S0-BSC-507

GERMANNA COMMUNITY COLLEGE
GERMANNA CENTER FOR ADVANCED TECHNOLOGY
18121 TECHNOLOGY DRIVE
CULPEPER, VA 22701

THE BOOK HOUSE

11/2/2013

THE WORLD ALMANAC®
AND BOOK OF FACTS
2013

WORLD ALMANAC BOOKS

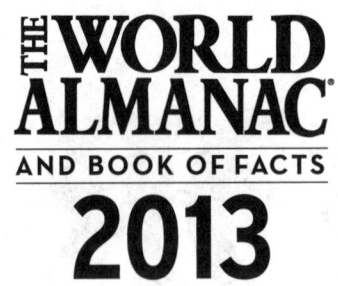

THE WORLD ALMANAC
AND BOOK OF FACTS
2013

Senior Editor: Sarah Janssen
Editor: M. L. Liu **Associate Editor:** Shmuel Ross
Index Editor: Nan Badgett
Contributors: Rachel Bozek, Andrea Brescia, Martin De Leon, Jeremy Eagle, Robert Famighetti, Marshall Gerometta, Jacqueline Laks Gorman, Sarah Hilliard, Geoffrey M. Horn, Michael J. Kaufman, Christopher Mari, John Mastroberardino, William A. McGeveran Jr., Lisa Renaud, Albert Rolls, John Rosenthal, Peter J. Schmidtke, George W. Smith, Peter N. Stearns, Steven Stern, Edward A. Thomas, Lori P. Wiesenfeld

Production: Newgen North America
Design and Production, Year in Pictures: Q2A/Bill Smith
Design, Cover: Takeshi Takahashi
Photo Research: Edward A. Thomas

For Infobase Learning:
Editorial Director: Laurie E. Likoff
Project Editor: Edward A. Thomas

Front cover: Hathaway, Romney, Obama: Shutterstock; Syrian rebels: Newscom: Youssef Boudal/Reuters; Phelps: Newscom: Fabrice Coffrini/AFP/Getty Images. **Back cover:** Curiosity: NASA/JPL-Caltech; *Costa Concordia*: Newscom: Polaris. **Tabs:** Shutterstock. **Interior pages:** Photos are from **AP Images** unless otherwise noted. **Jimmy Carter Library and Museum:** Carter, 533. **FEMA:** World Trade Center: Andrea Booher, 498; Katrina: Liz Roll, 498. **Gerald R. Ford Presidential Library and Museum:** Ford, 533. **Getty Images:** Costa: 2430/Gamma-Rapho, 193, 200; Obama/Biden: Saul Loeb/AFP, 194; Guangcheng: Saul Loeb/AFP, 196; Euro: Sakis Mitroldis/AFP, 198; Hitler: Bob Thomas/Popperfoto, 665; Mao: AFP, 667; Bhutto: Gamma-Rapho, 670; Mandela: Philip Littleton/AFP, 672; Banda Aceh, 674; Phelps: Martin Bureau/AFP, 810; James: Pool, 811; Murray: Erick W. Rasco/Sports Illustrated, 812; Woods: Patrick McDermott, 812; *Fifty Shades*: Saul Loeb/AFP, 814; Bradbury: Ulf Andersen, 815; Brown, Clark: WireImage/Ron Galella Collection, 815; Diller, Wells: Michael Ochs Archive, 815-16; Hamlisch: Harry Langdon, 815; Hemsley: CBS Photo Archive, 815; Houston, McGovern: Archive Photos, 816; James: Frederick M. Brown, 816. **iStockphoto:** 650. **Library of Congress:** 481, 483-85, 487-91, 526-36 (unless otherwise noted), 656, 662-63, 666. **Lyndon Baines Johnson Library and Museum:** Johnson, 532. **NASA:** Armstrong, 193, 815; *Challenger*, 495; *Apollo 11*, 668; Ride, 816; Venus: SDO, HMI, 193, 809; Mars: JPL-Caltech/MSSS, 809; *Discovery*: Rebecca Roth, 809. **National Archives:** 504, 506. **Newscom:** Primary: Paul Hennessy/Polaris, 193, 194; Obamacare: Christy Bowe/Polaris, 195; Green-on-Blue: Max Becherer/Polaris Image, 198; Libya: Mohammed Mohammed/Zuma Press, 198; Syria: Youssef Boudla/Reuters, 193, 198; Jong: KCNA/AFP/Getty Images, 198; *Deepsea Challenger*: Handout/Reuters, 809; *Homeland*: Danny Moloshok/UPI, 814; Hitchens: Zuma Press, 815; Sendak: Tricia Meadows/Globe-Zuma, 815; Vidal, 816; Wallace: Globe Photos/Zuma Press, 816. **Richard Nixon Presidential Library and Museum:** Nixon, 494. **Ronald Reagan Presidential Library:** Reagan/O'Connor, 495. **Shutterstock:** 649, 652, 654, 657. **Thinkstock:** Franklin: iStockphoto, 482; Alexander: Photos.com, 651; Spinning Jenny, 659. **U.S. Coast Guard:** Katrina: Petty Officer 2nd Class Kyle Niemi, 343; Mexico spill, 348; *Deepwater Horizon*, 501. **U.S. Dept. of Defense:** OK City bombing: Staff Sgt. Preston Chasteen, 497. **U.S. Dept. of Health and Human Services:** Sebelius: Chris Smith, 195. **U.S. Marine Corps:** Fallujah, 499. **White House:** Johnson: Cecil Stoughton, 492; Situation room: Pete Souza, 502; Bush: Eric Draper, 534; Obama: Pete Souza, 535.

Copyright © 2013 by Infobase Learning
The World Almanac® and The World Almanac and Book of Facts® are registered trademarks of Infobase Learning. All rights reserved. No part of this book may be reproduced or utilized in any form or by any means, electronic or mechanical, including photocopying, recording, or by any information storage or retrieval systems, without permission in writing from the publisher. For information, contact:

World Almanac® Books
An imprint of Infobase Learning
132 West 31st Street
New York, NY 10001

Hardcover	Paperback
ISBN-13: 978-1-60057-161-9	ISBN-13: 978-1-60057-162-6
ISBN-10: 1-60057-161-1	ISBN-10: 1-60057-162-X

The World Almanac® and Book of Facts is distributed in paperback to the trade by Simon & Schuster, and in paperback and hardcover to schools and libraries at special discounts by Infobase Learning. For further information, contact (800) 322-8755 or visit www.InfobaseLearning.com.

You can find The World Almanac® and Book of Facts on the Internet at www.worldalmanac.com.
Email: almanac@infobaselearning.com

The World Almanac® and Book of Facts 2013
Book printed and bound by IBT/Hamilton
Date printed: November 2012
Printed in the United States of America
RRD 10 9 8 7 6 5 4 3 2 1

CONTENTS

2012: SPECIAL FEATURES AND YEAR IN REVIEW

2012: YEAR IN PICTURES 193, 809

THE WORLD ALMANAC
AND BOOK OF FACTS 2013

Top 10 News Topics of 2012

1. Obama Wins Reelection. Pres. Barack Obama (D) won a narrow but clear victory over his Republican challenger, former Massachusetts Gov. Mitt Romney, on Nov. 6. Pending final official results, Obama apparently captured 332 electoral votes to Romney's 206 (270 are needed to win). Except for Indiana and North Carolina, Obama held onto all of the states he won in 2008, though often by reduced margins. His share of the popular vote was about 51% (to 48% for Romney), down from almost 53% in 2008. Obama became the first president since Franklin Roosevelt to win reelection when unemployment was as high as the 7.9% rate that prevailed on Election Day. The economy and the federal government's role were key campaign issues. Democrats held onto a majority in the Senate, while Republicans retained their majority in the House of Representatives.

2. Supreme Court Upholds "Obamacare." In a 5-4 ruling, the U.S. Supreme Court, June 28, upheld a key provision of the Patient Protection and Affordable Care Act. The 2010 law is intended to extend coverage to some 30 mil uninsured Americans. Opponents challenged the law's requirement that Americans either buy health insurance or pay a penalty to the federal government. The Obama administration defended it as a legitimate exercise of government power under the Constitution's commerce clause. Chief Justice John Roberts rejected that argument but joined the Court's liberal wing in a 5-4 decision upholding the requirement by relying on Congress's power to levy taxes. By a 7-2 majority, the Court struck down one provision of the law, which would have required states to participate in the act's expansion of Medicaid or lose their Medicaid funding.

3. Terrorism, Turmoil, and Transition Top Middle East News. In what was labeled an act of terrorism by U.S. officials, the U.S. consulate in Benghazi, Libya, was attacked Sept. 11, and four Americans, including ambassador to Libya J. Christopher Stevens, were killed. Elsewhere in the Middle East, what began as protests in Mar. 2011 against the autocratic regime of Syrian Pres. Bashar al-Assad had become a full-blown civil war by 2012. Government forces battled a loose coalition of military defectors, secular opposition groups, and Islamic jihadists. More than 36,000 Syrians had been killed in the escalating violence by Oct. 2012. In Egypt, where massive protests had brought down the government of Pres. Hosni Mubarak in 2011, a runoff presidential election June 16-17, 2012, was won by Mohammed Morsi of the Freedom and Justice Party, the political wing of the Muslim Brotherhood.

4. Storm Devastates U.S. Northeast. Sandy—a hurricane turned post-tropical cyclone—made landfall near Atlantic City, NJ, around 8 PM on Oct. 29, accompanied by a storm surge that flooded seaside towns up and down the New Jersey shore, low-lying areas of New York City, and other Northeast communities. An estimated 113 people in nine states died in the storm. Millions were left without power, many for more than a week, and tens of thousands were made homeless. Power outages and flooded rail and road tunnels crippled transportation in the New York City metropolitan area for days. Hurricane Sandy had wreaked havoc in the Caribbean Oct. 24-26, killing at least 69 people as it passed over or near Haiti, Cuba, the Bahamas, and other areas.

5. London Hosts 2012 Olympics. Some 10,500 athletes from 204 nations and territories took part in the XXX Summer Olympiad, July 27-Aug. 12. The Games, hosted by London, England, UK, included 302 medal events in 26 sports. The U.S. finished on top in both overall (104) and gold medals (46) won. China (88) and Russia (82) finished second and third in the overall medal count. Host nation Great Britain was fourth in total medals (65) and third in gold medals (29) won. American swimmer Michael Phelps added 4 gold and 2 silver medals to his career medal count, which at 22 is the highest for any athlete in Olympic history. After initial concerns about security and other preparations, the Games went off smoothly over a two-week period that, by British standards, saw very little rain.

6. Gun Violence Shocks the Nation. Twelve people were killed and 58 injured when a heavily armed gunman opened fire in an Aurora, CO, movie theater July 20, at a midnight premiere of *The Dark Knight Rises.* James E. Holmes was charged July 30 with murder and other crimes in connection with the attack, the largest mass shooting in U.S. history. In an act of domestic terrorism, a gunman opened fire Aug. 5 at a Sikh temple in Oak Creek,

WI. Six people were killed and three wounded by the attacker, Wade Page, who died of a self-inflicted gunshot wound to the head. On Oct. 21, Radcliffe F. Haughton opened fire at a day spa in Brookfield, WI, killing three (including his wife) and wounding four before taking his own life. Earlier in the year, in an incident with apparent racial overtones, unarmed black teenager Trayvon Martin was fatally shot in Sanford, FL, Feb. 26 by George Zimmerman, who was patrolling, in an unofficial capacity, his gated community.

7. U.S. Economy Continues Slow Growth. Leading indicators showed an economy that was recovering—but at a sluggish pace—from the severe recession of 2007-09. The Dept. of Commerce's estimate, released Oct. 26, was that the U.S. economy (as measured by real gross domestic product, or GDP) grew at an annual rate of 2.0% in the third quarter of 2012. This followed real GDP increases of 2.0% and 1.3% in the first and second quarters. Adding to the country's economic difficulties was a severe drought that affected more than 30 Midwestern and other states by Aug., the most widespread U.S. drought in more than half a century. The U.S. unemployment rate remained high, hovering above 8% for much of the year before dipping to 7.8% in Sept. and 7.9% in Oct. In an attempt to stimulate the economy and reduce unemployment, the Federal Reserve announced, Sept. 13, an open-ended program of monthly purchases of mortgage-backed and other securities.

8. U.S. Draws Down Troops in Afghanistan, Confronts Iran. In keeping with the Obama administration's timeline to remove all U.S. forces from Afghanistan by 2014, Defense Sec. Leon Panetta announced Sept. 21 that the U.S. had completed withdrawing the 33,000 "surge" troops sent to the country two years earlier; about 68,000 troops remained. U.S. Marine Gen. John Allen, the commander of U.S. and other coalition forces in Afghanistan, took steps Sept. 16 to limit joint training missions with coalition and Afghan security forces after a series of "green-on-blue" attacks by Afghan trainees on coalition personnel. By the end of Sept., more than 50 coalition troops had died in such attacks in 2012. Amid growing evidence that Iran was increasing its production of enriched uranium, the U.S. and the European Union tightened economic sanctions on Iran several times in 2012. The sanctions, intended to encourage Iran to engage in substantive negotiations, appeared to have significantly reduced Iran's oil exports and otherwise slowed its economy.

9. European Financial Woes Continue. Staggering levels of government debt and stagnant economies continued to plague some European Union members, in particular Greece, Spain, and Italy. EU finance ministers agreed Feb. 21 to a 130-bil-euro bailout package to help Greece restructure its debt. Greek elections June 17 brought to power a government committed to keeping the nation in the eurozone and to taking austerity measures demanded as a condition for financial aid. Sharp cuts in government spending by Greece and Spain contributed to unemployment rates around 25% and large-scale demonstrations in the summer and fall of 2012. The European Central Bank announced a program, Sept. 6, to buy Spanish and Italian government bonds to bring down the interest rates those governments would have to pay on new borrowing, but the bond-buying plan was tied to strict oversight of the countries' economic policies.

10. Penn State Football Program Sanctioned After Sandusky Conviction. In a scandal that rocked Penn State Univ.'s legendary football program, former assistant football coach Jerry Sandusky was convicted June 22 of sexually abusing 10 boys over a 15-year period. A number of the instances of abuse were found to have occurred on university property. Sandusky was sentenced Oct. 9 to 30-60 years in prison. An investigation commissioned by Penn State's board of trustees released a report July 12 that concluded that university officials, including longtime head football coach Joe Paterno, had concealed Sandusky's activities to avoid tarnishing the football program. Paterno's 46-year career as head coach—which included 37 bowl appearances and two national championships—had ended with his dismissal by the university Nov. 9, 2011; he died of lung cancer Jan. 22, 2012. On July 23, the NCAA fined Penn State $60 mil, voided the football team's victories for the previous 14 seasons, and barred it from postseason play for the next four seasons.

THE WORLD
AT A GLANCE

Surprising Facts

The number of U.S. households that owned **televisions** actually decreased in 2012 by 1.2 million, to 114.7 million. *(p. 282)*

Only 14.0 million **smartphones** were sold in the U.S. in 2006; an estimated 108.4 million were sold in 2012. *(p. 390)*

Sales of **LP and EP records** have steadily increased in the past half-decade, from $15.7 million in sales in 2006 to $119.4 million in sales in 2011. However, that is a small share of all music sales when compared to the $2.6 billion in digital music sales in 2011. *(p. 282)*

In 2010, 23.0% of Americans smoked **cigarettes**, down significantly from 38.7% of Americans in 1985. Yet Americans spent $96.1 billion on tobacco products in 2011—more than twice the $41.0 billion they spent in 1990. *(pp. 83, 175)*

In 1990, the average U.S. **movie ticket** cost $4.23; the average ticket in 2011 cost $7.93. *(p. 274)*

Americans paid an average of 22.8% of their total income in **income tax and Social Security** payments in 2011 (down from 24.7% in 2008); Belgians paid 42.2%. *(p. 737)*

U.S. **public debt** has more than tripled since 2000, from $3.4 trillion to $11.6 trillion in 2012. As a percentage of the U.S. gross domestic product, debt has doubled from 34.7% to 74.2%. *(p. 92)*

Since 1975, the **fuel efficiency** of U.S. cars has increased from 13.5 miles per gallon to 25.9 miles per gallon. *(p. 115)*

In almost half (45.4%) of **motor vehicle accidents** in 2010, state traffic authorities did not report that improper driving had occurred. *(p. 207)*

In the 2009-10 school year, 85.0% of undergraduates attending a four-year institution received **financial aid**. *(p. 418)*

Number Ones

Most-visited **social networking website** . . . . Facebook, 158.8 million unique visitors in Apr.-June 2012 *(p. 393)*

Most-used **search engine** . . . . .Google, 36.5 billion searches by 192.4 million unique visitors in Apr.-June 2012 *(p. 393)*

U.S. airline that carried the most passengers. . . . . .Southwest/AirTran, 135.2 million in 2011 *(p. 120)*

Busiest **U.S. airport** by passenger traffic . . . . . Hartsfield-Jackson Airport (Atlanta, GA), 92.4 million passengers in 2011 *(p. 120)*

Top U.S. state by **traveler spending** . . . . California, $95.6 billion in 2010 *(p. 119)*

Top-selling **light truck** in the U.S. . . . . Ford F-Series, 552,647 sold in 2011 *(p. 114)*

Most popular **light truck color** in the U.S. . . . . White/white pearl, 29% of 2011 model year light trucks *(p. 114)*

Top-selling **passenger car** in the U.S. . . . . Toyota Camry, 308,510 sold in 2011 *(p. 114)*

Most popular **compact/sports car color** in the U.S. . . . . Silver, 20% of 2011 model year compact/sports cars *(p. 114)*

Most popular **luxury car color** in the U.S. . . . . Black/black effect, 27% of 2011 model year luxury cars *(p. 114)*

Fastest **roller coaster** in the world . . . . Formula Rossa, 149.1 mph (Ferrari World Abu Dhabi, UAE) *(p. 121)*

Nations with the most **paid days off of work** per year . . . . .Austria and Malta, 38 paid days off *(p. 121)*

Nation with largest crude **oil reserves**. . . Saudi Arabia, 267.0 billion barrels in 2012 (U.S. reserves, 20.7 billion barrels) *(p. 144)*

Nation most dependent on **nuclear energy** . . . . France, 77.7% of electricity was nuclear-generated in 2011 *(p. 146)*

America: By the Numbers

49.3 million: number of students enrolled in U.S. public schools in 2009-10 school year *(p. 416)*

1.6 million: number of students enrolled in U.S. charter schools in 2009-10 school year *(p. 416)*

90.7%: public high school graduation rate in Wisconsin, the highest of any state in the U.S. *(p. 413)*

56.3%: public high school graduation rate in Nevada, the lowest of any state in the U.S. *(p. 413)*

28.7: median age at first marriage for U.S. men in 2011 (the highest it has ever been) *(p. 201)*

26.5: median age at first marriage for U.S. women in 2011 (the highest it has ever been) *(p. 201)*

49: average total hours of TV viewed per week by U.S. women age 55 and over *(p. 284)*

43: average total hours of TV viewed per week by U.S. men age 55 and over *(p. 284)*

23: average total hours of TV viewed per week by young adults ages 12-17 *(p. 284)*

18.3: average total hours U.S. Internet users age 12 and older spent online per week *(p. 394)*

80%: percentage of U.S. Internet users age 12 and older who checked their email at least once daily *(p. 394)*

91%: percentage of U.S. households with at least one cell phone in 2012 *(p. 395)*

23.8%: percentage of the population of Texas without health insurance in 2011, higher than any other U.S. state *(p. 171)*

24.1%: percentage of U.S. deaths in 2010 caused by heart disease, the leading cause of death *(p. 208)*

35.7%: percentage of U.S. population age 20 and over that was obese in 2009-10 *(p. 190)*

949.1%: change in U.S. annual per capita consumption of fresh broccoli since 1970 *(p. 125)*

−22.6%: change in U.S. annual per capita consumption of red meat since 1970 *(p. 126)*

111.7%: change in U.S. annual per capita consumption of chicken since 1970 *(p. 126)*

Money in America (pp. 76-105)

Median income for U.S. men in constant (2011) dollars . . . . .in 2005: $36,031 . . . . .in 2011: $32,986

Median income for U.S. women in constant (2011) dollars . . . . .in 2005: $21,401 . . . . .in 2011: $21,102

Amount of money that Americans put in savings . . . . .in 2005: $143.2 bil . . . . .in 2011: $489.4 bil

Percent of disposable income that Americans put in savings . . . . .in 2005: 1.5% . . . . .in 2011: 4.2%

If all circulating U.S. dollars and coins were equally distributed among the nation's population, in 2012 every American would receive $3,540.

Wealthiest American, 2012	Corporation with largest revenues, 2011
Bill Gates, $66.0 billion net worth	Exxon-Mobil, $452.9 billion

Top of the World, 2011

Top tourist destinations (millions of visitors, p. 118)	Top world airports (millions of passengers, p. 120)	Top cell phone usage (subscriptions per 100 pop., p. 395)
France 79.5	Beijing Capital 78.7	Saudi Arabia 191.24
U.S. 62.3	London Heathrow 69.4	Russia 179.31
China 57.6	Tokyo Haneda 62.6	Italy 151.84
Spain 56.7	Paris Charles de Gaulle 61.0	Vietnam 143.39
Italy 46.1	Frankfurt 56.4	Kazakhstan 142.55

Top personal computer usage (millions in use, p. 389)	Top gross domestic product (per capita, p. 736)	Top health care spenders (per capita of 50 most populous countries in 2009, p. 171)
U.S. 310.64	Liechtenstein $141,100	U.S. $7,960
China 195.14	Qatar $104,300	France $4,840
Japan 98.05	Luxembourg $81,100	Germany $4,723
Germany 71.49	Singapore $60,500	Canada $4,519
India 57.02	Norway $54,200	Australia $3,945

Milestone Birthdays in 2013

90

Chuck Yeager, Feb. 13

Richard Attenborough, Aug. 29

Bob Barker, Dec. 12

80

Michael Caine, Mar. 14

Quincy Jones, Mar. 14

Ruth Bader Ginsburg, Mar. 15

Philip Roth, Mar. 19

Willie Nelson, Apr. 30

Joan Collins, May 23

Joan Rivers, June 8

Larry King, Nov. 19

70

Bob Woodward, Mar. 26

Christopher Walken, Mar. 31

Newt Gingrich, June 17

Barry Manilow, June 17

Geraldo Rivera, July 4

Mick Jagger, July 26

Robert De Niro, Aug. 17

Chevy Chase, Oct. 8

Joni Mitchell, Nov. 7

Randy Newman, Nov. 28

Keith Richards, Dec. 18

60

Jim Jarmusch, Jan. 22

Michael Bolton, Feb. 26

Chaka Khan, Mar. 23

Pierce Brosnan, May 16

Cyndi Lauper, June 22

Hulk Hogan, Aug. 11

Kathie Lee Gifford, Aug. 16

John Malkovich, Dec. 9

Ben Bernanke, Dec. 13

Bill Pullman, Dec. 17

Meredith Vieira, Dec. 30

50

Michael Jordan, Feb. 17

Charles Barkley, Feb. 20

Vanessa Williams, Mar. 18

Quentin Tarantino, Mar. 27

Conan O'Brien, Apr. 18

Mike Myers, May 25

Johnny Depp, June 9

George Michael, June 25

Edie Falco, July 5

Lisa Kudrow, July 30

Brad Pitt, Dec. 18

40

Portia de Rossi, Jan. 31

Oscar De La Hoya, Feb. 4

Jim Parsons, Mar. 24

Heidi Klum, June 1

Neil Patrick Harris, June 15

Sergey Brin, Aug. 21

Kristen Wiig, Aug. 22

Dave Chappelle, Aug. 24

Tyra Banks, Dec. 4

Stephenie Meyer, Dec. 24

30

Justin Verlander, Feb. 20

Carrie Underwood, Mar. 10

Mila Kunis, Aug. 14

Jesse Eisenberg, Oct. 5

Aaron Rodgers, Dec. 2

Jonah Hill, Dec. 20

21

Taylor Lautner, Feb. 11

Josh Hutcherson, Oct. 12

Miley Cyrus, Nov. 23

18

Missy Franklin, May 10

Gabrielle "Gabby" Douglas, Dec. 31

U.S. ECONOMY: A STATISTICAL PORTRAIT

Annual Consumer Spending by Type of Expenditure, 1990, 2010

Source: Consumer Expenditure Survey, U.S. Bureau of Labor Statistics, U.S. Dept. of Commerce

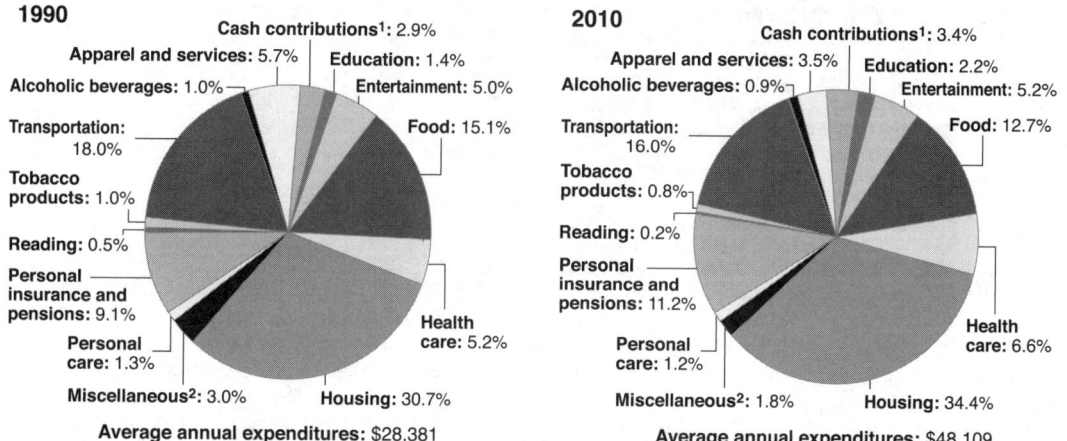

1990

- Cash contributions[1]: 2.9%
- Apparel and services: 5.7%
- Education: 1.4%
- Alcoholic beverages: 1.0%
- Entertainment: 5.0%
- Transportation: 18.0%
- Food: 15.1%
- Tobacco products: 1.0%
- Reading: 0.5%
- Personal insurance and pensions: 9.1%
- Health care: 5.2%
- Personal care: 1.3%
- Miscellaneous[2]: 3.0%
- Housing: 30.7%

Average annual expenditures: $28,381

2010

- Cash contributions[1]: 3.4%
- Apparel and services: 3.5%
- Education: 2.2%
- Alcoholic beverages: 0.9%
- Entertainment: 5.2%
- Transportation: 16.0%
- Food: 12.7%
- Tobacco products: 0.8%
- Reading: 0.2%
- Personal insurance and pensions: 11.2%
- Health care: 6.6%
- Personal care: 1.2%
- Miscellaneous[2]: 1.8%
- Housing: 34.4%

Average annual expenditures: $48,109

Note: Spending by consumer unit, defined as related members of a household; a person living alone or sharing a household but who is financially independent; or two or more persons living together who jointly decide expenditures. Percentages may not add up to 100 due to rounding. (1) Incl. alimony and charitable giving. (2) Incl. bank, legal, and accounting fees.

Dow Jones Industrial Average and Median Personal Income, 2000-11

Source: S&P Dow Jones Indices LLC; Current Population Survey, U.S. Census Bureau, U.S. Dept. of Commerce

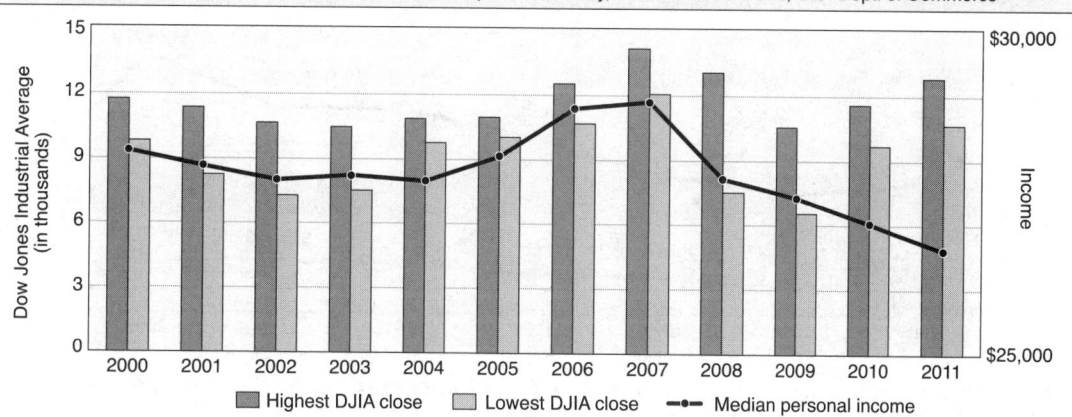

Highest DJIA close   Lowest DJIA close   Median personal income

Note: The Dow Jones Industrial Average (DJIA) consists of 30 component companies in all industries except Transportation and Utilities. Median personal income is in 2011 dollars for persons ages 14 and older.

Housing Affordability, 2000-12

Source: National Association of REALTORS®

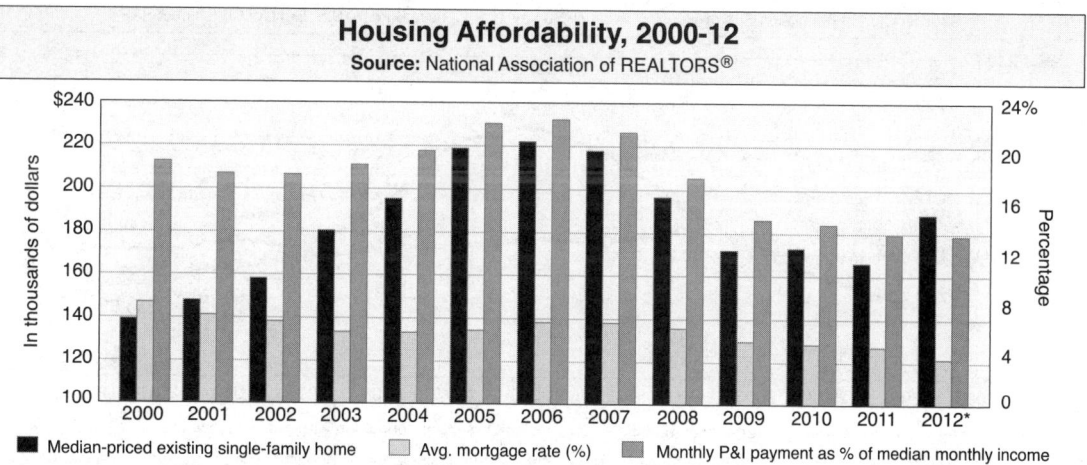

Median-priced existing single-family home   Avg. mortgage rate (%)   Monthly P&I payment as % of median monthly income

*Prelim. as of Aug. **Note:** Avg. mortgage rate assumes down payment of 20% of home price and qualifying ratio of 25% (i.e., monthly principal and interest [P&I] cannot exceed 25% of median monthly income); based on effective rate on loans closed on existing homes.

Employment Status, 2000-12

Source: Current Population Survey, U.S. Census Bureau, U.S. Dept. of Commerce; Bureau of Labor Statistics, U.S. Dept. of Labor

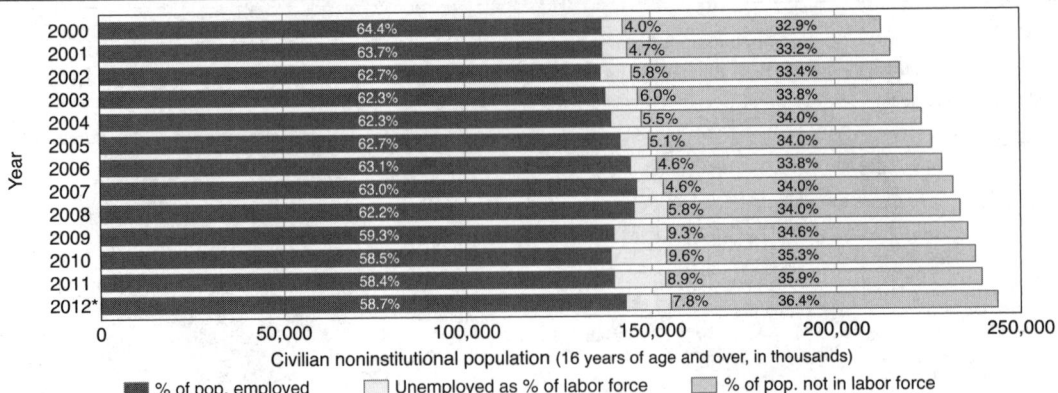

Civilian noninstitutional population (16 years of age and over, in thousands)

■ % of pop. employed   □ Unemployed as % of labor force   ▨ % of pop. not in labor force

*Sept. only. **Note:** The **labor force** is made up of the *employed* (incl. those with part-time or temporary work) and the *unemployed*, who were available for and tried to find work in the previous four weeks. Persons who are neither employed nor unemployed are said to be **not in the labor force**. That group incl. students and retirees as well as those *marginally attached to the labor force*, who have actively looked for work in the past 12 months but not the previous four weeks.

Median Family Income and Net Worth, 1989-2010

Source: Survey of Consumer Finances, Federal Reserve Board

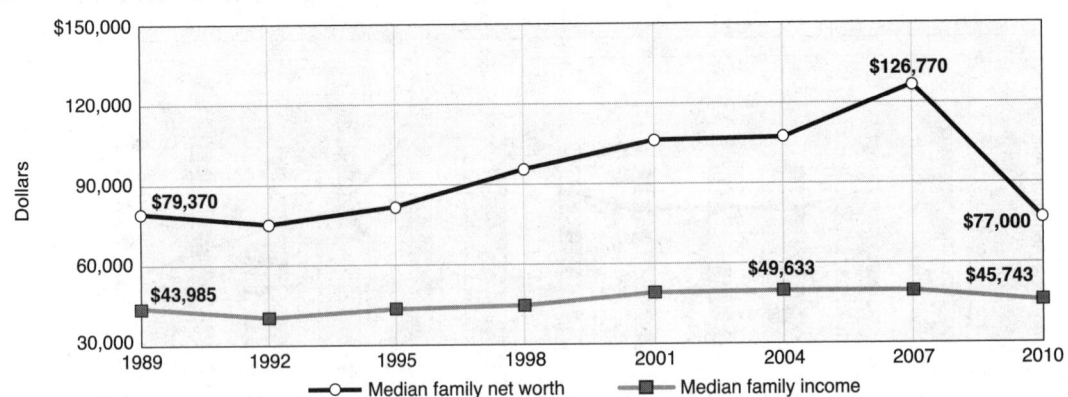

—○— Median family net worth   —■— Median family income

Note: Figures given are for total income before taxes for the calendar year preceding the survey. Numbers are in 2010 dollars. Most U.S. families base their wealth more upon housing than on financial assets.

Homeownership Rate and Home Price Index, 2000-12

Source: Current Population Survey/Housing Vacancy Survey, U.S. Census Bureau, U.S. Dept. of Commerce; S&P

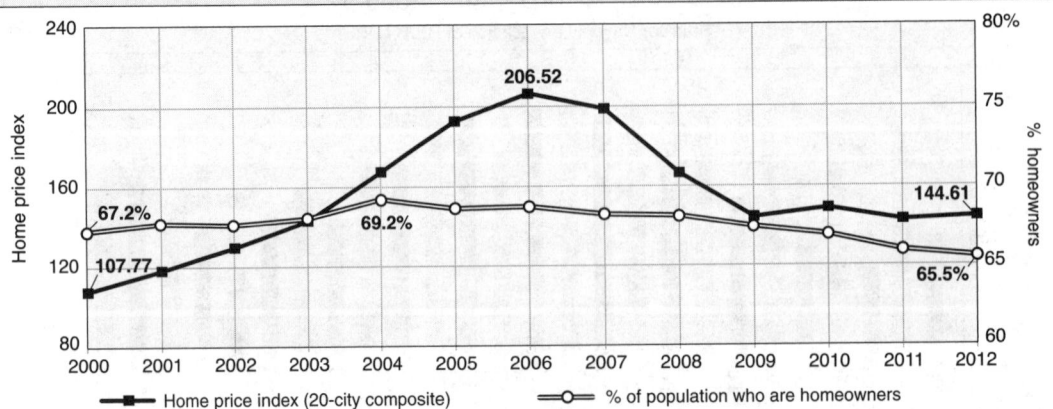

—■— Home price index (20-city composite)   —○— % of population who are homeowners

Note: The S&P/Case-Shiller Home Price Index tracks changes in the value of single-family housing. The 20-city index is a composite of home prices in 20 metro areas. The index has a base value of 100 (first quarter, 2000) and is for July of a given years. Homeownership rate is for the second quarter.

ELECTION, 2012

Obama Retains Presidency; Split Congress Continues

Incumbent Pres. Barack Obama (D) Nov. 6, 2012, won 332 electoral votes in 26 states and the District of Columbia (62 more than the 270 needed) to retain the White House, comfortably defeating his Republican challenger, former Massachusetts Gov. Mitt Romney. In Congress, Democrats kept control of the Senate, slightly increasing their majority, and Republicans held onto the House of Representatives.

The Obama Victory

Obama won an estimated 51% of the total popular vote (down from 53% in 2008), compared to Romney's 48%, with third-party and independent candidates winning the balance. About 30 mil people, in 34 states and the District of Columbia, voted early, either by mail or in person.

The president held onto all the states he had won in 2008, except for traditionally Republican North Carolina and Indiana. As expected, he swept the Northeast and the West Coast, while Romney won most of the other Western states and nearly the entire South. Throughout the campaign both candidates concentrated their resources on the few battleground states that analysts believed could go either way. Obama captured nearly all of them, including heavily contested Florida, Virginia, and Ohio.

Obama's victory reflected strong though somewhat reduced support from the demographic coalition that swept him into power in 2008. He remained overwhelmingly popular among African Americans, who turned out to give him 93% of their vote (vs. 95% in 2008), according to Pew Research Center exit poll data. He also captured 71% of the fast-growing Hispanic vote, up from 67%, an increase partly attributed to relatively hard-line policies on immigration espoused by Romney and the Republican platform. Despite concerns over an expected enthusiasm gap, young voters (ages 18 to 29) came out in high numbers, with 60% (down from 66%) supporting the president. Among non-Hispanic white voters, however, Obama fell well short of a majority, winning 39% (vs. 43% in 2008). There was a sizable decline in independents' support for Obama. He won 45% of their vote in 2012, down from 52% in 2008, but Democrats turned out in big enough numbers to offset the loss.

Obama continued to enjoy strong support from women, who backed him over Romney 55% to 44% (while 52% of men supported Romney). Romney's views opposing abortion (except in special circumstances), mandated insurance coverage of contraception, and funding for Planned Parenthood were cited in campaign rhetoric. At the same time, these views helped the GOP ticket win big (79%) among white Protestant evangelicals (73% in 2008). Catholics roughly mirrored the population at large, supporting Obama by 50% in 2012, down from 53% in 2008.

Both candidates focused strongly on energizing their bases. Democrats especially launched massive registration and get-out-the-vote efforts. Preliminary reports suggested, however, that overall turnout for 2012 was somewhat lower than in 2008.

The Fall Campaign

The economy was the biggest issue in the campaign. No president since Franklin D. Roosevelt (D) had been reelected with unemployment so high (7.9% in Oct.). Some 12 mil people remained out of work, while millions of others had dropped out of the labor force or had found only part-time work. The federal government continued to pile up trillion-dollar budget deficits and faced ballooning entitlement costs, with a "fiscal cliff"—consisting of tax increases and deep automatic spending cuts in government programs—looming at year's end if Congress and the White House did not act decisively to avert it.

Romney blamed Obama for a failed economy. But Obama blamed the fiscal crisis and recession that emerged under Pres. George W. Bush and claimed credit for 25 consecutive months of job growth and for slow but steady economic growth. Consumer confidence and housing sales were improving as the election approached, though serious challenges lay ahead.

Romney argued that his business experience and successes as governor of Massachusetts made him more capable than Obama of leading the nation out of its economic doldrums. But the Obama campaign put Romney on the defensive, portraying his business experience as devoted to profits at the expense of job creation and Romney himself as a multimillionaire out of touch with the needs of ordinary Americans. That image was reinforced in Sept. by a leaked video of a Romney speech to rich donors, in which he appeared to dismiss the 47% of the electorate who paid no income taxes as victims who believed they were entitled to government handouts.

There was a surge in support for Romney after the first presidential debate Oct. 3 in Denver, CO. He attacked Obama's record and sought to project a centrist image, stressing concern for the middle class and their economic future, while Obama turned in what was viewed as a lackluster performance. In the remaining debates, Oct. 16 and Oct. 22, Obama fought back aggressively and appeared to score points. Romney sought to keep the focus on the domestic economy and his determination to bring about change. Romney did not draw sharp contrasts with Obama foreign policy in the third debate, so much as present himself as competent and avoid being painted as an extremist.

Polls conducted shortly before the election predicted a tight race, with a modest Obama advantage in swing states.

Paths to Nomination

Obama had officially announced his candidacy for reelection in Apr. 2011 and had encountered no serious opposition. He again chose Vice Pres. Joe Biden as his running mate. The two were nominated Sept. 6 at the Democratic National Convention in Charlotte, NC.

Romney, who had run unsuccessfully for the 2008 GOP presidential nomination, officially announced his 2012 candidacy in June 2011. He was the presumed front-runner, but several generally more conservative rivals offered challenges. Rep. Michele Bachmann (MN) gained brief momentum after winning the Iowa straw poll in Aug. 2011. Texas Gov. Rick Perry then surged in opinion polls, emerging as a possible threat, but fumbled badly in Sept. 2011 debates. Businessman Herman Cain became a surprise favorite, but his campaign died out by early Dec. amid allegations of sexual misconduct, and former House Speaker Newt Gingrich (GA) rose in the polls. Gingrich gained traction with attacks on Romney's record at Bain Capital, a theme enthusiastically taken up by Democrats.

Romney placed first in the Jan. 10 New Hampshire primary, followed by maverick libertarian Rep. Ron Paul (TX) and moderate former Utah Gov. Jon Huntsman. Paul had respectable showings in some later primaries but never won, though he continued his candidacy. Huntsman soon dropped out. Gingrich revived his campaign with a win in South Carolina Jan. 21 but could not gain lasting traction. Romney's biggest rival through much of the primary season was former Sen. Rick Santorum (PA), an ardent social conservative, who had narrowly outpolled him in the Jan. 3 Iowa caucuses and scored several wins in Feb. and Mar. But he bowed out in Apr. after his fortunes declined.

Romney soon accumulated enough delegates to assure his nomination, but he had needed to woo a base that was more conservative than the electorate he would face in Nov. in order to win. As his running mate, he chose Rep. Paul Ryan (WI), the chairman of the House Budget Committee, who was especially popular among conservative Republicans. The two were nominated Aug. 28 at the Republican National Convention in Tampa, FL.

Big Money

The Center for Responsive Politics, a nonpartisan research group, estimated that total spending on the 2012 election would reach a record $6 bil (some $2.6 bil on the presidential race alone), most of it by the campaigns and political parties. But close to $1 bil of that total was spent by outside groups.

The explosion in that spending stemmed from a Jan. 2010 Supreme Court decision, *Citizens United v. Federal Election Commission*. It allowed corporations, labor unions, and other interest groups to use their funds to promote issues and candidates. They could also contribute indirectly to parties and campaigns through political action committees (PACs). A federal appellate court ruled soon after that PACs could receive unlimited contributions as long as they did not give the money to candidates and parties. Republicans created the first of these so-called super PACs with big contributions from corporations and wealthy individuals, but Democrats soon formed their own super PACs to attract big donors. Super PACs ran many of the highly charged negative ads that flooded the airwaves in battleground states. Because super PACs were not allowed to coordinate with candidates, the candidates were insulated from responsibility for their ads. Critics bemoaned the influence of PACs in the election; at the same time, the biggest Republican donors fell short of their goals. For example, billionaire casino magnate Sheldon Adelson spent at least $53 mil on Republican primary and general election candidates, but only one of those he backed was elected.

Congressional Contests

Republicans' early hopes of gaining control of the Senate faded as the election approached. With a reelected Vice Pres. Biden holding a deciding vote in case of ties, they would need a net gain of four seats in the chamber; instead they lost ground.

In one of the highest-profile races, incumbent Scott Brown (R, MA), who had won a special election in Jan. 2010 to take the seat formerly held by veteran liberal Sen. Edward "Ted" Kennedy (D), lost to Elizabeth Warren, a former Obama adviser and favorite of liberals.

Repeating a trend from 2010, extreme Tea Party candidates cost the Republicans Senate seats that had been regarded as safe. In Missouri, Rep. Todd Akin (R), who had won a crowded GOP primary, drew national attention after he claimed in a TV interview that women's bodies could avert pregnancies in cases of "legitimate" rape. He was defeated by Sen. Claire McCaskill (D), once considered among the most vulnerable incumbents. In Republican-leaning Indiana, Joe Donnelly, a moderate Democrat, defeated former state treasurer Richard Mourdock (R), a Tea Party candidate who upset veteran Sen. Richard Lugar in the primary. Mourdock was criticized late in the campaign for comments that pregnancies from rape were intended by God.

McCaskill was one of a few Democrats who distanced themselves from Obama as they competed in GOP strongholds. In North Dakota, former state attorney general Heidi Heitkamp (D) criticized environmental regulations and elements of Obama's health-care reform measure and defeated Rep. Rick Berg (R) for the seat vacated by Kent Conrad (D). Incumbent Sen. Jon Tester (D, MT), who bragged about votes against "Wall Street and auto bailouts," won a tight race against Rep. Denny Rehberg (R).

Rep. Tammy Baldwin (D) defeated former Gov. Tommy Thompson (R) in Wisconsin to become the first openly gay senator. The new Senate was set to have a record total of 20 women.

In the contest to succeed retiring Sen. Ben Nelson (D, NE), a well-known moderate, former Sen. Bob Kerrey (D) lost to Deb Fischer (R), a little-known state senator. Republicans held onto the seat of retiring Sen. Jon Kyl (AZ), as Rep. Jeff Flake (R) defeated Richard Carmona (D), who had served as George W. Bush's surgeon general (2002-06). In the swing state of Nevada, incumbent Sen. Dean Heller (R), who was appointed when Sen. John Ensign (R) resigned over a scandal in 2011, defeated Rep. Shelley Berkley (D) in a tight race.

In Connecticut, where independent Democrat Joe Lieberman was retiring, former wresting executive Linda McMahon (R) spent over $40 mil of her own money in her second Senate race but lost to Rep. Chris Murphy (D). In what was reportedly the costliest Senate race, former Virginia Gov. Tim Kaine (D) defeated former Sen. George Allen (R) to replace retiring centrist Jim Webb (D).

In the House, Republicans did not suffer heavy losses. Benefitting in part from favorable redistricting, they retained a comfortable majority. Vice-presidential nominee Paul Ryan, who ran for reelection in his district, was among those easily reelected. However, prominent Tea Party candidate Joe Walsh lost decisively in Illinois, and conservative firebrand Allen West appeared to have narrowly lost in Florida. Former presidential candidate Michele Bachmann fought hard to retain her Minnesota House seat. In other high-profile races, Joseph P. Kennedy III (D) won easily in the Massachusetts district held by retiring veteran Rep. Barney Frank (D). Rep. Jesse Jackson Jr. (D, IL) was reelected despite mental health problems that had caused him to be absent from his district since June.

Ballot Issues

Among prominent ballot issues, Maine, Maryland, and Washington became the first states to approve same-sex marriage through popular vote, while a measure in Minnesota to constitutionally block gay marriage was defeated. Colorado and Washington voted to legalize recreational use of marijuana. Californians backed a proposal to raise taxes to avoid education funding cuts and rejected a proposal to end the death penalty. In Puerto Rico, voters endorsed a proposal for the commonwealth to become the 51st U.S. state, subject to the approval of Congress.

Balance of Power, 2012

(as of Nov. 9, 2012)

	Senate		House		Governors	
	Before	After	Before	After	Before	After
Dem.	51	53	193	194	20	19
Rep.	47	45	242	233	29	30
Ind.	2[1]	2[2]	—	—	1	1

Note: Eight House seats were still pending. (1) Both independent senators chose to caucus with Democrats. (2) Both independent senators were expected to caucus with Democrats.

Campaign Trail Quotes, 2012

"I think it's been the worst campaign I've ever seen in my life."
—Former first lady Barbara Bush commenting Mar. 5 on the presidential campaign during primary season.

"If you were successful, somebody along the line gave you some help … Somebody helped to create this unbelievable American system that we have that allowed you to thrive. Somebody invested in roads and bridges. If you've got a business—you didn't build that. Somebody else made that happen."
—Pres. Barack Obama, in a July 13 speech to a VFW convention, interpreted by many opponents as denying people true credit for their own success.

"It seems to me, from what I understand from doctors, that's really rare. If it's a legitimate rape, the female body has ways to try to shut that whole thing down."
—Rep. Todd Akin (R), Senate candidate in Missouri, speaking of pregnancy from rape in a TV interview Aug. 19.

"So I … so I've got Mr. Obama sitting here. And he's … I was going to ask him a couple of questions."
—Actor-director Clint Eastwood, speaking to an empty chair, in an off-the-cuff riff at the GOP convention in Tampa, FL, Aug. 30.

"[I]nstead of inspiring us by reminding us of what makes us special, [Obama] divides us against each other. He tells Americans they're worse off because others are better off. That people got rich by making others poor. Hope and Change has become Divide and Conquer."
—Sen. Marco Rubio (R, FL), speaking at the GOP convention, Aug. 30.

"President Obama promised to begin to slow the rise of the oceans and heal the planet. My promise is to help you and your family."
—Former Gov. Mitt Romney, in his speech accepting the GOP presidential nomination, Aug. 30.

"No president—not me, not any of my predecessors—no one could have fully repaired all the damage that he found in just four years."
—Former Pres. Bill Clinton, at the Democratic National Convention in Charlotte, NC, Sept. 5.

"I'm sorry, Jim. I'm going to stop the subsidy to PBS. I'm going to stop other things. I like PBS. I love Big Bird. I actually like you too. But I'm not going to keep on spending money on things to borrow money from China to pay for it."
—Former Gov. Romney, in the first televised presidential debate Oct. 3 at Univ. of Denver, addressing moderator Jim Lehrer of PBS.

"Mr. Vice President, I know you're under a lot of duress to make up for lost ground, but I think people would be better served if we don't keep interrupting each other."
—Rep. Paul Ryan, in the vice-presidential debate Oct. 11 at Centre College in Danville, KY.

"With all due respect, that's a bunch of malarkey."
—Vice Pres. Joe Biden, responding to Rep. Ryan's criticism of administration foreign policy, in the vice-presidential debate Oct. 11.

"Gov. Romney was a very successful investor. If somebody came to you, Governor, with a plan that said, 'Here, I want to spend $7 or $8 trillion and we're going to pay for it but we can't tell you until maybe after the election how we're going to do it.' You wouldn't have taken such a sketchy deal and neither should you, the American people."
—Pres. Obama, in the second televised presidential debate Oct. 16 at Hofstra Univ. in Hempstead, NY.

"We took a concerted effort to go out and find women who had backgrounds that could be qualified to become members of our cabinet. I went to a number of women's groups and said, 'Can you help us find folks.' And they brought us whole binders full of women."
—Gov. Romney, in the second presidential debate, Oct. 16.

"I'm optimistic about the future. I'm excited about our prospects as a nation … We have an opportunity to have real leadership. America's going to have that kind of leadership and continue to promote principles of peace that'll make the world a safer place and make people in this country more confident that their future is secure."
—Gov. Romney, in the third presidential debate Oct. 22 at Lynn Univ. in Boca Raton, FL.

"You mentioned the Navy, for example, and that we have fewer ships than we did in 1916. Well, governor, we also have fewer horses and bayonets, because the nature of our military's changed ... And so the question is not a game of Battleship where we're counting ships, it's what are our capabilities."
—Pres. Obama, in the third presidential debate, Oct. 22.

Electoral and Popular Vote, 2008 and 2012

Source: © Associated Press; all rights reserved. 2012 results are preliminary as of Nov. 7, 2012. 2008 results, Federal Election Commission.

State	2012 Electoral vote Obama	Romney	2012 Popular vote Obama	Romney	Johnson[1]	2008 Electoral vote Obama	McCain	2008 Popular vote Obama	McCain	Nader[2]	State
AL	0	9	787,027	1,245,221	12,242	0	9	813,479	1,266,546	6,788	AL
AK	0	3	90,743	120,329	5,485	0	3	123,594	193,841	3,783	AK
AZ	0	11	712,868	902,631	20,738	0	10	1,034,707	1,230,111	11,301	AZ
AR	0	6	390,002	639,561	16,019	0	6	422,310	638,017	12,882	AR
CA	55	0	5,573,450	3,635,571	98,615	55	0	8,274,473	5,011,781	108,381	CA
CO	9	0	1,230,730	1,119,535	31,991	9	0	1,288,633	1,073,629	13,352	CO
CT	7	0	831,946	586,871	11,739	7	0	997,772	629,428	19,162	CT
DE	3	0	242,547	165,476	3,882	3	0	255,459	152,374	2,401	DE
DC	3	0	222,332	17,337	1,634	3	0	245,800	17,367	958	DC
FL	29	0	4,137,844	4,091,414	43,563	27	0	4,282,074	4,045,624	28,124	FL
GA	0	16	1,745,283	2,054,373	44,795	0	15	1,844,123	2,048,759	1,158	GA
HI	4	0	303,090	119,494	3,789	4	0	325,871	120,566	3,825	HI
ID	0	4	209,811	416,248	9,319	0	4	236,440	403,012	7,175	ID
IL	20	0	2,912,972	2,087,557	54,740	21	0	3,419,348	2,031,179	30,948	IL
IN	0	11	1,135,976	1,408,885	49,473	11	0	1,374,039	1,345,648	909	IN
IA	6	0	816,174	727,545	12,820	7	0	828,940	682,379	8,014	IA
KS	0	6	426,352	674,598	19,779	0	6	514,765	699,655	10,527	KS
KY	0	8	679,105	1,086,250	16,770	0	8	751,985	1,048,462	15,378	KY
LA	0	8	781,733	1,149,054	17,975	0	9	782,989	1,148,275	6,997	LA
ME	4	0	335,333	239,892	11,969	4	0	421,923	295,273	10,636	ME
MD	10	0	1,480,976	894,718	27,318	10	0	1,629,467	959,862	14,713	MD
MA	11	0	1,874,661	1,153,542	30,012	12	0	1,904,097	1,108,854	28,841	MA
MI	16	0	2,457,846	2,079,268	—	17	0	2,872,579	2,048,639	33,085	MI
MN	10	0	1,543,093	1,321,150	35,042	10	0	1,573,354	1,275,409	30,152	MN
MS	0	6	521,052	661,064	6,328	0	6	554,662	724,597	4,011	MS
MO	0	10	1,215,031	1,478,961	43,029	0	11	1,441,911	1,445,814	17,813	MO
MT	0	3	185,312	242,360	12,739	0	3	231,667	242,763	3,686	MT
NE[3]	0	5	289,154	462,972	10,610	1	4	333,319	452,979	5,406	NE[3]
NV	6	0	528,801	462,422	10,895	5	0	533,736	412,827	6,150	NV
NH	4	0	359,594	319,887	8,130	4	0	384,826	316,534	3,503	NH
NJ	14	0	1,916,190	1,356,792	19,202	15	0	2,215,422	1,613,207	21,298	NJ
NM	5	0	407,111	330,863	27,244	5	0	472,422	346,832	5,327	NM
NY	29	0	3,860,144	2,210,485	42,100	31	0	4,804,945	2,752,771	41,249	NY
NC	0	15	2,175,670	2,272,506	44,736	15	0	2,142,651	2,128,474	1,448	NC
ND	0	3	124,490	187,586	5,213	0	3	141,278	168,601	4,189	ND
OH	18	0	2,672,302	2,571,539	48,672	20	0	2,940,044	2,677,820	42,337	OH
OK	0	7	442,647	889,372	—	0	7	502,496	960,165	—	OK
OR	7	0	783,020	646,236	18,276	7	0	1,037,291	738,475	18,614	OR
PA	20	0	2,894,079	2,610,385	48,637	21	0	3,276,363	2,655,885	42,977	PA
RI	4	0	262,464	146,295	4,162	4	0	296,571	165,391	4,829	RI
SC	0	9	800,704	1,006,808	15,502	0	8	862,449	1,034,896	5,053	SC
SD	0	3	144,983	210,539	5,795	0	3	170,924	203,054	4,267	SD
TN	0	11	951,406	1,450,595	18,506	0	11	1,087,437	1,479,178	11,560	TN
TX	0	38	3,294,440	4,555,799	88,110	0	34	3,528,633	4,479,328	5,751	TX
UT	0	6	229,271	670,394	11,067	0	5	327,670	596,030	8,416	UT
VT	3	0	192,272	89,530	3,342	3	0	219,262	98,974	3,339	VT
VA	13	0	1,854,723	1,747,386	30,021	13	0	1,959,532	1,725,005	11,483	VA
WA	12	0	1,062,561	822,611	20,117	11	0	1,750,848	1,229,216	29,489	WA
WV	0	5	234,985	412,406	6,204	0	5	303,857	397,466	7,219	WV
WI	10	0	1,603,185	1,403,038	20,189	10	0	1,677,211	1,262,393	17,605	WI
WY	0	3	68,779	170,259	5,302	0	3	82,868	164,958	2,525	WY
Total	**332**	**206**	**59,989,422**	**57,319,405**	**1,153,783**	**365**	**173**	**69,498,516**	**59,948,323**	**739,034**	**Total**

— = Not listed on state's ballot. (1) Former New Mexico Gov. Gary Johnson (Libertarian). (2) Consumer advocate and political activist Ralph Nader (independent). (3) Nebraska is one of two states (the other is Maine) that may split its electoral votes between candidates.

Candidates' Closing Remarks

"And tonight, despite all the hardship we've been through, despite all the frustrations of Washington, I've never been more hopeful about our future. I have never been more hopeful about America. And I ask you to sustain that hope. I'm not talking about blind optimism, the kind of hope that just ignores the enormity of the tasks ahead or the roadblocks that stand in our path. I'm not talking about the wishful idealism that allows us to just sit on the sidelines or shirk from a fight. I have always believed that hope is that stubborn thing inside us that insists, despite all the evidence to the contrary, that something better awaits us so long as we have the courage to keep reaching, to keep working, to keep fighting.

"America, I believe we can build on the progress we've made and continue to fight for new jobs and new opportunity and new security for the middle class. I believe we can keep the promise of our founding, the idea that if you're willing to work hard, it doesn't matter who you are or where you come from or what you look like or where you love. It doesn't matter whether you're black or white or Hispanic or Asian or Native American or young or old or rich or poor, able, disabled, gay or straight, you can make it here in America if you're willing to try.

"I believe we can seize this future together because we are not as divided as our politics suggests. We're not as cynical as the pundits believe. We are greater than the sum of our individual ambitions, and we remain more than a collection of red states and blue states. We are and forever will be the United States of America. And together with your help and God's grace we will continue our journey forward and remind the world just why it is that we live in the greatest nation on Earth."
—Pres. Barack Obama, Chicago, IL, Nov. 7, 2012

"The nation, as you know, is at a critical point. At a time like this, we can't risk partisan bickering and political posturing. Our leaders have to reach across the aisle to do the people's work. And we citizens also have to rise to the occasion.

"We look to our teachers and professors. We count on you not just to teach, but to inspire our children with a passion for learning and discovery. We look to our pastors and priests and rabbis and counselors of all kinds to testify of the enduring principles upon which our society is built: honesty, charity, integrity, and family. We look to our parents, for in the final analysis everything depends on the success of our homes. We look to job creators of all kinds. We're counting on you to invest, to hire, to step forward. And we look to Democrats and Republicans in government at all levels to put the people before the politics.

"I believe in America. I believe in the people of America. And I ran for office because I'm concerned about America. This election is over, but our principles endure. I believe that the principles upon which this nation was founded are the only sure guide to a resurgent economy and to renewed greatness."
—Former Gov. Mitt Romney, Boston, MA, Nov. 7, 2012

Electoral Votes for President, 2012

Electoral votes based on the 2010 Census were in force beginning with the 2012 elections.

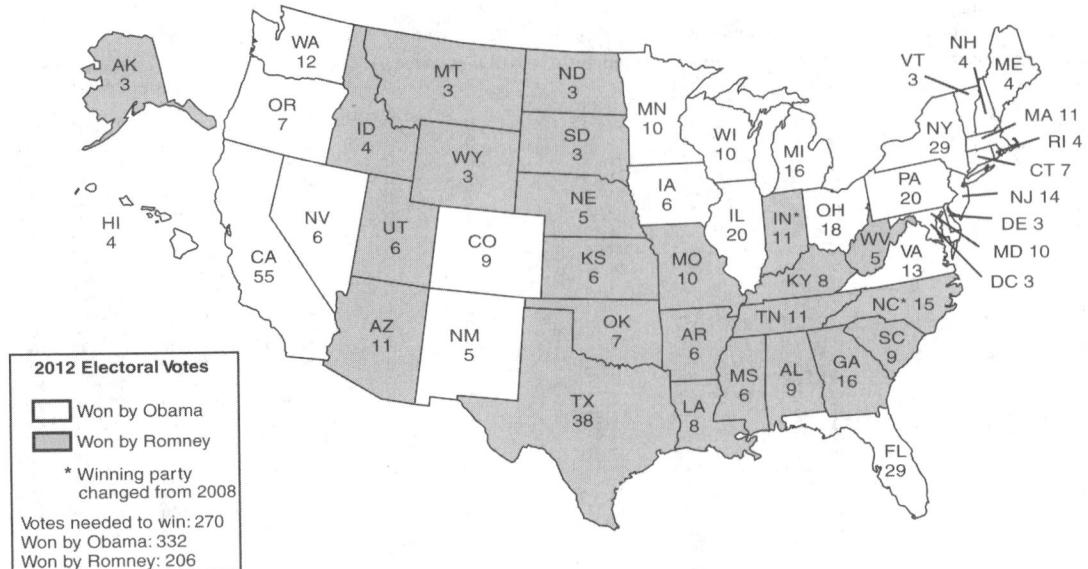

2012 Electoral Votes

☐ Won by Obama
▨ Won by Romney

* Winning party
changed from 2008

Votes needed to win: 270
Won by Obama: 332
Won by Romney: 206

Democratic Nominees

For President: Barack Obama

Born: Barack Hussein Obama, Aug. 4, 1961, Honolulu, HI. **Education:** BA, Columbia Univ., 1983; JD, Harvard Univ., 1991. **Career:** research assistant, Business Intl. Corp., NYC, 1983-84; community organizer, Chicago, 1985-88; lecturer, Univ. of Chicago Law School, 1992-2004; associate, then partner, Davis, Miner, Barnhill & Galland, Chicago, 1993-2004; Illinois state senator, 1997-2004; U.S. senator (D, IL), 2005-08; U.S. president, 2009-present. **Net worth:** $5.7 mil. **Religion:** Protestant. **Family:** married Michelle LaVaughn Robinson (b. 1964), 1992; children: Malia (b. 1998), Natasha (Sasha) (b. 2001).

Obama's father, Barack Obama Sr., a Kenyan economics student, met his mother, Stanley Ann Dunham, an American fellow student, at the Univ. of Hawaii. They married but separated soon after his birth and later divorced. After his mother married an Indonesian man, Obama lived with them in Indonesia from ages 6 to 10; he then lived with his maternal grandparents in Hawaii. Obama attended Occidental Coll. in Los Angeles before completing his degree at Columbia Univ. in New York. After working as a community organizer in Chicago, he went to Harvard Law School, becoming the first African-American president of the *Harvard Law Review*.

While a lecturer at the Univ. of Chicago Law School, Obama wrote a memoir, *Dreams From My Father: A Story of Race and Inheritance* (1995). He served eight years as an Illinois state senator. Obama lost a primary race for a U.S. House seat in 2000 but won the Democratic primary for U.S. Senate in 2004. After a stirring keynote address at that year's Democratic National Convention, he easily defeated his conservative Republican opponent in Nov. to become the Senate's only African-American member. He wrote a second book, *The Audacity of Hope: Thoughts on Reclaiming the American Dream* (2006).

Campaigning for the 2008 Democratic presidential nomination, Obama stressed his opposition to the Iraq war and determination to change Washington. He pulled ahead of Sen. Hillary Clinton (NY) to win the nomination. The economic crisis dominated the fall campaign. He took 53% of the popular vote, defeating Sen. John McCain (R, AZ) to become the first African-American president.

Obama's administration won passage in Feb. 2009 of a $787-bil stimulus package. The economy began to grow slowly, but unemployment rose, peaking at 10% in Oct. 2009. In Mar. 2010, Obama won passage of a controversial health-care reform bill (nicknamed "Obamacare"), which sought to expand coverage to the uninsured. The Dodd-Frank financial reform bill, aimed at changing regulations blamed for the 2007-09 recession, was enacted in July 2010. Obama took a conciliatory tone in foreign policy, as in a June 2009 speech in Cairo, calling for a "new beginning" in relations with the Muslim world, and received the 2009 Nobel Peace Prize. Over the next two years he gradually ended the presence of U.S. combat troops in Iraq while increasing, then reducing, U.S. troop strength in Afghanistan.

Following Nov. 2010 elections, Democrats lost their majority in the House and saw it reduced in the Senate. During the ensuing lame-duck session, Obama compromised with Republicans on an $858-bil spending plan that temporarily kept all Bush-era tax cuts while extending unemployment benefits and reducing the payroll tax. The bipartisan Simpson-Bowles commission, formed by the president, released a $4-tril deficit reduction plan in Dec. 2010, calling for steep entitlement and other spending cuts along with tax increases. Obama instead outlined a plan calling for no entitlement cuts and higher taxes on the wealthy. In summer 2011, a battle in Congress over raising the federal debt ceiling left the government threatened with default. A last-minute compromise raised the debt ceiling with compensating spending cuts, more than half of which were left to a bipartisan congressional committee. It deadlocked, leaving a "fiscal cliff" of automatic cuts in domestic programs and defense slated to go into effect in 2013.

As the Arab Spring uprisings unfolded, the U.S. joined in air strikes in Libya with the stated aim of protecting civilians, but resisted material involvement in the Syrian civil war and in other troubled nations. The killing of al-Qaeda leader Osama bin Laden in Pakistan in a May 2011 Navy SEAL operation proved to be a major achievement. Many other known or suspected terrorists were killed in U.S. drone attacks. But the fatal Sept. 11, 2012, terrorist attack on the U.S. consulate in Benghazi, Libya, along with Iran's nuclear development program and apparent tensions with Israel, brought criticism.

Republican presidential nominee Mitt Romney blamed Obama for continued high unemployment, trillion-dollar deficits, and "trickle-down" big-government economics. After losing traction in a first debate with Romney, Obama campaigned forcefully on several themes. He blamed the recession on failed Republican policy, defended the recovery as progressing well despite Republican obstruction in Congress, and faulted Romney's policies as favoring the rich at the expense of the middle class. Obama also highlighted concern for so-called women's issues, including access to abortion and insurance coverage for contraception.

For Vice President: Joe Biden

Born: Joseph Robinette Biden Jr., Nov. 20, 1942, Scranton, PA. **Education:** BA, Univ. of Delaware, 1965; JD, Syracuse Univ., 1968. **Career:** attorney/public defender, Wilmington, DE, 1969-72; member, New Castle County Council, 1970-72; U.S. senator (D, DE), 1973-2009; chair, Senate Judiciary Committee, 1987-95; chair, Foreign Relations Committee, 2001-03, 2007-09; contender for Dem. presidential nomination, 1988, 2008; U.S. vice president, 2009-present. **Net worth:** between –$1.2 mil and $191,000. **Religion:** Roman Catholic. **Family:** married Neilia Hunter (1942-72), 1966; children: Beau (b. 1969), Hunter (b. 1970), Naomi (1971-72); married Jill Tracy Jacobs (b. 1951), 1977; children: Ashley (b. 1981).

Biden was the oldest of four children in a working-class household. He went to law school, married as a student, and then practiced law while becoming active in the Democratic Party. In Nov. 1972, Biden won a U.S. Senate seat in an upset victory over the Republican incumbent. The following month, his wife and infant daughter were killed, and their two sons injured, in a car crash. Biden remarried in 1977.

In the Senate, Biden focused on foreign policy, judicial affairs, and criminal justice. As chairman of the Judiciary Committee, he presided over contentious Supreme Court nomination hearings that ended in the defeat of Robert Bork's nomination (1987) and in Clarence Thomas's confirmation (1991). He ran for the 1988 Democratic presidential nomination but withdrew, damaged by charges he had plagiarized parts of a speech. The following year he made a full recovery after emergency brain surgery.

Biden initially voted (2002) for use of force in Iraq, but later criticized the Bush administration's Iraq war policy. His son Beau

Biden became attorney general of Delaware in 2007 and was deployed to Iraq with the Delaware National Guard in 2008. Biden published a memoir, *Promises to Keep: On Life and Politics* (2007). He ran again for the party's presidential nomination in 2008 but dropped out after a poor finish in the Iowa caucus. Obama selected him as his running mate. As vice president, the sometimes-contrarian presidential adviser chaired a White House Task Force on Working Families, made frequent visits to Iraq, and served as a liaison to Congress. He played a key role in negotiations to resolve the federal debt crisis in 2011.

Known for his loquaciousness and occasional gaffes, Biden was nevertheless an effective campaigner. He gave a spirited defense of the administration at the 2012 Democratic National Convention and waged a strong attack on the Republican ticket in his debate Oct. 11 with GOP counterpart Paul Ryan, though some thought his effectiveness was undermined by a mocking attitude.

Republican Nominees

For President: Mitt Romney

Born: Willard Mitt Romney, Mar. 12, 1947, Detroit, MI. **Education:** BA, Brigham Young Univ., 1971; MBA, Harvard Business School, 1975; JD, Harvard Law School, 1975. **Career:** vice president, Bain & Co. consulting firm, 1978-84, CEO, 1991-92; founder and CEO, Bain Capital, 1984-2001; CEO, organizing committee, 2002 Olympic Games, Salt Lake City; Massachusetts governor, 2003-07; chair, Republican Governors' Assn., 2006; contender for Republican presidential nomination, 2008. **Net worth:** $230 mil. **Religion:** Mormon. **Family:** married Ann Lois Davies (b. 1949), 1969; children: Taggart (b. 1970), Matthew (b. 1971), Joshua (b. 1975), Benjamin (b. 1978), Craig (b. 1981).

Mitt Romney was the youngest of four children. His father, auto executive George Romney, was governor of Michigan (1963-69) and an unsuccessful contender for the 1968 Republican presidential nomination. His mother, Lenore LaFount Romney, ran unsuccessfully for a Senate seat in 1970. Romney began his undergraduate work at Stanford Univ. but left to serve for two years as a Mormon missionary in France. He married and finished college at Brigham Young Univ. before earning advanced degrees from Harvard. Afterward, he worked in management consulting in Boston. In 1984, after serving as vice president of Bain & Co., he cofounded a lucrative investment and venture capital firm, Bain Capital. He took a break from the firm to oversee a major restructuring at Bain & Co.

In 1994, Romney ran for a U.S. Senate seat from Massachusetts but lost to incumbent Sen. Ted Kennedy (D). As head of the organizing committee for the 2002 Winter Olympics in Salt Lake City, UT, which had been mired in an ethics scandal and deficits, he was credited with its successful turnaround. Courted by Massachusetts Republican officials, he ran unopposed for the gubernatorial nomination after the unpopular acting governor dropped out of the race; he went on to win in Nov. 2002. The Romney administration closed a $3 bil budget gap without income or sales tax increases. He claimed credit for rescuing the state's economy and led a bipartisan effort to reform the state's health care system, extending health insurance to almost all residents.

In Feb. 2007, Romney announced his candidacy for the 2008 Republican presidential nomination. Critics from the right objected to less conservative positions he had taken on issues such as abortion and gun control, as well as his health care plan in Massachusetts. Though he was considered a front-runner, he dropped out after losses in early primaries. Romney declared his candidacy for the party's 2012 presidential nomination in June 2011, citing his business and government experience. He vowed to repeal "Obamacare," arguing in part that health care reform should be determined at the state level. Competing with a large field of generally more conservative rivals, whom he outspent, Romney was accused of flip-flopping on issues to appear more conservative, but he clinched the nomination by May 2012.

Democrats faulted Romney's business experience as being focused on profits, not job creation, and depicted him as the candidate of the rich. This impression was reinforced by a video of a speech to wealthy donors, leaked in Sept. 2012, in which he appeared to dismiss 47% of Americans as looking for handouts from big government. Romney vowed to create 12 mil jobs through a 5-point plan stressing energy independence, trade promotion, education improvement, debt and deficit reduction, and reforms to aid small business, especially through reducing regulations and cutting tax rates.

Romney's campaign was lifted by a vigorous performance in his first debate with Obama: He blasted Obama's record while taking relatively centrist stands on some issues. He vowed not to support legislation that would increase taxes for the middle class or add to deficits. Democrats argued that Rom-

ney's program would benefit the rich and accused Romney of participating in a "war on women" with his stands on abortion and mandated insurance coverage for contraceptives. Romney initially questioned the administration's preparedness for and response to the Sept. 11, 2012, attack on the U.S. consulate in Benghazi, Libya. In the last presidential debate, on foreign policy, he attacked Obama's leadership but did not renew the Libya criticism.

For Vice President: Paul Ryan

Born: Paul Davis Ryan, Jan. 29, 1970, Janesville, WI. **Education:** BA, Miami Univ. of Ohio, 1992. **Career:** aide to Sen. Robert Kasten (R, WI), 1992; speechwriter/analyst, Empower America, 1993-95; legislative director for Sen. Sam Brownback (R, KS), 1995-97; U.S. representative (R, WI), 1999-present; chair, House Budget Committee, 2011-present. **Net worth:** $2.0-$7.7 mil. **Religion:** Roman Catholic. **Family:** married Janna Christine Little (b. 1969), 2000; children: Elizabeth (b. 2002), Charles (b. 2003), Samuel (b. 2004).

Paul Ryan was the youngest of four children born into a family with a long history in Janesville, WI. His great-grandfather started an earth-moving business there in 1884. Family members say Ryan became more serious and determined after his father died of a heart attack when he was 16. With the help of social security survivors benefits, he went to college, earning a degree in political science and economics. After working as a congressional aide, he took a job with conservative think tank Empower America and became a protégé of former HUD secretary and Rep. Jack Kemp (NY), a champion of so-called supply side economics, who was the Republican nominee for vice president in 1996. Ryan wrote speeches for Kemp and shared his belief that low taxes and small government were the keys to economic growth. Ryan has also cited the influence of author Ayn Rand, whose philosophy exalts individualism and free-market capitalism.

In 1998, Ryan won an open seat in Congress to become, at age 28, the second-youngest House member. He repeatedly won reelection by wide margins and devoted himself to budget issues. At the 2004 Republican National Convention, he gave a speech criticizing the tax plans of Democratic presidential nominee Sen. John Kerry (MA). In 2006 he was selected as ranking minority member on the House Budget Committee. Pres. Obama named him in 2010 to the bipartisan Simpson-Bowles commission on budget deficits and debt; he voted against the final report, which proposed a 2-1 mix of spending cuts and tax hikes. His own budget plans, beginning with his 2008 "Roadmap for America's Future," have proposed lower tax rates along with spending and entitlement cuts.

In Jan. 2011, Ryan, now Budget Committee chair, gave the Republican response to Obama's State of the Union address, stressing that the U.S. faced a crushing burden of debt. In Apr. 2011, he unveiled a budget plan that included controversial proposals to convert Medicaid to a program of block grants to states and Medicare to a program of vouchers for seniors to purchase private insurance (Medicare changes going into effect only for those reaching retirement age after 2021). In his 2012 budget plan, Ryan proposed savings of $5.3 tril over 10 years, with a proposal allowing retirees the option of using vouchers to purchase traditional Medicare coverage. Both plans passed the House but not the Democrat-controlled Senate.

In Aug. 2012, Romney named Ryan his running mate. The choice was popular among conservatives lukewarm toward Romney. Many fellow Catholics cited his consistent pro-life credentials, while other Catholics criticized his economic philosophy. Most pundits credited Ryan with an able, if not necessarily winning, performance in his Oct. 11 debate with an aggressive Vice Pres. Biden.

Members of the 113th Congress: Senate

Source: © Associated Press; all rights reserved. 2012 results are preliminary as of Nov. 7, 2012.

53 Democrats, 45 Republicans, 2 independents (who were both expected to caucus with Democrats). Boldface denotes the 2012 election winner. * = Incumbent. Third-party or independent candidates receiving fewer than 10,000 votes are not necessarily listed.

Terms are for 6 years and end Jan. 3 of the year preceding the senator's name in the following table. Annual salary, $174,000; President Pro Tempore, Majority Leader, and Minority Leader, $193,400. To be eligible to serve in the Senate, one must be at least 30 years old, a U.S. citizen for at least 9 years, and a resident of the state from which chosen.

D = Democrat; R = Republican; CP = Constitution Party; DFL = Dem.-Farmer-Labor; I = Independent; IP = Independence Party; LB = Libertarian; NPA = No party affiliation; Unaff. = Unaffiliated.

Term ends	Senator/candidate (party); service from[1]	2012 election results
Alabama		
2015	Jeff Sessions (R); 1/7/1997	
2017	Richard Shelby (R); 1/6/1987	
Alaska		
2015	Mark Begich (D); 1/6/2009	
2017	Lisa Murkowski (R); 12/20/2002	
Arizona		
2017	John McCain (R); 1/6/1987	
2019	**Jeff Flake (R)**	809,283
	Richard Carmona (D)	725,831
	Marc Victor (LB)	69,837
Arkansas		
2015	Mark Pryor (D); 1/7/2003	
2017	John Boozman (R); 1/5/2011	
California		
2017	Barbara Boxer (D); 1993	
2019	**Dianne Feinstein* (D); 11/10/1992**	5,613,610
	Elizabeth Emken (R)	3,528,510
Colorado		
2015	Mark Udall (D); 1/6/2009	
2017	Michael F. Bennet (D); 1/22/2009	
Connecticut		
2017	Richard Blumenthal (D); 1/5/2011	
2019	**Christopher S. Murphy (D)**	745,519
	Linda E. McMahon (R)	586,375
	Paul Passarelli (LB)	22,831
Delaware		
2015	Christopher Coons (D); 11/15/2010	
2019	**Thomas R. Carper* (D); 2001**	265,374
	Kevin Wade (R)	115,694
	Alexander Pires (Ind. Party of DE)	15,300
Florida		
2017	Marco Rubio (R); 1/5/2011	
2019	**Bill Nelson* (D); 2001**	4,415,463
	Connie Mack (R)	3,393,622
	Bill Gaylor (NPA)	124,090
	Chris Borgia (NPA)	80,182
Georgia		
2015	Saxby Chambliss (R); 1/7/2003	
2017	Johnny Isakson (R); 2005	
Hawaii		
2017	Daniel K. Inouye (D); 1963	
2019	**Mazie K. Hirono (D)**	266,435
	Linda Lingle (R)	159,002
Idaho		
2015	Jim Risch (R); 1/6/2009	
2017	Mike Crapo (R); 1/6/1999	
Illinois		
2015	Richard J. Durbin (D); 1/7/1997	
2017	Mark Kirk (R); 11/29/2010	
Indiana		
2017	Dan Coats (R); 1/5/2011	
2019	**Joe Donnelly (D)**	1,263,644
	Richard E. Mourdock (R)	1,123,872
	Andrew Horning (LB)	145,967
Iowa		
2015	Tom Harkin (D); 1985	
2017	Chuck Grassley (R); 1981	
Kansas		
2015	Pat Roberts (R); 1/7/1997	
2017	Jerry Moran (R); 1/5/2011	
Kentucky		
2015	Mitch McConnell (R); 1985	
2017	Rand Paul (R); 1/5/2011	
Louisiana		
2015	Mary L. Landrieu (D); 1/7/1997	
2017	David Vitter (R); 2005	
Maine		
2015	Susan M. Collins (R); 1/7/1997	
2019	**Angus King (I)**	314,740
	Charles E. Summers Jr. (R)	177,866
	Cynthia Ann Dill (D)	78,325
Maryland		
2017	Barbara Ann Mikulski (D); 1/6/1987	
2019	**Benjamin L. Cardin* (D); 2007**	1,237,336
	Daniel John Bongino (R)	626,351
	S. Rob Sobhani (Unaff.)	389,002
	Dean Ahmad (LB)	27,688
Massachusetts		
2015	John F. Kerry (D); 1/2/1985	
2019	**Elizabeth A. Warren (D)**	1,656,277
	Scott P. Brown* (R)	1,420,528
Michigan		
2015	Carl Levin (D); 1979	
2019	**Debbie Stabenow* (D); 2001**	2,625,394
	Pete Hoekstra (R)	1,733,133
	Scotty Boman (LB)	83,043
	Harley Mikkelson (Green)	27,412
	Richard A. Matkin (U.S. Taxpayers)	25,331
	John Litle (Natural Law)	11,000
Minnesota		
2015	Al Franken (DFL); 7/7/2009	
2019	**Amy Klobuchar* (DFL); 2007**	1,852,002
	Kurt Bills (R)	868,578
	Stephen Williams (IP)	73,539
	Tim Davis (Grassroots)	30,466
	Michael Cavlan (MN Open Progressives)	13,931
Mississippi		
2015	Thad Cochran (R); 12/27/1978	
2019	**Roger F. Wicker* (R); 12/31/2007**	660,289
	Albert N. Gore Jr. (D)	466,442
	Thomas Cramer (CP)	14,229
	Shawn O'Hara (Reform)	12,336
Missouri		
2017	Roy Blunt (R); 1/5/2011	
2019	**Claire McCaskill* (D); 2007**	1,484,683
	W. Todd Akin (R)	1,063,698
	Jonathan Dine (LB)	164,991
Montana		
2015	Max Baucus (D); 12/15/1978	
2019	**Jon Tester* (D); 2007**	216,100
	Denny Rehberg (R)	197,736
	Dan Cox (LB)	28,648
Nebraska		
2015	Mike Johanns (R); 1/6/2009	
2019	**Deb Fischer (R)**	444,319
	Bob Kerrey (D)	318,930
Nevada		
2017	Harry Reid (D); 1/6/1987	
2019	**Dean Heller* (R); 5/9/2011**	456,471
	Shelley Berkley (D)	444,337
	David Lory Van Der Beek (Independent American)	48,544
	None of these candidates	44,892
New Hampshire		
2015	Jeanne Shaheen (D); 1/6/2009	
2017	Kelly Ayotte (R); 1/5/2011	

Term ends	Senator/candidate (party); service from[1]	2012 election results
New Jersey		
2015	Frank Lautenberg (D); 1/7/2003	
2019	**Robert Menendez* (D); 1/18/2006**	**1,785,499**
	Joe Kyrillos (R)	1,221,012
	Kenneth R. Kaplan (LB)	14,816
	Ken Wolski (Green)	14,088
New Mexico		
2015	Tom Udall (D); 1/6/2009	
2019	**Martin Heinrich (D)**	**388,614**
	Heather A. Wilson (R)	346,305
	Jon R. Barrie (Independent American)	27,649
New York		
2017	Charles E. Schumer (D); 1/6/1999	
2019	**Kirsten E. Gillibrand* (D); 1/27/2009**	**4,168,017**
	Wendy Long (R)	1,534,532
	Colia Clark (Green)	36,070
	Chris Edes (LB)	27,753
	John Mangelli (Common Sense)	19,864
North Carolina		
2015	Kay Hagan (D); 1/6/2009	
2017	Richard Burr (R); 2005	
North Dakota		
2017	John Hoeven (R); 1/5/2011	
2019	**Heidi Heitkamp (D)**	**160,752**
	Rick Berg (R)	157,758
Ohio		
2017	Rob Portman (R); 1/5/2011	
2019	**Sherrod Brown* (D); 2007**	**2,621,380**
	Josh Mandel (R)	2,351,136
	Scott A. Rupert (I)	238,548
Oklahoma		
2015	James M. Inhofe (R); 11/21/1994	
2017	Tom Coburn (R); 2005	
Oregon		
2015	Jeff Merkley (D); 1/6/2009	
2017	Ron Wyden (D); 2/6/1996	
Pennsylvania		
2017	Pat Toomey (R); 1/5/2011	
2019	**Bob Casey Jr.* (D); 2007**	**2,930,117**
	Tom Smith (R)	2,445,789
	Rayburn Douglas Smith (LB)	94,261
Rhode Island		
2015	John F. Reed (D); 1/7/1997	
2019	**Sheldon Whitehouse* (D); 2007**	**253,693**
	Benjamin Barrett Hinckley III (R)	136,297
South Carolina		
2015	Lindsey Graham (R); 1/7/2003	
2017	Jim DeMint (R); 2005	

(1) Jan. 3, unless otherwise noted.

Term ends	Senator/candidate (party); service from[1]	2012 election results
South Dakota		
2015	Tim Johnson (D); 1/7/1997	
2017	John Thune (R); 2005	
Tennessee		
2015	Lamar Alexander (R); 1/7/2003	
2019	**Bob Corker* (R); 2007**	**1,494,230**
	Mark E. Clayton (D)	699,493
	Martin Pleasant (Green)	37,925
	Shaun E. Crowell (I)	20,796
	Kermit Steck (CP)	18,467
Texas		
2015	John Cornyn (R); 12/2/2002	
2019	**Ted Cruz (R)**	**4,456,599**
	Paul Sadler (D)	3,183,314
	John Jay Myers (LB)	161,462
	David B. Collins (Green)	67,791
Utah		
2017	Mike Lee (R); 1/5/2011	
2019	**Orrin G. Hatch* (R); 1977**	**594,796**
	Scott Howell (D)	275,592
	Shaun Lynn McCausland (CP)	28,302
Vermont		
2017	Patrick Leahy (D); 1975	
2019	**Bernard Sanders* (I); 2007**	**200,545**
	John MacGovern (R)	70,107
Virginia		
2015	Mark Warner (D); 1/6/2009	
2019	**Timothy M. Kaine (D)**	**1,886,993**
	George F. Allen (R)	1,715,298
Washington		
2017	Patty Murray (D); 1993	
2019	**Maria Cantwell* (D); 2001**	**1,129,609**
	Michael Baumgartner (R)	771,757
West Virginia		
2015	John D. "Jay" Rockefeller IV (D); 1/15/1985	
2019	**Joe Manchin III* (D); 11/15/2010**	**394,532**
	John R. Raese (R)	237,825
	Bob Henry Baber (Mountain)	19,231
Wisconsin		
2017	Ron Johnson (R); 1/5/2011	
2019	**Tammy Baldwin (D)**	**1,533,868**
	Tommy G. Thompson (R)	1,370,664
	Joseph Kexel (LB)	61,677
	Nimrod Y. U. Allen III (I)	16,240
Wyoming		
2015	Michael B. Enzi (R); 1/7/1997	
2019	**John Barrasso* (R); 6/22/2007**	**184,523**
	Tim Chesnut (D)	52,595

Members of the 113th Congress: The House of Representatives

Source: © Associated Press; all rights reserved. 2012 results are preliminary as of Nov. 7, 2012.

233 Republicans, 194 Democrats. Results in 8 races were still pending and are listed in italic. Boldface denotes the 2012 election winner. * = Incumbent. ** = Incumbent running in a different district. Third-party or independent candidates receiving fewer than 10,000 votes are not necessarily listed.

Terms are for 2 years ending Jan. 3, 2015. Annual salary, $174,000; Majority Leader and Minority Leader, $196,400; Speaker of the House, $223,500. To be eligible for membership, a person must be at least 25 years of age, a U.S. citizen for at least 7 years, and a resident of the state from which chosen.

D = Democrat; R = Republican; Amer. Const. = American Constitution; Amer. Ind. = American Independent Party; CP = Constitution Party; DFL = Dem.-Farmer-Labor; I = Independent; IP = Independence Party; LB = Libertarian; NPA = No party affiliation; NPD = No party designation; Prog. = Progressive; Unaff. = Unaffiliated.

Dist.	Representative/candidate (party)	2012 election results
Alabama		
1	**Jo Bonner* (R)**	**Unopposed**
2	**Martha Roby* (R)**	**180,339**
	Therese Ford (D)	102,836
3	**Mike Rogers* (R)**	**174,875**
	John Andrew Harris (D)	97,838
4	**Robert B. Aderholt* (R)**	**197,736**
	Daniel H. Boman (D)	69,427
5	**Mo Brooks* (R)**	**188,833**
	Charlie L. Holley (D)	101,504
6	**Spencer Bachus* (R)**	**215,966**
	Penny H. Bailey (D)	86,698
7	**Terri A. Sewell* (D)**	**230,077**
	Don Chamberlain (R)	73,292

Dist.	Representative/candidate (party)	2012 election results
Alaska		
	Don Young* (R)	**140,056**
	Sharon M. Cissna (D)	61,458
	Jim McDermott (LB)	10,951
Arizona		
1	**Ann Kirkpatrick (D)**	**100,443**
	Jonathan Paton (R)	93,939
	Kim Allen (LB)	12,155
2	*Martha McSally (R)*	*110,868*
	Ron Barber** (D)	*109,556*
3	**Raúl M. Grijalva** (D)**	**67,958**
	Gabriela Saucedo Mercer (R)	46,547
4	**Paul A. Gosar** (R)**	**136,079**
	Johnnie Robinson (D)	56,909

Dist.	Representative/candidate (party)	2012 election results
5	**Matt Salmon (R)**	**122,299**
	Spencer Morgan (D)	59,536
6	**David Schweikert** (R)	**124,849**
	Matt Jette (D)	66,529
7	**Ed Pastor** (D)	**60,241**
	Joe Cobb (LB)	15,442
8	**Trent Franks** (R)	**121,897**
	Gene Scharer (D)	65,991
9	*Kyrsten Sinema (D)*	*76,967*
	Vernon B. Parker (R)	*74,866*
	Powell Gammill (LB)	10,293
Arkansas		
1	**Rick Crawford* (R)**	**137,627**
	Scott Ellington (D)	95,233
2	**Tim Griffin* (R)**	**157,978**
	Herb Rule (D)	112,934
3	**Steve Womack* (R)**	**180,183**
	Rebekah J. Kennedy (Green)	39,551
	David Pangrac (LB)	19,257
4	**Tom Cotton (R)**	**152,730**
	Gene Jeffress (D)	94,383
California		
1	**Doug La Malfa (R)**	**126,936**
	Jim Reed (D)	92,728
2	**Jared Huffman (D)**	**159,287**
	Daniel W. Roberts (R)	67,882
3	**John Garamendi** (D)	**96,272**
	Kim Vann (R)	82,587
4	**Tom McClintock* (R)**	**155,165**
	Jack Uppal (D)	98,680
5	**Mike Thompson** (D)	**150,722**
	Randy Loftin (R)	52,817
6	**Doris O. Matsui** (D)	**100,579**
	Joseph McCray Sr. (R)	34,652
7	*Ami Bera (D)*	*88,406*
	*Dan Lungren** (R)*	*88,222*
8	**Paul Cook (R)**	**82,653**
	Gregg Imus (R)	60,732
9	**Jerry McNerney** (D)	**85,352**
	Ricky Gill (R)	72,340
10	**Jeff Denham** (R)	**80,885**
	Jose Hernandez (D)	69,336
11	**George Miller** (D)	**152,690**
	Virginia Fuller (R)	68,160
12	**Nancy Pelosi** (D)	**181,821**
	John Dennis (R)	32,809
13	**Barbara Lee** (D)	**161,302**
	Marilyn M. Singleton (NPD)	25,741
14	**Jackie Speier** (D)	**143,224**
	Debbie Bacigalupi (R)	50,983
15	**Eric Swalwell (D)**	**85,580**
	Fortney Pete Stark** (D)	75,669
16	**Jim Costa** (D)	**57,378**
	Brian Daniel Whelan (R)	47,964
17	**Mike Honda** (D)	**108,745**
	Evelyn Li (R)	39,835
18	**Anna G. Eshoo** (D)	**146,994**
	Dave Chapman (R)	63,211
19	**Zoe Lofgren** (D)	**107,414**
	Robert Murray (R)	40,897
20	**Sam Farr** (D)	**110,960**
	Jeff Taylor (R)	41,266
21	**David G. Valadao (R)**	**49,205**
	John Hernandez (D)	32,967
22	**Devin Nunes** (R)	**90,463**
	Otto Lee (D)	52,941
23	**Kevin McCarthy** (R)	**122,325**
	Terry Phillips (NPD)	43,386
24	**Lois Capps** (D)	**119,345**
	Abel Maldonado (R)	98,391
25	**Howard P. "Buck" McKeon* (R)**	**98,090**
	Lee C. Rogers (D)	79,597
26	**Julia Brownley (D)**	**105,734**
	Tony Strickland (R)	98,635
27	**Judy Chu** (D)	**115,910**
	Jack Orswell (R)	66,777
28	**Adam B. Schiff** (D)	**140,381**
	Phil Jennerjahn (R)	44,433
29	**Tony Cardenas (D)**	**82,233**
	David R. Hernandez (NPD)	28,564
30	**Brad Sherman** (D)	**109,311**
	Howard L. Berman** (D)	71,420

Dist.	Representative/candidate (party)	2012 election results
31	**Gary G. Miller** (R)	**68,892**
	Bob Dutton (R)	55,940
32	**Grace F. Napolitano** (D)	**94,920**
	David L. Miller (R)	50,297
33	**Henry A. Waxman** (D)	**126,880**
	Bill Bloomfield (NPD)	109,297
34	**Xavier Becerra** (D)	**90,579**
	Stephen C. Smith (R)	15,186
35	**Gloria Negrete McLeod (D)**	**60,866**
	Joe Baca** (D)	48,385
36	**Raul Ruiz (D)**	**83,402**
	Mary Bono Mack** (R)	78,845
37	**Karen Bass** (D)	**152,769**
	Morgan Osborne (R)	23,969
38	**Linda T. Sanchez** (D)	**109,080**
	Benjamin Campos (R)	53,291
39	**Ed Royce** (R)	**113,746**
	Jay Chen (D)	78,822
40	**Lucille Roybal-Allard** (D)	**57,716**
	David Sanchez (D)	39,494
41	**Mark Takano (D)**	**71,135**
	John Tavaglione (R)	55,081
42	**Ken Calvert** (R)	**99,110**
	Michael Williamson (D)	62,409
43	**Maxine Waters** (D)	**104,931**
	Bob Flores (D)	43,598
44	**Janice Hahn** (D)	**75,678**
	Laura Richardson** (D)	50,393
45	**John Campbell** (R)	**136,172**
	Sukhee Kang (D)	92,687
46	**Loretta Sanchez** (D)	**62,944**
	Jerry Hayden (R)	41,194
47	**Alan Lowenthal (D)**	**93,047**
	Gary DeLong (R)	74,952
48	**Dana Rohrabacher** (R)	**139,772**
	Ron Varasteh (D)	86,993
49	**Darrell E. Issa* (R)**	**118,145**
	Jerry Tetalman (D)	82,261
50	**Duncan D. Hunter Jr.** (R)	**125,833**
	David B. Secor (D)	57,978
51	**Juan Vargas (D)**	**74,716**
	Michael Crimmins (R)	32,223
52	*Scott Peters (D)*	*103,878*
	*Brian P. Bilbray** (R)*	*103,193*
53	**Susan A. Davis* (D)**	**111,654**
	Nick Popaditch (R)	73,135
Colorado		
1	**Diana L. DeGette* (D)**	**224,500**
	Danny Stroud (R)	88,955
	Frank Atwood (LB)	11,552
2	**Jared Polis* (D)**	**222,367**
	Kevin Lundberg (R)	153,305
	Randy Luallin (LB)	12,376
3	**Scott R. Tipton* (R)**	**177,285**
	Sal Pace (D)	135,163
	Tisha Casida (Unaff.)	10,237
4	**Cory Gardner* (R)**	**189,753**
	Brandon Shaffer (D)	118,918
5	**Doug Lamborn* (R)**	**189,649**
	Dave Anderson (Unaff.)	50,374
	Jim Pirtle (LB)	21,079
	Misha Luzov (Green)	17,016
	Kenneth R. Harvell (Amer. Const.)	12,151
6	**Mike Coffman* (R)**	**149,179**
	Joe Miklosi (D)	137,637
	Kathy Polhemus (Unaff.)	11,705
7	**Ed Perlmutter* (D)**	**171,874**
	Joe Coors (R)	132,727
Connecticut		
1	**John B. Larson* (D)**	**202,980**
	John Henry Decker (R)	80,747
2	**Joe Courtney* (D)**	**197,940**
	Paul M. Formica (R)	90,970
3	**Rosa L. DeLauro* (D)**	**181,625**
	Wayne Winsley (R)	66,646
4	**Jim Himes* (D)**	**134,559**
	Steve Obsitnik (R)	94,078
5	**Elizabeth Esty (D)**	**141,236**
	Andrew Roraback (R)	131,478
Delaware		
	John C. Carney Jr.* (D)	**249,905**
	Thomas H. Kovach (R)	129,749

Dist.	Representative/candidate (party)	2012 election results
Florida		
1	**Jeff Miller* (R)**	**237,361**
	Jim Bryan (D)	92,422
	Calen Fretts (LB)	11,087
2	**Steve Southerland II* (R)**	**174,957**
	Al Lawson (D)	156,290
3	**Ted Yoho (R)**	**203,795**
	J. R. Gaillot (D)	101,980
4	**Ander Crenshaw* (R)**	**235,942**
	Jim Klauder (NPA)	73,791
5	**Corrine Brown** (D)**	**187,457**
	LeAnne Kolb (R)	69,874
6	**Ron DeSantis (R)**	**195,596**
	Heather Beaven (D)	146,053
7	**John L. Mica* (R)**	**184,001**
	Jason H. Kendall (D)	128,469
8	**Bill Posey** (R)**	**202,475**
	Shannon Roberts (D)	128,714
	Richard Gillmor (NPA)	12,397
9	**Alan Grayson (D)**	**163,372**
	Todd Long (R)	98,060
10	**Daniel Webster** (R)**	**163,482**
	Val B. Demings (D)	152,188
11	**Richard B. Nugent** (R)**	**218,065**
	H. David Werder (D)	120,066
12	**Gus M. Bilirakis** (R)**	**207,745**
	Jonathan Michael Snow (D)	107,714
13	**C. W. Bill Young** (R)**	**185,867**
	Jessica Ehrlich (D)	136,472
14	**Kathy Castor** (D)**	**193,407**
	Evelio Otero (R)	82,061
15	**Dennis A. Ross** (R)**	**Unopposed**
16	**Vern Buchanan** (R)**	**186,743**
	Keith Fitzgerald (D)	161,349
17	**Tom Rooney** (R)**	**164,747**
	William Bronson (D)	115,986
18	*Patrick Murphy (D)*	*160,328*
	*Allen B. West** (R)*	*157,872*
19	**Trey Radel (R)**	**189,291**
	Jim Roach (D)	109,226
20	**Alcee L. Hastings** (D)**	**203,401**
	Randall Terry (NPA)	27,833
21	**Ted Deutch** (D)**	**207,898**
	Michael Trout (NPA)	35,601
	Cesar Henao (NPA)	23,934
22	**Lois Frankel (D)**	**160,617**
	Adam Hasner (R)	133,608
23	**Debbie Wasserman Schultz** (D)**	**166,548**
	Karen Harrington (R)	93,713
24	**Frederica S. Wilson** (D)**	**Unopposed**
25	**Mario Diaz-Balart** (R)**	**145,778**
	Stanley Blumenthal (NPA)	30,627
	VoteForEddie.com (NPA)	16,443
26	**Joe Garcia (D)**	**127,688**
	David Rivera** (R)	101,606
27	**Ileana Ros-Lehtinen** (R)**	**128,280**
	Manny Yevancey (D)	80,377
Georgia		
1	**Jack Kingston* (R)**	**153,791**
	Lesli Rae Messinger (D)	89,467
2	**Sanford D. Bishop Jr.* (D)**	**159,725**
	John House (R)	90,208
3	**Lynn A. Westmoreland* (R)**	**Unopposed**
4	**Henry "Hank" Johnson* (D)**	**208,395**
	J. Chris Vaughn (R)	74,909
5	**John Lewis* (D)**	**224,745**
	Howard Stopeck (R)	40,988
6	**Tom Price* (R)**	**182,371**
	Jeff Kazanow (D)	101,057
7	**Rob Woodall* (R)**	**156,484**
	Steve Reilly (D)	95,056
8	**Austin Scott* (R)**	**Unopposed**
9	**Doug Collins (R)**	**190,456**
	Jody Cooley (D)	59,449
10	**Paul C. Broun* (R)**	**Unopposed**
11	**Phil Gingrey* (R)**	**195,445**
	Patrick Thompson (D)	89,429
12	**John Barrow* (D)**	**138,965**
	Lee Anderson (R)	119,857
13	**David Scott* (D)**	**198,532**
	Shalid Malik (R)	78,370
14	**Tom Graves** (R)**	**159,698**
	Daniel Grant (D)	59,098

Dist.	Representative/candidate (party)	2012 election results
Hawaii		
1	**Colleen W. Hanabusa* (D)**	**114,756**
	Charles K. Djou (R)	95,431
2	**Tulsi Gabbard (D)**	**167,085**
	Kawika Crowley (R)	40,285
Idaho		
1	**Raul R. Labrador* (R)**	**195,264**
	Jimmy Farris (D)	94,850
	Rob Oates (LB)	11,935
2	**Mike Simpson* (R)**	**207,244**
	Nicole LeFavour (D)	110,817
Illinois		
1	**Bobby L. Rush* (D)**	**224,275**
	Donald E. Peloquin (R)	79,325
2	**Jesse Jackson Jr.* (D)**	**180,704**
	Brian Woodworth (R)	67,295
	Marcus Lewis (I)	38,658
3	**Daniel Lipinski* (D)**	**157,668**
	Richard L. Grabowski (R)	71,501
4	**Luis V. Gutierrez* (D)**	**129,165**
	Hector Concepcion (R)	26,170
5	**Mike Quigley* (D)**	**168,439**
	Dan Schmitt (R)	73,823
	Nancy Wade (Green)	14,549
6	**Peter J. Roskam* (R)**	**191,065**
	Leslie Coolidge (D)	131,410
7	**Danny K. Davis* (D)**	**228,531**
	Rita Zak (R)	29,329
	John Monaghan (I)	11,927
8	**Tammy Duckworth (D)**	**120,774**
	Joe Walsh* (R)	99,922
9	**Janice D. Schakowsky* (D)**	**184,850**
	Timothy C. Wolfe (R)	94,798
10	**Brad Schneider (D)**	**130,676**
	Robert J. Dold* (R)	128,129
11	**Bill Foster (D)**	**130,670**
	Judy Biggert** (R)	95,675
12	**William L. Enyart (D)**	**154,621**
	Jason Plummer (R)	128,582
	Paula Bradshaw (Green)	16,747
13	**Rodney Davis (R)**	**136,596**
	David M. Gill (D)	135,309
	John Hartman (I)	21,241
14	**Randy Hultgren* (R)**	**173,882**
	Dennis Anderson (D)	121,652
15	**John Shimkus** (R)**	**203,500**
	Angela Michael (D)	92,067
16	**Adam Kinzinger** (R)**	**179,123**
	Wanda Rohl (D)	110,378
17	**Cheri Bustos (D)**	**148,229**
	Bobby Schilling* (R)	129,970
18	**Aaron Schock* (R)**	**243,295**
	Steve Waterworth (D)	84,544
Indiana		
1	**Peter J. Visclosky* (D)**	**187,347**
	Joel Phelps (R)	91,072
2	**Jackie Walorski (R)**	**133,804**
	Brendan Mullen (D)	129,968
3	**Marlin A. Stutzman* (R)**	**187,610**
	Kevin R. Boyd (D)	92,179
4	**Todd Rokita* (R)**	**168,510**
	Tara E. Nelson (D)	92,992
	Benjamin Gehlhausen (LB)	10,553
5	**Susan Brooks (R)**	**194,350**
	Scott Reske (D)	125,127
	Chard Reid (LB)	13,420
6	**Luke Messer (R)**	**160,674**
	Bradley T. Bookout (D)	95,848
	Rex Bell (LB)	15,817
7	**André Carson* (D)**	**161,422**
	Carlos A. May (R)	95,521
8	**Larry Bucshon* (R)**	**151,416**
	Dave Crooks (D)	122,245
	Bart Gadau (LB)	10,125
9	**Todd C. Young* (R)**	**156,029**
	Shelli Yoder (D)	118,872
Iowa		
1	**Bruce L. Braley* (D)**	**220,795**
	Ben Lange (R)	161,854
2	**David Loebsack* (D)**	**209,551**
	John Archer (R)	160,717
3	**Tom Latham** (R)**	**201,016**
	Leonard Boswell* (D)	167,792
4	**Steve King** (R)**	**197,873**
	Christie Vilsack (D)	165,932

Dist.	Representative/candidate (party)	2012 election results
Kansas		
1	**Tim Huelskamp* (R)**	**Unopposed**
2	**Lynn Jenkins* (R)**	**157,450**
	Tobias Schlingensiepen (D)	108,936
	Dennis Hawver (LB)	11,730
3	**Kevin Yoder* (R)**	**197,266**
	Joel Balam (LB)	90,388
4	**Mike Pompeo* (R)**	**158,212**
	Robert Leon Tillman (D)	79,480
	Thomas Jefferson (LB)	15,587
Kentucky		
1	**Ed Whitfield* (R)**	**200,038**
	Charles Kendall Hatchett (D)	87,094
2	**Brett Guthrie* (R)**	**182,607**
	David Lynn Williams (D)	89,541
3	**John A. Yarmuth* (D)**	**206,368**
	Brooks Wicker (R)	111,446
4	**Thomas Massie (R)**	**185,614**
	William R. Adkins (D)	104,590
5	**Harold "Hal" Rogers* (R)**	**194,111**
	Kenneth S. Stepp (D)	54,166
6	**Garland "Andy" Barr (R)**	**153,348**
	Ben Chandler* (D)	141,496
Louisiana		
1	**Steve Scalise* (R)**	**192,406**
	M. V. "Vinny" Mendoza (D)	61,181
	Gary King (R)	24,677
2	**Cedric L. Richmond* (D)**	**137,444**
	Gary Landrieu (D)	67,385
	Dwayne Bailey (R)	37,442
	Josue Larose (R)	10,816
3	*Charles W. Boustany Jr.** (R)*	*139,113*
	Jeff Landry* (R)	*93,524*
	Ron Richard (D)	67,058
4	**John Fleming* (R)**	**187,783**
	Randall Lord (LB)	61,586
5	**Rodney Alexander* (R)**	**203,483**
	Ron Ceasar (NPA)	37,635
	Clay Steven Grant (LB)	20,519
6	**Bill Cassidy* (R)**	**243,594**
	Rufus Holt Craig Jr. (LB)	32,200
	Richard Torregano (NPA)	31,014
Maine		
1	**Chellie Pingree* (D)**	**203,840**
	Jonathan T. E. Courtney (R)	108,887
2	**Mike Michaud* (D)**	**156,581**
	Kevin L. Raye (R)	111,908
Maryland		
1	**Andy Harris* (R)**	**183,765**
	Wendy Rosen (D)	79,681
	Muir Boda (LB)	11,077
2	**C. A. Dutch Ruppersberger* (D)**	**181,191**
	Nancy C. Jacobs (R)	86,852
3	**John P. Sarbanes* (D)**	**193,993**
	Eric Delano Knowles (R)	87,245
	Paul Drgos (LB)	10,218
4	**Donna F. Edwards* (D)**	**195,067**
	Faith M. Loudon (R)	58,477
5	**Steny H. Hoyer* (D)**	**206,816**
	Tony O'Donnell (R)	119,768
6	**John Delaney (D)**	**164,264**
	Roscoe G. Bartlett* (R)	104,901
7	**Elijah E. Cummings* (D)**	**223,318**
	Frank C. Mirabile (R)	62,515
8	**Chris Van Hollen* (D)**	**180,693**
	Ken Timmerman (R)	80,022
Massachusetts		
1	**Richard E. Neal** (D)**	**Unopposed**
2	**James P. McGovern** (D)**	**Unopposed**
3	**Niki Tsongas** (D)**	**208,342**
	Jonathan A. Golnik (R)	106,574
4	**Joseph P. Kennedy III (D)**	**216,317**
	Sean Bielat (R)	126,754
	David Rosa (I)	10,208
5	**Edward J. Markey** (D)**	**252,895**
	Tom Tierney (R)	81,542
6	**John F. Tierney* (D)**	**179,603**
	Richard R. Tisei (R)	175,953
	Daniel Fishman (LB)	16,668
7	**Michael E. Capuano** (D)**	**206,424**
	Karla Romero (I)	40,438
8	**Stephen F. Lynch** (D)**	**262,565**
	Joe Selvaggi (R)	81,733

Dist.	Representative/candidate (party)	2012 election results
9	**Bill Keating** (D)**	**203,123**
	Christopher Sheldon (R)	108,850
	Daniel Botelho (I)	31,676
Michigan		
1	**Dan Benishek* (R)**	**166,833**
	Gary McDowell (D)	164,536
	Emily Salvette (LB)	10,917
2	**Bill Huizenga* (R)**	**192,430**
	Willie German (D)	107,963
3	**Justin Amash* (R)**	**172,282**
	Steve Pestka (D)	144,122
	Bill Gelineau (LB)	10,483
4	**Dave Camp* (R)**	**196,835**
	Debra Freidell Wirth (D)	104,601
5	**Daniel T. Kildee (D)**	**193,922**
	Jim Slezak (R)	98,289
6	**Fred Upton* (R)**	**163,355**
	Mike O'Brien (D)	122,357
7	**Tim Walberg* (R)**	**169,184**
	Kurt Richard Haskell (D)	136,508
8	**Mike Rogers* (R)**	**202,126**
	Lance Enderle (D)	128,622
9	**Sander M. Levin** (D)**	**208,834**
	Don Volaric (R)	114,746
10	**Candice S. Miller* (R)**	**226,151**
	Chuck Stadler (D)	98,058
11	**Kerry Bentivolio (R)**	**173,581**
	Syed Taj (D)	152,063
12	**John D. Dingell** (D)**	**203,392**
	Cynthia Kallgren (R)	83,272
13	**John Conyers Jr.** (D)**	**206,097**
	Harry T. Sawicki (R)	37,278
14	**Gary C. Peters** (D)**	**252,896**
	John Hauler (R)	50,470
Minnesota		
1	**Tim Walz* (DFL)**	**193,288**
	Allen Quist (R)	142,190
2	**John Kline* (R)**	**193,587**
	Mike Obermueller (DFL)	164,335
3	**Erik Paulsen* (R)**	**222,341**
	Brian Barnes (DFL)	159,941
4	**Betty McCollum* (DFL)**	**216,680**
	Tony Hernandez (R)	109,656
	Steve Carlson (IP)	21,132
5	**Keith Ellison* (DFL)**	**257,295**
	Chris Fields (R)	88,040
6	**Michele Bachmann* (R)**	**180,131**
	Jim Graves (DFL)	175,924
7	**Collin C. Peterson* (DFL)**	**197,736**
	Lee Byberg (R)	114,136
	Adam Steele (IP)	15,298
8	**Richard Nolan (DFL)**	**192,945**
	Chip Cravaack* (R)	161,203
Mississippi		
1	**Alan Nunnelee* (R)**	**176,708**
	Brad Morris (D)	106,121
2	**Bennie G. Thompson* (D)**	**197,771**
	Bill Marcy (R)	89,914
3	**Gregg Harper* (R)**	**218,372**
	John "Luke" Pannell (Reform)	54,976
4	**Steven M. Palazzo* (R)**	**168,666**
	Matthew Moore (D)	75,270
	Ron Williams (LB)	16,824
Missouri		
1	**Wm. Lacy Clay* (D)**	**264,836**
	Robyn Hamlin (R)	60,306
	Robb Cunningham (LB)	11,725
2	**Ann Wagner (R)**	**235,607**
	Glenn Koenen (D)	145,257
3	**Blaine Luetkemeyer** (R)**	**214,660**
	Eric C. Mayer (D)	111,116
	Steven Wilson (LB)	12,343
4	**Vicky Hartzler* (R)**	**192,166**
	Teresa Hensley (D)	113,044
	Thomas Holbrook (LB)	10,396
5	**Emanuel Cleaver* (D)**	**196,467**
	Jacob Turk (R)	121,437
6	**Sam Graves* (R)**	**216,721**
	Kyle Yarber (D)	108,414
7	**Billy Long* (R)**	**203,358**
	Jim Evans (D)	98,384
	Kevin Craig (LB)	16,656
8	**Jo Ann Emerson* (R)**	**215,975**
	Jack Rushin (D)	73,720
	Rick Vandeven (LB)	10,544

Dist. Representative/candidate (party)	2012 election results
Montana	
Steve Daines (R)	**231,584**
Kim Gillan (D)	187,698
David Kaiser (LB)	17,342
Nebraska	
1 Jeff Fortenberry* (R)	**171,385**
Korey L. Reiman (D)	78,732
2 Lee Terry* (R)	**127,119**
John W. Ewing Jr. (D)	121,165
3 Adrian Smith* (R)	**184,978**
Mark Sullivan (D)	64,257
Nevada	
1 Dina Titus (D)	**113,320**
Chris Edwards (R)	56,307
2 Mark E. Amodei* (R)	**161,915**
Samuel Koepnick (D)	101,594
Michael Haines (I)	11,082
3 Joe Heck* (R)	**136,829**
John Oceguera (D)	116,331
James Murphy (I)	12,783
4 Steven A. Horsford (D)	**120,037**
Danny Tarkanian (R)	101,093
New Hampshire	
1 Carol Shea-Porter (D)	**168,648**
Frank C. Guinta* (R)	155,354
Brendan Kelly (LB)	14,665
2 Ann McLane Kuster (D)	**165,231**
Charlie Bass* (R)	149,106
Hardy Macia (LB)	14,527
New Jersey	
1 Robert E. Andrews* (D)	**192,486**
Gregory W. Horton (R)	85,967
2 Frank A. LoBiondo* (R)	**154,736**
Cassandra Shober (D)	107,201
3 Jon Runyan* (R)	**155,770**
Shelley Adler (D)	131,417
4 Chris Smith* (R)	**185,969**
Brian P. Froelich (D)	84,905
5 Scott Garrett* (R)	**153,563**
Adam Gussen (D)	117,304
6 Frank Pallone Jr.* (D)	**140,038**
Anna Little (R)	78,437
7 Leonard Lance* (R)	**163,444**
Upendra J. Chivukula (D)	112,261
8 Albio Sires** (D)	**115,197**
Maria Karczewski (R)	28,031
9 Bill Pascrell Jr.** (D)	**146,819**
Shmuley Boteach (R)	50,726
10 Donald M. Payne Jr.* (D)	**172,498**
Brian C. Kelemen (R)	21,760
11 Rodney P. Frelinghuysen* (R)	**164,085**
John Arvanites (D)	109,506
12 Rush D. Holt* (D)	**172,763**
Eric A. Beck (R)	74,973
New Mexico	
1 Michelle Lujan Grisham (D)	**158,820**
Janice E. Arnold-Jones (R)	110,102
2 Steve Pearce* (R)	**131,895**
Evelyn Madrid Erhard (D)	91,421
3 Ben Ray Lujan* (D)	**164,612**
Jefferson L. Byrd (R)	96,825
New York	
1 Timothy H. Bishop* (D)	**132,525**
Randy Altschuler (R)	121,478
2 Peter T. King** (R)	**131,091**
Vivianne C. Falcone (D)	92,057
3 Steve Israel** (D)	**136,687**
Stephen A. Labate (R)	99,183
4 Carolyn McCarthy* (D)	**138,561**
Francis X. Becker Jr. (R)	72,673
Frank Scaturro (Conservative)	13,243
5 Gregory W. Meeks** (D)	**146,278**
Allan W. Jennings Jr. (R)	15,640
6 Grace Meng (D)	**100,571**
Daniel J. Halloran (R)	46,305
7 Nydia M. Velazquez** (D)	**116,873**
James Murray (Conservative)	6,823
8 Hakeem S. Jeffries (D)	**159,463**
Alan S. Bellone (R)	15,546
9 Yvette D. Clarke** (D)	**165,201**
Daniel J. Cavanagh (R)	21,984
10 Jerrold Nadler** (D)	**145,381**
Michael W. Chan (R)	34,848

Dist. Representative/candidate (party)	2012 election results
11 Mike Grimm** (R)	**94,102**
Mark S. Murphy (D)	82,401
12 Carolyn B. Maloney** (D)	**158,834**
Christopher R. Wight (R)	37,580
13 Charles B. Rangel** (D)	**152,592**
Craig Schley (R)	10,546
14 Joseph Crowley** (D)	**108,436**
William F. Gibbons Jr. (R)	19,934
15 Jose E. Serrano** (D)	**132,505**
Frank L. Della Valle (R)	3,983
16 Eliot L. Engel** (D)	**137,213**
Joseph McLaughlin (R)	37,860
17 Nita M. Lowey** (D)	**139,876**
Joe E. Carvin (R)	75,736
18 Sean Patrick Maloney (D)	**129,040**
Nan A. S. Hayworth** (R)	120,664
19 Christopher P. Gibson** (R)	**137,870**
Julian Schreibman (D)	120,060
20 Paul Tonko** (D)	**187,651**
Robert J. Dieterich (R)	86,640
21 Bill Owens** (D)	**113,921**
Matthew A. Doheny (R)	108,378
22 Richard L. Hanna** (R)	**133,143**
Dan Lamb (D)	87,710
23 Thomas Reed** (R)	**126,191**
Nate Shinagawa (D)	116,189
24 Daniel B. Maffei (D)	**130,508**
Ann Marie Buerkle** (R)	117,904
Ursula Rozum (Green)	21,291
25 Louise McIntosh Slaughter** (D)	**166,342**
Maggie Brooks (R)	124,585
26 Brian Higgins** (D)	**196,574**
Michael H. Madigan (R)	67,041
27 Chris Collins (R)	**150,446**
Kathleen C. Hochul** (D)	146,134
North Carolina	
1 G. K. Butterfield* (D)	**250,582**
Pete DiLauro (R)	76,449
2 Renee L. Ellmers* (R)	**174,562**
Steve Wilkins (D)	129,306
3 Walter B. Jones* (R)	**192,783**
Erik Anderson (D)	111,985
4 David E. Price* (D)	**265,410**
Tim D'Annunzio (R)	91,500
5 Virginia Foxx* (R)	**199,973**
Elisabeth Motsinger (D)	147,585
6 Howard Coble* (R)	**220,241**
Tony Foriest (D)	141,190
7 *Mike McIntyre* (D)	*166,750*
David Rouzer (R)	*166,372*
8 Richard Hudson (R)	**159,226**
Larry Kissell* (D)	134,891
9 Robert Pittenger (R)	**193,174**
Jennifer Roberts (D)	170,462
10 Patrick T. McHenry* (R)	**189,667**
Patsy Keever (D)	142,822
11 Mark Meadows (R)	**188,133**
Hayden Rogers (D)	139,614
12 Mel Watt* (D)	**246,451**
Jack Brosch (R)	62,924
13 George Holding (R)	**225,000**
Charles Malone (D)	169,246
North Dakota	
Kevin Cramer (R)	**172,905**
Pam Gulleson (D)	131,396
Eric Olson (LB)	10,215
Ohio	
1 Steve Chabot* (R)	**194,100**
Jeff Sinnard (D)	124,028
2 Brad Wenstrup (R)	**189,400**
William R. Smith (D)	131,256
3 Joyce Beatty (D)	**184,279**
Chris Long (R)	72,953
4 Jim Jordan* (R)	**177,861**
Jim Slone (D)	108,629
Chris Kalla (LB)	15,268
5 Bob Latta* (R)	**196,843**
Angela Zimmann (D)	132,886
Eric Eberly (LB)	11,906
6 Bill Johnson* (R)	**145,460**
Charlie Wilson (D)	127,147
7 Bob Gibbs** (R)	**172,121**
Joyce R. Healy-Abrams (D)	131,502

Dist.	Representative/candidate (party)	2012 election results
8	John Boehner* (R)	Unopposed
9	Marcy Kaptur* (D)	205,091
	Samuel J. Wurzelbacher (R)	66,351
	Sean Stipe (LB)	11,026
10	Mike Turner** (R)	195,022
	Sharen Swartz Neuhardt (D)	118,387
11	Marcia Fudge* (D)	Unopposed
12	Pat Tiberi* (R)	266,592
	Jim Reese (D)	155,489
13	Timothy Ryan** (D)	157,490
	Marisha G. Agana (R)	67,683
14	David P. Joyce (R)	179,704
	Dale Virgil Blanchard (D)	127,467
	Elaine Mastromatteo (Green)	12,546
	David Macko (LB)	11,088
15	Steve Stivers* (R)	243,913
	Pat Lang (D)	159,636
16	Jim Renacci* (R)	180,706
	Betty Sutton** (D)	165,248

Oklahoma

Dist.	Representative/candidate (party)	2012 election results
1	Jim Bridenstine (R)	180,886
	John Olson (D)	91,310
	Craig Allen (I)	12,786
2	Markwayne Mullin (R)	143,253
	Rob Wallace (D)	95,763
	Michael Fulks (I)	10,794
3	Frank D. Lucas* (R)	200,963
	Timothy Ray Murray (D)	53,295
	William Sanders (I)	12,756
4	Tom Cole* (R)	176,561
	Donna Marie Bebo (D)	71,755
	RJ Harris (I)	11,725
5	James Lankford* (R)	153,421
	Tom Guild (D)	97,359

Oregon

Dist.	Representative/candidate (party)	2012 election results
1	Suzanne Bonamici* (D)	146,277
	Delinda Morgan (R)	79,555
2	Greg Walden* (R)	206,759
	Joyce B. Segers (D)	85,408
3	Earl Blumenauer* (D)	184,903
	Ronald Green (R)	51,944
4	Peter A. DeFazio* (D)	196,969
	Art Robinson (R)	131,311
5	Kurt Schrader* (D)	159,333
	Fred Thompson (R)	126,340

Pennsylvania

Dist.	Representative/candidate (party)	2012 election results
1	Robert A. Brady* (D)	222,408
	John Featherman (R)	39,128
2	Chaka Fattah* (D)	299,567
	Robert Allen Mansfield Jr. (R)	31,466
3	Mike Kelly* (R)	160,238
	Missa Eaton (D)	120,144
	Steven Porter (I)	12,352
4	Scott Perry (R)	179,340
	Harry Perkinson (D)	103,387
	Wayne Wolff (I)	11,425
5	Glenn Thompson* (R)	172,042
	Charles Dumas (D)	101,624
6	Jim Gerlach* (R)	183,647
	Manan M. Trivedi (D)	138,688
7	Patrick Meehan* (R)	201,178
	George Badey (D)	137,231
8	Michael G. Fitzpatrick* (R)	199,283
	Kathy Boockvar (D)	152,515
9	Bill Shuster* (R)	165,858
	Karen Ramsburg (D)	103,298
10	Tom Marino* (R)	176,261
	Philip Scollo (D)	91,351
11	Lou Barletta* (R)	163,733
	Gene Stilp (D)	116,315
12	Keith J. Rothfus (R)	172,020
	Mark S. Critz* (D)	160,636
13	Allyson Y. Schwartz* (D)	203,072
	Joseph James Rooney (R)	91,887
14	Mike Doyle* (D)	248,905
	Hans Lessmann (R)	74,888
15	Charles W. Dent* (R)	165,629
	Rick Daugherty (D)	126,661
16	Joseph R. Pitts* (R)	154,337
	Aryanna C. Strader (D)	109,026
	John Murphy (I)	12,058

Dist.	Representative/candidate (party)	2012 election results
17	Matthew A. Cartwright (D)	157,629
	Laureen A. Cummings (R)	102,754
18	Tim Murphy* (R)	209,263
	Larry Maggi (D)	118,370

Rhode Island

Dist.	Representative/candidate (party)	2012 election results
1	David N. Cicilline* (D)	101,331
	Brendan P. Doherty (R)	77,632
	David Vogel (I)	11,690
2	Jim Langevin* (D)	116,573
	Michael G. Riley (R)	73,184
	Abel Collins (I)	19,247

South Carolina

Dist.	Representative/candidate (party)	2012 election results
1	Tim Scott* (R)	147,592
	Bobbie G. Rose (D)	78,091
2	Joe Wilson* (R)	Unopposed
3	Jeff Duncan* (R)	167,707
	Brian "Ryan B." Doyle (D)	83,899
4	Trey Gowdy* (R)	171,505
	Deb Morrow (D)	89,094
5	Mick Mulvaney* (R)	151,671
	Joyce Knott (D)	120,829
6	Jim Clyburn* (D)	195,943
	Nammu Y. Muhammad (Green)	11,855
7	Tom Rice (R)	147,654
	Gloria Bromell Tinubu (D)	121,002

South Dakota

Dist.	Representative/candidate (party)	2012 election results
	Kristi L. Noem* (R)	207,578
	Matt Varilek (D)	153,721

Tennessee

Dist.	Representative/candidate (party)	2012 election results
1	Phil Roe* (R)	182,186
	Alan Woodruff (D)	47,597
2	John J. Duncan Jr.* (R)	193,312
	Troy Christopher Goodale (D)	53,336
3	Chuck Fleischmann* (R)	157,725
	Mary M. Headrick (D)	91,031
4	Scott DesJarlais* (R)	126,751
	Eric Stewart (D)	99,823
5	Jim Cooper* (D)	166,999
	Brad Staats (R)	83,982
6	Diane Black* (R)	184,264
	Scott Beasley (I)	34,746
	Pat Riley (Green)	21,613
7	Marsha Blackburn* (R)	180,775
	Credo Amouzouvik (D)	61,050
8	Stephen Lee Fincher* (R)	190,571
	Timothy D. Dixon (D)	79,347
9	Steve Cohen* (D)	188,245
	George S. Flinn Jr. (R)	59,676

Texas

Dist.	Representative/candidate (party)	2012 election results
1	Louie Gohmert* (R)	182,621
	Shirley J. McKellar (D)	67,758
2	Ted Poe* (R)	159,369
	Jim Dougherty (D)	80,262
3	Sam Johnson* (R)	Unopposed
4	Ralph M. Hall* (R)	182,416
	VaLinda Hathcox (D)	60,124
5	Jeb Hensarling* (R)	134,005
	Linda S. Mrosko (D)	69,025
6	Joe Barton* (R)	144,892
	Kenneth Sanders (D)	97,933
7	John Abney Culberson* (R)	142,477
	James Cargas (D)	85,253
8	Kevin Brady* (R)	191,254
	Neil Burns (D)	50,077
9	Al Green* (D)	143,850
	Steve Mueller (R)	36,073
10	Michael T. McCaul* (R)	159,391
	Tawana W. Cadien (D)	95,316
11	Mike Conaway* (R)	177,166
	Jim Riley (D)	41,842
12	Kay Granger* (R)	175,298
	Dave Robinson (D)	65,991
13	Mac Thornberry* (R)	187,385
	John Robert Deek (LB)	12,671
14	Randy Weber (R)	130,937
	Nick Lampson (D)	109,264
15	Rubén Hinojosa* (D)	89,143
	Dale A. Brueggemann (R)	53,892
16	Beto O'Rourke (D)	100,804
	Barbara Carrasco (R)	50,478

Dist.	Representative/candidate (party)	2012 election results
17	**Bill Flores* (R)**	**143,126**
	Ben Easton (LB)	35,902
18	**Sheila Jackson Lee* (D)**	**145,893**
	Sean Seibert (R)	43,926
19	**Randy Neugebauer* (R)**	**160,067**
	Richard "Chip" Peterson (LB)	28,345
20	**Joaquin Castro (D)**	**118,719**
	David Rosa (R)	62,041
21	**Lamar Smith* (R)**	**186,525**
	Candace E. Duval (D)	108,852
	John-Henry Liberty (LB)	12,469
22	**Pete Olson* (R)**	**160,471**
	Kesha Rogers (D)	80,025
23	**Pete P. Gallego (D)**	**96,477**
	Francisco "Quico" Canseco* (R)	87,255
24	**Kenny Marchant* (R)**	**148,207**
	Tim Rusk (D)	87,347
25	**Roger Williams (R)**	**153,868**
	Elaine M. Henderson (D)	98,427
	Betsy Dewey (LB)	10,822
26	**Michael C. Burgess* (R)**	**175,669**
	David Sanchez (D)	73,661
27	**Blake Farenthold* (R)**	**120,490**
	Rose Meza Harrison (D)	83,280
28	**Henry Cuellar* (D)**	**112,262**
	William R. Hayward (R)	49,095
29	**Gene Green* (D)**	**85,920**
	Jamey Stanczak (LB)	4,988
30	**Eddie Bernice Johnson* (D)**	**169,889**
	Travis Washington Jr. (R)	40,841
31	**John R. Carter* (R)**	**145,096**
	Stephen M. Wyman (D)	82,791
32	**Pete Sessions* (R)**	**146,129**
	Katherine Savers McGovern (D)	98,867
33	**Marc Veasey (D)**	**84,940**
	Chuck Bradley (R)	30,152
34	**Filemon Vela (D)**	**88,781**
	Jessica Puente Bradshaw (R)	51,338
35	**Lloyd Doggett** (D)**	**105,260**
	Susan Narvaiz (R)	52,686
36	**Steve Stockman (R)**	**165,388**
	Max Martin (D)	62,052
Utah		
1	**Rob Bishop* (R)**	**161,546**
	Donna M. McAleer (D)	55,740
2	**Chris Stewart (R)**	**139,082**
	Jay Seegmiller (D)	75,261
3	**Jason Chaffetz* (R)**	**180,760**
	Soren D. Simonsen (D)	55,879
4	*Jim Matheson** (D)*	*108,075*
	Mia B. Love (R)	*105,257*
Vermont		
	Peter Welch* (D)	**201,476**
	Mark Donka (R)	65,208
Virginia		
1	**Robert J. Wittman* (R)**	**190,787**
	Adam M. Cook (D)	138,558
2	**E. Scott Rigell* (R)**	**152,719**
	Paul O. Hirschbiel Jr. (D)	130,989
3	**Bobby Scott* (D)**	**238,613**
	Dean J. Longo (R)	55,864
4	**Randy Forbes* (R)**	**190,412**
	Ella P. Ward (D)	139,453

Dist.	Representative/candidate (party)	2012 election results
5	**Robert Hurt* (R)**	**186,758**
	John Wade Douglass (D)	145,098
6	**Bob Goodlatte* (R)**	**209,254**
	Andy B. Schmookler (D)	109,916
7	**Eric Cantor* (R)**	**216,967**
	E. Wayne Powell (D)	153,306
8	**Jim Moran* (D)**	**198,396**
	J. Patrick Murray (R)	95,322
9	**H. Morgan Griffith* (R)**	**183,015**
	Anthony J. Flaccavento (D)	115,718
10	**Frank R. Wolf* (R)**	**196,784**
	Kristin A. Cabral (D)	129,179
11	**Gerry Connolly* (D)**	**167,694**
	Chris S. Perkins (R)	99,426
Washington		
1	**Suzan DelBene (D)**	**102,721**
	John Koster (R)	88,931
2	**Rick Larsen* (D)**	**113,694**
	Dan Matthews (R)	73,686
3	**Jaime Herrera Beutler* (R)**	**121,376**
	Jon T. Haugen (D)	84,114
4	**Doc Hastings* (R)**	**100,880**
	Mary Baechler (D)	50,367
5	**Cathy McMorris Rodgers* (R)**	**132,177**
	Rich Cowan (D)	82,367
6	**Derek Kilmer (D)**	**116,949**
	Bill Driscoll (R)	83,740
7	**Jim McDermott* (D)**	**169,860**
	Ron Bemis (R)	42,988
8	**Dave Reichert* (R)**	**107,121**
	Karen Porterfield (D)	73,295
9	**Adam Smith* (D)**	**112,157**
	Jim Postma (R)	44,949
10	**Denny Heck (D)**	**99,322**
	Richard "Dick" Muri (R)	70,486
West Virginia		
1	**David B. McKinley* (R)**	**130,783**
	Sue Thorn (D)	78,474
2	**Shelley Moore Capito* (R)**	**156,920**
	Howard Swint (D)	67,965
3	**Nick J. Rahall II* (D)**	**107,302**
	Rick Snuffer (R)	91,602
Wisconsin		
1	**Paul Ryan* (R)**	**199,715**
	Rob Zerban (D)	157,721
2	**Mark Pocan (D)**	**264,790**
	Chad Lee (R)	124,465
3	**Ron Kind* (R)**	**217,335**
	Ray Boland (R)	121,636
4	**Gwen Moore* (D)**	**228,534**
	Dan Sebring (R)	76,077
5	**Jim Sensenbrenner* (R)**	**249,267**
	Dave Heaster (D)	117,972
6	**Tom Petri* (R)**	**223,514**
	Joe Kallas (D)	136,146
7	**Sean P. Duffy* (R)**	**200,033**
	Pat Kreitlow (D)	155,068
8	**Reid J. Ribble* (R)**	**198,464**
	Jamie Wall (D)	156,371
Wyoming		
	Cynthia M. Lummis* (R)	**165,766**
	Chris Henrichsen (D)	57,146

Nonvoting Members of Congress

Representative/candidate (party)	2012 election results	Representative/candidate (party)	2012 election results
American Samoa		**Puerto Rico—Resident Commissioner[1]**	
Eni F.H. Faleomavaega* (D)	7,221	Pedro R. Pierluisi* (D)	881,274
Aumua Amata (Conservative)	4,420	Roberto Cox Alomar (Popular Dem. Party)	861,291
Rosie F. Tago Lancaster (I)	543	Juan Manuel "Juanchin" Mercado Nieves (Puerto Rican IP)	37,245
District of Columbia		**Virgin Islands**	
Eleanor Holmes Norton* (D)	206,664	Donna M. Christensen* (D)	11,512
Bruce Majors (LB)	13,462	Warren B. Mosler (I)	3,276
Natale Lino Stracuzzi (DC Statehood Green)	11,005	Holland Redfield (R)	2,131
Guam		Norma Pickard-Samuel (I)	1,927
Madeleine Z. Bordallo* (D)	20,174		
Frank Flores Blas Jr. (R)	13,160		

(1) The resident commissioner of Puerto Rico is the only member of the House of Representatives who serves a four-year term.

Governors of the 50 States

Source: © Associated Press; all rights reserved. 2012 results are preliminary as of Nov. 7, 2012.

Of the 50 state governors, 30 are Republicans, 19 are Democrats, and 1 is Independent. Election winners are listed in bold; results in pending races are in italic. Terms are for 4 years, with the exception of 2-year terms for governors of New Hampshire and Vermont. Governors for states not holding elections in Nov. 2012 are shown for reference. * = Incumbent. Third-party or independent candidates receiving fewer than 10,000 votes are not listed.

D = Democrat; R = Republican; Amer. Const. = American Constitution; Amer. Ind. = American Independent Party; CP = Constitution Party; DFL = Dem.-Farmer-Labor; I = Independent; IP = Independence Party; LB = Libertarian; Unaff. = Unaffiliated.

Term ends[1]	Governor/candidate (party)	2012 election results
Alabama		
2015	Robert Bentley (R)	
Alaska		
Dec. 2014	Sean Parnell (R)	
Arizona		
2015	Jan Brewer (R)	
Arkansas		
2015	Mike Beebe (D)	
California		
2015	Jerry Brown (D)	
Colorado		
2015	John Hickenlooper (D)	
Connecticut		
2015	Dan Malloy (D)	
Delaware		
2017	**Jack A. Markell* (D)**	275,991
	Jeffrey Cragg (R)	113,792
Florida		
2015	Rick Scott (R)	
Georgia		
2015	Nathan Deal (R)	
Hawaii		
Dec. 2014	Neil Abercrombie (D)	
Idaho		
2015	C. L. "Butch" Otter (R)	
Illinois		
2015	Patrick Quinn (D)	
Indiana		
2017	**Mike Pence (R)**	1,264,017
	John Gregg (D)	1,183,002
	Rupert Boneham (LB)	101,010
Iowa		
2015	Terry Branstad (R)	
Kansas		
2015	Sam Brownback (R)	
Kentucky		
Dec. 2015	Steven L. Beshear (D)	
Louisiana		
2016	Bobby Jindal (R)	
Maine		
2015	Paul LePage (R)	
Maryland		
2015	Martin O'Malley (D)	
Massachusetts		
2015	Deval Patrick (D)	
Michigan		
2015	Rick Snyder (R)	
Minnesota		
2015	Mark Dayton (D)	
Mississippi		
2016	Phil Bryant (R)	
Missouri		
2017	**Jay Nixon* (D)**	1,485,147
	Dave Spence (R)	1,157,475
	Jim Higgins (LB)	73,196
Montana		
2017	**Steve Bullock (D)**	216,608
	Rick Hill (R)	207,388
	Ron Vandevender (LB)	16,287

(1) Jan. unless otherwise noted.

Term ends[1]	Governor/candidate (party)	2012 election results
Nebraska		
2015	David Heineman (R)	
Nevada		
2015	Brian Sandoval (R)	
New Hampshire		
2015	**Maggie Hassan (D)**	368,554
	Ovide Lamontagne (R)	287,021
	John Babiarz (LB)	19,246
New Jersey		
2014	Chris Christie (R)	
New Mexico		
2015	Susana Martinez (R)	
New York		
2015	Andrew Cuomo (D)	
North Carolina		
2017	**Pat McCrory (R)**	2,444,447
	Walter Dalton (D)	1,929,330
	Barbara Howe (LB)	95,016
North Dakota		
Dec. 2016	**Jack Dalrymple* (R)**	199,769
	Ryan Taylor (D)	108,622
Ohio		
2015	John Kasich (R)	
Oklahoma		
2015	Mary Fallin (R)	
Oregon		
2015	John Kitzhaber (D)	
Pennsylvania		
2015	Tom Corbett (R)	
Rhode Island		
2015	Lincoln Chafee (I)	
South Carolina		
2015	Nikki R. Haley (R)	
South Dakota		
2015	Dennis Daugaard (R)	
Tennessee		
2015	Bill Haslam (R)	
Texas		
2015	Rick Perry (R)	
Utah		
2017	**Gary R. Herbert* (R)**	623,437
	Peter Cooke (D)	253,270
	Ken Larsen (LB)	19,938
	Kirk Pearson (CP)	15,497
Vermont		
2015	**Peter Shumlin* (D)**	163,337
	Randy Brock (R)	106,972
Virginia		
2014	Bob McDonnell (R)	
Washington		
2017	*Jay Inslee (D)*	*1,088,037*
	Rob McKenna (R)	*1,040,896*
West Virginia		
2017	**Earl Ray Tomblin* (D)**	331,116
	Bill Maloney (R)	299,682
Wisconsin		
2015	Scott Walker (R)	
Wyoming		
2015	Matthew Mead (R)	

Governors of U.S. Commonwealths and Territories

I = Independent; PNP = New Progressive Party; PDP = Popular Democratic Party.

Term ends	Governor/candidate (party)	2012 election results
American Samoa		
2017	*Lolo Matalasi Moliga (I)*	*4,372*
	Faoa Aitofele Sunia (D)	*4,315*
	Afoa L.S. Lutu (R)	2,521
Guam		
2015	Eddie Calvo (R)	

Term ends	Governor/candidate (party)	2012 election results
Northern Mariana Islands		
2015	Benígno Fitial (R)	
Puerto Rico		
2017	**Alejandro García Padilla (PDP)**	877,029
	Luis G. Fortuño* (PNP)	862,817
Virgin Islands		
2015	John deJongh Jr. (D)	

Presidential Election Results by State and County

Source: © Associated Press; all rights reserved. 2012 results are preliminary as of Nov. 7, 2012. Statewide totals may include votes and areas not listed separately. Results for New England states are for select cities and towns.

D = Democrat; R = Republican; Ind. = Independent; A3P = American Third Position; Amer. Ind. = American Independent/America's Party; Const. = Constitution Party; LB. = Libertarian; NPA = No party affiliation; Prohib. = Prohibition; RF. = Reform; Soc. = Socialist; unaff. = unaffiliated.

Alabama

County	2012 Obama (D)	Romney (R)	2008 Obama (D)	McCain (R)
Autauga	6,354	17,366	6,093	17,403
Baldwin	18,329	65,772	19,386	61,271
Barbour	5,873	5,539	5,697	5,866
Bibb	2,200	6,131	2,299	6,262
Blount	2,961	20,741	3,522	20,389
Bullock	4,058	1,250	4,011	1,391
Butler	4,367	5,081	4,188	5,485
Calhoun	15,462	30,210	16,334	32,348
Chambers	6,853	7,596	6,799	8,067
Cherokee	2,126	7,494	2,306	7,298
Chilton	3,391	13,910	3,674	13,960
Choctaw	3,785	4,150	3,636	4,223
Clarke	6,317	7,463	5,914	7,466
Clay	1,770	4,802	1,760	4,984
Cleburne	971	5,269	1,168	5,216
Coffee	4,899	14,638	5,079	14,919
Colbert	9,160	13,931	9,703	14,739
Conecuh	3,551	3,434	3,429	3,470
Coosa	2,188	3,028	2,273	3,248
Covington	3,155	12,148	3,240	12,444
Crenshaw	2,048	4,326	1,938	4,319
Cullman	4,855	27,930	5,864	28,896
Dale	5,283	13,105	5,270	13,886
Dallas	14,599	6,284	13,986	6,798
De Kalb	5,235	18,316	5,658	17,957
Elmore	8,940	26,223	8,301	25,777
Escambia	5,476	9,263	5,188	9,375
Etowah	12,792	29,102	13,497	30,595
Fayette	1,803	6,034	1,994	5,883
Franklin	3,171	7,567	3,469	8,048
Geneva	2,039	9,173	2,134	9,417
Greene	4,514	799	4,408	876
Hale	5,401	3,205	4,982	3,200
Henry	3,046	5,605	3,018	5,585
Houston	12,348	29,214	12,225	29,254
Jackson	5,817	14,422	6,374	14,083
Jefferson	156,182	138,070	166,121	149,921
Lamar	1,643	5,453	1,614	5,419
Lauderdale	12,504	23,902	13,329	24,068
Lawrence	5,055	8,855	5,164	9,277
Lee	21,274	32,062	21,498	32,230
Limestone	9,809	25,263	9,536	23,598
Lowndes	5,747	1,754	5,449	1,809
Macon	9,045	1,322	9,450	1,396
Madison	61,802	90,679	64,117	86,965
Marengo	6,154	5,321	5,926	5,516
Marion	2,249	9,696	2,600	9,536
Marshall	6,271	25,785	7,038	25,727
Mobile	75,338	90,739	82,181	98,049
Monroe	4,897	5,730	5,025	6,175
Montgomery	62,993	38,283	62,166	42,031
Morgan	13,401	35,309	13,895	36,014
Perry	4,536	1,504	4,457	1,679
Pickens	4,448	5,119	4,594	5,434
Pike	6,009	7,939	5,879	8,004
Randolph	3,076	7,219	3,064	7,175
Russell	10,495	8,276	10,085	8,705
St. Clair	5,790	29,001	6,091	27,649
Shelby	19,944	71,243	20,625	69,060
Sumter	5,420	1,585	5,264	1,731
Talladega	13,878	19,217	13,779	20,112
Tallapoosa	6,252	12,303	6,063	13,116
Tuscaloosa	32,003	45,703	32,796	45,405
Walker	6,551	21,633	7,420	20,722
Washington	2,971	5,749	3,067	5,654
Wilcox	4,867	1,676	4,612	1,868
Winston	1,286	8,310	1,757	8,103
Totals	**787,027**	**1,245,221**	**813,479**	**1,266,546**

All candidates, 2012: Romney, R., 1,245,221; Obama, D., 787,027; Johnson, Ind., 12,242; Stein, Ind., 3,366; Goode, Ind., 2,957.

Alaska

	2012 Obama (D)	Romney (R)	2008 Obama (D)	McCain (R)
Totals	90,743	120,329	123,594	193,841

All candidates, 2012: Romney, R., 120,329; Obama, D., 90,743; Johnson, LB., 5,485; Stein, Green, 2,089.

Arizona

County	2012 Obama (D)	Romney (R)	2008 Obama (D)	McCain (R)
Apache	14,519	6,802	15,390	8,551
Cochise	10,904	18,883	18,943	29,026
Coconino	23,250	17,200	31,433	22,186
Gila	6,604	11,520	7,884	14,095
Graham	3,429	7,724	3,487	8,376
Greenlee	1,310	1,590	1,165	1,712
La Paz	1,619	3,205	1,929	3,509
Maricopa	384,960	511,838	602,166	746,448
Mohave	16,737	42,403	22,092	44,333
Navajo	15,168	17,049	15,579	19,761
Pima	151,737	139,009	206,254	182,406
Pinal	32,410	46,982	44,254	59,421
Santa Cruz	8,133	3,708	8,683	4,518
Yavapai	29,049	56,479	36,889	61,192
Yuma	13,039	18,239	18,559	24,577
Totals	**712,868**	**902,631**	**1,034,707**	**1,230,111**

All candidates, 2012: Romney, R., 902,631; Obama, D., 712,868; Johnson, LB., 20,738; Stein, Green, 5,084.

Arkansas

County	2012 Obama (D)	Romney (R)	2008 Obama (D)	McCain (R)
Arkansas	2,454	3,892	2,619	4,185
Ashley	2,855	4,866	2,976	5,406
Baxter	5,172	13,688	6,539	12,852
Benton	20,913	50,486	23,331	51,124
Boone	3,627	10,787	4,435	10,575
Bradley	1,447	2,118	1,680	2,262
Calhoun	659	1,450	691	1,462
Carroll	3,691	6,121	4,172	6,083
Chicot	2,649	1,670	3,043	2,119
Clark	3,808	4,343	4,267	4,608
Clay	1,738	3,225	2,244	3,032
Cleburne	2,617	8,682	2,951	7,962
Cleveland	844	2,307	911	2,451
Columbia	3,557	5,790	3,554	5,861
Conway	3,003	4,511	3,149	4,691
Craighead	10,351	20,044	11,294	18,881
Crawford	4,872	15,125	5,238	14,688
Crittenden	9,092	6,192	10,330	7,650
Cross	2,279	4,268	2,580	4,393
Dallas	1,337	1,664	1,471	1,757
Desha	2,353	1,807	2,569	1,999
Drew	2,627	3,883	2,598	3,860
Faulkner	13,559	26,653	14,955	25,362
Franklin	1,720	4,610	1,869	4,411
Fulton	1,452	2,949	1,819	2,702
Garland	13,317	25,031	15,899	26,825
Grant	1,467	4,829	1,562	5,023
Greene	3,998	9,066	4,541	8,578
Hempstead	2,462	4,274	2,869	4,273
Hot Spring	3,824	7,087	4,288	7,209
Howard	1,460	2,862	1,746	2,957
Independence	3,279	8,724	3,688	8,255
Izard	1,563	3,571	1,792	3,193
Jackson	2,093	3,065	2,207	3,118
Jefferson	17,275	9,246	18,465	10,655
Johnson	2,784	5,014	3,034	4,922
Lafayette	1,173	1,712	1,133	1,685
Lawrence	1,786	3,535	2,138	3,357
Lee	2,107	1,280	2,263	1,454
Lincoln	1,424	2,199	1,710	2,513
Little River	1,552	3,385	1,753	3,247

County	2012 Obama (D)	Romney (R)	2008 Obama (D)	McCain (R)
Logan	2,009	5,078	2,286	5,350
Lonoke	5,237	17,450	5,968	17,242
Madison	2,099	4,262	2,144	3,972
Marion	2,024	4,771	2,384	4,524
Miller	4,517	10,619	4,869	9,913
Mississippi	6,445	6,599	6,667	6,976
Monroe	1,583	1,585	1,615	1,754
Montgomery	920	2,368	1,092	2,365
Nevada	1,314	1,996	1,474	2,062
Newton	993	2,508	1,182	2,588
Ouachita	4,626	5,516	4,346	5,427
Perry	1,187	2,580	1,352	2,743
Phillips	5,179	2,591	5,695	3,097
Pike	850	2,847	1,089	2,727
Poinsett	2,387	4,967	2,742	4,903
Polk	1,556	5,950	1,957	5,473
Pope	5,108	14,733	6,002	15,568
Prairie	877	2,149	1,048	2,223
Pulaski	87,055	68,856	88,854	70,212
Randolph	2,040	3,699	2,469	3,615
St. Francis	4,652	3,287	5,486	3,917
Saline	12,868	32,962	12,695	30,981
Scott	895	2,630	1,053	2,791
Searcy	803	2,668	961	2,726
Sebastian	13,080	29,151	13,673	28,637
Sevier	1,042	3,135	1,291	3,125
Sharp	2,091	4,919	2,436	4,535
Stone	1,356	3,773	1,598	3,534
Union	6,182	10,696	6,190	10,677
Van Buren	1,826	4,362	2,151	4,276
Washington	28,136	39,570	29,021	37,963
White	5,765	20,005	6,732	19,467
Woodruff	1,340	1,227	1,412	1,206
Yell	1,720	4,041	2,003	3,808
Totals	**390,002**	**639,561**	**422,310**	**638,017**

All candidates, 2012: Romney, R., 639,561; Obama, D., 390,002; Johnson, LB., 16,019; Stein, Green, 9,189; Lindsay, Socialism/Liberation, 1,722.

California

County	2012 Obama (D)	Romney (R)	2008 Obama (D)	McCain (R)
Alameda	308,478	76,794	489,106	119,555
Alpine	389	236	422	252
Amador	6,001	8,903	7,813	10,561
Butte	32,567	35,312	49,013	46,706
Calaveras	7,404	10,537	9,813	12,835
Colusa	2,070	3,381	2,569	3,733
Contra Costa	219,090	107,318	306,983	136,436
Del Norte	3,396	4,256	4,323	4,967
El Dorado	29,047	42,294	40,529	50,314
Fresno	75,313	80,859	136,706	131,015
Glenn	2,646	4,752	3,734	5,910
Humboldt	27,757	15,653	39,692	21,713
Imperial	17,464	9,545	24,162	14,008
Inyo	2,775	3,541	3,743	4,523
Kern	64,690	99,840	93,457	134,793
Kings	12,282	17,184	14,747	19,710
Lake	9,159	6,474	14,854	9,935
Lassen	2,469	5,830	3,586	7,483
Los Angeles	1,614,188	662,909	2,295,853	956,425
Madera	12,698	18,990	17,952	23,583
Marin	62,929	19,760	109,320	28,384
Mariposa	3,080	4,434	4,100	5,298
Mendocino	11,869	5,129	27,843	10,721
Merced	26,128	23,403	34,031	28,704
Modoc	1,113	2,779	1,313	2,981
Mono	2,574	2,202	3,093	2,354
Monterey	50,852	24,714	88,453	38,797
Napa	19,964	11,647	38,849	19,484
Nevada	14,261	15,696	28,617	25,663
Orange	377,684	458,590	549,558	579,064
Placer	49,126	74,460	75,112	94,647
Plumas	3,670	5,240	4,715	6,035
Riverside	237,914	246,944	325,017	310,041
Sacramento	184,515	132,919	316,506	213,583
San Benito	7,716	5,481	11,917	7,425
San Bernardino	231,028	208,331	315,720	277,408
San Diego	417,320	381,285	666,581	541,032
San Francisco	214,829	34,896	322,220	52,292
San Joaquin	80,005	66,742	113,974	91,607
San Luis Obispo	47,893	46,598	68,176	61,055
San Mateo	143,976	53,853	222,826	75,057
Santa Barbara	70,126	49,828	105,614	65,585
Santa Clara	300,889	121,501	462,241	190,039
Santa Cruz	61,106	17,132	98,745	25,244
Shasta	18,184	34,561	28,867	49,588
Sierra	652	1,056	743	1,158
Siskiyou	6,561	9,027	9,292	11,520
Solano	74,077	41,343	102,095	56,035
Sonoma	124,504	45,666	168,888	55,127
Stanislaus	52,504	53,593	80,279	77,497
Sutter	8,004	12,576	13,412	18,911
Tehama	6,032	10,791	8,945	14,843
Trinity	2,367	2,422	3,233	2,940
Tulare	27,430	40,012	43,634	59,765
Tuolumne	7,500	10,370	11,532	14,988
Ventura	130,512	118,156	187,601	145,853
Yolo	38,856	19,080	53,488	24,592
Yuba	5,817	8,746	8,866	12,007
Totals	**5,573,450**	**3,635,571**	**8,274,473**	**5,011,781**

All candidates, 2012: Obama, D., 5,573,450; Romney, R., 3,635,571; Johnson, LB., 98,615; Stein, Green, 57,748; Barr, Peace/Freedom, 36,914; Hoefling, Amer. Ind., 27,046.

Colorado

County	2012 Obama (D)	Romney (R)	2008 Obama (D)	McCain (R)
Adams	90,843	66,531	93,443	63,976
Alamosa	3,782	2,693	3,521	2,635
Arapahoe	132,584	112,399	148,218	113,866
Archuleta	2,637	3,831	2,836	3,638
Baca	462	1,554	536	1,572
Bent	778	1,053	799	1,077
Boulder	120,485	48,526	124,159	44,904
Broomfield	16,653	14,765	16,168	12,757
Chaffee	4,967	4,949	4,861	4,873
Cheyenne	162	858	198	890
Clear Creek	3,041	2,381	3,332	2,300
Conejos	2,180	1,794	2,154	1,653
Costilla	1,317	440	1,245	415
Crowley	535	924	552	976
Custer	862	1,776	912	1,672
Delta	4,542	10,762	5,084	10,067
Denver	209,759	69,755	204,882	62,567
Dolores	329	838	369	818
Douglas	54,093	93,930	61,960	88,108
Eagle	12,598	9,317	13,187	8,179
El Paso	103,481	162,281	108,899	160,318
Elbert	3,542	10,148	3,819	9,108
Fremont	6,644	13,087	6,844	12,668
Garfield	10,989	12,159	11,357	11,359
Gilpin	1,854	1,320	1,954	1,253
Grand	3,575	4,149	4,037	4,128
Gunnison	4,563	3,106	5,556	3,131
Hinsdale	228	352	240	344
Huerfano	1,897	1,615	1,989	1,580
Jackson	216	600	277	624
Jefferson	153,069	139,960	158,153	131,627
Kiowa	118	677	178	650
Kit Carson	789	2,664	912	2,455
La Plata	15,063	12,554	16,057	11,503
Lake	1,807	1,087	1,859	1,078
Larimer	83,103	74,603	89,822	73,641
Las Animas	3,282	3,105	3,562	3,086
Lincoln	537	1,663	546	1,717
Logan	2,675	6,124	2,846	6,002
Mesa	22,448	45,087	24,008	44,578
Mineral	291	344	270	334
Moffat	1,291	4,616	1,582	4,135
Montezuma	4,486	7,372	4,661	6,961
Montrose	5,852	12,789	6,495	12,199
Morgan	3,761	6,461	3,813	6,272
Otero	3,566	4,315	3,546	4,393
Ouray	1,640	1,470	1,636	1,367
Park	3,721	5,085	4,250	4,896
Phillips	588	1,637	622	1,612
Pitkin	6,648	2,941	7,349	2,484
Prowers	1,498	3,200	1,487	3,043
Pueblo	37,393	28,877	41,097	30,257
Rio Blanco	561	2,677	655	2,437
Rio Grande	2,256	2,553	2,448	2,930
Routt	7,389	5,361	8,270	4,725
Saguache	1,762	937	1,730	953
San Juan	266	212	264	218
San Miguel	2,961	1,144	3,349	933
Sedgwick	419	881	468	857
Summit	9,169	5,495	9,802	4,883

County	2012 Obama (D)	Romney (R)	2008 Obama (D)	McCain (R)
Teller	3,894	7,909	4,513	8,146
Washington	461	2,059	529	1,949
Weld	47,418	62,350	47,292	56,526
Yuma	950	3,433	1,117	3,286
Totals	**1,230,730**	**1,119,535**	**1,288,633**	**1,073,629**

All candidates, 2012: Obama, D., 1,230,730; Romney, R., 1,119,535; Johnson, LB., 31,991; Stein, Green, 6,850; Goode, Const., 5,761; Barr, Peace/Freedom, 4,478; Reed, unaff., 2,373; Anderson, Justice, 1,173; Tittle, We the People, 730; Hoefling, Amer. Ind., 625; La Riva, Socialism/Liberation, 282; Alexander, Soc. USA, 275; Miller, A3P, 247; Stevens, Objectivist, 211; Harris, Soc. Workers, 176; White, Soc. Equality, 171.

Connecticut

City	2012 Obama (D)	Romney (R)	2008 Obama (D)	McCain (R)
Bridgeport	32,135	5,168	33,976	6,507
Bristol	13,283	10,548	15,966	10,203
Danbury	15,290	10,590	16,028	10,732
East Hartford	13,000	4,272	14,811	5,195
Fairfield	15,282	14,352	17,236	13,071
Greenwich	11,137	14,368	16,233	13,937
Hamden	19,181	7,482	19,960	8,531
Hartford	31,735	2,138	31,741	2,686
Manchester	15,565	7,961	17,782	8,457
Meriden	14,886	6,880	15,913	7,363
Middletown	13,475	6,011	15,143	5,907
Milford	13,668	11,461	14,873	11,772
New Britain	14,938	4,466	16,742	5,442
New Haven	15,609	2,255	39,112	5,098
Norwalk	22,369	12,773	24,489	12,561
Shelton	8,362	10,327	9,655	10,428
Southington	10,727	10,452	12,066	9,845
Stamford	29,623	17,473	31,733	17,510
Stratford	13,483	9,324	14,626	10,199
Wallingford	11,559	9,259	12,833	9,372
Waterbury	32,495	11,019	22,599	12,821
West Hartford	21,080	10,538	23,576	10,021
West Haven	14,286	5,789	14,186	7,005
Other	458,401	399,438	546,493	414,675
Totals	**831,946**	**586,871**	**997,772**	**629,428**

All candidates, 2012: Obama, D., 831,946; Romney, R., 586,871; Johnson, LB., 11,739; Anderson, Ind., 5,127.

Delaware

County	2012 Obama (D)	Romney (R)	2008 Obama (D)	McCain (R)
Kent	35,525	32,134	36,392	29,827
New Castle	167,051	81,226	178,768	74,608
Sussex	39,971	52,116	40,299	47,939
Totals	**242,547**	**165,476**	**255,459**	**152,374**

All candidates, 2012: Obama, D., 242,547; Romney, R., 165,476; Johnson, LB., 3,882; Stein, Green, 1,939.

District of Columbia

	2012 Obama (D)	Romney (R)	2008 Obama (D)	McCain (R)
Totals	**222,332**	**17,337**	**245,800**	**17,367**

All candidates, 2012: Obama, D., 222,332; Romney, R., 17,337; Stein, DC Statehood Green, 2,045; Johnson, LB., 1,634.

Florida

County	2012 Obama (D)	Romney (R)	2008 Obama (D)	McCain (R)
Alachua	69,219	48,527	75,565	48,513
Baker	2,310	8,974	2,327	8,672
Bay	21,911	56,722	23,653	56,683
Bradford	3,324	8,216	3,430	8,136
Brevard	120,676	156,583	127,620	157,589
Broward	484,778	231,281	492,640	237,729
Calhoun	1,644	4,334	1,821	4,345
Charlotte	35,880	47,976	39,031	45,205
Citrus	28,347	44,530	31,460	43,706
Clay	25,604	69,826	26,697	67,203
Collier	51,531	96,342	54,450	86,379
Columbia	8,443	18,417	9,171	18,670
De Soto	4,158	5,577	4,383	5,632
Dixie	1,793	5,046	1,925	5,194
Duval	192,239	207,128	202,618	210,537
Escambia	57,700	87,974	61,572	91,411
Flagler	23,111	26,913	24,726	23,951
Franklin	1,845	3,568	2,134	3,818
Gadsden	15,706	6,614	15,582	6,811
Gilchrist	1,883	5,912	1,996	5,656
Glades	1,592	2,333	1,381	1,938

County	2012 Obama (D)	Romney (R)	2008 Obama (D)	McCain (R)
Gulf	2,001	4,986	2,149	4,980
Hamilton	2,216	3,130	2,364	3,179
Hardee	2,461	4,694	2,568	4,763
Hendry	4,735	5,352	4,998	5,780
Hernando	37,725	44,837	41,886	45,021
Highlands	16,036	25,828	18,135	26,221
Hillsborough	280,939	246,225	272,963	236,355
Holmes	1,262	6,891	1,446	7,033
Indian River	27,354	43,325	29,710	40,176
Jackson	7,299	13,372	7,671	13,717
Jefferson	3,937	3,805	4,088	3,797
Lafayette	687	2,668	642	2,679
Lake	61,697	87,534	62,948	82,802
Lee	109,550	153,668	119,701	147,608
Leon	89,834	55,245	91,747	55,705
Levy	6,089	12,027	6,711	11,754
Liberty	942	2,301	895	2,339
Madison	4,174	4,474	4,270	4,544
Manatee	66,276	85,455	70,034	80,721
Marion	66,793	93,010	70,839	89,628
Martin	30,051	48,136	33,508	44,143
Miami-Dade	521,329	317,382	499,831	360,551
Monroe	19,334	19,208	20,907	18,933
Nassau	10,205	29,849	10,618	27,403
Okaloosa	23,305	69,944	25,872	68,789
Okeechobee	4,843	7,314	5,108	7,561
Orange	268,478	185,490	273,009	186,832
Osceola	67,117	40,561	59,962	40,086
Palm Beach	323,862	228,611	361,271	226,037
Pasco	97,783	112,055	102,417	110,104
Pinellas	233,438	209,007	248,299	210,066
Polk	114,034	131,294	113,865	128,878
Putnam	11,609	19,287	13,226	19,637
St. Johns	35,056	78,360	35,791	69,222
St. Lucie	66,246	56,125	67,125	52,512
Santa Rosa	17,701	58,041	19,470	55,972
Sarasota	94,749	110,230	102,686	102,897
Seminole	95,640	109,456	99,335	105,070
Sumter	19,506	40,631	17,655	30,866
Suwannee	4,727	12,631	4,916	12,534
Taylor	2,749	6,237	2,803	6,457
Union	1,336	3,978	1,300	3,940
Volusia	114,446	117,299	127,795	113,938
Wakulla	5,156	9,257	5,311	8,877
Walton	6,646	21,433	7,174	19,561
Washington	2,797	7,978	2,863	8,178
Totals	**4,137,844**	**4,091,414**	**4,282,074**	**4,045,624**

All candidates, 2012: Obama, D., 4,137,844; Romney, R., 4,091,414; Johnson, LB., 43,563; Stein, Green, 8,703; Barr, Peace/Freedom, 7,981; Stevens, Objectivist, 3,797; Goode, Const., 2,528; Anderson, Justice, 1,714; Hoefling, Amer. Ind., 915; Barnett, RF., 793; Alexander, Soc., 779; Lindsay, Socialism/Liberation, 315.

Georgia

County	2012 Obama (D)	Romney (R)	2008 Obama (D)	McCain (R)
Appling	1,756	5,231	1,846	5,085
Atkinson	930	1,938	938	1,941
Bacon	791	3,092	817	3,089
Baker	790	784	846	828
Baldwin	8,469	7,585	8,587	7,823
Banks	779	5,353	1,027	5,120
Barrow	6,019	18,719	6,657	17,625
Bartow	8,383	26,847	9,662	25,976
Ben Hill	2,508	3,395	2,590	3,417
Berrien	1,268	4,837	1,471	4,901
Bibb	38,538	25,606	38,987	27,037
Bleckley	1,266	3,586	1,380	3,657
Brantley	939	4,963	1,119	5,080
Brooks	3,101	3,522	2,669	3,507
Bryan	3,695	9,537	3,636	9,112
Bulloch	9,572	14,159	9,586	14,174
Burke	5,403	4,298	5,233	4,344
Butts	2,966	6,306	3,065	5,947
Calhoun	1,297	883	1,342	862
Camden	6,358	11,318	6,482	10,502
Candler	1,155	2,344	1,209	2,286
Carroll	12,635	28,249	14,334	28,661
Catoosa	5,357	17,848	6,025	18,218
Charlton	1,197	2,527	1,197	2,466
Chatham	56,901	44,258	62,755	46,829
Chattahoochee	726	732	830	811
Chattooga	2,220	5,434	2,596	5,572
Cherokee	19,813	76,473	22,350	70,279
Clarke	25,386	13,804	29,591	15,333
Clay	858	535	879	558

County	2012 Obama (D)	Romney (R)	2008 Obama (D)	McCain (R)
Clayton	79,310	13,126	82,527	16,506
Clinch	852	1,598	989	1,678
Cobb	132,526	171,464	141,216	170,957
Coffee	5,048	9,242	4,811	8,872
Colquitt	3,971	9,240	4,139	9,185
Columbia	16,420	41,724	15,703	39,322
Cook	2,042	3,934	2,075	3,782
Coweta	15,156	39,633	15,521	37,571
Crawford	1,699	3,366	1,832	3,358
Crisp	3,160	4,179	3,085	4,424
Dade	1,404	4,458	1,612	4,703
Dawson	1,241	8,843	1,632	8,242
Decatur	4,580	5,816	4,424	5,890
DeKalb	237,704	64,308	254,594	65,581
Dodge	2,440	5,214	2,595	5,543
Dooly	2,278	1,983	2,138	1,991
Dougherty	26,209	11,441	26,135	12,547
Douglas	28,410	26,226	27,825	26,812
Early	2,762	2,556	2,603	2,711
Echols	173	917	201	981
Effingham	4,941	15,591	4,936	15,230
Elbert	3,179	4,857	3,366	4,868
Emanuel	2,919	5,086	3,068	5,110
Evans	1,266	2,267	1,374	2,462
Fannin	2,027	7,853	2,611	7,807
Fayette	19,703	38,046	20,313	38,501
Floyd	9,595	22,636	10,691	23,132
Forsyth	14,544	65,853	15,406	59,166
Franklin	1,499	6,112	1,914	6,069
Fulton	240,432	125,905	272,000	130,136
Gilmer	1,955	8,920	2,614	8,408
Glascock	176	1,135	210	1,202
Glynn	11,922	20,853	12,676	20,479
Gordon	3,436	13,174	4,268	13,113
Grady	3,419	5,922	3,539	5,775
Greene	3,195	5,067	3,339	4,532
Gwinnett	131,879	159,563	129,025	158,746
Habersham	2,297	12,148	2,900	11,766
Hall	12,489	45,918	14,457	44,962
Hancock	3,301	764	3,535	795
Haralson	1,787	8,439	2,248	8,658
Harris	3,900	10,572	4,184	10,648
Hart	2,869	6,516	3,365	6,537
Heard	947	3,155	1,042	3,133
Henry	43,374	46,299	40,567	47,157
Houston	22,643	34,631	22,094	33,392
Irwin	1,134	2,519	1,197	2,605
Jackson	4,236	19,122	4,950	17,776
Jasper	1,839	4,121	1,935	3,916
Jeff Davis	1,271	3,994	1,356	3,867
Jefferson	4,238	2,992	4,149	3,061
Jenkins	1,487	1,884	1,482	1,936
Johnson	1,305	2,440	1,198	2,426
Jones	4,272	7,740	4,572	7,782
Lamar	2,602	4,896	2,752	4,873
Lanier	1,108	1,812	1,062	1,787
Laurens	7,508	11,947	7,769	12,052
Lee	3,187	10,310	3,100	9,925
Liberty	10,427	5,558	10,474	5,828
Lincoln	1,586	2,806	1,650	2,731
Long	1,434	2,300	1,288	2,119
Lowndes	17,118	21,176	17,597	21,269
Lumpkin	2,049	8,633	2,586	8,326
Macon	3,211	1,545	3,251	1,712
Madison	2,486	8,441	2,965	8,226
Marion	1,411	1,731	1,381	1,772
McDuffie	4,041	5,475	3,989	5,400
McIntosh	2,860	3,405	2,905	3,282
Meriwether	4,163	4,676	4,465	4,982
Miller	848	1,904	818	1,899
Mitchell	4,081	4,153	3,872	4,201
Monroe	3,779	8,352	4,106	7,933
Montgomery	1,135	2,662	1,045	2,521
Morgan	2,751	6,178	3,091	5,987
Murray	2,542	8,439	3,026	8,180
Muscogee	40,500	25,301	44,158	29,568
Newton	21,844	20,979	20,827	20,337
Oconee	4,140	12,222	4,825	12,120
Oglethorpe	1,913	4,250	2,232	4,144
Paulding	15,779	40,771	17,229	39,192
Peach	6,141	5,280	5,927	5,173
Pickens	1,975	10,547	2,595	10,004
Pierce	1,124	5,666	1,253	5,500
Pike	1,355	6,660	1,575	6,547
Polk	3,608	9,798	4,052	9,850
Pulaski	1,219	2,444	1,377	2,553
Putnam	2,917	6,210	3,102	5,966

County	2012 Obama (D)	Romney (R)	2008 Obama (D)	McCain (R)
Quitman	612	510	597	509
Rabun	1,558	5,753	2,001	5,487
Randolph	1,749	1,249	1,833	1,370
Richmond	52,461	25,821	52,100	26,842
Rockdale	21,878	15,671	20,526	16,921
Schley	448	1,286	479	1,252
Screven	2,769	3,285	3,024	3,423
Seminole	1,475	2,244	1,660	2,315
Spalding	9,884	14,901	10,141	14,885
Stephens	2,123	7,207	2,705	7,689
Stewart	1,233	695	1,305	783
Sumter	6,370	5,372	6,454	5,717
Talbot	2,264	1,202	2,369	1,301
Taliaferro	636	321	643	339
Tattnall	1,894	4,702	1,932	4,730
Taylor	887	904	1,536	2,021
Telfair	1,804	2,479	1,862	2,486
Terrell	2,544	1,834	2,501	1,890
Thomas	7,651	11,153	7,720	10,642
Tift	4,640	9,171	4,749	9,431
Toombs	2,740	6,519	2,964	6,658
Towns	1,265	4,834	1,391	4,292
Treutlen	1,068	1,646	1,112	1,826
Troup	10,545	15,170	10,455	15,391
Turner	1,508	2,027	1,427	2,096
Twiggs	2,269	1,905	2,402	2,087
Union	2,137	8,771	2,486	8,013
Upson	3,955	7,229	4,061	7,291
Walker	5,269	16,245	6,095	17,110
Walton	8,139	29,018	8,469	27,253
Ware	3,892	7,933	4,034	8,311
Warren	1,525	990	1,554	1,087
Washington	4,705	4,033	4,607	4,216
Wayne	2,594	7,553	2,858	7,601
Webster	573	598	515	588
Wheeler	772	1,366	794	1,408
White	1,670	8,647	2,174	8,467
Whitfield	7,193	19,290	8,167	19,230
Wilcox	1,059	2,050	978	2,159
Wilkes	2,080	2,628	2,315	2,705
Wilkinson	2,180	2,245	2,298	2,349
Worth	2,486	5,864	2,542	5,780
Totals	**1,745,283**	**2,054,373**	**1,844,123**	**2,048,759**

All candidates, 2012: Romney, R., 2,054,373; Obama, D., 1,745,283; Johnson, LB., 44,795.

Hawaii

County	2012 Obama (D)	Romney (R)	2008 Obama (D)	McCain (R)
Hawaii	46,670	14,541	50,819	14,866
Honolulu	201,803	87,255	214,909	88,301
Kauai	18,638	6,121	20,416	6,245
Maui	35,979	11,577	39,727	11,154
Totals	**303,090**	**119,494**	**325,871**	**120,566**

All candidates, 2012: Obama, D., 303,090; Romney, R., 119,494; Johnson, LB., 3,789; Stein, Green, 3,121.

Idaho

County	2012 Obama (D)	Romney (R)	2008 Obama (D)	McCain (R)
Ada	77,043	97,471	82,236	93,328
Adams	577	1,413	728	1,517
Bannock	13,214	21,010	14,792	19,356
Bear Lake	302	2,489	502	2,377
Benewah	1,164	2,596	1,407	2,646
Bingham	3,822	13,440	4,424	12,230
Blaine	5,992	3,939	6,947	3,439
Boise	953	2,284	1,240	2,433
Bonner	4,963	8,319	7,840	11,145
Bonneville	9,929	32,336	11,417	29,334
Boundary	1,225	3,138	1,484	3,078
Butte	258	1,001	318	1,056
Camas	159	402	187	422
Canyon	19,866	44,369	20,147	42,752
Caribou	385	2,608	553	2,656
Cassia	1,093	7,150	1,332	6,309
Clark	66	235	64	305
Clearwater	1,032	2,541	1,211	2,569
Custer	530	1,744	611	1,694
Elmore	2,513	5,227	2,591	5,665
Franklin	325	5,195	600	4,246
Fremont	810	4,907	1,065	4,700
Gem	1,957	5,311	2,166	5,585
Gooding	1,287	3,696	1,489	3,765
Idaho	1,722	5,821	2,017	5,895
Jefferson	1,303	9,895	1,641	8,540

County	2012 Obama (D)	Romney (R)	2008 Obama (D)	McCain (R)
Jerome	1,699	4,804	1,794	4,897
Kootenai	18,824	39,347	22,120	38,387
Latah	7,094	6,135	9,195	7,988
Lemhi	960	3,029	1,061	2,938
Lewis	396	1,173	479	1,275
Lincoln	429	1,141	545	1,232
Madison	832	13,445	1,627	11,131
Minidoka	1,390	5,442	1,630	5,087
Nez Perce	6,451	9,967	7,123	10,357
Oneida	217	1,838	381	1,724
Owyhee	833	2,794	944	3,024
Payette	2,271	6,004	2,415	5,988
Power	982	1,870	1,027	1,754
Shoshone	2,277	2,699	2,521	2,953
Teton	1,926	2,458	2,302	2,263
Twin Falls	7,541	19,773	8,621	19,032
Valley	2,095	2,664	2,405	2,772
Washington	1,104	3,128	1,241	3,168
Totals	**209,811**	**416,248**	**236,440**	**403,012**

All candidates, 2012: Romney, R., 416,248; Obama, D., 209,811; Johnson, LB., 9,319; Stein, Ind., 4,330; Anderson, Ind., 2,451; Goode, Const., 2,169.

Illinois

County	2012 Obama (D)	Romney (R)	2008 Obama (D)	McCain (R)
Adams	9,627	20,371	11,794	18,711
Alexander	1,961	1,485	2,189	1,692
Bond	3,016	4,091	3,843	3,947
Boone	9,868	11,084	11,333	10,403
Brown	787	1,511	986	1,544
Bureau	8,118	8,151	8,889	7,911
Calhoun	1,079	1,439	1,423	1,221
Carroll	3,658	3,551	3,965	3,596
Cass	2,050	2,707	2,690	2,617
Champaign	40,378	35,086	48,597	33,871
Christian	5,487	8,873	6,918	7,872
Clark	2,587	5,138	3,742	4,409
Clay	1,581	4,184	2,425	3,926
Clinton	5,577	10,493	7,657	9,357
Coles	9,252	11,623	11,716	10,978
Cook	1,417,269	472,235	1,629,024	487,736
Crawford	2,855	5,577	3,883	5,070
Cumberland	1,640	3,506	2,055	3,156
DeKalb	21,171	18,906	25,784	18,266
DeWitt	2,598	4,576	3,308	4,348
Douglas	2,426	5,331	3,228	5,005
DuPage	197,441	193,333	228,698	183,626
Edgar	2,563	5,125	3,743	4,398
Edwards	754	2,402	1,140	2,137
Effingham	3,855	12,491	5,262	11,323
Fayette	2,848	5,950	3,967	5,499
Ford	1,654	4,225	2,227	4,079
Franklin	7,245	10,253	8,880	9,404
Fulton	8,324	6,622	9,732	6,251
Gallatin	1,028	1,492	1,587	1,212
Greene	2,023	3,446	2,619	3,053
Grundy	9,319	11,198	11,063	10,687
Hamilton	1,266	2,566	1,796	2,353
Hancock	3,246	4,810	4,141	5,161
Hardin	742	1,535	892	1,330
Henderson	1,977	1,538	2,215	1,541
Henry	12,316	11,564	13,181	11,263
Iroquois	3,408	9,115	4,643	8,695
Jackson	11,306	9,130	15,248	9,687
Jasper	1,434	3,511	2,063	2,964
Jefferson	6,080	9,805	7,462	9,302
Jersey	3,656	6,032	5,042	5,329
Jo Daviess	5,660	5,529	6,403	5,170
Johnson	1,571	3,959	1,871	3,912
Kane	91,120	89,502	106,756	83,963
Kankakee	21,574	23,115	24,750	22,527
Kendall	21,219	23,076	24,742	21,380
Knox	12,993	9,133	14,191	9,419
Lake	151,552	128,609	177,242	118,545
LaSalle	23,023	23,207	27,443	21,872
Lawrence	2,010	3,853	3,016	3,403
Lee	6,932	8,046	7,765	8,258
Livingston	5,014	9,745	6,189	9,191
Logan	3,974	7,835	5,250	7,429
Macon	22,688	25,249	25,487	24,948
Macoupin	9,440	10,909	12,090	9,891
Madison	58,813	60,481	68,979	57,177
Marion	6,210	9,229	8,345	8,691
Marshall	2,452	3,287	3,081	3,145
Mason	2,867	3,265	3,542	3,141
Massac	2,092	4,278	2,693	4,371

County	2012 Obama (D)	Romney (R)	2008 Obama (D)	McCain (R)
McDonough	5,957	6,142	6,783	6,055
McHenry	59,691	71,488	72,288	64,845
McLean	31,590	39,638	37,689	36,767
Menard	2,095	3,944	2,706	3,672
Mercer	4,503	3,874	4,887	3,833
Monroe	6,205	10,879	7,953	9,881
Montgomery	5,053	6,771	6,491	6,150
Morgan	5,792	7,962	7,467	7,591
Moultrie	2,142	3,781	2,668	3,471
Ogle	9,504	13,409	11,253	13,144
Peoria	40,050	36,617	45,906	34,579
Perry	3,813	5,497	4,701	5,086
Piatt	3,081	5,412	3,859	4,991
Pike	2,276	4,853	3,024	4,457
Pope	649	1,511	845	1,343
Pulaski	1,389	1,562	1,638	1,593
Putnam	1,558	1,500	1,900	1,378
Randolph	5,753	8,284	7,395	7,538
Richland	2,360	4,750	3,181	4,329
Rock Island	39,081	24,888	42,210	25,364
St. Clair	66,749	49,610	76,160	47,958
Saline	3,697	6,803	5,083	6,099
Sangamon	41,961	50,131	51,300	46,945
Schuyler	1,726	2,062	1,900	1,833
Scott	910	1,586	1,090	1,455
Shelby	3,336	6,837	4,245	6,396
Stark	1,095	1,527	1,357	1,513
Stephenson	7,954	8,742	11,349	9,909
Tazewell	24,385	35,266	29,384	33,247
Union	3,135	4,951	3,918	5,003
Vermilion	10,773	14,888	16,246	16,054
Wabash	1,588	3,473	2,462	3,254
Warren	3,893	3,460	4,286	3,637
Washington	2,448	4,787	3,342	4,473
Wayne	1,514	5,984	2,547	5,390
White	2,187	4,729	3,315	3,987
Whiteside	12,393	8,676	15,607	10,883
Will	127,522	118,366	160,406	122,597
Williamson	10,622	17,880	12,914	17,387
Winnebago	60,334	53,722	70,034	53,886
Woodford	5,564	12,947	6,999	12,191
Totals	**2,912,972**	**2,087,557**	**3,419,348**	**2,031,179**

All candidates, 2012: Obama, D., 2,912,972; Romney, R., 2,087,557; Johnson, LB., 54,740; Stein, Green, 29,298.

Indiana

County	2012 Obama (D)	Romney (R)	2008 Obama (D)	McCain (R)
Adams	3,800	8,936	4,928	8,404
Allen	59,834	84,378	71,263	77,793
Bartholomew	10,622	18,083	13,567	17,067
Benton	1,159	2,329	1,563	2,183
Blackford	1,927	2,710	2,677	2,690
Boone	8,326	18,807	9,752	16,622
Brown	3,056	4,330	3,854	4,060
Carroll	2,631	4,993	3,736	4,858
Cass	5,365	8,432	7,011	8,346
Clark	20,775	25,422	21,953	25,326
Clay	3,630	7,065	4,954	6,267
Clinton	3,307	6,338	5,307	6,919
Crawford	2,040	2,418	2,286	2,393
Daviess	2,437	7,638	3,370	7,098
Dearborn	6,387	15,216	7,123	14,886
Decatur	2,941	7,119	3,892	6,449
DeKalb	5,419	10,586	7,175	9,780
Delaware	22,630	21,231	28,384	20,916
Dubois	6,522	11,654	8,748	9,526
Elkhart	24,376	42,348	31,398	39,396
Fayette	3,553	5,044	4,389	4,917
Floyd	14,805	19,868	16,263	19,957
Fountain	2,233	4,660	3,094	4,158
Franklin	2,907	7,421	3,404	7,018
Fulton	2,621	5,315	3,702	5,147
Gibson	4,928	9,487	6,455	8,449
Grant	9,516	15,088	11,293	14,734
Greene	4,340	8,457	5,709	7,691
Hamilton	43,794	90,740	49,704	78,401
Hancock	8,526	21,053	11,874	22,008
Harrison	6,600	10,629	7,288	10,551
Hendricks	21,100	44,308	24,548	39,728
Henry	7,613	10,836	10,059	10,896
Howard	15,097	20,284	17,871	20,248
Huntington	4,596	10,862	5,843	10,291
Jackson	5,838	10,419	7,354	9,726
Jasper	4,672	7,955	5,044	7,669
Jay	3,063	4,643	3,748	4,401

County	2012 Obama (D)	Romney (R)	2008 Obama (D)	McCain (R)
Jefferson	5,728	7,096	6,255	7,053
Jennings	3,818	6,112	5,312	6,261
Johnson	17,080	39,136	21,553	36,487
Knox	5,228	9,612	7,569	8,639
Kosciusko	6,862	22,553	9,236	20,488
LaGrange	2,897	6,227	3,663	5,702
Lake	130,824	68,397	139,301	67,742
LaPorte	24,104	18,609	28,258	17,918
Lawrence	5,779	11,622	7,208	11,018
Madison	24,404	26,755	30,152	26,403
Marion	215,428	136,102	241,987	134,313
Marshall	6,136	11,260	7,889	10,406
Martin	1,351	3,262	1,706	3,122
Miami	4,220	8,163	5,564	8,312
Monroe	19,529	14,580	41,450	21,118
Montgomery	4,244	9,768	6,013	9,060
Morgan	7,969	19,591	10,330	18,129
Newton	2,212	3,291	2,625	3,301
Noble	5,229	10,680	7,064	9,673
Ohio	992	1,757	1,158	1,713
Orange	2,939	4,615	3,390	4,536
Owen	2,823	5,062	3,570	4,415
Parke	2,106	4,228	2,924	3,909
Perry	4,314	3,403	5,141	3,202
Pike	2,125	3,627	2,700	3,221
Porter	36,950	34,197	39,178	33,857
Posey	4,531	7,427	5,828	6,804
Pulaski	1,899	3,366	2,466	3,388
Putnam	4,504	9,004	6,334	8,086
Randolph	3,768	6,218	4,839	5,788
Ripley	3,241	7,484	4,187	7,794
Rush	2,221	4,633	3,229	4,271
St. Joseph	56,401	52,475	68,710	48,510
Scott	3,998	4,539	4,271	4,445
Shelby	5,357	10,972	6,987	10,333
Spencer	4,026	5,515	5,039	5,001
Starke	3,809	4,738	4,778	4,473
Steuben	4,846	8,542	6,284	7,674
Sullivan	3,191	4,902	4,284	4,343
Switzerland	1,437	1,872	1,638	1,940
Tippecanoe	26,642	28,708	37,781	29,822
Tipton	2,432	4,773	3,250	4,452
Union	1,018	2,022	1,224	2,061
Vanderburgh	31,659	39,504	39,423	37,512
Vermillion	2,979	3,426	4,003	3,010
Vigo	19,707	19,368	25,040	18,121
Wabash	3,929	8,528	5,456	8,238
Warren	1,324	2,377	1,755	2,166
Warrick	8,791	15,350	12,329	16,013
Washington	3,909	6,532	4,562	6,519
Wayne	10,591	14,321	13,459	14,558
Wells	3,434	9,255	4,403	8,504
White	3,635	5,970	4,839	5,731
Whitley	4,420	10,257	5,862	9,124
Totals	**1,135,976**	**1,408,885**	**1,374,039**	**1,345,648**

All candidates, 2012: Romney, R., 1,408,885; Obama, D., 1,135,976; Johnson, LB., 49,473.

Iowa

County	2012 Obama (D)	Romney (R)	2008 Obama (D)	McCain (R)
Adair	1,788	2,110	1,924	2,060
Adams	1,018	1,103	1,118	1,046
Allamakee	3,511	3,230	3,971	2,965
Appanoose	2,934	3,153	2,970	3,086
Audubon	1,608	1,800	1,739	1,634
Benton	6,850	6,935	7,058	6,447
Black Hawk	39,338	26,078	39,184	24,662
Boone	7,457	6,540	7,356	6,293
Bremer	6,710	6,383	6,940	5,741
Buchanan	5,903	4,443	6,050	4,139
Buena Vista	3,683	4,548	4,075	4,223
Butler	3,321	4,104	3,364	3,700
Calhoun	2,232	2,890	2,341	2,741
Carroll	4,912	5,577	5,302	4,922
Cass	2,856	4,212	3,211	4,006
Cedar	4,931	4,510	5,221	4,289
Cerro Gordo	13,204	10,084	14,405	9,375
Cherokee	2,623	3,656	2,890	3,372
Chickasaw	3,552	2,836	3,923	2,557
Clarke	2,187	2,124	2,218	2,118
Clay	3,363	4,934	3,925	4,355
Clayton	4,768	4,146	5,195	3,651

County	2012 Obama (D)	Romney (R)	2008 Obama (D)	McCain (R)
Clinton	15,123	9,423	15,018	9,324
Crawford	3,035	3,584	3,715	3,345
Dallas	16,211	20,538	15,149	16,954
Davis	1,518	2,133	1,680	2,029
Decatur	1,790	1,945	1,986	2,020
Delaware	4,605	4,628	4,649	4,113
Des Moines	11,873	8,130	12,462	7,721
Dickinson	4,088	5,911	4,625	5,162
Dubuque	28,600	21,265	28,611	18,651
Emmet	2,087	2,499	2,570	2,373
Fayette	5,709	4,484	5,908	4,205
Floyd	4,674	3,466	4,822	3,051
Franklin	2,256	2,818	2,575	2,501
Fremont	1,636	1,971	1,848	1,989
Greene	2,369	2,373	2,371	2,349
Grundy	2,615	4,205	2,790	3,945
Guthrie	2,565	3,164	2,625	3,074
Hamilton	3,776	3,986	4,018	3,913
Hancock	2,506	3,306	2,805	3,016
Hardin	4,021	4,647	4,393	4,315
Harrison	3,131	4,059	3,555	3,909
Henry	4,451	5,025	4,349	4,822
Howard	2,767	1,793	2,941	1,722
Humboldt	1,967	3,099	2,160	2,895
Ida	1,317	2,276	1,454	2,036
Iowa	4,118	4,551	4,202	4,188
Jackson	5,877	4,171	6,102	3,673
Jasper	10,240	8,868	10,250	8,794
Jefferson	4,772	3,429	5,070	3,324
Johnson	50,090	23,556	51,027	20,732
Jones	5,514	4,712	5,446	4,405
Keokuk	2,298	2,840	2,518	2,712
Kossuth	3,824	4,914	4,625	4,329
Lee	9,428	6,787	9,821	7,062
Linn	68,028	47,427	68,037	43,626
Louisa	2,449	2,416	2,523	2,314
Lucas	1,977	2,248	2,029	2,330
Lyon	1,416	4,965	1,675	4,471
Madison	3,508	4,492	3,733	4,579
Mahaska	4,207	6,420	4,464	6,271
Marion	7,478	9,810	7,421	9,256
Marshall	10,085	8,411	10,023	8,278
Mills	2,842	4,211	2,976	4,183
Mitchell	2,831	2,643	3,179	2,469
Monona	2,098	2,555	2,295	2,411
Monroe	1,729	2,022	1,798	2,000
Montgomery	1,919	2,999	2,326	2,887
Muscatine	11,213	8,152	10,920	7,929
O'Brien	1,964	5,259	2,338	4,894
Osceola	909	2,225	1,037	2,027
Page	2,588	4,338	2,900	4,351
Palo Alto	2,124	2,649	2,428	2,294
Plymouth	4,148	8,577	4,629	7,765
Pocahontas	1,518	2,388	1,800	2,138
Polk	128,264	96,029	120,984	89,668
Pottawattamie	19,347	21,751	20,436	21,237
Poweshiek	5,307	4,409	5,519	4,340
Ringgold	1,181	1,366	1,236	1,401
Sac	2,117	3,086	2,256	2,705
Scott	50,581	38,223	48,927	36,365
Shelby	2,468	3,903	2,863	3,488
Sioux	2,683	14,361	3,030	13,490
Story	25,940	19,557	26,548	18,995
Tama	4,737	4,076	4,899	3,820
Taylor	1,261	1,680	1,347	1,607
Union	3,029	2,800	3,000	2,781
Van Buren	1,398	2,058	1,546	1,986
Wapello	8,616	6,777	8,820	6,663
Warren	12,521	13,031	12,299	12,144
Washington	5,081	5,540	5,170	5,247
Wayne	1,251	1,583	1,357	1,565
Webster	9,458	8,453	9,917	8,337
Winnebago	2,895	2,897	3,254	2,730
Winneshiek	6,245	4,618	6,829	4,273
Woodbury	22,026	22,136	21,983	22,219
Worth	2,343	1,743	2,567	1,612
Wright	2,794	3,309	3,102	3,198
Totals	**816,174**	**727,545**	**828,940**	**682,379**

All candidates, 2012: Obama, D., 816,174; Romney, R., 727,545; Johnson, LB., 12,820; Stein, Green, 3,739; Goode, Const., 3,021; Litzel, Ind., 1,196; Harris, Soc. Workers, 465; La Riva, Socialism/Liberation, 364.

Kansas

County	2012 Obama (D)	Romney (R)	2008 Obama (D)	McCain (R)
Allen	1,449	2,586	2,189	3,552
Anderson	937	2,246	1,175	2,362
Atchison	2,486	3,836	3,241	3,791
Barber	473	1,753	598	1,833
Barton	2,693	9,132	3,027	7,802
Bourbon	1,951	4,022	2,394	4,240
Brown	1,039	2,738	1,317	2,985
Butler	7,124	17,764	9,159	18,155
Chase	343	857	383	976
Chautauqua	259	1,201	401	1,418
Cherokee	2,868	5,345	3,594	5,886
Cheyenne	231	1,157	323	1,148
Clark	171	791	245	897
Clay	811	2,715	1,009	2,998
Cloud	951	2,886	1,233	3,121
Coffey	884	2,860	1,121	3,054
Comanche	141	756	194	765
Cowley	4,219	7,932	5,012	8,492
Crawford	6,545	7,480	7,957	7,735
Decatur	266	1,219	343	1,189
Dickinson	1,962	5,709	2,422	6,081
Doniphan	885	2,397	1,115	2,372
Douglas	28,012	17,028	34,398	17,929
Edwards	291	1,048	333	995
Elk	277	1,040	363	1,042
Ellis	3,464	9,057	4,010	8,207
Ellsworth	696	1,905	851	2,021
Finney	2,307	5,108	3,275	6,926
Ford	2,468	5,459	2,991	5,730
Franklin	3,611	6,893	4,433	7,079
Geary	3,158	4,242	3,491	4,492
Gove	174	1,155	261	1,136
Graham	248	1,044	325	1,060
Grant	437	1,742	635	1,995
Gray	304	1,568	436	1,643
Greeley	112	539	151	591
Greenwood	653	1,986	622	1,619
Hamilton	159	678	233	844
Harper	536	1,723	736	1,999
Harvey	5,162	8,352	6,318	9,006
Haskell	202	1,131	278	1,277
Hodgeman	178	857	211	865
Jackson	1,871	3,477	2,308	3,811
Jefferson	2,883	4,647	3,542	5,220
Jewell	225	1,220	313	1,231
Johnson	107,651	155,442	127,091	152,627
Kearny	261	1,060	309	1,159
Kingman	731	2,371	963	2,603
Kiowa	160	970	200	912
Labette	3,074	4,668	3,839	5,001
Lane	170	732	193	814
Leavenworth	11,072	16,825	13,255	16,791
Lincoln	284	1,148	347	1,204
Linn	130	459	1,425	3,086
Logan	194	1,084	225	1,187
Lyon	4,972	6,358	5,924	6,698
Marion	1,371	3,865	1,801	4,159
Marshall	1,451	3,123	1,784	3,157
McPherson	3,384	8,399	4,218	8,937
Meade	254	1,394	357	1,540
Miami	4,632	9,721	5,742	9,382
Mitchell	576	2,293	701	2,440
Montgomery	3,406	8,417	4,338	9,309
Morris	705	1,750	907	1,875
Morton	180	1,050	229	1,153
Nemaha	988	3,878	1,432	3,817
Neosho	2,012	4,193	2,563	4,473
Ness	146	925	289	1,207
Norton	393	1,855	497	1,878
Osage	2,228	4,336	2,534	4,820
Osborne	320	1,448	403	1,490
Ottawa	548	2,260	704	2,323
Pawnee	704	1,808	882	1,946
Phillips	376	2,116	525	2,105
Pottawatomie	2,291	6,692	2,599	6,929
Pratt	974	2,730	1,294	2,822
Rawlins	184	1,207	273	1,247
Reno	7,888	15,398	9,916	16,112
Republic	470	2,098	640	1,978
Rice	899	2,631	1,163	2,780
Riley	8,587	11,157	10,495	12,111
Rooks	398	2,159	468	2,068

County	2012 Obama (D)	Romney (R)	2008 Obama (D)	McCain (R)
Rush	361	1,151	504	1,225
Russell	584	2,505	736	2,509
Saline	6,910	13,697	8,186	14,165
Scott	271	1,702	321	1,823
Sedgwick	69,373	104,411	82,337	106,849
Seward	1,393	3,495	1,493	3,791
Shawnee	35,959	37,226	41,235	41,476
Sheridan	165	1,136	254	1,108
Sherman	575	1,967	688	1,959
Smith	345	1,598	446	1,719
Stafford	403	1,382	542	1,495
Stanton	135	571	188	628
Stevens	241	1,724	283	1,815
Sumner	2,617	6,162	3,353	6,737
Thomas	576	2,729	787	2,837
Trego	289	1,230	420	1,225
Wabaunsee	908	2,230	1,036	2,395
Wallace	68	702	96	690
Washington	515	2,300	659	2,248
Wichita	157	821	163	840
Wilson	685	2,255	1,170	2,850
Woodson	377	1,030	512	1,055
Wyandotte	33,265	15,273	39,865	16,506
Totals	**426,352**	**674,598**	**514,765**	**699,655**

All candidates, 2012: Romney, R., 674,598; Obama, D., 426,352; Johnson, LB., 19,779; Baldwin, RF., 4,704.

Kentucky

County	2012 Obama (D)	Romney (R)	2008 Obama (D)	McCain (R)
Adair	1,508	6,345	1,668	5,512
Allen	1,808	5,184	2,024	5,258
Anderson	3,315	6,822	3,462	6,885
Ballard	1,189	2,647	1,427	2,537
Barren	5,400	10,922	5,434	11,133
Bath	1,770	2,275	2,210	2,234
Bell	2,224	7,127	2,782	6,681
Boone	15,628	35,920	16,292	33,812
Bourbon	3,075	4,692	3,385	4,820
Boyd	7,776	10,883	8,886	11,430
Boyle	4,471	7,703	4,769	7,701
Bracken	1,147	2,029	1,241	2,066
Breathitt	1,562	3,318	2,205	2,671
Breckinridge	2,825	5,025	3,110	5,281
Bullitt	9,971	21,306	10,177	20,102
Butler	1,293	3,716	1,555	3,696
Caldwell	1,852	3,904	2,212	3,866
Calloway	5,314	9,438	6,165	8,991
Campbell	15,080	24,240	15,622	24,046
Carlisle	750	1,835	879	1,699
Carroll	1,629	1,999	1,716	2,032
Carter	3,383	5,279	4,316	5,252
Casey	1,086	4,904	1,219	4,679
Christian	8,252	13,475	8,880	13,699
Clark	5,228	9,931	5,749	9,664
Clay	1,111	6,176	1,552	5,710
Clinton	752	3,569	761	3,366
Crittenden	960	2,839	1,254	2,604
Cumberland	599	2,216	697	2,056
Daviess	16,208	25,092	19,282	23,692
Edmonson	1,374	3,232	1,652	3,562
Elliott	1,186	1,126	1,535	902
Estill	1,356	3,749	1,555	3,685
Fayette	62,078	60,793	66,042	59,884
Fleming	1,911	3,780	2,279	3,432
Floyd	4,733	9,784	7,530	7,741
Franklin	11,535	11,345	11,767	11,911
Fulton	1,022	1,425	1,238	1,530
Gallatin	1,238	1,758	1,278	1,840
Garrard	1,661	5,310	2,012	5,118
Grant	2,810	5,664	3,112	5,510
Graves	4,547	10,699	5,843	10,056
Grayson	2,744	6,404	3,154	6,605
Green	1,165	3,634	1,204	3,785
Greenup	6,027	8,855	6,621	8,849
Hancock	1,833	2,212	2,135	1,928
Hardin	15,214	23,357	15,650	23,896
Harlan	1,830	8,652	2,586	7,165
Harrison	2,471	4,556	2,916	4,520
Hart	2,283	4,256	2,290	4,397
Henderson	8,091	10,296	10,049	9,523
Henry	2,529	3,940	2,725	4,081

County	2012 Obama (D)	Romney (R)	2008 Obama (D)	McCain (R)
Hickman	686	1,431	812	1,406
Hopkins	5,789	13,681	7,104	11,916
Jackson	612	4,365	743	4,407
Jefferson	186,164	148,415	196,435	153,957
Jessamine	6,001	14,232	6,236	13,711
Johnson	1,723	7,095	2,407	5,948
Kenton	24,743	40,979	26,480	40,714
Knott	1,420	4,130	2,612	3,070
Knox	2,484	8,467	3,074	8,150
LaRue	1,733	3,911	1,913	4,153
Laurel	3,906	18,151	4,618	17,660
Lawrence	1,520	3,995	2,036	3,503
Lee	595	1,977	752	1,978
Leslie	433	4,439	766	3,574
Letcher	1,702	6,811	2,623	5,367
Lewis	1,342	3,326	1,510	3,213
Lincoln	2,582	6,415	2,752	6,273
Livingston	1,346	3,089	1,622	2,890
Logan	3,469	6,899	3,811	6,925
Lyon	1,373	2,412	1,577	2,220
Madison	11,512	21,128	12,392	19,694
Magoffin	1,433	3,391	2,105	2,434
Marion	3,418	3,800	3,596	3,842
Marshall	5,022	10,402	5,683	9,512
Martin	574	3,180	808	2,824
Mason	2,592	4,197	2,891	4,102
McCracken	10,062	19,979	11,285	19,043
McCreary	1,069	4,564	1,258	4,078
McLean	1,432	2,705	1,963	2,386
Meade	4,122	6,606	4,343	6,691
Menifee	1,048	1,484	1,276	1,155
Mercer	2,966	6,820	3,159	6,781
Metcalfe	1,425	2,676	1,350	2,734
Monroe	936	3,762	1,067	3,537
Montgomery	3,701	6,398	4,234	5,947
Morgan	1,369	3,021	1,879	2,396
Muhlenberg	4,771	7,762	6,221	6,447
Nelson	7,611	10,673	7,654	10,139
Nicholas	948	1,583	1,272	1,634
Ohio	2,975	6,248	4,059	5,687
Oldham	9,240	20,179	10,000	18,997
Owen	1,501	2,971	1,694	2,969
Owsley	283	1,279	381	1,279
Pendleton	1,859	3,556	2,027	3,676
Perry	2,047	8,040	3,444	6,762
Pike	5,627	17,560	9,525	12,655
Powell	1,620	2,726	2,065	2,837
Pulaski	4,976	20,714	5,590	19,862
Robertson	340	579	451	533
Rockcastle	1,097	5,028	1,410	4,757
Rowan	3,438	4,035	4,074	3,907
Russell	1,445	6,346	1,569	5,779
Scott	7,532	12,679	7,712	11,782
Shelby	6,634	11,790	6,871	11,451
Simpson	2,650	4,355	2,775	4,437
Spencer	2,549	5,726	2,519	5,378
Taylor	3,284	7,551	3,165	7,568
Todd	1,403	3,247	1,543	3,336
Trigg	2,115	4,520	2,246	4,189
Trimble	1,355	2,133	1,484	2,239
Union	1,941	3,952	2,804	3,120
Warren	16,905	26,384	17,669	25,993
Washington	1,669	3,495	1,890	3,305
Wayne	1,855	5,289	2,201	4,868
Webster	1,765	3,607	2,390	3,037
Whitley	2,683	10,232	3,484	10,015
Wolfe	996	1,542	1,493	1,408
Woodford	4,883	7,218	5,027	7,130
Totals	**679,105**	**1,086,970**	**751,985**	**1,048,462**

All candidates, 2012: Romney, R., 1,086,970; Obama, D., 679,105; Johnson, LB., 16,770; Terry, Ind., 6,781; Stein, Green, 6,420.

Louisiana

Parish	2012 Obama (D)	Romney (R)	2008 Obama (D)	McCain (R)
Acadia	6,559	19,931	7,028	19,229
Allen	2,616	6,495	2,891	6,333
Ascension	16,343	33,846	14,625	31,239
Assumption	4,754	6,082	4,756	5,981
Avoyelles	6,075	10,667	6,327	10,236
Beauregard	2,827	11,111	3,071	10,718
Bienville	3,490	3,641	3,589	3,776
Bossier	12,955	34,986	12,703	32,713

Parish	2012 Obama (D)	Romney (R)	2008 Obama (D)	McCain (R)
Caddo	57,879	52,378	55,536	52,228
Calcasieu	28,357	51,844	30,244	50,449
Caldwell	1,016	3,640	1,118	3,696
Cameron	408	3,260	613	3,089
Catahoula	1,408	2,744	1,659	3,486
Claiborne	3,014	3,649	3,025	3,750
Concordia	3,833	5,450	3,766	5,668
DeSoto	5,552	7,353	5,242	6,883
E. Baton Rouge	102,460	92,235	99,652	95,390
East Carroll	2,244	1,122	2,267	1,254
East Feliciana	4,648	5,397	4,383	5,432
Evangeline	5,330	10,176	5,853	9,793
Franklin	2,921	6,294	2,961	6,278
Grant	1,421	7,082	1,474	6,907
Iberia	12,129	20,890	12,492	20,127
Iberville	9,548	7,271	9,023	7,185
Jackson	2,305	5,132	2,456	5,190
Jefferson	70,000	102,325	65,096	113,191
Jefferson Davis	3,483	10,014	3,923	9,278
Lafayette	31,766	64,989	32,145	62,055
Lafourche	9,543	28,332	9,662	27,089
LaSalle	764	5,726	860	5,602
Lincoln	7,947	10,731	8,292	10,680
Livingston	7,448	45,488	6,681	43,269
Madison	3,154	2,000	3,100	2,152
Morehouse	5,887	6,591	5,792	7,258
Natchitoches	7,941	9,077	7,801	9,054
Orleans	99,436	24,561	117,102	28,130
Ouachita	26,629	40,927	24,813	41,741
Plaquemines	3,597	6,469	3,380	6,894
Pointe Coupee	5,436	6,548	5,516	6,702
Rapides	20,040	37,187	20,127	36,611
Red River	2,253	2,483	2,080	2,484
Richland	4,074	7,316	3,311	5,751
Sabine	2,194	7,735	2,245	7,226
St. Bernard	5,052	8,497	3,491	9,643
St. Charles	8,894	15,936	8,522	16,457
St. Helena	4,233	2,756	3,567	2,522
St. James	7,055	5,209	6,994	5,432
St. John the Baptist	13,178	7,620	12,424	8,912
St. Landry	19,668	21,475	20,268	21,650
St. Martin	9,419	15,653	9,419	14,443
St. Mary	9,448	13,883	9,345	13,183
St. Tammany	25,723	84,710	24,596	83,078
Tangipahoa	17,720	31,583	16,438	31,434
Tensas	1,564	1,230	1,646	1,367
Terrebonne	12,071	29,500	11,581	28,210
Union	3,075	7,561	3,103	7,619
Vermilion	5,718	18,909	6,266	18,069
Vernon	3,173	12,146	3,534	11,946
Washington	6,351	11,470	6,122	12,215
Webster	6,802	11,397	6,610	11,417
W. Baton Rouge	5,692	6,920	5,043	6,654
West Carroll	853	3,628	878	4,045
W. Feliciana	2,441	3,257	2,415	3,150
Winn	1,919	4,539	2,047	4,632
Totals	**781,733**	**1,149,054**	**782,989**	**1,148,275**

All candidates, 2012: Romney, R., 1,149,054; Obama, D., 781,733; Johnson, LB., 17,975; Stein, Green, 6,873; Goode, Const., 2,461; Tittle, We the People, 1,748; Anderson, Justice, 1,319; Lindsay, Socialism/Liberation, 583; Fellure, Prohib., 503; Harris, Soc. Workers, 384; White, Soc. Equality, 352.

Maine

City	2012 Obama (D)	Romney (R)	2008 Obama (D)	McCain (R)
Auburn	6,503	4,462	6,866	4,686
Augusta	5,192	3,339	5,556	3,662
Bangor	4,618	3,150	9,406	6,258
Biddeford	6,618	3,047	6,840	2,903
Brunswick	7,853	3,654	7,845	3,692
Falmouth	4,149	3,319	4,189	2,861
Gorham	5,123	3,742	5,196	3,600
Kennebunk	3,935	2,798	4,237	2,685
Lewiston	9,550	5,778	10,629	5,961
Portland	27,490	7,439	28,317	7,844
Saco	6,146	3,556	6,457	3,374
Sanford	5,588	3,701	5,953	3,607
Scarborough	6,343	5,184	6,750	4,866

City	2012 Obama (D)	Romney (R)	2008 Obama (D)	McCain (R)
S. Portland	9,956	4,104	9,942	4,017
Waterville	4,677	2,103	5,080	2,109
Westbrook	5,504	3,042	5,590	3,030
Windham	3,817	3,427	5,086	4,000
York	4,888	3,594	5,107	3,314
Other	222,220	181,167	278,713	220,686
Totals	**335,333**	**239,892**	**421,923**	**295,273**

All candidates, 2012: Obama, D., 335,333; Romney, R., 239,892; Johnson, LB., 11,969; Stein, Green, 8,267.

Maryland

County	2012 Obama (D)	Romney (R)	2008 Obama (D)	McCain (R)
Allegany	9,001	18,158	10,693	18,405
Anne Arundel	115,960	118,165	125,015	129,682
Baltimore	202,733	144,686	214,151	158,714
Calvert	18,963	22,413	20,299	23,095
Caroline	4,621	7,674	4,971	8,015
Carroll	24,729	51,466	28,060	54,503
Cecil	15,489	23,660	17,665	23,855
Charles	45,621	23,637	43,635	25,732
Dorchester	6,570	7,514	6,912	8,168
Frederick	51,187	55,495	54,013	55,170
Garrett	2,792	9,102	3,736	8,903
Harford	46,390	69,496	48,552	71,751
Howard	84,017	54,094	87,120	55,393
Kent	4,453	4,533	4,953	4,905
Montgomery	286,493	110,940	314,444	118,608
Prince George's	279,156	28,148	332,396	38,833
Queen Anne's	7,898	14,879	8,575	15,087
St. Mary's	17,982	25,096	19,023	24,705
Somerset	4,478	4,706	4,779	5,037
Talbot	7,983	10,442	9,035	10,995
Washington	23,282	34,113	26,245	34,169
Wicomico	17,481	20,136	19,436	21,849
Worcester	8,399	11,615	11,374	15,607
City				
Baltimore	195,298	24,550	214,385	28,681
Totals	**1,480,976**	**894,718**	**1,629,467**	**959,862**

All candidates, 2012: Obama, D., 1,480,976; Romney, R., 894,718; Johnson, LB., 27,318; Stein, Green, 15,289.

Massachusetts

City	2012 Obama (D)	Romney (R)	2008 Obama (D)	McCain (R)
Arlington	18,580	6,659	18,365	6,407
Barnstable	12,842	12,290	13,559	11,084
Beverly	12,075	8,304	12,247	7,780
Boston	196,096	48,227	185,976	45,548
Brockton	25,140	8,668	23,299	9,646
Brookline	21,761	5,717	22,484	4,842
Cambridge	41,991	5,340	40,876	4,697
Chicopee	1,451	653	14,172	8,268
Fall River	21,724	7,323	22,591	7,933
Framingham	18,340	8,938	17,839	8,464
Haverhill	15,342	11,758	15,552	10,814
Lowell	22,597	10,586	20,646	10,393
Lynn	22,965	8,463	20,276	8,719
Malden	14,940	5,714	13,865	6,075
Medford	18,613	8,294	17,598	8,655
Methuen	11,048	10,168	11,263	9,303
New Bedford	25,205	7,541	24,881	8,201
Newton	32,099	12,154	33,360	10,283
Peabody	15,010	11,616	14,818	10,800
Pittsfield	15,600	4,044	15,665	4,404
Plymouth	15,106	14,258	15,180	13,139
Quincy	24,714	14,816	22,810	15,546
Somerville	28,467	4,865	26,665	5,215
Springfield	42,963	10,372	39,516	11,331
Taunton	13,479	8,783	13,243	8,677
Waltham	15,748	8,816	15,276	8,383
Weymouth	15,130	12,341	14,727	12,358
Worcester	40,568	17,155	41,352	18,474
Other	1,115,067	859,679	1,155,996	813,415
Totals	**1,874,661**	**1,153,542**	**1,904,097**	**1,108,854**

All candidates, 2012: Obama, D., 1,874,661; Romney, R., 1,153,542; Johnson, LB., 30,002; Stein, Green, 19,443.

Michigan

County	2012 Obama (D)	Romney (R)	2008 Obama (D)	McCain (R)
Alcona	2,462	3,571	2,896	3,404
Alger	2,212	2,329	2,472	2,188
Allegan	19,594	29,023	24,165	30,061
Alpena	6,549	7,298	7,705	7,125
Antrim	5,107	7,917	6,079	7,506
Arenac	3,669	4,054	4,155	3,807
Baraga	1,574	1,866	1,725	1,846
Barry	10,454	15,330	13,449	16,431
Bay	26,797	23,735	32,589	23,795
Benzie	4,683	5,071	5,451	4,687
Berrien	18,493	29,145	40,381	36,130
Branch	6,526	9,575	8,413	9,534
Calhoun	29,270	28,338	34,561	28,553
Cass	9,587	12,660	12,083	11,114
Charlevoix	5,936	7,997	6,817	7,306
Cheboygan	5,829	7,284	6,720	6,920
Chippewa	7,100	8,278	8,184	8,267
Clare	6,337	6,988	7,496	6,793
Clinton	18,187	20,630	20,005	19,726
Crawford	2,994	3,744	3,441	3,561
Delta	8,330	9,533	9,974	8,763
Dickinson	4,952	7,688	5,995	7,049
Eaton	27,912	26,193	30,742	25,900
Emmet	7,225	10,253	8,515	9,314
Genesee	113,391	66,918	143,927	72,451
Gladwin	5,760	6,661	6,590	6,391
Gogebic	4,058	3,444	4,757	3,330
Grand Traverse	20,875	26,532	23,258	24,716
Gratiot	7,606	8,236	9,105	8,322
Hillsdale	7,106	11,727	8,765	11,221
Houghton	6,530	8,040	7,476	8,101
Huron	6,432	8,686	8,367	8,434
Ingham	80,903	45,365	93,994	46,483
Ionia	11,016	14,319	12,565	14,156
Iosco	6,242	6,906	7,309	6,583
Iron	2,687	3,224	3,080	2,947
Isabella	13,038	10,800	16,679	11,220
Jackson	32,301	36,298	37,480	35,692
Kalamazoo	69,045	52,660	77,051	51,554
Kalkaska	3,268	4,897	3,780	4,527
Kent	134,560	157,801	149,909	148,336
Keweenaw	582	774	610	756
Lake	2,752	2,487	2,919	2,269
Lapeer	18,786	23,725	21,457	22,831
Leelanau	6,576	7,483	7,355	6,938
Lenawee	21,774	22,351	24,640	22,225
Livingston	37,186	60,000	42,349	55,592
Luce	951	1,501	1,191	1,490
Mackinac	2,652	3,396	3,027	3,268
Macomb	207,992	191,896	223,784	187,663
Manistee	6,467	5,736	7,235	5,510
Marquette	18,126	13,609	19,635	12,906
Mason	6,856	7,580	7,817	7,147
Mecosta	7,515	9,175	9,101	9,238
Menominee	5,244	5,565	5,981	4,855
Midland	17,480	23,942	20,701	22,263
Missaukee	2,274	4,665	2,898	4,469
Monroe	36,310	35,593	39,180	35,858
Montcalm	11,431	13,624	13,208	13,291
Montmorency	2,049	2,928	2,403	2,841
Muskegon	44,436	36,882	53,821	29,145
Newaygo	8,089	11,651	10,790	11,862
Oakland	349,055	296,531	372,566	276,956
Oceana	5,063	6,239	6,405	5,860
Ogemaw	4,791	5,437	5,391	5,133
Ontonagon	1,585	1,906	1,966	1,823
Osceola	3,981	6,140	4,855	5,973
Oscoda	1,654	2,308	1,887	2,320
Otsego	4,681	7,008	5,634	6,752
Ottawa	43,068	88,503	50,828	83,330
Presque Isle	3,192	3,794	3,722	3,606
Roscommon	6,198	6,701	7,082	6,727
Saginaw	51,040	41,920	60,276	42,225
St. Clair	33,845	39,076	40,677	38,536
St. Joseph	10,106	12,975	12,322	12,886
Sanilac	7,212	10,961	9,047	10,679
Schoolcraft	1,865	2,142	2,184	2,058
Shiawassee	17,191	15,962	19,397	16,268
Tuscola	11,643	14,517	13,503	13,740
Van Buren	16,288	16,140	18,588	15,534
Washtenaw	120,791	56,401	130,578	53,946

County	2012		2008	
	Obama (D)	Romney (R)	Obama (D)	McCain (R)
Wayne	526,749	191,058	660,085	219,582
Wexford	5,717	7,972	7,379	8,044
Totals	**2,457,846**	**2,079,268**	**2,872,579**	**2,048,639**

All candidates, 2012: Obama, D., 2,457,846; Romney, R., 2,079,268; Stein, Green, 20,855; Goode, U.S. Taxpayers, 16,463; Anderson, Natural Law, 5,045.

Minnesota

County	2012		2008	
	Obama (D)	Romney (R)	Obama (D)	McCain (R)
Aitkin	4,412	4,533	4,595	4,589
Anoka	88,611	93,430	86,976	91,357
Becker	6,829	9,204	7,687	8,851
Beltrami	11,818	9,637	12,019	9,762
Benton	8,173	10,849	8,454	10,338
Big Stone	1,345	1,385	1,552	1,362
Blue Earth	18,164	14,916	19,325	14,782
Brown	5,630	7,934	5,809	7,456
Carlton	11,389	6,586	11,501	6,549
Carver	20,745	31,155	20,654	28,156
Cass	6,858	8,957	7,276	8,660
Chippewa	3,083	2,967	3,280	2,907
Chisago	12,524	16,227	12,783	15,789
Clay	15,210	12,920	16,666	11,978
Clearwater	1,753	2,359	1,877	2,291
Cook	1,993	1,221	2,019	1,240
Cottonwood	2,433	3,316	2,759	3,157
Crow Wing	14,760	19,415	15,859	18,567
Dakota	116,253	109,514	116,778	104,364
Dodge	4,487	5,522	4,463	5,468
Douglas	8,665	11,905	9,256	11,241
Faribault	3,407	4,104	3,736	4,196
Fillmore	5,800	4,967	5,921	4,993
Freeborn	9,327	6,970	9,915	6,955
Goodhue	12,212	12,986	12,420	12,775
Grant	1,645	1,750	1,850	1,646
Hennepin	419,048	239,369	420,958	231,054
Houston	5,281	4,951	5,906	4,743
Hubbard	4,676	6,622	4,872	6,558
Isanti	8,024	11,675	8,248	11,324
Itasca	12,852	10,500	13,460	10,309
Jackson	2,268	3,044	2,618	2,858
Kanabec	3,586	4,319	3,743	4,479
Kandiyohi	9,806	11,239	10,125	11,319
Kittson	1,241	1,095	1,492	1,016
Koochiching	3,451	2,841	3,649	2,962
Lac Qui Parle	1,974	1,938	2,160	1,912
Lake	4,043	2,610	4,174	2,636
Lake of the Woods	859	1,306	971	1,278
Le Sueur	6,753	7,713	6,994	7,636
Lincoln	1,428	1,594	1,517	1,491
Lyon	5,462	6,588	6,110	6,315
Mahnomen	1,276	871	1,436	843
Marshall	1,998	2,569	2,311	2,285
Martin	4,054	6,657	4,413	6,053
McLeod	6,964	11,067	7,505	10,993
Meeker	4,969	6,917	5,380	6,737
Mille Lacs	5,829	6,951	6,072	7,049
Morrison	6,153	10,159	6,547	9,735
Mower	11,122	6,932	11,605	7,075
Murray	2,160	2,504	2,345	2,320
Nicollet	9,653	8,212	9,887	7,968
Nobles	3,793	4,581	4,244	4,368
Norman	1,730	1,384	2,129	1,204
Olmsted	39,341	36,837	38,711	36,202
Otter Tail	12,165	18,860	13,856	18,077
Pennington	3,024	3,303	3,394	3,248
Pine	6,891	6,914	7,084	6,862
Pipestone	1,728	2,828	2,023	2,652
Polk	6,735	7,583	7,850	7,148
Pope	2,981	3,142	3,317	3,069
Ramsey	184,936	86,799	182,974	88,942
Red Lake	928	978	1,120	983
Redwood	3,008	4,571	3,250	4,308
Renville	3,394	4,149	3,904	3,956
Rice	17,054	14,380	17,381	13,723
Rock	1,945	2,810	2,079	2,775
Roseau	2,772	4,409	3,097	4,438
St. Louis	74,223	39,700	77,351	38,742
Scott	29,714	40,321	29,208	36,724

County	2012		2008	
	Obama (D)	Romney (R)	Obama (D)	McCain (R)
Sherburne	17,597	27,848	17,957	26,140
Sibley	2,917	4,693	2,998	4,492
Stearns	33,553	43,007	35,690	41,194
Steele	8,705	9,903	9,016	10,068
Stevens	2,742	2,766	2,781	2,710
Swift	2,751	2,248	2,907	2,184
Todd	4,819	6,719	5,277	6,637
Traverse	942	860	1,043	933
Wabasha	5,415	6,049	5,646	5,935
Wadena	2,492	4,143	2,882	4,128
Waseca	4,370	5,116	4,401	5,211
Washington	70,203	69,137	70,277	64,334
Watonwan	2,482	2,508	2,562	2,526
Wilkin	1,258	1,884	1,550	1,786
Winona	14,980	11,480	16,308	10,975
Wright	26,584	41,460	26,343	37,779
Yellow Medicine	2,465	2,808	2,816	2,579
Totals	**1,543,093**	**1,321,150**	**1,573,354**	**1,275,409**

All candidates, 2012: Obama, D., 1,543,093; Romney, R., 1,321,150; Johnson, LB., 35,042; Stein, Green, 12,951; Goode, Const., 3,721; Carlson, Grassroots, 3,169; Anderson, Justice, 2,008; Morstad, Constitutional, 1,107; Harris, Soc. Workers, 1,058; Lindsay, Socialism/Liberation, 415.

Mississippi

County	2012		2008	
	Obama (D)	Romney (R)	Obama (D)	McCain (R)
Adams	7,999	5,542	9,021	6,566
Alcorn	3,449	11,027	4,130	10,805
Amite	3,218	4,393	3,348	4,245
Attala	3,368	4,452	3,849	5,273
Benton	2,026	2,030	2,227	2,329
Bolivar	9,772	4,346	10,334	4,891
Calhoun	2,250	3,961	2,522	4,467
Carroll	1,990	3,953	2,037	3,902
Chickasaw	3,914	3,601	4,588	4,395
Choctaw	1,283	2,533	1,459	2,624
Claiborne	4,633	608	4,682	748
Clarke	2,695	4,415	3,121	5,229
Clay	5,860	3,735	6,558	4,466
Coahoma	7,164	2,356	7,597	2,917
Copiah	7,201	5,714	7,710	6,701
Covington	3,800	5,282	3,852	5,523
DeSoto	20,979	42,399	19,627	44,222
Forrest	12,079	15,339	11,622	15,296
Franklin	1,706	2,705	1,733	2,909
George	1,279	7,721	1,532	7,700
Greene	1,065	3,929	1,366	4,361
Grenada	5,279	5,980	5,029	6,234
Hancock	3,879	12,859	3,768	13,020
Harrison	21,079	35,307	22,673	38,757
Hinds	70,512	26,450	75,401	32,949
Holmes	6,775	1,264	7,765	1,714
Humphreys	3,399	1,069	3,634	1,462
Issaquena	426	268	579	364
Itawamba	1,599	6,925	2,084	7,663
Jackson	15,452	33,262	17,781	35,993
Jasper	5,097	4,193	5,025	4,135
Jefferson	3,508	431	3,883	551
Jefferson Davis	4,094	2,439	4,454	2,871
Jones	9,146	20,635	8,846	20,157
Kemper	3,239	1,789	3,256	1,935
Lafayette	7,098	9,772	7,997	10,278
Lamar	5,037	17,472	5,159	18,497
Lauderdale	12,642	17,322	13,332	19,582
Lawrence	2,394	4,153	2,587	4,369
Leake	3,599	4,283	4,151	5,148
Lee	12,043	22,004	12,021	22,694
Leflore	8,423	3,115	8,914	4,105
Lincoln	4,879	9,333	5,505	10,781
Lowndes	12,037	12,399	13,209	13,994
Madison	19,133	26,037	19,831	27,203
Marion	3,833	7,118	4,422	8,513
Marshall	9,581	6,444	9,685	6,683
Monroe	6,990	9,661	7,169	10,184
Montgomery	2,245	2,543	2,609	3,071
Neshoba	3,030	7,772	3,114	8,209
Newton	3,069	5,909	3,218	6,579

County	2012 Obama (D)	Romney (R)	2008 Obama (D)	McCain (R)
Noxubee	4,920	1,325	5,030	1,525
Oktibbeha	8,030	7,728	9,326	9,320
Panola	8,175	6,810	8,690	7,620
Pearl River	3,813	15,836	4,320	17,881
Perry	1,519	4,110	1,533	4,067
Pike	9,304	7,986	9,276	8,651
Pontotoc	2,785	9,403	2,982	9,727
Prentiss	2,817	7,075	3,020	7,703
Quitman	2,837	1,116	2,803	1,334
Rankin	14,047	44,527	14,372	48,140
Scott	4,774	5,728	5,025	6,584
Sharkey	1,571	675	1,907	873
Simpson	4,330	6,683	4,817	7,641
Smith	1,979	6,049	1,968	6,265
Stone	1,794	4,924	1,996	5,149
Sunflower	7,989	2,907	7,838	3,245
Tallahatchie	3,838	2,480	4,105	2,786
Tate	4,572	6,666	5,003	7,678
Tippah	2,254	6,625	2,623	6,937
Tishomingo	1,623	6,070	1,962	6,249
Tunica	3,371	867	3,279	1,017
Union	2,481	7,759	2,985	9,072
Walthall	3,386	4,012	3,456	4,253
Warren	9,899	9,390	10,489	11,152
Washington	12,188	4,870	13,148	6,347
Wayne	3,747	5,297	3,890	6,070
Webster	1,087	3,684	1,349	4,072
Wilkinson	2,940	1,275	3,534	1,560
Winston	4,557	5,147	4,653	5,497
Yalobusha	2,984	3,261	3,151	3,628
Yazoo	6,220	4,560	6,116	5,290
Totals	**521,052**	**661,064**	**554,662**	**724,597**

All candidates, 2012: Romney, R., 661,064; Obama, D., 521,052; Johnson, LB., 6,328; Goode, Const., 2,506; Stein, Green, 1,516; Washer, RF., 950.

Missouri

County	2012 Obama (D)	Romney (R)	2008 Obama (D)	McCain (R)
Adair	4,218	5,648	5,735	5,891
Andrew	2,649	5,457	3,345	5,279
Atchison	756	1,902	1,000	1,936
Audrain	3,538	6,186	4,434	6,167
Barry	3,667	9,832	4,630	9,758
Barton	1,232	4,416	1,455	4,414
Bates	2,557	5,020	3,271	4,833
Benton	2,925	6,069	3,629	5,759
Bollinger	1,213	4,094	1,690	3,972
Boone	39,782	37,343	47,062	36,849
Buchanan	15,594	18,660	19,164	19,110
Butler	4,363	12,248	5,316	11,805
Caldwell	1,313	2,724	1,814	2,654
Callaway	6,070	11,742	7,580	11,389
Camden	6,458	15,089	7,773	14,074
Cape Girardeau	9,713	25,343	12,208	24,768
Carroll	1,154	3,072	1,535	2,955
Carter	754	1,978	984	1,840
Cass	17,044	30,912	19,844	29,695
Cedar	1,536	4,375	2,060	4,194
Chariton	1,339	2,402	1,799	2,339
Christian	9,809	27,465	11,883	25,382
Clark	1,398	1,730	1,572	1,782
Clay	47,250	56,131	53,761	54,516
Clinton	3,685	5,904	4,545	5,709
Cole	12,003	24,488	13,959	24,385
Cooper	2,474	4,887	2,996	4,902
Crawford	2,951	6,434	3,911	6,007
Dade	939	2,895	1,184	2,864
Dallas	2,122	4,992	2,656	4,895
Daviess	1,124	2,282	1,400	2,263
DeKalb	1,194	3,056	1,692	2,889
Dent	1,585	4,883	2,056	4,655
Douglas	1,709	4,649	2,140	4,405
Dunklin	3,635	6,849	4,540	7,044
Franklin	16,294	29,271	21,256	27,355
Gasconade	2,099	4,895	2,899	4,763
Gentry	937	1,986	1,235	1,964
Greene	46,130	76,786	56,181	77,683
Grundy	1,212	3,030	1,580	3,006

County	2012 Obama (D)	Romney (R)	2008 Obama (D)	McCain (R)
Harrison	984	2,624	1,287	2,512
Henry	3,604	6,229	4,869	6,095
Hickory	1,733	2,835	2,171	2,850
Holt	551	1,725	802	1,794
Howard	1,722	3,012	2,036	2,708
Howell	4,393	11,541	5,736	10,982
Iron	1,669	2,252	2,213	2,090
Jackson	180,100	121,891	210,824	124,687
Jasper	12,808	31,345	15,730	31,667
Jefferson	41,570	53,973	53,467	50,804
Johnson	7,661	12,750	9,480	12,183
Knox	698	1,205	759	1,212
Laclede	4,093	10,934	5,218	10,875
Lafayette	5,650	9,800	6,902	9,442
Lawrence	4,014	11,417	5,097	11,263
Lewis	1,507	2,677	1,837	2,594
Lincoln	7,733	14,330	10,234	12,924
Linn	2,031	3,331	2,638	3,140
Livingston	1,906	4,006	2,435	3,993
Macon	2,309	4,700	2,784	4,586
Madison	1,588	3,227	2,042	2,897
Maries	1,299	3,165	1,599	2,853
Marion	4,034	7,926	4,703	7,705
McDonald	1,920	5,694	2,454	5,499
Mercer	353	1,255	519	1,169
Miller	2,651	8,099	3,553	7,797
Mississippi	1,857	2,996	2,247	3,034
Moniteau	1,608	4,703	2,084	4,467
Monroe	1,398	2,564	1,703	2,533
Montgomery	1,734	3,486	2,347	3,428
Morgan	2,773	5,733	3,565	5,451
New Madrid	2,814	4,284	3,370	4,593
Newton	6,425	18,179	7,450	17,637
Nodaway	3,172	5,593	4,493	5,568
Oregon	1,419	2,886	1,811	2,652
Osage	1,472	5,330	1,907	5,062
Ozark	1,261	3,080	1,661	2,918
Pemiscot	2,671	3,596	3,029	3,954
Perry	2,184	5,669	3,005	5,527
Pettis	5,902	10,840	6,932	11,018
Phelps	5,798	11,893	7,394	11,706
Pike	2,581	4,576	3,487	4,268
Platte	19,171	25,617	21,459	24,460
Polk	3,580	9,252	4,553	8,956
Pulaski	4,199	9,092	5,249	9,552
Putnam	587	1,673	695	1,591
Ralls	1,736	3,231	2,041	2,987
Randolph	3,031	6,667	3,984	6,457
Ray	4,264	5,805	5,241	5,593
Reynolds	1,155	1,927	1,418	1,782
Ripley	1,396	3,743	1,795	3,407
St. Charles	71,798	110,732	84,183	102,550
St. Clair	1,460	3,019	1,886	2,981
St. Francois	8,837	13,248	11,540	12,660
St. Louis County	294,735	223,102	333,123	221,705
Ste. Genevieve	3,813	4,055	4,979	3,732
Saline	3,785	5,096	4,712	4,962
Schuyler	697	1,174	775	1,139
Scotland	643	1,246	793	1,249
Scott	5,122	11,623	6,258	11,563
Shannon	1,300	2,260	1,637	2,075
Shelby	966	2,188	1,114	2,166
Stoddard	3,153	9,496	3,899	9,172
Stone	3,920	11,780	5,029	11,147
Sullivan	908	1,610	1,173	1,607
Taney	5,462	15,713	6,683	14,736
Texas	2,871	7,618	3,410	7,215
Vernon	2,580	5,756	3,381	5,334
Warren	5,219	9,150	6,705	8,675
Washington	3,402	5,008	4,711	4,706
Wayne	1,811	3,790	2,243	3,784
Webster	4,407	10,702	5,685	10,431
Worth	341	664	427	707
Wright	1,953	5,831	2,557	5,784
City				
St. Louis	116,654	22,617	132,925	24,662
Totals	**1,215,031**	**1,478,961**	**1,441,911**	**1,445,814**

All candidates, 2012: Romney, R., 1,478,961; Obama, D., 1,215,031; Johnson, LB., 43,029; Goode, Const., 7,914.

Montana

County	2012 Obama (D)	Romney (R)	2008 Obama (D)	McCain (R)
Beaverhead	1,347	3,251	1,617	3,008
Big Horn	2,830	1,655	3,516	1,628
Blaine	1,598	1,169	1,702	1,139
Broadwater	761	2,150	857	1,875
Carbon	2,126	3,513	2,443	3,108
Carter	96	678	111	573
Cascade	14,949	18,039	17,664	16,857
Chouteau	969	1,751	1,122	1,634
Custer	1,824	3,353	2,267	3,047
Daniels	236	735	343	694
Dawson	1,219	3,024	1,593	2,639
Deer Lodge	2,829	1,431	3,402	1,502
Fallon	236	1,123	318	1,064
Fergus	1,628	4,243	1,933	4,108
Flathead	10,720	23,634	16,138	25,559
Gallatin	21,438	23,969	24,205	22,578
Garfield	66	622	110	598
Glacier	1,946	716	3,423	1,451
Golden Valley	110	351	124	343
Granite	533	1,107	601	1,013
Hill	3,372	3,133	3,596	2,787
Jefferson	2,256	4,042	2,582	3,538
Judith Basin	336	852	397	801
Lake	5,715	7,084	6,766	6,498
Lewis and Clark	15,479	16,673	17,114	14,966
Liberty	257	698	367	594
Lincoln	2,544	6,046	3,025	5,704
Madison	1,285	3,115	1,607	2,822
McCone	221	742	321	726
Meagher	269	670	298	624
Mineral	698	1,212	845	1,053
Missoula	34,380	23,285	36,531	20,743
Musselshell	482	1,852	636	1,581
Park	3,728	4,637	4,173	4,376
Petroleum	49	240	68	227
Phillips	471	1,688	638	1,423
Pondera	969	1,666	1,223	1,588
Powder River	170	833	208	802
Powell	884	1,798	1,021	1,683
Prairie	167	518	211	503
Ravalli	5,559	11,241	8,400	13,002
Richland	992	3,479	1,203	3,184
Roosevelt	2,044	1,503	2,564	1,473
Rosebud	1,478	2,035	1,919	1,768
Sanders	1,716	3,971	1,970	3,563
Sheridan	661	1,203	953	987
Silver Bow	10,782	5,374	11,676	4,818
Stillwater	1,209	3,237	1,512	2,991
Sweet Grass	473	1,584	541	1,494
Teton	1,073	2,091	1,294	1,874
Toole	582	1,440	737	1,317
Treasure	114	317	156	314
Valley	1,387	2,336	1,645	2,121
Wheatland	272	690	289	657
Wibaux	25	421	146	379
Yellowstone	15,752	24,140	32,038	36,483
Totals	**185,312**	**242,360**	**231,667**	**242,763**

All candidates, 2012: Romney, R., 242,360; Obama, D., 185,312; Johnson, LB., 12,739.

Nebraska

County	2012 Obama (D)	Romney (R)	2008 Obama (D)	McCain (R)
Adams	3,991	8,235	4,685	8,252
Antelope	571	2,585	757	2,383
Arthur	30	227	39	217
Banner	55	339	62	348
Blaine	29	268	43	266
Boone	615	2,136	742	2,042
Box Butte	1,634	2,795	1,886	2,932
Boyd	186	852	250	839
Brown	223	1,298	311	1,208
Buffalo	5,266	13,378	5,867	13,097
Burt	1,280	2,016	1,413	1,907
Butler	1,028	2,729	1,190	2,557
Cass	4,298	7,453	4,753	7,120
Cedar	952	3,231	1,190	2,912
Chase	252	1,573	341	1,477

County	2012 Obama (D)	Romney (R)	2008 Obama (D)	McCain (R)
Cherry	436	2,557	599	2,360
Cheyenne	983	3,134	1,173	3,572
Clay	662	2,213	780	2,177
Colfax	959	2,045	1,125	2,018
Cuming	1,015	2,858	1,274	2,732
Custer	1,066	4,251	1,192	4,301
Dakota	2,831	3,048	2,994	3,292
Dawes	1,102	2,435	1,285	2,376
Dawson	2,157	5,370	2,399	5,460
Deuel	215	763	243	732
Dixon	870	1,745	946	1,785
Dodge	5,588	8,937	6,689	8,557
Douglas	99,261	108,319	116,810	106,291
Dundy	176	791	218	783
Fillmore	794	1,972	962	1,913
Franklin	381	1,110	442	1,079
Frontier	381	1,005	349	1,034
Furnas	422	1,767	556	1,725
Gage	3,870	5,470	4,473	5,435
Garden	242	829	283	844
Garfield	147	762	212	800
Gosper	230	732	260	776
Grant	30	322	41	318
Greeley	340	820	458	715
Hall	6,971	12,412	7,855	12,977
Hamilton	1,136	3,582	1,332	3,389
Harlan	311	1,248	402	1,329
Hayes	50	473	85	461
Hitchcock	310	1,386	346	1,001
Holt	862	3,789	1,089	3,746
Hooker	59	330	75	355
Howard	914	1,890	1,083	1,847
Jefferson	1,185	2,156	1,520	2,103
Johnson	790	1,223	914	1,142
Kearney	761	2,341	876	2,224
Keith	920	3,036	974	2,942
Keya Paha	80	392	115	409
Kimball	391	1,222	439	1,346
Knox	1,055	2,878	1,255	2,728
Lancaster	59,970	61,177	65,734	59,398
Lincoln	4,350	10,545	5,046	10,817
Logan	68	356	81	327
Loup	62	290	86	302
Madison	3,368	9,874	4,142	9,655
McPherson	41	237	45	240
Merrick	921	2,477	986	2,375
Morrill	450	1,658	557	1,725
Nance	477	1,098	549	1,116
Nemaha	1,089	1,979	1,240	2,134
Nuckolls	567	1,563	657	1,498
Otoe	2,542	4,226	2,915	4,033
Pawnee	396	897	483	859
Perkins	237	1,133	310	1,092
Phelps	875	3,372	1,050	3,360
Pierce	637	2,707	783	2,385
Platte	3,095	9,963	3,796	9,373
Polk	527	1,886	668	1,822
Red Willow	940	3,855	1,216	3,735
Richardson	1,180	2,407	1,513	2,342
Rock	103	669	139	640
Saline	2,232	2,518	2,674	2,434
Sarpy	24,709	40,318	28,010	38,816
Saunders	3,279	6,725	3,767	6,188
Scotts Bluff	4,193	9,427	4,745	9,708
Seward	2,362	4,947	2,703	4,647
Sheridan	389	2,010	454	1,941
Sherman	549	919	585	950
Sioux	101	623	117	603
Stanton	607	1,945	664	1,781
Thayer	724	1,853	860	1,749
Thomas	42	360	51	331
Thurston	1,153	823	1,120	972
Valley	494	1,643	706	1,657
Washington	3,103	6,857	3,711	6,425
Wayne	1,074	2,493	1,249	2,503
Webster	440	1,255	552	1,233
Wheeler	93	345	96	334
York	1,352	4,814	1,607	4,848
Totals	**289,154**	**462,972**	**333,319**	**452,979**

All candidates, 2012: Romney, R., 462,972; Obama, D., 289,154; Johnson, LB., 10,610; Terry, petitioning cand., 2,347.

Nevada

County	2012 Obama (D)	Romney (R)	2008 Obama (D)	McCain (R)
Churchill	2,961	7,061	3,494	6,832
Clark	387,978	288,223	380,765	257,078
Douglas	9,288	16,264	10,672	14,648
Elko	3,510	12,013	4,541	10,969
Esmeralda	92	317	104	303
Eureka	107	663	144	564
Humboldt	1,737	3,810	1,909	3,586
Lander	534	1,580	577	1,466
Lincoln	400	1,691	518	1,498
Lyon	7,380	13,520	8,405	12,154
Mineral	863	1,080	1,082	1,131
Nye	6,320	10,566	7,226	9,537
Pershing	632	1,167	673	1,075
Storey	920	1,321	1,102	1,247
Washoe	94,806	88,151	99,671	76,880
White Pine	983	2,601	1,230	2,440
City				
Carson City	10,290	12,394	11,623	11,419
Totals	**528,801**	**462,422**	**533,736**	**412,827**

All candidates, 2012: Obama, D., 528,801; Romney, R., 462,422; Johnson, LB., 10,895; None of these candidates, 5,753; Goode, Ind. Amer., 3,234.

New Hampshire

City	2012 Obama (D)	Romney (R)	2008 Obama (D)	McCain (R)
Bedford	4,713	7,990	5,115	7,442
Concord	14,097	7,252	14,302	7,496
Derry	7,573	8,309	7,527	7,944
Dover	9,724	6,162	10,221	5,746
Hudson	5,451	5,174	5,807	6,351
Keene	8,667	3,592	9,427	3,641
Londonderry	5,660	7,295	6,107	6,879
Manchester	25,676	20,809	26,526	21,192
Merrimack	6,797	7,678	7,316	7,558
Nashua	23,213	17,506	22,902	17,325
Portsmouth	8,753	4,043	9,147	3,729
Rochester	6,230	5,556	7,947	6,483
Salem	6,026	8,285	6,838	8,073
Other	227,014	210,236	245,644	206,675
Totals	**359,594**	**319,887**	**384,826**	**316,534**

All candidates, 2012: Obama, D., 359,594; Romney, R., 319,887; Johnson, LB., 8,130; Goode, Const., 1,162.

New Jersey

County	2012 Obama (D)	Romney (R)	2008 Obama (D)	McCain (R)
Atlantic	59,509	41,918	67,830	49,902
Bergen	192,460	154,418	225,367	186,118
Burlington	115,951	79,110	131,219	89,626
Camden	136,009	62,275	159,259	73,819
Cape May	21,275	25,488	22,893	27,288
Cumberland	30,172	18,767	34,919	22,360
Essex	197,679	55,691	240,306	74,063
Gloucester	72,960	58,915	77,267	60,315
Hudson	136,239	38,082	154,140	55,360
Hunterdon	25,148	36,979	29,776	39,092
Mercer	94,300	43,155	107,926	50,223
Middlesex	175,354	100,180	193,812	123,695
Monmouth	125,471	140,376	148,737	160,433
Morris	90,313	114,265	112,275	132,331
Ocean	89,625	127,425	110,189	160,677
Passaic	104,057	59,181	113,257	72,552
Salem	14,456	14,214	16,044	14,816
Somerset	70,168	63,159	79,321	70,085
Sussex	23,406	37,215	28,840	44,184
Union	123,769	61,284	141,417	78,768
Warren	17,869	24,695	20,628	27,500
Totals	**1,916,190**	**1,356,792**	**2,215,422**	**1,613,207**

All candidates, 2012: Obama, D., 1,916,190; Romney, R., 1,356,792; Johnson, LB., 19,202; Stein, Green, 8,891; Goode, Const., 1,869; Anderson, Justice, 1,542; Boss, Ind., 885; Harris, Soc. Workers, 651; Miller, A3P, 609; Lindsay, Socialism/Liberation, 436.

New Mexico

County	2012 Obama (D)	Romney (R)	2008 Obama (D)	McCain (R)
Bernalillo	146,222	103,544	171,556	110,521
Catron	557	1,474	664	1,398
Chaves	6,621	13,271	8,197	13,651
Cibola	4,907	2,966	5,827	3,131
Colfax	2,879	2,763	3,490	2,805
Curry	3,956	9,150	4,670	9,599
De Baca	287	586	359	676
Doña Ana	36,778	26,988	40,282	28,068
Eddy	6,110	12,546	7,351	12,500
Grant	7,009	5,286	8,142	5,406
Guadalupe	1,388	518	1,557	620
Harding	260	326	260	358
Hidalgo	994	895	993	936
Lea	4,068	12,480	5,108	13,347
Lincoln	2,931	5,940	3,535	6,001
Los Alamos	5,191	4,796	5,824	5,064
Luna	3,333	3,300	4,311	3,870
McKinley	15,363	5,420	16,572	6,382
Mora	1,952	591	2,168	569
Otero	6,715	12,219	8,610	12,806
Quay	1,382	2,194	1,547	2,367
Rio Arriba	11,389	3,373	12,703	4,086
Roosevelt	1,719	4,032	2,303	4,311
San Juan	15,688	28,779	18,028	27,869
San Miguel	8,754	2,281	10,320	2,478
Sandoval	26,831	24,124	32,669	25,193
Santa Fe	49,668	15,145	55,567	15,807
Sierra	1,963	2,928	2,352	3,017
Socorro	3,983	2,698	4,696	3,032
Taos	11,855	2,710	13,816	2,866
Torrance	2,414	3,521	3,087	3,735
Union	471	1,231	492	1,227
Valencia	13,473	12,788	15,366	13,136
Totals	**407,111**	**330,863**	**472,422**	**346,832**

All candidates, 2012: Obama, D., 407,111; Romney, R., 330,863; Johnson, LB., 27,244; Stein, Green, 2,634; Anderson, Ind., 1,146; Goode, Const., 970.

New York

County	2012 Obama (D)	Romney (R)	2008 Obama (D)	McCain (R)
Albany	80,891	42,029	93,937	50,586
Allegany	5,658	9,609	7,016	11,013
Bronx[1]	288,378	26,304	338,261	41,683
Broome	38,315	34,878	47,204	40,077
Cattaraugus	11,695	15,406	14,307	17,770
Cayuga	14,162	11,355	18,128	15,243
Chautauqua	21,815	25,795	29,129	28,579
Chemung	15,285	16,207	18,888	19,364
Chenango	8,340	8,933	10,100	10,337
Clinton	17,123	10,054	20,216	12,579
Columbia	14,278	11,272	17,556	13,337
Cortland	9,445	7,886	11,861	9,678
Delaware	7,469	9,085	9,462	10,524
Dutchess	59,885	52,320	71,060	59,628
Erie	219,018	159,382	256,299	178,815
Essex	8,805	5,976	10,390	7,913
Franklin	9,065	5,248	10,571	6,676
Fulton	7,916	9,811	9,695	11,709
Genesee	8,886	13,701	10,762	15,705
Greene	7,911	9,935	9,850	12,059
Hamilton	955	1,652	1,225	2,141
Herkimer	128	299	12,094	14,619
Jefferson	15,345	16,279	18,166	20,220
Kings (Brooklyn)[1]	503,291	108,630	603,525	151,872
Lewis	4,263	5,083	4,986	5,969
Livingston	10,889	13,210	13,655	16,030
Madison	12,426	12,330	14,692	14,434
Monroe	178,491	124,769	207,371	144,262
Montgomery	7,881	8,622	9,080	10,711
Nassau	243,649	212,882	342,185	288,776
New York (Manhattan)[1]	417,861	72,300	572,126	89,906
Niagara	40,862	40,397	47,303	46,348
Oneida	37,388	41,639	43,506	49,256
Onondaga	112,664	72,807	129,317	84,972
Ontario	20,777	21,768	25,103	25,171
Orange	67,054	60,164	78,326	72,042
Orleans	5,411	8,076	6,614	9,708
Oswego	21,733	18,503	24,777	23,571
Otsego	10,975	10,527	13,570	12,026
Putnam	17,851	22,436	21,613	25,145
Queens[1]	399,970	103,193	480,692	155,221
Rensselaer	34,713	27,240	39,753	32,840
Richmond (Staten Island)[1]	67,524	66,420	79,311	86,062

County	2012 Obama (D)	Romney (R)	2008 Obama (D)	McCain (R)
Rockland	60,446	52,936	69,543	61,752
St. Lawrence	19,574	13,914	23,706	16,956
Saratoga	48,876	46,829	56,645	52,855
Schenectady	33,289	24,478	38,611	29,758
Schoharie	4,378	6,379	6,009	8,071
Schuyler	3,354	3,942	3,933	4,542
Seneca	6,526	5,405	7,422	7,038
Steuben	14,586	20,425	17,148	24,203
Suffolk	274,830	259,348	346,549	307,021
Sullivan	13,781	11,148	16,850	13,900
Tioga	8,263	11,278	10,172	12,536
Tompkins	24,019	10,080	29,826	11,927
Ulster	42,678	27,029	54,320	33,300
Warren	13,112	12,571	16,281	15,429
Washington	10,280	9,904	12,741	12,533
Wayne	14,558	17,704	18,184	22,239
Westchester	171,908	108,707	261,810	147,824
Wyoming	5,224	9,726	6,379	10,998
Yates	4,021	4,270	4,890	5,269
Totals	3,860,144	2,210,485	4,804,945	2,752,771

(1) Borough of New York City.
All candidates, 2012: Obama, D., 3,860,144; Romney, R., 2,210,485; Johnson, LB., 42,100; Stein, Green, 35,342; Goode, Const., 6,321; Lindsay, Socialism/Liberation, 2,107.

North Carolina

County	2012 Obama (D)	Romney (R)	2008 Obama (D)	McCain (R)
Alamance	28,297	37,638	28,918	34,859
Alexander	4,591	12,207	5,167	11,790
Alleghany	1,574	3,378	2,021	3,124
Anson	6,894	4,125	6,456	4,207
Ashe	4,100	8,207	4,872	7,916
Avery	1,861	5,708	2,178	5,681
Beaufort	9,399	13,918	9,454	13,460
Bertie	6,537	3,367	6,365	3,376
Bladen	8,277	7,947	7,853	7,532
Brunswick	21,932	34,587	21,331	30,753
Buncombe	70,066	54,429	69,716	52,494
Burke	13,025	21,056	14,901	22,102
Cabarrus	32,453	49,125	31,546	45,924
Caldwell	10,795	23,069	12,081	22,526
Camden	1,456	2,995	1,597	3,140
Carteret	10,197	24,598	11,130	23,131
Caswell	5,183	5,471	5,545	5,208
Catawba	23,954	44,386	25,656	42,993
Chatham	18,252	16,578	17,862	14,668
Cherokee	3,339	9,201	3,785	8,643
Chowan	3,507	3,872	3,688	3,773
Clay	1,573	3,952	1,734	3,707
Cleveland	16,734	25,440	17,363	26,078
Columbus	10,973	12,863	11,076	12,994
Craven	18,556	26,654	19,352	24,901
Cumberland	74,991	50,191	74,693	52,151
Currituck	3,521	7,431	3,737	7,234
Dare	7,258	10,102	8,074	9,745
Davidson	20,291	48,935	22,433	45,419
Davie	5,595	14,453	6,178	13,981
Duplin	8,923	11,330	8,958	10,834
Durham	109,185	33,326	103,456	32,353
Edgecombe	18,249	8,494	17,403	8,445
Forsyth	91,606	79,177	91,085	73,674
Franklin	13,317	14,480	13,085	13,273
Gaston	32,903	55,817	31,384	52,507
Gates	2,745	2,532	2,830	2,547
Graham	1,115	2,743	1,265	2,824
Granville	13,529	12,332	13,074	11,447
Greene	3,761	4,393	3,796	4,272
Guilford	145,483	103,904	142,101	97,718
Halifax	16,931	8,686	16,047	8,961
Harnett	16,858	25,070	16,785	23,579
Haywood	11,742	15,553	12,730	14,910
Henderson	18,457	32,772	20,082	30,930
Hertford	7,815	3,001	7,513	3,089
Hoke	9,915	6,721	9,227	6,293
Hyde	1,157	1,183	1,241	1,212
Iredell	25,952	49,071	27,318	45,148
Jackson	8,052	8,224	8,766	7,854
Johnston	27,052	48,206	26,795	43,622
Jones	2,335	2,825	2,378	2,817

County	2012 Obama (D)	Romney (R)	2008 Obama (D)	McCain (R)
Lee	10,577	13,000	10,784	12,775
Lenoir	13,350	13,763	13,378	13,401
Lincoln	10,980	25,184	11,713	23,631
Macon	5,692	10,817	6,620	10,317
Madison	4,466	5,379	5,026	5,192
Martin	6,514	5,963	6,539	5,957
McDowell	6,006	11,732	6,571	11,534
Mecklenburg	270,705	170,490	253,958	153,848
Mitchell	1,810	5,778	2,238	5,499
Montgomery	4,689	6,389	4,926	6,155
Moore	16,371	29,336	17,624	27,314
Nash	24,214	23,769	23,099	23,728
New Hanover	46,778	51,742	49,145	50,544
Northampton	7,210	3,474	6,903	3,671
Onslow	18,115	31,695	19,499	30,278
Orange	53,404	21,398	53,806	20,266
Pamlico	2,632	4,032	2,838	3,823
Pasquotank	9,970	7,216	10,272	7,778
Pender	9,455	14,368	9,907	13,618
Perquimans	2,747	3,814	2,772	3,678
Person	8,384	10,467	8,446	10,030
Pitt	40,701	35,534	40,501	33,927
Polk	4,000	6,219	4,396	5,990
Randolph	14,675	44,913	16,414	40,998
Richmond	9,747	9,236	9,713	9,424
Robeson	23,957	17,093	23,058	17,433
Rockingham	16,170	25,037	17,255	23,899
Rowan	22,529	38,622	23,391	37,451
Rutherford	9,277	18,797	9,641	18,769
Sampson	11,496	14,358	11,836	14,038
Scotland	8,131	5,799	8,151	6,005
Stanly	8,287	19,698	8,878	19,329
Stokes	5,969	15,142	6,875	14,488
Surry	9,005	19,753	10,475	18,730
Swain	2,618	2,976	2,806	2,900
Transylvania	6,740	9,522	7,275	9,401
Tyrrell	835	929	933	960
Union	32,032	60,468	31,189	54,123
Vance	13,286	7,406	13,166	7,606
Wake	286,939	232,933	250,891	187,001
Warren	6,635	3,111	7,086	3,063
Washington	3,811	2,615	3,748	2,670
Watauga	13,371	14,124	14,558	13,344
Wayne	23,154	27,536	22,671	26,952
Wilkes	8,089	20,410	8,934	20,288
Wilson	20,002	16,937	19,652	17,375
Yadkin	3,928	12,500	4,527	12,409
Yancey	3,954	5,249	4,486	5,045
Totals	2,175,670	2,272,506	2,142,651	2,128,474

All candidates, 2012: Romney, R., 2,272,506; Obama, D., 2,175,670; Johnson, LB., 44,736.

North Dakota

County	2012 Obama (D)	Romney (R)	2008 Obama (D)	McCain (R)
Adams	328	916	435	788
Barnes	2,389	2,953	2,741	2,826
Benson	1,232	867	1,569	773
Billings	89	472	114	375
Bottineau	1,163	2,246	1,387	2,059
Bowman	412	1,277	478	1,107
Burke	230	766	286	640
Burleigh	14,036	27,811	15,600	25,443
Cass	34,632	36,792	37,622	32,566
Cavalier	818	1,192	930	1,128
Dickey	849	1,601	1,044	1,525
Divide	382	731	464	630
Dunn	493	1,494	527	1,080
Eddy	484	631	583	548
Emmons	383	1,430	546	1,230
Foster	604	1,028	687	914
Golden Valley	161	740	210	642
Grand Forks	14,008	15,044	16,104	14,520
Grant	331	1,012	280	587
Griggs	535	770	598	682
Hettinger	313	998	406	893
Kidder	393	870	422	752
LaMoure	737	1,374	868	1,310
Logan	221	799	299	726
McHenry	924	1,651	981	1,374

County	2012 Obama (D)	Romney (R)	2008 Obama (D)	McCain (R)
McIntosh	456	1,028	579	916
McKenzie	926	2,450	933	1,740
McLean	1,660	3,130	1,867	2,767
Mercer	1,161	3,132	1,476	2,789
Morton	4,467	8,669	5,079	7,869
Mountrail	1,401	1,960	1,477	1,406
Nelson	766	862	907	800
Oliver	281	693	332	682
Pembina	1,245	1,893	1,494	1,722
Pierce	656	1,462	792	1,301
Ramsey	2,162	2,659	2,314	2,361
Ransom	1,341	1,008	1,371	998
Renville	398	850	505	799
Richland	3,190	4,213	3,513	3,900
Rolette	3,351	1,090	3,403	1,045
Sargent	1,073	876	1,115	778
Sheridan	161	637	229	555
Sioux	900	223	1,145	215
Slope	83	341	106	297
Stark	2,805	8,509	3,802	7,024
Steele	515	495	614	404
Stutsman	3,561	5,641	4,056	5,499
Towner	511	619	621	536
Traill	1,784	1,963	2,136	1,845
Walsh	2,118	2,809	2,325	2,415
Ward	8,412	16,176	10,144	15,061
Wells	671	1,646	841	1,468
Williams	2,288	7,087	2,921	6,291
Totals	**124,490**	**187,586**	**141,278**	**168,601**

All candidates, 2012: Romney, R., 187,586; Obama, D., 124,490; Johnson, LB., 5,213; Stein, Green, 1,357; Goode, Const., 1,179.

Ohio

County	2012 Obama (D)	Romney (R)	2008 Obama (D)	McCain (R)
Adams	3,857	6,691	4,170	6,914
Allen	16,869	28,802	19,521	29,941
Ashland	8,083	15,225	9,300	15,158
Ashtabula	22,964	17,890	25,027	18,949
Athens	17,268	8,118	20,722	9,742
Auglaize	5,643	16,802	6,727	16,395
Belmont	13,826	16,418	16,302	15,422
Brown	6,923	11,671	7,503	12,192
Butler	59,127	102,031	66,030	105,340
Carroll	5,396	7,177	6,423	7,097
Champaign	7,826	11,852	7,385	11,141
Clark	30,022	31,116	31,958	33,634
Clermont	29,334	62,527	31,611	62,559
Clinton	5,534	11,740	6,558	12,410
Columbiana	19,351	24,778	21,882	25,585
Coshocton	6,841	8,312	7,689	8,675
Crawford	7,207	11,561	8,288	12,316
Cuyahoga	420,953	184,475	458,204	199,864
Darke	6,610	17,745	7,964	17,290
Defiance	7,438	9,935	8,399	10,407
Delaware	36,117	58,966	36,653	54,778
Erie	20,969	16,655	23,148	17,432
Fairfield	28,831	40,134	29,250	41,580
Fayette	4,075	6,456	4,401	7,102
Franklin	316,356	201,939	334,684	218,478
Fulton	8,790	11,521	9,900	11,689
Gallia	3,418	5,912	4,777	8,247
Geauga	19,295	30,104	21,250	29,096
Greene	24,594	41,912	33,540	48,936
Guernsey	7,226	8,811	7,625	9,197
Hamilton	208,508	188,653	224,644	195,107
Hancock	12,192	22,077	13,870	22,420
Hardin	4,487	7,337	5,013	7,749
Harrison	2,895	3,936	3,683	3,872
Henry	5,513	8,111	6,320	8,239
Highland	5,772	11,032	6,857	11,908
Hocking	6,010	6,150	6,231	6,326
Holmes	2,562	8,540	3,141	7,720
Huron	8,421	10,341	12,076	12,884
Jackson	4,965	7,651	5,397	8,219
Jefferson	14,960	16,729	17,635	17,559
Knox	10,154	16,873	11,014	16,640
Lake	55,219	57,150	60,155	59,142
Lawrence	10,454	14,371	11,262	15,415
Licking	32,264	43,604	33,896	46,886
Logan	6,789	13,323	7,936	13,848
Lorain	75,798	56,376	85,276	59,068
Lucas	127,678	67,255	142,852	73,706
Madison	6,700	10,215	6,532	10,603
Mahoning	74,346	41,712	79,173	45,319
Marion	11,933	13,938	12,870	15,454
Medina	37,841	49,464	40,924	48,189
Meigs	3,911	5,782	4,094	6,015
Mercer	4,609	16,207	5,853	15,100
Miami	15,731	33,650	18,372	33,417
Monroe	3,007	3,540	3,705	3,066
Montgomery	128,983	121,188	145,997	128,679
Morgan	2,772	3,136	2,966	3,440
Morrow	5,780	9,662	6,177	10,067
Muskingum	16,327	18,826	17,730	20,549
Noble	2,082	3,498	2,474	3,450
Ottawa	11,214	10,323	12,049	10,618
Paulding	3,435	5,248	4,165	5,317
Perry	6,841	7,485	7,261	7,721
Pickaway	9,331	13,705	9,077	14,228
Pike	5,490	5,535	6,033	6,162
Portage	38,082	34,465	41,856	34,822
Preble	6,005	13,202	6,999	13,562
Putnam	4,238	13,563	5,281	13,072
Richland	21,766	33,010	25,727	34,034
Ross	13,895	14,582	14,455	16,759
Sandusky	14,035	13,491	15,601	14,190
Scioto	14,432	15,023	14,926	16,994
Seneca	10,962	13,025	13,087	13,823
Shelby	6,065	16,700	7,317	15,924
Stark	84,957	85,721	96,990	86,743
Summit	147,146	108,700	155,105	110,499
Trumbull	59,446	37,545	64,145	40,164
Tuscarawas	17,516	21,420	21,498	20,454
Union	8,546	15,947	8,761	15,744
Van Wert	3,923	9,433	5,178	9,168
Vinton	2,235	2,585	2,463	3,021
Warren	30,540	71,943	33,398	71,691
Washington	11,261	16,921	12,368	17,019
Wayne	18,932	29,450	21,712	29,342
Williams	7,045	9,863	8,174	9,880
Wood	31,596	28,997	34,285	29,648
Wyandot	3,962	6,054	4,461	6,270
Totals	**2,672,302**	**2,571,539**	**2,940,044**	**2,677,820**

All candidates, 2012: Obama, D., 2,672,302; Romney, R., 2,571,539; Johnson, LB., 48,672; Stein, Green, 17,657; Duncan, unaff., 12,032; Goode, Const., 7,838; Alexander, Soc., 2,858.

Oklahoma

County	2012 Obama (D)	Romney (R)	2008 Obama (D)	McCain (R)
Adair	2,110	4,362	2,052	4,638
Alfalfa	278	1,539	411	2,023
Atoka	1,241	3,534	1,370	3,511
Beaver	243	2,057	265	2,199
Beckham	1,413	5,496	1,625	5,772
Blaine	991	2,824	1,011	3,101
Bryan	3,533	9,188	4,426	9,307
Caddo	3,151	5,660	3,404	6,413
Canadian	10,533	35,615	11,426	36,428
Carter	4,907	12,213	5,603	13,241
Cherokee	6,137	8,151	7,194	9,186
Choctaw	1,494	3,572	1,860	3,730
Cimarron	115	1,082	152	1,119
Cleveland	34,701	59,019	39,681	64,749
Coal	648	1,709	600	1,672
Comanche	12,517	17,657	14,120	20,127
Cotton	657	1,796	690	1,793
Craig	1,746	3,552	2,073	3,858
Creek	7,114	18,964	8,318	20,187
Custer	2,358	7,442	2,660	7,842
Delaware	4,176	10,056	5,085	10,277
Dewey	301	1,769	346	1,857
Ellis	226	1,575	282	1,627
Garfield	4,732	15,176	5,545	17,067
Garvin	2,556	6,922	3,028	7,710
Grady	4,780	14,818	5,520	15,195
Grant	393	1,674	514	1,836
Greer	488	1,344	566	1,548
Harmon	264	659	333	757
Harper	173	1,261	221	1,342
Haskell	1,175	3,069	1,474	3,207
Hughes	1,370	2,836	1,709	3,134
Jackson	1,953	5,962	2,264	6,719

County	2012 Obama (D)	Romney (R)	2008 Obama (D)	McCain (R)
Jefferson	602	1,632	805	1,652
Johnston	1,134	2,644	1,249	2,708
Kay	4,624	11,498	5,463	13,230
Kingfisher	844	4,510	1,009	5,372
Kiowa	1,101	2,309	1,226	2,537
Latimer	1,169	2,620	1,313	2,860
Le Flore	4,658	11,172	5,136	11,605
Lincoln	3,265	9,542	3,504	10,470
Logan	4,686	12,297	5,717	12,556
Love	1,034	2,436	1,257	2,589
Major	446	2,700	515	2,956
Marshall	1,396	3,744	1,643	3,730
Mayes	4,822	9,634	5,749	10,234
McClain	3,191	11,108	3,551	11,193
McCurtain	2,440	7,633	2,794	7,745
McIntosh	2,767	4,498	3,320	4,903
Murray	1,540	3,606	1,592	3,746
Muskogee	9,943	13,392	11,294	15,289
Noble	1,142	3,484	1,174	3,881
Nowata	1,244	2,832	1,411	3,031
Okfuskee	1,251	2,328	1,480	2,643
Oklahoma	106,812	149,525	116,182	163,172
Okmulgee	5,416	7,712	6,191	8,727
Osage	6,695	11,218	7,498	12,160
Ottawa	3,508	6,465	4,268	6,905
Pawnee	1,813	4,228	2,063	4,533
Payne	9,193	16,467	10,601	18,435
Pittsburg	4,813	10,785	5,457	11,752
Pontotoc	3,934	8,921	4,512	9,750
Pottawatomie	7,182	16,240	7,910	17,753
Pushmataha	1,043	3,087	1,265	3,208
Roger Mills	272	1,402	287	1,502
Rogers	9,146	27,531	10,772	27,743
Seminole	2,597	4,852	2,977	5,600
Sequoyah	4,193	9,573	4,454	9,466
Stephens	3,939	12,907	4,538	14,394
Texas	854	4,908	923	5,336
Tillman	906	1,813	1,042	2,195
Tulsa	82,633	144,908	96,133	158,363
Wagoner	7,773	20,848	8,810	21,441
Washington	5,532	15,667	6,308	16,457
Washita	821	3,482	1,052	3,724
Woods	670	2,725	873	3,043
Woodward	1,129	5,936	1,350	6,404
Totals	**442,647**	**889,372**	**502,496**	**960,165**

All candidates, 2012: Romney, R., 889,372; Obama, D., 442,647.

Oregon

County	2012 Obama (D)	Romney (R)	2008 Obama (D)	McCain (R)
Baker	2,357	5,677	2,805	5,650
Benton	27,178	14,745	29,901	15,264
Clackamas	77,482	72,012	103,476	83,595
Clatsop	9,597	7,074	10,701	7,192
Columbia	8,376	7,413	13,390	10,413
Coos	11,209	12,679	14,401	15,354
Crook	3,081	6,769	3,632	6,371
Curry	4,611	6,577	5,230	6,646
Deschutes	27,547	32,659	38,819	39,064
Douglas	15,541	28,121	20,298	30,919
Gilliam	371	637	430	648
Grant	852	2,921	1,006	2,785
Harney	829	2,599	950	2,595
Hood River	5,977	3,400	6,302	3,265
Jackson	38,328	43,343	49,090	49,043
Jefferson	3,238	4,576	3,682	4,402
Josephine	14,473	22,968	17,412	22,973
Klamath	7,674	17,788	9,370	19,113
Lake	709	2,601	957	2,638
Lane	92,980	57,258	114,037	63,835
Lincoln	13,277	8,623	14,258	8,791
Linn	19,893	28,482	22,163	28,071
Malheur	2,701	6,751	2,949	7,157
Marion	53,944	58,032	61,816	59,059
Morrow	1,189	2,524	1,410	2,509
Multnomah	186,728	52,640	279,696	75,171
Polk	15,761	17,337	17,536	17,714
Sherman	317	677	385	634
Tillamook	6,249	5,670	7,072	5,757
Umatilla	8,499	15,425	9,484	15,254
Union	3,943	7,608	4,613	7,581
Wallowa	1,252	2,796	1,492	2,836
Wasco	5,066	5,152	5,906	5,103
Washington	100,814	70,130	141,544	89,185
Wheeler	262	542	281	498
Yamhill	10,715	11,990	20,797	21,390
Totals	**783,020**	**646,236**	**1,037,291**	**738,475**

All candidates, 2012: Obama, D., 783,020; Romney, R., 646,236; Johnson, LB., 18,276; Stein, Pacific Green, 14,692; Christensen, Const., 3,599; Anderson, OR Progressive, 2,559.

Pennsylvania

County	2012 Obama (D)	Romney (R)	2008 Obama (D)	McCain (R)
Adams	14,893	26,490	17,633	26,349
Allegheny	348,151	259,304	373,153	272,347
Armstrong	8,694	19,231	11,138	18,542
Beaver	36,833	42,118	40,499	42,895
Bedford	4,696	16,369	6,059	16,124
Berks	79,895	80,857	97,047	80,513
Blair	15,516	31,500	19,813	32,708
Bradford	8,285	13,822	10,306	15,057
Bucks	159,598	155,876	179,031	150,248
Butler	28,385	59,416	32,260	57,074
Cambria	23,181	33,464	32,451	31,995
Cameron	677	1,264	879	1,323
Carbon	11,040	12,710	13,464	12,957
Centre	33,677	33,697	41,950	32,992
Chester	122,232	123,280	137,833	114,421
Clarion	4,733	9,585	6,756	10,737
Clearfield	11,093	20,303	14,555	18,662
Clinton	5,503	6,941	7,097	7,504
Columbia	10,424	13,445	13,230	14,477
Crawford	13,024	19,497	16,780	20,750
Cumberland	43,983	64,365	48,306	63,739
Dauphin	64,209	56,838	69,975	58,238
Delaware	159,924	102,501	178,870	115,273
Elk	5,144	7,099	7,290	6,676
Erie	65,136	46,102	75,775	50,351
Fayette	21,841	25,845	25,866	26,081
Forest	894	1,381	1,038	1,366
Franklin	18,910	43,072	21,169	41,906
Fulton	1,297	4,780	1,576	4,642
Greene	5,564	7,985	7,829	7,889
Huntingdon	5,383	11,953	6,621	11,745
Indiana	14,403	21,187	17,065	19,727
Jefferson	4,535	12,288	6,447	12,057
Juniata	2,533	6,821	3,068	6,484
Lackawanna	61,309	34,730	67,520	39,488
Lancaster	87,108	129,364	99,586	126,568
Lawrence	17,427	20,915	19,711	21,851
Lebanon	18,975	34,010	23,310	34,314
Lehigh	77,029	66,091	87,089	63,382
Luzerne	63,974	57,969	72,492	61,127
Lycoming	15,104	30,490	18,381	30,280
McKean	5,260	9,494	6,465	9,224
Mercer	23,082	24,304	26,411	26,565
Mifflin	4,259	11,893	5,375	10,929
Monroe	33,431	25,100	39,453	28,293
Montgomery	227,561	169,903	253,393	165,552
Montour	3,026	4,636	3,364	4,574
Northampton	65,014	59,242	75,255	58,551
Northumber-land	12,392	18,516	14,329	19,018
Perry	5,430	12,511	6,396	13,058
Philadelphia	551,070	90,989	595,980	117,221
Pike	10,170	12,713	11,493	12,518
Potter	1,892	5,199	2,300	5,109
Schuylkill	24,453	32,156	28,300	33,767
Snyder	4,672	10,050	5,382	9,900
Somerset	9,420	23,935	12,878	21,686
Sullivan	1,028	1,859	1,233	1,841
Susquehanna	6,891	10,735	8,381	10,633
Tioga	5,053	10,599	6,390	11,326
Union	6,063	9,863	7,333	9,859
Venango	7,469	12,928	9,238	13,718
Warren	6,768	9,415	8,537	9,685
Washington	38,503	50,455	46,122	50,752
Wayne	8,138	12,531	9,892	12,702
Westmoreland	60,884	98,639	72,721	102,294
Wyoming	4,812	6,189	5,985	6,983
York	72,126	111,576	82,839	109,268
Totals	**2,894,079**	**2,610,385**	**3,276,363**	**2,655,885**

All candidates, 2012: Obama, D., 2,894,079; Romney, R., 2,610,385; Johnson, LB., 48,637; Stein, Green, 20,644.

Rhode Island

City	2012 Obama (D)	Romney (R)	2008 Obama (D)	McCain (R)
Bristol	5,974	3,450	6,833	3,834
Coventry	8,660	6,646	9,622	7,367
Cranston	20,322	12,302	22,520	13,981
Cumberland	8,863	6,751	9,707	6,941
East Providence	13,301	5,391	15,380	6,216
Johnston	7,117	5,176	7,763	6,066
Lincoln	5,754	4,608	6,264	4,831
Newport	5,656	2,648	6,989	3,215
North Kingstown	7,276	5,988	8,562	6,285
North Providence	9,183	5,152	9,954	5,933
Pawtucket	17,353	4,985	18,486	6,098
Providence	41,588	6,877	46,276	8,548
Smithfield	4,875	4,359	5,464	4,660
South Kingstown	7,970	4,361	9,336	4,689
Warwick	23,243	14,277	25,802	16,541
West Warwick	6,625	4,113	7,475	4,735
Westerly	5,537	3,938	6,490	4,710
Woonsocket	7,675	3,960	8,678	4,398
Other	55,492	41,313	64,970	46,343
Totals	**262,464**	**146,295**	**296,571**	**165,391**

All candidates, 2012: Obama, D., 262,464; Romney, R., 146,295; Johnson, LB., 4,162; Stein, Green, 2,261; Goode, Const., 437; Anderson, Justice, 379; Lindsay, Socialism/Liberation, 121.

South Carolina

County	2012 Obama (D)	Romney (R)	2008 Obama (D)	McCain (R)
Abbeville	4,507	5,923	4,593	6,264
Aiken	23,433	40,785	26,101	42,849
Allendale	3,335	894	3,029	947
Anderson	22,315	48,493	24,132	48,690
Bamberg	4,593	2,188	4,426	2,309
Barnwell	5,182	4,655	4,931	4,769
Beaufort	20,683	33,032	30,396	37,821
Berkeley	21,192	30,474	27,755	36,205
Calhoun	4,043	3,705	3,970	3,695
Charleston	59,765	61,612	82,698	69,822
Cherokee	7,219	13,306	7,215	13,305
Chester	7,421	6,054	7,478	6,318
Chesterfield	7,942	8,488	7,842	8,325
Clarendon	8,967	6,890	8,673	6,758
Colleton	8,470	8,439	8,616	8,525
Darlington	15,452	14,429	14,505	14,544
Dillon	7,623	5,477	7,408	5,874
Dorchester	23,037	32,367	21,806	29,929
Edgefield	4,965	6,511	5,075	6,334
Fairfield	7,743	3,996	7,591	3,912
Florence	28,508	28,825	28,012	29,861
Georgetown	14,119	16,476	14,199	15,790
Greenville	67,378	120,514	70,886	116,363
Greenwood	11,883	16,289	12,348	16,995
Hampton	5,814	3,310	5,816	3,439
Horry	38,530	66,539	38,879	64,609
Jasper	5,727	4,169	5,389	3,365
Kershaw	10,821	15,846	11,226	16,466
Lancaster	12,275	18,163	12,139	16,441
Laurens	10,297	14,726	10,578	15,334
Lee	5,972	2,829	5,960	3,074
Lexington	34,007	76,392	33,303	74,960
Marion	9,518	5,114	9,608	5,416
Marlboro	7,152	3,922	6,794	3,996
McCormick	2,637	2,460	2,755	2,437
Newberry	6,891	9,218	6,708	9,616
Oconee	8,537	21,573	9,481	21,164
Orangeburg	30,454	11,888	27,263	12,115
Pickens	10,659	32,320	11,691	32,552
Richland	84,023	37,636	105,656	57,941
Saluda	3,322	5,130	3,323	5,191
Spartanburg	40,920	65,951	41,632	65,042
Sumter	27,550	19,266	25,431	18,581
Union	5,748	6,566	5,935	7,449
Williamsburg	11,318	4,819	11,279	5,004
York	38,757	59,149	37,918	54,500
Totals	**800,704**	**1,006,808**	**862,449**	**1,034,896**

All candidates, 2012: Romney, R., 1,006,808; Obama, D., 800,704; Johnson, LB., 15,502; Stein, Green, 5,133; Goode, Const., 4,540.

South Dakota

County	2012 Obama (D)	Romney (R)	2008 Obama (D)	McCain (R)
Aurora	556	804	655	794
Beadle	2,880	4,230	3,493	4,054
Bennett	548	626	557	614
Bon Homme	1,167	1,830	1,367	1,712
Brookings	5,826	6,219	7,207	6,431
Brown	7,249	8,320	9,041	8,067
Brule	824	1,499	965	1,407
Buffalo	472	166	454	156
Butte	1,000	3,068	1,306	2,821
Campbell	153	616	243	591
Charles Mix	1,482	2,229	1,807	2,109
Clark	713	1,067	830	1,065
Clay	2,955	2,146	3,808	2,296
Codington	4,588	6,696	5,595	6,374
Corson	647	515	837	535
Custer	1,335	3,062	1,475	2,909
Davison	3,042	4,754	3,554	4,731
Day	1,497	1,320	1,785	1,372
Deuel	941	1,175	1,054	1,088
Dewey	1,207	663	1,328	659
Douglas	332	1,334	424	1,293
Edmunds	622	1,264	819	1,213
Fall River	1,137	2,256	1,338	2,348
Faulk	331	765	426	739
Grant	1,490	2,034	1,786	1,951
Gregory	599	1,507	771	1,423
Haakon	138	940	187	939
Hamlin	921	1,803	1,043	1,661
Hand	575	1,242	718	1,247
Hanson	760	1,627	961	1,426
Harding	82	638	135	575
Hughes	2,786	5,219	3,037	5,298
Hutchinson	923	2,451	1,242	2,285
Hyde	189	531	226	547
Jackson	426	661	435	668
Jerauld	452	538	542	546
Jones	108	490	147	463
Kingsbury	1,092	1,451	1,277	1,435
Lake	2,724	3,419	3,033	2,993
Lawrence	3,973	7,025	4,932	6,787
Lincoln	7,982	13,611	8,642	11,803
Lyman	605	933	710	894
Marshall	1,061	889	1,261	900
McCook	905	1,655	1,219	1,646
McPherson	272	921	441	915
Meade	2,928	7,560	3,751	7,515
Mellette	375	381	373	445
Miner	479	636	605	577
Minnehaha	34,668	40,330	39,838	39,251
Moody	1,429	1,535	1,663	1,508
Pennington	15,122	28,229	17,802	27,603
Perkins	319	1,205	499	1,102
Potter	339	1,029	482	937
Roberts	2,302	1,883	2,672	1,781
Sanborn	389	688	500	669
Shannon	2,922	188	2,971	331
Spink	1,300	1,670	1,550	1,660
Stanley	434	1,061	510	1,017
Sully	186	611	233	581
Todd	1,976	498	2,208	571
Tripp	737	1,905	914	1,859
Turner	1,411	2,715	1,681	2,538
Union	2,782	4,698	3,244	4,310
Walworth	671	1,731	923	1,668
Yankton	4,208	5,463	4,838	5,039
Ziebach	439	314	554	312
Totals	**144,983**	**210,539**	**170,924**	**203,054**

All candidates, 2012: Romney, R., 210,539; Obama, D., 144,983; Johnson, LB., 5,795; Goode, Const., 2,371.

Tennessee

County	2012 Obama (D)	Romney (R)	2008 Obama (D)	McCain (R)
Anderson	10,112	18,941	11,396	19,675
Bedford	4,207	10,026	5,027	10,217
Benton	2,255	3,850	2,645	3,696
Bledsoe	1,267	3,022	1,517	3,166
Blount	12,925	35,417	15,253	35,571

County	2012 Obama (D)	Romney (R)	2008 Obama (D)	McCain (R)
Bradley	8,035	27,417	9,357	28,333
Campbell	3,327	8,602	3,867	8,535
Cannon	1,560	3,308	2,011	3,322
Carroll	3,475	7,219	3,980	7,455
Carter	4,786	15,496	5,587	15,852
Cheatham	4,656	10,266	5,498	10,702
Chester	1,622	4,672	1,797	4,587
Claiborne	2,433	7,617	3,078	7,175
Clay	1,037	1,747	1,248	1,676
Cocke	2,804	8,459	3,340	8,945
Coffee	5,865	13,013	7,132	13,250
Crockett	1,669	3,782	1,967	3,994
Cumberland	6,260	18,651	7,889	17,436
Davidson	138,899	94,464	158,423	102,915
Decatur	1,302	2,873	1,566	3,101
DeKalb	2,168	4,134	2,832	4,085
Dickson	6,228	11,287	7,506	11,677
Dyer	3,757	9,921	4,411	9,859
Fayette	6,683	12,682	6,892	12,173
Fentress	1,559	5,240	1,831	4,789
Franklin	5,594	10,252	6,613	10,539
Gibson	6,564	12,883	7,406	13,516
Giles	3,759	6,914	4,614	6,902
Grainger	1,668	5,469	2,066	5,297
Greene	6,216	17,234	7,110	17,151
Grundy	1,637	2,502	1,971	2,563
Hamblen	5,229	14,515	6,807	15,508
Hamilton	58,794	79,877	64,246	81,702
Hancock	475	1,527	604	1,588
Hardeman	5,479	4,864	5,919	5,225
Hardin	2,467	7,886	2,794	7,077
Hawkins	5,086	14,376	5,930	14,756
Haywood	4,567	2,960	4,893	3,165
Henderson	2,516	7,418	3,021	7,669
Henry	4,337	8,187	5,153	8,182
Hickman	2,693	4,756	3,563	4,784
Houston	1,400	1,579	1,678	1,608
Humphreys	2,904	3,829	3,600	3,818
Jackson	1,736	2,380	2,224	2,185
Jefferson	4,230	13,037	5,178	13,092
Johnson	1,483	4,611	1,837	4,621
Knox	57,594	106,411	70,215	113,015
Lake	884	1,163	1,024	1,175
Lauderdale	4,010	4,616	4,322	4,933
Lawrence	4,237	10,770	5,161	10,566
Lewis	1,445	3,116	1,804	2,951
Lincoln	3,283	9,791	3,695	9,231
Loudon	5,057	16,701	6,058	15,815
Macon	1,552	5,259	2,060	5,145
Madison	18,360	21,989	20,209	23,290
Marion	3,952	6,268	4,506	6,746
Marshall	3,722	6,823	4,320	6,755
Maury	11,819	20,698	13,058	20,288
McMinn	4,603	12,958	5,541	12,989
McNairy	2,643	7,010	3,131	7,135
Meigs	1,163	2,728	1,372	2,797
Monroe	4,368	11,717	5,053	11,484
Montgomery	24,349	30,159	25,716	30,175
Moore	705	2,053	881	2,010
Morgan	1,722	4,668	1,969	4,717
Obion	3,320	8,814	4,308	8,873
Overton	2,802	4,772	3,419	4,497
Perry	992	1,578	1,329	1,596
Pickett	711	1,707	854	1,786
Polk	1,856	4,108	2,124	4,267
Putnam	7,793	17,242	9,739	17,101
Rhea	2,625	7,793	2,907	8,042
Roane	6,014	14,719	7,224	15,658
Robertson	8,289	17,641	9,318	17,903
Rutherford	36,400	60,829	40,460	59,892
Scott	1,452	5,117	1,720	4,931
Sequatchie	1,488	3,541	1,717	3,610
Sevier	7,415	25,979	8,604	24,922
Shelby	232,201	135,536	256,297	145,458
Smith	2,467	4,492	2,992	4,563
Stewart	2,069	2,963	2,470	2,956
Sullivan	15,303	43,528	18,354	44,808
Sumner	18,571	45,979	21,487	44,949
Tipton	7,020	16,395	7,931	17,165
Trousdale	1,238	1,610	1,475	1,688

County	2012 Obama (D)	Romney (R)	2008 Obama (D)	McCain (R)
Unicoi	1,909	5,028	2,107	5,011
Union	1,474	4,278	1,829	4,467
Van Buren	875	1,384	849	1,294
Warren	4,748	8,007	5,515	8,562
Washington	14,318	32,787	15,941	32,341
Wayne	1,163	4,251	1,355	4,076
Weakley	3,547	8,601	4,596	8,855
White	2,793	6,192	3,372	6,103
Williamson	24,328	68,090	27,886	64,858
Wilson	14,669	36,076	15,886	34,595
Totals	**951,406**	**1,450,595**	**1,087,437**	**1,479,178**

All candidates, 2012: Romney, R., 1,450,595; Obama, D., 951,406; Johnson, Ind., 18,506; Goode, Const., 7,278; Stein, Green, 6,443; Anderson, Ind., 2,617; Miller, Ind., 1,742.

Texas

County	2012 Obama (D)	Romney (R)	2008 Obama (D)	McCain (R)
Anderson	3,796	12,235	4,630	11,884
Andrews	794	3,636	790	3,816
Angelina	7,833	20,301	9,379	19,569
Aransas	2,703	6,829	3,006	6,693
Archer	525	3,599	740	3,595
Armstrong	98	828	128	856
Atascosa	5,128	7,451	4,415	5,462
Austin	2,252	9,260	2,821	8,786
Bailey	466	1,336	682	1,618
Bandera	1,859	7,423	2,250	6,935
Bastrop	9,860	14,019	11,687	13,817
Baylor	267	1,297	366	1,262
Bee	3,451	4,354	3,645	4,471
Bell	35,315	49,369	40,413	49,242
Bexar	263,871	240,519	275,527	246,275
Blanco	1,220	3,637	1,467	3,418
Borden	32	324	40	316
Bosque	1,366	5,873	1,797	5,762
Bowie	10,184	24,840	10,815	24,162
Brazoria	34,327	70,684	36,480	67,515
Brazos	17,440	37,152	20,502	37,465
Brewster	1,765	1,975	1,970	1,855
Briscoe	117	576	205	617
Brooks	1,886	507	1,747	556
Brown	1,904	11,894	2,822	12,052
Burleson	1,705	4,671	2,053	4,547
Burnet	3,672	12,828	4,608	12,059
Caldwell	4,787	6,018	5,403	6,107
Calhoun	2,510	4,145	2,729	4,106
Callahan	751	4,376	1,063	4,589
Cameron	49,159	24,955	48,480	26,671
Camp	1,428	2,878	1,734	2,798
Carson	292	2,450	406	2,548
Cass	2,921	8,747	3,490	8,279
Castro	630	1,470	719	1,562
Chambers	2,780	11,761	3,188	9,988
Cherokee	3,935	12,291	4,610	11,695
Childress	320	1,665	497	1,782
Clay	740	4,266	1,085	4,213
Cochran	256	648	284	758
Coke	179	1,216	299	1,252
Coleman	441	3,007	643	3,011
Collin	100,754	195,933	109,047	184,897
Collingsworth	177	962	234	943
Colorado	2,024	6,015	2,508	5,795
Comal	11,437	39,291	12,384	35,233
Comanche	890	3,940	1,334	3,813
Concho	194	793	257	807
Cooke	2,240	11,901	3,051	11,871
Coryell	5,141	11,193	6,619	11,550
Cottle	180	553	187	509
Crane	275	985	319	1,119
Crockett	480	957	512	1,026
Crosby	639	1,132	684	1,221
Culberson	566	294	492	257
Dallam	253	1,248	302	1,269
Dallas	403,170	294,339	422,989	310,000
Dawson	1,017	2,591	1,152	2,906
Deaf Smith	1,239	3,042	1,247	3,466

County	2012 Obama (D)	Romney (R)	2008 Obama (D)	McCain (R)	County	2012 Obama (D)	Romney (R)	2008 Obama (D)	McCain (R)
Delta	454	1,524	589	1,580	Kinney	522	880	633	907
Denton	79,917	156,105	91,160	149,935	Kleberg	4,752	4,056	5,256	4,540
DeWitt	1,463	5,114	1,716	4,888	Knox	332	1,160	367	986
Dickens	216	793	234	730	La Salle	965	669	1,052	714
Dimmit	2,141	762	2,692	874	Lamar	4,173	12,814	5,243	12,952
Donley	226	1,286	291	1,374	Lamb	998	3,056	1,156	3,344
Duval	3,331	979	3,298	1,076	Lampasas	1,457	5,583	1,903	5,651
Eastland	970	5,443	1,271	5,165	Lavaca	1,427	6,788	1,869	6,293
Ector	8,095	23,936	9,123	26,199	Lee	1,630	4,504	2,000	4,312
Edwards	232	641	346	673	Leon	1,061	5,812	1,418	5,566
El Paso	112,273	56,517	122,021	61,783	Liberty	5,196	17,304	5,991	15,448
Ellis	13,803	39,353	15,333	38,078	Limestone	2,208	5,288	2,516	5,079
Erath	1,965	10,325	3,128	10,768	Lipscomb	119	1,044	155	1,093
Falls	2,033	3,356	2,225	3,328	Live Oak	915	3,153	1,048	3,095
Fannin	2,482	8,143	3,464	8,092	Llano	1,818	7,560	2,250	7,281
Fayette	2,311	8,098	3,014	7,582	Loving	9	54	12	67
Fisher	512	1,094	687	1,083	Lubbock	26,088	63,133	30,486	66,304
Floyd	551	1,523	730	1,784	Lynn	464	1,377	627	1,473
Foard	140	346	198	327	Madison	964	3,028	1,146	2,891
Fort Bend	101,043	116,028	98,368	103,206	Marion	1,487	2,730	1,644	2,567
Franklin	750	3,446	1,036	3,392	Martin	247	1,338	314	1,389
Freestone	1,848	5,644	2,034	5,205	Mason	380	1,562	546	1,544
Frio	2,376	1,559	2,405	1,644	Matagorda	3,972	8,026	4,440	7,835
Gaines	535	3,484	650	3,385	Maverick	8,302	2,171	8,554	2,316
Galveston	39,162	68,594	41,805	62,258	McCulloch	537	2,419	728	2,263
Garza	276	1,262	375	1,356	McLennan	25,688	47,885	29,998	49,044
Gillespie	2,055	10,305	2,576	9,563	McMullen	67	436	132	400
Glasscock	44	526	52	502	Medina	4,760	11,016	5,147	10,480
Goliad	1,127	2,294	1,329	2,298	Menard	170	663	295	712
Gonzales	1,773	4,213	2,167	4,076	Midland	8,223	35,452	9,691	36,155
Gray	885	6,428	1,153	6,924	Milam	2,632	5,478	3,044	5,217
Grayson	10,665	30,907	13,900	31,136	Mills	279	1,882	398	1,753
Gregg	12,336	28,665	13,166	29,203	Mitchell	536	1,754	586	1,815
Grimes	2,339	6,141	2,704	5,562	Montague	1,116	6,539	1,597	6,245
Guadalupe	15,654	32,959	16,156	30,869	Montgomery	32,852	137,822	36,703	119,884
Hale	2,228	6,417	2,708	7,171	Moore	963	3,967	1,123	4,282
Hall	265	832	324	930	Morris	1,856	3,226	2,055	3,158
Hamilton	591	2,918	863	2,876	Motley	55	538	67	522
Hansford	158	1,787	240	1,847	Nacogdoches	6,441	13,910	8,393	14,828
Hardeman	302	1,176	373	1,199	Navarro	4,348	10,838	5,400	10,810
Hardin	3,358	17,744	3,939	16,603	Newton	1,721	4,399	1,751	3,446
Harris	585,451	584,866	590,982	571,883	Nolan	1,216	3,277	1,521	3,485
Harrison	8,431	17,471	8,887	17,103	Nueces	45,666	48,779	47,912	52,391
Hartley	183	1,700	250	1,711	Ochiltree	253	2,718	243	2,851
Haskell	551	1,422	699	1,388	Oldham	71	786	102	813
Hays	25,448	31,577	28,431	29,638	Orange	6,797	23,361	7,646	21,509
Hemphill	192	1,298	216	1,345	Palo Pinto	1,810	7,392	2,499	7,264
Henderson	6,094	21,202	7,913	20,857	Panola	2,211	7,941	2,586	7,582
Hidalgo	97,879	39,786	90,261	39,668	Parker	7,804	38,980	10,502	36,974
Hill	2,745	9,128	3,811	9,264	Parmer	528	2,005	719	2,969
Hockley	1,482	5,543	1,797	5,795	Pecos	1,591	2,512	1,476	2,480
Hood	3,829	18,341	5,087	17,299	Polk	4,836	14,019	6,230	13,731
Hopkins	2,775	9,834	3,530	9,299	Potter	7,114	18,905	8,939	20,761
Houston	2,235	5,839	2,656	5,872	Presidio	1,273	504	1,252	489
Howard	1,042	4,032	2,545	7,029	Rains	754	3,265	1,048	3,146
Hudspeth	379	471	430	458	Randall	7,553	41,366	9,468	41,948
Hunt	6,658	20,976	8,594	20,573	Reagan	158	676	197	795
Hutchinson	1,042	6,797	1,322	7,361	Real	277	1,236	375	1,238
Irion	112	668	164	644	Red River	1,482	3,549	1,539	3,461
Jack	303	2,580	470	2,528	Reeves	1,649	1,185	1,606	1,445
Jackson	1,068	3,903	1,301	3,723	Refugio	998	1,659	1,382	1,855
Jasper	3,402	9,924	3,658	9,022	Roberts	25	408	41	477
Jeff Davis	440	717	468	749	Robertson	2,792	4,416	2,675	3,980
Jefferson	44,626	43,214	44,888	42,905	Rockwall	8,112	27,098	8,492	23,300
Jim Hogg	1,301	356	1,336	472	Runnels	517	3,103	720	3,118
Jim Wells	6,492	4,595	6,706	4,841	Rusk	4,451	13,924	4,983	13,646
Johnson	10,481	37,609	12,912	36,685	Sabine	806	3,726	1,077	3,749
Jones	1,225	4,258	1,528	4,203	San Augustine	1,193	2,469	1,328	2,342
Karnes	1,324	2,823	1,760	2,736	San Jacinto	2,410	7,105	2,721	6,151
Kaufman	9,451	24,804	11,161	23,735	San Patricio	7,854	11,994	8,854	12,404
Kendall	3,035	14,467	3,599	12,971	San Saba	323	1,905	487	1,941
Kenedy	82	83	108	94	Schleicher	220	781	324	970
Kent	66	334	99	342	Scurry	837	4,121	1,088	4,414
Kerr	4,325	17,225	5,570	16,752	Shackelford	131	1,218	208	1,284
Kimble	217	1,667	342	1,487	Shelby	2,318	6,870	2,548	6,630
King	5	139	8	151	Sherman	121	908	127	884

County	2012 Obama (D)	Romney (R)	2008 Obama (D)	McCain (R)
Smith	22,101	61,858	23,726	55,187
Somervell	609	2,858	799	2,677
Starr	10,248	1,540	8,274	1,492
Stephens	475	2,891	626	2,869
Sterling	31	459	97	520
Stonewall	160	507	206	524
Sutton	369	1,110	381	1,189
Swisher	579	1,654	813	1,683
Tarrant	252,789	348,686	274,880	348,420
Taylor	9,725	32,853	12,690	34,317
Terrell	184	358	186	323
Terry	1,059	2,602	1,379	2,879
Throckmorton	109	700	166	671
Titus	2,638	6,062	3,145	6,028
Tom Green	9,246	26,749	11,158	27,362
Travis	231,540	139,503	254,017	136,981
Trinity	1,614	4,537	1,925	4,095
Tyler	1,659	5,889	2,166	5,644
Upshur	2,953	11,948	3,790	11,222
Upton	332	952	288	898
Uvalde	3,824	4,526	4,126	4,590
Val Verde	6,267	5,612	6,982	5,752
Van Zandt	3,083	15,790	4,505	15,734
Victoria	8,795	19,684	9,832	19,878
Walker	5,283	9,569	7,334	11,623
Waller	6,401	9,158	7,153	8,265
Ward	836	2,364	899	2,667
Washington	3,378	10,850	4,034	10,176
Webb	37,592	11,074	33,452	13,119
Wharton	4,235	9,750	4,937	9,431
Wheeler	232	1,878	314	1,918
Wichita	10,490	29,756	13,868	31,731
Wilbarger	971	2,956	1,196	3,283
Willacy	3,595	1,415	3,409	1,456
Williamson	61,812	96,910	67,691	88,323
Wilson	4,819	12,205	5,362	10,904
Winkler	398	1,331	477	1,529
Wise	3,219	17,178	4,471	15,973
Wood	3,052	14,317	4,010	13,658
Yoakum	409	1,698	450	1,989
Young	992	6,225	1,303	5,942
Zapata	2,517	993	1,939	919
Zavala	3,042	574	3,263	596
Totals	**3,294,440**	**4,555,799**	**3,528,633**	**4,479,328**

All candidates, 2012: Romney, R., 4,555,799; Obama, D., 3,294,440; Johnson, LB., 88,110; Stein, Green, 24,450.

Utah

County	2012 Obama (D)	Romney (R)	2008 Obama (D)	McCain (R)
Beaver	341	2,153	542	1,902
Box Elder	1,830	15,969	3,311	15,228
Cache	5,434	30,818	10,294	29,127
Carbon	2,204	4,834	3,468	4,091
Daggett	91	399	131	297
Davis	20,417	90,030	30,477	77,341
Duchesne	570	5,608	911	4,689
Emery	569	3,743	973	3,358
Garfield	306	1,811	405	1,710
Grand	1,678	1,917	2,067	1,871
Iron	1,720	11,172	3,258	12,518
Juab	436	3,400	741	2,683
Kane	718	2,463	856	2,212
Millard	424	4,421	758	3,653
Morgan	386	3,910	689	3,311
Piute	74	696	141	635
Rich	83	907	154	831
Salt Lake	132,686	198,739	176,988	176,692
San Juan	2,062	3,006	2,406	2,638
Sanpete	697	6,414	1,631	6,664
Sevier	701	6,961	1,359	6,394
Summit	7,656	8,464	9,532	6,956
Tooele	3,794	12,240	5,830	10,998
Uintah	962	10,001	1,462	8,441
Utah	15,791	142,337	29,567	122,224
Wasatch	2,097	6,852	2,892	5,430
Washington	7,762	41,104	10,826	37,311

County	2012 Obama (D)	Romney (R)	2008 Obama (D)	McCain (R)
Wayne	213	1,087	335	940
Weber	17,569	48,938	25,666	45,885
Totals	**229,271**	**670,394**	**327,670**	**596,030**

All candidates, 2012: Romney, R., 670,394; Obama, D., 229,271; Johnson, LB., 11,067; Anderson, Justice, 4,717; Stein, Green, 3,378; Goode, Const., 2,562; La Riva, unaff., 344.

Vermont

City	2012 Obama (D)	Romney (R)	2008 Obama (D)	McCain (R)
Barre	1,946	1,048	2,437	1,868
Bennington	4,503	1,753	4,702	1,941
Brattleboro	4,621	915	5,077	1,098
Burlington	14,322	2,591	17,257	3,086
Colchester	4,615	2,548	5,217	2,692
Essex	6,630	3,640	7,083	3,660
Hartford	3,315	1,405	3,585	1,517
Milton	2,586	1,966	2,789	2,056
Montpelier	3,692	700	3,901	810
Rutland	4,251	2,428	4,950	2,659
Shelburne	3,076	1,403	3,347	1,217
South Burlington	6,512	2,748	6,971	2,772
Springfield	2,331	1,339	2,746	1,436
Williston	3,329	1,697	3,507	1,645
Other	131,046	65,102	145,693	70,517
Totals	**192,272**	**89,530**	**219,262**	**98,974**

All candidates, 2012: Obama, D., 192,272; Romney, R., 89,530; Johnson, LB., 3,342; Anderson, Justice, 1,099; Lindsay, Socialism/Liberation, 666.

Virginia

County	2012 Obama (D)	Romney (R)	2008 Obama (D)	McCain (R)
Accomack	7,653	8,212	7,607	7,833
Albemarle	26,194	20,832	29,792	20,576
Alleghany	3,403	3,595	3,553	3,715
Amelia	2,488	4,324	2,488	3,970
Amherst	5,898	8,866	6,094	8,470
Appomattox	2,451	5,337	2,641	4,903
Arlington	81,176	34,432	78,994	29,876
Augusta	9,448	23,614	9,825	23,120
Bath	893	1,274	1,043	1,349
Bedford	10,925	29,281	11,017	24,420
Bland	735	2,144	864	2,031
Botetourt	5,449	12,471	5,693	11,471
Brunswick	4,993	2,965	4,973	2,877
Buchanan	3,094	6,433	4,063	4,541
Buckingham	3,747	3,569	3,489	3,428
Campbell	7,591	17,687	8,091	17,444
Caroline	7,258	6,148	7,163	5,617
Carroll	3,500	8,351	4,109	8,187
Charles City	2,772	1,396	2,838	1,288
Charlotte	2,502	3,311	2,705	3,372
Chesterfield	78,954	91,174	74,310	86,413
Clarke	3,237	4,295	3,457	3,840
Craig	830	1,757	877	1,695
Culpeper	8,265	11,549	8,802	10,711
Cumberland	2,422	2,538	2,255	2,418
Dickenson	2,472	4,274	3,278	3,324
Dinwiddie	6,425	6,769	6,246	6,526
Essex	3,009	2,602	2,934	2,379
Fairfax	260,835	173,786	310,359	200,994
Fauquier	13,891	20,955	14,616	19,227
Floyd	2,732	4,671	2,937	4,441
Fluvanna	5,740	6,405	6,185	6,420
Franklin	8,340	15,309	9,618	15,414
Frederick	11,761	21,298	12,961	20,149
Giles	2,702	4,634	3,192	4,462
Gloucester	6,759	12,129	6,916	12,089
Goochland	4,672	8,441	4,813	7,643
Grayson	2,094	4,801	2,480	4,540
Greene	3,284	5,555	3,174	4,980
Greensville	3,132	1,765	3,122	1,729
Halifax	7,760	8,699	8,126	8,600
Hanover	18,283	39,920	18,447	37,344
Henrico	89,116	70,248	86,323	67,381
Henry	10,312	13,978	11,118	13,758
Highland	459	924	590	930

County	2012 Obama (D)	Romney (R)	2008 Obama (D)	McCain (R)
Isle of Wight	8,754	11,797	8,573	11,258
James City	17,854	22,830	17,352	20,912
King and Queen	1,743	1,863	1,918	1,763
King George	4,475	6,601	4,473	5,888
King William	3,326	5,473	3,344	4,966
Lancaster	3,144	3,749	3,235	3,647
Lee	2,593	6,845	3,219	5,825
Loudoun	81,840	74,794	74,845	63,336
Louisa	6,949	9,207	6,978	8,182
Lunenburg	2,635	2,840	2,703	2,900
Madison	2,637	3,864	2,862	3,758
Mathews	1,807	3,485	1,934	3,456
Mecklenburg	6,786	7,855	7,127	7,817
Middlesex	2,367	3,619	2,391	3,545
Montgomery	19,903	20,036	21,031	19,028
Nelson	4,171	3,944	4,391	3,647
New Kent	3,554	7,244	3,493	6,385
Northampton	3,737	2,676	3,800	2,713
Northumberland	3,186	4,308	3,312	4,041
Nottoway	3,351	3,422	3,413	3,499
Orange	6,864	9,241	7,107	8,506
Page	3,721	6,340	4,235	6,041
Patrick	2,417	5,619	2,879	5,491
Pittsylvania	10,347	18,375	11,415	18,730
Powhatan	4,066	11,192	4,237	10,088
Prince Edward	5,132	3,952	5,101	4,174
Prince George	7,671	9,350	7,130	8,752
Prince William	90,676	67,192	93,435	67,621
Pulaski	5,287	8,917	5,918	8,857
Rappahannock	1,971	2,307	2,105	2,227
Richmond	1,572	2,160	1,618	2,092
Roanoke	19,589	33,344	19,812	30,571
Rockbridge	4,087	5,898	4,347	5,732
Rockingham	10,059	24,173	10,453	22,468
Russell	3,716	8,177	4,932	6,389
Scott	2,394	7,435	2,725	6,980
Shenandoah	6,462	12,526	6,912	12,005
Smyth	4,169	8,376	4,239	7,817
Southampton	4,148	4,437	4,402	4,583
Spotsylvania	19,404	24,789	24,897	28,610
Stafford	27,111	32,420	25,716	29,221
Surry	2,574	1,671	2,626	1,663
Sussex	3,350	2,021	3,301	2,026
Tazewell	3,652	13,823	5,596	11,201
Warren	6,449	9,865	6,997	8,879
Washington	6,990	17,888	8,063	16,077
Westmoreland	4,155	4,116	4,577	3,719
Wise	3,751	11,041	4,995	8,914
Wythe	3,780	8,324	4,107	8,207
York	13,165	20,182	13,700	19,833
City				
Alexandria	52,434	20,205	50,473	19,181
Bedford	1,225	1,527	1,208	1,497
Bristol	2,487	4,776	2,665	4,579
Buena Vista	904	1,545	1,108	1,282
Charlottesville	16,267	4,801	15,705	4,078
Chesapeake	47,881	48,685	53,994	52,625
Colonial Heights	2,541	5,937	2,562	6,161
Covington	1,077	796	1,304	1,020
Danville	12,215	7,756	12,352	8,361
Emporia	1,791	886	1,702	897
Fairfax	6,636	4,762	6,575	4,691
Falls Church	5,006	2,141	4,695	1,970
Franklin	2,830	1,496	2,819	1,576
Fredericksburg	7,114	4,054	6,155	3,413
Galax	899	1,331	1,052	1,317
Hampton	51,733	19,193	46,917	20,476
Harrisonburg	8,650	6,564	8,444	6,048
Hopewell	5,178	3,737	5,285	4,149
Lexington	1,484	1,146	1,543	914
Lynchburg	15,905	19,752	16,269	17,638
Manassas	8,477	6,461	7,518	5,975
Manassas Park	3,873	1,696	2,463	1,634
Martinsville	3,856	2,312	4,139	2,311
Newport News	47,187	25,356	51,972	28,667

County	2012 Obama (D)	Romney (R)	2008 Obama (D)	McCain (R)
Norfolk	57,373	21,366	62,819	24,814
Norton	566	892	743	744
Petersburg	11,920	1,209	13,774	1,583
Poquoson	1,679	5,309	1,748	5,229
Portsmouth	28,994	12,407	32,327	13,984
Radford	2,730	2,520	2,930	2,418
Richmond	69,783	18,557	73,623	18,649
Roanoke	22,179	14,116	24,934	15,394
Salem	4,756	7,289	5,164	7,088
Staunton	5,710	5,257	5,569	5,330
Suffolk	20,308	15,972	22,446	17,165
Virginia Beach	84,049	88,846	98,885	100,319
Waynesboro	3,836	4,789	3,906	4,815
Williamsburg	4,901	2,678	4,328	2,353
Winchester	5,089	4,943	5,268	4,725
Totals	**1,854,723**	**1,747,386**	**1,959,532**	**1,725,005**

All candidates, 2012: Obama, D., 1,854,723; Romney, R., 1,747,386; Johnson, LB., 30,021; Goode, Const., 13,458; Stein, Green, 8,366.

Washington

County	2012 Obama (D)	Romney (R)	2008 Obama (D)	McCain (R)
Adams	1,085	2,451	1,552	3,222
Asotin	3,453	4,855	4,139	5,451
Benton	18,473	34,163	26,288	45,345
Chelan	9,093	13,467	13,781	17,605
Clallam	12,930	12,977	19,470	18,199
Clark	67,438	66,624	95,356	84,212
Columbia	582	1,440	686	1,499
Cowlitz	14,452	13,006	24,597	19,554
Douglas	3,443	6,234	5,848	9,098
Ferry	1,192	1,877	1,467	1,916
Franklin	4,366	8,173	7,361	12,037
Garfield	317	878	385	968
Grant	6,815	13,912	9,601	17,153
Gray's Harbor	13,448	10,044	16,354	12,104
Island	17,845	16,516	22,058	19,426
Jefferson	9,737	5,041	13,252	6,330
King	378,779	162,578	648,230	259,716
Kitsap	41,415	33,314	68,624	53,297
Kittitas	4,110	5,363	8,030	9,471
Klickitat	2,905	3,611	4,965	4,944
Lewis	7,421	12,007	13,624	20,278
Lincoln	1,357	3,064	2,032	3,803
Mason	11,299	10,028	15,050	12,600
Okanogan	3,738	5,134	7,613	8,798
Pacific	4,981	3,982	6,094	4,555
Pend Oreille	2,219	3,442	2,562	3,717
Pierce	97,176	80,770	181,824	141,673
San Juan	5,861	2,659	7,374	2,958
Skagit	15,005	13,215	30,053	24,687
Skamania	2,129	2,233	2,817	2,524
Snohomish	111,015	79,477	187,294	126,722
Spokane	72,271	81,703	105,786	108,314
Stevens	4,605	8,343	8,499	13,132
Thurston	50,463	34,165	75,882	48,366
Wahkiakum	954	962	1,121	1,105
Walla Walla	4,741	7,599	10,081	14,182
Whatcom	31,528	25,303	58,236	40,205
Whitman	4,704	5,225	9,070	8,104
Yakima	19,216	26,776	33,792	41,946
Totals	**1,062,561**	**822,611**	**1,750,848**	**1,229,216**

All candidates, 2012: Obama, D., 1,062,561; Romney, R., 822,611; Johnson, LB., 20,117; Stein, Green, 10,442; Goode, Const., 4,592; Anderson, Justice, 2,415; Harris, Soc. Workers, 695; Lindsay, Socialism/Liberation, 667.

West Virginia

County	2012 Obama (D)	Romney (R)	2008 Obama (D)	McCain (R)
Barbour	1,761	3,804	2,419	3,685
Berkeley	14,122	21,956	15,994	20,841
Boone	2,777	5,414	4,529	3,632
Braxton	1,985	2,692	2,704	2,629
Brooke	3,984	5,014	4,717	4,961
Cabell	13,380	17,779	15,292	18,793
Calhoun	801	1,288	993	1,366
Clay	922	1,957	1,421	1,755
Doddridge	571	2,108	735	2,218

County	2012 Obama (D)	Romney (R)	2008 Obama (D)	McCain (R)
Fayette	5,368	8,304	7,242	7,658
Gilmer	830	1,580	1,004	1,445
Grant	713	3,775	997	3,166
Greenbrier	4,681	7,873	5,881	7,567
Hampshire	2,294	5,514	2,983	5,222
Hancock	4,571	7,159	5,504	7,518
Hardy	1,477	3,523	1,901	3,376
Harrison	9,660	15,755	13,582	17,824
Jackson	3,824	7,360	4,861	7,148
Jefferson	10,215	11,090	11,687	10,600
Kanawha	32,190	41,037	40,594	40,952
Lewis	1,779	4,349	2,109	4,335
Lincoln	2,204	4,336	3,029	3,637
Logan	3,461	8,186	5,873	7,326
Marion	8,905	11,981	11,618	11,501
Marshall	3,395	6,208	5,996	7,759
Mason	3,738	5,706	4,484	5,853
McDowell	2,086	3,931	3,430	2,882
Mercer	5,416	15,406	7,450	13,246
Mineral	2,836	7,687	3,750	7,616
Mingo	2,421	6,163	3,582	4,587
Monongalia	13,664	16,672	17,060	15,775
Monroe	1,441	3,571	2,014	3,397
Morgan	2,361	4,508	2,721	4,428
Nicholas	2,635	5,823	4,357	4,804
Ohio	6,623	10,577	8,593	10,694
Pendleton	1,067	2,087	1,310	2,035
Pleasants	942	1,805	1,142	1,772
Pocahontas	1,298	2,167	1,548	2,011
Preston	2,916	7,841	4,205	7,325
Putnam	7,198	15,926	9,334	15,162
Raleigh	7,651	20,375	10,237	17,548
Randolph	3,325	6,150	4,539	6,060
Ritchie	762	2,889	998	2,781
Roane	1,928	2,973	2,511	2,943
Summers	1,612	2,968	2,290	2,891
Taylor	1,933	3,827	2,462	3,605
Tucker	876	2,160	1,288	2,123
Tyler	880	2,291	1,241	2,415
Upshur	2,143	5,878	2,925	5,911
Wayne	4,915	8,673	6,137	8,947
Webster	939	1,708	1,552	1,386
Wetzel	2,194	3,449	2,942	3,342
Wirt	673	1,422	782	1,496
Wood	11,067	21,980	12,573	22,896
Wyoming	1,575	5,751	2,735	4,621
Totals	**234,985**	**412,406**	**303,857**	**397,466**

All candidates, 2012: Romney, R., 412,406; Obama, D., 234,985; Johnson, LB., 6,204; Stein, Mountain, 4,341; Terry, NPA, 3,767.

Wisconsin

County	2012 Obama (D)	Romney (R)	2008 Obama (D)	McCain (R)
Adams	5,537	4,643	5,806	3,974
Ashland	5,387	2,816	5,818	2,634
Barron	10,883	11,413	12,078	10,457
Bayfield	6,025	3,597	5,972	3,365
Brown	62,433	64,738	67,269	55,854
Buffalo	3,569	3,352	3,949	2,923
Burnett	3,981	4,541	4,337	4,200
Calumet	11,477	14,519	13,295	12,722
Chippewa	15,211	15,371	16,239	13,492
Clark	6,173	7,394	7,454	6,383
Columbia	17,158	13,014	16,661	12,193
Crawford	4,622	3,064	4,987	2,830
Dane	215,389	83,459	205,984	73,065
Dodge	18,745	25,190	19,183	23,015
Door	9,338	8,109	10,142	7,112
Douglas	12,207	6,414	15,830	7,835
Dunn	11,303	10,210	13,002	9,566
Eau Claire	30,618	23,218	33,146	20,959
Florence	952	1,643	1,134	1,512
Fond du Lac	22,356	30,329	23,463	28,164
Forest	2,421	2,172	2,673	1,963
Grant	13,574	10,255	14,875	9,068
Green	11,196	7,848	11,502	6,730
Green Lake	3,790	5,779	4,000	5,393
Iowa	8,099	4,302	7,987	3,829
Iron	1,783	1,788	1,914	1,464

County	2012 Obama (D)	Romney (R)	2008 Obama (D)	McCain (R)
Jackson	5,297	3,900	5,572	3,552
Jefferson	20,136	23,489	21,448	21,096
Juneau	6,237	5,400	6,186	5,148
Kenosha	44,838	34,942	45,836	31,609
Kewaunee	5,151	5,746	5,902	4,711
La Crosse	36,632	25,711	38,524	23,701
Lafayette	4,534	3,313	4,732	2,984
Langlade	4,569	5,810	5,182	5,081
Lincoln	7,543	7,444	8,424	6,519
Manitowoc	20,382	21,581	22,428	19,234
Marathon	32,330	36,568	36,367	30,345
Marinette	9,868	10,609	11,195	9,726
Marquette	4,112	3,758	4,068	3,654
Menominee	1,191	179	1,257	185
Milwaukee	320,654	153,635	319,819	149,445
Monroe	9,505	9,637	10,198	8,666
Oconto	8,810	10,691	9,927	8,755
Oneida	10,439	10,905	11,907	9,630
Outagamie	45,565	47,294	50,294	39,677
Ozaukee	19,075	35,991	20,579	32,172
Pepin	1,875	1,793	2,102	1,616
Pierce	10,213	10,383	11,803	9,812
Polk	9,373	11,447	10,876	11,282
Portage	22,052	16,599	24,817	13,810
Price	3,882	3,879	4,559	3,461
Racine	52,887	49,173	53,408	45,954
Richland	4,964	3,575	5,041	3,298
Rock	49,158	30,492	50,529	27,364
Rusk	3,391	3,673	3,855	3,253
St. Croix	19,874	25,475	21,177	22,837
Sauk	18,718	12,829	18,617	11,562
Sawyer	4,482	4,436	4,765	4,199
Shawano	8,990	11,017	10,259	9,538
Sheboygan	28,356	34,282	30,395	30,801
Taylor	3,761	5,597	4,563	4,586
Trempealeau	7,601	5,703	8,321	4,808
Vernon	8,031	5,935	8,463	5,367
Vilas	5,931	8,735	6,491	7,055
Walworth	22,512	28,962	24,177	25,485
Washburn	4,435	4,692	4,693	4,303
Washington	23,136	54,709	25,719	47,729
Waukesha	77,617	161,567	85,339	145,152
Waupaca	11,565	13,989	12,952	12,232
Waushara	5,330	6,558	5,868	5,770
Winnebago	45,410	42,073	48,167	37,946
Wood	18,546	19,684	21,710	16,581
Totals	**1,603,185**	**1,403,038**	**1,677,211**	**1,262,393**

All candidates, 2012: Obama, D., 1,603,185; Romney, R., 1,403,038; Johnson, LB., 20,189; Stein, Green, 7,556; Goode, Const., 5,051; White, Soc. Equality, 604; La Riva, Socialism/Liberation, 531.

Wyoming

County	2012 Obama (D)	Romney (R)	2008 Obama (D)	McCain (R)
Albany	7,445	7,851	8,644	7,936
Big Horn	868	4,269	1,108	4,045
Campbell	2,163	14,952	2,990	13,011
Carbon	2,109	4,152	2,336	4,331
Converse	1,089	5,043	1,380	4,922
Crook	426	3,109	612	2,967
Fremont	5,333	11,072	6,016	11,083
Goshen	1,458	4,178	1,832	3,942
Hot Springs	523	1,894	619	1,834
Johnson	749	3,362	908	3,334
Laramie	13,807	23,247	16,072	24,549
Lincoln	1,287	7,146	1,823	6,485
Natrona	8,960	22,129	10,475	21,906
Niobrara	200	1,022	244	1,017
Park	2,927	11,234	3,757	10,839
Platte	1,223	3,136	1,407	3,002
Sheridan	3,618	10,267	4,458	10,177
Sublette	767	3,472	936	3,316
Sweetwater	4,773	11,427	5,762	10,360
Teton	6,211	4,858	7,472	4,565
Uinta	1,627	6,605	2,317	5,763
Washakie	794	3,013	1,042	2,956
Weston	422	2,821	658	2,618
Totals	**68,779**	**170,259**	**82,868**	**164,958**

All candidates, 2012: Romney, R., 170,259; Obama, D., 68,779; Johnson, LB., 5,302; Goode, Const., 1,438.

The Chronology of Events reports the top National, International, and General news stories, month by month.

November 2011

National

Ballot Issues Highlight Off-Year Elections—In U.S. elections Nov. 8, voters rejected proposals in Ohio and Mississippi that had been favored by conservatives. In Ohio, a referendum campaign backed by labor unions and their Democratic allies succeeded in overturning a Mar. 2011 law that had restricted the collective-bargaining rights of public employees; the 62%-38% margin favoring repeal was widely viewed as a rebuke to Gov. John Kasich (R), who had pushed for the legislation. In Mississippi, by a margin of 58%-42%, voters rejected an amendment to the state constitution that defined persons to include "every human being from the moment of fertilization"; opponents said the so-called personhood amendment would have restricted not only abortion but also some forms of contraception along with in vitro fertilization. In notable state races for elective office, Steve Beshear (D) gained a second term as governor of Kentucky and Lieutenant Gov. Phil Bryant (R) won the race to succeed the term-limited incumbent Gov. Haley Barbour (R) in Mississippi. In San Francisco, interim Mayor Ed Lee (D) cruised to victory, becoming the first Chinese-American in the city's history to win a mayoral election.

Remains of War Dead Mishandled—Confirming earlier complaints by whistleblowers, the U.S. Office of Special Counsel, an independent federal agency, disclosed Nov. 8 that the mortuary at Dover Air Force Base in Delaware had mishandled body parts of slain military personnel between 2004 and 2008. A follow-up investigation published Dec. 7 in the *Washington Post* concluded that Air Force personnel had incinerated 976 fragments and 1,762 unidentified battlefield remains from at least 274 deceased U.S. troops and then dumped the ashes in a Virginia landfill, while concealing the unauthorized practice from the families of the deceased. A separate investigative panel headed by retired Army Gen. John P. Abizaid concluded Feb. 28, 2012, that mortuary officials at Dover had similarly mishandled body parts of some victims of the Sept. 11, 2001, terrorist attacks.

Idaho Man Accused of Attempting to Assassinate Pres. Obama—Oscar Ramiro Ortega-Hernandez, a 21-year-old Idaho resident, was charged by federal authorities Nov. 17 with using an assault rifle to fire shots at the White House six days earlier. Witnesses had reported hearing the gunfire and then seeing a car speeding away from the crime scene. An abandoned vehicle found later that night, containing a semiautomatic weapon, ammunition, and spent cartridges, was traced to Ortega-Hernandez, who was arrested Nov. 16. Neither the president nor first lady Michelle Obama were in the White House at the time of the shooting. Federal investigators alleged that Ortega-Hernandez believed the federal government was conspiring against him and that he needed to kill Obama because the president was "the Antichrist."

Alabama's Largest County Declares Bankruptcy; Other Economic Developments—Jefferson County, the most populous county in Alabama, filed for bankruptcy protection Nov. 9 after it was unable to reach a settlement with creditors over more than $3.1 bil in sewer-system debt. Jefferson County, with a population of about 660,000, includes Birmingham, the largest city in Alabama. A month earlier, Harrisburg, the Pennsylvania state capital, filed for bankruptcy because it was unable to deal with $300 mil in debt from a local incinerator project.

In the private sector, AMR Corp., the parent company of American Airlines, sought bankruptcy protection Nov. 29. AMR announced Feb. 1, 2012, that it would seek to slash $2 bil in annual expenses by making a 15% cut in its workforce and defaulting on pension obligations; when it declared bankruptcy, AMR had only $8.3 bil in assets to cover an estimated $18.5 bil in pensions owed to current and retired employees.

Overall, news on the employment front remained modestly positive; data released Dec. 2 showed that U.S. payrolls had added 120,000 jobs in Nov., and the unemployment rate had dipped to 8.6%. Buoyed by reports Nov. 30 that the Federal Reserve would work with other central banks to bolster the global economy, the Dow Jones Industrial Average jumped 490 points to finish at 12,045.68, a gain of 4.2% for the day but only 0.8% for the month. The S&P 500 closed at 1,246.96, for a monthly loss of 0.5%, and the Nasdaq Composite Index was 2,620.34, for a one-month decline of 2.4%.

International

Tensions Rise Over Iranian Nuclear Program—The International Atomic Energy Agency (IAEA) issued a report Nov. 8 offering evidence that Iran's nuclear program included activities "specific to nuclear weapons." Among the activities cited by the IAEA were development of bomb triggering devices and the installation of uranium centrifuges at the underground Fordo facility, which is protected by 250 ft of granite. As rumors circulated that Israel (which is believed to have a nuclear weapons stockpile) was planning air strikes at Iranian nuclear facilities, Iran reported Nov. 12 that a huge explosion at a munitions depot about 25 mi southwest of Tehran had killed at least 17 members of the Revolutionary Guard, including Major Gen. Hassan Tehrani Moghaddam, a key figure in the nation's ballistic missile program. Who was responsible for the attack was unclear, although the Israeli intelligence agency Mossad was widely suspected. Throughout the month, the U.S., the European Union, and allied countries all moved to tighten sanctions against Iran.

In Tehran on Nov. 29, student protesters stormed the British embassy, ransacking offices, while other protesters raided a British diplomatic residence. The UK retaliated by shutting its embassy in Tehran, pulling out its diplomatic staff, and expelling Iranian diplomats from Britain. The French government announced Dec. 3 that it was temporarily reducing its diplomatic presence in Iran. The U.S. has not had formal diplomatic relations with Iran since the hostage crisis of 1979-81.

Debt Crisis Topples European Leaders—The debt crisis that had plagued Europe since 2010 unseated governments in Greece, Italy, and Spain. Pressured by international lenders to implement unpopular austerity measures in exchange for a desperately needed bailout, Greek Prime Min. George Papandreou resigned Nov. 10 and was replaced by Lucas Papademos, an economist who had previously served as governor of the Bank of Greece and then as vice president of the European Central Bank. Debt pressures in Italy forced Prime Min. Silvio Berlusconi to step down Nov. 12 after his government had sought to reassure international credit markets by passing its own austerity program. Like Greece, Italy turned to an economist, Mario Monti, who on Nov. 16 appointed a cabinet of academics, business leaders, and bureaucrats. In Spain, another debt-ridden member of the eurozone, voters Nov. 20 ousted the Socialist Workers Party government that had held power since 2004. Former Deputy Prime Min. Mariano Rajoy, the leader of the conservative Popular Party, was sworn in as prime minister Dec. 21 and began implementing a program of tax increases and spending cuts. Meanwhile, labor unrest accompanied the tightening of austerity measures in Portugal and Great Britain. The Fitch credit-rating agency downgraded Portugal's debt to junk status on Nov. 24.

Saleh Agrees to Yield Power in Yemen; Other Post-Arab Spring Developments—Bowing to domestic and international pressures after nearly a year of antigovernment protests in Yemen, Pres. Ali Abdullah Saleh agreed Nov. 23 to surrender power. The accord, negotiated with the Gulf Cooperation Council and signed in Riyadh, Saudi Arabia, provided for Saleh to step down in exchange for immunity from prosecution. Saleh, who had ruled Yemen for more than three decades, transferred authority to his vice president, Abd al-Rab Mansur al-Hadi, who then named opposition leader Mohammed Basindwa as interim prime minister. Hadi was sworn in as president Feb. 25 following an uncontested election four days earlier. Yemen thus joined Tunisia, Egypt, and Libya as countries where autocratic leaders had been forced out by a wave of popular uprisings since early 2011.

Other North African and Middle Eastern countries continued to deal with the consequences of the Arab Spring protests. In Morocco, a moderate Islamist organization won parliamentary elections Nov. 25. Violent street clashes erupted in Cairo, Egypt, Nov. 19-23, on the eve of parliamentary elections, which were dominated by Islamist parties. In Syria, where thousands of antigovernment protesters had been killed since Mar., Pres. Bashar al-Assad maintained his brutal crackdown on dissidents. The Arab League voted Nov. 27 to impose sanctions against Syria, and Turkey issued its own sanctions three days later.

Errant NATO Air Strike Inflames Relations With Pakistan—A Nov. 26 attack on two Pakistani military checkpoints by NATO helicopters and fighter jets based in Afghanistan killed at least 24 Pakistani soldiers. Pakistani military officials portrayed the cross-border raid as irresponsible and unprovoked, while U.S. and NATO sources said that coalition troops in eastern Afghanistan had called in the air strike only after they took fire from the Pakistani outposts, which did not appear on coalition maps. Subsequent U.S. military inquiries concluded that poor coordination and communication between coalition forces and the Pakistani military had contributed to the incident, which outraged Pakistanis. Pakistan was an essential ally in the U.S.-led war against the Taliban and al-Qaeda in Afghanistan, which claimed the lives of 27 coalition troops (including 18 from the U.S.) during Nov.

General

Drug Firms Settle Multibillion-Dollar Claims—Glaxo-SmithKline agreed Nov. 3 to pay $3 bil to resolve U.S. civil and criminal probes of the British-based multinational pharmaceutical company's development and marketing practices. The settlement covered claims against some of the firm's best-known products, including Avandia, a diabetes drug, and Advair, a treatment for asthma. European and American regulators had imposed strict limits on Avandia in Sept. 2010 after it was linked to an elevated risk of heart attack, stroke, or heart failure. In a separate case, the U.S. Justice Dept. announced Nov. 22 that Merck, a global pharmaceutical firm with headquarters in New Jersey, would pay $950 mil and plead guilty to a criminal complaint over the marketing of Vioxx. The painkiller had been withdrawn from the market in 2004 after a study linked Vioxx to increased cardiac and stroke risk.

In another case involving a well-known drug, the U.S. Food and Drug Administration on Nov. 18 revoked its previous approval of Avastin as a treatment for breast cancer. The FDA held that Avastin, the world's top-selling cancer drug, had not proved effective in controlling breast tumor growth or substantially extending breast cancer patients' life expectancy, but had been linked to high blood pressure, hemorrhages, and heart attacks. Genentech, the drug's California-based manufacturer, would still be allowed to market Avastin for treating other types of cancers. The decision could cost Genentech and its parent firm, Switzerland's Roche Holding AG, up to $1 bil in sales annually.

Former Penn State Coach Charged With Abusing Boys—The arrest Nov. 5 of Gerald (Jerry) Sandusky, a former football coach at Pennsylvania State Univ., on charges that he had sexually abused young boys triggered a scandal that led to the departure of Penn State's longtime head football coach, Joe Paterno, and president, Graham Spanier. Sandusky, who had coached defense for Paterno from 1969 until his retirement in 1999, retained access to the school's football facilities long after he retired. Prosecutors alleged that between 1994 and 2009 he had sexually assaulted eight boys, all of whom he met through The Second Mile, a children's charity he founded in 1977. Also indicted were two university officials, athletic director Tim Curley and vice pres. Gary Schultz, who were accused of testifying falsely about the extent of their knowledge of Sandusky's illegal activities.

Some of the most incriminating testimony came from assistant football coach Mike McQueary, who told the grand jury that as a graduate assistant in 2002 he had witnessed Sandusky sexually assaulting a boy in the shower of a Penn State locker room. The next day, McQueary told Paterno what he had seen, and Paterno reported the incident to Curley. Other Penn State officials were informed of the event, but no police investigation was launched at that time.

On Nov. 9, Penn State's board of trustees voted to remove Spanier and Paterno, ending Paterno's 46-year head coaching career, which included 409 wins and 24 bowl championships. The 85-year-old Paterno, who had long been one of the most revered figures in college sports, died of lung cancer in State College Jan. 22, 2012.

Drosselmeyer Takes Breeders' Cup Classic—Drosselmeyer, a 14-1 long shot ridden by Mike Smith, put on a thrilling stretch run to overtake Game On Dude in the $5-mil Breeders' Cup Classic Nov. 5 at Churchill Downs in Louisville, KY. Drosselmeyer's victory foiled a bid by Game On Dude's rider, Chantal Sutherland, to become the first female jockey ever to win the prestigious 1.25-mi race.

Doctor Convicted in Michael Jackson Case—After 22 days of testimony and two days of deliberations, a Los Angeles jury Nov. 7 found Michael Jackson's personal physician, Dr. Conrad Murray, guilty of involuntary manslaughter for his role in the pop superstar's death in June 2009. The jury concluded that Murray had improperly provided a hospital anesthetic, the powerful sedative propofol, for home use as a sleep aid to Jackson. Calling Murray a disgrace who had practiced "money-for-medicine madness," Los Angeles Superior Court Judge Michael Pastor sentenced the physician to four years in prison; legal officials conceded that, under state guidelines intended to reduce prison overcrowding, Murray was likely to serve less than half that time. After consultations with the Jackson family and lawyers for the performer's estate, prosecutors told the court Jan. 18, 2012, that they were dropping a claim against Murray for more than $100 mil in restitution.

Duke Basketball Coach Sets Career Victory Record—Mike Krzyzewski, known to many players and fans as "Coach K," achieved a career basketball coaching milestone Nov. 15, as his Duke Univ. team defeated Michigan State, 74-69. The Blue Devils' victory at Madison Square Garden in New York City earned Coach K his 903rd win in 37 seasons (32 of them at Duke), eclipsing the former NCAA Division I mark set by Bob Knight, who had retired with 902 wins in 2008. Before coming to Duke, Krzyzewski had played college basketball for Knight at the U.S. Military Academy at West Point, NY, in the late 1960s and had served on Knight's coaching staff at Indiana Univ. in the mid-1970s.

Galaxy Wins MLS Championship—Dominant throughout the regular season, the Los Angeles Galaxy proved unstoppable during the playoffs, defeating the Houston Dynamo, 1-0, to win the Major League Soccer Cup final Nov. 20 before a hometown crowd at the Home Depot Center in Carson,

CA. The lone goal was scored in the 72nd minute of play by Landon Donovan, the MLS Cup MVP, on passes from Irish striker Robbie Keane and British star David Beckham.

NASA Launches Mars Mission—At 10:02 AM EST on Nov. 26, the National Aeronautics and Space Administration launched a Mars-bound rover from Cape Canaveral, FL. The nuclear-powered *Curiosity*, a mobile science laboratory equipped with a jackhammer and high-definition cameras, was designed to test the Martian soil for carbon-based compounds that might signal the presence of microbial life. Propelled into space by a United Launch Alliance Atlas V rocket, the one-ton rover was expected to complete its journey of 352 mil mi in Aug. 2012.

December 2011
National

Cain Drops Out of GOP Presidential Race—Stung by allegations that he had carried on a 13-year extramarital affair with Ginger White, an Atlanta businesswoman, Herman Cain announced Dec. 3 that he was suspending his campaign for the Republican presidential nomination. Cain, a radio talk-show host and former Godfather's Pizza executive, had led in several GOP presidential preference polls in late Oct. and early Nov., but his support ebbed after several women alleged that he sexually harassed them in the 1990s, while he headed the National Restaurant Association. A halting performance Nov. 14 in a *Milwaukee Journal Sentinel* newspaper interview, widely seen on YouTube, had raised further doubts about his qualifications. Disappointed Cain supporters turned mostly to former House Speaker Newt Gingrich (GA), who received Cain's endorsement Jan. 28, 2012, and to Rick Santorum, a former U.S. senator from Pennsylvania. Helped by a series of debate performances in which he adroitly skewered his Republican opponents, Pres. Barack Obama, and what he called the elite media, Gingrich surged ahead of former Massachusetts Gov. Mitt Romney in surveys of likely GOP primary voters. But both the Gingrich and Santorum campaigns failed to gather enough signatures to appear on the ballot in the delegate-rich Virginia primary, scheduled for Mar. 6.

Former Gov. Blagojevich Gets 14-Year Prison Sentence—In Chicago Dec. 7, U.S. District Court Judge James B. Zagel sentenced former Illinois Gov. Rod Blagojevich (D) to 14 years in prison for multiple felonies, including the attempted sale of the U.S. Senate seat vacated by Barack Obama after the Nov. 2008 presidential election. Impeached in Jan. 2009, Blagojevich had been convicted on a total of 18 felony corruption charges in trials Aug. 2010 and June 2011. The fourth former Illinois governor to serve a prison term since the 1960s, he reported to Federal Correctional Institution Englewood in Littleton, CO, on Mar. 15, 2012.

Federal Safety Agency Urges Ban on Phone Use While Driving—Citing the dangers of distracted driving, the National Transportation Safety Board (NTSB) called Dec. 13 for a ban on all phone use by anyone operating a vehicle. The NTSB issued a nonbinding recommendation that would not only bar drivers from talking and texting on handheld phones but also outlaw drivers' use of hands-free devices. In a statement, NTSB head Deborah A. P. Hersman noted that according to the National Highway Traffic Safety Administration, more than 3,000 people lost their lives in 2010 because of "distraction-related accidents." An analysis by the Governors' Highway Safety Association, which represents state traffic safety agencies, indicated that nine states and Washington, DC, already barred drivers from using handheld phones, and 35 states had laws against texting while driving.

Congress Passes Spending, Tax Cut, National Security Measures—Averting a government shutdown, congressional negotiators agreed on a $915 bil omnibus measure to fund the Defense, Education, Energy, Homeland Security, Labor, Health and Human Services, and Interior Departments and other federal agencies through the 2012 fiscal year. The measure—known as the Consolidated Appropriations Act, 2012—was passed Dec. 16 by the House of Representatives, 296-121, and Dec. 17 by the Senate, 67-32. The measure was signed into law by Pres. Obama on Dec. 23. Together with disaster relief and supplemental war funding measures, the spending approved by Congress exceeded $1 tril. The ranking Republican on the Senate Appropriations Committee, Sen. Thad Cochran (R, MS), stated that the legislation conformed with the federal spending levels and debt limits set by the Budget Control Act that had become law in Aug. 2011.

In a flurry of year-end activity, Congress also agreed to a two-month extension of a payroll tax break, affecting 160 mil workers, which had been scheduled to expire on Dec. 31. The measure, initially opposed by House Republicans but favored by Senate GOP leaders, also provided for an extension of benefits for the long-term unemployed and for a continuation of current Medicare reimbursement rates for physicians. Passed Dec. 23 without objection in the House and by unanimous consent in the Senate, the Temporary Payroll Tax Cut Continuation Act of 2011 was signed into law by Pres. Obama later that same day. Another major piece of legislation, the National Defense Authorization Act for Fiscal Year 2012, passed the House on Dec. 14, by a vote of 283-136, and the Senate Dec. 15, by 86-13. The bill authorized $662 bil in military spending, including $117 bil for the Afghanistan war and other overseas military operations; other legislative provisions called for tougher financial sanctions against Iran and, according to civil liberties groups, opened the door to the widespread, indefinite detention by the military of terrorist suspects, including U.S. citizens. Reversing an earlier veto threat, Obama signed the bill into law Dec. 31, but he appended a signing statement pledging that his administration would "not authorize the indefinite military detention without trial of American citizens."

Economy Ends Year on Upbeat Note—The Conference Board announced Dec. 27 that consumer confidence had rebounded to its highest level since Apr. 2011. Major U.S. retailers such as Macy's and Nordstrom reported robust holiday performance, and U.S. auto sales gained 10.3% over 2010. The Dow Jones Industrial Average closed Dec. 30 at 12,217.56, up 5.5% for the year, while the S&P 500 was nearly flat at 1,257.60, and the Nasdaq Composite Index (2,605.15) dropped 1.8%. The Dow Jones-UBS Commodity Index, which had peaked in Apr. 2011, fell during the next eight months, showing an annual decline of 13% by year's end. The price of gold, which flirted with $1,900 an ounce in Aug., stabilized at $1,566 by the close of 2011, but that still represented a rise of 10% over 2010 and the 11th consecutive year of annual gold price gains.

International

Putin's Party Wins Reduced Majority in Russian Elections; Fraud Alleged—A weak showing in Dec. 4 elections left Prime Min. Vladimir Putin's United Russia Party holding a slim majority in the Duma, the lower house of Russia's parliament. According to official results, United Russia captured 238 of the Duma's 450 seats, a drop of 77 seats from the previous election, while the party's share of the popular vote was 49%, down from 64% in Dec. 2007. Organizations increasing their representation in the Duma included the Communist Party (92 seats), A Just Russia (64 seats), and the Liberal Democratic Party (56 seats). Independent Russian observers uploaded videos documenting fraud by United Russia loyalists, including blatant ballot-box stuffing. Announcement of the results triggered large anti-Putin protests in Moscow, culminating in a Dec. 24 rally that attracted 30,000 protesters, according to a police estimate; rally organizers claimed the turnout was nearly four times that figure.

Former French Pres. Chirac Convicted of Corruption—A Paris court Dec. 15 found former French

Pres. Jacques Chirac guilty of embezzlement and misuse of public funds while he was mayor of France's capital city (1977-95). The 79-year-old Chirac, who was president for more than a decade (1995-2007), continued to maintain his innocence but declined to appeal his two-year suspended sentence. He had been excused from attending the trial because of severe memory loss and other health problems.

Tropical Storm Kills More Than 1,200 in Southern Philippines—Flash floods and mudslides from Tropical Storm Sendong (known internationally as Washi) devastated parts of the southern Philippine island of Mindanao Dec. 16-18. Contributing to the flood's lethal impact were high tides, deforestation, and erosion from illegal mining in the region. According to the final report issued Feb. 10, 2012, by the Philippines' National Disaster Risk Reduction and Management Council, the storm claimed the lives of 1,268 people and affected nearly 700,000.

North Korean Leader Kim Jong Il Dies; Youngest Son Named Successor—North Korea's state-run media announced Dec. 19 that "Dear Leader" Kim Jong Il had died while on a train trip two days earlier. Official reports listed a heart attack as the cause of death, but the reclusive dictator had reportedly been in poor health since suffering a stroke in 2008. He received a private funeral Dec. 28, accompanied by an elaborate, three-hour-long public procession involving 200,000 mourners, many of them in military uniforms. A nationally televised memorial service took place the following day.

Kim Jong Il had come to power following the death of his father Kim Il Sung in 1994. During Kim Jong Il's repressive 17-year rule, North Korea remained isolated and impoverished, as government policies emphasized a military buildup, including the development of nuclear weapons. Immediately after Kim Jong Il's death, his youngest son, Kim Jong Un, was anointed the "Great Successor." During the next two weeks, the younger Kim received a series of new titles, including supreme commander of the military.

Violence Flares in Iraq as U.S. Ends Military Mission—Formalities Dec. 12-15 marked the end of the U.S. military mission in Iraq. Public events included a visit by Iraqi Prime Min. Nouri al-Maliki to Washington, DC, where he met Dec. 12 with Pres. Obama; a speech by Obama Dec. 14 at Fort Bragg, NC; and a ceremony Dec. 15 at Baghdad International Airport attended by U.S. Defense Sec. Leon Panetta and high-ranking U.S. military officers. In the early morning hours on Dec. 18, a final convoy of U.S. troops crossed the border from Iraq into Kuwait. Seizing the opportunity presented by the U.S. pullout and by a government crisis that had heightened tensions between Iraq's Sunni and Shiite communities, insurgents Dec. 22 carried out more than a dozen coordinated attacks that killed 69 people in Baghdad. Al-Qaeda in Iraq claimed responsibility for the assaults, which struck markets, cafes, and government buildings in predominantly Shiite neighborhoods.

Since the U.S.-led invasion in Mar. 2003, nearly 4,500 U.S. service members had been killed and another 32,000 wounded. Tens of thousands of Iraqi civilians and combatants had lost their lives in the conflict, which cost American taxpayers more than $800 bil. After the troop pullout, the U.S. presence in Iraq was mostly confined to a fortress-like embassy complex in Baghdad staffed by 16,000 people, most of them federal contractors, at an estimated annual cost of $6 bil.

In Afghanistan, about 90,000 U.S. troops and 40,000 allied forces continued to support the government of Pres. Hamid Karzai against Taliban and al-Qaeda insurgents. According to the website iCasualties.org, a total of 566 coalition troops lost their lives during 2011 as part of Operation Enduring Freedom, including 418 from the U.S. and 46 from the UK. The Pakistan-based extremist group Lashkar-e-Jhangvi claimed responsibility for Dec. 6 bombings in Kabul, Kandahar, and

Mazar-i-Sharif that targeted Afghan Shiites as they gathered for the Ashura holiday. Pres. Karzai said Dec. 11 that the attacks had killed at least 80 people.

General

Griffin Wins Heisman Trophy; Other Football News—Robert Griffin III, who quarterbacked Baylor Univ. to a 10-3 season record, received the Heisman Trophy Dec. 10 as the nation's most outstanding college football player. Griffin, the first Baylor player ever to win the Heisman, also was named Associated Press College Football Player of the Year. On Dec. 29, he led Baylor to a 67-56 victory over the Washington Huskies in the Valero Alamo Bowl in San Antonio, TX.

In pro football, Carolina Panthers quarterback Cam Newton, the 2010 Heisman winner, finished the season with 14 TDs rushing and 21 TDs passing, along with a passing yardage total of 4,051, a record for a first-year quarterback. He was named Rookie of the Year. On Dec. 26, in a game against the Atlanta Falcons, New Orleans Saints quarterback Drew Brees broke one of pro football's most hallowed marks, eclipsing the single-season passing yardage record set by Dan Marino in 1984. Brees completed the season setting records for number of pass completions (468), completion rate (.712), and yardage (5,476). Another pro quarterback in the spotlight was Denver's Tim Tebow, a subpar passer but gifted field leader and exceptional runner, who led the Broncos into the playoffs with a series of heart-stopping 4th-quarter comebacks. Tebow, a devout Christian, also attracted nationwide attention with his on-field prayer rituals. With TV ratings rising, NFL owners on Dec. 14 approved $27.9 bil in contracts covering telecasts of NFL games on the Fox, CBS, and NBC networks from 2014 to 2022.

Pujols Signs $254-Million Free-Agent Deal—St. Louis Cardinals first baseman Albert Pujols, a three-time National League MVP, agreed Dec. 8 to a 10-year, $254-mil contract with the Los Angeles Angels of the American League. Pujols, generally regarded as the finest hitter of his generation, had led the Cardinals to the World Series championship in 2011. On Jan. 24, 2012, another slugging first baseman, Prince Fielder, agreed to jump from the Milwaukee Brewers of the National League to the Detroit Tigers of the American League, in a nine-year deal reportedly valued at $214 mil.

NBA Resolves Contract Issues, Starts Abbreviated Season—Delayed and shortened by a labor dispute, the 2011-12 National Basketball Association season opened Dec. 25 under an agreement reached a month earlier between team owners and player representatives. The owners had declared a lockout July 1 after negotiations for a new collective bargaining agreement broke down. The new contract covered a 10-year period, with either side permitted to opt out after the sixth year. The delayed start, which meant that each team would play only 66 regular-season games instead of the 82 originally planned, cost the league an estimated $500 mil.

January 2012
National

Battle for Republican Nomination Heats Up—Former Massachusetts Gov. Mitt Romney, the favorite to become the Republican nominee for president, appeared to emerge from the Iowa caucuses on Jan. 3 with a slim margin of victory. Endorsed by former Republican presidential nominee Sen. John McCain (R, AZ) in New Hampshire Jan. 4, Romney won the primary there Jan. 10, with 39% of the vote. Rep. Ron Paul (TX) finished in second, with 23%, followed by former Utah Gov. John Huntsman (17%). Former Sen. Rick Santorum (PA) retroactively appeared to emerge on top of Iowa (by 34 votes) when results were certified Jan. 19, weakening Romney's position. Romney lost further momentum when former House Speaker Newt Gingrich (GA) won the primary contest in South Carolina Jan. 21 with 40% of the vote. Romney placed second, with 28%. However, Romney quickly bounced back, decisively winning the Florida primary Jan. 31 with 46% of the vote to Gingrich's 32%.

The intraparty nomination process turned more contentious, as wealthy donors and super PACs funded attack ads. According to Kantar Media analysis, 92% of the campaign commercials in Florida the week before its primary were negative; 68% targeted Gingrich. Gingrich Jan. 19 was forced to respond to accusations by his second wife, Marianne Gingrich, that he had asked her to accept an "open marriage" in 1999 so that he could continue seeing a mistress (his third and current wife). Romney faced criticism over his income-tax returns, which he released after hesitation Jan. 24. Rep. Michele Bachmann (MN) announced Jan. 4 that she was withdrawing from the race. Huntsman dropped out of the race Jan. 16, endorsing Romney, and Texas Gov. Rick Perry, who had finished in a disappointing sixth place in New Hampshire, withdrew Jan. 19, throwing his support behind Gingrich.

Obama Appoints Consumer Financial Protection Agency Director in Disputed Recess Appointment—Pres. Barack Obama Jan. 4 appointed former Ohio Attorney Gen. Richard Cordray to be the first director of the new Consumer Financial Protection Agency, tasked with protecting consumers from predatory lending practices in compliance with the Dodd-Frank Wall Street Reform and Consumer Protection Act (2010). Obama nominated Cordray in July 2011, but Senate Republicans opposed to the new agency had blocked the nomination. To prevent Obama from making recess appointments, GOP legislators had held "pro forma" legislative sessions, some of which lasted no more than a minute. Obama made the appointment anyway, in a move that Republicans criticized as an unconstitutional power grab.

Supreme Court Expands Religious Exception to Discrimination Laws—Unanimously ruling Jan. 11 on *Hosanna-Tabor Church v. Equal Employment Opportunity Commission*, the Supreme Court expanded the "ministerial exception" to anti-discrimination laws. The case originated in 2005, when Cheryl Perich returned from disability leave to a Lutheran school in Redford, MI, where she had mostly taught secular subjects, to find her position had been filled. She threatened to sue and was fired for not abiding by the church's rule to settle disputes internally. With the support of the Equal Employment Opportunity Commission (EEOC), Perich's suit claimed the school discriminated against her because she was disabled. While acknowledging that churches were protected from anti-discrimination laws when assigning jobs to those who serve religious functions within a church, the EEOC argued that the primary function of Perich's job was not religious, and that she should therefore be protected from discrimination. The opinion of the Court noted that Perich spent a portion of her workdays teaching religion and had accepted "the formal call to religious service." The ruling thereby broadened the ministerial category to include ministers not exclusively serving in ministerial roles.

Obama Denies Keystone XL Pipeline Permit—Pres. Barack Obama Jan. 18 denied a Canadian company, Trans-Canada Pipelines Ltd., a permit to construct and manage the 1,700-mi Keystone XL oil pipeline. The proposed pipeline was expected to carry as much as 700,000 barrels of crude oil daily from oil-sand fields in Alberta, Canada, to refineries on the Gulf Coast. The project was supported by labor unions, business groups, and Republicans, who argued it would create jobs and increase the energy security of the U.S. Environmentalists opposed the project because of concerns over carbon emissions and possible spills. In announcing his decision, Obama did not reject the idea of building such a pipeline, but he objected to the arbitrary deadline, Feb. 21, 2012, that was imposed on the review of the project's environmental impact in an amendment to a payroll-tax bill passed in Dec. 2011.

Congress Postpones Online Antipiracy Bill Votes—Following online protests Jan. 18, the House of Representatives and the Senate announced on Jan. 20 that they would put aside bills intended to fight online piracy. The bills—the House's Stop Online Piracy Act (SOPA) and the Senate's Protect IP Act (PIPA)—would have given courts the power to block access to websites hosting or assisting in the theft of pirated material as well as to prevent payments for such material to be made from the U.S. to foreign websites.

Initially the bills, which were backed by content developers, garnered bipartisan support, but Google and other Internet companies lobbied in opposition, arguing that the bills were too broad in scope, risked curbing innovation, and would oblige web companies to police the Web. Civil liberties activists also raised concerns about free speech and over empowering the government to blackout websites without due process. In the weeks prior to the protest, millions signed petitions against the proposed measures, and Pres. Obama came out in opposition to many of the elements contained in the legislation, though he also made clear that piracy on the Internet was a problem that needed to be addressed. Many members of Congress withdrew support, and House Judiciary Committee Chairman Lamar Smith (R, TX) and Senate Majority Leader Harry Reid (D, NV) decided to postpone votes on the bills indefinitely.

Giffords Resigns From Congress—Rep. Gabrielle Giffords (D, AZ) announced Jan. 22 that she would resign from Congress Jan. 25, halfway through her third term. Giffords had been shot in the head during a mass shooting at a public event in Jan. 2011 and was leaving office to focus on recovering from her injuries. In her announcement, she suggested that she might return to politics once fully recovered. Ron Barber (D), a former Giffords aide who was also injured in the shooting, won a special election June 12 to fill the seat.

Obama Gives State of the Union Address—Obama delivered his State of the Union address to a joint session of Congress Jan. 24, drawing a sharp contrast between his vision for the country and that of Republicans in Congress and running for president. He urged Congress to adopt the so-called "Buffett rule," named for billionaire investor Warren Buffett, which called for households with annual incomes of at least $1 mil to pay higher tax rates. Drawing attention to the need to strengthen the economic recovery, he discussed bringing manufacturing jobs back to the U.S. and taking a tougher stand on China's unfair trade practices. He also addressed the importance of increasing the domestic production of oil and gas for both economic and security reasons.

In the official Republican response to the address, Indiana Gov. Mitch Daniels attacked Obama's economic policy and reckless spending during the previous three years, calling for smaller government to allow the private sector to grow the economy more quickly.

Report on Bungled Gun Probe Finds ATF Agents Responsible—A Jan. 31 report released by the House Government and Oversight Committee found that agents of the Bureau of Alcohol, Tobacco, Firearms, and Explosives (ATF) based in Phoenix, AZ, bungled a 2009-11 gun-trafficking sting known as Operation Fast and Furious. During the operation, ATF agents allowed around 2,000 guns bought in the U.S. to be smuggled into Mexico, a practice known as "gunwalking," with the intention of capturing gun smugglers. Some of the weapons were later used during crimes in the U.S. and Mexico, including an incident that led to the death of a U.S. Customs and Border Protection agent. Congressional Republicans had criticized the Justice Dept., specifically Attorney Gen. Eric Holder, for letting the guns to be used for criminal activities. The report asserted that Holder had not authorized the operation, but Republicans vowed to continue the investigation, threatening to hold Holder in contempt of Congress.

U.S. Economy Sees Modest Expansion in Fourth Quarter of 2011—The U.S. Dept. of Commerce announced Jan. 27 that the U.S. gross domestic product grew at a modest rate of 2.8% in the fourth quarter of 2011, an improvement over the 1.8% growth seen the previous quarter, but less than the 3% increase analysts had expected. The growth spurred hope that the pace of economic recovery from the 2007-09 recession was picking up. However, economists were cautious, noting that the improvement remained small and wasn't expected to be accompanied by significant gains in employment. Nonetheless, the Dow Jones Industrial Average and S&P 500 had their best Jan. since 1997, the Dow seeing a 3.4% increase, finishing the month at 12,632.91, and the S&P 500 having a 4.4% rise, closing on Jan. 31 at 1,312.41. The Nasdaq Composite Index also saw positive gains, climbing 8% to close at the end of the month at 2,813.84.

International

Afghan Taliban to Open Political Office—The Taliban, Afghanistan's primary insurgent group, announced Jan. 3 that it would open a political office in Qatar, in a move that was seen as a positive sign for future peace talks between the insurgent group and the U.S.-led coalition in Afghanistan. The announcement was the result of discussions the U.S. and Germany had held with Taliban representatives in the preceding months. While obstacles to negotiations remained— the Taliban's apparent refusal to engage with Afghan Pres. Hamid Karzai and their insistence on the release of detainees from the U.S. military prison in Guantánamo Bay, Cuba, among them—the Taliban's willingness to establish a neutral venue and reliable locale renewed optimism that future talks could be meaningful.

A video of four U.S. Marines urinating on three dead Afghans, probably made between Mar. and Sept. 2011, appeared on the Internet shortly thereafter, raising fears that efforts to begin negotiations with the Taliban would be derailed. The Marines' actions were denounced as inhuman by the Afghan government and the Taliban. The U.S. issued an apology on Jan. 12, and the Taliban stated the same day that it would not abandon talks. By the end of the month, talks were taking place in Qatar, though a Taliban office had yet to officially open. The Taliban, however, refused to characterize the negotiations as peace talks, insisting that they only involved demands for the release of prisoners and an attempt to build trust between the two parties. Coalition troop deaths in Afghanistan in Jan. totaled 34, of whom 26 were Americans.

Tensions With Iran Increase Over Nuclear Program; Other Developments—Iran announced Jan. 1 that it had produced its first nuclear fuel rod, which it said was already fueling a civilian nuclear research facility in Tehran. One week later, Iran revealed that it had begun to enrich uranium to 20% purity at its heavily fortified Fordo nuclear facility near Qom. The level of purity was high enough to fuel the Tehran research facility—consistent with Iran's insistence that its nuclear program was intended for peaceful purposes—but further enrichment of the uranium to make it weapons grade would not be difficult. Britain and France condemned the development as a violation of U.N. Security Council resolutions intended to curb Iran's nuclear ambitions, and France promised to negotiate tougher sanctions with its European partners. The governments of the EU announced Jan. 23 that they would ban all Iranian crude oil imports. The embargo was fully implemented July 1.

Iran Jan. 9 sentenced Amir Mirzaei Hekmati, an American citizen and former Marine arrested in Aug. 2011, to death for being a spy, a charge the U.S. government denied. Two days later, a bomb killed Mostafa Ahmadi-Roshan, an Iranian nuclear chemist who worked as a professor in Tehran and as an official at Iran's Natanz enrichment facility. Iran blamed the U.S., which condemned the assassination, and Israel, which neither denied nor confirmed its involvement.

Cruise Ship Capsizes Off Italian Coast—The cruise ship *Costa Concordia* Jan. 13 ran into a reef a few hundred yards off Giglio, a small island on the Italian coast, when its captain, Francesco Schettino, steered too close to the shore. Most of the more than 4,200 passengers and crew on board were evacuated safely, but 32 died. Schettino escaped to safety during the evacuation. He was arrested the next day on charges of manslaughter, causing a shipwreck, and abandoning ship.

Iraqiya Ends Boycott of Iraqi Parliament—Iraqiya, a Sunni Muslim-backed political coalition, signaled a lessening of tensions between Sunnis and Shiites within the Iraqi government when it announced Jan. 29 that it would end its boycott of the parliament. The boycott began in the middle of Dec. when Sunni frustration with Prime Min. Nouri al-Maliki reached its height amidst complaints that he was attempting to push Sunnis out of the government to increase the influence of Shiites. Such fears seemed to be confirmed when a warrant for the arrest of Sunni Vice Pres. Tariq al-Hashemi on terrorist charges was issued and a number of other Sunni politicians were arrested in the days after the boycott began. Iraqiya stated that their decision to re-engage was arrived at without any concessions from Maliki, to improve the political situation for a national summit to reconcile Iraqi Sunnis, Shiites, and Kurds.

General

Alabama Captures College Football Championship— Alabama's Crimson Tide won its second national title in three years, overwhelming LSU's Tigers in New Orleans, LA, Jan. 9 with a 21-0 victory in the Bowl Championship Series title game. The victory was credited to Alabama's defense, which prevented LSU's offense from crossing midfield until fewer than 8 minutes remained. Alabama offense accumulated 384 yards with 21 first downs but had trouble reaching the end zone, earning most of its points off the foot of placekicker Jeremy Shelley, who made 5 of 7 field goal attempts but missed the extra point after Heisman Trophy finalist Trent Richardson scored the game's only touchdown with 4:36 remaining.

Azarenka, Djokovic Win Australian Open Titles—Victoria Azarenka of Belarus, in her first appearance in a Grand Slam tennis final, defeated Maria Sharapova of Russia (6-3, 6-0) at Rod Laver Arena in Melbourne, Australia, Jan. 28. The following night, Serbian Novak Djokovic met Rafael Nadal of Spain in the men's finals for a match that did not end until early Monday morning. Djokovic defeated Nadal (5-7, 6-4, 6-2, 6-7 (5), 7-5) after 5 hours, 53 minutes of play, setting a new record for the longest-ever Grand Slam final.

February 2012

National

Republican Nomination Race Seesaws—Mitt Romney's status as the front-runner for the Republican presidential nomination seemed to be solidified Feb. 4 when he emerged from the Nevada caucuses with a clear victory, taking 50% of the votes to 21% by former House Speaker Newt Gingrich (GA). However, former Sen. Rick Santorum (R, PA) swept three contests Feb. 7. He won the Colorado caucuses with 40% of the vote, followed by Romney with 35%; the Minnesota caucuses with 45%, followed by Rep. Ron Paul (R, TX) with 27% and Romney with 17%; and the Missouri primary with 55%, followed by Romney with 25%, and Paul with 12%.

The victories seemed to establish Santorum as a viable conservative alternative to Romney, a status Gingrich had been trying to claim. Romney's triple defeat called attention to his failure to appeal to the conservative base of the party, raising questions about his ability to unite Republican support in the general election. Romney went on to win the Maine caucuses Feb. 11 with 39% of the vote, but the victory was underwhelming, as he was followed closely by Paul, with 36%. Romney reasserted his front-runner status with victories in the Arizona and Michigan primaries Feb. 28. He claimed a commanding win in Arizona, with 47% of the vote, 20 points ahead of his closest rival, Santorum. But his win in Michigan, his former home state, was less decisive: he claimed 41% of the vote, followed closely by Santorum, who had campaigned heavily in the state, with 38%.

California Same-Sex Marriage Ban Ruled Unconstitutional—A three-judge panel of the Ninth Circuit Court of Appeals in San Francisco, CA, ruled in a split decision Feb. 7 that a 2008 California ballot initiative known as Proposition 8—which amended the state constitution to recognize marriages only between a man and a woman—was unconstitutional. Judge Stephen Reinhardt wrote for the majority that Prop. 8 did not offer a legitimate reason for treating "different classes of people differently," as the constitution required. Implementation of the ruling was postponed pending an appeal to the full Ninth Circuit or the U.S. Supreme Court.

Major Banks Agree to $26-Billion Foreclosure Settlement—Five major U.S. banks (Bank of America, JPMorgan Chase, Citigroup, Wells Fargo, and Ally Financial), state attorneys general, and federal officials announced Feb. 9 that they had agreed to a $26 bil settlement over the controversial practice of "robo-signing" in the foreclosure process. In the wake of the housing crisis, banks had been accused of having employees rapidly approve foreclosures without properly checking the paperwork. The majority of the funds, $17 bil, was to be spent to reduce principal for troubled mortgage holders who owed far more than their homes were worth. An additional $5 bil was to be paid to state and federal programs to compensate homeowners.

Obama Alters Birth Control Insurance Mandate—Pres. Barack Obama announced Feb. 10 that he was altering an insurance mandate issued Jan. 20 that would have obliged employers, including institutions with religious affiliations other than houses of worship (such as universities or hospitals), to pay for birth control coverage at no cost to employees' health plans. The move came in response to critics, including the U.S. Conference of Catholic Bishops, who claimed the mandate, a part of the implementation of health-care reform signed into law in 2010, violated their religious liberty by requiring organizations to provide services that conflicted with their values. Instead, health insurers would be obliged to provide the coverage to female employees of organizations who chose to exclude it, at no cost to the employees. The Bishops' conference immediately pronounced the new terms unacceptable, though other critics, including the Catholic Health Assn., were satisfied with the compromise.

Congress Extends Payroll Tax Cut—Congress voted Feb. 17 to extend a temporary 2% payroll tax cut set to expire Mar. 1 through the end of 2012. The bill also maintained Medicare payment rates to doctors, which were set to drop 27%, and financed federal unemployment benefits. To offset the cost, the bill decreased governmental contributions to pension plans of new federal workers, requiring them to contribute 3.1% of their pay instead of 0.8%; auctioned off parts of the wireless spectrum to telecommunications companies; and cut $5 bil from a public health program that was part of the 2010 health care overhaul.

Supreme Court Rules Miranda Warnings Not a Prisoner Right—In a 6-3 decision Feb. 21, the Supreme Court ruled that officials were not necessarily required to inform inmates of their Miranda rights when questioning them about crimes not related to their confinement. Writing for the majority in *Howes v. Fields*, Justice Samuel A. Alito Jr. argued that removing Michigan state prisoner Randall Fields from his cell for questioning did not constitute custody for Miranda purposes, as he could reasonably have concluded that he was able to end the questioning and return to his cell. In her dissenting opinion, Justice Ruth Bader Ginsburg asserted that a statement telling a prisoner he is free to return to his cell "is no substitute for one ensuring that an individual is aware of his rights."

Unemployment Rate Falls to 8.3%; Other Economic Indicators Improve—The U.S. Dept. of Labor announced Feb. 3 that the national unemployment rate fell to 8.3% in Jan.—the lowest level since Feb. 2009—and 243,000 new jobs were created. The job growth suggested that employers were becoming more confident in the economy, but Federal Reserve Chairman Ben Bernanke cautioned that despite the positive employment report, the job market remained weak. Long-term unemployment persisted: 5.5 mil people, or 42.9% of the unemployed, had not worked for 27 weeks or longer. Furthermore, concern over Europe's economic crisis, slowing demand for U.S. goods, and the fact that U.S. incomes had not kept pace with inflation led economists to warn that economic growth would slow as the year progressed. During the month of Feb., the Dow Jones Industrial Average gained 2.5%, closing Feb. 29 at 12,952.07; the S&P 500 increased 4.1%, closing at 1,365.68; and the Nasdaq Composite Index was up 5.4% for the month, ending at 2,966.89.

International

Combat Mission in Afghanistan to End in 2013—U.S. Defense Sec. Leon Panetta announced Feb. 1 that the U.S. combat mission in Afghanistan would end as early as mid-2013, drawing criticism from U.S. lawmakers who prioritized defeating the insurgency and allies who were caught off guard. Of the 90,000 U.S. troops in the country, 22,000 were scheduled to withdraw in 2012, while the remaining 68,000 were to leave by the end of 2014. A timeline for withdrawal was not released, and Panetta added the next day that coalition troops would be "fully combat ready" and participating in combat as necessary through 2014. The same day as Panetta's announcement, a leaked NATO report found that Pakistan was supporting the Taliban in Afghanistan. The report threatened to derail renewed attempts to improve Pakistan's relations with Afghanistan and the U.S.

Deadly protests erupted Feb. 21 following reports that NATO soldiers at Bagram Air Base, near Kabul, had disposed of several copies of the Koran by burning them, an act forbidden in Islam. Pres. Barack Obama and other senior coalition officials apologized and said the burning was accidental, but the Taliban called for attacks on Western targets. Afghan Pres. Hamid Karzai condemned the incident Feb. 22 and called for the U.S. to turn over control of the Parwan detention facility, the origin of the disposed books.

Protests Erupt in Wake of Egyptian Soccer Violence—In the deadliest soccer violence since 1996, clashes of soccer fans in the northern Egyptian city of Port Said left more than 70 people dead and 200 others injured. Fans of the home team Al-Masry celebrated an upset victory over Cairo-based Al-Ahly Feb. 1 by attacking visiting players and fans, who found themselves trapped in the stadium by a locked gate, with clubs and knives. Police apparently did little to stop the violence, having failed to search fans entering the stadium for weapons and doing little to stop the attacks once they began. Critics of Egypt's military government asserted that the violence had been allowed to proceed to justify a strong military element in the transitioning government. Tens of thousands took to the streets to demonstrate against the government beginning the next day in Cairo, Port Said, and Suez, a city near the Red Sea, in Egypt's largest protests since the resignation of Pres. Hosni Mubarak Feb. 2011.

Russia, China Veto Syria Resolution as Violence Escalates—Frustrating the will of much of the international community, Russia and China vetoed a UN Security Council resolution Feb. 4 that sought to quicken the end of the 11-month conflict between the regime of Bashar al-Assad and Syrian opposition groups. An earlier version of the resolution, introduced by Morocco in late Jan., included an explicit call for Pres. Assad to step down, which had been removed in an attempt to appease Russia and China. The resolution supported the Arab League plan Assad had rejected in Jan., which called for him to grant power to Vice Pres. Farouk al-Sharaa so that a unity government could be formed in preparation for elections. The U.S. closed its embassy in Damascus Feb. 6, and a number of nations withdrew their ambassadors.

Conditions deteriorated on the ground. Syrian forces Feb. 3 began an assault on the city of Homs, an opposition stronghold, shelling the city while the Assad government blamed the violence on "armed terrorist groups." Government troops took the city by force, Feb. 29-Mar. 1. The U.S.-based Human Rights Watch said Mar. 2 that 700 people in Homs had been killed and thousands injured during the siege. Despite ongoing violence, the government held a nationwide referendum on a new constitution, claiming it had the support of 89% of voters. Opposition groups boycotted the voting, which was denounced by outside observers. According to UN estimates Feb. 28, more than 7,500 civilians had been killed since the Syrian uprising began in early 2011.

360 Die in Honduran Prison Fire—A fire broke out in an overcrowded prison in the Honduran city of Comayagua Feb. 14, killing at least 359 inmates and a visiting wife. The death toll was the highest in a prison fire in modern history. The incident brought attention to the prison crisis in Honduras, which has the world's highest murder rate, according to UN crime statistics. The prison, designed to house 500, held more than 850 prisoners. The following day, distressed relatives attempted to gain entrance to the prison but were repelled by security forces, who fired guns into the air and released tear gas. Frustrated family members Feb. 20 broke into a morgue in Tegucigalpa, the country's capital, trying to recover the remains of loved ones, only 32 of whom had been identified by Feb. 21.

EU Agrees to a Second Greek Bailout—European Union finance ministers, Feb. 21, agreed to a 130 bil euro ($172 bil) loan package to Greece to prevent a default. The package, which was to be financed by the Eurogroup, European Central Bank, and International Monetary Fund, included a debt swap that would allow Greece to write off 100 bil euro in debts; bonds owned by banks and private investors would lose as much as 75% of their value. In exchange, Greece agreed to reduce its sovereign debt to 120.5% of its GDP by 2020, down from a projected 160%, through government layoffs, reductions of government wages and pensions, and cuts in medical and defense spending.

Violence Kills 55 Across Iraq—Bombers and gunmen attacked civilian and government targets in more than a dozen Iraqi cities Feb. 23, primarily in Shiite neighborhoods, killing at least 55 and wounding more than 225. Civilian targets included an elementary school in Musayyib, a town about 40 mi south of Baghdad, where a car bomb killed three and wounded 73 others, mostly children; and a restaurant in northern Baghdad, where another car bomb killed nine and wounded 19. Some of the attacks targeted Iraqi security forces, including six killed in a shooting at a checkpoint in northern Baghdad and another two killed in a suicide bombing outside a police station in Baqouba, 35 mi northeast of Baghdad. The violence served to undermine Iraqi confidence in the government and its ability to protect civilians.

General

Giants Beat Packers in Super Bowl—In a matchup of two superstar quarterbacks Feb. 5, Eli Manning outlasted Tom Brady to lead the New York Giants to a 21-17 victory over the New England Patriots in Super Bowl XLVI at Lucas Oil Stadium in Indianapolis, IN. Down 17-15, the Giants gained control of the ball after Patriots receiver Wes Welker dropped an open pass and the team was forced to punt with under four minutes of play remaining. Starting from the Giants' 12th yard line, Manning threw a 38-yard pass to Mario Manningham, beginning a scoring drive that ended with a touchdown with 57 seconds left. In a last ditch effort with five seconds left on the clock, Brady threw a pass from midfield into the end zone. It fell to the ground beyond the reach of Rob Gronkowski, leaving Manning, who completed 30 of 40 passes for 296 yards, with his second Super Bowl ring and second Super Bowl MVP award.

An average audience of 53.9 mil households, or 111.3 mil viewers, tuned in for Super Bowl XLVI, making it the all-time most watched TV program. An estimated 114 mil people saw Madonna's halftime performance, which featured appearances by Cee Lo Green, LMFAO, Nicki Minaj, and M.I.A.

Adele Wins Big at Grammy Awards—The 23-year-old British soul singer Adele won six awards at the Grammy Awards ceremonies in Los Angeles, CA, Feb. 12, including Album of the Year for *21* and Song of the Year and Record of the Year for "Rolling in the Deep." Beating out Nicki Minaj and Skrillex, Bon Iver took home the award for Best New Artist in addition to Best Alternative Album.

***The Artist* Takes Best Picture at the Oscars**—*The Artist*, a black-and-white elegy to the silent era of film, took home five Academy Awards, including Best Picture, Best Director (Michel Hazanavicius), and Best Actor (Jean Dujardin) at ceremonies in Los Angeles, CA, Feb. 26. Actress Meryl Streep won her third Oscar for her leading role as Margaret Thatcher in *The Iron Lady*. Supporting Actress honors went to Octavia Spencer for *The Help*, and Christopher Plummer won Best Supporting Actor for *Beginners*. It was Plummer's first Oscar in a career that has spanned six decades.

Kenseth Wins Delayed Daytona 500—Matt Kenseth won his second Daytona 500 early in the morning Feb. 28 in Daytona Beach, FL, holding off a last-lap charge by Dale Earnhardt Jr., who placed second. Kenseth's win was almost lost in the drama of the event, which was postponed due to rain for the first time in the race's history, then delayed for two hours after Juan Pablo Montoya crashed into a truck loaded with fuel, setting the track on fire. The two rain delays—which moved the race from Sunday afternoon to Monday night—gave Fox the opportunity to air the race during primetime for the first time.

March 2012
National

Romney Extends Delegate Lead—Former Massachusetts Gov. Mitt Romney picked up momentum in the race for the Republican presidential nomination with a strong showing in the Washington state caucuses on Mar. 3 and again three days later on "Super Tuesday." Romney won six of the day's 10 primary contests—Alaska, Idaho, Massachusetts, Ohio, Vermont, and Virginia—and picked up 200 delegates. His status as the inevitable Republican nominee, however, remained precarious, as Southern voters seemed reluctant to offer their support. Former Sen. Rick Santorum (PA) won Tennessee and former House Speaker Newt Gingrich took Georgia, his home state. Santorum also picked up wins in Oklahoma and North Dakota and placed a close second in Ohio, despite being outspent four to one by Romney in that state.

Romney's inability to win over evangelical and Southern voters came to the fore in the following weeks. Santorum won the Kansas caucuses Mar. 10 as well as the Alabama and Mississippi primaries Mar. 13. Gingrich, who had hoped to regain momentum in the South, failed to win anywhere, though he placed second in Alabama and Mississippi. Romney took more low-profile contests, including Wyoming, Mar. 10, and Hawaii, Mar. 13; he also picked up victories in U.S. territories. He then enjoyed a decisive victory in delegate-rich Illinois Mar. 20, only to suffer a major defeat in Louisiana, which Santorum easily won four days later. This seemingly narrowed the nomination contest to a two-man race, despite Gingrich's insistence that he would remain in it until the end. Romney still led the Republican field at the end of Mar. with 568 delegates to Santorum's 273, Gingrich's 135, and Paul's 50, according to the AP count.

Maryland Legalizes Same-Sex Marriage—Maryland became the latest state to legally recognize gay marriage Mar. 1. Democratic Gov. Martin O'Malley signed the bill, which had passed the Maryland House of Representatives Feb. 17, 72-67, and the Senate Feb. 23, 25-22. The law was scheduled go into effect in Jan. 2013. Opponents of the bill gathered three times as many signatures as needed to force a referendum on the issue, and the Maryland Board of Elections announced July 10 that voters would have the chance to decide the issue on the ballot in Nov. 2012.

BP Civil Suit Settlement Announced—Oil-and-gas giant BP and the lawyers of more than 120,000 plaintiffs, victims of the *Deepwater Horizon* oil drilling rig explosion in the Gulf of Mexico in 2010, announced Mar. 2 that they had reached a settlement in a class-action lawsuit, which was set to begin trial three days later. BP agreed to pay medical expenses of those whose illnesses could be traced to the spill until 2033. The $20 bil escrow fund set up by BP in the aftermath of the explosion would be replaced by a fund administered by the court. According to BP's estimates, the settlement would cost $7.8 bil. The settlement did not resolve claims that the federal government or states were pursuing independently.

Justice Department Opens Investigation Into Teen's Shooting—The U.S. Justice Dept. revealed Mar. 19 that it had begun a civil rights investigation of the Feb. 26 shooting death of 17-year-old Trayvon Martin, an unarmed African-American high-school student, by 28-year-old George Zimmerman, in a Sanford, FL, gated community. The incident, initially investigated cursorily, had sparked nationwide protests and accusations of racial bias. Sanford Police Chief Bill Lee Jr. temporarily stepped down Mar. 22 amidst rising criticism over the handling of the case. Protestors believed that Zimmerman, who was on a neighborhood watch patrol at the time of the incident, had racially profiled Martin and was the aggressor; Zimmerman said he shot Martin in self-defense, and was therefore within his rights under Florida's "Stand Your Ground" law. A special prosecutor filed second-degree murder charges against Zimmerman Apr. 11. An FBI report released July 12 found no evidence that Zimmerman's actions were racially motivated.

U.S. Stocks Have Best First Quarter Since the 1990s—The Dow Jones Industrial Average closed at 13,212.04, Mar. 30, rising 8.1% since Jan. 1, and the S&P 500 closed at 1,408.47, a gain of 12% in the same period; neither had grown so much in the first quarter since 1998. The Nasdaq Composite Index finished at 3,091.57, for a gain of 18.7% and its best first quarter since 1991. Analysts credited increased consumer spending, as well as some abatement of concerns over the European debt crisis. The Labor Dept. announced Mar. 9 that 227,000 new jobs were added in Feb., though the unemployment rate held steady at 8.3%. In an indication of the banking industry's continuing recovery from the 2008 financial crisis, 15 of 19 major U.S. financial firms Mar. 13 passed the latest round of Federal Reserve stress tests, having enough capital to weather a hypothetical severe recession.

International

Putin Elected to Third Presidential Term—Russian Prime Min. Vladimir Putin (2008-12), who had served as president, 2000-08, won a third presidential term Mar. 4 with 64% of the vote. In the weeks before the election, large protests were staged in Moscow, mostly by young, urban professionals in opposition to Putin's government. But despite discontent with Putin among the middle class, opponents could not unite into a political force capable of challenging the ruling party. Those who voted for Putin—generally older, traditionally minded, and/or rural voters—feared that the country would descend into economic chaos without his leadership. International election monitors declared that the vote was flawed, noting that media coverage was strongly pro-Putin, that some candidates were denied the ability to run, and that Putin drew upon the country's treasury for campaign funds. There were also reports of companies intimidating employees to vote for Putin, and of voters being bused from poll site to poll site and instructed to vote for a particular candidate. Nevertheless, the election result stood, and Putin was inaugurated May 7.

Ethiopian Troops Battle Somali Islamic Militants—Al-Shabaab, an Islamic militant group that had recently declared ties to al-Qaeda, attacked Ethiopian troops in Yurkud, a town in southern Somalia, Mar. 10. Ethiopian, Kenyan, and African Union (AU) troops had been deployed in Somalia in 2011 to wrest control of the areas of the country (including the capital Mogadishu) that al-Shabaab had taken over in its attempt to impose a strict form of sharia law. The battle was the fiercest Ethiopian troops had faced since entering the country Nov. 2011. Witnesses said dozens died, though both sides claimed to have killed many while suffering few casualties themselves. The battle followed a Mar. 9 announcement that Ethiopian troops would withdraw from the country in Apr. and be replaced in the southern region by troops from Djibouti, Burundi, and Uganda under the AU flag.

Congolese Warlord Guilty of War Crimes—A three-judge panel at the International Criminal Court in The Hague, Netherlands, Mar. 14 handed down its first conviction since convening in 2002, pronouncing the Congolese warlord Thomas Lubanga Dyilo guilty of war crimes. The conviction stemmed from Lubanga's use (2002-03) of children under the age of 15 to fight in the Democratic Republic of the Congo's civil war (1998-2003). Lubanga was sentenced to 14 years in prison July 10. New attention had been paid to the issue of child soldiers in spring 2012, in part due to a video about Ugandan warlord Joseph Kony. The video, about Kony's abuse of child soldiers, went viral on video sharing sites, receiving 100 mil views by Mar. 16.

Karzai Demands U.S. Troops Leave Villages After Mass Shooting—After an American soldier reportedly killed 16 Afghan civilians, including 9 children, in Kandahar Province Mar. 11, Afghan Pres. Hamid Karzai demanded Mar. 15 that NATO troops withdraw to their bases and allow Afghan forces to take over the security in the country's villages. It was widely believed that agreeing to the demand would complicate NATO's counterinsurgency strategy and its ability to prepare for the transfer of security responsibilities to Afghan forces during the planned withdrawal of NATO troops at the end of 2013. Some observers felt his demands were made to appease domestic discontent with NATO's presence, and the Karzai government soon announced that it was in negotiations with NATO over the matter. In a separate setback for the coalition, the Taliban announced Mar. 15 that it was suspending negotiations because of the U.S.'s conditions on a planned prisoner exchange.

The shooting spree was allegedly carried out by U.S. Army Staff Sgt. Robert Bales, who was taken to Fort Leavenworth, KS, to await trial. U.S. officials announced Mar. 22 that Bales, a 38-year-old father who had served three tours of duty in Iraq before deploying to Afghanistan in Dec. 2011, would be charged with 17 counts of murder.

UN Approves Syrian Peace Plan—The United Nations Security Council Mar. 21 unanimously voted to approve a peace plan proposed by former UN Sec. Gen. Kofi Annan, whom the UN and Arab League had jointly appointed as special envoy to Syria in Feb. The six-point plan called for Pres. Bashar al-Assad's regime to allow "freedom of movement" for journalists, humanitarian aid to victims, and peaceful demonstrations to be held. It also called upon both the regime and the opposition to commit to a cease-fire. However, the agreement passed as a presidential statement and lacked the force of a UN resolution. Assad quickly declared he would accept the plan, but his commitment to its provisions remained uncertain, and violence in the country continued.

French Terrorist Dead After Police Standoff—Mohammed Merah, the alleged killer of seven unarmed people, was killed after a more than 30-hour standoff with French police Mar. 22. He was believed to have killed three unarmed French paratroopers—one in Toulouse Mar. 11, and two more in Montauban Mar. 15—and three children and a teacher at a Jewish school in Toulouse Mar. 19. According to police, Merah, who was under surveillance in France because of possible ties to Islamic terrorists, said he was a member of al-Qaeda and had carried out the attacks to protest the killing of Palestinian children and French involvement in Afghanistan.

Mali's Government Falls in Military Coup—A group of low-ranking military officers seized control of Mali's government Mar. 22, ousting democratically elected Pres. Amadou Toumani Touré, who had promised to step down following elections scheduled for Apr. The group suspended the constitution and blamed the coup on discontent with the government's response to a rebellion in the country's northern desert region, where mostly nomadic ethnic Tuaregs sought to create an independent state. The Tuaregs had gained an advantage using arms acquired while fighting for Muammar al-Qaddafi in Libya and had achieved a number of surprise victories. The ruling junta canceled the planned vote and read a new constitution on state TV Mar. 27. Response from the international community was mostly negative, as the EU and World Bank Mar. 22-23 and U.S. Mar. 26 halted development aid to Mali; the African Union suspended Mali's membership Mar. 23.

Iraq Takes Steps to Reassert Regional Power—Iraq hosted Mar. 27-29 its first Arab League summit since 1990 and began reestablishing its position as a regional force after a decade of occupation and turmoil. In the months leading up to the summit, Iraq sought to resolve lingering diplomatic issues with neighboring states, particularly Kuwait and Saudi Arabia. More than half the leaders of the Arab world, including Saudi Arabia's King Abdullah, failed to attend; they were said to be wary of Iraq's Shiite leadership. Discussions at the summit primarily focused on the violence in Syria, and the leaders in attendance endorsed the recently approved UN plan for peace there, retreating from earlier calls for Syrian Pres. Bashar al-Assad to step down.

Iraq reportedly spent $500 mil on the summit and mobilized 100,000 security forces to clean up the capital, eliminate insurgents, and block traffic nearby; few attacks occurred during the summit. But the country's security issues lingered: a series of coordinated attacks had killed dozens in the week leading up to the summit.

General

Archbishop of Canterbury Announces Plans to Resign—Rowan Williams, the 104th Archbishop of Canterbury and head of the Anglican church, announced Mar. 16 that he would resign from office at the end of the year to take a position at the Univ. of Cambridge. Williams, who had been confirmed as archbishop in 2002, made the announcement a few months before a vote was expected in favor of the consecration of female bishops. The issue had been debated throughout Williams's tenure, and he had attempted without success to forge a compromise on the question. A vote on the issue was again delayed at the church's General Synod in July.

Pope Benedict Visits Mexico, Cuba—In his first papal visit to either country, Pope Benedict XVI, the head of the Roman Catholic church, visited Mexico, Mar. 23-25, and Cuba, Mar. 26-28. While in Mexico, he met with Pres. Felipe Calderón Hinojosa and victims of drug-cartel violence, and celebrated mass before an estimated 350,000 near Guanajuato's Christ the King monument. In Cuba, he met Pres. Raúl Castro and former Pres. Fidel Castro, and said two open-air masses, including one attended by hundreds of thousands in Havana's Revolution Square.

April 2012
National

Santorum Suspends Campaign as Romney Tightens Hold on Nomination—By the end of Apr., former Massachusetts Gov. Mitt Romney's hold on the Republican presidential nomination was all but assured. Romney increased his lead Apr. 3, winning primaries in Wisconsin; Washington, DC; and Maryland; the latter two by wide margins. Former Sen. Rick Santorum (PA), widely regarded as Romney's only viable challenger, took 37% of the vote in Wisconsin and 29% in Maryland but had failed to make the ballot in Washington, DC, where Rep. Ron Paul (TX) won a slim second place with 12%, a percentage point ahead of former House Speaker Newt Gingrich (GA). All four candidates initially pledged to continue campaigning; Santorum, in particular, expected to do well in Apr. 24 primaries in Pennsylvania, his home state. But Santorum bowed out Apr. 10, apparently in response to calls from Republican leaders, who wished to shift the focus to defeating Pres. Barack Obama in the general election. Some noted that the former senator may also have wanted to avoid a potentially embarrassing loss in his home state, where Romney was gaining ground in polls. The Gingrich and Paul campaigns were ongoing, but Romney claimed a decisive victory in five state primaries Apr. 24 (Connecticut, Delaware, New York, Pennsylvania, Rhode Island).

Supreme Court Ruling Allows Increased Strip Searches—In a 5-4 vote, the Supreme Court ruled Apr. 2 in *Florence v. County of Burlington* that prison officials had the right to strip-search those being admitted to jail, regardless of the charges faced. The case arose out of the imprisonment of a New Jersey man, arrested after a traffic stop on an outstanding warrant issued for an unpaid fine (that had actually been paid), who had been subject to two strip searches during his seven-day imprisonment. The motorist, Albert Florence, argued that his Fourth Amendment protection against unreasonable search and seizure had been violated. Writing for the majority, Justice Anthony M. Kennedy cited *Bell v. Wolfish* (1979) and argued that security issues within prisons were more important than the individual rights of detainees, regardless of the invasiveness of the search. In concurring opinions, Chief Justice John G. Roberts Jr. and Justice Samuel A. Alito Jr. noted that the ruling did not apply to prisoners who would not interact with other inmates. In his dissent, Justice Stephen G. Breyer argued that strip searches were "a serious affront to human dignity and to individual privacy" and should be limited to those arrested for offenses involving drugs and violence.

Five Officers Sentenced for Post-Katrina Shootings—Five former New Orleans police officers received prison sentences in federal court Apr. 4 for their involvement in an infamous Sept. 2005 incident on Danziger Bridge in New Orleans, LA, in which a group of unarmed citizens fleeing the devastation of Hurricane Katrina were shot, resulting in two deaths. The Justice Dept. had taken over the case after state charges against the former officers were dropped in 2008 because of prosecutorial misconduct. Robert Faulcon was sentenced to 65 years in prison. Kenneth Bowen and Robert Gisevius were each sentenced to 40 years. Anthony Villavaso received a 38-year sentence, and Arthur Kaufman received a six-year sentence for conspiracy in covering up the incident. Five other New Orleans police officers involved in the Danziger Bridge shootings had agreed to plea bargains and testified against the five defendants.

Prostitution Scandal Engulfs U.S. Secret Service—A dozen agents for the U.S. Secret Service were implicated in a prostitution scandal while preparing for Pres. Barack Obama's Apr. 13 arrival in Cartagena, Colombia, for the Summit of the Americas. The agents allegedly met with prostitutes late Apr. 11 at their hotel after leaving a Cartagena nightclub. Prostitution is legal in some parts of Colombia, but local police were involved after one of the women got into a dispute over her payment. The police informed U.S. diplomats of the incident, and the agents were sent back to the U.S. and replaced by other agents. The Secret Service announced Apr. 18-24 that of the 12 agents implicated, six resigned, two were fired, one retired, and three were allowed to remain in their posts.

EPA Issues New Standards for Fracking—The Environmental Protection Agency (EPA) Apr. 18 set rules for releasing toxic or carcinogenic gases, such as hexane and benzene, during the drilling process known as hydraulic fracturing, or "fracking," which is used to extract otherwise inaccessible natural gas from rock formations. Energy companies will be required to install equipment to capture toxic gases released by fracking activities by 2015, reducing the amount being released into the air by 190,000 to 290,000 tons each year. The new rules did not explicitly cover greenhouse gas emissions but were still expected to cut up to 44 mil tons of greenhouse gas emissions per year.

Business Tax Cut Passes the House; Buffett Rule Fails—The Republican-controlled House passed a $46-bil one-year business tax cut Apr. 19, in a 235-173 vote mostly along party lines. The legislation would allow businesses employing fewer than 500 people to deduct 20% of business income from their taxes. The measure was opposed by most Democrats because the cuts were not tied to a hiring requirement and, according to the bipartisan Joint Committee on Taxation, would do little to spur the economy. That same day, Republicans defeated, by a vote of 234-179, a measure that would require a minimum tax of 30% on annual income exceeding $1 mil. Commonly called the "Buffett rule," after Warren Buffett, a billionaire business magnate who had publicly complained that his tax rate was lower than that of middle-class Americans, the measure was criticized as "class warfare" by Republicans, who argued it would bring in only enough funds to cover 1% of projected deficits over the next 10 years.

Signs of Slowing Economic Growth Offset by Positive Consumer Reports—A weaker than expected jobs report released Apr. 6 showed that the economy added 120,000 jobs in Mar., far fewer than the more than 200,000 that had been expected. The disappointing report undermined confidence in the strength of the economic recovery that the country had been experiencing over the previous months. A Commerce Dept. report Apr. 27 added to the gloomy economic picture, showing that the U.S. gross domestic product grew by only 2.2% in the first quarter, down from 3% in the previous quarter. The Dow Jones Industrial Average nonetheless held its ground, buoyed by strong consumer reports at the month's end, to close on Apr. 30 at 13,213.63, a 0.01% rise since Apr. 1. Meanwhile, the S&P 500 closed at 1,397.91, seeing a drop of 0.75% for the month. The Nasdaq Composite Index fared the worst, closing at 3,046.36, a loss of 1.46% from its opening on Apr. 1 and its first monthly loss of 2012.

International

Suu Kyi Victorious in Myanmar's Parliamentary Election—The National League for Democracy (NLD)—the opposition political party in Myanmar (Burma) led by Nobel Peace laureate Aung San Suu Kyi—won a majority of the seats up for grabs in Myanmar's Apr. 1 by-elections. Three days after the vote, state media announced the NLD had taken 43 of the 45 seats at stake. The victory would not change the balance of power in the country's 664-seat parliament, 80% of which was controlled by the military-supported Union Solidarity and Development Party (USDP). But it signaled a thaw in the ruling establishment, which had been controlled by a military junta between Mar. 1962 and Jan. 2011. The NLD had not been permitted to take part in elections since 1990, when it won a landslide victory that was ignored. Suu Kyi had been detained a year prior to that election; she spent more than 15 of the next 20 years under house arrest, gaining freedom only after a Nov. 2010 election resulted in USDP control of the nominally civil government that came to power. The 2012 elections, monitored by international observers, encouraged many in the international community to drop their opposition to the government. The U.S. eased some sanctions Apr. 4, while the EU suspended most of its sanctions for one year on Apr. 23, even as Suu Kyi and other NLD elected members initially refused to take the oath of office until the wording could be modified.

Afghan-U.S. Deal on Night Raids Reached Amid Continuing Violence—Under a deal signed Apr. 8, the Afghan government took control of night raids and other special operations missions. The deal was a major step in efforts to arrive at a broad agreement governing the future relationship between the two nations. Night raids had been a point of contention between the Afghan and U.S. governments, but under the agreement Afghan forces would take charge of such raids, while the U.S. would provide support, including air strikes, upon request. All such missions would also need approval from Afghan officials and a warrant from an Afghan court, which could be approved retroactively in some cases requiring immediate action.

Diplomatic progress did not dispel the threat of insurgent violence. Insurgents—either the Taliban or the Haqqani network—launched their most serious attacks since the Taliban was toppled in 2001, fighting an 18-hour battle with Afghan and NATO forces in Kabul Apr. 15-16 as well as staging coordinated attacks in the cities of Jalalabad, the capital of Nangarhar province; Gardez, the capital of Paktia province; and Pul-e-Alam, the capital of Logar province. A Taliban spokesman called the attacks the start of the Taliban's annual "spring offensive." Despite the coordinated attacks, only about eight security forces members and four civilians were believed to have been killed, along with 39 insurgents.

Chongqing Party Chief Bo Xilai Removed From Posts—Former Chongqing party chief Bo Xilai was removed from his positions on China's Central Committee and Politburo, Apr. 10, for committing "serious disciplinary violations." Bo's wife, Gu Kailai, and a domestic employee, Zhang Xiaojun, were arrested for allegedly poisoning British businessman Neil Heywood over a business dispute in 2011. Bo, who had been a strong contender for a top party position in an upcoming leadership shuffle, had been removed as Chongqing's party chief in Mar. in an unusually public political scandal involving the possible cover-up of the murder of Heywood. Gu was convicted of Heywood's murder Aug. 9 after a one-day trial and given a suspended death sentence, Aug. 20; Zhang received a nine-year sentence.

Worries Over Debt Intensify in Spain, Italy—Investors' concerns over the ability of Italy and Spain to handle their debts seemed to grow in Apr. Italy was obliged to pay 3.89% on three-year bonds auctioned Apr. 12, a rise of 1.3% from a similar auction in Mar., in spite of the country's announced spending cuts. The following day, the cost of financing existing 10-year bonds for Spain edged toward 6%, an unsustainable level that was surpassed Apr. 16, and the cost of insuring losses on Spain's debt for five years reached a record high of 4.98% per year. Spain found some relief after strong demand for its bonds at auction Apr. 19 seemed to allay fears that the Spanish bond market had dried up. Italy Apr. 18 forecast that its economy would shrink 1.2%, up from the 0.4% contraction it had predicted earlier in the year, and Prime Min. Mario

Monti acknowledged that the country's budget would not be balanced until 2015, not 2013 as had been previously forecast. An International Monetary Fund report was even less positive, predicting that the Italian economy would contract by 1.9% and that its budget would remain unbalanced until at least 2018.

Iraqi Insurgent Attacks Continue—In what was seen as part of a continuing effort to undermine confidence in Prime Min. Nouri al-Maliki's Shiite-led government, insurgents launched 12 attacks Apr. 19 in Baghdad and the northern city Kirkuk as well as in Diyala Province, killing approximately 30 and wounding nearly 100 more. The attacks targeted security patrols and Health Min. Majeed Hamad Amin, and were not necessarily seen as evidence of a deteriorating security situation. The Iraqi political situation, however, grew more complicated as tensions between the Shiite government and Kurds escalated over oil disputes. The Iraqi government threatened to withhold funds owed to Kurdistan over its entering an independent oil-exploration deal with ExxonMobil in 2011 that the central government considered illegal.

Former Liberian President Taylor Guilty of War Crimes—A three-judge panel of the Special Court for Sierra Leone in The Hague, Netherlands, convicted former Liberian Pres. Charles Taylor of 11 counts of aiding and abetting war crimes and crimes against humanity Apr. 26. The charges were related to Taylor's providing material support to the Revolutionary United Front (RUF)—which committed such crimes as murder, conscription of child soldiers, sexual slavery, rape, terror, and forced amputations—in exchange for diamonds during Sierra Leone's 1991-2002 civil war. Taylor was cleared of being directly responsible for the crimes carried out by the RUF, and was the first head of state to be convicted by an international court since the Nuremburg tribunals held in the wake of World War II.

General

Kentucky Wins NCAA Basketball Championship— The Univ. of Kentucky Wildcats beat the Univ. of Kansas Jayhawks 67-59 to win the school's eighth NCAA championship title Apr. 2 at the Mercedes-Benz Superdome in New Orleans, LA. Kentucky head coach John Calipari claimed his first career title after four trips to the Final Four with three different schools. Doron Lamb led the Wildcats with 22 points, but freshman Anthony Davis won the award for Most Outstanding Player in the Final Four. Despite making only 1 of 10 shots, he proved strong on defense with 6 of Kentucky's record-breaking 11 blocked shots and 16 rebounds. Kansas, trailing 59-44, had a 13-3 run with a little over 5 minutes left in the game, pulling within 5 points with 1:37 left. Kentucky's defense then retook control, denying Kansas the chance for a comeback.

Watson Wins Masters Golf Tournament—American golfer Bubba Watson defeated South African Louis Oosthuizen in a sudden-death playoff at Augusta (GA) National Golf Club, Apr. 8, to claim the Masters title. Watson shot a final round of 68 for a 10-under-par 278 total to tie Oosthuizen, who shot a final round of 69 and made only the fourth double-eagle, or albatross, in Masters history. Both players birdied the first sudden-death hole, but Oosthuizen failed to match Watson's par on the second, giving the 33-year-old Watson his first major championship.

May 2012

National

Romney Clinches Republican Nomination for President—Former Massachusetts Gov. Mitt Romney's position as the presumptive Republican nominee was secured May 29 with a win in the Texas primary that gave him a total of 1,191 pledged convention delegates. At least 1,144 delegates were needed to ensure his place on the Republican presidential ticket. Former House Speaker Newt Gingrich (GA) formally departed the Republican primary race May 2, and Rep. Ron Paul (TX) announced May 14 he would end his campaign but not his bid to win enough delegates to give him a platform at the Republican National Convention. Romney had won primaries in Indiana, North Carolina, and West Virginia, May 8; in Oregon and Nebraska, May 15; and in Arkansas and Kentucky, May 22.

Obama Voices Support for Same-Sex Marriage—Pres. Barack Obama became the first sitting president to endorse same-sex marriage during an ABC News interview May 9. During the 2008 presidential campaign, Obama supported civil unions but not marriage for same-sex couples, and he explained that his position on the issue had evolved over time. The announcement came just days after both Vice Pres. Joe Biden and Education Sec. Arne Duncan had voiced their support for such marriages.

Obama's announcement came during a month of action on same-sex marriage. North Carolina voters May 8 approved an amendment to the state constitution that defined marriage as between a man and a woman. Later in the month, a three-judge panel of the First Circuit Court of Appeals May 31 declared unconstitutional a provision of the 1996 Defense of Marriage Act (DOMA), which defines marriage as a union solely between a man and a woman, because it discriminated against married same-sex couples. The ruling was expected to be argued before the U.S. Supreme Court on appeal.

J.P. Morgan Reveals $2 Billion Trading Loss—J.P. Morgan Chase & Co. chairman and CEO Jamie Dimon revealed in a conference call with investors and analysts May 10 that the bank had suffered a surprise $2 bil trading loss over the previous six weeks. The loss originated in the bank's chief investment office in London and was the result of a poorly managed investment strategy. Dimon said it would not prevent the bank from remaining profitable, even though he estimated future losses of about $1 bil. (Total estimated losses grew to more than $7 bil by July 13.) Shares of the bank fell 9.3% the next day, and U.S. and British financial regulators opened investigations into the trades and the corporate decision-making process.

The announcement came as financial institutions, including J.P. Morgan, were lobbying Congress to weaken federal regulations implemented as part of the Dodd-Frank financial reform law passed in 2010, particularly the Volcker Rule, which is meant to put limits on banks' ability to invest their own funds in bonds, derivatives, and stocks.

Facebook Goes Public, Raises $16 Billion—Social networking giant Facebook Inc.'s initial public offering (IPO) raised $16 bil May 17 with the sale of 421 mil shares at $38 each. It was the third largest IPO in history behind General Motors Co. in 2010 and Visa Inc. in 2008. The stock broke the trade-volume record the following day, when 571 mil shares were traded publicly on the Nasdaq exchange, but failed to perform as well as expected. The price remained flat and banks underwriting the offering, including Morgan Stanley, had to intervene to prevent the share's price from falling below $38. Technical problems, which caused a half-hour delay in Facebook's Nasdaq debut, were in part blamed for the stock's poor performance. But share values continued to decline to $31 by May 22, the third full day of public trading. Estimates of the fortune of Mark Zuckerberg, the company's CEO and majority shareholder, thus decreased from $19 bil May 18 to $17.1 bil.

Edwards Acquitted of Campaign Finance Violations— After nine days of deliberations, a U.S. District Court jury in Greensboro, NC, acquitted 2004 Democratic vice presidential nominee and former Sen. John Edwards (D, NC) May 31 of one felony count of accepting illegal campaign contributions and deadlocked on five other counts. The cleared count was related to a $200,000 check that Rachel Mellon, a banking heiress, gave Edwards during his bid to claim the 2008 Democratic presidential nomination. A mistrial was declared on the five other counts, which included a conspiracy charge that alleged financial contributions were used to cover up Edwards's extramarital affair. The Justice Dept. announced June 13 that it would not retry Edwards on the five charges.

Economic Recovery Shows More Signs of Slowing—Jobs numbers released by the Labor Dept. May 4 were weak for a second consecutive month, adding to fears that the recovery from the 2007-09 recession was in trouble. The U.S. economy added only 115,000 jobs in Apr., while 342,000 people had ceased looking for jobs, a phenomenon that helped the unemployment rate decrease to 8.1% but that left only 63.6% of the working-age population participating in the job market, the lowest level since 1981. The numbers raised concerns over the volume of consumer activity, the reduction of which would limit the potential for growth in coming months. The stock market followed the negative trend. The Dow Jones Industrial Average fell 6.21%, or about 820 points, for the month, closing at 12,393.45 May 31. The S&P 500 saw a similar loss, falling 6.27%, to close at 1,310.33, while the Nasdaq Composite Index suffered a 7.19% decline, to end the month at 2,827.34.

International

Obama Visits Afghanistan to Sign Pact With Karzai; Other Regional Developments—Pres. Barack Obama visited Afghanistan May 1 to sign the U.S.'s new Strategic Partnership Agreement, agreed to Apr. 22, with Pres. Hamid Karzai. The pact outlines the U.S. role in Afghanistan after NATO forces withdraw from the country in 2014 and the scope of the relationship between the two countries through 2024. The agreement designates Afghanistan a major non-NATO ally, allows U.S. soldiers to remain in the country to train Afghan forces and conduct counterterrorism operations, and commits the U.S. to providing military and other kinds of aid. During his surprise visit, Obama gave a speech at Bagram Air Base on U.S. goals in the region, which he maintained were to defeat al-Qaeda and fight terrorism, not eradicate the Taliban or nation-build. The difficulty of establishing stability in Afghanistan was reinforced hours after Obama left May 2, when a compound in Kabul used by Western contractors suffered a sustained attack that left at least seven dead; the Taliban claimed responsibility. Later in the month, during a summit May 20-21 in Chicago, IL, NATO finalized a withdrawal plan that called for Afghan forces to assume security responsibilities by mid-2013 with NATO providing training and assistance as well as most of the funding to maintain the national security force.

Hollande Defeats Incumbent Sarkozy in French Presidential Runoff—Socialist Party candidate Francois Hollande defeated Pres. Nicolas Sarkozy of the center-right Union for a Popular Movement (UMP) 52%-48% in France's May 6 presidential election runoff, becoming the first Socialist French president since Francois Mitterrand left office in 1995. Hollande promised during the campaign to ease the austerity measures put in place in the wake of the Eurozone debt crisis, which Sarkozy had negotiated with German Chancellor Angela Merkel. Stressing job creation and economic growth over fiscal restraint, Hollande vowed to eliminate tax cuts for the wealthy, increase the tax rate for incomes over 1 mil euros, and introduce economic stimulus measures. Hollande was sworn into office May 15.

Greece Votes Against Austerity—In May 6 parliamentary elections in Greece, the majority of voters cast ballots rejecting the country's two dominant political parties—the conservative New Democracy and the socialist Pasok—raising fears that Greece would abandon the euro. New Democracy and Pasok had formed a coalition in Nov. 2011, sought the financial bailout Greece received in Feb., and accepted austerity demands along with it. The parties that benefited from the elections, including the leftist coalition Syriza and the extreme right Gold Dawn—regarded by many as a neo-Nazi

party—had campaigned against the bailout. No party, however, won a clear majority. After 10 days of negotiation failed to produce a coalition government, new elections were called for June 17. The uncertainty pushed the euro to a four-month low against the dollar, but the success of New Democracy in the June elections alleviated concerns.

Syrian Violence Continues Despite Cease-fire—Despite a UN-monitored cease-fire between the Syrian government and the opposition that nominally went into effect Apr. 12, the 14-month-old Syrian conflict raged on. Two suicide bombs exploded near a military intelligence compound in Damascus May 10, killing at least 55 people and wounding hundreds. The Syrian government blamed the rebels, who denied responsibility and accused the regime of Bashar al-Assad of staging the violence to justify continued crackdowns. Syrian forces attacked students demonstrating in Aleppo, Syria's biggest city, May 17. The United Nations reported May 26 that government forces and loyalist militias had carried out a massacre May 25-26 in Houla, northwest of the rebel city of Homs, killing 108 civilians, including 49 children and 34 women. The UN Security Council issued a nonbinding resolution May 27 that condemned the attack. It was approved by China and Russia, which had previously resisted attempts to condemn Syrian actions. Many Western governments, including the U.S., expelled senior Syrian diplomats in protest of the killings.

Chinese Activist Arrives in U.S. After Diplomatic Crisis—Chen Guangcheng, a blind Chinese legal activist, arrived at Newark Intl. Airport in New Jersey May 19, ending a drama that had enflamed tensions between the U.S. and China on the eve of economic talks between the two nations May 3-4. After fleeing house arrest, Chen had taken refuge Apr. 26 at the U.S. embassy in Beijing in pursuit of a deal that would allow him to safely remain in China and work as an activist. A U.S.-brokered compromise was reached May 2, and Chen left the embassy for a nearby hospital, only to change his mind within hours. He declared he would seek asylum in the U.S. and even made a public plea to be allowed to leave China on Sec. of State Hillary Clinton's plane. A new deal, which allowed Chen to apply for a passport to study abroad, was announced May 4. Upon arrival in the U.S., Chen took up residence in New York City, where he and his wife will attend New York Univ.'s law school as visiting scholars.

Headless Bodies Symbolize Cartel Violence—The decapitated bodies of 43 men and 6 women were found May 13 in Cadereyta Jiménez, Nuevo León, Mexico. The region had been the site of ongoing clashes between the rival Zetas and Gulf drug cartels, and banners claiming both groups were responsible appeared nearby in the following days. Mexican authorities were investigating the possibility that the murdered were migrant workers from other parts of Mexico or Central America, whom the cartels had kidnapped for ransom money. Mexico's army announced May 20 that Daniel "The Madman" Elizondo Ramirez, a member of the Zetas arrested two days earlier, had been charged with these and other cartel-related killings. According to Mexican government estimates released in Jan. 2012, cartel- and drug-related violence had killed 47,515 people between Dec. 2006 and Sept. 2011.

Former Ultranationalist Wins Serbian Presidency—Tomislav Nikolic, a politician who previously styled himself an ultranationalist but was running as a center-right populist with the Serbian Progressive Party (SNS), defeated former Pres. Boris Tadic of the liberal Democratic Party (DS) May 20 to win Serbia's presidential election runoff. The candidates were the top two finishers in the first round of voting May 6, when the SNS won the most seats—73 of 250—in parliamentary elections, though they did not have enough to form a single-party government. Tadic's DS, which won 67 seats, and the Socialist Party (SPS), which had won 44 seats, then said May 9 they would form a coalition government. That coalition gave rise to a cohabitation government in which parliament's governing coalition and the presidency were held by rival parties. SPS leader Ivica Dacic was sworn in as prime minister July 27.

General

I'll Have Another Wins Kentucky Derby and Preakness Stakes—I'll Have Another, bought for the modest price of $35,000 in 2011, surged in the homestretch to catch Bodemeister, the favorite who led much of the race, and win the 138th Kentucky Derby by a length and a half May 5 at Churchill Downs in Louisville, KY. I'll Have Another jockey Mario Gutierrez became the 42nd jockey to win the race in his first attempt. Two weeks later, May 19, at Pimlico in Baltimore, MD, I'll Have Another again caught up with race-leader Bodemeister in the homestretch to take the Preakness Stakes by a neck and set himself up for a chance to be the first Triple Crown winner in 34 years.

Drogba Plays Hero for Chelsea in UEFA Champions League Soccer Final—UK's Chelsea football club won a penalty shootout at the Allianz Arena in Munich, Germany, to win the European club soccer championship May 19 over Germany's Bayern Munich. Chelsea, down 1-0 with only a couple of minutes to play, tied the match when Didier Drogba headed a corner kick into the net. Juan Mata missed Chelsea's first penalty shot, but Bayern Munich's Ivica Olic and Bastian Schweinsteiger also failed to convert their penalties. The match's outcome was again left up to Drogba, who scored the decisive penalty to give Chelsea—which had lost the UEFA final in penalities in 2008—the first Champions League victory in club history.

Amid Wheldon Tribute, Franchitti Wins Third Indy 500—In an unusually competitive race that saw 10 drivers swap the lead a record-breaking 35 times, Dario Franchitti emerged victorious at Indianapolis Motor Speedway May 27 in a battle to the finish line with Takuma Sato, who slammed into the wall trying to pass on the final lap. The day also served as a tribute to Dan Wheldon, the previous year's Indy winner, who died in a crash during the IndyCar season finale in Oct. 2011. The tribute opened with car-owner Bryan Herta driving Wheldon's car in a parade lap and concluded with Franchitti donning Wheldon's trademark white sunglasses, facsimiles of which were also distributed to fans to wear on laps 26 and 98, in honor of Wheldon's Indy-winning car numbers.

June 2012
National

Romney and Obama Offer Competing Economic Plans—Having secured 1,480 delegates by June 14, more than enough to assure he would win the nomination for president at the Republican National Convention at the end of Aug., former Massachusetts Gov. Mitt Romney turned his attention to defeating Pres. Barack Obama. He and the Republican National Committee (RNC) out-fundraised Obama and the Democratic National Committee (DNC) in May, taking in $76.8 mil to the president's $60 mil, according to June 7 reports released by both campaigns. The contrast between the two candidates came to the fore in the battleground state of Ohio June 14, when each gave an economic policy speech. Romney reviewed his plan for stimulating growth by deregulating the business sector, instituting spending cuts, and pushing through tax reform. Obama, by contrast, largely avoided specific proposals and instead criticized Romney's proposals as comparable to the economic policies of Pres. George W. Bush's administration. The president also blamed Republicans in Congress for blocking his proposals, most significantly the American Jobs Act, which Obama had proposed in a joint session of Congress, Sept. 8, 2011. He highlighted his

administration's economic successes, including infrastructure projects, the automobile industry bailout, and his strengthening of public education. Many saw Obama's Ohio speech as an attempt to move beyond the controversy surrounding his statement that "the private sector is doing fine" during a White House news conference, June 8.

Wisconsin Governor Survives Recall—In what amounted to a gubernatorial election rematch, Wisconsin Gov. Scott Walker (R) defeated Milwaukee Mayor Tom Barrett 53%-46% in a recall election June 5. The victory was a rebuff to Democrats and labor unions, who had led the drive to remove Walker from office after he signed legislation that limited the collective bargaining rights of state employees. The election was the most expensive in Wisconsin's history: more than $63 mil was spent by the two campaigns, much of it from outside interest groups and super PACs. Lt. Gov. Rebecca Kleefisch and three out of four Republican state senators also survived the recall, but Democrats gained control of the state's senate, though it would not convene for a regular session until after the Nov. 2012 election.

New Immigration Policy Gives Young Undocumented Immigrants Chance to Remain in U.S.—Pres. Barack Obama June 15 announced an executive action that ended the deportation of qualified undocumented immigrants under the age of 30. Under the action, those who came to the U.S. illegally before they were 16, met certain education-related criteria or were honorably discharged military veterans, and had no significant criminal history would be able to apply for "deferred action" status. The measure would allow undocumented immigrants to stay in the U.S. and work legally though it did not provide a path to citizenship. Immigrants' rights groups called the move a step in the right direction. Former Gov. Mitt Romney, the presumptive Republican presidential nominee, criticized the action for not offering a permanent solution to the U.S. immigration problem.

Supreme Court Closes Term With Landmark Rulings on Immigration, Health Care—The U.S. Supreme Court June 25 ruled in *Arizona v. U.S.* that much of Arizona's immigration enforcement law first passed in 2010 was unconstitutional. The court ruled in a 5-3 vote that the state could not make it a crime for illegal immigrants to hold or seek jobs and could not authorize police to detain without a warrant immigrants that had, in their opinion, committed a crime for which they could be deported. The court, in a 6-2 vote, also ruled against a provision that made it illegal according to state law to violate federal immigration law. However, the provision requiring police to check the immigration status of people whom they had stopped or detained for other reasons was upheld in a unanimous vote. Justice Elena Kagan, who had worked to defend the Obama administration's position while serving as solicitor general, recused herself from the case.

In one of the most anticipated rulings of the term, the Supreme Court June 28 upheld most of the Patient Protection and Affordable Care Act, the health-care reform bill signed into law in 2010. In their decision, the justices upheld, 5-4, the individual mandate, a central provision requiring that almost all U.S. residents carry health insurance. But the Court struck down, 7-2, the provision that would have allowed the federal government to deny states Medicaid funding if they refused to comply with the program's expansion. The individual mandate was determined to be constitutional not under the Commerce Clause, as the solicitor general had argued before the Court, but as a permissible exercise of Congress's taxation power. Chief Justice John G. Roberts Jr., a George W. Bush appointee who generally votes with the court's conservative bloc, surprised many observers by providing the fifth vote that allowed the law to stand and writing the majority opinion.

Attorney General Holder Found in Contempt of Congress—By a vote of 255-67, the House of Representatives

June 28 found Attorney Gen. Eric Holder in contempt of Congress on both criminal and civil grounds, making Holder the first sitting cabinet member to be cited for contempt. Holder had refused to comply with a subpoena ordering the release of internal Justice Dept. documents related to the gun-trafficking sting Operation Fast and Furious. During the 2009-11 operation, Arizona-based agents of the Bureau of Alcohol, Tobacco, Firearms, and Explosives (ATF) allowed around 2,000 guns to be smuggled into Mexico. Some of the weapons were later used during crimes in the U.S. and Mexico, including an incident that led to the death of a U.S. Customs and Border Protection agent. A Jan. 2012 report by the House Oversight and Government Reform Committee had held the Arizona ATF agents responsible, but the committee voted June 20 along party lines, 23-17, to recommend the contempt citation. Committee chairman Rep. Darrell Issa (R, CA) said there was no evidence that Holder was involved in a cover-up but insisted that Congress had the right to access the documents. House Democrats regarded the investigation as politically motivated, and many boycotted the vote. The Justice Dept. refused to pursue the criminal case against Holder, citing Pres. Obama's June 20 assertion of executive privilege in the matter.

Unemployment Rises as Stocks Gain—Jobs numbers released June 1 showed that May was the weakest month of 2012, with only 69,000 jobs created, far below the 150,000 that analysts had predicted. The unemployment rate rose to 8.2%, a figure partially attributed to 642,000 people re-entering the job market, a sign of increased optimism over the economy among the long-term unemployed. Meanwhile, all three stock indexes saw gains during the month after a particularly bad May. The Dow Jones Industrial Average rose 3.93%, to close on June 29 at 12,880.09. The S&P 500 experienced slightly better gains, closing up 3.96% at 1,362.16, while the Nasdaq Composite Index lagged slightly behind, rising 3.81%, to end the month at 2,935.05.

International

Egypt Strides Toward Democracy—Deposed Egyptian Pres. Hosni Mubarak was convicted June 2 of being an accessory to murder and of attempted murder for failing to prevent the deaths of protestors during the demonstrations that toppled his regime in early 2011. Mubarak and former Interior Min. Habib el-Adly were sentenced to life in prison; six senior police officers were cleared of any wrongdoing. Many Egyptians who gathered outside the court to hear the verdicts reacted angrily, demanding the death penalty, and protestors filled Cairo's Tahrir Square over the next few days.

Egyptians voted in their first free presidential election May 23-24, but no candidate received the 50% of the vote needed to claim victory. Ahmed Shafiq, a former air force general and prime minister during the final days of Mubarak's regime, faced off against Mohammed Morsi, an Islamist from the Freedom and Justice Party (FJP)—the political wing of the Muslim Brotherhood—in a runoff election June 16-17; Morsi emerged the winner June 24. Between the runoff vote and the announcement, the Egyptian military leadership moved to hold onto powers it had assumed when it took over the government after Mubarak's fall. Morsi found himself with a dual challenge: he needed to allay fears that he would impose Islamic law on Egypt and assert his authority not only over the civilian population but also over the military.

UN Mission in Syria Undermined—Syrian opposition activists reported June 6 that Pres. Bashar al-Assad loyalists had killed 78 people in Qubair, a small village near the city of Hama. The next day, Syrian government forces reportedly fired on unarmed UN personnel, preventing UN observers tasked with monitoring the joint UN-Arab League sponsored cease-fire agreement from reaching the village. Monitors were allowed in the village June 9 but by then were unable to verify or disprove the activists' allegations. The

UN announced June 16 that it was suspending its mission in Syria because of increasing violence. Norwegian Major Gen. Robert Mood, the mission commander, noted that 300 monitors would remain in Syria so that the mission could quickly resume as conditions improved. According to UN estimates, as many as 10,000 Syrians had been killed since anti-Assad protests began in 2011.

Paraguayan President Lugo Removed From Office—Paraguay's senate voted, 39-4, to remove leftist Pres. Fernando Lugo from office June 22. The day before, the lower house of his country's parliament had voted, 76-1, to impeach him over his handling of a clash between police and landless peasants that resulted in 17 deaths. With only two hours to prepare his defense, Lugo was a no-show at his trial, sending instead his legal team with a request for a delay that was not granted. He accepted the senate's decision but criticized it as undemocratic. Vice Pres. Federico Franco was sworn in shortly after the vote.

Barclays Settles Over Libor Scandal, But Fallout Widens—The UK bank Barclays agreed June 27 to pay $450 mil to settle charges brought against it by U.S. and British regulators that it supplied inaccurate information regarding interest rates in order to manipulate the London Interbank Offered Rate (Libor). The Libor interest rate is used as an international benchmark for other interest rates, including those applied to commercial loans and mortgages. Barclays was accused of manipulating rates 2005-09 in order to increase traders' profits and give the bank the appearance of financial health during the 2008 financial crisis. By July 3 several of the bank's executives resigned, including CEO Robert Diamond and Chairman Marcus Agius. Several U.S. banks, including J.P. Morgan Chase, Bank of America, and Citigroup, were the focus of continuing investigations into Libor manipulation and more fines were expected to be levied. Meanwhile, British Prime Min. David Cameron declared July 2 that the parliament would investigate and release a report on the matter by year's end. The U.S. Congress opened its own investigation days later.

General

Sandusky Convicted of Sexual Abuse of Children—After a two-week trial, a jury in Bellafonte, PA, June 22 convicted Gerald "Jerry" Sandusky, a former assistant football coach at Penn State Univ., of 45 of 48 charges related to the sexual abuse of 10 boys over a period of 15 years. Now 18-28 years old, eight of the boys—whom Sandusky met through The Second Mile, the charity he founded for underprivileged children—testified during the trial that Sandusky had sexually abused them in hotels, on university property, and in Sandusky's home. The prosecution also relied on the testimony of former Penn State assistant football coach Mike McQueary, who said he saw Sandusky engaging in sexual acts with a boy in 2001 in a campus shower. Sandusky received a 30-60 year prison sentence Oct. 9.

The university's storied football program will likely see fallout for years to come. Louis Freeh, the former FBI director hired by Penn State's board of trustees to conduct an investigation into the university's response to the allegations, released a report July 12 that claimed senior officials, including Penn State head coach Joe Paterno, had concealed Sandusky's crimes to protect the school's football program. The NCAA July 23 fined the university $60 mil, capped football scholarships, banned Penn State's football team from the postseason for four years, and stripped the university of 14 years of victories.

Bradley Upsets Pacquiao to Become World Welterweight Champion—American Timothy Bradley defeated Filipino favorite Manny Pacquiao in a controversial split decision June 9 in Las Vegas, NV. Pacquiao dominated the first half of the match, but Bradley won five of the last six rounds. Pacquiao seemed to have done enough to retain his title, and the crowd was stunned when the winner was announced. Two judges scored the bout 115-113 in Bradley's favor, while the third put Pacquiao ahead, 115-113.

Sharapova, Nadal Win French Open—Russian Maria Sharapova easily defeated Italian Sara Errani at Roland Garros in Paris, France, June 9 to win her first French Open title, 6-3, 6-2. Spain's Rafael Nadal met the Serbian Novak Djokovic June 10, but the match was suspended in the fourth set due to rain. Nadal was leading 6-4, 6-3, 2-6, 1-2, but Djokovic turned things around, winning eight consecutive games as Nadal struggled with soggy conditions. When play resumed on June 11, Nadal won the fourth set 7-5 to become the first man to win seven French Open titles.

Union Rags Wins Belmont Stakes—Union Rags slipped through a slim opening along the rails and furiously battled Paynter over the last sixteenth of a mile to take the 144th Belmont Stakes June 9 in a photo finish at Belmont Park in Elmont, NY. It was jockey John Velazquez's second Belmont victory—perhaps aided by the absence of I'll Have Another, the winner of the Kentucky Derby and Preakness Stakes, who lost out on a chance for Triple Crown glory when a tendon injury two days before the race forced him to retire.

Once and *Peter and the Starcatcher* **Top Tony Awards**— Enda Walsh's *Once*, a musical based on a 2006 film about a Czech flower seller's romance with an Irish street musician, took home eight Tony Awards June 10, including Best Musical. Rick Elice's *Peter and the Starcatcher*, a play based on Dave Barry and Ridley Pearson's best-selling novel of the same name, took home five awards. The Tony for Best Play went to Bruce Norris's Pulitzer Prize-winning *Clybourne Park*.

L.A. Kings Claim Stanley Cup Crown—The L.A. Kings defeated the New Jersey Devils 6-1 at the Staples Center in Los Angeles, CA, June 11, to win the 45-year-old franchise's first Stanley Cup. Coming off two losses after taking a 3-0 lead in the best-of-seven series, the Kings took control of the game in the first period, scoring 3 goals during a five-minute power play after the ejection of the Devils' Steve Bernier. The lead was maintained thereafter, thanks in part to the goalkeeping skills of Jonathan Quick, who made 17 saves and was awarded the Conn Smythe Trophy as playoff MVP.

Miami Heat Win the NBA Championship—In the fifth and deciding game, June 21, the Miami Heat trounced the Oklahoma City Thunder, 121-106, at American Airlines Arena in Miami, FL, to give superstar LeBron James his first NBA championship (and seemingly justifying his decision to leave the Cleveland Cavaliers in 2010). With 26 points, 13 assists, and 11 rebounds on the night, James also took MVP honors.

Simpson Takes First U.S. Open—American golfer Webb Simpson won the U.S. Open at the Olympic Club in San Francisco, CA, June 17, to secure his first major championship. The 27-year-old came into the fourth round 4 shots down, but shot to the top of the leaderboard after making 4 birdies in 5 holes, for a final-round 2-under-par.

July 2012

National

Obama Administration Issues No Child Left Behind Waivers—Education Sec. Arne Duncan announced July 19 that Arizona, Kansas, Michigan, Mississippi, Oregon, South Carolina, and the District of Columbia had been added to the list of jurisdictions that would be exempt from a key requirement of the No Child Left Behind (NCLB) education law passed in 2002. In order to get the mandate—which required that all students achieve proficiency in reading and math by 2014—waived, states had to present alternative plans to improve schools and student achievement, tie teacher evaluations to students' standardized exam performance, and make a concerted effort to improve the worst schools. Congressional Republicans criticized Obama for an inappropriate use of executive authority in issuing the waivers to a total of 32

states plus the District of Columbia. Congress had failed to renew NCLB since 2007, the first year the legislation was up for renewal; it was widely agreed to be unrealistic in its current form.

Colorado Movie Theater Shooting Stuns—A man opened fire just after midnight in a crowded movie theater July 20 in Aurora, CO, killing 12 people and injuring 58. Police arrested 24-year-old James Holmes outside the theater right after the melee. Wearing body armor, a gas mask, and helmet, Holmes allegedly had entered the theater through an emergency exit about 30 minutes into a premiere showing of the highly anticipated Batman film *The Dark Knight Rises* and opened fire. Holmes was in possession of four guns, three of which were used in the shooting, and reportedly referred to himself as the Joker, one of Batman's nemeses. A graduate student who had recently withdrawn from a neuroscience program at the Univ. of Colorado's Anschutz Medical School, Holmes had also booby trapped his apartment with large amounts of explosives. Holmes was formally charged at Arapahoe County District Court July 30 and was eligible for the death penalty under Colorado state law.

Romney Tours England, Israel, and Poland—Seeking to demonstrate his ability to represent the U.S. on the world stage, presumptive Republican presidential nominee Mitt Romney visited England, Israel, and Poland, July 26-31. Even before he left the U.S., however, Romney's efforts at diplomacy floundered. Romney July 25 questioned London's preparedness to host the Summer Olympics set to begin July 27, earning him rebukes from British Prime Min. David Cameron and London Mayor Boris Johnson. Romney arrived in Israel July 28 and delivered a speech on Iran's nuclear program the next day, suggesting that his opposition to Iran's nuclear program would be stronger than Pres. Barack Obama's policies. On July 30, however, he offended Palestinian leaders, attributing the different economic status of Palestine and Israel to cultural differences.

Stock Markets Remain Steady Despite Signs of Slowing Recovery—For the third month in a row, the Labor Dept. announced disappointing job-creation numbers July 6; only 80,000 new jobs were created in June, not enough to significantly reduce unemployment, which held at 8.2%. More bad economic news followed at the end of the month. The Commerce Dept. reported July 27 that the U.S. gross domestic product had grown only 1.5% in the second quarter, down from 2% in the first quarter, leading economists to worry that the recovery from the 2007-09 recession was stalling. The stock markets, however, remained steady in the face of bad news. The Dow Jones Industrial Average closed at 13,008.68, July 31, up 1% or 128.59 for the month. The S&P 500 closed at 1,379.32, up 17.16 points, or 1.26%, while the Nasdaq Composite Index rose a mere 0.15%, or 47 points, to end the month at 2,939.52.

International

Peña Nieto Elected President of Mexico—Enrique Peña Nieto of the Institutional Revolutionary Party (PRI), won Mexico's July 1 presidential election, beating out Andrés Manuel López Obrador of the leftist Party of Democratic Revolution and Josefina Vazquez Mota of the conservative National Action Party (PAN). Peña Nieto's victory would bring PRI, Mexico's long-ruling party (1929-2000), back into power after 12 years in the opposition. The election was not without controversy. Reports of vote buying by PRI led López Obrador, who came in second, to challenge the results in Mexico's Federal Electoral Tribunal, which dismissed the case for lack of evidence, Aug. 30. Peña Nieto was scheduled to be sworn into office Dec. 1.

Pakistan Reopens NATO Supply Lines to Afghanistan—Pakistan agreed July 3 to reopen the North Atlantic Treaty Organization (NATO) supply lines along its borders into Afghanistan. The supply lines had been closed since 24

Pakistani soldiers were killed in a NATO air strike in Nov. 2011. Pakistan demanded an apology, which the U.S. had failed to give until July 3, when U.S. Sec. of State Hillary Clinton apologized to Pakistan Foreign Min. Hina Rabbani Khar. Without access to the supply lines on Pakistan's border, NATO was forced to use airlifts and supply lines along Afghanistan's northern border to keep troops in matériel, at a considerably greater cost.

Moderates Win Libya's First Democratic Elections Since 1964—Libyans July 7 voted for members of the parliament that would replace the unelected National Transitional Council—which had taken power after the fall of Muammar al-Qaddafi in 2011—in the first democratic elections held in Libya since 1964. Unlike Tunisia and Egypt, where Islamist parties topped post-Arab Spring elections, moderates came out on top in Libya. Former Interim Prime Min. Mahmoud Jibril's National Forces Alliance won 39 of the 80 contested seats, while the Justice and Construction Party, the political arm of Muslim Brotherhood, won 17. The other 120 seats were won by independent candidates, most of whom had not indicated their political affiliations. The parliament Aug. 9 selected the moderate Islamist Mohammed Magarief of the National Front Party—an outgrowth of Libya's oldest opposition movement—interim president. Mustafa Abu-Shakour, also of the National Front Party, was made prime minister Sept. 12.

Suicide Attack in Bulgaria Kills Six—A suicide bomber blew up a bus carrying Israeli tourists July 18 near the airport of Burgas, a popular resort city in Bulgaria. Five Israeli tourists and a Bulgarian bus driver were killed, and more than 30 others were injured. Israel and the U.S. blamed Iran-backed Islamic militant group Hezbollah for the attack, with one U.S. official claiming Iran was avenging the assassinations of its nuclear scientists, which it blamed on Israel. Israel promised to respond forcefully, though perhaps clandestinely, but both Iran and Hezbollah denied involvement.

Syrian Fighting Continues; Civil War Declared—A bomb hidden in a national security building in Damascus, Syria's capital, exploded July 18, killing three senior officials—Defense Min. Dawoud Rajiha; Pres. Bashar al-Assad's brother-in-law Assef Shawkat, who served as the deputy defense minister; and Hassan Turkmani, a former defense minister who headed the crisis group that was meeting and served as a military advisor to Vice Pres. Farouk al-Sharaa. Other officials were injured, including Interior Min. Mohammed Ibrahim al-Shaar, who later died as a result of his injuries. The Syrian opposition's successful attack illustrated a weakness in the security of Assad's government. Gen. Fahd Jassem al-Freij replaced Rajiha as defense minister the following day.

The International Red Cross declared the Syrian conflict a civil war July 15, and U.S. Defense Sec. Leon Panetta said July 18 that the situation in Syria was "rapidly spinning out of control." Opposition forces assaulted Damascus in July—forcing Assad to employ heavy weaponry, including tanks, in the capital for the first time—and had taken control of some of the city's neighborhoods until they retreated from a government counteroffensive July 20-23. The opposition also reportedly took control of posts along the border with Iraq and at least one on the border with Turkey. The international community could not agree on an appropriate response. Russia and China vetoed, July 19, a third UN Security Council resolution that would have imposed sanctions if Assad failed to withdraw his forces from populated areas and abide by the cease-fire plan accepted and subsequently ignored by both parties in Mar.

Terrorist Attacks in Iraq Kill 100—One day after al-Qaeda in Iraq declared a new offensive against the mainly Shiite Iraqi government, at least 100 people, most of them members of Iraqi security forces, were killed in attacks in at least 12 cities. It was the deadliest day since the withdrawal of U.S. forces in Dec. 2011. A gunman first opened fire July 23 at a military base near Dhuluiya in Salahuddin province, killing 15 Iraqi soldiers. That attack was followed

by bomb blasts at a number of sites, including in Taji, a city to the north of Baghdad, where 41 people died, and in Sadr City, a Shiite neighborhood within Baghdad, where 16 people died. More attacks followed in Baghdad and Diyala, raising questions about the effectiveness of Iraqi security.

India Suffers Worst Blackout in History—On July 30, India's northern power grid failed, leaving approximately 370 mil people—including the residents of Delhi, the country's capital—without power for most of the day. The next day, two more regional power grids failed, leaving about 670 mil people without power in the worst blackout in history, jamming traffic, trapping miners, and stranding trains and subways in at least 20 states across a 2,000-mi swath of the country. The exact cause of the grid failures was unknown, but India suffers from an 8%-12% power deficit at peak hours and often triggers rolling blackouts.

General

Spain Wins Euro Cup Soccer Championship—Spain, the 2010 World Cup champions, defeated Italy 4-0 at the Olympic Stadium in Kiev, Ukraine, to win the European 2012 football (soccer) championships July 1. Spain's David Silva claimed an early lead when he headed in a goal in the 14th minute; teammate Jordi Alba scored again in the 41st minute. Italy's hopes of a comeback faded when midfielder Thiago Motta was injured in the 64th minute and left Italy with only 10 players. Spain's Fernando Torres capitalized on the situation and put away a third goal in the 84th minute to become the first player to score a goal in two European Championship finals. Juan Mata put the game away in the 88th minute with another goal.

Scientists Uncover "God Particle"—Scientists at the European Organization for Nuclear Research (CERN) near Geneva, Switzerland, announced July 4 that they had discovered preliminary evidence of the existence of the Higgs boson particle, the so-called God particle, which British physicist Peter Higgs theorized in 1964 gave matter mass. If the discovery proved true, the Standard Model of particle physics would be confirmed. The Higgs boson was posited to explain something that was not understood: how elementary particles acquire mass. The paper explaining the discovery passed the peer-review process in Sept., overcoming the first obstacle toward acceptance as scientific fact.

Williams and Federer Win Wimbledon—After two years without a major title, American Serena Williams overcame Poland's Agnieszka Radwanska, 6-1, 5-7, 6-2, to win her fifth Wimbledon Championship and 14th tennis Grand Slam event at the All England Lawn Tennis Club July 7. The next day, Switzerland's Roger Federer defeated Andy Murray, 4-6, 7-5, 6-3, 6-4, for his seventh Wimbledon win and his record-breaking 17th Grand Slam title. In the process, Federer dashed British hopes that Murray would become the first British Wimbledon champion since Fred Perry in 1936.

Els Wins Dramatic British Open—Ernie Els of South Africa won the British Open at Royal Lytham & St Annes Golf Club in Lytham St Annes, Lancashire, England, July 22. As many as 7 strokes behind leader Adam Scott, over the first 9 holes, Els made birdies on the 14th and 18th holes to finish the day at 7-under-par, while Scott collapsed, dropping 4 strokes in the course's last 4 holes to finish second at 6-under par.

August 2012
National

Mass Shooting at Sikh Temple—In an incident described as an act of domestic terrorism, a gunman later identified as 40-year-old Wade Page opened fire Aug. 5 at a Sikh temple in Oak Creek, WI, leaving six dead, including two temple leaders and the center's president. Three more people were critically wounded, including a police officer. Page shot himself in the head after being wounded in a shootout with police officers following his refusal to put down his weapon. A former U.S. Army psychological operations specialist, Page reportedly reportedly had links with white supremacist rock bands. The incident rattled the U.S. Sikh community, which is estimated to number about 500,000.

Senate Candidate's Remarks on Rape Criticized—During an Aug. 19 interview with a St. Louis TV station, U.S. Rep. Todd Akin (R, MO), the Republican senate candidate challenging incumbent Sen. Claire McCaskill (D), justified his opposition to abortion in cases of rape by expressing doubt that a woman could become pregnant from a rape. Akin asserted that women's bodies could shut down their reproductive mechanisms in instances of "legitimate rape." The American Congress of Obstetricians and Gynecologists refuted the statement, calling it medically inaccurate and dangerous, and Democrats and Republicans alike condemned the remark. GOP leaders urged Akin to reconsider his candidacy, and the National Republican Senatorial Committee withdrew financial assistance, fearing that his comments would alienate female voters nationwide. Akin vowed to stay in the race, and allowed an Aug. 21 withdrawal deadline to pass.

Apple Wins $1.05 Billion From Samsung in Patent-Infringement Suit—A U.S. District Court jury in San Jose, CA, ruled Aug. 24 that Samsung Electronics Co. had infringed on six Apple Inc. smartphone and tablet patents. Samsung was ordered to pay Apple $1.05 bil in damages—among the highest figures ever awarded in an intellectual property suit. The jury also ruled against Samsung in its countersuit, finding that Apple had not infringed upon five Samsung patents. Samsung took action to have the decision overturned in post-trial motions or on appeal. The two companies were waging similar court battles in Asia, Europe, and Australia. The same day the blockbuster verdict was announced, a panel of South Korean judges ruled each company had infringed on the other's patents and awarded Apple 25 mil won ($22,400) and Samsung 40 mil won ($35,800).

Republican Convention Nominates Romney, Ryan—Meeting Aug. 27-30 at the Tampa Bay Times Forum in Tampa, FL, the Republican National Convention formally nominated former Massachusetts Gov. Mitt Romney for president and Rep. Paul Ryan (WI) for vice president. In his nomination acceptance speech Aug. 29, Ryan called attention to Pres. Barack Obama's economic record, particularly the high rate of unemployment among young college graduates, a demographic that largely had backed Obama in the 2008 election. The chairman of the House Budget Committee, Ryan also criticized the president for his failure to accept the deficit reduction recommendations of a bipartisan panel. Ryan portrayed Republicans as defenders of Medicare and denounced cuts to the program included in the health-care reform law championed by Pres. Obama; his remarks on that topic were criticized as disingenuous. Romney had named Ryan his running mate Aug. 11; the 42-year-old, seven-term congressman was best known for his fiscally conservative budget plan, which called for major changes to Medicaid and Medicare while sharply cutting taxes.

Gov. Romney formally accepted the nomination Aug. 30, in a speech that criticized the slow pace of the economic recovery from the 2007-09 recession. Romney touted his business credentials as head of Bain Capital, arguing that his success in the business sector qualified him to steer the economy in the right direction. Romney mentioned few policy details but promised to create 12 mil jobs over the next four years, reform the tax code, reduce the country's deficit, and repeal Obama's health-care reform law. He also promised to pursue foreign policy that would strengthen the U.S.'s position in the world, which he claimed had been weakened by Obama's policies.

After convening briefly Aug. 27 to open the convention, the rest of the day's events were cancelled as a precaution against Tropical Storm Isaac, which bypassed Tampa for the most part. New Jersey Gov. Chris Christie Aug. 28 gave the keynote speech, in which he accused Democrats of concealing the country's fiscal problems. Other convention speakers included Ann Romney, Romney's wife of 43 years; former Arkansas Gov. Mike Huckabee; former Sec. of State Condoleezza Rice; and Sen. John McCain (AZ), the 2008 presidential nominee. Few speeches received the attention garnered by actor and director Clint Eastwood Aug. 30, when he mockingly addressed an empty chair as though Obama were sitting in it.

Economy Remains Sluggish in Recession's Aftermath—The U.S. economic recovery continued to proceed at a sluggish pace, adding 163,000 jobs in July, according to the Labor Department's Aug. 3 report. The number was positive in one respect: economists had predicted that only 100,000 jobs would be added. But the new jobs number was not high enough to bring down the unemployment rate, which rose to 8.3% from 8.2% nationally. Nevertheless, the stock markets did not suffer, with all major indexes posting Aug. gains for the first time since 2009. The Nasdaq Composite Index closed at 3,066.96, a rise of 4.3% for the month; the Dow Jones Industrial Average closed up just 72 points at 13,090.84; and the S&P 500 saw a monthly gain of 1.98% when it closed at 1,406.58 Aug. 31.

International

European Central Bank Pledges to Intervene in Euro Crisis—European Central Bank (ECB) Pres. Mario Draghi announced Aug. 2 at a meeting of the bank's governing council in Frankfurt, Germany, that the ECB was willing to act to ease economic pressure of debt and high borrowing costs on countries in the eurozone. But Draghi did not list specific actions that would be taken, undercutting market speculation that the bank was ready to immediately step in based on a statement the week before. Some investors hoped that the ECB would resume its bond-buying program to relieve the pressure that Italy and Spain, the third- and fourth-largest economies in the eurozone, were suffering due to heavy debt burdens. Bundesbank, the German central bank, was opposed to ECB intervention in the bond market. The lack of a specific ECB plan and the apparent shelving of the bond-buying program sent interest rates of Spanish and Italian bonds soaring above 6%, the highest sustainable interest rate.

Syrian Forces Launch Offensive in Aleppo; Other Developments—The Syrian government launched a ground assault Aug. 8 in Aleppo, Syria's second largest city, in an attempt to retake control. Syrian rebels began their attack on Aleppo—a center of support for Pres. Bashar al-Assad for much of the rebellion—in late July and had been able to hold some neighborhoods even as Syrian troops employed jets, tanks, and helicopters to root them out. In the meantime, fighting again broke out in Damascus, Aug. 3, despite government claims that the rebels had been pushed out of the city. Former UN Sec. Gen. Kofi Annan announced, Aug. 2, that he was stepping down as joint UN-Arab League special envoy to Syria, placing the blame for his inability to find a resolution on Syrian government intransigence. Syrian Prime Min. Riyad Farid Hijab, who had only held office since June, defected to Jordan Aug. 8, becoming the highest-ranking official in Syria's former ruling class to revoke his support.

Green-on-Blue Attacks Rise in Afghanistan; Death Milestone Reached—Afghan police carried out two attacks in the southern province of Helmand against coalition forces, Aug. 10, killing six NATO soldiers. Attacks on coalition troops by Afghan security forces, commonly known as "green-on-blue" attacks, had increased considerably in 2012. In one attack, an Afghan police commander shot three members of the U.S. Special Forces after inviting them for a meal, then reportedly joined the Taliban. Another attack occurred at a joint Afghan-coalition facility, where someone working for the Afghan police shot three coalition soldiers. In the southwestern province of Nimruz the following day, another

Afghan police officer opened fire on his colleagues, killing 11 before being shot to death.

The U.S. mission in Afghanistan, which began as Operation Enduring Freedom in 2001, reached a grim milestone in Aug., when the U.S. military death toll surpassed 2,000.

WikiLeaks Founder Granted Asylum in Ecuador—Julian Assange, the founder of WikiLeaks, was granted political asylum by Ecuador, Aug. 16. Assange had been living in Ecuador's London Embassy since June 19, five days after Britain's Supreme Court rejected his appeal of a ruling that would have allowed him to be extradited to Sweden to face charges of rape and other sexual misconduct. Assange and his supporters claimed the charges were part of a conspiracy orchestrated by the U.S. to persecute him for releasing classified documents. However, the UK refused to grant Assange safe passage out of the country, so he remained at the Ecuadorean embassy indefinitely.

Russian Punk Group Jailed for Protests—A Moscow court Aug. 17 convicted three members of the punk group Pussy Riot—Nadezhda Tolokonnikova, Yekaterina Samutsevich, and Maria Alekhina—of hooliganism and inciting religious hatred. The trio was sentenced to two years in a penal colony. The charges stemmed from their Feb. 21 performance of a "punk prayer" at Christ the Savior Cathedral in Moscow as part of anti-Putin protests that took place in the run-up to the Mar. 4 election, which Putin won despite the objections of international voting observers. The case had won widespread international attention, and the U.S., European Union, and human rights groups denounced the sentences.

General

NASA's *Curiosity* Lands on Mars—After traveling 352 mil mi, the NASA rover *Curiosity* guided itself to a safe landing on the surface of Mars Aug. 6, successfully carrying out the most elaborate landing sequence ever attempted by a spacecraft. In the landing procedure, dubbed "seven minutes of terror," the Mars Science Laboratory craft slowed to 1,000 mph upon entering the Martian atmosphere, steered towards the Gale Crater with its thrusters, and deployed a 51-ft-wide parachute to slow its descent. The heat shield and parachute were then released while reverse rockets slowed the descent even more. The final delivery system, called the sky crane, used cables to carefully lower the rover to the surface. *Curiosity*'s mission was to explore Mars for signs of organic material, which would suggest that microbial life was once present on the planet.

XXX Summer Olympics Held in London, England—More than 10,500 athletes representing 204 nations and dependencies competed in 302 medal events at the XXX Summer Olympic Games, hosted July 27-Aug. 12 by the UK's capital. London reportedly spent $15-$20 bil preparing for the games, including $775 mil for its Olympic Stadium. The games were notable for being the first Olympics to which all countries sent female athletes. The U.S. led the medal count, with a total of 104 medals: 46 gold, 29 silver, and 29 bronze. China was second in the overall medal count, with 88: 38 gold, 27 silver, and 23 bronze. Other leading teams included Russia with 82 medals (24 gold), Great Britain (65 medals, 29 gold), Germany (44 medals, 11 gold), and Japan (38 medals, 7 gold).

American swimmer Michael Phelps turned in another dominant performance, winning four gold medals and two silver and bringing his career Olympic medal count to an unprecedented 22 over three Olympic Games. Jamaican track star Usain Bolt became the first man to successfully defend both 100-m and 200-m Olympic sprinting titles; Bolt also won gold anchoring Jamaica's 4x100-m relay team. Other American stars to emerge included 17-year-old U.S. swimmer Missy Franklin, who won four gold medals, and 16-year-old U.S. gymnast Gabrielle "Gabby" Douglas, who helped to earn the U.S. team competition gold medal and became the

first black gymnast to win gold in the women's individual all-around competition. Other marquee accomplishments included gold-medal performances by the U.S. women's and men's basketball teams; Misty May-Treanor and Kerry Walsh Jennings winning a third consecutive beach volleyball gold; and the victory of Andy Murray of Scotland, who beat top-ranked Roger Federer of Switzerland for the gold in men's tennis.

Armstrong Ends Battle Against Doping Charges—Seven-time Tour de France champion Lance Armstrong announced Aug. 23 that he would stop fighting the doping charges brought against him by the U.S. Anti-Doping Agency (USADA). Armstrong did not admit to doping and called the agency's pursuit of his case "an unconstitutional witch hunt," though the USADA had eyewitnesses, including some former Armstrong teammates, prepared to testify to his doping. He was subsequently banned from cycling for life and stripped of his seven Tour de France wins by the International Cycling Union Oct. 22.

September 2012
National

Democratic Convention Nominates Obama, Biden; Romney Fundraiser Video Leaked—Meeting Sept. 4-6 at Time Warner Cable Arena in Charlotte, NC, the Democratic National Convention formally nominated Pres. Barack Obama and Vice Pres. Joseph Biden. In his acceptance speech Sept. 6, Obama described the election as a "choice between two fundamentally different visions for the future." He went on to portray Republican presidential nominee Mitt Romney's economic plan as harmful to the middle class and as a return to the failed policies of Pres. George W. Bush. Obama's speech also spelled out specific goals for a second term. He promised to create 1 mil new manufacturing jobs, cut $4 tril from the federal budget deficit over the next decade, reduce the U.S.'s dependence on foreign oil, reduce the rise of college tuition, and end the war in Afghanistan by 2014. Vice Pres. Joe Biden used his acceptance speech Sept. 6 to introduce Obama, touting the president's character and his decision-making skills, drawing attention to the success of the government-mandated bankruptcies of U.S. automakers Chrysler Group and General Motors Co., and the U.S. Special Forces mission into Pakistan, which resulted in the death of Osama bin Laden.

Former Pres. Bill Clinton (1993-2001) nominated Obama Sept. 5 with a speech that defended Obama's economic record, attacked Republican economic policies, and decried bitter Washington partisanship. Other speakers included San Antonio Mayor Julian Castro, who gave the keynote speech, making him the first Hispanic American to be given that honor; Maryland Gov. Martin O'Malley; former Florida Gov. Charlie Crist (R); Senate Majority Leader Harry Reid (D, NV); and Elizabeth Warren, a Senate candidate in Massachusetts. Former Rep. Gabrielle Giffords (D, AZ), who retired from the House of Representatives Jan. 2012 after being hit in a 2011 mass shooting that left six dead, also appeared Sept. 6, to recite the Pledge of Allegiance.

In other campaign developments, leftist magazine *Mother Jones* Sept. 17 posted a video of Republican presidential nominee Mitt Romney that had been covertly recorded at a May 17 fundraising dinner. In the video, he said the 47% of the U.S. population who paid no income tax believed themselves to be victims who were entitled to government handouts. The next day, Romney confirmed the video's authenticity and described his remarks as inelegant, but he defended his point about the growing culture of dependency in the U.S. The Obama campaign seized on the remarks, asserting that they showed that Romney "had disdainfully written off half the nation." The controversy undermined the Romney campaign's attempts to get back on message as he lagged in the polls.

Chicago Teachers Strike Amid Stalled Contract Talks—Chicago's public school teachers walked off the job Sept. 10 after contract negotiations between the Chicago Teachers Union (CTU) and the nation's third largest school district failed to reach an agreement. At issue were the length of the school day, tying teacher evaluations to student performance, and potential job cuts. On Sept. 14, the CTU and Chicago Public Schools (CPS) reached a tentative agreement, but the strike continued into the following week as the union voted to give teachers time to look over the details, which included a pay increase of 17.6% over four years and linking a percentage of evaluations to student performance. After 350,000 students and 30,000 teachers had missed seven school days, CTU voted to suspend the strike Sept. 18 and returned to work the following day. CTU formally ratified the new agreement Oct. 4.

Federal Reserve to Buy Mortgage Bonds; Other Economic News—In an effort to stimulate the economy, the Federal Reserve announced Sept. 13 that it would begin buying mortgage-backed securities at a rate of $40 bil per month and continue to do so until the job market significantly improved, so long as inflation didn't spiral out of control. This bond-buying program was the third round of quantitative easing—bond-buying to stimulate the economy—since the recession began in 2007 and would be carried out in conjunction with the Federal Reserve's purchase of $45 bil of Treasury bonds per month through the end of 2012. The Fed also pledged to keep short-term interest rates near zero until mid-2015. Democrats praised the announcement, but Republican presidential nominee Mitt Romney described the move as further evidence that Obama's economic policies had failed.

The Labor Dept. reported Sept. 7 that 96,000 jobs had been added to the U.S. economy, a figure that failed to meet economists' expectations. The unemployment rate dropped from 8.3% to 8.1%, but some analysts believed the drop was due to 368,000 people ceasing to look for work. The labor-force participation rate—the percentage of the working-age population in the work force—fell to 63.5%, its lowest level since Sept. 1981. The stock markets, nonetheless, remained steady in Sept. The Dow Jones Industrial Average rose 2.65%, ending the month at 13,437.13, while the S&P 500 finished the month at 1,440.67, up 2.42%. The Nasdaq Composite Index rose 49.27 points, or 1.61%, to close at 3,116.23.

Justice Department Issues Report on Gun-Trafficking Program—Justice Dept. Inspector Gen. Michael Horowitz Sept 19 issued the final report on Operation Fast and Furious, the Bureau of Alcohol, Tobacco, Firearms, and Explosives' notorious failed gun-trafficking sting. Horowitz found that several Justice Dept. officials—including Assistant Deputy Attorney Gen. Jason Weinstein, who resigned Sept. 19, and the head of the Justice Dept.'s criminal division, Lanny Breuer—had allowed "a series of misguided strategies, tactics, errors in judgement, and management failures" to undermine the operation. Attorney Gen. Eric Holder, who had been held in contempt of Congress over their investigation earlier in the year, was largely exonerated by the report, which maintained he had been unaware of the tactics used during the operation.

International

Iraqi Vice President Sentenced to Death—Iraqi Vice Pres. Tariq al-Hashemi Sept. 9 was sentenced to death in absentia by the Central Criminal Court of Iraq for his alleged involvement in the murder of a lawyer and a security officer. Al-Hashemi, a Sunni Muslim, had been accused of being behind death squads, and a judicial panel found him responsible for 150 or more terrorist attacks in 2005-11, but neither of those accusations was related to his murder conviction. Sunnis condemned the sentence, discounting it as an effort of Prime Min. Nouri al-Maliki's Shiite-led government to marginalize Sunnis. From Turkey, al-Hashemi described the verdict as "false and unjust," and Turkey Pres. Recep Tayyip Erdogan Sept. 11 proclaimed al-Hashemi's innocence, vowing not to turn him over to Iraq.

Muslim World Responds to Anti-Islam Film; U.S. Ambassador to Libya Killed—Protests broke out Sept. 11 outside the U.S. embassy in Cairo in response to the broadcast on Egyptian TV of clips from a crude film called *The Innocence of Muslims*, which mocked Islam and the Prophet Muhammad and originated in the U.S. Demonstrations turned violent and unrest quickly spread. Protests erupted in Iran, Iraq, Yemen, Tunisia, Sudan, Lebanon, Afghanistan, Pakistan, and elsewhere.

The U.S. consulate in Benghazi, Libya, was stormed the night of Sept. 11-12, and U.S. ambassador to Libya J. Christopher Stevens and three other U.S. citizens—Sean Smith, Tyrone Woods, and Glen Doherty—were killed. U.S. officials later identified the attack as an act of terrorism by those using outrage over the video as a cover for the attack.

NATO Forces Curtail Joint Missions With Afghans; Other Developments—In response to a rise in insider attacks by Afghan security personnel on coalition forces—a quarter of which were traced to the Taliban—U.S. Marine Gen. John Allen, commander of coalition forces in Afghanistan, issued orders Sept. 16 that required missions involving Afghan and coalition forces to be preapproved by generals in charge of regional commands. Most joint missions had served to prepare Afghan troops for taking over of security in the country after the withdrawal of the coalition in 2014. The new orders raised concerns about the effectiveness of the coalition's training mission. U.S. Defense Sec. Leon Panetta further noted, Sept. 18, that changes to operational rules would not alter the coalition's withdrawal plan. More than 50 coalition troops had been killed by insider attacks—also known as "green-on-blue" attacks—by the end of Sept. 2012.

Syrian Military Headquarters Bombed in Damascus; Other Developments—Two large blasts struck the Syrian military headquarters in Damascus Sept. 26, killing four guards. The facility was then attacked by rebels with the Free Syrian Army, and a gun battle ensued. The incident demonstrated the strength of insurgency and the inability of Pres. Bashar al-Assad's regime to protect high profile targets. A day earlier, rebels bombed a Damascus school building, which the insurgency claimed was used as a government military base, killing dozens of Syrian government security personnel.

Elsewhere in Syria, government bombs in Aleppo damaged main water pipes, leaving hundreds of thousands without drinking water. The Syrian army Sept. 8 attacked Tel Shehab, where refugees waited to enter Jordan, and the Syrian air force, Sept. 19, pursued rebels into Lebanon. Rebel forces drove government forces out of Tal Abyad, a post along the Turkish border, and the next day, Syria's military killed at least 30 in an attack in nearby Ain Issa. Meanwhile, the Free Syrian Army, Sept. 22, moved its headquarters from Turkey into Syria, in an attempt to gain credibility with the myriad groups fighting in the against Assad's regime, and to quell the Turkish people's discontent with playing host to the Syrian opposition.

General

Williams, Murray Win U.S. Open Tennis Titles—Fresh off her gold-medal win at the Olympic Games in London, Serena Williams of the U.S. Sept. 9 beat top-ranked Victoria Azarenka of Belarus (6-2, 2-6, 7-5) to capture her fourth U.S. Open women's singles title at Arthur Ashe Stadium in Flushing, NY. Williams first won the U.S. Open in 1999; the 13 years between her first title and this year's win was the longest span between Grand Slam victories in the professional era. Andy Murray of Scotland defeated Novak Djokovic of Serbia (7-6 (10), 7-5, 2-6, 3-6, 6-2) to win his first Grand Slam title Sept. 11. Murray became the first British man to win a Grand Slam since Fred Perry won Wimbledon in 1936.

***Modern Family, Homeland* Take Top Emmy Honors—** ABC sitcom *Modern Family* was honored for the third year in a row as Outstanding Comedy Series, winning four Emmys in all, including supporting actor awards for Julie Bowen and Eric Stonestreet, at the Primetime Emmy Awards at Los Angeles's Nokia Theatre, Sept. 23. Showtime's *Homeland* was named Outstanding Drama Series, with Claire Danes and Damien Lewis from the show taking the top drama acting prizes. *The Daily Show With Jon Stewart* earned its 10th consecutive Emmy as Outstanding Variety Series. Critics' favorite *Mad Men*, which led all shows with 17 Emmy nominations, did not take home a single prize.

Europeans Retain Ryder Cup—The European Ryder Cup team made an historic comeback to beat the U.S. on the last day of the 39th Ryder Cup, Sept. 30, at Medinah Country Club in Medinah, IL. Going into the final day, the U.S. team was leading 10-6 and needed to win only 4½ of the 12 available points to take the cup back from Europe. At the end of the day, German Martin Kaymer sank a five-foot putt on the 18th green to get to 14 points, and Tiger Woods bogeyed on the final green to give Europe the improbable 14½-13½ win.

October 2012
National

Presidential Nominees Face Off in Debates—Pres. Barack Obama (D) and former Massachusetts Gov. Mitt Romney (R) met Oct. 3 at the Univ. of Denver in Denver, CO, in the first debate of the 2012 presidential campaign, to discuss domestic policy and economic issues. Romney took more moderate stances than those he had proposed on the campaign trail, criticizing Obama for believing "a bigger government, spending more, taxing more, regulating more—if you will, trickle-down government" would fix the economy. Obama, by contrast, characterized Romney's ideas as the same "top-down economic policies" that caused the 2008 financial crisis. The candidates also clashed over health care, as Romney reiterated his promise to repeal the Affordable Care Act of 2010. Romney's aggressive performance contrasted with Obama's somewhat listless presence, leading pundits to declare Romney the winner, re-energizing his campaign. The vice-presidential nominees met in their only scheduled debate Oct. 11 at Centre Coll. in Danville, KY. Vice Pres. Joe Biden squared off aggressively against Rep. Paul Ryan (R, WI) on foreign policy and economic philosophy, particularly on entitlement programs.

Obama and Romney met Oct. 16 for their second debate, a town hall-style forum in which they took questions from the audience at Hofstra Univ. in Hempstead, NY. Obama, who had fallen in recent polls, was more aggressive, defending his record and criticizing Romney's statement that 47% of Americans—those who pay no federal income tax—were freeloaders. Romney slammed Obama's economic policies while claiming that his own five-point economic plan would create 12 mil new jobs. This time, the pundits gave Obama the victory. Both candidates largely played it safe in a final debate on foreign policy Oct. 22 at Lynn Univ. in Boca Raton, FL. Romney agreed with many of Obama's foreign policy positions while criticizing the president for failing to display strong leadership.

Islamic Cleric Pleads Not Guilty to U.S. Terrorism Charges—Egyptian-born Islamic cleric Abu Hamza al-Masri Oct. 9 pleaded not guilty in U.S. District Court in New York, NY, to 11 counts of terrorism. Al-Masri, a British citizen, had been extradited to the U.S., Oct. 5-6. He faced allegations that he had conspired with two Seattle men to establish a terrorist training camp in Oregon, and aided in the abduction of 16 people—two of them American—in Yemen in 1998. His trial was set to begin Aug. 26, 2013. Four other men, Khaled al-Fawwaz, Adel Abdul Bary, Babar Ahmad,

and Seyla Talha Ahsan, were extradited from Britain to the U.S. along with al-Masri. Al-Fawwaz and Bary pleaded not guilty to their alleged involvement in the Aug. 1998 bombings of U.S. embassies in Tanzania and Kenya in a separate hearing in U.S. District Court that same day.

Federal Appeals Court Again Strikes Down DOMA— The federal Defense of Marriage Act (DOMA), which defined marriage as between a man and a woman, was ruled unconstitutional Oct. 18, in a 2-1 decision by the Second Circuit Court of Appeals in New York, NY. The case under consideration, *Windsor v. United States*, involved Edith Windsor, who sued the government after receiving an estate-tax bill for $363,053 related to the inheritance that she received from her wife, whom she married in Canada in 2007 and who died in 2009. No such tax would have been levied against a surviving opposite-sex spouse. Judge Dennis Jacobs argued in his majority opinion that DOMA violated the Constitution's 14th Amendment, which guarantees equal protection under the law. In his dissenting opinion, Judge Chester Straub asserted that the issue of same-sex marriage was "not for the courts to decide."

Hurricane Sandy Cripples the Northeast—The second-largest Atlantic storm on record (after 2001's Hurricane Olga) was technically a post-tropical cyclone when it made landfall near Atlantic City, NJ, on Oct. 29, but Sandy still packed 90-mph winds and caused massive devastation across New Jersey and the New York metropolitan area. Storm surges caused major damage and flooded towns along the New Jersey coast as well as New York's Staten Island, lower Manhattan, and parts of Brooklyn and Queens. Winds brought down trees, downed power lines, and damaged homes along the coast. Flood waters kept firefighters from devastating blazes, particularly in the Breezy Point neighborhood of Queens, NY, where more than 100 homes burned to the ground. Even after the storm passed, as many as 6.2 mil people remained without power throughout the Northeast; 113 were confirmed dead; and an estimated $50 bil in damage had been caused. Flooded tunnels and debris on the tracks between Manhattan, New Jersey, and Long Island crippled regional transit, including New York City's subway system, which had been shut down in advance of the storm.

Hurricane Sandy had formed as a tropical cyclone, Oct. 22, and passed through Jamaica, Cuba, and the Bahamas, killing at least 69 in the Caribbean. Reaching the U.S., it merged with an approaching cold front, which brought snow storms to parts of North Carolina, Pennsylvania, Virginia, and West Virginia.

Unemployment Rate Falls Below 8%—The U.S. Labor Dept. reported Oct. 5 that 114,000 jobs had been added to the U.S. economy, and the unemployment rate fell from 8.1% to 7.8%, its lowest monthly rate since Jan. 2009. Unlike previous decreases in unemployment, the Sept. decrease was not due to unemployed workers becoming discouraged and leaving the labor force altogether. However, some of the decline was attributed to job-seekers accepting part-time rather than full-time work. The stock markets reacted tepidly to the numbers. For the month, the Dow Jones Industrial Average fell 2.5%, losing 340.67 points and closing at 13,096.46; the S&P 500 fell 2.0%, losing 28.51 points and closing at 1,412.16; and the Nasdaq Composite Index declined 4.5%, losing 139 points and closing at 2,977.23.

International

Georgia Elections Choose New Prime Minister— A coalition of opposition parties called Georgian Dream won 55.1% of the vote in Georgia's Oct. 1 parliamentary elections, defeating Pres. Mikheil Saakashvili's United National Movement, which took 40.1%. The United National Movement had been ahead in the polls until Sept. 18, when videos of abused prisoners surfaced. (The prison population had quadrupled under Saakashvili's presidency.) Georgian Dream was backed by billionaire Bidzina Ivanishvili, who had only been active in politics for about a year but became prime minister Oct. 25. He had criticized Saakashvili, who had strengthened Georgia's ties to the U.S., for pursuing international aspirations at the expense of regional interests. But Ivanishvili promised his first international visit would be to the U.S., suggesting that he will maintain strong ties between the two countries.

EU Wins Nobel Peace Prize; Greeks Protest Merkel Visit to Athens—Norway's Nobel Committee Oct. 12 announced that the European Union (EU) was the Nobel Peace Prize winner. In its statement announcing the award, the Committee praised the EU for contributing "to the advancement of peace and reconciliation, democracy, and human rights in Europe" for over six decades. EU leaders welcomed the award, but critics felt the honor was inappropriate for a political body imposing unwanted austerity measures—which have been widely blamed for exacerbating the economic crisis that they were meant to alleviate—throughout Europe.

During an Oct. 9 visit to Athens, German Chancellor Angela Merkel urged Greece's parliament to continue implementing spending cuts and tax increases in order to combat the country's debt problem and ensure its continued membership in the European Union. Tens of thousands of protesters marched through the streets of Athens on Oct. 5, in advance of Merkel's visit, and again during the six hours she was in Greece. Police detained some 200 protesters and arrested more than 20. The country's largest unions staged a general strike Oct. 18, which corresponded with the beginning of a two-day EU summit on the economic crisis. Although the strike was largely peaceful, some protesters threw gas bombs and bottles at police.

Syria Conflict Spreads Beyond Its Borders—In response to Syria's shelling of the Turkish border town of Akcakale and the killing of five civilians, Turkey attacked military targets within Syria Oct. 3-8, and the Turkish parliament Oct. 4 authorized the use of ground forces within Syria if attacks on Turkey continued. The moves deepened Turkey's involvement in the Syrian conflict, as it demanded the UN Security Council act and called an emergency meeting with the rest of NATO. On Oct. 10, Turkey forced a Syrian Arab Airlines passenger jet traveling from Moscow to Damascus to land in Ankara and confiscated cargo allegedly containing missile components and military communications equipment.

A car bomb exploded Oct. 19 in Beirut, Lebanon, killing Wissam al-Hassan, the Lebanese intelligence chief. Lebanese officials immediately blamed the attack on Syrian Pres. Bashar al-Assad's government, which wanted to halt Hassan's investigation of an apparent Syrian plot to destabilize Lebanon through a campaign of terrorist bombings. The investigation had already led to the indictment of Michel Samaha, a former Lebanese information minister, and two Syrian officials.

Afghan Officials Set Date for Next Presidential Election—Noor Ahmad Noor, a spokesperson for Afghanistan's Independent Election Commission, announced Oct. 30 that Afghanistan's next presidential election would take place Apr. 5, 2014. There had been speculation that Pres. Hamid Karzai, who was constitutionally barred from a third term, would delay the vote because of security concerns surrounding the planned departure of foreign troops in 2014. The political opposition welcomed the announcement but urged the government to ensure that the vote would be free and fair; the previous election, in 2009, was widely seen as corrupt. Opposition leaders also feared that Pres. Karzai might veto a bill passed by the parliament's lower house that would mandate two UN-appointed foreigners on the country's five-person Electoral Complaints Commission. In the meantime, attacks on coalition forces continued, raising fears that international troops would pull out earlier than expected and be gone before the elections.

General

Brees Breaks Unitas's 52-Year-Old Record—New Orleans Saints quarterback Drew Brees Oct. 7 broke Hall of Fame quarterback Johnny Unitas's 52-year-old record for consecutive games with a touchdown pass. A 40-yard scoring toss to Devery Henderson in the first quarter of the Saints' 31-24 defeat of the San Diego Chargers marked Brees' 48th straight game with a touchdown pass; by Nov. 5, he had extended the streak to 51 games. The NFL allowed Saints coach Sean Payton, assistant head coach Joe Vitt, and general manager Mickey Loomis—all of whom had been suspended as a result of the NFL investigation into the Saints' alleged defensive "bounty" program—to attend the game per Brees's request.

Owners' Lockout Threatens 2012-13 Hockey Season—The National Hockey League Oct. 4 canceled the first two weeks of the season that had been scheduled to begin Oct. 11. Team owners had locked out their players Sept. 15 when the league's previous collective bargaining agreement expired. The league Oct. 26 canceled all games through the month of Nov. after the owners withdrew a contract proposal that would give the players a 50-50 split of hockey-related revenues. The players had already rejected the proposal, which offered them 7% less revenue than they had earned under the previous contract that expired in Sept. On Nov. 2, the NHL also canceled the Winter Classic—an outdoor game in Ann Arbor, MI, which had been slated for Jan. 1, 2013—causing fans to fear the cancellation of the entire season for the second time in a decade.

San Francisco Giants Win World Series; Cabrera Wins Triple Crown—With a 10-inning 4-3 win Oct. 28 in Game 4 of the World Series at Comerica Park in Detroit, MI, the San Francisco Giants completed a sweep of the Detroit Tigers to become world champions for the second time in three seasons. San Francisco's dominance of the Tigers was in marked contrast to the come-from-behind wins that brought the Giants to the World Series. In the Division Series, the Giants dropped the first two games at home against the Cincinnati Reds, only to take the next three on the road. In the National League Championship Series, San Francisco lost three of the first four games against the defending champion St. Louis Cardinals but rallied to win the last three contests. It was a turnabout for the Tigers as well, who had easily swept the NY Yankees in the American League Championship Series. Giants' third baseman Pablo Sandoval, who in Game 1 became only the fourth man in history to hit three home runs in a single World Series game, was named MVP of the Fall Classic.

Miguel Cabrera of the Detroit Tigers ended the 2012 regular season, Oct. 3, with the highest batting average (.330), the most home runs (44), and the most RBIs (139) in the American League. Those numbers made him the first player to win baseball's Triple Crown since 1967, when Carl Yastrzemski of the Boston Red Sox claimed it. Joining a list of such elite players as Mickey Mantle, Ted Williams, and Lou Gehrig, Cabrera became only the 15th player in MLB history to accomplish the feat.

Disney Acquires Lucasfilm—Walt Disney Co. announced Oct. 30 a deal to acquire Lucasfilm, the production studio owned by *Star Wars* creator George Lucas. Disney would pay approximately $4 bil, consisting of 40 mil new Disney shares and another $2 bil in cash, to take control of the *Star Wars* franchise—which had grossed approximately $4 bil worldwide since the first film's 1977 release—among other assets. Explaining the decision to sell, Lucas said, "I've always believed that *Star Wars* could live beyond me, and I thought it was important to set up the transition during my lifetime." Lucas had previously said he would never produce additional films in the *Star Wars* series, which currently stands at six episodes. But Disney immediately announced that it would release a new *Star Wars* film in 2015, with others following every two to three years after that.

OBITUARIES

(Nov. 1, 2011-Oct. 31, 2012)

A

Adler, Richard, 90, composer and lyricist; cowrote Tony Award-winning musicals *The Pajama Game* (1954) and *Damn Yankees* (1955); Southampton, NY, June 21, 2012.

Alou, Matty, 72, Dominican baseball player for San Francisco, Pittsburgh, others; made history playing in game with two brothers (1963); Miami, FL, Nov. 3, 2011.

Anderson, Bob, 89, British Olympic fencer and swordfight choreographer known for work on *Star Wars* films; West Sussex, Eng., UK, Jan. 1, 2012.

Anthony, Charles, 82, opera tenor who sang a record 57 seasons at the Metropolitan Opera (NY); Tampa, FL, Feb. 15, 2012.

Aramony, William, 84, United Way of America CEO; served prison time for misuse of funds; Alexandria, VA, Nov. 11, 2011.

Armstrong, Neil, 82, astronaut who was the first to make "one giant leap for mankind," by setting foot on the Moon (1969); Cincinnati, OH, Aug. 25, 2012.

Asher, William, 90, TV director best known for *Bewitched* (1964-72), starring wife Elizabeth Montgomery, and 100 episodes of *I Love Lucy* (1952-57); Palm Desert, CA, July 16, 2012.

Aubrac, Raymond, 97, French resistance leader in Nazi-occupied France; Paris, France, Apr. 10, 2012.

B

Baldrige, Letitia, 86, etiquette expert who served as Jacqueline Kennedy's social secretary; Bethesda, MD, Oct. 29, 2012.

Barzun, Jacques, 104, French-American historian and educator in cultural history; San Antonio, TX, Oct. 25, 2012.

Becher, Barry, 71, marketer best known for cocreating the Ginsu knife TV commercials; Ft. Lauderdale, FL, June 22, 2012.

Ben Bella, Ahmed, 93, Algerian revolutionary who became the first president of Algeria (1963-65); Algiers, Algeria, Apr. 11, 2012.

Berenstain, Jan(ice), 88, children's book writer who with her husband Stan wrote and illustrated book series the *Berenstain Bears*; Solebury, PA, Feb. 24, 2012.

Binchy, Maeve, 72, Irish novelist whose novels, typically set in midcentury Ireland, told stories of women's relationships and crises; Dublin, Ireland, July 30, 2012.

Bogart, Paul, 92, Emmy Award-winning TV director best known for *All in the Family* (1975-79); Chapel Hill, NC, Apr. 15, 2012.

Boozer, Bob, 75, basketball player; won Olympic gold (1960) and helped Milwaukee Bucks to NBA championship (1971); Omaha, NE, May 19, 2012.

Borgnine, Ernest, 95, actor best known for tough guy roles; he won an Oscar for *Marty* (1955) and starred in the TV sitcom *McHale's Navy* (1962-66); Los Angeles, CA, July 8, 2012.

Bormann, F(rederick) Herbert, 90, ecologist whose research discovered acid rain in North America; North Branford, CT, June 7, 2012.

Bouchard, Émile "Butch," 92, Canadian Hall of Fame hockey player whose defense helped the Montréal Canadiens (1941-56) win four Stanley Cups; Brossard, QC, Canada, Apr. 14, 2012.

Bradbury, Ray, 91, science-fiction writer whose works included *The Martian Chronicles* (1950) and *Fahrenheit 451* (1953); Los Angeles, CA, June 5, 2012.

Breitbart, Andrew, 43, conservative writer and blogger known for political exposés; Los Angeles, CA, Mar. 1, 2012.

Bridges, Steve, 48, impressionist best known for his mimicry of Pres. George W. Bush; Los Angeles, CA, Mar. 3, 2012.

Brown, Helen Gurley, 90, author and editor whose *Sex and the Single Girl* (1962) encouraged women's financial independence and sex outside of marriage; longtime editor of *Cosmopolitan* magazine (1965-97); New York, NY, Aug. 13, 2012.

Brown, Wesley, 85, U.S. naval officer who was the first African-American graduate of Annapolis (1949); Silver Spring, MD, May 22, 2012.

Browne, Malcolm, 81, Pulitzer Prize-winning journalist and photographer best known for "burning monk" images; Hanover, NH, Aug. 27, 2012.

Burke, Sarah, 29, Canadian freestyle skier who won five Winter X Game medals; died from injuries sustained in a superpipe crash; Salt Lake City, UT, Jan. 19, 2012.

C

Cady, Frank, 96, actor best known for the TV sitcoms *Petticoat Junction* (1963-70) and *Green Acres* (1965-71); Wilsonville, OR, June 8, 2012.

Carter, Don, 85, Hall of Fame bowler and first president of the Professional Bowlers Assn.; Miami, FL, Jan. 5, 2012.

Carter, Gary, 57, Hall of Fame catcher for the Montréal Expos and NY Mets who helped the Mets win the World Series (1986); West Palm Beach, FL, Feb. 16, 2012.

Carter, Robert, 94, attorney and federal judge; played key role in *Brown v. Board of Education* (1954); New York, NY, Jan. 3, 2012.

Cassie, Alex, 95, British RFA officer who helped Allied POWs escape from the Stalag Luft III camp during World War II; incident dramatized in the film *The Great Escape* (1963); Surrey, Eng., UK, Apr. 5, 2012.

Chamberlain, John, 84, sculptor best known for large-scale works made from automotive parts; New York, NY, Dec. 21, 2011.

Chertok, Boris, 99, Russian rocket engineer on early USSR spacecrafts; Moscow, Russia, Dec. 14, 2011.

Clark, Dick, 82, TV host and producer of *American Bandstand* (1956-89), *The $10,000 Pyramid* (1973-88), and *Dick Clark's New Year's Rockin' Eve* (1972-2011); Santa Monica, CA, Apr. 18, 2012.

Cockburn, Alexander, 71, Scottish-American left-wing columnist for *Village Voice* and *The Nation*; Bad Salzhausen, Germany, July 21, 2012.

Colson, Charles, 80, counsel to Pres. Richard Nixon who went to prison for obstructing justice in the Watergate scandal (1973); later became an evangelical leader; Fairfax, VA, Apr. 21, 2012.

Colvin, Marie, 56, journalist and war correspondent for UK's *Sunday Times*; died covering the siege of Homs, Syria; Feb. 22, 2012.

Commoner, Barry, 95, biologist whose study of ecology concluded that technology was a principal cause of environmental problems; New York, NY, Sept. 30, 2012.

Cornelius, Don, 75, TV host and producer best known for *Soul Train* (1970-2006); Sherman Oaks, CA, Feb. 1, 2012.

Covey, Stephen, 79, educator and consultant who wrote the best seller *The Seven Habits of Highly Effective People* (1989); Idaho Falls, ID, July 16, 2012.

Cowan, George, 92, chemist who helped build the first atomic bomb; worked at Los Alamos Natl. Laboratory for 40 years; Los Alamos, NM, Apr. 20, 2012.

Crews, Harry, 76, novelist who wrote darkly comic, Southern gothic tales; Gainesville, FL, Mar. 28, 2012.

Crist, Judith, 90, film critic and reviewer for the *Today* show (1963-73) and *TV Guide* (1966-88); New York, NY, Aug. 7, 2012.

Cunningham, Marion, 90, chef and food writer who revised *The Fannie Farmer Cookbook* in the late 1970s; Walnut Creek, CA, July 11, 2012.

D

David, Hal, 91, Oscar and Grammy Award-winning lyricist who with Burt Bacharach wrote "What the World Needs Now Is Love" and "Raindrops Keep Fallin' on My Head"; Los Angeles, CA, Sept. 1, 2012.

Davidson, Ben, 72, All-Pro football defensive end most associated with the Oakland Raiders (1964-71) and his handlebar mustache; San Diego, CA, July 2, 2012.

Dawson, Richard, 79, British-American TV actor best known for *Hogan's Heroes* (1965-71) and as host of game show *Family Feud* (1976-85); Los Angeles, CA, June 2, 2012.

Delaney, Shelagh, 72, British playwright and screenwriter best known for her first work, *A Taste of Honey* (1958); Suffolk, Eng., UK, Nov. 20, 2011.

Diller, Phyllis, 95, comedian and actress whose wild hair, loud clothing, and unusual laugh were trademarks during a 50-year career; Los Angeles, CA, Aug. 20, 2012.

Dokes, Michael, 54, world heavyweight boxing champion (1982) later convicted of attempting to murder his girlfriend; Akron, OH, Aug. 11, 2012.

Dulbecco, Renato, 97, Nobel Prize-winning Italian-American virologist who did work on how viruses invade cells and cause cancer; San Diego, CA, Feb. 19, 2012.

Duncan, Michael Clarke, 54, Oscar-nominated actor best known for his role in *The Green Mile* (1999); Los Angeles, CA, Sept. 3, 2012.

Dundee, Angelo, 90, boxing trainer who worked with Muhammad Ali and other champions during a 60-year career; Clearwater, FL, Feb. 1, 2012.

Dunn, Donald "Duck," 70, bass player with Booker T and the MGs, the Blues Brothers; Tokyo, Japan, May 13, 2012.

E

Ephron, Nora, 71, writer-director known for romantic comedies such as *When Harry Met Sally…* (1989), *Sleepless in Seattle* (1993); New York, NY, June 26, 2012.

Everett, Chad, 75, TV actor best known for *Medical Center* (1969-76); Los Angeles, CA, July 24, 2012.

F

Faas, Horst, 79, German Pulitzer Prize-winning war photographer and editor best known for Vietnam War images; Munich, Germany, May 10, 2012.

Fairfax, John, 74, British adventurer; first to row across the Atlantic Ocean alone (1969); Henderson, NV, Feb. 8, 2012.

Farentino, James, 73, actor in TV, film, and theater; pleaded no contest to stalking former girlfriend Tina Sinatra (1994); Los Angeles, CA, Jan. 24, 2012.

Fischer-Dieskau, Dietrich, 86, German operatic baritone best known for singing lieder; Starnberg, Germany, May 18, 2012.

Frankenthaler, Helen, 83, abstract painter known for use of color; pioneered a staining technique known as Color Field painting; Darien, CT, Dec. 27, 2011.

Frazier, "Smokin'" Joe, 67, world heavyweight boxing champion (1970-73) who beat rival Muhammad Ali in "Fight of the Century" (1971); Philadelphia, PA, Nov. 7, 2011.

Freeman, Al, Jr., 78, Emmy Award-winning TV, film, and theater actor; Washington, DC, Aug. 9, 2012.

Freeman, Von, 89, bebop tenor saxophonist whose fame as a jazz master came late in life; Chicago, IL, Aug. 11, 2012.

Frid, Jonathan, 87, Canadian actor best known for the gothic soap opera *Dark Shadows* (1966-71); Hamilton, ON, Canada, Apr. 14, 2012.

Fuentes, Carlos, 83, Mexican writer whose works centered on criticism of the government; Mexico City, Mexico, May 8, 2012.

Fussell, Paul, Jr., 88, literary scholar; National Book Award-winning author of *The Great War and Modern Memory* (1975); Medford, OR, May 23, 2012.

G

Gallup, George, Jr., 81, businessman who expanded his father's polling company; Princeton, NJ, Nov. 21, 2011.

Gazzara, Ben, 81, Emmy Award-winning actor known for his intense performances; New York, NY, Feb. 2, 2012.

Gibb, Robin, 62, British singer and songwriter best known as a member of the Bee Gees; London, Eng., UK, May 20, 2012.

Giraud, Jean, 73, French cartoonist whose science fiction and fantasy works were signed Moebius; Paris, France, Mar. 10, 2012.

Glazer, Samuel, 89, businessman who cofounded the company that manufactured Mr. Coffee coffee makers; Cleveland, OH, Mar. 12, 2012.

Green, Florence, 110, last known surviving veteran of World War I; Norfolk, Eng., UK, Feb. 4, 2012.

Griffith, Andy, 86, actor and Grammy Award-winning singer known for *The Andy Griffith Show* (1960-68) and *Matlock* (1986-95); Roanoke Island, VA, July 3, 2012.

H

Hamlisch, Marvin, 68, composer who received an Oscar for *The Way We Were* (1973) and a Pulitzer and Tony for *A Chorus Line* (1975); Los Angeles, CA, Aug. 6, 2012.

Havel, Vaclav, 75, playwright and activist who was the Czech Republic's first president (1993-2003); Hrádecek, Czech Republic, Dec. 18, 2011.

Heavy D (Dwight Myers), 44, Jamaican-American rapper, record producer, and actor; Los Angeles, CA, Nov. 8, 2011.

Heester, Johannes, 108, Dutch actor and singer whose work in Nazi entertainment caused controversy; Starnberg, Germany, Dec. 24, 2012.

Hegyes, Robert, 60, actor best known as Juan Epstein on *Welcome Back, Kotter* (1975-79); Edison, NJ, Jan. 26, 2012.

Helm, Levon, 71, singer and drummer for The Band; New York, NY, Apr. 19, 2012.

Hemsley, Sherman, 74, TV actor best remembered for *The Jeffersons* (1975-85); El Paso, TX, July 24, 2012.

Henze, Hans Werner, 86, German composer of operas and orchestral works; Dresden, Germany, Oct. 27, 2012.

Heymann, C. David, 67, best-selling biographer of Jacqueline Kennedy Onassis and Elizabeth Taylor; New York, NY, May 9, 2012.

Higham, Charles, 81, British celebrity biographer whose sensational charges created controversy; Los Angeles, CA, Apr. 21, 2012.

Hill, Henry, 69, gangster turned informant who inspired the Martin Scorsese film *Goodfellas* (1990); Los Angeles, CA, June 12, 2012.

Hirabayashi, Gordon, 93, sociologist imprisoned as a student for challenging the internment of Japanese Americans; Edmonton, AB, Canada, Jan. 2, 2012.

Hitchens, Christopher, 62, British-American writer whose work included scathing criticism of public figures and religion; Houston, TX, Dec. 15, 2011.

Holm, Celeste, 95, Oscar-winning actress best known for supporting roles; created the role of Ado Annie in *Oklahoma!* (1943); New York, NY, July 15, 2012.

Houston, Whitney, 48, Grammy Award-winning singer and actress who was the best-selling female R&B artist of the 20th century; Beverly Hills, CA, Feb. 11, 2012.

Huxley, Andrew, 94, British Nobel Prize-winning physiologist who discovered how nerve impulses are transmitted through cells; Cambridge, Eng., UK, May 30, 2012.

I

Ingle, John, 84, actor best known for the soap opera *General Hospital* (1993-2012); Los Angeles, CA, Sept. 16, 2012.

J

Jackson, Hal, 96, one of the first African-American disc jockeys, he had lengthy on-air career (1939-2012); New York, NY, May 23, 2012.

James, Etta, 73, R&B singer best known for signature song "At Last" (1961); Riverside, CA, Jan. 20, 2012.

Janklow, Bill, 72, four-time South Dakota governor; served in Congress (R, SD) until manslaughter conviction for killing a motorcyclist while speeding (2004); Sioux Falls, SD, Jan. 12, 2012.

Johansen, John, 96, architect who was the last surviving member of the "Harvard Five" group of Modernist architects; Brewster, MA, Oct. 26, 2012.

Jones, Davy, 66, British pop singer and actor who rose to fame as a member of The Monkees; Indiantown, FL, Feb. 29, 2012.

Joosten, Kathryn, 72, Emmy Award-winning character actress best known for *Desperate Housewives* (2005-12) and *The West Wing* (1999-2002); Westlake Village, CA, June 2, 2012.

Josephson, Erland, 88, Swedish actor who frequently worked with director Ingmar Bergman; Stockholm, Sweden, Feb. 25, 2012.

K

Kanter, Hal, 92, Emmy Award-winning screenwriter and director who created *Julia* (1968-71), the first TV show to feature a black woman as a working professional; Encino, CA, Nov. 6, 2011.

Karras, Alex, 77, NFL defensive tackle who became an actor; Los Angeles, CA, Oct. 10, 2012.

Katzenback, Nicholas, 90, lawyer who helped pass the Civil Rights Act (1964) and Voting Rights Act (1965); Skillman, NJ, May 8, 2012.

Keane, Bil, 89, cartoonist who created *The Family Circus*; Paradise Valley, AZ, Nov. 8, 2011.

Kennedy, Mary, 52, architect who was the estranged wife of Robert F. Kennedy Jr.; Bedford, NY, May 16, 2012.

Kim Jong Il, 69, North Korean dictator (1994-2011) who made his country a nuclear power while millions starved; also known for eccentric behavior; North Korea, Dec. 17, 2011.

King, Rodney, 47, African-American whose beating by Los Angeles police was caught on video (1991); acquittal of the officers touched off widespread riots (1992); Rialto, CA, June 17, 2012.

Kinkade, Thomas, 54, painter of sentimental scenes whose prints were owned by millions but disdained by art critics; Monte Sereno, CA, Apr. 6, 2012.

Kordek, Steve, 100, game designer who added two flippers to pinball machines and revolutionized the game; Park Ridge, IL, Feb. 19, 2012.

Kubert, Joe, 85, Poland-born cartoonist known for DC Comic characters Tor and Sgt. Rock; Morristown, NJ, Aug. 12, 2012.

L

Lauder, Evelyn, 75, Estée Lauder executive who cocreated the pink ribbon as a symbol of breast health; founded the Breast Cancer Research Foundation (1993); New York, NY, Nov. 12, 2011.

Lear, Evelyn, 86, operatic soprano known for versatility and musicianship; Sandy Spring, MD, July 1, 2012.

Ledley, Robert, 86, biophysicist who invented the full-body CT (computerized tomographic) scanner; Kensington, MD, July 24, 2012.

Lender, Murray, 81, businessman who expanded family business H. Lender & Sons, introducing frozen bagels and creating a nationwide brand; Miami, FL, Mar. 21, 2012.

Lenzi, Mark, 43, Olympic gold medalist in diving (1992); Greenville, NC, Apr. 9, 2012.

Lewis, Judy, 76, actress and writer who was the secret child of actors Clark Gable and Loretta Young (Young adopted and raised her); Gladwyne, PA, Nov. 24, 2011.

Lindsey, George, 83, actor best known as Goober Pyle on *The Andy Griffith Show* (1964-68), *Mayberry R.F.D.* (1968-71), and *Hee Haw* (1971-92); Nashville, TN, May 6, 2012.

Lom, Herbert, 95, Czech actor best remembered for his role as the chief inspector in the *Pink Panther* films (1963-93); London, Eng., UK, Sept. 27, 2012.

Lovell, Bernard, 98, British radio astronomer who cocreated the Jodrell Bank radio telescope; Cheshire, Eng., UK, Aug. 6, 2012.

M

Maas, Frederica Sagor, 111, screenwriter from the silent film era; La Mesa, CA, Jan. 5, 2012.

Macauley, Ed, 83, center for Boston Celtics who, at 32, was youngest Hall of Fame inductee; St. Louis, MO, Nov. 8, 2011.

Maletta, Lou, 74, activist who founded the Gay Cable Network (1982-2001); Kingston, NY, Nov. 2, 2011.

Mann, Theodore, 87, producer and director who cofounded the Circle in the Square Theatre (1951), which helped build an Off-Broadway movement; New York, NY, Feb. 24, 2012.

Marshall, Jim, 88, inventor of widely used Marshall amplifiers; known as the "Lord of Loud"; London, Eng., UK, Apr. 5, 2012.

Martin, Tony, 98, singer best remembered for ballads such as "There's No Tomorrow" (1969); Los Angeles, CA, July 27, 2012.

McGovern, George, 90, senator (D, SD, 1962-80) who as the Democratic nominee for president was defeated in a landslide (1972); Sioux Falls, SD, Oct. 21, 2012.

McGuire, Dorothy, 84, singer who performed with siblings as The McGuire Sisters; Paradise Valley, AZ, Sept. 7, 2012.

McKenzie, Scott, 73, singer best known for his rendition of "San Francisco (Be Sure to Wear Flowers in Your Hair)"; Los Angeles, CA, Aug. 18, 2012.

Means, Russell, 72, Oglala Sioux activist; one of the leaders of the months-long American Indian Movement occupation at Wounded Knee, SD (1973); Porcupine, SD, Oct. 22, 2012.

al-Megrahi, Abdel Basset Ali, 60, terrorist convicted in the 1988 bombing of an American jetliner over Lockerbie, Scotland, UK; Tripoli, Libya, May 20, 2012.

Milano, Fred, 72, singer with Dion and the Belmonts, best known for "A Teenager in Love" (1959); New York, NY, Jan. 2, 2012.

Modell, Art, 87, football team owner of Cleveland Browns (1961-95) and Baltimore Ravens (1996-2004) who negotiated TV coverage; Baltimore, MD, Sept. 6, 2012.

Moon, Rev. Sun Myung, 92, Korean evangelist and self-declared Messiah who founded the Unification Church; Gapyeong, South Korea, Sept. 3, 2012.

Morgan, Harry, 96, actor best remembered for *Dragnet* (1967-70) and *M*A*S*H* (1975-83); Los Angeles, CA, Dec. 7, 2011.

N

Neiman, LeRoy, 91, expressionist painter known for quick renditions of sporting events; New York, NY, June 20, 2012.

Nelson, Jerry, 78, puppeteer best known for his work with The Muppets, most notably Count von Count; Cape Cod, MA, Aug. 23, 2012.

Noble, Gil, 80, TV journalist who hosted the New York public affairs show *Like It Is* (1968-2011); Wayne, NJ, Apr. 5, 2012.

O

O'Donnell, Mark, 58, Tony Award-winning writer as co-author of Broadway's *Hairspray* (2003); New York, NY, Aug. 6, 2012.

Opel, John, 86, executive who worked at I.B.M. for 44-year period, during which the company entered the personal computer market; Fort Meyers, FL, Nov. 3, 2011.

Osborne Dupont, Margaret, 94, tennis player who won six Grand Slam singles titles in the 1940s and '50s; El Paso, TX, Oct. 24, 2012.

Ostrom, Elinor, 78, political scientist who won a Nobel Prize in economics (2009) for her work on economic governance; Bloomington, IN, June 12, 2012.

Otis, Johnny, 90, R&B singer who was instrumental in promoting black music to white audiences; Altadena, CA, Jan. 17, 2012.

Owens, Everett "Cotton," 88, Hall of Fame NASCAR driver and team owner; Spartanburg, SC, June 7, 2012.

P

Palillo, Ron, 63, actor best known as Arnold Horshack on the sitcom *Welcome Back, Kotter* (1975-79); Palm Beach Gardens, FL, Aug. 14, 2012.

Paterno, Joe, 85, Penn St. coach (1966-2011) who won more games than anyone in college football; wins from 1998-2011 were vacated in aftermath of child sex abuse scandal; State College, PA, Jan. 22, 2012.

Pesky, Johnny, 92, Red Sox shortstop, manager, broadcaster, and coach; Danvers, MA, Aug. 13, 2012.

Peters, Lana (Svetlana Stalina Alliluyeva), 85, daughter of Soviet dictator Joseph Stalin; defected to the U.S. (1967); Richland County, WI, Nov. 22, 2011.

Piaggi, Anna, 81, Italian writer, editor, and fashion icon, known for unique style; Milan, Italy, Aug. 7, 2012.

Pockriss, Lee, 87, songwriter known for "Johnny Angel" and "Itsy Bitsy Teenie Weenie Yellow Polka Dot Bikini"; Bridgewater, CT, Nov. 14, 2011.

Polley, Eugene, 96, engineer for Zenith Electronics Corp. who invented the wireless TV remote control; Downers Grove, IL, May 20, 2012.

Porsche, Ferdinand A., 76, German designer best known for the Porsche 911 sports car; Salzburg, Austria, Apr. 5, 2012.

Price, Kenneth, 77, sculptor best known for ceramics works; Arroyo Hondo, NM, Feb. 24, 2012.

Puccio, Thomas, 67, defense attorney best known for the 1985 acquittal of socialite Claus von Bülow, who had been accused of attempting to murder his wife; New Haven, CT, Mar. 12, 2012.

R

Rakoff, David, 47, Canadian-American writer and humorist whose essays focused on his experiences as a gay Jewish New Yorker; New York, NY, Aug. 9, 2012.

Ramsey, Norman, 96, Nobel Prize-winning physicist whose work led to construction of atomic clocks; Wayland, MA, Nov. 4, 2011.

Raspberry, William, 76, Pulitzer Prize-winning columnist for the *Washington Post* for 39 years; Washington, DC, July 17, 2012.

Reed, Herb, 83, founding member of The Platters, whose songs included "The Great Pretender" (1955); Boston, MA, June 4, 2012.

Rich, Adrienne, 82, poet whose work addressed struggles of women and lesbians; Santa Cruz, CA, Mar. 27, 2012.

Ride, Sally, 61, astronaut and physicist who was the first U.S. woman in space (1983); La Jolla, CA, July 23, 2012.

Rivers, Sam, 88, multi-instrument jazz musician, best known as a saxophonist and composer; Orlando, FL, Dec. 26, 2011.

Rooney, Andy, 92, radio and TV journalist best remembered for acerbic commentaries on *60 Minutes* (1978-2011); New York, NY, Nov. 4, 2011.

Ross, Al, 100, cartoonist whose work appeared in the *New Yorker* for more than 60 years; Bronx, NY, Mar. 22, 2012.

Rosset, Barney, Jr., 89, owner of Grove Press; efforts to publish Henry Miller's *Tropic of Cancer* led to a landmark U.S. Supreme Court decision on freedom of speech (1964); New York, NY, Feb. 21, 2012.

Russell, Ken, 84, British film director best known for *Women in Love* (1969) and *The Devils* (1971); London, Eng., UK, Nov. 27, 2011.

Rutherford, Ann, 94, Canadian-American actress best known for roles in Andy Hardy movies and in *Gone With the Wind* (1939); Beverly Hills, CA, June 11, 2012.

S

Sabol, Steve, 69, filmmaker who was president of NFL Films, which produced weekly highlight films promoting football; Moorestown, NJ, Sept. 18, 2012.

Sams, Doris, 85, outfielder/pitcher for the All-American Girls Professional Baseball League (1946-53); Knoxville, TN, June 28, 2012.

Sarris, Andrew, 83, film critic for *Village Voice* known for popularizing auteur theory; New York, NY, June 20, 2012.

Sassoon, Vidal, 84, British hair stylist who had a major influence on styles of the 1960s and '70s; Los Angeles, CA, May 9, 2012.

Scaglietti, Sergio, 91, Italian designer of Ferraris in the 1950s and '60s; Modena, Italy, Nov. 20, 2011.

Schwartz, Anna, 96, economist known for collaboration with Milton Friedman on *A Monetary History of the United States, 1867-1960* (1963); New York, NY, June 21, 2012.

Scott, Barbara Ann, 84, Canadian figure skater; only Canadian woman to win Olympic gold (1948) in singles skating; Fernandina Beach, FL, Sept. 30, 2012.

Scott, Tony, 68, British film director best remembered for action films including *Top Gun* (1986) and *Crimson Tide* (1995); San Pedro, CA, Aug. 19, 2012.

Scruggs, Earl, 88, bluegrass banjoist who popularized the three-finger picking style; Nashville, TN, Mar. 28, 2012.

Searle, Ronald, 91, British cartoonist best known for *St. Trinian's* drawings and the *Molesworth* book series; Draguignan, France, Dec. 30, 2011.

Seau, Tiaina "Junior," 43, NFL Pro Bowl linebacker who played for the San Diego Chargers for 13 years; Oceanside, CA, May 2, 2012.

Sendak, Maurice, 83, children's writer and illustrator best known for dark tales, including *Where the Wild Things Are* (1963); Danbury, CT, May 8, 2012.

Shadid, Anthony, 43, Pulitzer Prize-winning foreign correspondent who focused on the Middle East; Syria, Feb. 16, 2012.

Shamir, Yitzhak, 96, Israeli prime minister (1983-84, 1986-92) and leader of the conservative Likud party; Tel Aviv, Israel, June 30, 2012.

Shelby, Carroll, 89, auto racer and designer who created the Cobra sports car; Dallas, TX, May 10, 2012.

Sherman, Robert, 86, Oscar-winning lyricist who cowrote songs for *Mary Poppins* (1964) and *Chitty Chitty Bang Bang* (1968); London, Eng., UK, Mar. 6, 2012.

Sihanouk, Norodom, 89, king of Cambodia (1941-55, 1993-2004) who abdicated the throne to win democratic election as ruler (1955-70); Beijing, China, Oct. 15, 2012.

Simon, Joe, 98, cartoonist who cocreated the superhero Captain America; New York, NY, Dec. 14, 2011.

Sklarek, Norma Merrick, 83, architect who was the first black woman licensed in her profession in the U.S.; designed Terminal One of Los Angeles Intl. Airport; Pacific Palisades, CA, Feb. 6, 2012.

Solomon, Freddie, 59, wide receiver for the Miami Dolphins and San Francisco 49ers; Tampa, FL, Feb. 13, 2012.

Specter, Arlen, 82, long-serving senator (R, PA, 1981-2011) who became a Democrat in 2009 in a failed re-election bid; Philadelphia, PA, Oct. 14, 2012.

Stevens, J(ohn) Christopher, 52, U.S. ambassador to Libya; died in an attack on the U.S. consulate; Benghazi, Libya, Sept. 11, 2012.

Stewart, Bob (Isadore Steinberg), 91, TV producer who created game shows including *The $10,000 Pyramid* and *The Price Is Right*; Los Angeles, CA, May 4, 2012.

Strange, Billy, 81, guitarist and arranger who worked with Elvis Presley and Chubby Checker; Franklin, TN, Feb. 22, 2012.

Strobos, Tina, 91, Dutch psychiatrist who sheltered Jews during the Nazi occupation of Holland; Rye, NY, Feb. 27, 2012.

Sues, Alan, 85, comedian best known for *Rowan & Martin's Laugh-In* (1968-72); Los Angeles, CA, Dec. 1, 2011.

Sulzberger, Arthur "Punch" Ochs, 86, publisher of the *NY Times* (1963-92) who decided to publish the Pentagon Papers (1971); Southampton, NY, Sept. 29, 2012

Sumlin, Hubert, 80, blues guitarist and singer who was a member of Howlin' Wolf's band; Wayne, NJ, Dec. 4, 2012.

Summer, Donna, 63, Grammy Award-winning singer and songwriter best known for 1970s disco hits; Naples, FL, May 17, 2012.

Szymborska, Wisława, 88, Polish Nobel Prize-winning poet; Krakow, Poland, Feb. 1, 2012.

T

Tàpies, Antoni, 88, Spanish painter and sculptor of abstract and avant-garde art; Barcelona, Spain, Feb. 6, 2012.

Thomas, E. Donnall, 92, Nobel Prize-winning physician who developed techniques to transplant bone marrow; Seattle, WA, Oct. 20, 2012.

Tramiel, Jack, 83, Polish-American tech. pioneer who founded Commodore Computers, which popularized home computing; Palo Alto, CA, Apr. 8, 2012.

Tufeld, Dick, 85, radio and TV announcer best known as the voice of the robot on *Lost in Space* (1965-68); Studio City, CA, Jan. 22, 2012.

V

Vidal, Gore, 86, writer and gadfly of social and cultural life whose literary career spanned 60 years; Hollywood Hills, CA, July 31, 2012.

Vogel, Herbert, 89, postal worker who with his wife Dorothy, a librarian, amassed a surprising collection of minimalist and conceptual art; New York, NY, July 22, 2012.

W

Wallace, Mike, 93, TV journalist known for probing interviews on *60 Minutes* (1968-2008); New Canaan, CT, Apr. 7, 2012.

Watson, Arthel "Doc," 89, guitarist and singer of bluegrass and country music; Winston-Salem, NC, May 29, 2012.

Welch, Bob, 66, guitarist with Fleetwood Mac (1971-74); solo career included the hit "Sentimental Lady" (1977); Nashville, TN, June 7, 2012.

Wells, Kitty (Muriel Ellen Deason), 92, singer whose "It Wasn't God Who Made Honky Tonk Angels" (1952) made her the first female country music superstar; Madison, TN, July 16, 2012.

White, Kevin, 82, politician best known as the mayor of Boston (1968-84); Boston, MA, Jan 27, 2012.

Whitman, George, 98, American-born owner of the Parisian bookstore Shakespeare & Co.; Paris, France, Dec. 14, 2011.

Wicker, Tom, 85, political reporter and commentator for the *NY Times* (1960-91); Rochester, VT, Nov. 26, 2011.

Williams, Andy, 84, easygoing pop singer best known for "Moon River" (1962); Branson, MO, Sept. 25, 2012.

Williams, Camilla, 92, lyric soprano who was the first black woman to have a contract with a major U.S. opera company; Bloomington, IN, Jan. 29, 2012.

Wilson, James Q., 80, political scientist who co-authored the broken windows theory; Boston, MA, Mar. 2, 2012.

Windom, William, 88, Emmy Award-winning TV actor known mainly for supporting roles; Woodacre, CA, Aug. 16, 2012.

Woods, Sylvia, 86, founder of the Harlem, NY, soul food restaurant that bore her name; Mount Vernon, NY, July 19, 2012.

Y

Yauch, Adam "MCA," 47, rapper and founding member of hip-hop group Beastie Boys; Brooklyn, NY, May 4, 2012.

Yoovidhya, Chaleo, 80?, Thai businessman who cocreated the energy drink Red Bull; Bangkok, Thailand, Mar. 17, 2012.

Z

Zanuck, Richard, 77, Oscar-winning film producer for *Driving Miss Daisy* (1989); Beverly Hills, CA, July 13, 2012.

Zeisel, Eva, 105, Hungarian-American ceramic artist who designed eccentric dinnerware; New City, NY, Dec. 30, 2011.

Zenawi, Meles, 57, Ethiopian prime minister (1995-2012) whose government was both repressive and reforming; Brussels, Belgium, Aug. 20, 2012.

CONGRESS

Key Information on the 112th Congress

The 112th Congress convened Jan. 5, 2011, with the Senate under Democratic control (51-47, 2 ind.) and the House of Representatives led by Republicans (242-193). The 112th Congress was the first since the 107th (2001-03) in which the House and Senate were led by different parties. Ninety-two women were serving in Congress, of whom 75 were in the House and 17 in the Senate. The House had 44 African-American members; 26 Hispanic members; 11 members of Asian, Native Hawaiian, or Pacific Islander heritage; and one American Indian member. The Senate had two Hispanic members and two Asian members. Rep. Gabrielle Giffords (D, AZ) resigned Jan. 25, 2012, after sustaining severe injuries in a shooting in early 2011. Ron Barber (D, AZ) took over her seat following a special election in June. Rep. Donald M. Payne (D), New Jersey's first African-American congressman, died Mar. 6, 2012.

Leadership. The top-ranking members of the Senate were Majority Leader Harry Reid (D, NV), Minority Leader Mitch McConnell (R, KY), Majority Whip Richard Durbin (D, IL), and Minority Whip Jon Kyl (R, AZ). John Boehner (R, OH) took over the office of speaker of the House when the 112th Congress convened. Other leading House members were Majority Leader Eric Cantor (R, VA), Minority Leader Nancy Pelosi (D, CA), Majority Whip Kevin McCarthy (R, CA), and Minority Whip Steny Hoyer (D, MD). The all-time longest continuously serving member of the House was John Dingell (D, MI), in office since 1955.

Ethics. Second-term Rep. Christopher Lee (R, NY) resigned his seat Feb. 9, 2011, after admitting he emailed a shirtless photo of himself to a woman with whom he was seeking an extramarital relationship. Rep. Anthony Weiner (D, NY), a married 7-term congressman, left office June 21, 2011, after admitting he sent lewd photos of himself to women over Facebook and Twitter. Rep. David Wu (D, OR) resigned Aug. 3, 2011, after being accused of sexually assaulting the 18-year-old daughter of a campaign contributor. Third-term Sen. John Ensign (R, NV) resigned May 3, 2011. He faced accusations of improperly helping a former legislative aide develop lobbying contacts and business after Ensign engaged in an extramarital affair with the aide's wife. The Senate Ethics Committee May 12, 2011, concluded he had violated federal civil and criminal laws relating to post-employment lobbying, discrimination, obstruction of justice, and campaign finance. Rep. Laura Richardson (D, CA) was fined and reprimanded by the House Aug. 2, 2012, for ordering her congressional staff to campaign for her, destroying evidence, and attempting to influence witness testimony. On Sept. 25, 2012, the House Ethics Committee wrapped up a three-year investigation of Rep. Maxine Waters (D, CA), clearing her of allegations of using her position to steer $12 mil in bailout funds to a failing bank in which her husband owned stock worth approximately $200,000.

Unfinished Business. The House Sept. 21, 2012, and Senate Sept. 22, 2012, adjourned for the election campaign season, leaving a number of measures unfunded. Congress failed to pass a 5-year extension of comprehensive farm relief programs that expired on Sept. 30. In addition, it had not yet enacted postal service reform or reauthorized the Violence Against Women Act, which expired last year. At the time of adjournment, Congress was facing what was dubbed a "fiscal cliff" at the end of 2012: if a deal was not reached, $1.2 tril in automatic, indiscriminate spending cuts would begin to go into effect Jan. 1, 2013, and the Bush-era tax cuts, payroll tax cut, and a number of tax deductions would all expire.

For Further Information. Detailed legislative information can be accessed at thomas.loc.gov.

Major Actions of Congress, 2011

Federal Budget, Defense Funding. 2011 U.S. Federal Budget (Department of Defense and Full-Year Continuing Appropriations Act, 2011) averts government shutdown, cutting $38.5 bil in spending and providing $3.8 tril for federal operations through Sept. 2011; blocks use of funds to move Guantánamo detainees into the U.S. Passed by the House Apr. 14, 260-167; passed by the Senate Apr. 14, 81-19; signed by Pres. Obama Apr. 15 (PL 112-10).

National Debt. Budget Control Act of 2011 resolves debt-ceiling crisis by reducing spending by $917 bil over 10 years and raising $14.3 tril debt limit by up to $2.4 tril through 2013. Establishes 12-member bipartisan Joint Select Committee on Deficit Reduction to draft legislation reducing deficit by additional $1.5 tril; increases Pell Grant funding but reduces other educational financial aid. Passed by the Senate Feb. 17, unanimous consent; passed by the House (as amended) Aug. 1, 269-161; final vote by the Senate on resolving differences Aug. 2, 74-26; signed by Pres. Obama Aug. 2. (PL 112-25).

Patent Reform. Leahy-Smith America Invents Act (AIA) reforms U.S. patent system by changing rights to future patents from a first-to-invent to a first-to-file basis; expands ability to contest patents and the definition of "prior art." Passed by the House June 23, 304-117; passed by the Senate Sept. 8, 89-9. Signed by Pres. Obama Sept. 16 (PL 112-29).

Defense. National Defense Authorization Act authorizes $662 bil for the nation's defense; adds new sanctions against Iran; broadens cap on compensation for executive contractors; and affirms power of the executive branch, through the armed forces, to indefinitely detain anyone (including U.S. citizens) who supports or is a part of terrorist organizations. Passed by the House Dec. 14, 283-136; passed by the Senate Dec. 15, 86-13; signed by Pres. Obama Dec. 31 (PL 112-81).

Major Actions of Congress, 2012

Tax and Unemployment Relief. Middle Class Tax Relief and Job Creation Act, a $143 bil measure, extends a 2% payroll tax reduction rate; extends unemployment insurance benefits for up to 99 weeks (depending on state); provides grants to states for short-term "work sharing" programs; and saves $15 bil over 10 years by increasing federal employees' share of pension contributions. Passed by the House Feb. 17, 293-132; passed by the Senate Feb. 17, 60-36; signed by Pres. Obama Feb. 22 (PL 112-96).

Financial Ethics. Stop Trading on Congressional Knowledge (STOCK) Act prohibits members of Congress, congressional employees, and federal officials from using non-public information for personal financial gain. Requires Congress members to report financial transactions over $1,000 within 45 days; stipulates officials must disclose terms of home mortgages. Passed by the House Feb. 9, 417-2; passed by the Senate Feb. 2, 96-3; signed by Pres. Obama Apr. 4 (PL 112-105).

Small Business. Jumpstart Our Business Startups (JOBS) Act streamlines process by which small businesses and startups can raise capital by permitting companies to utilize Internet "crowdfunding," raising threshold for funds raised in mini-public offerings valued $5-$50 mil, and extending to five years the amount of time new companies have to comply with specific public company disclosure requirements. Passed by the Senate Mar. 22, 73-26; passed by the House Mar. 8, 390-23; signed by Pres. Obama Apr. 5 (PL 112-106).

Veterans in the Workplace. Veterans Skills to Jobs Act requires federal employers to consider relevant military training in place of federal certification requirements. Passed by the House July 9, unanimous consent; passed by the Senate July 11, unanimous consent; signed by Pres. Obama July 23 (PL 112-147).

Leadership of Selected Congressional Committees

House

Appropriations: Hal Rogers (R, KY)
Armed Services: Buck McKeon (R, CA)
Budget: Paul Ryan (R, WI)
Education and Workforce: John Kline (R, MN)
Energy and Commerce: Fred Upton (R, MI)
Financial Services: Spencer Bachus (R, AL)
Foreign Affairs: Ileana Ros-Lehtinen (R, FL)
Intelligence: Mike Rogers (R, MI)
Judiciary: Lamar Smith (R, TX)
Natural Resources: Doc Hastings (R, WA)
Transportation and Infrastructure: John L. Mica (R, FL)
Ways and Means: Dave Camp (R, MI)

Senate

Appropriations: Daniel K. Inouye (D, HI)
Armed Services: Carl Levin (D, MI)
Banking, Housing, and Urban Affairs: Tim Johnson (D, SD)
Budget: Kent Conrad (D, ND)
Commerce, Science, and Transportation: John D. Rockefeller IV (D, WV)
Energy and Natural Resources: Jeff Bingaman (D, NM)
Finance: Max Baucus (D, MT)
Foreign Relations: John Kerry (D, MA)
Health, Education, Labor, and Pensions: Tom Harkin (D, IA)
Judiciary: Patrick Leahy (D, VT)

Joint Committees

Joint Economic Committee: Roger P. Casey Jr. (D, PA)
Joint Committee on Taxation: Max Baucus (D, MT)

U.S. SUPREME COURT

The U.S. Supreme Court's 2011-12 term began Oct. 3, 2011, and concluded June 28, 2012, for its summer recess. The justices decided 75 cases (65 of which carried signed opinions) and issued 15 rulings (20%) by a 5-4 majority.

Membership. Chief Justice John G. Roberts Jr. presided over his seventh full term on the court. The eight associate justices, by order of seniority, were Antonin Scalia, Anthony M. Kennedy, Clarence Thomas, Ruth Bader Ginsburg, Stephen G. Breyer, Samuel A. Alito Jr., Sonia Sotomayor, and Elena Kagan.

In 2011-12, Roberts, Scalia, Thomas, and Alito tended to vote together as a conservative bloc, while Ginsburg, Breyer, Sotomayor, and Kagan composed the court's liberal wing. Kennedy was the swing vote on 10 out of 15, or two-thirds of, split decisions. Associate Justice Kennedy was in the majority 93% of the time; Chief Justice Roberts was in the majority 92% of the time.

Notable Supreme Court Decisions, 2011-12

Note: The columns on the right provide information on how each justice voted. Gray shading indicates a justice who was part of the majority; black indicates a justice recused herself. MO = justice authored majority opinion; CO = justice authored concurring opinion; DO = justice authored dissenting opinion; CD in part = justice authored opinion containing both concurring and dissenting opinions; JD = justices jointly authored a dissenting opinion.

Campaign Finance
The Supreme Court June 25 ruled, 5-4, that a century-old Montana law, which prohibited corporations from making contributions to candidates or political parties, ran afoul of the court's 2010 ruling in the case of *Citizens United v. FEC*. The unsigned, two-paragraph ruling was a summary judgment made without oral arguments in *American Tradition Partnership v. Bullock*.

Criminal Law
The court June 25 ruled, 5-4, that state statutes imposing mandatory sentences of life imprisonment without parole were unconstitutional when applied to juvenile offenders. The court did not say that judges could never give juveniles such sentences, only that minimum sentencing laws requiring such sentences violated the 8th Amendment's ban on cruel and unusual punishment. The ruling addressed two separate cases, *Miller v. Alabama* and *Jackson v. Hobbs*.

The court Jan. 23 ruled unanimously in *U.S. v. Jones* that police had violated 4th Amendment protections against unreasonable search and seizure when they attached a GPS tracking device to a suspect's car without a valid search warrant. The case was widely considered one of the first major cases dealing with privacy rights in the digital age.

In *Florence v. County of Burlington*, the court decided Apr. 2, 5-4, to allow strip searches of anyone admitted to a jail's general population, regardless of the charges. The court ruled that officials were allowed to visually inspect a prisoner without clothing, as long as no physical contact or abusive gestures were involved in the search.

The Supreme Court June 21 ruled in *Dorsey v. U.S.*, 5-4, that a federal law reducing the disparity between the federal mandatory minimum prison sentences for individuals convicted of possessing crack cocaine and those convicted of possessing powder cocaine could be applied to any defendant sentenced after the law went into effect.

Defendants' Rights
The Supreme Court Mar. 21 ruled, 5-4, that defendants had a right to effective counsel during the plea bargaining process under the 6th Amendment. The ruling stemmed from two cases: *Missouri v. Frye* and *Lafler v. Cooper*.

Free Speech
In *U.S. v. Alvarez*, the court June 28 ruled, 6-3, to strike down a law making it illegal to lie about being the recipient of a military medal of honor, saying the law violated the 1st Amendment's free-speech protections. The Stolen Valor Act, which Congress passed in 2006, prohibited individuals from falsely claiming that they had been "awarded any decoration or medal authorized by Congress for the armed forces of the United States."

The court June 21 ruled, 8-0, to overturn fines and citations that the Federal Communications Commission (FCC) issued for the airing of unscripted profanities and brief nudity. The court did not rule on whether the FCC's broadcast decency rules violated the 1st Amendment's free-speech guarantees. The decision was *FCC v. Fox Television Stations*.

Health Care
The Supreme Court June 28 ruled to uphold most of the Patient Protection and Affordable Care Act. The justices upheld, 5-4, a central provision known as the individual mandate, which required that almost all U.S. residents carry health insurance or pay a fine. The court rejected the federal government's argument that the individual mandate fell within the powers allotted to Congress under the Constitution's commerce clause, but it found that the mandate was a permissible exercise of Congress's taxation power. The justices also upheld an expansion of Medicaid contained in the law while striking down, 7-2, a provision of the Medicaid expansion that allowed the federal government to withhold Medicaid funding from some states for noncompliance. The court had consolidated three cases into a ruling known as *Natl. Federation of Independent Business v. Sebelius*.

Immigration
The Supreme Court June 25 voided three sections of Arizona's 2010 state immigration law and upheld one provision in *Arizona v. U.S.* The court unanimously upheld the law's centerpiece, a provision requiring law enforcement officials to check the immigration status of those they stopped or detained who they suspected were in the U.S. illegally. In separate split votes, the court voided provisions that made it a crime for illegal immigrants to hold jobs or to seek work; that gave police the authority to detain without a warrant any immigrant they believed had committed an offense that could merit deportation; and that made it a state crime to violate federal immigration law.

Religion
The Supreme Court Jan. 11 ruled unanimously that certain employment discrimination laws did not protect church ministers, affirming that religious groups were free to choose and dismiss their leaders without interference from the federal government. The case was *Hosanna-Tabor Church v. Equal Employment Opportunity Commission*.

Case	Kagan	Sotomayor	Breyer	Ginsburg	Kennedy	Scalia	Thomas	Roberts	Alito
Campaign Finance (*American Tradition Partnership v. Bullock*)			DO						
Criminal Law – *Miller v. Alabama* / *Jackson v. Hobbs*	MO		CO				DO	DO	DO
U.S. v. Jones		CO				MO			CO
Florence v. County of Burlington			DO		MO			CO	CO
Dorsey v. U.S.			MO			DO			
Defendants' Rights (*Missouri v. Frye* / *Lafler v. Cooper*)					MO	DO			DO
U.S. v. Alvarez			CO		MO				DO
FCC v. Fox Television Stations		(recused)		CO	MO				
Health Care (*Natl. Federation of Independent Business v. Sebelius*)				CO	JD	JD	JD/DO	MO	JD
Immigration (*Arizona v. U.S.*)	(recused)				MO	CD in part	CD in part		CD in part
Religion (*Hosanna-Tabor Church v. EEOC*)							CO	MO	CO

Around the World

"Get back on board, for f— sake!"
—Gregorio De Falco, Italian coast guard official, speaking by telephone to the captain of the cruise ship *Costa Concordia*, after it ran aground off an Italian island Jan. 13; more than 30 lives were lost.

"My eyes sting with tears . . . he provided us with such a comfortable home and always worried so much about us year after year."
—Ro Chang Hae, North Korean citizen, mourning Kim Jong Il, the nation's recently deceased longtime Supreme Leader, amid Lunar New Year crowds in Pyongyang Jan. 23.

"When you have to choose between bad and worse, you will pick what is bad to avoid what is worse."
—Greek Finance Min. Evangelos Venizelos, Feb. 13, after Greece's parliament passed harsh austerity measures in an effort to avert government default.

"Pressures, sanctions, and assassinations will bear no fruit. No obstacles can stop Iran's nuclear work."
—Iran's Supreme Leader Ayatollah Ali Khamenei, on state TV Feb. 22, referring to actions by other countries aimed at curbing Iran's nuclear program, which the regime claims is for peaceful purposes.

"I will never let my people live in the shadow of annihilation."
—Israeli Prime Min. Benjamin Netanyahu, referring to threat to Israel posed by Iran's nuclear program, Mar. 5 in Washington, DC.

"It was like throwing a lighted match into a gasoline-filled room."
—Paul S. Keim, a microbial geneticist, in a remark reported Mar. 31; referring to Haiti's deadly cholera epidemic, believed to have been sparked by infected UN peacekeepers under unsanitary conditions worsened by the Jan. 2010 earthquake.

"It is not so much our triumph as a triumph of the people, who have decided that they have to be involved in the political process in this country."
—Aung San Suu Kyi, long-suppressed democracy activist in Myanmar (Burma), after her party's landslide victory in by-elections Apr. 1.

"Austerity need not be Europe's fate."
—François Hollande, French Socialist politician, after defeating conservative Pres. Nicolas Sarkozy in presidential runoff elections, May 5-6.

"We've been waiting for it for 7,000 years. For the first time in history we have our own president, elected by us."
—Egyptian MP Abdul Mawgoud Dardery, referring to presidential elections held May 23-24; Muslim Brotherhood-affiliated candidate Mohammed Morsi was declared the winner.

"We cannot believe that the world is watching us being killed."
—Ahmad, Syrian activist (not fully named for security reasons), June 11, after one of many instances in which Syrian government troops fired on rebels and civilians alike, in the midst of civil war.

"It's a triumphant day for fundamental physics. Now some fun begins."
—Nima Arkani-Hamed, physicist at the Institute for Advanced Study in Princeton, after the July 4 announcement that a new subatomic particle had been discovered.

"We are holding an Olympic Games in one of the busiest, most active, bustling cities anywhere in the world. Of course it's easier if you hold an Olympic Games in the middle of nowhere."
—British Prime Min. David Cameron, July 26, after U.S. presidential contender Mitt Romney expressed doubts about the London Olympics; alluding to Salt Lake City, which hosted the Games Romney oversaw in 2002.

"Some have sought to justify this vicious behavior as a response to inflammatory material posted on the Internet. The United States deplores any intentional effort to denigrate the religious beliefs of others . . . But let me be clear: There is never any justification for violent acts of this kind."
—Sec. of State Hillary Clinton, Sept. 11, on an attack on the U.S. consulate in Benghazi, Libya, that day, which killed the U.S. ambassador and three other Americans.

"This is not acceptable to the Libyan people; this is not acceptable to our values. We are taking this very, very seriously."
—Libyan Prime Min.-elect Mustafa Abushagur, referring to the Sept. 11 attack in Benghazi.

"I don't mind if I have to sit on the floor at school. All I want is education. And I am afraid of no one."
—Pakistani schoolgirl Malala Yousafzai speaking in 2009, when she was 11; she was shot and seriously wounded Oct. 9, 2012, by a Taliban gunman in retaliation for her outspoken views in defense of female education.

National News

"If I had a son, he'd look like Trayvon."
—Pres. Barack Obama, when asked about the fatal shooting of unarmed black teenager Trayvon Martin by a neighborhood watch volunteer, Feb. 26, in Sanford, FL.

"Decisions about medical care should be made by a woman and her doctor, not a woman and her boss."
—Health and Human Services Sec. Kathleen Sebelius, in a statement Feb. 29 opposing legislation that would exempt employers from providing contraceptive coverage in their health care plans if they object on moral or religious grounds.

"We have made it clear in no uncertain terms to the government that we are not at peace with its invasive attempt to curtail the religious freedom we cherish as Catholics and Americans."
—Cardinal Timothy Dolan, in a Mar. 2 letter to Catholic bishops protesting mandated coverage of contraception in employee health insurance plans.

"At a certain point, I've just concluded that, for me personally it is important to go ahead and affirm that same-sex couples should be able to get married."
—Pres. Obama, in a May 9 interview with ABC News; he became the first sitting president to declare support for same-sex marriage.

"We know we were sloppy. We know we were stupid. We know there was bad judgment."
—Jamie Dimon, JPMorgan Chase CEO, on NBC's *Meet the Press* May 13, after the bank disclosed a loss of $2 bil on investments made by its traders.

"It is not our job to protect the people from the consequences of their political choices."
—Chief Justice John Roberts, in majority Supreme Court decision, June 28, upholding the mandate to purchase health insurance as constitutional, if not necessarily good policy.

"We all have to remember that we can't let our love of the games get ahead of the core values, and we know that happens often. This is a painful, painful reminder that awful things can happen when that occurs."
—NCAA Pres. Mark Emmert, in a July 23 interview with the *NY Times*, after announcing sanctions against Penn State Univ. for the institution's response to a child sex abuse scandal.

"Freedom of religion is a fundamental tenet of democracy, and it's incredibly sad that victims were shot down while exercising that right."
—Sapreet Kaur, executive director of the Sikh Coalition, after a gunman, Aug. 5, killed six worshippers at a Sikh temple near Milwaukee.

"The devastation on the Jersey shore is some of the worst we've ever seen. The cost of the storm is incalculable at this point."
—New Jersey Gov. Chris Christie, Oct. 30, on the damage caused by former-hurricane Sandy.

People

"I don't remember much from that horrible day, but I will never forget the trust you placed in me to be your voice."
—Rep. Gabrielle Giffords (D, AZ), announcing her resignation from Congress, Jan. 22, just over a year after she was seriously wounded in an assassination attempt.

"It's a rite of passage in this new era."
—Jorge Cauz, Encyclopædia Britannica president, in an interview with the *NY Times*, Mar. 13, after announcing the company's decision to stop publishing print editions.

"Even though I wasn't the one who caused him to jump off the bridge, I did do things wrong, and I was stupid about a lot of stuff."
—Dharun Ravi, former Rutgers Univ. student convicted on 15 charges related to his spying on gay roommate Tyler Clementi, who committed suicide; in an interview for ABC's *20/20* broadcast Mar. 23.

"My tears are hidden behind goggles. Yours are streaming down your face."
—Swimmer Michael Phelps, speaking to his trainer at the Summer Olympics in London, Aug. 4, prior to the 4x100-m medley relay, in which he won his 22nd Olympic medal.

"My mother used to tell us in the mornings, 'Carl, put on your shoes. Oscar, you put on your prosthetic legs . . .' So I grew up not really thinking I had a disability. I grew up thinking I had different shoes."
—Oscar Pistorius, South African sprinter who, Aug. 4, became the first double amputee ever to compete in an Olympic track and field event.

"Nobody needs to cry for me. I'm going to be great."
—Cyclist Lance Armstrong, speaking publicly, Aug. 25, after dropping his appeal of doping charges. He was subsequently banned for life from cycling and stripped of all seven Tour de France titles Oct. 22.

Cannonball Myth: Confirmed

The Discovery Channel's *MythBusters* is known for two things: using scientific experiments to check the plausibility of physical phenomena and blowing things up. The cast members frequently note that they're professionals and that most of their experiments shouldn't be tried at home. But even professionals need to exercise caution, especially when explosives are involved. A team from the show Dec. 6, 2011, was setting up an experiment to test whether a stone cannonball could penetrate a stone castle wall. They were firing cannonballs into water barrels at a Dublin, CA, police firing range to calibrate a homemade cannon when the muzzle lifted upon firing. The 30-lb cannonball banked off a safety berm and launched 700 yds into a suburban neighborhood. The runaway projectile hit the sidewalk, bounded through the front door of a house, and crashed through the wall of a second-story bedroom where a woman and her toddler were sleeping. The cannonball continued across a busy road and ricocheted off the roof of another house before coming to rest inside a minivan. Luckily, no one was hurt. The *MythBusters* hosts apologized, promised to take more care in the future, and pledged never to air footage of the incident on the show.

Please Rise and Paste Hymn 1337

Intellectual property issues are increasingly central in today's world, and Sweden has long been at the forefront of such issues. Popular file-sharing site The Pirate Bay is based in Sweden, and its political spinoff, the Swedish Pirate Party, has two seats in European Parliament. Now comes the world's first religion for the post-Napster generation. The Swedish government officially recognized the Church of Kopimism—the name derives from "copy me"—as a religious organization in Jan. 2012. Founded in 2010 by 19-year-old philosophy student Isak Gerson, the church posits that information is holy, that copying is a sacrament, and that all file-sharing should be legal. Sacred symbols include "Ctrl + C" and "Ctrl + V," the keystroke shortcuts to copy and paste. The movement is spreading: the First United Church of Kopimism registered with the state of Illinois in Apr. 2012. Worldwide, the Church of Kopimism claims upward of 8,000 members and branches in 18 countries.

Spot the Pig

In hindsight, having prisoners work on elements of police cruisers might have been asking for trouble. The Vermont State Police logo is a modified version of the state's seal and coat of arms. It includes a pine tree, some sheaves of grain, and a red Holstein cow. While the cow is supposed to be solid red, the cows on police vehicles have spots. A Vermont state trooper cleaning his patrol car Feb. 1, 2012, noticed that one of the spots on the cow was shaped like a pig. ("Pig" is a derogatory term for a police officer.) Investigations found that the logo decals had been made at a print shop at the Northwest State Correctional Facility in 2009, and that an inmate had modified the computer file with the logo to add the pig. Despite a Facebook petition to "Save the Vermont Pigs" or auction the logo decals for charity, they were destroyed and replaced, at a cost of $780.

How to Live on $30 a Month

Eric Simons lived in AOL's offices in Palo Alto, CA, rent-free for two months before anyone was the wiser. Simons, a 19-year-old with an educational software startup, participated in a 3½-month incubator program on the AOL campus. Simons didn't have enough money for rent after the program was over, but he did still have an active AOL security badge. They had everything he needed: free food (cereal, ramen, and trail mix), a gym with showers, and even a laundromat. During the day, he worked on his startup. Workers who saw him in the morning assumed he got there early; those who saw him at the end of the day figured he was working late. He spent only $30 during the first month of his residence, but eventually, word got out and he was expelled. By then he had made enough progress to get capital to cover the rent on a house in Palo Alto … where he promptly sublet the use of bunk beds to two other programmers.

Knight of the Elm

One might not expect a professional logger to become famous for saving a tree, but logger Frank Knight of Yarmouth, ME, didn't fit preconceptions. While he made his living felling and selling trees, he also worked to protect trees in his neighborhood. He tried hardest to save a 110-ft-tall elm planted in 1793, nicknamed "Herbie." In 1956, when Herbie and other Yarmouth elms were first threatened by Dutch elm disease, Knight came to the rescue. He carefully pruned the tree for decades, but by Jan. 2010, Herbie could no longer be saved. Knight, then 101 years old, told the Associated Press that Herbie's "time has come, and mine is about due, too." Herbie's wood was supplied to local artisans, who used it to make tables, ornaments, and even an electric guitar. Some of these items were auctioned off, raising more than $45,000 to pay for the planting of more trees in Yarmouth.

Knight died May 14, 2012, at the age of 103 and was laid to rest in a casket made from Herbie's wood. His son, Dick Knight, told the *Boston Herald*, "Frank cared for Herbie for 52 years, and now Herbie will care for Frank forever."

Dust in the Wind

When thunderstorms meet desert sand, they can kick up massive dust storms, called "haboobs" by meteorologists. Comparable to a dust tsunami, a haboob can suddenly engulf an area. They're quite dangerous: 48 vehicle crashes—including two fatalities and 41 injuries—were caused by dust storms in Arizona in 2010. So the Arizona Dept. of Transportation started a campaign to convince drivers to pull over when a storm hits. They asked people to use Twitter to submit haiku (17-syllable poems in a 5/7/5-syllable pattern) about haboobs, like "Drive with care in dust / Pull aside and stay alive / Wait for dust to pass." Hundreds submitted entries, even though there were no prizes (except bragging rights), and the "Pull Aside, Stay Alive" campaign was widely reported. The winning entry, announced June 29, 2012, came from Twitter user @Lisa4LFA, or Lisa Fullam: "Dust blows, swirls and grows / Roadways become danger zones / Pull over, lights off."

Monkey Shines

Elías García Martínez painted a fresco of Jesus Christ known as "Ecce Homo" (Behold the Man) at the Santuario de Misericodia Church in Borja, Spain, around a century ago. Neither the artist nor the painting were particularly noteworthy, but the painting had sentimental value, and some of Martínez's descendants arranged to have the fresco professionally restored. But when their expert arrived, it was too late: an 81-year-old parishioner, Cecilia Giménez, admitted to fixing the painting herself in Aug. 2012. Unfortunately, Giménez wasn't a painter. The heartfelt but awful result was described as "a furry alien Neanderthal," "Ewok Jesus," and, ultimately, "Ecce Mono" (Behold the Monkey). Martínez's descendants and the church were distressed, but the story endeared the world to "Ecce Mono." The image spread on social media and appeared on T-shirts, wine bottles, and coffee mugs. The church began charging admission to see the painting and took in more than $2,500 in just four days.

By Oct. 2012, many questions remained unresolved: Could the "restoration" be undone? Could the top layer be lifted off to preserve both the original and Giménez's work? Would Giménez be sued for ruining Martínez's fresco? Could Giménez sue those making T-shirts and other merchandise—or even the church—for a cut of the profits? Who owns the rights to "Ecce Mono"? All parties have retained counsel.

Ev'rybody Wants to See a Cat

Cat videos are a mainstay of Internet culture, so they seemed to qualify for the Walker Art Center's Open Field initiative for experimental public programming. The museum, in Minneapolis, MN, decided to host the first Internet Cat Video Film Festival, for which they winnowed 10,000 video submissions to 79. They wondered if the online community would really turn out for an offline event. But on Aug. 30, 2012, an estimated 10,000 people attended the festival—some in cat costumes, some with cats in tow. There were even a few dogs. The "Golden Kitty," a people's choice award, went to "Henri 2, Paw de Deux," a black-and-white short in which Henri the cat expresses his ennui in French (with English subtitles). The video—one of five starring Henri as of Oct. 2012—has led to sales of Henri-related merchandise, and Random House plans to publish a book starring the bored *chat* in 2013.

HISTORICAL ANNIVERSARIES

1913 – 100 Years Ago

The 16th Amendment to the U.S. Constitution, authorizing federal income tax, is ratified Feb. 3.

Mexican Pres. Francisco Madero is ousted in a military coup Feb. 18 and assassinated Feb. 22.

Springtime flooding kills more than 700 people in Indiana and Ohio in Mar.

The 17th Amendment to the U.S. Constitution, providing for direct popular election of U.S. senators, is ratified Apr. 8.

The First Balkan War ends with treaty signing May 30. The Second Balkan War is fought (treaty signed Aug. 10). The conflicts destabilize much of southeastern Europe, setting the stage for World War I.

A "peace jubilee" reunites more than 53,000 veterans of the Civil War at Gettysburg on the occasion of that battle's 50th anniversary July 1-4.

After 30 years of construction, the tugboat *Gatun* is the first vessel to travel through the locks of the Panama Canal Sept. 26.

A coal mine explosion Oct. 22 kills 263 people in Dawson, NM.

The Great Lakes Storm Nov. 7-10 batters the region with hurricane force winds and whiteout blizzard conditions; more than a dozen ships sink and at least 250 people are killed.

Ford Motor Co.'s moving assembly line begins operations Dec. 1, enabling a massive surge in automobile production.

The Federal Reserve System is authorized Dec. 23 in a major reform of U.S. banking and finance.

Art. The Armory Show in New York City introduces a large exhibition of international modern art to U.S., Feb. 17-Mar. 15. Leonardo da Vinci's *Mona Lisa*, stolen in 1911, is recovered. Marcel Duchamp's *Bicycle Wheel*.

Film. *Caprice* and *In the Bishop's Carriage* starring Mary Pickford; Alice Guy-Blaché's *Matrimony's Speed Limit*; D. W. Griffith's *Oil and Water*; *Traffic in Souls*.

Literature. First volume of Marcel Proust's *In Search of Lost Time* is published in France as *Du côté de chez Swann*. Willa Cather's *O Pioneers!*; D. H. Lawrence's *Sons and Lovers*.

Music. Igor Stravinsky's *The Rite of Spring*, a ballet with choreography by Vaslav Nijinsky, premieres in Paris.

Nonfiction. Third and final volume of Alfred North Whitehead and Bertrand Russell's *Principia Mathematica* is published.

Pop music. Alfred Bryan and Fred Fisher's "Peg o' My Heart"; Joseph McCarthy and James V. Monaco's "You Made Me Love You (I Didn't Want to Do It)"; Frederic Weatherly's "Danny Boy."

Science and technology. Niels Bohr revises Ernest Rutherford's atomic model to produce a quantum model of the atom.

Sports. Jack Johnson, the first black heavyweight champion boxer, is convicted of violating the Mann Act (or White Slave Traffic Act), in what is widely regarded as a sham trial. The Brooklyn Dodgers play the first game in Ebbets Field Apr. 9. The Wimbledon tennis tournament includes championships for women and mixed doubles for the first time.

Theater. *A Good Little Devil* starring Mary Pickford; *The Honeymoon Express* starring Al Jolson; "Potash and Perlmutter" characters debut in their eponymous show.

Miscellaneous. New York City's Grand Central Terminal and Woolworth Building (the world's tallest skyscraper through 1930) open to the public. First crossword puzzle for adults is published in the *New York World* newspaper. Gideon Sundback perfects the design for the modern zipper.

1963 – 50 Years Ago

Alabama Gov. George C. Wallace proclaims "segregation now, segregation tomorrow, segregation forever," in his inaugural address Jan. 14.

In *Gideon v. Wainwright*, Mar. 18, the U.S. Supreme Court unanimously rules that all criminal defendants charged with serious crimes must have counsel.

Atomic-powered U.S. Navy submarine *Thresher* sinks in the North Atlantic Apr. 10 with 129 aboard.

Two black students enroll at Univ. of Alabama June 11, desegregating the institution after federally deployed National Guard troops ask Gov. George Wallace, who was blocking the entrance, to step aside. Civil rights leader Medgar Evers is assassinated June 12 in Jackson, MS, a few hours after Pres. John F. Kennedy addresses the nation on civil rights.

The U.S. Supreme Court holds June 17 that school rules and local laws that required recitation of the Lord's Prayer or Bible verses in public schools were unconstitutional.

Soviet Union and U.S. agree June 20 to establish a hotline for direct communication between the White House and the Kremlin.

Pres. John F. Kennedy speaks about freedom before a huge crowd in West Berlin, Germany, June 26, saying, "I take pride in the words 'Ich bin ein Berliner.'"

More than 200,000 attend massive march on Washington, DC, Aug. 28 in support of black civil rights and equality; Rev. Martin Luther King Jr. gives "I Have a Dream" speech.

Four black girls are killed when 16th St. Baptist Church is bombed in Birmingham, AL, Sept. 15.

Hurricane Flora strikes the Caribbean Sept. 26-Oct. 12, killing more than 7,000 in Cuba, the Dominican Republic, and Haiti.

Great Britain, Soviet Union, and U.S. agree on a limited nuclear test-ban treaty that enters into force Oct. 10.

After military coup Nov. 1, South Vietnam Pres. Ngo Dinh Diem is executed Nov. 2.

Pres. John F. Kennedy is shot and fatally wounded Nov. 22 while riding in a motorcade through downtown Dallas, TX; Vice Pres. Lyndon B. Johnson is sworn in as president aboard Air Force One. Arrested and charged with murder for Kennedy's assassination, Lee Harvey Oswald is shot and fatally wounded Nov. 24 while in custody.

Zanzibar and Kenya are granted independence from Great Britain in Dec.; both remain in the Commonwealth of Nations.

Art. Leonardo da Vinci's *Mona Lisa* is on view in the U.S. for the first time. New York's Guggenheim Museum holds *Six Painters and the Object* exhibition, the first large museum show of Pop Art. Roy Lichtenstein's *Drowning Girl* and *Whaam!*; Andy Warhol's *Double Elvis*.

Film. *Dr. No* starring Sean Connery, the first James Bond film, is released in U.S. Elia Kazan's *America, America*; Alfred Hitchcock's *The Birds*; Stanley Donen's *Charade* starring Cary Grant and Audrey Hepburn; *Cleopatra* starring Richard Burton, Elizabeth Taylor, and Rex Harrison; Federico Fellini's *8½*; *The Great Escape* starring Richard Attenborough, James Garner, and Steve McQueen; Akira Kurosawa's *High and Low*; *Hud* starring Melvyn Douglas, Patricia Neal, and Paul Newman; *Lilies of the Field* starring Sidney Poitier; Jerry Lewis's *The Nutty Professor*; *Shock Corridor*; *Tom Jones* starring Albert Finney.

Literature. James Baldwin's *The Fire Next Time*; John le Carré's *The Spy Who Came in From the Cold*; Sylvia Plath's *The Bell Jar*; Thomas Pynchon's *V.*; Maurice Sendak's *Where the Wild Things Are*; Mario Vargas Llosa's *The Time of the Hero*.

Music. Leonard Bernstein's *Kaddish* (Symphony No. 3).

Nonfiction. Shelby Foote's *Fredericksburg to Meridian*; Betty Friedan's *The Feminine Mystique*; Richard Hofstadter's *Anti-Intellectualism in American Life*; Martin Luther King Jr.'s "Letter From Birmingham Jail."

Pop music. The Beach Boys' "Surfin' USA"; Johnny Cash's "Ring of Fire"; Jimmy Gilmer and the Fireballs' "Sugar Shack"; Lesley Gore's "It's My Party"; The Kingsmen's "Louie Louie"; Peter, Paul, and Mary's "Blowin' in the Wind"; and The Ronettes' "Be My Baby." The British Invasion begins with the U.S. release of The Beatles' "I Want to Hold Your Hand," with "I Saw Her Standing There" as the B-side.

Science and technology. Astronaut L. Gordon Cooper makes final *Mercury* mission and is first American to travel in space for more than a day; Soviet cosmonaut Valentina Tereshkova becomes the first woman to travel to space. Stanley Milgram publishes initial findings from his experiments on obedience to authority figures. The first successful lung and liver transplants are performed.

Sports. Pro Football Hall of Fame opens in Canton, OH, with 17 charter members. Jack Nicklaus wins the Masters Tournament and PGA Championship for the first time.

Television. Daytime soap opera *General Hospital* debuts. *Beverly Hillbillies* is top-rated show. *Dick Van Dyke Show* and *The Defenders* win Emmy Awards.

Theater. Neil Simon's *Barefoot in the Park*, Bertolt Brecht's *Mother Courage and Her Children*, and *Oliver!* debut on Broadway. Guthrie Theater opens in Minneapolis.

Miscellaneous. The U.S. postal system begins using ZIP codes. Coca-Cola Co. introduces Tab, its first diet-cola soft drink. The Second Session of Vatican Council II, which adjourns Dec. 4, decrees that Mass may be conducted in English and other languages instead of in Latin.

1988 – 25 Years Ago

The U.S. Justice Dept. Feb. 5 unseals indictments that charge Panama leader Manuel Noriega with violating U.S. racketeering and drug trafficking laws.

Anthony M. Kennedy is sworn in to the U.S. Supreme Court Feb. 18.

U.S. Lt. Col. Oliver North, Rear Adm. John Poindexter, and two others are indicted in the ongoing Iran-Contra scandal Mar. 16.

The Soviet army begins withdrawing its 115,000 troops from Afghanistan May 15 after more than eight years of fighting.

Congress approves June 8 expansion of Medicare benefits to protect the elderly and disabled against "catastrophic" medical costs. (The provision was repealed in Nov. 1989.)

Much of the U.S. suffers the worst drought in over 50 years; by late June many of the nation's agricultural counties have been declared disaster areas. Drought contributes to major wildfires in the West, including fires that burn in Yellowstone National Park for several months.

The U.S. Navy warship *Vincennes* in the Persian Gulf mistakes a commercial Iranian airliner for an attacking fighter jet and shoots it down with a missile July 3, killing all 290 aboard.

Pres. Reagan Aug. 10 signs into law an act offering reparations to Japanese Americans forcibly relocated to internment camps during World War II.

The Iran-Iraq War officially ends in a UN-brokered cease-fire Aug. 20 after eight years of fighting; Iraqi leader Saddam Hussein uses chemical weapons in his campaign against Kurds in northern Iraq.

Communist Party Gen. Sec. Mikhail Gorbachev assumes the Soviet presidency Oct. 1.

Former Philippines Pres. Ferdinand Marcos, his wife Imelda Marcos, and eight associates are indicted on racketeering charges Oct. 21.

Vice Pres. George H. W. Bush (R) decisively defeats Massachusetts Gov. Michael Dukakis (D) Nov. 8 to become the 41st U.S. president.

Benazir Bhutto Dec. 1 becomes the first woman elected to lead a majority-Muslim nation as prime minister of Pakistan.

An earthquake strikes Armenia Dec. 7; approximately 25,000 are killed.

En route from London to New York City, Pan Am Flight 103 crashes into Lockerbie, Scotland, Dec. 21, killing all 259 people aboard and 11 on the ground; investigators confirm Dec. 28 that the crash was caused by a bomb on the plane.

Art. Francis Bacon's *Second Version of Triptych 1944*; Jeff Koons's *Banality* series. Jean-Michel Basquiat dies at age 27.

Film. *The Accidental Tourist* starring Geena Davis, William Hurt, and Kathleen Turner; *The Accused* starring Jodie Foster; *Beaches*; Tim Burton's *Beetlejuice*; *Big* starring Tom Hanks; *Bull Durham* starring Kevin Costner and Susan Sarandon; *Coming to America* starring Eddie Murphy; *Dangerous Liaisons*; *Die Hard* starring Bruce Willis; *A Fish Called Wanda*; *Rain Man* starring Tom Cruise and Dustin Hoffman; *Stand and Deliver*; Errol Morris's *The Thin Blue Line*; Pixar's short film *Tin Toy*; *Twins*; *Willow*; *Who Framed Roger Rabbit*; *Working Girl* starring Harrison Ford and Melanie Griffith.

Literature. Peter Carey's *Oscar and Lucinda*; Roald Dahl's *Matilda*; Pete Dexter's *Paris Trout*; Salman Rushdie's *The Satanic Verses*; Anne Tyler's *Breathing Lessons*.

Music. Roger Reynolds's *Whispers Out of Time*.

Nonfiction. Taylor Branch's *Parting the Waters: America in the King Years, 1954-63*; Stephen Hawking's *A Brief History of Time*; Neil Sheehan's *A Bright Shining Lie: John Paul Vann and America in Vietnam*.

Pop music. "Man in the Mirror" and "Dirty Diana" are the fourth and fifth No. 1 singles from Michael Jackson's *Bad* album. Guns 'n' Roses' "Sweet Child o' Mine" and "Paradise City"; Bobby McFerrin's "Don't Worry, Be Happy"; George Michael's *Faith*; New Kids on the Block's *Hangin' Tough*; Public Enemy's *It Takes a Nation of Millions to Hold Us Back*; Sonic Youth's *Daydream Nation*; U2's *Rattle and Hum*.

Science and technology. NASA resumes shuttle flights for the first time since the 1986 *Challenger* disaster. A "worm" crafted by Cornell Univ. computer science graduate student Robert Tappan Morris infects thousands of computers, shutting many down and causing perhaps millions of dollars of damage—the first known case of large-scale damage caused by a computer virus spread via the Internet.

Sports. Olympic Games are held in Calgary, AB, Canada, and Seoul, South Korea. The Chicago Cubs host their first night game at Wrigley Field. Mike Tyson knocks out Michael Spinks 91 seconds into the first round.

Television. *The Wonder Years* and *Roseanne* premiere; *The Cosby Show* and *A Different World* are among highest-rated shows.

Theater. *M. Butterfly* and *Phantom of the Opera* win Tony Awards (*Phantom* has been on Broadway ever since). David Mamet's *Speed-the-Plow* debuts on Broadway starring Madonna, Joe Mantegna, and Ron Silver.

Miscellaneous. Use of fax machines increases sharply. Roman Catholic Church announces that carbon dating performed on the Shroud of Turin showed that the linen dated only to the Middle Ages, not (as popularly believed) to the burial date of Jesus Christ.

WORLD ALMANAC EDITORS' PICKS
2012 Time Capsule

The editors of *The World Almanac* have selected the following items as representative of the year 2012.

- A life preserver from the *Costa Concordia* luxury cruise ship, which sank Jan. 13 off an Italian island.

- A hooded sweatshirt representing those worn by activists protesting the shooting death of Trayvon Martin, an African-American teenager, by a neighborhood watch volunteer in Florida Feb. 26.

- The 32-volume, 2012 edition of *Encyclopædia Britannica*, which the company announced Mar. 13 would be its last in print.

- A Higgs boson—the so-called "God particle"—the existence of which scientists at Switzerland's Large Hadron Collider confirmed for the first time July 4.

- Penn State's famed 7-ft-tall Joe Paterno statue, which the university took down July 22 in the continuing aftermath of the Jerry Sandusky child sex abuse scandal.

- A copy of E. L. James's *Fifty Shades of Grey*, the runaway best seller that topped fiction charts in 2012.

- A stock certificate from Facebook's problematic May 18 initial public offering.

- One of Michael Phelps's record-setting 22 Olympic medals, along with the July 26 video of the U.S. Olympic swim team lip-synching Carly Rae Jepsen's "Call Me Maybe."

- The parachutes used to slow the descents of the *Curiosity* rover to the Martian surface, Aug. 6, and skydiver Felix Baumgartner's supersonic fall from a record 24 miles above Earth's surface Oct. 14.

- The empty chair Clint Eastwood addressed as Pres. Obama in an impromptu speech at the Republican National Convention in Tampa, FL, Aug. 30.

- Republican presidential nominee Mitt Romney's 2011 tax returns, which the candidate released Sept. 21.

- Game balls from each of the record seven no-hitters thrown during the 2012 Major League Baseball season (including three perfect games) and a baseball bat belonging to Detroit Tiger Miguel Cabrera, who became the first to win the Triple Crown since 1967.

- A plank from the Seaside Heights, NJ, boardwalk, one of many destroyed in Northeast coastal towns when former-hurricane Sandy made landfall Oct. 29.

ECONOMICS

Index of Leading Economic Indicators

Source: The Conference Board

The index of leading economic indicators is used to project the U.S. economy's performance. The index is made up of 10 measurements of economic activity that tend to change direction in advance of the overall economy. The index has predicted economic downturns from 8 to 20 months in advance and recoveries from 1 to 10 months in advance. It can be inconsistent, however, and has occasionally shown false signals of recessions. In 2012, the Conference Board made significant changes to the composition of the Leading Economic Index for the first time since 1996. As a result, data from 2012 forward are not directly comparable with those from prior years. The components are listed below.

- Average weekly hours of production workers in manufacturing
- Institute for Supply Management index of new orders in manufacturing
- Consumer expectations for business conditions (surveys by Conference Board and Reuters/Univ. of Michigan)
- Interest rate spread (10-yr Treasury bonds less federal funds)
- Building permits for new private housing units
- Manufacturers' new orders for consumer goods and materials, adjusted for inflation
- Leading Credit Index, a proprietary Conference Board measure of credit conditions
- Stock prices, 500 common stocks
- Manufacturers' new orders for nondefense capital goods, excluding aircraft, adjusted for inflation
- Average weekly initial claims for unemployment insurance

U.S. Gross Domestic Product, Gross National Product, Net National Product, National Income, and Personal Income, 1970-2011

Source: Bureau of Economic Analysis, U.S. Dept. of Commerce

(in billions of current dollars, revised)

	1970	1980	1990	2000	2005	2009	2010	2011
Gross domestic product	$1,038.3	$2,788.1	$5,800.5	$9,951.5	$12,623.0	$13,973.7	$14,498.9	$15,075.7
Gross national product	1,044.7	2,822.3	5,835.0	9,989.2	12,720.1	14,117.2	14,708.2	15,327.5
Less: Consumption of fixed capital	108.3	344.1	691.2	1,184.3	1,541.4	1,866.3	1,873.4	1,936.8
Net national product	936.4	2,478.2	5,143.7	8,804.9	11,178.7	12,250.9	12,834.8	13,390.8
Less: Statistical discrepancy	6.9	45.3	84.2	−134.0	−95.1	118.3	23.3	31.9
Equals: National income	929.5	2,433.0	5,059.5	8,938.9	11,273.8	12,132.6	12,811.4	13,358.9
Less: Corporate profits with inventory valuation and capital consumption adjustments	82.5	201.4	434.4	819.2	1,456.1	1,342.3	1,702.4	1,827.0
Taxes on production and imports less subsidies[1]	86.6	190.5	398.0	662.7	869.3	963.5	998.0	1,036.2
Contributions for government social insurance	46.4	166.2	410.1	705.8	872.7	963.1	983.3	919.3
Net interest and miscellaneous payments on assets	39.1	181.8	444.2	539.3	543.0	640.5	567.9	527.4
Business current transfer payments (net)	4.5	14.7	40.1	87.0	95.9	133.4	140.0	132.6
Current surplus of government enterprises	0.0	−5.1	1.6	9.1	−3.5	−15.6	−19.5	−26.5
Wage accruals less disbursements	0.0	0.0	0.1	0.0	5.0	5.0	0.0	0.0
Plus: Personal income receipts on assets	93.5	338.7	920.8	1,360.7	1,542.0	1,626.5	1,598.3	1,685.1
Personal current transfer receipts	74.7	279.5	594.9	1,083.0	1,508.6	2,140.1	2,284.3	2,319.2
Equals: Personal income	838.6	2,301.5	4,846.7	8,559.4	10,485.9	11,867.0	12,321.9	12,947.3

(1) Subsidies are included net of the current surplus of government enterprises.

U.S. Gross Domestic Product, 2000-11

Source: Bureau of Economic Analysis, U.S. Dept. of Commerce

	Billions of current dollars				Billions of constant (2005) dollars			
	2000	2005	2010	2011	2000	2005	2010	2011
Gross domestic product	$9,951.5	$12,623.0	$14,498.9	$15,075.7	$11,216.4	$12,623.0	$13,063.0	$13,299.1
Personal consumption expenditures	6,830.4	8,803.5	10,215.7	10,729.0	7,604.6	8,803.5	9,196.2	9,428.8
Goods	2,459.1	3,076.7	3,364.9	3,624.8	2,518.2	3,076.7	3,209.1	3,331.0
Durable goods	915.8	1,123.4	1,079.4	1,146.4	818.0	1,123.4	1,178.3	1,262.6
Nondurable goods	1,543.4	1,953.4	2,285.5	2,478.4	1,714.5	1,953.4	2,029.3	2,075.2
Services	4,371.2	5,726.8	6,850.9	7,104.2	5,093.6	5,726.8	5,987.6	6,101.5
Gross private domestic investment	1,772.2	2,172.3	1,737.3	1,854.9	1,963.1	2,172.3	1,658.0	1,744.0
Fixed investment	1,717.7	2,122.3	1,679.0	1,818.3	1,906.8	2,122.3	1,598.7	1,704.5
Nonresidential	1,268.7	1,347.3	1,338.4	1,479.6	1,311.3	1,347.3	1,268.5	1,378.2
Structures	318.1	351.8	376.3	404.8	440.0	351.8	310.6	319.2
Equipment and software	950.5	995.6	962.1	1,074.7	889.2	995.6	963.9	1,070.0
Residential	449.0	775.0	340.6	338.7	580.0	775.0	332.2	327.6
Change in private inventories	54.5	50.0	58.4	36.6	60.2	50.0	50.9	31.0
Net exports of goods and services	−382.1	−722.7	−511.6	−568.1	−451.3	−722.7	−419.7	−408.0
Exports	1,093.2	1,305.1	1,844.4	2,094.2	1,187.4	1,305.1	1,665.6	1,776.9
Goods	784.3	906.1	1,278.5	1,474.5	843.4	906.1	1,164.1	1,247.6
Services	308.9	399.0	565.9	619.7	343.5	399.0	501.9	529.8
Imports	1,475.3	2,027.8	2,356.1	2,662.3	1,638.7	2,027.8	2,085.2	2,184.9
Goods	1,246.5	1,708.0	1,947.0	2,229.2	1,366.7	1,708.0	1,730.3	1,820.0
Services	228.8	319.8	409.1	433.0	271.7	319.8	356.6	366.6
Government consumption expenditures and gross investment	1,731.0	2,369.9	3,057.5	3,059.8	2,097.8	2,369.9	2,605.8	2,523.9
Federal	576.1	876.3	1,223.1	1,222.1	698.1	876.3	1,076.8	1,047.0
National defense	371.0	589.0	817.7	820.8	453.5	589.0	717.6	699.1
Nondefense	205.0	287.3	405.3	401.3	244.4	287.3	359.2	347.9
State and local	1,154.9	1,493.6	1,834.4	1,837.7	1,400.1	1,493.6	1,534.1	1,482.0

U.S. Gross Domestic Product, 1930-2011

Source: Bureau of Economic Analysis, U.S. Dept. of Commerce

(in billions of current dollars)

1930	1935	1940	1945	1950	1960	1965	1970	1975	1980	1985	1990	1995	2000	2005	2010	2011
91	73	101	223	294	526	719	1,038	1,638	2,788	4,218	5,801	7,415	9,952	12,623	14,999	15,076

U.S. National Income by Type, 1930-2011

Source: Bureau of Economic Analysis, U.S. Dept. of Commerce

(in billions of current dollars)

	1930	1940	1950	1960	1970	1980	1990	2000	2010	2011
NATIONAL INCOME[1,2]	$83.1	$90.9	$263.9	$473.9	$929.5	$2,433.0	$5,059.5	$8,938.9	$12,811.4	$13,358.9
Employee compensation	46.9	52.2	155.3	296.4	617.2	1,647.6	3,326.3	5,788.8	7,970.0	8,295.2
Wage and salary accruals	46.2	49.9	147.3	272.9	551.6	1,373.4	2,741.2	4,827.7	6,404.6	6,661.3
Government	5.2	8.5	22.6	49.2	117.2	261.5	519.0	779.7	1,191.3	1,195.3
Supplements to wages and salaries	0.7	2.3	8.0	23.6	65.7	274.2	585.1	961.2	1,565.4	1,633.9
Employer contributions for employee pension and insurance funds	0.6	0.9	4.7	14.3	41.8	185.2	378.6	615.9	1,097.3	1,139.0
Employer contributions for government social insurance	0.0	1.4	3.4	9.3	23.8	88.9	206.5	345.2	468.1	494.9
Proprietors' income with inventory valuation and capital consumption adjustments	11.1	12.3	37.5	50.7	78.5	173.5	365.1	817.5	1,103.4	1,157.3
Farm	4.0	4.1	12.9	10.6	12.9	11.7	32.2	29.6	44.3	54.6
Nonfarm	7.0	8.2	24.6	40.1	65.6	161.8	333.0	787.8	1,059.1	1,102.8
Rental income of persons with capital consumption adjustment	5.5	3.9	9.1	17.0	21.1	28.5	49.8	215.3	349.2	409.7
Corporate profits with inventory valuation and capital consumption adjustment	7.5	9.6	35.6	53.1	82.5	201.4	434.4	819.2	1,702.4	1,827.0
Taxes on corporate income	0.8	2.8	17.9	22.8	34.8	87.2	145.4	265.1	373.3	379.0
Profits after tax with inventory valuation and capital consumption adjustments	6.6	6.8	17.7	30.3	47.7	114.2	289.0	554.1	1,329.1	1,447.9
Net dividends	5.5	4.0	8.8	13.4	24.3	64.1	169.1	377.9	600.9	697.2
Undistributed profits with inventory valuation and capital consumption adjustments	1.1	2.8	8.9	16.9	23.4	50.2	120.0	176.3	728.2	750.7
Net interest and miscellaneous payments	4.8	3.3	3.2	10.6	39.1	181.8	444.2	539.3	567.9	527.4

(1) Numbers may not add up to totals because of rounding and incomplete enumeration. (2) National income is the aggregate of labor and property earnings that arise in the production of goods and services. It is the sum of employee compensation, proprietors' income, rental income, adjusted corporate profits, and net interest. It measures the total factor costs of goods and services produced by the economy. Income is measured before deduction of taxes. Total national income figures include adjustments not itemized.

U.S. National Income by Industry, 2000-11

Source: Bureau of Economic Analysis, U.S. Dept. of Commerce

(in billions of current dollars)

	2000	2005	2007	2008	2009	2010	2011
National income without capital consumption adjustment	$8,817.9	$11,353.9	$12,500.0	$12,532.1	$12,099.7	$12,740.4	$13,135.1
Domestic industries	8,780.2	11,256.8	12,376.7	12,363.0	11,956.2	12,531.1	12,883.2
Private industries	7,762.4	9,921.4	10,908.1	10,819.7	10,362.8	10,897.9	11,239.4
Agriculture, forestry, fishing, and hunting	71.4	92.8	110.5	120.7	110.9	119.0	131.6
Arts, entertainment, recreation, accommodation, and food services	339.4	434.8	490.3	475.6	459.1	487.1	508.9
Construction	478.0	657.0	685.8	629.0	547.6	539.4	552.0
Educ. services, health care, social assistance	692.2	993.5	1,114.8	1,189.4	1,251.6	1,308.0	1,343.5
Finance, insurance, real estate, rental, and leasing	1,539.3	1,998.5	2,160.3	2,130.5	2,158.8	2,178.4	2,175.7
Information	296.0	408.1	452.6	439.2	417.6	425.4	441.0
Manufacturing	1,194.6	1,304.8	1,409.1	1,333.0	1,168.6	1,296.8	1,372.0
Durable goods	723.8	744.0	800.9	750.1	631.9	722.3	768.8
Nondurable goods	470.9	560.8	608.2	583.0	536.6	574.5	603.2
Mining	92.5	163.1	204.5	251.8	148.2	177.1	202.8
Professional and business services	1,120.7	1,490.3	1,684.9	1,752.6	1,683.2	1,823.9	1,889.5
Retail trade	674.1	859.6	902.1	837.0	838.5	876.2	893.3
Transportation and warehousing	272.7	332.9	361.0	362.6	340.8	371.7	387.4
Utilities	136.2	161.3	198.4	183.2	174.7	184.4	180.4
Wholesale trade	570.8	688.4	769.1	754.8	701.1	733.5	771.8
Other services, except government	284.5	336.3	364.8	360.3	362.1	377.2	389.5
Government	1,017.8	1,335.3	1,468.6	1,543.2	1,593.3	1,633.3	1,643.8
Rest of the world	37.7	97.1	123.3	169.2	143.5	209.3	251.9

Consumer Price Index

The Consumer Price Index (CPI) is a measure of the change in prices over time of one or more kinds of basic consumer goods and services.

Beginning in Jan. 1978, the Bureau of Labor Statistics began publishing CPIs for two population groups: (1) a CPI for all urban consumers (CPI-U), which covers about 87% of the total U.S. population; and (2) a CPI for urban wage earners and clerical workers (CPI-W), which covers about 32% of the total U.S. population. In addition to wage earners and clerical workers, the CPI-U includes professional, managerial, and technical workers; the self-employed; short-term workers; the unemployed; retirees; and others not in the labor force.

The CPI is based on the price of food, clothing, shelter, and fuels; transportation fares; charges for doctors' and dentists' services; drug prices; and the cost of other goods and services bought for day-to-day living. The index currently measures price changes from a designated reference period, 1982-84, which equals 100.0. Use of this reference period began in Jan. 1988.

U.S. Consumer Price Index by Major Group, 1915-2011

Source: Bureau of Labor Statistics, U.S. Dept. of Labor

For all urban consumers. **1982-84 = 100**, unless otherwise noted.

Year	All items	Apparel	Food & beverages	Housing	Transportation	Medical care	Entertainment & recreation[1]	Educ. & communication[1]	Other goods & services
1915	10.1	15.3	—	—	—	—	—	—	—
1920	20.0	43.1	—	—	—	—	—	—	—
1930	16.7	24.2	—	—	—	—	—	—	—
1940	14.0	21.8	—	—	14.2	10.4	—	—	—
1945	18.0	31.4	—	—	15.9	11.9	—	—	—
1950	24.1	40.3	—	—	22.7	15.1	—	—	—
1955	26.8	42.9	—	—	25.8	18.2	—	—	—
1960	29.6	45.7	—	—	29.8	22.3	—	—	—
1965	31.5	47.8	—	—	31.9	25.2	—	—	—
1970	38.8	59.2	40.1	36.4	37.5	34.0	—	—	40.9
1975	53.8	72.5	60.2	50.7	50.1	47.5	—	—	53.9
1980	82.4	90.9	86.7	81.1	83.1	74.9	—	—	75.2
1985	107.6	105.0	105.6	107.7	106.4	113.5	—	—	114.5
1990	130.7	124.1	132.1	128.5	120.5	162.8	—	—	159.0
1995	152.4	132.0	148.9	148.5	139.1	220.5	94.5	92.2	206.9
2000	172.2	129.6	168.4	169.6	153.3	260.8	103.3	102.5	271.1
2005	195.3	119.5	191.2	195.7	173.9	323.2	109.4	113.7	313.4
2006	201.6	119.5	195.7	203.2	180.9	336.2	110.9	116.8	321.7
2007	207.3	119.0	203.3	209.6	184.7	351.1	111.4	119.6	333.3
2008	215.3	118.9	214.2	216.2	195.5	364.1	113.3	123.6	345.4
2009	214.5	120.0	218.2	217.1	179.3	375.6	114.3	127.4	368.6
2010	218.1	119.5	220.0	216.3	193.4	388.4	113.3	129.9	381.3
2011	224.9	122.1	227.9	219.1	212.4	400.3	113.4	131.5	387.2

— = Comparable data not available. (1) Dec. 1997 = 100.

U.S. Consumer Price Index, 1915-2011

Source: Bureau of Labor Statistics, U.S. Dept. of Labor

Annual averages of monthly figures, specified for all urban consumers. **1982-84 = 100**.

Excluding 2009, prices as measured by the U.S. Consumer Price Index have risen steadily since World War II. What cost $1.00 in 1982-84 cost about $0.10 in 1913, $0.18 in 1945, and $2.25 in 2011.

U.S. Consumer Price Indexes for Selected Items and Groups, 1970-2011

Source: Bureau of Labor Statistics, U.S. Dept. of Labor

Annual averages of monthly figures, specified for all urban consumers. **1982-84 = 100**, unless otherwise noted.

	1970	1975	1980	1985	1990	1995	2000	2005	2009	2010	2011
ALL ITEMS....................	38.8	53.8	82.4	107.6	130.7	152.4	172.2	195.3	214.5	218.1	224.9
Food and beverages.............	40.1	60.2	86.7	105.6	132.1	148.9	168.4	191.2	218.2	220.0	227.9
Food.......................	39.2	59.8	86.8	105.6	132.4	148.4	167.8	190.7	218.0	219.6	227.8
Food at home............	39.9	61.8	88.4	104.3	132.3	148.8	167.9	189.8	215.1	215.8	226.2
Cereals and bakery products	37.1	62.9	83.9	107.9	140.0	167.5	188.3	209.0	252.6	250.4	260.3
Meats, poultry, fish, eggs	44.6	67.0	92.0	100.1	130.0	138.8	154.5	184.7	203.8	207.7	223.2
Dairy products	44.7	62.6	90.9	103.2	126.5	132.8	160.7	182.4	197.0	199.2	212.7
Fruits and vegetables.......	37.8	56.9	82.1	106.4	149.0	177.7	204.6	241.4	272.9	273.5	284.7
Nonalcoholic beverages.....	27.1	41.3	91.4	104.3	113.5	131.7	137.8	144.4	163.0	161.6	166.8
Sugar and sweets........	30.5	65.3	90.5	105.8	124.7	137.5	154.0	165.2	196.9	201.2	207.8
Fats and oils............	39.2	73.5	89.3	106.9	126.3	137.3	147.4	167.7	201.2	200.6	219.2
Other foods.............	39.6	58.9	83.6	106.4	131.2	151.1	172.2	182.5	205.5	204.6	209.3
Food away from home	37.5	54.5	83.4	108.3	133.4	149.0	169.0	193.4	223.3	226.1	231.4
Alcoholic beverages............	52.1	65.9	86.4	106.4	129.3	153.9	174.7	195.9	220.8	223.3	226.7
Housing......................	36.4	50.7	81.1	107.7	128.5	148.5	169.6	195.7	217.1	216.3	219.1
Shelter	35.5	48.8	81.0	109.8	140.0	165.7	193.4	224.4	249.4	248.4	251.6
Rent of primary residence	46.5	58.0	80.9	111.8	138.4	157.8	183.9	217.3	248.8	249.4	253.6
Fuels and utilities	29.1	45.4	75.4	106.5	111.6	123.7	137.9	179.0	210.7	214.2	220.4
Household furnishings and operations	46.8	63.4	86.3	103.8	113.3	123.0	128.2	126.1	128.7	125.5	124.9

	1970	1975	1980	1985	1990	1995	2000	2005	2009	2010	2011
Apparel	59.2	72.5	90.9	105.0	124.1	132.0	129.6	119.5	120.1	119.5	122.1
Men's and boys'	62.2	75.5	89.4	105.0	120.4	126.2	129.7	116.1	113.6	111.9	114.7
Women's and girls'	71.8	85.5	96.0	104.9	122.6	126.9	121.5	110.8	108.1	107.1	109.2
Footwear	56.8	69.6	91.8	102.3	117.4	125.4	123.8	122.6	126.9	128.0	128.5
Transportation	37.5	50.1	83.1	106.4	120.5	139.1	153.3	173.9	179.3	193.4	212.4
Private	37.5	50.6	84.2	106.2	118.8	136.3	149.1	170.2	174.8	188.7	207.6
New vehicles	53.0	62.9	88.4	106.1	121.4	139.0	142.8	137.9	135.6	138.0	141.9
Used cars and trucks	31.2	43.8	62.3	113.7	117.6	156.5	155.8	139.4	127.0	143.1	149.0
Gasoline	27.9	45.1	97.5	98.6	101.0	99.8	128.6	194.7	201.6	238.6	301.7
Public	35.2	43.5	69.0	110.5	142.6	175.9	209.6	217.3	236.3	251.4	269.4
Medical care	34.0	47.5	74.9	113.5	162.8	220.5	260.8	323.2	375.6	388.4	400.3
Entertainment/recreation[1]	47.5	62.0	83.6	107.9	132.4	153.9	103.3	109.4	114.3	113.3	113.4
Other goods and services	40.9	53.9	75.2	114.5	159.0	206.9	271.1	313.4	368.6	381.3	387.2
Tobacco products	43.1	54.7	72.0	116.7	181.5	225.7	394.9	502.8	730.3	807.3	834.8
Personal care	43.5	57.9	81.9	106.3	130.4	147.1	165.6	185.6	204.6	206.6	208.6
Personal care products	42.7	58.0	79.6	107.6	128.2	143.1	153.7	154.4	162.6	161.1	160.5
Personal care services	44.2	57.7	83.7	108.9	132.8	151.5	178.1	203.9	227.6	229.6	230.8

(1) Dec. 1997 = 100. Entertainment was reclassified as Recreation in 1997.

Consumer Price Indexes by Region and Major Cities, 1990-2011

Source: Bureau of Labor Statistics, U.S. Dept. of Labor
For all urban consumers; % change not annualized. **1982-84 = 100**, unless otherwise noted.

Region and city	1990	1995	2000	2005	2008	2009	2010	2011
U.S. city average	130.7	152.4	172.2	195.3	215.3	214.5	218.1	224.9
Northeast urban	136.3	159.1	179.4	207.5	229.3	229.3	233.9	241.0
Boston-Brockton-Nashua, MA-NH-ME-CT	138.9	158.6	183.6	216.4	235.4	233.8	237.4	243.9
New York-Northern New Jersey-Long Island, NY-NJ-CT-PA	138.5	162.2	182.5	212.7	235.8	236.8	240.9	247.7
Philadelphia-Wilmington-Atlantic City, PA-NJ-DE-MD	135.8	158.7	176.5	204.2	224.1	223.3	227.7	233.8
Pittsburgh, PA	126.2	149.2	168.0	189.8	211.3	212.1	215.4	225.1
Midwest urban	127.4	148.4	168.3	188.4	205.4	204.1	208.0	214.7
Chicago-Gary-Kenosha, IL-IN-WI	131.7	153.3	173.8	194.3	212.5	210.0	212.9	218.7
Cincinnati-Hamilton, OH-KY-IN	126.5	146.2	164.8	181.6	201.5	200.6	204.7	211.1
Cleveland-Akron, OH	129.0	147.9	168.0	187.9	203.0	200.5	204.6	211.0
Detroit-Ann Arbor-Flint, MI	128.6	148.6	169.8	190.8	204.7	203.5	205.1	211.8
Kansas City, MO-KS	126.0	145.3	166.6	185.3	201.2	201.0	205.4	213.5
Milwaukee-Racine, WI	126.2	151.0	168.6	185.2	203.0	203.0	209.6	216.9
Minneapolis-St. Paul, MN-WI	127.0	147.0	170.1	193.1	209.0	207.9	211.7	219.3
St. Louis, MO-IL	128.1	145.2	163.1	186.2	198.7	198.5	203.2	209.8
South urban	127.9	149.0	167.2	188.3	208.7	207.8	211.3	218.6
Atlanta, GA	131.7	150.9	170.6	188.9	206.5	201.0	203.5	209.1
Dallas-Fort Worth, TX	125.1	144.9	164.7	184.7	201.8	200.5	201.6	207.9
Houston-Galveston-Brazoria, TX	120.6	139.8	154.2	175.6	190.0	190.5	194.2	200.5
Miami-Fort Lauderdale, FL	128.0	148.9	167.8	194.3	222.1	221.4	223.1	230.9
Tampa-St. Petersburg-Clearwater, FL[1]	111.7	129.7	145.7	168.5	190.1	189.9	193.5	198.9
Washington-Baltimore, DC-MD-VA-WV[2]	NA	NA	107.6	124.3	139.5	139.8	142.2	147.0
West urban	131.5	153.5	174.8	198.9	219.6	218.8	221.2	227.5
Anchorage, AK	118.6	138.9	150.9	171.8	189.5	191.7	195.1	201.4
Denver-Boulder-Greeley, CO	120.9	147.9	173.2	190.9	209.9	208.5	212.4	220.3
Honolulu, HI	138.1	168.1	176.3	197.8	228.9	230.0	234.9	243.6
Los Angeles-Riverside-Orange County, CA	135.9	154.6	171.6	201.8	225.0	223.2	225.9	231.9
Phoenix-Mesa, AZ[3]	NA	NA	NA	108.3	119.3	117.6	118.2	121.5
Portland-Salem, OR-WA	127.4	153.2	178.0	196.0	215.4	215.6	218.3	224.6
San Diego, CA	138.4	156.8	182.8	220.6	242.3	242.3	245.5	252.9
San Francisco-Oakland-San Jose, CA	132.1	151.6	180.2	202.7	222.8	224.4	227.5	233.4
Seattle-Tacoma-Bremerton, WA	126.8	152.3	179.2	200.2	224.7	226.0	226.7	232.8

NA = Not available. (1) 1987 = 100. (2) Nov. 1996 = 100. (3) Dec. 2001 = 100.

Distribution of U.S. Total Personal Income, 1930-2011

Source: Bureau of Economic Analysis, U.S. Dept. of Commerce
(in billions of current dollars)

Year	Personal income	Personal taxes and nontax payments	Disposable personal income	Personal outlays	Personal savings	Savings as % of income[1]
1930	$76.1	$1.6	$74.6	$71.6	$2.9	4.0%
1940	78.4	1.7	76.8	72.4	4.3	5.7
1950	228.0	18.9	209.9	195.0	14.9	7.1
1960	411.3	46.1	365.2	338.9	26.3	7.2
1970	838.6	103.1	735.5	666.1	69.4	9.4
1980	2,301.5	298.9	2,002.7	1,806.4	196.3	9.8
1990	4,846.7	592.7	4,254.0	3,977.3	276.7	6.5
2000	8,559.4	1,232.3	7,327.2	7,114.1	213.1	2.9
2005	10,485.9	1,208.6	9,277.3	9,149.6	143.2	1.5
2006	11,268.1	1,352.4	9,915.7	9,659.1	256.6	2.6
2007	11,912.3	1,488.7	10,423.6	10,174.9	248.7	2.4
2008	12,460.2	1,435.7	11,024.5	10,432.2	592.3	5.4
2009	11,867.0	1,144.6	10,722.4	10,214.3	508.2	4.7
2010	12,321.9	1,194.8	11,127.1	10,560.4	566.7	5.1
2011	12,947.3	1,398.0	11,549.3	11,059.9	489.4	4.2

Note: Personal income minus taxes/nontax payments equals disposable income; disposable income minus outlays equals savings. Figures may not add up to totals because of rounding. (1) Personal savings as a percentage of disposable personal income.

Median Income by Race, Hispanic Origin, and Sex, 1947-2011

Source: *Current Population Survey*, U.S. Census Bureau, U.S. Dept. of Commerce

Race, Hispanic origin, and year		Male			Female		
		Number with income (thous.)	Median income Current dollars	Median income 2011 dollars	Number with income (thous.)	Median income Current dollars	Median income 2011 dollars
All races	2011	106,228	$32,986	$32,986	108,332	$21,102	$21,102
	2010	105,191	32,205	33,221	107,220	20,775	21,430
	2009	105,025	32,184	33,747	106,229	20,957	21,975
	2005	102,986	31,275	36,031	104,245	18,576	21,401
	2000	98,504	28,343	37,017	101,704	16,063	20,979
	1990	88,220	20,293	33,852	92,245	10,070	16,799
	1980	78,661	12,530	32,562	80,826	4,920	12,786
	1970	65,008	6,670	34,477	51,647	2,237	11,563
	1960	55,172	4,080	27,115	36,526	1,261	8,380
	1950	47,585	2,570	20,960	24,651	953	7,772
	1947	46,813	2,230	19,642	21,479	1,017	8,958
White	2011	87,083	35,344	35,344	85,993	21,379	21,379
	2010	86,368	34,374	35,458	85,486	20,896	21,555
	2009	87,400	33,748	35,387	85,760	21,118	22,144
	2005	85,996	32,179	37,073	84,768	18,669	21,508
	2000	83,372	29,797	38,916	84,123	16,079	21,000
	1990	76,480	21,170	35,315	78,566	10,317	17,211
	1980	69,420	13,328	34,636	70,573	4,947	12,856
	1970	58,447	7,011	36,240	45,288	2,266	11,713
	1960	49,788	4,296	28,551	32,001	1,352	8,985
	1950	NA	2,709	22,093	NA	1,060	8,645
	1948	NA	2,510	20,470	NA	1,133	9,240
White, not Hispanic	2011	72,902	38,148	38,148	74,206	22,226	22,226
	2010	72,723	37,154	38,326	73,995	21,715	22,400
	2009	73,485	36,785	38,572	74,693	21,939	23,005
	2005	73,219	35,345	40,720	75,014	19,451	22,409
	2000	72,530	31,508	41,151	75,206	16,665	21,765
	1990	69,987	21,958	36,630	72,939	10,581	17,651
	1980	65,564	13,681	35,553	67,084	4,980	12,942
Black	2011	11,562	23,584	23,584	14,411	19,561	19,561
	2010	11,433	23,086	23,814	14,212	19,548	20,165
	2009	11,064	23,674	24,824	13,793	19,413	20,356
	2005	10,651	22,609	26,047	13,237	17,595	20,271
	2000	9,905	21,343	27,875	12,461	15,881	20,741
	1990	8,820	12,868	21,466	10,687	8,328	13,893
	1980	7,387	8,009	20,813	8,596	4,580	11,902
	1970	5,844	4,157	21,488	5,844	2,063	10,664
	1960	5,384	2,260	15,020	4,525	837	5,563
	1950	NA	1,471	11,997	NA	474	3,866
	1949	NA	1,196	9,876	NA	495	4,087
	1948	NA	1,363	11,116	NA	492	4,013
Asian	2011	5,556	35,835	35,835	5,820	22,013	22,013
	2010	5,406	35,121	36,229	5,604	23,552	24,295
	2009	4,828	36,886	38,678	4,923	24,170	25,344
	2005	4,518	33,036	38,060	4,520	21,623	24,911
	2000	4,303	30,833	40,269	4,192	17,356	22,668
	1990	2,235	19,394	32,353	2,333	11,086	18,493
Hispanic	2011	15,665	23,731	23,731	13,278	16,829	16,829
	2010	15,106	22,420	23,127	12,947	16,292	16,806
	2009	14,919	22,256	23,337	12,035	16,210	16,997
	2005	13,714	22,089	25,448	10,638	15,036	17,323
	2000	11,343	19,498	25,465	9,431	12,248	15,996
	1990	6,767	13,470	22,470	5,903	7,532	12,565
	1980	3,996	9,659	25,101	3,617	4,405	11,447

NA = Not available. **Note:** Income for persons 15 years of age and over beginning in Mar. 1980; 14 years of age and over as of Mar. of the following year for previous years. Beginning in 2005, Black and Asian totals include those who identified themselves as being black or Asian in combination with some other race. Asian category includes Pacific Islanders before 2005.

Consumer Credit Outstanding, 2009-11

Source: Federal Reserve System

(in billions of dollars as of Dec. of year shown, not seasonally adjusted)

	2009	2010	2011		2009	2010	2011
TOTAL	$2,438.7	$2,545.3	$2,631.5	Credit unions	$35.4	$36.3	$37.9
Major holders				Federal government[1]	—	—	—
Depository institutions	906.3	1,185.5	1,192.6	Nonfinancial business	32.3	32.8	32.8
Finance companies	471.9	708.4	690.6	Pools of securitized assets[2] . . .	441.9	31.4	29.8
Credit unions	237.1	226.5	223.0	**Nonrevolving**[3]	1,516.9	1,695.1	1,780.1
Federal government[1]	178.6	308.8	417.4	Depository institutions	532.3	520.8	528.7
Nonfinancial business	51.7	53.1	53.1	Finance companies	433.6	623.5	603.6
Pools of securitized assets[2] . . .	593.2	63.0	54.8	Credit unions	201.7	190.1	185.1
Major types of credit				Federal government[1]	178.6	308.8	417.4
Revolving.	921.9	850.2	851.4	Nonfinancial business	19.4	20.3	20.3
Depository institutions	373.9	664.7	663.9	Pools of securitized assets[2] . . .	151.3	31.7	25.0
Finance companies	38.3	85.0	87.1				

— = Not available. (1) Includes loans originated by the Dept. of Education under the Federal Direct Loan Program, as well as Federal Family Education Loan Program loans that the government purchased from depository institutions and finance companies. (2) Outstanding balances of pools upon which securities have been issued; these balances are no longer carried on the balance sheets of the loan originators. (3) Includes estimates for holders that do not separately report consumer credit holding by type.

Financial Assets of U.S. Families, 1989-2010

Source: *Survey of Consumer Finances* (triennial), Federal Reserve System

Category	1989	1992	1995	1998	2001	2004	2007	2010
Median net worth (thous.)	$59.7	$56.5	$60.9	$71.6	$106.1	$107.2	$126.4	$77.3
Average net worth (thous.)	236.9	212.7	224.8	282.5	487.0	517.1	584.6	498.8
Financial assets								
Transaction accounts	19.1%	17.5%	14.0%	11.4%	11.4%	13.1%	10.9%	13.3%
Certificates of deposit	10.2	8.1	5.7	4.3	3.1	3.7	4.0	3.9
Savings bonds	1.5	1.1	1.3	0.7	0.7	0.5	0.4	0.3
Bonds	10.2	8.4	6.3	4.3	4.5	5.3	4.1	4.4
Stocks	15.0	16.5	15.7	22.7	21.5	17.5	17.8	14.0
Mutual funds (excluding money market funds)	5.3	7.7	12.7	12.5	12.1	14.6	15.8	15.0
Retirement accounts	21.5	25.5	27.9	27.5	29.0	32.4	35.1	38.1
Cash value of life insurance	6.0	6.0	7.2	6.4	5.3	2.9	3.2	2.5
Other managed assets	6.6	5.4	5.9	8.6	10.5	7.9	6.5	6.2
Other	4.8	3.8	3.4	1.7	1.9	2.1	2.1	2.3
Financial assets as % of total assets	30.4	31.5	36.6	40.6	42.2	35.8	34.0	37.9

Wealthiest Americans, 2012

Source: *Forbes* magazine
(as of Sept. 1, 2012; ranked by 2012 net worth)

The 20 wealthiest Americans saw their net worth increase by a combined $85.7 bil in 2012. Only two of the top 20 lost money, while the top 10 all increased their holdings by more than $3 bil each.

		Net worth (bil)		% change,			
Rank	Name	2011	2012	2011-12	Age	Residence	Source of wealth
1.	Bill Gates	$59.0	$66.0	11.9%	56 . . .	Medina, WA	Microsoft
2.	Warren Buffett	39.0	46.0	17.9	82 . . .	Omaha, NE	Berkshire Hathaway
3.	Lawrence Ellison	33.0	41.0	24.2	68 . . .	Woodside, CA	Oracle
4.	Charles Koch	25.0	31.0	24.0	76 . . .	Wichita, KS	Manufacturing, energy
	David Koch	25.0	31.0	24.0	72 . . .	New York, NY	Manufacturing, energy
6.	Christy Walton	24.5	27.9	13.9	57 . . .	Jackson, WY	Wal-Mart
7.	Jim C. Walton	21.1	26.8	27.0	64 . . .	Bentonville, AR	Wal-Mart
8.	Alice Walton	20.9	26.3	25.8	62 . . .	Fort Worth, TX	Wal-Mart
9.	S. Robson Walton	20.5	26.1	27.3	68 . . .	Bentonville, AR	Wal-Mart
10.	Michael Bloomberg	19.5	25.0	28.2	70 . . .	New York, NY	Bloomberg, LP
11.	Jeff Bezos	19.1	23.2	21.5	48 . . .	Seattle, WA	Amazon.com
12.	Sheldon Adelson	21.5	20.5	−4.7	79 . . .	Las Vegas, NV	Sands casinos
13.	Sergey Brin	16.7	20.3	21.6	39 . . .	Los Altos, CA	Google
	Larry Page	16.7	20.3	21.6	39 . . .	Palo Alto, CA	Google
15.	George Soros	22.0	19.0	−13.6	82 . . .	Katonah, NY	Hedge funds
16.	Forrest Mars Jr.	13.8	17.0	23.2	81 . . .	Big Horn, WY	Mars candy
	Jacqueline Mars	13.8	17.0	23.2	73 . . .	The Plains, VA	Mars candy
	John Mars	13.8	17.0	23.2	76 . . .	Jackson, WY	Mars candy
19.	Steve Ballmer	13.9	15.9	14.4	56 . . .	Hunts Point, WA.	Microsoft
20.	Paul Allen	13.2	15.0	13.6	59 . . .	Mercer Island, WA	Microsoft

Poverty Rate

Source: U.S. Census Bureau, U.S. Dept. of Commerce

The poverty rate is the proportion of the population whose income falls below the government's official poverty level, which is adjusted each year for inflation. The national poverty rate dropped slightly from 15.1% in 2010 to 15.0% in 2011. More than 46 mil people in the U.S. were in poverty in 2011, up from 31.6 mil in 2000. In 2010, 21.9% of children under 18 and 8.7% of people aged 65 and older were defined as poor.

Persons Below Poverty Level, 1960-2011

Source: U.S. Census Bureau, U.S. Dept. of Commerce

	Number below poverty level (mil)					% of subgroup below poverty level					Avg. income cut-off, family of 4 at poverty level[4]
Year	All races[1]	Asian[2]	White	Black[2]	Hispanic[3]	All races[1]	Asian[2]	White	Black[2]	Hispanic[3]	
1960	39.9	NA	28.3	NA	NA	22.2%	NA	17.8%	NA	NA	$3,022
1970	25.4	NA	17.5	7.5	NA	12.6	NA	9.9	33.5%	NA	3,968
1980	29.3	NA	19.7	8.6	3.5	13.0	NA	10.2	32.5	25.7%	8,414
1990	33.6	0.9	22.3	9.8	6.0	13.5	12.2%	10.7	31.9	28.1	13,359
1995	36.4	1.4	24.4	9.9	8.6	13.8	14.6	11.2	29.3	30.3	15,569
2000	31.6	1.3	21.6	8.0	7.7	11.3	9.9	9.5	22.5	21.5	17,604
2001	32.9	1.3	22.7	8.1	8.0	11.7	10.2	9.9	22.7	21.4	18,104
2002	34.6	1.2	23.5	8.9	8.6	12.1	10.0	10.2	23.9	21.8	18,392
2003	35.9	1.5	24.3	9.1	9.1	12.5	11.8	10.5	24.3	22.5	18,810
2004	37.0	1.3	25.3	9.4	9.1	12.7	9.7	10.8	24.7	21.9	19,307
2005	37.0	1.5	24.9	9.5	9.4	12.6	10.9	10.6	24.7	21.8	19,971
2006	36.5	1.4	24.4	9.5	9.2	12.3	10.1	10.3	24.2	20.6	20,614
2007	37.3	1.5	25.1	9.7	9.9	12.5	10.2	10.5	24.4	21.5	21,203
2008	39.8	1.7	27.0	9.9	11.0	13.2	11.6	11.2	24.6	23.2	22,025
2009	43.6	1.9	29.8	10.6	12.4	14.3	12.4	12.3	25.9	25.3	21,954
2010	46.3	2.1	31.1	11.6	13.5	15.1	12.0	13.0	27.4	26.5	22,315
2011	46.2	2.2	30.8	11.7	13.2	15.0	12.3	12.8	27.5	25.3	23,021

NA = Not available. **Note:** Because of a change in the definition of poverty, data prior to 1980 are not directly comparable to data since 1980. (1) Includes other races not shown separately. (2) Beginning in 2002, totals include those who identified themselves as being Asian or black in combination with some other race. Asian includes Pacific Islanders 1990-2000. (3) Persons of Hispanic origin may be of any race. (4) Figures for 1960-80 for nonfarm families only.

Poverty Thresholds by Family Size, 1980-2011
Source: U.S. Census Bureau, U.S. Dept. of Commerce

	1980	1990	2000	2010	2011		1980	1990	2000	2010	2011
1 person	$4,190	$6,652	$8,791	$11,137	$11,484	3 people	$6,565	$10,419	$13,740	$17,373	$17,916
Under age 65. . . .	4,290	6,800	8,959	11,344	11,702	4 people	8,414	13,359	17,604	22,315	23,021
Age 65 or older . .	3,949	6,268	8,259	10,458	10,788	5 people	9,966	15,792	20,815	26,442	27,251
2 people	5,363	8,509	11,235	14,216	14,657	6 people	11,269	17,839	23,533	29,904	30,847
Householder						7 people	12,761	20,241	26,750	34,019	35,085
under age 65 . .	5,537	8,794	11,589	14,676	15,139	8 people	14,199	22,582	29,701	37,953	39,064
Householder age						9 or more people . .	16,896	26,848	35,150	45,224	46,572
65 or older.	4,983	7,905	10,418	13,194	13,609						

Note: Weighted averages; not used for computing poverty data.

Families Below Poverty Level by Status, Race, and Sex, 1990-2011
Source: U.S. Census Bureau, U.S. Dept. of Commerce
(numbers in thousands)

Year and race	All families			Married-couple families			Male householder, no wife present			Female householder, no husband present		
		Below poverty level			Below poverty level			Below poverty level			Below poverty level	
	Total	Number	Percent	Total	Number	Percent	Total	Number	Percent	Total	Number	Percent
All races												
1990	66,322	7,098	10.7%	52,147	2,981	5.7%	2,907	349	12.0%	11,268	3,768	33.4%
1995	69,597	7,532	10.8	53,570	2,982	5.6	3,513	493	14.0	12,514	4,057	32.4
2000	73,778	6,400	8.7	56,598	2,637	4.7	4,277	485	11.3	12,903	3,278	25.4
2005	77,418	7,657	9.9	58,189	2,944	5.1	5,134	669	13.0	14,095	4,044	28.7
2009	78,867	8,792	11.1	58,428	3,409	5.8	5,582	942	16.9	14,857	4,441	29.9
2010	79,559	9,400	11.8	58,667	3,681	6.3	5,649	892	15.8	15,243	4,827	31.7
2011	80,529	9,497	11.8	58,963	3,652	6.2	5,888	950	16.1	15,678	4,894	31.2
White[1]												
1990	56,803	4,622	8.1	47,014	2,386	5.1	2,277	226	9.9	7,512	2,010	26.8
1995	58,872	4,994	8.5	47,877	2,443	5.1	2,711	351	12.9	8,284	2,200	26.6
2000	61,330	4,333	7.1	49,473	2,181	4.4	3,283	332	10.1	8,574	1,820	21.2
2005	63,414	5,068	8.0	50,369	2,317	4.6	3,906	439	11.2	9,139	2,312	25.3
2009	64,145	5,994	9.3	50,180	2,694	5.4	4,196	629	15.0	9,769	2,671	27.3
2010	63,976	6,305	9.9	50,016	2,921	5.8	4,176	563	13.5	9,784	2,822	28.8
2011	64,625	6,334	9.8	50,061	2,863	5.7	4,348	614	14.1	10,216	2,857	28.0
Black[1]												
1990	7,471	2,193	29.3	3,569	448	12.6	472	97	20.6	3,430	1,648	48.1
1995	8,055	2,127	26.4	3,713	314	8.5	573	112	19.5	3,769	1,701	45.1
2000	8,731	1,686	19.3	4,214	266	6.3	732	120	16.3	3,785	1,300	34.3
2005	9,051	1,997	22.1	4,128	341	8.3	806	170	21.1	4,117	1,486	36.1
2009	9,367	2,125	22.7	4,276	366	8.6	939	234	25.0	4,152	1,524	36.7
2010	9,571	2,311	24.1	4,267	377	8.8	916	236	25.7	4,387	1,698	38.7
2011	9,656	2,334	24.2	4,362	408	9.4	956	234	24.4	4,338	1,693	39.0

(1) Data are for one race only. The Census Bureau revised race categories in 2002, so data after 2002 are not directly comparable with data for previous years.

Poverty Rates by State, 1990-2011
Source: U.S. Census Bureau, U.S. Dept. of Commerce

State	1990	2000	2005	2010	2011	State	1990	2000	2005	2010	2011
Alabama	19.2%	13.3%	16.7%	17.2%	15.4%	Montana	16.3%	14.1%	13.8%	14.5%	16.5%
Alaska.	11.4	7.6	10.0	12.5	11.7	Nebraska	10.3	8.6	9.5	10.2	10.2
Arizona	13.7	11.7	15.2	18.8	17.2	Nevada	9.8	8.8	10.6	16.6	15.5
Arkansas.	19.6	16.5	13.8	15.3	18.7	New Hampshire	6.3	4.5	5.6	6.5	7.6
California	13.9	12.7	13.2	16.3	16.9	New Jersey.	9.2	7.3	6.8	11.1	11.4
Colorado.	13.7	9.8	11.4	12.3	13.2	New Mexico	20.9	17.5	17.9	18.3	22.2
Connecticut.	6.0	7.7	9.3	8.6	10.1	New York	14.3	13.9	14.5	16.0	16.0
Delaware	6.9	8.4	9.2	12.2	13.7	North Carolina . .	13.0	12.5	13.1	17.4	15.4
Dist. of Columbia	21.1	15.2	21.3	19.5	19.9	North Dakota . . .	13.7	10.4	11.2	12.6	9.9
Florida.	14.4	11.0	11.1	16.0	14.9	Ohio	11.5	10.0	12.3	15.4	15.1
Georgia.	15.8	12.1	14.4	18.8	18.4	Oklahoma	15.6	14.9	15.6	16.3	13.9
Hawaii.	11.0	8.9	8.6	12.4	12.1	Oregon	9.2	10.9	12.0	14.3	14.4
Idaho.	14.9	12.5	9.9	13.8	15.7	Pennsylvania . . .	11.0	8.6	11.2	12.2	12.6
Illinois	13.7	10.7	11.5	14.1	14.2	Rhode Island . . .	7.5	10.2	12.1	14.0	13.4
Indiana	13.0	8.5	12.6	16.3	15.6	South Carolina . .	16.2	11.1	15.0	16.9	19.0
Iowa	10.4	8.3	11.3	10.3	10.4	South Dakota . . .	13.3	10.7	11.8	13.6	14.5
Kansas	10.3	8.0	12.5	14.5	14.3	Tennessee	16.9	13.5	14.9	16.7	16.3
Kentucky.	17.3	12.6	14.8	17.7	16.0	Texas	15.9	15.5	16.2	18.4	17.4
Louisiana	23.6	17.2	18.3	21.5	21.1	Utah	8.2	7.6	9.2	10.0	11.0
Maine	13.1	10.1	12.6	12.6	13.4	Vermont	10.9	10.0	7.6	10.8	11.6
Maryland.	9.9	7.4	9.7	10.9	9.3	Virginia	11.1	8.3	9.2	10.7	11.4
Massachusetts . .	10.7	9.8	10.1	10.9	10.6	Washington.	8.9	10.8	10.2	11.6	12.5
Michigan	14.3	9.9	12.0	15.7	15.0	West Virginia . . .	18.1	14.7	15.4	16.8	17.5
Minnesota	12.0	5.7	8.1	10.8	10.0	Wisconsin	9.3	9.3	10.2	10.1	13.1
Mississippi	25.7	14.9	20.1	22.5	17.4	Wyoming.	11.0	10.8	10.6	9.6	10.7
Missouri	13.4	9.2	11.6	15.0	15.4	**United States** . .	**13.5**	**11.3**	**12.6**	**15.1**	**15.0**

Selected Personal Consumption Expenditures in the U.S., 1990-2011

Source: Bureau of Economic Analysis, U.S. Dept. of Commerce

(in billions of dollars)

	1990	1995	2000	2005	2009	2010	2011
Personal consumption expenditures	$3,835.5	$4,987.3	$6,830.4	$8,803.5	$9,845.9	$10,215.7	$10,729.0
GOODS	1,491.3	1,815.5	2,459.1	3,076.7	3,194.4	3,364.9	3,624.8
Durable goods	497.1	635.7	915.8	1,123.4	1,029.6	1,079.4	1,146.4
Motor vehicles and parts	205.1	255.7	363.2	408.2	316.0	342.7	373.6
New motor vehicles	134.7	147.5	210.7	248.9	165.6	177.8	203.0
Motor vehicle parts and accessories	28.3	35.4	41.8	46.6	46.2	49.6	53.3
Furniture and durable household equipment	120.9	146.7	208.1	261.3	235.4	241.3	251.7
Furniture and furnishings	69.2	83.4	121.7	153.0	135.7	139.2	144.8
Household appliances	23.7	26.6	34.1	43.3	39.8	40.4	41.6
Recreational goods and vehicles	105.6	153.7	234.1	312.8	317.3	326.7	340.1
Video, audio, photo, and information processing equipment	56.1	84.7	130.9	182.9	199.0	208.4	214.9
Sporting equipment, guns, and ammunition	19.9	27.2	39.1	50.7	51.4	51.8	55.1
Sports and recreational vehicles	16.6	22.5	34.9	45.7	33.5	32.2	33.8
Recreational books	10.9	16.4	24.4	28.1	28.7	29.5	31.3
Other durable goods	65.5	79.6	110.4	141.1	160.8	168.7	181.0
Jewelry and watches	30.3	37.8	49.1	58.1	58.4	60.8	67.3
Therapeutic appliances and equipment	18.4	21.0	32.2	41.5	49.8	52.6	55.2
Nondurable goods	994.2	1,179.8	1,543.4	1,953.4	2,164.8	2,285.5	2,478.4
Food and beverages purchased for off-premise consumption	391.2	443.7	537.5	644.5	742.3	760.6	810.2
Food and nonalcoholic beverages purchased for off-premises consumption	341.2	388.3	463.1	558.2	642.4	654.5	698.2
Alcoholic beverages purchased for off-premises consumption	49.3	55.0	74.0	86.0	99.5	105.8	111.6
Clothing and footwear	195.2	231.2	280.8	314.0	317.0	331.6	349.2
Women's and girls' clothing	94.5	108.9	132.7	152.5	153.2	160.6	169.5
Men's and boys' clothing	57.4	72.2	85.9	91.0	90.7	94.5	99.6
Footwear	35.3	41.2	50.8	57.7	55.8	58.7	61.6
Gasoline and other energy goods	124.2	133.4	188.8	303.8	299.3	352.4	428.3
Motor vehicle fuels, lubricants, and fluids	111.4	120.4	172.9	283.8	278.7	330.1	403.8
Other nondurable goods	283.6	371.4	536.2	691.1	806.1	840.8	890.7
Pharmaceutical and medical products	59.1	85.1	159.0	254.7	315.4	328.5	348.1
Recreational items	50.9	68.9	93.7	119.1	134.5	138.8	147.2
Household supplies	54.2	70.4	86.7	102.2	109.8	112.8	118.0
Personal care products	39.3	50.2	68.5	81.5	92.2	96.7	103.1
Tobacco	41.0	49.2	68.5	71.1	87.9	94.5	96.1
Magazines, newspapers, and stationery	36.5	46.1	56.6	57.5	58.4	63.0	70.2
SERVICES	2,344.2	3,171.7	4,371.2	5,726.8	6,651.5	6,850.9	7,104.2
Housing	570.4	756.2	1,010.5	1,328.9	1,576.2	1,586.6	1,623.3
Rental of tenant-occupied nonfarm housing	150.7	186.2	227.9	264.7	353.1	360.2	377.6
Imputed rental of owner-occupied housing	412.8	559.8	768.9	1,044.5	1,202.3	1,205.1	1,222.8
Household utilities	125.9	157.6	188.1	253.7	295.4	305.3	306.7
Water supply and sanitation	27.1	39.3	50.4	63.7	80.0	83.7	87.2
Electricity	71.8	87.6	98.4	128.7	157.4	167.2	168.4
Natural gas	27.0	30.7	39.3	61.2	58.0	54.5	51.1
Health care	506.2	719.9	918.4	1,308.9	1,601.6	1,663.0	1,751.6
Physician services	134.8	177.8	229.2	330.5	386.9	396.9	412.6
Dental services	32.4	45.4	63.6	89.1	104.6	107.0	113.9
Paramedical services	64.9	113.4	143.8	206.3	255.9	267.0	279.9
Hospital and nursing home services	274.1	383.3	481.8	683.0	854.2	892.2	945.2
Transportation services	126.4	177.9	262.3	286.0	284.5	287.6	302.0
Motor vehicle services	87.2	129.1	189.3	209.6	206.5	207.5	217.2
Public transportation	39.2	48.8	73.0	76.3	78.0	80.1	84.8
Ground transportation	12.9	16.7	21.6	26.2	29.7	30.5	32.1
Air transportation	25.9	31.1	49.2	47.7	45.8	47.0	49.8
Recreation services	121.8	181.1	255.5	328.2	370.7	378.5	394.5
Membership clubs, sports centers, parks, theaters, and museums	49.7	69.5	91.9	115.2	131.6	135.1	141.1
Audio-video, photographic, and information processing equipment services	37.9	50.0	70.1	85.4	100.5	102.0	106.9
Gambling	23.7	45.4	67.6	92.9	97.8	98.1	101.5
Food services and accommodations	262.7	316.7	410.1	533.9	607.2	631.0	670.9
Food services	235.1	280.2	354.9	461.3	523.8	541.0	573.4
Accommodations	27.6	36.6	55.2	72.7	83.5	90.0	97.5
Financial services and insurance	253.2	364.7	570.0	698.4	741.8	796.3	807.1
Financial services	141.5	212.5	370.0	424.0	477.3	512.5	518.1
Insurance	111.7	152.2	199.9	274.4	264.4	283.8	289.0
Other services	297.9	390.5	591.1	777.1	894.7	922.8	956.2
Communication	68.3	95.9	156.6	184.4	215.7	223.6	232.8
Telecommunication services	60.7	85.2	130.2	145.9	159.1	161.5	169.0
Internet access	0.1	1.6	16.4	29.9	48.0	53.7	55.6
Education services	60.7	85.5	125.2	170.3	221.2	237.0	252.2
Higher education	34.7	51.9	76.8	108.7	145.0	156.7	167.5
Nursery, elementary, secondary schools	14.8	19.2	24.1	31.7	38.8	39.4	41.4
Commercial and vocational schools	11.1	14.4	24.3	29.9	37.5	40.9	43.3
Professional and other services	67.7	82.8	113.0	148.6	163.2	164.6	166.9
Personal care and clothing services	44.9	56.5	80.2	102.5	109.2	110.9	117.2
Social services and religious activities	41.2	58.1	85.0	121.0	147.4	153.5	159.1
Household maintenance	25.4	34.5	47.7	55.3	57.4	56.0	59.9
Net foreign travel	−10.3	−23.0	−16.5	−5.0	−19.4	−22.8	−31.9
Foreign travel by U.S. residents	42.7	54.7	84.3	99.8	107.1	114.8	120.8
Less: Expenditures in the U.S. by nonresidents	53.0	77.7	100.8	104.7	126.5	137.6	152.7

Note: Subtotals may not add up to totals due to rounding or incomplete enumeration.

Leading U.S. Businesses, 2011

Source: *Fortune* magazine

(in millions of revenue-dollars; rank among all businesses by 2011 revenue)

Company (rank)	Revenue
Advertising, Marketing	
Omnicom Group (196)	$13,873
Interpublic Group (358)	7,015
Aerospace and Defense	
Boeing (39)	$68,735
United Technologies (48)	58,190
Lockheed Martin (58)	46,692
Honeywell International (77)	37,059
General Dynamics (92)	32,677
Northrop Grumman (104)	28,058
Raytheon (117)	24,857
L-3 Communications (174)	15,169
Textron (236)	11,275
Goodrich (319)	8,075
Precision Castparts (387)	6,267
Airlines	
United Continental Holdings (76)	$37,110
Delta Air Lines (83)	35,115
AMR (123)	23,979
Southwest Airlines (167)	15,658
US Airways Group (208)	13,055
Apparel	
Nike (136)	$20,862
VF (277)	9,459
Automotive Retailing, Services	
AutoNation (197)	$13,832
Penske Automotive Group (222)	11,870
CarMax (279)	9,402
Hertz Global Holdings (309)	8,298
Sonic Automotive (330)	7,871
Beverages	
Coca-Cola (59)	$46,542
Coca-Cola Enterprises (324)	7,939
Chemicals	
Dow Chemical (47)	$59,985
DuPont (72)	38,719
PPG Industries (180)	14,885
Monsanto (224)	11,822
Huntsman (237)	11,259
Praxair (238)	11,252
Air Products & Chemicals (265)	10,082
Mosaic (268)	9,938
Sherwin-Williams (293)	8,766
Ashland (307)	8,370
Eastman Chemical (346)	7,283
Ecolab (365)	6,799
Avery Dennison (367)	6,787
Celanese (368)	6,763
Commercial Banks	
Bank of America Corp. (13)	$115,074
J.P. Morgan Chase & Co. (16)	110,838
Citigroup (20)	102,939
Wells Fargo (26)	87,597
Morgan Stanley (68)	39,376
Goldman Sachs Group (80)	36,793
American Express (95)	32,282
U.S. Bancorp (132)	21,399
Capital One Financial (148)	18,525
PNC Financial Services Group (165)	15,820
Bank of New York Mellon Corp. (166)	15,804
Ally Financial (201)	13,642
State Street Corp. (262)	10,207
BB&T Corp. (267)	9,998
SunTrust Banks (271)	9,602
Discover Financial Services (300)	8,550
Regions Financial (343)	7,427
Fifth Third Bancorp (372)	6,673
Computer Peripherals	
EMC (139)	$20,008
Western Digital (276)	9,526
Computer Software	
Microsoft (37)	$69,943
Oracle (82)	35,622
Symantec (391)	6,190
Computers, Office Equipment	
Hewlett-Packard (10)	$127,245
Apple (17)	108,249
Dell (44)	62,071
Xerox (127)	22,626

Company (rank)	Revenue
Construction and Farm Machinery	
Caterpillar (46)	$60,138
Deere (97)	32,013
Cummins (150)	18,048
AGCO (292)	8,773
Terex (379)	6,505
Diversified Financials	
General Electric (6)	$147,616
Fannie Mae (8)	137,451
Freddie Mac (25)	88,262
INTL FCStone (30)	75,498
Marsh & McLennan (231)	11,526
Aon (235)	11,287
Ameriprise Financial (248)	10,621
Diversified Outsourcing	
Aramark (204)	$13,245
Automatic Data Processing (269)	9,880
Electronics, Electrical Equipment	
Emerson Electric (120)	$24,234
Whirlpool (147)	18,666
Energy	
American Electric Power (176)	$15,116
Constellation Energy (199)	13,758
NRG Energy (284)	9,079
Williams (325)	7,930
Energy Future Holdings (357)	7,040
Calpine (364)	6,800
Engineering, Construction	
Fluor (124)	$23,381
Jacobs Engineering Group (254)	10,382
Peter Kiewit Sons' (255)	10,381
URS (275)	9,545
KBR (280)	9,261
AECOM Technology (322)	8,037
Entertainment	
Walt Disney (66)	$40,893
News Corp. (91)	33,405
Time Warner (103)	28,974
Viacom (177)	14,963
CBS (188)	14,245
CC Media Holdings (394)	6,161
Financial Data Services	
First Data (243)	$10,714
Visa (281)	9,188
MasterCard (370)	6,714
Food Consumer Products	
PepsiCo (41)	$66,504
Kraft Foods (50)	54,365
General Mills (181)	14,880
Kellogg (205)	13,198
Dean Foods (207)	13,056
Land O'Lakes (210)	12,849
ConAgra Foods (215)	12,395
Sara Lee (220)	12,103
H.J. Heinz (244)	10,707
Hormel Foods (327)	7,895
Campbell Soup (334)	7,719
Dole Food (349)	7,224
Food and Drug Stores	
CVS Caremark (18)	$107,750
Kroger (23)	90,374
Walgreen (32)	72,184
Safeway (63)	43,630
Supervalu (75)	37,534
Publix Super Markets (106)	27,179
Rite Aid (113)	25,215
Whole Foods Market (264)	10,108
Great Atlantic & Pacific Tea (317)	8,079
Winn-Dixie Stores (363)	6,930
Food Production	
Archer Daniels Midland (28)	$80,676
Tyson Foods (96)	32,266
Smithfield Foods (218)	12,203
Corn Products International (390)	6,219
Food Services	
McDonald's (107)	$27,006
Yum Brands (213)	12,626
Starbucks (227)	11,700
Darden Restaurants (342)	7,500
Forest and Paper Products	
International Paper (111)	$26,034
Weyerhaeuser (374)	6,618

Company (rank)	Revenue
General Merchandisers	
Wal-Mart Stores (2)	$446,950
Target (38)	69,865
Sears Holdings (65)	41,567
Macy's (110)	26,405
Kohl's (146)	18,804
J.C. Penney (153)	17,260
Dollar General (183)	14,807
Nordstrom (242)	10,877
Family Dollar Stores (301)	8,548
Dillard's (383)	6,400
Health Care: Insurance and Managed Care	
UnitedHealth Group (22)	$101,862
WellPoint (45)	60,711
Humana (79)	36,832
Aetna (89)	33,780
Cigna (130)	21,998
Coventry Health Care (219)	12,187
Health Net (221)	11,901
Amerigroup (385)	6,318
Health Care: Medical Facilities	
HCA Holdings (94)	$32,506
Community Health Systems (198)	13,817
Tenet Healthcare (272)	9,601
Universal Health Services (339)	7,534
DaVita (359)	6,999
Health Care: Pharmacy and Other Services	
Medco Health Solutions (36)	$70,063
Express Scripts Holding (60)	46,128
Quest Diagnostics (341)	7,511
Omnicare (389)	6,240
Home Equipment, Furnishings	
Stanley Black & Decker (252)	$10,438
Masco (338)	7,560
Jarden (371)	6,680
Hotels, Casinos, Resorts	
Marriott International (217)	$12,317
Las Vegas Sands (278)	9,411
Caesars Entertainment (288)	8,835
MGM Resorts International (331)	7,849
Household and Personal Products	
Procter & Gamble (27)	$82,559
Kimberly-Clark (137)	20,846
Colgate-Palmolive (155)	16,734
Avon Products (234)	11,292
Estée Lauder (290)	8,810
Industrial Machinery	
Illinois Tool Works (149)	$18,257
Eaton (163)	16,049
Parker Hannifin (216)	12,346
Dover (304)	8,502
Information Technology Services	
IBM (19)	$106,916
Computer Sciences (162)	16,144
SAIC (245)	10,657
CDW (270)	9,602
Cognizant Technology Solutions (398)	6,121
Insurance: Life, Health (Mutual)	
New York Life Insurance (86)	$34,394
TIAA-CREF (88)	34,079
Northwestern Mutual (116)	24,861
Massachusetts Mutual Life Insurance (121)	24,226
Guardian Life Ins. Co. of America (250)	10,571
Thrivent Financial for Lutherans (332)	7,843
Insurance: Life, Health (Stock)	
MetLife (34)	$70,641
Prudential Financial (55)	49,045
Aflac (128)	22,171
Lincoln National (247)	10,636
Genworth Financial (258)	10,344
Unum Group (260)	10,278
Reinsurance Group of America (289)	8,830
Principal Financial (295)	8,710

Company (rank)	Revenue
Insurance: Property and Casualty (Mutual)	
State Farm Insurance Cos. (43)	$64,305
Nationwide (100)	30,698
Insurance: Property and Casualty (Stock)	
Berkshire Hathaway (7)	$143,688
American International Group (33)	71,730
Liberty Mutual Insurance Group (84)	34,671
Allstate (93)	32,654
Travelers Cos. (112)	25,446
Hartford Financial Services Group (131)	21,918
United Services Automobile Assn. (144)	19,036
Progressive (169)	15,508
Loews (190)	14,127
Chubb (202)	13,585
Assurant (310)	8,273
American Family Insurance Group (382)	6,400
Internet Services and Retailing	
Amazon.com (56)	$48,077
Google (73)	37,905
eBay (228)	11,652
Liberty Interactive (230)	11,624
Mail, Package, Freight Delivery	
United Parcel Service (52)	$53,105
FedEx (70)	39,304
Medical Products and Equipment	
Medtronic (164)	$15,933
Baxter International (195)	13,893
Stryker (308)	8,307
Becton Dickinson (333)	7,832
Boston Scientific (335)	7,622
Metals	
Alcoa (115)	$24,951
Nucor (138)	20,024
United States Steel (140)	19,884
Reliance Steel & Aluminum (315)	8,135
Steel Dynamics (323)	7,998
Commercial Metals (326)	7,920
AK Steel Holding (381)	6,468
Mining, Crude Oil Production	
Occidental Petroleum (122)	$24,216
Freeport-McMoRan Copper & Gold (135)	20,880
Apache (154)	16,888
Marathon Oil (173)	15,282
Anadarko Petroleum (192)	13,967
Chesapeake Energy (229)	11,635
Devon Energy (232)	11,497
Newmont Mining (257)	10,358
EOG Resources (263)	10,126
Peabody Energy (316)	8,096
Alpha Natural Resources (356)	7,109
Cliffs Natural Resources (366)	6,794
Consol Energy (399)	6,117
Miscellaneous	
3M (102)	$29,611
Spectrum Group International (352)	7,203
Mohawk Industries (432)	5,642
Motor Vehicles and Parts	
General Motors (5)	$150,276
Ford Motor (9)	136,264
Johnson Controls (67)	40,833
Goodyear Tire & Rubber (126)	22,767
Paccar (159)	16,355
TRW Automotive Holdings (161)	16,244
Lear (189)	14,157
Navistar International (193)	13,958
Icahn Enterprises (223)	11,855
Autoliv (313)	8,232
Visteon (321)	8,047
Dana Holding (336)	7,592
Oshkosh (337)	7,585
Tenneco (350)	7,205
BorgWarner (355)	7,115
Network and Other Communications Equipment	
Cisco Systems (64)	$43,218

Company (rank)	Revenue
Qualcomm (178)	14,962
Motorola Mobility Holdings (206)	13,064
Motorola Solutions (274)	9,549
Corning (328)	7,890
Oil and Gas Equipment, Services	
Halliburton (118)	$24,829
Baker Hughes (141)	19,831
National Oilwell Varco (184)	14,658
Cameron International (362)	6,959
Packaging, Containers	
Crown Holdings (296)	$8,644
Ball (297)	8,631
Owens-Illinois (345)	7,358
Petroleum Refining	
Exxon Mobil (1)	$452,926
Chevron (3)	245,621
ConocoPhillips (4)	237,272
Valero Energy (12)	125,095
Marathon Petroleum (31)	73,645
Sunoco (61)	45,765
Hess (74)	37,871
Murphy Oil (98)	31,446
Tesoro (101)	29,927
HollyFrontier (170)	15,440
Western Refining (285)	9,071
Pharmaceuticals	
Pfizer (40)	$67,932
Johnson & Johnson (42)	65,030
Merck (57)	48,047
Abbott Laboratories (71)	38,851
Eli Lilly (119)	24,287
Bristol-Myers Squibb (134)	21,244
Amgen (168)	15,582
Gilead Sciences (306)	8,385
Mylan (396)	6,130
Pipelines	
Enterprise Products Partners (62)	$44,313
Plains All American Pipeline (87)	34,275
Oneok (175)	15,119
Enbridge Energy Partners (282)	9,110
Kinder Morgan (311)	8,265
Energy Transfer Equity (312)	8,241
Targa Resources (361)	6,995
NuStar Energy (377)	6,575
Spectra Energy (438)	5,602
El Paso (488)	4,860
Publishing, Printing	
R.R. Donnelley & Sons (249)	$10,611
McGraw-Hill (384)	6,336
Gannett (465)	5,240
Railroads	
Union Pacific (143)	$19,557
CSX (226)	11,743
Norfolk Southern (241)	11,172
Real Estate	
CBRE Group (416)	$5,912
Host Hotels & Resorts (479)	5,003
Scientific, Photo, Control Equipment	
Danaher (158)	$16,476
Thermo Fisher Scientific (225)	11,780
Agilent Technologies (375)	6,615
Eastman Kodak (408)	6,022
Securities	
BlackRock (283)	$9,081
Franklin Resources (353)	7,140
Charles Schwab (485)	4,884
Semiconductors and Other Electronic Components	
Intel (51)	$53,999
Jabil Circuit (157)	16,519
Texas Instruments (200)	13,735
Applied Materials (251)	10,517
Micron Technology (291)	8,788
Broadcom (344)	7,389
Sanmina-SCI (376)	6,602
Advanced Micro Devices (378)	6,568
SanDisk (430)	5,662
Specialty Retailers: Apparel	
TJX (125)	$23,192
Gap (185)	14,549
Limited Brands (256)	10,364
Ross Stores (299)	8,608
Specialty Retailers: Other	
Costco Wholesale (24)	$88,915
Home Depot (35)	70,395
Best Buy (53)	50,272

Company (rank)	Revenue
Lowe's (54)	50,208
Staples (114)	25,022
Toys "R" Us (194)	13,909
Office Depot (233)	11,490
GameStop (273)	9,551
Bed Bath & Beyond (294)	8,759
AutoZone (320)	8,073
TravelCenters of America (329)	7,889
Pantry (347)	7,272
OfficeMax (354)	7,121
Barnes & Noble (360)	6,999
Dollar Tree (373)	6,631
Advance Auto Parts (392)	6,171
PetSmart (400)	6,113
Telecommunications	
AT&T (11)	$126,723
Verizon Communications (15)	110,875
Comcast (49)	55,842
Sprint Nextel (90)	33,679
DirecTV (105)	27,226
Time Warner Cable (142)	19,675
CenturyLink (171)	15,351
DISH Network (191)	14,048
Liberty Global (261)	10,247
Cablevision Systems (348)	7,252
Charter Communications (351)	7,204
NII Holdings (369)	6,719
Temporary Help	
Manpower (129)	$22,006
Tobacco	
Philip Morris International (99)	$31,097
Altria Group (156)	16,619
Reynolds American (302)	8,541
Transportation and Logistics	
C.H. Robinson Worldwide (259)	$10,336
Expeditors International of Washington (395)	6,151
Utilities: Gas and Electric	
Exelon (145)	$18,924
AES (151)	17,759
Southern (152)	17,657
FirstEnergy (160)	16,258
NextEra Energy (172)	15,341
PG&E Corp. (179)	14,956
Duke Energy (186)	14,529
Dominion Resources (187)	14,379
Consolidated Edison (209)	12,938
Edison International (211)	12,760
PPL (212)	12,756
Entergy (239)	11,229
Public Service Enterprise Group (240)	11,191
Xcel Energy (246)	10,655
Sempra Energy (266)	10,036
Progress Energy (286)	8,907
DTE Energy (287)	8,897
CenterPoint Energy (305)	8,450
Ameren (340)	7,531
CMS Energy (380)	6,503
Waste Management	
Waste Management (203)	$13,378
Republic Services (314)	8,193
Wholesalers: Diversified	
World Fuel Services (85)	$34,623
Global Partners (182)	14,836
Genuine Parts (214)	12,459
W. W. Grainger (318)	8,078
Anixter International (386)	6,270
Wesco International (397)	6,126
Wholesalers: Electronics and Office Equipment	
Ingram Micro (81)	$36,329
Avnet (108)	26,534
Tech Data (109)	26,488
Arrow Electronics (133)	21,390
Synnex (253)	10,410
Wholesalers: Food and Grocery	
Sysco (69)	$39,324
CHS (78)	36,916
Core-Mark Holding (393)	6,163
Wholesalers: Health Care	
McKesson (14)	$112,084
Cardinal Health (21)	102,644
AmerisourceBergen (29)	80,218
Owens & Minor (298)	8,628
Henry Schein (303)	8,530

100 U.S. Corporations With Largest Revenues, 2011

Source: *Fortune* magazine

(in millions of dollars; ranked by 2011 revenues)

Rank	Company (2010 rank)	Revenues	Profits	Rank	Company (2010 rank)	Revenues	Profits
1.	Exxon Mobil (2)	$452,926.0	$41,060.0	51.	Intel (56)	$53,999.0	$12,942.0
2.	Wal-Mart Stores (1)	446,950.0	15,699.0	52.	United Parcel Service (48)	53,105.0	3,804.0
3.	Chevron (3)	245,621.0	26,895.0	53.	Best Buy (47)	50,272.0	1,277.0
4.	ConocoPhillips (4)	237,272.0	12,436.0	54.	Lowe's (50)	50,208.0	1,839.0
5.	General Motors (8)	150,276.0	9,190.0	55.	Prudential Financial (64)	49,045.0	3,666.0
6.	General Electric (6)	147,616.0	14,151.0	56.	Amazon.com (78)	48,077.0	631.0
7.	Berkshire Hathaway (7)	143,688.0	10,254.0	57.	Merck (53)	48,047.0	6,272.0
8.	Fannie Mae (5)	137,451.0	−16,855.0	58.	Lockheed Martin (52)	46,692.0	2,655.0
9.	Ford Motor (10)	136,264.0	20,213.0	59.	Coca-Cola (70)	46,542.0	8,572.0
10.	Hewlett-Packard (11)	127,245.0	7,074.0	60.	Express Scripts Holding (55)	46,128.3	1,275.8
11.	AT&T (12)	126,723.0	3,944.0	61.	Sunoco (68)	45,765.0	−1,684.0
12.	Valero Energy (24)	125,095.0	2,090.0	62.	Enterprise Products Partners (80)	44,313.0	2,046.9
13.	Bank of America Corp. (9)	115,074.0	1,446.0	63.	Safeway (60)	43,630.2	516.7
14.	McKesson (15)	112,084.0	1,202.0	64.	Cisco Systems (62)	43,218.0	6,490.0
15.	Verizon Communications (16)	110,875.0	2,404.0	65.	Sears Holdings (57)	41,567.0	−3,140.0
16.	J.P. Morgan Chase & Co. (13)	110,838.0	18,976.0	66.	Walt Disney (65)	40,893.0	4,807.0
17.	Apple (35)	108,249.0	25,922.0	67.	Johnson Controls (76)	40,833.0	1,624.0
18.	CVS Caremark (21)	107,750.0	3,461.0	68.	Morgan Stanley (63)	39,376.0	4,110.0
19.	International Business Machines (18)	106,916.0	15,855.0	69.	Sysco (67)	39,323.5	1,152.0
20.	Citigroup (14)	102,939.0	11,067.0	70.	FedEx (73)	39,304.0	1,452.0
21.	Cardinal Health (19)	102,644.2	959.0	71.	Abbott Laboratories (69)	38,851.3	4,728.4
22.	UnitedHealth Group (22)	101,862.0	5,142.0	72.	DuPont (84)	38,719.0	3,474.0
23.	Kroger (25)	90,374.0	602.0	73.	Google (92)	37,905.0	9,737.0
24.	Costco Wholesale (28)	88,915.0	1,462.0	74.	Hess (74)	37,871.0	1,703.0
25.	Freddie Mac (20)	88,262.0	−5,266.0	75.	Supervalu (61)	37,534.0	−1,510.0
26.	Wells Fargo (23)	87,597.0	15,869.0	76.	United Continental Holdings (114)	37,110.0	840.0
27.	Procter & Gamble (26)	82,559.0	11,797.0	77.	Honeywell International (81)	37,059.0	2,067.0
28.	Archer Daniels Midland (39)	80,676.0	2,036.0	78.	CHS (103)	36,915.8	961.4
29.	AmerisourceBergen (27)	80,217.6	706.6	79.	Humana (79)	36,832.0	1,419.0
30.	INTL FCStone (51)	75,497.6	37.3	80.	Goldman Sachs Group (54)	36,793.0	4,442.0
31.	Marathon Petroleum (NA)	73,645.0	2,389.0	81.	Ingram Micro (75)	36,328.7	244.2
32.	Walgreen (32)	72,184.0	2,714.0	82.	Oracle (96)	35,622.0	8,547.0
33.	American International Group (17)	71,730.0	17,798.0	83.	Delta Air Lines (88)	35,115.0	854.0
34.	MetLife (46)	70,641.0	6,981.0	84.	Liberty Mutual Insurance Group (82)	34,671.0	365.0
35.	Home Depot (30)	70,395.0	3,883.0	85.	World Fuel Services (133)	34,622.9	194.0
36.	Medco Health Solutions (34)	70,063.3	1,455.7	86.	New York Life Insurance (71)	34,393.5	557.3
37.	Microsoft (38)	69,943.0	23,150.0	87.	Plains All American Pipeline (99)	34,275.0	966.0
38.	Target (33)	69,865.0	2,929.0	88.	TIAA-CREF (87)	34,079.0	2,388.4
39.	Boeing (36)	68,735.0	4,018.0	89.	Aetna (77)	33,779.4	1,985.7
40.	Pfizer (31)	67,932.0	10,009.0	90.	Sprint Nextel (85)	33,679.0	−2,890.0
41.	PepsiCo (43)	66,504.0	6,443.0	91.	News Corp. (83)	33,405.0	2,739.0
42.	Johnson & Johnson (40)	65,030.0	9,672.0	92.	General Dynamics (86)	32,677.0	2,526.0
43.	State Farm Insurance Cos. (37)	64,305.1	845.0	93.	Allstate (89)	32,654.0	788.0
44.	Dell (41)	62,071.0	3,492.0	94.	HCA Holdings (90)	32,506.0	2,465.0
45.	WellPoint (42)	60,710.7	2,646.7	95.	American Express (91)	32,282.0	4,935.0
46.	Caterpillar (58)	60,138.0	4,928.0	96.	Tyson Foods (93)	32,266.0	750.0
47.	Dow Chemical (45)	59,985.0	2,742.0	97.	Deere (98)	32,012.5	2,799.9
48.	United Technologies (44)	58,190.0	4,979.0	98.	Murphy Oil (113)	31,446.3	872.7
49.	Comcast (66)	55,842.0	4,160.0	99.	Philip Morris International (94)	31,097.0	8,591.0
50.	Kraft Foods (49)	54,365.0	3,527.0	100.	Nationwide (127)	30,697.8	−793.1

NA = Not available.

Top U.S. Franchises, 2012

Source: *Entrepreneur* magazine

Rank	Company (2011 rank)	Type of business	Locations	Startup costs[1]
1.	Hampton Hotels (1)	Mid-priced hotels	1,909	$3.75 mil-$13.52 mil
2.	Subway (9)	Submarine sandwiches & salads	37,199	$85,200-$260,350
3.	7-Eleven Inc. (4)	Convenience store	47,298	$30,800-$1.6 mil
4.	Servpro (8)	Insurance/disaster restoration & cleaning	1,615	$133,050-$181,450
5.	Days Inn (6)	Hotels	1,865	$202,170-$6.8 mil
6.	McDonald's (3)	Hamburgers, chicken, salads	33,427	$1 mil-$2.2 mil
7.	Denny's Inc. (10)	Full-service family restaurant	1,684	$1.18 mil-$2.4 mil
8.	H&R Block (27)	Tax preparation	11,578	$32,510-$138,700
9.	Pizza Hut Inc. (13)	Pizza, pasta, wings	13,432	$295,000-$2.2 mil
10.	Dunkin' Donuts (15)	Coffee, doughnuts, baked goods	10,020	$368,900-$1.7 mil
11.	Anytime Fitness (18)	Fitness center	1,906	$46,300-$321,900
12.	Stratus Building Solutions (20)	Commercial cleaning	5,148	$3,450-$57,750
13.	Jazzercise Inc. (17)	Dance fitness classes	8,181	$2,980-$76,500
14.	Supercuts (5)	Hair salon	2,260	$103,560-$196,500
15.	Jiffy Lube Intl. Inc. (30)	Fast oil change	1,973	$196,500-$331,500
16.	ampm (2)	Convenience store & gas station	2,420	$1.85 mil-$7.76 mil
17.	KFC Corp. (16)	Chicken	16,853	$1.31 mil-$2.47 mil
18.	Kumon Math & Reading Centers (14)	Supplemental education	25,431	$67,760-$145,320
19.	Miracle-Ear Inc. (44)	Hearing instruments	1,339	$122,500-$450,000
20.	Taco Bell Corp. (NA)	Quick-service Mexican restaurant	5,896	$1.3 mil-$2.5 mil

NA = Not available. **Note:** Franchises are ranked by a combination of factors, including financial strength and stability, growth rate, number of locations, startup costs, and whether the company provides financing. (1) Does not include franchise fee, which varies.

United States Mint

Source: United States Mint, U.S. Dept. of the Treasury

The United States Mint was created on Apr. 2, 1792, by an act of Congress, which established the U.S. national coinage system. In 1799, the mint became an independent agency reporting directly to the president. It was made a statutory bureau of the Treasury Department in 1873, with a director appointed by the president. The mint manufactures and ships all U.S. coins for circulation to Federal Reserve banks and branches, which in turn issue coins to the public and business community through depository institutions. The mint also safeguards the Treasury Department's stored gold and silver, as well as other monetary assets.

The composition of dimes, quarters, and half dollars, traditionally produced from silver, was changed by the Coinage Act of 1965, which mandated that these coins from then on be minted from a cupronickel-clad alloy and reduced the silver content of the half dollar to 40%. In 1970, legislative action mandated that the half dollar and a dollar coin be minted from the same alloy.

Mint headquarters are in Washington, DC. Mint production facilities are in Philadelphia, Denver, San Francisco, and West Point, NY. In addition, the mint is responsible for the U.S. Bullion Depository at Fort Knox, KY.

The mint offers free public tours and operates sales centers at the U.S. mints in Denver and Philadelphia. Further information is available from the U.S. Mint, Customer Care Center, 801 9th St. NW, Washington, DC 20220; (800) USA-MINT. **Website:** www.usmint.gov.

New Circulating and Commemorative Coins

Source: United States Mint, U.S. Dept. of the Treasury

Dollar coins. A large, unwieldy dollar coin featuring the likeness of Pres. Dwight D. Eisenhower was minted 1971-78. The smaller Susan B. Anthony dollar, minted 1979-81, marked the first time that a woman other than a mythical figure appeared on a generally circulated U.S. coin. A golden dollar coin was first minted in 2000. It depicts Sacagawea, a Shoshone woman who helped guide explorers Lewis and Clark, on the obverse. The reverse shows an eagle and 17 stars, one for each of the states at the time of the Lewis and Clark expedition. In 2007, the mint began issuing a series of golden dollar coins featuring U.S. presidents on the front and the Statue of Liberty on the back. Each includes the president's name, likeness, and years of service. Four are to be issued each year in the order in which the presidents served. Andrew Johnson, Ulysses S. Grant, Rutherford B. Hayes, and James Garfield were honored in 2011; Chester A. Arthur, Grover Cleveland, and Benjamin Harrison were honored in 2012. Cleveland will appear on two coins because he served nonconsecutive terms as president. Only presidents deceased more than two years will be honored, so the program is currently slated to end in 2016 with coins commemorating Richard Nixon, Gerald Ford, and Ronald Reagan. From 2009-11, the mint also issued golden dollar coins whose reverse sides celebrated the important contributions made by American Indian tribes to the development of the U.S. The 2009 coin featured a woman planting seeds; the 2010 issue depicted the Hiawatha belt binding five arrows; and the 2011 coin celebrated the Wampanoag Treaty of 1621.

America the Beautiful quarters. In 2010, the U.S. Mint began an initiative to honor 56 national parks and other sites of national importance. Five new reverse designs appear on the quarter-dollar each year in 2010-21; the order of issuance corresponds to the order in which the featured site was first established. The 2011 quarters commemorated Gettysburg Military National Park, PA; Glacier National Park, MT; Olympic National Park, WA; Vicksburg Military National Park, MS; and Chickasaw National Recreation Area, OK. The 2012 coins commemorated El Yunque National Forest, PR; Chaco Culture National Historical Park, NM; Acadia National Park, ME; Hawai'i Volcanoes National Park, HI; and Denali National Park, AK. The 2013 coins will commemorate White Mountain National Forest, NH; Perry's Victory and International Peace Memorial, OH; Great Basin National Park, NV; Fort McHenry National Monument and Historic Shrine, MD; and Mount Rushmore National Memorial, SD.

Commemorative coins. From 1892 to 1954, and again since 1982, Congress has authorized the mint to produce more than 50 different commemorative coins. Recent issues include the 2007 Little Rock Central High School Desegregation silver dollar coin; the 2009 Louis Braille Bicentennial-Braille Literacy silver dollar; the 2010 Boy Scouts of America Centennial silver dollar; the 2011 Medal of Honor gold 5-dollar coin and silver dollar coin; and the 2012 Infantry Soldier silver dollar.

Bureau of Engraving and Printing

Source: Bureau of Engraving and Printing, U.S. Dept. of the Treasury

The Bureau of Engraving and Printing manufactures the financial and other securities of the United States. It designs and prints a variety of products, including Federal Reserve notes (bills in various denominations), Treasury securities, identification cards, naturalization certificates, and other special security documents. Denominations of the various types of printings produced by the bureau range from a 1/5-cent wine stamp to a $100,000,000 International Monetary Fund special note. Among its products are all hand-engraved invitations issued by the White House.

The first general circulation of paper money by the federal government dates back to 1861, prior to the establishment of the bureau, when Congress authorized the U.S. Treasury to issue non-interest-bearing demand notes, nicknamed "greenbacks" because of their color, to finance the Civil War. A portrait of Pres. Abraham Lincoln appeared on the face of the first $10 notes. By 1862, the design of U.S. currency incorporated fine-line engraving, intricate geometric lathe work patterns, a Treasury seal, and engraved signatures to aid in counterfeit

deterrence. All U.S. currency issued since 1861 remain valid and redeemable at full face value.

The Bureau of Engraving and Printing began operations by 1862, originally separating and sealing bank notes that were printed by private companies. In 1877, the bureau became the sole producer of U.S. currency. In 1894, it also began producing postage stamps. On June 10, 2005, the bureau printed its last stamps, a roll of 37-cent flag stamps; stamps are now produced by private printers.

The Federal Reserve Act of 1913 created the Federal Reserve as the nation's central bank and provided for currency called Federal Reserve notes. The first notes, issued the following year, were $10 notes bearing a portrait of Pres. Andrew Jackson. In 1929, the look of U.S. currency was standardized. The national motto, "In God We Trust," was added to paper money in 1957.

The Bureau of Engraving and Printing currently operates two facilities, one in Washington, DC, opened in 1914, and one in Fort Worth, TX, which began operations in 1991.

Denominations of U.S. Currency

Since 1969 the largest denomination of U.S. currency that has been issued is the $100 bill. As larger-denomination bills reach the Federal Reserve Bank, they are removed from circulation. Because some discontinued currency is expected to be in the hands of holders for many years, the description of the various denominations below is continued.

Note	Portrait	Embellishment on back	Note	Portrait	Embellishment on back
$1	George Washington	Great Seal of U.S.	$500	William McKinley	Ornate denominational marking
2	Thomas Jefferson	Signers of Declaration	1,000	Grover Cleveland	Ornate denominational marking
5	Abraham Lincoln	Lincoln Memorial			Washington resigning as Army
10	Alexander Hamilton	U.S. Treasury	5,000	James Madison	commander
20	Andrew Jackson	White House	10,000	Salmon Chase	Embarkation of the Pilgrims
50	Ulysses S. Grant	U.S. Capitol	100,000*	Woodrow Wilson	Ornate denominational marking
100	Benjamin Franklin	Independence Hall			

*For use only in transactions between Federal Reserve System and Treasury Department.

Portraits on U.S. Treasury Bills, Bonds, Notes, and Savings Bonds

The U.S. Treasury discontinued issuing treasury bill, bond, and note certificates in 1986. Since then, all issues of marketable treasury securities have been available only in book-entry form, although some certificates remain in circulation.

Denomination	EE savings bonds	Treasury bills	Treasury bonds	Treasury notes
$50	George Washington		Thomas Jefferson	
75	John Adams			
100	Thomas Jefferson		Andrew Jackson	
200	James Madison			
500	Alexander Hamilton (Treasury Sec., 1789-95)		George Washington	
1,000	Benjamin Franklin	Hugh McCulloch (Treasury Sec., 1865-69; 1884-85)	Abraham Lincoln	Abraham Lincoln
5,000	Paul Revere	John G. Carlisle (Treasury Sec., 1893-97)	James Monroe	James Monroe
10,000	James Wilson (Supreme Court Justice, 1789-98)	John Sherman (Treasury Sec., 1877-81)	Grover Cleveland	Grover Cleveland
50,000	Carter Glass (Treasury Sec., 1918-20)			
100,000		Albert Gallatin (Treasury Sec., 1801-14)	Ulysses S. Grant	Ulysses S. Grant
1,000,000		Oliver Wolcott (Treasury Sec., 1795-1800)	Theodore Roosevelt	Theodore Roosevelt
100,000,000				James Madison
500,000,000				William McKinley

U.S. Currency Designs

The U.S. Dept. of the Treasury, the Board of Governors of the Federal Reserve System, and the U.S. Secret Service unveiled a new design for the $100 note Apr. 21, 2010. A number of new security and anti-counterfeiting features were included in the redesign, including a blue 3-D security ribbon and the image of a bell in an inkwell on the front of the note. The security ribbon contains images of bells and the numeral 100 that change from one to the other as the note is tilted. The bell in the copper-colored inkwell changes color from copper to green when the note is tilted. The new notes were initially scheduled for release in Feb. 2011, but problems in the printing process has postponed the release indefinitely. Upon the issue date of the new currency, older $100 notes will remain legal tender.

The new $100 bill is considered the last denomination of the major currency redesign that the Treasury launched in 2003. On Oct. 9, 2003, the U.S. Treasury introduced a new $20 note, using background colors for the first time since 1905. The notes have a vertical security thread on one side, with "USA TWENTY" and a small U.S. flag; the thread glows green under UV light. Other security features include color-shifting ink in the number 20 in the lower right corner on the note's face. A new $50 note with similar security features was released Sept. 28, 2004, followed by a $10 note on Mar. 2, 2006, and a $5 note Mar. 13, 2008.

Website: www.newmoney.gov.

The U.S. $1 Bill

Plate position: Shows where on the 32-note plate this bill was printed.

Serial number: Each bill has its own.

Federal Reserve District number: Shows which district issued the bill.

Federal Reserve District seal: The name of the Federal Reserve Bank that issued the bill is printed in the seal. The letter tells you where the bill is from. Here are the letter codes for the 12 Federal Reserve Districts:

A: Boston
B: New York
C: Philadelphia
D: Cleveland
E: Richmond
F: Atlanta
G: Chicago
H: St. Louis
I: Minneapolis
J: Kansas City
K: Dallas
L: San Francisco

Treasurer of the U.S. signature

Series indicator: Year note's design was first used.

Secretary of the Treasury signature

Treasury Department seal: The balancing scales represent justice. The pointed stripe across the middle has 13 stars for the original 13 colonies. The key represents authority.

Plate serial number: Shows which printing plate was used for the face of the bill.

Plate serial number: Shows which plate was used for the back.

Reverse of the Great Seal of the United States: The pyramid symbolizes something that endures for ages. The eye, known as the Eye of Providence, probably comes from anancient Egyptian symbol. The pyramid has 13 levels; at its base are the Roman numerals for 1776, the year of American independence. "Annuit Coeptis" is Latin for "God has favored our undertaking." "Novus Ordo Seclorum" is Latin for "a new order of the ages." Both phrases are from the works of the Roman poet Virgil.

Front of the Great Seal of the United States: The bald eagle is the national bird. The shield has 13 stripes for the 13 original colonies. The eagle holds 13 arrows (symbol of war) and an olive branch (symbol of peace). Above the eagle is the motto "E Pluribus Unum," Latin for "out of many, one," and a constellation of 13 stars.

U.S. Currency and Coin

Source: Financial Management Service, U.S. Dept. of the Treasury; as of June 30, 2012

Total Money in Circulation, 1955-2012

Date	Dollars (mil)	Per capita[1]	Date	Dollars (mil)	Per capita[1]	Date	Dollars (mil)	Per capita[1]
June 30, 1955.....	$30,229	$183	Sept. 30, 1985.....	$187,337	$782	June 30, 2008	$826,314	$2,676
June 30, 1960.....	32,064	177	Sept. 30, 1990.....	278,903	1,105	June 30, 2009.....	909,697	2,963
June 30, 1965.....	39,719	204	Sept. 30, 1995.....	409,272	1,553	June 30, 2010.....	945,138	3,051
June 30, 1970.....	54,351	265	Sept. 30, 2000.....	568,614	2,061	June 30, 2011.....	1,028,910	3,302
June 30, 1975.....	81,196	380	Sept. 30, 2005.....	766,487	2,578	June 30, 2012.....	1,111,901	3,540
Sept. 30, 1980	129,916	581						

(1) Based on U.S. Census Bureau population estimates.

Currency in Circulation by Denomination, 2012

Denomination	Total currency in circulation	Federal Reserve notes[1]	U.S. notes	Currency no longer issued
$1	$10,021,909,418	$9,880,157,298	$143,503	$141,608,617
$2	1,916,156,274	1,784,204,480	131,939,218	12,576
$5	11,647,015,220	11,513,229,005	108,336,010	25,450,205
$10	16,742,814,360	16,722,252,430	6,300	20,555,630
$20	140,112,775,380	140,092,669,560	3,840	20,101,980
$50	69,188,001,000	69,176,506,100	500	11,494,400
$100	820,155,828,300	820,133,848,800	NA	21,979,500
$500	142,118,500	141,923,500	5,500	189,500
$1,000.....................................	165,464,000	165,252,000	5,000	207,000
$5,000.....................................	1,765,000	1,710,000	NA	55,000
$10,000...................................	3,460,000	3,360,000	NA	100,000
Fractional notes[2].....................	600	NA	90	510
Total currency.....................	**$1,070,097,308,052**	**$1,069,615,113,173**	**$240,439,961**	**$241,754,918**

NA = Not applicable. (1) Issued on or after July 1, 1929. (2) Represents the value of certain partial denominations not presented for redemption.

Budget Receipts and Outlays, 1789-1940

Source: U.S. Dept. of the Treasury
(in thousands of dollars; annual statements for years ending June 30, unless otherwise noted)

Yearly average	Receipts	Outlays	Yearly average	Receipts	Outlays	Yearly average	Receipts	Outlays
1789-1800[1]......	$5,717	$5,776	1866-1870	$447,301	$377,642	1906-1910	$628,507	$639,178
1801-1810[2]......	13,056	9,086	1871-1875	336,830	287,460	1911-1915	710,227	720,252
1811-1820[2]......	21,032	23,943	1876-1880	288,124	255,598	1916-1920	3,483,652	8,065,333
1821-1830[2]......	21,928	16,162	1881-1885	366,961	257,691	1921-1925	4,306,673	3,578,989
1831-1840[2]......	30,461	24,495	1886-1890	375,448	279,134	1926-1930	4,069,138	3,182,807
1841-1850[2]......	28,545	34,097	1891-1895	352,891	363,599	1931-1935	2,770,973	5,214,874
1851-1860	60,237	60,163	1896-1900	434,877	457,451	1936-1940	4,960,614	10,192,367
1861-1865 160,907		683,785	1901-1905	559,481	535,559			

(1) Average for period Mar. 4, 1789, to Dec. 31, 1800. (2) Years 1801-42 end Dec. 31; average for 1841-50 is for the period Jan. 1, 1841, to June 30, 1850.

U.S. Budget Receipts and Outlays, Fiscal Years 2000-11

Source: Congressional Budget Office; *Budget of the U.S. Government*, Office of Mgt. and Budget, Exec. Office of the President

A $236 bil surplus in 2000 turned into a $1.3 tril deficit as of 2011. Over the past decade, the total amount of money the government receives in taxes declined, while outlays have more than doubled for national defense, Medicare, and other health and income security programs.

(in millions of current dollars; numbers may not add up to totals because of independent rounding or omitted subcategories, including some subcategories with negative values.)

Function and subfunction	2000	2005	2008	2009	2010	2011
NET RECEIPTS	$2,025,191	$2,153,611	$2,523,991	$2,104,989	$2,162,724	$2,303,466
Individual income taxes..................	1,004,462	927,222	1,145,747	915,308	898,549	1,091,473
Corporation income taxes	207,289	278,282	304,346	138,229	191,437	181,085
Social insurance and retirement receipts	652,852	794,125	900,155	890,917	864,814	818,792
Employment and general retirement	620,451	747,664	856,459	848,885	815,894	758,516
Old-age and survivors insurance (off-budget)	411,677	493,646	562,519	559,067	539,996	483,683
Disability insurance (off-budget)...........	68,907	83,830	95,527	94,942	91,691	82,105
Hospital insurance	135,529	166,068	193,980	190,663	180,068	188,490
Railroad retirement/pension fund	2,688	2,284	2,404	2,301	2,285	2,415
Railroad social security equivalent account ...	1,650	1,836	2,029	1,912	1,854	1,823
Unemployment insurance	27,640	42,002	39,527	37,889	44,823	56,241
Other retirement	4,761	4,459	4,169	4,143	4,097	4,035
Excise taxes	68,865	73,094	67,334	62,483	66,909	72,381
Federal funds	22,692	22,547	15,726	13,854	18,256	18,904
Alcohol	8,140	8,111	9,283	9,903	9,229	9,294
Tobacco	7,221	7,920	7,639	12,841	17,160	16,685
Telephone............................	5,670	6,047	1,048	1,115	993	930
Transportation fuels	819	−770	−5,127	−10,324	−11,030	−8,644
Trust funds	46,173	50,547	51,608	48,629	48,653	53,477
Transportation........................	34,972	37,892	36,385	34,961	34,992	36,906
Airport and airway	9,739	10,314	11,992	10,569	10,612	11,532
Black lung disability	518	610	653	645	595	623
Inland waterway	101	91	88	76	74	84
Oil spill liability	182	—	333	447	476	501
Aquatic resources......................	342	429	595	576	580	593
Leaking underground storage tank..........	184	189	171	169	169	152
Tobacco assessments	—	899	1,140	951	937	932
Vaccine injury compensation	133	123	251	235	218	278
Other receipts	91,723	80,888	106,409	98,052	141,015	139,735

Function and subfunction	2000	2005	2008	2009	2010	2011
OUTLAYS	$1,788,950	$2,471,957	$2,982,544	$3,517,677	$3,456,213	$3,603,061
National defense	294,363	495,308	616,073	661,049	693,586	705,625
Department of Defense—Military	281,029	474,071	594,632	636,742	666,703	678,064
Military personnel	75,950	127,463	138,940	147,348	155,690	161,608
Operation and maintenance	105,812	188,118	244,836	259,312	275,988	291,038
Procurement	51,696	82,294	117,398	129,218	133,603	128,003
Research, development, test, and evaluation	37,602	65,694	75,120	79,030	76,990	74,871
Military construction	5,109	5,331	11,563	17,614	21,169	19,917
Family housing	3,413	3,720	3,590	2,721	3,173	3,432
Atomic energy defense activities	12,138	18,042	17,126	17,552	19,315	20,410
Defense-related activities	1,196	3,195	4,315	6,755	7,568	7,151
International affairs	17,213	34,565	28,857	37,529	45,195	45,685
International development and humanitarian assistance	6,516	17,696	14,074	22,095	19,014	21,255
International security assistance	6,387	7,895	9,480	6,247	11,363	12,042
Conduct of foreign affairs	4,708	9,148	10,388	12,152	13,557	12,486
Foreign information and exchange activities	817	1,129	1,330	1,330	1,485	1,575
International financial programs	−1,215	−1,303	−6,415	−4,295	−224	−1,673
General science, space, and technology	23,597	25,525	29,449	31,047	23,597	29,466
General science and basic research	8,819	10,267	11,052	12,677	8,819	12,434
Space flight, research, and supporting activities	14,778	15,258	18,397	18,370	14,778	17,032
Energy	−761	429	628	4,749	11,613	12,174
Energy supply	−1,818	−940	−416	2,045	5,796	8,084
Energy conservation	666	883	409	1,432	4,997	6,736
Emergency energy preparedness	162	162	179	754	199	−3,263
Energy information, policy, and regulation	229	324	456	518	621	617
Natural resources and environment	25,003	27,980	31,817	35,568	43,662	45,470
Water resources	5,078	5,723	6,071	8,063	11,656	11,618
Conservation and land management	6,762	6,226	8,718	9,813	10,783	11,955
Recreational resources	2,540	2,990	3,208	3,550	3,911	4,157
Pollution control and abatement	7,395	8,065	8,079	8,270	10,842	10,946
Agriculture	36,458	26,565	18,387	22,237	21,356	20,661
Farm income stabilization	33,446	22,048	13,762	17,635	16,605	16,016
Agricultural research and services	3,012	4,517	4,625	4,602	4,751	4,645
Commerce and housing credit	3,207	7,566	27,870	291,535	−82,298	−12,575
Mortgage credit	−3,335	−862	17	99,760	35,804	14,156
Postal Service	2,129	−1,223	−3,074	−978	−682	909
Deposit insurance	−3,053	−1,371	18,760	22,573	−32,033	−8,697
Transportation	46,853	67,894	77,616	84,289	91,972	92,965
Ground transportation	31,697	42,317	49,978	54,103	60,784	60,902
Air transportation	10,571	18,807	19,399	20,799	21,431	21,353
Water transportation	4,394	6,439	8,121	9,093	9,351	10,358
Community and regional development	10,623	26,262	23,952	27,650	23,804	23,816
Community development	5,480	5,861	10,198	7,719	9,901	9,605
Area and regional development	2,538	2,745	2,584	3,221	3,249	4,050
Disaster relief and insurance	2,605	17,656	11,170	16,710	10,654	10,161
Education, training, employment, and social services	53,764	97,555	91,287	79,749	127,710	101,233
Elementary, secondary, and vocational education	20,578	38,271	38,918	53,206	73,261	66,476
Higher education	10,115	31,442	23,566	−3,258	20,023	1,108
Research and general education aids	2,543	3,124	3,194	3,456	3,631	3,710
Training and employment	6,777	6,852	7,181	7,652	9,854	9,139
Social services	12,557	16,251	16,805	17,047	19,176	18,931
Health	154,504	250,548	280,599	334,335	369,054	372,500
Health care services	136,201	219,559	247,739	300,013	330,710	332,210
Health research and training	15,979	28,050	29,883	30,570	34,200	36,194
Consumer and occupational health and safety	2,324	2,939	2,977	3,752	4,144	4,096
Medicare	197,113	298,638	390,758	430,093	451,636	485,653
Income security	253,724	345,847	431,313	533,224	622,210	597,352
Retirement and disability insurance (excl. social security)	5,189	6,976	8,899	8,218	6,564	6,697
Federal employee retirement and disability	77,152	93,351	108,998	118,119	119,867	124,450
Unemployment compensation	23,012	35,435	45,340	122,537	160,145	120,556
Housing assistance	28,949	37,899	40,556	50,913	58,651	55,440
Food and nutrition assistance	32,483	50,833	60,673	79,080	95,110	103,199
Social security	409,423	523,305	617,027	682,963	706,737	730,811
Veterans benefits and services	46,989	70,120	84,653	95,429	108,384	127,189
Income security for veterans	24,907	35,767	41,338	45,952	49,163	58,747
Veterans education, training, and rehabilitation	1,285	2,790	2,730	3,495	8,089	10,683
Hospital and medical care for veterans	19,516	28,754	36,974	41,882	45,714	50,062
Veterans housing	364	860	−419	−578	540	1,262
Administration of justice	28,499	40,019	47,138	51,549	53,436	56,055
Federal law enforcement activities	12,121	19,912	24,615	27,552	27,766	29,801
Federal litigative and judicial activities	7,762	9,641	11,781	12,083	13,073	13,565
Federal correctional activities	3,707	5,862	6,888	7,298	7,748	8,057
Criminal justice assistance	4,909	4,604	3,854	4,616	4,849	4,632
General government	13,013	16,997	20,323	22,017	23,031	25,507
Legislative functions	2,223	3,451	3,658	3,815	4,089	3,960
Executive direction and management	456	569	525	535	528	446
Central fiscal operations	8,285	9,515	10,553	10,752	11,906	11,631
General property and records management	−32	472	570	554	1,194	2,304
Central personnel management	184	101	−12	102	338	124
General purpose fiscal assistance	2,084	3,333	4,089	4,097	5,082	7,475
Deductions for offsetting receipts	−2,383	−2,841	−462	−1,012	−1,704	−3,448
Net interest	222,949	183,986	252,757	186,902	196,194	229,968
Undistributed offsetting receipts	−42,581	−65,224	−86,242	−92,639	−82,116	−86,494
Employer share, employee retirement (on-budget)	−30,214	−47,977	−53,033	−56,431	−62,100	−64,581
TOTAL SURPLUS/DEFICIT	236,241	−318,346	−458,553	−1,412,688	−1,293,489	−1,299,595

Federal Receipts, Outlays, and Surpluses or Deficits, 1901-2013

Source: *Budget of the U.S. Government*, Fiscal Year 2013, Office of Management and Budget, Exec. Office of the President
(in millions of current dollars)

Fiscal year	Receipts	Outlays	Surplus or deficit (–)	Fiscal year	Receipts	Outlays	Surplus or deficit (–)	Fiscal year	Receipts	Outlays	Surplus or deficit (–)
1901	$588	$525	**$63**	1939	$6,295	$9,141	–$2,846	1977	$355,559	$409,218	–$53,659
1902	562	485	**77**	1940	6,548	9,468	–2,920	1978	399,561	458,746	–59,185
1903	562	517	**45**	1941	8,712	13,653	–4,941	1979	463,302	504,028	–40,726
1904	541	584	–43	1942	14,634	35,137	–20,503	1980	517,112	590,941	–73,830
1905	544	567	–23	1943	24,001	78,555	–54,554	1981	599,272	678,241	–78,968
1906	595	570	**25**	1944	43,747	91,304	–47,557	1982	617,766	745,743	–127,977
1907	666	579	**87**	1945	45,159	92,712	–47,553	1983	600,562	808,364	–207,802
1908	602	659	–57	1946	39,296	55,232	–15,936	1984	666,438	851,805	–185,367
1909	604	694	–89	1947	38,514	34,496	**4,018**	1985	734,037	946,344	–212,308
1910	676	694	–18	1948	41,560	29,764	**11,796**	1986	769,155	990,382	–221,227
1911	702	691	**11**	1949	39,415	38,835	**580**	1987	854,288	1,004,017	–149,730
1912	693	690	**3**	1950	39,443	42,562	–3,119	1988	909,238	1,064,416	–155,178
1913	714	715	—	1951	51,616	45,514	**6,102**	1989	991,105	1,143,744	–152,639
1914	725	726	—	1952	66,167	67,686	–1,519	1990	1,031,958	1,252,994	–221,036
1915	683	746	–63	1953	69,608	76,101	–6,493	1991	1,054,988	1,324,226	–269,238
1916	761	713	**48**	1954	69,701	70,855	–1,154	1992	1,091,208	1,381,529	–290,321
1917	1,101	1,954	–853	1955	65,451	68,444	–2,993	1993	1,154,335	1,409,386	–255,051
1918	3,645	12,677	–9,032	1956	74,587	70,640	**3,947**	1994	1,258,566	1,461,753	–203,186
1919	5,130	18,493	–13,363	1957	79,990	76,578	**3,412**	1995	1,351,790	1,515,742	–163,952
1920	6,649	6,358	**291**	1958	79,636	82,405	–2,769	1996	1,453,053	1,560,484	–107,431
1921	5,571	5,062	**509**	1959	79,249	92,098	–12,849	1997	1,579,232	1,601,116	–21,884
1922	4,026	3,289	**736**	1960	92,492	92,191	**301**	1998	1,721,728	1,652,458	**69,270**
1923	3,853	3,140	**713**	1961	94,388	97,723	–3,335	1999	1,827,452	1,701,842	**125,610**
1924	3,871	2,908	**963**	1962	99,676	106,821	–7,146	2000	2,025,191	1,788,950	**236,241**
1925	3,641	2,924	**717**	1963	106,560	111,316	–4,756	2001	1,991,082	1,862,846	**128,236**
1926	3,795	2,930	**865**	1964	112,613	118,528	–5,915	2002	1,853,136	2,010,894	–157,758
1927	4,013	2,857	**1,155**	1965	116,817	118,228	–1,411	2003	1,782,314	2,159,899	–377,585
1928	3,900	2,961	**939**	1966	130,835	134,532	–3,698	2004	1,880,114	2,292,841	–412,727
1929	3,862	3,127	**734**	1967	148,822	157,464	–8,643	2005	2,153,611	2,471,957	–318,346
1930	4,058	3,320	**738**	1968	152,973	178,134	–25,161	2006	2,406,869	2,655,050	–248,181
1931	3,116	3,577	–462	1969	186,882	183,640	**3,242**	2007	2,567,985	2,728,686	–160,701
1932	1,924	4,659	–2,735	1970	192,807	195,649	–2,842	2008	2,523,991	2,982,544	–458,553
1933	1,997	4,598	–2,602	1971	187,139	210,172	–23,033	2009	2,104,989	3,517,677	–1,412,688
1934	2,955	6,541	–3,586	1972	207,309	230,681	–23,373	2010	2,162,724	3,456,213	–1,293,489
1935	3,609	6,412	–2,803	1973	230,799	245,707	–14,908	2011	2,303,466	3,603,061	–1,299,595
1936	3,923	8,228	–4,304	1974	263,224	269,359	–6,135	2012E	2,468,599	3,795,547	–1,326,948
1937	5,387	7,580	–2,193	1975	279,090	332,332	–53,242	2013E	2,901,956	3,803,364	–901,408
1938	6,751	6,840	–89	1976	298,060	371,792	–73,732				

— = $500,000 or less. E = Estimate, as of Feb. 1, 2012. Figures in **bold** denote annual surpluses. **Note:** Budget figures prior to 1933 are based on "Administrative Budget" concepts rather than "Unified Budget" concepts. Through 1976, fiscal years end June 30; after 1976, fiscal years end Sept. 30. Surplus or deficit column may not equal difference between figures because of rounding.

Budget Deficits as Percent of GDP in Selected Countries, 1995-2013

Source: *OECD Economic Outlook*, Organization for Economic Cooperation and Development

Country	1995	2000	2005	2007	2008	2009	2010	2011	2012	2013
Australia	–3.9%	0.4%	1.2%	1.8%	–0.8%	–4.5%	–4.7%	–3.9%	–2.2%	0.4%
Austria	–5.9	–1.9	–1.8	–1.0	–1.0	–4.2	–4.5	–2.6	–2.9	–2.3
Belgium	–4.5	–0.1	–2.8	–0.1	–1.0	–5.7	–3.9	–3.9	–2.8	–2.2
Canada	–5.3	2.9	1.5	1.4	–0.4	–4.9	–5.6	–4.5	–3.5	–2.4
Czech Republic	–13.4	–3.7	–3.6	–0.7	–2.2	–5.8	–4.8	–3.1	–2.5	–2.2
Denmark	–2.9	2.2	5.0	4.8	3.3	–2.7	–2.7	–1.9	–3.9	–2.0
Estonia	1.1	–0.2	1.6	2.4	–2.9	–2.0	0.3	1.0	–2.0	–0.3
Finland	–6.2	6.8	2.5	5.3	4.2	–2.7	–2.9	–0.9	–0.7	0.0
France	–5.5	–1.5	–3.0	–2.7	–3.3	–7.6	–7.1	–5.2	–4.5	–3.0
Germany	–9.7	1.3	–3.3	0.2	–0.1	–3.2	–4.3	–1.0	–0.9	–0.6
Greece	–9.1	–3.7	–5.3	–6.8	–9.9	–15.6	–10.5	–9.2	–7.4	–4.9
Hungary	–8.7	–3.0	–7.9	–5.1	–3.7	–4.5	–4.3	4.2	–3.0	–2.9
Iceland	–3.0	1.7	4.9	5.4	–13.5	–10.0	–10.1	–4.4	–2.6	–1.4
Ireland	–2.1	4.8	1.6	0.1	–7.3	–14.0	–31.2	–13.0	–8.4	–7.6
Israel	NA	–4.0	–4.9	–1.5	–3.8	–6.4	–5.0	–4.4	–4.3	–4.2
Italy	–7.4	–0.9	–4.4	–1.6	–2.7	–5.4	–4.5	–3.8	–1.7	–0.6
Japan	–4.7	–7.6	–6.7	–2.1	–1.9	–8.8	–8.4	–9.5	–9.9	–10.1
Korea, South	3.5	5.4	3.4	4.7	3.0	–1.1	1.3	1.8	2.3	2.8
Luxembourg	2.4	6.0	0.0	3.7	3.0	–0.8	–0.9	–0.6	–1.4	–1.1
Netherlands	–9.2	2.0	–0.3	0.2	0.5	–5.5	–5.0	–4.6	–4.3	–3.0
New Zealand	2.5	1.8	4.7	4.5	0.4	–2.6	–4.2	–8.2	–4.4	–2.9
Norway	3.2	15.4	15.1	17.3	18.8	10.6	11.2	13.6	15.1	16.3
Poland	–4.4	–3.0	–4.1	–1.9	–3.7	–7.4	–7.9	–5.1	–2.9	–2.2
Portugal	–5.0	–2.9	–5.9	–3.2	–3.7	–10.2	–9.8	–4.2	–4.6	–3.5
Slovakia	–3.4	–12.3	–2.8	–1.8	–2.1	–8.0	–7.7	–4.8	–4.6	–2.9
Slovenia	–8.4	–3.7	–1.5	0.0	–1.9	–6.1	–6.0	–6.4	–3.9	–3.0
Spain	–6.5	–1.0	1.0	1.9	–4.5	–11.2	–9.3	–8.5	–5.4	–3.3
Sweden	–7.3	3.6	1.9	3.6	2.2	–1.0	–0.1	0.1	–0.3	0.3
Switzerland	–2.0	0.1	–0.7	1.7	2.3	1.0	0.6	0.8	0.6	0.6
United Kingdom	–5.8	3.7	–3.3	–2.8	–5.0	–11.0	–10.3	–8.4	–7.7	–6.6
United States	–3.3	1.5	–3.3	–2.9	–6.6	–11.6	–10.7	–9.7	–8.3	–6.5
Euro area	–7.5	–0.1	–2.6	–0.7	–2.1	–6.4	–6.2	–4.1	–3.0	–2.0
Total OECD	**–4.8**	**0.1**	**–2.8**	**–1.3**	**–3.4**	**–8.1**	**–7.5**	**–6.3**	**–5.3**	**–4.2**

NA = Not available.

Public Debt of the U.S., 1946-2012

Source: *Budget of the U.S. Government*, Office of Management and Budget, Exec. Office of the President

Year	Debt held by public — Current dollars (bil)	Debt held by public — FY 2011 dollars (bil)	Debt held by public — As % of GDP	Interest on public debt as % of— Total federal outlays	Interest on public debt as % of— GDP	Year	Debt held by public — Current dollars (bil)	Debt held by public — FY 2011 dollars (bil)	Debt held by public — As % of GDP	Interest on public debt as % of— Total federal outlays	Interest on public debt as % of— GDP
1946	$241.9	$2,324.7	108.7%	7.4%	1.8%	2001	$3,319.6	$4,145.5	32.5%	11.6%	2.1%
1950	219.0	1,712.9	80.2	11.4	1.8	2002	3,540.4	4,349.4	33.6	8.9	1.7
1955	226.6	1,557.3	57.2	7.6	1.3	2003	3,913.4	4,711.4	35.6	7.5	1.5
1960	236.8	1,444.9	45.6	8.5	1.5	2004	4,295.5	5,043.6	36.8	7.3	1.4
1965	260.8	1,487.7	37.9	8.1	1.4	2005	4,592.2	5,222.2	36.9	7.7	1.5
1970	283.2	1,343.4	28.0	7.9	1.5	2006	4,829.0	5,311.0	36.6	8.9	1.8
1975	394.7	1,377.8	25.3	7.5	1.6	2007	5,035.1	5,378.6	36.3	9.2	1.8
1980	711.9	1,718.7	26.1	10.6	2.3	2008	5,803.1	6,058.4	40.5	8.7	1.8
1985	1,507.3	2,773.7	36.4	16.2	3.7	2009	7,544.7	7,764.6	54.1	5.7	1.4
1990	2,411.6	3,800.7	42.1	16.2	3.5	2010	9,018.9	9,196.4	62.8	6.6	1.6
1995	3,604.4	5,004.6	49.1	15.8	3.3	2011	10,128.2	10,128.2	67.7	7.4	1.8
2000	3,409.8	4,358.5	34.7	13.0	2.4	2012[E]	11,578.1	11,367.7	74.2	7.1	1.7

E = Estimate. **Note:** As of end of fiscal year. Through 1976, the fiscal year ended June 30. From 1977 on, the fiscal year ended Sept. 30.

State Finances: Revenues, Taxes, Expenditures, and Debt, 2010

Source: U.S. Census Bureau, U.S. Dept. of Commerce

(in thousands of dollars; fiscal year)

State	Revenues — Total revenue	Revenues — General revenues	Revenues — Intergovt. revenue	Taxes	Total expenditures	Debt at end of fiscal year
Alabama	$26,823,681	$22,989,680	$9,369,725	$8,185,563	$27,699,687	$8,785,245
Alaska	12,374,672	11,035,812	2,961,501	4,517,927	10,996,963	6,380,597
Arizona	32,841,609	26,324,126	12,577,215	10,199,338	33,015,591	13,956,433
Arkansas	19,595,441	16,221,062	5,978,147	7,279,215	17,353,711	4,260,547
California	278,494,901	196,643,170	67,805,353	104,840,520	257,248,691	148,929,107
Colorado	27,990,510	19,930,978	6,371,099	8,586,401	27,660,864	16,709,540
Connecticut	26,840,365	21,924,404	6,229,831	12,285,994	27,437,324	30,215,550
Delaware	7,975,651	7,233,570	2,035,019	2,769,731	7,826,826	5,515,150
Florida	91,653,258	71,341,309	25,447,682	31,498,998	81,629,113	40,403,855
Georgia	44,878,023	36,479,685	16,193,428	14,782,779	44,482,208	13,788,833
Hawaii	11,565,500	9,627,041	2,592,047	4,837,862	11,178,392	7,700,654
Idaho	8,859,444	6,726,503	2,672,926	2,951,703	8,514,075	3,872,453
Illinois	73,274,871	55,674,264	19,345,760	27,511,933	75,269,674	61,411,694
Indiana	35,575,267	29,801,851	10,400,713	13,796,427	35,474,194	23,634,564
Iowa	21,265,049	17,113,161	6,743,091	6,809,344	19,108,588	5,140,385
Kansas	16,545,579	14,215,169	4,624,104	6,492,996	16,583,949	6,478,228
Kentucky	26,993,403	22,861,951	9,149,028	9,531,108	29,097,531	14,393,269
Louisiana	32,188,166	27,440,627	13,255,001	8,757,557	33,615,486	17,442,967
Maine	9,539,306	8,247,985	3,212,892	3,489,953	9,024,322	6,034,227
Maryland	37,394,440	31,184,749	10,534,111	15,223,923	37,487,628	24,474,671
Massachusetts	50,471,792	42,208,719	13,326,217	20,050,292	51,730,861	73,939,716
Michigan	65,971,789	52,667,317	19,527,609	22,205,870	63,917,651	32,146,344
Minnesota	39,887,029	31,462,337	10,024,802	17,208,877	37,942,727	11,682,878
Mississippi	20,978,550	17,427,242	8,807,805	6,268,804	20,022,653	6,467,833
Missouri	33,915,612	26,111,659	11,798,319	9,708,463	30,771,516	20,421,226
Montana	7,141,352	6,008,627	2,504,673	2,142,809	7,052,380	4,373,930
Nebraska	10,062,763	8,675,960	3,202,752	3,809,266	9,584,493	2,330,277
Nevada	14,053,177	9,937,131	2,917,112	5,835,963	12,934,509	4,435,774
New Hampshire	7,827,936	6,221,852	2,360,687	2,124,984	7,705,787	8,347,216
New Jersey	66,740,281	51,182,545	15,476,911	25,927,891	67,971,367	60,958,345
New Mexico	17,566,599	14,010,955	6,247,462	4,413,988	17,996,038	8,739,878
New York	195,460,010	139,965,783	55,725,570	63,529,354	174,307,538	129,529,501
North Carolina	57,467,430	44,057,698	15,698,831	21,517,254	52,189,891	18,853,155
North Dakota	6,118,449	5,415,249	1,741,931	2,645,695	5,134,130	2,198,282
Ohio	89,664,151	57,507,853	22,461,873	23,583,596	76,730,622	31,177,155
Oklahoma	23,692,058	19,486,441	8,007,066	7,079,985	22,639,978	9,963,419
Oregon	28,703,267	19,000,510	6,857,718	7,289,362	26,978,154	13,510,005
Pennsylvania	83,287,051	63,884,140	21,338,641	30,169,122	87,285,286	44,737,622
Rhode Island	8,809,270	7,087,779	2,966,972	2,568,851	8,211,203	9,498,115
South Carolina	28,867,808	21,511,929	7,933,502	7,312,534	28,927,120	15,770,780
South Dakota	4,492,586	3,974,366	1,794,047	1,304,487	4,429,197	3,483,142
Tennessee	29,719,569	25,517,396	11,371,391	10,513,788	29,675,372	5,835,113
Texas	120,389,837	99,923,805	41,450,202	39,399,251	119,604,888	42,033,571
Utah	16,022,191	13,227,809	4,373,886	5,092,415	16,262,957	6,477,933
Vermont	6,001,197	5,330,512	1,904,907	2,511,387	5,726,034	3,492,873
Virginia	46,356,567	37,103,065	9,779,654	16,411,055	43,457,150	24,966,916
Washington	44,298,597	33,710,587	11,176,371	16,106,154	46,238,022	27,478,320
West Virginia	13,564,289	11,561,249	4,426,116	4,655,034	12,343,051	7,144,323
Wisconsin	48,088,136	30,845,174	10,403,378	14,368,569	38,589,815	22,318,551
Wyoming	7,411,311	5,585,873	2,456,605	2,117,100	5,756,937	1,514,359
United States[1]	**$2,035,699,790**	**$1,563,628,659**	**$575,561,683**	**$702,221,472**	**$1,942,822,144**	**$1,113,354,521**

(1) Figures may not add up to totals because of rounding.

State and Local Government Receipts and Current Expenditures, 1980-2011

Source: Bureau of Economic Analysis, U.S. Dept. of Commerce

(in billions of current dollars; as of Sept. 2012)

	1980	1990	1995	2000	2005	2008	2009	2010	2011
Receipts	$338.2	$738.0	$991.9	$1,322.6	$1,730.4	$1,944.8	$1,961.4	$2,042.4	$2,064.4
Current tax receipts	230.0	519.1	672.1	893.2	1,163.1	1,326.4	1,264.9	1,304.6	1,360.8
Personal current taxes	48.9	122.6	158.1	236.7	276.7	334.4	287.6	300.6	322.8
Income taxes	42.6	109.6	141.7	217.4	251.7	307.7	259.3	270.1	291.2
Other.	6.3	13.0	16.4	19.4	25.0	26.7	28.3	30.4	31.6
Taxes on production and imports	166.7	374.1	482.4	621.3	831.4	944.6	931.8	959.5	990.4
Sales taxes.	82.9	184.3	242.7	316.8	402.2	444.0	422.3	442.6	461.5
Property taxes.	68.8	161.5	202.6	254.7	346.9	408.3	431.2	433.5	439.8
Other.	15.0	28.3	37.0	49.8	82.3	92.3	78.3	83.4	89.2
Taxes on corporate income	14.5	22.5	31.7	35.2	54.9	47.4	45.5	44.5	47.6
Contributions for government social									
insurance	3.6	10.0	13.6	10.8	24.8	19.0	19.0	18.4	18.3
Income receipts on assets	26.3	68.5	68.5	94.3	88.3	106.8	95.0	88.8	86.4
Interest receipts	23.1	64.1	63.0	86.7	76.4	91.9	81.8	75.7	73.0
Dividends	0.1	0.2	1.0	1.4	2.1	2.9	2.1	2.2	2.2
Rents and royalties	3.1	4.2	4.5	6.3	9.8	12.0	11.1	10.9	11.2
Current transfer receipts.	79.5	133.5	224.2	313.9	454.3	505.0	593.6	643.2	612.7
Federal grants-in-aid.	72.3	111.4	184.2	247.3	361.2	395.5	482.6	531.1	497.8
From business (net)	2.5	7.1	13.5	28.6	36.5	44.3	45.0	44.8	45.5
From persons	4.7	14.9	26.5	38.0	56.5	65.2	66.0	67.3	69.4
Current surplus of government									
enterprises	−1.2	6.9	13.5	10.4	0.1	−12.3	−11.1	−12.5	−13.8
Expenditures.	**329.4**	**731.8**	**982.7**	**1,281.3**	**1,704.5**	**2,017.0**	**2,074.6**	**2,132.1**	**2,166.3**
Consumption expenditures	258.4	547.0	701.3	930.6	1,212.0	1,449.2	1,473.3	1,496.2	1,518.0
Government social benefit payments to									
persons	51.2	127.7	217.6	271.4	404.8	456.7	495.1	528.3	538.5
Interest payments	19.4	56.8	63.5	78.8	87.3	108.1	104.8	106.0	109.2
Subsidies	0.4	0.4	0.3	0.5	0.4	3.0	1.4	1.6	0.5
Net state and local government saving	8.8	6.2	9.2	41.3	25.9	−72.2	−113.2	−89.7	−102.0
Social insurance funds	1.3	2.0	4.0	2.0	7.4	1.2	1.7	2.2	2.8
Other.	7.5	4.2	5.1	39.3	18.5	−73.4	−115.0	−91.9	−104.7
Addenda:									
Total receipts	356.8	762.9	1,024.2	1,366.4	1,786.7	2,007.6	2,027.9	2,118.0	2,136.9
Current receipts	338.2	738.0	991.9	1,322.6	1,730.4	1,944.8	1,961.4	2,042.4	2,064.4
Capital transfer receipts	18.6	25.0	32.4	43.8	56.2	62.8	66.5	75.6	72.5
Total expenditures.	363.3	801.7	1,060.1	1,404.5	1,852.6	2,188.8	2,238.8	2,278.6	2,285.1
Current expenditures	329.4	731.8	982.7	1,281.3	1,704.5	2,017.0	2,074.6	2,132.1	2,166.3
Gross government investment	64.0	127.2	154.0	224.3	281.6	348.8	350.3	338.2	319.7
Capital transfer payments	0.0	0.0	0.0	0.0	6.4	0.0	0.0	0.0	0.0
Net purchases of nonproduced									
assets	1.8	5.7	6.6	8.6	10.3	14.1	12.7	11.6	11.5
Less: Consumption of fixed capital . .	31.8	63.0	83.1	109.7	150.1	191.2	198.8	203.3	212.4
Net lending or net borrowing (−)	**−6.6**	**−38.8**	**−35.9**	**−38.1**	**−66.0**	**−181.1**	**−210.9**	**−160.5**	**−148.2**

Federal Deposit Insurance Corporation (FDIC)

The Federal Deposit Insurance Corporation (FDIC) was created by Congress during the height of the Depression to maintain stability and public confidence in the nation's banking system. It covered depositors for up to $2,500 in case of bank failure in 1934; the limit today is 100 times that much, or $250,000. In its unique role as deposit insurer of banks and savings associations, and in cooperation with other federal and state regulatory agencies, the FDIC seeks to promote the safety and soundness of insured depository institutions in the U.S. financial system.

The quarterly premiums on deposit insurance are paid by the banks rather than by consumers. The amount of the premium is based on the institution's balance of insured deposits for the preceding quarter and the institution's risk to the insurance fund. In 2009, Congress permanently increased the limit that the FDIC may borrow from the U.S. Treasury from $30 bil to $100 bil.

U.S. Banks, 1935-2012

Source: *Summary of Deposits*, Federal Deposit Insurance Corp.

Comprises all FDIC-insured commercial and savings banks, including savings and loan institutions (S&Ls).

	Total number of banks					Total deposits (mil dollars)				
		Commercial banks[1]		Savings			Commercial banks[1]		Savings	
Year	All banks	National charter	State charter	Non-members	banks, total	All deposits	National charter	State charter	Non-members	banks, total
1935[2]	15,295	5,386	1,001	7,735	1,173	$45,102	$24,802	$13,653	$5,669	$978
1940	15,772	5,144	1,342	6,956	2,330	67,494	35,787	20,642	7,040	4,025
1950	16,500	4,958	1,912	6,576	3,054	171,963	84,941	41,602	19,726	25,694
1960	17,549	4,530	1,641	6,955	4,423	310,262	120,242	65,487	34,369	90,164
1970	18,205	4,621	1,147	7,743	4,694	686,901	285,436	101,512	95,566	204,367
1980	18,763	4,425	997	9,013	4,328	1,832,716	656,752	191,183	344,311	640,470
1990	15,158	3,979	1,009	7,355	2,815	3,637,292	1,558,915	397,797	693,438	987,142
1995	12,289	2,941	995	6,230	2,082	3,214,678	1,337,105	439,430	696,108	735,856
2000	10,119	2,302	996	5,180	1,622	4,003,744	1,792,773	707,562	793,275	706,461
2005	8,855	1,864	906	4,779	1,293	5,933,742	2,946,589	765,673	1,191,977	1,023,620
2006	8,767	1,780	903	4,796	1,276	6,449,864	3,190,482	818,565	1,311,720	1,118,948
2007	8,605	1,676	888	4,786	1,244	6,702,053	3,273,531	831,116	1,425,412	1,165,119
2008	8,441	1,585	874	4,744	1,227	7,025,791	3,596,712	857,003	1,432,614	1,132,356
2009	8,185	1,505	858	4,632	1,180	7,559,590	4,141,792	962,232	1,512,677	936,101
2010	7,821	1,427	836	4,413	1,135	7,676,878	4,305,697	1,002,425	1,464,022	891,159
2011	7,523	1,349	824	4,240	1,100	8,249,233	4,708,210	1,120,747	1,491,112	909,912
2012	7,255	1,285	836	4,101	1,023	8,947,239	5,250,842	1,220,930	1,576,616	874,850

Note: Figures are for the end of the year shown through 1990 and for June 30 thereafter. (1) Nonmembers are banks that are not members of the Federal Reserve System; national charter and state charter institutions are Federal Reserve members. (2) Figures for 1935 do not include S&Ls, the data for which are not available.

U.S. Bank Failures, 1934-2012

Source: Federal Deposit Insurance Corp.

Covers all FDIC-insured commercial and savings banks, including savings and loan institutions (S&Ls) 1980 and after. As of Oct. 21, 2012.

Year	Closed or assisted	Year	Closed or assisted	Year	Closed or assisted	Year	Closed or assisted	Year	Closed or assisted	Year	Closed or assisted
1934	9	1960-69 ..	44	1988	470	1997	1	2006	0		
1935	25	1970-79 ..	79	1989	534	1998	3	2007	3		
1936	69	1980	22	1990	382	1999	8	2008	30		
1937	75	1981	40	1991	271	2000	7	2009	148		
1938	74	1982	119	1992	181	2001	4	2010	157		
1939	60	1983	99	1993	50	2002	11	2011	92		
1940	43	1984	106	1994	15	2003	3	2012	43		
1941	15	1985	180	1995	8	2004	4	**Total,**			
1942	20	1986	204	1996	6	2005	0	**1934-2012**	**4,025**		
1950-59 ..	28	1987	262								

Largest U.S. Bank Holding Companies, 2012

Source: National Information Center, Federal Financial Institutions Examination Council
(as of June 30, 2012; ranked by total assets, in thousands of dollars)

Rank	Institution name, location	Total assets	Rank	Institution name, location	Total assets
1.	JPMorgan Chase & Co., New York, NY ..	$2,290,146	15.	Ally Financial Inc., Detroit, MI	$178,560
2.	Bank of America Corporation,		16.	BB&T Corporation, Winston-Salem, NC ..	178,529
	Charlotte, NC	2,162,083	17.	SunTrust Banks, Inc., Atlanta, GA	178,307
3.	Citigroup Inc., New York, NY...........	1,916,451	18.	Principal Financial Group, Inc.,	
4.	Wells Fargo & Company,			Des Moines, IA..................	152,051
	San Francisco, CA	1,336,204	19.	American Express Company,	
5.	Goldman Sachs Group, Inc., New York, NY	948,981		New York, NY	146,890
6.	MetLife, Inc., New York, NY	825,188	20.	Ameriprise Financial, Inc., Minneapolis, MN	135,271
7.	Morgan Stanley, New York, NY.........	748,517	21.	RBS Citizens Financial Group, Inc.,	
8.	U.S. Bancorp, Minneapolis, MN	353,136		Providence, RI	129,314
9.	Bank of New York Mellon Corporation,		22.	Regions Financial Corp., Birmingham, AL	122,345
	New York, NY	330,490	23.	Fifth Third Bancorp, Cincinnati, OH	117,543
10.	HSBC North America Holdings Inc.,		24.	BMO Financial Corp., Wilmington, DE ...	112,166
	New York, NY	317,482	25.	Charles Schwab Corp., San Francisco, CA	111,816
11.	PNC Financial Services Group, Inc.,		26.	United Services Automobile Association,	
	Pittsburgh, PA...................	299,712		San Antonio, TX	110,563
12.	Capital One Financial Corporation,		27.	Northern Trust Corp., Chicago, IL.......	94,456
	McLean, VA	296,698	28.	UnionBanCal Corp., San Francisco, CA ..	87,940
13.	TD Bank US Holding Company,		29.	KeyCorp, Cleveland, OH.	86,741
	Portland, ME....................	207,333	30.	Santander Holdings USA, Inc.,	
14.	State Street Corporation, Boston, MA ...	200,369		Boston, MA.....................	82,944

Note: Includes foreign-owned banks with a strong presence in the U.S.

Status of Top Recipients of Treasury Department Bailout Funds, 2012

Source: ProPublica

Since Oct. 2008, the federal government has spent more than $600 bil to bail out more than 900 institutions severely affected by the financial crisis. Companies that failed to repay the government and have resulted in a loss to the taxpayers are listed in **bold italics**. All other investments either returned a profit to the government or may still be repaid.

(in billions of dollars; as of Oct. 21, 2012)

Recipient	Disbursed	Repaid[1]	Net profit or amount still outstanding[2]	Recipient	Disbursed	Repaid[1]	Net profit or amount still outstanding[2]
Fannie Mae..............	$116.1	$25.5	−$90.6	AllianceBernstein Legacy			
Freddie Mac	71.3	20.1	−51.2	Securities Master Fund,			
AIG	67.8	65.2	−2.6	L.P.................	$3.3	$3.7	$0.5
General Motors..........	50.7	23.5	−27.2	BB&T	3.1	3.3	0.2
Bank of America	45.0	49.6	4.6	Bank of New York Mellon ..	3.0	3.2	0.2
Citigroup	45.0	57.3	12.4	KeyCorp	2.5	2.9	0.4
JPMorgan Chase	25.0	26.7	1.7	*CIT Group*	*2.3*	*—*	*−2.3*
Wells Fargo.............	25.0	27.3	2.3	Comerica Incorporated	2.3	2.6	0.3
GMAC (now Ally Financial)	16.3	5.5	−10.8	State Street............	2.0	2.1	0.1
Chrysler	*10.7*	*9.4*	*−1.3*	RLJ Western Asset Public/			
Goldman Sachs	10.0	11.4	1.4	Private Master Fund, L.P.	1.9	1.8	−0.1
Morgan Stanley..........	10.0	11.3	1.3	Invesco Legacy Securities			
PNC Financial Services ...	7.6	8.3	0.7	Master Fund, L.P.	1.7	2.3	0.6
U.S. Bancorp	6.6	6.9	0.3	Marshall & Ilsley	1.7	1.9	0.2
SunTrust	4.9	5.4	0.5	Oaktree PPIP Fund, L.P....	1.7	—	−1.3
Capital One Financial Corp.	3.6	3.8	0.3	Blackrock PPIF, L.P.	1.6	—	−1.2
Regions Financial Corp....	3.5	4.1	0.6	Northern Trust...........	1.6	1.7	0.1
Fifth Third Bancorp	3.4	4.0	0.6	Chrysler Financial Services	1.5	1.5	—
Hartford Financial Services	3.4	4.2	0.8	Zions Bancorp	1.4	1.6	0.2
American Express	3.4	3.8	0.4	Huntington Bancshares ...	1.4	1.6	0.2
AG GECC PPIF Master				Marathon Legacy Securities			
Fund, L.P.	3.4	1.7	−1.6	Public-Private Investment			
Wellington Management				Partnership, L.P........	1.4	—	−1.1
Legacy Securities PPIF				Discover Financial Services	1.2	1.5	0.2
Master Fund, LP	3.3	0.8	−2.5	**Total**	**$603.8**	**$430.1**	**−$173.7**

— = less than $0.1 bil. **Note:** Total includes other disbursements not shown. (1) Amounts repaid include principal, dividends, interest, warrants, and other proceeds. (2) Negative number represents outstanding debt.

Federal Reserve System

The Federal Reserve System is the central bank for the U.S. The system was established on Dec. 23, 1913, originally to give the country an elastic currency, provide facilities for discounting commercial paper, and improve the supervision of banking. Since then, the system's responsibilities have been broadened. Over the years, stability and growth of the economy, a high level of employment, stability in the purchasing power of the dollar, and reasonable balance in transactions with other countries have come to be recognized as primary objectives of governmental economic policy.

The Federal Reserve System consists of the Board of Governors, the 12 District Reserve Banks and their branch offices, and the Federal Open Market Committee. Several advisory councils help the board meet its varied responsibilities.

The hub of the system is the 7-member Board of Governors in Washington, DC. The members of the board are appointed by the president and confirmed by the Senate to 14-year terms. The president also appoints the chairman and vice chairman of the board from among the board members for 4-year, renewable terms. As of Sept. 2012, the board members were Ben S. Bernanke, chair; Janet L. Yellen, vice-chair; Elizabeth A. Duke; Daniel K. Tarullo; Sarah Bloom Raskin; Jeremy C. Stein; and Jerome H. Powell.

The 12 **District Reserve Banks** and their branch offices serve as the decentralized portion of the system, carrying out day-to-day operations such as circulating currency and coin and providing fiscal agency functions and payments mechanism services. The 12 are in Boston, New York, Philadelphia, Cleveland, Richmond, Atlanta, Chicago, St. Louis, Minneapolis, Kansas City, Dallas, and San Francisco.

The system's principal function is monetary policy, which it controls using three tools: reserve requirements, the discount rate, and open market operations.

Uniform **reserve requirements**, set by the board, are applied to the transaction accounts and nonpersonal time deposits of all depository institutions. Responsibility for setting the **discount rate** (the interest rate at which depository institutions can borrow money from the Reserve Banks) is shared by the Board of Governors and the Reserve Banks. Changes in the discount rate are recommended by the individual boards of directors of the Reserve Banks and are subject to approval by the Board of Governors.

The most important tool of monetary policy is **open market operations**, or the purchase and sale of government securities. Responsibility for influencing the cost and availability of money and credit through the purchase and sale of government securities lies with the **Federal Open Market Committee** (FOMC), which is composed of the seven members of the Board of Governors, the president of the Federal Reserve Bank of New York, and four other Federal Reserve Bank presidents, who each serve 1-year terms on a rotating basis. The committee bases its decisions on economic and financial developments and outlook, setting yearly growth objectives for key measures of money supply and credit. The decisions of the committee are carried out by the domestic trading desk of the Federal Reserve Bank of New York.

A Federal Advisory Council meets with the Federal Reserve Board four times a year to discuss business and financial conditions, as well as to make recommendations.

Website: www.federalreserve.gov.

Federal Reserve Board Discount Rates, 1955-2012

The interest rate that the Federal Reserve charges its member banks to borrow money overnight is often referred to as the discount rate. On Jan. 9, 2003, the Fed divided the discount window into two categories: primary credit, for banks in sound financial condition, and secondary credit, for banks that do not qualify for primary credit. The secondary credit rate is ½ a percentage point higher than the primary credit rate. Banks typically raise or lower the rates they extend to their customers to track changes in the discount rate.

Effective date	Rate	Effective date	Rate	Effective date	Rate	Effective date	Rate	Effective date	Rate
1955:		**1970:**		**1979:**		**1990:**		**2003:**	
Jan. 3	1½	Nov. 13	5¾	July 20	10	Dec. 18	6½	Jan. 9	2¼[1]
Apr. 15	1¾	Dec. 4	5½	Aug. 17	10½	**1991:**		June 25	2
Aug. 5	2	**1971:**		Sept. 19	11	Apr. 30	5½	**2004:**	
Sept. 9	2¼	Jan. 8	5¼	Oct. 8	12	Sept. 13	5	June 30	2¼
Nov. 18	2½	Jan. 22	5	**1980:**		Nov. 6	4½	Aug. 10	2½
1956:		Feb. 19	4¾	Feb. 15	13	Dec. 20	3½	Sept. 21	2¾
Apr. 13	2¾	July 16	5	May 30	12	**1992:**		Nov. 10	3
Aug. 24	3	Nov. 19	4¾	June 13	11	July 2	3	Dec. 14	3¼
1957:		Dec. 17	4½	July 28	10	**1994:**		**2005:**	
Aug. 23	3½	**1973:**		Sept. 26	11	May 17	3½	Feb. 2	3½
Nov. 15	3	Jan. 15	5	Nov. 17	12	Aug. 16	4	Mar. 22	3¾
1958:		Feb. 26	5½	Dec. 5	13	Nov. 15	4¾	May 3	4
Jan. 24	2¾	May 4	5¾	**1981:**		**1995:**		June 30	4¼
Mar. 7	2¼	May 11	6	May 5	14	Feb. 1	5	Aug. 9	4½
Apr. 18	1¾	June 11	6½	Nov. 2	13	**1996:**		Sept. 20	4¾
Sept. 12	2	July 2	7	Dec. 4	12	Jan. 31	5	Nov. 1	5
Nov. 7	2½	Aug. 14	7½	**1982:**		**1998:**		Dec. 13	5¼
1959:		**1974:**		July 20	11½	Oct. 15	4¾	**2006:**	
Mar. 6	3	Apr. 25	8	Aug. 2	11	Nov. 17	4½	Jan. 31	5½
May 29	3½	Dec. 9	7¾	Aug. 16	10	**1999:**		Mar. 28	5¾
Sept. 11	4	**1975:**		Aug. 27	10	Aug. 24	4¾	May 10	6
1960:		Jan. 10	7¼	Oct. 12	9½	Nov. 16	5	June 29	6¼
June 10	3½	Feb. 5	6¾	Dec. 15	8½	**2000:**		**2007:**	
Aug. 12	3	Mar. 19	6¼	**1984:**		Feb. 2	5¼	Aug. 17	5¾
1963:		May 16	6	Apr. 9	9	Mar. 21	5½	Sept.18	5¼
July 17	3½	**1976:**		Nov. 21	8½	May 16	6	Nov. 1	5
1964:		Jan. 19	5½	Dec. 24	8	**2001:**		Dec. 12	4¾
Nov. 24	4	Nov. 22	5¼	**1985:**		Jan. 3	5¾	**2008:**	
1965:		**1977:**		May 20	7½	Jan. 31	5	Jan. 22	4
Dec. 6	4½	Aug. 31	5¾	**1986:**		Mar. 20	4½	Jan. 30	3½
1967:		Oct. 26	6	Mar. 7	7	Apr. 18	4	Mar. 17	3¼
Apr. 7	4	**1978:**		Apr. 21	6½	May 15	3½	Mar. 18	2½
Nov. 20	4½	Jan. 9	6½	July 11	6	June 27	3¼	Apr. 30	2¼
1968:		May 11	7	Aug. 21	5½	Aug. 21	3	Oct. 8	1¾
Mar. 22	5	July 3	7¼	**1987:**		Sept. 17	2½	Oct. 29	1¼
Apr. 19	5½	Aug. 21	7¾	Sept. 4	6	Oct. 2	2	Dec. 16	½
Aug. 30	5¼	Sept. 22	8	**1988:**		Dec. 11	1¼	**2010:**	
Dec. 18	5½	Oct. 16	8½	Aug. 9	6½	**2002:**		Feb. 19	¾
1969:		Nov. 1	9½	**1989:**		Nov. 6	¾		
Apr. 4	6			Feb. 24	7				

Note: As of Oct. 10, 2012, rate effective Feb. 19, 2010, was unchanged. (1) Adjustment credit rate replaced with primary credit rate. See note above.

Standard & Poor's 500 Index, 1997-2012

Monthly closing levels; record high daily closing was 1,565.15 on Oct. 9, 2007.

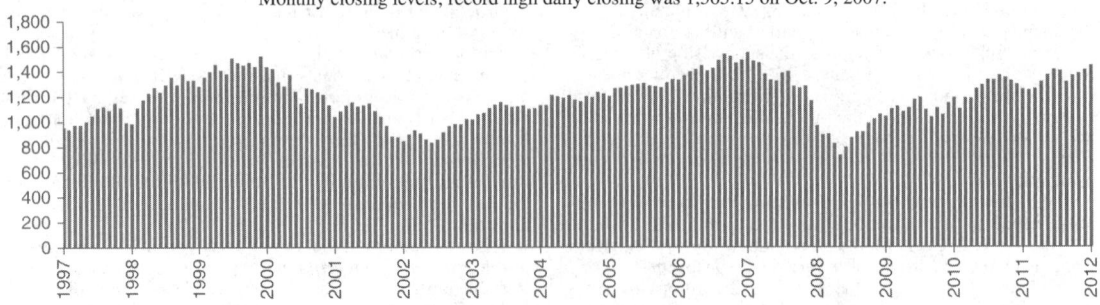

U.S. Holdings of Foreign Securities, 2006-11

Source: *U.S. Portfolio Holdings of Foreign Securities*, U.S. Dept. of the Treasury
(in billions of dollars)

	2006	2008	2009	2010	2011[P]		2006	2008	2009	2010	2011[P]
Europe	$3,129	$2,172	$3,001	$3,154	$2,978	Latin America and					
United	1,076	647	958	1,001	989	Caribbean	$946	$733	$965	$1,064	$1,393
Kingdom						Cayman Islands . . .	376	315	373	366	709
France	402	285	362	366	306	Brazil	110	91	213	235	196
Switzerland.	264	218	305	327	292	Bermuda.	208	163	148	160	161
Germany.	292	255	294	299	266	Mexico	108	65	88	109	108
Netherlands	234	169	233	233	242	Netherlands Antilles	58	38	57	83	70
Ireland	121	63	120	132	149	Asia	1,166	775	1,053	1,343	1,232
Sweden.	102	59	76	122	115	Japan	596	403	419	519	509
Luxembourg	60	60	94	100	93	South Korea	124	56	105	148	146
Spain	111	93	113	87	76	Hong Kong	88	65	93	135	116
Canada.	478	378	540	695	736	China, mainland . . .	75	55	102	102	77
Africa	57	43	67	99	88	Taiwan	74	41	77	95	72
South Africa	43	32	54	78	71	India	49	32	65	91	59
Australia	173	146	276	323	334	Total holdings.	$5,991	$4,291	$5,977	$6,763	$6,841

P = Preliminary.

Record One-Day Gains and Losses of the Dow Jones Industrial Average

Source: Dow Jones & Co., Inc.
(Ranked by largest one-day losses and gains for two terms; as of Oct. 3, 2012.)

		Greatest % losses					Greatest point losses		
Rank	Date	Close	Net chg.	% chg.	Rank	Date	Close	Net chg.	% chg.
1.	10/19/1987	1,738.74	−508.00	−22.61%	1.	9/29/2008	10,365.45	−777.68	−6.98%
2.	10/28/1929	260.64	−38.33	−12.82	2.	10/15/2008	8,577.91	−733.08	−7.87
3.	10/29/1929	230.07	−30.57	−11.73	3.	9/17/2001	8,920.70	−684.81	−7.13
4.	11/6/1929	232.13	−25.55	−9.92	4.	12/1/2008	8,149.09	−679.95	−7.70
5.	12/18/1899	58.27	−5.57	−8.72	5.	10/9/2008	8,579.19	−678.92	−7.33
		Greatest % gains					**Greatest point gains**		
Rank	Date	Close	Net chg.	% chg.	Rank	Date	Close	Net chg.	% chg.
1.	3/15/1933	62.10	8.26	15.34%	1.	10/13/2008	9,387.61	936.42	11.08%
2.	10/6/1931	99.34	12.86	14.87	2.	10/28/2008	9,065.12	889.35	10.88
3.	10/30/1929	258.47	28.40	12.34	3.	11/13/2008	8,835.25	552.60	6.67
4.	9/21/1932	75.16	7.67	11.36	4.	3/16/2000	10,630.61	499.19	4.93
5.	10/13/2008	9,387.61	936.42	11.08	5.	3/23/2009	7,775.86	497.48	6.84

Dow Jones Industrial Average, 1965-2012

Source: Dow Jones & Co., Inc.
(as of Oct. 10, 2012)

Year	Highest close		Lowest close		Year	Highest close		Lowest close	
1965	Dec. 31	969.26	June 28	840.59	1999	Dec. 31	11,497.12	Jan. 22	9,120.67
1970	Dec. 29	842.00	May 6	631.16	2000	Jan. 14	11,722.98	Mar. 7	9,796.03
1975	July 15	881.81	Jan. 2	632.04	2001	May 21	11,337.92	Sept. 21	8,235.81
1980	Nov. 20	1,000.17	Apr. 21	759.13	2002	Mar. 19	10,635.25	Oct. 9	7,286.27
1985	Dec. 16	1,553.10	Jan. 4	1,184.96	2003	Dec. 31	10,453.90	Mar. 11	7,524.06
1990	July 16	2,999.75	Oct. 11	2,365.10	2004	Dec. 28	10,854.54	Oct. 25	9,749.99
1991	Dec. 31	3,168.83	Jan. 9	2,470.30	2005	Mar. 4	10,940.50	Apr. 20	10,012.36
1992	June 1	3,413.21	Oct. 9	3,136.58	2006	Dec. 27	12,510.57	Jan. 20	10,667.39
1993	Dec. 29	3,794.33	Jan. 20	3,241.95	2007	Oct. 9	14,164.53*	Mar. 5	12,050.41
1994	Jan. 31	3,978.36	Apr. 4	3,593.35	2008	Jan. 3	13,056.72	Nov. 20	7,552.29
1995	Dec. 13	5,216.47	Jan. 30	3,832.08	2009	Dec. 30	10,548.51	Mar. 9	6,547.05
1996	Dec. 27	6,560.91	Jan. 10	5,032.94	2010	Dec. 29	11,585.38	July 2	9,686.48
1997	Aug. 6	8,259.31	Apr. 11	6,391.69	2011	Apr. 29	12,810.54	Oct. 3	10,655.30
1998	Nov. 23	9,374.27	Aug. 31	7,539.07	2012	Oct. 5	13,610.15	June 4	12,101.46

*Record high closing.

Milestones of the Dow Jones Industrial Average
(as of Oct. 3, 2012)

First close over—		First close over—		First close over—		First close over—		First close over—	
100	Jan. 12, 1906	3000	Apr. 17, 1991	6000	Oct. 14, 1996	9000	Apr. 6, 1998	12000	Oct. 19, 2006
500	Mar. 12, 1956	3500	May 19, 1993	6500	Nov. 25, 1996	9500	Jan. 6, 1999	12500	Dec. 27, 2006
1000	Nov. 14, 1972	4000	Feb. 23, 1995	7000	Feb. 13, 1997	10000	Mar. 29, 1999	13000	Apr. 25, 2007
1500	Dec. 11, 1985	4500	June 16, 1995	7500	June 10, 1997	10500	Apr. 21, 1999	13500	May 18, 2007
2000	Jan. 8, 1987	5000	Nov. 21, 1995	8000	July 16, 1997	11000	May 3, 1999	14000	July 19, 2007
2500	July 17, 1987	5500	Feb. 8, 1996	8500	Feb. 27, 1998	11500	Jan. 7, 2000		

Components of the Dow Jones Averages
(as of Oct. 3, 2012)

Dow Jones Industrial Average

Company name (ticker symbol)
Alcoa (AA)
American Express Co. (AXP)
AT&T Inc. (T)
Bank of America Corp. (BAC)
Boeing Co. (BA)
Caterpillar Inc. (CAT)
Chevron Corp. (CVX)
Cisco Systems, Inc. (CSCO)
Coca-Cola Co. (KO)
E. I. DuPont de Nemours & Co. (DD)
Exxon Mobil Corp. (XOM)

Company name (ticker symbol)
General Electric Co. (GE)
Hewlett-Packard Co. (HPQ)
Home Depot Inc. (HD)
Intel Corp. (INTC)
International Business Machines Corp. (IBM)
Johnson & Johnson (JNJ)
JPMorgan Chase & Co. (JPM)
McDonald's Corp. (MCD)
Merck & Co., Inc. (MRK)

Company name (ticker symbol)
Microsoft Corp. (MSFT)
Pfizer Inc. (PFE)
Procter & Gamble Co. (PG)
Travelers Companies, Inc. (TRV)
3M Co. (MMM)
United Technologies Corp. (UTX)
UnitedHealth Group Inc. (UNH)
Verizon Communications Inc. (VZ)
Wal-Mart Stores Inc. (WMT)
Walt Disney Co. (DIS)

Dow Jones Utility Average

Company name (ticker symbol)
AES Corp. (AES)
American Electric Power Co. Inc. (AEP)
CenterPoint Energy (CNP)
Consolidated Edison Inc. (ED)
Dominion Resources Inc. (Virginia) (D)

Company name (ticker symbol)
Duke Energy Corp. (DUK)
Edison International (EIX)
Exelon Corp. (EXC)
FirstEnergy Corp. (FE)
NextEra Energy, Inc. (NEE)
NiSource Inc. (NI)

Company name (ticker symbol)
PG&E Corp. (PCG)
Public Service Enterprise Group Inc. (PEG)
Southern Co. (SO)
Williams Cos. (WMB)

Dow Jones Transportation Average

Company name (ticker symbol)
Alaska Air Group, Inc. (ALK)
C.H. Robinson Worldwide Inc. (CHRW)
Con-way Inc. (CNW)
CSX Corp. (CSX)
Delta Air Lines, Inc. (DAL)
Expeditors Intl. of Washington Inc. (EXPD)

Company name (ticker symbol)
FedEx Corp. (FDX)
GATX Corp. (GMT)
J.B. Hunt Transport Services Inc. (JBHT)
JetBlue Airways Corp. (JBLU)
Kansas City Southern (KSU)
Landstar System Inc. (LSTR)
Matson Inc. (MATX)

Company name (ticker symbol)
Norfolk Southern Corp. (NSC)
Overseas Shipholding Group Inc. (OSG)
Ryder System Inc. (R)
Southwest Airlines Co. (LUV)
Union Pacific Corp. (UNP)
United Continental Holdings (UAL)
United Parcel Service Inc. ClB (UPS)

Record One-Day Gains and Losses on the Nasdaq Stock Market
Source: Nasdaq Stock Market
(Ranked by largest one-day losses and gains for two terms; as of Oct. 4, 2012.)

	Greatest point gains			Greatest % gains			Greatest point losses			Greatest % losses	
Rank	Date	Change	Rank	Date	% change	Rank	Date	Change	Rank	Date	% change
1.	1/3/2001	324.83	1.	1/3/2001	14.17%	1.	4/14/2000	−355.49	1.	10/19/1987	−11.35%
2.	12/5/2000	274.05	2.	10/13/2008	11.81	2.	4/3/2000	−349.15	2.	4/14/2000	−9.67
3.	4/18/2000	254.41	3.	12/5/2000	10.48	3.	4/12/2000	−286.27	3.	9/29/2008	−9.14
4.	5/30/2000	254.37	4.	10/28/2008	9.53	4.	4/10/2000	−258.25	4.	10/20/1987	−9.00
5.	10/19/2000	247.04	5.	4/5/2001	8.92	5.	1/4/2000	−229.46	5.	10/26/1987	−9.00
6.	10/13/2000	242.09	6.	4/18/2001	8.12	6.	3/14/2000	−200.61	6.	12/1/2008	−8.95
7.	6/2/2000	230.88	7.	5/30/2000	7.94	7.	5/10/2000	−200.28	7.	8/31/1998	−8.56
8.	4/25/2000	228.75	8.	10/13/2008	7.87	8.	5/23/2000	−199.66	8.	10/15/2008	−8.47
9.	4/17/2000	217.87	9.	10/19/2000	7.79	9.	9/29/2008	−199.61	9.	4/3/2000	−7.64
10.	10/13/2008	194.74	10.	5/8/2002	7.78	10.	10/25/2000	−190.22	10.	1/2/2001	−7.23

Nasdaq Stock Market Closing Prices, 1971-2012
Source: Nasdaq Stock Market

Year	High	Low	Year	High	Low	Year	High	Low	Year	High	Low
1971	114.12	99.68	1982	241.63	158.92	1993	790.56	645.02	2003	2,009.88	1,271.47
1972	135.15	113.65	1983	329.11	229.88	1994	803.93	691.23	2004	2,178.00	1,752.00
1973	136.84	88.67	1984	288.41	223.91	1995	1,072.82	740.53	2005	2,273.37	1,904.18
1974	96.53	54.87	1985	325.53	245.82	1996	1,328.45	978.17	2006	2,465.98	2,020.39
1975	88.00	60.70	1986	411.21	322.14	1997	1,748.62	1,194.39	2007	2,811.61	2,340.68
1976	97.88	78.06	1987	456.27	288.49	1998	2,200.63	1,357.09	2008	2,609.63	1,505.90
1977	105.05	93.66	1988	397.54	329.00	1999	4,090.61	2,193.13	2009	2,167.70	1,265.52
1978	139.25	99.09	1989	487.60	376.87	2000	5,048.62*	2,332.78	2010	2,671.48	2,091.79
1979	152.29	117.84	1990	470.30	322.93	2001	2,892.36	1,387.06	2011	2,873.54	2,335.83
1980	208.29	124.09	1991	586.35	352.85	2002	2,059.38	1,114.11	2012	3,183.95	2,648.36
1981	223.96	170.80	1992	676.95	545.85						

*Record high closing, Mar. 10, 2000; as of Oct. 4, 2012.

Average Yields of Long-Term Treasury, Corporate, and Municipal Bonds, 1986-2012

Source: Office of Market Finance, U.S. Dept. of the Treasury; Federal Reserve System

Period	Treasury 30-year bonds[1]	New Aa corporate bonds[2]	New Aa municipal bonds[3]	Period	Treasury 30-year bonds[1]	New Aa corporate bonds[2]	New Aa municipal bonds[3]	Period	Treasury 30-year bonds[1]	New Aa corporate bonds[2]	New Aa municipal bonds[3]
1986				**1995**				**2004**			
June	7.57%	9.39%	7.87%	June	6.57%	7.42%	5.84%	June	5.45%	6.01%	5.05%
Dec.	7.37	8.87	6.87	Dec.	6.06	7.02	5.45	Dec.	4.88	5.47	4.49
1987				**1996**				**2005**			
June	8.57	9.64	7.79	June	7.06	8.00	6.02	June	4.35	4.96	4.23
Dec.	9.12	10.22	7.96	Dec.	6.55	7.45	5.64	Dec.	4.73	5.37	4.46
1988				**1997**				**2006**			
June	9.00	10.08	7.78	June	6.77	7.71	5.53	June	5.15	5.89	4.60
Dec.	9.01	10.05	7.61	Dec.	5.99	6.68	5.19	Dec.	4.68	5.32	4.11
1989				**1998**				**2007**			
June	8.27	9.24	7.02	June	5.70	6.43	5.12	June	5.20	5.79	4.60
Dec.	7.90	9.23	6.98	Dec.	5.06	6.13	4.98	Dec.	4.53	5.49	4.42
1990				**1999**				**2008**			
June	8.46	9.69	7.24	June	6.04	7.21	5.37	June	4.69	5.68	4.69
Dec.	8.24	9.55	7.09	Dec.	6.35	7.55	5.95	Dec.	2.87	5.05	5.56
1991				**2000**				**2009**			
June	8.47	9.37	7.13	June	5.93	7.75	5.80	June	4.52	5.61	4.81
Dec.	7.70	8.55	6.69	Dec.	5.49	7.21	5.22	Dec.	4.49	5.26	4.21
1992				**2001**				**2010**			
June	7.84	8.45	6.49	June	5.67	7.11	5.20	June	4.13	4.88	4.36
Dec.	7.44	8.12	6.22	Dec.	5.48	6.80	5.25	Dec.	4.42	5.02	4.92
1993				**2002**				**2011**			
June	6.81	7.48	5.63	June	5.65	6.57	5.09	June	4.23	4.99	4.51
Dec.	6.25	7.22	5.35	Dec.	5.01	5.93	4.85	Dec.	2.98	3.93	3.95
1994				**2003**				**2012**			
June	7.40	8.16	6.11	June	4.34	4.97	4.33	June	2.70	3.64	3.94
Dec.	7.87	8.66	6.80	Dec.	5.11	5.62	4.65				

(1) On Feb. 18, 2002, the U.S. treasury discontinued the 30-year constant maturity yield and reintroduced it on Feb. 9, 2006; rates in the interim are for 20-year yields. (2) Treasury series based on 3-week moving average of reoffering yields of new corporate bonds rated Aa by Moody's Investors Service with an original maturity of at least 20 years. Treasury discontinued yield index after Jan. 31, 2003. Rates thereafter are for Moody's seasoned Aaa corporate bonds as listed by Federal Reserve. (3) Index of new reoffering yields on 20-year general obligations rated Aa by Moody's Investors Service; discontinued by Treasury Jan. 31, 2003; rates thereafter are from Bond Buyer Index of general obligation, 20-year-to-maturity, mixed quality state and local bonds.

Ownership of U.S. Treasury Securities, 2001-11

Source: *Treasury Bulletin, June 2012*, Financial Management Service, U.S. Dept. of the Treasury
(in billions of dollars)

In 2001, 17.5% of U.S. treasury securities were held by foreign and international investors. By 2011, the total public debt had nearly tripled, while the portion held by investors outside the U.S. had nearly doubled, to 32.8%.

	2001	2003	2004	2005	2006	2007	2008	2009	2010	2011
Total public debt........	$5,943.4	$6,998.0	$7,596.1	$8,170.4	$8,680.2	$9,229.2	$10,699.8	$12,311.3	$14,025.2	$15,222.8
Federal Reserve and intra-governmental holdings ...	3,123.9	3,620.1	3,905.6	4,199.8	4,558.1	4,833.5	4,806.4	5,276.9	5,656.2	6,439.6
Total privately held	2,819.5	3,377.9	3,690.5	3,970.6	4,122.1	4,395.7	5,893.4	7,034.4	8,368.9	8,783.3
Depository institutions	181.5	153.1	125.0	117.1	114.8	129.8	105.0	202.4	319.1	279.7
U.S. savings bonds........	190.3	203.9	204.5	205.2	202.4	196.5	194.1	191.3	187.9	185.2
Private pension funds[1].....	145.8	172.2	173.7	184.9	207.5	257.6	297.2	429.8	520.2	583.4
Pension funds of state and local governments.......	155.1	148.6	151.0	153.8	156.2	141.6	146.4	174.5	185.6	188.9
Insurance companies	105.7	136.5	188.5	202.3	197.9	141.9	171.4	222.0	248.4	256.2
Mutual funds............	261.9	280.9	254.1	251.3	250.7	362.9	768.8	666.2	637.9	800.8
State and local governments	328.4	364.2	389.1	475.0	506.8	525.1	475.1	493.9	503.6	444.6
Foreign and international ...	1,040.1	1,523.1	1,849.3	2,033.9	2,103.1	2,353.2	3,077.2	3,685.1	4,435.6	4,996.6
Other investors[2]	410.7	395.4	355.4	347.0	382.7	287.2	658.3	969.2	1,330.7	1,047.8

(1) Includes securities held by the Federal Employees Retirement System Thrift Savings Plan G Fund. (2) Includes individuals, government-sponsored enterprises, brokers and dealers, bank personal trusts and estates, corporate and noncorporate businesses, and other investors.

2012 Federal Corporate Tax Rates

Personal service corporations (used by incorporated professionals such as attorneys and doctors) pay a flat rate of 35%.

Taxable income amount	Tax rate	Taxable income amount	Tax rate
Not more than $50,000........................	15%	$335,001 to $10,000,000......................	34%
$50,001 to $75,000..........................	25	$10,000,001 to $15,000,000..................	35
$75,001 to $100,000.........................	34	$15,000,001 to $18,333,333..................	38
$100,001 to $335,000........................	39	More than $18,333,333	35

Characteristics of Mutual Fund Investors, 2011

Source: *2012 Investment Company Fact Book*; Investment Company Institute

Median age	50	Employed........................	71%
Median annual household income..............	$80,000	Married or living with a partner	74
Median household financial assets..............	$200,000	Four-year college degree or more...............	47
Median mutual fund assets	$120,000	Investing to save for retirement	94
Median number of funds owned	4	Own Individual Retirement Accounts (IRAs)........	65

Performance of Mutual Funds by Type, 2012

Source: *Kiplinger* magazine
(as of Sept. 30, 2012)

Fund type/fund objective	Average annual return 1-year	3-year	5-year	Fund type/fund objective	Average annual return 1-year	3-year	5-year
Large-Company				**Sector**			
Growth	26.85%	11.93%	1.13%	Financial	31.16%	3.42%	−6.35%
Blend	27.07	10.93	0.02	Precious Metals	−1.77	7.92	4.96
Value	27.19	10.50	−0.78	Health	34.50	15.09	6.63
Midsize-Company				Natural Resources	16.37	4.32	−3.28
Growth	24.29	12.71	1.44	Realty	31.94	19.69	1.83
Blend	26.07	11.32	0.92	Technology	22.88	11.39	1.22
Value	27.17	11.48	1.18	Utilities	16.65	11.32	1.26
Small-Company				Hybrid	17.23	8.37	1.61
Growth	28.60	13.45	1.78	**International**			
Blend	29.95	12.51	1.53	Diversified	15.66	2.80	−5.00
Value	29.22	11.44	2.20	Small/Midsize Diversified	18.11	7.85	−2.59
Taxable Government Bond				Specialized	17.55	3.57	−4.49
Short-Term	1.43	2.19	3.27	**Corporate Bond**			
Intermediate-Term	3.79	5.18	5.72	High Yield	17.58	11.39	7.14
Long-Term	7.85	9.05	7.58	Short-Term	3.49	3.16	3.08
Tax-Free Government Bond				Intermediate-Term	7.72	7.17	6.35
Long-Term Municipal	10.27	6.13	5.21	Long-Term	13.80	11.44	8.15
Intermediate Municipal	7.32	5.21	5.09				
Short-Term Municipal	2.33	2.30	2.90				
High-Yield Municipal	13.60	7.98	3.95				

Mutual Fund Ownership, 1940-2011

Source: *2012 Investment Company Fact Book*; Investment Company Institute

Year	Mutual funds	Mutual fund accounts (thous.)	Households owning mutual funds (thous.)	Total net assets (bil.)	Exchange-traded funds (ETFs) Number of funds	Total net assets (bil.)
1940	68	296	NA	$0.45	NA	NA
1950	98	939	NA	2.53	NA	NA
1960	161	4,898	NA	17.03	NA	NA
1970	361	10,690	NA	47.62	NA	NA
1980	564	12,088	4,600	134.76	NA	NA
1990	3,079	61,948	NA	1,065.19	NA	NA
2000	8,155	244,705	51,700	6,964.63	80	$65.59
2005	7,974	275,479	53,700	8,891.11	204	300.82
2006	8,118	288,596	54,900	10,397.94	359	422.55
2007	8,026	292,555	51,000	12,001.46	629	608.42
2008	8,022	264,529	52,500	9,603.65	728	531.29
2009	7,684	269,224	50,400	11,120.15	797	777.13
2010	7,580	290,885	51,600	11,820.65	923	991.99
2011	7,637	299,715	52,300	11,621.60	1,134	1,048.13

NA = Not available. **Note:** Does not include data for funds that invest primarily in other mutual funds. Mutual fund accounts data include both individual and omnibus accounts.

Chicago Futures and Options, 2010-11

Source: Chicago Mercantile Exchange Group, Inc.

Futures group	2010	2011	% change, 2010-11	Futures group	2010	2011	% change, 2010-11
Futures	2,638,080,808	2,900,914,065	10.0	Interest rate	268,726,554	274,011,450	2.0
Commodities & alternative				Metals	9,411,086	12,351,645	31.2
investments	188,628,792	218,156,249	15.6	Energy	71,185,792	74,176,489	4.2
Equity index	697,580,318	755,636,901	8.3	**Combined futures and**			
FX	221,551,655	222,467,404	0.4	**options**	3,080,497,016	3,386,986,678	9.9
Interest rate	1,109,855,510	1,245,645,034	12.2	Commodities & alternative			
Metals	70,449,506	85,240,389	21.0	investments	230,402,225	273,197,405	18.6
Energy	350,015,027	373,768,088	6.8	Equity index	737,877,536	816,262,095	10.6
Options	442,416,208	486,072,613	9.9	FX	232,573,780	232,334,083	−0.1
Commodities & alternative				Interest rate	1,378,582,064	1,519,656,484	10.2
investments	41,773,433	55,041,156	31.8	Metals	79,860,592	97,592,034	22.2
Equity index	40,297,218	60,625,194	50.4	Energy	421,200,819	447,944,577	6.4
FX	11,022,125	9,866,679	−10.5				

Gold Owned by the U.S, 2012

Source: *Status Report of U.S. Treasury-Owned Gold*, Financial Management Service, U.S. Dept. of the Treasury
(as of Sept. 30, 2012)

	Fine troy ounces	Book value		Fine troy ounces	Book value
Total Treasury-owned gold	261,498,926	$11,041,059,958	**Held by the Federal Reserve**		
Gold bullion	258,641,878	10,920,429,099	**Bank**	13,452,811	$568,007,258
Gold coins, blanks,			Gold bullion	13,378,981	564,890,013
miscellaneous	2,857,048	120,630,859	Federal Reserve Banks–NY		
Held by the U.S. Mint	248,046,116	10,473,052,701	vault	13,376,988	564,805,851
Denver, CO, deep storage	43,853,707	1,851,599,996	Federal Reserve Banks–display	1,993	84,162
Fort Knox, KY, deep storage	147,341,858	6,221,097,413	Gold coins	73,830	3,117,245
West Point, NY, deep storage	54,067,331	2,282,841,677	Federal Reserve Banks–NY		
Gold coins, blanks,			vault	73,809	3,116,392
miscellaneous	2,783,219	117,513,615	Federal Reserve Banks–display	20	853

World's Leading Gold Producers, 1980-2011

Source: *Minerals Yearbook*, U.S. Geological Survey, U.S. Dept. of the Interior
(in thousands of troy ounces; ranked by 2011 production)

Country	1980	1990	2000	2005	2006	2007	2008	2009	2010[1]	2011[1]
China[1]	225	3,215	5,787	7,234	7,877	8,841	9,163	10,288	11,092	11,413
Australia	548	7,845	9,530	8,423	7,941	7,941	6,912	7,202	8,391	8,681
United States	970	9,452	11,349	8,231	8,102	7,652	7,491	7,170	7,427	7,620
Russia[2]	8,300	9,710	4,598	5,279	5,123	5,047	5,531	6,200	6,174	6,430
South Africa	21,669	19,451	13,767	9,474	8,749	8,121	6,840	6,354	6,067	6,109
Peru[3]	134	293	4,263	6,682	6,521	5,473	5,783	5,864	5,275	4,823
Canada	1,627	5,433	5,022	3,844	3,328	3,286	3,054	3,130	2,926	3,537
Indonesia[4]	60	360	4,006	4,200	2,996	3,789	2,070	4,180	3,858	3,215
Ghana	353	540	2,318	2,149	2,245	2,322	2,346	2,568	2,636	3,215
Uzbekistan[1]	NA	NA	2,733	2,894	2,733	2,733	2,733	2,894	2,894	2,894
Mexico	196	311	848	976	1,253	1,265	1,619	1,652	2,334	2,733
World total	**39,197**	**70,089**	**82,949**	**79,412**	**76,197**	**75,554**	**73,304**	**79,091**	**82,306**	**86,807**

NA = Not applicable. **Note:** 1 kilogram is equal to 32.1507 troy ounces. (1) Estimated. (2) 1980-90 figures for USSR as constituted prior to Dec. 1991; after 1990, Russia only. Includes gold recovered as a byproduct, but excludes secondary production. (3) Includes documented production from placer artisanal production. (4) Excludes production from "people's mines," which may add more than 600,000 troy oz. to the total.

Prices of Precious Metals, 1990-2011

Source: *Minerals Yearbook* and *Mineral Industry Surveys*, U.S. Geological Survey, U.S. Dept. of the Interior

Year	Dollars per troy ounce			Dollars per pound			
	Platinum[1]	Gold	Silver	Copper[2]	Lead	Tin[3]	Zinc[4]
1990	$467	$385	$4.82	$1.23	$0.46	$3.86	$0.75
1995	425	386	5.15	1.38	0.42	4.16	0.56
1996	398	389	5.19	1.09	0.49	4.12	0.51
1997	397	332	4.89	1.07	0.47	3.81	0.65
1998	375	295	5.54	0.79	0.45	3.73	0.51
1999	379	280	5.25	0.76	0.44	3.66	0.53
2000	549	280	5.00	0.88	0.44	3.70	0.56
2001	533	272	4.39	0.77	0.44	3.15	0.44
2002	543	311	4.62	0.76	0.44	2.92	0.39
2003	694	365	4.91	0.85	0.44	3.40	0.41
2004	849	411	6.69	1.34	0.55	5.47	0.52
2005	900	446	7.34	1.74	0.61	4.83	0.67
2006	1,144	606	11.57	3.15	0.77	5.65	1.59
2007	1,308	699	13.41	3.28	1.24	8.99	1.54
2008	1,578	874	15.00	3.19	1.20	11.29	0.89
2009	1,208	975	14.69	2.41	0.87	8.37	0.78
2010	1,616	1,228	20.20	3.48	1.09	12.40	1.02
2011	1,725	1,571	35.12	4.06	1.22	12.15	1.06

(1) Average annual dealer prices. (2) U.S. producer price for cathode copper. (3) Platt's Metals Week price. (4) Platt's Metals Week price for North American special high grade zinc except for 1990, which shows average prices for high grade zinc.

Economic and Financial Glossary

Reviewed by William M. Gentry, Graduate School of Business, Columbia University

Annuity contract: An investment vehicle sold by insurance companies. Annuity buyers can elect to receive periodic payments for the rest of their lives. Annuities provide insurance against outliving one's wealth.

Arbitrage: A form of hedged investment meant to capture slight differences in the prices of two related securities—for example, buying gold in London and selling it at a higher price in New York.

Balance of payments: The difference between all payments, for some categories of transactions, made to and from foreign countries over a set period of time. A favorable balance of payments exists when more payments are coming in than going out; an unfavorable balance of payments obtains when the reverse is true. Payments may include gold, the cost of merchandise and services, interest and dividend payments, money spent by travelers, and repayment of principal on loans.

Balance of trade (trade gap): The difference between exports and imports, in both actual funds and credit. A nation's balance of trade is favorable when exports exceed imports and unfavorable when the reverse is true.

Balanced budget: A budget is balanced when receipts equal expenditures. When receipts exceed expenditures, there is a **surplus**; when they fall short of expenditures, there is a **deficit**.

Bear market: A market in which prices are falling.

Bearer bond: A bond issued in bearer form rather than being registered in a specific owner's name. Ownership is determined by possession.

Bond: A written promise, or IOU, by the issuer to repay a fixed amount of borrowed money on a specified date and generally to pay interest at regular intervals in the interim.

Bull market: A market in which prices are on the rise.

Capital gain (loss): An increase (decrease) in the market value of an asset over some period of time. For tax purposes, capital gains are typically calculated from when an asset is bought to when it is sold.

Commercial paper: An extremely short-term corporate IOU, generally due in 270 days or less.

Consumer price index (CPI): A statistical measure of the change in the price of consumer goods.

Convertible bond: A corporate bond (see below) that may be converted into a stated number of shares of common stock. Its price tends to fluctuate along with fluctuations in the price of the stock and with changes in interest rates.

Corporate bond: A bond issued by a corporation. The bond normally has a stated life and pays a fixed rate of interest. Considered safer than the common or preferred stock of the same company.

Cost of living: The cost of maintaining a standard of living measured in terms of purchased goods and services. Inflation typically measures changes in the cost of living.

Cost-of-living adjustments: Changes in promised payments, such as retirement benefits, to account for changes in the cost of living.

Credit crunch (liquidity crisis): A situation in which cash for lending is in short supply.

Debenture: An unsecured bond backed only by the general credit of the issuing corporation.

Deficit spending: Government spending in excess of revenues, generally financed with the sale of bonds. A deficit increases the government debt.

Deflation: A decrease in the level of prices.

Depression: A long period of economic decline marked by low prices, high unemployment, and many business failures.

Derivatives: Financial contracts, such as options, whose values are based on, or derived from, the price of an underlying financial asset or indicator such as a stock or an interest rate.

Devaluation: The official lowering of a nation's currency, decreasing its value in relation to foreign currencies.

Discount rate: The rate of interest set by the Federal Reserve that member banks are charged when borrowing money through the Federal Reserve System.

Disposable income: Income after taxes that is available to persons for spending and saving.

Diversification: Investing in more than one asset in order to reduce the riskiness of the overall asset portfolio. By holding more than one asset, losses on some assets may be offset by gains realized on other assets.

Dividend: Discretionary payment by a corporation to its shareholders, usually in the form of cash or stock shares.

Dow Jones Industrial Average: An index of stock market prices, based on the prices of 30 companies, 27 of which are on the New York Stock Exchange.

Econometrics: The use of statistical methods to study economic and financial data.

Federal Deposit Insurance Corp. (FDIC): A U.S. government-sponsored corporation that insures accounts in national banks and other qualified institutions against bank failures.

Federal Reserve System: The entire banking system of the U.S., incorporating 12 Federal Reserve banks (one in each of 12 Federal Reserve districts), 25 Federal Reserve branch banks, all national banks, and state-chartered commercial banks and trust companies that have been admitted to its membership. The governors of the system greatly influence the nation's monetary and credit policies.

Full employment: The economy is said to be at full employment when everyone who wishes to work at the going wage-rate for his or her type of labor is employed, save only for the small amount of unemployment due to the time it takes to switch from one job to another.

Futures: A futures contract is an agreement to buy or sell a specific amount of a commodity or financial instrument at a particular price at a set date in the future. For example, futures based on a stock index (such as the Dow Jones Industrial Average) are bets on the future price of that group of stocks.

Golden parachute: Provisions in contracts of some high-level executives guaranteeing substantial severance benefits if they lose their position in a corporate takeover.

Government bond: A bond issued by the U.S. Treasury, considered a safe investment. These are divided into 2 categories—marketable and not marketable. Savings bonds cannot be bought and sold once the original purchase is made. Marketable bonds fall into several categories. Treasury bills are short-term U.S. obligations, maturing in 3, 6, or 12 months. Treasury notes mature in up to 10 years. Treasury bonds mature in 10 to 30 years. Indexed bonds are adjusted for inflation.

Greenmail: A company buying back its own shares for more than the going market price to avoid a threatened hostile takeover.

Gross domestic product (GDP): The market value of all goods and services that have been bought for final use during a period of time. It became the official measure of the size of the U.S. economy in 1991, replacing gross national product (GNP), in use since 1941. GDP covers workers and capital employed within the nation's borders. GNP covers production by U.S. residents regardless of where it takes place. The switch aligned U.S. terminology with that of most other industrialized countries.

Hedge fund: A flexible investment fund for a limited number of large investors (the minimum investment is typically $1 mil). Hedge funds use a variety of investment techniques, including those forbidden to mutual funds, such as short-selling and heavy leveraging.

Hedging: Taking two positions whose gains and losses will offset each other if prices change, in order to limit risk.

Individual retirement account (IRA): A self-funded tax-advantaged retirement plan that allows employed individuals to contribute up to a maximum yearly sum. With a traditional IRA, individuals contribute pre-tax earnings and defer income taxes until retirement. With a Roth IRA, individuals contribute after-tax earnings but do not pay taxes on future withdrawals (the interest is never taxed). 401(k) plans are employer-sponsored plans similar to traditional IRAs but having higher contribution limits.

Inflation: An increase in the level of prices.

Insider information: Important facts about the condition or plans of a corporation that have not been released to the general public.

Interest: The cost of borrowing money.

Investment bank: A financial institution that arranges the initial issuance of stocks and bonds and offers companies advice about acquisitions and divestitures.

Junk bonds: Bonds issued by companies with low credit ratings. They typically pay relatively high interest rates because of the fear of default.

Leading indicators: A series of 11 indicators from different segments of the economy used by the U.S. Commerce Department to predict when changes in the level of economic activity will occur.

Leverage: The extent to which a purchase was paid for with borrowed money. Amplifies the potential gain or loss for the purchaser.

Leveraged buyout (LBO): An acquisition of a company in which much of the purchase price is borrowed, with the debt to be repaid from future profits or by subsequently selling off company assets. A leveraged buyout is typically carried out by a small group of investors, often including incumbent management.

Liquid assets: Assets consisting of cash and/or items that are easily converted into cash.

Margin account: A brokerage account that allows a person to trade securities on credit. A **margin call** is a demand for more collateral on the account.

Money supply: The currency held by the public, plus checking accounts in commercial banks and savings institutions.

Mortgage-backed securities: Created when a bank, builder, or government agency gathers together a group of mortgages and then sells bonds to other institutions and the public. The investors receive their proportionate share of the interest payments on the loans as well as the principal payments. Usually, the mortgages in question are guaranteed by the government.

Municipal bond: Issued by governmental units such as states, cities, local taxing authorities, and other agencies. Interest is exempt from U.S.—and sometimes state and local—income tax. Municipal bond unit investment trusts offer a portfolio of many different municipal bonds chosen by professionals. The income is exempt from federal income taxes.

Mutual fund: A portfolio of professionally bought and managed financial assets in which you pool your money along with that of many other people. A share price is based on net asset value, or the value of all the investments owned by the funds, less any debt, and divided by the total number of shares. The major advantage, relative to investing individually in only a small number of stocks, is less risk—the holdings are spread out over many assets, and if one or two badly the remainder may shield you from the losses. Bond funds are mutual funds that deal in the bond market exclusively. Money market mutual funds buy in the so-called money market—institutions that need to borrow large sums of money for short terms. These funds often offer special checking account advantages.

National debt: The debt of the national government, as distinguished from the debts of political subdivisions of the nation and of private business and individuals.

National debt ceiling: Total borrowing limit set by Congress beyond which the U.S. national debt cannot rise. This limit is periodically raised by congressional vote.

Option: A type of contractual agreement between a buyer and a seller to buy or sell shares of a security. A **call** option contract gives the right to purchase shares of a specific stock at a stated price within a given period of time. A **put** option contract gives the buyer the right to sell shares of a specific stock at a stated price within a given period of time.

Per capita income: The total income of a group divided by the number of people in the group.

Prime interest rate: The rate charged by banks on short-term loans to large commercial customers with the highest credit rating.

Producer price index: A statistical measure of the change in the price of wholesale goods. It is reported for 3 different stages of the production chain: crude, intermediate, and finished goods.

Program trading: Trading techniques involving large numbers and large blocks of stocks, usually used in conjunction with computer programs. Techniques include index arbitrage, in which traders profit from price differences between stocks and futures contracts on stock indexes, and portfolio insurance, which is the use of stock-index futures to protect stock investors from potentially large losses when the market drops.

Public debt: The total of a nation's debts owed by state, local, and national government. Increases in this sum, reflected in public-sector deficits, indicate how much of the nation's spending is being financed by borrowing rather than by taxation.

Recession: A mild decrease in economic activity marked by a decline in real (inflation-adjusted) GDP, employment, and trade, usually lasting from six months to a year, and marked by widespread decline in many sectors of the economy.

Savings Association Insurance Fund (SAIF): Created in 1989 to insure accounts in savings and loan associations up to $100,000.

Seasonal adjustment: Statistical changes made to compensate for regular fluctuations in data that are so great they tend to distort the statistics and make comparisons meaningless. For instance, seasonal adjustments are made for a slowdown in housing construction in midwinter and for the rise in farm income in the fall after summer crops are harvested.

Short-selling: Borrowing shares of stock from a brokerage firm and selling them, hoping to buy the shares back at a lower price, return them, and realize a profit from the decline in prices.

Stagnation: Economic slowdown in which there is little growth in the GDP, capital investment, and real income.

Stock: Common stocks are shares of ownership in a corporation. For publicly held firms, the stock typically trades on an exchange, such as the New York Stock Exchange; for closely held firms, the founders and managers own most of the stock. There can be wide swings in the prices of this kind of stock. Preferred stock is a type of stock on which a fixed dividend must be paid before holders of common stock are issued their share of the issuing corporation's earnings. Preferred stock is less risky than common stock. Convertible preferred stock can be converted into the common stock of the company that issued the preferred. Over-the-counter stock is not traded on the major or regional exchanges but bought directly from dealers. Blue-chip stocks are so called because they have been leading stocks for a long time. Growth stocks are from companies that reinvest their earnings, rather than pay dividends, with the expectation of future stock price appreciation.

Supply-side economics: A school of thinking about economic policy holding that lowering income tax rates will inevitably lead to enhanced economic growth and general revitalization of the economy.

Takeover: Acquisition of one company by another company or group by sale or merger. A friendly takeover occurs when the acquired company's management is agreeable to the merger; when management is opposed to the merger, it is a hostile takeover.

Tender offer: A public offer to buy a company's stock; usually priced at a premium above the market.

Zero coupon bond: A corporate or government bond that is issued at a deep discount from the maturity value and pays no interest during the life of the bond. It is redeemable at face value.

Top Brands in Selected Categories, 2011-12

Source: Information Resources, Inc., a Chicago-based marketing research company

Figures for 52-week period ending Sept. 9, 2012. Percent change represents dollar sales change in 2011-12 over same period in 2010-11.

Baby food	Sales (mil)	% change	Market share
Gerber Second Foods Nature Select	$116.1	1,725.7%	12.5%
Gerber Second Foods	92.4	−59.5	9.9
Gerber	88.6	−2.9	9.5
Gerber Graduates	79.9	−6.5	8.6
Beechnut Stage 2	42.4	−14.9	4.5
Total sales	**977.1**	**4.1**	
Batteries (alkaline)			
Duracell Coppertop	$473.5	2.6%	42.5%
Energizer Max	315.6	−5.0	28.3
Private label	214.3	2.8	19.3
Ray O Vac	24.9	10.0	2.2
Duracell	21.3	48.8	1.9
Total sales	**1,113.4**	**1.0**	
Beer			
Bud Light	$1,567.5	−1.3%	17.9%[1]
Coors Light	827.4	2.3	9.5[1]
Miller Lite	713.2	−1.7	8.2[1]
Budweiser	649.3	−4.8	7.4[1]
Corona Extra	461.3	2.1	21.1[2]
Total sales	**11,004.3**	**3.4**	
Bottled water			
Private label	$961.6	9.6%	24.3%
Dasani	333.3	8.5	8.4
Aquafina	323.0	−7.4	8.2
Poland Spring	260.9	1.3	6.6
Glaceau Vitamin Water	250.1	−10.2	6.3
Total sales	**3,957.3**	**2.6**	
Cat food (dry)			
Purina Cat Chow Complete	$75.5	−13.9%	7.0%
Private label	75.2	−14.7	7.0
Purina Cat Chow Indoor	67.6	−11.0	6.3
Purina Kit & Kaboodle	62.9	9.7	5.9
Meow Mix	60.6	−25.9	5.6
Total sales	**1,075.4**	**−3.8**	
Chocolate candies			
M&M's	$318.5	0.6%	14.1%
Hershey's	163.1	−1.7	7.2
Reese's	120.4	−1.6	5.3
Dove Promises	100.0	8.5	4.4
Hershey's Kisses	93.1	−2.9	4.1
Total sales	**2,266.9**	**3.4**	
Coffee (ground)			
Folgers	$812.5	4.6%	28.0%
Maxwell House	458.7	5.0	15.8
Private label	290.8	4.4	10.0
Starbucks	254.5	4.3	8.8
Dunkin' Donuts	190.0	6.3	6.6
Total sales	**2,901.5**	**7.2**	
Coffee (decaf)			
Folgers	$60.6	−3.3%	24.0%
Private label	43.0	−2.4	17.0
Maxwell House	23.1	−7.4	9.1
Starbucks	22.5	7.5	8.9
Dunkin' Donuts	21.1	3.3	8.3
Total sales	**252.8**	**0.1**	
Cold cereals (ready-to-eat)			
Private label	$668.0	5.7%	10.5%
General Mills Honey Nut Cheerios	338.8	−0.6	5.3
Post Honey Bunches of Oats	285.0	−6.0	4.5
General Mills Cheerios	263.3	−1.7	4.1
Kelloggs Frosted Flakes	254.3	−0.1	4.0
Total sales	**6,372.0**	**−0.9**	

Cookies	Sales (mil)	% change	Market share
Private label	$641.3	2.5%	14.8%
Nabisco Oreo	341.9	7.0	7.9
Nabisco Chips Ahoy	330.7	1.9	7.6
Nabisco Oreo Double Stuf	153.0	3.5	3.5
Lofthouse	130.4	−4.5	3.0
Total sales	**4,340.8**	**2.9**	
Dog food (dry)			
Private label	$182.6	−4.7%	8.7%
Pedigree	140.1	−16.7	6.7
Purina Dog Chow Healthy Life Nutrition	130.9	−12.8	6.2
Purina One Smart Blend	128.1	115.4	6.1
Purina Beneful	128.0	−2.0	6.1
Total sales	**2,097.6**	**−0.6**	
Ice cream			
Private label	$1,064.1	8.0%	25.6%
Breyers	364.6	−8.8	8.8
Blue Bell	356.4	7.4	8.6
Häagen-Dazs	274.8	5.1	6.6
Ben & Jerry's	267.1	7.5	6.4
Total sales	**4,580.8**	**4.1**	
Pizza (frozen)			
DiGiorno	$676.6	−4.4%	22.4%
Private label	336.6	9.0	11.1
Red Baron	275.8	−1.0	9.1
Tombstone	215.6	−9.8	7.1
Totino's Party Pizza	165.4	−2.3	5.5
Total sales	**3,022.6**	**−3.4**	
Potato chips			
Lay's	$1,042.3	2.6%	28.2%
Ruffles	347.6	1.8	9.4
Wavy Lay's	292.6	−2.6	7.9
Private label	272.9	11.2	7.4
Pringles Super Stack	214.4	4.7	5.8
Total sales	**3,699.7**	**2.2**	
Salad dressing			
Kraft	$265.3	−3.0%	18.9%
Hidden Valley Ranch	236.2	2.4	16.8
Private label	207.4	12.8	14.8
Wishbone	171.3	0.3	12.2
Ken's Steak House	161.2	4.1	11.5
Total sales	**1,517.9**	**2.4**	
Soft drinks			
Coke Classic	$1,780.6	−1.4%	21.7%
Pepsi	1,237.2	−2.9	15.1
Mountain Dew	795.7	2.9	9.7
Dr Pepper	632.1	−0.4	7.7
Private label	581.7	−0.5	7.1
Total sales	**8,215.5**	**−1.4**	
Soft drinks (low calorie)			
Diet Coke	$1,137.9	−2.3%	24.4%
Diet Pepsi	637.7	−4.1	13.7
Coke Zero	349.1	4.8	7.5
Diet Mountain Dew	331.6	0.9	7.1
Diet Dr Pepper	290.6	−4.6	6.2
Total sales	**4,661.7**	**−2.5**	

Note: For all categories, brands are ranked by dollar sales at supermarkets, drugstores, and mass merchandisers, excluding Walmart. "Private label" represents the aggregated sales figures for store-branded products in that category. Total category sales include other brands not listed here. (1) Share of domestic beer sales, not total beer market. (2) Share of imported beer sales, not total beer market.

Who Owns What: Familiar Consumer Products and Services

The following is a partial list of well-known consumer brands with their (U.S.) parent companies as of Oct. 2012. Among brands not listed are many whose parent companies have the same or a similar name (e.g., Colgate is owned by Colgate-Palmolive Co.).

ABC broadcasting: Walt Disney
Advil: Pfizer
Ajax cleanser: Colgate-Palmolive
Altoids mints: Mars
Amana appliances: Whirlpool
American Girl: Mattel
Aquafina water: PepsiCo
Arm & Hammer: Church & Dwight
Band-Aid bandages: Johnson & Johnson
Barbie dolls: Mattel
Betty Crocker prods.: General Mills
Bounty paper towels: Procter & Gamble
Braun appliances: Procter & Gamble
Brillo soap pads: Armaly Brands
Brita water systems: Clorox
Calphalon cookware: Newell Rubbermaid
Canada Dry ginger ale: Dr Pepper Snapple
  Group
Cap'n Crunch cereal: PepsiCo
ChapStick: Pfizer
Charmin toilet tissue: Procter & Gamble
Cheer detergent: Procter & Gamble
Cheerios cereal: General Mills
Cheez Whiz: Kraft
Chips Ahoy!: Kraft
Clairol hair products: Procter & Gamble
Claritin allergy products: Merck
Coppertone sunscreen: Merck
Crest toothpaste: Procter & Gamble
Crisco shortening: J.M. Smucker
Dasani water: Coca-Cola
Doritos chips: PepsiCo
Dove soap: Unilever
Drake's cakes: HostessBrands
Dreyer's ice cream: Nestlé
Duracell batteries: Procter & Gamble
Fantastik: S.C. Johnson
Febreze: Procter & Gamble
Fisher-Price toys: Mattel
Folger's coffee: J.M. Smucker
Formula 409 spray cleaner: Clorox
Friskies cat food: Nestlé
Frito-Lay's snacks: PepsiCo
Fruit of the Loom apparel: Berkshire
  Hathaway
Gatorade: PepsiCo
Gerber baby food: Nestlé
Gillette razors: Procter & Gamble
Glad products: Clorox
Glade air fresheners: S.C. Johnson
Green Giant vegetables: General Mills

Häagen-Dazs: General Mills
Halls cough drops: Kraft
Head & Shoulders shampoo: Procter &
  Gamble
Healthy Choice meals: ConAgra
Hellmann's mayonnaise: Unilever
Hillshire Farm meats: Sara Lee
Hot Wheels/Matchbox cars: Mattel
Huggies diapers: Kimberly-Clark
Hunt's tomatoes: ConAgra
Iams pet food: Procter & Gamble
Irish Spring soap: Colgate-Palmolive
Ivory soap: Procter & Gamble
Jell-O: Kraft
Jennie-O turkey: Hormel
Jif peanut butter: J.M. Smucker
Jimmy Dean sausages: Sara Lee
Keebler cookies: Kellogg Co.
KFC restaurants: Yum! Brands
Kibbles 'n Bits pet food: Del Monte
Kingsford charcoal: Clorox
Kit Kat candy: Hershey
KitchenAid appliances: Whirlpool
Kleenex: Kimberly-Clark
Knorr soups: Unilever
Kool-Aid: Kraft
Lipton tea: Unilever
Listerine mouthwash: Johnson & Johnson
Maxwell House coffee: Kraft
Maytag appliances: Whirlpool
Minute Maid juices: Coca-Cola
Mr. Clean: Procter & Gamble
Mountain Dew soda: PepsiCo
Neosporin: Johnson & Johnson
Neutrogena soap: Johnson & Johnson
9 Lives cat food: Del Monte
OFF! insect repellents: S.C. Johnson
Olay: Procter & Gamble
Old Navy clothing: Gap
Oreo cookies: Kraft
Oscar Mayer meats: Kraft
Pampers: Procter & Gamble
Pantene shampoo: Procter & Gamble
Paper Mate pens: Newell Rubbermaid
Parker Bros. games: Hasbro
Pedigree pet food: Mars
Pepperidge Farm prods.: Campbell Soup
Pepto-Bismol: Procter & Gamble
Perrier water: Nestlé
Pillsbury: General Mills
Pine-Sol cleaner: Clorox

Pizza Hut restaurants: Yum! Brands
Planters nuts: Kraft
Prego pasta sauce: Campbell Soup
Pringles snacks: Kellogg Co.
Prozac: Eli Lilly
Purina pet foods: Nestlé
Q-Tips: Unilever
Ragu sauce: Unilever
Raid insecticide: S.C. Johnson
Reese's candy: Hershey
Rice-A-Roni: PepsiCo
Right Guard deodorant: Henkel
Ritz crackers: Kraft
Robitussin: Pfizer
Rogaine hair-growth aide: Johnson &
  Johnson
Saran wrap: S.C. Johnson
Schick razors: Energizer
Scope mouthwash: Procter & Gamble
Scotch tape: 3M
Scott tissue: Kimberly-Clark
Skippy peanut butter: Unilever
SlimFast: Unilever
S.O.S. soap pads: Clorox
Splenda sweetener: Johnson & Johnson
Sprite soda: Coca-Cola
Sudafed: Johnson & Johnson
Swanson broth: Campbell Soup
Taco Bell restaurants: Yum! Brands
Tampax tampons: Procter & Gamble
Tide detergent: Procter & Gamble
Timberland apparel: V.F. Corp.
Trident gum: Kraft
Triscuit crackers: Kraft
Trojan condoms: Church & Dwight
Tropicana juice: PepsiCo
Twizzlers candy: Hershey
Tylenol: Johnson & Johnson
V8 vegetable juice: Campbell Soup
Vans apparel: V.F. Corp.
Vaseline: Unilever
Velveeta cheese products: Kraft
Viagra: Pfizer
Vicks cold medicines: Procter & Gamble
Visine eye drops: Johnson & Johnson
Wheaties cereal: General Mills
Windex: S.C. Johnson
Wonder bread: Hostess Brands
Wrigley's candy and gum: Mars
Xanax: Pfizer
Ziploc storage bags: S.C. Johnson

U.S. Home Ownership Rates, by Selected Characteristics, 2005, 2012

Source: U.S. Census Bureau, U.S. Dept. of Commerce

Region	2005	2012	Age	2005	2012	Race/ethnicity[1]	2005	2012	Income	2005	2012
Northeast	64.7%	63.7%	Under 35	42.8%	36.5%	White, non-			Median family		
Midwest	73.4	69.6	35-44	68.7	62.2	Hispanic	75.6%	73.5%	income or more	84.0%	80.5%
South	70.4	67.4	45-54	76.3	71.4	Black	48.0	43.8	Below median		
West	63.8	59.7	55-64	81.3	77.1	Hispanic	49.2	46.5	family income	52.7	50.6
			65+	80.3	81.6	Other	58.0	55.0	**Total U.S.**	**68.6**	**65.5**

Note: Figures are for 2nd quarter of the year shown. Not seasonally adjusted. (1) Hispanic householders may be of any race. "Other" includes householders self-identifying as Asian, Native Hawaiian/Pacific Islander, and Native American/Alaska Native, as well as combinations of two or more races/ethnicities.

U.S. Housing Affordability, 1990-2012

Source: National Association of REALTORS®

Year	Median-priced existing home	Avg. mortgage rate[1]	Monthly principal & interest payment	Payment as % of median monthly income	Year	Median-priced existing home	Avg. mortgage rate[1]	Monthly principal & interest payment	Payment as % of median monthly income
1990	$92,000	10.04%	$648	22.0%	2006	$221,900	6.58%	$1,131	23.2%
1995	110,500	7.85	639	18.9	2007	217,900	6.52	1,104	21.7
2000	139,000	8.03	818	19.3	2008	196,600	6.15	958	18.1
2001	147,800	7.03	789	18.4	2009	172,100	5.14	751	14.8
2002	158,100	6.55	804	18.3	2010	173,100	4.89	734	14.4
2003	180,200	5.74	840	19.1	2011	166,200	4.67	687	13.6
2004	195,200	5.73	909	20.2	2012[2]	188,100	3.78	699	13.7
2005	219,000	5.91	1,040	22.4					

(1) All figures assume a down payment of 20% of the home price. Based on effective rate on loans closed on existing homes for the period shown. (2) Preliminary figures, as of July 2012.

Median Price of Existing Single-Family Homes, by Metropolitan Area, 2010-12

Source: National Association of REALTORS®

Median prices are in thousands of dollars and based on all transactions within time period shown. 2nd qtr. 2012 figures are preliminary.

Metropolitan area	2010	2011	2nd qtr. 2012	Metropolitan area	2010	2011	2nd qtr. 2012
Akron, OH	$108.9	$90.9	$116.7	Little Rock-North Little Rock, AR	$132.5	$129.8	$137.8
Albany-Schenectady-Troy, NY	195.7	193.8	197.5	Los Angeles-Long Beach-Santa Ana, CA	323.3	307.7	296.8
Albuquerque, NM	178.7	167.9	174.3	Louisville, KY-IN	134.6	130.4	139.6
Allentown-Bethlehem-Easton, PA-NJ	224.0	185.4	191.7	Madison, WI	217.7	213.2	216.6
Amarillo, TX	124.7	128.2	137.2	Manchester-Nashua, NH	232.0	213.5	212.7
Anaheim-Santa Ana-Irvine, CA	546.4	512.5	542.0	Memphis, TN-MS-AR	120.2	112.3	123.5
Atlanta-Sandy Springs-Marietta, GA	114.8	98.6	103.2	Miami-Fort Lauderdale-Miami Beach, FL	201.9	181.1	206.7
Atlantic City, NJ	226.4	223.2	218.7	Milwaukee-Waukesha-West Allis, WI	205.9	185.2	189.7
Austin-Round Rock, TX	193.6	193.1	214.9	Minneapolis-St. Paul-Bloomington, MN-WI	170.6	154.7	174.5
Baltimore-Towson, MD	246.1	230.0	255.0	Mobile, AL	121.0	103.2	107.8
Barnstable Town, MA	326.0	311.5	333.6	Montgomery, AL	129.0	128.2	132.5
Baton Rouge, LA	169.6	163.4	168.4	Nashville-Davidson–Murfreesboro, TN	153.8	151.9	159.8
Beaumont-Port Arthur, TX	125.1	124.2	127.4	New Haven-Milford, CT.	231.0	223.1	223.5
Birmingham-Hoover, AL	143.0	139.8	154.1	New Orleans-Metairie-Kenner, LA	159.7	153.0	165.1
Bismarck, ND	163.4	166.9	194.0	New York-Northern New Jersey-			
Bloomington-Normal, IL	157.9	155.1	154.5	Long Island, NY-NJ-PA	393.7	378.7	377.6
Boise City-Nampa, ID	136.2	115.4	138.2	New York-Wayne-White Plains, NY-NJ	450.0	442.6	429.9
Boston-Cambridge-Quincy, MA-NH	357.3	346.2	362.1	NY: Edison, NJ	345.4	313.9	297.5
Boulder, CO	358.1	353.1	NA	NY: Nassau-Suffolk, NY	387.0	375.9	385.0
Bridgeport-Stamford-Norwalk, CT	408.6	390.6	374.9	NY: Newark-Union, NJ-PA	379.2	370.5	385.7
Buffalo-Niagara Falls, NY	121.2	119.2	131.6	Norwich-New London, CT	204.7	184.1	186.6
Burlington-South Burlington, VT	261.2	272.0	266.4	Oklahoma City, OK	145.7	141.6	139.1
Canton-Massillon, OH	90.9	NA	NA	Omaha, NE-IA	137.3	135.7	143.0
Cape Coral-Fort Myers, FL	88.9	102.9	130.7	Orlando, FL	134.7	124.9	136.1
Cedar Rapids, IA	144.7	138.8	149.8	Palm Bay-Melbourne-Titusville, FL	103.0	108.5	121.4
Champaign-Urbana, IL	141.9	143.9	154.7	Pensacola-Ferry Pass-Brent, FL	141.0	134.6	142.9
Charleston, WV	129.1	129.8	126.7	Peoria, IL	116.9	119.8	128.9
Charleston-North Charleston, SC	200.5	197.0	212.3	Philadelphia-Camden-Wilmington, PA-NJ-DE-MD	214.9	210.1	219.7
Charlotte-Gastonia-Concord, NC-SC	191.0	NA	NA	Phoenix-Mesa-Scottsdale, AZ	139.2	115.5	148.4
Chattanooga, TN-GA	121.4	121.4	128.7	Pittsfield, MA	195.5	188.3	182.2
Chicago-Naperville-Joliet, IL	191.4	176.5	187.7	Portland-South Portland-Biddeford, ME	218.0	213.7	226.0
Cincinnati-Middletown, OH-KY-IN	128.0	122.3	135.4	Portland-Vancouver-Beaverton, OR-WA	237.3	219.5	233.9
Cleveland-Elyria-Mentor, OH	114.5	105.1	103.9	Providence-New Bedford-Fall River, RI-MA	228.5	217.2	217.5
Colorado Springs, CO	195.5	187.2	205.4	Raleigh-Cary, NC	217.6	NA	NA
Columbia, MO	146.3	150.3	159.6	Reading, PA	153.3	143.1	144.9
Columbia, SC	142.6	140.6	143.4	Reno-Sparks, NV	179.5	158.0	165.3
Columbus, OH	136.4	123.9	142.1	Riverside-San Bernardino-Ontario, CA	179.3	172.3	183.0
Corpus Christi, TX	135.1	134.2	146.9	Rochester, NY	118.9	119.7	122.9
Cumberland, MD-WV	100.3	88.8	102.7	Sacramento–Arden-Arcade–Roseville, CA	184.2	167.1	170.2
Dallas-Fort Worth-Arlington, TX	143.8	148.9	163.0	Saint Louis, MO-IL	131.1	121.8	134.7
Davenport-Moline-Rock Island, IA-IL	112.2	109.9	117.8	Salem, OR	173.5	146.2	142.5
Dayton, OH	103.6	93.3	NA	Salt Lake City, UT	206.5	182.2	NA
Deltona-Daytona Beach-Ormond Beach, FL	115.6	104.8	113.1	San Antonio, TX	151.0	152.5	162.8
Denver-Aurora, CO	232.4	231.4	260.7	San Diego-Carlsbad-San Marcos, CA	385.7	370.3	379.1
Des Moines, IA	150.9	151.1	162.6	San Francisco-Oakland-Fremont, CA	525.6	483.4	552.6
Detroit-Warren-Livonia, MI	NA	53.8	60.2	San Jose-Sunnyvale-Santa Clara, CA	595.0	570.0	660.0
Dover, DE	193.3	170.8	171.5	Sarasota-Bradenton-Venice, FL	164.6	156.2	173.4
Durham, NC	177.9	NA	NA	Seattle-Tacoma-Bellevue, WA	295.7	285.0	290.7
El Paso, TX	134.3	134.3	135.0	Shreveport-Bossier City, LA	156.6	156.2	158.0
Erie, PA	107.7	109.7	119.6	Sioux Falls, SD	143.3	141.4	150.8
Eugene-Springfield, OR	196.3	NA	NA	Spartanburg, SC	118.2	117.0	123.0
Fort Wayne, IN	97.4	95.4	106.9	Spokane, WA	172.2	162.3	168.1
Gainesville, FL	161.6	148.6	147.1	Springfield, IL	124.0	117.2	125.2
Gary-Hammond, IN	122.9	120.6	131.9	Springfield, MA	190.0	181.4	178.5
Glens Falls, NY	147.5	156.2	159.0	Springfield, MO	109.1	104.7	111.8
Grand Rapids, MI	91.5	99.5	112.6	Syracuse, NY	125.1	122.9	124.9
Green Bay, WI	130.4	134.8	129.8	Tallahassee, FL	152.8	143.0	146.1
Greensboro-High Point, NC	129.8	123.8	127.8	Tampa-St. Petersburg-Clearwater, FL	134.2	127.8	144.3
Greenville, SC	145.3	144.5	152.3	Toledo, OH	81.5	75.7	84.0
Gulfport-Biloxi, MS	125.0	104.8	100.6	Topeka, KS	107.2	101.5	113.2
Hagerstown-Martinsburg, MD-WV	144.4	131.3	134.8	Trenton-Ewing, NJ	250.7	240.1	258.3
Hartford-West Hartford-East Hartford, CT	235.8	227.6	226.3	Tucson, AZ	156.6	134.5	147.8
Honolulu, HI	607.6	597.0	629.7	Tulsa, OK	132.3	129.7	136.5
Houston-Baytown-Sugar Land, TX	155.0	155.7	168.3	Virginia Beach-Norfolk-Newport News, VA-NC	205.0	182.9	195.0
Indianapolis, IN	123.3	123.9	135.1	Washington-Arlington-Alexandria, DC-VA-MD-WV	325.3	325.4	367.0
Jackson, MS	133.2	135.9	146.5	Wichita, KS	118.7	115.6	118.8
Jacksonville, FL	137.7	123.6	133.0	Worcester, MA	223.3	209.6	213.5
Kansas City, MO-KS	141.6	133.2	148.4				
Knoxville, TN	140.9	141.0	144.4				
Lansing-East Lansing, MI	84.4	77.5	92.5				
Las Vegas-Paradise, NV	138.0	124.7	130.7				
Lexington-Fayette, KY	143.2	138.6	146.6				
Lincoln, NE	133.6	133.0	139.5				

NA = Not available.

Characteristics of American Housing Units, 2009

Source: *American Housing Survey, 2009*, U.S. Dept. of Housing and Urban Development

Characteristic	Number of homes (thous.)	% of all homes	Characteristic	Number of homes (thous.)	% of all homes
Total units	130,112	100.0%	3	53,734	123.9%
Units in structure			4 or more	25,909	19.9
1, detached	82,472	63.4	**Number of complete bathrooms**		
1, attached	7,053	5.4	None	1,678	1.3
2-4.	10,160	7.8	1	46,977	36.1
5-9.	6,347	4.9	1-1/2	17,233	13.2
10-19.	5,722	4.4	2 or more	64,223	49.4
20-49.	4,525	3.5	**Square footage of unit[1]**		
50 or more.	5,063	3.9	Less than 500	988	1.1
Manufactured/mobile home or			500-749	2,765	3.0
trailer.	8,769	6.7	750-999	6,440	7.0
Cooperatives.	844	0.6	1,000-1,499	21,224	23.3
Condominiums	8,741	6.7	1,500-1,999	20,636	22.6
Year built			2,000-2,499	14,361	15.7
2005-09.	7,324	5.6	2,500-2,999	7,589	8.3
2000-04.	9,158	7.0	3,000-3,999	7,252	8.0
1995-99.	8,821	6.8	4,000 or more	4,456	4.9
1990-94.	7,060	5.4	Not reported or don't know	5,529	6.1
1985-89.	8,804	6.8	Median square footage	1,700	
1980-84.	7,478	5.8	**Equipment**		
1975-79.	13,731	10.6	Lacking full kitchen facilities	5,586	4.3
1970-74.	11,068	8.5	Kitchen sink	128,769	99.0
1960-69.	15,261	11.7	Refrigerator	126,534	97.2
1950-59.	13,222	10.2	Cooking stove or range	126,744	97.4
1940-49.	7,945	6.1	Dishwasher	82,397	63.3
1930-39.	5,840	4.5	Washing machine	101,387	77.9
1920-29.	5,164	4.0	Clothes dryer	98,657	75.8
1919 or earlier.	9,235	7.1	Disposal in kitchen sink.	63,776	49.0
Median year built.	1974	1.5	Trash compactor	4,511	3.5
Location			Air conditioning	109,325	84.1
Inside metropolitan statistical areas	102,679	78.9	Central air	82,475	63.4
In central cities	37,604	28.9	**Main source of heating[2]**		
Suburbs	65,075	50.0	Piped gas	63,361	49.0
Outside metropolitan statistical			Fuel oil	9,065	7.0
areas.	27,433	21.0	Bottled gas	7,366	5.7
Number of bedrooms			Wood	2,215	1.7
None	1,265	1.0	Kerosene or other liquid fuel	732	0.6
1	14,690	11.3	Coal or coke	126	0.1
2	34,514	53.0	Solar energy	18	0.0
			Other	359	0.3

(1) Percentages based on 91,241 single detached homes and trailers. (2) Percentages based on 129,181 homes with heat.

Fair Market Rents for Selected Metropolitan Areas, 2013

Source: *Fair Market Rents 2013*, U.S. Dept. of Housing and Urban Development

Metropolitan area	Number of bedrooms 0	1	2	3	4	Metropolitan area	Number of bedrooms 0	1	2	3	4
Atlanta-Sandy Springs-Marietta, GA	$676	$737	$874	$1,158	$1,406	Nashville-Davidson–Murfreesboro–Franklin, TN	$593	$684	$819	$1,089	$1,168
Austin-Round Rock-San Marcos, TX.	681	834	1,050	1,421	1,723	New Orleans-Metairie-Kenner, LA	637	755	935	1,173	1,420
Baltimore-Towson, MD	846	1,000	1,251	1,598	1,740	New York, NY	1,191	1,243	1,474	1,895	2,124
Birmingham-Hoover, AL	554	662	785	1,031	1,160	Oklahoma City, OK.	503	584	748	1,024	1,229
Boston-Cambridge-Quincy, MA-NH	1,035	1,156	1,444	1,798	1,955	Orlando-Kissimmee-Sanford, FL	697	825	983	1,311	1,586
Buffalo-Niagara Falls, NY	557	591	736	941	1,065	Philadelphia-Camden-Wilmington, PA-NJ-DE-MD	788	929	1,119	1,394	1,496
Charlotte-Gastonia-Rock Hill, NC-SC.	607	669	793	1,069	1,326	Phoenix-Mesa-Glendale, AZ. .	593	748	925	1,363	1,592
Chicago-Joliet-Naperville, IL. .	717	815	966	1,231	1,436	Pittsburgh, PA	540	619	772	969	1,032
Cincinnati-Middleton, OH-KY-IN	445	557	740	1,025	1,129	Portland-Vancouver-Hillsboro, OR-WA	659	766	912	1,344	1,615
Cleveland-Elyria-Mentor, OH	487	585	741	993	1,025	Providence-Fall River, RI-MA	675	762	930	1,158	1,386
Columbus, OH	484	601	782	1,008	1,166	Richmond, VA.	786	826	979	1,287	1,560
Dallas, TX	585	701	887	1,183	1,429	Riverside-San Bernardino-Ontario, CA	763	879	1,116	1,577	1,924
Denver-Aurora-Broomfield, CO	588	726	940	1,379	1,599	Sacramento–Arden-Arcade–Roseville, CA.	717	855	1,073	1,581	1,900
Detroit-Warren-Livonia, MI . . .	495	629	821	1,095	1,196	St. Louis, MO-IL	543	643	830	1,081	1,227
Hartford-West Hartford-East Hartford, CT	704	883	1,101	1,371	1,593	Salt Lake City, UT.	564	677	839	1,197	1,408
Honolulu, HI	1,276	1,392	1,833	2,701	3,100	San Antonio-New Braunfels, TX	550	693	870	1,134	1,244
Houston-Baytown-Sugar Land, TX	636	765	945	1,290	1,595	San Diego-Carlsbad-San Marcos, CA	959	1,054	1,382	2,009	2,448
Indianapolis, IN.	499	615	765	1,020	1,190	San Francisco, CA	1,093	1,423	1,795	2,438	2,948
Jacksonville, FL	614	757	910	1,200	1,468	San Jose-Sunnyvale-Santa Clara, CA	1,079	1,262	1,610	2,270	2,574
Kansas City, MO-KS.	491	632	783	1,073	1,195	San Juan-Guaynabo, PR	484	526	584	773	915
Las Vegas-Paradise, NV.	691	864	1,064	1,568	1,861	Seattle-Bellevue, WA	758	897	1,104	1,627	1,955
Los Angeles-Long Beach, CA	911	1,101	1,421	1,921	2,140	Tampa-St. Petersburg-Clearwater, FL.	582	730	915	1,221	1,462
Louisville, KY-IN	503	588	731	1,012	1,144	Washington-Arlington-Alexandria, DC-VA-MD	1,130	1,191	1,412	1,890	2,374
Memphis, TN-MS-AR	567	648	768	1,049	1,170						
Miami-Miami Beach, FL	719	876	1,122	1,539	1,799						
Milwaukee-Waukesha-West Allis, WI	535	659	828	1,056	1,142						
Minneapolis-St. Paul-Bloomington, MN-WI.	592	736	920	1,296	1,529						

Note: Figures are projections made in the previous year.

TRADE

U.S. Trade With Selected Countries and Major Areas, 2011

Source: U.S. Census Bureau and U.S. Bureau of Economic Analysis, U.S. Dept. of Commerce

(in millions of dollars; top 25 countries as ranked by amount of total trade with U.S.)

Rank	Country	Total trade with U.S.	U.S. exports to	Rank[1]	U.S. imports from	Rank[1]	U.S. trade balance with	Rank[2]
1.	Canada	$596,236.1	$280,889.6	1	$315,346.5	2	−$34,456.9	5
2.	China[3]	503,301.3	103,939.4	3	399,361.9	1	−295,422.5	1
3.	Mexico	461,242.0	198,377.6	2	262,864.4	3	−64,486.9	2
4.	Japan	194,630.7	65,706.1	4	128,924.6	4	−63,218.5	3
5.	Germany	147,818.4	49,155.8	6	98,662.6	5	−49,506.9	4
6.	United Kingdom	107,116.8	55,880.7	5	51,236.1	7	4,644.6	225
7.	South Korea	100,075.7	43,414.5	7	56,661.2	6	−13,246.7	16
8.	Brazil	74,680.1	42,943.9	8	31,736.2	17	11,207.7	230
9.	France	67,842.6	27,803.0	13	40,039.6	11	−12,236.6	19
10.	Taiwan	67,293.5	25,888.7	15	41,404.8	10	−15,516.1	12
11.	Netherlands	65,801.8	42,350.6	9	23,451.2	21	18,899.4	235
12.	Saudi Arabia	61,305.8	13,829.5	25	47,476.3	8	−33,646.8	6
13.	India	57,654.1	21,501.3	17	36,152.8	13	−14,651.5	13
14.	Venezuela	55,599.8	12,343.4	26	43,256.4	9	−30,913.1	8
15.	Singapore	50,336.6	31,223.3	11	19,113.3	24	12,110.0	231
16.	Italy	49,957.1	16,006.6	18	33,950.5	15	−17,943.9	11
17.	Switzerland	48,782.7	24,425.2	16	24,357.5	20	67.8	152
18.	Belgium	47,329.4	29,898.7	12	17,430.7	27	12,468.0	232
19.	Ireland	47,013.9	7,644.3	34	39,369.6	12	−31,725.4	7
20.	Russia	42,905.1	8,286.1	31	34,619.0	14	−26,332.8	10
21.	Hong Kong	40,850.2	36,448.9	10	4,401.3	52	32,047.6	236
22.	Malaysia	40,023.2	14,246.5	23	25,776.7	18	−11,530.2	22
23.	Nigeria	38,766.0	4,911.8	44	33,854.2	16	−28,942.4	9
24.	Australia	37,782.9	27,541.8	14	10,241.1	33	17,300.7	234
25.	Colombia	37,433.9	14,320.5	22	23,113.4	22	−8,793.0	24

Major area/group

Country	Total trade with U.S.	U.S. exports to	U.S. imports from	U.S. trade balance with
North America	$1,057,478.2	$479,267.2	$578,211.0	−$98,943.8
Europe	777,229.7	328,741.7	448,488.0	−119,746.3
Euro Area	480,847.0	195,904.2	284,942.8	−89,038.6
EU	636,828.8	268,473.9	368,354.9	−99,881.0
Africa	125,856.9	32,848.3	93,008.6	−60,160.4
OECD	2,105,219.0	926,595.2	1,178,623.8	−252,028.6
Pacific Rim Countries	1,085,458.7	367,877.6	717,581.1	−349,703.5
Asia/Near East	162,146.2	58,358.6	103,787.6	−45,429.0
Asia/NICS	258,556.0	136,975.4	121,580.6	15,394.8
Asia/South	74,946.9	27,898.7	47,048.2	−19,149.6
ASEAN	194,498.8	76,241.6	118,257.2	−42,015.6
APEC	2,282,964.0	894,670.5	1,388,293.5	−493,623.1
South/Central America	343,057.7	168,781.9	174,275.8	−5,493.9
Twenty Latin American Republics	773,773.4	351,955.2	421,818.2	−69,863.0
SICA	47,199.8	22,779.6	24,420.2	−1,640.6
ALADI	704,263.4	312,187.6	392,075.8	−79,888.2
NATO Allies	1,180,906.5	548,486.1	632,420.4	−83,934.3
OPEC	256,123.6	64,620.1	191,503.5	−126,883.4
World total	**$3,688,255.8**	**$1,480,431.9**	**$2,207,823.9**	**− $727,392.0**

Note: Figures may not equal totals due to rounding. Country grouping data reflect the groups as they were at the time of reporting. (1) Rank shown is for column to the left. Ranking includes territories as well as nations. (2) Rank by size of U.S. trade deficit. Ranking includes territories as well as nations. (3) Not including Hong Kong, Macao, and Taiwan. **Definitions of major areas/groups used in table, as provided by source: North America**—Canada, Mexico. **Europe**—Albania, Andorra, Armenia, Austria, Azerbaijan, Belarus, Belgium, Bosnia-Herzegovina, Bulgaria, Croatia, Cyprus, Czech Republic, Denmark, Estonia, Faroe Isls., Finland, France, Georgia, Germany, Gibraltar, Greece, Hungary, Iceland, Ireland, Italy, Kazakhstan, Kosovo, Kyrgyzstan, Latvia, Liechtenstein, Lithuania, Luxembourg, Macedonia, Malta, Moldova, Monaco, Montenegro, Netherlands, Norway, Poland, Portugal, Romania, Russia, San Marino, Serbia, Slovakia, Slovenia, Spain, Svalbard, Jan Mayen Isl., Sweden, Switzerland, Tajikistan, Turkey, Turkmenistan, Ukraine, United Kingdom, Uzbekistan, Vatican City. **Euro Area**—Austria, Belgium, Cyprus, Estonia, Finland, France, Germany, Greece, Ireland, Italy, Luxembourg, Malta, Netherlands, Portugal, Slovakia, Slovenia, Spain. **EU (European Union)**—Euro Area plus Bulgaria, Czech Republic, Denmark, Hungary, Latvia, Lithuania, Poland, Romania, Sweden, United Kingdom. **Africa**—Algeria, Angola, Benin, Botswana, British Indian Ocean Territories, Burkina Faso, Burundi, Cameroon, Cape Verde, Central African Republic, Chad, Comoros, Congo (Brazzaville), Congo (Kinshasa), Djibouti, Egypt, Equatorial Guinea, Eritrea, Ethiopia, French Southern and Antarctic Lands, Gabon, The Gambia, Ghana, Guinea, Guinea-Bissau, Ivory Coast, Kenya, Lesotho, Liberia, Libya, Madagascar, Malawi, Mali, Mauritania, Mauritius, Mayotte, Morocco, Mozambique, Namibia, Niger, Nigeria, Réunion, Rwanda, St. Tomé and Príncipe, Senegal, Seychelles, Sierra Leone, Somalia, South Africa, South Sudan, Sudan, Swaziland, Tanzania, Togo, Tunisia, Uganda, Western Sahara, Zambia, Zimbabwe. **OECD (Org. for Economic Cooperation and Development)**—Australia, Austria, Belgium, Canada, Chile, Czech Republic, Denmark, Estonia, Finland, France, Germany, Greece, Hungary, Iceland, Ireland, Israel, Italy, Japan, Korea (South), Luxembourg, Mexico, Netherlands, New Zealand, Norway, Poland, Portugal, Slovakia, Spain, Sweden, Switzerland, Turkey, United Kingdom. **Pacific Rim Countries**—Australia, Brunei, China, Hong Kong, Indonesia, Japan, Korea, Macao, Malaysia, New Zealand, Papua New Guinea, Philippines, Singapore, Taiwan. **Asia/Near East**—Bahrain, Iran, Iraq, Israel, Jordan, Kuwait, Lebanon, Oman, Qatar, Saudi Arabia, Syria, United Arab Emirates, Yemen. **Asia/NICS (Newly Industrialized Countries)**—Hong Kong, South Korea, Singapore, Taiwan. **Asia/South**—Afghanistan, Bangladesh, India, Nepal, Pakistan, Sri Lanka. **ASEAN (Assn. of South East Asia Nations)**—Brunei, Cambodia, Indonesia, Laos, Malaysia, Myanmar, Philippines, Singapore, Thailand, Vietnam. **APEC (Asia-Pacific Economic Cooperation)**—Australia, Brunei, Canada, Chile, China, Hong Kong, Indonesia, Japan, Korea (South), Malaysia, Mexico, New Zealand, Papua New Guinea, Peru, Philippines, Russia, Singapore, Taiwan, Thailand, Vietnam. **South/Central America**—Anguilla, Antigua and Barbuda, Argentina, Aruba, The Bahamas, Barbados, Belize, Bermuda, Bolivia, Brazil, British Virgin Isls., Cayman Isls., Chile, Colombia, Costa Rica, Cuba, Dominica, Dominican Republic, Ecuador, El Salvador, Falkland Isls., French Guiana, Grenada, Guadeloupe, Guatemala, Guyana, Haiti, Honduras, Jamaica, Martinique, Montserrat, Netherlands Antilles, Nicaragua, Panama, Paraguay, Peru, St. Kitts and Nevis, St. Lucia, St. Vincent and the Grenadines, Suriname, Trinidad and Tobago, Turks and Caicos Isls., Uruguay, Venezuela. **Twenty Latin American Republics**—Argentina, Bolivia, Brazil, Chile, Colombia, Costa Rica, Cuba, Dominican Republic, Ecuador, El Salvador, Guatemala, Haiti, Honduras, Mexico, Nicaragua, Panama, Paraguay, Peru, Uruguay, Venezuela. **SICA (Central American Integration System)**—Costa Rica, El Salvador, Guatemala, Honduras, Nicaragua. **ALADI (Latin American Integration Assn.)**—Argentina, Bolivia, Brazil, Chile, Colombia, Cuba, Ecuador, Mexico, Paraguay, Peru, Uruguay, Venezuela. **NATO (North Atlantic Treaty Org.) Allies**—Albania, Belgium, Bulgaria, Canada, Croatia, Czech Republic, Denmark, Estonia, France, Germany, Greece, Hungary, Iceland, Italy, Latvia, Lithuania, Luxembourg, Netherlands, Norway, Poland, Portugal, Romania, Slovakia, Slovenia, Spain, Turkey, United Kingdom. **OPEC (Org. of Petroleum Exporting Countries)**—Algeria, Angola, Ecuador, Iran, Iraq, Kuwait, Libya, Nigeria, Qatar, Saudi Arabia, United Arab Emirates, Venezuela.

U.S. Exports and Imports by Principal Commodity Groupings, 2011
Source: U.S. Census Bureau and U.S. Bureau of Economic Analysis, U.S. Dept. of Commerce
(in millions of dollars)

Item	Exports	Imports	Item	Exports	Imports
TOTAL[1]	$1,480,432	$2,207,824	Live animals	$1,023	$2,300
Manufactured goods[2]	971,671	1,611,456	Meat and preparations	16,627	5,734
Agricultural commodities[2]	136,351	99,124	Metal manufactures[3]	20,256	29,614
Mineral fuels[2]	128,564	453,872	Metal ores; scrap	32,838	9,423
Selected commodities[2]			Metalworking machines	6,246	8,619
ADP equipment; office machinery	21,906	116,490	Mineral fuels, other	10,119	4,548
Airplanes, engines, and parts	82,550	25,393	Natural gas	6,432	13,567
Alcoholic beverages, distilled	1,285	6,248	Nickel	1,582	3,718
Aluminum	6,433	11,896	Oils/fats, vegetable	2,532	6,099
Animal feeds	9,288	1,929	Optical goods	3,262	5,896
Artwork/antiques	3,112	6,903	Paper and paperboard	15,988	15,795
Basketware, etc.	8,699	14,458	Petroleum preparations	90,458	92,281
Cereal flour	3,379	5,055	Photographic equipment	3,259	2,183
Chemicals-cosmetics	13,244	10,613	Plastic articles[3]	10,439	17,402
Chemicals-dyeing	8,542	3,458	Platinum	1,036	5,555
Chemicals-fertilizers	5,133	9,165	Pottery	99	1,504
Chemicals-inorganic	13,345	17,019	Power generating machines	36,341	52,074
Chemicals-medicinal	40,011	69,678	Printed materials	5,859	4,512
Chemicals-organic	43,571	54,367	Pulp and waste paper	9,709	4,020
Chemicals-plastics	46,195	20,744	Records/magnetic media	4,368	5,716
Chemicals[3]	27,127	13,294	Rice	2,100	631
Cigarettes	383	181	Rubber articles[3]	2,332	3,763
Clothing	3,339	85,559	Rubber tires and tubes	5,155	13,377
Coal	16,204	2,133	Scientific instruments	48,247	43,527
Coffee	4	6,906	Ships, boats	2,466	1,179
Copper	3,644	10,154	Silver and bullion	3,094	8,577
Cork, wood, and lumber	5,498	4,452	Soybeans	17,581	219
Corn	14,064	399	Spacecraft	1	51
Cotton, raw and linters	8,468	17	Specialized industrial machines	51,655	41,407
Crude fertilizers	2,619	2,848	Sugar	72	1,637
Crude oil	1,463	336,687	Televisions, VCRs, etc.	23,397	137,952
Electrical machinery	77,799	137,937	Textile yarn, fabric	12,880	24,135
Fish and preparations	5,279	16,519	Tobacco, unmanufactured	1,149	752
Footwear	832	22,652	Toys, games, and sporting goods	4,334	28,650
Furniture and bedding	5,259	32,365	Travel goods	526	9,033
Gem diamonds	3,092	22,299	Vegetables and fruits	17,967	23,595
General industrial machines	60,082	74,175	Vehicles	106,196	198,707
Glass[3]	3,657	2,665	Watches, clocks, and parts	460	4,829
Glassware	1,026	2,566	Wheat	11,150	644
Gold, nonmonetary	33,675	16,394	Wood manufactures	2,092	6,783
Hides and skins	2,301	55	**Re-exports**	**182,017**	**NA**
Iron and steel mill products	18,467	32,894	Agricultural commodities	3,995	NA
Jewelry	5,222	11,091	Manufactured goods	174,972	NA
Lighting, plumbing	2,848	8,018	Mineral fuels	1,310	NA
Liquefied propane/butane	3,459	2,629			

NA = Not available. **Note:** Commodity group totals include products not listed here. Figures may not equal totals due to rounding. (1) Both domestic and foreign exports (re-exports). (2) Domestic exports. (3) Not specified elsewhere.

Trends in U.S. Foreign Trade, 1790-2011
Source: U.S. Census Bureau and U.S. Bureau of Economic Analysis, U.S. Dept. of Commerce
In 1790, U.S. exports and imports combined came to $43 mil, and there was a $3 mil trade deficit. The global recession caused total U.S. trade and the overall trade deficit to fall in 2009, but they both resumed the ever-upward path they had been following since the last recorded surplus in 1975.
(in millions of dollars)

Year	Exports	Imports	Trade balance	Year	Exports	Imports	Trade balance	Year	Exports	Imports	Trade balance
1790	$20	$23	-$3	1890	$858	$789	$69	1985	$213,133	$345,276	-$132,143
1795	48	70	-22	1895	808	732	76	1990	394,030	495,042	-101,012
1800	71	91	-20	1900	1,394	850	545	1995	584,742	743,445	-158,703
1805	96	121	-25	1905	1,519	1,118	401	1996	625,075	795,289	-170,214
1810	67	85	-19	1910	1,745	1,557	188	1997	689,182	870,671	-181,489
1815	53	113	-60	1915	2,769	1,674	1,094	1998	682,138	911,896	-229,758
1820	70	74	-5	1920	8,228	5,278	2,950	1999	695,797	1,024,618	-328,821
1825	91	90	1	1925	4,910	4,227	683	2000	781,918	1,218,022	-436,104
1830	72	63	9	1930	3,843	3,061	782	2001	729,100	1,140,999	-411,899
1835	115	137	-22	1935	2,283	2,047	235	2002	693,103	1,161,366	-468,263
1840	124	98	25	1940	4,021	2,625	1,396	2003	724,771	1,257,121	-532,350
1845	106	113	-7	1945	9,806	4,159	5,646	2004	818,775	1,469,704	-650,930
1850	144	174	-29	1950	9,997	8,954	1,043	2005	905,978	1,673,455	-767,477
1855	219	258	-39	1955	14,298	11,566	2,732	2006	1,036,635	1,853,939	-817,304
1860	334	354	-20	1960	19,659	15,073	4,586	2007	1,162,479	1,956,962	-794,483
1865	166	239	-73	1965	26,742	21,520	5,222	2008	1,287,442	2,103,641	-816,199
1870	393	436	-43	1970	42,681	40,356	2,325	2009	1,056,043	1,559,625	-503,582
1875	513	533	-20	1975	107,652	98,503	9,149	2010	1,278,263	1,913,160	-634,897
1880	836	668	168	1980	220,626	244,871	-24,245	2011	1,480,432	2,207,824	-727,392
1885	742	578	165								

World Trade Organization (WTO)
The World Trade Organization is an international body that seeks to promote free trade by eliminating barriers to trade. Founded in 1995, the WTO had grown to 155 member countries as of Aug. 2012, with 29 others, including Russia and Vatican City, granted observer status. International intergovernmental organizations, such as the International Monetary Fund and the World Bank, may also be granted observer status. With the exception of Vatican City, observers must start accession negotiations within five years of becoming observers.

Foreign Exchange Rates, 1970-2011

Source: Federal Reserve Board

One U.S. dollar was worth the following amounts in each country's national currency; exchange rates are annual averages.

Year	Australia (dollar)	Austria (schilling; euro)	Belgium (franc; euro)	Canada (dollar)	China (yuan)	Denmark (krone)	France (franc; euro)	Germany[1] (deutsche mark; euro)	Greece (drachma; euro)
1970	0.8980	25.8800	49.6800	1.0103	NA	7.4890	5.5200	3.6480	30.0000
1980	0.8772	12.9450	29.2370	1.1693	NA	5.6340	4.2250	1.8175	42.6200
1990	1.2799	11.3700	33.4180	1.1668	NA	6.1890	5.4453	1.6157	158.5100
1995	1.3486	10.0810	29.4800	1.3724	8.3700	5.6020	4.9915	1.4331	231.6600
2000	1.7197	1.0832	1.0832	1.4855	8.2784	8.0950	1.0832	1.0832	365.9200
2005	1.3111	0.8033	0.8033	1.2115	8.1936	5.9953	0.8033	0.8033	0.8033
2006	1.3271	0.7960	0.7960	1.1340	7.9723	5.9422	0.7960	0.7960	0.7960
2007	1.1918	0.7293	0.7293	1.0734	7.6058	5.4413	0.7293	0.7293	0.7293
2008	1.1714	0.6791	0.6791	1.0660	6.9477	5.0885	0.6791	0.6791	0.6791
2009	1.2615	0.7176	0.7176	1.1412	6.8307	5.3574	0.7176	0.7176	0.7176
2010	1.0870	0.7541	0.7541	1.0298	6.7696	5.6266	0.7541	0.7541	0.7541
2011	0.9679	0.7178	0.7178	0.989	6.463	5.353	0.7178	0.7178	0.7178

Year	Hong Kong (dollar)	India (rupee)	Ireland (pound; euro)	Italy (lira; euro)	Japan (yen)	Malaysia (ringgit)	Mexico (new peso)	Netherlands (guilder; euro)	Norway (krone)
1970	NA	7.576	2.3959	623.0000	357.60	3.0900	NA	3.5970	7.1400
1980	NA	7.887	2.0577	856.0000	226.63	2.1767	NA	1.9875	4.9381
1990	NA	17.504	1.6585	1,198.0000	144.79	2.7049	2.812	1.8209	6.2597
1995	7.7357	32.427	1.6038	1,628.9000	94.06	2.5044	6.419	1.6057	6.3352
2000	7.7925	45.000	1.0832	1.0832	107.80	3.8000	9.459	1.0832	8.8131
2005	7.7775	44.000	0.8033	0.8033	110.11	3.7869	10.894	0.8033	6.4412
2006	7.7681	45.190	0.7960	0.7960	116.31	3.6661	10.906	0.7960	6.4095
2007	7.8016	41.180	0.7293	0.7293	117.76	3.4354	10.928	0.7293	5.8557
2008	7.7862	43.390	0.6791	0.6791	103.39	3.3292	11.143	0.6791	5.6365
2009	7.7514	48.330	0.7176	0.7176	93.68	3.5231	13.498	0.7176	6.2908
2010	7.7687	45.65	0.7541	0.7541	87.78	3.2175	12.623	0.7541	6.0451
2011	7.784	46.58	0.7178	0.7178	79.70	3.0564	12.427	0.7178	5.6022

Year	Portugal (escudo; euro)	Singapore (dollar)	South Korea (won)	Spain (peseta; euro)	Sweden (krona)	Switzerland (franc)	Taiwan (dollar)	Thailand (baht)	UK (pound)
1970	28.7500	3.0800	310.57	69.7200	5.1700	4.3160	NA	21.000	0.4174
1980	50.0800	2.1412	607.43	71.7600	4.2309	1.6772	NA	20.476	0.4302
1990	142.5500	1.8125	707.76	101.9300	5.9188	1.3892	NA	25.585	0.5603
1995	151.1100	1.4174	771.27	124.6900	7.1333	1.1825	26.495	24.915	0.6335
2000	1.0832	1.7250	1,130.90	1.0832	9.1735	1.6904	31.260	40.210	0.6598
2005	0.8033	1.6639	1,023.75	0.8033	7.4710	1.2459	32.131	40.252	0.5493
2006	0.7960	1.5882	954.32	0.7960	7.3718	1.2532	32.506	37.876	0.5425
2007	0.7293	1.5065	928.97	0.7293	6.7550	1.1999	32.852	32.203	0.4995
2008	0.6791	1.4140	1,098.71	0.6791	6.5846	1.0816	31.521	32.962	0.5392
2009	0.7176	1.4543	1,274.63	0.7176	7.6539	1.0860	33.020	34.310	0.6385
2010	0.7541	1.3629	1,155.74	0.7541	7.2053	1.0432	31.498	31.700	0.6472
2011	0.7178	1.2565	1,106.94	0.7178	6.4878	0.8862	29.382	30.462	0.6233

NA = Not available. **Note:** The euro, the European Union's single currency, replaced the national currencies in the EU nations shown above. Since 1999 (or 2001 in the case of Greece), the euro has been fixed at the following conversion rates: 13.7603 Austrian schillings, 40.3399 Belgian francs, 6.55957 French francs, 1.95583 German marks, 340.750 Greek drachmas, 787564 Irish pounds, 1936.27 Italian lire, 2.20371 Netherlands guilders, 200.482 Portuguese escudos, and 166.386 Spanish pesetas. (1) West Germany before 1991.

North American Free Trade Agreement (NAFTA)

NAFTA, a free trade pact between the U.S., Canada, and Mexico, took effect Jan. 1, 1994. Major provisions, which were fully implemented Jan. 1, 2008, are as follows:

Agriculture: With limited exceptions, tariffs on all agricultural products eliminated over 15 years. Domestic price-support systems may continue provided they do not distort trade.

Automobiles: At least 62.5% of an automobile's value must be produced in North America for it to qualify for duty-free status.

Disputes: Special judges have jurisdiction to resolve disagreements within strict timetables.

Energy: Mexico bars foreign ownership of its oil fields, but U.S. and Canadian companies could bid on contracts offered by Mexico's state-owned oil and electricity monopolies.

Environment: The trade agreement cannot be used to overrule national and state environmental, health, or safety laws.

Finance: Limits on ownership of banks, insurance companies, and brokerages eliminated by Jan. 1, 2000.

Jobs: Barriers to limit Mexican migration unaffected by NAFTA.

Patent and copyright protection: Mexico strengthened its intellectual property laws and agreed to honor pharmaceutical patents for 20 years.

Tariffs: Tariffs on 10,000 goods eliminated over 15 years. One-half of U.S. exports to Mexico were duty-free by 1999.

Textiles: A provision requires most garments to be made from yarn and fabric produced in North America.

Trucking: Trucks to have free access throughout the three countries by 1999, but the U.S. restricted Mexican trucks to a 20-mi comm. zone at the border. In 2001, an arbitration panel ruled the restrictions were in violation of NAFTA.

U.S. Trade With Mexico and Canada, 1996-2011

Source: U.S. Census Bureau and U.S. Bureau of Economic Analysis, U.S. Dept. of Commerce

(in millions of dollars)

WITH MEXICO				WITH CANADA			
Year	Exports	Imports	U.S. trade balance[1]	Year	Exports	Imports	U.S. trade balance[1]
1996	$56,792	$74,297	−$17,506	1996	$134,210	$155,893	−$21,682
1998	78,773	94,629	−15,857	1998	156,603	173,256	−16,653
2000	111,349	135,926	−24,577	2000	178,941	230,838	−51,897
2002	97,470	134,616	−37,146	2002	160,923	209,088	−48,165
2003	97,412	138,060	−40,648	2003	169,924	221,595	−51,671
2004	110,835	155,902	−45,067	2004	189,880	256,360	−66,480
2005	120,365	170,109	−49,744	2005	211,899	290,384	−78,486
2006	133,979	198,253	−64,274	2006	230,656	302,438	−71,782
2007	136,092	210,714	−74,622	2007	248,888	317,057	−68,169
2008	151,220	215,942	−64,722	2008	261,150	339,491	−78,342
2009	128,892	176,654	−47,762	2009	204,658	226,248	−21,591
2010	163,473	229,908	−66,435	2010	249,105	277,648	−28,543
2011	198,378	262,864	−64,487	2011	280,890	315,346	−34,457

(1) Figures may not add up to totals due to rounding.

Central American Free Trade Agreement (CAFTA)

CAFTA (also known as CAFTA-DR) is a free trade agreement between the U.S. and Costa Rica, Dominican Republic, El Salvador, Guatemala, Honduras, and Nicaragua. The U.S. and El Salvador approved the agreement Mar. 1, 2006; Nicaragua joined a month later, and Guatemala entered into the accord July 1, 2006. The Dominican Republic approved CAFTA Mar. 1, 2007, and Costa Rica completed the treaty by signing on Jan. 1, 2009. Some highlights of the agreement:

Agriculture: Tariffs on 50% of U.S. farm goods eliminated; other goods deemed "sensitive"—including corn, milk, and potatoes—to have tariffs reduced to zero over 20 years. Sugar imports to the U.S. allowed to rise to 1.2% of annual U.S. production, up to 1.7% over 15 years.

Automobiles: Tariffs on autos and auto parts to be phased out over five years.

Environment and labor: Party nations agree to enforce local labor and environmental protections, although no mechanisms to monitor enforcement currently exist.

Intellectual property: Party nations agree to uphold international standards of trademark, copyright, and patent protection to which the U.S. is a signatory. This includes seizing pirated and counterfeit goods and prosecuting those who traffic in them.

Manufacturing: Tariffs eliminated on 80% of U.S. goods.

Market barriers: Barriers for services such as telecommunications, insurance, and financial services eliminated or reduced.

Pharmaceuticals: U.S. pharmaceuticals given five-year patent protection from their date of introduction to CAFTA markets, regardless of date introduced in U.S.

Textiles and clothing: Elimination of duties on nearly all textiles and clothing instituted, retroactive to Jan. 1, 2004.

Busiest U.S. Ports, 2010

Source: U.S. Army Corps of Engineers, Dept. of the Army, U.S. Dept. of Defense
(figures in tons; ranked by total tonnage handled)

Rank	Port	Total	Domestic	Foreign	Imports	Exports
1.	South Louisiana, LA	236,262,069	121,110,982	115,151,087	41,167,427	73,983,660
2.	Houston, TX	227,133,231	67,572,638	159,560,593	88,507,605	71,052,988
3.	New York, NY-NJ	139,198,215	55,483,848	83,714,367	63,884,008	19,830,359
4.	Beaumont, TX	76,958,592	25,176,606	51,781,986	44,309,994	7,471,992
5.	Long Beach, CA	75,434,788	12,869,965	62,564,823	38,816,457	23,748,366
6.	Corpus Christi, TX	73,663,432	18,840,615	54,822,817	41,654,989	13,167,828
7.	New Orleans, LA	72,410,730	38,331,450	34,079,280	15,721,133	18,358,147
8.	Los Angeles, CA	62,386,603	6,443,068	55,943,535	34,648,808	21,294,727
9.	Huntington WV-KY-OH	61,521,942	61,521,942	0	0	0
10.	Texas City, TX	56,590,856	16,515,074	40,075,782	32,553,419	7,522,363
11.	Plaquemines, LA	55,836,687	36,927,933	18,908,754	1,357,043	17,551,711
12.	Mobile, AL	55,713,273	26,356,690	29,356,583	15,060,887	14,295,696
13.	Baton Rouge, LA	55,536,987	34,768,822	20,768,165	14,126,050	6,642,115
14.	Lake Charles, LA	54,614,895	21,614,336	33,000,559	26,928,081	6,072,478
15.	Norfolk Harbor, VA	41,569,373	6,180,239	35,389,134	8,794,958	26,594,176
16.	Baltimore, MD	39,629,187	9,462,226	30,166,961	13,516,079	16,650,882
17.	Pascagoula, MS	37,275,809	10,677,578	26,598,231	20,026,182	6,572,049
18.	Duluth-Superior, MN-WI	36,598,247	26,936,111	9,662,136	331,330	9,330,806
19.	Savannah, GA	34,681,656	1,789,004	32,892,652	17,504,770	15,387,882
20.	Tampa, FL	34,202,079	23,005,959	11,196,120	5,757,363	5,438,757
21.	Philadelphia, PA	34,036,094	12,565,092	21,471,002	20,986,570	484,432
22.	Pittsburgh, PA	33,843,362	33,843,362	0	0	0
23.	Valdez, AK	31,902,056	31,902,056	0	0	0
24.	St. Louis, MO-IL	30,772,951	30,772,951	0	0	0
25.	Port Arthur, TX	30,231,786	10,766,872	19,464,914	10,782,699	8,682,215
26.	Seattle, WA	27,191,675	5,094,265	22,097,410	8,606,657	13,490,753
27.	Freeport, TX	26,675,842	4,347,395	22,328,447	20,083,819	2,244,628
28.	Portland, OR	25,949,307	8,178,736	17,770,571	3,472,804	14,297,767
29.	Richmond, CA	24,177,521	11,412,369	12,765,152	10,667,556	2,097,596
30.	Tacoma, WA	22,399,200	5,354,244	17,044,956	4,861,472	12,183,484
31.	Marcus Hook, PA	21,940,459	9,530,805	12,409,654	12,155,728	253,926
32.	Newport News, VA	20,839,227	4,280,717	16,558,510	320,030	16,238,480
33.	Port Everglades, FL	20,233,197	10,156,174	10,077,023	6,822,724	3,254,299
34.	Jacksonville, FL	19,117,823	7,400,936	11,716,887	9,618,481	2,098,406
35.	Boston, MA	19,091,378	6,138,578	12,952,800	11,721,627	1,231,173
36.	Oakland, CA	18,609,728	2,265,063	16,344,665	6,734,892	9,609,773
37.	Chicago, IL	18,534,237	15,381,973	3,152,264	2,079,695	1,072,569
38.	Portland, ME	18,158,230	1,628,500	16,529,730	16,509,276	20,454
39.	Charleston, SC	17,985,995	2,885,976	15,100,019	8,916,147	6,183,872
40.	Paulsboro, NJ	17,499,056	7,238,991	10,260,065	9,535,925	724,140
41.	Galveston, TX	13,948,896	5,934,427	8,014,469	1,877,503	6,136,966
42.	Two Harbors, MN	13,877,097	13,391,512	485,585	17,334	468,251
43.	Detroit, MI	13,406,493	10,792,960	2,613,533	2,413,966	199,567
44.	Cincinnati, OH	12,708,524	12,708,524	0	0	0
45.	Kalama, WA	12,254,997	489,260	11,765,737	480,010	11,285,727
46.	Memphis, TN	12,155,049	12,155,049	0	0	0
47.	San Juan, PR	11,395,499	6,604,262	4,791,237	4,008,155	783,082
48.	Cleveland, OH	10,791,326	9,218,274	1,573,052	1,509,430	63,622
49.	Toledo, OH	10,720,187	3,927,139	6,793,048	3,803,648	2,989,400
50.	Indiana Harbor, IN	10,168,960	9,901,838	267,122	0	267,122
51.	New Haven, CT	9,987,285	7,221,889	2,765,396	2,223,797	541,599
52.	Barbers Point, Oahu, HI	9,170,554	1,620,451	7,550,103	7,336,838	213,265
53.	Honolulu, HI	8,903,468	7,773,385	1,130,083	836,902	293,181
54.	Matagorda, TX	8,879,191	2,154,222	6,724,969	4,652,207	2,072,762
55.	Presque Isle, MI	8,720,506	6,447,080	2,273,426	16,550	2,256,876
56.	Anacortes, WA	8,455,447	6,668,158	1,787,289	436,534	1,350,755
57.	Vancouver, WA	8,390,485	2,019,272	6,371,213	916,330	5,454,883
58.	St. Clair, MI	7,988,201	7,988,201	0	0	0
59.	Gary, IN	7,831,215	7,607,812	223,403	164,980	58,423
60.	Wilmington, NC	7,428,160	2,617,086	4,811,074	3,580,702	1,230,372

U.S. Railroad Freight and Miles, 1890-2011

Source: Assn. of American Railroads; Bureau of Transportation Statistics, Research and Innovative Technology Admin., U.S. Dept. of Transportation

(in billion ton-miles)

Year	Class I freight[1]	All freight	Miles[2]	Year	Class I freight[1]	All freight	Miles[2]	Year	Class I freight[1]	All freight	Miles[2]
1890...	NA	76	163,597	1960...	572	575	217,552	2006...	1,772	1,856	140,490
1900...	NA	142	193,346	1970...	765	771	205,782	2007...	1,771	1,820	140,695
1910...	NA	255	240,293	1980...	919	932	178,056	2008...	1,777	1,730	139,326
1920...	410	414	252,845	1990...	1,034	1,064	145,979	2009...	1,532	NA	139,118
1930...	383	386	249,052	2000...	1,466	1,546	144,473	2010...	1,691	NA	138,624
1940...	373	375	233,670	2005...	1,696	1,733	140,810	2011...	1,729	NA	NA
1950...	589	592	223,779								

NA = Not available. **Note:** A ton-mile equals one ton of freight transported one statute mile. (1) Largest class of freight railroad companies, determined by annual operating revenue. (2) Aggregate length of operating roadway in U.S., excluding yard tracks, sidings, and parallel tracks.

Merchant Fleets of the World, 2010

Source: Maritime Administration, U.S. Dept. of Transportation

(tonnage in thousands; self-propelled oceangoing vessels of 10,000 gross deadweight tons or more, ranked by total tons, all vessels)

By flag of registry	All vessels No.	All vessels Tons (thous.)	Tanker No.	Tanker Tons (thous.)	Dry bulk carrier No.	Dry bulk carrier Tons (thous.)	Container No.	Container Tons (thous.)	Other[1] No.	Other[1] Tons (thous.)
Panama	4,506	283,730	875	71,169	2,257	164,985	691	35,216	669	12,196
Liberia................	2,309	156,438	748	69,084	533	45,078	868	38,886	160	3,389
Marshall Islands	1,255	92,563	566	53,565	438	31,288	201	6,536	50	1,174
Hong Kong	1,218	85,779	235	21,675	634	49,095	233	11,752	116	3,258
Greece	622	70,250	325	44,368	257	23,319	34	2,456	6	106
Singapore.............	1,074	61,674	461	32,091	190	15,347	308	11,377	115	2,858
Bahamas	861	60,079	357	38,277	239	14,366	43	1,687	204	5,545
Malta.................	941	56,115	278	21,471	497	29,441	83	3,520	79	1,636
China[2]...............	830	37,252	130	8,890	427	20,516	126	5,418	147	2,428
Cyprus	572	30,703	113	10,370	263	14,796	147	4,530	—	—
Isle of Man	213	18,296	144	12,560	48	5,429	5	111	—	—
Italy..................	344	17,561	169	8,754	77	6,327	21	1,054	74	1,395
Korea, South	266	17,347	36	1,733	167	14,409	29	674	34	531
Norway Intl. (NIS)[3]	321	17,040	189	10,290	51	4,105	—	—	—	—
Germany..............	319	17,024	22	667	5	823	276	15,267	16	267
Japan	155	15,774	49	6,815	81	8,355	1	100	24	505
United Kingdom	321	15,434	54	2,141	29	2,693	171	9,557	66	1,023
Denmark Intl. (DIS)[4]	217	13,133	119	5,712	4	401	84	6,882	10	139
Antigua and Barbuda	458	9,641	1	10	34	1,277	296	6,678	127	1,676
Bermuda..............	113	9,612	63	5,552	22	3,320	15	577	—	—
United States	192	9,123	60	4,184	13	581	77	3,446	42	913
Malaysia..............	131	8,387	88	7,215	9	356	23	682	11	135
India	132	8,361	66	4,756	58	3,487	6	91	—	—
France International (FIS)[5]	75	7,709	46	5,295	2	345	26	2,055	1	14
Indonesia	188	6,606	85	3,806	51	2,076	28	421	—	—
Top 25 (as ranked above)	17,633	1,125,633	5,279	450,451	6,386	462,217	3,792	168,971	1,951	39,190
World total.............	20,050	1,213,701	5,794	477,602	7,167	496,781	4,014	175,426	2,279	44,972
Top 25 as % of total	87.9%	92.7%	91.1%	94.3%	89.1%	93.0%	94.5%	96.3%	85.6%	87.1%

— = Not available. (1) Includes roll-on/roll-off, gas carriers, general cargo carriers, partial container ships, refrigerated cargo ships, barge carriers, and specialized cargo ships. (2) Excludes Hong Kong. (3) Norwegian Intl. Shipping Registry (4) Danish Intl. Shipping Registry (5) French Intl. Shipping Registry.

U.S. International Transactions, 1970-2011

Source: U.S. Bureau of Economic Analysis, U.S. Dept. of Commerce

(in millions of dollars; revised as of June 2012)

	1970	1980	1990	2000	2005	2009	2010	2011
CURRENT ACCT.								
Exports of goods and services, and income receipts	$68,387	$344,440	$706,975	$1,425,260	$1,824,780	$2,180,553	$2,518,767	$2,847,988
Goods, BOP basis[1]	42,469	224,250	387,401	784,781	911,686	1,069,733	1,288,882	1,497,406
Services	14,171	47,584	147,832	288,002	375,755	509,212	553,603	605,961
Income receipts on U.S.-owned assets abroad	11,748	72,606	170,570	348,083	532,542	596,131	670,641	738,810
Imports of goods and services and income payments	−59,901	−333,774	−759,290	−1,782,832	−2,464,813	−2,439,990	−2,829,645	−3,180,861
Goods, BOP basis[1]	−39,866	−249,750	−498,438	−1,230,568	−1,692,416	−1,575,491	−1,934,006	−2,235,819
Services	−14,520	−41,491	−117,659	−218,964	−303,649	−382,608	−403,216	−427,428
Income payments on foreign-owned assets in U.S.	−5,515	−42,532	−139,728	−322,345	−453,800	−468,579	−479,624	−503,796
Unilateral current transfers, net	−6,156	−8,349	−26,654	−58,767	−105,741	−122,459	−131,074	−133,053
CAPITAL ACCT.: Transactions, net ..	NA	NA	−7,220	−1	13,116	−140	−157	−1,212
FINANCIAL ACCT.								
U.S.-owned assets abroad (decrease/financial outflow [−])[2] ...	−9,337	−86,967	−81,234	−560,523	−546,631	−119,535	−939,484	−483,653
U.S. official reserve assets.......	2,481	−8,155	−2,158	−290	14,096	−52,256	−1,834	−15,877
U.S. govt. assets, other than official reserve assets	−1,589	−5,162	2,317	−941	5,539	541,342	7,540	−103,666
U.S. private assets...............	−10,229	−73,651	−81,393	−559,292	−566,266	−608,622	−945,189	−364,110
Foreign-owned assets in U.S. (increase/financial inflow [+])[2]	7,226	62,037	139,357	1,038,224	1,247,347	314,390	1,308,279	1,000,990
Statistical discrepancy (sum of above with sign reversed)	−219	22,613	28,066	−61,361	31,942	142,365	59,237	−89,208
BALANCE ON CURRENT ACCT.	2,331	2,317	−78,968	−416,338	−745,774	−381,896	−441,951	−465,926

NA = Not available or applicable. (1) BOP = Balance of payments. Excl. exports of goods under U.S. military agency sales contracts identified in Census export documents, excl. imports of goods under direct defense expenditures identified in Census import documents, and reflects various other adjustments. (2) Excl. financial derivatives.

Foreign Direct Investment in the U.S. by Selected Countries and Territories, 2000-2011

Source: U.S. Bureau of Economic Analysis, U.S. Dept. of Commerce
(in millions of dollars)

	2011	2010	2000
All countries[1]	$2,547,828	$2,342,829	$1,256,867
Canada	210,864	206,139	114,309
Europe[1]	1,811,875	1,697,196	887,014
Austria	4,781	4,353	3,007
Belgium	86,021	43,236	14,787
Denmark	7,854	9,285	4,025
Finland	5,511	6,558	8,875
France	198,741	184,762	125,740
Germany	215,938	212,915	122,412
Ireland	24,974	30,583	25,523
Italy	23,021	15,689	6,576
Liechtenstein	NA	NA	319
Luxembourg	190,380	181,203	58,930
Netherlands	240,306	217,050	138,894
Norway	18,056	10,356	2,665
Spain	44,750	40,723	5,068
Sweden	42,313	40,758	21,991
Switzerland	211,700	192,231	64,719
United Kingdom	442,179	432,488	277,613
Latin America and other Western Hemisphere[1]	85,695	60,074	53,691
South and Central America[1]	25,010	19,206	13,384
Brazil	5,038	1,093	882
Mexico	13,763	12,591	7,462
Panama	1,098	1,485	3,819
Venezuela	3,784	2,857	792
Other Western Hemisphere[1]	$60,686	$40,869	$40,307
Bahamas, The	473	128	1,254
Bermuda	1,406	5,142	18,336
Netherlands Antilles	NA	3,680	3,807
UK isls., Caribbean	53,493	31,150	15,191
Africa[1]	4,281	2,010	2,700
South Africa	932	687	704
Middle East[1]	25,363	15,407	6,506
Israel	15,007	7,231	3,012
Kuwait	NA	347	908
Lebanon	NA	NA	1
United Arab Emirates	1,371	591	64
Asia and Pacific[1]	409,749	362,003	192,647
Australia	55,862	49,543	18,775
China	3,815	3,150	NA
Hong Kong	4,854	4,272	1,493
India	4,888	3,344	NA
Japan	289,490	257,273	159,690
Korea, South	18,421	15,213	3,110
Malaysia	646	362	310
New Zealand	1,660	556	395
Philippines	NA	NA	47
Singapore	23,528	21,831	5,087
Taiwan	5,180	5,180	3,174
European Union[1,2]	1,573,371	1,484,806	814,033
OPEC[1,3]	14,407	11,437	4,330

NA = Not available. **Note:** On a historical cost basis for comparison purposes. Foreign direct investment in all industries. Book value of foreign direct investors' equity in, and net outstanding loans to, their U.S. affiliates. A U.S. affiliate is a U.S. business enterprise in which a single foreign direct investor owns at least 10% of the voting securities or the equivalent. (1) May include countries or territories not shown in table. (2) EU members in 2011: Austria, Belgium, Bulgaria, Cyprus, Czech Republic, Denmark, Estonia, Finland, France, Germany, Greece, Hungary, Ireland, Italy, Latvia, Lithuania, Luxembourg, Malta, Netherlands, Poland, Portugal, Romania, Slovakia, Slovenia, Spain, Sweden, and the United Kingdom. (3) Org. of the Petroleum Exporting Countries in 2011: Algeria, Angola, Ecuador, Iran, Iraq, Kuwait, Libya, Nigeria, Qatar, Saudi Arabia, United Arab Emirates, and Venezuela.

U.S. Direct Investment Abroad in Selected Countries and Territories, 2000-2011

Source: U.S. Bureau of Economic Analysis, U.S. Dept. of Commerce
(in millions of dollars)

	2011	2010	2000
All countries[1]	$4,155,551	$3,908,231	$1,316,247
Canada	318,964	296,691	132,472
Europe[1]	2,307,697	2,185,898	687,320
Austria	20,852	16,876	2,872
Belgium	52,888	73,526	17,973
Czech Republic	5,261	5,909	1,228
Denmark	14,034	9,828	5,270
Finland	1,504	1,472	1,342
France	89,293	92,820	42,628
Germany	106,887	105,828	55,508
Greece	1,252	1,798	795
Hungary	3,263	4,863	1,920
Ireland	188,274	190,478	35,903
Italy	25,338	29,015	23,484
Luxembourg	335,279	274,923	27,849
Netherlands	595,139	521,427	115,429
Norway	28,462	33,843	4,379
Poland	12,327	12,684	3,884
Portugal	2,879	2,639	2,664
Russia	9,733	9,880	1,147
Spain	58,619	58,053	21,236
Sweden	26,953	29,444	25,959
Switzerland	124,964	143,627	55,377
Turkey	5,203	5,693	1,826
United Kingdom	549,339	508,369	230,762
Latin America and other Western Hemisphere[1]	831,151	724,405	266,576
South America[1]	148,386	136,401	84,220
Argentina	13,309	12,111	17,488
Brazil	71,101	66,021	36,717
Chile	34,187	26,260	10,052
Colombia	6,874	6,574	3,693
Ecuador	1,201	1,250	832
Peru	7,753	7,907	3,130
Venezuela	12,110	13,693	10,531
Central America[1]	$103,752	$104,127	$73,841
Costa Rica	1,542	1,651	1,716
Honduras	930	1,027	399
Mexico	91,402	90,304	39,352
Panama	5,692	6,040	30,758
Other Western Hemisphere[1]	579,014	483,877	108,515
Barbados	10,889	5,710	2,141
Bermuda	327,185	264,442	60,114
Dominican Republic	1,710	1,344	1,143
UK isls., Caribbean	180,761	149,039	33,451
Africa[1]	56,632	53,522	11,891
Egypt	14,581	11,746	1,998
Nigeria	4,994	5,224	470
South Africa	6,546	6,503	3,562
Middle East[1]	35,905	36,573	10,863
Israel	9,562	9,694	3,735
Saudi Arabia	8,659	8,005	3,661
United Arab Emirates	5,785	4,271	683
Asia and Pacific[1]	605,202	611,143	207,125
Australia	136,244	133,990	34,838
China	54,234	60,452	11,140
Hong Kong	52,542	54,035	27,447
India	24,663	27,066	2,379
Indonesia	11,591	15,502	8,904
Japan	116,533	113,263	57,091
Korea, South	NA	30,165	8,968
Malaysia	13,903	15,982	7,910
New Zealand	6,741	6,872	4,271
Philippines	5,321	6,579	3,638
Singapore	116,533	106,042	24,133
Taiwan	15,803	20,977	7,836
Thailand	11,308	12,701	5,824
European Union[1,2]	2,094,413	1,945,326	609,674
OPEC[1,3]	54,400	56,379	28,545

NA = Not available. **Note:** On a historical cost basis for comparison purposes. U.S. direct investment in all industries. Book value of U.S. direct investors' equity in, and net outstanding loans to, their foreign affiliates. A foreign affiliate is a foreign business enterprise in which a single U.S. investor owns at least 10% of the voting securities or the equivalent. (1) May include countries or territories not shown in table. (2) EU members in 2011: Austria, Belgium, Bulgaria, Cyprus, Czech Republic, Denmark, Estonia, Finland, France, Germany, Greece, Hungary, Ireland, Italy, Latvia, Lithuania, Luxembourg, Malta, Netherlands, Poland, Portugal, Romania, Slovakia, Slovenia, Spain, Sweden, and the United Kingdom. (3) Org. of the Petroleum Exporting Countries in 2011: Algeria, Angola, Ecuador, Iran, Iraq, Kuwait, Libya, Nigeria, Qatar, Saudi Arabia, United Arab Emirates, and Venezuela.

TRANSPORTATION AND TRAVEL

Top Motor Vehicle Producing Nations, 2011

Source: R.L. Polk

(numbers in thousands of units; ranked by total production)

	Total motor vehicles	Cars	Trucks[1]	% change, 2010-11[2]		Total motor vehicles	Cars	Trucks[1]	% change, 2010-11[2]
China[3]	16,510	12,251	4,259	2.27%	South Africa	527	320	206	8.21%
U.S.	8,462	3,072	5,391	10.88	Malaysia	514	385	129	−6.55
Japan	7,901	7,159	743	−14.09	Taiwan	335	290	46	12.42
Germany	6,109	5,872	237	7.18	Romania	335	310	25	−22.27
South Korea	4,564	4,222	342	9.08	Australia	229	196	33	−4.18
India	3,511	3,106	405	11.39	Uzbekistan	222	222	NA	1.83
Brazil	3,112	2,493	618	−8.60	Hungary	218	218	NA	−2.68
Mexico	2,551	1,659	892	13.03	Sweden	206	206	NA	7.85
Spain	2,330	1,836	494	−1.69	Portugal	188	142	46	22.08
France	2,241	1,929	312	2.75	Slovenia	174	169	5	−17.92
Canada	2,127	991	1,137	2.56	Colombia	136	132	4	NA
Russia	1,897	1,747	149	42.42	Austria	130	130	NA	49.43
Iran	1,562	1,392	170	30.17	Philippines	98	47	51	NA
UK	1,447	1,344	103	4.70	**Asia-Pacific/**				
Thailand	1,437	538	899	6.92	**Middle East**	37,321	29,655	7,665	0.95
Czech Republic	1,199	1,196	3	14.19	**Western Europe**	13,992	12,552	1,440	4.03
Turkey	1,145	640	505	8.12	**NAFTA**	13,140	5,721	7,419	8.75
Poland	827	724	103	−6.76	**Central & Eastern**				
Argentina	820	577	243	14.37	**Europe**	6,717	5,926	791	13.44
Italy	734	486	248	−8.93	**South America**	4,203	3,289	914	−2.84
Indonesia	661	70	590	NA	**Africa**	653	443	210	16.61
Slovakia	578	578	NA	9.06	**World total**	76,027	57,587	18,440	3.70
Belgium	562	562	NA	7.25					

NA = Not available. **Note:** Regional and world totals include countries or territories not listed. (1) Light commercial vehicles (pickup trucks and vans). (2) Percent change in number of total motor vehicles. (3) Not including Taiwan.

World Motor Vehicle Production, 1950-2011

Source: For 1950-97, American Automobile Manufacturers Assn.; for 1998 and on, Automotive News Data Center and R.L. Polk

(in thousands of units)

Year	United States	Canada	Europe[1]	Japan	Other	World total	U.S. % of world total
1950	8,006	388	1,991	32	160	10,577	75.7%
1960	7,905	398	6,837	482	866	16,488	47.9
1970	8,284	1,160	13,049	5,289	1,637	29,419	28.2
1980	8,010	1,324	15,496	11,043	2,692	38,565	20.8
1985	11,653	1,933	16,113	12,271	2,939	44,909	25.9
1990	9,783	1,928	18,866	13,487	4,496	48,554	20.1
1995	11,985	2,408	17,045	10,196	8,349	49,983	24.0
2000	12,832	2,952	17,678	10,145	16,098	59,704	21.5
2001	11,518	2,535	17,825	9,777	16,170	57,705	19.7
2002	12,328	2,624	17,419	10,240	16,975	59,587	20.7
2003	12,145	2,547	16,943	10,286	19,641	61,562	19.7
2004	12,021	2,698	20,850	10,512	16,573	65,654	18.3
2005	12,018	2,665	20,855	10,800	20,691	67,892	17.7
2006	11,351	2,545	21,490	11,486	23,180	70,992	16.0
2007	10,611	2,602	22,858	11,596	26,019	74,647	14.2
2008	8,503	2,046	21,608	10,969	31,224	67,602	12.6
2009	5,591	1,476	17,075	7,648	32,374	59,096	9.5
2010	7,632	2,074	19,371	9,197	35,036	73,311	10.4
2011	8,462	2,127	20,709	7,901	36,828	76,027	11.1

Note: Data for 1998 and on are not fully comparable with earlier years because they are derived from different sources. Number of units may not add up to totals due to rounding. (1) Prior to 2004, numbers exclude Eastern European production.

New and Used Passenger Cars Imported into the U.S. by Country of Origin, 1970-2011

Source: Foreign Trade Division, U.S. Census Bureau

(in number of units)

Year	Japan	Germany[1]	Italy	UK	Sweden	France	S. Korea	Mexico	Canada	Total[2]
1970	381,338	674,945	42,523	76,257	57,844	37,114	NA	NA	692,783	2,013,420
1975	695,573	370,012	102,344	67,106	51,993	15,647	NA	0	733,766	2,074,653
1980	1,991,502	338,711	46,899	32,517	61,496	47,386	NA	1	594,770	3,116,448
1985	2,527,467	473,110	8,689	24,474	142,640	42,882	NA	13,647	1,144,805	4,397,679
1990	1,867,794	245,286	11,045	27,271	93,084	1,976	201,475	215,986	1,220,221	3,944,602
1995	1,114,360	204,932	1,031	42,450	82,593	14	131,718	462,800	1,552,691	3,624,428
1996	1,190,896	234,909	1,365	44,373	86,619	27	225,623	550,867	1,690,733	4,069,113
1997	1,387,812	300,489	1,912	43,691	79,780	67	222,568	544,075	1,731,209	4,378,295
1998	1,456,081	373,330	2,104	49,891	84,543	56	211,650	584,795	1,837,615	4,673,418
1999	1,707,277	461,061	1,697	68,394	83,399	186	372,965	639,878	2,170,427	5,639,616
2000	1,839,093	488,323	3,125	81,196	86,707	134	568,121	934,000	2,138,811	6,324,284
2001	1,790,346	494,131	2,580	82,487	92,439	92	633,769	861,853	1,855,789	6,065,138
2002	2,046,902	574,455	3,504	157,633	87,709	150	627,881	845,181	1,882,660	6,477,659
2003	1,770,355	561,482	2,943	207,158	119,773	298	692,863	680,214	1,811,892	6,127,485
2004	1,727,065	547,008	3,373	185,621	98,131	2,417	860,424	652,509	2,035,345	6,521,248
2005	1,832,534	547,191	5,377	184,716	93,736	412	730,500	693,149	1,967,985	6,564,844
2006	2,347,532	532,022	5,469	148,014	81,008	567	697,061	947,824	1,963,922	7,380,077
2007	2,300,913	466,458	5,650	108,576	92,600	1,746	676,594	889,474	1,912,744	7,220,792
2008	2,190,013	502,971	5,783	110,737	59,638	28,198	612,300	928,273	1,609,005	6,525,836
2009	1,238,773	348,093	3,067	78,999	27,017	16,909	476,912	649,740	1,164,849	4,276,163
2010	1,569,190	506,053	4,298	96,689	38,749	4,153	515,601	902,565	1,741,493	5,668,081
2011	1,436,515	537,178	5,390	95,759	26,878	5,018	587,574	968,403	1,836,166	5,819,826

NA = Not available. **Note:** Excludes cars assembled in U.S. foreign trade zones. (1) Figures prior to 1991 are for West Germany. (2) Includes units imported from countries not shown in table.

Passenger Car Production in U.S. Plants, 2010-11

Source: WardsAuto Group, a division of Penton Media Inc.

(in number of units)

	2011	2010
AUTOALLIANCE[1] TOTAL	**117,836**	**122,754**
Ford Mustang	78,286	77,586
Mazda6	39,550	45,168
CHRYSLER TOTAL	**250,417**	**169,398**
Chrysler 200 Series	122,625	2,197
Chrysler Sebring	—	39,986
Chrysler total	**122,625**	**42,183**
Dodge Avenger	75,951	59,170
Dodge Caliber	51,841	67,586
Dodge Viper	—	459
Dodge total	**127,792**	**127,215**
FORD TOTAL	**311,814**	**298,639**
Ford Focus	221,514	199,502
Ford Taurus	77,664	83,052
Ford total	**299,178**	**282,554**
Lincoln MKS	12,636	16,085
GENERAL MOTORS TOTAL	**721,501**	**600,703**
Buick LaCrosse	64,729	73,480
Buick Lucerne	15,882	29,654
Buick Verano	4,471	—
Buick total	**85,082**	**103,134**
Cadillac CTS	64,935	60,688
Cadillac DTS	6,515	21,023
Cadillac STS	1,907	4,792
Cadillac total	**73,357**	**86,503**
Chevrolet Cobalt	—	91,796
Chevrolet Corvette	13,222	15,791
Chevrolet Cruze	281,810	66,303
Chevrolet Malibu	214,388	235,956
Chevrolet Sonic	36,527	—
Chevrolet Volt	14,510	1,219
Chevrolet total	**560,457**	**411,065**

	2011	2010
Opel Ampera	2,605	—
Pontiac G6	—	1
HONDA TOTAL	**349,969**	**426,119**
Acura TL	35,763	35,294
Honda Accord	229,439	295,709
Honda Civic	84,767	95,116
HYUNDAI TOTAL	**338,127**	**238,387**
Hyundai Elantra	112,665	19,780
Hyundai Sonata	225,462	218,607
KIA MOTORS TOTAL	**35,132**	**—**
Kia Optima	35,132	—
MITSUBISHI TOTAL	**26,583**	**22,969**
Mitsubishi Eclipse	7,142	6,424
Mitsubishi Galant	19,441	16,545
NISSAN TOTAL	**385,109**	**346,891**
Nissan Altima	319,203	275,115
Nissan Maxima	65,906	71,776
NUMMI[2] TOTAL	**—**	**63,319**
Toyota Corolla	—	63,319
SUBARU[3] TOTAL	**125,738**	**131,522**
Subaru Legacy	46,568	43,791
Toyota Camry	79,170	87,731
TOYOTA TOTAL	**268,314**	**310,404**
Toyota Avalon	38,684	40,155
Toyota Camry	227,663	270,249
Toyota Corolla	1,967	—
VOLKSWAGEN TOTAL	**45,857**	**—**
Volkswagen Passat	45,857	—
TOTAL CARS	**2,976,397**	**2,731,105**

— = No production. (1) Joint venture between Ford and Mazda. (2) NUMMI (New United Motor Manufacturing, Inc.) was a joint venture between GM and Toyota (1984-2010). (3) SIA (Subaru of Indiana Automotive) also builds the Toyota Camry in a collaboration with Toyota.

Domestic and Imported Retail Car Sales in the U.S., 1980-2011

Source: WardsAuto Group, a division of Penton Media Inc.

(in number of units)

Year	Cars Domestic[1]	Imports	Total cars	Light trucks Domestic[1]	Imports	Total light trucks	All vehicles Domestic[1]	Imports	Total vehicles
1980	6,579,778	2,369,457	8,949,235	1,750,735	478,887	2,229,622	8,330,513	2,848,344	11,178,857
1981	6,180,784	2,308,418	8,489,202	1,591,575	461,975	2,053,550	7,772,359	2,770,393	10,542,752
1982	5,756,658	2,199,802	7,956,460	1,968,534	430,330	2,398,864	7,725,192	2,630,132	10,355,324
1983	6,795,299	2,352,739	9,148,038	2,477,259	496,969	2,974,228	9,272,558	2,849,708	12,122,266
1984	7,951,523	2,372,172	10,323,695	3,208,371	674,153	3,882,524	11,159,894	3,046,325	14,206,219
1985	8,204,670	2,774,517	10,979,187	3,629,080	832,186	4,461,266	11,833,750	3,606,703	15,440,453
1986	8,215,017	3,189,222	11,404,239	3,675,914	977,920	4,653,834	11,890,931	4,167,142	16,058,073
1987	7,085,279	3,106,598	10,191,877	3,791,882	921,698	4,713,580	10,877,161	4,028,296	14,905,457
1988	7,543,116	3,003,692	10,546,808	4,199,643	710,661	4,910,304	11,742,759	3,714,353	15,457,112
1989	7,098,098	2,680,419	9,778,517	4,113,441	641,387	4,754,828	11,211,539	3,321,806	14,533,345
1990	6,918,869	2,384,346	9,303,215	3,956,756	611,941	4,568,697	10,875,625	2,996,287	13,871,912
1991	6,161,573	2,023,406	8,184,979	3,605,633	538,008	4,143,641	9,767,206	2,561,414	12,328,620
1992	6,285,916	1,927,197	8,213,113	4,247,097	408,003	4,655,100	10,533,013	2,335,200	12,868,213
1993	6,741,667	1,776,192	8,517,859	5,000,482	377,639	5,378,121	11,742,149	2,153,831	13,895,980
1994	7,255,303	1,735,214	8,990,517	5,658,302	409,759	6,068,061	12,913,605	2,144,973	15,058,578
1995	7,113,902	1,506,257	8,620,159	5,705,708	402,181	6,107,889	12,819,610	1,908,438	14,728,048
1996	7,206,349	1,272,196	8,478,545	6,179,881	438,757	6,618,638	13,386,230	1,710,953	15,097,183
1997	6,862,175	1,355,305	8,217,480	6,324,758	579,483	6,904,241	13,186,933	1,934,788	15,121,721
1998	6,705,208	1,379,781	8,084,989	6,802,016	656,002	7,458,018	13,507,224	2,035,783	15,543,007
1999	6,918,781	1,718,927	8,637,708	7,480,607	775,223	8,255,830	14,399,388	2,494,150	16,893,538
2000	6,761,603	2,016,120	8,777,723	7,719,707	852,325	8,572,032	14,481,310	2,868,445	17,349,755
2001	6,254,371	2,097,629	8,352,000	7,789,089	981,280	8,770,369	14,043,460	3,078,909	17,122,369
2002	5,816,671	2,225,584	8,042,255	7,707,738	1,066,375	8,774,113	13,524,409	3,291,959	16,816,368
2003	5,472,500	2,083,051	7,555,551	7,856,322	1,227,180	9,083,502	13,328,822	3,310,231	16,639,053
2004	5,333,496	2,149,059	7,482,555	8,138,107	1,246,258	9,384,365	13,471,603	3,395,317	16,866,920
2005	5,473,450	2,186,533	7,659,983	8,072,456	1,215,315	9,287,771	13,545,906	3,401,848	16,947,754
2006	5,416,828	2,344,764	7,761,592	7,396,058	1,346,750	8,742,808	12,812,886	3,691,514	16,504,400
2007	5,197,271	2,365,063	7,562,334	7,138,803	1,388,085	8,526,888	12,336,074	3,753,148	16,089,222
2008	4,490,836	2,278,271	6,769,107	5,329,165	1,096,469	6,425,634	9,820,001	3,374,740	13,194,741
2009	3,557,608	1,843,282	5,400,890	4,116,550	884,242	5,000,792	7,674,158	2,727,524	10,401,682
2010	3,791,877	1,843,556	5,635,433	5,020,441	898,644	5,919,085	8,812,318	2,742,200	11,554,518
2011	4,156,587	1,932,835	6,089,422	5,662,578	982,443	6,645,021	9,819,165	2,915,278	12,734,443

Note: Vehicles are cars and light trucks belonging to Gross Vehicle Weight (GWV) classes 1-3 (under 14,001 lbs). (1) Includes the U.S., Canada, and Mexico.

U.S. Retail Car Sales by Vehicle Size, 1985-2011

Source: WardsAuto Group, a division of Penton Media Inc.
(percent of total U.S. sales)

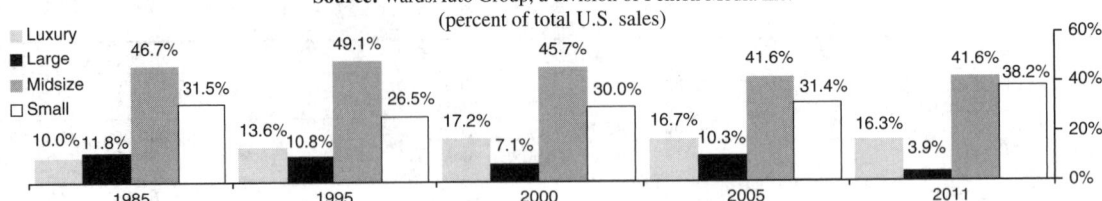

U.S. Light Truck Sales by Type, 1985-2011

Source: WardsAuto Group, a division of Penton Media Inc.
(percent of total U.S. sales)

Note: Comm. chassis sales (not shown) were 1.0% for 1985, 0.7% for 1995, 0.2% for 2000, 0.1% for 2005, and 0.4% for 2011.

Top-Selling Passenger Cars in the U.S., 2008-11

Source: Ward's Automotive Group, a division of Penton Media Inc.
(ranked by number of vehicles sold)

Rank, car	2011 sales	Rank, car	2011 sales	Rank, car	2011 sales
1. Toyota Camry	308,510	8. Honda Civic	221,235	15. Nissan Sentra	114,991
2. Nissan Altima	268,981	9. Chevrolet Malibu	204,808	16. Mazda3	102,417
3. Ford Fusion	248,067	10. Hyundai Elantra	186,361	17. Kia Soul	102,267
4. Toyota Corolla	240,259	11. Volkswagen Jetta	177,360	18. Nissan Versa	99,730
5. Honda Accord	235,625	12. Ford Focus	175,717	19. BMW 3 Series	94,371
6. Chevrolet Cruze	231,732	13. Chevrolet Impala	171,434	20. Chevrolet Camaro	88,249
7. Hyundai Sonata	225,961	14. Toyota Prius	136,463		

Rank, car	2010 sales	Rank, car	2009 sales	Rank, car	2008 sales
1. Toyota Camry	327,804	1. Toyota Camry	356,824	1. Toyota Camry	436,617
2. Honda Accord	282,530	2. Toyota Corolla/Matrix	296,874	2. Honda Accord	372,789
3. Toyota Corolla/Matrix	266,082	3. Honda Accord	287,492	3. Toyota Corolla/Matrix	351,007
4. Honda Civic	260,218	4. Honda Civic	259,722	4. Honda Civic	339,289
5. Nissan Altima	229,263	5. Nissan Altima	203,568	5. Nissan Altima	269,668
6. Ford Fusion	219,219	6. Ford Fusion	180,671	6. Chevrolet Impala	265,840
7. Chevrolet Malibu	198,770	7. Chevrolet Impala	165,565	7. Ford Focus	195,823
8. Hyundai Sonata	196,623	8. Chevrolet Malibu	161,568	8. Chevrolet Cobalt	188,045
9. Ford Focus	172,421	9. Ford Focus	160,433	9. Chevrolet Malibu	178,253
10. Chevrolet Impala	172,078	10. Toyota Prius	139,682	10. Toyota Prius	158,884

Top-Selling Light Trucks in the U.S., 2009-11

Source: WardsAuto Group, a division of Penton Media Inc.
(ranked by number of vehicles sold)

Rank, truck	2011 sales	Rank, truck	2010 sales	Rank, truck	2009 sales
1. Ford F-Series	552,647	1. Ford F-Series	502,125	1. Ford F-Series	392,112
2. Chevrolet Silverado	415,130	2. Chevrolet Silverado	370,135	2. Chevrolet Silverado	316,544
3. Ford Escape	254,293	3. Honda CR-V	203,714	3. Honda CR-V	191,214
4. Ram Pickup	237,236	4. Ram Pickup	194,175	4. Ram Pickup	173,066
5. Honda CR-V	218,373	5. Ford Escape	191,026	5. Ford Escape	173,044
6. Chevrolet Equinox	193,274	6. Toyota RAV4	170,877	6. Toyota RAV4	149,088
7. GMC Sierra	149,170	7. Chevrolet Equinox	149,979	7. GMC Sierra	111,842
8. Ford Explorer	135,704	8. GMC Sierra	129,794	8. Toyota Tacoma	111,824
9. Toyota RAV4	132,237	9. Ford Edge	118,637	9. Honda Odyssey	100,133
10. Kia Sorento	130,235	10. Chrysler Town & Country	112,275	10. Lexus RX	93,379

Most Popular Colors, by Vehicle Type, 2011

Source: WardsAuto Group, a division of Penton Media Inc.; Du Pont Automotive Products; for 2011 model year

Luxury cars/SUVs		Intermediate cars/CUVs		Compact/sports cars		Light trucks	
Color	Percent	Color	Percent	Color	Percent	Color	Percent
Black/black effect	27%	White/white pearl	18%	Silver	20%	White/white pearl	29%
White/white pearl	22	Black/black effect	18	Black/black effect	19	Black/black effect	17
Silver	15	Silver	17	White/white pearl	18	Silver	14
Red	10	Gray	16	Gray	17	Red	11
Gray	8	Blue	10	Red	10	Gray	11
Beige/brown	8	Red	10	Blue	9	Blue	8
Yellow/gold	5	Beige/brown	6	Beige/brown	5	Beige/brown	4
Blue	4	Yellow/gold	4	Green	1	Green	3
Green	<1	Green	1	Yellow/gold	<1	Yellow/gold	3
Other	<1	Other	<1	Other	<1	Other	<1

U.S. Light-Duty Vehicle Fuel Efficiency, 1975-2011

Source: Natl. Vehicle and Fuel Emissions Laboratory, Office of Transportation and Air Quality, U.S. Environmental Protection Agency

Cars and light-duty trucks (SUVs, minivans, passenger vans, and pickup trucks) showed significant fuel-efficiency improvements from 1975 through 1987, when the fuel economy for both reached a high of 22 miles per gallon (mpg). After 1987, the fuel economy value entered a long-term decline, reaching 19.3 mpg in 2004 before the trend reversed itself. Since 2005, fuel economy has increased. Most of this increase has been due to higher truck fuel economy.

In Dec. 2006, the EPA changed its method of calculating adjusted real-world fuel economy values due to changed driving habits, including more aggressive driving and increased air conditioning use, among other factors. Data from 1986 on were revised under this method. Comparing laboratory 55/45 fuel economy values, however, shows an all-time high was reached in 2011.

Sales of light-duty trucks, which in recent years have had an average fuel efficiency 5-7 mpg less than cars, accounted for only 19% of the market in 1975 but have been at about 40% since 1998. This increase has been a major factor in the leveling off in the fuel efficiency of the average light-duty vehicle. But technological innovations have helped to boost fuel efficiency in recent years.

Year[1]	Cars (mpg)	Light-duty trucks (mpg)	All light-duty vehicles (mpg)	Year[1]	Cars (mpg)	Light-duty trucks (mpg)	All light-duty vehicles (mpg)
1975	13.5	11.6	13.1	2002	22.3	16.4	19.5
1980	20.0	15.8	19.2	2003	22.7	16.6	19.6
1985	23.0	17.5	21.3	2004	22.5	16.4	19.3
1990	23.3	17.4	21.2	2005	22.9	16.9	19.9
1995	23.2	17.0	20.5	2006	22.8	17.1	20.1
1996	22.9	17.2	20.4	2007	23.5	17.3	20.6
1997	22.9	16.9	20.1	2008	23.7	17.7	21.0
1998	22.9	17.1	20.1	2009	24.8	18.4	22.4
1999	22.5	16.6	19.7	2010	25.5	18.7	22.6
2000	22.4	16.9	19.8	2011	25.9	18.9	22.8
2001	22.4	16.4	19.6				

Note: Adjusted mpg composite values (city and highway fuel efficiency combined in a 55%/45% ratio) are used for all vehicles and are intended to reflect real-world use. (1) Because of changes in methodology, mpg figures prior to 1986 are not entirely comparable with later values.

Registered Cars in the U.S., 1900-2010

Source: Office of Highway Policy Information, Federal Highway Administration, U.S. Dept. of Transportation

(includes automobiles for public and private use)

Year	Reg. cars	Year	Reg. cars	Year	Reg. cars	Year	Reg. cars	Year	Reg. cars
1900	8,000	1940	27,465,826	1980	121,600,843	1996	129,728,311	2003	135,669,897
1905	77,400	1945	25,796,985	1985	127,885,193	1997	129,748,704	2004	136,430,651
1910	458,377	1950	40,339,077	1990	133,700,497	1998	131,838,538	2005	136,568,083
1915	2,332,426	1955	52,144,739	1991	128,299,601	1999	132,432,044	2006	135,399,945
1920	8,131,522	1960	61,671,390	1992	126,581,148	2000	133,621,420	2007	135,932,930
1925	17,481,001	1965	75,257,588	1993	127,327,189	2001	137,633,467	2008	137,079,843
1930	23,034,753	1970	89,243,557	1994	127,883,469	2002	135,920,677	2009	134,879,600
1935	22,567,827	1975	106,705,934	1995	128,386,775	2002	135,920,677	2010	130,892,240

Note: There were no publicly owned vehicles before 1925; statistics also exclude military vehicles for all years. Alaska and Hawaii data included since 1960.

Licensed Drivers, by Age and Sex, 1980-2010

Source: Office of Highway Policy Information, Federal Highway Administration, U.S. Dept. of Transportation

(numbers in thousands)

Age	1980 Total	1990 Total	2000 Male	2000 Female	2000 Total[1]	2010 Male	2010 Female	2010 Total[1]	2010 % total drivers
Under 16	93	43	14	13	27	199	198	398	0.2%
16	1,823	1,443	755	715	1,470	608	605	1,213	0.6
17	2,790	2,132	1,201	1,130	2,331	1,025	1,004	2,028	1.0
18	3,247	2,595	1,471	1,368	2,839	1,408	1,323	2,731	1.3
19	3,542	3,037	1,589	1,488	3,077	1,641	1,546	3,187	1.5
19 and under	**11,496**	**9,249**	**5,029**	**4,714**	**9,744**	**4,880**	**4,676**	**9,556**	**4.5**
20	3,636	3,229	1,611	1,530	3,140	1,744	1,682	3,426	1.6
21	3,733	3,249	1,620	1,552	3,172	1,756	1,717	3,474	1.7
22	3,811	3,262	1,624	1,557	3,182	1,757	1,725	3,483	1.7
23	3,938	3,398	1,656	1,591	3,247	1,767	1,748	3,515	1.7
24	3,915	3,758	1,648	1,577	3,225	1,792	1,779	3,571	1.7
20-24	19,032	16,897	8,159	7,807	15,966	8,817	8,651	17,469	8.3
25-29	18,925	19,895	8,988	8,598	17,586	9,179	9,253	18,431	8.8
30-34	17,369	20,578	9,767	9,387	19,155	8,934	8,915	17,849	8.5
35-39	13,696	19,055	10,622	10,438	21,059	9,079	9,082	18,161	8.6
40-44	11,134	16,905	10,577	10,516	21,093	9,613	9,565	19,178	9.1
45-49	10,076	13,020	9,578	9,575	19,154	10,381	10,433	20,814	9.9
50-54	10,090	10,484	8,448	8,420	16,868	10,241	10,388	20,628	9.8
55-59	9,770	9,438	6,394	6,366	12,760	9,127	9,313	18,440	8.8
60-64	8,232	9,235	4,970	4,944	9,915	7,847	8,011	15,858	7.5
65-69	6,580	8,375	4,183	4,203	8,386	5,652	5,816	11,468	5.5
70-74	NA	NA	3,645	3,823	7,468	4,029	4,202	8,231	3.9
75-79	NA	NA	2,820	3,091	5,911	2,966	3,192	6,158	2.9
80-84	NA	NA	1,657	1,854	3,511	2,090	2,373	4,464	2.1
85 and over	**NA**	**NA**	**958**	**1,093**	**2,050**	**1,541**	**1,870**	**3,411**	**1.6**
Total	**145,295**	**167,015**	**95,796**	**94,829**	**190,625**	**104,374**	**105,740**	**210,115**	**100.0**

NA = Not available. (1) Numbers may not add up to totals due to rounding.

Selected Motor Vehicle Statistics

Source: Federal Highway Admin., U.S. Dept. of Transportation; Insurance Inst. for Highway Safety; American Petroleum Inst.

Driver's license age requirements, state gas tax, and safety belt use laws (incl. laws passed, but not in effect) as of 2012. Other figures are for 2010.

STATE	Driver's license age requirements Learner's permit	Regular[1]	State gas tax (cents/gal)	Safety belt use law[5]	Licensed drivers Per 1,000 resident pop.	Per reg. motor vehicle	Reg. motor vehicles per 1,000 pop.	Fuel use per reg. motor vehicle (gallons)	Annual miles driven Per gal used	Per reg. vehicle	Per lic. driver
Alabama	15	17	16.0	P	796	0.83	974	731	18.87	13,787	16,859
Alaska	14	16y, 6m	8.0	P	725	0.74	1,000	717	9.42	6,754	9,313
Arizona	15y, 6m	16y, 6m	18.0	S	695	1.04	676	794	17.52	13,903	13,517
Arkansas	14	18	21.5	P	713	1.02	711	1,006	16.06	16,159	16,125
California	15y, 6m	17	36.0	P	638	0.71	833	568	18.32	10,410	13,592
Colorado	15	17	22.0	S	751	2.49	831	642	17.50	11,229	12,420
Connecticut	16	18[2]	25.0	P	821	0.97	862	579	17.53	10,154	10,664
Delaware	16	17[2]	23.0	P	774	0.88	890	645	17.35	11,198	12,874
Dist. of Columbia	16	18[3]	23.5	P	640	1.93	352	689	24.63	16,965	9,328
Florida	15	18	4.0	P	742	0.99	764	668	20.39	13,620	14,033
Georgia	15	18[2]	7.5	P	672	0.78	795	799	18.16	14,506	17,167
Hawaii	15y, 6m	17[2]	17.0	P	669	1.03	665	523	21.14	11,050	10,990
Idaho	14y, 6m	16[2]	25.0	S	682	0.82	845	717	16.62	11,926	14,774
Illinois	15	18[2]	19.0	P	653	0.84	786	628	16.71	10,496	12,633
Indiana	15	18[2]	18.0	P	856	0.99	879	763	17.42	13,296	13,649
Iowa	14	17[2]	21.0	P	711	0.66	1,087	711	13.32	9,475	14,486
Kansas	14	16y, 6m	24.0	S(a)	713	0.85	854	700	17.52	12,273	14,706
Kentucky	16	17[2]	28.5	P	680	0.83	827	838	15.96	13,376	16,272
Louisiana	15	17[2]	20.0	P	691	0.79	901	744	14.94	11,120	14,500
Maine	15	16y, 9m[2]	30.0	P	768	0.99	793	836	16.51	13,806	14,268
Maryland	15y, 9m	18	23.5	P	679	0.87	789	716	17.19	12,316	14,324
Massachusetts	16	18[2]	21.0	S	701	0.87	815	599	17.02	10,192	11,837
Michigan	14y, 9m	17[2]	19.0	P	717	0.92	940	578	18.16	10,507	13,775
Minnesota	15	17[2]	28.5	P	619	0.68	914	662	17.64	11,682	17,258
Mississippi	15	16y, 6m	18.0	P	650	0.97	679	1,100	17.97	19,763	20,659
Missouri	15	17y, 11m	17.0	S(b)	709	0.83	860	816	16.84	13,751	16,689
Montana	14y, 6m	16[2]	27.0	S	752	0.83	936	806	14.99	12,086	15,048
Nebraska	15	17	26.2	S	740	0.77	987	713	15.12	10,784	14,382
Nevada	15y, 6m	18[2]	23.0	S	626	1.27	504	1,031	15.04	15,510	12,487
New Hampshire	15y, 6m	18[2]	18.0	None	788	0.87	914	675	16.08	10,861	12,598
New Jersey	16	18	10.5	P(a)	677	0.92	754	752	14.65	11,018	12,268
New Mexico	15	16y, 6m[2]	17.0	P	683	0.90	783	867	18.12	15,706	18,013
New York	16	18[2,4]	8.1	P	582	1.04	529	696	18.38	12,799	11,630
North Carolina	15	16y, 6m[2]	37.5	P(a)	686	1.16	602	957	18.63	17,828	15,663
North Dakota	14	16	23.0	S	718	0.67	1,094	855	13.14	11,232	17,103
Ohio	15y, 6m	18[2]	28.0	S	690	0.72	850	666	17.14	11,411	14,044
Oklahoma	15y, 6m	17[4]	16.0	P	626	0.72	895	805	17.66	14,221	20,329
Oregon	15	17[2]	30.0	P	723	0.93	796	673	16.44	11,073	12,194
Pennsylvania	16	17	12.0	S(b)	688	0.89	787	656	15.31	10,042	11,483
Rhode Island	16	17y, 6m[2]	32.0	P	711	0.97	743	570	18.57	10,583	11,072
South Carolina	15	16y, 6m	16.0	P	722	0.93	791	922	14.55	13,419	14,720
South Dakota	14	16	22.0	S	740	0.67	1,137	712	13.46	9,579	14,721
Tennessee	15	17	20.0	P	696	0.88	806	803	17.15	13,774	15,943
Texas	15	18[4]	20.0	P	603	0.83	684	944	14.42	13,611	15,439
Utah	15	17[2]	24.5	S(b)	601	0.62	961	551	18.16	10,014	16,017
Vermont	15	16y, 6m[2]	19.0	S	821	0.93	906	690	18.53	12,790	14,115
Virginia	15y, 6m	18[2]	17.5	S	675	0.89	769	821	16.29	13,364	15,210
Washington	15	17[2]	37.5	S	759	0.94	696	712	17.15	12,213	11,200
West Virginia	15	17	20.5	S	651	0.86	775	800	16.71	13,377	15,923
Wisconsin	15y, 6m	16y, 9m[2]	30.9	P	727	0.84	874	664	18.01	11,961	14,376
Wyoming	15	16y, 6m[2]	13.0	S	744	0.66	1,177	1,067	13.52	14,426	22,810
U.S. AVERAGE			21.0		681	0.87	784	721	17.01	12,255	14,118

Note: Most states have graduated licensing systems that phase in full driving privileges. During the learner's stage, driving generally is not permitted without adult supervision. In an intermediate stage, young licensees may be allowed to drive unsupervised only under certain conditions. (1) Min. age at which all restrictions may be lifted on private passenger car operation. (2) Applicants under a specified age (typically between 17 and 19) must complete driver education. Some states allow applicants to substitute home training, state-sponsored traffic school, or a number of hrs. of supervised driving for driver ed. (3) Learner's stage mandatory for all license applicants regardless of age. (4) Minimum age for an unrestricted driver's license may be lower if the applicant has completed driver education. (5) P = Officer may stop vehicle for violation (primary); S = officer may issue seat belt citation only when vehicle is stopped for another moving violation (secondary). (a) Secondary enforcement for rear seat occupants. (b) Primary enforcement for children under a specified age.

Handheld Phone and Texting Device Laws for Drivers, 2012
Source: Insurance Institute for Highway Safety; as of July 2012

State	Handheld ban	Texting ban	Enforcement	State	Handheld ban	Texting ban	Enforcement	State	Handheld ban	Texting ban	Enforcement
AL	(1)	Yes	P	KY	No	Yes	P	ND	No	Yes	P
AK	No	Yes	P	LA	(7)	Yes	P	OH	No	Yes	P10
AZ	No	No	NA	ME	No	Yes	P	OK	(9)	(11)	P
AR	(2)	Yes	(3)	MD	Yes	Yes	S8	OR	Yes	Yes	P
CA	Yes	Yes	P4	MA	No	Yes	P	PA	No	Yes	P
CO	No	Yes	P	MI	No	Yes	P	RI	No	Yes	P
CT	Yes	Yes	P	MN	No	Yes	P	SC	No	No	NA
DE	Yes	Yes	P	MS	No	(9)	P	SD	No	No	NA
DC	Yes	Yes	P	MO	No	(2)	P	TN	No	Yes	P
FL	No	No	NA	MT	No	No	NA	TX	(12)	(13)	P
GA	No	Yes	P	NE	No	Yes	S	UT	No14	Yes	P
HI	No	No	NA	NV	Yes	Yes	P	VT	No	Yes	P
ID	No	Yes	P	NH	No	Yes	P	VA	No	Yes	S
IL	(5)	Yes	P	NJ	Yes	Yes	P	WA	Yes	Yes	P
IN	No	Yes	P	NM	No	(9)	P	WV	Yes	Yes	P15
IA	No	Yes	(6)	NY	Yes	Yes	P	WI	No	Yes	P
KS	No	Yes	P	NC	No	Yes	P	WY	No	Yes	P

NA = Not available. P = Officer may stop vehicle for violation (primary); S = officer may issue citation only when vehicle is stopped for another moving violation (secondary). **Note:** Laws shown for licensed passenger car drivers. Different laws and regulations apply to school bus, municipal transit, and other mass transit operators. (1) Drivers ages 16 and 17 who have held an intermediate license for fewer than 6 months. (2) Drivers 21 and younger. (3) Primary for texting by all drivers; secondary for cell phone use by young drivers. (4) Secondary for hands-free cell phone use by young drivers. (5) Drivers in construction and school speed zones. (6) Primary for learner's permit and intermediate license holders; secondary for texting. (7) All learner's permit holders and all intermediate license holders are prohibited from driving while using a handheld cell phone, and all drivers younger than 18 are prohibited from using any cell phone. All drivers issued a first driver's license are prohibited from using a cell phone for one year. The cell phone ban is secondary for novice drivers age 18 and older. (8) Primary for texting. (9) Learner's permit and intermediate license holders. (10) Primary for drivers younger than 18; secondary for texting. (11) Learner's permit holders and intermediate license holders. (12) Drivers in school crossing zones. (13) Drivers in school crossing zones and drivers younger than 18. (14) A person is not prohibited from using a handheld wireless device while operating a motor vehicle while making or receiving a telephone call. (15) Secondary for handheld ban until July 1, 2013; then primary.

Tourism Trends

World tourist arrivals decreased 3.9% between 2008 and 2009 but increased 6.4% between 2009 and 2010, according to the World Tourism Organization's (UNWTO) *Barometer* publication. The number of international tourist arrivals in 2011 was an estimated 982 mil, an increase of 4.6% over the previous year. Worldwide tourism receipts, as measured in constant U.S. dollars, increased 7.7% from 2010 to 2011, to a value of $1.03 tril. Europe as a region again commanded the largest share of international tourist arrivals (51%) and receipts (45%) in 2011. Asia and the Pacific posted the second-largest share in each category, with 22% of international tourist arrivals and 28% of receipts worldwide. With 150 mil arrivals, the Americas held a 16% share of the world total. All regions showed an increase in the number of international tourist arrivals in 2011 compared to 2010 except for the Middle East, which had a decrease of 8.4%.

The International Air Transport Association (IATA) reported a 5.9% increase in international passenger traffic (as measured in revenue passenger kilometers) in 2011. It expected a decrease in the global airline industry's net profits in 2012. The price of fuel remains a challenge, having risen from 13% of airline operating costs in 2001 to 30% in 2011, although this is lower than the high of 33% three years earlier. IATA forecasted that fuel will account for 33% of operating costs in 2012.

World Tourism Receipts, 1990-2011
Source: World Tourism Organization (UNWTO), © UNWTO
(in billions of U.S. dollars)

Year	Receipts[1]	Year	Receipts[1]	Year	Receipts[1]	Year	Receipts[1]	Year	Receipts[1]	Year	Receipts[1]
1990	$262	1994	$356	1998	$445	2002	$484	2006	$744	2009	$853
1991	278	1995	403	1999	458	2003	533	2007	859	2010	928
1992	317	1996	439	2000	475	2004	634	2008	942	2011	1,030*
1993	323	1997	443	2001	466	2005	679				

*Preliminary. (1) Total of all transactions made by or on behalf of visitors for the duration of their visit. Does not include receipts from international passenger transport contracted from companies outside a traveler's country of residence.

Top 10 Countries in Tourism Earnings, 2011
Source: World Tourism Organization (UNWTO), © UNWTO
(in billions of U.S. dollars; ranked by receipts from most recent year)

Rank	Country	Receipts[1] 2011*	2010	% change, 2010-11	Rank	Country	Receipts[1] 2011*	2010	% change, 2010-11
1.	United States	$116.3	$103.5	12.3%	6.	Germany	$38.8	$34.7	6.7%
2.	Spain	59.9	52.5	8.6	7.	United Kingdom	35.9	32.4	6.9
3.	France	53.8	46.6	10.1	8.	Australia	31.4	29.8	-6.2
4.	China[2]	48.5	45.8	5.8	9.	Macao	NA	27.8	NA
5.	Italy	43.0	38.8	5.6	10.	Hong Kong	27.2	22.2	22.7

*Preliminary. NA = Not available. (1) Excluding receipts from international passenger transport contracted from companies outside a traveler's country of residence. (2) Not including Hong Kong, Macao, and Taiwan.

World's Top 10 Tourist Destinations, 2011
Source: World Tourism Organization (UNWTO), © UNWTO
(ranked by number of arrivals in millions; preliminary)

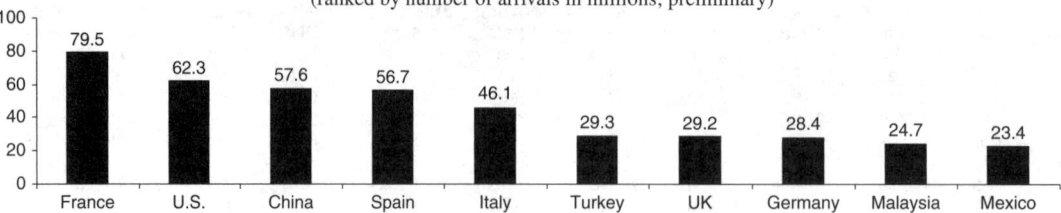

France	U.S.	China	Spain	Italy	Turkey	UK	Germany	Malaysia	Mexico
79.5	62.3	57.6	56.7	46.1	29.3	29.2	28.4	24.7	23.4

International Travel to the U.S., 1986-2011
Source: Office of Travel and Tourism Industries, Intl. Trade Admin., U.S. Dept. of Commerce; World Tourism Organization
(visitors in millions)

*Preliminary figure.

International Visitors to the U.S. by Top Countries of Origin, 2011
Source: Office of Travel and Tourism Industries, Intl. Trade Admin., U.S. Dept. of Commerce
(ranked by number of visitors)

Country of origin	Visitors	Expenditures (mil)[1]	Expenditures per visitor	Country of origin	Visitors	Expenditures (mil)[1]	Expenditures per visitor
1. Canada........	21,028,000	$23,964	$1,139.62	12. Spain	700,183	NA	NA
2. Mexico	13,414,000	9,249	689.50	13. India	663,465	$4,418	$6,658.98
3. UK............	3,835,300	11,974	3,122.05	14. Netherlands	601,013	2,081	3,462.49
4. Japan	3,249,569	14,755	4,540.60	15. Venezuela......	561,080	2,939	5,238.11
5. Germany.......	1,823,797	6,338	3,475.17	16. Argentina	512,258	2,787	5,440.62
6. Brazil..........	1,508,279	8,453	5,604.40	17. Colombia	496,814	NA	NA
7. France	1,504,182	4,980	3,310.77	18. Switzerland.....	476,502	NA	NA
8. South Korea	1,145,216	3,797	3,315.53	19. Sweden........	438,972	NA	NA
9. China[1]........	1,089,405	7,740	7,104.80	20. Ireland.........	346,879	NA	NA
10. Australia	1,037,852	4,963	4,781.99	All countries.......	62,325,157	152,746	2,450.79
11. Italy...........	891,571	3,680	4,127.55				

NA = Not available. (1) Not including Hong Kong and Taiwan.

Traveler Spending in the U.S., 1987-2011
Source: Office of Travel and Tourism Industries, Intl. Trade Admin., U.S. Dept. of Commerce; U.S. Travel Assn.
(in billions of dollars)

Year	Traveler spending Domestic	International	Year	Traveler spending Domestic	International	Year	Traveler spending Domestic	International
1987	$235	$31	1996	$385	$70	2004	$532	$75
1988	258	38	1997	406	73	2005	572	82
1989	273	47	1998	425	71	2006	610	86
1990	291	43	1999	458	75	2007	641	97
1991	296	48	2000	503	82	2008	662	110
1992	306	55	2001	484	72	2009	606	94
1993	323	58	2002	478	67	2010	644	103
1994	340	58	2003	496	65	2011	697	116
1995	360	63						

U.S. Domestic Leisure Travel Volume, 1995-2010
Source: U.S. Travel Assn.
(in billions of person-trips of 50 mi or more, one-way)

1995	1996	1997	1998	1999	2000	2001	2002	2003	2004	2005	2006	2007	2008	2009	2010
1.23	1.22	1.22	1.23	1.30	1.33	1.32	1.41	1.39	1.44	1.48	1.49	1.51	1.50	1.46	1.51

Note: Method of collecting travel data has been revised; data for earlier years have been adjusted to maintain comparability.

Top 10 U.S. States by Traveler Spending, 2010

Source: U.S. Travel Assn.

(domestic and international traveler spending within state, in billions of dollars)

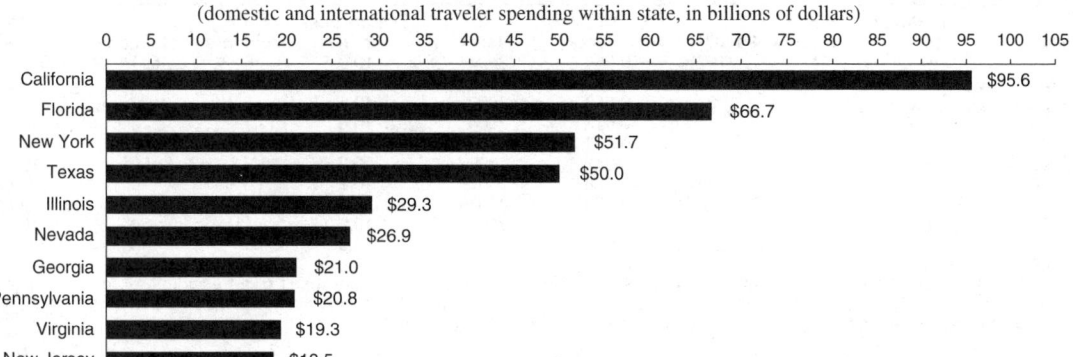

State	Spending
California	$95.6
Florida	$66.7
New York	$51.7
Texas	$50.0
Illinois	$29.3
Nevada	$26.9
Georgia	$21.0
Pennsylvania	$20.8
Virginia	$19.3
New Jersey	$18.5

Characteristics of U.S. Travelers Visiting Overseas Destinations, 2011

Source: Survey of Intl. Air Travelers, Office of Travel and Tourism Industries, Intl. Trade Admin., U.S. Dept. of Commerce

Total U.S. resident travelers	27,023,000
Males (adults)........................	49%
Females (adults)......................	51%
Avg. age of males (yrs.).................	45.9
Avg. age of females (yrs.)..............	44.2
Median annual household income	$96,500
Avg. total trip expend. per visitor (incl. airfare)..	$2,936
Avg. expend. outside the U.S. per visitor per day	$67
Median number of nights	11.0

Region of residence	% of travelers
Middle Atlantic	27%
South Atlantic (incl. Florida, DC metro area)	23
Pacific (incl. California, Washington)	13
East North Central (incl. Illinois, Ohio)	8
West South Central (incl. Texas)	8
New England	7
Mountain	5
West North Central........................	5
East South Central	2

Main purpose of trip	% of travelers
Leisure/recreation/holiday	39%
Visit friends/relatives...........................	35
Business.......................................	18
Study/teaching	4
Religion/pilgrimage..............................	2
Convention/conference..........................	1
Health treatment................................	1

Occupation	% of travelers
Professional/technical.	37%
Manager/executive............................	21
Retired	14
Student.......................................	11
Homemaker	6
Clerical/sales	4
Craftsman/factory worker	3
Government/military	3

Leisure/recreational activities[1]	% of travelers
Dining in restaurants............................	82%
Shopping	70
Visit historical places	50
Visit small towns/villages	43
Sightseeing in cities	40
Touring the countryside	34
Cultural heritage sights..........................	33
Water sports/sunbathing.........................	25
Art gallery, museum	22
Nightclub/dancing...............................	19
Guided tours...................................	17
Ethnic heritage sites............................	13
Visit national parks	12
Amusement/theme parks	11
Concert, play, musical	11

(1) Percentages based on multiple responses.

U.S. Resident Travel Abroad, 1997-2011

Source: Office of Travel and Tourism Industries, Intl. Trade Admin., U.S. Dept. of Commerce

(numbers in thousands; regions ranked by most recent numbers)

Region/country[1]	2011	2000	1997	Region/country[1]	2011	2000	1997
Total outbound[2]	**58,702**	**61,327**	**52,735**	Caribbean..............	6,134	3,867	NA
Mexico	20,084	19,285	17,909	Jamaica.............	1,486	886	1,341
Canada...............	11,595	15,189	13,401	Asia.................	5,107	4,914	NA
Overseas subtotal[3]	**27,023**	**26,853**	**21,634**	China[4]...............	1,108	644	476
Europe	9,674	13,373	NA	South America	1,973	2,095	NA
Western Europe	9,053	12,916	NA	Central America	1,946	886	NA
United Kingdom	2,405	4,189	3,570	Middle East.............	1,756	1,370	NA
France.............	1,756	2,927	2,098	Eastern Europe..........	1,054	806	NA
Italy..............	1,702	2,148	1,471	Africa	892	483	NA
Germany..........	1,594	2,309	1,796	Oceania	486	1,047	NA
Spain	1,081	1,262	714				

NA = Not available. **Note:** Visits of one or more nights. Visitation estimates for Canada and Mexico include all modes of transportation used. Estimates for all other countries are available only for air travel to that country and are based upon data from the airlines that voluntarily provided it. (1) Only individual countries that received more than 1 mil visitors in 2011 are shown. Region figures include U.S. resident travelers to all countries in region. (2) To Canada, Mexico, and overseas. (3) To all countries except Canada and Mexico. (4) Not including Hong Kong, Macao, and Taiwan.

Airline Safety, U.S. Scheduled Commercial Carriers, 1985-2011

Source: National Transportation Safety Board; Federal Aviation Administration, U.S. Dept. of Transportation

Year	Departures (mil)	Fatal accidents	Fatalities[1]	Rate of fatal accidents[2]	Year	Departures (mil)	Fatal accidents	Fatalities[1]	Rate of fatal accidents[2]
1985	6.1	4	197	0.066	2001[3]	10.6	6	531	0.019
1990	7.8	6	39	0.077	2002	10.3	0	0	0.000
1992	7.5	4	33	0.053	2003	10.2	2	22	0.020
1993	7.7	1	1	0.013	2004	10.8	1	13	0.009
1994[3]	7.8	4	239	0.051	2005	10.9	3	22	0.027
1995	8.1	1	160	0.012	2006	10.6	2	50	0.019
1996	7.9	3	342	0.038	2007	10.7	0	0	—
1997	9.9	3	3	0.030	2008	10.3	0	0	—
1998	10.5	1	1	0.009	2009	10.2	1	50	0.010
1999	10.9	2	12	0.018	2010	9.5	0	0	—
2000	11.1	2	89	0.018	2011*	8.9	0	0	—

— = Not applicable. *Preliminary. (1) Includes deaths that occurred on the ground as a result of an accident, except for fatalities resulting from the Sept. 11, 2001, terrorist attacks. (2) Per 100,000 departures. (3) An illegal act, such as suicide or sabotage, was counted among fatal accidents and fatalities for this year but was not used in the calculation of accident rates.

U.S. Scheduled Airline Traffic, 2000-11

Source: Airlines for America
(in millions, except where otherwise noted)

	2000	2005	2006	2007	2008	2009	2010	2011
Passengers enplaned	666.1	738.6	744.7	769.6	743.3	703.9	720.5	730.8
Revenue passenger miles[1]	692,757	779,035	797,434	829,441	812,377	769,412	798,043	814,353
Available seat miles[2]	956,950	1,003,364	1,006,351	1,037,691	1,021,330	957,105	972,601	992,669
Cargo revenue (ton miles)[1]	23,888	28,039	29,340	29,571	28,119	24,970	27,885	28,123
% of seating utilized	72.4	77.6	79.2	79.9	79.5	80.4	82.1	82.0
Passenger revenue	$93,638	$93,633	$101,968	$107,678	$111,511	$91,443	$103,978	$113,992
Net profit[3]	$2,533	−$27,220	$18,186	$7,691	−$23,750	−$2,610	$3,666	$1,481
Total employment[4]	673.9	562.2	545.1	556.7	553.3	522.8	514.2	527.7

(1) One fare-paying passenger or one ton of revenue cargo transported one mile. (2) One seat transported one mile. (3) For all years except 2009, excludes bankruptcy-related charges (reorganization expenses and fresh-start accounting gains). (4) Figures are of avg. full-time equivalents (FTE), i.e., the number of full-time employees that could have been employed if the reported number of hours worked by part-time employees had been worked by full-time employees. In this table, part-time employees are treated as 0.5 FTEs.

Top 25 U.S. Passenger Airlines, 2011

Source: Airlines for America
(in millions; ranked by number of passengers)

Rank Airline	Passengers	Rank Airline	Passengers	Rank Airline	Passengers	Rank Airline	Passengers
1. Southwest/ AirTran	135.2	6. ExpressJet	30.4	13. Republic	10.5	20. Mesaba	5.7
2. Delta	113.5	7. JetBlue	26.4	14. Hawaiian	8.7	21. Comair	5.5
3. United/ Continental	95.6	8. SkyWest	24.4	15. Mesa	8.4	22. Chautauqua	5.3
		9. Alaska	17.8	16. Spirit	8.3	23. Virgin America	5.0
4. American	86.0	10. American Eagle	17.3	17. Horizon	6.6	24. Shuttle America	4.9
5. US Airways	52.9	11. Frontier	10.6	18. Air Wisconsin	6.0	25. PSA	4.9
		12. Pinnacle	10.5	19. Allegiant	5.8		

Note: Domestic and international. Does not include passengers on flights with both origin and destination in a foreign country.

Top North American Airports by Passenger Traffic, 2011

Source: *2011 World Annual Traffic Report*, Airports Council Intl.

City/airport name (airport code)	Total passengers[1]
1. Hartsfield-Jackson Atlanta Intl. (ATL)	92,389,023
2. Chicago O'Hare Intl. (ORD)	66,701,241
3. Los Angeles Intl. (LAX)	61,862,052
4. Dallas/Fort Worth Intl. (DFW)	57,803,439
5. Denver Intl. (DEN)	52,849,132
6. New York John F. Kennedy Intl. (JFK)	47,683,529
7. San Francisco Intl. (SFO)	40,927,786
8. Phoenix Sky Harbor Intl. (PHX)	40,591,948
9. Las Vegas McCarran Intl. (LAS)	40,560,285
10. Houston George Bush Intercontinental (IAH)	40,128,953
11. Charlotte Douglas Intl. (CLT)	39,043,708
12. Miami Intl. (MIA)	38,314,389
13. Orlando Intl. (MCO)	35,426,006
14. Newark Liberty Intl. (EWR)	33,711,372
15. Toronto Pearson Intl. (YYZ)	33,435,280
16. Minneapolis-St. Paul Intl. (MSP)	33,118,499
17. Seattle-Tacoma Intl. (SEA)	32,467,007
18. Detroit Metro. Wayne County (DTW)	32,406,159
19. Philadelphia Intl. (PHL)	30,839,175
20. Boston Logan Intl. (BOS)	28,907,938
21. New York LaGuardia (LGA)	24,122,478
22. Fort Lauderdale-Hollywood Intl. (FLL)	23,349,835
23. Washington Dulles Intl. (IAD)	23,056,291
24. Baltimore/Wash. Intl. Thurgood Marshall (BWI)	22,395,908
25. Salt Lake City Intl. (SLC)	20,389,474

Top World Airports by Passenger Traffic, 2011

Source: *2011 World Annual Traffic Report*, Airports Council Intl.

City/airport name (country; airport code)	Total passengers[1]
1. Beijing Capital Intl. (China; PEK)	78,675,058
2. London Heathrow (UK; LHR)	69,433,565
3. Tokyo Haneda Intl. (Japan; HND)	62,584,826
4. Paris Charles De Gaulle (France; CDG)	60,970,551
5. Frankfurt Intl. (Germany; FRA)	56,436,255
6. Hong Kong Intl. (China; HKG)	53,328,613
7. Jakarta Soekarno-Hatta Intl. (Indonesia; CGK)	51,178,188
8. Dubai Intl. (United Arab Emirates; DXB)	50,977,960
9. Amsterdam Schiphol (Netherlands; AMS)	49,755,252
10. Madrid-Barajas (Spain; MAD)	49,644,680
11. Bangkok Intl. Suvarnabhumi (Thailand; BKK)	47,910,904
12. Singapore Changi (Singapore; SIN)	46,543,845
13. Guangzhou Baiyun Intl. (China; CAN)	45,040,340
14. Shanghai Pudong Intl. (China; PVG)	41,447,730
15. Munich (Germany; MUC)	37,763,701
16. Kuala Lumpur Intl. (Malaysia; KUL)	37,704,510
17. Rome Leonardo Da Vinci-Fiumicino (Italy; FCO)	37,651,222
18. Istanbul Ataturk Intl. (Turkey; IST)	37,406,025
19. Sydney Intl. (Australia; SYD)	36,016,533
20. Seoul Incheon Intl. (South Korea; ICN)	35,191,825
21. Delhi Indira Gandhi Intl. (India; DEL)	35,001,742
22. Barcelona El Prat (Spain; BCN)	34,388,254
23. London Gatwick (UK; LGW)	33,681,493
24. Shanghai Hongqiao Intl. (China; SHA)	33,112,442
25. Mumbai Chhatrapati Shivaji Intl. (India; BOM)	30,439,121

Note: World list excludes North American airports and airports that do not participate in ACI's Airport Traffic Statistics collection. (1) Arriving and departing passengers and direct transit passengers counted once.

Top Travel Websites, 2012

Source: comScore Media Metrix
(ranked by number of visitors)

Rank	Website	Visitors (thous.)[1]	% of all travel websites	Rank	Website	Visitors (thous.)[1]	% of all travel websites
1.	Expedia Inc.	21,020	17.5%	10.	Travelocity	6,767	5.6%
2.	TripAdvisor Media Group	18,392	15.3	11.	Delta Airlines	5,821	4.8
3.	Travora Media	14,299	11.9	12.	Marriott	5,518	4.6
4.	Priceline.com Incorporated	14,008	11.6	13.	United Airlines	5,274	4.4
5.	Yahoo! Travel	11,443	9.5	14.	Hilton Hotels	5,193	4.3
6.	Orbitz Worldwide	10,980	9.1	15.	About.com Travel	4,937	4.1
7.	Southwest Airlines Co.	9,114	7.6	**Total travel audience[2]**		**120,355**	**100.0**
8.	Kayak.com Network	7,769	6.5	**Total Internet audience[2]**		**221,342**	**—**
9.	Fareportal Media Group	6,855	5.7				

(1) Average monthly unique users who visited at least once in 2nd quarter 2012 (Apr.-June). (2) Audience comprises all persons older than two years of age, at U.S. home/work locations.

Number of Paid Days Off Per Year in Selected Countries

Source: *2011 Worldwide Benefit and Employment Guidelines*, Mercer

The figures are based on statutory entitlements for an employee working five days a week, with 10 years' service. Ranked by total paid days off.

Country	Paid vacation days	Paid holidays	Total paid days off	Country	Paid vacation days	Paid holidays	Total paid days off	Country	Paid vacation days	Paid holidays	Total paid days off
Austria	25	13	38	Denmark	25	9	34	Germany	20	9	29
Malta	24	14	38	South Korea	19	15	34	Ireland	20	9	29
Poland	26	11	37	Brazil	22	11	33	Switzerland	20	9	29
Bolivia	25	12	37	Colombia	15	18	33	Taiwan	15	13	28
Greece	25	12	37	Argentina	20	12	32	India	12	16	28
UK.	28	8	36	Russia	20	12	32	South Africa	15	12	27
France	25	11	36	Malaysia	16	16	32	Hong Kong	14	12	26
Sweden	25	11	36	United Arab Emirates	22	9	31	Mexico	16	7	23
Venezuela	24	12	36	Norway	21	10	31	Vietnam	14	9	23
Spain	22	14	36	Italy	20	11	31	Thailand	6	16	22
Portugal	22	13	35	Lebanon	15	16	31	China	10	11	21
Japan	20	15	35	Australia	20	10	30	Philippines	5	15	20
Slovakia	20	15	35					Canada	10	9	19

Note: The U.S. has no nationwide statutory entitlement that mandates paid days off.

Record-Breaking Roller Coasters

Source: UltimateRollerCoaster.com; speeds measured in mph, lengths and heights in ft

Steel-Tracked Roller Coasters

Fastest	Roller coaster	Theme park, location
149.1 mph	Formula Rossa	Ferrari World Abu Dhabi, United Arab Emirates
128	Kingda Ka	Six Flags Great Adventure, Jackson, NJ
120	Top Thrill Dragster	Cedar Point, Sandusky, OH
106.8	Dodonpa	Fuji-Q High Land, Fujiyoshida-shi, Japan
100	Tower of Terror	Dreamworld, Gold Coast, Australia
100	Superman the Escape	Six Flags Magic Mountain, Valencia, CA

Tallest

456 ft	Kingda Ka	Six Flags Great Adventure, Jackson, NJ
420	Top Thrill Dragster	Cedar Point, Sandusky, OH
415	Superman the Escape	Six Flags Magic Mountain, Valencia, CA
377	Tower of Terror	Dreamworld, Gold Coast, Australia
318	Steel Dragon 2000	Nagashima Spa Land, Mie, Japan

Largest drop

418 ft	Kingda Ka	Six Flags Great Adventure, Jackson, NJ
400	Top Thrill Dragster	Cedar Point, Sandusky, OH
306	Steel Dragon 2000	Nagashima Spa Land, Mie, Japan
300	Millennium Force	Cedar Point, Sandusky, OH
300	Intimidator 305	Kings Dominion, Doswell, VA

Longest

8,133 ft	Steel Dragon 2000	Nagashima Spa Land, Mie, Japan
7,450	The Ultimate	Lightwater Valley, UK
6,709	Fujiyama	Fuji-Q High Land, Fujiyoshida-shi, Japan
6,595	Millennium Force	Cedar Point, Sandusky, OH
6,562	Formula Rossa	Ferrari World Abu Dhabi, United Arab Emirates

Wood-Tracked Roller Coasters

Fastest	Roller coaster	Theme park, location
74.6 mph	Colossos	Heide Park, Soltau, Germany
70	El Toro	Six Flags Great Adventure, Jackson, NJ
67.4	The Voyage	Holiday World & Splashin' Safari, Santa Claus, IN
66.3	The Boss	Six Flags St. Louis, Eureka, MO
66	American Eagle	Six Flags Great America, Gurnee, IL

Tallest

197 ft	Colossos	Heide Park, Soltau, Germany
183	T Express	Everland, Yongin, S. Korea
181	El Toro	Six Flags Great Adventure, Jackson, NJ
179	The Rattler	Six Flags Fiesta Texas, San Antonio, TX
173	The Voyage	Holiday World & Splashin' Safari, Santa Claus, IN

Largest drop

176 ft	El Toro	Six Flags Great Adventure, Jackson, NJ
159	Colossos	Heide Park, Soltau, Germany
155	Mean Streak	Cedar Point, Sandusky, OH
154	The Voyage	Holiday World & Splashin' Safari, Santa Claus, IN
151	T Express	Everland, Yongin, S. Korea

Longest

7,400 ft	The Beast	Kings Island, Cincinnati, OH
6,442	The Voyage	Holiday World & Splashin' Safari, Santa Claus, IN
5,578	White Cyclone	Nagashima Spa Land, Mie, Japan
5,427	Mean Streak	Cedar Point, Sandusky, OH
5,384	Shivering Timbers	Michigan's Adventure, Muskegon, MI

Passports, Health Regulations, and Travel Warnings for Foreign Travel

Source: Bureau of Consular Affairs, U.S. Dept. of State; Centers for Disease Control and Prevention (CDC), U.S. Dept. of Health and Human Services; World Health Organization (WHO); Transportation Security Administration (TSA), U.S. Dept. of Homeland Security

Passports, Visas

Passports are issued by the Dept. of State to U.S. citizens and nationals to provide documentation for foreign travel. As of Sept. 2012, the fees for a new passport for persons ages 16 and over total $165; provided certain criteria are met, passports can be renewed for $140.

In July 2008, the U.S. government began issuing passport cards. Travelers arriving by land or sea from Canada, Mexico, the Caribbean (17 nations), and Bermuda may present a passport card to enter the U.S. Passport cards may not be used for air travel, however. The fees for a new passport card for persons ages 16 and over total $55.

A U.S. passport is often sufficient for U.S. citizens to gain admission for a limited stay in another country. Some countries also require a visa to enter. Each country has its own specific guidelines concerning length and purpose of visit, among other considerations. Visitors may need to provide proof of sufficient funds for their intended stay, onward/return tickets, and/or at least six months remaining validity on their U.S. passports.

All persons traveling by air outside of the U.S. (excluding direct travel to and from a U.S. territory) are required to present a passport or other valid document upon reentering the U.S.

For up-to-date passport and international travel information, visit the Consular Affairs website (travel.state.gov) or call the National Passport Information Center at 1-877-4USA-PPT (1-877-487-2778).

Health Regulations

Under WHO regulations, first instituted in 1969, member countries agree to abide by resolutions meant to contain the spread of disease. For example, some countries require travelers to provide proof of vaccination against yellow fever before entering.

Detailed information can be found in *Health Information for International Travel*, or the "yellow book," published every two years by the CDC. The book is written primarily for health care providers but may be of use to other travelers. The CDC also issues travel notices on outbreaks, health precautions, and health warnings. For current notices and more on travelers' health, visit wwwnc.cdc.gov/travel/.

WHO publishes a more technical guide, *International Travel and Health*, which can be found online at www.who.int/ith/.

Travel Warnings and Alerts

The State Dept. issues travel warnings as recommendations that Americans avoid travel to certain countries. Long-term conditions in such countries may be dangerous or unstable; because of an embassy closure or limited personnel, the U.S. government's ability to assist U.S. citizens is also reduced. As of Oct. 2012, travel warnings were in effect for the following countries: Afghanistan, Algeria, Burundi, Central African Republic, Chad, Colombia, Côte d'Ivoire, Dem. Rep. of the Congo, Eritrea, Guinea, Haiti, Iran, Iraq, Israel (incl. West Bank and Gaza), Kenya, Lebanon, Libya, Mali, Mauritania, Mexico, Niger, Nigeria, North Korea, Pakistan, Philippines, Saudi Arabia, Somalia, South Sudan, Sudan, Syria, Tunisia, and Yemen.

The department issues travel alerts when it has concerns about short-term conditions—natural disasters, terrorist attacks, anniversaries of attacks, election-related demonstrations, and regional sporting events, among others. For the latest travel warnings and alerts, see travel.state.gov.

Summary of TSA Regulations

Airplane carry-ons. TSA promotes the "3-1-1" rule regarding carry-on items. Containers with liquids, gels, or aerosols may hold only **3.4** oz or less; these containers should be packed inside a single **1**-quart, clear plastic, zip-top bag; and this **1** bag must be X-rayed when going through security. Exceptions to the 3-1-1 rule include medication, baby formula and food, and breast milk. Travelers must declare any exceptions at security.

Security checkpoint identification. Adult travelers (18 years of age and over) must present a U.S. federal or state-issued photo ID. The ID must have name, date of birth, sex, expiration date, and a tamper-resistant feature. Acceptable documents: U.S. passport or passport card; foreign government-issued passport; state-issued driver's license; permanent resident card; or U.S. military ID, among others.

Screening process. Travelers may wear loose fitting or religious garments (incl. head coverings) through security. They may be subject to additional screening if clothing could potentially conceal prohibited items. Travelers may request a private area if selected for personal screening. In most cases, travelers will be screened by someone of the same gender.

Disability-related permitted carry-on items:
- Wheelchairs
- Crutches, canes, and walkers
- Personal supplemental oxygen
- Slate and stylus
- Medications and associated supplies
- Service animals

Permitted carry-on items:
- Safety razors (incl. disposable razors)
- Eye drops and saline solution (amounts greater than 3.4 oz must be declared)
- Nail clippers, tweezers
- Blunt-tipped plastic or metal scissors
- Mobile phones
- Umbrellas (must be inspected at security)
- Common lighters
- Beverages (any size) purchased after security screening
- Musical instruments (one per traveler going through security, though some airlines prohibit musical instruments as carry-ons)

Prohibited carry-on items:
- Knives (except for plastic or round-bladed butter knives), incl. knives that are religious objects
- Baseball bats, golf clubs
- Flares
- Realistic firearm replicas
- Hammers, screwdrivers, wrenches, pliers, and other tools more than 7 in. in length
- Brass knuckles
- Lighter fluid
- Liquid bleach
- Spray paint
- Snow globes

For complete travel information, visit www.tsa.gov/traveler-information.

Air Distances Between Selected World Cities

Point-to-point measurements, in miles, are usually from City Hall or its equivalent.

	Bangkok	Beijing	Berlin	Cairo	Cape Town	Caracas	Chicago	Hong Kong	Honolulu	Lima
Bangkok.........	...	2,046	5,352	4,523	6,300	10,555	8,570	1,077	6,609	12,244
Beijing...........	2,046	...	4,584	4,698	8,044	8,950	6,604	1,217	5,077	10,349
Berlin...........	5,352	4,584	...	1,797	5,961	5,238	4,414	5,443	7,320	6,896
Cairo...........	4,523	4,698	1,797	...	4,480	6,342	6,141	5,066	8,848	7,726
Cape Town......	6,300	8,044	5,961	4,480	...	6,366	8,491	7,376	11,535	6,072
Caracas.........	10,555	8,950	5,238	6,342	6,366	...	2,495	10,165	6,021	1,707
Chicago.........	8,570	6,604	4,414	6,141	8,491	2,495	...	7,797	4,256	3,775
Hong Kong......	1,077	1,217	5,443	5,066	7,376	10,165	7,797	...	5,556	11,418
Honolulu........	6,609	5,077	7,320	8,848	11,535	6,021	4,256	5,556	...	5,947
London.........	5,944	5,074	583	2,185	5,989	4,655	3,958	5,990	7,240	6,316
Los Angeles.....	7,637	6,250	5,782	7,520	9,969	3,632	1,745	7,240	2,557	4,171
Madrid..........	6,337	5,745	1,165	2,087	5,308	4,346	4,189	6,558	7,872	5,907
Melbourne.......	4,568	5,643	9,918	8,675	6,425	9,717	9,673	4,595	5,505	8,059
Mexico City......	9,793	7,753	6,056	7,700	8,519	2,234	1,690	8,788	3,789	2,639
Montreal........	8,338	6,519	3,740	5,427	7,922	2,438	745	7,736	4,918	3,970
Moscow.........	4,389	3,607	1,006	1,803	6,279	6,177	4,987	4,437	7,047	7,862
New York, NY....	8,669	6,844	3,979	5,619	7,803	2,120	714	8,060	4,969	3,639
Paris..........	5,877	5,120	548	1,998	5,786	4,732	4,143	5,990	7,449	6,370
Rio de Janeiro	9,994	10,768	6,209	6,143	3,781	2,804	5,282	11,009	8,288	2,342
Rome...........	5,494	5,063	737	1,326	5,231	5,195	4,824	5,774	8,040	6,750
San Francisco.....	7,931	5,918	5,672	7,466	10,248	3,902	1,859	6,905	2,398	4,518
Singapore........	883	2,771	6,164	5,137	6,008	11,402	9,372	1,605	6,726	11,689
Stockholm........	5,089	4,133	528	2,096	6,423	5,471	4,331	5,063	6,875	7,166
Tokyo..........	2,865	1,307	5,557	5,958	9,154	8,808	6,314	1,791	3,859	9,631
Warsaw.........	5,033	4,325	322	1,619	5,935	5,559	4,679	5,147	7,366	7,215
Washington, DC ...	8,807	6,942	4,181	5,822	7,895	2,047	596	8,155	4,838	3,509

	London	Los Angeles	Madrid	Melbourne	Mexico City	Montreal	Moscow	New Delhi	New York, NY	Paris
Bangkok..........	5,944	7,637	6,337	4,568	9,793	8,338	4,389	1,813	8,669	5,877
Beijing...........	5,074	6,250	5,745	5,643	7,753	6,519	3,607	2,353	6,844	5,120
Berlin...........	583	5,782	1,165	9,918	6,056	3,740	1,006	3,598	3,979	548
Cairo...........	2,185	7,520	2,087	8,675	7,700	5,427	1,803	2,758	5,619	1,998
Cape Town........	5,989	9,969	5,308	6,425	8,519	7,922	6,279	5,769	7,803	5,786
Caracas	4,655	3,632	4,346	9,717	2,234	2,438	6,177	8,833	2,120	4,732
Chicago	3,958	1,745	4,189	9,673	1,690	745	4,987	7,486	714	4,143
Hong Kong	5,990	7,240	6,558	4,595	8,788	7,736	4,437	2,339	8,060	5,990
Honolulu	7,240	2,557	7,872	5,505	3,789	4,918	7,047	7,412	4,969	7,449
London	...	5,439	785	10,500	5,558	3,254	1,564	4,181	3,469	214
Los Angeles	5,439	...	5,848	7,931	1,542	2,427	6,068	7,011	2,451	5,601
Madrid...........	785	5,848	...	10,758	5,643	3,448	2,147	4,530	3,593	655
Melbourne.........	10,500	7,931	10,758	...	8,426	10,395	8,950	6,329	10,359	10,430
Mexico City........	5,558	1,542	5,643	8,426	...	2,317	6,676	9,120	2,090	5,725
Montreal	3,254	2,427	3,448	10,395	2,317	...	4,401	7,012	331	3,432
Moscow	1,564	6,068	2,147	8,950	6,676	4,401	...	2,698	4,683	1,554
New York, NY......	3,469	2,451	3,593	10,359	2,090	331	4,683	7,318	...	3,636
Paris............	214	5,601	655	10,430	5,725	3,432	1,554	4,102	3,636	...
Rio de Janeiro	5,750	6,330	5,045	8,226	4,764	5,078	7,170	8,753	4,801	5,684
Rome	895	6,326	851	9,929	6,377	4,104	1,483	3,684	4,293	690
San Francisco......	5,367	347	5,803	7,856	1,887	2,543	5,885	7,691	2,572	5,577
Singapore.........	6,747	8,767	7,080	3,759	10,327	9,203	5,228	2,571	9,534	6,673
Stockholm.........	942	5,454	1,653	9,630	6,012	3,714	716	3,414	3,986	1,003
Tokyo...........	5,959	5,470	6,706	5,062	7,035	6,471	4,660	3,638	6,757	6,053
Warsaw..........	905	5,922	1,427	9,598	6,337	4,022	721	3,277	4,270	852
Washington, DC	3,674	2,300	3,792	10,180	1,885	489	4,876	7,500	205	3,840

	Rio de Janeiro	Rome	San Francisco	Singapore	Stockholm	Tehran	Tokyo	Vienna	Warsaw	Wash., DC
Bangkok	9,994	5,494	7,931	883	5,089	3,391	2,865	5,252	5,033	8,807
Beijing...........	10,768	5,063	5,918	2,771	4,133	3,490	1,307	4,648	4,325	6,942
Berlin	6,209	737	5,672	6,164	528	2,185	5,557	326	322	4,181
Cairo...........	6,143	1,326	7,466	5,137	2,096	1,234	5,958	1,481	1,619	5,822
Cape Town........	3,781	5,231	10,248	6,008	6,423	5,241	9,154	5,656	5,935	7,895
Caracas	2,804	5,195	3,902	11,402	5,471	7,320	8,808	5,372	5,559	2,047
Chicago	5,282	4,824	1,859	9,372	4,331	6,502	6,314	4,698	4,679	596
Hong Kong	11,009	5,774	6,905	1,605	5,063	3,843	1,791	5,431	5,147	8,155
Honolulu	8,288	8,040	2,398	6,726	6,875	8,070	3,859	7,632	7,366	4,838
London	5,750	895	5,367	6,747	942	2,743	5,959	771	905	3,674
Los Angeles	6,330	6,326	347	8,767	5,454	7,682	5,470	6,108	5,922	2,300
Madrid...........	5,045	851	5,803	7,080	1,653	2,978	6,706	1,128	1,427	3,792
Melbourne.........	8,226	9,929	7,856	3,759	9,630	7,826	5,062	9,790	9,598	10,180
Mexico City........	4,764	6,377	1,887	10,327	6,012	8,184	7,035	6,320	6,337	1,885
Montreal	5,078	4,104	2,543	9,203	3,714	5,880	6,471	4,009	4,022	489
Moscow	7,170	1,483	5,885	5,228	716	1,532	4,660	1,043	721	4,876
New York, NY......	4,801	4,293	2,572	9,534	3,986	6,141	6,757	4,234	4,270	205
Paris............	5,684	690	5,577	6,673	1,003	2,625	6,053	645	852	3,840
Rio de Janeiro	...	5,707	6,613	9,785	6,683	7,374	11,532	6,127	6,455	4,779
Rome	5,707	...	6,259	6,229	1,245	2,127	6,142	477	820	4,497
San Francisco......	6,613	6,259	...	8,448	5,399	7,362	5,150	5,994	5,854	2,441
Singapore	9,785	6,229	8,448	...	5,936	4,103	3,300	6,035	5,843	9,662
Stockholm.........	6,683	1,245	5,399	5,936	...	2,173	5,053	780	494	4,183
Tokyo...........	11,532	6,142	5,150	3,300	5,053	4,775	...	5,689	5,347	6,791
Warsaw..........	6,455	820	5,854	5,843	494	1,879	5,689	347	...	4,472
Washington, DC	4,779	4,497	2,441	9,662	4,183	6,341	6,791	4,438	4,472	...

AGRICULTURE

Number and Acreage of Farms by State, 2000, 2011

Source: National Agricultural Statistics Service, U.S. Dept. of Agriculture

State	No. of farms (thous.) 2011	No. of farms (thous.) 2000	Acreage in farms (mil) 2011	Acreage in farms (mil) 2000	Acreage per farm 2011	Acreage per farm 2000	State	No. of farms (thous.) 2011	No. of farms (thous.) 2000	Acreage in farms (mil) 2011	Acreage in farms (mil) 2000	Acreage per farm 2011	Acreage per farm 2000
AL.....	47.5	47.0	9.0	9.0	188	191	NE.....	46.8	46.1	45.5	46.1	972	887
AK.....	0.7	0.6	0.9	0.9	1,294	1,569	NV.....	3.0	3.1	5.9	6.4	1,983	2,065
AZ.....	15.5	10.7	26.1	26.9	1,684	2,518	NH	4.2	3.3	0.5	0.4	113	133
AR.....	48.3	48.0	13.5	14.6	280	304	NJ.....	10.3	9.7	0.7	0.8	71	86
CA.....	81.5	83.1	25.4	28.0	312	337	NM	23.0	18.0	43.4	44.9	1,887	2,494
CO	36.7	30.0	31.3	31.6	853	1,060	NY.....	36.0	37.5	7.0	7.7	194	205
CT.....	4.9	4.2	0.4	0.4	82	86	NC	50.4	55.5	8.5	9.2	169	166
DE.....	2.5	2.6	0.5	0.6	196	215	ND	31.9	30.8	39.6	39.4	1,241	1,279
FL.....	47.5	44.0	9.3	10.4	195	238	OH	73.7	79.0	13.6	14.8	185	187
GA	47.0	49.1	10.3	10.9	219	223	OK	85.5	84.5	34.7	33.8	406	401
HI	7.5	5.5	1.1	1.4	148	251	OR	38.3	40.0	16.3	17.3	426	433
ID	24.7	24.5	11.4	11.9	462	486	PA.....	62.2	59.0	7.7	7.7	123	130
IL	74.6	77.0	26.6	27.5	357	357	RI	1.2	0.8	0.1	0.1	57	75
IN	62.0	63.4	14.7	15.2	237	240	SC	26.5	24.2	4.9	4.9	185	203
IA	92.3	94.0	30.7	32.5	333	346	SD	31.3	32.4	43.7	44.0	1,395	1,358
KS.....	65.5	64.5	46.0	47.5	702	736	TN	77.3	88.0	10.8	11.8	140	134
KY.....	85.3	90.0	14.0	13.7	164	152	TX	245.0	228.3	130.0	130.9	531	573
LA.....	29.0	29.0	8.0	8.0	274	277	UT	16.6	15.5	11.1	11.6	669	747
ME	8.1	7.1	1.4	1.4	167	190	VT	7.0	6.6	1.2	1.3	174	192
MD	12.8	12.4	2.1	2.1	160	172	VA	46.4	48.5	8.0	8.7	171	180
MA	7.7	6.1	0.5	0.5	68	89	WA	39.5	37.0	14.8	15.6	375	420
MI	54.9	53.0	10.0	10.2	182	192	WV	22.5	20.8	3.7	3.6	162	173
MN	79.8	81.0	26.9	27.9	336	344	WI	77.0	77.5	15.0	16.0	195	206
MS	42.4	42.0	11.2	11.2	263	266	WY	11.0	9.2	30.2	34.5	2,745	3,750
MO	106.5	109.0	28.9	30.2	271	277	**U.S. ....**	**2,181.0**	**2,166.8**	**917.0**	**945.1**	**420**	**436**
MT	29.3	27.8	60.5	59.3	2,065	2,133							

Number and Average Size of U.S. Farms, 1940-2011

Source: National Agricultural Statistics Service, U.S. Dept. of Agriculture

The number of farms in the United States in 2011 was estimated at 2.2 mil, about 11,000 fewer than in 2010. Total land in farms decreased 1.9 mil acres between 2010 and 2011 to 917 mil acres. The average farm size in 2011 was 420 acres, a slight increase from the previous year.

U.S. Federal Food Assistance Programs, 1990-2011

Source: Food and Nutrition Service (FNS), U.S. Dept. of Agriculture
(in millions of dollars; for fiscal years ending on Sept. 30)

Program	1990	1995	2000	2005	2007	2008	2009	2010	2011
Supplemental Nutrition Assistance Program (SNAP)[1]	$15,491	$24,620	$17,054	$31,073	$33,191	$37,640	$53,633	$68,295	$75,674
Puerto Rico nutrition assistance[2]	937	1,131	1,268	1,495	1,551	1,623	2,001	2,001	2,001
Natl. school lunch[3]	3,834	5,160	6,149	8,031	8,739	9,318	9,992	10,878	11,305
School breakfast[3,4]	596	1,048	1,393	1,927	2,163	2,366	2,583	2,859	3,034
WIC (Women, Infants, and Children)[5]...	2,122	3,440	3,982	4,994	5,410	6,189	6,472	6,683	7,169
Summer food service[6]	164	237	267	267	290	326	348	359	373
Child and adult care[7]	813	1,464	1,683	2,111	2,237	2,403	2,535	2,639	2,725
Special milk[4]......................	19	17	15	16	14	15	14	12	12
Nutrition for the elderly (NSIP)[8]	142	148	137	4	3	2	2	3	2
Food distrib. to Indian reserv.[9]	66	65	76	76	81	96	100	95	94
Commodity supp. food prog.[9]	85	99	98	156	142	161	155	165	198
Food dist. to charitable inst.[10]	104	64	2	4	0	0	0	1	0
Emergency food assistance[11]	334	135	225	373	255	283	617	631	531
Total	**$24,707**	**$37,628**	**$32,317**	**$50,673**	**$54,254**	**$60,625**	**$78,995**	**$95,327**	**$103,562**

Note: 2011 data are preliminary. All data subject to revision by the FNS. Figures may not add up to totals because of rounding and administrative costs not shown. (1) Formerly known as the Food Stamp Program. Includes benefits and admin. expenses. (2) Provides benefits analogous to SNAP. (3) Data are nine-month averages (summer months excluded). (4) Costs are cash payments or federal reimbursements to states. (5) Includes food benefits, nutrition services and admin. funds, Farmers' Market Nutrition Program, infrastructure, breastfeeding promotion and peer counseling, program evaluation, and technical assistance. (6) Includes cash payments, commodity costs, and admin. expenditures. Similar services provided by natl. school lunch and breakfast programs. (7) Includes cash payments, entitlement and bonus commodities, cash-in-lieu of commodities, sponsor admin. costs, start-up costs, and audits. (8) For years 2003 and on, program was administered by the Agency on Aging; FNS costs limited to value of commodities distributed. (9) Includes commodity distribution costs and admin. expenses. (10) Includes summer camps. (11) Food made available to hunger relief orgs. such as food banks and soup kitchens.

U.S. Cost of Food, 2012

Source: Center for Nutrition Policy and Promotion, U.S. Dept. of Agriculture

	Weekly cost[1]				Monthly cost[1]			
	Thrifty plan	Low-cost plan	Mod.-cost plan	Liberal plan	Thrifty plan	Low-cost plan	Mod.-cost plan	Liberal plan
Individual child, age[2]								
1 year	$21.30	$28.30	$32.10	$39.10	$92.20	$122.50	$139.00	$169.40
2-3 years	23.30	29.30	35.60	43.30	100.90	127.10	154.10	187.60
4-5 years	24.20	30.60	37.70	46.00	104.80	132.40	163.30	199.30
6-8 years	30.90	42.50	51.50	60.80	133.90	184.30	223.00	263.40
9-11 years	35.00	46.40	59.60	69.50	151.80	201.00	258.10	301.10
Individual male, age[2]								
12-13 years	37.80	53.40	66.80	78.10	163.60	231.20	289.50	338.30
14-18 years	38.90	54.50	68.90	78.80	168.50	236.20	298.60	341.60
19-50 years	41.80	54.00	67.60	83.20	181.10	234.00	292.80	360.50
51-70 years	38.20	50.90	62.80	76.00	165.70	220.60	272.30	329.10
71+ years	38.50	50.70	62.40	77.20	166.90	219.80	270.40	334.40
Individual female, age[2]								
12-13 years	37.80	46.10	55.00	67.40	163.90	199.90	238.40	292.00
14-18 years	37.20	46.30	56.10	69.00	161.40	200.50	243.30	299.10
19-50 years	37.20	46.90	58.00	74.00	161.10	203.00	251.40	320.60
51-70 years	36.70	45.80	56.80	68.00	159.00	198.30	246.00	294.70
71+ years	35.70	45.50	56.20	67.60	154.90	197.30	243.50	292.90
2-person family[3], age								
19-50 years	86.90	110.90	138.10	172.90	376.40	480.70	598.60	749.20
51-70 years	82.40	106.30	131.60	158.40	357.20	460.80	570.10	686.20
4-person family[4] **2 children, ages**								
2-3 and 4-5 years	126.50	160.70	198.80	246.50	547.90	696.50	861.60	1,068.00
6-8 and 9-11 years	144.90	189.80	236.60	287.50	627.90	822.30	1,025.30	1,245.60

Note: The Food Plans represent a nutritious diet at four different cost levels. The nutritional bases of the Food Plans are the 1997-2005 Dietary Reference Intakes, 2005 Dietary Guidelines for Americans, and 2005 MyPyramid food intake recommendations. In addition to cost, differences among plans are in specific foods and quantities of foods. Another basis of the Food Plans is that all meals and snacks are prepared at home. For specific foods and quantities in the Food Plans, see *Thrifty Food Plan, 2006* and *The Low-Cost, Moderate-Cost, and Liberal Food Plans, 2007* from the source. All four food plans are based on 2001-02 data and updated to current dollars using the consumer price index for specific food items. (1) All costs are rounded to nearest 10 cents. (2) The costs given are for individuals in 4-person families. (3) Ten percent added for family size adjustment. (4) Defined as a couple, 19-50 years old, and two children.

U.S. Annual Per Capita Consumption of Selected Foods, 1970-2010

Source: Economic Research Service, U.S. Dept. of Agriculture; Distilled Spirits Council of the U.S., Inc.; Beer Institute; Wine Institute
(fruits and vegetables in pounds, beverages in gallons)

	1970	1990	2010	% change, 1970-2010		1970	1990	2010	% change, 1970-2010
Fresh fruit	96.0	111.0	121.5	26.6%	**Fresh vegetables**	144.5	163.9	172.6	19.4%
Apples	16.3	18.8	14.8	–9.2	Bell peppers	2.0	5.4	9.1	358.3
Avocados	0.4	1.3	3.2	674.5	Broccoli	0.5	3.1	5.1	949.1
Bananas	17.4	24.3	25.6	47.4	Cabbage	8.1	7.8	6.9	–14.0
Cherries	0.5	0.4	1.2	167.8	Carrots	5.8	8.0	7.4	27.5
Grapes	2.6	7.1	7.4	183.6	Cauliflower	0.7	2.0	1.2	80.6
Melons	19.6	22.3	23.2	19.5	Celery	6.8	6.7	5.8	–14.0
Grapefruit	8.0	4.3	2.7	–66.4	Cucumbers	2.6	4.3	6.2	140.4
Oranges	15.7	12.0	9.4	–40.1	Garlic	0.4	1.1	1.9	428.5
Peaches/nectarines	5.5	5.3	4.5	–18.7	Head lettuce	20.8	25.8	15.0	–27.9
Pears	1.8	3.1	2.8	52.6	Mushrooms	0.3	1.9	2.3	779.1
Pineapples	0.7	1.9	5.4	714.4	Onions	9.5	14.2	18.7	95.8
Plums/prunes	1.4	1.5	0.7	–47.0	Potatoes	59.3	44.9	34.2	–42.4
Strawberries	1.6	3.0	6.7	319.7	Snap beans	1.5	1.0	1.8	21.2
					Squash	1.2	3.2	3.9	224.7
Canned vegetables	100.4	110.3	99.1	–1.3	Sweet corn	7.2	6.2	8.5	18.9
Carrots	2.0	1.2	0.8	–62.3	Tomatoes	10.3	13.2	17.7	71.7
Green peas	3.1	2.0	1.2	–62.7	**Beverages**				
Snap beans	4.7	3.7	3.7	–21.4					
Sweet corn	14.3	11.0	6.8	–52.0	Bottled water	NA	8.8	NA	NA
Tomatoes	62.1	75.3	71.0	14.4	Carbonated soft drinks	24.3	46.2	NA	NA
					Regular	22.2	35.6	NA	NA
Frozen vegetables	43.7	66.7	70.2	60.7	Diet	2.1	10.7	NA	NA
Broccoli	1.0	2.2	2.4	154.0	Coffee	33.4	26.8	23.2	–30.6
Carrots	1.4	2.3	1.5	4.2	Fruit juice	5.5	7.0	7.2	30.5
Green peas	1.9	2.2	1.6	–18.1	Beer	18.5	23.9	20.7	11.9
Potatoes	28.5	46.4	49.3	72.9	Wine	1.3	2.0	2.5	93.9
Sweet corn	5.7	8.6	8.5	48.5	Distilled spirits	1.8	1.5	1.5	–16.7

NA = Not available. **Note:** All figures are rounded. Percent change based on unrounded raw data.

U.S. Meat Production and Consumption, 1940-2012

Source: Economic Research Service, U.S. Dept. of Agriculture

(in millions of pounds)

Year	Beef Prod.	Beef Cons.	Veal Prod.	Veal Cons.	Lamb and mutton Prod.	Lamb and mutton Cons.	Pork Prod.	Pork Cons.	All red meats[1] Prod.	All red meats[1] Cons.	All poultry Prod.	All poultry Cons.
1940	7,175	7,257	981	981	876	873	10,044	9,701	19,076	18,812	NA	NA
1950	9,534	9,529	1,230	1,206	597	596	10,714	10,390	22,075	21,721	3,174	3,097
1960	14,728	15,465	1,109	1,118	769	857	13,905	14,057	30,511	31,497	6,310	6,168
1970	21,684	23,451	588	613	551	669	14,699	14,957	37,522	39,689	10,193	9,981
1980	21,643	23,560	400	420	318	351	16,617	16,838	38,978	41,170	14,173	13,525
1990	22,743	24,030	327	325	363	397	15,354	16,025	38,787	40,778	23,468	22,152
1995	25,222	25,534	319	319	285	346	17,849	17,768	43,675	43,967	30,393	25,944
2000	26,888	27,338	225	225	234	354	18,952	18,643	46,299	46,560	36,073	30,508
2005	26,787	27,754	165	164	191	355	20,705	19,112	45,848	47,385	40,935	34,947
2007	26,523	28,144	145	144	188	384	21,962	19,763	48,817	48,435	42,117	35,667
2008	26,663	27,302	152	150	180	343	23,367	19,415	50,361	47,210	43,235	35,379
2009	25,965	26,904	147	147	177	338	22,999	19,839	49,274	47,227	41,673	34,116
2010	26,304	26,392	145	150	168	317	22,437	19,072	49,039	45,931	43,058	35,201
2011	26,195	25,545	138	139	153	295	22,758	18,384	49,232	44,363	43,513	35,548
2012*	25,178	25,188	128	128	153	284	23,298	18,615	48,744	44,215	43,388	34,976

*Preliminary. NA = Not available. (1) Numbers may not add up to totals because of rounding.

U.S. Per Capita Consumption of Meat and Dairy, 1910-2010

Source: Economic Research Service, U.S. Dept. of Agriculture

(in pounds per capita, unless otherwise noted)

Meat	1910	1930	1950	1970	1990	2000	2010	% change, 1910-2010
Beef	48.5	33.7	44.6	79.6	63.9	64.5	56.7	16.9%
Chicken	11.0	11.1	14.3	27.4	42.4	54.2	58.0	428.5
Fish/shellfish	11.2	10.2	11.9	11.7	14.9	15.2	15.8	40.9
Pork	38.2	41.1	43.0	48.1	46.4	47.8	44.3	16.0
Red meat	96.0	83.6	95.8	131.9	112.2	113.7	102.1	6.4
Dairy								
Butter	18.4	17.6	10.9	5.4	4.0	4.5	4.9	−73.6
Cheese, American	2.8	3.2	5.5	7.0	11.1	12.7	13.3	380.3
Cheese, other	1.5	1.5	2.2	4.4	13.5	17.1	20.0	1,217.0
Ice cream	1.9	9.3	16.4	16.7	14.8	15.6	13.3	584.3
Milk, skim/lower fat (gallons)	7.1	5.0	2.9	5.8	15.2	14.4	14.6	106.3
Milk, whole (gallons)	25.2	28.2	34.3	25.5	10.5	8.1	5.6	−77.8

Note: All figures are rounded. Percent change based on unrounded raw data.

U.S. Organic Farmland and Animals, 1995-2008

Source: Economic Research Service, U.S. Dept. of Agriculture

Crop	Organic acreage[1] 1995	Organic acreage[1] 2000	Organic acreage[1] 2002	Organic acreage[1] 2003	Organic acreage[1] 2004	Organic acreage[1] 2005	Organic acreage[1] 2008	% change, 2000-08	Total U.S. farmland[2]
Grains									
Corn	32,650	77,912	96,270	105,574	99,111	130,672	194,637	149.8%	93,600,000
Wheat	120,820	206,474	217,611	234,221	214,244	293,824	415,902	101.4	60,433,000
Oats	13,250	29,771	53,459	46,074	42,616	46,465	57,374	92.7	3,760,000
Barley	17,150	41,904	34,031	30,265	26,629	39,271	46,954	12.1	4,020,000
Rice	8,400	26,870	22,381	20,152	22,173	26,428	49,638	84.7	2,761,000
Beans									
Soybeans	47,200	136,071	126,540	122,403	114,239	122,217	125,621	−7.7	63,631,000
Dry beans	NA	14,010	2,430	9,836	7,642	10,561	16,465	17.5	1,526,900
Dry peas & lentils	5,900	10,144	7,476	16,188	15,893	17,757	16,987	67.5	571,000
Hay and silage	84,100	231,207	267,827	327,538	356,590	411,342	793,442	243.2	61,625,000
All vegetables	NA	62,342	69,887	78,905	86,822	98,525	177,049	184.0	2,045,020
All fruits	NA	43,481	60,693	77,989	80,707	97,277	121,066	178.4	3,839,300
Other crops									
Cotton	32,850	15,027	10,551	9,875	9,213	9,537	15,377	2.3	10,830,300
Peanuts	NA	2,085	5,134	5,698	9,514	11,940	16,776	704.6	1,230,000
Potatoes	NA	5,433	6,593	6,569	7,300	6,581	8,273	52.3	1,148,800
Trees for maple syrup	10,200	11,965	1,121	1,514	13,357	12,247	31,340	161.9	NA
Fallow land	NA	57,688	64,668	83,003	116,582	198,650	194,428	237.0	37,968,749
Total cropland	638,500	1,218,905	1,299,632	1,451,601	1,452,353	1,723,271	2,655,382	117.8	370,653,755
Total pasture and rangeland	276,300	557,167	625,902	745,273	1,592,756	2,331,158	2,160,577	287.8	473,212,960
Total farmland	914,800	1,776,073	1,925,534	2,196,874	3,045,109	4,054,429	4,815,959	171.2	843,866,715

Animal	Number of organic animals[1] 1995	Number of organic animals[1] 2000	Number of organic animals[1] 2002	Number of organic animals[1] 2003	Number of organic animals[1] 2004	Number of organic animals[1] 2005	Number of organic animals[1] 2008	% change, 2000-08	Total U.S. animals
Total livestock	NA	56,028	108,362	124,346	157,253	196,506	475,829	749.3%	167,512,858
Beef cows	NA	13,829	23,384	27,285	36,662	36,113	63,680	360.5	32,834,801
Milk cows	NA	38,196	67,207	74,435	74,840	87,082	249,766	553.9	9,266,574
Other cows[3]	NA	NA	10,103	11,501	36,598	58,822	144,817	NA	54,246,483
Hogs and pigs	NA	1,724	2,753	6,564	4,883	10,018	10,111	486.5	65,110,000
Sheep and lambs	NA	2,279	4,915	4,561	4,270	4,471	7,455	227.1	6,055,000
Total poultry	NA	3,159,050	6,270,181	8,780,152	7,304,566	13,757,270	15,518,075	391.2	9,632,362,000
Layer hens	NA	1,113,746	1,052,272	1,591,181	1,787,901	2,415,056	5,538,011	397.2	377,492,000
Broilers	NA	1,924,807	3,032,189	6,301,014	4,769,104	10,405,879	9,015,984	368.4	8,882,000,000
Turkeys	NA	9,138	305,605	217,353	164,292	144,086	398,531	4,261.2	262,460,000
Other/unclassified	NA	111,359	1,880,115	670,604	583,269	792,249	565,549	407.9	110,410,000

NA = Not available. (1) Based on information from USDA-accredited state and private organic certifiers. (2) Total acreage of organic and nonorganic land used for agricultural purposes. (3) Includes breeding stock, replacement heifers, and unclassified cows.

Production of Principal U.S. Crops, 1990-2011

Source: National Agricultural Statistics Service, U.S. Dept. of Agriculture

Year	Corn for grain (1,000 bu)	Oats (1,000 bu)	Barley (1,000 bu)	Sorghum for grain (1,000 bu)	All wheat (1,000 bu)	Rye (1,000 bu)	Flaxseed (1,000 bu)	Cotton (upland) (1,000 b)	Cottonseed (1,000 t)
1990	7,934,028	357,654	422,196	573,303	2,729,778	10,176	3,812	15,505.4	5,968.5
1995	7,373,876	162,027	359,562	460,373	2,182,591	10,064	2,211	17,532.2	6,848.7
1998	9,758,685	165,981	352,125	519,933	2,547,321	12,161	6,708	13,475.9	5,365.4
1999	9,430,612	146,193	280,292	595,166	2,299,010	11,038	7,864	16,293.7	6,354.0
2000	9,915,051	149,545	318,728	470,526	2,232,460	8,386	10,730	16,799.2	6,435.6
2001	9,506,840	117,024	249,420	514,524	1,957,043	6,971	11,455	19,602.4	7,452.2
2002	8,966,787	116,002	226,906	360,713	1,605,878	6,488	11,863	16,530.3	6,183.9
2003	10,089,222	144,383	278,283	411,237	2,344,760	8,634	10,516	17,822.9	6,664.6
2004	11,807,086	115,695	279,743	453,654	2,158,245	8,255	10,368	22,505.1	8,242.1
2005	11,114,082	114,878	211,896	392,933	2,104,690	7,537	19,695	23,259.7	8,172.1
2006	10,534,868	93,638	180,165	277,538	1,812,036	7,193	11,019	20,822.4	7,347.9
2007	13,037,875	90,430	210,110	497,445	2,051,088	6,311	5,896	18,355.1	6,588.7
2008	12,091,648	89,135	240,193	472,342	2,499,164	7,979	5,716	12,384.5	4,300.3
2009	13,091,862	93,081	227,323	382,983	2,218,061	6,993	7,423	11,787.6	4,148.8
2010	12,446,865	81,190	180,268	345,625	2,206,916	7,431	9,056	17,600.0	6,098.1
2011	12,358,412	53,649	155,780	214,443	1,999,347	6,326	2,791	14,828.0	5,267.0

Year	Tobacco (1,000 lb)	All hay (1,000 t)	Beans, dry edible (1,000 cwt)	Peas, dry edible (1,000 cwt)	Peanuts[1] (1,000 lb)	Soybeans[2] (1,000 bu)	Potatoes (1,000 cwt)	Sweet potatoes (1,000 cwt)
1990	1,626,380	146,212	32,379	2,372	3,602,770	1,925,947	402,110	12,594
1995	1,268,538	154,166	30,812	4,765	4,247,455	2,176,814	443,606	12,906
1998	1,479,867	151,780	30,418	5,934	3,963,440	2,741,014	475,771	12,382
1999	1,292,692	159,707	33,085	4,773	3,829,490	2,653,758	478,216	12,234
2000	1,052,999	151,921	26,409	3,474	3,265,505	2,757,810	513,621	13,794
2001	991,223	156,764	19,583	3,763	4,276,704	2,890,682	437,888	14,637
2002	871,122	149,467	30,312	4,727	3,321,040	2,756,147	458,171	12,799
2003	802,560	157,585	22,492	5,202	4,144,150	2,453,665	457,814	15,891
2004	881,973	158,247	17,788	11,419	4,288,200	3,123,686	456,041	16,112
2005	645,015	151,017	26,772	14,003	4,869,860	3,063,237	423,926	15,730
2006	727,347	142,336	24,247	13,203	3,464,250	3,188,247	441,348	16,248
2007	787,653	146,901	25,586	16,287	3,672,250	2,667,117	444,875	18,070
2008	800,504	146,270	25,558	12,270	5,162,400	2,967,007	415,055	18,443
2009	822,581	147,700	25,427	17,137	3,691,650	3,359,011	432,601	19,469
2010	718,190	145,624	31,801	14,221	4,156,840	3,329,181	404,273	23,845
2011	601,029	131,144	19,833	5,625	3,636,320	3,056,032	427,406	27,041

Year	Rice (1,000 cwt)	Sugarcane (1,000 t)	Sugar beets (1,000 t)	Pecans[3] (1,000 lb)	Apples (1,000 t)	Grapes (1,000 t)	Peaches (1,000 t)	Oranges[4] (1,000 bx)	Grapefruit[4] (1,000 bx)
1990	156,088	28,136	27,513	205,000	4,828	5,660	1,121	184,415	49,300
1995	173,871	30,944	27,954	268,000	5,293	5,922	1,150	263,605	71,050
1998	184,443	32,743	32,499	146,400	5,823	5,820	1,190	315,525	63,150
1999	206,027	35,299	33,420	406,100	5,316	6,236	1,252	224,580	61,200
2000	190,872	36,114	32,541	209,850	5,291	7,688	1,276	299,760	66,980
2001	215,270	34,587	25,764	338,500	4,712	6,569	1,204	280,935	59,750
2002	210,960	35,553	27,707	172,900	4,262	7,339	1,268	283,760	58,660
2003	199,897	33,858	30,710	282,100	4,397	6,664	1,260	267,040	50,080
2004	232,362	29,013	30,021	185,800	5,220	6,240	1,307	294,620	52,540
2005	223,235	26,606	27,433	280,250	4,853	7,814	1,185	216,500	25,640
2006	193,736	29,564	34,064	207,300	4,912	6,378	1,010	210,750	30,600
2007	198,388	29,969	31,834	387,305	4,545	7,057	1,127	177,280	39,900
2008	203,733	27,603	26,881	202,080	4,817	7,319	1,135	234,376	37,900
2009	219,850	30,432	29,783	302,020	4,853	7,307	1,104	210,709	32,025
2010	243,104	27,360	32,034	293,740	4,641	7,471	1,150	192,835	30,400
2011	185,009	28,279	28,789	269,700	4,710	7,378	1,072	203,749	30,150

b = bale; bu = bushel; bx = box; cwt = hundred weight. **Note:** Some 2011 figures are preliminary estimates. (1) Harvested for nuts. (2) Harvested for beans. (3) Utilized production only. (4) Crop year ending in year cited.

Livestock on Farms in the U.S., 1900-2012

Source: National Agricultural Statistics Service, U.S. Dept. of Agriculture
(in thousands)

Year (on Jan. 1)	All cattle[1]	Milk cows	Sheep and lambs	Hogs and pigs[2]	Year (on Jan. 1)	All cattle[1]	Milk cows	Sheep and lambs	Hogs and pigs[2]
1900	59,739	16,544	48,105	51,055	1995	102,755	9,487	8,886	57,150
1910	58,993	19,450	50,239	48,072	2000	98,199	9,183	7,036	59,335
1920	70,400	21,455	40,743	60,159	2001	97,298	9,172	6,908	59,110
1930	61,003	23,032	51,565	55,705	2002	96,723	9,106	6,623	59,722
1940	68,309	24,940	52,107	61,165	2003	96,100	9,142	6,321	59,554
1950	77,963	23,853	29,826	58,937	2004	94,888	8,990	6,105	60,444
1955	96,592	23,462	31,582	50,474	2005	95,838	9,005	6,135	60,975
1960	96,236	19,527	33,170	59,026	2006	96,702	9,063	6,230	61,449
1965	109,000	16,981	25,127	56,106	2007	97,003	9,132	6,165	62,490
1970	112,369	12,091	20,423	57,046	2008	96,035	9,257	5,950	66,963
1975	132,028	11,220	14,515	54,693	2009	94,521	9,333	5,747	66,768
1980	111,242	10,758	12,699	67,318	2010	93,881	9,086	5,620	65,327
1985	109,582	10,777	10,716	54,073	2011	100,000	9,200	5,480	64,625
1990	95,816	10,015	11,358	53,788	2012	97,800	9,200	5,345	66,361

(1) Includes milk cows and heifers that have calved since 1970. (2) As of Dec. 1 of preceding year.

Animal Products: Average Prices Received by U.S. Farmers, 1940-2011

Source: National Agricultural Statistics Service, U.S. Dept. of Agriculture

Figures below represent dollars per 100 lb for beef cattle, veal calves, hogs, lambs, milk (wholesale), and sheep; dollars per head for milk cows; cents per lb for broilers, chickens, turkeys, and wool; cents per dozen for eggs; weighted calendar year prices for livestock and livestock products other than wool. For 1943-63, wool prices were weighted on marketing year basis. The marketing year was changed in 1964 from a calendar year to a Dec.-Nov. basis for broilers, chickens, eggs, and hogs.

Year	Broilers	Calves (veal)	Cattle (beef)	Chickens (excl. broilers)	Eggs	Hogs	Lambs	Milk cows	Milk	Sheep	Turkeys	Wool
1940	17.3	8.83	7.56	13.0	18.0	5.39	8.10	61	1.82	3.95	15.2	28.4
1950	27.4	26.30	23.30	22.2	36.3	18.00	25.10	198	3.89	11.60	32.8	62.1
1960	16.9	22.90	20.40	12.2	36.1	15.30	17.90	223	4.21	5.61	25.4	42.0
1970	13.6	34.50	27.10	9.1	39.1	22.70	26.40	332	5.71	7.51	22.6	35.4
1980	27.7	76.80	62.40	11.0	56.3	38.00	63.60	1,190	13.05	21.30	41.3	88.1
1985	30.1	62.10	53.70	14.8	57.1	44.00	67.70	860	12.76	23.90	49.1	63.3
1990	32.6	95.60	74.60	9.3	70.9	53.70	55.50	1,160	13.74	23.20	39.4	80.0
1995	34.4	73.10	61.80	6.5	62.4	40.50	78.20	1,130	12.78	28.00	41.6	104.0
2000	33.6	104.00	68.60	5.7	61.8	42.30	79.80	1,340	12.40	34.30	40.7	33.0
2001	39.3	106.00	71.30	4.5	62.2	44.30	66.90	1,500	15.04	34.60	39.0	36.0
2002	30.5	96.40	66.50	4.8	58.9	33.40	73.80	1,600	12.18	27.90	36.5	53.0
2003	34.6	102.00	79.70	4.9	73.2	37.20	94.40	1,340	12.55	34.90	36.1	73.0
2004	44.6	119.00	85.80	5.8	71.4	49.30	101.00	1,580	16.13	38.80	42.0	80.0
2005	43.6	135.00	89.70	6.5	54.0	50.20	110.00	1,770	15.19	45.10	44.9	71.0
2006	36.3	133.00	87.20	5.8	58.2	46.00	95.50	1,730	12.96	35.20	47.9	68.0
2007	43.6	119.00	89.90	5.6	88.5	46.60	98.50	1,830	19.21	31.00	52.3	87.0
2008	45.8	110.00	89.10	6.6	109.0	47.00	99.60	1,950	18.45	27.20	56.5	99.0
2009	45.7	105.00	80.30	7.2	81.7	41.60	99.60	1,390	12.93	32.50	50.0	79.0
2010	48.2	117.00	92.20	8.1	85.7	54.10	125.00	1,330	16.35	49.70	61.5	115.0
2011	46.6	142.00	113.00	8.7	96.2	65.30	NA	1,420	20.25	NA	68.2	167.0

NA = Not available.

Crops: Average Prices Received by U.S. Farmers, 1940-2011

Source: National Agricultural Statistics Service, U.S. Dept. of Agriculture

Figures below represent cents per lb for apples, cotton, and peanuts; dollars per bushel for barley, corn, oats, soybeans, and wheat; dollars per 100 lb for potatoes, rice, and sorghum; dollars per ton for cottonseed and baled hay; weighted crop year prices. The marketing year is described as follows: apples, June-May; barley, hay, oats, potatoes, and wheat, July-June; cotton, cottonseed, peanuts, and rice, Aug.-July; soybeans, Sept.-Aug.; and corn and sorghum grain, Oct.-Sept.

Year	Apples	Barley	Corn	Cotton-seed	Cotton (upland)*	Hay	Oats	Peanuts	Pota-toes	Rice	Sor-ghum	Soy-beans	Wheat
1940	NA	0.39	0.62	21.70	9.8	9.78	0.30	3.7	0.85	1.80	0.87	0.89	0.67
1950	NA	1.19	1.52	86.60	39.9	21.10	0.79	10.9	1.50	5.09	1.88	2.47	2.00
1960	2.7	0.84	1.00	42.50	30.1	21.70	0.60	10.0	2.00	4.55	1.49	2.13	1.74
1970	6.5	0.97	1.33	56.40	21.9	26.10	0.62	12.8	2.21	5.17	2.04	2.85	1.33
1980	12.1	2.86	3.11	129.00	74.4	71.00	1.79	25.1	6.55	12.80	5.25	7.57	3.91
1985	17.3	1.98	2.23	66.00	56.8	67.60	1.23	24.4	3.92	6.53	3.45	5.05	3.08
1990	20.9	2.14	2.28	121.00	67.1	80.60	1.14	34.7	6.08	6.68	3.79	5.74	2.61
1995	24.0	2.89	3.24	106.00	75.4	82.20	1.67	29.3	6.77	9.15	5.69	6.72	4.55
2000	17.8	2.11	1.85	105.00	49.8	84.60	1.10	27.4	5.08	5.61	3.37	4.54	2.62
2001	22.9	2.22	1.97	90.50	29.8	96.50	1.59	23.4	6.99	4.25	4.25	4.38	2.78
2002	25.6	2.72	2.32	101.00	44.5	92.40	1.81	18.2	6.69	4.49	4.14	5.53	3.56
2003	29.4	2.83	2.42	117.00	61.8	85.50	1.48	19.3	5.89	8.08	4.26	7.34	3.40
2004	21.8	2.48	2.06	107.00	41.6	92.00	1.48	18.9	5.67	7.33	3.19	5.74	3.40
2005	24.4	2.53	2.00	96.00	47.7	98.20	1.63	17.3	7.06	7.65	3.33	5.66	3.42
2006	31.7	2.85	3.04	111.00	46.5	110.00	1.87	17.7	7.33	9.96	5.88	6.43	4.26
2007	28.8	4.02	4.20	162.00	59.3	128.00	2.63	20.5	7.51	12.80	7.28	10.10	6.48
2008	23.2	5.37	4.06	223.00	47.8	152.00	3.15	23.0	9.09	16.80	5.72	9.97	6.78
2009	23.1	4.66	3.55	158.00	62.9	108.00	2.02	21.7	8.25	14.40	5.75	9.59	4.87
2010	25.2	3.86	5.18	161.00	81.5	114.00	2.52	22.5	9.20	12.70	8.96	11.30	5.70
2011[1]	29.2	5.40	6.20	260.00	91.3	175.00	3.40	28.0	9.37	14.20	10.90	11.70	7.30

*Beginning in 1964, 480-lb net weight bales. NA = Not available. (1) Preliminary data.

Value of U.S. Agricultural Exports and Imports, 1978-2011

Source: Economic Research Service, U.S. Dept. of Agriculture

(in billions of dollars, unless otherwise noted)

Year[1]	Agric. trade surplus	Agric. exports	% of all exports	Agric. imports	% of all imports	Year[1]	Agric. trade surplus	Agric. exports	% of all exports	Agric. imports	% of all imports
1978	$13.4	$27.3	21%	$13.9	8%	1995	$26.0	$56.3	10%	$30.3	4%
1979	15.8	32.0	19	16.2	8	1996	26.8	60.3	10	33.5	4
1980	23.2	40.5	19	17.3	7	1997	21.7	57.3	9	35.7	4
1981	26.4	43.8	19	17.3	7	1998	16.8	53.7	8	36.8	4
1982	23.6	39.1	18	15.5	6	1999	11.8	49.1	8	37.3	4
1983	18.5	34.8	18	16.3	7	2000	11.9	50.8	7	38.9	3
1984	19.1	38.0	18	18.9	6	2001	13.7	52.7	8	39.0	3
1985	11.5	31.2	15	19.7	6	2002	12.4	53.3	8	41.0	4
1986	5.4	26.3	13	20.9	6	2003	10.3	56.0	9	45.7	4
1987	7.2	27.9	12	20.7	5	2004	9.7	62.4	9	52.7	4
1988	14.3	35.3	12	21.0	5	2005	4.8	62.5	8	57.7	4
1989	18.1	39.7	12	21.6	5	2006	4.6	68.6	8	64.0	4
1990	16.6	39.5	11	22.9	5	2007	12.2	82.2	8	70.1	4
1991	16.4	39.3	10	22.9	5	2008	35.6	114.9	10	79.3	4
1992	18.3	43.1	10	24.8	5	2009	22.9	96.3	10	73.4	5
1993	17.7	42.9	10	25.1	4	2010	29.6	108.6	10	79.0	4
1994	19.2	46.2	10	27.0	4	2011	42.9	137.4	11	94.5	4

(1) Fiscal year (Oct.-Sept.).

World Meat Production, 2000, 2010

Source: UN Food and Agriculture Organization; in thousands of metric tons; ranked by top producers in 2010

	Top beef producers				Top pork producers				Top poultry producers		
Rank	Country	2000	2010	Rank	Country	2000	2010	Rank	Country	2000	2010
1.	U.S.	12,298	12,047	1.	China	40,752	51,677	1.	U.S.	16,416	19,584
2.	Brazil	6,579	6,977	2.	U.S.	8,597	10,186	2.	China	12,689	16,987
3.	China	5,156	6,546	3.	Germany	3,982	5,488	3.	Brazil	6,125	11,142
4.	Argentina	2,718	2,630	4.	Spain	2,905	3,369	4.	Mexico	1,868	2,722
5.	India	2,237	2,549	5.	Brazil	2,600	3,078	5.	Russia	775	2,580
6.	Australia	1,988	2,108	6.	Vietnam	1,409	3,036	6.	India	904	2,338
7.	Mexico	1,409	1,745	7.	Russia	1,569	2,308	7.	France	2,220	1,791
8.	Russia	1,894	1,711	8.	France	2,312	2,260	8.	Indonesia	818	1,678
9.	France	1,528	1,550	9.	Canada	1,640	1,926	9.	Iran	815	1,662
10.	Sudan (former)	296	1,505	10.	Poland	1,923	1,895	10.	Argentina	1,000	1,643
11.	Pakistan	886	1,490	11.	Italy	1,479	1,673	11.	UK.	1,513	1,558
12.	Canada	1,263	1,272	12.	Denmark	1,625	1,668	12.	South Africa	821	1,478
13.	Germany	1,304	1,205	13.	Philippines	1,213	1,613	13.	Turkey	661	1,459
14.	Italy	1,153	1,075	14.	Japan	1,256	1,291	14.	Malaysia	714	1,412
15.	Colombia	745	930	15.	Netherlands	1,623	1,287	15.	Japan	1,195	1,401
16.	UK.	705	925	16.	Mexico	1,030	1,175	16.	Germany	790	1,380
17.	South Africa	625	884	17.	Belgium	1,042	1,124	17.	Thailand	1,149	1,301
18.	Egypt	544	743	18.	South Korea	916	1,097	18.	Poland	589	1,221
19.	Uzbekistan	390	665	19.	Thailand	693	862	19.	Canada	1,065	1,216
20.	New Zealand	572	635	20.	UK.	899	774	20.	Italy	1,092	1,181
21.	Spain	651	607	21.	Indonesia	413	637	21.	Spain	987	1,141
22.	Ireland	577	558	22.	Ukraine	676	631	22.	Peru	542	1,020
23.	Uruguay	453	524	23.	Austria	620	542	23.	Colombia	504	1,000
24.	Japan	530	513	24.	Chile	261	498	24.	Ukraine	193	953
25.	Venezuela	429	466	25.	Myanmar	123	459	25.	Australia	643	923
	Africa	4,327	6,922		Africa	770	1,232		Africa	2,999	4,640
	Asia	13,004	16,462		Asia	48,007	61,916		Asia	22,884	34,488
	Central America	1,766	2,211		Central America	1,140	1,341		Central America	2,371	3,493
	Europe	11,777	11,041		Europe	25,377	26,968		Europe	11,863	16,074
	North America	13,561	13,319		North America	10,237	12,112		North America	17,481	20,800
	Oceania	2,581	2,764		Oceania	489	474		Oceania	767	1,093
	South America	11,846	12,785		South America	3,774	4,847		South America	9,741	16,904
	World total	**59,087**	**65,737**		**World total**	**90,002**	**109,215**		**World total**	**68,597**	**98,090**

World Corn, Rice, and Wheat Production, 2000, 2010

Source: UN Food and Agriculture Organization; in millions of metric tons; ranked by top producers in 2010

	Top corn producers				Top rice producers				Top wheat producers		
Rank	Country	2000	2010	Rank	Country	2000	2010	Rank	Country	2000	2010
1.	U.S.	251.9	316.2	1.	China	189.8	197.2	1.	China	99.6	115.2
2.	China	106.2	177.5	2.	India	127.5	120.6	2.	India	76.4	80.7
3.	Brazil	31.9	56.1	3.	Indonesia	51.9	66.4	3.	U.S.	60.6	60.1
4.	Mexico	17.6	23.3	4.	Bangladesh	37.6	49.4	4.	Russia	34.5	41.5
5.	Argentina	16.8	22.7	5.	Vietnam	32.5	40.0	5.	France	37.4	38.2
6.	Indonesia	9.7	18.4	6.	Myanmar	21.3	33.2	6.	Germany	21.6	24.1
7.	India	12.0	14.1	7.	Thailand	25.8	31.6	7.	Pakistan	21.1	23.3
8.	France	16.0	14.0	8.	Philippines	12.4	15.8	8.	Canada	26.5	23.2
9.	South Africa	11.4	12.8	9.	Brazil	11.1	11.3	9.	Australia	22.1	22.1
10.	Ukraine	3.8	12.0	10.	U.S.	8.7	11.0	10.	Turkey	21.0	19.7
11.	Canada	7.0	11.7	11.	Japan	11.9	10.6	11.	Ukraine	10.2	16.9
12.	Romania	4.9	9.0	12.	Cambodia	4.0	8.2	12.	Iran	8.1	15.0
13.	Italy	10.1	8.8	13.	Pakistan	7.2	7.2	13.	Argentina	16.1	14.9
14.	Nigeria	4.1	7.3	14.	South Korea	7.2	5.8	14.	UK.	16.7	14.9
15.	Serbia	—	7.2	15.	Madagascar	2.5	4.7	15.	Kazakhstan	9.1	9.6
16.	Egypt	6.5	7.0	16.	Egypt	6.0	4.3	16.	Poland	8.5	9.5
17.	Hungary	5.0	7.0	17.	Sri Lanka	2.9	4.3	17.	Egypt	6.6	7.2
18.	Philippines	4.5	6.4	18.	Nepal	4.2	4.0	18.	Italy	7.5	6.9
19.	Vietnam	2.0	4.6	19.	Nigeria	3.3	3.2	19.	Uzbekistan	3.5	6.7
20.	Tanzania	2.0	4.5	20.	Laos	2.2	3.0	20.	Brazil	1.7	6.0
21.	Thailand	4.5	4.5	21.	Peru	1.9	2.8	21.	Romania	4.5	5.8
22.	Ethiopia	2.7	4.4	22.	Malaysia	2.1	2.5	22.	Spain	7.3	5.6
23.	Turkey	2.3	4.3	23.	North Korea	1.7	2.4	23.	Denmark	4.7	5.1
24.	Germany	3.3	4.1	24.	Colombia	2.7	2.4	24.	Morocco	1.4	4.9
25.	Malawi	2.5	3.8	25.	Mali	0.7	2.3	25.	Afghanistan	1.5	4.5
	Africa	44.3	64.3		Africa	17.5	22.9		Africa	14.3	22.0
	Asia	149.1	246.1		Asia	545.5	607.3		Asia	254.5	292.4
	Central America	20.3	27.3		Central America	1.2	1.3		Central America	3.5	3.7
	Europe	55.4	92.2		Europe	3.2	4.4		Europe	183.6	201.1
	North America	258.8	327.9		North America	8.7	11.0		North America	87.2	83.3
	Oceania	63.5	85.6		Oceania	1.1	0.2		Oceania	22.4	22.6
	South America	0.6	0.5		South America	20.9	23.4		South America	20.2	25.7
	World total	**592.5**	**844.4**		**World total**	**599.4**	**672.0**		**World total**	**585.7**	**650.9**

Crop Consumption Per Capita in Selected Nations, 1980-2009

Source: UN Food and Agriculture Organization

(in kg per capita per year)

Country	Corn 1980	Corn 1990	Corn 2009	Corn % change, 1980-2009	Rice 1980	Rice 1990	Rice 2009	Rice % change, 1980-2009	Wheat 1980	Wheat 1990	Wheat 2009	Wheat % change, 1980-2009
Australia	2	4	5	121.7%	8	8	12	51.3%	81	70	79	−1.9%
Bangladesh	0	0	8	NA	148	163	173	17.4	29	22	16	−45.4
Brazil	22	22	25	10.4	39	41	35	−12.0	50	44	54	7.9
Cambodia	11	8	17	46.5	138	158	160	16.3	4	0	2	−60.5
Canada	4	3	20	429.7	3	5	10	185.3	76	78	86	12.2
Chad	5	4	11	130.6	7	11	7	9.1	2	4	11	378.3
China	5	4	7	38.8	76	83	76	0.7	59	79	66	13.5
Congo Republic	5	3	3	−44.7	2	5	8	382.4	33	33	51	55.0
Cuba	0	0	28	NA	51	48	62	22.2	78	74	49	−36.8
Egypt	49	57	60	24.1	26	31	39	46.2	129	149	145	12.4
France	2	13	12	572.2	4	4	5	31.4	96	92	102	6.8
Germany	3	7	15	374.2	2	2	5	152.6	69	68	78	11.7
India	8	8	5	−36.3	64	78	68	7.1	45	41	58	28.8
Indonesia	23	28	38	68.0	121	127	127	5.6	9	9	21	123.4
Iran	1	1	2	266.7	30	31	23	−23.1	155	169	157	1.2
Israel	12	23	30	164.3	6	8	10	58.3	138	124	108	−21.7
Italy	5	3	4	−20.0	5	5	6	28.3	174	149	144	−17.0
Japan	15	19	11	−22.6	73	65	54	−26.4	44	44	48	9.6
Kenya	114	88	77	−32.3	2	1	8	233.3	20	18	25	23.2
Korea, North	43	56	44	2.1	72	70	76	6.3	32	22	18	−44.0
Korea, South	2	13	14	768.8	138	97	81	−40.9	49	48	50	0.6
Mexico	121	127	121	−0.1	5	4	6	20.8	43	43	32	−25.3
New Zealand	1	3	3	153.8	2	4	10	295.8	78	69	76	−3.3
Nigeria	6	32	29	398.3	14	20	21	46.2	15	3	21	36.2
Pakistan	7	6	8	20.9	22	14	17	−24.1	113	127	110	−2.6
Philippines	22	19	7	−70.3	98	94	123	26.5	17	20	24	39.1
Rwanda	14	15	17	16.0	2	1	10	464.7	2	3	10	363.6
Saudi Arabia	12	13	23	97.4	33	18	36	6.6	88	105	89	1.5
South Africa	120	108	104	−13.7	4	8	15	236.4	56	57	61	8.4
Spain	1	1	2	150.0	6	7	12	101.8	98	93	86	−12.5
Thailand	0	1	4	1,950.0	132	104	133	1.1	4	6	17	312.5
Turkey	8	21	16	86.9	3	7	9	173.5	209	222	200	−4.4
United Arab Emirates	1	1	1	12.5	34	41	47	38.0	86	127	123	42.8
United Kingdom	3	3	3	−6.3	2	3	6	221.1	82	82	99	19.8
United States	8	13	13	60.8	4	7	8	112.8	70	81	81	15.4
Uruguay	23	28	29	28.3	8	10	19	146.2	105	96	124	18.2
Venezuela	76	54	64	−14.8	21	13	32	53.6	51	51	49	−3.4
Vietnam	7	7	11	60.3	131	132	141	8.2	17	3	14	−16.5
Africa	37	41	42	13.8	15	17	21	44.5	47	47	50	6.0
Asia	8	9	9	17.9	78	83	77	−1.2	53	60	63	20.0
Central America	109	115	106	−3.2	8	7	10	31.6	38	39	33	−14.8
Europe	4	5	7	97.3	5	4	5	4.0	118	118	108	−8.4
North America	8	12	13	78.7	4	7	9	123.7	71	81	82	15.1
Oceania	2	4	4	131.6	9	10	14	61.2	79	69	78	−1.6
South America	23	23	27	19.7	30	32	31	6.4	58	53	57	−2.7
World per capita consumption	13	15	17	31.5%	50	54	53	6.4%	64	68	66	2.5%

NA = Not applicable. **Note:** All figures are rounded. Percent change based on unrounded raw data.

Meat Consumption Per Capita in Selected Nations, 1980-2009

Source: UN Food and Agriculture Organization

(in kg per capita per year)

Country	Beef 1980	Beef 1990	Beef 2009	Beef % change, 1980-2009	Pork 1980	Pork 1990	Pork 2009	Pork % change, 1980-2009	Poultry 1980	Poultry 1990	Poultry 2009	Poultry % change, 1980-2009
Australia	53	47	39	−26.4%	15	18	22	48.6%	21	24	38	84.6%
Bangladesh	2	1	1	−13.3	0	0	0	NA	1	1	1	85.7
Brazil	23	28	38	68.4	8	7	12	46.3	10	14	35	247.5
Cambodia	2	4	5	157.1	1	6	9	1,012.5	1	2	2	155.6
Canada	40	36	31	−23.3	35	28	26	−25.7	22	28	37	65.6
Chad	7	12	8	13.7	0	0	0	NA	1	1	1	−28.6
China	0	1	5	1,100.0	12	20	37	209.2	2	3	13	641.2
Congo Republic	4	1	1	−75.0	1	2	1	42.9	2	5	3	55.0
Cuba	15	13	7	−55.7	5	10	22	363.8	10	12	20	108.4
Egypt	7	8	12	75.7	0	0	0	−100.0	4	5	10	163.2
France	33	33	26	−22.0	38	34	31	−17.3	16	21	22	38.5
Germany	23	22	13	−45.1	61	61	55	−10.0	10	11	17	76.5
India	2	2	2	−30.4	0	1	0	−25.0	0	1	2	750.0
Indonesia	2	2	2	29.4	1	3	3	125.0	1	3	6	400.0
Iran	6	6	7	14.5	0	0	0	NA	6	7	22	282.8
Israel	13	14	25	91.6	3	2	3	8.0	35	39	67	89.0
Italy	26	27	24	−9.9	25	32	43	71.9	18	20	17	−4.4
Japan	5	8	9	76.0	14	15	20	47.4	10	14	17	67.3
Kenya	12	9	12	3.4	0	0	0	NA	2	1	1	−70.0
Korea, North	2	2	1	−50.0	10	11	5	−52.1	2	3	2	−14.3
Korea, South	3	6	12	376.0	8	13	29	273.1	3	6	13	412.0
Mexico	11	14	17	61.1	18	10	15	−17.0	7	10	30	353.8
New Zealand	57	39	28	−51.9	12	14	22	89.6	10	17	30	216.7

Country	Beef 1980	1990	2009	% change, 1980-2009	Pork 1980	1990	2009	% change, 1980-2009	Poultry 1980	1990	2009	% change, 1980-2009
Nigeria	5	2	2	−63.5%	1	1	2	200.0%	2	2	2	−5.6%
Pakistan	5	6	8	76.6	0	0	0	NA	1	1	4	533.3
Philippines	3	2	4	57.1	9	12	18	108.0	5	4	10	108.3
Rwanda	2	2	3	41.7	1	0	1	40.0	0	0	0	0.0
Saudi Arabia	6	5	6	−4.8	0	0	0	NA	24	29	42	75.0
South Africa	20	17	15	−21.8	3	4	7	126.7	8	15	32	310.3
Spain	11	13	14	25.4	31	48	49	57.2	21	23	28	33.5
Thailand	6	6	3	−50.0	6	6	11	100.0	7	9	12	68.1
Turkey	3	7	5	40.6	0	0	0	NA	6	8	17	191.2
United Arab Emirates	14	13	9	−35.5	0	0	0	NA	43	39	49	13.2
United Kingdom	23	21	20	−12.8	26	25	26	−0.8	14	19	32	136.8
United States	47	44	40	−16.0	33	29	30	−8.8	26	40	49	85.6
Uruguay	76	47	18	−76.9	9	7	16	82.6	5	7	19	310.9
Venezuela	22	18	24	10.4	6	5	8	26.7	18	13	36	106.9
Vietnam	2	2	4	126.3	5	11	35	546.3	2	3	10	466.7
Africa	7	6	6	−9.9	1	1	1	100.0	2	3	6	200.0
Asia	2	3	4	121.1	6	10	15	146.8	2	3	9	319.0
Central America	11	13	15	43.8	15	8	13	−13.8	6	9	27	355.9
Europe	23	25	16	−30.9	32	35	34	5.9	12	15	22	87.2
North America	47	43	39	−16.7	33	28	30	−10.8	26	38	48	83.8
Oceania	50	43	35	−31.0	14	17	21	53.3	18	22	36	98.3
South America	28	27	31	11.0	7	6	10	41.7	9	12	30	228.3
World per capita consumption	11	10	10	−9.4%	12	13	16	32.8%	6	8	14	134.5%

NA = Not applicable. **Note:** All figures are rounded. Percent change based on unrounded raw data.

Trade in Wheat, Rice, Corn, and Meat, 1999, 2009

Source: UN Food and Agriculture Organization; in thousands of dollars

Wheat exports

Rank	Country	1999	Country	2009
1.	U.S.	$3,580,990	U.S.	$5,380,050
2.	Canada	2,286,000	Canada	5,291,980
3.	France	2,260,410	Australia	3,838,690
4.	Australia	2,136,990	France	3,761,000
5.	Argentina	998,527	Russia	2,753,000
6.	Germany	655,916	Germany	2,203,500
7.	Ukraine	588,000	Ukraine	1,778,020
8.	UK	390,162	Argentina	1,001,970
9.	Kazakhstan	270,141	Kazakhstan	632,854
10.	Belgium-Luxembourg	202,822	UK	475,356

Wheat imports

Rank	Country	1999	Country	2009
1.	Japan	$1,074,140	Algeria	$1,830,350
2.	Italy	932,883	Italy	1,724,940
3.	Brazil	832,136	Egypt	1,576,060
4.	Iran	801,301	Japan	1,562,140
5.	Algeria	662,202	Indonesia	1,316,110
6.	Egypt	605,810	Spain	1,306,030
7.	South Korea	533,237	Brazil	1,208,680
8.	Spain	476,466	Iran	1,076,050
9.	Belgium-Luxembourg	452,727	Pakistan	1,040,470
10.	Netherlands	430,486	Netherlands	1,004,090

Rice exports

Rank	Country	1999	Country	2009
1.	U.S.	$156,860	U.S.	$552,799
2.	Argentina	51,091	China	48,660
3.	Uruguay	20,148	Argentina	28,234
4.	Australia	16,649	India	18,026
5.	France	11,393	Italy	13,737
6.	China	6,373	Russia	13,570
7.	Italy	6,160	Paraguay	12,002
8.	Spain	6,086	Greece	10,669
9.	Greece	2,388	France	10,557
10.	Kazakhstan	2,000	Brazil	10,079

Rice imports

Rank	Country	1999	Country	2009
1.	Brazil	$116,082	Mexico	$288,316
2.	Mexico	97,114	Saudi Arabia	69,946
3.	Turkey	43,775	Honduras	46,001
4.	Costa Rica	16,334	Nicaragua	42,248
5.	Nicaragua	14,500	Costa Rica	41,194
6.	Portugal	14,026	Guatemala	27,931
7.	Honduras	10,320	El Salvador	26,702
8.	Botswana	8,112	Turkey	26,188
9.	El Salvador	7,464	Brazil	24,813
10.	Guatemala	6,092	Italy	23,186

Corn exports

Rank	Country	1999	Country	2009
1.	U.S.	$5,126,990	U.S.	$9,086,410
2.	France	1,401,450	France	1,847,590
3.	Argentina	812,293	Argentina	1,612,530
4.	China	450,018	Brazil	1,302,150
5.	Hungary	176,824	Ukraine	1,012,750
6.	Canada	95,823	Hungary	849,909
7.	Germany	79,766	India	527,884
8.	Chile	61,895	South Africa	453,462
9.	South Africa	59,803	Romania	347,678
10.	Ukraine	48,150	Serbia	288,129

Corn imports

Rank	Country	1999	Country	2009
1.	Japan	$1,883,090	Japan	$3,709,510
2.	South Korea	883,663	South Korea	1,637,990
3.	Mexico	648,192	Mexico	1,436,750
4.	Egypt	643,900	China	975,989
5.	China	557,150	Spain	930,467
6.	Spain	406,904	Egypt	833,724
7.	Netherlands	299,068	Netherlands	770,131
8.	Malaysia	259,903	Colombia	671,171
9.	Italy	248,453	Iran	652,278
10.	Germany	234,160	Germany	620,698

Meat exports

Rank	Country	1999	Country	2009
1.	U.S.	$5,733,279	Brazil	$11,252,375
2.	Netherlands	4,428,153	U.S.	10,796,293
3.	France	3,610,112	Germany	9,353,374
4.	Denmark	3,253,079	Netherlands	8,394,367
5.	Australia	2,545,782	Australia	4,855,203
6.	Germany	2,163,550	Denmark	4,798,635
7.	Belgium-Luxembourg	2,047,426	France	4,606,309
8.	Canada	1,999,466	Belgium	4,316,288
9.	Brazil	1,909,744	Spain	3,752,828
10.	Ireland	1,819,993	Canada	3,440,184

Meat imports

Rank	Country	1999	Country	2009
1.	Japan	$7,156,948	Japan	$9,968,322
2.	Germany	3,669,515	UK	7,644,901
3.	UK	3,487,291	Germany	7,464,076
4.	U.S.	3,329,185	Italy	5,883,480
5.	Italy	3,056,422	France	5,619,995
6.	France	2,803,773	Russia	5,594,973
7.	Hong Kong	1,377,314	U.S.	4,635,671
8.	Netherlands	1,336,485	Netherlands	4,504,299
9.	Russia	1,183,461	Hong Kong	2,775,277
10.	Mexico	1,068,873	Mexico	2,526,216

Note: Data for China excludes Hong Kong and Macao.

World Capture of Fish, Crustaceans, and Mollusks, 2001-10

Source: UN Food and Agriculture Organization

(in thousands of metric tons; ranked by 2010 captures; total includes nations not shown)

Country	2001	2005	2008	2009	2010	Country	2001	2005	2008	2009	2010
China	14,176	14,589	14,791	14,920	15,419	Philippines . . .	1,949	2,270	2,561	2,603	2,612
Indonesia	4,259	4,696	4,997	5,104	5,380	Vietnam	1,725	1,988	2,136	2,281	2,421
India	3,777	3,691	4,099	4,067	4,695	Thailand	2,834	2,814	1,873	1,871	1,827
U.S.	4,944	4,893	4,350	4,222	4,370	South Korea . .	1,994	1,646	1,957	1,859	1,733
Peru	7,986	9,388	7,395	6,914	4,261	Bangladesh. . .	1,068	1,334	1,558	1,822	1,727
Russia.	3,629	3,198	3,384	3,826	4,070	Mexico	1,399	1,320	1,581	1,611	1,524
Japan	4,714	4,312	4,302	4,116	4,044	Malaysia	1,235	1,214	1,399	1,398	1,433
Myanmar						Morocco	1,096	1,026	997	1,165	1,136
(Burma). . . .	1,188	1,732	2,494	2,767	3,063	Iceland	1,984	1,665	1,284	1,142	1,061
Chile	3,798	4,328	3,555	3,454	2,680	Spain	1,094	853	918	918	969
Norway	2,687	2,393	2,431	2,524	2,675	**World total. . .**	**90,781**	**92,329**	**89,699**	**89,630**	**88,604**

World Aquaculture Production, 2001-10

Source: UN Food and Agriculture Organization

Country	Metric tons (thous.) 2001	2005	2008	2009	2010	Value (mil) 2001	2005	2008	2009	2010
China	22,702	28,121	32,731	34,780	36,734	$23,050	$30,509	$51,346	$55,142	$59,142
India	2,120	2,967	3,851	3,792	4,649	2,393	3,763	6,240	5,648	9,085
Vietnam	588	1,437	2,462	2,556	2,672	1,346	2,931	4,606	4,803	5,150
Indonesia	864	1,197	1,690	1,733	2,305	2,397	1,999	2,814	3,206	4,895
Bangladesh.	713	882	1,006	1,064	1,309	1,065	1,246	1,766	2,351	2,840
Thailand	814	1,304	1,331	1,417	1,286	1,752	1,741	2,346	2,623	2,817
Norway	511	662	848	962	1,008	1,020	2,136	3,139	3,590	5,020
Egypt	343	540	694	705	920	757	792	1,251	1,356	1,546
Myanmar (Burma).	121	485	675	778	851	320	959	817	912	956
Philippines	435	557	741	737	745	661	794	1,576	1,486	1,563
Japan	800	746	730	787	718	2,846	2,892	3,149	3,601	3,532
Chile	566	724	843	793	701	1,725	3,229	4,503	4,668	3,753
U.S.	480	514	500	480	495	804	896	976	953	1,016
Brazil.	206	258	365	416	479	325	445	737	806	949
South Korea	294	437	474	473	476	484	1,195	1,287	1,361	1,482
Malaysia	158	176	243	333	373	318	339	564	676	839
Taiwan	297	305	324	286	310	895	969	1,069	910	1,116
Ecuador	58	139	172	218	272	272	610	765	1,010	1,247
Spain	309	219	250	267	252	339	308	557	519	520
France	252	245	238	234	224	454	674	1,018	959	871
World total[1]	**34,614**	**44,296**	**52,946**	**55,714**	**59,873**	**$48,554**	**$65,933**	**$100,693**	**$106,498**	**$119,444**

Note: Does not include aquatic plants or marine mammals. (1) Includes nations not shown.

U.S. Commercial Landings of Fish and Shellfish, 1990-2011

Source: Natl. Marine Fisheries Service, Natl. Oceanic and Atmospheric Admin., U.S. Dept. of Commerce

Year	Landings for human food Weight (mil lbs)	Value (mil)	Landings for industrial purposes[1] Weight (mil lbs)	Value (mil)	Total Weight (mil lbs)	Value (mil)
1990	7,041	$3,366	2,363	$156	9,404	$3,522
1995	7,667	3,625	2,121	145	9,788	3,770
1996	7,474	3,355	2,091	132	9,565	3,487
1997	7,244	3,285	2,598	163	9,842	3,448
1998	7,173	3,009	2,021	119	9,194	3,128
1999	6,832	3,265	2,507	202	9,339	3,467
2000	6,912	3,398	2,157	152	9,069	3,550
2001	7,311	3,064	2,178	154	9,489	3,218
2002	7,205	2,940	2,192	152	9,397	3,092
2003	7,521	3,185	1,986	157	9,507	3,347
2004	7,794	3,611	1,889	145	9,683	3,756
2005	7,997	3,825	1,710	117	9,707	3,942
2006	7,842	3,911	1,641	113	9,483	4,024
2007	7,490	4,015	1,819	177	9,309	4,192
2008	6,633	4,231	1,692	152	8,325	4,383
2009	6,198	3,733	1,833	158	8,031	3,891
2010	6,526	4,356	1,705	164	8,231	4,520
2011[2]	7,911	5,116	2,179	187	10,090	5,303

Note: Does not include products of aquaculture, except oysters and clams. Statistics on landings are shown in round (live) weight for all items except univalve and bivalve mollusks such as clams, oysters, and scallops, which are shown in weight of meats (excluding the shell). (1) Processed into meal, oil, solubles, and shell products or used as bait or animal food. (2) Preliminary.

U.S. Domestic Landings by Region, 2005, 2011

Source: Natl. Marine Fisheries Service, Natl. Oceanic and Atmospheric Admin., U.S. Dept. of Commerce

Region	2005 Weight (thous. lbs)	Value (thous.)	2011[1] Weight (thous. lbs)	Value (thous.)
New England	684,090	$971,663	623,606	$1,117,048
Middle Atlantic	199,937	221,505	207,572	256,659
Chesapeake	508,953	218,933	571,564	268,386
South Atlantic	122,422	125,117	124,582	176,477
Gulf	1,196,355	620,987	1,984,244	797,000
Pacific Coast incl. Alaska	6,950,647	1,700,927	6,530,947	2,579,607
Great Lakes[2]	16,732	12,434	17,811	17,241
Hawaii.	28,139	70,811	29,289	91,565
Total	**9,707,275**	**$3,942,376**	**10,089,615**	**$5,303,983**

Note: Landings reported in round (live) weight for all items except univalve and bivalve mollusks (e.g., clams, oysters, scallops), which are reported in weight of meats (excluding the shell). (1) Preliminary. (2) Data for the Great Lakes states lag by one year.

EMPLOYMENT

Employment and Unemployment in the U.S., 1900-2011

Source: Bureau of Labor Statistics, U.S. Dept. of Labor

(civilian labor force, persons 16 years of age and older; annual averages, in thousands)

Year[1]	Employed	Unemployed Number	Unemployed Rate	Year[1]	Employed	Unemployed Number	Unemployed Rate	Year[1]	Employed	Unemployed Number	Unemployed Rate
1900[2]	26,956	1,420	5.0%	1986	109,597	8,237	7.0%	1999	133,488	5,880	4.2%
1910[2]	34,599	2,150	5.9	1987	112,440	7,425	6.2	2000	136,891	5,692	4.0
1920[2]	39,208	2,132	5.2	1988	114,968	6,701	5.5	2001	136,933	6,801	4.7
1930[2]	44,183	4,340	8.9	1989	117,342	6,528	5.3	2002	136,485	8,378	5.8
1940[2]	47,520	8,120	14.6	1990	118,793	7,047	5.6	2003	137,736	8,774	6.0
1950	58,918	3,288	5.0	1991	117,718	8,628	6.8	2004	139,252	8,149	5.5
1955	62,170	2,852	4.4	1992	118,492	9,613	7.5	2005	141,730	7,591	5.1
1960	65,778	3,852	5.5	1993	120,259	8,940	6.9	2006	144,427	7,001	4.6
1965	71,088	3,366	4.5	1994	123,060	7,996	6.1	2007	146,047	7,078	4.6
1970	78,678	4,093	4.9	1995	124,900	7,404	5.6	2008	145,362	8,924	5.8
1975	85,846	7,929	8.5	1996	126,708	7,236	5.4	2009	139,877	14,265	9.3
1980	99,303	7,637	7.1	1997	129,558	6,739	4.9	2010	139,064	14,825	9.6
1985	107,150	8,312	7.2	1998	131,463	6,210	4.5	2011	139,869	13,747	8.9

Note: Because of revisions in population controls, data for a given year may not be strictly comparable to other years. (1) **Other unemployment rates (1905-45)**, 14 years of age and older: 1905, 4.3; 1915, 8.5; 1925, 3.2; 1935, 20.3; 1936, 16.9; 1937, 14.3; 1938, 19.0; 1939, 17.2; 1945, 1.9. (2) Persons 14 years of age and older.

Unemployment Insurance Data by State, 2011

Source: Employment and Training Admin., U.S. Dept. of Labor; state programs only

State/ terr.	Unemployment rate	Monetarily eligible claimants	Number of first payments	Number of final payments	Initial claims	Benefits paid	Average weekly benefit	Employers subject to state law
AL	9.0%	177,212	125,782	52,943	332,737	$352,986,355	$205	85,805
AK	7.6	57,075	36,572	21,941	88,625	153,614,082	242	17,434
AZ	9.5	201,485	155,153	89,239	299,447	535,483,579	211	122,156
AR	8.0	144,250	93,341	42,905	226,110	340,841,826	279	67,248
CA	11.7	1,715,118	1,344,208	771,000	3,324,747	6,698,272,600	293	1,224,939
CO	8.3	157,069	128,688	78,278	197,852	673,106,781	335	147,856
CT	8.8	203,378	161,793	70,276	282,382	792,859,936	327	96,641
DE	7.3	38,404	25,678	13,486	60,644	120,503,109	241	25,640
DC	10.2	28,535	27,678	16,223	23,002	148,254,922	296	29,289
FL	10.5	602,643	375,451	264,520	926,660	1,508,695,064	231	456,235
GA	9.6	375,309	269,412	143,310	710,192	873,186,263	269	204,453
HI	6.7	46,650	36,057	16,592	104,080	245,334,253	413	30,562
ID	8.7	80,854	63,945	30,553	144,848	203,819,519	250	47,552
IL	9.8	413,709	418,422	205,376	763,319	2,261,305,469	309	299,210
IN	9.0	253,505	196,561	107,339	400,709	764,141,917	295	129,260
IA	5.9	133,704	107,937	42,490	199,073	448,211,518	316	73,932
KS	6.7	99,959	85,415	42,284	170,725	312,052,901	322	69,619
KY	9.5	176,818	121,705	44,280	318,166	518,771,521	287	84,662
LA	7.3	147,775	101,979	49,298	202,313	360,814,644	196	104,890
ME	7.5	58,707	44,103	19,903	92,507	174,982,681	274	41,812
MD	7.0	178,517	139,460	69,388	345,317	749,315,322	323	136,680
MA	7.4	298,495	254,786	127,150	420,308	1,579,387,719	388	203,583
MI	10.3	410,517	360,769	160,278	768,447	1,466,032,922	290	201,823
MN	6.4	240,076	172,235	80,044	331,626	797,922,675	346	129,515
MS	10.7	98,329	71,498	34,281	158,203	203,983,404	190	54,080
MO	8.6	250,594	168,199	85,523	478,291	635,338,170	238	137,223
MT	6.8	47,541	30,547	16,701	76,507	130,711,751	262	36,403
NE	4.4	57,685	46,255	25,774	102,106	158,071,890	256	48,457
NV	13.5	129,688	107,143	63,743	233,278	563,848,437	307	56,337
NH	5.4	50,800	32,528	9,894	77,222	126,686,477	275	39,838
NJ	9.3	412,791	360,053	207,926	604,780	2,368,911,602	392	228,646
NM	7.4	94,419	49,564	29,705	100,525	268,167,436	293	44,339
NY	8.2	832,119	628,495	312,839	1,353,796	3,082,644,555	302	497,380
NC	10.5	452,908	308,535	172,412	745,960	1,315,695,624	291	195,000
ND	3.5	21,150	15,601	6,718	26,638	66,421,150	320	21,751
OH	8.6	317,886	270,404	111,799	676,561	1,278,336,195	292	218,152
OK	6.2	96,779	65,322	36,563	167,916	273,026,888	268	82,953
OR	9.5	215,581	174,409	81,515	451,277	816,627,930	288	109,588
PA	7.9	616,214	530,009	228,135	1,333,868	2,969,089,630	335	298,203
PR	15.7	117,011	100,999	58,028	160,298	226,147,581	117	47,302
RI	11.3	53,967	45,019	24,657	93,219	283,636,925	378	32,653
SC	10.3	188,404	128,341	73,582	308,533	422,815,729	237	96,519
SD	4.7	14,952	10,751	2,514	22,708	38,776,845	253	25,610
TN	9.2	228,435	175,581	88,353	391,895	572,680,399	235	111,816
TX	7.9	679,986	494,340	268,863	921,153	2,242,812,887	316	461,572
UT	6.7	84,514	62,857	30,276	111,716	257,338,918	313	67,917
VT	5.6	30,563	25,381	7,110	47,893	105,638,714	297	21,415
VA	6.2	243,768	136,022	74,601	344,284	606,552,912	284	191,111
VI	NA	3,468	3,151	1,567	4,340	18,035,275	308	3,505
WA	9.2	304,065	235,620	95,667	554,996	1,336,749,612	374	210,606
WV	8.0	67,987	48,886	17,338	86,736	188,052,825	250	35,766
WI	7.5	337,203	283,624	103,449	699,368	1,013,754,828	270	130,920
WY	6.0	23,846	18,181	8,645	30,491	86,822,007	329	21,763
U.S.	8.9	12,312,417	9,474,445	4,837,274	21,098,394	43,737,274,174	296	7,557,616

NA = Not available.

Unemployed Persons in the U.S. by Industry and Duration of Unemployment, 2011

Source: Bureau of Labor Statistics, U.S. Dept. of Labor

Occupation	Total	Less than 5 weeks	5 to 14 weeks	15 to 26 weeks	27 weeks and over	Average (mean) duration	Median duration
		Number of unemployed persons (thous.)				Weeks of unemployment	
Management, professional, and related.............	2,458	466	510	361	1,121	41.6	22.8
Management, business, and financial operations	1,067	157	215	164	531	45.1	27.2
Professional and related	1,392	309	295	197	591	39.0	20.0
Service	2,727	587	639	415	1,086	36.1	18.4
Sales and office	3,135	545	641	463	1,486	40.6	24.7
Sales and related...........................	1,481	277	310	211	683	40.0	23.3
Office and administrative support..............	1,653	267	331	252	803	41.2	26.0
Natural resources, construction, and maintenance	2,000	421	430	295	855	39.2	20.4
Farming, fishing, and forestry.....................	181	45	58	36	42	23.8	12.0
Construction and extraction......................	1,414	315	292	196	611	39.5	20.6
Installation, maintenance, and repair..................	406	60	80	63	202	44.9	27.4
Production, transportation, and material moving	2,099	383	426	317	973	41.4	23.5
Production	1,025	180	204	142	499	43.8	25.9
Transportation and material moving..................	1,073	203	222	175	474	39.0	21.8
Industry[1]							
Agriculture and related industries.......................	195	49	60	38	48	25.0	12.3
Mining, quarrying, and oil and gas extraction	52	11	11	9	22	40.4	21.3
Construction.................................	1,407	293	292	205	617	39.7	21.3
Manufacturing..............................	1,391	218	251	197	725	47.1	29.9
Durable goods	899	131	157	125	486	48.3	33.2
Nondurable goods	492	86	94	72	239	44.9	26.2
Wholesale and retail trade	1,861	333	410	285	833	39.8	22.4
Transportation and utilities......................	533	88	102	78	265	43.8	26.9
Information	230	43	41	30	116	43.6	27.8
Financial activities	601	85	105	96	315	45.4	29.1
Professional and business services....................	1,475	278	320	237	641	38.6	21.4
Education and health services....................	1,642	352	380	239	671	36.2	18.8
Leisure and hospitality	1,588	359	399	234	596	33.5	16.3
Other services	559	111	112	87	249	41.3	22.5
Public administration	279	43	51	45	140	40.6	27.4
No previous work experience......................	1,284	270	335	203	474	35.1	16.9

(1) Includes wage and salary workers only.

Persons Not in the U.S. Labor Force, 2011

Source: Bureau of Labor Statistics, U.S. Dept. of Labor

The Labor Dept.'s unemployment rate, based on its household survey, shows the number of people out of work as a percentage of U.S. adults age 16 and older in the labor force. That rate excludes, however, the millions of adults considered not to be in the labor force. (in thousands)

	Total	16 to 24	25 to 54	55 and over	Men	Women
		Age in years			Sex	
Total not in the labor force	86,001	17,201	22,961	45,839	34,343	51,658
Do not want a job now[1]..............	79,564	15,177	20,107	44,280	31,298	48,266
Want a job[1].......................	6,437	2,023	2,854	1,560	3,045	3,392
Did not search for work in previous year	3,268	1,010	1,303	955	1,463	1,804
Searched for work in previous year[2]...	3,169	1,014	1,551	605	1,582	1,587
Not available to work now	597	262	262	73	236	361
Available to work now	2,573	752	1,289	532	1,346	1,227
Reason not currently looking[3]						
Discouragement over job prospects[4].....	989	222	519	248	579	410
Reasons other than discouragement.....	1,584	530	770	284	767	817
Family responsibilities	215	30	139	45	48	166
In school or training	323	245	75	4	183	140
Ill health or disability...............	169	18	93	58	86	83
Other[5]............................	877	238	463	177	449	428

(1) Includes some persons who were not asked if they want a job. (2) Persons who had a job in the prior 12 months must have searched since the end of that job to be considered unemployed. (3) Of those available to work now. (4) Includes believing no work is available, not being able to find work, lacking necessary schooling or training, thought of as too young or old by employers, and other types of discrimination. (5) Includes those who did not actively look for work in the prior four weeks for such reasons as child care and transportation problems, as well as a small number for which reason for nonparticipation was not ascertained.

U.S. Displaced Workers, 2012

Source: Bureau of Labor Statistics, U.S. Dept. of Labor

	Total (thous.)	Plant or company closed down or moved	Insufficient work	Position or shift abolished
		Reason for job loss		
Total displaced workers..........	6,121	30.8%	39.5%	29.7%
Age: 20 to 24 years...............	128	40.5	39.3	20.3
25 to 54 years...............	4,268	31.8	40.2	28.0
55 to 64 years...............	1,338	27.8	37.0	35.2
65 years and over............	386	26.7	40.8	32.5
Sex: Men	3,440	31.1	43.2	25.7
Women.....................	2,681	30.4	34.8	34.8
Race: White	5,027	30.2	38.9	30.9
Black.......................	662	33.5	41.0	25.5
Asian.......................	230	30.5	46.9	22.7
Hispanic or Latino...........	901	35.9	50.1	14.0

Note: As of Jan. 2012. Displaced workers are persons 20 years or older who lost or left jobs they had held for at least three years. Workers in this table were displaced between Jan. 2009 and Dec. 2011. Hispanic or Latino persons may be of any race.

U.S. Unemployment Rates by Selected Characteristics, 1995-2012
Source: Bureau of Labor Statistics, U.S. Dept. of Labor

	1995	2000	2005	2007	2008	2009	2010	2011 Jan.	2011 June	2011 Yr.	2012 Jan.	2012 June
Total (all civilian workers)	5.6%	4.0%	5.1%	4.6%	5.8%	9.3%	9.6%	9.8%	9.3%	8.9%	8.8%	8.4%
Men, 20 years and older	4.8	3.3	4.4	4.1	5.4	9.6	9.8	10.2	8.7	8.7	8.7	7.5
Women, 20 years and older	4.9	3.6	4.6	4.0	4.9	7.5	8.0	8.1	8.2	7.9	7.8	7.6
Both sexes, 16 to 19 years	17.3	13.1	16.6	15.7	18.7	24.3	25.9	26.3	27.6	24.4	24.2	26.5
White	4.9	3.5	4.4	4.1	5.2	8.5	8.7	8.8	8.2	7.9	8.0	7.5
Black	10.4	7.6	10.0	8.3	10.1	14.8	16.0	16.5	16.5	15.8	14.2	14.8
Asian	—	3.6	4.0	3.2	4.0	7.3	7.5	6.9	6.8	7.0	6.7	6.3
Hispanic (of any race)	9.3	5.7	6.0	5.6	7.6	12.1	12.5	13.2	11.5	11.5	11.5	11.0
Married men, spouse present	3.3	—	—	—	3.4	6.6	6.8	5.9	6.2	5.8	5.1	4.9
Married women, spouse present	3.9	—	—	—	3.6	5.5	5.9	5.6	5.6	5.6	5.6	5.4
Women who maintain families	8.0	5.9	7.8	6.5	8.0	11.5	12.3	12.7	12.8	12.4	12.0	11.8
Occupation												
Management, professional, and related	2.4	1.8	2.3	2.1	2.7	4.6	4.7	4.7	4.7	4.5	4.3	4.4
Service	7.5	5.2	6.4	5.9	6.7	9.6	10.3	10.4	9.6	9.9	10.6	9.0
Sales and office	5.0	3.8	4.8	4.3	5.3	8.5	9.0	9.1	9.2	8.7	8.2	8.1
Nat. resources, constr., and maintenance	—	5.3	6.5	6.3	8.8	15.6	16.1	17.7	12.5	13.3	14.6	10.0
Prod., transp., and material moving	—	5.1	6.5	5.8	7.6	13.3	12.8	12.9	11.4	11.3	10.8	9.8
Industry												
Nonagricultural, private wage, and salary workers	5.8	4.1	5.2	4.7	5.9	9.8	9.9	10.0	9.0	9.0	9.0	7.9
Mining	5.2	4.4	3.1	3.4	3.1	11.6	9.4	8.5	5.2	6.1	9.4	4.8
Construction	11.5	6.2	7.4	7.4	10.6	19.0	20.6	22.5	15.6	16.4	17.7	12.8
Manufacturing	4.9	3.5	4.9	4.3	5.8	12.1	10.6	9.9	9.2	9.0	8.4	6.9
Durable goods	4.4	3.2	4.6	4.2	5.6	12.9	11.2	9.9	9.7	9.2	8.3	6.8
Nondurable goods	5.7	4.0	5.3	4.5	6.0	10.6	9.6	9.9	8.3	8.5	8.6	7.0
Wholesale and retail trade	6.5	4.3	5.4	4.7	5.9	9.0	9.5	9.1	9.7	8.9	9.3	8.3
Transportation and utilities	4.5	3.4	4.1	3.9	5.1	8.9	8.4	8.8	8.2	8.2	7.0	7.2
Information	—	3.2	5.0	3.6	5.0	9.2	9.7	7.3	7.9	7.3	7.9	7.1
Financial activities	3.3	2.4	2.9	3.0	3.9	6.4	6.9	7.2	6.8	6.4	4.9	5.6
Professional and business services	—	4.8	6.2	5.3	6.5	10.8	10.8	10.2	9.1	9.7	9.5	8.9
Education and health services	—	2.5	3.4	3.0	3.5	5.3	5.8	5.8	5.8	5.6	5.5	6.2
Leisure and hospitality	—	6.6	7.8	7.4	8.6	11.7	12.2	13.8	10.9	11.6	12.6	9.8
Other services	8.4	3.9	4.8	3.9	5.3	7.5	8.5	8.8	8.7	8.8	9.3	7.5
Agriculture and related	11.1	9.0	8.3	6.3	9.2	14.3	13.9	16.0	9.0	12.5	17.6	8.4
Government	2.9	2.1	2.6	2.3	2.4	3.6	4.4	5.0	5.8	4.7	4.2	5.2
Self-employed and unpaid family workers	—	2.1	2.7	2.8	3.6	5.5	5.9	6.8	5.7	6.0	5.8	5.0

— = Not available. **Note:** All monthly rates are unadjusted, except for married men and women, which are seasonally adjusted.

Employed Persons in the U.S. by Occupation and Sex, 2010-11
Source: Bureau of Labor Statistics, U.S. Dept. of Labor
(persons 16 years of age and older; in thousands)

	Total 2010	Total 2011	Men 2010	Men 2011	Women 2010	Women 2011
Total	139,064	139,869	73,359	74,290	65,705	65,579
Management, professional, and related occupations	51,743	52,547	25,070	25,552	26,673	26,995
Management, business, and financial operations	20,938	21,589	11,945	12,275	8,993	9,314
Management	15,001	15,250	9,266	9,439	5,735	5,812
Business and financial operations	5,937	6,339	2,679	2,837	3,258	3,503
Professional and related	30,805	30,957	13,125	13,277	17,680	17,681
Computer and mathematical	3,531	3,608	2,620	2,705	911	903
Architecture and engineering	2,619	2,785	2,282	2,406	337	379
Life, physical, and social science	1,409	1,303	755	687	655	616
Community and social services	2,337	2,352	836	835	1,500	1,518
Legal	1,716	1,770	878	889	838	881
Education, training, and library	8,628	8,619	2,261	2,274	6,367	6,345
Arts, design, entertainment, sports, and media	2,759	2,779	1,484	1,499	1,276	1,281
Healthcare practitioner and technical	7,805	7,740	2,009	1,982	5,796	5,758
Service occupations	24,634	24,787	10,652	10,929	13,982	13,858
Healthcare support	3,332	3,359	370	413	2,962	2,945
Protective service	3,289	3,210	2,587	2,546	703	664
Food preparation and serving related	7,660	7,747	3,439	3,534	4,221	4,213
Building and grounds cleaning and maintenance	5,328	5,492	3,164	3,359	2,164	2,133
Personal care and service	5,024	4,979	1,092	1,077	3,932	3,902
Sales and office occupations	33,433	33,066	12,419	12,450	21,015	20,616
Sales and related	15,386	15,330	7,703	7,733	7,683	7,597
Office and administrative support	18,047	17,736	4,716	4,717	13,331	13,019
Natural resources, construction, and maintenance occupations	13,073	13,009	12,467	12,457	606	552
Farming, fishing, and forestry	987	1,001	755	785	231	216
Construction and extraction	7,175	7,125	6,990	6,962	185	163
Installation, maintenance, and repair	4,911	4,883	4,721	4,710	190	173
Production, transportation, and material moving occupations	16,180	16,461	12,751	12,902	3,429	3,558
Production	7,998	8,142	5,792	5,826	2,206	2,316
Transportation and material moving	8,182	8,318	6,959	7,076	1,224	1,242

Note: Numbers may not add up to totals because of independent rounding.

Projected Openings for Selected High-Paying Occupations, 2010-20
Source: Employment Projections Program, Bureau of Labor Statistics, U.S. Dept. of Labor

Job openings shown below represent the average number expected each year for workers in the U.S. who are entering these occupations for the first time.

Occupation	Annual avg. job openings[1]	Median annual earnings[2]	Occupation	Annual avg. job openings[1]	Median annual earnings[2]
Registered nurses	1,207,400	$64,690	Accountants and auditors	452,100	$61,690
Truck drivers, heavy and tractor-trailer	649,400	37,770	Gen. and operations mgrs.	410,100	94,400
Postsecondary teachers	586,100	62,050	Carpenters	408,300	39,530
First-line office and admin. support supvrs.	584,400	47,460	Gen. maintenance and repair workers	379,100	34,730
Elementary school teachers[3]	573,200	51,660	Lic. practical and voc. nurses	369,200	40,380
Sales representatives[4]	559,900	52,440	Secondary school teachers[3]	355,600	53,230
First-line retail supvrs.	513,700	35,820	Business operations specialists[5]	327,200	62,450
Bookkeeping, accounting, auditing clerks	467,800	34,030			

(1) As a result of growth and net replacement needs. (2) For 2010. (3) Except special and vocation education. (4) Wholesale and manufacturing, except technical and scientific products. (5) Except agents, business mgrs. of artists, performers, and athletes; buyers and purchasing agents; claims adjusters, appraisers, examiners, and investigators; compliance officers; cost estimators; human resource workers; logisticians; management analysts; meeting, convention, and event planners; compensation, benefits, and job analysis specialists; training and development specialists; and market research analysts and specialists.

Top-Paying U.S. Counties by Average Weekly Wage, 2011
Source: Bureau of Labor Statistics, U.S. Dept. of Labor

County	Avg. weekly wage	% change, 2010-11	County	Avg. weekly wage	% change, 2010-11
New York, NY	$1,889	−2.3%	Fairfax, VA	$1,519	−1.5%
Santa Clara, CA	1,836	−5.7	Alexandria City, VA	1,434	0.4
Washington, DC	1,668	−1.2	Morris, NJ	1,400	−1.5
Suffolk, MA	1,599	−2.9	Somerset, NJ	1,393	−5.0
San Francisco, CA	1,597	0.8	Middlesex, MA	1,376	−3.0
Arlington, VA	1,591	−5.0	Montgomery, MD	1,324	−0.5
Fairfield, CT	1,589	−4.6	Chester, PA	1,284	1.3
San Mateo, CA	1,556	0.1	**United States**	**955**	**−1.7**

Note: Figures shown are for 4th quarter, from among the 323 largest U.S. counties, which comprise 70.7% of total covered workers. Horry County, SC, recorded the lowest average weekly earnings among the largest counties, with an average weekly wage of $569 in the 4th quarter of 2011. It was followed by Cameron County, TX ($597); Hidalgo County, TX ($601); Yakima County, WA ($648); Lake County, FL ($649); and Webb County, TX ($651). Data include all workers covered by state and federal unemployment insurance programs.

Federal Minimum Hourly Wage Rates
Source: Bureau of Labor Statistics, U.S. Dept. of Labor

Effective date	Minimum wage	% avg. earnings[1]	In 2012 dollars	Effective date	Minimum wage	% avg. earnings[1]	In 2012 dollars
Oct. 24, 1938	$0.25	40%	$4.08	Jan. 1, 1978	$2.65	43%	$9.36
Oct. 24, 1939	0.30	48	4.97	Jan. 1, 1979	2.90	43	9.20
Oct. 24, 1945	0.40	39	5.12	Jan. 1, 1980	3.10	43	8.67
Jan. 25, 1950	0.75	52	7.17	Jan. 1, 1981	3.35	42	8.49
Mar. 1, 1956	1.00	51	8.47	Apr. 1, 1990	3.80	35	6.70
Sept. 3, 1961	1.15	50	8.86	Apr. 1, 1991	4.25	38	7.19
Sept. 3, 1963	1.25	51	9.41	Oct. 1, 1996	4.75	37	6.67
Feb. 1, 1967	1.40	49	9.66	Sept. 1, 1997	5.15	39	7.39
Feb. 1, 1968	1.60	53	10.59	July 24, 2007	5.85	34	6.50
May 1, 1974	2.00	45	9.35	July 24, 2008	6.55	37	7.01
Jan. 1, 1975	2.10	43	8.99	July 24, 2009	7.25	40	7.79
Jan. 1, 1976	2.30	44	9.31				

Note: Before 1961, the minimum wage applied primarily to employees engaged in, or producing goods for, interstate commerce. Coverage was added 1961-64 primarily to employees in large retail and service enterprises and to local transit, construction, and gas station employees. Coverage was added 1966-77 (at reduced rates) to farm workers; federal, state, and local government employees; workers in various retail and service trades; and certain domestic workers. Starting in 1978, the minimum wage applied equally to all covered, nonexempt workers. At present, exceptions apply under specific circumstances to workers with disabilities, full-time students, youth under age 20 in their first 90 consecutive calendar days of employment, tipped employees, and student-learners. (1) Percent of gross hourly earnings of production workers in manufacturing.

Fatal Occupational Injuries, 2010
Source: Census of Fatal Occupational Injuries, Bureau of Labor Statistics, U.S. Dept. of Labor, in cooperation with other agencies

	Fatalities Number	%		Fatalities Number	%
Total	4,547	100%	Contact with objects and equipment	732	16%
			Struck by object or equipment	402	9
Transportation incidents	1,766	39	Struck by falling object or equipment	263	6
Highway	968	21	Struck by flying object or equipment	36	1
Collision bet. vehicles, mobile equipment	501	11	Caught in or compressed by equipment or objects	224	5
Vehicle struck object on side of road	244	5	Caught in running equipment or machinery	90	2
Noncollision	195	4	Caught in or crushed in collapsing materials	91	2
Jackknifed or overturned	173	4			
Nonhighway (farm, industrial premises)	272	6	**Falls**	**635**	**14**
Overturned	154	3			
Worker struck by vehicle	277	6	**Exposure to harmful substances or environments**	**409**	**9**
Railway accident	44	1	Contact with electric current	163	4
Water vehicle accident	52	1	Contact with overhead power lines	76	2
Aircraft accident	151	3	Contact with temperature extremes	45	1
			Exposure to caustic, noxious, or allergenic substances	139	3
Assaults and violent acts	808	18	Inhalation of substance	57	1
Homicides	506	11	Oxygen deficiency	60	1
Shooting	401	9	Drowning, submersion	45	1
Stabbing	34	1	**Fires and explosions**	**187**	**4**
Self-inflicted injuries	258	6			

Note: Totals for categories may include subcategories not shown separately. Percentages show incidence rate per total fatalities.

U.S. Occupational Injuries and Illnesses by Worker Characteristics, 2010

Source: Bureau of Labor Statistics, U.S. Dept. of Labor

Characteristic	Total			Female			Male		
	Number	Percent	Days away from work[1]	Number	Percent	Days away from work[1]	Number	Percent	Days away from work[1]
Total	1,191,100	100.0%	8	472,520	100.0%	7	712,080	100.0%	9
Occupation									
Management, business, and financial occupations..........	29,050	2.4	5	17,010	3.6	5	12,030	1.7	5
Professional and related occupations.................	135,620	11.4	6	101,020	21.4	6	34,370	4.8	6
Service occupations	371,410	31.2	7	192,930	40.8	7	177,250	24.9	7
Sales and related occupations	67,040	5.6	8	41,400	8.8	8	25,610	3.6	8
Office and administrative support occupations.................	79,170	6.6	7	50,980	10.8	7	28,040	3.9	8
Farming, fishing, and forestry occupations.................	12,280	1.0	7	2,710	0.6	8	9,570	1.3	7
Construction and extraction occupations.................	88,670	7.4	12	2,120	0.4	20	85,760	12.0	12
Installation, maintenance, and repair occupations...........	93,100	7.8	9	3,010	0.6	14	89,500	12.6	9
Production occupations.........	111,800	9.4	8	27,990	5.9	9	83,800	11.8	8
Transportation and material moving occupations...........	200,150	16.8	12	32,930	7.0	11	165,280	23.2	12
Age									
14-15.........................	220	(2)	3	120	(2)	3	100	(2)	2
16-19.........................	23,690	2.0	4	8,890	1.9	4	14,790	2.1	4
20-24.........................	96,620	8.1	5	36,890	7.8	4	59,640	8.4	5
25-34.........................	243,820	20.5	6	87,500	18.5	5	155,650	21.9	7
35-44.........................	273,790	23.0	8	101,950	21.6	7	170,850	24.0	9
45-54.........................	318,510	26.7	10	130,440	27.6	8	187,100	26.3	11
55-64.........................	180,080	15.1	12	83,810	17.7	10	95,490	13.4	14
65 and over...................	34,560	2.9	16	15,680	3.3	14	18,850	2.6	18
Nature of injury, illness									
Sprains, strains, tears	474,000	39.8	10	190,690	40.4	8	280,720	39.4	11
Fractures.....................	85,480	7.2	28	33,510	7.1	24	51,600	7.2	30
Cuts, lacerations, punctures	92,210	7.7	4	20,850	4.4	3	71,080	10.0	4
Cuts, lacerations	81,260	6.8	4	18,780	4.0	3	62,230	8.7	4
Punctures	10,950	0.9	3	2,080	0.4	3	8,850	1.2	3
Amputations	5,540	0.5	21	630	0.1	15	4,890	0.7	21
Bruises, contusions............	100,380	8.4	4	50,060	10.6	4	49,630	7.0	4
Heat burns, scalds	16,380	1.4	5	6,740	1.4	4	9,620	1.4	7
Chemical burns................	4,660	0.4	3	1,340	0.3	2	3,310	0.5	4
Carpal tunnel syndrome	10,060	0.8	27	6,450	1.4	27	3,600	0.5	25
Tendonitis	4,820	0.4	14	3,060	0.6	14	1,750	0.2	13
Multiple traumatic injuries and disorders	57,650	4.8	9	26,370	5.6	7	31,260	4.4	10
With fractures, burns, and other injuries	9,270	0.8	25	3,000	0.6	25	6,270	0.9	26
With sprains and bruises	21,780	1.8	8	12,630	2.7	7	9,160	1.3	10
Soreness, pain, including back	134,060	11.3	8	59,580	12.6	7	74,400	10.4	9
Back pain only...............	40,910	3.4	8	16,250	3.4	6	24,650	3.5	10
All other natures	205,860	17.3	6	73,230	15.5	5	130,220	18.3	7
Part of body affected									
Head........................	76,460	6.4	2	27,030	5.7	3	49,190	6.9	2
Eye(s)	25,230	2.1	2	5,440	1.2	2	19,720	2.8	2
Neck, including throat	16,980	1.4	8	7,800	1.7	7	9,050	1.3	8
Trunk.......................	386,550	32.5	10	145,380	30.8	8	239,340	33.6	11
Shoulder, incl. clavicle, scapula	87,040	7.3	21	32,680	6.9	14	53,890	7.6	24
Back, including spine, spinal cord	227,730	19.1	7	90,520	19.2	7	136,240	19.1	8
Upper extremities	253,450	21.3	7	94,810	20.1	7	157,800	22.2	7
Arm(s)......................	53,200	4.5	10	20,170	4.3	10	32,800	4.6	9
Wrist(s)	47,140	4.0	14	25,610	5.4	14	21,430	3.0	15
Hand(s), except finger(s)........	48,280	4.1	5	16,380	3.5	5	31,730	4.5	5
Finger(s), fingernail(s)..........	87,990	7.4	5	24,580	5.2	4	63,090	8.9	6
Lower extremities	274,210	23.0	10	107,170	22.7	8	165,560	23.3	12
Knee(s)	110,040	9.2	15	44,350	9.4	12	65,040	9.1	18
Ankle(s)	63,180	5.3	8	26,340	5.6	6	36,470	5.1	9
Foot, toe	49,100	4.1	7	18,240	3.9	6	30,620	4.3	8
Body systems	23,150	1.9	4	8,840	1.9	5	14,180	2.0	4
Multiple body parts	151,480	12.7	10	77,830	16.5	8	73,400	10.3	13
All other parts of body..........	8,820	0.7	5	3,650	0.8	5	3,550	0.5	8
Source of injury, illness									
Chemicals and chemical products	16,130	1.4	3	5,840	1.2	3	10,280	1.4	4
Containers....................	129,210	10.8	10	47,620	10.1	8	81,400	11.4	11
Furniture and fixtures	48,420	4.1	6	24,800	5.2	6	23,530	3.3	7
Machinery....................	58,720	4.9	7	14,690	3.1	5	44,010	6.2	8
Parts and materials............	88,160	7.4	8	9,590	2.0	7	78,400	11.0	8
Floors, walkways, ground surfaces	257,560	21.6	10	132,180	28.0	8	124,560	17.5	14
Handtools	49,160	4.1	5	9,580	2.0	3	39,360	5.5	5
Vehicles.....................	101,970	8.6	9	29,990	6.3	7	71,300	10.0	10
Person, injured or ill worker.......	178,090	15.0	12	71,730	15.2	12	106,080	14.9	11
Bodily motion or position of injured, ill worker	165,070	13.9	12	67,110	14.2	12	97,700	13.7	12
Person, other than injured or ill worker	105,560	8.9	7	73,350	15.5	7	31,860	4.5	8
Health care patient	72,750	6.1	7	57,910	12.3	7	14,580	2.0	7
All other sources	158,120	13.3	5	53,160	11.3	4	101,290	14.2	5

Note: Because of rounding and classifications not shown, percentages may not add up to 100. All injuries and illnesses reported involved days away from work. All types of ownership included (private sector, state government, and local government). (1) The measure used to summarize the varying lengths of absences. Half the cases involved more days away from work and half involved fewer days away from work. (2) Data too small to be displayed.

Civilian Employment of the Executive Branch, 1940-2010

Source: U.S. Office of Personnel Management

(in thousands)

Year	Total executive branch	Dept. of Defense	Civilian agencies/depts.									
			Total employees	Agricul-ture	HHS, Education, Social Sec.[1]	Homeland Sec.	Interior	Justice	Transpor-tation	Treasury	Veterans Affairs	Other
1940	699	256	443	98	9	18	46	11	NA	45	40	176
1945	3,370	2,635	736	82	11	20	45	19	NA	84	65	409
1950	1,439	753	686	84	13	20	66	20	NA	76	188	219
1955	1,860	1,187	673	86	40	21	54	24	NA	65	178	206
1960	1,808	1,047	761	99	62	21	56	24	NA	62	172	265
1965	1,901	1,034	867	113	87	21	71	27	NA	74	167	307
1970	2,203	1,219	983	118	112	23	75	33	62	84	169	308
1975	2,149	1,042	1,107	121	147	31	80	47	69	101	213	297
1980	2,161	960	1,201	129	163	40	77	48	66	102	228	346
1985	2,252	1,107	1,145	122	147	40	80	55	56	110	247	286
1990	2,250	1,034	1,216	123	129	49	78	71	61	132	248	326
1991	2,243	1,013	1,230	126	135	50	82	77	64	139	256	302
1992	2,225	952	1,274	128	136	56	85	82	64	133	260	329
1993	2,157	891	1,266	124	135	56	85	82	63	127	268	326
1994	2,085	850	1,235	120	133	55	81	83	59	128	262	315
1995	2,012	802	1,210	113	132	56	76	87	58	128	264	297
2000	1,778	651	1,127	104	126	70	74	98	58	113	220	265
2001	1,792	647	1,145	109	129	73	76	99	59	117	226	258
2002	1,818	645	1,173	98	130	76	77	96	96	118	223	258
2003	1,867	636	1,231	100	131	153	72	102	58	132	226	257
2004	1,882	644	1,238	111	130	153	77	104	57	111	236	257
2005	1,872	649	1,224	108	131	147	76	105	56	108	235	258
2006	1,880	653	1,227	105	129	154	72	107	54	107	239	260
2007	1,888	651	1,237	103	129	159	72	107	54	104	254	254
2008	1,960	670	1,289	104	132	172	76	109	55	106	274	261
2009	2,094	737	1,357	104	139	180	75	113	57	109	297	283
2010	2,133	773	1,360	107	144	183	70	118	58	110	305	265

NA = Not available. **Note:** End-of-fiscal-year count; postal service excluded. (1) Estimated, 1940-50.

Median Earnings by Industry and Sex, 2010

Source: 2010 Census, U.S. Census Bureau, U.S. Dept. of Commerce

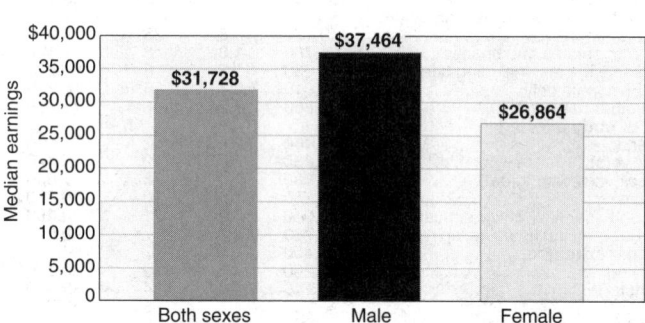

Industry	Total employed	Male (%)	Female (%)	Median earnings	Median earnings (male)	Median earnings (female)
Agriculture; forestry; fishing, hunting; mining	2,646,975	82.2%	17.8%	$27,790	$30,545	$18,906
Arts, entertainment, recreation; accommodation, food services	12,859,572	48.7	51.3	15,009	17,518	12,402
Construction	8,686,813	90.8	9.2	32,068	32,127	31,454
Educational services; health care, social assistance	32,311,107	25.3	74.7	32,509	42,252	30,845
Finance, insurance; real estate, rental, leasing	9,275,465	44.6	55.4	41,446	52,360	36,135
Information	3,015,521	56.6	43.4	43,874	51,360	36,208
Manufacturing	14,439,691	70.7	29.3	40,237	43,339	31,001
Other services, except public administration	6,913,449	47.0	53.0	21,586	29,451	16,570
Professional, scientific, management; administrative, waste management services	14,710,089	57.9	42.1	39,197	45,915	31,940
Public administration	7,187,193	55.1	44.9	48,331	55,225	41,077
Retail trade	16,203,408	50.2	49.8	21,098	26,143	17,151
Transportation, warehousing; utilities	6,843,579	75.8	24.2	41,313	43,600	34,196
Wholesale trade	3,941,066	70.2	29.8	39,367	41,821	31,690

Note: For the civilian employed population 16 years of age and over including workers not employed full-time.

U.S. Median Weekly Earnings, 2012

Source: Bureau of Labor Statistics, U.S. Dept. of Labor

AGE, RACE, OR ETHNICITY	Total Number of workers (thous.)	Total Median weekly earnings	Men Number of workers (thous.)	Men Median weekly earnings	Women Number of workers (thous.)	Women Median weekly earnings
All workers, by age						
16 years and over	102,769	$771	57,319	$865	45,450	$689
16 to 24 years	9,098	429	5,200	460	3,897	409
16 to 19 years	1,068	357	648	372	420	322
20 to 24 years	8,029	453	4,552	477	3,477	418
25 years and over	93,672	821	52,119	918	41,553	727
25 to 54 years	74,267	810	41,749	902	32,518	722
25 to 34 years	24,648	722	14,036	751	10,611	680
35 to 44 years	24,136	861	13,731	953	10,405	749
45 to 54 years	25,484	884	13,982	1,003	11,502	733
55 years and over	19,405	873	10,370	991	9,034	748
55 to 64 years	16,340	897	8,671	1,015	7,669	760
65 years and over	3,065	712	1,699	780	1,366	661
White						
16 years and over	82,045	792	46,765	891	35,280	701
16 to 24 years	7,188	451	4,179	471	3,009	421
25 years and over	74,857	846	42,586	943	32,271	736
25 to 54 years	58,671	833	33,829	925	24,843	731
55 years and over	16,186	893	8,757	1,020	7,428	758
Black						
16 years and over	12,198	637	5,785	668	6,413	616
16 to 24 years	1,211	382	599	392	612	369
25 years and over	10,987	682	5,186	704	5,801	658
25 to 54 years	9,004	673	4,270	693	4,734	652
55 years and over	1,984	752	916	792	1,067	727
Asian						
16 years and over	5,540	930	3,101	1,092	2,439	771
16 to 24 years	321	492	201	514	120	417
25 years and over	5,219	957	2,900	1,137	2,319	807
25 to 54 years	4,360	982	2,393	1,157	1,967	849
55 years and over	859	805	507	980	352	625
Hispanic[1]						
16 years and over	16,325	576	9,995	600	6,330	525
16 to 24 years	2,036	403	1,242	422	794	381
25 years and over	14,289	608	8,753	632	5,536	569
25 to 54 years	12,595	607	7,794	633	4,800	564
55 years and over	1,694	615	958	624	736	602
OCCUPATION						
Managerial, professional, and related	40,782	1,102	19,720	1,342	21,062	945
Management, business, and financial	16,884	1,174	9,163	1,410	7,721	979
Professional and related	23,898	1,036	10,557	1,269	13,341	928
Service	14,836	485	7,642	529	7,194	435
Sales and office	23,536	659	9,515	764	14,021	615
Sales and related	9,394	696	5,504	843	3,890	509
Office and administrative support	14,142	646	4,011	692	10,131	636
Natural resources, construction, and maintenance	9,732	745	9,383	756	349	586
Farming, fishing, and forestry	699	444	578	453	121	428
Construction and extraction	5,040	762	4,946	766	94	647
Installation, maintenance, and repair	3,993	800	3,859	802	134	709
Production, transportation, and material moving	13,883	651	11,059	696	2,824	512
Production	7,407	647	5,433	716	1,974	505
Transportation and material moving	6,475	656	5,626	676	850	551

Note: Not seasonally adjusted; figures are median usual weekly earnings of full-time wage and salary workers for 2nd quarter 2012. (1) May be of any race.

Average Hours and Earnings of U.S. Production Workers, 1969-2011

Source: Bureau of Labor Statistics, U.S. Dept. of Labor
(annual averages)

	Weekly hours	Hourly earnings	Weekly earnings		Weekly hours	Hourly earnings	Weekly earnings		Weekly hours	Hourly earnings	Weekly earnings
1969	37.5	$3.22	$120.75	1984	35.1	$8.49	$298.00	1998	34.5	$13.01	$448.56
1970	37.0	3.40	125.80	1985	34.9	8.74	305.03	1999	34.3	13.49	463.15
1971	36.8	3.63	133.58	1986	34.7	8.93	309.87	2000	34.3	14.02	481.01
1972	36.9	3.90	143.91	1987	34.7	9.14	317.16	2001	34.0	14.54	493.79
1973	36.9	4.14	152.77	1988	34.6	9.44	326.62	2002	33.9	14.97	506.75
1974	36.4	4.43	161.25	1989	34.5	9.80	338.10	2003	33.7	15.37	518.06
1975	36.0	4.73	170.28	1990	34.3	10.20	349.75	2004	33.7	15.69	529.09
1976	36.1	5.06	182.67	1991	34.1	10.52	358.51	2005	33.8	16.13	544.33
1977	35.9	5.44	195.30	1992	34.2	10.77	368.25	2006	33.9	16.76	567.87
1978	35.8	5.88	210.50	1993	34.3	11.05	378.89	2007	33.9	17.43	590.04
1979	35.6	6.34	225.70	1994	34.5	11.34	391.22	2008	33.6	18.08	607.95
1980	35.2	6.85	241.12	1995	34.3	11.65	400.07	2009	33.1	18.63	617.18
1981	35.2	7.44	261.89	1996	34.3	12.04	413.28	2010	33.4	19.07	636.92
1982	34.7	7.87	273.09	1997	34.5	12.51	431.86	2011	33.6	19.47	654.87
1983	34.9	8.20	286.18								

Note: Data refer to production workers in natural resources, mining, and manufacturing; construction workers; and non-supervisory workers in the service industries.

Elderly in U.S. Labor Force, 1890-2011

Source: U.S. Census Bureau, U.S. Dept. of Commerce

(labor force participation rate of persons age 65 and older; 1910 figures not available)

Median Weekly Earnings of Wage and Salary Workers in the U.S. by Union Affiliation, 1996, 2011

Source: Bureau of Labor Statistics, U.S. Dept. of Labor

Sex and age	1996				2011			
	Total	Union member[1]	Represented by unions[2]	Non-union	Total	Union member[1]	Represented by unions[2]	Non-union
Total, 16 years and older	**$490**	**$615**	**$610**	**$462**	**$756**	**$938**	**$934**	**$729**
16 to 24 years	298	371	362	294	440	552	550	432
25 years and older	520	625	621	498	797	954	950	766
25 to 34 years	463	554	548	447	693	852	848	671
35 to 44 years	559	636	632	530	837	992	983	805
45 to 54 years	594	687	686	552	866	988	987	832
55 to 64 years	535	620	616	505	881	992	992	845
65 years and older	384	510	510	367	742	849	855	728
Men, 16 years and older	**557**	**653**	**651**	**520**	**832**	**982**	**981**	**798**
16 to 24 years	307	375	369	303	455	577	575	447
25 years and older	599	669	668	580	886	1,000	999	857
25 to 34 years	499	591	587	485	717	876	876	699
35 to 44 years	632	683	683	617	935	1,030	1,022	912
45 to 54 years	698	718	721	682	979	1,036	1,038	964
55 to 64 years	643	667	664	633	997	1,062	1,066	977
65 years and older	477	589	593	424	821	897	910	813
Women, 16 years and older	**418**	**549**	**543**	**398**	**684**	**879**	**871**	**653**
16 to 24 years	284	358	339	280	421	520	518	416
25 years and older	444	560	555	420	718	895	888	688
25 to 34 years	415	497	495	405	662	829	823	637
35 to 44 years	463	561	556	439	734	936	925	702
45 to 54 years	481	620	616	445	744	925	922	715
55 to 64 years	420	524	523	395	749	917	916	724
65 years and older	334	417	413	321	664	820	819	645

Note: Data refer to the sole or principal job of full- and part-time workers. Excluded are self-employed workers regardless of whether or not their businesses are incorporated. (1) Including members of an employee association similar to a union. (2) Including members of a labor union or employee association similar to a union, and others whose jobs are covered by a union or an employee-association contract.

Work Stoppages (Strikes and Lockouts) in the U.S., 1950-2011

Source: Bureau of Labor Statistics, U.S. Dept. of Labor; involving 1,000 workers or more

Year	No.	Workers (thous.)	Days idle (thous.)	Year	No.	Workers (thous.)	Days idle (thous.)	Year	No.	Workers (thous.)	Days idle (thous.)
1950	424	1,698	30,390	1984	62	376	8,499	1998	34	387	5,116
1955	363	2,055	21,180	1985	54	324	7,079	1999	17	73	1,996
1960	222	896	13,260	1986	69	533	11,861	2000	39	394	20,419
1965	268	999	15,140	1987	46	174	4,481	2001	29	99	1,151
1970	381	2,468	52,761	1988	40	118	4,381	2002	19	46	660
1975	235	965	17,563	1989	51	452	16,996	2003	14	129	4,091
1976	231	1,519	23,962	1990	44	185	5,926	2004	17	171	3,344
1977	298	1,212	21,258	1991	40	392	4,584	2005	22	100	1,736
1978	219	1,006	23,774	1992	35	364	3,989	2006	20	70	2,688
1979	235	1,021	20,409	1993	35	182	3,981	2007	21	189	1,265
1980	187	795	20,844	1994	45	322	5,020	2008	15	72	1,954
1981	145	729	16,908	1995	31	192	5,771	2009	5	13	124
1982	96	656	9,061	1996	37	273	4,889	2010	11	45	302
1983	81	909	17,461	1997	29	339	4,497	2011	19	113	1,020

Note: Numbers cover stoppages that began in the year indicated. Workers are counted more than once if they are involved in more than one stoppage during the year. For work stoppages ongoing at the end of a calendar year, days idle include only the days for the calendar year.

U.S. Union Membership, 1930-2011

Source: Bureau of Labor Statistics, U.S. Dept. of Labor

(numbers in thousands)

Year	Total employed[1]	% in union	Union members[2]	Year	Total employed[1]	% in union	Union members[2]	Year	Total employed[1]	% in union	Union members[2]
1930	29,424	11.6%	3,401	1970	70,920	27.3%	19,381	2005	125,889	12.5%	15,685
1935	27,053	13.2	3,584	1975	76,945	25.5	19,611	2006	128,237	12.0	15,359
1940	32,376	26.9	8,717	1980	90,564	21.9	19,843	2007	129,767	12.1	15,670
1945	40,394	35.5	14,322	1985	94,521	18.0	16,996	2008	129,377	12.4	16,098
1950	45,222	31.5	14,267	1990	103,905	16.1	16,740	2009	124,490	12.3	15,327
1955	50,675	33.2	16,802	1995	110,038	14.9	16,360	2010	124,073	11.9	14,715
1960	54,234	31.4	17,049	2000	120,786	13.5	16,258	2011	125,187	11.8	14,764
1965	60,815	28.4	17,299								

(1) Does not include agricultural employment; from 1985 on, does not include self-employed or unemployed persons. (2) From 1930 to 1980, includes dues-paying members of traditional trade unions, regardless of employment status; after 1980, includes employed only. From 1985 on, includes members of employee associations that engage in collective bargaining with employers.

ENERGY

U.S. Energy Overview, 1960-2011

Source: *Annual Energy Review 2011*, Energy Information Administration (EIA), U.S. Dept. of Energy; in quadrillion Btu

	1960	1970	1975	1980	1985	1990	1995	2000	2005	2010	2011P
Production	42.80	63.50	61.36	67.23	67.80	70.87	71.32	71.49	69.59	74.82	78.17
Fossil fuels	39.87	59.19	54.73	59.01	57.54	58.56	57.54	57.37	55.04	58.25	60.67
Coal[1]	10.82	14.61	14.99	18.60	19.33	22.49	22.13	22.74	23.19	22.04	22.18
Natural gas (dry)	12.66	21.67	19.64	19.91	16.98	18.33	19.08	19.66	18.56	21.82	23.51
Crude oil[2]	14.93	20.40	17.73	18.25	18.99	15.57	13.89	12.36	10.96	11.61	12.06
Natural gas plant liquids (NGPL)	1.46	2.51	2.37	2.25	2.24	2.17	2.44	2.61	2.33	2.78	2.93
Nuclear electric power	0.01	0.24	1.90	2.74	4.08	6.10	7.08	7.86	8.16	8.43	8.26
Renewable energy	2.93	4.08	4.72	5.49	6.18	6.21	6.70	6.26	6.39	8.14	9.24
Conventional hydroelectric power[3]	1.61	2.63	3.15	2.90	2.97	3.05	3.21	2.81	2.70	2.54	3.17
Biomass[4]	1.32	1.43	1.50	2.48	3.02	2.74	3.10	3.01	3.12	4.34	4.51
Geothermal energy	(*)	0.01	0.07	0.11	0.20	0.34	0.29	0.32	0.34	0.21	0.23
Solar	NA	NA	NA	NA	(*)	0.06	0.07	0.07	0.07	0.13	0.16
Wind	NA	NA	NA	NA	(*)	0.03	0.03	0.06	0.18	0.92	1.17
Imports	4.19	8.34	14.03	15.80	11.78	18.82	22.26	28.97	34.71	29.88	28.59
Coal	0.01	(*)	0.02	0.03	0.05	0.07	0.24	0.31	0.76	0.48	0.33
Natural gas	0.16	0.85	0.98	1.01	0.95	1.55	2.90	3.87	4.45	3.83	3.54
All crude oil and petroleum prods.[5]	4.00	7.47	12.95	14.66	10.61	17.12	18.88	24.53	29.25	25.37	24.49
Electricity[6]	0.02	0.02	0.04	0.09	0.16	0.06	0.15	0.17	0.15	0.15	0.18
Exports	1.48	2.63	2.32	3.69	4.20	4.75	4.51	4.01	4.56	8.23	10.36
Coal	1.02	1.94	1.76	2.42	2.44	2.77	2.32	1.53	1.27	2.10	2.75
Natural gas	0.01	0.07	0.07	0.05	0.06	0.09	0.16	0.25	0.74	1.15	1.52
All crude oil and petroleum prods.[5]	0.43	0.55	0.44	1.16	1.66	1.82	1.99	2.15	2.44	4.84	5.90
Electricity[6]	(*)	0.01	0.02	0.01	0.02	0.06	0.01	0.05	0.07	0.65	0.51
Consumption	45.09	67.84	72.00	78.12	76.49	84.65	91.17	98.97	100.44	97.67	97.18
Fossil fuels	42.14	63.52	65.35	69.83	66.09	72.33	77.26	84.73	85.79	81.05	79.66
Coal	9.84	12.26	12.66	15.42	17.48	19.17	20.09	22.58	22.80	20.79	19.57
Natural gas[7]	12.39	21.80	19.95	20.24	17.70	19.60	22.67	23.82	22.56	24.26	24.80
Petroleum[8]	19.92	29.52	32.73	34.20	30.92	33.55	34.44	38.26	40.39	36.01	35.28
Nuclear electric power	0.01	0.24	1.90	2.74	4.08	6.10	7.08	7.86	8.16	8.43	8.26
Renewable energy	2.93	4.08	4.72	5.49	6.18	6.21	6.71	6.26	6.41	8.09	9.14
Conventional hydroelectric power[3]	1.61	2.63	3.15	2.90	2.97	3.05	3.21	2.81	2.70	2.54	3.17
Biomass[4]	1.32	1.43	1.50	2.48	3.02	2.74	3.10	3.01	3.12	4.29	4.41
Geothermal energy	(*)	0.01	0.07	0.11	0.20	0.34	0.29	0.32	0.34	0.21	0.23
Solar	NA	NA	NA	NA	(*)	0.06	0.07	0.07	0.07	0.13	0.16
Wind	NA	NA	NA	NA	(*)	0.03	0.03	0.06	0.18	0.92	1.17

NA = Not available. P = preliminary. (*) = Less than 0.005 quadrillion Btu. **Note:** Some numbers may not add up to totals because of rounding. (1) Incl. waste coal supplied beginning in 1989 and refuse recovery beginning in 2001. (2) Incl. lease condensate. (3) Starting in 1990, pumped storage was removed and expanded coverage of industrial use of hydroelectric power was included. (4) Category known as "wood, waste, and alcohol" for years prior to 2000. Includes wood, waste, and alcohol fuels (ethanol blended into motor gasoline). Ethanol is included in both Petroleum and Biomass categories but is only counted once in totals. (5) Incl. imports of crude oil for the Strategic Petroleum Reserve, which began in 1977. (6) Small amts. transmitted across borders with Canada and Mexico. (7) Incl. supplemental gaseous fuels. (8) Petroleum products supplied, incl. natural gas plant liquids and crude oil burned as fuel.

U.S. Energy Flow, 2011

Source: *Annual Energy Review 2011*, Energy Information Administration (EIA), U.S. Dept. of Energy; in quadrillion Btu

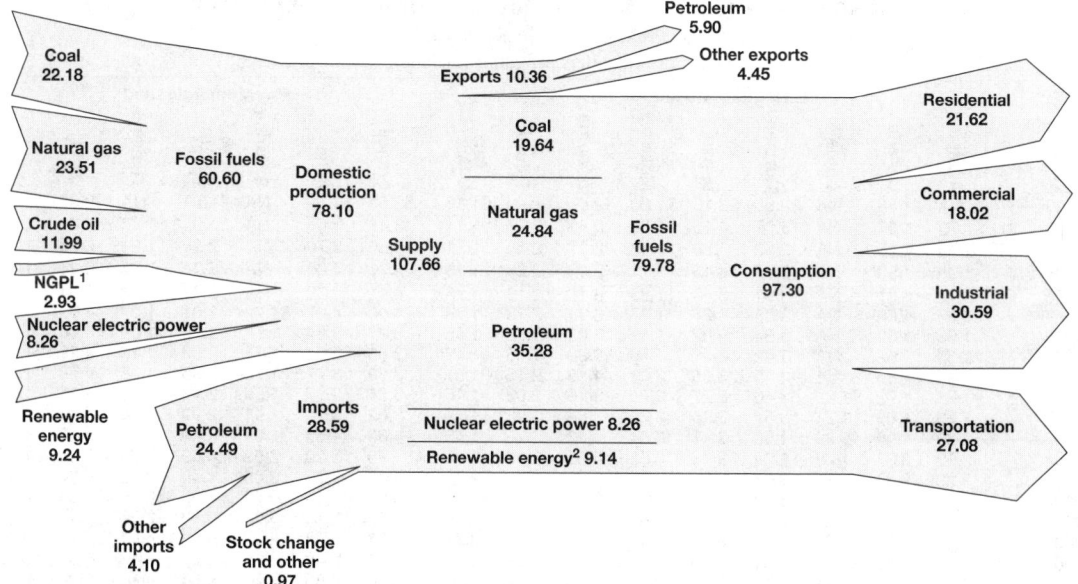

Note: Preliminary figures. Some numbers may not add up to totals because of rounding. (1) Natural gas plant liquids. (2) Conventional hydroelectric power, biomass, geothermal, solar thermal and photovoltaic, and wind.

U.S. Energy Consumption by Source, 1949-2011

Source: *Annual Energy Review 2011*, Energy Information Administration (EIA), U.S. Dept. of Energy

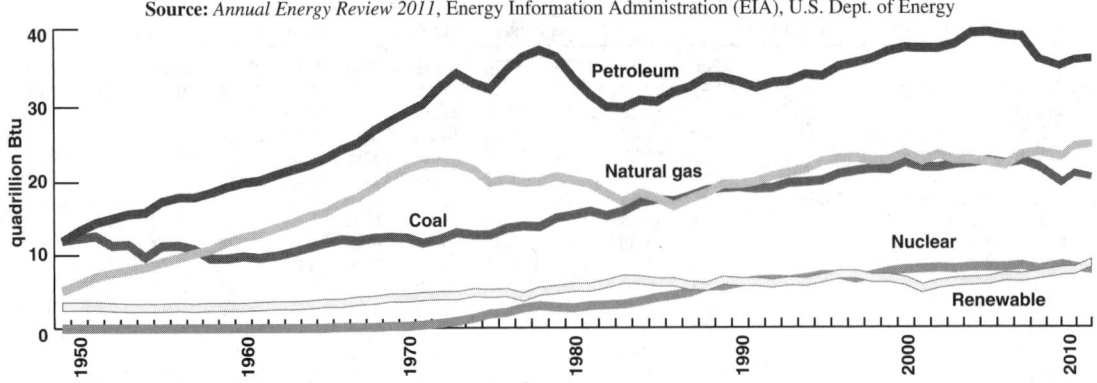

World's Largest Energy Producers and Consumers, 1980-2009

Source: Energy Information Administration (EIA), U.S. Dept. of Energy

(primary energy in quadrillion Btu; ranked by top producers/consumers in 2009)

Production	1980	1985	1990	1995	2000	2005	2008	2009	% change, 1980-2009
1. China	18.122	24.303	29.385	35.045	34.200	64.448	78.348	81.887	351.9%
2. United States	67.233	67.798	70.870	71.317	71.485	69.427	73.114	72.648	8.1
3. Russia.	NA	NA	NA	41.418	43.002	50.717	52.178	49.514	NA
4. Saudi Arabia	22.434	8.642	15.920	20.659	21.593	25.508	25.245	22.912	2.1
5. Canada.	10.276	12.020	13.404	16.830	18.124	18.894	19.020	18.246	77.6
6. India	3.101	5.266	6.821	9.484	9.832	11.734	13.597	14.585	370.3
7. Iran	3.944	5.587	7.670	9.347	10.400	13.115	13.357	14.260	261.6
8. Indonesia	4.227	4.201	5.313	6.971	7.735	9.036	11.935	12.707	200.6
9. Australia	3.245	4.997	6.155	7.429	9.655	11.056	11.926	12.264	277.9
10. Norway	2.929	3.771	5.804	8.347	10.270	10.656	10.125	9.886	237.5
Total world production	287.482	307.079	349.860	363.486	394.257	456.399	488.553	484.147	68.4%

Consumption	1980	1985	1990	1995	2000	2005	2008	2009	% change, 1980-2009
1. United States	78.124	77.164	85.040	91.815	99.823	100.281	99.278	94.547	21.0%
2. China	17.287	22.006	26.999	34.756	36.352	68.247	84.673	90.258	422.1
3. Russia.	NA	NA	NA	27.941	27.219	27.677	29.367	26.816	NA
4. India	4.041	5.914	7.879	11.443	13.462	16.363	19.992	21.689	436.7
5. Japan	15.210	15.706	18.779	20.965	22.436	22.656	21.863	20.598	35.4
6. Germany[1]	14.864	14.828	14.856	14.383	14.261	14.400	14.355	13.461	−9.4
7. Canada.	9.695	10.152	10.979	12.211	13.062	14.167	13.951	13.042	34.5
8. France.	8.389	8.350	9.125	10.052	10.850	11.353	11.290	10.658	27.0
9. Brazil.	4.022	4.593	5.751	7.017	8.526	9.347	10.313	10.288	155.8
10. Korea, South.	1.758	2.306	3.841	6.362	7.839	9.228	9.887	9.959	466.5
Total world consumption	283.194	308.968	347.686	365.393	397.536	458.692	490.841	482.972	70.5%

NA = Not available. (1) Data for 1980-90 represents sum of figures for East and West Germany and may not be directly comparable.

Gasoline Retail Prices in Selected Countries, 1990-2011

Source: *Energy Prices and Taxes,* International Energy Agency

(average price in dollars per gallon, including taxes)

Year	Regular unleaded									Premium unleaded						
	Australia	Canada	China	Germany	Japan	Mexico	S. Korea	Taiwan	U.S.	France	Italy	S. Africa	Spain	Thailand	UK	U.S.
1990	NA	$1.86	NA	$2.65	$3.16	$1.00	$2.05	$2.49	$1.16	$3.63	$4.59	NA	NA	NA	$2.82	$1.35
1993	$1.73	1.57	NA	3.07	4.16	1.56	2.88	2.27	1.11	3.41	3.68	NA	$3.01	$1.26	2.84	1.30
1994	1.84	1.45	NA	3.52	4.36	1.48	2.87	2.14	1.11	3.59	3.70	NA	2.99	1.21	2.98	1.31
1995	1.95	1.53	NA	3.96	4.43	1.11	2.93	2.23	1.15	4.26	4.00	NA	3.24	1.25	3.21	1.34
1996	2.12	1.61	NA	3.94	3.64	1.25	3.18	2.15	1.23	4.41	4.39	NA	3.32	1.49	3.34	1.41
1997	2.05	1.62	NA	3.53	3.26	1.47	3.34	2.23	1.23	4.00	4.07	$1.72	3.01	1.27	3.83	1.42
1998	1.63	1.38	NA	3.34	2.82	1.49	3.03	1.86	1.06	3.87	3.84	1.51	2.80	1.09	4.06	1.25
1999	1.72	1.52	NA	3.42	3.27	1.79	3.80	1.86	1.17	3.85	3.87	1.55	2.82	1.22	4.29	1.36
2000	1.94	1.86	NA	3.45	3.65	2.01	4.18	2.15	1.51	3.80	3.77	1.78	2.86	1.38	4.58	1.69
2001	1.71	1.72	$1.22	3.40	3.27	2.20	3.75	2.02	1.46	3.51	3.57	1.59	2.73	1.33	4.13	1.66
2002	1.76	1.69	1.21	3.67	3.15	2.24	3.84	1.93	1.36	3.62	3.74	1.41	2.90	1.35	4.16	1.56
2003	2.20	1.99	1.26	4.59	3.47	2.04	4.12	2.16	1.59	4.35	4.53	1.91	3.49	1.52	4.70	1.66
2004	2.72	2.37	1.48	5.24	3.93	2.03	4.51	2.46	1.88	4.99	5.30	2.58	4.09	1.76	5.56	1.95
2005	3.23	2.89	1.70	5.66	4.28	2.22	5.28	2.76	2.30	5.46	5.73	3.05	4.49	2.25	5.97	2.37
2006	3.54	3.26	2.11	6.03	4.47	2.31	5.92	3.05	2.59	5.87	6.10	3.42	4.85	2.76	6.36	2.67
2007	3.85	3.59	2.29	6.88	4.49	2.40	6.21	3.20	2.80	6.60	6.73	3.64	5.36	3.20	7.15	2.91
2008	4.45	4.08	3.11	7.75	5.74	2.45	5.83	3.53	3.27	7.51	7.64	4.13	6.13	4.01	7.42	3.37
2009	3.79	3.15	3.26	6.81	4.86	2.14	4.70	3.01	2.35	6.35	6.48	NA	5.27	4.13	5.86	2.48
2010	4.37	3.79	NA	7.10	5.73	2.46	5.60	NA	2.78	6.74	6.83	NA	5.84	NA	6.83	2.90
2011	5.58	4.78	NA	NA	6.91	2.79	6.59	NA	3.52	7.90	8.18	NA	6.95	NA	8.08	3.65

NA = Not available. **Note:** Some countries report only premium averages, and some do not sell regular unleaded gasoline.

Average U.S. Gasoline Prices, 1973-2012

Source: *Monthly Energy Review*, Sept. 2012; *Short-Term Energy Outlook*, Sept. 2012; Energy Information Administration (EIA); U.S. Dept. of Energy

(in dollars per gallon, including taxes; constant dollars is price in Aug. 2012 dollars)

Year	Leaded regular	Current dollars Unleaded regular	Current dollars Unleaded premium	All types[1]	Constant dollars, all types[1]	Year	Leaded regular	Current dollars Unleaded regular	Current dollars Unleaded premium	All types[1]	Constant dollars, all types[1]
1973	$0.39	NA	NA	NA	NA	1993	NA	$1.11	$1.30	$1.17	$1.87
1974	0.53	NA	NA	NA	NA	1994	NA	1.11	1.31	1.17	1.82
1975	0.57	NA	NA	NA	NA	1995	NA	1.15	1.34	1.21	1.82
1976	0.59	$0.61	NA	NA	NA	1996	NA	1.23	1.41	1.29	1.89
1977	0.62	0.66	NA	NA	NA	1997	NA	1.23	1.42	1.29	1.85
1978	0.63	0.67	NA	$0.65	$2.30	1998	NA	1.06	1.25	1.12	1.58
1979	0.86	0.90	NA	0.88	2.79	1999	NA	1.17	1.36	1.22	1.69
1980	1.19	1.25	NA	1.22	3.41	2000	NA	1.51	1.69	1.56	2.09
1981[2]	1.31	1.38	$1.47	1.35	3.43	2001	NA	1.46	1.66	1.53	1.99
1982	1.22	1.30	1.42	1.28	3.06	2002	NA	1.36	1.56	1.44	1.85
1983	1.16	1.24	1.38	1.23	2.83	2003	NA	1.59	1.78	1.64	2.05
1984	1.13	1.21	1.37	1.20	2.66	2004	NA	1.88	2.07	1.92	2.35
1985	1.12	1.20	1.34	1.20	2.56	2005	NA	2.30	2.49	2.34	2.76
1986	0.86	0.93	1.09	0.93	1.96	2006	NA	2.59	2.81	2.64	3.01
1987	0.90	0.95	1.09	0.96	1.94	2007	NA	2.80	3.03	2.85	3.17
1988	0.90	0.95	1.11	0.96	1.88	2008	NA	3.27	3.52	3.32	3.55
1989	1.00	1.02	1.20	1.06	1.97	2009	NA	2.35	2.61	2.40	2.58
1990	1.15	1.16	1.35	1.22	2.15	2010	NA	2.79	3.05	2.84	3.00
1991	NA	1.14	1.32	1.20	2.02	2011	NA	3.53	3.79	3.58	3.58
1992	NA	1.13	1.32	1.19	1.95	2012 (Aug.)	NA	3.71	3.99	3.76	3.76

NA = Not applicable. **Note:** Until unleaded gas became available in 1976, leaded was the only type used in automobiles. Starting in Sept. 1981, the Bureau of Labor Statistics included gasohol in average for all types, and unleaded premium is weighted more heavily. Average retail prices (in cents per gallon) for selected years preceding 1973 were as follows: 1950: 27; 1955: 29; 1960: 31; 1965: 31; 1970: 36. (1) Also includes types of motor gasoline not shown separately.

Energy Consumption, Total and Per Capita, by State, 2010

Source: State Energy Data System, Energy Information Administration (EIA), U.S. Dept. of Energy

Total Consumption

Rank, state	Trillion Btu	Rank, state	Trillion Btu
1. Texas	11,769.9	27. Arizona	1,399.6
2. California	7,825.7	28. Massachusetts	1,396.9
3. Florida	4,381.9	29. Mississippi	1,189.2
4. Louisiana	4,065.4	30. Kansas	1,165.3
5. Illinois	3,936.7	31. Arkansas	1,125.6
6. Ohio	3,833.7	32. Oregon	977.1
7. Pennsylvania	3,758.8	33. Nebraska	843.8
8. New York	3,728.4	34. Utah	763.7
9. Georgia	3,155.7	35. Connecticut	754.0
10. Indiana	2,871.1	36. West Virginia	738.9
11. Michigan	2,798.1	37. New Mexico	680.1
12. North Carolina	2,705.2	38. Nevada	646.1
13. Virginia	2,502.1	39. Alaska	641.7
14. New Jersey	2,447.5	40. Wyoming	535.3
15. Tennessee	2,250.6	41. Idaho	533.8
16. Washington	2,036.5	42. North Dakota	480.7
17. Kentucky	1,976.5	43. Maine	407.3
18. Alabama	1,959.7	44. Montana	401.4
19. Missouri	1,928.4	45. South Dakota	379.6
20. Minnesota	1,867.3	46. New Hampshire	295.5
21. Wisconsin	1,800.1	47. Hawaii	272.2
22. South Carolina	1,661.6	48. Delaware	256.2
23. Oklahoma	1,551.6	49. Rhode Island	197.2
24. Colorado	1,516.9	50. District of Columbia	185.5
25. Iowa	1,492.3	51. Vermont	147.6
26. Maryland	1,481.1	**United States**	**97,710.6**

Consumption per Capita

Rank, state	Trillion Btu	Rank, state	Trillion Btu
1. Wyoming	948.1	27. Virginia	311.8
2. Alaska	898.5	28. Maine	306.8
3. Louisiana	894.4	29. District of Columbia	306.6
4. North Dakota	712.6	30. Illinois	306.5
5. Iowa	489.3	31. Washington	302.0
6. Texas	466.1	32. Colorado	300.5
7. South Dakota	464.9	33. Pennsylvania	295.6
8. Nebraska	461.1	34. Delaware	284.7
9. Kentucky	454.7	35. Michigan	283.3
10. Indiana	442.3	36. North Carolina	283.0
11. Oklahoma	412.6	37. New Jersey	278.1
12. Alabama	409.5	38. Utah	275.2
13. Kansas	407.6	39. Maryland	256.0
14. Montana	405.1	40. Oregon	254.6
15. Mississippi	400.4	41. Nevada	238.9
16. West Virginia	398.4	42. Vermont	235.9
17. Arkansas	385.3	43. Florida	232.6
18. South Carolina	358.3	44. New Hampshire	224.4
19. Tennessee	354.0	45. Arizona	218.2
20. Minnesota	351.6	46. Massachusetts	213.1
21. Idaho	339.7	47. Connecticut	210.9
22. Ohio	332.3	48. California	209.6
23. New Mexico	329.2	49. Hawaii	199.6
24. Georgia	324.9	50. New York	192.2
25. Missouri	321.6	51. Rhode Island	187.4
26. Wisconsin	316.3	**United States**	**315.9**

Note: U.S. total includes –6.2 tril Btu in coal coke imports not allocated to states.

U.S. Production of Crude Oil by State, 2011

Source: *Petroleum Supply Annual 2011*, Energy Information Administration (EIA), U.S. Dept. of Energy

(in thousands of barrels)

Rank, state	Total	Rank, state	Total	Rank, state	Total	Rank, state	Total
1. Texas	529,951	9. Kansas	41,486	17. Arkansas	5,877	25. South Dakota	1,613
2. Alaska	208,749	10. Colorado	39,056	18. Ohio	4,891	26. Nevada	408
3. California	196,189	11. Utah	26,286	19. Pennsylvania	3,304	27. New York	370
4. North Dakota	152,985	12. Mississippi	24,212	20. Nebraska	2,504	28. Tennessee	246
5. Oklahoma	74,645	13. Montana	24,150	21. Kentucky	2,323	29. Missouri	118
6. New Mexico	71,426	14. Illinois	9,239	22. West Virginia	2,146	30. Arizona	37
7. Louisiana	68,945	15. Alabama	8,374	23. Florida	2,023	31. Virginia	10
8. Wyoming	54,755	16. Michigan	6,557	24. Indiana	1,987	**U.S. total**	**2,065,172**

Note: One barrel is equal to 42 U.S. gallons. U.S. total includes 500,649 thousand barrels of federal offshore production.

U.S. Petroleum Trade, 1976-2012

Source: *Monthly Energy Review*, Aug. 2012, Energy Information Administration (EIA), U.S. Dept. of Energy
(in thousands of barrels per day; average for the year)

Year	Imports from Persian Gulf[1]	Total imports	Total exports	Net imports[2]	Petroleum products supplied[3]	Year	Imports from Persian Gulf[1]	Total imports	Total exports	Net imports[2]	Petroleum products supplied[3]
1976	1,840	7,313	223	7,090	17,461	2000	2,488	11,459	1,040	10,419	19,701
1980	1,519	6,909	544	6,365	17,056	2001	2,761	11,871	971	10,900	19,649
1985	311	5,067	781	4,286	15,726	2002	2,269	11,530	984	10,546	19,761
1990	1,966	8,018	857	7,161	16,988	2003	2,501	12,264	1,027	11,238	20,034
1991	1,845	7,627	1,001	6,626	16,714	2004	2,493	13,145	1,048	12,097	20,731
1992	1,778	7,888	950	6,938	17,033	2005	2,334	13,714	1,165	12,549	20,802
1993	1,782	8,620	1,003	7,618	17,237	2006	2,211	13,707	1,317	12,390	20,687
1994	1,728	8,996	942	8,054	17,718	2007	2,163	13,468	1,433	12,036	20,680
1995	1,573	8,835	949	7,886	17,725	2008	2,370	12,915	1,802	11,114	19,498
1996	1,604	9,478	981	8,498	18,309	2009	1,689	11,691	2,024	9,667	18,771
1997	1,755	10,162	1,003	9,158	18,620	2010	1,771	11,793	2,353	9,441	19,180
1998	2,136	10,708	945	9,764	18,917	2011	1,862	11,360	2,924	8,436	18,835
1999	2,464	10,852	940	9,912	19,519	2012[4]	NA	10,860	3,022	7,839	18,611

NA = Not available. **Note:** U.S. exports include shipments to U.S. territories; imports include receipts from U.S. territories. Numbers may not add up to totals because of rounding. (1) Bahrain, Iran, Iraq, Kuwait, Qatar, Saudi Arabia, United Arab Emirates, and the Neutral Zone between Kuwait and Saudi Arabia. (2) Total imports minus total exports. (3) Includes domestic production and imports minus change in stocks, refinery imports, and exports. (4) Estimated annualized 7-month average, for Jan.-July.

World Fossil Fuel Reserves

Source: International Energy Statistics Database, Energy Information Administration (EIA), U.S. Dept. of Energy

	Crude oil (bil barrels), 2012	Natural gas (tril cu ft), 2012	Coal (mil short tons), 2008		Crude oil (bil barrels), 2012	Natural gas (tril cu ft), 2012	Coal (mil short tons), 2008
North America[1] ..	**209.3**	**343.6**	**269,343**	Middle East	799.6	2,800.0	1,326
Canada	173.6	61.0	7,255	Bahrain	0.1	3.3	NA
Greenland	0.0	0.0	202	Iran	151.2	1,168.0	1,326
Mexico........	10.2	17.3	1,335	Iraq	143.1	111.5	NA
United States[1] ..	20.7	272.5	260,551	Israel	0.0	9.6	NA
Central & South				Kuwait	104.0	63.5	NA
America[2]	**238.8**	**268.5**	**13,788**	Oman..........	5.5	30.0	NA
Argentina......	2.5	13.4	551	Qatar.........	25.4	890.0	NA
Bolivia	0.2	9.9	1	Saudi Arabia ...	267.0	283.5	NA
Brazil.........	14.0	14.7	5,025	Syria	2.5	8.5	NA
Chile	0.2	3.5	171	United Arab			
Colombia......	2.0	4.7	7,436	Emirates.....	97.8	215.0	NA
Cuba	0.1	2.5	NA	Yemen	3.0	16.9	NA
Ecuador.......	7.2	0.3	26	**Africa ....**	**124.2**	**509.4**	**34,934**
Peru..........	0.6	12.5	49	Algeria........	12.2	159.0	65
Trinidad and				Angola........	9.5	10.9	NA
Tobago......	0.7	13.5	NA	Congo	0.2	0.0	97
Venezuela	211.2	195.1	528	Egypt.........	4.4	77.2	18
Europe	**11.9**	**146.9**	**84,202**	Libya	47.1	52.8	NA
Albania	0.2	0.0	875	Mozambique ...	0.0	4.5	234
Bosnia and				Namibia.......	0.0	2.2	NA
Herzegovina..	0.0	0.0	3,145	Niger	0.0	0.0	77
Bulgaria.......	0.0	0.2	2,608	Nigeria........	37.2	180.5	209
Czech Republic	0.0	0.1	1,213	South Africa....	0.0	NA	33,241
Germany.......	0.3	6.2	44,863	Sudan[3].......	5.0	3.0	NA
Greece........	0.0	0.0	3,329	Swaziland ....'	0.0	0.0	159
Hungary.......	0.0	0.3	1,830	Tanzania	0.0	0.2	220
Italy..........	0.5	2.3	11	Zimbabwe	0.0	0.0	553
Macedonia.....	0.0	0.0	366	**Asia & Oceania[2]**	**45.4**	**537.5**	**293,042**
Montenegro....	0.0	0.0	157	Afghanistan....	0.0	1.8	73
Norway	5.3	70.9	6	Australia	1.4	27.9	84,217
Poland........	0.2	3.4	6,293	Bangladesh....	0.0	6.5	323
Romania	0.6	2.2	321	Brunei	1.1	13.8	NA
Serbia	0.1	1.7	15,179	China.........	20.4	107.0	126,215
Slovakia.......	0.0	0.5	289	India..........	8.9	40.7	66,800
Slovenia.......	0.0	0.0	246	Indonesia......	3.9	141.1	6,095
Spain.........	0.2	0.1	584	Japan.........	0.0	0.7	386
Turkey........	0.3	0.2	2,583	Korea, North ...	0.0	0.0	661
United Kingdom	2.8	8.9	251	Korea, South ...	0.0	0.3	139
Eurasia.........	**98.9**	**2,164.8**	**251,364**	Laos..........	0.0	0.0	554
Armenia.......	0.0	0.0	180	Malaysia	4.0	83.0	4
Azerbaijan.....	7.0	30.0	NA	Mongolia	0.0	0.0	2,778
Belarus	0.2	0.1	110	Myanmar			
Georgia	0.0	0.3	222	(Burma)	0.1	10.0	2
Kazakhstan	30.0	85.0	37,038	New Zealand ...	0.1	1.0	629
Kyrgyzstan.....	0.0	0.2	895	Pakistan......	0.3	26.6	2,282
Russia........	60.0	1,680.0	173,074	Philippines.....	0.1	3.5	348
Tajikistan	0.0	0.2	413	Thailand.......	0.4	10.6	1,366
Turkmenistan...	0.6	265.0	NA	Vietnam.......	4.4	24.7	165
Ukraine	0.4	39.0	37,339	**World[1] ....**	**1,341.6**	**6,289.1**	**948,000**
Uzbekistan.....	0.6	65.0	2,094				

NA = Not reported separately but included in regional and world totals. **Note:** Regional and world totals may include countries not shown. Proved reserves only. Some countries omitted for lack of appreciable reserves. (1) Figures for crude oil and natural gas are from 2009, the latest year available. (2) Figures for natural gas are from 2011, the latest year available. (3) Includes South Sudan.

U.S. Crude Oil Imports by Selected Countries, 1990-2011
Source: *Petroleum Supply Annual*, Energy Information Administration (EIA); U.S. Dept. of Energy
(in thousands of barrels per day; ranked by 2011 imports)

The United States' dependence on foreign oil declined dramatically in 2011, thanks to increased production of crude oil, natural gas, and domestic biofuels like ethanol and biodiesel. Imports fell to fewer than 9,000 barrels a day, a level not seen since the 20th century. Since 2005, Canada has been the largest supplier of U.S. oil by far, responsible for nearly a quarter of all U.S. imports. Western Hemisphere nations provide more than half of the oil that the U.S. imports. Increases in imports from Iraq and Saudi Arabia raised total imports from the Persian Gulf, but overall imports from OPEC countries fell to their lowest levels since 2002. Sanctions do not permit the U.S. to import oil from Iran.

Country	1990	1995	2000	2005	2006	2007	2008	2009	2010	2011
Canada...............	643	1,040	1,348	1,633	1,802	1,888	1,956	1,943	1,970	2,225
Saudi Arabia#..........	1,195	1,260	1,523	1,445	1,423	1,447	1,503	980	1,082	1,186
Mexico	689	1,027	1,313	1,556	1,577	1,409	1,187	1,092	1,152	1,102
Venezuela#...........	666	1,151	1,223	1,241	1,142	1,148	1,039	951	912	868
Nigeria#	784	621	875	1,077	1,037	1,084	922	776	983	767
Iraq#................	514	0	620	527	553	484	627	449	415	459
Colombia	140	207	318	156	141	137	178	251	338	397
Angola#[1].............	236	360	295	456	513	498	504	448	383	335
Brazil...............	0	0	5	94	133	165	231	295	255	232
Russia[2].............	1	14	7	199	108	112	116	230	269	223
Ecuador[3]............	0	96	125	276	272	198	214	181	210	203
Kuwait#..............	79	213	263	227	179	175	206	180	195	191
Algeria#	63	27	1	228	362	443	312	281	328	178
Norway	96	258	302	119	98	56	30	58	25	53
Congo Republic	NA	20	42	25	27	63	67	64	70	53
Chad................	NA	NA	NA	74	95	77	102	65	18	49
Oman	0	20	2	22	35	32	17	30	12	41
United Kingdom	155	341	291	224	130	101	78	103	120	36
Azerbaijan............	NA	NA	NA	NA	27	57	73	75	55	36
Cameroon............	NA	2	4	3	2	26	10	38	50	36
Gabon[4]	NA	229	143	127	60	63	58	63	47	34
Trinidad and Tobago	76	62	56	64	67	48	23	40	45	33
Argentina	NA	44	53	56	29	33	29	53	29	28
Indonesia	98	64	36	19	16	15	16	15	33	20
Equatorial Guinea........	NA	NA	6	68	57	55	74	89	50	19
Non-OPEC imports......	**NA**	**3,660**	**4,526**	**5,310**	**5,335**	**4,643**	**4,369**	**4,658**	**4,661**	**4,727**
OPEC imports..........	**3,514**	**3,570**	**4,544**	**4,816**	**4,783**	**5,388**	**5,415**	**4,355**	**4,553**	**4,209**
Persian Gulf Country imports.............	**1,801**	**1,479**	**2,409**	**2,207**	**2,160**	**2,115**	**2,340**	**1,656**	**1,694**	**1,849**
TOTAL	**5,894**	**7,230**	**9,071**	**10,126**	**10,118**	**10,031**	**9,783**	**9,013**	**9,213**	**8,935**

= OPEC member. NA = Not available. (1) Angola became a member of OPEC as of Jan. 1, 2007, and is not included in OPEC totals from before that year. (2) May include oil from USSR states before 1992. (3) Ecuador suspended its OPEC membership Dec. 1992-Nov. 2007. Ecuador's imports between 1993 and 2007, inclusive, appear in non-OPEC totals. (4) Gabon withdrew from OPEC Dec. 31, 1994. Imports after Jan. 1, 1995, appear in non-OPEC totals.

U.S. Coal Production and Consumption, 1950-2011
Source: *Annual Energy Review 2011* and *Annual Coal Report, 2011*, Energy Information Administration (EIA), U.S. Dept. of Energy
(in thousand short tons)

Year	Coal production[1]			Coal consumption				
	Surface mining	Underground mining	Total production	Residential	Commercial	Industrial	Electric power[2]	Total consumption
1950....	139,388	421,000	560,388	51,562	63,021	224,637	91,871	494,102
1960....	141,745	292,584	434,329	24,159	16,789	177,402	176,685	398,081
1970....	272,131	340,530	612,661	9,024	7,090	186,637	320,182	523,231
1975....	361,174	293,467	654,641	2,823	6,587	147,244	405,962	562,640
1980....	492,192	337,508	829,700	1,355	5,097	127,004	569,274	702,730
1985....	532,838	350,800	883,638	1,711	6,068	116,429	693,841	818,049
1990....	604,529	424,546	1,029,076	1,345	5,379	115,207	782,567	904,498
1995....	636,725	396,249	1,032,974	755	5,052	106,067	850,230	962,104
2000....	699,953	373,659	1,073,612	454	3,673	94,147	985,821	1,084,095
2005....	762,887	368,612	1,131,498	378	4,342	83,774	1,037,485	1,125,978
2006....	803,728	359,022	1,162,750	290	2,936	82,429	1,026,636	1,112,292
2007....	794,845	351,790	1,146,635	353	3,173	79,331	1,045,141	1,127,998
2008....	814,729	357,079	1,171,809	351	3,155	76,463	1,040,580	1,120,548
2009....	742,862	332,062	1,074,923	353	2,857	60,641	933,627	997,478
2010....	745,357	337,155	1,084,368	339	2,742	70,381	975,052	1,048,514
2011[3]...	NA	NA	1,095,628	307	2,485	67,671	928,558	999,022

NA = Not available. (1) A small amount of refuse recovery has been included in coal production figures since 2001. (2) Electricity-only and combined-heat-and-power (CHP) plants whose primary business is to sell electricity, or electricity and heat, to the public. Through 1988, data are for electric utilities only; beginning in 1989, data are for electric utilities and independent power producers. (3) Estimated or based on preliminary figures.

World Nuclear Power Summary, 2011

Source: *Nuclear Power Reactors in the World*, International Atomic Energy Agency; as of Dec. 31, 2011

Country	Reactors in operation No. of units	Reactors in operation Total MW(e)	Reactors under construction No. of units	Reactors under construction Total MW(e)	Nuclear electricity supplied in 2011 TW(e).h[1]	Nuclear electricity supplied in 2011 % of nation's total	Total operating experience[2] Years	Total operating experience[2] Months
Argentina	2	935	1	692	5.9	5.0	66	7
Armenia	1	375	—	—	2.4	33.2	37	8
Belgium	7	5,927	—	—	45.9	54.0	247	7
Brazil	2	1,884	1	1,245	14.8	3.2	41	3
Bulgaria	2	1,906	—	—	15.3	32.6	151	3
Canada	18	12,604	—	—	88.3	15.3	618	2
China	16	11,816	26	26,620	82.6	1.9	125	6
Czech Republic	6	3,766	—	—	26.7	33.0	122	10
Finland	4	2,736	1	1,600	22.3	31.6	131	4
France	58	63,130	1	1,600	423.5	77.7	1,816	4
Germany	9	12,068	—	—	102.3	17.8	782	9
Hungary	4	1,889	—	—	14.7	43.3	106	2
India	20	4,391	7	4,824	28.9	3.7	357	3
Iran	1	915	—	—	0.1	0.0	0	4
Japan	50	44,215	2	2,650	156.2	18.1	1,546	4
Korea, South	23	20,671	4	4,980	147.8	34.6	381	1
Mexico	2	1,300	—	—	9.3	3.6	39	11
Netherlands	1	482	—	—	3.9	3.6	67	0
Pakistan	3	725	2	630	3.8	3.8	52	8
Romania	2	1,300	—	—	10.8	19.0	19	11
Russia	33	23,643	11	9,297	162.0	17.6	1,056	4
Slovakia	4	1,816	2	782	14.3	54.0	140	7
Slovenia	1	688	—	—	5.9	41.7	30	3
South Africa	2	1,830	—	—	12.9	5.2	54	3
Spain	8	7,560	—	—	55.1	19.5	285	6
Sweden	10	9,378	—	—	58.1	39.6	392	6
Switzerland	5	3,263	—	—	25.7	40.9	184	11
Taiwan	6	5,018	2	2,600	40.4	19.0	182	1
Ukraine	15	13,107	2	1,900	84.9	47.2	398	6
United Kingdom	16	9,246	—	—	62.7	17.8	1,495	2
United States	104	101,465	1	1,165	790.4	19.3	3,707	11
TOTAL	**435**	**370,049**	**64**	**61,930**	**2,518.0**	**NA**	**14,792**	**3**

MW(e) = Megawatt electricity. (1) 1 terawatt-hour [TW(e).h] = 10[6] megawatt-hour [MW(e).h]. For an average power plant, 1 TW(e).h = 0.39 megaton of coal equivalent (input) and 0.23 megaton of oil equivalent (input). (2) Through Dec. 31, 2011. Total includes shutdown plants for countries not listed here: Italy (81 years), Kazakhstan (25 years, 10 months), and Lithuania (43 years, 6 months).

Nations Most Reliant on Nuclear Energy, 2011

Source: *Nuclear Share in Electricity Generation*, International Atomic Energy Agency

(nuclear electricity generation as % of total electricity generated within country)

Rank	Country	Nuclear share	Rank	Country	Nuclear share	Rank	Country	Nuclear share	Rank	Country	Nuclear share
1.	France......	77.7%	8.	Sweden.........	39.6%	15.	United States ...	19.3%	22.	Canada.....	15.3%
2.	Belgium.....	54.0	9.	Korea, South.....	34.6	16.	Romania.......	19.0	23.	South Africa	5.2
	Slovakia	54.0	10.	Armenia	33.2		Taiwan	19.0	24.	Argentina ...	5.0
4.	Ukraine.....	47.2	11.	Czech Republic. ..	33.0	18.	Japan	18.1	25.	Pakistan	3.8
5.	Hungary	43.3	12.	Bulgaria	32.6	19.	Germany	17.8	26.	India	3.7
6.	Slovenia	41.7	13.	Finland	31.6		United Kingdom	17.8	27.	Mexico	3.6
7.	Switzerland..	40.9	14.	Spain	19.5	21.	Russia..:......	17.6		Netherlands	3.6

U.S. Nuclear Reactors and Power Plant Operations, 1955-2011

Source: *Annual Energy Review 2011*, Energy Information Administration (EIA), U.S. Dept. of Energy

Years	Ordered[1]	Cancelled	Construction permits issued[2]	Low-power licenses issued[3]	Full-power licenses issued[4]	Shutdown[5]	Operable units[6]	Capacity factor[6,7]	Nuclear electricity generation (bil net KW-hrs)[6]	Nuclear share of domestic electricity generation[6]
1955-59	14	0	8	2	2	0	2	NA	0.2	NA
1960-64	7	0	12	13	12	1	13	NA	3.3	0.3%
1965-69	81	0	50	8	9	5	17	NA	13.9	1.0
1970-74	143	16	59	41	41	3	55	47.8%	114.0	6.1
1975-79	13	43	48	17	17	3	69	58.4	255.2	11.3
1980-84	0	54	0	24	19	1	87	56.3	327.6	13.5
1985-89	0	7	0	24	28	4	111	62.2	529.4	17.8
1990-94	0	15	0	49	58	9	109	73.8	640.4	19.7
1995-99	0	2	0	1	1	6	104	85.3	728.3	19.7
2000-04	0	0	0	0	0	0	104	90.1	788.5	19.9
2005-09	0	0	0	0	0	0	104	90.3	798.9	20.2
2010-11	0	0	0	0	0	0	104	89.1	790.2	19.2
Total	**259**	**124**	**177**	**132**	**132**	**28**	**NA**	**NA**	**NA**	**NA**

NA = Not applicable. **Note:** The permit/license categories shown here are historic. The Nuclear Regulatory Commission anticipates 16 or more new combined license applications under current regulations over the next few years—the first of which was submitted in Sept. 2007—which may amount to 25 or more new reactor units. (1) Order placed by a utility or government agency for a nuclear steam supply system. (2) Permits issued in a given period, not extant permits. (3) Permission to conduct testing but not operate at full power. (4) Permission to operate at full power. (5) Permanently ceased operation. (6) As of the last year of designated period. (7) The ratio of electric energy produced to the amount that could be produced at continuous full-power operation.

U.S. Nuclear Reactors Generating the Most Electricity, 2010
Source: U.S. Nuclear Statistics Database, Energy Information Administration (EIA), U.S. Dept. of Energy
(in thousand net megawatt-hours)

Rank	Reactor, location	Electricity generated	Capacity[1]	Rank	Reactor, location	Electricity generated	Capacity[1]
1.	Palo Verde-2, Wintersburg, AZ	11,652,972	101%	14.	LaSalle-2, Seneca, IL........	9,925,542	101%
2.	South Texas-1, Bay City, TX ...	11,304,107	101	15.	Catawba-1, Lake Wylie, SC ...	9,889,074	100
3.	Seabrook-1, Portsmouth, NH ..	10,910,055	100	16.	Limerick-2, Pottstown, PA	9,879,131	99
4.	Perry-1, Dothan, OH........	10,619,711	98	17.	South Texas-2, Bay City, TX ...	9,822,674	88
5.	Comanche Peak-2,			18.	Peach Bottom-3,		
	Glen Rose, TX	10,531,748	104		Lancaster, PA	9,759,275	100
6.	Byron-1, Byron, IL..........	10,337,288	101	19.	Diablo Canyon-2, San Luis		
7.	Waterford-3, Taft, LA	10,276,184	100		Obispo, CA	9,752,476	100
8.	Vogtle-1, Waynesboro, GA	10,247,423	102	20.	Watts Bar-1, Spring City, TN ...	9,738,457	99
9.	Palo Verde-3, Wintersburg, AZ	10,238,992	89	21.	Comanche Peak-1,		
10.	Susquehanna-2, Berwick, PA ..	10,221,221	98		Glen Rose, TX	9,676,719	91
11.	McGuire-2, Cowens			22.	Grand Gulf-1, Port Gibson, MS	9,643,241	88
	Ford Dam, NC............	10,014,695	104	23.	Wolf Creek-1, Burlington, KS ..	9,555,712	94
12.	Braidwood-2, Braidwood, IL ...	10,003,246	99	24.	Sequoyah-2, Chattanooga, TN	9,536,672	97
13.	Salem-2, Salem, NJ	9,954,772	98	25.	Byron-2, Byron, IL..........	9,518,424	96

(1) The ratio of power generated to the maximum potential generation expressed as a percentage.

Renewable Energy Sources
Source: U.S. Dept. of Energy

Concern over the environmental impact of burning fossil fuels has helped spur interest in alternative fuels that are less polluting. And because the supply of fossil fuels is finite and diminishing, there is interest in "renewable" sources that do not deplete existing supplies. However, renewable energy sources still make up only a small share of U.S. domestic energy production (about 9% in 2011). The main reason for this is their relatively higher cost (in some cases two to four times that of power obtained from traditional fuels). The following are the major renewable energy sources available.

Biomass is plant-derived material usable as an energy source. It includes wood energy crops such as hybrid poplars and willow trees, agricultural crops including soybeans and corn, and animal and other wastes. Biomass is one of the two most common renewable energy sources in the U.S. today, along with hydropower. Biomass such as wood can be burned to produce heat and generate electricity. Agricultural crops can be chemically converted into fuels such as ethanol and biodiesel; these are the only known renewable liquid energy sources and may one day replace petroleum and fossil-fuel-produced diesel. But bringing ethanol and biodiesel into wide use would require more energy-efficient methods of production and transportation. Overall, biomass fuels burn much cleaner than fossil fuels, though biomass fuels still produce carbon dioxide and other pollutants.

Geothermal energy is generated from heat inside of the Earth. This form of energy is both clean and renewable. The technology has caught on in countries with substantial geothermal activity such as Iceland, where it accounted for 66% of primary energy use in 2009. In the U.S., the best sources for geothermal power are in the West, where there are many underground heated lakes. Large-scale access, however, would require drilling. A major goal in this field is to find a way to harness energy directly from magma (molten rock material), which has great potential because of its high temperatures.

Hydrogen is the third most abundant element on Earth. It does not naturally occur on Earth as a pure gas or liquid but is always combined with other elements (such as oxygen, to form water, or carbon, to form methane). If hydrogen is to be used for energy, it must be separated from these other elements. That can be achieved through methods involving heat, photosynthesis, sunlight, or electricity.

Hydrogen batteries, or fuel cells, were used by NASA's space shuttles. Within a fuel cell, a chemical reaction occurs in which electrons are released from hydrogen atoms. These electrons flow through an external circuit as electricity. The hydrogen atoms' protons combine with oxygen (and some of the electrons in the electric current) to produce heat and water suitable for drinking. Fuel cells do not run down but work as long as hydrogen is supplied. Some experts think hydrogen will be the power source of the future. However, an infrastructure would need to be created for safe and cost-effective transportation and storage of hydrogen.

Hydropower, or hydroelectric power, is generated by water flowing through turbines. Along with biomass fuels, it is one of the two most common renewable energy sources in the U.S. today. A dam on a river is a common hydropower producer. No harmful greenhouse gases are produced, but the dams needed to generate power can harm river ecosystems. Researchers are working on turbine technologies to maximize use of hydropower and reduce adverse environmental effects.

Ocean energy can be generated in two ways. Thermal ocean energy uses heat that the ocean absorbs from the sun to power generators, sometimes producing drinkable desalinated water as a by-product. Mechanical ocean energy is generated by the movement of tides and waves through turbines. In both cases, power generation is not very efficient with current technology. Much more research is needed. Mechanical ocean energy requires the building of large dams or breakwater-type structures called tidal barrages, which could harm coastal ecosystems.

Solar energy is generated using heat and light from the sun. Solar energy is an increasingly common source of electricity. Photovoltaic (PV) solar cells are made of semiconducting materials that can directly convert sunlight to electricity without producing any harmful waste. Arrays of mirrors can concentrate the sun's rays onto PV panels, making solar collectors more efficient. Sunlight can also be used to heat water directly. According to the Dept. of Energy, homes incorporating solar heating designs can save as much as 50% on heating bills. The downside to solar energy is that it depends heavily on a range of factors including location, time of year, and weather.

Wind energy uses wind turbines to produce energy. They are perched on high towers, usually 100 ft tall or higher, and often placed in large groups ("farms") to generate electricity for towns and cities. Farmers and homeowners sometimes use stand-alone turbines to generate supplemental electricity. In the past 20 years, tax credits to producers and government incentives for homeowners have helped lower the price of wind power by 85%, making it a more feasible option. Some people object to wind farms, however, because of their appearance or the noise the turbines make. Wind power raises few other environmental problems, but the turbines can pose a danger to birds. In addition, because weather is involved, consistent energy generation can be a challenge.

CRIME

Measuring Crime

The U.S. Dept. of Justice administers two statistical programs to measure trends in crime in the U.S. Because of differences in focus and methodology, their results are not strictly comparable.

The Federal Bureau of Investigation (FBI) conducts the **Uniform Crime Report (UCR)** program, which aims to provide statistics for law enforcement administration, operation, and management. It collects actual counts on the crimes of homicide, forcible rape, robbery, aggravated assault, burglary, larceny-theft, motor vehicle theft, and arson as they are reported to law enforcement agencies. Each year, the program releases a preliminary report in the spring, followed by a more detailed, final report in the fall.

The **National Crime Victimization Survey (NCVS)** is conducted annually by the Bureau of Justice Statistics through interviews with members of a nationally representative sample of households about their experiences with crime. The survey complements the UCR by providing alternative and previously unavailable data, including information about the victims of crime and their offenders (e.g., age, sex, ethnicity, victim-offender relationship) and information on crimes not reported to law enforcement. In contrast to the UCR, the NCVS does not cover homicide, arson, commercial crimes, or crimes against children under age 12.

Further explanation of the UCR and NCVS is available at bjs.ojp.usdoj.gov/content/pub/pdf/ntcm.pdf.

Uniform Crime Report, 2010

Source: *Crime in the United States, 2010*, Federal Bureau of Investigation (FBI), U.S. Dept. of Justice

In 2010, the latest year for which statistics are available, more than 18,000 city, county, college and university, state, tribal, and federal agencies—representing more than 308 mil U.S. inhabitants—voluntarily participated in the UCR program.

Although crime tends to rise in hard economic times, the number of reported violent crimes dropped 6.0% between 2009 and 2010, marking the fourth straight year violent crime declined. The number of property crimes reported was also down, by 2.7% from 2009, making it the eighth year in a row property crime reports declined.

The biggest decrease in violent crime was in robberies, down 10.0% from 2009. However, the total amount lost by victims of all property crimes, excluding arson, increased slightly from 2009 levels to $15.7 bil. Although arson is considered a property crime, it is not included in estimates of totals because of variations in the level of participation by reporting agencies.

Additional highlights from the 2010 report:

- Males accounted for 78% of all murder victims whose gender was known. Men committed 90% of the murders in which the offender's gender was known.
- Firearms were known to be used in 68% of all murders.
- Of the 7,272 murder victims whose relation to the offender was known, 24.8% were killed by a family member, and 22.2% were killed by a stranger. The other 53% were killed by an acquaintance (e.g., friend, neighbor, employee, romantic partner). Wives were more than five times as likely to kill their spouses as husbands; girlfriends were responsible for almost four times as many murders as boyfriends.
- The majority of property crimes reported were larceny-thefts (68%). Among all larceny-thefts, 26% involved non-accessory items taken from motor vehicles, 17% were shoplifting incidents, 11% were of property from buildings, and 3% were of bikes.

National Crime Victimization Survey, 2010

Source: *Criminal Victimization, 2010*, Bureau of Justice Statistics, U.S. Dept. of Justice

Victimizations of U.S. residents age 12 and over continued to decline to historic lows, according to the NCVS estimates for 2010. The violent crime rate—14.9 victimizations per 1,000 persons—was down sharply from the 2009 estimate of 17.1, and has dropped more than 40 percent since 2001. The property crime rate fell a bit more gradually to 120

victimizations per 1,000 households from 127 in 2009 and 167 in 2001. After declining 38% between 2008 and 2009, the numbers of rapes or sexual assaults increased nearly 50% in 2010. The Bureau of Justice Statistics cautions that rape and sexual assault statistics are based on a small number of incidents.

Criminal Victimization, 2001-10

Source: *Criminal Victimization, 2010*, Bureau of Justice Statistics, U.S. Dept. of Justice

A crime committed against an individual or single household counts as one **victimization**. Because a personal crime may involve more than one victim, the number of victimizations may be greater than the number of personal crime incidents. In property crimes, the affected household is considered one victim.

Victimization rates measure the frequency with which victimizations occur. Personal crime victimization rates are based on the number of victimizations per 1,000 persons in the U.S. resident population age 12 and over. Property crime victimization rates are calculated per 1,000 of total households.

Type of crime	Number of victimizations			Percent change, 2001-10	Percent change, 2009-10	Average annual change, 2001-09
	2001	2009	2010			
All crimes	24,215,700	20,057,180	18,725,710	−22.7%	−6.6%	−2.1%
Crimes of violence[1]	5,743,820	4,343,450	3,817,380	−33.5	−12.1	−3.1
Rape/sexual assault[2]	248,250	125,920	188,380	−24.1	49.6	−7.5
Robbery	630,690	533,790	480,750	−23.8	−9.9	−1.9
Assault......................	4,864,890	3,683,750	3,148,250	−35.3	−14.5	−3.1
Aggravated.................	1,222,160	823,340	725,180	−40.7	−11.9	−4.4
Simple.....................	3,642,720	2,860,410	2,423,060	−33.5	−15.3	−2.7
Personal theft[3]	188,370	133,210	138,340	−26.6	3.9	−3.9
Property crimes	18,283,510	15,580,520	14,769,990	−19.2	−5.2	−1.8
Household burglary	3,139,700	3,134,930	2,923,430	−6.9	−6.7	<0.5
Motor vehicle theft	1,008,730	735,770	606,990	−39.8	−17.5	−3.5
Theft........................	14,135,090	11,709,830	11,239,560	−20.5	−4.0	−2.1
Total population age 12 and over ..	229,215,290	254,105,610	255,961,940			
Total households	109,568,450	122,327,660	122,885,160			

Note: Details may not add up to totals due to rounding. (1) Excludes murder because the NCVS is based on interviews with victims. (2) Includes male as well as female victims and both heterosexual and homosexual rape. (3) Includes pocket picking, completed purse snatching, and attempted purse snatching.

Crime in the U.S., 1989-2010

Source: *Crime in the United States, 2010*, Federal Bureau of Investigation (FBI), U.S. Dept. of Justice

In the FBI's Uniform Crime Reporting (UCR) Program, offenses are classified as **violent crimes** if they involve force or the threat of force: murder and nonnegligent manslaughter, forcible rape, robbery, and aggravated assault. The following offenses are considered **property crimes**: burglary, larceny-theft, motor vehicle theft, and arson. Arson data is excluded from this table because of variations in the level of participation by reporting agencies. That data is presented separately online at www.fbi.gov/ about-us/cjis/ucr/.

		Violent crime					Property crime			
Year(s)	Population[1]	All violent crimes	Murder and nonnegligent manslaughter	Forcible rape[2]	Robbery	Aggravated assault[3]	All property crimes	Burglary	Larceny-theft[4]	Motor vehicle theft
NUMBER OF OFFENSES										
1989	246,819,230	1,646,037	21,500	94,504	578,326	951,707	12,605,412	3,168,170	7,705,872	7,872,442
1990	249,464,396	1,820,127	23,438	102,555	639,271	1,054,863	12,655,486	3,073,909	7,945,670	1,635,907
1995	262,803,276	1,798,792	21,606	97,470	580,509	1,099,207	12,063,935	2,593,784	7,997,710	1,472,441
1997	267,783,607	1,636,096	18,208	96,153	498,534	1,023,201	11,558,475	2,460,526	7,743,760	1,354,189
1998	270,248,003	1,533,887	16,974	93,144	447,186	976,583	10,951,827	2,332,735	7,376,311	1,242,781
1999	272,690,813	1,426,044	15,522	89,411	409,371	911,740	10,208,334	2,100,739	6,955,520	1,152,075
2000	281,421,906	1,425,486	15,586	90,178	408,016	911,706	10,182,584	2,050,992	6,971,590	1,160,002
2001[5]	285,317,559	1,439,480	16,037	90,863	423,557	909,023	10,437,189	2,116,531	7,092,267	1,228,391
2002	287,973,924	1,423,677	16,229	95,235	420,806	891,407	10,455,277	2,151,252	7,057,379	1,246,646
2003	290,788,976	1,383,676	16,528	93,883	414,235	859,030	10,442,862	2,154,834	7,026,802	1,261,226
2004	293,656,842	1,360,088	16,148	95,089	401,470	847,381	10,319,386	2,144,446	6,937,089	1,237,851
2005	296,507,061	1,390,745	16,740	94,347	417,438	862,220	10,174,754	2,155,448	6,783,447	1,235,859
2006	299,398,484	1,435,123	17,309	94,472	449,246	874,096	10,019,601	2,194,993	6,626,363	1,198,245
2007	301,621,157	1,422,970	17,128	92,160	447,324	866,358	9,882,212	2,190,198	6,591,542	1,100,472
2008	304,059,724	1,394,461	16,465	90,750	443,563	843,683	9,774,152	2,228,887	6,586,206	959,059
2009	307,006,550	1,325,896	15,399	89,241	408,742	812,514	9,337,060	2,203,313	6,338,095	795,652
2010	308,745,538	1,246,248	14,748	84,767	367,832	778,901	9,082,887	2,159,878	6,185,867	737,142
PERCENT CHANGE: NUMBER OF OFFENSES										
2010/2009.		−6.0%	−4.2%	−5.0%	−10.0%	−4.1%	−2.7%	−2.0%	−2.4%	−7.4%
2010/2006.		−13.2	−14.8	−10.3	−18.1	−10.9	−9.3	−1.6	−6.6	−38.5
2010/2001.		−13.4	−8.0	−6.7	−13.2	−14.3	−13.0	2.0	−12.8	−40.0
RATE PER 100,000 RESIDENTS										
1989		666.9	8.7	38.3	234.3	385.6	5,107.1	1,283.6	3,189.6	634.0
1990		729.6	9.4	41.1	256.3	422.9	5,073.1	1,232.2	3,185.1	655.8
1995		684.5	8.2	37.1	220.9	418.3	4,590.5	987.0	3,043.2	560.3
1997		611.0	6.8	35.9	186.2	382.1	4,316.3	918.8	2,891.8	505.7
1998		567.6	6.3	34.5	165.5	361.4	4,052.5	863.2	2,729.5	459.9
1999		523.0	5.7	32.8	150.1	334.3	3,743.6	770.4	2,550.7	422.5
2000		506.5	5.5	32.0	145.0	324.0	3,618.3	728.8	2,477.3	412.2
2001		504.5	5.6[5]	31.8	148.5	318.6	3,658.1	741.8	2,485.7	430.5
2002		494.4	5.6	33.1	146.1	309.5	3,630.6	747.0	2,450.7	432.9
2003		475.8	5.7	32.3	142.5	295.4	3,591.2	741.0	2,416.5	433.7
2004		463.2	5.5	32.4	136.7	288.6	3,514.1	730.3	2,362.3	421.5
2005		469.0	5.6	31.8	140.8	290.8	3,431.5	726.9	2,287.8	416.8
2006		479.3	5.8	31.6	150.0	292.0	3,346.6	733.1	2,213.2	400.2
2007		471.8	5.7	30.6	148.3	287.2	3,276.4	726.1	2,185.4	364.9
2008		458.6	5.4	29.8	145.9	277.5	3,214.6	733.0	2,166.1	315.4
2009		431.9	5.0	29.1	133.1	264.7	3,041.3	717.7	2,064.5	259.2
2010		403.6	4.8	27.5	119.1	252.3	2,941.9	699.6	2,003.5	238.8
PERCENT CHANGE: RATE PER 100,000 RESIDENTS										
2010/2009.		−6.5%	−4.8%	−5.5%	−10.5%	−4.7%	−3.3%	−2.5%	−3.0%	−7.9%
2010/2006.		−15.8	−17.4	−13.0	−20.6	−13.6	−12.1	−4.6	−9.5	−40.3
2010/2001.		−20.0	−15.0	−13.8	−19.7	−20.8	−19.6	−5.7	−19.4	−44.5

Note: Figures for 2006-10 have been revised from previous reports. (1) U.S. Census Bureau estimates for July 1 of each year except for 1990, 2000, and 2010, which show Apr. 1 decennial census counts. (2) Does not include statutory rape (i.e., rape not involving force) and other offenses of a sexual nature. Also does not include sexual attacks on males, which are considered aggravated assaults or sex offenses, depending on circumstances and extent of injuries. (The FBI revised its definition of rape in 2012 to be more inclusive.) (3) Attack upon another with the intent of doing serious bodily harm; usually accompanied by the use of a weapon or other means likely to produce death or great bodily harm. (4) The unlawful taking of another's property not involving force or fraud (e.g., theft of motor vehicle parts, shoplifting). Excludes crimes such as embezzlement and check fraud. (5) The murder and nonnegligent homicides that occurred as a result of the Sept. 11, 2001, terrorist attacks are not included.

Law Enforcement Civilian Employees and Officers, 2010

Source: *Crime in the United States, 2010*; *Law Enforcement Officers Killed and Assaulted, 2009*; Federal Bureau of Investigation (FBI), U.S. Dept. of Justice

As of Oct. 31, 2010, 14,744 city, county, state, college and university, and tribal agencies around the country collectively employed 1,013,608 full-time law enforcement workers. About 69.6% of employees were sworn officers. The FBI's UCR program defines a sworn law enforcement officer as a person who ordinarily carries a firearm and badge, has full arrest powers, and is paid from government funds specifically dedicated to law enforcement. Civilians (e.g., clerks, radio dispatchers, correctional officers) made up the remaining 30.4% of law enforcement employees.

Altogether, they provided service to an estimated 291.4 mil people around the country, meaning there were 3.5 full-time law enforcement employees (civilian and sworn officers) and 2.4 sworn officers per 1,000 residents.

The great majority of sworn officers (88.2%) are male, but females make up 60.8% of civilian employees. Not surprisingly, the most populous state, California, employed the greatest number of full-time law enforcement workers (118,884). Washington, DC, had the highest rate, with 7.4 full-time law enforcement employees (and 6.6 sworn officers) for every 1,000 residents in its population.

Nationwide, 48 law enforcement officers were killed in the line of duty in 2009, the latest year for which data is available. Of that number, 15 died in ambush situations, 8 were attacked during arrests, 8 were performing traffic stops, 5 were killed during tactical situations, and 4 died while investigating suspicious persons or circumstances. Almost all (45 of the 48 officers) were killed with firearms. The majority of these firearms (28) were handguns. Another 47 officers died accidentally while performing official duties.

U.S. Crime Rates by Region, Geographic Division, and State, 2010

Source: *Crime in the United States, 2010*, Federal Bureau of Investigation, U.S. Dept. of Justice

(per 100,000 residents, as estimated by U.S. Census Bureau for July 1 of year)

	Violent crime				Property crime[1]			
	All violent crimes	Murder and nonnegligent manslaughter	Forcible rape[2]	Robbery	Aggra-vated assault[3]	All property crimes	Burglary	Larceny-theft[4]	Motor vehicle theft
Total U.S.[5,6]	403.6	4.8	27.5	119.1	252.3	2,941.9	699.6	2,003.5	238.8
Northeast.	357.0	4.2	19.4	124.4	209.1	2,115.8	423.2	1,555.9	136.7
New England	331.9	2.9	24.6	84.1	220.3	2,320.5	520.8	1,640.8	158.9
Connecticut.	281.4	3.6	16.3	99.4	162.0	2,193.2	424.5	1,581.0	187.7
Maine	122.0	1.8	29.3	31.2	59.8	2,479.3	554.0	1,850.8	74.5
Massachusetts	466.6	3.2	26.7	105.0	331.8	2,350.5	576.8	1,598.8	174.9
New Hampshire	167.0	1.0	31.3	34.3	100.4	2,186.3	413.3	1,699.5	73.5
Rhode Island.	256.6	2.8	28.1	74.1	151.6	2,556.6	581.5	1,747.2	227.9
Vermont	130.2	1.1	21.1	11.8	96.2	2,282.3	537.9	1,673.9	70.5
Middle Atlantic	365.9	4.6	17.5	138.6	205.1	2,043.5	388.7	1,525.9	128.8
New Jersey	307.7	4.2	11.2	134.4	157.9	2,081.9	440.5	1,464.5	176.9
New York	392.1	4.5	14.3	146.9	226.4	1,941.2	335.3	1,500.4	105.4
Pennsylvania.	366.2	5.2	26.9	128.8	205.3	2,173.0	434.3	1,607.4	131.2
Midwest[5]	362.5	4.4	31.1	107.7	219.3	2,833.6	668.6	1,958.5	206.5
East North Central .	377.4	4.7	30.9	126.6	215.2	2,857.4	709.7	1,935.4	212.2
Illinois	435.2	5.5	23.6	156.3	249.7	2,681.0	587.6	1,868.9	224.4
Indiana	314.5	4.5	27.2	95.9	186.9	3,042.4	726.7	2,113.4	202.3
Michigan	490.3	5.7	47.3	116.3	321.0	2,713.6	747.4	1,689.5	276.8
Ohio	315.2	4.1	32.1	142.8	136.2	3,245.2	923.3	2,138.8	183.1
Wisconsin	248.7	2.7	20.9	79.2	145.9	2,507.7	467.1	1,897.5	143.1
West North Central[5]	328.9	3.6	31.6	65.1	228.6	2,779.6	575.4	2,010.6	193.6
Iowa	273.5	1.3	27.4	33.2	211.6	2,242.5	546.8	1,571.8	124.0
Kansas	369.1	3.5	38.8	54.1	272.7	3,119.9	680.1	2,229.2	210.6
Minnesota[5]	236.0	1.8	33.9	63.9	136.4	2,572.3	460.3	1,950.0	161.9
Missouri.	455.0	7.0	23.9	102.4	321.7	3,346.4	735.4	2,343.0	268.0
Nebraska.	279.5	3.0	36.8	56.1	183.6	2,673.2	455.9	2,019.4	197.9
North Dakota.	225.0	1.5	35.2	13.4	174.8	1,768.5	292.3	1,348.5	127.7
South Dakota	268.5	2.8	47.9	18.9	198.9	1,852.4	390.7	1,364.1	97.6
South[6]	452.0	5.6	27.9	122.4	296.1	3,438.8	886.4	2,315.1	237.3
South Atlantic[6]	454.1	5.6	24.4	128.4	295.8	3,331.2	843.7	2,251.3	236.2
Delaware.	620.9	5.3	34.7	203.7	377.1	3,448.2	836.9	2,396.5	214.8
District of Columbia[6]	1,330.2	21.9	31.1	718.8	558.4	4,778.9	703.1	3,238.9	836.9
Florida.	542.4	5.2	28.6	138.7	369.8	3,558.4	899.5	2,438.4	220.5
Georgia.	403.3	5.8	21.6	127.7	248.2	3,640.5	998.4	2,329.3	312.8
Maryland	547.7	7.4	21.3	191.5	327.5	2,997.3	632.9	2,051.7	312.6
North Carolina.	363.4	5.0	21.1	100.8	236.5	3,447.3	1,076.9	2,178.4	192.0
South Carolina	597.7	6.1	31.7	107.7	452.3	3,900.4	997.9	2,617.2	285.3
Virginia	213.6	4.6	19.1	70.7	119.1	2,327.2	382.8	1,812.5	131.8
West Virginia	314.6	3.3	19.1	44.7	247.5	2,239.6	580.5	1,531.7	127.4
East South Central	409.6	5.6	31.4	106.6	266.0	3,252.4	906.1	2,145.6	200.8
Alabama	377.8	5.7	28.2	99.6	244.2	3,516.8	879.4	2,415.6	221.8
Kentucky	242.6	4.3	31.8	86.4	120.1	2,551.3	698.5	1,709.7	143.1
Mississippi.	269.7	7.0	31.2	93.7	137.8	2,985.0	1,026.0	1,778.4	180.6
Tennessee	613.3	5.6	33.7	131.8	442.2	3,657.9	1,012.2	2,411.9	233.8
West South Central	470.0	5.8	32.0	120.4	311.9	3,710.2	946.5	2,506.0	257.7
Arkansas	505.3	4.7	45.0	81.3	374.3	3,558.9	1,114.9	2,253.8	190.1
Louisiana.	549.0	11.2	27.2	114.9	395.6	3,647.5	1,002.2	2,427.1	218.2
Oklahoma	479.5	5.2	38.7	89.0	346.7	3,415.5	999.0	2,144.8	271.6
Texas	450.3	5.0	30.3	130.6	284.4	3,783.0	909.1	2,603.3	270.5
West.	400.8	4.2	29.5	120.6	246.4	2,886.5	643.4	1,893.6	349.5
Mountain	386.7	4.2	37.4	84.7	260.4	3,012.7	668.4	2,083.4	260.9
Arizona	408.1	6.4	33.9	108.5	259.3	3,534.0	794.3	2,403.2	336.5
Colorado	320.8	2.4	43.7	62.3	212.4	2,684.2	520.0	1,940.5	223.6
Idaho.	221.0	1.3	33.5	13.7	172.6	1,995.8	414.8	1,496.7	84.3
Montana	272.2	2.6	32.4	15.9	221.2	2,543.8	369.3	2,020.3	154.2
Nevada	660.6	5.9	35.7	196.2	422.9	2,774.7	823.0	1,574.5	377.1
New Mexico	588.9	6.9	46.5	78.4	457.1	3,435.4	1,020.5	2,160.1	254.8
Utah	212.7	1.9	34.3	45.9	130.6	3,179.6	543.3	2,421.0	215.2
Wyoming.	195.9	1.4	29.1	13.5	151.9	2,461.6	381.3	1,975.4	104.9
Pacific[2]	407.0	4.2	26.1	136.5	240.2	2,830.7	632.4	1,809.6	388.7
Alaska.	638.8	4.4	75.0	83.6	475.8	2,852.5	437.2	2,187.3	228.0
California.	440.6	4.9	22.4	156.0	257.4	2,635.8	614.3	1,612.1	409.4
Hawaii.	262.7	1.8	26.8	77.5	156.7	3,314.2	636.8	2,302.4	374.9
Oregon[2].	252.0	2.4	31.7	62.4	155.6	3,012.9	512.6	2,267.7	232.6
Washington.	313.8	2.3	38.1	88.2	185.3	3,706.6	820.3	2,503.7	382.6
Puerto Rico[7]	403.6	4.8	27.5	119.1	252.3	2,941.9	699.6	2,003.5	238.8

Note: Offense totals are based on all reporting agencies and estimates for unreported areas. Figures may not add up to totals due to rounding. (1) Data for arson, considered a property crime, are not included in this table. (2) Does not include statutory rape (i.e., rape not involving force) and other offenses of a sexual nature. Also does not include sexual attacks on males, which are considered aggravated assaults or sex offenses, depending on circumstances and extent of injuries. (The FBI revised its definition of rape in 2012 to be more inclusive.) (3) Attack upon another with the intent of doing serious bodily harm; usually accompanied by the use of a weapon or other means likely to produce death or great bodily harm. (4) The unlawful taking of another's property not involving force or fraud (e.g., theft of motor vehicle parts, shoplifting). Excludes crimes such as embezzlement and check fraud. (5) Minnesota, with the exception of Minneapolis and St. Paul, collects data on forcible rape offenses using methodology not consistent with national UCR guidelines. Forcible rape offenses in the state, with the exception of data from the previously mentioned cities, are not included in this table. (6) Includes offenses reported by the National Zoological Park Police and Washington Metro Transit Police. (7) Data are from 2009 and are not included in U.S. totals.

State and Federal Prison Population; Death Penalty, 2000-10

Source: *Prisoners in 2010*; *Capital Punishment, 2010*; Bureau of Justice Statistics, U.S. Dept. of Justice

The prison population declined in 2010 for the first time since 1972. As of Dec. 31, 2010, 1,612,395 prisoners were under the jurisdiction, or legal authority, of state (87.0%) or federal (13.0%) correctional authorities. Jails, which are locally operated, typically hold persons awaiting trial or sentencing as well as those sentenced to one year or less.

The imprisonment rate, or number of prisoners per 100,000 U.S. residents, also declined in 2010, from 504 to 500, largely because of an increase in the U.S. population. The rate was still significantly higher than the 470 at year-end 2001. Black males (3,074 per 100,000 U.S. residents) were incarcerated at 6.7 times the rate of white males (459 per 100,000) and more than twice as often as Hispanic males (1,258 per 100,000).

There were 3,158 persons under sentence of death at year-end 2010; 12 states executed a total of 46 inmates (17 in Texas alone). Twenty inmates died of other causes, and 53 were removed from death row. A total of 104 inmates were received on death row in 2010, the lowest number since 1973. Since 2000, the death row population has decreased every year, but the composition has changed little: 98% were male; 55% were white, and 42% were black. This population continues to linger longer on death row, as average time between sentencing and execution hit a record high 14 years, 10 months.

New Mexico repealed its death penalty law for crimes committed after July 1, 2009; the repeal was not retroactive. All 36 death penalty states authorize lethal injection as a method of execution; nine also permit electrocution; three permit the gas chamber, three hanging, and two (Oklahoma and Utah) authorize firing squads.

	Prisoners				Death penalty[1]				
					Death penalty statute?	Under sentence of death, year-end 2010	Executed in 2010	Executed, as of 2010[2]—	
Region/jurisdiction	Year-end 2000	Year-end 2009	Year-end 2010	% change 2009-10				Since 1930	Since 1977
U.S. total	1,391,261	1,617,970	1,612,395	−0.3%	—	3,158	46	5,093[3]	1,234
Federal[4]	145,416	208,118	209,771	0.8	Y	58	0	36	3
State	1,245,845	1,409,852	1,402,624	−0.5	36[5]	3,100	46	5,017	1,231
Northeast	174,826	177,361	173,911	−1.9	—	226	0	612	4
Connecticut[6]	18,355	19,716	19,321	−2.0	Y	10	0	22	1
Maine	1,679	2,206	2,154	−2.4	N	—	—	—	—
Massachusetts	10,722	11,316	11,312	0.0	N	—	—	27	—
New Hampshire	2,257	2,731	2,761	1.1	Y	1	0	1	0
New Jersey	29,784	25,382	25,007	−1.5	N	—	—	74	0
New York	70,199	58,687	56,656	−3.5	Y	0	0	329	0
Pennsylvania	36,847	51,429	51,264	−0.3	Y	215	0	155	3
Rhode Island[6]	3,286	3,674	3,357	−8.6	N	—	—	—	—
Vermont[6]	1,697	2,220	2,079	−6.4	N	—	—	4	—
Midwest	237,378	261,615	263,428	0.7	—	256	8	539	144
Illinois	45,281	45,161	48,418	7.2	Y	15	0	102	12
Indiana	20,125	28,808	28,028	−2.7	Y	13	0	60	20
Iowa	7,955	8,813	9,455	7.3	N	—	—	18	—
Kansas	8,344	8,641	9,051	4.7	Y	8	0	15	0
Michigan	47,718	45,478	44,113	−3.0	N	—	—	—	—
Minnesota	6,238	9,986	9,796	−1.9	N	—	—	—	—
Missouri[7]	27,543	30,563	30,623	0.2	Y	49	0	129	67
Nebraska	3,895	4,474	4,587	2.5	Y	12	0	7	3
North Dakota	1,076	1,486	1,487	0.1	N	—	—	—	—
Ohio	45,833	51,606	51,712	0.2	Y	157	8	213	41
South Dakota	2,616	3,434	3,434	0.0	Y	2	0	2	1
Wisconsin	20,754	23,165	22,724	−1.9	N	—	—	—	—
South	561,214	653,819	654,142	0.0	—	1,630	35	3,279	1,013
Alabama	26,332	31,874	31,764	−0.3	Y	201	5	178	49
Arkansas	11,915	15,208	16,204	6.5	Y	42	0	145	27
Delaware[6]	6,921	6,794	6,598	−2.9	Y	17	0	26	14
Florida	71,319	103,915	104,306	0.4	Y	392	1	239	69
Georgia	44,232	56,986	56,432	−1.0	Y	100	2	411	48
Kentucky	14,919	21,638	20,544	−5.1	Y	34	0	106	3
Louisiana	35,207	39,780	39,445	−0.8	Y	84	1	161	28
Maryland	23,538	22,255	22,645	1.8	Y	5	0	73	5
Mississippi	20,241	21,482	21,067	−1.9	Y	60	3	167	13
North Carolina	31,266	40,529	40,116	−1.0	Y	158	0	306	43
Oklahoma	23,181	26,397	26,252	−0.5	Y	71	3	154	94
South Carolina	21,778	24,288	23,578	−2.9	Y	56	0	204	42
Tennessee	22,166	26,965	27,451	1.8	Y	86	0	99	6
Texas	166,719	171,249	173,649	1.4	Y	315	17	761	464
Virginia	30,168	38,092	37,410	−1.8	Y	9	3	200	108
West Virginia	3,856	6,367	6,681	4.9	N	—	—	40	—
West	272,427	317,057	311,143	−1.9	—	988	3	579	70
Alaska[6]	4,173	5,285	5,597	5.9	N	—	—	—	—
Arizona[7]	26,510	40,627	40,130	−1.2	Y	133	1	62	24
California	163,001	171,275	165,062	−3.6	Y	699	0	305	13
Colorado	16,833	22,795	22,815	0.1	Y	3	0	48	1
Hawaii[6]	5,053	5,891	5,912	0.4	N	—	—	—	—
Idaho	5,535	7,400	7,431	0.4	Y	16	0	4	1
Montana	3,105	3,605	3,716	3.1	Y	2	0	9	3
Nevada	10,063	12,482	12,653	1.4	Y	81	0	41	12
New Mexico	5,342	6,448	6,659	3.3	N	2	0	9	1
Oregon	10,580	14,403	14,014	−2.7	Y	34	0	21	2
Utah	5,637	6,538	6,807	4.1	Y	9	1	20	7
Washington	14,915	18,233	18,235	0.0	Y	8	1	52	5
Wyoming	1,680	2,075	2,112	1.8	Y	1	0	8	1

— = Not available or applicable. (1) Figures do not include persons held under Armed Forces jurisdiction with a military death sentence for murder. (2) Military authorities carried out an additional 160 executions between 1930 and 1961. (3) Total executed includes 40 executions performed under the District of Columbia's jurisdiction since 1930. (4) Prisoners sentenced under DC's criminal code are housed in federal facilities. (5) The death penalty is legally authorized by 36 states. (6) Prisons and jails form one integrated system. Data includes total jail and prison population. (7) Prisoner population based on custody count.

Prison Situation Under Correctional Authorities' Jurisdiction, 2010

Source: *Prisoners in 2010*, Bureau of Justice Statistics, U.S. Dept. of Justice

Largest prison populations		Imprisonment rates of sentenced prisoners		% change in prison population, 2009-10		Avg. annual % change in prison population, 2000-09	
Jurisdiction	Number	Jurisdiction	Rate[1]	Jurisdiction	% change	Jurisdiction	% change
U.S. total	1,612,395	U.S. total	500	U.S. total	−0.3%	U.S. total	1.7%
Federal[2]	209,771	Federal[2]	61	Federal[2]	0.8	Federal[2]	4.1
State.........	1,402,624	State.........	439	State.........	−0.5	State.........	1.4
1. Texas	173,649	1. Louisiana	867	1. Iowa	7.3	1. West Virginia ..	5.7
2. California	165,062	2. Mississippi	686	2. Illinois	7.2	2. Minnesota.....	5.4
3. Florida.......	104,306	3. Oklahoma.....	654	3. Arkansas	6.5	3. Arizona[3]	4.9
4. New York	56,656	4. Alabama......	648	4. Alaska[4].......	5.9	4. Florida........	4.3
5. Georgia.......	56,432	5. Texas	648	5. West Virginia ..	4.9	5. Kentucky	4.2
6. Ohio	51,712	6. Arizona[3]	572	6. Kansas	4.7	6. Indiana	4.1
7. Pennsylvania ..	51,264	7. Florida........	556	7. Utah	4.1	7. Pennsylvania ..	3.8
8. Illinois	48,418	8. Arkansas.....	552	8. New Mexico ...	3.3	8. North Dakota ..	3.7
9. Michigan......	44,113	9. Georgia.......	549	9. Montana	3.1	9. Oregon........	3.5
10. Arizona[3]	40,130	10. Missouri[3].....	508	10. Nebraska	2.5	10. Colorado......	3.4

Note: Excludes jail population unless otherwise noted. (1) Prisoners sentenced to more than one year. Rates are per 100,000 U.S. residents, based upon Census Bureau population estimates for Jan. 1, 2010. (2) Includes prisoners sentenced under DC's criminal code. (3) Population based on custody count (number of prisoners held in its facilities) as opposed to jurisdiction count (number of prisoners under its legal authority). Some states are unable to provide both counts. (4) Prisons and jails form one integrated system. Data includes total jail and prison population.

Arrests by Race, 2010

Source: *Crime in the United States, 2010*, Federal Bureau of Investigation, U.S. Dept. of Justice

Each instance in which a person is arrested, cited, or summoned for an offense is counted as one arrest. The figures below therefore do not represent the number of individuals arrested but the number of times persons were arrested, as an individual may be arrested multiple times in one year. Arrest estimates are based on statistics from law enforcement agencies that reported 12 months of arrest data.

Offense charged	Total	Number of arrests where arrestee was—				% distrib. for offense charged[1]			
		White	Black	Amer. Indian/ Alaska Native	Asian/ Pacific Islander	White	Black	Amer. Indian/ Alaska Native	Asian/ Pacific Islander
PART I OFFENSES[2]									
Violent crime..............	429,166	254,620	163,670	5,776	5,100	59.3%	38.1%	1.3%	1.2%
Murder and nonnegligent manslaughter..........	8,641	4,261	4,209	91	80	49.3	48.7	1.1	0.9
Forcible rape.............	15,503	10,178	4,925	214	186	65.7	31.8	1.4	1.2
Robbery	87,587	37,906	48,154	617	910	43.3	55.0	0.7	1.0
Aggravated assault........	317,435	202,275	106,382	4,854	3,924	63.7	33.5	1.5	1.2
Property crime	1,288,295	881,420	372,562	17,080	17,233	68.4	28.9	1.3	1.3
Burglary	225,775	152,210	69,541	1,961	2,063	67.4	30.8	0.9	0.9
Larceny-theft.............	998,476	687,609	282,246	14,323	14,298	68.9	28.3	1.4	1.4
Motor vehicle theft	55,278	35,009	18,797	696	776	63.3	34.0	1.3	1.4
Arson	8,766	6,592	1,978	100	96	75.2	22.6	1.1	1.1
PART II OFFENSES[3]									
Other assaults[4]...........	1,004,273	659,171	318,117	14,848	12,137	65.6	31.7	1.5	1.2
Forgery and counterfeiting	60,538	40,167	19,350	342	679	66.4	32.0	0.6	1.1
Fraud	144,214	95,126	46,493	1,253	1,342	66.0	32.2	0.9	0.9
Embezzlement	12,930	8,568	4,037	88	237	66.3	31.2	0.7	1.8
Stolen property: buying, receiving, possessing......	74,122	48,303	24,494	598	727	65.2	33.0	0.8	1.0
Vandalism................	197,015	145,284	46,306	3,279	2,146	73.7	23.5	1.7	1.1
Weapons: carrying, possessing, etc.	123,278	71,772	49,443	874	1,189	58.2	40.1	0.7	1.0
Prostitution and commercialized vice.......	48,154	26,156	20,405	342	1,251	54.3	42.4	0.7	2.6
Sex offenses (except forcible rape and prostitution)	56,125	41,406	13,182	744	793	73.8	23.5	1.3	1.4
Drug abuse violations........	1,270,443	846,736	404,609	8,766	10,332	66.6	31.8	0.7	0.8
Gambling	7,512	2,160	5,071	32	249	28.8	67.5	0.4	3.3
Offenses against the family and children	84,812	56,233	26,470	1,533	576	66.3	31.2	1.8	0.7
Driving under the influence....	1,082,301	927,516	124,467	13,980	16,338	85.7	11.5	1.3	1.5
Liquor laws................	396,942	329,895	47,529	14,129	5,389	83.1	12.0	3.6	1.4
Drunkenness	440,688	362,396	66,837	8,583	2,872	82.2	15.2	1.9	0.7
Disorderly conduct	480,080	305,154	162,521	8,415	3,990	63.6	33.9	1.8	0.8
Vagrancy	24,759	14,092	9,935	567	165	56.9	40.1	2.3	0.7
All other offenses (except traffic violations)	2,877,687	1,905,436	893,018	43,634	35,599	66.2	31.0	1.5	1.2
Suspicion[5]................	903	582	310	5	6	64.5	34.3	0.6	0.7
Curfew and loitering law violations...............	73,670	43,961	28,036	744	929	59.7	38.1	1.0	1.3
TOTAL ARRESTS	**10,177,907**	**7,066,154**	**2,846,862**	**145,612**	**119,279**	**69.4**	**28.0**	**1.4**	**1.2**

(1) Percentages may not add up to 100 due to rounding. (2) In the UCR program, serious crimes that occur in all areas of the country and are likely to be reported to police are classified as part I offenses. See Crime in the U.S. table footnotes for offense definitions. (3) Arrest data only is collected for UCR program-designated part II offenses. (4) Simple assaults, where no weapons were used and where the victim did not sustain serious injury (e.g., stalking). (5) Arrested for no specific offense and released without formal charges being placed against a person.

Imprisonment Rate by Gender, Race, Hispanic Origin, and Age, 2010

Source: *Prisoners in 2010*, Bureau of Justice Statistics, U.S. Dept. of Justice

(number of prisoners sentenced to more than one year per 100,000 of each group in the U.S. resident population)

	Male					Female			
Age	All races[1]	White	Black	Hispanic	Age	All races[1]	White	Black	Hispanic
18-19	462	149	1,555	563	18-19	20	11	40	31
20-24	1,511	638	4,618	1,908	20-24	102	72	182	122
25-29	2,098	980	6,349	2,707	25-29	168	125	299	202
30-34	2,261	1,061	7,299	2,808	30-34	175	136	309	189
35-39	2,014	995	6,600	2,486	35-39	158	124	289	153
40-44	1,752	916	5,637	2,146	40-44	147	106	290	156
45-49	1,489	788	4,751	1,901	45-49	115	81	238	117
50-54	1,051	552	3,441	1,495	50-54	68	45	150	88
55-59	650	347	2,239	1,031	55-59	34	22	76	55
60-64	391	233	1,262	679	60-64	17	12	33	29
65 or older	143	95	418	294	65 or older	4	3	7	8
Total[2]	943	459	3,074	1,258	Total[2]	67	47	133	77

Note: Rates are based on Census Bureau population estimates for Jan. 1. Detailed categories exclude persons who reported being of two or more races. Hispanics may be of any race but are not included in white and black populations here. (1) Includes races not shown. (2) Includes persons under age 18.

Hate Crimes by Offense Type, Bias Motivation, 2010

Source: *Hate Crime Statistics, 2010*, Federal Bureau of Investigation (FBI), U.S. Dept. of Justice

Hate crimes are defined as crimes in which victims are chosen because of one or more personal characteristics, such as race, ethnicity, or religion. Congress enacted the Hate Crime Statistics Act of 1990, which led to the collection of hate crime data as part of the FBI's Uniform Crime Report (UCR) program beginning in 1992. Not all agencies that participate in the UCR program submit hate crime data, so the data presented is not representative of the nation as a whole. The hate crime data for 2010 covered about 285 mil U.S. residents.

Bias motivation	Total offenses	Crimes against persons[1]						Crimes against property[2]						Total crimes against society[3]
		Aggravated assault	Simple assault	Intimidation	Other	Total crimes against persons	Robbery	Burglary	Larceny-theft	Destruction/ damage/vandalism	Other	Total crimes against property	
SINGLE-BIAS INCIDENTS	7,690	886	1,679	2,231	24	4,820	146	125	173	2,318	94	2,856	14
Race.............	3,725	444	755	1,227	8	2,434	53	61	84	1,045	37	1,280	11
Anti-White.............	679	92	192	157	5	446	32	22	49	111	16	230	3
Anti-Black.............	2,600	315	486	933	3	1,737	19	25	16	781	17	858	5
Anti-American Indian/ Alaskan Native........	45	3	12	2	0	17	1	1	17	5	3	27	1
Anti-Asian/Pacific Islander	190	15	42	73	0	130	0	7	1	52	0	60	0
Anti-multiple races, group	211	19	23	62	0	104	1	6	1	96	1	105	2
Religion...............	1,409	35	133	321	4	493	11	29	38	816	22	916	0
Anti-Jewish............	922	12	65	201	0	278	9	6	8	619	2	644	0
Anti-Catholic...........	61	0	5	7	0	12	0	6	10	31	2	49	0
Anti-Protestant	46	0	1	3	0	4	0	5	3	33	1	42	0
Anti-Islamic..........	186	17	46	69	0	132	1	1	3	47	2	54	0
Anti-other religion........	134	4	11	25	4	44	1	9	8	59	13	90	0
Anti-multiple religions, group	53	2	5	15	0	22	0	1	5	23	2	31	0
Anti-atheism/ agnosticism/etc........	7	0	0	1	0	1	0	1	1	4	0	6	0
Sexual orientation......	1,470	247	495	331	9	1,082	56	19	24	273	16	388	0
Anti-male homosexual ...	851	158	301	190	4	653	39	6	12	134	7	198	0
Anti-female homosexual	167	23	40	52	4	119	2	4	2	39	1	48	0
Anti-homosexual........	403	58	139	84	0	281	15	8	3	92	4	122	0
Anti-heterosexual	21	3	7	1	0	11	0	0	1	8	1	10	0
Anti-bisexual...........	28	5	8	4	1	18	0	1	6	0	3	10	0
Ethnicity/national origin...	1,040	154	276	347	2	779	23	15	20	183	18	259	2
Anti-Hispanic	681	112	183	227	2	524	16	9	11	105	15	156	1
Anti-other ethnicity/ national origin	359	42	93	120	0	255	7	6	9	78	3	103	1
Disability...............	46	6	20	5	1	32	3	1	7	1	1	13	1
Anti-physical..........	22	4	8	5	1	18	0	0	3	0	0	3	1
Anti-mental...........	24	2	12	0	0	14	3	1	4	1	1	10	0
MULTIPLE-BIAS INCIDENTS[4]...........	9	2	2	0	0	4	0	0	2	3	0	5	0
Total offenses...........	7,699	888	1,681	2,231	24	4,824	146	125	175	2,321	94	2,861	14

(1) Includes murder, non-negligent manslaughter, forcible rape, and additional offenses not shown here in details. (2) Includes arson, motor vehicle theft, and additional offenses not shown here in detail. (3) Includes drug or narcotic, gambling, and prostitution offenses and weapon law violations where society as a whole is considered the victim. (4) More than one offense type must occur, and at least two offense types must be motivated by different biases to count as a multiple-bias incident.

Notable Assassinations Since 1865

1865—Apr. 14: U.S. Pres. Abraham Lincoln shot by John Wilkes Booth, well-known actor with Confederate sympathies, at Ford's Theater in Washington, DC; died Apr. 15.

1881—Mar. 13: Alexander II of Russia. **July 2:** U.S. Pres. James A. Garfield shot by Charles J. Guiteau, disappointed office seeker, in Washington, DC; died Sept. 19.

1894—June 24: French Pres. Sadi Carnot by Sante Caserio, Italian anarchist, in Lyon.

1898—Sept. 10: Empress Elizabeth of Austria stabbed by Luigi Lucheni, Italian anarchist.

1900—July 29: Umberto I, king of Italy, by an anarchist.

1901—Sept. 6: U.S. Pres. William McKinley shot by Leon Czolgosz, anarchist, in Buffalo, NY; died Sept. 14.

1908—Feb. 1: King Carlos I of Portugal and his son Luís Filipe in Lisbon.

1913—Feb. 23: Mexican Pres. Francisco I. Madero and Vice Pres. José María Pino Suárez. **Mar. 18:** King George of Greece.

1914—June 28: Archduke Francis Ferdinand of Austria-Hungary and his wife shot by Gavrilo Princip, Serb nationalist, in Sarajevo, Bosnia.

1916—Dec. 30: Grigory Rasputin, Russian mystic and court figure, by group of aristocrats.

1918—July 12: Grand Duke Michael of Russia, at Perm. **July 16:** Nicholas II, former (abdicated) czar of Russia; his wife, Czarina Alexandra; their son, Czarevitch Alexis; their daughters, Grand Duchesses Olga, Tatiana, Marie, Anastasia; and 4 members of household executed by Bolsheviks at Ekaterinburg.

1920—May 20: Mexican Pres. Gen. Venustiano Carranza in Tlaxcalantongo.

1922—Aug. 22: Michael Collins, Irish revolutionary, in ambush in West Cork. **Dec. 16:** Polish Pres. Gabriel Narutowicz in Warsaw.

1923—July 20: Gen. Francisco "Pancho" Villa, ex-rebel leader, in Parral, Mexico.

1928—July 17: Gen. Alvaro Obregon, president-elect of Mexico, in San Angel.

1932—May 6: French Pres. Paul Doumer shot by Russian émigré, Pavel Gorgulov, in Paris.

1934—July 25: Austrian Chancellor Engelbert Dollfuss by Nazis, in Vienna.

1935—Sept. 8: Sen. Huey P. Long, former Louisiana governor, shot by Dr. Carl Austin Weiss, son-in-law of political opponent, in Baton Rouge; died Sept. 10.

1940—Aug. 20: Leon Trotsky (Lev Bronstein), exiled Soviet commissar of war, fatally wounded with ice ax by Soviet agent near Mexico City.

1948—Jan. 30: Leader of movement for Indian independence Mohandas K. Gandhi (Mahatma) shot by Hindu fanatic in New Delhi. **Sept. 17:** Count Folke Bernadotte, UN mediator for Palestine, by Jewish extremists in Jerusalem.

1951—July 20: Jordanian King Abdullah ibn Hussein. **Oct. 16:** Prime Min. Liaquat Ali Khan of Pakistan shot, in Rawalpindi.

1956—Sept. 21: Pres. Anastasio Somoza of Nicaragua shot in Leon; died Sept. 29.

1957—July 26: Guatemalan Pres. Carlos Castillo Armas, in Guatemala City by one of his guards.

1958—July 14: King Faisal of Iraq, Crown Prince Abdullah, and **July 15,** Prem. Nuri as-Said, by rebels in Baghdad.

1959—Sept. 25: Prime Min. Solomon Bandaranaike of Ceylon, by Buddhist monk in Colombo.

1961—Jan. 17: First elected prime min. of the Congo, Patrice Lumumba, in Katanga Prov., by political rivals. **May 30:** Dominican dictator Rafael Leónidas Trujillo Molina, nr. Ciudad Trujillo.

1963—June 12: Medgar Evers, NAACP's Mississippi field secretary, shot by Byron De La Beckwith in Jackson, MS. **Nov. 2:** Pres. Ngo Dinh Diem of South Vietnam and his brother, Ngo Dinh Nhu, in military coup. **Nov. 22:** U.S. Pres. John F. Kennedy shot while riding in motorcade through downtown Dallas, TX; accused gunman Lee Harvey Oswald murdered by nightclub owner Jack Ruby while awaiting trial.

1965—Jan. 21: Iranian Prem. Hassan Ali Mansour in Tehran. **Feb. 21:** Malcolm X, black nationalist leader, shot by three men linked to Nation of Islam at New York City rally.

1966—Sept. 6: Prime Min. Hendrik F. Verwoerd of South Africa stabbed to death in parliament at Cape Town.

1968—Apr. 4: Rev. Martin Luther King Jr. fatally shot in Memphis, TN; James Earl Ray convicted of crime. **June 5:** Sen. Robert F. Kennedy (D, NY) shot in Los Angeles; died June 6. Sirhan Sirhan convicted of crime.

1971—Nov. 28: Jordanian Prime Min. Wasfi Tal by Palestinian guerrillas, in Cairo.

1973—Mar. 2: U.S. Amb. Cleo A. Noel Jr., U.S. Charge d'Affaires George C. Moore, and Belgian Charge d'Affaires Guy Eid by Palestinian guerrillas in Khartoum, Sudan. **Dec. 20:** Spanish Prem. Luis Carrero Blanco in car bombing by Basque separatist group ETA, in Madrid.

1974—Aug. 19: U.S. Amb. to Cyprus, Rodger P. Davies, by sniper's bullet in Nicosia.

1975—Feb. 11: Pres. Richard Ratsimandrava of Madagascar shot in Tananarive. **Mar. 25:** Saudi Arabian King Faisal shot by nephew Prince Musad Abdel Aziz, in Riyadh. **Aug. 15:** Bangladesh Pres. Sheik Mujibur Rahman killed in coup.

1976—Feb. 13: Nigerian head of state, Gen. Murtala Ramat Mohammed, by self-styled young revolutionaries.

1977—Mar. 16: Kamal Jumblat, Lebanese Druse chieftain, shot near Beirut. **Mar. 18:** Congo Pres. Marien Ngouabi shot in Brazzaville.

1978—May 9: Former Italian Prem. Aldo Moro killed by Red Brigades terrorists who abducted him Mar. 16 in Rome, held him hostage for several weeks. **July 9:** Former Iraqi Prem. Abdul Razak Al-Naif shot in London.

1979—Feb. 14: U.S. Amb. Adolph Dubs shot by Afghan Muslim extremists in Kabul. **Aug. 27:** Lord Mountbatten, WWII hero, and 2 others killed when a bomb exploded on his fishing boat off coast of Co. Sligo, Ireland. IRA claimed responsibility. **Oct. 26:**

S. Korean Pres. Park Chung Hee and 6 bodyguards fatally shot by Kim Jae Kyu, head of S. Korean CIA.

1980—Apr. 12: Liberian Pres. William R. Tolbert in military coup. **Sept. 17:** Former Nicaraguan Pres. Anastasio Somoza Debayle shot in Paraguay.

1981—Oct. 6: Egyptian Pres. Anwar al-Sadat shot by commandos while reviewing military parade in Cairo; 7 others killed, 28 wounded.

1982—Sept. 14: Lebanese Pres.-elect Bashir Gemayel killed by bomb in east Beirut.

1983—Aug. 21: Philippine opposition leader Benigno Aquino Jr. shot by gunman at Manila Intl. Airport.

1984—Oct. 31: Indian Prime Min. Indira Gandhi shot and killed by 2 Sikh bodyguards, in New Delhi.

1986—Feb. 28: Swedish Prime Min. Olof Palme shot by gunman on Stockholm street for unknown reasons.

1987—June 1: Lebanese Prem. Rashid Karami killed when bomb exploded aboard helicopter.

1988—Apr. 16: PLO military chief Khalil Wazir (Abu Jihad) gunned down by Israeli commandos in Tunisia.

1989—Aug. 18: Colombian pres. candidate Luis Carlos Galán killed by Medellín cartel drug traffickers at campaign rally in Bogotá. **Nov. 22:** Lebanese Pres. Rene Moawad killed when bomb exploded next to his motorcade.

1990—Mar. 22: Colombian pres. candidate Bernardo Jaramillo Ossa shot by gunman at airport in Bogotá.

1991—May 21: Former Indian Prime Min. Rajiv Gandhi killed by bomb during election rally in Madras.

1992—June 29: Algerian Pres. Mohammed Boudiaf shot by gunman in Annaba.

1993—May 1: Sri Lankan Pres. Ranasinghe Premadasa killed by bomb in Colombo.

1994—Mar. 23: Mexican pres. candidate Luis Donaldo Colosio shot by gunman Mario Aburto Martinez. **Apr. 6:** Burundian Pres. Cyprien Ntaryamira and Rwandan Pres. Juvénal Habyarimana killed with 8 others when their plane was shot down.

1995—Nov. 4: Israeli Prime Min. Yitzhak Rabin shot by Yigal Amir, Jewish extremist, at peace rally in Tel Aviv.

1996—Oct. 2: Andrei Lukanov, former Bulgarian prime min., shot outside home by unidentified gunman.

1998—Feb. 6: Prefect of Corsica, Claude Erignac, shot in the back by 2 unidentified gunmen while walking to concert. **Apr. 26:** Guatemalan Roman Catholic Bishop Juan Gerardi Conedera, human rights champion, found beaten to death in Guatemala City.

1999—Mar. 23: Paraguayan Vice Pres. Luis María Argaña, ambushed and shot to death along with his driver, by 4 unidentified assailants, in Asunción. **Apr. 9:** Niger Pres. Ibrahim Bare Mainassara ambushed and killed by dissident soldiers. **Oct. 27:** Armenian Prime Min. Vazgen Sarkissian, along with 7 others, shot to death during session of parliament.

2000—Jan. 15: Serbian paramilitary leader Zeljko Raznjatovic (Arkan), with 2 others, shot and killed by unidentified gunman in Belgrade. **June 8:** Brig. Gen. Stephen Saunders, Britain's senior military representative in Greece, fatally shot by 2 men on motorcycle, while driving car in Athens suburb.

2001—Jan. 16: Dem. Rep. of the Congo Pres. Laurent Kabila shot to death by bodyguard at pres. palace in Kinshasa. **June 1:** Nepal's King Birendra, Queen Aiswarya, and 7 other royals fatally shot by Crown Prince Dipendra, who also fatally wounded himself. **Oct. 14:** Abdel Rahman Hamad, a leader of Palestinian militant group Hamas, shot by Israeli military snipers. **Oct. 17:** Israeli tourism min. Rehavam Zeevifatally shot; Popular Front for the Liberation of Palestine claimed responsibility.

2002—Mar. 16: Colombian cleric Isaías Duarte Cancino, critic of Colombian guerrillas and drug traffickers, shot by unidentified gunmen outside of church in Cali. **May 6:** Dutch right-wing politician Pim Fortuyn shot outside radio station in Hilversum. **July 6:** Afghan Vice Pres. Haji Abdul Qadir shot outside his office in Kabul.

2003—Mar. 12: Serbian Prime Min. Zoran Djindjic shot by snipers (paramilitary) outside govt. headquarters in Belgrade. **Apr. 10:** Shiite Muslim cleric Abdul Majid al-Khoei attacked by crowd, hacked to death at Imam Ali mosque, Najaf, Iraq. **Apr. 17:** Sergei Yushenkov, former Russian legislator and Liberal Party head, shot outside apartment in Moscow. **Sept. 10:** Swedish Foreign Min. Anna Lindh stabbed in Stockholm dept. store by mentally ill man; died Sept. 11.

2004—Feb. 13: Former Chechen Pres. Zelimkhan Yandarbiyev killed after car exploded in Qatar. **Mar. 22:** Sheik Ahmed Yassin, spiritual leader of Hamas, by Israeli missile attack in Gaza City. **Apr. 17:** Hamas leader Abdel Aziz Rantisi by Israeli missile strike, in Gaza City. **May 9:** Chechen Pres. Akhmad Kadyrov by bomb explosion at WWII memorial service in Grozny. **May 17:** Iraqi Gov. Council Pres. Ezzedine Salim, by car bomb explosion at Green Zone checkpoint in Baghdad. **Nov. 2:** Filmmaker Theo van Gogh, critic of Islam and great-grandnephew of painter Vincent van Gogh, shot and stabbed by Muslim militant in Amsterdam.

2005—Jan. 4: Baghdad Gov. Ali al-Haidari gunned down by insurgents in Baghdad, Iraq. **Feb. 14:** Former Lebanese Prime Min. Rafik al-Hariri killed when motorcade bombed in Beirut. **Mar. 8:** Former Chechen pres. Aslan Maskhadov killed in raid by Russian special forces, in village outside Grozny.

2006—Feb. 11: Leading Kazakhstan opposition politician Altynbek Sarsenbayev (Sarsenbaiuly) kidnapped, found murdered outside Almaty. **Sept. 14:** Andrei Kozlov, Russian central banker active in reforming industry, shot by unidentified gunmen in Moscow. **Oct. 7:** Anna Politkovskaya, reporter critical of Kremlin's Chechnya policies, fatally shot by unidentified gunman in apartment building in Moscow.

2007—June 13: Walid Eido, Lebanese parliament member who was part of anti-Syria coalition, killed by car bomb in Beirut. **Aug. 2:** *Oakland Post* editor Chauncey Bailey, who was investigating financial status of black Muslim organization, shot dead in downtown Oakland, CA. **Dec. 27:** Benazir Bhutto, former Pakistani prime min. and first female elected leader of a Muslim state, by gunfire and/or bomb as she was leaving political rally for Pakistan People's Party.

2008—Feb. 12: Imad Mughniyeh, top Hezbollah commander, by car bomb in Syria. Mughniyeh had been on FBI's Most Wanted Terrorist list and was believed to have orchestrated the 1983 bombing of U.S. embassy in Beirut. **May 8:** Edgar Eusebio Millán Gómez, Mexico's acting national police chief, by gunmen outside his home in Mexico City. **Aug. 1:** Syrian brig. gen. and top presidential aide Mohammed Suleiman reportedly shot by sniper nr. Tartus; Suleiman had been Syria's primary contact with investigators from Intl. Atomic Energy Agency. **Oct. 23:** Ivo Pukanic, owner and editor-in-chief of Croatian political newspaper *Nacional*, killed in Zagreb when bomb exploded near his car, widely attributed to organized crime groups.

2009—Jan.: Six candidates for elected office killed in several regions of Iraq shortly before scheduled provincial elections.

Mar. 2: Rocket grenades launched into home of Guinea-Bissau's longtime Pres. João Bernardo Vieira and Gen. Batista Tagme Na Waie, killing both men. **Mar. 31:** Sulim Yamadeyev, former Chechen general and enemy of the Kremlin-installed president, killed by gunmen in Dubai. **May 31:** Dr. George Tiller, one of the few doctors in U.S. to perform abortions late in pregnancy, shot to death in his Wichita, KS, church by anti-abortion activist. **June 12:** Harith al-Obaidi, Sunni member of Iraq's Parliament, shot at point-blank range. **June 13:** Bashir Aushev, former vice prem. of Ingushetia region of Russia, killed by gunmen. **Sept. 2:** Abdullah Lahgmani, deputy director of Afghanistan's National Directorate for Security, and at least 15 others killed by suicide bomber in Mehtar Lam. **Sept. 27:** Two officials from Russian republic of Dagestan, Alimsultan Alkhamatov and Alimsultan Atuyev, shot dead in separate incidents.

2010—Jan. 19: Mahmoud al-Mabhouh, senior commander for Hamas, found drugged and suffocated in his Dubai, United Arab Emirates, hotel room; Israel's Mossad spy agency suspected. **Aug. 2:** Raza Haider, member of Pakistan's parliament, and his bodyguard shot dead by four gunmen in mosque in Karachi, Pakistan, unleashing violence that killed at least 78 others.

2011—Mar. 2: Shahbaz Bhatti, only Christian minister in Pakistani govt. and opponent of nation's blasphemy laws, shot in Islamabad. **July 12:** Ahmed Wali Karzai, power-wielding half-brother of Afghan Pres. Hamid Karzai, shot dead in Kandahar home by a long-time confidante. Three other Karzai allies, including Kandahar mayor Ghulam Hamidi, assassinated over the next two weeks. **July 28:** Gen. Abdul Fattah Younes, Libya's top rebel commander, and two other officers killed in Benghazi. **Sept. 20:** Burhanuddin Rabbani, a former pres. and then-leader of Afghanistan's High Peace Council, killed in home by assassin with explosives hidden in turban.

2012—Jan. 11: Iranian nuclear scientist Mostafa Ahmadi Roshan and driver killed by car bomb. **July 18:** Three senior Syrian officials, including Defense Min. Dawoud Rajiha and Assef Shawkat, brother-in-law to Pres. Bashar al-Assad, killed by bomb.

Notable Assassination Attempts Since 1912

1912—Oct. 14: Former U.S. Pres. Theodore Roosevelt shot and wounded by mentally ill man in Milwaukee, WI.

1933—Feb. 15: In Miami, FL, anarchist Joseph Zangara shot at Pres.-elect Franklin D. Roosevelt, but a woman seized his arm; bullet fatally wounded Chicago Mayor Anton J. Cermak, who died Mar. 6.

1944—July 20: Adolf Hitler injured when bomb, planted by German officer, exploded in his headquarters; one aide killed,12 injured.

1950—Nov. 1: In attempt to assassinate Pres. Harry Truman, 2 members of Puerto Rican nationalist movement—Griselio Torresola and Oscar Collazo—tried to shoot their way into Blair House, across the street from White House. Torresola killed. Pvt. Leslie Coffelt, White House policeman, fatally shot.

1970—Nov. 27: Pope Paul VI unharmed by knife-wielding assailant who attempted to attack him in airport in Manila, Philippines.

1972—May 15: Alabama Gov. George Wallace seriously wounded when shot in Laurel, MD, by fame-seeking Arthur Bremer.

1975—Sept. 5: Pres. Gerald R. Ford unharmed when Secret Service agent grabbed pistol aimed at him by Lynette "Squeaky" Fromme, follower of cult leader Charles Manson, in Sacramento, CA. **Sept. 22:** Pres. Ford unharmed when bystander grabbed arm of Sara Jane Moore as she fired upon Ford in San Francisco.

1980—May 29: Civil rights leader Vernon E. Jordan Jr. shot and wounded in Ft. Wayne, IN.

1981—Mar. 30: Pres. Ronald Reagan, along with Press Sec. James Brady, Secret Service agent Timothy J. McCarthy, and Washington, DC, policeman Thomas Delahanty shot and seriously wounded by John W. Hinckley Jr. in Washington, DC. **May 13:** Pope John Paul II and two bystanders shot and wounded by Mehmet Ali Agca, an escaped Turkish prisoner, in St. Peter's Square, Rome.

1982—May 12: Pope John Paul II wounded by ultra-conservative priest wielding bayonet, in Fatima, Portugal.

1984—Oct. 12: British Prime Min. Margaret Thatcher unharmed when a bomb, said to have been planted by the IRA, exploded at the Grand Hotel in Brighton, England, during a Party conference; four died, incl. a member of Parliament.

1986—Sept. 7: Chilean Pres. Gen. Augusto Pinochet Ugarte unharmed after motorcade was attacked by rebels.

1995—June 26: Egyptian Pres. Hosni Mubarak unharmed when gunmen fired on his motorcade in Addis Ababa, Ethiopia; 4 died, incl. two Ethiopian police officers.

1997—Feb. 12: Colombian Pres. Ernesto Samper Pizano unharmed when bomb exploded on runway in Barranquilla as his plane was preparing to land. **Apr. 30:** Tajik Pres. Imamali Rakhmanov injured when a grenade was thrown at him.

1998—Feb. 9: Georgian Pres. Eduard A. Shevardnadze unharmed when gunmen fired on his motorcade in Tbilisi.

2002—Apr. 14: Leading Colombian pres. candidate Álvaro Uribe Vélez unharmed after bomb exploded under parked bus as his motorcade passed in Barranquilla; three bystanders killed. **July 14:** French Pres. Jacques Chirac unharmed after Maxime Brunerie, gunman with ties to neo-Nazi groups, fired at his open-top jeep during Bastille Day parade in Paris. **Sept. 5:** Afghan Pres. Hamid Karzai unharmed after militant shot at car in Kandahar. **Nov. 25:** Turkmenistan Pres. Saparmurat Niyazov unharmed after gunmen opened fire on his motorcade in Ashgabat.

2003—Dec. 14: Pakistani Pres. Pervez Musharraf unharmed after bomb detonated on bridge in Rawalpindi seconds after his motorcade crossed.

2004—Mar. 19: Taiwanese Pres. Chen Shui-bian shot while campaigning in motorcade; minor injuries. **July 13:** Separatists bombed motorcade of Sergei Abramov, Chechnya's acting pres. **Sept. 5:** Ukrainian opposition presidential candidate Viktor Yushchenko, who later won office, fell ill after meeting; diagnosed with dioxin poisoning. **Sept. 16:** Rocket fired at helicopter carrying Afghan Pres. Hamid Karzai, near Gardez.

2005—Mar. 15: Kosovo Pres. Ibrahim Rugova survived bombing of his motorcade as it traveled through Pristina.

2007—June 29: Rockets hit plane carrying former rebel chief and Côte d'Ivoire Prime Min. Guillaume Soro, shortly after plane landed in Bouake; Soro unhurt.

2008—Feb. 11: Pres. José Ramos-Horta shot in attack led by fugitive former army official, in Dili, Timor-Leste. Ambush of Prime Min. Xanana Gusmão's motorcade a short time later unsuccessful. **Apr. 27:** Afghan Pres. Hamid Karzai unharmed after Taliban gunmen fired on military parade in Kabul where Karzai was in attendance.

2009—Apr. 30: After shootout, Bolivian police killed three men and captured two others whom they accused of plotting to assassinate Pres. Evo Morales. **June 22:** Yunus-Bek Yevkurov, president of Ingushetia region of Russia, seriously wounded when suicide bomber in car packed with explosives crashed into his motorcade.

2010—May 14: Indonesian National Police announced they broke up plot by terrorists calling themselves al-Qaeda in Aceh to assassinate Pres. Susilo Bambang Yudhoyono. **Sept. 23:** Alexander Ankvab, vice pres. of Georgian region of Ankhazia, survived fourth assassination attempt in five years, a grenade fired into his Gudauta home.

2011—Jan. 8: U.S. Rep. Gabrielle Giffords (D, AZ) severely wounded by lone gunman at public meeting near an Arizona supermarket; six others killed, including a federal judge. **June 3:** Yemeni Pres. Ali Abdullah Saleh survived bombing of presidential palace. **Nov. 11:** Gunman fired shots from assault rifle in direction of White House, piercing a window; the president was not in the building.

2012—May 18: Taliban soldiers killed seven in attempt to kill governor of the Afghanistan prov. of Farah. **Sept. 12:** Hassan Sheik Mohamud survived suicide bombing attack on his home two days after being elected Somalia's president

Notable U.S. Kidnappings Since 1924

Bobby Franks, 14, in Chicago, **May 21, 1924**, by 2 youths from wealthy families—Richard Loeb, 18, and Nathan Leopold, 19—who killed boy. Demand for $10,000 ignored. Loeb killed in prison; Leopold paroled 1958.

Charles A. Lindbergh Jr., 20 mos. old, nr. Hopewell, NJ, **Mar. 1, 1932**; found dead **May 12**. Ransom of $50,000 paid to man identified as Bruno Richard Hauptmann, 35, paroled German convict who entered U.S. illegally. Hauptmann convicted, electrocuted in Trenton, NJ, prison, Apr. 3, 1936.

William A. Hamm Jr., 39, brewing company pres. in St. Paul, **June 15, 1933**, by Karpis-Barker gang. $100,000 paid. Alvin Karpis given life, paroled in 1969.

Charles F. Urschel, in Oklahoma City, **July 22, 1933**. Released **July 31** after $200,000 paid. George "Machine Gun" Kelly and 5 others sentenced to life.

Brooke L. Hart, 22, in San Jose, CA. Thomas Thurmond and John Holmes arrested after demanding $40,000. When Hart's body was found in San Francisco Bay, **Nov. 26, 1933**, a mob forced its way into jail and lynched the 2 kidnappers.

June Robles, 6, abducted in Tucson, AZ, **Apr. 25, 1934**. Missing for 19 days after ransom note sent to parents. Found alive in iron cage buried in desert. No arrests ever made.

George Weyerhaeuser, 9, of Weyerhaeuser lumber company, in Tacoma, WA, **May 24, 1935**. Returned home **June 1** after $200,000 paid. Kidnappers given 20 to 60 years.

Charles Mattson, 10, in Tacoma, WA, **Dec. 27, 1936**. Kidnapper initially asked for $28,000 but subsequent communication with parents was confusing. Charles found dead **Jan. 11, 1937**.

Robert C. Greenlease, 6, son of wealthy car dealer, taken from Kansas City, MO, school **Sept. 28, 1953**; held for $600,000. Body was found **Oct. 7**. Bonnie Brown Heady and Carl A. Hall pleaded guilty, were executed.

Lee Crary, 8, in Everett, WA, **Sept. 22, 1957**; $10,000 ransom not paid. Crary escaped after 3 days and led police to George E. Collins, who was convicted.

Frank Sinatra Jr., 19, from hotel room in Lake Tahoe, CA, **Dec. 8, 1963**. Released **Dec. 11** after his father paid $240,000 ransom. Three men sentenced to prison.

Barbara Jane Mackle, 20, abducted **Dec. 17, 1968**, from Atlanta, GA, motel; found unharmed 3 days later, buried in coffin-like box 18 in. underground, after her father paid $500,000 ransom. Gary Steven Krist sentenced to life, Ruth Eisenmann-Schier to 7 years.

Virginia Piper, 49, abducted **July 27, 1972**, from her home in suburban Minneapolis; found unharmed near Duluth 2 days later after husband, retired banker, paid $1 mil ransom, then largest ransom ever reported in U.S.

J. Paul Getty III, 17, grandson of the oil billionaire, disappeared **July 10, 1973**, in Italy. Reported payment of $2.8 mil ransom not made until after Getty's ear was sent to a newspaper with a warning that other parts of his body would be mutilated unless ransom was paid. Getty freed **Dec. 15**; 2 men sentenced to prison.

Patricia "Patty" Hearst, 19, taken from her Berkeley, CA, apartment **Feb. 4, 1974**; "Symbionese Liberation Army" captors demanded her father, publisher Randolph Hearst, give millions to area poor. Patty implicated in San Francisco bank holdup, **Apr. 15**. The FBI, **Sept. 18, 1975**, captured her and others. She was convicted of bank robbery, Mar. 20, 1976; released from prison under executive clemency, Feb. 1, 1979. In 1978, William and Emily Harris were sentenced to 10 years to life for the kidnapping; both were paroled in 1983.

J. Reginald Murphy, 40, an editor of *Atlanta Constitution* (GA), kidnapped **Feb. 20, 1974**; freed **Feb. 22** after newspaper paid $700,000 ransom. William A. H. Williams arrested; most of the money recovered.

Jack Teich, Kings Point, NY, steel executive, seized **Nov. 12, 1974**; released **Nov. 19** after payment of $750,000.

Adam Walsh, 6, abducted from Hollywood, FL, dept. store, **July 27, 1981**. Severed head found 2 weeks later. John Walsh, Adam's father, became active in raising awareness about missing children.

Terry Anderson, 37, Middle East bureau chief for Associated Press, in Beirut, Lebanon, by members of Islamic fundamentalist group Hezbollah on **Mar. 16, 1985**. Freed **Dec. 4, 1991**. Anderson had been held hostage with **William Buckley**, 55, CIA station chief in Beirut who was kidnapped **Mar. 16, 1984**, and died in captivity.

Jaycee Dugard, 11, kidnapped near her home in South Lake Tahoe, CA, **June 10, 1991**; held for 18 years by Nancy and Philip Garrido, who fathered two girls with Dugard during her captivity. Dugard, along with her 11- and 15-year-old daughters, was reunited with her family **Aug. 27, 2009**, after police arrested the Garridos.

Sidney J. Reso, oil company exec., seized **Apr. 29, 1992**; died **May 3**. Arthur D. Seale—former security official at oil company—and his wife, Irene, arrested June 19. Arthur pleaded guilty, sentenced to life in prison; Irene sentenced to 20-year prison term.

Polly Klaas, 12, Petaluma, CA, abducted at knife point, **Oct. 1, 1993**, during slumber party at her home. Police arrested Richard Allen Davis on **Nov. 30**; he led them to her body, found **Dec. 4** in wooded area of Cloverdale, CA. Davis found guilty June 18, 1996, and sentenced to death Sept. 26.

Tionda Z. Bradley, 10, and sister **Diamond Yvette Bradley**, 3, went missing **July 6, 2001**, in Chicago, IL. Note left by Tionda at home stated the 2 girls were going to the store and playground. Disappearance still unsolved.

Daniel Pearl, 38, reporter for *Wall Street Journal*, disappeared **Jan. 23, 2002**, while researching story in Karachi, Pakistan. British-born militant Ahmad Omar Saeed Sheikh **Feb. 14** admitted to organizing the kidnapping and said Pearl was dead. Sheikh and 3 others convicted July 15 of kidnapping and murder by judge in Hyderabad.

Elizabeth Smart, 14, abducted from her home in Salt Lake City, UT, **June 5, 2002**, by Brian D. Mitchell, and forced to live with Mitchell and wife Wanda for 9 months in various U.S. cities; found walking down street with captors in Sandy, UT, 15 mi from Smart family home, **Mar. 12, 2003**.

Jill Carroll, 28, freelance journalist, in Baghdad by group called the Revenge Brigade, **Jan. 7, 2006**. She was on assignment for the *Christian Science Monitor* when she was seized. She was released **Mar. 30**; 4 Iraqis arrested in connection with her kidnapping.

Steve Centanni, 60, a Fox News reporter released **Aug. 26, 2006** (along with a colleague), after being held hostage for 13 days by Palestinian militant group Holy Jihad Brigades. The group had demanded that the U.S. release all Muslims held in its prisons.

Reigh Storrow Mills, 7, abducted **July 27, 2008**, by her father Christian Gerhartsreiter (who used the alias Clark Rockefeller); reunited with her mother **Aug. 2, 2008**, by FBI agents who took Gerhartsreiter into custody.

Felix Batista, 55, Cuban-American who negotiated the release of numerous kidnapping victims in Latin America, was abducted in Mexico in early **Dec. 2008**.

Melissa Roxas, 31, a volunteer health worker released **May 24, 2009**, five days after being kidnapped in the Philippines.

David Rohde, 41, a *New York Times* reporter captured by the Taliban in Afghanistan **Nov. 10, 2008**, escaped **June 19, 2009**.

Jessica Buchanan, 32, aid worker for the Danish Refugee Council, taken hostage by Somali pirates **Oct. 25, 2011**; rescued by U.S. Navy SEALs **Jan. 25, 2012**.

Notable Terrorist Incidents Worldwide Since 1971

Source: U.S. Dept. of State; *Facts On File World News Digest @ Facts.com*; World Almanac research

Selected noteworthy incidents, excluding most assassinations, kidnappings, and military targets. Does not include all incidents in Iraq or Afghanistan, 2001-present; see Chronology of the Year's Events.

1971—Mar. 1: Senate wing of U.S. Capitol Building in Wash., DC, bombed by Weather Underground; no deaths.

1972—July 21: "Bloody Friday." Provisional IRA exploded 20+ bombs across Belfast, N. Ireland; 9 killed, hundreds injured. **Sept. 5:** Members of Palestinian group Black September killed 2 Israeli athletes and seized 9 others at Olympic Village in Munich, W. Germany, during Summer Olympics. 9 hostages, 5 militants, 1 Ger. officer died in botched rescue.

1973—Dec. 17: Palestinian gunmen attacked Rome airport and bombed plane on tarmac; hijacked Lufthansa plane with 5 Italian hostages to Athens, Greece, then to Kuwait; 31 killed in all.

1974—June 17: Houses of Parliament in London, England, bombed by Provisional IRA; 11 injured.

1975—Jan. 27: Puerto Rican FALN nationalists bombed Fraunces Tavern in New York City; 4 killed, 53 injured. **Jan. 29:** U.S. State Dept. building in Wash., DC, bombed by Weather Underground; no deaths.

1976—June 27: Palestinian and Baader-Meinhof militants forced Air France jet to land at Entebbe, Uganda. Israeli army rescued 103 hostages from airport terminal in battle with terrorists and Ugandan troops, July 3-4; 32 killed in all.

1978—Mar. 11: Palestinian militants landed on beach near Haifa, Israel. Shot civilians and hijacked bus with hostages to Tel Aviv. Exploded at roadblock; 43 killed.

1979—Nov. 4: Iranian radicals seized U.S. embassy in Tehran, taking 66 Americans hostage. 52 were held until Jan. 20, 1981. **Nov. 20:** 200 Islamic terrorists seized Grand Mosque in Mecca, Saudi Arabia, and held hundreds of pilgrims hostage. Saudi forces retook mosque Dec. 4; about 250 died.

1980—Feb. 27: Members of leftist guerrilla group April 19 Movement (M-19) seized Dominican Republic embassy in Bogota, Colombia; 80 hostages taken, 18 held until Apr. 27.

1983—Apr. 18: Hezbollah suicide truck bomb at U.S. embassy in Beirut, Lebanon, killed 63. **Oct. 9:** N. Korean agents ambushed a S. Korean govt. delegation in Rangoon, Burma, killing 21. **Oct. 23:** Hezbollah suicide truck bombings of U.S. and French military bases, Beirut, Lebanon; 242 Americans, 58 French killed.

1984—Sept. 20: U.S. embassy annex nr. Beirut, Lebanon, bombed, killing approx. 20.

1985—June 14: Hezbollah members hijacked TWA Flight 847 with 153 passengers and crew to Beirut, Lebanon; 39 held for 17 days; 1 U.S. Navy sailor killed. **June 23:** Air India Flight 182 destroyed by bomb off coast of Ireland; 329 killed. Blamed on Sikh terrorists. **Apr. 12:** Bomb blast at restaurant nr. Air Force base in Torrejon, Spain; 18 killed. **Oct. 7:** Four Palestinians hijacked Italian cruise ship *Achille Lauro*; 1 passenger killed. **Nov. 23:** EgyptAir Flight 648 from Athens to Cairo hijacked to Malta by Palestinian group Abu Nidal; 60 killed in rescue. **Dec. 27:** Palestinian militants opened fire at El-Al airline counters at Rome and Vienna airports; 19 killed.

1986—Apr. 5: Nightclub in Berlin, W. Germany, bombed; 3 killed, incl. 2 U.S. servicemen, 200+ hurt. 3 Libyan embassy workers in Germany convicted in bombing.

1987—Apr. 17: Bomb in Sri Lankan capital killed 100+; blamed on Tamil rebels who, 4 days later, attacked Sinhalese travelers on highway, killing 127. **June 19:** Basque group ETA bombed supermarket garage in Barcelona, Spain; 21 killed, 45 injured. **Nov. 29:** Bomb planted by N. Korean agents exploded on Korean Air Lines Flight 858 over Indian Ocean; 115 killed.

1988—Dec. 21: Pan Am Flight 103 exploded over Lockerbie, Scotland, killing all 259 aboard and 11 on ground; Libya took responsibility for bombing in Aug. 2003.

1989—Sept. 19: French UTA Flight 722 from Congo to Paris destroyed by bomb in midair over Niger; 171 killed. Several Libyan officials convicted in absentia; no official admission.

1992—Mar. 17: Israeli embassy in Buenos Aires, Argentina, bombed; 28 killed, 200+ injured. Hezbollah suspected.

1993—Feb. 26: Truck bomb exploded in World Trade Center garage in New York City; 6 killed. Blast later linked to al- Qaeda. **Mar. 12-19:** At least 11 bombs ripped through Bombay and Calcutta, India; 300+ killed.

1994—Feb. 25: U.S.-born Israeli settler Baruch Goldstein opened fire in mosque in Hebron, West Bank; about 30 Muslim worshippers killed. **July 18:** Buenos Aires Jewish center bombed; 87 killed. Blamed on Hezbollah.

1995—Mar. 20: Twelve killed and over 5,000 injured when Japanese Aum Shinri-kyu cult members released Sarin nerve gas in several Tokyo subway cars. **Apr. 19:** Murrah Federal Building in Oklahoma City bombed, killing 168 and injuring 500+. Timothy McVeigh and Terry Nichols convicted in bombing. McVeigh executed in 2001; Nichols sentenced to life in prison, 1998 on state charges, 2004 on federal charges. **Nov. 13:** U.S. miltary compound in Riyadh, Saudi Arabia, bombed by Islamic Movement of Change; 7 killed.

1996—Jan. 31: Tamil Tigers drove explosives-laden truck into Central Bank in Colombo, Sri Lanka; 90 killed. **June 25:** Bomb-laden fuel truck exploded outside Khobar Towers, a U.S. military complex in Dhahran, Saudi Arabia; killed 19. **July 27:** Bomb exploded at Centennial Olympic Park in Atlanta, GA, during Summer Games; killed 2, injured 100+. Suspect Eric Robert Rudolph arrested in 2003, pleaded guilty; sentenced to life in prison, 2005. **Dec. 3:** Bomb exploded on subway train in Paris; 4 killed, 86 injured. Blamed on Algerian extremists.

1997—Nov. 17: Gamaa al-Islamiya gunmen killed 58 tourists and 4 Egyptians in Valley of the Kings near Luxor, Egypt.

1998—Aug. 7: U.S. embassies in Nairobi, Kenya, and Dar-es-Salaam, Tanzania, bombed; 257 people killed. Al-Qaeda blamed. **Aug. 15:** IRA car bomb exploded outside courthouse in Omagh, N. Ireland; killed 29, injured 300+. **Oct. 18:** National Liberation Army of Colombia blew up Ocensa oil pipeline; about 71 killed, 100+ injured.

1999—Sept. 9-16: Three apt. buildings bombed in Moscow and Volgodonsk, Russia; about 300 killed. Chechen rebels blamed.

2000—Oct. 12: Small boat assisting in docking of U.S.S. *Cole* exploded while alongside it in Aden, Yemen; 17 U.S. sailors killed, 39 injured. Blamed on al-Qaeda.

2001—Sept. 11: 19 al-Qaeda terrorists hijacked 4 U.S. domestic flights, including 2 planes that crashed into World Trade Center towers and 1 into Pentagon. Total dead minus hijackers: 2,973; deadliest attack of terrorism yet on U.S. soil. **Sept.-Nov. 7:** Letters tainted with deadly anthrax bacteria mailed through U.S. postal system killed 5.

2002—Mar. 27: Suicide bombing at hotel in Netanya, Israel, during Passover celebration; 27 killed. **Oct 12:** Resort in Bali, Indonesia, bombed; 202 dead. Jemaah Islamiah blamed. **Oct. 23:** Chechen guerrillas seized theater in Moscow, held 700+ hostages. Russian authorities gassed theater; most guerrillas and about 128 hostages killed. **Dec. 27:** Chechen rebels plowed truck bomb into pro-Russian govt. headquarters in Grozny, Chechnya; 80 killed, 152 injured.

2003—May 12-13: Al-Qaeda militants detonated car bombs at 3 residential complexes used by Westerners in Riyadh, Saudi Arabia; 34 killed. **May 16:** Five explosions in Casablanca, Morocco; 44 killed, 100+ wounded. Blamed on al-Qaeda. **Aug. 19:** UN headquarters in Baghdad bombed by truck; 22 killed, incl. UN envoy to Iraq. **Aug. 25:** 2 bombs exploded in taxis in Mumbai (Bombay), India; 46 killed, 100+ injured. Islamic militants suspected. **Oct. 27:** Suicide bombings at Intl. Red Cross and police stations; 40 killed. **Nov. 15:** Two synagogues in Istanbul, Turkey, bombed; 25 killed. **Nov. 20:** British consulate and offices of British bank HSBC bombed in Istanbul, Turkey; 27 killed incl. Br. cons. gen. Blamed on al-Qaeda. **Dec. 5:** Suicide bombing on commuter train in Yessentuki, Russia; 44 killed, 150 injured. Blamed on Chechen rebels.

2004—Feb. 6: Bomb exploded on Moscow subway; 39 killed, 130 injured. Chechen rebels blamed. **Mar. 11:** Al-Qaeda cell bombed 4 commuter trains during morning rush hour in Madrid, Spain; 191 killed, about 1,200 injured. **May 29:** Al-Qaeda militants stormed foreigner compound in Khobar, Saudi Arabia, taking hostages; 22 killed. **Aug. 24:** Two Russian passenger planes crashed nearly simultaneously in diff. parts of Russia; 90 killed. Blamed on Chechen rebels. **Sept. 1:** Militants seized school in Beslan, in northern Ossetia, Russia; held 1,000+ hostage for 3 days before Russian troops stormed school. About 330 killed, incl. 27 hostage-takers; Chechen militants suspected.

2005—July 7: Four bombs exploded on 3 separate subways and a bus in central London, UK; 52 killed, incl. bombers, about 700 injured. **July 21:** Four bombs placed on 3 subways and a bus in London malfunction. **July 23:** Three car bombs explode nr. resorts at Sharm el Sheik, Egypt; about 90 killed. **Nov. 9:** 3 suicide bombings targeting hotels in Amman, Jordan; killed 56+, injured about 100. Al-Qaeda in Iraq took responsibility.

2006—July 11: 8 explosions struck 7 different trains and 1 station of public commuter rail system in Mumbai, India; 207 killed, 700+ wounded. Lashkar-e-Qahhar (Army of Terror) claimed responsibility.

2007—Feb. 19: Train traveling between New Delhi and border with Pakistan caught fire, 68 killed; Indian ministers blamed Muslim militants for trying to disrupt peace talks between India and Pakistan. **June 30:** In apparent attempt at suicide attack, two men crashed their SUV into main terminal of Scotland's Glasgow Airport; driver later died of burns sustained in attack. **Dec. 11:** Two coordinated car bombs went off outside govt. building and UN office building in Algiers, Algeria; 41 killed, incl. 17 UN employees, 170 wounded.

2008—Sept. 20: Suicide bomber in truck set off explosion outside of Marriott Hotel in Islamabad, Pakistan. Hotel was popular among foreigners and wealthy residents and was located nr. prime min.'s house and parliament building; 53 killed, 271 wounded. **Nov. 26-29:** Series of attacks and bombings on luxury hotels and high-profile targets in Mumbai, India; 171 killed, 300 injured.

2009—Feb. 20: Suicide bomber targeted Shiite funeral in Dera Ismail Khan, Pakistan; 30 killed, 50+ wounded. **Dec. 25:** Umar Farouk Abdulmutallab, a 23-year-old Nigerian, failed in his attempt to blow up a Northwest Airlines flight from Amsterdam to Detroit with a bomb in his underpants.

2010—Jan. 1: Taliban suicide bomber killed more than 100 people on a playground in NW Pakistan. **Mar. 29:** Two female Chechen separatists detonated suicide bombs at two landmark subway stations in Moscow, killing at least 40 people. **July 9:** Suicide bombers attacked group of tribal elders in Mohmand, Pakistan, killing more than 100. **July 11:** Several bombs exploded simultaneously in Kampala, Uganda, killing more than 70 people who had gathered to watch the broadcast of the World Cup final.

2011—Jan. 24: Suicide bomber killed 35 people in international arrivals hall in Moscow's Domodedovo Airport, a location chosen to maximize deaths of foreigners. **July 22:** Anders Behring Breivik, a right-wing Norwegian extremist, set off car bomb outside govt. buildings in Oslo, then donned a police uniform and traveled 25 mi to a summer camp on Tyrifjorden Lake, where he massacred dozens of young people, bringing death toll to 77. **Oct. 4:** Suicide bomber belonging to Al-Shabab insurgent group killed more than 100 people in Mogadishu, Somalia.

2012—May 21: Suicide bomber claimed by al-Qaeda in the Arabian Peninsula killed more than 100 soldiers and wounded 200 during military parade rehearsal nr. Yemeni presidential palace.

MILITARY AFFAIRS

Chief Commanding Officers of the U.S. Military

Chairman, Joint Chiefs of Staff: Gen. Martin E. Dempsey (U.S. Army)
Vice Chairman: Adm. James A. Winnefeld Jr. (USN)

The **Joint Chiefs of Staff** consists of the Chairman and Vice Chairman of the Joint Chiefs of Staff; the Senior Enlisted Advisor of the Chairman; the Chief of Staff, U.S. Army; the Chief of Staff, U.S. Air Force; the Chief of Naval Operations; and the Commandant of the Marine Corps. Date of rank is date when the individual achieved his or her current rank. While serving in any of these positions, or as commander of a unified or specified combatant command, basic pay is $20,587.80 per month. Officers hold positions listed as of Sept. 15, 2012.

Army

Chief of Staff	Date of rank
Odierno, Raymond T.	Aug. 2, 2011

Other Generals	
Alexander, Keith B.	May 7, 2010
Austin III, Lloyd J.	July 29, 2010
Cone, Robert W.	Apr. 14, 2011
Grass, Frank J.	Sept. 7, 2012
Ham, Carter F.	July 23, 2008
Jacoby Jr., Charles H.	Aug. 2, 2011
Rodriguez, David M.	Apr. 14, 2011
Thurman, James D.	Mar. 19, 2010
Via, Dennis L.	Aug. 7, 2012

Air Force

Chief of Staff	Date of rank
Welsh III, Mark A.	Dec. 13, 2010

Other Generals	
Breedlove, Philip M.	Jan. 14, 2011
Carlisle, Herbert J.	Aug. 3, 2012
Fraser, Douglas M.	June 25, 2009
Fraser III, William M.	Oct. 8, 2008
Hostage III, Gilmary M.	Sept. 13, 2011
Johns Jr., Raymond E.	Nov. 20, 2009
Kehler, C. Robert "Bob".	Oct. 12, 2007
McKinley, Craig R.	Nov. 17, 2008
Rice Jr., Edward A.	Nov. 17, 2010
Selva, Paul J.	July 26, 2012
Shelton, William L.	Jan. 5, 2011
Spencer, Larry O.	July 27, 2012
Wolfenbarger, Janet C.	June 5, 2012

Navy

Chief of Naval Operations	Date of rank
Greenert, Jonathan W. (submariner).	Sept. 23, 2011

Other Admirals	
Clingan, Bruce W. (aviator)	Feb. 24, 2012
Donald, Kirkland H. (submariner)	Jan. 1, 2005
Ferguson III, Mark E. (surface warfare).	Aug. 2, 2011
Gortney, William E. (aviator)	May 24, 2012
Haney, Cecil D. (surface warfare).	Jan. 20, 2012
Harvey Jr., John C. (nuclear propulsion).	July 24, 2009
Locklear III, Samuel J. (surface warfare).	Mar. 9, 2012
McRaven, William H. (special operations).	June 30, 2011
Richardson, John M. (submariner).	July 26, 2012
Stavridis, James G. (surface warfare).	Oct. 19, 2006
Winnefeld Jr., James A. "Sandy" (aviator)	May 7, 2010

Marine Corps

Commandant of the Marine Corps (CMC)	Date of rank
Amos, James F.	Oct. 22, 2010

Other Generals	
Allen, John R.	June 30, 2011
Dunford Jr., Joseph F.	Aug. 4, 2010
Kelly, John F.	July 26, 2012
Mattis, James N.	Nov. 9, 2007

Coast Guard

Commandant, with rank of Admiral	Date of rank
Papp Jr., Robert J.	Apr. 22, 2010

Vice Commandant, with rank of Vice Admiral	
Currier, John P.	May 18, 2012

Unified Combatant Commands Commanders-in-Chief

U.S. European Command, Stuttgart-Vaihingen, Germany: Adm. James G. Stavridis (USN)
U.S. Pacific Command, Honolulu, Hawaii: Adm. Samuel J. Locklear III (USN)
U.S. Special Operations Command, MacDill AFB, Florida: Adm. William H. McRaven (USN)
U.S. Transportation Command, Scott AFB, Illinois: Gen. William M. Fraser III (USAF)
U.S. Central Command, MacDill AFB, Florida: Gen. James N. Mattis (USMC)
U.S. Southern Command, Miami, Florida: Gen. Douglas M. Fraser (USAF)
U.S. Northern Command, Peterson AFB, Colorado: Gen. Charles H. Jacoby Jr. (U.S. Army)
U.S. Strategic Command, Offutt AFB, Nebraska: Gen. C. Robert "Bob" Kehler (USAF)
U.S. Africa Command, Kelley Barracks, Stuttgart, Germany: Gen. Carter F. Ham (U.S. Army)

North Atlantic Treaty Organization (NATO) International Commands

NATO Headquarters: Chairman, NATO Military Committee: Gen. Knud Bartels (Danish Army)
Strategic Commands:
  Allied Command Operations (ACO): Adm. James G. Stavridis (USN), Supreme Allied Commander, Europe
  Allied Command Transformation (ACT): Gen. Stéphane Abrial (French Air Force), Supreme Allied Commander Transformation
ACO Subordinate Commands:
  Joint Force Command Brunssum (JFC Brunssum): Gen. Wolf Langheld (German Army), Commander
  Joint Force Command Naples (JFC Naples): Adm. Bruce W. Clingan (USN), Commander
  Joint Force Command Lisbon (JHQ Lisbon): Lt. Gen. Philippe Stoltz (French Army), Commander

Chairmen of the Joint Chiefs of Staff, 1949-2012

Gen. of the Army Omar N. Bradley, USA	.8/16/1949-8/15/1953	Gen. John W. Vessey Jr., USA	6/18/1982-9/30/1985
Adm. Arthur W. Radford, USN.	8/15/1953-8/15/1957	Adm. William J. Crowe Jr., USN	10/1/1985-9/30/1989
Gen. Nathan F. Twining, USAF.	8/15/1957-9/30/1960	Gen. Colin L. Powell, USA.	10/1/1989-9/30/1993
Gen. Lyman L. Lemnitzer, USA.	10/1/1960-9/30/1962	Gen. John M. Shalikashvili, USA.	10/25/1993-9/30/1997
Gen. Maxwell D. Taylor, USA	10/1/1962-7/1/1964	Gen. Henry H. Shelton, USA.	9/30/1997-9/30/2001
Gen. Earle G. Wheeler, USA.	7/3/1964-7/2/1970	Gen. Richard B. Myers, USAF.	10/1/2001-9/30/2005
Adm. Thomas H. Moorer, USN	7/2/1970-7/1/1974	Gen. Peter Pace, USMC.	9/30/2005-9/30/2007
Gen. George S. Brown, USAF.	7/1/1974-6/20/1978	Adm. Michael G. Mullen, USN.	10/1/2007-9/30/2011
Gen. David C. Jones, USAF	.6/21/1978-6/18/1982	Gen. Martin E. Dempsey, USA	10/1/2011-

Directors of the Central Intelligence Agency

In 1942, Pres. Franklin D. Roosevelt established the Office of Strategic Services (OSS); it was disbanded in 1945. In 1946, Pres. Harry Truman established the Central Intelligence Group (CIG) to operate under the National Intelligence Authority (NIA). A 1947 law replaced the NIA with the National Security Council (NSC) and the CIG with the Central Intelligence Agency (CIA).

Director	Served	Appointed by President	Director	Served	Appointed by President
Adm. Sidney W. Souers	1946	Truman	Adm. Stansfield Turner	1977-1981	Carter
Gen. Hoyt S. Vandenberg	1946-1947	Truman	William J. Casey	1981-1987	Reagan
Adm. Roscoe H. Hillenkoetter	1947-1950	Truman	William H. Webster	1987-1991	Reagan
Gen. Walter Bedell Smith	1950-1953	Truman	Robert M. Gates	1991-1993	Bush, G. H. W.
Allen W. Dulles	1953-1961	Eisenhower	R. James Woolsey	1993-1995	Clinton
John A. McCone	1961-1965	Kennedy	John M. Deutch	1995-1997	Clinton
Adm. William F. Raborn Jr.	1965-1966	Johnson, L. B.	George J. Tenet	1997-2004	Clinton
Richard Helms	1966-1973	Johnson, L. B.	Porter Goss	2004-2006	Bush, G. W.
James R. Schlesinger	1973	Nixon	Gen. Michael V. Hayden	2006-2009	Bush, G. W.
William E. Colby	1973-1976	Nixon	Leon E. Panetta	2009-2011	Obama
George H. W. Bush	1976-1977	Ford	Gen. David H. Petraeus	2011-	Obama

U.S. Army and Air Force Units

Army Units. Squad: In infantry, usually 8-16 enlisted personnel under a staff sergeant. **Platoon:** In infantry, 2-4 squads under a lieutenant. **Company:** Headquarters and 3-5 platoons under a captain. (Company-size unit in the artillery is a battery; in the cavalry, a troop.) **Battalion:** Hdqts. and 4-6 companies under a lieutenant colonel. (In cavalry, battalion-size unit is a squadron.) **Brigade:** Hdqts. and 2-5 battalions under a colonel. (Brigade-size unit in the cavalry and rangers is a regiment; in the special forces, a group.) **Division:** Hdqts. and 3 brigades with artillery, combat support, and combat service support units under a major general. **Corps:** Two or more divisions with corps troops under a lieutenant general. **Army:** Hdqts. and 2 or more corps with operational and support responsibilities under a general.

Air Force Units. Flight: Numerically designated flights are the lowest level unit. They are used primarily where there is a need for small mission elements to be incorporated into an organized unit. **Squadron:** The basic unit. Designates specific operational or support capability like mission units in operational commands. **Group:** Flexible unit composed of 2 or more squadrons whose functions may be operational, support, or administrative in nature. **Wing:** Primary group with supporting groups on a distinct mission with significant scope such as combat, flying training, or airlift. **Numbered Air Force (NAF):** Normally operationally oriented, the numbered air force is designed for the control of subordinate units with the same mission and/or geographical location. **Major Command (MAJCOM):** A major subdivision with full staff that manages a major segment of the USAF mission. Major command is composed of 3 or more numbered air forces.

Active Duty U.S. Military Personnel Strength Worldwide, 2011
Source: U.S. Dept. of Defense
(as of Dec. 31, 2011)

TOTAL WORLDWIDE[1] 1,414,149

U.S. TERRITORIES & SPEC. LOCATIONS
U.S., 48 contiguous states	1,017,418
Alaska	21,308
Hawaii	42,502
Guam	4,272
Puerto Rico	179
Transients	50,627
Afloat	81,588
Regional total[2]	**1,217,901**

OTHER WESTERN HEMISPHERE
Canada	135
Colombia	58
Cuba (Guantánamo)	954
Haiti	14
Honduras	357
Afloat	10
Regional total[2]	**1,970**

EUROPE
Belgium	1,207
Germany	53,526
Greece	379
Greenland	122
Italy	10,817
Netherlands	392
Portugal	700
Spain	1,481
Turkey	1,504
United Kingdom	9,317
Afloat	408
Regional total[2]	**80,370**

SUB-SAHARAN AFRICA
Djibouti	192
Regional total[2]	**509**

FORMER SOVIET UNION
Total	146

EAST ASIA & PACIFIC
Australia	185
Japan	36,708
Korea, South	NA
Philippines	174
Singapore	150
Thailand	125
Afloat	13,618
Regional total[2]	**51,170**

NORTH AFRICA, NEAR EAST, & SOUTH ASIA*
Afghanistan[3]	102,200
Bahrain	2,135
Diego Garcia	303
Egypt	238
Iraq[3]	49,800
Qatar	596
Saudi Arabia	270
United Arab Emirates	175
Afloat	600
Regional total[2,4]	**4,604**

NA = Not available. *Special Forces personnel involved in Operation Enduring Freedom in Afghanistan not reported by Dept. of Defense. (1) Includes undistributed personnel. (2) Most countries and areas with fewer than 100 assigned U.S. military members not listed; regional totals include personnel stationed in those countries and areas not shown. (3) Rounded strengths for Operation Enduring Freedom (OEF) and Operation New Dawn (OND) deployment; includes troops in surrounding areas and deployed Reserve/National Guard. (4) Excludes troops deployed for OEF/OND.

U.S. Army Personnel on Active Duty
Source: Dept. of the Army, U.S. Dept. of Defense
(as of midyear, except where noted)

Date	Total strength[1]	Commissioned officers Total	Male	Female[2]	Warrant officers[3] Male	Female	Enlisted personnel Total	Male	Female
1940	267,767	17,563	16,624	939	763	—	249,441	249,441	—
1942	3,074,184	203,137	190,662	12,475	3,285	—	2,867,762	2,867,762	—
1943	6,993,102	557,657	521,435	36,222	21,919	—	6,413,526	6,358,200	55,325
1944	7,992,868	740,077	692,351	47,726	36,893	10	7,215,888	7,144,601	71,287
1945	8,266,373	835,403	772,511	62,892	56,216	44	7,374,710	7,283,930	90,780
1946	1,889,690	257,300	240,658	16,642	9,826	18	1,622,546	1,605,847	16,699
1950	591,487	67,784	63,375	4,409	4,760	22	518,921	512,370	6,551
1955	1,107,606	111,347	106,196	5,151	10,552	48	985,659	977,943	7,716
1960	871,348	91,056	86,832	4,224	10,141	39	770,112	761,833	8,279
1965	967,049	101,812	98,029	3,783	10,285	23	854,929	846,409	8,520
1970	1,319,735	143,704	138,469	5,235	23,005	13	1,153,013	1,141,537	11,476
1975	781,316	89,756	85,184	4,572	13,214	22	678,324	640,621	37,703
1980 (Sept. 30)	772,661	85,339	77,843	7,496	13,265	113	673,944	612,593	61,351
1985 (Sept. 30)	776,244	94,103	83,563	10,540	15,296	288	666,557	598,639	67,918
1990 (Mar. 31)	746,220	91,330	79,520	11,810	15,177	470	639,713	567,015	72,698
1995	521,036	72,646	62,250	10,396	12,053	599	435,807	377,832	57,975
2000	471,633	66,344	56,391	9,953	10,608	781	393,900	333,947	59,953
2002	485,536	66,446	55,715	10,731	10,900	812	404,363	341,794	62,569
2003 (Sept. 30)	499,301	68,198	56,980	11,218	11,273	854	414,769	351,921	62,848
2004 (Sept. 30)	499,543	68,640	57,245	11,395	11,414	914	414,438	354,043	60,395
2005 (Sept. 30)	492,728	69,174	57,675	11,499	11,506	976	406,923	346,194	57,354
2006 (Sept. 30)	505,402	68,742	57,318	11,424	11,931	1,035	419,353	361,528	57,825
2007 (Sept. 30)	522,017	70,657	58,854	11,803	13,844	1,160	433,109	374,989	58,120
2008 (Sept. 30)	539,170	72,650	60,357	12,293	13,428	1,246	451,846	392,163	59,683
2009 (Sept. 30)	553,044	75,337	63,146	12,191	13,815	1,348	457,980	398,579	59,401
2010 (Sept. 30)	566,045	78,588	64,952	13,636	14,106	1,434	467,248	406,871	60,377
2011 (Sept. 30)	565,463	81,395	67,140	14,255	14,373	1,472	463,605	403,381	60,224
2012 (Mar. 31)	557,780	81,479	NA	NA	15,909*	NA	455,860	NA	NA

NA = Not available. * = 2012 figure for male warrant officers includes female officers. **Note:** Represents strength of active Army, including Philippine Scouts (1940-46), ret. Regular Army personnel on extended active duty, and National Guard and Reserve personnel on extended active duty; excl. U.S. Military Academy cadets, contract surgeons, and National Guard and Reserve personnel not on extended active duty. (1) Includes categories not listed, e.g., West Point cadets. Data for 1940-46 include personnel in the Army Air Forces and its predecessors (Air Service and Air Corps). (2) Includes Army Nurse Corps for all years, Women's Army Corps (1942-78), and Medical Specialists Corps (1949 and after). (3) Act of Congress approved Apr. 27, 1926, directed the appointment as warrant officers of field clerks still in active service. Includes flight officers as follows: 1943, 5,700; 1944, 13,615; 1945, 31,117; 1946, 2,580.

U.S. Navy Personnel on Active Duty
Source: U.S. Dept. of Defense
(as of midyear, except where noted)

Year	Officers	Nurses[1]	Enlisted	Officer candidates[1]	Total[2]	Year	Officers	Nurses[1]	Enlisted	Officer candidates[1]	Total[2]
1940	13,162	442	144,824	2,569	160,997	1999	55,726	—	322,372	—	378,098
1945	320,293	11,086	2,988,207	61,231	3,380,817	2000 (Oct.)	53,698	—	320,212	—	373,910
1950	42,687	1,964	331,860	5,037	381,538	2005	54,039	—	305,368	—	363,858
1960	67,456	2,103	544,040	4,385	617,984	2006	53,209	—	295,773	—	353,496
1970	78,488	2,273	605,899	6,000	692,660	2007 (Sept.)	51,385	—	281,772	—	337,547
1980	63,100	—	464,100	—.	527,200	2008	52,184	—	276,346	—	331,785
1990 (Sept.)	74,429	—	530,133	—	604,562	2009	52,233	—	274,858	—	331,637
1995 (May)	61,075	—	402,626	—	463,701	2010	53,071	—	273,609	—	330,065
1996	60,013	—	376,595	—	436,608	2011	53,620	—	270,425	—	328,648
1997	57,341	—	340,616	—	397,957	2012 (Mar.)	52,558	—	263,928	—	320,961
1998 (Sept.)	55,007	—	326,196	—	381,203						

(1) Starting in 1980, "Nurses" are included with "Officers," and "Officer candidates" are included with "Enlisted." (2) May include categories not shown, e.g., midshipmen.

U.S. Air Force Personnel on Active Duty
Source: U.S. Dept. of Defense
(as of midyear, except where noted)

Year[1]	Strength	Year[1]	Strength	Year[1]	Strength	Year[1]	Strength	Year[1]	Strength	Year[1]	Strength
1918 . . .	195,023	1943 . . .	2,197,114	1980 . . .	557,969	1994 . . .	426,327	2000 . . .	357,777	2009 . . .	334,009
1920 . . .	9,050	1944 . . .	2,372,292	1986 . . .	608,200	1995 . . .	400,051	2005 . . .	358,705	2010 . . .	337,505
1930 . . .	13,531	1945 . . .	2,282,259	1990 . . .	535,233	1996 . . .	389,400	2006 . . .	352,620	2011 . . .	333,729
1940 . . .	51,165	1950 . . .	411,277	1991 . . .	510,432	1997 . . .	378,681	2007 . . .	340,596	2012	
1941 . . .	152,125	1960 . . .	814,213	1992 . . .	470,315	1998 . . .	363,479	2008 . . .	328,771	(Mar.)	332,709
1942 . . .	764,415	1970 . . .	791,078	1993 . . .	444,351	1999 . . .	357,929				

(1) Prior to 1947, data are for U.S. Army Air Corps and Air Service of the Signal Corps.

U.S. Marine Corps Personnel on Active Duty
Source: U.S. Dept. of Defense
(as of midyear, except where noted)

Year	Officers	Enlisted	Total	Year	Officers	Enlisted	Total	Year	Officers	Enlisted	Total
1940	1,800	26,545	28,345	1994	18,430	159,949	178,379	2006	19,218	159,705	178,923
1945	37,067	437,613	474,680	1995	18,017	153,929	171,946	2007	19,456	162,085	181,541
1950	7,254	67,025	74,279	1996	18,146	154,141	172,287	2008	20,137	172,903	193,040
1960	16,203	154,418	170,621	1997	18,089	154,240	172,329	2009	21,031	183,243	204,274
1970	24,941	234,796	259,737	1998	17,984	154,648	172,632	2010	21,680	179,446	201,126
1980	18,198	170,271	188,469	1999	17,892	155,250	173,142	2011	22,281	178,546	200,827
1990	19,958	176,694	196,652	2000	17,897	154,744	172,641	2012 (Mar.) . .	22,253	176,174	198,427
1993	18,878	161,205	180,083	2005	19,118	159,113	178,231				

U.S. Coast Guard Personnel on Active Duty
Source: U.S. Dept. of Defense
(as of midyear, except where noted)

Year	Total	Officers	Cadets	Enlisted	Year	Total	Officers	Cadets	Enlisted
1970	37,689	5,512	653	31,524	2006	40,639	8,032	1,004	32,001
1980	39,381	6,463	877	32,041	2007	41,265	8,231	720	32,314
1985	38,595	6,775	733	31,087	2008	42,424	8,282	1,005	33,137
1990	37,308	6,475	820	29,860	2009	43,514	8,497	993	34,024
1995	36,731	7,489	841	28,401	2010	43,135	8,678	744	33,713
2000	35,712	7,154	863	27,695	2011	43,327	8,659	1,053	33,615
2005	40,814	7,908	1,006	31,900	2012 (Mar.)	43,062	8,316	988	33,758

Women in the U.S. Armed Forces
Source: U.S. Dept. of Defense; U.S. Census Bureau; Women in Military Service for America Memorial Foundation

Women in the Army, Navy, Air Force, Marines, and Coast Guard are fully integrated with male personnel. All enlisted jobs were open to women when the draft ended June 30, 1973. Admission to service academies began in 1976. Under rules instituted in 1993, women were allowed to fly combat aircraft and serve aboard warships. By the mid-1990s, 80% of all jobs and more than 90% of all career fields had been opened to women. The first woman achieved the rank of four-star general in 2009. In Apr. 2010, the Navy announced that women would be placed on submarine crews by Jan. 2012. Women remain restricted from service in ground combat units.

(on active duty as of Sept. 30 in year shown)

Women Active Duty Troops, 2011

Service	% women
Army	13.6%
Navy	16.4
Marines	6.8
Air Force	19.1
Coast Guard	15.7

Women on Active Duty, All Services, 1973-2011

Year	% women	Year	% women
1973	2.5%	1997	13.6%
1975	4.6	2000	14.4
1981	8.9	2005	14.6
1987	10.2	2010	14.5
1993	11.6	2011	14.6

African American Service in U.S. Wars
Source: U.S. Dept. of Defense; U.S. Census Bureau

American Revolution. About 5,000 served in the Continental Army, mostly in integrated units, some in all-black combat units.
Civil War. Some 180,000 served in 163 units of the Union Army's U.S. Colored Troops, 200,000 worked in service units—10% of the Union Army in all; about 37,000 died, 31,000 wounded.
World War I. 350,000-400,000 served in the armed forces, 100,000 in France. Some 40,000 fought.
World War II. Some 1 mil served in the armed forces—8% of all troops—mostly in Army service units; all-black fighter and bomber Army Air Force units and infantry divisions gave distinguished service.
Korean War. More than 600,000 served in the military; 3,075 lost their lives in combat. By 1954, armed forces were completely desegregated.
Vietnam War. 274,937 served in the armed forces (1965-74)—9.8% of all troops; 7,243 were killed in combat.
Persian Gulf War. About 104,000 served in the Kuwaiti theater—20% of all U.S. troops. 66 died in combat.
Operation Enduring Freedom. 159 military deaths and 1,133 wounded in Afghanistan and other locations (as of Aug. 16, 2012).
Operation Iraqi Freedom/Operation New Dawn. 444 military deaths and 2,766 wounded (as of Aug. 16, 2012).

Monthly Military Pay Scale

Source: U.S. Dept. of Defense

(effective Jan. 1, 2012; salaries rounded to nearest dollar)

	<2	2	3	4	6	8	10	12	14	16	18	20	22	24	26
Commissioned officers															
O-10[1]	NA	NA	NA	NA	NA	NA	NA	NA	NA	NA	NA	15,647	15,723	16,051	16,620
O-9[1]	NA	NA	NA	NA	NA	NA	NA	NA	NA	NA	NA	13,685	13,883	14,167	14,664
O-8[1]	9,683	10,000	10,211	10,270	10,532	10,971	11,073	11,490	11,609	11,968	12,488	12,967	13,286	13,286	13,286
O-7[1]	8,046	8,420	8,593	8,730	8,979	9,225	9,509	9,793	10,077	10,971	11,726	11,726	11,726	11,726	11,785
O-6[2]	5,963	6,552	6,981	6,981	7,008	7,309	7,348	7,348	7,766	8,504	8,938	9,371	9,617	9,867	10,351
O-5	4,971	5,600	5,988	6,061	6,303	6,448	6,766	6,999	7,301	7,763	7,982	8,199	8,446	8,446	8,446
O-4	4,289	4,966	5,297	5,371	5,678	6,008	6,419	6,738	6,961	7,088	7,162	7,162	7,162	7,162	7,162
O-3	3,771	4,275	4,615	5,031	5,272	5,537	5,708	5,989	6,136	6,136	6,136	6,136	6,136	6,136	6,136
O-2	3,259	3,711	4,274	4,419	4,510	4,510	4,510	4,510	4,510	4,510	4,510	4,510	4,510	4,510	4,510
O-1	2,828	2,944	3,559	3,559	3,559	3,559	3,559	3,559	3,559	3,559	3,559	3,559	3,559	3,559	3,559
Commissioned officers with over 4 years' active duty service as enlisted member or warrant officer															
O-3[3]	NA	NA	NA	5,031	5,272	5,537	5,708	5,989	6,226	6,362	6,548	6,548	6,548	6,548	6,548
O-2[3]	NA	NA	NA	4,419	4,510	4,653	4,896	5,083	5,222	5,222	5,222	5,222	5,222	5,222	5,222
O-1[3]	NA	NA	NA	3,559	3,800	3,941	4,085	4,226	4,419	4,419	4,419	4,419	4,419	4,419	4,419
Warrant officers															
W-5	NA	NA	NA	NA	NA	NA	NA	NA	NA	NA	NA	6,930	7,282	7,544	7,833
W-4	3,898	4,193	4,313	4,431	4,635	4,837	5,041	5,349	5,618	5,874	6,084	6,289	6,589	6,836	7,118
W-3	3,559	3,707	3,860	3,909	4,069	4,383	4,709	4,863	5,041	5,224	5,554	5,776	5,909	6,051	6,243
W-2	3,149	3,447	3,539	3,602	3,806	4,124	4,281	4,436	4,625	4,773	4,907	5,068	5,173	5,257	5,257
W-1	2,765	3,062	3,142	3,311	3,511	3,806	3,944	4,136	4,325	4,474	4,611	4,777	4,777	4,777	4,777
Enlisted members															
E-9[4]	NA	NA	NA	NA	NA	NA	4,709	4,816	4,950	5,108	5,268	5,524	5,740	5,967	6,315
E-8	NA	NA	NA	NA	NA	3,855	4,025	4,131	4,257	4,394	4,642	4,767	4,980	5,098	5,390
E-7	2,680	2,925	3,037	3,185	3,301	3,500	3,612	3,811	3,976	4,089	4,209	4,256	4,412	4,496	4,816
E-6	2,318	2,550	2,663	2,772	2,886	3,143	3,243	3,437	3,496	3,539	3,590	3,590	3,590	3,590	3,590
E-5	2,123	2,266	2,375	2,488	2,662	2,845	2,995	3,013	3,013	3,013	3,013	3,013	3,013	3,013	3,013
E-4	1,947	2,046	2,157	2,267	2,363	2,363	2,363	2,363	2,363	2,363	2,363	2,363	2,363	2,363	2,363
E-3	1,757	1,868	1,981	1,981	1,981	1,981	1,981	1,981	1,981	1,981	1,981	1,981	1,981	1,981	1,981
E-2	1,671	1,671	1,671	1,671	1,671	1,671	1,671	1,671	1,671	1,671	1,671	1,671	1,671	1,671	1,671
E-1[5]	1,491	NA	NA	NA	NA	NA	NA	NA	NA	NA	NA	NA	NA	NA	NA

NA = Not applicable. **Notes:** Basic pay rate for Academy cadets/midshipmen and ROTC members/applicants is $990. In 2007, the military pay scale was expanded to 40 years. **Over 30 years**—O-10: 17,451; O-9: 15,398; O-8: 13,619; O-7: 12,021; O-6: 10,557; W-5: 8,225; W-4: 7,260; E-9: 6,631; E-8: 5,498. **Over 34 years**—O-10: 18,323; O-9: 16,168; O-8: 13,959; W-5: 8,636; E-9: 6,962. **Over 38 years**—O-10: 19,240; O-9: 16,976; W-5: 9,069; E-9: 7,311. (1) Basic pay for an O-7 to O-10 is limited by Level II of the Executive Schedule which is $14,975.10. Basic pay for O-6 and below is limited by Level V of the Executive Schedule which is $12,141.60. (2) While serving as Chairman, Joint Chief of Staff/Vice Chairman, Joint Chief of Staff, Chief of Navy Operations, Commandant of the Marine Corps, Army/Air Force Chief of Staff, Commander of a unified or specified combatant command, basic pay is $20,587.80. (See footnote 1.) (3) Applicable to O-1 to O-3 with at least 4 years and 1 day of active duty or more than 1,460 points as a warrant and/or enlisted member. See Dept. of Defense Financial Management Regulations for more details on who is eligible for this special basic pay rate. (4) For the Master Chief Petty Officer of the Navy, Chief Master Sergeant of the Air Force, Sergeant Major of the Army or Marine Corps, or Senior Enlisted Advisor of the JCS, basic pay is $7,609.50. Combat Zone Tax Exclusion for O-1 and above is based on this basic pay rate plus Hostile Fire Pay/Imminent Danger Pay which is $225.00. (5) Applicable to E-1 with 4 months or more of active duty. Basic pay for an E-1 with less than 4 months of active duty is $1,378.80.

Outlays for Individual Payments to Veterans, 1940-2013

Source: White House Office of Management and Budget

(in millions of dollars)

Year	Total	Compensation	Pensions	Hospital, medical	Education	Insurance & burial	Year	Total	Compensation	Pensions	Hospital, medical	Education	Insurance & burial
1940...	$578	$244	$185	$69	—	$80	2004...	$55,021	$26,297	$3,334	$21,590	$2,408	$1,392
1950...	8,827	1,533	476	764	$2,739	3,315	2005...	62,206	30,877	3,663	23,073	3,224	1,369
1960...	5,355	2,049	1,263	931	392	720	2006...	63,658	30,991	3,547	24,445	3,325	1,350
1970...	8,808	2,980	2,255	1,723	1,002	848	2007...	69,740	31,055	3,376	30,537	3,427	1,345
1980...	20,927	7,446	3,585	6,290	2,418	1,188	2008...	76,113	36,256	3,790	31,096	3,607	1,364
1990...	28,545	10,735	3,594	12,021	795	1,400	2009...	85,501	40,399	4,161	35,264	4,308	1,369
1995...	36,822	14,842	3,024	16,196	1,386	1,374	2010...	95,997	43,377	4,359	38,216	8,727	1,318
2000...	46,086	20,775	2,969	19,343	1,636	1,363	2011...	111,100	52,914	4,664	41,299	11,088	1,135
2001...	45,435	18,579	2,760	20,966	1,783	1,347	2012*...	113,154	51,986	4,207	43,297	12,528	1,136
2002...	50,969	22,418	3,166	22,384	1,681	1,320	2013*...	124,729	59,607	4,914	44,980	14,145	1,083
2003...	55,792	24,696	3,229	24,487	2,049	1,331							

*Estimate. **Note:** Compensation is service-connected; pension is not.

U.S. Veteran Population, 2012

Source: U.S. Dept. of Veterans Affairs

(population projection, in thousands, as of Sept. 30)

TOTAL VETERANS IN CIVILIAN LIFE[1] **21,806.4**	
Total wartime veterans[2] **16,122.1**	
Total Gulf War[3] 6,038.9	
Gulf War with no prior wartime service.......... 5,696.3	
Gulf War with service in Vietnam era............... 337.7	
Gulf War with service in Vietnam and Korea........... 4.3	
Gulf War with service in Vietnam, Korea, and WWII ... 0.5	
Total Vietnam era[3] 7,247.4	
Vietnam era with no prior wartime service 6,693.2	
Vietnam era with service in Korean conflict 159.9	
Vietnam era with service in Korea and WWII 51.7	

Total Korean conflict[3] 2,100.7
  Korean conflict with no prior wartime service......... 1,767.8
  Korean conflict with service in WWII 116.4
Total World War II[3] 1,462.8
  WWII only.. 1,294.1
Total peacetime veterans[4] **5,684.4**
  Post Gulf War...................................... 105.4
  Service between Vietnam era and Gulf War only...... 3,384.3
  Service between Korean conflict and Vietnam
    era only 2,099.1
  Pre-Korean conflict without service in WWII 95.6

Note: Figures are for U.S. veterans worldwide. (1) Includes those who served on active duty in Army, Navy, Air Force, Marines, Coast Guard, uniformed Public Health Service and NOAA, and reservists called to federal active duty. Excludes those dishonorably discharged, those whose only active duty was training, and those currently on active duty. (2) Veterans serving in more than one period are counted only once in total. (3) Total includes veterans who also served in previous periods. (4) Veterans with both wartime and peacetime service are counted only as "wartime veterans."

Nations With Largest Armed Forces, by Active-Duty Troop Strength

Source: *The Military Balance 2012*, International Institute for Strategic Studies, published by Routledge Journals, Taylor & Francis, UK
(as of Nov. 2011 except defense expenditure, which is for 2010)

		Troop strength				Navy		Combat aircraft	
		Active troops	Reserve troops	Defense expend.	Tanks (MBT)	Cruisers/ frigates/	Sub-	FGA	FTR
Rank	Country	(thous.)		($ bil)	(army only)	destroyers	marines	(air force only)	
1.	China	2,285	510	$76,361	7,400+	65F/13D	71	415+	890
2.	United States	1,569	865	693,600	5,855	22C/20F/61D*	71	833	277
3.	India	1,325	1,155	30,865	3,233+	10F/10D*	15	698	64
4.	Korea, North	1,190	600	—	3,500+	3F	72	48	441+
5.	Russia	956	20,000	41,944	2,800+	6C/8F/18D*	65	356	786
6.	Korea, South	655	4,500	25,069	2,414	2C/12F/6D	23	286	176
7.	Pakistan	642	0	5,599	2,411+	10F	8	170	223
8.	Iran	523	350	10,564	1,663+	0	23	108	189+
9.	Turkey	511	379	17,445	4,503	18F	14	284+	54
10.	Vietnam	482	5,000	2,573	1,315	2F	2	231	0
11.	Egypt	439	479	4,129	2,412	8F	4	310	82
12.	Myanmar	406	0	1,762	160	1F	0	0	69
13.	Brazil	318	1,340	33,385	267	11F/3D*	5	61	57
14.	Thailand	306	200	4,821	283	10F*	0	6	88
15.	Indonesia	302	400	7,182	0	11F	2	10	22
16.	Syria	295	314	2,296	4,950	0	0	240	85
17.	Taiwan	290	1,657	8,979	565	4C/22F	4	128	291
18.	Colombia	283	62	10,353	0	4F	4	23	0
19.	Mexico	280	87	5,410	0	7F	0	0	10
20.	Iraq	271	0	4,848	336+	0	0	0	0
21.	Germany	251	40	44,057	350	11F/7D	4	51	89
22.	Japan	248	56	54,357	806	2C/15F/29D*	18	146	202
23.	France	239	34	52,005	254	11F/13D*	9	181	73
24.	Saudi Arabia	234	0	45,170	565	4F/3D	0	163	82
25.	Eritrea	202	120	—	270	0	0	10	6
26.	Morocco	196	150	3,163	380	3F	0	31	22
27.	Italy	185	42	21,908	320	12F/4D*	4	127	71
28.	Israel	177	565	14,043	480	0	3	251	143
29.	United Kingdom	174	82	57,796	227	13F/5D	11	220	0
30.	Afghanistan	171	0	277	0	0	0	0	0

— = Not available. MBT = Main battle tank. FGA = Fighter, ground attack. FTR = Fighter. * = Navy with aircraft carrier(s), as follows: Brazil 1, China 1, France 1, India 1, Italy 2, Japan 2, Russia 1, Thailand 1, U.S. 11.

Budget for Global War on Terror Operations, 2001-11

Source: Congressional Research Service, Library of Congress
(in billions of dollars)

	2001/02[1]	2003	2004	2005	2006	2007	2008	2009	2010	2011[2]	Total
Total: All missions	$33.8	$81.1	$94.1	$107.6	$121.5	$170.9	$185.6	$155.1	$165.3	$168.1	$1,283.3
Dept. of Defense.	33.0	77.4	72.4	102.6	116.8	164.9	179.2	148.3	154.3	159.1	1,208.1
Foreign aid and diplomacy[3]	0.8	3.7	21.7	4.8	4.3	5.0	5.4	5.4	9.1	6.5	66.7
Veterans Affairs medical. . . .	0.0	0.0	0.0	0.2	0.4	1.0	1.0	1.5	1.9	2.4	8.4
Op. Iraqi Freedom/New Dawn[4]	0.0	53.0	75.9	85.6	101.7	131.3	142.1	95.5	71.3	49.3	805.5
Dept. of Defense.	0.0	50.0	56.4	83.4	98.1	127.2	138.5	92.0	66.5	45.7	757.8
Foreign aid and diplomacy[3]	0.0	3.0	19.5	2.0	3.2	3.2	2.7	2.2	3.3	2.3	41.4
Veterans Affairs medical. . . .	0.0	0.0	0.0	0.2	0.4	0.9	0.9	1.2	1.5	1.3	6.3
Op. Enduring Freedom[5]	20.8	14.7	14.6	20.0	19.0	39.2	43.4	59.5	93.8	118.6	443.5
Dept. of Defense.	20.0	14.0	12.4	17.2	17.9	37.2	40.6	56.1	87.7	113.3	416.2
Foreign aid and diplomacy[3]	0.8	0.7	2.2	2.8	1.1	1.9	2.7	3.1	5.7	4.1	25.1
Veterans Affairs medical. . . .	0.0	0.0	0.0	0.0	0.0	0.1	0.1	0.2	0.5	1.1	2.1
Op. Noble Eagle[6].	13.0	8.0	3.7	2.1	0.8	0.5	0.1	0.1	0.1	0.1	28.6
Dept. of Defense unallocated	0.0	5.5	0.0	0.0	0.0	0.0	0.0	0.0	0.0	0.0	5.5

(1) Fiscal year (FY) 2001 and FY2002 funds combined because most were obligated in FY2002 after the Sept. 11, 2001, attacks at the end of FY2001, on Sept. 30, 2001. (2) FY2011 Continuing Resolution, signed by Pres. Obama Mar. 18, 2011, extended funding for all agencies through Apr. 8, 2011. (3) Foreign aid and diplomacy figures include monies for reconstruction, development and humanitarian aid, embassy operations, counternarcotics, initial training of the Afghan and Iraqi armies, foreign military sales credits, and Economic Support Funds. (4) Began in fall 2002 with the buildup of troops for the Mar. 2003 invasion of Iraq and continues with counterinsurgency and stability operations. (5) Covers Afghanistan and other ongoing Global War on Terror (GWOT) operations, ranging from the Philippines to Djibouti, that began immediately after the Sept. 11, 2001, attacks. (6) Dept. of Defense funds that rebuilt the Pentagon and provide higher security at U.S. military bases and other homeland security, including combat air patrol.

Leading Purchasers of U.S. Defense Articles and Services

Source: Congressional Research Service, Library of Congress
(in current U.S. dollars)

	Worldwide Deliveries, 2003-06					Worldwide Deliveries, 2007-10				
Rank	Country	Value	Rank	Country	Value	Rank	Country	Value	Rank	Country	Value
1.	Egypt	$6.3 bil	6.	South Korea . . .	$2.4 bil	1.	Saudi Arabia . . .	$5.3 bil	6.	Australia	$2.7 bil
2.	Israel.	5.3 bil	7.	Japan	2.0 bil	2.	Israel.	4.5 bil	7.	South Korea	2.7 bil
3.	Saudi Arabia . . .	4.2 bil	8.	UK.	1.6 bil	3.	Egypt	4.0 bil	8.	Greece	2.3 bil
4.	Taiwan	4.1 bil	9.	Australia	1.3 bil	4.	Taiwan	3.0 bil	9.	Poland	2.2 bil
5.	Greece	3.2 bil	10.	Kuwait.	1.1 bil	5.	Japan	2.9 bil	10.	Iraq	2.0 bil

Note: Total dollar value of all U.S. defense articles and services actually delivered to top 10 purchasers worldwide. Figures include government-to-government sales through the Foreign Military Sales system (which accounts for the overwhelming majority of U.S. conventional arms deliveries) concluded in calendar years listed, as well as commercially licensed exports concluded in pertinent fiscal years.

U.S. Foreign Military Financing, 2002-10

Source: Defense Security Cooperation Agency, U.S. Dept. of Defense, for 2002-09; Office of the Director of U.S. Foreign Assistance, U.S. Dept. of State, for 2010

(in thousands of U.S. dollars)

	2010	2002-09		2010	2002-09
Near East and South Asia	**$4,853,810**	**$34,991,358**	**Europe**	**$137,855**	**$1,419,639**
Afghanistan	0	1,051,877	Bosnia and Herzegovina	4,000	55,882
Bahrain	19,000	204,588	Bulgaria	9,000	76,403
Egypt	1,300,000	10,349,950	Czech Republic	6,000	62,768
Israel	2,775,000	18,833,604	Georgia	16,000	128,384
Jordan	300,000	2,162,317	Poland	47,000	261,527
Lebanon	100,000	99,606	Romania	13,000	106,645
Morocco	9,000	65,423	Turkey	0	170,977
Oman	8,848	189,756	Ukraine	11,000	50,902
Pakistan	294,169	1,863,630	**Africa**	**17,950**	**155,287**
Tunisia	18,000	66,677	Djibouti	2,000	37,589
Yemen	12,500	72,122	Liberia	6,000	9,299
East Asia and Pacific	**59,100**	**348,656**	**Americas**	**352,990**	**666,641**
Indonesia	20,000	36,952	Colombia	55,000	497,400
Philippines	29,000	268,977	El Salvador	0	42,291
			Mexico	265,250	33,150
			World total	**5,476,169**	**37,581,582**

Note: Grants extended to foreign governments in a fiscal year to pay for military equipment and services. May be from U.S. Dept. of Defense (DOD) or, for specific countries, negotiated directly with U.S. commercial suppliers with DOD approval.

Defense Contracts, 2012

Source: U.S. Dept. of Defense
(in millions of U.S. dollars)

Listed are the 50 companies or organizations receiving the largest dollar volume of prime contract awards from the U.S. Dept. of Defense during fiscal year 2012 (Oct. 1, 2011-Sept. 30, 2012).

Rank Contractor	Contracts awarded[1]	% of total	Rank Contractor	Contracts awarded[1]	% of total
1. The Boeing Co.	$22,897.1	8.90%	27. Northrop Grumman Systems Corp.	$1,492.3	0.58%
2. Lockheed Martin Corp.	22,081.6	8.58	28. Booz Allen Hamilton Holding Corp.	1,459.5	0.57
3. General Dynamics Corp.	11,029.3	4.29	29. FedEx Corp.	1,210.6	0.47
4. Raytheon Co.	10,590.4	4.12	30. Refinery Associates of Texas Inc.	1,193.4	0.46
5. United Technologies Corp.	6,209.6	2.41	31. Honeywell International Inc.	1,169.2	0.45
6. L-3 Communications Holdings Inc.	4,879.2	1.90	32. CACI International Inc.	1,159.0	0.45
7. BAE Systems PLC	3,754.6	1.46	33. ManTech International Corp.	1,154.0	0.45
8. Humana Inc.	3,304.7	1.28	34. World Fuel Cayman Holding Co. I	1,151.7	0.45
9. SAIC Inc.	3,272.3	1.27	35. Royal Dutch Shell PLC	1,116.0	0.43
10. TriWest Healthcare Alliance Corp.	2,920.8	1.14	36. Fluor Corp.	1,113.9	0.43
11. Northrop Grumman Corp.	2,878.3	1.12	37. BP PLC	1,096.8	0.43
12. Health Net Inc.	2,849.2	1.11	38. Northrop Grumman Corp.	1,090.2	0.42
13. Bell-Boeing Joint Project Office	2,756.5	1.07	39. Alliant Techsystems Inc.	1,071.4	0.42
14. Northrop Grumman Corp.	2,731.2	1.06	40. Amerisourcebergen Corp.	1,060.3	0.41
15. Huntington Ingalls Industries Inc.	2,639.0	1.03	41. Huntington Ingalls Inc.	1,053.8	0.41
16. Bechtel Group Inc.	2,207.3	0.86	42. Oshkosh Corp.	1,043.6	0.41
17. Supreme Group Holding SARL	2,102.4	0.82	43. Computershare Limited	1,034.1	0.40
18. Miscellaneous foreign contractors	2,045.8	0.79	44. Harris Corp.	1,005.4	0.39
19. United Launch Alliance LLC	1,839.9	0.71	45. A.P. Moller - Maersk A/S	983.7	0.38
20. General Electric Co.	1,806.6	0.70	46. Valero Energy Corp.	935.4	0.36
21. The Veritas Capital Fund II LP.	1,768.9	0.69	47. McDonnell Douglas Helicopter Co.	879.8	0.34
22. Textron Inc.	1,715.8	0.67	48. Navistar International Corp.	856.0	0.33
23. General Atomic Technologies Corp.	1,664.5	0.65	49. Lockheed Martin Corp.	838.6	0.33
24. ITT Corp.	1,618.0	0.63	50. World Fuel Services Corp.	814.6	0.32
25. URS Corp.	1,600.6	0.62	Other	107,717.9	
26. Computer Sciences Corp.	1,578.0	0.61	**Total**	**258,442.8**	

Note: Contractors listed more than once represent different company locations or facilities. Contractor totals are for amounts reported by Oct. 1, 2012. Total is sum of all contracts to top 50,000 contractors. (1) Amounts include contracts awarded to subsidiaries of each company.

Arms Transfer Agreements With the World by Supplier, 2004-11

Source: Congressional Research Service, Library of Congress
(in millions of current U.S. dollars)

Supplier	2004	2005	2006	2007	2008	2009	2010	2011	2004-11
United States	$12,368	$12,099	$15,435	$23,691	$36,323	$22,002	$21,103	$66,274	$209,295
Russia	8,800	8,400	15,400	10,400	6,600	13,300	8,800	4,800	76,500
France	2,900	6,300	7,700	2,200	3,800	9,600	1,800	4,400	38,700
United Kingdom	4,200	2,900	4,100	9,500	300	1,400	1,500	400	24,300
China	1,000	2,700	2,000	2,500	2,100	2,500	1,600	2,100	16,500
Germany	4,100	2,000	2,800	1,800	5,500	3,600	100	100	20,000
Italy	400	1,500	1,200	1,400	4,100	1,600	1,900	1,200	13,300
All other European	5,200	7,400	5,600	6,700	5,300	6,500	4,200	3,300	44,200
All others	3,300	1,900	3,400	2,800	3,100	5,000	2,900	2,700	25,100
Total	**42,268**	**45,199**	**57,635**	**60,991**	**67,123**	**65,502**	**43,903**	**85,274**	**467,895**

Note: All data are for the calendar year given except for U.S. MAP (Military Assistance Program), IMET (International Military Education, and Training), and Excess Defense Article data, which are included for the particular fiscal year. All amounts given include the values of all categories of weapons, spare parts, construction, all associated services, military assistance, excess defense articles, and training programs. Statistics for foreign countries are based upon estimated selling prices. All foreign data are rounded to the nearest $100 mil.

Personal Salutes and Honors

The U.S. **national salute**, 21 guns, is also the salute to a national flag. U.S. independence is commemorated by the salute to the Union—one gun for each state—fired at noon July 4, at all military posts provided with suitable artillery.

A 21-gun salute on arrival and departure, with 4 ruffles and flourishes, is rendered to the **president** of the, to a former president, and to a president-elect. The national anthem or "Hail to the Chief," as appropriate, is played for the president, and the national anthem for the others. A 21-gun salute on arrival and departure, with 4 ruffles and flourishes, also is rendered to the **sovereign or chief of state of a foreign country** or a member of a reigning royal family, and the national anthem of his or her country is played. The music is considered an inseparable part of the salute and immediately follows the ruffles and flourishes without pause. For the Honors March, generals receive the "General's March," admirals receive the "Flag Officer's March," and all others receive the 32-bar medley of "The Stars and Stripes Forever."

GRADE, TITLE, OR OFFICE	SALUTE (IN GUNS) Arriving	Leaving	Ruffles and flourishes	Music
Vice President of U.S.	19	—	4	Hail, Columbia
Speaker of the House.	19	—	4	Honors March
U.S. or foreign ambassador in country to which accredited	19	—	4	Natl. anthem of official
Premier or prime minister	19	—	4	Natl. anthem of official
Secretary of Defense, Army, Navy, or Air Force	19	19	4	Honors March
Other cabinet members, Senate president pro tempore, governor, or chief justice of U.S.	19	—	4	Honors March
Chairman, Joint Chiefs of Staff.	19	19	4	Honors March
Army chief of staff, chief of naval operations, Air Force chief of staff, Marine commandant.	19	19	4	Honors March
General of the Army, general of the Air Force, fleet admiral	19	19	4	Honors March
Generals, admirals	17	17	4	Honors March
Assistant secretaries of Defense, Army, Navy, or Air Force.	17	17	4	Honors March
Chair of a committee of Congress	17	—	4	Honors March

Other salutes (on arrival only, with Honors March) include 17 guns, with 3 ruffles and flourishes, for U.S. ambassadors returning to the U.S. on official business; 15 guns, with 3 ruffles and flourishes, for U.S. envoys or ministers, foreign envoys or ministers accredited to the U.S., and lieutenant generals or vice admirals; 13 guns, with 2 ruffles and flourishes, for a major general or rear admiral (upper half) and for U.S. ministers resident and ministers resident accredited to the U.S.; 11 guns, with 1 ruffle and flourish, for a brigadier general or rear admiral (lower half) and for U.S. chargés d'affaires and like officials accredited to the U.S.; 11 guns, no ruffles and flourishes, for consuls general accredited to the U.S.

Medal of Honor

Source: Congressional Medal of Honor Society; U.S. Army, U.S. Dept. of Defense

(as of Oct. 1, 2012)

The Medal of Honor is the highest military award for bravery that can be given to any individual in the U.S. The first Army Medals were awarded on Mar. 25, 1863; the first Navy Medals went to sailors and Marines on Apr. 3, 1863.

On Dec. 21, 1861, Pres. Abraham Lincoln signed a bill to create the Navy Medal of Honor. Lincoln, on July 14, 1862, approved a resolution providing for the presentation of Medals of Honor to enlisted men of the Army and Voluntary Forces. The law was amended on Mar. 3, 1863, so that officers as well as enlisted men were eligible.

The Medal of Honor is awarded in the name of Congress to a person who, while a member of the armed forces, distinguishes himself or herself conspicuously by gallantry and intrepidity at the risk of life above and beyond the call of duty while engaged in an action against any enemy of the U.S.; while engaged in military operations involving conflict with an opposing foreign force; or while serving with friendly foreign forces engaged in an armed conflict against an opposing armed force in which the U.S. is not a belligerent party.

The deed performed must have been one of personal bravery or self-sacrifice so conspicuous as to clearly distinguish the individual above his or her comrades and must have involved risk of life. Incontestable proof of the performance of service is required, and each recommendation for award of this decoration is considered on the standard of extraordinary merit.

Prior to World War I, the 2,625 Army Medal of Honor awards up to that time were reviewed to determine which met new stringent criteria. The Army removed 911 names from the list, most of them former members of a Civil War volunteer infantry group who had been induced to extend their enlistments when they were promised the medal. However, in 1977, a medal was restored to Dr. Mary Walker, and in 1989, medals were restored to Buffalo Bill Cody and seven other Indian scouts.

Medals of Honor were awarded posthumously for actions during the Battle of Mogadishu (Somalia), Oct. 3, 1993, to Army Master Sgt. Gary I. Gordon and to Sgt. First Class Randall D. Shughart. Both received the medal for voluntarily guarding a helicopter crash site and its downed crew while under heavy enemy fire until relief could arrive.

Seven African American soldiers were awarded Medals of Honor for service in World War II (six of them posthumously) in Jan. 1997. Previously, no black soldier had received the medal for World War II service; an Army inquiry begun in 1993 concluded that the prevailing political climate and Army practices of the time had prevented proper recognition of heroism on the part of black soldiers in that war. In 1996, Congress authorized a review of Asian American and Pacific Islander recipients of the Distinguished Service Cross whose award should be upgraded. Twenty-two Asian Americans received the Medal of Honor for World War II service in June 2000.

Iraq. Four Medals of Honor have been awarded for actions in Operation Iraqi Freedom. On Apr. 4, 2003, Army Sgt. First Class Paul R. Smith was mortally wounded while holding an exposed position, near Baghdad Intl. Airport, against enemy attack. On Apr. 14, 2004, Marine Cpl. Jason L. Dunham was mortally wounded at Karbala when he covered a live grenade with his helmet and body to protect his fellow Marines. On Sept. 29, 2006, Navy Petty Officer Second Class (SEAL) Michael A. Monsoor was mortally wounded at Ar Ramadi when he threw himself onto a grenade, saving the lives of two teammates. Army Private First Class Ross A. McGinnis, whose posthumous award was presented June 5, 2008, covered a grenade with his body, saving his four Humvee crew members from serious injury.

Afghanistan. Six Medals of Honor have been awarded for actions in Afghanistan. The Medal was awarded posthumously to Navy Lt. Michael P. Murphy, whose SEAL team came under attack by Taliban fighters June 28, 2005. Heavily outnumbered and with all four team members wounded, Lt. Murphy left cover to radio for help and was shot in the back. On June 21, 2006, Army Sgt. First Class Jared C. Monti and his patrol were ambushed. Monti repeatedly tried to rescue a wounded soldier despite overwhelming gunfire. Monti was killed by a grenade on his third attempt and received the Medal of Honor posthumously. Special Forces Staff Sgt. Robert Miller received the Medal of Honor after dying while saving the lives of 7 U.S. and 15 Afghan Army soldiers during a battle against more than 100 insurgents on Jan. 25, 2008.

Army Staff Sgt. Salvatore Giunta on Oct. 25, 2007, advanced in the face of persistent Taliban fire to give aid to comrades injured in an ambush; he became the first surviving Medal of Honor recipient since the Vietnam War Nov. 16, 2010. A wounded Staff Sgt. Leroy Petry May 26, 2008, protected fellow injured rangers by throwing a live enemy grenade, losing his right hand as it detonated. On Sept. 8, 2009, Marine Corps Cpl. Dakota Meyer helped rescue 13 American and 23 Afghan soldiers from an ambush, manning a Humvee gun turret on five trips into enemy fire over six hours.

Other Selected Awards

Source: U.S. Army Institute of Heraldry, Navy Department Awards Web Service, Air Force Personnel Center

Distinguished Service Cross

Established in Congress July 9, 1918, on recommendation of Gen. John J. "Black Jack" Pershing, and awarded for extraordinary heroism not justifying the award of a Medal of Honor. The act or acts of heroism must have been so notable and have involved risk of life so extraordinary as to set the individual apart from his or her comrades.

Silver Star

An earlier version of this award, the Citation Star, was established by Congress on July 19, 1918, and retroactively awarded to soldiers for "gallantry in action," back to the Spanish-American War. The Silver Star medal replaced the Citation Star in 1932 and is awarded for gallantry in action which, while of a lesser degree than that required for award of the Distinguished Service Cross, must nevertheless have been performed with marked distinction.

Legion of Merit

Established by Congress on July 20, 1942, and awarded to individuals who have distinguished themselves by exceptionally meritorious conduct in the performance of outstanding services. There are different designs depending on the level of command of the award recipient.

Distinguished Flying Cross

Established by Congress July 2, 1926, and awarded for heroism or extraordinary achievement while participating in aerial flight. Awards are made only to recognize single acts of heroism or extraordinary achievement, not sustained operational activities against an armed enemy. Initial awards were given to persons who made record-breaking long-distance and endurance flights or who set altitude records. The first DFC was awarded to Cpt. Charles A. Lindbergh on May 31, 1927. DFCs were awarded retroactively to Orville and Wilbur Wright.

Soldier's Medal

Established by Congress July 2, 1926, to recognize acts of heroism not involving actual conflict with an enemy. The same degree of heroism is required as for the award of the Distinguished Flying Cross. The performance must have involved personal hazard or danger and the voluntary risk of life under conditions not involving conflict with an armed enemy. Awards are not made solely on the basis of having saved a life.

Bronze Star

Established by Executive Order Feb. 4, 1944, largely to raise the morale of ground troops in WWII, on the recommendation of Gen. George C. Marshall. It is awarded to any person who, while serving in any capacity in or with the U.S. military, distinguishes himself or herself by heroic or meritorious achievement or service, not involving participation in aerial flight.

Purple Heart

The original Purple Heart, designated as the Badge of Military Merit, was established by Gen. George Washington on Aug. 7, 1782. Following the American Revolution, the badge fell into disuse until 1932, the 200th anniversary of Washington's birth. During WWII, the Order of the Purple Heart was awarded for both wounds received in action and for meritorious service. Following the introduction of the Legion of Merit, the Purple Heart was awarded only for combat wounds. Today, it is awarded to any armed forces member who, while serving with the U.S. Armed Services, has been wounded or killed, or who has died or may hereafter die after being wounded in action against an enemy of the U.S. or in an armed conflict in which the U.S. or friendly foreign forces are engaged; as the result of an act of any hostile foreign force; as a result of an international terrorist attack against the U.S. or a friendly foreign nation; or as a result of military operations outside the U.S. as part of a peacekeeping force. Wounds must be inflicted by weapon fire while directly engaged in armed conflict, regardless of the fire causing the wound, or while held as a prisoner of war or while being taken captive.

Air Medal

Authorized by Pres. Franklin D. Roosevelt on May 11, 1942, and awarded for heroism or meritorious achievement while participating in aerial flight. Awards may be made to recognize single acts of merit or heroism or for meritorious service. Awards are not made to individuals who use air transportation solely for the purpose of moving from point to point in a combat zone.

Army Commendation

Established Dec. 18, 1945, and awarded for heroism, meritorious achievement, or meritorious service. It may also be awarded to a member of the armed forces of a friendly foreign nation who distinguishes him- or herself by an act of heroism, extraordinary achievement, or meritorious service which has been of mutual benefit to a friendly nation and the U.S.

U.S. Military Awards in Selected Wars and Conflicts

Source: U.S. Army Human Resources Command, U.S. Dept. of Defense

Award	Civil War	WWI	WWII	Korea	Vietnam	Gulf War	OEF[1]	Iraq[2]
Medal of Honor............	1,522	119	467	136	249	0	6	4
Distinguished Service Cross....	NA	6,430	4,434	724	848	0	9	16
Silver Star.............	NA	NA	73,654	10,061	21,634	75	253	409
Legion of Merit.............	NA	NA	20,273	NA	10,356	158	102	133
Distinguished Flying Cross.....	NA	NA	126,318	NA	21,697	108	195	118
Soldier's Medal.............	NA	NA	12,485	581	5,402	43	37	111
Bronze Star (total)[3]..........	NA	NA	395,380	30,359	719,968	27,967	51,422	111,435
Purple Heart.............	NA	NA	NA	NA	220,516	504	7,588	21,898
Air Medal (total)[3]............	NA	NA	1,166,471	0	1,039,124	6,399	13,258	21,875
Army Commendation (total)[3] ...	NA	NA	0	0	837,037	81,979	126,387	388,200

NA = Not available or applicable. **Note:** Numbers for the individual decorations shown here represent only those awards that were properly processed and reported to Headquarters, Dept. of the Army. The actual number of individual decorations awarded under combat conditions, when award approval authority is delegated to field commanders, cannot be stated with absolute certainty. Numbers here reflect the current statistics recorded by the Military Awards Branch, as of Sept. 25, 2012, except for MOH, which is as reported by the Congressional Medal of Honor Society as of Oct. 1, 2012. (1) Operation Enduring Freedom (primarily Afghanistan). (2) Operation Iraqi Freedom and Operation New Dawn. (3) Includes awards for valor/heroism and for meritorious service or achievement.

Federal Service Academies

U.S. Military Academy, West Point, NY. Founded 1802. Awards BS degree and Army commission for a 5-year service obligation. For admissions information, write West Point Admissions, Bldg. 606, West Point, NY 10996. **Website:** www.usma.edu

U.S. Naval Academy, Annapolis, MD. Founded 1845. Awards BS degree and Navy or Marine Corps commission for a 5-year service obligation. For admissions information, write Candidate Guidance Office, United States Naval Academy, 117 Decatur Rd., Annapolis, MD 21402-5018. **Website:** www.usna.edu

U.S. Air Force Academy, Colorado Springs, CO. Founded 1954. Awards BS degree and Air Force commission for a 6-year service obligation. For admissions information, write HQ USAFA/RRS, 2304 Cadet Dr., Ste. 2300, USAF Academy, CO 80840-5025. **Website:** www.usafa.edu

U.S. Coast Guard Academy, New London, CT. Founded 1876. Awards BS degree and Coast Guard commission for a 5-year service obligation. For admissions information, write Director of Admissions, U.S. Coast Guard Academy, 31 Mohegan Ave., New London, CT 06320-8103. **Website:** www.cga.edu

U.S. Merchant Marine Academy, Kings Point, NY. Founded 1943. Awards BS degree, a license as a deck, engineer, or dual officer, and a U.S. Naval Reserve commission. Service obligations vary according to options taken by the graduate. For admissions information, write Admissions Office, U.S. Merchant Marine Academy, 300 Steamboat Rd., Kings Point, NY 11024-1699. **Website:** www.usmma.edu

Casualties in Principal Wars of the U.S.

Source: U.S. Dept. of Defense, U.S. Coast Guard

Data prior to World War I are based on incomplete records in many cases. Casualty data are confined to dead and wounded personnel and, therefore, exclude personnel captured or missing in action who were subsequently returned to military control. (—) = Not available. Off. = Officers.

	Branch of service	Number serving	CASUALTIES Battle deaths	CASUALTIES Other deaths	CASUALTIES Wounds not mortal[7]	Total[13]
Revolutionary War	Total	—	4,435	—	6,188	10,623
1775-83	Army	184,000	4,044	—	6,004	10,048
	Navy	to	342	—	114	456
	Marines	250,000[11]	49	—	70	119
War of 1812	Total	286,730[8]	2,260	—	4,505	6,765
1812-15	Army	—	1,950	—	4,000	5,950
	Navy	—	265	—	439	704
	Marines	—	45	—	66	111
Mexican War	Total	78,718[8]	1,733	11,550	4,152	17,435
1846-48	Army	—	1,721	11,550	4,102	17,373
	Navy	—	1	—	3	4
	Marines	—	11	—	47	58
	Coast Guard[12]	71 off.	—	—	—	—
Civil War 1861-65						
Union forces[1]	Total	2,213,363	140,414	224,097	281,881	646,392
	Army	2,128,948[8]	138,154	221,374	280,040	639,568
	Navy	84,415	2,112	2,411	1,710	6,233
	Marines	(in Navy total)	148	312	131	591
	Coast Guard[12]	219 off.	1	—	—	1
Confederate forces (estimate)[1]	Total	—	74,524	59,297	—	133,821
	Army	600,000	—	—	—	—
	Navy	to	—	—	—	—
	Marines	1,500,000	—	—	—	—
Spanish-American War	Total	306,760	385	2,061	1,662	4,108
1898	Army[3]	280,564	369	2,061	1,594	4,024
	Navy	22,875	10	—	47	57
	Marines	3,321	6	—	21	27
	Coast Guard[12]	660	0	—	—	—
World War I	Total	4,734,991	53,402	63,114	204,002	320,518
Apr. 6, 1917-Nov. 11, 1918	Army[4]	4,057,101	50,510	55,868	193,663	300,041
	Navy	599,051	431	6,856	819	8,106
	Marines	78,839	2,461	390	9,520	12,371
	Coast Guard	8,835	111	81	—	192
World War II	Total	16,112,566	291,557	113,842	670,846	1,076,245
Dec. 7, 1941-Dec. 31, 1946[2]	Army[5]	11,260,000	234,874	83,400	565,861	884,135
	Navy[6]	4,183,466	36,950	25,664	37,778	100,392
	Marines	669,100	19,733	4,778	67,207	91,718
	Coast Guard	241,093	574	1,343	—	1,917
Korean War[9]	Total	5,720,000	33,739	2,835	103,284	139,858
June 25, 1950-July 27, 1953	Army	2,834,000	27,731	2,125	77,596	107,452
	Navy	1,177,000	503	154	1,576	2,233
	Marines	424,000	4,267	242	23,744	28,253
	Air Force	1,285,000	1,238	314	368	1,920
	Coast Guard	44,143	—	—	—	—
Vietnam War[10]	Total	8,744,000	47,434	10,786	153,303	211,523
Aug. 4, 1964-Jan. 27, 1973	Army	4,368,000	30,963	7,261	96,802	135,026
	Navy	1,842,000	1,631	935	4,178	6,744
	Marines	794,000	13,095	1,749	51,392	66,236
	Air Force	1,740,000	1,745	841	931	3,517
	Coast Guard	8,000	7	2	60	69
Persian Gulf War	Total	2,225,000	148	235	467	850
1991	Army	782,000	98	126	354	578
	Navy	669,000	6	50	12	68
	Marines	213,000	24	44	92	160
	Air Force	561,000	20	15	9	44
	Coast Guard	400	—	—	—	—
Iraq War[14]	Total	269,363[15]	3,517	958	32,227	36,702
Mar. 19, 2003-Dec. 15, 2011	Army	99,664[15]	2,573	720	22,517	25,810
	Navy	61,018[15]	64	41	636	741
	Marines	66,166[15]	851	171	8,625	9,647
	Air Force	42,515[15]	29	26	449	504
	Coast Guard	1,250[15]	1	—	—	1

Note: As of Aug. 28, 2012, there have been 1,662 battle deaths, 436 non-hostile deaths, and 17,420 wounded in Op. Enduring Freedom, mostly in Afghanistan and the Persian Gulf area. (1) From the final report of the Provost Marshal General, 1863-66. Authoritative statistics for the Confederate forces are not available. In addition, an estimated 26,000-31,000 Confederate personnel died in Union prisons. New estimates published in *Civil War History* in 2012 recalculated the death toll for both sides and determined that it was 20% higher than previously thought, at 750,000. (2) Data are for Dec. 1, 1941, through Dec. 31, 1946, when hostilities were officially terminated by presidential proclamation; few battle deaths or wounds not mortal were incurred after Japanese acceptance of Allied peace terms on Aug. 14, 1945. Numbers serving Dec. 1, 1941-Aug. 31, 1945: Total—14,903,213; Army—10,420,000; Navy—3,883,520; Marine Corps—599,693. (3) Number serving Apr. 21-Aug. 13, 1898, while dead and wounded data are for May 1-Aug. 31, 1898. Active hostilities ceased on Aug. 13, 1898, but the U.S. and Spain did not exchange ratifications of the treaty of peace until Apr. 11, 1899. (4) Includes Army Air Forces battle deaths and other deaths, as well as casualties suffered by American forces in northern Russia to Aug. 25, 1919, and in Siberia to Apr. 1, 1920. Other deaths cover Apr. 1, 1917-Dec. 31, 1918. (5) Includes Army Air Forces. (6) Battle deaths and wounds not mortal include casualties incurred in Oct. 1941 due to hostile action. (7) Marine Corps data for Iraq War, World War II, the Spanish-American War, and prior wars represent the number of individuals wounded, whereas all other data in this column represent the total number (incidence) of wounds. (8) As reported by Commissioner of Pensions in his Annual Report for Fiscal Year 1903. (9) As a result of an ongoing Dept. of Defense review of available Korean War casualty record information, updates have been made to previously reported figures for battle deaths and other deaths. (10) Number serving Aug. 5, 1964-Jan. 27, 1973 (date of cease-fire). Includes casualties incurred in Mayaguez incident. Wounds not mortal exclude 150,341 persons not requiring hospital care. (11) Estimated. (12) Then known as the U.S. Revenue Cutter Services, predecessor to the U.S. Coast Guard. (13) Totals do for all branches not include categories for which no data are listed. (14) Military deaths during the invasion phase, which ended Apr. 30, 2003, totaled 115 combat-related and 23 other. (15) Number serving as of Mar. 31, 2003, i.e., does not include numbers of troops deployed since then.

U.S. Army, Navy, Air Force, Marine Corps, and Coast Guard Insignia

Source: Dept. of the Army, Dept. of the Navy, Dept. of the Air Force, U.S. Dept. of Defense; U.S. Coast Guard, U.S. Dept. of Homeland Security

Army

General of the Armies—Gen. John J. Pershing (1860-1948), the only person to have held this rank while living, was authorized to prescribe his own insignia but never wore in excess of four stars. Congress established the rank in 1799 to be bestowed posthumously on George Washington; Washington was finally promoted to the rank by joint resolution of Congress, approved by Pres. Gerald Ford, Oct. 19, 1976.

General of the Army—Five silver stars fastened together in a circle and the coat of arms of the U.S. in gold color metal with shield and crest enameled. Reserved for wartime use only.

Rank	Insignia
General of the Army*	Five silver stars
General	Four silver stars
Lieutenant General	Three silver stars
Major General	Two silver stars
Brigadier General	One silver star
Colonel	Silver eagle
Lieutenant Colonel	Silver oak leaf
Major	Gold oak leaf
Captain	Two silver bars
First Lieutenant	One silver bar
Second Lieutenant	One gold bar

Warrant Officers
Grade Five—Silver bar with enamel black line.
Grade Four—Silver bar with 4 enamel black squares.
Grade Three—Silver bar with 3 enamel black squares.
Grade Two—Silver bar with 2 enamel black squares.
Grade One—Silver bar with 1 enamel black square.

Noncommissioned Officers
Sergeant Major of the Army (E-9)—Three chevrons above 3 arcs, with a U.S. coat of arms centered on the chevrons, flanked by 2 stars—one star on each side of the eagle. Also wears distinctive red-and-white shield collar insignia.
Command Sergeant Major (E-9)—Three chevrons above 3 arcs with a 5-pointed star with a wreath around the star between the chevrons and arcs.
Sergeant Major (E-9)—Three chevrons above 3 arcs with a 5-pointed star between the chevrons and arcs.
First Sergeant (E-8)—Three chevrons above 3 arcs with a lozenge between the chevrons and arcs.
Master Sergeant (E-8)—Three chevrons above 3 arcs.
Sergeant First Class (E-7)—Three chevrons above 2 arcs.
Staff Sergeant (E-6)—Three chevrons above 1 arc.
Sergeant (E-5)—Three chevrons.
Corporal (E-4)—Two chevrons.

Specialists
Specialist (E-4)—Eagle device only.

Other Enlisted
Private First Class (E-3)—One chevron above 1 arc.
Private (E-2)—One chevron.
Private (E-1)—None.
*Rank reserved for wartime use only.

Air Force
Insignia for Air Force officers are identical to those of the Army. Insignia for enlisted personnel are worn on both sleeves and consist of a star and an appropriate number of rockers. Chevrons appear above 5 rockers for the top 3 noncommissioned officer ranks, as follows (in ascending order): Master Sergeant, 1 chevron; Senior Master Sergeant, 2 chevrons; and Chief Master Sergeant, 3 chevrons. The insignia of the Chief Master Sergeant of the Air Force has 3 chevrons and a wreath around the star design. General of the Air Force is reserved for wartime use only.

Navy
The following stripes are worn on the lower sleeves of the Service Dress Blue uniform. They are of gold embroidery.

Rank	Insignia
Fleet Admiral*	1 two inch with 4 one-half inch
Admiral	1 two inch with 3 one-half inch
Vice Admiral	1 two inch with 2 one-half inch
Rear Admiral (upper half)	1 two inch with 1 one-half inch
Rear Admiral (lower half)	1 two inch
Captain	4 one-half inch
Commander	3 one-half inch
Lieutenant Commander	2 one-half inch with 1 one-quarter inch between
Lieutenant	2 one-half inch
Lieutenant (jr. grade)	1 one-half inch with one-quarter inch above
Ensign	1 one-half inch
Warrant Officer W-4	½" stripe with 1 break
Warrant Officer W-3	½" stripe with 2 breaks, 2" apart
Warrant Officer W-2	½" stripe with 3 breaks, 2" apart

Enlisted personnel (noncommissioned petty officers)—A rating badge worn on the upper left sleeve consisting of a spread eagle, appropriate number of chevrons, and centered specialty mark.

*Rank reserved for wartime use only.

Marine Corps
Marine Corps' distinctive cap and collar ornament is the Marine Corps emblem—a combination of the American eagle, a globe, and an anchor. Marine Corps and Army officer insignia are similar. Marine Corps enlisted insignia, although basically similar to the Army's, feature crossed rifles beneath the chevrons. Marine Corps enlisted rank insignia are as follows:

Sergeant Major of the Marine Corps (E-9)—Same as Sergeant Major (below) but with Marine Corps emblem in the center with a 5-pointed star on both sides of the emblem.
Sergeant Major (E-9)—Three chevrons above 4 rockers with a 5-pointed star in the center.
Master Gunnery Sergeant (E-9)—Three chevrons above 4 rockers with a bursting bomb insignia in the center.
First Sergeant (E-8)—Three chevrons above 3 rockers with a diamond in the middle.
Master Sergeant (E-8)—Three chevrons above 3 rockers with crossed rifles in the middle.
Gunnery Sergeant (E-7)—Three chevrons above 2 rockers with crossed rifles in the middle.
Staff Sergeant (E-6)—Three chevrons above 1 rocker with crossed rifles in the middle.
Sergeant (E-5)—Three chevrons above crossed rifles.
Corporal (E-4)—Two chevrons above crossed rifles.
Lance Corporal (E-3)—One chevron above crossed rifles.
Private First Class (E-2)—One chevron.
Private (E-1)—None.

Coast Guard
Coast Guard insignia follow Navy custom, with certain minor changes such as the officer cap insignia. The Coast Guard shield is worn on both sleeves of officers and on the right sleeve of all enlisted personnel.

For Further Information on the U.S. Armed Forces

Additional information on all the U.S. Armed Forces branches, as well as many other related organizations, can be accessed through the official website of the Dept. of Defense: www.defense.gov.

Army—Office of the Chief of Public Affairs, Media Relations Division—MRD, 1500 Army Pentagon, Washington, DC 20310-1500. **Website:** www.army.mil

Navy—Chief of Information, 1200 Navy Pentagon, Washington, DC 20350-1200. **Website:** www.navy.mil

Air Force—Office of Public Affairs, 1690 Air Force Pentagon, Washington, DC 20330-1690. **Website:** www.af.mil

Marine Corps—Marine Corps Headquarters, Division of Public Affairs, 3000 Marine Corps, Pentagon, Washington, DC 20350-3000. **Website:** www.usmc.mil

Coast Guard—Commandant (CG-09222), Attn: Chief of Media Relations, U.S. Coast Guard, 2100 2nd St. SW, Stop 7362, Washington, DC 20593-7362. **Website:** www.uscg.mil

Timeline of Major Wars Since 1066

Norman Conquest
1066-71

William I, duke of Normandy, landed on the English coast near Hastings on Sept. 28, 1066, and defeated Harold II, Saxon king of England, at Battle of Hastings Oct. 14. William crowned king Dec. 25 in Westminster Abbey. Most revolts were suppressed by 1071. **Conquest linked England's interests with those of the continent and led to its rise as a powerful monarchy.**

Crusades
1095-1270/1291

Military expeditions undertaken by **Western European Christians** usually at the behest of the **papacy**, to recover **Jerusalem** and other Biblical places of pilgrimage from **Muslim** control; in the long term, stimulated trade and flow of ideas between East and West. Pope Urban II called Nov. 27, 1095, for the **First Crusade**; Crusaders took Jerusalem on July 15, 1099, massacred inhabitants, and founded four temporary states: Antioch, Edessa, Jerusalem, and Tripoli. The failed **Second Crusade** was prompted by Muslims' capture of Edessa in 1144. Jerusalem was captured by Ayyubid sultan Saladin on Oct. 2, 1187, launching the **Third Crusade**, which involved the Holy Roman emperor, Frederick I (Barbarossa); the French king, Philip II (Augustus); and the English king, Richard I (Lion-Heart) but did not lead to a Crusader victory. The **Fourth Crusade** sacked Constantinople on Apr. 13, 1204. The **Fifth Crusade** began with capture of Damietta in Egypt (1219) but failed at Cairo. A **Sixth Crusade** led to the Treaty of Jaffa in 1229, giving Jerusalem to the Crusaders until 1244, when it was taken by the Khwarizmians, launching a **Seventh Crusade**. The last crusade abruptly ended when its leader, French King Louis IX, died in 1270. The last major Crusader stronghold, Acre, was lost on May 18, 1291.

Hundred Years
War
1337-1453

Series of armed conflicts over rival claims to the French throne, broken by a number of truces and peace treaties. Edward III declared self king of France in 1338 and invaded, with victories at Crécy in 1346 and Poitiers in 1356. **Treaty of Brétigny** signed May 8, 1360, but French king Charles V renewed fighting in 1369. Truce from 1396 until **Henry V** of England invaded in 1415 and **defeated French army at Agincourt**, capturing land north of Loire River including Paris. **Treaty of Troyes** in 1420 made Henry VI heir of both thrones. The siege of French stronghold Orléans, lifted in 1429 with help from **Joan of Arc**, turned the tide in favor of French. **War ended English claims to France, paved way for French absolute monarchy.**

Wars of the Roses
1455-85

Series of dynastic civil wars in England fought by the **rival houses of Lancaster and York for the throne**. Richard, third duke of York, in conflict with the Lancastrian King **Henry VI**, won victories at St. Albans (1455) and Northampton (1460); Richard died at battle of Wakefield on Dec. 30, 1460, before coronation, leaving his son to become King Edward IV. Henry VI imprisoned in tower of London, 1465. Edward died in 1483; his brother became **Richard III** after usurping throne from Edward V. Henry Tudor defeated Richard III at the Battle of Bosworth Field (1485). As Henry VII, he married Edward's daughter Elizabeth, 1486, finally **uniting the houses.**

Thirty Years War
1618-48

A series of religious and political conflicts involving **most countries of western Europe**; most fighting in Germany, devastating it. Protestants stormed Hapsburg palace in the "Defenestration of Prague" (May 23, 1618). Major conflicts included defeat of King Christian IV of Denmark and Norway by Catholic League (1626); victories by Lutheran King Gustav II Adolph of Sweden at Breitenfeld (1631) and Lützen (1632). France, under cardinal and statesman **Richelieu**, chief minister of King Louis XIII, declared war on the Hapsburgs in May 1635; defeated Austro-Bavarian army (Aug. 3, 1645), leading to Truce of Ulm. **Peace of Westphalia** signed at Münster on Oct. 24, 1648, bringing peace by recognizing the rulers' sovereignty within their lands and their right to determine the religious beliefs of their subjects.

English Civil Wars
1638-60

Series of conflicts between followers of King Charles (Cavaliers) and Parliament (Roundheads), over divine right of king versus Parliament's right to control national finances. Presbyterian Scots, allied with Parliament, rioted and in 1640 occupied the northern counties of England. **Oliver Cromwell**, second in command of Parliament's New Model Army, destroyed the king's army at Battle of Naseby (June 14, 1645); first civil war ended May 1646 when Charles surrendered to the Scots. Charles later allied with Scots but was defeated by Cromwell at Preston Aug. 17-19, 1648, and executed Jan. 30, 1649. Parliament abolished monarchy and House of Lords. Cromwell suppressed Irish and Scottish rebellions, was briefly succeeded by son Richard after death (1658); **Charles II restored to the throne** by the "Long Parliament," May 1660.

War of the
Spanish
Succession
1701-14

War fought by the Grand Alliance (originally England, Netherlands, Denmark, and Austria; later also Portugal), against coalition of France, Spain, and a number of small Italian and German principalities to preserve balance of power after death of Spanish king Charles II. Opened with invasion of Italy, via Venice, by an Austrian army under Prince Eugène of Savoy in May 1701. French forced to withdraw from Netherlands and Italy in 1706 and finally defeated 1709 in bloodiest battle of the war at the French village of Malplaquet. Treaty of Rastatt and Baden signed in 1714; gave **Austria control of Spanish Netherlands and settled peace between Austria and France.**

War of the
Austrian
Succession
1740-48

Conflict over rival claims for the **hereditary dominions of the Habsburg family**, following death (1740) of Charles VI, Holy Roman emperor and archduke of Austria. An alliance of Bavaria, France, Spain, Sardinia, Prussia, and Saxony fought against Austria, allied with Holland and Great Britain. King Frederick the Great of Prussia captured Silesia from Austria in the First (1740-42) and Second Silesian Wars (1744-45). British king George II defeated French army at Battle of Dettingen am Main (June 27, 1743). French conquered Austrian Netherlands (1745-46). Treaty of Aix-la-Chapelle Oct. 18, 1748, **restored most original borders, and Prussia became a significant force.**

Seven Years War
1756-63

Worldwide conflicts fought for the **control of Germany** and for **supremacy in colonial N America and India**. French defeated British Gen. Edward Braddock on the Monongahela in 1754, leading to formal declaration of **French-Indian War**, May 1756. Frederick II of Prussia invaded Saxony on Aug. 29, 1756; defeated French at Rossbach (1757), Austrians at Leuthen (1757), Russians at Zorndorf (1758). By 1760, British conquered French Canada. Peter III signed armistice with Prussia, 1762. Treaty of Paris Feb. 10, 1763; Peace of Hubertusburg Feb. 15, 1763, between Prussia and Austria. **England emerged as leading world naval power.**

American
Revolution
1775-83

Conflict between Great Britain and 13 British colonies in eastern North America. George Washington took command of the Continental Army, July 2, 1775, and King George III declared colonies traitors on Aug. 23. **Independence of colonies declared July 4, 1776.** France recognized the colonies' independence Feb. 6, 1778, followed by Spain on June 21, 1779; both pledged support. French fleet drove British fleet under Adm. Thomas Graves from Chesapeake Bay on Sept. 5, 1781. French and Americans laid siege to Yorktown, VA, Sept. 28-Oct. 19, forcing British Gen. Cornwallis to surrender. **Treaty of Paris** (Sept. 3, 1783) recognized U.S. independence.

Wars of French
Revolution and
Napoleonic Wars
1792-1815

Large-scale wars fought between France and two multinational coalitions. France declared war on the Austrian part of the Holy Roman Empire for aiding King Louis XVI, Apr. 20, 1792. Newly created French Republic declared war on monarchs of Britain and Holland, Feb. 1, 1793, and Spain, Mar. 7. **Napoleon Bonaparte** defeated Austria in N Italy (1796-97), captured Egypt from Britain (1798-99; Battle of the Pyramids, July 21, 1798), and became First Consul after coup d'état of Nov. 9-10, 1799. French Grande Armée later swept through Europe using innovative and aggressive tactics. French navy defeated by British under Adm. Horatio Nelson at **Trafalgar** (Oct. 21, 1805), but Napoleon defeated Austro-Russian forces at Austerlitz (Dec. 2) and controlled most of Europe except Russia and Great Britain by 1808. France suffered its first major defeat by Austria at Aspern-Essling, May 21-22, 1809. **Napoleon invaded Russia**, captured Moscow Sept. 14, 1812, but was forced to flee the bitter Russian winter and abandoned Germany after defeat at Leipzig, Oct. 16-19, 1813. Paris captured by Allied armies Mar. 30-31, 1814. Napoleon exiled to Elba May 4 but returned for "Hundred Days" reign, Mar. 20-June 28, 1815; **final defeat at Waterloo** by British and Prussian troops (June 18). The **Bourbon monarchy was restored under Louis XVIII**, and Britain, Prussia, Russia, and Austria maintained European peace.

Crimean War
1853-56

Conflict between **Russia** and coalition of **Great Britain, France, Sardinia, and Turkey for influence over Balkans** and the straits between the Black Sea and the Mediterranean. Russia destroyed Turkish fleet at Sinope on Nov. 30, 1853. Britain and France declared war in Mar. 1854 and with Turkish troops defeated Russians at Battle of Alma River on Sept. 20. Lord Lucan of Britain prevented Russia from capturing Balaklava on Oct. 25 ("Charge of the Light Brigade"). Siege of Sevastopol ended when Russia evacuated Sept. 8, 1855. Treaty of Paris signed Mar. 30, 1856; **curbed Russian expansion and loosened European power alignments.**

American Civil War
1861-65

Conflict between the U.S. (the Union) and 11 secessionist Southern states, organized as the Confederate States of America. Union garrison at Fort Sumter off Charleston, SC, surrendered to Brig. Gen. Pierre Beauregard (Apr. 12-13, 1861). 22,000 Confederates under Beauregard repelled 35,000 Union troops under Gen. Irvin McDowell along Bull Run stream near Manassas, VA (July 21). The *Merrimack* (renamed the *Virginia*) battled the *Monitor* Mar. 9, 1862. In **Battle of Antietam** (Sept. 17), some 12,000 Northerners and 12,700 Southerners were killed or wounded. Pres. Abraham Lincoln announced **Emancipation Proclamation** on Sept. 22. Confederate Gen. Robert E. Lee's forces numbering 75,000 battled 88,000 Union troops under Gen. George Meade at **Gettysburg** July 1-3, 1863; Lee's army forced back across the Potomac River. Lee surrendered to Ulysses S. Grant at **Appomattox Court House** (Apr. 9, 1865). **The Union was preserved and slavery abolished.**

Franco-Prussian War
1870-71

German states led by Prussia defeated France, seizing Alsace and part of Lorraine. French defeated in several major battles, culminating at **Sedan** Sept. 1, 1870, when Prussian forces decisively defeated the French army and captured emperor Napoleon III. Prussian king crowned William I, emperor of unified Germany, Jan 18, 1871. **France surrendered** Jan. 28. Final treaty signed May 10; set the stage for later **German imperialistic expansion.**

Spanish-American War
1898

War waged by the U.S. to **liberate Cuba from Spanish rule.** A mysterious explosion, blamed on Spain by American newspapers, sank the U.S. battleship *Maine* in Havana's harbor (Feb. 15, 1898), killing 260. The U.S. called for Spain's withdrawal from Cuba, and Spain declared war (Apr. 24). Rufus Shafter led 17,000 U.S. troops from Daiquirí to Santiago de Cuba, taking **San Juan Hill** with help of the Rough Riders under Teddy Roosevelt. Santiago de Cuba surrendered July 17. The Treaty of Paris (Dec. 10, 1898) provided for the **independence of Cuba** and the cession by Spain to the U.S. of **Puerto Rico, Guam, and for a $20 mil payment, the Philippine Islands.**

World War I
1914-18

Local European war that grew into a global war involving 32 nations: the Allies and the Associated Powers—28 nations including Great Britain, France, Russia, Italy, and the U.S.—versus the Central Powers of Germany, Austria-Hungary, Turkey, and Bulgaria. Archduke Francis Ferdinand assassinated at Sarajevo, Bosnia (June 28, 1914). Germany invaded France through Belgium and the Netherlands; advance on Paris halted by the French under Gen. Joseph Jacques Césaire Joffre at the **First Battle of the Marne**, Sept. 5-12. Germany checked the Russian army at the Battle of Tannenberg, Aug. 26-30. The British suffered 57,470 casualties (19,240 dead) in the opening day of the **First Battle of the Somme** (July 1-Nov. 18, 1916); first of 12 battles that forced Germany back to Hindenburg Line. **U.S. declared war on Germany Apr. 6, 1917.** Russian involvement ended when Bolshevik party seized power on Nov. 7; signed armistice Dec. 15. German offensive halted by U.S. and French troops at **Second Battle of the Marne** (July 15-Aug. 5, 1918), turning point of the war. Allied counteroffensive broke the Hindenburg Line, and an armistice was signed Nov. 11.

World War II
1939-45

Global military conflict stemming from European unrest after World War I and Japan's aggressive expansion into Asia and the Pacific. **War in Europe:** The Nazi-Soviet nonaggression pact (Aug. 23, 1939) freed Germany and the Soviet Union to attack Poland in Sept. **Britain and France declared war on Germany** Sept. 3. German forces raced through Europe (Apr.-June 1940), capturing Paris June 14. **Italy declared war on France and Britain** June 10; German-Italian campaigns won the Balkans and N Africa by June 1941. U.S. entered war Dec. 1941. Three million Axis troops invaded Russia June 22, 1941, but Russian counterthrusts stopped the German advance (**Stalingrad**, Aug. 20, 1942-Feb. 2, 1943), and Allies took N Africa (Nov. 8, 1942-May 13, 1943), Italy (July 10, 1943-May 2, 1945). Normandy invaded on **D-Day**, June 6, 1944; Paris liberated Aug. 25. Yalta Conference (Feb. 4-11, 1945) to defeat and split Germany into quarters. Adolf Hitler committed suicide Apr. 30. **Germany surrendered unconditionally** May 7. **War in the Pacific:** Japan invaded China (July 7, 1937), joined alliance with Germany and Italy (Sept. 27, 1940) and signed nonaggression pact with Russia (Apr. 13, 1941); attacked Hawaii's Pearl Harbor, Dec. 7, 1941; U.S. declared war on Japan Dec. 8. **Battle of Midway** (June 4-7, 1942) repulsed the Japanese advance. Marines landed on Guadalcanal Aug. 7. Navy defeated Japanese fleet at **Leyte Gulf**, Oct. 23-26, 1944. B-29 bombing raids on Japan began in Nov. Marines invaded Iwo Jima (Feb. 19-Mar. 16, 1945) with heavy casualties, then Okinawa (Apr. 1-June 21). **U.S. atom bombs dropped** on Hiroshima (Aug. 6) and Nagasaki (Aug. 9) and the Soviet invasion of Manchuria (Aug. 8) **forced Japan to agree, on Aug. 14, to surrender;** formal surrender on Sept. 2.

Korean War
1950-53

Military struggle fought on the Korean Peninsula between the Democratic Peoples' Republic of Korea (N Korea) and the Republic of Korea (S Korea) that developed into an international war involving China allied with N Korea against the U.S. and other nations under the UN flag. DPRK army crossed the 38th parallel and invaded S Korea (June 25, 1950), entering Seoul (June 26). Amphibious assault launched at **Inchon** by Gen. Douglas MacArthur (Sept. 15) helped U.S. forces rout DPRK close to Yalu River by Nov. 24. Chinese counterattack retook Seoul (Jan. 4, 1951), but forced back to the 38th parallel by Apr. 22. Armistice was signed (July 27, 1953) by the UN, DPRK, and China, but not ROK, **leaving the peninsula partitioned at about the 38th parallel.**

Vietnam War
1959-75

Struggle primarily in S Vietnam that widened into a war between S Vietnam supported mainly by the U.S. and N Vietnam supported by the USSR and China. Viet Minh, led by Communist leader Ho Chi Minh, formed the Democratic Republic of Vietnam (Sept. 2, 1945). Colonial power France withdrew after fortress at Dien Bien Phu fell (May 8, 1954). Pres. John F. Kennedy pledged U.S. commitment to S Vietnamese independence Dec. 14, 1961. USS *Maddox* destroyer damaged in **Gulf of Tonkin** (Aug. 2, 1964) prompted Congress to increase involvement. Regular bombing of N Vietnam began (Feb. 24, 1965) and the first U.S. combat ground forces arrived (Mar. 6). N Vietnamese Army siege of **Khe Sanh** (Jan. 21-Apr. 7, 1968) and the **"Tet" offensive** (Jan. 30) aimed to cause insurrection in the S. **My Lai Massacre** by U.S. soldiers against civilians (Mar. 16, 1968) created scandal, fueled U.S. disaffection with war. U.S. forces peaked at 543,400 in Apr. 1969. NVA **"Easter Offensive"** (Mar. 30, 1972) rebuffed, and U.S. responded with aerial bombings in May and Dec. U.S. withdrew after ceasefire, Jan. 1973. **NVA offensive captured Saigon, Apr. 30, 1975, and unified Vietnam under Communist rule.**

Persian Gulf Wars
1991, 2003-10

Conflicts fought principally between Iraq and the U.S. concerning Iraq's influence in the Middle East and its development of weapons of mass destruction. **First Gulf War:** Iraq under dictator Saddam Hussein invaded Kuwait Aug 2, 1990, and annexed it; UN Security Council ordered Iraqi forces to withdraw by Jan. 15, 1991. Beginning Jan. 17, a multinational force (**Operation Desert Storm**) led by U.S. bombed military targets in Iraq and Kuwait. A coordinated air-land offensive (**Operation Desert Sabre**, begun Feb. 24) retook Kuwait City Feb. 26, and permanent ceasefire was signed on Apr. 6. Iraq was ordered to pay reparations to Kuwait, reveal locations of biological and chemical weapons, and eliminate weapons of mass destruction. **Second Gulf War:** The U.S. and UK mistakenly asserted that Iraq was still producing WMD and posed an imminent threat. The UN passed Resolution 1441, Nov. 8, 2002, warning Iraq of "serious consequences" if it failed to cooperate fully and unconditionally with UN weapons inspectors. Iraq rejected a Mar. 17, 2003, U.S. ultimatum demanding Hussein and his sons leave Iraq; U.S. launched **Operation Iraqi Freedom** Mar. 19, 2003, with support from UK and other allies, but without full UN Security Council support. Baghdad fell Apr. 9, and major combat operations declared over May 1. Hussein was captured Dec. 13, but guerrilla opposition to U.S. troops and insurgent violence continued. U.S. combat operations in Iraq formally ended Aug. 31, 2010.

HEALTH

U.S. Health Expenditures, 1960-2009

Source: *Health, United States, 2011*, National Center for Health Statistics, Centers for Disease Control and Prevention

	1960	1970	1980	1990	2000	2005	2007	2008	2009
					Amount in billions				
National health expenditures	$27.3	$74.8	$255.7	$724.0	$1,378.0	$2,021.0	$2,283.5	$2,391.4	$2,486.3
					Percent distribution				
Health consumption expenditures	90.6%	89.6%	92.1%	93.3%	93.5%	93.5%	93.5%	93.4%	93.7%
Personal health care	85.4	84.3	84.9	85.2	84.5	83.7	83.4	83.5	84.1
Hospital care	32.9	36.3	39.3	34.6	30.2	30.0	30.1	30.2	30.5
Professional services	29.2	26.4	25.2	28.7	28.2	27.7	27.1	27.3	27.1
Physician and clinical services	20.6	19.2	18.7	22.0	21.0	20.8	20.3	20.3	20.3
Other professional services	1.4	1.0	1.4	2.4	2.7	2.6	2.6	2.7	2.7
Dental services	7.2	6.2	5.2	4.4	4.5	4.3	4.3	4.3	4.1
Other personal care	1.6	1.8	3.3	3.4	4.7	4.8	4.7	4.7	4.9
Home health care[1]	0.2	0.3	0.9	1.7	2.4	2.4	2.5	2.6	2.7
Nursing care facilities and retirement communities[1]	3.0	5.4	6.0	6.2	6.2	5.5	5.5	5.6	5.5
Retail outlet sales of medical products	18.4	14.1	10.1	10.6	12.9	13.3	13.4	13.2	13.2
Prescription drugs	9.8	7.3	4.7	5.6	8.8	10.0	10.1	9.9	10.1
Durable medical equipment	2.7	2.3	1.6	1.9	1.8	1.5	1.5	1.5	1.4
Nondurable medical products	5.9	4.4	3.8	3.1	2.3	1.8	1.8	1.8	1.7
Government administration[2]	0.2	0.3	1.0	0.9	1.2	1.3	1.3	1.2	1.2
Net cost of health insurance	3.7	2.6	3.7	4.5	4.6	5.7	5.8	5.6	5.4
Government public health activities	1.4	1.8	2.5	2.8	3.1	2.8	3.0	3.1	3.1
Investment	9.4	10.4	7.9	6.7	6.5	6.5	6.5	6.6	6.3
Research[3]	2.5	2.6	2.1	1.8	1.8	2.0	1.8	1.8	1.8
Structures and equipment	6.8	7.8	5.7	5.0	4.7	4.5	4.7	4.8	4.5
				Average annual percent change from previous year shown					
National health expenditures	—	10.6%	13.1%	11.0%	6.6%	8.0%	6.1%	4.7%	4.0%
Health consumption expenditures	—	10.5	13.4	11.1	6.7	8.0	5.9	4.6	4.3
Personal health care	—	10.4	13.2	11.0	6.6	7.8	5.9	4.9	4.6
Hospital care	—	11.7	14.0	9.6	5.2	7.9	5.9	5.2	5.1
Professional services	—	9.5	12.6	12.4	6.5	7.5	5.3	5.3	3.5
Physician and clinical services	—	9.8	12.8	12.8	6.2	7.7	4.8	5.2	4.0
Other professional services	—	6.3	17.0	17.5	7.8	7.5	7.4	6.6	5.3
Dental services	—	9.1	11.1	9.0	7.0	7.0	6.5	5.1	-0.1
Other personal care	—	11.4	20.4	11.1	10.3	8.3	6.1	4.6	8.3
Home health care[1]	—	14.5	26.9	18.1	9.9	8.5	9.9	7.5	10.0
Nursing care facilities and retirement communities[1]	—	17.4	14.2	11.4	6.6	5.7	8.1	5.0	3.1
Retail outlet sales of medical products	—	7.7	9.4	11.4	8.8	8.7	5.2	3.0	4.2
Prescription drugs	—	7.5	8.2	12.8	11.6	10.8	4.7	3.1	5.3
Durable medical equipment	—	9.0	8.8	13.0	6.2	3.9	7.6	2.3	-0.8
Nondurable medical products	—	7.4	11.4	8.6	3.5	3.4	6.0	3.1	2.2
Government administration[2]	—	16.7	25.9	9.5	10.6	9.4	3.1	0.1	2.0
Net cost of health insurance	—	6.9	17.0	13.1	7.0	12.4	4.4	1.5	-1.2
Government public health activities	—	13.8	16.9	12.0	8.0	5.5	9.9	6.0	5.9
Investment	—	11.7	10.0	9.2	6.3	7.9	9.8	6.0	-0.6
Research[3]	—	10.9	10.8	8.9	7.2	9.6	1.3	3.1	4.8
Structures and equipment	—	12.0	9.7	9.4	5.9	7.1	13.5	7.1	-2.7

— = Not applicable. **Note:** Numbers may not add up to totals because of rounding. (1) Freestanding facilities only. Additional services of this type provided in hospital-based facilities are counted as hospital care. (2) Includes personal care services delivered by government public health agencies. (3) Excludes research and development expenditures of drug companies, other mfrs. and providers of medical equipment, and supplies. They are included in the expenditure class in which a product falls.

Health Coverage for Persons Under 65, 1984-2010

Source: *Health, United States, 2011*, National Center for Health Statistics, Centers for Disease Control and Prevention

	Private insurance				Medicaid[1]				Not covered[2]			
	1984[3]	1995[3]	2000	2010	1984[3]	1995[3]	2000	2010	1984[3]	1995[3]	2000	2010
					Percent of each population group							
Total	76.8%	71.3%	71.5%	61.7%	6.8%	11.5%	9.5%	16.9%	14.5%	16.1%	17.0%	18.2%
Age												
Under 18 years	72.6	65.2	66.6	54.1	11.9	21.5	19.6	36.4	13.9	13.4	12.6	7.8
18-44 years	76.5	70.9	70.5	60.0	5.1	7.8	5.6	10.9	17.1	20.4	22.4	27.1
45-64 years	83.3	80.1	78.7	71.3	3.4	5.6	4.5	6.8	9.6	10.9	12.6	15.7
Race and Hispanic origin[4,5]												
White, non-Hispanic	82.4	78.6	79.5	72.0	3.7	7.1	6.1	11.0	11.9	13.0	12.5	13.7
Black, non-Hispanic	58.2	53.4	56.0	45.1	20.7	28.1	21.0	30.0	19.7	17.9	19.5	20.7
Hispanic, any race	55.7	46.4	47.8	36.8	13.3	21.9	15.5	28.6	29.5	31.4	35.6	32.0
Percent of poverty level[4]												
Below 100%	32.2	22.6	25.2	16.0	33.0	48.4	38.4	50.8	33.9	29.6	34.2	30.3
100%-199%	70.3	55.3	50.1	34.8	5.3	14.4	16.2	28.5	21.8	28.3	31.0	32.4
200%-399%	89.3	86.4	78.1	70.7	0.8	2.3	4.0	8.4	7.6	10.0	15.4	17.4
400% or more	95.4	93.2	91.9	89.9	0.2	0.4	0.9	2.0	3.2	5.4	5.9	5.6
Geographic region[4]												
Northeast	80.5	75.4	76.2	68.2	8.6	11.7	10.6	17.9	10.2	13.3	12.2	12.4
Midwest	80.6	77.3	78.8	66.7	7.4	10.5	8.0	17.3	11.3	12.2	12.3	14.1
South	74.3	66.9	66.8	57.5	5.1	11.3	9.4	16.0	17.7	19.4	20.5	21.9
West	71.9	67.5	66.5	58.9	7.0	12.9	10.4	17.1	18.2	17.9	20.7	20.6

Note: Data based on household interviews of a sample of the civilian noninstitutionalized population. Percents may not add up to 100 because other types of health insurance (e.g., Medicare, military) are not shown, and persons with both private insurance and Medicaid appear in both sections. (1) Includes Medicaid and other public assistance. (2) Includes persons not covered by private insurance, Medicaid or other public assistance, Medicare, or military plans. (3) A change in the questionnaire in 1997 prevents direct comparison with later years. (4) Age adjusted. (5) Changed reporting methods make race percentages before 1999 not strictly comparable with those from 1999 on.

Spending on Health in the 50 Most Populous Countries, 2009

Source: *World Health Statistics 2012*, World Health Organization

Country	As % of GDP	Per capita[1]	Country	As % of GDP	Per capita[1]	Country	As % of GDP	Per capita[1]	Country	As % of GDP	Per capita[1]
Afghanistan[2]	7.6%	$34	Germany	11.7%	$4,723	Myanmar			Tanzania	5.5%	$27
Algeria	4.6	181	Ghana	5.0	54	(Burma)	2.1%	$14	Thailand	4.2	160
Argentina	9.5	734	India	4.2	44	Nepal	5.5	24	Turkey	6.7	575
Australia	8.7	3,945	Indonesia	2.5	56	Nigeria	6.1	67	Uganda	8.5	44
Bangladesh	3.4	21	Iran	5.7	287	Pakistan	2.2	20	Ukraine	7.8	200
Brazil	8.8	734	Iraq[3]	8.4	200	Peru	5.3	236	United		
Canada	11.4	4,519	Italy	9.4	3,323	Philippines	3.6	66	Kingdom	9.8	3,440
China	5.1	191	Japan	9.5	3,754	Poland	7.4	829	United States	17.6	7,960
Colombia	7.6	392	Kenya	4.8	36	Russia	5.6	476	Uzbekistan	5.9	73
Congo, Dem.			Korea, South	6.9	1,184	Saudi Arabia	4.4	608	Venezuela	6.0	688
Rep. of	2.8	67	Malaysia	4.6	316	South Africa	9.2	521	Vietnam	6.9	77
Egypt	4.8	114	Mexico	6.5	525	Spain	9.6	3,032	Yemen	5.5	63
Ethiopia	4.4	16	Morocco	5.2	152	Sudan	7.3	94	**World**[4]	**9.4**	**900**
France	11.9	4,840	Mozambique	5.4	23						

(1) At average exchange rate. (2) GDP also includes illicit GDPs (e.g., opium). Govt. expenditures include external assistance (ext. budget). (3) Not including expenditures for Northern Iraq. (4) Includes other nations not shown.

Population Not Covered by Health Insurance, by State, 1990-2011

Source: Annual Social and Economic Supplements, Current Population Survey, U.S. Census Bureau, U.S. Dept. of Commerce
(numbers in thousands)

	2011 No. not covered	2011 % pop. not covered	2000 No. not covered	2000 % pop. not covered	1990 No. not covered	1990 % pop. not covered		2011 No. not covered	2011 % pop. not covered	2000 No. not covered	2000 % pop. not covered	1990 No. not covered	1990 % pop. not covered
AL	622	13.0%	557	12.7%	710	17.4%	MT	180	18.3%	146	16.4%	115	14.0%
AK	130	18.2	114	18.3	77	15.4	NE	225	12.3	140	8.3	138	8.5
AZ	1,137	17.3	834	16.0	547	15.5	NV	607	22.6	336	16.4	201	16.5
AR	508	17.5	367	13.8	421	17.4	NH	163	12.5	99	8.0	107	9.9
CA	7,425	19.7	6,154	18.1	5,683	19.1	NJ	1,336	15.4	985	11.7	773	10.0
CO	788	15.7	598	13.8	495	14.7	NM	399	19.6	426	23.7	339	22.2
CT	303	8.6	313	9.3	226	6.9	NY	2,355	12.2	3,001	16.0	2,176	12.1
DE	90	10.0	69	8.9	96	13.9	NC	1,550	16.3	1,046	13.1	883	13.8
DC	52	8.4	75	13.6	109	19.2	ND	61	9.1	66	10.7	40	6.3
FL	3,765	19.8	2,727	17.0	2,376	18.0	OH	1,549	13.7	1,191	10.7	1,123	10.3
GA	1,862	19.2	1,145	14.1	971	15.3	OK	636	16.9	624	18.4	574	18.6
HI	105	7.8	110	9.1	81	7.3	OR	532	13.8	417	12.2	360	12.4
ID	266	16.9	194	15.0	159	15.2	PA	1,375	10.8	963	8.0	1,218	10.1
IL	1,873	14.7	1,632	13.3	1,272	10.9	RI	125	12.0	74	7.1	105	11.1
IN	764	12.0	650	10.8	587	10.7	SC	877	19.0	473	11.9	550	16.2
IA	303	10.0	239	8.4	225	8.1	SD	105	13.0	77	10.5	81	11.6
KS	380	13.5	274	10.3	272	10.8	TN	841	13.3	585	10.4	673	13.7
KY	621	14.4	521	13.0	480	13.2	TX	6,080	23.8	4,650	22.4	3,569	21.1
LA	938	20.8	755	17.3	797	19.7	UT	412	14.6	259	11.5	156	9.0
ME	133	10.0	135	10.6	139	11.2	VT	53	8.6	50	8.3	54	9.5
MD	802	13.8	511	9.7	601	12.7	VA	1,066	13.4	747	10.7	996	15.7
MA	219	3.4	527	8.4	530	9.1	WA	986	14.5	772	13.2	557	11.4
MI	1,209	12.5	838	8.5	865	9.4	WV	273	14.9	247	13.9	249	13.8
MN	487	9.2	368	7.5	389	8.9	WI	589	10.4	398	7.5	321	6.7
MS	476	16.2	361	12.9	531	19.9	WY	100	17.8	74	15.3	58	12.5
MO	877	14.9	511	9.3	665	12.7	**U.S.**	**48,613**	**15.7**	**38,426**	**13.7**	**34,719**	**13.9**

Persons Not Covered by Health Insurance, by Selected Characteristics, 2011

Source: Annual Social and Economic Supplements, Current Population Survey, U.S. Census Bureau, U.S. Dept. of Commerce
(numbers in thousands)

Race and Hispanic origin[1]	Number not covered	% of pop. specified at left	Region	Number not covered	% of pop. specified at left
White	35,991	14.9%	Northeast	6,061	11.0%
Non-Hispanic	21,681	11.1	Midwest	8,425	12.7
Black	7,722	19.5	South	21,059	18.3
Asian	2,696	16.8	West	13,067	18.0
Hispanic	15,776	30.1	**Household income**		
Nativity			Less than $25,000	14,923	25.4
Native born	35,436	13.2	$25,000 to $49,999	15,442	21.5
Foreign born	13,177	33.0	$50,000 to $74,999	8,811	15.4
Naturalized citizen	3,431	19.1	$75,000 or more	9,437	7.8
Not a citizen	9,746	44.2	**Work experience**[2]		
Age			Worked at least one week	27,863	19.3
Under 65 years	47,923	17.9	Worked full-time year-round	14,926	15.3
Under 18 years	6,964	9.4	Worked less than full-time		
18 to 24 years	7,649	25.4	year-round	12,937	27.7
25 to 34 years	11,529	28.0	Did not work	13,096	26.7
35 to 44 years	8,399	21.0	**Total**	**48,613**	**15.7**
45 to 54 years	7,853	17.9			
55 to 64 years	5,529	14.6			
65 years and over	690	1.7			

(1) Persons of Hispanic origin may be of any race. (2) Persons 18 to 64 years of age only.

Provisions of the Patient Protection and Affordable Care Act (PPACA)

Source: U.S. Dept. of Health and Human Services

On Mar. 23, 2010, Pres. Barack Obama signed a sweeping health-care reform measure into law that would extend medical insurance to more than 30 mil uninsured people. The legislation—the Patient Protection and Affordable Care Act (PPACA)—is projected to still leave some 23 mil people in the U.S., one-third of whom were undocumented immigrants, without insurance in 2019. The Congressional Budget Office released a Mar. 2010 report which projected that the final reform package would cost $938 bil over 10 years and reduce the budget deficit by $138 bil during the same period.

Upon signing, the PPACA activated provisions allowing health insurance tax credits to small businesses; a $15 bil fund invested in prevention and public health programs; increased payments to rural health care providers; and efforts to crack down on health care fraud, expand primary care, and hold insurance companies accountable for rate hikes. Beginning Apr. 1, 2010, more people were covered under state Medicaid programs. Beginning June 2010, coverage to early retirees was expanded, and seniors who reached the gap in Medicare prescription drug coverage known as the "donut hole" received a $250 rebate check from Medicare to pay for prescriptions. Beginning July 2010, new health insurance options were made available online, and access to insurance was extended for uninsured individuals with pre-existing conditions.

For health plan years beginning on or after Sept. 23, 2010: Insurance companies were prevented from denying coverage to children under age 19 due to a pre-existing condition and from rescinding coverage. Lifetime dollar limits on insurance coverage were eliminated, annual dollar limits on coverage were regulated, and insurance company decisions could be appealed by consumers. Insurance companies were required to cover certain preventive services for free, and young adults could stay on their parents' plan until age 26. Beginning Oct. 2010, grants were awarded to states to fund consumer assistance programs.

After the PPACA was challenged by 26 states, the U.S. Supreme Court on June 28, 2012, upheld the health-care law.

Note: Provisions go into effect Jan. 1 of year shown, unless otherwise noted.

2011
- Prescription drug discounts offered.
- Senior citizens: free preventive care; improved care after they leave the hospital.
- At least 85% of all premium dollars collected by insurance companies for large employer plans must be spent on health care services and health care quality improvement.
- The new Community First Choice Option allows states to offer home and community-based services to disabled individuals through Medicaid rather than institutional care in nursing homes. (Oct. 1)

2012
- Incentives for physicians to join together to form integrated health systems.
- Federal health programs required to collect and report racial, ethnic, and language data, to help reduce health disparities. (Mar.)
- Financial incentives to hospitals to improve quality of care. (Oct. 1)
- Health plans required to use electronic records. (Oct. 1)

2013
- New funding to state Medicaid programs that choose to cover preventive services for patients at little or no cost.

- Authority expanded to bundle payments to hospitals, doctors, and other providers.
- Medicaid payments increased for primary care doctors.
- Additional funding for Children's Health Insurance Program. (Oct. 1)

2014
- Those who can afford it will be required to obtain basic health insurance coverage or pay a fine.
- Strong reforms prohibiting discrimination due to pre-existing conditions or gender.
- Annual limits on insurance coverage eliminated.
- Coverage ensured for people in clinical trials.
- Tax credits to help those in the middle class not eligible for other affordable coverage.
- Affordable insurance exchanges for those whose employers do not offer insurance.
- Small-business tax credit increased.
- Access to Medicaid for those who earn less than 133% of the poverty level.

2015
- Physicians to be paid based on value, not volume.

Health Care Visits by Selected Characteristics, 1997-2010

Source: National Health Interview Survey; *Health, United States*; National Center for Health Statistics; Centers for Disease Control and Prevention

Characteristic	Zero visits			1-3 visits			4-9 visits			10 or more visits		
	1997	2000	2010	1997	2000	2010	1997	2000	2010	1997	2000	2010
	Percent distribution											
All persons	16.5%	16.7%	15.6%	46.2%	45.4%	45.4%	23.6%	24.6%	25.8%	13.7%	13.3%	13.2%
Age												
Under 6 years	5.0	6.3	3.7	44.9	44.5	48.9	37.0	38.1	36.8	13.0	11.1	10.6
6-17 years	15.3	15.2	10.4	58.7	58.2	59.1	19.3	20.6	23.6	6.8	6.0	6.9
18-44 years	21.7	23.5	24.2	46.7	45.2	43.9	19.0	19.1	20.6	12.6	12.2	11.3
45-64 years	16.9	15.0	14.8	42.9	43.4	42.8	24.7	25.7	26.1	15.5	15.9	16.4
65-74 years	9.8	9.0	6.3	36.9	34.5	36.1	31.6	34.5	35.7	21.6	22.1	21.9
75 years and over	7.7	5.8	4.1	31.8	29.3	31.0	33.8	39.3	38.0	26.6	25.6	27.0
Sex												
Male	21.3	21.7	20.4	47.1	45.9	46.4	20.6	22.3	22.7	11.0	10.1	10.5
Female	11.8	11.9	10.9	45.4	44.8	44.4	26.5	27.0	28.8	16.3	16.3	15.9
Race and Hispanic origin												
White, not Hispanic	14.7	14.5	13.2	46.6	45.4	45.3	24.4	25.9	27.1	14.3	14.1	14.4
Black, not Hispanic	16.9	17.1	15.6	46.1	46.8	47.3	23.1	23.5	24.9	13.8	12.6	12.2
Hispanic[1]	24.9	26.8	23.5	42.3	41.8	43.2	20.3	19.8	22.6	12.5	11.6	10.7
Health insurance status[2]												
Insured continuously	14.1	14.0	12.1	49.2	48.8	48.6	23.6	24.6	26.2	13.0	12.6	13.0
Uninsured for any period	18.9	20.6	18.5	46.0	44.5	47.8	20.8	20.8	22.0	14.4	14.1	11.6
Uninsured	39.0	43.2	43.8	41.4	39.6	39.7	13.2	12.1	12.6	6.4	5.1	3.9

Note: Covers visits to doctor's offices, emergency departments, and home visits in the 12-month period prior to interview. Estimates are age-adjusted to the year 2000 standard population. Totals include persons of races not shown separately and of unknown health insurance status. (1) Persons of Hispanic origin may be of any race. (2) In 12 months prior to interview, for under-65 population only; persons having both Medicaid and private coverage are classified as having private coverage.

Reasons Given by Patients for Outpatient Visits, 2009

Source: National Hospital Ambulatory Medical Care Survey, National Center for Health Statistics, Centers for Disease Control and Prevention

Rank	Reason	Number of visits (thous.)	% of all visits	Rank	Reason	Number of visits (thous.)	% of all visits
1.	Progress visit, not otherwise specified	9,052	9.4%	11.	Fever	1,341	1.4%
2.	General medical examination	5,762	6.0	12.	Knee symptoms	1,331	1.4
3.	Cough	2,638	2.7	13.	Earache or ear infection	1,326	1.4
4.	Counseling, not otherwise specified	2,550	2.7	14.	Stomach pain, cramps, and spasms	1,231	1.3
5.	Prenatal examination, routine	2,410	2.5	15.	Well-baby examination	1,198	1.2
6.	Medication, other and unspecified kinds	2,282	2.4	16.	Headache, pain in head	1,091	1.1
				17.	Low back symptoms	1,078	1.1
7.	Symptoms referable to throat	1,773	1.8	18.	Hypertension	1,078	1.1
8.	Back symptoms	1,630	1.7	19.	Skin rash	1,053	1.1
9.	Postoperative visit	1,593	1.7	20.	Gynecological examination	1,032	1.1
10.	Diabetes mellitus	1,568	1.6		**All other reasons**	**53,115**	**55.3**
					All visits	**96,132**	**100.0**

Emergency Room Visits by Diagnosis, 2009

Source: National Hospital Ambulatory Medical Care Survey, National Center for Health Statistics, Centers for Disease Control and Prevention

Rank	Principal diagnosis group	Number of visits (thous.)	% of all visits	Rank	Principal diagnosis group	Number of visits (thous.)	% of all visits
1.	Heart disease, excluding ischemic	1,067	6.2%	12.	Fractures, excluding lower limb	260	1.5%
2.	Chest pain	927	5.4	13.	Malignant neoplasms	241	1.4
3.	Pneumonia	732	4.3	14.	Disorder of gallbladder and biliary tract	239	1.4
4.	Ischemic heart disease	513	3.0	15.	Abdominal pain	232	1.4
5.	Cerebrovascular disease	477	2.8	16.	Gastrointestinal hemmorhage	230	1.3
6.	Psychoses, excluding major depressive disorder	445	2.6	17.	Urinary tract infection, site not specified	224	1.3
7.	Chronic and unspecified bronchitis	324	1.9	18.	Diabetes mellitus	219	1.3
8.	Syncope and collapse	316	1.8	19.	Anemia	197	1.1
9.	Fracture of the lower limb	305	1.8	20.	Essential hypertension	192	1.1
10.	Cellulitis and abscess	296	1.7		**All other diagnoses[1]**	**9,421**	**55.0**
11.	Complications of pregnancy, childbirth, and the puerperium	262	1.5		**All visits**	**17,119**	**100.0**

(1) Includes blanks and discharges in which diagnosis was unknown.

Most Frequently Mentioned Drugs at Outpatient Department Visits, 2009

Source: National Hospital Ambulatory Medical Care Survey, National Center for Health Statistics, Centers for Disease Control and Prevention

Rank	Therapeutic drug category[1]	No. of mentions (thous.)	% of total[2]	Rank	Therapeutic drug category[1]	No. of mentions (thous.)	% of total[2]
1.	Analgesics	32,498	12.7%	11.	Antiplatelet agents	7,337	2.9%
2.	Antidepressants	11,736	4.6	12.	Proton pump inhibitors	7,289	2.9
3.	Antidiabetic agents	10,956	4.3	13.	ACE[3] inhibitors	6,833	2.7
4.	Antihyperlipidemic agents	10,615	4.2	14.	Antihistamines	6,770	2.7
5.	Anxiolytics, sedatives, and hypnotics	9,086	3.6	15.	Antiemetic or antivertigo agents	5,714	2.2
6.	Bronchodilators	8,644	3.4	16.	Viral vaccines	5,365	2.1
7.	Anticonvulsants	8,456	3.3	17.	Adrenal cortical steroids	5,039	2.0
8.	Beta-adrenergic blocking agents	7,941	3.1	18.	Calcium channel blocking agents	4,640	1.8
9.	Dermatological agents	7,550	3.0	19.	Penicillins	4,090	1.6
10.	Diuretics	7,360	2.9	20.	Sex hormones	4,009	1.6

(1) Based on the Multum Lexicon second-level therapeutic drug category. (2) Based on an estimated 255,022,000 drugs provided, prescribed, or continued at outpatient department visits in 2009. (3) Angiotensin-converting enzyme.

U.S. Organ Transplants

Source: Organ Procurement and Transplantation Network (OPTN), United Network for Organ Sharing (UNOS)

Waiting List, June 2012

Type of transplant	Patients waiting	% of total
Any organ[1]	**124,681**	**100.0%**
Kidney	99,164	79.5
Liver	16,795	13.5
Heart	3,218	2.6
Kidney-pancreas	2,238	1.8
Lung	1,670	1.3
Pancreas	1,287	1.0
Intestine	258	0.2
Heart-lung	51	0.0

Transplants Performed, 2011

Type of transplant	Number	% of total
Any organ	**28,537**	**100.0%**
Kidney	16,813	58.9
Liver	6,342	22.2
Heart	2,322	8.1
Lung	1,822	6.4
Kidney-pancreas	795	2.8
Pancreas	287	1.0
Intestine	129	0.5
Heart-lung	27	0.1

Note: Waiting list as of June 29, 2012. (1) Figures may not add up to total because patients waiting for more than one organ are included in multiple categories.

Drug Use in the General U.S. Population, 2010

Source: Substance Abuse and Mental Health Services Administration (SAMHSA), U.S. Dept. of Health and Human Services

According to SAMHSA's 2010 annual survey, an estimated 119.5 mil Americans 12 years of age and older (or 47.1% of that population) had used an illicit drug at least once in their lifetimes. Of that number, an estimated 76.2 mil (30% of persons 12 or older) had used an illicit drug other than marijuana at least once in their lives. About 15.3% of the 12-and-older population had used an illicit drug in the previous year; 8.9% had used one in the month prior to their participation in the survey. The rate of current illicit drug use (i.e.,

within the past month) in 2010 was 11.2% for men and 6.8% for women.

SAMHSA's Drug Abuse Warning Network (DAWN) reported 2.1 mil drug abuse or misuse-related visits to hospital emergency departments in 2009. Nearly half of all visits where alcohol was not also a factor (47%) involved an illicit drug. Cocaine was a factor in 20% of these. Alcohol in combination with illegal drug use was involved in 10% of emergency visits.

Illicit Drug Use Among Persons 12 or Older, 2005-10

Source: National Survey on Drug Use and Health, Substance Abuse and Mental Health Services Admin. (SAMHSA), U.S. Dept. of Health and Human Services

(numbers in thousands)

	2005 No.	2005 %	2006 No.	2006 %	2007 No.	2007 %	2008 No.	2008 %	2009 No.	2009 %	2010 No.	2010 %
Used in lifetime												
Illicit drugs[1]	112,085	46.1	111,774	45.4	114,275	46.1	117,325	47.0	118,705	47.1	119,508	47.1
Illicit drugs other than marijuana[1]	71,822	29.5	72,906	29.6	73,494	29.7	75,573	30.3	75,780	30.1	76,203	30.0
Used in past month												
Illicit drugs[1]	19,720	8.1	20,357	8.3	19,857	8.0	20,077	8.0	21,813	8.7	22,622	8.9
Illicit drugs other than marijuana[1]	8,963	3.7	9,615	3.9	9,270	3.7	8,565	3.4	9,157	3.6	9,017	3.6
Used in past year												
Illicit drugs[1]	35,041	14.4	35,775	14.5	35,692	14.4	35,525	14.2	37,954	15.1	38,806	15.3
Marijuana and hashish	25,375	10.4	25,378	10.3	25,085	10.1	25,768	10.3	28,521	11.3	29,206	11.5
Illicit drugs other than marijuana[1]	20,109	8.3	21,254	8.6	21,144	8.5	19,990	8.0	21,000	8.3	20,576	8.1
Cocaine	5,523	2.3	6,069	2.5	5,738	2.3	5,255	2.1	4,797	1.9	4,499	1.8
Crack	1,381	0.6	1,479	0.6	1,451	0.6	1,109	0.4	1,016	0.4	871	0.3
Heroin	379	0.2	560	0.2	366	0.1	453	0.2	605	0.2	618	0.2
Hallucinogens	3,809	1.6	3,956	1.6	3,762	1.5	3,678	1.5	4,509	1.8	4,517	1.8
LSD	563	0.2	666	0.3	620	0.3	802	0.3	779	0.3	874	0.3
PCP	164	0.1	187	0.1	137	0.1	99	0.0	122	0.0	95	0.0
Ecstasy	1,960	0.8	2,130	0.9	2,132	0.9	2,139	0.9	2,799	1.1	2,645	1.0
Inhalants	2,187	0.9	2,218	0.9	2,080	0.8	2,047	0.8	2,090	0.8	2,030	0.8
Nonmedical use of psychotherapeutics[2]	15,346	6.3	16,482	6.7	16,280	6.6	15,166	6.1	16,006	6.4	16,031	6.3
Pain relievers	11,815	4.9	12,649	5.1	12,466	5.0	11,885	4.8	12,405	4.9	12,213	4.8
OxyContin®	1,226	0.5	1,323	0.5	1,422	0.6	1,459	0.6	1,677	0.7	1,869	0.7
Tranquilizers	5,249	2.2	5,058	2.1	5,282	2.1	5,103	2.0	5,460	2.2	5,581	2.2
Stimulants	3,088	1.3	3,791	1.5	2,998	1.2	2,639	1.1	3,060	1.2	2,887	1.1
Sedatives	750	0.3	926	0.4	864	0.3	621	0.2	811	0.3	907	0.4

(1) Includes marijuana/hashish, cocaine (including crack), heroin, hallucinogens, inhalants, or prescription-type psychotherapeutics used nonmedically. (2) Includes the nonmedical use of pain relievers, tranquilizers, stimulants, or sedatives but not over-the-counter drugs.

Lifetime Prevalence of Drug Use in 12th Graders, 1975-2011

Source: Monitoring the Future study, Univ. of Michigan Inst. for Social Research; National Institute on Drug Abuse
(percent who have ever used)

Drug	1975	1980	1985	1990	1995	2000	2005	2007	2008	2009	2010	2011	2010-11 change
Any illicit drug[1,2]	55.2%	65.4%	60.6%	47.9%	48.4%	54.0%	50.4%	46.8%	47.4%	46.7%	48.2%	49.9%	1.7%
Marijuana/hashish	47.3	60.3	54.2	40.7	41.7	48.8	44.8	41.8	42.6	42.0	43.8	45.5	1.7
Inhalants[3]	—	17.3	18.1	18.5	17.8	14.6	11.9	11.0	10.1	10.2	9.0	8.1	−0.9
Amyl/butyl nitrites[4]	—	11.1	7.9	2.1	1.5	0.8	1.1	1.2	0.6	1.1	—	—	—
Hallucinogens[5,6]	—	15.6	12.1	9.7	13.1	13.6	9.3	8.9	9.0	8.0	8.6	8.3	−0.2
LSD	11.3	9.3	7.5	8.7	11.7	11.1	3.5	3.4	4.0	3.1	4.0	4.0	0.0
PCP[4]	—	9.6	4.9	2.8	2.7	3.4	2.4	2.1	1.8	1.7	1.8	2.3	0.5
Ecstasy (MDMA)	—	—	—	—	—	11.0	5.4	6.5	6.2	6.5	7.3	8.0	0.7
Cocaine	9.0	15.7	17.3	9.4	6.0	8.6	8.0	7.8	7.2	6.0	5.5	5.2	−0.3
Crack	—	—	—	3.5	3.0	3.9	3.5	3.2	2.8	2.4	2.4	1.9	−0.5
Heroin (with and without a needle)	2.2	1.1	1.2	1.3	1.6	2.4	1.5	1.5	1.3	1.2	1.6	1.4	−0.1
Narcotics other than heroin[7,8]	9.0	9.8	10.2	8.3	7.2	10.6	12.8	13.1	13.2	13.2	13.0	13.0	0.0
Amphetamines[2,7]	22.3	26.4	26.2	17.5	15.3	15.6	13.1	11.4	10.5	9.9	11.1	12.2	1.1
Methamphetamine	—	—	—	—	—	7.9	4.5	3.0	2.8	2.4	2.3	2.1	−0.2
Crystal meth. (ice)	—	—	—	2.7	3.9	4.0	4.0	3.4	2.8	2.1	1.8	2.1	0.3
Sedatives (barbiturates)[7]	18.2	14.9	11.8	7.5	7.6	9.3	11.0	9.6	8.9	8.4	7.5	7.0	−0.5
Methaqualone[7]	8.1	9.5	6.7	2.3	1.2	0.8	1.3	1.0	0.8	0.7	0.4	0.6	0.2
Tranquilizers[5,7]	17.0	15.2	11.9	7.2	7.1	8.9	9.9	9.5	8.9	9.3	8.5	8.7	0.1
Alcohol[9]	90.4	93.2	92.2	89.5	80.7	80.3	75.1	72.2	71.9	72.3	71.0	70.0	−1.0
Cigarettes	73.6	71.0	68.8	64.4	64.2	62.5	50.0	46.2	44.7	43.6	42.2	40.0	−2.3
Smokeless tobacco	—	—	—	—	30.9	23.1	17.5	15.1	15.6	16.3	17.6	16.9	−0.8
Steroids[7]	—	—	—	2.9	2.3	2.5	2.6	2.2	2.2	2.2	2.0	1.8	−0.2

— = Not available. (1) Includes marijuana, LSD, other hallucinogens, crack, other cocaine, or heroin; or any use of narcotics other than heroin, amphetamines, sedatives (barbiturates), methaqualone (excluded since 1990), or tranquilizers not under a doctor's orders. (2) Because of changes to question wording, data from 1982 on are not directly comparable to data from prior years. (3) Not adjusted for underreporting of amyl and butyl nitrites. (4) Because of changes to question wording, data from 1987 on are not directly comparable to data from prior years. (5) Because of changes to question wording, data from 2001 on are not directly comparable to data from prior years. (6) Not adjusted for underreporting of PCP. (7) Includes only drug use not under a doctor's orders. (8) Because of changes to question wording, data from 2002 on are not directly comparable to data from prior years. (9) Because of changes to question wording, data from 1993 on are not directly comparable to data from prior years.

Cigarette Use in the U.S., 1985-2010

Source: National Survey on Drug Use and Health, Substance Abuse and Mental Health Services Admin. (SAMHSA), U.S. Dept. of Health and Human Services

(percentage reporting use in the month prior to the survey)

	1985	2000	2005	2008	2009	2010		1985	2000	2005	2008	2009	2010
Total[1]	38.7	24.9	24.9	23.9	23.3	23.0	**Race/ethnicity**						
							White, not Hispanic	38.9	25.9	26.0	25.2	24.5	24.3
Sex							Black, not Hispanic	38.0	23.3	24.5	24.8	22.8	22.6
Male	43.4	26.9	27.4	26.3	25.3	25.4	Hispanic	40.0	20.7	22.1	19.4	21.2	20.1
Female	34.5	23.1	22.5	21.7	21.4	20.7							
							Education[2]						
Age group							Non-high school graduate	37.3	32.4	34.8	34.4	35.4	34.3
12-17 years	29.4	13.4	10.8	9.1	8.9	8.3	High school graduate	37.0	31.1	31.8	30.6	30.0	29.6
18-25	47.4	38.3	39.0	35.7	35.8	34.2	Some college	32.6	27.7	28.1	26.6	25.4	25.8
26 years and older	45.7[3]	24.2	24.3	23.8	23.0	22.8	College graduate	23.0	13.9	13.8	14.0	13.1	12.8

(1) Persons 12 years of age and older. (2) Persons aged 18 and older. (3) Persons aged 26 to 34 only.

Daily Use of Cigarettes by 8th, 10th, and 12th Graders, 1995-2011

Source: Monitoring the Future study, Univ. of Michigan Inst. for Social Research; National Inst. on Drug Abuse
(percent who smoked daily in last 30 days)

	8th grade						10th grade						12th grade					
	1995	2000	2005	2010	2011	2010-11 change	1995	2000	2005	2010	2011	2010-11 change	1995	2000	2005	2010	2011	2010-11 change
Total	9.3%	7.4%	4.0%	2.9%	2.4%	−0.5%	16.3%	14.0%	7.5%	6.6%	5.5%	−1.0%	21.6%	20.6%	13.6%	10.7%	10.3%	−0.5%
Sex																		
Male	9.2	7.0	3.9	3.5	2.5	−1.1	16.3	13.7	7.2	7.2	6.4	−0.8	21.7	20.9	14.6	12.3	11.6	−0.7
Female	9.2	7.5	4.0	2.3	2.2	−0.1	16.1	14.1	7.7	5.9	4.5	−1.4	20.8	19.7	11.9	8.7	8.6	−0.1
College plans																		
None or under 4 yrs.	22.5	21.7	14.4	12.8	8.1	−4.7	32.7	28.8	19.2	19.1	17.1	−2.0	33.7	31.7	24.9	21.6	21.0	−0.6
Complete 4 yrs.	7.5	5.6	2.9	2.0	1.9	−0.1	13.3	11.6	5.9	5.0	4.2	−0.9	17.4	16.6	10.5	8.2	7.9	−0.3
Region																		
Northeast	9.2	6.9	3.2	2.4	1.4	−0.9	15.8	14.1	7.6	5.7	6.3	0.6	22.5	22.8	13.3	10.3	10.2	0.0
Midwest	11.0	9.0	4.8	3.3	2.3	−1.0	17.6	16.3	8.6	7.3	5.7	−1.6	25.7	23.6	16.3	12.5	11.7	−0.9
South	9.4	7.8	5.0	3.8	2.9	−0.9	19.3	15.7	8.8	7.9	6.6	−1.3	21.7	19.4	15.4	12.3	10.8	−1.4
West	7.0	4.9	2.4	1.4	2.3	0.9	9.4	7.8	4.0	4.4	3.0	−1.3	14.5	16.9	7.6	6.7	7.9	1.3
Race/ethnicity[1]																		
White	10.5	9.0	4.6	3.2	3.0	−0.2	23.9	25.7	17.1	7.4	7.1	−0.3	23.9	25.7	17.1	13.5	13.0	−0.5
Black	2.8	3.2	2.1	1.9	1.5	−0.4	6.1	8.0	5.6	3.5	3.5	0.0	6.1	8.0	5.6	5.3	4.9	−0.5
Hispanic	9.2	7.1	3.1	2.3	2.4	0.1	11.6	15.7	7.7	4.4	3.8	−0.6	11.6	15.7	7.7	5.7	5.3	−0.4

Note: Figures may not add up to totals because of rounding. (1) For each of these groups, data for the specified year and previous year have been combined to increase sample size and thus provide a more reliable estimate.

Alcohol Use by 8th and 12th Graders, 1980-2011

Source: Monitoring the Future study, Univ. of Michigan Inst. for Social Research; National Inst. on Drug Abuse

	1980	1990	1995	2000	2005	2007	2008	2009	2010	2011	2010-11 change
Alcohol use[1]			Percent using alcohol in the month before the survey								
All 12th graders	72.0%	57.1%	51.3%	50.0%	47.0%	44.4%	43.1%	43.5%	41.2%	40.0%	−1.2%
Male	77.4	61.3	55.7	54.0	50.7	47.1	45.8	47.8	44.2	42.1	−2.1
Female	66.8	52.3	47.0	46.1	43.3	41.4	40.9	38.9	37.9	37.5	−0.4
White	75.4	63.8	54.5	55.1	52.3	49.3	48.6	47.2	45.4	43.8	−1.6
Black	47.6	35.8	35.2	30.0	29.0	28.7	28.6	30.5	31.4	30.1	−1.3
Hispanic	63.6	49.1	48.7	51.2	43.3	41.4	38.9	40.1	40.1	39.7	−0.4
All 8th graders	—	—	24.6	22.4	17.1	15.9	15.9	14.9	13.8	12.7	−1.1
Male	—	—	25.0	22.5	16.2	15.6	15.4	14.7	13.2	12.1	−1.1
Female	—	—	24.0	22.0	17.9	16.0	16.4	14.9	14.3	12.8	−1.5
White	—	—	25.4	24.7	17.9	15.6	15.2	15.4	13.9	12.3	−1.6
Black	—	—	18.7	16.0	14.9	12.3	12.9	12.3	11.8	11.6	−0.2
Hispanic	—	—	32.4	26.7	20.6	23.0	21.5	19.2	18.1	18.0	−0.1
Heavy alcohol use[2]			Percent heavily using in the 2 weeks before the survey								
All 12th graders	41.2%	32.2%	29.8%	30.0%	27.1%	25.9%	24.6%	25.2%	23.2%	21.6%	−1.5%
Male	52.1	39.1	36.9	36.7	32.6	30.7	28.4	30.5	28.0	25.5	−2.6
Female	30.5	24.4	23.0	23.5	21.6	21.5	21.3	20.2	18.4	17.6	−0.8
White	44.3	36.6	32.3	34.6	32.5	29.7	29.9	29.0	27.6	25.9	−1.7
Black	17.7	14.4	14.9	11.5	11.3	11.5	10.9	12.0	13.1	11.3	−1.8
Hispanic	33.1	25.6	26.6	31.0	23.9	22.5	21.5	22.6	22.1	20.8	−1.3
All 8th graders	—	—	12.3	11.7	8.4	8.3	8.1	7.8	7.2	6.4	−0.7
Male	—	—	12.5	11.7	8.2	8.2	8.1	7.8	6.5	6.1	−0.4
Female	—	—	12.1	11.3	8.6	8.2	8.0	7.7	7.8	6.5	−1.3
White	—	—	12.1	13.0	9.0	8.0	7.8	7.7	7.1	6.2	−0.8
Black	—	—	8.3	7.3	6.1	5.6	5.7	5.2	5.3	5.1	−0.1
Hispanic	—	—	18.4	16.0	12.1	12.5	12.3	11.5	10.8	10.4	−0.4

— = Data not available. **Note:** Monitoring the Future study excludes high school dropouts (about 3%-6% of the class group) and absentees (about 16%-17% of 12th graders and 9%-10% of 8th graders). These pops. have higher alcohol usage than those surveyed. (1) Since 1993 the alcohol question has indicated that a "drink" is defined as "more than a few sips." (2) Five or more drinks in a row at least once in the prior 2-week period.

Acquired Immune Deficiency Syndrome (AIDS)

Source: Centers for Disease Control and Prevention

AIDS (Acquired Immune Deficiency Syndrome) is caused by the human immunodeficiency virus (**HIV**). HIV kills or disables crucial immune cells, progressively destroying the body's ability to fight disease.

HIV is commonly **spread** through unprotected sexual contact with an infected partner's semen or vaginal fluids. It is also spread through contact with infected blood. Where modern screening techniques are used, it is rare to contract HIV from transfusion or organ/tissue transplants. But it can be contracted when intravenous drug users share syringes and similar equipment with others. A woman can also transmit HIV to her child during pregnancy or delivery or through breastfeeding. With treatment, a woman can reduce her transmission rate from about 25% to less than 2%. There is no evidence HIV can spread through saliva or casual contact such as in the sharing of food utensils, towels and bedding, telephones, or toilet seats.

Some people experience flu-like symptoms a short time after infection with HIV. Even when symptoms are not present, HIV is active in the body, multiplying, infecting, and killing crucial CD4+ T cells, also known as T-lymphocytes or T-helper cells, which signal other immune cells to perform their functions.

The term AIDS applies to the most advanced stages of HIV infection. According to the official case definition issued by the Centers for Disease Control and Prevention (CDC), an HIV-infected person with fewer than 200 CD4+ T cells per cubic millimeter of blood can be said to have AIDS. (Healthy adults usually have 1,000 or more per cubic millimeter.) An HIV-infected person, regardless of T cell count, is diagnosed with AIDS if he or she develops 1 of 26 conditions that typically affect people with advanced HIV. Most of these conditions are opportunistic infections that occur when the immune system is so ravaged by HIV that the body cannot fight off certain bacteria, viruses, and microbes.

Months or years prior to the onset of AIDS, people may experience such **symptoms** as swollen glands, lack of energy, fevers and sweats, and skin rashes. People diagnosed with AIDS may develop infections of the intestinal tract, lungs, brain, eyes, and other organs and become severely debilitated. They also are prone to developing certain cancers, especially those caused by viruses, such as Kaposi's sarcoma, cervical cancer, and lymphoma. Children with AIDS may have delayed development or fail to thrive.

HIV is primarily **detected** by testing a person's blood for the presence of antibodies (disease-fighting proteins of the immune system) to HIV. In very rare cases, HIV antibodies may take more than six months after exposure to reach detectable levels. But in 97% of infected individuals, the antibodies are detectable in the first three months. HIV testing may also be performed on oral fluid and urine samples. Rapid HIV tests can provide preliminary results in about 20 minutes.

Patients are typically given a combination of different **drugs** to prevent the HIV virus from becoming resistant to any single one. While these drugs extend the period of time between HIV infection and the development of serious illness, they do not prevent the spread of the disease to others and can have severe side effects.

The U.S. Food and Drug Administration (FDA) has approved a number of drugs that may slow the growth of HIV in the body and treat AIDS-related infections and cancers. The first group of drugs used to treat HIV—nucleoside reverse transcriptase inhibitors (NRTIs)—include the drug zidovudine (commonly known as AZT). Non-nucleoside reverse transcriptase inhibitors (NNRTIs), as well as a third class of drugs, called protease inhibitors, have also been approved for HIV treatment. In 2003, the FDA granted accelerated approval of Fuzeon for use with other anti-HIV drugs. Fuzeon was the first among a new class of medications called fusion inhibitors; drugs in this class interfere with HIV's entry into cells by hindering the fusion of viral and cellular membranes.

The FDA in July 2006 approved Atripla, the first once-a-day, single-pill drug combination treatment for HIV. The pill combined three previously approved drugs and was regarded as a significant milestone in HIV treatment. FDA officials said complicated drug regimens dissuaded patients from taking their pills as directed.

In 2007, the FDA approved raltegravir, the first of a new class of HIV drugs called integrase inhibitors. Raltegravir is taken with other anti-HIV medications.

Since there is no vaccine or cure for AIDS, the only **protection** is to avoid activities that carry a risk. The CDC recommends abstinence (the only certain protection) if a potential partner's HIV status is unknown, mutual monogamy with an uninfected partner, or correct and consistent use of male latex condoms.

New AIDS Diagnoses in the U.S., by Transmission Category, 1985-2010

Source: *HIV Surveillance Report, 2010*; National Center for HIV/AIDS, Viral Hepatitis, STD, and TB Prevention; Centers for Disease Control and Prevention

Transmission category	All years[1]	1985	1990	2000	2005	2007	2008	2009	2010
All males 13 years of age and older	**893,058**	**7,504**	**36,193**	**30,251**	**27,436**	**24,979**	**24,735**	**24,507**	**24,749**
Male-to-male sexual contact.....................	541,330	5,348	23,658	13,648	16,824	15,966	15,908	16,317	16,796
Injection drug use............................	186,122	1,103	6,923	5,554	4,350	3,332	3,103	2,738	2,745
Male-to-male sexual contact and injection drug use	79,048	661	2,943	1,587	2,085	1,786	1,713	1,543	1,446
Heterosexual contact[2].......................	74,708	32	715	2,537	3,920	3,747	3,846	3,771	3,629
Other[3].....................................	11,851	—	—	—	256	148	164	138	133
All females 13 years of age and older	**226,593**	**524**	**4,547**	**9,979**	**9,799**	**9,304**	**8,839**	**8,421**	**8,242**
Injection drug use............................	88,400	287	2,347	2,545	2,724	2,306	2,097	1,878	1,752
Heterosexual contact[2].......................	131,904	119	1,538	4,025	6,856	6,835	6,624	6,410	6,364
Other[3].....................................	6,289	—	—	—	219	163	117	133	127
All children, under 13 years of age	**9,475**	**—**	**—**	**—**	**55**	**36**	**39**	**14**	**23**
Perinatal....................................	8,617	—	—	—	50	34	34	13	18
Other[4].....................................	859	—	—	—	5	2	5	1	4

Note: The definition of AIDS cases for reporting purposes was expanded in 1985, 1987, and 1993, as more was learned about the spectrum of human immunodeficiency virus-associated diseases. (1) Includes cases for years not shown, from the beginning of the epidemic (1981) through 2010. (2) Heterosexual contact with a person known to have or be at high risk for HIV infection. (3) Includes hemophilia, blood transfusion, perinatal exposure, and risk factors not reported or not identified. (4) Includes hemophilia, blood transfusion, and risk factors not reported or not identified.

AIDS Deaths and New AIDS Diagnoses in the U.S., 1981-2010

Source: HIV/AIDS Surveillance Supplemental Report; *Health, United States*; Office of Analysis and Epidemiology, National Center for Health Statistics, Centers for Disease Control and Prevention

	% of total, all years	All years[1]	2006	2007	2008	2009
DEATHS OF PERSONS DIAGNOSED WITH AIDS, BY YEAR[2]	—	602,340	NA	15,681	14,600	13,050
CASES, BY YEAR AIDS FIRST DIAGNOSED						
All persons[3]	100.0%	1,108,611	36,151	35,434	34,755	34,247
All males, 13 years of age and older	79.2%	878,366	26,473	25,871	25,612	25,587
Race/origin						
Not of Hispanic origin						
White	43.5	381,898	8,923	8,511	8,239	8,121
Black	36.9	323,872	11,093	10,968	11,042	11,093
Asian[4]	0.8	7,068	348	370	399	349
Native Hawaiian or other Pacific Islander	0.1	695	35	42	35	43
American Indian or Alaska Native	0.3	2,879	115	100	137	127
Hispanic[5]	17.3	152,310	5,483	5,418	5,313	5,359
Age diagnosed						
13-14 years	0.1	712	27	31	27	25
15-24 years	4.0	34,949	1,454	1,728	1,795	2,031
25-34 years	31.0	272,485	5,404	5,386	5,452	5,648
35-44 years	39.5	346,798	10,043	9,168	8,550	7,864
45-54 years	18.4	161,665	6,712	6,870	6,837	7,060
55-64 years	5.5	48,138	2,209	2,124	2,343	2,358
65 years and over	1.6	13,618	625	564	610	603
All females, 13 years of age and older	19.9%	220,795	9,639	9,531	9,102	8,647
Race/origin						
Not of Hispanic origin						
White	19.3	42,602	1,558	1,534	1,421	1,344
Black	61.9	136,690	6,177	6,179	6,000	5,639
Asian[4]	0.5	1,208	73	84	88	80
Native Hawaiian or other Pacific Islander	0.1	136	15	10	5	7
American Indian or Alaska Native	0.4	789	30	41	39	28
Hispanic[5]	16.3	36,091	1,578	1,490	1,385	1,357
Age diagnosed						
13-14 years	0.3	609	51	50	31	33
15-24 years	6.9	15,185	580	601	554	548
25-34 years	32.3	71,302	2,227	2,088	2,124	1,871
35-44 years	36.7	81,013	3,371	3,253	3,038	2,718
45-54 years	16.8	37,042	2,439	2,460	2,342	2,389
55-64 years	5.2	11,518	759	852	823	844
65 years and over	1.9	4,125	211	228	190	243
All children, under 13 years of age	0.9%	9,448	39	31	40	13
Race/origin						
Not of Hispanic origin						
White	17.0	1,602	3	4	7	1
Black	61.3	5,787	30	22	23	8
Asian[4]	0.5	48	1	0	2	0
Native Hawaiian or other Pacific Islander	0.1	7	0	0	0	0
American Indian or Alaska Native	0.3	31	0	0	0	0
Hispanic[5]	19.7	1,862	4	4	3	3

NA = Not available. **Note:** Data are for the 50 states and DC and are based on reporting by state and DC health departments. (1) Based on cases reported to the CDC from the beginning of the epidemic (1981) through June 30, 2010. (2) Deaths may be due to any cause. (3) Total for all years includes 306 persons of unknown races and 2 persons of unknown sex. (4) Includes persons formerly classified as "Asian or Pacific Islander," before new race categories were implemented in 2003. (5) May be of any race.

Allergies and Asthma

Source: Asthma and Allergy Foundation of America

An estimated one in five Americans suffers from **allergies**. People with allergies have immune systems that react to defend the body against normally harmless substances. Common allergens—the substances that may trigger such a response—include plant pollens, dust mites, or animal dander; plants such as poison ivy; certain drugs, such as penicillin; and foods such as eggs, milk, wheat, nuts, or seafood.

The **tendency to develop allergies** is usually inherited. While allergies typically manifest in childhood, they can show up at any age. Food allergies and eczema (patches of dry skin) are common allergies among infants. Older children and adults may develop allergic rhinitis, or hay fever, in reaction to an inhaled allergen. Allergic rhinitis symptoms include nasal congestion, runny nose, and sneezing.

People with allergies should avoid contact with an allergen, if feasible. **Medications**, such as antihistamines and nasal steroids, may be used to decrease an allergic reaction. Other effective allergy treatments include decongestants, eye drops, and ointments. There are also treatments aimed at gradually desensitizing a patient to an allergen.

Some allergy sufferers also have **asthma**. Asthma, which can develop at any age, is a chronic inflammation disease affecting the passageways that carry air into and out of the lungs. During what is known as an asthma attack, these inflamed, supersensitive airways tighten and fill with mucus. A person may experience wheezing, difficulty breathing, tightening of the chest, and coughing. Exposure to an allergen can set off an attack. Asthma can become life-threatening if not controlled in its early stages. The following **symptoms** may be indicative of an emergency: the patient shows no improvement minutes after initial treatment; struggles to breathe while hunched over with his or her chest and neck pulled in; has trouble walking or talking; and develops gray or blue lips or fingernails.

Besides common allergens, tobacco smoke, cold air, and pollution can trigger an asthma attack, as can viral infections or physical exercise. An accurate diagnosis by a physician is important. Although there is no cure for asthma or allergies, they can be controlled through lifestyle changes and medications.

Website: www.aafa.org

Alzheimer's Disease

Source: Alzheimer's Association

Alzheimer's disease, the most common form of dementia, is a progressive, degenerative brain disease in which nerve cells deteriorate and die. Its first symptoms usually involve impaired memory and confusion about recent events. As the disease advances, it results in greater impairment of memory, thinking, judgment, language, behavior, and physical health.

The **rate of progression** of Alzheimer's varies, ranging from 4 to 20 years. The average length of time from onset of symptoms until death is five years. As they become progressively debilitated, affected individuals grow increasingly susceptible to infections of the lungs, urinary tract, and other organs.

Alzheimer's disease affects an estimated 5.4 mil Americans, striking men and women of all races and ethnicities. Almost two-thirds of all Americans living with Alzheimer's are women. Although most people are older than age 65 when diagnosed with Alzheimer's, younger-onset, or early-onset, cases occur in people in their 40s and 50s. An estimated 13% of the U.S. population over age 65 has Alzheimer's.

Diagnosis involves a comprehensive evaluation that may include a complete health history, physical examination, neurological and mental status assessments, and other tests. Skilled health care professionals can generally diagnose Alzheimer's with more than 90% accuracy. Depression, drug interactions, nutritional imbalances, and infections such as AIDS, meningitis, and syphilis can cause similar symptoms. Other forms of dementia, such as those associated with stroke, Huntington's disease, Parkinson's disease, frontotemporal dementia, and vascular disease, can also appear to be Alzheimer's. Absolute confirmation of diagnosis requires a brain biopsy or autopsy.

Treatments for cognitive and behavioral symptoms are available, but no intervention has yet been developed to prevent Alzheimer's or reverse its course. The U.S. Food and Drug Administration has approved five drugs that temporarily slow worsening of symptoms for about six to twelve months. They are effective for only about half of the individuals who take them. Some research suggests that risk factors for heart disease, such as high blood pressure, elevated cholesterol, diabetes, and excess body weight, may increase a person's risk of developing Alzheimer's. Staying physically and mentally active and socially connected may be associated with a lower risk for the disease.

Providing **care** for people with Alzheimer's is physically and psychologically demanding. About 60%-70% of affected individuals live at home, where family or friends tend to them without pay. In the disease's advanced stages, many individuals require long-term residential care. Nearly half of all nursing home residents in the U.S. have Alzheimer's.

The costs of diagnosing, treating, and providing long-term care in this country for Alzheimer's patients are estimated to be $200 bil in 2012. People with Alzheimer's need a safe, stable environment and a regular daily schedule offering appropriate stimulation. Physical exercise and social interaction are important, as are proper nutrition and adequate pain management. Security is also a consideration, because many people with Alzheimer's tend to wander. An identification bracelet with the person's name, address, and condition may help ensure the safe return of an individual who wanders.

Website: www.alz.org

Warning Signs of Alzheimer's Disease

- Memory loss that disrupts daily life
- Challenges in planning or solving problems
- Difficulty completing familiar tasks at home, at work, or at leisure
- Confusion with time or place
- Trouble understanding visual images and spatial relationships
- New problems with words in speaking or writing
- Misplacing things and losing the ability to retrace steps
- Decreased or poor judgment
- Withdrawal from work or social activities
- Changes in mood and personality

Arthritis

Source: Arthritis Foundation; Centers for Disease Control and Prevention

The term arthritis refers to more than 100 different diseases that cause pain, stiffness, swelling, and restricted movement in joints. The condition is usually chronic. The CDC estimates that 50 mil adults in the United States report being told by a doctor that they had arthritis. Arthritis annually results in 44 mil ambulatory care visits and an estimated 992,100 hospitalizations. The **cause** for most types of arthritis is unknown; scientists are studying the roles played by genetics, lifestyle, and environment.

Symptoms may develop slowly or suddenly. A visit to the doctor is indicated when pain, stiffness, swelling in a joint, or difficulty in moving a joint persists for more than two weeks. To **diagnose** arthritis, the doctor records the patient's symptoms and examines his or her joints, looking for any swelling or limited movement. In addition, the doctor checks for other signs often seen with arthritis, such as rashes, mouth sores, or eye involvement. The doctor may test blood, urine, or joint fluid, or take X-rays of the joints.

Of the three most prevalent forms of arthritis, **osteoarthritis** is the most common, affecting approximately 27 mil Americans. It usually occurs after age 45. In patients with osteoarthritis, also called degenerative arthritis, the protective cartilage of joints is lost and changes occur in the bone, leading to pain and stiffness. It usually occurs in the fingers, knees, feet, hips, neck, and back.

Fibromyalgia, another common arthritis condition, affects about 5 mil Americans. People suffering from fibromyalgia experience widespread pain and tenderness in muscles and their attachments to bone. Common symptoms include fatigue, disturbed sleep, stiffness, and psychological distress. More women than men are afflicted with this type of arthritis.

Rheumatoid arthritis, which affects an estimated 1.5 mil in the U.S., is one of the most serious and disabling forms of the disease. In this type—which is also more common and more degenerative in women—inflammation of the joints leads to cartilage and bone damage. The areas of the body that can be affected are the hands, wrists, feet, knees, ankles, and elbows.

Other forms of arthritis and related conditions include lupus, gout, ankylosing spondylitis, and scleroderma. Bursitis and tendinitis, which may result from injuring or overusing a joint, are also related.

Medications that relieve pain and swelling, such as analgesics, anti-inflammatory drugs, biologic response modifiers, glucocorticoids, and antirheumatic drugs, can be used to treat arthritis. They also tend to slow the disease process. Most treatment programs call for exercise, use of heat or cold, and joint-protection techniques, such as avoidance of excess stress on the joints, the use of assistive devices, and weight loss and control. In some cases, surgery may help.

Website: www.arthritis.org

Cancer Prevention

Source: American Cancer Society, Inc., www.cancer.org

PRIMARY PREVENTION: Modifiable determinants of cancer risk.

Smoking	The risk of developing lung cancer is about 23 times higher for current male smokers and 13 times higher for current female smokers than for those who have never smoked. Smoking accounts for at least 30% of all U.S. cancer deaths. Tobacco use is responsible for nearly 1 in 5 deaths in the U.S. Smoking increases the risk of the following types of cancer: nasopharynx, nasal cavity and paranasal sinuses, lip, oral cavity (mouth, tongue, lips), pharynx, larynx, lung, esophagus, pancreas, cervix, ovary (mucinous), kidney, bladder, stomach, colorectum, and acute myeloid leukemia.
Diet and physical activity	Overweight and obesity are associated with increased risk for developing many cancers, including cancers of the breast in postmenopausal women, colon and rectum, endometrium, kidney, pancreas, and adenocarcinoma of the esophagus. Over-weight and obesity may also be associated with increased risk of cancers of the liver, non-Hodgkin lymphoma, multiple myeloma, cervix, ovary, and aggressive prostate cancer. Obesity likely increases the risk of cancer of the gallbladder. In addition, abdominal fatness is convincingly associated with colorectal cancer, and probably related to higher risk of pancreatic, endometrial, and postmenopausal breast cancers. It's not yet known for certain how diet, nutrition intake, and the amount and distribution of body fat factor into the development of certain cancers. But eating a mostly plant-based diet, with grains and beans and five or more servings of fruits and vegetables each day, and regular physical activity can help one achieve and maintain a healthy weight. That in turn may reduce the risk for many cancers.
Sunlight	Many of the more than 3.5 mil skin cancers diagnosed annually in the U.S. could have been prevented by protection from the sun's rays and avoiding indoor tanning. Epidemiological evidence shows that sun exposure is a major factor in the development of melanoma and that incidence rates are increasing worldwide.
Alcohol	Alcohol consumption increases the risk of cancers of the mouth, pharynx, larynx, esophagus, liver, colorectum, and breast. Alcohol consumption combined with tobacco use increases the risk of cancers of the mouth, larynx, and esophagus far more than either drinking or smoking alone.
Smokeless tobacco	Use of chewing tobacco, snuff, and other tobacco products that are not smoked causes oral, esophageal, and pancreatic cancers. The excess risk of cancer of the cheek and gum is especially high among long-term snuff users.
Estrogen	Menopausal hormone therapy (MHT, formerly called hormone replacement therapy) without the use of progestin can increase the risk of endometrial and ovarian cancer. Combining progestin with estrogen MHT may help minimize that risk. Studies, however, suggest that use of MHT increases the risk of breast cancer. The benefits and risks of the use of estrogen by menopausal women should be discussed carefully with one's doctor.
Radiation	Excessive exposure to ionizing radiation can increase cancer risk. Medical and dental X-rays are adjusted to deliver the lowest dose possible without sacrificing image quality. Excessive radon exposure in the home may increase lung cancer risk, especially in cigarette smokers.
Environmental hazards	Exposure to various chemicals (including benzene, asbestos, vinyl chloride, arsenic, and aflatoxin) increases risk of various cancers. Risk of lung cancer from asbestos is greatly increased among smokers.
Vaccination	There are two vaccines approved for the prevention of the most common types of HPV infection that cause cervical cancer; Gardasil is recommended for use in females 9-26 years of age and Cervarix in females 9-25 years of age.

Screening Guidelines for Early Detection of Cancer

SECONDARY PREVENTION: Steps to diagnose a cancer or precursor as early as possible after it has developed in asymptomatic people.

Cancer site	Population	Test or procedure	Frequency
Breast	Women, age 20+	Breast self-examination (BSE)	Beginning in their early 20s: women should be told about BSE. Prompt reporting of any new breast symptoms to a health professional should be emphasized. Women should receive instruction and have their technique reviewed at a periodic health exam.
		Clinical breast examination (CBE)	Women in their 20s and 30s: CBE should be part of a periodic health exam, preferably at least every 3 years. Asymptomatic women aged 40+ should continue to receive a CBE as part of a periodic health exam, preferably annually.
		Mammography	At age 40: begin annual mammography. A clinical breast examination should be performed prior to mammography.
Cervix	Women, age 21+	Pap test, HPV DNA test	All women, including those vaccinated against HPV, should begin screening by age 21. Women ages 21-29 should have a Pap test every 3 years. From ages 30-65, the preferred way to screen is with a Pap test combined with an HPV test every 5 years. Another option is to get tested every 3 years with just the Pap test. (Women who are at high risk of cervical cancer may need to be screened more often.) Women ages 65+ who have had regular screening in the previous 10 years should consult a physician; health history may allow them to stop cervical cancer screening. Women who have had a total hysterectomy may stop screening, unless the hysterectomy was done as a treatment for cervical cancer or precancer.
Colorectal	Men and women, age 50+	Fecal occult blood test (FOBT) with at least 50% test sensitivity for cancer, or fecal immunochemical test (FIT) with at least 50% test sensitivity for cancer, **or**	Annual, starting at age 50. Testing at home with adherence to manufacturer's recommendation for collection techniques and number of samples is recommended. FOBT with the single stool sample collected on the clinician's fingertip during a digital rectal examination in a health care setting is not recommended. Guaiac-based toilet bowl FOBT tests also are not recommended. In comparison with guaiac-based tests for the detection of occult blood, immunochemical tests are more patient-friendly and are likely to be equal or better in sensitivity and specificity. There is no need to repeat an FOBT in response to an initial positive finding.
		Stool DNA test, **or**	Interval uncertain, starting at age 50
		Flexible sigmoidoscopy (FSIG), **or**	Every 5 years, starting at age 50. FSIG can be performed alone, or consideration can be given to combining FSIG performed every 5 years with a highly sensitive gFOBT or FIT performed annually.
		Double contrast barium enema (DCBE), **or**	Every 5 years, starting at age 50
		Colonoscopy	Every 10 years, starting at age 50
		CT Colonography	Every 5 years, starting at age 50
Endometrial	Women, at menopause	Women at average risk should be informed about risks and symptoms of endometrial cancer and strongly encouraged to report any unexpected bleeding or spotting to their physicians.	
Prostate	Men, age 50+	Digital rectal examination (DRE) and prostate-specific antigen test (PSA)	Men who have at least a 10-year life expectancy should make an informed decision with their health care provider about whether to be screened for prostate cancer after receiving information about the potential benefits, risks, and uncertainties associated with prostate cancer screening. Screening should not occur without an informed decision-making process.
Cancer-related checkup	Men and women, age 20+	On the occasion of a periodic health exam, the cancer-related checkup should include examination for cancers of the thyroid, testicles, ovaries, lymph nodes, oral cavity, and skin, as well as health counseling about tobacco, sun exposure, diet and nutrition, risk factors, sexual practices, and environmental and occupational exposures.	

Estimated New U.S. Cancer Cases and Deaths for Leading Sites, 2012

Source: *Cancer Facts & Figures 2012*, American Cancer Society, Inc.

The following estimates exclude basal and squamous cell skin cancers and in situ carcinomas (i.e., noninvasive cancers), except of the urinary bladder. In 2012, an estimated 63,300 new cases of carcinoma in situ of the breast and 55,560 cases of melanoma in situ are expected to be diagnosed. More than 2 mil cases of basal cell and squamous cell cancer are diagnosed yearly. They are highly curable forms of skin cancer.

Estimated New Cases

Both sexes		Male		Female	
Prostate	241,740	Prostate	241,740	Breast	226,870
Breast	229,060	Lung and bronchus	116,470	Lung and bronchus	109,690
Lung and bronchus	226,160	Urinary bladder	55,600	Colon	53,250
Colon	103,170	Colon	49,920	Uterine corpus	47,130
Melanoma—skin	76,250	Melanoma—skin	44,250	Thyroid	43,210
Urinary bladder	73,510	Kidney and renal pelvis	40,250	Melanoma—skin	32,000
Non-Hodgkin lymphoma	70,130	Non-Hodgkin lymphoma	38,160	Non-Hodgkin lymphoma	31,970
Kidney and renal pelvis	64,770	Rectum	23,500	Kidney and renal pelvis	24,520
Thyroid	56,460	Pancreas	22,090	Ovary	22,280
Uterine corpus	47,130	Liver and intrahepatic bile duct	21,370	Pancreas	21,830
All sites	**1,638,910**	**All sites**	**848,170**	**All sites**	**790,740**

Estimated Deaths

Both sexes		Male		Female	
Lung and bronchus	160,340	Lung and bronchus	87,750	Lung and bronchus	72,590
Colon and rectum	51,690	Prostate	28,170	Breast	39,510
Breast	39,920	Colon and rectum	26,470	Colon and rectum	25,220
Pancreas	37,390	Pancreas	18,850	Pancreas	18,540
Prostate	28,170	Liver and intrahepatic bile duct	13,980	Ovary	15,500
Liver and intrahepatic bile duct	20,550	Esophagus	12,040	Non-Hodgkin lymphoma	8,620
Non-Hodgkin lymphoma	18,940	Urinary bladder	10,510	Uterine corpus	8,010
Ovary	15,500	Non-Hodgkin lymphoma	10,320	Liver and intrahepatic bile duct	6,570
Esophagus	15,070	Kidney and renal pelvis	8,650	Brain and other nervous system	5,980
Urinary bladder	14,880	Brain and other nervous system	7,720	Kidney and renal pelvis	4,920
All sites	**577,190**	**All sites**	**301,820**	**All sites**	**275,370**

U.S. Cancer Survival Rates by Year of Diagnosis, 1960-2008

Source: SEER (Surveillance, Epidemiology, and End Results) Cancer Statistics Review, 1975-2009, National Cancer Institute, National Institutes of Health

	All Races			White			Black		
Year	% Total	% Male	% Female	% Total	% Male	% Female	% Total	% Male	% Female
1960-63	—	—	—	39.0%	—	—	27.0%	—	—
1970-73	—	—	—	43.0	—	—	31.0	—	—
1975-77	49.1%	42.0%	56.0%	50.0	42.9%	56.7%	39.2	32.9%	46.4%
1978-80	49.2	43.3	55.1	50.1	44.5	55.7	39.0	33.4	45.7
1981-83	50.4	45.4	55.3	51.5	46.8	56.2	39.0	34.3	44.6
1984-86	52.5	47.3	57.7	53.8	48.8	58.7	40.2	35.6	45.5
1987-89	55.5	51.4	59.8	56.8	53.0	60.8	43.1	39.0	47.8
1990-92	60.1	59.3	61.0	61.5	61.0	62.2	47.9	47.7	48.3
1993-95	61.4	61.0	61.9	62.5	62.2	63.0	52.8	54.4	50.7
1996-98	63.4	63.1	63.8	64.5	64.2	64.8	55.1	57.8	52.1
1999-2001	66.1	66.4	65.8	67.3	67.6	66.9	57.8	60.9	54.1
2002-08	67.7	68.5	66.9	68.9	69.7	68.0	59.9	63.6	55.8

— = Statistic could not be calculated. **Note:** The geographic areas of surveillance may vary for different years. Rates are five-year relative (estimated) survival rates for all invasive cancer sites; based on follow-up of patients into 2009.

U.S. Cancer Survival Rates by Age at Diagnosis, 2002-08

Source: SEER (Surveillance, Epidemiology, and End Results) Cancer Statistics Review, 1975-2009, National Cancer Institute, National Institutes of Health

	All Races			White			Black		
Age	% Total	% Male	% Female	% Total	% Male	% Female	% Total	% Male	% Female
Under age 45	80.0%	75.0%	83.2%	81.6%	77.1%	84.6%	67.9%	60.7%	72.2%
Ages 45-54	72.0	66.3	76.7	73.6	67.8	78.5	60.6	58.8	62.4
Ages 55-64	69.0	68.9	69.0	69.8	69.6	70.2	61.6	64.7	56.7
Under age 65	72.3	69.2	75.3	73.5	70.4	76.6	62.5	62.2	62.9
Ages 65 and older	58.3	62.9	52.8	58.8	63.0	53.9	52.3	60.4	42.7
Ages 65-74	64.6	68.0	59.7	65.1	68.2	60.8	59.1	65.9	48.9
Ages 75 and older	52.0	56.8	47.4	52.7	57.0	48.6	42.8	50.3	36.4

Note: Rates are five-year relative (estimated) survival rates for all invasive cancer sites; based on follow-up of patients into 2009.

Breast Cancer

Source: American Cancer Society, Inc.

In 2012, an estimated 226,870 women and 2,190 men in the U.S. will be newly diagnosed with breast cancer, and about 39,920 women and 410 men will die from it. Currently, an estimated 2.6 mil women are living with a history of breast cancer, the second biggest cause of cancer death for women in the U.S. (lung cancer ranks first). But mortality rates have been declining, especially among younger women, probably because of earlier detection and improved treatment.

The **risk** for breast cancer increases with age. It is higher for women with a personal or family history of cancer, a long menstrual history (menstrual periods that started early and ended later in life), recent use of birth control pills, recent and long-term use of menopausal hormone therapy containing estrogen and progestin, and who have no children or had no live birth until age 30 or older. Other risk factors include alcohol consumption and obesity. Inherited mutations such as in the BRCA1 and BRCA2 genes greatly increase risk, but these probably account for 5% to 10% of all breast cancers. By far the majority of women who develop breast cancer have no family history of it.

Breast cancer often manifests first as an abnormality on a mammogram X-ray. Physical symptoms that show up later, which may be detectable by a woman or her doctor, include a breast lump and, less commonly, breast pain or heaviness; persistent changes to the breast, such as swelling, thickening, or redness of the breast's skin; and nipple abnormalities such as spontaneous discharge, erosion, inversion, or tenderness. Breast pain can result from benign conditions and is not an early symptom of breast cancer.

Studies show that early detection increases survival and treatment options. Although most detected breast lumps are noncancerous, any suspicious lump should be biopsied.

Treatment for breast cancer may involve lumpectomy (local removal of a tumor), mastectomy (surgical removal of the breast), radiation therapy, targeted therapy, chemotherapy, and/or hormone therapy. Long-term **survival rates** following lumpectomy plus radiation therapy are the same as survival rates after a mastectomy; however, there is a higher risk of local recurrence (cancer returning to the breast) with lumpectomy.

Website: www.cancer.org

Prostate Cancer

Source: Prostate Cancer Foundation; American Cancer Society, Inc.

The prostate is a male gland located between the bladder and scrotum that secretes seminal fluid. Prostate cancer is the most common non-skin cancer in the U.S., and the second-most common cause, after lung cancer, of cancer deaths in American men. In 2012, an estimated 241,740 men will be diagnosed with prostate cancer, and about 28,170 will die from the disease. Currently, more than 2.5 mil men in the U.S. are living with a history of prostate cancer.

The exact cause of prostate cancer is unknown. The most identifiable **risk factors** are age, family history, and race. About 60% of all prostate cancers are diagnosed in men over the age of 65, and the chances of developing the disease rise dramatically with age. Having a single first-degree relative with a history of prostate cancer more than doubles a man's risk of developing the disease, and those with several affected relatives have a much higher risk. African-American men are much more likely to develop prostate cancer than non-Hispanic white men and are more than twice as likely to die from it. The cause for this disparity remains unclear.

Usually, the disease has no **symptoms** in its early stages. With more advanced disease, men may experience weak or interrupted urine flow; inability to urinate or difficulty starting or stopping the urine flow; the need to urinate frequently, especially at night; blood in the urine; or pain or burning with urination. Advanced prostate cancer commonly spreads to the bones, which can cause pain in the hips, spine, ribs, or other areas.

The American Cancer Society recommends that once they reach 50, men at average risk of prostate cancer should speak with their health care provider about the benefits and risks of being screened through a prostate-specific antigen (PSA) blood test or digital rectal exam (DRE). African-American men or those with a family history of the disease should be aware of their screening options beginning at age 40 or 45. Men under 40 seldom get prostate cancer.

Prostate cancer **treatment** may include surgery, radiation, hormonal therapy, chemotherapy, or some combination. If caught early on, while tumor cells are localized within the prostate, the five-year relative **survival rate** approaches 100%.

Websites: www.pcf.org; www.cancer.org

Skin Cancer

Source: American Cancer Society, Inc.

Skin cancer is generally divided into two main classes, **nonmelanomas** and **melanomas**, both types affecting different types of skin cells. Melanoma develops in skin cells called melanocytes, which produce melanin, a pigment that gives skin a tan or brown color and helps to protect the deeper layers of skin from the harmful effects of the sun. Melanoma is the most dangerous type of skin cancer because it can easily spread to other parts of the body.

Although skin cancer is the most common type of cancer diagnosed in the U.S., melanoma accounts for less than 5% of all skin cancers. The American Cancer Society estimates that in 2012, 76,250 new cases of melanoma will be diagnosed in the U.S., and about 9,180 people will die from melanoma, while 12,190 will die from any skin cancer.

The exact causes of melanoma are unclear, but there are several **risk factors** that have been associated with the disease:

- Overexposure to UV light (sunlight)
- Presence of moles; moles themselves are not harmful but are associated with an increased risk for skin cancer.
- Fair skin, freckling, and light hair
- Family history
- Use of immune suppression drugs
- Age; although melanoma is more likely to occur in older people, it is one of the most common cancers in people younger than 30.
- Gender; men get melanoma more often than women.
- Past history of melanoma
- Xeroderma pigmentosum (XP), a rare, genetic condition in which people are less able to repair damage caused by sunlight

Melanomas generally look like abnormal moles on the surface of the skin. Normal moles are most often an evenly colored brown, tan, or black spot on the skin that can be flat or raised. They normally have a distinct border that separates them from normal skin cells. Moles can be present at birth, form over time, or even disappear. Abnormal moles differ from regular skin cells and may be a sign of skin cancer. An irregular mole should be examined as soon as possible. Irregular moles generally have the following characteristics:

- Asymmetry—one half of the mole does not match the other half.
- Border—the edges are irregular, ragged, notched, or blurred.
- Color—not uniform; there may be shades of tan, brown, black, and sometimes patches of pink, red, blue, or white.
- Diameter—moles wider than ¼ inch are abnormal (however, melanomas can be smaller).

If a melanoma is suspected, the doctor will perform a biopsy using cells extracted from the suspected cancer or by removing the whole mass and examining it. If a melanoma is found, doctors will often check to see if the cancer has spread to other parts of the body. This is called staging and is represented by Roman numerals I through IV (1-4). The lower the number, the less the cancer has spread. This will determine what course of treatment is necessary.

If caught early, melanoma is highly curable. The five-year **survival rates** for the various stages are as follows:

- All stages   91%
- Local   98%
- Regional   62%
- Distant   15%

Treatment may include simple removal of the melanoma; amputation if the cancer is found on a finger or toe; or chemotherapy, immunotherapy, and/or radiation if the melanoma has spread to other parts of the body.

Website: www.cancer.org

Depression

Source: National Institute of Mental Health, National Institutes of Health, U.S. Dept. of Health and Human Services

Depression is a serious illness that affects thoughts, feelings, and the ability to function in everyday life. It strikes all age groups and often goes unrecognized or is inadequately treated. The National Institute of Mental Health (NIMH) estimates that about 20.9 mil American adults age 18 and older suffer from depression or some other mood or depressive disorder in any given year; more than 16% of all Americans will have had depression at some point in life. Young people are at particular risk; in a one-year period, three times as many persons with depression were 18 to 29 years old as were 60 or older.

Nearly twice as many women as men suffer from a depressive illness in a given year. Although conventional wisdom holds that depression is most closely associated with menopause, the childbearing years, followed by the years prior to menopause, are marked by the highest rates of depression. The influence of hormones on depression in women has been an active area of NIMH research.

In a given year, 1%-5% of people age 65 and older living in the community (i.e., residing outside of institutions) suffer from major depression. Depression frequently occurs with other physical illnesses including heart disease, stroke, cancer, HIV/AIDS, diabetes, and Parkinson's disease. It is not a normal part of aging.

Available **treatments** can alleviate symptoms, and with awareness growing, more people with depression are seeking help. But many depressed people—and those around them—still fail to realize that they have an illness or could benefit from medical help.

Symptoms and Types of Depression

- Persistent sad, anxious, or "empty" feelings
- Feelings of hopelessness and/or pessimism
- Feelings of guilt, worthlessness, and/or helplessness
- Irritability, restlessness
- Loss of interest in activities or hobbies once pleasurable, including sex
- Fatigue and decreased energy
- Difficulty concentrating, remembering details, and making decisions
- Insomnia, early-morning wakefulness, or excessive sleeping
- Overeating, or appetite loss
- Thoughts of suicide, suicide attempts
- Aches or pains, headaches, cramps, or digestive problems that do not ease even with treatment

A diagnosis of **major depressive disorder** (or **unipolar major depression**) is made if an individual reports experiencing five or more of these symptoms in the same two-week period.

Bipolar disorder (or **manic-depressive illness**) is characterized by episodes of major depression alternating with periods of mania, when a person experiences a persistent,

abnormally elevated mood or irritability, accompanied by feelings of inflated self-esteem, less need for sleep, increased talkativeness, racing thoughts, distractibility, agitation, and excessive involvement in pleasurable activities that have a high potential for painful consequences. While it shares some of the features of major depression, bipolar disorder is a distinct illness.

Dysthymic disorder (or **dysthymia**), a less severe yet more chronic form of depression, is diagnosed when a depressed mood persists for at least two years in adults (one year in children or adolescents) and is accompanied by at least two other depressive symptoms. Many people with dysthymic disorder also experience major depressive episodes.

In contrast to normal experiences of sadness, depression is extreme and persistent and can interfere significantly with an individual's ability to function. A study sponsored by the World Health Organization and the World Bank found unipolar major depression to be the leading cause of disability in the U.S. and worldwide.

Treatments for Depression

A variety of **medicines** are used to treat depression. These drugs influence the functioning of certain neurotransmitters in the brain, primarily serotonin and norepinephrine, known as monoamines. Older drugs—tricyclic antidepressants (TCAs) and monoamine oxidase inhibitors (MAOIs)—affect the functioning of both of these neurotransmitters. But they can have strong side effects or, in the case of MAOIs, require dietary restrictions. Newer medications, such as selective serotonin reuptake inhibitors (SSRIs), have fewer side effects. All of these medications can be effective, but some people respond to one type and not another.

NIMH research has shown that certain types of **psychotherapy**, particularly cognitive-behavioral therapy (CBT) and interpersonal therapy (IPT), can help relieve depression. CBT helps patients change the negative thinking and behaving patterns often associated with depression. IPT focuses patients on working through personal relationships that may contribute to depression. Studies of adults have shown that a combination of psychotherapy and antidepressant medication is most effective in treating moderate-to-severe depression.

Electroconvulsive therapy (ECT) has been found effective in treating some cases of severe depression, particularly those that have not responded to other forms of treatment. ECT involves producing a seizure in the brain of a patient under general anesthesia by applying electrical stimulation through electrodes placed on the scalp. Memory loss and other cognitive problems, though common side effects, are typically short-lived.

Website: www.nimh.nih.gov

Diabetes

Source: American Diabetes Association; Centers for Disease Control and Prevention

Diabetes is a chronic disease in which the body does not produce or properly use the hormone **insulin**. Insulin is needed to convert sugar, starches, and other foods into energy. Both genetics and environment appear to play roles in the onset of diabetes. This disease, which has no cure, is the seventh leading cause of death by disease in the U.S. According to death certificate data, 68,905 people in the U.S. died as a result of diabetes in 2010. In 2011, an estimated 25.8 mil Americans had diabetes, 7 mil of whom were undiagnosed.

The American Diabetes Association supports studies proving that detection at an earlier stage and modest lifestyle changes, such as eating better and exercising more, will help prevent or delay complications.

There are two major types of diabetes:

Type 1 (formerly known as insulin dependent, or juvenile diabetes). The body does not produce insulin; the disease is usually diagnosed in children and young adults. People with type 1 diabetes must take daily insulin injections to stay alive.

Type 2 (formerly known as non-insulin dependent, or adult-onset diabetes). The body does not produce enough or cannot properly use insulin. It is the most common form of the disease (90%-95% of diabetes cases in people over age 20) and often begins later in life.

Prediabetes

There are 79 mil people in the U.S. who have prediabetes, the state that occurs when a person's blood glucose levels are higher than normal but not high enough for a diagnosis of diabetes. One study indicated that about 11% of people with prediabetes developed type 2 diabetes each year during the average three-year study follow-up period. Other studies showed that most people with prediabetes develop type 2 diabetes within 10 years.

Complications From Diabetes

People often have diabetes many years before it is diagnosed. During that time, serious complications may develop. Potential complications include the following:

Blindness. Diabetes is the leading cause of new cases of blindness in people ages 20-74. Each year, 12,000 to 24,000 people lose their eyesight because of diabetes.

Kidney disease. 10% to 21% of all people with diabetes develop kidney disease. In 2008, a total of 48,374 people in the U.S. initiated treatment for end-stage renal disease (kidney failure) because of diabetes.

Amputations. Diabetes is the most frequent cause for nontraumatic lower limb amputations. The risk of a leg amputation is 15 to 40 times greater for a person with diabetes than for the average American. In 2006, approximately 65,700 lower-limb amputations were performed as a result of complications brought on by diabetes.

Heart disease and stroke. People with diabetes are two to four times more likely to have heart disease. They are also two to four times more likely to suffer a stroke.

Warning Signs of Diabetes

Type 1 diabetes (signs usually occur suddenly):

- frequent urination
- unusual thirst
- extreme hunger
- unusual weight loss
- extreme fatigue
- irritability

Type 2 diabetes (signs occur less suddenly):

- any type 1 symptoms
- frequent infections
- blurred vision
- cuts/bruises slow to heal
- tingling/numbness in hands or feet
- recurring skin, gum, or bladder infections

Gestational Diabetes

Gestational diabetes is a form of diabetes that affects about 18% of pregnant women. Usually there are no symptoms, or the symptoms are mild. Because the condition usually appears around the 24th week, it is recommended that all pregnant women receive a glucose tolerance test between the 24th and 28th week. Pregnancy hormones can cause insulin resistance, making blood glucose levels rise. The goal of treatment is to keep blood glucose levels within normal limits, mainly through diet and exercise; treatment may also include daily blood glucose testing and insulin injections. Women with gestational diabetes tend to have larger babies at birth, which can increase the chance of problems at the time of delivery. Glucose levels usually return to normal after delivery, but odds of recurrence in future pregnancies are two-in-three.

Website: www.diabetes.org

Eating Disorders

Source: National Institute of Mental Health, National Institutes of Health, U.S. Dept. of Health and Human Services

Eating disorders involve serious disturbances in eating behavior, usually in the forms of extreme and unhealthy reduction of food intake or severe overeating. They are not due to a failure of will; rather, they are real and treatable medical illnesses in which certain behavior patterns get out of control. The main types are anorexia nervosa, bulimia nervosa, and binge-eating disorder (technically categorized with "eating disorders not otherwise specified"). These disorders usually develop in adolescence or early adulthood and often occur with other illnesses such as depression, substance abuse, and anxiety disorders. They are much more common among females; only about 5% to 15% of anorexia or bulimia patients and 35% of binge eaters are male.

If not treated, eating disorders can lead to serious complications, including heart conditions and kidney failure, which may result in death.

Anorexia nervosa affects an estimated 0.9% of all females. Symptoms include resistance to maintaining weight at minimally healthy levels, intense fear of gaining weight, exaggerated importance of body weight or shape in one's self image, and infrequent or absent menstrual periods. Anorexics see themselves as overweight even when they are dangerously thin. In response, they avoid food and take other extreme measures to lose weight, such as exercising compulsively or purging by means of vomiting or laxatives and enemas. While some anorexics fully recover after a single episode, others may relapse frequently or experience chronic deterioration.

Bulimia nervosa affects an estimated 0.5% of females. It is characterized by recurrent uncontrolled binge-eating episodes followed by what is believed to be compensatory behavior to prevent weight gain, such as self-induced vomiting, exercising excessively, or fasting. Persons with bulimia can weigh within the normal range for their age and height, but they still fear gaining weight and are intensely dissatisfied with their bodies. They often perform their behaviors in secret, feeling shame when they binge and relief when they purge.

Binge-eating disorder, which is not officially approved as a psychiatric diagnosis, affects an estimated 2% to 3.5% of males and females in the U.S. As with bulimia, a binge-eating disorder involves episodes of excessive eating during which the sufferer may feel a complete lack of control. But individuals with this disorder do not compensate by purging, exercising, or fasting. Many are thus overweight, and the shame they feel can lead to further binge-eating.

Eating disorder sufferers may not admit they are ill. Early diagnosis and a comprehensive **treatment** program are essential to recovery. Some patients may need immediate hospitalization. For anorexia, treatment usually follows three established steps: weight restoration, usually in an inpatient hospital setting; treatment of any accompanying psychological disturbances, including the use of medications; and achieving long-term remission or recovery by reducing or eliminating negative thoughts and behaviors.

Heart and Blood Vessel Disease

Source: American Heart Association; National Center for Chronic Disease Prevention and Health Promotion, Centers for Disease Control and Prevention; National Heart, Blood, and Lung Institute, National Institutes of Health, U.S. Dept. of Health and Human Services

Warning Signs of Heart Attack

- Chest discomfort. Most heart attacks involve discomfort in the center of the chest that lasts more than a few minutes or that goes away and then returns. It can feel like uncomfortable pressure, squeezing, fullness, or pain.
- Discomfort in other areas of the upper body. Symptoms can include pain or discomfort in one or both arms, the back, neck, jaw, or stomach.
- Shortness of breath. This feeling may occur with or without chest discomfort.
- Other signs may include breaking out in a cold sweat, nausea, or lightheadedness.
- The American Heart Association advises immediate action at onset of symptoms, as more than half of heart attack victims die within an hour of symptoms first manifesting. Call 9-1-1. Get to a hospital right away.

Warning Signs of Stroke

- Sudden numbness or weakness of the face, arm, or leg, especially on one side of the body.
- Sudden confusion, trouble speaking, or understanding.
- Sudden trouble seeing in one or both eyes.
- Sudden trouble walking, dizziness, loss of balance or coordination.
- Sudden severe headache with no known cause.
- Prompt treatment of a stroke can be a major factor in controlling the effects. If you have one or more stroke symptoms that last more than a few minutes, call 9-1-1 or the emergency medical service number immediately so an ambulance, ideally one with advanced life support, can be sent for you quickly.

Major Modifiable Risk Factors

High blood pressure. High blood pressure, or hypertension, increases the risk of stroke, heart attack, kidney failure, and congestive heart failure. It affects men and women of all races, ethnic origins, and ages. Obesity, physical inactivity, and an unhealthy diet can contribute to this often symptomless disease. Individuals should have a blood pressure reading at least once every two years or more often if advised by a physician.

A blood pressure reading is really two measurements, with one value written above the other, such as 122/78 mmHg. The upper number (systolic pressure) represents the amount of pressure in the arteries when the heart contracts (beats) and pushes blood through the circulatory system. The lower number (diastolic pressure) represents the pressure in the arteries between beats, when the heart is resting. According to recent National Institutes of Health (NIH) guidelines, a blood pressure reading below 120/80 is considered normal, while readings from 120/80 to 139/89 are considered prehypertension.

High blood pressure is divided into two stages:
Stage 1 is 140-159 (systolic) over 90-99 (diastolic);
Stage 2 is 160+ (systolic) over 100+ (diastolic).
The diagnosis can be based on either the systolic or the diastolic reading.

High blood pressure usually cannot be cured, but it can be controlled in a variety of ways, including lifestyle modifications and medication. **Treatment** always should be at the direction and under the supervision of a physician. The treatment goal for patients with hypertension is blood pressure below 140/90. Individuals with hypertension and diabetes or chronic kidney disease should aim for blood pressure lower than 130/80.

High blood cholesterol. Cholesterol is a waxy fat-like substance found in all cells of the body. It is produced by the body and also comes in some foods. The body needs some cholesterol, but excess levels increase the risk of heart disease. High cholesterol in itself usually does not cause **symptoms**, so many people are unaware that they have a problem.

There are two major kinds of cholesterol: LDL (low-density lipoprotein), often called "bad" cholesterol, leads to narrowing of the arteries. HDL (high-density lipoprotein), known as "good" cholesterol, helps reduce that risk.

NIH guidelines classify total cholesterol levels (determined by a blood test) of less than 200 mg/dl as desirable, 200-239 as borderline high, and 240 and higher as high. About 14% of Americans have a cholesterol level of 240 mg/dl or higher. LDL levels of less than 100 are considered optimal, 130-159 as borderline high, 160-189 as high, and 190 and higher as very high. For HDL, levels of 60 mg/dl and higher are considered protective against heart disease, while levels under 40 mg/dl are considered a risk factor.

As with high blood pressure, high blood cholesterol can be controlled by lifestyle changes and medication and should be treated by a physician.

Triglycerides, another form of fat in the blood, can also raise the risk of heart disease. Levels that are borderline high (150-199) or high (200 or more) may need treatment.

Diabetes. Diabetes is a major risk factor for heart disease; at least 65% of people with diabetes mellitus die of some form of heart or blood vessel disease.

Smoking. Cigarette smokers are two to four times more likely to develop coronary heart disease (CHD). Smoking is also associated with the risk of sudden cardiac death.

Obesity. Using a body mass index (BMI) of 25 and higher for overweight and 30 and higher for obesity, between 60% and 70% of Americans are either overweight or obese. Of these, more than 78 mil are obese.

Physical inactivity. A sedentary lifestyle is a risk factor for CHD. The risk increase is comparable to that observed for high blood cholesterol, high blood pressure, or cigarette smoking.

Women and Cardiovascular Disease

The American Heart Association reports that diseases of the heart and stroke, respectively, are the number one and number three killers of women over the age of 25. (Cancer is the second leading cause.) More than one in three women died of some form of cardiovascular disease in 2008. Because heart disease was long viewed as a "man's" disease, many of the major cardiovascular studies were conducted only on men. Recent attention has been directed toward understanding the influence of gender on cardiovascular disease risk and prevention, but important gaps in knowledge remain.

Women often present some of the same classic symptoms of heart attack as men, such as chest pain that spreads to the shoulders and arms. But women may more often report atypical chest pain or complain of abdominal pain, difficulty breathing (dyspnea), and nausea. Another problem in **diagnosis** is that women tend to have heart attacks later in life than men, so symptoms may be masked by other age-related diseases such as arthritis or osteoporosis. Even certain diagnostic tests and procedures such as the exercise stress test may not be as accurate in women, with the result that disease process leading to heart attack or stroke may not be detected early on, with potentially serious consequences.

Website: www.heart.org

Irritable Bowel Syndrome
Source: National Institute of Diabetes and Digestive and Kidney Diseases, National Institutes of Health

Irritable Bowel Syndrome (IBS)—a functional disorder, not a disease, in the large intestine—is one of the most common disorders diagnosed by physicians. Nearly one in five Americans has IBS symptoms, and it accounts for more than 1 out of every 10 doctor visits in the U.S. IBS occurs more frequently in women than in men, and it usually begins before the age of 35 for about 50% of those affected. Though IBS causes discomfort and may even be painful, it does not damage the bowel.

Many people are uncomfortable discussing IBS because of its embarrassing **symptoms**. They may include the following:
- Abdominal pain
- Bloating
- Discomfort
- Constipation
- Mucus in the stool
- Diarrhea
- Alternating between constipation and diarrhea

For most people, IBS is a chronic condition, and there will likely be times when the symptoms may worsen or disappear altogether only to reappear in the future. Most **complications** are derived from the symptoms, such as hemorrhoids, which may form as a result of diarrhea and constipation. People with chronic IBS may also go through periods of depression because of the constant discomfort and the symptoms' interference in work and personal relationships.

The specific **causes** for IBS are unknown. The walls of the intestines are lined with layers of muscle that contract and relax in a coordinated manner as they move food through the digestive system. When a person has IBS, the contractions cause food to either speed up or slow down as it moves though the bowel, subsequently causing gas, bloating, diarrhea, or constipation. Some researchers believe that people who suffer from IBS have a colon that is particularly sensitive to certain foods. Milk products, alcohol, caffeine, carbonated drinks, chocolate, and fatty foods in particular can trigger IBS symptoms. Another common factor is a low tolerance for stretching of the large intestine. Women tend to get IBS more often than men and usually have more severe symptoms during menstrual periods, leading researchers to believe that IBS may have a hormonal trigger. Recent research has shown that serotonin, a neurotransmitter hormone, may be linked with gastrointestinal functioning.

IBS can sometimes result from infection or other problems in the body. Researchers have found that people who have had gastroenteritis later develop IBS. But because IBS symptoms can match those of many serious diseases, it is important for chronic sufferers to consult their doctors. If symptoms began early in life and have remained stable, one may need to get a colonoscopy to rule out inflammatory bowel disease, such as Crohn's disease or ulcerative colitis, or even colon cancer. Those with IBS over 50 years of age should be regularly screened for colon cancer.

Despite the uncertainty over what causes IBS, there are known **precautionary measures** that people with sensitive digestive systems can take. Keeping a well-balanced diet is the best possible preventive. Eating foods with dietary fiber, such as whole-grain bread and cereal, as well as vegetables and beans as part of a daily diet can reduce IBS symptoms, although high-fiber diets may cause gas and bloating. Eating large meals has been shown to worsen the condition, so IBS sufferers may want to eat several smaller meals.

There is no cure for IBS. **Treatment** usually involves lessening the symptoms so that they don't interfere as much in a person's life.

Common Infectious Diseases

Source: National Institutes of Health, Centers for Disease Control and Prevention, U.S. Dept. of Health and Human Services; World Health Organization

The following is a list of major infectious diseases. It is meant to be used for reference purposes only and not as a tool for diagnosis. Statistics may appear uneven because of the different reporting methods used by the various agencies and because not all diseases are surveyed in the same year.

Chicken pox

(*Varicella simplex*) Usually nonthreatening viral disease commonly associated with children. In adults, the disease can be serious. **Transmission:** highly contagious. Transmitted by direct contact with rash, coughing, or sneezing of infected persons. **Symptoms:** blister-like rash, discomfort, high fever. Infected people may develop shingles later in life. **Vaccine:** became available in 1995. **Treatment:** none; antibiotics in some severe cases. **Annual U.S. cases:** before 1995, about 4 mil, mostly children; 15,427 reported in 2010.

Chlamydia

(*Chlamydia trachomatis*) One of the most widely spread sexually transmitted diseases (STDs). **Transmission:** sexually transmitted. **Symptoms:** about 70% of those infected show no symptoms. In women, vaginal discharge, infection of the cervix and urinary tract, can cause pelvic inflammatory disease. In men, infection of urinary tract and epididymitis (inflammation of testicular duct); can also infect the throat, rectum, and eyes. **Treatment:** curable with antibiotics. **Annual U.S. cases:** 1,307,893 in 2010.

Common cold

(More than 200 different viruses) An upper respiratory viral infection. **Transmission:** touching one's nose, eyes, or mouth after touching something contaminated by the virus; inhalation of airborne virus. **Symptoms:** irritated nose or scratchy throat, sneezing and watery green or yellow nasal discharge, coughing, muscle aches, headache, postnasal drip, decreased appetite. **Treatment:** no cure. Over-the-counter remedies can relieve symptoms; effectiveness of antiviral drugs uncertain. **Est. annual U.S. cases:** about 1 bil.

Gonorrhea

(*Neisseria gonorrhoeae*) Common bacterial STD. **Transmission:** sexually transmitted. **Symptoms:** in men, discomfort in urethra, yellow or green discharge, burning during urination. In women, pelvic pain, bleeding associated with intercourse, burning during urination, yellow or bloody discharge. **Treatment:** highly curable with antibiotics. **Annual U.S. cases:** 309,341 in 2010.

Hepatitis

A viral disease that causes inflammation of the liver. In the U.S., five forms are endemic: A, B, C, D, and E. Forms A, B, and C are the most common. **Symptoms:** all forms have generally similar symptoms including jaundice, fatigue, abdominal pain, loss of appetite, nausea, mild flu-like symptoms. Many cases cause no symptoms. In extreme cases, liver transplants may be necessary.

Hepatitis A (*Hepatovirus picornaviridae*). **Transmission:** food or water contaminated with feces from infected persons. **Vaccine:** effective; travelers are advised to not drink tap water in countries where disease is common. **Treatment:** disease usually resolves on its own; alcohol consumption should be avoided. **Est. annual U.S. cases:** 17,000 infections in 2010; 1,670 acute lab-confirmed cases reported in 2010.

Hepatitis B (*Orthohepadnavirus hepadnaviridae*). **Transmission:** unsterilized needle sharing; contaminated blood transfusions; sexual contact. **Vaccine:** highly effective. **Treatment:** for chronic cases, drug treatment is necessary. For acute cases, disease usually resolves itself. Severe cases treated with lamivudine. **Est. annual U.S. cases:** 35,000 infections in 2010; 3,374 acute lab-confirmed cases reported in 2010.

Hepatitis C (*Hepacivirus flavinviridae*). **Transmission:** unsterilized needle sharing; contaminated blood transfusions; sexual contact. **Vaccine:** none. **Treatment:** chronic cases treated with drugs, which eliminates virus in about 50% of patients. For acute cases, treatment recommended if disease present after two to three months. **Est. annual U.S. cases:** 17,000 infections in 2010; 849 acute lab-confirmed cases reported in 2010.

HPV infection

(More than 100 strains of human papillomavirus) Common viral infection; leading cause of cervical cancer. **Transmission:** sexually transmitted. **Symptoms:** most of those infected have no symptoms but can still transmit virus. In some cases, genital warts and precancerous bumps on anus, cervix or vulva, or penis. **Vaccine:** Gardasil and Cervarix. **Treatment:** while there is no cure, a healthy immune system can usually fight off HPV naturally. Women with HPV should have a Pap smear and pelvic exam every six months. **Est. annual U.S. cases:** 6 mil new cases; approximately 20 mil currently infected with HPV.

Influenza

(Various influenza viruses) Highly contagious viral respiratory infection. **Transmission:** airborne; contact with face after touching infected surface. **Symptoms:** chills, fatigue, fever, headache, sore throat, sinus congestion, coughing. ("Stomach flu" is not influenza.) **Vaccine:** yearly vaccinations recommended; available as injection or nasal spray. **Treatment:** antiviral drugs; disease normally runs its course in a matter of days. **Est. annual U.S. cases:** 5%-20% of population; more than 200,000 flu-related hospitalizations, 36,000 flu-related deaths.

Lyme disease

(*Borrelia burgdorferi*) Bacterial inflammatory disease, first identified 1975 in Old Lyme, CT. Found across the U.S., usually in areas with large deer populations. **Transmission:** bite from infected deer ticks. Mice and deer are most common tick hosts. **Symptoms:** mimic those of other diseases. Flu-like symptoms: fatigue, stiff neck, joint inflammation, skin rash may appear at site of tick bite. **Treatment:** antibiotics in early stages; anti-inflammation drugs to relieve symptoms. Without treatment, long-term complications (some fatal) involving joints, heart, and nervous system. **Annual U.S. cases:** from 9,895 reported cases in 1992 to 30,158 confirmed and probable cases in 2010.

Malaria

(*Plasmodium* parasite) Infectious disease known from as early as 2700 BCE. Virtually eradicated in developed countries; still a major killer in tropical regions. **Transmission:** bite from infected mosquito. **Symptoms:** high fever, shaking chills, heavy sweating, headache, fatigue, enlarged spleen. If left untreated, organ damage and death. **Treatment:** antimalarial drugs, including chloroquine, for treatment and prevention. **Annual cases:** 1,773 in the U.S. in 2010; worldwide, an estimated 216 mil cases and 655,000 deaths, most young children in sub-Saharan Africa, in 2010.

Measles

(*Rubeola* virus) Once-common viral infection; today almost nonexistent in U.S. and Canada. **Transmission:** airborne transmission by infected persons. **Symptoms:** itchy and raised rash, sore throat, cough, pink eye, high fever. In rare cases, encephalitis, seizures, permanent deafness, death. **Vaccine:** highly effective. **Treatment:** no specific treatment; symptoms relieved with bed rest, acetaminophen, humidified air. **Annual U.S. cases:** 63 in 2010.

Mumps

(Mumps virus) Acute and contagious viral infection. **Transmission:** direct contact with mucus or saliva of infected persons. **Symptoms:** painful, visible swelling of the salivary or parotid glands in the face. Chills, headache, fever, painful swallowing. In some cases, inflammation of testes, pancreas, ovaries. In severe cases, brain swelling and symptoms ranging from nausea and drowsiness to seizures and permanent deafness. **Vaccine:** MMR (measles, mumps, and rubella) vaccine is effective. **Treatment:** no specific treatment; symptoms may be relieved by applying ice or heat to swollen glands. **Annual U.S. cases:** 2,612 in 2010.

Peptic ulcer

(Most from *Helicobacter pylori* [*H. pylori*] bacteria; also overuse of aspirin or other anti-inflammatory drugs) Weakening of the stomach's protective mucous coating, allowing stomach acid and bacteria to irritate stomach lining. **Transmission:** *H. pylori* may be transmitted through food and water. **Symptoms:** indigestion; bloating; dull, transient abdominal pain or discomfort; nausea; vomiting. **Treatment:** antibiotics, acid-suppressing drugs. **Est. annual U.S. cases:** about 20% of the population under 40 years of age and half of those over 60 may be infected with *H. pylori*. An estimated 500,000 to 850,000 develop peptic ulcers each year.

Pertussis or Whooping cough

(*Bordetella pertussis* or *B. parepertussis*) Upper respiratory bacterial infection. **Transmission:** airborne transmission by infected persons; highly contagious. **Symptoms:** initially, mild cold-like symptoms, fever, diarrhea, difficulty breathing; later, violent coughing with characteristic "whooping" heard when patient tries to breathe between coughs, vomiting. In severe cases, apnea, pneumonia, seizures, encephalopathy. **Vaccine:** available as part of combination vaccine that also prevents diphtheria and tetanus. **Treatment:** antibiotics in early cases; otherwise, disease must run its course. **Annual U.S. cases:** 27,550 in 2010.

Salmonella or Salmonellosis

(*Salmonella enteritidis*) Bacterial infection. **Transmission:** eating foods contaminated by feces carrying the bacteria or undercooked meats or raw eggs contaminated by bacteria. Contact with feces of infected animal or pet. **Symptoms:** fever, diarrhea, abdominal cramps 12 to 72 hours after infection. **Treatment:** no standard treatment.

Runs its course in four to seven days. Antibiotics in severe cases. **Annual U.S. cases:** 54,424 in 2010.

Shigellosis

(Four species of *Shigella*: *boydii*, *dysenteriae*, *flexneri*, and *sonnei*) Bacterial infection and a form of dysentery, an intestinal disease. **Transmission:** consuming food contaminated by infected feces or vegetables grown in fields containing contaminated sewage. Swimming in contaminated water. **Symptoms:** watery or bloody diarrhea one to four days after infection, high fever, vomiting, painful bowel movements, severe diarrhea. In extreme cases, seizures in children, intestinal perforation. **Treatment:** mild infection allowed to run its course; replacement of fluids and salts lost through excessive diarrhea. Antibiotics in severe cases. Although severe diarrhea is symptomatic, antidiarrheal medicines may make illness worse. **Annual U.S. cases:** 14,786 in 2010.

Syphilis

(*Treponema pallidum*) Bacterial infection known since ancient times that spread rampantly throughout Europe in the Middle Ages. **Transmission:** sexually transmitted. **Symptoms:** primary stage: painless sore, called a chancre, where bacteria enters the body; usually heals in 3 to 12 weeks with or without treatment. Without treatment, disease enters secondary stage: skin rash as chancre is healing or weeks after it is healed. Without treatment, enters tertiary stage: mouth sores, fever, fatigue, loss of appetite, weight loss, hair loss, jaundice, syphilitic meningitis, aortal aneurysms, lesions, damage to nervous system, heart, and eyes. Most infected do not progress beyond primary or secondary stage. **Treatment:** curable with antibiotics (mostly penicillin). **Annual U.S. cases:** 45,834 in 2010; 13,774 primary and secondary.

Tetanus or Lockjaw

(*Clostridium tetani*) Bacterial infection. **Transmission:** bacteria, found in soil, enters body through broken skin. **Symptoms:** muscle stiffness and spasms or "locking" of muscles of the jaw, neck, and limbs. **Vaccine:** four forms of immunization. **Treatment:** tetanus immune globulin to fight infection. With treatment, less than 10% of cases are fatal. **Annual U.S. cases:** 26 in 2010.

Tuberculosis

(*Mycobacterium tuberculosis*) Bacterial infection that primarily affects the lungs. **Transmission:** airborne transmission by persons with active TB infection. **Symptoms:** weight loss, fever, cough with discharge (sometimes with bloody sputum), night sweats, growing shortness of breath over time, chest pains. **Vaccine/treatment:** BCG (Bacille Calmette Guerin) vaccine only effective in protecting young children and used where TB is prevalent. Not recommended by health experts for use in the U.S. because of the low risk of infection and its variable effectiveness. **Annual U.S. cases:** 11,182 in 2010.

Yellow fever

(Yellow fever virus, in *flavivirus* group) Viral infection that has caused large epidemics in South America, the Caribbean, and Africa. **Transmission:** bite from mosquitoes carrying the virus. **Symptoms:** headaches, muscle aches, fever, jaundice (yellowing skin), nausea and vomiting, kidney failure, severe generalized pain. In severe cases, shock, coma, and death. **Vaccine:** available, safe, and effective. **Treatment:** symptoms treated until disease runs its course. **Annual U.S. cases:** 0 in the U.S.; an estimated 200,000 new cases, 30,000 deaths worldwide.

Dietary Guidelines for Americans, 2010: Key Recommendations

Source: *Dietary Guidelines for Americans 2010*, U.S. Dept. of Agriculture; U.S. Dept. of Health and Human Services

Balancing Calories to Manage Weight

- Prevent and/or reduce overweight and obesity through improved eating and physical activity behaviors.
- Control total calorie intake to manage body weight.
- Increase physical activity and reduce time spent in sedentary behaviors.
- Maintain appropriate calorie balance during each stage of life.

Foods and Food Components to Reduce

- Reduce daily sodium intake to less than 2,300 mg. Further reduce intake to 1,500 mg among persons who are 51 and older and those of any age who are African American or have hypertension, diabetes, or chronic kidney disease.
- Consume less than 10% of calories from saturated fats by replacing them with monounsaturated and polyunsaturated fats.
- Consume less than 300 mg per day of dietary cholesterol.
- Keep trans fat consumption as low as possible by limiting foods that contain synthetic sources of trans fats, such as partially hydrogenated oils.
- Reduce the intake of calories from solid fats and added sugars.
- Limit the consumption of foods that contain refined grains, especially refined grain foods that contain solid fats, added sugars, and sodium.
- If alcohol is consumed, it should be consumed in moderation—up to 1 drink per day for women and 2 drinks per day for men.

Website: www.health.gov/dietaryguidelines/

Foods and Nutrients to Increase

- Increase vegetable and fruit intake.
- Eat a variety of vegetables (especially dark-green, red, and orange vegetables), beans, and peas.
- Consume at least half of all grains as whole grains. Replace refined grains with whole grains.
- Increase intake of fat-free or low-fat milk and milk products, such as milk, yogurt, cheese, or fortified soy beverages.
- Choose a variety of protein foods, which include seafood, lean meat/poultry, eggs, beans and peas, soy products, and unsalted nuts and seeds.
- Increase seafood consumed by choosing seafood in place of some meat and poultry.
- Replace protein foods that are higher in solid fats with choices that are lower in solid fats and calories and/or are sources of oils.
- Use oils to replace solid fats where possible.
- Choose foods that provide more potassium, dietary fiber, calcium, and vitamin D, which are nutrients of concern in American diets. These foods include vegetables, fruits, whole grains, and milk and milk products.

Building Healthy Eating Patterns

- Select an eating pattern that meets nutrient needs over time at an appropriate calorie level.
- Account for all foods and beverages consumed and assess how they fit within a total healthy eating pattern.
- Follow food safety recommendations when preparing and eating foods to reduce the risk of foodborne illnesses.

Understanding Food Components

Protein

Proteins, composed of amino acids, are essential to good nutrition. They build, maintain, and repair the body. Best sources: eggs, milk, fish, meat, poultry, soybeans, nuts. High-quality proteins such as eggs, meat, or fish supply all eight amino acids needed in a diet. Plant foods—whole grain breads and cereals, rice, oats, soybeans, other beans, split peas, and nuts—can be combined to meet protein needs as well.

Fats

Fats provide energy by furnishing calories to the body. They also contain vitamins A, D, E, and K. They are the most concentrated source of energy in a diet. Best sources of polyunsaturated and monounsaturated fats: margarine, vegetable/plant oils, nuts. Concentrated sources of saturated fats: meats, cheeses, butter, cream, egg yolks, lard.

Carbohydrates

Carbohydrates provide energy to the body by supplying immediate calories. The carbohydrate group includes sugars, starches, fiber, and starchy vegetables. Best sources: grains, legumes, potatoes, vegetables, fruits.

Fiber

The portion of plant foods that our bodies cannot digest is known as fiber. There are two basic types: insoluble ("roughage") and soluble. Insoluble fibers help move food materials through the digestive tract; soluble fibers tend to slow them down. Both types absorb water, thus preventing and treating constipation by softening and increasing the bulk of the undigested food components passing through the digestive tract. Soluble fibers may also be helpful in reducing blood cholesterol levels. Best sources: beans, bran, fruits, whole grains, vegetables.

Water

Water dissolves and transports other nutrients throughout the body, aiding in the processes of digestion, absorption, circulation, and excretion. It helps regulate body temperature.

Vitamins

Vitamin A—promotes good eyesight; helps keep skin and mucous membranes resistant to infection. Best sources: liver, sweet potatoes, carrots, kale, cantaloupe, turnip greens, collard greens, broccoli, fortified milk.

Vitamin B_1 (thiamine)—prevents beriberi. Essential to carbohydrate metabolism and nervous system health. Best sources: pork, enriched cereals, grains, soybeans, nuts.

Vitamin B_2 (riboflavin)—protects the skin, mouth, eyes, eyelids, and mucous membranes. Essential to protein and energy metabolism. Best sources: milk, meat, poultry, cheese, broccoli, spinach.

Vitamin B_6 (pyridoxine)—important in the regulation of the central nervous system and in protein metabolism. Best sources: whole grains, meats, fish, poultry, nuts, brewers' yeast.

Vitamin B_{12} (cobalamin)—needed to form red blood cells. Best sources: meat, fish, poultry, eggs, dairy products.

Niacin—maintains health of skin, the tongue, and the digestive system. Best sources: poultry, peanuts, fish, enriched flour, bread.

Folic acid (folacin)—required for normal blood cell formation, growth, and reproduction and for important chemical reactions in body cells. Best sources: yeast, orange juice, green leafy vegetables, wheat germ, asparagus, broccoli, nuts.

Other B vitamins—biotin, pantothenic acid.

Vitamin C (ascorbic acid)—maintains collagen, a protein necessary for the formation of skin, ligaments, and bones. Helps heal wounds and mend fractures. Aids in resisting some types of viral and bacterial infections. Best sources: citrus fruits and juices, cantaloupe, broccoli, Brussels sprouts, potatoes and sweet potatoes, tomatoes, cabbage.

Vitamin D—important for bone development. Best sources: sunlight, fortified milk and milk products, fish-liver oils, egg yolks.

Vitamin E (tocopherol)—helps protect red blood cells. Best sources: vegetable oils, wheat germ, whole grains, eggs, peanuts, margarine, green leafy vegetables.

Vitamin K—necessary for formation of prothrombin, which helps blood to clot. Also made by intestinal bacteria. Best dietary sources: green leafy vegetables, tomatoes.

Minerals

Calcium—works with phosphorus to build and maintain bones and teeth. Best sources: milk and milk products, cheese, blackstrap molasses, some types of tofu.

Phosphorus—performs more functions than any other mineral and plays a part in nearly every chemical reaction in the body. Best sources: cheese, milk, meats, poultry, fish, tofu.

Iron—necessary for the formation of myoglobin, which is a reservoir of oxygen for muscle tissue, and hemoglobin, which transports oxygen within blood. Best sources: lean meats, beans, green leafy vegetables, shellfish, enriched breads and cereals, whole grains.

Other minerals—chromium, cobalt, copper, fluorine, iodine, magnesium, manganese, molybdenum, potassium, selenium, sodium, sulfur, zinc.

Understanding Food Label Claims

Source: Center for Food Safety and Applied Nutrition, Food and Drug Admin., U.S. Dept. of Health and Human Services

The federal Nutrition Labeling and Education Act of 1990 provides that manufacturers can make certain claims on processed food labels only if they meet the definitions specified here.

Sugar

Sugar free: less than 0.5 g per serving

No added sugars; Without added sugars: no sugars or sugar-containing ingredients added during processing; must state if food is not "low" or "reduced calorie"

Unsweetened; No added sweeteners: remain as factual statements

Reduced sugar: at least 25% less sugar than reference food

Fat

Fat free: less than 0.5 g of fat per serving

Saturated fat free: less than 0.5 g of saturated fat and less than 0.5 g of trans fatty acids per serving

Low fat: 3 g or less per serving and, if the serving is 30 g or less or 2 tbs or less, per 50 g of the food

Low saturated fat: 1 g or less per serving and not more than 15% of calories from saturated fat

Reduced fat; Less fat: at least 25% less per serving than reference food

Fiber

High fiber: 5 g or more per serving (must also meet low-fat definition or state level of total fat)

Good source of fiber: 2.5 g to 4.9 g per serving

More fiber; Added fiber: at least 2.5 g more per serving than reference food

Sodium

Sodium free: less than 5 mg per serving

Low sodium: 140 mg or less per serving and, if the serving is 30 g or less or 2 tbs or less, per 50 g of the food

Very low sodium: 35 mg or less per serving and, if the serving is 30 g or less or 2 tbs or less, per 50 g of the food

Reduced sodium; Less sodium: at least 25% less per serving than reference food

Calories

Calorie free: under 5 calories per serving

Low calorie: 40 calories or less per serving; if the serving is 30 g or less or 2 tbs or less, 40 calories or less per 50 g of food

Reduced calories; Fewer calories: at least 25% fewer calories than reference food

Cholesterol

Cholesterol free: less than 2 mg of cholesterol and 2 g or less of saturated fat per serving

Low cholesterol: 20 mg or less and 2 g or less of saturated fat per serving and, if the serving is 30 g or less or 2 tbs or less, per 50 g of the food

Reduced cholesterol; Less cholesterol: at least 25% less than reference food

Other Food Label Claims

Source: Food Safety and Inspection Service, Agricultural Marketing Service, U.S. Dept. of Agriculture

The FDA allows food producers and marketers to use language on their packaging that advertises the health benefits and production methods of their products. Products marked *certified* have been formally evaluated for class, grade, or other quality characteristics by the U.S. Dept. of Agriculture's (USDA) Food Safety and Inspection Service. Below are some common packaging terms and their meanings.

Organic: Produced by farmers who use environmentally friendly methods to raise their crops or animals. Before a product can be labeled organic, the farm where the food is grown must pass a special inspection by a USDA official. Organic foods must be produced without conventional pesticides; fertilizers made with synthetic ingredients or sewage sludge; bioengineering; or ionizing radiation.

The official *USDA organic* label may appear on vegetables, fruit, packages of meat, cartons of milk, eggs, cheese, and other single-ingredient foods. Foods with more than one ingredient can place the official seal on their packaging if at least 95% of the ingredients are organic. Products with at least 70% organic ingredients may advertise prominently on the front of the package that the item contains organic ingredients. Products with less than 70% organic ingredients may not make any organic claims on the front of the package but may list organic ingredients on the side panel. Foods that contain 100% organic ingredients may advertise that fact on the front of the packaging along with the organic seal.

Natural: A minimally processed product that does not contain any artificial ingredient or added color. The label must explain the specific use of the term *natural* with regard to the product, such as "no added colorings," "no artificial ingredients," or "minimally processed."

Free range or **free roaming:** Producers must demonstrate to the USDA that the poultry has been allowed access to the outside.

Halal and **Zabiah Halal:** Produced in federally inspected meat packing plants and handled in accordance with Islamic law and under Islamic authority.

Kosher: Meat and poultry products prepared under Rabbinical supervision.

Minimal processing: Produced using traditional physical processes that do not fundamentally alter the raw products in order to make food edible, to preserve it, or to make it safe for human consumption.

No hormones administered: Hormones are not allowed in raising hogs or poultry, so those products may not make this claim. If sufficient documentation is provided to the USDA proving that hormones were not used, this term may appear on packages of beef.

No antibiotics added: Claim may be made on a package (red meat and poultry) if sufficient documentation is provided to the USDA showing that the animals were raised without antibiotics.

Recommended Levels for Elements (Minerals)

Source: Food and Nutrition Board, Institute of Medicine, National Academy of Sciences, 2010

(in milligrams per day (mg/d) or micrograms per day (µg/d); asterisk denotes level defined as "adequate intake" (AI))

Life stage group		Calcium (mg/d)	Chromium (µg/d)	Copper (µg/d)	Fluoride (mg/d)	Iodine (µg/d)	Iron (mg/d)	Magnesium (mg/d)	Manganese (mg/d)	Molybdenum (µg/d)	Phosphorus (mg/d)	Selenium (µg/d)	Zinc (mg/d)
Infants	0-6 mos.	200*	0.2*	200*	0.01*	110*	0.27*	30*	0.003*	2*	100*	15*	2*
	6-12 mos.	260*	5.5*	220*	0.5*	130*	11	75*	0.6*	3*	275*	20*	3
Children	1-3 yrs.	700	11*	340	0.7*	90	7	80	1.2*	17	460	20	3
	4-8 yrs.	1,000	15*	440	1*	90	10	130	1.5*	22	500	30	5
Males	9-13 yrs.	1,300	25*	700	2*	120	8	240	1.9*	34	1,250	40	8
	14-18 yrs.	1,300	35*	890	3*	150	11	410	2.2*	43	1,250	55	11
	19-30 yrs.	1,000	35*	900	4*	150	8	400	2.3*	45	700	55	11
	31-50 yrs.	1,000	35*	900	4*	150	8	420	2.3*	45	700	55	11
	51-70 yrs.	1,000	30*	900	4*	150	8	420	2.3*	45	700	55	11
	over 70 yrs.	1,200	30*	900	4*	150	8	420	2.3*	45	700	55	11
Females	9-13 yrs.	1,300	21*	700	2*	120	8	240	1.6*	34	1,250	40	8
	14-18 yrs.	1,300	24*	890	3*	150	15	360	1.6*	43	1,250	55	9
	19-30 yrs.	1,000	25*	900	3*	150	18	310	1.8*	45	700	55	8
	31-50 yrs.	1,000	25*	900	3*	150	18	320	1.8*	45	700	55	8
	51-70 yrs.	1,200	20*	900	3*	150	8	320	1.8*	45	700	55	8
	over 70 yrs.	1,200	20*	900	3*	150	8	320	1.8*	45	700	55	8
Pregnancy	14-18 yrs.	1,300	29*	1,000	3*	220	27	400	2.0*	50	1,250	60	12
	19-30 yrs.	1,000	30*	1,000	3*	220	27	350	2.0*	50	700	60	11
	31-50 yrs.	1,000	30*	1,000	3*	220	27	360	2.0*	50	700	60	11
Lactation	14-18 yrs.	1,300	44*	1,300	3*	290	10	360	2.6*	50	1,250	70	13
	19-30 yrs.	1,000	45*	1,300	3*	290	9	310	2.6*	50	700	70	12
	31-50 yrs.	1,000	45*	1,300	3*	290	9	320	2.6*	50	700	70	12

Note: For healthy breastfed infants, the AI is the mean intake. The AI for other life stage and gender groups is believed to cover needs of all individuals in the group, but lack of data or uncertainty in the data prevent being able to specify with confidence the percentage of individuals covered by this intake.

Recommended Levels for Vitamins

Source: Food and Nutrition Board, Institute of Medicine, National Academy of Sciences, 2010

(in milligrams per day (mg/d) or micrograms per day (µg/d); asterisk denotes level defined as "adequate intake" (AI))

Life stage group		Vitamin A (µg/d)[1]	Vitamin C (mg/d)	Vitamin D (µg/d)[2]	Vitamin E (mg/d)	Vitamin K (µg/d)	Thiamin (mg/d)	Riboflavin (mg/d)	Niacin (mg/d)[3]	Vitamin B6 (mg/d)	Folate (µg/d)[4]	Vitamin B12 (µg/d)	Pantothenic acid (mg/d)	Biotin (µg/d)	Choline (mg/d)[5]
Infants	0-6 mos.	400*	40*	10	4*	2.0*	0.2*	0.3*	2*	0.1*	65*	0.4*	1.7*	5*	125*
	6-12 mos.	500*	50*	10	5*	2.5*	0.3*	0.4*	4*	0.3*	80*	0.5*	1.8*	6*	150*
Children	1-3 yrs.	300	15	15	6	30*	0.5	0.5	6	0.5	150	0.9	2*	8*	200*
	4-8 yrs.	400	25	15	7	55*	0.6	0.6	8	0.6	200	1.2	3*	12*	250*
Males	9-13 yrs.	600	45	15	11	60*	0.9	0.9	12	1.0	300	1.8	4*	20*	375*
	14-18 yrs.	900	75	15	15	75*	1.2	1.3	16	1.3	400	2.4	5*	25*	550*
	19-30 yrs.	900	90	15	15	120*	1.2	1.3	16	1.3	400	2.4	5*	30*	550*
	31-50 yrs.	900	90	15	15	120*	1.2	1.3	16	1.3	400	2.4	5*	30*	550*
	51-70 yrs.	900	90	15	15	120*	1.2	1.3	16	1.7	400	2.4[6]	5*	30*	550*
	over 70 yrs.	900	90	20	15	120*	1.2	1.3	16	1.7	400	2.4[6]	5*	30*	550*
Females	9-13 yrs.	600	45	15	11	60*	0.9	0.9	12	1.0	300	1.8	4*	20*	375*
	14-18 yrs.	700	65	15	15	75*	1.0	1.0	14	1.2	400[7]	2.4	5*	25*	400*
	19-30 yrs.	700	75	15	15	90*	1.1	1.1	14	1.3	400[7]	2.4	5*	30*	425*
	31-50 yrs.	700	75	15	15	90*	1.1	1.1	14	1.3	400[7]	2.4	5*	30*	425*
	51-70 yrs.	700	75	15	15	90*	1.1	1.1	14	1.5	400	2.4[6]	5*	30*	425*
	over 70 yrs.	700	75	20	15	90*	1.1	1.1	14	1.5	400	2.4[6]	5*	30*	425*
Pregnancy	14-18 yrs.	750	80	15	15	75*	1.4	1.4	18	1.9	600[8]	2.6	6*	30*	450*
	19-30 yrs.	770	85	15	15	90*	1.4	1.4	18	1.9	600[8]	2.6	6*	30*	450*
	31-50 yrs.	770	85	15	15	90*	1.4	1.4	18	1.9	600[8]	2.6	6*	30*	450*
Lactation	14-18 yrs.	1,200	115	15	19	75*	1.4	1.6	17	2.0	500	2.8	7*	35*	550*
	19-30 yrs.	1,300	120	15	19	90*	1.4	1.6	17	2.0	500	2.8	7*	35*	550*
	31-50 yrs.	1,300	120	15	19	90*	1.4	1.6	17	2.0	500	2.8	7*	35*	550*

Note: For healthy breastfed infants, the AI is the mean intake. The AI for other life stage and gender groups is believed to cover needs of all individuals in the group, but lack of data or uncertainty in the data prevent being able to specify with confidence the percentage of individuals covered by this intake. (1) As retinol activity equivalents (RAEs). (2) Under the assumption of minimal sunlight. (3) As niacin equivalents (NEs). (4) As dietary folate equivalents (DFEs). (5) Although AIs have been set for choline, there are few data to assess whether a dietary supply of choline is needed at all stages of the life cycle. (6) Because 10%-30% of older people may malabsorb food-bound B12, it is advisable for those older than 50 years to meet their RDA mainly by consuming foods fortified with B12 or a supplement containing B12. (7) In view of evidence linking folate intake with neural tube defects in the fetus, it is recommended that all women capable of becoming pregnant consume 400 µg from supplements or fortified foods in addition to intake of food folate from a varied diet. (8) It is assumed that women will continue consuming 400 µg from supplements or fortified food until their pregnancy is confirmed and they enter prenatal care, which ordinarily occurs after the end of the periconceptional period—the critical time for formation of the neural tube.

Dietary Requirements

The Food and Nutrition Board of the National Academy of Sciences' Institute of Medicine, in reports published between 1997 and 2005, established **Dietary Reference Intakes (DRIs)**. DRIs establish daily consumption values for vitamins and elements (often called minerals) that aim to optimize health, not just guard against nutritional deficiencies, at all stages of life.

There are four DRI categories. The **Recommended Dietary Allowance (RDA)** gives intake values that meet the nutrient requirements of almost all (97%-98%) healthy individuals in a specified group. The **Estimated Average Requirement (EAR)** specifies the average daily nutrient intake level estimated to meet the requirement of half the healthy individuals in a specified group. **Adequate Intake (AI)** values are given when there's inadequate scientific evidence to calculate an RDA. For healthy breastfed infants, the AI is the mean intake; for other life stage groups, the AI is thought to cover the needs of all group individuals, but lack of data or uncertainty in the data prevents the percentage of individuals covered from being specified with confidence. The **Tolerable Upper Intake Level (UL)** designates the maximum intake amount that is unlikely to pose a risk of adverse health effects in almost all healthy individuals in a group. RDAs and AIs may both be used as individual intake goals.

Weight Guidelines for Adults

Source: Dietary Guidelines for Americans, 2010, U.S. Dept. of Agriculture; National Center for Health Statistics, CDC

Guidelines on identification, evaluation, and treatment of overweight and obesity in adults were released in June 1998 by the National Heart, Lung, and Blood Institute (NHLBI), in cooperation with the National Institute of Diabetes and Digestive and Kidney Diseases (NIDDK). The guidelines, based on research into risk factors contributing to heart disease, stroke, and other conditions, define overweight and obesity in terms of **body mass index (BMI)**. BMI is based on a person's weight and height and is strongly correlated with total body fat content. A BMI of 25-29 is said to indicate **overweight**; a BMI of 30 or higher indicates **obesity**. Weight reduction is advised for persons with a BMI of 25 or higher. Factors such as a large waist circumference, high blood pressure or cholesterol, and family medical history may increase a person's risk of developing an obesity-related disease.

The National Center for Health Statistics notes that in 2009-10, 35.7% of American adults were obese. Over the past three decades, childhood obesity rates in America have almost tripled, and in 2009-10, 16.9% of children (ages 2-19) were obese. Based on directly measured weight and height, between 1988-94 and 2009-10, the proportion of adults ages 20 years and over who were obese rose by 56.5%, from 23% to 36%. During the same period, obesity increased by 63.6% in children ages 6-11, from 11% to 18%, and by 63.6% in adolescents ages 12-19, from 11% to 18%.

A high prevalence of overweight and obesity is a public health concern because excess body fat has been associated with type 2 diabetes, hypertension, dyslipidemia, cardiovascular disease, stroke, gall bladder disease, respiratory dysfunction, gout, osteoarthritis, and certain kinds of cancers.

The table below shows the BMI for certain heights and weights. For weight reduction help, contact the Weight-control Information Network, 1 WIN Way, Bethesda, MD 20892-3665; (877) 946-4627; www.win.niddk.nih.gov.

Body Mass Index (BMI) by Height and Weight
Weight (lbs)

Height	HEALTHY						OVERWEIGHT					OBESE									
4'10"	91	96	100	105	110	115	119	124	129	134	138	143	148	153	158	162	167	172	177	181	186
4'11"	94	99	104	109	114	119	124	128	133	138	143	148	153	158	163	168	173	178	183	188	193
5'0"	97	102	107	112	118	123	128	133	138	143	148	153	158	163	168	174	179	184	189	194	199
5'1"	100	106	111	116	122	127	132	137	143	148	153	158	164	169	174	180	185	190	195	201	206
5'2"	104	109	115	120	126	131	136	142	147	153	158	164	169	175	180	186	191	196	202	207	213
5'3"	107	113	118	124	130	135	141	146	152	158	163	169	175	180	186	191	197	203	208	214	220
5'4"	110	116	122	128	134	140	145	151	157	163	169	174	180	186	192	197	204	209	215	221	227
5'5"	114	120	126	132	138	144	150	156	162	168	174	180	186	192	198	204	210	216	222	228	234
5'6"	118	124	130	136	142	148	155	161	167	173	179	186	192	198	204	210	216	223	229	235	241
5'7"	121	127	134	140	146	153	159	166	172	178	185	191	198	204	211	217	223	230	236	242	249
5'8"	125	131	138	144	151	158	164	171	177	184	190	197	203	210	216	223	230	236	243	249	256
5'9"	128	135	142	149	155	162	169	176	182	189	196	203	209	216	223	230	236	243	250	257	263
5'10"	132	139	146	153	160	167	174	181	188	195	202	209	216	222	229	236	243	250	257	264	271
5'11"	136	143	150	157	165	172	179	186	193	200	208	215	222	229	236	243	250	257	265	272	279
6'0"	140	147	154	162	169	177	184	191	199	206	213	221	228	235	242	250	258	265	272	279	287
6'1"	144	151	159	166	174	182	189	197	204	212	219	227	235	242	250	257	265	272	280	288	295
6'2"	148	155	163	171	179	186	194	202	210	218	225	233	241	249	256	264	272	280	287	295	303
6'3"	152	160	168	176	184	192	200	208	216	224	232	240	248	256	264	272	279	287	295	303	311
6'4"	156	164	172	180	189	197	205	213	221	230	238	246	254	263	271	279	287	295	304	312	320
BMI[1]	19	20	21	22	23	24	25	26	27	28	29	30	31	32	33	34	35	36	37	38	39

(1) The BMI numbers apply to both men and women. Some very muscular people may have a high BMI without health risks.

Estimated Calorie Requirements

Source: *Dietary Guidelines for Americans, 2010*, U.S. Dept. of Agriculture; U.S. Dept. of Health and Human Services

Estimated amounts of calories, rounded to the nearest 200, needed to maintain energy balance by sex, for various age groups and levels of physical activity.

	Age (years)	Sedentary[1]	Moderately active[2]	Active[3]		Age (years)	Sedentary[1]	Moderately active[2]	Active[3]
Child	2-3	1,000-1,200	1,000-1,400	1,000-1,400					
Female[4]	4-8	1,200-1,400	1,400-1,600	1,400-1,800	**Male**	4-8	1,200-1,400	1,400-1,600	1,600-2,000
	9-13	1,400-1,600	1,600-2,000	1,800-2,200		9-13	1,600-2,000	1,800-2,200	2,000-2,600
	14-18	1,800	2,000	2,400		14-18	2,000-2,400	2,400-2,800	2,800-3,200
	19-30	1,800-2,000	2,000-2,200	2,400		19-30	2,400-2,600	2,600-2,800	3,000
	31-50	1,800	2,000	2,200		31-50	2,200-2,400	2,400-2,600	2,800-3,000
	51+	1,600	1,800	2,000-2,200		51+	2,000-2,200	2,200-2,400	2,400-2,800

Note: Based on Estimated Energy Requirements (EER) equations, using reference heights (average) and reference weights (healthy) for each age/gender group. For children and adolescents, reference height and weight vary. For adults, the reference man is 5 ft 10 in. tall and weighs 154 lbs. The reference woman is 5 ft 4 in. tall and weighs 126 lbs. (1) Engaging only in the light activities associated with ordinary day-to-day life. (2) Includes physical activity equivalent to walking 1.5 to 3 miles per day at 3-4 mph. (3) Includes physical activity equivalent to walking more than 3 miles per day at 3-4 mph. (4) Excludes women who are pregnant or breastfeeding.

Calories Used During Physical Activity

Source: Center for Nutrition Policy and Promotion, U.S. Dept. of Agriculture

Amounts of calories burned during physical activities are estimates for a 154-pound man. The more an individual weighs, the more calories he or she will burn by exercising at the same intensity.

Moderate physical activities	In 1 hr.	In 30 mins.	Vigorous physical activities	In 1 hr.	In 30 mins.
Hiking	370	185	Running/jogging (5 miles per hour)	590	295
Light gardening/yard work	330	165	Bicycling (more than 10 miles per hour)	590	295
Dancing	330	165	Swimming (slow freestyle laps)	510	255
Golf (walking and carrying clubs)	330	165	Aerobics	480	240
Bicycling (less than 10 miles per hour)	290	145	Walking (4½ miles per hour)	460	230
Walking (3½ miles per hour)	280	140	Heavy yard work (e.g., chopping wood)	440	220
Weight training (general light workout)	220	110	Weight lifting (vigorous effort)	440	220
Stretching	180	90	Basketball (vigorous)	440	220

Finding Your Target Heart Rate

Source: Carole Casten, EdD, *Aerobics Today*; Peg Jordan, RN, Aerobics and Fitness Assn. of America

The target heart rate is the rate of heartbeats a person should aim for during aerobic exercise (e.g., running, cycling, or cross-country skiing) to get the full benefit for cardiovascular conditioning.

First, determine the intensity level at which one would like to exercise. Someone who's led a sedentary lifestyle may want to begin an exercise regimen at the 60% level and work up to the 70% level. Athletes and highly fit individuals must work at an 85% or higher level to receive benefits. Second, calculate the target heart rate. One common way is by using the American College of Sports Medicine Method.

An individual should subtract his or her age from 220, then multiply that number by the desired intensity level of the workout. Divide the answer by 6 for a 10-second pulse count. (The 10-second pulse count is useful for checking whether the target heart rate is being achieved during the workout. One can easily check one's pulse—on the inside of the wrist or side of the neck—by counting the number of beats in 10 seconds.)

For example, a 20-year-old wishing to exercise at 70% intensity would do the following calculations to figure out his or her target heart rate:

Maximum heart rate	$220 - 20 = 200$
Target heart rate	$200 \times 0.70 = 140$
10-second pulse count	$140/6 = 23.33$

To work out at 70% intensity, this 20-year-old would strive for a target heart rate of 140 beats per minute, or a 10-second pulse count of 23.

To obtain cardiovascular fitness benefits from aerobic exercise, an individual should participate in an aerobic activity at least three to five times a week for 20-30 minutes each session. Cardiac patients and very sedentary individuals can obtain benefits with shorter periods (15-20 minutes per session). Generally, training changes occur within four to six weeks, but they can occur in as little as two weeks.

Obesity Among Adults in the U.S., 2009-10

Source: National Health and Nutrition Examination Survey, National Center for Health Statistics, CDC

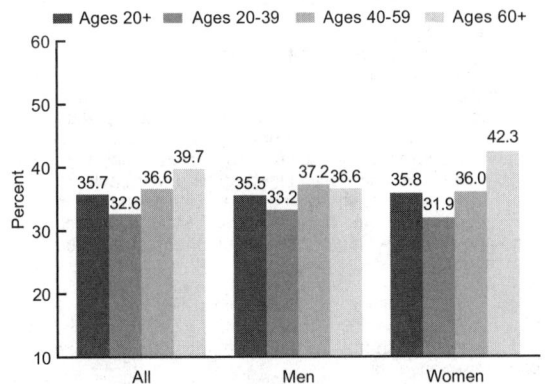

Obesity Among Children and Adolescents in the U.S., 2009-10

Source: National Health and Nutrition Examination Survey, National Center for Health Statistics, CDC

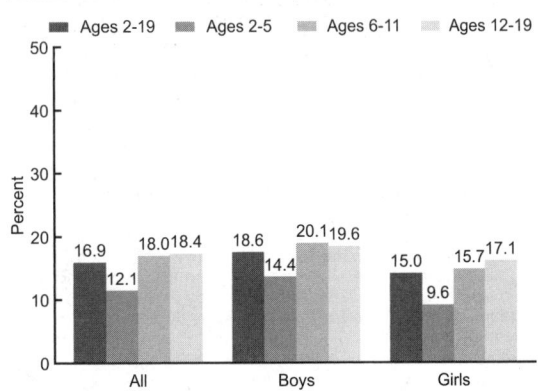

Basic First Aid

Source: Courtesy of the American National Red Cross, www.redcross.org. All rights reserved in all countries.

Note: This information is not intended to be a substitute for formal training. It is recommended that you contact your local American Red Cross chapter to sign up for a First Aid/CPR/AED course.

In an emergency, it is important to get medical assistance as soon as possible, but knowing what to do until a doctor or other trained person gets to the scene can save a life, especially in cases of severe bleeding, choking, poisoning, and shock.

People with special medical problems, such as diabetes, cardiovascular disease, epilepsy, or allergies, are urged to wear some sort of emblem identifying the problem as a safeguard against receiving medication that might be harmful or even fatal. Emblems may be obtained from Medic Alert Foundation, 2323 Colorado Ave., Turlock, CA 95382; (888) 633-4298; www.medicalert.org.

Animal bite: Call 9-1-1 or the local emergency number if the wound is bleeding seriously or if you suspect the animal might have rabies. Control any bleeding. Wash minor wounds with soap under running water and apply antibiotic ointment and a dressing. When possible, proper authorities should test the animal for rabies.

Asphyxiation: Call 9-1-1 or the local emergency number.

Bleeding: Use a barrier between your hand and the wound to help prevent infection. Cover wound with a sterile dressing. Apply direct pressure until bleeding stops. Cover compress with a bandage. Call 9-1-1 or the local emergency number if bleeding is severe.

Burn: Check for life-threatening conditions. If the burn is mild, with skin unbroken and no blisters, flush with cold running water for at least 20 minutes. Gently wash with soap and water and pat dry. Apply a thin layer of antibiotic ointment. Apply a loose, sterile dry dressing to prevent infection. If the burn is severe, call 9-1-1 or the local emergency number. Care for shock (see below). Keep the person from getting chilled or overheated until advanced medical assistance arrives. Do not try to clean a severe burn or break blisters.

Chemical in eye: Call 9-1-1 or the local emergency number. Turn the person's head to the side so that the affected eye is lower than the unaffected eye. Flush the affected eye with large amounts of water for at least 20 minutes.

Choking: See **First Aid for Choking** below.

Convulsions (seizures): Remove nearby objects that might cause injury. Protect the person's head by placing a thin folded towel or item of clothing under it. Roll him or her on one side to drain fluids from the mouth. Do not place anything between the person's teeth. Stay with the person until he or she is fully conscious. If convulsions do not stop, get medical attention immediately.

Cut (minor): Use a clean barrier between your hand and the wound to prevent infection. Apply direct pressure for a few minutes to control any bleeding. Wash the wound thoroughly with soap and water and apply a thin layer of antibiotic ointment or a microthin film dressing. Cover the wound with a sterile dressing and a bandage.

Foreign object in eye: If an object is impaled in someone's eye, do not remove it. If not impaled, try to remove the object by having the person blink several times. If the object doesn't come out, gently flush the eye with saline solution or water. Do not rub the eye. If the object still doesn't come out, the person should receive professional medical attention.

Frostbite: Handle the frostbitten area gently. Do not rub. If there is no danger of the affected area refreezing, soak it in warm water (not warmer than 105°F). Do not allow the frostbitten area to touch the side of the water container. Keep the frostbitten part in the water until normal color returns and it feels warm. Loosely bandage the area with dry, sterile dressings. If fingers or toes are frostbitten, put cotton or gauze between them. Do not break any blisters. Call 9-1-1 or seek emergency help as soon as possible.

Heart attack and stroke: See **Heart and Blood Vessel Disease** earlier in chapter.

Heat stroke: Remove the person from the heat. Loosen any tight clothing. Immerse person in cold water until he or she becomes alert. If a large enough source of water is not available, drench the person with cold water and fan constantly. If the person is conscious, have him or her slowly drink some cool water. Call 9-1-1 if the person's condition does not improve.

Hypothermia: Call 9-1-1 or the local emergency number. For mild hypothermia, cover all exposed skin. Replace wet clothes with something dry. If the person is alert, give him or her simple carbohydrates to eat and warm, nonalcoholic and decaffeinated liquids to drink. Apply heat pads or other heat sources if available but do not place against bare skin.

Loss of limb: Call 9-1-1 or the local emergency number and care for any life-threatening conditions. If a limb is severed, it is important to properly protect the limb so that it can possibly be reattached. After the victim is cared for, the limb should be wrapped in sterile gauze and placed in a plastic bag. Place bag in a larger bag or container of an ice and water slurry, not ice alone. Be sure the limb is taken to the hospital with the person.

Poisoning: Care for any life-threatening conditions. Call the National Capital Poison Center (800-222-1222), 9-1-1, or the local emergency number and follow their directions. Do not give the person any food or drink or induce vomiting unless specified to do so by medical professionals.

Shock (injury-related): Monitor breathing and consciousness. Have the person lie down and keep him or her as comfortable as possible. Maintain an open airway. Give sips of cool water if he or she tolerates fluids. Elevate his or her legs about 12 inches unless you suspect injuries to the head or lower extremities. Maintain normal body temperature. If the weather is cold or damp, place blankets or extra clothing over and under the person; if the weather is hot, provide shade.

Snakebite: Call 9-1-1 or the local emergency number. Gently wash the injury. Splint bitten extremities, and keep the area at approximately the level of the heart. Keep the person calm. Do not cut, suck, apply a constricting band, or apply cold to a bite from a pit viper (such as a rattlesnake, copperhead, or cottonmouth). For a bite from an elapid snake, such as a coral snake, apply an elastic roller bandage after washing the wound.

Sprains and strains: Splint any injured bone or joint that the person cannot use.

Sting from bee or wasp: If possible, remove the stinger by scraping it away with your finger or a plastic card (like a credit card) or using tweezers. If you use tweezers, grasp the stinger, not the venom sac. Wash the area with soap and water. Cover it to keep it clean. Apply cold to the area. Call 9-1-1 or the local emergency number immediately if the wound does not stop swelling, the person collapses, or he or she is known to be allergic to the sting.

Unconsciousness: Call 9-1-1 or the local emergency number immediately. Do not move the person if a spinal injury is suspected.

First Aid for Choking

The recommended first aid for a conscious choking victim who is unable to speak, cough, or breathe, is to deliver a series of five blows to the back and five thrusts to the abdomen. Have another person call 9-1-1 or the local emergency number. Obtain consent from the victim to treat him or her. Lean the victim forward and apply five blows to his or her back with the heel of your hand. Then stand or kneel behind the victim and wrap your arms around his or her waist. Make a fist with one hand and place the thumb side against the middle of the person's abdomen, just above the navel and well below the lower tip of the breastbone. Grasp your fist in your other hand and quickly thrust upwards into the abdomen five times. Continue back blows and abdominal thrusts until the object is dislodged, and the person can breathe or cough forcefully, or the person loses consciousness.

YEAR IN PICTURES

Campaign Trail Pres. Barack Obama and Vice Pres. Joe Biden defended their record in office while campaigning in Iowa, Sept. 7, 2012.

Republican Ticket Former Gov. Mitt Romney and running mate Rep. Paul Ryan campaigned for votes in swing state Ohio, Aug. 25, 2012.

Last Men Standing Republican primary candidates Rick Santorum, Mitt Romney, Newt Gingrich, and Ron Paul were the last contenders in the long presidential primary process.

Captive Audience Actor/director Clint Eastwood addressed an empty chair as though it were the president in an impromptu speech Aug. 30, 2012, at the Republican National Convention.

Immigration Policy Shift Thousands of young undocumented immigrants Aug. 15, 2012, applied for deportation deferrals and work permits under a new Obama administration policy.

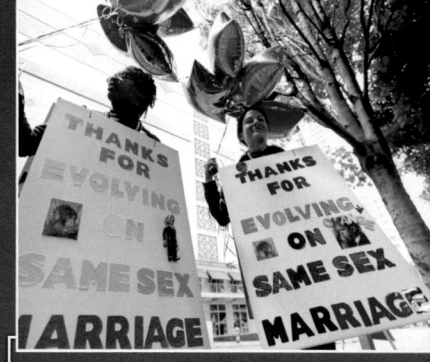

Marriage Equality Pres. Barack Obama became the first sitting president to affirm support for same-sex marriage May 9, 2012.

"Obamacare" Stands The U.S. Supreme Court June 28, 2012, upheld the controversial health care reform act signed into law in 2010.

Contraceptive Controversy After a new rule requiring institutions to cover contraception in their insurance plans faced strong opposition from religious leaders, including New York Archbishop Timothy Dolan, in Feb. 2012, Health and Human Services Sec. Kathleen Sebelius and the Obama administration announced a compromise measure.

New Home
Chinese dissident and civil-rights activist Chen Guangcheng arrived in the U.S. May 19, 2012, after a series of tense negotiations with the Chinese government that had U.S. diplomats scrambling.

Held in Contempt
The House of Representatives June 28, 2012, voted to hold Attorney Gen. Eric Holder in contempt of Congress in connection with Operation Fast and Furious, a flawed gun-trafficking sting.

Stand Your Ground The fatal shooting of teenager Trayvon Martin by a neighborhood watch volunteer in Florida Feb. 26, 2012, touched off a national debate on racial bias.

School's Out
Chicago public school teachers went on strike in Sept. 2012 for the first time in 25 years; 26,000 teachers and 350,000 students were out of classrooms for seven school days.

Dark Night Former neuroscience graduate student James Holmes was charged July 30, 2012, with killing 12 people and wounding 58 others at a movie theater in Aurora, CO.

Facebook's Public Profile Social networking behemoth Facebook made its stock market debut May 18, 2012.

Temple Tragedy
A gunman fatally shot six people and wounded four more at a Sikh temple in Oak Creek, WI, Aug. 5, 2012.

Penn State Scandal
Fallout from a child sex abuse scandal continued to shake Penn State even after longtime assistant coach Jerry Sandusky's conviction; an independent inquiry July 12, 2012, faulted head coach Joe Paterno (right) and university leadership for concealing the abuse.

Parched Earth The worst U.S. drought in decades threatened farms across the U.S. in 2012.

WORLD

Civil War in Syria
Syrian Pres. Bashar al-Assad's government troops and the rebelling Free Syrian Army battled in Syria's cities and countryside throughout 2012; an estimated 20,000 had been killed since conflicts began in 2011.

Green-on-Blue Violence
In response to growing numbers of insider attacks, in which Afghan security personnel attacked coalition forces, U.S. Marine Gen. John Allen issued orders curtailing their joint operations Sept. 16, 2012.

Euro Crisis Europeans in Greece, Spain, and other EU countries protested 2012 budget cuts and austerity measures required in exchange for loans intended to bailout their struggling economies.

Consulates Attacked A crude film denigrating the Prophet Muhammad sparked anti-U.S. protests in mor than 20 countries in Sept. 2012. U.S. ambassador to Libya J. Christopher Stevens was killed Sept. 11, 201 in Benghazi in what initially appeared to be a related incident, but was later described by the State Dept. as a terrorist attack.

Balance of Power Vladimir Putin (right) assumed the Russian presidency for a third term May 7, 2012, and named Dmitri Medvedev his prime minister; each had held the other office for four years.

Departed Dear Leader Funeral services were held for North Korean dictator Kim Jong Il Dec. 28, 2011; son Kim Jong Un was appointed the nation's military leader Dec. 30.

Egyptian Elections Just a year after Hosni Mubarak's regime was toppled, the Muslim Brotherhood's Mohammed Morsi June 24, 2012, was declared the first democratically elected Egyptian president.

Myanmar Transition? Nobel Peace Prize laureate and former political prisoner Daw Aung San Suu Kyi took a parliamentary seat after by-elections Apr. 1, 2012.

Criminal Justice Former Liberian Pres. Charles Taylor was convicted Apr. 26, 2012, of war crimes and crimes against humanity for his role in atrocities committed during Sierra Leone's 1991-2002 civil war.

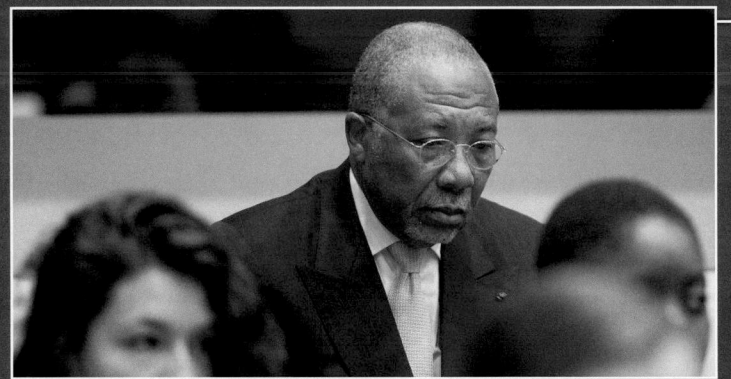

Record Blackout
Major grid collapses July 30-31, 2012, left 670 million people across India without power.

Diamond Jubilee
The UK's Queen Elizabeth and Prince Philip celebrated the 60th anniversary of her accession to the throne June 3, 2012, amid fanfare and pageantry.

Bizarre Crime   Gu Kailai, wife of disgraced political leader Bo Xilai, received a suspended death sentence Aug. 20, 2012, for her role in the murder of a British businessman.

***Costa* Disaster**   Luxury cruise ship *Costa Concordia* capsized Jan. 13, 2012, killing 32 people; the ship's captain, who had abandoned ship, was charged with manslaughter.

VITAL STATISTICS

Recent Trends in Vital Statistics

Source: National Center for Health Statistics (NCHS), U.S. Dept. of Health and Human Services

Births
An estimated 3,961,000 babies were born in the U.S. in 2011, a decrease from 4,007,000 in 2010. The birth rate decreased to 12.7 per 1,000 total population, a new record low.

The fertility rate (number of live births per 1,000 women aged 15-44 years) decreased to an estimated 63.4 for 2011, down from the 2010 rate of 64.2.

Deaths
The number of deaths during 2011 was estimated at 2,508,000 according to provisional data, up from 2,452,000 in 2010. The death rate in 2011 decreased to 8.3 deaths per 1,000 population, down from 8.4 in 2010. The death rate for infants under 1 year of age was 5.7 deaths per 1,000 live births in 2011, the same as in 2010.

Natural Increase
As a result of natural increase (the excess of births over deaths), an estimated 1,453,000 persons were added to the population in 2011.

Marriages
An estimated 2,096,000 marriages were performed in 2010, compared to 2,080,000 in 2009. The provisional marriage rate for 2010 (6.8 per 1,000 population) remained the same as in 2009.

Divorces
The divorce rate increased slightly from 3.5 per 1,000 population in 2009 to 3.6 per 1,000 population in 2010, according to provisional data. Data are incomplete however. The NCHS does not include divorce data for California, Georgia, Hawaii, Indiana, Louisiana, and Minnesota.

Births and Deaths in the U.S., 1960-2011

Source: National Center for Health Statistics (NCHS), U.S. Dept. of Health and Human Services

Year	BIRTHS Total number	Rate	DEATHS Total number	Rate	Year	BIRTHS Total number	Rate	DEATHS Total number	Rate
1960	4,257,850	23.7	1,711,982	9.5	2000	4,058,814	14.4	2,403,351	8.5
1970	3,731,386	18.4	1,921,031	9.5	2001	4,025,933	14.1	2,416,425	8.5
1980	3,612,258	15.9	1,989,841	8.8	2002	4,021,726	13.9	2,443,387	8.5
1990	4,092,994	16.7	2,148,463	8.6	2003	4,089,950	14.1	2,448,288	8.4
1992	4,049,024	15.8	2,175,613	8.5	2004	4,112,052	14.0	2,397,615	8.2
1993	4,000,240	15.4	2,268,553	8.7	2005	4,138,349	14.0	2,448,017	8.3
1994	3,952,767	15.0	2,278,994	8.7	2006	4,265,555	14.2	2,426,264	8.1
1995	3,899,589	14.6	2,312,132	8.7	2007	4,316,233	14.3	2,423,712	8.0
1996	3,891,494	14.4	2,314,690	8.6	2008	4,247,694	14.0	2,471,984	8.1
1997	3,880,894	14.2	2,314,245	8.5	2009	4,130,665	13.5	2,437,163	7.9
1998	3,941,553	14.3	2,337,256	8.5	2010[1]	4,000,279	13.0	2,465,936	8.0
1999	3,959,417	14.2	2,391,399	8.6	2011[2]	3,961,000	12.7	2,508,000	8.3

Note: Statistics cover only events occurring within the U.S. and exclude fetal deaths. Rates per 1,000 population; enumerated as of Apr. 1 for decennial census years; estimated as of July 1 for all other years. Beginning 1970, statistics exclude births and deaths occurring among nonresidents of the U.S. (1) Preliminary. (2) Provisional.

Marriage and Divorce Rates in the U.S., 1920-2010

Source: National Center for Health Statistics (NCHS), U.S. Dept. of Health and Human Services

(Divorce rates for 2006-10 were calculated excluding data and populations from the nonreporting states California, Georgia, Hawaii, Indiana, Louisiana, and Minnesota. Some data are provisional.)

The U.S. marriage rate dipped during the Depression and peaked sharply just after World War II; the trend after that has been more gradual. The divorce rate generally rose from the 1920s through 1981, when it peaked at 5.3 per 1,000 population, before declining somewhat. The graph below shows marriage and divorce rates since 1920.

U.S. Median Age at First Marriage, 1890-2011

Source: U.S. Census Bureau, U.S. Dept. of Commerce

Year[1]	Men	Women	Year[1]	Men	Women	Year[1]	Men	Women	Year[1]	Men	Women	Year[1]	Men	Women
1890	26.1	22.0	1960	22.8	20.3	1991	26.3	24.1	1998	26.7	25.0	2005	27.1	25.3
1900	25.9	21.9	1965	22.8	20.6	1992	26.5	24.4	1999	26.9	25.1	2006	27.5	25.5
1910	25.1	21.6	1970	23.2	20.8	1993	26.5	24.5	2000	26.8	25.1	2007	27.5	25.6
1920	24.6	21.2	1975	23.5	21.1	1994	26.7	24.5	2001	26.9	25.1	2008	27.6	25.9
1930	24.3	21.3	1980	24.7	22.0	1995	26.9	24.5	2002	26.9	25.3	2009	28.1	25.9
1940	24.3	21.5	1985	25.5	23.3	1996	27.1	24.8	2003	27.1	25.3	2010	28.2	26.1
1950	22.8	20.3	1990	26.1	23.9	1997	26.8	25.0	2004	27.4	25.3	2011	28.7	26.5

(1) Figures after 1947 based on Current Population Survey data; earlier figures based on decennial censuses.

Divorce Rates by State, 2010

Source: National Center for Health Statistics (NCHS), U.S. Dept. of Health and Human Services

State	Divorce rate	State	Divorce rate	State	Divorce rate
Alabama	4.4	Louisiana	NA	Ohio	3.4
Alaska	4.7	Maine	4.2	Oklahoma	5.2
Arizona	3.5	Maryland	2.8	Oregon	4.0
Arkansas	5.7	Massachusetts	2.5	Pennsylvania	2.7
California	NA	Michigan	3.5	Rhode Island	3.2
Colorado	4.3	Minnesota	NA	South Carolina	3.1
Connecticut	2.9	Mississippi	4.3	South Dakota	3.4
Delaware	3.5	Missouri	3.9	Tennessee	4.2
District of Columbia	2.8	Montana	3.9	Texas	3.3
Florida	4.4	Nebraska	3.6	Utah	3.7
Georgia	NA	Nevada	5.9	Vermont	3.8
Hawaii	NA	New Hampshire	3.8	Virginia	3.8
Idaho	5.2	New Jersey	3.0	Washington	4.2
Illinois	2.6	New Mexico	4.0	West Virginia	5.1
Indiana	NA	New York	2.9	Wisconsin	3.0
Iowa	2.4	North Carolina	3.8	Wyoming	5.1
Kansas	3.7	North Dakota	3.1	**United States**	**3.5**
Kentucky	4.5				

NA = Not available. **Note:** Rate per 1,000 population. Rate includes annulments and may also include divorce petitions filed and legal separations for some counties and states.

Birth Rates and Fertility Rates by Age of Mother, 1950-2010

Source: National Center for Health Statistics (NCHS), U.S. Dept. of Health and Human Services

Live births per 1,000 women by age of mother

Year	Birth rate[1]	Fertility rate[2]	10-14 years	15-19 years	15-17 years	18-19 years	20-24 years	25-29 years	30-34 years	35-39 years	40-44 years	45-49 years
1950	24.1	106.2	1.0	81.6	40.7	132.7	196.6	166.1	103.7	52.9	15.1	1.2
1960	23.7	118.0	0.8	89.1	43.9	166.7	258.1	197.4	112.7	56.2	15.5	0.9
1970	18.4	87.9	1.2	68.3	38.8	114.7	167.8	145.1	73.3	31.7	8.1	0.5
1980	15.9	68.4	1.1	53.0	32.5	82.1	115.1	112.9	61.9	19.8	3.9	0.2
1990	16.7	70.9	1.4	59.9	37.5	88.6	116.5	120.2	80.8	31.7	5.5	0.2
1992	15.8	68.4	1.4	60.3	37.6	93.6	113.7	115.7	79.6	32.3	5.9	0.3
1993	15.4	67.0	1.4	59.0	37.5	91.1	111.3	113.2	79.9	32.7	6.1	0.3
1994	15.0	65.9	1.4	58.2	37.2	90.2	109.2	111.0	80.4	33.4	6.4	0.3
1995	14.6	64.6	1.3	56.0	35.5	87.7	107.5	108.8	81.1	34.0	6.6	0.3
1996	14.4	64.1	1.2	53.5	33.3	84.7	107.8	108.6	82.1	34.9	6.8	0.3
1997	14.2	63.6	1.1	51.3	31.4	82.1	107.3	108.3	83.0	35.7	7.1	0.4
1998	14.3	64.3	1.0	50.3	29.9	80.9	108.4	110.2	85.2	36.9	7.4	0.4
1999	14.2	64.4	0.9	48.8	28.2	79.1	107.9	111.2	87.1	37.8	7.4	0.4
2000	14.4	65.9	0.9	47.7	26.9	78.1	109.7	113.5	91.2	39.7	8.0	0.5
2001	14.1	65.3	0.8	45.3	24.7	76.1	106.2	113.4	91.9	40.6	8.1	0.5
2002	13.9	64.8	0.7	43.0	23.2	72.8	103.6	113.6	91.5	41.4	8.3	0.5
2003	14.1	66.1	0.6	41.6	22.4	70.7	102.6	115.6	95.1	43.8	8.7	0.5
2004	14.0	66.3	0.7	41.1	22.1	70.0	101.7	115.5	95.3	45.4	8.9	0.5
2005	14.0	66.7	0.7	40.5	21.4	69.9	102.2	115.5	95.8	46.3	9.1	0.6
2006	14.2	68.5	0.6	41.9	22.0	73.0	105.9	116.7	97.7	47.3	9.4	0.6
2007	14.3	69.5	0.6	42.5	22.1	73.9	106.3	117.5	99.9	47.5	9.5	0.6
2008	14.0	68.6	0.6	41.5	21.7	70.6	103.0	115.1	99.3	46.9	9.8	0.7
2009	13.5	66.2	0.5	37.9	19.6	64.0	96.2	111.5	97.5	46.1	10.0	0.7[4]
2010[3]	13.0	64.1	0.4	34.3	17.3	58.3	90.0	108.3	96.6	45.9	10.2	0.7[4]

(1) Live births per 1,000 population. (2) Live births per 1,000 women 15-44 years of age. (3) Preliminary. (4) Women 45-54 years of age.

Cesarean Delivery Rates by State, 1996-2009

Source: National Center for Health Statistics (NCHS), U.S. Dept. of Health and Human Services

State	1996	2009	Percent change, 1996-2009	State	1996	2009	Percent change, 1996-2009
Alabama	23.3%	35.4%	52%	Missouri	20.4%	31.4%	54%
Alaska	16.7	23.2	39	Montana	19.1	29.5	54
Arizona	16.1	27.2	69	Nebraska	19.8	31.7	60
Arkansas	25.3	34.4	36	Nevada	19.3	33.3	73
California	20.6	33.0	60	New Hampshire	20.3	30.8	52
Colorado	15.1	26.4	75	New Jersey	24.0	39.0	63
Connecticut	19.8	35.5	79	New Mexico	17.2	22.8	33
Delaware	21.0	35.6	70	New York	22.9	34.7	52
District of Columbia	21.3	32.0	50	North Carolina	21.1	31.0	47
Florida	21.6	38.1	76	North Dakota	18.9	29.3	55
Georgia	20.9	33.4	60	Ohio	19.0	31.0	63
Hawaii	17.5	26.8	53	Oklahoma	22.5	34.5	53
Idaho	16.0	24.5	53	Oregon	16.9	29.4	74
Illinois	19.3	31.2	62	Pennsylvania	19.4	31.8	64
Indiana	20.3	30.5	50	Rhode Island	17.7	32.5	84
Iowa	18.6	30.3	63	South Carolina	22.6	35.3	56
Kansas	19.2	30.1	57	South Dakota	20.8	26.3	26
Kentucky	21.3	35.9	69	Tennessee	21.7	33.8	56
Louisiana	26.4	39.5	50	Texas	23.1	35.3	53
Maine	20.8	29.5	42	Utah	15.9	22.9	44
Maryland	21.6	33.2	54	Vermont	16.5	27.8	68
Massachusetts	19.8	33.2	68	Virginia	21.1	34.1	62
Michigan	20.2	32.1	59	Washington	16.8	29.2	74
Minnesota	16.9	27.2	61	West Virginia	22.8	35.8	57
Mississippi	26.6	37.6	41	Wisconsin	15.6	25.8	65
				Wyoming	18.3	28.1	54
				United States	**20.7**	**32.8**	**58**

Note: The cesarean rate is the percentage of all live births by cesarean delivery.

Assisted Reproductive Technology (ART) Pregnancy Success Rates, 2010

Source: Centers for Disease Control and Prevention (CDC), U.S. Dept. of Health and Human Services

Type of cycle	Under 35	35-37	Age of woman[1] 38-40 Number	41-42	43-44
Fresh embryos from nondonor eggs	41,741	21,366	21,739	10,120	4,501
Average number of embryos transferred	2.0	2.2	2.6	3.0	3.2
Frozen embryos from nondonor eggs	12,631	6,195	4,682	1,591	710
Average number of embryos transferred	2.0	1.9	2.1	2.2	2.2
Fresh embryos from nondonor eggs			Percent distribution		
Cycles resulting in pregnancies	47.6%	38.8%	29.9%	19.9%	10.6%
Cycles resulting in live births[2]	41.5	31.9	22.1	12.4	5.0
Retrievals resulting in live births[2]	44.4	35.4	25.3	14.8	6.3
Transfers resulting in live births[2]	47.6	38.3	28.1	16.7	7.4
Transfers resulting in singleton live births	31.4	27.3	21.5	13.7	6.6
Pregnancies with twins	32.9	27.3	21.6	15.0	8.1
Pregnancies with triplets or more.	2.6	3.1	3.7	3.0	0.6
Live births having multiple infants[2]	34.0	28.7	23.3	18.0	10.2
Cancellations	6.6	9.9	12.8	16.4	20.6
Frozen embryos from nondonor eggs					
Transfers resulting in live births[2]	38.4%	34.7%	28.4%	21.5%	16.8%

Donor eggs (all ages)	Fresh embryos[3]	Frozen embryos[3]
Number of transfers	9,866	6,665
Average number of embryos transferred	2.0	2.0
Percentage of transfers resulting in live births[2].	55.8%	34.9%

Note: Data are preliminary. 443 ART clinics in the U.S. submitted data in 2010. A total of 154,417 cycles were reported. There were 47,102 live-birth deliveries and 61,561 infants born resulting from ART cycles in 2010. (1) Clinic-specific outcome rates are unreliable for women older than 44 undergoing ART cycles using fresh or frozen embryos with nondonor eggs. (2) A multiple-infant birth is counted as one live birth. (3) All ages (including ages over 44) are reported together because previous data show that patient age does not materially affect success with donor eggs.

Numbers of Multiple Births in the U.S., 1990-2009

Source: National Center for Health Statistics (NCHS), U.S. Dept. of Health and Human Services

The general upward trend in multiple births reflects greater numbers of births to older women and increased use of fertility drugs.

Year	Twins	Triplets	Quadruplets	Quintuplets[1]	Year	Twins	Triplets	Quadruplets	Quintuplets[1]
1990	93,865	2,830	185	13	2002	125,134	6,898	434	69
1995	96,736	4,551	365	57	2003	128,665	7,110	468	85
1996	100,750	5,298	560	81	2004	132,219	6,750	439	86
1997	104,137	6,148	510	79	2005	133,122	6,208	418	68
1998	110,670	6,919	627	79	2006	137,085	6,118	355	67
1999	114,307	6,742	512	67	2007	138,961	5,967	369	91
2000	118,916	6,742	506	77	2008	138,660	5,877	345	46
2001	121,246	6,885	501	85	2009	137,217	5,905	355	80

(1) Quintuplets and other multiple births of five or more.

Origin Countries for U.S. Foreign Adoptions, 2000-11

Source: Office of Immigration Statistics, U.S. Dept. of Homeland Security
(ranked by 2011 adoptions)

Country	2011	2010	2009	2008	2007	2006	2005	2003	2002	2001	2000
China	2,589	3,401	2,990	3,852	5,453	6,493	7,906	6,859	6,119	4,681	5,053
Ethiopia.	1,727	2,513	2,221	1,666	1,255	732	441	135	105	158	95
Russia.	970	1,082	1,580	1,859	2,310	3,706	4,639	5,209	4,939	4,279	4,269
South Korea	736	863	1,106	1,038	939	1,376	1,630	1,790	1,779	1,870	1,794
Ukraine.	632	445	605	487	606	460	821	702	1,106	1,246	659
Philippines	230	214	292	279	265	245	271	214	221	219	173
India	228	243	298	306	416	320	323	472	464	543	503
Colombia	216	235	237	308	310	344	291	272	334	407	246
Uganda.	207	62	69	55	54	12	17	3	18	3	1
Taiwan	205	285	254	262	184	187	141	107	41	44	24
Total[1]	**9,320**	**11,059**	**12,782**	**17,229**	**19,741**	**20,705**	**22,710**	**21,320**	**20,100**	**19,087**	**18,120**

(1) Includes countries not shown.

Leading Causes of Infant Death in the U.S., 2010

Source: National Center for Health Statistics (NCHS), U.S. Dept. of Health and Human Services

Cause	Number	Percent of total deaths	Mortality rate[1]
Congenital malformations, deformations, and chromosomal abnormalities	5,077	20.7%	126.9
Disorders related to short gestation and low birth weight, not elsewhere classified	4,130	16.8	103.2
Sudden infant death syndrome.	1,890	7.7	47.2
Newborn affected by maternal complications of pregnancy	1,555	6.3	38.9
Accidents (unintentional injuries)	1,043	4.2	26.1
Newborn affected by complications of placenta, cord, and membranes.	1,030	4.2	25.7
Bacterial sepsis[2] of newborn	569	2.3	14.2
Respiratory distress of newborn.	499	2.0	12.5
Diseases of the circulatory system	496	2.0	12.4
Neonatal hemorrhage.	470	1.9	11.7
All other causes	7,789	31.7	194.7
All causes	**24,548**	**100.0**	**613.7**

(1) Infant deaths during the first year of life per 100,000 live births. (2) Toxic condition resulting from the spread of bacteria.

Nonmarital Childbearing in the U.S., 1970-2009
Source: National Center for Health Statistics (NCHS), U.S. Dept. of Health and Human Services

	1970	1975	1980	1985	1990	1995	2000	2005	2006	2007	2008	2009
Births to unmarried mothers (thous.) . . .	399	448	666	828	1,165	1,254	1,347	1,527	1,642	1,715	1,727	1,694
Race/Hispanic origin of mother					Percent of live births to unmarried mothers							
All races and origins.	10.7%	14.3%	18.4%	22.0%	28.0%	32.2%	33.2%	36.9%	38.5%	39.7%	40.6%	41.0%
White.	5.5	7.1	11.2	14.7	20.4	25.3	27.1	31.7	—	34.8	35.7	36.0
Black.	37.5	49.5	56.1	61.2	66.5	69.9	68.5	69.3	—	71.2	71.8	72.3
American Indian or Alaska Native.	22.4	32.7	39.2	46.8	53.6	57.2	58.4	63.5	64.6	65.3	65.8	65.4
Asian or Pacific Islander	—	—	7.3	9.5	13.2	16.3	14.8	16.2	16.3	16.6	16.9	17.2
Hispanic origin (selected states)[1,2]	—	—	23.6	29.5	36.7	40.8	42.7	48.0	49.9	51.3	52.6	53.2
Maternal age					Percent distribution of live births to unmarried mothers							
Under 20 years.	50.1%	52.1%	40.8%	33.8%	30.9%	30.9%	28.0%	23.1%	22.7%	22.5%	22.2%	21.4%
20-24 years.	31.8	29.9	35.6	36.3	34.7	34.5	37.4	38.3	38.1	37.6	37.1	36.9
25 years and over.	18.1	18.0	23.5	29.9	34.4	34.7	34.6	38.6	39.2	39.9	40.7	41.7
Race/Hispanic origin of mother					Live births per 1,000 unmarried women 15-44 years of age[3]							
All races and origins.	26.4	24.5	29.4	32.8	43.8	44.3	44.0	47.5	—	52.3	52.5	50.5
White[4]	13.9	12.4	18.1	22.5	32.9	37.0	38.2	43.0	—	48.1	48.2	46.3
Black[4]	95.5	84.2	81.1	77.0	90.5	74.5	70.5	67.8	—	72.6	72.5	69.9
Hispanic origin (selected states)[1,2]	—	—	—	89.6	88.7	87.2	100.3	—	108.4	105.1	96.8

— = Not available. (1) Hispanic origin data prior to 1995 is not directly comparable to more recent years due to differences in reporting area. (2) Includes mothers of all races. (3) Rates computed by relating births to unmarried mothers, regardless of mother's age, to unmarried women 15-44 years of age. (4) For 1970 and 1975, birth rates are by race of child.

Number, Ratio, and Rate of Legal Abortions in U.S., 1970-2008
Source: *Abortion Surveillance—United States, 2008*, Centers for Disease Control and Prevention, U.S. Dept. of Health and Human Services

Year	Legal abortions	Ratio[1]	Rate[2]	Year	Legal abortions	Ratio[1]	Rate[2]	Year	Legal abortions	Ratio[1]	Rate[2]
1970	193,491	52	5	1991	1,388,937	338	24	2000	857,475	251	16
1971	485,816	137	11	1992	1,359,146	334	23	2001	853,485	251	16
1972	586,760	180	13	1993	1,330,414	333	23	2002	854,122	252	16
1973	615,831	196	14	1994	1,267,415	321	21	2003	848,163	247	16
1974	763,476	242	17	1995	1,210,883	311	20	2004	839,226	243	16
1975	854,853	272	18	1996	1,225,937	315	21	2005	820,151	238	16
1980	1,297,606	359	25	1997	1,186,039	306	20	2006	852,385	238	16
1985	1,328,570	354	24	1998	884,273	270	17	2007	827,609	231	16
1990	1,429,247	344	24	1999	861,789	261	17	2008	825,564	234	16

Note: After 1998, reporting area varies. (1) Number of abortions per 1,000 live births. (2) Number of abortions per 1,000 women aged 15-44 years.

Reported Abortions by Age, Race, and Marital Status, 2008
Source: *Abortion Surveillance—United States, 2008*, Centers for Disease Control and Prevention, U.S. Dept. of Health and Human Services

Characteristic	White		Black		Other		Total, all races	
Age[1]	No.	%	No.	%	No.	%	No.	%
Under 15 years	1,088	0.4%	1,384	0.7%	113	0.3%	2,585	0.5%
15-19 years.	41,158	16.5	32,680	17.3	4,507	13.0	78,345	16.6
20-24 years.	83,822	33.6	61,187	32.4	9,632	27.8	154,641	32.7
25-29 years.	58,671	23.5	47,412	25.1	8,716	25.1	114,799	24.3
30-34 years.	33,854	13.6	27,522	14.6	6,007	17.3	67,383	14.2
35-39 years.	22,585	9.0	14,563	7.7	4,095	11.8	41,243	8.7
40 years and over	8,427	3.4	4,147	2.2	1,628	4.7	14,202	3.0
Total	249,605	100.0	188,895	100.0	34,698	100.0	473,198	100.0
Marital status[2]								
Married	38,595	17.3	16,991	9.8	10,643	32.3	66,229	15.4
Unmarried	184,959	82.7	157,144	90.2	22,320	67.7	364,423	84.6
Total	223,554	100.0	174,135	100.0	32,963	100.0	430,652	100.0

(1) Data from 33 reporting areas; excludes 19 areas (CA, CT, DC, FL, HI, IL, LA, MD, MA, NE, NV, NH, NM, RI, TX, UT, WA, WI, and WY) that did not report, did not report by race or age, or did not meet reporting standards for race or for age. (2) Data from 31 reporting areas; excludes 21 areas (AR, CA, CT, DC, FL, HI, IL, LA, MD, MA, NE, NV, NH, NM, NY, RI, TX, UT, WA, WI, and WY) that did not report, did not report by race or marital status, or did not meet reporting standards for race or for marital status.

Lifetime and Median Number of Sexual Partners by Age and Race, 2008
Source: *Sexual Behavior, Sexual Attraction, and Sexual Identity in the United States*, National Center for Health Statistics (NCHS), U.S. Dept. of Health and Human Services

	No. of opposite-sex partners in lifetime, % distrib.						Median		No. of opposite-sex partners in lifetime, % distrib.						Median
	0	1	2	3-6	7-14	15+	no.[2]		0	1	2	3-6	7-14	15+	no.[2]
Male, 15-44 years[1]	11.4	15.0	7.6	26.5	18.1	21.4	5.1	**Female, 15-44 years[1]**	11.3	22.2	10.7	31.6	16.0	8.3	3.2
Age								**Age**							
15-19 years.	43.3	21.2	9.4	17.6	5.4	3.1	1.8	15-19 years.	48.1	22.7	8.2	15.7	4.1	1.1	1.4
20-24 years.	14.4	19.1	8.0	26.1	18.1	14.2	4.1	20-24 years.	12.6	24.5	12.5	31.6	11.7	7.2	2.6
25-44 years.	2.4	12.3	7.0	28.9	21.5	27.9	6.1	25-44 years.	1.6	21.4	10.9	35.6	20.1	10.4	3.6
Race/Hispanic origin								**Race/Hispanic origin**							
White, non-Hispanic	11.6	16.1	7.3	25.7	18.4	20.9	5.1	White, non-Hispanic	11.7	19.2	9.7	31.4	18.9	8.9	3.7
Black, non-Hispanic	9.6	8.3	5.0	25.6	21.6	30.0	6.9	Black, non-Hispanic	10.5	12.3	8.3	40.9	16.7	11.3	4.4
Hispanic or Latino . . .	7.9	12.5	10.2	32.6	17.8	19.1	4.6	Hispanic or Latina . . .	10.7	35.0	16.7	26.6	6.6	4.4	1.6

(1) Includes people of other or multiple races and origin groups, not shown separately. (2) Excludes people who have never had sex with a partner.

Number of Opposite-Sex Partners in Past Year, 2008

Source: *Sexual Behavior, Sexual Attraction, and Sexual Identity in the United States,* National Center for Health Statistics (U.S. males and females 15-44 years of age)

Number of Opposite-Sex Partners in Lifetime by Age, 2008

Source: *Sexual Behavior, Sexual Attraction, and Sexual Identity in the United States,* National Center for Health Statistics (U.S. males and females 15-44 years of age)

Contraceptive Use in the U.S. by Race and Marital Status, 2006-08

Source: National Survey of Family Growth, National Center for Health Statistics (NCHS), U.S. Dept. of Health and Human Services

		Race and Hispanic origin[2]				Marital and cohabitation status			
	Hispanic	White, single race	Black, single race	Total other or multiple races	Asian, single race	Currently married	Currently cohabiting	Formerly married	Never married
All women (thous.; aged 15-44 years)....	10,377	37,660	8,452	5,375	2,493	27,006	6,821	5,190	22,847
Contraceptive status and method					Percent distribution				
Using contraception[1]	58.5%	64.7%	54.5%	59.2%	63.9%	78.6%	71.2%	60.6%	39.3%
Female sterilization.................	19.6	14.9	21.8	16.1	11.6	23.6	16.3	35.3	4.5
Male sterilization...................	3.4	8.3	1.1	3.9	4.5	12.7	2.2	2.3	0.3
Pill...............................	11.4	21.2	11.4	10.9	11.1	16.3	23.2	11.4	18.1
Implant, Lunelle™, or patch	1.5	0.5	0.6	1.0	0.0	0.7	1.0	—	0.6
3-month injectable (Depo-Provera™)	2.6	1.4	4.1	1.8	—	1.4	3.1	2.6	2.2
Contraceptive ring.................	1.2	1.6	1.7	0.8	—	1.0	3.7	0.8	1.5
Intrauterine device (IUD).............	4.8	3.3	2.8	2.2	1.9	5.3	4.7	2.1	1.1
Condom	9.4	9.5	8.8	16.2	26.1	11.7	10.2	4.1	9.1
Periodic abstinence—calendar rhythm ...	0.6	0.5	—	1.0	2.1	1.0	0.4	—	0.2
Withdrawal	3.0	3.3	2.1	5.1	4.8	4.5	5.3	1.4	1.5
Not using contraception	41.5	35.3	45.5	40.8	36.1	21.4	28.8	39.4	60.7
Surgically sterile–female (noncontraceptive)	0.7	0.2	0.4	—	0.0	0.3	—	1.0	0.4
Nonsurgically sterile–female or male	1.8	1.6	1.8	1.9	1.2	1.0	2.2	2.7	2.1
Pregnant or postpartum	8.3	4.9	5.7	3.4	2.9	7.2	10.5	2.6	2.6
Seeking pregnancy	6.2	3.5	4.4	4.1	3.0	6.4	7.1	0.8	1.3
Never had intercourse or no intercourse in last 3 months	18.8	18.3	22.6	21.2	23.1	0.9	1.8	21.1	45.6
Had intercourse without contraception in last 3 months	5.8	6.7	10.6	9.5	5.9	5.5	6.9	11.3	8.7

— = Figure does not meet standard of reliability or precision. **Note:** Data was collected in interviews 2006-08. For all methods shown, the reported standard error was less than 3.1%. (1) Includes categories not shown with use rates under 0.5%, including diaphragm, emergency contraception, natural family planning. (2) Hispanics may be of any race. Other columns below are for non-Hispanic persons of single or multiple race.

Sexual Activity of Older Adults, 1999-2009

Source: *Sex, Romance, and Relationships–AARP Survey of Midlife and Older Adults,* Apr. 2010

	Total			Men			Women		
Sexual activity[1]	1999	2004	2009	1999	2004	2009	1999	2004	2009
Kissing and hugging..............	65%	69%	58%	74%	76%	67%	58%	62%	49%
Sexual touching or caressing	55	53	44	63	61	54	47	46	35
Sexual intercourse	38	36	28	42	41	33	35	31	23
Oral sex	13	14	16	14	19	20	11	10	12
Anal sex	—	—	3	—	—	4	—	—	2
Self stimulation...................	12	20	22	23	34	34	3	8	12

(1) Sexual activities engaged in at least once a week by persons ages 45 and older in the six months prior to the survey.

Frequency of Older Adults' Sexual Activity, 2009

Source: *Sex, Romance, and Relationships–AARP Survey of Midlife and Older Adults,* Apr. 2010

	Frequency of sexual intercourse[1]					Frequency of sexual intercourse[1]			
Men, ages	Weekly	Monthly	Less than monthly	Never	Women, ages	Weekly	Monthly	Less than monthly	Never
45-49 years........	50%	9%	10%	31%	45-49 years........	26%	12%	20%	42%
50-59 years........	41	22	9	28	50-59 years........	32	10	9	49
60-69 years........	24	18	18	40	60-69 years........	24	8	13	55
45+ years	33	16	13	37	45+ years	23	9	10	58
70+ years	15	7	18	60	70+ years	5	6	3	87

(1) During the six months prior to the survey.

Sexual Activity of High School Students, 2011

Source: *Youth Risk Behavior Surveillance—United States, 2011*, Centers for Disease Control and Prevention

	Ever had sexual intercourse			First sexual intercourse before age 13			Currently sexually active[1]			Condom use during last sexual intercourse[2]		
	Female	Male	Total	Female	Male	Total	Female	Male	Total	Female	Male	Total
Race/ethnicity												
White[3]	44.5%	44.0%	44.3%	2.6%	5.2%	3.9%	35.0%	30.0%	32.4%	53.4%	66.3%	59.5%
Black[3]	53.6	66.9	60.0	7.0	21.2	13.9	36.9	46.0	41.3	53.8	75.4	65.3
Hispanic........	43.9	53.0	48.6	2.9	11.1	7.1	31.6	35.3	33.5	53.0	63.4	58.4
Grade												
9	27.8	37.8	32.9	4.1	13.3	8.8	19.0	23.6	21.3	56.3	67.0	62.2
10	43.0	44.5	43.8	3.9	8.6	6.3	31.4	29.1	30.3	56.7	69.9	63.3
11	51.9	54.5	53.2	3.0	6.8	4.9	38.9	38.5	38.7	55.5	67.0	61.1
12	63.6	62.6	63.1	2.2	6.2	4.2	50.7	44.4	47.5	48.9	64.7	56.3
Total............	**45.6**	**49.2**	**47.4**	**3.4**	**9.0**	**6.2**	**34.2**	**33.3**	**33.7**	**53.6**	**67.0**	**60.2**

(1) Sexual intercourse during the 3 months preceding the survey. (2) Among the 33.7% who were sexually active. (3) Non-Hispanic.

Risk Behaviors in High School Students, 2011

Source: *Youth Risk Behavior Surveillance—United States, 2011*, Centers for Disease Control and Prevention

		Percent rarely or never wore seat belts[1]			Percent rarely or never wore bicycle helmets[2]			Percent who rode with a driver who had been drinking alcohol[3]		
		Female	Male	Total	Female	Male	Total	Female	Male	Total
Race	White, non-Hispanic	5.1%	7.3%	6.3%	83.9%	87.1%	85.7%	23.8%	20.5%	22.1%
	Black, non-Hispanic	8.0	12.6	10.3	89.4	94.4	92.3	23.2	22.5	22.8
	Hispanic	8.4	10.1	9.3	92.0	92.2	92.1	30.7	30.7	30.7
Grade	9	8.4	10.3	9.5	85.8	87.2	86.6	22.9	20.7	21.8
	10	5.9	9.0	7.5	85.2	87.9	86.7	23.5	23.1	23.3
	11	4.9	7.0	6.0	85.7	89.2	87.7	25.2	22.4	23.8
	12	5.5	8.5	7.1	87.3	92.0	89.9	28.0	27.4	27.7
Total		**6.3**	**8.9**	**7.7**	**85.9**	**88.8**	**87.5**	**24.9**	**23.3**	**24.1**

(1) When riding in a car driven by someone else. (2) Among the 70.2% of students who rode a bicycle during the 12 months preceding the survey. (3) In a car or other vehicle one or more times in the 30 days preceding the survey.

Risky Driving Behaviors by High School Students, 2011

Source: *Youth Risk Behavior Surveillance–United States, 2011*, Centers for Disease Control and Prevention

		Percent who drove when drinking alcohol[1]			Percent who texted or emailed while driving[2]		
		Female	Male	Total	Female	Male	Total
Race	White, non-Hispanic	7.0%	8.9%	8.0%	35.4%	36.9%	36.2%
	Black, non-Hispanic	4.0	7.8	5.9	19.0	29.3	24.1
	Hispanic	7.8	11.5	9.7	26.3	35.2	30.9
Grade	9	3.3	6.1	4.7	9.4	13.9	11.7
	10	5.2	6.0	5.6	20.6	25.6	23.2
	11	7.8	10.4	9.1	40.6	45.0	42.9
	12	11.2	16.0	13.6	55.9	60.0	58.0
Total		**6.7**	**9.5**	**8.2**	**30.4**	**34.9**	**32.8**

(1) Drove a car or other vehicle when they had been drinking alcohol, one or more times during the 30 days before the survey. (2) On at least one day during the 30 days before the survey.

U.S. Motor Vehicle Crashes, 2009

Source: National Safety Council (NSC); Natl. Highway Traffic Safety Admin. (NHTSA)

An estimated 35,500 people in the U.S. were killed in motor vehicle crashes in 2010, down 2% from the total for 2009. Although the number of drivers (212 mil) increased in 2010, the vehicle miles driven (3 tril) stayed the same, and the death rate per 100 mil vehicle miles decreased 4% to 1.18, the lowest on record.

Motor vehicle deaths per 10,000 registered vehicles dropped from 1.43 in 2009 to 1.39 in 2010 and were down from 1.92 in 2000. The rate of fatalities per 100,000 population declined 27% between 2000 and 2010 and 3% between 2009 and 2010.

Male drivers were involved in about 5.4 mil crashes, whereas female drivers were in 4.1 mil. Male drivers were also involved in 73% of fatal crashes, or about 31,965, compared with 11,811 accidents involving female drivers.

In 2010, 10,228 traffic fatalities, or 31%, involved an intoxicated (blood alcohol concentration of 0.08 or greater) driver or motorcycle operator, a decline of 4.9% from 2009.

Seat belt use was 84% in 2011. In 2010, safety belts and child restraints saved an estimated 12,849 lives. Another 2,306 lives were saved by frontal air bags. Women used safety belts (88%) more often than men (83%). The least likely safety belt users were rural drivers (81%) and drivers of pickup trucks (74%).

Crashes	Deaths	Injuries
All motor vehicle crashes	35,500	3,600,000
Collision between motor vehicles	13,900	2,690,000
Collision with fixed object	11,400	510,000
Collision with pedestrian	5,400	150,000
Noncollision accidents (e.g., rollovers)	3,700	130,000
Collision with pedal cycle	800	110,000
Collision with railroad train	200	1,000
Other (mostly collisions with animals)..	100	9,000

Note: NSC numbers are rounded and preliminary.

Improper Driving Reported in Accidents, 2000-10

Source: National Safety Council

Type	Percentage of fatal accidents			Percentage of injury accidents			Percentage of all accidents		
	2010	2005	2000	2010	2005	2000	2010	2005	2000
Improper driving..................	55.9%	62.7%	61.6%	55.6%	62.7%	60.3%	54.6%	58.5%	57.8%
Speed too fast or unsafe.............	13.6	18.1	23.7	10.0	15.0	16.3	9.5	12.7	13.6
Right of way	10.6	12.2	18.6	14.7	17.5	19.9	12.5	14.3	20.1
Failed to yield	7.0	8.0	10.1	10.2	12.5	12.5	9.2	10.8	12.7
Disregarded signal	1.4	1.4	4.6	2.4	2.5	3.6	1.6	1.7	5.3
Passed stop sign.................	2.2	2.8	3.8	2.2	2.5	1.3	1.7	1.8	2.2
Drove left of center	6.3	8.0	8.2	1.0	2.2	1.1	0.9	1.6	1.0
Improper overtaking	1.0	1.4	0.9	0.7	0.6	0.6	0.7	0.8	0.9
Made improper turn	3.2	4.5	0.7	2.9	4.2	2.0	3.1	4.5	2.4
Followed too closely	0.8	1.0	0.5	4.8	6.8	4.3	6.2	8.7	5.7
Other improper driving	20.4	17.5	9.0	21.5	16.4	16.1	21.7	15.9	14.1
No improper driving stated	44.1	37.3	38.4	44.4	37.3	39.7	45.4	41.5	42.2

Note: Based on reports from state traffic authorities. When a driver was under the influence of alcohol or drugs, the accident was considered a result of the driver's physical condition—not a driving error. For this reason, accidents in which the driver was reported to be under the influence are included under "no improper driving stated."

U.S. Passenger Deaths and Death Rates, 1999-2009

Source: National Safety Council

Year	Passenger automobiles[1]		Vans, SUVs, pickup trucks		Buses[2]		Railroad passenger trains		Scheduled airlines[3]	
	Deaths	Rate[4]	Deaths	Rate[4]	Deaths	Rate[4]	Deaths	Rate[4]	Deaths	Rate[4]
1999	20,851	0.84	11,295	0.76	40	0.07	14	0.10	24	0.005
2000	20,689	0.81	11,545	0.76	3	0.01	4	0.03	94	0.02
2001	20,310	0.78	11,736	0.76	11	0.02	3	0.02	279	0.06
2002	20,564	0.78	12,278	0.78	36	0.06	7	0.05	0	0.00
2003	19,723	0.74	12,551	0.78	30	0.05	3	0.02	24	0.005
2004	19,183	0.71	12,678	0.75	27	0.05	3	0.02	13	0.002
2005	18,509	0.68	13,043	0.76	43	0.07	16	0.10	22	0.004
2006	17,792	0.66	12,723	0.72	15	0.02	2	0.01	52	0.01
2007	29,075	0.66	NA	NA	18	0.03	5	0.03	0	0.00
2008	25,344	0.59	NA	NA	50	0.08	24	0.13	0	0.00
2009	23,376	0.53	NA	NA	21	0.04	3	0.02	49	0.01

NA = Not available. (1) Drivers of passenger automobiles are considered passengers. Includes taxi passengers. Starting in 2007, passenger automobiles includes vans, SUVs, and pickup trucks. (2) Excludes school buses. (3) Excludes charter, cargo, and on-demand service and suicide/sabotage. (4) Deaths per 100 mil passenger miles.

Death Rates for Suicide at Selected Ages, 1960-2008

Source: Health, United States, 2011, National Center for Health Statistics (NCHS), U.S. Dept. of Health and Human Services

Age	2008			2000			1980			1960		
	Both sexes	Male	Female	Both sexes	Male	Female	Both sexes	Male	Female	Both sexes	Male	Female
15-24 years..................	10.1	16.3	3.6	10.2	17.1	3.0	12.3	20.2	4.3	5.2	8.2	2.2
25-44 years..................	14.4	22.3	6.3	13.4	21.3	5.4	15.6	24.0	7.7	12.2	17.9	6.6
45-64 years..................	17.6	27.5	8.2	13.5	21.3	6.2	15.9	23.7	8.9	22.0	34.4	10.2
65 years and older	14.8	29.4	4.1	15.2	31.1	4.0	17.6	35.0	6.1	24.5	44.0	8.4
All ages	11.6	18.9	4.8	10.4	17.7	4.0	12.2	19.9	5.7	12.5	20.0	5.6

Note: Rate is per 100,000 population. Rates for all ages include ages not shown here.

U.S. Fires, 2011

Source: National Fire Protection Association

Fires

- Public fire departments responded to 1,389,500 fires in 2011, an increase of 4.4% from 2010.
- Every 23 seconds, a fire department responds to a fire somewhere in the United States.
- There were 484,500 structure fires in 2011, a very slight increase of 0.5% from 2010. Of those fires, 76% (370,000 fires) occurred in homes.
- Fires in vehicles increased 1.6% from the previous year, totaling 219,000 in 2011.
- There were 686,000 fires in outside properties, an increase of 8.2% from 2010.

Civilian deaths

- There were an estimated 3,005 civilian fire deaths in 2011. This was a 3.7% decrease from the year before.
- The number of civilian fire deaths that occurred in home structure fires decreased 4.5% to 2,520 and fires in the home caused 84% of all fire deaths.
- Fires caused an average of one civilian death every 175 minutes.

Civilian injuries

- There were an estimated 17,500 civilian fire injuries reported in 2011, a 1.2% decrease from 2010. Nationwide, a civilian was injured in a fire every 30 minutes.

- Home structure fires were the site of 13,910 civilian fire injuries in 2011, and non-home structure fires accounted for 1,275 civilian injuries.

Property damage

- Direct property damage from fires amounted to an estimated $11.7 bil in 2011, a very slight increase of 0.6% from 2010. Structure fires accounted for $9.7 bil of property damage.
- Property loss associated with home fires came to $6.9 bil for 2011.

Intentionally set fires

- There were an estimated 26,500 intentionally set structure fires in 2011, a decrease of 3.6% from 2010.
- Intentionally set structure fires are believed to have resulted in 190 civilian deaths in 2011, a decrease of 5.0% from the year before. Property damage from intentionally set structure fires totaled $601 mil, an increase of 2.7% from the 2010 figure.
- The number of intentionally set vehicle fires in 2011 was 14,000, no change from a year ago. Intentionally set vehicle fires caused an estimated $88 mil in property damage, a slight decrease of 1.1% from 2010.

Leading Causes of Death in the U.S., 2010

Source: National Center for Health Statistics (NCHS), U.S. Dept. of Health and Human Services

	Number	% of total deaths	Death rate[1]		Number	% of total deaths	Death rate[1]
All causes	2,465,932	100.0%	798.7	10. Intentional self-harm (suicide)...	37,793	1.5%	12.2
1. Diseases of the heart	595,444	24.1	192.9	11. Septicemia	34,843	1.4	11.3
2. Cancer	573,855	23.3	185.9	12. Chronic liver disease and cirrhosis	31,802	1.3	10.3
3. Chronic lower respiratory diseases	137,789	5.6	44.6	13. Hypertension and hypertensive			
4. Stroke	129,180	5.2	41.8	renal disease..............	26,577	1.1	8.6
5. Accidents (unintentional injuries)	118,043	4.8	38.2	14. Parkinson's disease	21,963	0.9	7.1
6. Alzheimer's diseases	83,308	3.4	27.0	15. Pneumonitis due to solids and			
7. Diabetes	68,905	2.8	22.3	liquids	17,001	0.7	5.5
8. Kidney disease	50,472	2.0	16.3	All other causes (residual)	488,954	19.8	158.5
9. Influenza and pneumonia	50,003	2.0	16.2				

(1) Per 100,000 population.

Principal Types of Accidental Deaths in the U.S., 1970-2010

Source: National Safety Council

Year[1]	Total	Motor vehicle	Falls	Poisoning	Drowning	Fires, flames, smoke	Suffocation: ingestion of food, object	Firearms	Mechanical suffocation
1970	NA	54,633	16,926	5,299	7,860	6,718	2,753	2,406	NA
1980	105,718	53,172	13,294	4,331	7,257	5,822	3,249	1,955	NA
1985	93,457	45,901	12,001	5,170	5,316	4,938	3,551	1,649	NA
1990	91,983	46,814	12,313	5,803	4,685	4,175	3,303	1,416	NA
1995	93,320	43,363	13,986	9,072	4,350	3,761	3,185	1,225	NA
2000	97,900	43,354	13,322	12,757	3,482	3,377	4,313	776	1,335
2001	101,537	43,788	15,019	14,078	3,281	3,309	4,185	802	1,370
2002	106,742	45,380	16,257	17,550	3,447	3,159	4,128	762	1,389
2003	109,277	44,757	17,229	19,457	3,306	3,369	4,272	730	1,309
2004	112,012	44,933	18,807	20,950	3,308	3,229	4,470	649	1,421
2005	117,809	45,343	19,656	23,617	3,582	3,197	4,386	789	1,514
2006	121,599	45,316	20,823	27,531	3,579	3,109	4,332	642	1,580
2007	123,706	43,945	22,631	29,846	3,443	3,286	4,344	613	1,653
2008	121,902	39,790	24,013	31,116	3,548	2,912	4,366	592	1,759
2009	122,600	36,300	26,000	33,500	3,600	3,100	4,500	590	1,800
2010[2]	126,100	35,500	28,000	35,600	3,600	3,100	4,700	570	1,900
Death rates per 100,000 population									
1970	NA	26.8	8.3	2.6	3.9	3.3	1.4	1.2	NA
1980	47.8	23.4	5.9	1.9	3.2	2.6	1.4	0.9	NA
1985	39.3	19.3	5.0	2.2	2.2	2.1	1.5	0.7	NA
1990	36.9	18.8	4.9	2.3	1.9	1.7	1.3	0.6	NA
1995	35.5	16.5	5.3	3.4	1.7	1.4	1.2	0.5	NA
2000	35.6	15.7	4.8	4.6	1.3	1.2	1.6	0.3	0.5
2001	35.6	15.4	5.3	4.9	1.2	1.2	1.5	0.3	0.5
2002	37.1	15.8	5.6	6.4	1.2	1.1	1.4	0.3	0.5
2003	37.6	15.4	5.9	6.7	1.1	1.2	1.5	0.3	0.4
2004	38.1	15.3	6.4	7.1	1.1	1.1	1.5	0.2	0.5
2005	39.7	15.3	6.6	8.0	1.2	1.1	1.5	0.3	0.5
2006	40.8	15.2	7.0	9.2	1.2	1.0	1.5	0.2	0.5
2007	41.1	14.6	7.5	9.9	1.1	1.1	1.4	0.2	0.5
2008	40.0	13.1	7.9	10.2	1.2	1.0	1.4	0.2	0.6
2009	40.0	11.8	8.5	10.9	1.2	1.0	1.5	0.2	0.6
2010[2]	40.7	11.5	9.0	11.5	1.2	1.0	1.5	0.2	0.6

NA = Not available. **Note:** All figures include on-the-job deaths. (1) Data after 1999 are not comparable with earlier data because of classification changes. (2) Preliminary. Totals include 13,700 other accidental deaths in 2010.

Deaths in the U.S. Involving Firearms by Age and Sex, 2008

Source: National Safety Council

Type and sex	All ages	Under 5	5-14	15-19	20-24	25-44	45-64	65-74	75 & older
Total firearms deaths	31,593	88	288	2,590	4,095	11,161	8,801	2,191	2,379
Male	27,336	55	209	2,331	3,684	9,591	7,367	1,930	2,169
Female	4,257	33	79	259	411	1,570	1,434	261	210
Unintentional..............	592	21	41	61	71	174	156	37	31
Male	510	16	34	59	65	143	134	34	25
Female	82	5	7	2	6	31	22	3	6
Suicide..................	18,223	—	50	698	1,311	5,153	6,868	1,933	2,210
Male	15,931	—	41	640	1,181	4,399	5,848	1,754	2,068
Female	2,292	—	9	58	130	754	1,020	179	142
Homicide.................	12,179	65	187	1,785	2,609	5,578	1,635	196	124
Male	10,361	37	126	1,588	2,339	4,815	1,269	123	64
Female	1,818	28	61	197	270	763	366	73	60
Legal intervention.........	326	0	0	19	61	167	70	7	2
Male	314	0	0	18	61	160	66	7	2
Female	12	0	0	1	0	7	4	0	0
Undetermined[1]	273	2	10	27	43	89	72	18	12
Male	220	2	8	26	38	74	50	12	10
Female	53	0	2	1	5	15	22	6	2

— = Not applicable. (1) The intention involved (whether accident, suicide, or homicide) could not be determined.

U.S. Infant Mortality Rates by Race and Sex, 1960-2010

Source: National Center for Health Statistics (NCHS), U.S. Dept. of Health and Human Services

Year	All races[1] Both sexes	Male	Female	White Both sexes	Male	Female	Black Both sexes	Male	Female
1960	26.0	29.3	22.6	22.9	26.0	19.6	44.3	49.1	39.4
1970	20.0	22.4	17.5	17.8	20.0	15.4	32.6	36.2	29.0
1980	12.6	13.9	11.2	11.0	12.3	9.6	21.4	23.3	19.4
1985	10.6	11.9	9.3	9.3	10.6	8.0	18.2	19.9	16.5
1990	9.2	10.3	8.1	7.6	8.5	6.6	18.0	19.6	16.2
1995	7.6	8.3	6.8	6.3	7.0	5.6	15.1	16.3	13.9
1996	7.3	8.0	6.6	6.1	6.7	5.4	14.7	16.0	13.3
1997	7.2	8.0	6.5	6.0	6.7	5.4	14.2	15.5	12.8
1998	7.2	7.8	6.5	6.0	6.5	5.4	14.3	15.7	12.8
1999	7.1	7.7	6.4	5.8	6.4	5.2	14.6	15.9	13.2
2000	6.9	7.6	6.2	5.7	6.2	5.1	14.1	15.5	12.6
2001	6.8	7.5	6.1	5.7	6.2	5.1	14.0	15.5	12.5
2002	7.0	7.6	6.3	5.8	6.4	5.1	14.4	15.4	13.3
2003	6.9	7.6	6.1	5.7	6.3	5.0	14.0	15.5	12.4
2004	6.8	7.5	6.1	5.7	6.2	5.1	13.8	15.2	12.3
2005	6.9	7.6	6.2	5.7	6.3	5.1	13.7	15.2	12.3
2006	6.7	7.3	6.0	5.6	6.1	5.0	13.3	14.4	12.2
2007	6.8	7.4	6.1	5.6	6.2	5.1	13.2	14.5	11.9
2008	6.6	7.2	6.0	5.6	6.1	5.0	12.7	13.9	11.5
2009	6.4	NA	NA	5.3	NA	NA	12.6	NA	NA
2010[2]	6.1	NA	NA	5.2	NA	NA	11.6	NA	NA

NA = Not available. **Note:** Rates per 1,000 live births in specified group. (1) Includes races other than white and black. (2) Preliminary.

Years of Life Expected at Birth in U.S., 1900-2010

Source: National Center for Health Statistics (NCHS), U.S. Dept. of Health and Human Services

Year[2]	All races[1] Both sexes	Male	Female	White Both sexes	Male	Female	Black Both sexes	Male	Female
1900	47.3	46.3	48.3	47.6	46.6	48.7	NA	NA	NA
1910	50.0	48.4	51.8	50.3	48.6	52.0	NA	NA	NA
1920	54.1	53.6	54.6	54.9	54.4	55.6	NA	NA	NA
1930	59.7	58.1	61.6	61.4	59.7	63.5	NA	NA	NA
1940	62.9	60.8	65.2	64.2	62.1	66.6	NA	NA	NA
1950	68.2	65.6	71.1	69.1	66.5	72.2	NA	NA	NA
1960	69.7	66.6	73.1	70.6	67.4	74.1	NA	NA	NA
1970	70.8	67.1	74.7	71.7	68.0	75.6	64.1	60.0	68.3
1975	72.6	68.8	76.6	73.4	69.5	77.3	68.8	62.4	71.3
1980	73.7	70.0	77.5	74.4	70.7	78.1	68.1	63.8	72.5
1985	74.7	71.2	78.2	75.3	71.9	78.7	69.3	65.0	73.4
1990	75.4	71.8	78.8	76.1	72.7	79.4	69.1	64.5	73.6
1995	75.8	72.5	78.9	76.5	73.4	79.6	69.6	65.2	73.9
1996	76.1	73.1	79.1	76.8	73.9	79.7	70.2	66.1	74.2
1997	76.5	73.6	79.4	77.1	74.3	79.9	71.1	67.2	74.7
1998	76.7	73.8	79.5	77.3	74.5	80.0	71.3	67.6	74.8
1999	76.7	73.9	79.4	77.3	74.6	79.9	71.4	67.8	74.7
2000	76.8	74.1	79.3	77.3	74.7	79.9	71.8	68.2	75.1
2001	76.9	74.2	79.4	77.4	74.8	79.9	72.0	68.4	75.2
2002	76.9	74.3	79.5	77.4	74.9	79.9	72.1	68.6	75.4
2003	77.1	74.5	79.6	77.6	75.0	80.0	72.3	68.8	75.6
2004	77.5	74.9	79.9	77.9	75.4	80.4	72.8	69.3	76.0
2005	77.4	74.9	79.9	77.9	75.4	80.4	72.8	69.3	76.1
2006	77.7	75.1	80.2	78.2	75.7	80.6	73.2	69.7	76.5
2007	77.9	75.4	80.4	78.4	75.9	80.8	73.6	70.0	76.8
2008	78.1	75.6	80.6	78.5	76.1	80.9	74.0	70.6	77.2
2009	78.6	76.0	80.9	78.8	76.4	81.2	74.7	71.4	77.7
2010[3]	78.7	76.2	81.1	79.0	76.5	81.3	75.1	71.8	78.0

NA = Not available. (1) Includes races other than white and black. (2) Data prior to 1940 does not include all states. (3) Preliminary.

U.S. Life Expectancy at Selected Ages, 2010

Source: National Center for Health Statistics (NCHS), U.S. Dept. of Health and Human Services

Exact age in years	All races[1] Both sexes	Male	Female	White Both sexes	Male	Female	Black Both sexes	Male	Female
0	78.7	81.1	80.6	79.0	76.5	81.3	75.1	71.8	78.0
1	78.2	80.5	80.0	78.4	76.0	80.7	75.0	71.8	77.8
5	74.3	76.6	76.1	74.4	72.1	76.8	71.1	67.9	73.9
10	69.3	71.6	71.2	69.5	67.1	71.8	66.1	62.9	69.0
15	64.4	66.7	66.2	64.5	62.2	66.8	61.2	58.0	64.0
20	59.5	61.8	61.3	59.7	57.3	61.9	56.4	53.3	59.1
25	54.8	56.9	56.4	54.9	52.7	57.1	51.7	48.8	54.3
30	50.0	52.0	51.6	50.2	48.0	52.2	47.1	44.3	49.5
35	45.3	47.2	46.8	45.4	43.3	47.4	42.4	39.7	44.7
40	40.6	42.5	42.0	40.7	38.7	42.6	37.9	35.2	40.1
45	36.0	37.8	37.3	36.1	34.1	37.9	33.4	30.8	35.5
50	31.5	33.2	32.8	31.6	29.7	33.3	29.1	26.6	31.2
55	27.2	28.8	28.4	27.3	25.5	28.9	25.1	22.7	27.0
60	23.1	24.5	24.1	23.1	21.6	24.5	21.4	19.2	23.1
65	19.2	20.3	20.0	19.2	17.8	20.4	17.8	15.9	19.3
70	15.5	16.5	16.1	15.5	14.2	16.5	14.6	12.9	15.8
75	12.2	12.9	12.5	12.1	11.0	12.9	11.6	10.2	12.5
80	9.2	9.7	9.4	9.1	8.2	9.7	9.0	7.8	9.6
85	6.6	7.0	6.8	6.5	5.8	6.9	6.8	5.9	7.2
90	4.7	4.9	4.8	4.6	4.0	4.8	5.1	4.4	5.3
95	3.3	3.4	3.3	3.2	2.8	3.3	3.8	3.3	3.9
100	2.4	2.4	2.2	2.3	2.1	2.3	2.9	2.5	2.9

Note: Data is preliminary. (1) Includes races other than white and black.

NOTED PERSONALITIES

Widely Known Americans of the Present

Political leaders, journalists, other prominent living persons. As of Oct. 2012. Excludes most who fall in categories listed elsewhere in Noted Personalities, such as Writers of the Present and Entertainment Personalities of the Present, or in Sports Personalities. Includes some figures who are active in American life but are not U.S. citizens.

Roger Ailes, b 5/15/40 (Warren, OH), TV exec.

Madeleine K. Albright, b 5/15/37 (Prague, Czech.), former sec. of state.

Edwin "Buzz" Aldrin, b 1/20/30 (Montclair, NJ), former astronaut, 2nd person to walk on the Moon.

Samuel A. Alito Jr., b 4/1/50 (Trenton, NJ), Supreme Court justice.

Paul Allen, b 1/21/53 (Seattle, WA), co-founder of Microsoft.

Christiane Amanpour, b 1/12/58 (London, Eng., UK), TV journalist.

Marc Andreessen, b 1971 (New Lisbon, IA), co-author of web browser Mosaic, cofounder of Netscape.

Richard K. Armey, b 7/7/40 (Cando, ND), former U.S. rep. (R, TX), House majority leader.

John Ashcroft, b 5/9/42 (Chicago, IL), former MO gov., U.S. attorney gen.

David Axelrod, b 2/22/55 (New York, NY), sr. adviser to Pres. Obama, political strategist.

Michele Bachmann, b 4/6/56 (Waterloo, IA), U.S. rep (R, MN), former 2012 pres. contender.

F. Lee Bailey, b 6/10/33 (Waltham, MA), attorney.

Russell Baker, b 8/14/25 (Morrisonville, VA), columnist.

Dave Barry, b 7/3/47 (Armonk, NY), humorist.

Marion Barry, b 3/6/36 (Itta Bena, MS), DC city council member; former Wash., DC, mayor.

Max Baucus, b 12/11/41 (Helena, MT), senator (D, MT), Finance Committee chair.

Gary Bauer, b 5/4/46 (Covington, KY), domestic policy adviser to Pres. Reagan; founder, Campaign for Working Families.

Glenn Beck, b 2/10/64 (Mount Vernon, WA), political commentator.

William Bennett, b 7/31/43 (Brooklyn, NY), author, former education secretary.

Chris Berman, b 5/10/55 (Greenwich, CT), sportscaster.

Ben Bernanke, b 12/13/53 (Augusta, GA), Federal Reserve Chairman.

Carl Bernstein, b 2/14/44 (Washington, DC), journalist; with Bob Woodward cracked Watergate scandal.

Jeff Bezos, b 1/12/64 (Albuquerque, NM), founder and CEO of Amazon.com.

Jill Biden, b 6/5/51 (Hammonton, NJ), English college professor, wife of vice pres. Joe Biden.

Joseph R. Biden Jr., b 11/20/42 (Scranton, PA), U.S. vice pres.; former sen. (D, DE).

James H. Billington, b 6/1/29 (Bryn Mawr, PA), librarian of U.S. Congress.

Rod Blagojevich, b 12/10/56 (Chicago, IL), former IL governor (D).

Lloyd Blankfein, b 9/20/54 (Bronx, NY), CEO and chairman of Goldman Sachs.

Wolf Blitzer, b 3/22/48 (Augsburg, Germany), TV journalist.

Harold Bloom, b 7/11/30 (New York, NY), literary critic.

Michael R. Bloomberg, b 2/14/42 (Brighton, MA), NYC mayor, financial information/media entrepreneur.

Roy Blunt, b 1/10/50 (Niangua, MO), senator (R, MO); former U.S. rep., House minority whip.

John Boehner, b 11/17/49 (Cincinnati, OH), U.S. rep. (R, OH), speaker of the House.

Charles F. Bolden, b 8/19/46 (Columbia, SC), NASA head.

Julian Bond, b 1/14/40 (Nashville, TN), civil rights leader, former NAACP chairman.

Cory Booker, b 4/27/69 (Washington, DC), Newark, NJ, mayor.

Barbara Boxer, b 11/11/40 (Brooklyn, NY), senator (D, CA).

Bill Bradley, b 7/28/43 (Crystal City, MO), former senator (D, NJ), basketball player, pres. candidate.

James Brady, b 8/29/40 (Centralia, IL), gun control advocate; former pres. press sec.

L. Paul Bremer III, b 9/30/41 (Hartford, CT), diplomat, former top U.S. civilian administrator in Iraq.

Jimmy Breslin, b 10/17/30 (Jamaica, Queens, NY), columnist, author.

Stephen Breyer, b 8/15/38 (San Francisco, CA), Supreme Court justice.

Sergey Brin, b 8/21/73 (Moscow, Russia), cofounder of Google.

Roslyn M. Brock, b 5/30/65 (Fort Pierce, FL), NAACP chair.

Tom Brokaw, b 2/6/40 (Webster, SD), TV journalist, retired NBC anchor.

David Brooks, b 8/11/61 (Toronto, ON, Can.), columnist, political commentator.

Joyce Brothers, b 10/20/29 (New York, NY), psychologist.

Aaron Brown, b 11/10/48 (Hopkins, MN), broadcast journalist.

Jerry (Edmund G.) Brown Jr., b 4/7/38 (San Francisco, CA), CA gov (1975-83, 2011-), former atty. gen. (CA), pres. candidate.

Scott Brown, b 9/12/59 (Wakefield, MA), senator (R, MA).

Pat Buchanan, b 11/2/38 (Washington, DC), journalist, former pres. candidate.

Warren Buffett, b 8/30/30 (Omaha, NE), investor, leading philanthropist.

Barbara Bush, b 6/8/25 (Flushing, NY), former first lady.

Barbara Bush, b 11/25/81 (Dallas, TX), daughter of former Pres. George W. Bush.

George H. W. Bush, b 6/12/24 (Milton, MA), former U.S. president.

George W. Bush, b 7/6/46 (New Haven, CT), former U.S. president.

Laura Bush, b 11/4/46 (Midland, TX), former first lady.

Herman Cain, b 12/13/45 (Memphis, TN), former chairman and CEO of Godfather's Pizza; former 2012 pres. contender.

Eric Cantor, b 6/6/63 (Richmond, VA), U.S. rep. (R, VA), House majority leader.

Tucker Carlson, b 5/16/69 (San Francisco, CA), journalist, TV commentator.

Jay Carney, b 5/22/65 (Washington, DC), White House press secretary.

Jimmy Carter, b 10/1/24 (Plains, GA), former U.S. president; 2002 Nobel Peace Prize winner.

Rosalynn Carter, b 8/18/27 (Plains, GA), former first lady.

James Carville Jr., b 10/25/44 (Fort Benning, GA), TV political commentator.

Steve Case, b 8/21/58 (Honolulu, HI), former AOL Time Warner chairman.

Julie Chen, b 1/6/70 (New York, NY), host of *The Talk* and *Big Brother*.

Dick Cheney, b 1/30/41 (Lincoln, NE), former U.S. vice president.

Lynne Cheney, b 8/14/41 (Casper, WY), political commentator, wife of Dick Cheney.

Noam Chomsky, b 12/7/28 (Philadelphia, PA), linguist; activist.

Chris Christie, b 9/6/62 (Newark, NJ), NJ governor (R).

Steven Chu, b 2/28/48 (St. Louis, MO), energy secretary, atomic physicist.

Connie Chung, b 8/20/46 (Washington, DC), TV journalist.

James R. Clapper, b 1941, director of national intelligence.

Bill Clinton, b 8/19/46 (Hope, AR), former U.S. president.

Chelsea Clinton, b 2/27/80 (Little Rock, AR), daughter of former pres. Bill Clinton and Hillary Rodham Clinton.

Hillary Rodham Clinton, b 10/26/47 (Chicago, IL), sec. of state, former senator (D, NY), former first lady, 2008 pres. contender.

James Clyburn, b 7/21/40 (Sumter, SC), U.S. rep. (D, SC), former House majority whip.

Kenneth Cole, b 3/23/54 (Brooklyn, NY), fashion designer.

Gail Collins, b 11/25/45 (Cincinnati, OH), newspaper columnist.

Tim Cook, b 11/1/60 (Robertdale, AZ), CEO of Apple, Inc.

Anderson Cooper, b 6/3/67 (New York, NY), CNN anchor.

Jon Corzine, b 1/1/47 (Willey's Station, IL), former sen. (D, NJ) and NJ governor.

Bob Costas, b 3/22/52 (Queens, NY), TV sports journalist.

Ann Coulter, b 12/8/61 (New Canaan, CT), political commentator, author.

Katie Couric, b 1/7/57 (Arlington, VA), TV journalist, host of *Katie*, former *Today* show news anchor, former anchor of *CBS Evening News*.

Candy Crowley, b 12/12/48 (Kalamazoo, MI), CNN senior political correspondent.

Mark Cuban, b 7/31/58 (Pittsburgh, PA), entrepreneur, Dallas Mavericks (NBA) owner.

Andrew Cuomo, b 12/6/57 (New York, NY), NY governor (D), former state atty. gen.

Mario Cuomo, b 6/15/32 (Jamaica, Queens, NY), former NY governor.

Ann Curry, b 11/19/56 (Guam), former *Today* show news anchor.

Richard M. Daley, b 4/24/42 (Chicago, IL), former Chicago mayor.

William Daley, b 8/9/48 (Chicago, IL), former White House chief of staff.

Thomas Daschle, b 12/9/47 (Aberdeen, SD), former senator (D, SD) and Senate minority leader.

Howard Dean, b 11/17/48 (New York, NY), former VT gov., former Dem. Natl. Committee chair.

Oscar de la Renta, b 7/22/36 (Santo Domingo, Dominican Rep.), fashion designer.
Tom DeLay, b 4/8/47 (Laredo, TX), former U.S. rep. (R, TX), House Majority leader.
Michael Dell, b 2/23/65 (Houston, TX), founder, chairman, and CEO of Dell computers.
Martin Dempsey, b 3/14/52 (Bayonne, NJ), chairman, Joint Chiefs of Staff.
Alan Dershowitz, b 9/1/38 (Brooklyn, NY), attorney.
Barry Diller, b 2/2/42 (San Francisco, CA), media exec.
John Dingell, b 7/8/26 (Colorado Springs, CO), U.S. rep. (D, MI), Dean of the House.
Lou Dobbs, b 9/24/45 (Childress, TX), TV journalist.
James Dobson, b 4/21/36 (Shreveport, LA), evangelical Christian leader, chairman of Focus on the Family.
Christopher Dodd, b 5/27/44 (Willimantic, CT), Motion Picture Assn. of America chair/CEO; former senator (D, CT), 2008 pres. contender.
Timothy Dolan, b 2/6/50 (St. Louis, MO), Rom. Cath. cardinal.
Elizabeth Hanford Dole, b 7/29/36 (Salisbury, NC), former senator (R, NC), Red Cross pres., cabinet member.
Robert Dole, b 7/22/23 (Russell, KS), former Senate majority leader (R, KS), 1996 pres. nominee.
Sam Donaldson, b 3/11/34 (El Paso, TX), TV journalist.
Elizabeth Drew, b 11/16/35 (Cincinnati, OH), journalist.
Matt Drudge, b 10/27/66 (Takoma Park, MD), Internet journalist.
Michael S. Dukakis, b 11/3/33 (Brookline, MA), former MA gov. (D), pres. nominee.
Arne Duncan, b 11/6/64 (Chicago, IL), education secretary.
Dick Durbin, b 11/21/44 (East St. Louis, IL), Senate majority whip (D, IL).
Bernard Ebbers, b 8/27/41 (Edmonton, AB, Can.), former WorldCom CEO; jailed for fraud.
Roger Ebert, b 6/18/42 (Urbana, IL), film critic.
Marian Wright Edelman, b 6/6/39 (Bennettsville, SC), pres. and founder of Children's Defense Fund.
John Edwards, b 6/10/53 (Seneca, SC), former senator (D, NC), 2004 vice-pres. candidate, 2008 pres. contender.
Edward Egan, b 4/2/32 (Oak Park, IL), Rom. Cath. cardinal, archbishop emeritus of New York.
Michael Eisner, b 3/7/42 (Mt. Kisco, NY), former Disney Co. CEO.
Lawrence J. Ellison, b 8/17/44 (New York, NY), Oracle Corp. founder, CEO.
Rahm Emanuel, b 11/29/59 (Chicago, IL), Chicago mayor; former White House chief of staff, U.S. rep. (D, IL).
Myrlie Evers-Williams, b 3/17/33 (Vicksburg, MS), civil rights activist.
Louis Farrakhan, b 5/11/33 (Roxbury, MA), Nation of Islam leader.
Russell Feingold, b 3/2/53 (Janesville, WI), former senator (D, WI).
Dianne Feinstein, b 6/22/33 (San Francisco, CA), senator (D, CA).
Carly (Carleton) S. Fiorina, b 9/6/54 (Austin, TX), former CEO of Hewlett-Packard, 2010 Senate candidate (R, CA).
Larry Flynt, b 11/1/42 (Lakeville, KY), publisher.
Steve (Malcolm) Forbes Jr., b 7/18/47 (Morristown, NJ), publisher, former pres. contender.
Tom Ford, b 8/27/61 (Austin, TX), fashion designer.
Barney Frank, b 3/31/40 (Bayonne, NJ), attorney, long-serving U.S. rep. (D, MA).
Al Franken, b 5/21/51 (New York, NY), senator (D, MN); humorist, political writer, radio host.
Thomas Friedman, b 7/20/53 (Minneapolis, MN), columnist, author.
Bill Gates, b 10/28/55 (Seattle, WA), software pioneer; Microsoft exec.
Henry Louis Gates Jr., b 9/16/50 (Keyser, WV), African American studies scholar.

Robert M. Gates, b 9/25/43 (Wichita, KS), former sec. of defense.
David Geffen, b 2/21/43 (Brooklyn, NY), entertainment exec.
Timothy Geithner, b 8/18/61 (New York, NY), Treasury secretary, former CEO of Federal Reserve Bank of NY.
Robert Gibbs, b 3/29/71 (Auburn, AL), former White House press secretary.
Charles Gibson, b 3/4/43 (Evanston, IL), TV journalist, former host of ABC's *World News*.
Gabrielle Giffords, b 6/8/70 (Tucson, AZ), former U.S. rep. (D, AZ), shot in 2011 assassination attempt.
Kirsten Gillibrand, b 12/9/66 (Albany, NY), senator (D, NY), attorney.
Newt Gingrich, b 6/17/43 (Harrisburg, PA), former House speaker (R, GA), former 2012 pres. contender.
Ruth Bader Ginsburg, b 3/15/33 (Brooklyn, NY), Supreme Court justice.
Rudolph Giuliani, b 5/28/44 (Brooklyn, NY), former NYC mayor.
John Glenn, b 7/18/21 (Cambridge, OH), former senator (D, OH), astronaut.
Alberto Gonzales, b 8/4/55 (San Antonio, TX), former U.S. attorney general.
Roger Goodell, b 2/19/59 (Jamestown, NY), NFL commissioner.
Ellen Goodman, b 4/11/41 (Newton, MA), columnist.
Doris Kearns Goodwin, b 1/4/43 (Brooklyn, NY), historian, TV commentator.
Berry Gordy, b 11/28/29 (Detroit, MI), Motown record label founder.
Al Gore Jr., b 3/31/48 (Washington, DC), former sen. (D, TN), U.S. vice pres., 2000 pres. candidate; 2007 Nobel Peace Prize winner.
Tipper Gore, b 8/19/48 (Washington, DC), former wife of Al Gore.
Rev. Billy Graham, b 11/7/18 (Charlotte, NC), evangelist.
(William) Franklin Graham III, b 7/14/52 (Asheville, NC), evangelist, son of Billy Graham.
Andrew Greeley, b 2/5/28 (Oak Park, IL), Rom. Cath. priest, sociologist, writer.
Jeff Greenfield, b 6/10/43 (New York, NY), TV journalist.
Alan Greenspan, b 3/6/26 (New York, NY), former Federal Reserve chairman.
Jenna Bush Hager, b 11/25/81 (Dallas, TX), daughter of former Pres. George W. Bush.
Pete Hamill, b 6/24/35 (Brooklyn, NY), journalist, author.
Lee Hamilton, b 4/20/31 (Daytona Beach, FL), 9/11 commission vice-chair, former U.S. rep. (D, IN).
Sean Hannity, b 12/30/61 (New York, NY), radio and TV host, author, political commentator.
J. Dennis Hastert, b 1/2/42 (Aurora, IL), former House speaker, U.S. rep. (R, IL).
Reed Hastings, b 10/8/60 (Boston, MA), founder, pres., CEO and board chair, Netflix, Inc.
Orrin Hatch, b 3/22/34 (Homestead Park, PA), senator (R, UT).
Hugh Hefner, b 4/9/26 (Chicago, IL), publisher.
Tommy Hilfiger, b 3/24/51 (Elmira, NY), fashion designer.
Anita Hill, b 7/30/56 (Morris, OK), legal scholar; complainant against Clarence Thomas.
Paris Hilton, b 2/17/81 (New York, NY), heiress; actress.
Perez Hilton, b 3/23/78 (Miami, FL), gossip columnist.
James P. Hoffa, b 5/19/41 (Detroit, MI), Teamsters Union head.
Eric Holder Jr., b 1/21/51 (Bronx, NY), first African American U.S. atty. gen.
David Horowitz, b 1/10/39 (New York, NY), consumer advocate, columnist, author.
Steny H. Hoyer, b 6/14/39 (New York, NY), House minority whip, former majority leader (D, MD).
Mike Huckabee, b 8/24/55 (Hope, AR), former gov. (R, AR), minister, 2008 pres. contender, TV host.

Arianna Huffington, b 7/15/50 (Athens, Greece), political commentator.
H. Wayne Huizenga, b 12/29/39 (Evergreen Park, IL), entrepreneur, sports exec.
Brit Hume, b 6/22/43 (Washington, DC), TV journalist on FOX.
Jon Huntsman Jr., b 3/26/60 (Palo Alto, CA), former UT gov. (R), ambassador to China, 2012 pres. contender.
Kay Bailey Hutchison, b 7/22/43 (Galveston, TX), senator (R, TX).
Lee Iacocca, b 10/15/24 (Allentown, PA), former auto exec.
Carl Icahn, b 2/16/36 (Queens, NY), financier.
Gwen Ifill, b 9/29/55 (Queens, NY), TV journalist, moderator on PBS.
Don Imus, b 7/23/40 (Riverside, CA), talk-show host.
Daniel Inouye, b 9/7/24 (Honolulu, HI), senator (D, HI), president pro tempore.
Patricia Ireland, b 10/19/45 (Oak Park, IL), feminist leader.
Rev. Jesse Jackson, b 10/8/41 (Greenville, SC), civil rights leader, former pres. contender.
Lisa Jackson, b 2/8/62 (Philadelphia, PA), EPA administrator.
Marc Jacobs, b 4/9/64 (New York, NY), fashion designer.
Valerie Jarrett, b 11/14/56 (Shiraz, Iran), sr. adviser to Pres. Obama.
Bobby Jindal, b 6/10/71 (Baton Rouge, LA), LA governor (R), first elected Indian American governor.
Jasper Johns, b 5/15/30 (Augusta, GA), artist.
Gary Johnson, b 1/1/53 (Minot, ND), former NM governor (R); 2012 Libertarian pres. nominee.
Robert L. Johnson, b 4/8/46 (Hickory, MS), Black Entertainment Television founder and CEO.
Vernon E. Jordan Jr., b 8/15/35 (Atlanta, GA), attorney, former pres. adviser, civil rights leader.
Elena Kagan, b 4/28/60 (New York, NY), Supreme Court justice.
Tim Kaine, b 2/26/58 (St. Paul, MN), former Dem Natl. Committee chair, VA governor.
Donna Karan, b 10/2/48 (Forest Hills, Queens, NY), fashion designer.
Jeffrey Katzenberg, b 12/21/50 (New York, NY), entertainment exec.
Thomas Kean, b 4/21/35 (New York, NY), 9/11 commission chair, former Drew Univ. pres., former NJ gov.
Garrison Keillor, b 8/7/42 (Anoka, MN), author, broadcaster.
Mark Kelly, b 2/21/64 (Orange, NJ), U.S. Navy capt., former NASA shuttle commander.
Anthony M. Kennedy, b 7/23/36 (Sacramento, CA), Supreme Court justice.
Kirk Kerkorian, b 6/6/17 (Fresno, CA), pres. and CEO of investment firm Tracinda Corp.
John Kerry, b 12/11/43 (Aurora, CO), senator (D, MA), Foreign Relations Committee chair, 2004 pres. candidate.
Larry King, b 11/19/33 (Brooklyn, NY), TV talk show host.
Michael Kinsley, b 3/9/51 (Detroit, MI), editor, political commentator.
Calvin Klein, b 11/19/42 (Bronx, NY), fashion designer.
Philip H. Knight, b 2/24/38 (Portland, OR), founder and chairman of the board of Nike.
Charles G. Koch, b 5/3/40 (Wichita, KS), Koch Industries executive; philanthropist.
David H. Koch, b 11/1/35 (Wichita, KS), Koch Industries executive; philanthropist.
Edward I. Koch, b 12/12/24 (Bronx, NY), former NYC mayor.
Ted Koppel, b 2/8/40 (Lancashire, Eng., UK), former ABC network TV journalist; former anchor of *Nightline*.
Larry Kramer, b 6/25/35 (Bridgeport, CT), AIDS activist, writer.
Nicholas D. Kristof, b 4/27/59 (Chicago, IL), Pulitzer Prize winning columnist, author.

William Kristol, b 12/23/52 (New York, NY), editor, columnist.
Steve Kroft, b 8/22/45 (Kokomo, IN), TV journalist.
Paul Krugman, b 2/28/53 (Long Island, NY), economist, columnist.
Dennis Kucinich, b 10/8/46 (Cleveland, OH), U.S. rep. (D, OH), pres. contender.
Jon Kyl, b 4/25/42 (Oakland, NE), senator (R, AZ), Senate minority whip.
Brian Lamb, b 10/9/41 (Lafayette, IN), cable TV exec., journalist.
Matt Lauer, b 12/30/57 (New York, NY), TV journalist; NBC *Today* show co-host.
Ralph Lauren, b 10/14/39 (Bronx, NY), fashion designer.
Bernard F. Law, b 11/4/31 (Torreon, Mexico), cardinal archbishop emeritus of Boston.
Patrick Leahy, b 3/31/40 (Montpelier, VT), senator (D, VT), Judiciary Committee chair.
Norman Lear, b 7/27/22 (New Haven, CT), TV producer, political activist.
Jim Lehrer, b 5/19/34 (Wichita, KS), TV journalist, author.
Carl Levin, b 6/28/34 (Detroit, MI), senator (D, MI), Armed Services Committee chair.
Jacob Lew, b 8/29/55 (New York, NY), White House chief of staff.
Monica Lewinsky, b 7/23/73 (San Francisco, CA), former White House intern.
Joseph Lieberman, b 2/24/42 (Stamford, CT), senator (ind., CT), former vice pres. candidate, 2004 pres. contender.
Rush Limbaugh, b 1/12/51 (Cape Girardeau, MO), radio talk-show host.
Gary Locke, b 1/21/50 (Seattle, WA), first Chinese-Amer. U.S. ambassador to China, former commerce sec., WA governor (D).
Trent Lott, b 10/9/41 (Grenada, MS), former senator (R, MS) and majority leader.
Shannon Lucid, b 1/14/43 (Shanghai, China), NASA scientist, astronaut.
Richard Lugar, b 4/4/32 (Indianapolis, IN), senator (R, IN).
Rachel Maddow, b 4/1/73 (Castro Valley, CA), TV/radio host, political commentator.
Bernie Madoff, b 4/29/38 (Queens, NY), financier who swindled investors; sentenced to 150 years in prison.
Mary Matalin, b 8/19/53 (Chicago, IL), political commentator.
Chris Matthews, b 12/18/45 (Philadelphia, PA), TV journalist.
John McCain, b 8/29/36 (Panama Canal Zone), senator (R, AZ), 2008 Republican presidential candidate.
Kevin McCarthy, b 1/26/65 (Bakersfield, CA), U.S. rep. (R, CA), House majority whip.
Mitch McConnell, b 2/20/42 (Tuscumbia, AL), senator (R, KY), Senate minority leader.
David McCullough, b 7/7/33 (Pittsburgh, PA), historian, biographer.
George McGovern, b 7/19/22 (Avon, SD), former senator (D, SD), 1972 pres. nominee.
Dr. Phil McGraw, b 9/1/50 (Vinita, OK), talk-show host, motivational speaker, author.
James McGreevey, b 8/6/57 (Jersey City, NJ), former NJ governor (D); resigned amid allegations of sexual harassment.
John McLaughlin, b 3/29/27 (Providence, RI), TV journalist.
Russell Means, b 11/10/39 (Pine Ridge Indian Reserv., SD), Native American activist.
Kate Michelman, b 8/4/42 (NJ), abortion-rights activist.
Kate Millett, b 9/14/34 (St. Paul, MN), author, feminist.
George Mitchell, b 8/20/33, (Waterville, ME), former spec. envoy for Middle East peace, Senate majority leader (D, ME), diplomat, Disney Co. chair.
Walter Mondale, b 1/5/28 (Ceylon, MN), former vice pres., senator (D, MN), 1984 pres. nominee.

Michael Moore, b 4/23/54 (Davison, MI), activist, documentary filmmaker, author.
Bill Moyers, b 6/5/34 (Hugo, OK), TV journalist, author.
Robert S. Mueller III, b 8/7/44 (New York, NY), FBI director.
Michael Mullen, b 10/4/46 (Los Angeles, CA), former chairman of Joint Chiefs of Staff.
Rupert Murdoch, b 3/11/31 (Melbourne, Aust.), media exec.
Ralph Nader, b 2/27/34 (Winsted, CT), consumer advocate, independent pres. cand. in 1996, 2000, 2004, and 2008.
Janet Napolitano, b 11/29/57 (New York, NY), homeland security sec., former AZ governor.
John Negroponte, b 7/21/39 (London, Eng., UK), former director of National Intelligence, U.S. rep. to UN.
Craig Newmark, b 12/6/52 (Morristown, NY), founder of Craigslist.com.
Peggy Noonan, b 9/7/50 (Brooklyn, NY), columnist, speechwriter.
Oliver North, b 10/7/43 (San Antonio, TX), talk-show host, former Natl. Sec. Council aide, figure in Iran-contra scandal.
Eleanor Holmes Norton, b 6/13/37 (Washington, DC), U.S. House delegate for Washington, DC (D).
Sam Nunn, b 9/8/38 (Perry, GA), former senator (D, GA).
Barack Obama, b 8/4/61 (Honolulu, HI), U.S. president, former senator (D, IL).
Michelle Obama, b 1/17/64 (Chicago, IL), first lady, lawyer.
Soledad O'Brien, b 9/19/66 (Smithtown, NY), TV journalist.
Sandra Day O'Connor, b 3/26/30 (El Paso, TX), former Supreme Court justice.
Keith Olbermann, b 1/27/59 (New York, NY), political commentator, former ESPN/MSNBC host.
Todd Oldham, b 11/22/61 (Corpus Christi, TX), fashion designer.
Bill O'Reilly, b 9/10/49 (New York, NY), TV commentator, host.
Joel Osteen, b 3/5/63 (Houston, TX), televangelist, author.
Michael Ovitz, b 12/14/46 (Encino, CA), entertainment exec.
Clarence Page, b 6/2/47 (Dayton, OH), journalist, TV commentator.
Lawrence Page, b 9/26/73 (East Lansing, MI), cofounder of Google.
Camille Paglia, b 4/2/47 (Endicott, NY), scholar, author.
Sarah Palin, b 2/11/64 (Sandpoint, ID), former AK governor, 2008 Republican vice-pres. nominee.
Leon E. Panetta, b 6/28/38 (Monterey, CA), sec. of defense; former CIA director, White House chief of staff, U.S. rep. (D, CA).
Richard Parsons, b 4/4/48 (Brooklyn, NY), Citigroup chairman, former Time Warner CEO.
David Paterson, b 5/20/54 (Brooklyn, NY), attorney, former NY governor (D).
Ron Paul, b 8/20/35 (Pittsburgh, PA), physician, U.S. rep. (R, TX), pres. contender (2008, 2012).
Jane Pauley, b 10/31/50 (Indianapolis, IN), TV journalist.
Henry Paulson, b 3/28/46 (Palm Beach, FL), former sec. of treasury, former CEO/chairman of Goldman Sachs.
Tim Pawlenty, b 11/27/60 (St. Paul, MN), former MN governor (R).
Nancy Pelosi, b 3/26/40 (Baltimore, MD), U.S. rep. (D, CA); House minority leader; former House speaker.
Ross Perot, b 6/27/30 (Texarkana, TX), entrepreneur, former pres. nominee.
Rick Perry, b 3/4/50 (Paint Creek, TX), TX governor (R), former 2012 pres. contender.
David Petraeus, b 11/7/52 (Cornwall-on-Hudson, NY), CIA director; former U.S. Forces Afghanistan cmdr., CENTCOM cmdr.
Colin Powell, b 4/5/37 (New York, NY), former sec. of state, natl. security adviser, Joint Chiefs of Staff chairman.

Reince Priebus, b 3/18/72 (Kenosha, WI), Rep. Natl. Committee chair.
Dan Quayle, b 2/4/47 (Indianapolis, IN), former U.S. vice pres., senator (R, IN), pres. contender.
Anna Quindlen, b 7/8/53 (Philadelphia, PA), author, columnist.
Martha Raddatz, b1953 (Salt Lake City, UT), ABC news correspondent.
Dan Rather, b 10/31/31 (Wharton, TX), TV journalist, retired CBS anchor.
Nancy Reagan, b 7/6/21 (Flushing, Queens, NY), former first lady.
Sumner Redstone, b 5/27/23 (Boston, MA), Viacom/CBS chairman.
Ralph Reed Jr., b 6/24/61 (Portsmouth, VA), political adviser.
Robert B. Reich, b 6/24/46 (Scranton, PA), economist, author, former labor sec.
Harry Reid, b 12/2/39 (Searchlight, NV), Senate majority leader (D, NV).
Janet Reno, b 7/21/38 (Miami, FL), former U.S. attorney gen.
Condoleezza Rice, b 11/14/54 (Birmingham, AL), former sec. of state, former natl. security adviser.
Susan Rice, b 11/17/64 (Washington, DC), U.S. ambassador to UN.
Frank Rich, b 6/2/49 (Washington, DC), essayist, columnist.
Cecile Richards, b 1958, pres. of Planned Parenthood.
Bill Richardson, b 11/15/47 (Pasadena, CA), former energy sec., UN rep., U.S. rep. (D, NM), NM gov.; 2008 pres. contender.
Tom Ridge, b 8/26/45 (Munhall, PA), former sec. of homeland security, former PA gov.
Geraldo Rivera, b 7/4/43 (New York, NY), TV journalist.
Cokie Roberts, b 12/27/43 (New Orleans, LA), TV journalist.
John G. Roberts, b 1/27/55 (Buffalo, NY), Supreme Court chief justice.
Robin Roberts, b 11/23/60 (Tuskegee, AL), *Good Morning America* co-host.
Rev. Pat Robertson, b 3/22/30 (Lexington, VA), religious broadcasting exec., former pres. contender.
V. Gene Robinson, b 5/29/47 (Lexington, KY), first openly gay Episcopal bishop.
David Rockefeller, b 6/12/15 (New York, NY), banker.
Buddy Roemer, b 10/4/43 (Shreveport, LA), former LA governor, U.S. rep (D); former 2012 pres. contender.
Al Roker, b 8/20/54 (Queens, NY), TV weather person.
Mitt Romney, b 3/12/47 (Detroit, MI), Rep. pres. nominee (2012); former MA governor, Olympics organizer.
Charlie Rose, b 1/5/42 (Henderson, NC), TV journalist.
Karl Rove, b 12/25/50 (Denver, CO), former adviser to Pres. G. W. Bush, political commentator.
Marco Rubio, b 5/28/71 (Miami, FL), senator (R, FL).
Donald Rumsfeld, b 7/9/32 (Chicago, IL), former sec. of defense.
Paul Ryan, b 1/29/70 (Janesville, WI), 2012 vice pres. nominee; U.S. rep. (R, WI).
Morley Safer, b 11/8/31 (Toronto, ON, Can.), TV journalist.
Ken Salazar, b 3/2/55 (Alamosa, CO), interior sec., former sen. (D, CO), rancher.
Rick Santorum, b 5/10/58 (Winchester, VA), former sen. (R, PA), U.S. rep; 2012 pres. contender.
Diane Sawyer, b 12/22/45 (Glasgow, KY), TV journalist, anchor of ABC *World News With Diane Sawyer*.
Antonin Scalia, b 3/11/36 (Trenton, NJ), Supreme Court justice.
Bob Schieffer, b 2/25/37 (Austin, TX), CBS TV news anchor.
Phyllis Schlafly, b 8/15/24 (St. Louis, MO), political activist.
Caroline Kennedy Schlossberg, b 11/27/57 (New York, NY), author, daughter of Pres. Kennedy.

Eric Schmidt, b 4/27/55 (Washington, DC), Google CEO.

Rev. Robert Schuller, b 9/16/26 (Alton, IA), TV evangelist.

Charles Schumer, b 11/23/50 (Brooklyn, NY), senator (D, NY).

Arnold Schwarzenegger, b 7/30/47 (Thal, Styria, Austria), actor, former CA governor.

H. Norman Schwarzkopf, b 8/22/34 (Trenton, NJ), former military leader.

Willard Scott, b 3/7/34 (Alexandria, VA), former TV weather person.

Kathleen Sebelius, b 5/15/58 (Cincinnati, OH), health and human services sec., former KS governor.

Allan H. (Bud) Selig, b 7/30/34 (Milwaukee, WI), MLB commissioner.

Richard Serra, b 11/2/39 (San Francisco, CA), sculptor.

Rev. Al Sharpton, b 10/3/54 (Brooklyn, NY), activist, civil rights leader, TV personality.

Eric Shinseki, b 11/28/42 (Lihue, HI), veterans affairs sec., former Army chief of staff.

Will Shortz, b 8/26/52 (Crawfordsville, IN), puzzle editor.

Maria Shriver, b 11/6/55 (Chicago, IL), TV journalist, former CA first lady.

George P. Shultz, b 12/13/20 (New York, NY), former sec. of state, other cabinet posts.

Russell Simmons, b 10/4/57 (Queens, NY), music producer.

Bob Simon, b 5/29/41 (Bronx, NY), TV journalist.

O. J. Simpson, b 7/9/47 (San Francisco, CA), former football star, murder defendant.

Harry Smith, b 8/21/51 (Lansing, IL), NBC TV journalist, former CBS morning anchor.

Liz Smith, b 2/2/23 (Ft. Worth, TX), gossip columnist.

Hilda Solis, b 10/20/57 (Los Angeles, CA), labor sec., former U.S. rep. (D, CA).

George Soros, b 8/12/30 (Budapest, Hungary), financier, philanthropist.

Sonia Sotomayor, b 6/25/54 (Bronx, NY), Supreme Court justice.

David H. Souter, b 9/17/39 (Melrose, MA), former Supreme Court justice.

Kate Spade, b 1962 (Kansas City, MO), fashion designer.

Steven Spielberg, b 12/18/46 (Cincinnati, OH), movie director, producer.

Eliot Spitzer, b 6/10/59 (Bronx, NY), former NY gov. (D); resigned after involvement with prostitutes exposed.

Lesley Stahl, b 12/16/41 (Swampscott, MA), TV journalist.

Kenneth Starr, b 7/21/46 (Vernon, TX), former Whitewater indep. counsel.

Michael Steele, b 10/19/58 (Prince George's Co., MD), former Rep. Natl. Committee chair, MD lt. gov.

Shelby Steele, b 1/1/46 (Chicago, IL), scholar, critic.

Ben Stein, b 11/25/44 (Washington, DC), attorney, columnist, former speechwriter, actor, TV personality.

Gloria Steinem, b 3/25/34 (Toledo, OH), author, feminist.

Frank Stella, b 5/12/36 (Malden, MA), painter.

George Stephanopoulos, b 2/10/61 (Fall River, MA), TV journalist, former pres. adviser; *Good Morning America* co-host.

David J. Stern, b 9/22/42 (New York, NY), NBA commissioner.

Howard Stern, b 1/12/54 (Roosevelt, NY), radio talk show host.

John Paul Stevens, b 4/20/20 (Chicago, IL), former Supreme Court justice.

Martha Stewart, b 8/3/41 (Nutley, NJ), homemaking adviser, entrepreneur, TV personality.

Biz Stone, b 3/10/74 (Boston, MA), cofounder of Twitter.

Chesley (Sully) Sullenberger III, b 1/23/51 (Denison, TX), US Airways pilot who safely landed a jet in the Hudson River.

Andrew Sullivan, b 8/10/63 (Eng.), political commentator and blogger.

Arthur Ochs Sulzberger Jr., b 9/22/51 (Mt. Kisco, NY), newspaper publisher.

Lawrence H. Summers, b 11/30/54 (New Haven, CT), economist; former Natl. Economic Council dir., Harvard Univ. pres., sec. of treasury.

George Tenet, b 1/5/53 (Flushing, Queens, NY), former CIA director.

Clarence Thomas, b 6/23/48 (Savannah, GA), Supreme Court justice.

Helen Thomas, b 8/4/20 (Winchester, KY), former journalist.

Richard Trumka, b 7/24/49 (Waynesburg, PA), pres. of AFL-CIO.

Donald Trump, b 6/14/46 (Jamaica, Queens, NY), real estate exec., TV personality.

Ted Turner, b 11/19/38 (Cincinnati, OH), TV exec., philanthropist.

Neil deGrasse Tyson, b 10/5/58 (New York, NY), astrophysicist, director of NYC's Hayden Planetarium, author, TV host.

Abigail Van Buren, b 7/4/18 (Sioux City, IA), retired advice columnist.

Gloria Vanderbilt, b 2/20/24 (New York, NY), fashion designer, heiress.

Greta Van Susteren, b 6/11/54 (Appleton, WI), attorney, TV journalist.

Jesse Ventura, b 7/15/51 (Minneapolis, MN), former wrestler, former MN governor; radio talk show host.

Meredith Vieira, b 12/30/53 (Providence, RI), former *Today* show co-host.

Antonio Villaraigosa, b 1/23/53 (East Los Angeles, CA), 1st Hispanic mayor of L.A. since 1870s.

Paul Volcker, b 9/5/27 (Cape May, NJ), economist, former Federal Reserve chairman.

Jimmy Wales, b 8/8/66 (Huntsville, AL), cofounder of Wikipedia.

Barbara Walters, b 9/25/31 (Boston, MA), TV journalist.

Vera Wang, b 6/27/49 (New York, NY), fashion designer.

Rick Warren, b 1/28/54 (San Jose, CA), evangelical Christian pastor, founder of Saddleback Church, author.

Debbie Wasserman Schultz, b 9/27/66 (Forest Hills, NY), U.S. rep. (D, FL), Dem. Natl. Committee chair.

James Watson, b 4/6/28 (Chicago, IL), biochemist, DNA pioneer, co-winner of the 1962 Nobel Prize.

Dr. Andrew Weil, b 6/8/42 (Philadelphia, PA), health adviser.

Anthony Weiner, b 9/4/64 (Brooklyn, NY), former U.S. rep. (D, NY); resigned after 2011 scandal.

Harvey Weinstein, b 3/19/52 (Flushing, Queens, NY), movie exec.

Jack Welch, b 11/19/35 (Peabody, MA), former General Electric CEO.

Jann Wenner, b 1/7/46 (New York, NY), publisher, founder of *Rolling Stone*.

Cornel West, b 6/23/53 (Tulsa, OK), African American scholar, critic.

Ruth Westheimer, b 6/4/28 (Frankfurt am Main, Germany), human sexuality expert.

Meg Whitman, b 8/4/56 (Cold Spring Harbor, NY), 2010 CA gubernatorial candidate (R), former eBay CEO; HP CEO.

Elie Wiesel, b 9/30/28 (Sighet, Romania), scholar, author, 1986 Nobel Peace Prize winner.

George Will, b 5/4/41 (Champaign, IL), journalist, author.

Brian Williams, b 5/5/59 (Elmira, NY), NBC TV news anchor.

Evan Williams, b 3/31/72 (Clarks, NE), cofounder and CEO of Twitter.

Jody Williams, b 10/9/50 (Brattleboro, VT), peace activist, 1997 Nobel Peace Prize winner.

Oprah Winfrey, b 1/29/54 (Kosciusko, MS), TV and media personality, businesswoman, actress.

Bob Woodward, b 3/26/43 (Geneva, IL), journalist; with Bernstein cracked Watergate scandal.

Steve Wynn, b 1/27/42 (New Haven, CT), casino developer.

Paula Zahn, b 2/24/56 (Omaha, NE), TV journalist.

Mark Zuckerberg, b 5/14/84 (Dobbs Ferry, NY), founder of Facebook.

Mortimer Zuckerman, b 6/4/37 (Montreal, QC, Can.), publisher, columnist.

Widely Known World Personalities of the Present

Living non-Americans only. Generally excludes current heads of state or government (see Nations chapter) and excludes most others covered elsewhere, such as in Widely Known Americans, Entertainment and Writers lists, or Sports Personalities.

Mahmoud Abbas (Abu Mazen), b 3/26/35 (Safed, Palestine [now Israel]), president of the Palestinian National Authority.

Gerry Adams, b 10/6/48 (Belfast, N. Ireland, UK), Sinn Fein leader.

Viswanathan Anand, b 12/11/69 (Chennai, Madras, India), world chess champion.

Prince Andrew, b 2/19/60 (London, Eng., UK), Duke of York (2nd son of Queen Elizabeth II).

Kofi Annan, b 4/8/38 (Kumasi, Ghana), former UN sec.-gen.; 2001 Nobel laureate.

Princess Anne, b 8/15/50 (London, Eng., UK), Princess Royal (daughter of Queen Elizabeth II).

Michael Arad, b 1969 (Jerusalem, Israel), designer of the Natl. 9/11 Memorial in NYC.

Oscar Arias Sánchez, b 9/13/41 (Heredia, Costa Rica), former Costa Rican pres., peace negotiator, 1987 Nobel laureate.

Giorgio Armani, b 7/30/34 (Piacenza, Italy), fashion designer.

Julian Assange, b 7/3/71 (Townsville, Queensland, Australia), editor-in-chief and founder of WikiLeaks media organization.

Ban Ki-Moon, b 6/13/44 (Umsong, [now] South Korea), UN sec.-gen.

Ehud Barak, b 2/12/42 (Mishmar Ha-Sharon Kibbutz, Israel), Israeli minister of defense, former Israeli prime min.

Benedict XVI (Joseph Ratzinger), b 4/16/27 (Marktl am Inn, Germany), pope of Rom. Cath. Church, elected 2005.

Boris Berezovsky, b 1/23/46 (Moscow, USSR), businessman, politician.

Tim Berners-Lee, b 6/8/55 (London, Eng., UK), World Wide Web inventor.

Tony Blair, b 5/6/53 (Edinburgh, Scot., UK), former British prime minister.

Hans Blix, b 6/28/28 (Uppsala, Swed.), former UN weapons inspector.

Bono (Paul David Hewson), b 5/20/60 (Glasnevin, Dublin, Ire., UK), musician, social activist, philanthropist.

Fernando Botero, b 4/19/32 (Medellín, Col.), Colombian artist.

Boutros Boutros-Ghali, b 11/14/22 (Cairo, Egypt), former UN sec.-gen.

Richard Branson, b 7/18/50 (S. London, Eng., UK), British Virgin Records and Airways founder.

Gordon Brown, b 2/20/51 (Glasgow, Scot., UK), former British prime minister.

Tina Brown, b 11/21/53 (Maidenhead, Eng., UK), journalist, TV talk show host, author.

Carla Bruni, b 12/23/67 (Turin, Italy), former first lady of France, musician, actress, model.

Mark Burnett, b 7/17/60 (Myland, Eng., UK), reality TV producer.

Rhonda Byrne, b 3/12/51 (Australia), author, TV writer and producer.

Kim Campbell, b 3/10/47 (Port Alberni, BC, Can.), former Canadian prime min.

Pierre Cardin, b 7/7/22 (San Biaggio di Callalta, Italy), fashion designer.

Princess Caroline, b 1/23/57 (Monte Carlo, Monaco), Monaco royal (eldest daughter of Prince Rainier and Princess Grace).

Fidel Castro, b 8/13/26 (Birán, Cuba), former prime minister of Cuba.

Prince Charles, b 11/14/48 (London, Eng., UK), Prince of Wales (eldest son of Queen Elizabeth II); heir to British throne.

Chen Guangcheng, b 11/12/71 (Dongshigu, China), civil rights activist.

Jacques Chirac, b 11/29/32 (Paris, France), former French pres.

Deepak Chopra, b 1946 (New Delhi, India), new age writer.

Jean Chrétien, b 1/11/34 (Shawinigan, QC, Can.), former Canadian prime min.

Christo (Javacheff), b 6/13/35 (Gabrovo, Bulg.), artist.

Joe (Charles Joseph) Clark, b 6/5/39 (High River, AB, Can.), former Canadian prime min.

King Constantine II, b 6/2/40 (Psychiko, Greece), former king of Greece.

Simon Cowell, b 10/7/59 (Brighton, East Sussex, Eng., UK), music exec., TV producer, former *American Idol* host.

Dalai Lama (Tenzin Gyatso), b 7/6/35 (Taktser, Amdo, Tibet), Buddhist leader; 1989 Nobel Peace Prize laureate.

Richard Dawkins, b 3/26/41 (Nairobi, Kenya), ethologist, evolutionary biologist, author.

Mario Draghi, b 9/3/47 (Rome, Italy), European Central Bank pres.

Shirin Ebadi, b 6/21/47 (Hamadan, Iran), human rights activist, 2003 Nobel Peace Prize winner.

Prince Edward, b 3/10/64 (London, Eng., UK), Earl of Essex (3rd son of Queen Elizabeth II).

Mohamed ElBaradei, b 6/17/42 (Cairo, Egypt), former director general of the International Atomic Energy Agency (IAEA); 2005 Nobel Peace Prize winner.

Prince Felipe, b 1/30/68 (Madrid, Spain), heir to Spanish throne.

Sarah Ferguson, b 10/15/58 (London, Eng., UK), Duchess of York, ex-wife of Prince Andrew.

John Galliano, b 11/28/60 (Gibraltar, UK terr.), fashion designer.

Wael Ghonim, b 12/23/80 (Cairo, Egypt), computer engineer and Internet activist who sparked Egyptian revolution (2011).

Valery Giscard d'Estaing, b 2/2/26 (Koblenz, Ger.), former French pres.

Jane Goodall, b 4/3/34 (London, Eng., UK), anthropologist, primatologist.

Mikhail Gorbachev, b 3/2/31 (Privolnoye, USSR), former Soviet pres.; 1990 Nobel Peace Prize winner.

Jürgen Habermas, b 6/18/29 (Dusseldorf, Ger.), philosopher.

Stephen Hawking, b 1/8/42 (Oxford, Eng., UK), physicist, author.

Prince Henry (Harry) (of Wales), b 9/15/84 (London, Eng., UK), son of Prince Charles; 3rd in line to British throne.

Damien Hirst, b 6/7/65 (Bristol, Eng., UK), artist.

David Hockney, b 7/9/37 (Bradford, Eng., UK), artist.

Jiang Zemin, b 8/17/26 (Yangzhou, Jiangsu Prov., China), former pres. of China.

Garry Kasparov, b 4/13/63 (Baku, Azerbaijan, USSR), former world chess champion; Russian pro-democracy leader.

Ayatollah Ali Khamenei, b 7/17/39 (Mashhad, Iran), Supreme Leader and former president of Iran, cleric, author.

F. W. (Frederik Willem) de Klerk, b 3/18/36 (Johannesburg, S. Africa), former S. African pres.; 1993 Nobel Peace Prize winner.

Helmut Kohl, b 4/3/30 (Ludwigshafen, Ger.), former German chancellor.

Hans Kung, b 3/19/28 (Sursee, Switz.), Rom. Cath. theologian.

Christine Lagarde, b 1/1/56 (Paris, France), Intl. Monetary Fund managing dir.

Karl Lagerfeld, b 9/10/38 (Hamburg, Germany), fashion designer.

Richard Leakey, b 12/19/44 (Nairobi, Kenya), anthropologist, paleontologist, conservationist.

Tzipi Livni, b 7/5/58 (Tel Aviv, Israel), attorney, former head of Israeli Kadima party, foreign affairs minister of Israel.

John Major, b 3/29/43 (Wimbledon, Eng., UK), former British prime min.

Nelson Mandela, b 7/18/18 (Transkei, S. Africa), former pres. of S. Africa; 1993 Nobel Peace Prize winner.

Imelda Marcos, b 7/2/29 (Manila, Philip.), former first lady of Philippines; Philip. House of Rep. member.

Paul Martin, b 8/28/38 (Windsor, ON, Can.), former prime minister of Canada.

Peter Max, b 10/19/37 (Berlin, Ger.), artist, designer.

Stella McCartney, b 9/13/71 (London, Eng., UK), fashion designer.

Angela Merkel, b 7/17/54 (Hamburg, Ger.), 1st woman chancellor of Germany.

Jean-Marie Messier, b 12/13/56 (Grenoble, Fr.), former CEO of Vivendi Universal.

Empress Michiko, b 10/20/34 (Tokyo, Japan), empress of Japan.

Kate Middleton (Catherine, Duchess of Cambridge), b 1/9/82 (Reading, UK), wife of Prince William.

Pippa Middleton, b 9/6/83 (Reading, UK), event planner; socialite sister of Catherine, Duchess of Cambridge.

Kate Moss, b 1/16/74 (Addiscombe, Surrey, Eng., UK), model.

Mir Hussein Moussavi, b 9/29/41 (Khameneh, Iran), challenger in Iran's 2009 presidential election.

Hosni Mubarak, b 5/4/28 (Kafre al-Musailha, Egypt), deposed Egyptian president.

Brian Mulroney, b 3/20/39 (Baie-Corneau, QC, Can.), former Canadian prime min.

Prince Naruhito, b 2/23/60 (Tokyo, Japan), crown prince of Japan.

Hassan Nasrallah, b 8/31/60 (Qarantina, Lebanon), leader of the Hezbollah in Lebanon.

Queen Noor (Lisa Halaby), b 8/23/51 (Washington, DC), American-born widow of Jordan's King Hussein.

Ehud Olmert, b 9/30/45 (Binyamina, Palestine), former prime minister of Israel.

Daniel Ortega Saavedra, b 11/11/45 (La Libertad, Nicar.), Nicaraguan pres., Sandinista leader.

Camilla Parker-Bowles, Duchess of Cornwall, b 7/17/47 (London, Eng., UK), wife of Prince Charles.

Jean-Marie le Pen, b 6/20/28 (La Trinite-sur-Mer, Fr.), French right-wing politician.

Marine Le Pen, b 8/5/68 (Neuilly-sur-Seine, France), head of France's National Front Party.

Javier Perez de Cuellar, b 1/19/20 (Lima, Peru), former UN sec.-gen.

Prince Philip, b 6/10/21 (Corfu, Greece), Duke of Edinburgh (husband of Queen Elizabeth II).

Gerhard Richter, b 2/9/32 (Dresden, Ger.), artist.

Mary Robinson, b 5/21/44 (Ballina, Co. Mayo, Ireland), former Irish pres., former UN High Commissioner for Human Rights.

Ségolène Royal, b 9/22/53 (Dakar, Senegal), French socialist politician, 2007 candidate for president of France.

Muqtada al-Sadr, b 8/12/73? (Najaf, Iraq), extremist Shiite cleric.

Carlos Salinas de Gortari, b 4/3/48 (Mexico City, Mex.), former Mexican pres.

Nicolas Sarkozy, b 1/28/55 (Paris, France), former French pres.

Helmut Schmidt, b 12/23/18 (Hamburg, Germany), former German chancellor.

Gerhard Schröder, b 4/7/44 (Mossenburg, Germany), former German chancellor.

Yitzhak Shamir, b 10/22/15 (Kuzinoy, Poland), former Israeli prime minister.

Ariel Sharon, b 2/26/28 (Kfar Malal, Palestine), former Israeli prime minister.

Eduard Shevardnadze, b 1/25/28 (Mamati, Georgia, USSR), former Georgian pres.

Ayatollah Ali al-Sistani, b 8/4/30 (Mashhad, Iran), major Iraqi Shiite religious leader.

Carlos Slim Helú, b 1/28/40 (Mexico City, Mexico), chairman and CEO of Telmex, Telcel and América Móvil.

Princess Stephanie, b 2/1/65 (Monte Carlo, Monaco), youngest child of Prince Rainier and Princess Grace.

Dominique Strauss-Kahn, b 4/25/49 (Neuilly-sur-Seine, France), former Intl. Monetary Fund managing dir.

Aung San Suu Kyi, b 6/19/45 (Rangoon, Myanmar), member of parliament, pro-democracy political activist, 1991 Nobel Peace Prize winner.

Valentina Tereshkova, b 3/6/37 (Maslennikovo, Russia, USSR), 1st woman in space.

Margaret Thatcher, b 10/13/25 (Grantham, Eng., UK), former British prime min.

John Napier Turner, b 6/7/29 (Richmond, Surrey, Eng., UK), former Canadian prime min.

Desmond Tutu, b 10/7/31 (Klerksdorp, Transvaal, S. Africa), former S. African archbishop; 1984 Nobel Peace Prize winner.

Lech Walesa, b 9/29/43 (Popowo, Pol.), Solidarity leader; 1983 Nobel Peace Prize winner; former president of Poland.

Prince William (of Wales), b 6/21/82 (London, Eng., UK), son of Prince Charles; 2nd in line to British throne.

Rowan Williams, b 6/14/50 (Ystradgynlais, Wales, UK), Archbishop of Canterbury.

Xi Jinping, b 6/1/53 (Shaanxi, Fuping, China), Communist party leader.

Muhammad Yunus, b 6/28/40 (Chittagong, India), 2006 Nobel Peace prize winner, economics professor.

Ayman al-Zawahiri, b 6/19/51 (Cairo, Egypt), reputed high-ranking al-Qaeda leader.

Architects

Alvar Aalto, 1898-1976, Säynätsalo, Jyväskylä, Finland; Vuoksenniska Church, Vuoksenniska, Finland.

Max Abramovitz, 1908-2004, Avery Fisher Hall, New York, NY; U.S. Steel Bldg. (now USX Towers), Pittsburgh, PA.

Tadao Ando, b 1941, Modern Art Museum, Ft. Worth, TX; Stone Hill Center, MA.

Michael Arad, b 1969, World Trade Center Memorial, New York, NY.

Henry Bacon, 1866-1924, Lincoln Memorial, Washington, DC.

Benjamin Banneker, 1731-1806, African American inventor, astronomer, mathematician; helped design and lay out Washington, DC.

Pietro Belluschi, 1899-1994, Juilliard School, Lincoln Center, Pan Am Bldg. (now MetLife Bldg.) with Walter Gropius, New York, NY.

Marcel Breuer, 1902-81, Whitney Museum of American Art (with Hamilton Smith), New York, NY.

Charles Bulfinch, 1763-1844, State House, Boston, MA; Capitol (part), Wash., DC.

Gordon Bunshaft, 1909-90, Lever House, Park Ave., New York, NY; Hirshhorn Museum, Washington, DC.

Daniel H. Burnham, 1846-1912, Union Station, Washington, DC; Flatiron Bldg., New York, NY.

Irwin Chanin, 1892-1988, theaters, skyscrapers, New York, NY.

David Childs, b 1941, Washington Mall Master Plan/Constitution Gardens, Washington, DC; WTC Freedom Tower, New York, NY.

Lucio Costa, 1902-98, master plan for city of Brasilia, Brazil (with Oscar Niemeyer).

Ralph Adams Cram, 1863-1942, Cath. of St. John the Divine, New York, NY; U.S. Military Acad. (part), West Point, NY.

Norman Foster, b 1935, Commerzbank Headquarters, Frankfurt-am-Main, Ger.; London Millennium Bridge, Eng., UK; 30 St. Mary Axe, Eng., UK.

James Ingo Freed, 1930-2005, Holocaust Memorial Museum, Washington, DC; Jacob K. Javits Center, New York, NY.

R. Buckminster Fuller, 1895-1983, U.S. Pavilion (geodesic domes), Expo 67, Montreal, QC, Can.

Frank O. Gehry, b 1929, Guggenheim Museum, Bilbao, Spain; Experience Music Project, Seattle, WA; Walt Disney Concert Hall, Los Angeles, CA.

Cass Gilbert, 1859-1934, Custom House, Woolworth Bldg., New York, NY; Supreme Court Bldg., Washington, DC.

Bertram G. Goodhue, 1869-1924, Capitol, Lincoln, NE; St. Thomas's Church, St. Bartholomew's Church, New York, NY.

Michael Graves, b 1934, Portland Bldg., Portland, OR; Humana Bldg., Louisville, KY.

Walter Gropius, 1883-1969, Pan Am Bldg. (now MetLife Bldg.) (with Pietro Belluschi), New York, NY.

Zaha Hadid, b 1950, Rosenthal Center for Contemporary Art, Cincinnati, OH; London Aquatics Centre, Eng., UK.

Lawrence Halprin, 1916-2009, Ghirardelli Sq., San Francisco, CA; Nicollet Mall, Minneapolis, MN; FDR Memorial, Washington, DC.

Peter Harrison, 1716-75, Touro Synagogue, Redwood Library, Newport, RI.

Wallace K. Harrison, 1895-1981, Metropolitan Opera House, Lincoln Center, New York, NY.

Thomas Hastings, 1860-1929, NY Public Library (with John Carrère), Frick Mansion, New York, NY.

James Hoban, 1762-1831, White House, Washington, DC.

Raymond Hood, 1881-1934, Rockefeller Center (part), Daily News Bldg., New York, NY; Tribune Tower, Chicago, IL.

Richard M. Hunt, 1827-95, Metropolitan Museum (part), New York, NY; Biltmore Estate, Asheville, NC.

Helmut Jahn, b 1940, United Airlines Terminal, O'Hare Airport, Chicago, IL.

William Le Baron Jenney, 1832-1907, Home Insurance Bldg. (demolished 1931), Chicago, IL.

Philip C. Johnson, 1906-2005, AT&T headquarters (now 550 Madison Ave.), New York, NY; Transco (now Williams) Tower, Houston, TX.

Albert Kahn, 1869-1942, General Motors Bldg., Detroit, MI.

Louis Kahn, 1901-74, Salk Laboratory, La Jolla, CA; Yale Art Gallery, New Haven, CT.

Rem Koolhaas, b 1944, Seattle Central Library, Seattle, WA.

Christopher Grant LaFarge, 1862-1938, Roman Catholic Chapel, West Point, NY.

Benjamin H. Latrobe, 1764-1820, Capitol (part), Washington, DC; State Capitol Bldg., Richmond, VA.

Le Corbusier (Charles-Edouard Jeanneret), 1887-1965, Salvation Army Hostel, Swiss Dormitory, Paris, France; master plan for cities of Algiers and Buenos Aires.

William Lescaze, 1896-1969, Philadelphia Savings Fund Society, PA; Borg-Warner Bldg., Chicago, IL.

Daniel Libeskind, b 1946, primary architect for the rebuilding World Trade Center site, New York, NY.

Maya Lin, b 1959, Vietnam Veterans Mem., Washington, DC.

Charles Rennie Mackintosh, 1868-1928, Glasgow School of Art; Hill House, Helensburgh, Scot., UK.

Bernard R. Maybeck, 1862-1957, Hearst Hall, Univ. of CA, Berkeley; First Church of Christ Scientist, Berkeley, CA.

Charles F. McKim, 1847-1909, Boston Public Library; Columbia Univ. (part), New York, NY.

Charles M. McKim, b 1920, KUHT-TV Transmitter Bldg., Lutheran Church of the Redeemer, Houston, TX.

Richard Meier, b 1934, Getty Center Museum, Los Angeles, CA; High Museum of Art, Atlanta, GA.

Ludwig Mies van der Rohe, 1886-1969, Seagram Bldg. (with Philip C. Johnson), New York, NY; National Gallery, Berlin, Ger.

Robert Mills, 1781-1855, Washington Monument, Washington, DC.

Charles Moore, 1925-93, Sea Ranch, nr. San Francisco, CA; Piazza d'Italia, New Orleans, LA.

Julia Morgan, 1872-1957, San Simeon, CA.

John Nash, 1752-1835, Buckingham Palace, London, Eng., UK.

Richard J. Neutra, 1892-1970, Mathematics Park, Princeton, NJ; Orange Co. Courthouse, Santa Ana, CA.

Oscar Niemeyer, b 1907, government buildings, Brasilia Palace Hotel, all Brasilia, Braz.

Gyo Obata, b 1923, Natl. Air and Space Museum, Smithsonian Inst., Washington, DC; Dallas-Ft. Worth Airport, TX.

Frederick L. Olmsted, 1822-1903, Central Park, New York, NY; Fairmount Park, Philadelphia, PA.

I(eoh) M(ing) Pei, b 1917, East Wing, Natl. Gallery of Art, Washington, DC; Pyramid, The Louvre, Paris, Fr.; Rock & Roll Hall of Fame and Museum, Cleveland, OH.

Cesar Pelli, b 1926, World Financial Center, Carnegie Hall Tower, New York, NY; Petronas Twin Towers, Malaysia.

William Pereira, 1909-85, Cape Canaveral, FL; Transamerica Bldg., San Francisco, CA.

Renzo Piano, b 1937, Pompidou Centre, Paris, Fr.; New York Times Bldg., New York, NY.

John Russell Pope, 1874-1937, National Gallery, Jefferson Memorial, Wash., DC.

John Portman, b 1924, Peachtree Center, Atlanta, GA.

George Browne Post, 1837-1913, NY Stock Exchange, New York, NY; Capitol, Madison, WI.

James Renwick Jr., 1818-95, Grace Church, St. Patrick's Cathedral, New York, NY; Smithsonian Institution (Castle), Washington, DC.

Henry H. Richardson, 1838-86, Trinity Church, Boston, MA.

Kevin Roche, b 1922, Oakland Museum, Oakland, CA; Fine Arts Center, University of Massachusetts, Amherst, MA.

James Gamble Rogers, 1867-1947, Columbia-Presbyterian Medical Ctr., New York, NY; Northwestern Univ., Evanston, IL.

John Wellborn Root, 1887-1963, Palmolive Bldg., Chicago, IL; Hotel Statler, Washington, DC.

Paul Rudolph, 1918-97, Jewitt Art Center, Wellesley College, MA; Art & Architecture Bldg., Yale Univ., New Haven, CT.

Eero Saarinen, 1910-61, Gateway to the West Arch, St. Louis, MO; Trans World Airlines Flight Center, New York, NY.

Kazuyo Sejima, b 1956, 21st Century Museum of Contemporary Art, Kanazawa, Japan (with Ryue Nishizawa).

Louis Skidmore, 1897-1962, Atomic Energy Commission town site, Oak Ridge, TN; Terrace Plaza Hotel, Cincinnati, OH.

Norma Merrick Sklarek, 1928-2012, Terminal One at Los Angeles International Airport, CA.

Clarence S. Stein, 1882-1975, Temple Emanu-El, New York, NY.

Edward Durell Stone, 1902-78, interior of Radio City Music Hall, Museum of Modern Art, New York, NY.

Louis H. Sullivan, 1856-1924, Auditorium Bldg., Chicago, IL.

Kenzo Tange, 1913-2005, Hiroshima Peace Park, 1964 Tokyo Olympics twin stadiums, Japan.

Richard Upjohn, 1802-78, Trinity Church, New York, NY.

Max O. Urbahn, 1912-95, Vehicle Assembly Bldg., Cape Canaveral, FL.

Joern Utzon, 1918-2008, Sydney Opera House, Australia.

William Van Alen, 1883-1954, Chrysler Building, New York, NY.

Robert Venturi, b 1925, Gordon Wu Hall, Princeton, NJ; Mielparque Nikko Kirifuri Resort, Japan.

Ralph T. Walker, 1889-1973, NY Telephone Bldg., New York, NY; IBM Research Lab, Poughkeepsie, NY.

Roland A. Wank, 1898-1970, Cincinnati Union Terminal, OH; head architect (1933-44), Tennessee Valley Authority.

Stanford White, 1853-1906, Washington Arch in Washington Square Park, first Madison Square Garden, New York, NY.

Christopher Wren, 1632-1723, St. Paul's Cathedral, London, Eng., UK.

Frank Lloyd Wright, 1867-1959, Imperial Hotel, Tokyo, Jpn.; Guggenheim Museum, New York, NY; Kaufmann "Fallingwater" house, Bear Run, PA; Taliesin West, Scottsdale, AZ.

William Wurster, 1895-1973, Ghirardelli Sq., San Francisco, CA.

Minoru Yamasaki, 1912-86, World Trade Center (destroyed 2001), New York, NY.

Artists, Photographers, and Sculptors of the Past

Artists are painters unless otherwise indicated.

Berenice Abbott, 1898-1991, (U.S.) photographer. Documentary of New York City, *Changing New York* (1939).

Ansel Easton Adams, 1902-84, (U.S.) photographer. Landscapes of the American Southwest.

Washington Allston, 1779-1843, (U.S.) landscapist. *Belshazzar's Feast*.

Albrecht Altdorfer, 1480-1538, (Ger.) landscapist.

Fra Angelico, c. 1400-55, (It.) Renaissance muralist. *Madonna of the Linen Drapers' Guild*.

Diane Arbus, 1923-71, (U.S.) photographer. Disturbing images.

Alexsandr Archipenko, 1887-1964, (U.S.) sculptor. *Boxing Match, Medranos*.

Jean Arp, 1887-1966, (Fr.) sculptor and painter, founder of Dada movement.

Eugène Atget, 1856-1927, (Fr.) photographer. Paris life.

John James Audubon, 1785-1851, (U.S.) *Birds of America*.

Richard Avedon, 1923-2004, (U.S.) fashion and celebrity photographer.

Hans Baldung-Grien, 1484-1545, (Ger.) *Todentanz*.

Ernst Barlach, 1870-1938, (Ger.) Expressionist sculptor. *Man Drawing a Sword*.

Frédéric-Auguste Bartholdi, 1834-1904, (Fr.) *Liberty Enlightening the World* (Statue of Liberty), *Lion of Belfort*.

Fra Bartolommeo, 1472-1517, (It.) *Vision of St. Bernard*.

Romare Bearden, 1911-88, (U.S.) collage and other media. *The Visitation*.

Aubrey Beardsley, 1872-98, (Br.) illustrator. *Salome, Lysistrata, Morte d'Arthur, Volpone*.

Cecil Beaton, 1904-80, (Br.) fashion and celebrity photographer.

Max Beckmann, 1884-1950, (Ger.) Expressionist. *The Descent From the Cross*.

Gentile Bellini, 1426-1507, (It.) Renaissance. *Procession in St. Mark's Square*.

Giovanni Bellini, 1428-1516, (It.) Renaissance. *St. Francis in Ecstasy*.

Jacopo Bellini, 1400-70, (It.) Renaissance. *Crucifixion*.

George Wesley Bellows, 1882-1925, (U.S.) sports artist, portraitist, landscapist. *Stag at Sharkey's, Edith Clavell*.

Thomas Hart Benton, 1889-1975, (U.S.) American regionalist. *Threshing Wheat, Arts of the West*.

Ruth Bernhard, 1905-2006, (Ger.-U.S.) photographer. Black-and-white studies of female nudes.

Gianlorenzo Bernini, 1598-1680, (It.) Baroque sculptor. *The Assumption*.

Albert Bierstadt, 1830-1902, (U.S.) landscapist. *The Rocky Mountains, Mount Corcoran*.

George Caleb Bingham, 1811-79, (U.S.) American frontier. *Fur Traders Descending the Missouri*.

William Blake, 1757-1827, (Br.) engraver. *Book of Job*, *Songs of Innocence*, *Songs of Experience*.

Rosa Bonheur, 1822-99, (Fr.) realist. *The Horse Fair*.

Pierre Bonnard, 1867-1947, (Fr.) Intimist. *The Breakfast Room*, *Girl in a Straw Hat*.

Gutzon Borglum, 1867-1941, (U.S.) sculptor. Mt. Rushmore Memorial.

Hieronymus Bosch, 1450-1516, (Flem.) religious allegories. *The Crowning With Thorns*.

Sandro Botticelli, 1444-1510, (It.) Renaissance. *Birth of Venus*, *Adoration of the Magi*, *Guiliano de'Medici*.

Louise Bourgeois, 1911-2010, (Fr.) sculptor. *Maman*.

Margaret Bourke-White, 1904-71, (U.S.) photographer, photojournalist. WWII, USSR, rural South during the Depression.

Mathew Brady, c. 1823-96, (U.S.) official photographer of the Civil War.

Constantin Brancusi, 1876-1957, (Romania-Fr.) Nonobjective sculptor. *Flying Turtle*, *The Kiss*.

Georges Braque, 1882-1963, (Fr.) Cubist. *Violin and Palette*.

Pieter Bruegel the Elder, c. 1525-69, (Flem.) Renaissance. *The Peasant Dance*, *Hunters in the Snow*, *Magpie on the Gallows*.

Pieter Bruegel the Younger, 1564-1638, (Flem.) Baroque. *Village Fair*, *The Crucifixion*.

Edward Burne-Jones, 1833-98, (Br.) Pre-Raphaelite artist-craftsman. *The Mirror of Venus*.

Alexander Calder, 1898-1976, (U.S.) sculptor. *Lobster Trap and Fish Tail*.

Julia Margaret Cameron, 1815-79, (Br.) photographer, prominent portraitist.

Robert Capa (Endre Friedmann), 1913-54, (Hung.-U.S.) photographer, war photojournalist. Invasion of Normandy.

Michelangelo Merisi da Caravaggio, 1573-1610, (It.) Baroque. *The Supper at Emmaus*.

Emily Carr, 1871-1945, (Can.) landscapist. *Blunden Harbour*, *Big Raven*, *Rushing Sea of Undergrowth*.

Carlo Carrà, 1881-1966, (It.) Metaphysical school. *Lot's Daughters*, *The Enchanted Room*.

Henri Cartier-Bresson, 1908-2004, (Fr.) photographer. *Imagenes à la sauvette*.

Leonora Carrington, 1917-2011, (Br.) Surrealist. *The Inn of the Dawn Horse (Self-Portrait)*.

Mary Cassatt, 1844-1926, (U.S.) Impressionist. *The Cup of Tea*, *Woman Bathing*, *The Boating Party*.

George Catlin, 1796-1872, (U.S.) American Indian life. *Gallery of Indians*, *Buffalo Dance*.

Benvenuto Cellini, 1500-71, (It.) Mannerist sculptor, goldsmith. *Perseus and Medusa*.

Paul Cézanne, 1839-1906, (Fr.) Post-Impressionist. *Card Players*, *Mont-Sainte-Victoire With Large Pine Trees*.

Marc Chagall, 1887-1985, (Russ.) Jewish life and folklore. *I and the Village*, *The Praying Jew*.

John Chamberlain, 1927-2011, (U.S.) sculptor of automobile metal.

Jean Simeon Chardin, 1699-1779, (Fr.) still lifes. *The Kiss*, *The Grace*.

Giorgio de Chirico, 1888-1978, (It.) founded the Metaphysical school. *Enigma of an Autumn Night*.

Frederick Church, 1826-1900, (U.S.) Hudson River school. *Niagara*, *Andes of Ecuador*.

Giovanni Cimabue, 1240-1302, (It.) Byzantine mosaicist. *Madonna Enthroned With St. Francis*.

Claude (Lorrain) (Claude Gellée), 1600-82, (Fr.) Ideal-landscapist. *The Enchanted Castle*.

Thomas Cole, 1801-48, (U.S.) Hudson River school. *The Ox-Bow*, *In the Catskills*.

John Constable, 1776-1837, (Br.) landscapist. *Salisbury Cathedral From the Bishop's Grounds*.

John Singleton Copley, 1738-1815, (U.S.) portraitist. *Samuel Adams*, *Watson and the Shark*.

Lovis Corinth, 1858-1925, (Ger.) Expressionist. *Apocalypse*.

Jean-Baptiste-Camille Corot, 1796-1875, (Fr.) landscapist. *Souvenir de Mortefontaine*, *Pastorale*.

Correggio, 1494-1534, (It.) Renaissance muralist. *Mystic Marriages of St. Catherine*.

Gustave Courbet, 1819-77, (Fr.) Realist. *The Artist's Studio*.

Lucas Cranach the Elder, 1472-1553, (Ger.) Protestant Reformation portraitist. *Luther*.

Imogen Cunningham, 1883-1976, (U.S.) photographer, portraitist. Plant photography.

Nathaniel Currier, 1813-88, and **James M. Ives**, 1824-95, (both U.S.) lithographers. *A Midnight Race on the Mississippi*, *American Forest Scene—Maple Sugaring*.

John Steuart Curry, 1897-1946, (U.S.) Americana, murals. *Baptism in Kansas*.

Edward S. Curtis, 1868-1952, (U.S.) photographer. *The Native American Indian*.

Salvador Dalí, 1904-89, (Sp.) Surrealist. *Persistence of Memory*, *The Crucifixion*.

Honoré Daumier, 1808-79, (Fr.) caricaturist. *The Third-Class Carriage*.

Jacques-Louis David, 1748-1825, (Fr.) Neoclassicist. *The Oath of the Horatii*.

Arthur Davies, 1862-1928, (U.S.) Romantic landscapist. *Unicorns*, *Leda and the Dioscuri*.

Edgar Degas, 1834-1917, (Fr.) realist/Impressionist. *The Ballet Class*.

Willem de Kooning, 1904-97, (Neth.-U.S.) Abstract Expressionist. *Excavation*, *Woman I*, *Door to the River*.

Eugène Delacroix, 1798-1863, (Fr.) Romantic. *Massacre at Chios*, *Liberty Leading the People*.

Paul Delaroche, 1797-1856, (Fr.) historical themes. *Children of Edward IV*.

Luca Della Robbia, 1400-82, (It.) Renaissance terracotta. *Cantoria* (singing gallery), Florence cathedral.

Donatello, 1386-1466, (It.) Renaissance sculptor. *David*, *Gattamelata*.

Aaron Douglas, 1899-79, (U.S.) Harlem Renaissance illustrator and muralist.

Jean Dubuffet, 1902-85, (Fr.) painter, sculptor, printmaker. *Group of Four Trees*.

Marcel Duchamp, 1887-1968, (Fr.) Dadaist. *Nude Descending a Staircase, No. 2*.

Raoul Dufy, 1877-1953, (Fr.) Fauvist. *Chateau and Horses*.

Asher Brown Durand, 1796-1886, (U.S.) Hudson River school. *Kindred Spirits*.

Albrecht Dürer, 1471-1528, (Ger.) Renaissance painter, engraver, woodcuts. *St. Jerome in His Study*, *Melencolia I*.

Anthony van Dyck, 1599-1641, (Flem.) Baroque portraitist. *Portrait of Charles I Hunting*.

Thomas Eakins, 1844-1916, (U.S.) Realist. *The Gross Clinic*.

Alfred Eisenstaedt, 1898-1995, (Ger.-U.S.) photographer, photojournalist. Famous photo, V-J Day, Aug. 14, 1945.

Peter Henry Emerson, 1856-1936, (Br.) photographer. Promoted photography as an independent art form.

Jacob Epstein, 1880-1959, (Br.) religious and allegorical sculptor. *Genesis*, *Ecce Homo*.

Erté (Romain de Tiertoff), 1892-1990, (Fr.) painter, fashion and stage designer.

Walker Evans, 1903-75, (U.S.) photographer. Documented Great Depression.

Jan van Eyck, c. 1390-1441, (Flem.) naturalistic panels. *Adoration of the Lamb*.

Horst Faas, 1933-2012, (Ger.) Vietnam War photographer.

Roger Fenton, 1819-69, (Br.) photographer. Crimean War.

Anselm Feuerbach, 1829-80, (Ger.) Romantic Classicist. *Judgment of Paris*, *Iphigenia*.

John Bernard Flannagan, 1895-1942, (U.S.) animal sculptor. *Triumph of the Egg*.

Jean-Honoré Fragonard, 1732-1806, (Fr.) Rococo. *The Swing*.

Helen Frankenthaler, 1928-2011, (U.S.) abstract expressionist. *Mountains and Sea*.

Daniel Chester French, 1850-1931, (U.S.) sculptor. *The Minute Man of Concord*;

seated *Lincoln*, Lincoln Memorial, Washington, DC.

Lucian Freud, 1922-2011, (Ger.-Br.) portraitist. *Girl With Roses*.

Caspar David Friedrich, 1774-1840, (Ger.) Romantic landscapist. *Man and Woman Gazing at the Moon*.

Thomas Gainsborough, 1727-88, (Br.) portraitist. *The Blue Boy*, *The Watering Place*, *Orpin the Parish Clerk*.

Alexander Gardner, 1821-82, (U.S.) photographer. Civil War, railroad construction, Great Plains Indians.

Paul Gauguin, 1848-1903, (Fr.) Post-Impressionist. *The Tahitians*, *Spirit of the Dead Watching*.

Lorenzo Ghiberti, 1378-1455, (It.) Renaissance sculptor. "Gates of Paradise" baptistery doors, Florence, It.

Alberto Giacometti, 1901-66, (Switz.) attenuated sculptures of solitary figures. *Man Pointing*.

Giorgione, c. 1477-1510, (It.) Renaissance. *The Tempest*.

Giotto di Bondone, 1267-1337, (It.) Renaissance. *Presentation of Christ in the Temple*.

François Girardon, 1628-1715, (Fr.) Baroque sculptor of classical themes. *Apollo Tended by the Nymphs*.

Vincent van Gogh, 1853-90, (Neth.) *The Starry Night*, *L'Arlesienne*, *Bedroom at Arles*, *Self-Portrait*.

Edward Gorey, 1925-2000, (U.S.) illustrator. *The Doubtful Guest*.

Arshile Gorky, 1905-48, (U.S.) Surrealist. *The Liver Is the Cock's Comb*.

Francisco de Goya y Lucientes, 1746-1828, (Sp.) painter, printmaker. *The Naked Maja*, *The Disasters of War* (etchings).

El Greco (Domenikos Theotokopoulos), 1541-1614, (Gr.-Sp.) painter, sculptor. *View of Toledo*, *Assumption of the Virgin*.

Horatio Greenough, 1805-52, (U.S.) Neo-Classical sculptor.

Matthias Grünewald, 1480-1528, (Ger.) mystical religious themes. *The Resurrection*.

Frans Hals, c. 1580-1666, (Neth.) portraitist. *Laughing Cavalier*, *Gypsy Girl*.

Richard Hamilton, 1922-2011, (Br.) Pop artist. *Just What Is It That Makes Today's Homes So Different, So Appealing?*

Austin Hansen, 1910-96, (U.S.) photographer. Harlem, NY, life.

Childe Hassam, 1859-1935, (U.S.) Impressionist. *Southwest Wind*, *July 14 Rue Daunon*.

Edward Hicks, 1780-1849, (U.S.) folk. *The Peaceable Kingdom*.

Lewis Wickes Hine, 1874-1940, (U.S.) photographer. Studies of immigrants, children in industry.

Hans Hofmann, 1880-1966, (U.S.) early Abstract Expressionist. *Spring*, *The Gate*.

William Hogarth, 1697-1764, (Br.) caricaturist. *The Rake's Progress*.

Katsushika Hokusai, 1760-1849, (Jpn.) printmaker. *Crabs*.

Hans Holbein the Elder, 1460-1524, (Ger.) late Gothic. *Presentation of Christ in the Temple*.

Hans Holbein the Younger, 1497-1543, (Ger.) portraitist. *Henry VIII*, *The French Ambassadors*.

Winslow Homer, 1836-1910, (U.S.) naturalist, marine themes. *Marine Coast*, *High Cliff*.

Edward Hopper, 1882-1967, (U.S.) realistic urban scenes. *Nighthawks*, *House by the Railroad*.

Horst P. Horst, 1906-99, (Ger.) fashion, celebrity photographer.

Jean-Auguste-Dominique Ingres, 1780-1867, (Fr.) Classicist. *Valpincon Bather*.

George Inness, 1825-94, (U.S.) luminous landscapist. *Delaware Water Gap*.

William Henry Jackson, 1843-1942, (U.S.) photographer. American West, building of Union Pacific Railroad.

Jeanne-Claude (Javacheff), 1935-2009, (Moroc.), created large-scale, temporary installations in public places with her husband, Christo.

Donald Judd, 1928-94, (U.S.) sculptor, major Minimalist.

Frida Kahlo, 1907-54, (Mex.) folkloric stylist. *Self-Portrait With Monkey.*

Wassily Kandinsky, 1866-1944, (Russ.) Abstractionist. *Capricious Forms, Improvisation 28 (second version).*

Paul Klee, 1879-1940, (Switz.) Abstractionist. *Twittering Machine, Pastoral, Death and Fire.*

Gustav Klimt, 1862-1918, (Austria) cofounder of Vienna Secession Movement. *The Kiss.*

Oscar Kokoschka, 1886-1980, (Austria) Expressionist. *View of Prague, Harbor of Marseilles.*

Kathe Kollwitz, 1867-1945, (Ger.) printmaker, social justice themes. *The Peasant War.*

Gaston Lachaise, 1882-1935, (U.S.) figurative sculptor. *Standing Woman.*

John La Farge, 1835-1910, (U.S.) muralist. *Red and White Peonies, The Ascension.*

Sir Edwin (Henry) Landseer, 1802-73, (Br.) painter, sculptor. *Shoeing, Rout of Comus.*

Dorothea Lange, 1895-1965, (U.S.) photographer. Great Depression, migrant farm workers.

Fernand Léger, 1881-1955, (Fr.) Machine art. *The Cyclists.*

Leonardo da Vinci, 1452-1519, (It.) Renaissance. *Mona Lisa, Last Supper, The Annunciation.*

Emanuel Leutze, 1816-68, (U.S.) historical themes. *Washington Crossing the Delaware.*

Roy Lichtenstein, 1923-97, (U.S.) Pop Art.

Jacques Lipchitz, 1891-1973, (Fr.) Cubist sculptor. *Harpist.*

Filippino Lippi, 1457-1504, (It.) Renaissance. *Adoration of the Magi.*

Fra Filippo Lippi, 1406-69, (It.) Renaissance. *Coronation of the Virgin, Madonna and Child With Angels.*

Morris Louis, 1912-62, (U.S.) Abstract Expressionist. *Signa, Stripes, Alpha-Phi.*

René Magritte, 1898-1967, (Belg.) Surrealist. *The Descent of Man, The Betrayal of Images.*

Aristide Maillol, 1861-1944, (Fr.) sculptor. *L'Harmonie.*

Édouard Manet, 1832-83, (Fr.) forerunner of Impressionism. *Luncheon on the Grass, Olympia.*

Andrea Mantegna, 1431-1506, (It.) Renaissance frescoes. *Triumph of Caesar.*

Robert Mapplethorpe, 1946-89, (U.S.) photographer.

Franz Marc, 1880-1916, (Ger.) Expressionist. *Blue Horses.*

John Marin, 1870-1953, (U.S.) Expressionist seascapes. *Maine Island.*

Reginald Marsh, 1898-1954, (U.S.) satire. *Tattoo and Haircut.*

Agnes Martin, 1912-2004, (U.S.) abstract artist. *Night Sea.*

Masaccio, 1401-28, (It.) Renaissance. *The Tribute Money.*

Henri Matisse, 1869-1954, (Fr.) Fauvist. *Woman With the Hat.*

John McCracken, 1934-2011, (U.S.) minimalist sculptor.

Michelangelo Buonarroti, 1475-1564, (It.) Renaissance. *Pietà, David, Moses, The Last Judgment*, Sistine Chapel ceiling.

Jean-Francois Millet, 1814-75, (Fr.) peasants. *The Gleaners, The Man With a Hoe.*

Joan Miró, 1893-1983, (Sp.) exuberant colors, playful images. *Catalan landscape, Dutch Interior.*

Amedeo Modigliani, 1884-1920, (It.) figurative works. *Reclining Nude.*

Piet Mondrian, 1872-1944, (Neth.) Abstractionist. *Composition With Red, Yellow and Blue.*

Claude Monet, 1840-1926, (Fr.) Impressionist. *The Bridge at Argenteuil, Haystacks, Bridge Over a Pond of Water Lillies.*

Henry Moore, 1898-1986, (Br.) sculptor of large-scale, abstract works. *Reclining Figure* (several).

Gustave Moreau, 1826-98, (Fr.) Symbolist. *The Apparition, Dance of Salome.*

James Wilson Morrice, 1865-1924, (Can.) landscapist. *The Ferry, Quebec, Venice, Looking Over the Lagoon.*

William Morris, 1834-96, (Br.) decorative artist, leader of Arts and Crafts movement.

Grandma Moses (Anna Mary Robertson Moses), 1860-1961, (U.S.) folk. *Out for the Christmas Tree, Catching the Thanksgiving Turkey.*

Edvard Munch, 1863-1944, (Nor.) Expressionist. *The Cry.*

Bartolome Murillo, 1618-82, (Sp.) Baroque religious artist. *Vision of St. Anthony, The Two Trinities.*

Elizabeth Murray, 1940-2007, (U.S.) abstract colors. *Kitchen Party.*

Eadweard Muybridge, 1830-1904, (Br.-U.S.) photographer. Studies of motion, *Animal Locomotion.*

Nadar (Gaspar-Félix Tournachon), 1820-1910, (Fr.) photographer, caricaturist, portraitist. Invented photo-essay.

LeRoy Neiman, 1921-2012, (U.S.) sports expressionist painter.

Arnold Newman, 1918-2006, (U.S.) portrait photographer.

Barnett Newman, 1905-70, (U.S.) Abstract Expressionist. *Stations of the Cross.*

Isamu Noguchi, 1904-88, (U.S.) abstract sculptor, designer. *Kouros, BirdC(MU)*, sculptural gardens.

Kenneth Noland, 1924-2010, (U.S.) American color field painter, abstract.

Georgia O'Keeffe, 1887-1986, (U.S.) Southwest motifs. *Cow's Skull: Red, White, and Blue; The Shelton With Sunspots.*

José Clemente Orozco, 1883-1949, (Mex.) frescoes. *House of Tears, Pre-Columbian Golden Age.*

Timothy H. O'Sullivan, 1840-82, (U.S.) Civil War photographer.

Gordon Parks, 1912-2006, (U.S.) African American photographer, filmmaker. *Life* photographer, 1948-68.

Charles Willson Peale, 1741-1827, (U.S.) Amer. Revolutionary portraitist. *The Staircase Group*, U.S. presidents.

Rembrandt Peale, 1778-1860, (U.S.) portraitist. *Thomas Jefferson.*

Irving Penn, 1917-2009, (U.S.) portraitist, fashion photographer.

Pietro Perugino, 1446-1523, (It.) Renaissance. *Delivery of the Keys to St. Peter.*

Pablo Picasso, 1881-1973, (Sp.) painter, sculptor. *Guernica; Dove; Head of a Woman; Head of a Bull, Metamorphosis.*

Piero della Francesca, c. 1415-92, (It.) Renaissance. *Duke of Urbino, Flagellation of Christ.*

Camille Pissarro, 1830-1903, (Fr.) Impressionist. *Boulevard des Italiens, Morning, Sunlight; Bather in the Woods.*

Jackson Pollock, 1912-56, (U.S.) Abstract Expressionist. *Autumn Rhythm.*

Nicolas Poussin, 1594-1665, (Fr.) Baroque pictorial classicism. *St. John on Patmos.*

Maurice B. Prendergast, c. 1860-1924, (U.S.) Postimpressionist watercolorist. *Umbrellas in the Rain.*

Pierre-Paul Prud'hon, 1758-1823, (Fr.) Romanticist. *Crime Pursued by Vengeance and Justice.*

Pierre Cecile Puvis de Chavannes, 1824-98, (Fr.) muralist. *The Poor Fisherman.*

Raphael Sanzio, 1483-1520, (It.) Renaissance. *Disputa, School of Athens, Sistine Madonna.*

Robert Rauschenberg, 1925-2008, (U.S.) printmaker. *Combine, Bed, Revolvers, Outpost.*

Man Ray (Emmanuel Radnitsky), 1890-1976, (U.S.) Dadaist and Surrealist. *Observing Time, The Lovers, Marquis de Sade.*

Odilon Redon, 1840-1916, (Fr.) Symbolist painter, lithographer. *In the Dream, Vase of Flowers.*

Rembrandt van Rijn, 1606-69, (Neth.) painter, printmaker. *The Bridal Couple, The Night Watch.*

Frederic Remington, 1861-1909, (U.S.) painter, sculptor. Portrayer of the American West, *Bronco Buster.*

Pierre-Auguste Renoir, 1841-1919, (Fr.) Impressionist. *The Luncheon of the Boating Party, Dance in the Country.*

Joshua Reynolds, 1723-92, (Br.) portraitist. *Mrs. Siddons as the Tragic Muse.*

Herb Ritts, 1952-2002, (U.S.) photographer. Nudes, celebrities.

Diego Rivera, 1886-1957, (Mex.) frescoes. *The Fecund Earth.*

Larry Rivers, 1923-2002, (U.S.) painter, sculptor, often realistic. Dutch Masters series.

Henry Peach Robinson, 1830-1901, (Br.) photographer. A leader of "high art" photography.

Norman Rockwell, 1894-1978, (U.S.) painter, illustrator. *Saturday Evening Post* covers.

Auguste Rodin, 1840-1917, (Fr.) sculptor. *The Thinker.*

Milton Rogovin, 1909-2011, (U.S.) documentary photographer.

Willy Ronis, 1910-2009, (Fr.) photographer. Post-war Paris.

Joe Rosenthal, 1911-2006, (U.S.) photojournalist; photographed six marines raising the U.S. flag over Iwo Jima in WWII.

Mark Rothko, 1903-70, (U.S.) Abstract Expressionist. *Light, Earth and Blue.*

Georges Rouault, 1871-1958, (Fr.) Expressionist. *Three Judges.*

Henri Rousseau, 1844-1910, (Fr.) primitive exotic themes. *The Snake Charmer.*

Theodore Rousseau, 1812-67, (Switz.-Fr.) landscapist. *Under the Birches, Evening.*

Peter Paul Rubens, 1577-1640, (Flem.) Baroque. *Mystic Marriage of St. Catherine.*

Jacob van Ruisdael, c. 1628-82, (Neth.) landscapist. *Jewish Cemetery.*

Charles M. Russell, 1866-1926, (U.S.) Western life.

Salomon van Ruysdael, c. 1600-70, (Dutch) landscapist. *River With Ferry-Boat.*

Albert Pinkham Ryder, 1847-1917, (U.S.) seascapes, allegories. *Toilers of the Sea.*

Augustus Saint-Gaudens, 1848-1907, (U.S.) memorial statues. *Farragut, Mrs. Henry Adams (Grief).*

Niki de Saint Phalle, 1930-2002, (Fr.) paintings, sculptures, prints, large public installations.

Andrea Sansovino, 1460-1529, (It.) Renaissance sculptor. *Baptism of Christ.*

Jacopo Sansovino, 1486-1570, (It.) Renaissance sculptor. *St. John the Baptist.*

John Singer Sargent, 1856-1925, (U.S.) Edwardian society portraitist. *The Wyndham Sisters, Madam X.*

Andrea del Sarto, 1486-1530, (It.) frescoes. *Madonna of the Harpies.*

George Segal, 1924-2000, (U.S.) sculptor. Life-sized figures realistically depicting daily life.

Georges Seurat, 1859-91, (Fr.) Pointillist. *Sunday Afternoon on the Island of La Grande Jatte.*

Gino Severini, 1883-1966, (It.) Futurist and Cubist. *Dynamic Hieroglyph of the Bal Tabarin.*

Ben Shahn, 1898-1969, (U.S.) social and political themes. Sacco and Vanzetti series, *Seurat's Lunch, Handball.*

Charles Sheeler, 1883-1965, (U.S.) abstractionist.

David Alfaro Siqueiros, 1896-1974, (Mex.) political muralist. *March of Humanity.*

David Smith, 1906-65, (U.S.) welded metal sculpture. *Hudson River Landscape, Zig, Cubi* series.

Edward Steichen, 1879-1973, (U.S.) photographer. Credited with transforming photography into an art form.

Alfred Stieglitz, 1864-1946, (U.S.) photographer, editor. Helped create acceptance of photography as art.

Paul Strand, 1890-1976, (U.S.) photographer. People, nature, landscapes.

Gilbert Stuart, 1755-1828, (U.S.) portraitist. George Washington, Thomas Jefferson, James Madison.

Thomas Sully, 1783-1872, (U.S.) portraitist. *Col. Thomas Handasyd Perkins, The Passage of the Delaware.*

William Henry Fox Talbot, 1800-77, (Br.) photographer. *Pencil of Nature*, early photographically illustrated book.

George Tames, 1919-94, (U.S.) photographer. Presidents, political leaders.

Yves Tanguy, 1900-55, (Fr.) Surrealist. *Rose of the Four Winds; Mama, Papa Is Wounded!*

Giovanni Battista Tiepolo, 1696-1770, (It.) Rococo frescoes. *The Crucifixion.*

Jacopo Tintoretto, 1518-94, (It.) Mannerist. *The Last Supper*.

Titian (Tiziano Vecellio), c. 1488-1576, (It.) Renaissance. *Venus and the Lute Player*, *The Bacchanal*.

Jose Rey Toledo, 1916-94, (U.S.) Native American life. Tribal dances.

George Tooker, 1920-2011, (U.S.) Magic realist. *Subway*.

Henri de Toulouse-Lautrec, 1864-1901, (Fr.) Postimpressionist. *At the Moulin Rouge*.

John Trumbull, 1756-1843, (U.S.) historical themes. *The Declaration of Independence*.

J(oseph) M(allord) W(illiam) Turner, 1775-1851, (Br.) Romantic landscapist. *Snow Storm*.

Cy Twombly, 1928-2011, (U.S.) painter and sculptor. *Leda and the Swan*.

Paolo Uccello, 1397-1475, (It.) Gothic-Renaissance. *The Rout of San Romano*.

Maurice Utrillo, 1883-1955, (Fr.) Impressionist. *Sacre-Coeur de Montmartre*.

John Vanderlyn, 1775-1852, (U.S.) Neo-classicist. *Ariadne Asleep on the Island of Naxos*.

Diego Velázquez, 1599-1660, (Sp.) Baroque. *Las Meninas*, *Portrait of Juan de Pareja*.

Jan Vermeer, 1632-75, (Neth.) interior genre subjects. *Young Woman With a Water Jug*.

Paolo Veronese, 1528-88, (It.) devotional themes, vastly peopled canvases. *The Temptation of St. Anthony*.

Andrea del Verrocchio, 1435-88, (It.) sculptor. *Colleoni*.

Maurice de Vlaminck, 1876-1958, (Fr.) Fauvist landscapist. *Red Trees*.

Andy Warhol, 1928-87, (U.S.) Pop Art. *Campbell's Soup Cans*, *Marilyn Diptych*.

Antoine Watteau, 1684-1721, (Fr.) Rococo "scenes of gallantry." *The Embarkation for Cythera*.

George Frederic Watts, 1817-1904, (Br.) painter and sculptor. Grandiose allegorical themes. *Hope*.

Benjamin West, 1738-1820, (U.S.) realistic historical themes. *Death of General Wolfe*.

Edward Weston, 1886-1958, (U.S.) photographer. Landscapes of American West.

James Abbott McNeill Whistler, 1834-1903, (U.S.) *Arrangement in Grey and Black, No. 1: The Artist's Mother*.

Archibald M. Willard, 1836-1918, (U.S.) murals. *The Spirit of '76*.

Grant Wood, 1891-1942, (U.S.) Midwestern regionalist. *American Gothic*, *Daughters of Revolution*.

Andrew Wyeth, 1917-2009, (U.S.) regionalist. *Christina's World*.

Ossip Zadkine, 1890-1967, (Russ.) School of Paris sculptor. *The Destroyed City*, *Musicians*, *Christ*.

Business Leaders and Philanthropists of the Past

Giovanni Agnelli, 1921-2003, (It.) industrialist; principal shareholder of Fiat.

Walter Annenberg, 1908-2002, (U.S.) publisher, founder of *TV Guide*, philanthropist.

Elizabeth Arden (F. N. Graham), 1884-1966, (U.S.) Canadian-born founder of cosmetics empire.

Philip D. Armour, 1832-1901, (U.S.) industrialist; streamlined meatpacking.

Brooke Astor, 1902-2007, (U.S.) philanthropist; president of Vincent Astor Foundation.

John Jacob Astor, 1763-1848, (U.S.) German-born fur trader, banker, real estate magnate; at death, richest in U.S.

Francis W. Ayer, 1848-1923, (U.S.) ad industry pioneer.

August Belmont, 1816-90, (U.S.) German-born financier.

James B. (Diamond Jim) Brady, 1856-1917, (U.S.) financier, philanthropist, legendary bon vivant.

Adolphus Busch, 1839-1913, (U.S.) German-born businessman; established brewery empire.

Asa Candler, 1851-1929, (U.S.) founded Coca-Cola Co.

Andrew Carnegie, 1835-1919, (U.S.) Scottish-born industrialist, philanthropist; founded Carnegie Steel Co.

Tom Carvel, 1908-89, (Gr.-U.S.) founded ice cream chain.

William Colgate, 1783-1857, (Br.-U.S.) businessman, philanthropist; founded soap-making empire.

Jay Cooke, 1821-1905, (U.S.) financier; sold $1 billion in Union bonds during Civil War.

Peter Cooper, 1791-1883, (U.S.) industrialist, inventor, philanthropist; founded Cooper Union (1859).

Ezra Cornell, 1807-74, (U.S.) businessman, philanthropist; headed Western Union, established university.

Erastus Corning, 1794-1872, (U.S.) financier; headed New York Central Railroad.

Charles Crocker, 1822-88, (U.S.) railroad builder, financier.

Samuel Cunard, 1787-1865, (Can.) pioneered transatlantic steam navigation.

Marcus Daly, 1841-1900, (U.S.) Irish-born copper magnate.

W. Edwards Deming, 1900-93, (U.S.) quality-control expert who revolutionized Japanese manufacturing.

Walt Disney, 1901-66, (U.S.) pioneer in cinema animation; built entertainment empire.

Herbert H. Dow, 1866-1930, (U.S.) founder of chemical co.

Anthony Drexel, 1826-93, (U.S.) banker, philanthropist, university founder.

James Duke, 1856-1925, (U.S.) founded American Tobacco, Duke Univ.

Eleuthere I. du Pont, 1771-1834, (Fr.-U.S.) gunpowder manufacturer; founded one of the largest business empires.

Thomas C. Durant, 1820-85, (U.S.) railroad official, financier.

William C. Durant, 1861-1947, (U.S.) industrialist; formed General Motors.

George Eastman, 1854-1932, (U.S.) inventor; manufacturer of photographic equipment.

Marshall Field, 1834-1906, (U.S.) merchant; founded Chicago's largest department store.

Harvey Firestone, 1868-1938, (U.S.) founded tire company.

Avery Fisher, 1906-94, (U.S.) industrialist, philanthropist; founded Fisher electronics.

Henry M. Flagler, 1830-1913, (U.S.) financier; helped form Standard Oil, developed FL as resort state.

Malcolm Forbes, 1919-90, (U.S.) magazine publisher.

Henry Ford, 1863-1947, (U.S.) automaker; developed first popular low-priced car.

Henry Ford II, 1917-87, (U.S.) headed auto company founded by grandfather.

Henry C. Frick, 1849-1919, (U.S.) steel and coke magnate; had prominent role in development of U.S. Steel.

Jakob Fugger (Jakob the Rich), 1459-1525, (Ger.) headed leading banking, trading house, in 16th-cent. Europe.

Alfred C. Fuller, 1885-1973, (U.S.) Canadian-born businessman; founded brush company.

Elbert H. Gary, 1846-1927, (U.S.) one of the organizers of U.S. Steel; chaired board of directors, 1903-27.

Jean Paul Getty, 1892-1976, (U.S.) founded oil empire.

Amadeo Giannini, 1870-1949, (U.S.) founded Bank of America.

Stephen Girard, 1750-1831, (U.S.) French-born financier, philanthropist; richest man in U.S. at time of death.

Leonard H. Goldenson, 1905-99, (U.S.) turned ABC into major TV network.

Jay Gould, 1836-92, (U.S.) railroad magnate, financier.

Hetty Green, 1834-1916, (U.S.) financier, the "witch of Wall St."; richest woman in U.S. in her day.

William Gregg, 1800-67, (U.S.) launched textile industry in the South.

Meyer Guggenheim, 1828-1905, (U.S.) Swiss-born merchant, philanthropist; built merchandising, mining empires.

Armand Hammer, 1898-1990, (U.S.) headed Occidental Petroleum, promoted U.S.-Soviet ties.

Elliot Handler, 1916-2011, (U.S.) cofounder of Mattel; introduced the Barbie doll.

Edward H. Harriman, 1848-1909, (U.S.) railroad financier, administrator; headed Union Pacific.

Henry J. Heinz, 1844-1919, (U.S.) founded food empire.

Leona Helmsley, 1920-2007, (U.S.) real estate magnate, philanthropist.

Milton Snavely Hershey, 1857-1945, (U.S.) chocolate co. founder, philanthropist.

James J. Hill, 1838-1916, (U.S.) Canadian-born railroad magnate, financier; founded Great Northern Railway.

Conrad N. Hilton, 1888-1979, (U.S.) hotel chain founder.

Howard Hughes, 1905-76, (U.S.) industrialist, aviator, filmmaker.

H. L. Hunt, 1889-1974, (U.S.) oil magnate.

Collis P. Huntington, 1821-1900, (U.S.) railroad magnate.

Henry E. Huntington, 1850-1927, (U.S.) railroad builder, philanthropist.

Walter L. Jacobs, 1898-1985, (U.S.) founder of the first rental car agency, which later became Hertz.

Steve Jobs, (1955-2011), (U.S.) Apple cofounder and exec; Pixar exec.

Howard Johnson, 1896-1972, (U.S.) founded restaurants.

John H. Johnson, 1918-2005, (U.S.) built publishing empire based on *Ebony* and *Jet*.

Samuel Curtis Johnson, 1928-2004, (U.S.) headed S.C. Johnson & Sons.

Henry J. Kaiser, 1882-1967, (U.S.) industrialist; built empire in steel, aluminum.

Minor C. Keith, 1848-1929, (U.S.) railroad magnate; founded United Fruit Co.

Will K. Kellogg, 1860-1951, (U.S.) businessman, philanthropist; founded breakfast food co.

Richard King, 1825-85, (U.S.) cattleman; founded half-million-acre King Ranch in Texas.

John W. Kluge, 1914-2010, (Ger.-U.S.) Metromedia chair; philanthropist.

William S. Knudsen, 1879-1948, (U.S.) Danish-born auto industry executive.

Samuel H. Kress, 1863-1955, (U.S.) businessman, art collector, philanthropist; founded "dime store" chain.

Ray A. Kroc, 1902-84, (U.S.) original CEO of McDonald's Corp.; oversaw company's vast expansion.

Alfred Krupp, 1812-87, (Ger.) armaments magnate.

Estée Lauder, 1908-2004, (U.S.) cofounder of Estée Lauder companies.

Kenneth L. Lay, 1942-2006, (U.S.), former CEO of Enron; indicted on fraud charges.

William Levitt, 1907-94, (U.S.) industrialist; "suburb maker."

Thomas Lipton, 1850-1931, (Scot.) merchant; tea empire.

James McGill, 1744-1813, (Scot.-Can.) founded university.

Andrew W. Mellon, 1855-1937, (U.S.) financier, industrialist; benefactor of National Gallery of Art.

Charles E. Merrill, 1885-1956, (U.S.) financier; developed firm of Merrill Lynch.

John Pierpont Morgan, 1837-1913, (U.S.) most powerful figure in finance and industry at turn of the century.

Akio Morita, 1921-99, (Jpn.) cofounded Sony Corp.

Malcolm Muir, 1885-1979, (U.S.) created *Business Week* magazine; headed *Newsweek*, 1937-61.

Roy Neuberger, 1903-2010, (U.S.) financier and art patron.

Samuel Newhouse, 1895-1979, (U.S.) publishing and broadcasting magnate; built communications empire.

Aristotle Onassis, 1906-75, (Gr.) shipping magnate.

William S. Paley, 1901-90, (U.S.) built CBS communications empire.

Frederick D. Patterson, 1901-88, (U.S.) founder of United Negro College Fund, 1944.

George Peabody, 1795-1869, (U.S.) merchant, financier, philanthropist.

James C. Penney, 1875-1971, (U.S.) businessman; developed department store chain.

Frank Perdue, 1920-2005, (U.S.) founder of Perdue Farms, chicken-processing company.

William C. Procter, 1862-1934, (U.S.) headed soap co.

John D. Rockefeller, 1839-1937, (U.S.) industrialist; established Standard Oil.

John D. Rockefeller Jr., 1874-1960, (U.S.) philanthropist; established foundation, provided land for UN.

Laurance S. Rockefeller, 1910-2004, (U.S.) philanthropist, conservationist.

Meyer A. Rothschild, 1743-1812, (Ger.) founded international banking house.

Thomas Fortune Ryan, 1851-1928, (U.S.) financier; a founder of American Tobacco.

Edmond J. Safra, 1932-99, (U.S.) banker.

David Sarnoff, 1891-1971, (U.S.) broadcasting pioneer; established first radio network, NBC.

Richard Sears, 1863-1914, (U.S.) founded mail-order co.

Werner von Siemens, 1816-92, (Ger.) industrialist, inventor.

Alfred P. Sloan, 1875-1966, (U.S.) industrialist, philanthropist; headed General Motors.

A. Leland Stanford, 1824-93, (U.S.) railroad official, philanthropist; founded university.

Frank Stanton, 1908-2006, (U.S.) president of CBS network, 1946-71.

Larry Stewart, 1948-2007, (U.S.) "Kansas City's Secret Santa."

Nathan Straus, 1848-1931, (U.S.) German-born merchant, philanthropist; headed Macy's.

Levi Strauss, c. 1829-1902, (U.S.) pants manufacturer.

Clement Studebaker, 1831-1901, (U.S.) wagon, carriage maker.

Gustavus Swift, 1839-1903, (U.S.) pioneer meatpacker.

Gerard Swope, 1872-1957, (U.S.) industrialist, economist; headed General Electric.

Dave Thomas, 1932-2002, (U.S.) Wendy's founder.

James Walter Thompson, 1847-1928, (U.S.) ad executive.

Alice Tully, 1902-93, (U.S.) philanthropist, arts patron.

Theodore N. Vail, 1845-1920, (U.S.) organized Bell Telephone system, headed AT&T.

Cornelius Vanderbilt, 1794-1877, (U.S.) financier; established steamship, railroad empires.

Henry Villard, 1835-1900, (U.S.) German-born railroad executive, financier.

Charles R. Walgreen, 1873-1939, (U.S.) founded drugstore chain.

Madame C. J. Walker, 1867-1919, (U.S.) African-American hair care entrepreneur and philanthropist.

DeWitt Wallace, 1889-1981, (U.S.) and **Lila Wallace**, 1889-1984, (U.S.) cofounders of *Reader's Digest* magazine.

Sam Walton, 1918-92, (U.S.) founder of Wal-Mart stores.

John Wanamaker, 1838-1922, (U.S.) department-store merchandising pioneer.

Aaron Montgomery Ward, 1843-1913, (U.S.) established first mail-order firm.

Thomas J. Watson, 1874-1956, (U.S.) IBM head, 1914-56.

George Westinghouse, 1846-1914, (U.S.) inventor, manufacturer; organized Westinghouse Electric Co., 1886.

John Hay Whitney, 1905-82, (U.S.) publisher, sportsman, philanthropist.

Charles E. Wilson, 1890-1961, (U.S.) auto exec.; public official.

Frank W. Woolworth, 1852-1919, (U.S.) created five and dime chain.

William Wrigley Jr., 1861-1932, (U.S.) founded Wrigley chewing gum company.

American Cartoonists

Reviewed by Lucy Shelton Caswell, Professor and Curator, Cartoon Research Library, Ohio State University.

Scott Adams, b 1957, Dilbert.

Charles Addams, 1912-88, macabre cartoons.

Brad Anderson, b 1924, Marmaduke.

Sergio Aragones, b 1937, *MAD* magazine.

Peter Arno, 1904-68, *The New Yorker*.

Tex Avery, 1908-80, animator; Bugs Bunny, Porky Pig.

George Baker, 1915-75, The Sad Sack.

Carl Barks, 1901-2000, Donald Duck comic books.

C. C. Beck, 1910-89, Captain Marvel.

Dave Berg, 1920-2002, *Mad* magazine.

Jim Berry, b 1932, Berry's World.

Herb Block (Herblock), 1909-2001, political cartoonist.

George Booth, b 1926, *The New Yorker*.

Berkeley Breathed, b 1957, Bloom County.

Dik Browne, 1917-89, Hi & Lois, Hagar the Horrible.

Marjorie Buell, 1904-93, Little Lulu.

Ernie Bushmiller, 1905-82, Nancy.

Milton Caniff, 1907-88, Terry & the Pirates, Steve Canyon.

Al Capp, 1909-79, Li'l Abner.

Roz Chast, b 1954, *The New Yorker*.

Gene Colan, 1926-2011, *Daredevil*.

Paul Conrad, 1924-2010, political cartoonist.

Roy Crane, 1901-77, Captain Easy, Buz Sawyer.

R(obert) Crumb, b 1943, underground cartoonist.

Shamus Culhane, 1908-96, animator.

Jay N. "Ding" Darling, 1876-1962, political cartoonist.

Jack Davis, b 1924, *MAD* magazine.

Jim Davis, b 1945, Garfield.

Billy DeBeck, 1890-1942, Barney Google.

Rudolph Dirks, 1877-1968, The Katzenjammer Kids.

Walt Disney, 1901-66, produced animated cartoons; created Mickey Mouse, Donald Duck.

Steve Ditko, b 1927, Spider-Man.

Mort Drucker, b 1929, *MAD* magazine.

Will Eisner, 1917-2005, the Spirit.

Jules Feiffer, b 1929, political cartoonist.

Bud Fisher, 1884-1954, Mutt & Jeff.

Ham Fisher, 1900-55, Joe Palooka.

Max Fleischer, 1883-1972, Betty Boop.

Hal Foster, 1892-1982, Tarzan, Prince Valiant.

Fontaine Fox, 1884-1964, Toonerville Folks.

Isadore "Friz" Freleng, 1905-95, animator; Yosemite Sam, Porky Pig, Sylvester and Tweety Bird.

Rube Goldberg, 1883-1970, Boob McNutt.

Chester Gould, 1900-85, Dick Tracy.

Harold Gray, 1894-1968, Little Orphan Annie.

Matt Groening, b 1954, Life in Hell, The Simpsons.

Cathy Guisewite, b 1950, Cathy.

Bill Hanna, 1910-2001, and **Joe Barbera**, 1911-2006, animators; Tom & Jerry, Yogi Bear, Flintstones.

Oliver Harrington, 1912-95, Bootsie.

Johnny Hart, 1931-2007, BC, Wizard of Id.

Alfred Harvey, 1913-94, created Casper the Friendly Ghost.

Jimmy Hatlo, 1898-1963, Little Iodine.

John Held Jr., 1889-1958, Jazz Age.

George Herriman, 1881-1944, Krazy Kat.

Harry Hershfield, 1885-1974, Abie the Agent.

Stephen Hillenburg, b 1961, SpongeBob SquarePants.

Al Hirschfeld, 1903-2003, *NY Times* theater caricaturist.

Burne Hogarth, 1911-96, Tarzan.

Helen Hokinson, 1900-49, *The New Yorker*.

Nicole Hollander, b 1939, Sylvia.

Lynn Johnston, b 1947 (Can.), For Better or For Worse.

Oliver Johnston, 1912-2008, Disney animator.

Chuck Jones, 1912-2002, animator; Bugs Bunny, Porky Pig.

Mike Judge, b 1962, Beavis and Butt-head, King of the Hill.

Bob Kane, 1916-98, Batman.

Bil Keane, 1922-2011, The Family Circus.

Walt Kelly, 1913-73, Pogo.

Hank Ketcham, 1920-2001, Dennis the Menace.

Ted Key, 1912-2008, Hazel.

Frank King, 1883-1969, Gasoline Alley.

Jack Kirby, 1917-94, Fantastic Four, The Incredible Hulk.

Rollin Kirby, 1875-1952, political cartoonist.

B(ernard) Kliban, 1935-90, cat books.

Edward Koren, b 1935, *The New Yorker*.

John Kricfalusi, b 1955, Ren & Stimpy.

Joe Kubert, 1926-2012, Sgt. Rock.

Harvey Kurtzman, 1921-93, *MAD* magazine.

Walter Lantz, 1900-94, Woody Woodpecker.

Gary Larson, b 1950, The Far Side.

Mell Lazarus, b 1927, Momma, Miss Peach.

Stan Lee, b 1922, Marvel Comics.

David Levine, 1926-2009, *NY Review of Books* caricatures.

Seth MacFarlane, b 1973, Family Guy.

Jeff MacNelly, 1947-2000, political cartoonist; Shoe.

Doug Marlette, 1949-2007, political cartoonist; Kudzu.

Don Martin, 1931-2000, *MAD* magazine.

Bill Mauldin, 1921-2003, political cartoonist.

Winsor McCay, 1872-1934, Little Nemo.

John T. McCutcheon, 1870-1949, political cartoonist.

Dwayne McDuffie, 1962-2011, *Justice League*.

Aaron McGruder, b 1974, The Boondocks.

George McManus, 1884-1954, Bringing Up Father.

Dale Messick, 1906-2005, Brenda Starr.

Norman Mingo, 1896-1980, Alfred E. Neuman.

Bob Montana, 1920-75, Archie.

Dick Moores, 1909-86, Gasoline Alley.

Willard Mullin, 1902-78, sports cartoonist; Dodgers "Bum," Mets "Kid."

Russell Myers, b 1938, Broom Hilda.

Thomas Nast, 1840-1902, political cartoonist; Republican elephant, Democratic donkey.

Pat Oliphant, b 1935, political cartoonist.

Frederick Burr Opper, 1857-1937, Happy Hooligan.

Richard Outcault, 1863-1928, Yellow Kid, Buster Brown.

Brant Parker, 1920-2007, Wizard of Id.

Trey Parker, b 1969, animator, co-creator of South Park.

Harvey Pekar, 1939-2010, American Splendor.

Mike Peters, b 1943, cartoonist; Mother Goose & Grimm.

George Price, 1901-95, *The New Yorker*.

Antonio Prohias, 1921-98, Spy vs. Spy.

Alex Raymond, 1909-56, Flash Gordon, Jungle Jim.

Forrest (Bud) Sagendorf, 1915-94, Popeye.

Art Sansom, 1920-91, The Born Loser.

Charles Schulz, 1922-2000, Peanuts.

Elzie C. Segar, 1894-1938, Popeye.

Joe Shuster, 1914-92, and **Jerry Siegel**, 1914-96, Superman.

Sidney Smith, 1887-1935, The Gumps.

Otto Soglow, 1900-75, Little King.

Art Spiegelman, b 1948, Raw, Maus.

William Steig, 1907-2003, *The New Yorker*.

Matt Stone, b 1971, animator, co-creator of South Park.

James Swinnerton, 1875-1974, Little Jimmy, Canyon Kiddies.

Paul Szep, b 1941, political cartoonist.

Paul Terry, 1887-1971, animator of Mighty Mouse.

Bob Thaves, 1924-2006, Frank and Ernest.

James Thurber, 1894-61, *The New Yorker*.

Garry Trudeau, b 1948, Doonesbury.

Jim Unger, 1937-2012, Herman.

Mort Walker, b 1923, Beetle Bailey.

Bill Watterson, b 1958, Calvin and Hobbes.

Russ Westover, 1887-1966, Tillie the Toiler.

Signe Wilkinson, b 1950, political cartoonist.

Frank Willard, 1893-1958, Moon Mullins.

J. R. Williams, 1888-1957, The Willets Family, Out Our Way.

Gahan Wilson, b 1930, *The New Yorker*.

Tom Wilson, 1931-2011, Ziggy.

Art Young, 1866-1943, political cartoonist.

Chic Young, 1901-73, Blondie.

Economists, Educators, Historians, and Social Scientists of the Past

For Psychologists, see Scientists of the Past.

Brooks Adams, 1848-1927, (U.S.) historian, political theoretician; *The Law of Civilization and Decay*.

Henry Adams, 1838-1918, (U.S.) historian, autobiographer; *The Education of Henry Adams*.

Stephen Ambrose, 1936-2002, (U.S.) historian; *Eisenhower*.

Francis Bacon, 1561-1626, (Eng.) philosopher, essayist, statesman; championed observation and induction.

George Bancroft, 1800-91, (U.S.) historian; 10-volume *History of the United States*.

Jack Barbash, 1910-94, (U.S.) labor economist; helped create the AFL-CIO.

Henry Barnard, 1811-1900, (U.S.) public school reformer.

Charles A. Beard, 1874-1948, (U.S.) historian; *The Economic Basis of Politics*.

(St.) Bede (the Venerable), c. 673-735, (Br.) scholar, historian; *Ecclesiastical History of the English People*.

Daniel Bell, 1919-2011, (U.S.) sociologist; *The End of Ideology*.

Ruth Benedict, 1887-1948, (U.S.) anthropologist; studied Indian tribes of the Southwest.

Sir Isaiah Berlin, 1909-97, (Br.) philosopher, historian; *The Age of Enlightenment*.

Leonard Bloomfield, 1887-1949, (U.S.) linguist; *Language*.

Franz Boas, 1858-1942, (U.S.) German-born anthropologist; studied American Indians.

Van Wyck Brooks, 1886-1963, (U.S.) historian; critic of New England culture, especially literature.

Edmund Burke, 1729-97, (Ire.) British parliamentarian and political philosopher; *Reflections on the Revolution in France*.

Nicholas Murray Butler, 1862-1947, (U.S.) educator; headed Columbia Univ., 1902-45; Nobel Peace Prize, 1931.

Joseph Campbell, 1904-87, (U.S.) author, editor, teacher; wrote books on mythology, folklore.

Thomas Carlyle, 1795-1881, (Scot.) historian, critic; *Sartor Resartus, Past and Present, The French Revolution*.

(Charles) Bruce Catton, 1899-1978, (U.S.) historian; *A Stillness at Appomattox*.

Edward Channing, 1856-1931, (U.S.) historian; 6-volume *History of the United States*.

Henry Steele Commager, 1902-98, (U.S.) historian, educator; *The Growth of the American Republic*.

John R. Commons, 1862-1945, (U.S.) economist, labor historian; *Legal Foundations of Capitalism*.

James B. Conant, 1893-1978, (U.S.) educator, diplomat; *The American High School Today*.

Benedetto Croce, 1866-1952, (It.) philosopher, statesman, historian; *Philosophy of the Spirit*.

Bernard A. De Voto, 1897-1955, (U.S.) historian; wrote trilogy on American West, edited Mark Twain manuscripts.

Melvil Dewey, 1851-1931, (U.S.) devised decimal system of library-book classification.

Donald Herbert Donald, 1920-2009, (U.S.) Pulitzer Prize-winning Civil War and Lincoln historian.

St. Clair Drake, 1911-90, (U.S.) sociologist, black studies pioneer; *Black Metropolis* (1945), with Horace R. Cayton.

W(illiam) E(dward) B(urghardt) Du Bois, 1868-1963, (U.S.) historian, sociologist; NAACP founder, 1909.

Will(iam), 1885-1981 (U.S.) and **Ariel Durant**, 1898-1981 (Ukraine), historians; *The Story of Civilization*.

Emile Durkheim, 1858-1917, (Fr.) a founder of modern sociology; *The Rules of Sociological Method*.

Jean Baptiste Point du Sable, c. 1750-1818, (U.S.) pioneer trader and first settler of Chicago, 1779.

Charles Eliot, 1834-1926, (U.S.) educator, Harvard president.

Friedrich Engels, 1820-95, (Ger.) political writer; with Marx wrote the *Communist Manifesto*.

Irving Fisher, 1867-1947, (U.S.) economist; contributed to the development of modern monetary theory.

John Fiske, 1842-1901, (U.S.) historian and lecturer; popularized Darwinian theory of evolution.

Charles Fourier, 1772-1837, (Fr.) utopian socialist.

John Hope Franklin, 1915-2009, (U.S.) historian; *From Slavery to Freedom: A History of African Americans*.

Sir James George Frazer, 1854-1941, (Br.) anthropologist; studied myth in religion; *The Golden Bough*.

Milton Friedman, 1912-2006, (U.S.) economist.

Paul Fussell, 1924-2012, (U.S.) literary historian; *The Great War and Modern Memory*.

John Kenneth Galbraith, 1908-2006, (Can.-U.S.) economist, author, professor, former amb. to India.

Giovanni Gentile, 1875-1944, (It.) philosopher, educator; reformed Italian educational system.

Henry George, 1839-97, (U.S.) economist, reformer; led single-tax movement.

Edward Gibbon, 1737-94, (Br.) historian; *The History of the Decline and Fall of the Roman Empire*.

Francesco Guicciardini, 1483-1540, (It.) historian; *Storia d'Italia*, principal historical work of the 16th cent.

Thomas Hobbes, 1588-1679, (Eng.) philosopher, political theorist; *Leviathan*.

Richard Hofstadter, 1916-70, (U.S.) historian; *The Age of Reform*.

Charles Hamilton Houston, 1895-1950, (U.S.) African American lawyer, Howard University instructor; champion of minority rights.

Samuel Huntington, 1927-2008, (U.S.), political scientist, Harvard University professor; *The Clash of Civilizations*.

Alfred Kahn, 1917-2010, (U.S.) economist; deregulated the U.S. airline industry.

John Keegan, 1934-2012, (Br.) war historian; *The Face of Battle*.

George F. Kennan, 1904-2005, (U.S.) diplomat, historian; main architect of U.S. Cold War "containment" strategy.

John Maynard Keynes, 1883-1946, (Br.) economist; principal advocate of deficit spending.

Alfred Kinsey, 1894-1956, (U.S.) zoologist; pioneering human sex researcher.

Russell Kirk, 1918-94, (U.S.) social philosopher; *The Conservative Mind*.

Alfred L. Kroeber, 1876-1960, (U.S.) cultural anthropologist; studied Indians of North and South America.

Elisabeth Kubler-Ross, 1926-2004, (Switz.) psychiatrist, author; *On Death and Dying*.

Christopher Lasch, 1932-94, (U.S.) social critic, historian; *The Culture of Narcissism*.

James L. Laughlin, 1850-1933, (U.S.) economist; helped establish Federal Reserve System.

Margaret Leech, 1893-1974 (U.S.) historian; *Reveille in Washington, 1860-1865*.

Lucien Lévy-Bruhl, 1857-1939, (Fr.) philosopher; studied the psychology of primitive societies; *Primitive Mentality*.

John Locke, 1632-1704, (Eng.) philosopher, political theorist; *Two Treatises of Government*.

Thomas B. Macaulay, 1800-59, (Br.) historian, statesman.

Niccolò Machiavelli, 1469-1527, (It.) writer, statesman; *The Prince*.

Bronislaw Malinowski, 1884-1942, (Pol.) considered the father of social anthropology.

Thomas R. Malthus, 1766-1834, (Br.) economist; *Essay on the Principle of Population*.

Horace Mann, 1796-1859, (U.S.) pioneered modern public school system.

Karl Mannheim, 1893-1947, (Hung.) sociologist, historian; *Ideology and Utopia*.

Harriet Martineau, 1802-76, (Eng.) writer, feminist; *Society in America*.

Karl Marx, 1818-83, (Ger.) political theorist, proponent of Communism; *Communist Manifesto, Das Kapital*.

Benjamin Mays, 1895-1984, (U.S.) minister, educator, civil rights leader; headed Morehouse College, 1940-67.

Giuseppe Mazzini, 1805-72, (It.) political philosopher.

William H. McGuffey, 1800-73, (U.S.) his *Reader* was a mainstay of 19th-cent. U.S. public education.

George H. Mead, 1863-1931, (U.S.) philosopher, social psychologist.

Margaret Mead, 1901-78, (U.S.) cultural anthropologist; popularized field; *Coming of Age in Samoa*.

Alexander Meiklejohn, 1872-1964, (U.S.) Br.-born educator; championed academic freedom and experimental curricula.

James Mill, 1773-1836, (Scot.) philosopher, historian, economist; a proponent of utilitarianism.

John Stuart Mill, 1806-73, (Eng.) philosopher, economist; *Utilitarianism*; eldest son of James Mill.

Perry G. Miller, 1905-63, (U.S.) historian; interpreted 17th-cent. New England.

Theodor Mommsen, 1817-1903, (Ger.) historian; *The History of Rome*.

Ashley Montagu, 1905-99, (Eng.) anthropologist; *The Natural Superiority of Women*.

Charles-Louis Montesquieu, 1689-1755, (Fr.) social philosopher; *The Spirit of Laws*.

Maria Montessori, 1870-1952, (It.) educator, physician; started Montessori method of student self-motivation.

Samuel Eliot Morison, 1887-1976, (U.S.) historian; chronicled voyages of early explorers.

Lewis Mumford, 1895-1990, (U.S.) sociologist, critic; *The Culture of Cities*.

Gunnar Myrdal, 1898-1987, (Swed.) economist, social scientist; *Asian Drama: An Inquiry Into the Poverty of Nations*.

Allan Nevins, 1890-1971, (U.S.) historian, biographer; *The Ordeal of the Union*.

José Ortega y Gasset, 1883-1955, (Sp.) philosopher; advocated control by elite; *The Revolt of the Masses*.

Elinor Ostrom, 1933-2012, (U.S.) political economist.

Robert Owen, 1771-1858, (Br.) political philosopher, reformer; pioneer in cooperative movement.

Thomas Paine, 1737-1809, (Br.-U.S.) political theorist, writer; *Common Sense*.

Vilfredo Pareto, 1848-1923, (It.) economist, sociologist.

Francis Parkman, 1823-93, (U.S.) historian; *France and England in North America*.

Elizabeth P. Peabody, 1804-94, (U.S.) education pioneer; founded 1st kindergarten in U.S., 1860.

William Prescott, 1796-1859, (U.S.) early American historian; *The Conquest of Peru*.

Pierre Joseph Proudhon, 1809-65, (Fr.) social theorist; father of anarchism; *The Philosophy of Property*.

François Quesnay, 1694-1774, (Fr.) economic theorist.

David Ricardo, 1772-1823, (Br.) economic theorist; advocated free international trade.

David Riesman, 1909-2002, (U.S.) sociologist; co-author, *The Lonely Crowd*.

Jacqueline de Romilly, 1913-2010, (Fr.) scholar of Greek civilization and language.

Theodore Roszak, 1933-2011, (U.S.) historian; *The Making of a Counter Culture*.

Jean-Jacques Rousseau, 1712-78, (Fr.) social philosopher; the father of romantic sensibility; *Confessions*.

Paul Samuelson, 1915-2009, (U.S.) economist, famed for modern mathematical approach to economics.

Edward Sapir, 1884-1939, (Ger.-U.S.) anthropologist; studied ethnology and linguistics of U.S. Indian groups.

Ferdinand de Saussure, 1857-1913, (Switz.) a founder of modern linguistics.

Arthur Schlesinger Jr., 1917-2007, (U.S.) historian, author; *The Imperial Presidency*.

Joseph Schumpeter, 1883-1950, (Czech.-U.S.) economist, sociologist.

Elizabeth Seton, 1774-1821, (U.S.) nun; est. parochial school education in U.S., first native-born American saint.

Georg Simmel, 1858-1918, (Ger.) sociologist, philosopher; helped establish German sociology.

Robert Sklar, 1936-2011, (U.S.) film scholar.

Adam Smith, 1723-90, (Br.) economist; advocated laissez-faire economy, free trade; *The Wealth of Nations*.

Jared Sparks, 1789-1866, (U.S.) historian, educator, editor; *The Library of American Biography*.

Oswald Spengler, 1880-1936, (Ger.) philosopher, historian; *The Decline of the West*.

Leo Steinberg, 1920-2011, (Rus.-Am.) art historian.

William G. Sumner, 1840-1910, (U.S.) social scientist, economist; laissez-faire economy, Social Darwinism.

Hippolyte Taine, 1828-93, (Fr.) historian; basis of naturalistic school; *The Origins of Contemporary France*.

A(lan) J(ohn) P(ercivale) Taylor, 1906-90, (Br.) historian; *The Origins of the Second World War*.

Nikolaas Tinbergen, 1907-88, (Neth.-Br.) ethologist; pioneer in study of animal behavior.

Alexis de Tocqueville, 1805-59, (Fr.) political scientist, historian; *Democracy in America*.

Francis E. Townsend, 1867-1960, (U.S.) led old-age pension movement, 1933.

Arnold Toynbee, 1889-1975, (Br.) historian; *A Study of History*, sweeping analysis of hist. of civilizations.

George Trevelyan, 1876-1962, (Br.) historian, statesman; favored "literary" over "scientific" history; *History of England*.

Henri Troyat, 1911-2007 (Russ.-Fr.), biographies of major figures in Russian history.

Frederick J. Turner, 1861-1932, (U.S.) historian, educator; *The Frontier in American History*.

Thorstein B. Veblen, 1857-1929, (U.S.) economist, social philosopher; *The Theory of the Leisure Class*.

Giovanni Vico, 1668-1744, (It.) historian, biographer; regarded by many as first modern historian; *New Science*.

Izaak Walton, 1593-1683, (Eng.) biographer; political-philosophical study of fishing, *The Compleat Angler*.

Booker T. Washington, 1856-1915, (U.S.) founder, 1881, and first pres. of Tuskegee Institute; *Up From Slavery*.

Sidney J., 1859-1947, and **Beatrice Webb**, 1858-1943, (Br.) leading figures in Fabian Society and Labor Party.

Max Weber, 1864-1920, (Ger.) sociologist; *The Protestant Ethic and the Spirit of Capitalism*.

Walter White, 1893-1955, (U.S.) exec. sec., NAACP, 1931-55.

Roy Wilkins, 1901-81, (U.S.) exec. director, NAACP, 1955-77.

Emma Hart Willard, 1787-1870, (U.S.) pioneered higher education for women.

James Q. Wilson, 1931-2012, (U.S.) political scientist; co-authored broken windows theory.

Carter G. Woodson, 1875-1950, (U.S.) historian; founded Assn. for the Study of Negro Life and History.

C. Vann Woodward, 1908-99, (U.S.) historian; *The Strange Career of Jim Crow*.

American Journalists of the Past

Reviewed by Dean Mills, Dean, Missouri School of Journalism.

See also Business Leaders and Philanthropists, American Cartoonists, Writers of the Past.

Franklin P. Adams (F.P.A.), 1881-1960, humorist; wrote column "The Conning Tower."

Joseph W. Alsop, 1910-89, and **Stewart Alsop**, 1914-74, Washington-based political analysts, columnists.

Jack Anderson, 1922-2006, muckraking Washington, DC, syndicated columnist.

Brooks Atkinson, 1894-1984, theater critic.

Robert L. Bartley, 1937-2003, editorial-page editor for *Wall Street Journal*.

James Gordon Bennett, 1795-1872, editor and publisher; founded *NY Herald*.

James Gordon Bennett, 1841-1918, succeeded father, financed expeditions, founded afternoon paper.

Nellie Bly (Elizabeth Cochrane), 1867-1922, pioneer woman journalist, investig. reporter; noted for series on trip around the world.

Elias Boudinot, c. 1803-39, founding editor of first Native American newspaper in U.S., *Cherokee Phoenix* (1828-34).

Ed Bradley, 1941-2006, TV journalist (*60 Minutes*); one of the first African American journalists to report on the Vietnam War.

Andrew Breitbart, 1969-2012, conservative commentator and blogger.

David Brinkley, 1920-2003, co-anchor of NBC's *Huntley-Brinkley Report*, host of ABC's *This Week With David Brinkley*.

Arthur Brisbane, 1864-1936, editor; helped introduce "yellow journalism" with sensational, simply written articles.

David Broder, 1929-2011, political journalist for *The Washington Post*.

Heywood Broun, 1888-1939, author, columnist; founded American Newspaper Guild.

Helen Gurley Brown, 1922-2012, author; editor-in-chief of *Cosmopolitan* magazine (1965-97).

Art Buchwald, 1925-2007, journalist, humorist, syndicated columnist.

William F. Buckley Jr., 1925-2008, columnist and commentator; founder of *National Review*.

Herb Caen, 1916-97, longtime columnist for *San Francisco Chronicle* and *Examiner*.

John Campbell, 1653-1728, published *Boston News-Letter*, first continuing newspaper in the American colonies.

Jimmy Cannon, 1909-73, syndicated sports columnist.

John Chancellor, 1927-96, NBC reporter, anchor.

Harry Chandler, 1864-1944, *Los Angeles Times* publisher (1917-41); made it a dominant force.

Otis Chandler, 1928-2006, *Los Angeles Times* publisher (1960-80).

Marquis Childs, 1903-90, reporter and columnist for *St. Louis Post-Dispatch* and United Feature syndicate.

Craig Claiborne, 1920-2000, *NY Times* food editor and critic; key in internationalizing American tastes.

Alexander Cockburn, 1941-2012, left-wing journalist.

Charles Collingwood, 1917-85, CBS news correspondent.

Alistair Cooke, 1908-2004, journalist, TV narrator; naturalized American citizen, "Letter From America" series.

Howard Cosell, 1920-95, TV and radio sportscaster.

Gardner Cowles, 1861-1946, founded newspaper chain.

Judith Crist, 1922-2012, film critic.

Walter Cronkite, 1916-2009, CBS evening news anchor, TV journalist.

Evelyn Cunningham, 1916-2010, African American civil rights reporter.

Cyrus Curtis, 1850-1933, publisher of *Saturday Evening Post*, *Ladies' Home Journal*, *Country Gentleman*.

John Charles Daly, 1914-91, war correspondent, TV journalist; Voice of America head.

Charles Anderson Dana, 1819-97, editor, publisher; made *NY Sun* famous for its news reporting.

Elmer (Holmes) Davis, 1890-1958, *NY Times* editorial writer, radio commentator.

Richard Harding Davis, 1864-1916, war correspondent, travel writer, fiction writer.

Benjamin Day, 1810-89, published *NY Sun* beginning in 1833, introducing penny press to the U.S.

Dorothy Dix (Elizabeth Meriwether Gilmer), 1861-1951, reporter; pioneer of the advice column genre.

Finley Peter Dunne, 1867-1936, humorist, social critic; wrote "Mr. Dooley" columns.

Mary Baker Eddy, 1821-1910, founded Christian Science movement and *Christian Science Monitor*.

Rowland Evans Jr., 1921-2001, Washington columnist.

Fanny Fern (Sara Willis Parton), 1811-72, newspaper columnist, author.

Marshall Field III, 1893-1956, retail magnate, *Chicago Sun* founder.

Doris Fleeson, 1901-70, war correspondent, columnist.

Benjamin Franklin, 1706-90, publisher of *Poor Richards Almanack*.

James Franklin, 1697-1735, printer, pioneer journalist; publisher of *New England Courant* and *Rhode Island Gazette*.

Fred W. Friendly, 1915-98, radio, TV reporter, producer, executive; collaborator with Edward R. Murrow.

Margaret Fuller, 1810-50, social reformer, transcendentalist, critic and foreign correspondent for *NY Tribune*.

Frank E. Gannett, 1876-1957, founded newspaper chain.

Mary Ellen Garber, 1916-2008, sports journalist.

William Lloyd Garrison, 1805-79, abolitionist; publisher of *The Liberator*.

Edwin Lawrence Godkin, 1831-1902, founder of *The Nation*, editor of *NY Evening Post*.

Katharine Graham, 1917-2001, *Washington Post* publisher.

Sheilah Graham, 1904-89, Hollywood gossip columnist.

Horace Greeley, 1811-72, editor, politician; founded *NY Tribune*.

Meg Greenfield, 1930-99, *Newsweek* columnist, *Washington Post* editorial page editor.

Gilbert Hovey Grosvenor, 1875-1966, longtime editor of *National Geographic* magazine.

John Gunther, 1901-70, *Chicago Daily News* foreign correspondent, author.

David Halberstam, 1934-2007, journalist, sports reporter, author; *The Best and the Brightest*, *Summer of '49*.

Sarah Josepha Buell Hale, 1788-1879, first female magazine editor; *Ladies' Magazine*, later *Godey's Lady's Book*.

Paul Harvey, 1918-2009, radio broadcaster and commentator.

William Randolph Hearst, 1863-1951, founder of Hearst newspaper chain, one of the pioneers of yellow journalism.

Gabriel Heatter, 1890-1972, radio commentator.

John Hersey, 1914-98, foreign correspondent for *Time*, *Life*, and *The New Yorker*; author.

Marguerite Higgins, 1920-66, reporter, war correspondent.

Christopher Hitchens, 1949-2011, columnist and literary critic.

Hedda Hopper, 1885-1966, Hollywood gossip columnist.

Roy Howard, 1883-1964, editor, executive; Scripps-Howard papers and United Press (later United Press International).

Chet (Chester Robert) Huntley, 1911-74, co-anchor of NBC's *Huntley-Brinkley Report*.

Ralph Ingersoll, 1900-85, editor; *Fortune*, *Time*, *Life* exec.

Molly Ivins, 1944-2007, author, syndicated political columnist.

Peter Jennings, 1938-2005, ABC correspondent, anchor.

Pauline Kael, 1919-2001, film critic.

H. V. (Hans von) Kaltenborn, 1878-1965, radio commentator, reporter.

Murray Kempton, 1917-97, reporter, columnist for magazines and newspapers, including *NY Post*.

Dorothy Kilgallen, 1913-65, crime reporter, columnist.

James J. Kilpatrick, 1920-2010, political columnist, author and television personality.

John S. Knight, 1894-1981, editor, publisher; founded Knight newspaper group, which merged into Knight-Ridder.

Joseph Kraft, 1942-86, foreign policy columnist.

Irving Kristol, 1920-2009, columnist, commentator.

Arthur Krock, 1886-1974, *NY Times* political writer, Washington bureau chief.

Charles Kuralt, 1934-97, TV anchor; host of CBS "On the Road" featuring stories about life in the U.S.

Ann Landers (Eppie Lederer), 1918-2002, advice columnist.

David Lawrence, 1888-1973, reporter, columnist, publisher; founded *U.S. News & World Report*.

Frank Leslie, 1821-80, engraver, publisher of newspapers and magazines, notably *Leslie's Illustrated Newspaper*.

Alexander Liberman, 1912-99, editorial director for Condé Nast magazines.

A(bbott) J(oseph) Liebling, 1904-63, foreign correspondent, critic; principally with *The New Yorker*.

Walter Lippmann, 1889-1974, political analyst, social critic, columnist, author.

Peter Lisagor, 1915-76, Washington bureau chief, *Chicago Daily News*; broadcast commentator.

David Ross Locke, 1833-88, humorist, satirist under pseudonym P.V. Nasby; owned *Toledo (Ohio) Blade*.

Elijah Parish Lovejoy, 1802-37, abolitionist editor in St. Louis and in Alton, IL; killed by proslavery mob.

Clare Booth Luce, 1903-87, war correspondent for *Life*, diplomat, playwright.

Henry R. Luce, 1898-1967, founded *Time*, *Fortune*, *Life*, *Sports Illustrated*.

Dwight Macdonald, 1906-82, reporter, social critic.

Don Marquis, 1878-1937, humor columnist for *NY Sun* and *NY Tribune*; wrote "Archy and Mehitabel" stories.

Nancy Hicks Maynard, 1946-2008, African American publisher, journalist.

Robert Maynard, 1937-97, first African American editor and then owner of major U.S. paper, the *Oakland Tribune*.

C(harles) K(enny) McClatchy, 1858-1936, founder of McClatchy newspaper chain.

Sarah McClendon, 1910-2003, veteran White House correspondent.

Samuel McClure, 1857-1949, founder (1893) of *McClure's Magazine*, famous for its investigative reporting.

Anne O'Hare McCormick, 1889-1954, foreign correspondent; first woman on *NY Times* editorial board.

Robert R. McCormick, 1880-1955, editor, publisher, executive of *Chicago Tribune* and *NY Daily News*.

Ralph McGill, 1893-1969, crusading editor, publisher of *Atlanta Constitution*.

Mary McGrory, 1918-2004, Washington columnist.

O(scar) O(dd) McIntyre, 1884-1938, feature writer, syndicated columnist on everyday life in New York City.

Joseph Medill, 1823-99, longtime editor of the *Chicago Tribune*.

H(enry) L(ouis) Mencken, 1880-1956, reporter, editor, columnist with *Baltimore Sun* papers; anti-establishment viewpoint.

Edwin Meredith, 1876-1928, founder of magazine company.

Frank A. Munsey, 1854-1925, owner, editor, and publisher of newspapers and magazines, including *Munsey's Magazine*.

Edward R. Murrow, 1908-65, broadcast reporter, executive; reported from Britain in WWII; hosted *See It Now*, *Person to Person*.

Edwin Newman, 1919-2010, NBC news correspondent.

Louella Parsons, 1881-1972, Hollywood gossip columnist.

Ethel L. Payne, 1911-91, African American civil rights reporter.

Daniel Pearl, 1963-2002, American journalist; kidnapped and murdered in Pakistan.

Drew (Andrew Russell) Pearson, 1897-1969, investigative reporter, columnist.

(James) Westbrook Pegler, 1894-1969, reporter, columnist.

Shirley Povich, 1905-98, sports columnist.

Joseph Pulitzer, 1847-1911, *NY World* publisher; founded Columbia Journalism School, Pulitzer Prizes.

Joseph Pulitzer II, 1885-1955, longtime *St. Louis Post-Dispatch* editor, publisher; built it into major paper.

Ernie Pyle, 1900-45, reporter, war correspondent; killed in WWII.

William Raspberry, 1935-2012, public affairs columnist.

Henry Raymond, 1820-69, cofounder, editor, *NY Times*.

Harry Reasoner, 1923-91, ABC and CBS news reporter, anchor.

John Reed, 1887-1920, reporter; foreign correspondent famous for coverage of Bolshevik Revolution; buried at the Kremlin.

Whitelaw Reid, 1837-1912, longtime editor, *NY Tribune*.

James Reston, 1909-95, *NY Times* political reporter, columnist.

Frank Reynolds, 1923-83, ABC reporter, anchor.

(Henry) Grantland Rice, 1880-1954, sportswriter.

Jacob Riis, 1849-1914, reporter, photographer; exposed slum conditions in *How the Other Half Lives*.

Max Robinson, 1939-88, first African American to anchor network news (ABC), 1978.

Andy Rooney, 1919-2011, radio and TV commentator (*60 Minutes*).

A. M. Rosenthal, 1922-2006, reporter, editor for *NY Times* (1943-99).

Harold Ross, 1892-1951, founder, editor, *The New Yorker*.

Carl T. Rowan, 1925-2000, reporter, columnist, author.

Mike Royko, 1932-97, Chicago newspaper columnist; wrote *Boss*, biography of Mayor Richard J. Daley (1902-76).

Louis Rukeyser, 1933-2006, TV journalist, financial analyst; hosted *Wall Street Week* on public television.

(Alfred) Damon Runyon, 1884-1946, sportswriter, columnist; stories collected in *Guys and Dolls*.

Tim Russert, 1950-2008, TV journalist; moderator of *Meet the Press* (NBC).

John B. Russwurm, 1799-1851, cofounded (1827) nation's first black newspaper, *Freedom's Journal*, in New York, NY.

William Safire, 1929-2009, Pulitzer Prize-winning columnist, *NY Times*.

Adela Rogers St. Johns, 1894-1988, reporter, sportswriter for Hearst newspapers.

Pierre Salinger, 1925-2004, press sec. under Pres. Kennedy and Johnson, foreign correspondent.

Harrison Salisbury, 1908-93, reporter, foreign correspondent; a Soviet specialist.

Andrew Sarris, 1928-2012, film critic, *Village Voice*.

Daniel Schorr, 1916-2010, broadcast and print journalist.

E(dward) W(illis) Scripps, 1854-1926, founded first large U.S. newspaper chain, pioneered syndication.

Eric Sevareid, 1912-92, war correspondent, radio newscaster, CBS commentator.

Anthony Shadid, 1968-2012, foreign correspondent.

Randy Shilts, 1951-94, journalist; author of *And the Band Played On*.

William L. Shirer, 1904-93, broadcaster, foreign correspondent; wrote *The Rise and Fall of the Third Reich*.

Howard K. Smith, 1914-2002, ABC news reporter, anchor.

Red (Walter) Smith, 1905-82, sportswriter.

Edgar P. Snow, 1905-71, correspondent; expert on Chinese Communist movement.

Tony Snow, 1955-2008, columnist, radio/TV journalist, White House press sec.

Tom Snyder, 1936-2007, television journalist.

Lawrence Spivak, 1900-94, co-creator, moderator, producer of *Meet the Press*.

(Joseph) Lincoln Steffens, 1866-1936, muckraking journalist.

I(sidor) F(einstein) Stone, 1907-89, one-man editor of *I. F. Stone's Weekly*.

Arthur Hays Sulzberger, 1891-1968, long-time publisher of *NY Times* (1935-61).

Arthur Ochs "Punch" Sulzberger, 1926-2012, long-time publisher of *NY Times* (1963-92).

C(yrus) L(eo) Sulzberger, 1912-93, *NY Times* foreign correspondent, columnist.

David Susskind, 1920-87, TV producer, public affairs talk-show host (*Open End*).

John Cameron Swayze, 1906-95, early TV newscaster (NBC).

Herbert Bayard Swope, 1882-1958, war correspondent, editor of *NY World*.

Ida Tarbell, 1857-1944, muckraking journalist.

Isaiah Thomas, 1750-1831, printer, publisher; cofounder of revolutionary journal, *Massachusetts Spy*.

Lowell Thomas, 1892-1981, radio newscaster, world traveler.

Dorothy Thompson, 1894-1961, foreign correspondent, columnist, radio commentator.

Hunter S. Thompson, 1937-2005, political journalist, author; *Fear and Loathing on the Campaign Trail* (1972).

Kenneth Thompson, 1923-2006, Canadian media magnate; owned Toronto *Globe and Mail* newspaper.

Mike Wallace, 1918-2012, TV journalist (*60 Minutes*).

Ida Bell Wells-Barnett, 1862-1931, African American reporter, editor, anti-lynching crusader.

William Allen White, 1868-1944, newspaper editor, publisher.

Tom Wicker, 1926-2011, *NY Times* political reporter, columnist.

Walter Winchell, 1897-1972, reporter, columnist, broadcaster of celebrity news.

John Peter Zenger, 1697-1746, printer, journalist; acquitted in precedent-setting libel suit (1735).

Military and Naval Leaders of the Past

Reviewed by Alan C. Aimone, USMA Library.

Alexander the Great, 356-323 BCE, (Maced.) conquered Persia and much of the world known to Europeans.

Harold Alexander, 1891-1969, (Br.) led Allied invasion of Italy, 1943, WWII.

Ethan Allen, 1738-89, (U.S.) headed Green Mountain Boys; captured Ft. Ticonderoga, 1775, Amer. Rev.

Edmund Allenby, 1861-1936, (Br.) in Boer War, WWI; led Egyptian expeditionary force, 1917-18.

Benedict Arnold, 1741-1801, (U.S.) victorious at Saratoga; tried to betray West Point to British, Amer. Rev.

Henry "Hap" Arnold, 1886-1950, (U.S.) commanded Army Air Force in WWII.

Ashurnasirpal II, 884-859 BCE, (Assyria) king; began Assyrian conquest of Middle East.

John Barry, 1745-1803, (U.S.) won numerous sea battles during Amer. Rev.

Pierre Beauregard, 1818-93, (U.S.) Confed. general; ordered bombardment of Ft. Sumter that began Civil War.

Belisarius, c. 505-565, (Byzant.) won remarkable victories for Byzantine emperor Justinian I.

Gebhard von Blücher, 1742-1819, (Ger.) helped defeat Napoleon at Waterloo.

Simón Bolívar, 1783-1830, (Venez.) S. Amer. revolutionary who liberated much of the continent from Spanish rule.

Napoleon Bonaparte, 1769-1821, (Fr.) defeated Russia and Austria at Austerlitz, 1805; invaded Russia, 1812; defeated at Waterloo, 1815.

Edward Braddock, 1695-1755, (Br.) commanded forces in French and Indian War.

Omar N. Bradley, 1893-1981, (U.S.) headed U.S. ground troops in Normandy invasion, 1944, WWII.

John Burgoyne, 1722-92, (Br.) general; defeated at Saratoga, Amer. Rev.

Julius Caesar, 100-44 BCE, (Rom.) general and politician; conquered northern Gaul, overthrew Roman Republic.

Charlemagne, 742-814, (Fr.) king of the Franks, Holy Roman Emperor; conquered most of Western Europe.

Claire Lee Chennault, 1893-1958, (U.S.) headed Flying Tigers in WWII.

El Cid (Rodrigo Diaz de Vivar), 1040-99, (Sp.) renowned knight; captured Valencia (1094), hero of "Song of Cid" epic.

Mark W. Clark, 1896-1984, (U.S.) helped plan N African invasion in WWII; commander of UN forces, Korean War.

Karl von Clausewitz, 1780-1831, (Prus.) military theorist.

Lucius D. Clay, 1897-1978, (U.S.) led Berlin airlift, 1948-49.

Henry Clinton, 1738-95, (Br.) commander of forces in Amer. Rev., 1778-81.

Cochise, c. 1815-74, (Nat. Am.) chief of Chiricahua band of Apache Indians in Southwest U.S.

Charles Cornwallis, 1738-1805, (Br.) victorious at Brandywine, 1777; surrendered at Yorktown, Amer. Rev.

Hernán Cortés, 1485-1547, (Sp.) led Spanish conquistadors in the defeat of the Aztec empire, 1519-28.

Crazy Horse, 1849-77, (Nat. Am.) Sioux war chief victorious at Battle of Little Bighorn.

George Armstrong Custer, 1839-76, (U.S.) army officer defeated and killed at Battle of Little Bighorn.

Benjamin O. Davis Jr., 1912-2002, (U.S.) leader of WWII black aviators; first African American general in U.S. Air Force.

Benjamin O. Davis Sr., 1877-1970, (U.S.) first African American general in U.S. Army (1940).

Moshe Dayan, 1915-81, (Isr.) directed campaigns in the 1967, 1973 Arab-Israeli wars.

Stephen Decatur, 1779-1820, (U.S.) naval hero of Barbary wars, War of 1812.

Anton Denikin, 1872-1947, (Russ.) led White forces in Russian civil war.

George Dewey, 1837-1917, (U.S.) destroyed Spanish fleet at Manila, 1898, Span.-Amer. War.

Karl Doenitz, 1891-1980, (Ger.) submarine cmdr. in chief and naval cmdr., WWII; last pres. of Third Reich.

Jimmy Doolittle, 1896-1993, (U.S.) led 1942 air raid on Tokyo and other Japanese cities in WWII.

Hugh Dowding, 1882-1970, (Br.) headed RAF Fighter Command, 1936-40, WWII.

Jubal Early, 1816-94, (U.S.) Confed. general; led raid on Washington, 1864, Civil War.

Dwight D. Eisenhower, 1890-1969, (U.S.) commanded Allied forces in Europe, WWII.

Erich von Falkenhayn, 1861-1922, (Ger.) minister of war, general, commander at Verdun in WWI.

David Farragut, 1801-70, (U.S.) Union admiral; captured New Orleans, Mobile Bay, Civil War.

John Arbuthnot Fisher, 1841-1920, (Br.) WWI admiral; naval reformer.

Ferdinand Foch, 1851-1929, (Fr.) headed victorious Allied armies, 1918, WWI.

Nathan Bedford Forrest, 1821-77, (U.S.) Confed. general; led raids against Union supply lines, Civil War.

Frederick the Great, 1712-86, (Prus.) led Prussia in Seven Years War.

Horatio Gates, 1728-1806, (U.S.) commanded army at Saratoga, Amer. Rev.

Genghis Khan, 1162-1227, (Mongol) unified Mongol tribes, subjugated much of Asia, 1206-21.

Geronimo, 1829-1909, (Nat. Am.) leader of Chiricahua band of Apache Indians.

Charles G. Gordon, 1833-85, (Br.) led forces in China, Crimean War; killed at Khartoum.

Ulysses S. Grant, 1822-85, (U.S.) headed Union army, Civil War, 1864-65; forced Robert E. Lee's surrender, 1865.

Nathanael Greene, 1742-86, (U.S.) defeated British in Southern campaign, 1780-81, Amer. Rev.

Heinz Guderian, 1888-1954, (Ger.) tank theorist; led panzer forces in Poland, France, Russia, WWII.

Gustavus Adolphus, 1594-1632, (Swed.) king, military tactician, reformer; led forces in Thirty Years' War.

Douglas Haig, 1861-1928, (Br.) led British armies in France, 1915-18, WWI.

William F. Halsey, 1882-1959, (U.S.) defeated Japanese fleet at Leyte Gulf, 1944, WWII.

Hannibal, 247-183 BCE, (Carthage) invaded Rome, crossing Alps, in Second Punic War, 218-201 BCE.

Sir Arthur Travers Harris, 1895-1984, (Br.) led Britain's WWII bomber command.

Paul von Hindenburg, 1847-1934, (Ger.) chief of general staff, WWI; 2nd pres. of Weimar Republic.

Richard Howe, 1726-99, (Br.) commanded navy in Amer. Rev., 1776-78; June 1 victory against French, 1794.

William Howe, 1729-1814, (Br.) commanded forces in Amer. Rev., 1776-78.

Isaac Hull, 1773-1843, (U.S.) sunk British frigate *Guerriere*, War of 1812.

Thomas "Stonewall" Jackson, 1824-63, (U.S.) Confed. general; led Shenandoah Valley campaign, Civil War.

Daniel James Jr., 1920-78, (U.S.) first black 4-star general (1975); commander, N. American Air Defense Command.

Joseph Joffre, 1852-1931, (Fr.) headed Allied armies; won Battle of the Marne, 1914, WWI.

John Paul Jones, 1747-92, (U.S.) commanded *Bonhomme Richard* in victory over *Serapis*, Amer. Rev., 1779.

Chief Joseph, c. 1840-1904, (Nat. Am.) chief of the Nez Percé; forced by army to retreat and surrender.

Stephen Kearny, 1794-1848, (U.S.) headed Army of the West in Mexican War.

Albert Kesselring, 1885-1960, (Ger.) field marshal who led the defense of Italy in WWII.

Ernest J. King, 1878-1956, (U.S.) key WWII naval strategist.

Horatio H. Kitchener, 1850-1916, (Br.) led forces in Boer War, victorious at Khartoum; organized army in WWI.

Henry Knox, 1750-1806, (U.S.) general in Amer. Rev.; first sec. of war under U.S. Constitution.

Lavrenti Kornilov, 1870-1918, (Russ.) commander-in-chief, 1917; led counterrevolutionary march on Petrograd.

Thaddeus Kosciusko, 1746-1817, (Pol.) aided Amer. Rev.

Walter Krueger, 1881-1967, (U.S.) led Sixth Army in WWII in Southwest Pacific.

Mikhail Kutuzov, 1745-1813, (Russ.) fought at Borodino, Napol. Wars, 1812; abandoned Moscow, forced French retreat.

Marquis de Lafayette, 1757-1834, (Fr.) fought in, secured French aid for Amer. Rev.

T(homas) E. Lawrence (of Arabia), 1888-1935, (Br.) organized revolt of Arabs against Turks in WWI.

William Daniel Leahy, 1875-1959, (U.S.) chief of staff to Pres. Roosevelt in WWII, Fleet Admiral.

Henry (Light-Horse Harry) Lee, 1756-1818, (U.S.) cavalry officer in Amer. Rev.

Robert E. Lee, 1807-70, (U.S.) Confed. general; defeated at Gettysburg, Civil War; surrendered to Grant, 1865.

Curtis LeMay, 1906-90, (U.S.) Air Force cmdr. in WWII, Korean War, Vietnam War.

Lyman Lemnitzer, 1899-1988, (U.S.) WWII hero; later general, chairman of Joint Chiefs of Staff.

James Longstreet, 1821-1904, (U.S.) aided Lee at Gettysburg, Civil War.

Erich Ludendorff, 1865-1937, (Ger.) general; victor at Tannenberg, WWI.

Douglas MacArthur, 1880-1964, (U.S.) commanded forces in SW Pacific in WWII; headed occupation forces in Japan, 1945-51; UN commander in Korean War.

Carl Gustaf Mannerheim, 1867-1951, (Fin.) army officer and pres. of Finland, 1944-46.

Erich von Manstein, 1887-1973, (Ger.) served WWI, WWII; planned inv. of France (1940); convicted of war crimes.

Francis Marion, 1733-95, (U.S.) led guerrilla actions in South Carolina during Amer. Rev.

Duke of Marlborough, 1650-1722, (Br.) led forces against Louis XIV in War of the Spanish Succession.

George C. Marshall, 1880-1959, (U.S.) chief of staff in WWII; authored Marshall Plan.

Maurice, Count of Nassau, 1567-1625, (Neth.) military innovator; led forces in Thirty Years' War.

George B. McClellan, 1826-85, (U.S.) Union general; commanded Army of the Potomac, 1861-62, Civil War.

George Meade, 1815-72, (U.S.) commanded Union forces at Gettysburg, Civil War.

Doris "Dorie" Miller, 1919-43, (U.S.) Navy hero of Pearl Harbor attack; first African American awarded Navy Cross.

Billy Mitchell, 1879-1936, (U.S.) WWI air-power advocate; court-martialed for insubordination, later vindicated.

Helmuth von Moltke, 1800-91, (Ger.) victorious in Austro-Prussian, Franco-Prussian wars.

Louis de Montcalm, 1712-59, (Fr.) headed troops in Canada, French and Indian War; defeated at Quebec, 1759.

Bernard Law Montgomery, 1887-1976, (Br.) stopped German offensive at Alamein, 1942, WWII; helped plan Normandy invasion.

Daniel Morgan, 1736-1802, (U.S.) victorious at Cowpens, 1781, Amer. Rev.

Louis Mountbatten, 1900-79, (Br.) Supreme Allied Commander of SE Asia, 1943-46, WWII.

Joachim Murat, 1767-1815, (Fr.) led cavalry at Marengo, Austerlitz, and Jena, Napoleonic Wars.

Horatio Nelson, 1758-1805, (Br.) naval commander; destroyed French fleet at Trafalgar.

Michel Ney, 1769-1815, (Fr.) commanded forces in Switz., Austria, Russ., Napoleonic Wars; defeated at Waterloo.

Chester Nimitz, 1885-1966, (U.S.) cmdr. of naval forces in Pacific in WWII.

George S. Patton, 1885-1945, (U.S.) led assault on Sicily, 1943, Third Army invasion of Europe, WWII.

Oliver Perry, 1785-1819, (U.S.) won Battle of Lake Erie in War of 1812.

John Pershing, 1860-1948, (U.S.) commanded Mexican border campaign, 1916; Amer. Expeditionary Force, WWI.

Henri Philippe Pétain, 1856-1951, (Fr.) defended Verdun, 1916; headed Vichy government in WWII.

George E. Pickett, 1825-75, (U.S.) Confed. general famed for "charge" at Gettysburg, Civil War.

Charles Portal, 1893-1971, (Br.) chief of staff, Royal Air Force, 1940-45; led in Battle of Britain.

Manfred Frieherr von Richthofen (Red Baron), 1892-1918, (Ger.) WWI flying ace, led elite fighter squadron.

Hyman Rickover, 1900-86, (U.S.) father of nuclear navy.

Matthew Bunker Ridgway, 1895-1993, (U.S.) commanded Allied ground forces in Korean War.

Erwin Rommel, 1891-1944, (Ger.) headed Afrika Korps, WWII.

Gerd von Rundstedt, 1875-1953, (Ger.) supreme cmdr. in West, 1942-45, WWII.

Saladin, 1138-93, (Kurdish Muslim) recaptured Jerusalem from Crusaders.

Aleksandr Samsonov, 1859-1914, (Russ.) led invasion of E Prussia, WWI; defeated at Tannenberg, 1914.

Antonio Lopez de Santa Anna, 1794-1876, (Mex.) defeated Texans at the Alamo; defeated in Mexican War.

Maurice, Count of Saxe, 1696-1750, (Fr.) general, noted tactician; War of Austrian Succession, War of Pol. Succession.

Scipio Africanus the Elder, 234?-183 BCE, (Rom.) hero of 2nd Punic War; defeated Hannibal, invaded N Africa.

Winfield Scott, 1786-1866, (U.S.) hero of War of 1812; headed forces in Mexican War, took Mexico City.

Philip Sheridan, 1831-88, (U.S.) Union cavalry officer; headed Army of the Shenandoah, 1864-65, Civil War.

William T. Sherman, 1820-91, (U.S.) Union general; sacked Atlanta during "march to the sea," 1864, Civil War.

Carl Spaatz, 1891-1974, (U.S.) directed strategic bombing against Germany, later Japan, in WWII.

Raymond Spruance, 1886-1969, (U.S.) victorious at Midway Island, 1942, WWII.

Joseph W. Stilwell, 1883-1946, (U.S.) headed forces in the China, Burma, India theater in WWII.

J.E.B. Stuart, 1833-64, (U.S.) Confed. cavalry commander, Civil War.

Sun Tzu, 6th? cent. BCE, (China) general; author of *The Art of War*.

Aleksandr Suvorov, 1729-1800, (Russ.) commanded Allied Russian and Austrian armies, Russo-Turkish War.

Tamerlane, 1336-1405, (Turkoman Mongol) conqueror; established empire from India to Mediterranean Sea.

George H. Thomas, 1816-70, (U.S.) saved Union army at Chattanooga, 1863; won at Nashville, 1864, Civil War.

Semyon Timoshenko, 1895-1970, (USSR) defended Moscow, Stalingrad, WWII; led winter offensive, 1942-43.

Alfred von Tirpitz, 1849-1930, (Ger.) responsible for submarine blockade in WWI.

Henri de la Tour d'Auvergne, Viscount of Turenne, 1611-75, (Fr.) marshal; Thirty Years' War, Fronde, War of Devolution.

Sebastien Le Prestre de Vauban, 1633-1707, (Fr.) innovative military engineer, theorist.

Jonathan M. Wainwright, 1883-1953, (U.S.) forced to surrender on Corregidor, Philippines, 1942, WWII.

George Washington, 1732-99, (U.S.) led Continental army, 1775-83, Amer. Rev.

Archibald Wavell, 1883-1950, (Br.) commanded forces in N and E Africa, SE Asia in WWII.

Anthony Wayne, 1745-96, (U.S.) captured Stony Point, NY, 1779, Amer. Rev.

Duke of Wellington, 1769-1852, (Br.) defeated Napoleon at Waterloo, 1815.

William Westmoreland, 1914-2005, (U.S.) commanded forces in Vietnam, 1964-68.

William I (The Conqueror), 1027-87, (Br.) victor, Battle of Hastings, 1066; became first Norman king of England.

James Wolfe, 1727-59, (Br.) captured Quebec from French, 1759, French and Indian War.

Isoroku Yamamoto, 1884-1943, (Jpn.) cmdr. in chief of Japanese fleet, naval planner before and during WWII.

Georgi Zhukov, 1895-1974, (Russ.) defended Moscow, 1941; led assault on Berlin, 1945, WWII.

Philosophers and Religious Figures of the Past

Excludes most biblical figures and popes (see Religion). For Greeks and Romans, see also Historical Figures chapter.

Lyman Abbott, 1835-1922, (U.S.) clergyman, reformer; advocate of Christian Socialism.

Pierre Abelard, 1079-1142, (Fr.) philosopher, theologian, teacher; used dialectic method to support Christian beliefs.

Felix Adler, 1851-1933, (U.S.) German-born founder of the Ethical Culture Soc.

Mortimer Adler, 1902-2001, (U.S.) philosopher; helped create "Great Books" program.

(St.) Anselm, c. 1033-1109, (It.) philosopher-theologian, church leader; "ontological argument" for God's existence.

(St.) Thomas Aquinas, 1225-74, (It.) preeminent medieval philosopher-theologian; *Summa Theologica*.

Aristotle, 384-322 BCE, (Gr.) pioneering wide-ranging philosopher, logician, ethician, naturalist.

(St.) Augustine, 354-430, (N Africa) philosopher, theologian, bishop; *Confessions*, *City of God*, *On the Trinity*.

J. L. Austin, 1911-60, (Br.) ordinary-language philosopher.

Averroes (Ibn Rushd), 1126-98, (Sp.) Islamic philosopher, physician.

Avicenna (Ibn Sina), 980-1037, (Iran) Islamic philosopher, scientist.

A(lfred) J(ules) Ayer, 1910-89, (Br.) philosopher, logical positivist; *Language, Truth, and Logic*.

Roger Bacon, c. 1214-94, (Eng.) philosopher, scientist.

Bahá'u'lláh (Mirza Husayn Ali), 1817-92, (Pers.) founder of Bahá'í faith.

Karl Barth, 1886-1968, (Switz.) theologian; a leading force in 20th-cent. Protestantism.

Thomas à Becket, 1118-70, (Eng.) archbishop of Canterbury; opposed Henry II, murdered by King's men.

(St.) Benedict, c. 480-547, (It.) founded the Benedictines.

Jeremy Bentham, 1748-1832, (Br.) philosopher, reformer; enunciated utilitarianism.

Henri Bergson, 1859-1941, (Fr.) philosopher of evolution.

George Berkeley, 1685-1753, (Ire.) idealist philosopher, bishop.

John Biddle, 1615-62, (Eng.) founder of English Unitarianism.

Jakob Boehme, 1575-1624, (Ger.) theosophist, mystic.

Dietrich Bonhoeffer, 1906-45, (Ger.) Lutheran theologian, pastor; executed as opponent of Nazis.

William Brewster, 1567-1644, (Eng.) led Pilgrims.

Emil Brunner, 1889-1966, (Switz.) Protestant theologian.

Giordano Bruno, 1548-1600, (It.) philosopher, pantheist.

Martin Buber, 1878-1965, (Ger.) Jewish philosopher, theologian; *I and Thou*.

Buddha (Siddhartha Gautama), c. 563-c. 483 BCE, (India) philosopher; founded Buddhism.

John Calvin, 1509-64, (Fr.) theologian; a key figure in the Protestant Reformation.

Rudolph Carnap, 1891-1970, (U.S.) German-born analytic philosopher; a founder of logical positivism.

William Ellery Channing, 1780-1842, (U.S.) clergyman; early spokesman for Unitarianism.

Auguste Comte, 1798-1857, (Fr.) philosopher; originated positivism.

Confucius, 551-479 BCE, (China) founder of Confucianism.

John Cotton, 1584-1652, (Eng.) Puritan theologian.

Thomas Cranmer, 1489-1556, (Eng.) Anglican churchman; wrote much of *Book of Common Prayer*.

Jacques Derrida, 1930-2004, (Fr.) deconstructionist philosopher.

René Descartes, 1596-1650, (Fr.) philosopher, mathematician; "father of modern philosophy"; *Discourse on Method*, *Meditations on First Philosophy*.

John Dewey, 1859-1952, (U.S.) philosopher, educator; instrumentalist theory of knowledge, progressive education.

Denis Diderot, 1713-84, (Fr.) philosopher, encyclopedist.

John Duns Scotus, c. 1266-1308, (Sc.) Franciscan philosopher, theologian.

Mary Baker Eddy, 1821-1910, (U.S.) founder of Christian Science; *Science and Health*.

Jonathan Edwards, 1703-58, (U.S.) preacher, theologian; "Sinners in the Hands of an Angry God."

(Desiderius) Erasmus, c. 1466-1536, (Neth.) Renaissance humanist; *On the Freedom of the Will*.

Jerry Falwell, 1933-2007, (U.S.) TV evangelist, religious commentator.

Johann Fichte, 1762-1814, (Ger.) idealist philosopher.

Michel Foucault, 1926-84, (Fr.) structuralist philosopher, historian.

George Fox, 1624-91, (Br.) founder of Society of Friends (Quakers).

(St.) Francis of Assisi, 1182-1226, (It.) espoused voluntary poverty, founded Franciscans.

al-Ghazali, 1058-1111, ([now] Iran) Islamic philosopher.

Billy James Hargis, 1925-2004, (U.S.) anti-Communist televangelist; founder of the Church of the Christian Crusade.

Georg W. F. Hegel, 1770-1831, (Ger.) idealist philosopher; *Phenomenology of Mind*.

Martin Heidegger, 1889-1976, (Ger.) existentialist philosopher; affected many fields; *Being and Time*.

Johann G. Herder, 1744-1803, (Ger.) philosopher, cultural historian; a founder of German Romanticism.

Thomas Hobbes, 1588-1679, (Eng.) philosopher, political theorist; *Leviathan*.

David Hume, 1711-76, (Scot.) empiricist philosopher; *Enquiry Concerning Human Understanding*.

Jan Hus, 1369-1415, (Czech.) religious reformer.

Edmund Husserl, 1859-1938, (Ger.) philosopher; founded the phenomenological movement.

Thomas Huxley, 1825-95, (Br.) philosopher, educator.

William Ralph Inge, 1860-1954, (Br.) theologian; explored mystic aspects of Christianity.

William James, 1842-1910, (U.S.) philosopher, psychologist, pragmatist; studied religious experience.

Karl Jaspers, 1883-1969, (Ger.) existentialist philosopher.

Joan of Arc, 1412-31, (Fr.) national heroine, a patron saint of France; key figure in the Hundred Years' War.

Immanuel Kant, 1724-1804, (Ger.) philosopher; founder of modern critical philosophy; *Critique of Pure Reason.*

Thomas à Kempis, c. 1380-1471, (Ger.) monk, devotional writer; *Imitation of Christ* attributed to him.

Soren Kierkegaard, 1813-55, (Den.) religious philosopher, pre-existentialist; *Either/Or, The Sickness Unto Death.*

John Knox, 1505-72, (Scot.) leader of Protestant Reformation in Scotland.

Lao-Tzu, 604-531 BCE, (China) philosopher; considered the founder of the Taoist religion.

Gottfried von Leibniz, 1646-1716, (Ger.) rationalistic philosopher, logician, mathematician.

John Locke, 1632-1704, (Eng.) political theorist, empiricist philosopher; *Essay Concerning Human Understanding.*

(St.) Ignatius Loyola, 1491-1556, (Sp.) founder of the Jesuits; *Spiritual Exercises.*

Martin Luther, 1483-1546, (Ger.) leader of the Protestant Reformation; founded Lutheran church.

Jean-Francois Lyotard, 1924-98, (Fr.) postmodern philosopher, lecturer; *The Post-Modern Condition.*

Maimonides, 1135-1204, (Sp.) major Jewish philosopher.

Gabriel Marcel, 1889-1973, (Fr.) Rom. Cath. existentialist philosopher, dramatist.

Jacques Maritain, 1882-1973, (Fr.) neo-Thomist philosopher.

Cotton Mather, 1663-1728, (U.S.) defender of orthodox Puritanism; founded Yale, 1701.

Aimee Semple McPherson, 1890-1944, (Can.) Pentecostal evangelist.

Philipp Melanchthon, 1497-1560, (Ger.) theologian, humanist; an important voice in the Reformation.

Maurice Merleau-Ponty, 1908-61, (Fr.) existentialist philosopher; *Phenomenology of Perception.*

Thomas Merton, 1915-68, (U.S.) Trappist monk, spiritual writer; *The Seven Storey Mountain.*

Dwight Moody, 1837-99, (U.S.) evangelist.

Rev. Sun Myung Moon, 1920-2012, (N. Kor.) Unification Church founder.

G(eorge) E(dward) Moore, 1873-1958, (Br.) philosopher; *Principia Ethica,* "A Defense of Common Sense."

Muhammad, c. 570-632, (Arab.) prophet of Islam.

Elijah Muhammad, 1897-1975, (U.S.) founder of Black Muslim group, Nation of Islam.

Heinrich Muhlenberg, 1711-87, (Ger.) organized the Lutheran Church in America.

John H. Newman, 1801-90, (Br.) Rom. Cath. convert, cardinal; led Oxford Movement; *Apologia pro Vita Sua.*

Reinhold Niebuhr, 1892-1971, (U.S.) Protestant theologian.

Richard Niebuhr, 1894-1962, (U.S.) Protestant theologian.

Friedrich Nietzsche, 1844-1900, (Ger.) philosopher; *The Birth of Tragedy, Beyond Good and Evil, Thus Spake Zarathustra.*

Robert Nozick, 1938-2002, (U.S.) political philosopher; *Anarchy, State, and Utopia.*

Blaise Pascal, 1623-62, (Fr.) philosopher, mathematician; *Pensées.*

(St.) Patrick, c. 389-c. 461, (Br.) brought Christianity to Ireland.

Norman Vincent Peale, 1898-1993, (U.S.) minister, author; *The Power of Positive Thinking.*

C(harles) S. Peirce, 1839-1914, (U.S.) philosopher, logician; originated concept of pragmatism, 1878.

Plato, c. 428-347 BCE, (Gr.) philosopher; wrote Socratic dialogues; argued for immortality of soul, indep. reality of ideas or forms; *Republic, Meno, Phaedo, Apology.*

Plotinus, 205-70, (Rom.) a founder of neo-Platonism; *Enneads.*

W(illard) V(an) O(rman) Quine, 1908-2001, (U.S.) philosopher, logician; "On What There Is."

John Rawls, 1922-2002, (U.S.) political philosopher; *A Theory of Justice.*

Oral Roberts, 1918-2009, (U.S.) televangelist, university founder.

Moishe Rosen, 1932-2010, (U.S.) Jews for Jesus founder.

Josiah Royce, 1855-1916, (U.S.) idealist philosopher.

Bertrand Russell, 1872-1970, (Br.) philosopher, logician; one of the founders of modern logic; a prolific popular writer.

Charles T. Russell, 1852-1916, (U.S.) founder of Jehovah's Witnesses.

Gilbert Ryle, 1900-76, (Br.) analytic philosopher; *The Concept of Mind.*

George Santayana, 1863-1952, (U.S.) philosopher, writer, critic; *The Sense of Beauty, The Realms of Being.*

Jean-Paul Sartre, 1905-80, (Fr.) philosopher, novelist, playwright; *Nausea, No Exit, Being and Nothingness.*

Friedrich von Schelling, 1775-1854, (Ger.) philosopher of romantic movement.

Friedrich Schleiermacher, 1768-1834, (Ger.) theologian; a founder of modern Protestant theology.

Arthur Schopenhauer, 1788-1860, (Ger.) philosopher; *The World as Will and Idea.*

Albert Schweitzer, 1875-1965, (Ger.) theologian, social philosopher, medical missionary.

Joseph Smith, 1805-44, (U.S.) founded Latter-Day Saints (Mormon) movement, 1830.

Socrates, 469-399 BCE, (Gr.) philosopher immortalized by Plato.

Herbert Spencer, 1820-1903, (Br.) philosopher of evolution.

Herbert Spiegel, 1914-2009, (U.S.) psychiatrist who popularized hypnosis.

Baruch de Spinoza, 1632-77, (Neth.) rationalist philosopher; *Ethics.*

John Stott, 1921-2011, (Br.) evangelical Anglican cleric.

Billy Sunday, 1862-1935, (U.S.) evangelist.

Emanuel Swedenborg, 1688-1772, (Swed.) philosopher, mystic; *Principia.*

Pierre Teilhard de Chardin, 1881-1955, (Fr.) Jesuit priest, paleontologist, philosopher-theologian; *The Divine Milieu.*

Daisetz Teitaro Suzuki, 1870-1966, (Jpn.) Buddhist scholar.

(St.) Therese of Lisieux, 1873-97, (Fr.) Carmelite nun ("Little Flower"), revered for everyday sanctity; *The Story of a Soul.*

Paul Tillich, 1886-1965, (U.S.) German-born philosopher, theologian; brought depth psychology to Protestantism.

John Wesley, 1703-91, (Br.) theologian, evangelist; founded Methodism.

Alfred North Whitehead, 1861-1947, (Br.) philosopher, mathematician; *Process and Reality.*

William of Occam, c. 1285-c. 1349, (Eng.) medieval scholastic philosopher, nominalist.

Roger Williams, c. 1603-83, (U.S.) clergyman; championed religious freedom and separation of church and state.

Ludwig Wittgenstein, 1889-1951, (Austria) philosopher; major influence on contemporary language philosophy; *Tractatus Logico-Philosophicus, Philosophical Investigations.*

John Woolman, 1720-72, (U.S.) Quaker social reformer, abolitionist, writer; *The Journal.*

John Wycliffe, 1320-84, (Eng.) theologian, reformer.

(St.) Francis Xavier, 1506-52, (Sp.) Jesuit missionary; "Apostle of the Indies."

Brigham Young, 1801-77, (U.S.) Mormon leader after Joseph Smith's assassination; colonized Utah.

Huldrych Zwingli, 1484-1531, (Switz.) theologian; led Swiss Protestant Reformation.

Political Leaders of the Past

U.S. presidents, vice presidents, Supreme Court justices, and signers of the Declaration of Independence listed elsewhere.

Abu Bakr, 573-634, (Arab.) Muslim leader, first caliph, chosen successor to Muhammad.

Dean Acheson, 1893-1971, (U.S.) sec. of state; architect of Cold War foreign policy.

Samuel Adams, 1722-1803, (U.S.) patriot; Boston Tea Party firebrand.

Konrad Adenauer, 1876-1967, (Ger.) first West German chancellor.

Emilio Aguinaldo, 1869-1964, (Philip.) revolutionary; fought against Spain and the U.S.

Corazon Aquino, 1933-2009, (Philip.) pres. of the Philippines, 1986-92.

Akbar, 1542-1605, Mogul emperor of India.

Carl Albert, 1908-2000, (U.S.) House rep. (D, OK), Speaker, 1971-76.

Salvador Allende Gossens, 1908-73, (Chile) Marxist pres., 1970-73; ousted and died in coup.

Idi Amin, 1925-2003, (Uganda) Ugandan ruler, 1971-79; blamed for hundreds of thousands of deaths.

Yasir Arafat, 1929-2004, (Egypt) leader of the Palestine Liberation Organization (PLO).

Herbert H. Asquith, 1852-1928, (Br.) Liberal prime min.; instituted major social reforms.

Hafez al Assad, 1930-2000, (Syr.) Syrian ruler from 1970.

Atahualpa, 1500?-1533, (Inca) ruling chief of Peru.

Kemal Ataturk, 1881-1938, (Turk.) founded modern Turkey.

Clement Attlee, 1883-1967, (Br.) Labour party leader, prime min.; enacted natl.

health care system, nationalized many industries.

Stephen F. Austin, 1793-1836, (U.S.) led Texas colonization.

Mikhail Bakunin, 1814-76, (Russ.) revolutionary; leading exponent of anarchism.

Arthur J. Balfour, 1848-1930, (Br.) foreign sec. under Lloyd George; issued Balfour Declaration backing Zionism.

Bernard M. Baruch, 1870-1965, (U.S.) financier, govt. adviser.

Fulgencio Batista y Zaldívar, 1901-73, (Cub.) Cuban pres., 1940-44, 1952-59; overthrown by Castro.

Lord Beaverbrook, 1879-1964, (Br.) financier, statesman, newspaper owner.

Menachem Begin, 1913-92, (Isr.) Israeli prime min.; shared 1978 Nobel Peace Prize.

Ahmed Ben Bella, 1918-2012, (Alg.) first Algerian pres., 1963-65.

Eduard Benes, 1884-1948, (Czech.) pres. during interwar and post-WWII eras.

David Ben-Gurion, 1886-1973, (Isr.) first prime min. of Israel, 1948-53, 1955-63.

Thomas Hart Benton, 1782-1858, (U.S.) MO senator; championed agrarian interests and westward expansion.

Aneurin Bevan, 1897-1960, (Br.) Labour party leader.

Ernest Bevin, 1881-1951, (Br.) Labour party leader, foreign minister; helped lay foundation for NATO.

Benazir Bhutto, 1953-2007, (Pak.) former prime minister of Pakistan.

Otto von Bismarck, 1815-98, (Ger.) statesman known as the Iron Chancellor; uniter of Germany, 1870.

James G. Blaine, 1830-93, (U.S.) Republican politician, diplomat; influential in Pan-American movement.

Léon Blum, 1872-1950, (Fr.) socialist leader, writer; headed first Popular Front government.

William E. Borah, 1865-1940, (U.S.) isolationist senator; helped block U.S. membership in League of Nations.

Cesare Borgia, 1476-1507, (It.) soldier, politician; an outstanding figure of the Italian Renaissance.

P. W. Botha, 1916-2006, (S. Africa) S. African president, prime minister.

Tom Bradley, 1917-98, (U.S.) first African American mayor of L.A.

Willy Brandt, 1913-92, (Ger.) statesman, chancellor of West Germany, 1969-74; promoted East/West peace, *Ostpolitik*.

Leonid Brezhnev, 1906-82, (USSR) Soviet leader, 1964-82.

Aristide Briand, 1862-1932, (Fr.) foreign min.; chief architect of Locarno Pact and anti-war Kellogg-Briand Pact.

William Jennings Bryan, 1860-1925, (U.S.) Democratic, populist leader, orator; 3 times lost race for presidency.

Ralph Bunche, 1904-71, (U.S.) first black person to win the Nobel Peace Prize, 1950; undersecretary of the UN, 1950.

Robert Byrd, 1917-2010, (U.S.) longest serving senator (D, WV).

John C. Calhoun, 1782-1850, (U.S.) political leader; champion of states' rights and a symbol of the Old South.

James Callaghan (Baron Callaghan), 1912-2005, (Br.) Labour party politician, prime min., 1976-79.

Robert Castlereagh, 1769-1822, (Br.) foreign sec.; guided Grand Alliance against Napoleon.

Camillo Benso Cavour, 1810-61, (It.) statesman; largely responsible for uniting Italy under the House of Savoy.

Nicolae Ceausescu, 1918-89, (Roman.) Communist leader, head of state, 1967-89; executed.

Austen Chamberlain, 1863-1937, (Br.) statesman; helped finalize Locarno Treaties, both 1925.

Neville Chamberlain, 1869-1940, (Br.) Conservative prime min. whose appeasement of Hitler led to Munich Pact.

Chiang Kai-shek, 1887-1975, (China) Nationalist Chinese pres. whose government was driven from mainland to Taiwan.

Madame Chiang Kai-shek (Mayling Soong), 1898-2003, (China) highly influential wife of Nationalist Chinese leader Chiang Kai-shek.

Shirley Chisholm, 1924-2005, (U.S.) first black woman elected to U.S. House (1968, D, NY); pres. contender, 1972.

Warren Christopher, 1925-2011, (U.S.) secretary of state, diplomat.

Winston Churchill, 1874-1965, (Br.) prime min., soldier, author; guided Britain through WWII.

Galeazzo Ciano, 1903-44, (It.) Fascist foreign minister; helped create Rome-Berlin Axis; executed by Benito Mussolini.

Henry Clay, 1777-1852, (U.S.) "The Great Compromiser"; one of the most influential pre-Civil War political leaders.

Georges Clemenceau, 1841-1929, (Fr.) twice prem.; Woodrow Wilson's antagonist at Paris Peace Conference after WWI.

DeWitt Clinton, 1769-1828, (U.S.) political leader; responsible for promoting the Erie Canal.

Robert Clive, 1725-74, (Br.) first administrator of Bengal; laid foundation for British Empire in India.

Jean Baptiste Colbert, 1619-83, (Fr.) statesman; influential under Louis XIV; created the French navy.

Bettino Craxi, 1934-2000, (It.) Italy's first post-WWII Socialist premier.

David Crockett, 1786-1836, (U.S.) frontiersman, congressman; died defending the Alamo.

Oliver Cromwell, 1599-1658, (Br.) Lord Protector of England; led parliamentary forces during Civil War.

Curzon of Kedleston, 1859-1925, (Br.) viceroy of India, foreign sec.; major force in post-WWI world.

Édouard Daladier, 1884-1970, (Fr.) Radical Socialist politician, arrested by Vichy, interned by Germans until 1945.

Richard J. Daley, 1902-76, (U.S.) Chicago mayor.

Georges Danton, 1759-94, (Fr.) leading French Rev. figure.

Jefferson Davis, 1808-89, (U.S.) pres. of the Confederacy.

Charles G. Dawes, 1865-1951, (U.S.) statesman, banker; advanced plan to stabilize post-WWI German finances.

William L. Dawson, 1886-1970, (U.S.) IL congressman; first black chairman of a major U.S. House committee.

Alcide De Gasperi, 1881-1954, (It.) prime min.; founder of Christian Democratic party.

Charles De Gaulle, 1890-1970, (Fr.) general, statesman; first pres. of the Fifth Republic.

Deng Xiaoping, 1904-97, (China) "paramount leader" of China; backed economic modernization.

Eamon De Valera, 1882-1975, (Ire.-U.S.) statesman; led fight for Irish independence.

Thomas E. Dewey, 1902-71, (U.S.) NY governor (R); twice lost in try for presidency.

Ngo Dinh Diem, 1901-63, (Viet.) South Vietnamese pres.; assassinated in government takeover.

Everett M. Dirksen, 1896-1969, (U.S.) Senate Republican minority leader, orator.

Benjamin Disraeli, 1804-81, (Br.) prime min.; considered founder of modern Conservative party.

Anatoly Dobrynin, 1919-2010, (Russ.) diplomat and Soviet amb. to U.S. (1962-86).

Engelbert Dollfuss, 1892-1934, (Austria) chancellor; assassinated by Austrian Nazis.

Andrea Doria, 1466-1560, (It.) Genoese admiral, statesman; called "Father of Peace" and "Liberator of Genoa."

Stephen A. Douglas, 1813-61, (U.S.) Democratic leader, orator; ran against Lincoln for IL sen. seat, presidency.

Alexander Dubcek, 1921-92, (Czech.) statesman whose attempted liberalization was crushed, 1968.

John Foster Dulles, 1888-1959, (U.S.) sec. of state under Eisenhower; Cold War policy maker.

Lawrence Eagleburger, 1930-2011, (U.S.) diplomat and foreign policy advisor.

Abba Eban, 1915-2002, (Isr.) diplomat; foreign min., 1966-74.

Friedrich Ebert, 1871-1925, (Ger.) Social Democratic movement leader; 1st pres., Weimar Republic, 1919-25.

Sir Anthony Eden, 1897-1977, (Br.) foreign sec., prime min. during Suez invasion of 1956.

Ludwig Erhard, 1897-1977, (Ger.) economist, West German chancellor; led nation's economic rise after WWII.

King Fahd, 1923-2005, (Saudi Arabia) monarch from 1982 but inactive after 1995 stroke; encouraged U.S. relations.

Geraldine Ferraro, 1935-2011 (U.S.) former U.S. rep. (D, NY), vice-pres. nominee.

Joao Baptista de Figueiredo, 1918-99, (Braz.) president of Brazil; restored the nation's democracy.

Hamilton Fish, 1808-93, (U.S.) sec. of state; successfully mediated disputes with Great Britain, Latin America.

James V. Forrestal, 1892-1949, (U.S.) sec. of navy, first sec. of defense.

Francisco Franco, 1892-1975, (Sp.) leader of rebel forces during Spanish Civil War, longtime ruler of Spain.

Benjamin Franklin, 1706-90, (U.S.) printer, publisher, author, inventor, scientist, diplomat.

Louis de Frontenac, 1620-98, (Fr.) governor of New France (Canada); encouraged explorations, fought Iroquois.

J. William Fulbright, 1905-95, (U.S.) senator (D, AR); leading figure in U.S. foreign policy during Cold War years.

Hugh Gaitskell, 1906-63, (Br.) Labour party leader; major force in reversing its stand for unilateral disarmament.

Albert Gallatin, 1761-1849, (U.S.) sec. of treasury; instrumental in negotiating end of War of 1812.

Léon Gambetta, 1838-82, (Fr.) statesman, politician; one of the founders of the Third Republic.

Indira Gandhi, 1917-84, (In.) daughter of Jawaharlal Nehru; prime min. of India, 1966-77, 1980-84; assassinated.

Mohandas K. Gandhi, 1869-1948, (In.) political leader, ascetic; led movement against British rule; assassinated.

Giuseppe Garibaldi, 1807-82, (It.) patriot, soldier; a leader in the Risorgimento, Italian unification movement.

William E. Gladstone, 1809-98, (Br.) prime min. 4 times; dominant force of Liberal party 1868-94.

Paul Joseph Goebbels, 1897-1945, (Ger.) Nazi propagandist; master of mass psychology.

Barry Goldwater, 1909-98, (U.S.) conservative U.S. senator (AZ), 1964 Republican pres. nominee.

Klement Gottwald, 1896-1953, (Czech.) Communist leader; ushered Communism into his country.

Alexander Hamilton, 1755-1804, (U.S.) first treasury sec.; champion of strong central government.

Dag Hammarskjold, 1905-61, (Swed.) statesman; UN sec.-general.

King Hassan II, 1929-99, (Moroc.) ruler of Morocco, 1962-99.

Vaclav Havel, 1936-2011, (Czech.) first president of Czech Republic, 1989-92.

John Hay, 1838-1905, (U.S.) sec. of state; primarily associated with Open Door Policy toward China.

Sir Edward Heath, 1916-2005, (Br.) Conservative prime min., 1970-74; promoted European unity.

Jesse Helms, 1921-2008, (U.S.) conservative senator (R, NC).

Patrick Henry, 1736-99, (U.S.) major Revolutionary War figure, orator.

Édouard Herriot, 1872-1957, (Fr.) Radical Socialist leader; twice prem., pres. of National Assembly.

Theodor Herzl, 1860-1904, (Hung.) founded modern Zionism.

Heinrich Himmler, 1900-45, (Ger.) head of Nazi SS and Gestapo.

Paul von Hindenburg, 1847-1934, (Ger.) field marshal, WWI; 2nd pres. of Weimar Republic, 1925-34.

Adolf Hitler, 1889-1945, (Ger.) dictator; built Nazism, launched WWII, presided over the Holocaust.

Ho Chi Minh, 1890-1969, (Viet.) N. Vietnamese pres., Vietnamese Communist leader.

Harry L. Hopkins, 1890-1946, (U.S.) New Deal administrator; closest adviser to Franklin D. Roosevelt during WWII.

Edward M. House, 1858-1938, (U.S.) diplomat; confidential adviser to Woodrow Wilson.

Samuel Houston, 1793-1863, (U.S.) leader of struggle for Texas independence.

Cordell Hull, 1871-1955, (U.S.) sec. of state, 1933-44; initiated reciprocal trade to lower tariffs, helped organize UN.

Hubert H. Humphrey, 1911-78, (U.S.) senator (D, MN), vice pres., pres. candidate.

King Hussein, 1935-99, (Jordan) peacemaker; ruler of Jordan, 1952-99.

Saddam Hussein, 1937-2006, (Iraq) Iraqi ruler; put to death for crimes against humanity.

Muhammad Ali Jinnah, 1876-1948, (Pak.) founder, first gov.-gen. of Pakistan.

Barbara Jordan, 1936-96, (U.S.) congresswoman, orator, educator; first black woman to win a seat in the TX senate, 1966.

Benito Juarez, 1806-72, (Mex.) rallied his country against foreign threats; sought to create democratic, federal republic.

Constantine Karamanlis, 1907-98, (Gr.) Greek prime min.; restored democracy, later president.

Frank B. Kellogg, 1856-1937, (U.S.) sec. of state; negotiated Kellogg-Briand Pact to outlaw war.

Jack Kemp, 1935-2009, (U.S.) sec. of HUD, U.S. rep. (R, NY), football player.

Edward M. Kennedy, 1932-2009, (U.S.) senator (D, MA); championed progressive causes.

Robert F. Kennedy, 1925-68, (U.S.) attorney general, sen. (D, NY); assassinated while seeking presidency.

Aleksandr Kerensky, 1881-1970, (Russ.) headed provisional government after Feb. 1917 revolution.

Ayatollah Ruhollah Khomeini, 1900-89, (Iran), religious-political leader; spearheaded overthrow of Shah, 1979.

Nikita Khrushchev, 1894-1971, (USSR) prem., first sec. of Communist party; initiated de-Stalinization.

Kim Dae Jung, 1925-2009, (Korea) S. Korean dissident, opposition leader, pres.; 2000 Nobel Peace Prize winner.

Kim Jong Il, 1942-2011, (Korea) N. Korean dictator, 1994-2011.

Kim Il Sung, 1912-94, (Korea) N. Korean dictator, 1948-94.

Lajos Kossuth, 1802-94, (Hung.) principal figure in 1848 Hungarian revolution.

Pyotr Kropotkin, 1842-1921, (Russ.) anarchist; championed the peasants but opposed Bolshevism.

Kublai Khan, c. 1215-94, (Mongol) emperor; founder of Yüan dynasty in China.

Béla Kun, 1886-c. 1939, (Hung.) member of 3rd Communist International; tried to foment worldwide revolution.

Robert M. LaFollette, 1855-1925, (U.S.) WI public official; leader of progressive movement.

Fiorello La Guardia, 1882-1947, (U.S.) New York City reform mayor.

Pierre Laval, 1883-1945, (Fr.) politician, Vichy foreign min.; executed for treason.

Andrew Bonar Law, 1858-1923, (Br.) Conservative party politician; led opposition to Irish home rule.

Vladimir Ilyich Lenin (Ulyanov), 1870-1924, (Russ.) revolutionary; founded Bolshevism; Soviet leader, 1917-24.

Ferdinand de Lesseps, 1805-94, (Fr.) diplomat, engineer; conceived idea of Suez Canal.

Rene Levesque, 1922-87, (Can.) prem. of Quebec, 1976-85; led unsuccessful separatist campaign.

Trygve Lie, 1896-1968, (Nor.) first UN sec.-gen.

Maxim Litvinov, 1876-1951, (Pol.-Russ.) revolutionary, commissar of foreign affairs; favored cooperation with West.

Liu Shaoqi, c. 1898-1969, (China) Communist leader; fell from grace during Cultural Revolution.

David Lloyd George, 1863-1945, (Br.) Liberal party prime min.; laid foundations for modern welfare state.

Henry Cabot Lodge, 1850-1924, (U.S.) Republican senator; led opposition to participation in League of Nations.

Huey P. Long, 1893-1935, (U.S.) Louisiana political demagogue, governor, U.S. senator; assassinated.

Rosa Luxemburg, 1871-1919, (Ger.) revolutionary; leader of the German Social Democratic party and Spartacus party.

J. Ramsay MacDonald, 1866-1937, (Br.) first Labour party prime min. of Great Britain.

Harold Macmillan, 1895-1986, (Br.) prime min. of Great Britain, 1957-63.

Makarios III, 1913-77, (Cyprus) Greek Orthodox archbishop; first pres. of Cyprus.

Wilma Mankiller, 1945-2010, (U.S.) first female Chief of the Cherokee Nation.

Mao Zedong, 1893-1976, (China) chief Chinese Marxist theorist, revolutionary, political leader; led revolution establishing his nation as Communist state.

Jean Paul Marat, 1743-93, (Fr.) revolutionary, politician; identified with radical Jacobins; assassinated.

Thurgood Marshall, 1908-93, (U.S.) first black U.S. solicitor general, 1965; first black justice of U.S. Supreme Court, 1967-91.

José Martí, 1853-95, (Cub.) patriot, poet; leader of Cuban struggle for independence.

Jan Masaryk, 1886-1948, (Czech.) foreign min.; died under mysterious circumstances, allegedly committed suicide following Communist coup.

Thomas G. Masaryk, 1850-1937, (Czech.) statesman, philosopher; first pres. of Czechoslovakia.

Jules Mazarin, 1602-61, (Fr.) cardinal, statesman; prime min. under Louis XIII and queen regent Anne of Austria.

Giuseppe Mazzini, 1805-72, (It.) reformer dedicated to Risorgimento movement for renewal of Italy.

Tom Mboya, 1930-69, (Kenya) political leader; instrumental in securing independence for Kenya.

Eugene McCarthy, 1916-2005, (U.S.) political leader, author; 1968 Dem. presidential contender.

Joseph R. McCarthy, 1908-57, (U.S.) senator (R, WI); extremist in searching out alleged Communists and pro-Communists.

Cosimo I de' Medici, 1519-74, (It.) Duke of Florence, grand duke of Tuscany.

Lorenzo de' Medici, the Magnificent, 1449-92, (It.) merchant prince; a towering figure in Italian Renaissance.

Catherine de Médicis, 1519-89, (Fr.) queen consort of Henry II, regent of France; influential in Catholic-Huguenot wars.

Golda Meir, 1898-1978, (Isr.) a founder of the state of Israel; prime min., 1969-74.

Klemens W. N. L. Metternich, 1773-1859, (Austria) statesman; arbiter of post-Napoleonic Europe.

Slobodan Milosevic, 1941-2006, (Serbia/Yugoslavia) former Yugoslav pres.; tried for war crimes.

François Mitterrand, 1916-96, (Fr.) pres. of France, 1981-95.

Mobutu Sese Seko, 1930-97, (Zaire) longtime ruler of Zaire (now Dem. Rep. of Congo), 1965-97; exiled after rebellion.

Guy Mollet, 1905-75, (Fr.) socialist politician, resistance leader.

Henry Morgenthau Jr., 1891-1967, (U.S.) sec. of treasury; fundraiser for New Deal and U.S. WWII activities.

Gouverneur Morris, 1752-1816, (U.S.) statesman, diplomat, financial expert; helped plan decimal coinage.

Daniel Patrick Moynihan, 1927-2003, (U.S.) senator (D, NY), diplomat, social scientist, author.

Benito Mussolini, 1883-1945, (It.) leader of the Italian fascist state; assassinated.

Imre Nagy, c. 1896-1958, (Hung.) Communist prem.; assassinated after Soviets crushed 1956 uprising.

Gamal Abdel Nasser, 1918-70, (Egypt) leader of Arab unification, 2nd Egyptian pres.

Jawaharlal Nehru, 1889-1964, (In.) prime min.; guided India through its early years of independence.

Kwame Nkrumah, 1909-72, (Ghana) 1st prime min., 1957-60; pres., 1960-66, of Ghana.

Frederick North, 1732-92, (Br.) prime min.; his inept policies led to loss of American colonies.

Julius K. Nyerere, 1922-99, (Tanz.) founding father; 1st pres., 1962-85, of Tanzania.

Daniel O'Connell, 1775-1847, (Ire.) nationalist political leader; known as The Liberator.

Omar, c. 581-644, Muslim leader; 2nd caliph, led Islam to become an imperial power.

Thomas P. (Tip) O'Neill Jr., 1912-94, (U.S.) U.S. rep. (D, MA), Speaker of the House, 1977-86.

Ignace Paderewski, 1860-1941, (Pol.) statesman, pianist, composer, briefly prime min.; ardent patriot.

Viscount Palmerston, 1784-1865, (Br.) Whig-Liberal prime min., foreign min.; embodied British nationalism.

Andreas George Papandreou, 1919-96, (Gr.) leftist politician; served twice as prem., 1981-89, 1993-96.

Georgios Papandreou, 1888-1968, (Gr.) Republican politician; served 3 times as prime min.

Franz von Papen, 1879-1969, (Ger.) politician; major role in overthrow of Weimar Republic and rise of Hitler.

Charles Stewart Parnell, 1846-1891, (Ire.) nationalist leader; "uncrowned king of Ireland."

Lester Pearson, 1897-1972, (Can.) diplomat, Liberal party leader, prime min.

Robert Peel, 1788-1850, (Br.) reformist prime min.; founder of Conservative party.

Frances Perkins, 1882-1965, (U.S.) first female cabinet member (sec. of labor).

Eva (Evita) Perón, 1919-52, (Arg.) highly influential 2nd wife of Juan Perón.

Juan Perón, 1895-1974, (Arg.) dynamic pres. of Argentina, 1946-55, 1973-74.

Joseph Pilsudski, 1867-1935, (Pol.) statesman; instrumental in reestablishing Polish state in the 20th cent.

Charles Pinckney, 1757-1824, (U.S.) founding father; his Pinckney plan largely incorporated into Constitution.

Christian Pineau, 1905-95, (Fr.) leader of French Resistance during WWII; French foreign min., 1956-58.

Augusto Pinochet (Ugarte), 1915-2006, (Chile) former Chilean ruler; indicted for human rights abuses while in office.

William Pitt the Elder, 1708-78, (Br.) statesman; the "Great Commoner," transformed Britain into imperial power.

William Pitt the Younger, 1759-1806, (Br.) prime min. during French Revolutionary wars.

Georgi Plekhanov, 1857-1918, (Russ.) revolutionary, social philosopher; called "father of Russian Marxism."

Raymond Poincaré, 1860-1934, (Fr.) 9th pres. of the Republic; advocated harsh punishment of Germany after WWI.

Pol Pot, 1925-98, (Camb.) leader of Khmer Rouge; ruled Cambodia, 1975-79; responsible for mass deaths.

Georges Pompidou, 1911-74, (Fr.) Gaullist political leader; pres., 1969-74.

Grigori Potemkin, 1739-91, (Russ.) field marshal; favorite of empress Catherine II.

Adam Clayton Powell Jr., 1908-72, (U.S.) civil rights leader; U.S. rep. (D, NY), 1945-69.

Muammar al-Qaddafi, 1942-2011, (Libya) Libyan ruler, 1969-2011.

Yitzhak Rabin, 1922-95, (Isr.) military, political leader; prime min. of Israel, 1974-77, 1992-95; assassinated.

Joseph H. Rainey, 1832-87, (U.S.) first black person elected to U.S. House (1869), from SC.

Edmund Randolph, 1753-1813, (U.S.) attorney; prominent in drafting, ratification of Constitution.

John Randolph, 1773-1833, (U.S.) Southern planter; strong advocate of states' rights.

Jeannette Rankin, 1880-1973, (U.S.) pacifist; first woman member of U.S. Congress (R, MT).

Walter Rathenau, 1867-1922, (Ger.) industrialist, statesman.

Sam Rayburn, 1882-1961, (U.S.) U.S. rep. (D, TX) for 47 years, House Speaker for 17.

Hiram R. Revels, 1822-1901, (U.S.) first African American U.S. senator; elected in MS, served 1870-71.

Paul Reynaud, 1878-1966, (Fr.) statesman; prem. in 1940 at time of France's defeat by Germany.

Syngman Rhee, 1875-1965, (Korea) first pres. of S. Korea.

Cecil Rhodes, 1853-1902, (Br.) imperialist, industrial magnate; established Rhodes scholarships in his will.

Ann Richards, 1933-2006, (U.S.) former TX gov.

Cardinal de Richelieu, 1585-1642, (Fr.) statesman, known as "red eminence"; chief minister to Louis XIII.

Maximilien Robespierre, 1758-94, (Fr.) leading figure in French Revolution and Reign of Terror.

Nelson Rockefeller, 1908-79, (U.S.) Republican governor of NY, 1959-73; U.S. vice pres., 1974-77.

Eleanor Roosevelt, 1884-1962, (U.S.) influential first lady, humanitarian, UN diplomat.

Elihu Root, 1845-1937, (U.S.) lawyer, statesman, diplomat; leading Republican supporter of the League of Nations.

Dean Rusk, 1909-95, (U.S.) statesman; sec. of state, 1961-69.

John Russell, 1792-1878, (Br.) Liberal prime min. during the Irish potato famine.

Anwar al-Sadat, 1918-81, (Egypt) pres., 1970-81; promoted peace with Israel; Nobel laureate; assassinated.

António de Oliveira Salazar, 1889-1970, (Port.) longtime dictator.

José de San Martin, 1778-1850, S. Amer. revolutionary; protector of Peru.

Eisaku Sato, 1901-75, (Jpn.) prime min.; presided over Japan's post-WWII emergence as major world power.

Abdul Aziz Ibn Saud, c.1880-1953, (Saudi Arabia) king of Saudi Arabia, 1932-53.

Robert Schuman, 1886-1963, (Fr.) statesman; founded European Coal and Steel Community.

Carl Schurz, 1829-1906, (U.S.) German-American political leader, journalist, orator, dedicated reformer.

Kurt Schuschnigg, 1897-1977, (Austria) chancellor; unsuccessful in stopping Austria's annexation by Germany.

William H. Seward, 1801-72, (U.S.) antislavery activist; as U.S. sec. of state purchased Alaska.

Carlo Sforza, 1872-1952, (It.) foreign min., anti-Fascist.

Yitzhak Shamir, 1915-2012, (Isr.) prime min. of Israel, 1983-84, 1986-92.

Norodom Sihanouk, 1922-2012, (Camb.) King of Cambodia (1941-55, 1993-2004).

Sitting Bull, c.1831-90, (Nat. Am.) Sioux leader in Battle of Little Bighorn against George A. Custer, 1876.

Alfred E. Smith, 1873-1944, (U.S.) NY Democratic governor; first Roman Catholic to run for president.

Margaret Chase Smith, 1897-1995, (U.S.) congresswoman, senator (R, ME); 1st woman elected to both houses of Congress.

Jan C. Smuts, 1870-1950, (S. Africa) statesman, philosopher, soldier, prime min.

Paul Henri Spaak, 1899-1972, (Belg.) statesman, socialist leader.

Joseph Stalin, 1879-1953, (USSR) Soviet dictator, 1924-53; instituted forced collectivization, massive purges, and labor camps, causing millions of deaths.

Edwin M. Stanton, 1814-69, (U.S.) sec. of war, 1862-68.

Alexander Stephens, 1812-1883, (U.S.) vice pres. of the Confederacy.

Edward R. Stettinius Jr., 1900-49, (U.S.) industrialist; sec. of state who coordinated aid to WWII allies.

Adlai E. Stevenson, 1900-65, (U.S.) Democratic leader, diplomat, governor (IL), presidential candidate.

Henry L. Stimson, 1867-1950, (U.S.) statesman; served in 5 administrations, foreign policy adviser in 1930s and 1940s.

Carl Stokes, 1927-96, (U.S.) first black mayor of a major American city (Cleveland, 1967-72).

Suharto, 1921-2008, (Indon.) former longtime Indonesian ruler.

Sukarno, 1901-70, (Indon.) dictatorial first pres. of the Indonesian republic.

Sun Yat-sen, 1866-1925, (China) revolutionary; leader of Kuomintang pol. party, regarded as father of modern China.

Robert A. Taft, 1889-1953, (U.S.) conservative Senate leader (OH); called "Mr. Republican."

Charles de Talleyrand, 1754-1838, (Fr.) statesman, diplomat; the major force of the Congress of Vienna of 1814-15.

U Thant, 1909-74, (Burma) statesman, UN sec.-general.

Norman M. Thomas, 1884-1968, (U.S.) social reformer; 6 times Socialist party presidential candidate.

Josip Broz Tito, 1892-1980, (Yug.) pres. of Yugoslavia from 1953; WWII guerrilla chief, postwar rival of Stalin.

Palmiro Togliatti, 1893-1964, (It.) major Italian Communist leader.

Hideki Tojo, 1885-1948, (Jpn.) statesman, soldier; prime min. during most of WWII.

François Toussaint L'Ouverture, c.1744-1803, (Haiti) patriot, martyr; thwarted French colonial aims.

Leon Trotsky, 1879-1940, (Russ.) revolutionary; founded Red Army, expelled from party in conflict with Stalin; assassinated.

Pierre Elliott Trudeau, 1919-2000, (Can.) longtime liberal prime min. of Canada, 1968-79, 1980-84; achieved native Canadian constitution.

Rafael L. Trujillo Molina, 1891-1961, (Dominican) dictator of Dominican Republic, 1930-61; assassinated.

Moise K. Tshombe, 1919-69, (Congo) pres. of secessionist Katanga prov., prem. of Congo (now Dem. Rep. of the Congo).

William M. Tweed, 1823-78, (U.S.) political boss of Tammany Hall, New York City's Democratic political machine.

Walter Ulbricht, 1893-1973, (Ger.) Communist leader of German Democratic Republic.

Arthur H. Vandenberg, 1884-1951, (U.S.) senator (R, MI); proponent of bipartisan anti-Communist foreign policy.

Eleutherios Venizelos, 1864-1936, (Gr.) most prominent Greek statesman of early 20th cent.

Hendrik F. Verwoerd, 1901-66, (S. Africa) prime min.; rigorously applied apartheid policy despite protest.

Kurt Waldheim, 1918-2007, (Austria) UN sec.-gen., Austrian pres.

George Wallace, 1919-98, (U.S.) former segregationist governor of Alabama, pres. candidate.

Robert Walpole, 1676-1745, (Br.) statesman; generally considered Britain's first prime min.

Harold Washington, 1922-87, (U.S.) first black mayor of Chicago.

Robert C. Weaver, 1907-97, (U.S.) first African American appointed to cabinet; sec. of Housing and Urban Development.

Daniel Webster, 1782-1852, (U.S.) orator, politician; advocate of business interests during Jacksonian agrarianism.

Caspar Weinberger, 1917-2006, (U.S.) business exec., former defense sec., other cabinet posts.

Chaim Weizmann, 1874-1952, (Russ.-Isr.) Zionist leader, scientist; first Israeli pres.

Kevin White, 1929-2012, (U.S.) Boston mayor, 1967-84.

Wendell L. Willkie, 1892-1944, (U.S.) Republican who tried to unseat Franklin D. Roosevelt when he ran for his 3rd term.

Harold Wilson, 1916-95, (Br.) Labour party leader; prime min., 1964-70, 1974-76.

Boris Yeltsin, 1931-2007, (USSR-Russia) first freely elected president of post-Soviet Russia.

Coleman A. Young, 1918-97, (U.S.) first African-American mayor of Detroit, 1974-93.

Emiliano Zapata, c.1879-1919, (Mex.) revolutionary; major influence on modern Mexico.

Todor Zhivkov, 1911-98, (Bulg.) Communist ruler of Bulgaria from 1954 until ousted in a 1989 coup.

Zhou Enlai, 1898-1976, (China) diplomat, prime min.; a leading figure of the Chinese Communist party.

Scientists of the Past

Revised by Peter Barker, Prof. and Chair, Dept. of the History of Science, Univ. of Oklahoma.

For pre-modern scientists, see also Philosophers and Religious Figures of the Past and Historical Figures chapters.

Albertus Magnus, c.1200-80, (Ger.) theologian, philosopher; helped found medieval study of natural science.

Alhazen (Ibn al-Haytham), c. 965-c. 1040, mathematician, astronomer, optical theorist.

Andre-Marie Ampère, 1775-1836, (Fr.) mathematician, chemist; founder of electrodynamics.

Neil Armstrong, 1930-2012, (U.S.) astronaut, 1st man to walk on the moon.

John V. Atanasoff, 1903-95, (U.S.) physicist; co-invented Atanasoff-Berry Computer (1939-41).

Amedeo Avogadro, 1776-1856, (It.) chemist, physicist; proposed that equal volumes of gas contain equal numbers of molecules, permitting determination of molecular weights.

John Bardeen, 1908-91, (U.S.) double Nobel laureate in physics (transistor, 1956; superconductivity, 1972).

A. H. Becquerel, 1852-1908, (Fr.) physicist; discovered radioactivity in uranium (1896).

Alexander Graham Bell, 1847-1922, (U.S.) inventor; first to patent and commercially exploit the telephone (1876).

Daniel Bernoulli, 1700-82, (Switz.) mathematician; developed fluid dynamics and kinetic theory of gases.

Clifford Berry, 1918-63, (U.S.) collaborated with John V. Atanasoff on the ABC computer (1939-41).

Jöns Jakob Berzelius, 1779-1848, (Swed.) chemist; developed modern chemical symbols and formulas.

Henry Bessemer, 1813-98, (Br.) engineer; invented Bessemer steel-making process.

Hans Bethe, 1906-2005, (Ger.-U.S.) physicist; won Nobel Prize in 1967 for describing how stars generate energy.

Bruno Bettelheim, 1903-90, (Austria-U.S.) psychoanalyst; studied disturbed children; *Uses of Enchantment* (1976).

Louis Blériot, 1872-1936, (Fr.) engineer; monoplane pioneer, first Channel flight (1909).

Franz Boas, 1858-1942, (Ger.-U.S.) founded modern anthropology; studied Pacific Coast tribes.

Niels Bohr, 1885-1962, (Den.) atomic and nuclear physicist; founded quantum mechanics.

Norman Borlaug, 1914-2009, (U.S.) plant pathologist and geneticist; father of "green" (agricultural) revolution.

Max Born, 1882-1970, (Ger.) atomic and nuclear physicist; helped develop quantum mechanics.

Satyendranath Bose, 1894-1974, (India) physicist; forerunner of modern quantum theory for integral-spin particles.

Louis de Broglie, 1892-1987, (Fr.) physicist; proposed quantum wave-particle duality.

Robert Bunsen, 1811-99, (Ger.) chemist; pioneered spectroscopic analysis; discovered rubidium, caesium.

Luther Burbank, 1849-1926, (U.S.) naturalist; developed plant breeding into a modern science.

Vannevar Bush, 1890-1974, (U.S.) electrical engineer; developed differential analyzer, an early analogue computer; headed WWII Office of Scientific Res. and Dev.

Marvin Camras, 1916-95, (U.S.) inventor, electrical engineer; invented magnetic tape recording.

Alexis Carrel, 1873-1944, (Fr.) surgeon, biologist; developed methods of suturing blood vessels, transplanting organs.

Rachel Carson, 1907-64, (U.S.) marine biologist, environmentalist; *Silent Spring* (1962).

James Chadwick, 1891-1974, (Br.) physicist; discovered the neutron (1932); led Brit. Manhattan Project group in U.S.

Albert Claude, 1898-1983, (Belg.-U.S.) a founder of modern cell biology; determined role of mitochondria.

Samuel Cohen, 1921-2010, (U.S.) physicist who invented the neutron bomb.

Barry Commoner, 1917-2012, biologist; noted environmentalist.

Nicolaus Copernicus, 1473-1543, (Pol.) first modern astronomer to propose Sun as center of the planets' motions.

Jacques Yves Cousteau, 1910-97, (Fr.) oceanographer; co-inventor, with Emile Gagnan, of the Aqualung (1943).

Seymour Cray, 1925-96, (U.S.) computer industry pioneer; developed supercomputers.

Francis Crick, 1916-2004, (Br.) biophysicist; co-discoverer of genetic code; shared 1962 Nobel Prize.

Marie, 1867-1934, (Pol.-Fr.) and **Pierre Curie**, 1859-1906, (Fr.) physical chemists; pioneer investigators of radioactivity; discovered radium and polonium (1898).

Gottlieb Daimler, 1834-1900, (Ger.) engineer, inventor; pioneer automobile manufacturer.

John Dalton, 1766-1844, (Br.) chemist, physicist; formulated atomic theory, made first table of atomic weights.

Charles Darwin, 1809-82, (Br.) naturalist; established theory of organic evolution; *Origin of Species* (1859).

Lee De Forest, 1873-1961, (U.S.) inventor of triode; pioneer in wireless telegraphy, sound pictures, television.

Pierre-Gilles de Gennes, 1932-2007, (Fr.) physicist whose research aided development of liquid-crystal-display (LCD); awarded Nobel Prize for Physics, 1991.

Max Delbrück, 1906-81, (Ger.-U.S.) founded molecular biology.

Rudolf Diesel, 1858-1913, (Ger.) mechanical engineer; patented Diesel engine (1892).

Theodosius Dobzhansky, 1900-75, (Russ.-U.S.) biologist; reconciled genetics and natural selection.

Christian Doppler, 1803-53, (Austria) physicist; showed change in wave frequency caused by motion of source, now known as Doppler effect.

J. Presper Eckert Jr., 1919-95, (U.S.) co-inventor, with John W. Mauchly, of the ENIAC computer (1943-45).

Thomas A. Edison, 1847-1931, (U.S.) inventor; held more than 1,000 patents, including incandescent electric lamp.

Paul Ehrlich, 1854-1915, (Ger.) medical researcher in immunology and bacteriology; pioneered antitoxin production.

Albert Einstein, 1879-1955, (Ger.-U.S.) theoretical physicist; founded relativity theory.

John F. Enders, 1897-1985, (U.S.) virologist; helped discover vaccines against polio, measles, mumps and chicken pox.

Erik Erikson, 1902-94, (U.S.) psychoanalyst, author; theory of developmental stages of life; *Childhood and Society* (1950).

Leonhard Euler, 1707-83, (Switz.) mathematician, physicist; pioneer of calculus, revived ideas of Fermat.

Gabriel Fahrenheit, 1686-1736, (Ger.) physicist; improved thermometers and introduced Fahrenheit temperature scale.

Michael Faraday, 1791-1867, (Br.) chemist, physicist; discovered electrical induction and invented dynamo (1831).

Philo T. Farnsworth, 1906-71, (U.S.) inventor; built first television system (San Francisco, 1928).

Pierre de Fermat, 1601-65, (Fr.) mathematician; founded modern theory of numbers.

Enrico Fermi, 1901-54, (It.-U.S.) nuclear physicist; demonstrated first controlled chain reaction (Chicago, 1942).

Richard Feynman, 1918-88, (U.S.) theoretical physicist, author; founder of Quantum Electrodynamics (QED).

Alexander Fleming, 1881-1955, (Br.) bacteriologist; discovered penicillin (1928).

Jean B. J. Fourier, 1768-1830, (Fr.) introduced Fourier Series, method of analysis in math and physics.

Sigmund Freud, 1856-1939, (Austria) psychiatrist; founder of psychoanalysis; *Interpretation of Dreams* (1901).

Erich Fromm, 1900-80, (U.S.) psychoanalyst; *Man for Himself* (1947).

Galileo Galilei, 1564-1642, (It.) physicist; used telescope to vindicate Copernicus, founded modern science of motion.

Carl Friedrich Gauss, 1777-1855, (Ger.) math. physicist; completed work of Fermat and Euler in number theory.

Josiah W. Gibbs, 1839-1903, (U.S.) theoretical physicist, chemist; founded chemical thermodynamics.

Robert H. Goddard, 1882-1945, (U.S.) physicist; invented liquid fuel rocket (1926).

George W. Goethals, 1858-1928, (U.S.) chief engineer who completed Panama Canal (1907-14).

William C. Gorgas, 1854-1920, (U.S.) physician; pioneer in prevention of yellow fever and malaria.

Stephen Jay Gould, 1941-2002, (U.S.) paleontologist, evolutionary biologist, writer.

Ernest Haeckel, 1834-1919, (Ger.) zoologist, evolutionist; early Darwinist, introduced concept of "ecology."

Otto Hahn, 1879-1968, (Ger.) chemist; with Lise Meitner discovered nuclear fission (1938).

Edmund Halley, 1656-1742, (Br.) astronomer; predicted return of 1682 comet (Halley's Comet) in 1759.

William Harvey, 1578-1657, (Br.) physician, anatomist; discovered circulation of the blood (1628).

Werner Heisenberg, 1901-76, (Ger.) physicist; developed matrix mechanics and uncertainty principle (1927).

Hermann von Helmholtz, 1821-94, (Ger.) physicist, physiologist; formulated principle of conservation of energy.

William Herschel, 1738-1822, (Ger.-Br.) astronomer; discovered Uranus (1781).

Heinrich Hertz, 1857-94, (Ger.) physicist; discovered radio waves and photo-electric effect (1886-87).

David Hilbert, 1862-1943, (Ger.) mathematician; contributed to algebra, calculus, and foundational studies (formalism).

Albert Hofmann, 1906-2008, (U.S.) father of LSD.

Edwin P. Hubble, 1889-1953, (U.S.) astronomer; discovered observational evidence of expanding universe.

Alexander von Humboldt, 1769-1859, (Ger.) naturalist, author; explored S. America, created ecology.

Edward Jenner, 1749-1823, (Br.) physician; pioneered vaccination, introduced term "virus."

James Joule, 1818-89, (Br.) physicist; found relation between heat and mechanical energy (conservation of energy).

Carl Jung, 1875-1961, (Switz.) psychiatrist; founder of analytical psychology.

Ernest Everett Just, 1883-1941, (U.S.) marine biologist; studied egg development; *Biology of Cell Surfaces* (1941).

Johannes Kepler, 1571-1630, (Ger.) astronomer; discovered laws of planetary motion.

Al-Khawarizmi, early 9th cent., (Arab.) mathematician; regarded as founder of algebra.

Robert Koch, 1843-1910, (Ger.) bacteriologist; isolated bacterial causes of tuberculosis and other diseases.

Georges Köhler, 1946-95, (Ger.) immunologist; with Cesar Milstein, developed monoclonal antibody technique.

Willem Kolff, 1911-2009, (Neth.-U.S.) physician, biomedical engineer; developed first practical kidney dialysis machine; considered the "father of artificial organs."

Jacques Lacan, 1901-81, (Fr.) influential psychoanalyst.

Joseph Lagrange, 1736-1813, (Fr.) geometer, astronomer; showed that gravity of Earth and Moon cancel, creating stable points in space around them.

Jean B. Lamarck, 1744-1829, (Fr.) naturalist; forerunner of Darwin in evolutionary theory.

Pierre Simon de Laplace, 1749-1827, (Fr.) astronomer, physicist; proposed nebular origin for solar system.

Lewis H. Latimer, 1848-1928, (U.S.) African American scientist; associate of Edison; supervised installation of first electric street lighting in New York City.

Antoine Lavoisier, 1743-94, (Fr.) a founder of modern chemistry.

Ernest O. Lawrence, 1901-58, (U.S.) physicist; invented the cyclotron.

Louis, 1903-72, and **Mary Leakey**, 1913-96, (Br.) early hominid paleoanthropologists; discovered remains in Africa.

Anton van Leeuwenhoek, 1632-1723, (Neth.) founder of microscopy.

Jerome Lejeune, 1927-94, (Fr.) geneticist; discovered chromosomal cause of Down syndrome (1959).

Claude Levi-Strauss, 1908-2009, (Belg.-Fr.) cultural anthropologist, sociologist, philosopher.

Kurt Lewin, 1890-1947, (Ger.-U.S.) social psychologist; studied human motivation and group dynamics.

Justus von Liebig, 1803-73, (Ger.) founded quantitative organic chemistry.

Joseph Lister, 1827-1912, (Br.) physician; pioneered antiseptic surgery.

Hendrik Lorentz, 1853-1928, (Neth.) physicist; developed electron theory of matter, contrib. to relativity theory.

Konrad Lorenz, 1903-89, (Austria) ethologist; pioneer in study of animal behavior.

Bernard Lovell, 1913-2012, (Br.) physicist and radio astronomer.

Percival Lowell, 1855-1916, (U.S.) astronomer; predicted the existence of Pluto.

Louis, 1864-1948, and **Auguste Lumière**, 1862-1954, (Fr.) invented cinematograph, made first motion picture (1895).

Theodore H. Maiman, 1927-2007, (U.S.) physicist; invented the first workable laser, which he displayed in 1960.

Guglielmo Marconi, 1874-1937, (It.) physicist; developed wireless telegraphy.

John W. Mauchly, 1907-80, (U.S.) co-inventor, with J. Presper Eckert Jr., of computer ENIAC (1943-45).

James Clerk Maxwell, 1831-79, (Br.) physicist; unified electricity and magnetism, electromagnetic theory of light.

Maria Goeppert Mayer, 1906-72, (Ger.-U.S.) physicist; developed shell model of atomic nuclei.

Barbara McClintock, 1902-92, (U.S.) geneticist; showed that some genetic elements are mobile.

Lise Meitner, 1878-1968, (Austria) co-discoverer, with Otto Hahn, of nuclear fission (1938).

Gregor J. Mendel, 1822-84, (Austria) botanist, monk; his experiments became the foundation of modern genetics.

Dmitri Mendeleyev, 1834-1907, (Russ.) chemist; established Periodic Table of the Elements.

Bruce R. Merrifield, 1921-2006, (U.S.) chemist; discovered how to synthesize proteins quickly and efficiently.

Franz Mesmer, 1734-1815, (Ger.) physician; introduced hypnotherapy.

Albert A. Michelson, 1852-1931, (U.S.) physicist; invented interferometer.

Robert A. Millikan, 1868-1953, (U.S.) physicist; measured electronic charge.

Thomas Hunt Morgan, 1866-1945, (U.S.) geneticist, embryologist; established role of chromosomes in heredity.

Isaac Newton, 1642-1727, (Br.) natural philosopher; discovered laws of gravitation, motion; with Gottfried Wilhelm Leibniz, founded calculus.

Robert N. Noyce, 1927-90, (U.S.) invented microchip.

J. Robert Oppenheimer, 1904-67, (U.S.) physicist; scientific director of Manhattan Project.

Wilhelm Ostwald, 1853-1932, (Ger.) chemist, philosopher; main founder of modern physical chemistry.

Louis Pasteur, 1822-95, (Fr.) chemist; showed that germs cause disease and fermentation; originated pasteurization.

Linus C. Pauling, 1901-94, (U.S.) chemist; studied chemical bonds; campaigned for nuclear disarmament.

Jean Piaget, 1896-1980, (Switz.) psychologist; four-stage theory of intellectual development in children.

Max Planck, 1858-1947, (Ger.) physicist; introduced quantum hypothesis (1900).

Jules Henri Poincaré, 1854-1912, (Fr.) mathematician; founded algebraic topology, many other discoveries.

Walter S. Reed, 1851-1902, (U.S.) Army physician; proved mosquitoes transmit yellow fever.

Theodor Reik, 1888-1969, (Austria-U.S.) psychoanalyst; major Freudian disciple.

Sally Ride, 1951-2012, (U.S.) astronaut, 1st U.S. woman in space.

Bernhard Riemann, 1826-66, (Ger.) mathematician; developed non-Euclidean geometry used by Einstein.

Norbert Rillieux, 1806-94, (U.S.) African American inventor of a vacuum pan evaporator (1846); revolutionized sugar-refining industry.

Wilhelm Roentgen, 1845-1923, (Ger.) physicist; discovered X-rays (1895).

Carl Rogers, 1902-87, (U.S.) psycho-therapist, author; originated nondirective therapy.

Ernest Rutherford, 1871-1937, (Br.) physicist; pioneer investigator of radioactivity, identified the atomic nucleus.

Albert B. Sabin, 1906-93, (Russ.-U.S.) developed oral polio live-virus vaccine.

Carl Sagan, 1934-96, (U.S.) astronomer, author.

Jonas Salk, 1914-95, (U.S.) developed first successful polio vaccine, widely used in U.S. after 1955.

Allan Sandage, 1926-2010, (U.S.) astronomer; refined the Hubble Constant, a measure of the universe's expansion.

Giovanni Schiaparelli, 1835-1910, (It.) astronomer; reported canals on Mars.

Erwin Schrödinger, 1887-1961, (Austria) physicist; developed wave equation for quantum systems.

Glenn T. Seaborg, 1912-99, (U.S.) chemist; Nobel Prize winner (1951); co-discoverer of plutonium.

Harlow Shapley, 1885-1972, (U.S.) astronomer; mapped galactic clusters and position of Sun in our own galaxy.

Norman E. Shumway, 1923-2006, (U.S.) surgeon; performed world's first successful heart-lung transplant.

B. F. Skinner, 1904-90, (U.S.) psychologist; leading advocate of behaviorism.

Richard E. Smalley, 1943-2005, (U.S.) chemist; with three other scientists, discovered buckminsterfullerenes, a previously unknown class of carbon molecules.

Roger W. Sperry, 1913-94, (U.S.) neurobiologist; established different functions of right and left sides of brain.

Benjamin Spock, 1903-98, (U.S.) pediatrician, child care expert; *Common Sense Book of Baby and Child Care.*

Charles P. Steinmetz, 1865-1923, (Ger.-U.S.) electrical engineer; developed basic ideas on alternating current.

Ernst Stuhlinger, 1913-2008, (Ger.) rocket scientist; electric propulsion for NASA in early space age.

Leo Szilard, 1898-1964, (Hung.-U.S.) physicist; helped on Manhattan Project, later opposed nuclear weapons.

Edward Teller, 1908-2003, (Hung.-U.S.) physicist; aided on Manhattan Project, had key role in development of H-bomb.

Nikola Tesla, 1856-1943, (Serb.-U.S.) invented electrical devices including AC dynamos, transformers, and motors.

William Thomson (Lord Kelvin), 1824-1907, (Br.) physicist; aided in success of transatlantic telegraph cable (1865); proposed Kelvin absolute temperature scale.

Alan Turing, 1912-54, (Br.) mathematician; helped develop basis for computers.

James Van Allen, 1914-2006, (U.S.) physicist; discovered the presence of radiation belts around Earth (Van Allen belts).

Rudolf Virchow, 1821-1902, (Ger.) pathologist; pioneered the modern theory that diseases affect the body through cells.

Alessandro Volta, 1745-1827, (It.) physicist; electricity pioneer.

Werner von Braun, 1912-77, (Ger.-U.S.) developed rockets for warfare and space exploration.

John Von Neumann, 1903-57, (Hung.-U.S.) mathematician; originated game theory; basic design for modern computers.

Alfred Russell Wallace, 1823-1913, (Br.) naturalist; proposed concept of evolution independently of Darwin.

John B. Watson, 1878-1958, (U.S.) psychologist; a founder of behaviorism.

James E. Watt, 1736-1819, (Br.) mechanical engineer, inventor; invented modern steam engine (1765).

Alfred L. Wegener, 1880-1930, (Ger.) meteorologist, geophysicist; postulated continental drift.

Norbert Wiener, 1894-1964, (U.S.) mathematician; founder of cybernetics.

Daniel Hale Williams, 1858-1931, (U.S.) African American surgeon; performed one of first two open-heart operations (1893).

Sewall Wright, 1889-1988, (U.S.) evolutionary theorist; helped found population genetics.

Wilhelm Wundt, 1832-1920, (Ger.) founder of experimental psychology.

Qian Xuesen (Tsien Hsue-shen), 1911-2009, (China) rocket scientist; father of China's space program.

Rosalyn Yalow, 1921-2011, (U.S.), physicist; co-developer of radioimmunoassay.

Ferdinand von Zeppelin, 1838-1917, (Ger.) soldier, aeronaut, airship designer.

Social Reformers, Activists, and Humanitarians of the Past

Ralph David Abernathy, 1926-90, (U.S.) black civil rights activist; pres., 1968, Southern Christian Leadership Conf.

Jane Addams, 1860-1935, (U.S.) cofounder of Hull House; won Nobel Peace Prize, 1931.

Susan B. Anthony, 1820-1906, (U.S.) a leader in temperance, antislavery, and woman suffrage movements.

Thomas Barnardo, 1845-1905, (Br.) social reformer; pioneer in care of destitute children.

Clara Barton, 1821-1912, (U.S.) organized American Red Cross.

Daisy Bates, 1914-99, (U.S.) black civil rights leader who fought for integration; advocate for the "Little Rock 9" during Arkansas desegregation crisis in 1957.

Henry Ward Beecher, 1813-87, (U.S.) clergyman, abolitionist.

Peter Benenson, 1921-2005, (Br.) activist; founded Amnesty International, 1961.

Mary McLeod Bethune, 1875-1955, (U.S.) black educator, civil rights activist; adviser to FDR and Truman; founder, pres., Bethune-Cookman College.

Amelia Bloomer, 1818-94, (U.S.) suffragette, social reformer.

Yelena Bonner, 1923-2011, (Russ.) human rights activist in former Soviet Union.

William Booth, 1829-1912, (Br.) founded Salvation Army.

John Brown, 1800-59, (U.S.) abolitionist who led murder of 5 pro-slavery men; hanged.

Frances Xavier (Mother) Cabrini, 1850-1917, (It.-U.S.) Italian-born nun; founded charitable institutions; first American canonized as a saint, 1946.

Stokely Carmichael (Kwame Toure), 1941-98, (U.S.) black power activist; major proponent of Pan-Africanism; prime min. Black Panthers.

Carrie Chapman Catt, 1859-1947, (U.S.) suffragette.

Cesar Chavez, 1927-93, (U.S.) labor leader; helped establish United Farm Workers of America.

Eldridge Cleaver, 1935-98, (U.S.) revolutionary social critic; former minister of information for Black Panthers; *Soul on Ice*.

Clarence Darrow, 1857-1938, (U.S.) lawyer; defender of underdog, opponent of capital punishment.

Ossie Davis, 1917-2005, (U.S.) black civil rights activist, actor, director.

Dorothy Day, 1897-1980, (U.S.) founder of Catholic Worker movement.

Eugene V. Debs, 1855-1926, (U.S.) labor leader; led Pullman strike, 1894; 4-time Socialist presidential candidate.

Vine Deloria Jr., 1933-2005, (U.S.) Native American activist, author; *Custer Died for Your Sins*.

Dorothea Dix, 1802-87, (U.S.) crusader for mentally ill.

Thomas Dooley, 1927-61, (U.S.) "jungle doctor"; noted for efforts to supply medical aid to developing countries.

Marjory Stoneman Douglas, 1890-1998, (U.S.) writer, environmentalist; campaigned to save Florida Everglades.

Frederick Douglass, 1817-95, (U.S.) slave, author, editor, orator, diplomat; edited abolitionist weekly *The North Star*.

Andrea Dworkin, 1946-2005, (U.S.) radical feminist, antipornography crusader.

Medgar Evers, 1925-63, (U.S.) black civil rights leader; campaigned to register black voters; assassinated.

James Farmer, 1920-99, (U.S.) black civil rights leader; founded Congress of Racial Equality (CORE).

Betty Friedan, 1921-2006, (U.S.) author, feminist; *The Feminine Mystique*.

Millard Fuller, 1935-2009, (U.S.) founder of Habitat for Humanity.

William Lloyd Garrison, 1805-79, (U.S.) abolitionist.

Miep Gies, 1909-2010, (Neth.) protector of Anne Frank and her family during WWII.

Emma Goldman, 1869-1940, (Russ.-U.S.) published anarchist *Mother Earth*; birth-control advocate.

Samuel Gompers, 1850-1924, (U.S.) labor leader; first president of the American Federation of Labor (AFL).

Prince Hall, 1735-1807, (U.S.) activist; founded black Freemasonry; served in American Revolutionary war.

Michael Harrington, 1928-89, (U.S.) exposed poverty in affluent U.S. in *The Other America*, 1963.

Dorothy Height, 1912-2010, (U.S.) civil rights activist; pres. of the National Council of Negro Women, 1957-97.

Sidney Hillman, 1887-1946, (U.S.) labor leader; helped organize CIO.

Benjamin Hooks, 1925-2010, (U.S.) civil rights activist; exec. dir. NAACP, 1977-92.

Samuel G. Howe, 1801-76, (U.S.) social reformer; changed public attitudes toward the handicapped.

Franklin Kameny, 1925-2011, (U.S.) gay rights activist.

Helen Keller, 1880-1968, (U.S.) crusader for better treatment for the handicapped; deaf and blind herself.

Jack Kevorkian 1928-2011, (U.S.) pathologist; assisted-suicide activist.

Coretta Scott King, 1927-2006, (U.S.) black civil rights leader; wife of Rev. Martin Luther King Jr.

Rev. Martin Luther King Jr., 1929-68, (U.S.) civil rights leader; led 1955-56 Montgomery, AL, boycott; founder, pres., Southern Christian Leadership Conference, 1957; Nobel laureate, 1964; assassinated.

Maggie Kuhn, 1905-95, (U.S.) founded Gray Panthers, 1970.

William Kunstler, 1919-95, (U.S.) civil liberties attorney.

John L. Lewis, 1880-1969, (U.S.) labor leader; headed United Mine Workers, 1920-60.

Almena Lomax, 1915-2011, (U.S.) civil rights activist; journalist who founded *The Los Angeles Tribune*.

Clara Luper, 1923-2011, (U.S.) civil rights activist.

Wangari Maathai, 1940-2011, (Kenya), environmental activist; 2004 Nobel Peace Prize winner.

Robert Macauley, 1923-2010, (U.S.) founder of AmeriCares.

Malcolm X (Little), 1925-65, (U.S.) Black Muslim, black nationalist leader; promoted black pride; assassinated.

Karl Menninger, 1893-1990, (U.S.) with brother William, founded Menninger Clinic and Menninger Foundation.

Lucretia Mott, 1793-1880, (U.S.) reformer, pioneer feminist.

Philip Murray, 1886-1952, (U.S.) Scottish-born labor leader.

Huey P. Newton, 1942-89, (U.S.) co-founded Black Panther Party, 1966.

Florence Nightingale, 1820-1910, (Br.) founder of modern nursing.

Emmeline Pankhurst, 1858-1928, (Br.) woman suffragist.

Rosa Parks,1913-2005, (U.S.) black civil rights activist; her actions sparked 1955-56 Montgomery, AL, bus boycott.

A. Philip Randolph, 1889-1979, (U.S.) organized Brotherhood of Sleeping Car Porters, 1925; an organizer of 1941 and 1963 March on Washington movements.

Walter Reuther, 1907-70, (U.S.) labor leader; headed UAW.

Jacob Riis, 1849-1914, (U.S.) crusader for urban reforms.

Paul Robeson, 1898-1976, (U.S.) actor, singer, black civil rights activist.

Bayard Rustin, 1910-87, (U.S.) an organizer of the 1963 March on Washington; exec. director, A. Philip Randolph Institute.

Margaret Sanger, 1883-1966, (U.S.) social reformer; pioneered the birth-control movement.

Earl of Shaftesbury (A. A. Cooper), 1801-85, (Br.) social reformer.

Eunice Kennedy Shriver, 1921-2009, (U.S.) cofounder of Special Olympics for mentally challenged athletes.

Sargent Shriver, 1915-2011, (U.S.) founding director of Peace Corps; founder of Job Corps, Head Start.

Fred Shuttlesworth, 1922-2011, (U.S.) civil rights activist.

Albertina Sisulu, 1918-2011, (S. Africa), anti-apartheid activist.

Elizabeth Cady Stanton, 1815-1902, (U.S.) woman suffrage pioneer.

Lucy Stone, 1818-93, (U.S.) feminist, abolitionist.

Mother Teresa of Calcutta, 1910-97, (Alban.) nun; founded order to care for sick, dying poor; 1979 Nobel Peace Prize.

Willard Townsend, 1895-1957, (U.S.) organized the United Transport Service Employees (Red Caps), 1935.

Sojourner Truth (Isabella Baumfree), 1797-1883, (U.S.) preacher, abolitionist; worked for black educ. opportunity.

Harriet Tubman, 1823-1913, (U.S.) prominent figure in the Underground Railroad, which helped runaway slaves in the South reach safety in the North; nurse, spy for Union Army in the Civil War.

Nat Turner, 1800-31, (U.S.) slave who led the most significant of more than 200 slave revolts in U.S., in Southampton, VA; hanged.

Philip Vera Cruz, 1905-94, (Philip.-U.S.) helped found the United Farm Workers Union.

Edgar Wayburn, 1906-2010, (U.S.) conservationist; Sierra Club pres.

William Wilberforce, 1759-1833, (Br.) social reformer; prominent in struggle to abolish slave trade.

Frances E. Willard, 1839-98, (U.S.) temperance, women's rights leader.

Mary Wollstonecraft, 1759-97, (Br.) *Vindication of the Rights of Women*.

Sports Personalities of the Past and Present

Henry (Hank) Aaron, b 1934, Milwaukee-Atlanta outfielder; hit record 755 home runs, led NL 4 times; record 2,297 RBI.

Kareem Abdul-Jabbar, b 1947, Milwaukee, L.A. Lakers center; MVP 6 times; all-time leading NBA scorer, 38,387 points.

Andre Agassi, b 1970, won Wimbledon (1992); U.S. Open ('94, '99), Austral. Open ('95, 2000-01, '03), French Open ('99).

Troy Aikman, b 1966, quarterback; led Dallas Cowboys to Super Bowl wins in 1993-94, '96; Super Bowl MVP, 1993.

Ben Ainslie, b 1977, (Br.) most decorated Olympic sailor; gold, 2000, '04, '08, '12. silver, 1996.

Amy Alcott, b 1956, golfer; 33 career wins (5 majors); inducted into Hall of Fame, 1999.

Grover Cleveland "Pete" Alexander, 1887-1950, pitcher; won 373 NL games; pitched 16 shutouts, 1916.

Muhammad Ali, b 1942, 3-time heavyweight champion.

Fernando Alonso, b 1981, (Sp.) Formula 1 racer; youngest ever to win a World Grand Prix championship, 2005; defended title, 2006.

Morten Andersen, b 1960, (Den.) kicker; NFL's career points leader, with 2,544 (1982-2007).

Gary Anderson, b 1959, (S. Afr.) kicker; NFL's 2nd in career points, with 2,434.

Sparky Anderson, 1934-2010, first manager to win World Series in the NL (Cincinnati, 1975-76) and AL (Detroit, 1984).

Mario Andretti, b 1940, (Ital.) race-car driver; won Daytona 500 (1967), Indy 500 (1969); Formula 1 world title (1978).

Earl Anthony, 1938-2001, bowler; won record 6 PBA Championships (1973-75, 1981-83), 43 career PBA tournaments.

Eddie Arcaro, 1916-97, only jockey to win racing's Triple Crown twice, 1941, '48; rode to 4,779 wins in his career.

Lance Armstrong, b 1971, cyclist; record 7-time winner of Tour de France (1999-2005); stripped of victories in 2012 for use of performance-enhancing drugs.

Arthur Ashe, 1943-93, tennis player; won U.S. Open (1968); Wimbledon (1975).

Evelyn Ashford, b 1957, sprinter; won 100m gold (1984) and silver (1988); member of 5 U.S. Olympic teams.

Red Auerbach, 1917-2006, coached Boston to 9 NBA titles.

Tracy Austin, b 1962, youngest player to win U.S. Open tennis title (age 16 in 1979).

Victoria Azarenka, b 1989, (Belarus) tennis player; won Australian Open (2012).

Ernie Banks, b 1931, Chicago Cubs slugger; hit 512 NL homers; twice MVP.

Roger Bannister, b 1929, (Br.) physician; ran 1st sub-4-minute mile, May 6, 1954 (3 min. 59.4 sec.).

Charles Barkley, b 1963, NBA MVP, 1993; 4th player ever to surpass 20,000 points, 10,000 rebounds, 4,000 assists.

Rick Barry, b 1944, NBA scoring leader, 1967; ABA scoring leader, 1969.

Sammy Baugh, 1914-2008, Washington Redskins quarterback; held numerous records upon retirement after 16 seasons.

Elgin Baylor, b 1934, L.A. Lakers forward; 11-time all-star.

Bob Beamon, b 1946, Olympic long jump gold medalist, 1968; world record jump of 29 ft 2½ in. stood until 1991.

Boris Becker, b 1967, (Ger.) tennis star; won U.S. Open 1989; Wimbledon champ 1985, '86, '89.

David Beckham, b 1975, (Br.) soccer star; captain of 2002 World Cup team; joined L.A. Galaxy, 2007, with record-breaking $250 mil contract.

Bill Belichick, b 1952, NFL coach; led New England Patriots to 3 Super Bowl wins (2001, '03, '04); best all-time postseason coaching record.

Jean Béliveau, b 1931, (Can.) Montréal Canadiens center; scored 507 goals; twice MVP.

Johnny Bench, b 1947, Cincinnati Reds catcher; twice MVP; led league in home runs twice, RBIs 3 times.

Patty Berg, 1918-2006, 80+ golf tournament wins; AP Woman Athlete of the Year 3 times.

Chris Berman, b 1955, sportscaster, anchor for ESPN and ABC Sports.

Yogi Berra, b 1925, Yankee catcher (1946-63); 3-time MVP.

Abebe Bikila, 1932-73, (Eth.) runner; won consecutive Olympic marathon gold medals in 1960 (barefoot), 1964.

Matt Biondi, b 1965, swimmer; won 5 golds, 1988 Olympics.

Larry Bird, b 1956, Boston Celtics forward (1979-92); NBA MVP, 1984-86; 1998 coach of the year with Indiana Pacers.

Bonnie Blair, b 1964, speed skater; won 5 individual gold medals in 3 Olympics (1988, '92, '94).

George Blanda, 1927-2010, quarterback, kicker; 26 years as active player, scored 2,002 career points.

Fanny Blankers-Koen, 1918-2004, (Neth.) track star; won 4 golds in 1948 Olympics.

Wade Boggs, b 1958, AL batting champ, 1983, 1985-88; reached 3,000 career hits, 1999 (3,010).

Usain Bolt, b 1986, (Jam.) Olympic sprinter, gold medalist, 2008, '12; world record for men's 100m, 200m runs.

Barry Bonds, b 1964, outfielder; hit record 73 homers, 2001; NL MVP, 1990, 1992-93, 2001-04; 1st all-time in HRs (762); indicted in steroid scandal, 2007; convicted of obstruction of justice, 2011.

Björn Borg, b 1956, (Swed.) led Sweden to first Davis Cup, 1975; 6-time French Open, 5-time Wimbledon champion.

Ray Bourque, b 1960, (Can.) Boston defenseman,1979-2000; 5-time Norris Trophy winner; won Stanley Cup with Colorado, 2001.

Bill Bradley, b 1943, All-American at Princeton; led NY Knicks to 2 NBA titles (1970, '73); U.S. senator, 1979-97.

Donald Bradman, 1908-2001, (Austral.) widely regarded as greatest cricketer ever; set several batting records.

Terry Bradshaw, b 1948, quarterback; led Pittsburgh to 4 Super Bowl wins, 1975-76, 1979-80; NFL MVP, 1978.

Tom Brady, b 1977, quarterback; led New England Patriots to 3 Super Bowl titles, 2002, '04, '05; Super Bowl MVP, 2002, '04; NFL MVP, 2007, '11; most single-season TD passes (50), 2007.

Ryan Braun, b 1983, Milwaukee Brewers left fielder; NL MVP, 2011.

Drew Brees, b 1979, New Orleans Saints quarterback; Super Bowl MVP, 2010; single-season record-holder for passing yards (5,476), 2011.

Christine Brennan, b 1958, sports journalist for *USA Today*, radio and TV commentator specializing in figure skating.

George Brett, b 1953, Kansas City Royals infielder; led AL in batting, 1976, '80, '90; MVP, 1980.

Lou Brock, b 1939, St. Louis Cardinals outfielder; stole NL single-season record 118 bases, 1974; led NL 8 times.

Jim Brown, b 1936, Cleveland fullback; 12,312 career yds.; NFL MVP 1957, '58, '65.

Paul Brown, 1908-91, football team-owner, coach; led eponymous Cleveland Browns to 3 NFL championships.

Bob Bryan and **Mike Bryan**, b 1978, doubles tennis players; won French Open (2003); U.S. Open, (2005, '08, '10, '12); Wimbledon, (2006, '11); Austral. Open. (2006-07, '09-'12); Olympic gold, 2012.

Kobe Bryant, b 1978, guard; won 3 straight titles with Lakers (2000-02); leading NBA scorer, 2005-06 and 2006-07; 2007-08 NBA MVP; NBA Finals MVP 2009, '10; member of U.S. Olympic gold medal team (2008, '12).

Paul "Bear" Bryant, 1913-83, college football coach with 323 wins; led Alabama to 6 national titles (1961, '64, '65, '73, '78, '79).

Sergei Bubka, b 1963, (Ukr.) pole vaulter; first to clear 20 ft.; gold medal, 1988 Olympics.

Don Budge, 1915-2000, won numerous amateur and pro tennis titles; Grand Slam, 1938.

Reggie Bush, b 1985, NFL running back; helped USC to 2 national titles (2003-04; '04 vacated).

Dick Butkus, b 1942, Chicago Bears linebacker; NFL defensive player of the year (1969, '70).

Dick Button, b 1929, figure skater; won 1948, 1952 Olympic gold medals; world titleholder, 1948-52.

Miguel Cabrera, b 1983, (Venez.) 7-time All-Star; won AL triple crown (2012).

Walter Camp, 1859-1925, Yale football player, coach, athletic director; established many rules for modern football.

Roy Campanella, 1921-93, Hall of Fame catcher for the Brooklyn Dodgers (1948-57); 3-time NL MVP.

Earl Campbell, b 1955, NFL running back; MVP 1978-79.

Jose Canseco, b 1964, outfielder; led Oakland A's to World Series, 1988; wrote book about steroids in baseball, 2005.

Eric Cantona, b 1966, (Fr.) soccer star; Manchester United (1992-97).

Rod Carew, b 1945, AL infielder; 7 batting titles, 1977 MVP.

Steve Carlton, b 1944, NL pitcher; won 20 games 6 times, Cy Young award 4 times; 4,136 career strikeouts.

Pete Carroll, b 1951, college and pro football coach; coached the USC Trojans to 2 championships (2003-04).

Billy Casper, b 1931, PGA Player of the Year 2 times; U.S. Open champ twice.

Wilt Chamberlain, 1936-99, center; NBA leading scorer 7 times, MVP 4 times; scored 100 pts. in a game, 1962.

Bobby Clarke, b 1949, (Can.) Philadelphia Flyers center; led team to 2 Stanley Cup championships; MVP 3 times.

Roger Clemens, b 1962, pitcher; 1986 AL MVP; only 7-time Cy Young winner (1986-87, '91, '97-'98, 2001, '04); twice recorded record 20 Ks in a game; 354 wins, 4,672 Ks (3rd all-time); indicted, accused of lying to Congress about using steroids, 2011.

Roberto Clemente, 1934-72, Pittsburgh Pirates outfielder; won 4 batting titles; MVP, 1966; 3,000 career hits; killed in plane crash.

Kim Clijsters, b 1983, (Belg.) tennis player; U.S. Open winner (2005, '09-'10), Austral. Open (2011).

Ty Cobb, 1886-1961, Detroit Tigers outfielder; record .367 lifetime batting average, 12 batting titles.

Sebastian Coe, b 1956, (Br.) runner; won Olympic 1,500m gold medal and 800m silver medal in 1980 and '84.

Nadia Comaneci, b 1961, (Rom.) gymnast; won 3 gold medals, achieved 7 perfect scores, 1976 Olympics; 9 Olympic medals overall.

Maureen Connolly, 1934-69, won tennis Grand Slam, 1953; AP Woman Athlete of the Year 3 times.

Jimmy Connors, b 1952, tennis player; 5 U.S. Open, 2 Wimbledon titles.

Alberto Contador, b 1982, (Sp.) cyclist; won Tour de France 2007, '09; stripped of '10 title because of doping offense.

Cynthia Cooper, b 1963, basketball; 4-time MVP of WNBA finals; 2-time league MVP for the Houston Comets.

James J. Corbett, 1866-1933, heavyweight champion, 1892-97; credited with being the first "scientific" boxer.

Angel Cordero Jr., b 1942, jockey; leading money winner, 1976, 1982-83; rode 3 Kentucky Derby winners.

Margaret Smith Court, b 1942, (Austral.) tennis great; won 24 Grand Slam events.

Bob Cousy, b 1928, Boston guard; 6 NBA titles, 1957 MVP.

Mark Cuban, b 1958, Dallas Mavericks owner; known for criticism of NBA.

Bjoern Daehlie, b 1967, (Nor.) cross-country skier; won record 8 Winter Olympic gold medals.

Lindsay Davenport, b 1976, tennis player; won Olympic gold, 1996; U.S. Open, 1998; Wimbledon, 1999; Austral. Open, 2000.

Al Davis, 1929-2011, Oakland Raiders owner, former coach.

Dizzy Dean, 1910-74, pitcher; St. Louis Cardinals' "Gashouse Gang" in the '30s.

Mary Decker Slaney, b 1958, runner; has held 6 separate American records from the 800m to 10,000m.

Frank Deford, b 1938, sr. contributing writer for *Sports Illustrated*; author, commentator.

Oscar De La Hoya, b 1973, won IBF lightweight (1995); WBC super lightweight (1996); welterweight (1997-99, 2000) titles.

Juan Martin del Potro, b 1988, (Arg.) tennis player; won U.S. Open, 2009.

Jack Dempsey, 1895-1983, heavyweight champ, 1919-26.

Donna de Varona, b 1947, swimmer; won 2 Olympic golds, 1964; 1st female sportscaster at a major network, 1965.

Gail Devers, b 1966, Olympic 100m gold medalist (1992, '96).

Joe DiMaggio, 1914-99, NY Yankees outfielder; hit safely in record 56 consecutive games, 1941; AL MVP 3 times.

Novak Djokovic, b 1987, (Serb.) tennis player; won Austral. Open (2008, '11, '12); Wimbledon (2011), U.S. Open (2011).

Landon Donovan, b 1982, forward for L.A. Galaxy; all-time leading U.S. international goal scorer with 46; MLS MVP, 2009.

Tony Dorsett, b 1954, Heisman winner who led the Dallas Cowboys to an NFL title in his rookie year, 1977.

Gabrielle Douglas, b 1995, first African-American gymnast to win Olympic gold in all-around (2012).

Tim Duncan, b 1976, San Antonio center; 3-time NBA Finals MVP, 1999, 2003, 2005; NBA MVP, 2002-03.

Roberto Duran, b 1951, (Pan.) boxer; held titles at 3 weights; lost 1980 "no mas" fight to Sugar Ray Leonard.

Leo Durocher, 1905-91, manager; won 3 NL pennants (Brooklyn, 1941; NY Giants, 1951, '54), 1954 World Series.

Dale Earnhardt Jr., b 1974, 2004 Daytona 500 winner.

Dale Earnhardt Sr., 1951-2001, 7-time NASCAR Winston Cup champ; died in a last-lap crash at 2001 Daytona 500.

Stefan Edberg, b 1966, (Swed.) tennis player; U.S. Open (1991, '92), Wimbledon (1988, '90), Austral. Open (1985, '87).

Gertrude Ederle, 1905-2003, first woman to swim English Channel; broke existing men's record, 1926.

Teresa Edwards, b 1964, 5-time basketball Olympian; gold medalist, 1984, '88, '96, 2000; bronze medalist, 1992.

Hicham El Guerrouj, b 1974, (Morocco) runner; holds world records in mile (3:43.13) and 1,500m (3:26); won gold medals in 1,500m and 5,000m, 2004 Olympics.

John Elway, b 1960, quarterback; led Denver Broncos to 2 Super Bowl wins, 1998, '99; NFL MVP, 1987; Super Bowl MVP, 1999.

Julius "Dr. J" Erving, b 1950, 3-time ABA MVP, 1981 NBA MVP.

Phil Esposito, b 1942, (Can.) NHL scoring leader 5 times.

Janet Evans, b 1971, 4 Olympic swimming golds, 1988, '92.

Lee Evans, b 1947, Olympic 400m gold medalist in 1968 with 43.86-sec. world record not broken until 1988.

Chris Evert, b 1954, 6-time U.S. Open tennis champ, 3-time Wimbledon champ.

Ray Ewry, 1873-1937, track-and-field star; won 8 Olympics gold medals (1900, '04, '08).

Nick Faldo, b 1957, (Br.) golfer; won Masters, British Open 3 times each.

Juan Manuel Fangio, 1911-95 (Arg.), 5-time World Grand Prix driving champ (1951, 1954-57).

Marshall Faulk, b 1973, 2000 NFL MVP; scored then-record 26 TDs, 2001; 3-time Off. Player of the Year (1999-2001).

Brett Favre, b 1969, quarterback; led Green Bay to Super Bowl win, 1997; NFL MVP, 1995, '96; co-MVP, 1997; left retirement to play for NY Jets, 2008; Minnesota Vikings, 2009-10.

Roger Federer, b 1981, (Switz.) tennis star; won Austral. Open (2004, '06-'07, '10), Wimbledon (2003-07, '09, '12), U.S. Open (2004-08), French Open (2009).

Bob Feller, 1918-2010, Cleveland Indians pitcher; won 266 games; pitched 3 no-hitters, 12 one-hitters.

Rollie Fingers, b 1946, pitcher; 341 career saves; AL MVP, Cy Young Award, 1981; World Series MVP, 1974.

Peggy Fleming, b 1948, world figure skating champion, 1966-68; gold medalist, 1968 Olympics.

Whitey Ford, b 1928, NY Yankees pitcher; won record 10 World Series games.

George Foreman, b 1949, heavyweight champion, 1973-74, 1994-95; at 45, oldest to win a heavyweight title; gold medalist, 1968 Olympics.

Dick Fosbury, b 1947, high jumper; won 1968 Olympic gold medal; developed the "Fosbury Flop."

Jimmie Foxx, 1907-67, Red Sox, Athletics slugger; MVP 3 times; triple crown, 1933.

A. J. Foyt, b 1935, won Indy 500 4 times; U.S. Auto Club champ 7 times.

Dario Franchitti, b 1973, (Scot.) 3-time Indy 500 winner, 2007, '10, '12.

Missy Franklin, b 1995, won 4 Olympic swimming golds, 2012.

Joe Frazier, 1944-2011, heavyweight champion, 1970-73; gold medalist, 1964 Olympics.

Walt Frazier, b 1945, Hall of Fame guard for NY Knicks' NBA championship teams (1970, '73).

Peter Gammons, b 1945, sportswriter, broadcaster; named to Baseball Hall of Fame.

Lou Gehrig, 1903-41, NY Yankees 1st baseman; MVP, 1927, '36; triple crown,

1934; AL record 184 RBIs, 1931; played in 2,130 straight games (1925-39), a record that stood until 1995.

Althea Gibson, 1927-2003, 2-time U.S. and Wimbledon champ.

Bob Gibson, b 1935, St. Louis Cardinals pitcher; won Cy Young award twice; struck out 3,117 batters.

Josh Gibson, 1911-47, Hall of Fame catcher; known as "Babe Ruth of the Negro Leagues"; credited with as many as 84 homers in 1 season, about 800 in his career.

Marc Girardelli, b 1963, (Lux.) skier; won 5 World Cup titles.

Raul Gonzalez, b 1977, (Sp.) soccer player; led Real Madrid to 3 Champions League titles (1998, 2000, '02); all-time top UEFA goal scorer (71).

Jeff Gordon, b 1971, race-car driver; youngest to win NASCAR title 4 times (1995, '97 '98, 2001).

Steffi Graf, b 1969, (Ger.) won tennis Grand Slam 1988; U.S. Open champ 5 times; Wimbledon, 7 times; Austral. 4 times; French 6 times.

Otto Graham, 1921-2003, Cleveland quarterback; 4-time all-pro.

Red Grange, 1903-91, All-American at Univ. of Illinois, 1923-25; played for Chicago Bears, 1925-35.

"Mean" Joe Greene, b 1946, Pittsburgh Steelers lineman; twice NFL outstanding defensive player.

Wayne Gretzky, b 1961, (Can.) top scorer in NHL history with record 894 goals, 1,963 assists, 2,857 points; MVP, 1980-87, '89.

Bob Griese, b 1945, All-Pro quarterback; led Miami Dolphins to 17-0 season, 1972, 2 Super Bowl titles, 1973-74.

Ken Griffey Jr., b 1969, outfielder; led AL in homers 1994, '97-'99; 1997 AL MVP; 10 gold gloves.

Archie Griffin, b 1954, Ohio State running back; only 2-time winner of the Heisman Trophy (1974-75).

Florence Griffith Joyner, 1959-98, sprinter; won 3 gold medals at 1988 Olympics; world and Olympic record for 100m.

Lefty Grove, 1900-75, pitcher; won 300 AL games.

Vladimir Guerrero, b 1975, (Dom. Rep.) right fielder; 2004 American League MVP award.

Janet Guthrie, b 1938, 1st woman driver in Indy 500 (1977).

Tony Gwynn, b 1960, 8-time NL batting champ (1984, '87-'89, '94-'97); 3,141 career hits.

Walter Hagen, 1892-1969, golfer; 5 PGA, 4 British Open titles.

Mika Hakkinen, b 1968, (Fin.) Formula One racing driver; Formula One champion, 1998, '99.

George Halas, 1895-1983, founder/player/coach of Chicago Bears; won 6 NFL championships as coach.

Roy Halladay, b 1977, pitcher; Cy Young Award, 2003, '10; pitched perfect game, 2010.

Dorothy Hamill, b 1956, figure skater; gold medalist at the Olympics and World championships, 1976.

Josh Hamilton, b 1981, Texas Rangers outfielder; AL MVP, 2010.

Scott Hamilton, b 1958, U.S. and world figure skating champion, 1981-84; Olympic gold medalist, 1984.

Mia Hamm, b 1972, soccer player; led U.S. to World Cup (1991, '99) and Olympic (1996, 2004) titles; most career intl. goals (158).

Franco Harris, b 1950, running back; 4 Super Bowls with Steelers (1975-76, 1979-80); 1,000+ yds. in a season 8 times.

Marvin Harrison, b 1972, Indianapolis Colts wide receiver; NFL record for single-season receptions (143), 2002.

Bill Hartack, 1932-2007, jockey; rode 5 Kentucky Derby winners.

Dominik Hasek, b 1965, (Czech.) NHL goaltender; won Vezina Trophy, 1994-95, '97-'99, 2001; NHL MVP, 1997-98.

John Havlicek, b 1940, Boston Celtics forward; scored 26,395 career pts.

Eric Heiden, b 1958, speed skater; won 5 Olympic golds, 1980.

Rickey Henderson, b 1958, outfielder; 1990 AL MVP; record 130 stolen bases, 1982; all-time leader in steals, runs.

Sonja Henie, 1912-69, (Nor.) world champion figure skater, 1927-36; Olympic gold medalist, 1928, '32, '36.

Martina Hingis, b 1980, (Switz.) won Austral. and U.S. Opens, Wimbledon; youngest number one player (16 yrs., 6 mos.), 1997.

Trevor Hoffman, b 1967, relief pitcher (601 career saves).

Ben Hogan, 1912-97, golfer; won 4 U.S. Open titles, 2 PGA Championships, 2 Masters.

Santonio Holmes, b 1984, wide receiver; Super Bowl MVP, 2009.

Evander Holyfield, b 1962, 4-time heavyweight champion.

Rogers Hornsby, 1896-1963, NL 2nd baseman; batted record .424, 1924; twice won triple crown.

Paul Hornung, b 1935, Green Bay Packers running back, placekicker; scored record 176 points, 1960.

Ryan Howard, b 1979, first baseman for Philadelphia Phillies; known for his hitting; 2006 NL MVP.

Gordie Howe, b 1928, (Can.) hockey forward; NHL MVP 6 times; scored 801 goals in 26 NHL seasons.

Carl Hubbell, 1903-88, NY Giants pitcher; 20-game winner 5 consecutive years, 1933-37.

Bobby Hull, b 1939, (Can.) NHL all-star 10 times; MVP, 1965-66.

Brett Hull, b 1964, (Can.) St. Louis Blues forward; led NHL in goals, 1990-92; MVP, 1991.

Catfish Hunter, 1946-99, pitched perfect game, 1968; 20-game winner 5 times.

Don Hutson, 1913-97, Packers receiver; caught 99 TD passes; 2-time NFL MVP.

Juli Inkster, b 1960, Hall of Fame golfer; 2nd to win all 4 of LPGA's modern majors; won 7 career major titles.

Bo Jackson, b 1962, NFL running back (1987-90) and MLB outfielder (1986-91, '93-'94); 1985 Heisman Trophy winner.

Phil Jackson, b 1945, won 11 NBA titles as coach of Bulls and Lakers; 1970, '73 title as player with NY Knicks.

Reggie Jackson, b 1946, slugger; led AL in home runs 4 times; MVP, 1973; hit 5 World Series home runs, 1977.

"Shoeless" Joe Jackson, 1889-1951, outfielder; 3rd highest career batting average (.356); one of the "Black Sox" banned for allegedly throwing 1919 World Series.

Jaromir Jagr, b 1972, (Czech.) hockey player; NHL MVP, 1999; Art Ross Trophy (leading scorer), 1995, 1998-2001.

LeBron James, b 1984, NBA forward; Rookie of the Year, 2004; member of 2008, '12 U.S. Olympic gold medal teams; NBA MVP, 2008-09, '09-'10, '11-'12.

Ron Jaworski, b 1951, former NFL quarterback (1974-89); NFL analyst on ESPN.

Sally Jenkins, b 1960, sports journalist and writer for *The Washington Post*.

Bruce Jenner, b 1949, Olympic decathlon gold medalist, 1976.

Lynn Jennings, b 1960, runner; 3-time World, 9-time U.S. cross country champ; bronze (10,000m), 1992 Olympics.

Derek Jeter, b 1974, shortstop; led NY Yankees to 5 World Series titles; World Series MVP, 2000; 1st Yankee to reach 3,000 hits, 2011.

Earvin "Magic" Johnson, b 1959, NBA MVP, 1987, '89, '90; playoff MVP, 1980, '82, '87; 4th in career assists.

Jack Johnson, 1878-1946, heavyweight champion, 1908-15.

Jimmie Johnson, b 1975, 5-time NASCAR Sprint Cup Series champ, 2006-10; Daytona 500 winner, 2006.

Michael Johnson, b 1967, 4-time Olympic gold medalist (1992, '96, 2000); world and Olympic record, 400m and 4 × 400m.

Randy Johnson, b 1963, 5-time Cy Young winner; strikeout leader, 1992-95, 1999-2002, 2004; 4,875 strikeouts (2nd all-time); pitched perfect game, 2004.

Walter Johnson, 1887-1946, Washington Senators pitcher; won 417 games; record 110 shutouts.

Bobby Jones, 1902-71, won golf's Grand Slam, 1930; U.S. amateur champ 5 times, U.S. Open champ 4 times.

Cobi Jones, b 1970, soccer player; most U.S. national team appearances with 164.

David "Deacon" Jones, b 1938, 5-time All-Pro with L.A. Rams (1965-69); "sack" specialist credited with inventing the term.

Marion Jones, b 1975, 2000 Olympic 100m, 200m, 1,600m relay gold medalist, bronze in long jump and 400m relay; stripped of medals in 2007 after admitting use of performance-enhancing drugs.

Roy Jones Jr., b 1969, light heavyweight champ, 1999-2004.

Michael Jordan, b 1963, guard; leading NBA scorer, 1987-93, '96-'98; MVP, 1988, 1991-'92, '96, '98; playoff MVP, 1991-93, '96-'98; ESPN Athlete of the Century.

Dorothy Kamenshek, 1925-2010, led Rockford (IL) Peaches to 4 All-American Girls Baseball League titles in the 1940s.

Jackie Joyner-Kersee, b 1962, Olympic gold medalist in heptathlon (1988, '92), long jump (1988).

Clayton Kershaw, b 1988, pitcher; NL Cy Young Award (2011).

Harmon Killebrew, 1936-2011, Minnesota Twins slugger; led AL in home runs 6 times; 573 lifetime.

Jean Claude Killy, b 1943, (Fr.) skier; 3 Olympic golds, 1968.

Kim Yu-Na, b 1990, (S. Kor.) figure skater; Olympic gold medal winner, 2010; world champion, 2009.

Ralph Kiner, b 1922, Pittsburgh Pirates slugger; led NL in home runs 7 consecutive years, 1946-52.

Billie Jean King, b 1943, U.S. singles champ 4 times; Wimbledon champ 6 times; beat Bobby Riggs, 1973.

Peter King, b 1957, senior writer for *Sports Illustrated*.

Bob Knight, b 1940, ESPN studio analyst, ret. basketball coach; led Indiana U. to NCAA title in 1976, '81, '87; winningest men's college basketball coach (902).

Olga Korbut, b 1955, (Belarus) gymnast; 3 Olympic golds, 1972.

Sandy Koufax, b 1935, 3-time Cy Young winner; lowest ERA in NL, 1962-66; pitched 4 no-hitters, 1 perfect game.

Jack Kramer, 1921-2009, world's number one tennis player, 1946-53; first at Wimbledon to compete in shorts.

Ingrid Kristiansen, b 1956, (Nor.) only runner to have held world records in 5,000m, 10,000m, and marathon.

Julie Krone, b 1963, winningest female jockey; only woman to ride a winner in a Triple Crown race (Belmont, 1993).

Michelle Kwan, b 1980, figure skater; 9 U.S., 5 World titles; silver medalist at 1998 Olympics, bronze in 2002.

Guy Lafleur, b 1951, (Can.) 3-time NHL scoring leader; 1977-78 MVP.

Alexi Lalas, b 1970, soccer player; first modern-era American to play in Italian League Serie A.

Kenesaw Mountain Landis, 1866-1944, 1st commissioner of baseball (1920-44);

banned the 8 "Black Sox" involved in fixing 1919 World Series.

Tom Landry, 1924-2000, Dallas Cowboys head coach, 1960-88; won 2 Super Bowls (1972, '78); 3rd in career wins (270).

Dick "Night Train" Lane, 1928-2002, Hall of Fame defensive back; intercepted an NFL season record 14 passes (1952).

Don Larsen, b 1929, as NY Yankee, pitched only World Series perfect game, Oct. 8, 1956—2-0 win over Brooklyn.

Rod Laver, b 1938, (Austral.) won tennis Grand Slam, 1962, 1969; Wimbledon champ 4 times.

Mario Lemieux, b 1965, (Can.) 6-time NHL leading scorer; MVP, 1988, '93, '96; playoff MVP, 1991-92.

Greg Lemond, b 1961, cyclist; 3-time Tour de France winner (1986, '89-'90); first American to win the event.

Ivan Lendl, b 1960, (Czech.) 8 Grand Slam tennis titles, including U.S. Open, 1985-87.

Sugar Ray Leonard, b 1956, boxer; held titles in 5 different weight classes.

Lisa Leslie, b 1972, L.A. Sparks center; 3-time WNBA MVP (2001, '04, '06).

Carl Lewis, b 1961, track-and-field star; won 9 Olympic gold medals in sprinting and long jump.

Lennox Lewis, b 1965, (Br.) heavyweight champ, 1994, 1997-2004, retired undefeated; gold medalist, 1998 Olympics.

Ray Lewis, b 1975, linebacker for the Baltimore Ravens; Super Bowl MVP, 2001.

Tim Lincecum, b 1984, S.F. Giants pitcher; NL Cy Young Award, 2008-09.

Tara Lipinski, b 1982, youngest figure skater to win U.S., world championships, 1997, and Winter Olympic gold, 1998.

Ryan Lochte, b 1984, swimmer; 11-time Olympic medalist, incl. 5 gold (2004, '08, '12).

Vince Lombardi, 1913-70, Green Bay Packers coach; led team to 5 NFL championships, 2 Super Bowl victories.

Nancy Lopez, b 1957, Hall of Fame golfer; 4-time LPGA Player of the Year, 3-time winner of the LPGA Championship.

Greg Louganis, b 1960, won Olympic gold medals in both springboard and platform diving, 1984, 1988.

Joe Louis, 1914-81, heavyweight champion, 1937-49.

Sid Luckman, 1916-98, Chicago Bears quarterback; led team to 4 NFL championships; MVP, 1943.

Evan Lysacek, b 1985, figure skater; world champion, 2009, Olympic gold winner, 2010.

Connie Mack, 1862-1956, Philadelphia Athletics manager, 1901-50; won 9 pennants, 5 championships.

John Madden, b 1936, won Super Bowl as coach of Oakland Raiders (1977); former NFL TV analyst.

Greg Maddux, b 1966, NL pitcher; won 4 consecutive Cy Young awards, 1992-95; 355 career wins.

Karl Malone, b 1963, Utah Jazz, L.A. Lakers forward; MVP, 1997, '99; 14-time All-Star; 36,928 career points (2nd all-time).

Moses Malone, b 1955, NBA center; MVP, 1979, '82-'83.

Eli Manning, b 1981, NY Giants quarterback; Super Bowl MVP, 2008, '12.

Peyton Manning, b 1976, Indianapolis Colts quarterback; most NFL MVP awards, 2003-04, '08-'09; Super Bowl MVP, 2007; highest single-season passer rating (121.1), 2004.

Mickey Mantle, 1931-95, NY Yankees outfielder; triple crown, 1956; 18 World Series home runs; MVP 3 times.

Diego Maradona, b 1960, (Arg.) soccer player; led Argentina to World Cup, 1986.

"Pistol" Pete Maravich, 1947-88, guard; scored NCAA record 44.2 ppg during collegiate career; led NBA in scoring, 1977.

Rocky Marciano, 1923-69, heavyweight champion, 1952-56; retired undefeated.

Dan Marino, b 1961, Miami quarterback; NFL record single-season yards passing (5,084), 1984.

Roger Maris, 1934-85, NY Yankees outfielder; hit AL record 61 home runs, 1961, record held 37 years; MVP, 1960, '61.

Marta (Marta Vieira da Silva), b 1986, (Braz.) soccer forward; FIFA World Player of the Year, 2006-10.

Curtis Martin, b 1973, Jets running back; 5-time Pro-Bowler; 4th in all-time rushing yards with 14,101.

Eddie Mathews, 1931-2001, Milwaukee-Atlanta Braves 3rd baseman; hit 512 career home runs.

Christy Mathewson, 1880-1925, pitcher; won 373 games.

Bob Mathias, 1930-2006, decathlon gold, 1948, '52 Olympics.

Hideki Matsui, b 1974, (Jpn.) designated hitter/outfielder; 1st Japanese-born World Series MVP, 2009.

Misty May-Treanor, b 1977, beach volleyball player; 3-time Olympic gold medalist with Kerri Walsh Jennings (2004, '08, '12).

Willie Mays, b 1931, NY-S.F. Giants center fielder; hit 660 home runs, led NL 4 times; had 3,283 hits; twice MVP.

Willie McCovey, b 1938, S.F. Giants slugger; hit 521 home runs; led NL 3 times; MVP, 1969.

John McEnroe, b 1959, U.S. Open tennis champ (1979-81, '84); Wimbledon champ (1981, '83-'84).

John McGraw, 1873-1934, NY Giants manager; led team to 10 pennants, 3 championships.

Mark McGwire, b 1963, hit then-record 70 home runs in 1998; 583 career home runs (10th); admitted career steroid use, 2010.

Rory McIlroy, b 1989, (N. Ire.) golfer; won U.S. Open 16 under par, 2011; won PGA Championship, 2012.

Tamara McKinney, b 1962, 1st U.S. skier to win overall Alpine World Cup championship (1983).

Andrea Mead Lawrence, 1932-2009, skier; first woman to win 2 gold medals in alpine skiing at one Olympics (1952).

Lionel Messi, b 1987, (Arg.) forward for FC Barcelona; FIFA World Player of the Year, 2009-10.

Mark Messier, b 1961, (Can.) center; NHL MVP, 1990, '92; Conn Smythe Trophy, 1984.

Debbie Meyer, b 1952, 1st swimmer to win 3 individual Olympic golds (1968).

Al Michaels, b 1944, *NBC Sunday Night Football* announcer; 5-time Outstanding Sports Personality Emmy winner.

George Mikan, 1924-2005, Minn. Lakers center; considered the best basketball player of first half of 20th cent.

Stan Mikita, b 1940, (Czech.) Chicago Blackhawks center; led NHL in scoring 4 times; MVP twice.

Billy Mills, b 1938, runner; upset winner of the 1964 Olympic 10,000m; only American man ever to win the event.

Joe Montana, b 1956, S.F. 49ers quarterback; Super Bowl MVP, 1982, 1985, 1990.

Archie Moore, 1913-98, light-heavyweight champ, 1952-62.

Howie Morenz, 1902-37, (Can.) Montreal Canadiens forward; considered best hockey player of first half of 20th cent.

Edwin Moses, b 1955, undefeated in 122 consecutive 400m hurdles races, 1977-87; Olympic gold medalist, 1976, '84.

Shirley Muldowney, b 1940, 1st woman to race Natl. Hot Rod Assn. Top Fuel dragsters; 3-time NHRA points champ.

Eddie Murray, b 1956, 3rd player with both 3,000+ hits and 500+ home runs.

Stan Musial, b 1920, St. Louis Cardinals star; won 7 NL batting titles; MVP 3 times.

Rafael Nadal, b 1986, (Sp.) tennis player; won French Open (2005-08, '10-'12), Wimbledon (2008, '10), Australian Open (2009), U.S. Open (2010); Olympic gold medal in men's singles (2008).

Bronko Nagurski, 1908-90, (Can.) Chicago Bears fullback and tackle; gained more than 4,000 yds. rushing.

Joe Namath, b 1943, Jets quarterback; 1969 Super Bowl MVP.

Steve Nash, b 1974, (Can.) Phoenix Suns point guard; NBA MVP, 2005, '06.

Martina Navratilova, b 1956, (Czech.) Wimbledon champ 9 times; U.S. Open champ (1983-84, '86-'87); Austral. 3 times, French 2 times.

Byron Nelson, 1912-2006, won 11 consecutive golf tournaments in 1945; twice Masters and PGA titlist.

Ernie Nevers, 1903-76, Stanford football star; selected as best college fullback to play between 1919 and 1969.

Paula Newby-Fraser, b 1962, ([now] Zimbabwe) 8-time Ironman Triathlon world champ; holds women's course record.

John Newcombe, b 1944, (Austral.) twice U.S. Open tennis champ; Wimbledon champ 3 times.

Jack Nicklaus, b 1940, PGA Player of the Year, 1967, 1972; leading money winner 8 times; won 18 majors (6 Masters).

Chuck Noll, b 1932, Pittsburgh coach; won 4 Super Bowls.

Dirk Nowitzki, b 1978, (Ger.) NBA forward; led Mavericks to NBA title, 2011; NBA MVP, 2007.

Paavo Nurmi, 1897-1973, (Fin.) distance runner; won 9 Olympic gold medals, 1920, 1924, 1928.

Lorena Ochoa, b 1981, (Mex.) LPGA Player of the Year, 2006-09, money leader 2006-08.

Al Oerter, 1936-2007, discus thrower; won gold medal at 4 consecutive Olympics, 1956, '60, '64, '68.

Apolo Anton Ohno, b 1982, speed skater; most decorated American Winter Olympic athlete with 2 gold, 2 silver, 4 bronze (2002, '06, '10).

Hakeem Olajuwon, b 1963, (Nigeria) Houston center; NBA MVP, 1994, playoff MVP, 1994-95; career blocked shots leader (3,830).

Barney Oldfield, 1878-1946, pioneer auto racer; was first to drive a car 60 mph, 1903.

Shaquille O'Neal, b 1972, center; led L.A. Lakers to NBA titles, 2000-02, and Miami Heat to NBA title, 2006; Finals MVP 2000-02; NBA MVP 2000.

Bobby Orr, b 1948, (Can.) Boston Bruins defenseman; 8-time Norris Trophy winner; led NHL in scoring twice, assists 5 times.

Mel Ott, 1909-58, NY Giants right fielder; hit 511 home runs; led NL 6 times.

Jesse Owens, 1913-80, track and field; 4 1936 Olympic golds.

Terrell Owens, b 1973, wide receiver; NFL record for single-game receptions with 20 in 2000.

Satchel Paige, 1906-82, pitcher; starred in Negro leagues, 1924-48; entered major leagues at age 42.

Arnold Palmer, b 1929, golf's first $1 mil winner; won 4 Masters, 2 British Opens.

Jim Palmer, b 1945, Baltimore Orioles pitcher; won Cy Young award 3 times; 20-game winner 8 times.

Candace Parker, b 1986, L.A. Sparks forward; first woman to dunk in an NCAA tournament game; 2008 WNBA MVP award, Rookie of the Year.

Joe Paterno, 1926-2012, Penn St. football coach; national title-winner 1982, '86; had most wins in NCAA Div. I coaching history until 111 Penn St. wins (1998-2011) were vacated as penalty for the child sex abuse scandal.

Danica Patrick, b 1982, race car driver; 4th woman to race at Indy 500, 1st to lead, 2005.

Floyd Patterson, 1935-2006, 2-time heavyweight champion; first to ever regain the title after losing it.

Walter Payton, 1954-99, Chicago Bears running back; 2nd most rushing yards in NFL history; top NFC rusher, 1976-80.

Pelé (Edson Arantes do Nascimento), b 1940, (Braz.) soccer player; led Brazil to 3 World Cups (1958, '62, '70); scored 1,281 goals.

Bob Pettit, b 1932, first NBA player to score 20,000 points; twice NBA scoring leader.

Richard Petty, b 1937, NASCAR national champ 7 times; 7-time Daytona 500 winner.

Michael Phelps, b 1985, swimmer; holds record for most Olympic medals (22) and gold medals (18) won by single athlete; won 8 medals at 2004 Olympics; 8 gold in 2008; 6 medals in 2012.

Laffit Pincay Jr., b 1946, (Pan.) jockey; leading money-winner, 1970-74, '79, '85.

Oscar Pistorius, b 1986, (S. Afr.) sprinter, 1st double-leg amputee to compete in Olympics, 2012.

Jacques Plante, 1929-86, (Can.) NHL goaltender; 7 Vezina trophies; first goalie to wear mask in a game.

Gary Player, b 1935, (S. Afr.) golfer; won 3 Masters, 3 British Opens, 2 PGA Championships, and U.S. Open.

Mike Powell, b 1963, track and field athlete; holds world record for long jump (29 ft, 4.5 in.).

Steve Prefontaine, 1951-75, runner; 1st to win 4 NCAA titles in same event (5,000m, 1970-73).

Kirby Puckett, 1960-2006, Minnesota Twins center fielder (1984-95); led team to World Series titles in 1987, '91.

Albert Pujols, b 1980, St. Louis first baseman; NL MVP, 2005, '08-'09.

Paula Radcliffe, b 1973, British runner; set marathon world record of 2:15:25 in London, 2003.

Kimi Räikkönen, b 1979, (Fin.) Formula One race car driver; 2007 Formula One World Drivers' Champion.

Manny Ramirez, b 1972, (Dom. Rep.) outfielder; 2004 World Series MVP; suspended for violating MLB performance-enhancing drug policy, 2009; retired after testing positive for P.E.D.s, 2011.

Willis Reed, b 1942, NY Knicks center; MVP, 1970; playoff MVP, 1970, '73.

Mary Lou Retton, b 1968, gymnast; won all-around gold medal at 1984 Olympics; also won 2 silvers, 2 bronzes.

Claudio Reyna, b 1973, midfielder; U.S. National Team; named to the FIFA World Cup All-Star team, 2002.

Jerry Rice, b 1962, receiver; 1989 Super Bowl MVP; NFL record for career touchdowns (208), receptions (1,549).

Maurice Richard, 1921-2000, (Can.) Montreal Canadiens forward; scored 544 regular season goals, 82 playoff goals.

Branch Rickey, 1881-1965, MLB exec. helped break baseball's color barrier, 1947; initiated farm system, 1919.

Cal Ripken Jr., b 1960, Baltimore shortstop; AL MVP, 1983, '91; most consecutive games played (2,632).

Mariano Rivera, b 1969, (Pan.) relief pitcher; helped NY Yankees to 5 World Series titles; World Series MVP, 1999; all-time MLB leader in postseason saves with 42.

Oscar Robertson, b 1938, NBA guard; averaged career 25.7 points per game; 5th in career assists (9,887); MVP, 1964.

Brooks Robinson, b 1937, Baltimore Orioles 3rd baseman; played in 4 World Series; MVP, 1964; 16 gold gloves.

Frank Robinson, b 1935, MVP in both NL and AL; triple crown, 1966; 586 career home runs; first black manager in majors.

Jackie Robinson, 1919-72, broke baseball's color barrier with Brooklyn Dodgers, 1947; NL MVP, 1949.

Sugar Ray Robinson, 1921-89, boxer; middleweight champion 5 times; welterweight champion, 1946-51.

Knute Rockne, 1888-1931, Notre Dame football coach, 1918-31; revolutionized game by stressing forward pass.

Aaron Rodgers, b 1983, Green Bay quarterback; led Packers to victory in Super Bowl XLV; Super Bowl MVP, 2011; NFL MVP, 2011.

Bill Rodgers, b 1947, runner; won Boston and New York City marathons 4 times each between 1975 and 1980.

Alex Rodriguez, b 1975, NY Yankees third baseman; AL MVP in 2003, '05, '07; 14-time All Star; youngest player to ever hit 500 HRs; admitted steroid use 2001-03.

Juan "Chi Chi" Rodriguez, b 1935, champion golfer; 8 PGA tour wins, 22 Champions tour wins.

Ben Roethlisberger, b 1982, Pittsburgh Steelers quarterback; youngest to win Super Bowl, 2005.

Ronaldinho, b 1980, (Braz.) soccer midfielder; led Brazil to World Cup Finals in 2006; FIFA World Player of the Year, 2004, '05.

Ronaldo (Ronaldo Luiz Nazario de Lima), b 1976, (Braz.) soccer forward; led Brazil to 2002 World Cup title; 3-time FIFA world player of the year, 1996-97, 2002; most World Cup goals, 15.

Art Rooney, 1901-88, NFL owner; bought Pittsburgh Pirates in 1933, renamed Steelers, 1940.

Pete Rose, b 1941, won 3 NL batting titles; hit in 44 consecutive games, 1978; most career hits, 4,256; banned for gambling, 1989; admitted betting on his team, 2004.

Ken Rosewall, b 1934, (Austral.) tennis player; 2-time U.S. champ; 8 Grand Slam singles titles.

Patrick Roy, b 1965, (Can.) Montréal-Colorado goalie; only 3-time NHL playoffs MVP (Conn Smythe Trophy), 1986, '93, 2001.

Wilma Rudolph, 1940-94, sprinter; won 3 1960 Olympic golds.

Adolph Rupp, 1901-77, NCAA basketball coach; led Kentucky to 4 national titles, 1948-49, '51, '58.

Bill Russell, b 1934, Boston Celtics center; led team to 11 NBA titles; MVP 5 times; first black coach of major pro sports team.

Babe Ruth, 1895-1948, NY Yankees outfielder; hit 60 home runs, 1927, 714 lifetime (3rd all-time); led AL 12 times.

Johnny Rutherford, b 1938, auto racer; won 3 Indy 500s.

Nolan Ryan, b 1947, pitcher; holds season (383), career (5,714) strikeout records; won 324 games (7 no-hitters).

Pete Sampras, b 1971, tennis star; 1st man in Open era to win 7 Wimbledons; 2nd-most career Grand Slam wins (14).

Joan Benoit Samuelson, b 1957, won 1st Olympic women's marathon (1984), Boston Marathon (1979, '83).

Barry Sanders, b 1968, rushed for 2,053 yards in 1997; led NFL in rushing, 1990, '94, '96, '97.

Deion Sanders, b 1967, NFL cornerback (1989-2000, '04-'05) and MLB outfielder (1989-95, '97, 2005).

Gale Sayers, b 1943, Chicago running back; twice led NFL in rushing.

Mike Schmidt, b 1949, Phillies 3rd baseman; led NL in home runs 8 times; 548 lifetime; NL MVP, 1980, '81, '86.

Michael Schumacher, b 1969, (Ger.) race-car driver; 7-time Formula 1 world champ (1994-95, 2000-04).

Tom Seaver, b 1944, pitcher; won NL Cy Young award 3 times; won 311 major league games.

Monica Seles, b 1973, (Yug.) tennis player; won U.S. (1991-92), Austral. (1991-93, '96), French (1990-92) Opens; stabbed on court by spectator, 1993.

Maria Sharapova, b 1987, (Russ.) tennis star; won Wimbledon (2004), U.S. Open (2006), Australian Open (2008), French Open (2012); Olympic silver, 2012.

Patty Sheehan, b 1956, Hall of Fame golfer; 3 LPGA Championships (1983-84, '93).

Willie Shoemaker, 1931-2003, jockey; rode 4 Kentucky Derby, 5 Belmont Stakes winners.

Frank Shorter, b 1947, runner; only American to win men's Olympic marathon (1972) since 1908; silver medalist (1976).

Don Shula, b 1930, all-time winningest NFL coach (347 games).

Bill Simmons, b 1969, online columnist known as "The Sports Guy."

O. J. Simpson, b 1947, running back; rushed for 2,003 yds., 1973; AFC leading rusher 4 times; acquitted of murder, 1995; jailed after being found guilty of robbery and kidnapping, 2008.

Webb Simpson, b 1985, golfer; won U.S. Open, 2012.

Dean Smith, b 1931, retired basketball coach; 879 Division I wins; led North Carolina to 2 NCAA titles (1982, '93).

Emmitt Smith, b 1969, running back; NFL and Super Bowl MVP, 1993; rushed for career record 18,355 yds.

Conn Smythe, 1895-1980, (Can.) won 7 Stanley Cups as Toronto GM (1929-61); playoff MVP award named in his honor.

Sam Snead, 1912-2002, PGA and Masters champ 3 times each; record 82 PGA tournament victories.

Annika Sorenstam, b 1970, (Swed.) golfer; set LPGA 18-hole record of 59 (−13), 72-hole record of 27-under-par, 2001; won 10 LPGA majors, including career Grand Slam.

Sammy Sosa, b 1968, (Dom. Rep.) right fielder; 66 homers, NL MVP, 1998; 1st to hit 60+ homers 3 times (1998, '99, 2001).

Warren Spahn, 1921-2003, pitcher; won 363 NL games; 20-game winner 13 times; Cy Young award, 1957.

Tris Speaker, 1888-1958, AL outfielder; batted .345 over 22 seasons; hit record 792 career doubles.

Mark Spitz, b 1950, swimmer; won 7 golds at 1972 Olympics.

Amos Alonzo Stagg, 1862-1965, football innovator; Univ. of Chicago football coach for 41 years, 5 undefeated seasons.

Bart Starr, b 1934, Green Bay Packers quarterback; led team to 5 NFL titles, 2 Super Bowl victories.

Roger Staubach, b 1942, Dallas Cowboys quarterback; leading NFC passer 5 times.

George Steinbrenner, 1930-2010, NY Yankees owner.

Casey Stengel, 1890-1975, managed Yankees to 10 pennants, 7 World Series wins between 1949 and 1960.

Jackie Stewart, b 1939, (Scot.) auto racer; 27 Grand Prix wins.

John Stockton, b 1962, Utah Jazz guard; NBA career leader in assists, steals; NBA assists leader, 1988-96.

Samantha Stosur, b 1984, (Austral.) tennis player; won U.S. Open, 2011, French Open, 2012.

Picabo Street, b 1971, skier; 2-time World Cup downhill champion (1995-96); Olympic super G gold medalist, 1998.

Louise Suggs, b 1923, golfer; U.S. Women's Open champ, 1949, '52; 11 major victories, ranks 3rd all-time.

John L. Sullivan, 1858-1918, last bareknuckle heavyweight champion, 1882-92.

Pat Summitt, b 1952, women's basketball coach; led Tennessee Lady Vols to 8 NCAA titles (1987, '89, '91, '96-'98, 2007-08); all-time winningest NCAA coach.

Ichiro Suzuki, b 1973, (Japan) center fielder for the Seattle Mariners; Pacific League MVP, 1994, '95, '96; American League MVP, 2001; single-season hits record (262), 2004.

Sheryl Swoopes, b 1971, guard/forward; 1st player named WNBA MVP 3 times (2000, '02, '05).

Fran Tarkenton, b 1940, Minnesota, NY Giants quarterback; 4th in career TD passes (342); 1975 Player of the Year.

Diana Taurasi, b 1982, WNBA shooting guard, Phoenix Mercury; Olympic gold medalist, 2008, '12; WNBA MVP, 2009.

Lawrence Taylor, b 1959, linebacker; led NY Giants to 2 Super Bowl titles; played in 10 Pro Bowls.

Jenny Thompson, b 1973, swimmer; most decorated U.S. female Olympian; 12 medals (8 gold) in 1992, '96, 2000, '04.

Daley Thompson, b 1958, (Br.) decathlete; Olympic gold medalist in 1980, '84.

Bobby Thomson, 1923-2010, outfielder/3B; known for pennant-clinching "Shot Heard 'Round the World" for the NY Giants, 1951.

Jim Thorpe, 1888-1953, football All-American, 1911, '12; won pentathlon and decathlon, 1912 Olympics.

Bill Tilden, 1893-1953, won 7 U.S. tennis titles, 3 Wimbledon.

Y. A. Tittle, b 1926, NY Giants quarterback; MVP, 1961, '63.

Alberto Tomba "La Bomba," b 1966, (It.) skier; 5 Olympic alpine medals (3 golds, 2 silver) in 1988, '92, '94.

LaDainian "L.T." Tomlinson, b 1979, running back; NFL records for single season touchdowns (31), rushing touchdowns (28), most points scored in a single season (186).

Joe Torre, b 1940, former MLB player; managed L.A. Dodgers, NY Yankees, St. Louis Cardinals, Atlanta Braves, and NY Mets.

Lee Trevino, b 1939, golfer; won U.S., British Open twice.

Bryan Trottier, b 1956, (Can.) Islanders, Penguins center for 6 Stanley Cup champs.

Gene Tunney, 1897-1978, heavyweight champion, 1926-28.

Mike Tyson, b 1966, undisputed heavyweight champ, 1987-90; at 20, youngest to win a heavyweight title (WBC, 1986).

Wyomia Tyus, b 1945, Olympic 100m gold medalist, 1964, '68.

Johnny Unitas, 1933-2002, Baltimore Colts quarterback; passed for more than 40,000 yds.; MVP, 1957, '67.

Al Unser, b 1939, Indy 500 winner 4 times.

Bobby Unser, b 1934, Indy 500 winner 3 times.

Brian Urlacher, b 1978, Chicago Bears linebacker; Defensive Rookie of the Year, 2000; 7-time Pro Bowler.

Norm Van Brocklin, 1926-83, quarterback; passed for game record 554 yds., 1951; MVP, 1960.

Amy Van Dyken, b 1973, swimmer; first American woman to win 4 gold medals in one Olympics (1996).

Justin Verlander, b 1983, pitcher; won AL MVP and Cy Young, 2011.

Michael Vick, b 1980, quarterback; suspended and convicted (2007) of illegal dog fighting, gambling activities.

Lasse Viren, b 1949, (Fin.) runner; Olympic 5,000m and 10,000m gold medalist in 1972, 1976.

Lindsey Vonn, b 1984; 1st U.S. woman to win the world super-G championship, gold medal in downhill, 2010 Olympics; 3 World Cup titles 2008-10.

Joey Votto, b 1983, (Can.) Cincinnati Reds 1st baseman; NL MVP, 2010.

Dwyane Wade, b 1982, guard; led Miami Heat to NBA title, 2006; finals MVP, 2006; NBA scoring title, 2009.

Honus Wagner, 1874-1955, Pittsburgh Pirates shortstop; 8 NL batting titles.

Grete Waitz, 1953-2011, (Nor.) 9-time winner of the New York City Marathon (1978-80, '82-'86, '88).

"Jersey" Joe Walcott, 1914-94, boxer; became heavyweight champion at age 37, 1951-52.

Kerri Walsh Jennings, b 1978, beach volleyball player; 3-time Olympic gold medalist with Misty May-Treanor (2004, '08, '12).

Bill Walton, b 1952, center; led Portland Trail Blazers to 1977 NBA title; MVP, 1978; NBA TV commentator.

Kurt Warner, b 1971, Rams, Giants, Cardinals quarterback; NFL MVP, 1999, 2001; Super Bowl MVP, 2000.

Tom Watson, b 1949, golfer; 6-time PGA Player of the Year; won 5 British Opens, 2 Masters, U.S. Open.

Karrie Webb, b 1974, (Austral.) golfer; youngest woman (26 yrs., 6 mos.) to win career Grand Slam, 1999-2001.

Johnny Weissmuller, 1903-84, swimmer; won 52 national championships, 5 Olympic gold medals; set 67 world records.

Jerry West, b 1938, L.A. Lakers guard; had career average 27 pts. per game; first team all-star 10 times.

Dan Wheldon, 1978-2011, (Br.) race-car driver; 2-time Indy 500 winner (2005, 2011).

Byron "Whizzer" White, 1917-2002, running back; led NCAA in scoring and rushing at Colorado, 1937; led NFL in rushing twice, 1938, '40; Supreme Court justice, 1962-93.

Shaun White, b 1986, snowboarder/skateboarder; Olympic gold medalist in halfpipe (2006, '10).

Kathy Whitworth, b 1939, 7-time LPGA Player of the Year (1966-69, '71-'73); 88 tour wins, most on LPGA or PGA tour.

Michelle Wie, b 1989, golfer; in 2002 became youngest-ever qualifier for LPGA event; turned pro at age 15.

Michael Wilbon, b 1958, commentator/analyst for ESPN and ABC.

Bradley Wiggins, b 1980, (Br.) cyclist; Tour de France winner, 2012; 4-time Olympic gold medalist (2004, '08, '12).

Lenny Wilkens, b 1937, 2nd winningest coach in NBA history; Hall of Fame player and coach.

Serena Williams, b 1981, tennis champ; won at Wimbledon (2002-03, '09-'10, '12), U.S. Open (1999, 2002, '08, '12), Australian Open (2003, '05, '07, '09, '10), French Open (2002); Olympic gold medals in singles (2012) and doubles (2000, '08, '12) with sister Venus.

Ted Williams, 1918-2002, Boston Red Sox outfielder; won 6 batting titles, 2 triple crowns; hit .406 in 1941.

Venus Williams, b 1980, tennis champ at Wimbledon (2000, '01, '05, '07, '08), U.S. Open (2000, '01); Olympic gold medals in singles (2000) and doubles with sister Serena (2000, '08, '12).

Helen Wills Moody, 1905-98, tennis star; won U.S. Open 7 times, Wimbledon 8 times.

Katarina Witt, b 1965, (Ger.) figure skater; won Olympic gold medal, 1984, '88; world champ, 1984-85, '87-'88.

John Wooden, 1910-2010, UCLA basketball coach; 10 NCAA titles.

Tiger Woods, b 1975, golfer; youngest to win career Grand Slam, at age 24 (1997-2000); 14 career major titles.

Mickey Wright, b 1935, golfer; won LPGA and U.S. Open championship 4 times; 82 career wins, including 13 majors.

Eric Wynalda, b 1969, soccer; 2nd leading U.S. international goal scorer with 34.

Kristi Yamaguchi, b 1971, figure skater; won national, world, Olympic titles in 1992.

Yao Ming, b 1980, (China) center for Houston Rockets; 8-time NBA All-Star.

Carl Yastrzemski, b 1939, Boston Red Sox slugger; won 3 batting titles; triple crown, 1967.

Cy Young, 1867-1955, pitcher; won record 511 games.

Steve Young, b 1961, 49ers quarterback; led NFL in passing, 1991-94, '96, '97; NFL MVP, 1992, '94; Super Bowl MVP, 1995.

Babe Didrikson Zaharias, 1911-56, all-around athlete; 3 track-and-field medals (2 golds), 1932 Olympics; won 10 golf majors; also played baseball; 6-time AP Female Athlete of the Year.

Emil Zátopek, 1922-2000, (Czech.) runner; won 3 gold medals at 1952 Olympics (5,000m, 10,000m, marathon).

Zinedine Zidane, b 1972, (Fr.) soccer midfielder; led France to 1998 World Cup title; named top player in 2006; 3-time FIFA world player of the year (1998, 2000, '03).

Writers of the Present

Name	Birthplace	Birthdate
Chinua Achebe	Ogidi, Nigeria	11/16/30
Richard Adams	Newbury, England, UK	5/9/20
Edward Albee	Washington, DC	3/12/28
Mitch Albom	Passaic, NJ	5/23/58
Elizabeth Alexander	New York, NY	5/30/62
Isabel Allende	Lima, Peru	8/2/42
Dorothy Allison	Greenville, SC.	4/11/49
Martin Amis	Oxford, England, UK.	8/25/49
Maya Angelou	St. Louis, MO	4/4/28
Piers Anthony	Oxford, England, UK.	8/6/34
Jeffrey Archer	Somerset, England, UK	4/15/40
John Ashbery	Rochester, NY	7/28/27
Margaret Atwood	Ottawa, ON, Canada.	11/18/39
David Auburn	Chicago, IL	1969
Jean Auel	Chicago, IL	2/18/36
Paul Auster	Newark, NJ	2/3/47
Alan Ayckbourn	Hampstead, England, UK.	4/12/39
Nicholson Baker	New York, NY	1/7/57
David Baldacci	Richmond, VA.	8/5/60
Russell Banks	Newton, MA	3/28/40
John Barth	Cambridge, MD	5/27/30
Ann Beattie	Washington, DC	9/8/47
Alan Bennett	Leeds, UK.	5/9/34
John Berendt	Syracuse, NY	12/5/39
Elizabeth Berg	St. Paul, MN	12/2/48
Thomas Berger	Cincinnati, OH	7/20/24
Judy Blume	Elizabeth, NJ	2/12/38
T. Coraghessan Boyle	Peekskill, NY.	12/2/48
Barbara Taylor Bradford	Leeds, England, UK	5/10/33
Christopher Bram	Buffalo, NY	2/22/52
Geraldine Brooks	Sydney, Australia	9/14/55
Dan Brown	Exeter, NH	6/22/64
Rita Mae Brown	Hanover, PA	11/28/44
Christopher Buckley	New York, NY	5/5/05
James Lee Burke	Houston, TX	12/5/36
Augusten Burroughs	Pittsburgh, PA.	10/23/65
Robert Olen Butler	Granite City, IL	1/20/45
A. S. Byatt	Sheffield, England, UK	8/24/36
Ethan Canin	Ann Arbor, MI	7/19/60
Peter Carey	Bacchus-Marsh, Victoria, Australia	5/7/43
Robert A. Caro	New York, NY	10/30/35
Caleb Carr	New York, NY	8/2/55
Michael Chabon	Washington, DC	5/24/63
Tracy Chevalier	Washington, DC	10/19/62
Sandra Cisneros	Chicago, IL	12/20/54
Tom Clancy	Baltimore, MD.	4/12/47
Mary Higgins Clark	Bronx, NY	12/24/27
Beverly Cleary	McMinnville, OR	4/12/16
Harlan Coben	Newark, NJ	1/4/62
Paulo Coelho	Rio de Janeiro, Brazil	8/24/47
J(ohn) M(axwell) Coetzee	Capetown, S. Africa	2/9/40
Billy Collins	New York, NY	3/22/41
Jackie Collins	London, England, UK	10/4/41
Suzanne Collins	Hartford, CT	8/10/62
Evan S. Connell	Kansas City, MO.	8/17/24
Pat Conroy	Atlanta, GA	10/26/45
Robin Cook	New York, NY	5/4/40
Patricia Cornwell	Miami, FL	6/9/56
Michael Cunningham	Cincinnati, OH	11/6/52
Clive Cussler	Aurora, IL	7/15/31
Don DeLillo	Bronx, NY.	11/20/36
Nelson DeMille	New York, NY	8/23/43
Junot Díaz	Santo Domingo, Dominican Republic	12/31/68
Joan Didion	Sacramento, CA	12/5/34
Annie Dillard	Pittsburgh, PA	4/30/45
E. L. Doctorow	Bronx, NY.	1/6/31
Emma Donoghue	Dublin, Ireland.	10/24/69
Rita Dove	Akron, OH.	8/28/52
Roddy Doyle	Dublin, Ireland.	5/8/58
Carol Ann Duffy	Glasgow, Scotland, UK.	12/23/55
Umberto Eco	Alessandria, Italy	1/5/32
Jennifer Egan	Chicago, IL	9/7/62
Dave Eggers	Boston, MA.	3/12/70
Bret Easton Ellis	Los Angeles, CA	3/7/64
James Ellroy	Los Angeles, CA	3/4/48
Louise Erdrich	Little Falls, MN	6/7/54
Laura Esquivel	Mexico City, Mexico	9/30/50
Jeffrey Eugenides	Detroit, MI.	3/8/60
Janet Evanovich	South River, NJ.	4/22/43
Lawrence Ferlinghetti	Yonkers, NY	3/24/19
Helen Fielding	Morley, Yorkshire, England, UK	2/19/58
Fannie Flagg	Birmingham, AL	9/21/44
Vince Flynn	St. Paul, MN	4/6/66
Dario Fo	San Giano, Italy	3/26/26
Ken Follett	Cardiff, Wales, UK.	6/5/49
Richard Ford	Jackson, MS	2/16/44
Frederick Forsyth	Ashford, England, UK.	8/25/38
Paula Fox	New York, NY	4/22/23

Name	Birthplace	Birthdate
Jonathan Franzen	Western Springs, IL	8/17/59
Michael Frayn	London, England, UK	9/8/33
Charles Frazier	Asheville, NC	11/4/50
Brian Friel	Killyclogher, N. Ireland, UK	1/9/29
Ernest J. Gaines	Oscar, LA	1/15/33
Gabriel Garcia Marquez	Aracataca, Colombia	3/6/27
Frank Gilroy	Bronx, NY.	10/13/25
Malcolm Gladwell	Fareham, Hampshire, Eng., UK	9/3/63
Robert Goddard	Fareham, Hampshire, Eng., UK	11/13/54
Gail Godwin	Birmingham, AL	6/18/37
William Goldman	Highland Park, IL	8/12/31
Nadine Gordimer	Springs, S. Africa	11/20/23
Mary Gordon	Far Rockaway, NY.	12/8/49
Sue Grafton	Louisville, KY	4/24/40
Günter Grass	Danzig [now Gdansk], Poland	10/16/27
Shirley Ann Grau	New Orleans, LA	7/8/29
John Grisham	Jonesboro, AR	2/8/55
John Guare	New York, NY	2/5/38
Pete Hamill	Brooklyn, NY.	6/24/35
David Handler	Los Angeles, CA	9/14/52
Paul Harding	Wenham, MA	12/19/67
David Hare	St. Leonards, Sussex, England, UK	6/5/47
Jim Harrison	Grayling, MI	12/11/37
Robert Hass	San Francisco, CA	3/1/41
Seamus Heaney	Mossbaum, Co. Derry, N. Ire., UK	4/13/39
Mark Helprin	New York, NY	6/28/47
Carl Hiaasen	Plantation, FL	3/12/53
Oscar Hijuelos	New York, NY.	8/24/51
Laura Hillenbrand	Fairfax, VA.	5/15/67
S. E. Hinton	Tulsa, OK	7/22/48
Alice Hoffman	New York, NY	3/16/52
Alan Hollinghurst	Stroud, Gloucestershire, UK	5/26/54
Khaled Hosseini	Kabul, Afghanistan	3/4/65
John Irving	Exeter, NH	3/2/42
Walter Isaacson	New Orleans, LA	5/20/52
Kazuo Ishiguro	Nagasaki, Japan	11/8/54
John Jakes	Chicago, IL	3/31/32
E. L. James	London, England, UK	1963
P. D. James	Oxford, England, UK.	8/3/20
Elfriede Jelinek	Müzzuschlag, Austria	10/20/46
Ha Jin	Liaoning, China.	2/21/56
Edward P. Jones	Washington, DC	10/5/50
Erica Jong	New York, NY	3/26/42
Sebastian Junger	Boston, MA.	1/17/62
Jan Karon	Lenoir, NC.	3/14/37
Garrison Keillor	Anoka, MN	8/7/42
Thomas Keneally	Sydney, Australia	10/7/35
William Kennedy	Albany, NY	1/16/28
Sue Monk Kidd	Sylvester, GA	8/12/48
Jamaica Kincaid	St. John's, Antigua	5/25/49
Stephen King	Portland, ME.	9/21/47
Barbara Kingsolver	Annapolis, MD	4/8/55
Maxine Hong Kingston	Stockton, CA.	10/27/40
Galway Kinnell	Providence, RI	2/1/27
Dean Koontz	Everett, PA	7/9/45
Ted Kooser	Ames, IA.	4/25/39
Jon Krakauer	Brookline, MA.	4/12/54
Judith Krantz	New York, NY	1/9/28
Maxine Kumin	Philadelphia, PA	6/6/25
Milan Kundera	Brno, Czechoslovakia	4/1/29
Tony Kushner	New York, NY	7/16/56
Jhumpa Lahiri	London, England, UK	1967
Erik Larson	Brooklyn, NY.	1/3/54
David Leavitt	Pittsburgh, PA	6/23/61
John Le Carré	Poole, England, UK	10/19/31
Jean Marie Gustave Le Clézio	Nice, France	4/13/40
Ursula K. Le Guin	Berkeley, CA.	10/21/29
Harper Lee	Monroeville, AL	4/28/26
Elmore Leonard	New Orleans, LA	10/11/25
Doris Lessing	Kermanshah, Persia	10/22/19
Jonathan Lethem	Brooklyn, NY.	2/19/64
David Lodge	South London, England, UK.	1/28/35
Alison Lurie	Chicago, IL	9/3/26
Gregory Maguire	Albany, NY	6/9/54
David Malouf	Brisbane, Queensland, Australia	3/20/34
Thomas Mallon	Glen Cove, NY	11/2/51
David Mamet	Chicago, IL	11/30/47
Yann Martel	Salamanca, Spain	6/25/63
George R.R. Martin	Bayonne, NJ	9/20/48
Bobbie Ann Mason	nr. Mayfield, KY.	5/1/40
Peter Matthiessen	New York, NY	5/22/27
Armistead Maupin	Washington, DC	4/13/44
Cormac McCarthy	Providence, RI	7/20/33
Colleen McCullough	Wellington, NSW, Australia	6/1/37
David McCullough	Pittsburgh, PA.	7/7/33
Alice McDermott	Brooklyn, NY.	6/27/53

Name	Birthplace	Birthdate	Name	Birthplace	Birthdate
Ian McEwan	Aldershot, England, UK	6/21/48	Marilynne Robinson	Sandpoint, IL	11/26/43
Thomas McGuane	Wyandotte, MI	12/11/39	Philip Roth	Newark, NJ	3/19/33
Terry McMillan	Port Huron, MI	10/18/51	J. K. Rowling	Chipping Sodbury, Eng., UK	7/31/65
Larry McMurtry	Wichita Falls, TX	6/3/36	Norman Rush	Oakland, CA	10/24/33
Terrence McNally	St. Petersburg, FL	11/3/39	Salman Rushdie	Bombay, India	6/19/47
John McPhee	Princeton, NJ	3/8/31	Richard Russo	Johnstown, NY	7/15/49
W(illiam) S(tanley)			Alice Sebold	Madison, WI	9/6/63
Merwin	New York, NY	9/30/27	David Sedaris	Johnson City, NY	12/26/56
Stephenie Meyer	Hartford, CT	12/24/73	Vikram Seth	Calcutta, India	6/20/52
Steven Millhauser	New York, NY	8/3/43	John Patrick Shanley	New York, NY	10/13/50
Toni Morrison	Lorain, OH	2/18/31	Sam Shepard	Ft. Sheridan, IL	11/5/43
Walter Mosley	Los Angeles, CA	1/12/52	Anne Rivers Siddons	Atlanta, GA	1/9/36
Andrew Motion	London, England, UK	10/26/52	Neil Simon	Bronx, NY	7/4/27
Bharati Mukherjee	Calcutta, India	7/27/40	Jane Smiley	Los Angeles, CA	9/26/49
Herta Müller	Nitzkydorf, Banat, Romania	8/17/53	Wole Soyinka	Abeokuta, Nigeria	7/13/34
Alice Munro	Wingham, ON, Canada	7/10/31	Nicholas Sparks	Omaha, NE	12/31/65
Haruki Murakami	Kyoto, Japan	1/12/49	Danielle Steel	New York, NY	8/14/47
V. S. Naipaul	Chaguanas, Trinidad	8/17/32	Richard Stern	New York, NY	2/25/28
Joyce Carol Oates	Lockport, NY	6/16/38	Mary Stewart	Sunderland, England, UK	9/17/16
Edna O'Brien	Tuamgraney, Ireland	12/15/32	R(obert) L(awrence)		
Tim O'Brien	Austin, MN	10/1/46	Stine	Columbus, OH	10/8/43
Kenzaburo Oe	Uchiko, Japan	1/31/35	Kathryn Stockett	Jackson, MS	1969
Michael Ondaatje	Colombo, Sri Lanka	9/12/43	Tom Stoppard	Zlin, Czechoslovakia	7/3/37
Cynthia Ozick	New York, NY	4/17/28	Mark Strand	Summerside, PE, Canada	4/11/34
Orhan Pamuk	Istanbul, Turkey	6/7/52	Elizabeth Strout	Portland, ME	1/6/56
Suzan-Lori Parks	Fort Knox, KY	5/10/63	Amy Tan	Oakland, CA	2/19/52
Ann Patchett	Los Angeles, CA	12/2/63	Donna Tartt	Greenwood, MS	12/23/63
James Patterson	Newburgh, NY	3/22/47	Paul Theroux	Medford, MA	4/10/41
Jodi Picoult	New York, NY	5/19/66	Calvin Trillin	Kansas City, MO	12/5/35
Marge Piercy	Detroit, MI	3/31/36	Scott F. Turow	Chicago, IL	4/12/49
Robert Pinsky	Long Branch, NJ	10/20/40	Anne Tyler	Minneapolis, MN	10/25/41
Michael Pollan	New York, NY	2/6/55	Mario Vargas Llosa	Arequipa, Peru	3/28/36
Richard Powers	Evanston, IL	6/18/57	Paula Vogel	Washington, DC	11/16/51
Richard Price	Bronx, NY	10/12/49	Sarah Vowell	Muskogee, OK	12/27/69
E. Annie Proulx	Norwich, CT	8/22/35	Derek Walcott	Castries, Saint Lucia	1/23/30
Philip Pullman	Norwich, England, UK	10/19/46	Alice Walker	Eatonton, GA	2/9/44
Thomas Pynchon	Glen Cove, NY	5/8/37	Joseph Wambaugh	East Pittsburgh, PA	1/22/37
David Rabe	Dubuque, IA	3/10/40	Edmund White	Cincinnati, OH	1/13/40
Ishmael Reed	Chattanooga, TN	2/22/38	Elie Wiesel	Sighet, Romania	9/30/28
Ruth Rendell	London, England, UK	2/17/30	Tom Wolfe	Richmond, VA	3/2/31
Anne Rice	New Orleans, LA	10/4/41	Tobias Wolff	Birmingham, AL	6/19/45
Mary Roach	Etna, NH	3/20/59	Herman Wouk	New York, NY	5/27/15
Nora Roberts	Silver Spring, MD	10/10/50	Yevgeny Yevtushenko	Zima, Russia	7/18/33

Writers of the Past

See also Journalists, and Greeks and Romans in Historical Figures chapter.

Alice Adams, 1926-99, (U.S.) novelist, short-story writer. *Superior Woman*.

James Agee, 1909-55, (U.S.) novelist. *A Death in the Family*.

S(hmuel) Y(osef) Agnon, 1888-1970, (Isr.) Hebrew novelist. *Only Yesterday*.

Conrad Aiken, 1889-1973, (U.S.) poet, critic. *Ushant*.

Anna Akhmatova, 1889-1966, (Russ.) poet. *Requiem*.

Louisa May Alcott, 1832-88, (U.S.) novelist. *Little Women*.

Sholom Aleichem, 1859-1916, (Russ.) Yiddish writer. *Tevye's Daughters, The Old Country*.

Vicente Aleixandre, 1898-1984, (Sp.) poet. *La destrucción o el amor, Dialogolos del conocimiento*.

Horatio Alger, 1832-99, (U.S.) "rags-to-riches" books.

Jorge Amado, 1912-2001, (Brazil) novelist. *Dona Flor and Her Two Husbands, The Violent Land*.

Eric Ambler, 1909-98, (Br.) suspense novelist. *A Coffin for Dimitrios*.

Kingsley Amis, 1922-95, (Br.) novelist, critic. *Lucky Jim*.

Hans Christian Andersen, 1805-75, (Den.) author of fairy tales. *The Ugly Duckling*.

Maxwell Anderson, 1888-1959, (U.S.) playwright. *What Price Glory?, High Tor, Winterset, Key Largo*.

Sherwood Anderson, 1876-1941, (U.S.) short-story writer. "Death in the Woods," *Winesburg, Ohio*.

Reinaldo Arenas, 1943-90, (Cuba) short-story writer, novelist. *Before Night Falls*.

Ludovico Ariosto, 1474-1533, (It.) poet. *Orlando Furioso*.

Matthew Arnold, 1822-88, (Br.) poet, critic. "Thrysis," "Dover Beach," "Culture and Anarchy."

Isaac Asimov, 1920-92, (U.S.) versatile writer, espec. of science-fiction. *I Robot*.

Miguel Angel Asturias, 1899-1974, (Guatemala) novelist. *El Señor Presidente*.

Louis Auchincloss, 1917-2010, (U.S.) novelist, memoirist, short-story writer. *The Rector of Justin*.

W(ystan) H(ugh) Auden, 1907-73, (Br.) poet, playwright, literary critic. "The Age of Anxiety."

Jane Austen, 1775-1817, (Br.) novelist. *Pride and Prejudice, Sense and Sensibility, Emma, Mansfield Park*.

Isaac Babel, 1894-1941, (Russ.) short-story writer, playwright. *Odessa Tales, Red Cavalry*.

James Baldwin, 1924-87, (U.S.) author, playwright. *The Fire Next Time, Blues for Mister Charlie*.

Honoré de Balzac, 1799-1850, (Fr.) novelist. *Le Père Goriot, Cousine Bette, Eugénie Grandet*.

James M. Barrie, 1860-1937, (Br.) playwright, novelist. *Peter Pan, Dear Brutus, What Every Woman Knows*.

Charles Baudelaire, 1821-67, (Fr.) poet. *Les Fleurs du Mal*.

L(yman) Frank Baum, 1856-1919, (U.S.) *Wizard of Oz* series.

Simone de Beauvoir, 1908-86, (Fr.) novelist, essayist. *The Second Sex, Memoirs of a Dutiful Daughter*.

Samuel Beckett, 1906-89, (Ire.) novelist, playwright. *Waiting for Godot, Endgame* (plays); *Murphy, Watt, Molloy* (novels).

Brendan Behan, 1923-64, (Ire.) playwright. *The Quare Fellow, The Hostage, Borstal Boy*.

Saul Bellow, 1915-2005, (U.S.) novelist. *The Adventures of Augie March, Humboldt's Gift*.

Robert Benchley, 1889-1945, (U.S.) humorist.

Stephen Vincent Benét, 1898-1943, (U.S.) poet, novelist. *John Brown's Body*.

Jan Berenstain, 1923-2012, and **Stan Berenstain**, 1923-2005, (U.S.) co-writers and illustrators of *Berenstain Bears* series of children's books.

John Berryman, 1914-72, (U.S.) poet. *Homage to Mistress Bradstreet*.

Ambrose Bierce, 1842-1914, (U.S.) short-story writer, journalist. *In the Midst of Life, The Devil's Dictionary*.

Maeve Binchy, 1940-2012, (Ire.) novelist, short-story writer, *Circle of Friends, Tara Road*.

Elizabeth Bishop, 1911-79, (U.S.) poet. *North and South—A Cold Spring*.

William Blake, 1757-1827, (Br.) poet, artist. *Songs of Innocence, Songs of Experience*.

Aleksandr Blok, 1880-1921, (Russ.) poet. "The Twelve," "The Scythians."

Giovanni Boccaccio, 1313-75, (It.) poet. *Decameron*.

Heinrich Böll, 1917-85, (Ger.) novelist, short-story writer. *Group Portrait With Lady*.

Jorge Luis Borges, 1900-86, (Arg.) short-story writer, poet, essayist. *Labyrinths*.

James Boswell, 1740-95, (Scot.) biographer. *The Life of Samuel Johnson*.

Pierre Boulle, 1913-94, (Fr.) novelist. *The Bridge Over the River Kwai, Planet of the Apes*.

Paul Bowles, 1910-99, (U.S.) novelist, short-story writer. *The Sheltering Sky*.

Ray Bradbury, 1920-2012, (U.S.) novelist, short-story writer. *Fahrenheit 451, The Martian Chronicles.*

Anne Bradstreet, c. 1612-72, (U.S.) poet. *The Tenth Muse Lately Sprung Up in America.*

Bertolt Brecht, 1898-1956, (Ger.) dramatist, poet. *The Threepenny Opera, Mother Courage and Her Children.*

Joseph Brodsky, 1940-96, (Russ.-U.S.) poet. *A Part of Speech, Less Than One, To Urania.*

Charlotte Brontë, 1816-55, (Br.) novelist. *Jane Eyre.*

Emily Brontë, 1818-48, (Br.) novelist. *Wuthering Heights.*

Sterling A. Brown, 1901-89, (U.S.) poet, literature professor. *Southern Road.*

William Wells Brown, 1815-84, (U.S.) writer, memoirist; first African American to publish a novel, *Clotel*, 1853.

Elizabeth Barrett Browning, 1806-61, (Br.) poet. *Sonnets From the Portuguese, Aurora Leigh.*

Robert Browning, 1812-89, (Br.) poet. "My Last Duchess," "Fra Lippo Lippi," *The Ring and the Book.*

Pearl S. Buck, 1892-1973, (U.S.) novelist. *The Good Earth.*

Charles Bukowski, 1920-94, (U.S.) novelist, poet. *Ham on Rye, Women.*

Mikhail Bulgakov, 1891-1940, (Russ.) novelist, playwright. *The Heart of a Dog, The Master and Margarita.*

John Bunyan, 1628-88, (Br.) writer. *Pilgrim's Progress.*

Anthony Burgess, 1917-93, (Br.) author. *A Clockwork Orange.*

Frances Hodgson Burnett, 1849-1924, (Br.-U.S.) novelist. *The Secret Garden.*

Robert Burns, 1759-96, (Scot.) poet. "Flow Gently, Sweet Afton," "My Heart's in the Highlands," "Auld Lang Syne."

Edgar Rice Burroughs, 1875-1950, (U.S.) "Tarzan" books.

William S. Burroughs, 1914-97, (U.S.) novelist. *Naked Lunch.*

George Gordon, Lord Byron, 1788-1824, (Br.) poet. *Don Juan, Childe Harold, Manfred, Cain.*

Pedro Calderon de la Barca, 1600-81, (Sp.) playwright. *Life Is a Dream.*

Hortense Calisher, 1911-2009, (U.S.) novelist, short-story writer. *False Entry.*

Italo Calvino, 1923-85, (It.) novelist, short-story writer. *If on a Winter's Night a Traveler.*

Luis Vaz de Camoes, 1524?-80 (Port.) poet. *The Lusiads.*

Albert Camus, 1913-60, (Fr.) writer. *The Stranger, The Fall.*

Elias Canetti, 1905-94, (Bulg.) novelist, essayist. *Auto-Da-Fe.*

Karel Capek, 1890-1938, (Czech.) playwright, novelist, essayist. *R.U.R. (Rossum's Universal Robots).*

Truman Capote, 1924-84, (U.S.) author. *Other Voices, Other Rooms; Breakfast at Tiffany's; In Cold Blood.*

Lewis Carroll (Charles Dodgson), 1832-98, (Br.) writer, mathematician. *Alice's Adventures in Wonderland.*

Barbara Cartland 1901-2000, (Br.) romance novelist.

Giacomo Casanova, 1725-98, (It.) adventurer, memoirist.

Willa Cather, 1873-1947, (U.S.) novelist. *O Pioneers!, My Antonia, Death Comes for the Archbishop.*

Constantine Cavafy, 1863-1933, (Gr.) poet. "Ithaka," "Sensual Pleasures."

Camilo Jose Cela, 1916-2001, (Sp.) novelist. *The Family of Pascual Duarte, The Hive.*

Miguel de Cervantes Saavedra, 1547-1616, (Sp.) novelist, dramatist, poet. *Don Quixote.*

Raymond Chandler, 1888-1959, (U.S.) writer of detective fiction. Philip Marlowe series.

Geoffrey Chaucer, c. 1340-1400, (Br.) poet. *The Canterbury Tales, Troilus and Criseyde.*

John Cheever, 1912-82, (U.S.) novelist, short-story writer. *The Wapshot Scandal*, "The Country Husband."

Anton Chekhov, 1860-1904, (Russ.) short-story writer, dramatist. *Uncle Vanya, The Cherry Orchard, The Three Sisters.*

Charles Waddell Chesnutt, 1858-1932, (U.S.) author known for his short stories. *The Conjure Woman.*

G(ilbert) K(eith) Chesterton, 1874-1936, (Br.) critic, novelist, relig. apologist. Father Brown series of mysteries.

Kate Chopin, 1851-1904, (U.S.) writer. *The Awakening.*

Agatha Christie, 1890-1976, (Br.) mystery writer; created Miss Marple, Hercule Poirot. *And Then There Were None, Murder on the Orient Express, Murder of Roger Ackroyd.*

James Clavell, 1924-94, (Br.-U.S.) novelist. *Shogun, King Rat.*

Arthur C. Clarke, 1917-2008, (Br.) science fiction writer. *2001: A Space Odyssey.*

Jean Cocteau, 1889-1963, (Fr.) writer, visual artist, filmmaker. *The Beauty and the Beast, Les Enfants Terribles.*

Samuel Taylor Coleridge, 1772-1834, (Br.) poet, critic. "Kubla Khan," "The Rime of the Ancient Mariner."

(Sidonie) Colette, 1873-1954, (Fr.) novelist. *Claudine, Gigi.*

Wilkie Collins, 1824-89, (Br.) novelist. *The Moonstone.*

Joseph Conrad, 1857-1924, (Br.) novelist. *Lord Jim, Heart of Darkness, The Secret Agent.*

James Fenimore Cooper, 1789-1851, (U.S.) novelist. *Leatherstocking Tales, The Last of the Mohicans.*

Pierre Corneille, 1606-84, (Fr.) dramatist. *Medeé, Le Cid.*

Hart Crane, 1899-1932, (U.S.) poet. "The Bridge."

Stephen Crane, 1871-1900, (U.S.) novelist, short-story writer. *The Red Badge of Courage*, "The Open Boat."

Harry Crews, 1935-2012, (U.S.) novelist. *A Feast of Snakes.*

Michael Crichton, 1942-2008, (U.S.) writer. *The Andromeda Strain, Jurassic Park.*

Countee Cullen, 1903-46, (U.S.) poet, prominent in the Harlem Renaissance of the 1920s. *The Black Christ.*

E. E. Cummings, 1894-1962, (U.S.) poet. *Tulips and Chimneys.*

Roald Dahl, 1916-90, (Br.-U.S.) writer. *Charlie and the Chocolate Factory, James and the Giant Peach.*

Gabriele D'Annunzio, 1863-1938, (It.) poet, novelist, dramatist. *The Child of Pleasure, The Intruder, The Victim.*

Dante Alighieri, 1265-1321, (It.) poet. *The Divine Comedy.*

Robertson Davies, 1913-95, (Can.) novelist, playwright, essayist. Salterton, Deptford, and Cornish trilogies.

Daniel Defoe, 1660-1731, (Br.) writer. *Robinson Crusoe, Moll Flanders, Journal of the Plague Year.*

Charles Dickens, 1812-70, (Br.) novelist. *David Copperfield, Oliver Twist, Great Expectations, A Tale of Two Cities.*

Philip K. Dick, 1928-82, (U.S.) science fiction writer. *Do Androids Dream of Electric Sheep?*

James Dickey, 1923-97, (U.S.) poet, novelist. *Deliverance.*

Emily Dickinson, 1830-86, (U.S.) lyric poet. "Because I could not stop for Death . . .," "Success is counted sweetest . . ."

Isak Dinesen (Karen Blixen), 1885-1962, (Den.) author. *Out of Africa, Seven Gothic Tales, Winter's Tales.*

John Donne, 1573-1631, (Br.) poet. *Songs and Sonnets.*

José Donoso, 1924-96, (Chile) surreal novelist and short-story writer. *The Obscene Bird of Night.*

John Dos Passos, 1896-1970, (U.S.) novelist. *U.S.A.*

Fyodor Dostoyevsky, 1821-81, (Russ.) novelist. *Crime and Punishment, The Brothers Karamazov, The Possessed.*

Arthur Conan Doyle, 1859-1930, (Br.) novelist. Sherlock Holmes mystery stories.

Theodore Dreiser, 1871-1945, (U.S.) novelist. *An American Tragedy, Sister Carrie.*

John Dryden, 1631-1700, (Br.) poet, dramatist, critic. *All for Love, Mac Flecknoe, Absalom and Achitophel.*

Alexandre Dumas (père), 1802-70, (Fr.) novelist, dramatist. *The Three Musketeers, The Count of Monte Cristo.*

Alexandre Dumas (fils), 1824-95, (Fr.) dramatist, novelist. *La Dame aux Camélias, Le Demi-Monde.*

Paul Laurence Dunbar, 1872-1906, (U.S.) poet, novelist. *Lyrics of Lowly Life.*

Lawrence Durrell, 1912-90, (Br.) novelist, poet. *Alexandria Quartet.*

Ilya G. Ehrenburg, 1891-1967, (Russ.) writer. *The Thaw.*

George Eliot (Mary Ann or Marian Evans), 1819-80, (Br.) novelist. *Silas Marner, Middlemarch.*

T(homas) S(tearns) Eliot, 1888-1965, (Br.) poet, critic. *The Waste Land*, "The Love Song of J. Alfred Prufrock."

Stanley Elkin, 1930-95, (U.S.) novelist, short-story writer. *George Mills.*

Ralph Ellison, 1914-94, (U.S.) writer. *Invisible Man.*

Ralph Waldo Emerson, 1803-82, (U.S.) poet, essayist. "Brahma," "Nature," "The Over-Soul," "Self-Reliance."

James T. Farrell, 1904-79, (U.S.) novelist. *Studs Lonigan.*

Howard Fast, 1914-2003, (U.S.) novelist. *Spartacus, The Immigrants.*

William Faulkner, 1897-1962, (U.S.) novelist. *Sanctuary; Light in August; The Sound and the Fury; Absalom, Absalom!*

Edna Ferber, 1887-1968, (U.S.) novelist, short-story writer, playwright. *So Big, Cimarron, Show Boat.*

Henry Fielding, 1707-54, (Br.) novelist. *Tom Jones.*

F(rancis) Scott Fitzgerald, 1896-1940, (U.S.) short-story writer, novelist. *The Great Gatsby, Tender Is the Night.*

Gustave Flaubert, 1821-80, (Fr.) novelist. *Madame Bovary.*

Ian Fleming, 1908-64, (Br.) novelist; James Bond spy thrillers. *Dr. No, Goldfinger.*

Horton Foote, 1916-2009, (U.S.) playwright, screenwriter. *The Trip to Bountiful.*

Ford Madox Ford, 1873-1939, (Br.) novelist, critic, poet. *The Good Soldier.*

C(ecil) S(cott) Forester, 1899-1966, (Br.) writer. Horatio Hornblower books.

E(dward) M(organ) Forster, 1879-1970, (Br.) novelist. *A Passage to India, Howards End.*

Anatole France, 1844-1924, (Fr.) writer. *Penguin Island, My Friend's Book, The Crime of Sylvestre Bonnard.*

Dick Francis, 1920-2010, (Br.) crime novelist.

Marilyn French, 1929-2009, (U.S.) novelist. *The Women's Room.*

Robert Frost, 1874-1963, (U.S.) poet. "Birches," "Fire and Ice," "Stopping by Woods on a Snowy Evening."

Carlos Fuentes, 1928-2012, (Pan.) novelist, essayist. *The Old Gringo.*

William Gaddis, 1922-98, (U.S.) novelist. *The Recognitions.*

John Galsworthy, 1867-1933, (Br.) novelist, dramatist. *The Forsyte Saga.*

Federico Garcia Lorca, 1898-1936, (Sp.) poet, dramatist. *Blood Wedding.*

Erle Stanley Gardner, 1889-1970, (U.S.) mystery writer; created Perry Mason.

Jean Genet, 1911-86, (Fr.) playwright, novelist. *The Maids*.

Kahlil Gibran, 1883-1931, (Leban.-U.S.) mystical novelist, essayist, poet. *The Prophet*.

André Gide, 1869-1951, (Fr.) writer. *The Immoralist*, *The Pastoral Symphony*, *Strait Is the Gate*.

Allen Ginsberg, 1926-97, (U.S.) Beat poet. "Howl."

Jean Giraudoux, 1882-1944, (Fr.) novelist, dramatist. *Electra*, *The Madwoman of Chaillot*, *Ondine*, *Tiger at the Gate*.

Johann Wolfgang von Goethe, 1749-1832, (Ger.) poet, dramatist, novelist. *Faust*, *Sorrows of Young Werther*.

Nikolai Gogol, 1809-52, (Russ.) short-story writer, dramatist, novelist. *Dead Souls*, *The Inspector General*.

William Golding, 1911-93, (Br.) novelist. *Lord of the Flies*.

Oliver Goldsmith, 1728-74, (Br.-Ire.) dramatist, novelist. *The Vicar of Wakefield*, *She Stoops to Conquer*.

Maxim Gorky, 1868-1936, (Russ.) dramatist, novelist. *The Lower Depths*.

Robert Graves, 1895-1985, (Br.) poet, classical scholar, novelist. *I, Claudius*; *The White Goddess*.

Thomas Gray, 1716-71, (Br.) poet. "Elegy Written in a Country Churchyard," "The Progress of Poesy."

Julien Green, 1900-98, (U.S.-Fr.) expatriate American, French novelist. *Moira*, *Each Man in His Darkness*.

Graham Greene, 1904-91, (Br.) novelist. *The Power and the Glory*, *The Heart of the Matter*, *The Ministry of Fear*.

Zane Grey, 1872-1939, (U.S.) writer of Western stories.

Jakob Grimm, 1785-1863, (Ger.) philologist, folklorist; with brother **Wilhelm Grimm**, 1786-1859, collected *Grimm's Fairy Tales*.

Alex Haley, 1921-92, (U.S.) author. *Roots*.

Dashiell Hammett, 1894-1961, (U.S.) detective-story writer; created Sam Spade. *The Maltese Falcon*.

Jupiter Hammon, c. 1720-1800, (U.S.) poet; first African American to have his works published, 1761.

Knut Hamsun, 1859-1952, (Nor.) novelist. *Hunger*.

Lorraine Hansberry, 1930-65, (U.S.) playwright. *A Raisin in the Sun*.

Thomas Hardy, 1840-1928, (Br.) novelist, poet. *The Return of the Native*, *Tess of the D'Urbervilles*, *Jude the Obscure*.

E. Lynn Harris, 1955-2009, (U.S.) novelist. *Invisible Life*, *Basketball Jones*.

Joel Chandler Harris, 1848-1908, (U.S.) writer. Uncle Remus stories.

Moss Hart, 1904-61, (U.S.) playwright. *Once in a Lifetime*, *You Can't Take It With You*, *The Man Who Came to Dinner*.

Bret Harte, 1836-1902, (U.S.) short-story writer, poet. *The Luck of Roaring Camp*.

Jaroslav Hasek, 1883-1923, (Czech.) writer, playwright. *The Good Soldier Schweik*.

Vaclav Havel, 1936-2011, (Czech.) essayist, poet, playwright. *The Power of the Powerless*.

John Hawkes, 1925-98, (U.S.) experimental fiction writer. *The Goose on the Grave*, *Blood Oranges*.

Nathaniel Hawthorne, 1804-64, (U.S.) novelist, short-story writer. *The Scarlet Letter*, "Young Goodman Brown."

Heinrich Heine, 1797-1856, (Ger.) poet. *Book of Songs*.

Robert Heinlein, 1907-88, (U.S.) science-fiction writer. *Stranger in a Strange Land*.

Joseph Heller, 1923-99, (U.S.) novelist. *Catch-22*.

Lillian Hellman, 1905-84, (U.S.) playwright, memoirist. *The Little Foxes*, *An Unfinished Woman*, *Pentimento*.

Ernest Hemingway, 1899-1961, (U.S.) novelist, short-story writer. *A Farewell to Arms*, *For Whom the Bell Tolls*.

O. Henry (W. S. Porter), 1862-1910, (U.S.) short-story writer. "The Gift of the Magi."

George Herbert, 1593-1633, (Br.) poet. "The Altar," "Easter Wings."

Zbigniew Herbert, 1924-98, (Pol.) poet. "Apollo and Marsyas."

Robert Herrick, 1591-1674, (Br.) poet. "To the Virgins to Make Much of Time."

John Hersey, 1914-93, (U.S.) novelist, journalist. *Hiroshima*, *A Bell for Adano*.

Hermann Hesse, 1877-1962, (Ger.) novelist, poet. *Death and the Lover*, *Steppenwolf*, *Siddhartha*.

Tony Hillerman, 1925-2008, (U.S.) novelist. *Dance Hall of the Dead*.

James Hilton, 1900-54, (Br.) novelist. *Lost Horizon*.

Chester Himes, 1909-84, (U.S.) novelist. *Cotton Comes to Harlem*.

Oliver Wendell Holmes, 1809-94, (U.S.) poet, novelist. *The Autocrat of the Breakfast-Table*.

Gerard Manley Hopkins, 1844-89, (Br.) poet. "Pied Beauty," "God's Grandeur."

A(lfred) E. Housman, 1859-1936, (Br.) poet. *A Shropshire Lad*.

William Dean Howells, 1837-1920, (U.S.) novelist, critic. *The Rise of Silas Lapham*.

Langston Hughes, 1902-67, (U.S.) poet, lyric writer, author; a major influence in 1920s Harlem Renaissance.

Ted Hughes, 1930-98, (Br.) British poet laureate, 1984-98. *Crow*, *The Hawk in the Rain*.

Victor Hugo, 1802-85, (Fr.) poet, dramatist, novelist. *Notre Dame de Paris*, *Les Misérables*.

Zora Neale Hurston, 1903-60, (U.S.) novelist, folklorist. *Their Eyes Were Watching God*, *Mules and Men*.

Aldous Huxley, 1894-1963, (Br.) writer. *Brave New World*.

Henrik Ibsen, 1828-1906, (Nor.) dramatist, poet. *A Doll's House*, *Ghosts*, *The Wild Duck*, *Hedda Gabler*.

William Inge, 1913-73, (U.S.) playwright. *Picnic*; *Come Back, Little Sheba*; *Bus Stop*.

Eugene Ionesco, 1910-94, (Fr.) surrealist dramatist. *The Bald Soprano*, *The Chairs*.

Washington Irving, 1783-1859, (U.S.) writer. "Rip Van Winkle," "The Legend of Sleepy Hollow."

Christopher Isherwood, 1904-86, (Br.) novelist, playwright. *The Berlin Stories*.

Shirley Jackson, 1919-65, (U.S.) short-story writer. "The Lottery."

Henry James, 1843-1916, (U.S.) novelist, short-story writer, critic. *The Portrait of a Lady*, *The Ambassadors*, *Daisy Miller*.

Robinson Jeffers, 1887-1962, (U.S.) poet, dramatist. *Tamar and Other Poems*, *Medea*.

James Weldon Johnson, 1871-1938, (U.S.) poet, novelist, diplomat; lyricist for *Lift Every Voice and Sing*.

Samuel Johnson, 1709-84, (Br.) author, scholar, critic. *Dictionary of the English Language*, *Vanity of Human Wishes*.

Ben Jonson, 1572-1637, (Br.) dramatist, poet. *Volpone*.

James Joyce, 1882-1941, (Ire.) writer. *Ulysses*, *Dubliners*, *A Portrait of the Artist as a Young Man*, *Finnegans Wake*.

Ernst Junger, 1895-1998, (Ger.) novelist, essayist. *The Peace*, *On the Marble Cliff*.

Franz Kafka, 1883-1924, (Austria-Hung./Czech.) novelist, short-story writer. *The Trial*, *The Castle*, "The Metamorphosis."

George S. Kaufman, 1889-1961, (U.S.) playwright. *The Man Who Came to Dinner*, *You Can't Take It With You*.

Yasunari Kawabata, 1899-1972, (Jpn.) novelist. *The Sound of the Mountains*.

Nikos Kazantzakis, 1883-1957, (Gr.) novelist. *Zorba the Greek*, *A Greek Passion*.

Alfred Kazin, 1915-98 (U.S.) author, critic, teacher. *On Native Grounds*.

John Keats, 1795-1821, (Br.) poet. "Ode on a Grecian Urn," "Ode to a Nightingale," "La Belle Dame Sans Merci."

Jack Kerouac, 1922-69, (U.S.) author, Beat poet. *On the Road*, *The Dharma Bums*, "Mexico City Blues."

Joyce Kilmer, 1886-1918, (U.S.) poet. "Trees."

Rudyard Kipling, 1865-1936, (Br.) author, poet. "The White Man's Burden," "Gunga Din," *The Jungle Book*.

Jean de la Fontaine, 1621-95, (Fr.) poet. *Fables choisies*.

Pär Lagerkvist, 1891-1974, (Swed.) poet, dramatist, novelist. *Barabbas*, *The Sybil*.

Selma Lagerlöf, 1858-1940, (Swed.) novelist. *Jerusalem*, *The Ring of the Lowen-skolds*.

Alphonse de Lamartine, 1790-1869, (Fr.) poet, novelist, statesman. *Méditations poétiques*.

Charles Lamb, 1775-1834, (Br.) essayist. *Specimens of English Dramatic Poets*, *Essays of Elia*.

Louis L'Amour, 1908-88, (U.S.) Western author, screenwriter. *Hondo*, *The Cherokee Trail*.

Giuseppe di Lampedusa, 1896-1957, (It.) novelist. *The Leopard*.

William Langland, c. 1332-1400, (Br.) poet. *Piers Plowman*.

Ring Lardner, 1885-1933, (U.S.) short-story writer, humorist.

Steig Larsson, 1954-2004, (Swed.) novelist. *The Girl With the Dragon Tattoo*.

Arthur Laurents, 1917-2011, (U.S.) playwright and director. *West Side Story*.

D(avid) H(erbert) Lawrence, 1885-1930, (Br.) novelist. *Sons and Lovers*, *Women in Love*, *Lady Chatterley's Lover*.

Halldór Laxness, 1902-98, (Iceland) novelist. *Iceland's Bell*.

Madeleine L'Engle, 1918-2007, (U.S.) novelist of young adult fiction. *A Wrinkle in Time*.

Mikhail Lermontov, 1814-41, (Russ.) novelist, poet. "Demon," *Hero of Our Time*.

Alain-René Lesage, 1668-1747, (Fr.) novelist. *Gil Blas de Santillane*.

Gotthold Lessing, 1729-81, (Ger.) dramatist, philosopher, critic. *Miss Sara Sampson*, *Minna von Barnhelm*.

Ira Levin, 1929-2007, (U.S.) novelist, playwright. *Deathtrap*.

C(live) S(taples) Lewis, 1898-1963, (Br.) critic, novelist, religious writer. *Allegory of Love*; *The Lion, the Witch and the Wardrobe*; *Out of the Silent Planet*.

Sinclair Lewis, 1885-1951, (U.S.) novelist. *Babbitt*, *Main Street*, *Arrowsmith*, *Dodsworth*.

Vachel Lindsay, 1879-1931, (U.S.) poet. *General William Booth Enters Into Heaven*, *The Congo*.

Li Po, 701-762, (China) poet. "Song Before Drinking," "She Spins Silk."

Hugh Lofting, 1886-1947, (Br.) writer. Dr. Doolittle series.

Jack London, 1876-1916, (U.S.) novelist, journalist. *Call of the Wild*, *The Sea-Wolf*, *White Fang*.

Henry Wadsworth Longfellow, 1807-82, (U.S.) poet. *Evangeline*, *The Song of Hiawatha*.

Lope de Vega, 1562-1635, (Sp.) playwright. *Noche de San Juan*, *Maestro de Danzar*.

H(oward) P(hillips) Lovecraft, 1890-1937, (U.S.) novelist, short-story writer. "At the Mountains of Madness."

Amy Lowell, 1874-1925, (U.S.) poet, critic. "Lilacs."

James Russell Lowell, 1819-91, (U.S.) poet, editor. *Poems*, *The Biglow Papers*.

Robert Lowell, 1917-77, (U.S.) poet. "Lord Weary's Castle."

Joaquim Maria Machado de Assis, 1839-1908, (Brazil) novelist, poet. *The Posthumous Memoirs of Bras Cubas.*

Archibald MacLeish, 1892-1982, (U.S.) poet. *Conquistador.*

Naguib Mahfouz, 1911-2006, (Egypt) novelist; first Arabic-language writer to win the Nobel Prize for Literature. *Cairo Trilogy.*

Norman Mailer, 1923-2007, (U.S.) novelist, essayist, journalist. *The Naked and the Dead.*

Bernard Malamud, 1914-86, (U.S.) short-story writer, novelist. "The Magic Barrel," *The Assistant, The Fixer.*

Stéphane Mallarmé, 1842-98, (Fr.) poet. *Poésies.*

Sir Thomas Malory, c. 1410-71, (Br.) writer. *Morte d'Arthur.*

Andre Malraux, 1901-76, (Fr.) novelist. *Man's Fate.*

Osip Mandelstam, 1891-1938, (Russ.) poet. *Stone, Tristia.*

Thomas Mann, 1875-1955, (Ger.) novelist, essayist. *Buddenbrooks, The Magic Mountain,* "Death in Venice."

Katherine Mansfield, 1888-1923, (Br.) short-story writer. "Bliss."

Christopher Marlowe, 1564-93, (Br.) dramatist, poet. *Tamburlaine the Great, Dr. Faustus, The Jew of Malta.*

Andrew Marvell, 1621-78, (Br.) poet. "To His Coy Mistress."

John Masefield, 1878-1967, (Br.) poet. "Sea Fever," "Cargoes," *Salt Water Ballads.*

Edgar Lee Masters, 1869-1950, (U.S.) poet, biographer. *Spoon River Anthology.*

W(illiam) Somerset Maugham, 1874-1965, (Br.) author. *Of Human Bondage, The Moon and Sixpence.*

Guy de Maupassant, 1850-93, (Fr.) novelist, short-story writer. "A Life," "Bel-Ami," "The Necklace."

François Mauriac, 1885-1970, (Fr.) novelist, dramatist. *Viper's Tangle, The Kiss to the Leper.*

Vladimir Mayakovsky, 1893-1930, (Russ.) poet, dramatist. *The Cloud in Trousers.*

Mary McCarthy, 1912-89, (U.S.) critic, novelist, memoirist. *Memories of a Catholic Girlhood.*

Frank McCourt, 1930-2009, (U.S.) memorist. *Angela's Ashes, 'Tis, Teacher Man.*

Carson McCullers, 1917-67, (U.S.) novelist. *The Heart Is a Lonely Hunter, Member of the Wedding.*

Herman Melville, 1819-91, (U.S.) novelist, poet. *Moby-Dick, Typee, Billy Budd, Omoo.*

George Meredith, 1828-1909, (Br.) novelist, poet. *The Ordeal of Richard Feverel, The Egoist.*

Prosper Mérimée, 1803-70, (Fr.) author. *Carmen.*

James Merrill, 1926-95, (U.S.) poet. *Divine Comedies.*

James Michener, 1907-97, (U.S.) novelist. *Tales of the South Pacific.*

Edna St. Vincent Millay, 1892-1950, (U.S.) poet. *The Harp Weaver and Other Poems.*

Arthur Miller, 1915-2005, (U.S.) playwright. *The Crucible, After the Fall, Death of a Salesman.*

Henry Miller, 1891-1980, (U.S.) erotic novelist. *Tropic of Cancer.*

A(lan) A(lexander) Milne, 1882-1956, (Br.) author. *Winnie-the-Pooh.*

Czeslaw Milosz, 1911-2004, (Pol.) essayist, poet. "Esse," "Encounter."

John Milton, 1608-74, (Br.) poet, writer. *Paradise Lost, Comus, Lycidas, Areopagitica.*

Mishima Yukio (Hiraoka Kimitake) 1925-70, (Jpn.) writer. *Confessions of a Mask.*

Gabriela Mistral, 1889-1957, (Chile) poet. *Sonnets of Death.*

Margaret Mitchell, 1900-49, (U.S.) novelist. *Gone With the Wind.*

Jean Baptiste Molière, 1622-73, (Fr.) dramatist. *Tartuffe, Le Misanthrope, Le Bourgeois Gentilhomme.*

Ferenc Molnár, 1878-1952, (Hung.) dramatist, novelist. *Liliom, The Guardsman, The Swan.*

Michel de Montaigne, 1533-92, (Fr.) essayist. *Essais.*

Eugenio Montale, 1896-1981, (It.) poet.

Brian Moore, 1921-99, (Ire.-U.S.) novelist. *The Lonely Passion of Judith Hearne.*

Clement C. Moore, 1779-1863, (U.S.) poet, educator. "A Visit From Saint Nicholas."

Marianne Moore, 1887-1972, (U.S.) poet.

Alberto Moravia, 1907-90, (It.) novelist, short-story writer. *The Time of Indifference.*

Sir Thomas More, 1478-1535, (Br.) writer, statesman, saint. *Utopia.*

Wright Morris, 1910-98, (U.S.) novelist. *My Uncle Dudley.*

Murasaki Shikibu, c. 978-1026, (Jpn.) novelist. *The Tale of Genji.*

Iris Murdoch, 1919-99, (Br.) novelist, philosopher. *The Sea, The Sea.*

Alfred de Musset, 1810-57, (Fr.) poet, dramatist. *La Confession d'un Enfant du Siècle.*

Vladimir Nabokov, 1899-1977, (Russ.-U.S.) novelist. *Lolita, Pale Fire.*

R. K. Narayan, 1906-2001, (India) novelist. *The Guide.*

Ogden Nash, 1902-71, (U.S.) poet of light verse.

Irène Némirovsky, 1903-42, (Ukraine) novelist. *David Golder, Suite Française.*

Pablo Neruda, 1904-73, (Chile) poet. *Twenty Love Poems and One Song of Despair, Toward the Splendid City.*

Patrick O'Brian, 1914-2000, (Br.) historical novelist. *Master and Commander, Blue at the Mizzen.*

Sean O'Casey, 1884-1964, (Ire.) dramatist. *Juno and the Paycock, The Plough and the Stars.*

Flannery O'Connor, 1925-64, (U.S.) novelist, short-story writer. *Wise Blood,* "A Good Man Is Hard to Find."

Frank O'Connor (Michael Donovan), 1903-66, (Ire.) short-story writer. "Guests of a Nation."

Clifford Odets, 1906-63, (U.S.) playwright. *Waiting for Lefty, Awake and Sing, Golden Boy, The Country Girl.*

John O'Hara, 1905-70, (U.S.) novelist, short-story writer. *From the Terrace, Appointment in Samarra, Pal Joey.*

Omar Khayyam, c. 1028-1122, (Per.) poet. *Rubaiyat.*

Eugene O'Neill, 1888-1953, (U.S.) playwright. *Emperor Jones, Anna Christie, Long Day's Journey Into Night.*

George Orwell (Eric Arthur Blair), 1903-50, (Br.) novelist, essayist. *Animal Farm, Nineteen Eighty-Four.*

John Osborne, 1929-95, (Br.) dramatist, novelist. *Look Back in Anger, The Entertainer.*

Wilfred Owen, 1893-1918, (Br.) poet. "Dulce et Décorum Est."

Grace Paley, 1922-2007, (U.S.) short-story writer, poet. *The Little Disturbances of Man.*

Dorothy Parker, 1893-1967, (U.S.) poet, short-story writer. *Enough Rope, Laments for the Living.*

Robert B. Parker, 1932-2010, (U.S.) crime novelist. "Spenser" novels.

Boris Pasternak, 1890-1960, (Russ.) poet, novelist. *Doctor Zhivago.*

Alan Paton, 1903-88, (S. Africa) novelist. *Cry, the Beloved Country.*

Octavio Paz, 1914-98, (Mex.) poet, essayist. *The Labyrinth of Solitude, They Shall Not Pass!, The Sun Stone.*

Samuel Pepys, 1633-1703, (Br.) public official, diarist.

S(idney) J(oseph) Perelman, 1904-79, (U.S.) humorist. *The Road to Miltown, Under the Spreading Atrophy.*

Charles Perrault, 1628-1703, (Fr.) writer. *Tales From Mother Goose (Sleeping Beauty, Cinderella).*

Petrarch (Francesco Petrarca), 1304-74, (It.) poet. *Africa, Trionfi, Canzoniere.*

Harold Pinter, 1930-2008, (Br.) playwright. *The Birthday Party, The Caretaker, The Homecoming.*

Luigi Pirandello, 1867-1936, (It.) novelist, dramatist. *Six Characters in Search of an Author.*

Sylvia Plath, 1932-63, (U.S.) author, poet. *The Bell Jar.*

Edgar Allan Poe, 1809-49, (U.S.) poet, short-story writer, critic. "Annabel Lee," "The Raven," "The Purloined Letter."

Alexander Pope, 1688-1744, (Br.) poet. *The Rape of the Lock, The Dunciad, An Essay on Man.*

Katherine Anne Porter, 1890-1980, (U.S.) novelist, short-story writer. *Ship of Fools.*

Chaim Potok, 1929-2002, (U.S.) novelist. *The Chosen.*

Ezra Pound, 1885-1972, (U.S.) poet. *Cantos.*

Anthony Powell, 1905-2000, (Br.) novelist. *A Dance to the Music of Time* series.

Reynolds Price, 1933-2011, (U.S.) novelist, short-story writer, poet. *A Long and Happy Life.*

J(ohn) B(oynton) Priestley, 1894-1984, (Br.) novelist, dramatist. *The Good Companions.*

Marcel Proust, 1871-1922, (Fr.) novelist. *Remembrance of Things Past.*

Aleksandr Pushkin, 1799-1837, (Russ.) poet, novelist. *Boris Godunov, Eugene Onegin.*

Mario Puzo, 1920-99, (U.S.) novelist. *The Godfather.*

François Rabelais, 1495-1553, (Fr.) writer. *Gargantua.*

Jean Racine, 1639-99, (Fr.) dramatist. *Andromaque, Phèdre, Bérénice, Britannicus.*

David Rakoff, 1964-2012, (Can.-U.S.) essayist. *Fraud, Don't Get Too Comfortable.*

Ayn Rand, 1905-82, (Russ.-U.S.) novelist, moral theorist. *The Fountainhead, Atlas Shrugged.*

Terence Rattigan, 1911-77, (Br.) playwright. *Separate Tables, The Browning Version.*

Erich Maria Remarque, 1898-1970, (Ger.-U.S.) novelist. *All Quiet on the Western Front.*

Mary Renault, 1905-1983, (Br.) novelist. *The Last of the Wine.*

Adrienne Rich, 1929-2012, (U.S.) poet. *Diving Into the Wreck: Poems, 1971-1972.*

Samuel Richardson, 1689-1761, (Br.) novelist. *Pamela; or Virtue Rewarded.*

Rainer Maria Rilke, 1875-1926, (Ger.) poet. *Life and Songs, Duino Elegies, Poems From the Book of Hours.*

Arthur Rimbaud, 1854-91, (Fr.) poet. *A Season in Hell.*

Harold Robbins, 1916-97, (U.S.) novelist, *The Carpetbaggers.*

Edwin Arlington Robinson, 1869-1935, (U.S.) poet. "Richard Cory," "Miniver Cheevy," *Merlin.*

Theodore Roethke, 1908-63, (U.S.) poet. *Open House, The Waking, The Far Field.*

Romain Rolland, 1866-1944, (Fr.) novelist, biographer. *Jean-Christophe.*

Pierre de Ronsard, 1524-85, (Fr.) poet. *Sonnets pour Hélène, La Franciade.*

Christina Rossetti, 1830-94, (Br.) poet. "When I Am Dead, My Dearest."

Dante Gabriel Rossetti, 1828-82, (Br.) poet, painter. *The Blessed Damozel*.

Edmond Rostand, 1868-1918, (Fr.) poet, dramatist. *Cyrano de Bergerac*.

Damon Runyon, 1880-1946, (U.S.) short-story writer, journalist. *Guys and Dolls*, *Blue Plate Special*.

John Ruskin, 1819-1900, (Br.) critic, social theorist. *Modern Painters*, *The Seven Lamps of Architecture*.

François Sagan (Françoise Quoirez), 1935-2004, (Fr.) novelist. *Bonjour Tristesse*.

Antoine de Saint-Exupéry, 1900-44, (Fr.) writer. *Wind, Sand and Stars*; *The Little Prince*.

Saki (or H[ector] H[ugh] Munro), 1870-1916, (Br.) writer. *The Chronicles of Clovis*.

J. D. Salinger, 1919-2010, (U.S.) novelist. *The Catcher in the Rye*.

George Sand (Amandine Lucie Aurore Dupin), 1804-76, (Fr.) novelist. *Indiana*, *Consuelo*.

Carl Sandburg, 1878-1967, (U.S.) poet. *The People, Yes*; *Chicago Poems*; *Smoke and Steel*; *Harvest Poems*.

Jose Saramago, 1922-2010, (Port.) novelist. *Blindness*.

William Saroyan, 1908-81, (U.S.) playwright, novelist. *The Time of Your Life*, *The Human Comedy*.

Nathalie Sarraute, 1900-99, (Fr.) Nouveau Roman novelist. *Tropisms*.

May Sarton, 1914-95, (Belg.-U.S.) poet, novelist. *Encounter in April*, *Anger*.

Dorothy L. Sayers, 1893-1957, (Br.) mystery writer; created Lord Peter Wimsey.

Richard Scarry, 1920-94, (U.S.) author of children's books. *Richard Scarry's Best Story Book Ever*.

Friedrich von Schiller, 1759-1805, (Ger.) dramatist, poet, historian. *Don Carlos*, *Maria Stuart*, *Wilhelm Tell*.

Sir Walter Scott, 1771-1832, (Scot.) novelist, poet. *Ivanhoe*.

Gil Scott-Heron, 1949-2011, (U.S.) poet. "The Revolution Will Not Be Televised."

Jaroslav Seifert, 1902-86, (Czech.) poet.

Maurice Sendak, 1928-2012, (U.S.) children's book author and illustrator. *Where the Wild Things Are*.

Dr. Seuss (Theodor Seuss Geisel), 1904-91, (U.S.) children's book author and illustrator. *The Cat in the Hat*.

William Shakespeare, 1564-1616, (Br.) dramatist, poet. *Romeo and Juliet*, *Hamlet*, *King Lear*, *Julius Caesar*, sonnets.

Karl Shapiro, 1913-2000, (U.S.) poet. "Elegy for a Dead Soldier."

George Bernard Shaw, 1856-1950, (Ire.- Br.) playwright, critic. *St. Joan*, *Pygmalion*, *Major Barbara*, *Man and Superman*.

Sidney Sheldon, 1917-2007, (U.S.) screenwriter, novelist. *Rage of Angels*, *Memories of Midnight*.

Mary Wollstonecraft Shelley, 1797-1851, (Br.) novelist, feminist. *Frankenstein*, *The Last Man*.

Percy Bysshe Shelley, 1792-1822, (Br.) poet. *Prometheus Unbound*, *Adonais*, "Ode to the West Wind," "To a Skylark."

Richard B. Sheridan, 1751-1816, (Br.) dramatist. *The Rivals*, *School for Scandal*.

Robert Sherwood, 1896-1955, (U.S.) playwright, biographer. *The Petrified Forest*, *Abe Lincoln in Illinois*.

Mikhail Sholokhov, 1906-84, (Russ.) writer. *The Silent Don*.

Shel Silverstein, 1932-99, (U.S.) poet, writer. *The Giving Tree*, *Where the Sidewalk Ends*.

Georges Simenon (Georges Sims), 1903-89, (Belg.-Fr.) mystery writer; created Inspector Maigret.

Upton Sinclair, 1878-1968, (U.S.) novelist. *The Jungle*.

Isaac Bashevis Singer, 1904-91, (Pol.-U.S.) novelist, short-story writer, in Yiddish. *The Magician of Lublin*.

C(harles) P(ercy) Snow, 1905-80, (Br.) novelist, scientist. *Strangers and Brothers*, *Corridors of Power*.

Aleksandr Solzhenitsyn, 1918-2008, (Russ.) novelist, dramatist. *One Day in the Life of Ivan Denisovich*.

Susan Sontag, 1933-2004, (U.S.) critic, essayist, novelist. *Notes on Camp*, *The Volcano Lover*, *In America*.

Stephen Spender, 1909-95, (Br.) poet, critic, novelist. *Twenty Poems*, "Elegy for Margaret."

Edmund Spenser, 1552-99, (Br.) poet. *The Faerie Queen*.

Mickey Spillane, 1918-2006, (U.S.) novelist; series of novels with the character detective Mike Hammer. *The Killing Man*.

Johanna Spyri, 1827-1901, (Switz.) children's author. *Heidi*.

Christina Stead, 1903-83, (Austral.) novelist, short-story writer. *The Man Who Loved Children*.

Richard Steele, 1672-1729, (Br.) essayist, playwright; began the *Tatler* and *Spectator*.*The Conscious Lovers*.

Gertrude Stein, 1874-1946, (U.S.) writer. *Three Lives*.

John Steinbeck, 1902-68, (U.S.) novelist. *The Grapes of Wrath*, *Of Mice and Men*, *The Winter of Our Discontent*.

Stendhal (Marie Henri Beyle), 1783-1842, (Fr.) novelist. *The Red and the Black*, *The Charterhouse of Parma*.

Laurence Sterne, 1713-68, (Br.) novelist. *Tristram Shandy*.

Wallace Stevens, 1879-1955, (U.S.) poet. *Harmonium*, *The Man With the Blue Guitar*, *Notes Toward a Supreme Fiction*.

Robert Louis Stevenson, 1850-94, (Br.) novelist, poet, essayist. *Treasure Island*, *A Child's Garden of Verses*.

Bram Stoker, 1847-1912, (Br.) writer. *Dracula*.

Rex Stout, 1886-1975, (U.S.) mystery writer; created Nero Wolfe.

Harriet Beecher Stowe, 1811-96, (U.S.) novelist. *Uncle Tom's Cabin*.

Lytton Strachey, 1880-1932, (Br.) biographer, critic. *Eminent Victorians*, *Queen Victoria*, *Elizabeth and Essex*.

August Strindberg, 1849-1912, (Swed.) dramatist, novelist. *The Father*, *Miss Julie*, *The Creditors*.

William Styron, 1925-2006, (U.S.) novelist, essayist. *The Confessions of Nat Turner*, *Sophie's Choice*, *Darkness Visible: A Memoir of Madness*.

Jonathan Swift, 1667-1745, (Br.) satirist, poet. *Gulliver's Travels*, "A Modest Proposal."

Algernon C. Swinburne, 1837-1909, (Br.) poet, dramatist. *Atalanta in Calydon*.

John M. Synge, 1871-1909, (Ire.) poet, dramatist. *Riders to the Sea*, *The Playboy of the Western World*.

Wislawa Szymborska, 1923-2012, (Pol.) poet. "Cat in an Empty Apartment."

Rabindranath Tagore, 1861-1941, (India) author, poet. *Sadhana*, *The Realization of Life*, *Gitanjali*.

Booth Tarkington, 1869-1946, (U.S.) novelist. *Seventeen*.

Peter Taylor, 1917-94, (U.S.) novelist. *A Summons to Memphis*.

Sara Teasdale, 1884-1933, (U.S.) poet. *Helen of Troy and Other Poems*, *Rivers to the Sea*.

Alfred, Lord Tennyson, 1809-92, (Br.) poet. *Idylls of the King*, *In Memoriam*, "The Charge of the Light Brigade."

William Makepeace Thackeray, 1811-63, (Br.) novelist. *Vanity Fair*, *Henry Esmond*, *Pendennis*.

Dylan Thomas, 1914-53, (Wales) poet. *Under Milk Wood*, *A Child's Christmas in Wales*.

Hunter S. Thompson, 1937-2005, (U.S.) author, journalist. *Hell's Angels*, *Fear and Loathing in Las Vegas*.

Henry David Thoreau, 1817-62, (U.S.) writer, philosopher, naturalist. *Walden*, "Civil Disobedience."

James Thurber, 1894-1961, (U.S.) humorist. "The Secret Life of Walter Mitty," *My Life and Hard Times*.

J(ohn) R(onald) R(euel) Tolkien, 1892-1973, (Br.) writer. *The Hobbit*, *Lord of the Rings* trilogy.

Leo Tolstoy, 1828-1910, (Russ.) novelist, short-story writer. *War and Peace*, *Anna Karenina*, "The Death of Ivan Ilyich."

Lionel Trilling, 1905-75, (U.S.) critic, author, teacher. *The Liberal Imagination*.

Anthony Trollope, 1815-82, (Br.) novelist. *The Warden*, *Barchester Towers*, the Palliser novels.

Ivan Turgenev, 1818-83, (Russ.) novelist, short-story writer. *Fathers and Sons*, *First Love*, *A Month in the Country*.

Amos Tutuola, 1920-97, (Nigeria) novelist. *The Palm-Wine Drunkard*, *My Life in the Bush of Ghosts*.

Mark Twain (Samuel Clemens), 1835-1910, (U.S.) novelist, humorist. *The Adventures of Huckleberry Finn*.

Sigrid Undset, 1881-1949, (Nor.) novelist. *Kristin Lavransdatter*.

John Updike, 1932-2009, (U.S.) novelist, literary critic. *Rabbit is Rich*, *The Witches of Eastwick*.

Paul Valéry, 1871-1945, (Fr.) poet, critic. *La Jeune Parque*, *The Graveyard by the Sea*.

Paul Verlaine, 1844-96, (Fr.) Symbolist poet. *Songs Without Words*.

Jules Verne, 1828-1905, (Fr.) novelist. *Twenty Thousand Leagues Under the Sea*.

Gore Vidal, 1925-2012, (U.S.) novelist. *The City and the Pillar*.

François Villon, 1431-c. 1463, (Fr.) poet. *The Lays*, *The Grand Testament*.

Voltaire (F. M. Arouet), 1694-1778, (Fr.) writer of "philosophical romances"; philosopher, historian. *Candide*.

Kurt Vonnegut Jr., 1922-2007, (U.S.) novelist, essayist. *Cat's Cradle*, *Slaughterhouse-Five*, *Breakfast of Champions*.

David Foster Wallace, 1962-2008, (U.S.) novelist, essayist. *Infinite Jest*, *A Supposedly Fun Thing I'll Never Do Again*.

Robert Penn Warren, 1905-89, (U.S.) novelist, poet, critic. *All the King's Men*.

Wendy Wasserstein, 1950-2006, (U.S.) playwright. *The Heidi Chronicles*.

Evelyn Waugh, 1903-66, (Br.) novelist. *The Loved One*, *Brideshead Revisited*, *A Handful of Dust*.

H(erbert) G(eorge) Wells, 1866-1946, (Br.) novelist. *The Time Machine*, *The Invisible Man*, *The War of the Worlds*.

Eudora Welty, 1909-2001, (U.S.) southern short-story writer, novelist. "Why I Live at the P.O.," "The Ponder Heart."

Rebecca West, 1893-1983, (Br.) novelist, critic, journalist. *Black Lamb and Grey Falcon*.

Edith Wharton, 1862-1937, (U.S.) novelist. *The Age of Innocence*, *The House of Mirth*, *Ethan Frome*.

Phillis Wheatley, c. 1753-84, (U.S.) poet; 2nd American woman and first black woman to be published, 1770.

E(lwyn) B(rooks) White, 1899-1985, (U.S.) essayist, novelist. *Charlotte's Web*, *Stuart Little*.

Patrick White, 1912-90, (Austral.) novelist. *The Tree of Man*.

T(erence) H(anbury) White, 1906-64, (Br.) author. *The Once and Future King*, *A Book of Beasts*.

Walt Whitman, 1819-92, (U.S.) poet. *Leaves of Grass*.

John Greenleaf Whittier, 1807-92, (U.S.) poet, journalist. *Snow-Bound*.

Oscar Wilde, 1854-1900, (Ire.) novelist, playwright. *The Picture of Dorian Gray*, *The Importance of Being Earnest*.

Laura Ingalls Wilder, 1867-1957, (U.S.) novelist. Little House on the Prairie series of children's books.

Thornton Wilder, 1897-1975, (U.S.) playwright. Our Town, The Skin of Our Teeth, The Matchmaker.

Tennessee Williams, 1911-83, (U.S.) playwright. A Streetcar Named Desire, Cat on a Hot Tin Roof, The Glass Menagerie.

William Carlos Williams, 1883-1963, (U.S.) poet, physician. Tempers, Al Que Quiere! Paterson, "This Is Just to Say."

Edmund Wilson, 1895-1972, (U.S.) critic, novelist. Axel's Castle, To the Finland Station.

Lanford Wilson, 1937-2011, (U.S.) playwright. Talley's Folly, Fifth of July.

P(elham) G(renville) Wodehouse, 1881-1975, (Br.-U.S.) humorist. "Jeeves" novels, Anything Goes.

Thomas Wolfe, 1900-38, (U.S.) novelist. Look Homeward, Angel; You Can't Go Home Again.

Virginia Woolf, 1882-1941, (Br.) novelist, essayist. Mrs. Dalloway, To the Lighthouse, A Room of One's Own.

William Wordsworth, 1770-1850, (Br.) poet. "Tintern Abbey," "Ode: Intimations of Immortality," The Prelude.

Richard Wright, 1908-60, (U.S.) novelist, short-story writer. Native Son, Black Boy, Uncle Tom's Children.

Elinor Wylie, 1885-1928, (U.S.) poet. Nets to Catch the Wind.

William Butler Yeats, 1865-1939, (Ire.) poet, playwright. "The Second Coming," The Wild Swans at Coole.

Frank Yerby, 1916-91, (U.S.) first best-selling African American novelist. The Foxes of Harrow.

Émile Zola, 1840-1902, (Fr.) novelist. Nana, Thérèsè Raquin.

Poets Laureate

There is no record of the origin of the office of Poet Laureate of England. Henry III (1216-72) reportedly had a Versificator Regis, or King's Poet, paid 100 shillings per year. Other poets said to have filled the role include Geoffrey Chaucer (d 1400), Edmund Spenser (d 1599), Ben Jonson (d 1637), and Sir William d'Avenant (d 1668). The first official English poet laureate was John Dryden, appointed 1668, for life (as was customary). Then came Thomas Shadwell, in 1689; Nahum Tate, 1692; Nicholas Rowe, 1715; Rev. Laurence Eusden, 1718; Colley Cibber, 1730; William Whitehead, 1757; Rev. Thomas Warton, 1785; Henry James Pye, 1790; Robert Southey, 1813; William Wordsworth, 1843; Alfred, Lord Tennyson, 1850; Alfred Austin, 1896; Robert Bridges, 1913; John Masefield, 1930; C. Day Lewis, 1968; Sir John Betjeman, 1972; Ted Hughes, 1984; Andrew Motion, 1999; and Carol Ann Duffy, 2009.

In the U.S., appointment is by the Librarian of Congress and is not for life: Robert Penn Warren, appointed 1986; Richard Wilbur, 1987; Howard Nemerov, 1988; Mark Strand, 1990; Joseph Brodsky, 1991; Mona Van Duyn, 1992; Rita Dove, 1993; Robert Hass, 1995; Robert Pinsky, 1997; Stanley Kunitz, 2000; Billy Collins, 2001; Louise Gluck, 2003; Ted Kooser, 2004; Donald Hall, 2006; Charles Simic, 2007; Kay Ryan, 2008; W. S. Merwin, 2010; Philip Levine, 2011; Natasha Trethewey, 2012.

Composers of Classical and Avant Garde Music

John Adams, b 1947, (U.S.) Nixon in China, The Death of Klinghoffer.

Milton Babbitt, 1916-2011, (U.S.) serial and electronic music.

Carl Philipp Emanuel Bach, 1714-88, (Ger.) cantatas, passions, numerous keyboard and instrumental works.

Johann Christian Bach, 1735-82, (Ger.) concertos, operas, sonatas. Known as the "English" Bach.

Johann Sebastian Bach, 1685-1750, (Ger.) St. Matthew Passion, The Well-Tempered Clavier.

Samuel Barber, 1910-81, (U.S.) Adagio for Strings, Vanessa.

Béla Bartók, 1881-1945, (Hung.) Concerto for Orchestra, The Miraculous Mandarin.

Amy Beach (Mrs. H. H. A. Beach), 1867-1944, (U.S.) The Year's at the Spring, Fireflies, The Chambered Nautilus.

Ludwig van Beethoven, 1770-1827, (Ger.) concertos (Emperor), sonatas (Moonlight, Pathétique), 9 symphonies.

Vincenzo Bellini, 1801-35, (It.) I Puritani, La Sonnambula, Norma.

Alban Berg, 1885-1935, (Austria) Wozzeck, Lulu.

Hector Berlioz, 1803-69, (Fr.) Damnation of Faust, Symphonie Fantastique, Requiem.

Leonard Bernstein, 1918-90, (U.S.) Chichester Psalms, Jeremiah Symphony, Mass.

Georges Bizet, 1838-75, (Fr.) Carmen, Pearl Fishers.

Ernest Bloch, 1880-1959, (Switz.-U.S.) Macbeth (opera), Schelomo, Voice in the Wilderness.

Luigi Boccherini, 1743-1805, (It.) chamber music and guitar pieces.

Alexander Borodin, 1833-87, (Russ.) Prince Igor, In the Steppes of Central Asia, Polovtzian Dances.

Pierre Boulez, b 1925, (Fr.) Le Visage nuptial, Edats/Multiple, Domaines.

Johannes Brahms, 1833-97, (Ger.) Liebeslieder Waltzes, Acad. Festival Overture, chamber music, 4 symphonies.

Henry Brant, 1913-2008, (Can.) spatial music.

Benjamin Britten, 1913-76, (Br.) Peter Grimes, Turn of the Screw, A Ceremony of Carols, War Requiem.

Anton Bruckner, 1824-96, (Austria) 9 symphonies.

Dietrich Buxtehude, 1637-1707, (Den.) organ works, vocal music.

William Byrd, 1543-1623, (Br.) masses, motets.

John Cage, 1912-92, (U.S.) Winter Music, Fontana Mix.

Elliott Carter, b 1908, (U.S.) Second String Quartet, Third String Quartet.

Emmanuel Chabrier, 1841-94, (Fr.) Le Roi Malgré Lui, España.

Gustave Charpentier, 1860-1956, (Fr.) Louise.

Frédéric Chopin, 1810-49, (Pol.) mazurkas, waltzes, etudes, nocturnes, polonaises, sonatas.

Aaron Copland, 1900-90, (U.S.) Appalachian Spring, Fanfare for the Common Man, Lincoln Portrait.

John Corigliano, b 1938, (U.S.) Symphony No. 2.

Paul Creston, 1906-1985, (U.S.) Walt Whitman.

Claude Debussy, 1862-1918, (Fr.) Pelleas et Melisande, La Mer, Prelude to the Afternoon of a Faun.

David Del Tredici, b 1937, (U.S.) Child Alice, In Memory of a Summer Day.

Gaetano Donizetti, 1797-1848, (It.) Elixir of Love, Lucia di Lammermoor, Daughter of the Regiment.

Paul Dukas, 1865-1935, (Fr.) Sorcerer's Apprentice.

Antonín Dvořák, 1841-1904, (Czech.) Songs My Mother Taught Me, Symphony in E Minor (From the New World).

Edward Elgar, 1857-1934, (Br.) Enigma Variations, Pomp and Circumstance.

Manuel de Falla, 1876-1946, (Sp.) El Amor Brujo, La Vida Breve, The Three-Cornered Hat.

Gabriel Faurè, 1845-1924, (Fr.) Requiem, Elègie for Cello and Piano.

Cesar Franck, 1822-90, (Belg.) Symphony in D minor, Violin Sonata.

George Gershwin, 1898-1937, (U.S.) Rhapsody in Blue, An American in Paris, Porgy and Bess.

Philip Glass, b 1937, (U.S.) Einstein on the Beach, The Voyage.

Mikhail Glinka, 1804-57, (Russ.) A Life for the Tsar, Ruslan and Ludmilla.

Christoph W. Gluck, 1714-87, (Ger.) Alceste, Iphigènie en Tauride.

Henryk Gorecki, 1933-2010, (Pol.) Symphony no. 3 (Symphony of Sorrowing Songs).

Charles Gounod, 1818-93, (Fr.) Faust, Romeo and Juliet.

Percy Grainger, 1882-1961, (Austral.) Country Gardens.

Edvard Grieg, 1843-1907, (Nor.) Peer Gynt Suite, Concerto in A minor for piano.

George Frideric Handel, 1685-1759, (Ger.-Br.) Messiah, Water Music.

Howard Hanson, 1896-1981, (U.S.) Symphonies No. 1 (Nordic) and No. 2 (Romantic).

Roy Harris, 1898-1979, (U.S.) symphonies.

(Franz) Joseph Haydn, 1732-1809, (Austria) symphonies (Clock, London, Toy), chamber music, oratorios.

Hildegard von Bingen, 1098-1179, (Ger.) Ordo virtutum.

Paul Hindemith, 1895-1963, (U.S.) Mathis der Maler.

Gustav Holst, 1874-1934, (Br.) The Planets.

Arthur Honegger, 1892-1955, (Fr.) Judith, Le Roi David, Pacific 231.

Alan Hovhaness, 1911-2000, (U.S.) symphonies, Magnificat.

Engelbert Humperdinck, 1854-1921, (Ger.) Hansel and Gretel.

Charles Ives, 1874-1954, (U.S.) Concord Sonata, symphonies.

Aram Khachaturian, 1903-78, (Russ.) ballets, piano pieces, Sabre Dance.

Zoltán Kodaly, 1882-1967, (Hung.) Háry János, Psalmus Hungaricus.

Fritz Kreisler, 1875-1962, (Austria) Caprice Viennois, Tambourin Chinois.

Edouard Lalo, 1823-92, (Fr.) Symphonie Espagnole.

David Lang, b 1957, (U.S.) The Little Match Girl Passion.

Morten Lauridsen, 1943 (U.S.) Lux Aeterna.

Ruggero Leoncavallo, 1857-1919, (It.) Pagliacci.

György Ligeti, 1923-2006, (Rom.) Atmosphères, Requiem.

Franz Liszt, 1811-86, (Hung.) 20 Hungarian rhapsodies, symphonic poems.

Edward MacDowell, 1861-1908, (U.S.) To a Wild Rose.

Gustav Mahler, 1860-1911, (Austria) Das Lied von der Erde; 9 complete symphonies.

Pietro Mascagni, 1863-1945, (It.) Cavalleria Rusticana.

Jules Massenet, 1842-1912, (Fr.) *Manon, Le Cid, Thaïs*.

Felix Mendelssohn, 1809-47, (Ger.) *A Midsummer Night's Dream, Songs Without Words*, violin concerto.

Gian Carlo Menotti, 1911-2007, (It.-U.S.) *The Medium, The Consul, Amahl and the Night Visitors*.

Olivier Messiaen, 1908-1992, (Fr.) *Apparition de l'Église Éternelle*.

Claudio Monteverdi, 1567-1643, (It.) opera, masses, madrigals.

Wolfgang Amadeus Mozart, 1756-91, (Austria) chamber music, concertos, operas (*Magic Flute, Marriage of Figaro*), 41 symphonies.

Modest Mussorgsky, 1839-81, (Russ.) *Boris Godunov, Pictures at an Exhibition*.

Carl Nielsen, 1865-1931, (Den.) *Saul og David*.

Jacques Offenbach, 1819-80, (Fr.) *Tales of Hoffmann*.

Carl Orff, 1895-1982, (Ger.) *Carmina Burana*.

Johann Pachelbel, 1653-1706, (Ger.) Canon and Fugue in D major.

Ignacy Paderewski, 1860-1941, (Pol.) Minuet in G.

Niccolò Paganini, 1782-1840, (It.) Caprices for violin solo.

Giovanni Palestrina, c. 1525-94, (It.) masses, madrigals.

Arvo Pärt, b 1935, (Eston.) sacred music. *Fratres, Cantus in memoriam Benjamin Britten, Tabula Rasa*.

Krzysztof Penderecki, b 1933, (Pol.) *Psalmus, Polymorphia, De natura sonoris*.

Francis Poulenc, 1899-1963, (Fr.) *Dialogues des Carmèlites*.

Mel Powell, 1923-98, (U.S.) *Duplicates: A Concerto for Two Pianos and Orchestra, Cantilena Concertante*.

Sergei Prokofiev, 1891-1953, (Russ.) Classical Symphony, *Love for Three Oranges, Peter and the Wolf*.

Giacomo Puccini, 1858-1924, (It.) *La Boheme, Manon Lescaut, Tosca, Madama Butterfly*.

Henry Purcell, 1659-95, (Eng.) *Dido and Aeneas*.

Sergei Rachmaninoff, 1873-1943, (Russ.) concertos, preludes (Prelude in C sharp minor), symphonies.

Maurice Ravel, 1875-1937, (Fr.) *Bolèro, Daphnis et Chloè*, Piano Concerto in D for Left Hand Alone.

Steve Reich, b 1936, (U.S.) *Double Sextet, Three Tales*.

Nikolai Rimsky-Korsakov, 1844-1908, (Russ.) *Golden Cockerel, Scheherazade, Flight of the Bumblebee*.

Gioacchino Rossini, 1792-1868, (It.) *Barber of Seville, Otello, William Tell*.

John Rutter, b 1945, (Br.) *Magnificat, Requiem*.

Camille Saint-Saëns, 1835-1921, (Fr.) *Carnival of Animals (The Swan), Samson and Delilah, Danse Macabre*.

Alessandro Scarlatti, 1660-1725, (It.) cantatas, oratorios, operas.

Domenico Scarlatti, 1685-1757, (It.) harpsichord works.

Alfred Schnittke, 1934-98 (Sov.-Ger.) *Life With an Idiot*.

Arnold Schoenberg, 1874-1951, (Austria) *Pelleas and Melisande, Pierrot Lunaire, Verklärte Nacht*.

Franz Schubert, 1797-1828, (Austria) chamber music (*Trout Quintet*), lieder, symphonies ("Unfinished").

Robert Schumann, 1810-56, (Ger.) *Die Frauenliebe und Leben, Träumerei*.

Dmitri Shostakovich, 1906-75, (Russ.) symphonies, *Lady Macbeth of the District Mzensk*.

Jean Sibelius, 1865-1957, (Fin.) *Finlandia*.

Bedrich Smetana, 1824-84, (Czech.) *The Bartered Bride*.

Karlheinz Stockhausen, 1928-2008, (Ger.) *Kontra-Punkte, Kontakte for Electronic Instruments*.

Richard Strauss, 1864-1949, (Ger.) *Salome, Elektra, Der Rosenkavalier, Thus Spake Zarathustra*.

Igor Stravinsky, 1882-1971, (Russ.) *Noah and the Flood, The Rake's Progress, The Rite of Spring*.

Toru Takemitsu, 1930-96, (Jpn.) *Requiem for Strings, Dorian Horizon*.

Thomas Tallis, 1515?-85, (Br.) anthems, motets.

Peter I. Tchaikovsky, 1840-93, (Russ.) *Nutcracker, Swan Lake, The Sleeping Beauty*.

Georg Philipp Telemann, 1681-1767, (Ger.) church music, orchestral suites, chamber music.

Virgil Thomson, 1896-1989, (U.S.) opera, film music, *Four Saints in Three Acts*.

Dmitri Tiomkin, 1894-1979, (Russ.-U.S.) film scores, including *High Noon*.

Sir Michael Tippett, 1905-98, (Br.) *A Child of Our Time, The Midsummer Marriage, The Knot Garden*.

Michael Torke, b 1961, (U.S.) *Bright Blue Music, Ecstatic Orange*.

Eric Whitacre, b 1970, (U.S.) *Cloudburst*.

Ralph Vaughan Williams, 1872-1958, (Br.) *Fantasia on a Theme by Thomas Tallis*, symphonies, vocal music.

Giuseppe Verdi, 1813-1901, (It.) *Aida, Rigoletto, Don Carlo, Il Trovatore, La Traviata, Falstaff, Macbeth*.

Heitor Villa-Lobos, 1887-1959, (Braz.) *Bachianas Brasileiras*.

Antonio Vivaldi, 1678-1741, (It.) Concerto grossos (*The Four Seasons*).

Richard Wagner, 1813-83, (Ger.) *Rienzi, Tannhäuser, Lohengrin, Tristan und Isolde*.

William Walton, 1902-83, (Br.) *Façade, Belshazzar's Feast*.

Carl Maria von Weber, 1786-1826, (Ger.) *Der Freischutz*.

Composers of Operettas, Musicals, and Popular Music

Richard Adler, 1921-2012, (U.S.) *Pajama Game; Damn Yankees*.

Milton Ager, 1893-1979, (U.S.) "I Wonder What's Become of Sally"; "Hard-Hearted Hannah"; "Ain't She Sweet?"

Leroy Anderson, 1908-75, (U.S.) "Sleigh Ride"; "Blue Tango"; "Syncopated Clock."

Paul Anka, b 1941, (Can.) "My Way"; *Tonight Show* theme.

Harold Arlen, 1905-86, (U.S.) "Stormy Weather"; "Over the Rainbow"; "Blues in the Night"; "That Old Black Magic."

Burt Bacharach, b 1928, (U.S.) "Raindrops Keep Fallin' on My Head"; "Walk on By"; "What the World Needs Now Is Love."

Ernest Ball, 1878-1927, (U.S.) "Mother Machree"; "When Irish Eyes Are Smiling."

John Barry, 1933-2011, (U.S.) *Born Free; Lion in Winter; Out of Africa*.

Irving Berlin, 1888-1989, (U.S.) *Annie Get Your Gun; Call Me Madam*; "God Bless America"; "White Christmas."

Leonard Bernstein, 1918-90, (U.S.) *On the Town; Wonderful Town; Candide; West Side Story*.

Eubie Blake, 1883-1983, (U.S.) *Shuffle Along*; "I'm Just Wild About Harry."

Jerry Bock, 1928-2010, (U.S.) *Mr. Wonderful; Fiorello; Fiddler on the Roof; The Rothschilds*.

Carrie Jacobs Bond, 1862-1946, (U.S.) "I Love You Truly."

Nacio Herb Brown, 1896-1964, (U.S.) "Singing in the Rain"; "You Were Meant for Me"; "All I Do Is Dream of You."

Hoagy Carmichael, 1899-1981, (U.S.) "Stardust"; "Georgia on My Mind"; "Old Buttermilk Sky."

James Cleveland, 1931-91, (U.S.) composer, musician, singer; first black gospel artist to appear at Carnegie Hall.

George M. Cohan, 1878-1942, (U.S.) "Give My Regards to Broadway"; "You're a Grand Old Flag"; "Over There."

Cy Coleman, 1929-2004, (U.S.) *Sweet Charity*; "Witchcraft."

John Frederick Coots, 1895-1985, (U.S.) "Santa Claus Is Coming to Town"; "You Go to My Head"; "For All We Know."

Noël Coward, 1899-1973, (Br.) *Bitter Sweet*; "Mad Dogs and Englishmen"; "Mad About the Boy."

Neil Diamond, b 1941, (U.S.) "I'm a Believer"; "Sweet Caroline."

Walter Donaldson, 1893-1947, (U.S.) "My Buddy"; "Carolina in the Morning"; "Makin' Whoopee."

Vernon Duke, 1903-69, (U.S.) "April in Paris."

Bob Dylan, b 1941, (U.S.) "Blowin' in the Wind"; "Like a Rolling Stone."

Gus Edwards, 1879-1945, (U.S.) "School Days"; "By the Light of the Silvery Moon"; "In My Merry Oldsmobile."

Sherman Edwards, 1919-81, (U.S.) "See You in September"; "Wonderful! Wonderful!"

Duke Ellington, 1899-1974, (U.S.) "Sophisticated Lady"; "Satin Doll"; "It Don't Mean a Thing"; "Solitude."

Sammy Fain, 1902-89, (U.S.) "I'll Be Seeing You"; "Love Is a Many-Splendored Thing."

Fred Fisher, 1875-1942, (U.S.) "Peg O' My Heart"; "Chicago."

Stephen Collins Foster, 1826-64, (U.S.) "My Old Kentucky Home"; "Old Folks at Home"; "Beautiful Dreamer."

Rudolf Friml, 1879-1972, (Czech.-U.S.) *The Firefly; Rose Marie; Vagabond King; Bird of Paradise*.

John Gay, 1685-1732, (Br.) *The Beggar's Opera*.

George Gershwin, 1898-1937, (U.S.) "Someone to Watch Over Me"; "I've Got a Crush on You"; "Embraceable You."

Morton Gould, 1913-96, (U.S.) "Fall River Suite"; "Holocaust Suite"; "Spirituals for Orchestra"; "Stringmusic."

Ferde Grofe, 1892-1972, (U.S.) "Grand Canyon Suite."

Marvin Hamlisch, 1944-2012, (U.S.) "The Way We Were"; "Nobody Does It Better"; *A Chorus Line*.

Ray Henderson, 1896-1970, (U.S.) *George White's Scandals*; "That Old Gang of Mine"; "Five Foot Two, Eyes of Blue."

Victor Herbert, 1859-1924, (Ire.-U.S.) *Mlle. Modiste; Babes in Toyland; The Red Mill; Naughty Marietta; Sweethearts*.

Jerry Herman, b 1931, (U.S.) *Hello Dolly; Mame*.

Brian Holland, b 1941, **Lamont Dozier** b 1941, **Eddie Holland**, b 1939, (all U.S.) "Heat Wave"; "Stop! In the Name of Love"; "Baby, I Need Your Loving."

Rupert Holmes, b 1947, (Eng.-U.S.) *The Mystery of Edwin Drood; Curtains*.

Antonio Carlos Jobim, 1927-94, (Brazil) "The Girl From Ipanema"; "Desafinado"; "One Note Samba."

Billy Joel (William Martin), b 1949, (U.S.) "Just the Way You Are"; "Honesty"; "Piano Man."

Elton John, b 1947, (Br.) *The Lion King*; "Candle in the Wind"; "Your Song."

Scott Joplin, 1868-1917, (U.S.) Maple Leaf Rag; *Treemonisha*.

John Kander, b 1927, (U.S.) *Cabaret; Chicago; Funny Lady*.

Jerome Kern, 1885-1945, (U.S.) *Sally; Sunny; Show Boat*.

Carole King, b 1942, (U.S.) "Will You Love Me Tomorrow?"; "Natural Woman"; "One Fine Day"; "Up on the Roof."

Burton Lane, 1912-97, (U.S.) *Finian's Rainbow*.

Jonathan Larson, 1960-96, (U.S.) *tick, tick... BOOM!; Rent*.

Franz Lehar, 1870-1948, (Hung.) *Merry Widow*.

Jerry Leiber (1933-2011) and **Mike Stoller**, b 1933, (both U.S.) "Hound Dog"; "Searchin'"; "Yakety Yak"; "Love Me Tender."

Mitch Leigh, b 1928, (U.S.) *Man of La Mancha*.

John Lennon, 1940-80, and **Paul McCartney**, b 1942, (both Br.) "I Want to Hold Your Hand"; "She Loves You."

Jay Livingston, 1915-2001, (U.S.) "Mona Lisa"; "Que Sera, Sera."

Andrew Lloyd Webber, b 1948, (Br.) *Jesus Christ Superstar; Evita; Cats; The Phantom of the Opera.*

Frank Loesser, 1910-69, (U.S.) *Guys and Dolls; Where's Charley?; The Most Happy Fella; How to Succeed in Business....*

Frederick Loewe, 1901-88, (Austria-U.S.) *Brigadoon; Paint Your Wagon; My Fair Lady; Camelot.*

Henry Mancini, 1924-94, (U.S.) "Moon River"; "Days of Wine and Roses"; "Pink Panther Theme."

Barry Mann, b 1939, and **Cynthia Weil**, b 1937, (both U.S.) "You've Lost That Loving Feeling."

Hugh Martin, 1914-2011, (U.S.) "Have Yourself a Merry Little Christmas"; "The Trolley Song."

Jimmy McHugh, 1894-1969, (U.S.) "Don't Blame Me"; "I'm in the Mood for Love"; "I Feel a Song Coming On."

Alan Menken, b 1949, (U.S.) *Little Shop of Horrors; Beauty and the Beast.*

Joseph Meyer, 1894-1987, (U.S.) "If You Knew Susie"; "California, Here I Come"; "Crazy Rhythm."

Chauncey Olcott, 1858-1932, (U.S.) "Mother Machree."

Jerome "Doc" Pomus, 1925-91, (U.S.) "Save the Last Dance for Me"; "A Teenager in Love."

Cole Porter, 1893-1964, (U.S.) *Anything Goes; Kiss Me Kate; Can Can; Silk Stockings.*

Smokey Robinson, b 1940, (U.S.) "Shop Around"; "My Guy"; "My Girl"; "Get Ready."

Richard Rodgers, 1902-79, (U.S.) *Oklahoma!; Carousel; South Pacific; The King and I; The Sound of Music.*

Sigmund Romberg, 1887-1951, (Hung.) *Maytime; The Student Prince; Desert Song; Blossom Time.*

Harold Rome, 1908-93, (U.S.) *Pins and Needles; Call Me Mister; Wish You Were Here; Fanny; Destry Rides Again.*

Vincent Rose, 1880-1944, (U.S.) "Avalon"; "Whispering"; "Blueberry Hill."

Harry Ruby, 1895-1974, (U.S.) "Three Little Words"; "Who's Sorry Now?"

Arthur Schwartz, 1900-84, (U.S.) *The Band Wagon;* "Dancing in the Dark"; "By Myself"; "That's Entertainment."

Steven Schwartz, b 1948, (U.S.) *Godspell; Pippin; Wicked.*

Neil Sedaka, b 1939, (U.S.) "Breaking Up Is Hard to Do."

Marc Shaiman, b 1959, (U.S.) *Hairspray.*

Paul Simon, b 1942, (U.S.) "Sounds of Silence"; "I Am a Rock"; "Mrs. Robinson"; "Bridge Over Troubled Waters."

Stephen Sondheim, b 1930, (U.S.) *A Little Night Music; Company; Sweeney Todd; Sunday in the Park With George.*

John Philip Sousa, 1854-1932, (U.S.) *El Capitan;* "Stars and Stripes Forever."

Oskar Straus, 1870-1954, (Austrian) *Chocolate Soldier.*

Johann Strauss, 1825-99, (Austrian) *Gypsy Baron; Die Fledermaus;* waltzes: *Blue Danube; Artist's Life.*

Charles Strouse, b 1928, (U.S.) *Bye Bye, Birdie; Annie.*

Jule Styne, 1905-94, (Br.-U.S.) *Gentlemen Prefer Blondes; Bells Are Ringing; Gypsy; Funny Girl.*

Arthur S. Sullivan, 1842-1900, (Br.) *H.M.S. Pinafore; Pirates of Penzance; The Mikado.*

Deems Taylor, 1885-1966, (U.S.) *Peter Ibbetson.*

Harry Tobias, 1905-94, (U.S.) *I'll Keep the Lovelight Burning.*

Egbert van Alstyne, 1882-1951, (U.S.) "In the Shade of the Old Apple Tree"; "Memories"; "Pretty Baby."

Jimmy Van Heusen, 1913-90, (U.S.) "Moonlight Becomes You"; "Swinging on a Star"; "All the Way"; "Love and Marriage."

Albert von Tilzer, 1878-1956, (U.S.) "I'll Be With You in Apple Blossom Time"; "Take Me Out to the Ball Game."

Harry von Tilzer, 1872-1946, (U.S.) "Only a Bird in a Gilded Cage"; "On a Sunday Afternoon."

Fats Waller, 1904-43, (U.S.) "Honeysuckle Rose"; "Ain't Misbehavin."

Harry Warren, 1893-1981, (U.S.) "You're My Everything"; "We're in the Money"; "I Only Have Eyes for You."

Jimmy Webb, b 1946, (U.S.) "Up, Up and Away"; "By the Time I Get to Phoenix"; "Didn't We?"; "Wichita Lineman."

Kurt Weill, 1900-50, (Ger.-U.S.) *Threepenny Opera; Lady in the Dark; Knickerbocker Holiday; One Touch of Venus.*

Percy Wenrich, 1887-1952, (U.S.) "When You Wore a Tulip"; "Moonlight Bay"; "Put On Your Old Gray Bonnet."

Richard A. Whiting, 1891-1938, (U.S.) "Till We Meet Again"; "Sleepytime Gal"; "Beyond the Blue Horizon"; "My Ideal."

Fred Wildhorn, b 1959, (U.S.) *Jekyll and Hyde; Victor/Victoria; The Civil War.*

John Williams, b 1932, (U.S.) *Jaws; E.T.; Star Wars* series; *Raiders of the Lost Ark* series.

Meredith Willson, 1902-84, (U.S.) *The Music Man.*

Stevie Wonder, b 1950, (U.S.) "You Are the Sunshine of My Life"; "Signed, Sealed, Delivered, I'm Yours."

Vincent Youmans, 1898-1946, (U.S.) *Two Little Girls in Blue; Wildflower; No, No, Nanette; Hit the Deck; Rainbow; Smiles.*

Lyricists

Howard Ashman, 1950-91, (U.S.) *Little Shop of Horrors; The Little Mermaid.*

Johnny Burke, 1908-84, (U.S.) "Misty"; "Imagination."

Irving Caesar, 1895-1996, (U.S.) "Swanee"; "Tea for Two"; "Just a Gigolo."

Sammy Cahn, 1913-93, (U.S.) "High Hopes"; "Love and Marriage"; "The Second Time Around"; "It's Magic."

Leonard Cohen, b 1934, (Can.) "Suzanne"; "Stranger Song."

Betty Comden, 1917-2006, (U.S.) and **Adolph Green**, 1915-2002, (U.S.) "The Party's Over"; "New York, New York."

Hal David, 1921-2012, (U.S.) "What the World Needs Now Is Love."

Buddy De Sylva, 1895-1950, (U.S.) "When Day Is Done"; "Look for the Silver Lining"; "April Showers."

Howard Dietz, 1896-1983, (U.S.) "Dancing in the Dark"; "That's Entertainment."

Al Dubin, 1891-1945, (U.S.) "Tiptoe Through the Tulips"; "Lullaby of Broadway."

Fred Ebb, 1936-2004, (U.S.) *Cabaret; Zorba; Woman of the Year; Chicago.*

Ray Evans, 1915-2007, (U.S.) "Mona Lisa"; "Que Sera, Sera."

Dorothy Fields, 1905-74, (U.S.) "On the Sunny Side of the Street"; "Don't Blame Me"; "The Way You Look Tonight."

Ira Gershwin, 1896-1983, (U.S.) "The Man I Love"; "S'Wonderful"; "Embraceable You."

William S. Gilbert, 1836-1911, (Br.) *H.M.S. Pinafore; Pirates of Penzance.*

Gerry Goffin, b 1939, (U.S.) "Will You Love Me Tomorrow"; "Take Good Care of My Baby"; "Up on the Roof."

Mack Gordon, 1905-59, (Pol.-U.S.) "You'll Never Know"; "The More I See You"; "Chattanooga Choo-Choo."

Oscar Hammerstein II, 1895-1960, (U.S.) *Ol' Man River; Oklahoma!; Carousel.*

E. Y. (Yip) Harburg, 1898-1981, (U.S.) "Brother, Can You Spare a Dime"; "April in Paris"; "Over the Rainbow."

Sheldon Harnick, b 1924, (U.S.) *Fiddler on the Roof; She Loves Me.*

Lorenz Hart, 1895-1943, (U.S.) "Isn't It Romantic"; "Blue Moon"; "Lover"; "Manhattan"; "My Funny Valentine."

DuBose Heyward, 1885-1940, (U.S.) "Summertime."

Gus Kahn, 1886-1941, (U.S.) "Memories"; "Ain't We Got Fun."

Alan J. Lerner, 1918-86, (U.S.) *Brigadoon; My Fair Lady; Camelot; Gigi; On a Clear Day You Can See Forever.*

Johnny Mercer, 1909-76, (U.S.) "Blues in the Night"; "Come Rain or Come Shine"; "Laura"; "That Old Black Magic."

Bob Merrill, 1921-98, (U.S.) "People"; "(How Much Is That) Doggie in the Window."

Jack Norworth, 1879-1959, (U.S.) "Take Me Out to the Ball Game"; "Shine On Harvest Moon."

Mitchell Parish, 1901-93, (U.S.) "Stardust"; "Stairway to the Stars."

Andy Razaf, 1895-1973, (U.S.) "Honeysuckle Rose"; "Ain't Misbehavin."

Leo Robin, 1900-84, (U.S.) "Thanks for the Memory"; "Diamonds Are a Girl's Best Friend."

Robert Sherman, 1925-2012, (U.S.) *Mary Poppins, The Jungle Book.*

Bernie Taupin, b 1947 (Br.) "Rocket Man"; "Your Song."

Paul Francis Webster, 1907-84, (U.S.) "Secret Love"; "The Shadow of Your Smile"; "Love Is a Many-Splendored Thing."

Jack Yellen, 1892-1991, (U.S.) "Ain't She Sweet"; "Happy Days Are Here Again."

Blues and Jazz Artists of the Past

Julian "Cannonball" Adderley, 1928-75, alto sax.

Nat Adderley, 1931-2000, cornet.

Henry "Red" Allen, 1908-67, trumpet.

Louis "Satchmo" Armstrong, 1901-71, trumpet, singer, bandleader.

Albert Ayler, 1936-70, tenor sax, alto sax.

Mildred Bailey, 1907-51, singer.

Chet Baker, 1929-88, trumpet, singer.

Ray Barretto, 1930-2006, conga drummer.

William "Count" Basie, 1904-84, bandleader, piano, composer.

Sidney Bechet, 1897-1959, soprano sax, clarinet.

Bix Beiderbecke, 1903-31, cornet, composer, piano.

Rowland "Bunny" Berigan, 1908-42, trumpet.

Barney Bigard, 1906-80, clarinet.

Eubie Blake, 1883-1983, composer, piano.

Art Blakey, 1919-90, drums, bandleader.

Jimmy Blanton, 1921-42, bass.

Charles "Buddy" Bolden, 1877-1931, cornet, pioneer bandleader.

Lester Bowie, 1941-99, trumpet, composer, bandleader.

Michael Brecker, 1949-2007, saxophone.

Big Bill Broonzy, 1893-1958, blues singer, guitar.

Clarence "Gatemouth" Brown, 1924-2005, guitar, singer.

Clifford Brown, 1930-56, trumpet.

Ray Brown, 1926-2002, bass.

Don Byas, 1912-72, tenor sax.

Charlie Byrd, 1925-99, guitar; popularized bossa nova.

Cab Calloway, 1907-94, bandleader, singer.

Harry Carney, 1910-74, baritone sax, clarinet.

Benny Carter, 1907-2003, alto sax.

Betty Carter, 1930-98, jazz singer.

Sidney "Big Sid" Catlett, 1910-51, drums.

Adolphus Anthony "Doc" Cheatham, 1905-97, trumpet.

Don Cherry, 1936-95, trumpet.

Charlie Christian, 1916-42, guitar.

Kenny "Klook" Clarke, 1914-85, drums.

Buck Clayton, 1911-91, trumpet.

Al Cohn, 1925-88, tenor sax.

Nat "King" Cole, 1919-65, piano, singer.

William "Cozy" Cole, 1909-81, drums.

Alice Coltrane, 1937-2007, piano, composer.

John Coltrane, 1926-67, tenor sax, soprano sax, composer.

Eddie Condon, 1905-73, guitar, bandleader.

Tadd Dameron, 1917-65, piano, composer.

Eddie "Lockjaw" Davis, 1921-86, tenor sax.

Miles Davis, 1926-91, trumpet, composer.

Wild Bill Davison, 1906-89, cornet.

Blossom Dearie, 1924-2009, singer.

Paul Desmond, 1924-77, alto sax.

Vic Dickenson, 1906-84, trombone.

Willie Dixon, 1915-92, composer, bass.

Johnny Dodds, 1892-1940, clarinet.

Warren "Baby" Dodds, 1898-1959, drums.

Eric Dolphy, 1928-64, alto sax, bass clarinet, flute.

Jimmy Dorsey, 1904-57, alto sax, bandleader.

Tommy Dorsey, 1905-56, trombone, bandleader.

Billy Eckstine, 1914-93, singer, bandleader.

Harry "Sweets" Edison, 1915-99, trumpet.

David "Honeyboy" Edwards, 1915-2011, guitar, singer.

Roy Eldridge, 1911-89, trumpet, singer.

Duke Ellington, 1899-1974, piano, bandleader, composer.

Bill Evans, 1929-80, piano.

Gil Evans, 1912-88, composer, arranger, piano.

Art Farmer, 1928-99, trumpet, flugelhorn.

Maynard Ferguson, 1926-2006, trumpet, bandleader.

Ella Fitzgerald, 1917-96, singer.

Tommy Flanagan, 1930-2001, piano.

Erroll Garner, 1921-77, piano, composer.

Stan Getz, 1927-91, tenor sax.

Dizzy Gillespie, 1917-93, trumpet, composer, singer.

Benny Goodman, 1909-86, clarinet, bandleader.

Dexter Gordon, 1923-90, tenor sax.

Stéphane Grappelli, 1908-97, violin.

Bobby Hackett, 1915-76, trumpet, cornet.

Lionel Hampton, 1908-2002, vibraphone, bandleader.

W. C. Handy, 1873-1958, composer.

Jimmy Harrison, 1900-31, trombone.

Coleman Hawkins, 1904-69, tenor sax.

Percy Heath, 1923-2005, bass.

Fletcher Henderson, 1898-1952, bandleader, arranger.

Woody Herman, 1913-87, clarinet, alto sax, bandleader.

Jay C. Higginbotham, 1906-73, trombone.

Ruiz Hilton, 1952-2006, piano, composer.

Earl "Fatha" Hines, 1903-83, piano.

Milt Hinton, 1910-2000, bass.

Al Hirt, 1922-99, trumpet.

Johnny Hodges, 1906-70, alto sax.

Billie Holiday, 1915-59, singer.

John Lee Hooker, 1917-2001, blues guitar, singer.

Sam "Lightnin'" Hopkins, 1912-82, blues singer, guitar.

Shirley Horn, 1934-2005, piano, singer.

Howlin' Wolf (Chester Burnett), 1910-1976, blues singer, harmonica, guitar.

Alberta Hunter, 1895-1984, singer.

Mahalia Jackson, 1911-72, gospel singer.

Milt Jackson, 1923-99, vibraphone.

Elmore James, 1918-63, blues singer, guitar.

Etta James, 1938-2012, blues singer.

"Blind" Lemon Jefferson, 1897-1929, blues singer, guitar.

William "Bunk" Johnson, 1879-1949, trumpet.

J. J. Johnson, 1924-2001, trombone.

James P. Johnson, 1891-1955, piano, composer.

Robert Johnson, 1912-38, blues singer, guitar.

Elvin Jones, 1927-2004, drums.

Jo Jones, 1911-85, drums.

Philly Joe Jones, 1923-85, drums.

Thad Jones, 1923-86, cornet, bandleader, composer.

Scott Joplin, 1868-1917, ragtime composer.

Louis Jordan, 1908-75, singer, alto sax.

Stan Kenton, 1911-79, bandleader, composer, piano.

Barney Kessel, 1923-2004, guitar.

Albert King, 1923-92, blues guitar.

John Kirby, 1908-52, bandleader, bass.

Rahsaan Roland Kirk, 1936-77, saxophone, composer.

Gene Krupa, 1909-73, drums, bandleader.

Scott LaFaro, 1936-61, bass.

Lead Belly (Huddie Ledbetter), 1888-1949, folk and blues singer, guitar.

Peggy Lee, 1920-2002, singer.

John Lewis, 1920-2001, piano, Modern Jazz Quartet founder.

Mel Lewis, 1929-90, drums, bandleader.

Jimmie Lunceford, 1902-47, bandleader.

Machito (Frank Grillo), 1908-84, Latin percussion, singer, bandleader.

Shelly Manne, 1920-84, drums, bandleader.

Jackie McLean, 1931-2006, saxophone, composer.

Jimmy McPartland, 1907-91, trumpet.

Carmen McRae, 1920-94, singer.

Glenn Miller, 1904-44, trombone, bandleader.

Charles Mingus, 1922-79, bass, composer, bandleader.

Thelonious Monk, 1917-82, piano, composer.

Wes Montgomery, 1925-68, guitar.

James Moody, 1925-2010, saxophone.

Ferdinand "Jelly Roll" Morton, 1885-1941, composer, piano.

Bennie Moten, 1894-1935, piano, bandleader.

Gerry Mulligan, 1927-96, baritone sax, composer.

Theodore "Fats" Navarro, 1923-50, trumpet.

Red Nichols, 1905-65, cornet, bandleader.

Red Norvo, 1908-99, vibraphone, xylophone, bandleader.

Anita O'Day, 1919-2006, singer.

Arturo "Chico" O'Farrill, 1921-2001, Latin composer, arranger.

King Oliver, 1885-1938, cornet, band-leader.

Sy Oliver, 1910-88, arranger, composer.

Edward "Kid" Ory, 1886-1973, trombone, bandleader.

Johnny Otis, 1921-2012, blues singer.

Oran "Hot Lips" Page, 1908-54, trumpet, singer.

Charlie "Bird" Parker, 1920-55, alto sax, composer.

Joe Pass, 1929-94, guitar.

Art Pepper, 1925-82, alto sax.

Pinetop Perkins, 1913-2011, piano.

Oscar Peterson, 1925-2007, piano.

Oscar Pettiford, 1922-60, bass.

Earl "Bud" Powell, 1924-66, piano.

Chano Pozo, 1915-48, Cuban percussion, singer.

Louis Prima, 1911-78, singer, bandleader.

Tito Puente, 1923-2000, Latin percussion, bandleader.

Gertrude "Ma" Rainey, 1886-1939, blues singer.

Lou Rawls, 1933-2006, singer.

Dewey Redman, 1931-2006, tenor sax.

Don Redman (Robert Rodney Chudnick), 1900-64, composer, arranger.

Django Reinhardt, 1910-53, guitar.

Buddy Rich, 1917-87, drums.

Max Roach, 1924-2007, drums, composer.

Red Rodney (Robert Chudnick), 1927-94, trumpet.

Jimmy Rowles, 1918-96, piano.

Jimmy Rushing, 1903-72, blues and jazz singer.

Charles "Pee Wee" Russell, 1906-69, clarinet.

Artie Shaw, 1910-2004, swing-era bandleader, clarinet.

George Shearing, 1919-2011, piano.

Nina Simone (Eunice Waymon), 1933-2003, singer.

John "Zoot" Sims, 1925-85, tenor sax.

Zutty Singleton, 1898-1975, drums.

Bessie Smith, 1894-1937, blues singer.

Clarence "Pinetop" Smith, 1904-29, piano, singer, boogie woogie pioneer.

Willie "The Lion" Smith, 1897-1973, piano, composer.

Francis "Muggsy" Spanier, 1906-67, cornet.

Edward "Sonny" Stitt, 1924-82, tenor sax, alto sax.

Billy Strayhorn, 1915-67, composer, piano, Duke Ellington collaborator.

Sun Ra (Herman Blount), 1915?-93, bandleader, piano, composer.

Art Tatum, 1910-56, piano.

Art Taylor, 1929-95, drums.

Billy Taylor, 1921-2010, piano.

Jack Teagarden, 1905-64, trombone, singer.

Mel Tormé, 1925-99, singer ("The Velvet Fog").

Dave Tough, 1908-48, drums.

Lennie Tristano, 1919-78, piano, composer.

Joe Turner, 1911-85, blues singer.

Sarah Vaughan, 1924-90, singer.

Joe Venuti, 1903-78, violin.

Aaron "T-Bone" Walker, 1910-75, blues guitar.

Thomas "Fats" Waller, 1904-43, piano, singer, composer.

Dinah Washington (Ruth Jones), 1924-63, singer.

Grover Washington Jr., 1943-99, pop-jazz sax, composer.

Ethel Waters, 1896-1977, jazz and blues singer.

Muddy Waters (McKinley Morganfield), 1915-83, blues singer, songwriter.

Julius Watkins, 1921-77, French horn.

William "Chick" Webb, 1902-39, bandleader, drums.

Ben Webster, 1909-73, tenor sax.

Junior Wells (Amos Blackmore), 1934-98, blues singer, harmonica.

Paul Whiteman, 1890-1967, bandleader.

Margaret Whiting, 1924-2011, singer.

Charles "Cootie" Williams, 1910-85, trumpet, bandleader.

Joe Williams, 1918-99, singer.

Mary Lou Williams, 1910-81, piano, composer.

Tony Williams, 1945-97, drums.

John Lee "Sonny Boy" Williamson, 1914-48, blues singer, harmonica.

Sonny Boy Williamson (Aleck "Rice" Miller), 1900?-65, blues singer, harmonica.

Teddy Wilson, 1912-86, piano.

Kai Winding, 1922-83, trombone.

Jimmy Yancey, 1894-1951, piano.

Lester "Pres" Young, 1909-59, tenor sax.

Country Music Artists of the Past and Present

Roy Acuff, 1903-92, fiddler, singer, songwriter; "Wabash Cannon Ball."

Alabama (Jeff Cook, b 1949; Teddy Gentry, b 1952; Mark Herndon, b 1955; Randy Owen, b 1949); "Feels So Right."

Jason Aldean, b 1977, singer; "Don't You Wanna Stay."

James "Whispering Bill" Anderson, b 1937, singer, songwriter; "Make Mine Night Time."

Eddy Arnold, 1918-2008, singer, guitarist, known as the "Tennessee Plowboy."

Chet Atkins, 1924-2001, guitarist, composer, producer; helped create the "Nashville sound."

Gene Autry, 1907-98, first great singing movie cowboy; "Back in the Saddle Again."

Clint Black, b 1962, singer, songwriter; "Killin' Time."

Garth Brooks, b 1962, singer, songwriter; "Friends in Low Places."

Brooks & Dunn (Kix Brooks, b 1955; Ronnie Dunn, b 1953); "Hard Workin' Man."

Luke Bryan, b 1976, singer, songwriter; "Someone Else Calling You Baby."

Boudleaux, 1920-87, and **Felice Bryant**, 1925-2003, songwriting team; "Hey Joe."

Glen Campbell, b 1936, singer, guitarist; "Gentle on My Mind."

Mary Chapin Carpenter, b 1958, singer, songwriter; "I Feel Lucky."

Carter Family (original members A. P., 1891-1960; "Mother" Maybelle, 1909-78; Sara, 1898-1979); "Wildwood Flower."

Johnny Cash, 1932-2003, singer, songwriter; "I Walk the Line," "Ring of Fire," "Folsom Prison Blues."

Kenny Chesney, b 1968, guitarist, singer, songwriter; "You Had Me From Hello."

Roy Clark, b 1933, guitarist, banjoist, singer, co-host of *Hee Haw*; "Yesterday, When I Was Young."

Patsy Cline, 1932-63, singer; "Walkin' After Midnight," "Crazy," "Sweet Dreams."

Billy Ray Cyrus, b 1961, singer, songwriter; "Achy Breaky Heart."

Charlie Daniels, b 1936, guitarist, fiddler; "The Devil Went Down to Georgia."

Jimmy Dean, 1928-2010, singer; "Big Bad John."

John Denver, 1943-97, singer, songwriter; "Rocky Mountain High."

Dixie Chicks (Natalie Maines, b 1974; Emily Erwin Robison, b 1972; Martie Seidel, b 1969); "Wide Open Spaces."

Dale Evans, 1912-2001, singer, actress, married Roy Rogers.

Sara Evans, b 1971, singer, songwriter; "Born to Fly."

Flatt & Scruggs (Lester Flatt, 1914-79; Earl Scruggs, 1924-2012), guitar-banjo duo and soloists; "Foggy Mountain Breakdown."

Red Foley, 1910-68, singer; "Chattanoogie Shoe Shine Boy."

Tennessee Ernie Ford, 1919-91, singer, TV host; "Sixteen Tons."

William "Lefty" Frizzell, 1928-75, singer, guitarist; "Long Black Veil."

Vince Gill, b 1957, singer, songwriter; "When I Call Your Name."

Merle Haggard, b 1937, singer, songwriter; "Okie From Muskogee."

Emmylou Harris, b 1947, singer, songwriter, folk-country crossover artist; "If I Could Only Win Your Love."

Faith Hill, b 1967, singer, songwriter; "Breathe."

Alan Jackson, b 1958, singer, songwriter; "Where Were You (When the World Stopped Turning)."

Waylon Jennings, 1937-2002, singer, songwriter, "outlaw country" pioneer; "Luckenbach, Texas."

George Jones, b 1931, singer; "He Stopped Loving Her Today."

The Judds (Naomi, b 1946; Wynonna, b 1964), mother-daughter duo; Wynonna also a solo act.

Toby Keith, b 1961, singer, songwriter; guitarist; "Should've Been a Cowboy."

Alison Krauss, b 1971, bluegrass fiddler, singer, bandleader; "When You Say Nothing at All."

Kris Kristofferson, b 1936, singer, songwriter, actor; "Me and Bobby McGee."

Lady Antebellum (Dave Haywood, b 1982; Charles Kelley, b 1981; Hillary Scott, b 1984); "I Run to You."

Miranda Lambert, b. 1983, singer, guitarist; "The House That Built Me."

Louvin Brothers (Charlie, 1927-2011; Ira, 1924-65), singers; "If I Could Only Win Your Love."

Patty Loveless, b 1957, singer, songwriter; "How Can I Help You Say Goodbye."

Lyle Lovett, b 1957, singer, songwriter, bandleader, actor; "Cowboy Man."

Loretta Lynn, b 1935?, singer; "Coal Miner's Daughter."

Barbara Mandrell, b 1948, singer; "I Was Country When Country Wasn't Cool."

Kathy Mattea, b 1959, singer, songwriter; "Eighteen Wheels and a Dozen Roses."

Martina McBride, b 1966, singer, songwriter; "Independence Day."

Reba McEntire, b 1955, singer, songwriter, actress; "Whoever's in New England."

Tim McGraw, b 1967, singer; "It's Your Love," "I Like It, I Love It."

Roger Miller, 1936-92, singer, songwriter; "King of the Road."

Ronnie Milsap, b 1944, singer, songwriter; "There's No Gettin' Over Me."

Bill Monroe, 1911-96, singer, songwriter, mandolin player, "father of bluegrass music"; "Mule Skinner Blues."

Anne Murray, b 1945, singer; "You Needed Me."

Willie Nelson, b 1933, singer, songwriter, actor; "On the Road Again."

Mark O'Connor, b 1961, fiddler, country-classical crossover composer.

Buck Owens, 1929-2006, singer, guitarist; "Act Naturally."

Brad Paisley, b 1972, singer, songwriter; "Whiskey Lullaby," "When I Get Where I'm Going."

Dolly Parton, b 1946, singer, songwriter, actress; "Here You Come Again," "9 to 5."

Johnny Paycheck, (Don Lytle), 1938-2003, singer, guitarist; "Take This Job and Shove It."

Minnie Pearl, 1912-96, comedienne, Grand Ole Opry star.

Kellie Pickler, b 1986, singer, songwriter.

Ray Price, b 1926, country singer, guitarist, and songwriter; "Crazy Arms."

Charley Pride, b 1938, singer, 1st African American country star; "Kiss an Angel Good Mornin'."

Eddie Rabbit, 1941-98, singer, songwriter; "I Love A Rainy Night."

Rascal Flatts (Jay DeMarcus, b 1971; Gary LeVox, b 1970; Joe Don Rooney, b 1975); "Life Is a Highway."

Jim Reeves, 1923-64, singer, songwriter; "Four Walls."

Charlie Rich, 1932-95, singer, songwriter called the "Silver Fox"; "The Most Beautiful Girl."

LeAnn Rimes, b 1982, singer; "Blue."

Tex Ritter, 1905-74, singer, songwriter; "Jingle, Jangle, Jingle."

Marty Robbins, 1925-82, singer, songwriter; "A White Sport Coat and a Pink Carnation."

Jimmie Rodgers, 1897-1933, singer, songwriter; "T for Texas."

Kenny Rogers, b 1938, singer, songwriter; "The Gambler."

Roy Rogers (Leonard Slye), 1911-98, singer, actor, "King of the Cowboys," sang with Sons of the Pioneers.

Fred Rose, 1898-1954, songwriter, singer, producer; "Blue Eyes Cryin' in the Rain."

Blake Shelton, b 1976, singer; "Home."

Ricky Skaggs, b 1954, singer, songwriter, bandleader; "Don't Cheat in Our Hometown."

Ralph Stanley, b 1927, singer, banjo player; "Man of Constant Sorrow."

George Strait, b 1952, singer, bandleader; "Ace in the Hole."

Sugarland (Kristian Bush, b 1970; Jennifer Nettles, b 1974); "Stay."

Taylor Swift, b 1989, singer, songwriter; "You Belong With Me."

Lonnie "Mel" Tillis, b 1932, singer, songwriter, bandleader; "I Ain't Never."

Merle Travis, 1917-83, singer, guitarist, songwriter; "Divorce Me C.O.D."

Randy Travis, b 1959, singer, songwriter; "Forever and Ever, Amen."

Ernest Tubb, 1914-84, singer, songwriter, guitarist; "Walking the Floor Over You."

Josh Turner, b 1977, singer; "Why Don't We Just Dance."

Shania Twain, b 1965, singer, songwriter; "You're Still the One."

Conway Twitty, 1933-93, singer, songwriter; "Hello Darlin'."

Carrie Underwood, b 1983, singer, songwriter; *American Idol* winner.

Keith Urban, b 1967, guitarist, singer, songwriter; "It's a Love Thing."

Porter Wagoner, 1927-2007, singer, songwriter, guitarist; "I Will Always Love You."

Kitty Wells (Ellen Deason), 1919-2012, singer, songwriter; "It Wasn't God Who Made Honky-Tonk Angels."

Dottie West, 1932-91, singer, songwriter; "Here Comes My Baby."

Hank Williams Jr., b 1949, singer, songwriter; "Bocephus"; "All My Rowdy Friends (Have Settled Down)."

Hank Williams Sr., 1923-53, singer, songwriter; "Your Cheatin' Heart."

Bob Wills, 1905-75, Western Swing fiddler, singer, bandleader, songwriter; "New San Antonio Rose."

Lee Ann Womack, b 1966, singer, songwriter; "I Hope You Dance."

Tammy Wynette, 1942-98, singer; "Stand By Your Man."

Trisha Yearwood, b 1964, singer, songwriter; "How Do I Live."

Dwight Yoakam, b 1957, singer, songwriter, actor; "Ain't That Lonely Yet."

Zac Brown Band (Coy Bowles, b 1979; Zac Brown, b 1978; Clay Cook, Jimmy De Martini, Chris Fryar, b 1970; John Driskell Hopkins, b 1971); "Chicken Fried."

Dance Figures of the Past

Alvin Ailey, 1931-89, (U.S.) modern dancer, choreographer; melded modern dance and Afro-Caribbean techniques.

Frederick Ashton, 1904-88, (Br.) ballet choreographer; director of Great Britain's Royal Ballet, 1963-70.

Fred Astaire, 1899-1987, (U.S.) dancer, actor; teamed with dancer/actress **Ginger Rogers**, 1911-95, (U.S.) in movie musicals.

George Balanchine, 1904-83, (Russ.-U.S.) ballet choreographer, teacher; most influential exponent of neoclassical style; founded, with Lincoln Kirstein, School of American Ballet and New York City Ballet.

Pina Bausch, 1940-2009, (Ger.) modern dance choreographer influencing the Tanztheater style of dance.

Carlo Blasis, 1795-1878, (It.) ballet dancer, choreographer, writer; his teaching methods are standards of classical dance.

August Bournonville, 1805-79, (Den.) ballet dancer, choreographer, teacher; exuberant, light style.

Fernando Bujones, 1955-2005, (Cuba-U.S.) ballet dancer.

Gisella Caccialanza, 1914-98, (U.S.) ballerina; charter member of Balanchine's American Ballet.

Irene, 1893-1969, (U.S.) and **Vernon Castle**, 1887-1918, (Br.) husband-and-wife ballroom dancers.

Enrico Cecchetti, 1850-1928, (It.) ballet dancer, leading dancer of Russia's Imperial Ballet; his technique was basis for Britain's Imperial Soc. of Teachers of Dancing.

Gower Champion, 1921-80, (U.S.) dancer, choreographer, director; with wife **Marge**, b 1923, (U.S.) choreographed, danced in Broadway musicals and films.

John Cranko, 1927-73, (S. Africa) choreographer; created narrative ballets based on literary works.

Merce Cunningham, 1919-2009, (U.S.) dancer, choreographer of avant-garde dance.

Agnes de Mille, 1905-93, (U.S.) ballerina, choreographer; known for using American themes, she choreographed the ballet *Rodeo* and the musical *Oklahoma!*

Alexandra Danilova, 1903-97, (Russ.) ballerina; noted teacher at the School of American Ballet.

Dame Ninette De Valois, 1898-2001, (Br.) choreographer, founding director of London's Royal Ballet; *The Rake's Progress.*

Sergei Diaghilev, 1872-1929, (Russ.) impresario; founded Les Ballet Russes; saw ballet as art unifying dance, drama, music, and decor.

Isadora Duncan, 1877-1927, (U.S.) expressive dancer who united free movement with serious music; one of the founders of modern dance.

Katherine Dunham, 1910-2006, (U.S.) dancer, choreographer; internationally known for African, Caribbean, and African American dance forms.

Fanny Elssler, 1810-84, (Austria) ballerina of the Romantic era; known for dramatic skill, sensual style.

Michel Fokine, 1880-1942, (Russ.) ballet dancer, choreographer, teacher; rejected strict classicism in favor of dramatically expressive style.

Margot Fonteyn, 1919-91, (Br.) prima ballerina, Royal Ballet of Great Britain; famed performance partner of Rudolf Nureyev.

Bob Fosse, 1927-87, (U.S.) jazz dancer, choreographer, director; Broadway musicals and film.

Serge Golovine, 1924-98, (Fr.) ballet dancer with Grand Ballet du Marquis de Cuevas, choreographer.

Martha Graham, 1894-1991, (U.S.) modern dancer, choreographer; created and codified her own dramatic technique.

Melissa Hayden, 1923-2006, (Can.) ballet dancer.

Martha Hill, 1900-95, (U.S.) educator; leading figure in modern dance; founded American Dance Festival.

Gregory Hines, 1946-2003, (U.S.) tap-dance innovator; master of improvisation.

Doris Humphrey, 1895-1958, (U.S.) modern dancer, choreographer, writer, teacher.

Michael Jackson, 1958-2009, (U.S.) singer and dancer who perfected the "moonwalk."

Robert Joffrey, 1930-88, (U.S.) ballet dancer, choreographer; cofounded with **Gerald Arpino**, 1928-2008, (U.S.) the Joffrey Ballet.

Kurt Jooss, 1901-79, (Ger.) choreographer, teacher; created expressionist works using modern and classical techniques.

Tamara Karsavina, 1885-1978, (Russ.) prima ballerina of Russia's Imperial Ballet and Diaghilev's Ballets Russes; partner of Nijinsky.

Nora Kaye, 1920-87, (U.S.) ballerina with Metropolitan Opera Ballet and Ballet Theater (now American Ballet Theatre).

Gene Kelly, 1912-96, (U.S.) dancer, actor in movie musicals.

Michael Kidd, 1915-2003, (U.S.) dancer, film and theater choreographer.

Lincoln Kirstein, 1907-96 (U.S.) brought ballet as an art form to U.S.; founded, with George Balanchine, School of American Ballet and New York City Ballet.

Serge Lifar, 1905-86, (Russ.-Fr.) prem. danseur, choreographer; director of dance at Paris Opera, 1930-45, 1947-58.

José Limón, 1908-72, (Mex.-U.S.) modern dancer, choreographer, teacher; developed technique based on Humphrey.

Catherine Littlefield, 1908-51, (U.S.) ballerina, choreographer, teacher; pioneer of American ballet.

Kenneth MacMillan, 1929-92, (Br.) dancer, choreographer; directed Royal Ballet of Great Britain, 1970-77.

Dame Alicia Markova, 1910-2004, (Br.) ballerina; helped popularize ballet in U.S. and Britain; known for title role in *Giselle*.

Léonide Massine, 1896-1979, (Russ.-U.S.) ballet dancer, choreographer; known for his "symphonic ballet."

Fayard Nicholas, 1914-2006, (U.S.) tap dancer, choreographer, actor; together with brother **Harold Nicholas**, 1921-2000, (U.S.) formed the "Nicholas Brothers."

Vaslav Nijinsky, 1890-50, (Russ.) prem. danseur, choreographer; leading member of Diaghilev's Ballets Russes; his ballets were revolutionary for their time.

Alwin Nikolais, 1910-93, (U.S.) modern choreographer; created dance theater utilizing mixed media effects.

Jean-George Noverre, 1727-1810, (Fr.) ballet choreographer, teacher, writer; "Shakespeare of the Dance."

Rudolf Nureyev, 1938-93, (Russ.) prem. danseur, choreographer; leading male dancer of his generation; director of dance at Paris Opera, 1983-89.

Ruth Page, 1899-1991, (U.S.) ballerina, choreographer; danced, directed ballet at Chicago Lyric Opera.

Anna Pavlova, 1881-1931, (Russ.) prima ballerina; toured with her own company to world acclaim.

Marius Petipa, 1818-1910, (Fr.) ballet dancer, choreographer; ballet master of the Imperial Ballet; established Russian classicism as leading style of late 19th cent.

Roland Petit, 1924-2011, (Fr.) dancer, choreographer; founder Les Ballets de Paris.

Pearl Primus, 1919-95, (Trinidad-U.S.) modern dancer, choreographer, scholar; combined African, Caribbean, and African American styles.

Jerome Robbins, 1918-98, (U.S.) choreographer, director, dancer; *The King and I, West Side Story, Fiddler on the Roof.*

Bill "Bojangles" Robinson, 1878-1949, (U.S.) famed tap dancer; called "King of Tapology" on stage and screen.

Ruth St. Denis, 1877-1968, (U.S.) influential interpretive dancer, choreographer, teacher.

Ted Shawn, 1891-1972, (U.S.) modern dancer, choreographer; formed dance company and school with Ruth St. Denis; established Jacob's Pillow Dance Festival.

Marie Taglioni, 1804-84, (It.) ballerina, teacher; in title role of *La Sylphide* established image of the ethereal ballerina.

Glen Tetley, 1926-2007, (U.S.) dancer, choreographer, ballet director; fused elements of modern dance with ballet.

Antony Tudor, 1908-87, (Br.) choreographer, teacher; exponent of the "psychological ballet."

Galina Ulanova, 1910-98, (Russ.) revered ballerina with Bolshoi Ballet.

Agrippina Vaganova, 1879-1951, (Russ.) ballet teacher, director; codified Soviet ballet technique; called "queen of variations."

Mary Wigman, 1886-1973, (Ger.) modern dancer, choreographer, teacher; influenced European expressionist dance.

Opera Singers of the Past

Frances Alda, 1883?-1952, (N.Z.) soprano.

Pasquale Amato, 1878-1942, (It.) baritone.

Marian Anderson, 1897-1993, (U.S.) contralto.

Charles Anthony, 1929-2012, (U.S.) tenor.

Jussi Björling, 1911-60, (Swed.) tenor.

Lucrezia Bori, 1887-1960, (It.) soprano.

Maria Callas, 1923-77, (U.S.) soprano.

Emma Calvé, 1858-1942, (Fr.) soprano.

Enrico Caruso, 1873-1921, (It.) tenor.

Feodor Chaliapin, 1873-1938, (Russ.) bass.

Lili Chookasian, 1921-2012, (U.S.) contralto.

Boris Christoff, 1914-93, (Bulg.) bass.

Franco Corelli, 1921-2003, (It.) tenor.

Hughes Cuenod, 1902-2010, (Switz.) tenor.

Victoria De Los Angeles, 1923-2005, (Sp.) soprano.

Giuseppe De Luca, 1876-1950, (It.) baritone.

Fernando De Lucia, 1860-1925, (It.) tenor.

Edouard De Reszke, 1853-1917, (Pol.) bass.

Jean De Reszke, 1850-1925, (Pol.) tenor.

Emmy Destinn, 1878-1930, (Czech.) soprano.

Emma Eames, 1865-1952, (U.S.) soprano.

(Carlo Broschi) Farinelli, 1705-82, (It.) castrato.

Geraldine Farrar, 1882-1967, (U.S.) soprano.

Eileen Farrell, 1920-2002, (U.S.) soprano.

Kathleen Ferrier, 1912-53, (Eng.) contralto.

Dietrich Fischer-Dieskau, 1925-2012, (Ger.) baritone.

Kirsten Flagstad, 1895-1962, (Nor.) soprano.
Olive Fremstad, 1871-1951, (Swed.-U.S.) soprano.
Amelita Galli-Curci, 1882-1963, (It.) soprano.
Mary Garden, 1874-1967, (Br.) soprano.
Nicolai Ghiaurov, 1929-2004, (Bulg.) bass.
Beniamino Gigli, 1890-1957, (It.) tenor.
Tito Gobbi, 1913-84, (It.) baritone.
Giulia Grisi, 1811-69, (It.) soprano.
Frieda Hempel, 1885-1955, (Ger.) soprano.
Jerome Hines, 1921-2003, (U.S.) bass.
Hans Hotter, 1909-2003, (Ger.) bass-baritone.
Maria Jeritza, 1887-1982, (Czech.) soprano.
Sena Jurinac, 1921-2011, (Yugo.) soprano.
Alexander Kipnis, 1891-1978, (Russ.-U.S.) bass.
Dorothy Kirsten, 1910-92, (U.S.) soprano.
Alfredo Kraus, 1927-99, (Sp.) tenor.
Luigi Lablache, 1794-1858, (It.) bass.
Lilli Lehmann, 1848-1929, (Ger.) soprano.
Lotte Lehmann, 1888-1976, (Ger.-U.S.) soprano.
Jenny Lind, 1820-87, (Swed.) soprano.
Cornell MacNeil, 1922-2011, (U.S.) baritone.
Maria Malibran, 1808-36, (Sp.) mezzo-soprano.

Giovanni Martinelli, 1885-1969, (It.) tenor.
John McCormack, 1884-1945, (Ire.) tenor.
Nellie Melba, 1861-1931, (Austral.) soprano.
Lauritz Melchior, 1890-1973, (Den.) tenor.
Robert Merrill, 1919-2004, (U.S.) baritone.
Zinka Milanov, 1906-89, (Yugo.) soprano.
Patricia Neway, 1919-2012, (U.S.) soprano.
Birgit Nilsson, 1918-2005, (Swed.) soprano.
Lillian Nordica, 1857-1914, (U.S.) soprano.
Giuditta Pasta, 1797-1865, (It.) soprano.
Adelina Patti, 1843-1919, (It.) soprano.
Luciano Pavarotti, 1935-2007, (It.) tenor.
Peter Pears, 1910-86, (Eng.) tenor.
Jan Peerce, 1904-84, (U.S.) tenor.
Ezio Pinza, 1892-1957, (It.) bass.
Lily Pons, 1898-1976, (Fr.) soprano.
Rosa Ponselle, 1897-1981, (U.S.) soprano.
Hermann Prey, 1929-98, (Ger.) baritone.
Margaret Price, 1941-2011, (U.K.) soprano.
Elisabeth Rethberg, 1894-1976, (Ger.) soprano.
Giovanni Battista Rubini, 1794-1854, (It.) tenor.
Leonie Rysanek, 1926-98, (Austria) soprano.
Dorothy Sarnoff, 1914-2008, (U.S.) soprano.
Bidú Sayão, 1902-99, (Braz.) soprano.

Friedrich Schorr, 1888-1953, (Hung.) bass-baritone.
Elisabeth Schwarzkopf, 1915-2006, (Ger.) soprano.
Marcella Sembrich, 1858-1935, (Pol.) soprano.
Cesare Siepi, 1923-2010, (It.) bass.
Beverly Sills, 1929-2007, (U.S.) soprano.
Elisabeth Söderström, 1927-2009, (Swed.) soprano.
Eleanor Steber, 1914-90, (U.S.) soprano.
Joan Sutherland, 1926-2010, (Austral.) soprano.
Ferrucio Tagliavini, 1913-95, (It.) tenor.
Renata Tebaldi, 1922-2004 (It.) soprano.
Luisa Tetrazzini, 1871-1940, (It.) soprano.
Lawrence Tibbett, 1896-1960, (U.S.) baritone.
Giorgio Tozzi, 1923-2011, (U.S.) bass-baritone.
Tatiana Troyanos, 1938-93, (U.S.) mezzo-soprano.
Richard Tucker, 1913-75, (U.S.) tenor.
Pauline Viardot, 1821-1910, (Fr.) mezzo-soprano.
Shirley Verrett, 1931-2010, (U.S.) mezzo-soprano.
William Warfield, 1920-2002, (U.S.) bass-baritone.
Leonard Warren, 1911-60, (U.S.) baritone.
Ljuba Welitsch, 1913-96, (Bulg.) soprano.
Camilla Williams, 1919-2012, (U.S.) soprano.
Wolfgang Windgassen, 1914-74, (Ger.) tenor.

Rock and Roll, Rhythm and Blues, and Rap Artists

Titles in quotation marks are singles; others are albums. *Inducted into Rock and Roll Hall of Fame as performer between 1986 and 2012; year is in parentheses.

Aaliyah: "More than a Woman"
*ABBA (2010): "Dancing Queen"
Paula Abdul: "Straight Up"
*AC/DC (2003): "Back in Black"
Bryan Adams: "Cuts Like a Knife"
Adele: "Rolling in the Deep"
*Aerosmith (2001): "Sweet Emotion"
Christina Aguilera: "What a Girl Wants"
Alice in Chains: "Heaven Beside You"
*The Allman Brothers Band (1995): "Ramblin' Man"
*The Animals (1994): "House of the Rising Sun"
Paul Anka: "Lonely Boy"
Fiona Apple: "Criminal"
Ashanti: "Foolish"
Frankie Avalon: "Venus"
The B-52s: "Love Shack"
Bachman Turner Overdrive: "Takin' Care of Business"
Backstreet Boys: "I Want It That Way"
Bad Company: "Can't Get Enough"
Erykah Badu: "On and On"
*La Vern Baker (1991): "I Cried a Tear"
*Hank Ballard[1] and the Midnighters (1990): "Work With Me, Annie"
*The Band (1994): "The Weight"
Barenaked Ladies: "One Week"
*The Beach Boys (1988): "Good Vibrations"
*Beastie Boys (2012): "(You Gotta) Fight for Your Right (to Party)"
*The Beatles (1988): Sgt. Pepper's Lonely Hearts Club Band
Beck: "Loser"
*Jeff Beck (2009): "Escape"
*The Bee Gees (1997): "Stayin' Alive"
Pat Benatar: "Hit Me With Your Best Shot"
Ben Folds Five: "Brick"
*Chuck Berry (1986): "Johnny B. Goode"
Beyoncé: "Crazy in Love"
The Big Bopper: "Chantilly Lace"
Björk: "Human Behavior"
The Black Crowes: "Hard to Handle"
Black Eyed Peas: Elephunk
*Black Sabbath (2006): "Paranoid"
*Bobby "Blue" Bland (1992): "Turn On Your Love Light"
Mary J. Blige: My Life
Blind Faith: "Can't Find My Way Home"
Blink-182: "All the Small Things"
*Blondie (2006): "Heart of Glass"
Blood, Sweat, and Tears: "Spinning Wheel"
Blues Traveler: "Run-Around"
Gary "U.S." Bonds: "Quarter to Three"

Bon Jovi: "Livin' on a Prayer"
*Booker T. and the M.G.'s (1992): "Green Onions"
Earl Bostic: "Flamingo"
Boston: "More Than A Feeling"
*David Bowie (1996): "Space Oddity"
Boyz II Men: "I'll Make Love to You"
Toni Braxton: "Un-Break My Heart"
Chris Brown: "Kiss Kiss"
*James Brown (1986): "Papa's Got a Brand New Bag"
*Ruth Brown (1993): "Lucky Lips"
*Jackson Browne (2004): "Doctor My Eyes"
*Buffalo Springfield (1997): "For What It's Worth"
Jimmy Buffett: "Margaritaville"
*Solomon Burke (2001): "Over and Over (Huggin' and Lovin')"
Bush: "Glycerine"
*The Byrds (1991): "Turn! Turn! Turn!"
Mariah Carey: "Vision of Love"
The Carpenters: "(They Long to Be) Close to You"
The Cars: "Shake It Up"
*Johnny Cash (1992): "I Walk the Line"
*Ray Charles (1986): "Georgia on My Mind"
Cheap Trick: "Surrender"
Chubby Checker: "The Twist"
Chicago: "Saturday in the Park"
*Eric Clapton (2000): "Layla"
Kelly Clarkson: "Since U Been Gone"
*The Clash (2003): "Rock the Casbah"
*Jimmy Cliff (2010): "I Can See Clearly Now"
*The Coasters (1987): "Yakety Yak"
*Eddie Cochran (1987): "Summertime Blues"
Joe Cocker: "With a Little Help From My Friends"
*Leonard Cohen (2008): "Suzanne"
Coldplay: "Clocks"
Collective Soul: "The World I Know"
Phil Collins: "Against All Odds"
*Sam Cooke (1986): "You Send Me"
Coolio: "Gangsta's Paradise"
*Alice Cooper (2011): "School's Out"
*Elvis Costello and the Attractions (2003): "Alison"
Counting Crows: "Mr. Jones"
*Cream (1993): "Sunshine of Your Love"
Creed: "Arms Wide Open"
*Creedence Clearwater Revival (1993): "Proud Mary"
*Crosby, Stills, and Nash (1997): "Suite: Judy Blue Eyes"

Sheryl Crow: "All I Want to Do"
The Crystals: "Da Doo Ron Ron"
The Cult: "She Sells Sanctuary"
The Cure: "Boys Don't Cry"
Cypress Hill: "Insane in the Brain"
Danny and the Juniors: "At the Hop"
*Bobby Darin (1990): "Splish Splash"
Daughtry: "It's Not Over"
*The Dave Clark Five (2008): "Glad All Over"
Dave Matthews Band: "Don't Drink the Water"
*Miles Davis (2006): Bitches Brew
Spencer Davis Group: "Gimme Some Lovin'"
Deep Purple: "Smoke on the Water"
Def Leppard: "Photograph"
*The Dells (2004): "Oh, What a Night"
Depeche Mode: "Strange Love"
Destiny's Child: "Survivor"
*Neil Diamond (2011): "Cracklin' Rosie"
*Bo Diddley (1987): "Who Do You Love?
*Dion[1] and the Belmonts (1989): "A Teenager in Love"
Celine Dion: "Because You Loved Me"
Dire Straits: "Money for Nothing"
DMX: "What's My Name"
*Fats Domino (1986): "Blueberry Hill"
*Donovan (2012): "Mellow Yellow"
The Doobie Brothers: "What a Fool Believes"
*The Doors (1993): "Light My Fire"
Drake: "Over"
Dr. Dre: "Nothin' But a 'G' Thang"
*The Drifters (1988): "Save the Last Dance for Me"
*Dr. John (2011): "Right Place, Wrong Time"
Duran Duran: "Hungry Like the Wolf"
*Bob Dylan (1988): "Like a Rolling Stone"
*The Eagles (1998): "Hotel California"
*Earth, Wind, and Fire (2000): "Shining Star"
*Duane Eddy (1994): "Rebel-Rouser"
Missy Elliott: "Sock It 2 Me"
Eminem: "The Real Slim Shady"
En Vogue: "Hold On"
The Eurythmics: "Sweet Dreams (Are Made of This)"
Everclear: "Father Of Mine"
*The Everly Brothers (1986): "Wake Up, Little Susie"
50 Cent (Curtis Jackson): Get Rich or Die Tryin'
The Five Satins: "In the Still of the Night"

Roberta Flack: "The First Time Ever I Saw Your Face"
*The Flamingos (2001): "I Only Have Eyes for You"
*Fleetwood Mac (1998): *Rumours*
The Foo Fighters: "I'll Stick Around"
Foreigner: "Double Vision"
*The Four Seasons (1990): "Sherry"
*The Four Tops (1990): "I Can't Help Myself (Sugar Pie, Honey Bunch)"
*Aretha Franklin (1987): "Respect"
Nelly Furtado: "I'm Like a Bird"
Peter Gabriel: "Shock the Monkey"
*Gamble (Kenny) and Huff (Leon) (2008): "If You Don't Know Me By Now"
*Marvin Gaye (1987): "I Heard It Through the Grapevine"
*Genesis (2010): "No Reply at All"
Goo Goo Dolls: "Iris"
Grand Funk Railroad: "We're an American Band"
*Grandmaster Flash and the Furious Five (2007): "The Message"
*The Grateful Dead (1994): "Uncle John's Band"
*Al Green (1995): "Let's Stay Together"
Green Day: "Boulevard of Broken Dreams"
The Guess Who: "American Woman"
*Guns N' Roses (2012): "Sweet Child o' Mine"
*Buddy Guy (2005): *A Man and His Blues*
*Bill Haley[1] and His Comets (1987): "Rock Around the Clock"
Hall and Oates: "Kiss on My List"
Hanson: "MMMBop"
*George Harrison (2004): "My Sweet Lord"
*Isaac Hayes (2002): "Theme From 'Shaft'"
Heart: "Barracuda"
*Jimi Hendrix (1992): "Purple Haze"
Lauryn Hill: "Doo-Wop (That Thing)"
Hole: "Doll Parts"
*The Hollies (2010): "Long Cool Woman (In a Black Dress)"
*Buddy Holly (1986): "Peggy Sue"
*John Lee Hooker (1991): "Boogie Chillen"
Hootie and the Blowfish: *Cracked Rear View*
Whitney Houston: "I Will Always Love You"
*The Impressions (1991): "For Your Precious Love"
Indigo Girls: "Closer to Fine"
INXS: "Need You Tonight"
*The Isley Brothers (1992): "It's Your Thing"
*The Jackson Five (1997): "ABC"
Janet Jackson: *Rhythm Nation*
*Michael Jackson (2001): *Thriller*
*Etta James (1993): "At Last"
Tommy James and the Shondells: "Crimson and Clover"
Jane's Addiction: "Jane Says"
Ja Rule: *Venni, Vetti, Vecci*
Jay and the Americans: "This Magic Moment"
Jay-Z: "Can I Live"
*Jefferson Airplane (1996): "White Rabbit"
Jethro Tull: *Aqualung*
Joan Jett: "I Love Rock 'n' Roll"
Jewel: "You Were Meant For Me"
*Billy Joel (1999): "Piano Man"
*Elton John (1994): "Candle in the Wind"
*Little Willie John (1996): "Sleep"
Norah Jones: *Come Away With Me*
*Janis Joplin (1995): "Me and Bobby McGee"
Journey: "Don't Stop Believin'"
K.C. and the Sunshine Band: "Get Down Tonight"
R. Kelly: "I Can't Sleep Baby (If I)"
Alicia Keys: "Fallin'"
Kid Rock: "Cowboy"
*B.B. King (1987): "The Thrill Is Gone"
Carole King: *Tapestry*
*The Kinks (1990): "You Really Got Me"
Kiss: "Rock 'n' Roll All Night"
*Gladys Knight and the Pips (1996): "Midnight Train to Georgia"
Korn: "Blind"
Lenny Kravitz: "Are You Gonna Go My Way?"
Lady Gaga: "Poker Face"
*Led Zeppelin (1995): "Stairway to Heaven"
*Brenda Lee (2002): "I'm Sorry"
John Legend: "Ordinary People"
*John Lennon (1994): "Imagine"

*Jerry Lee Lewis (1986): "Whole Lotta Shakin' Going On"
Lil' Kim: "No Matter What They Say"
Lil Wayne: *The Block Is Hot.*
Limp Bizkit: "Break Stuff"
Linkin Park: "One Step Closer"
*Little Anthony and the Imperials (2009): "Tears on My Pillow"
*Little Richard (1986): "Tutti Frutti"
*Little Walter (2008): "Juke"
Live: "Lightning Crashes"
L.L. Cool J: "Mama Said Knock You Out"
Jennifer Lopez: "Love Don't Cost a Thing"
*Darlene Love (2011): "He's a Rebel"
*The Lovin' Spoonful (2000): "Summer in the City"
Ludacris: "Money Maker"
*Frankie Lymon and the Teenagers (1993): "Why Do Fools Fall in Love?"
*Lynyrd Skynyrd (2006): "Free Bird"
*Madonna (2008): "Material Girl"
*The Mamas and the Papas (1998): "Monday, Monday"
Aimee Mann: "Save Me"
Marilyn Manson: "Beautiful People"
*Bob Marley (1994): *Exodus*
Maroon 5: *Songs About Jane*
Bruno Mars: "Just the Way You Are"
*Martha and the Vandellas (1995): "Dancin' in the Streets"
The Marvelettes: "Please, Mr. Postman"
Matchbox 20: "Push"
John Mayer: "Daughters"
*Curtis Mayfield (1999): "Superfly"
*Paul McCartney (1999): "Band on the Run"
Don McLean: "American Pie"
*Clyde McPhatter (1987): "A Lover's Question"
Meat Loaf: "Paradise by the Dashboard Light"
*John (Cougar) Mellencamp (2008): "Jack and Diane"
Men at Work: "Who Can It Be Now?"
*Metallica (2009): "Enter Sandman"
George Michael: "Faith"
Nicki Minaj: *Pink Friday.*
*Joni Mitchell (1997): "Both Sides Now"
Moby: "Bodyrock"
The Monkees: "I'm a Believer"
Moody Blues: "Nights in White Satin"
*The Moonglows (2000): "Blue Velvet"
Alanis Morissette: "Ironic"
*Van Morrison (1993): "Brown-Eyed Girl"
Mötley Crüe: "Live Wire"
Motörhead: "Ace of Spades"
Jason Mraz: "I'm Yours"
Nelly: *Country Grammar*
*Ricky Nelson (1987): "Hello, Mary Lou"
Nickelback: "Photograph"
Nine Inch Nails: "Closer"
Nirvana: *Nevermind*
No Doubt: *Rock Steady*
The Notorious B.I.G.: "Mo Money Mo Problems"
'N Sync: "Bye, Bye, Bye"
Ted Nugent: "Strangehold"
N.W.A.: "Straight Outta Compton"
Oasis: "Wonderwall"
The Offspring: "Pretty Fly (For a White Guy)"
*The O'Jays (2005): "Back Stabbers"
*Roy Orbison (1987): "Oh, Pretty Woman"
Ozzy Osbourne: "Crazy Train"
OutKast: *Speakerboxxx/The Love Below*
*Parliament/Funkadelic (1997): "One Nation Under a Groove"
Pearl Jam: "Jeremy"
*Carl Perkins (1987): "Blue Suede Shoes"
Katy Perry: "I Kissed a Girl"
Peter, Paul, and Mary: "Leaving on a Jet Plane"
*Tom Petty and the Heartbreakers (2002): "Refugee"
Liz Phair: *Exile in Guyville*
Phish: "Sample in a Jar"
*Wilson Pickett (1991): "Land of 1,000 Dances"
Pink: *Missundaztood!*
*Pink Floyd (1996): *The Wall*
*Gene Pitney (2002): "Only Love Can Break a Heart"
*The Platters (1990): "The Great Pretender"
The Pointer Sisters: "I'm So Excited"
*The Police (2003): "Every Breath You Take"

Iggy Pop: "Lust for Life"
*Elvis Presley (1986): "Love Me Tender"
*The Pretenders (2005): "Back on the Chain Gang"
*Lloyd Price (1998): "Stagger Lee"
*Prince (The Artist) (2004): "Purple Rain"
Public Enemy: "Fight the Power"
Puff Daddy and the Family: *No Way Out*
*Queen (2001): "Bohemian Rhapsody"
Radiohead: *OK Computer*
Rage Against the Machine: "Bulls on Parade"
*Bonnie Raitt (2000): "Something to Talk About"
*The Ramones (2002): "I Wanna Be Sedated"
*Otis Redding (1989): "(Sittin' on) The Dock of the Bay"
*Red Hot Chili Peppers (2012): "Under the Bridge"
*Jimmy Reed (1991): "Ain't That Loving You, Baby?"
Lou Reed: "Walk on the Wild Side"
*R.E.M. (2007): "Losing My Religion"
REO Speedwagon: "Can't Fight This Feeling"
Busta Rhymes: "What's It Gonna Be?"
*The Righteous Brothers (2003): "You've Lost That Lovin' Feelin'"
Rihanna: "Rude Boy"
Johnny Rivers: "Poor Side of Town"
*Smokey Robinson[1] and the Miracles (1987): "Shop Around"
*The Rolling Stones (1989): "Satisfaction"
*The Ronettes (2007): "Be My Baby"
Linda Ronstadt: "You're No Good"
Diana Ross: "I'm Coming Out"
*Run-D.M.C. (2009): "Raisin' Hell"
Rush: "Tom Sawyer"
Sade: "Smooth Operator"
Salt-N-Pepa: "Shoop"
*Sam and Dave (1992): "Soul Man"
*Santana (1998): "Black Magic Woman"
Seal: "Kiss From a Rose"
Neil Sedaka: "Breaking Up Is Hard to Do"
*Bob Seger (2004): "Old Time Rock & Roll"
*Sex Pistols (2006): "Anarchy in the UK"
Shaggy: "It Wasn't Me"
Shakira: "Whenever, Wherever"
Tupac Shakur: "How Do U Want It"
*Del Shannon (1999): "Runaway"
*The Shirelles (1996): "Soldier Boy"
Carly Simon: "You're So Vain"
*Paul Simon (2001): "50 Ways to Leave Your Lover"
*Simon and Garfunkel (1990): "Bridge Over Troubled Water"
*Percy Sledge (2005): "When a Man Loves a Woman"
*Sly and the Family Stone (1993): "Everyday People"
Smashing Pumpkins: "Today"
*Patti Smith (2007): "Because the Night"
Will Smith: "Gettin' Jiggy With It"
The Smiths: "This Charming Man"
Snoop Lion (née Dogg): "Gin and Juice"
Sonic Youth: "Bull in the Heather"
Soundgarden: "Black Hole Sun"
Britney Spears: "Hit Me Baby One More Time"
Spice Girls: "Wannabe"
*Dusty Springfield (1999): "I Only Want to Be With You"
*Bruce Springsteen (1999): "Born to Run"
Squeeze: "Tempted"
*Staple Singers (1999): "I'll Take You There"
*Steely Dan (2001): "Rikki Don't Lose That Number"
Gwen Stefani: "Hollaback Girl"
Steppenwolf: "Born to Be Wild"
*Rod Stewart (1994): "Maggie Mae"
Sting: "If You Love Somebody, Set Them Free"
Stone Temple Pilots: "Plush"
*The Stooges (2010): "I Wanna Be Your Dog"
Styx: "Come Sail Away"
Sublime: "What I Got"
The Sugar Hill Gang: "Rapper's Delight"
Donna Summer: "Bad Girls"
*The Supremes (1988): "Stop! In the Name of Love"

Taj Mahal: "Going Up to the Country, Paint My Mailbox Blue"
*Talking Heads (2002): "Once in a Lifetime"
*James Taylor (2001): "You've Got a Friend"
*The Temptations (1989): "My Girl"
Three Dog Night: "Joy to the World"
Justin Timberlake: "SexyBack"
TLC: "Waterfalls"
T. Rex: "Bang a Gong (Get It On)"
*Traffic (2004): Traffic
*Big Joe Turner (1987): "Shake, Rattle & Roll"
*Ike and Tina Turner (1991): "Proud Mary"
*Tina Turner (1991): "What's Love Got to Do With It?"
The Turtles: "Happy Together"
*U2 (2005): "With or Without You"

Usher: "You Make Me Wanna"
*Ritchie Valens (2001): "La Bamba"
*Van Halen (2007): "Running With the Devil"
Stevie Ray Vaughan: "Crossfire"
*The Velvet Underground (1996): "Sweet Jane"
*The Ventures (2008): "Walk, Don't Run"
*Gene Vincent (1998): "Be-Bop-A-Lula"
*Tom Waits (2011): "Downtown Train"
The Wallflowers: "One Headlight"
Dionne Warwick: "I Say a Little Prayer"
*Muddy Waters (1987): "I Can't Be Satisfied"
Mary Wells: "My Guy"
Kanye West: "Gold Digger"
The White Stripes: "Seven Nation Army"
Whitesnake: "Here I Go Again"
*The Who (1990): Tommy

Lucinda Williams: Car Wheels on a Gravel Road
*Jackie Wilson (1987): "That's Why"
*Bobby Womack (2009): "Lookin' for a Love"
*Stevie Wonder (1989): "You Are the Sunshine of My Life"
Wu-Tang Clan: "Protect Ya Neck"
Weird Al Yankovic: Dare to Be Stupid
*The Yardbirds (1992): "For Your Love"
Yes: "Roundabout"
*Neil Young (1995): "Down by the River"
*The Young Rascals/The Rascals (1997): "Good Lovin' "
*Frank Zappa[1]/Mothers of Invention (1995): Hot Rats
John Zorn: News for Lulu
*ZZ Top (2004): "Legs"

(1) Only individual performer is in Rock and Roll Hall of Fame.

Entertainment Personalities of the Present

Living actors, musicians, dancers, singers, producers, directors, and radio-TV performers.

Name	Birthplace	Birthdate	Name	Birthplace	Birthdate
Abbado, Claudio	Milan, Italy	6/26/33	Arnaz, Lucie	Hollywood, CA	7/17/51
Abdul, Paula	San Fernando, CA	6/19/62	Arnett, Will	Toronto, ON, Canada	5/4/70
Abraham, F. Murray	Pittsburgh, PA	10/24/39	Arnold, Tom	Ottumwa, IA	3/6/59
Abrams, J(effrey) J(acob)	New York, NY	6/27/66	Arquette, David	Winchester, VA	9/8/71
Adams, Amy	Aviano, Italy	8/20/74	Arquette, Patricia	Chicago, IL	4/8/68
Adams, Bryan	Kingston, ON, Canada	11/5/59	Arquette, Rosanna	New York, NY	8/10/59
Adams, Yolanda	Houston, TX	8/27/61	Arroyo, Martina	New York, NY	2/2/37
Adele	London, England, UK	5/5/88	Ashanti (Douglas)	Glen Cove, NY.	10/13/80
Adjani, Isabelle	Paris, France	6/27/55	Ashley, Elizabeth	Ocala, FL	8/30/39
Ad-Rock	South Orange, NJ	10/31/66	Asner, Ed	Kansas City, KS.	11/15/29
Affleck, Ben	Berkeley, CA	8/15/72	Assante, Armand	New York, NY	10/4/49
Affleck, Casey	Falmouth, MA	8/12/75	Astin, John	Baltimore, MD	3/30/30
Aghdashloo, Shohreh	Tehran, Iran	5/11/52	Astin, Sean	Santa Monica, CA	2/25/71
Agron, Dianna	Savannah, GA	4/30/86	Atkins, Eileen	London, England, UK	6/16/34
Aguilera, Christina	Staten Island, NY.	12/18/80	Atkins, Sharif	Pittsburgh, PA	1/29/75
Aiello, Danny	New York, NY	6/20/33	Atkinson, Rowan	Newcastle upon Tyne, England, UK	1/6/55
Aiken, Clay	Raleigh, NC.	11/30/78			
Aimee, Anouk	Paris, France	4/27/32	Attenborough, Richard	Cambridge, England, UK.	8/29/23
Alba, Jessica	Pomona, CA	4/28/81	Auberjonois, Rene	New York, NY	6/1/40
Albanese, Licia	Bari, Italy	7/22/13	Austin, Patti	New York, NY	8/10/48
Alberghetti, Anna Maria	Pesaro, Italy	5/15/36	Autry, Alan	Shreveport, LA	7/31/52
Albert, Marv	Brooklyn, NY	6/12/41	Avalon, Frankie	Philadelphia, PA	9/18/40
Alda, Alan	New York, NY	1/28/36	Aykroyd, Dan	Ottawa, ON, Canada	7/1/52
Alexander, Jane	Boston, MA	10/28/39	Azaria, Hank	Forest Hills, Queens, NY	4/25/64
Alexander, Jason	Newark, NJ	9/23/59	Aznavour, Charles	Paris, France	5/22/24
Allen, Debbie	Houston, TX	1/16/50	Babyface	Indianapolis, IN	4/10/59
Allen, Joan	Rochelle, IL	8/20/56	Bacall, Lauren	Bronx, NY	9/16/24
Allen, Karen	Carrollton, IL	10/5/51	Bacon, Kevin	Philadelphia, PA	7/8/58
Allen, Kris	Jacksonville, AR	6/21/85	Badalucco, Michael	Brooklyn, NY	12/20/54
Allen, Ted	Columbus, OH.	5/20/65	Bader, Diedrich	Alexandria, VA	12/24/66
Allen, Tim	Denver, CO	6/13/53	Badu, Erykah	Dallas, TX	2/26/71
Allen, Woody	Brooklyn, NY	12/1/35	Baez, Joan	Staten Island, NY.	1/9/41
Alley, Kirstie	Wichita, KS	1/12/51	Bain, Conrad	Lethbridge, AB, Canada	2/4/23
Allman, Gregg	Nashville, TN.	12/8/47	Baio, Scott	Brooklyn, NY	9/22/61
Alonso, Maria Conchita	Cienfuegos, Cuba	6/29/57	Baker, Anita	Toledo, OH	1/26/58
Alpert, Herb	Los Angeles, CA	3/31/35	Baker, Carroll	Johnstown, PA.	5/28/31
Almodóvar, Pedro	Calzada de Calatrava, Spain	9/24/49	Baker, Diane	Hollywood, CA.	2/25/38
Ambrose, Lauren	New Haven, CT.	2/20/78	Baker, Joe Don	Groesbeck, TX.	2/12/36
Ames, Ed	Malden, MA.	7/9/27	Baker, Kathy	Midland, TX.	6/8/50
Amos, John	Newark, NJ	12/27/41	Baker, Simon	Launceston, Tasmania, Australia	7/30/69
Amos, Tori	Newton, NC.	8/22/63			
Anderson, Gillian	Chicago, IL	8/9/68	Bakula, Scott	St. Louis, MO.	10/9/54
Anderson, Harry	Newport, RI.	10/14/52	Baldwin, Alec	Massapequa, NY.	4/3/58
Anderson, Ian	Dunfermline, Scotland, UK	8/10/47	Baldwin, Daniel	Massapequa, NY.	10/5/60
Anderson, Kevin	Gurnee, IL	1/13/60	Baldwin, Stephen	Massapequa, NY.	5/12/66
Anderson, Loni	St. Paul, MN	8/5/46	Baldwin, William	Massapequa, NY.	2/21/63
Anderson, Lynn	Grand Forks, ND	9/26/47	Bale, Christian	Pembrokeshire, Wales, UK	1/30/74
Anderson, Melissa Sue	Berkeley, CA	9/26/62	Ballard, Kaye	Cleveland, OH.	11/20/26
Anderson, Pamela	Ladysmith, BC, Canada	7/1/67	Bana, Eric	Melbourne, Australia	8/9/68
Anderson, Richard	Long Branch, NJ	8/8/26	Banderas, Antonio	Málaga, Spain	8/10/60
Anderson, Richard Dean	Minneapolis, MN	1/23/50	Banks, Elizabeth	Pittsfield, MA	2/10/74
Anderson, Wes	Houston, TX	5/1/69	Banks, Tyra	Los Angeles, CA	12/4/73
Andersson, Bibi	Stockholm, Sweden.	11/11/35	Baranski, Christine	Buffalo, NY	5/2/52
André 3000	Atlanta, GA	5/27/75	Barbeau, Adrienne	Sacramento, CA	6/11/45
Andress, Ursula	Bern, Switzerland	3/19/36	Bardem, Javier	Las Palmas, Canary Islands, Spain	3/1/69
Andrews, Julie	Walton-on-Thames, Surrey, England, UK	10/1/35			
Andrews, Naveen	London, England, UK	1/17/69	Bardot, Brigitte	Paris, France	9/28/34
Andrews, Patty	Mound, MN	2/16/18	Barker, Bob	Darrington, WA	12/12/23
Aniston, Jennifer	Sherman Oaks, CA	2/11/69	Barkin, Ellen	Bronx, NY	4/16/55
Anka, Paul	Ottawa, ON, Canada	7/30/41	Barrie, Barbara	Chicago, IL	5/23/31
Ann-Margret	Stockholm, Sweden	4/28/41	Barrino, Fantasia	High Point, NC.	6/30/84
Anthony, Marc	New York, NY	9/16/68	Barrymore, Drew	Los Angeles, CA	2/22/75
Apatow, Judd	Syosset, NY.	12/6/67	Bartoli, Cecilia	Rome, Italy	6/4/66
Apple, Fiona	New York, NY	9/13/77	Barton, Misha	London, England, UK	1/24/86
Applegate, Christina	Los Angeles, CA	11/25/71	Baryshnikov, Mikhail	Riga, Latvia	1/28/48
Archer, Anne	Los Angeles, CA	8/25/47	Basinger, Kim	Athens, GA	12/8/53
Archuleta, David	Miami, FL	12/28/90	Bass, Lance	Laurel, MS.	5/4/79
Arkin, Adam	Brooklyn, NY	8/19/56	Bassett, Angela	New York, NY	8/16/58
Arkin, Alan	New York, NY	3/26/34	Bassey, Shirley	Cardiff, Wales, UK	1/8/37
Armisen, Fred	Hattiesburg, MS	12/4/66	Bateman, Jason	Rye, NY.	1/14/69
Arnaz, Desi, Jr.	Hollywood, CA.	1/19/53	Bateman, Justine	Rye, NY.	2/19/66
			Bates, Kathy	Memphis, TN.	6/28/48

Name	Birthplace	Birthdate
Batt, Bryan	New Orleans, LA	3/1/63
Battle, Kathleen	Portsmouth, OH	8/13/48
Baxter, Meredith	South Pasadena, CA	6/21/47
Bean, Orson	Burlington, VT	7/22/28
Bean, Sean	Sheffield, England, UK	4/17/59
Beatty, Ned	Louisville, KY	7/6/37
Beatty, Warren	Richmond, VA	3/30/37
Beauvais, Garcelle	St. Marc, Haiti	11/26/66
Beck	Los Angeles, CA	7/8/70
Beck, Jeff	Wallington, Surrey, Eng., UK	6/24/44
Beckham, Victoria	Hertfordshire, England, UK	4/17/74
Beckinsale, Kate	London, England, UK	7/26/73
Bedelia, Bonnie	New York, NY	3/25/48
Begley, Ed, Jr.	Los Angeles, CA	9/16/49
Behar, Joy	Brooklyn, NY	10/7/43
Belafonte, Harry	New York, NY	3/1/27
Bell, Art	Camp Lejeune, NC	6/17/45
Bell, Catherine	London, England, UK	8/14/68
Bell, Kristen	Huntington Woods, MI	7/18/80
Bello, Maria	Norristown, PA	4/18/67
Belmondo, Jean-Paul	Neuilly-sur-Seine, France	4/9/33
Belushi, Jim	Chicago, IL	6/15/54
Belzer, Richard	Bridgeport, CT	8/4/44
Benanti, Laura	Kinnelon, NJ	7/15/79
Benatar, Pat	Brooklyn, NY	1/10/53
Benedict, Dirk	Helena, MT	3/1/45
Benigni, Roberto	Misericordia, Italy	10/27/52
Bening, Annette	Topeka, KS	5/29/58
Benjamin, Richard	New York, NY	5/22/38
Bennett, Alan	Leeds, England, UK	5/9/34
Bennett, Tony	Astoria, Queens, NY	8/3/26
Benson, George	Pittsburgh, PA	3/22/43
Benson, Robby	Dallas, TX	1/21/56
Berenger, Tom	Chicago, IL	5/31/50
Bergen, Candice	Beverly Hills, CA	5/9/46
Bergen, Polly	Knoxville, TN	7/14/30
Bergeron, Tom	Haverhill, MA	5/6/55
Berman, Shelley	Chicago, IL	2/3/26
Bernard, Crystal	Garland, TX	9/30/61
Bernhard, Sandra	Flint, MI	6/6/55
Bernsen, Corbin	N. Hollywood, CA	9/7/54
Berry, Chuck	St. Louis, MO	10/18/26
Berry, Halle	Cleveland, OH	8/14/66
Berry, Ken	Moline, IL	11/3/33
Bertinelli, Valerie	Wilmington, DE	4/23/60
Bertolucci, Bernardo	Parma, Italy	3/16/40
Bettany, Paul	London, England, UK	5/27/71
Biafra, Jello	Boulder, CO	6/17/58
Bialik, Mayim	San Diego, CA	12/12/75
Bichir, Demián	Mexico City, Mexico	8/1/63
Bieber, Justin	Stratford, ON, Canada	3/1/94
Biel, Jessica	Ely, MN	3/3/82
Big Boi	Savannah, GA	2/1/75
Bigelow, Kathryn	San Carlos, CA	11/27/51
Biggs, Jason	Pompton Plains, NJ	5/12/78
Bikel, Theodore	Vienna, Austria	5/2/24
Bilson, Rachel	Los Angeles, CA	8/25/81
Binoche, Juliette	Paris, France	3/9/64
Birch, Thora	Beverly Hills, CA	3/11/82
Birney, David	Washington, DC	4/23/39
Bisset, Jacqueline	Weybridge, England, UK	9/13/44
Bissett, Josie	Seattle, WA	10/5/70
Björk	Reykjavik, Iceland	11/21/65
Black, Clint	Long Branch, NJ	2/4/62
Black, Jack	Santa Monica, CA	4/7/69
Black, Karen	Park Ridge, IL	7/1/42
Black, Lewis	Washington, DC	8/30/48
Blades, Ruben	Panama City, Panama	7/16/48
Blair, Linda	St. Louis, MO	1/22/59
Blair, Selma	Southfield, MI	6/23/72
Blake, Robert	Nutley, NJ	9/18/33
Blanchett, Cate	Melbourne, Australia	5/14/69
Bledsoe, Tempestt	Chicago, IL	8/1/73
Bleeth, Yasmine	New York, NY	6/14/68
Blethyn, Brenda	Ramsgate, Kent, Eng., UK	2/20/46
Blige, Mary J.	Bronx, NY	1/11/71
Bloom, Claire	London, England, UK	2/15/31
Bloom, Orlando	Canterbury, England, UK	1/13/77
Blyth, Ann	Mt. Kisco, NY	8/16/28
Bochco, Steven	New York, NY	12/16/43
Bocelli, Andrea	Lajatico, Italy	9/22/58
Bogdanovich, Peter	Kingston, NY	7/30/39
Bogosian, Eric	Woburn, MA	4/24/53
Bologna, Joseph	Brooklyn, NY	12/30/38
Bolton, Michael	New Haven, CT	2/26/53
Bonet, Lisa	San Francisco, CA	11/16/67
Bonham Carter, Helena	London, England, UK	5/26/66
Bon Jovi, Jon	Sayreville, NJ	3/2/62
Bono	Dublin, Ireland	5/10/60
Boone, Debby	Hackensack, NJ	9/22/56
Boone, Pat	Jacksonville, FL	6/1/34
Boreanaz, David	Buffalo, NY	5/16/69
Bosco, Philip	Jersey City, NJ	9/26/30
Bostwick, Barry	San Mateo, CA	2/24/45
Bosworth, Kate	Los Angeles, CA	1/2/83
Bottoms, Timothy	Santa Barbara, CA	8/30/51

Name	Birthplace	Birthdate
Bow Wow	Columbus, OH	3/9/87
Bowen, Julie	Baltimore, MD	3/3/70
Bowie, David	London, England, UK	1/8/47
Bowles, Peter	London, England, UK	10/16/36
Boxleitner, Bruce	Elgin, IL	5/12/50
Boy George	Bexleyheath, England, UK	6/14/61
Boyle, Lara Flynn	Davenport, IA	3/24/70
Bracco, Lorraine	Brooklyn, NY	10/2/55
Brady, Wayne	Orlando, FL	6/2/72
Braff, Zach	S. Orange, NJ	4/6/75
Branagh, Kenneth	Belfast, N. Ireland, UK	12/10/60
Brand, Russell	Grays, Essex, UK	6/4/75
Brandauer, Klaus Maria	Steiermark, Austria	6/22/44
Brandy (Norwood)	McComb, MS	2/11/79
Braschi, Nicoletta	Cesena, Italy	4/19/60
Bratt, Benjamin	San Francisco, CA	12/16/63
Braugher, Andre	Chicago, IL	7/1/62
Braxton, Toni	Severn, MD	10/7/66
Bremner, Ewen	Edinburgh, Scotland, UK	1/23/72
Brendon, Nicholas	Los Angeles, CA	4/12/71
Brennan, Eileen	Los Angeles, CA	9/3/35
Brenneman, Amy	Glastonbury, CT	6/22/64
Brenner, David	Philadelphia, PA	2/4/45
Bridges, Beau	Los Angeles, CA	12/9/41
Bridges, Jeff	Los Angeles, CA	12/4/49
Brightman, Sarah	Berkhamsted, England, UK	8/14/60
Brimley, Wilford	Salt Lake City, UT	9/27/34
Brinkley, Christie	Malibu, CA	2/2/54
Britton, Connie	Boston, MA	3/6/67
Broadbent, Jim	Lincolnshire, England, UK	5/24/49
Broderick, Matthew	New York, NY	3/21/62
Brody, Adam	San Diego, CA	12/15/79
Brody, Adrien	New York, NY	4/14/73
Brolin, James	Los Angeles, CA	7/18/40
Brolin, Josh	Los Angeles, CA	2/12/68
Brooks, Albert	Beverly Hills, CA	7/22/47
Brooks, Garth	Tulsa, OK	2/7/62
Brooks, James L.	North Bergen, NJ	5/9/40
Brooks, Mel	Brooklyn, NY	6/28/26
Brosnan, Pierce	Navan, Co. Meath, Ireland	5/16/53
Brown, Blair	Washington, DC	4/23/46
Brown, Bobby	Roxbury, MA	2/5/69
Brown, Bryan	Panania, Australia	6/23/47
Brown, Chris	Tappahannock, VA	5/5/89
Brown, Foxy	Brooklyn, NY	9/6/79
Browne, Jackson	Heidelberg, Germany	10/9/48
Brubeck, Dave	Concord, CA	12/6/20
Bryson, Peabo	Greenville, SC	4/13/51
Bublé, Michael	Burnaby, BC, Canada	9/9/75
Buckley, Betty	Big Spring, TX	7/3/47
Buffett, Jimmy	Pascagoula, MS	12/25/46
Bujold, Geneviève	Montreal, QC, Canada	7/1/42
Bullock, Sandra	Arlington, VA	7/26/64
Bumbry, Grace	St. Louis, MO	1/4/37
Bündchen, Gisele	Horizontina, Brazil	7/20/80
Burghoff, Gary	Bristol, CT	5/24/43
Burke, Delta	Orlando, FL	7/30/56
Burnett, Carol	San Antonio, TX	4/26/33
Burns, Edward	Woodside, Queens, NY	1/29/68
Burrell, Ty	Grants Pass, OR	8/22/67
Burstyn, Ellen	Detroit, MI	12/7/32
Burton, LeVar	Landstuhl, Germany	2/16/57
Burton, Tim	Burbank, CA	8/25/58
Buscemi, Steve	Brooklyn, NY	12/13/57
Busey, Gary	Goose Creek, TX	6/29/44
Busfield, Timothy	Lansing, MI	6/12/57
Butler, Brett	Montgomery, AL	1/30/58
Butler, Dan	Fort Wayne, IN	12/2/54
Butler, Gerard	Glasgow, Scot., UK	11/13/69
Butz, Norbert Leo	St. Louis, MO	1/30/67
Buzzi, Ruth	Westerly, RI	7/24/36
Bynes, Amanda	Thousand Oaks, CA	4/3/86
Byrne, David	Dumbarton, Scotland, UK	5/14/52
Byrne, Gabriel	Dublin, Ireland	5/12/50
Byrne, Rose	Sydney, NSW, Australia	7/24/79
Caan, James	Bronx, NY	3/26/40
Caballe, Montserrat	Barcelona, Spain	4/12/33
Caesar, Sid	Yonkers, NY	9/8/22
Cage, Nicolas	Long Beach, CA	1/7/64
Cain, Dean	Mt. Clemens, MI	7/31/66
Caine, Michael	London, England, UK	3/14/33
Caldwell, Zoe	Hawthorn, Australia	9/14/33
Callow, Simon	London, England, UK	6/15/49
Cameron, James	Kapuskasing, ON, Canada	8/16/54
Cameron, Kirk	Panorama City, CA	10/12/70
Campanella, Joseph	New York, NY	11/21/27
Campbell, Bruce	Royal Oak, MI	6/22/58
Campbell, Glen	Delight, AR	4/22/36
Campbell, Naomi	South London, Eng., UK	5/22/70
Campbell, Neve	Guelph, ON, Canada	10/3/73
Campion, Jane	Waikanae, New Zealand	4/30/54
Cannavale, Bobby	Union City, NJ	5/3/71
Cannell, Stephen J.	Pasadena, CA	2/5/41
Cannon, Dyan	Tacoma, WA	1/4/37
Cannon, Nick	San Diego, CA	10/8/80
Capshaw, Kate	Ft. Worth, TX	11/3/53

Name	Birthplace	Birthdate
Cara, Irene	New York, NY	3/18/59
Cardellini, Linda	Redwood City, CA	6/25/75
Cardinale, Claudia	Tunis, Tunisia	4/15/38
Carell, Steve	Concord, MA	8/16/62
Carey, Drew	Cleveland, OH	5/23/58
Carey, Harry, Jr.	Saugus, CA	5/16/21
Carey, Mariah	Huntington, NY	3/27/70
Cariou, Len	St. Boniface, MB, Canada	9/30/39
Carlton, Vanessa	Milford, PA	8/16/80
Carlyle, Robert	Glasgow, Scotland, UK	4/14/61
Carmen, Eric	Cleveland, OH	8/11/49
Caron, Leslie	Boulogne, France	7/1/31
Carpenter, John	Carthage, NY	1/16/48
Carpenter, Mary Chapin	Princeton, NJ	2/21/58
Carr, Vikki	El Paso, TX	7/19/41
Carreras, Jose	Barcelona, Spain	12/5/46
Carrere, Tia	Honolulu, HI	1/2/67
Carrey, Jim	Newmarket, ON, Canada	1/17/62
Carroll, Diahann	Bronx, NY	7/17/35
Carroll, Pat	Shreveport, LA	5/5/27
Carter, Jack	Brooklyn, NY	6/24/23
Carter, Lynda	Phoenix, AZ	7/24/51
Carter, Nick	Jamestown, NY	1/28/80
Carter, Ron	Ferndale, MI	5/4/37
Cartwright, Nancy	Kettering, OH	10/25/59
Caruso, David	Forest Hills, Queens, NY	1/17/56
Carvey, Dana	Missoula, MT	6/2/55
Case, Sharon	Detroit, MI	2/9/71
Cash, Rosanne	Memphis, TN	5/24/55
Cassidy, David	New York, NY	4/12/50
Castellaneta, Dan	Chicago, IL	10/29/57
Castle-Hughes, Keisha	Donnybrook, Australia	3/24/90
Cates, Phoebe	New York, NY	7/16/63
Cattrall, Kim	Liverpool, England, UK	8/21/56
Cavanagh, Tom	Ottawa, ON, Canada	10/26/63
Cavett, Dick	Gibbon, NE	11/19/36
Cavill, Henry	Jersey, Channel Islands	5/5/83
Cedric the Entertainer	Jefferson City, MO	4/24/64
Cera, Michael	Brampton, ON, Canada	6/7/88
Chabert, Lacey	Purvis, MS	9/30/82
Chalke, Sarah	Ottawa, ON, Canada	8/27/76
Chamberlain, Richard	Beverly Hills, CA	3/31/34
Chambers, Justin	Springfield, OH	7/11/70
Chan, Jackie	Hong Kong	4/7/54
Chance, Greyson	Wichita Falls, TX	8/16/97
Chandler, Kyle	Buffalo, NY	9/17/65
Channing, Carol	Seattle, WA	1/31/21
Channing, Stockard	New York, NY	2/13/44
Chaplin, Geraldine	Santa Monica, CA	7/31/44
Chapman, Tracy	Cleveland, OH	3/30/64
Chappelle, Dave	Washington, DC	8/24/73
Charles, Josh	Baltimore, MD	9/15/71
Charo	Murcia, Spain	1/15/51?
Chase, Chevy	New York, NY	10/8/43
Chasez, J.C. (Joshua)	Washington, DC	8/8/76
Chastain, Jessica	Sacramento, CA	3/29/81
Cheadle, Don	Kansas City, MO	11/29/64
Checker, Chubby	Spring Gulley, SC	10/3/41
Chenoweth, Kristin	Broken Arrow, OK	7/24/68
Cher	El Centro, CA	5/20/46
Chesney, Kenny	Lutrelle, TN	3/26/68
Chianese, Dominic	Bronx, NY	2/24/31
Chiba, Sonny	Fukuoka, Kyushu, Japan	1/23/39
Chiklis, Michael	Lowell, MA	8/30/63
Cho, Margaret	San Francisco, CA	12/5/68
Chong, Thomas	Edmonton, AB, Canada	5/24/38
Chow Yun-Fat	Lamma Island, Hong Kong	5/18/55
Christensen, Hayden	Vancouver, BC, Canada	4/19/81
Christie, Julie	Chukua, Assam, India	4/14/41
Christopher, William	Evanston, IL	10/20/32
Chuck D	Roosevelt, NY	8/1/60
Church, Charlotte	Llandaff, Cardiff, Wales, UK	2/21/86
Church, Thomas Haden	El Paso, TX	6/17/61
C.K., Louis	Washington, DC	9/12/67
Clapp, Gordon	North Conway, NH	9/24/48
Clapton, Eric	Ripley, Surrey, England, UK	3/30/45
Clark, Anthony	Lynchburg, VA	4/4/64
Clark, Petula	Epson, Surrey, England, UK	11/15/32
Clark, Roy	Meherrin, VA	4/15/33
Clarkson, Kelly	Burleson, TX	4/24/82
Clarkson, Patricia	New Orleans, LA	12/29/59
Clay, Andrew Dice	Brooklyn, NY	9/29/57
Cleese, John	Weston-super-Mare, Eng., UK	10/27/39
Cliburn, Van	Shreveport, LA	7/12/34
Clooney, George	Lexington, KY	5/6/61
Close, Glenn	Greenwich, CT	3/19/47
Cocker, Joe	Sheffield, England, UK	5/20/44
Coen, Ethan	St. Louis Park, MN	9/21/57
Coen, Joel	St. Louis Park, MN	11/29/54
Cohen, Leonard	Montreal, QC, Canada	9/21/34
Cohen, Sacha Baron	London, England, UK	10/13/71
Colbert, Stephen	Charleston, SC	5/13/64
Cole, Gary	Park Ridge, IL	9/20/56
Cole, Natalie	Los Angeles, CA	2/6/50
Cole, Olivia	Memphis, TN	11/26/42
Cole, Paula	Rockport, MA	4/5/68

Name	Birthplace	Birthdate
Coleman, Dabney	Austin, TX	1/3/32
Coleman, Ornette	Fort Worth, TX	3/19/30
Colfer, Chris	Fresno, CA	5/27/90
Collette, Toni	Blacktown, Australia	11/1/72
Collins, Joan	London, England, UK	5/23/33
Collins, Judy	Seattle, WA	5/1/39
Collins, Pauline	Exmouth, England, UK	9/3/40
Collins, Phil	London, England, UK	1/30/51
Collins, Stephen	Des Moines, IA	10/1/47
Colvin, Shawn	Vermillion, SD	1/10/56
Combs, Sean	New York, NY	11/4/69
Connelly, Jennifer	Round Top, NY	12/12/70
Connery, Sean	Edinburgh, Scotland, UK	8/25/30
Connick, Harry, Jr.	New Orleans, LA	9/11/67
Connolly, Kevin	Patchogue, NY	3/5/74
Connors, Mike	Fresno, CA	8/15/25
Conrad, Robert	Chicago, IL	3/1/35
Conroy, Frances	Monroe, GA	11/13/53
Constantine, Michael	Reading, PA	5/22/27
Conti, Tom	Paisley, Scotland, UK	11/22/41
Conway, Tim	Willoughby, OH	12/15/33
Cook, Barbara	Atlanta, GA	10/25/27
Cook, David	Houston, TX	12/20/82
Coolidge, Rita	Nashville, TN	5/1/45
Coolio	Compton, CA	8/1/63
Cooper, Alice	Detroit, MI	2/4/48
Cooper, Bradley	Philadelphia, PA	1/5/75
Cooper, Chris	Kansas City, MO	7/9/51
Copperfield, David	Metuchen, NJ	9/16/56
Coppola, Francis Ford	Detroit, MI	4/7/39
Coppola, Sofia	New York, NY	5/14/71
Corbett, John	Wheeling, WV	5/9/61
Corbin, Barry	Lamesa, TX	10/16/40
Corea, Chick	Chelsea, MA	6/12/41
Corgan, Billy	Elk Grove, IL	3/17/67
Cornell, Chris	Seattle, WA	7/20/64
Corwin, Jeff	Norwell, MA	7/11/67
Cosby, Bill	Philadelphia, PA	7/12/37
Cosgrove, Miranda	Los Angeles, CA	5/14/93
Costas, Bob	Astoria, Queens, NY	3/22/52
Costello, Elvis	London, England, UK	8/25/54
Costner, Kevin	Compton, CA	1/18/55
Cotillard, Marion	Paris, France	9/30/75
Courtenay, Tom	Hull, England, UK	2/25/37
Cowell, Simon	London, England, UK	10/7/59
Cox, Brian	Dundee, Scotland, UK	6/1/46
Cox, Courteney	Birmingham, AL	6/15/64
Cox, Ronny	Cloudcroft, NM	7/23/38
Coyote, Peter	New York, NY	10/10/42
Craig, Daniel	Chester, England, UK	3/2/68
Cranston, Bryan	San Fernando Valley, CA	3/7/56
Crawford, Cindy	DeKalb, IL	2/20/66
Crawford, Michael	Salisbury, England, UK	1/19/42
Criss, Darren	San Francisco, CA	2/5/87
Cromwell, James	Los Angeles, CA	1/27/40
Crosby, David	Los Angeles, CA	8/14/41
Cross, Ben	London, England, UK	12/16/47
Cross, Marcia	Marlborough, MA	3/25/62
Crouse, Lindsay	New York, NY	5/12/48
Crow, Sheryl	Kennett, MO	2/11/62
Crowe, Cameron	Palm Springs, CA	7/13/57
Crowe, Russell	Wellington, New Zealand	4/7/64
Crowell, Rodney	Houston, TX	8/17/50
Crudup, Billy	Manhasset, NY	7/8/68
Cruise, Tom	Syracuse, NY	7/3/62
Cruz, Penelope	Madrid, Spain	4/28/74
Cryer, Jon	New York, NY	4/16/65
Crystal, Billy	Long Beach, NY	3/14/47
Culkin, Kieran	New York, NY	9/30/82
Culkin, Macaulay	New York, NY	8/26/80
Culkin, Rory	New York, NY	7/21/89
Cullum, John	Knoxville, TN	3/2/30
Cumming, Alan	Aberfeldy, Perthshire, Scotland, UK	1/27/65
Cuoco, Kaley	Camarillo, CA	11/30/85
Curry, Tim	Grappenhall, Cheshire, England, UK	4/19/46
Curtin, Jane	Cambridge, MA	9/6/47
Curtis, Jamie Lee	Los Angeles, CA	11/22/58
Cusack, Joan	New York, NY	10/11/62
Cusack, John	Evanston, IL	6/28/66
Cyrus, Billy Ray	Flatwoods, KY	8/25/61
Cyrus, Miley	Nashville, TN	11/23/92
Dafoe, Willem	Appleton, WI	7/22/55
Dahl, Arlene	Minneapolis, MN	8/11/28
Dale, Jim	Rothwell, England, UK	8/15/35
Dalton, Timothy	Colwyn Bay, Wales, UK	3/21/46
Daltrey, Roger	London, England, UK	3/1/44
Daly, Carson	Santa Monica, CA	6/22/73
Daly, Timothy	New York, NY	3/1/56
Daly, Tyne	Madison, WI	2/21/46
Damon, Matt	Cambridge, MA	10/8/70
Damone, Vic	Brooklyn, NY	6/12/28
Dane, Eric	San Francisco, CA	11/9/72
Danes, Claire	New York, NY	4/12/79
D'Angelo	Richmond, VA	2/11/74

Name	Birthplace	Birthdate
D'Angelo, Beverly	Columbus, OH	11/15/54
Daniels, Anthony	Salisbury, England, UK	2/21/46
Daniels, Charlie	Wilmington, NC	10/28/36
Daniels, Jeff	Athens, GA	2/19/55
Daniels, William	Brooklyn, NY	3/31/27
Danner, Blythe	Rosemont, PA	2/3/43
Danson, Ted	San Diego, CA	12/29/47
Danza, Tony	Brooklyn, NY	4/21/51
Darby, Kim	Hollywood, CA	7/8/48
Daughtry, Chris	Roanoke Rapids, NC	12/26/79
David, Larry	Brooklyn, NY	7/2/47
Davidson, John	Pittsburgh, PA	12/13/41
Davis, Ann B.	Schenectady, NY	5/5/26
Davis, Clifton	Chicago, IL	10/4/45
Davis, Geena	Wareham, MA	1/21/56
Davis, Hope	Englewood, NJ	3/23/64
Davis, Judy	Perth, Australia	4/23/55
Davis, Kristin	Boulder, CO	2/24/65
Davis, Mac	Lubbock, TX	1/21/42
Davis, Viola	Saint Matthews, SC	8/11/65
Dawber, Pam	Farmington Hills, MI	10/18/51
Dawson, Rosario	New York, NY	5/9/79
Day, Doris	Cincinnati, OH	4/3/24
Day-Lewis, Daniel	London, England, UK	4/29/57
De Havilland, Olivia	Tokyo, Japan	7/1/16
De la Rocha, Zack	Long Beach, CA	1/12/70
De Mornay, Rebecca	Santa Rosa, CA	8/29/62
De Niro, Robert	New York, NY	8/17/43
De Rossi, Portia	Melbourne, Victoria, Austral.	1/31/73
Dee, Ruby	Cleveland, OH	10/27/24
DeFranco, Buddy	Camden, NJ	2/17/23
DeGeneres, Ellen	Metairie, LA	1/26/58
DeHaven, Gloria	Los Angeles, CA	7/23/25
Del Toro, Benicio	Santurce, Puerto Rico	2/19/67
Delaney, Kim	Philadelphia, PA	11/29/61
Delany, Dana	New York, NY	3/13/56
Delon, Alain	Sceaux, France	11/8/35
Demme, Jonathan	Baldwin, NY	2/22/44
Dempsey, Patrick	Lewiston, ME	1/13/66
Dench, Judi	York, England, UK	12/9/34
Deneuve, Catherine	Paris, France	10/22/43
Dennehy, Brian	Bridgeport, CT	7/9/38
DePalma, Brian	Newark, NJ	9/11/40
Depardieu, Gerard	Chateauroux, France	12/27/48
Depp, Johnny	Owensboro, KY	6/9/63
Derek, Bo	Long Beach, CA	11/20/56
Dern, Bruce	Winnetka, IL	6/4/36
Dern, Laura	Santa Monica, CA	2/10/67
Deschanel, Zooey	Los Angeles, CA	1/17/80
Devine, Loretta	Houston, TX	8/21/49
DeVito, Danny	Neptune, NJ	11/17/44
DeWitt, Joyce	Wheeling, WV	4/23/49
DeWyze, Lee	Mount Prospect, IL	4/2/86
Dey, Susan	Pekin, IL	12/10/52
Diamond, Neil	Brooklyn, NY	1/24/41
Diaz, Cameron	San Diego, CA	8/30/72
DiCaprio, Leonardo	Hollywood, CA	11/11/74
Dick, Andy	Charleston, SC	12/21/65
Dickinson, Angie	Kulm, ND	9/30/31
Diesel, Vin	New York, NY	7/18/67
Diggs, Taye	Essex Co., NJ	1/2/72
Dillahunt, Garret	Castro Valley, CA	11/24/64
Dillman, Bradford	San Francisco, CA	4/14/30
Dillon, Kevin	Mamaroneck, NY	8/19/65
Dillon, Matt	New Rochelle, NY	2/18/64
Dinklage, Peter	Mendham, NJ	6/11/69
Dion, Celine	Charlemagne, QC, Canada	3/30/68
DioGuardi, Kara	Scarsdale, NY	12/9/70
Djalili, Omid	London, England, UK	9/30/65
Dobrev, Nina	Sofia, Bulgaria	1/9/89
Dobson, Kevin	Jackson Heights, Queens, NY	3/18/43
Doherty, Shannen	Memphis, TN	4/12/71
Dolenz, Mickey	Los Angeles, CA	3/8/45
Domingo, Placido	Madrid, Spain	1/21/41
Domino, Fats	New Orleans, LA	2/26/28
Donahue, Phil	Cleveland, OH	12/21/35
D'Onofrio, Vincent	Brooklyn, NY	6/30/59
Donovan (Leitch)	Glasgow, Scotland, UK	5/10/46
Donovan, Tate	Tenafly, NJ	9/25/63
Dorn, Michael	Luling, TX	12/9/52
Dorough, Howie	Orlando, FL	8/22/73
Dotrice, Roy	Guernsey, England, UK	5/26/23
Douglas, Kirk	Amsterdam, NY	12/9/16
Douglas, Michael	New Brunswick, NJ	9/25/44
Dourdan, Gary	Philadelphia, PA	12/11/66
Dow, Tony	Hollywood, CA	4/13/45
Down, Lesley-Anne	London, England, UK	3/17/54
Downey, Robert, Jr.	New York, NY	4/4/65
Downey, Roma	Derry, N. Ireland, UK	5/6/60
Downs, Hugh	Akron, OH	2/14/21
Drake	Toronto, ON, Canada	10/24/86
Drescher, Fran	Flushing, Queens, NY	9/30/57
Dreyfuss, Richard	Brooklyn, NY	10/29/47
Driver, Minnie	London, England, UK	1/31/70
Dryer, Fred	Hawthorne, CA	7/6/46
Duchovny, David	New York, NY	8/7/60

Name	Birthplace	Birthdate
Duff, Haylie	Houston, TX	2/19/85
Duff, Hilary	Houston, TX	9/28/87
Duffy (Aimee Anne)	Bangor, Gwynedd, Wales, UK	6/23/84
Duffy, Julia	Minneapolis, MN	6/27/51
Duffy, Patrick	Townsend, MT	3/17/49
Duhamel, Josh	Minot, ND	11/14/72
Dujardin, Jean	Rueil-Malmaison, France	6/19/72
Dukakis, Olympia	Lowell, MA	6/20/31
Duke, Patty	Elmhurst, Queens, NY	12/14/46
Dullea, Keir	Cleveland, OH	5/30/36
Dunaway, Faye	Bascom, FL	1/14/41
Duncan, Lindsay	Edinburgh, Scotland, UK	11/7/50
Duncan, Sandy	Henderson, TX	2/20/46
Dunham, Lena	New York, NY	5/13/86
Dunne, Griffin	New York, NY	6/8/55
Dunst, Kirsten	Point Pleasant, NJ	4/30/82
Durbin, Deanna	Winnipeg, MB, Canada	12/4/21
Durning, Charles	Highland Falls, NY	2/28/23
Dussault, Nancy	Pensacola, FL	6/30/36
Dutton, Charles S.	Baltimore, MD	1/30/51
Duvall, Robert	San Diego, CA	1/5/31
Duvall, Shelley	Houston, TX	7/7/49
Dylan, Bob	Duluth, MN	5/24/41
Dylan, Jakob	New York, NY	12/9/69
Dysart, Richard	Brighton, MA	3/30/29
Dzundza, George	Rosenheim, Germany	7/19/45
Eads, George	Fort Worth, TX	3/1/67
Easton, Sheena	Bellshill, Scotland, UK	4/27/59
Eastwood, Clint	San Francisco, CA	5/31/30
Ebersole, Christine	Chicago, IL	2/21/53
Ebert, Roger	Urbana, IL	6/18/42
Eckhart, Aaron	Cupertino, CA	3/12/68
Eden, Barbara	Tucson, AZ	8/23/34
Edwards, Anthony	Santa Barbara, CA	7/19/62
Efron, Zac	San Luis Obispo, CA	10/18/87
Ehle, Jennifer	Winston-Salem, NC	12/29/69
Eichhorn, Lisa	Reading, PA	2/4/52
Eikenberry, Jill	New Haven, CT	1/21/47
Eisenberg, Jesse	Bayside, NY	10/5/83
Ekberg, Anita	Malmo, Sweden	9/29/31
Ekland, Britt	Stockholm, Sweden	10/6/42
Electra, Carmen	Cincinnati, OH	4/20/72
Elfman, Jenna	Los Angeles, CA	9/30/71
Elizondo, Hector	New York, NY	12/22/36
Elliott, Bob	Boston, MA	3/26/23
Elliott, Chris	New York, NY	5/31/60
Elliott, Missy	Portsmouth, VA	7/1/71
Elliott, Sam	Sacramento, CA	8/9/44
Elvira	Manhattan, KS	9/17/51
Emerson, Michael	Cedar Rapids, IA	9/7/54
Eminem	St. Joseph, MO	10/17/72
Enberg, Dick	Mt. Clemens, MI	1/9/35
Englund, Robert	Glendale, CA	6/6/49
Enya	Gweedore, Ireland	5/17/61
Ermey, R. Lee	Emporia, KS	3/24/44
Estefan, Gloria	Havana, Cuba	9/1/57
Estevez, Emilio	New York, NY	5/12/62
Estrada, Erik	New York, NY	3/16/49
Etheridge, Melissa	Leavenworth, KS	5/29/61
Evans, Chris	Framingham, MA	6/13/81
Evans, Linda	Hartford, CT	11/18/42
Evans, Robert	New York, NY	6/29/30
Everett, Rupert	Norfolk, England, UK	5/29/59
Everly, Don	Brownie, KY	2/1/37
Everly, Phil	Chicago, IL	1/19/39
Evigan, Greg	South Amboy, NJ	10/14/53
Fabares, Shelley	Santa Monica, CA	1/19/44
Fabian	Philadelphia, PA	2/6/43
Fabio	Milan, Italy	3/15/61
Fabolous	Brooklyn, NY	11/18/77
Fairchild, Morgan	Dallas, TX	2/3/50
Faison, Donald	New York, NY	6/22/74
Falana, Lola	Philadelphia, PA	9/11/42
Falco, Edie	Brooklyn, NY	7/5/63
Fallon, Jimmy	Brooklyn, NY	9/19/74
Fanning, Dakota	Conyers, GA	2/23/94
Fargo, Donna	Mt. Airy, NC	11/10/49
Farina, Dennis	Chicago, IL	2/29/44
Farr, Jamie	Toledo, OH	7/1/34
Farrell, Colin	Dublin, Ireland	5/31/76
Farrell, Mike	St. Paul, MN	2/6/39
Farrell, Perry	Bayside, Queens, NY	3/29/59
Farrelly, Bobby	Cumberland, RI	6/17/58
Farrelly, Peter	Phoenixville, PA	12/17/56
Farrow, Mia	Los Angeles, CA	2/9/45
Fassbender, Michael	Heidelberg, Germany	4/2/77
Fatone, Joey	Brooklyn, NY	1/28/77
Feinstein, Michael	Columbus, OH	9/7/56
Feldon, Barbara	Bethel Park, PA	3/12/32
Feldshuh, Tovah	New York, NY	12/27/52
Feliciano, Jose	Lares, Puerto Rico	9/10/45
Fenn, Sherilyn	Detroit, MI	2/1/65
Fergie	Hacienda Heights, CA	3/27/75
Ferguson, Craig	Glasgow, Scotland, UK	5/17/62
Ferguson, Jesse Tyler	Missoula, MT	10/22/75
Ferrara, Jerry	Brooklyn, NY	11/29/79

Name	Birthplace	Birthdate
Ferrell, Conchata	Charleston, WV	3/28/43
Ferrell, Will	Irvine, CA	7/16/67
Ferrera, America	Los Angeles, CA	4/18/84
Feuerstein, Mark	New York, NY	6/8/71
Fey, Tina	Upper Darby, PA	5/18/70
Field, Sally	Pasadena, CA	11/6/46
Fiennes, Joseph	Salisbury, England, UK	5/27/70
Fiennes, Ralph	Suffolk, England, UK	12/22/62
Fierstein, Harvey	Brooklyn, NY	6/6/54
50 Cent	Jamaica, Queens, NY	7/6/76
Fillion, Nathan	Edmonton, AB, Canada	3/27/71
Fincher, David	Denver, CO	5/10/62
Finney, Albert	Salford, England, UK	5/9/36
Fiorentino, Linda	Philadelphia, PA	3/9/60
Firth, Colin	Grayshott, England, UK	9/10/60
Firth, Peter	Bradford, Yorkshire, Eng., UK	10/27/53
Fischer, Jenna	Ft. Wayne, IN	3/7/74
Fishburne, Laurence	Augusta, GA	7/30/61
Fisher, Carrie	Beverly Hills, CA	10/21/56
Flack, Roberta	Black Mountain, NC	2/10/39
Flanagan, Fionnula	Dublin, Ireland	12/10/41
Flavor Flav	Roosevelt, NY	3/16/59
Fleetwood, Mick	Redruth, Cornwall, Eng., UK	6/24/42
Fleming, Rhonda	Hollywood, CA	8/10/23
Fletcher, Louise	Birmingham, AL	7/22/34
Flockhart, Calista	Freeport, IL	11/11/64
Florek, Dann	Flat Rock, MI	5/1/50
Fogerty, John	Berkeley, CA	5/28/45
Foley, Dave	Etobicoke, ON, Canada	1/4/63
Fonda, Bridget	Los Angeles, CA	1/27/64
Fonda, Jane	New York, NY	12/21/37
Fonda, Peter	New York, NY	2/23/40
Fontaine, Joan	Tokyo, Japan	10/22/17
Ford, Faith	Alexandria, LA	9/14/64
Ford, Harrison	Chicago, IL	7/13/42
Forman, Milos	Caslav, Czechoslovakia	2/18/32
Forte, Will	Alameda Co., CA	6/17/70
Foster, Jodie	Los Angeles, CA	11/19/62
Foster, Sutton	Statesboro, GA	3/18/75
Fox, James	London, England, UK	5/19/39
Fox, Jorja	New York, NY	7/7/68
Fox, Matthew	Crowheart, WY	7/14/66
Fox, Megan	Rockwood, TN	5/16/86
Fox, Michael J.	Edmonton, AB, Canada	6/9/61
Fox, Vivica A.	South Bend, IN	7/30/64
Foxworth, Robert	Houston, TX	11/1/41
Foxworthy, Jeff	Atlanta, GA	9/6/58
Foxx, Jamie	Terrell, TX	12/13/67
Frampton, Peter	Kent, England, UK	4/22/50
Francis, Connie	Newark, NJ	12/12/38
Franco, James	Palo Alto, CA	4/19/78
Franken, Al	New York, NY	5/21/51
Franklin, Aretha	Memphis, TN	3/25/42
Franklin, Bonnie	Santa Monica, CA	1/6/44
Franz, Dennis	Maywood, IL	10/28/44
Fraser, Brendan	Indianapolis, IN	12/3/68
Freeman, Mona	Baltimore, MD	6/9/26
Freeman, Morgan	Memphis, TN	6/1/37
French, Dawn	Holyhead, Wales, UK	10/11/57
Fricker, Brenda	Dublin, Ireland	2/17/45
Friedkin, William	Chicago, IL	8/29/39
Frost, David	Tenterden, England, UK	4/7/39
Fry, Stephen	London, England, UK	8/24/57
Fuentes, Daisy	Havana, Cuba	11/17/66
Fuller, Robert	Troy, NY	7/29/34
Funicello, Annette	Utica, NY	10/22/42
Furlong, Edward	Pasadena, CA	8/2/77
Furtado, Nelly	Victoria, BC, Canada	12/2/78
Gabor, Zsa Zsa	Budapest, Hungary	2/6/17
Gabriel, Peter	Surrey, England, UK	2/13/50
Gaines, Boyd	Atlanta, GA	5/11/53
Galecki, Johnny	Bree, Belgium	4/30/75
Galifianakis, Zach	Wilkesboro, NC	10/1/69
Gallagher, Peter	Armonk, NY	8/19/55
Gallo, Vincent	Buffalo, NY	4/11/62
Galway, James	Belfast, N. Ireland, UK	12/8/39
Gandolfini, James	Westwood, NJ	9/18/61
Garagiola, Joe	St. Louis, MO.	2/12/26
Garber, Victor	London, ON, Canada	3/16/49
Garcia, Andy	Havana, Cuba	4/12/56
Garfield, Andrew	Los Angeles, CA	8/20/83
Garfunkel, Art	Forest Hills, Queens, NY	11/5/41
Garlin, Jeff	Chicago, IL	6/5/62
Garner, James	Norman, OK	4/7/28
Garner, Jennifer	Houston, TX	4/17/72
Garofalo, Janeane	Newton, NJ	9/28/64
Garr, Teri	Lakewood, OH	12/11/49
Garrett, Brad	Woodland Hills, CA	4/14/60
Garth, Jennie	Urbana, IL	4/3/72
Gatlin, Larry	Seminole, TX	5/2/48
Gavin, John	Los Angeles, CA	4/8/31
Gayle, Crystal	Paintsville, KY	1/9/51
Gaynor, Mitzi	Chicago, IL	9/4/31
Geary, Anthony	Coalville, UT	5/29/47
Gedda, Nicolai	Stockholm, Sweden	7/11/25
Gellar, Sarah Michelle	New York, NY	4/14/77

Name	Birthplace	Birthdate
Gere, Richard	Philadelphia, PA	8/31/49
Gervais, Ricky	Reading, England, UK	6/25/61
Giannini, Giancarlo	La Spezia, Italy	8/1/42
Gibb, Barry	Isle of Man, England, UK	9/1/46
Gibbons, Leeza	Hartsville, SC	3/26/57
Gibbs, Marla	Chicago, IL	6/14/31
Gibson, Deborah	Brooklyn, NY	8/31/70
Gibson, Mel	Peekskill, NY	1/3/56
Gibson, Thomas	Charleston, SC	7/3/62
Gifford, Frank	Santa Monica, CA	8/16/30
Gifford, Kathie Lee	Neuilly-sur-Seine, France	8/16/53
Gilbert, Melissa	Los Angeles, CA	5/8/64
Gilbert, Sara	Santa Monica, CA	1/29/75
Gilberto, Astrud	Salvador, Brazil	3/30/40
Gill, Vince	Norman, OK	4/12/57
Gillette, Anita	Baltimore, MD	8/16/36
Gilley, Mickey	Natchez, MS	3/9/36
Gilliam, Terry	Minneapolis, MN	11/22/40
Gilmour, David	Cambridge, England, UK	3/6/46
Gilpin, Peri	Waco, TX	5/27/61
Gilsig, Jessalyn	Montreal, QC, Canada	11/30/71
Ginty, Robert	Brooklyn, NY	11/14/48
Givens, Robin	New York, NY	11/27/64
Glaser, Paul Michael	Cambridge, MA	3/25/43
Gleeson, Brendan	Belfast, N. Ireland, UK	11/9/55
Glenn, Scott	Pittsburgh, PA	1/26/42
Gless, Sharon	Los Angeles, CA	5/31/43
Glover, Crispin	New York, NY	4/20/64
Glover, Danny	San Francisco, CA	7/22/47
Glover, John	Kingston, NY	8/7/44
Glover, Julian	London, England, UK	3/27/35
Glover, Savion	Newark, NJ	11/19/73
Godard, Jean Luc	Paris, France	12/3/30
Goldberg, Whoopi	New York, NY	11/13/55
Goldblum, Jeff	Pittsburgh, PA	10/22/52
Goldthwait, Bobcat	Syracuse, NY	5/26/62
Goldwyn, Tony	Los Angeles, CA	5/20/60
Gooding, Cuba, Jr.	Bronx, NY	1/2/68
Goodman, John	Affton, MO	6/20/52
Gordon-Levitt, Joseph	Los Angeles, CA	2/17/81
Gorme, Eydie	Bronx, NY	8/16/28
Gosling, Ryan	London, ON, Canada	11/12/80
Gosselaar, Mark-Paul	Panorama City, CA	3/1/74
Gossett, Louis, Jr.	Brooklyn, NY	5/27/36
Gould, Elliott	Brooklyn, NY	8/29/38
Grace, Topher	New York, NY	7/12/78
Graham, Heather	Milwaukee, WI	1/29/70
Grammer, Kelsey	St. Thomas, U.S. Virgin Isls.	2/21/55
Grant, Amy	Augusta, GA	11/25/60
Grant, Hugh	London, England, UK	9/9/60
Grant, Lee	New York, NY	10/31/27
Gray, Linda	Santa Monica, CA	9/12/40
Gray, Macy	Canton, OH	9/9/70
Green, Al	Forrest City, AR	4/13/46
Green, Cee Lo	Atlanta, GA	5/30/74
Green, Seth	Philadelphia, PA	2/8/74
Green, Tom	Pembroke, ON, Canada	7/30/71
Greene, Shecky	Chicago, IL	4/8/26
Greenfield, Max	Dobbs Ferry, NY	9/4/80
Greenwood, Bruce	Noranda, QC, Canada	8/12/56
Gregory, Cynthia	Los Angeles, CA	7/8/46
Gregory, Dick	St. Louis, MO.	10/12/32
Grenier, Adrian	Brooklyn, NY	7/10/76
Grey, Jennifer	New York, NY	3/26/60
Grey, Joel	Cleveland, OH	4/11/32
Grier, David Alan	Detroit, MI	6/30/55
Grier, Pam	Winston-Salem, NC	5/26/49
Gries, Jon	Glendale, CA	6/17/57
Griffin, Kathy	Oak Park, IL	11/4/61
Griffith, Melanie	New York, NY	8/9/57
Griffiths, Rachel	Melbourne, Australia	12/18/68
Griffiths, Richard	Stockton-on-Tees, Eng., UK	7/31/47
Grimes, Tammy	Lynn, MA	1/30/34
Grint, Rupert	Walton-at-Stone, Hertfordshire, Eng., UK	8/24/88
Groban, Josh	Los Angeles, CA	2/27/81
Grodin, Charles	Pittsburgh, PA	4/21/35
Groff, Jonathan	Lancaster, PA	3/26/85
Grohl, David	Warren, OH	1/14/69
Gross, Michael	Chicago, IL	6/21/47
Guest, Christopher	New York, NY	2/5/48
Guillaume, Robert	St. Louis, MO.	11/30/37
Gumbel, Greg	New Orleans, LA	5/3/46
Gunn, Anna	Santa Fe, NM	8/11/68
Gunn, Tim	Washington, DC	7/29/53
Guthrie, Arlo	Brooklyn, NY	7/10/47
Guttenberg, Steve	Brooklyn, NY	8/24/58
Guy, Buddy	Lettsworth, LA	7/30/36
Guy, Jasmine	Boston, MA	3/10/64
Gyllenhaal, Jake	Los Angeles, CA	12/19/80
Gyllenhaal, Maggie	New York, NY	11/16/77
Hackman, Gene	San Bernardino, CA.	1/30/30
Hader, Bill	Tulsa, OK	6/7/78
Hagerty, Julie	Cincinnati, OH.	6/15/55
Haggard, Merle	Bakersfield, CA	4/6/37
Hagman, Larry	Fort Worth, TX	9/21/31

Name	Birthplace	Birthdate
Haid, Charles	San Francisco, CA	6/2/43
Hale, Barbara	DeKalb, IL	4/18/22
Hale, Tony	West Point, NY	9/30/70
Hall, Anthony Michael	West Roxbury, MA	4/14/68
Hall, Arsenio	Cleveland, OH	2/12/55
Hall, Daryl	Pottstown, PA	10/11/49
Hall, Deidre	Milwaukee, WI	10/31/47
Hall, Michael C.	Raleigh, NC	2/1/71
Hall, Monty	Winnipeg, MB, Canada	8/25/21
Hall, Tom T.	Olive Hill, KY	5/25/36
Halliwell, Geri	Watford, England, UK	8/6/72
Hamill, Mark	Oakland, CA	9/25/51
Hamilton, George	Memphis, TN	8/12/39
Hamilton, Linda	Salisbury, MD	9/26/56
Hamlin, Harry	Pasadena, CA	10/30/51
Hamm, Jon	St. Louis, MO.	3/10/71
Hammer, Armie	Los Angeles, CA	8/28/86
Hammer (M.C.)	Oakland, CA	3/30/63
Hammond, Darrell	Melbourne, FL	10/8/55
Hancock, Herbie	Chicago, IL	4/12/40
Handler, Chelsea	Livingston, NJ	2/25/75
Hanks, Tom	Concord, CA	7/9/56
Hannah, Daryl	Chicago, IL	12/3/60
Hannigan, Alyson	Washington, DC	3/24/74
Hanson, Curtis	Reno, NV	3/24/45
Hanson, Isaac	Tulsa, OK	11/17/80
Hanson, Taylor	Tulsa, OK	3/14/83
Hanson, Zac	Tulsa, OK	10/22/85
Harden, Marcia Gay	La Jolla, CA	8/14/59
Harewood, Dorian	Dayton, OH	8/6/50
Hargitay, Mariska	Los Angeles, CA	1/23/64
Harmon, Angie	Highland Park, TX	8/10/72
Harmon, Mark	Burbank, CA	9/2/51
Harper, Ben	Claremont, CA	10/28/69
Harper, Tess	Mammoth Spring, AR	8/15/50
Harper, Valerie	Suffern, NY	8/22/40
Harrelson, Woody	Midland, TX	7/23/61
Harrington, Pat	New York, NY	8/13/29
Harris, Barbara	Evanston, IL	7/25/35
Harris, Ed	Tenafly, NJ.	11/28/50
Harris, Emmylou	Birmingham, AL	4/2/47
Harris, Julie	Grosse Pointe Park, MI	12/2/25
Harris, Neil Patrick	Albuquerque, NM.	6/15/73
Harris, Rosemary	Ashby, England, UK.	9/19/27?
Harris, Steve	Chicago, IL	12/3/65
Harrison, Gregory	Avalon, CA	5/31/50
Harry, Deborah	Miami, FL	7/1/45
Hart, Mary	Madison, SD	11/8/50
Hart, Melissa Joan	Smithtown, NY.	4/18/76
Hartley, Hal	Lindenhurst, NY.	11/3/59
Hartley, Mariette	New York, NY	6/21/40
Hartman, David	Pawtucket, RI	5/19/35
Hartman Black, Lisa	Houston, TX	6/1/56
Hartnett, Josh	San Francisco, CA.	7/21/78
Harvey, P. J.	Yeovil, Somerset, Eng., UK	10/9/69
Harvey, Steve	Welch, WV.	11/23/56
Hasselbeck, Elisabeth	Cranston, RI	5/28/77
Hasselhoff, David	Baltimore, MD	7/17/52
Hatcher, Teri	Sunnyvale, CA.	12/8/64
Hatfield, Juliana	Wiscasset, ME.	7/27/67
Hathaway, Anne	Brooklyn, NY	11/12/82
Hauer, Rutger	Breukelen, Netherlands	1/23/44
Hawke, Ethan	Austin, TX	11/6/70
Hawn, Goldie	Washington, DC	11/21/45
Hayek, Salma	Coatzacoalcos, Mexico	9/2/66
Hayes, Sean	Glen Ellyn, IL	6/26/70
Haynes, Roy	Roxbury, MA	3/13/25
Hays, Robert	Bethesda, MD	7/24/47
Head, Anthony	Camden Town, Eng., UK	2/20/54
Heard, John	Washington, DC	3/7/45
Hearn, George	St. Louis, MO.	6/18/34
Heaton, Patricia	Bay Village, OH	3/4/58
Heche, Anne	Aurora, OH	5/25/69
Heder, Jon	Fort Collins, CO.	10/26/77
Hedren, Tippi	New Ulm, MN	1/19/30?
Heigl, Katherine	Washington, DC	11/24/78
Helfgott, David	Melbourne, Australia	5/19/47
Helgenberger, Marg	Fremont, NE	11/16/58
Helmond, Katherine	Galveston, TX	7/5/34
Helms, Ed	Atlanta, GA	1/24/74
Hemingway, Mariel	Mill Valley, CA	11/22/61
Hemsworth, Chris	Melbourne, Victoria, Australia	8/11/83
Hemsworth, Liam	Melbourne, Victoria, Australia	1/13/90
Henderson, Florence	Dale, IN	2/14/34
Hendricks, Christina	Knoxville, TN	5/3/75
Henley, Don	Gilmer, TX	7/22/47
Henner, Marilu	Chicago, IL	4/6/52
Hennessy, Jill	Edmonton, AB, Canada	11/25/68
Henry, Buck	New York, NY	12/9/30
Herman, Pee-Wee	Peekskill, NY.	8/27/52
Herrmann, Edward	Washington, DC	7/21/43
Hershey, Barbara	Hollywood, CA.	2/5/48
Hesseman, Howard	Lebanon, OR.	2/27/40
Hetfield, James	Downey, CA.	8/3/63
Hewitt, Jennifer Love	Waco, TX.	2/21/79
Hicks, Catherine	Scottsdale, AZ	8/6/51

Name	Birthplace	Birthdate
Higgins, John Michael	Boston, MA	2/12/63
Hill, Dulé	Orange, NJ	5/3/75
Hill, Faith	Jackson, MS	9/21/67
Hill, Jonah	Los Angeles, CA	12/20/83
Hill, Lauryn	South Orange, NJ	5/25/75
Hill, Steven	Seattle, WA	2/24/22
Hillerman, John	Denison, TX.	12/20/32
Hilton, Paris	New York, NY	2/17/81
Hines, Cheryl	Miami Beach, FL	9/21/65
Hirsch, Emile	Palms, CA	3/13/85
Hirsch, Judd	New York, NY	3/15/35
Hodgman, John	Cambridge, MA	6/3/71
Hoffman, Dustin	Los Angeles, CA	8/8/37
Hoffman, Philip Seymour	Fairport, NY.	7/23/67
Hogan, Hulk	Augusta, GA	8/11/53
Hogan, Paul	Lightning Ridge, NSW, Australia	10/8/39
Holbrook, Hal	Cleveland, OH.	2/17/25
Holder, Geoffrey	Port of Spain, Trinidad	8/1/30
Holliday, Polly	Jasper, AL	7/2/37
Holliman, Earl	Delhi, LA	9/11/28
Holloway, Josh	San Jose, CA.	7/20/69
Holly, Lauren	Bristol, PA	10/28/63
Holm, Ian	Ilford, England, UK	9/12/31
Holmes, Katie	Toledo, OH	12/18/78
Hooks, Jan	Decatur, GA.	4/23/57
Hopkins, Anthony	Port Talbot, South Wales, UK	12/31/37
Hopkins, Bo	Greenville, SC	2/2/42
Hopkins, Telma	Louisville, KY.	10/28/48
Horne, Marilyn	Bradford, PA	1/16/34
Hornsby, Bruce	Williamsburg, VA	11/23/54
Horsley, Lee	Muleshoe, TX	5/15/55
Hoskins, Bob	Suffolk, England, UK	10/26/42
Hounsou, Djimon	Cotonou, Benin	4/24/64
Howard, Ken	El Centro, CA.	3/28/44
Howard, Ron	Duncan, OK.	3/1/54
Howard, Terrence	Chicago, IL	3/11/69
Howell, C. Thomas	Van Nuys, CA	12/7/66
Howes, Sally Ann	St. John's Wood, London, England, UK	7/20/30
Hudgens, Vanessa	Salinas, CA	12/14/88
Hudson, Jennifer	Chicago, IL	9/12/81
Hudson, Kate	Los Angeles, CA	4/19/79
Huffman, Felicity	Bedford, NY.	12/9/62
Hughley, D. L.	Los Angeles, CA	3/6/63
Hulce, Tom	Whitewater, WI.	12/6/53
Humperdinck, Engelbert	Madras, India.	5/2/36
Humphries, Barry	Melbourne, Australia	2/17/34
Hunt, Bonnie	Chicago, IL	9/22/64
Hunt, Helen	Culver City, CA	6/15/63
Hunt, Linda	Morristown, NJ	4/2/45
Hunter, Holly	Conyers, GA	3/20/58
Hunter, Tab	New York, NY	7/11/31
Hurley, Elizabeth	Hampshire, England, UK	6/10/65
Hurt, John	Chesterfield, England, UK	1/22/40
Hurt, Mary Beth	Marshalltown, IA	9/26/48
Hurt, William	Washington, DC	3/20/50
Huston, Anjelica	Santa Monica, CA	7/8/51
Hutcherson, Josh	Union, KY	10/12/92
Hutton, Lauren	Charleston, SC	11/17/43
Hutton, Timothy	Malibu, CA.	8/16/60
Hyman, Earle	Rocky Mount, NC	10/11/26
Ian, Janis	New York, NY	4/7/51
Ice Cube	Los Angeles, CA	6/15/69
Ice-T	Newark, NJ	2/16/58
Idle, Eric	S. Shields, England, UK.	3/29/43
Idol, Billy	Middlesex, England, UK	11/30/55
Iglesias, Enrique	Madrid, Spain	5/8/75
Iglesias, Julio	Madrid, Spain	9/23/43
Iler, Robert	New York, NY	3/2/85
Iman	Mogadishu, Somalia	7/25/55
Imbruglia, Natalie	Sydney, Australia	2/4/75
Imperioli, Michael	Mount Vernon, NY	1/1/66
Imus, Don	Riverside, CA.	7/23/40
Ingram, James	Akron, OH	2/16/56
Innes, Laura	Pontiac, MI	8/16/59
Ireland, Kathy	Glendale, CA.	3/20/63
Irons, Jeremy	Cowes, Isle of Wight, England, UK	9/19/48
Irving, Amy	Palo Alto, CA.	9/10/53
Irving, George S.	Springfield, MA	11/1/22
Irwin, Bill	Santa Monica, CA	4/11/50
Ivanek, Željko	Ljubljana, Yugoslavia	8/15/57
Ivey, Judith	El Paso, TX	9/4/51
Ivory, James	Berkeley, CA	6/7/28
Izzard, Eddie	Aden, Yemen.	2/7/62
Jackée (Harry)	Winston-Salem, NC	8/14/56
Jackman, Hugh	Sydney, Australia	10/12/68
Jackson, Anne	Allegheny, PA	9/3/26
Jackson, Cheyenne	Newport, WA.	7/12/75
Jackson, Glenda	Birkenhead, England, UK	5/9/36
Jackson, Janet	Gary, IN	5/16/66
Jackson, Jermaine	Gary, IN.	12/11/54
Jackson, Jonathan	Orlando, FL	5/11/82
Jackson, Joshua	Vancouver, BC, Canada.	6/11/78
Jackson, Kate	Birmingham, AL.	10/29/48

Name	Birthplace	Birthdate
Jackson, La Toya	Gary, IN.	5/29/56
Jackson, Peter	Wellington, New Zealand	10/31/61
Jackson, Samuel L.	Chattanooga, TN	12/21/48
Jacobi, Derek	London, England, UK	10/22/38
Jagger, Mick	Dartford, England, UK	7/26/43
James, Kevin	Mineola, NY.	4/26/65
Janis, Conrad	New York, NY	2/11/28
Janney, Allison	Dayton, OH	11/19/60
Janssen, Famke	Amsterdam, Netherlands	11/5/65
Jardine, Al	Lima, OH.	9/3/42
Jarmusch, Jim	Akron, OH	1/22/53
Jarreau, Al	Milwaukee, WI	3/12/40
Jarrett, Keith	Allentown, PA	5/8/45
Ja Rule	Hollis, Queens, NY	2/29/76
Jay Z	Brooklyn, NY	12/4/69
Jeffreys, Anne	Goldsboro, NC	1/26/23
Jepsen, Carly Rae	Mission, BC, Can.	11/21/85
Jett, Joan	Philadelphia, PA	9/22/60
Jewel	Payson, UT	5/23/74
Jewison, Norman	Toronto, ON, Canada.	7/21/26
Jillette, Penn	Greenfield, MA	3/5/55
Jillian, Ann	Cambridge, MA	1/29/50
Joel, Billy	Bronx, NY	5/9/49
Johansson, Scarlett	New York, NY	11/22/84
John, Elton	Pinner, Middlesex, Eng., UK	3/25/47
Johns, Glynis	Durban, S. Africa	10/5/23
Johnson, Arte	Benton Harbor, MI	1/20/34
Johnson, Beverly	Buffalo, NY	10/13/52
Johnson, Don	Flatt Creek, MO	12/15/49
Johnson, Dwayne "The Rock"	Hayward, CA	5/2/72
Johnston, Bruce	Los Angeles, CA	6/24/42
Johnston, Kristen	Washington, DC	9/20/67
Jolie, Angelina	Los Angeles, CA	6/4/75
Jonas, Joe	Casa Grande, AZ.	8/15/89
Jonas, Kevin	Teaneck, NJ	11/5/87
Jonas, Nick	Dallas, TX	9/16/92
Jones, Cherry	Paris, TN	11/21/56
Jones, Dean	Decatur, AL	1/25/31
Jones, Gemma	London, England, UK	12/4/42
Jones, George	Saratoga, TX	9/12/31
Jones, Grace	Spanish Town, Jamaica	5/19/48
Jones, Jack	Hollywood, CA.	1/14/38
Jones, James Earl	Arkabutla, MS	1/17/31
Jones, January	Sioux Falls, SD	1/5/78
Jones, Mick	London, England, UK	6/26/55
Jones, Norah	New York, NY	3/30/79
Jones, Quincy	Chicago, IL	3/14/33
Jones, Shirley	Charleroi, PA	3/31/34
Jones, Star	Badin, NC	3/24/62
Jones, Tom	Pontypridd, Wales, UK.	6/7/40
Jones, Tommy Lee	San Saba, TX	9/15/46
Jonze, Spike	Rockville, MD	10/22/69
Jourdan, Louis	Marseilles, France	6/19/19
Jovovich, Milla	Kiev, Ukraine	12/17/75
Judd, Ashley	Granada Hills, CA	4/19/68
Judd, Naomi	Ashland, KY	1/11/46
Judd, Wynonna	Ashland, KY	5/30/64
Kaczmarek, Jane	Milwaukee, WI	12/21/55
Kanaly, Steve	Burbank, CA	3/14/46
Kane, Carol	Cleveland, OH.	6/18/52
Kaplan, Gabe	Brooklyn, NY	3/31/45
Kardashian, Khloe	Los Angeles, CA	6/27/84
Kardashian, Kim	Los Angeles, CA	10/21/80
Kardashian, Kourtney	Los Angeles, CA	4/18/79
Karlen, John	New York, NY	5/28/33
Karn, Richard	Seattle, WA	2/17/56
Kasem, Casey	Detroit, MI	4/27/32
Kattan, Chris	Sherman Oaks, CA	10/19/70
Kavner, Julie	Burbank, CA	9/7/51
Kaye, Judy	Phoenix, AZ.	12/11/48
Kazan, Lainie	New York, NY	5/15/42
Ke$ha	Los Angeles, CA	3/1/87
Keach, Stacy	Savannah, GA	6/2/41
Keaton, Diane	Santa Ana, CA.	1/5/46
Keaton, Michael	Coraopolis, PA.	9/9/51
Keener, Catherine	Miami, FL	3/23/59
Keillor, Garrison	Anoka, MN	8/7/42
Keitel, Harvey	Brooklyn, NY	5/13/39
Keith, David	Knoxville, TN	5/8/54
Keith, Penelope	Sutton, Surrey, Eng., UK	4/2/40
Kellerman, Sally	Long Beach, CA	6/2/37
Kelly, Minka	Los Angeles, CA	6/24/80
Kelly, R(obert)	Chicago, IL	1/8/67
Kennedy, George	New York, NY	2/18/25
Kennedy, Jamie	Upper Darby, PA	5/25/70
Kennedy, Jayne	Washington, DC	10/27/51
Kenny G	Seattle, WA.	6/5/56
Kent, Allegra	Santa Monica, CA.	8/11/37
Keoghan, Phil	Christchurch, New Zealand	5/31/67
Kercheval, Ken	Wolcottville, IN.	7/15/35
Kerns, Joanna	San Francisco, CA.	2/12/53
Keys, Alicia	New York, NY	1/25/81
Khan, Chaka	Great Lakes, IL	3/23/53
Kidder, Margot	Yellowknife, NT, Canada	10/17/48
Kidman, Nicole	Honolulu, HI	6/20/67
Kiel, Richard	Detroit, MI	9/13/39
Kilborn, Craig	Kansas City, KS.	8/24/62
Kilmer, Val	Los Angeles, CA	12/31/59
Kim, Daniel Dae	Pusan, S. Korea	8/4/68
Kimmel, Jimmy	Brooklyn, NY	11/13/67
King, B. B.	Itta Bena, MS.	9/16/25
King, Carole	Brooklyn, NY	2/9/42
King, Larry	Brooklyn, NY	11/19/33
King, Perry	Alliance, OH	4/30/48
Kingsley, Ben	Scarborough, England, UK	12/31/43
Kingston, Alex	London, England, UK	3/11/63
Kinnear, Greg	Logansport, IN.	6/17/63
Kinney, Kathy	Stevens Point, WI	11/3/53
Kinski, Nastassja	Berlin, W. Germany	1/24/60
Kirkland, Gelsey	Bethlehem, PA.	12/29/52
Kirkpatrick, Chris	Clarion, PA	10/17/71
Kirshner, Mia	Toronto, ON, Canada.	1/25/75
Klein, Robert	Bronx, NY	2/8/42
Kline, Kevin	St. Louis, MO.	10/24/47
Klugman, Jack	Philadelphia, PA	4/27/22
Klum, Heidi	Bergish-Gladbach, Germany..	6/1/73
Knight, Gladys	Atlanta, GA	5/28/44
Knight, Shirley	Goessel, KS	7/5/36
Knight, T. R.	Minneapolis, MN	3/26/73
Knight, Wayne	New York, NY	8/7/55
Knightley, Keira	Teddington, England, UK	3/26/85
Knopfler, Mark	Glasgow, Scotland, UK	8/12/49
Knowles, Beyoncé	Houston, TX	9/4/81
Knoxville, Johnny	Knoxville, TN	3/11/71
Konitz, Lee	Chicago, IL	10/13/27
Kopell, Bernie	Brooklyn, NY	6/21/33
Kotto, Yaphet	New York, NY	11/15/37
Krakowski, Jane	Parsippany, NJ.	10/11/68
Krasinski, John	Newton, MA.	10/20/79
Krause, Peter	Alexandria, MN	8/12/65
Kressley, Carson	Allentown, PA	11/11/69
Kretschmann, Thomas	Dessau, E. Germany	9/8/62
Kristofferson, Kris	Brownsville, TX	6/22/36
Kudrow, Lisa	Encino, CA	7/30/63
Kunis, Mila	Kiev, Ukraine	8/14/83
Kuriyama, Chiaki	Tsuchiura, Ibaraki, Japan.	10/10/84
Kurtz, Swoosie	Omaha, NE	9/6/44
Kutcher, Ashton	Cedar Rapids, IA	2/7/78
Kwan, Nancy	Hong Kong	5/19/39
LaBelle, Patti	Philadelphia, PA	5/24/44
LaBeouf, Shia	Los Angeles, CA	6/11/86
Lachey, Nick	Harlan, KY.	11/9/73
Ladd, Cheryl	Huron, SD	7/12/51
Ladd, Diane	Meridian, MS	11/29/32
Lady Gaga	New York, NY	3/28/86
Lagasse, Emeril	Fall River, MA	10/15/59
Lahti, Christine	Birmingham, MI	4/4/50
Laine, Cleo	Southall, England, UK	10/28/27
Lake, Ricki	Hastings-on-Hudson, NY	9/21/68
Lamas, Lorenzo	Santa Monica, CA	1/20/58
Lambert, Adam	Indianapolis, IN	1/29/82
Lambert, Christopher	Great Neck, NY	3/29/57
Lambert, Miranda	Longview, TX	11/10/83
Landau, Martin	Brooklyn, NY	6/20/28
Landis, John	Chicago, IL	8/3/50
Lane, Diane	New York, NY	1/22/65
Lane, Nathan	Jersey City, NJ.	2/3/56
lang, k.d.	Consort, AB, Canada.	11/2/61
Lang, Stephen	Jamaica Estates, Queens, NY	7/11/52
Lange, Jessica	Cloquet, MN	4/20/49
Langella, Frank	Bayonne, NJ	1/1/40
Lansbury, Angela	London, England, UK	10/16/25
LaPaglia, Anthony	Adelaide, Australia	1/31/59
Larroquette, John	New Orleans, LA	11/25/47
LaSalle, Eriq	Hartford, CT	6/23/62
Lauper, Cyndi	Ozone Park, Queens, NY	6/22/53
Laurie, Hugh	Oxford, England, UK	6/11/59
Laurie, Piper	Detroit, MI	1/22/32
Lautner, Taylor	Grand Rapids, MI	2/11/92
Lavigne, Avril	Belleville, ON, Canada.	9/27/84
Lavin, Linda	Portland, ME	10/15/37
Law, Jude	London, England, UK	12/29/72
Lawless, Lucy	Mount Albert, New Zealand	3/29/68
Lawrence, Carol	Melrose Park, IL	9/5/34
Lawrence, Jennifer	Louisville, KY.	8/15/90
Lawrence, Joey	Montgomery, PA	4/20/76
Lawrence, Martin	Frankfurt, Germany	4/16/65
Lawrence, Steve	Brooklyn, NY	7/8/35
Lawrence, Vicki	Inglewood, CA.	3/26/49
Leach, Robin	London, England, UK	8/29/41
Leachman, Cloris	Des Moines, IA	4/30/26
Lear, Norman	New Haven, CT	7/27/22
Learned, Michael	Washington, DC	4/9/39
Leary, Denis	Worcester, MA.	8/18/57
LeBlanc, Matt	Newton, MA.	7/25/67
LeBon, Simon	Bushey, England, UK.	10/27/58
Lee, Ang	Pingtung, Taiwan	10/23/54
Lee, Brenda	Lithonia, GA	12/11/44
Lee, Christopher	London, England, UK	5/27/22
Lee, Jason	Huntington Beach, CA	4/25/70
Lee, Michele	Los Angeles, CA	6/24/42

Name	Birthplace	Birthdate
Lee, Spike	Atlanta, GA	3/20/57
Leeves, Jane	Ilford, England, UK	4/18/61
Legrand, Michel	Paris, France	2/24/32
Leguizamo, John	Bogotá, Colombia	7/22/64
Lehmkuhl, Reichen	Cincinnati, OH	12/26/73
Leibman, Ron	New York, NY	10/11/37
Leigh, Jennifer Jason	Hollywood, CA	2/5/62
Leighton, Laura	Iowa City, IA	7/24/68
Lennox, Annie	Aberdeen, Scotland, UK	12/25/54
Leno, Jay	New Rochelle, NY	4/28/50
Leo, Melissa	New York, NY	9/14/60
Leonard, Robert Sean	Westwood, NJ	2/28/69
Leoni, Tea	New York, NY	2/25/66
Leslie, Joan	Detroit, MI	1/26/25
Leto, Jared	Bossier City, LA	12/26/71
Letterman, David	Indianapolis, IN	4/12/47
Levine, Adam	Los Angeles, CA	3/18/79
Levine, James	Cincinnati, OH	6/23/43
Levine, Ted	Bellaire, OH	5/29/57
Levinson, Barry	Baltimore, MD	4/6/42
Levy, Eugene	Hamilton, ON, Canada	12/17/46
Lewis, Damian	London, Eng., UK	2/11/71
Lewis, Huey	New York, NY	7/5/50
Lewis, Jason	Newport Beach, CA	6/25/71
Lewis, Jerry	Newark, NJ	3/16/26
Lewis, Jerry Lee	Ferriday, LA	9/29/35
Lewis, Juliette	San Fernando Valley, CA	6/21/73
Lewis, Leona	London, England, UK	4/3/85
Lewis, Richard	Brooklyn, NY	6/29/47
Li, Jet	Beijing, China	4/26/63
Light, Judith	Trenton, NJ	2/9/49
Lightfoot, Gordon	Orillia, ON, Canada	11/17/38
Lil' Kim	Brooklyn, NY	7/11/75
Lil' Romeo	New Orleans, LA	8/19/89
Lilly, Evangeline	Fort Saskatchewan, AB, Can.	8/3/79
Linden, Hal	Bronx, NY	3/20/31
Ling, Lisa	Sacramento, CA	8/30/73
Linn-Baker, Mark	St. Louis, MO.	6/17/54
Linney, Laura	New York, NY	2/5/64
Liotta, Ray	Newark, NJ	12/18/54
Lithgow, John	Rochester, NY	10/19/45
Little, Rich	Ottawa, ON, Canada	11/26/38
Little Richard	Macon, GA	12/5/32
Littrell, Brian	Lexington, KY	2/20/75
Liu, Lucy	Jackson Heights, Queens, NY	12/2/68
Lively, Blake	Tarzana, CA.	8/25/87
L. L. Cool J	St. Albans, Queens, NY	1/14/68
Lloyd, Christopher	Stamford, CT.	10/22/38
Lloyd, Emily	North London, Eng., UK	9/29/70
Lloyd Webber, Andrew	London, England, UK	3/22/48
Locke, Sondra	Shelbyville, TN.	5/28/47
Lockhart, June	New York, NY	6/25/25
Locklear, Heather	Westwood, CA.	9/25/61
Loggia, Robert	Staten Island, NY.	1/3/30
Loggins, Kenny	Everett, WA	1/7/48
Lohan, Lindsay	New York, NY	7/2/86
Lollobrigida, Gina	Subiaco, Italy	7/4/27
Lonergan, Kenneth	New York, NY	10/16/62
Long, Nia	Brooklyn, NY	10/30/70
Long, Shelley	Ft. Wayne, IN.	8/23/49
Longoria, Eva	Corpus Christi, TX.	3/15/75
Lopez, George	Mission Hills, CA	4/23/61
Lopez, Jennifer	Bronx, NY	7/24/70
Lopez, Mario	San Diego, CA.	10/10/73
Loren, Sophia	Rome, Italy	9/20/34
Loring, Gloria	New York, NY	12/10/46
Louis C.K.	Washington, DC	9/12/67
Louis-Dreyfus, Julia	New York, NY	1/13/61
Lovato, Demi	Dallas, TX	8/20/92
Love, Courtney	San Francisco, CA.	7/9/64
Love, Mike	Baldwin Hills, CA.	3/15/41
Loveless, Patty	Pikeville, KY	1/4/57
Lovett, Lyle	Klein, TX.	11/1/57
Lovitz, Jon	Tarzana, CA.	7/21/57
Lowe, Rob	Charlottesville, VA	3/17/64
Lowell, Carey	Huntington, NY	2/11/61
Lucas, George	Modesto, CA.	5/14/44
Lucci, Susan	Scarsdale, NY.	12/23/46
Luckinbill, Laurence	Ft. Smith, AR.	11/21/34
Ludacris	Champaign, IL.	9/11/77
Ludwig, Christa	Berlin, Germany	3/16/24
Luhrmann, Baz	Sydney, Australia	9/17/62
LuPone, Patti	Northport, NY	4/21/49
Lynch, David	Missoula, MT.	1/20/46
Lynch, Jane	Dolton, IL.	7/14/60
Lynch, Susan	Corrinshego, N. Ireland, UK.	6/5/71
Lynley, Carol	New York, NY	2/13/42
Lynn, Loretta	Butcher Hollow, KY	4/14/32
Lynn, Vera	London, England, UK	3/20/17
Lynne, Shelby	Quantico, VA	10/22/68
Ma, Yo-Yo	Paris, France	10/7/55
Maazel, Lorin	Neuilly-sur-Seine, France.	3/6/30
Macchio, Ralph	Huntington, NY	11/4/62
MacDonald, Kelly	Glasgow, Scotland, UK	2/23/76
MacDowell, Andie	Gaffney, SC	4/21/58
MacFarlane, Seth	Kent, CT	11/26/73

Name	Birthplace	Birthdate
MacGowan, Shane	Tunbridge, Kent, Eng., UK	12/25/57
MacGraw, Ali	Pound Ridge, NY	4/1/38
MacLachlan, Kyle	Yakima, WA.	2/22/59
MacLaine, Shirley	Richmond, VA	4/24/34
MacLeod, Gavin	Mt. Kisco, NY.	2/28/31
MacNee, Patrick	London, England, UK	2/6/22
MacNicol, Peter	Dallas, TX	4/10/54
MacPherson, Elle	Sydney, Australia	3/29/64
Macy, Bill	Revere, MA	5/18/22
Macy, William H.	Miami, FL	3/13/50
Madden, John	Austin, MN.	4/10/36
Madigan, Amy	Chicago, IL	9/11/50
Madonna (Ciccone)	Bay City, MI	8/16/58
Madsen, Michael	Chicago, IL	9/25/58
Maguire, Tobey	Santa Monica, CA	6/27/75
Maher, Bill	New York, NY	1/20/56
Mahoney, John	Blackpool, Lancashire, England, UK	6/20/40
Majors, Lee	Wyandotte, MI	4/23/39
Malick, Terrence	Ottawa, IL	11/30/43
Malick, Wendie	Buffalo, NY	12/13/50
Malina, Joshua	New York, NY	1/17/66
Malkovich, John	Christopher, IL.	12/9/53
Malone, Dorothy	Chicago, IL	1/30/25
Mamet, David	Chicago, IL	11/30/47
Manchester, Melissa	Bronx, NY	2/15/51
Mandel, Howie	Toronto, ON, Canada.	11/29/55
Mandrell, Barbara	Houston, TX	12/25/48
Mangione, Chuck	Rochester, NY	11/29/40
Manheim, Camryn	Caldwell, NJ	3/8/61
Manilow, Barry	Brooklyn, NY	6/17/43
Mann, Aimee	Richmond, VA	8/9/60
Manoff, Dinah	New York, NY	1/25/58
Manson, Marilyn	Canton, OH	1/5/69
Mantegna, Joe	Chicago, IL	11/13/47
Mantello, Joe	Rockford, IL.	12/27/62
Mara, Rooney	Bedford, NY.	4/17/85
Marcil, Vanessa	Indio, CA	10/15/69
Margulies, Julianna	Spring Valley, NY.	6/8/66
Marie, Constance	Hollywood, CA.	9/9/69
Marin, Cheech	Los Angeles, CA	7/13/46
Marinaro, Ed	New York, NY	3/31/50
Marriner, Neville	Lincoln, England, UK.	4/15/24
Mars, Bruno	Honolulu, HI	10/8/85
Marsalis, Branford	New Orleans, LA	8/26/60
Marsalis, Wynton	New Orleans, LA	10/18/61
Marsh, Jean	London, England, UK	7/1/34
Marshall, Garry	Bronx, NY	11/13/34
Marshall, Penny	Bronx, NY	10/15/42
Marshall, Peter	Huntington, WV	3/30/27
Martin, Chris	Devon, England, UK	3/22/77
Martin, Jesse L.	Rocky Mount, VA	1/18/69
Martin, Kellie	Riverside, CA.	10/16/75
Martin, Ricky	San Juan, Puerto Rico	12/24/71
Martin, Steve	Waco, TX.	8/14/45
Martindale, Margo	Jacksonville, TX.	7/18/51
Martins, Peter	Copenhagen, Denmark	10/27/46
Mason, Jackie	Sheboygan, WI	6/9/31
Mason, Marsha	St. Louis, MO.	4/3/42
Masterson, Christopher	Long Island, NY.	1/22/80
Masterson, Mary Stuart	New York, NY	6/28/66
Mastrantonio, Mary Elizabeth	Lombard, IL.	11/17/58
Masur, Kurt	Brieg, Germany	7/18/27
Masur, Richard	New York, NY	11/20/48
Mathers, Jerry	Sioux City, IA.	6/2/48
Matheson, Tim	Glendale, CA.	12/31/47
Mathis, Johnny	Gilmer, TX.	9/30/35
Matlin, Marlee	Morton Grove, IL	8/24/65
Matthews, Dave	Johannesburg, S. Africa.	1/9/67
May, Elaine	Philadelphia, PA	4/21/32
Mayer, John	Bridgeport, CT.	10/16/77
Mays, Jayma	Bristol, TN.	7/16/79
Mazar, Debi	Jamaica, Queens, NY	8/13/64
Mazursky, Paul	Brooklyn, NY	4/25/30
McAdams, Rachel	London, ON, Canada.	10/7/86
McArdle, Andrea	Abington, PA	11/5/63
McAvoy, James	Glasgow, Scotland, UK	1/1/79
McBride, Patricia	Teaneck, NJ	8/23/42
McCallum, David	Glasgow, Scotland, UK	9/19/33
McCarthy, Andrew	Westfield, NJ	11/29/62
McCarthy, Jenny	Chicago, IL.	11/1/72
McCarthy, Melissa	Plainfield, IL.	8/26/70
McCartney, Paul	Liverpool, England, UK	6/18/42
McCarver, Tim	Memphis, TN.	10/16/41
McConaughey, Matthew	Uvalde, TX.	11/4/69
McCoo, Marilyn	Jersey City, NJ.	9/30/43
McCormack, Eric	Toronto, ON, Canada.	4/18/63
McCormack, Mary	Plainsfield, NJ	2/8/69
McCrane, Paul	Philadelphia, PA	1/19/61
McCreery, Scotty	Garner, NC	10/9/93
McDaniel, James	Washington, DC	3/25/58
McDermott, Dylan	Waterbury, CT	10/26/61
McDiarmid, Ian	Carnoustie, Tayside, Scot., UK	4/17/47
McDonald, Audra	Berlin, Germany	7/3/70
McDonnell, Mary	Wilkes-Barre, PA	4/28/52

Name	Birthplace	Birthdate
McDormand, Frances	Chicago, IL	6/23/57
McDowell, Malcolm	Leeds, England, UK	6/13/43
McEntire, Reba	McAlester, OK	3/28/55
McFerrin, Bobby	New York, NY	3/11/50
McGillis, Kelly	Newport Beach, CA	7/9/57
McGovern, Elizabeth	Evanston, IL	7/18/61
McGovern, Maureen	Youngstown, OH	7/27/49
McGraw, Tim	Delhi, LA	5/1/67
McGregor, Ewan	Crieff, Scotland, UK	3/31/71
McHale, Joel	Rome, Italy	11/20/71
McHale, Kevin	Plano, TX	6/14/88
McKean, Michael	New York, NY	10/17/47
McKechnie, Donna	Pontiac, MI	11/16/42
McKellen, Ian	Burnley, England, UK	5/25/39
McKenzie, Benjamin	Austin, TX	9/12/78
McKidd, Kevin	Elgin, UK	8/9/73
McLachlan, Sarah	Halifax, NS, Canada	1/28/68
McLean, A. J.	West Palm Beach, FL	1/9/78
McNichol, Kristy	Los Angeles, CA	9/11/62
McPartland, Marian	Stough, England, UK	3/20/18
McRaney, Gerald	Collins, MS	8/19/47
McShane, Ian	Blackburn, England, UK	9/29/42
Meadows, Jayne	Wu Chang, China	9/27/20
Meara, Anne	Brooklyn, NY	9/20/29
Meat Loaf	Dallas, TX	9/27/47
Meester, Leighton	Marco Island, FL	4/9/86
Mehta, Zubin	Bombay, India	4/29/36
Mellencamp, John	Seymour, IN	10/7/51
Meloni, Christopher	Washington, DC	4/2/61
Mendes, Sam	Redding, England, UK	8/1/65
Mendes, Sergio	Niteroi, Brazil	2/11/41
Menzel, Idina	Syosset, NY	5/30/71
Merchant, Natalie	Jamestown, NY	10/26/63
Merkerson, S. Epatha	Saginaw, MI	11/28/52
Merrill, Dina	New York, NY	12/9/25
Messing, Debra	Brooklyn, NY	8/15/68
Metcalf, Laurie	Carbondale, IL	6/16/55
Meyers, Seth	Bedford, NH	12/28/73
Michael, George	London, England, UK	6/25/63
Michaels, Al	Brooklyn, NY	11/12/44
Michaels, Bret	Pittsburgh, PA	3/15/63
Michaels, Lorne	Toronto, ON, Canada	11/17/44
Michele, Lea	Bronx, NY	8/29/86
Midler, Bette	Honolulu, HI	12/1/45
Midori (Goto)	Osaka, Japan	10/25/71
Mike D	Brooklyn, NY	11/20/65
Milano, Alyssa	Brooklyn, NY	12/19/72
Miles, Sarah	Ingatestone, England, UK	12/31/41
Miles, Vera	nr. Boise City, OK	8/23/29
Miller, Dennis	Pittsburgh, PA	11/3/53
Miller, Penelope Ann	Santa Monica, CA	1/13/64
Mills, Donna	Chicago, IL	12/11/43
Mills, Hayley	London, England, UK	4/18/46
Milner, Martin	Detroit, MI	12/28/27
Milnes, Sherrill	Downers Grove, IL	1/10/35
Milsap, Ronnie	Robinsville, NC	1/16/44
Mimieux, Yvette	Hollywood, CA	1/8/42
Ming-Na (Wen)	Macao	11/20/63
Minnelli, Liza	Los Angeles, CA	3/12/46
Minogue, Kylie	Melbourne, Australia	5/28/68
Mirren, Helen	London, England, UK	7/26/45
Mitchell, Brian Stokes	Seattle, WA	10/31/57
Mitchell, Elizabeth	Los Angeles, CA	3/27/70
Mitchell, Jerry	Paw Paw, MI	1/15/60
Mitchell, Joni	Fort McLeod, AB, Canada	11/7/43
Moby	New York, NY	9/11/65
Modine, Matthew	Loma Linda, CA	3/22/59
Moffat, Donald	Plymouth, England, UK	12/26/30
Molina, Alfred	London, England, UK	5/24/53
Molinaro, Al	Kenosha, WI	6/24/19
Moll, Richard	Pasadena, CA	1/13/43
Moloney, Janel	Woodland Hills, CA	10/3/69
Monaghan, Dominic	Berlin, Germany	12/8/76
Monica (Arnold)	College Park, GA	10/24/80
Mo'Nique	Woodlawn, MD	12/11/67
Monteith, Cory	Calgary, AB, Canada	5/11/82
Moody, Ron	London, England, UK	1/8/24
Moore, Demi	Roswell, NM	11/11/62
Moore, Julianne	Fort Bragg, NC	12/3/60
Moore, Mandy	Nashua, NH	4/10/84
Moore, Mary Tyler	Brooklyn, NY	12/29/36
Moore, Melba	New York, NY	10/29/45
Moore, Michael	Flint, MI	4/23/54
Moore, Roger	London, England, UK	10/14/27
Moore, Terry	Los Angeles, CA	1/7/29
Morales, Esai	Brooklyn, NY	10/1/62
Moranis, Rick	Toronto, ON, Canada	4/18/54
Moreau, Jeanne	Paris, France	1/23/28
Moreno, Rita	Humacao, Puerto Rico	12/11/31
Morgan, Piers	Guildford, Surrey, UK	3/30/65
Morgan, Tracy	Bronx, NY	11/10/68
Moriarty, Michael	Detroit, MI	4/5/41
Morris, Garrett	New Orleans, LA	2/1/37
Morissette, Alanis	Ottawa, ON, Canada	6/1/74
Morrison, Matthew	Fort Ord, CA	10/30/78
Morrison, Van	Belfast, N. Ireland, UK	8/31/45

Name	Birthplace	Birthdate
Morrissey (Steven Patrick)	Manchester, England, UK	5/22/59
Morrow, Rob	New Rochelle, NY	9/21/62
Morse, David	Beverly, MA	10/11/53
Morse, Robert	Newton, MA	5/18/31
Mortensen, Viggo	New York, NY	10/20/58
Mortimer, Emily	London, England, UK	12/1/71
Morton, Joe	New York, NY	10/18/47
Morton, Samantha	Nottingham, England, UK	5/13/77
Moses, William	Los Angeles, CA	11/17/59
Moss, Carrie-Anne	Vancouver, BC, Canada	8/21/67
Moss, Elisabeth	Los Angeles, CA	7/24/82
Moss, Kate	Croydon, Surrey, Eng., UK	1/16/74
Moyer, Stephen	Brentwood, UK	10/11/69
Mueller-Stahl, Armin	Tilsit, E. Prussia	12/17/30
Muldaur, Diana	Brooklyn, NY	8/19/38
Mulgrew, Kate	Dubuque, IA	4/29/55
Mull, Martin	Chicago, IL	8/18/43
Mullally, Megan	Los Angeles, CA	11/12/58
Mullan, Peter	Peterhead, Scotland, UK	11/2/59
Mulroney, Dermot	Alexandria, VA	10/31/63
Muniz, Frankie	Ridgewood, NJ	12/5/85
Munsel, Patrice	Spokane, WA	5/14/25
Murphy, Ben	Jonesboro, AR	3/6/42
Murphy, Donna	Corona, Queens, NY	3/7/58
Murphy, Eddie	Brooklyn, NY	4/3/61
Murphy, Michael	Los Angeles, CA	5/5/38
Murray, Anne	Springhill, NS, Canada	6/20/45
Murray, Bill	Wilmette, IL	9/21/50
Murray, Don	Hollywood, CA	7/31/29
Musburger, Brent	Portland, OR	5/26/39
Muti, Riccardo	Naples, Italy	7/28/41
Myers, Mike	Scarborough, ON, Canada	5/25/63
Nabors, Jim	Sylacauga, AL	6/12/30
Nagra, Parminder	Leicester, England, UK	10/5/75
Nash, Graham	Blackpool, England, UK	2/2/42
Naughton, James	Middletown, CT	12/6/45
Navarro, Dave	Santa Monica, CA	6/7/67
Nealon, Kevin	St. Louis, MO	11/18/53
Neeson, Liam	Ballymena, N. Ireland, UK	6/7/52
Neff, Lucas	Chicago, IL	11/7/85
Neill, Sam	Ulster, N. Ireland, UK	9/14/47
Nelligan, Kate	London, ON, Canada	3/16/51
Nelly	Austin, TX	11/2/74
Nelson, Craig T.	Spokane, WA	4/4/44
Nelson, Ed	New Orleans, LA	12/21/28
Nelson, Judd	Portland, ME	11/28/59
Nelson, Tracy	Santa Monica, CA	10/25/63
Nelson, Willie	Abbott, TX	4/30/33
Nero, Peter	Brooklyn, NY	5/22/34
Nesmith, Mike	Houston, TX	12/30/42
Neuwirth, Bebe	Newark, NJ	12/31/58
Neville, Aaron	New Orleans, LA	1/24/41
Newhart, Bob	Oak Park, IL	9/5/29
Newman, Randy	New Orleans, LA	11/28/43
Newton, Wayne	Norfolk, VA	4/3/42
Newton-John, Olivia	Cambridge, England, UK	9/26/48
Nicholas, Denise	Detroit, MI	7/12/44
Nichols, Mike	Berlin, Germany	11/6/31
Nicholson, Jack	Neptune, NJ	4/22/37
Nicks, Stevie	Phoenix, AZ	5/26/48
Nielsen, Connie	Frederikshavn, Denmark	7/3/65
Nighy, Bill	Caterham, Surrey, Eng., UK	12/12/49
Nimoy, Leonard	Boston, MA	3/26/31
Nixon, Cynthia	New York, NY	4/9/66
Nolte, Nick	Omaha, NE	2/8/41
Noone, Peter	Manchester, England, UK	11/5/47
Norman, Jessye	Augusta, GA	9/15/45
Norris, Chuck	Ryan, OK	3/10/40
Northam, Jeremy	Cambridge, England, UK	12/1/61
Norton, Edward	Boston, MA	8/18/69
Noth, Christopher	Madison, WI	11/13/54
Novak, Kim	Chicago, IL	2/13/33
Nuyen, France	Marseilles, France	7/31/39
Oates, John	New York, NY	4/7/49
O'Brian, Hugh	Rochester, NY	4/19/25
O'Brien, Conan	Brookline, MA	4/18/63
O'Brien, Margaret	San Diego, CA	1/15/37
Ocean, Billy	Fyzabad, Trinidad	1/21/50
O'Connor, Sinead	Glenageary, Ireland	12/8/66
O'Donnell, Chris	Winnetka, IL	6/26/70
O'Donnell, Rosie	Commack, NY	3/21/62
O'Grady, Gail	Detroit, MI	1/23/63
Oh, Sandra	Nepean, ON, Canada	7/20/71
O'Hara, Catherine	Toronto, ON, Canada	3/4/54
O'Hara, Maureen	Dublin, Ireland	8/17/20
O'Hare, Denis	Kansas City, MO	1/17/62
Oka, Masi	Tokyo, Japan	12/27/74
Oldman, Gary	South London, Eng., UK	3/21/58
Olin, Ken	Chicago, IL	7/30/54
Olin, Lena	Stockholm, Sweden	3/22/55
Olmos, Edward James	E. Los Angeles, CA	2/24/47
Olsen, Ashley	Sherman Oaks, CA	6/13/86
Olsen, Mary-Kate	Sherman Oaks, CA	6/13/86
Olson, Nancy	Milwaukee, WI	7/14/28
Olyphant, Timothy	Honolulu, HI	5/20/68
O'Malley, Mike	Boston, MA	10/31/69

Name	Birthplace	Birthdate
O'Neal, Ryan	Los Angeles, CA	4/20/41
O'Neal, Tatum	Los Angeles, CA	11/5/63
O'Neill, Ed.	Youngstown, OH	4/12/46
Ontkean, Michael	Vancouver, BC, Canada.	1/24/46
O'Quinn, Terry	Newbury, MI	7/15/52
Orlando, Tony	New York, NY	4/3/44
Ormond, Julia	Epsom, England, UK.	1/4/65
Osbourne, Jack	London, England, UK	11/8/85
Osbourne, Kelly	London, England, UK	10/27/84
Osbourne, Ozzy	Birmingham, England, UK.	12/3/48
Osbourne, Sharon	London, England, UK	10/9/52
O'Shea, Milo	Dublin, Ireland	6/2/26
Oslin, K.T.	Crossett, AR	5/15/42
Osment, Haley Joel	Los Angeles, CA	4/10/88
Osmond, Donny	Ogden, UT	12/9/57
Osmond, Marie	Ogden, UT	10/13/59
O'Toole, Annette	Houston, TX	4/1/51
O'Toole, Peter.	Connemara, Ireland.	8/2/32
Owen, Clive	Keresley, England, UK.	10/3/64
Oz, Frank	Herford, England, UK.	5/25/44
Ozawa, Seiji	Shenyang, China.	9/1/35
Pacino, Al	New York, NY	4/25/40
Packer, Billy	Wellsville, NY	2/25/40
Page, Ellen	Halifax, NS, Canada	2/21/87
Page, Jimmy	Heston, England, UK.	1/9/44
Page, Patti	Claremore, OK	11/8/27
Paget, Debra.	Denver, CO	8/19/33
Paige, Janis	Tacoma, WA	9/16/22
Paisley, Brad.	Glen Dale, WV.	10/28/72
Palin, Michael	Sheffield, England, UK.	5/5/43
Palmer, Betsy	East Chicago, IN	11/1/26
Palmer, Geoffrey	London, England, UK	6/4/27
Palminteri, Chazz	Bronx, NY	5/15/51
Paltrow, Gwyneth	Los Angeles, CA	9/28/72
Panettiere, Hayden	Palisades, NY	8/21/89
Panjabi, Archie	Edgware, England, UK	5/31/73
Pantoliano, Joe	Hoboken, NJ	9/12/51
Papas, Irene	Chiliomodi, Greece	9/3/26
Paquin, Anna	Winnipeg, MB, Canada.	7/24/82
Parker, Alan	Islington, England, UK.	2/14/44
Parker, Eleanor.	Cedarville, OH.	6/26/22
Parker, Jameson	Baltimore, MD	11/18/47
Parker, Mary-Louise	Fort Jackson, SC	8/2/64
Parker, Sarah Jessica	Nelsonville, OH	3/25/65
Parsons, Estelle	Marblehead, MA	11/20/27
Parsons, Jim	Houston, TX	3/24/73
Parton, Dolly	Sevierville, TN	1/19/46
Pasdar, Adrian	Pittsfield, MA	4/30/65
Patinkin, Mandy	Chicago, IL	11/30/52
Patric, Jason	Queens, NY.	6/17/66
Pattinson, Robert	London, England, UK	5/13/86
Patton, Will	Charleston, SC	6/14/54
Paul, Aaron	Emmett, ID	8/27/79
Paul, Adrian	London, England, UK	5/29/59
Paulson, Sarah	Tampa, FL	12/17/75
Paxton, Bill .	Fort Worth, TX	5/17/55
Pearce, Guy	Ely, England, UK	10/5/67
Peet, Amanda	New York, NY	1/11/72
Penn, Kal	Montclair, NJ	4/23/77
Penn, Sean	Burbank, CA	8/17/60
Pepper, Barry	Campbell River, BC, Can.	4/4/70
Perez, Rosie	Brooklyn, NY	9/6/64
Perkins, Elizabeth	Queens, NY.	11/18/60
Perlman, Itzhak	Tel Aviv, Israel	8/31/45
Perlman, Rhea	Brooklyn, NY	3/31/48
Perlman, Ron	New York, NY	4/13/50
Perrine, Valerie	Galveston, TX	9/3/43
Perry, Katy	Santa Barbara, CA.	10/25/84
Perry, Luke	Mansfield, OH	10/11/65
Perry, Matthew	Williamstown, MA	8/19/69
Persoff, Nehemiah	Jerusalem, Israel.	8/2/20
Pesci, Joe	Newark, NJ	2/9/43
Peters, Bernadette	Ozone Park, Queens, NY	2/28/48
Peters, Roberta	Bronx, NY	5/4/30
Petersen, Wolfgang.	Emden, Germany	3/14/41
Petty, Lori	Chattanooga, TN	3/23/63
Petty, Tom	Gainesville, FL	10/20/50
Pfeiffer, Michelle	Santa Ana, CA.	4/29/58
Phair, Liz.	New Haven, CT	4/17/67
Philbin, Regis	New York, NY	8/25/31
Phillippe, Ryan	New Castle, DE	9/10/74
Phillips, Lou Diamond	Subic Bay, Philippines	2/17/62
Phillips, Mackenzie	Alexandria, VA.	11/10/59
Phillips, Michelle	Long Beach, CA	6/4/44
Phillips, Phillip.	Leesburg, GA	9/20/90
Phillips, Sian	Bettws, Wales, UK.	5/14/34
Phoenix, Joaquin	San Juan, Puerto Rico.	10/28/74
Pierce, David Hyde	Albany, NY.	4/3/59
Pinchot, Bronson	New York, NY	5/20/59
Pink.	Doylestown, PA	9/8/79
Pinkett Smith, Jada.	Baltimore, MD	9/18/71
Pirner, David	Green Bay, WI	4/16/64
Piscopo, Joe	Passaic, NJ .	6/17/51
Pitt, Brad.	Shawnee, OK	12/18/63
Piven, Jeremy	New York, NY	7/26/65
Plant, Robert	W. Bromwich, England, UK	8/20/48
Plimpton, Martha	New York ,NY	11/16/70
Plowright, Joan	Brigg, England, UK	10/28/29
Plummer, Amanda	New York, NY	3/23/57
Plummer, Christopher.	Toronto, ON, Canada.	12/13/27
Poehler, Amy.	Burlington, MA.	9/16/71
Poitier, Sidney.	Miami, FL	2/20/27
Polanski, Roman.	Paris, France.	8/18/33
Pompeo, Ellen	Everett, MA	11/10/69
Pop, Iggy.	Ann Arbor, MI	4/21/47
Portman, Natalie.	Jerusalem, Israel.	6/9/81
Posey, Parker	Baltimore, MD	11/8/68
Post, Markie	Palo Alto, CA.	11/4/50
Potente, Franka.	Dulmen bei Munster, Germany	7/22/74
Potts, Annie.	Nashville, TN.	10/28/52
Povich, Maury.	Washington, DC	1/17/39
Powell, Jane	Portland, OR.	4/1/28
Powers, Stefanie.	Hollywood, CA.	11/2/42
Prentiss, Paula	San Antonio, TX.	3/4/39
Prepon, Laura	Watchung, NJ	3/7/80
Presley, Priscilla	Brooklyn, NY	5/24/45
Pressly, Jaime.	Kinston, NC.	7/30/77
Previn, Andre	Berlin, Germany	4/6/29
Price, Leontyne.	Laurel, MS.	2/10/27
Price, Molly	North Plainfield, NJ	12/15/66
Price, Ray.	Perryville, TX.	1/12/26
Pride, Charley.	Sledge, MS	3/18/38
Priestley, Jason.	Vancouver, BC, Canada.	8/28/69
Prince (The Artist).	Minneapolis, MN	6/7/58
Prince, Faith	Augusta, GA	8/5/57
Principal, Victoria	Fukuoka, Japan.	1/3/50
Prinze, Freddie, Jr.	Albuquerque, NM.	3/8/76
Probst, Jeff	Wichita, KS	11/4/62
Proctor, Emily	Raleigh, NC.	10/8/68
Pryce, Jonathan	Holywell, N. Wales, UK.	6/1/47
Puck, Wolfgang	St. Veit, Austria	1/8/49
Pulliam, Keshia Knight	Newark, NJ	4/9/79
Pullman, Bill	Hornell, NY	12/17/53
Purcell, Sarah	Richmond, IN	10/8/48
Quaid, Dennis	Houston, TX	4/9/54
Quaid, Randy	Houston, TX	10/1/50
Queen Latifah	Newark, NJ	3/18/70
Quinn, Aidan	Chicago, IL	3/8/59
Quinn, Colin	Brooklyn, NY	6/6/59
Quinn, Martha	Albany, NY.	5/11/59
Quinto, Zachary	Pittsburgh, PA	6/2/77
Rachins, Alan	Cambridge, MA	10/3/42
Radcliffe, Daniel	London, England, UK	7/23/89
Rae, Charlotte.	Milwaukee, WI	4/22/26
Raffi	Cairo, Egypt.	7/8/48
Rainer, Luise.	Düsseldorf, Germany.	1/12/1910
Raitt, Bonnie	Burbank, CA	11/8/49
Ramey, Samuel.	Colby, KS.	3/28/42
Ramirez, Efren	Los Angeles, CA.	10/2/73
Ramirez, Sara.	Mazatlan, Mexico.	8/31/75
Ramone, Tommy	Budapest, Hungary.	1/29/52
Rancic, Giuliana	Naples, Italy.	8/17/75
Randolph, Joyce.	Detroit, MI	10/21/24
Raphael, Sally Jessy	Easton, PA.	2/25/35
Rashad, Phylicia	Houston, TX	6/19/48
Ratzenberger, John	Bridgeport, CT.	4/6/47
Raver, Kim	New York, NY	3/15/69
Ray, Rachael	Glen Falls, NY.	8/25/68
Reddy, Helen	Melbourne, Australia	10/25/41
Redford, Robert	Santa Monica, CA	8/18/36
Redgrave, Vanessa.	London, England, UK	1/30/37
Reed, Lou	Brooklyn, NY	3/2/42
Reed, Rex.	Ft. Worth, TX.	10/2/38
Reese, Della	Detroit, MI	7/6/31
Reeves, Keanu	Beirut, Lebanon.	9/2/64
Reeves, Martha	Eufaula, AL	7/18/41
Regalbuto, Joe	New York, NY	8/24/49
Reid, Tara	Wyckoff, NJ	11/8/75
Reid, Tim	Norfolk, VA	12/19/44
Reid, Vernon	London, England, UK	8/22/58
Reilly, John C.	Chicago, IL	5/24/65
Reiner, Carl.	Bronx, NY	3/20/22
Reiner, Rob.	Bronx, NY	3/6/47
Reinhold, Judge	Wilmington, DE	5/21/57
Reinking, Ann	Seattle, WA.	11/10/49
Reiser, Paul	New York, NY	3/30/57
Reitman, Ivan	Komarno, Czechoslovakia	10/26/46
Remini, Leah	Brooklyn, NY	6/15/70
Renner, Jeremy	Modesto, CA	1/7/71
Resnik, Regina	New York, NY	8/30/22
Reynolds, Burt	Waycross, GA	2/11/36
Reynolds, Debbie	El Paso, TX.	4/1/32
Reynolds, Ryan	Vancouver, BC, Canada.	10/23/76
Reznor, Trent	Mercer, PA.	5/17/65
Rhames, Ving	New York, NY	5/12/59
Rhymes, Busta.	Brooklyn, NY.	5/20/72
Rhys Meyers, Jonathan	Dublin, Ireland.	7/27/77
Ribisi, Giovanni.	Los Angeles, CA.	12/17/74
Ricci, Christina	Santa Monica, CA .	2/12/80
Richards, Denise	Downers Grove, IL.	2/17/71
Richards, Keith	Dartford, Kent, Eng., UK	12/18/43
Richards, Michael	Culver City, CA	7/24/49

Name	Birthplace	Birthdate	Name	Birthplace	Birthdate
Richardson, Kevin	Lexington, KY	10/3/71	Samberg, Andy	Berkeley, CA	8/18/78
Richardson, Miranda	Lancashire, England, UK	3/3/58	Samms, Emma	London, England, UK	8/28/60
Richardson, Patricia	Bethesda, MD	2/23/51	San Giacomo, Laura	Hoboken, NJ	11/14/62
Richie, Lionel	Tuskegee, AL	6/20/49	Sandler, Adam	Brooklyn, NY	9/9/66
Richie, Nicole	Berkeley, CA	9/21/81	Sands, Julian	West Yorkshire, Eng., UK	1/15/58
Richter, Andy	Grand Rapids, MI	10/28/66	Santana, Carlos	Autlan, Mexico	7/20/47
Rickles, Don	Jackson Heights, Queens, NY	5/8/26	Sara, Mia	Brooklyn, NY	6/19/67
Rickman, Alan	Hammersmith, Eng., UK	2/21/46	Sarandon, Susan	New York, NY	10/4/46
Riegert, Peter	New York, NY	4/11/47	Sartain, Gailard	Tulsa, OK	9/18/46
Rigg, Diana	Doncaster, England, UK	7/20/38	Savage, Ben	Highland Park, IL	9/13/80
Rihanna	St. Michael, Barbados	2/20/88	Savage, Fred	Highland Park, IL	7/9/76
Riley, Amber	Long Beach, CA	2/15/86	Sawa, Devon	Vancouver, BC, Canada	9/7/78
Rimes, LeAnn	Flowood, MS	8/28/82	Saxon, John	Brooklyn, NY	8/5/36
Ringwald, Molly	Roseville, CA	2/18/68	Sayles, John	Schenectady, NY	9/28/50
Ripa, Kelly	Stratford, NJ	10/2/70	Scacchi, Greta	Milan, Italy	2/18/60
Rivera, Chita	Washington, DC	1/23/33	Scaggs, Boz	Canton, OH	6/8/44
Rivera, Geraldo	New York, NY	7/4/43	Scales, Prunella	Sutton Abinger, Eng., UK	6/22/32
Rivers, Joan	Brooklyn, NY	6/8/33	Scalia, Jack	Brooklyn, NY	11/10/51
Robbins, Tim	W. Covina, CA	10/16/58	Schallert, William	Los Angeles, CA	7/6/22
Roberts, Doris	St. Louis, MO	11/4/30	Schell, Maximilian	Vienna, Austria	12/8/30
Roberts, Eric	Biloxi, MS	4/18/56	Schiff, Richard	Bethesda, MD	5/27/55
Roberts, Julia	Smyrna, GA	10/28/67	Schiffer, Claudia	Rheinbach, Germany	8/25/70
Roberts, Tony	New York, NY	10/22/39	Schneider, John	Mt. Kisco, NY	4/8/54
Robertson, Dale	Harrah, OK	7/14/23	Schneider, Rob	San Francisco, CA	10/31/63
Robinson, Smokey	Detroit, MI	2/19/40	Schram, Bitty	New York, NY	7/17/68
Rochon, Lela	Torrance, CA	4/17/64	Schreiber, Liev	San Francisco, CA	10/4/67
Rock, Chris	Andrews, SC	2/7/65	Schroder, Rick	Staten Island, NY	4/13/70
Rodgers, Jimmy	Camas, WA	9/18/33	Schwarzenegger, Arnold	Thal, Austria	7/30/47
Rodriguez, Johnny	Sabinal, TX	12/10/51	Schwimmer, David	Astoria, Queens, NY	11/2/66
Rodriguez, Michelle	Bexar County, TX	7/12/78	Sciorra, Annabella	Wethersfield, CT	3/24/64
Rogan, Joe	Newark, NJ	8/11/67	Scolari, Peter	New Rochelle, NY	9/12/54
Rogen, Seth	Vancouver, BC, Canada	4/15/82	Scorsese, Martin	Flushing, Queens, NY	11/17/42
Rogers, Kenny	Houston, TX	8/21/38	Scott, Lizabeth	Scranton, PA	9/29/22
Rogers, Mimi	Coral Gables, FL	1/27/56	Scott, Ridley	South Shields, England, UK	11/30/37
Rogers, Wayne	Birmingham, AL	4/7/33	Scott, Seann William	Cottage Grove, MN	10/3/76
Rohm, Elisabeth	Dusseldorf, Germany	4/28/73	Scott-Heron, Gil	Chicago, IL	4/1/49
Rollins, Henry	Washington, DC	2/13/61	Scott Thomas, Kristin	Redruth, England, UK	5/24/60
Rollins, Sonny	New York, NY	9/7/30	Scotto, Renata	Savona, Italy	2/24/34
Romano, Ray	Forest Hills, Queens, NY	12/21/57	Scully, Vin	Bronx, NY	11/29/27
Romijn, Rebecca	Berkeley, CA	11/6/72	Seacrest, Ryan	Atlanta, GA	12/24/74
Ronstadt, Linda	Tucson, AZ	7/15/46	Seagal, Steven	Lansing, MI	4/10/51
Rooney, Mickey	Brooklyn, NY	9/23/20	Secor, Kyle	Tacoma, WA	5/31/57
Root, Stephen	Sarasota, FL	11/17/51	Sedaka, Neil	Brooklyn, NY	3/13/39
Rose, Axl	Lafayette, IN	2/6/62	Sedgwick, Kyra	New York, NY	8/19/65
Roseanne	Salt Lake City, UT	11/3/52	Seeger, Pete	New York, NY	5/3/19
Rose Marie	New York, NY	8/15/23	Segal, George	Great Neck, NY	2/13/34
Ross, Charlotte	Winnetka, IL	1/21/68	Seidelman, Susan	Abington, PA	12/11/52
Ross, Diana	Detroit, MI	3/26/44	Seinfeld, Jerry	Brooklyn, NY	4/29/54
Ross, Katharine	Hollywood, CA	1/29/40	Seldes, Marian	New York, NY	8/23/28
Ross, Marion	Albert Lea, MN	10/25/28	Sellecca, Connie	Bronx, NY	5/25/55
Rossdale, Gavin	London, England, UK	10/30/65	Selleck, Tom	Detroit, MI	1/29/45
Rossellini, Isabella	Rome, Italy	6/18/52	Severinsen, Doc	Arlington, OR	7/7/27
Rossum, Emmy	New York, NY	9/12/86	Sevigny, Chloë	Springfield, MA	11/18/74
Roth, David Lee	Bloomington, IN	10/10/55	Sewell, Rufus	Twickenham, Middlesex, England, UK	10/29/67
Roth, Tim	London, England, UK	5/14/61	Seymour, Jane	Hillingdon, England, UK	2/15/51
Rotten, Johnny	London, England, UK	1/31/56	Shackelford, Ted	Oklahoma City, OK	6/23/46
Rourke, Mickey	Schenectady, NY	9/16/56	Shaffer, Paul	Thunder Bay, ON, Canada	11/28/49
Routh, Brandon	Des Moines, IA	10/9/79	Shakira (Mebarak Ripoll)	Barranquilla, Colombia	2/2/77
Routledge, Patricia	Birkenhead, England, UK	2/17/29	Shalhoub, Tony	Green Bay, WI	10/9/53
Rowan, Kelly	Ottawa, ON, Canada	10/26/65	Shandling, Garry	Chicago, IL	11/29/49
Rowlands, Gena	Cambria, WI	6/19/30	Shankar, Ravi	Benares, India	4/7/20
Rubinstein, John	Beverly Hills, CA	12/8/46	Shannon, Molly	Shaker Heights, OH	9/16/64
Rudd, Paul	Passaic, NJ	4/6/1969	Sharif, Omar	Alexandria, Egypt	4/10/32
Rudner, Rita	Miami, FL	9/17/56	Shatner, William	Montreal, QC, Canada	3/22/31
Rudolph, Maya	Gainesville, FL	7/27/72	Shaughnessy, Charles	London, England, UK	2/9/55
Ruehl, Mercedes	Jackson Heights, Queens, NY	2/28/48	Shaver, Helen	St. Thomas, ON, Canada	2/24/51
Ruffalo, Mark	Kenosha, WI	11/22/67	Shawkat, Alia	Riverside, CA	4/18/89
Rupp, Debra Jo	Glendale, CA	2/24/51	Shea, John	N. Conway, NH	4/14/49
Rush, Barbara	Denver, CO	1/4/27	Shearer, Harry	Los Angeles, CA	12/23/43
Rush, Geoffrey	Toowoomba, Australia	7/6/51	Sheedy, Ally	New York, NY	6/13/62
Russell, Keri	Fountain Valley, CA	3/23/76	Sheen, Charlie	Los Angeles, CA	9/3/65
Russell, Kurt	Springfield, MA	3/17/51	Sheen, Martin	Dayton, OH	8/3/40
Russell, Leon	Lawton, OK	4/2/41	Sheen, Michael	Newport, Wales, UK	2/5/69
Russell, Mark	Buffalo, NY	8/23/32	Sheindlin, Judy	Brooklyn, NY	10/21/42
Russell, Theresa	San Diego, CA	3/20/57	Shelley, Carole	London, England, UK	8/16/39
Russo, Rene	Burbank, CA	2/17/54	Shelton, Blake	Ada, OK	6/18/76
Ruttan, Susan	Oregon City, OR	9/16/50	Shepard, Sam	Ft. Sheridan, IL	11/5/43
Ryan, Meg	Fairfield, CT	11/19/61	Shepherd, Cybill	Memphis, TN	2/18/50
Ryan, Roz	Detroit, MI	7/7/51	Shepherd, Sherri	Chicago, IL	4/22/67
Rydell, Bobby	Philadelphia, PA	4/26/42	Sheridan, Nicollette	Worthing, England, UK	11/21/63
Ryder, Winona	Winona, MN	10/29/71	Shields, Brooke	New York, NY	5/31/65
Sabato, Antonio, Jr.	Rome, Italy	2/29/72	Shire, Talia	Lake Success, NY	4/25/46
Sade (Adu)	Ibadan, Nigeria	1/16/59	Short, Martin	Hamilton, ON, Canada	3/26/50
Sagal, Katey	Hollywood, CA	1/19/54	Shortz, Will	Crawfordsville, IN	8/26/52
Saget, Bob	Philadelphia, PA	5/17/56	Show, Grant	Detroit, MI	2/27/62
Sagnier, Ludivine	La Celle-St.-Cloud, France	7/3/79	Shue, Andrew	S. Orange, NJ	2/20/67
Sahl, Mort	Montreal, QC, Canada	5/11/27	Shue, Elisabeth	Wilmington, DE	10/6/63
Saint, Eva Marie	Newark, NJ	7/4/24	Shyamalan, M. Night	Pondicherry, India	8/6/70
St. James, Susan	Hollywood, CA	8/14/46	Sidibe, Gabourey	Brooklyn, NY	5/6/83
St. John, Jill	Los Angeles, CA	8/19/40	Sigler, Jamie-Lynn	Jericho, NY	5/15/81
St. Patrick, Mathew	Philadelphia, PA	3/17/68	Sikking, James B.	Los Angeles, CA	3/5/34
Sajak, Pat	Chicago, IL	10/26/46	Silverman, Jonathan	Beverly Hills, CA	8/5/66
Saks, Gene	New York, NY	11/8/21	Silverman, Sarah	Bedford, NH	12/1/70
Saldana, Zoë	Passaic, NJ	6/19/78	Silverstone, Alicia	San Francisco, CA	10/4/76
Salling, Mark	Dallas, TX	8/17/82	Simmons, Gene	Haifa, Israel	8/25/49
Salonga, Lea	Manila, Philippines	2/22/71			

Name	Birthplace	Birthdate
Simmons, Henry	Stamford, CT	7/1/70
Simmons, Richard	New Orleans, LA	7/12/48
Simon, Carly	New York, NY	6/25/45
Simon, Paul	Newark, NJ	10/13/41
Simpson, Ashlee	Waco, TX	10/3/84
Simpson, Jessica	Abilene, TX	7/10/80
Sinatra, Nancy	Jersey City, NJ	6/8/40
Sinbad	Benton Harbor, MI	11/10/56
Singleton, John	Los Angeles, CA	1/6/68
Sinise, Gary	Blue Island, IL	3/17/55
Sirico, Tony	Brooklyn, NY	7/29/42
Sisto, Jeremy	Grass Valley, CA	10/6/74
Sizemore, Tom	Detroit, MI	9/29/64
Skerritt, Tom	Detroit, MI	8/25/33
Slater, Christian	New York, NY	8/18/69
Slater, Helen	Massapequa, NY	12/15/63
Slattery, John	Boston, MA	8/13/63
Sledge, Percy	Leighton, AL	11/25/40
Slezak, Erika	Hollywood, CA	8/5/46
Slick, Grace	Evanston, IL	10/30/39
Smirnoff, Yakov	Odessa, Ukraine	1/24/51
Smith, Allison	New York, NY	12/9/69
Smith, Jaclyn	Houston, TX	10/26/47
Smith, Jaden	Malibu, CA	7/8/98
Smith, Keely	Norfolk, VA	3/9/32
Smith, Kevin	Red Bank, NJ	8/2/70
Smith, Maggie	Ilford, England, UK	12/28/34
Smith, Patti	Chicago, IL	12/30/46
Smith, Robert	Blackpool, England, UK	4/21/59
Smith, Will	Philadelphia, PA	9/25/68
Smits, Jimmy	Brooklyn, NY	7/9/55
Smothers, Dick	Governor's Island, NY	11/20/38
Smothers, Tom	Governor's Island, NY	2/2/37
Snipes, Wesley	Orlando, FL	7/31/62
Snooki (Nicole Polizzi)	Santiago, Chile	11/23/87
Snoop Lion (née Snoop Dogg)	Long Beach, CA	10/20/72
Soderbergh, Steven	Atlanta, GA	1/14/63
Somers, Suzanne	San Bruno, CA	10/16/46
Sommer, Elke	Berlin, Germany	11/5/40
Sorbo, Kevin	Mound, MN	9/24/58
Sorvino, Mira	Tenafly, NJ	9/28/67
Sorvino, Paul	Brooklyn, NY	4/13/39
Soul, David	Chicago, IL	8/28/43
Spacek, Sissy	Quitman, TX	12/25/49
Spacey, Kevin	S. Orange, NJ	7/26/59
Spade, David	Birmingham, MI	7/22/64
Spader, James	Boston, MA	2/7/60
Spalding, Esperanza	Portland, OR	10/18/84
Spano, Joe	San Francisco, CA	7/7/46
Sparks, Jordin	Phoenix, AZ	12/22/89
Spears, Britney	Kentwood, LA	12/2/81
Spears, Jamie-Lynn	McComb, MS	4/4/91
Spector, Phil	Bronx, NY	12/26/40
Spelling, Tori	Los Angeles, CA	5/16/73
Spencer, Octavia	Montgomery, AL	5/25/72
Spielberg, Steven	Cincinnati, OH	12/18/46
Spiner, Brent	Houston, TX	2/2/49
Springer, Jerry	London, England, UK	2/13/44
Springfield, Rick	Sydney, Australia	8/23/49
Springsteen, Bruce	Long Branch, NJ	9/23/49
Spurlock, Morgan	Parksburg, WV	11/7/70
Stahl, Nick	Harlingen, TX	12/5/79
Stallone, Sylvester	New York, NY	7/6/46
Stamos, John	Cypress, CA	8/19/63
Stamp, Terence	Stepney, England, UK	7/22/39
Stanton, Harry Dean	West Irvine, KY	7/14/26
Stapleton, Jean	New York, NY	1/19/23
Starr, Ringo	Liverpool, England, UK	7/7/40
Steenburgen, Mary	Newport, AR	2/8/53
Stefani, Gwen	Fullerton, CA	10/3/69
Stein, Ben	Washington, DC	11/25/44
Stephens, James	Mt. Kisco, NY	5/18/51
Stern, Daniel	Bethesda, MD	8/28/57
Stern, Howard	Roosevelt, NY	1/12/54
Sternhagen, Frances	Washington, DC	1/13/30
Stevens, Andrew	Memphis, TN	6/10/55
Stevens, Cat (Yusef Islam)	London, England, UK	7/21/48
Stevens, Connie	Brooklyn, NY	8/8/38
Stevens, Rise	Bronx, NY	6/11/13
Stevens, Stella	Hot Coffee, MS	10/1/36
Stevenson, Parker	Philadelphia, PA	6/4/52
Stewart, French	Albuquerque, NM	2/20/64
Stewart, Jon	New York, NY	11/28/62
Stewart, Kristen	Los Angeles, CA	4/9/90
Stewart, Patrick	Mirfield, England, UK	7/13/40
Stewart, Rod	London, England, UK	1/10/45
Stiers, David Ogden	Peoria, IL	10/31/42
Stiles, Julia	New York, NY	3/28/81
Stiller, Ben	New York, NY	11/30/65
Stiller, Jerry	Brooklyn, NY	6/8/27
Stills, Stephen	Dallas, TX	1/3/45
Sting	Newcastle upon Tyne, England, UK	10/2/51
Stipe, Michael	Decatur, GA	1/4/60
Stockwell, Dean	North Hollywood, CA	3/5/36

Name	Birthplace	Birthdate
Stoltz, Eric	Whittier, CA	9/30/61
Stone, Dee Wallace	Kansas City, KS	12/14/48
Stone, Emma	Scottsdale, AZ	11/6/88
Stone, Oliver	New York, NY	9/15/46
Stone, Sharon	Meadville, PA	3/10/58
Stonestreet, Eric	Kansas City, KS	9/9/71
Stookey, Paul	Baltimore, MD	12/30/37
Storch, Larry	New York, NY	1/8/23
Stowe, Madeleine	Eagle Rock, CA	8/18/58
Strait, George	Pearsall, TX	5/18/52
Strasser, Robin	New York, NY	5/7/45
Stratas, Teresa	Toronto, ON, Canada	5/26/38
Strathairn, David	San Francisco, CA	1/26/49
Strauss, Peter	Croton-on-Hudson, NY	2/20/47
Streep, Meryl	Summit, NJ	6/22/49
Streisand, Barbra	Brooklyn, NY	4/24/42
Stringfield, Sherry	Colorado Springs, CO	6/24/67
Stritch, Elaine	Detroit, MI	2/2/26
Stroman, Susan	Wilmington, DE	10/17/54
Struthers, Sally	Portland, OR	7/28/48
Studdard, Ruben	Frankfurt, Germany	9/12/78
Suchet, David	London, England, UK	5/2/46
Sullivan, Erik Per	Worcester, MA	7/12/91
Sullivan, Susan	New York, NY	11/18/42
Sutherland, Donald	St. John, NB, Canada	7/17/34
Sutherland, Kiefer	London, England, UK	12/21/66
Suvari, Mena	Newport, RI	2/9/79
Swank, Hilary	Bellingham, WA	7/30/74
Swift, Taylor	Wyomissing, PA	12/13/89
Swinton, Tilda	London, England, UK	11/5/60
Swit, Loretta	Passaic, NJ	11/4/37
Sykes, Wanda	Portsmouth, VA	3/7/64
Szmanda, Eric	Milwaukee, WI	7/24/75
T, Mr.	Chicago, IL	5/21/52
Takei, George	Los Angeles, CA	4/20/37
Tallchief, Maria	Fairfax, OK	1/24/25
Tamblyn, Amber	Santa Monica, CA	5/14/83
Tamblyn, Russ	Los Angeles, CA	12/30/34
Tambor, Jeffrey	San Francisco, CA	7/8/44
Tarantino, Quentin	Knoxville, TN	3/27/63
Tatum, Channing	Cullman, AL	4/26/80
Tautou, Audrey	Beaumont, France	8/9/78
Taylor, Buck	Hollywood, CA	5/13/38
Taylor, James	Boston, MA	3/12/48
Taylor, Rip	Washington, DC	1/13/34
Taylor, Rod	Sydney, Australia	1/11/30
Taymor, Julie	Newton, MA	12/15/52
Te Kanawa, Kiri	Gisborne, New Zealand	3/6/44
Teller	Philadelphia, PA	2/14/48
Temple Black, Shirley	Santa Monica, CA	4/23/28
Tennant, Victoria	London, England, UK	9/30/50
Tennille, Toni	Montgomery, AL	5/8/43
Tesh, John	Garden City, NY	7/9/52
Tharp, Twyla	Portland, IN	7/1/41
Theron, Charlize	Benoni, South Africa	8/7/75
Thicke, Alan	Kirkland Lake, ON, Canada	3/1/47
Thiessen, Tiffani	Long Beach, CA	1/23/74
Thomas, Jay	Kermit, TX	7/12/48
Thomas, Jonathan Taylor	Bethlehem, PA	9/8/81
Thomas, Marlo	Deerfield, MI	11/21/37
Thomas, Michael Tilson	Hollywood, CA	12/21/44
Thomas, Philip Michael	Columbus, OH	5/26/49
Thomas, Richard	New York, NY	6/13/51
Thomas, Sean Patrick	Wilmington, DE	12/17/70
Thompson, Emma	London, England, UK	4/15/59
Thompson, Jack	Sydney, Australia	8/31/40
Thompson, Lea	Rochester, MN	5/31/61
Thorne-Smith, Courtney	San Francisco, CA	11/8/67
Thornton, Billy Bob	Hot Springs, AR	8/4/55
Thurman, Uma	Boston, MA	4/29/70
Tiegs, Cheryl	Breckenridge, MN	9/25/47
Tierney, Maura	Boston, MA	2/3/65
Tillis, Mel	Tampa, FL	8/8/32
Tilly, Jennifer	Harbor City, CA	9/16/58
Tilly, Meg	Long Beach, CA	2/14/60
Timberlake, Justin	Memphis, TN	1/31/81
Tisdale, Ashley	West Deal, NJ	7/2/85
Tomei, Marisa	Brooklyn, NY	12/4/64
Tomlin, Lily	Detroit, MI	9/1/39
Tork, Peter	Washington, DC	2/13/42
Torn, Rip	Temple, TX	2/6/31
Townsend, Robert	Chicago, IL	2/6/57
Townshend, Peter	Chiswick, England, UK	5/19/45
Travanti, Daniel J.	Kenosha, WI	3/7/40
Travis, Nancy	Astoria, Queens, NY	9/21/61
Travis, Randy	Marshville, NC	5/4/59
Travolta, John	Englewood, NJ	2/18/54
Trebek, Alex	Sudbury, ON, Canada	7/22/40
Tripplehorn, Jean	Tulsa, OK	6/10/63
Tritt, Travis	Marietta, GA	2/9/63
Tucci, Stanley	Katonah, NY	1/11/60
Tucker, Chris	Decatur, GA	8/31/72
Tucker, Michael	Baltimore, MD	2/6/44
Tucker, Tanya	Seminole, TX	10/10/58
Tune, Tommy	Wichita Falls, TX	2/28/39

Name	Birthplace	Birthdate
Turlington, Christy	Walnut Creek, CA	1/2/69
Turner, Janine	Lincoln, NE	12/6/62
Turner, Kathleen	Springfield, MO	6/19/54
Turner, Tina	Brownsville, TN	11/26/39
Turturro, John	Brooklyn, NY	2/28/57
Twain, Shania	Windsor, ON, Canada	8/28/65
Twiggy (Lawson)	London, England, UK	9/19/49
Tyler, Liv	New York, NY	7/1/77
Tyler, Steven	Yonkers, NY	3/26/48
Tyson, Cicely	New York, NY	12/19/33
Uecker, Bob	Milwaukee, WI	1/26/35
Uggams, Leslie	New York, NY	5/25/43
Ullman, Tracey	Slough, England, UK	12/30/59
Ullmann, Liv	Tokyo, Japan	12/16/38
Ulrich, Skeet	Lynchburg, VA	1/20/70
Underwood, Blair	Tacoma, WA	8/25/64
Underwood, Carrie	Checotah, OK	3/10/83
Urban, Keith	Whangarei, North Island, New Zealand	10/26/67
Urie, Michael	Dallas, TX	8/8/80
Usher (Raymond IV)	Chattanooga, TN	10/14/78
Vaccaro, Brenda	Brooklyn, NY	11/18/39
Vale, Jerry	Bronx, NY	7/8/32
Valente, Caterina	Paris, France	1/14/31
Valley, Mark	Ogdensburg, NY	12/24/64
Valli, Frankie	Newark, NJ	5/3/37
Van Ark, Joan	New York, NY	6/16/43
Van Damme, Jean-Claude	Brussels, Belgium	10/18/60
Van Der Beek, James	Cheshire, CT	3/8/77
Van Doren, Mamie	Rowena, SD	2/6/31
Van Dyke, Dick	West Plains, MO	12/13/25
Van Dyke, Jerry	Danville, IL	7/27/31
Van Halen, Eddie	Nijmegen, Netherlands	1/26/55
Van Patten, Dick	Kew Gardens, Queens, NY	12/9/28
Van Peebles, Mario	Mexico City, Mexico	1/15/57
Van Sant, Gus	Louisville, KY	7/24/52
Van Zandt, Steven	Winthrop, MA	11/22/50
VanCamp, Emily	Port Perry, ON, Canada	5/12/86
Vance, Courtney B.	Detroit, MI	3/12/60
Vardalos, Nia	Winnipeg, MB, Canada	9/24/62
Vaughn, Robert	New York, NY	11/22/32
Vaughn, Vince	Minneapolis, MN	3/28/70
Vedder, Eddie	Evanston, IL	12/23/64
Vega, Alexa	Miami, FL	8/27/88
Ventimiglia, Milo	Anaheim, CA	7/8/77
Vereen, Ben	Miami, FL	10/10/46
Vergara, Sofia	Barranquilla, Colombia	7/10/72
Vickers, Jon	Prince Albert, SK, Canada	10/29/26
Vieira, Meredith	Providence, RI	12/30/53
Vigoda, Abe	New York, NY	2/24/21
Vincent, Jan-Michael	Denver, CO	7/15/44
Vinton, Bobby	Canonsburg, PA.	4/16/35
Visnjic, Goran	Sibenik, Yugo. (Croatia)	9/9/72
Vitale, Dick	East Rutherford, NJ	6/9/39
Voight, Jon	Yonkers, NY	12/29/38
Von Stade, Frederica	Somerville, NJ	6/1/45
Von Sydow, Max	Lund, Sweden	4/10/29
Von Trier, Lars	Copenhagen, Denmark	4/30/56
Wagner, Jack	Washington, MO	10/3/59
Wagner, Lindsay	Los Angeles, CA	6/22/49
Wagner, Robert	Detroit, MI	2/10/30
Wahl, Ken	Chicago, IL	10/31/54
Wahlberg, Mark	Dorchester, MA	6/5/71
Wain, Bea	Bronx, NY	4/30/17
Waite, Ralph	White Plains, NY	6/22/28
Waits, Tom	Pomona, CA	12/7/49
Walden, Robert	New York, NY	9/25/43
Walken, Christopher	Astoria, Queens, NY	3/31/43
Walker, Clint	Hartford, IL	5/30/27
Wallace, Marcia	Creston, IA	11/1/42
Wallach, Eli	Brooklyn, NY	12/7/15
Walsh, Kate	San Jose, CA	10/13/67
Walter, Jessica	Brooklyn, NY	1/31/41
Ward, Fred	San Diego, CA	12/30/42
Ward, Sela	Meridian, MS	7/11/56
Ward, Simon	Kent, London, Eng., UK	10/19/41
Warfield, Marsha	Chicago, IL	3/5/54
Warner, Malcolm-Jamal	Jersey City, NJ	8/18/70
Warren, Lesley Ann	New York, NY	8/16/46
Warwick, Dionne	East Orange, NJ	12/12/40
Washington, Denzel	Mt. Vernon, NY	12/28/54
Washington, Isaiah	Houston, TX	8/3/63
Wasikowska, Mia	Canberra, Australia	10/14/89
Watanabe, Ken	Koide, Niigata, Japan	10/21/59
Waters, John	Baltimore, MD	4/22/46
Waters, Roger	Great Bookham, Eng., UK	9/6/43
Waterston, Sam	Cambridge, MA	11/15/40
Watson, Emily	London, England, UK	1/14/67
Watson, Emma	Paris, France	4/15/90
Watts, Andre	Nuremberg, Germany	6/20/46
Watts, Naomi	Shoreham, England, UK	9/28/68
Wayans, Damon	New York, NY	9/4/60
Wayans, Keenen Ivory	Brooklyn, NY	6/8/58
Wayans, Marlon	New York, NY	7/23/72
Wayans, Shawn	New York, NY	1/19/71
Weathers, Carl	New Orleans, LA	1/14/48

Name	Birthplace	Birthdate
Weaver, Fritz	Pittsburgh, PA	1/19/26
Weaver, Sigourney	New York, NY	10/8/49
Weiland, Scott	Santa Cruz, CA	10/27/67
Weir, Peter	Sydney, Australia	8/21/44
Weisz, Rachel	London, England, UK	3/7/71
Weitz, Bruce	Norwalk, CT	5/27/43
Welch, Raquel	Chicago, IL	9/5/40
Weld, Tuesday	New York, NY	8/27/43
Weller, Peter	Stevens Point, WI	6/24/47
Welling, Tom	Putnam Valley, NY	4/26/77
Wendt, George	Chicago, IL	10/17/48
Wentz, Pete	Wilmette, IL	6/5/79
West, Adam	Walla Walla, WA	9/19/28
West, Kanye	Atlanta, GA	6/8/77
West, Shane	Baton Rouge, LA	6/10/78
Wettig, Patricia	Cincinnati, OH	12/4/51
Whalley, Joanne	Manchester, England, UK	8/25/64
Wheaton, Wil	Burbank, CA	7/29/72
Whitaker, Forest	Longview, TX	7/15/61
White, Betty	Oak Park, IL	1/17/22
White, Jack	Detroit, MI	7/9/75
White, Jaleel	Pasadena, CA	11/27/76
White, Vanna	N. Myrtle Beach, SC	2/18/57
Whitford, Bradley	Madison, WI	10/10/59
Whitman, Stuart	San Francisco, CA	2/1/28
Wiest, Dianne	Kansas City, MO	3/28/48
Wiig, Kristen	Canandaigua, NY	8/22/73
Wilde, Olivia	New York, NY	3/10/84
Wilder, Gene	Milwaukee, WI	6/11/33
Wilkinson, Tom	Leeds, England, UK	12/12/48
Williams, Armstrong	Marion, SC	2/5/59
Williams, Barry	Santa Monica, CA	9/30/54
Williams, Billy Dee	New York, NY	4/6/37
Williams, Cindy	Van Nuys, CA	8/22/47
Williams, Esther	Los Angeles, CA	8/8/21
Williams, Hal	Columbus, OH	12/14/38
Williams, Hank, Jr.	Shreveport, LA	5/26/49
Williams, JoBeth	Houston, TX	12/6/48
Williams, Kimberly	Rye, NY	9/14/71
Williams, Lucinda	Lake Charles, LA	1/26/53
Williams, Michelle	Kalispell, MT	9/9/80
Williams, Montel	Baltimore, MD	7/3/56
Williams, Paul	Omaha, NE	9/19/40
Williams, Robin	Chicago, IL	7/21/51
Williams, Treat	Rowayton, CT	12/1/51
Williams, Vanessa	Millwood, NY	3/18/63
Williamson, Kevin	New Bern, NC	3/14/65
Williamson, Nicol	Hamilton, Scotland, UK	9/14/38
Willis, Bruce	Idar-Oberstein, W. Ger.	3/19/55
Wilson, Brian	Inglewood, CA	6/20/42
Wilson, Cassandra	Jackson, MS	12/4/55
Wilson, Chandra	Houston, TX	8/27/69
Wilson, Demond	Valdosta, GA	10/13/46
Wilson, Elizabeth	Grand Rapids, MI	4/4/21
Wilson, Luke	Dallas, TX	9/21/71
Wilson, Nancy	Chillicothe, OH	2/20/37
Wilson, Owen	Dallas, TX	11/18/68
Wilson, Rainn	Seattle, WA	1/20/66
Winfrey, Oprah	Kosciusko, MS	1/29/54
Winger, Debra	Cleveland, OH	5/16/55
Winkler, Henry	New York, NY	10/30/45
Winningham, Mare	Phoenix, AZ	5/16/59
Winokur, Marissa Jaret	New York, NY	2/2/73
Winslet, Kate	Reading, England, UK	10/5/75
Winter, Johnny	Beaumont, TX	2/23/44
Winters, Jonathan	Dayton, OH	11/11/25
Winwood, Steve	Birmingham, England, UK	5/12/48
Withers, Jane	Atlanta, GA	4/12/26
Witherspoon, Reese	New Orleans, LA	3/22/76
Witt, Alicia	Worcester, MA	8/21/75
Wolf, Scott	Boston, MA	6/4/68
Wonder, Stevie	Saginaw, MI	5/13/50
Wong, Faye	Beijing, China	8/8/69
Woo, John	Guangzhou, China	5/1/46
Wood, Elijah	Cedar Rapids, IA	1/28/81
Woodard, Alfre	Tulsa, OK	11/8/53
Woods, James	Vernal, UT	4/18/47
Woodward, Joanne	Thomasville, GA	2/27/30
Wopat, Tom	Lodi, WI	9/9/51
Worthington Sam	Godalming, Surrey, Eng., UK	8/2/76
Wright, Jeffrey	Washington, DC	12/7/65
Wright, Max	Detroit, MI	8/2/43
Wright, Robin	Dallas, TX	4/8/66
Wright, Steven	New York, NY	12/6/55
Wyle, Noah	Hollywood, CA	6/4/71
Wyman, Bill	London, England, UK	10/24/36
Yankovic, Weird Al	Lynwood, CA	10/23/59
Yanni (Chrysomallis)	Kalamata, Greece	11/14/54
Yarrow, Peter	New York, NY	5/31/38
Yearwood, Trisha	Monticello, GA	9/19/64
Yoakam, Dwight	Pikesville, KY	10/23/56
York, Michael	Fulmer, England, UK	3/27/42
Young, Alan	North Shields, England, UK	11/19/19
Young, Burt	New York, NY	4/30/40
Young, Neil	Toronto, ON, Canada	11/12/45

Name	Birthplace	Birthdate	Name	Birthplace	Birthdate
Young, Sean	Louisville, KY	11/20/59	Zimbalist, Efrem, Jr.	New York, NY	11/30/18
Zane, Billy	Chicago, IL	2/24/66	Zimbalist, Stephanie	New York, NY	10/8/56
Zeffirelli, Franco	Florence, Italy	2/12/23	Zimmer, Kim	Grand Rapids, MI	2/2/55
Zellweger, Renée	Katy, TX	4/25/69	Zhang, Ziyi	Beijing, China	2/9/79
Zemeckis, Robert	Chicago, IL	5/14/52	Zukerman, Pinchas	Tel Aviv, Israel	7/16/48
Zerbe, Anthony	Long Beach, CA	5/20/36	Zuniga, Daphne	Berkeley, CA	10/28/62
Zeta-Jones, Catherine	Swansea, Wales, UK	9/25/69			

Entertainment Personalities of the Past

See also other lists for some deceased entertainers not included here.

Name	Born	Died	Name	Born	Died	Name	Born	Died
Aaliyah	1979	2001	Bates, Alan	1934	2003	Bridges, Lloyd	1913	1998
Abbott, Bud	1895	1974	Bavier, Francis	1902	1989	Broderick, Helen	1891	1959
Abbott, George	1887	1995	Baxter, Anne	1923	1985	Bronson, Charles	1921	2003
Acuff, Roy	1903	1992	Baxter, Warner	1889	1951	Brooks, Foster	1912	2001
Adams, Don	1923	2005	Beaumont, Hugh	1909	1982	Brooks, Louise	1906	1985
Adams, Edie	1927	2008	Beavers, Louise	1902	1962	Brown, Clarence	1890	1987
Adams, Joey	1911	1999	Beery, Noah, Jr.	1913	1994	Brown, James	1933	2006
Adams, Maude	1872	1953	Beery, Noah, Sr.	1884	1946	Brown, Joe E.	1892	1973
Adler, Jacob P.	1855	1926	Beery, Wallace	1885	1949	Brown, Les	1912	2001
Adoree, Renee	1898	1933	Begley, Ed	1901	1970	Browne, Roscoe Lee	1925	2007
Agar, John	1921	2002	Bel Geddes, Barbara	1922	2005	Bruce, Lenny	1925	1966
Aherne, Brian	1902	1986	Bellamy, Ralph	1904	1991	Bruce, Nigel	1895	1953
Ailey, Alvin	1931	1989	Belushi, John	1949	1982	Bruce, Virginia	1910	1982
Akins, Claude	1918	1994	Benaderet, Bea	1906	1968	Brynner, Yul	1915	1985
Albert, Eddie	1906	2005	Bendix, William	1906	1964	Buchanan, Edgar	1903	1979
Albertson, Frank	1909	1964	Bennett, Constance	1904	1965	Buchholz, Horst	1933	2003
Albertson, Jack	1907	1981	Bennett, Joan	1910	1990	Buñuel, Luis	1900	1983
Alda, Robert	1914	1986	Bennett, Michael	1943	1987	Buono, Victor	1938	1982
Allen, Fred	1894	1956	Benny, Jack	1894	1974	Burke, Billie	1885	1970
Allen, Gracie	1906	1964	Berg, Gertrude	1899	1966	Burnette, Smiley	1911	1967
Allen, Mel	1913	1996	Bergen, Edgar	1903	1978	Burns, George	1896	1996
Allen, Peter	1944	1992	Bergman, Ingmar	1918	2007	Burr, Raymond	1917	1993
Allen, Steve	1921	2000	Bergman, Ingrid	1915	1982	Burton, Richard	1925	1984
Allgood, Sara	1883	1950	Berkeley, Busby	1895	1976	Busch, Mae	1897	1946
Allyson, June	1917	2006	Berle, Milton	1908	2002	Bushman, Francis X.	1883	1966
Altman, Robert	1925	2006	Berlin, Irving	1888	1989	Buttons, Red	1919	2006
Ameche, Don	1908	1993	Bernardi, Herschel	1923	1986	Byington, Spring	1893	1971
Ames, Leon	1903	1993	Bernhardt, Sarah	1844	1923	Cabot, Bruce	1904	1972
Amsterdam, Morey	1908	1996	Bernstein, Leonard	1918	1990	Cabot, Sebastian	1918	1977
Anderson, G. M. "Bronco Billy"	1882	1971	Berry, Jan	1941	2004	Cagney, James	1899	1986
Anderson, Judith	1897	1992	Bessell, Ted	1939	1996	Caldwell, Sarah	1924	2006
Anderson, Marian	1897	1993	Bickford, Charles	1889	1967	Calhern, Louis	1895	1956
Andre the Giant	1946	1993	Big Bopper, The	1930	1959	Calhoun, Rory	1922	1999
Andrews, Dana	1909	1992	Billingsley, Barbara	1915	2010	Callas, Charlie	1927	2011
Andrews, Laverne	1913	1967	Bing, Rudolf	1902	1997	Callas, Maria	1923	1977
Andrews, Maxene	1916	1995	Bishop, Joey	1918	2007	Calloway, Cab	1907	1994
Angeli, Pier	1932	1971	Bitzer, Billy	1872	1944	Cambridge, Godfrey	1933	1976
Antonioni, Michelangelo	1912	2007	Bixby, Bill	1934	1993	Campbell, Mrs. Patrick	1865	1940
Arbuckle, Fatty (Roscoe)	1887	1933	Blackstone, Harry, Jr.	1934	1997	Candy, John	1950	1994
Archerd, Army	1922	2009	Blackstone, Harry, Sr.	1885	1965	Cantinflas	1911	1993
Arden, Eve	1908	1990	Blaine, Vivian	1921	1995	Cantor, Eddie	1892	1964
Arlen, Richard	1900	1976	Blake, Amanda	1931	1989	Capra, Frank	1897	1991
Arliss, George	1868	1946	Blake, Eubie	1883	1983	Carey, Harry	1878	1947
Armstrong, Louis	1901	1971	Blanc, Mel	1908	1989	Carey, Macdonald	1913	1994
Arnaz, Desi	1917	1986	Blocker, Dan	1928	1972	Carle, Frankie	1903	2001
Arness, James	1923	2011	Blondell, Joan	1909	1979	Carlin, George	1937	2008
Arnold, Eddy	1918	2008	Blondin, Charles	1824	1897	Carlisle Hart, Kitty	1910	2007
Arnold, Edward	1890	1956	Blore, Eric	1887	1959	Carney, Art	1918	2003
Arquette, Cliff	1905	1974	Blue, Ben	1901	1975	Carpenter, Karen	1950	1983
Arthur, Beatrice	1922	2009	Blyden, Larry	1925	1975	Carradine, David	1936	2009
Arthur, Jean	1900	1991	Bogarde, Dirk	1921	1999	Carradine, John	1906	1988
Ashcroft, Peggy	1907	1991	Bogart, Humphrey	1899	1957	Carrillo, Leo	1880	1961
Astaire, Fred	1899	1987	Boland, Mary	1880	1965	Carroll, Leo G.	1892	1972
Astor, Mary	1906	1987	Boles, John	1895	1969	Carroll, Madeleine	1906	1987
Atkins, Chet	1924	2001	Bolger, Ray	1904	1987	Carson, Jack	1910	1963
Atwill, Lionel	1885	1946	Bond, Ward	1903	1960	Carson, Johnny	1925	2005
Auer, Mischa	1905	1967	Bondi, Beulah	1888	1981	Carter, Benny	1907	2003
Aumont, Jean-Pierre	1911	2001	Bono, Sonny	1935	1998	Carter, Dixie	1939	2010
Austin, Gene	1900	1972	Boone, Richard	1917	1981	Carter, Nell	1948	2003
Autry, Gene	1907	1998	Booth, Edwin	1833	1893	Caruso, Enrico	1873	1921
Axton, Hoyt	1938	1999	Booth, John Wilkes	1838	1865	Casals, Pablo	1876	1973
Ayres, Lew	1908	1996	Booth, Junius Brutus	1796	1852	Cash, Johnny	1932	2003
Backus, Jim	1913	1989	Booth, Shirley	1898	1992	Cash, June Carter	1929	2003
Bailey, Pearl	1918	1990	Borge, Victor	1909	2000	Cass, Peggy	1924	1999
Bainter, Fay	1892	1968	Borgnine, Ernest	1917	2012	Cassavetes, John	1929	1989
Baker, Josephine	1906	1975	Borzage, Frank	1893	1962	Cassidy, Jack	1927	1976
Balanchine, George	1904	1983	Bosley, Tom	1927	2010	Castle, Irene	1893	1969
Ball, Lucille	1911	1989	Bow, Clara	1905	1965	Castle, Vernon	1887	1918
Balsam, Martin	1919	1996	Bowes, Maj. Edward	1874	1946	Chaliapin, Feodor	1873	1938
Bancroft, Anne	1931	2005	Bowman, Lee	1914	1979	Champion, Gower	1919	1980
Bankhead, Tallulah	1902	1968	Boxcar Willie	1931	1999	Chandler, Jeff	1918	1961
Bara, Theda	1885?	1955	Boyd, Stephen	1928	1977	Chaney, Lon	1883	1930
Barnett, Etta Moten	1902	2004	Boyd, William	1898	1972	Chaney, Lon, Jr.	1905	1973
Barnum, Phineas T.	1810	1891	Boyer, Charles	1899	1978	Chapin, Harry	1942	1981
Barrett, Syd	1946	2006	Boyle, Peter	1935	2006	Chaplin, Charles	1889	1977
Barry, Gene	1919	2009	Bracken, Eddie	1915	2002	Chapman, Graham	1941	1989
Barrymore, Ethel	1879	1959	Brady, Alice	1892	1939	Charisse, Cyd	1921	2008
Barrymore, John	1882	1942	Brando, Marlon	1924	2004	Charles, Ray	1930	2004
Barrymore, Lionel	1878	1954	Branigan, Laura	1957	2004	Chase, Ilka	1905	1978
Barrymore, Maurice	1848	1905	Brazzi, Rossano	1916	1994	Chatterton, Ruth	1893	1961
Barthelmess, Richard	1895	1963	Brennan, Walter	1894	1974	Cherrill, Virginia	1908	1996
Bartholomew, Freddie	1924	1992	Brent, George	1904	1979	Chevalier, Maurice	1888	1972
Barty, Billy	1924	2000	Brett, Jeremy	1935	1995	Child, Julia	1912	2004
Basehart, Richard	1914	1984	Brewer, Teresa	1931	2007	Clair, René	1898	1981
Basie, Count	1904	1984	Brice, Fanny	1891	1951	Clark, Dick	1929	2012

Name	Born	Died
Clayburgh, Jill	1944	2010
Clayton, Jan	1917	1983
Clemons, Clarence	1942	2011
Clift, Montgomery	1920	1966
Cline, Patsy	1932	1963
Clooney, Rosemary	1928	2002
Clyde, Andy	1892	1967
Cobain, Kurt	1967	1994
Cobb, Lee J.	1911	1976
Coburn, Charles	1877	1961
Coburn, James	1928	2002
Coca, Imogene	1908	2001
Coco, James	1930	1987
Cody, Buffalo Bill	1846	1917
Cody, Iron Eyes	1907	1999
Cohan, George M.	1878	1942
Cohen, Myron	1902	1986
Colbert, Claudette	1903	1996
Cole, Nat "King"	1919	1965
Coleman, Gary	1968	2010
Collins, Gary	1938	2012
Collins, Ray	1890	1965
Colman, Ronald	1891	1958
Columbo, Russ	1908	1934
Comden, Betty	1917	2006
Como, Perry	1912	2001
Conniff, Ray	1916	2002
Connors, Chuck	1921	1992
Conrad, William	1920	1994
Conried, Hans	1917	1982
Conte, Richard	1911	1975
Convy, Bert	1933	1991
Conway, Tom	1904	1967
Coogan, Jackie	1914	1984
Cook, Elisha, Jr.	1904	1995
Cooke, Alistair	1908	2004
Cooke, Sam	1931	1964
Cooper, Gary	1901	1961
Cooper, Gladys	1888	1971
Cooper, Jackie	1922	2011
Cooper, Melville	1896	1973
Copland, Aaron	1900	1990
Corby, Ellen	1913	1999
Corelli, Franco	1921	2003
Corey, Jeff	1914	2002
Corio, Ann	1914	1999
Corley, Pat	1930	2006
Cornelius, Don	1936	2012
Cornell, Katharine	1893	1974
Correll, Charles ("Andy")	1890	1972
Costello, Dolores	1905	1979
Costello, Lou	1906	1959
Cotten, Joseph	1905	1994
Coward, Noel	1899	1973
Cox, Wally	1924	1973
Crabbe, Buster	1908	1983
Crain, Jeanne	1925	2003
Crane, Bob	1928	1978
Crawford, Broderick	1911	1986
Crawford, Joan	1904	1977
Crenna, Richard	1926	2003
Crews, Laura Hope	1880	1942
Crisp, Donald	1880	1974
Crisp, Quentin	1908	1999
Croce, Jim	1942	1973
Cronyn, Hume	1911	2003
Crosby, Bing	1903	1977
Crothers, Scatman	1910	1986
Cruz, Celia	1925	2003
Cugat, Xavier	1900	1990
Cukor, George	1899	1983
Cullen, Bill	1920	1990
Culp, Robert	1930	2010
Cummings, Constance	1910	2005
Cummings, Robert	1908	1990
Curtis, Ken	1916	1991
Curtis, Tony	1925	2010
Curtiz, Michael	1888	1962
Cushing, Peter	1913	1994
Dailey, Dan	1915	1978
Dandridge, Dorothy	1923	1965
Dangerfield, Rodney	1921	2004
Daniell, Henry	1894	1963
Daniels, Bebe	1901	1971
Darin, Bobby	1936	1973
Darnell, Linda	1923	1965
Darwell, Jane	1879	1967
Da Silva, Howard	1909	1986
Davenport, Harry	1866	1949
Davies, Marion	1897	1961
Davis, Bette	1908	1989
Davis, Joan	1907	1961
Davis, Ossie	1917	2005
Davis, Sammy, Jr.	1925	1990
Dawson, Richard	1932	2012
Day, Dennis	1917	1988
Day, Laraine	1920	2007
Dean, James	1931	1955
Dean, Jimmy	1928	2010
Dearie, Blossom	1924	2009
De Carlo, Yvonne	1922	2007
Dee, Frances	1907	2004
Dee, Sandra	1942	2005
Defore, Don	1917	1993
Dekker, Albert	1905	1968
De Laurentiis, Dino	1919	2010
Del Rio, Dolores	1905	1983
DeLuise, Dom	1933	2009
Demarest, William	1892	1983
de Mille, Agnes	1905	1993
De Mille, Cecil B.	1881	1959
Dennis, Sandy	1937	1992
Denny, Reginald	1891	1967
Denver, Bob	1935	2005
Denver, John	1943	1997
Derek, John	1926	1998
DeSica, Vittorio	1901	1974
Devine, Andy	1905	1977
Dewhurst, Colleen	1924	1991
De Wilde, Brandon	1942	1972
De Wolfe, Billy	1907	1974
Diamond, Selma	1920	1985
Diddley, Bo	1928	2008
Dietrich, Marlene	1901	1992
Diller, Phyllis	1917	2012
Disney, Walt	1901	1966
Dix, Richard	1894	1949
Dmytryk, Edward	1908	1999
Donahue, Troy	1936	2001
Donat, Robert	1905	1958
Donlevy, Brian	1901	1972
Dors, Diana	1931	1984
Dorsey, Jimmy	1904	1957
Dorsey, Tommy	1905	1956
Douglas, Melvyn	1901	1981
Douglas, Paul	1907	1959
Dove, Billie	1900	1998
Downey, Morton, Jr.	1933	2001
Doyle, David	1929	1997
Drake, Alfred	1914	1992
Draper, Ruth	1884	1956
Dressler, Marie	1869	1934
Drew, Ellen	1915	2003
Drew, Mrs. John	1820	1897
Dru, Joanne	1923	1996
Duchin, Eddy	1909	1951
Duff, Howard	1917	1990
Duggan, Andrew	1923	1988
Dumbrille, Douglass	1890	1974
Dumont, Margaret	1889	1965
Duncan, Isadora	1878	1927
Duncan, Michael Clarke	1957	2012
Dunham, Katherine	1910	2006
Dunn, James	1905	1967
Dunne, Irene	1898	1990
Dunnock, Mildred	1901	1991
Durante, Jimmy	1893	1980
Duryea, Dan	1907	1968
Duse, Eleanora	1858	1924
Dvorak, Ann	1912	1979
Eagels, Jeanne	1894	1929
Ebsen, Buddy	1908	2003
Eckstine, Billy	1914	1993
Eddington, Paul	1927	1995
Eddy, Nelson	1901	1967
Edelman, Herb	1933	1996
Edwards, Blake	1922	2010
Edwards, Cliff	1895	1971
Edwards, Ralph	1913	2005
Edwards, Vince	1928	1996
Egan, Richard	1923	1987
Eisenstein, Sergei	1898	1948
Elam, Jack	1916	2003
Ellington, Duke	1899	1974
Elliot, Cass	1941	1974
Elliott, Denholm	1922	1992
Ellis, Mary	1897	2003
Elman, Mischa	1891	1967
Ephron, Nora	1941	2012
Errol, Leon	1881	1951
Evans, Dale	1912	2001
Evans, Edith	1888	1976
Evans, Maurice	1901	1989
Everett, Chad	1936?	2012
Ewell, Tom	1909	1994
Fadiman, Clifton	1904	1999
Fairbanks, Douglas	1883	1939
Fairbanks, Douglas, Jr.	1909	2000
Falk, Peter	1927	2011
Farentino, James	1938	2012
Farley, Chris	1964	1997
Farmer, Frances	1913	1970
Farnsworth, Richard	1920	2000
Farnum, Dustin	1874	1929
Farnum, William	1876	1953
Farrar, Geraldine	1882	1967
Farrell, Charles	1901	1990
Farrell, Eileen	1920	2002
Fassbinder, Rainer Werner	1946	1982
Fawcett, Farrah	1947	2009
Faye, Alice	1915	1998
Fazenda, Louise	1895	1962
Feld, Fritz	1900	1993
Feldman, Marty	1933	1982
Fell, Norman	1924	1998
Fellini, Federico	1920	1993
Fenneman, George	1919	1997
Ferrer, Jose	1912	1992
Ferrer, Mel	1917	2008
Fetchit, Stepin	1898	1985
Fiedler, Arthur	1894	1979
Fiedler, John	1925	2005
Fields, Gracie	1898	1979
Fields, Totie	1930	1978
Fields, W. C.	1879	1946
Finch, Peter	1916	1977
Fine, Larry	1902	1975
Firkusny, Rudolf	1912	1994
Fisher, Eddie	1928	2010
Fiske, Minnie Maddern	1865	1932
Fitzgerald, Barry	1888	1961
Fitzgerald, Ella	1917	1996
Fitzgerald, Geraldine	1913	2005
Flagstad, Kirsten	1895	1962
Fleischer, Richard	1916	2006
Fleming, Art	1924	1995
Fleming, Victor	1889	1949
Flynn, Errol	1909	1959
Flynn, Joe	1925	1974
Foch, Nina	1924	2008
Fogelberg, Dan	1951	2007
Foley, Red	1910	1968
Fonda, Henry	1905	1982
Fontaine, Frank	1920	1978
Fontanne, Lynn	1887	1983
Fonteyn, Margot	1919	1991
Ford, Glenn	1916	2006
Ford, John	1895	1973
Ford, Paul	1901	1976
Ford, Tennessee Ernie	1919	1991
Forrest, Helen	1917	1999
Forsythe, John	1918	2010
Fosse, Bob	1927	1987
Foster, Phil	1914	1985
Foster, Preston	1901	1970
Foxx, Redd	1922	1991
Foy, Eddie	1856	1928
Franchi, Sergio	1926	1990
Franciosa, Anthony	1928	2006
Francis, Anne	1930	2011
Francis, Arlene	1907	2001
Francis, Kay	1905	1968
Franciscus, James	1934	1991
Frankenheimer, John	1930	2002
Frann, Mary	1943	1998
Frawley, William	1887	1966
Frederick, Pauline	1885	1938
Freed, Alan	1921	1965
Freeman, Al, Jr.	1934	2012
French, Victor	1934	1989
Friganza, Trixie	1870	1955
Froman, Jane	1907	1980
Funt, Allen	1914	1999
Furness, Betty	1916	1994
Gabin, Jean	1904	1976
Gable, Clark	1901	1960
Gabor, Eva	1920	1995
Garbo, Greta	1905	1990
Garcia, Jerry	1942	1995
Gardenia, Vincent	1922	1992
Gardner, Ava	1922	1990
Garfield, John	1913	1952
Garland, Beverly	1926	2008
Garland, Judy	1922	1969
Garrett, Betty	1919	2011
Garson, Greer	1904	1996
Gassman, Vittorio	1922	2000
Gaye, Marvin	1939	1984
Gaynor, Janet	1906	1984
Gazzara, Ben	1930	2012
Gebel-Williams, Gunther	1934	2001
Geer, Will	1902	1978
George, Gladys	1904	1954
Gershwin, George	1898	1937
Getty, Estelle	1923	2008
Ghostley, Alice	1926	2007
Gibb, Andy	1958	1988
Gibb, Maurice	1949	2003

Name	Born	Died	Name	Born	Died	Name	Born	Died
Gibb, Robin	1949	2012	Hayes, Gabby	1885	1969	Jackson, Michael	1958	2009
Gibson, Henry	1935	2009	Hayes, Helen	1900	1993	Jackson, Milt	1923	1999
Gibson, Hoot	1892	1962	Hayes, Isaac	1942	2008	Jaeckel, Richard	1926	1997
Gielgud, John	1904	2000	Hayward, Leland	1902	1971	Jaffe, Sam	1891	1984
Gilbert, Billy	1894	1971	Hayward, Louis	1909	1985	Jagger, Dean	1903	1991
Gilbert, John	1895	1936	Hayward, Susan	1917	1975	Jam Master Jay	1965	2002
Gilford, Jack	1907	1990	Hayworth, Rita	1918	1987	James, Dennis	1917	1997
Gillespie, Dizzy	1917	1993	Head, Edith	1897	1981	James, Etta	1938	2012
Gillette, William	1853	1937	Healy, Ted	1896	1937	James, Harry	1916	1983
Gingold, Hermione	1897	1987	Heckart, Eileen	1919	2001	James, Rick	1948	2004
Gish, Dorothy	1898	1968	Heflin, Van	1910	1971	Janis, Elsie	1889	1956
Gish, Lillian	1893	1993	Heifetz, Jascha	1901	1987	Jannings, Emil	1886	1950
Giulini, Carlo Maria	1914	2005	Held, Anna	1873	1918	Janssen, David	1930	1980
Gleason, Jackie	1916	1987	Helm, Levon	1940	2012	Jenkins, Allen	1900	1974
Gleason, James	1886	1959	Hemingway, Margaux	1955	1996	Jennings, Waylon	1937	2002
Gluck, Alma	1884	1938	Hemmings, David	1941	2003	Jessel, George	1898	1981
Gobel, George	1919	1991	Hemsley, Sherman	1938	2012	Jeter, Michael	1952	2003
Goddard, Paulette	1905?	1990	Henderson, Skitch	1918	2005	Johnson, Ben	1918	1996
Godfrey, Arthur	1903	1983	Hendrix, Jimi	1942	1970	Johnson, Celia	1908	1982
Godunov, Alexander	1949	1995	Henie, Sonja	1912	1969	Johnson, Chic	1892	1962
Goldwyn, Samuel	1882	1974	Henreid, Paul	1908	1992	Johnson, J.J.	1924	2001
Goodman, Benny	1909	1986	Henson, Jim	1936	1990	Johnson, Robert	1911	1938
Gorcey, Leo	1917	1969	Hepburn, Audrey	1929	1993	Johnson, Van	1916	2008
Gordon, Gale	1906	1995	Hepburn, Katharine	1907	2003	Jolson, Al	1886	1950
Gordon, Ruth	1896	1985	Hersholt, Jean	1886	1956	Jones, Brian	1942	1969
Gorshin, Frank	1934	2005	Heston, Charlton	1923	2008	Jones, Buck	1889	1942
Gosden, Freeman ("Amos")	1899	1982	Hewett, Christopher	1922	2001	Jones, Carolyn	1933	1983
Gottschalk, Louis	1829	1869	Hickey, William	1928	1997	Jones, Charlie	1930	2008
Gould, Glenn	1932	1982	Hickson, Joan	1906	1998	Jones, Davy	1945	2012
Gould, Harold	1923	2010	Hildegarde	1906	2005	Jones, Elvin	1927	2004
Gould, Morton	1913	1996	Hill, Arthur	1922	2006	Jones, Henry	1912	1999
Goulet, Robert	1933	2007	Hill, Benny	1925	1992	Jones, Jennifer	1919	2009
Grable, Betty	1916	1973	Hill, George Roy	1921	2002	Jones, Spike	1911	1965
Graham, Martha	1894	1991	Hiller, Wendy	1912	2003	Joplin, Janis	1943	1970
Graham, Virginia	1912	1998	Hines, Gregory	1946	2003	Joplin, Scott	1868	1917
Grahame, Gloria	1925	1981	Hines, Jerome	1921	2003	Jordan, Richard	1937	1993
Granger, Farley	1925	2011	Hingle, Pat	1924	2009	Jory, Victor	1902	1982
Granger, Stewart	1913	1993	Hirt, Al	1922	1999	Joslyn, Allyn	1905	1981
Grant, Cary	1904	1986	Hitchcock, Alfred	1899	1980	Julia, Raul	1940	1994
Granville, Bonita	1923	1988	Ho, Don	1930	2007	Jump, Gordon	1932	2003
Grapewin, Charley	1869	1956	Hobson, Valerie	1917	1998	Jurado, Katy	1924	2002
Graves, Peter	1926	2010	Hodiak, John	1914	1955	Jurgens, Curt	1915	1982
Gray, Dolores	1924	2002	Holden, William	1918	1981	Kahn, Madeline	1942	1999
Gray, Spalding	1941	2004	Holiday, Billie	1915	1959	Kane, Helen	1904	1966
Grayson, Kathryn	1922	2010	Holliday, Judy	1921	1965	Kanin, Garson	1912	1999
Greco, Jose	1918	2000	Holloway, Sterling	1905	1992	Karloff, Boris	1887	1969
Green, Adolph	1915	2002	Holly, Buddy	1936	1959	Karns, Roscoe	1893	1970
Greene, Lorne	1915	1987	Holm, Celeste	1919	2012	Karras, Alex	1935	2012
Greenstreet, Sydney	1879	1954	Holt, Jack	1888	1951	Kaufman, Andy	1949	1984
Greenwood, Charlotte	1890	1978	Holt, Tim	1918	1973	Kaye, Danny	1913	1987
Gregory, James	1911	2002	Homolka, Oscar	1898	1978	Kaye, Stubby	1918	1997
Griffin, Merv	1925	2007	Hooker, John Lee	1917	2001	Kazan, Elia	1909	2003
Griffith, Andy	1926	2012	Hoon, Shannon	1967	1995	Kean, Charles	1811	1868
Griffith, David Wark	1874	1948	Hope, Bob	1903	2003	Kean, Mrs. Charles	1806	1880
Griffith, Hugh	1912	1980	Hopkins, Miriam	1902	1972	Kean, Edmund	1787	1833
Grizzard, George	1928	2007	Hopper, Dennis	1936	2010	Keaton, Buster	1895	1966
Guardino, Harry	1925	1995	Hopper, DeWolf	1858	1935	Keel, Howard	1919	2004
Guinness, Sir Alec	1914	2000	Hopper, Hedda	1885	1966	Keeler, Ruby	1910	1993
Guthrie, Woody	1912	1967	Hopper, William	1915	1970	Keeshan, Bob (Captain		
Gwenn, Edmund	1875	1959	Horowitz, Vladimir	1904	1989	Kangaroo)	1927	2004
Gwynne, Fred	1926	1993	Horne, Lena	1917	2010	Keith, Brian	1921	1997
Hackett, Buddy	1924	2003	Horton, Edward Everett	1886	1970	Kellaway, Cecil	1893	1973
Hackett, Joan	1934	1983	Houdini, Harry	1874	1926	Kelley, DeForest	1920	1999
Hagen, Uta	1919	2004	Houseman, John	1902	1988	Kelly, Emmett	1898	1979
Haines, William	1900	1973	Houston, Whitney	1963	2012	Kelly, Gene	1912	1996
Hale, Alan, Jr.	1918	1990	Howard (Horwitz), Curly	1903	1952	Kelly, Grace	1929	1982
Hale, Alan, Sr.	1892	1950	Howard, Leslie	1890	1943	Kelly, Jack	1927	1992
Haley, Bill	1925	1981	Howard (Horwitz), Moe	1897	1975	Kelly, Patsy	1910	1981
Haley, Jack	1899	1979	Howard (Horwitz), Shemp	1895	1955	Kennedy, Arthur	1914	1990
Hall, Huntz	1919	1999	Howard, Trevor	1916	1988	Kennedy, Edgar	1890	1948
Hall, Jon	1915	1979	Hudson, Rock	1925	1985	Kerr, Deborah	1921	2007
Hamilton, Margaret	1902	1985	Hughes, Bernard	1915	2006	Kibbee, Guy	1886	1956
Hammerstein, Oscar	1847	1919	Hughes, John	1950	2009	Kilbride, Percy	1888	1964
Hammerstein II, Oscar	1895	1960	Hull, Henry	1890	1977	Kiley, Richard	1922	1999
Hampton, Lionel	1908	2002	Hull, Josephine	1886	1957	King, Alan	1927	2004
Hardwicke, Cedric	1893	1964	Humphrey, Doris	1895	1958	King, Henry	1896	1982
Hardy, Oliver	1892	1957	Hunter, Jeffrey	1926	1969	Kinski, Klaus	1926	1991
Harlow, Jean	1911	1937	Hunter, Kim	1922	2002	Kirby, Bruno	1949	2006
Harris, Phil	1904	1995	Hunter, Ross	1920	1996	Kirby, George	1923	1995
Harris, Richard	1930	2002	Hussey, Ruth	1911	2005	Kirby, Durward	1912	2000
Harrison, George	1943	2001	Huston, John	1906	1987	Kirsten, Dorothy	1910	1992
Harrison, Rex	1908	1990	Huston, Walter	1884	1950	Kitt, Eartha	1927	2008
Hart, William S.	1864	1946	Hutchence, Michael	1960	1997	Klemperer, Werner	1920	2000
Hartman, Phil	1948	1998	Hutton, Betty	1921	2007	Knight, Ted	1923	1986
Harvey, Laurence	1928	1973	Hutton, Jim	1934	1979	Knotts, Don	1924	2006
Harvey, Paul	1918	2009	Hyde-White, Wilfrid	1903	1991	Korman, Harvey	1927	2008
Harwell, Ernie	1918	2010	Ingram, Rex	1895	1969	Kostelanetz, Andre	1901	1980
Hatfield, Bobby	1940	2003	Ireland, Jill	1936	1990	Kovacs, Ernie	1919	1962
Haver, June	1926	2005	Ireland, John	1915	1992	Kramer, Stanley	1913	2001
Havoc, June	1912	2010	Irving, Henry	1838	1905	Kruger, Otto	1885	1974
Hawkins, Jack	1910	1973	Ives, Burl	1909	1995	Kubrick, Stanley	1928	1999
Hawkins, Screamin' Jay	1929	2000	Irwin, Steve	1962	2006	Kulp, Nancy	1921	1991
Hawks, Howard	1896	1977	Iturbi, Jose	1895	1980	Kurosawa, Akira	1910	1998
Hawthorne, Nigel	1929	2001	Jack, Wolfman	1938	1995	Kyser, Kay	1906	1985
Hayakawa, Sessue	1890	1973	Jackson, Joe	1875	1942	Ladd, Alan	1913	1964
Hayden, Sterling	1916	1986	Jackson, Mahalia	1911	1972	Lahr, Bert	1895	1967

Name	Born	Died	Name	Born	Died	Name	Born	Died
Laine, Frankie	1913	2007	MacMurray, Fred	1908	1991	Mills, Sir John	1908	2005
Lake, Arthur	1905	1987	MacRae, Gordon	1921	1986	Mineo, Sal	1939	1976
Lake, Veronica	1919	1973	Macready, George	1909	1973	Miner, Jan	1917	2004
LaLanne, Jack	1914	2011	Madison, Guy	1922	1996	Minghella, Anthony	1954	2008
Lamarr, Hedy	1913	2000	Magnani, Anna	1908	1973	Mingus, Charles	1922	1979
Lamas, Fernando	1915	1982	Mancini, Henry	1924	1994	Minnelli, Vincente	1903	1986
Lamour, Dorothy	1914	1996	Main, Marjorie	1890	1975	Miranda, Carmen	1909	1955
Lancaster, Burt	1913	1994	Malden, Karl	1912	2009	Mitchell, Cameron	1918	1994
Lanchester, Elsa	1902	1986	Malle, Louis	1932	1995	Mitchell, Thomas	1892	1962
Landis, Carole	1919	1948	Mamoulian, Rouben	1897	1987	Mitchum, Robert	1917	1997
Landis, Jessie Royce	1904	1972	Mankiewicz, Joseph	1909	1993	Mix, Tom	1880	1940
Landon, Michael	1936	1991	Mann, Herbie	1930	2003	Monica, Corbett	1930	1998
Lane, Priscilla	1917	1995	Mansfield, Jayne	1932	1967	Moffo, Anna	1932	2006
Lang, Fritz	1890	1976	Mantovani, Annunzio	1905	1980	Monroe, Marilyn	1926	1962
Langdon, Harry	1884	1944	Marais, Jean	1913	1998	Monroe, Vaughn	1911	1973
Lange, Hope	1931	2003	March, Fredric	1897	1975	Montalban, Ricardo	1920	2009
Langford, Frances	1914	2005	March, Hal	1920	1970	Montand, Yves	1921	1991
Langtry, Lillie	1853	1929	Marchand, Nancy	1928	2000	Montez, Maria	1917	1951
Lanza, Mario	1921	1959	Markova, Alicia	1910	2004	Montgomery, Elizabeth	1933	1995
LaRue, Lash (Alfred)	1917	1996	Marley, Bob	1945	1981	Montgomery, George	1916	2000
Lauder, Harry	1870	1950	Marshall, E.G.	1910	1998	Montgomery, Robert	1904	1981
Laughton, Charles	1899	1962	Marshall, Herbert	1890	1966	Moore, Clayton	1914	1999
Laurel, Stan	1890	1965	Martin, Barney	1923	2005	Moore, Colleen	1900	1988
Lawford, Peter	1923	1984	Martin, Dean	1917	1995	Moore, Dudley	1935	2002
Lawrence, Florence	1886	1938	Martin, Dick	1922	2008	Moore, Garry	1915	1993
Lawrence, Gertrude	1898	1952	Martin, Mary	1913	1990	Moore, Grace	1898	1947
Lean, David	1908	1991	Martin, Ross	1920	1981	Moorehead, Agnes	1906	1974
Ledger, Heath	1979	2008	Martin, Tony	1913	2012	Moreland, Mantan	1902	1973
Lee, Anna	1913	2004	Marvin, Lee	1924	1987	Morgan, Dennis	1910	1994
Lee, Bernard	1908	1981	Marx, Harpo (Arthur)	1888	1964	Morgan, Frank	1890	1949
Lee, Bruce	1940	1973	Marx, Zeppo (Herbert)	1901	1979	Morgan, Harry	1915	2011
Lee, Canada	1907	1952	Marx, Groucho (Julius)	1890	1977	Morgan, Helen	1900	1941
Lee, Gypsy Rose	1914	1970	Marx, Chico (Leonard)	1887	1961	Morgan, Henry	1915	1994
Lee, Peggy	1920	2002	Marx, Gummo (Milton)	1893	1977	Morita, Pat	1932	2005
LeGallienne, Eva	1899	1991	Mason, James	1909	1984	Morley, Robert	1908	1992
Lehmann, Lotte	1888	1976	Massey, Raymond	1896	1983	Morris, Chester	1901	1970
Leigh, Janet	1927	2004	Mastroianni, Marcello	1924	1996	Morris, Greg	1934	1996
Leigh, Vivien	1913	1967	Matthau, Walter	1920	2000	Morris, Howard	1919	2005
Leighton, Margaret	1922	1976	Mature, Victor	1913	1999	Morris, Wayne	1914	1959
Lemmon, Jack	1925	2001	Maxwell, Marilyn	1921	1972	Morrison, Jim	1943	1971
Lennon, John	1940	1980	Mayer, Louis B.	1885	1957	Morrow, Vic	1929	1982
Lenya, Lotte	1898	1981	Mayfield, Curtis	1942	1999	Morton, Jelly Roll	1885	1941
Leonard, Eddie	1870	1941	Mayo, Virginia	1920	2005	Mostel, Zero	1915	1977
Leonard, Sheldon	1907	1997	Mazurki, Mike	1909	1990	Mowbray, Alan	1897	1969
Leone, Sergio	1929	1989	MCA (Adam Yauch)	1964	2012	Mulhare, Edward	1923	1997
LeRoy, Mervyn	1900	1987	McCambridge, Mercedes	1916	2004	Mulligan, Gerry	1927	1996
Levant, Oscar	1906	1972	McCarey, Leo	1898	1969	Mulligan, Richard	1932	2000
Levene, Sam	1905	1980	McCarthy, Kevin	1914	2010	Muni, Paul	1895	1967
Levenson, Sam	1911	1980	McCartney, Linda	1941	1998	Munshin, Jules	1915	1970
Lewis, Al	1923	2006	McClanahan, Rue	1934	2010	Murnau, F. W.	1888	1931
Lewis, Joe E.	1902	1971	McClure, Doug	1935	1995	Murphy, Audie	1924	1971
Lewis, Shari	1934	1998	McCormack, John	1884	1945	Murphy, Brittany	1977	2009
Lewis, Ted	1892	1971	McCrary, Tex	1910	2003	Murphy, George	1902	1992
Liberace	1919	1987	McCrea, Joel	1905	1990	Murray, Arthur	1895	1991
Lillie, Beatrice	1894	1989	McDaniel, Hattie	1895	1952	Murray, Kathryn	1906	1999
Lincoln, Elmo	1889	1952	McDowall, Roddy	1928	1998	Murray, Mae	1889	1965
Lind, Jenny	1820	1887	McFarland, Spanky (George)	1928	1993	Nagel, Conrad	1897	1970
Lindfors, Viveca	1920	1995	McGoohan, Patrick	1928	2009	Naish, J. Carroll	1900	1973
Lindley, Audra	1918	1997	McGuire, Al	1931	2001	Naldi, Nita	1898	1961
Linkletter, Art	1912	2010	McGuire, Dorothy	1916	2001	Nance, Jack	1943	1996
Linville, Larry	1939	2000	McHugh, Frank	1898	1981	Natwick, Mildred	1908	1994
Little, Cleavon	1939	1992	McIntire, John	1907	1991	Nazimova, Alla	1879	1945
Llewelyn, Desmond	1914	1999	McKern, Leo	1920	2002	Neal, Patricia	1926	2010
Lloyd, Harold	1893	1971	McLaglen, Victor	1886	1959	Negri, Pola	1897	1987
Lloyd, Marie	1870	1922	McMahon, Ed	1923	2009	Nelson, David	1936	2011
Lockhart, Gene	1891	1957	McNeill, Don	1907	1996	Nelson, Harriet (Hilliard)	1909	1994
Logan, Ella	1913	1969	McQueen, Butterfly	1911	1995	Nelson, Ozzie	1906	1975
Lom, Herbert	1917	2012	McQueen, Steve	1930	1980	Nelson, Rick	1940	1985
Lombard, Carole	1908	1942	Meader, Vaughn	1936	2004	Nesbit, Evelyn	1884	1967
Lombardo, Guy	1902	1977	Meadows, Audrey	1924	1996	Nettleton, Lois	1927	2008
Long, Richard	1927	1974	Meek, Donald	1880	1946	Newley, Anthony	1931	1999
Lopes, Lisa	1971	2002	Meeker, Ralph	1920	1988	Newman, Edwin	1919	2010
Lopez, Vincent	1895	1975	Melba, Nellie	1861	1931	Newman, Paul	1925	2008
Lord, Jack	1920	1998	Melchior, Lauritz	1890	1973	Newton, Robert	1905	1956
Lorne, Marion	1888	1968	Menjou, Adolphe	1890	1963	Nicholas, Fayard	1914	2006
Lorre, Peter	1904	1964	Menken, Helen	1902	1966	Nicholas, Harold	1924	2000
Loudon, Dorothy	1933	2003	Menuhin, Yehudi	1916	1999	Nielsen, Leslie	1926	2010
Lowe, Edmund	1890	1971	Mercer, Marian	1935	2011	Nijinsky, Vaslav	1890	1950
Loy, Myrna	1905	1993	Mercouri, Melina	1925	1994	Nilsson, Anna Q.	1888	1974
Lubitsch, Ernst	1892	1947	Mercury, Freddie	1946	1991	Niven, David	1910	1983
Ludden, Allen	1918	1981	Meredith, Burgess	1909	1997	Nolan, Lloyd	1902	1985
Lugosi, Bela	1882	1956	Merman, Ethel	1908	1984	Normand, Mabel	1894	1930
Lukas, Paul	1894	1971	Merrick, David	1911	2000	North, Sheree	1933	2005
Lumet, Sidney	1924	2011	Merrill, Gary	1915	1990	Notorious B.I.G.	1972	1997
Lunt, Alfred	1892	1977	Milestone, Lewis	1895	1980	Novarro, Ramon	1899	1968
Lupino, Ida	1918	1995	Mifune, Toshiro	1920	1997	Nureyev, Rudolf	1938	1993
Lymon, Frankie	1942	1968	Milland, Ray	1905	1986	Oakie, Jack	1903	1978
Lynde, Paul	1926	1982	Miller, Ann	1923	2004	Oakley, Annie	1860	1926
Lynn, Diana	1926	1971	Miller, Glenn	1904	1944	Oates, Warren	1928	1982
Mac, Bernie	1957	2008	Miller, Marilyn	1898	1936	Oberon, Merle	1911	1979
MacArthur, James	1937	2010	Miller, Mitch	1911	2010	O'Brien, Edmond	1915	1985
MacCorkindale, Simon	1952	2010	Miller, Roger	1936	1992	O'Brien, Pat	1899	1983
MacDonald, Jeanette	1903	1965	Mills, Donald	1915	1999	O'Connell, Arthur	1908	1981
Mack, Ted	1904	1976	Mills, Harry	1913	1982	O'Connell, Helen	1921	1993
MacKenzie, Gisele	1927	2003	Mills, Herbert	1912	1989	O'Connor, Carroll	1924	2001
MacLane, Barton	1902	1969	Mills, John	1889	1967	O'Connor, Donald	1925	2003

Name	Born	Died
O'Connor, Una	1880	1959
Odetta	1930	2008
O'Herlihy, Daniel	1919	2005
O'Keefe, Dennis	1908	1968
Oland, Warner	1880	1938
Olcott, Chauncey	1860	1932
Oliver, Edna May	1883	1942
Olivier, Laurence	1907	1989
Olsen, Merlin	1940	2010
Olsen, Ole	1892	1963
O'Neal, Ron	1937	2004
O'Neill, James	1849	1920
Ophuls, Max	1902	1957
Orbach, Jerry	1935	2004
Orbison, Roy	1936	1988
Ormandy, Eugene	1899	1985
O'Sullivan, Maureen	1911	1998
Ouspenskaya, Maria	1876	1949
Owen, Reginald	1887	1972
Owens, Buck	1929	2006
Paar, Jack	1918	2004
Paderewski, Ignace	1860	1941
Page, Bettie	1923	2008
Page, Geraldine	1924	1987
Pakula, Alan	1928	1998
Palance, Jack	1919	2006
Pallette, Eugene	1889	1954
Palmer, Lilli	1914	1986
Palmer, Robert	1949	2003
Pangborn, Franklin	1894	1958
Parker, Fess	1925	2010
Parker, Jean	1915	2005
Parks, Bert	1914	1992
Parks, Larry	1914	1975
Pasternack, Josef A.	1881	1940
Pastor, Tony (vaudevillian)	1837	1908
Pastor, Tony (bandleader)	1907	1969
Patrick, Gail	1911	1980
Patti, Adelina	1843	1919
Patti, Carlotta	1840	1889
Paul, Les	1915	2009
Pavarotti, Luciano	1935	2007
Pavlova, Anna	1885	1931
Paycheck, Johnny	1938	2003
Payne, John	1912	1989
Pearl, Minnie	1912	1996
Peck, Gregory	1916	2003
Peckinpah, Sam	1925	1984
Peerce, Jan	1904	1984
Pendergrass, Teddy	1950	2010
Penn, Arthur	1922	2010
Penn, Chris	1965	2006
Penner, Joe	1905	1941
Peppard, George	1928	1994
Perkins, Anthony	1932	1992
Perkins, Carl	1932	1998
Perkins, Marlin	1905	1986
Peters, Brock	1927	2005
Peters, Jean	1926	2000
Peters, Susan	1921	1952
Peterson, Oscar	1925	2007
Phillips, John	1935	2001
Phoenix, River	1970	1993
Piaf, Edith	1915	1963
Pickens, Slim	1919	1983
Pickett, Wilson	1941	2006
Pickford, Mary	1893	1979
Picon, Molly	1898	1992
Pidgeon, Walter	1897	1984
Pinza, Ezio	1892	1957
Pitney, Gene	1941	2006
Pitts, Zasu	1898	1963
Plato, Dana	1964	1999
Pleasence, Donald	1919	1995
Pleshette, Suzanne	1937	2008
Pollack, Sydney	1934	2008
Pons, Lily	1904	1976
Ponselle, Rosa	1897	1981
Ponti, Carlo	1912	2007
Porter, Edwin S.	1870	1941
Porter, Eric	1928	1995
Porter, Nyree Dawn	1940	2001
Postlethwaite, Pete	1946	2011
Poston, Tom	1921	2007
Powell, Dick	1904	1963
Powell, Eleanor	1912	1982
Powell, William	1892	1984
Power, Tyrone	1914	1958
Preminger, Otto	1905	1986
Presley, Elvis	1935	1977
Preston, Billy	1946	2006
Preston, Robert	1918	1987
Price, Vincent	1911	1993
Prima, Louis	1911	1978
Prinze, Freddie	1954	1977
Prosky, Robert	1930	2008
Provine, Dorothy	1937	2010
Prowse, Juliet	1936	1996
Pryor, Richard	1940	2005
Puente, Tito	1923	2000
Pyle, Denver	1920	1997
Quayle, Anthony	1913	1989
Questel, Mae	1908	1998
Quinn, Anthony	1915	2001
Quintero, José	1924	1999
Rabb, Ellis	1930	1998
Rabbit, Eddie	1941	1998
Radner, Gilda	1946	1989
Rafferty, Gerry	1947	2011
Raft, George	1895	1980
Rains, Claude	1889	1967
Raitt, John	1917	2005
Ralston, Esther	1902	1994
Ramone, Dee Dee	1952	2002
Ramone, Joey	1951	2001
Ramone, Johnny	1948	2004
Rampal, Jean-Pierre	1922	2000
Randall, Tony	1920	2004
Randolph, John	1915	2004
Rathbone, Basil	1892	1967
Ratoff, Gregory	1897	1960
Rawls, Lou	1933	2006
Ray, Aldo	1926	1991
Ray, Johnnie	1927	1990
Ray, Nicholas	1911	1979
Rayburn, Gene	1917	1999
Raye, Martha	1916	1994
Raymond, Gene	1908	1998
Reagan, Ronald	1911	2004
Redding, Otis	1941	1967
Redgrave, Corin	1939	2010
Redgrave, Lynn	1943	2010
Redgrave, Michael	1908	1985
Reed, Donna	1921	1986
Reed, Jerry	1937	2008
Reed, Oliver	1938	1999
Reed, Robert	1932	1992
Reeve, Christopher	1952	2004
Reeves, George	1914	1959
Reeves, Steve	1926	2000
Reid, Wallace	1891	1923
Reilly, Charles Nelson	1931	2007
Reinhardt, Max	1873	1943
Remick, Lee	1935	1991
Renaldo, Duncan	1904	1980
Rennie, Michael	1909	1971
Renoir, Jean	1894	1979
Rettig, Tommy	1941	1996
Reynolds, Marjorie	1921	1997
Rich, Charlie	1932	1995
Richardson, Ian	1934	2007
Richardson, Natasha	1963	2009
Richardson, Ralph	1902	1983
Riddle, Nelson	1921	1985
Riefenstahl, Leni	1902	2003
Ripperton, Minnie	1947	1979
Ritchard, Cyril	1898	1977
Ritter, John	1948	2003
Ritter, Tex	1905	1974
Ritter, Thelma	1905	1969
Ritz, Al	1901	1965
Ritz, Harry	1906	1986
Ritz, Jimmy	1903	1985
Roach, Hall	1892	1992
Roach, Max	1924	2007
Robards, Jason	1922	2000
Robbins, Jerome	1918	1998
Robbins, Marty	1925	1982
Roberts, Pernell	1928	2010
Roberts, Rachel	1927	1980
Robertson, Cliff	1925	2011
Robeson, Paul	1898	1976
Robinson, Bill	1878	1949
Robinson, Edward G.	1893	1973
Robson, Flora	1902	1984
Roche, Eugene	1928	2004
Rochester (Eddie Anderson)	1905	1977
Roddenberry, Gene	1921	1991
Rodgers, Jimmie	1897	1933
Rogers, Buddy	1904	1999
Rogers, Fred	1928	2003
Rogers, Ginger	1911	1995
Rogers, Roy	1911	1998
Rogers, Will	1879	1935
Roland, Gilbert	1905	1994
Rolle, Esther	1920?	1998
Rollins, Howard	1950	1996
Roman, Ruth	1924	1999
Romero, Cesar	1907	1994
Rose, Billy	1899	1966
Rossellini, Roberto	1906	1977
Rostropovich, Mstislav	1927	2007
Rowan, Dan	1922	1987
Rubinstein, Artur	1887	1982
Rubenstein, Zelda	1933	2010
Ruggles, Charles	1886	1970
Russell, Harold	1914	2002
Russell, Jane	1921	2011
Russell, Ken	1927	2011
Russell, Lillian	1861	1922
Russell, Nipsey	1923	2005
Russell, Rosalind	1911	1976
Rutherford, Ann	1917	2012
Rutherford, Margaret	1892	1972
Ryan, Irene	1903	1973
Ryan, Robert	1909	1973
Sabu (Dastagir)	1924	1963
St. Cyr, Lili	1917	1999
St. Denis, Ruth	1877	1968
Sakall, S. Z.	1883	1955
Sale (Chic), Charles	1885	1936
Sales, Soupy	1926	2009
Sanders, George	1906	1972
Sanford, Isabel	1917	2004
Sargent, Dick	1933	1994
Sarrazin, Michael	1940	2011
Savalas, Telly	1924	1994
Scheider, Roy	1935	2008
Schell, Maria	1926	2005
Schenkel, Chris	1923	2005
Schiavelli, Vincent	1948	2005
Schildkraut, Joseph	1896	1964
Schipa, Tito	1888	1965
Schlesinger, John	1926	2003
Schnabel, Artur	1882	1951
Schneider, Maria	1952	2011
Schneider, Romy	1938	1982
Schwartzkopf, Elizabeth	1915	2006
Scofield, Paul	1922	2008
Scott, George C.	1927	1999
Scott, Gordon	1926	2007
Scott, Hazel	1920	1981
Scott, Martha	1914	2003
Scott, Randolph	1898	1987
Scott, Zachary	1914	1965
Scott-Siddons, Mrs.	1843	1896
Seberg, Jean	1938	1979
Seeley, Blossom	1892	1974
Segovia, Andres	1893	1987
Selena	1971	1995
Sellers, Peter	1925	1980
Selznick, David O.	1902	1965
Sennett, Mack	1880	1960
Señor Wences	1896	1999
Serling, Rod	1924	1975
Shakur, Tupac	1971	1996
Shaw, Artie	1910	2004
Shaw, Robert (actor)	1927	1978
Shaw, Robert (conductor)	1916	1999
Shawn, Ted	1891	1972
Shean, Al	1868	1949
Shearer, Moira	1926	2006
Shearer, Norma	1902	1983
Shearing, George	1919	2011
Sheppard, Bob	1910	2010
Sheridan, Ann	1915	1967
Shore, Dinah	1917	1994
Short, Bobby	1924	2005
Shubert, Lee	1875	1953
Shull, Richard B.	1929	1999
Siddons, Sarah	1755	1831
Sidney, Sylvia	1910	1999
Siegel, Don	1912	1991
Signoret, Simone	1921	1985
Sills, Beverly	1929	2007
Silver, Ron	1946	2009
Silverheels, Jay	1912	1980
Silvers, Phil	1912	1985
Sim, Alastair	1900	1976
Simmons, Jean	1929	2010
Simone, Nina	1933	2003
Sinatra, Frank	1915	1998
Sinclair, Madge	1938	1995
Singleton, Penny	1908	2003
Sirk, Douglas	1900	1987
Siskel, Gene	1946	1999
Sitka, Emil	1914	1998
Sjostrom, Victor	1879	1960
Skelton, Red	1913	1997
Skinner, Otis	1858	1942
Smith, Alexis	1921	1993
Smith, Bessie	1894?	1937
Smith, Buffalo Bob	1917	1998
Smith, C. Aubrey	1863	1948
Smith, Elliott	1969	2003
Smith, Jeff	1939	2004
Smith, Kate	1907	1986
Smith, Kent	1907	1985

Name	Born	Died	Name	Born	Died	Name	Born	Died
Snodgress, Carrie	1946	2004	Thompson, Sada	1927	2011	Weaver, Dennis	1924	2006
Snow, Hank	1914	1999	Thorndike, Sybil	1882	1976	Webb, Clifton	1891	1966
Snyder, Tom	1936	2007	Thulin, Ingrid	1926	2004	Webb, Jack	1920	1982
Solti, George	1912	1997	Tibbett, Lawrence	1896	1960	Weems, Ted.	1901	1963
Sondergaard, Gale	1899	1985	Tierney, Gene	1920	1991	Weissmuller, Johnny	1904	1984
Sothern, Ann	1909	2001	Tiny Tim.	1932	1996	Welk, Lawrence	1903	1992
Sousa, John Philip.	1854	1932	Tippett, Sir Michael	1905	1998	Welles, Orson	1915	1985
Sparks, Ned	1884	1957	Todd, Michael	1909	1958	Wellman, William	1896	1975
Spelling, Aaron	1923	2006	Todd, Richard	1919	2009	Wells, Kitty.	1919	2012
Spencer, John	1946	2005	Tomlinson, David	1917	2000	Werner, Oskar	1922	1984
Sperber, Wendy Jo	1958	2005	Tone, Franchot	1905	1968	West, Mae.	1893	1980
Springfield, Dusty	1939	1999	Torme, Mel	1925	1999	Weston, Jack	1924	1996
Stack, Robert	1919	2003	Toscanini, Arturo	1867	1957	Whale, James	1889	1957
Stafford, Jo	1917	2008	Tracy, Lee.	1898	1968	Wheeler, Bert	1895	1968
Stander, Lionel	1908	1994	Tracy, Spencer	1900	1967	White, Barry	1944	2003
Stang, Arnold	1918	2009	Traubel, Helen.	1899	1972	White, Jesse	1919	1997
Stanley, Kim	1925	2001	Travers, Henry.	1874	1965	White, Pearl.	1889	1938
Stanwyck, Barbara.	1907	1990	Travers, Mary	1936	2009	Whiteman, Paul	1891	1967
Stapleton, Maureen	1925	2006	Treacher, Arthur	1894	1975	Whiting, Margaret	1924	2011
Steiger, Rod	1925	2002	Tree, Herbert Beerbohm	1853	1917	Whitmore, James.	1921	2009
Sterling, Jan	1921	2004	Trevor, Claire.	1909	2000	Whitty, May	1865	1948
Stern, Isaac.	1920	2001	Truex, Ernest.	1890	1973	Wickes, Mary.	1910	1995
Stevens, Craig.	1918	2000	Truffaut, Francois.	1932	1984	Widmark, Richard	1914	2008
Stevens, George	1904	1975	Tucker, Forrest.	1919	1986	Wilde, Cornel.	1915	1989
Stevens, Inger	1934	1970	Tucker, Richard	1913	1975	Wilder, Billy	1906	2002
Stevens, Mark	1916	1994	Tucker, Sophie.	1884	1966	Wilding, Michael	1912	1979
Stevenson, McLean	1929	1996	Turner, Big Joe	1911	1985	Williams, Andy.	1927	2012
Stewart, James	1908	1997	Turner, Ike	1931	2008	Williams, Bert	1874	1922
Stickney, Dorothy.	1896	1998	Turner, Lana	1920	1995	Williams, Guy	1924	1989
Stokowski, Leopold	1882	1977	Turpin, Ben	1869	1940	Williams, Hank, Sr.	1923	1953
Stone, Fred	1873	1959	Twelvetrees, Helen	1908	1958	Wills, Bob	1905	1975
Stone, Lewis	1879	1953	Twitty, Conway	1933	1993	Wills, Chill	1902	1978
Stone, Milburn	1904	1980	Urich, Robert.	1946	2002	Wilson, Carl.	1946	1998
Storm, Gale	1922	2009	Ustinov, Peter	1921	2004	Wilson, Dennis	1944	1983
Straight, Beatrice.	1918	2001	Valens, Ritchie.	1941	1959	Wilson, Dooley	1894	1953
Strasberg, Lee.	1901	1982	Valentino, Rudolph.	1895	1926	Wilson, Flip	1933	1998
Strasberg, Susan.	1938	1999	Vallee, Rudy	1901	1986	Wilson, Jackie	1934	1984
Strode, Woody.	1914	1994	Van, Bobby	1928	1980	Wilson, Marie	1917	1972
Strummer, Joe	1952	2002	Vance, Vivian.	1912	1979	Windom, William	1923	2012
Stuart, Gloria.	1910	2010	Van Cleef, Lee.	1925	1989	Windsor, Marie	1919	2000
Stuarti, Enzo	1919	2005	Vandross, Luther	1951	2005	Winehouse, Amy	1983	2011
Sturges, Preston	1898	1959	Van Fleet, Jo	1922	1996	Winfield, Paul.	1941	2004
Sullavan, Margaret.	1911	1960	Varney, Jim	1949	2000	Winninger, Charles	1884	1969
Sullivan, Barry	1912	1994	Vaughan, Sarah.	1924	1990	Winters, Shelley.	1920	2006
Sullivan, Ed.	1902	1974	Veidt, Conrad.	1893	1943	Wise, Robert	1914	2005
Sullivan, Francis L.	1903	1956	Velez, Lupe.	1908	1944	Wiseman, Joseph	1918	2009
Sumac, Yma	1922	2008	Vera-Ellen (Rohe)	1926	1981	Wong, Anna May	1907	1961
Summer, Donna	1948	2012	Verdon, Gwen	1925	2000	Wood, Natalie	1938	1981
Summerville, Slim	1892	1946	Vernon, Jackie.	1925	1987	Wood, Peggy	1892	1978
Sutherland, Joan	1926	2010	Vernon, John.	1932	2005	Wood, Sam	1884	1949
Swanson, Gloria	1899	1983	Verrett, Shirley	1931	2010	Woodard, Edward	1930	2009
Swarthout, Gladys	1904	1969	Vidor, King.	1894	1982	Wooley, Sheb	1921	2003
Swayze, Patrick.	1952	2009	Villechaize, Herve	1943	1993	Woolley, Monty	1888	1963
Sweet, Blanche	1896	1986	Vincent, Gene	1935	1971	Worth, Irene	1916	2002
Switzer, Carl "Alfalfa"	1927	1959	Vicious, Sid	1957	1979	Wray, Fay.	1907	2004
Talbot, Lyle	1902	1996	Vinson, Helen	1907	1999	Wright, Teresa	1918	2005
Talmadge, Constance	1900	1973	Von Stroheim, Erich.	1885	1957	Wyatt, Jane	1910	2006
Talmadge, Norma	1893	1957	Von Zell, Harry	1906	1981	Wyler, William	1902	1981
Tamiroff, Akim	1899	1972	Walker, Junior	1942	1995	Wyman, Jane	1914?	2007
Tandy, Jessica	1909	1994	Walker, Nancy	1922	1992	Wynette, Tammy	1942	1998
Tanguay, Eva	1878	1947	Walker, Robert.	1918	1951	Wynn, Ed.	1886	1966
Tati, Jacques	1908	1982	Wallenda, Karl	1905	1978	Wynn, Keenan.	1916	1986
Taylor, Billy	1921	2010	Walsh, J. T.	1943	1998	Yankovic, Frank.	1915	1998
Taylor, Deems	1885	1966	Walsh, Raoul.	1887	1980	York, Dick	1928	1992
Taylor, Dub	1907	1994	Walston, Ray	1914	2001	York, Susannah.	1939	2011
Taylor, Elizabeth	1932	2011	Walter, Bruno.	1876	1962	Young, Clara Kimball.	1890	1960
Taylor, Estelle	1899	1958	Ward, Helen	1916	1998	Young, Gig	1913	1978
Taylor, Laurette	1887	1946	Warden, Jack.	1920	2006	Young, Loretta.	1913	2000
Taylor, Robert	1911	1969	Waring, Fred	1900	1984	Young, Robert	1907	1998
Tebaldi, Renata	1922	2004	Warner, H. B.	1876	1958	Young, Roland.	1887	1953
Terry, Ellen	1847	1928	Warrick, Ruth.	1915	2005	Youngman, Henny.	1906	1998
Thalberg, Irving	1899	1936	Washington, Dinah	1924	1963	Zanuck, Darryl F.	1902	1979
Thaw, John	1942	2002	Waters, Ethel.	1896	1977	Zappa, Frank.	1940	1993
Thaxter, Phyllis	1919	2012	Waters, Muddy	1915	1983	Zevon, Warren.	1947	2003
Thigpen, Lynne	1948	2003	Waxman, Al.	1935	2001	Ziegfeld, Florenz	1869	1932
Thomas, Danny	1912	1991	Wayne, David	1914	1995	Zinneman, Fred	1907	1997
Thomas, John Charles.	1891	1960	Wayne, John	1907	1979	Zukor, Adolph	1873	1976

Original Names of Selected Entertainers

Aaliyah: Aaliyah Haughton
Adele: Adele Laurie Blue Adkins
Ad-Rock: Adam Horovitz
Clay Aiken: Clayton Grissom
Eddie Albert: Edward Albert Heimberger
Alan Alda: Alphonso D'Abruzzo
Jason Alexander: Jay Greenspan
Ali G: Sacha Baron Cohen
Fred Allen: John Sullivan
Woody Allen: Allen Konigsberg
June Allyson: Ella Geisman
André 3000: Andre Benjamin
Julie Andrews: Julia Wells
Criss Angel: Christopher Sarantakos
Eve Arden: Eunice Quedens
Beatrice Arthur: Bernice Frankel
Jean Arthur: Gladys Greene
Ashanti: Ashanti Douglas

Fred Astaire: Frederick Austerlitz
Babyface: Kenneth Edmonds
Lauren Bacall: Betty Joan Perske
Erykah Badu: Erica Wright
Eric Bana: Eric Banadinovich
Anne Bancroft: Anna Maria Italiano
Theda Bara: Theodosia Goodman
Beck: Beck Hensen
Pat Benatar: Patricia Andrejewski
Tony Bennett: Anthony Benedetto
Jack Benny: Benjamin Kubelsky
Milton Berle: Mendel Berlinger
Irving Berlin: Israel Baline
Sarah Bernhardt: Henriette-Rosine Bernard
Jello Biafra: Eric Reed Boucher
Big Boi: Antwan Patton
The Big Bopper: Jiles Perry "J.P." Richardson
Joey Bishop: Joseph Gottlieb

Robert Blake: Michael James Vijencio Gubitosi
Jon Bon Jovi: John Francis Bongiovi
Björk: Björk Gudmundsdottir
Bono: Paul Hewson
Bow Wow: Shad Gregory Moss
David Bowie: David Robert Jones
Boy George: George Alan O'Dowd
Fanny Brice: Fanny Borach
Charles Bronson: Charles Buchinski
Albert Brooks: Albert Einstein
Mel Brooks: Melvin Kaminsky
Foxy Brown: Inga Marchand
George Burns: Nathan Birnbaum
Ellen Burstyn: Edna Gilhooley
Richard Burton: Richard Jenkins
Red Buttons: Aaron Chwatt
Nicolas Cage: Nicholas Coppola
Michael Caine: Maurice Micklewhite

Maria Callas: Maria Kalogeropoulos
Cedric The Entertainer: Cedric Kyles
Jackie Chan: Chan Kwong-Sung
Cyd Charisse: Tula Finklea
Ray Charles: Ray Charles Robinson
Charo: Maria Rosario Pilar Martinez Molina Baeza
Chubby Checker: Ernest Evans
Cher: Cherilyn Sarkisian
Chuck D: Carlton Ridenhour
Patsy Cline: Virginia Patterson Hensley
Claudette Colbert: Lily Chauchoin
Coolio: Artis Leon Ivey Jr.
Alice Cooper: Vincent Furnier
David Copperfield: David Kotkin
Howard Cosell: Howard Cohen
Elvis Costello: Declan McManus
Lou Costello: Louis Cristillo
Peter Coyote: Peter Cohon
Quentin Crisp: Denis Pratt
Tom Cruise: Thomas Cruise Mapother IV
Tony Curtis: Bernard Schwartz
Miley Cyrus: Destiny Hope Cyrus
Vic Damone: Vito Farinola
D'Angelo: Michael D'Angelo Archer
Rodney Dangerfield: Jacob Cohen
Bobby Darin: Walden Robert Cassotto
Doris Day: Doris von Kappelhoff
Yvonne De Carlo: Peggy Middleton
Portia de Rossi: Amanda Lee Rogers
Sandra Dee: Alexandra Zuck
John Denver: Henry John Deutschendorf Jr.
Bo Derek: Mary Cathleen Collins
Danny DeVito: Daniel Michaeli
Angie Dickinson: Angeline Brown
Bo Diddley: Elias Bates
Vin Diesel: Mark Vincent
Phyllis Diller: Phyllis Driver
Divine: Harris Glenn Milstead
DMX: Earl Simmons
Troy Donahue: Merle Johnson Jr.
Kirk Douglas: Issur Danielovitch
Melvyn Douglas: Melvyn Hesselberg
Drake: Aubrey Drake Graham
Duffy: Aimee Anne Duffy
Bob Dylan: Robert Zimmerman
Barbara Eden: Barbara Huffman
Carmen Electra: Tara Leigh Patrick
Elvira: Cassandra Peterson
Eminem: Marshall Mathers
Enya: Eithne Ni Bhraonian
Dale Evans: Frances Smith
Chad Everett: Raymon Cramton
Fabian: Fabian Anthony Forte
Fabio: Fabio Lanzoni
Fabolous: John Jackson
Douglas Fairbanks: Douglas Ullman
Morgan Fairchild: Patsy McClenny
Jamie Farr: Jameel Farah
Alice Faye: Alice Jeanne Leppert
Fergie: Stacy Ferguson
Stepin Fetchit: Lincoln Perry
W. C. Fields: William Claude Dukenfield
50 Cent: Curtis Jackson
Barry Fitzgerald: William Shields
Flavor Flav: William Drayton
Joan Fontaine: Joan de Havilland
Jodie Foster: Alicia Christian Foster
Redd Foxx: John Sanford
Arlene Francis: Arlene Kazanjian
Connie Francis: Concetta Franconero
Kenny G: Kenneth Gorelick
Greta Garbo: Greta Gustafsson
Vincent Gardenia: Vincent Scognamiglio
John Garfield: Julius Garfinkle
Judy Garland: Frances Gumm
James Garner: James Bumgarner
Crystal Gayle: Brenda Gail Webb
George Gershwin: Jacob Gershowitz
Kathie Lee Gifford: Kathie Epstein
Whoopi Goldberg: Caryn Johnson
Eydie Gorme: Edith Garmezano
Stewart Granger: James Stewart
Cary Grant: Archibald Leach
Lee Grant: Lyova Rosenthal
Robert Guillaume: Robert Williams
Buddy Hackett: Leonard Hacker
Hammer: Stanley Kirk Burrell
Jean Harlow: Harlean Carpenter
Rex Harrison: Reginald Carey Harrison
Laurence Harvey: Larushka Skikne
Helen Hayes: Helen Brown
Susan Hayward: Edythe Marrener
Rita Hayworth: Margarita Cansino
Pee-Wee Herman: Paul Reubenfeld
Charlton Heston: John Charles Carter
Perez Hilton: Mario Armando Lavandeira Jr.
Hulk Hogan: Terry Gene Bollea
William Holden: William Beedle
Billie Holiday: Eleanora Fagan

Buddy Holly: Charles Hardin Holley
Judy Holliday: Judith Tuvim
Bob Hope: Leslie Townes Hope
Harry Houdini: Erik Weisz
Leslie Howard: Leslie Stainer
Howlin' Wolf: Chester Burnett
Rock Hudson: Roy Scherer Jr. (later Fitzgerald)
Engelbert Humperdinck: Arnold Dorsey
Kim Hunter: Janet Cole
Ice Cube: O'Shea Jackson
Ice-T: Tracy Morrow
Billy Idol: William Broad
Etta James: Jamesetta Hawkins
Ja Rule: Jeffrey Atkins
Jay-Z: Shawn Carter
Jewel: Jewel Kilcher
Elton John: Reginald Dwight
Angelina Jolie: Angelina Jolie Voight
Al Jolson: Asa Yoelson
Jennifer Jones: Phylis Isley
Tom Jones: Thomas Woodward
Spike Jonze: Adam Spiegel
Louis Jourdan: Louis Gendre
Wynonna Judd: Christina Ciminella
Boris Karloff: William Henry Pratt
Danny Kaye: David Kaminsky
Ke$ha: Kesha Rose Sebert
Diane Keaton: Diane Hall
Michael Keaton: Michael Douglas
Alicia Keys: Alicia Augello Cook
Chaka Khan: Yvette Stevens
Carole King: Carole Klein
Larry King: Larry Zeiger
Ben Kingsley: Krishna Banji
Ted Knight: Tadewurz Wladziu Konopka
Cheryl Ladd: Cheryl Stoppelmoor
Lady Gaga: Stefani Germanotta
Veronica Lake: Constance Ockleman
Hedy Lamarr: Hedwig Kiesler
Dorothy Lamour: Mary Leta Dorothy Slaton
Michael Landon: Eugene Orowitz
k.d. lang: Kathryn Dawn Lang
Mario Lanza: Alfredo Cocozza
Queen Latifah: Dana Owens
Stan Laurel: Arthur Jefferson
Steve Lawrence: Sidney Leibowitz
Brenda Lee: Brenda Mae Tarpley
Gypsy Rose Lee: Rose Louise Hovick
Michelle Lee: Michelle Dusiak
Peggy Lee: Norma Egstrom
Janet Leigh: Jeanette Morrison
Vivien Leigh: Vivian Hartley
Huey Lewis: Hugh Cregg
Jerry Lewis: Joseph Levitch
Lil' Kim: Kimberly Denise Jones
Lil' Romeo: Percy Romeo Miller Jr.
Little Richard: Richard Penniman
L.L. Cool J: James Todd Smith
Carole Lombard: Jane Peters
Sophia Loren: Sophia Scicolone
Peter Lorre: Laszlo Lowenstein
Myrna Loy: Myrna Williams
Bela Lugosi: Bela Ferenc Blasko
Moms Mabley: Loretta Mary Aiken
Shirley Maclaine: Shirley Beaty
Elle Macpherson: Eleanor Gow
Madonna: Madonna Louise Veronica Ciccone
Lee Majors: Harvey Lee Yeary
Karl Malden: Mladen Sekulovich
Barry Manilow: Barry Alan Pincus
Jayne Mansfield: Vera Jane Palmer
Marilyn Manson: Brian Warner
Fredric March: Frederick Bickel
Bruno Mars: Peter Gene Hernandez
Dean Martin: Dino Crocetti
Ricky Martin: Enrique Jose Martin Morales
Groucho Marx: Julius Henry Marx
MCA: Adam Yauch
Meat Loaf: Marvin Lee Aday
Freddie Mercury: Frederick Bulsara
Ethel Merman: Ethel Zimmermann
George Michael: Georgios Panayiotou
Midori: Midori Goto
Mike D: Michael Diamond
Ray Milland: Reginald Truscott-Jones
Ann Miller: Lucille Collier
Helen Mirren: Ilynea Lydia Mironoff
Joni Mitchell: Roberta Joan Anderson
Moby: Richard Melville Hall
Mo'Nique: Monique Imes
Marilyn Monroe: Norma Jean Mortenson (later Baker)
Yves Montand: Ivo Livi
Demi Moore: Demetria Guynes
Rita Moreno: Rosita Alverio
Harry Morgan: Harry Bratsburg
Morrissey: Steven Patrick Morrissey
Mr.T: Lawrence Tureaud
Paul Muni: Mehilem Weisenfreund

Nelly: Cornell Haynes Jr.
Mike Nichols: Michael Igor Peschowsky
Chuck Norris: Carlos Ray Norris
Notorious B.I.G.: Christopher Wallace
Hugh O'Brian: Hugh Krampke
Odetta: Odetta Holmes
Maureen O'Hara: Maureen FitzSimons
Ozzy Osbourne: John Michael Osbourne
Jack Palance: Vladimir Palanuik
Minnie Pearl: Sarah Ophelia Cannon
Katy Perry: Kathryn Hudson
Bernadette Peters: Bernadette Lazzara
Joaquin Phoenix: Joaquin Bottom
Edith Piaf: Edith Gassion
Slim Pickens: Louis Lindley
Mary Pickford: Gladys Smith
Pink: Alecia Moore
Iggy Pop: James Newell Osterberg
Natalie Portman: Natalie Hershlag
Robert Preston: Robert Preston Meservey
Prince: Prince Rogers Nelson
Raffi: Raffi Cavoukian
Dee Dee Ramone: Douglas Colvin
Joey Ramone: Jeffrey Hyman
Johnny Ramone: John Cummings
Tommy Ramone: Tom Erdelyi
Tony Randall: Leonard Rosenberg
Martha Raye: Margaret O'Reed
Della Reese: Delloreese Patricia Early
Busta Rhymes: Trevor Smith Jr.
Joan Rivers: Joan Sandra Molinsky
Edward G. Robinson: Emmanuel Goldenberg
The Rock: Dwayne Johnson
Ginger Rogers: Virginia McMath
Roy Rogers: Leonard Franklin Slye
Mickey Rooney: Joe Yule Jr.
Johnny Rotten: John Lydon
Lillian Russell: Helen Leonard
Meg Ryan: Margaret Hyra
Winona Ryder: Winona Horowitz
Sabu: Sabu Dastagir
Sade: Helen Folsade Abu
Soupy Sales: Milton Supman
Susan Sarandon: Susan Tomaling
Randolph Scott: George Randolph Crane
Seal: Seal Henry Olusegun Olumide Adeola Samuel
Selena: Selena Quintanilla
Jane Seymour: Joyce Frankenberg
Shakira: Shakira Isabel Mebarak Ripoll
Omar Sharif: Michael Shalhoub
Charlie Sheen: Carlos Irwin Estevez
Martin Sheen: Ramon Estevez
Talia Shire: Talia Coppola
Beverly Sills: Belle Silverman
Phil Silvers: Philip Silversmith
Gene Simmons: Chaim Witz
Sinbad: David Adkins
Anna Nicole Smith: Vickie Lynn Hogan
Snoop Dogg: Calvin Broadus
Ann Sothern: Harriette Lake
Barbara Stanwyck: Ruby Stevens
Jean Stapleton: Jeanne Murray
Ringo Starr: Richard Starkey
Cat Stevens: Stephen Demetre Georgiou
Connie Stevens: Concetta Ingolia
Jon Stewart: Jonathan Stuart Leibowitz
Sting: Gordon Sumner
Joe Strummer: John Graham Mellor
Donna Summer: La Donna Gaines
Rip Taylor: Charles Elmer Taylor Jr.
Robert Taylor: Spangler Brugh
Teller: Robert Joseph Teller
Danny Thomas: Muzyad Yakhoob (later Amos Jacobs)
Tiny Tim: Herbert Khaury
Rip Torn: Elmore Rual Torn Jr.
Randy Travis: Randy Traywick
Sophie Tucker: Sophia Kalish
Tina Turner: Annie Mae Bullock
Shania Twain: Eilleen Regina Edwards
Twiggy: Lesley Hornby
Conway Twitty: Harold Lloyd Jenkins
Steven Tyler: Stephen Tallarico
Usher: Usher Raymond IV
Rudolph Valentino: Rudolpho D'Antonguolla
Frankie Valli: Frank Castelluccio
Eddie Vedder: Edward Louis Seversen III
Sid Vicious: John Simon Ritchie
John Wayne: Marion Morrison
Raquel Welch: Raquel Tejada
Gene Wilder: Jerome Silberman
Shelley Winters: Shirley Schrift
Stevie Wonder: Stevland Morris
Jane Wyman: Sarah Jane Mayfield
Yanni: Yanni Chrysomallis
Loretta Young: Gretchen Michaels Young
Buckwheat Zydeco: Stanley Dural Jr.

ARTS AND MEDIA

Some Notable Movies, Sept. 2011-Aug. 2012

Film (rating)	Stars	Director(s)
21 Jump Street (R)	Jonah Hill, Channing Tatum, Ice Cube	Phil Lord, Chris Miller
Abraham Lincoln: Vampire Hunter (R)	Benjamin Walker, Rufus Sewell, Dominic Cooper	Timur Bekmambetov
The Adventures of Tintin (PG)	Jamie Bell, Andy Serkis, Daniel Craig	Steven Spielberg
The Amazing Spider-Man (PG-13)	Andrew Garfield, Emma Stone, Rhys Ifans	Marc Webb
The Artist (PG-13)	Jean Dujardin, Bérénice Bejo, John Goodman	Michel Hazanavicius
The Avengers (PG-13)	Robert Downey Jr., Chris Evans, Scarlett Johansson	Joss Whedon
The Best Exotic Marigold Hotel (PG-13)	Judi Dench, Bill Nighy, Maggie Smith	John Madden
The Bourne Legacy (PG-13)	Jeremy Renner, Rachel Weisz, Edward Norton	Tony Gilroy
Brave (PG)	Kelly Macdonald, Billy Connolly, Emma Thompson	Mark Andrews, Brenda Chapman, Steve Purcell
The Cabin in the Woods (R)	Kristen Connolly, Chris Hemsworth, Anna Hutchison	Drew Goddard
The Campaign (R)	Will Ferrell, Zach Galifianakis, Jason Sudeikis	Jay Roach
Contagion (PG-13)	Matt Damon, Kate Winslet, Jude Law	Steven Soderbergh
Coriolanus (R)	Ralph Fiennes, Gerard Butler, Brian Cox	Ralph Fiennes
Cosmopolis (R)	Robert Pattinson, Juliette Binoche, Sarah Gadon	David Cronenberg
A Dangerous Method (R)	Michael Fassbender, Keira Knightley, Viggo Mortensen	David Cronenberg
The Dark Knight Rises (PG-13)	Christian Bale, Tom Hardy, Anne Hathaway	Christopher Nolan
Dark Shadows (PG-13)	Johnny Depp, Michelle Pfeiffer, Eva Green	Tim Burton
The Descendants (R)	George Clooney, Shailene Woodley, Amara Miller	Alexander Payne
The Dictator (R)	Sacha Baron Cohen, Anna Faris, Ben Kingsley	Larry Charles
Dolphin Tale (PG)	Morgan Freeman, Ashley Judd, Harry Connick Jr.	Charles Martin Smith
Dream House (PG-13)	Daniel Craig, Rachel Weisz, Naomi Watts	Jim Sheridan
Drive (R)	Ryan Gosling, Carey Mulligan, Bryan Cranston	Nicolas Refn
Extremely Loud and Incredibly Close (PG-13)	Thomas Horn, Tom Hanks, Sandra Bullock	Stephen Daldry
The Five-Year Engagement (R)	Jason Segel, Emily Blunt, Chris Pratt	Nicholas Stoller
The Girl With the Dragon Tattoo (R)	Daniel Craig, Rooney Mara, Christopher Plummer	David Fincher
The Grey (R)	Liam Neeson, Dermot Mulroney, Frank Grillo	Joe Carnahan
Haywire (R)	Gina Carano, Ewan McGregor, Michael Fassbender	Steven Soderbergh
Hope Springs (PG-13)	Meryl Streep, Tommy Lee Jones, Steve Carell	David Frankel
Hugo (PG)	Asa Butterfield, Chloë Grace Moretz	Martin Scorsese
The Hunger Games (PG-13)	Jennifer Lawrence, Josh Hutcherson, Liam Hemsworth	Gary Ross
The Ides of March (R)	Paul Giamatti, George Clooney, Philip Seymour Hoffman	George Clooney
In Time (PG-13)	Justin Timberlake, Amanda Seyfried, Cillian Murphy	Andrew Niccol
The Iron Lady (PG-13)	Meryl Streep, Jim Broadbent, Richard E. Grant	Phyllida Lloyd
J. Edgar (R)	Leonardo DiCaprio, Armie Hammer, Naomi Watts	Clint Eastwood
Jack and Jill (PG)	Adam Sandler, Katie Holmes, Al Pacino	Dennis Dugan
Jiro Dreams of Sushi (PG)	documentary	David Gelb
John Carter (PG-13)	Taylor Kitsch, Lynn Collins, Willem Dafoe	Andrew Stanton
Katy Perry: Part of Me (PG)	documentary	Dan Cutforth, Jane Lipsitz
Killer Elite (R)	Jason Statham, Clive Owen, Robert De Niro	Gary McKendry
Lawless (R)	Tom Hardy, Shia LaBeouf, Guy Pearce	John Hillcoat
Lockout (PG-13)	Guy Pearce, Maggie Grace, Peter Stormare	James Mather, Stephen St. Leger
The Lucky One (PG-13)	Zac Efron, Taylor Schilling, Blythe Danner	Scott Hicks
Magic Mike (R)	Channing Tatum, Alex Pettyfer, Olivia Munn	Steven Soderbergh
Melancholia (R)	Kirsten Dunst, Charlotte Gainsbourg, Kiefer Sutherland	Lars von Trier
Men in Black 3 (PG-13)	Will Smith, Tommy Lee Jones, Josh Brolin	Barry Sonnenfeld
Mirror Mirror (PG)	Lily Collins, Julia Roberts, Armie Hammer	Tarsem Singh
Mission: Impossible—Ghost Protocol (PG-13)	Tom Cruise, Jeremy Renner, Simon Pegg	Brad Bird
Moneyball (PG-13)	Brad Pitt, Robin Wright, Jonah Hill	Bennett Miller
Moonrise Kingdom (PG-13)	Jared Gilman, Kara Hayward, Bruce Willis	Wes Anderson
The Muppets (PG)	Jason Segel, Amy Adams, Chris Cooper	James Bobin
ParaNorman (PG)	Kodi Smit-McPhee, Anna Kendrick, Christopher Mintz-Plasse	Chris Butler, Sam Fell
Prometheus (R)	Noomi Rapace, Logan Marshall-Green, Michael Fassbender	Ridley Scott
Puss in Boots (PG)	Antonio Banderas, Salma Hayek, Zach Galifianakis	Chris Miller
Red Tails (PG-13)	Cuba Gooding Jr., Gerald McRaney, David Oyelowo	Anthony Hemingway
Rock of Ages (PG-13)	Julianne Hough, Diego Boneta, Tom Cruise	Adam Shankman
The Rum Diary (R)	Johnny Depp, Giovanni Ribisi, Aaron Eckhart	Bruce Robinson
Safe (R)	Jason Statham, Catherine Chan, Chris Sarandon	Boaz Yakin
Savages (R)	Aaron Taylor-Johnson, Taylor Kitsch, Blake Lively	Oliver Stone
The Skin I Live In (R)	Antonio Banderas, Elena Anaya, Jan Cornet	Pedro Almodóvar
Snow White and the Huntsman (PG-13)	Kristen Stewart, Chris Hemsworth, Charlize Theron	Rupert Sanders
Straw Dogs (R)	James Marsden, Kate Bosworth, Alexander Skarsgård	Rod Lurie
Ted (R)	Mark Wahlberg, Mila Kunis, Seth MacFarlane	Seth MacFarlane
That's My Boy (R)	Adam Sandler, Andy Samberg, Leighton Meester	Sean Anders
The Three Stooges (PG)	Sean Hayes, Chris Diamantopoulos, Will Sasso	Bobby Farrelly, Peter Farrelly
Tinker Tailor Soldier Spy (R)	Gary Oldman, Colin Firth, Tom Hardy	Tomas Alfredson
Total Recall (PG-13)	Colin Farrell, Bokeem Woodbine, Bryan Cranston	Len Wiseman
Tower Heist (PG-13)	Eddie Murphy, Ben Stiller, Casey Affleck	Brett Ratner
The Vow (PG-13)	Rachel McAdams, Channing Tatum, Sam Neill	Michael Sucsy
Wanderlust (R)	Jennifer Aniston, Paul Rudd, Malin Akerman	David Wain
War Horse (PG-13)	Jeremy Irvine, Emily Watson, David Thewlis	Steven Spielberg
The Watch (R)	Ben Stiller, Vince Vaughn, Jonah Hill	Akiva Schaffer
We Bought a Zoo (PG)	Matt Damon, Scarlett Johansson, Thomas Haden Church	Cameron Crowe
We Need to Talk About Kevin (R)	Tilda Swinton, John C. Reilly, Ezra Miller	Lynne Ramsay
What's Your Number? (R)	Anna Faris, Chris Evans, Ari Graynor	Mark Mylod
The Woman in Black (PG-13)	Daniel Radcliffe, Janet McTeer, Ciarán Hinds	James Watkins
The Words (PG-13)	Bradley Cooper, Dennis Quaid, Olivia Wilde	Brian Klugman, Lee Sternthal
Wrath of the Titans (PG-13)	Sam Worthington, Liam Neeson, Rosamund Pike	Jonathan Liebesman
Young Adult (R)	Charlize Theron, Patrick Wilson, Patton Oswalt	Jason Reitman

50 Top-Grossing Movies, 2011
Source: Rentrak Corporation

Rank	Title	Gross (mil)	Rank	Title	Gross (mil)
1.	Harry Potter and the Deathly Hallows: Part 2	$381.0	26.	Paranormal Activity 3	$104.0
2.	Transformers: Dark of the Moon	352.4	27.	Just Go With It	103.0
3.	The Twilight Saga: Breaking Dawn—Part 1	276.1	28.	Bad Teacher	100.3
4.	The Hangover 2	254.5	29.	Cowboys and Aliens	100.2
5.	Pirates of the Caribbean: On Stranger Tides	241.1	30.	Gnomeo and Juliet	99.8
6.	Fast Five	209.8	31.	The Green Hornet	98.8
7.	Cars 2	191.5	32.	Alvin and the Chipmunks: Chipwrecked	97.8
8.	Thor	181.0	33.	The Lion King	94.2
9.	Rise of the Planet of the Apes	176.8	34.	Real Steel	84.6
10.	Captain America: The First Avenger	176.7	35.	True Grit	84.6
11.	The Help	169.5	36.	Crazy, Stupid, Love.	84.4
12.	Bridesmaids	169.1	37.	The Muppets	83.6
13.	Kung Fu Panda 2	165.2	38.	Battle: Los Angeles	83.6
14.	X-Men: First Class	146.4	39.	Immortals	82.7
15.	Puss in Boots	145.7	40.	Zookeeper	80.4
16.	Rio	143.6	41.	Limitless	79.2
17.	The Smurfs	142.6	42.	Tower Heist	76.8
18.	Mission: Impossible—Ghost Protocol	140.6	43.	Contagion	75.7
19.	Sherlock Holmes: A Game of Shadows	136.9	44.	Moneyball	75.0
20.	Super 8	127.0	45.	Justin Bieber: Never Say Never	73.0
21.	Rango	123.5	46.	Dolphin Tale	72.0
22.	Horrible Bosses	117.5	47.	Jack and Jill	71.8
23.	Green Lantern	116.6	48.	No Strings Attached	70.7
24.	The King's Speech	115.9	49.	Mr. Popper's Penguins	68.2
25.	Hop	108.1	50.	Unknown	63.7

Note: Box-office grosses in the U.S. and Canada Jan. 3, 2011-Jan. 2, 2012; some films may have had 2010 release dates.

All-Time Top-Grossing American Movies
Source: Rentrak Corporation

Rank	Title (original release)	Gross (mil)	Rank	Title (original release)	Gross (mil)
1.	Avatar (2009)	$760.5	28.	Transformers (2007)	$319.2
2.	The Avengers (2012)	617.8	29.	Iron Man (2008)	318.6
3.	Titanic (1997)	600.8	30.	Harry Potter and the Sorcerer's Stone (2001)	317.6
4.	The Dark Knight (2008)	533.3	31.	Indiana Jones and the Kingdom of the Crystal Skull (2008)	317.1
5.	Star Wars (1977)	461.0			
6.	Shrek 2 (2004)	436.7	32.	The Lord of the Rings: Fellowship of the Ring (2001)	314.2
7.	E.T. the Extra-Terrestrial (1982)	435.0	33.	The Lion King (1994)	312.9
8.	Star Wars: Episode I—The Phantom Menace (1999)	431.0	34.	Iron Man 2 (2010)	312.4
9.	The Dark Knight Rises (2012)	424.0	35.	Star Wars: Episode II—Attack of the Clones (2002)	310.7
10.	Pirates of the Caribbean: Dead Man's Chest (2006)	423.3	36.	Pirates of the Caribbean: At World's End (2007)	309.4
11.	Toy Story 3 (2010)	415.0	37.	Star Wars: Episode VI—Return of the Jedi (1983)	309.2
12.	The Hunger Games (2012)	407.9	38.	Independence Day (1996)	306.1
13.	Spider-Man (2002)	403.7	39.	Pirates of the Caribbean: The Curse of the Black Pearl (2003)	305.4
14.	Transformers: Revenge of the Fallen (2009)	402.1			
15.	Harry Potter and the Deathly Hallows: Part 2 (2011)	381.0	40.	Harry Potter and the Half Blood Prince (2010)	302.0
16.	Star Wars: Episode III—Revenge of the Sith (2005)	380.2	41.	The Twilight Saga: Eclipse (2010)	300.5
17.	The Lord of the Rings: Return of the King (2003)	377.0	42.	The Twilight Saga: New Moon (2009)	296.6
18.	Spider-Man 2 (2004)	373.3	43.	Harry Potter and the Deathly Hallows: Part 1 (2010)	296.0
19.	The Passion of the Christ (2004)	370.3	44.	The Sixth Sense (1999)	293.5
20.	Jurassic Park (1993)	357.0	45.	Up (2009)	293.0
21.	Transformers: Dark of the Moon (2011)	352.4	46.	Inception (2010)	292.6
22.	The Lord of the Rings: Two Towers (2002)	341.7	47.	Harry Potter and the Order of the Phoenix (2007)	292.6
23.	Finding Nemo (2003)	339.7	48.	The Chronicles of Narnia: The Lion, The Witch, and the Wardrobe (2005)	291.7
24.	Spider-Man 3 (2007)	336.5			
25.	Alice in Wonderland (2010)	334.2	49.	Star Wars: Episode V—The Empire Strikes Back (1980)	290.3
26.	Forrest Gump (1994)	329.7			
27.	Shrek the Third (2007)	322.7	50.	Harry Potter and the Goblet of Fire (2005)	290.0

Note: Box-office grosses in the U.S. and Canada through Aug. 30, 2012, in absolute dollars. Rising ticket prices favor newer films. Revenues from re-releases are included.

100 Best American Movies of All Time
Source: American Film Institute

First unveiled in 1998 based on ballots sent to 1,500 individuals, mostly from the film world, in 1997. Updated in 2007 (the version shown here) to include newly eligible films and reflect shifting cultural perspectives. Criteria for judging included historical significance, cultural impact, critical recognition and awards, and popularity. The year each film was first released is in parentheses.

1. Citizen Kane (1941)
2. The Godfather (1972)
3. Casablanca (1942)
4. Raging Bull (1980)
5. Singin' in the Rain (1952)
6. Gone With the Wind (1939)
7. Lawrence of Arabia (1962)
8. Schindler's List (1993)
9. Vertigo (1958)
10. The Wizard of Oz (1939)
11. City Lights (1931)
12. The Searchers (1956)
13. Star Wars (1977)
14. Psycho (1960)
15. 2001: A Space Odyssey (1968)
16. Sunset Boulevard (1950)
17. The Graduate (1967)
18. The General (1927)
19. On the Waterfront (1954)
20. It's a Wonderful Life (1946)
21. Chinatown (1974)
22. Some Like It Hot (1959)
23. The Grapes of Wrath (1940)
24. E.T. the Extra-Terrestrial (1982)
25. To Kill a Mockingbird (1962)
26. Mr. Smith Goes to Washington (1939)
27. High Noon (1952)
28. All About Eve (1950)
29. Double Indemnity (1944)
30. Apocalypse Now (1979)
31. The Maltese Falcon (1941)
32. The Godfather Part II (1974)
33. One Flew Over the Cuckoo's Nest (1975)
34. Snow White and the Seven Dwarfs (1937)
35. Annie Hall (1977)
36. The Bridge on the River Kwai (1957)
37. The Best Years of Our Lives (1946)

38. The Treasure of the Sierra Madre (1948)
39. Dr. Strangelove (1964)
40. The Sound of Music (1965)
41. King Kong (1933)
42. Bonnie and Clyde (1967)
43. Midnight Cowboy (1969)
44. The Philadelphia Story (1940)
45. Shane (1953)
46. It Happened One Night (1934)
47. A Streetcar Named Desire (1951)
48. Rear Window (1954)
49. Intolerance (1916)
50. The Lord of the Rings: The Fellowship of the Ring (2001)
51. West Side Story (1961)
52. Taxi Driver (1976)
53. The Deer Hunter (1978)
54. M*A*S*H (1970)
55. North by Northwest (1959)
56. Jaws (1975)
57. Rocky (1976)

58. The Gold Rush (1925)
59. Nashville (1975)
60. Duck Soup (1933)
61. Sullivan's Travels (1941)
62. American Graffiti (1973)
63. Cabaret (1972)
64. Network (1976)
65. The African Queen (1951)
66. Raiders of the Lost Ark (1981)
67. Who's Afraid of Virginia Woolf? (1966)
68. Unforgiven (1992)
69. Tootsie (1982)
70. A Clockwork Orange (1971)
71. Saving Private Ryan (1998)
72. The Shawshank Redemption (1994)
73. Butch Cassidy and the Sundance Kid (1969)
74. The Silence of the Lambs (1991)
75. In the Heat of the Night (1967)
76. Forrest Gump (1994)
77. All the President's Men (1976)
78. Modern Times (1936)

79. The Wild Bunch (1969)
80. The Apartment (1960)
81. Spartacus (1960)
82. Sunrise (1927)
83. Titanic (1997)
84. Easy Rider (1969)
85. A Night at the Opera (1935)
86. Platoon (1986)
87. 12 Angry Men (1957)
88. Bringing Up Baby (1938)
89. The Sixth Sense (1999)
90. Swing Time (1936)
91. Sophie's Choice (1982)
92. Goodfellas (1990)
93. The French Connection (1971)
94. Pulp Fiction (1994)
95. The Last Picture Show (1971)
96. Do the Right Thing (1989)
97. Blade Runner (1982)
98. Yankee Doodle Dandy (1942)
99. Toy Story (1995)
100. Ben-Hur (1959)

National Film Registry, 2011

Source: National Film Registry, Library of Congress

The National Film Registry adds 25 "culturally, historically, or aesthetically significant" American films annually.

Allures (1961)	A Cure for Pokeritis (1912)	I, an Actress (1977)	Norma Rae (1979)
Bambi (1942)	El Mariachi (1992)	The Iron Horse (1924)	Porgy and Bess (1959)
The Big Heat (1953)	Faces (1968)	The Kid (1921)	The Silence of the Lambs
A Computer Animated Hand	Fake Fruit Factory (1986)	The Lost Weekend (1945)	(1991)
(1972)	Forrest Gump (1994)	The Negro Soldier (1944)	Stand and Deliver (1988)
Crisis: Behind a Presidential	Growing Up Female (1971)	Nicholas Brothers Family	Twentieth Century (1934)
Commitment (1963)	Hester Street (1975)	Home Movies (1930s-40s)	War of the Worlds (1953)
The Cry of the Children (1912)			

Film and Television Production by State, 2010-11

Source: Motion Picture Association of America

State	Number of productions, examples	State	Number of productions, examples
Alabama*	12, The One Warrior, The Man in the Maze	New Jersey*	46, Gimme Shelter, Drama Class, Bad Parents, Brick City (TV)
Alaska*	17, Big Miracle, Deadliest Catch (TV)	New Mexico*	42, The Avengers, Gambit, The Last Stand, Breaking Bad (TV)
Arizona	31, Under the Bridge, The Coalition		
Arkansas*	5, Mud, Then the Night Comes	New York*	470, Extremely Loud and Incredibly Close, The Bourne Legacy, Damages (TV)
California*	1,117, The Avengers, Drive, The Big Bang Theory (TV)		
		North Carolina*	29, The Hunger Games, Piranha 3DD, Homeland (TV), One Tree Hill (TV)
Colorado*	15, The Girl With the Dragon Tattoo, Unwrapped (TV)		
		North Dakota	4, The Legend of Hell's Gate: An American Conspiracy, The Aviators (TV)
Connecticut*	32, The Big C (TV), Maury (TV)		
Delaware	2, Infamous, Punkin Chunkin (TV)	Ohio*	24, The Avengers, Fun Size, Liberal Arts, One Born Every Minute (TV)
Florida*	42, Magic Mike, Parker, Burn Notice (TV)		
Georgia*	103, Lawless, Flight, The Vampire Diaries (TV)	Oklahoma*	10, The Killer Inside Me, A Christmas Snow, Yellow
Hawaii*	16, Rise of the Planet of the Apes, Battleship		
		Oregon*	27, Gone, ParaNorman, Shiver, Grimm (TV)
Idaho*	1, Leap	Pennsylvania*	37, The Dark Knight Rises, Learning to Fly, One Shot
Illinois*	53, Man of Steel, Lincoln, The Rosie Show (TV)		
		Rhode Island*	9, Moonrise Kingdom, Hall Pass, Body of Proof (TV)
Indiana*	6, Transformers: Dark of the Moon, Resurrection		
		South Carolina*	4, The Bay, Little Red Wagon, Army Wives (TV)
Iowa	2, At Any Price, Scribble		
Kansas*	3, The Casserole Club, Earthwork	South Dakota	2, The Great Mystery, Full Throttle Saloon (TV)
Kentucky*	9, The Ides of March, Land of Tomorrow		
Louisiana*	125, 21 Jump Street, Treme (TV)	Tennessee*	18, Country Strong, Water for Elephants, Fall Away
Maine*	7, Anatomy of the Tide, Black Rock, American Loggers (TV)		
		Texas*	86, Abel's Field, The Ghost of Goodnight Lane, Friday Night Lights (TV)
Maryland*	10, Dead Money, The Haunting of Pearson Place, Ace of Cakes (TV)		
		Utah*	16, John Carter, 127 Hours, My Girlfriend's Boyfriend
Massachusetts*	30, R.I.P.D., That's My Boy, Ted, Frontline (TV)		
		Vermont	1, Dug Up
Michigan*	61, The Five-Year Engagement, The Ides of March, Detroit 1-8-7 (TV)	Virginia*	12, Lincoln, J. Edgar, To Have and to Hold
		Washington*	21, Dancing on the Edge, Desert Cathedral, 21 and Over
Minnesota*	18, Fun Size, Young Adult, Thin Ice		
Mississippi*	8, The Help, The Dynamiter, Mud	Wash., DC*	19, Safe House, J. Edgar, The Chris Matthews Show (TV)
Missouri*	10, A Horrible Way to Die, Small Pond, Turbine		
		West Virginia*	6, Super 8, Cut, Pilgrim Song, Jamie Oliver's Food Revolution (TV)
Montana*	6, Winter in the Blood, Treasure State, Frontier Force (TV)		
		Wisconsin*	4, Transformers: Dark of the Moon, House of Purgatory
Nebraska	3, Vino Veritas, Geocachers, Trunk'd		
Nevada	34, My Mother's Curse, Pretty Obsession, Bachelor Pad (TV)	Wyoming*	5, Django Unchained, Tree Fight, Deeper
New Hampshire	9, The Resurrection of Victor Jara, The A Plate, Joy and the Apocalypse (TV)		

* = State has enacted incentives to increase production.

Movie Theaters, 1946-2011
Source: Motion Picture Association of America; Rentrak Corporation

Year	Box office (mil)	Admissions (mil)	Admissions per week (mil)	Screens	Avg. ticket price	Films produced	Films released
1946	$1,692.0	4,067.3	78.2	NA	$0.42	NA	400
1950	1,379.0	3,017.5	58.0	NA	0.46	NA	483
1955	1,204.0	2,072.3	39.9	NA	0.58	NA	319
1960	984.4	1,304.5	25.1	NA	0.76	NA	248
1965	1,041.8	1,031.5	19.8	NA	1.01	NA	279
1970	1,429.2	920.6	17.7	NA	1.55	279	306
1975	2,114.8	1,032.8	19.9	15,030	2.05	258	233
1980	2,748.5	1,021.5	19.6	17,590	2.69	214	233
1985	3,749.4	1,056.1	20.3	21,147	3.55	264	470
1990	5,021.8	1,188.6	22.9	23,689	4.23	346	410
1995	5,269.0	1,211.0	23.3	27,805	4.35	631	411
2000	7,468.0	1,383.0	26.6	37,396	5.39	683	475
2001	8,125.0	1,438.0	27.7	36,764	5.66	611	454
2002	9,272.0	1,599.0	30.8	35,280	5.81	546	475
2003	9,165.0	1,521.0	29.3	35,786	6.03	593	455
2004	9,215.0	1,484.0	28.5	36,594	6.21	611	489
2005	8,832.0	1,376.0	26.5	38,852	6.41	920	507
2006	9,138.0	1,395.0	26.8	38,415	6.55	928	594
2007	9,629.0	1,400.0	26.9	38,974	6.88	789	611
2008	9,791.0	1,364.0	26.2	38,834	7.18	773	638
2009	10,543.6	1,415.0	27.2	39,233	7.50	751	558
2010	10,741.0	1,341.0	25.8	39,547	7.89	795	569
2011	10,186.1	1,285.0	24.7	39,641	7.93	817	610

NA = Not available.

Top Film Websites, 2012
Source: comScore Media Metrix, Inc.

Rank	Website	Visitors[1]	% change[2]	Rank	Website	Visitors[1]	% change[2]
1.	IMDb.com	35,417	−13.5%	11.	UGO Film-TV	2,870	−37.5%
2.	Yahoo! Movies	26,269	−1.7	12.	Disney Movies	2,415	33.4
3.	Moviefone	14,242	6.2	13.	SolarMovie.eu	2,409	NA
4.	Fandango Movies Portfolio	12,200	−16.6	14.	AMC Entertainment Inc.	2,168	23.8
5.	MSN Movies	11,941	−3.7	15.	WarnerBros.com	1,575	−4.6
6.	Flixster.com	9,684	7.5	16.	Cinemablend.com	1,543	284.6
7.	Rogue Movie Network	6,697	−0.8	17.	WatchSeries.eu	1,541	325.0
8.	Hollywood.com Sites	5,478	−29.0	18.	ScreenRant.com	1,448	31.8
9.	1Channel.ch	4,223	NA	19.	NextMovie.com	1,429	127.7
10.	Hark.com	4,213	103.4	20.	Cinemark.com	1,245	17.4

NA = Not available. (1) Number of unique visitors, in thousands, who visited website at least once in Apr.-June 2012. (2) Percent change over Apr.-June 2011.

Most Popular DVDs, 2011
Source: Rentrak Corporation

Top Rentals, 2011

Rank	Movie	Rank	Movie
1.	Red	12.	Just Go With It
2.	Due Date	13.	The Green Hornet (2011)
3.	Little Fockers	14.	Rango
4.	Unstoppable	15.	Transformers: Dark of the Moon
5.	The Social Network		
6.	Bridesmaids	16.	The Dilemma (2011)
7.	The Tourist	17.	Horrible Bosses
8.	The Lincoln Lawyer	18.	The Town
9.	The Fighter	19.	Harry Potter and the Deathly Hallows: Part 1
10.	Dinner for Schmucks		
11.	Limitless	20.	Inception

Top-Selling DVDs, 2011

Rank	Movie	Rank	Movie
1.	Harry Potter and the Deathly Hallows: Part 1	10.	The Help
		11.	Due Date
2.	Tangled	12.	Fast Five
3.	Harry Potter and the Deathly Hallows: Part 2	13.	Rise of the Planet of the Apes
4.	Cars	14.	Secretariat
5.	Rio	15.	Beverly Hills Chihuahua 2
6.	The Hangover 2	16.	X-Men: First Class
7.	Bridesmaids	17.	Red
8.	Megamind	18.	Tron: Legacy
9.	Transformers: Dark of the Moon	19.	Gnomeo and Juliet
		20.	Yogi Bear

Note: Top-selling DVDs exclude units sold into the rental channel, online, and in Canada. Top rental DVDs exclude kiosk and online/by-mail channels.

Top-Selling Video Games, 2011
Source: The NPD Group/Retail Tracking Service; ranked by retail units sold

The video game industry (which includes hardware, software, and accessories) generated U.S. retail sales (including digital sales) in 2011 of $24.8 bil, a 1.2% decrease from $25.1 bil in 2010.

Rank	Game (console)	Rank	Game (console)
1.	Call of Duty: Modern Warfare 3* (360, NDS, PC, PS3, Wii)	6.	NBA 2K12 (360, iOS, PS2, PS3, PSP, Wii)
2.	Just Dance 3 (360, PS3, Wii)	7.	Batman: Arkham City* (360, PC, PS3, Wii)
3.	Madden NFL 12 (360, iOS, PS2, PS3, PSP, Wii)	8.	Gears of War 3* (360)
4.	Battlefield 3 (360, iOS, PC, PS3)	9.	Assassin's Creed: Revelations* (360, PC, PS3)
5.	The Elder Scrolls V: Skyrim* (360, PC, PS3)	10.	FIFA Soccer 12 (360, iOS, PC, PS2, PS3, PSP, Wii)

* = Includes collector's, limited, legendary, and bundled editions. 360 = Microsoft Xbox 360; iOS = Apple mobile operating system devices (iPad, iPhone); NDS = Nintendo DS; PC = personal computer; PSP = PlayStation Portable; PS3 = PlayStation 3; PS2 = PlayStation 2; Wii = Nintendo Wii.

Film and TV Content Ratings

The Motion Picture Association of America (MPAA) began rating movies in 1968. The system was heavily revised in 1984 and again in 1990. The MPAA, National Cable Television Association, and National Association of Broadcasters developed and revised the TV ratings system in 1997, in accordance with the Telecommunications Act of 1996; it was implemented in Oct. 1997.

Film Ratings

G: General Audience. All ages admitted. Does not contain themes, language, nudity, sex, or violence that the MPAA ratings board believes would offend parents whose younger children see the film. Does not necessarily denote a certificate of approval nor children's movie. No nudity, sex scenes, or drug use depicted.

PG: Parental Guidance Suggested. Some material may not be suited for children. The MPAA ratings board recommends that parents determine whether the content of the film is appropriate for their children. The film may contain more mature themes, some profanity, violence, or brief nudity. No drug use depicted.

PG-13: Parents Strongly Cautioned. Some material may be inappropriate for children under 13. The MPAA urges more strongly that parents vet the movie to see if its content is appropriate for their children. Any movie depicting drug use or more than brief nudity is automatically rated at least PG-13. Violence is permitted, though it is generally not both realistic or extreme and persistent violence. The single use of one sexually-derived expletive rates a PG-13; more than one use requires at least an R rating.

R: Restricted. Under 17 requires accompanying parent or adult guardian. Movies given R ratings contain some adult material, defined as adult themes or activity, hard language, intense or persistent violence, sexually-oriented nudity, or drug abuse.

NC-17: No One 17 and Under Admitted. The ratings board considers NC-17 films those that most parents would consider too adult for children under 17. An NC-17 rating does not mean the film is obscene or pornographic. The rating can be based on violence, sex, aberrational behavior, drug abuse, or any other element that most parents would consider too adult for children.

TV Ratings

TV-Y: All Children. Program designed to be acceptable for children of all ages. Its themes and elements are designed for a very young audience.

TV-Y7: Directed to Older Children. Program designed for children ages 7 and older, and more appropriate for those who have the skills to distinguish between make-believe and reality. May include mild fantasy/comedic violence. Programs with more than mild fantasy violence are denoted with FV.

TV-G: General Audience. Program not necessarily designed for children, but most parents would find it suitable for all ages. Little or no violence, no strong language, and little or no sexual dialogue or situations.

TV-PG: Parental Guidance Suggested. Program might contain material that parents would consider inappropriate for children, such as an adult theme or one or more of the following: suggestive dialogue (D), infrequent coarse language (L), some sexual situations (S), or moderate violence (V).

TV-14: Parents Strongly Cautioned. Program contains material that many parents would consider inappropriate for children under 14, such as one or more of the following: intensely suggestive dialogue (D), strong coarse language (L), intense sexual situations (S), or intense violence (V).

TV-MA: Mature Audience Only. Program specifically designed for adults and may be unsuitable for children under 17. Contains one or more of the following: crude indecent language (L), explicit sexual activity (S), or graphic violence (V).

Longest-Running Broadway Plays

Source: The Broadway League, New York, NY

Rank	Title (run)[1]	Performances[2]	Rank	Title (run)[1]	Performances[2]	Rank	Title (run)[1]	Performances[2]
1.	*The Phantom of the Opera (1988-)	10,121	17.	Tobacco Road (1933-41)	3,182	35.	Gemini (1977-81)	1,819
2.	Cats (1982-2000)	7,485	18.	Hello Dolly! (1964-70)	2,844	36.	Deathtrap (1978-82)	1,793
3.	Les Misérables (1987-2003)	6,680	19.	My Fair Lady (1956-62)	2,717	37.	Harvey (1944-49)	1,775
4.	*Chicago (revival, 1996-)	6,448	20.	*Jersey Boys (2005-)	2,710	38.	Dancin' (1978-82)	1,774
5.	A Chorus Line (1975-90)	6,137	21.	Hairspray (2002-09)	2,642	39.	La Cage aux Folles (1983-87)	1,761
6.	*The Lion King (1997-)	6,035	22.	Avenue Q (2003-09)	2,534	40.	Hair (1968-72)	1,750
7.	Oh! Calcutta! (revival, 1976-89)	5,959	23.	The Producers (2001-07)	2,502	41.	The Wiz (1975-79)	1,672
			24.	Cabaret (revival, 1998-2004)	2,377	42.	Born Yesterday (1946-49)	1,642
8.	Beauty and the Beast (1994-2007)	5,461	24.	Annie (1977-83)	2,377	43.	Crazy For You (1992-96)	1,622
9.	Rent (1996-2008)	5,123	26.	Man of La Mancha (1965-71)	2,328	44.	Ain't Misbehavin' (1978-82)	1,604
10.	*Mamma Mia! (2001-)	4,398	27.	Abie's Irish Rose (1922-27)	2,327	45.	The Best Little Whorehouse in Texas (1978-82)	1,584
11.	Miss Saigon (1991-2001)	4,092	28.	*Mary Poppins (2006-)	2,303			
12.	*Wicked (2003-)	3,556	29.	Oklahoma! (1943-48)	2,212	46.	Spamalot (2005-09)	1,575
13.	42nd Street (1980-89)	3,486	30.	Smokey Joe's Cafe (1995-2000)	2,036	47.	Mary, Mary (1961-64)	1,572
14.	Grease (1972-80)	3,388	31.	Pippin (1972-77)	1,944	48.	Evita (1979-83)	1,567
15.	Fiddler on the Roof (1964-72)	3,242	32.	South Pacific (1949-54)	1,925	49.	The Voice of the Turtle (1943-48)	1,557
16.	Life With Father (1939-47)	3,224	33.	The Magic Show (1974-78)	1,920	50.	Jekyll & Hyde (1997-2001)	1,543
			34.	Aida (2000-04)	1,852			

* = Still running as of Sept. 1, 2012. (1) Unless noted, listings reflect a play's first run on Broadway. (2) Number of performances through May 27, 2012.

Broadway Season Statistics, 1959-2012

Source: The Broadway League, New York, NY

Season	Gross (mil $)	Attendance (mil)	Playing weeks	New productions	Season	Gross (mil $)	Attendance (mil)	Playing weeks	New productions
1959-1960	$46	7.9	1,156	58	2004-2005	$769	11.5	1,494	39
1964-1965	50	8.2	1,250	67	2005-2006	862	12.0	1,501	39
1969-1970	53	7.1	1,047	62	2006-2007	939	12.3	1,509	35
1974-1975	57	6.6	1,101	54	2007-2008	938	12.3	1,560	36
1979-1980	146	9.6	1,540	61	2008-2009	943	12.2	1,548	43
1984-1985	209	7.3	1,078	33	2009-2010	1,020	11.9	1,464	39
1989-1990	282	8.0	1,070	40	2010-2011	1,080	12.5	1,588	42
1994-1995	406	9.0	1,120	33	2011-2012	1,139	12.3	1,522	41
1999-2000	603	11.4	1,464	37					

Notable U.S. Museums

This unofficial list of some of the largest (by budget) museums in the U.S. was compiled with the assistance of the American Association of Museums, a national association representing the concerns of the museum community. Association members also include zoos, aquariums, arboretums, botanical gardens, and planetariums, but these are not included in *The World Almanac* listings.

Museum	City	State
American Museum of Natural History	New York	NY
Amon Carter Museum of Western Art	Ft. Worth	TX
The Art Institute of Chicago	Chicago	IL
Boston Children's Museum	Boston	MA
Brooklyn Museum of Art	Brooklyn	NY
Busch-Reisinger Museum	Cambridge	MA
California Academy of Sciences	San Francisco	CA
California Science Center	Los Angeles	CA
Carnegie Museums of Pittsburgh	Pittsburgh	PA
Children's Museum of Indianapolis	Indianapolis	IN
Cincinnati Art Museum	Cincinnati	OH
Cincinnati Museum Center	Cincinnati	OH
Cleveland Museum of Art	Cleveland	OH
Colonial Williamsburg	Williamsburg	VA
Corning Museum of Glass	Corning	NY
Crystal Bridges Museum of American Art	Bentonville	AR
Dallas Museum of Art	Dallas	TX
Denver Art Museum	Denver	CO
Denver Museum of Nature and Science	Denver	CO
Detroit Institute of Arts	Detroit	MI
Exploratorium	San Francisco	CA
The Field Museum	Chicago	IL
Fine Arts Museums of San Francisco	San Francisco	CA
Franklin Institute	Philadelphia	PA
The Frick Collection	New York	NY
J. Paul Getty Museum	Los Angeles	CA
Solomon R. Guggenheim Museum of Art	New York	NY
Harvard University Art Museums	Cambridge	MA
Henry F. Dupont Winterthur Museum	Winterthur	DE
Henry Ford Museum/Greenfield Village	Dearborn	MI
High Museum of Art	Atlanta	GA
Houston Museum of Natural Science	Houston	TX
Jamestown-Yorktown Foundation	Williamsburg	VA
Jewish Museum	New York	NY
L.A. County Museum of Art	Los Angeles	CA
Liberty Science Center, Liberty State Park	Jersey City	NJ
Maryland Science Center	Baltimore	MD
Mashantucket Pequot Museum and Research Center	Mashantucket	CT
Metropolitan Museum of Art	New York	NY
Milwaukee Public Museum	Milwaukee	WI
Minneapolis Institute of Arts	Minneapolis	MN
Museum of African American History	Detroit	MI
Museum of the American West	Los Angeles	CA
Museum of Contemporary Art	Los Angeles	CA
Museum of Fine Arts	Boston	MA
Museum of Fine Arts	Houston	TX
Museum of Modern Art	New York	NY
Museum of New Mexico	Santa Fe	NM
Museum of Science	Boston	MA
Museum of Science and Industry	Chicago	IL
Musical Instrument Museum	Phoenix	AZ
Mystic Seaport Museum	Mystic	CT
National Air and Space Museum	Washington	DC
National Baseball Hall of Fame and Museum, Inc.	Cooperstown	NY
National Constitution Center	Philadelphia	PA
National Gallery of Art	Washington	DC
National Museum of American History	Washington	DC
National Museum of the American Indian	Washington	DC
National Museum of Natural History	Washington	DC
Nelson-Atkins Museum of Art	Kansas City	MO
New York Historical Society	New York	NY
New York State Museum	Albany	NY
Peabody Essex Museum	Salem	MA
Philadelphia Museum of Art	Philadelphia	PA
Rock and Roll Hall of Fame and Museum, Inc.	Cleveland	OH
St. Louis Science Center	St. Louis	MO
San Diego Museum of Art	San Diego	CA
San Francisco Museum of Modern Art	San Francisco	CA
Science Museum of Minnesota	St. Paul	MN
Toledo Museum of Art	Toledo	OH
U.S. Holocaust Memorial Museum	Washington	DC
Univ. of Pennsylvania Museum of Archaeology and Anthropology	Philadelphia	PA
Virginia Museum of Fine Arts	Richmond	VA
Wadsworth Atheneum	Hartford	CT
Walker Art Center	Minneapolis	MN
Whitney Museum of American Art	New York	NY

Symphony Orchestras: Most Performed Composers, 2009-10

Source: League of American Orchestras

Composer	Performances	Composer	Performances	Composer	Performances
Ludwig Van Beethoven	457	Maurice Ravel	123	Samuel Barber	94
Wolfgang Amadeus Mozart	450	Sergei Rachmaninoff	121	Richard Wagner	92
Piotr Ilyich Tchaikovsky	252	Felix Mendelssohn	107	Hector Berlioz	85
Johannes Brahms	229	Jean Sibelius	106	George Frederic Handel	83
Igor Stravinsky	165	Sergei Prokofiev	104	Bela Bartok	80
Richard Strauss	145	Gustav Mahler	95	Antonio Vivaldi	78
Franz Joseph Haydn	144	Dmitri Shostakovich	95	Robert Schumann	77
Antonin Dvořák	123				

Note: Scheduled performances of a given composer's work(s) during the 2009-10 season (generally Oct.-Sept.) by members of the League of American Orchestras.

Opera: Most Produced Works, 2011-12

Source: OPERA America

Work, composer	Productions	Work, composer	Productions	Work, composer	Productions
Madama Butterfly, Giacomo Puccini	13	*Lucia di Lammermoor*, Gaetano Donizetti	8	*La traviata*, Giuseppe Verdi	7
Aida, Giuseppe Verdi	9	*Don Giovanni*, Wolfgang Amadeus Mozart	8	*Pagliacci*, Ruggiero Leoncavallo	7
La bohème, Giacomo Puccini	8	*Tosca*, Giacomo Puccini	8	*Le nozze di Figaro [The Marriage of Figaro]*, Wolfgang Amadeus Mozart	7
Carmen, Georges Bizet	8				

Note: Scheduled productions of a given work (not individual performances) during the 2011-12 season (generally Oct.-Sept.) by members of OPERA America and Opera.ca.

Best-Selling U.S. Magazines, 2012

Source: Audit Bureau of Circulations (ABC)

General magazines, exclusive of comics; also excluding magazines that failed to file reports to ABC by press time. Based on total average paid and verified circulation during the six months ending June 30, 2012, ranked by paid circulation size.

Publication	Paid circ.	Publication	Paid circ.	Publication	Paid circ.
1. AARP The Magazine	22,528,478	8. Family Circle	4,100,977	16. Prevention	2,930,730
2. AARP Bulletin	22,283,411	9. People	3,563,035	17. Southern Living	2,841,331
3. Game Informer Magazine	8,169,524	10. Woman's Day	3,449,692	18. AAA Via	2,590,421
4. Better Homes and Gardens	7,617,038	11. Time	3,276,822	19. Maxim	2,518,827
5. Reader's Digest	5,577,717	12. Taste of Home	3,231,697	20. AAA Living	2,459,089
6. Good Housekeeping	4,346,757	13. Ladies' Home Journal	3,205,302	21. O, The Oprah Magazine	2,444,934
7. National Geographic	4,232,205	14. Sports Illustrated	3,204,945	22. AAA Going Places	2,439,257
		15. Cosmopolitan	3,017,834	23. Glamour	2,374,291

Publication	Paid circ.	Publication	Paid circ.	Publication	Paid circ.
24. American Legion Magazine	2,284,729	32. Seventeen	2,025,299	42. Every Day With Rachael Ray	1,709,309
25. Parenting	2,232,588	33. TV Guide Magazine	2,010,879	43. American Rifleman	1,696,922
26. Redbook	2,222,177	34. FamilyFun	1,985,827	44. Gold Digest	1,677,098
27. Smithsonian	2,138,931	35. Us Weekly	1,977,251	45. Country Living	1,641,000
28. ESPN the Magazine	2,132,897	36. Men's Health	1,918,387	46. Shape	1,635,933
29. Martha Stewart Living	2,082,348	37. Money	1,908,509	47. Women's Health	1,617,737
		38. Cooking Light	1,814,471	48. Food Network Magazine	1,597,796
30. Parents	2,058,281	39. Entertainment Weekly	1,781,934	49. Bon Appetit	1,541,469
31. Real Simple	2,031,596	40. Guideposts	1,774,250	50. Self	1,528,583
		41. In Style	1,767,248		

Most Challenged Books, 2011

Source: Office for Intellectual Freedom, American Library Association (ALA)

A challenge is a formal, written complaint filed with a library or school requesting that materials be removed because of content or appropriateness.

Rank	Title, author	Common reasons given for challenge
1.	*ttyl; ttfn; l8r, g8r* (series), Lauren Myracle	Offensive language; religious viewpoint; sexually explicit; unsuited to age group
2.	*The Color of Earth* (series), Kim Dong Hwa	Nudity; sex education; sexually explicit; unsuited to age group
3.	*The Hunger Games* trilogy, Suzanne Collins	Anti-ethnic; anti-family; insensitivity; offensive language; occult/satanic; violence
4.	*My Mom's Having a Baby! A Kid's Month-by-Month Guide to Pregnancy*, Dori Hillestad Butler	Nudity; sex education; sexually explicit; unsuited to age group
5.	*The Absolutely True Diary of a Part-Time Indian*, Sherman Alexie	Offensive language; racism; religious viewpoint; sexually explicit; unsuited to age group
6.	*Alice* (series), Phyllis Reynolds Naylor	Nudity; offensive language; religious viewpoint
7.	*Brave New World*, Aldous Huxley	Insensitivity; nudity; racism; religious viewpoint; sexually explicit
8.	*What My Mother Doesn't Know*, Sonya Sones	Nudity; offensive language; sexually explicit
9.	*Gossip Girl* (series), Cecily Von Ziegesar	Drugs; offensive language; sexually explicit
10.	*To Kill a Mockingbird*, Harper Lee	Offensive language; racism

Some Notable New Books, 2012

Source: Reference and User Services Association, American Library Association (ALA)

Fiction

Lost Memory of Skin, Russell Banks
The Sense of an Ending, Julian Barnes
The Sisters Brothers, Patrick deWitt
Say Her Name, Francisco Goldman
The Art of Fielding, Chad Harbach
Light Lifting, Alexander MacLeod
The Tiger's Wife, Téa Obreht
The Cat's Table, Michael Ondaatje
The Tragedy of Arthur, Arthur Phillips
Swamplandia!, Karen Russell
We the Animals, Justin Torres
Selected Stories, William Trevor

Poetry

Illuminations, Arthur Rimbaud, John Ashbery (trans.)
Beauty Is a Verb: The New Poetry of Disability, Jennifer Bartlett, Sheila Black, and Michael Northen

Nonfiction

Right Turn at Machu Picchu: Rediscovering the Lost City One Step at a Time, Mark Adams
The Memory Palace, Mira Bartók
The Information: A History, a Theory, a Flood, James Gleick
The Swerve: How the World Became Modern, Stephen Greenblatt
Unbroken: A World War II Story of Survival, Resilience, and Redemption, Laura Hillenbrand
Arguably: Essays, Christopher Hitchens
Apollo's Angels: A History of Ballet, Jennifer Homans
Thinking, Fast and Slow, Daniel Kahneman
Malcolm X: A Life of Reinvention, Manning Marable
Destiny of the Republic: A Tale of Madness, Medicine, and the Murder of a President, Candace Millard
Emperor of All Maladies: A Biography of Cancer, Siddhartha Mukherjee
Inside Scientology: The Story of America's Most Secretive Religion, Janet Reitman

Some Notable New Books for Children, 2012

Source: Association for Library Service to Children, American Library Association (ALA)

Younger Readers

All the Water in the World, George Ella Lyon, Katherine Tillotson (illus.)
A Ball for Daisy, Chris Raschka
Blackout, John Rocco
Bring on the Birds, Susan Stockdale
The Cazuela That the Farm Maiden Stirred, Samantha R. Vamos, Rafael López (illus.)
Chirchir Is Singing, Kelly Cunnane, Jude Daly (illus.)
Do You Know Which Ones Will Grow?, Susan A. Shea, Tom Slaughter (illus.)
Dot, Patricia Intriago
Goodnight, Goodnight, Construction Site, Sherri Duskey Rinker, Tom Lichtenheld (illus.)
Grandpa Green, Lane Smith
Harry and Hopper, Margaret Wild, Freya Blackwood (illus.)
I Broke My Trunk, Mo Willems
I Want My Hat Back, Jon Klassen
King Jack and the Dragon, Peter Bently, Helen Oxenbury (illus.)
Little Treasures: Endearments From Around the World, Jacqueline K. Ogburn, Chris Raschka (illus.)

Little White Rabbit, Kevin Henkes
Me... Jane, Patrick McDonnell
Mouse & Lion, Rand Burkert, Nancy Ekholm Burkert (illus.)
Naamah and the Ark at Night, Susan Campbell Bartoletti, Holly Meade (illus.)
A New Year's Reunion: A Chinese Story, Yu Li-Qiong, Zhu Cheng-Liang (illus.)
Over and Under the Snow, Kate Messner, Christopher Silas Neal (illus.)
Prudence Wants a Pet, Cathleen Daly, Stephen Michael King (illus.)
See Me Run, Paul Meisel
Should I Share My Ice Cream?, Mo Willems
Stars, Mary Lyn Ray, Marla Frazee (illus.)
Tales for Very Picky Eaters, Josh Schneider
Tell Me the Day Backwards, Albert Lamb, David McPhail (illus.)
Ten Little Caterpillars, Bill Martin Jr., Lois Ehlert (illus.)
These Hands, Margaret H. Mason, Floyd Cooper (illus.)
Tía Isa Wants a Car, Meg Medina, Claudio Muñoz (illus.)
Where's Walrus?, Stephen Savage
Who Has What?: All About Girls' Bodies and Boys' Bodies, Robie H. Harris, Nadine Bernard Westcott (illus.)

Middle Readers

America Is Under Attack: September 11, 2001: The Day the Towers Fell, Don Brown
Balloons Over Broadway: The True Story of the Puppeteer of Macy's Parade, Melissa Sweet
Breaking Stalin's Nose, Eugene Yelchin,
The Cheshire Cheese Cat: A Dickens of a Tale, Carmen Agra Deedy and Randall Wright, Barry Moser (illus.)
Diego Rivera: His World and Ours, Duncan Tonatiuh
Dream Something Big: The Story of the Watts Towers, Dianna Hutts Aston, Susan L. Roth (illus.)
E-mergency!, Tom Lichtenheld, Ezra Fields-Meyer (illus.)
Emma Dilemma: Big Sister Poems, Kristine O'Connell George, Nancy Carpenter (illus.)
The Great Migration: Journey to the North, Eloise Greenfield, Jan Spivey Gilchrist (illus.)
Inside Out and Back Again, Thanhha Lai
Junonia, Kevin Henkes
Lemonade, and Other Poems Squeezed From a Single Word, Bob Raczka, Nancy Doniger (illus.)
The Lily Pond, Annika Thor, Linda Schenck (trans.)
The Mangrove Tree: Planting Trees to Feed Families, Susan L. Roth and Cindy Trumbore, Susan L. Roth (illus.)
Marisol McDonald Doesn't Match/Marisol McDonald no combina, Monica Brown, Sara Palacios (illus.)
Maximilian and the Mystery of the Guardian Angel: A Bilingual Lucha Libre Thriller, Xavier Garza
Migrant, Maxine Trottier, Isabelle Arsenault (illus.)
Night Flight: Amelia Earhart Crosses the Atlantic, Robert Burleigh, Wendell Minor (illus.)
No Ordinary Day, Deborah Ellis
Nursery Rhyme Comics: 50 Timeless Rhymes From 50 Celebrated Cartoonists, Chris Duffy (ed.)
Soldier Bear, Bibi Dumon Tak, Philip Hopman (illus.), Laura Watkinson (trans.)
The Third Gift, Linda Sue Park, Bagram Ibatoulline (illus.)
Thunder Birds: Nature's Flying Predators, Jim Arnosky
Treasury of Greek Mythology: Classic Stories of Gods, Goddesses, Heroes, & Monsters, Donna Jo Napoli, Christina Balit (illus.)
The Trouble With May Amelia, Jennifer L. Holm
Underground, Shane Evans
The Unforgotten Coat, Frank Cottrell Boyce, Carl Hunter and Clare Heney (illus.)
The Watcher: Jane Goodall's Life With the Chimps, Jeanette Winter
Wonderstruck, Brian Selznick
Won-Ton: A Cat Tale Told in Haiku, Lee Wardlaw, Eugene Yelchin (illus.)
Young Fredle, Cynthia Voigt, Louise Yates (illus.)
Zita the Spacegirl, Ben Hatke

Older Readers

Amelia Lost: The Life and Disappearance of Amelia Earhart, Candace Fleming
Anya's Ghost, Vera Brosgol

Between Shades of Gray, Ruta Sepetys
Billions of Years, Amazing Changes: The Story of Evolution, Laurence Pringle, Steve Jenkins (illus.)
Black & White: The Confrontation Between Reverend Fred L. Shuttlesworth and Eugene "Bull" Connor, Larry Dane Brimner
Blizzard of Glass: The Halifax Explosion of 1917, Sally M. Walker
Bluefish, Pat Schmatz
Bootleg: Murder, Moonshine, and the Lawless Years of Prohibition, Karen Blumenthal
Dead End in Norvelt, Jack Gantos
Drawing From Memory, Allen Say
The Elephant Scientist, Caitlin O'Connell and Donna M. Jackson, Caitlin O'Connell and Timothy Rodwell (illus.)
The Fingertips of Duncan Dorfman, Meg Wolitzer
Flyaway, Lucy Christopher
Hidden, Helen Frost
The House Baba Built: An Artist's Childhood in China, Ed Young and Libby Koponen, Ed Young (illus.)
How They Croaked: The Awful Ends of the Awfully Famous, Georgia Bragg, Kevin O'Malley (illus.)
Hurricane Dancers: The First Caribbean Pirate Shipwreck, Margarita Engle
Into the Unknown: How Great Explorers Found Their Way by Land, Sea, and Air, Stuart Ross, Stephen Biesty (illus.)
Jefferson's Sons: A Founding Father's Secret Children, Kimberly Brubaker Bradley
Lost & Found, Shaun Tan
A Monster Calls: A Novel, Patrick Ness
Music Was It: Young Leonard Bernstein, Susan Goldman Rubin
Okay for Now, Gary D. Schmidt
Queen of Hearts, Martha Brooks
Raggin', Jazzin', Rockin': A History of American Musical Instrument Makers, Susan VanHecke
The Scorpio Races, Maggie Stiefvater
Sita's Ramayana, Samhita Arni, Moyna Chitrakar (illus.)
Space, Stars, and the Beginning of Time: What the Hubble Telescope Saw, Elaine Scott
Stones for My Father, Trilby Kent
Tall Story, Candy Gourlay
Terezin: Voices From the Holocaust, Ruth Thomson
Under the Mesquite, Guadalupe Garcia McCall
Witches! The Absolutely True Tale of Disaster in Salem, Rosalyn Schanzer

All Ages

Can We Save the Tiger?, Martin Jenkins, Vicky White (illus.)
Heart and Soul: The Story of America and African Americans, Kadir Nelson
If Rocks Could Sing: A Discovered Alphabet, Leslie McGuirk
Never Forgotten, Patricia McKissack, Leo and Diane Dillon (illus.)
Press Here, Hervé Tullet
Swirl by Swirl: Spirals in Nature, Joyce Sidman, Beth Krommes (illus.)

Best-Selling Books, 2011

Source: Publishers Weekly

Hardcover Fiction

1. *The Litigators*, John Grisham
2. *11/23/1963*, Stephen King
3. *The Best of Me*, Nicholas Sparks
4. *Smokin' Seventeen*, Janet Evanovich
5. *A Dance With Dragons*, George R. R. Martin
6. *Explosive Eighteen*, Janet Evanovich
7. *Kill Alex Cross*, James Patterson
8. *Micro*, Michael Crichton
9. *Dead Reckoning*, Charlaine Harris
10. *Locked On*, Tom Clancy with Mark Greaney

Hardcover Nonfiction

1. *Steve Jobs*, Walter Isaacson
2. *Unbroken: A World War II Story of Survival, Resilience, and Redemption*, Laura Hillenbrand
3. *Killing Lincoln: The Shocking Assassination That Changed America Forever*, Bill O'Reilly and Martin Dugard
4. *The 17 Day Diet: A Doctor's Plan Designed for Rapid Results*, Dr. Mike Moreno
5. *Stolen Life: A Memoir*, Jaycee Dugard
6. *Bossypants*, Tina Fey
7. *Go the F**k to Sleep*, Adam Mansbach, Ricardo Cortes (illus.)

8. *Every Day a Friday: How to Be Happier 7 Days a Week*, Joel Osteen
9. *Gabby: A Story of Courage and Hope*, Gabrielle Gifford and Mark Kelly with Jeffrey Zaslow
10. *In the Garden of Beasts: Love, Terror, and an American Family in Hitler's Berlin*, Erik Larson

Mass Market Fiction

1. *A Feast for Crows*, George R. R. Martin
2. *The Confession*, John Grisham
3. *A Game of Thrones*, George R. R. Martin
4. *A Clash of Kings*, George R. R. Martin
5. *A Storm of Swords*, George R. R. Martin
6. *The Search*, Nora Roberts
7. *Sizzling Sixteen*, Janet Evanovich
8. *Worth Dying For*, Lee Child
9. *Big Girl*, Danielle Steel
10. *Smokin' Seventeen*, Janet Evanovich

Trade Paperbacks

1. *The Help*, Kathryn Stockett
2. *Heaven Is for Real*, Todd Burpo
3. *Water for Elephants*, Sara Gruen

4. *The Girl With the Dragon Tattoo*, Stieg Larsson
5. *The Next Always*, Nora Roberts
6. *Sarah's Key*, Tatiana de Rosnay
7. *Cutting for Stone*, Abraham Verghese
8. *One Day*, David Nicholls
9. *Safe Haven*, Nicholas Sparks
10. *Inside of a Dog: What Dogs See, Smell, and Know*, Alexandra Horowitz

E-books

1. *The Help*, Kathryn Stockett
2. *Heaven Is for Real*, Todd Burpo
3. *Unbroken*, Laura Hillenbrand
4. *Steve Jobs*, Walter Isaacson
5. *The Lincoln Lawyer*, Michael Connelly
6. *Explosive Eighteen*, Janet Evanovich
7. *Stolen Life*, Jaycee Dugard
8. *Bossypants*, Tina Fey
9. *Now You See Her*, James Patterson
10. *Something Borrowed*, Emily Giffin

Children's and Young Adult Hardcover

1. *Cabin Fever (Diary of a Wimpy Kid #6)*, Jeff Kinney
2. *Inheritance (Inheritance Cycle #4)*, Christopher Paolini
3. *The Son of Neptune (Heroes of Olympus #2)*, Rick Riordan

4. *The Throne of Fire (Kane Chronicles #2)*, Rick Riordan
5. *Destined (House of Night #9)*, P.C. and Kristin Cast
6. *Middle School: The Worst Years of My Life*, James Patterson and Chris Tebbetts, Laura Park (illus.)
7. *Every Thing on It*, Shel Silverstein
8. *If You Give a Dog a Donut*, Laura Numeroff, Felicia Bond (illus.)
9. *City of Fallen Angels (Mortal Instruments #4)*, Cassandra Clare
10. *Tales From a Not-So-Talented Pop Star (Dork Diaries #3)*, Rachel Renée Russell

Children's and Young Adult Paperback

1. *Breaking Dawn (Twilight Saga #4)*, Stephenie Meyer
2. *Witch & Wizard*, James Patterson and Gabrielle Charbonnet
3. *Phineas and Ferb: Across the 2nd Dimension*
4. *Pinkalicious: Pinkie Promise*, Victoria Kann
5. *The Last Olympian (Percy Jackson and the Olympians #5)*, Rick Riordan
6. *Phineas and Ferb: Agent P's Top-Secret Joke Book*
7. *Race Around the World (Disney/Pixar Cars 2)*
8. *Fang (Maximum Ride #6)*, James Patterson
9. *African Cats: A Lion's Pride*
10. *Beastly*, Alex Flin

U.S. Daily Newspapers, 2011

Source: *Editor & Publisher International Data Book*, 2012

As of Feb. 1, 2012, the number of U.S. daily newspapers had fallen to 1,382, for a net loss of 15 since Feb. 1, 2010. The number of Sunday papers fell by 19, to 900. Average daily circulation fell by 1.9 mil, from 46.3 mil in 2009 to about 44.4 mil in 2011. Average Sunday circulation rose by 1.6 mil, from 46.9 mil in 2009 to 48.5 mil in 2011.

(ranked by circulation as of Sept. 30, 2011; m = morning, d = all day)

Rank	Newspaper (edition)	Circulation	Rank	Newspaper (edition)	Circulation
1.	New York (NY) *Wall Street Journal* (m)	2,096,169	27.	San Diego (CA) *Union-Tribune* (m)	219,347
2.	McLean (VA) *USA Today* (m)	1,784,242	28.	Las Vegas (NV) *Review-Journal* (m)	213,078
3.	New York (NY) *Times* (m)	1,150,589	29.	Newark (NJ) *Star-Ledger* (m)	210,586
4.	New York (NY) *Daily News* (m)	605,677	30.	Boston (MA) *Globe* (m)	205,939
5.	Los Angeles (CA) *Times* (m)	572,998	31.	Sacramento (CA) *Bee* (m)	199,921
6.	San Jose (CA) *Mercury News* (m)	527,568	32.	Kansas City (MO) *Star* (m)	199,222
7.	New York (NY) *Post* (m)	512,067	33.	St. Louis (MO) *Post-Dispatch* (m)	191,631
8.	Washington (DC) *Post* (m)	507,465	34.	Fort Worth (TX) *Star-Telegram* (m)	189,795
9.	Chicago (IL) *Tribune* (m)	425,370	35.	Milwaukee (WI) *Journal Sentinel* (m)	188,819
10.	Dallas (TX) *Morning News* (m)	409,642	36.	St. Paul (MN) *Pioneer Press* (m)	188,081
11.	Long Island (NY) *Newsday* (m)	404,542	37.	Pittsburgh (PA) *Tribune-Review* (m)	187,875
12.	Chicago (IL) *Sun-Times* (m)	389,353	38.	Little Rock (AR) *Democrat-Gazette* (m)	179,134
13.	Houston (TX) *Chronicle* (m)	369,710	39.	Honolulu (HI) *Star-Advertiser* (m)	178,082
14.	Denver (CO) *Post* (m)	353,115	40.	San Juan (PR) *Nuevo Día* (m)	178,005
15.	Philadelphia (PA) *Inquirer* (m)	331,134	41.	Atlanta (GA) *Journal-Constitution* (m)	173,884
16.	Minneapolis (MN) *Star Tribune* (m)	298,147	42.	Pittsburgh (PA) *Post-Gazette* (m)	173,160
17.	Phoenix (AZ) *Republic* (m)	292,838	43.	Indianapolis (IN) *Star* (m)	171,662
18.	Orange County (CA) *Register* (m)	270,809	44.	Orlando (FL) *Sentinel* (d)	171,418
19.	New York (NY) *am New York* (m)	266,852	45.	Baltimore (MD) *Sun* (m)	170,510
20.	Washington (DC) *Examiner* (m)	259,906	46.	Miami (FL) *Herald* (m)	160,505
21.	Cleveland (OH) *Plain Dealer* (m)	243,299	47.	Buffalo (NY) *News* (m)	152,074
22.	Seattle (WA) *Times* (m)	242,814	48.	Ft. Lauderdale (FL) *South Florida Sun-Sentinel* (m)	147,860
23.	Portland (OR) *Oregonian* (d)	242,784	49.	Woodland Park (NJ) *Record, Herald News* (m)	146,523
24.	St. Petersburg (FL) *Times* (m)	240,024	50.	Norfolk (VA) *Virginian-Pilot* (m)	145,785
25.	Detroit (MI) *Free Press* (m)	234,579			
26.	San Francisco (CA) *Chronicle* (m)	220,515			

Paid U.S. Newspaper Circulation, 1940-2011

Source: *Editor & Publisher International Data Book*, 2012

(circulation figures in thousands)

Year	Number of daily newspapers			Circulation of daily newspapers			Sunday newspapers	
	Morning	Evening	Total	Morning	Evening	Total	Number	Circulation
1940	380	1,498	1,878	16,114	25,018	41,132	525	32,371
1945	330	1,419	1,749	19,240	29,144	48,384	485	39,860
1950	322	1,450	1,772	21,266	32,563	53,829	549	46,582
1955	316	1,454	1,760	22,183	33,964	56,147	541	46,448
1960	312	1,459	1,763	24,029	34,853	58,882	563	47,699
1965	320	1,444	1,751	24,107	36,251	60,358	562	48,600
1970	334	1,429	1,748	25,934	36,174	62,108	586	49,217
1975	339	1,436	1,756	25,490	35,165	60,655	639	51,096
1980	387	1,388	1,745	29,414	32,787	62,202	736	54,676
1985	482	1,220	1,676	36,362	26,405	62,766	798	58,826
1990	559	1,084	1,611	41,311	21,017	62,328	863	62,635
1995	656	891	1,533	44,310	13,883	58,193	888	61,229
2000	766	727	1,480	46,772	9,000	55,773	917	59,421
2005	817	645	1,452	46,122	7,222	53,345	914	55,270
2006	833	614	1,437	45,441	6,888	52,329	907	53,179
2007	867	565	1,422	44,548	6,194	50,742	907	51,246
2008	872	546	1,408	42,758	5,840	48,598	902	49,115
2009	869	528	1,397	40,796	5,482	46,278	919	46,850
2011	931	451	1,382	40,321	4,100	44,421	900	48,510

Newspaper Advertising Revenues, 1950-2011

Source: Research Dept., Newspaper Association of America

Year	National ad revenue (mil $)	Retail ad revenue (mil $)	Classified ad revenue (mil $)	Print advertising total revenue (mil $)	% change[1]	Online advertising total revenue (mil $)	% change	Total advertising revenue (mil $)	% change
1950	$518	$1,175	$377	$2,070	—	—	—	—	—
1955	712	1,755	610	3,077	48.7%	—	—	—	—
1960	778	2,100	803	3,681	19.6	—	—	—	—
1965	783	2,429	1,214	4,426	20.2	—	—	—	—
1970	891	3,292	1,521	5,704	28.9	—	—	—	—
1975	1,109	4,966	2,159	8,234	44.4	—	—	—	—
1980	1,963	8,609	4,222	14,794	79.7	—	—	—	—
1985	3,352	13,443	8,375	25,170	70.1	—	—	—	—
1990	4,122	16,652	11,506	32,280	28.3	—	—	—	—
1995	4,251	18,099	13,742	36,092	11.8	—	—	—	—
2000	7,653	21,409	19,608	48,670	5.1	—	—	—	—
2005	7,910	22,187	17,312	47,408	1.5	$2,027	31.5%	$49,435	2.5%
2006	7,505	22,121	16,986	46,611	−1.7	2,664	31.4	49,275	−0.3
2007	7,005	21,018	14,186	42,209	−9.4	3,166	18.8	45,375	−7.9
2008	5,996	18,769	9,975	34,740	−17.7	3,109	−1.8	37,848	−16.6
2009	4,424	14,218	6,179	24,821	−28.6	2,743	−11.8	27,564	−27.2
2010	4,221	12,926	5,648	22,795	−8.2	3,042	10.9	25,838	−6.3
2011	3,777	11,887	5,028	20,692	−9.2	3,249	6.8	23,941	−7.3

(1) Percent change for years 1950-2000 refers to the rate of change over the preceding five-year period; 2005-11 figures represent the rate of change over the past year.

Canadian Daily Newspapers, 2011

Source: *Editor & Publisher International Data Book*, 2012

(ranked by circulation as of Sept. 30, 2011; all morning papers)

Newspaper	Circulation	Newspaper	Circulation
1. Toronto (ON) *Globe and Mail*	309,154	6. Toronto (ON) *National Post*	146,245
2. Toronto (ON) *Star*	266,143	7. Vancouver (BC) *Province*	144,996
3. Montreal (QC) *Le Journal de Montréal*	206,490	8. Toronto (ON) *Sun*	141,144
4. Montreal (QC) *La Presse*	205,411	9. Calgary (AB) *Herald*	124,559
5. Vancouver (BC) *Sun*	156,769	10. Montreal (QC) *Gazette*	116,446

Top Newspaper Websites, 2012

Source: comScore Media Metrix, Inc.

Rank Website	Visitors[1]	% change[2]	Rank Website	Visitors[1]	% change[2]
1. The New York Times	27,756	−15.0%	12. NYPost.com	6,317	1.6%
2. Tribune Newspapers	25,340	−11.9	13. Boston.com	6,134	−2.2
3. Advance Digital	17,450	−5.6	14. CSMonitor.com	5,084	−12.0
4. WashingtonPost.com	16,796	−4.3	15. Scripps Interactive Newspaper Group	4,685	3.3
5. Hearst Newspapers	14,816	−2.4	16. Telegraph Media Group	4,534	38.9
6. McClatchy Corporation	13,669	−1.9	17. Journal Register Company	3,950	19.5
7. MediaNews Group	12,464	−0.9	18. The Atlanta Journal-Constitution	3,415	−6.3
8. NYDailyNews.com	10,355	−2.2	19. Sun-Times Media/Chicago Region-Wide Network (CRWN)	3,411	−25.3
9. The Guardian	8,770	NA	20. Philly.com	2,959	27.4
10. Lee Enterprises, Incorporated	6,966	56.5			
11. Topix.com	6,605	NA			

NA = Not available. (1) Number of unique visitors, in thousands, who visited website at least once in Apr.-June 2012. (2) Percent change over Apr.-June 2011.

Top News/Information Websites, 2012

Source: comScore Media Metrix, Inc.

Rank Website	Visitors[1]	% change[2]	Rank Website	Visitors[1]	% change[2]
1. Yahoo!-ABC News Network	84,876	NA	11. The Washington Post Company	23,509	−5.9%
2. New York Times Digital	70,926	10.1%	12. WeatherBug Property	21,244	−23.0
3. HPMG News	59,095	4.7	13. WorldNow sites	20,821	8.2
4. CNN Network	56,599	−26.3	14. Advance Digital	17,450	−5.6
5. MSNBC Network	53,973	5.7	15. DFM Network	17,301	NA
6. The Weather Channel	50,447	24.0	16. Mail Online: CA/US	16,085	NA
7. Gannett sites	46,791	11.0	17. Hearst Newspapers	14,816	−2.4
8. CBS News	36,446	124.7	18. McClatchy Corporation	13,669	−1.9
9. Fox News Digital Network	28,046	7.9	19. BBC	12,576	−9.3
10. Tribune Newspapers	25,340	−11.9	20. NYDailyNews.com	10,355	−2.2

NA = Not available. (1) Number of unique visitors, in thousands, who visited website at least once in Apr.-June 2012. (2) Percent change over Apr.-June 2011.

Top-Selling Albums of All-Time

Source: Recording Industry Assn. of America

(As of Sept. 1, 2012. Sales figures represent RIAA multi-platinum certifications; albums ranked by latest sales certification.)

Rank	Title, artist	Unit sales (mil)	Rank	Title, artist	Unit sales (mil)
1.	*Thriller*, Michael Jackson	29.0	9.	*Rumours*, Fleetwood Mac	19.0
	Eagles/Their Greatest Hits 1971-1975, Eagles	29.0		*The Beatles*, The Beatles	19.0
3.	*Greatest Hits Volume I & Volume II*, Billy Joel	23.0	11.	*Appetite for Destruction*, Guns N' Roses	18.0
	Led Zeppelin IV, Led Zeppelin	23.0	12.	*The Beatles 1967-1970*, The Beatles	17.0
	The Wall, Pink Floyd	23.0		*No Fences*, Garth Brooks	17.0
6.	*Back in Black*, AC/DC	22.0		*Boston*, Boston	17.0
7.	*Double Live*, Garth Brooks	21.0		*The Bodyguard* (soundtrack), Whitney Houston	17.0
8.	*Come on Over*, Shania Twain	20.0			

Rank	Title, artist	Unit sales (mil)
16.	*Hotel California*, Eagles	16.0
	Greatest Hits, Elton John	16.0
	Cracked Rear View, Hootie & the Blowfish	16.0
	Physical Graffiti, Led Zeppelin	16.0
	Jagged Little Pill, Alanis Morissette	16.0
21.	*The Beatles 1962-1966*, The Beatles	15.0

Rank	Title, artist	Unit sales (mil)
	Saturday Night Fever (soundtrack), Bee Gees	15.0
	Greatest Hits, Journey	15.0
	Metallica, Metallica	15.0
	Dark Side of the Moon, Pink Floyd	15.0
	Born in the U.S.A., Bruce Springsteen	15.0
	Supernatural, Santana	15.0

U.S. Commercial Radio Stations by Format, 2002-12

Source: The Radio Book by Inside Radio © 2012

(ranked by 2012 numbers)

Primary format	2012	2011	2010	2009	2008	2007	2006	2005	2004	2003	2002
1. Country	2,020	1,988	1,996	1,996	2,024	2,032	2,034	2,014	2,049	2,077	2,123
2. News/Talk	1,503	1,453	1,436	1,414	1,367	1,363	1,335	1,329	1,285	1,225	1,205
3. Spanish	816	812	806	801	799	781	705	704	665	633	627
4. Sports	692	677	661	634	595	560	530	501	466	433	413
5. Classic Hits	657	656	624	572	519	468	425	269	234	236	249
6. Oldies	597	622	642	665	702	712	729	763	816	812	800
7. Adult Contemporary	597	609	635	627	668	664	660	683	700	680	683
8. Top 40	559	522	492	482	470	473	485	504	506	487	492
9. Classic Rock	477	478	482	479	474	456	455	461	452	427	415
10. Hot Adult Contemporary	420	434	421	408	372	377	375	373	420	409	400
11. Religion (Teaching, Variety)	342	332	324	327	298	288	313	319	335	350	340
12. Rock	295	302	296	295	288	281	279	271	280	275	269
13. Adult Standards	240	253	270	328	359	372	369	408	457	492	519
14. Black Gospel	214	226	233	242	244	252	266	284	273	268	251
15. Southern Gospel	170	188	194	212	211	208	208	208	206	207	217
Stations off the air	NA	265	242	206	132	92	91	72	76	124	103
Total operating stations[1]	**11,434**	**11,351**	**11,360**	**11,310**	**11,224**	**11,161**	**11,039**	**10,916**	**10,857**	**10,906**	**10,923**

NA = Not available. (1) As of June 2012. Totals include stations that are changing or did not report format, as well as formats not listed here.

Multi-Platinum and Platinum Awards for Recorded Music and Music Videos, 2011-12

Source: Recording Industry Assn. of America

To achieve platinum status, an **album** must reach minimum total sales of 1 mil units in LPs, CDs, and digital with a manufacturer's dollar volume of at least $2 mil based on one-third of the suggested retail list price for each record, CD, or digital copy sold. To achieve multi-platinum status, an album must reach minimum total sales of at least 2 mil units in LPs, CDs, and digital with a manufacturer's dollar volume of at least $4 mil based on one-third of the list price.

Singles must sell 1 mil units to achieve a platinum award and 2 mil to achieve a multi-platinum award. **Digital singles** are certified at the same levels; the digital sales award was first created in 2004. **Music videos** (longform) must sell 100,000 units to qualify for a platinum award, more than 200,000 units for a multi-platinum award.

Awards listed here are for albums, digital singles, and music videos (released Sept. 2010-Aug. 2012) that were certified Sept. 2011-Aug. 2012. Number in parentheses represents number of millions sold. Alphabetized by artist name.

Albums, Multi-Platinum

21, Adele (9)
My Kinda Party, Jason Aldean (2)
Born This Way, Lady Gaga (2)
Tha Carter IV, Lil Wayne (2)
Drama y Luz, Mana (2)
Formula Vol. 1, Romeo Santos (3)
Speak Now, Taylor Swift (4)

Albums, Platinum

The Band Perry, The Band Perry
Duets II, Tony Bennett
Believe, *Under the Mistletoe*, Justin Bieber
Tailgates & Tanlines, Luke Bryan
Chief, Eric Church
Mylo Xyloto, Coldplay
Take Care, Drake
Watch the Throne, Jay-Z and Kanye West
Own the Night, Lady Antebellum
Hands All Over, Maroon 5
Clear As Day, Scotty McCreery
Number One Hits, Tim McGraw
Pink Friday: Roman Reloaded, Nicki Minaj
Up All Night, One Direction
Entre Dios y el Diablo, Gerardo Ortiz
Greatest Hits: So Far!!!, Pink
Tuskegee, Lionel Richie

Longform Videos, Multi-Platinum

Live at the Royal Albert Hall, Adele (9)
Controlled Chaos, Jeff Dunham (5)
Up All Night: The Live Tour, One Direction (3)

Digital Singles, Platinum and Multi-Platinum

"Rolling in the Deep" (7), "Rumour Has It," "Set Fire to the Rain" (4), "Someone Like You" (5), Adele
"Dirt Road Anthem" (3), "Don't You Wanna Stay" (2), Jason Aldean
"Lighters" (2), Bad Meets Evil
"Boyfriend" (2), Justin Bieber
"Dance (A$$)" (2), Big Sean

"So Good," "Strange Clouds," B.O.B.
"A Woman Like You," Lee Brice
"Country Girl (Shake It for Me)" (2), "Don't Want This Night to End," "Drunk On You," Luke Bryan
"Brigher Than the Sun," Colbie Caillat
"You and Tequila," Kenny Chesney feat. Grace Potter
"Springsteen," Eric Church
"Too Close," Alex Clare
"You Make Me Feel" (2), Cobra Starship
"Paradise," Coldplay
"Work Out," J. Cole
"Higher," Taio Cruz
"Not Over You," Gavin DeGraw
"In the Dark," Dev
"I Need a Doctor" (2), Dr. Dre
"Headlines," "Make Me Proud," "The Motto" (2), "Take Care," Drake
"Crazy Girl," Eli Young Band
"Love the Way You Lie" (5), Eminem feat. Rihanna
"Good Feeling" (3), "Wild Ones" (3), Flo Rida
"Pumped Up Kicks" (4), Foster the People
"We Are Young" (5), Fun
"Love You Like a Love Song" (2), Selena Gomez & the Scene
"Somebody That I Used to Know" (6), Gotye
"Lights" (2), Ellie Goulding
"Titanium," "Turn Me On" (2), "Where Them Girls At," "Without You" (2), David Guetta
"Ass Back Home," "Stereo Hearts" (3), Gym Class Heroes
"Feel So Close," Calvin Harris
"Wanted," Hunter Hayes
"I Like It Like That," "Tonight Tonight" (2), Hot Chelle Rae
"Ni**as in Paris" (2), Jay-Z and Kanye West
"Call Me Maybe" (5), Carly Rae Jepsen
"Domino," Jesse J
"Brokenhearted," Karmin
"Red Solo Cup" (2), Toby Keith
"No Sleep," Wiz Khalifa
"Just a Kiss," Lady Antebellum

"You and I" (2), Lady Gaga
"How to Love" (2), "Mirror," "She Will," Lil Wayne
"Pontoon," Little Big Town
"Want U Back," Cher Lloyd
"Party Rock Anthem" (7), "Sexy and I Know It" (5), "Shots" (2), LMFAO
"I Just Had Sex," The Lonely Island
"On the Floor" (3), Jennifer Lopez
"Dance Again," Jennifer Lopez feat. Pitbull
"Give Your Heart a Break," "Skyscraper," Demi Lovato
"Moves Like Jagger" (5), "Payphone" (3), Maroon 5
"Grenade" (5), "It Will Rain" (2), Bruno Mars
"Fly," "Starships" (3), "Super Bass" (4), Nicki Minaj
"Somethin' bout a Truck," Kip Moore
"Everybody Talks," Neon Trees
"What Makes You Beautiful" (3), One Direction
"Tonight Is the Night," Outasight
"Barefoot Blue Jean Night," Jake Owen
"Remind Me," Brad Paisley and Carrie Underwood
"A Thousand Years," Christina Perri
"Home," Phillip Phillips
"I Won't Let Go," Rascal Flatts
"Cheers (Drink to That)," "Only Girl (In the World)" (3), "S&M" (3), "We Found Love" (4), "Where Have You Been," "You Da One," Rihanna
"God Gave Me You," "Honey Bee" (2), Blake Shelton
"Young, Wild and Free," Snoop Dogg and Wiz Khalifa
"Mean," "Ours," "Safe & Sound," Taylor Swift
"Drive By" (2), Train
"Bottoms Up" (3), Trey Songz
"Rack City" (2), Tyga
"Good Girl," Carrie Underwood
"Glad You Came" (3), The Wanted
"Mercy," "All of the Lights," Kanye West
"Tomorrow," Chris Young

Top-Grossing North American Concert Tours, 1985-2011

Source: Pollstar

Rank Artist (year)	Total gross[1]	Cities/ shows	Rank Artist (year)	Total gross[1]	Cities/ shows
1. The Rolling Stones (2005)	$162.0	38/42	14. Bruce Springsteen & The E Street Band (2009)	$94.5	44/58
2. U2 (2005)	138.9	43/78	15. Céline Dion (2008)	94.0	31/47
3. The Rolling Stones (2006)	138.5	35/39	16. Barbra Streisand (2006)	92.5	16/20
4. The Police (2007)	133.2	41/54	17. Roger Waters (2010)	89.5	36/56
5. U2 (2009)	123.0	16/20	18. The Rolling Stones (1997)	89.3	26/33
6. The Rolling Stones (1994)	121.2	43/60	19. Tim McGraw/Faith Hill (2006)	88.8	55/73
7. Bruce Springsteen & The E Street Band (2003)	115.9	30/47	20. Elton John and Billy Joel (2009)	88.0	27/31
8. U2 (2001)	109.7	56/80	21. The Rolling Stones (2002)	87.9	33/34
9. Bon Jovi (2010)	108.2	38/51	22. Prince (2004)	87.4	69/96
10. Madonna (2008)	105.3	19/30	23. 'N Sync (2001)	86.8	36/43
11. Pink Floyd (1994)	103.5	39/59	24. Madonna (2006)	85.9	14/34
12. Paul McCartney (2002)	103.3	43/53	25. Britney Spears (2009)	82.5	51/61
13. The Rolling Stones (1989)	98.0	33/60			

(1) In millions. Not adjusted for inflation.

Sales of Recorded Music and Music Videos, by Units Shipped and Value, 2000-11

Source: Recording Industry Assn. of America
(in millions, net after returns)

	2000	2005	2006	2007	2008	2009	2010	2011	% change, 2010-11
Physical units shipped	1,079.2	748.7	648.2	543.9	385.5	309.2	233.0	222.0	−4.7%
Dollar value	$14,323.7	11,195.0	9,868.6	7,985.8	5,758.5	4,555.9	3,438.7	3,170.9	−7.8
Compact discs (CDs)	942.5	705.4	619.7	511.1	368.4	292.9	253.0	240.8	−4.8
Dollar value	$13,214.5	10,520.2	9,372.6	7,452.3	5,471.3	4,274.1	3,389.4	3,100.7	−8.5
Cassettes	76.0	2.5	0.7	0.4	0.1	—	—	—	
Dollar value	$626.0	13.1	3.7	3.0	0.9	—	—	—	
LP/EP	2.2	1.0	0.9	1.3	2.9	3.2	4.2	5.5	31.5
Dollar value	$27.7	14.2	15.7	22.9	56.7	60.2	88.9	119.4	34.2
CD singles	34.2	2.8	1.7	2.6	0.7	0.9	1.0	1.3	28.3
Dollar value	$142.7	10.9	7.7	12.2	3.5	3.1	2.9	3.5	18.4
Vinyl singles	4.8	2.3	1.5	0.6	0.4	0.3	0.3	0.4	19.7
Dollar value	$26.3	13.2	9.9	4.0	2.9	2.5	2.3	4.6	99.6
Music videos[1]	18.2	33.8	23.2	27.5	12.8	11.8	9.1	7.7	−15.0
Dollar value	$281.9	602.2	451.1	484.9	218.9	212.0	177.6	151.0	−15.0
Digital formats[2]	—	383.1	625.3	868.4	1,128.6	1,236.8	1,283.4	1,428.6	11.3
Dollar value	—	$503.6	878.0	1,257.5	1,711.5	2,030.7	2,232.9	2,619.7	17.3
Download albums	—	13.6	27.6	42.5	63.6	76.4	85.8	104.8	22.1
Dollar value	—	$135.7	275.9	424.9	635.3	763.4	872.4	1,091.4	25.1
Download singles	—	366.9	586.4	809.9	1,042.7	1,138.3	1,177.4	1,306.2	10.9
Dollar value	—	$363.3	580.6	801.6	1,032.2	1,220.3	1,317.4	1,492.7	13.3
Music videos	—	1.9	9.9	14.2	20.8	20.4	18.4	16.3	−11.6
Dollar value	—	$3.7	19.7	28.2	41.3	40.6	36.6	32.4	−11.6
Mobile formats[3]	—	170.0	315.0	362.0	405.1	305.8	188.5	115.9	−38.5
Dollar value	—	$421.6	773.8	880.8	977.1	728.8	448.0	277.4	−38.1
Subscription formats[4]	—	1.3	1.3	1.8	1.6	1.2	1.5	1.8	18.9
Dollar value	—	$149.2	206.2	201.3	221.4	213.1	212.4	241.0	13.5
Digital performances[5]	—	27.4	31.5	47.0	100.0	155.5	249.2	292.0	17.2
Total units[6]	1,079.2	1,301.8	1,588.5	1,774.3	1,919.2	1,851.8	1,739.6	1,800.2	3.5
Total value	$14,323.7	12,296.9	11,758.2	10,372.1	8,768.4	7,683.9	6,995.0	7,007.7	0.2

— = Not available or not applicable. (1) Includes DVD videos. (2) Includes kiosk singles and albums. (3) Includes master ringtones, ringbacks, music videos, full-length downloads, and other mobile music. (4) Weighted annual average. (5) Estimated royalty payments in dollars to artists and copyright holders distributed by SoundExchange. (6) Includes albums and singles; excludes subscriptions and royalties.

Top Cable TV Networks, 2011

Source: SNL Kagan

Rank	Network (year began)	Subscribers (mil)	Rank	Network (year began)	Subscribers (mil)
1.	CNN (1980)	101.0		Lifetime Television (1984)	99.5
2.	The Weather Channel (1982)	100.6	12.	HGTV (1994)	99.4
3.	Discovery Channel (1985)	100.4		Spike TV (2003)	99.4
4.	Nickelodeon/Nick at Nite (1979)	100.2		Disney Channel (1983)	99.4
5.	Food Network (1993)	100.1	15.	Cartoon Network (1992)	99.3
6.	USA Network (1980)	100.0		TLC (1980)	99.3
7.	TNT (1988)	99.9		C-SPAN (1979)	99.3
8.	A&E (1984)	99.7	18.	MTV (1981)	99.2
	ESPN (1979)	99.7	19.	Comedy Central (1991)	98.9
10.	ESPN2 (1993)	99.5		HLN (1982)	98.9

U.S. Television Set Owners, 2012

Source: Nielsen Media Research, Sept. 2012

Of the 114.7 mil U.S. households that owned at least one TV set in 2012:

84.7% had 2 or more TV sets	54.6% had a VCR	91.3% received basic cable
32.7% had 4 or more TV sets	84.0% had a DVD player	31.0% received premium cable

U.S. Households With Cable Television, 1979-2012

Source: Nielsen Media Research

Year[1]	Subscribers[2] (mil)	As % of house-holds with TVs	Year[1]	Subscribers[2] (mil)	As % of house-holds with TVs	Year[1]	Subscribers[2] (mil)	As % of house-holds with TVs
1979	14.9	19.4%	1991	56.1	60.3%	2002	87.8	83.8%
1980	17.7	22.6	1992	56.2	61.1	2003	88.4	82.9
1981	23.2	28.3	1993	57.6	61.9	2004	92.4	85.3
1982	27.4	33.4	1994	59.7	63.4	2005	94.0	85.7
1983	31.8	37.9	1995	62.1	65.1	2006	95.0	86.2
1984	35.8	42.5	1996	63.6	66.3	2007	94.5	83.8
1985	38.7	45.3	1997	65.1	67.2	2008	99.7	88.2
1986	40.9	47.4	1998	65.9	67.2	2009	103.0	89.7
1987	43.3	49.2	1999	76.4	76.9	2010	104.1	90.6
1988	46.3	52.0	2000	78.6	77.9	2011	104.8	90.4
1989	50.2	55.6	2001	81.5	79.8	2012	104.7	91.3
1990	53.9	58.6						

(1) After 1998, figures include wired-cable households as well as households that receive TV programming via alternate delivery systems (including satellite receivers, SMATV, MMDS). (2) Households that subscribe to basic cable service.

Selected Reality TV Show Winners, 2000-12

Numbers in parentheses represent the season, edition, or cycle of the show. As of Oct. 2012.

The Amazing Race. Debuted Aug. 2001 on CBS. Rob Frisbee & Brennan Swain (1); Chris Luca & Alex Boylan (2); Flo Pesenti & Zach Behr (3); Reichen Lehmkuhl & Chip Arndt (4); Chip & Kim McAllister (5); Freddy Holliday & Kendra Bentley (6); Uchenna & Joyce Agu (7); The Linz Family (8); B. J. Averell & Tyler MacNiven (9); Tyler Denk & James Branaman (10); All-Stars: Eric Sanchez & Danielle Turner (11); TK Erwin & Rachel Morales (12); Nick & Starr Spangler (13); Tammy & Victor Jih (14); Meghan Rickey & Cheyne Whitney (15); Dan & Jordan Pious (16); Natalie Strand & Katherine Chang (17); LaKisha & Jennifer Hoffman (18); Ernie Halvorsen & Cindy Chiang (19); Rachel Brown & Dave Brown Jr. (20).

American Idol. Debuted July 2002 on Fox. Kelly Clarkson (1); Ruben Studdard (2); Fantasia Barrino (3); Carrie Underwood (4); Taylor Hicks (5); Jordin Sparks (6); David Cook (7); Kris Allen (8); Lee DeWyze (9); Scotty McCreery (10); Phillip Phillips (11).

America's Got Talent. Debuted June 2006 on NBC. Bianca Ryan (1); Terry Fator (2); Neil E. Boyd (3); Kevin Skinner (4); Michael Grimm (5); Landau Eugene Murphy Jr. (6); Olate Dogs (7).

America's Next Top Model. Debuted May 2003. Adrianne Curry (1); Yoanna House (2); Eva Pigford (3); Naima Mora (4); Nicole Linkletter (5); Danielle Evans (6); CariDee English (7); Jaslene Gonzalez (8); Saleisha Stowers (9); Whitney Thompson (10); McKey Sullivan (11); Teyona Anderson (12); Nicole Fox (13); Krista White (14); Ann Ward (15); Brittani Kline (16); Lisa D'Amato (17); Sophie Sumner (18).

The Apprentice. Debuted Jan. 2004 on NBC. Bill Rancic (1); Kelly Perdew (2); Kendra Todd (3); Randal Pinkett (4); Sean Yazbeck (5); Stefani Schaeffer (6); Brandy Kuentzel (7). *Celebrity Apprentice*: Piers Morgan (1); Joan Rivers (2); Bret Michaels (3); John Rich (4); Arsenio Hall (5).

The Bachelor. Debuted Mar. 2002 on ABC. Alex Michel chose Amanda Marsh (1); Aaron Buerge chose Helene Eksterowicz (2); Andrew Firestone chose Jen Schefft (3); Bob Guiney chose Estella Gardinier (4); Jesse Palmer chose Jessica Bowlin (5); Byron Velvick chose Mary Delgado (6); Charlie O'Connell chose Sarah Brice (7); Travis Stork chose Sarah Stone (8); Lorenzo Borghese chose Jennifer Wilson (9); Andy Baldwin chose Tessa Horst (10); Brad Womack chose no one (11); Matt Grant chose Shayne Lamas (12); Jason Mesnick chose Melissa Rycroft (13); Jake Pavelka chose Vienna Girardi (14); Brad Womack chose Emily Maynard (15); Ben Flajnik chose Courtney Robertson (16).

The Bachelorette. Debuted Jan. 2003 on ABC. Trista Rehn chose Ryan Sutter (1); Meredith Phillips chose Ian McKee (2); Jen Schefft chose Jerry Ferris (3); DeAnna Pappas chose Jesse Csincsak (4); Jillian Harris chose Ed Swiderski (5); Ali Fedotowsky chose Roberto Martinez (6); Ashley Hebert chose J. P. Rosenbaum (7); Emily Maynard chose Jef Holm (8).

The Biggest Loser. Debuted Oct. 2004 on NBC. Ryan Benson (1); Matt Hoover (2); Erik Chopin (3); Bill Germanakos (4); Ali Vincent (5); Michelle Aguilar (6); Helen Phillips (7);

Danny Cahill (8); Michael Ventrella (9); Patrick House (10); Olivia Ward (11); John Rhode (12); Jeremy Britt (13).

Big Brother. Debuted July 2000 on CBS. Eddie McGee (1); Will Kirby (2); Lisa Donahue (3); Jun Song (4); Drew Daniel (5); Maggie Ausburn (6); Mike Malinto (7); Dick Donato (8); Adam Jasinski (9); Dan Gheesling (10); Jordan Lloyd (11); Hayden Moss (12); Rachel Reilly (13); Ian Terry (14).

Dancing With the Stars. Debuted June 2005 on ABC. Kelly Monaco & Alex Mazo (1); Drew Lachey & Cheryl Burke (2); Emmitt Smith & Cheryl Burke (3); Apolo Anton Ohno & Julianne Hough (4); Helio Castroneves & Julianne Hough (5); Kristi Yamaguchi & Mark Ballas (6); Brooke Burke & Derek Hough (7); Shawn Johnson & Mark Ballas (8); Donny Osmond & Kym Johnson (9); Nicole Scherzinger & Derek Hough (10); Jennifer Grey & Derek Hough (11); Hines Ward & Kym Johnson; J.R. Martinez & Karina Smirnoff (13); Donald Driver & Peta Murgatroyd (14).

Food Network Star. Debuted June 2005 on Food Network. Steve McDonagh & Dan Smith (1); Guy Fieri (2); Amy Finley (3); Aaron McCargo Jr. (4); Melissa d'Arabian (5); Aarti Sequeria (6); Jeff Mauro (7); Justin Warner (8).

Hell's Kitchen. Debuted Mar. 2005 on FOX. Michael Wray (1); Heather West (2); Rock Harper (3); Christina Machamer (4); Danny Veltri (5); Dave Levey (6); Holli Ugalde (7); Nona Sivley (8); Paul Niedermann (9); Christina Wilson (10).

Project Runway. Debuted Dec. 2004 on Bravo. Jay McCarroll (1); Chloe Dao (2); Jeffrey Sebelia (3); Christian Siriano (4); Leanne Marshall (5); Irina Shabayeva (6); Seth Aaron Henderson (7); Gretchen Jones (8); Anya Ayoung-Chee (9); Dmitry Sholokhov (10). All-Stars: Mondo Guerra.

So You Think You Can Dance. Debuted July 2005 on FOX. Nick Lazzarini (1); Benji Schwimmer (2); Sabra Johnson (3); Joshua Allen (4); Jeanine Mason (5); Russell Ferguson (6); Lauren Froderman (7); Melanie Moore (8); Eliana Girard & Chehon Wespi-Tschopp (9).

Survivor. Debuted May 2000 on CBS. Borneo: Richard Hatch (1); Outback: Tina Wesson (2); Africa: Ethan Zohn (3); Marquesas: Vecepia Towery (4); Thailand: Brian Heidik (5); The Amazon: Jenna Morasca (6); Pearl Islands: Sandra Diaz-Twine (7); All-Stars, Panama: Amber Brkich (8); Vanuatu: Chris Daugherty (9); Palau: Tom Westman (10); Guatemala: Danni Boatwright (11); Panama: Aras Baskauskas (12); Cook Islands: Yul Kwon (13); Fiji: Earl Cole (14); China: Todd Herzog (15); Micronesia: Parvati Shallow (16); Gabon: Robert Crowley (17); Tocantins: James "JT" Thomas (18); Samoa: Natalie White (19); Heroes vs. Villains: Sandra Diaz-Twine (20); Nicaragua: Jud Birza (21); Redemption Island: Rob Mariano (22); South Pacific: Sophie Clarke (23); One World: Kim Spradlin (24).

Top Chef. Debuted Mar. 2006 on Bravo. Harold Dieterle (1); Ilan Hall (2); Hung Huynh (3); Stephanie Izard (4); Hosea Rosenberg (5); Michael Voltaggio (6); Kevin Sbraga (7); Richard Blais (8); Paul Qui (9). *Top Chef Masters*: Rick Bayless (1); Marcus Samuelsson (2); Floyd Cardoz (3); Chris Cosentino (4).

The Voice. Debuted Apr. 2011 on NBC. Javier Colon (1); Jermaine Paul (2).

Average U.S. Television Viewing Time, 2011-12

Source: Nielsen Media Research (hours: minutes per week)

Group	Age	Total per week	M-F 7-10 AM	M-F 10 AM-4 PM	M-Sun. 8-11 PM	M-F 11:30 PM-1 AM	Sat. 7 AM-1 PM	Sun. 1-7 PM
Men	18+	34:36	1:59	4:27	8:27	1:45	1:01	1:55
	18-24	23:14	1:02	3:17	4:52	1:27	0:35	1:12
	25-54	32:26	1:46	3:46	7:60	1:48	0:59	1:49
	55+	43:06	2:45	6:08	10:45	1:47	1:14	2:22
Women	18+	38:55	2:30	5:52	9:17	1:55	1:07	1:47
	18-24	26:13	1:17	4:14	5:40	1:33	0:40	1:10
	25-54	35:22	2:17	4:52	8:33	1:53	1:03	1:39
	55+	48:36	3:16	7:54	11:38	2:05	1:22	2:13
Children	2-11	25:16	1:49	4:10	5:09	0:49	1:12	1:18
Teens	12-17	23:07	0:59	2:41	5:22	1:12	0:45	1:11
All viewers		**34:03**	**2:05**	**4:50**	**8:04**	**1:38**	**1:03**	**1:43**

Note: For viewing period Sept. 19, 2011-Aug. 26, 2012. Includes DVR playback.

Favorite Prime-Time Television Programs, 2011-12

Source: Nielsen Media Research

Data are for regularly scheduled network programs Sept. 19, 2011-Aug. 26, 2012; ranked by average audience percentage. Average audience percentages, or ratings, are estimates of the percentage of all TV-owning households that are watching a particular program live, or on DVR within seven days of broadcast. Audience share percentages are estimates of the percentage of those watching TV that are tuned into a particular program.

Rank	Program, network	Avg. audience	Audience share	Rank	Program, network	Avg. audience	Audience share
1.	Dancing With the Stars, ABC	12.0%	18%	27.	Survivor: One World, CBS	6.9%	11%
2.	American Idol-Wednesday, FOX	11.8	19	28.	Football Night in America, NBC	6.9	11
3.	American Idol-Thursday, FOX	11.0	18	29.	Modern Family, ABC	6.8	11
4.	Dancing With the Stars-Results, ABC	10.6	16	30.	The Voice-Results, NBC	6.8	10
5.	NCIS, CBS	10.6	17	31.	Hawaii Five-0, CBS	6.8	11
6.	The Voice, NBC	9.2	14	32.	CSI: Miami, CBS	6.8	11
7.	NCIS: Los Angeles, CBS	8.8	13	33.	The Good Wife, CBS	6.7	10
8.	The Big Bang Theory, CBS	8.5	14	34.	The Amazing Race 19, CBS	6.7	10
9.	The Mentalist, CBS	8.5	14	35.	Body of Proof, ABC	6.6	11
10.	Two and a Half Men, CBS	8.0	12	36.	Blue Bloods CBS	6.6	12
11.	The OT, FOX	8.0	13	37.	America's Got Talent-Wednesday, NBC	6.5	11
12.	Unforgettable, CBS	7.9	13	38.	Mike & Molly, CBS	6.3	10
13.	Person of Interest, CBS	7.8	12	39.	Smash, NBC	6.2	10
14.	Castle, ABC	7.7	12	40.	2 Broke Girls, CBS	6.1	9
15.	Survivor: South Pacific, CBS	7.6	12	41.	Revenge, ABC	6.1	10
16.	Grey's Anatomy, ABC	7.6	12	42.	Scandal, ABC	6.1	10
17.	Criminal Minds, CBS	7.5	12	43.	The Amazing Race 20, CBS	6.0	9
18.	X-Factor-Thursday, FOX	7.4	12	44.	Terra Nova, FOX	6.0	9
19.	X-Factor-Wednesday, FOX	7.4	12	45.	Rules of Engagement, CBS	6.0	10
20.	60 Minutes, CBS	7.4	13	46.	The Bachelor, ABC	6.0	9
21.	America's Got Talent-Monday, NBC	7.2	12	47.	Missing, ABC	5.9	10
22.	America's Got Talent-Tuesday, NBC	7.2	12	48.	Bones, FOX	5.9	9
23.	Rob, CBS	7.2	11	49.	Private Practice, ABC	5.9	10
24.	CSI, CBS	7.0	12	50.	The Bachelorette, ABC	5.9	10
25.	Desperate Housewives, ABC	7.0	11				
26.	Once Upon a Time, ABC	7.0	11				

Favorite Syndicated Programs, 2011-12

Source: Nielsen Media Research

Average audience percentages, or ratings, are estimates of the percentage of TV-owning households watching a program live or on DVR within seven days of broadcast, Sept. 19, 2011-Aug. 26, 2012.

Rank	Program	Avg. audience	Rank	Program	Avg. audience
1.	Judge Judy	7.0%	14.	Criminal Minds	3.0%
2.	Wheel of Fortune	6.8	15.	Dr. Phil	3.0
3.	The Big Bang Theory	6.6	16.	How I Met Your Mother (weekend)	2.9
4.	Two and a Half Men	5.9	17.	Law & Order	2.9
5.	Jeopardy	5.7	18.	Wheel of Fortune (weekend)	2.9
6.	The Big Bang Theory (weekend B)	4.9	19.	The Dr. Oz Show	2.8
7.	The Big Bang Theory (weekend A)	4.3	20.	Judge Joe Brown	2.7
8.	Family Guy	4.1	21.	Law & Order: Criminal Intent	2.6
9.	Family Guy (weekend)	4.0	22.	Two and a Half Men (weekend B)	2.6
10.	Entertainment Tonight	3.7	23.	Live With Kelly	2.6
11.	How I Met Your Mother	3.1	24.	Monk	2.5
12.	Inside Edition	3.0	25.	Seinfeld	2.5
13.	Family Feud	3.0			

Favorite Basic Cable Programs, 2011-12

Source: Nielsen Media Research

Data are for regularly scheduled basic cable programs Sept. 19, 2011-Aug. 26, 2012; excludes miniseries. Average audience percentages, or ratings, are estimates of the percentage of TV-owning households watching a program live or on DVR within seven days of broadcast. The top-rated cable program for the period was The History Channel's miniseries *Hatfields & McCoys* with a 9.9% average audience.

Rank	Program, network	Avg. audience	Rank	Program, network	Avg. audience
1.	Jersey Shore Season 4, MTV	5.6%	16.	White Collar, USA	3.1%
2.	The Closer, TNT	5.3	17.	Teen Mom II, MTV	3.1
3.	Jersey Shore Season 5, MTV	5.1	18.	World Wrestling Entertainment, USA	3.0
4.	Rizzoli & Isles, TNT	5.1	19.	Franklin & Bash, TNT	2.9
5.	Walking Dead, AMC	5.1	20.	Necessary Roughness, USA	2.8
6.	Perception, TNT	4.3	21.	Psych, USA	2.8
7.	Dallas, TNT	3.9	22.	Anger Management, FX	2.8
8.	Suits, USA	3.9	23.	Fairly Legal, USA	2.7
9.	Royal Pains, USA	3.7	24.	Legend of Korra, Nickelodeon	2.7
10.	Burn Notice, USA	3.5	25.	Mad Men, AMC	2.7
11.	Covert Affairs, USA	3.4	26.	Real Housewives of New Jersey, Bravo	2.6
12.	In Plain Sight, USA	3.4	27.	NASCAR Post-Race Show, TNT	2.6
13.	Falling Skies, TNT	3.4	28.	Mountain Men, The History Channel	2.5
14.	Longmire, A&E	3.3	29.	Hell on Wheels, AMC	2.5
15.	Comedy Central Roast, Comedy Central	3.2	30.	Tosh.0, Comedy Central	2.5

Favorite Premium Cable Programs, 2011-12

Source: Nielsen Media Research

Average audience percentages, or ratings, are estimates of the percentage of TV-owning households watching a program live or on DVR within seven days of broadcast, Sept. 19, 2011-Aug. 26, 2012.

Top-Rated Series

Rank	Program, network	Avg. audience
1.	Game of Thrones, HBO	2.9%
2.	True Blood, HBO	2.5
3.	The Newsroom, HBO	1.8
4.	Shameless, Showtime	1.3
5.	House of Lies, Showtime	0.8
6.	Weeds, Showtime	0.8
7.	Californication, Showtime	0.8
8.	Nurse Jackie, Showtime	0.7
9.	Boardwalk Empire, HBO	0.7
10.	Luck, HBO	0.7
11.	Veep, HBO	0.6
12.	The Borgias, Showtime	0.6
13.	The Big C, Showtime	0.6
14.	Girls, HBO	0.6
15.	Real Time With Bill Maher, HBO	0.4
16.	Episodes, Showtime	0.4
17.	Eastbound & Down, HBO	0.4
18.	Dexter, Showtime	0.4

Top-Rated Movies

Rank	Program, network	Avg. audience
1.	The Hangover Part II, HBO	1.1%
2.	Mr. Popper's Penguins, HBO	0.6
3.	Crazy, Stupid, Love, HBO	0.6
4.	The Change-Up, HBO	0.5
5.	Cowboys & Aliens, Cinemax	0.5
6.	Puss in Boots, HBO	0.5
7.	Fast Five, HBO	0.5
8.	Just Go With It, STARZ	0.4
9.	Hall Pass, HBO	0.4
10.	Happy Feet Two, HBO	0.4
11.	Rio, HBO	0.4
12.	Hemingway & Gellhorn, HBO	0.3
13.	Horrible Bosses, HBO	0.3
14.	Red Riding Hood, HBO	0.3
15.	The Blind Side, HBO	0.3

All-Time Most Watched Television Programs

Source: Nielsen Media Research, Jan. 1961-Aug. 2012

Estimates exclude unsponsored or joint network telecasts (e.g., presidential addresses) or programs under 30 minutes long. Ranked by number of TV-owning households tuned in to the program.

Rank	Program	Telecast date	Network	Rating	Avg. audience (thous.)
1.	Super Bowl XLVI	2/5/2012	NBC	47.0%	53,910
2.	Super Bowl XLV	2/6/2011	FOX	46.1	53,435
3.	Super Bowl XLIV	2/7/2010	CBS	45.2	51,873
4.	M*A*S*H (last episode)	2/28/1983	CBS	60.2	50,150
5.	Super Bowl XLII	2/3/2008	FOX	43.2	48,721
6.	Super Bowl XLIII	2/1/2009	NBC	42.0	48,139
7.	Super Bowl XLI	2/4/2007	CBS	42.7	47,535
8.	Super Bowl XL	2/5/2006	ABC	41.6	45,869
9.	XVII Winter Olympics (Women's figure skating)	2/23/1994	CBS	48.5	45,690
10.	Super Bowl XXXIX	2/6/2005	FOX	41.1	45,080
11.	Super Bowl XXXVIII	2/1/2004	CBS	41.4	44,910
12.	Super Bowl XXX	1/28/1996	NBC	46.0	44,150
13.	Super Bowl XXXII	1/25/1998	NBC	44.5	43,630
14.	Super Bowl XXXIV	1/30/2000	ABC	43.3	43,620
15.	Super Bowl XXXVII	1/26/2003	ABC	40.7	43,430
16.	Super Bowl XXVIII	1/30/1994	NBC	45.5	42,860
17.	Super Bowl XXXVI	2/3/2002	FOX	40.4	42,660
18.	Cheers (last episode)	5/20/1993	NBC	45.5	42,360
19.	Super Bowl XXXI	1/26/1997	FOX	43.3	42,000
20.	Super Bowl XXVII	1/31/1993	NBC	45.1	41,990
21.	XVII Winter Olympics (Women's figure skating)	2/25/1994	CBS	44.1	41,540
22.	Super Bowl XX	1/26/1986	NBC	48.3	41,490

Highest-Rated Television Programs by Season, 1950-2012

Source: Nielsen Media Research; regular series programs, Sept.-May season

Rating is percentage of TV-owning households tuned in to the program. Data prior to 1988-89 exclude Alaska and Hawaii.

Season	Program	Rating	TV-owning households (thous.)	Season	Program	Rating	TV-owning households (thous.)
1950-51	Texaco Star Theatre	61.6%	10,320	1981-82	Dallas	28.4%	81,500
1951-52	Godfrey's Talent Scouts	53.8	15,300	1982-83	60 Minutes	25.5	83,300
1952-53	I Love Lucy	67.3	20,400	1983-84	Dallas	25.7	83,800
1953-54	I Love Lucy	58.8	26,000	1984-85	Dynasty	25.0	84,900
1954-55	I Love Lucy	49.3	30,700	1985-86	Cosby Show	33.8	85,900
1955-56	$64,000 Question	47.5	34,900	1986-87	Cosby Show	34.9	87,400
1956-57	I Love Lucy	43.7	38,900	1987-88	Cosby Show	27.8	88,600
1957-58	Gunsmoke	43.1	41,920	1988-89	Roseanne	25.5	90,400
1958-59	Gunsmoke	39.6	43,950	1989-90	Roseanne	23.4	92,100
1959-60	Gunsmoke	40.3	45,750	1990-91	Cheers	21.6	93,100
1960-61	Gunsmoke	37.3	47,200	1991-92	60 Minutes	21.7	92,100
1961-62	Wagon Train	32.1	48,555	1992-93	60 Minutes	21.6	93,100
1962-63	Beverly Hillbillies	36.0	50,300	1993-94	Home Improvement	21.9	94,200
1963-64	Beverly Hillbillies	39.1	51,600	1994-95	Seinfeld	20.5	95,400
1964-65	Bonanza	36.3	52,700	1995-96	E.R.	22.0	95,900
1965-66	Bonanza	31.8	53,850	1996-97	E.R.	21.2	97,000
1966-67	Bonanza	29.1	55,130	1997-98	Seinfeld	22.0	98,000
1967-68	Andy Griffith	27.6	56,670	1998-99	E.R.	17.8	99,400
1968-69	Rowan & Martin's Laugh-In	31.8	58,250	1999-2000	Who Wants to Be a Millionaire	18.6	100,800
1969-70	Rowan & Martin's Laugh-In	26.3	58,500	2000-01	Survivor II	17.4	102,200
1970-71	Marcus Welby, M.D.	29.6	60,100	2001-02	Friends	15.3	105,500
1971-72	All in the Family	34.0	62,100	2002-03	CSI	16.1	106,700
1972-73	All in the Family	33.3	64,800	2003-04	CSI	15.9	108,400
1973-74	All in the Family	31.2	66,200	2004-05	CSI	16.3	106,900
1974-75	All in the Family	30.2	68,500	2005-06	American Idol-Tuesday	17.6	110,200
1975-76	All in the Family	30.1	69,600	2006-07	American Idol-Wednesday	17.3	112,800
1976-77	Happy Days	31.5	71,200	2007-08	American Idol-Tuesday	16.1	113,050
1977-78	Laverne & Shirley	31.6	72,900	2008-09	American Idol-Wednesday	15.1	114,900
1978-79	Laverne & Shirley	30.5	74,500	2009-10	American Idol-Tuesday	13.7	114,900
1979-80	60 Minutes	28.2	76,300	2010-11	American Idol-Wednesday	14.5	115,900
1980-81	Dallas	31.2	79,900	2011-12	Dancing With the Stars	12.0	114,700

All-Time Highest-Rated Television Programs

Source: Nielsen Media Research, Jan. 1961-Aug. 2012

Estimates exclude unsponsored or joint network telecasts (e.g., presidential addresses) and programs under 30 minutes long. Ranked by rating (percentage of TV-owning households tuned in to the program). Average audience is number of TV-owning households tuned in.

Rank	Program	Telecast date	Network	Rating	Avg. audience (thous.)
1.	M*A*S*H (last episode)	2/28/1983	CBS	60.2%	50,150
2.	Dallas ("Who Shot J.R.?" episode)	11/21/1980	CBS	53.3	41,470
3.	Roots-Pt. 8	1/30/1977	ABC	51.1	36,380
4.	Super Bowl XVI	1/24/1982	CBS	49.1	40,020
5.	Super Bowl XVII	1/30/1983	NBC	48.6	40,480
6.	XVII Winter Olympics (Women's figure skating)	2/23/1994	CBS	48.5	45,690
7.	Super Bowl XX	1/26/1986	NBC	48.3	41,490
8.	Gone With the Wind-Pt. 1	11/7/1976	NBC	47.7	33,960
9.	Gone With the Wind-Pt. 2	11/8/1976	NBC	47.4	33,750
10.	Super Bowl XII	1/15/1978	CBS	47.2	34,410
11.	Super Bowl XIII	1/21/1979	NBC	47.1	35,090
12.	Super Bowl XLVI	2/5/2012	NBC	47.0	53,910
13.	Bob Hope Christmas Show	1/15/1970	NBC	46.6	27,260
14.	Super Bowl XIX	1/20/1985	ABC	46.4	39,390
15.	Super Bowl XVIII	1/22/1984	CBS	46.4	38,800
16.	Super Bowl XIV	1/20/1980	CBS	46.3	35,330
17.	Super Bowl XLV	2/6/2011	FOX	46.1	53,435
18.	Super Bowl XXX	1/28/1996	NBC	46.0	44,150
19.	ABC Theater (The Day After)	11/20/1983	ABC	46.0	38,550
20.	Roots-Pt. 6	1/28/1977	ABC	45.9	32,680
21.	The Fugitive (last episode)	8/29/1967	ABC	45.9	25,700
22.	Super Bowl XXI	1/25/1987	CBS	45.8	40,030
23.	Roots-Pt. 5	1/27/1977	ABC	45.7	32,540
24.	Super Bowl XXVIII	1/30/1994	NBC	45.5	42,860
25.	Cheers (last episode)	5/20/1993	NBC	45.5	42,360
26.	The Ed Sullivan Show (First live U.S. TV appearance of The Beatles.)	2/9/1964	CBS	45.3	23,240
27.	Super Bowl XLIV	2/7/2010	CBS	45.2	51,873

AWARDS — MEDALS — PRIZES

Alfred B. Nobel Prizes, 1901-2012

Alfred B. Nobel (1833-96) bequeathed $9 mil, the interest on which was to be distributed yearly to those judged to have most benefited humankind in chemistry, literature, promotion of peace, physics, and physiology or medicine. Prizes were first awarded in 1901. The first prize in economics was awarded in 1969, funded by Sweden's central bank. Each prize is now worth 8 mil Swedish krona (about $1.2 mil). If year is omitted, no award was given. The Royal Swedish Academy selects prize winners for chemistry, economics, and physics; the Nobel Assembly at Karolinska Institutet, physiology or medicine; the Swedish Academy, literature; and the Norwegian Nobel Committee, the peace prize. The 2012 Nobel Prizes were announced Oct. 8-15. Winners sharing a prize are generally listed in alphabetical order, except when the awarding body has given a larger proportion of a shared prize to one or more recipients.

Nobel Prizes, 2012

Chemistry: Americans Robert J. Lefkowitz and Brian K. Kobilka shared the prize "for studies of G-protein-coupled receptors." The research contributed to understanding how the human body senses the outside world and sends messages to cells.

Economics: Americans Alvin E. Roth and Lloyd S. Shapley were awarded the prize for their work on matching theory, especially in markets without prices.

Literature: Chinese author Mo Yan, "who with hallucinatory realism merges folk tales, history and the contemporary."

Peace: European Union, for contributions to advance "peace and reconciliation, democracy and human rights in Europe."

Physics: Serge Haroche of France and David J. Wineland of the U.S. shared the prize for developing techniques that enable scientists to measure and manipulate quantum particles.

Physiology or Medicine: Sir John B. Gurdon, UK, and Shinya Yamanaka, Japan-U.S., were awarded the prize "for the discovery that mature cells can be reprogrammed to become pluripotent."

Physics

1901 Wilhelm C. Röntgen, Ger.	**1951** Sir John D. Cockcroft, UK; Ernest T. S. Walton, Ire.	**1985** Klaus von Klitzing, Ger.
1902 Hendrik A. Lorentz, Pieter Zeeman, Neth.	**1952** Felix Bloch, Edward M. Purcell, U.S.	**1986** Ernst Ruska, Gerd Binnig, Ger.; Heinrich Rohrer, Switz.
1903 Antoine Henri Becquerel, Pierre Curie, Fr.; Marie Curie, Pol.-Fr.	**1953** Frits Zernike, Neth.	**1987** J. Georg Bednorz, Ger.; K. Alex Müller, Switz.
1904 Lord Rayleigh (John W. Strutt), UK	**1954** Max Born, UK; Walter Bothe, Ger.	**1988** Leon M. Lederman, Melvin Schwartz, Jack Steinberger, U.S.
1905 Philipp E. A. von Lenard, Ger.	**1955** Polykarp Kusch, Willis E. Lamb, U.S.	
1906 Sir Joseph J. Thomson, UK	**1956** John Bardeen, Walter H. Brattain, William Shockley, U.S.	**1989** Norman F. Ramsey, U.S.; Hans G. Dehmelt, Ger.-U.S.; Wolfgang Paul, Ger.
1907 Albert A. Michelson, U.S.	**1957** Tsung-Dao Lee, Chen Ning Yang, U.S.-China	
1908 Gabriel Lippmann, Fr.		**1990** Jerome I. Friedman, Henry W. Kendall, U.S.; Richard E. Taylor, Can.
1909 Carl F. Braun, Ger.; Guglielmo Marconi, Ital.	**1958** Pavel Cherenkov, Il'ja Frank, Igor Y. Tamm, USSR	
1910 Johannes D. van der Waals, Neth.	**1959** Owen Chamberlain, Emilio G. Segre, U.S.	**1991** Pierre-Gilles de Gennes, Fr.
1911 Wilhelm Wien, Ger.	**1960** Donald A. Glaser, U.S.	**1992** Georges Charpak, Pol.-Fr.
1912 Nils G. Dalén, Swed.	**1961** Robert Hofstadter, U.S.; Rudolf L. Mossbauer, Ger.	**1993** Russell A. Hulse, Joseph H. Taylor, U.S.
1913 Heike Kamerlingh Onnes, Neth.	**1962** Lev D. Landau, USSR	**1994** Bertram N. Brockhouse, Can.; Clifford G. Shull, U.S.
1914 Max von Laue, Ger.	**1963** Maria Goeppert-Mayer, Eugene P. Wigner, U.S.; J. Hans D. Jensen, Ger.	**1995** Martin Perl, Frederick Reines, U.S.
1915 Sir William H. Bragg, William L. Bragg, UK	**1964** Nicolay G. Basov, Aleksandr M. Prokhorov, USSR; Charles H. Townes, U.S.	**1996** David M. Lee, Douglas D. Osheroff, Robert C. Richardson, U.S.
1917 Charles G. Barkla, UK		**1997** Steven Chu, William D. Phillips, U.S.; Claude Cohen-Tannoudji, Fr.
1918 Max K. E. L. Planck, Ger.	**1965** Richard P. Feynman, Julian S. Schwinger, U.S.; Sin-Itiro Tomonaga, Jpn.	
1919 Johannes Stark, Ger.		**1998** Robert B. Laughlin, U.S.; Horst L. Störmer, Ger.-U.S; Daniel C. Tsui, China-U.S.
1920 Charles E. Guillaume, Fr.-Switz.	**1966** Alfred Kastler, Fr.	
1921 Albert Einstein, Ger.-U.S.	**1967** Hans A. Bethe, U.S.	**1999** Gerardus 't Hooft, Martinus J. G. Veltman, Neth.
1922 Niels Bohr, Den.	**1968** Luis W. Alvarez, U.S.	
1923 Robert A. Millikan, U.S.	**1969** Murray Gell-Mann, U.S.	**2000** Jack S. Kilby, U.S.; Herbert Kroemer, Ger.-U.S.; Zhores I. Alferov, Russ.
1924 Karl M. G. Siegbahn, Swed.	**1970** Hannes Alfvén, Swed.; Louis Néel, Fr.	
1925 James Franck, Gustav Hertz, Ger.		**2001** Eric A. Cornell, Carl E. Wieman, U.S.; Wolfgang Ketterle, Ger.
1926 Jean B. Perrin, Fr.	**1971** Dennis Gabor, UK	
1927 Arthur H. Compton, U.S.; Charles T. R. Wilson, UK	**1972** John Bardeen, Leon N. Cooper, John R. Schrieffer, U.S.	**2002** Raymond Davis Jr., Riccardo Giacconi, U.S.; Masatoshi Koshiba, Jpn.
1928 Owen W. Richardson, UK	**1973** Brian D. Josephson, UK; Leo Esaki, Jpn.; Ivar Giaever, U.S.	
1929 Prince Louis-Victor de Broglie, Fr.	**1974** Antony Hewish, Sir Martin Ryle, UK	**2003** Alexei A. Abrikosov, Vitaly L. Ginzburg, Russ.; Anthony J. Leggett, UK
1930 Sir Chandrasekhara V. Raman, India	**1975** Aage Bohr, Den.; Ben Mottelson, U.S.-Den.; Leo James Rainwater, U.S.	
1932 Werner Heisenberg, Ger.		**2004** David J. Gross, H. David Politzer, Frank Wilczek, U.S.
1933 Paul A. M. Dirac, UK; Erwin Schrödinger, Austria	**1976** Burton Richter, Samuel C. C. Ting, U.S.	
1935 Sir James Chadwick, UK	**1977** Philip W. Anderson, John H. van Vleck, U.S.; Sir Nevill F. Mott, UK	**2005** Roy J. Glauber, John L. Hall, U.S.; Theodor W. Hänsch, Ger.
1936 Carl D. Anderson, U.S.; Victor F. Hess, Austria		**2006** John C. Mather, George F. Smoot, U.S.
1937 Clinton J. Davisson, U.S.; Sir George P. Thomson, UK	**1978** Pyotr Kapitsa, USSR; Arno Penzias, Robert Wilson, U.S.	**2007** Albert Fert, Fr.; Peter Grünberg, Ger.
1938 Enrico Fermi, Ital.-U.S.	**1979** Sheldon L. Glashow, Steven Weinberg, U.S.; Abdus Salam, Pakistan	**2008** Yoichiro Nambu, U.S.; Makoto Kobayashi, Toshihide Maskawa, Jpn.
1939 Ernest O. Lawrence, U.S.		
1943 Otto Stern, U.S.	**1980** James W. Cronin, Val L. Fitch, U.S.	
1944 Isidor Isaac Rabi, U.S.	**1981** Nicolaas Bloembergen, Arthur Schawlow, U.S.; Kai M. Siegbahn, Swed.	**2009** Charles K. Kao, U.S.-UK; Willard S. Boyle, U.S.-Can.; George E. Smith, U.S.
1945 Wolfgang Pauli, U.S.-Austria		
1946 Percy W. Bridgman, U.S.	**1982** Kenneth G. Wilson, U.S.	**2010** Andre Geim, Russ.-Neth.; Konstantin Novoselov, Russ.-UK
1947 Sir Edward V. Appleton, UK	**1983** Subramanyan Chandrasekhar, William A. Fowler, U.S.	
1948 Patrick M. S. Blackett, UK	**1984** Carlo Rubbia, Ital.; Simon van der Meer, Neth.	**2011** Saul Perlmutter, Adam G. Riess, U.S.; Brian P. Schmidt, Austral.-U.S.
1949 Hideki Yukawa, Jpn.		
1950 Cecil F. Powell, UK		

Chemistry

1901	Jacobus H. van 't Hoff, Neth.	1951	Edwin M. McMillan, Glenn T. Seaborg, U.S.	1986	Dudley Herschbach, Yuan T. Lee, U.S.; John C. Polanyi, Can.

1901 Jacobus H. van 't Hoff, Neth.
1902 Emil Fischer, Ger.
1903 Svante A. Arrhenius, Swed.
1904 Sir William Ramsay, UK
1905 Adolf von Baeyer, Ger.
1906 Henri Moissan, Fr.
1907 Eduard Buchner, Ger.
1908 Ernest Rutherford, UK
1909 Wilhelm Ostwald, Ger.
1910 Otto Wallach, Ger.
1911 Marie Curie, Pol.-Fr.
1912 Victor Grignard, Paul Sabatier, Fr.
1913 Alfred Werner, Switz.
1914 Theodore W. Richards, U.S.
1915 Richard M. Willstätter, Ger.
1918 Fritz Haber, Ger.
1920 Walther H. Nernst, Ger.
1921 Frederick Soddy, UK
1922 Francis W. Aston, UK
1923 Fritz Pregl, Austria
1925 Richard A. Zsigmondy, Ger.
1926 Theodor Svedberg, Swed.
1927 Heinrich O. Wieland, Ger.
1928 Adolf O. R. Windaus, Ger.
1929 Sir Arthur Harden, UK;
Hans von Euler-Chelpin, Swed.
1930 Hans Fischer, Ger.
1931 Friedrich Bergius, Carl Bosch, Ger.
1932 Irving Langmuir, U.S.
1934 Harold C. Urey, U.S.
1935 Frédéric Joliot, Irene Joliot-Curie, Fr.
1936 Peter J. W. Debye, Neth.
1937 Walter N. Haworth, UK;
Paul Karrer, Switz.
1938 Richard Kuhn, Ger.
1939 Adolf F. J. Butenandt, Ger.;
Leopold Ruzicka, Switz.
1943 George de Hevesy, Hung.
1944 Otto Hahn, Ger.
1945 Artturi I. Virtanen, Fin.
1946 James B. Sumner, John H.
Northrop, Wendell M. Stanley, U.S.
1947 Sir Robert Robinson, UK
1948 Arne W. K. Tiselius, Swed.
1949 William F. Giauque, U.S.
1950 Kurt Alder, Otto P. H. Diels, Ger.

1951 Edwin M. McMillan,
Glenn T. Seaborg, U.S.
1952 Archer J. P. Martin,
Richard L. M. Synge, UK
1953 Hermann Staudinger, Ger.
1954 Linus C. Pauling, U.S.
1955 Vincent du Vigneaud, U.S.
1956 Sir Cyril N. Hinshelwood, UK;
Nikolay N. Semenov, USSR
1957 Lord (Alexander R.) Todd, UK
1958 Frederick Sanger, UK
1959 Jaroslav Heyrovsky, Czech.
1960 Willard F. Libby, U.S.
1961 Melvin Calvin, U.S.
1962 John C. Kendrew, Max F. Perutz, UK
1963 Giulio Natta, Ital.; Karl Ziegler, Ger.
1964 Dorothy C. Hodgkin, UK
1965 Robert B. Woodward, U.S.
1966 Robert S. Mulliken, U.S.
1967 Manfred Eigen, Ger.; Ronald G. W.
Norrish, George Porter, UK
1968 Lars Onsager, U.S.
1969 Derek H. R. Barton, UK;
Odd Hassel, Nor.
1970 Luis F. Leloir, Arg.
1971 Gerhard Herzberg, Can.
1972 Christian B. Anfinsen, Stanford
Moore, William H. Stein, U.S.
1973 Ernst Otto Fischer, Ger.;
Geoffrey Wilkinson, UK
1974 Paul J. Flory, U.S.
1975 John Cornforth, Austral.-UK;
Vladimir Prelog, Bosnia-Switz.
1976 William N. Lipscomb, U.S.
1977 Ilya Prigogine, Belg.
1978 Peter Mitchell, UK
1979 Herbert C. Brown, U.S.;
Georg Wittig, Ger.
1980 Paul Berg, Walter Gilbert, U.S.;
Frederick Sanger, UK
1981 Kenichi Fukui, Jpn.;
Roald Hoffmann, U.S.
1982 Aaron Klug, UK-Lith.
1983 Henry Taube, Can.
1984 Robert Bruce Merrifield, U.S.
1985 Herbert A. Hauptman,
Jerome Karle, U.S.

1986 Dudley Herschbach, Yuan T. Lee,
U.S.; John C. Polanyi, Can.
1987 Donald J. Cram,
Charles J. Pedersen, U.S.;
Jean-Marie Lehn, Fr.
1988 Johann Deisenhofer, Robert Huber,
Hartmut Michel, Ger.
1989 Sidney Altman,
Thomas R. Cech, U.S.
1990 Elias James Corey, U.S.
1991 Richard R. Ernst, Switz.
1992 Rudolph A. Marcus, Can.-U.S.
1993 Kary B. Mullis, U.S.;
Michael Smith, UK-Can.
1994 George A. Olah, U.S.
1995 Paul Crutzen, Neth.; Mario Molina,
Mex.-U.S.; Sherwood Rowland, U.S.
1996 Robert F. Curl Jr.,
Richard E. Smalley, U.S.;
Sir Harold W. Kroto, UK
1997 Paul D. Boyer, U.S.; John E. Walker,
UK; Jens C. Skou, Den.
1998 Walter Kohn, U.S.;
John A. Pople, UK
1999 Ahmed H. Zewail, U.S.
2000 Alan J. Heeger, U.S.;
Alan G. MacDiarmid, N. Zea.-U.S.;
Hideki Shirakawa, Jpn.
2001 K. Barry Sharpless,
William S. Knowles, U.S.;
Ryoji Noyori, Jpn.
2002 John B. Fenn, U.S.;
Koichi Tanaka, Jpn.;
Kurt Wüthrich, Switz.
2003 Peter Agre,
Roderick MacKinnon, U.S.
2004 Aaron Ciechanover, Avram Hershko,
Isr.; Irwin Rose, U.S.
2005 Yves Chauvin, Fr.; Robert H.
Grubbs, Richard R. Schrock, U.S.
2006 Roger D. Kornberg, U.S.
2007 Gerhard Ertl, Ger.
2008 Martin Chalfie, Osamu Shimomura,
Roger Y. Tsien, U.S.
2009 Venkatraman Ramakrishnan, UK;
Thomas A. Steitz, U.S.;
Ada E. Yonath, Isr.
2010 Richard F. Heck, U.S.; Ei-ichi
Negishi, Jpn.-U.S.; Akira Suzuki, Jpn.
2011 Dan Shechtman, Isr.

Physiology or Medicine

1901 Emil A. von Behring, Ger.
1902 Sir Ronald Ross, UK
1903 Niels R. Finsen, Den.
1904 Ivan P. Pavlov, Russ.
1905 Robert Koch, Ger.
1906 Camillo Golgi, Ital.;
Santiago Ramon y Cajal, Spain
1907 Charles L. A. Laveran, Fr.
1908 Paul Ehrlich, Ger.;
Ilya Mechnikov, Fr.
1909 Emil T. Kocher, Switz.
1910 Albrecht Kossel, Ger.
1911 Allvar Gullstrand, Swed.
1912 Alexis Carrel, Fr.
1913 Charles R. Richet, Fr.
1914 Robert Bárány, Austria
1919 Jules Bordet, Belg.
1920 Schack A. S. Krogh, Den.
1922 Archibald V. Hill, UK;
Otto F. Meyerhof, Ger.
1923 Frederick G. Banting, Can.;
John J. R. Macleod, UK
1924 Willem Einthoven, Neth.
1926 Johannes A. G. Fibiger, Den.
1927 Julius Wagner-Jauregg, Austria
1928 Charles J. H. Nicolle, Fr.
1929 Christiaan Eijkman, Neth.;
Sir Frederick G. Hopkins, UK
1930 Karl Landsteiner, U.S.

1931 Otto H. Warburg, Ger.
1932 Edgar D. Adrian,
Sir Charles S. Sherrington, UK
1933 Thomas H. Morgan, U.S.
1934 George R. Minot, William P. Murphy,
G. H. Whipple, U.S.
1935 Hans Spemann, Ger.
1936 Sir Henry H. Dale, UK;
Otto Loewi, U.S.
1937 Albert Szent-Gyorgyi, Hung.-U.S.
1938 Corneille J. F. Heymans, Belg.
1939 Gerhard Domagk, Ger.
1943 Henrik C. P. Dam, Den.;
Edward A. Doisy, U.S.
1944 Joseph Erlanger,
Herbert S. Gasser, U.S.
1945 Ernst B. Chain, Sir Alexander
Fleming, Sir Howard W. Florey, UK
1946 Hermann J. Muller, U.S.
1947 Carl F. Cori, Gerty T. Cori, U.S.;
Bernardo A. Houssay, Arg.
1948 Paul H. Müller, Switz.
1949 Walter R. Hess, Switz.;
Antonio Moniz, Port.
1950 Philip S. Hench, Edward C. Kendall,
U.S.; Tadeus Reichstein, Switz.
1951 Max Theiler, U.S.
1952 Selman A. Waksman, U.S.
1953 Hans A. Krebs, UK;
Fritz A. Lipmann, U.S.

1954 John F. Enders, Frederick C.
Robbins, Thomas H. Weller, U.S.
1955 Alex H. T. Theorell, Swed.
1956 André F. Cournand,
Dickinson W. Richards, U.S.;
Werner Forssmann, Ger.
1957 Daniel Bovet, Ital.
1958 George W. Beadle, Edward L.
Tatum, Joshua Lederberg, U.S.
1959 Arthur Kornberg,
Severo Ochoa, U.S.
1960 Sir Frank Macfarlane Burnet,
Austral.; Peter B. Medawar, UK
1961 Georg von Békésy, U.S.
1962 Francis H. C. Crick,
Maurice H. F. Wilkins, UK;
James D. Watson, U.S.
1963 Sir John C. Eccles, Austral.;
Alan L. Hodgkin,
Andrew F. Huxley, UK
1964 Konrad E. Bloch, U.S.;
Feodor Lynen, Ger.
1965 François Jacob, André Lwoff,
Jacques Monod, Fr.
1966 Charles B. Huggins,
Peyton Rous, U.S.
1967 Ragnar Granit, Swed.;
Haldan Keffer Hartline,
George Wald, U.S.

1968 Robert W. Holley,
H. Gobind Khorana,
Marshall W. Nirenberg, U.S.
1969 Max Delbrück, Alfred D. Hershey,
Salvador Luria, U.S.
1970 Julius Axelrod, U.S.;
Sir Bernard Katz, UK;
Ulf von Euler, Swed.
1971 Earl W. Sutherland Jr., U.S.
1972 Gerald M. Edelman, U.S.;
Rodney R. Porter, UK
1973 Konrad Lorenz, Austria;
Nikolaas Tinbergen, UK;
Karl von Frisch, Ger.
1974 Albert Claude, Lux.-U.S.;
Christian de Duve, Belg.;
George Emil Palade, Rom.-U.S.
1975 David Baltimore,
Howard Temin, U.S.;
Renato Dulbecco, Ital.-U.S.
1976 Baruch S. Blumberg,
Daniel Carleton Gajdusek, U.S.
1977 Rosalyn S. Yalow,
Roger C.L. Guillemin,
Andrew V. Schally, U.S.
1978 Werner Arber, Switz.;
Daniel Nathans,
Hamilton O. Smith, U.S.
1979 Allan M. Cormack, U.S.;
Godfrey N. Hounsfield, UK
1980 Baruj Benacerraf, George Snell,
U.S.; Jean Dausset, Fr.

1981 Roger W. Sperry, David H. Hubel,
Torsten N. Wiesel, U.S.
1982 Sune K. Bergström,
Bengt I. Samuelsson, Swed.;
John R. Vane, UK
1983 Barbara McClintock, U.S.
1984 Niels K. Jerne, UK-Den.;
Georges J. F. Köhler, Ger.;
César Milstein, UK-Arg.
1985 Michael S. Brown,
Joseph L. Goldstein, U.S.
1986 Stanley Cohen, U.S.;
Rita Levi-Montalcini, Ital.-U.S.
1987 Susumu Tonegawa, Jpn.
1988 Sir James W. Black, UK;
Gertrude B. Elion,
George H. Hitchings, U.S.
1989 J. Michael Bishop,
Harold E. Varmus, U.S.
1990 Joseph E. Murray,
E. Donnall Thomas, U.S.
1991 Edwin Neher, Bert Sakmann, Ger.
1992 Edmond H. Fisher,
Edwin G. Krebs, U.S.
1993 Richard J. Roberts, UK;
Phillip A. Sharp, U.S.
1994 Alfred G. Gilman,
Martin Rodbell, U.S.
1995 Edward B. Lewis,
Eric F. Wieschaus, U.S.;
Christiane Nüsslein-Volhard, Ger.
1996 Peter C. Doherty, Austral.;
Rolf M. Zinkernagel, Switz.

1997 Stanley B. Prusiner, U.S.
1998 Robert F. Furchgott,
Louis J. Ignarro, Ferid Murad, U.S.
1999 Günter Blobel, U.S.
2000 Arvid Carlsson, Swed.;
Paul Greengard, U.S.;
Eric R. Kandel, Austria-U.S.
2001 Leland H. Hartwell, U.S.;
R. Timothy (Tim) Hunt,
Sir Paul M. Nurse, UK
2002 Sydney Brenner, John E. Sulston,
UK; H. Robert Horvitz, U.S.
2003 Paul C. Lauterbur, U.S.;
Sir Peter Mansfield, UK
2004 Richard Axel, Linda B. Buck, U.S.
2005 Barry J. Marshall,
J. Robin Warren, Austral.
2006 Andrew Z. Fire, Craig C. Mello, U.S.
2007 Mario R. Capecchi,
Oliver Smithies, U.S.;
Sir Martin J. Evans, UK
2008 Harald zur Hausen, Ger.;
Françoise Barré-Sinoussi,
Luc Montagnier, Fr.
2009 Elizabeth H. Blackburn,
Carol W. Greider,
Jack W. Szostak, U.S.
2010 Robert G. Edwards, UK
2011 Bruce A. Beutler, U.S.;
Jules A. Hoffmann, Fr.;
Ralph M. Steinman, Can.-U.S.

Literature

1901 Rene F. A. Sully Prudhomme, Fr.
1902 Theodor Mommsen, Ger.
1903 Bjørnstjerne Bjørnson, Nor.
1904 José Echegaray y Eizaguirre, Spain;
Fréderic Mistral, Fr.
1905 Henryk Sienkiewicz, Pol.
1906 Giosuè Carducci, Ital.
1907 Rudyard Kipling, UK
1908 Rudolf C. Eucken, Ger.
1909 Selma Lagerlöf, Swed.
1910 Paul J. L. Heyse, Ger.
1911 Maurice Maeterlinck, Belg.
1912 Gerhart Hauptmann, Ger.
1913 Rabindranath Tagore, India
1915 Romain Rolland, Fr.
1916 Verner von Heidenstam, Swed.
1917 Karl A. Gjellerup,
Henrik Pontoppidan, Den.
1919 Carl F. G. Spitteler, Switz.
1920 Knut Hamsun, Nor.
1921 Anatole France, Fr.
1922 Jacinto Benavente, Spain
1923 William Butler Yeats, Ire.
1924 Wladyslaw S. Reymont, Pol.
1925 George Bernard Shaw, Ire.-UK
1926 Grazia Deledda, Ital.
1927 Henri Bergson, Fr.
1928 Sigrid Undset, Nor.
1929 Thomas Mann, Ger.
1930 Sinclair Lewis, U.S.
1931 Erik A. Karlfeldt, Swed.
1932 John Galsworthy, UK
1933 Ivan A. Bunin, USSR
1934 Luigi Pirandello, Ital.
1936 Eugene O'Neill, U.S.
1937 Roger Martin du Gard, Fr.

1938 Pearl S. Buck, U.S.
1939 Frans E. Sillanpää, Fin.
1944 Johannes V. Jensen, Den.
1945 Gabriela Mistral, Chile
1946 Hermann Hesse, Ger.-Switz.
1947 André Gide, Fr.
1948 T. S. Eliot, UK
1949 William Faulkner, U.S.
1950 Bertrand Russell, UK
1951 Pär F. Lagerkvist, Swed.
1952 François Mauriac, Fr.
1953 Sir Winston Churchill, UK
1954 Ernest Hemingway, U.S.
1955 Halldór K. Laxness, Ice.
1956 Juan Ramón Jiménez, Spain
1957 Albert Camus, Fr.
1958 Boris L. Pasternak, USSR
(declined)
1959 Salvatore Quasimodo, Ital.
1960 Saint-John Perse, Fr.
1961 Ivo Andric, Yugo.
1962 John Steinbeck, U.S.
1963 Giorgos Seferis, Greece
1964 Jean-Paul Sartre, Fr. (declined)
1965 Mikhail Sholokhov, USSR
1966 Shmuel Yosef Agnon, Isr.;
Nelly Sachs, Swed.
1967 Miguel Angel Asturias, Guat.
1968 Yasunari Kawabata, Jpn.
1969 Samuel Beckett, Ire.
1970 Aleksandr I. Solzhenitsyn, USSR
1971 Pablo Neruda, Chile
1972 Heinrich Böll, Ger.
1973 Patrick White, Austral.
1974 Eyvind Johnson,
Harry Edmund Martinson, Swed.

1975 Eugenio Montale, Ital.
1976 Saul Bellow, U.S.
1977 Vicente Aleixandre, Spain
1978 Isaac Bashevis Singer, U.S.
1979 Odysseus Elytis, Greece
1980 Czeslaw Milosz, Pol.-U.S.
1981 Elias Canetti, Bulg.-UK
1982 Gabriel García Márquez, Colombia
1983 William Golding, UK
1984 Jaroslav Siefert, Czech.
1985 Claude Simon, Fr.
1986 Wole Soyinka, Nigeria
1987 Joseph Brodsky, USSR-U.S.
1988 Naguib Mahfouz, Egypt
1989 Camilo José Cela, Spain
1990 Octavio Paz, Mex.
1991 Nadine Gordimer, S. Afr.
1992 Derek Walcott, St. Lucia
1993 Toni Morrison, U.S.
1994 Kenzaburo Oe, Jpn.
1995 Seamus Heaney, Ire.
1996 Wislawa Szymborska, Pol.
1997 Dario Fo, Ital.
1998 Jose Saramago, Por.
1999 Günter Grass, Ger.
2000 Gao Xingjian, China-Fr.
2001 Sir V. S. Naipaul, UK
2002 Imre Kertész, Hung.
2003 J. M. Coetzee, S. Afr.
2004 Elfriede Jelinek, Austria
2005 Harold Pinter, UK
2006 Orhan Pamuk, Turk.
2007 Doris Lessing, UK
2008 Jean-Marie Gustave Le Clézio, Fr.
2009 Herta Müller, Ger.
2010 Mario Vargas Llosa, Peru
2010 Mario Vargas Llosa, Peru
2011 Tomas Tranströmer, Swed.

Peace

1901 Jean H. Dunant, Switz.;
Frédéric Passy, Fr.
1902 Élie Ducommun,
Charles A. Gobat, Switz.
1903 Sir William R. Cremer, UK
1904 Institute of International Law
1905 Baroness Bertha von Suttner,
Austria
1906 Theodore Roosevelt, U.S.
1907 Ernesto T. Moneta, Ital.;
Louis Renault, Fr.

1908 Klas P. Arnoldson, Swed.;
Fredrik Bajer, Den.
1909 Auguste M. F. Beernaert, Belg.;
Paul H. B. B. d'Estournelles
de Constant, Fr.
1910 Permanent Intl. Peace Bureau
1911 Tobias M. C. Asser, Neth.;
Alfred H. Fried, Austria
1912 Elihu Root, U.S.
1913 Henri La Fontaine, Belg.
1917 International Red Cross

1919 Woodrow Wilson, U.S.
1920 Léon V. A. Bourgeois, Fr.
1921 Karl H. Branting, Swed.;
Christian L. Lange, Nor.
1922 Fridtjof Nansen, Nor.
1925 Sir J. Austen Chamberlain, UK;
Charles G. Dawes, U.S.
1926 Aristide Briand, Fr.;
Gustav Stresemann, Ger.
1927 Ferdinand E. Buisson, Fr.;
Ludwig Quidde, Ger.

1929	Frank B. Kellogg, U.S.	1965	UN Children's Fund (UNICEF)	1991	Aung San Suu Kyi, Burma
1930	Nathan Söderblom, Swed.	1968	René Cassin, Fr.	1992	Rigoberta Menchú Tum, Guat.

1929 Frank B. Kellogg, U.S.
1930 Nathan Söderblom, Swed.
1931 Jane Addams,
        Nicholas Murray Butler, U.S.
1933 Sir Norman Angell, UK
1934 Arthur Henderson, UK
1935 Carl von Ossietzky, Ger.
1936 Carlos Saavedra Lamas, Arg.
1937 Viscount Cecil of Chelwood, UK
1938 Nansen Intl. Office for Refugees
1944 International Red Cross
1945 Cordell Hull, U.S.
1946 Emily G. Balch, John R. Mott, U.S.
1947 Friends Service Council, UK; Amer.
        Friends Service Committee, U.S.
1949 Lord John Boyd Orr of Brechin, UK
1950 Ralph J. Bunche, U.S.
1951 Léon Jouhaux, Fr.
1952 Albert Schweitzer, Fr.
1953 George C. Marshall, U.S.
1954 Office of UN High Commissioner for
        Refugees
1957 Lester B. Pearson, Can.
1958 Georges Pire, Belg.
1959 Philip J. Noel-Baker, UK
1960 Albert J. Lutuli, S. Afr.
1961 Dag Hammarskjöld, Swed.
1962 Linus C. Pauling, U.S.
1963 International Red Cross,
        League of Red Cross Societies
1964 Martin Luther King Jr., U.S.

1965 UN Children's Fund (UNICEF)
1968 René Cassin, Fr.
1969 Intl. Labor Organization
1970 Norman E. Borlaug, U.S.
1971 Willy Brandt, Ger.
1973 Henry Kissinger, U.S.;
        Le Duc Tho, N. Viet. (Tho declined)
1974 Seán MacBride, Ire.;
        Eisaku Sato, Jpn.
1975 Andrei Sakharov, USSR
1976 Mairead Corrigan,
        Betty Williams, N. Ire.
1977 Amnesty International
1978 Anwar al-Sadat, Egypt;
        Menachem Begin, Isr.
1979 Mother Teresa of Calcutta,
        Alb.-India
1980 Adolfo Pérez Esquivel, Arg.
1981 Office of UN High Commissioner for
        Refugees
1982 Alfonso García Robles, Mex.;
        Alva Myrdal, Swed.
1983 Lech Walesa, Pol.
1984 Bishop Desmond Tutu, S. Afr.
1985 Intl. Physicians for the Prevention
        of Nuclear War, U.S.
1986 Elie Wiesel, Rom.-U.S.
1987 Oscar Arias Sánchez, Costa Rica
1988 UN Peacekeeping Forces
1989 Dalai Lama (Tenzin Gyatso), Tibet
1990 Mikhail S. Gorbachev, USSR

1991 Aung San Suu Kyi, Burma
1992 Rigoberta Menchú Tum, Guat.
1993 Frederik W. de Klerk,
        Nelson Mandela, S. Afr.
1994 Yasser Arafat, Pal.; Shimon Peres,
        Yitzhak Rabin, Isr.
1995 Joseph Rotblat, Pol.-UK;
        Pugwash Conferences
1996 Bishop Carlos Ximenes Belo,
        José Ramos-Horta, Timor-Leste
1997 Jody Williams, U.S.; Intl. Campaign
        to Ban Landmines
1998 John Hume, David Trimble, N. Ire.
1999 Doctors Without Borders
        (Médecins Sans Frontières), Fr.
2000 Kim Dae-Jung, S. Kor.
2001 UN; Kofi Annan, Ghana
2002 Jimmy Carter, U.S.
2003 Shirin Ebadi, Iran
2004 Wangari Maathai, Kenya
2005 Mohamed ElBaradei, Egypt;
        Intl. Atomic Energy Agency, Austria
2006 Muhammad Yunus,
        Grameen Bank, Bangl.
2007 Intergovernmental Panel on Climate
        Change, Switz.;
        Albert Arnold Gore Jr., U.S.
2008 Martti Ahtisaari, Fin.
2009 Barack H. Obama, U.S.
2010 Liu Xiaobo, China
2011 Leymah Gbowee, Ellen Johnson
        Sirleaf, Liberia; Tawakkol Karman,
        Yemen

Nobel Memorial Prize in Economic Sciences

1969 Ragnar Frisch, Nor.;
        Jan Tinbergen, Neth.
1970 Paul A. Samuelson, U.S.
1971 Simon Kuznets, U.S.
1972 Kenneth J. Arrow, U.S.;
        John R. Hicks, UK
1973 Wassily Leontief, U.S.
1974 Gunnar Myrdal, Swed.;
        Friedrich A. von Hayek, Austria
1975 Leonid Kantorovich, USSR;
        Tjalling Koopmans, Neth.-U.S.
1976 Milton Friedman, U.S.
1977 James E. Meade, UK;
        Bertil Ohlin, Swed.
1978 Herbert A. Simon, U.S.
1979 Sir Arthur Lewis, UK;
        Theodore W. Schultz, U.S.
1980 Lawrence R. Klein, U.S.
1981 James Tobin, U.S.
1982 George J. Stigler, U.S.
1983 Gerard Debreu, Fr.-U.S.
1984 Richard Stone, UK
1985 Franco Modigliani, Ital.-U.S.

1986 James M. Buchanan, U.S.
1987 Robert M. Solow, U.S.
1988 Maurice Allais, Fr.
1989 Trygve Haavelmo, Nor.
1990 Harry M. Markowitz,
        Merton H. Miller,
        William F. Sharpe, U.S.
1991 Ronald H. Coase, UK-U.S.
1992 Gary S. Becker, U.S.
1993 Robert W. Fogel,
        Douglass C. North, U.S.
1994 John C. Harsanyi, John F. Nash,
        U.S.; Reinhard Selten, Ger.
1995 Robert E. Lucas Jr., U.S.
1996 James A. Mirrlees, UK;
        William Vickrey, Can.-U.S.
1997 Robert C. Merton, U.S.;
        Myron S. Scholes, Can.-U.S.
1998 Amartya Sen, India
1999 Robert A. Mundell, Can.
2000 James J. Heckman,
        Daniel L. McFadden, U.S.

2001 George A. Akerlof, A. Michael
        Spence, Joseph E. Stiglitz, U.S.
2002 Daniel Kahneman, U.S.-Isr.;
        Vernon L. Smith, U.S.
2003 Robert F. Engle, U.S.;
        Clive W. J. Granger, UK
2004 Finn E. Kydland, Nor.;
        Edward C. Prescott, U.S.
2005 Robert J. Aumann, Isr.-U.S.;
        Thomas C. Schelling, U.S.
2006 Edmund S. Phelps, U.S.
2007 Leonid Hurwicz, Eric S. Maskin,
        Roger B. Myerson, U.S.
2008 Paul Krugman, U.S.
2009 Elinor Ostrom,
        Oliver E. Williamson, U.S.
2010 Peter A. Diamond, Dale T.
        Mortensen, U.S.; Christopher A.
        Pissarides, Cyprus-UK.
2011 Thomas J. Sargent, Christopher A.
        Sims, U.S.

Pulitzer Prizes in Journalism, Letters, and Music, 1917-2012

Endowed by Joseph Pulitzer (1847-1911), publisher of the *New York World*, in a bequest to Columbia Univ. and awarded annually, in years shown, for work published the previous year. Prizes are currently $10,000 in each category except Public Service (in Journalism), for which a gold medal is given. The prize board began considering submissions from online-only publications in 2009. For letters and music, prizes in past years are listed; if a year is omitted, no award was given that year.

Pulitzer Prizes in Journalism, 2012

Public Service: *Philadelphia Inquirer* for its exploration of pervasive violence in the city's schools.

Breaking News Reporting: *Tuscaloosa News* (AL) staff, for tornado coverage that used social media and traditional methods.

Investigative Reporting (two prizes): Matt Apuzzo, Adam Goldman, Chris Hawley, and Eileen Sullivan, Associated Press, for investigations of the NYPD's clandestine program that monitored life in Muslim communities. Michael J. Berens and Ken Armstrong, *Seattle Times*, for examination of how Washington state transferred vulnerable patients from a safer pain-control medication to methadone.

Explanatory Reporting: David Kocieniewski, *NY Times*, for series explaining how the wealthiest U.S. citizens and corporations exploit tax code loopholes and avoid paying taxes.

Local Reporting: Sara Ganim and *Patriot-News* (Harrisburg, PA) staff, for covering the Penn State sexual assault scandal involving former assistant football coach Jerry Sandusky.

National Reporting: David Wood, *Huffington Post*, for exploration of the physical and emotional challenges facing American soldiers severely wounded during a decade of war.

International Reporting: Jeffrey Gettleman, *NY Times*, for stories on famine and conflict in Africa, reported at personal peril.

Feature Writing: Eli Sanders, *The Stranger* (Seattle, WA), for story on a woman who survived a brutal attack that took her partner's life.

Commentary: Mary Schmich, *Chicago Tribune*, for down-to-earth columns that reflect the character and culture of Chicago.

Criticism: Wesley Morris, *Boston Globe*, for smart, inventive film criticism.

Editorial Writing: No award.

Editorial Cartooning: Matt Wuerker, *Politico*, for consistently fresh, funny cartoons.

Breaking News Photography: Massoud Hossaini, Agence France-Presse, for photo of a girl at a crowded Kabul shrine after a suicide bombing.

Feature Photography: Craig F. Walker, *Denver Post* (CO), for compassionate chronicle of an Iraq war veteran struggling with severe post-traumatic stress.

Pulitzer Prizes in Letters, 1917-2012

Fiction

1918 Ernest Poole, *His Family*
1919 Booth Tarkington, *The Magnificent Ambersons*
1921 Edith Wharton, *The Age of Innocence*
1922 Booth Tarkington, *Alice Adams*
1923 Willa Cather, *One of Ours*
1924 Margaret Wilson, *The Able McLaughlins*
1925 Edna Ferber, *So Big*
1926 Sinclair Lewis, *Arrowsmith* (refused)
1927 Louis Bromfield, *Early Autumn*
1928 Thornton Wilder, *Bridge of San Luis Rey*
1929 Julia M. Peterkin, *Scarlet Sister Mary*
1930 Oliver LaFarge, *Laughing Boy*
1931 Margaret Ayer Barnes, *Years of Grace*
1932 Pearl S. Buck, *The Good Earth*
1933 T. S. Stribling, *The Store*
1934 Caroline Miller, *Lamb in His Bosom*
1935 Josephine W. Johnson, *Now in November*
1936 Harold L. Davis, *Honey in the Horn*
1937 Margaret Mitchell, *Gone With the Wind*
1938 John P. Marquand, *The Late George Apley*
1939 Marjorie Kinnan Rawlings, *The Yearling*
1940 John Steinbeck, *The Grapes of Wrath*
1942 Ellen Glasgow, *In This Our Life*
1943 Upton Sinclair, *Dragon's Teeth*
1944 Martin Flavin, *Journey in the Dark*
1945 John Hersey, *A Bell for Adano*
1947 Robert Penn Warren, *All the King's Men*
1948 James A. Michener, *Tales of the South Pacific*
1949 James Gould Cozzens, *Guard of Honor*
1950 A. B. Guthrie Jr., *The Way West*
1951 Conrad Richter, *The Town*
1952 Herman Wouk, *The Caine Mutiny*
1953 Ernest Hemingway, *The Old Man and the Sea*
1955 William Faulkner, *A Fable*
1956 MacKinlay Kantor, *Andersonville*
1958 James Agee, *A Death in the Family*
1959 Robert Lewis Taylor, *The Travels of Jaimie McPheeters*
1960 Allen Drury, *Advise and Consent*
1961 Harper Lee, *To Kill a Mockingbird*
1962 Edwin O'Connor, *The Edge of Sadness*
1963 William Faulkner, *The Reivers*
1965 Shirley Ann Grau, *The Keepers of the House*
1966 Katherine Anne Porter, *Collected Stories*
1967 Bernard Malamud, *The Fixer*
1968 William Styron, *The Confessions of Nat Turner*
1969 N. Scott Momaday, *House Made of Dawn*
1970 Jean Stafford, *Collected Stories*
1972 Wallace Stegner, *Angle of Repose*
1973 Eudora Welty, *The Optimist's Daughter*
1975 Michael Shaara, *The Killer Angels*
1976 Saul Bellow, *Humboldt's Gift*
1978 James Alan McPherson, *Elbow Room*
1979 John Cheever, *The Stories of John Cheever*
1980 Norman Mailer, *The Executioner's Song*
1981 John Kennedy Toole, *A Confederacy of Dunces*
1982 John Updike, *Rabbit Is Rich*
1983 Alice Walker, *The Color Purple*
1984 William Kennedy, *Ironweed*
1985 Alison Lurie, *Foreign Affairs*
1986 Larry McMurtry, *Lonesome Dove*
1987 Peter Taylor, *A Summons to Memphis*
1988 Toni Morrison, *Beloved*
1989 Anne Tyler, *Breathing Lessons*
1990 Oscar Hijuelos, *The Mambo Kings Play Songs of Love*
1991 John Updike, *Rabbit at Rest*
1992 Jane Smiley, *A Thousand Acres*
1993 Robert Olen Butler, *A Good Scent From a Strange Mountain*
1994 E. Annie Proulx, *The Shipping News*
1995 Carol Shields, *The Stone Diaries*
1996 Richard Ford, *Independence Day*
1997 Steven Millhauser, *Martin Dressler: The Tale of an American Dreamer*
1998 Philip Roth, *American Pastoral*
1999 Michael Cunningham, *The Hours*
2000 Jhumpa Lahiri, *Interpreter of Maladies*
2001 Michael Chabon, *The Amazing Adventures of Kavalier & Clay*
2002 Richard Russo, *Empire Falls*
2003 Jeffrey Eugenides, *Middlesex*
2004 Edward P. Jones, *The Known World*
2005 Marilynne Robinson, *Gilead*
2006 Geraldine Brooks, *March*
2007 Cormac McCarthy, *The Road*
2008 Junot Díaz, *The Brief Wondrous Life of Oscar Wao*
2009 Elizabeth Strout, *Olive Kitteridge*
2010 Paul Harding, *Tinkers*
2011 Jennifer Egan, *A Visit From the Goon Squad*
2012 No award

Drama

1918 Jesse Lynch Williams, *Why Marry?*
1920 Eugene O'Neill, *Beyond the Horizon*
1921 Zona Gale, *Miss Lulu Bett*
1922 Eugene O'Neill, *Anna Christie*
1923 Owen Davis, *Icebound*
1924 Hatcher Hughes, *Hell-Bent for Heaven*
1925 Sidney Howard, *They Knew What They Wanted*
1926 George Kelly, *Craig's Wife*
1927 Paul Green, *In Abraham's Bosom*
1928 Eugene O'Neill, *Strange Interlude*
1929 Elmer Rice, *Street Scene*
1930 Marc Connelly, *The Green Pastures*
1931 Susan Glaspell, *Alison's House*
1932 George S. Kaufman, Morrie Ryskind, and Ira Gershwin, *Of Thee I Sing*
1933 Maxwell Anderson, *Both Your Houses*
1934 Sidney Kingsley, *Men in White*
1935 Zoe Akins, *The Old Maid*
1936 Robert E. Sherwood, *Idiot's Delight*
1937 George S. Kaufman and Moss Hart, *You Can't Take It With You*
1938 Thornton Wilder, *Our Town*
1939 Robert E. Sherwood, *Abe Lincoln in Illinois*
1940 William Saroyan, *The Time of Your Life*
1941 Robert E. Sherwood, *There Shall Be No Night*
1943 Thornton Wilder, *The Skin of Our Teeth*
1945 Mary Chase, *Harvey*
1946 Russel Crouse and Howard Lindsay, *State of the Union*
1948 Tennessee Williams, *A Streetcar Named Desire*
1949 Arthur Miller, *Death of a Salesman*
1950 Richard Rodgers, Oscar Hammerstein II, and Joshua Logan, *South Pacific*
1952 Joseph Kramm, *The Shrike*
1953 William Inge, *Picnic*
1954 John Patrick, *Teahouse of the August Moon*
1955 Tennessee Williams, *Cat on a Hot Tin Roof*
1956 Frances Goodrich and Albert Hackett, *The Diary of Anne Frank*
1957 Eugene O'Neill, *Long Day's Journey Into Night*
1958 Ketti Frings, *Look Homeward, Angel*
1959 Archibald MacLeish, *J. B.*
1960 George Abbott, Jerome Weidman, Sheldon Harnick, and Jerry Bock, *Fiorello!*
1961 Tad Mosel, *All the Way Home*
1962 Frank Loesser and Abe Burrows, *How to Succeed in Business Without Really Trying*
1965 Frank D. Gilroy, *The Subject Was Roses*
1967 Edward Albee, *A Delicate Balance*
1969 Howard Sackler, *The Great White Hope*
1970 Charles Gordone, *No Place to Be Somebody*
1971 Paul Zindel, *The Effect of Gamma Rays on Man-in-the-Moon Marigolds*
1973 Jason Miller, *That Championship Season*
1975 Edward Albee, *Seascape*
1976 Michael Bennett, James Kirkwood, Nicholas Dante, Marvin Hamlisch, and Edward Kleban, *A Chorus Line*
1977 Michael Cristofer, *The Shadow Box*
1978 Donald L. Coburn, *The Gin Game*
1979 Sam Shepard, *Buried Child*
1980 Lanford Wilson, *Talley's Folly*
1981 Beth Henley, *Crimes of the Heart*
1982 Charles Fuller, *A Soldier's Play*
1983 Marsha Norman, *'night, Mother*
1984 David Mamet, *Glengarry Glen Ross*
1985 Stephen Sondheim and James Lapine, *Sunday in the Park With George*
1987 August Wilson, *Fences*
1988 Alfred Uhry, *Driving Miss Daisy*
1989 Wendy Wasserstein, *The Heidi Chronicles*
1990 August Wilson, *The Piano Lesson*
1991 Neil Simon, *Lost in Yonkers*
1992 Robert Schenkkan, *The Kentucky Cycle*
1993 Tony Kushner, *Angels in America: Millennium Approaches*
1994 Edward Albee, *Three Tall Women*
1995 Horton Foote, *The Young Man From Atlanta*
1996 Jonathan Larson, *Rent*
1998 Paula Vogel, *How I Learned to Drive*
1999 Margaret Edson, *Wit*
2000 Donald Margulies, *Dinner With Friends*
2001 David Auburn, *Proof*
2002 Suzan-Lori Parks, *Topdog/Underdog*
2003 Nilo Cruz, *Anna in the Tropics*
2004 Doug Wright, *I Am My Own Wife*
2005 John Patrick Shanley, *Doubt, a parable*
2007 David Lindsay-Abaire, *Rabbit Hole*
2008 Tracy Letts, *August: Osage County*
2009 Lynn Nottage, *Ruined*
2010 Tom Kitt and Brian Yorkey, *Next to Normal*
2011 Bruce Norris, *Clybourne Park*
2012 Quiara Alegría Hudes, *Water by the Spoonful*

History (U.S.)

1917 J. J. Jusserand, *With Americans of Past and Present Days*
1918 James Ford Rhodes, *History of the Civil War*
1920 Justin H. Smith, *The War With Mexico*
1921 William Sowden Sims, *The Victory at Sea*
1922 James Truslow Adams, *The Founding of New England*
1923 Charles Warren, *The Supreme Court in United States History*
1924 Charles Howard McIlwain, *The American Revolution: A Constitutional Interpretation*
1925 Frederick L. Paxton, *A History of the American Frontier*
1926 Edward Channing, *A History of the U.S.*
1927 Samuel Flagg Bemis, *Pinckney's Treaty*
1928 V. L. Parrington, *Main Currents in American Thought*
1929 Fred A. Shannon, *The Organization and Administration of the Union Army, 1861-65*
1930 Claude H. Van Tyne, *The War of Independence*
1931 Bernadotte E. Schmitt, *The Coming of the War, 1914*
1932 Gen. John J. Pershing, *My Experiences in the World War*
1933 Frederick J. Turner, *The Significance of Sections in American History*
1934 Herbert Agar, *The People's Choice*
1935 Charles McLean Andrews, *The Colonial Period of American History*
1936 Andrew C. McLaughlin, *The Constitutional History of the United States*
1937 Van Wyck Brooks, *The Flowering of New England*
1938 Paul Herman Buck, *The Road to Reunion, 1865-1900*
1939 Frank Luther Mott, *A History of American Magazines*
1940 Carl Sandburg, *Abraham Lincoln: The War Years*
1941 Marcus Lee Hansen, *The Atlantic Migration, 1607-1860*
1942 Margaret Leech, *Reveille in Washington*
1943 Esther Forbes, *Paul Revere and the World He Lived In*
1944 Merle Curti, *The Growth of American Thought*
1945 Stephen Bonsal, *Unfinished Business*
1946 Arthur M. Schlesinger Jr., *The Age of Jackson*
1947 James Phinney Baxter III, *Scientists Against Time*
1948 Bernard De Voto, *Across the Wide Missouri*
1949 Roy F. Nichols, *The Disruption of American Democracy*
1950 O. W. Larkin, *Art and Life in America*
1951 R. Carlyle Buley, *The Old Northwest: Pioneer Period 1815-1840*
1952 Oscar Handlin, *The Uprooted*
1953 George Dangerfield, *The Era of Good Feelings*
1954 Bruce Catton, *A Stillness at Appomattox*
1955 Paul Horgan, *Great River: The Rio Grande in North American History*
1956 Richard Hofstadter, *The Age of Reform*
1957 George F. Kennan, *Russia Leaves the War*
1958 Bray Hammond, *Banks and Politics in America—From the Revolution to the Civil War*
1959 Leonard D. White and Jean Schneider, *The Republican Era, 1869-1901*
1960 Margaret Leech, *In the Days of McKinley*
1961 Herbert Feis, *Between War and Peace: The Potsdam Conference*
1962 Lawrence H. Gibson, *The Triumphant Empire: Thunderclouds Gather in the West*
1963 Constance McLaughlin Green, *Washington: Village and Capital, 1800-1878*
1964 Sumner Chilton Powell, *Puritan Village: The Formation of a New England Town*
1965 Irwin Unger, *The Greenback Era*
1966 Perry Miller, *Life of the Mind in America*
1967 William H. Goetzmann, *Exploration and Empire: The Explorer and Scientist in the Winning of the American West*
1968 Bernard Bailyn, *The Ideological Origins of the American Revolution*
1969 Leonard W. Levy, *Origin of the Fifth Amendment*
1970 Dean Acheson, *Present at the Creation: My Years in the State Department*
1971 James McGregor Burns, *Roosevelt: The Soldier of Freedom*
1972 Carl N. Degler, *Neither Black nor White*
1973 Michael Kammen, *People of Paradox: An Inquiry Concerning the Origins of American Civilization*
1974 Daniel J. Boorstin, *The Americans: The Democratic Experience*
1975 Dumas Malone, *Jefferson and His Time*
1976 Paul Horgan, *Lamy of Santa Fe*
1977 David M. Potter, *The Impending Crisis*
1978 Alfred D. Chandler Jr., *The Visible Hand: The Managerial Revolution in American Business*
1979 Don E. Fehrenbacher, *The Dred Scott Case: Its Significance in American Law and Politics*
1980 Leon F. Litwack, *Been in the Storm So Long*

1981 Lawrence A. Cremin, *American Education: The National Experience, 1783-1876*
1982 C. Vann Woodward, ed., *Mary Chesnut's Civil War*
1983 Rhys L. Issac, *The Transformation of Virginia, 1740-1790*
1985 Thomas K. McCraw, *Prophets of Regulation*
1986 Walter A. McDougall, *The Heavens and the Earth*
1987 Bernard Bailyn, *Voyagers to the West*
1988 Robert V. Bruce, *The Launching of Modern American Science, 1846-1876*
1989 Taylor Branch, *Parting the Waters: America in the King Years, 1954-63*; James M. McPherson, *Battle Cry of Freedom: The Civil War Era*
1990 Stanley Karnow, *In Our Image: America's Empire in the Philippines*
1991 Laurel Thatcher Ulrich, *A Midwife's Tale: The Life of Martha Ballard, based on her diary, 1785-1812*
1992 Mark E. Neely Jr., *The Fate of Liberty: Abraham Lincoln and Civil Liberties*
1993 Gordon S. Wood, *The Radicalism of the American Revolution*
1995 Doris Kearns Goodwin, *No Ordinary Time: Franklin and Eleanor Roosevelt: The Home Front in World War II*
1996 Alan Taylor, *William Cooper's Town: Power and Persuasion on the Frontier of the Early American Republic*
1997 Jack N. Rakove, *Original Meanings: Politics and Ideas in the Making of the Constitution*
1998 Edward J. Larson, *Summer for the Gods: The Scopes Trial and America's Continuing Debate Over Science and Religion*
1999 Edwin G. Burrows and Mike Wallace, *Gotham: A History of New York City to 1898*
2000 David M. Kennedy, *Freedom From Fear: The American People in Depression and War, 1929-1945*
2001 Joseph J. Ellis, *Founding Brothers: The Revolutionary Generation*
2002 Louis Menand, *The Metaphysical Club: A Story of Ideas in America*
2003 Rick Atkinson, *An Army at Dawn: The War in North Africa, 1942-1943*
2004 Steven Hahn, *A Nation Under Our Feet: Black Political Struggles in the Rural South From Slavery to the Great Migration*
2005 David Hackett Fischer, *Washington's Crossing*
2006 David M. Oshinsky, *Polio: An American Story*
2007 Gene Roberts and Hank Klibanoff, *The Race Beat: The Press, the Civil Rights Struggle, and the Awakening of a Nation*
2008 Daniel Walker Howe, *What Hath God Wrought: The Transformation of America, 1815-1848*
2009 Annette Gordon-Reed, *The Hemingses of Monticello: An American Family*
2010 Liaquat Ahamed, *Lords of Finance: The Bankers Who Broke the World*
2011 Eric Foner, *The Fiery Trial: Abraham Lincoln and American Slavery*
2012 Manning Marable, *Malcolm X: A Life of Reinvention*

Biography or Autobiography

1917 Laura E. Richards and Maude Howe Elliott, assisted by Florence Howe Hall, *Julia Ward Howe*
1918 William Cabell Bruce, *Benjamin Franklin, Self-Revealed*
1919 Henry Adams, *The Education of Henry Adams*
1920 Albert J. Beveridge, *The Life of John Marshall*
1921 Edward Bok, *The Americanization of Edward Bok*
1922 Hamlin Garland, *A Daughter of the Middle Border*
1923 Burton J. Hendrick, *The Life and Letters of Walter H. Page*
1924 Michael Pupin, *From Immigrant to Inventor*
1925 M. A. DeWolfe Howe, *Barrett Wendell and His Letters*
1926 Harvey Cushing, *Life of Sir William Osler*
1927 Emory Holloway, *Whitman: An Interpretation in Narrative*
1928 Charles Edward Russell, *The American Orchestra and Theodore Thomas*
1929 Burton J. Hendrick, *The Training of an American: The Earlier Life and Letters of Walter H. Page*
1930 Marquis James, *The Raven* (Sam Houston)
1931 Henry James, *Charles W. Eliot*
1932 Henry F. Pringle, *Theodore Roosevelt*
1933 Allan Nevins, *Grover Cleveland*
1934 Tyler Dennett, *John Hay*
1935 Douglas Southall Freeman, *R. E. Lee*
1936 Ralph Barton Perry, *The Thought and Character of William James*
1937 Allan Nevins, *Hamilton Fish: The Inner History of the Grant Administration*
1938 Odell Shepard, *Pedlar's Progress*; Marquis James, *Andrew Jackson, 2 vols.*
1939 Carl Van Doren, *Benjamin Franklin*
1940 Ray Stannard Baker, *Woodrow Wilson, Life and Letters*
1941 Ola Elizabeth Winslow, *Jonathan Edwards*
1942 Forrest Wilson, *Crusader in Crinoline* (Harriet Beecher Stowe)

1943 Samuel Eliot Morison, *Admiral of the Ocean Sea* (Christopher Columbus)
1944 Carleton Mabee, *The American Leonardo: The Life of Samuel F. B. Morse*
1945 Russell Blaine Nye, *George Bancroft: Brahmin Rebel*
1946 Linny Marsh Wolfe, *Son of the Wilderness*
1947 William Allen White, *Autobiography of William Allen White*
1948 Margaret Clapp, *Forgotten First Citizen: John Bigelow*
1949 Robert E. Sherwood, *Roosevelt and Hopkins*
1950 Samuel Flagg Bemis, *John Quincy Adams and the Foundations of American Foreign Policy*
1951 Margaret Louise Coit, *John C. Calhoun: American Portrait*
1952 Merlo J. Pusey, *Charles Evans Hughes*
1953 David J. Mays, *Edmund Pendleton, 1721-1803*
1954 Charles A. Lindbergh, *The Spirit of St. Louis*
1955 William S. White, *The Taft Story*
1956 Talbot F. Hamlin, *Benjamin Henry Latrobe*
1957 John F. Kennedy, *Profiles in Courage*
1958 Douglas Southall Freeman, *George Washington*, Vols. I-VI
1959 Arthur Walworth, *Woodrow Wilson: American Prophet*
1960 Samuel Eliot Morison, *John Paul Jones*
1961 David Donald, *Charles Sumner and the Coming of the Civil War*
1963 Leon Edel, *Henry James: Vols. 2-3*
1964 Walter Jackson Bate, *John Keats*
1965 Ernest Samuels, *Henry Adams*
1966 Arthur M. Schlesinger Jr., *A Thousand Days* (JFK)
1967 Justin Kaplan, *Mr. Clemens and Mark Twain*
1968 George F. Kennan, *Memoirs (1925-1950)*
1969 B. L. Reid, *The Man From New York: John Quinn and His Friends*
1970 T. Harry Williams, *Huey Long*
1971 Lawrence Thompson, *Robert Frost: The Years of Triumph, 1915-1938*
1972 Joseph P. Lash, *Eleanor and Franklin*
1973 W. A. Swanberg, *Luce and His Empire*
1974 Louis Sheaffer, *O'Neill, Son and Artist*
1975 Robert A. Caro, *The Power Broker: Robert Moses and the Fall of New York*
1976 R. W. B. Lewis, *Edith Wharton: A Biography*
1977 John E. Mack, *A Prince of Our Disorder: The Life of T. E. Lawrence*
1978 Walter Jackson Bate, *Samuel Johnson*
1979 Leonard Baker, *Days of Sorrow and Pain: Leo Baeck and the Berlin Jews*
1980 Edmund Morris, *The Rise of Theodore Roosevelt*
1981 Robert K. Massie, *Peter the Great: His Life and World*
1982 William S. McFeely, *Grant: A Biography*
1983 Russell Baker, *Growing Up*
1984 Louis R. Harlan, *Booker T. Washington*
1985 Kenneth Silverman, *The Life and Times of Cotton Mather*
1986 Elizabeth Frank, *Louise Bogan: A Portrait*
1987 David J. Garrow, *Bearing the Cross: Martin Luther King Jr. and the Southern Christian Leadership Conference*
1988 David Herbert Donald, *Look Homeward: A Life of Thomas Wolfe*
1989 Richard Ellmann, *Oscar Wilde*
1990 Sebastian de Grazia, *Machiavelli in Hell*
1991 Steven Naifeh and Gregory White Smith, *Jackson Pollock: An American Saga*
1992 Lewis B. Puller Jr., *Fortunate Son: The Healing of a Vietnam Vet*
1993 David McCullough, *Truman*
1994 David Levering Lewis, *W.E.B. DuBois: Biography of a Race, 1868-1919*
1995 Joan D. Hedrick, *Harriet Beecher Stowe: A Life*
1996 Jack Miles, *God: A Biography*
1997 Frank McCourt, *Angela's Ashes: A Memoir*
1998 Katharine Graham, *Personal History*
1999 A. Scott Berg, *Lindbergh*
2000 Stacy Schiff, *Véra (Mrs. Vladimir Nabokov)*
2001 David Levering Lewis, *W.E.B. Du Bois: The Fight for Equality and the American Century, 1919-1963*
2002 David McCullough, *John Adams*
2003 Robert Caro, *The Years of Lyndon Johnson: Master of the Senate*
2004 William Taubman, *Khrushchev: The Man and His Era*
2005 Mark Stevens and Annalyn Swan, *de Kooning: An American Master*
2006 Kai Bird and Martin J. Sherwin, *American Prometheus: The Triumph and Tragedy of J. Robert Oppenheimer*
2007 Debby Applegate, *The Most Famous Man in America: The Biography of Henry Ward Beecher*
2008 John Matteson, *Eden's Outcasts: The Story of Louisa May Alcott and Her Father*
2009 Jon Meacham, *American Lion: Andrew Jackson in the White House*
2010 T. J. Stiles, *The First Tycoon: The Epic Life of Cornelius Vanderbilt*
2011 Ron Chernow, *Washington: A Life*
2012 John Lewis Gaddis, *George F. Kennan: An American Life*

American Poetry

1922 Edwin Arlington Robinson, *Collected Poems*
1923 Edna St. Vincent Millay, *The Ballad of the Harp-Weaver*; *A Few Figs From Thistles*; other works
1924 Robert Frost, *New Hampshire: A Poem With Notes and Grace Notes*
1925 Edwin Arlington Robinson, *The Man Who Died Twice*
1926 Amy Lowell, *What's O'Clock*
1927 Leonora Speyer, *Fiddler's Farewell*
1928 Edwin Arlington Robinson, *Tristram*
1929 Stephen Vincent Benet, *John Brown's Body*
1930 Conrad Aiken, *Selected Poems*
1931 Robert Frost, *Collected Poems*
1932 George Dillon, *The Flowering Stone*
1933 Archibald MacLeish, *Conquistador*
1934 Robert Hillyer, *Collected Verse*
1935 Audrey Wurdemann, *Bright Ambush*
1936 Robert P. Tristram Coffin, *Strange Holiness*
1937 Robert Frost, *A Further Range*
1938 Marya Zaturenska, *Cold Morning Sky*
1939 John Gould Fletcher, *Selected Poems*
1940 Mark Van Doren, *Collected Poems*
1941 Leonard Bacon, *Sunderland Capture*
1942 William Rose Benet, *The Dust Which Is God*
1943 Robert Frost, *A Witness Tree*
1944 Stephen Vincent Benet, *Western Star*
1945 Karl Shapiro, *V-Letter and Other Poems*
1947 Robert Lowell, *Lord Weary's Castle*
1948 W. H. Auden, *The Age of Anxiety*
1949 Peter Viereck, *Terror and Decorum*
1950 Gwendolyn Brooks, *Annie Allen*
1951 Carl Sandburg, *Complete Poems*
1952 Marianne Moore, *Collected Poems*
1953 Archibald MacLeish, *Collected Poems*
1954 Theodore Roethke, *The Waking*
1955 Wallace Stevens, *Collected Poems*
1956 Elizabeth Bishop, *Poems, North and South*
1957 Richard Wilbur, *Things of This World*
1958 Robert Penn Warren, *Promises: Poems 1954-1956*
1959 Stanley Kunitz, *Selected Poems 1928-1958*
1960 W. D. Snodgrass, *Heart's Needle*
1961 Phyllis McGinley, *Times Three: Selected Verse From Three Decades*
1962 Alan Dugan, *Poems*
1963 William Carlos Williams, *Pictures From Breughel*
1964 Louis Simpson, *At the End of the Open Road*
1965 John Berryman, *77 Dream Songs*
1966 Richard Eberhart, *Selected Poems*
1967 Anne Sexton, *Live or Die*
1968 Anthony Hecht, *The Hard Hours*
1969 George Oppen, *Of Being Numerous*
1970 Richard Howard, *Untitled Subjects*
1971 William S. Merwin, *The Carrier of Ladders*
1972 James Wright, *Collected Poems*
1973 Maxine Winokur Kumin, *Up Country*
1974 Robert Lowell, *The Dolphin*
1975 Gary Snyder, *Turtle Island*
1976 John Ashbery, *Self-Portrait in a Convex Mirror*
1977 James Merrill, *Divine Comedies*
1978 Howard Nemerov, *Collected Poems*
1979 Robert Penn Warren, *Now and Then: Poems 1976-1978*
1980 Donald Justice, *Selected Poems*
1981 James Schuyler, *The Morning of the Poem*
1982 Sylvia Plath, *The Collected Poems*
1983 Galway Kinnell, *Selected Poems*
1984 Mary Oliver, *American Primitive*
1985 Carolyn Kizer, *Yin*
1986 Henry Taylor, *The Flying Change*
1987 Rita Dove, *Thomas and Beulah*
1988 William Meredith, *Partial Accounts*
1989 Richard Wilbur, *New and Collected Poems*
1990 Charles Simic, *The World Doesn't End*
1991 Mona Van Duyn, *Near Changes*
1992 James Tate, *Selected Poems*
1993 Louise Glück, *The Wild Iris*
1994 Yusef Komunyakaa, *Neon Vernacular*
1995 Philip Levine, *The Simple Truth*
1996 Jorie Graham, *The Dream of the Unified Field*
1997 Lisel Mueller, *Alive Together: New and Selected Poems*
1998 Charles Wright, *Black Zodiac*
1999 Mark Strand, *Blizzard of One*
2000 C. K. Williams, *Repair*
2001 Stephen Dunn, *Different Hours*
2002 Carl Dennis, *Practical Gods*
2003 Paul Muldoon, *Moy Sand and Gravel*
2004 Franz Wright, *Walking to Martha's Vineyard*
2005 Ted Kooser, *Delights & Shadows*
2006 Claudia Emerson, *Late Wife*

2007 Natasha Trethewey, *Native Guard*
2008 Robert Hass, *Time and Materials*; Philip Schultz, *Failure*
2009 W. S. Merwin, *The Shadow of Sirius*
2010 Rae Armantrout, *Versed*
2011 Kay Ryan, *The Best of It: New and Selected Poems*
2012 Tracy K. Smith, *Life on Mars*

General Nonfiction

1962 Theodore H. White, *The Making of the President 1960*
1963 Barbara W. Tuchman, *The Guns of August*
1964 Richard Hofstadter, *Anti-Intellectualism in American Life*
1965 Howard Mumford Jones, *O Strange New World*
1966 Edwin Way Teale, *Wandering Through Winter*
1967 David Brion Davis, *The Problem of Slavery in Western Culture*
1968 Will and Ariel Durant, *Rousseau and Revolution*
1969 Norman Mailer, *The Armies of the Night*;
     Rene Jules Dubos, *So Human an Animal: How We Are Shaped by Surroundings and Events*
1970 Eric H. Erikson, *Gandhi's Truth*
1971 John Toland, *The Rising Sun*
1972 Barbara W. Tuchman, *Stilwell and the American Experience in China, 1911-1945*
1973 Frances FitzGerald, *Fire in the Lake: The Vietnamese and the Americans in Vietnam*;
     Robert Coles, *Children of Crisis, Vols. II and III*
1974 Ernest Becker, *The Denial of Death*
1975 Annie Dillard, *Pilgrim at Tinker Creek*
1976 Robert N. Butler, *Why Survive? Being Old in America*
1977 William W. Warner, *Beautiful Swimmers*
1978 Carl Sagan, *The Dragons of Eden*
1979 Edward O. Wilson, *On Human Nature*
1980 Douglas R. Hofstadter, *Gödel, Escher, Bach: An Eternal Golden Braid*
1981 Carl E. Schorske, *Fin-de-Siecle Vienna: Politics and Culture*
1982 Tracy Kidder, *The Soul of a New Machine*
1983 Susan Sheehan, *Is There No Place on Earth for Me?*
1984 Paul Starr, *Social Transformation of American Medicine*
1985 Studs Terkel, *The Good War*
1986 Joseph Lelyveld, *Move Your Shadow*;
     J. Anthony Lukas, *Common Ground*
1987 David K. Shipler, *Arab and Jew*
1988 Richard Rhodes, *The Making of the Atomic Bomb*
1989 Neil Sheehan, *A Bright Shining Lie: John Paul Vann and America in Vietnam*
1990 Dale Maharidge and Michael Williamson, *And Their Children After Them*
1991 Bert Holldobler and Edward O. Wilson, *The Ants*
1992 Daniel Yergin, *The Prize: The Epic Quest for Oil*
1993 Garry Wills, *Lincoln at Gettysburg*

1994 David Remnick, *Lenin's Tomb: The Last Days of the Soviet Empire*
1995 Jonathan Weiner, *The Beak of the Finch: A Story of Evolution in Our Time*
1996 Tina Rosenberg, *The Haunted Land: Facing Europe's Ghosts After Communism*
1997 Richard Kluger, *Ashes to Ashes: America's Hundred-Year Cigarette War, the Public Health, and the Unabashed Triumph of Philip Morris*
1998 Jared Diamond, *Guns, Germs, and Steel: The Fates of Human Societies*
1999 John McPhee, *Annals of the Former World*
2000 John W. Dower, *Embracing Defeat: Japan in the Wake of World War II*
2001 Herbert P. Bix, *Hirohito and the Making of Modern Japan*
2002 Diane McWhorter, *Carry Me Home: Birmingham, Alabama, the Climactic Battle of the Civil Rights Revolution*
2003 Samantha Power, *A Problem From Hell: America and the Age of Genocide*
2004 Anne Applebaum, *Gulag: A History*
2005 Steve Coll, *Ghost Wars*
2006 Caroline Elkins, *Imperial Reckoning: The Untold Story of Britain's Gulag in Kenya*
2007 Lawrence Wright, *The Looming Tower: Al-Qaeda and the Road to 9/11*
2008 Saul Friedländer, *The Years of Extermination: Nazi Germany and the Jews, 1939-1945*
2009 Douglas A. Blackmon, *Slavery by Another Name: The Re-Enslavement of Black Americans From the Civil War to World War II*
2010 David E. Hoffman, *The Dead Hand: The Untold Story of the Cold War Arms Race and Its Dangerous Legacy*
2011 Siddhartha Mukherjee, *The Emperor of All Maladies: A Biography of Cancer*
2012 Stephen Greenblatt, *The Swerve: How the World Became Modern*

Special Citation in Letters

1944 Richard Rodgers and Oscar Hammerstein II, for *Oklahoma!*
1957 Kenneth Roberts, for his historical novels
1960 *The Armada*, by Garrett Mattingly
1961 *American Heritage Picture History of the Civil War*
1973 *George Washington, Vols. I-IV*, by James Thomas Flexner
1977 Alex Haley, for *Roots*
1978 E. B. White
1984 Theodore Seuss Geisel (Dr. Seuss)
1992 Art Spiegelman, for *Maus*
2006 Edmund S. Morgan
2007 Ray Bradbury

Pulitzer Prizes in Music, 1943-2012

1943 William Schuman, *Secular Cantata No. 2, A Free Song*
1944 Howard Hanson, *Symphony No. 4, Op. 34*
1945 Aaron Copland, *Appalachian Spring*
1946 Leo Sowerby, *The Canticle of the Sun*
1947 Charles E. Ives, *Symphony No. 3*
1948 Walter Piston, *Symphony No. 3*
1949 Virgil Thomson, *Louisiana Story*
1950 Gian-Carlo Menotti, *The Consul*
1951 Douglas Moore, *Giants in the Earth*
1952 Gail Kubik, *Symphony Concertante*
1954 Quincy Porter, *Concerto for Two Pianos and Orchestra*
1955 Gian-Carlo Menotti, *The Saint of Bleecker Street*
1956 Ernest Toch, *Symphony No. 3*
1957 Norman Dello Joio, *Meditations on Ecclesiastes*
1958 Samuel Barber, *Vanessa*
1959 John La Montaine, *Concerto for Piano and Orchestra*
1960 Elliott Carter, *Second String Quartet*
1961 Walter Piston, *Symphony No. 7*
1962 Robert Ward, *The Crucible*
1963 Samuel Barber, *Piano Concerto No. 1*
1966 Leslie Bassett, *Variations for Orchestra*
1967 Leon Kirchner, *Quartet No. 3*
1968 George Crumb, *Echoes of Time and the River*
1969 Karel Husa, *String Quartet No. 3*
1970 Charles W. Wuorinen, *Time's Encomium*
1971 Mario Davidovsky, *Synchronisms No. 6*
1972 Jacob Druckman, *Windows*
1973 Elliott Carter, *String Quartet No. 3*
1974 Donald Martino, *Notturno*
1975 Dominick Argento, *From the Diary of Virginia Woolf*
1976 Ned Rorem, *Air Music*
1977 Richard Wernick, *Visions of Terror and Wonder*
1978 Michael Colgrass, *Deja Vu for Percussion and Orchestra*
1979 Joseph Schwantner, *Aftertones of Infinity*
1980 David Del Tredici, *In Memory of a Summer Day*
1982 Roger Sessions, *Concerto for Orchestra*
1983 Ellen T. Zwilich, *Three Movements for Orchestra*
1984 Bernard Rands, *Canti del Sole*
1985 Stephen Albert, *Symphony, RiverRun*
1986 George Perle, *Wind Quintet IV*

1987 John Harbison, *The Flight Into Egypt*
1988 William Bolcom, *12 New Etudes for Piano*
1989 Roger Reynolds, *Whispers Out of Time*
1990 Mel Powell, *Duplicates: A Concerto for Two Pianos and Orchestra*
1991 Shulamit Ran, *Symphony*
1992 Wayne Peterson, *The Face of the Night, The Heart of the Dark*
1993 Christopher Rouse, *Trombone Concerto*
1994 Gunther Schuller, *Of Reminiscences and Reflections*
1995 Morton Gould, *Stringmusic*
1996 George Walker, *Lilacs for Voice and Orchestra*
1997 Wynton Marsalis, *Blood on the Fields*
1998 Aaron Jay Kernis, *String Quartet No. 2 (musica instrumentalis)*
1999 Melinda Wagner, *Concerto for Flute, Strings, and Percussion*
2000 Lewis Spratlan, *Life is a Dream, Opera in Three Acts: Act II, Concert Version*
2001 John Corigliano, *Symphony No. 2 for String Orchestra*
2002 Henry Brant, *Ice Field*
2003 John Adams, *On the Transmigration of Souls*
2004 Paul Moravec, *Tempest Fantasy*
2005 Steven Stucky, *Second Concerto for Orchestra*
2006 Yehudi Wyner, *Piano Concerto: "Chiavi in Mano"*
2007 Ornette Coleman, *Sound Grammar*
2008 David Lang, *The Little Match Girl Passion*
2009 Steve Reich, *Double Sextet*
2010 Jennifer Higdon, *Violin Concerto*
2011 Zhou Long, *Madame White Snake*
2012 Kevin Puts, *Silent Night: Opera in Two Acts*

Special Citation in Music

1974 Roger Sessions
1976 Scott Joplin
1982 Milton Babbitt
1985 William Schuman
1998 George Gershwin
1999 Edward Kennedy "Duke" Ellington
2006 Thelonious Monk
2007 John Coltrane
2008 Bob Dylan
2010 Hank Williams

Man Booker Prize for Fiction, 1969-2012

The Booker Prize for fiction, established in 1968, is awarded annually in Oct. for what is judged the best full-length novel written in English by a citizen of the UK, the Commonwealth, or the Irish Republic. In 2002, sponsorship of the award was taken over by Man Group PLC, the name was changed to the Man Booker Prize, and the amount was increased from £20,000 to £50,000 (about $80,000).

Year	Author, book	Year	Author, book
1969	P. H. Newby, *Something to Answer For*	1991	Ben Okri, *The Famished Road*
1970	Bernice Rubens, *The Elected Member*	1992	Michael Ondaatje, *The English Patient*;
1971	V. S. Naipaul, *In a Free State*		Barry Unsworth, *Sacred Hunger*
1972	John Berger, *G*	1993	Roddy Doyle, *Paddy Clarke Ha Ha Ha*
1973	J. G. Farrell, *The Siege of Krishnapur*	1994	James Kelman, *How Late It Was, How Late*
1974	Nadine Gordimer, *The Conservationist*;	1995	Pat Barker, *The Ghost Road*
	Stanley Middleton, *Holiday*	1996	Graham Swift, *Last Orders*
1975	Ruth Prawer Jhabvala, *Heat and Dust*	1997	Arundhati Roy, *The God of Small Things*
1976	David Storey, *Saville*	1998	Ian McEwan, *Amsterdam*
1977	Paul Scott, *Staying On*	1999	J. M. Coetzee, *Disgrace*
1978	Iris Murdoch, *The Sea, The Sea*	2000	Margaret Atwood, *The Blind Assassin*
1979	Penelope Fitzgerald, *Offshore*	2001	Peter Carey, *True History of the Kelly Gang*
1980	William Golding, *Rites of Passage*	2002	Yann Martel, *Life of Pi*
1981	Salman Rushdie, *Midnight's Children*[1]	2003	DBC Pierre, *Vernon God Little*
1982	Thomas Keneally, *Schindler's Ark*	2004	Alan Hollinghurst, *The Line of Beauty*
1983	J. M. Coetzee, *Life and Times of Michael K*	2005	John Banville, *The Sea*
1984	Anita Brookner, *Hotel du Lac*	2006	Kiran Desai, *The Inheritance of Loss*
1985	Keri Hulme, *The Bone People*	2007	Anne Enright, *The Gathering*
1986	Kingsley Amis, *The Old Devils*	2008	Aravind Adiga, *The White Tiger*
1987	Penelope Lively, *Moon Tiger*	2009	Hilary Mantel, *Wolf Hall*
1988	Peter Carey, *Oscar and Lucinda*	2010	Howard Jacobson, *The Finkler Question*
1989	Kazuo Ishiguro, *The Remains of the Day*	2011	Julian Barnes, *The Sense of an Ending*
1990	A. S. Byatt, *Possession*	2012	Hilary Mantel, *Bring up the Bodies*

(1) Rushdie's *Midnight's Children* also won the Booker of Booker prize in 1993 and the Best of the Booker prize in 2008.

Newbery Medal, 1922-2012

The Newbery Medal is awarded annually by the Association for Library Service to Children, a division of the American Library Association, to the author of the most distinguished contribution to American literature for children.

Year	Book, author	Year	Book, author
1922	*The Story of Mankind*, Hendrik Willem van Loon	1968	*From the Mixed-Up Files of Mrs. Basil E. Frankweiler*, E. L. Konigsburg
1923	*The Voyages of Dr. Dolittle*, Hugh Lofting	1969	*The High King*, Lloyd Alexander
1924	*The Dark Frigate*, Charles Boardman Hawes	1970	*Sounder*, William H. Armstrong
1925	*Tales From Silver Lands*, Charles Joseph Finger	1971	*The Summer of the Swans*, Betsy Byars
1926	*Shen of the Sea*, Arthur Bowie Chrisman	1972	*Mrs. Frisby and the Rats of NIMH*, Robert C. O'Brien
1927	*Smoky, the Cowhorse*, Will James	1973	*Julie of the Wolves*, Jean George
1928	*Gay-Neck*, Dhan Gopal Mukerji	1974	*The Slave Dancer*, Paula Fox
1929	*The Trumpeter of Krakow*, Eric P. Kelly	1975	*M. C. Higgins the Great*, Virginia Hamilton
1930	*Hitty, Her First Hundred Years*, Rachel Field	1976	*Grey King*, Susan Cooper
1931	*The Cat Who Went to Heaven*, Elizabeth Coatsworth	1977	*Roll of Thunder, Hear My Cry*, Mildred D. Taylor
1932	*Waterless Mountain*, Laura Adams Armer	1978	*Bridge to Terabithia*, Katherine Paterson
1933	*Young Fu of the Upper Yangtze*, Elizabeth Foreman Lewis	1979	*The Westing Game*, Ellen Raskin
1934	*Invincible Louisa*, Cornelia Lynde Meigs	1980	*A Gathering of Days*, Joan Blos
1935	*Dobry*, Monica Shannon	1981	*Jacob Have I Loved*, Katherine Paterson
1936	*Caddie Woodlawn*, Carol Ryrie Brink	1982	*A Visit to William Blake's Inn: Poems for Innocent and Experienced Travelers*, Nancy Willard
1937	*Roller Skates*, Ruth Sawyer	1983	*Dicey's Song*, Cynthia Voigt
1938	*The White Stag*, Kate Seredy	1984	*Dear Mr. Henshaw*, Beverly Cleary
1939	*Thimble Summer*, Elizabeth Enright	1985	*The Hero and the Crown*, Robin McKinley
1940	*Daniel Boone*, James Daugherty	1986	*Sarah, Plain and Tall*, Patricia MacLachlan
1941	*Call It Courage*, Armstrong Sperry	1987	*The Whipping Boy*, Sid Fleischman
1942	*The Matchlock Gun*, Walter D. Edmonds	1988	*Lincoln: A Photobiography*, Russell Freedman
1943	*Adam of the Road*, Elizabeth Janet Gray	1989	*Joyful Noise: Poems for Two Voices*, Paul Fleischman
1944	*Johnny Tremain*, Esther Forbes	1990	*Number the Stars*, Lois Lowry
1945	*Rabbit Hill*, Robert Lawson	1991	*Maniac Magee*, Jerry Spinelli
1946	*Strawberry Girl*, Lois Lenski	1992	*Shiloh*, Phyllis Reynolds Naylor
1947	*Miss Hickory*, Carolyn S. Bailey	1993	*Missing May*, Cynthia Rylant
1948	*Twenty-One Balloons*, William Pène Du Bois	1994	*The Giver*, Lois Lowry
1949	*King of the Wind*, Marguerite Henry	1995	*Walk Two Moons*, Sharon Creech
1950	*The Door in the Wall*, Marguerite de Angeli	1996	*The Midwife's Apprentice*, Karen Cushman
1951	*Amos Fortune, Free Man*, Elizabeth Yates	1997	*The View From Saturday*, E. L. Konigsburg
1952	*Ginger Pye*, Eleanor Estes	1998	*Out of the Dust*, Karen Hesse
1953	*Secret of the Andes*, Ann Nolan Clark	1999	*Holes*, Louis Sachar
1954	*...And Now Miguel*, Joseph Krumgold	2000	*Bud, Not Buddy*, Christopher Paul Curtis
1955	*The Wheel on the School*, Meindert DeJong	2001	*A Year Down Yonder*, Richard Peck
1956	*Carry On, Mr. Bowditch*, Jean Lee Latham	2002	*A Single Shard*, Linda Sue Park
1957	*Miracles on Maple Hill*, Virginia Sorensen	2003	*Crispin: The Cross of Lead*, Avi
1958	*Rifles for Watie*, Harold Keith	2004	*The Tale of Despereaux*, Kate DiCamillo
1959	*The Witch of Blackbird Pond*, Elizabeth George Speare	2005	*Kira-Kira*, Cynthia Kadohata
1960	*Onion John*, Joseph Krumgold	2006	*Criss Cross*, Lynne Rae Perkins
1961	*Island of the Blue Dolphins*, Scott O'Dell	2007	*The Higher Power of Lucky*, Susan Patron
1962	*The Bronze Bow*, Elizabeth George Speare	2008	*Good Masters! Sweet Ladies! Voices From a Medieval Village*, Laura Amy Schlitz
1963	*A Wrinkle in Time*, Madeleine L'Engle	2009	*The Graveyard Book*, Neil Gaiman
1964	*It's Like This, Cat*, Emily Cheney Neville	2010	*When You Reach Me*, Rebecca Stead
1965	*Shadow of a Bull*, Maja Wojciechowska	2011	*Moon Over Manifest*, Clare Vanderpool
1966	*I, Juan de Pareja*, Elizabeth Borton de Trevino	2012	*Dead End in Norvelt*, Jack Gantos
1967	*Up a Road Slowly*, Irene Hunt		

Caldecott Medal, 1938-2012

The Caldecott Medal is awarded annually by the Association for Library Service to Children, a division of the American Library Association, to the illustrator of the most distinguished American picture book for children.

Year	Book, illustrator
1938	*Animals of the Bible*, Dorothy P. Lathrop
1939	*Mei Li*, Thomas Handforth
1940	*Abraham Lincoln*, Ingri and Edgar Parin d'Aulaire
1941	*They Were Strong and Good*, Robert Lawson
1942	*Make Way for Ducklings*, Robert McCloskey
1943	*The Little House*, Virginia Lee Burton
1944	*Many Moons*, Louis Slobodkin
1945	*Prayer for a Child*, Elizabeth Orton Jones
1946	*The Rooster Crows*, Maude and Miska Petersham
1947	*The Little Island*, Leonard Weisgard
1948	*White Snow, Bright Snow*, Roger Duvoisin
1949	*The Big Snow*, Berta and Elmer Hader
1950	*Song of the Swallows*, Leo Politi
1951	*The Egg Tree*, Katherine Milhous
1952	*Finders Keepers*, Nicolas, pseud. (Nicholas Mordvinoff)
1953	*The Biggest Bear*, Lynd Ward
1954	*Madeline's Rescue*, Ludwig Bemelmans
1955	*Cinderella, or the Little Glass Slipper*, Marcia Brown
1956	*Frog Went A-Courtin'*, Feodor Rojankovsky
1957	*A Tree Is Nice*, Marc Simont
1958	*Time of Wonder*, Robert McCloskey
1959	*Chanticleer and the Fox*, Barbara Cooney
1960	*Nine Days to Christmas*, Marie Hall Ets
1961	*Baboushka and the Three Kings*, Nicolas Sidjakov
1962	*Once a Mouse*, Marcia Brown
1963	*The Snowy Day*, Ezra Jack Keats
1964	*Where the Wild Things Are*, Maurice Sendak
1965	*May I Bring a Friend?*, Beni Montressor
1966	*Always Room for One More*, Nonny Hogrogian
1967	*Sam, Bang, and Moonshine*, Evaline Ness
1968	*Drummer Hoff*, Ed Emberley
1969	*The Fool of the World and the Flying Ship*, Uri Shulevitz
1970	*Sylvester and the Magic Pebble*, William Steig
1971	*A Story A Story*, Gail E. Haley
1972	*One Fine Day*, Nonny Hogrogian
1973	*The Funny Little Woman*, Blair Lent
1974	*Duffy and the Devil*, Margot Zemach
1975	*Arrow to the Sun*, Gerald McDermott

Year	Book, illustrator
1976	*Why Mosquitoes Buzz in People's Ears*, Leo & Diane Dillon
1977	*Ashanti to Zulu: African Traditions*, Leo & Diane Dillon
1978	*Noah's Ark*, Peter Spier
1979	*The Girl Who Loved Wild Horses*, Paul Goble
1980	*Ox-Cart Man*, Barbara Cooney
1981	*Fables*, Arnold Lobel
1982	*Jumanji*, Chris Van Allsburg
1983	*Shadow*, Marcia Brown
1984	*The Glorious Flight: Across the Channel With Louis Bleriot*, Alice and Martin Provensen
1985	*Saint George and the Dragon*, Trina Schart Hyman
1986	*The Polar Express*, Chris Van Allsburg
1987	*Hey, Al*, Richard Egielski
1988	*Owl Moon*, John Schoenherr
1989	*Song and Dance Man*, Stephen Grammell
1990	*Lon Po Po: A Red-Riding Hood Story From China*, Ed Young
1991	*Black and White*, David Macaulay
1992	*Tuesday*, David Wiesner
1993	*Mirette on the High Wire*, Emily Arnold McCully
1994	*Grandfather's Journey*, Allen Say
1995	*Smoky Night*, David Diaz
1996	*Officer Buckle and Gloria*, Peggy Rathmann
1997	*Golem*, David Wisniewski
1998	*Rapunzel*, Paul O. Zelinsky
1999	*Snowflake Bentley*, Mary Azarian
2000	*Joseph Had a Little Overcoat*, Simms Taback
2001	*So You Want to be President?*, David Small
2002	*The Three Pigs*, David Wiesner
2003	*My Friend Rabbit*, Eric Rohmann
2004	*The Man Who Walked Between the Towers*, Mordicai Gerstein
2005	*Kitten's First Full Moon*, Kevin Henkes
2006	*The Hello, Goodbye Window*, Chris Raschka
2007	*Flotsam*, David Wiesner
2008	*The Invention of Hugo Cabret*, Brian Selznick
2009	*The House in the Night*, Beth Krommes
2010	*The Lion & the Mouse*, Jerry Pinkney
2011	*A Sick Day for Amos McGee*, Erin E. Stead
2012	*A Ball for Daisy*, Chris Raschka

National Book Awards, 1950-2011

The National Book Awards (known as American Book Awards 1980-86) are administered by the National Book Foundation and have been given annually in the years shown, since 1950. The prizes, each valued at $10,000, are awarded to U.S. citizens for works published in the U.S. In some years, multiple awards were given for nonfiction in various categories; in such cases, the history and biography (if any) or biography winner is listed. Selected additional awards in nonfiction are listed in footnotes.

Other National Book Awards, 2011: Poetry: Nikky Finney, *Head Off & Split*. Young People's Literature: Thanhha Lai, *Inside Out & Back Again*. Distinguished Contribution to American Letters: John Ashbery. Literarian Award: Mitchell Kaplan.

Fiction

Year	Author, book
1950	Nelson Algren, *The Man With the Golden Arm*
1951	William Faulkner, *The Collected Stories*
1952	James Jones, *From Here to Eternity*
1953	Ralph Ellison, *Invisible Man*
1954	Saul Bellow, *The Adventures of Augie March*
1955	William Faulkner, *A Fable*
1956	John O'Hara, *Ten North Frederick*
1957	Wright Morris, *The Field of Vision*
1958	John Cheever, *The Wapshot Chronicle*
1959	Bernard Malamud, *The Magic Barrel*
1960	Philip Roth, *Goodbye, Columbus*
1961	Conrad Richter, *The Waters of Kronos*
1962	Walker Percy, *The Moviegoer*
1963	J. F. Powers, *Morte d'Urban*
1964	John Updike, *The Centaur*
1965	Saul Bellow, *Herzog*
1966	Katherine Anne Porter, *The Collected Stories*
1967	Bernard Malamud, *The Fixer*
1968	Thornton Wilder, *The Eighth Day*
1969	Jerzy Kosinski, *Steps*
1970	Joyce Carol Oates, *Them*
1971	Saul Bellow, *Mr. Sammler's Planet*
1972	Flannery O'Connor, *The Complete Stories*
1973	John Barth, *Chimera*
1974	Thomas Pynchon, *Gravity's Rainbow*
1974	Isaac Bashevis Singer, *A Crown of Feathers*
1975	Robert Stone, *Dog Soldiers*
1976	William Gaddis, *JR*
1977	Wallace Stegner, *The Spectator Bird*
1978	Mary Lee Settle, *Blood Ties*
1979	Tim O'Brien, *Going After Cacciato*
1980	William Styron, *Sophie's Choice*

Year	Author, book
1981	Wright Morris, *Plains Song*
1982	John Updike, *Rabbit Is Rich*
1983	Alice Walker, *The Color Purple*
1984	Ellen Gilchrist, *Victory Over Japan*
1985	Don DeLillo, *White Noise*
1986	E. L. Doctorow, *World's Fair*
1987	Larry Heinemann, *Paco's Story*
1988	Pete Dexter, *Paris Trout*
1989	John Casey, *Spartina*
1990	Charles Johnson, *Middle Passage*
1991	Norman Rush, *Mating*
1992	Cormac McCarthy, *All the Pretty Horses*
1993	E. Annie Proulx, *The Shipping News*
1994	William Gaddis, *A Frolic of His Own*
1995	Philip Roth, *Sabbath's Theater*
1996	Andrea Barrett, *Ship Fever and Other Stories*
1997	Charles Frazier, *Cold Mountain*
1998	Alice McDermott, *Charming Billy*
1999	Ha Jin, *Waiting*
2000	Susan Sontag, *In America*
2001	Jonathan Franzen, *The Corrections*
2002	Julia Glass, *Three Junes*
2003	Shirley Hazzard, *The Great Fire*
2004	Lily Tuck, *The News From Paraguay*
2005	William T. Vollmann, *Europe Central*
2006	Richard Powers, *The Echo Maker*
2007	Denis Johnson, *Tree of Smoke*
2008	Peter Matthiessen, *Shadow Country*
2009	Colum McCann, *Let the Great World Spin*
2010	Jaimy Gordon, *Lord of Misrule*
2011	Jesmyn Ward, *Salvage the Bones*

Nonfiction

Year	Author, book
1950	Ralph L. Rusk, *Ralph Waldo Emerson*
1951	Newton Arvin, *Herman Melville*
1952	Rachel Carson, *The Sea Around Us*
1953	Bernard A. De Voto, *The Course of an Empire*
1954	Bruce Catton, *A Stillness at Appomattox*
1955	Joseph Wood Krutch, *The Measure of Man*
1956	Herbert Kubly, *An American in Italy*
1957	George F. Kennan, *Russia Leaves the War*
1958	Catherine Drinker Bowen, *The Lion and the Throne*
1959	J. Christopher Herold, *Mistress to an Age: A Life of Madame De Stael*
1960	Richard Ellman, *James Joyce*
1961	William L. Shirer, *The Rise and Fall of the Third Reich*
1962	Lewis Mumford, *The City in History: Its Origins, Its Transformations, and Its Prospects*
1963	Leon Edel, *Henry James: Vol. II: The Conquest of London and Vol. III: The Middle Years*
1964	WIlliam H. McNeill, *The Rise of the West: A History of the Human Community*
1965	Louis Fisher, *The Life of Lenin*
1966	Arthur M. Schlesinger Jr., *A Thousand Days: John F. Kennedy in the White House*
1967	Peter Gay, *The Enlightenment, An Interpretation, Vol I: The Rise of Modern Paganism*
1968	George F. Kennan, *Memoirs: 1925-1950*[1]
1969	Winthrop D. Jordan, *White Over Black: American Attitudes Toward the Negro, 1550-1812*[2]
1970	T. Harry Williams, *Huey Long*[3]
1971	James MacGregor Burns, *Roosevelt: The Soldier of Freedom*
1972	Joseph P. Lash, *Eleanor and Franklin: The Story of Their Relationship, Based on Eleanor Roosevelt's Private Papers*
1973	James Thomas Flexner, *George Washington, Vol. IV: Anguish and Farewell, 1793-1799*[4]
1974	John Clive, *Macaulay, The Shaping of the Historian*; Douglas Day, *Malcolm Lowry: A Biography*[5]
1975	Richard B. Sewall, *The Life of Emily Dickinson*[6]
1976	David Brion Davis, *The Problem of Slavery in the Age of Revolution, 1770-1823*
1977	W. A. Swanberg, *Norman Thomas: The Last Idealist*[7]
1978	W. Jackson Bate, *Samuel Johnson*
1979	Arthur M. Schlesinger Jr., *Robert Kennedy and His Times*
1980	Tom Wolfe, *The Right Stuff*
1981	Maxine Hong Kingston, *China Men*
1982	Tracy Kidder, *The Soul of a New Machine*
1983	Fox Butterfield, *China: Alive in the Bitter Sea*
1984	Robert V. Remini, *Andrew Jackson and the Course of American Democracy, 1833-1845*
1985	J. Anthony Lukas, *Common Ground: A Turbulent Decade in the Lives of Three American Families*
1986	Barry Lopez, *Arctic Dreams*
1987	Richard Rhodes, *The Making of the Atom Bomb*
1988	Neil Sheehan, *A Bright Shining Lie: John Paul Vann and America in Vietnam*
1989	Thomas L. Friedman, *From Beirut to Jerusalem*
1990	Ron Chernow, *The House of Morgan: An American Banking Dynasty and the Rise of Modern Finance*
1991	Orlando Patterson, *Freedom*
1992	Paul Monette, *Becoming a Man: Half a Life Story*
1993	Gore Vidal, *United States: Essays 1952-1992*
1994	Sherwin B. Nuland, *How We Die: Reflections on Life's Final Chapter*
1995	Tina Rosenberg, *The Haunted Land: Facing Europe's Ghosts After Communism*
1996	James Carroll, *An American Requiem: God, My Father, and the War That Came Between Us*
1997	Joseph J. Ellis, *American Sphinx: The Character of Thomas Jefferson*
1998	Edward Ball, *Slaves in the Family*
1999	John W. Dower, *Embracing Defeat: Japan in the Wake of World War II*
2000	Nathaniel Philbrick, *In the Heart of the Sea: The Tragedy of the Whaleship Essex*
2001	Andrew Solomon, *The Noonday Demon: An Atlas of Depression*
2002	Robert A. Caro, *Master of the Senate: The Years of Lyndon Johnson*
2003	Carlos Eire, *Waiting for Snow in Havana: Confessions of a Cuban Boy*
2004	Kevin Boyle, *Arc of Justice: A Saga of Race, Civil Rights, and Murder in the Jazz Age*
2005	Joan Didion, *The Year of Magical Thinking*
2006	Timothy Egan, *The Worst Hard Time: The Untold Story of Those Who Survived the Great American Dust Bowl*
2007	Tim Weiner, *Legacy of Ashes: The History of the CIA*
2008	Annette Gordon-Reed, *The Hemingses of Monticello: An American Family*
2009	T. J. Stiles, *The First Tycoon: The Epic Life of Cornelius Vanderbilt*
2010	Patti Smith, *Just Kids*
2011	Stephen Greenblatt, *The Swerve: How the World Became Modern*

(1) Science, Philosophy, & Religion: Jonathan Kozol, *Death at an Early Age*. (2) Arts & Letters: Norman Mailer, *The Armies of the Night: History as a Novel, the Novel as History*. (3) Arts & Letters: Lillian Hellman, *An Unfinished Woman: A Memoir*. (4) Contemp. Affairs: Frances FitzGerald, *Fire in the Lake: The Vietnamese and the Americans in Vietnam*. (5) Arts & Letters: Pauline Kael, *Deeper Into the Movies*. (6) Arts & Letters: Roger Shattuck, *Marcel Proust*; Lewis Thomas, *The Lives of a Cell: Notes of a Biology Watcher*. (7) Contemp. Thought: Bruno Bettelheim, *The Uses of Enchantment: The Meaning and Importance of Fairy Tales*.

Journalism Awards, 2012

National Journalism Awards, by Scripps Howard Foundation. Breaking News: *Arizona Republic* (Phoenix). Business/Economics Reporting: ProPublica. Commentary: Brian McGrory, *Boston Globe*. Community Journalism: *Patriot-News* (Harrisburg, PA). Editorial Cartooning: Jack Ohman, *Oregonian* (Portland). Editorial Writing: Jamie Lucke, *Lexington* (KY) *Herald-Leader*. Environmental Reporting: *Pittsburgh Post-Gazette*. Human Interest Writing: Corinne Reilly, *Virginian-Pilot* (Norfolk). Investigative Reporting: *NY Times*. Photojournalism: Lara Solt, *Dallas Morning News*. Public Service Reporting: California Watch and Center for Investigative Reporting. Radio In-Depth Reporting: WLRN-*Miami Herald* News. TV/Cable In-Depth Reporting: Al Jazeera English. Washington Reporting: Damian Paletta, *Wall Street Journal*.

Distinguished Service to the First Amendment: *Yancey County News* (Burnsville, NC). Journalism Teacher of the Year: Douglas B. Ward, Univ. of Kansas. Journalism Admin. of the Year: John Lavine, Northwestern Univ.

National Magazine Awards, by American Society of Magazine Editors and Columbia Univ. Graduate School of Journalism, honoring excellence in print and on digital platforms. Magazine of the Year: *Time*. General Excellence: Active- and Special-Interest, *Inc.*; General Interest, *Bloomberg Businessweek*; Lifestyle, *House Beautiful*; Thought-Leader, *IEEE Spectrum*; Women's, *O, The Oprah Magazine*. Columns and Commentary: *Vanity Fair*. Design: *GQ*. Essays and Criticism: *New York*. Feature Photography: *NY Times Magazine*. Feature Writing: *Esquire*. Fiction: *Zoetrope: All-Story*. Leisure Interests: *Saveur*. Magazine Section: *New York*. News and Documentary Photography: *Harper's Magazine*. Personal Service: *Glamour*. Photography: *Vogue*. Profile Writing: *D Magazine*. Public Interest: *New Yorker*. Reporting: *New Yorker*. Single-Topic Issue: *New York*. **Digital** awards: General Excellence: *New York*. Website: *New York*. Tablet Edition: *National Geographic*.

George Foster Peabody Awards, by Univ. of Georgia, awarded to the best in electronic media. "Peace Corps—A Trust Betrayed," *ABC News Brian Ross Investigates*, ABC. Arab Awakening coverage, Al Jazeera English. "Somalia: Land of Anarchy," *BBC Current Affairs* and BBC.com; BBC News. "Inside Syria," *CBS Evening News With Scott Pelley*, CBS. Arab Spring reporting; *CNN Heroes: An All-Star Tribute*; "Interpretation and Commentary on Iran" and "Restoring the American Dream: Fixing Education," *Fareed Zakaria GPS*; CNN. Super PAC segments, *The Colbert Report*, Comedy Central. *The Untold Stories of the Tsunami in Japan*, Fuji Television. *On Location*, GlobalPost.com. *Earth Made of Glass*, *Game of Thrones*, *Treme*, HBO. *Acting Up: Russia's Civil Society* and *Gold's Costly Dividend: The Porgera Joint Venture*, Human Rights Watch/*New Yorker*. *Portlandia*, IFC. "Who Killed Chea Vichea?", KBDI-TV, Denver. "Their Crime, Your Dime," KING-TV, Seattle. "Desert Underwater," KLAS-TV, Las Vegas. "Toxic Secrets," KPHO-TV, Phoenix. *Parks and Recreation*, NBC. *Surviving the Tsunami*, NHK. "Native Foster Care: Lost Children, Shattered Families" and "Arab Spring From Egypt to Libya," NPR. *StoryCorps 9/11*, NPR Morning Edition. *American Experience*; "Eames—The Architect and the Painter," *American Masters*; *Austin City Limits*; *Bhutto*; "My Perestroika," *POV*; PBS. *Intersexions*, SABC 1. *A Year in the Clouds*, PTS. *Homeland*, *Rebirth*; Showtime. *Jeopardy!*, Sony Pictures Television. TED. com, TED. "People's Republic of Cheating and Misjudged Cases," *News Magazine*, Television Broadcasts Ltd. "Operation Deep Freeze," WEWS-TV, Cleveland.

Reuben Award, by National Cartoonists Society. Outstanding Cartoonist of the Year: Tom Richmond.

Miscellaneous Book Awards, 2012

(Awarded in 2012 unless otherwise noted.)

Academy of American Poets Awards. Wallace Stevens Award, for poetry mastery, $100,000: Gary Snyder. Academy Fellowship, $25,000: Brenda Hillman. Lenore Marshall Poetry Prize, $25,000: David Wojahn, *World Tree*. James Laughlin Award, $5,000: Catherine Barnett, *The Game of Boxes*. Walt Whitman Award, $5,000: Matt Rasmussen, *Black Aperture*. Raiziss/de Palchi Translation Prizes: Book, $10,000: Jennifer Scappettone, *Locomotrix: Selected Poetry and Prose* by Amelia Rosselli; Fellowship, $25,000 (2011): Dominic Siracusa, *Oramai* by Emilio Villa. Harold Morton Landon Translation Award, $1,000: Jen Hofer, *Negro Marfil/Ivory Black* by Myriam Moscona.

American Academy of Arts and Letters. Academy Awards in Literature, $7,500 each: Andre Dubus III, Adam Hochschild, David Lindsay-Abaire, Christopher Middleton, Julie Otsuka, Michael Palmer, Frederick Seidel, Timothy Snyder. E. M. Forster Award, $20,000: David Mitchell. Harold D. Vursell Memorial Award, $10,000: Peter Carey. Katherine Anne Porter Award, $20,000 (biennial): Maureen Howard. Michael Braude Award for Light Verse, $5,000: Roger Angell. Morton Dauwen Zabel Award, $10,000: Andrew Sarris. Rome Fellowships in Literature: Lucy Corin, Jessica Fisher. Rosenthal Family Foundation Award, $10,000: Teju Cole, *Open City*. Sue Kaufman Prize for First Fiction, $5,000: Ismet Prcic, *Shards*. Thornton Wilder Prize for Translation, $20,000: Michael Hofmann.

Bollingen Prize in American Poetry, by the Yale Univ. Library, $100,000 (biennial) (2011): Susan Howe.

Coretta Scott King Awards, by American Library Assn., for African American authors and illustrators of outstanding books for children and young adults. Author: Kadir Nelson, *Heart and Soul: The Story of America and African Americans*. Illustrator: Shane W. Evans, *Underground: Finding the Light to Freedom*. Lifetime Achievement: Ashley Bryan.

Costa Book Awards: Book of the Year (formerly Whitbread Award): Andrew Miller, *Pure*. Novel: Andrew Miller, *Pure*. First Novel: Christie Watson, *Tiny Sunbirds Far Away*. Biography: Matthew Hollis, *Now All Roads Lead to France: The Last Years of Edward Thomas*. Poetry: Carol Ann Duffy, *The Bees*. Children's Book: Moira Young, *Blood Red Road*.

Edgar Awards, by the Mystery Writers of America. Novel: *Gone*, Mo Hayder. First Novel: *Bent Road*, Lori Roy. Paperback Original: *The Company Man*, Robert Jackson Bennett. Fact Crime: *Destiny of the Republic: A Tale of Madness, Medicine and the Murder of a President*, Candice Millard. Critical/Biographical: *On Conan Doyle: Or, the Whole Art of Storytelling*, Michael Dirda. Short Story: "The Man Who Took His Hat Off to the Driver

of the Train," Peter Turnbull. Juvenile: *Icefall*, Matthew J. Kirby. Young Adult: *The Silence of Murder*, Dandi Daley Mackall. Play: *The Game's Afoot*, Ken Ludwig. TV Episode: "Pilot," *Homeland*, Showtime. Grandmaster: Martha Grimes.

Golden Kite Awards, by the Society of Children's Book Writers and Illustrators. Fiction: *Between Shades of Gray*, Ruta Sepetys. Nonfiction: *Amelia Lost: The Life and Disappearance of Amelia Earhart*, Candace Fleming. Picture Book Text: *Over and Under the Snow*, Kate Messner. Picture Book Illustration: *Balloons Over Broadway*, Melissa Sweet.

Hugo Awards, by the World Science Fiction Society (WSFS). Novel: *Among Others*, Jo Walton. Novella: "The Man Who Bridged the Mist," Kij Johnson. Novelette: "Six Months, Three Days," Charlie Jane Anders. Short Story: "The Paper Menagerie," Ken Liu. Related Work: *The Encyclopedia of Science Fiction, 3rd Ed.*, edited by John Clute, David Langford, Peter Nicholls, Graham Sleight. Graphic Story: *Digger*, Ursula Vernon. Dramatic Presentation, long form: *Game of Thrones*, HBO. Dramatic Presentation, short form: "The Doctor's Wife," *Doctor Who*, BBC Wales. Best New Writer (not a Hugo but admin. by WSFS): E. Lily Yu.

Lincoln Prize, by Gettysburg College and the Gilder Lehrman Inst. of American History, $25,000 each: William C. Harris, *Lincoln and the Border States: Preserving the Union*, and Elizabeth D. Leonard, *Lincoln's Forgotten Ally: Judge Advocate General Joseph Holt of Kentucky*.

National Book Critics Circle Awards. Fiction: Edith Pearlman, *Binocular Vision: New & Selected Stories*. Nonfiction: Maya Jasanoff, *Liberty's Exiles: American Loyalists in the Revolutionary World*. Biography: John Lewis Gaddis, *George F. Kennan: An American Life*. Autobiography: Mira Bartók, *The Memory Palace: A Memoir*. Criticism: Geoff Dyer, *Otherwise Known as the Human Condition: Selected Essays and Reviews*. Poetry: Laura Kasischke, *Space, in Chains*. Ivan Sandrof Lifetime Achievement Award: Robert B. Silvers. Nona Balakian Citation for Excellence in Reviewing: Kathryn Schulz.

Nebula Awards, by the Science Fiction and Fantasy Writers of America. Novel: *Among Others*, Jo Walton. Novella: "The Man Who Bridged the Mist," Kij Johnson. Novelette: "What We Found," Geoff Ryman. Short Story: "The Paper Menagerie," Ken Liu. Ray Bradbury Award: "The Doctor's Wife," *Doctor Who*. Andre Norton Award: *The Freedom Maze*, Delia Sherman. Damon Knight Grand Master Award: Connie Willis. Solstice Award: Octavia Butler (posthumous) and John Clute.

PEN/Faulkner Award, for fiction, $15,000: Julie Otsuka, *The Buddha in the Attic*.

Spingarn Medal, 1915-2011

The Spingarn Medal has been awarded annually since 1915 (except in 1938) by the National Assn. for the Advancement of Colored People for outstanding achievement by an African American.

1915 Ernest E. Just	1941 Richard Wright	1964 Roy Wilkins	1988 Frederick D. Patterson
1916 Charles Young	1942 A. Philip Randolph	1965 Leontyne Price	1989 Jesse Jackson
1917 Harry T. Burleigh	1943 William H. Hastie	1966 John H. Johnson	1990 L. Douglas Wilder
1918 William S. Braithwaite	1944 Charles Drew	1967 Edward W. Brooke	1991 Gen. Colin L. Powell
1919 Archibald H. Grimké	1945 Paul Robeson	1968 Sammy Davis Jr.	1992 Barbara Jordan
1920 W. E. B. Du Bois	1946 Thurgood Marshall	1969 Clarence M. Mitchell Jr.	1993 Dorothy I. Height
1921 Charles S. Gilpin	1947 Dr. Percy L. Julian	1970 Jacob Lawrence	1994 Maya Angelou
1922 Mary B. Talbert	1948 Channing H. Tobias	1971 Leon H. Sullivan	1995 John Hope Franklin
1923 George W. Carver	1949 Ralph J. Bunche	1972 Gordon Parks	1996 A. Leon Higginbotham
1924 Roland Hayes	1950 Charles H. Houston	1973 Wilson C. Riles	1997 Carl T. Rowan
1925 James W. Johnson	1951 Mabel K. Staupers	1974 Damon Keith	1998 Myrlie Evers-Williams
1926 Carter G. Woodson	1952 Harry T. Moore	1975 Henry (Hank) Aaron	1999 Earl G. Graves Sr.
1927 Anthony Overton	1953 Paul R. Williams	1976 Alvin Ailey	2000 Oprah Winfrey
1928 Charles W. Chesnutt	1954 Theodore K. Lawless	1977 Alex Haley	2001 Vernon E. Jordan Jr.
1929 Mordecai W. Johnson	1955 Carl Murphy	1978 Andrew Young	2002 John Lewis
1930 Henry A. Hunt	1956 Jack R. Robinson	1979 Rosa L. Parks	2003 Constance Baker Motley
1931 Richard B. Harrison	1957 Martin Luther King Jr.	1980 Dr. Rayford W. Logan	2004 Robert L. Carter
1932 Robert R. Moton	1958 Daisy Bates and the	1981 Coleman Young	2005 Oliver W. Hill
1933 Max Yergan	Little Rock Nine	1982 Dr. Benjamin E. Mays	2006 Dr. Benjamin S. Carson
1934 William T. B. Williams	1959 Duke Ellington	1983 Lena Horne	2007 John Conyers Jr.
1935 Mary McLeod Bethune	1960 Langston Hughes	1984 Thomas Bradley	2008 Ruby Dee
1936 John Hope	1961 Kenneth B. Clark	1985 Bill Cosby	2009 Julian Bond
1937 Walter White	1962 Robert C. Weaver	1986 Dr. Benjamin L. Hooks	2010 Cicely Tyson
1939 Marian Anderson	1963 Medgar W. Evers	1987 Percy E. Sutton	2011 Frankie Muse Freeman
1940 Louis T. Wright			

Miscellaneous Awards, 2012

(Awarded in 2012, unless otherwise noted.)

American Academy of Arts and Letters Architecture Awards. Arthur W. Brunner Memorial Prize, $5,000: Kathryn Gustafson. Academy Awards, $7,500 each: Hilary Ballon, Marlon Blackwell, Elizabeth Gray and Alan Organschi, Michael Maltzan.

American Academy of Arts and Letters Art Awards. Award of Merit Medal for Painting, $10,000: Joyce Pensato. Academy Awards, $7,500 each: Jim Campbell, John Newman, Michael E. Smith, Rebecca Smith, Karl Wirsum. John Koch Award in Art, $10,000: Nicole Wittenberg. Jimmy Ernst Award, $10,000: Forrest Myers. Rosenthal Family Foundation Award in Painting, $10,000: Nathlie Provosty. Willard L. Metcalf Award in Art: Elisa Soliven.

American Academy of Arts and Letters Music Awards. Academy Awards, $7,500 each: Paul Moravec, Frank Ticheli, Dan Welcher, John Zorn. Andrew Imbrie Award, $10,000: Louis Karchin. Charles Ives Fellowships, $15,000 each: Haralabos Stafylakis, Xi Wang. Charles Ives Scholarships, $7,500 each: Niccolo Athens, Sean Friar, David Hertzberg, Takuma Itoh, Wang Jie, Chris Rogerson. Goddard Lieberson Fellowships, $15,000 each: Edmund Campion, Huck Hodge. Marc Blitzstein Memorial Award for Musical Theater: John Kander. Walter Hinrichsen Award: Reena Esmail. Wladimir and Rhoda Lakond Award, $10,000: Christopher Theofanidis. Richard Rodgers Award for Musical Theater: *Witness Uganda*, Matt Gould, Griffin Matthews.

Congressional Gold Medal, by Congress: Montford Point Marines, Nov. 11, 2011; Victims of the Sept. 11, 2001, terrorist attacks, Dec. 23, 2011; Raoul Wallenberg, July 26, 2012; Daw Aung San Suu Kyi, Sept. 19, 2012 (awarded May 6, 2008).

Intel Science Talent Search. First place, $100,000: Nithin Tumma, Fort Gratiot, MI; second place, $75,000: Andrey Sushko, Richland, WA; third place, $50,000: Mimi Yen, Brooklyn, NY.

John F. Kennedy Center Honors. 2011: Barbara Cook, Neil Diamond, Yo-Yo Ma, Sonny Rollins, Meryl Streep. 2012: Buddy Guy, Dustin Hoffman, Led Zeppelin, David Letterman, Natalia Makarova.

Library of the Year Award, by Gale and *Library Journal*, $10,000: San Diego County Library, CA.

MacArthur Fellows, by the John D. and Catherine T. MacArthur Foundation, $500,000 each: Natalia Almada, Uta Barth, Claire Chase, Raj Chetty, Maria Chudnovsky, Eric Coleman, Junot Díaz, David Finkel, Olivier Guyon, Elissa Hallem, An-My Lê, Sarkis Mazmanian, Dinaw Mengestu, Maurice Lim Miller, Dylan C. Penningroth, Terry Plank, Laura Poitras, Nancy Rabalais, Benoît Rolland, Daniel Spielman, Melody Swartz, Chris Thile, Benjamin Warf.

National Humanities Medal, by National Endowment for the Humanities (2011): Kwame Anthony Appiah, John Ashbery, Robert Darnton, Andrew Delbanco, National History Day, Charles Rosen, Teofilo Ruiz, Ramón Saldívar, Amartya Sen.

National Medal of the Arts, by the National Endowment for the Arts and the White House: Will Barnet, Rita Dove, Al Pacino, Emily Rauh Pulitzer, Martin Puryear, Mel Tillis, United Service Organizations (USO), André Watts.

Presidential Medal of Freedom, by the White House, May 29, Madeleine Albright, John Doar, Bob Dylan, Dr. William Foege, John Glenn, Gordon Hirabayashi, Dolores Huerta, Jan Karski, Juliette Gordon Low, Toni Morrison, John Paul Stevens, Pat Summitt; June 13: Shimon Peres.

Pritzker Architecture Prize, by the Hyatt Foundation, $100,000: Wang Shu, China.

Teacher of the Year, by Council of Chief State School Officers: Rebecca Mieliwocki, English, Luther Burbank Middle School, Burbank, CA.

Templeton Prize, by Templeton Foundation, £1.1 mil (about $1.8 mil): Dalai Lama.

Miss America Winners, 1921-2012

Year	Winner, hometown	Year	Winner, hometown
1921	Margaret Gorman, Washington, DC	1971	Phyllis Ann George, Denton, Texas
1922-23	Mary Campbell, Columbus, Ohio	1972	Laurie Lea Schaefer, Columbus, Ohio
1924	Ruth Malcolmson, Philadelphia, Pennsylvania	1973	Terry Anne Meeuwsen, DePere, Wisconsin
1925	Fay Lamphier, Oakland, California	1974	Rebecca Ann King, Denver, Colorado
1926	Norma Smallwood, Tulsa, Oklahoma	1975	Shirley Cothran, Fort Worth, Texas
1927	Lois Delander, Joliet, Illinois	1976	Tawney Elaine Godin, Yonkers, New York
1933	Marion Bergeron, West Haven, Connecticut	1977	Dorothy Kathleen Benham, Edina, Minnesota
1935	Henrietta Leaver, Pittsburgh, Pennsylvania	1978	Susan Perkins, Columbus, Ohio
1936	Rose Coyle, Philadelphia, Pennsylvania	1979	Kylene Barker, Galax, Virginia
1937	Bette Cooper, Bertrand Island, New Jersey	1980	Cheryl Prewitt, Ackerman, Mississippi
1938	Marilyn Meseke, Marion, Ohio	1981	Susan Powell, Elk City, Oklahoma
1939	Patricia Donnelly, Detroit, Michigan	1982	Elizabeth Ward, Russellville, Arkansas
1940	Frances Marie Burke, Philadelphia, Pennsylvania	1983	Debra Maffett, Anaheim, California
1941	Rosemary LaPlanche, Los Angeles, California	1984[1]	Suzette Charles, Mays Landing, New Jersey
1942	Jo-Caroll Dennison, Tyler, Texas	1985	Sharlene Wells, Salt Lake City, Utah
1943	Jean Bartel, Los Angeles, California	1986	Susan Akin, Meridian, Mississippi
1944	Venus Ramey, Washington, DC	1987	Kellye Cash, Memphis, Tennessee
1945	Bess Myerson, New York City, New York	1988	Kaye Lani Rae Rafko, Monroe, Michigan
1946	Marilyn Buferd, Los Angeles, California	1989	Gretchen Carlson, Anoka, Minnesota
1947	Barbara Walker, Memphis, Tennessee	1990	Debbye Turner, Columbia, Missouri
1948	BeBe Shopp, Hopkins, Minnesota	1991	Marjorie Vincent, Oak Park, Illinois
1949	Jacque Mercer, Litchfield, Arizona	1992	Carolyn Suzanne Sapp, Honolulu, Hawaii
1951	Yolande Betbeze, Mobile, Alabama	1993	Leanza Cornett, Jacksonville, Florida
1952	Coleen Kay Hutchins, Salt Lake City, Utah	1994	Kimberly Aiken, Columbia, South Carolina
1953	Neva Jane Langley, Macon, Georgia	1995	Heather Whitestone, Birmingham, Alabama
1954	Evelyn Margaret Ay, Ephrata, Pennsylvania	1996	Shawntel Smith, Muldrow, Oklahoma
1955	Lee Meriwether, San Francisco, California	1997	Tara Dawn Holland, Overland Park, Kansas
1956	Sharon Ritchie, Denver, Colorado	1998	Kate Shindle, Evanston, Illinois
1957	Marian McKnight, Manning, South Carolina	1999	Nicole Johnson, Roanoke, Virginia
1958	Marilyn Van Derbur, Denver, Colorado	2000	Heather Renee French, Maysville, Kentucky
1959	Mary Ann Mobley, Brandon, Mississippi	2001	Angela Perez Baraquio, Honolulu, Hawaii
1960	Lynda Lee Mead, Natchez, Mississippi	2002	Katie Harman, Gresham, Oregon
1961	Nancy Fleming, Montague, Michigan	2003	Erika Harold, Urbana, Illinois
1962	Maria Fletcher, Asheville, North Carolina	2004	Ericka Dunlap, Orlando, Florida
1963	Jacquelyn Mayer, Sandusky, Ohio	2005[2]	Deidre Downs, Birmingham, Alabama
1964	Donna Axum, El Dorado, Arkansas	2006	Jennifer Berry, Tulsa, Oklahoma
1965	Vonda Kay Van Dyke, Phoenix, Arizona	2007	Lauren Nelson, Lawton, Oklahoma
1966	Deborah Irene Bryant, Overland Park, Kansas	2008	Kirsten Haglund, Farmington Hills, Michigan
1967	Jane Anne Jayroe, Laverne, Oklahoma	2009	Katie Stam, Seymour, Indiana
1968	Debra Dene Barnes, Moran, Kansas	2010	Caressa Cameron, Fredricksburg, Virginia
1969	Judith Anne Ford, Belvidere, Illinois	2011	Teresa Scanlan, Gering, Nebraska
1970	Pamela Anne Eldred, Birmingham, Michigan	2012	Laura Kaeppeler, Kenosha, Wisconsin

(1) Miss New York, Vanessa Williams, resigned July 23, 1984. (2) The Sept. 2005 Miss America Pageant and award were postponed until Jan. 2006, when the pageant was broadcast from Las Vegas, NV, by Country Music Television (CMT).

Entertainment Awards
Tony (Antoinette Perry) Awards, 2012

Play: *Clybourne Park*, Bruce Norris
Musical: *Once*
Book of a musical: *Once*, Enda Walsh
Original score: *Newsies*, Alan Menken, Jack Feldman
Play revival: *Arthur Miller's Death of a Salesman*
Musical revival: *The Gershwins' Porgy and Bess*
Actor, play: James Corden, *One Man, Two Guvnors*
Actress, play: Nina Arianda, *Venus in Fur*
Actor, musical: Steve Kazee, *Once*
Actress, musical: Audra McDonald, *The Gershwins' Porgy and Bess*
Featured actor, play: Christian Borle, *Peter and the Starcatcher*
Featured actress, play: Judith Light, *Other Desert Cities*
Featured actor, musical: Michael McGrath, *Nice Work If You Can Get It*
Featured actress, musical: Judy Kaye, *Nice Work If You Can Get It*

Director, play: Mike Nichols, *Arthur Miller's Death of a Salesman*
Director, musical: John Tiffany, *Once*
Choreography: Christopher Gattelli, *Newsies*
Orchestrations: Martin Lowe, *Once*
Scenic design, play: Donyale Werle, *Peter and the Starcatcher*
Scenic design, musical: Bob Crowley, *Once*
Costume design, play: Paloma Young, *Peter and the Starcatcher*
Costume design, musical: Gregg Barnes, *Follies*
Regional theater: Shakespeare Theatre Company, Washington, DC
Special Tony Award, lifetime achievement: Emanuel Azenberg
Isabelle Stevenson Award: Bernadette Peters
Tony Honors for Excellence in the Theatre: Freddie Gershon; Artie Siccardi; TDF Open Doors
Special Tony Award: Actors' Equity Association; Hugh Jackman

Tony Awards, 1948-2012

Year	Play	Musical	Year	Play	Musical
1948	*Mister Roberts*	No award	1981	*Amadeus*	*42nd Street*
1949	*Death of a Salesman*	*Kiss Me Kate*	1982	*The Life and Adventures of Nicholas Nickelby*	*Nine*
1950	*The Cocktail Party*	*South Pacific*	1983	*Torch Song Trilogy*	*Cats*
1951	*The Rose Tattoo*	*Guys and Dolls*	1984	*The Real Thing*	*La Cage aux Folles*
1952	*The Fourposter*	*The King and I*	1985	*Biloxi Blues*	*Big River*
1953	*The Crucible*	*Wonderful Town*	1986	*I'm Not Rappaport*	*The Mystery of Edwin Drood*
1954	*The Teahouse of the August Moon*	*Kismet*	1987	*Fences*	*Les Miserables*
1955	*The Desperate Hours*	*The Pajama Game*	1988	*M. Butterfly*	*Phantom of the Opera*
1956	*The Diary of Anne Frank*	*Damn Yankees*	1989	*The Heidi Chronicles*	*Jerome Robbins' Broadway*
1957	*Long Day's Journey Into Night*	*My Fair Lady*	1990	*The Grapes of Wrath*	*City of Angels*
1958	*Sunrise at Campobello*	*The Music Man*	1991	*Lost in Yonkers*	*The Will Rogers Follies*
1959	*J.B.*	*Redhead*	1992	*Dancing at Lughnasa*	*Crazy for You*
1960	*The Miracle Worker*	*Fiorello!*, *The Sound of Music*	1993	*Angels in America: Millennium Approaches*	*Kiss of the Spider Woman*
1961	*Becket*	*Bye, Bye Birdie*	1994	*Angels in America: Perestroika*	*Passion*
1962	*A Man for All Seasons*	*How to Succeed in Business Without Really Trying*	1995	*Love! Valour! Compassion!*	*Sunset Boulevard*
1963	*Who's Afraid of Virginia Woolf?*	*A Funny Thing Happened on the Way to the Forum*	1996	*Master Class*	*Rent*
			1997	*The Last Night of Ballyhoo*	*Titanic*
1964	*Luther*	*Hello, Dolly!*	1998	*Art*	*The Lion King*
1965	*The Subject Was Roses*	*Fiddler on the Roof*	1999	*Side Man*	*Fosse*
1966	*Marat/Sade*	*Man of La Mancha*	2000	*Copenhagen*	*Contact*
1967	*The Homecoming*	*Cabaret*	2001	*Proof*	*The Producers*
1968	*Rosencrantz and Guildenstern Are Dead*	*Hallelujah, Baby!*	2002	*Edward Albee's The Goat or Who Is Sylvia?*	*Thoroughly Modern Millie*
1969	*The Great White Hope*	*1776*	2003	*Take Me Out*	*Hairspray*
1970	*Borstal Boy*	*Applause*	2004	*I Am My Own Wife*	*Avenue Q*
1971	*Sleuth*	*Company*	2005	*Doubt*	*Monty Python's Spamalot*
1972	*Sticks and Bones*	*Two Gentlemen of Verona*	2006	*The History Boys*	*Jersey Boys*
1973	*That Championship Season*	*A Little Night Music*	2007	*The Coast of Utopia*	*Spring Awakening*
1974	*The River Niger*	*Raisin*	2008	*August: Osage County*	*In the Heights*
1975	*Equus*	*The Wiz*	2009	*God of Carnage*	*Billy Elliot, The Musical*
1976	*Travesties*	*A Chorus Line*	2010	*Red*	*Memphis*
1977	*The Shadow Box*	*Annie*	2011	*War Horse*	*The Book of Mormon*
1978	*Da*	*Ain't Misbehavin'*	2012	*Clybourne Park*	*Once*
1979	*The Elephant Man*	*Sweeney Todd*			
1980	*Children of a Lesser God*	*Evita*			

Selected Daytime Emmy Awards, 2012

Drama: *General Hospital*, ABC
Game show: *Jeopardy!*, synd.
Animated children's show: *Penguins of Madagascar*, Nickelodeon
Culinary show: *Bobby Flay's Barbecue Addiction*, Food Network
Legal/courtroom show: *Last Shot With Judge Gunn*, synd.
Morning show: *Today*, NBC
Talk show, entertainment: *Live With Regis and Kelly*, synd.

Talk show, informative: *The Dr. Oz Show*, synd.
Actress: Heather Tom, *The Bold and the Beautiful*, CBS
Actor: Anthony Geary, *General Hospital*, ABC
Game show host: Todd Newton, *Family Game Night*, The Hub
Lifestyle/culinary host: Sandra Lee, *Semi-Homemade Cooking With Sandra Lee*, Food Network
Talk show host: Regis Philbin and Kelly Ripa, *Live With Regis and Kelly*, synd.

Selected Prime-Time Emmy Awards, 2012

Drama series: *Homeland*, Showtime
Comedy series: *Modern Family*, ABC
Miniseries or movie: *Game Change*, HBO
Variety series: *The Daily Show With Jon Stewart*, Comedy Central
Lead actor, drama: Damian Lewis, *Homeland*, Showtime
Lead actress, drama: Claire Danes, *Homeland*, Showtime
Lead actor, comedy: Jon Cryer, *Two and a Half Men*, CBS
Lead actress, comedy: Julia Louis-Dreyfus, *Veep*, HBO
Lead actor, miniseries/movie: Kevin Costner, *Hatfields & McCoys*, History Channel
Lead actress, miniseries/movie: Julianne Moore, *Game Change*, HBO
Sup. actor, drama: Aaron Paul, *Breaking Bad*, AMC
Sup. actress, drama: Maggie Smith, *Downton Abbey*, PBS

Sup. actor, comedy: Eric Stonestreet, *Modern Family*, ABC
Sup. actress, comedy: Julie Bowen, *Modern Family*, ABC
Sup. actor, miniseries/movie: Tom Berenger, *Hatfields & McCoys*, History Channel
Sup. actress, miniseries/movie: Jessica Lange, *American Horror Story*, FX
Reality-competition program: *The Amazing Race*, CBS
Director, drama: Tim Van Patten, *Boardwalk Empire*, HBO
Director, comedy: Steven Levitan, *Modern Family*, ABC
Writing, drama: Alex Gansa, Howard Gordon, Gideon Raff, *Homeland*, Showtime
Writing, comedy: Louis C.K., *Louis*, FX
Writing, variety: *The Daily Show With Jon Stewart*, Comedy Central

Primetime Emmy Awards, 1952-2012

The Academy of Television Arts and Sciences presented the first Emmy Awards in 1949. Through the years, award categories have changed, but since 1952, the Academy has given out an outstanding comedy and drama award annually.

Year	Comedy	Drama	Year	Comedy	Drama
1952	*Red Skelton Show*, NBC	*Studio One*, CBS	1978	*All in the Family*, CBS	*The Rockford Files*, NBC
1953	*I Love Lucy*, CBS	*Robert Montgomery Presents*, NBC	1979	*Taxi*, ABC	*Lou Grant*, CBS
			1980	*Taxi*, ABC	*Lou Grant*, CBS
1954	*I Love Lucy*, CBS	*The U.S. Steel Hour*, ABC	1981	*Taxi*, ABC	*Hill Street Blues*, NBC
1955	*Make Room for Daddy*, ABC	*The U.S. Steel Hour*, ABC	1982	*Barney Miller*, ABC	*Hill Street Blues*, NBC
1956	*Phil Silvers Show*, CBS	*Producers' Showcase*, NBC	1983	*Cheers*, NBC	*Hill Street Blues*, NBC
1957	*Phil Silvers Show*, CBS	"Requiem for a Heavyweight," CBS[1]	1984	*Cheers*, NBC	*Hill Street Blues*, NBC
			1985	*The Cosby Show*, NBC	*Cagney & Lacey*, CBS
1958	*Phil Silvers Show*, CBS	*Gunsmoke*, CBS	1986	*Golden Girls*, NBC	*Cagney & Lacey*, CBS
1959[2]	*Jack Benny Show*, CBS	(3)	1987	*Golden Girls*, NBC	*L.A. Law*, NBC
1960	*Art Carney Special*, NBC	*Playhouse 90*, CBS	1988	*The Wonder Years*, ABC	*thirtysomething*, ABC
1961	*Jack Benny Show*, CBS	*Hallmark Hall of Fame: Macbeth*, NBC	1989	*Cheers*, NBC	*L.A. Law*, NBC
			1990	*Murphy Brown*, CBS	*L.A. Law*, NBC
1962	*Bob Newhart Show*, CBS	*The Defenders*, CBS	1991	*Cheers*, NBC	*L.A. Law*, NBC
1963	*Dick Van Dyke Show*, CBS	*The Defenders*, CBS	1992	*Murphy Brown*, CBS	*Northern Exposure*, CBS
1964	*Dick Van Dyke Show*, CBS	*The Defenders*, CBS	1993	*Seinfeld*, NBC	*Picket Fences*, CBS
1965	*Dick Van Dyke Show*, CBS	*Hallmark Hall of Fame: The Magnificent Yankee*, NBC	1994	*Frasier*, NBC	*Picket Fences*, CBS
			1995	*Frasier*, NBC	*NYPD Blue*, ABC
			1996	*Frasier*, NBC	*ER*, NBC
1966	*Dick Van Dyke Show*, CBS	*The Fugitive*, ABC	1997	*Frasier*, NBC	*Law & Order*, NBC
1967	*The Monkees*, NBC	*Mission: Impossible*, CBS	1998	*Frasier*, NBC	*The Practice*, ABC
1968	*Get Smart*, NBC	*Mission: Impossible*, CBS	1999	*Ally McBeal*, FOX	*The Practice*, ABC
1969	*Get Smart*, NBC	*NET Playhouse*, NET	2000	*Will & Grace*, NBC	*The West Wing*, NBC
1970	*My World and Welcome to It*, NBC	*Marcus Welby, M.D.*, ABC	2001	*Sex and the City*, HBO	*The West Wing*, NBC
			2002	*Friends*, NBC	*The West Wing*, NBC
1971	*All in the Family*, CBS	*The Bold Ones: The Senator*, NBC	2003	*Everybody Loves Raymond*, CBS	*The West Wing*, NBC
1972	*All in the Family*, CBS	*Masterpiece Theatre: Elizabeth R*, PBS	2004	*Arrested Development*, FOX	*The Sopranos*, HBO
1973	*All in the Family*, CBS	*The Waltons*, CBS	2005	*Everybody Loves Raymond*, CBS	*Lost*, ABC
1974	*M*A*S*H*, CBS	*Masterpiece Theatre: Upstairs, Downstairs*; PBS	2006	*The Office*, NBC	*24*, FOX
1975	*Mary Tyler Moore Show*, CBS	*Masterpiece Theatre: Upstairs, Downstairs*; PBS	2007	*30 Rock*, NBC	*The Sopranos*, HBO
			2008	*30 Rock*, NBC	*Mad Men*, AMC
1976	*Mary Tyler Moore Show*, CBS	*Police Story*, NBC	2009	*30 Rock*, NBC	*Mad Men*, AMC
1977	*Mary Tyler Moore Show*, CBS	*Masterpiece Theatre: Upstairs, Downstairs*; PBS	2010	*Modern Family*, ABC	*Mad Men*, AMC
			2011	*Modern Family*, ABC	*Mad Men*, AMC
			2012	*Modern Family*, ABC	*Homeland*, Showtime

(1) Best single program of the year; shown on *Playhouse 90*, which was named best new series. (2) Beginning in 1959, Emmys awarded for work in the season encompassing the previous and current year. (3) *Playhouse 90* (CBS) was best dramatic series of one hour or longer, *Alcoa-Goodyear Theatre* (NBC) of less than one hour.

Golden Globe Awards, 2012

The Hollywood Foreign Press Association (then the Hollywood Foreign Correspondents Association) presented its first awards for achievement in film in 1944; television was considered for the first time in 1955.

Film
Drama: *The Descendants*
Comedy/musical: *The Artist*
Actress, drama: Meryl Streep, *The Iron Lady*
Actor, drama: George Clooney, *The Descendants*
Actress, comedy/musical: Michelle Williams, *My Week With Marilyn*
Actor, comedy/musical: Jean Dujardin, *The Artist*
Sup. actress: Octavia Spencer, *The Help*
Sup. actor: Christopher Plummer, *Beginners*
Director: Martin Scorsese, *Hugo*
Screenplay: Woody Allen, *Midnight in Paris*
Animated film: *The Adventures of Tintin*
Foreign-language film: *A Separation*, Iran
Original score: Ludovic Bource, *The Artist*

Original song: "Masterpiece," *W.E.*, w/m by Madonna, Julie Frost, and Jimmy Harry
Cecil B. DeMille Award: Morgan Freeman

Television
Series, drama: *Homeland*, Showtime
Series, comedy/musical: *Modern Family*, ABC
Actress, drama: Claire Danes, *Homeland*, Showtime
Actor, drama: Kelsey Grammer, *Boss*, Starz
Actress, comedy/musical: Laura Dern, *Enlightened*, HBO
Actor, comedy/musical: Matt LeBlanc, *Episodes*, Showtime
Miniseries/made-for-TV movie: *Downton Abbey (Masterpiece)*, PBS
Actress, miniseries/movie: Kate Winslet, *Mildred Pierce*, HBO
Actor, miniseries/movie: Idris Elba, *Luther*, BBC America
Sup. actress: Jessica Lange, *American Horror Story*, FX
Sup. actor: Peter Dinklage, *Game of Thrones*, HBO

People's Choice Awards, 2012

The first People's Choice Awards were presented in 1975. Sponsored by Procter & Gamble, the nominees and awards were initially selected by a Gallup Poll. Since 2005, winners have been selected by Internet voting.

Film
Movie: *Harry Potter and the Deathly Hallows: Part 2*
Actor: Johnny Depp
Actress: Emma Stone
Action movie: *Harry Potter and the Deathly Hallows: Part 2*
Action movie star: Hugh Jackman
Comedy: *Bridesmaids*
Comedy actor: Adam Sandler
Comedy actress: Emma Stone
Drama: *Water for Elephants*
Animated voice: Johnny Depp, *Rango*
Book adaptation: *Harry Potter and the Deathly Hallows: Part 2*
Ensemble cast: *Harry Potter and the Deathly Hallows: Part 2*
Icon: Morgan Freeman
Star Under 25: Chloë Grace Moretz
Superhero: Ryan Reynolds, *The Green Lantern*

Music
Band: Maroon 5
Female artist: Katy Perry
Male artist: Bruno Mars
Album: *Born This Way*, Lady Gaga
Song: "E.T.," Katy Perry feat. Kanye West
Country artist: Taylor Swift

Hip hop artist: Eminem
Pop artist: Demi Lovato
R&B artist: Rihanna
Music video: "Last Friday Night (T.G.I.F.)," Katy Perry
Tour headliner: Katy Perry

Television
Drama: *Supernatural*
Drama actor: Nathan Fillion
Drama actress: Nina Dobrev
Comedy: *How I Met Your Mother*
Comedy actor: Neil Patrick Harris
Comedy actress: Lea Michele
Cable comedy: *Hot in Cleveland*
Cable drama: *Pretty Little Liars*
Competition show: *American Idol*
Crime drama: *Castle*
New drama: *Person of Interest*
New comedy: *2 Broke Girls*
Sci-Fi/fantasy show: *Supernatural*
Daytime host: Ellen DeGeneres, *The Ellen DeGeneres Show*
Late night host: Jimmy Fallon, *Late Night With Jimmy Fallon*
Celebreality star: Kim Kardashian
Guest star: Katy Perry, *How I Met Your Mother*

Academy Awards (Oscars), 1927-2011

Year	Picture	Actor	Actress	Supporting actor[1]	Supporting actress[1]	Director
1927 -28	Wings	Emil Jannings *The Way of All Flesh*	Janet Gaynor *Seventh Heaven*	NA	NA	Frank Borzage *Seventh Heaven*; Lewis Milestone *Two Arabian Knights*
1928 -29	Broadway Melody	Warner Baxter *In Old Arizona*	Mary Pickford *Coquette*	NA	NA	Frank Lloyd *The Divine Lady*
1929 -30	All Quiet on the Western Front	George Arliss *Disraeli*	Norma Shearer *The Divorcee*	NA	NA	Lewis Milestone *All Quiet on the Western Front*
1930 -31	Cimarron	Lionel Barrymore *Free Soul*	Marie Dressler *Min and Bill*	NA	NA	Norman Taurog *Skippy*
1931 -32	Grand Hotel	Fredric March *Dr. Jekyll and Mr. Hyde*; Wallace Beery *The Champ*	Helen Hayes *The Sin of Madelon Claudet*	NA	NA	Frank Borzage *Bad Girl*
1932 -33	Cavalcade	Charles Laughton *The Private Life of Henry VIII*	Katharine Hepburn *Morning Glory*	NA	NA	Frank Lloyd *Cavalcade*
1934	It Happened One Night	Clark Gable *It Happened One Night*	Claudette Colbert *It Happened One Night*	NA	NA	Frank Capra *It Happened One Night*
1935	Mutiny on the Bounty	Victor McLaglen *The Informer*	Bette Davis *Dangerous*	NA	NA	John Ford *The Informer*
1936	The Great Ziegfeld	Paul Muni *Story of Louis Pasteur*	Luise Rainer *The Great Ziegfeld*	Walter Brennan *Come and Get It*	Gale Sondergaard *Anthony Adverse*	Frank Capra *Mr. Deeds Goes to Town*
1937	Life of Emile Zola	Spencer Tracy *Captains Courageous*	Luise Rainer *The Good Earth*	Joseph Schildkraut *Life of Emile Zola*	Alice Brady *In Old Chicago*	Leo McCarey *The Awful Truth*
1938	You Can't Take It With You	Spencer Tracy *Boys Town*	Bette Davis *Jezebel*	Walter Brennan *Kentucky*	Fay Bainter *Jezebel*	Frank Capra *You Can't Take It With You*
1939	Gone With the Wind	Robert Donat *Goodbye Mr. Chips*	Vivien Leigh *Gone With the Wind*	Thomas Mitchell *Stage Coach*	Hattie McDaniel *Gone With the Wind*	Victor Fleming *Gone With the Wind*
1940	Rebecca	James Stewart *The Philadelphia Story*	Ginger Rogers *Kitty Foyle*	Walter Brennan *The Westerner*	Jane Darwell *The Grapes of Wrath*	John Ford *The Grapes of Wrath*
1941	How Green Was My Valley	Gary Cooper *Sergeant York*	Joan Fontaine *Suspicion*	Donald Crisp *How Green Was My Valley*	Mary Astor *The Great Lie*	John Ford *How Green Was My Valley*
1942	Mrs. Miniver	James Cagney *Yankee Doodle Dandy*	Greer Garson *Mrs. Miniver*	Van Heflin *Johnny Eager*	Teresa Wright *Mrs. Miniver*	William Wyler *Mrs. Miniver*
1943	Casablanca	Paul Lukas *Watch on the Rhine*	Jennifer Jones *The Song of Bernadette*	Charles Coburn *The More the Merrier*	Katina Paxinou *For Whom the Bell Tolls*	Michael Curtiz *Casablanca*
1944	Going My Way	Bing Crosby *Going My Way*	Ingrid Bergman *Gaslight*	Barry Fitzgerald *Going My Way*	Ethel Barrymore *None But the Lonely Heart*	Leo McCarey *Going My Way*
1945	The Lost Weekend	Ray Milland *The Lost Weekend*	Joan Crawford *Mildred Pierce*	James Dunn *A Tree Grows in Brooklyn*	Anne Revere *National Velvet*	Billy Wilder *The Lost Weekend*
1946	The Best Years of Our Lives	Fredric March *The Best Years of Our Lives*	Olivia de Havilland *To Each His Own*	Harold Russell *The Best Years of Our Lives*	Anne Baxter *The Razor's Edge*	William Wyler *The Best Years of Our Lives*
1947	Gentleman's Agreement	Ronald Colman *A Double Life*	Loretta Young *The Farmer's Daughter*	Edmund Gwenn *Miracle on 34th Street*	Celeste Holm *Gentleman's Agreement*	Elia Kazan *Gentleman's Agreement*
1948	Hamlet	Laurence Olivier *Hamlet*	Jane Wyman *Johnny Belinda*	Walter Huston *Treasure of Sierra Madre*	Claire Trevor *Key Largo*	John Huston *Treasure of Sierra Madre*
1949	All the King's Men	Broderick Crawford *All the King's Men*	Olivia de Havilland *The Heiress*	Dean Jagger *Twelve O'Clock High*	Mercedes McCambridge *All the King's Men*	Joseph L. Mankiewicz *Letter to Three Wives*
1950	All About Eve	Jose Ferrer *Cyrano de Bergerac*	Judy Holliday *Born Yesterday*	George Sanders *All About Eve*	Josephine Hull *Harvey*	Joseph L. Mankiewicz *All About Eve*
1951	An American in Paris	Humphrey Bogart *The African Queen*	Vivien Leigh *A Streetcar Named Desire*	Karl Malden *A Streetcar Named Desire*	Kim Hunter *A Streetcar Named Desire*	George Stevens *A Place in the Sun*
1952	The Greatest Show on Earth	Gary Cooper *High Noon*	Shirley Booth *Come Back Little Sheba*	Anthony Quinn *Viva Zapata!*	Gloria Grahame *The Bad and the Beautiful*	John Ford *The Quiet Man*
1953	From Here to Eternity	William Holden *Stalag 17*	Audrey Hepburn *Roman Holiday*	Frank Sinatra *From Here to Eternity*	Donna Reed *From Here to Eternity*	Fred Zinnemann *From Here to Eternity*

Year	Picture	Actor	Actress	Supporting actor[1]	Supporting actress[1]	Director
1954	On the Waterfront	Marlon Brando *On the Waterfront*	Grace Kelly *The Country Girl*	Edmond O'Brien *The Barefoot Contessa*	Eva Marie Saint *On the Waterfront*	Elia Kazan *On the Waterfront*
1955	*Marty*	Ernest Borgnine *Marty*	Anna Magnani *The Rose Tattoo*	Jack Lemmon *Mister Roberts*	Jo Van Fleet *East of Eden*	Delbert Mann *Marty*
1956	*Around the World in 80 Days*	Yul Brynner *The King and I*	Ingrid Bergman *Anastasia*	Anthony Quinn *Lust for Life*	Dorothy Malone *Written on the Wind*	George Stevens *Giant*
1957	*The Bridge on the River Kwai*	Alec Guinness *The Bridge on the River Kwai*	Joanne Woodward *The Three Faces of Eve*	Red Buttons *Sayonara*	Miyoshi Umeki *Sayonara*	David Lean *The Bridge on the River Kwai*
1958	*Gigi*	David Niven *Separate Tables*	Susan Hayward *I Want to Live*	Burl Ives *The Big Country*	Wendy Hiller *Separate Tables*	Vincente Minnelli *Gigi*
1959	*Ben-Hur*	Charlton Heston *Ben-Hur*	Simone Signoret *Room at the Top*	Hugh Griffith *Ben-Hur*	Shelley Winters *Diary of Anne Frank*	William Wyler *Ben-Hur*
1960	*The Apartment*	Burt Lancaster *Elmer Gantry*	Elizabeth Taylor *Butterfield 8*	Peter Ustinov *Spartacus*	Shirley Jones *Elmer Gantry*	Billy Wilder *The Apartment*
1961	*West Side Story*	Maximilian Schell *Judgment at Nuremberg*	Sophia Loren *Two Women*	George Chakiris *West Side Story*	Rita Moreno *West Side Story*	Jerome Robbins, Robert Wise *West Side Story*
1962	*Lawrence of Arabia*	Gregory Peck *To Kill a Mockingbird*	Anne Bancroft *The Miracle Worker*	Ed Begley *Sweet Bird of Youth*	Patty Duke *The Miracle Worker*	David Lean *Lawrence of Arabia*
1963	*Tom Jones*	Sidney Poitier *Lilies of the Field*	Patricia Neal *Hud*	Melvyn Douglas *Hud*	Margaret Rutherford *The V.I.P.s*	Tony Richardson *Tom Jones*
1964	*My Fair Lady*	Rex Harrison *My Fair Lady*	Julie Andrews *Mary Poppins*	Peter Ustinov *Topkapi*	Lila Kedrova *Zorba the Greek*	George Cukor *My Fair Lady*
1965	*The Sound of Music*	Lee Marvin *Cat Ballou*	Julie Christie *Darling*	Martin Balsam *A Thousand Clowns*	Shelley Winters *A Patch of Blue*	Robert Wise *The Sound of Music*
1966	*A Man for All Seasons*	Paul Scofield *A Man for All Seasons*	Elizabeth Taylor *Who's Afraid of Virginia Woolf?*	Walter Matthau *The Fortune Cookie*	Sandy Dennis *Who's Afraid of Virginia Woolf?*	Fred Zinnemann *A Man for All Seasons*
1967	*In the Heat of the Night*	Rod Steiger *In the Heat of the Night*	Katharine Hepburn *Guess Who's Coming to Dinner*	George Kennedy *Cool Hand Luke*	Estelle Parsons *Bonnie and Clyde*	Mike Nichols *The Graduate*
1968	*Oliver!*	Cliff Robertson *Charly*	Katharine Hepburn *The Lion in Winter*; Barbra Streisand *Funny Girl*	Jack Albertson *The Subject Was Roses*	Ruth Gordon *Rosemary's Baby*	Sir Carol Reed *Oliver!*
1969	*Midnight Cowboy*	John Wayne *True Grit*	Maggie Smith *The Prime of Miss Jean Brodie*	Gig Young *They Shoot Horses Don't They?*	Goldie Hawn *Cactus Flower*	John Schlesinger *Midnight Cowboy*
1970	*Patton*	George C. Scott *Patton* (refused)	Glenda Jackson *Women in Love*	John Mills *Ryan's Daughter*	Helen Hayes *Airport*	Franklin Schaffner *Patton*
1971	*The French Connection*	Gene Hackman *The French Connection*	Jane Fonda *Klute*	Ben Johnson *The Last Picture Show*	Cloris Leachman *The Last Picture Show*	William Friedkin *The French Connection*
1972	*The Godfather*	Marlon Brando *The Godfather* (refused)	Liza Minnelli *Cabaret*	Joel Grey *Cabaret*	Eileen Heckart *Butterflies Are Free*	Bob Fosse *Cabaret*
1973	*The Sting*	Jack Lemmon *Save the Tiger*	Glenda Jackson *A Touch of Class*	John Houseman *The Paper Chase*	Tatum O'Neal *Paper Moon*	George Roy Hill *The Sting*
1974	*The Godfather Part II*	Art Carney *Harry and Tonto*	Ellen Burstyn *Alice Doesn't Live Here Anymore*	Robert DeNiro *The Godfather Part II*	Ingrid Bergman *Murder on the Orient Express*	Francis Ford Coppola *The Godfather Part II*
1975	*One Flew Over the Cuckoo's Nest*	Jack Nicholson *One Flew Over the Cuckoo's Nest*	Louise Fletcher *One Flew Over the Cuckoo's Nest*	George Burns *The Sunshine Boys*	Lee Grant *Shampoo*	Milos Forman *One Flew Over the Cuckoo's Nest*
1976	*Rocky*	Peter Finch *Network*	Faye Dunaway *Network*	Jason Robards *All the President's Men*	Beatrice Straight *Network*	John G. Avildsen *Rocky*
1977	*Annie Hall*	Richard Dreyfuss *The Goodbye Girl*	Diane Keaton *Annie Hall*	Jason Robards *Julia*	Vanessa Redgrave *Julia*	Woody Allen *Annie Hall*
1978	*The Deer Hunter*	Jon Voight *Coming Home*	Jane Fonda *Coming Home*	Christopher Walken *The Deer Hunter*	Maggie Smith *California Suite*	Michael Cimino *The Deer Hunter*
1979	*Kramer vs. Kramer*	Dustin Hoffman *Kramer vs. Kramer*	Sally Field *Norma Rae*	Melvyn Douglas *Being There*	Meryl Streep *Kramer vs. Kramer*	Robert Benton *Kramer vs. Kramer*
1980	*Ordinary People*	Robert DeNiro *Raging Bull*	Sissy Spacek *Coal Miner's Daughter*	Timothy Hutton *Ordinary People*	Mary Steenburgen *Melvin and Howard*	Robert Redford *Ordinary People*
1981	*Chariots of Fire*	Henry Fonda *On Golden Pond*	Katharine Hepburn *On Golden Pond*	John Gielgud *Arthur*	Maureen Stapleton *Reds*	Warren Beatty *Reds*
1982	*Gandhi*	Ben Kingsley *Gandhi*	Meryl Streep *Sophie's Choice*	Louis Gossett Jr. *An Officer and a Gentleman*	Jessica Lange *Tootsie*	Richard Attenborough *Gandhi*
1983	*Terms of Endearment*	Robert Duvall *Tender Mercies*	Shirley MacLaine *Terms of Endearment*	Jack Nicholson *Terms of Endearment*	Linda Hunt *The Year of Living Dangerously*	James L. Brooks *Terms of Endearment*

Year	Picture	Actor	Actress	Supporting actor[1]	Supporting actress[1]	Director
1984	Amadeus	F. Murray Abraham *Amadeus*	Sally Field *Places in the Heart*	Haing S. Ngor *The Killing Fields*	Peggy Ashcroft *A Passage to India*	Milos Forman *Amadeus*
1985	Out of Africa	William Hurt *Kiss of the Spider Woman*	Geraldine Page *The Trip to Bountiful*	Don Ameche *Cocoon*	Anjelica Huston *Prizzi's Honor*	Sydney Pollack *Out of Africa*
1986	Platoon	Paul Newman *The Color of Money*	Marlee Matlin *Children of a Lesser God*	Michael Caine *Hannah and Her Sisters*	Dianne Wiest *Hannah and Her Sisters*	Oliver Stone *Platoon*
1987	The Last Emperor	Michael Douglas *Wall Street*	Cher *Moonstruck*	Sean Connery *The Untouchables*	Olympia Dukakis *Moonstruck*	Bernardo Bertolucci *The Last Emperor*
1988	Rain Man	Dustin Hoffman *Rain Man*	Jodie Foster *The Accused*	Kevin Kline *A Fish Called Wanda*	Geena Davis *The Accidental Tourist*	Barry Levinson *Rain Man*
1989	Driving Miss Daisy	Daniel Day-Lewis *My Left Foot*	Jessica Tandy *Driving Miss Daisy*	Denzel Washington *Glory*	Brenda Fricker *My Left Foot*	Oliver Stone *Born on the Fourth of July*
1990	Dances With Wolves	Jeremy Irons *Reversal of Fortune*	Kathy Bates *Misery*	Joe Pesci *Goodfellas*	Whoopi Goldberg *Ghost*	Kevin Costner *Dances With Wolves*
1991	The Silence of the Lambs	Anthony Hopkins *The Silence of the Lambs*	Jodie Foster *The Silence of the Lambs*	Jack Palance *City Slickers*	Mercedes Ruehl *The Fisher King*	Jonathan Demme *The Silence of the Lambs*
1992	Unforgiven	Al Pacino *Scent of a Woman*	Emma Thompson *Howards End*	Gene Hackman *Unforgiven*	Marisa Tomei *My Cousin Vinny*	Clint Eastwood *Unforgiven*
1993	Schindler's List	Tom Hanks *Philadelphia*	Holly Hunter *The Piano*	Tommy Lee Jones *The Fugitive*	Anna Paquin *The Piano*	Steven Spielberg *Schindler's List*
1994	Forrest Gump	Tom Hanks *Forrest Gump*	Jessica Lange *Blue Sky*	Martin Landau *Ed Wood*	Dianne Wiest, *Bullets Over Broadway*	Robert Zemeckis *Forrest Gump*
1995	Braveheart	Nicolas Cage *Leaving Las Vegas*	Susan Sarandon *Dead Man Walking*	Kevin Spacey *The Usual Suspects*	Mira Sorvino *Mighty Aphrodite*	Mel Gibson *Braveheart*
1996	The English Patient	Geoffrey Rush *Shine*	Frances McDormand *Fargo*	Cuba Gooding Jr. *Jerry Maguire*	Juliette Binoche *The English Patient*	Anthony Minghella *The English Patient*
1997	Titanic	Jack Nicholson *As Good As It Gets*	Helen Hunt *As Good As It Gets*	Robin Williams *Good Will Hunting*	Kim Basinger *L.A. Confidential*	James Cameron *Titanic*
1998	Shakespeare in Love	Roberto Benigni *Life Is Beautiful*	Gwyneth Paltrow *Shakespeare in Love*	James Coburn *Affliction*	Judi Dench *Shakespeare in Love*	Steven Spielberg *Saving Private Ryan*
1999	American Beauty	Kevin Spacey *American Beauty*	Hilary Swank *Boys Don't Cry*	Michael Caine, *The Cider House Rules*	Angelina Jolie *Girl Interrupted*	Sam Mendes *American Beauty*
2000	Gladiator	Russell Crowe *Gladiator*	Julia Roberts *Erin Brockovich*	Benicio Del Toro *Traffic*	Marcia Gay Harden *Pollock*	Steven Soderbergh *Traffic*
2001	A Beautiful Mind	Denzel Washington *Training Day*	Halle Berry *Monster's Ball*	Jim Broadbent *Iris*	Jennifer Connelly *A Beautiful Mind*	Ron Howard *A Beautiful Mind*
2002	Chicago	Adrien Brody *The Pianist*	Nicole Kidman *The Hours*	Chris Cooper *Adaptation*	Catherine Zeta-Jones, *Chicago*	Roman Polanski *The Pianist*
2003	The Lord of the Rings: The Return of the King	Sean Penn *Mystic River*	Charlize Theron *Monster*	Tim Robbins *Mystic River*	Renée Zellweger *Cold Mountain*	Peter Jackson *The Lord of the Rings: The Return of the King*
2004	Million Dollar Baby	Jamie Foxx *Ray*	Hilary Swank *Million Dollar Baby*	Morgan Freeman *Million Dollar Baby*	Cate Blanchett *The Aviator*	Clint Eastwood *Million Dollar Baby*
2005	Crash	Philip Seymour Hoffman *Capote*	Reese Witherspoon *Walk the Line*	George Clooney *Syriana*	Rachel Weisz *The Constant Gardener*	Ang Lee *Brokeback Mountain*
2006	The Departed	Forest Whitaker *The Last King of Scotland*	Helen Mirren *The Queen*	Alan Arkin *Little Miss Sunshine*	Jennifer Hudson *Dreamgirls*	Martin Scorsese *The Departed*
2007	No Country for Old Men	Daniel Day-Lewis *There Will Be Blood*	Marion Cotillard *La Vie en Rose*	Javier Bardem *No Country for Old Men*	Tilda Swinton *Michael Clayton*	Joel Coen and Ethan Coen, *No Country for Old Men*
2008	Slumdog Millionaire	Sean Penn *Milk*	Kate Winslet *The Reader*	Heath Ledger *The Dark Knight*	Penelope Cruz, *Vicky Cristina Barcelona*	Danny Boyle *Slumdog Millionaire*
2009	The Hurt Locker	Jeff Bridges *Crazy Heart*	Sandra Bullock *The Blind Side*	Christoph Waltz *Inglourious Basterds*	Mo'Nique *Precious*	Kathryn Bigelow *The Hurt Locker*
2010	The King's Speech	Colin Firth *The King's Speech*	Natalie Portman *Black Swan*	Christian Bale *The Fighter*	Melissa Leo *The Fighter*	Tom Hooper *The King's Speech*
2011	The Artist	Jean Dujardin *The Artist*	Meryl Streep *The Iron Lady*	Christopher Plummer, *Beginners*	Octavia Spencer *The Help*	Michel Hazanavicius *The Artist*

(1) Award not given until 1936.

Other Oscar Winners, 2011

Animated film: *Rango*
Art direction: *Hugo*
Cinematography: *Hugo*
Costume design: *The Artist*
Documentary: *Undefeated*
Film editing: *The Girl With the Dragon Tattoo*
Foreign language film: *A Separation*, Iran
Makeup: *The Iron Lady*
Original score: *The Artist*, Ludovic Bource
Original song: "Man or Muppet," *The Muppets*, Bret McKenzie

Screenplay, adapted: *The Descendants*, Alexander Payne, Nat Faxon, Jim Rash
Screenplay, original: *Midnight in Paris*, Woody Allen
Short films: *The Fantastic Flying Books of Mr. Morris Lessmore* (animated), *Saving Face* (documentary), *The Shore* (live-action)
Sound editing: *Hugo*
Sound mixing: *Hugo*
Visual effects: *Hugo*

Other Film Awards, 2012
(Awarded in 2012, unless otherwise noted.)

Berlin International Film Festival
Best film (Golden Bear): Cesare deve morire [Caesar Must Die], Italy
Jury grand prix (Silver Bear): Csak a szél [Just the Wind], Hungary/Germany/France
Director: Christian Petzold, Barbara, Germany
Actress: Rachel Mwanza, Rebelle [War Witch], Canada
Actor: Mikkel Boe Følsgaard, En Kongelig Affære [A Royal Affair], Denmark/Czech Rep./Sweden/Germany
Artistic contribution: Lutz Reitemeier, Bai lu yuan [White Deer Plain], China
Script: Nikolaj Arcel, Rasmus Heisterberg, En Kongelig Affære [A Royal Affair], Denmark/Czech Rep./Sweden/Germany
Special award Silver Bear: L'enfant d'en haut [Sister], Switzerland/France
Alfred Bauer Prize: Tabu, Portugal/Germany/Brazil/France

British Academy of Film and Television Awards (BAFTAs)
Awarded in 2012 to films released in the UK in 2011.
Best film: The Artist
British film: Tinker Tailor Soldier Spy
Director: Michel Hazanavicius, The Artist
Original screenplay: Michel Hazanavicius, The Artist
Adapted screenplay: Bridget O'Connor, Peter Straughan, Tinker Tailor Soldier Spy
Foreign language film: The Skin I Live In, Spain
Animated film: Rango
Actor: Jean Dujardin, The Artist
Actress: Meryl Streep, The Iron Lady
Supporting actor: Christopher Plummer, Beginners
Supporting actress: Octavia Spencer, The Help

Cannes International Film Festival Awards
Palme d'Or: Amour [Love], France/Germany/Austria
Grand Prix: Reality, Italy/France
Best Director: Carlos Reygadas, Post Tenebras Lux, Mexico
Best Screenplay: Cristian Mungiu, Dupā Dealuri [Beyond the Hills], Romania/France/Belgium
Best Actress: Cristina Flutur, Cosmina Stratan, Dupā Dealuri [Beyond the Hills], Romania/France/Belgium
Best Actor: Mads Mikkelsen, Jagten [The Hunt], Denmark
Jury Prize: The Angels' Share, UK/France/Belgium/Italy
Palme d'Or, short film: Sessiz-Be Deng [Silent], Turkey

Genie Awards
Awarded to Canadian-produced or Canadian-coproduced films.
Motion picture: Monsieur Lazhar
Actor: Fellag, Monsieur Lazhar
Actress: Vanessa Paradis, Café de Flore
Supporting actor: Viggo Mortensen, A Dangerous Method
Supporting actress: Sophie Nélisse, Monsieur Lazhar
Documentary: La nuit, elles dancert [At Night, They Dance]
Director: Philippe Falardeau, Monsieur Lazhar

Director's Guild of America Awards
Feature film: Michel Hazanavicius, The Artist
Documentary: James Marsh, Project Nim

Sundance Film Festival Awards
Grand Jury Prize: Beasts of the Southern Wild, Benh Zeitlin (drama); The House I Live In, Eugene Jarecki (doc.)
World Cinema Jury Prize: Violeta se Fue a Los Cielos [Violeta Went to Heaven], Andrés Wood, Chile/Argentina/Brazil/Spain (drama); The Law in These Parts, Ra'anan Alexandrowicz, Israel (doc.)
Audience Award: The Surrogate, Ben Lewin (drama); The Invisible War, Kirby Dick (doc.)
World Cinema Audience Award: Valley of Saints, Musa Syeed, India/U.S. (drama); Searching for Sugar Man, Malik Bendjelloul, Sweden/UK (doc.)
Best of Next Audience Award: Sleepwalk With Me, Mike Birbiglia
Directing: Ava DuVernay, Middle of Nowhere (drama); Lauren Greenfield, The Queen of Versailles (doc.)
World Cinema Directing Award: Mads Matthiesen, Teddy Bear, Denmark (drama); Emad Burnat, Guy Davidi, 5 Broken Cameras, Palestine/Israel/France (doc.)
Waldo Salt Screenwriting Award: Derek Connolly, Safety Not Guaranteed
World Cinema Screenwriting Award: Marialy Rivas, Camila Gutiérrez, Pedro Peirano, Sebastián Sepúlveda, Young & Wild, Chile
Documentary editing: Detropia
World Cinema Doc. Editing Award: Indie Game: The Movie, Canada
Cinematography: Beasts of the Southern Wild (drama); Chasing Ice (doc.)
World Cinema Cinematography Award: My Brother the Devil, UK (drama); Putin's Kiss, Denmark (doc.)
Special Jury Prizes: Andrea Sperling and Jonathan Schwartz for Smashed and Nobody Walks (drama; producing); The Surrogate (drama; ensemble); Ai Weiwei: Never Sorry (doc.; spirit of defiance); Love Free or Die (doc.; agent of change)
World Cinema Special Jury Prize: Can, Rasit Celikezer, Turkey (drama; artistic vision); Searching for Sugar Man, Malik Bendjelloul, Sweden/UK (doc.; artistic spirit)

Toronto International Film Festival
Prize of the International Critics (FIPRESCI Prize) for Discovery: Call Girl, Mikael Marcimain, Sweden/Ireland/Norway/Finland
FIPRESCI Prize for Special Presentations: In the House, François Ozon, France
People's Choice Award: Silver Linings Playbook, David O. Russell, U.S.
People's Choice Award (documentary): Artifact, Bartholomew Cubbins, U.S.
People's Choice Award (Midnight Madness): Seven Psychopaths, Martin McDonagh, U.S./UK
Canadian Feature Film: Laurence Anyways, Xavier Dolan, Canada/France
Canadian Short Film: Keep a Modest Head, Deco Dawson
Canadian First Feature Film: Antiviral, Brandon Cronenberg; Blackbird, Jason Buxton

MTV Video Music Awards, 2012
Video of the year: "We Found Love," Rihanna feat. Calvin Harris
New artist: "What Makes You Beautiful," One Direction
Female video: "Starships," Nicki Minaj
Male video: "Turn Up the Music," Chris Brown
Video with a message: "Skyscraper," Demi Lovato
Electronic dance video: "Feel So Close," Calvin Harris
Hip-hop video: "HYFR," Drake feat. Lil Wayne
Pop video: "What Makes You Beautiful," One Direction
Rock video: "Paradise," Coldplay
Shareworthy video: "What Makes You Beautiful," One Direction
Art direction: "Wide Awake," Katy Perry
Choreography: "Turn Up the Music," Chris Brown
Cinematography: "Bad Girls," M.I.A.
Direction: "Bad Girls," M.I.A.
Editing: "Countdown," Beyoncé
Visual effects: "First of the Year (Equinox)," Skrillex

Academy of Country Music Awards, 2012
Entertainer of the year: Taylor Swift
Male vocalist: Blake Shelton
Female vocalist: Miranda Lambert
Vocal duo: Thompson Square
Vocal group: Lady Antebellum
New artist: Scotty McCreery
Album: Four the Record, Miranda Lambert
Record (single): "Don't You Wanna Stay," Jason Aldean, Kelly Clarkson
Song: "Crazy Girl," Eli Young Band
Vocal event: "Don't You Wanna Stay," Jason Aldean, Kelly Clarkson
Songwriter: Dallas Davidson
Video: "Red Solo Cup," Toby Keith

Selected Grammy Awards, 2011

Source: National Academy of Recording Arts and Sciences
For albums released Oct. 1, 2010-Sept. 30, 2011, awarded in Feb. 2012.

Record of the year (single): "Rolling in the Deep," Adele
Album of the year: *21*, Adele
Song of the year: "Rolling in the Deep," Adele
New artist: Bon Iver
Pop perf., solo: "Someone Like You," Adele
Pop perf., duo/group: "Body and Soul," Tony Bennett and Amy Winehouse
Pop album, instrumental: *The Road From Memphis*, Booker T. Jones
Pop album, vocal: *21*, Adele
Dance recording: "Scary Monsters and Nice Sprites," Skrillex
Dance/electronic album: *Scary Monsters and Nice Sprites*, Skrillex
Rock perf.: "Walk," Foo Fighters
Hard rock perf.: "White Limo," Foo Fighters
Rock song: "Walk," Foo Fighters
Rock album: *Wasting Light*, Foo Fighters
Alternative album: *Bon Iver*, Bon Iver
R&B perf.: "Is This Love," Corinne Bailey Rae
R&B perf., traditional: "Fool for You," Cee Lo Green and Melanie Fiona
R&B song: "Fool for You," Cee Lo Green and Melanie Fiona
R&B album: *F.A.M.E.*, Chris Brown

Rap perf.: "Otis," Jay-Z and Kanye West
Rap/sung collaboration: "All of the Lights," Kanye West, Rihanna, Kid Cudi, Fergie
Rap song: "All of the Lights," Kanye West, Rihanna, Kid Cudi, Fergie
Rap album: *My Beautiful Dark Twisted Fantasy*, Kanye West
Country perf., solo: "Mean," Taylor Swift
Country perf., duo/group: "Barton Hollow," The Civil Wars
Country song: "Mean," Taylor Swift
Country album: *Own the Night*, Lady Antebellum
Bluegrass album: *Paper Airplane*, Alison Krauss and Union Station
New age album: *What's It All About*, Pat Metheny
Comedy album: *Hilarious*, Louis C.K.
Spoken-word album: *If You Ask Me (And Of Course You Won't)*, Betty White
Soundtrack album, compilation: *Boardwalk Empire: Vol. 1*, various artists
Soundtrack album, score: *The King's Speech*, Alexandre Desplat
Song, visual media: "I See the Light," *Tangled*
Music video, short form: "Rolling in the Deep," Adele
Music video, long form: *Back and Forth*, Foo Fighters

Grammy Awards, 1958-2011

Record of the Year (single)	Year	Album of the Year
Domenico Modugno, "Nel Blu Dipinto di Blu (Volare)"	1958	Henry Mancini, *The Music From Peter Gunn*
Bobby Darin, "Mack the Knife"	1959	Frank Sinatra, *Come Dance With Me*
Percy Faith, "Theme From a Summer Place"	1960	Bob Newhart, *Button Down Mind*
Henry Mancini, "Moon River"	1961	Judy Garland, *Judy at Carnegie Hall*
Tony Bennett, "I Left My Heart in San Francisco"	1962	Vaughn Meader, *The First Family*
Henry Mancini, "The Days of Wine and Roses"	1963	Barbra Streisand, *The Barbra Streisand Album*
Stan Getz and Astrud Gilberto, "The Girl From Ipanema"	1964	Stan Getz and João Gilberto, *Getz/Gilberto*
Herb Alpert, "A Taste of Honey"	1965	Frank Sinatra, *September of My Years*
Frank Sinatra, "Strangers in the Night"	1966	Frank Sinatra, *A Man and His Music*
5th Dimension, "Up, Up and Away"	1967	The Beatles, *Sgt. Pepper's Lonely Hearts Club Band*
Simon and Garfunkel, "Mrs. Robinson"	1968	Glen Campbell, *By the Time I Get to Phoenix*
5th Dimension, "Aquarius/Let the Sunshine In"	1969	Blood, Sweat & Tears, *Blood, Sweat & Tears*
Simon and Garfunkel, "Bridge Over Troubled Water"	1970	Simon and Garfunkel, *Bridge Over Troubled Water*
Carole King, "It's Too Late"	1971	Carole King, *Tapestry*
Roberta Flack, "The First Time Ever I Saw Your Face"	1972	George Harrison and Friends, *The Concert for Bangla Desh*
Roberta Flack, "Killing Me Softly With His Song"	1973	Stevie Wonder, *Innervisions*
Olivia Newton-John, "I Honestly Love You"	1974	Stevie Wonder, *Fulfillingness' First Finale*
Captain & Tennille, "Love Will Keep Us Together"	1975	Paul Simon, *Still Crazy After All These Years*
George Benson, "This Masquerade"	1976	Stevie Wonder, *Songs in the Key of Life*
Eagles, "Hotel California"	1977	Fleetwood Mac, *Rumours*
Billy Joel, "Just the Way You Are"	1978	Bee Gees, *Saturday Night Fever*
The Doobie Brothers, "What a Fool Believes"	1979	Billy Joel, *52nd Street*
Christopher Cross, "Sailing"	1980	Christopher Cross, *Christopher Cross*
Kim Carnes, "Bette Davis Eyes"	1981	John Lennon and Yoko Ono, *Double Fantasy*
Toto, "Rosanna"	1982	Toto, *Toto IV*
Michael Jackson, "Beat It"	1983	Michael Jackson, *Thriller*
Tina Turner, "What's Love Got to Do With It"	1984	Lionel Richie, *Can't Slow Down*
USA for Africa, "We Are the World"	1985	Phil Collins, *No Jacket Required*
Steve Winwood, "Higher Love"	1986	Paul Simon, *Graceland*
Paul Simon, "Graceland"	1987	U2, *The Joshua Tree*
Bobby McFerrin, "Don't Worry, Be Happy"	1988	George Michael, *Faith*
Bette Midler, "Wind Beneath My Wings"	1989	Bonnie Raitt, *Nick of Time*
Phil Collins, "Another Day in Paradise"	1990	Quincy Jones, *Back on the Block*
Natalie Cole, with Nat "King" Cole, "Unforgettable"	1991	Natalie Cole, with Nat "King" Cole, *Unforgettable*
Eric Clapton, "Tears in Heaven"	1992	Eric Clapton, *Unplugged*
Whitney Houston, "I Will Always Love You"	1993	Whitney Houston, *The Bodyguard*
Sheryl Crow, "All I Wanna Do"	1994	Tony Bennett, *MTV Unplugged*
Seal, "Kiss From a Rose"	1995	Alanis Morissette, *Jagged Little Pill*
Eric Clapton, "Change the World"	1996	Celine Dion, *Falling Into You*
Shawn Colvin, "Sunny Came Home"	1997	Bob Dylan, *Time Out of Mind*
Celine Dion, "My Heart Will Go On"	1998	Lauryn Hill, *The Miseducation of Lauryn Hill*
Santana feat. Rob Thomas, "Smooth"	1999	Santana, *Supernatural*
U2, "Beautiful Day"	2000	Steely Dan, *Two Against Nature*
U2, "Walk On"	2001	Various artists, *O Brother, Where Art Thou?*
Norah Jones, "Don't Know Why"	2002	Norah Jones, *Come Away With Me*
Coldplay, "Clocks"	2003	OutKast, *Speakerboxxx/The Love Below*
Ray Charles and Norah Jones, "Here We Go Again"	2004	Ray Charles and various artists, *Genius Loves Company*
Green Day, "Boulevard of Broken Dreams"	2005	U2, *How to Dismantle an Atomic Bomb*
Dixie Chicks, "Not Ready to Make Nice"	2006	Dixie Chicks, *Taking the Long Way*
Amy Winehouse, "Rehab"	2007	Herbie Hancock, *River: The Joni Letters*
Robert Plant and Alison Krauss, "Please Read the Letter"	2008	Robert Plant and Alison Krauss, *Raising Sand*
Kings Of Leon, "Use Somebody"	2009	Taylor Swift, *Fearless*
Lady Antebellum, "Need You Now"	2010	Arcade Fire, *The Suburbs*
Adele, "Rolling in the Deep"	2011	Adele, *21*

SCIENCE AND TECHNOLOGY

Science and Technology News, 2012

The following were some of the more newsworthy developments in science and technology in the past year.

"God Particle" Revealed

Scientists at the European Organization for Nuclear Research (CERN) July 4, 2012, announced that they had observed what they believe to be the Higgs boson, the long-sought subatomic particle that purportedly dictates how other particles acquire mass. They said the findings of experiments carried out at CERN's Large Hadron Collider in Switzerland, had less than a one-in-three-million chance of being due to chance.

The Higgs boson is one of the final pieces of the puzzle known as the Standard Model of physics. This model posits the existence of an invisible force field throughout the universe. Particles pass through this so-called Higgs field at different speeds depending on their characteristics. Particles that are slowed down by the field have a large mass, while those that stream through it have a small mass. The Higgs boson is the only manifestation of this force field; being crucial and elusive, it was nicknamed the "God particle." For comparison's sake, imagine two people trying to get across a paparazzi-filled room. An ordinary person moves quickly through the crowd, but a celebrity is swarmed by the photographers, acquiring "mass." The boson is named for Peter Higgs, a professor at the Univ. of Edinburgh, who was one of the first physicists to suggest its existence back in 1964. For the past 50 years, a generation of scientists has believed in the boson's existence without ever seeing it.

The $10-bil Large Hadron Collider was built from 1998-2008, partially for the purpose of identifying the Higgs boson. It works by firing subatomic particles at each other at nearly the speed of light. When the particles collide, they release a flood of new particles. By repeating collisions billions of times, scientists amassed enough data to provide evidence of a boson fitting the description of the Higgs.

Red Rover, Red Rover

After an eight-month, 350-mil mile voyage, the NASA rover known as *Curiosity* successfully landed on Mars Aug. 6, 2012, and began exploring for signs of whether the red planet has or could sustain microbial life. Twice as long and three times as heavy as the two rovers that landed on Mars in Jan. 2004, *Curiosity* is armed with a laser and other scientific instruments for analyzing rock and soil samples. Over the course of one Martian year, or 687 Earth days, the Mars Science Laboratory mission (as it is officially named) will investigate whether Mars holds organic molecules and other chemical elements essential to life, such as oxygen, nitrogen, and sulfur.

Just the act of landing the vehicle on Mars's surface required technical innovation by NASA's Jet Propulsion Laboratory. *Curiosity*'s one-ton mass made it impossible to use proven landing systems like the air bags used to land the 2004 rovers. Instead, engineers devised a parachute to slow the spacecraft's descent, before a rocket-powered sky crane lowered the rover to the ground. The rover landed in an area called Gale Crater, formed by a meteor crash at least 3.5 bil years ago. The six-wheeled vehicle can travel up to 200 meters per day, and can roll over obstacles up to 25 inches high. *Curiosity* began returning photographs almost immediately after landing, and made its first test drive on the Martian surface on Aug. 22.

Shedding Light on Dark Matter

Because it neither emits nor absorbs light, dark matter is impossible to see. But astronomers inferred its existence 80 years ago from its gravitational effect on light and visible matter surrounding it. Physicists estimate that 80% of the universe's matter is made up of dark matter, theorizing that it is the cosmic web or skeleton responsible for shaping galaxies.

A report by an international team of scientists in the July 12 edition of *Nature* provides evidence for this cosmic web. Using data from the Subaru telescope in Hawaii and the XMM-Newton space telescope, the scientists discovered a filament of dark matter connecting Abell 222 and 223, two clusters of galaxies nearly 3 bil light years from Earth. "It's a resounding confirmation of the standard theory of structure formation of the universe," said the paper's lead author, Jörg Dietrich at the Univ. Observatory Munich. "The galaxy clusters and the filaments are mostly made up of dark matter. The normal matter just follows the distribution of dark matter."

Global Warming Heats Up

With an average temperature of 77.6°F, July 2012 ranked as the hottest month in the lower 48 states since the U.S. started keeping records in 1895, according to the Natl. Oceanic and Atmospheric Admin. The high temperatures combined with a lack of rainfall to cause severe droughts across more than 60% of the U.S., ruining crops and raising prices. A report by 10 researchers in the July 29 issue of *Nature Geoscience* suggested that this kind of heat and drought could be the "new normal" for the foreseeable future. The study, funded by the National Science Foundation, NASA, and the U.S. Dept. of Energy, found that the 2000-04 drought in the Western U.S. was the most severe in 800 years, worse even than the Dust Bowl of the 1930s. In Aug., the Natl. Snow and Ice Center reported that the amount of Arctic sea ice had fallen to its lowest level since the government-sponsored agency started measuring it in 1979.

Meanwhile, scientists and politicians continued to debate human contributions to the changing climate. Physicist Richard Muller, one of the more prominent scientists who had been a global warming skeptic, confessed "a total turnaround" in a July 28 editorial in the *NY Times*. The co-founder of the Berkeley Earth Surface Temperature project said the empirical evidence had persuaded him that global warming is real, and that "humans are almost entirely the cause."

Why Zebras Have Stripes

Scientists have long believed the zebra's stripes camouflage it in tall grass from larger predators like lions. But according to a report in the Mar. 2012 issue of *The Journal of Experimental Biology*, the stripes also protect them from parasites like blood-sucking horseflies. From their previous work, Susanne Åkesson, a professor of evolutionary ecology at Sweden's Lunds Univ., and her colleagues knew that flies were attracted to darker fur because it reflected polarized light, making it look more like water, where the flies lay their eggs. But they were surprised when their experiments demonstrated that black-and-white stripes were even less attractive to horseflies than an all-white pattern. Narrower stripes were more repellent to flies than wider ones. That may explain why zebras have their narrowest stripes on their faces and legs, where they are most vulnerable because their skin is thinnest. The study did not take into account the flies' sense of smell. Nor does it explain why all horses did not evolve the same way zebras did.

Arsenic-Based Life? Maybe Not

Around 18 months after NASA-funded researchers reported in Dec. 2010 finding a strain of bacteria that survived on arsenic, the scientific community rebutted their study. The research, published on the *Science* website and led by Felisa Wolfe-Simon of NASA's Astrobiology Institute, seemed to contradict the conventional wisdom that organisms could not survive without phosphorus, among such building blocks of life as carbon, hydrogen, nitrogen, oxygen, and sulfur. If arsenic could sustain life, rather than poison it, there might be all kinds of life-forms on other planets and even on Earth.

But two subsequent studies using the same bacterium as the original research failed to replicate the results. A team led by Rosemary Redfield at the Univ. of British Columbia found that they could not get the bacterium to grow on arsenic alone. It wasn't until they added phosphorous that they got the kind of growth that the NASA team reported. Redfield's team suggested that the bacteria used by the NASA researchers may have been unwittingly contaminated by trace amounts of phosphorous. Another team of scientists in Switzerland found that the bacterium could resist high concentrations of arsenic, but not without at least a trace amount of phosphorous. Both studies appeared first in the July 8, 2012, online edition of *Science*.

Science Glossary

This glossary covers some concepts that come up frequently in the news, in biology, chemistry, geology, and physics.

Biology

Amino acid: one of about 20 similar small molecules that are the building blocks of proteins.

Antibiotic: a substance produced by or derived from a bacterium, fungus, or other organism that battles infections and diseases caused by microorganisms, especially bacteria; it works by killing the microorganism or halting its growth.

Archaea: a group of single-celled microorganisms; they are prokaryotes, like bacteria, but they share some similarities with eukaryotes.

Autoimmunity: a condition in which an individual's immune system reacts against his or her own tissues; leads to diseases such as lupus, some forms of diabetes, inflammatory bowel disease, and rheumatoid arthritis.

Bacterium (plural, bacteria): one of a large, varied class of microscopic and simple, single-celled organisms; bacteria live almost everywhere—some forms cause disease, while others are useful in digestion and other natural processes.

Biodiversity: richness of variety of life-forms—both plant and animal—in a given environment.

Cell: the smallest unit of life capable of living independently, or with other cells; usually bounded by a membrane. May include a nucleus and other specialized parts.

Cholesterol: a fatty substance in animal tissues. It is produced by the liver in humans; is found in foods such as butter, eggs, and meat; and is an essential body constituent.

Chromosome: one of the rod-like structures in cell nuclei that carry genetic material (DNA).

Cloning: the process of copying a particular piece of DNA to allow it to be sequenced, studied, or used in some other way; can also refer to producing a genetic copy of an organism.

DNA (deoxyribonucleic acid): the double-stranded chemical substance that carries genetic information, which determines the form and functioning of all living things.

Ecosystem: an interdependent community of living organisms and their climatic and geographical habitat.

Enzyme: a protein that promotes a particular chemical reaction in the body.

Estrogen: one of a group of hormones that promote development of female secondary sex characteristics and the growth and health of the female reproductive system; males also produce small amounts of estrogen.

Eukaryote: any of the group of single- or multi-celled organisms whose cells have distinct nuclei.

Evolution: the process of gradual change that may occur as a species adapts to its environment; natural selection is the process by which evolution occurs.

Gene: a portion of a DNA molecule that provides the blueprint for the assembly of a protein.

Gene pool: the collection and total diversity of genes in an interbreeding population.

Gene therapy: a treatment in which scientists try to implant functioning genes into a person's cells so the genes can produce proteins that the person lacks or that help the person fight disease.

Genetic sequencing: the process of finding the order of subunits in a gene or the order of all an organism's genes.

Genome: the complete set of an organism's genetic material.

Hormone: a substance secreted in one part of an organism that regulates the functioning of other tissues or organs.

Meiosis: the process of cell division that results in gametes (sperm or egg cells), all of which contain half the number of chromosomes as their precursor.

Metabolism: the sum total of the body's chemical processes providing energy for vital functions and enabling new material to be synthesized.

Mitosis: the process by which a cell divides its nucleus and other cell materials into two duplicate daughter cells with the same DNA.

Neuron or **nerve cell:** any of the cells in the nervous system that send electrical and chemical messages to other cells.

Nucleus (plural, nuclei): the center of an atom; or the portion of a eukaryotic cell that contains genetic material and regulates growth and metabolism.

Organism: a living entity, capable of growth, metabolism, and usually reproduction.

Phenotype: the observable properties and characteristics of an organism arising at least in part from its genetic makeup.

Pheromone: a chemical secreted by an animal or plant to influence the behavior of other members of its species.

Placebo effect: a phenomenon in which patients show improvements even though they have taken a medically inactive substance, called a placebo.

Prokaryote: a single-celled organism that does not have a distinct nucleus, such as a bacterium or archaeon.

Protein: a complex molecule made up of one or more chains of amino acids; essential to the structure and function of all cells.

RNA (ribonucleic acid): a complex molecule similar to the genetic material DNA but usually single-stranded; several forms of RNA translate the genetic code of DNA and use that code to assemble proteins for structural and biological functions in the body. RNA also serves as the genetic material of some viruses.

Species: a population of organisms that breed with each other in nature and produce fertile offspring; other definitions of species exist to accommodate the diversity of life on Earth.

Stem cell: a cell that can give rise to other types of cells; for instance, bone marrow stem cells may divide and produce different types of blood cells.

Steroid: a type of chemical substance with a certain molecular structure. Some steroids are hormones that can suppress immune response or influence stress reaction, blood pressure, or sexual development.

Testosterone: a steroid hormone that stimulates the development and maintenance of male sexual characteristics and the production of sperm; women also produce small amounts of testosterone.

Virus: a microscopic, often disease-causing, "organism" made of genetic material surrounded by a protein shell; can only reproduce inside a living cell.

Chemistry

Acid: a class of compound that contrasts with bases. Acids taste sour, turn litmus red/pink, and often produce hydrogen gas in contact with some metals. Acids donate protons (hydrogen atoms minus the electron) in chemical reactions.

Base: a substance that yields hydroxyl ions (OH-) when dissolved in water; any of a class of compounds whose aqueous solutions taste bitter, feel slippery, turn litmus blue, and react with acids to form salts; also known as **alkaline**.

Carbon fiber: an extremely strong, thin fiber made by pyrolyzing (decomposing by heat) synthetic fibers, such as rayon, until charred; used to make high-strength composites.

Chlorofluorocarbon (CFC): one of a group of industrial chemicals that contain chlorine, fluorine, and carbon and have been found to damage Earth's ozone layer.

Element: a substance that cannot be chemically decomposed into simpler substances; the atoms of an element all have the same number of protons and electrons.

Isotope: an atom of a chemical element with the same number of protons in its nucleus as other atoms of that element, but with a different number of neutrons.

Molecule: the basic unit of a chemical compound, composed of two or more atoms bound together.

Noble gases or **inert gases:** a group of gases including helium, neon, argon, krypton, xenon, and radon that are not reactive except in rare and limited instances.

Osmosis: the transfer of a fluid across a semipermeable membrane, usually from an area of higher concentration to one of lower concentration.

Phase: any of the possible states of matter—solid, liquid, gas, or plasma—that change according to temperature and pressure.

Polymer: a huge molecule containing hundreds or thousands of smaller molecules arranged in repeating units.

Salt: a neutral compound produced by the reaction of an acid and a base.

Geology

Fault, tectonic: a crack or break in Earth's crust, often due to the slippage of tectonic plates past or over one another; usually geologically unstable.

Igneous: a type of rock formed by solidification from a molten state, especially from molten magma.

Magma: hot liquid rock material under Earth's crust, from which igneous rock is formed by cooling.

Metamorphic: in geology, the name given to rocks or minerals that have recrystallized under the influence of heat and pressure since their original formation.

Pangaea: a single supercontinent that scientists believe began to break apart at least 200 mil years ago to form the current continents.

Plate tectonics: theory that Earth's lithosphere—the uppermost layer that includes the crust—is made up of many separate rigid plates of rock that float on top of hot semi-liquid rock.

Sedimentary: a type of rock formed by the buildup of material at the bottoms of bodies of water.

Physics

Absolute zero: the theoretical temperature at which all motion within a molecule stops, corresponding to $-273.15°C$ ($-459.67°F$).

Antimatter: matter that consists of antiparticles, such as antiprotons, that have an opposite charge from normal particles; when matter meets antimatter, both are destroyed, and their combined mass is converted to energy. Antimatter is created in certain radioactive decay processes but appears to be present in only small amounts in the universe.

Atom: the basic unit of a chemical element.

Atomic mass: the total mass of an atom of a given element; atoms of the same element with different atomic masses (different numbers of neutrons, not protons) are called **isotopes**.

Atomic number: the number of protons in an atom of a given element of the periodic table; the characteristic that sets atoms of different elements apart.

Axion: a hypothetical subatomic particle with low mass and energy that is thought to exist because of the properties of the strong nuclear force.

Bose-Einstein condensate (BEC): a "super-atom" comprising thousands of atoms super-cooled to within a few hundred millionths of a degree of absolute zero and thus condensed into the lowest energy state. Atoms bound in the BEC behave synchronously, giving the BEC wavelike properties.

Boson: force-carrying particles including photons, gluons, and the W and Z particles; one of the two primary categories of particles in the Standard Model, the other being fermions.

Dark energy: a mysterious, undefined energy leading to a repulsive force pervading all of space-time; proposed by cosmologists as counteracting gravity and accelerating the expansion of the universe; predicted to make up 73% of the universe's composition.

Dark matter: hypothetical, invisible matter that some scientists believe makes up 83% of the matter in the universe (excluding dark energy). Its existence was proposed to account for otherwise inexplicable gravitational forces observed in space.

Doppler effect: a change in the frequency of sound, light, or radio waves caused by the motion of the source emitting the waves or the motion of the person or instrument perceiving the waves.

Electron: negatively charged particle that is the least massive electrically charged fundamental particle; the most common charged lepton in the Standard Model.

Energy: capacity to perform work. Energy can take various forms, such as potential energy, kinetic energy, and chemical energy.

Entropy: a measure of disorder in a system.

Fermion: any one of a number of matter particles including electrons, protons, neutrons, and quarks; one of the two primary categories of particles in the Standard Model, the other being bosons.

Field: the effects of forces (gravitational, electric, etc.) are visualized and described mathematically by physicists in terms of fields, which show the strength and direction of a force at a given position.

Fission: a nuclear reaction that occurs when the nuclei of large, unstable atoms break apart, releasing large amounts of energy.

Fluorescence: luminescence that is caused by the absorption of radiation at one wavelength followed by an almost immediate re-radiation, usually at a different wavelength, that stops almost immediately when the radiation stops.

Force: in classical physics, something that causes acceleration in a body; can be thought of as a push or pull.

Fusion: a nuclear reaction occurring when atomic nuclei collide at high temperatures and combine to form one heavier atomic nucleus, releasing enormous energy in the process.

Gravity: an attractive force between any two objects or particles, proportional to the mass (or energy) of the objects; strength of the force decreases with greater distance; the only fundamental force still unaccounted for by the Standard Model.

Half-life: the time it takes for half of a given amount of a radioactive element to decay.

Hertz (Hz): a measure of frequency, or how many times a given event occurs per second; applied to sound waves, electrical current, and microchip clock speeds.

Laser: light consisting of a cascade of photons all having the same wavelength; stands for Light Amplification by Stimulated Emission of Radiation.

Light-emitting diode (LED): a semiconductor that emits light when an electrical current is passed through it. The color of the light depends on the material used in making the diode.

Neutrino: a tiny fundamental particle with no electrical charge and very small mass that moves very quickly through the universe; comes in three varieties, or flavors, called electron, muon, and tau.

Neutron: a neutral particle found in the nuclei of atoms.

Particle accelerator: a large machine with a circular or long, straight tunnel in which atoms smash into each other at high speeds. Physicists use these machines to study subatomic particles.

Phosphorescence: luminescence that is caused by the absorption of radiation at one wavelength followed by a delayed re-radiation, usually at a different wavelength, that continues for at least a hundredth of a second after the radiation stops.

Photon: the elementary unit, or quantum, of light or electromagnetic radiation having no mass or electrical charge; one of the fundamental force-carrying particles, or bosons, described by the Standard Model.

Plasma: a high-energy state of matter different from solid, liquid, or gas in which atomic nuclei and the electrons orbiting them separate from each other.

Proton: a positively charged subatomic particle found in the nuclei of atoms.

Quantum: a natural unit of some physically measurable property, such as energy or electrical charge.

Quark: a fermion and a fundamental matter particle that makes up neutrons and protons, forming atomic nuclei; there are six different varieties, or flavors, of quarks grouped in pairs: up and down, charm and strange, top and bottom.

Radiation: energy emitted as rays or particles. Radiation includes heat, light, ultraviolet rays, gamma rays, X-rays, cosmic rays, alpha particles, and beta particles.

Relativity, general theory of: a theory of space-time proposed by Albert Einstein in 1915; gravitational and other forces are transmitted through the effects of the curvature of space-time.

Relativity, special theory of: Einstein's theory of space and time: all laws of physics are valid in all uniformly moving frames of reference, and the speed of light in a vacuum is always the same, so long as the source and the observer are moving uniformly (not accelerating).

Standard Model: prevailing theory of the interaction of subatomic particles. Matter particles are fermions: either leptons or quarks; force-carrying particles are bosons: either gluons, W or Z bosons, or photons; successfully explains three of the four elementary forces acting on particles (strong, weak, electromagnetic) but thus far has not incorporated gravity.

String theory: a theory that seeks to unify quantum mechanics and general relativity, positing that the basic constituents of matter can best be understood not as point objects but as tiny oscillating "strings."

Subatomic particle: one of the small particles, such as electrons, neutrons, and protons, which make up an atom.

Superconductivity: the property of certain materials, usually metals and chemically complex ceramics, to conduct electricity without resistance, generally at very cold temperatures.

Thermodynamics: the branch of physics that describes how energy, heat, and temperature flow in physical systems.

Ultraviolet radiation: a form of light, invisible to the human eye, that has a shorter wavelength and greater energy than visible light but a longer wavelength and less energy than X-rays.

Virtual particle: subatomic particles that rapidly pop into and out of existence and can exert real forces; usually occur in particle-antiparticle pairs and are rapidly annihilated.

Mohs Scale of Hardness

Hardness is the ability of a solid substance to resist abrasion or deformation on its surface. Soft minerals scratch more easily than hard ones. For example, a diamond will scratch graphite because the graphite is softer. In 1812, German mineralogist Frederich Mohs (1773-1839) created the arbitrary scale shown below to measure relative hardness using 10 minerals that were readily available at that time. The numbers in the Mohs scale are arranged in order of increasing hardness. An item's hardness is obtained by determining which mineral in the Mohs scale can scratch it.

Mohs Scale		Selected items and their relative hardness	
1. . . . . . Talc	6. . . . . Orthoclase feldspar	2.5 . . . . . .Fingernail	5.5 . . . . . .Knife blade
2. . . . . . Gypsum	7. . . . . Quartz	2.5-3 . . . .Gold, silver	6-7 . . . . .Glass
3. . . . . . Calcite	8. . . . . Topaz	3 . . . . . . .Copper penny	6.5 . . . . .Iron pyrite
4. . . . . . Fluorite	9. . . . . Corundum	4-4.5 . . . . .Platinum	7+. . . . . .Hardened steel file
5. . . . . . Apatite	10. . . . . Diamond	4-5 . . . . . .Iron	

Chemical Elements, Atomic Numbers, Year Discovered

See Periodic Table of the Elements on the following page for atomic weights.

Element	Symbol	Atomic number	Year discov.	Element	Symbol	Atomic number	Year discov.	Element	Symbol	Atomic number	Year discov.
Actinium	Ac	89	1899	Gold	Au	79	BCE	Protactinium	Pa	91	1917
Aluminum	Al	13	1825	Hafnium	Hf	72	1923	Radium	Ra	88	1898
Americium	Am	95	1944	Hassium	Hs	108	1984	Radon	Rn	86	1900
Antimony	Sb	51	1450	Helium	He	2	1868	Rhenium	Re	75	1925
Argon	Ar	18	1894	Holmium	Ho	67	1878	Rhodium	Rh	45	1803
Arsenic	As	33	13th cent.	Hydrogen	H	1	1766	Roentgenium	Rg	111	1995
Astatine	At	85	1940	Indium	In	49	1863	Rubidium	Rb	37	1861
Barium	Ba	56	1808	Iodine	I	53	1811	Ruthenium	Ru	44	1845
Berkelium	Bk	97	1949	Iridium	Ir	77	1804	Rutherfordium	Rf	104	1969
Beryllium	Be	4	1798	Iron	Fe	26	BCE	Samarium	Sm	62	1879
Bismuth	Bi	83	15th cent.	Krypton	Kr	36	1898	Scandium	Sc	21	1879
Bohrium	Bh	107	1981	Lanthanum	La	57	1839	Seaborgium	Sg	106	1974
Boron	B	5	1808	Lawrencium	Lr	103	1961	Selenium	Se	34	1817
Bromine	Br	35	1826	Lead	Pb	82	BCE	Silicon	Si	14	1823
Cadmium	Cd	48	1817	Lithium	Li	3	1817	Silver	Ag	47	BCE
Calcium	Ca	20	1808	Livermorium	Lv	116	2000	Sodium	Na	11	1807
Californium	Cf	98	1950	Lutetium	Lu	71	1907	Strontium	Sr	38	1790
Carbon	C	6	BCE	Magnesium	Mg	12	1829	Sulfur	S	16	BCE
Cerium	Ce	58	1803	Manganese	Mn	25	1774	Tantalum	Ta	73	1802
Cesium	Cs	55	1860	Meitnerium	Mt	109	1982	Technetium	Tc	43	1937
Chlorine	Cl	17	1774	Mendelevium	Md	101	1955	Tellurium	Te	52	1782
Chromium	Cr	24	1797	Mercury	Hg	80	BCE	Terbium	Tb	65	1843
Cobalt	Co	27	1735	Molybdenum	Mo	42	1782	Thallium	Tl	81	1861
Copernicium	Cn	112	1996	Neodymium	Nd	60	1885	Thorium	Th	90	1828
Copper	Cu	29	BCE	Neon	Ne	10	1898	Thulium	Tm	69	1879
Curium	Cm	96	1944	Neptunium	Np	93	1940	Tin	Sn	50	BCE
Darmstadtium	Ds	110	1995	Nickel	Ni	28	1751	Titanium	Ti	22	1791
Dubnium (Hahnium)[1]	Db (Ha)	105	1970	Niobium[2]	Nb	41	1801	Tungsten (Wolfram)	W	74	1783
Dysprosium	Dy	66	1886	Nitrogen	N	7	1772	*Ununoctium	Uuo	118	2006
Einsteinium	Es	99	1952	Nobelium	No	102	1958	*Ununpentium	Uup	115	2004
Erbium	Er	68	1843	Osmium	Os	76	1804	*Ununseptium	Uus	117	2010
Europium	Eu	63	1901	Oxygen	O	8	1774	*Ununtrium	Uut	113	2004
Fermium	Fm	100	1953	Palladium	Pd	46	1803	Uranium	U	92	1789
Flerovium	Fl	114	1999	Phosphorus	P	15	1669	Vanadium	V	23	1830
Fluorine	F	9	1771	Platinum	Pt	78	1735	Xenon	Xe	54	1898
Francium	Fr	87	1939	Plutonium	Pu	94	1941	Ytterbium	Yb	70	1878
Gadolinium	Gd	64	1886	Polonium	Po	84	1898	Yttrium	Y	39	1794
Gallium	Ga	31	1875	Potassium	K	19	1807	Zinc	Zn	30	BCE
Germanium	Ge	32	1886	Praseodymium	Pr	59	1885	Zirconium	Zr	40	1789
				Promethium	Pm	61	1945				

Note: 118 elements are listed here; only 114 have been independently confirmed. (*) Indicates element whose existence has been reported or hypothesized, but not yet confirmed. Between 2004 and 2010, observation of isotopes of elements 113, 115, 117, and 118 were reported in refereed journals. These reports all await confirmation and are shown in italics in the periodic table. (1) The name Dubnium (Db) has been approved by IUPAC for element 105, but the name Hahnium (Ha) was used in most of the scientific literature before 1998 and is still sometimes used in the U.S. (2) Formerly Columbium.

Periodic Table of the Elements

Source: Lawrence Berkeley National Laboratory; International Union of Pure and Applied Chemistry (IUPAC)

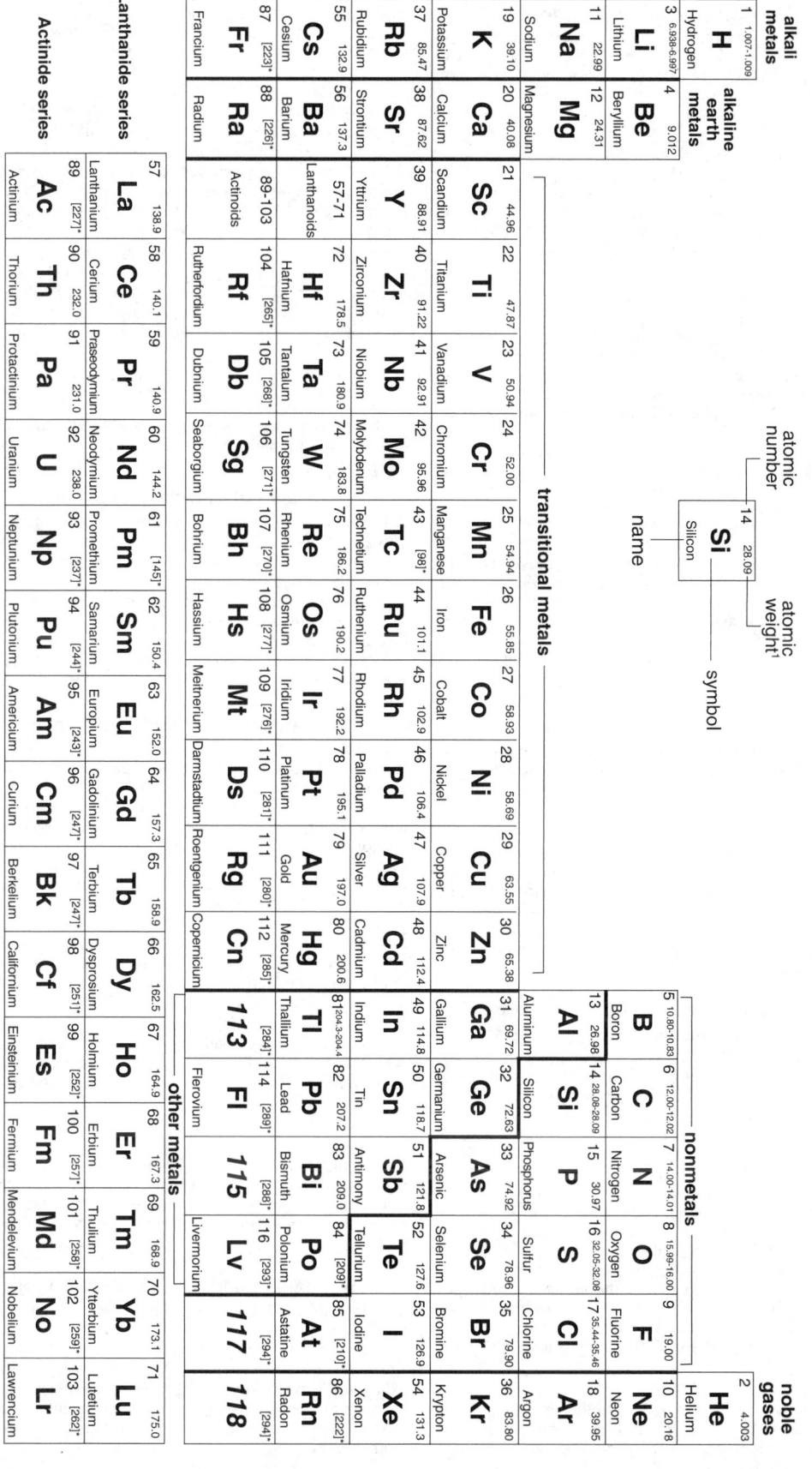

* Element has no stable nuclides. The value enclosed in brackets, e.g. [209], indicates the mass number of the longest-lived isotope of the element. However, three such elements (Th, Pa, and U) do have a characteristic terrestrial isotopic composition, and for these an atomic weight is tabulated. (1) For elements whose atomic weight varies, a range is shown.

Basic Laws of Physics

Newton's Laws of Motion

1. An object in motion moves at a constant velocity in a straight line unless acted upon by a force. Likewise, an object at rest will stay at rest. These two properties are known as inertia.

2. The acceleration of an object is proportional to the force acting on it and inversely proportional to the mass of an object.

Force (F) equals mass (m) times acceleration (a):

$$F = ma$$

3. For every action, there is an equal and opposite reaction. For example, if a force of 1 ton pushes down on an object, the object pushes up with an equal force. As per the second law, the amount of movement (acceleration) produced in the object will depend on the object's mass.

Law of Gravity

In common usage, gravity refers to the gravitational force between planets and objects on or near them. But in scientific parlance, gravitation represents one of four basic forces controlling the interactions of matter. The others are the strong and weak nuclear forces and electromagnetic force. The gravitational force (F) between objects is proportional to the product of their masses (m_1 and m_2) and inversely proportional to the square of the distance (d) between them. G represents the gravitational constant in Newton's law of gravity, a fixed ratio of approximately 6.67384×10^{-11} newton m^2/kg^2.

The basic law of gravity is:

$$F = G\frac{m_1 m_2}{d_2}$$

Near Earth's surface, Earth's gravitational force is considered to pull objects downward at a constant acceleration of $g = 9.8$ m/s^2. This allows calculation of the vertical velocity (v) of an object with an initial vertical velocity of v_0 in free fall at a given point in time (t) and calculation of the distance (d) of an object from Earth at any given time with a given initial velocity (v_0) and a known initial height (a) via the following equations:

$$v = v_0 - gt$$

$$d = -\tfrac{1}{2}g(t^2) + v_0 t + a$$

Assuming that height is measured in feet and speeds in feet per second, the maximum height (H) reached by an object with a positive v_0 is expressed as:

$$H = a + \frac{v_0^2}{64}$$

For motion not near Earth's surface, more complicated equations are required. Also, if the object's upward velocity is very great, the object may escape Earth's gravity. Even near Earth's surface, there are slight complications. Gravity is lessened by the centrifugal force of the Earth's rotation. At the poles, where centrifugal force is absent, acceleration due to gravity is greater.

Gravity is weaker on a mountaintop than at sea level because the mountaintop is farther from Earth's center.

Conservation Laws

In physics, laws of conservation state that in a closed system, where neither mass nor energy is added or subtracted, certain measurable quantities remain constant.

Conservation of Mass: Mass is neither created nor destroyed within a closed system except when converted to energy.

Conservation of Momentum: All moving objects have momentum, and in a closed system, total momentum is always conserved. Linear momentum is the product of the mass of an object and its velocity. In the following equation, M and V represent the initial total mass and velocity of objects within a closed system. After a collision between those objects, the mass and velocity of individual objects may change (for example, one object breaks into smaller pieces, each traveling at a different velocity), but the product of the total mass and velocity in the system after the collision (mv) will remain the same.

$$MV = mv$$

Any object moving in a circle has another kind of momentum—angular momentum. This is because circular motion requires acceleration toward the center of the circle. The amount of acceleration depends on the speed of the object and the square of the radius of the circle. (Angular momentum is the product of this speed, the mass of the object, and the square of the radius.)

Conservation of Energy: The total amount of energy in a closed system will not change except when converted to mass.

Conservation of Mass-Energy: Although mass and energy can be converted into one another, the total amount of mass and energy together must be conserved. This is reflected in Einstein's famous equation, where m is mass, E is energy, and c is the speed of light in a vacuum (which is constant):

$$E = mc^2$$

Relativistic mass can describe how mass increases with velocity. The following equation—where m is the mass of a moving object, m_0 is the object's mass when not moving, v is its velocity in relation to a stationary observer, and c is the speed of light—shows the relationship:

$$m = \frac{m_0}{\sqrt{1 - \dfrac{v^2}{c^2}}}$$

The theory that no object can travel faster than the speed of light is based in this equation. As an object approaches c, so much energy is converted to mass that it no longer accelerates.

Laws of Thermodynamics

1. Heat is a form of energy. Within a closed system energy must be conserved except in nuclear reactions or other extreme conditions. It is neither created nor destroyed.

2. Within a self-sustaining system, heat can never go from an area of low temperature to an area of high temperature, for this would require added energy. Without added energy, disorder, or entropy, can only increase.

3. Absolute zero cannot be attained by any procedure in a finite number of steps. Although it can be approached asymptotically, it can never be reached.

Laws of Current Electricity

Electric current generally represents the flow of electrons through a conductor. The rate at which electrons flow can be measured in amperes, defined as the number of electrons (measured in a unit called the coulomb, equal to about 6.24 quintillion or 6.24×10^{18} electrons) moving past a particular point every second. One ampere is equal to 1 coulomb of charge passing each second. Like water, electrons tend to move from areas of high pressure to low pressure. The difference between these two pressures is known as potential difference and is measured in volts.

Certain substances, such as copper and carbon, allow electric currents to pass more readily than others—that is, they have greater conductivity. Resistance to conductivity is measured in ohms.

Ohm's Law: Electric current is directly proportional to the potential difference and inversely proportional to the total resistance of the circuit. I is electric current (measured in amperes), V is the potential difference (measured in volts), and R is resistance (measured in ohms):

$$I = \frac{V}{R}$$

Law of Electric Power: Electric power (P), measured in watts, represents the rate at which electricity is converted into some other form of energy (such as light, in the case of a lightbulb). For a direct-current circuit, P is the product of current and potential difference:

$$P = IV$$

Two Basic Laws of Quantum Physics

1. Heisenberg's uncertainty principle: Certain pairs of observable quantities like energy and time or position and momentum cannot be measured with complete accuracy simultaneously. Also known as the indeterminacy principle.

2. Pauli's exclusion principle: Two electrons in an atom cannot simultaneously occupy the same quantum or energy state. This has since been shown to be true for many subatomic particles.

Breaking the Sound Barrier; Speed of Sound

The prefix **Mach** is used to describe supersonic speed. It was named for Ernst Mach (1838-1916), a Czech-born Austrian physicist. Mach may be defined as the ratio of the velocity of an object to the velocity of sound in a particular medium. A plane moving at the speed of sound moves at Mach 1. At twice the speed of sound, it moves at Mach 2.

When a plane passes the sound barrier—flying faster than sound travels—people in the area, though not the people on the plane, hear what seem to be thunderclaps. These sounds are sometimes called sonic booms.

Sound is produced by vibrations of an object and is transmitted by the alternating increase and decrease in pressure radiating outward through a material medium of molecules, like waves spreading out on a pond after a rock has been tossed in.

The **frequency of sound** is determined by the number of times the vibrating waves undulate per second and is measured in cycles per second. The slower the cycle of waves, the lower the frequency. As the frequency increases, the sound becomes higher in pitch. The human ear is sensitive to frequencies between 20 and 20,000 vibrations per second, although this range varies among individuals.

Intensity, or loudness, is the strength of the pressure of these radiating waves and is measured in decibels. (See Weights and Measures.)

The **speed of sound** varies depending on temperature and altitude. It moves faster in water than in air, for example. At sea level and a temperature of 59°F (15°C), the speed of sound is approximately 761 mph, or 1,100 ft per sec.

Light; Colors of the Spectrum

Light, a form of electromagnetic radiation similar to radiant heat, radio waves, and X-rays, is emitted from a source in straight lines and spreads out over larger areas as it travels. For emission from a point source, light per unit area diminishes in proportion to the square of the distance.

The English mathematician and physicist Isaac Newton (1642-1727) described light as an **emission of particles**; the Dutch astronomer, mathematician, and physicist Christiaan Huygens (1629-95) and others developed the theory that light travels in a **wave motion**. It is now believed that these two theories are essentially complementary. The development of quantum theory has led to results where light acts like a series of particles in some experiments and like a wave in others.

The first relatively accurate measurement of the **speed of light** in a laboratory experiment was made by the French physicist Armand Hippolyte Louis Fizeau (1819-96). Today the speed of light is known very precisely as 299,792.458 km per sec (or 186,282.397 mi per sec) in a vacuum. In water the speed of light is about 25% less, and in glass, 33% less.

Color sensations are produced through the excitation of the retina of the eye by light vibrating at different frequencies. The different colors of the spectrum may be seen by viewing light refracted by passage through a prism, which separates the light into its wavelengths.

Customarily, the basic colors are taken to be the six monochromatic (single) colors that occupy relatively large areas of the spectrum: red, orange, yellow, green, blue, and violet. So-called primary colors can be combined to produce the sensation of other colors. However, scientists disagree about how many and what primary colors to recognize. The color sensation of **black** is due to complete lack of stimulation of the retina, that of **white** to complete stimulation.

Infrared and **ultraviolet rays**, which are below the red (long) end and above the violet (short) end of the visible spectrum, respectively, are invisible to the naked eye. Heat is the principal effect of infrared rays, and chemical action that of ultraviolet rays.

Discoveries and Innovations: Biology, Chemistry, Medicine, Physics

Discovery	Date	Discoverer(s)	Nationality
Acetylene gas	1862	Berthelot	French
ACTH	1927	Evans, Long	U.S.
Adrenaline	1901	Takamine	Japanese
Aluminum, electrolytic process	1886	Hall	U.S.
Aluminum, isolated	1825	Oersted	Danish
Anesthesia, ether	1842	Long	U.S.
Anesthesia, local	1885	Koller	Austrian
Anesthesia, spinal	1898	Bier	German
Aniline dye	1856	Perkin	English
Anti-rabies	1885	Pasteur	French
Antiseptic surgery	1867	Lister	English
Antitoxin, diphtheria	1891	Von Behring	German
Argyrol	1897	Bayer	German
Arsphenamine	1910	Ehrlich	German
Aspirin	1853	Gerhardt	French
Atabrine	1932	Mietzsch, et al.	German
Atomic numbers	1913	Moseley	English
Atomic theory	1803	Dalton	English
Atomic time clock	1948	Lyons	U.S.
Atomic time clock, cesium beam	1948	Essen	English
Atom-smashing theory	1919	Rutherford	English
Bacitracin	1943	Johnson, Meleneyl	U.S.
Bacteria, description	1676	Leeuwenhoek	Dutch
Bleaching powder	1798	Tennant	English
Blood, circulation	1628	Harvey	English
Blood plasma storage (blood bank)	1940	Drew	U.S.
Bordeaux mixture	1885	Millardet	French
Bromine from the sea	1826	Balard	French
Calcium carbide	1888	Wilson	U.S.
Calculus	1670	Newton	English
Camphor synthetic	1896	Haller	French
Canning (food)	1804	Appert	French
Carbon oxides	1925	Fisher	German
Chemotherapy	1909	Ehrlich	German
Chloramphenicol	1947	Burkholder	U.S.
Chlorine	1774	Scheele	Swedish
Chloroform	1831	Guthrie, S.	U.S.
Chlortetracycline	1948	Duggen	U.S.
Classification of plants and animals	1735	Linnaeus	Swedish

Discovery	Date	Discoverer(s)	Nationality
Cloning, DNA	1973	Boyer, Cohen	U.S.
Cloning, mammal	1996	Wilmut, et al.	Scottish
Cocaine	1860	Niermann	German
Combustion explained	1777	Lavoisier	French
Conditioned reflex	1914	Pavlov	Russian
Cortisone	1936	Kendall	U.S.
Cortisone, synthesis	1946	Sarett	U.S.
Cosmic rays	1910	Gockel	Swiss
Cyanamide	1905	Frank, Caro	German
Cyclotron	1930	Lawrence	U.S.
DDT (not applied as insecticide until 1939)	1874	Zeidler	German
Deuterium	1932	Urey, Brickwedde, Murphy	U.S.
DNA (structure)	1953	Crick, Wilkins	English
		Watson	U.S.
Electric resistance, law of	1827	Ohm	German
Electric waves	1888	Hertz	German
Electrolysis	1852	Faraday	English
Electromagnetism	1819	Oersted	Danish
Electron	1897	Thomson, J.	English
Electron diffraction	1936	Thomson	English
		Davisson, G.	U.S.
Electroshock treatment	1938	Cerletti, Bini	Italian
Erythromycin	1952	McGuire	U.S.
Evolution, natural selection	1858	Darwin	English
Falling bodies, law of	1590	Galileo	Italian
Gases, law of combining volumes	1808	Gay-Lussac	French
Geometry, analytic	1619	Descartes	French
Gold, cyanide process for extraction	1887	MacArthur, Forest.	British
Gravitation, law	1687	Newton	English
HIV (human immuno-deficiency virus)	1984	Montagnier	French
		Gallo	U.S.
Holograph	1948	Gabor	British
Human heart transplant	1967	Barnard	S. African
Indigo, synthesis of	1880	Baeyer	German
Induction, electric	1830	Henry	U.S.
Insulin	1922	Banting, Best	Canadian
		Macleod	Scottish
Intelligence testing	1905	Binet, Simon	French
In vitro fertilization	1978	Steptoe, Edwards	English

Discovery	Date	Discoverer(s)	Nationality
Isotopes, theory	1912	Soddy	English
Laser	1957	Gould	U.S.
Light, velocity	1675	Roemer	Danish
Light, wave theory	1690	Huygens	Dutch
Lithography	1796	Senefelder	Bohemian
Logarithms	1614	Napier	Scottish
LSD-25	1943	Hoffman	Swiss
Mendelian laws	1866	Mendel	Austrian
Mercator projection (map)	1568	Mercator (Kremer)	Flemish
Methanol	1661	Boyle	Irish
Milk condensation	1853	Borden	U.S.
Molecular hypothesis	1811	Avogadro	Italian
Motion, laws of	1687	Newton	English
Neomycin	1949	Waksman, Lechevalier	U.S.
Neutrino	1956	Reines, Cowan	U.S.
Neutron	1932	Chadwick	English
Nitric acid	1648	Glauber	German
Nitric oxide	1772	Priestley	English
Nitroglycerin	1846	Sobrero	Italian
Oil cracking process	1891	Dewar	U.S.
Oxygen	1774	Priestley	English
Oxytetracycline	1950	Finlay, et al.	U.S.
Ozone	1840	Schonbein	German
Paper, sulfite process	1867	Tilghman	U.S.
Paper, wood pulp, sulfate process	1884	Dahl	German
Penicillin	1928	Fleming	Scottish
Penicillin, practical use	1941	Florey, Chain	English
Periodic law and table of elements	1869	Mendeleyev	Russian
Physostigmine synthesis	1935	Julian	U.S.
Pill, birth-control	1954	Pincus, Rock	U.S.
Planetary motion, laws	1609	Kepler	German
Plutonium fission	1940	Kennedy, Wahl, Seaborg, Segre	U.S.
Polymyxin	1947	Ainsworth	English
Positron	1932	Anderson	U.S.
Proton	1919	Rutherford	N. Zealand
Psychoanalysis	1900	Freud	Austrian
Pulsars	1967	Bell	English
Quantum theory	1900	Planck	German
Quasars	1963	Matthews, Sandage	U.S.
Quinine synthetic	1946	Woodward, Doering	U.S.
Radioactivity	1896	Becquerel	French
Radiocarbon dating	1947	Libby	U.S.
Radium	1898	Curie, Pierre	French
		Curie, Marie	Pol.-Fr.
Relativity theory	1905	Einstein	German
Reserpine	1949	Jal Vaikl	Indian

Discovery	Date	Discoverer(s)	Nationality
Schick test	1913	Schick	U.S.
Silicon	1823	Berzelius	Swedish
Smallpox eradication	1979	World Health Org.	UN
Streptomycin	1944	Waksman, et al.	U.S.
Sulfanilamide	1935	Bovet, Trefouel	French
Sulfanilamide theory	1908	Gelmo	German
Sulfapyridine	1938	Ewins, Phelps	English
Sulfathiazole	1939	Fosbinder, Walter	U.S.
Sulfuric acid	1831	Phillips	English
Sulfuric acid, lead	1746	Roebuck	English
Superconductivity	1911	Onnes	Dutch
Superconductivity theory	1957	Bardeen, Cooper, Schreiffer	U.S.
Superconductors, high-temp.	1986	Bednorz, Muller	Ger., Swiss
Syphilis test	1906	Wassermann	German
Transplant, heart	1967	Barnard	S. African
Tuberculin	1890	Koch	German
Uranium fission, atomic reactor	1942	Fermi, Szilard	U.S.
Uranium fission theory	1939	Hahn, Meitner, Strassmann	German
		Bohr	Danish
		Fermi	Italian
		Einstein, Pegram, Wheeler	U.S.
Vaccine, measles	1963	Enders	U.S.
Vaccine, measles-mumps-rubella	1971	Hilleman	U.S.
Vaccine, meningitis (first conjugate)	1987	Gordon, et al., Connaught Labs	U.S.
Vaccine, polio	1954	Salk	U.S.
Vaccine, polio, oral	1960	Sabin	U.S.
Vaccine, rabies	1885	Pasteur	French
Vaccine, smallpox	1796	Jenner	English
Vaccine, typhus	1909	Nicolle	French
Vaccine, varicella	1974	Takahashi	Japanese
Van Allen belts, radiation	1958	Van Allen	U.S.
Vitamin A	1913	McCollum, Davis	U.S.
Vitamin B	1916	McCollum	U.S.
Vitamin C	1928	Szent-Gyorgyi	Hungarian
		King	U.S.
Vitamin D	1922	McCollum	U.S.
Vitamin K	1935	Dam, Doisy	U.S.
Xerography	1938	Carlson	U.S.
X-ray	1895	Roentgen	German

Inventions

Invention	Date	Inventor(s)	Nationality
Adding machine	1642	Pascal	French
Adding machine	1885	Burroughs	U.S.
Aerosol spray	1926	Rotheim	Norwegian
Air brake	1868	Westinghouse	U.S.
Air conditioning	1902	Carrier	U.S.
Air pump	1654	Guericke	German
Airbag	1952	Hetrick	U.S.
Airplane, automatic pilot	1912	Sperry	U.S.
Airplane, experimental	1896	Langley	U.S.
Airplane, hydro	1911	Curtiss	U.S.
Airplane jet engine	1939	Ohain	German
Airplane with motor	1903	Wright Bros.	U.S.
Airship	1852	Giffard	French
Aqua-Lung	1943	Cousteau, Gagnan	French
Arc welder	1919	Thomson	U.S.
Aspartame	1965	Schlatter	U.S.
Autogyro	1920	de la Cierva	Spanish
Automobile, differential gear	1885	Benz	German
Automobile, electric	1892	Morrison	U.S.
Automobile, exp'mtl	1864	Marcus	Austrian
Automobile, gasoline	1889	Daimler	German
Automobile, gasoline	1892	Duryea	U.S.
Automobile magneto	1897	Bosch	German
Automobile muffler	1904	Pope	U.S.
Automobile self-starter	1911	Kettering	U.S.
Bakelite	1907	Baekeland	Belg., U.S.
Balloon	1783	Montgolfier	French
Barometer	1643	Torricelli	Italian
Bicycle, modern	1885	Starley	English
Bifocal lens	1780	Franklin	U.S.
Bottle machine	1895	Owens	U.S.
Braille printing	1829	Braille	French
Brassiere, modern	1913	Jacob	U.S
Bubble gum	1928	Diemer	U.S.
Burner, gas	1855	Bunsen	German
Calculating machine	1833	Babbage	English
Calculator, electronic pocket	1972	Merryman, Van Tassel	U.S.

Invention	Date	Inventor(s)	Nationality
Camera, digital	1977	Lloyd, Sasson	U.S.
Camera, Kodak	1888	Eastman, Walker	U.S.
Camera, Polaroid Land	1948	Land	U.S.
Can, pop-top	1959	Fraze	U.S.
Car coupler	1873	Janney	U.S.
Carburetor, gasoline	1893	Maybach	German
Carding machine	1797	Whittemore	U.S.
Carpet sweeper	1876	Bissell	U.S.
Cash register	1879	Ritty	U.S.
Cassette, audio	1963	Philips Co.	Dutch
Cassette, videotape	1969	Sony	Japanese
CAT, or CT, scan	1973	Hounsfield	English
Cathode-ray tube	1897	Braun	German
Cellophane	1908	Brandenberger	Swiss
Celluloid	1870	Hyatt	U.S.
Cement, Portland	1824	Aspdin	English
Chronometer	1735	Harrison	English
Circuit breaker	1925	Hilliard	U.S.
Circuit, integrated	1959	Kilby, Noyce, Texas Instr.	U.S.
Clock, pendulum	1657	Huygens	Dutch
Coaxial cable system	1929	Affel, Espensched	U.S.
Coca-Cola	1885	Pemberton	U.S.
Coffeemaker, automatic drip	1963	Bunn Corp.	U.S.
Compressed air rock drill	1871	Ingersoll	U.S.
Comptometer	1887	Felt	U.S.
Computer, automatic sequence	1944	Aiken, et al.	U.S.
Computer, electronic	1942	Atanasoff, Berry	U.S.
Computer, laptop	1987	Sinclair	English
Computer, mini	1960	Digital Corp.	U.S.
Condenser microphone (telephone)	1916	Wente	U.S.
Contact lens, corneal	1948	Tuohy	U.S.
Contraceptive, oral	1954	Pincus, Rock	U.S.
Corn, hybrid	1917	Jones	U.S.
Cotton gin	1793	Whitney	U.S.
Cream separator	1878	DeLaval	Swedish

Invention	Date	Inventor(s)	Nationality
Cultivator, disc	1878	Mallon	U.S.
Cyclotron	1931	Lawrence	U.S.
Cystoscope	1878	Nitze	German
Diapers, disposable	1950	Donovan	U.S.
Diesel engine	1895	Diesel	German
Disc, compact	1972	RCA	U.S.
Disc player, compact	1979	Sony, Philips Co.	Japanese, Dutch
Dishwasher	1893	Cochrane	U.S.
Disk, floppy	1970	IBM	U.S.
Disk, video	1972	Philips Co.	Dutch
Dynamite	1866	Nobel	Swedish
Dynamo, contin. current	1871	Gramme	Belgian
Electric battery	1800	Volta	Italian
Electric fan	1882	Wheeler	U.S.
Electrocardiograph	1903	Einthoven	Dutch
Electroencephalograph	1929	Berger	German
Electromagnet	1824	Sturgeon	English
Electronic paper (e-ink)	1974	Sheridon	U.S.
Electron microscope	1931	Ruska, Knoll	German
Electron spectrometer	1944	Deutsch, Elliott, Evans	U.S.
Electron tube multigrid	1913	Langmuir	U.S.
Electroplating	1805	Brugnatelli	Italian
Electrostatic generator	1929	Van de Graaff	U.S.
Elevator brake	1852	Otis	U.S.
Elevator, push button	1922	Larson	U.S.
Engine, automatic transmission	1910	Fottinger	German
Engine, coal-gas 4-cycle	1876	Otto	German
Engine, compression ignition	1883	Daimler	German
Engine, electric ignition	1883	Benz	German
Engine, gas, compound	1926	Eickemeyer	U.S.
Engine, gasoline	1872	Brayton, Geo.	U.S.
Engine, gasoline	1889	Daimler	German
Engine, jet	1930	Whittle	English
Engine, steam, piston	1705	Newcomen	English
Engine, steam, piston	1769	Watt	Scottish
Engraving, half-tone	1852	Talbot	English
Ferris wheel	1893	Ferris	U.S.
Fiberglass	1938	Owens-Corning	U.S.
Fiber optics	1955	Kapany	English
Fiber optic wire	1970	Keck, Maurer Schulz	U.S.
Filament, tungsten	1913	Coolidge	U.S.
Flanged rail	1831	Stevens	U.S.
Flatiron, electric	1882	Seely	U.S.
Food, frozen	1923	Birdseye	U.S.
Freon	1930	Midgley, et al.	U.S.
Furnace (for steel)	1858	Siemens	German
Galvanometer	1820	Sweigger	German
Garbage bag, polyethylene	1950	Wasylyk	Canadian
Gas discharge tube	1922	Hull	U.S.
Gas lighting	1792	Murdoch	Scottish
Gas mantle	1885	Welsbach	Austrian
Gasoline, cracked	1913	Burton	U.S.
Gasoline, high octane	1930	Ipatieff	Russian
Gasoline (lead ethyl)	1922	Midgley	U.S.
Geiger counter	1913	Geiger	German
Geodesic dome	1948	Fuller	U.S.
Glass, laminated safety	1909	Benedictus	French
Glider	1853	Cayley	English
Google search software	1996	Brin, Page	U.S.
Gun, breechloader	1811	Thornton	U.S.
Gun, Browning	1897	Browning	U.S.
Gun, magazine	1875	Hotchkiss	U.S.
Gun, silencer	1908	Maxim, H. P.	U.S.
Guncotton	1847	Schoenbein	German
Gyrocompass	1911	Sperry	U.S.
Gyroscope	1852	Foucault	French
Hard drive, computer	1955	Johnson	U.S.
Harvester-thresher	1818	Lane	U.S.
Heart, artificial	1982	Jarvik	U.S.
Helicopter	1939	Sikorsky	U.S.
Hovercraft	1955	Cockerell	English
Hydrometer	1768	Baume	French
Ice resurfacing machine	1949	Zamboni	U.S.
Iron lung	1928	Drinker, Slaw	U.S.
Jet Ski	1973	Jacobsen	U.S.
Kaleidoscope	1817	Brewster	Scottish
Kevlar	1965	Kwolek, Blades	U.S.
Kidney dialysis machine	1941	Kolff	Dutch
Kinetoscope	1889	Edison	U.S.
Lamp, arc	1847	Staite	English
Lamp, fluorescent	1938	General Electric, Westinghouse	U.S.

Invention	Date	Inventor(s)	Nationality
Lamp, incandescent	1879	Edison	U.S.
Lamp, incand., gas	1913	Langmuir	U.S.
Lamp, klieg	1911	Kliegl, A. and J.	U.S.
Lamp, mercury vapor	1912	Hewitt	U.S.
Lamp, miner's safety	1816	Davy	English
Lamp, neon	1909	Claude	French
Lathe, turret	1845	Fitch	U.S.
Launderette	1934	Cantrell	U.S.
Lens, achromatic	1758	Dollond	English
Lens, fused bifocal	1908	Borsch	U.S.
Leyden jar (condenser)	1745	von Kleist	German
Lightning rod	1752	Franklin	U.S.
Linoleum	1860	Walton	English
Linotype	1884	Mergenthaler	U.S.
Linux	1991	Torvalds	Finnish
Liquid Paper	c.1951	Graham	U.S.
Lock, cylinder	1851	Yale	U.S.
Locomotive, electric	1851	Vail	U.S.
Locomotive, exp'mtl	1802	Trevithick	English
Locomotive, exp'mtl	1812	Fenton, et al.	English
Locomotive, exp'mtl	1814	Stephenson	English
Locomotive, 1st U.S.	1830	Cooper, P.	U.S.
Locomotive, practical	1829	Stephenson	English
Loom, power	1785	Cartwright	English
Loudspeaker, dynamic	1924	Rice, Kellogg	U.S.
Machine gun	1862	Gatling	U.S.
Machine gun, improved	1872	Hotchkiss	U.S.
Machine gun (Maxim)	1883	Maxim, H. S.	U.S.-Eng.
Magnet, electro	1828	Henry	U.S.
Magnetic Resonance Imaging (MRI)	1971	Damadian	U.S.
Maser	1953	Townes	U.S.
Mason jar	1858	Mason, J.	U.S.
Match, friction	1827	Walker, J.	English
Mercerized textiles	1843	Mercer, J.	English
Meter, induction	1888	Shallenberger	U.S.
Metronome	1816	Malezel	German
Microcomputer	1973	Truong, et al.	French
Micrometer	1636	Gascoigne	English
Microphone	1877	Berliner	U.S.
Microprocessor	1971	Intel Corp.	U.S.
Microscope, compound	1590	Janssen	Dutch
Microscope, electronic	1931	Knoll, Ruska	German
Microscope, field ion	1951	Mueller	German
Microwave oven	1947	Spencer	U.S.
Monitor, warship	1861	Ericsson	U.S.
Monotype	1887	Lanston	U.S.
Motor, AC	1892	Tesla	U.S.
Motor, DC	1837	Davenport	U.S.
Motor, induction	1887	Tesla	U.S.
Motorcycle	1885	Daimler	German
Mouse, computer	1968	Engelbart	U.S.
Movie machine	1894	Jenkins	U.S.
Movie, panoramic	1952	Waller	U.S.
Movie, talking	1927	Warner Bros.	U.S.
Mower, lawn	1831	Budding, Ferrabee	English
Mowing machine	1822	Bailey	U.S.
Neoprene	1930	Carothers	U.S.
Nylon	1937	DuPont lab	U.S.
Oil cracking furnace	1891	Gavrilov	Russian
Oil filled power cable	1921	Emanueli	Italian
Oleomargarine	1869	Mege-Mouries	French
Ophthalmoscope	1851	Helmholtz	German
Pacemaker	1952	Zoll	U.S.
Pacemaker, implantable cardiac	1958	Greatbatch	U.S.
Paper	105	Ts'ai	Chinese
Paper clip	1900	Waaler	Norwegian
Paper machine	1809	Dickinson	U.S.
Parachute	1785	Blanchard	French
Pen, ballpoint	1888	Loud	U.S.
Pen, fountain	1884	Waterman	U.S.
Pen, steel	1780	Harrison	English
Pendulum	1583	Galileo	Italian
Percussion cap	1807	Forsythe	Scottish
Phonograph	1877	Edison	U.S.
Photo film, celluloid	1893	Reichenbach	U.S.
Photo film, transparent	1884	Eastman, Goodwin	U.S.
Photo, color	1892	Ives	U.S.
Photocopier	1938	Carlson	U.S.
Photoelectric cell	1895	Elster	German
Photographic paper	1835	Talbot	English
Photography	1816	Niepce	French
Photography	1835	Talbot	English
Photography	1835	Daguerre	French

Invention	Date	Inventor(s)	Nationality
Photophone	1880	Bell	U.S.-Scot.
Phototelegraphy	1925	Bell Labs	U.S.
Piano	1709	Cristofori	Italian
Piano, player	1863	Fourneaux	French
Pin, safety	1849	Hunt	U.S.
Pistol (revolver)	1836	Colt	U.S.
Plow, cast iron	1785	Ransome	English
Plow, disc	1896	Hardy	U.S.
Pneumatic hammer	1890	King	U.S.
Post-it note	1980	Fry, Silver	U.S.
Potato chip	1853	Crum	U.S.
Powder, smokeless	1884	Vieille	French
Printing press, rotary	1845	Hoe	U.S.
Printing press, web	1865	Bullock	U.S.
Propeller, screw	1804	Stevens	U.S.
Propeller, screw	1837	Ericsson	Swedish
Punch card accounting	1889	Hollerith	U.S.
Radar	1940	Watson-Watt	Scottish
Radio, magnetic detector	1902	Marconi	Italian
Radio, signals	1895	Marconi	Italian
Radio amplifier	1906	De Forest	U.S.
Radio beacon	1928	Donovan	U.S.
Radio crystal oscillator	1918	Nicolson	U.S.
Radio FM, 2-path	1933	Armstrong	U.S.
Radio receiver, cascade tuning	1913	Alexanderson	U.S.
Radio receiver, heterodyne	1913	Fessenden	Canadian
Radio transmitter triode modulation	1914	Alexanderson	U.S.
Radio tube diode	1904	Fleming	English
Radio tube oscillator	1915	De Forest	U.S.
Radio tube triode	1906	De Forest	U.S.
Rayon (acetate)	1895	Cross	English
Rayon (cuprammonium)	1890	Despeissis	French
Rayon (nitrocellulose)	1884	Chardonnet	French
Razor, electric	1917	Schick	U.S.
Razor, safety	1895	Gillette	U.S.
Reaper	1834	McCormick	U.S.
Record, cylinder	1887	Bell, Tainter	U.S.
Record, disc	1887	Berliner	U.S.
Record, long playing	1947	Goldmark	U.S.
Record, wax cylinder	1888	Edison	U.S.
Refrigerator car	1868	David	U.S.
Remote control	1898	Tesla	U.S.
Resin, synthetic	1931	Hill	English
Richter scale	1935	Richter	U.S.
Rifle, repeating	1860	Henry	U.S.
Rocket, liquid fuel	1926	Goddard	U.S.
Rollerblades	1980	Olson	U.S.
Rubber, vulcanized	1839	Goodyear	U.S.
Saccharin	1879	Remsen, Fahlberg	U.S.
Saw, circular	1777	Miller	English
Scotch tape	1930	Drew	U.S.
Seat belt	1959	Volvo	Swedish
Segway human transporter	2001	Kamen	U.S.
Seismograph	1880	Milne, Ewing, Gray	Eng.-Scot.
Sewing machine	1846	Howe	U.S.
Shoe-lasting machine	1883	Matzeliger	U.S.
Shoe-sewing machine	1860	McKay	U.S.
Shrapnel shell	1784	Shrapnel	English
Shuttle, flying	1733	Kay	English
Skates, in-line	1759	Merlin	Belgian
Sleeping-car	1865	Pullman	U.S.
Slide rule	1620	Oughtred	English
Slinky	1943	James	U.S.
Smoke detector	1969	Smith, House	U.S.
Soap, hardwater	1928	Bertsch	German
Spectroscope	1859	Kirchoff, Bunsen	German
Spectroscope (mass)	1918	Dempster	U.S.
Spinning jenny	c.1764	Hargreaves	English
Spinning mule	1779	Crompton	English
Steam car	1770	Cugnot	French
Steam turbine	1884	Parsons	English
Steamboat, exp'mtl	1778	Jouffroy	French
Steamboat, exp'mtl	1785	Fitch	U.S.
Steamboat, exp'mtl	1787	Rumsey	U.S.
Steamboat, exp'mtl	1803	Fulton	U.S.
Steamboat, exp'mtl	1804	Stevens	U.S.
Steamboat, practical	1802	Symington	Scottish
Steamboat, practical	1807	Fulton	U.S.
Steel (converter)	1856	Bessemer	English

Invention	Date	Inventor(s)	Nationality
Steel alloy	1891	Harvey	U.S.
Steel alloy, high-speed	1901	Taylor, White	U.S.
Steel, manganese	1884	Hadfield	English
Steel, stainless	1916	Brearley	English
Stereoscope	1838	Wheatstone	English
Stethoscope	1819	Laennec	French
Stethoscope, binaural	1840	Cammann	U.S.
Stock ticker	1870	Edison	U.S.
Storage battery, rechargeable	1859	Plante	French
Stove, electric	1896	Hadaway	U.S.
Submarine	1891	Holland	U.S.
Submarine, even keel	1894	Lake	U.S.
Submarine, torpedo	1776	Bushnell	U.S.
Synthesizer	1964	Moog	U.S.
Tank, military	1914	Swinton	English
Tape recorder, magnetic	1899	Poulsen	Danish
Teflon	1938	Du Pont	U.S.
Telegraph, magnetic	1837	Morse	U.S.
Telegraph, quadruplex	1864	Edison	U.S.
Telegraph, railroad	1887	Woods	U.S.
Telegraph, wireless high frequency	1895	Marconi	Italian
Telephone[1]	1871	Meucci	U.S.-Italian
Telephone[1]	1876	Bell	U.S.-Scot.
Telephone amplifier	1912	De Forest	U.S.
Telephone answering machine (1st practical)	1954	Hashimoto	Japanese
Telephone, automatic	1891	Strowger	U.S.
Telephone, cellular	1947	Bell Labs	U.S.
Telephone, cordless[2]	1950	Gross	U.S.
Telephone, radio	1900	Poulsen	Danish
		Fessenden	Canadian
Telephone, radio	1906	De Forest	U.S.
Telephone, radio, long dist.	1915	AT&T	U.S.
Telephone, recording	1898	Poulsen	Danish
Telescope	1608	Lippershey	Dutch
Telescope	1609	Galileo	Italian
Telescope, astronomical	1611	Kepler	German
Telescope, reflecting	1668	Newton	English
Teletype	1928	Morkrum, Kleinschmidt	U.S.
Television, color	1928	Baird	Scottish
Television, electronic	1927	Farnsworth	U.S.
Television, iconoscope	1923	Zworykin	U.S.
Television, mech. scanner	1923	Baird	Scottish
Tesla Coil	1891	Tesla	U.S.
Thermometer	1593	Galileo	Italian
Thermometer	1730	Reaumur	French
Thermometer, mercury	1714	Fahrenheit	German
Time recorder	1890	Bundy	U.S.
Tire, double-tube	1845	Thomson	Scottish
Tire, pneumatic	1888	Dunlop	Scottish
Toaster, automatic	1918	Strite	U.S.
Toilet, flush	1589	Harington	English
Tool, pneumatic	1865	Law	English
Torpedo, marine	1804	Fulton	U.S.
Tractor, crawler	1904	Holt	U.S.
Transformer, AC	1885	Stanley	U.S.
Transistor	1947	Shockley, Brattain, Bardeen	U.S.
Trolley car, electric	1884-87	Van DePoele, Sprague	U.S.
Tungsten, ductile	1912	Coolidge	U.S.
Tupperware®	1945	Tupper	U.S.
Turbine, gas	1849	Bourdin	French
Turbine, hydraulic	1849	Francis	U.S.
Turbine, steam	1884	Parsons	English
Type, movable	1447	Gutenberg	German
Typewriter	1867	Sholes, Soule, Glidden	U.S.
Universal Serial Bus (USB)	1994	Bhatt et al.	U.S.
Vacuum cleaner, electric	1907	Spangler	U.S.
Vacuum evaporating pan	1846	Rillieux	U.S.
Velcro	1948	de Mestral	Swiss
Video game ("Pong")	1972	Bushnell	U.S.
Video home system (VHS)	1975	Matsushita, JVC	Japanese

Invention	Date	Inventor(s)	Nationality	Invention	Date	Inventor(s)	Nationality
Vinyl	1926	Semon	U.S.	Windshield wiper	1903	Anderson	U.S.
Washer, electric	1901	Fisher	U.S.	Wind tunnel	1912	Eiffel	French
Welding, atomic hydrogen	1924	Langmuir, Palmer	U.S.	Wire, barbed	1874	Glidden	U.S.
Welding, electric	1877	Thomson	U.S.	World Wide Web	1989	Berners-Lee	English
Wheelchair, multiterrain	1986	Twitchell	U.S.	Wrench, double-acting	1913	Owen	U.S.
Wheelchair, stair-climbing	1962	Blanco	U.S.	X-ray tube	1913	Coolidge	U.S.
Wiki software	1995	Cunningham	U.S.	Zeppelin	1900	Zeppelin	German
				Zipper, early model	1893	Judson	U.S.
				Zipper, improved	1913	Sundback	Canadian

(1) While Alexander Graham Bell has traditionally been credited with invention of the telephone, which he patented, Antonio Meucci developed a working model before Bell. (2) Al Gross held a number of important early patents in the field of wireless communication; other people were also involved in the development of practical cordless telephones.

U.S. Patent-Receiving Corporations, 2011

Source: U.S. Patent and Trademark Office, U.S. Dept. of Commerce

(ranked by number of patents granted)

Rank	Company	No. of patents	Rank	Company	No. of patents
1.	International Business Machines Corp.	6,148	11.	LG Electronics Inc.	1,404
2.	Samsung Electronics Co., Ltd.	4,868	12.	Fujitsu Limited.	1,382
3.	Canon Kabushiki Kaisha.	2,818	13.	Hewlett-Packard Development Company, L.P.	1,307
4.	Panasonic Corp.	2,533	14.	Ricoh Company, Ltd.	1,246
5.	Toshiba Corp.	2,451	15.	Intel Corp.	1,244
6.	Microsoft Corp.	2,309	16.	Broadcom Corp.	1,164
7.	Sony Corp.	2,265	17.	GM Global Technology Operations, Inc.	1,092
8.	Seiko Epson Corp.	1,525	18.	Renesas Electronics Corp.	984
9.	Hitachi, Ltd	1,455	19.	Cisco Technology, Inc.	979
10.	General Electric Co.	1,444	20.	Fujifilm Corp.	963

Note: Reflects patent ownership at time of patent grant. Changes may occur after patent grant. Where more than one assignee exists, patents are attributed to first-named assignee.

U.S. Patents by Country, 2011

Source: U.S. Patent and Trademark Office, U.S. Dept. of Commerce

Rank	Country	Patents	% change, 2010-11	Share of total issued	Rank	Country	Patents	% change, 2010-11	Share of total issued
1.	Japan	46,139	3.0%	20.6%	7.	UK	4,307	0.1%	1.9%
2.	South Korea	12,262	5.1	5.5	8.	China	3,174	19.5	1.4
3.	Germany	11,920	−3.6	5.3	9.	Israel	1,981	8.9	0.9
4.	Taiwan	8,781	6.6	3.9	10.	Australia	1,919	9.8	0.9
5.	Canada	5,012	3.3	2.2		United States	108,626	0.8	48.4
6.	France	4,531	1.8	2.0		All countries	224,505	2.2	100.0

Note: Country of origin is determined by residence of first-named inventor in patent.

U.S. Patents by Category, 1991-2011

Source: U.S. Patent and Trademark Office, U.S. Dept. of Commerce

(ranked by number of patents issued in 2011)

Rank	Category	Pre-1991	1991	2000	2010	2011	% change, 1991-2011
1.	Multiplex Communications	3,402	362	1,832	7,415	7,720	2,032.6%
2.	Active Solid-State Devices (e.g., Transistors, Solid-State Diodes)	5,576	1,245	2,716	6,901	7,028	464.5
3.	Semiconductor Device Manufacturing: Process	5,474	802	4,486	6,143	5,909	636.8
4.	Telecommunications	2,784	291	1,876	4,311	5,578	1,816.8
5.	Electrical Computers and Digital Processing Systems: Multicomputer Data Transferring	302	56	1,161	4,647	4,877	8,608.9
6.	Drug, Bio-Affecting and Body Treating Compositions	23,801	2,533	3,949	4,712	4,597	81.5
7.	Data Processing: Database and File Management or Data Structures	278	54	849	4,452	4,245	7,761.1
8.	Data Processing: Financial, Business Practice, Management, or Cost/Price Determination	726	96	735	4,056	4,062	4,131.2
9.	Image Analysis	1,960	475	1,245	3,370	3,744	688.2
10.	Chemistry: Molecular Biology and Microbiology	7,331	970	3,451	3,711	3,733	284.8
11.	Computer Graphics Processing and Selective Visual Display Systems	3,076	402	1,635	3,321	3,525	776.9
12.	Pulse or Digital Communications	2,962	439	1,346	3,024	3,073	600.0
13.	Drug, Bio-Affecting and Body Treating Compositions	7,756	1,145	2,788	2,843	2,899	153.2
14.	Television	7,158	824	1,036	2,338	2,779	237.3
15.	Static Information Storage and Retrieval	4,007	495	1,929	2,738	2,764	458.4
16.	Stock Material or Miscellaneous Articles	17,113	1,698	2,772	2,497	2,757	62.4
17.	Electricity: Electrical Systems and Devices	6,746	592	1,391	2,498	2,602	339.5
18.	Recording, Communication, or Information Retrieval Equipment	5,021	792	1,564	2,698	2,458	210.4
19.	Error Detection/Correction and Fault Detection/Recovery	2,711	284	986	2,385	2,379	737.7
20.	Communications: Electrical	7,130	659	1,542	2,209	2,297	248.6

Geologic Time Scale

Our understanding of Earth's ancient history is largely a result of geoscientists' study of climate, rock strata, ice samples, mineral deposits, and fossils from around the world; clues to the planet's origin have also been found through the study of extraterrestrial bodies. Geologists divide Earth's history into the following units (MYA = million years ago):

PRECAMBRIAN TIME (4,600-541 MYA)

HADEAN EON (4,600-4,000 MYA) Earth has no continents, oceans, or life; surface conditions are defined by intense volcanic activity and widespread meteorite impact. Oldest known minerals and rocks, many of meteoric origin, date to this era.

ARCHEAN EON (4,000-2,500 MYA) Earth's surface cools and water vapor in atmosphere condenses to form early oceans, which define small protocontinents; the first single-celled organisms, bacteria and archaea, appear in these oceans.

PROTEROZOIC EON (2,500-541 MYA) Protocontinents merge into larger landmasses as Earth's crust continues to shift. Atmospheric oxygen levels increase, and first known multicellular life appears. Later, soft-bodied marine animals emerge.

PHANEROZOIC EON (541 MYA-present)

Paleozoic Era (541-251 MYA)

Cambrian Period (541-485 MYA) The supercontinent known as Gondwana, or Gondwanaland, dominates the Southern Hemisphere. Seas experience an explosion of invertebrate animal life, including thousands of species of trilobites, and the first known vertebrates appear. There is no life on land.

Ordovician Period (485-443 MYA) Gondwanaland extends from South Pole to tropic regions; Northern Hemisphere is mostly open ocean. Average global temperatures are warmer than present era. First primitive land plants, early ancestors of starfish and mollusks, and first armored, jawless fishes appear. The period ends in extinction of a majority of species, possibly a result of a global drop in sea level due to glaciation.

Silurian Period (443-419 MYA) South Pole remains covered by supercontinent, but precursors of present-day N America, Europe, and Asia coalesce around the equator and middle latitudes. Appearance of first known vascular land plants, first freshwater fish, first jawed fish, first coral reefs, and first air-breathing animals (certain eurypterids, a scorpion-like creature).

Devonian Period (419-359 MYA) Collisions between Gondwanaland and ancestral landmasses of N America and Eurasia produce mountains visible today as northern Appalachians. Newly-formed ozone layer offers protection from sun's rays, allowing first air-breathing spiders and mites to appear on dry land; emergence of fish with fins and scales and first amphibians.

Carboniferous Period (359-299 MYA) Precursors of modern N America and Northern Europe lie in tropical latitudes north of the equator; warm and humid conditions there facilitate spread of lush forests and peat swamps that later form most of the world's coal and limestone. Later period sees emergence of first true conifers, Lepidodendrales ("scale trees") as tall as 100 ft, and first true reptiles.

Permian Period (299-252 MYA) All major landmasses collide to form the supercontinent Pangaea, surrounded by the world ocean Panthalassa. Gradual warming through much of the Permian allows for initial flourishing of species—including dinosaur precursors (up to 10 ft in length) and marine species in shallow inland seas. The period ended with a mass extinction of as much as 95% of all marine species and most land species.

Mesozoic Era (252-66 MYA)

Triassic Period (252-201 MYA) Pangea separates into supercontinents of Laurasia and Gondwana; subtropical conditions extend as far north as present-day Wyoming and New England. Emergence of icthyosaurs and plesiosaurs (large marine reptiles), several species of dinosaurs (up to 15 ft long), first true mammals, and first insects to undergo metamorphosis from larva to pupa to adult.

Jurassic Period (201-145 MYA) N American continent drifts westward, opening Gulf of Mexico; rift forms between S America and Africa. Warm, moist climate contributes to flourishing of coral reefs and temperate and subtropical forests. Appearance of first angiosperms (flowering plants), pterosaurs (winged reptiles), the earliest known birds, and huge dinosaurs such as the carnivorous *Allosaurus* and herbivorous *Apatosaurus*.

Cretaceous Period (145-66 MYA) African continental plate drifts north, creating roots of European Alps; gap between S America and Africa broadens; western movement of N America drives formation of Sierra Nevada and Rocky Mountains, turning the western interior of continent into a vast swamp. Later, sea levels rise and cover about one-third of Earth's present land area; global climate is warm and mild. The period ends in a mass extinction of plant and animal species (including dinosaurs), likely caused by the impact of one or more asteroids or comet fragments.

Cenozoic Era (66 MYA-present)

Paleogene Period (66-23 MYA)

• Paleocene Epoch (66-56 MYA) Australia begins to separate from Antarctica; N America and Greenland begin to spread apart. Mammalian life predominates, including early marsupials, insectivores, creodonts (carnivorous relatives of cats and dogs), and primitive hoofed mammals.

• Eocene Epoch (56-33.9 MYA) Australia drifts farther from Antarctica; the Indian subcontinent becomes welded to Asia, and tectonic forces drive the upheaval of the Alpine-Himalayan system. Climate in N America and Europe is subtropical and moist, with temperate forests as far north as Greenland and Siberia. Ancestors of modern horses, elephants, rhinoceroses, camels, bats, primates, and squirrel-like rodents emerge; earliest known marine mammals appear in later Eocene.

• Oligocene Epoch (33.9-23 MYA) San Andreas fault develops between N American and Pacific plates. Mammalian species continue to diversify, producing modern horse and multiple rodent, camel, and rhinoceros-like species, as well as first known species of great ape. Long-term cooling trend begins that would later cause Pleistocene ice ages.

Neogene Period (23 MYA-2.6 MYA)

• Miocene Epoch (23-5.3 MYA) Crustal plate collisions continue to drive uplift of Alps, Himalayas, and Cordilleran Ranges in Americas; eroded sediment is deposited in shallow marine basins, forming reservoirs for oil fields of California, Romania, and Caspian Sea. Ocean currents prevent Antarctica from receiving warmer waters, fostering growth of Antarctic ice sheet; northern forests become grassy prairies. Large apes related to the orangutan live in Asia and southern Europe; oldest hominid fossils from Africa date to this epoch.

• Pliocene Epoch (5.3-2.6 MYA) Alps continue to rise in Europe, and subduction of the Pacific tectonic plate elevates the Sierra Nevada and volcanic Cascade Range. Climate becomes cooler and drier, driving formation of permanent Arctic ice cap. Rapid primate evolution produces *Australopithecus*, earliest direct ancestor of *Homo sapiens*.

Quarternary Period (2.6 MYA-present)

• Pleistocene Epoch (2.6 MYA-11,700 years ago) Glacier ice covers as much as 25% or more of Earth's land surface, carving numerous present-day features including the Great Lakes; increased rainfall in lower latitudes allows plant and animal life to flourish in northern and eastern Africa. Late Pleistocene brings worldwide extinction of many large mammals, including the mastodon, saber-toothed tiger, and ground sloth. Evidence of Neanderthals dates from the latter part of the Pleistocene.

• Holocene Epoch (11,700 years ago to present-day) Melting ice caused sea levels to rise 100 ft or more in early Holocene, covering large areas of land and extending continental shelf of N America. Humans proliferate, and civilization begins.

Classification

Source: *Funk & Wagnalls New Encyclopedia*

In biology, classification is the identification, naming, and grouping of organisms into a formal system. The two fields that are most directly concerned with classification are taxonomy and systematics. Although they overlap, taxonomy is more concerned with nomenclature (naming) and with constructing hierarchical systems, and systematics with uncovering evolutionary relationships. Two kingdoms of living forms, Plantae and Animalia, have been recognized since Aristotle established the first taxonomy in the 4th century BCE. Plants and animals are examples of eukaryotes; their cells have nuclei bound by membranes. Two other kingdoms of eukaryotes that have been identified are Protista (one-celled organisms) and Fungi. The single-celled bacteria and archaea lack such nuclei. They are referred to as prokaryotes (or procaryotes) and are commonly placed in separate kingdoms. The seven basic categories of classification (from most general to most specific) are kingdom, phylum (or division), class, order, family, genus, and species. (In addition, many scientists group all eukaryotes together in a single "domain." The bacteria and archaea are also often treated as separate domains.) Below are two examples of classification:

ZOOLOGICAL HIERARCHY

Kingdom	Phylum	Class	Order	Family	Genus	Species name	Common name
Animalia	Chordata	Mammalia	Primates	Hominidae	*Homo*	*Homo sapiens*	Human

BOTANICAL HIERARCHY

Kingdom	Division*	Class	Order	Family	Genus	Species name	Common name
Plantae	Magnoliophyta	Magnoliopsida	Magnoliales	Magnoliaceae	*Magnolia*	*M. virginiana*	Sweet Bay

*In botany, the division is generally used in place of the phylum.

Gestation, Longevity, and Incubation of Selected Animals

Information reviewed by Ronald M. Nowak, author of *Walker's Mammals of the World* (6th ed., Johns Hopkins University Press, 1999). Average longevity figures supplied by Ronald T. Reuther. These apply to animals in captivity; the potential life span of animals is rarely attained in nature. Figures on gestation and incubation are averages based on estimates.

Animal	Gestation (days)	Average longevity (yrs.)	Maximum longevity (yrs.-mos.)	Animal	Gestation (days)	Average longevity (yrs.)	Maximum longevity (yrs.-mos.)
Ass	365	12	47	Leopard	98	12	23
Baboon	187	20	45	Lion	100	15	30
Bear (black)	219	18	36-10	Monkey (rhesus)	166	15	37
Bear (grizzly)	225	25	50	Moose	240	12	27
Bear (polar)	240	20	45	Mouse (domestic white)	19	3	6
Beaver	105	5	50	Mouse (meadow)	21	3	4
Bison	285	15	40	Opossum (American)	13	1	5
Camel	406	12	50	Pig (domestic)	112	10	27
Cat (domestic)	63	12	38	Puma	90	12	20
Chimpanzee	230	20	60	Rabbit (domestic)	31	5	18-10
Chipmunk	31	6	10	Rhinoceros (black)	450	15	45-10
Cow	284	15	30	Rhinoceros (white)	480	20	50
Deer (white-tailed)	201	8	20	Sea lion (California)	350	12	34
Dog (domestic)	61	12	21	Sheep (domestic)	154	12	23
Elephant (African)	660	35	70	Squirrel (gray)	44	10	23-6
Elephant (Asian)	645	40	77	Tiger	105	16	26-3
Elk	250	15	26-8	Wolf (maned)	63	5	15-8
Fox (red)	52	7	14	Zebra (Grant's)	365	15	50
Giraffe	457	10	36-2				
Goat (domestic)	151	8	18			**Incubation time (days)**	
Gorilla	258	20	54	Chicken			21
Guinea pig	68	4	8	Duck			30
Hippopotamus	238	41	61	Goose			30
Horse	330	20	50	Pigeon			18
Kangaroo (gray)	36	7	24	Turkey			26

Major Venomous Animals

Snakes

Asian pit viper—2 ft to 5 ft long; throughout Asia; reactions and mortality vary, but most bites cause tissue damage, and mortality is generally low.

Australian brown snake—4 ft to 7 ft long; very slow onset of cardiac or respiratory distress; moderate mortality, but because death can be sudden and unexpected, it is the most dangerous of the Australian snakes; antivenom.

Barba Amarilla or fer-de-lance—up to 7 ft long; from tropical Mexico to Brazil; severe tissue damage common; moderate mortality; antivenom.

Black mamba—up to 14 ft long, fast-moving; S and central Africa; rapid onset of dizziness, difficulty breathing, erratic heartbeat; mortality high, nears 100% without antivenom.

Boomslang—less than 6 ft long; African savannahs; rapid onset of nausea and dizziness, often followed by slight recovery and then sudden death from internal hemorrhaging; bites rare, mortality high; antivenom.

Bushmaster—up to 12 ft long; wet tropical forests of Central and S America; few bites occur, but mortality rate is high.

Common, or Asian, cobra—4 ft to 8 ft long; throughout southern Asia; considerable tissue damage, sometimes paralysis; mortality probably not more than 10%; antivenom.

Copperhead—less than 4 ft long; from New England to Texas; pain and swelling; very seldom fatal; antivenom seldom needed.

Coral snake—2 ft to 5 ft long; in Americas south of Canada; bite may be painless; slow onset of paralysis, impaired breathing; mortalities rare, but high without antivenom and mechanical respiration.

Cottonmouth water moccasin—up to 5 ft long; wetlands of southern U.S. from Virginia to Texas; rapid onset of severe pain, swelling; mortality low, but tissue destruction can be extensive; antivenom.

Death adder—less than 3 ft long; Australia; rapid onset of faintness, cardiac and respiratory distress; at least 50% mortality without antivenom.

Desert horned viper—up to 2 ft long; dry areas of Africa and western Asia; swelling and tissue damage; low mortality; antivenom.

European viper—1 ft to 3 ft long; throughout Europe; bleeding and tissue damage; mortality low; antivenom.

Gaboon viper—more than 6 ft long, fat, 2-in. fangs; S of the Sahara; massive tissue damage, internal bleeding; few recorded bites.

King cobra—up to 16 ft long; throughout southern Asia; rapid swelling, dizziness, loss of consciousness, difficulty breathing, erratic heartbeat; mortality varies sharply with amount of venom involved, but most bites involve nonfatal amounts; antivenom.

Krait—up to 5 ft long; SE Asia; rapid onset of sleepiness, numbness; up to 50% mortality even with use of antivenom.

Puff adder—up to 5 ft long, fat; S of the Sahara, throughout the Middle East; rapid large swelling, great pain, dizziness; moderate mortality, often from internal bleeding; antivenom.

Rattlesnake—2 ft to 6 ft long; throughout W Hemisphere; rapid onset of severe pain, swelling; mortality low, but amputation of affected digits is sometimes necessary; antivenom. Mojave rattler may produce temporary paralysis.

Ringhals, or spitting, cobra—5 ft to 7 ft long; southern Africa; squirts venom through holes in front of fangs as a defense; venom is severely irritating, can cause blindness.

Russell's viper or tic-polonga—more than 5 ft long; throughout Asia; internal bleeding; bite reports common; moderate mortality rate; antivenom.

Saw-scaled, or carpet, viper—up to 2 ft long; dry areas from India to Africa; severe bleeding, fever; high mortality, causes more human fatalities than any other snake; antivenom.

Sea snakes—3 ft to 10 ft long; throughout Pacific, Indian Oceans except NE Pacific; almost painless bite; variety of muscle pain, paralysis; mortality rate low, many bites not envenomed; some antivenoms.

Sharp-nosed pit viper or one hundred pace snake—up to 5 ft long; S Vietnam, Taiwan, and China; the most toxic of Asian pit vipers; very rapid onset of swelling and tissue damage, internal bleeding; moderate mortality; antivenom.

Taipan—up to 11 ft long; Australia and New Guinea; rapid paralysis with severe breathing difficulty; mortality nears 100% without antivenom.

Tiger snake—2 ft to 6 ft long; S Australia; pain, numbness, mental disturbances with rapid paralysis; may be deadliest of all land snakes, but antivenom is quite effective.

Yellow, or cape, cobra—7 ft long; southern Africa; most toxic venom of any cobra; rapid onset of swelling, breathing and cardiac difficulties; mortality is high without treatment; antivenom.

Note: Not all bites by venomous snakes are actually envenomed. Any animal bite, however, carries the danger of tetanus, and anyone suffering a venomous snake bite should seek medical attention. Antivenoms do not cure; they are only an aid in the treatment of bites. Mortality rates above are for envenomed bites; low mortality, c. 2% or less; moderate, 2%-5%; high, 5%-15%.

Lizards

Gila monster—up to 24 in. long, with heavy body and tail; in high desert in SW U.S. and N Mexico; immediate severe pain and transient low blood pressure; no recent mortality.

Mexican beaded lizard—similar to Gila monster; Mexican west coast; reaction and mortality rate similar to Gila monster.

Insects

Ants, bees, wasps, hornets—global distribution; usual reaction is piercing pain in area of sting; not directly fatal, except in cases of massive multiple stings, though many people suffer allergic reactions—swelling and rashes—and a few may die within minutes from severe sensitivity to the venom (anaphylactic shock).

Spiders, scorpions

Black widow—small, round-bodied with red hourglass marking; the widow and its relatives are found in tropical and temperate zones; severe musculoskeletal pain, weakness, breathing difficulty, convulsions; may be more serious in small children; low mortality; antivenom. The **redback** spider of Australia has the hourglass marking on its back, rather than on its front, but is otherwise identical to the black widow.

Brown recluse, or fiddleback, spider—small, oblong body; throughout U.S.; pain with later ulceration, which may last months, at place of bite; in severe cases fever, nausea, and stomach cramps; very low mortality.

Funnel web spider—several varieties, often large; Australia; slow onset of breathing, circulation difficulties; low mortality; antivenom.

Scorpion—crablike body with stinger in tail, various sizes; many varieties throughout tropical and subtropical areas; symptoms may include severe pain spreading from the wound, numbness, severe agitation, cramps; severe reaction may include respiratory failure; low mortality, usually in children; antivenoms.

Tarantula—large, hairy spider found around the world; the American tarantula, and probably all other tarantulas, are harmless to humans, though their bite may cause some pain and swelling.

Sea life

Cone-shell—mollusk in small shell; S Pacific and Indian Oceans; shoots barbs into victims; paralysis; low mortality.

Octopus—global distribution, usually in warm waters; rapid onset of paralysis with breathing difficulty; all varieties produce venom, but only a few can cause death.

Portuguese man-of-war—jellyfish-like, with tentacles up to 100 ft long; in most warm water areas; immediate severe pain; not directly fatal, though shock may cause death in rare cases.

Sea wasp—jellyfish, with tentacles up to 30 ft long; S Pacific; very rapid onset of circulatory problems; high mortality because of speed of toxic reaction; antivenom.

Stingray—several varieties of differing sizes; tropical and temperate seas and some freshwater; severe pain, rapid onset of nausea, vomiting, breathing difficulties; wound area may ulcerate, gangrene may appear; seldom fatal.

Stonefish—brownish fish that lies motionless on bottom of shallow waters; throughout S Pacific and Indian Oceans; extraordinary pain, rapid paralysis; low mortality; antivenom available, amount determined by number of puncture wounds; warm water relieves pain.

Speeds of Selected Animals

Source: *Natural History* magazine. © American Museum of Natural History

Animal	mph	Animal	mph	Animal	mph
Cheetah	70	Mongolian wild ass	40	Human	27.89
Pronghorn antelope	61	Greyhound	39.35	Elephant	25
Wildebeest	50	Whippet	35.50	Black mamba snake	20
Lion	50	Rabbit (domestic)	35	Six-lined race runner (lizard)	18
Thomson's gazelle	50	Mule deer	35	Wild turkey	15
Quarterhorse	47.5	Jackal	35	Squirrel	12
Elk	45	Reindeer	32	Pig (domestic)	11
Cape hunting dog	45	Giraffe	32	Chicken	9
Coyote	43	White-tailed deer	30	Spider (*Tegenaria atrica*)	1.17
Gray fox	42	Wart hog	30	Giant tortoise	0.17
Hyena	40	Grizzly bear	30	Three-toed sloth	0.15
Zebra	40	Cat (domestic)	30	Garden snail	0.03

Note: Most of these measurements are for maximum speeds over approximate quarter-mile distances. Exceptions are the lion and elephant, whose speeds were clocked in the act of charging; the whippet, which was timed over a 200-yd course; the cheetah, timed over a 100-yd distance; a human, timed over a 15-yd segment of a 100-yd run; and the black mamba, six-lined race runner, spider, giant tortoise, three-toed sloth, and garden snail, which were measured over various small distances.

Top American Kennel Club Breed Registrations, 2001-11

Source: American Kennel Club (AKC)

Breed	Rank 2011	2010	2006	2001	Breed	Rank 2011	2010	2006	2001
Labrador Retrievers	1	1	1	1	Chihuahuas	14	13	11	9
German Shepherd Dogs	2	2	3	3	German Shorthaired Pointers	15	16	20	22
Beagles	3	4	5	5	Siberian Huskies	16	18	25	21
Golden Retrievers	4	5	4	2	Pomeranians	17	15	14	12
Yorkshire Terriers	5	3	2	6	French Bulldogs	18	21	36	64
Bulldogs	6	6	12	19	Great Danes	19	17	24	28
Boxers	7	7	7	8	Shetland Sheepdogs	20	19	19	16
Poodles	8	9	8	7	Cavalier King Charles Spaniels	21	23	27	44
Dachshunds	9	8	6	4	Boston Terriers	22	20	15	18
Rottweilers	10	11	17	11	Maltese	23	22	18	20
Shih Tzu	11	10	9	10	Australian Shepherds	24	26	34	35
Miniature Schnauzers	12	12	10	13	Pembroke Welsh Corgis	25	27	22	26
Doberman Pinschers	13	14	21	24					

Dog Breeds by Type

Source: American Kennel Club (AKC)

The AKC currently recognizes 175 breeds and uses the following seven groups to classify breeds, according to functions and other distinctive traits.

Herding Group: Australian Cattle Dog, Australian Shepherd, Bearded Collie, Beauceron, Belgian Malinois, Belgian Sheepdog, Belgian Tervuren, Border Collie, Bouvier des Flandres, Briard, Canaan Dog, Cardigan Welsh Corgi, Collie, Entlebucher Mountain Dog, Finnish Lapphund, German Shepherd Dog, Icelandic Sheepdog, Norwegian Buhund, Old English Sheepdog, Pembroke Welsh Corgi, Polish Lowland Sheepdog, Puli, Pyrenean Shepherd, Shetland Sheepdog, Swedish Vallhund.

Hound Group: Afghan Hound, American English Coonhound, American Foxhound, Basenji, Basset Hound, Beagle, Black and Tan Coonhound, Bloodhound, Bluetick Coonhound, Borzoi, Dachshund, English Foxhound, Greyhound, Harrier, Ibizan Hound, Irish Wolfhound, Norwegian Elkhound, Otterhound, Petit Basset Griffon Vendéen, Pharaoh Hound, Plott, Redbone Coonhound, Rhodesian Ridgeback, Saluki, Scottish Deerhound, Treeing Walker Coonhound, Whippet.

Non-Sporting Group: American Eskimo Dog, Bichon Frise, Boston Terrier, Bulldog, Chinese Shar-Pei, Chow Chow, Dalmatian, Finnish Spitz, French Bulldog, Keeshond, Lhasa Apso, Löwchen, Norwegian Lundehund, Poodle (standard and miniature), Schipperke, Shiba Inu, Tibetan Spaniel, Tibetan Terrier, Xoloitzcuintli.

Sporting Group: American Water Spaniel, Boykin Spaniel, Brittany, Chesapeake Bay Retriever, Clumber Spaniel, Cocker Spaniel, Curly-Coated Retriever, English Cocker Spaniel, English Setter, English Springer Spaniel, Field Spaniel, Flat-Coated Retriever, German Shorthaired Pointer, German Wirehaired Pointer, Golden Retriever, Gordon Setter, Irish Red and White Setter, Irish Setter, Irish Water Spaniel, Labrador Retriever, Nova Scotia Duck Tolling Retriever, Pointer, Spinone Italiano, Sussex Spaniel, Vizsla, Weimaraner, Welsh Springer Spaniel, Wirehaired Pointing Griffon.

Terrier Group: Airedale Terrier, American Staffordshire Terrier, Australian Terrier, Bedlington Terrier, Border Terrier, Bull Terrier, Cairn Terrier, Cesky Terrier, Dandie Dinmont Terrier, Glen of Imaal Terrier, Irish Terrier, Kerry Blue Terrier, Lakeland Terrier, Manchester Terrier, Miniature Bull Terrier, Miniature Schnauzer, Norfolk Terrier, Norwich Terrier, Parson Russell Terrier, Russell Terrier, Scottish Terrier (standard), Sealyham Terrier, Skye Terrier, Smooth Fox Terrier, Soft Coated Wheaten Terrier, Staffordshire Bull Terrier, Welsh Terrier, West Highland White Terrier, Wire Fox Terrier.

Toy Group: Affenpinscher, Brussels Griffon, Cavalier King Charles Spaniel, Chihuahua, Chinese Crested, English Toy Spaniel, Havanese, Italian Greyhound, Japanese Chin, Maltese, Manchester Terrier (toy), Miniature Pinscher, Papillon, Pekingese, Pomeranian, Poodle (toy), Pug, Shih Tzu, Silky Terrier, Toy Fox Terrier, Yorkshire Terrier.

Working Group: Akita, Alaskan Malamute, Anatolian Shepherd Dog, Bernese Mountain Dog, Black Russian Terrier, Boxer, Bullmastiff, Cane Corso, Doberman Pinscher, Dogue de Bordeaux, German Pinscher, Giant Schnauzer, Great Dane, Great Pyrenees, Greater Swiss Mountain Dog, Komondor, Kuvasz, Leonberger, Mastiff, Neapolitan Mastiff, Newfoundland, Portuguese Water Dog, Rottweiler, Saint Bernard, Samoyed, Siberian Husky, Standard Schnauzer, Tibetan Mastiff.

Registrations for Pedigreed Cats, 2010

Source: The Cat Fanciers' Association

(ranked by total registrations)

Rank	Breed	Rank	Breed	Rank	Breed	Rank	Breed	Rank	Breed
1.	Persian	9.	Cornish Rex	17.	Burmese	26.	Manx	34.	Chartreux
2.	Maine Coon	10.	Birman	18.	Siberian	27.	American Curl	35.	Bombay
3.	Exotic	11.	Norwegian Forest Cat	19.	Ocicat	28.	Colorpoint Shorthair	36.	European Burmese
4.	Ragdoll			20.	Russian Blue			37.	LaPerm
5.	Sphynx	12.	British Shorthair	21.	Egyptian Mau	29.	Singapura	38.	American Bobtail
6.	Siamese	13.	Tonkinese	22.	Japanese Bobtail	30.	Balinese/Javanese	39.	Turkish Van
7.	Abyssinian	14.	Oriental	23.	Somali	31.	Havana Brown	40.	American Wirehair
8.	American Shorthair	15.	Devon Rex	24.	Selkirk Rex	32.	Korat	41.	Chinese Li Hua
		16.	Scottish Fold	25.	Turkish Angora	33.	RagaMuffin		

Note: In Feb. 2011, the Cat Fanciers' Association accepted for registration the Burmilla, a 42nd breed.

Trees of the U.S.

Source: American Forests

More than 870 native and naturalized species of trees grow in the U.S. The trunk of the world's largest known living tree, the General Sherman giant sequoia in California, weighs almost 1,400 tons—about as much as 15 adult blue whales. To determine the country's largest trees, American Forests uses a point system whereby trunk circumference (in inches) + height (in feet) + ¼ average crown spread (in feet) = total points. As of Apr. 1, 2012.

10 Largest National Champion Trees

Tree type	Girth at 4.5 ft (in.)	Height (ft)	Crown spread (ft)	Total points	Location
Giant sequoia (Gen. Sherman tree)	1,020	274	107	1,321	Sequoia National Park, CA
Coast redwood	950	321	75	1,290	Jedediah Smith Redwoods State Park, CA
Coast redwood	895	307	83	1,223	Jedediah Smith Redwoods State Park, CA
Coast redwood	844	349	89	1,216	Redwood National Park, CA
Coast redwood	867	299	101	1,191	Prairie Creek Redwoods State Park, CA
Western red cedar	761	159	45	931	Olympic National Park, WA
Sitka spruce	668	191	96	883	Olympic National Park, WA
Coast Douglas-fir	505	281	71	804	Olympic National Forest, WA
Port-Orford-cedar	522	242	35	773	Coos, OR
Common baldcypress	647	96	74	762	Cat Island, LA

ENVIRONMENT

U.S. Greenhouse Gas Emissions From Human Activities, 1990-2010

Source: U.S. Environmental Protection Agency

Gas and major source(s)	1990	1995	2000	2007	2008	2009	2010	% change, 2000-10
Carbon dioxide (CO_2)......	5,100.5	5,421.5	5,975.0	6,118.6	5,924.3	5,500.5	5,706.4	–4.5%
Fossil fuel combustion	4,738.3	5,037.7	5,586.2	5,757.8	5,571.5	5,206.2	5,387.8	–3.6
Methane (CH_4)	668.3	677.8	650.6	656.2	667.9	672.2	666.5	2.4
Landfills	147.7	146.6	111.1	111.7	113.1	111.2	107.8	–3.0
Enteric fermentation[1]	133.8	142.5	138.8	143.8	143.4	142.6	141.3	1.8
Natural gas systems........	189.6	197.5	209.2	205.3	212.7	220.9	215.4	3.0
Coal mining	84.1	68.1	60.4	57.8	66.9	70.1	72.6	20.2
Nitrous oxide (N_2O)	316.2	336.2	340.6	334.9	317.1	304.0	306.2	–10.1
Agricultural soil management......	200.0	205.3	208.8	211.1	212.9	207.3	207.8	–0.5
Hydrofluorocarbons, etc.	90.1	90.2	137.6	143.1	139.1	131.6	142.6	3.6
Total U.S. emissions	**6,175.2**	**6,457.4**	**7,103.8**	**7,252.8**	**7,048.3**	**6,608.3**	**6,821.8**	**–4.0**
Net U.S. emissions[2]	**5,293.4**	**5,562.5**	**6,424.1**	**6,144.5**	**5,960.9**	**5,545.7**	**5,747.1**	**–10.5**

Note: Emissions given in terms of equivalent emissions of carbon dioxide (CO_2), using units of teragrams of carbon dioxide equivalents (Tg CO_2 eq.). (1) Digestive process of ruminant animals, such as cattle and sheep, producing methane as a by-product. (2) Total emissions minus carbon dioxide absorbed by forests or other means.

U.S. Carbon Dioxide Emissions From Fossil Fuel Combustion, 1990-2010

Source: U.S. Environmental Protection Agency; in teragrams of carbon dioxide equivalents (Tg CO_2 eq.)

The concept of Global Warming Potential (GWP) was developed by the Intergovernmental Panel on Climate Change (IPCC) to compare the ability of each greenhouse gas to trap heat in the atmosphere relative to another gas. Carbon dioxide (CO_2) from fossil fuel combustion is the largest source of U.S. greenhouse gas emissions, accounting for approximately 78% of GWP weighted emissions since 1990.

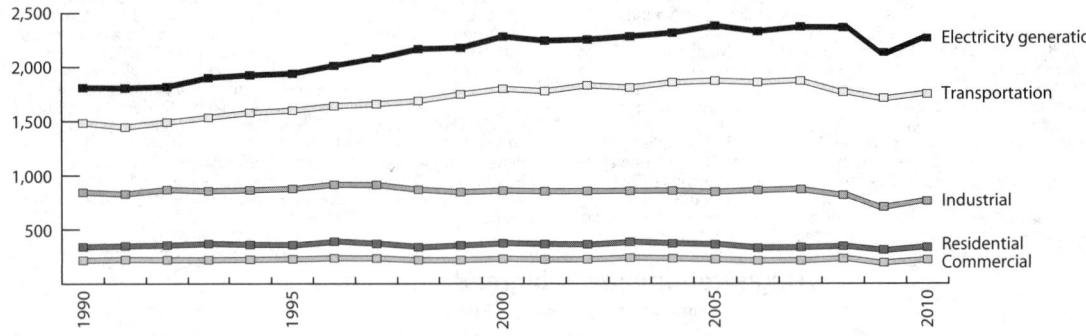

Top 15 Nations Producing Carbon Dioxide Emissions, 1980-2010

Source: U.S. Dept. of Energy

(in million metric tons of carbon dioxide emitted from the consumption of energy; ranked by 2010 totals)

Country	1980	1990	1995	2000	2005	2010	% change, 1980-2010	% change, 1990-2010
China	1,448.46	2,269.71	2,861.68	2,849.75	5,512.70	8,320.96	474%	267%
United States	4,776.83	5,040.59	5,319.78	5,861.32	5,991.76	5,610.11	17	11
India	291.22	578.62	870.23	1,002.95	1,183.28	1,695.62	482	193
Russia[1].............	3,081.87	3,820.85	1,603.06	1,498.77	1,574.16	1,633.80	NA	NA
Japan	947.01	1,046.98	1,116.24	1,201.43	1,241.26	1,164.47	23	11
Germany[2]...........	759.25	698.14	890.82	854.66	847.36	793.65	NA	NA
Korea, South	131.74	242.13	381.43	438.83	493.80	578.97	339	139
Iran	116.83	202.11	262.20	321.68	451.05	560.33	380	177
Canada..............	457.45	470.59	508.73	573.27	623.75	548.75	20	17
United Kingdom	613.57	601.82	560.13	560.34	583.06	532.44	–13	–12
Saudi Arabia..........	176.92	208.02	235.29	290.54	405.54	478.41	170	130
South Africa	235.03	297.98	347.47	386.01	432.53	465.10	98	56
Brazil	185.66	237.33	289.09	344.36	369.74	453.87	144	91
Mexico	240.33	302.16	321.37	383.04	397.81	445.28	85	47
Italy................	371.79	415.41	431.43	447.72	471.88	416.37	12	0
World total[3]	**18,434.18**	**21,615.45**	**22,149.34**	**23,738.59**	**28,291.50**	**31,780.36**	**72**	**47**

NA = Not applicable. (1) Numbers for 1980-90 are for the former Soviet Union. (2) Numbers for 1980-90 are for former West Germany. (3) Includes nations not listed.

Air Pollution in Selected World Cities

Source: *World Development Indicators 2012*, The World Bank

Particulate matter in the following table refers to smoke, soot, dust, and liquid droplets from combustion that are in the air—specifically, to particulates less than 10 microns in diameter (PM10) capable of reaching deep into the respiratory tract. The level of particulates, an important indicator of air quality, is significantly affected by the state of technology and pollution controls. Particulate pollution causes an estimated 500,000 premature deaths each year. **Sulfur dioxide** is a pollutant formed when fossil fuels containing sulfur are burned. **Nitrogen dioxide** is a poisonous, pungent gas formed when nitric oxide combines with hydrocarbons and sunlight, producing a photochemical reaction. Nitrogen oxides are emitted by bacteria, nitrogenous fertilizers, aerobic decomposition of organic matter, biomass combustion, and, especially, burning fuel for vehicles and industrial activities. Emissions of sulfur dioxide and nitrogen oxides lead to **acid rain**.

Data in the table are average concentrations based on reports from urban monitoring sites, measured in micrograms per cubic meter (mpcm); the figures give a general indication of air quality, but results should be interpreted with caution. World Health Organization standards for acceptable air quality are annual mean concentrations of 20 mpcm for particulate matter less than 10 microns in diameter and 40 mpcm for nitrogen dioxide and daily mean concentrations of 20 mpcm for sulfur dioxide.

City, country	Particulate matter[1]	Sulfur dioxide[2]	Nitrogen dioxide[2]	City, country	Particulate matter[1]	Sulfur dioxide[2]	Nitrogen dioxide[2]
Accra, Ghana	21	NA	NA	Montréal, Canada	15	10	42
Amsterdam, Netherlands	30	10	58	Moscow, Russia	16	109	NA
Athens, Greece	33	34	64	Mumbai, India	50	33	39
Bangkok, Thailand	60	11	23	Nairobi, Kenya	31	NA	NA
Barcelona, Spain	27	11	43	New York, NY, U.S.	17	26	79
Beijing, China	73	90	122	Oslo, Norway	19	8	43
Berlin, Germany	18	18	26	Paris, France	10	14	57
Cairo, Egypt	112	69	NA	Prague, Czech Republic	17	14	33
Cape Town, South Africa	16	21	72	Quito, Ecuador	24	22	NA
Caracas, Venezuela	13	33	57	Rio de Janeiro, Brazil	25	129	NA
Chicago, IL, U.S.	20	14	57	Rome, Italy	23	NA	NA
Delhi, India	118	24	41	São Paulo, Brazil	28	43	83
Jakarta, Indonesia	70	NA	NA	Seoul, South Korea	35	44	60
Kolkata, India	101	49	34	Shanghai, China	60	53	73
London, United Kingdom	17	25	77	Sofia, Bulgaria	49	39	122
Los Angeles, CA, U.S.	28	9	74	Tokyo, Japan	32	18	68
Manila, Philippines	24	33	NA	Toronto, Canada	18	17	43
Mexico City, Mexico	43	74	130	Warsaw, Poland	38	16	32
Milan, Italy	24	31	248				

NA = Not available. (1) Urban-population weighted PM10 data as of 2009. (2) As of 2001.

Air Quality of Selected U.S. Urban Areas, 2000-11

Source: Office of Air Quality Planning and Standards, U.S. Environmental Protection Agency

Data indicate the number of days metropolitan statistical areas or corresponding core based statistical areas failed to meet acceptable air-quality standards.

Urban area	2000	2005	2007	2008	2009	2010	2011
Atlanta-Sandy Springs-Marietta, GA	26	5	15	4	0	2	0
Bakersfield, CA	62	33	29	40	23	14	10
Baltimore-Towson, MD	7	6	5	4	1	6	5
Baton Rouge, LA	19	9	5	0	0	3	1
Boston-Cambridge-Quincy, MA-NH	1	3	2	0	0	0	0
Chicago-Naperville-Joliet, IL-IN-WI	1	6	2	0	1	0	1
Cincinnati-Middletown, OH-KY-IN	3	5	4	0	0	0	3
Cleveland-Elyria-Mentor, OH	2	6	2	0	0	1	0
Dallas-Fort Worth-Arlington, TX	17	16	3	1	3	0	6
Denver-Aurora, CO	0	0	2	0	0	0	1
Detroit-Warren-Livonia, MI	1	7	4	1	0	0	0
Fresno, CA	69	19	19	17	10	11	22
Houston-Sugar Land-Baytown, TX	30	19	5	3	6	1	7
Indianapolis-Carmel, IN	6	1	0	0	0	1	0
Kansas City, MO-KS	6	4	2	0	0	0	2
Las Vegas-Paradise, NV	1	3	2	0	0	0	0
Los Angeles-Long Beach-Santa Ana, CA	36	29	18	31	18	4	11
Memphis, TN-MS-AR	6	4	2	1	0	0	0
Miami-Fort Lauderdale-Pompano Beach, FL	0	1	0	0	0	0	1
Minneapolis-St. Paul-Bloomington, MN-WI	1	2	0	0	0	0	0
Nashville-Davidson–Murfreesboro–Franklin, TN	5	1	2	0	0	0	0
New Orleans-Metairie-Kenner, LA	5	0	1	0	0	16	26
New York-Northern New Jersey-Long Island, NY-NJ-PA	7	12	7	2	0	1	3
Philadelphia-Camden-Wilmington, PA-NJ-DE-MD	9	9	7	4	0	3	3
Phoenix-Mesa-Scottsdale, AZ	2	1	92	84	17	3	45
Pittsburgh, PA	7	13	8	2	3	10	3
Riverside-San Bernardino-Ontario, CA	65	50	52	57	47	31	35
Sacramento–Arden-Arcade–Roseville, CA	22	22	4	19	8	4	3
Salt Lake City, UT	9	2	9	1	4	5	1
San Francisco-Oakland-Fremont, CA	1	0	0	1	0	1	0
Seattle-Tacoma-Bellevue, WA	1	0	2	0	1	0	0
Tucson, AZ	0	0	0	0	1	0	0
Washington-Arlington-Alexandria, DC-VA-MD-WV	5	4	3	3	0	3	3
Winston-Salem, NC	4	0	2	0	1	0	0

U.S. Greenhouse Gas Emissions, 2010
Source: U.S. Environmental Protection Agency

HFCs, PFCs, and sulfur hexafluoride, 2.1%
Methane, 9.8%
Nitrous oxide, 4.5%
Carbon dioxide, 83.6%

World Carbon Dioxide Emissions From the Use of Fossil Fuels, 2010
Source: U.S. Energy Information Administration

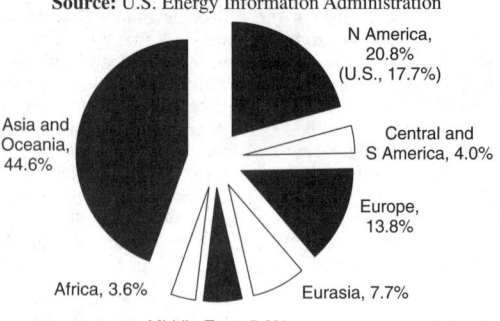

N America, 20.8% (U.S., 17.7%)
Central and S America, 4.0%
Asia and Oceania, 44.6%
Europe, 13.8%
Eurasia, 7.7%
Africa, 3.6%
Middle East, 5.6%

HFC = hydrofluorocarbon. PFC = perfluorocarbon. **Note:** Emissions sources are independently rounded; percentages may not add up to 100.

Atmospheric Concentration of Carbon Dioxide, 1744-2011
Source: Carbon Dioxide Information Analysis Center, U.S. Dept. of Energy

Year[1]	CO_2 in ppm[2]	Year[1]	CO_2 in ppm[2]	Year[1]	CO_2 in ppm[2]	Year[1]	CO_2 in ppm[2]	Year[1]	CO_2 in ppm[2]
1744	277	1878	290	1960	317	2000	369	2008	386
1791	280	1903	295	1970	326	2005	380	2009	387
1816	284	1915	301	1980	339	2006	382	2010	390
1843	287	1927	306	1990	354	2007	384	2011	392
1869	289	1943	308						

(1) Measurements for the years 1744-1943 were derived from a 200-m ice core sample drilled near Siple Station in Antarctica in 1983-84. Measurements from 1960-2011 were taken directly from the atmosphere at Mauna Loa Observatory in Hawaii. (2) Parts per million.

Emissions of Principal Air Pollutants in the U.S., 1970-2008
Source: Office of Air Quality Planning and Standards, U.S. Environmental Protection Agency; in est. million tons

Pollutant	1970	1975	1980	1985	1990	1995	2000	2005	2008
Carbon monoxide	204.0	188.4	185.4	176.8	154.2	126.8	114.5	93.0	77.7
Nitrogen oxides[1]	26.9	26.4	27.1	25.8	25.5	25.0	22.6	19.1	16.3
Particulate matter[2]									
PM10	13.0	7.6	7.0	41.3	27.8	25.8	23.0	18.3	11.9
PM2.5	NA	NA	NA	NA	7.6	6.9	6.5	3.0	2.4
Sulfur dioxide	31.2	28.0	25.9	23.3	23.1	18.6	16.3	14.8	11.4
Volatile org. compounds[1]	3.5	30.8	31.1	27.4	24.1	22.1	17.5	18.4	15.9
Lead	0.221	0.160	0.074	0.022	0.005	0.004	0.003	0.001	0.001
Total[3]	278.8	281.4	276.5	294.6	254.7	91.5	193.9	163.6	133.2

NA = Not available. (1) Ozone, a major air pollutant and the primary constituent of smog, is not emitted directly to the air but is formed by sunlight acting on emissions of nitrogen oxides and volatile organic compounds. (2) PM10, particulates 10 microns or smaller in diameter. PM2.5, particulates 2.5 microns or smaller in diameter. (3) Totals are rounded, as are components of totals.

Carbon Monoxide Emission Estimates, 1970-2008
(in thousand tons)

Source	1970	1975	1980	1985	1990	1995	2000	2006	2007	2008
Fuel combustion, elec. util.	237	276	322	291	363	372	484	661	680	699
Industrial processes[1]	10,610	8,304	7,700	5,894	5,572	5,631	3,628	3,143	3,213	3,283
Transportation[2]	174,602	167,884	160,512	153,216	131,702	107,755	92,239	65,111	61,007	56,902
Total[3]	204,042	188,398	185,408	176,845	154,188	126,778	114,465	87,915	82,801	77,685

(1) Industrial fuel combustion, chemical and allied manufacturing, metals processing, and petroleum and other industrial sectors. (2) Highway and off-highway vehicles. (3) Numbers may not add up to totals because not all categories are listed.

Nitrogen Oxides Emission Estimates, 1970-2008
(in thousand tons)

Source	1970	1975	1980	1985	1990	1995	2000	2006	2007	2008
Fuel combustion, elec. util.	4,900	5,694	7,024	6,127	6,663	6,384	5,330	3,446	3,320	3,006
Industrial processes[1]	5,100	4,546	4,110	4,009	3,831	3,909	3,518	2,769	2,755	2,741
Transportation[2]	15,276	15,029	14,846	14,508	13,373	12,989	12,561	10,740	10,101	9,461
Total[3]	26,882	26,378	27,080	25,757	25,527	24,955	22,599	18,110	17,321	16,339

(1) Industrial fuel combustion, chemical and allied manufacturing, metals processing, and petroleum and other industrial sectors. (2) Highway and off-highway vehicles. (3) Numbers may not add up to totals because not all categories are listed.

Sulfur Dioxide Emission Estimates, 1970-2008
(in thousand tons)

Source	1970	1975	1980	1985	1990	1995	2000	2006	2007	2008
Fuel combustion, elec. util.	17,398	18,268	17,469	16,272	15,909	12,080	11,396	9,404	8,941	7,552
Industrial processes[1]	11,661	7,993	6,725	5,597	5,402	4,945	3,516	2,701	2,683	2,663
Transportation[2]	551	635	717	809	874	741	697	827	673	520
Total[3]	31,218	28,044	25,926	23,307	23,077	18,619	16,348	13,655	13,006	11,429

(1) Industrial fuel combustion, chemical and allied manufacturing, metals processing, and petroleum and other industrial sectors. (2) Highway and off-highway vehicles. (3) Numbers may not add up to totals because not all categories are listed.

Average Global Temperatures, 1900-2011

Source: National Oceanic and Atmospheric Administration, U.S. Dept. of Commerce; in degrees Fahrenheit

Period	Avg. °F	Period	Avg. °F	Period	Avg. °F	Period	Avg. °F	Period	Avg. °F
1900-09	56.58	1950-59	56.98	2000	57.67	2004	57.98	2008	57.88
1910-19	56.56	1960-69	57.04	2001	57.90	2005	58.11	2009	57.99
1920-29	56.76	1970-79	57.06	2002	58.02	2006	57.99	2010	58.11
1930-39	57.01	1980-89	57.35	2003	58.02	2007	58.01	2011	57.92
1940-49	57.13	1990-99	57.64						

Note: In 2005 and 2010, the average global temperature reached 58.11°F, making them the warmest years on record. The next warmest year on record was 1998.

Toxics Release Inventory in the U.S., 2009-10

Source: U.S. Environmental Protection Agency

Releases of toxic chemicals into the environment, by manner of release and industry sector; pollutant transfers by destination of transfer. Numbers may not add up to totals because of rounding.

Pollutant releases	2009 mil lbs	2010 mil lbs	Top industries, total releases	2009 %	2010 %
Air releases	918	860	Metal mining	34%	41%
Surface water discharges	207	226	Electric utilities	24	18
Underground injection	181	229	Chemicals	12	13
On-site land releases	1,727	2,205	Primary metals	9	10
Off-site releases	357	410	Paper	5	5
Total on- and off-site releases	**3,389**	**3,929**	All others	16	14

Pollutant transfers	mil lbs	mil lbs	Top carcinogens, air/water/land releases	mil lbs	mil lbs
To recycling	1,631	1,889	Lead compounds	369	555
To energy recovery	367	429	Arsenic compounds	97	222
To treatment	229	250	Chromium compounds	35	54
To publicly owned treatment works	218	231	Nickel compounds	23	32
Other transfers	<1	<1	Styrene	21	25
Off-site to disposal	392	444	Formaldehyde	15	19
Total	**2,837**	**3,244**			

Note: This information does not indicate whether or to what degree the public has been exposed to toxic chemicals.

Total Toxics Releases by State, 2010

Source: U.S. Environmental Protection Agency

State	Total lbs	State	Total lbs	State	Total lbs	State	Total lbs
Alaska	835,742,316	Texas	205,855,905	Louisiana	135,525,059	Kentucky	95,148,528
Nevada	476,873,463	Indiana	155,309,692	Pennsylvania	116,446,353		
Utah	211,955,455	Ohio	154,765,946	Illinois	101,796,012	**U.S. total***	**3,929,326,530**

*Includes states not shown, District of Columbia, Puerto Rico, American Samoa, Guam, Northern Marianas, and the U.S. Virgin Islands.

Hazardous Waste Sites in the U.S., 2012

Source: *National Priorities List*, U.S. Environmental Protection Agency; as of Sept. 2012

State/territory	Proposed Gen.	Proposed Fed.	Final Gen.	Final Fed.	Total	State/territory	Proposed Gen.	Proposed Fed.	Final Gen.	Final Fed.	Total
Alabama	1	0	11	3	15	Nebraska	0	0	12	1	13
Alaska	0	0	1	5	6	Nevada	0	0	1	0	1
Arizona	0	0	7	2	9	New Hampshire	1	0	19	1	21
Arkansas	0	0	9	0	9	New Jersey	3	0	105	8	116
California	1	0	74	24	99	New Mexico	1	0	13	1	15
Colorado	2	0	15	3	20	New York	1	0	83	4	88
Connecticut	1	0	13	1	15	North Carolina	0	0	36	2	38
Delaware	1	0	12	1	14	North Dakota	0	0	0	0	0
District of Columbia	0	0	0	1	1	Ohio	4	2	34	3	43
Florida	1	0	49	6	56	Oklahoma	1	0	7	1	9
Georgia	2	0	13	2	17	Oregon	1	0	12	2	15
Guam	0	0	1	1	2	Pennsylvania	2	0	90	6	98
Hawaii	0	0	1	2	3	Puerto Rico	0	0	15	1	16
Idaho	3	0	4	2	9	Rhode Island	0	0	10	2	12
Illinois	3	1	41	4	49	South Carolina	0	0	25	2	27
Indiana	0	0	33	0	33	South Dakota	0	0	1	1	2
Iowa	1	0	10	1	12	Tennessee	1	0	12	3	15
Kansas	2	0	10	1	13	Texas	1	0	46	4	51
Kentucky	0	0	13	1	14	Utah	3	1	11	4	18
Louisiana	3	0	8	1	12	Vermont	0	0	11	0	11
Maine	0	0	10	3	13	Virgin Islands	0	0	1	0	1
Maryland	1	0	10	10	21	Virginia	0	0	20	11	31
Massachusetts	3	0	24	6	33	Washington	0	0	36	13	49
Michigan	1	1	66	0	68	West Virginia	0	0	7	2	9
Minnesota	0	0	23	2	25	Wisconsin	1	0	38	0	39
Mississippi	1	0	8	0	9	Wyoming	0	0	1	1	2
Missouri	0	0	30	3	33	**Total**	**49**	**5**	**1,158**	**158**	**1,370**
Montana	1	0	16	0	17						

Note: Fed. = Hazardous waste produced by federal agency; Gen. = Non-fed. sites. Sites that have been proposed for federal Superfund financing are listed under Proposed; sites that have qualified for Superfund financing are under Final.

Renewable Water Resources, 2010

Source: Food and Agriculture Organization, United Nations

Globally, water supplies are abundant, but they are unevenly distributed among and within countries. In some areas, water withdrawals are so high, relative to supply, that surface water supplies are shrinking, and groundwater reserves are being depleted faster than they can be replenished by precipitation. The U.S. (including Alaska and Hawaii) has 9,079 cubic meters per capita and 2,818 cubic kilometers of internal renewable water resources total.

These numbers, and those in the tables below, were published by the Food and Agriculture Organization. The tables, which take into account countries for which data are available, draw upon studies done over a number of years and use 2010 population data. Numbers represent each country's internal resources.

Countries With Greatest Internal Water Resources

Country	Cubic m per capita	Total cubic km
Iceland	531,250	170.0
Guyana	319,629	241.0
Suriname	167,619	88.0
Papua New Guinea	116,798	801.0
Gabon	108,970	164.0
Bhutan	107,438	78.0
Canada	83,782	2,850.0
Solomon Islands	83,086	44.7
Norway	78,231	382.0
New Zealand	74,863	327.0

Countries With Lowest Internal Water Resources

Country	Cubic m per capita	Total cubic km
Kuwait	0	0
Bahrain	3.17	0.004
United Arab Emirates	19.97	0.15
Egypt	22.19	1.8
Qatar	31.84	0.056
Bahamas, The	58.31	0.02
Yemen	87.31	2.1
Saudi Arabia	87.44	2.4
Maldives	94.94	0.03
Israel	101.10	0.75

Top 50 Countries by Forest Area, 1990-2010

Source: Food and Agriculture Organization, United Nations
(in square kilometers; ranked by 2010 area)

Country	Forest area, 1990	Forest area, 2010	% change, 1990-2010	% of land area covered by forest in 2010	Country	Forest area, 1990	Forest area, 2010	% change, 1990-2010	% of land area covered by forest in 2010
Russia	8,089,500	8,090,900	0.0%	49.0%	Congo Rep.	227,260	224,110	−1.4%	66.0%
Brazil	5,748,390	5,195,220	−9.6	62.0	Finland	218,890	221,570	1.2	73.0
Canada	3,101,340	3,101,340	0.0	34.0	Gabon	220,000	220,000	0.0	85.0
United States	2,963,350	3,040,220	2.6	33.0	Malaysia	223,760	204,560	−8.6	62.0
China	1,571,410	2,068,610	31.6	22.0	Cameroon	243,160	199,160	−18.1	42.0
Congo, Dem. Rep.	1,603,630	1,541,350	−3.9	68.0	Thailand	195,490	189,720	−3.0	37.0
Australia	1,545,000	1,493,000	−3.4	19.0	Spain	138,180	181,730	31.5	36.0
Indonesia	1,185,450	944,320	−20.3	52.0	Paraguay	211,570	175,820	−16.9	44.0
Sudan	763,810	699,490	−8.4	29.0	Chile	152,630	162,310	6.3	22.0
India	639,390	684,340	7.0	23.0	France	145,370	159,540	9.7	29.0
Peru	701,560	679,920	−3.1	53.0	Laos	173,140	157,510	−9.0	68.0
Mexico	702,910	648,020	−7.8	33.0	Zimbabwe	221,640	156,240	−29.5	40.0
Colombia	625,190	604,990	−3.2	55.0	Guyana	152,050	152,050	0.0	77.0
Angola	609,760	584,800	−4.1	47.0	Suriname	147,760	147,580	−0.1	95.0
Bolivia	627,950	571,960	−8.9	53.0	Vietnam	93,630	137,970	47.4	44.0
Zambia	528,000	494,680	−6.3	67.0	Madagascar	136,920	125,530	−8.3	22.0
Venezuela	520,260	462,750	−11.1	52.0	Mali	140,720	124,900	−11.2	10.0
Mozambique	433,780	390,220	−10.0	50.0	Ethiopia	151,140	122,960	−18.6	11.0
Tanzania	414,950	334,280	−19.4	38.0	Chad	131,100	115,250	−12.1	9.0
Myanmar (Burma)	392,180	317,730	−19.0	48.0	Botswana	137,180	113,510	−17.3	20.0
Argentina	347,930	294,000	−15.5	11.0	Turkey	96,800	113,340	17.1	15.0
Papua New Guinea	315,230	287,260	−8.9	63.0	Germany	107,410	110,760	3.1	32.0
Sweden	272,810	282,030	3.4	69.0	Iran	110,750	110,750	0.0	7.0
Japan	249,500	249,790	0.1	69.0	Mongolia	125,360	108,980	−13.1	7.0
Central African Rep.	232,030	226,050	−2.6	36.0	Côte d'Ivoire	102,220	104,030	1.8	33.0
					World	**41,684,000**	**40,330,620**	**−3.2**	**NA**

NA = Not available.

Selected Endangered Animal Species

Source: Fish and Wildlife Service, U.S. Dept. of the Interior

Common name	Scientific name	Range
Albatross, Amsterdam	Diomedia amsterdamensis	Amsterdam Island, Indian Ocean
Antelope, giant sable	Hippotragus niger variani	Angola
Armadillo, giant	Priodontes maximus	Venezuela, Guyana to Argentina
Babirusa	Babyrousa babyrussa	Indonesia
Bandicoot, desert	Perameles eremiana	Australia
Bat, gray	Myotis grisescens	Central, southeastern U.S.
Bear, Mexican grizzly	Ursus arctos	Mexico
Bobcat, Mexican	Lynx rufus escuinapae	Central Mexico
Caiman, black	Melanosuchus niger	Amazon Basin
Camel, Bactrian	Camelus bactrianus	Mongolia, China
Caribou, woodland	Rangifer tarandus caribou	Canada, northern U.S.

Common name	Scientific name	Range
Cheetah	Acinonyx jubatus	Africa to India
Chimpanzee, pygmy	Pan paniscus	Dem. Rep. of the Congo
Condor, California	Gymnogyps californianus	U.S. (AZ, CA, OR), Mexico (Baja California)
Crane, whooping	Grus americana	Canada, Mexico, U.S. (Rocky Mts. to Carolinas)
Crocodile, American	Crocodylus acutus	U.S. (FL), Mexico, Caribbean Sea, Central and South America
Deer, Columbian white-tailed	Odocoileus virginianus leucurus	U.S. (OR, WA)
Dolphin, Chinese river	Lipotes vexillifer	China
Dugong	Dugong dugon	East Africa to southern Japan, Palau
Elephant, Asian	Elephas maximus	South-central and southeastern Asia
Fox, northern swift	Vulpes velox hebes	U.S. (northern Great Plains), Canada
Frog, mountain yellow-legged	Rana muscosa	Western U.S. (CA, NV)
Gorilla	Gorilla gorilla	Central and West Africa
Hartebeest, Tora	Alcelaphus buselaphus tora	Egypt, Ethiopia, Sudan
Hawk, Hawaiian	Buteo solitarius	U.S. (HI)
Hyena, brown	Parahyaena brunnea	Southern Africa
Impala, black-faced	Aepyceros melampus petersi	Angola, Namibia
Kangaroo, Tasmanian forester	Macropus giganteus tasmaniensis	Australia (Tasmania)
Leopard	Panthera pardus	Africa, Asia
Lion, Asiatic	Panthera leo persica	Turkey to India
Manatee, West Indian	Trichechus manatus	Southeastern U.S., Caribbean Sea, Mexico
Monkey, spider	Ateles geoffroyi frontatus	Costa Rica, Nicaragua
Ocelot	Leopardus pardalis	U.S. (AZ, TX) to Central and S America
Orangutan	Pongo pygmaeus	Borneo, Sumatra
Ostrich, West African	Struthio camelus spatzi	Western Sahara
Otter, marine	Lontra felina	Peru south to Straits of Magellan
Panda, giant	Ailuropoda melanoleuca	China
Panther, Florida	Puma concolor coryi	U.S. (LA and AR to SC and FL)
Parakeet, golden	Aratinga guarouba	Brazil
Parrot, imperial	Amazona imperialis	West Indies (Dominica)
Penguin, Galapagos	Spheniscus mendiculus	Ecuador (Galapagos Islands)
Puma, eastern	Puma concolor couguar	Eastern N America (presumed extinct in wild)
Python, Indian	Python molurus molurus	Sri Lanka, India
Rat-kangaroo, brush-tailed	Bettongia penicillata	Australia
Rhinoceros, black	Diceros bicornis	Sub-Saharan Africa
Rhinoceros, northern white	Ceratotherium simum cottoni	Dem. Rep. of the Congo, Sudan, Uganda, Central African Rep.
Salamander, Chinese giant	Andrias davidianus	Western China
Sea-lion, Steller	Eumetopias jubatus	U.S. (AK, CA, OR), Russia
Squirrel, Carolina northern flying	Glaucomys sabrinus coloratus	U.S. (NC, TN)
Tiger	Panthera tigris	Asia
Tortoise, Galapagos	Geochelone nigra	Ecuador (Galapagos Islands)
Whale, gray	Eschrichtius robustus	Northern Pacific Ocean
Whale, humpback	Megaptera novaeangliae	All major oceans
Wolf, red	Canis rufus	Southeastern U.S.
Woodpecker, ivory-billed	Campephilus principalis	South-central and southeastern U.S., Cuba
Yak, wild	Bos mutus	China (Tibet), India
Zebra, mountain	Equus zebra zebra	South Africa

List of Endangered and Threatened Species, 2012
Source: Fish and Wildlife Service, U.S. Dept. of the Interior; as of Sept. 2012

Group	Endangered U.S.	Endangered Foreign	Threatened U.S.	Threatened Foreign	Total species[1]	U.S. species with recovery plans
Mammals	70	256	14	16	356	63
Birds	78	208	13	15	314	86
Reptiles	14	69	20	17	120	35
Amphibians	15	8	9	1	33	17
Fishes	82	11	65	1	159	102
Clams	68	2	8	0	78	70
Snails	28	1	12	0	41	29
Insects	53	4	10	0	67	40
Arachnids	12	0	0	0	12	12
Crustaceans	19	0	3	0	22	18
Corals	0	0	2	0	2	0
Animal subtotal	**439**	**559**	**156**	**50**	**1,204**	**472**
Flowering plants	616	1	147	0	764	640
Conifers and cycads	2	0	1	2	5	3
Ferns and allies	27	0	2	0	29	26
Lichens	2	0	0	0	2	2
Plant subtotal	**647**	**1**	**150**	**2**	**800**	**671**
Grand total	**1,086**	**560**	**306**	**52**	**2,004**	**1,143**

(1) Some species are classified as both endangered and threatened. The table tallies these dual status species only once, as endangered. The dual status species, all tallied as endangered, are (U.S.) California tiger salamander, chinook salmon, chum salmon, coho salmon, green sea turtle, piping plover, roseate tern, sockeye salmon, steelhead, Steller sea-lion; (non-U.S.) argali, chimpanzee, dugong, leopard, saltwater crocodile.

METEOROLOGY

National Weather Service Watches and Warnings

Source: National Weather Service, National Oceanic and Atmospheric Admin. (NOAA), U.S. Dept. of Commerce; *Glossary of Meteorology*, American Meteorological Society

The National Weather Service issues watches, warnings, and advisories for specific geographic areas to alert people to the possibility or imminent arrival of severe weather or of flooding. Often the weather hazard is a convective storm (a storm involving upward and downward movement of heat and moisture). A severe thunderstorm or tornado watch is issued when a severe convective storm, covering a relatively small geographic area or moving in a narrow path, is sufficiently intense to threaten life and property. Excessive localized convective rains are not classified as severe storms but are often the product of severe local storms. Such rainfall may result in phenomena, such as flash floods, that threaten life and property. Lightning occurs with all thunderstorms and, along with flash floods, is a leading cause of storm deaths and injuries.

Cyclone: atmospheric circulation of winds rotating counterclockwise in the Northern Hemisphere and clockwise in the Southern Hemisphere. Tornadoes, hurricanes, and the lows shown on weather maps are all examples of cyclones. Cyclones are usually accompanied by precipitation or stormy weather.

Severe thunderstorm: thunderstorm (any local atmospheric disturbance) that produces a tornado, winds of at least 50 knots (58 mph), and/or hail at least 1 in. in diameter. A severe thunderstorm watch indicates conditions are favorable for the development of a severe thunderstorm within 4 to 8 hours. A severe thunderstorm warning indicates a severe thunderstorm has been sighted by radar or reported by a spotter.

Tornado: violent rotating column of air that extends from the base of a thunderstorm to the ground. On a local scale, it is the most destructive of all atmospheric phenomena. Tornado paths range from a few feet to more than 100 mi long (average 5 mi) and from a few feet to more than 1 mi in diameter (avg. 220 yds). The average forward speed is 30 mph, and wind speeds can reach to more than 200 mph. A rotating column of air over water, whether or not linked to a thunderstorm, is called a **waterspout**.

Tropical storm: cyclone that develops over tropical or subtropical waters with 1-min. sustained surface winds between 34 and 63 knots (39-73 mph). A tropical storm watch is issued when tropical storm conditions pose a threat to specified coastal areas within 48 hours. A tropical storm warning is issued when such conditions are expected in a specified coastal area within 36 hours.

Hurricane: tropical cyclone having 1-min. sustained surface winds of 64 knots (74 mph) or more. (In the northwest Pacific Ocean, west of the international date line, such storms are known as **typhoons**.) The hurricane-force winds form a circle or oval, sometimes as wide as 300 mi in diameter. In the lower latitudes, hurricanes usually move W or NW at 10-15 mph. When the center approaches 25° to 30° N lat., the direction of motion often changes to the NE, with increased forward speed. In the Atlantic, hurricane season is June 1-Nov. 30. Hurricane season is May 15-Nov. 30 in the eastern Pacific. A hurricane warning is issued when a hurricane is forecast for an area within 36 hours.

Winter storm and **blizzard:** A winter storm watch is issued when there is a potential for heavy snow or significant ice accumulations, usually at least 24-36 hours in advance. A winter storm warning is issued when a winter storm is producing or is forecast to produce heavy snow or significant ice accumulations. A blizzard warning is issued for winter storm conditions where winds are 35 mph or more, there is sufficient falling and/or blowing snow to frequently reduce visibility to less than ¼ mi, and the conditions are expected to prevail for at least 3 hours.

Floods take many forms. **River flooding:** occurs when rains, sometimes coupled with melting snow, quickly fill river basins with an excess of water. Torrential rains from decaying hurricanes or tropical systems are also a major cause. **Coastal flooding:** tropical storm and hurricane winds or intense offshore low-pressure systems can drive ocean water inland. Coastal floods can also be produced by sea waves called **tsunamis**, produced by earthquakes or underwater volcanic eruptions or landslides. **Flash flooding:** usually due to copious amounts of rain falling in a short time. Ice can also cause flash flooding. When ice accumulates at natural or artificial obstructions, it can stop the flow of water. The resulting buildup of water can lead to flooding upstream. If the jam suddenly gives way, a flash flood can occur downstream. Flash flooding typically occurs within 6 hours of the causative event.

Flash floods account for the majority of flood deaths in the U.S. and are the leading cause of deaths associated with thunderstorms. Urbanization significantly increases runoff because less rain is absorbed by the terrain, making flash flooding in urban areas extremely dangerous. Streets can become swift-moving rivers, and basements can fill with water.

A (flash) flood watch indicates flooding or flash flooding is possible within a designated area. A (flash) flood warning indicates flooding is in progress, imminent, or highly likely.

National Weather Service Marine Warnings and Advisories

Primary sources of dissemination are commercial radio, TV, U.S. Coast Guard radio stations, and NOAA VHF radio broadcasts. The NOAA Weather Radio All Hazards (NWR) network broadcasts on seven frequencies between 162.40 and 162.55 MHz. These broadcasts can usually be received within at least 25 nautical mi of the transmission site using a special radio receiver. The following are examples of the warnings and advisories that may be addressed to mariners.

Small craft advisory: alerts mariners to sustained weather and/or sea conditions, present or forecast, potentially hazardous to small boats, including winds 20-33 knots (23-38 mph) and/or dangerous wave conditions. The advisory is also issued when sea or lake ice exists that could be hazardous to small boats. Criteria vary depending on region and type of marine environment.

Special marine warning: indicates potentially hazardous weather conditions not covered by existing marine warnings. The conditions are usually of short duration (2 hours or less) and involve wind speeds of 34 knots (39 mph) or more, and/or hail at least ¾ in. in diameter or waterspouts.

Gale warning: indicates winds of 34-47 knots (39-54 mph) not directly associated with a tropical storm are forecast for the area.

Storm warning: indicates winds 48-63 knots (55-73 mph) not directly associated with a tropical storm are forecast for the area.

Monthly Normal Mean Temperatures, Precipitation in U.S. Cities

Source: National Climatic Data Center, NESDIS, NOAA, U.S. Dept. of Commerce

Normals are averages covering a 30-year period. The temperature and precipitation normals given here are based on records for 1981-2010. Temperatures listed below represent means of the normal daily maximum and normal daily minimum temperatures for each month. For stations that did not have continuous records from the same site for the entire 30 years, the means have been adjusted to the record at the present site. (*) = city station. Other figures are for airport stations. T = Temperature in Fahrenheit; P = Precipitation in inches.

Station	Jan. T	Jan. P	Feb. T	Feb. P	Mar. T	Mar. P	Apr. T	Apr. P	May T	May P	June T	June P	July T	July P	Aug. T	Aug. P	Sept. T	Sept. P	Oct. T	Oct. P	Nov. T	Nov. P	Dec. T	Dec. P
Albany, NY	23	2.6	26	2.2	35	3.2	48	3.2	58	3.6	67	3.8	72	4.1	70	3.5	62	3.3	50	3.7	40	3.3	29	2.9
Albuquerque, NM	36	0.4	41	0.5	48	0.5	56	0.6	66	0.5	75	0.7	78	1.5	76	1.6	69	1.1	58	1.0	45	0.6	36	0.5
Anchorage, AK	17	0.7	20	0.7	27	0.6	37	0.5	48	0.7	55	1.0	59	1.8	57	3.3	49	3.0	35	2.0	22	1.2	19	1.1
Asheville, NC	37	3.7	40	3.8	47	3.8	55	3.3	63	3.7	71	4.7	74	4.3	73	4.4	66	3.8	56	2.9	47	3.7	39	3.6
Atlanta, GA	43	4.2	47	4.7	54	4.8	62	3.4	70	3.7	77	4.0	80	5.3	79	3.9	74	4.5	63	3.4	54	4.1	45	3.9
Atlantic City, NJ	33	3.2	35	2.9	42	4.2	52	3.6	61	3.4	71	3.1	76	3.7	74	4.1	67	3.2	56	3.4	47	3.3	37	3.7
Baltimore, MD	33	3.1	36	2.9	44	3.9	54	3.2	64	4.0	72	3.5	77	4.1	75	3.3	68	4.0	56	3.3	47	3.3	37	3.4
Barrow, AK	-13	0.1	-14	0.1	-13	0.1	2	0.2	21	0.2	36	0.3	41	1.0	39	1.1	32	0.1	17	0.4	-2	0.2	-8	0.1
Birmingham, AL	44	4.8	48	4.5	55	5.2	63	4.4	71	5.0	78	4.4	81	4.8	81	3.9	75	3.9	64	3.4	54	4.9	46	4.5
Bismarck, ND	13	0.4	18	0.5	30	0.9	44	1.3	56	2.4	65	3.2	71	2.9	70	2.3	59	1.6	45	1.3	29	0.7	16	0.5
Boise, ID	31	1.2	37	1.0	45	1.4	51	1.2	59	1.4	68	0.7	76	0.3	75	0.2	65	0.6	53	0.8	40	1.4	31	1.6
Boston, MA	29	3.4	32	3.3	38	4.3	48	3.7	58	3.5	68	3.7	73	3.4	72	3.4	65	3.4	54	3.9	45	4.0	35	3.8
Buffalo, NY	25	3.2	26	2.5	34	2.9	46	3.0	57	3.5	66	3.7	71	3.2	70	3.3	62	3.9	51	3.5	41	4.0	30	3.9
Burlington, VT	19	2.1	22	1.8	31	2.2	45	2.8	56	3.5	66	3.7	71	4.2	69	3.9	61	3.6	48	3.6	38	3.1	26	2.4
Caribou, ME	10	2.7	14	2.2	25	2.5	39	2.7	52	3.3	61	3.5	66	4.1	64	3.8	55	3.3	43	3.5	32	3.6	18	3.3
Charleston, SC	48	3.7	52	3.0	58	3.7	65	2.9	73	3.0	79	5.7	82	6.5	81	7.2	76	6.1	67	3.8	59	2.4	51	3.1
Charleston, WV	34	3.0	38	3.2	46	3.9	56	3.2	64	4.8	72	4.3	75	4.9	74	3.7	67	3.3	57	2.7	47	3.7	37	3.3
Chicago, IL	24	1.7	28	1.8	38	2.5	49	3.4	59	3.7	69	3.5	74	3.7	72	4.9	65	3.2	53	3.2	40	3.2	28	2.3
Cleveland, OH	28	2.7	31	2.3	38	2.9	50	3.5	60	3.7	69	3.4	73	3.5	72	3.5	65	3.8	54	3.1	44	3.6	32	3.1
Columbus, OH	30	2.7	33	2.3	42	3.0	53	3.4	63	4.2	72	4.0	75	4.8	74	3.3	67	2.8	55	2.6	44	3.2	34	3.0
Dallas-Ft. Worth, TX	46	2.1	50	2.7	58	3.5	66	3.1	74	4.9	81	3.8	85	2.2	86	1.9	78	2.6	68	4.2	57	2.7	47	2.6
Denver, CO	31	0.4	33	0.3	40	0.9	47	1.7	57	2.2	67	2.0	74	3.0	73	1.6	63	1.0	51	1.0	38	0.6	30	0.3
Des Moines, IA	23	1.0	27	1.3	39	2.3	52	3.9	62	4.7	72	4.9	76	4.5	74	4.1	66	3.1	53	2.6	39	2.2	26	1.4
Detroit, MI	26	2.0	28	2.0	37	2.3	49	2.9	60	3.4	69	3.5	74	3.4	72	3.0	64	3.3	52	2.5	42	2.8	30	2.4
Dodge City, KS	32	0.6	36	0.7	44	1.6	54	1.8	64	2.9	74	3.2	80	3.1	78	2.8	69	1.7	57	1.7	43	0.8	33	0.8
Duluth, MN	10	1.0	15	0.8	26	1.5	40	2.4	51	3.2	60	4.2	66	3.9	64	3.7	56	4.1	43	2.9	29	2.1	15	1.2
Fairbanks, AK	-8	0.6	-1	0.4	11	0.3	33	0.3	49	0.6	60	1.4	63	2.2	56	1.9	45	1.1	24	0.8	3	0.7	-4	0.6
Fresno, CA	47	2.2	52	2.0	57	2.0	62	1.0	70	0.4	77	0.2	83	0.0	82	0.0	76	0.2	66	0.6	54	1.1	47	1.8
Galveston, TX*	53	3.7	55	3.0	61	2.9	68	2.2	76	3.0	82	4.8	84	3.9	84	3.4	80	5.4	73	4.2	64	3.4	56	3.4
Grand Rapids, MI	24	2.1	27	1.8	36	2.4	48	3.4	59	4.0	68	3.8	72	3.8	71	3.6	63	4.3	51	3.3	40	3.5	29	2.5
Helena, MT	23	0.4	28	0.3	36	0.6	45	1.0	54	1.9	62	2.1	70	1.2	68	1.2	58	1.1	46	0.7	33	0.5	22	0.4
Honolulu, HI	73	2.3	73	2.0	75	2.0	76	0.6	78	0.6	80	0.3	81	0.5	82	0.6	82	0.7	80	1.8	78	2.4	75	3.2
Houston, TX	53	3.4	56	3.2	63	3.4	70	3.3	77	5.1	82	5.9	84	3.8	85	3.8	80	4.1	72	5.7	62	4.3	54	3.7
Huron, SD	17	0.5	22	0.6	33	1.5	47	2.3	58	3.1	68	3.9	74	2.9	72	2.4	62	2.5	48	1.8	33	0.9	19	0.5
Indianapolis, IN	28	2.7	32	2.3	42	3.6	53	3.8	63	5.1	72	4.3	75	4.6	74	3.1	67	3.1	55	3.1	44	3.7	32	3.2
Jackson, MS	46	5.0	50	4.8	57	5.0	64	5.0	72	4.4	79	4.1	82	4.8	81	4.2	76	3.0	65	3.9	56	4.8	48	5.2
Jacksonville, FL	53	3.3	56	3.2	62	4.0	67	2.6	74	2.5	80	6.5	82	6.6	82	6.8	78	8.2	70	3.9	62	2.1	55	2.8
Juneau, AK	28	5.4	30	4.1	34	3.8	41	2.9	49	3.4	55	3.2	57	4.6	56	5.7	50	8.6	42	8.6	33	6.0	30	5.8
Kansas City, MO	29	1.1	34	1.5	44	2.4	55	3.7	65	5.2	74	5.2	78	4.5	77	3.9	68	4.6	56	3.2	44	2.2	32	1.5
Knoxville, TN	38	4.3	42	4.3	50	4.3	59	4.0	67	4.5	75	3.8	78	5.1	78	3.3	71	3.2	60	2.5	50	4.0	41	4.5
Lander, WY	22	0.4	26	0.6	36	1.2	44	1.9	53	2.2	63	1.3	71	0.8	70	0.6	59	1.1	46	1.3	31	0.9	21	0.6
Lexington, KY	33	3.2	37	3.2	46	4.1	55	3.6	64	5.3	73	4.4	76	4.7	75	3.3	68	2.9	57	3.1	46	3.5	36	3.9
Little Rock, AR	41	3.6	45	3.7	53	4.7	62	5.1	71	4.9	79	3.7	83	3.3	83	2.6	75	3.2	64	4.9	53	5.3	43	5.0
Los Angeles, CA*	58	3.1	59	3.8	61	2.4	63	0.9	66	0.3	69	0.1	73	0.0	74	0.0	73	0.2	69	0.7	62	1.0	58	2.3
Louisville, KY	35	3.2	39	3.2	48	4.2	58	4.0	67	5.3	76	3.8	79	4.2	78	3.3	71	3.1	60	3.2	49	3.6	38	3.8
Marquette, MI*	19	1.8	21	1.3	29	2.0	40	2.5	51	2.5	60	2.7	67	2.8	67	2.6	59	3.2	47	3.1	35	2.6	24	2.0
Memphis, TN	41	4.0	46	4.4	54	5.2	63	5.5	72	5.3	80	3.6	83	4.6	82	2.9	75	3.1	64	4.0	53	5.5	44	5.7
Miami, FL	68	1.6	70	2.3	73	3.0	76	3.1	80	5.3	83	9.7	84	6.5	84	8.9	83	9.9	80	6.3	75	3.3	71	2.0
Milwaukee, WI	22	1.8	26	1.7	35	2.3	46	3.6	56	3.4	66	3.9	72	3.7	71	4.0	63	3.2	51	2.7	39	2.7	27	2.0
Minneapolis, MN	16	0.9	21	0.8	33	1.9	48	2.7	59	3.4	69	4.2	74	4.0	71	4.3	62	3.1	49	2.4	34	1.8	20	1.2
Mobile, AL	50	5.7	54	5.1	60	6.1	66	4.8	74	5.1	80	6.1	82	7.2	82	7.0	78	5.1	68	3.7	60	5.1	52	5.1
Moline, IL	23	1.5	27	1.6	39	2.9	51	3.6	62	4.3	72	4.5	75	4.3	74	4.5	65	3.1	53	3.0	40	2.6	27	2.2
Nashua, NH	24	3.7	27	3.2	35	4.3	46	4.0	57	2.9	66	4.3	71	3.7	70	4.5	62	3.4	50	4.7	40	4.1	30	3.7
Nashville, TN	38	3.8	42	3.9	50	4.1	59	4.0	68	5.5	76	4.1	79	3.6	79	3.2	72	3.4	60	3.0	50	4.3	40	4.2
Newark, NJ	32	3.5	35	2.9	42	4.2	53	4.2	63	4.1	72	4.0	77	4.8	76	3.7	68	3.8	57	3.6	47	3.7	37	3.8
New Orleans, LA	53	5.2	57	5.3	63	4.6	69	4.6	77	4.6	82	8.1	83	5.9	83	6.0	80	5.1	71	3.6	63	4.5	56	5.3
New York, NY*	33	3.7	35	3.1	43	4.4	53	4.5	62	4.2	71	4.4	77	4.6	75	4.4	68	4.3	57	4.4	48	4.0	38	4.0
Norfolk, VA	40	3.4	43	3.1	50	3.7	58	3.4	67	3.4	75	4.3	80	5.1	78	5.5	72	4.8	62	3.4	53	3.2	44	3.3
Oklahoma City, OK	39	1.4	44	1.6	52	3.1	61	3.1	70	4.7	78	4.9	83	2.9	82	3.3	74	4.1	63	3.7	51	2.0	41	1.9
Omaha, NE	24	0.7	28	0.9	40	2.0	52	3.0	62	4.8	72	4.2	77	3.8	75	3.8	66	2.7	53	2.2	39	1.6	26	1.0
Philadelphia, PA	33	3.0	36	2.7	44	3.8	54	3.6	64	3.7	73	3.4	78	4.4	77	3.5	69	3.8	58	3.2	48	3.0	38	3.6
Phoenix, AZ	56	0.9	60	0.9	65	1.0	73	0.3	82	0.1	91	0.0	95	1.1	94	1.0	88	0.6	77	0.6	64	0.7	55	0.9
Pittsburgh, PA	29	2.7	32	2.7	40	3.1	52	3.2	61	4.2	69	4.0	73	3.8	72	3.5	65	3.4	53	2.5	43	3.4	33	2.9
Portland, ME	22	3.4	26	3.3	34	4.2	44	4.3	54	4.0	63	3.8	69	3.6	68	3.1	60	3.7	49	4.9	39	4.9	29	4.0
Portland, OR	41	4.9	44	3.7	48	3.7	52	2.7	58	2.5	64	1.7	69	0.7	70	0.7	65	1.5	55	3.0	47	5.6	40	5.5
Providence, RI	29	3.9	32	3.3	39	5.0	49	4.4	59	3.6	68	3.4	73	3.3	72	3.6	65	3.9	54	3.9	45	4.5	34	4.2
Raleigh, NC	41	3.5	45	3.2	52	4.1	60	2.9	68	3.3	76	3.5	80	4.7	79	4.3	72	4.4	61	3.3	52	3.1	43	3.1
Rapid City, SD	25	0.3	27	0.4	35	0.9	45	1.8	55	3.2	65	2.5	73	1.9	72	1.6	61	1.3	48	1.4	35	0.5	25	0.4
Reno, NV	36	1.0	40	1.0	46	0.8	51	0.5	60	0.6	68	0.5	75	0.2	73	0.2	65	0.4	54	0.5	43	0.8	35	1.0
Richmond, VA	38	3.0	41	2.8	49	4.0	58	3.3	66	3.8	75	3.9	79	4.5	78	4.7	71	4.1	60	3.0	50	3.2	41	3.3
St. Louis, MO	32	2.4	36	2.2	46	3.3	57	3.7	67	4.7	76	4.3	80	4.1	79	3.0	70	3.1	59	3.3	47	3.9	35	2.8
Salt Lake City, UT	30	1.3	34	1.3	44	1.8	51	2.0	60	2.0	70	1.0	79	0.6	77	0.7	66	1.2	53	1.5	40	1.5	30	1.4
San Antonio, TX	52	1.8	56	1.8	62	2.3	69	2.1	77	4.0	82	4.1	85	2.7	85	2.1	80	3.0	71	4.1	61	2.3	53	1.9
San Diego, CA	57	2.0	58	2.3	59	1.8	62	0.8	64	0.1	66	0.1	70	0.0	72	0.0	71	0.2	67	0.6	61	1.0	57	1.5
San Francisco, CA	50	4.2	53	4.1	55	3.0	57	1.3	60	0.5	62	0.1	64	0.0	65	0.0	65	0.2	62	1.0	56	2.4	51	4.0
San Juan, PR	78	3.8	78	2.4	79	2.0	80	4.7	82	5.9	83	4.4	83	5.1	84	5.5	84	5.8	83	5.6	81	6.4	79	5.0
Santa Fe, NM	32	0.6	36	0.5	43	0.8	50	0.7	60	0.9	69	1.1	73	1.8	71	2.6	64	1.6	53	1.4	40	0.7	31	0.8
Savannah, GA	50	3.7	53	2.8	59	3.7	66	3.1	73	3.0	80	6.0	83	5.6	82	6.6	77	4.6	68	3.7	59	2.4	52	3.0
Seattle, WA	42	5.6	43	3.5	47	3.7	50	2.7	56	1.9	61	1.6	66	0.7	66	0.9	61	1.5	53	3.5	45	6.6	41	5.4
Spokane, WA	30	1.8	33	1.3	40	1.6	47	1.3	55	1.6	62	1.3	70	0.6	69	0.6	60	0.7	48	1.2	36	2.3	27	2.3
Springfield, MO	33	2.5	37	2.5	46	3.6	56	4.3	65	5.1	73	4.9	78	3.7	78	3.6	69	4.6	58	3.6	46	4.2	35	3.0
Tampa, FL	61	2.2	63	2.8	67	3.0	72	2.0	78	2.1	82	6.7	83	7.1	83	7.8	82	6.3	76	2.3	69	1.6	63	2.5
Washington, DC	36	2.8	39	2.6	47	3.5	57	3.1	66	4.0	75	3.8	80	3.7	78	2.9	71	3.7	60	3.4	50	3.0	40	3.1
Wilmington, DE	32	3.0	35	2.7	43	3.9	53	3.5	63	4.0	72	3.9	77	4.6	75	3.2	68	4.3	56	3.4	47	3.1	37	3.5
Windsor Locks, CT	26	3.2	30	2.9	38	3.6	49	3.7	60	4.4	69	4.4	74	4.2	72	3.9	64	3.9	52	4.4	42	3.9	32	3.4

Normal High and Low Temperatures, Precipitation in U.S. Cities

Source: National Climatic Data Center, NESDIS, NOAA, U.S. Dept. of Commerce

The normal temperatures and precipitation data given here are based on records for the period 1981-2010. The extreme temperatures are based on records from the time of each station's installation. (*) = city station. Other figures are for airport stations.

State	Station	NORMAL TEMPERATURE (°F) January Max.	January Min.	July Max.	July Min.	EXTREME TEMPERATURE (°F) Highest	Lowest	AVG. ANNUAL PRECIPITATION (in.)
Alabama	Mobile	61	40	91	73	105	3	66.15
Alaska	Anchorage	23	11	65	52	85	−34	16.58
Alaska	Barrow	−7	−20	47	35	79	−56	4.53
Alaska	Juneau	33	24	64	50	90	−22	62.27
Arizona	Phoenix	67	46	106	78	122	17	8.03
Arkansas	North Little Rock	50	33	92	73	111	−6	50.03
California	Los Angeles	65	49	74	64	110	23	12.82
California	San Francisco	56	44	72	55	106	20	20.65
Colorado	Denver	44	17	89	59	105	−19	14.92
Connecticut	Windsor Locks	35	18	85	63	102	−26	45.85
Delaware	Wilmington	40	25	86	68	103	11	43.08
District of Columbia	Washington–Reagan	43	29	88	71	105	−5	39.74
Florida	Jacksonville	65	41	92	73	105	7	52.39
Florida	Miami	76	60	91	77	98	30	61.90
Georgia	Atlanta	52	34	89	71	105	−8	49.71
Georgia	Savannah	60	39	92	73	105	3	47.96
Hawaii	Honolulu	80	66	88	75	95	53	17.10
Idaho	Boise	38	25	91	60	111	−25	11.73
Illinois	Chicago	31	17	84	64	104	−27	36.89
Indiana	Indianapolis	36	21	85	66	104	−27	42.44
Iowa	Des Moines	31	14	86	67	108	−26	36.01
Kansas	Dodge City	44	20	93	66	110	−21	21.60
Kentucky	Lexington	41	25	86	66	103	−21	45.17
Kentucky	Louisville	43	27	89	70	106	−22	44.91
Louisiana	New Orleans	62	45	91	75	102	11	62.66
Maine	Caribou	20	1	76	55	96	−41	38.49
Maine	Portland	31	13	79	59	103	−39	47.25
Maryland	Baltimore	41	24	87	67	105	−7	41.88
Massachusetts	Boston	36	22	81	65	102	−12	43.77
Michigan	Detroit	32	19	83	64	104	−21	33.47
Michigan	Grand Rapids	31	18	83	62	100	−22	38.27
Michigan	Sault Ste. Marie	23	8	76	54	98	−36	32.95
Minnesota	Duluth	19	2	76	55	97	−39	30.96
Minnesota	Minneapolis	24	8	83	64	105	−34	30.61
Mississippi	Jackson	56	35	92	72	107	2	54.14
Missouri	Kansas City	38	20	88	68	109	−23	38.86
Missouri	St. Louis	40	24	89	71	107	−18	40.96
Montana	Helena	33	13	86	54	105	−42	11.22
Nebraska	Omaha	33	14	87	66	114	−23	30.62
Nevada	Reno	46	25	92	58	108	−16	7.40
New Hampshire	Concord	31	10	82	58	102	−37	40.61
New Jersey	Atlantic City	42	25	86	67	106	−11	41.75
New Mexico	Albuquerque	47	26	90	66	107	−17	9.45
New York	Albany	31	15	82	61	100	−28	39.35
New York	Buffalo	31	19	80	62	99	−20	40.48
New York	New York–Central Park*	38	27	84	69	106	−15	49.94
North Carolina	Raleigh	51	31	90	70	105	−9	43.34
North Dakota	Bismarck	23	2	85	57	112	−44	17.85
Ohio	Cleveland	34	22	83	64	104	−20	39.14
Ohio	Columbus	37	23	85	66	102	−22	39.31
Oklahoma	Oklahoma City	50	29	94	72	110	−8	36.52
Oregon	Portland	47	36	81	58	107	−3	36.03
Pennsylvania	Philadelphia	40	26	87	69	104	−7	41.53
Pennsylvania	Pittsburgh	36	21	83	63	103	−22	38.19
Puerto Rico	San Juan	83	72	89	78	98	60	56.35
Rhode Island	Providence	37	21	83	64	104	−13	47.18
South Carolina	Charleston	59	38	91	73	105	6	51.03
South Dakota	Huron	27	7	86	61	112	−41	22.90
South Dakota	Rapid City	37	13	87	58	111	−31	16.29
Tennessee	Memphis	50	33	92	74	108	−13	53.68
Tennessee	Nashville	47	28	89	68	107	−17	47.25
Texas	Dallas-Fort Worth	56	36	96	75	113	−1	36.14
Texas	Houston	63	43	94	75	109	7	49.77
Utah	Salt Lake City	37	22	93	65	107	−30	16.10
Vermont	Burlington	27	10	81	60	101	−30	36.82
Virginia	Norfolk	48	33	87	72	105	−3	46.53
Virginia	Richmond	47	28	90	69	105	−12	43.60
Washington	Seattle-Tacoma	47	37	76	56	103	0	37.49
Washington	Spokane	34	25	83	56	108	−25	16.56
West Virginia	Charleston	43	26	85	66	104	−16	44.03
Wisconsin	Milwaukee	29	16	80	64	103	−26	34.76
Wyoming	Lander	33	10	87	56	101	−37	12.66

Mean annual snowfall (in.): Based on climate normals 1981-2010: Albany, NY, 59.1; Anchorage, AK, 74.5; Boston, MA, 43.8; Burlington, VT, 81.2; Lander, WY, 91.4; Sault Ste. Marie, MI, 123.4.

World's wettest spot: Quibdo, Colombia, may be the rainiest place in the world. It has a recorded average annual rainfall of 354 in.

Temperature extremes: The world's highest temperature ever recorded under standard conditions was 134°F in Death Valley, CA, on July 10, 1913. The world record low of −128.5°F was recorded at the Soviet station of Vostok in Antarctica on July 21, 1983. The record low in the U.S. was −80°F at Prospect Creek, AK, Jan. 23, 1971.

Annual Climatological Data for U.S. Cities, 2011

Source: National Climatic Data Center, NESDIS, NOAA, U.S. Dept. of Commerce

Station	Elev. (ft)	TEMPERATURE (°F) Highest	Date	Lowest	Date	PRECIPITATION[1] Total (in.)	Greatest in 24 hrs. (in.)	Date	Snowfall[2] Total snow-fall (in.)	Greatest in 24 hrs. (in.)	Date	FASTEST[3] WIND MPH	Date	NO. OF DAYS Prec. 0.01 in. or more	Snow, sleet 1 in. or more
Albany, NY	281	99	7/21	−13	1/24	53.68	4.81	8/27-28	80.3	12.8	1/12	40	2/19	142	16
Albuquerque, NM	5,308	100	6/26+	−7	2/3	4.72	0.98	10/4-5	5.1	1.4	12/19	54	12/1	40	2
Anchorage, AK	222	72	7/22	−12	1/16	17.16	1.00	12/11-12	93.1	6.8	12/12	35	11/16	139	32
Asheville, NC	2,174	93	8/8+	4	1/14	46.04	2.59	11/28	10.0	7.7	1/10	41	6/18	123	2
Atlanta, GA	974	99	8/26	19	1/9	39.23	3.02	3/26-27	5.6	3.7	1/9	40	6/26	108	2
Atlantic City, NJ	117	105	7/23+	5	1/24	48.52	5.75	8/27-28	17.1	7.7	1/8	46	2/25	122	5
Baltimore, MD	196	106	7/22	8	1/24	56.52	4.69	8/27-28	13.2	7.6	1/26	45	2/25	133	3
Barrow, AK	38	62	7/19	−45	1/24	6.59	0.41	7/12-13	77.1	6.5	12/4	49	2/23	127	26
Birmingham, AL	630	100	8/26+	16	1/14+	58.32	7.20	9/4-5	2.0	1.0	2/9	46	4/27	102	2
Bismarck, ND	1,654	97	7/19	−32	2/2	23.22	2.48	8/15-16	54.8	7.0	3/22	56	8/15	119	16
Boise, ID	2,861	103	7/24	9	1/1	10.49	0.81	1/15-16	6.7	1.5	2/17	41	7/7	91	3
Boston, MA	180	103	7/22	−2	1/24	52.39	2.48	12/7-8	60.0	14.6	1/12	46	8/28	138	12
Buffalo, NY	717	95	7/22	−8	1/24	49.56	2.07	5/14-15	82.0	8.0	2/25	46	4/28	177	26
Burlington, VT	348	97	7/21	−19	1/24	50.92	3.38	8/28	112.1	17.1	3/7	38	8/28	165	24
Caribou, ME	626	87	7/23+	−16	3/4	55.36	4.04	6/8-9	108.2	15.9	3/7	52	7/22	169	25
Charleston, SC	48	102	7/21+	19	1/14	37.01	2.98	8/13	T	T	4/21	45	7/13	93	0
Chicago, IL	658	99	7/21+	−9	2/10	49.83	8.21	7/22-23	43.4	13.6	2/1	55	6/21	142	8
Cleveland, OH	805	97	7/21	−1	2/10	65.32	3.85	8/14-15	64.7	8.9	2/25	46	4/28	170	18
Columbus, OH	812	97	9/3+	−2	1/22	54.96	2.17	9/11	21.9	5.7	1/20	46	2/28	160	6
Dallas-Ft. Worth, TX	562	110	8/2	13	2/2	25.88	2.84	6/21	4.3	2.6	2/4	46	6/18	64	1
Denver, CO	5,382	99	8/25	−17	2/2	17.31	1.95	5/11-12	47.5	8.0	10/26	51	7/13	80	16
Des Moines, IA	971	99	8/2+	−9	2/8	37.20	4.87	6/9-10	34.3	6.4	2/1	44	6/26	111	11
Detroit, MI	631	100	7/21	−5	2/10	47.70	3.51	7/27-28	66.1	8.2	2/20	46	7/2	164	17
Duluth, MN	1,429	92	7/18	−25	1/21	26.07	2.57	8/1-2	51.5	4.4	1/14	43	6/1	134	21
Fairbanks, AK	464	88	6/25	−44	2/15	9.52	0.92	2/20-21	63.6	17.1	2/20	37	2/25	106	17
Fresno, CA	375	107	6/22	28	12/24	10.92	1.89	3/20-21	T	T	3/23	31	12/1	37	0
Grand Rapids, MI	788	97	7/20	−9	1/23	45.09	4.16	7/27-28	67.7	11.1	2/2	43	7/11	152	24
Helena, MT	3,867	99	7/18	−19	2/26+	13.28	1.65	6/6-7	31.7	6.9	11/18	45	12/29	94	10
Honolulu, HI	18	90	10/8+	59	1/11	15.69	2.44	1/12-13	—	—	—	39	3/4	108	—
Houston, TX	107	109	8/27	21	2/2	24.57	3.02	10/9	T	T	7/6	47	9/29	66	0
Huron, SD	1,284	100	8/1	−25	2/8	22.71	2.72	6/20-21	52.0	10.0	2/20	48	8/11	99	14
Indianapolis, IN	797	100	9/3	−3	1/21	49.63	3.31	4/19-20	23.3	4.4	1/11	44	4/19	136	8
Jackson, MS	296	102	7/10	18	2/11	49.46	10.69	9/4-5	—	—	—	39	11/22	88	—
Jacksonville, FL	34	99	8/27+	22	1/13	47.96	2.64	1/25	—	—	—	41	5/14	93	—
Kansas City, MO	1,008	107	8/2	−12	2/3	36.92	2.40	8/20	34.1	8.9	2/1	49	8/20	101	6
Knoxville, TN	982	99	8/3	12	1/14+	56.64	5.98	9/5-6	7.4	4.3	1/10	46	6/21	124	2
Lander, WY	5,560	97	7/25	−20	2/2	15.42	3.21	5/18-19	80.9	8.4	12/21	54	6/6	71	23
Lexington, KY	984	98	9/3+	−2	1/22	66.35	3.69	4/11-12	15.0	3.3	1/20+	45	4/12	145	6
Los Angeles, CA	326	92	10/13	40	12/23	9.87	2.47	3/20-21	—	—	—	32	11/30	32	—
Louisville, KY	484	102	9/3	6	1/22	68.02	3.66	4/11-12	11.4	3.6	1/20	47	7/20	133	4
Marquette, MI	1,415	94	7/20+	−18	2/11	29.43	2.90	9/29	161.8	11.4	11/9	—	—	158	43
Memphis, TN	254	106	8/3	11	2/11	58.36	4.98	12/4-5	10.8	3.1	2/9	45	6/16	108	5
Miami, FL	29	97	7/17	44	1/23	63.78	5.37	10/7-8	—	—	—	46	6/30	131	—
Milwaukee, WI	680	98	7/20	−7	2/10	32.59	1.65	4/25-26	54.8	9.1	2/2	46	2/2	61	16
Minneapolis, MN	872	103	6/7	−16	1/21	26.91	2.92	7/15-16	53.5	11.8	2/20	37	9/29	116	18
Mobile, AL	212	103	6/4	21	1/13	50.42	6.92	9/3-4	T	T	2/5+	44	8/24	106	0
Moline, IL	607	100	7/19	−17	2/3	34.83	1.76	5/25-26	30.7	14.8	2/1	44	4/10	118	7
Nashville, TN	600	102	8/3	7	2/11	52.14	2.34	9/4-5	8.0	2.5	1/10	40	4/27	116	4
Newark, NJ	28	108	7/22	5	1/24	69.91	8.92	8/27-28	48.9	11.0	1/26	45	8/28	127	10
New Orleans, LA	7	100	7/2	28	1/14+	54.63	7.00	9/2-3	—	—	—	47	3/9	90	—
New York, NY	161	104	7/22	6	1/24	72.81	6.86	8/27-28	44.7	12.3	1/26	32	8/28	126	12
Norfolk, VA	69	103	7/23	19	2/11+	51.10	7.92	8/27	4.0	3.3	2/10	45	8/27	110	1
North Little Rock, AR	565	111	8/3	12	2/10	62.98	4.50	11/21	17.9	6.2	2/9	—	—	101	6
Oklahoma City, OK	1,284	110	8/6+	−5	2/10	30.37	5.86	5/19-20	19.6	11.8	2/1	51	4/15	66	3
Philadelphia, PA	62	103	7/22	8	1/24	64.33	5.70	8/27-28	31.6	14.2	1/26	53	8/18	130	7
Phoenix, AZ	1,106	118	7/2	30	2/4+	4.66	0.76	7/24-25	—	—	—	46	7/10	33	—
Pittsburgh, PA	1,175	96	7/22	−1	1/22	43.51	1.39	2/27-28	47.3	7.9	2/21	43	4/20	173	13
Portland, ME	72	100	7/22	−13	1/24	51.77	2.97	7/29-30	74.2	13.0	1/12	40	8/28	139	18
Portland, OR	223	96	8/20	18	2/26	37.10	2.40	11/22-23	—	—	—	40	3/13	165	—
Providence, RI	53	101	7/22	−2	1/24	5.72	2.40	7/8-9	45.2	12.2	1/12	43	12/22	126	12
Raleigh-Durham, NC	430	104	7/29	16	1/23	43.70	4.31	8/6	0.7	0.4	2/10	38	4/5	100	0
Rapid City, SD	3,153	103	7/31	−20	2/2	19.42	2.45	5/19-20	76.3	9.7	2/20	54	4/30	108	20
Reno, NV	4,407	100	7/29	10	12/24	4.92	0.57	2/18	24.4	6.3	1/28	49	2/14	39	7
Richmond, VA	167	103	7/29	11	1/23	47.54	5.37	8/27-28	2.8	2.0	1/7	51	12/7	111	1
St. Louis, MO	710	104	9/1	0	1/21	47.17	4.45	6/25-26	30.7	5.7	1/20	52	2/27	126	10
Salt Lake City, UT	4,224	101	7/3	5	1/1	19.14	1.24	10/5-6	39.8	3.7	2/16	52	4/21	100	17
San Antonio, TX	821	110	8/28	19	2/2	17.58	3.12	10/8-9	0.4	0.4	2/4	37	2/1	54	0
San Diego, CA	81	97	9/6	41	12/24+	9.08	1.40	11/12	—	—	—	32	3/20	39	—
San Francisco, CA	89	90	9/28	35	2/26	16.59	1.52	3/23-24	—	—	—	49	5/22	71	—
San Juan, PR	10	94	9/12	69	5/21	88.14	5.91	8/21-22	0.0	0.0	—	45	8/22	226	0
Sault Ste. Marie, MI	727	88	7/17	−22	1/23	38.18	1.49	4/26-27	71.1	4.1	3/3	38	5/11	159	26
Savannah, GA	143	102	6/13	18	1/14	34.85	4.90	6/29	T	T	1/22+	47	7/31	84	0
Scottsbluff, NE	3,949	102	8/23	−20	2/2	18.85	1.97	5/11-12	38.5	4.7	3/6	46	6/16	103	14
Seattle, WA	434	87	8/21	19	2/26	36.39	2.06	11/22-23	4.8	2.8	1/11	38	12/25	166	2
Spokane, WA	2,384	94	8/20	−10	2/26+	15.40	0.90	4/25-26	34.7	6.8	2/23	45	2/28	123	9
Springfield, MO	1,280	108	8/2	−10	2/10	40.61	3.53	4/24-25	19.3	10.0	2/1	44	7/24	119	5
Tampa, FL	40	95	7/6	31	1/13	53.22	4.82	7/7-8	0.0	0.0	—	39	1/25	90	—
Washington, DC	3	104	7/29	17	1/24+	46.89	3.83	8/27-28	8.0	5.0	1/26	47	8/28	126	2
Wilmington, DE	77	102	7/22	8	1/24	56.58	6.94	8/27-28	23.4	10.3	1/26	45	2/25	126	5
Windsor Locks, CT	165	103	7/22	−7	1/24	69.23	5.20	8/27-28	84.5	24.0	1/12	44	2/19	131	16

(+) = Indicates value for extreme also occurred on an earlier date(s). (T) = Trace amount. — = Data not available or unreported. (1) Where one value is shown, it is the starting date of the storm. (2) Comprises all forms of frozen precipitation, including hail and sleet. (3) Sustained for at least 2 mins., not peak gust.

Record Temperatures by State

Source: National Climatic Data Center, NESDIS, NOAA, U.S. Dept. of Commerce
(through 2011)

		LOWEST TEMPERATURE		Approx. elevation (ft)		HIGHEST TEMPERATURE		Approx. elevation (ft)
State	°F	Latest date	Station		°F	Latest date	Station	
Alabama	−27	Jan. 30, 1966	New Market	732	112	Sept. 6, 1925	Centerville	220
Alaska	−80	Jan. 23, 1971	Prospect Creek Camp	955	100	June 27, 1915	Fort Yukon	445
Arizona	−40	Jan. 7, 1971	Hawley Lake	8,180	128	June 29, 1994	Lake Havasu City	505
Arkansas	−29	Feb. 13, 1905	Brook Farm Pond	1,260	120	Aug. 10, 1936	Ozark	390
California	−45	Jan. 20, 1937	Boca	5,575	134	July 10, 1913	Greenland Ranch	−194
Colorado	−61	Feb. 1, 1985	Maybell	5,944	114	July 11, 1954[1]	Sedgwick	3,584
Connecticut	−32	Jan. 22, 1961[1]	Coventry	480	106	July 15, 1995[1]	Danbury	405
Delaware	−17	Jan. 17, 1893	Millsboro	20	110	July 21, 1930	Millsboro	20
Florida	−2	Feb. 13, 1899	Tallahassee	192	109	June 29, 1931	Monticello	98
Georgia	−17	Jan. 27, 1940	CCC Fire Camp F-16	1,000	112	Aug. 20, 1983[1]	Greenville	960
Hawaii	12	May 17, 1979	Mauna Kea Observ.	13,773	100	Apr. 27, 1931	Pahala	840
Idaho	−60	Jan. 18, 1943	Island Park Dam	6,290	118	July 28, 1934	Orofino	1,320
Illinois	−36	Jan. 5, 1999	Congerville	635	117	July 14, 1954	East St. Louis	410
Indiana	−36	Jan. 19, 1994	New Whiteland	785	116	July 14, 1936	Collegeville	650
Iowa	−47	Feb. 3, 1996[1]	Elkader	788	118	July 20, 1934	Keokuk	651
Kansas	−40	Feb. 13, 1905	Lebanon	1,874	121	July 24, 1936[1]	Alton	1,591
Kentucky	−37	Jan. 19, 1994	Shelbyville	730	114	July 28, 1930	Greensburg	590
Louisiana	−16	Feb. 13, 1899	Minden	200	114	Aug. 10, 1936	Plain Dealing	290
Maine	−50	Jan. 16, 2009	Big Black River	885	105	July 10, 1911[1]	North Bridgton	449
Maryland	−40	Jan. 13, 1912	Oakland	2,420	109	July 10, 1936[1]	Cumberland	899
							Frederick	380
Massachusetts	−35	Jan. 12, 1981[1]	Chester	640	107	Aug. 2, 1975	Chester	640
							New Bedford	70
Michigan	−51	Feb. 9, 1934	Vanderbilt	905	112	July 13, 1936	Mio	960
							Stanwood	830
Minnesota	−60	Feb. 2, 1996	Tower	1,485	115	July 29, 1917	Beardsley	1,089
Mississippi	−19	Jan. 30, 1966	Corinth	420	115	July 29, 1930	Holly Springs	502
Missouri	−40	Feb. 13, 1905	Warsaw	705	118	July 14, 1954	Warsaw	705
							Union	540
Montana	−70	Jan. 20, 1954	Rogers Pass	5,545	117	July 5, 1937[1]	Medicine Lake	1,942
Nebraska	−47	Dec. 22, 1989[1]	Oshkosh	3,390	118	July 24, 1936[1]	Minden	2,160
Nevada	−50	Jan. 8, 1937	San Jacinto	5,203	125	June 29, 1994	Laughlin	605
New Hampshire	−46	Jan. 8, 1968	Mt. Washington	6,267	106	July 4, 1911	Nashua	140
New Jersey	−34	Jan. 5, 1904	River Vale	70	110	July 10, 1936	Runyon	20
New Mexico	−50	Feb. 1, 1951	Gavilan	7,425	122	June 27, 1994	Waste Isolat. Pilot Plant	3,411
New York	−52	Feb. 18, 1979	Old Forge	1,748	108	July 22, 1926	Troy	35
North Carolina	−34	Jan. 21, 1985	Mt. Mitchell	6,240	110	Aug. 21, 1983	Fayetteville	186
North Dakota	−60	Feb. 15, 1936	Parshall	1,952	121	July 6, 1936	Steele	1,885
Ohio	−39	Feb. 10, 1899	Milligan	875	113	July 21, 1934	Gallipolis (near)	669
Oklahoma	−27	Jan. 4, 1947[1]	Guthrie	1,110	120	June 27, 1994[1]	Tipton	1,269
Oregon	−54	Feb. 10, 1933[1]	Seneca	4,660	119	Aug. 10, 1898[1]	Pendleton	1,040
Pennsylvania	−42	Jan. 5, 1904	Smethport	1,469	111	July 10, 1936[1]	Phoenixville	105
Rhode Island	−28	Jan. 11, 1942	Wood River Junction	49	104	Aug. 2, 1975	Providence	60
South Carolina	−19	Jan. 21, 1985	Caesars Head	3,200	111	June 28, 1954[1]	Camden	140
South Dakota	−58	Feb. 17, 1936	McIntosh	2,175	120	July 15, 2006[1]	Fort Pierre	1,590
Tennessee	−32	Dec. 30, 1917	Mountain City	2,503	113	Aug. 9, 1930[1]	Perryville	371
Texas	−23	Feb. 8, 1933	Seminole	3,336	120	June 28, 1994[1]	Monahans	2,547
Utah	−50	Jan. 5, 1913	Strawberry Tunnel E.	7,615	117	July 5, 1985	Saint George	2,770
Vermont	−50	Dec. 30, 1933	Bloomfield	1,040	107	July 7, 1912	Vernon	226
Virginia	−30	Jan. 21, 1985	Mountain Lake Bio. Station	3,870	110	July 15, 1954[1]	Balcony Falls	732
Washington	−48	Dec. 30, 1968	Mazama Winthrop	2,106 1,749	118	Aug. 5, 1961[1]	Ice Harbor Dam	368
West Virginia	−37	Dec. 30, 1917	Lewisburg	2,251	112	July 10, 1936[1]	Martinsburg	534
Wisconsin	−55	Feb. 4, 1996[1]	Couderay	1,300	114	July 13, 1936	Wisconsin Dells	835
Wyoming	−66	Feb. 9, 1933	Riverside Ranger Sta.	6,500	115	July 15, 1988[1]	Diversion Dam	5,575

(1) Also on earlier dates at the same or other places.

Hurricane and Tornado Classifications

Source: National Weather Service, NOAA, U.S. Dept. of Commerce

The Saffir-Simpson Hurricane Wind Scale rates a hurricane's intensity from 1 to 5. The scale, updated in 2012, provides examples of the type of damage and impacts associated with winds of the indicated intensity. The Fujita (or F) Scale was created by T. Theodore Fujita in 1971 to classify tornadoes. The Enhanced Fujita Scale, an update to the original, was implemented in the U.S. in 2007. It uses 3-sec. gusts estimated at the point of damage based on a judgment of several levels of damage to 28 indicators.

Saffir-Simpson Wind Scale (Hurricanes)			Enhanced Fujita Scale (Tornadoes)	
Category	Winds[1]	Summary of damage	Rank	3-sec. gust
1	74-95 mph	Very dangerous winds will produce some damage.	EF-0	65-85 mph
2	96-110 mph	Extremely dangerous winds will cause extensive damage.	EF-1	86-110 mph
3	111-129 mph	Devastating damage will occur.	EF-2	111-135 mph
4	130-156 mph	Catastrophic damage will occur.	EF-3	136-165 mph
5	Over 156 mph	Catastrophic damage will occur.	EF-4	166-200 mph
(1) 1-min. sustained winds.			EF-5	Over 200 mph

Tropical Cyclone Names in 2013

Source: National Weather Service, NOAA, U.S. Dept. of Commerce

Atlantic: Andrea, Barry, Chantal, Dorian, Erin, Fernand, Gabrielle, Humberto, Ingrid, Jerry, Karen, Lorenzo, Melissa, Nestor, Olga, Pablo, Rebekah, Sebastien, Tanya, Van, Wendy. If there are more than 21 named Atlantic storms in one season, remaining storms take names from the Greek alphabet, starting with Alpha. (This has only been necessary once, in 2005.)

Eastern North Pacific: Alvin, Barbara, Cosme, Dalila, Erick, Flossie, Gil, Henriette, Ivo, Juliette, Kiko, Lorena, Manuel, Narda, Octave, Priscilla, Raymond, Sonia, Tico, Velma, Wallis, Xina, York, Zelda.

World Temperature and Precipitation

Source: World Meteorological Organization

Average daily maximum and minimum temperatures and annual precipitation based on records for the period 1961-90. Records of extreme temperatures include all available years of data for a given location and are usually for a longer period. Surface elevations are supplied by the WMO and may differ from figures in other sections of *The World Almanac*. NA = Not available.

Station	Surface elevation (ft)	Temperature (°F) AVERAGE DAILY January Max.	January Min.	July Max.	July Min.	EXTREME Max.	EXTREME Min.	Avg. annual precipitation (in.)
Algiers, Algeria	82	61.7	42.6	87.1	65.3	NA	NA	27.0
Athens, Greece	49	56.1	44.6	88.9	73.0	NA	NA	14.6
Auckland, New Zealand	20	74.8	61.2	58.5	46.4	NA	NA	49.4
Bangkok, Thailand	66	89.6	69.8	90.9	77.0	104	51	59.0
Berlin, Germany	190	35.2	26.8	73.6	55.2	107	−4	23.3
Bogotá, Colombia	8,357	67.3	41.7	64.6	45.5	75	21	32.4
Bucharest, Romania	298	34.7	22.1	83.8	60.1	105	−18	23.4
Budapest, Hungary	456	34.2	24.8	79.7	59.7	103	−10	20.3
Buenos Aires, Argentina	82	85.8	67.3	59.7	45.7	104	22	45.2
Cairo, Egypt	243	65.8	48.2	93.9	71.1	118	34	1.0
Cape Town, South Africa	138	79.0	60.3	63.3	44.6	105	28	20.5
Caracas, Venezuela	2,739	79.9	60.8	81.3	66.0	96	45	36.1
Casablanca, Morocco	203	62.8	47.1	77.7	66.7	NA	NA	16.8
Copenhagen, Denmark	16	35.6	28.4	68.9	55.0	NA	NA	NA
Damascus, Syria	2,004	54.3	32.9	97.2	61.9	NA	NA	5.6
Dublin, Ireland	279	45.7	36.5	66.0	52.5	86	8	28.8
Geneva, Switzerland	1,364	38.3	27.9	76.3	53.2	101	−3	35.6
Havana, Cuba	164	78.4	65.5	88.3	74.8	NA	NA	46.9
Hong Kong, China	203	65.5	56.5	88.7	79.9	97	32	87.2
Istanbul, Turkey	108	47.8	37.2	82.8	65.3	105	7	27.4
Jerusalem, Israel	2,483	53.4	39.4	83.8	63.0	107	26	23.2
Lagos, Nigeria	125	90.0	72.3	82.8	72.1	NA	NA	59.3
Lima, Peru	43	79.0	66.9	66.4	59.4	NA	NA	0.2
London, England	203	44.1	32.7	71.1	52.3	99	2	29.7
Manila, Philippines	79	85.8	74.8	89.1	76.8	NA	NA	49.6
Mexico City, Mexico	7,570	70.3	43.7	73.8	53.2	NA	NA	33.4
Montreal, Canada	118	21.6	5.2	79.2	59.7	100	−36	37.0
Mumbai (Bombay), India	36	85.3	66.7	86.2	77.5	110	46	85.4
Nairobi, Kenya	5,897	77.9	50.9	71.6	48.6	NA	NA	41.9
Paris, France	213	42.8	33.6	75.2	55.2	105	−1	25.6
Prague, Czech Republic	1,197	32.7	22.5	73.9	53.2	98	−16	20.7
Reykjavik, Iceland	200	35.4	26.6	55.9	46.9	76	−3	31.5
Rome, Italy	79	53.8	35.4	88.2	62.1	NA	NA	33.0
San Salvador, El Salvador	2,037	86.5	61.3	86.2	66.4	105	45	68.3
São Paulo, Brazil	2,598	81.1	65.7	71.2	53.1	NA	NA	57.4
Shanghai, China	23	45.9	32.9	88.9	76.6	104	10	43.8
Singapore	52	85.8	73.6	87.4	75.6	NA	NA	84.6
Stockholm, Sweden	171	30.7	23.0	71.4	56.1	97	−26	21.2
Sydney, Australia	10	79.5	65.5	62.4	43.9	114	32	46.4
Tehran, Iran	3,906	45.0	30.0	98.2	75.2	109	−5	9.1
Tokyo, Japan	118	49.1	34.2	83.8	72.1	NA	NA	55.4
Toronto, Canada	567	27.5	12.0	80.2	57.6	105	−26	30.8

Speed of Winds in the U.S.

Source: National Climatic Data Center, NESDIS, NOAA, U.S. Dept. of Commerce

Based on available records through 2011. Average and maximum speeds are annual. Max. speeds are highest 1-min. average.

Station	Avg. mph	Max. mph	Station	Avg. mph	Max. mph	Station	Avg. mph	Max. mph
Albuquerque, NM	8.9	54	Helena, MT[2]	7.7	73	Oklahoma City, OK	12.2	74
Anchorage, AK[1,2]	7.1	75	Honolulu, HI	11.2	46	Omaha, NE	10.5	70
Atlanta, GA	9.1	60	Houston, TX	7.6	51	Philadelphia, PA[2]	9.5	73
Baltimore, MD[2]	8.7	80	Indianapolis, IN	9.6	60	Phoenix, AZ	6.2	54
Birmingham, AL[2]	7.1	65	Jackson, MS	6.8	55	Pittsburgh, PA	8.9	58
Bismarck, ND	10.2	64	Jacksonville, FL	7.8	57	Portland, ME	8.7	57
Boise, ID[2]	8.7	61	Little Rock, AR[2]	7.7	65	Portland, OR[2]	7.9	88
Boston, MA	12.3	54	Los Angeles, CA[2]	4.9	49	Providence, RI	10.4	90
Buffalo, NY[2]	11.8	91	Louisville, KY	8.3	56	Richmond, VA	7.7	51
Burlington, VT	9.0	39	Miami, FL	9.2	86	St. Louis, MO	9.6	53
Charleston, SC	8.6	52	Milwaukee, WI	11.5	54	Salt Lake City, UT[2]	8.8	71
Chicago, IL	10.3	58	Minn.-St. Paul, MN	10.5	51	San Francisco, CA[2]	8.7	47
Cleveland, OH	10.5	53	Mobile, AL	8.7	66	San Juan, PR	8.3	79
Dallas-Ft. Worth, TX	10.7	73	Mount Washington, NH[1,2]	35.1	231	Seattle, WA[2]	8.8	66
Denver, CO	8.7	54	Nashville, TN	7.9	58	Sioux Falls, SD	11.0	70
Des Moines, IA[2]	10.7	76	Newark, NJ	10.2	82	Washington, DC	9.4	49
Detroit, MI	10.1	61	New Orleans, LA	8.2	69	Wichita, KS	12.2	70
Hartford, CT	8.4	46	New York, NY	9.1	40	Wilmington, DE	9.0	58

(1) Max. speed based on short gusts. (2) Max. speed calculated from minimum time during which 1 mi of wind passed the station.

Wind Chill Temperature

Source: National Weather Service, NOAA, U.S. Dept. of Commerce

Temperature and wind combine to cause heat loss from body surfaces. For example, a temperature of 5°F, plus a 10-mph wind, causes body heat loss equal to that which would occur in –10°F with no wind. In other words, a 10-mph wind makes 5°F feel like –10°F. Wind speeds greater than 45 mph have little additional chilling effect. Direct sunlight can increase the wind chill temperature 10° to 15°F. When the wind chill temperature falls within the shaded area, frostbite can occur in 30 mins. or less.

Calm	\multicolumn{17}{c}{Air temperature (°F)}
Wind speed (mph)	40	35	30	25	20	15	10	5	0	–5	–10	–15	–20	–25	–30	–35	–40	–45
	\multicolumn{18}{c}{Wind chill temperature (°F)}
5	36	31	25	19	13	7	1	–5	–11	–16	–22	–28	–34	–40	–46	–52	–57	–63
10	34	27	21	15	9	3	–4	–10	–16	–22	–28	–35	–41	–47	–53	–59	–66	–72
15	32	25	19	13	6	0	–7	–13	–19	–26	–32	–39	–45	–51	–58	–64	–71	–77
20	30	24	17	11	4	–2	–9	–15	–22	–29	–35	–42	–48	–55	–61	–68	–74	–81
25	29	23	16	9	3	–4	–11	–17	–24	–31	–37	–44	–51	–58	–64	–71	–78	–84
30	28	22	15	8	1	–5	–12	–19	–26	–33	–39	–46	–53	–60	–67	–73	–80	–87
35	28	21	14	7	0	–7	–14	–21	–27	–34	–41	–48	–55	–62	–69	–76	–82	–89
40	27	20	13	6	–1	–8	–15	–22	–29	–36	–43	–50	–57	–64	–71	–78	–84	–91
45	26	19	12	5	–2	–9	–16	–23	–30	–37	–44	–51	–58	–65	–72	–79	–86	–93

(Rows labeled under "Wind speed (mph)": 5, 10, 15, 20, 25, 30, 35, 40, 45)

Heat Index

Source: National Weather Service, NOAA, U.S. Dept. of Commerce

The heat index, or apparent temperature, is a measure of how hot it feels when the relative humidity is added to the actual air temperature. For example, when air temperature is 100°F, and relative humidity is 50%, it feels as if it's 118°F with no humidity. Full sunlight can make one feel even hotter. On the chart, the shaded area above 103°-105°F apparent temperature corresponds to a level that may cause increasingly severe heat disorders with continued exposure and/or physical activity.

Relative humidity %	\multicolumn{16}{c}{Temperature (°F)}
	80	82	84	86	88	90	92	94	96	98	100	102	104	106	108	110
	\multicolumn{16}{c}{Apparent temperature (°F)}
40	80	81	83	85	88	91	94	97	101	105	109	114	119	124	130	136
45	80	82	84	87	89	93	96	100	104	109	114	119	124	130	137	
50	81	83	85	88	91	95	99	103	108	113	118	124	131	137		
55	81	84	86	89	93	97	101	106	112	117	124	130	137			
60	82	84	88	91	95	100	105	110	116	123	129	137				
65	82	85	89	93	98	103	108	114	121	128	136					
70	83	86	90	95	100	105	112	119	126	134						
75	84	88	92	97	103	109	116	124	132							
80	84	89	94	100	106	113	121	129								
85	85	90	96	102	110	117	126	135								
90	86	91	98	105	113	122	131									
95	86	93	100	108	117	127										
100	87	95	103	112	121	132										

(Rows labeled under "Relative humidity %": 40, 45, 50, 55, 60, 65, 70, 75, 80, 85, 90, 95, 100)

☐ Caution　　☐ Extreme caution　　☐ Danger　　☐ Extreme danger

Ultraviolet (UV) Index Forecast

Source: National Weather Service, NOAA, U.S. Dept. of Commerce; U.S. Environmental Protection Agency; U.S. Food and Drug Administration, U.S. Dept. of Health and Human Services

The National Weather Service (NWS) and the Environmental Protection Agency (EPA) developed and began offering a UV index in 1994 in response to increasing incidences of skin cancer, cataracts, and other effects from exposure to the sun's harmful rays. In 2004, they adapted their index to the Global Solar UV Index sponsored by the World Health Organization. The UV index is now a regular element of NWS atmospheric forecasts.

The UV index, ranging from 0 to 11+, is an indication of the expected intensity of UV radiation reaching the Earth's surface during the solar noon hour (the time of day when the sun appears to have reached its highest point in the sky; it depends on location and the time of year). The lower the UV index value, the less the radiation. The UV index forecast is produced daily for 58 cities by the NWS Climate Prediction Center and uses the following scale.

UV index	Exposure	Minimum precautions
0-2	Low	Sunscreen with an SPF of at least 15
3-5	Moderate	Sunscreen, covering up
6-7	High	Sunscreen, hat, UV-blocking sunglasses, avoid sun 10 AM-4 PM
8-10	Very high	Same as above
11+	Extreme	Same as above

The index value is valid for a radius of about 30 miles around a listed city and is based on several factors:

Ozone. Ozone, a form of oxygen, the molecules of which consist of three atoms rather than two, blocks UV radiation. The more ozone, the lower the UV radiation at the surface.

Sun height. The higher the sun is in the sky, the higher the UV radiation level.

Cloudiness. UV radiation levels are highest under cloudless skies. Even with cloud cover, UV radiation levels can be high due to the scattering of UV radiation by water molecules and fine particles in the atmosphere.

Reflectivity. Reflective surfaces intensify UV exposure. White sand reflects about 15% of UV radiation reaching the surface; sea foam, 25%; snow, as much as 80%; water, up to 100% depending on reflection angle.

Elevation. At higher elevations, UV radiation travels a shorter distance to reach Earth's surface so there is less atmosphere to absorb the rays. For every 1,000 m (3,281 ft) one travels above sea level, UV levels increase by 10%-12%. Snow and lack of pollutants intensify UV exposure at higher altitudes.

Latitude. The closer a location is to the equator, the higher the UV radiation level.

SPF (sun protection factor) number. The UV index is not linked in any way to the SPF number on sunscreens. The Centers for Disease Control and Prevention recommends using a sunscreen with at least SPF 15. Under a Food and Drug Administration rule that took effect in 2012, sunscreens that protect against cancer and early skin aging as well as sunburn will be labeled as "broad spectrum."

Further information. For precautions to take after learning the UV index value, call the EPA's Stratospheric Ozone Hotline (800-296-1996). For questions on scientific aspects, visit the NWS Climate Prediction Center online at www.cpc.ncep.noaa.gov.

Lightning

Source: National Weather Service, NOAA, U.S. Dept. of Commerce

Lightning is a powerful electric discharge, or spark, that can occur in the atmosphere when an imbalance of positive and negative charges develops. It may travel within a cloud, between clouds, between a cloud and clear air, or between a cloud and the ground. Lightning generally accompanies rainstorms, but it sometimes is also seen with snowstorms, volcano eruption clouds, and violent forest fires. In a common form of cloud-to-ground lightning, a negatively charged area in a thunderstorm sends charges down toward positively charged objects. Lightning can travel miles away from the area of a storm.

The transfer of charges in lightning generates a huge amount of heat, sending the temperature in the channel to 50,000°F or more and causing the air within it to expand rapidly. The sound of that expansion is thunder. Sound travels more slowly than light, so lightning is usually observed before thunder is heard.

An estimated 25 mil cloud-to-ground lightning bolts happen in the U.S. each year. They killed an annual average of 54 people in 1982-2011. This is a small number compared to U.S. deaths from fire (about 3,000 a year) and motor vehicle accidents (more than 30,000 in recent years), but it is still significant. In comparison, tornadoes caused an average of 74 deaths a year and hurricanes an average of 47 over the same 30-year time period. According to preliminary figures from the National Weather Service, 26 people were struck and killed by lightning in 2011; 187 more were injured.

Most lightning deaths and injuries occur in summer when people are outdoors. If outdoors, one should run to a safe building or vehicle when thunder is first heard, lightning is seen, or dark threatening clouds are observed developing overhead. Even while indoors, one is advised to stay away from windows and doors and to avoid contact with anything conducting electricity, including corded phones, computers, and tubs, showers, and other plumbing. One should stay inside until 30 min. after the last clap of thunder is heard.

More information about lightning can be found online at www.lightningsafety.noaa.gov.

Global Temperature Extremes and Precipitation Records

Source: World Weather/Climate Extremes Archive, World Meteorological Organization (WMO) Commission for Climatology

(records in each category ranked from most to least extreme)

Highest Temperature Extremes

Continent	Highest temp. (°F)	Place	Elevation (ft)	Date
Africa	131	Kebili, Tunisia[1]	125	July 7, 1931
North America	134	Death Valley, CA, U.S. (Furnace Creek Ranch)	−179	July 10, 1913
Asia	129.2	Tirat Tsvi, Israel	−722	June 21, 1942
Australia	123	Oodnadatta, South Australia	367	Jan. 2, 1960
South America	120	Rivadavia, Argentina	2,192	Dec. 11, 1905
Europe	118.4	Athens, Greece (and Elefsina, Greece)	774	July 10, 1977
Oceania	108	Tuguegarao, Philippines	676	Apr. 29, 1912
Antarctica	59	Vanda Station (New Zealand), Wright Valley	49	May 1, 1974

(1) Previous record of 136.4°F set on Sept. 13, 1922, in El Azizia, Libya, was invalidated in Sept. 2012 after the WMO determined that an error had been made in recording the temperature.

Lowest Temperature Extremes

Continent	Lowest temp. (°F)	Place	Elevation (ft)	Date
Antarctica	−129	Vostok Station (Russia)	11,220	July 21, 1983
Asia	−90	Verkhoyansk, Russia	350	Feb. 5 and 7, 1892
	−90	Oimekon, Russia	2,625	Feb. 6, 1933
North America	−81.4	Snag, Yukon Territory, Canada	2,120	Feb. 3, 1947
Europe	−72.6	Ust'-Shchugor, Russia	279	Dec. 31, 1978
South America	−27	Sarmiento, Argentina	879	June 1, 1907
Africa	−11	Ifrane, Morocco	5,364	Feb. 11, 1935
Australia	−9.4	Charlotte Pass, New South Wales	5,758	June 29, 1994

(1) Previous record of 136.4°F set on Sept. 13, 1922, in El Azizia, Libya, was invalidated in Sept. 2012 after the WMO determined that an error had been made in recording the temperature.

Highest Measured Average Annual Precipitation Extremes

Continent	Highest avg. (in.)[1]	Place	Elevation (ft)	Years in averaging period
Asia	467.4	Mawsynram, India	4,695	38
Oceania	460.	Mt. Waialeale, Kauai, HI, U.S.	5,148	30
Africa	405.	Debundscha, Cameroon	30	32
South America	354.	Quibdo, Colombia	230	29
Australia	316.3	Bellenden Ker, Queensland	5,102	34
North America	276.	Henderson Lake, British Columbia, Canada	12	15
Europe	183.	Crkvica, Bosnia-Herzegovina	4,298	22
Antarctica	>31.5[2]	Along coast of E and W and over the Antarctic Peninsula		3[3]

(1) Official greatest average annual precipitation. The frequently cited record of 523.6 in. in Lloro, Colombia (14 mi SE and at a higher elevation than Quibdo) is an estimate. (2) Water equivalent. (3) July 1996-June 1999.

Lowest Measured Average Annual Precipitation Extremes

Continent	Lowest avg. (in.)	Place	Elevation (ft)	Years in averaging period
South America	0.03	Arica, Chile	213	59
Antarctica	0.08	Amundsen-Scott South Pole Station (U.S.)	9,301	10
Africa	<0.1	Wadi Halfa, Sudan	590	39
North America	1.2	Batagues, Mexico	69	14
Asia	1.8	Aden, Yemen	63	50
Australia	4.05	Troudaninna, South Australia	46	42
Europe	6.4	Astrakhan, Russia	66	25
Oceania	7.41	Mauna Kea Observatory, HI, U.S.	13,780	11[1]

(1) 1972-82.

OCEANOGRAPHY

Tides and Their Causes

Source: National Ocean Service, NOAA, U.S. Dept. of Commerce

The tides are natural phenomena involving the movement of waves in the Earth's large fluid bodies as a result of the gravitational attraction of the sun and moon. These two variable influences combined produce the complex recurrent cycle of the tides. Tides may occur in both oceans and seas; to a limited extent in large lakes and in the atmosphere; and, to a very minute degree, in the Earth itself. The length of time between succeeding tides can vary.

The tide-generating force represents the difference between (1) the centrifugal force produced by Earth's revolution around the common center-of-gravity of the Earth-moon system and (2) the gravitational attraction of the moon acting upon the Earth's overlying waters. The moon is about 390 times closer to Earth than is the sun. So despite its smaller mass, the moon's tide-raising force is two times greater.

The tide-generating forces of the moon and sun acting tangentially to the Earth's surface tend to cause a maximum accumulation of waters at two diametrically opposite points on the Earth's surface and to withdraw compensating amounts of water from all points 90° removed from these tidal bulges. As the Earth rotates beneath the maxima and minima of these tide-generating forces, a sequence of two high tides, separated by two low tides, is produced each lunar day (the time it takes for a specific site on the Earth to rotate from an exact point under the moon to the same point under the moon, 24 hours and 50 minutes) in what is called a **semidiurnal tide**. Each ocean basin reacts differently to tidal forces.

Twice each month, when the sun, moon, and Earth are directly aligned—the moon between the Earth and sun (at new moon) or on the opposite side of Earth from the sun (at full moon)—the sun and moon exert gravitational forces in a mutual or additive fashion. The highest high tides and lowest low tides, called **spring tides**, are produced at these times. At two positions 90° in between, the moon and sun's gravitational forces—imposed at right angles—counteract each other to the greatest extent, and the range between high and low tides is reduced, resulting in **neap tides**.

The inclination of the moon's monthly orbit and of the sun to the equator during Earth's yearly passage through its orbit produce a difference in the height of succeeding high and low tides, known as the diurnal inequality. In most cases, this produces a so-called **mixed tide**. In extreme cases, these phenomena may result in a **diurnal tide**, with only one high tide and one low tide each day. There are other monthly and yearly variations in the tides because of the elliptical shape of the orbits.

The range of tides in the open ocean is generally less than in the coastal regions, where the incoming tide can be augmented by the continental shelves, as well as by bays and estuaries. The largest tidal ranges in the world occur in the Bay of Fundy and in Ungava Bay, Canada, where the range of tide reaches 53 ft. In New Orleans, the periodic rise and fall of the diurnal tide is affected by the seasonal stages of the Mississippi River, being about 10 in. at low stage and 0 at high.

In every case, actual high or low tide can vary considerably from the average as a result of weather conditions such as strong winds, abrupt barometric pressure changes, or prolonged periods of extreme high or low pressure.

Mean Ranges of Tide

Place	Ft	In.	Place	Ft	In.	Place	Ft	In.
Baltimore, MD	1	2	Key West, FL	1	3	Provincetown, MA	9	3
Biloxi, MS	1	6	Los Angeles, CA	3	10	St. Petersburg, FL	1	7
Boston, MA	9	6	Miami Beach, FL	2	6	San Diego, CA	4	1
Charleston, SC	5	3	New London, CT	2	7	Sandy Hook, NJ	4	8
Eastport, ME	18	4	Newport, RI	3	6	San Francisco, CA	4	1
Ft. Pulaski, GA	6	11	New York, NY	4	6	San Juan, PR	1	1
Galveston, TX	1	0	Philadelphia, PA	6	1	Seattle, WA	7	8
Honolulu, HI	1	3	Portland, ME	9	1	Washington, DC	2	9

Note: Mean range is the difference in height between mean high water and mean low water.

El Niño and La Niña

Source: National Weather Service, NOAA, U.S. Dept. of Commerce

El Niño is a climatically significant disruption of the ocean-atmosphere system characterized by large-scale weakening of trade winds and warming of the surface layers in the central and eastern equatorial Pacific. The term *El Niño*, Spanish for "the little boy" or "the Christ Child," was originally used by fishermen to refer to a warm ocean current that appeared around Christmas off the west coasts of Ecuador and Peru lasting several months. The term has come to be reserved for exceptionally strong, warm currents that bring heavy rains.

El Niño events generally occur at irregular intervals of 2 to 7 years, at an average of once every 3 to 4 years. They typically last 12 to 18 months. The intensity of El Niño events varies depending on the area encompassed by the abnormally warm ocean temperatures. Some are strong, such as in 1982-83 and 1997-98. Others are considerably weaker, such as the 2009-10 event. The eastward extent of warmer than normal water varies from episode to episode.

El Niño influences weather around the globe, and its impacts are most clearly seen in the winter. During El Niño years, winter temperatures in the continental U.S. tend to be warmer than normal in the North and West Coast states and cooler than normal in the Southeast. Conditions tend to be wetter than normal over central and southern California, the Southwest states and across much of the South, and drier than normal over the northern portions of the Rocky Mountains and in the Ohio Valley. Globally, El Niño brings wetter than normal conditions to Peru and Chile and dry conditions to Australia and Indonesia. It should be noted that El Niño is only one of a number of factors influencing seasonal variations of climate.

La Niña ("the little girl") is characterized by colder than normal sea surface temperatures in the equatorial Pacific. La Niña typically brings wetter, cooler conditions to the Pacific Northwest and drier, warmer conditions to much of the southern U.S. El Niño and La Niña are opposite phases of the El Niño-Southern Oscillation (ENSO) cycle, which involves a shift in tropical sea-level pressure between the Eastern and Western Hemispheres.

The National Oceanographic and Atmospheric Administration and other agencies monitor these events using satellites, weather balloons, and buoys in the Pacific Ocean. Highly sophisticated numerical computer models of the ocean and atmosphere use these data to predict the onset and evolution of El Niño and La Niña.

DISASTERS

Some Notable Aircraft Disasters Since 1937

Source: National Transportation Safety Board; World Almanac research. As of Sept. 2012.

Particularly notable disasters are in bold. Asterisk (*) indicates number of deaths includes people on ground.

Date	Aircraft	Site of accident	Deaths
1937, May 6	**German zeppelin Hindenburg**	**Burned at mooring, Lakehurst, NJ**	**36***
1944, Aug. 23	U.S. Air Force B-24 Liberator bomber	Hit school, Freckleton, England	61*
1945, July 28	U.S. Army B-25.	Hit Empire State Building after getting lost in fog, New York, NY.	14*
1952, Dec. 20	U.S. Air Force C-124	Crashed at Moses Lake, WA	87
1953, Mar. 3	**Canadian Pacific DH-106 Comet**	**Crashed on takeoff from Karachi, Pakistan; world's first fatal commercial passenger jet crash**	**11**
1953, June 18	U.S. Air Force C-124	Crashed, burned near Tokyo, Japan	129
1955, Oct. 6	United Airlines DC-4	Crashed in Medicine Bow Peak, WY	66
1955, Nov. 1	United Airlines DC-6.	Bomb on board exploded near Longmont, CO.	44[1]
1956, June 20	Venezuelan Super Constellation	Crashed into Atlantic off Asbury Park, NJ	74
1956, June 30	TWA Super Const., United DC-7	Collided over Grand Canyon, AZ	128
1960, Dec. 16	United DC-8, TWA Super Const.	Collided over New York, NY, killing all 128 on planes, 6 on ground.	134*
1962, Mar. 16	Flying Tiger Super Constellation	Vanished in W Pacific en route to Philippines from Guam	107
1962, June 3	Air France Boeing 707	Crashed on takeoff from Paris, France.	130
1962, June 22	Air France Boeing 707	Crashed in storm, Guadeloupe, French W Indies	113
1963, Feb. 1	Lebanese Middle East Airlines Vickers Viscount 754, Turkish Mil. Douglas C-47	Collided over Ankara, Turkey, killing all 17 on planes, 87 on ground	104*
1963, June 3	Northwest Airlines DC-7	Crashed into Pacific off British Columbia, Canada.	101
1963, Nov. 29	Trans-Canada Air Lines DC-8	Crashed after takeoff from Montreal, QC, Canada.	118
1965, May 20	Pakistani Boeing 720	Crashed at airport in Cairo, Egypt	121
1966, Jan. 24	Air India Boeing 707	Crashed on Mont Blanc, France-Italy.	117
1966, Feb. 4	All-Nippon Boeing 727	Plunged into Tokyo Bay, Japan	133
1966, Mar. 5	BOAC Boeing 707	Crashed into Mt. Fuji, Japan, after encountering severe turbulence	124
1966, Dec. 24	U.S. military-chartered CL-44.	Crashed into village in S Vietnam.	129*
1967, Apr. 20	Globe Air Bristol Britannia	Crashed on approach to airport, Nicosia, Cyprus.	126
1967, July 19	Piedmont Boeing 727, Cessna 310	Collided over Hendersonville, NC.	82
1968, Apr. 20	S. African Airways Boeing 707	Crashed on takeoff from Windhoek, Namibia.	122
1968, May 3	Braniff International Electra	Crashed in storm near Dawson, TX	85
1969, Mar. 16	Venezuelan DC-9	Crashed after takeoff from Maracaibo, Venezuela.	155[2]
1969, Dec. 8	Olympic Airways DC-6B	Crashed in storm near Athens, Greece	93
1970, Feb. 15	Dominicana DC-9	Crashed into sea on takeoff from Santo Domingo, Dominican Rep.	102
1970, July 3	British-chartered DH-106 Comet	Crashed near Barcelona, Spain.	112
1970, July 5	Air Canada DC-8	Crashed near Toronto Intl. Airport, ON, Canada	108
1970, Aug. 9	LANSA Lockheed L-188A Electra	Crashed on takeoff from Cuzco, Peru	101*
1970, Nov. 14	Southern Airways DC-9	Crashed into mountains near Huntington, WV	75[3]
1971, July 30	All-Nippon Boeing 727, Japan Air Force F-86 fighter	Collided over Morioka, Japan.	162[4]
1971, Sept. 4	Alaska Airlines Boeing 727.	Crashed into mountain near Juneau, AK	111
1972, Aug. 14	East German IL-62	Crashed on takeoff from East Berlin.	156
1972, Oct. 13	Aeroflot IL-62	Crashed near Moscow, U.S.S.R.	176
1972, Dec. 3	Spanish-chartered Convair CV-990	Crashed on takeoff from Canary Islands, Spain.	155
1972, Dec. 29	Eastern Airlines Lockheed Tristar.	Crashed on approach to Miami Intl. Airport, FL	101
1973, Jan. 22	Nigerian-chartered Boeing 707.	Burst into flames upon landing at Kano Airport, Nigeria.	176
1973, Feb. 21	**Libyan Arab Boeing 727**	**Flew off course, shot down by Israeli fighter planes over Sinai Desert**	**108**
1973, Apr. 10	British Vickers Vanguard	Crashed during snowstorm on approach to Basel, Switzerland	104
1973, June 3	Soviet Supersonic Tu-144	Crashed near Goussainville, France	14[5]
1973, July 11	Brazilian Boeing 707.	Crashed on approach to Orly Airport, Paris, France	122
1973, July 31	Delta Airlines DC-9.	Crashed while attempting landing in fog, Logan Airport, Boston, MA	89
1974, Mar. 3	Turkish DC-10	Crashed in Ermenonville, near Paris, France.	346
1974, Apr. 22	Pan American Boeing 707	Crashed in Bali, Indonesia	107
1974, Dec. 1	TWA Boeing 727	Crashed on approach in storm, Upperville, VA	92
1974, Dec. 4	Dutch-chartered DC-8	Crashed in storm near Colombo, Sri Lanka	191
1975, Apr. 4	Air Force Galaxy C-5A	Crashed on takeoff nr. Saigon, S Vietnam; carried orphans	172
1975, June 24	Eastern Airlines 727	Crashed in storm, JFK Airport, New York, NY	113
1975, Aug. 3	Alia Royal Jordanian Boeing 707	Hit mountainside in heavy fog near Agadir, Morocco	188
1976, Sept. 10	Brit. Airways Trident, Yug. DC-9.	Collided near Zagreb, Yugoslavia	176
1976, Sept. 19	Turkish 727.	Hit mountain in S Turkey	155
1976, Oct. 13	LAB Boeing 707	Crashed after takeoff from Santa Cruz, Bolivia	100[6]
1977, Mar. 27	**KLM 747, Pan American 747**	**Collided on runway, Tenerife, Canary Islands, Spain; world's worst airline disaster**	**583**
1977, Nov. 19	TAP Portugal Boeing 727.	Crashed in Madeira, Portugal.	130
1977, Dec. 4	Malaysian Airlines Boeing 737.	Hijacked and forced to fly to Singapore, crashed near Johor Strait.	100
1977, Dec. 13	National Jet Service DC-3	Crashed after takeoff from Evansville, IN; passengers incl. Univ. of Evansville men's basketball team	29
1978, Jan. 1	Air India 747	Crashed into sea after takeoff from Bombay, India	213
1978, Sept. 25	Boeing 727, Cessna 172	Collided over San Diego, CA	150
1978, Nov. 15	Indonesian-chartered DC-8	Crashed on approach to airport, Colombo, Sri Lanka	183
1979, May 25	**American Airlines DC-10**	**Crashed after takeoff from O'Hare Airport, Chicago, IL; highest death toll in U.S. aviation history**	**275***
1979, Aug. 11	Aeroflot/Moldova Tu-134, Aeroflot Tu-134	Collided over Ukraine.	178
1979, Nov. 26	Pakistani Boeing 707	Crashed near Jidda, Saudi Arabia	156
1979, Nov. 28	Air New Zealand DC-10	Crashed into mountain after takeoff from Antarctica	257
1980, Mar. 14	PLL LOT IL-62	Crashed making emergency landing, Warsaw, Poland	87[7]
1980, Aug. 19	Saudi Arabian Tristar	Burned after emergency landing in Riyadh, Saudi Arabia	301
1981, Dec. 1	Inex Adria DC-9	Crashed into mountain on island of Corsica, France	180
1982, Jan. 13	Air Florida Boeing 737	Crashed into Potomac R. after takeoff from Washington, DC	78
1982, July 9	Pan Am Boeing 727	Crashed after takeoff from Kenner, LA, near New Orleans	153*
1983, Sept. 1	**S. Korean Boeing 747**	**Shot down after violating Soviet airspace near Sakhalin; plane apparently misidentified**	**269**
1983, Nov. 27	Avianca Boeing 747	Crashed near Barajas Airport, Madrid, Spain.	183
1984, Oct. 11	Aeroflot/East Siberia Tu-154	Crashed into vehicles on runway while landing in poor weather, Omsk, Russia.	178*

Date	Aircraft	Site of accident	Deaths
1985, Feb. 19	Spanish Boeing 727	Crashed into Mt. Oiz, Spain	148
1985, June 23	Air India Boeing 747	Crashed into Atlantic off Ireland after bomb detonated on board	329
1985, Aug. 2	Delta Air Lines L-1011	Crashed at Dallas-Ft. Worth Airport, TX	137
1985, Aug. 12	**Japan Air Lines Boeing 747**	**Crashed into Mt. Ogura, Japan; world's worst single-plane disaster**	**520**
1985, Dec. 12	Arrow Air DC-8	Crashed after takeoff from Gander, NL, Canada	256[8]
1986, Mar. 31	Mexican Boeing 727	Crashed NW of Mexico City	166
1986, Aug. 31	Aeromexico DC-9, Piper PA-28	Collided over Cerritos, CA	82*
1987, May 9	Polish IL-62M	Crashed after takeoff from Warsaw, Poland	183
1987, Aug. 16	Northwest Airlines MD-82	Crashed after takeoff from Romulus, MI	156
1987, Nov. 28	S. African Boeing 747	Crashed into Indian Ocean near Mauritius	159
1987, Nov. 29	S. Korean Boeing 707	Bomb planted by 2 N. Korean agents exploded while plane over Thai-Burmese border	155
1988, Mar. 17	Colombian Boeing 707	Crashed into mountainside near Venezuela border	137
1988, July 3	**Iran Air Airbus A300**	**Misidentified as hostile aircraft, shot down by U.S. Navy warship *Vincennes* over Persian Gulf**	**290**
1988, Dec. 21	**Pan Am Boeing 747**	**Libyan agent planted bomb on board; exploded over Lockerbie, Scotland**	**270[9]**
1989, Feb. 8	U.S.-chartered Boeing 707	Crashed into mountain on Azores Isls., off Portugal	144
1989, June 7	Suriname DC-8	Crashed near Paramaribo Airport, Suriname	168
1989, July 19	United Airlines DC-10	Crashed on landing in Sioux City, IA	111
1989, Sept. 19	**UTA DC-10**	**Bomb exploded on board flight from Chad to France while over desert in Niger**	**171**
1989, Nov. 27	Avianca Boeing 727	Bomb exploded on flight from Bogotá, Colombia	107
1990, Jan. 25	Avianca Air Boeing 707	Crashed on landing at JFK Airport, New York, NY	73
1990, Feb. 14	Indian Airlines Airbus 320	Crashed and burned on landing in Bangalore, India	91
1990, Oct. 2	Xiamen Airlines Boeing 737	Hijacked after takeoff from Xiamen; struck empty 707, then 757 on runway, Guangzhou, China	132
1991, May 26	Lauda-Air Boeing 767-300	Exploded over rural Thailand	223
1991, July 11	Nigerian DC-8	Crashed on landing at Jidda, Saudi Arabia	261
1991, Oct. 5	Air Force Lockheed C-130 Hercules	Crashed after takeoff from Jakarta, Indonesia	137*
1992, July 31	Thai Airbus A300-310	Crashed into mountain N of Kathmandu, Nepal	113
1992, Oct. 4	**El Al Boeing 747-200F**	**Crashed into 2 apartment bldgs., Amsterdam, Netherlands**	**120***
1993, Feb. 8	Iran Air Tu-154, Iranian Air Force jet	Collided after military jet took off from Tehran, Iran	133
1993, Mar. 5	Macedonian Pal Air Fokker 100	Crashed after takeoff in snowstorm from Skopje, Macedonia	83
1994, Jan. 3	Aeroflot Tu-154	Crashed and exploded after takeoff from Irkhutsk, Russia	125*
1994, Apr. 26	China Airlines Airbus A300	Crashed on approach to Nagoya Airport, Japan	264
1994, June 6	China Northwest Airlines Tu-154	Crashed near Xian, China	160
1994, Sept. 8	USAir Boeing 737-300	Crashed near Pittsburgh Intl. Airport, Aliquippa, PA	132
1994, Oct. 31	American Eagle ATR-72-210	Crashed in field near Roselawn, IN	68
1995, Aug. 11	Aviateca Boeing 737	Crashed into Chichontepec volcano, El Salvador	65
1995, Dec. 20	American Airlines Boeing 757	Crashed into mountain N of Cali, Colombia	160
1996, Jan. 8	Antonov-32 cargo plane	Crashed into central market in Kinshasa, Zaire	350+*
1996, Feb. 6	Turkish Boeing 757	Crashed into Atlantic off Dominican Republic	189
1996, Apr. 3	U.S. Air Force Boeing T-43A	Crashed into mountain near Dubrovnik, Croatia	35[10]
1996, May 11	ValuJet DC-9	Crashed into Florida Everglades after takeoff	110
1996, July 17	Trans World Airlines Boeing 747	Exploded and crashed into Atlantic off Long Island, NY	230
1996, Aug. 29	Vnukovo Tu-154	Crashed into mountain on Arctic island of Spitsbergen	141
1996, Oct. 2	Aeroperu Boeing 757	Crashed into Pacific after takeoff from Lima, Peru	70
1996, Oct. 31	Brazilian TAM Fokker-100	Crashed shortly after takeoff from São Paulo, Brazil	97*
1996, Nov. 7	ADG Boeing 727	Crashed into lagoon SE of Lagos, Nigeria	143
1996, Nov. 12	**Saudi Arabian Boeing 747, Kazakh IL-76 cargo plane**	**Collided near New Delhi, India; world's worst midair collision**	**349**
1996, Nov. 23	Ethiopian Airlines Boeing 767	Hijacked, then crashed into Indian Ocean off the Comoros	127
1997, Aug. 6	Korean Air Boeing 747-300	Crashed into jungle on Guam on approach to airport	228
1997, Sept. 26	Indonesian Airbus A300	Crashed near airport, Medan, Indonesia	234
1997, Oct. 10	Austral Airlines DC-9-32	Crashed and exploded near Neuvo Berlin, Uruguay	74
1997, Dec. 15	Tajik Air Tu-154	Crashed in desert near airport, Sharja, UAE	85
1997, Dec. 17	AeroSvit Airlines Yakovlev-42	Crashed into mountains near Katerini, Greece	70
1997, Dec. 19	SilkAir Boeing 737-300	Crashed into Musi R., Sumatra, Indonesia	104
1998, Feb. 2	Cebu Pacific Air DC-9-32	Crashed into mountain near Cagayan de Oro, Philippines	104
1998, Feb. 16	China Airlines Airbus A300	Crashed on approach to airport in Taipei, Taiwan	203*
1998, Sept. 2	Swissair MD-11	Crashed into Atlantic off Nova Scotia, Canada	229
1998, Dec. 11	Thai Airways Airbus A310	Crashed on third landing attempt at Surat Thani Airport, Thailand	101
1999, Sept. 1	LAPA Boeing 737-200	Crashed on takeoff from airport, Buenos Aires, Argentina	74*
1999, Oct. 31	EgyptAir Boeing 767	Crashed off Nantucket, MA; result of deliberate actions by copilot, motives unknown	217
2000, Jan. 30	Kenya Airways Airbus A310	Crashed into Atlantic after takeoff from Abidjan, Ivory Coast	169
2000, Jan. 31	Alaska Airlines MD-83	Crashed into Pacific off coast of Southern CA	88
2000, Apr. 19	Air Philippines Boeing 737-200	Crashed on approach to airport, Davao, Philippines	131
2000, July 25	**Air France Concorde**	**Crashed into hotel after takeoff from Paris; world's first Concorde crash**	**113***
2000, Aug. 23	Gulf Air Airbus A320	Crashed into Persian Gulf on approach to airport in Bahrain	143
2000, Oct. 31	Singapore Airlines Boeing 747	Crashed immediately after takeoff from Taipei, Taiwan	81
2001, July 3	Vladivostokavia Tu-154	Crashed on approach to airport, Irkutsk, Russia	145
2001, Sept. 11	**2 Boeing 767s, 2 Boeing 757s**	**September 11 terrorist attacks**	**265[11]**
2001, Oct. 4	Sibir Airlines Tu-154	Crashed into Black Sea off Russia after hit by errant Ukrainian missile	78
2001, Oct. 8	Cessna 525A Citation, Scandinavian Airlines System (SAS) MD-87	Collided in heavy fog on takeoff from Milan, Italy	118*
2001, Nov. 12	**American Airlines Airbus A300**	**Crashed after takeoff from JFK Airport, New York, NY**	**265***
2002, Jan. 28	TAME Ecuador Boeing 727	Crashed into Andes mountains, S Colombia	92
2002, Feb. 12	Iran Air Tours Tu-154	Crashed in Khorramabad, Iran	119
2002, Apr. 15	Air China Boeing 767	Crashed into mountainside in rain and fog on approach to airport, Pusan, S. Korea	129
2002, May 4	EAS Airlines BAC 1-11	Crashed shortly after takeoff from Kano, Nigeria	149

Date	Aircraft	Site of accident	Deaths
2002, May 7	China Northern Airlines MD-82.	Plunged into sea, apparently after a passenger started fire in cabin, NE China	112
2002, May 25	China Airlines Boeing 747	Broke apart in midair, plunged into Taiwan Strait en route to Hong Kong airport	225
2002, July 27	**Ukraine Air Force Sukhoi Su-27 . . . .**	**Crashed while performing, Lviv, Ukraine; world's worst air-show crash**	**77[12]**
2002, Aug. 19	Russian Mi-26 transport helicopter.	Hit by Chechen missile near Grozny, Chechnya	127
2003, Jan. 8	Turkish Airlines British Aerospace RJ-100	Crashed on approach to airport in Diyarbakir, Turkey	75
2003, Feb. 19	Iranian Revolutionary Guard Il-76.	Crashed into mountain near Kerman, Iran; passengers were Revolutionary Guard members.	275
2003, Mar. 6	Air Algérie Boeing 737-200.	Crashed on takeoff from Tamanrasset, Algeria	102
2003, May 26	Ukrain.-Medit. Airlines Yak-42	Crashed into mountain in fog approaching Trabzon, Turkey; passengers incl. Spanish peacekeepers returning from Afghan. . .	75
2003, July 8	Sudan Airways Boeing 737-200	Mechanical problems reported shortly after takeoff; crashed upon return to Port Sudan Airport	115
2003, Dec. 25	Union Transp. Africains Boeing 727.	Overloading caused crash on takeoff from Cotonou, Benin.	138
2004, Jan. 3	Flash Airlines Boeing 737-300	Crashed into Red Sea after takeoff from Sharm el-Sheik, Egypt. . . .	148
2004, Aug. 24	Volga-Aviaexpress Tu-134, Sibir Airlines Tu-154.	2 planes that took off from Moscow crashed within minutes of each other; brought down by Chechen suicide bombers	90
2005, Feb. 3	Kam Air Boeing 737-200	Crashed on approach to airport in Kabul, Afghan.	104
2005, Aug. 14	Helios Airways Boeing 737-300	Crashed after air pressure failure on board, near Athens, Greece. . .	121
2005, Aug. 16	West Caribbean Airways MD-82	Crashed after engine failure, near Machiques, Venezuela.	160
2005, Sept. 5	Mandala Airlines Boeing 737-200.	Crashed shortly after takeoff from Medan, Sumatra, Indonesia.	145*
2005, Oct. 22	Bellview Airlines Boeing 737-200	Crashed during heavy electrical storm near Lagos, Nigeria.	117
2005, Dec. 6	Islamic Rep. of Iran Air Force Lockheed C-130	Crashed into apartment building after reportedly attempting emergency landing back at airport, Tehran, Iran	116*
2005, Dec. 10	Sosoliso Airlines DC-9-30.	Crashed during storm on approach to Port Harcourt, Nigeria	107
2006, May 3	Armavia Airbus A320	Crashed into Black Sea on approach to airport, Sochi, Russia	113
2006, July 9	S7 Airlines Airbus A310	Skidded off runway, crashed into concrete barrier after landing, Irkutsk, Russia	125
2006, Aug. 22	Pulkovo Aviation Tu-154.	Crashed after encountering storm, near Donetsk, Ukraine	170
2006, Aug. 27	Comair Bombardier CRJ-100	Crashed after takeoff from Lexington, KY	49
2006, Sept. 29	Gol Airlines Boeing 737	Crashed into Amazon jungle after midair collision with Embraer Legacy jet, Brazil	154
2006, Oct. 29	ADC Airlines Boeing 737-200.	Crashed in stormy weather shortly after takeoff from Abuja, Nigeria . .	96
2007, Jan. 1	Adam Air Boeing 737-400	Crashed into sea off coast, Makassar, Indonesia.	102
2007, May 5	Kenya Airways Boeing 737-800	Crashed shortly after takeoff from Douala, Cameroon.	114
2007, July 17	TAM Airlines Airbus 320	Crashed into cargo depot, gas station after skidding off airport runway, São Paulo, Brazil	199*
2007, Sept. 16	One-Two-Go Airlines Boeing-MD-82	Skidded off runway, caught fire after landing, Phuket, Thailand	89
2008, Aug. 20	Spanair Boeing-MD-82.	Swerved off runway, caught fire on takeoff attempt, Madrid, Spain . .	154
2008, Sept. 14	Aeroflot-Nord Boeing 737-500	Crashed on approach to airport, Perm, Russia	88
2009, Feb. 12	Colgan Air Bombardier Dash 8 Q400	Crashed into house near airport, Buffalo, NY	50*
2009, May 20	Indonesian military C-130 Hercules	Crashed into houses and a rice field, Java, Indonesia.	98*
2009, June 1	**Air France Airbus A330 . . . .**	**Plunged into Atlantic Ocean en route from Rio de Janeiro, Brazil, to Paris, France**	**228**
2009, June 29	Yemenia Airbus A310-300	Fell into Indian Ocean on approach to Moroni, Comoros.	152
2009, July 15	Caspian Airlines Tupolev 154.	Crashed after takeoff from Tehran, Iran	168
2010, Jan. 25	Ethiopian Airlines Boeing 737-800	Crashed into Mediterranean after takeoff from Beirut, Lebanon	90
2010, Apr. 10	Polish Air Force Tupolev 154M	Crashed on approach to Smolensk Air Base, killing Pres. Lech Kaczynski, his wife, and several members of Poland's Parliament	96
2010, May 12	Afriqiyah Airways Airbus A330-200	Crashed short of runway in Tripoli, Libya	103
2010, May 22	Air India Express Boeing 737-800	Overran runway on landing at Mangalore, India.	158
2010, July 28	Airblue Airbus 321-231.	Crashed into Margalla Hills near Islamabad, Pakistan.	152
2011, Jan. 9	Iran Air Boeing 727-200	Crashed during forced landing 5 mi from Orumiyeh Airport, Iran. . . .	77
2011, July 8	Hewa Bora Airways Boeing 727-022	Crashed on landing at Kisangani Airport, Dem. Rep. of Congo	77
2011, July 26	Royal Moroccan Air Force C-130H Hercules	Crashed on approach to Goulimime Airport, Morocco	80
2012, Apr. 20	Bhoja Airlines Boeing 737-236.	Crashed on approach to airport in Islamabad, Pakistan.	127
2012, June 3	Dana Air MD-83	Crashed into residential area of Lagos, Nigeria	163*

(1) Bomb was planted by Jack G. Graham in insurance plot to kill his mother, Daisie E. King, a passenger. (2) 84 on plane, 71 on ground killed. (3) Incl. 43 Marshall Univ. (WV) football players and coaches. (4) Fighter pilot parachuted to safety. (5) First supersonic plane crash; killed 8 on ground. (6) Crew of 3, 97 on ground killed. (7) Incl. 22 members of U.S. amateur boxing team. (8) Incl. 248 members of U.S. 101st Airborne Division. (9) Incl. 11 on ground. (10) Incl. U.S. Sec. of Commerce Ron Brown. (11) 4 planes were hijacked and crashed, with all on board killed (265, incl. 19 hijackers). American Airlines Flight 11, a Boeing 767-200, with 81 passengers, 11 crew, crashed into Tower 1 of World Trade Center; United Airlines Flight 175, a Boeing 767-200, with 56 passengers, 9 crew, crashed into Tower 2 of World Trade Center; American Airlines Flight 77, a Boeing 757-200, with 58 passengers, 6 crew, crashed into Pentagon outside Washington, DC; United Air lines Flight 93, a Boeing 757-200, with 37 passengers, 7 crew, crashed near Shanksville, PA. The official death toll of 2,753 (as of Aug. 9, 2011) includes all those who perished on the ground at the Pentagon and the World Trade Center, as well as those who died as many as 10 years later from pulmonary sarcoidosis, a lung disease caused by exposure to toxic dust created by the disaster. (12) The two pilots ejected to safety. All spectator deaths.

Disaster Averted

Date: Jan. 15, 2009. **Location:** Hudson River, NY-NJ. **Fatalities:** 0.

Chesley B. "Sully" Sullenberger III, the captain of U.S. Airways Flight 1549, made a spectacular emergency landing on the surface of a chilly Hudson River after apparent bird strikes took out both of the plane's engines shortly after takeoff from New York's LaGuardia Airport. Ferry boats and other nearby watercrafts safely evacuated the five crew members and all 150 passengers to shore soon after the emergency water landing. Some passengers were treated for hypothermia, but no major injuries were reported.

Some Notable Shipwrecks Since 1854

Figures are estimated deaths. Does not include most wartime disasters.

Date—vessel(s)	Incident	Deaths
1854, Mar. 1—City of Glasgow	British steamer left Liverpool for Philadelphia, never heard from again	480
1854, Sept. 27—Arctic and Vesta	U.S. Collins Line steamer sunk in collision with French steamer nr. Cape Race, Canada	285-351
1856, Jan. 23—Pacific	U.S. Collins Line steamer went missing in N Atlantic	186-286
1857, Sept. 12—Central America	U.S. mail steamship sank off Florida coast with $1.5 mil in gold	427
1858, Sept. 23—Austria	German steamer destroyed by fire in N Atlantic	471
1863, Apr. 27—Anglo-Saxon	British steamer wrecked at Cape Race, Canada	238
1865, Apr. 27—Sultana	Mississippi R. steamer carrying 2,300 released Civil War prisoners exploded nr. Memphis, TN. Worst maritime disaster in U.S. history	1,700+
1869, Feb. 20—Radetzky	Austrian steam frigate exploded in Adriatic Sea	345
1869, Oct. 27—Stonewall	U.S. steamer burned, Mississippi R. below Cairo, IL	200
1872, Nov. 7—Mary Celeste	U.S. half-brig sailing from New York to Genoa, Italy, found abandoned	Unknown
1873, Jan. 22—Northfleet	British steamer rammed by Spanish steamer *Murillo* off Dungeness, England	300
1873, Apr. 1—Atlantic	British White Star steamer off Halifax, Nova Scotia, Canada	585
1873, Nov. 23—Ville du Havre and Loch Earn	French steamer sank after collision with British sailing ship	226
1874, Nov. 17—Cospatrick	Burned off Auckland, New Zealand	468
1875, May 7—Schiller	German steamer off Scilly Isles, UK	312
1875, Nov. 4—Pacific	U.S. steamer sank after collision off Cape Flattery, WA	236
1878, Mar. 24—Eurydice	British frigate sank off Isle of Wight	398
1878, Sept. 3—Princess Alice	British steamer sank after collision with *Bywell Castle* in Thames R.	700
1878, Dec. 18—Byzantin and Rinaldo	French and British steamers collided in Dardanelles, off Turkey	210
1883, Jan. 19—Cimbria and Sultan	German steamer sank in collision with British steamer in North Sea	389
1887, Nov. 15—Wah Yeung	Chinese steamer burned in Canton R., Hong Kong	400
1890, Feb. 17—Duburg	British steamer wrecked, China Sea	400
1890, Sept. 19—Ertogrul	Turkish frigate off Japan	540
1891, Mar. 17—Utopia and Anson	British steamer sank in collision with British ironclad off Gibraltar	562
1893, June 22—Victoria	British battleship sank after collision with warship *Camperdown*, off Syrian coast	358
1895, Jan. 30—Elbe and Craithie	German steamer sank in collision with British steamer in North Sea	332
1895, Mar. 11—Reina Regenta	Spanish cruiser foundered nr. Gibraltar	400
1898, Feb. 15—USS Maine	Explosion caused battleship to sink in Havana Harbor, Cuba	260
1898, July 4—La Bourgogne and Cromartyshire	French steamer sank in collision with British sailing ship off Nova Scotia, Canada	549
1904, May 15—Yoshino	Japanese cruiser sank after collision with cruiser *Kasuga* in fog off Liao-Tung Peninsula, China	329
1904, June 15—General Slocum	Excursion steamer burned off N. Brother Isl., New York, NY	1,021
1904, June 28—Norge	Danish steamer wrecked on Rockall Isl., Scotland	620
1906, Aug. 4—Sirio	Italian steamer wrecked off Cape Palos, Spain	350
1907, Feb. 11—Larchmont	U.S. steamer sank after collision with U.S. schooner *Harry Knowlton* nr. Block Island, RI	131
1908, Mar. 23—Mutsu Maru	Japanese steamer sank in collision with another steamer nr. Hakodate, Japan	300
1909, Aug. 1—Waratah	British steamer vanished en route from Sydney to London	300
1911, Sept. 25—Liberté	French battleship exploded at Toulon	285
1912, Apr. 14-15—Titanic	British White Star steamer hit iceberg in N Atlantic	1,503
1912, Sept. 28—Kichemaru	Japanese steamer sank off Japan coast	1,000
1914, May 29—Empress of Ireland	Canadian Pacific steamer collided with Norwegian coal transporter *Storstad* in St. Lawrence R., Canada	1,014
1914, Nov. 26—Bulwark	British battleship exploded in Sheerness harbor, England	788
1915, May 7—Lusitania	British Cunard Line steamer torpedoed and sunk by German submarine off Ireland	1,198
1915, July 24—Eastland	Steamer capsized, Chicago R., IL	844
1916, Feb. 26—Provence	French cruiser sank in Mediterranean; then-worst disaster in maritime history	3,100
1916, Mar. 5—Principe de Asturias	Spanish steamer wrecked nr. Santos, Brazil	558
1917, Dec. 6—Mont Blanc and Imo	French ammunition ship and Belgian steamer collided in Halifax Harbor, Canada	1,600
1918, Apr. 25—Kiang-Kwan	Chinese steamer sank after collision with Chinese gunboat *Chutai* off Hankow, China	500
1918, July 12—Kawachi	Japanese battleship blew up in Tokayama Bay	500
1918, Oct. 25—Princess Sophia	Canadian-Pacific steamer sank off Vanderbilt reef, Alaska	398
1919, Jan. 17—Chaonia	French steamer lost in Straits of Messina, Italy	460
1919, Sept. 9—Valbanera	Spanish steamer lost off FL coast	500
1920, Jan. 11—Afrique	French liner sank nr. La Rochelle, France	553
1921, Mar. 18—Hong Kong	Chinese steamer wrecked, S China Sea	1,000
1922, Aug. 26—Niitaka	Japanese cruiser sank in storm off Kamchatka, USSR	300
1927, Sept. 20—Gentoku Maru	Japanese steamer capsized in Tsingtao Bay, China	278
1927, Oct. 25—Principessa Mafalda	Italian steamer blew up, sank off Porto Seguro, Brazil	314
1934, Sept. 8—Morro Castle	U.S. steamer en route from Havana to New York, burned off Asbury Park, NJ	134
1940, June 17—Lancastria	Nazi forces sank Cunard liner evacuating British troops from France	2,500-6,000
1940, July 24—Meknes	French liner torpedoed by Nazis in English Channel	350
1942, Feb. 18—USS Truxtun and USS Pollux	Destroyer and cargo ship ran aground, sank off Newfoundland, Canada	204
1942, Oct. 2—Curacao and Queen Mary	British cruiser sank after collision with liner	338
1944, Dec. 17-18—Spence, Monaghan, Hull	3 U.S. destroyers sank during typhoon, Philippine Sea	790
1945, Jan. 30—Wilhelm Gustloff	Liner with German refugees, soldiers sunk by Soviet submarine in Baltic	5,000-9,000
1945, Apr. 16—Goya	Cargo ship carrying German refugees, soldiers sunk by Soviet submarine in Baltic	6,000-7,000
1945, May 3—Cap Arcona and Thielbeck	German liners carrying concentration camp inmates sunk by British warplanes in Lubeck Bay, Germany	7,000-8,000

Date—vessel(s)	Incident	Deaths
1947, Jan. 19—Himera	Greek steamer hit mine off Athens, Greece	392
1947, Apr. 16—Grandcamp	Ammonium nitrate explosion aboard French freighter caused fires throughout port, Texas City, TX	576+
1948, Dec. 3—Kiangya	Chinese refugee ship wrecked in explosion S of Shanghai	1,100+
1954, Sept. 26—Toya Maru	Japanese ferry sank, Tsugaru Strait, Japan	1,172
1956, July 26—Andrea Doria and Stockholm	Italian liner and Swedish liner collided off Nantucket Isl., MA	51
1957, July 14—Eshghabad	Soviet fishing boat ran aground in Caspian Sea	270
1961, Apr. 8—Dara	British liner exploded in Persian Gulf	236
1961, July 8—Save	Portuguese ship ran aground off Mozambique	259
1965, Nov. 13—Yarmouth Castle	Cruise ship burned and sank off Nassau, Bahamas	89
1970, Dec. 15—Namyong-Ho	S. Korean ferry sank in Korea Strait	308
1975, Nov. 10—Edmund Fitzgerald	U.S. cargo ship sank during storm on Lake Superior	29
1980, Apr. 22—Don Juan	Sank off Mindoro Isl., Philippines, after colliding with barge	1,000+
1981, Jan. 27—Tamponas II	Indonesian car ferry caught fire and sank in Java Sea	580
1983, May 25—10th of Ramadan	Nile steamer caught fire and sank in Lake Nasser, Egypt	357
1986, May 25—Shamia	Ferry capsized in storm, Meghna R., Bangladesh	500+
1986, Sept. 1—Admiral Nakhimov and Pyotr Vasev	Soviet cruise ship collided with Soviet freighter in Black Sea	425
1987, Dec. 20—Doña Paz and Victor	Philippine ferry and oil tanker collided in Tablas Strait, Philippines	4,341
1988, Aug. 6	Indian ferry capsized on Ganges R.	400+
1988, Oct. 24—Doña Marilyn	Philippine ferry sank by typhoon near Leyte Isl.	350+
1991, Dec. 14—Salem Express	Ferry rammed coral reef nr. Safaga, Egypt	462
1993, Feb. 17—Neptune	Ferry capsized off Port-au-Prince, Haiti	500+
1993, Oct. 10—Seohae	S. Korean ferry capsized in Yellow Sea during storm	292
1994, Sept. 28—Estonia	Ferry sank in Baltic Sea off Finland	850+
1996, May 21—Bukoba	Overcrowded Tanzanian ferry sank in Lake Victoria	500+
1997, Sept. 8—Pride of la Gonâve	Haitian ferry sank off Montrouis, Haiti	200+
1999, Feb. 6—Harta Rimba	Cargo ship sank off Indonesia	280+
1999, May 1—Miss Majestic	"Duck" boat on tour sank, Lake Hamilton, AR	13
1999, Nov. 24—Dashun	Passenger ferry capsized nr. Yantai, China	280
2000, June 29—Cahaya Bahari	Overloaded ferry carrying refugees from religious strife capsized in storm off Sulawesi Isl., Indonesia	500+
2001, Oct. 19	Fishing boat overloaded with refugees, mainly from Middle East, sank off Indonesia	350+
2002, May 4—Salahuddin-2	Overloaded Bangladesh ferry sank in Meghna R.	300+
2002, Sept. 26—Joola	Overloaded Senegalese ferry capsized in ocean off The Gambia	1,863
2003, July 8—MV-Nasrin 1	Overcrowded ferry sank nr. Chandpur in Bangladesh R.	400
2003, Oct. 15—Andrew J. Barberi	NYC ferry crashed into dock on approach to Staten Isl.	11
2006, Feb. 3—Al-Salam Boccaccio 98	Ferry caught fire, sank in Red Sea off Egypt	1,000+
2006, Dec. 30—Senopati Nusantara	High waves capsized ferry en route to Java, Indonesia	400+
2007, Nov. 23—Explorer	Canadian cruise ship hit Antarctic iceberg; first commercial passenger ship to sink in region	0
2008, June 23—Princess of the Stars	Philippine ferry capsized during Typhoon Fengshen nr. Manila	800
2011, July 10—Bulgaria	Riverboat carrying two dozen children capsized in Volga R., Russia	122
2012, Jan 17—Costa Concordia	Cruise ship ran aground off Italian coast; captain abandoned ship before passengers	32

Some Notable Railroad Disasters Since 1925

Date	Location	Deaths	Date	Location	Deaths
1925, June 16	Hackettstown, NJ	50	1962, Jan. 8	Woerden, Netherlands	91
1926, Sept. 5	Waco, CO	30	1962, May 3	Tokyo, Japan	163
1937, July 16	Bhita, India	107	1963, Nov. 9	Yokohama, Japan	120+
1938, June 19	Saugus, MT	47	1964, July 26	Porto, Portugal	94
1939, Dec. 22	Near Magdeburg, Germany	132	1967, July 6	Madgeburg, Germany	94
1939, Dec. 22	Near Friedrichshafen, Germany	99	1970, Feb. 1	Buenos Aires, Argentina	236
1940, Apr. 19	Little Falls, NY	31	1972, June 16	Vierzy, France	107
1940, July 31	Cuyahoga Falls, OH	43	1972, July 21	Seville, Spain	76
1943, Sept. 6	Frankford Junction, Philad., PA	79	1972, Oct. 6	Saltillo, Mexico	208
1943, Dec. 16	Between Rennert and Buie, NC	72	1972, Oct. 30	Chicago, IL	45
1944, Jan. 16	León Province, Spain	500	1974, Aug. 30	Zagreb, Yugoslavia	153
1944, Mar. 2	Salerno, Italy	521	1977, Jan. 18	Granville, Australia	83
1944, July 6	High Bluff, TN	35	1981, June 6	Bihar, India	800+
1944, Aug. 4	Near Stockton, GA	47	1982, Jan. 27	El Asnam, Algeria	130
1944, Dec. 31	Bagley, UT	50	1982, July 11	Tepic, Mexico	120
1945, Aug. 9	Michigan, ND	34	1983, Feb. 19	Empalme, Mexico	100
1946, Mar. 20	Aracaju, Mexico	185	1985, Feb. 23	Madhya Pradesh state, India	50
1946, Apr. 25	Naperville, IL	45	1987, July 2	Kasumbalesha Shaba, Zaire	125
1949, Oct. 22	Near Dwor, Poland	200+	1988, June 27	Gare de Lyon train station, Paris	57
1950, Feb. 17	Rockville Centre, NY	31	1989, Jan. 15	Maizdi Khan, Bangladesh	110+
1950, Sept. 11	Coshocton, OH	33	1990, Jan. 4	Sindh Province, Pakistan	210+
1950, Nov. 22	Richmond Hill, NY	79	1993, Sept. 22	Big Bayou Conot, AL	47
1951, Feb. 6	Woodbridge, NJ	84	1994, Mar. 8	Near Durban, South Africa	63
1952, Mar. 4	Near Rio de Janeiro, Brazil	119	1994, Sept. 22	Tolunda, Angola	300
1952, July 9	Rzepin, Poland	160	1995, Aug. 20	Firozabad, India	358
1952, Oct. 8	Harrow, England	112	1997, Mar. 3	Punjab Province, Pakistan	125
1953, Dec. 24	Tangiwai, New Zealand	151	1997, Apr. 29	Rongjiawan, China	58
1955, Apr. 3	Guadalajara, Mexico	300	1997, May 4	Rwandan refugees on overcrowded trains, Kisangani, Zaire	100+
1956, Jan. 22	Los Angeles, CA	30	1997, Sept. 14	Madhya Pradesh state, India	77
1957, Sept. 1	Kendal, Jamaica	178	1998, Feb. 19	Yaounde, Cameroon	100+
1957, Sept. 29	Montgomery, W Pakistan	250	1998, June 3	Eschede, Germany	102
1957, Dec. 4	London, England	90	1998, Nov. 26	Khanna, India	200+
1958, May 8	Rio de Janeiro, Brazil	128	1999, Aug. 2	Gauhati, India	285+
1958, Sept. 15	Elizabethport, NJ	48	2000, Nov. 11	Kaprun, Austria	155
1960, Nov. 14	Pardubice, Czechoslovakia	110			

Date	Location	Deaths	Date	Location	Deaths
2001, June 22	Cochin, India	64	2008, Sept. 12	Commuter train collided head-on with freight train, Los Angeles, CA	25
2002, Feb. 20	S of Cairo, Egypt	373	2010, May 28	W Bengal, India	148
2002, Feb. 27	Train fire, Godhra, India	59	2010, July 19	Express train crashed into stationary train in W Bengal, India	66
2002, May 25	Muamba, Mozambique	196+			
2002, June 24	Igandu, Tanzania	281+	2010, July 21	Derailment between Brazzaville and Pointe-Noire, Congo Republic	76
2002, Sept. 10	Bihar, India	118			
2003, Feb. 1	NW Zimbabwe	46	2011, July 7	Train crashed into bus carrying wedding guests, Uttar Pradesh, India	38+
2004, Feb. 18	Neyshabur, NE Iran	300+			
2004, Apr. 22	Ryongchon, N. Korea	161	2011, July 23	High-speed train crashed into stationary train near Wenzhou, China	40
2005, Apr. 25	Near Amagasaki, Japan	107+			
2005, July 13	Ghotki, Pakistan	133	2012, Feb. 22	Commuter train crashed into station in suburb of Buenos Aires, Argentina	51
2005, Oct. 29	Near Veligonda, India	114+			
2006, Jan. 23	Podgorica, Montenegro	46	2012, July 30	Train caught fire in Andhra Pradesh, India	32+
2007, Aug. 2	Nr. Benaleka, Dem. Rep. of Congo	70+			

Principal U.S. Mine Disasters Since 1900

Source: Bureau of Mines, U.S. Dept. of the Interior; Mine Safety and Health Admin., U.S. Dept. of Labor; World Almanac research
All are bituminous coal mines unless otherwise noted.

Date	Location	Deaths	Date	Location	Deaths	Date	Location	Deaths
1900, May 1	Scofield, UT	200	1913, Oct. 22	Dawson, NM	263	1940, Mar. 16	St. Clairesville, OH	72
1902, May 19	Coal Creek, TN	184	1914, Apr. 28	Eccles, WV	181	1942, Mar. 26	Allentown, PA[4]	31
1902, July 10	Johnstown, PA	112	1915, Mar. 2	Layland, WV	115	1943, Feb. 27	Washoe, MT	74
1903, June 30	Hanna, WY	169	1917, Apr. 27	Hastings, CO	121	1947, Mar. 25	Centralia, IL	111
1904, Jan. 25	Cheswick, PA	179	1917, June 8	Butte, MT[1]	163	1951, Dec. 21	West Frankfort, IL	119
1905, Feb. 20	Virginia City, AL	112	1919, June 5	Wilkes-Barre, PA[2]	92	1968, Mar. 6	Belle Isle, LA[5]	21
1907, Jan. 29	Stuart, WV	84	1922, Nov. 6	Spangler, PA	79	1968, Nov. 20	Farmington, WV	78
1907, Dec. 6	Monongah, WV	362	1922, Nov. 22	Dolomite, AL	90	1970, Dec. 30	Hyden, KY	38
1907, Dec. 19	Jacobs Creek, PA	239	1923, Feb. 8	Dawson, NM	120	1972, May 2	Kellogg, ID[6]	91
1908, Nov. 28	Marianna, PA	154	1923, Aug. 14	Kemmerer, WY	99	1976, Mar. 9	Oven Fork, KY	15
1909, Nov. 13	Cherry, IL	259	1924, Mar. 8	Castle Gate, UT	172	1981, Apr. 15	Redstone, CO	15
1910, Jan. 31	Primero, CO	75	1924, Apr. 28	Benwood, WV	119	1981, Dec. 8	Whitwell, TN	13
1910, May 5	Palos, AL	84	1926, Jan. 13	Wilburton, OK	91	1984, Dec. 19	Orangeville, UT	27
1910, Nov. 8	Delagua, CO	79	1926, Nov. 3	Ishpeming, MI[3]	51	1989, Sept. 13	Wheatcroft, KY	10
1911, Apr. 8	Littleton, AL	128	1927, Apr. 30	Everettville, WV	97	2001, Sept. 23	Brookwood, AL	13
1911, Dec. 9	Briceville, TN	84	1928, May 19	Mather, PA	195	2006, Jan. 2	Buckhannon, WV	12
1912, Mar. 26	Jed, WV	81	1930, Nov. 5	Millfield, OH	82	2010, Apr. 5	Montcoal, WV	29
1913, Apr. 23	Finleyville, PA	98	1940, Jan. 10	Bartley, WV	91			

Note: The world's worst mine disaster killed 1,549 workers in Manchuria, China, Apr. 25, 1942. (1) Copper mine. (2) Anthracite mine. (3) Iron mine. (4) Limestone mine. (5) Salt mine. (6) Silver mine.

Some Notable U.S. Tornadoes Since 1925

Date	Location	Deaths	Date	Location	Deaths
1925, Mar. 18	MO, IL, IN	747	1971, Feb. 21	Mississippi Delta: MS, LA, AR, TN	110
1927, Apr. 12	Rocksprings, TX	74	1973, May 26-27	South, Midwest	47
1927, May 9	AR; Poplar Bluff, MO	92	1974, Apr. 3-4	AL; GA; KY; Xenia, OH; other states	315
1927, Sept. 29	St. Louis, MO	90	1977, Apr. 4	AL, MS, GA	22
1930, May 6	Hill, Navarro, Ellis Cos., TX	41	1979, Apr. 10	TX, OK	60
1932, Mar. 21	Alabama	268	1984, Mar. 28	NC, SC	57
1936, Apr. 5-6	Tupelo, MS; Gainesville, GA	454	1985, May 31	NY; PA; OH; Ontario, Can.	75
1938, Sept. 29	Charleston, SC	32	1987, May 22	Saragosa, TX	30
1942, Mar. 16	Central to NE Mississippi	75	1989, Nov. 15	Huntsville, AL	18
1942, Apr. 27	Rogers and Mayes Cos., OK	52	1990, Aug. 28	Northern IL	25
1944, June 23	OH, PA, WV, MD	150	1991, Apr. 26	KS, OK	23
1945, Apr. 12	OK, AR	102	1992, Nov. 21-23	South, Midwest	26
1947, Apr. 9	TX; Woodward, OK; KS	181	1994, Mar. 27-28	AL, TN, GA, NC, SC	52
1948, Mar. 19	Bunker Hill and Gillespie, IL	33	1995, May 6-7	S Oklahoma, N Texas	23
1949, Jan. 3	LA, AR	58	1997, Mar. 1	Central AR	26
1952, Mar. 21-22	AR, MO, TN	208	1997, May 27	Jarrell, TX	27
1953, May 11	Waco, TX	114	1998, Feb. 22-23	Central FL	42
1953, June 8	Flint-Beecher, MI; OH	142	1998, Apr. 8	AL, GA, MS	39
1953, June 9	Worcester and vicinity, MA	90	1999, May 3	OK, KS	54
1953, Dec. 5	Vicksburg, MS	38	2000, Feb. 14	SW Georgia	22+
1955, May 25	Udall, KS; MO; Blackwell, OK; TX	115	2001, Nov. 23-24	AL, AR, MS	13
1957, May 20	KS, MO	48	2002, Nov. 10-11	AL, MS, TN, IN, OH, PA	36
1958, June, 4	NW Wisconsin	30	2003, May 4-11	TN, MO, KS, IL, OK, WV, AL	48
1959, Feb. 10	St. Louis, MO	21	2005, Nov. 6	KY, IN	22
1960, May 5-6	Southeastern OK, AR	30	2007, Mar. 1	AL, GA, MO, Midwest	20
1962, Mar. 31	Milton, FL	17	2008, Feb. 25	"Super Tuesday"—TN, AR, KY, AL, MO	57
1965, Apr. 11	IA, IN, IL, OH, MI, WI	271	2008, May 10	MS, OK, GA	23
1966, Mar. 3	Jackson, MS; AL	57	2011, Apr. 14-16	Southeast, Midwest U.S., OK to VA	38
1967, Apr. 21	IL, MO, IA, MI	33	2011, Apr. 25-28	U.S.; 305 funnels reported from TX to NY	321
1968, May 15	Midwest	71	2011, May 22	Joplin, MO	162
1969, Jan. 23	Mississippi	32	2012, Mar. 2-3	IL, IN, KY	40
1970, May 11	Lubbock, TX	23			

A Record Year for Tornadoes

Date: 2011. **Location:** Primarily Midwest, SE U.S.
Fatalities: 551. **Damages:** $28 bil.

The spring and summer of 2011 proved to be one of the most active, destructive, and deadly tornado years in U.S. history. The United States from Oklahoma to Virginia was plagued Apr. 14-16 by hundreds of tornadoes. At least 343 twisters tracked across the eastern half of the country Apr. 25-28, killing at least 321 people, including 248 in Alabama. Tuscaloosa and Birmingham, AL, suffered some of the greatest damage in that cluster, with 65 deaths, over 1,000 injured, and damages estimated at $100 mil. But the deadliest single 2011 tornado struck May 22 in Joplin, MO, and caused 162 deaths and $3 bil in damages.

Some Notable Hurricanes, Typhoons, Blizzards, Other Storms

C.—cyclone; H.—hurricane; TS.—tropical storm; T.—typhoon[1]

Date	Location	Deaths	Date	Location	Deaths
1881, Aug. 24-29	H., GA, SC	700	1990, May 6-11	C. (mult.), SE India	450
1888, Mar. 11-14	Blizzard, eastern U.S.	400	1991, Apr. 30	C., Bangladesh	139,000
1893, Aug. 15-Sept. 2	H., GA, SC	1,000+	1991, Nov. 5	TS. Thelma, flash floods,	
1893, Oct. 1	H., LA	1,100+		central Philippines	7,000+
1900, Sept. 8	H., Galveston, TX	8,000+	1992, Aug. 24-26	H. Andrew, southern FL, LA	65
1906, Sept. 18	T., Hong Kong	10,000+	1993, Mar. 12-14	Blizzard, eastern U.S.	270+
1906, Sept. 19-24	H., LA, MS	350	1993, June	Monsoon, Bangladesh	2,000
1909, Sept. 20	H., LA	350+	1994, Nov. 8-18	TS. Gordon, Caribbean, FL	830
1915, Aug. 16	H., Galveston, TX	275	1995, Oct. 2-4	H. Opal, S Mexico, FL, AL	59
1915, Sept. 29	H., LA	275	1995, Nov. 2-3	T. Angela, Philippines	600+
1919, Sept. 6-14	H., Carib., FL Keys, Gulf, TX	600+[2]	1996, Jan. 7-8	Blizzard, northeastern U.S.	100
1926, Sept. 11-22	H., FL, AL, MS	370+	1996, Aug. 22	Blizzard, Himalayas, N India	239
1926, Oct. 20	H., Cuba	600	1996, Aug. 29-Sept. 6	H. Fran, Carib., NC, VA, WV	30
1928, Sept. 6-20	H., southern FL	2,500+	1996, Sept. 9	T. Sally, S China	114
1930, Sept. 3	H., Dominican Republic	2,000	1996, Nov. 6	C., Andhra Pradesh, India	1,000+
1935, Aug. 29-Sept. 10	H., Caribbean, SE U.S.	400+	1996, Nov. 24-25	Ice storms, TX to MO	26
1937, Sept. 2	T., "The Great Typhoon,"		1996, Dec. 25	TS. Greg, E Malaysia	100+
	Hong Kong	10,000+	1997, May 19	C., Bangladesh	108
1938, Sept. 21	H., "Long Isl. Express," NY;		1997, Aug. 18-21	T. Winnie, Taiwan, E China	140+
	New England	682	1997, Oct. 8-10	H. Pauline, SW Mexico	230
1940, Nov. 11-12	Blizzard, NE, Midwest U.S.	144	1998, June 9	C., Gujarat, India	1,320
1942, Oct. 15-16	H., Bengal, India	40,000	1998, Aug.	Monsoon, Bangladesh	326
1947, Dec. 26	Blizzard, NYC, N Atl. states	55	1998, Sept. 21-23	H. Georges, Carib., FL, U.S. Gulf	600+
1952, Oct. 22	T., Philippines	440	1998, Oct. 27-29	H. Mitch, Honduras, Nicaragua,	
1954, Aug. 30	H. Carol, northeastern U.S.	68		Guatemala, El Salvador	10,866+
1954, Oct. 5-18	H. Hazel, E Canada, U.S., Haiti	347	1999, Sept. 4-17	H. Floyd, Baha., E seaboard U.S.	56
1955, Aug. 7-21	H. Diane, eastern U.S.	400	1999, Oct. 29	C., E India	9,392
1955, Sept. 19	H. Hilda, Mexico	200	1999, Dec. 26-29	Gales, France, Switz., Germany	120
1956, Feb. 1-29	Blizzard, W Europe	1,000	2000, Dec. 27	Winter storm, TX, OK, AR	40+
1957, June 25-30	H. Audrey, TX to AL	390	2001, July 30	T. Toraji, Taiwan	200
1958, Feb. 15-16	Blizzard, northeastern U.S.	171	2001, Nov. 6-12	T. Lingling, S Philip., Vietnam	220+
1959, Sept. 17-19	T. Sarah, Japan, S. Korea	2,000	2002, Aug.-Sept.	T. Rusa, N. and S. Korea	115+
1959, Sept. 26-27	T. Vera, Honshu, Japan	4,466	2003, Feb. 16-17	Blizzard, E seaboard U.S.	59
1960, Sept. 4-12	H. Donna, Caribbean, E U.S.	148	2003, Sept. 7-19	H. Isabel, NC, VA, E seaboard	40+
1961, Oct. 31	H. Hattie, Brit. Honduras	400	2003, Sept. 12	T. Maemi, S. Korea	130
1962, Sept. 1	T. Wanda, Hong Kong	130-200	2004, Mar. 7-19	C. Gafilo, Madagascar	198
1963, May 28-29	Windstorm, Bangladesh	22,000	2004, May 19	C., Myanmar	220
1963, Oct. 4-8	H. Flora, Caribbean	6,000	2004, Aug. 12-15	T. Rananim, E China	164
1964, June 30	T. Winnie, N Philippines	107	2004, Aug. 13-14	H. Charley, FL, SC	36
1964, Sept. 5	T. Ruby, Hong Kong, China	735	2004, Sept. 5-6	H. Frances, Bahamas, FL.	35
1965, May 11-12	Windstorm, Bangladesh	17,000	2004, Sept. 7-16	H. Ivan, Barbados, Grenada,	
1965, June 1-2	Windstorm, Bangladesh	30,000		U.S. Gulf Coast	115
1965, Sept. 7-12	H. Betsy, FL, MS, LA	74	2004, Sept. 16-26	H. Jeanne, Dom. Rep., Haiti, FL.	1,500+
1965, Dec. 15	Windstorm, Bangladesh	10,000	2005, July 7-11	H. Dennis, Jamaica, Haiti, Cuba,	
1966, June 4-10	H. Alma, Honduras, SE U.S.	51		FL	50
1966, Sept. 24-30	H. Inez, Carib., FL, Mexico	293	2005, Aug. 25-29	H. Katrina, LA, MS, FL, AL, GA	1,833+[3]
1967, July 9	T. Billie, SW Japan	347	2005, Aug. 31-Sept. 1	T. Talim, Taiwan, E China	129+
1967, Sept. 5-23	H. Beulah, Carib., Mex., TX	54	2005, Sept. 21-24	H. Rita, TX, LA	62[4]
1967, Dec. 12-20	Blizzard, SW U.S.	51	2005, Sept. 21-28	T. Damrey, SE Asia; Philippines;	
1969, Aug. 17-18	H. Camille, MS, LA	256		Hainan, China	145
1970, Sept. 15	T. Georgia, Philippines	300	2005, Oct. 4	H. Stan, Central Amer., Mex.	1,000+[5]
1970, Oct. 14	T. Sening, Philippines	583	2006, Jul. 14	TS. Bilis, SE China	612
1970, Oct. 15	T. Titang, Philippines	526	2006, Aug. 10	T. Saomai, SE China	295
1970, Nov. 13	C., Bay of Bengal, Bangladesh	300,000	2006, Nov. 30	T. Durian, Philippines	450-1,000+
1971, Aug. 1	T. Rose, Hong Kong	130	2007, June 6-7	C. Gonu, Oman, Iran	54[6]
1972, June 19-29	H. Agnes, FL to NY	118	2007, Nov. 15	C. Sidr, S Bangladesh	3,363
1972, Dec. 3	T. Theresa, Philippines	169	2008, May 2-3	C. Nargis, S Myanmar	84,500-125,000
1973, June-Aug.	Monsoon rains, India	1,217	2008, June 20-25	T. Fengshen, Philippines, China	233
1974, July 11	T. Gilda, Japan, S. Korea	108	2008, Aug. 26-Sept. 1	H. Gustav, Haiti, Dom. Rep., U.S.	138
1974, Sept. 19-20	H. Fifi, Honduras	2,000	2008, Sept. 1-4	TS. Hanna, Haiti	529
1975, Sept. 13-27	H. Eloise, Caribbean, NE U.S.	71	2008, Sept. 7-13	H. Ike, Haiti; Cuba; Galveston, TX	164
1976, May 20	T. Olga, floods, Philippines	215	2009, May 23-26	C. Alia, India, Bangladesh	260
1976, Sept. 25-Oct. 2	H. Liza, W Mexico	630	2009, Aug. 7-9	T. Morakot, mudslides, Taiwan	700+
1978, Oct. 27	T. Rita, Philippines	400	2009, Sept. 23-30	T. Ketsana, Philippines, Vietnam,	
1979, Aug. 30-Sept. 7	H. David, Caribbean, E U.S.	1,100		Cambodia, Laos	498+
1980, Aug. 4-11	H. Allen, Caribbean, TX	272	2009, Oct. 3-10	T. Parma, Philippines	375
1981, Nov. 25	T. Irma, Luzon Isl., Philippines	176	2009, Oct. 30-Nov. 3	T. Mirinae, Philippines, Vietnam	159+
1983, June	Monsoon, India	900	2009, Dec. 11-22	Snowstorms, central Europe	90+
1984, Sept. 2	T. Ike, S Philippines	1,363	2010, Apr. 13	C., India, Bangladesh	137
1985, May 25	C., Bangladesh	10,000	2010, May 29	TS. Agatha, Guatemala,	
1985, Oct. 26-Nov. 6	H. Juan, SE U.S.	97		El Salvador, Honduras	184
1987, Nov. 25	T. Nina, Philippines	650	2010, July 13-17	T. Conson, Luzon Isl., Philippines	105+
1988, Sept. 10-17	H. Gilbert, Carib., Gulf of Mex.	260	2011, Dec. 16	TS. Washi, Philippines	1,257
1989, Sept. 16-22	H. Hugo, Caribbean, SE U.S.	86	2012, Jan. 24-Feb. 14	Blizzard/cold snap, E Europe	650+

(1) What hurricanes are called W of intl. date line and N of equator. (2) Incl. about 500 lost on ships at sea. (3) Official toll as of Aug. 2006 was 1,577 in LA, 238 in MS, 14 in FL, and 2 each in AL and GA. (4) Incl. 55 indirect deaths, among them 20 people, mostly elderly evacuees from a nursing home, whose bus exploded and caught fire outside Dallas. (5) Incl. deaths from floods and landslides generated by heavy rainstorms. (6) First documented super cyclone in Arabian Sea.

Hurricane Katrina

Dates: Aug. 25-29, 2005. **Location:** FL, LA, MS, AL, other inland states.
Fatalities: 1,833+. **Damages:** $125 bil.

The costliest storm to date in U.S. history first made landfall in SE Florida, Aug. 25, as a Category 1 hurricane. Katrina brought heavy rains that led to flooding in the Florida peninsula. Katrina then weakened slightly, strengthened over the Gulf of Mexico, but was downgraded again to Category 3 status before hitting land south of Buras, LA, on Aug. 29. Despite weakening, Katrina caused massive storm surges measuring up to 25-28 ft throughout SE Louisiana, S Mississippi, and SW Alabama. These storm surges, combined with strong winds and heavy rainfall, contributed to the failure of New Orleans's levee system Aug. 30. About 80% of the city eventually flooded. Approximately 1 mil were displaced from their homes.

Some Notable Floods, Tidal Waves

Date	Location	Deaths	Date	Location	Deaths
1703	Awa, Japan	100,000+	1997, Mar.	Ohio R. Valley	35
1889, May 31	Johnstown, PA	2,200+	1997, July	Poland, Czech Republic	98
1903, June 15	Heppner, OR	325	1997, Nov.	Bardera, Somalia	1,300+
1911	Chang Jiang R., China	100,000	1998, Mar.	SW Pakistan	300+
1913, Mar. 25-27	OH, IN	732	1998, July 17	Papua New Guinea	3,000
1915, Aug. 17	Galveston, TX	275	1998, July-Aug.	China	4,150
1927, Jan.-July	Mississippi Valley	246+	1998, July-Sept.	Bangladesh	1,441
1928, Mar. 13	Dam collapse, Saugus, CA	450	1999, Aug. 1-4	Philippines, SE Asia	188+
1928, Sept. 16	Lake Okeechobee, FL	1,770+	1999, Sept.-Oct.	NE Mexico	350+
1931, Aug.	Huang He R., China	3,700,000	1999, Oct.-Dec.	Central Vietnam	700+
1937, Jan. 22	OH, MS valleys	250	1999, Dec. 15-17	NW Venezuela	9,000+
1939	N China	200,000	2000, Feb.-Mar.	Madagascar	150+
1946, Apr. 1	HI, AK	159	2000, Feb.-Mar.	Mozambique	700
1947, Sept. 20	Honshu Isl., Japan	1,900	2000, Aug. 2	Himachal Pradesh, India	120+
1951, Aug.	Manchuria	1,800	2000, Aug. 2	Bhutan	200+
1953, Jan. 31	W Europe	2,000	2000, Sept. 19-30	India, Bangladesh	1,000+
1954, Aug. 17	Farahzad, Iran	2,000	2001, Aug. 1-6	Taiwan	100+
1955, Oct. 7-12	India, Pakistan	1,700	2001, Aug. 10-12	NE Iran	247
1959, Nov. 1	W Mexico	2,000	2001, Aug.	N Thailand	170
1959, Dec. 2	Frejus, France	412	2001, Aug.-Nov.	S Vietnam, Cambodia	360+
1960, Oct. 10	Bangladesh	6,000	2001, Nov. 9-10	N Algeria	711+
1960, Oct. 31	Bangladesh	4,000	2002, Jan. 30-Feb. 15	Java Isl., Indonesia	147
1962, Feb. 17	North Sea coast, Germany	343	2002, Apr.-May	E Africa	150+
1962, Sept. 27	Barcelona, Spain	445	2002, Apr.-Aug.	China	800+
1963, Oct. 9	Dam collapse, Vaiont, Italy	1,800	2002, July-Aug.	India, Nepal, Bangladesh	1,100+
1966, Nov. 3-4	Florence, Venice, Italy	113	2002, Aug.	Russia	110
1967, Jan. 18-24	E Brazil	894	2002, Aug.	Germany, Hungary, Austria, Czech Rep.	100+
1967, Mar. 19	Rio de Janeiro, Brazil	436	2003, May 17-27	Sri Lanka	250
1967, Nov. 26	Lisbon, Portugal	464	2003, Aug.-mid-Sept.	E India	200+
1968, Aug. 7-14	Gujarat state, India	1,000	2003, Dec. 10-		
1968, Oct. 7	NE India	780	Jan. 23, 2004	Sumatra, Indonesia	148
1969, Jan. 18-26	Southern CA	100	2003, Dec. 19-		
1969, Mar. 17	Mundau Valley, Alagoas, Brazil	218	Jan. 7, 2004	Central Philippines	200
1969, Aug. 20-22	Western VA	189	2004, Jan. 10-Mar. 8	E Brazil	161
1969, Sept. 15	South Korea	250	2004, May 23-25	Dom. Republic, Haiti	2,000
1969, Oct. 1-8	Tunisia	500	2004, June-Sept.	Banglad., India, Myanmar, Nepal	2,000+
1970, May 20	Central Romania	160	2004, June-Sept.	China	500
1970, July 22	Himalayas, India	500	2004, Nov.-Dec.	Philippines	1,060+
1971, Feb. 26	Rio de Janeiro, Brazil	130	2004, Dec. 26	12 Indian Ocean nations	226,328[1]
1972, Feb. 26	Buffalo Creek, WV	118	2005, July 26-Aug. 2	W Maharashtra state, India	1,000+
1972, June 9	Rapid City, SD	238	2006, Feb. 17	Leyte Isl., Philippines	1,000
1972, Aug. 7	Luzon Isl., Philippines	454	2006, July 17	S of Java, Indonesia	530+
1972, Aug. 19-31	Pakistan	1,500	2008, Sept.	E Orissa, India	173
1974, Mar. 29	Tubaro, Brazil	1,000	2008, Oct. 24-25	Hadramaut, Mahaura, Yemen	100
1974, Aug. 12	Monty-Long, Bangladesh	2,500	2008, Nov. 22-Dec. 3	Santa Catarina, S Brazil	116
1976, July 31	Big Thompson Canyon, CO	140	2009, Mar. 27	Jakarta, Indonesia	77+
1976, Nov. 17	E Java, Indonesia	136	2009, Mar.-Apr.	Zambia, Namibia	92
1977, July 19-20	Johnstown, PA	68	2009, Sept. 29	Amer. Samoa, Samoa, Tonga	170+
1977, Nov. 6	Toccoa, GA	39	2009, Sept. 29-Oct. 14	S India	355
1978, June-Sept.	N India	1,200	2009, Nov. 4-6	El Salvador	192+
1979, Jan.-Feb.	Brazil	204	2009, Nov. 25	Jeddah, Saudi Arabia	106
1979, July 17	Lomblem Isl., Indonesia	539	2010, May 1-7	Afghanistan, Tajikistan	124+
1979, Aug. 11	Morvi, India	15,000	2010, June 13-24	Cenxi, China	377+
1981, Apr.	N China	550	2010, June 28	Dazhai, China	99
1981, July	Sichuan, Hubei Prov., China	1,300	2010, July 1-7	Qinghai, China	118
1982, Jan. 23	Near Lima, Peru	600	2010, July-Aug.	Pakistan	1,600+
1982, May 12	Guangdong, China	430	2010, July-Nov.	Pakistan	1,985+
1982, Sept. 17-21	El Salvador, Guatemala	1,300+	2010, Aug.	Sahel region, W Africa	200+
1984, Aug.-Sept.	South Korea	200+	2010, Oct.	West Papua, Indonesia	145
1985, July 19	Dam collapse, N Italy	361	2011, Jan.	SE Brazil	830+
1987, Aug.-Sept.	N Bangladesh	1,000+	2011, Mar. 11	NE Japan	20,896+
1988, Sept.	N India	1,000+	2011, Apr.-May	N Colombia	425+
1993, July-Aug.	Midwest, U.S.	47	2011, July-Dec.	Cambodia, Myanmar, Philippines, Thailand	2,000
1995, July	NE China	1,200	2011, Oct. 11-20	Central America	105
1995, Aug. 19	SW Morocco	136	2012, June	Bangladesh	110+
1995, Dec. 25	KwaZulu Natal, South Africa	166	2012, July	Russia	171+
1996, Feb. 17	Biak Isl., Indonesia	105	2012, July	North Korea	169
1996, Apr.	Afghanistan	100+			
1996, June-July	S China	950+			

(1) Based on official estimates assembled by the Intl. Fed. of Red Cross and Red Crescent Societies, including 50,773 missing; as reported Dec. 15, 2005. The nearly 176,300 listed as dead include 128,645 from Indonesia; 31,147 from Sri Lanka; 10,749 from India; and 5,395 from Thailand.

Earthquake, Tsunami, Meltdown

Dates: Beg. Mar. 11, 2011. **Location:** NE Japan.
Fatalities: 20,896+. **Damages:** $245-$600 bil (est.).

Japan experienced one of the worst disasters in its history when it was struck by a 9.0-magnitude temblor. But the earthquake was just the beginning of the tragedy. An ensuing tsunami wiped out entire towns in the northeastern provinces of Iwate, Miyagi, and Fukushima, and flooded the Fukushima Daiichi nuclear power plant. Officials released nearly 12,000 tons of radioactive water into the ocean in hopes of preventing even more toxic water from escaping the plant but could not avoid partial meltdowns in three of the plant's reactors. Some officials put the disaster on par with the 1986 Chernobyl explosion in Ukraine.

Some Major Earthquakes

Source: Global Volcanism Network, Smithsonian Institution; U.S. Geological Survey, U.S. Dept. of the Interior; World Almanac research
Magnitude of earthquakes (mag.) is a relative measurement of an earthquake's energy.

Date	Location	Deaths	Mag.	Date	Location	Deaths	Mag.
526, May 20	Antioch, Syria	250,000	NA	1950, Aug. 15	Assam, India	1,526	8.6
856	Corinth, Greece	45,000	NA	1951, Aug. 2	Cosiguina, Nicaragua	1,000	5.8
856, Dec. 22	Damghan, Iran	200,000	NA	1953, Mar. 18	NW Turkey	1,070	7.3
893, Mar. 23	Ardabil, Iran	150,000	NA	1954, Sept. 9	Orleansville, Algeria	1,250	6.8
1057	Chihli, China	25,000	NA	1956, June 10-17	N Afghanistan	2,000	7.7
1138, Aug. 9	Aleppo, Syria	230,000	NA	1957, July 2	N Iran	1,200	7.1
1169, Feb. 11	Nr. Mt. Etna, Sicily	15,000	NA[1]	1957, Dec. 13	W Iran	1,130	7.1
1268	Silicia, Asia Minor	60,000	NA	1960, Feb. 29	Agadir, Morocco	12,000	5.7
1290, Sept. 27	Chihli, China	100,000	NA	1960, May 21-30	S Chile	1,655	9.5[5]
1293, May 20	Kamakura, Japan	30,000	NA	1962, Sept. 1	NW Iran	12,255	7.1
1531, Jan. 26	Lisbon, Portugal	30,000	NA	1963, July 26	Skopje, Yugoslavia	1,100	6.0
1556, Jan. 24	Shaanxi, China	830,000	NA	1964, Mar. 27	Prince Wm. Sound, AK	131	9.2[6]
1667, Nov.	Shemakha, Caucasia	80,000	NA	1966, Mar. 7	Hebei, China	1,000	7.0
1693, Jan. 11	Catania, Italy	60,000	NA	1966, Mar. 22	Hebei, China	1,000	6.9
1737, Oct. 11	India, Calcutta	300,000	NA	1966, Aug. 19	E Turkey	2,529	6.8
1755, June 7	N Persia (current-day Iran)	40,000	NA	1968, Aug. 31	NE Iran	12,000	7.3
1755, Nov. 1	Lisbon, Portugal	60,000	8.75[2]	1969, July 25	Guangdong, China	3,000	5.9
1783, Feb. 4	Calabria, Italy	30,000	NA	1970, Jan. 5	Yunnan Prov., China	10,000	7.5
1797, Feb. 4	Quito, Ecuador	41,000	NA	1970, Mar. 28	W Turkey	1,086	6.9
1822, Sept. 5	Asia Minor, Aleppo	22,000	NA	1970, May 31	Chimbote, Peru	70,000	7.9
1828, Dec. 28	Echigo, Japan	30,000	NA	1971, Feb. 9	San Fernando Valley, CA	65	6.6
1868, Aug. 13-15	Peru, Ecuador	40,000	NA	1971, May 22	SE of Ankara, Turkey	1,000	6.9
1875, May 16	Venezuela, Colombia	16,000	NA	1972, Apr. 10	S Iran	5,054	7.1
1886, Aug. 31	Charleston, SC	60	6.6	1972, Dec. 23	Managua, Nicaragua	5,000	6.2
1896, June 15	Sanriku, Japan (tsunami)	27,120	8.5	1974, May 10	China	20,000	6.8
1902, Apr. 19	Quezaltenango and San Marcos, Guatemala	2,000	7.5	1974, Dec. 28	N Pakistan	5,300	6.2
1902, Dec. 16	Uzbekistan, Russia	4,700	6.4	1975, Feb. 4	Haicheng, China	2,000	7.0
1903, Apr. 28	Malazgirt, Turkey	3,500	7.0	1975, Sept. 6	E Turkey	2,300	6.7
1903, May 28	Gole, Turkey	1,000	5.8	1976, Feb. 4	Guatemala	23,000	7.5
1905, Apr. 4	Kangra, India	19,000	7.5	1976, May 6	NE Italy	1,000	6.5
1906, Jan. 31	Off coast of Esmeraldas, Ecuador	1,000	8.8	1976, June 25	Irian Jaya, New Guinea	422	7.1
1906, Mar. 16	Chia-i, Taiwan	1,250	6.8	1976, July 28	Tangshan, China	242,769	7.5
1906, Apr. 18-19	San Francisco, CA	3,000+	7.7[3]	1976, Aug. 16	Mindanao, Philippines	8,000	7.9
1906, Aug. 17	Valparaiso, Chile	3,882	8.6	1976, Nov. 24	NW Iran-Turkey border	5,000	7.3
1907, Oct. 21	Central Asia	12,000	8.1	1977, Mar. 4	Romania	1,500	7.2
1908, Dec. 28	Messina, Italy	72,000	7.2	1978, Sept. 16	NE Iran	15,000	7.8
1909, Jan. 23	Silakhor, Iran	5,000-6,000	7.3	1980, Oct. 10	NW Algeria	5,000	7.7
				1980, Nov. 23	S Italy	2,735	6.5
1912, Aug. 9	Murefte, Turkey	2,800	7.4	1981, June 11	S Iran	3,000	6.9
1914, Oct. 3	Burdur, Turkey	4,000	7.0	1981, July 28	S Iran	1,500	7.3
1915, Jan. 13	Avezzano, Italy	32,610	7.0	1982, Dec. 13	W Arabian Peninsula	2,800	6.0
1917, July 30	Yunnan, China	1,800	7.5	1983, Oct. 30	E Turkey	1,342	6.9
1918, Feb. 13	Guangdong, China	1,000	7.4	1985, Sept. 19	Michoacan, Mexico	9,500	8.0
1920, Dec. 16	Gansu, China	200,000	7.8[4]	1986, Oct. 10	El Salvador	1,000+	5.5
1923, Mar. 24	Sichuan, China	3,500	7.3	1987, Mar. 6	Colombia-Ecuador	1,000	7.0
1923, Mar. 25	Torbat-e Heydariyeh, Iran	2,200	5.7	1988, Aug. 20	India-Nepal border	1,000	6.8
1923, Sept. 1	Yokohama, Japan	142,800	7.9	1988, Dec. 7	Spitak, Armenia	25,000	6.8
1925, Mar. 16	Yunnan, China	5,800	7.0	1989, Oct. 17	San Francisco Bay area, CA	63	6.9
1927, Mar. 7	Tango, Japan	3,020	7.6	1990, June 20	W Iran	40,000+	7.4
1927, May 22	Gansu, China	40,900	7.6	1990, July 16	Luzon, Philippines	1,621	7.7
1929, May 1	Koppeh Dagh, Iran	3,800	7.2	1991, Feb. 1	Pakistan-Afgh. border	1,200	6.8
1930, May 6	Salmas, Iran	2,500	7.2	1991, Oct. 19	N India	2,000	7.0
1930, July 23	Irpinia, Italy	1,404	6.5	1992, Dec. 12	Flores Isl., Indonesia	2,500	7.5
1931, Mar. 31	Managua, Nicaragua	2,500	6.0	1993, Sept. 30	Maharashtra, S India	9,748	6.2
1931, Apr. 27	Armenia-Azerbaijan border	2,800	5.7	1994, Jan. 17	Northridge, CA	61	6.8
1931, Aug. 10	Xinjiang, China	10,000	8.0	1994, June 6	Cauca, SW Colombia	1,000	6.8
1933, Mar. 2	Sanriku, Japan (tsunami)	2,990	8.4	1995, Jan. 16	Kobe, Japan	5,502	6.9
1933, Mar. 10	Long Beach, CA	115	6.2	1995, May 27	Sakhalin Isl., Russia	1,989	7.5
1933, Aug. 25	Sichuan, China	9,300	7.5	1997, Feb. 28	NW Iran	1,000+	6.1
1934, Jan. 15	Bihar, India-Nepal	10,700	8.1	1997, May 10	N Iran	1,567	7.3
1935, Apr. 21	Miao-li, Taiwan	3,270	7.1	1998, Feb. 4, 8	Hindu Kush, Afghanistan	2,323	5.9
1935, May 30	Quetta, Pakistan	30,000	7.6	1998, May 30	Afghanistan-Tajikistan border	4,000+	6.6
1939, Jan. 25	Chillan, Chile	28,000	7.8	1998, July 17	Papua New Guinea	2,183	7.0
1939, Dec. 26	Erzincan, Turkey	32,700	7.8	1999, Jan. 25	Armenia, Colombia	1,185+	6.1
1940, Nov. 10	Vrancea, Romania	1,000	7.3	1999, Aug. 17	Izmit, W Turkey	17,118+	7.6
1942, Dec. 20	Erbaa, Turkey	1,100	7.3	1999, Sept. 20	Taichung, Taiwan	2,400	7.6
1943, Sept. 10	Tottori, Japan	1,190	7.4	2001, Jan. 26	Gujarat, India	20,085	7.6
1943, Nov. 26	Ladik, Turkey	4,000	7.6	2002, Mar. 25-26	Hindu Kush, Afghanistan	1,000+	6.1
1944, Jan. 15	San Juan, Argentina	8,000	7.4	2003, May 21	N Algeria	2,266	6.8
1944, Feb. 1	Gerede, Turkey	2,790	7.4	2003, Dec. 26	Bam, SE Iran	31,000	6.6
1945, Jan. 12	Mikawa, Japan	1,961	7.1	2004, Dec. 26	Sumatra-Andaman Isls., Indonesia	227,898	9.1[7]
1945, Nov. 27	Makran Coast, Pakistan	4,000	8.0	2005, Mar. 28	N. Sumatra, Indonesia	1,313	8.6
1946, May 31	Ustukran, Turkey	1,300	5.9	2005, Oct. 8	Kashmir, Pakistan, India	86,000	7.6
1946, Nov. 10	Ancash, Peru	1,400	7.3	2006, May 26	Java, Indonesia	5,749	6.3
1946, Dec. 21	Honshu, Japan	1,362	8.1	2008, May 12	E Sichuan Prov., China	87,857	7.9
1948, June 28	Fukui, Japan	3,769	7.3	2009, Sept. 30	Sumatra, Indonesia	1,117	7.5
1948, Oct. 5	Ashgabat, Turkmenistan	110,000	7.3	2010, Jan. 12	Haiti	316,000	7.0
1949, July 10	Khait, Tajikistan	12,000	7.5	2010, Feb. 27	Chile	800	8.8
1949, Aug. 5	Pelileo, Ecuador	5,050	6.8	2010, Apr. 13	S Qinghai, China	2,220	6.9
				2011, Mar. 11	NE Japan	20,896	9.0[8]

NA = Not available. (1) Once thought to have been a volcanic eruption; evidence indicates a destructive earthquake and tsunami occurred on this date. (2) This earthquake caused the most deadly tsunami to date in the Atlantic Ocean. (3) Incl. deaths from resulting fires; revised estimates of magnitude range from 7.7 to 7.9. (4) Commonly referred to as the Gansu quake; actually located within the Ningxia autonomous region. (5) The largest recorded earthquake; caused a deadly tsunami that spread across the Pacific Ocean as far as Japan. (6) The "Good Friday" earthquake sent a tsunami that hit British Columbia, Canada, and the U.S. Pacific coast. (7) This undersea earthquake triggered devastating tsunamis that hit 12 Indian Ocean nations. (8) The most powerful earthquake in Japan's history set off a tsunami that inundated much of the coast and caused a partial meltdown of the Fukushima nuclear power plant.

Some Notable Fires Since 1930

See also Some Notable Explosions Since 1920.

Date	Location	Deaths
1930, Apr. 21	Penitentiary, Columbus, OH	320
1931, July 24	Home for aged, Pittsburgh, PA	48
1934, Dec. 11	Hotel Kerns, Lansing, MI	34
1938, May 16	Terminal Hotel, Atlanta, GA	35
1940, Apr. 23	Nightclub, Natchez, MS	198
1942, Nov. 28	Cocoanut Grove Nightclub, Boston, MA	492
1942, Dec. 12	Hostel, St. John's, NL, Canada	100
1943, Sept. 7	Gulf Hotel, Houston, TX	55
1944, July 6	Ringling Circus, Hartford, CT	168
1946, June 5	LaSalle Hotel, Chicago, IL	61
1946, Dec. 7	Winecoff Hotel, Atlanta, GA	119
1946, Dec. 12	Ice plant, tenement, New York, NY	37
1949, Apr. 5	Hospital, Effingham, IL	77
1950, Jan. 7	Mercy Hospital, Davenport, IA	41
1953, Mar. 29	Nursing home, Largo, FL	35
1953, Apr. 16	Metalworking plant, Chicago, IL	35
1957, Feb. 17	Home for aged, Warrenton, MO	72
1958, Mar. 19	Loft building, New York, NY	24
1958, Dec. 1	Parochial school, Chicago, IL	95
1958, Dec. 16	Store, Bogotá, Colombia	83
1959, June 23	Resort hotel, Stalheim, Norway	34
1960, Mar. 12	Chemical plant, Pusan, Korea	68
1960, July 14	Mental hospital, Guatemala City	225
1960, Nov. 10	Movie theater, Amude, Syria	152
1960, Dec. 19	USS *Constellation*, Brooklyn, NY	49
1961, Jan. 6	Thomas Hotel, San Francisco, CA	20
1961, Dec. 17	Circus, Niteroi, Brazil	323
1963, May 4	Theater, Diourbel, Senegal	64
1963, Nov. 18	Surfside Hotel, Atlantic City, NJ	25
1963, Nov. 23	Rest home, Fitchville, OH	63
1963, Dec. 29	Roosevelt Hotel, Jacksonville, FL	22
1964, May 8	Apt. bldg., Manila, Philippines	30
1964, Dec. 18	Nursing home, Fountaintown, IN	20
1965, Mar. 1	Apartment, LaSalle, QC, Can.	28
1965, Aug. 11-16	Watts riot fires, Los Angeles, CA	30+
1966, Mar. 11	2 ski resorts, Numata, Japan	31
1966, Oct. 17	Bldg. (firefighters), New York, NY	12
1966, Dec. 7	Barracks, Erzurum, Turkey	68
1967, Feb. 7	Restaurant, Montgomery, AL	25
1967, May 22	Dept. store, Brussels, Belgium	322
1967, July 16	State prison, Jay, FL	37
1967, July 29	USS *Forrestal*, off N Vietnam	134
1968, May 11	Wedding hall, Vijayawada, India	58
1969, Dec. 2	Nursing home, Notre Dame, QC, Can.	54
1970, Jan. 9	Nursing home, Marietta, OH	27
1970, Nov. 1	Dance hall, Grenoble, France	145
1970, Dec. 20	Hotel, Tucson, AZ	28
1971, Dec., 25	Hotel, Seoul, S. Korea	162
1972, May 13	Nightclub, Osaka, Japan	116
1972, July 5	Hospital, Sherborne, England	30
1973, June 24	Bar, New Orleans, LA	32
1973, Aug. 3	Amusement park, Isle of Man, Eng.	51
1973, Sept. 1	Hotel, Copenhagen, Denmark	35
1973, Nov. 29	Dept. store, Kumamoto, Japan	107
1973, Dec. 2	Theater, Seoul, S. Korea	50
1974, Feb. 1	Bank building, São Paulo, Brazil	189
1974, June 30	Discotheque, Port Chester, NY	24
1974, Nov. 3	Hotel, disco, Seoul, S. Korea	88
1975, Dec. 12	Tent city, Mina, Saudi Arabia	138
1976, Oct. 24	Social club, Bronx, NY	25
1977, Feb. 25	Rossiya Hotel, Moscow, Russia	45
1977, May 28	Nightclub, Southgate, KY	164
1977, June 9	Nightclub, Abidjan, Ivory Coast	41
1977, June 26	Jail, Columbia, TN	42
1977, Nov. 14	Hotel, Manila, Philippines	47
1978, Jan. 28	Coates House Hotel, Kansas City, MO	16
1978, Aug. 19	Movie theater, Abadan, Iran	425+
1979, July 14	Hotel, Saragossa, Spain	80
1979, Dec. 31	Social club, Chapais, QC, Can.	42
1980, May 20	Nursing home, Kingston, Jamaica	157
1980, Nov. 21	MGM Grand Hotel, Las Vegas, NV	84
1980, Dec. 4	Stouffer Inn, Harrison, NY	26
1981, Jan. 9	Boarding home, Keansburg, NJ	30
1981, Feb. 10	Las Vegas Hilton, Las Vegas, NV	8

Date	Location	Deaths
1981, Feb. 14	Discotheque, Dublin, Ireland	44
1982, Nov. 8	County jail, Biloxi, MS	29
1983, Feb. 13	Movie theater, Turin, Italy	64
1983, Dec. 17	Discotheque, Madrid, Spain	83
1984, May 11	Great Adventure Amusement Pk., Jackson Twp., NJ	8
1985, Apr. 21	Movie theaters, Tabaco, Philippines	44
1985, Apr. 26	Hospital, Buenos Aires, Argentina	79
1985, May 11	Soccer stadium, Bradford, England	53
1985, May 13	MOVE headquarters, row houses, Philadelphia, PA	11
1986, Dec. 31	Dupont Plaza Hotel, Puerto Rico	96
1987, May 6-June 2	Forest fire, N China	193
1987, Nov. 17	Subway, London, England	30
1988, Mar. 20	About 2,000 buildings, Lashio, Myan.	134
1990, Mar. 25	Social club, Bronx, NY	87
1991, Mar. 3	Munitions dump, Addis Ababa, Ethiopia	260+
1991, Sept. 3	Processing plant, Hamlet, NC	25
1991, Oct. 20-21	Wildfire, Oakland, Berkeley, CA	24
1993, Apr. 19	Cult compound, Waco, TX	72
1994, May 10	Toy factory, Bangkok, Thailand	213
1994, July 4-10	(Firefighters) Glenwood Springs, CO	14
1994, Nov. 2	Burning fuel flood, Durunka, Egypt	500
1994, Dec. 10	Theater, Karamay, China	300
1995, Oct. 28	Subway train, Baku, Azerbaijan	300
1995, Dec. 23	School, Mandi Dabwali, India	500+
1996, Mar. 19	Nightclub, Quezon City, Philippines	150+
1996, Mar. 28	Shopping mall, Bogor, Indonesia	78
1996, Nov. 20	Building, Hong Kong	39
1997, Feb. 23	Worship site, Baripada, India	164
1997, Apr. 15	Encampment, Mina, Saudi Arabia	343
1997, June 7	Temple, Thanjavur, India	60+
1997, June 13	Movie theater, New Delhi, India	60
1997, July 11	Hotel, Pattaya, Thailand	90
1997, Sept. 29	Children's home, nr. Colina, Chile	30
1998, Dec. 3	Orphanage, Manila, Philippines	28
1999, Mar. 24	Mt. Blanc Tunnel, France, Italy	40
1999, Oct. 30	Karaoke salon, Inchon, S. Korea	55+
2000, Mar. 17	Church, Kanungu, Uganda	530
2000, Oct. 20	Nightclub, Mexico City, Mexico	20
2000, Nov. 11	Cable car, Kaprun, Austria	155
2000, Dec. 25	Shopping center, Luoyang, China	309
2001, Mar. 6	School, central China	41
2001, Mar. 26	School, Machakos, Kenya	64
2001, Aug. 18	Hotel, Quezon City, Philippines	73
2001, Sept. 1	Nightclub, Tokyo, Japan	44
2001, Dec. 29	Fireworks accident, Lima, Peru	291
2002, Mar. 11	Girls' school, Mecca, Saudi Arabia	15
2002, June 16	Internet cafe, Beijing, China	24
2002, July 7	Coal mine, Donetsk region, Ukraine	34+
2002, July 20	Disco, Lima, Peru	25+
2002, July 31	Coal mine, Donetsk region, Ukraine	20
2003, Feb. 18	Subway train, Taegu, S. Korea	198
2003, Feb. 20	Pyrotechnics in nightclub, Warwick, RI	100
2003, Sept. 15	Prison, Riyadh, Saudi Arabia	94
2003, Nov. 24	Students' hostel, Moscow, Russia	36
2004, May 17	Prison, San Pedro Sula, Honduras	104
2004, July 16	Pvt. school, Kumbakonam, India	80+
2004, Aug. 1	Market, Asunción, Paraguay	400+
2004, Dec. 30	Club, Buenos Aires, Argentina	194
2005, Feb. 14	Mosque, Tehran, Iran	59
2005, Mar. 7	Prison, Higuey, Dom. Republic	159
2005, Apr. 15	Hotel, Paris, France	22
2005, Sept. 5	Theater, Beni Suef, Egypt	32
2006, Dec. 9	Drug treatment center, Moscow, Russ.	45
2007, Mar. 20	Nursing home for elderly and disabled, Kamyshevatskaya, Russia	62
2007, Aug. 24-Sept. 2	Wildfires (arson), Greece	65
2008, Apr. 26	Factory fire, Casablanca, Morocco	55
2008, Sept.	Wildfires, Mozambique, S. Africa, Swaziland	89
2009, Jan.-Feb.	Wildfires (arson), Victoria, Australia	173
2012, Feb. 14	Prison fire, Comayagua, Honduras	360+

Some Notable Explosions Since 1920

See also Principal U.S. Mine Disasters Since 1900. Some bombings related to political conflicts and terrorism are not included.

Date	Location	Deaths
1920, Sept. 16	Wall Street, New York, NY	30
1921, Sept. 21	Chem. storage facility, Oppau, Ger.	561
1924, Jan. 3	Food plant, Pekin, IL.	42
1927, May 18	Bath school, Lansing, MI	38
1928, Apr. 13	Dance hall, West Plains, MO	40
1937, Mar. 18	School, New London, TX	311
1940, Sept. 12	Hercules Powder factory, Kenvil, NJ	55
1942, June 5	Ordnance plant, Elwood, IL	49
1944, Apr. 14	Harbor, Bombay, India	700
1944, July 17	Munitions ships, depot, Port Chicago, CA	322
1944, Oct. 21	Liquid gas tank, Cleveland, OH	135
1947, Apr. 16	Freighter, chemical co. plant, Texas City, TX.	576
1948, July 28	Farben works, Ludwigshafen, Ger.	184
1950, May 19	Munitions barges, S. Amboy, NJ	30
1954, May 26	USS *Bennington*, off RI	103
1956, Aug. 7	Dynamite trucks, Cali, Colombia	1,100
1958, Apr. 18	Sunken munitions ship, Okinawa, Japan	40
1958, May 22	Nike missiles, Leonardo, NJ.	10
1959, Apr. 10	WWII bomb, Philippines	38
1959, June 28	Rail tank cars, Meldrim, GA	25
1959, Aug. 7	Dynamite truck, Roseburg, OR.	13
1959, Nov. 2	Explosives, Jamuri Bazar, India	46
1959, Dec. 13	2 apt. bldgs., Dortmund, Ger.	26
1960, Mar. 4	Belgian munitions ship, Havana, Cuba.	100
1962, Oct. 3	New York Telephone Co. office, New York, NY	23
1963, Jan. 2	Packing plant, Terre Haute, IN.	17
1963, Mar. 9	Dynamite plant, S. Africa	45
1963, Aug. 13	Explosives dump, Gauhaiti, India	32
1963, Oct. 31	State Fair Coliseum, Indianapolis, IN.	73
1964, July 23	Harbor munitions, Bone, Algeria.	100
1965, Aug. 9	Missile silo, Searcy, AR	53
1965, Oct. 21	Bridge, Tila Bund, Pakistan	80
1965, Nov. 24	Armory, Keokuk, IA.	20
1967, Dec. 25	Apartment bldg., Moscow, USSR.	20
1968, Apr. 6	Sports store, Richmond, IN.	43
1969, Mar. 31	Coal mine, nr. Barroteran, Mexico	180
1970, Apr. 8	Subway construction, Osaka, Japan	73
1971, June 24	Tunnel, Sylmar, CA	17
1973, Feb., 10	Liquid gas tank, Staten Island, NY	40
1975, Dec. 27	Coal mine, Chasnala, India	431
1976, Apr. 13	Munitions works, Lapua, Finland	40
1977, Nov. 11	Freight train, Iri, S. Korea	57
1977, Dec. 22	Grain elevator, Westwego, LA	35
1978, Feb. 24	Derailed tank car, Waverly, TN.	12
1978, July 11	Propylene truck, Tarragona, Spain.	150
1980, Oct. 23	School, Ortuella, Spain.	64
1982, Apr. 25	Antiques exhibition, Todi, Italy	33
1982, Nov. 2	Salang Tunnel, Afghanistan	1,000+
1984, Feb. 25	Oil pipeline, Cubatao, Brazil.	508
1984, June 21	Naval supply depot, Severomorsk, USSR	200+
1984, Nov. 19	Gas storage area, NE Mexico City	334
1984, Dec. 3	Chemical plant, Bhopal, India.	3,849
1984, Dec. 5	Coal mine, Taipei, Taiwan	94
1985, June 25	Fireworks factory, Hallett, OK.	21
1988, Apr. 10	Army ammunitions dump nr. Rawalpindi and Islamabad, Pakistan	100
1988, July 6	Oil rig, North Sea off NE Scotland	167
1989, June 3	Gas pipeline, between Ufa, Asha, USSR	650+
1992, Mar. 3	Coal mine, Kozlu, Turkey	270+
1992, Apr. 22	Gas leak in sewers, Guadalajara, Mexico	200+
1992, May 9	Coal mine, Plymouth, Nova Scotia.	26
1993, Feb. 26	World Trade Center, New York, NY	6
1994, July 18	Jewish comm. center, Buenos Aires, Arg.	100
1995, Apr. 19	Fed. office building, Oklahoma City, OK.	168
1995, Apr. 29	Subway construction, S. Korea	110
1996, Jan. 31	Bank, Colombo, Sri Lanka	53
1996, Mar. 3-4	Jerusalem and Tel Aviv, Israel	33
1996, June 25	U.S. military housing complex, nr. Dhahran, Saudi Arabia	19
1996, July 24	Train, Colombo, Sri Lanka	86
1996, Nov. 16	Military apt., Dagestan region, Russia	68

Date	Location	Deaths
1996, Nov. 21	Propane gas leak in bldg., San Juan, Puerto Rico.	33
1996, Nov. 27	Coal mine, Shanxi Prov., China	91+
1996, Dec. 30	Train, Assam, India.	59+
1997, Dec. 2	Coal mine, Novokuznetsk, Siberia	68
1998, Feb. 14	2 oil tankers, Yaounde, Cameroon.	120
1998, Feb. 14	17 bombs, Coimbatore, India	50
1998, Apr. 4	Coal mine, Donetsk, Ukraine	63
1998, Aug. 7	Bomb, U.S. emb., Nairobi, Kenya.	213
1998, Aug. 7	Bomb, U.S. emb., Dar-es-Salaam, Tanz.	11
1998, Sept. 8	2 buses, São Paulo, Brazil	59
1998, Oct. 17	Oil pipeline, Jesse, Nigeria.	700+
1999, May 16	Fuel truck, Punjab Prov., Pakistan	75
1999, Sept. 10	Apartment building, Moscow, Russia	94
1999, Sept. 13	Apartment building, Moscow, Russia	118
1999, Sept. 16	Apartment building, Moscow, Russia	18
1999, Sept. 26	Fireworks factory, Celaya, Mexico	56
2000, Feb. 25	Bombs on 2 buses, Ozamis, Philippines	41
2000, Mar. 11	Coal mine, Krasnodon, Ukraine	80
2000, Apr. 16	Airport hangar, Dem. Rep. of Congo	100+
2000, July16	Oil pipeline, Warri, Nigeria	30
2000, Sept. 9	Truck explosion, Urumqi, China	60
2000, Oct. 12	U.S. destroyer, Yemen	17
2001, Mar. 6	School, Wanzai Co., China.	41
2001, Apr. 21	Coal mine, Shaanxi, China.	51
2001, June 1	Dance club, Tel Aviv, Israel	21
2001, July17	Coal mine, Guanxi, China.	76+
2001, Aug. 19	Coal mine, Donetsk region, Ukraine.	52
2001, Sept. 21	Chem. plant, Toulouse, France	29
2002, Jan. 21	Volcanic lava caused gas station blast, Goma, Dem. Rep. of Congo.	50+
2002, Jan. 27	Munitions dump, Lagos, Nigeria.	1,000+
2002, May 9	Land mine at parade, Kaspiisk, Russia	34+
2002, June 14	Car bomb outside U.S. consulate, Karachi, Pakistan	12
2002, June 18	Bomb on bus, Jerusalem, Israel.	20
2002, July 5	Bomb in market, Larba, Algeria	35+
2002, Aug. 9	Explosion, Jalalabad, Afghanistan	25+
2002, Sept. 5	Car bomb, Kabul, Afghanistan	30
2002, Oct. 12	Nightclub bombings, Bali, Indonesia	202
2003, Aug. 25	Bombs in 2 taxis, Mumbai, India.	52
2003, Dec. 5	Bomb on train, Yessentuki, Russia.	45
2003, Dec. 23	Gas well explosion, Chongqing, China.	233
2004, Jan. 19	Natural gas facility, Skikda, Algeria	27
2004, Feb. 6	Bomb on subway car, Moscow, Russia	39
2004, Mar. 11	Bombs on commuter trains, Madrid, Spain	191
2005, Feb. 14	Coal mine, NE China	214
2005, Mar. 23	Oil refinery, Texas City, TX.	15
2005, May 2	Arms cache, Baghlan Prov., Afghan.	34+
2005, July 7	Bombs in mass transit, London, Eng.	56
2005, Oct. 1	Bombings of restaurants, Bali, Indonesia	26
2005, Nov. 27	Coal mine, NE China	161+
2006, May 12	Oil pipeline, nr. Lagos, Nigeria	200
2006, July 1	Bombings of trains, station, Mumbai, India	207
2007, Mar. 19	Coal mine, Siberia, Russia.	108
2007, Mar. 22	Natl. weapons depot, Maputo, Mozambique.	117
2007, June 9	Oil pipeline, Pyongan Prov., N. Korea	110
2007, Nov. 18	Methane gas buildup in coal mine, E Ukraine	90
2008, May 15	Pipeline explosion in Lagos, Nigeria.	100+
2008, Sept. 20	Truck bomb outside hotel, Islamabad, Pakistan	40+
2009, Feb. 22	Coal mine, N China	74
2010, Apr. 5	Coal mine, Montcoal, WV	29
2010, Apr. 20	Oil rig, Gulf of Mexico, U.S.	11
2010, May 8-9	Coal mine, Siberia, Russia	91
2010, June 17	Coal mine, Amaga, Colombia.	73
2010, Nov. 19	Coal mine, Ataru, New Zealand	29
2011, Mar. 28	Munitions factory, Abyan, Yemen.	150+
2011, July 13	Bombs in three locations in Mumbai, India	27
2012, Mar. 4	Arms depot, Brazzaville, Congo Republic	250+

World's Largest Blackout

Dates: July 31-Aug. 1, 2012. **Location:** Northern India

670 mil people—nearly one-tenth of the world's population—lost power simultaneously in 2012 when three interconnected power grids in India shut down, jamming traffic, trapping miners, and stranding trains and subways in 14 states across a 2,000-mi swath of the country. More than half of India's 1.2 bil people experienced the blackout, but there were no reported fatalities as a result of it.

Notable Nuclear Accidents

Oct. 7, 1957: Fire in the Windscale plutonium production reactor N of Liverpool, England, released radioactive material; later blamed for 39 cancer deaths.

Jan. 3, 1961: Reactor explosion at a federal installation near Idaho Falls, ID, killed 3 workers. Radiation contained.

Oct. 5, 1966: Sodium cooling system malfunction caused a partial core meltdown at the Enrico Fermi demonstration breeder reactor, near Detroit, MI. Radiation contained.

Jan. 21, 1969: Coolant malfunction from an experimental underground reactor at Lucens Vad, Switzerland, released radiation into a cavern, which was then sealed.

Mar. 22, 1975: Fire at the Brown's Ferry reactor in Decatur, AL, caused dangerous lowering of cooling water levels.

Mar. 28, 1979: Worst commercial nuclear accident in the U.S. occurred as equipment failures and human mistakes led to a loss of coolant and a partial core meltdown at the Three Mile Island reactor in Middletown, PA.

Feb. 11, 1981: 8 workers were contaminated when 100,000 gallons of radioactive coolant fluid leaked into the containment building of TVA's Sequoyah 1 plant near Chattanooga, TN.

Apr. 25, 1981: Some 100 workers were exposed to radiation during repairs of a nuclear plant at Tsuruga, Japan.

Jan. 6, 1986: Cylinder of nuclear material burst after being improperly heated at a Kerr-McGee plant at Gore, OK. One worker died; 100 were hospitalized.

Apr. 26, 1986: In the worst nuclear accident in the history of nuclear power, fires and explosions resulting from an unauthorized experiment at the Chernobyl nuclear power plant near Kiev, USSR (now in Ukraine), left at least 31 dead in the immediate aftermath and spread radioactive material over much of Europe. An estimated 135,000 people were evacuated from the region, some of which was uninhabitable for years. As a result of the radiation released, tens of thousands of excess cancer deaths (as well as increased birth defects) were expected.

Mar. 11, 2011: A 9.0-magnitude earthquake caused a devastating tsunami that inundated the Fukushima Daiichi nuclear power plant on Japan's NE coast. Three of the plant's reactors suffered partial meltdowns, and more than 12,000 tons of radioactive water was released into the sea.

Record Oil Spills

The exact number of barrels in a ton varies with the type of oil, but a good approximation is 7 barrels per ton. Each barrel contains 42 gallons.

Name, location	Date	Cause	Tons
BP *Deepwater Horizon* rig, Gulf of Mexico, U.S.	Apr. 20-July 15, 2010	Explosion	700,000[1]
Ixtoc I oil well, S Gulf of Mexico	June 3, 1979	Blowout	600,000
Nowruz oil field, Persian Gulf	Feb. 1983	Blowout	600,000 (est.)
Atlantic Empress and *Aegean Captain*, off Trinidad and Tobago	July 19, 1979	Collision	300,000
ABT Summer, off Angola	May 28, 1991	Explosion	260,000
Castillo de Bellver, off Cape Town, South Africa	Aug. 6, 1983	Fire	250,000
Amoco Cadiz, near Portsall, France	Mar. 16, 1978	Grounding	223,000
Torrey Canyon, off Land's End, England	Mar. 18, 1967	Grounding	119,000
Sea Star, Gulf of Oman	Dec. 19, 1972	Collision	115,000
Urquiola, La Coruna, Spain	May 12, 1976	Grounding	100,000

Other Notable Oil Spills

Name, location	Date	Cause	Gallons
Persian Gulf	Began Jan. 21, 1991	Intentional spillage by Iraq	130,000,000[2]
Braer, off Shetland Islands, UK	Jan. 5, 1993	Grounding	26,000,000
Prestige, off N Spain	Nov. 13-19, 2002	Ship broke in half	22,600,000
Aegean Sea, off N Spain	Dec. 3, 1992	Grounding	21,500,000
Sea Empress, off SW Wales	Feb. 15, 1996	Grounding	18,000,000
Newtown Creek, Greenpoint, Brooklyn, NY	Oct. 5, 1950-present	Industrial explosion, preceded by leaks in 1940s-50s	17,000,000
World Glory, off South Africa	June 13, 1968	Hull failure	13,524,000
Exxon Valdez, Prince William Sound, AK	Mar. 24, 1989	Grounding	10,080,000
Ashland Oil facility, Floreffe, PA; Monongahela R.	Jan. 2, 1988	Storage tank collapse	3,850,000

(1) The Dept. of Energy estimated the spill at 4.9 mil barrels, or more than 200 mil gallons. (2) Est. by Saudi Arabia. Some estimates as low as 25 mil gal.

Gulf of Mexico Oil Spill

Dates: Beg. Apr. 20, 2010. **Location:** Gulf of Mexico, off the coast of LA. **Fatalities:** 11. **Damages:** $20 bil.

The worst oil spill in history began with a gas explosion on the *Deepwater Horizon* platform 50 mi off Venice, LA. When the rig burned and sank, oil started gushing unabated from the ruptured pipes. After 86 days and several failed efforts, BP, the well's owner, finally capped the leak. Approximately 4.9 mil barrels of oil had spilled into the water—nearly 20 times the amount released in the 1989 Exxon *Valdez* disaster. But while a few tar balls washed up on beaches from Florida to Texas, a fast-moving current kept most oil swirling out to sea. By 2011, fish, shrimp, and even oysters from the Gulf were deemed safe to eat.

Some Notable Miscellaneous Disasters Since 1950

Date	Event	Location	Details	Est. deaths
1952, Dec.	Pollution	London, England	Heavy smog blanketed city; caused breathing difficulties	4,000
1973-74	Drought and famine	Ethiopia	Caused by 6-year drought	200,000
1974	Famine	Bangladesh	Caused by flooding	26,000+
1974-75	Famine	Sub-Saharan Africa	Drought in some regions, torrential rains in others, compounded by government mismanagement	40,000+
1980, summer	Heat wave	United States	June through Sept.	1,265
1984, Dec. 3	Industrial accident	Bhopal, India	Toxic gas leaked from a Union Carbide factory	16,000
1984	Famine	Africa, espec. Ethiopia	Several years of drought compounded by government mismanagement	800,000-1 mil
1986, Aug. 21	Gas	Nr. Lake Nyos, Cameroon	Volcanic lake released cloud of carbon dioxide gas	1,700
1990, July 2	Stampede	Mecca, Saudi Arabia	Pilgrims panicked in tunnel leading to the holy city	1,426
2003, summer	Heat wave	Europe	Abnormally high temperatures from Russia to Britain; France suffered most, with 14,800 dead	35,000
2005, Aug. 31	Stampede	Baghdad, Iraq	Fear of suicide bomber caused bridge stampede	1,000

AEROSPACE

Memorable Moments in Human Spaceflight

Source: National Aeronautics and Space Administration (NASA); Congressional Research Service; World Almanac research

The spaceflights listed are a selection of notable U.S. missions by NASA, unless otherwise noted, plus non-U.S. missions (shown with an asterisk). The non-U.S missions were sponsored by the USSR—later, the Commonwealth of Independent States (CIS) and, from 1997, Russia—or by China. Launch dates are Eastern standard time. EVA = extravehicular activity. ASTP = Apollo-Soyuz Test Project. STS = Space Transportation System, NASA's name for the overall shuttle program.

For shuttle flights, mission name is in parentheses following name of orbiter. Duration of flight is listed in hours:minutes for 1961-Apr. 1970; days (d.), hours (hr.), and minutes (min.) for June 1970-Apr. 1981; days only thereafter. Number of total flights taken by each crew member is given in parentheses when flight listed is not the person's first.

4/12/1961: *Vostok 1*; 1:48; Yuri A. Gagarin. **1st human orbital flight.**

5/5/1961: *Mercury-Redstone 3*; 0:15; Alan B. Shepard Jr. **1st American in space.**

7/21/1961: *Mercury-Redstone 4*; 0:15; Virgil I. Grissom. Flight successful but spacecraft sank shortly after splashdown; Grissom rescued.

8/6/1961: *Vostok 2*; 25:18; Gherman S. Titov. 1st spaceflight of more than 24 hours.

2/20/1962: *Mercury-Atlas 6*; 4:55; John H. Glenn Jr. **1st American in orbit**; 3 orbits.

5/24/1962: *Mercury-Atlas 7*; 4:56; M. Scott Carpenter. Manual retrofire error caused 250-mi landing overshoot.

8/11/1962: *Vostok 3*; 94:22; Andrian G. Nikolayev. *Vostok 3* and 4 made 1st group flight.

8/12/1962: *Vostok 4*; 70:57; Pavel R. Popovich. On 1st orbit, it came within 3 mi of *Vostok 3*.

10/3/1962: *Mercury-Atlas 8*; 9:13; Walter M. Schirra Jr. Landed 5 mi from target; 6 orbits.

5/15/1963: *Mercury-Atlas 9*; 34:19; L. Gordon Cooper. 1st U.S. evaluation of effects of one day in space on a person; 22 orbits.

6/14/1963: *Vostok 5*; 119:06; Valery F. Bykovsky. *Vostok 5* and 6 made 2nd group flight.

6/16/1963: *Vostok 6*; 70:50; Valentina V. Tereshkova. **1st woman in space**; passed within 3 mi of *Vostok 5*.

10/12/1964: *Voskhod 1*; 24:17; Vladimir M. Komarov, Konstantin P. Feoktistov, Boris B. Yegorov. 1st 3-person orbital flight; 1st without space suits.

3/18/1965: *Voskhod 2*; 26:02; Pavel I. Belyayev, Aleksei A. Leonov. Leonov made **1st spacewalk** (10 min.).

3/23/1965: *Gemini-Titan 3*; 4:53; Virgil I. Grissom (2), John W. Young. 1st piloted spacecraft to change its orbital path.

6/3/1965: *Gemini-Titan 4*; 97:56; James A. McDivitt, Edward H. White II. White was **1st American to "walk in space"** (36 min.).

8/21/1965: *Gemini-Titan 5*; 190:55; L. Gordon Cooper (2), Charles Conrad Jr. Longest-duration human flight to date.

12/4/1965: *Gemini-Titan 7*; 330:35; Frank Borman, James A. Lovell. Longest-duration *Gemini* flight.

12/15/1965: *Gemini-Titan 6A*; 25:51; Walter M. Schirra Jr. (2), Thomas P. Stafford. Completed 1st U.S. space rendezvous, with *Gemini 7*.

3/16/1966: *Gemini-Titan 8*; 10:41; Neil A. Armstrong, David R. Scott. **1st docking of one space vehicle with another**; mission aborted, control malfunction; 1st Pacific landing.

6/3/1966: *Gemini-Titan 9A*; 72:21; Thomas P. Stafford (2), Eugene A. Cernan. Performed simulation of lunar module rendezvous.

7/18/1966: *Gemini-Titan 10*; 70:47; John W. Young (2), Michael Collins. 1st use of Agena target vehicle's propulsion systems; 1st orbital docking.

9/12/1966: *Gemini-Titan 11*; 71:17; Charles Conrad Jr. (2), Richard F. Gordon Jr. 1st tethered flight; highest Earth-orbit altitude (850 mi).

11/11/1966: *Gemini-Titan 12*; 94:34; James A. Lovell (2), Edwin E. "Buzz" Aldrin Jr. Final *Gemini* mission; 5-hr. EVA.

4/23/1967: *Soyuz 1*; 26:40; Vladimir M. Komarov (2). Crashed on reentry, killing Komarov; **1st space fatality**.

10/11/1968: *Apollo-Saturn 7*; 260:09; Walter M. Schirra Jr. (3), Donn F. Eisele, R. Walter Cunningham. **1st piloted flight of Apollo** spacecraft command-service module only; live TV footage of crew.

12/21/1968: *Apollo-Saturn 8*; 147:00; Frank Borman (2), James A. Lovell (3), William A. Anders. **1st lunar orbit** and piloted lunar return reentry (command-service module only); views of lunar surface televised to Earth.

1/14/1969: *Soyuz 4*; 71:21; Vladimir A. Shatalov. Docked with *Soyuz 5*.

1/15/1969: *Soyuz 5*; 72:54; Boris V. Volyanov, Aleksei S. Yeliseyev, Yevgeny V. Khrunov. Docked with *Soyuz 4*; Yeliseyev and Khrunov transferred to *Soyuz 4* via a spacewalk.

3/3/1969: *Apollo-Saturn 9*; 241:00; James A. McDivitt (2), David R. Scott (2), Russell L. Schweickart. 1st piloted flight of lunar module.

5/18/1969: *Apollo-Saturn 10*; 192:03; Thomas P. Stafford (3), John W. Young (3), Eugene A. Cernan (2). 1st lunar module orbit of Moon, 50,000 ft from Moon's surface.

7/16/1969: *Apollo-Saturn 11*; 195:18; Neil A. Armstrong (2), Michael Collins (2), Edwin E. "Buzz" Aldrin Jr. (2). **1st Moon landing** made by Armstrong and Aldrin (7/20); collected 48.5 lbs of soil, rock samples; lunar stay time 21:36.

10/11/1969: *Soyuz 6*; 118:43; Georgi S. Shonin, Valery N. Kubasov. 1st welding of metals in space.

10/12/1969: *Soyuz 7*; 118:40; Anatoly V. Flipchenko, Vladislav N. Volkov, Viktor V. Gorbatko. Space lab construction test made; *Soyuz 6, 7,* and *8:* 1st time 3 spacecraft, 7 crew members orbited the Earth at once.

10/13/1969: *Soyuz 8*; 118:51; Vladimir A. Shatalov (2), Aleksei S. Yeliseyev (2). Part of space lab construction team.

11/14/1969: *Apollo-Saturn 12*; 244:36; Charles Conrad Jr. (3), Richard F. Gordon Jr. (2), Alan L. Bean. Conrad and Bean made **2nd Moon landing** (11/18); collected 74.7 lbs of samples; lunar stay time 31:31.

4/11/1970: *Apollo-Saturn 13*; 142:54; James A. Lovell (4), Fred W. Haise Jr., John L. Swigert Jr. Aborted after service module oxygen tank ruptured; crew returned in lunar module.

6/1/1970: *Soyuz 9*; 17 d., 16 hr., 59 min.; Andrian G. Nikolayev (2), Vitaly I. Sevastyanov. Longest human spaceflight to date.

1/31/1971: *Apollo-Saturn 14*; 9 d., 2 min.; Alan B. Shepard Jr. (2), Stuart A. Roosa, Edgar D. Mitchell. Shepard and Mitchell made **3rd Moon landing** (2/3); collected 96 lbs of lunar samples; lunar stay 33:31.

4/19/1971: *Salyut 1*; launched without crew. **1st space station**.

4/22/1971: *Soyuz 10*; 1 d., 23 hr., 46 min.; Vladimir A. Shatalov (3), Aleksei S. Yeliseyev (3), Nikolay N. Rukavishnikov. **1st successful docking with a space station**; failed to enter space station.

6/6/1971: *Soyuz 11*; 23 d., 28 hr., 22 min.; Georgi T. Dobrovolskiy, Vladislav N. Volkov (2), Viktor I. Patsayev. Docked and entered *Salyut 1* space station; **crew died** during reentry from loss of pressurization.

7/26/1971: *Apollo-Saturn 15*; 12 d., 17 hr., 12 min.; David R. Scott (3), James B. Irwin, Alfred M. Worden. Scott and Irwin made **4th Moon landing** (7/30). 1st lunar rover use; 1st deep spacewalk; 170 lbs of samples; 66:55 stay.

4/16/1972: *Apollo-Saturn 16*; 11 d., 1 hr., 51 min.; John W. Young (4), Charles M. Duke Jr., Thomas K. Mattingly II. Young and Duke made **5th Moon landing** (4/20); collected 213 lbs of lunar samples; lunar stay 71:02.

12/7/1972: *Apollo-Saturn 17*; 12 d., 13 hr., 52 min.; Eugene A. Cernan (3), Ronald E. Evans, Harrison H. Schmitt. Cernan and Schmitt made 6th and **last lunar landing** (12/11); collected 243 lbs of samples; record lunar stay over 75 hrs.

5/14/1973: *Skylab 1*; launched without crew. **1st U.S. space station**; fell out of orbit 7/11/1979.

5/25/1973: *Skylab 2*; 28 d., 49 min.; Charles Conrad Jr. (4), Joseph P. Kerwin, Paul J. Weitz. 1st U.S.-piloted orbiting space station; crew repaired damage caused in boost.

7/28/1973: *Skylab 3*; 59 d., 11 hr., 1 min.; Alan L. Bean (2), Owen K. Garriott, Jack R. Lousma. Crew systems and operational tests; scientific activities; 3 EVAs, 13:44.

11/16/1973: *Skylab 4*; 84 d., 1 hr., 16 min.; Gerald P. Carr, Edward G. Gibson, William R. Pogue. Final *Skylab* mission.

7/15/1975: *Soyuz 19 (ASTP)*; 6 d., 11 hr., 31 min.; Aleksei A. Leonov (2), Valery N. Kubasov (2). U.S.-USSR joint flight; crews linked up in space (7/17), conducted experiments, shared meals, held a joint news conference.

7/15/1975: *Apollo (ASTP)*; 9 d., 7 hr., 28 min.; Vance D. Brand, Thomas P. Stafford (4), Donald K. Slayton. Joint flight with *Soyuz 19*.

12/10/1977: *Soyuz 26*; 96 d., 10 hr.; Yuri V. Romanenko, Georgiy M. Grechko (2). 1st multiple docking at a space station (*Soyuz 26* and *27* docked at *Salyut 6*).

1/10/1978: *Soyuz 27*; 5 d., 22 hr., 59 min.; Vladimir A. Dzhanibekov. See *Soyuz 26*.

3/2/1978: *Soyuz 28*; 7 d., 22 hr., 16 min.; Aleksei A. Gubarev (2), Vladimir Remek. 1st international crew launch; Remek was 1st Czech in space.

4/12/1981: *Columbia (STS-1)*; 2 d., 6 hr., 21 min.; John W. Young (5), Robert L. Crippen. **1st reusable space shuttle** to fly into Earth's orbit.

11/12/1981: *Columbia (STS-2)*; 3 days; Joe H. Engle, Richard H. Truly. 1st scientific payload; 1st reuse of space shuttle.

11/11/1982: *Columbia (STS-5)*; 6 days; Vance D. Brand (2), Robert F. Overmyer, William Lenoir, Joseph Allen. 1st 4-person crew.

6/18/1983: *Challenger (STS-7)*; 7 days; Robert L. Crippen (2), Frederick Hauck, Sally K. Ride, John M. Fabian, Norman E. Thagard. Ride was **1st U.S. woman in space**; 1st 5-person crew.

6/27/1983: *Soyuz T-9*; 150 days; Vladimir A. Lyakhov (2), Aleksandr Pavlovich. Docked at *Salyut 7*. 1st construction in space.

8/30/1983: *Challenger (STS-8)*; 7 days; Richard H. Truly (2), Daniel Brandenstein, William Thornton, Guion Bluford, Dale Gardner. Bluford was **1st African American in space**; **1st night launch**.

11/28/1983: *Columbia (STS-9)*; 11 days; John W. Young (6), Brewster Shaw Jr., Robert Parker, Owen K. Garriott (2), Byron Lichtenberg, Ulf Merbold. 1st 6-person crew; 1st Spacelab mission.

2/3/1984: *Challenger (41-B)*; 8 days; Vance Brand (3), Robert Gibson, Ronald McNair, Bruce McCandless, Robert Stewart. 1st untethered EVA.

2/8/1984: *Soyuz T-10B*; 63 days; Leonid Kizim, Vladimir Solovyov, Oleg Atkov. Docked with *Salyut 7*; crew set space duration record of 237 days.

4/3/1984: *Soyuz T-11*; 182 days; Yury Malyshev (2), Gennady Strekalov (3), Rakesh Sharma. Docked with *Salyut 7*; Sharma was 1st Indian in space.

4/6/1984: *Challenger (41-C)*; 7 days; Robert L. Crippen (3), Francis R. Scobee, George D. Nelson, Terry J. Hart, James D. van Hoften. 1st in-orbit satellite repair.

7/17/1984: *Soyuz T-12*; 12 days; Vladimir A. Dzhanibekov (4), Svetlana Y. Savitskaya (2), Igor P. Volk. Docked at *Salyut 7*; Savitskaya was 1st woman to perform EVA.

8/30/1984: *Discovery (41-D)*; 7 days; Henry W. Hartsfield (2), Michael L. Coats, Richard M. Mullane, Steven A. Hawley, Judith A. Resnik, Charles D. Walker. 1st flight of U.S. non-astronaut (Walker).

10/5/1984: *Challenger (41-G)*; 9 days; Robert L. Crippen (4), Jon A. McBride, Kathryn D. Sullivan, Sally K. Ride (2), Marc Garneau, David C. Leestma, Paul D. Scully-Power. 1st 7-person crew.

11/8/1984: *Discovery (51-A)*; 8 days; Frederick Hauck (2), David M. Walker, Dr. Anna L. Fisher, Joseph Allen (2), Dale Gardner (2). 1st satellite retrieval/repair.

4/12/1985: *Discovery (51-D)*; 7 days; Karol J. Bobko, Donald E. Williams, Jake Garn, Charles D. Walker (2), Jeffrey A. Hoffman, S. David Griggs, M. Rhea Seddon. Garn (R, UT) was **1st U.S. senator in space**.

6/17/1985: *Discovery (51-G)*; 8 days; Daniel Brandenstein (2), John O. Creighton, Shannon W. Lucid, Steven R. Nagel, John M. Fabian (2), Prince Sultan Salman al-Saud, Patrick Baudry. Launched 3 satellites; Salman al-Saud was 1st Arab in space; Baudry was 1st French person on U.S. mission.

10/3/1985: *Atlantis (51-J)*; 5 days; Karol J. Bobko (3), Ronald J. Grabe, David C. Hilmers, Robert Stewart (2), William A. Pailes. 1st *Atlantis* flight.

10/30/1985: *Challenger (61-A)*; 8 days; Henry W. Hartsfield (3), Steven R. Nagel (2), James F. Buchli (2), Guion Bluford (2), Bonnie J. Dunbar, Wubbo J. Ockels, Richard Furrer, Ernst Messerschmid. 1st 8-person crew; 1st German Spacelab mission.

1/12/1986: *Columbia (61-C)*; 7 days; Robert Gibson (2), Charles F. Bolden Jr., Steven A. Hawley (2), George D. Nelson (2), Franklin R. Chang Díaz, Robert J. Cenker, Bill Nelson. Nelson (D, FL) was **1st U.S. representative in space**.

1/28/1986: *Challenger (51-L)*; 73 seconds; Francis R. Scobee (2), Michael J. Smith, Judith A. Resnik (2), Ellison S. Onizuka (2), Ronald E. McNair, Gregory B. Jarvis, Christa McAuliffe. **Exploded 73 seconds after liftoff; all aboard were killed**, including McAuliffe, a New Hampshire schoolteacher who won a national competition to become 1st private citizen in space.

2/20/1986: *Mir*[1]; launched without crew. **Space station** with 6 docking ports launched.

3/13/1986: *Soyuz T-15*; 125 days; Leonid Kizim (3), Vladimir Solovyov (2). Ferry between stations; docked at *Mir*.

2/5/1987: *Soyuz TM-2*; 327 days; Yuri V. Romanenko (3), Aleksandr I. Laveikin. Romanenko set endurance record, since broken.

7/22/1987: *Soyuz TM-3*; 161 days; Aleksandr Viktorenko, Aleksandr Pavlovich Aleksandrov (2), Mohammed Faris. Docked with *Mir*; Faris was 1st Syrian in space.

9/29/1988: *Discovery (STS-26)*; 4 days; Frederick Hauck (3), Richard O. Covey (2), David C. Hilmers (2), George D. Nelson (3), John M. Lounge (2). **1st shuttle flight since *Challenger* explosion** 1/28/1986.

5/4/1989: *Atlantis (STS-30)*; 4 days; David M. Walker (2), Ronald J. Grabe (2), Norman E. Thagard (3), Mary L. Cleave (2), Mark C. Lee. Launched Venus orbiter *Magellan*.

10/18/1989: *Atlantis (STS-34)*; 5 days; Donald E. Williams (2), Michael J. McCulley, Shannon W. Lucid (2), Franklin R. Chang Díaz (2), Ellen S. Baker. Launched Jupiter probe and orbiter *Galileo*.

4/24/1990: *Discovery (STS-31)*; 6 days; Loren J. Shriver (2), Charles F. Bolden Jr. (2), Steven A. Hawley (2), Bruce McCandless (2), Kathryn D. Sullivan (2). **Launched Hubble Space Telescope**.

10/6/1990: *Discovery (STS-41)*; 5 days; Richard N. Richards (2), Robert D. Cabana, Bruce E. Melnick, William M. Shepherd (2), Thomas D. Akers. Launched *Ulysses* spacecraft to investigate interstellar space and the Sun.

5/18/1991: *Soyuz TM-12*; 145 days; Anatoly Artsebarsky, Sergei Krikalev (2) (to *Mir*), Helen Sharman. Docked with *Mir*; Sharman was 1st Briton in space.

3/17/1992: *Soyuz TM-14*; 146 days; Aleksandr Viktorenko (3) (to *Mir*), Alexandr Kaleri (to *Mir*), Klaus-Dietrich Flade, Aleksandr

Volkov (3) (from *Mir*), Sergei Krikalev (2) (from *Mir*). 1st human CIS space mission; docked with *Mir* 3/19; Krikalev was in space 313 days.

5/7/1992: *Endeavour (STS-49)*; 9 days; Daniel Brandenstein (4), Thomas D. Akers (2), Kevin C. Chilton, Richard J. Hieb (2), Bruce E. Melnick (2), Kathryn Thornton (2), Pierre J. Thuot (2). 1st 3-person EVA; satellite recovery and redeployment.

9/12/1992: *Endeavour (STS-47)*; 8 days; Robert Gibson (4), Jay Apt (2), Curtis L. Brown Jr., N. Jan Davis, Mae Carol Jemison, Mark C. Lee (2), Mamoru Mohri. Jemison was **1st black woman in space**; Lee and Davis were **1st married couple to travel together in space**; 1st Japanese Spacelab.

6/21/1993: *Endeavour (STS-57)*; 10 days; Ronald J. Grabe (4), Brian J. Duffy (2), G. David Low (3), Nancy J. Sherlock, Janice E. Voss, Peter J. K. Wisoff. Carried Spacelab commercial payload module.

12/2/1993: *Endeavour (STS-61)*; 11 days; Richard O. Covey (3), Kenneth D. Bowersox (2), Claude Nicollier (2), F. Story Musgrave (5), Thomas D. Akers (3), Kathryn Thornton (3), Jeffrey A. Hoffman (4). Hubble Space Telescope repaired; Akers set new U.S. EVA duration record (29 hr., 40 min.).

2/3/1994: *Discovery (STS-60)*; 9 days; Charles F. Bolden Jr. (3), Kenneth S. Reightler Jr. (2), N. Jan Davis (2), Franklin R. Chang Díaz (3), Ronald M. Sega, Sergei Krikalev (3). Krikalev was 1st Russian on U.S. shuttle.

7/1/1994: **Soyuz TM-19*; 126 days; Yuri I. Malenchenko, Talgat A. Musabayev, Ulf Merbold (2) (from *Mir*). Docked with *Mir*.

9/9/1994: *Discovery (STS-64)*; 11 days; Richard N. Richards (4), L. Blaine Hammond Jr. (2), Jerry M. Linenger, Susan J. Helms (2), Carl J. Meade (3), Mark C. Lee (3). Performed atmospheric research; 1st untethered EVA in more than 10 years.

2/3/1995: *Discovery (STS-63)*; 9 days; James D. Wetherbee (3), Eileen M. Collins, Bernard A. Harris (2), C. Michael Foale (3), Janice E. Voss (2), Vladimir Titov (4). *Discovery* and Russian space station rendezvous.

3/2/1995: *Endeavour (STS-67)*; 17 days; Stephen S. Oswald (3), William G. Gregory, Samuel T. Durrance (2), Ronald Parise (2), Wendy B. Lawrence, Tamara E. Jernigan (3), John M. Grunsfeld. Shuttle data made available on the Internet.

3/14/1995: **Soyuz TM-21*; 112 days; Norman E. Thagard (5), Vladimir Dezhurov, Gennady Strekalov (5). Docked with *Mir* 3/16. Thagard was 1st American onboard Russian spacecraft; Valery Polyakov returned to Earth, 3/22/1995, after record stay in space (439 days).

6/27/1995: *Atlantis (STS-71)*; 10 days; Robert Gibson (5), Charles J. Precourt (2), Ellen S. Baker (3), Gregory J. Harbaugh (3), Bonnie J. Dunbar (4), Anatoly Solovyev (4) (to *Mir*), Nikolai M. Budarin (to *Mir*), Norman E. Thagard (5) (from *Mir*), Gennady Strekalov (from *Mir*), Vladimir Dezhurov (from *Mir*). **1st shuttle-*Mir* docking**; exchanged crew members with *Mir*.

11/12/1995: *Atlantis (STS-74)*; 9 days; Kenneth D. Cameron (3), James D. Halsell Jr. (2), Chris Hadfield, Jerry L. Ross (5), William S. McArthur (2). 2nd shuttle-*Mir* docking (11/15-11/18); erected a 15-ft permanent docking tunnel to *Mir* for future use by U.S. orbiters.

2/22/1996: *Columbia (STS-75)*; 16 days; Andrew M. Allen (3), Scott J. Horowitz, Franklin R. Chang Díaz (5), Umberto Guidoni, Jeffrey A. Hoffman (5), Maurizio Cheli, Claude Nicollier (3). Lost an Italian satellite when its tether was severed; microgravity experiments performed; singe marks found on 2 O-rings.

3/22/1996: *Atlantis (STS-76)*; 10 days; Kevin C. Chilton (3), Richard A. Searfoss (2), Ronald M. Sega (2), Michael R. Clifford (3), Linda Godwin (3), Shannon W. Lucid (5) (to *Mir*). 3rd shuttle-*Mir* docking (5 days); 2-person EVA.

9/16/1996: *Atlantis (STS-79)*; 11 days; Jay Apt (4), Terry W. Wilcutt (2), William Readdy (3), Thomas D. Akers (4), Carl E. Walz (3), Shannon W. Lucid (5) (from *Mir*), John E. Blaha (5) (to *Mir*).

Docked with *Mir* 9/18; exchanged crew members; Lucid set **U.S. and women's duration in space record** (188 days).

11/19/1996: *Columbia (STS-80)*; 18 days; Kenneth D. Cockrell (3), Kent V. Rominger (2), Tamara E. Jernigan (4), Thomas D. Jones (3), F. Story Musgrave (6). Longest-duration shuttle flight; Musgrave, 61, oldest thus far to fly in space; 2 science satellites deployed, retrieved.

1/12/1997: *Atlantis (STS-81)*; 11 days; Michael A. Baker (4), John M. Grunsfeld (2), Marsha Ivins (4), Brent W. Jett (2), Peter J. K. Wisoff (3), Jerry M. Linenger (2) (to *Mir*), John E. Blaha (5) (from *Mir*). Docked with *Mir* 1/14-1/19; Blaha spent 128 days in space.

2/11/1997: *Discovery (STS-82)*; 10 days; Kenneth D. Bowersox (4), Gregory J. Harbaugh (4), Steven A. Hawley (4), Scott J. Horowitz (2), Mark C. Lee (4), Steve Smith (2), Joe Tanner (2). Increased capabilities of Hubble Space Telescope; 5 EVAs conducted to service it.

5/15/1997: *Atlantis (STS-84)*; 10 days; Charles J. Precourt (3), Jean-François Clervoy (2), Eileen M. Collins (2), Elena Kondakova, Edward T. Lu, Carlos Noriega, C. Michael Foale (4) (to *Mir*), Jerry M. Linenger (2) (from *Mir*). Docked with *Mir* 5/16-5/21. Foale's stay on *Mir* marked by major collision with cargo ship 6/25/1997.

8/5/1997: **Soyuz TM-26*; 198 days; Anatoly Solovyev (5), Pavel Vinogradov. Docked with *Mir* 8/7; repaired damaged space station.

8/7/1997: *Discovery (STS-85)*; 12 days; Curtis L. Brown Jr. (4), Robert L. Curbeam Jr., N. Jan Davis (3), Stephen K. Robinson, Kent V. Rominger (3), Bjarni V. Tryggvason. Deployed and retrieved satellite designed to study Earth's middle atmosphere; demonstrated robotic arm.

9/25/1997: *Atlantis (STS-86)*; 11 days; James D. Wetherbee (4), Michael J. Bloomfield, Vladimir Titov (4), Scott Parazynski (2), Jean-Loup Chrétien (3), Wendy B. Lawrence (2), David A. Wolf (2) (to *Mir*), C. Michael Foale (4) (from *Mir*). Docked with *Mir* 9/27-10/3; delivered new computer to *Mir*.

4/17/1998: *Columbia (STS-90)*; 16 days; Richard A. Searfoss (3), Scott D. Altman, Richard M. Linnehan (2), Dave R. Williams, Kathryn P. Hire, Jay C. Buckey, James A. Pawelczyk. Studied effects of microgravity on the nervous systems of the crew and more than 2,000 live animals; 1st surgery in space on animals meant to survive.

6/2/1998: *Discovery (STS-91)*; 10 days; Charles J. Precourt (4), Dominic L. Gorie, Wendy B. Lawrence (3), Franklin R. Chang Díaz (6), Janet L. Kavandi, Valery Ryumin (4), Andrew S.W. Thomas (2) (from *Mir*). Final docking mission with *Mir*; Thomas from *Mir*, 141 days in space.

10/29/1998: *Discovery (STS-95)*; 10 days; Curtis L. Brown Jr. (5), Steven W. Lindsey (2), Scott Parazynski (3), Stephen K. Robinson (2), Pedro Duque, Chiaki Mukai (2), John H. Glenn Jr. (2). The 77-year-old Glenn, one of the original *Mercury* astronauts, and at that point a senator (D, OH), became **oldest person to fly in space**; Duque was 1st Spaniard in space; experiments to study aging performed on Glenn.

12/4/1998: *Endeavour (STS-88)*; 12 days; Robert D. Cabana (4), Frederick W. Sturckow, Nancy J. Currie (3), Jerry L. Ross (6), James H. Newman (3), Sergei Krikalev (4). **1st assembly of International Space Station (ISS)**; attached U.S.-built *Unity* connecting module to Russian-built *Zarya* control module; 1st crew to enter ISS.

7/23/1999: *Columbia (STS-93)*; 5 days; Eileen M. Collins (3), Jeffrey S. Ashby, Steven A. Hawley (5), Catherine G. Coleman (2), Michel Tognini (2). Collins was **1st woman space shuttle commander**; deployed Chandra X-ray Observatory telescope.

2/11/2000: *Endeavour (STS-99)*; 12 days; Kevin R. Kregel (4), Dominic L. Gorie, Janet L. Kavandi (2), Janice E. Voss (5), Mamoru Mohri (2), Gerhard P.J. Thiele. Used radar to make most complete topographic map of Earth's surface ever produced.

9/8/2000: *Atlantis (STS-106)*; 12 days; Terry W. Wilcutt (4), Scott D. Altman (2), Edward T. Lu (2), Richard A. Mastracchio, Daniel C. Burbank, Yuri I. Malenchenko (2), Boris V. Morukov. Prepared ISS for 1st permanent crew; 1 EVA by all 7 crew members.

10/31/2000: **Soyuz TM-31*; William M. Shepherd (4), Yuri Gidzenko (2), Sergei Krikalev (5). Established **1st permanent manning of ISS** with 3-person crew for a 4-month stay.

3/8/2001: *Discovery (STS-102)*; 13 days; James D. Wetherbee (5), James M. Kelly, Susan J. Helms (4) (to ISS), James S. Voss (5) (to ISS), Paul Richards, Andrew S.W. Thomas (2), Yuri V. Usachev (4) (to ISS), William M. Shepherd (4) (from ISS), Yuri Gidzenko (2) (from ISS), Sergei Krikalev (5) (from ISS). Transported 2nd permanent crew to ISS and returned 1st crew to Earth; 2 EVAs.

7/12/2001: *Atlantis (STS-104)*; 13 days; Steven W. Lindsey (3), Charles O. Hobaugh, Michael L. Gernhardt (4), Janet L. Kavandi (3), James F. Reilly II (2). Installed a Joint Airlock, with nitrogen and oxygen tanks to permit future spacewalks from the ISS; 3 EVAs.

3/1/2002: *Columbia (STS-109)*; 11 days; Scott D. Altman (3), Duane G. Carey, John M. Grunsfeld (4), Nancy J. Currie (4), Richard M. Linnehan (3), James H. Newman (4), Michael J. Massimino. Installed powerful new camera and upgraded other equipment on Hubble Space Telescope; 5 EVAs.

4/8/2002: *Atlantis (STS-110)*; 11 days; Michael J. Bloomfield (3), Stephen N. Frick, Rex J. Walheim, Ellen Ochoa (4), Lee M.E. Morin, Jerry L. Ross (7), Steven L. Smith (4). Installed S0 Truss, backbone for expansion of ISS; Ross set records with 7th spaceflight, 9th spacewalk.

10/30/2002: **Soyuz TMA-1*[2]; Sergei Zalyotin (2), Frank De Winne, Yuri Lonchakov (2). 1st launch of *Soyuz TMA* (crew returned 11/10/2002 on *Soyuz TM-34* already docked at ISS).

1/16/2003: *Columbia (STS 107)*; 16 days; Rick Husband (2), William McCool, Michael Anderson (2), David Brown, Kalpana Chawla (2), Laurel Clark, Ilan Ramon. **Entire crew lost when** *Columbia* **burned** during reentry, 2/1; Ramon was 1st Israeli astronaut.

10/15/2003: **Shenzhou 5*; 21 hr.; Yang Liwei. **1st Chinese manned spacecraft**.

6/21/2004: *SpaceShipOne*; 90 min.; Mike Melvill. **1st privately funded manned spaceflight**[3].

7/26/2005: *Discovery (STS-114)*; 14 days; Charles Camarda, Eileen M. Collins (4), James M. Kelly (2), Wendy B. Lawrence (4), Soichi Noguchi, Stephen K. Robinson (3), Andrew S.W. Thomas (3). **1st space shuttle flight since** *Columbia* **disaster**; tested new safety modifications to craft.

7/4/2006: *Discovery (STS-121)*; 13 days; Steven W. Lindsey (4), Mark E. Kelly, Michael E. Fossum, Piers J. Sellers (2), Lisa M. Nowak, Thomas Reiter (to ISS), Stephanie D. Wilson. 1st shuttle to launch on Independence Day; conducted more safety tests to craft; brought supplies to and performed maintenance on ISS.

4/7/2007: **Soyuz TMA-10*[2]; Oleg Kotov (to ISS), Sheikh Muszaphar Shukor (from ISS), Charles Simonyi (U.S.) Fyodor Yurchikhin (to ISS). Kotov and Yurchikhin joined ISS expedition 15; Simonyi became **5th space tourist** (returned on *TMA-9*); Shukor was 1st Malaysian in space (arrived on *TMA-11*).

6/8/2007: *Atlantis (STS-117)*; 14 days; Frederick Sturckow (3), Lee Archambault, Patrick Forrester (2), John "Danny" Olivas, Jim Reilly (3), Steven Swanson, Clayton Anderson (to ISS), Sunita L. Williams (from ISS). Delivered truss segments and

solar arrays to ISS; Williams set record for **longest spaceflight by a woman**.

8/8/2007: *Endeavour (STS-118)*; 13 days; Scott Kelly (2), Alvin Drew, Barbara R. Morgan, Charles O. Hobaugh (2), Tracy Caldwell, Rick Mastracchio (2), Dave R. Williams (2). Brought **Teacher in Space** project participant Morgan to ISS; attached new truss segment; repaired faulty gyroscope.

10/10/2007: **Soyuz TMA-11*[2]; Yuri I. Malenchenko (3), Sheikh Muszaphar Shukor (to ISS), Peggy A. Whitson (2) (from ISS), Yi So-yeon (from ISS). Delivered and installed components of ISS; malfunctioned on return to Earth, landing short of its touchdown area but causing no fatalities.

10/23/2007: *Discovery (STS-120)*; 16 days; Pamela A. Melroy (3), Paolo Nespoli, Scott Parazynski (5), Douglas Wheelock, Stephanie Wilson, George Zamka, Daniel M. Tani (2) (to ISS), Clayton Anderson (from ISS). Installed living space (Harmony Node 2) on ISS.

2/7/2008: *Atlantis (STS-122)*; 13 days; Stephen N. Frick (2), Stanley G. Love, Leland D. Melvin, Alan G. Poindexter, Hans Schlegel (2), Léopold Eyharts (to ISS), Daniel M. Tani (from ISS), Rex J. Walheim (2). Installed European Space Agency's Columbus laboratory on the ISS; minor damage to a thermal plate caused concern about the shuttle's safety during reentry, but *Atlantis* landed safely.

3/11/2008: *Endeavor (STS-123)*; 16 days; Dominic L. Gorie (4), Robert L. Behnken, Takao Doi (2), Michael J. Foreman, Gregory H. Johnson, Richard M. Linnehan (4), Léopold Eyharts (from ISS), Garrett Reisman (to ISS). Delivered and installed components of the Japanese Kibo science laboratory.

4/8/2008: **Soyuz TMA-12*[2]; Oleg Kononenko, Sergei Volkov, Yi So-yeon (to ISS), Richard Garriott (from ISS). Yi became 1st S. Korean in space.

5/31/2008: *Discovery (STS-124)*; 14 days; Mark E. Kelly (3), Michael E. Fossum (2), Ronald J. Garan Jr., Kenneth T. Ham, Akihiko Hoshide, Karen Nyberg, Gregory E. Chamitoff (to ISS), Garrett Reisman (from ISS). Delivered and installed pressurized and experimental modules of Kibo.

9/25/2008: **Shenzhou 7*; 68 hr.; Jing Haipeng, Liu Boming, Zhai Zhigang. Zhai completed 1st Chinese spacewalk.

10/12/2008: **Soyuz TMA-13*[2]; Richard Garriott (to ISS), Yuri V. Lonchakov (3), Michael Fincke. Garriott became 6th space tourist.

3/15/2009: *Discovery (STS-119)*; 13 days; Lee J. Archambault (2), Joseph M. Acaba, Dominic A. Antonelli, Richard R. Arnold, John L. Phillips, Steven Swanson (2), Koichi Wakata (to ISS), Sandra H. Magnus (from ISS). Delivered final solar panels and last U.S.-made truss segment.

5/11/2009: *Atlantis (STS-125)*; 13 days; Scott D. Altman (4), Andrew J. Feustel, Michael T. Good, John M. Grunsfeld (5), Gregory C. Johnson, Michael J. Massimino (2), K. Megan McArthur. Final Hubble Space Telescope servicing mission.

11/16/2009: *Atlantis (STS-129)*; 11 days; Charles O. Hobaugh (3), Randolph J. Bresnik, Michael J. Foreman (2), Leland D. Melvin (2), Robert L. Satcher Jr., Barry E. Wilmore, Nicole P. Stott (from ISS). Final Space Shuttle crew rotation flight.

6/15/2010: **Soyuz TMA-19*[2]; Fyodor Yurchikhin (3), Shannon Walker, Douglas H. Wheelock (2). 100th mission since launching of the International Space Station.

7/8/2011: *Atlantis (STS-135)*; 13 days; Christopher Ferguson (3), Doug Hurley (2), Sandy Magnus (3), Rex Walheim (3). **Final Space Shuttle mission**.

Note: Four Soviet cosmonauts have died during spaceflight: Vladimir Komarov was killed on *Soyuz 1* (1967) when parachute lines tangled during descent; the 3-person *Soyuz 11* crew (1971) was asphyxiated. Six Americans and an Israeli astronaut died aboard the *Columbia*; 7 Americans died in the *Challenger* explosion; and 3 astronauts—Virgil I. Grissom, Edward H. White, and Roger B. Chaffee—died in the Jan. 27, 1967, *Apollo 1* fire on the ground at Cape Canaveral, FL. (1) Space stations, such as the *Salyuts* and *Mir*, were used to house crews starting in 1971. (2) *Soyuz* crew often return from the ISS on spacecraft that launched and were docked at the station before their arrival. (3) Date of first successful flight; later, *SpaceShipOne* flew at least 100 km (62 mi) into space, 9/29/2004, piloted by Mike Melvill, and 10/4/2004, piloted by Brian Binnie, winning the $10 mil Ansari Prize for first private venture to accomplish this feat twice within two weeks.

U.S. Manned Space Program

Source: National Aeronautics and Space Administration (NASA)

After 50 years of sending men and women into space, the United States ended its manned space program with the safe landing of the *Atlantis* space shuttle on July 21, 2011, at Florida's Kennedy Space Center. U.S. astronauts currently travel to and from the International Space Station (ISS) on Russian rockets, but NASA is hopeful that private companies will someday carry passengers to the ISS.

Pres. Barack Obama announced Apr. 15, 2010, a new blueprint for NASA's efforts in the human exploration of space. NASA's plans include development of a heavy-lift rocket with the ability to efficiently send into orbit crew capsules, propulsion systems, and large quantities of supplies needed to reach deep space. By 2025, a new spacecraft designed for long journeys will carry astronauts to long-range destinations, including asteroids and Mars.

The era of the reusable space shuttle (1981-2011) was tempered by two tragedies: the Jan. 28, 1986, *Challenger* explosion, in which six astronauts and schoolteacher Christa McAuliffe were killed 73 seconds after liftoff; and the Feb. 1, 2003, accident in which all seven astronauts aboard died when the *Columbia* burned up on reentry.

The surviving space shuttles are now on display at museums around the country. In Apr. 2012, *Discovery* was placed at the Smithsonian National Air and Space Museum's Udvar-Hazy Center at Washington-Dulles Intl. Airport in Virginia. It replaced *Enterprise*, which performed test runs but never went into space. A week later, *Enterprise* was moved to New York City's Intrepid Air, Sea, and Space Museum. *Endeavour* was scheduled to go on display at the California Science Center in Los Angeles on Oct. 30, 2012. *Atlantis* remained on permanent display at the Kennedy Space Center.

International Space Station

Source: National Aeronautics and Space Administration (NASA)

The International Space Station (ISS) is considered the largest cooperative scientific project in history. Construction began in 1998; it has been inhabited by international crew members since 2000.

16 cooperating nations: Brazil, Belgium, Canada, Denmark, France, Germany, Italy, Japan, Netherlands, Norway, Russia, Spain, Sweden, Switzerland, United Kingdom, United States.

The station when completed:
- Mass of 925,000 lbs
- 361 ft long, with almost an acre of solar panels
- Internal volume roughly equivalent to one-and-a-half 747 jumbo jets
- 6 laboratories
- Living space for up to 7 people

Examples of research conducted or planned:
- Studying the effects of long-term exposure to reduced gravity on plants, crystals, plant and animal cells, and pathogens
- Studying the effects on humans of long-term exposure to reduced gravity
- Recording large-scale long-term changes in Earth's environment by observing the planet from orbit
- Testing recycling technologies for human life support

Summary of Worldwide Successful Launches, 1957-2012

Source: National Aeronautics and Space Administration (NASA), World Almanac research

Year	Total[1]	Russia[2]	U.S.	ESA[3]	China	Japan	France	India	UK	Germany	Canada	Israel	Iran	S. Korea
1957-59	24	6	18	—	—	—	—	—	—	—	—	—	—	—
1960-69	1,035	399	614	2	—	—	4	—	1	—	—	—	—	—
1970-79	1,366	1,028	247	5	8	18	14	1	6	3	4	—	—	—
1980-89	1,431	1,132	191	14	16	26	5	9	4	7	5	—	—	—
1990-99	1,045	542	300	55	33	23	16	11	7	6	4	—	—	—
2000-09	603	246	206	63	52	18	0	13	0	0	0	3	1	1
2010-12[4]	180	70	38	15	43	6	(3)	5	(3)	(3)	0	1	0	0
Total	**5,684**	**3,423**	**1,614**	**154**	**152**	**91**	**39**	**39**	**18**	**16**	**13**	**4**	**1**	**1**

(1) Includes launches sponsored by countries not shown. (2) Data for 1957-91 apply to the Soviet Union, for 1992-96 to the Commonwealth of Independent States, after 1996 to Russia. (3) European Space Agency. Member states as of Sept. 2012 are Austria, Belgium, Czech Republic, Denmark, Finland, France, Germany, Greece, Ireland, Italy, Luxembourg, the Netherlands, Norway, Portugal, Romania, Spain, Sweden, Switzerland, and the UK. Canada, Hungary, Poland, Estonia, and Slovenia also participate in some projects under cooperation agreements. (4) As of July 9, 2012.

Notable Lunar and Planetary Science Missions

Source: National Aeronautics and Space Administration (NASA)

Spacecraft	Launch date[1]	Mission	Remarks
Mariner 2	Aug. 27, 1962	Venus	Passed within 22,000 mi of Venus 12/14/1962; confirmed high surface temperature on planet; contact lost 1/3/1963 at 54 mil mi.
Ranger 7	July 28, 1964	Moon	Yielded over 4,000 photos of lunar surface.
Mariner 4	Nov. 28, 1964	Mars	1st probe to fly by Mars; passed behind planet 7/14/1965; took 22 photos from 6,000 mi above surface.
Ranger 8	Feb. 17, 1965	Moon	Yielded over 7,000 photos of lunar surface.
Venera 3	Nov. 16, 1965	Venus	Soviet probe; 1st artificial probe to impact on the surface of another planet, 3/1/1966; probe failed to send back data.
Surveyor 3	Apr. 17, 1967	Moon	Scooped and tested lunar soil.
Mariner 5	June 14, 1967	Venus	In solar orbit; closest Venus flyby 10/19/1967; allowed scientists to obtain accurate readings on the composition of the Venusian atmosphere.
Mariner 6	Feb. 24, 1969	Mars	Came within 2,000 mi of Mars 7/31/1969; collected data, photos.
Mariner 7	Mar. 27, 1969	Mars	Came within 2,000 mi of Mars 8/5/1969.
Venera 7	Aug. 17, 1970	Venus	Soviet probe; 1st probe to land safely on the surface of another planet; because of high atmospheric temperatures, probe is thought to have melted.
Mariner 9	May 30, 1971	Mars	1st craft to orbit Mars 11/13/1971; sent back over 7,000 photos.
Pioneer 10	Mar. 2, 1972	Jupiter	Passed Jupiter 12/4/1973; took readings on Jupiter's composition and found that the planet is composed mostly of hydrogen. Exited the planetary system 6/13/1983; transmission ended 3/31/1997 at 6.39 bil mi.
Pioneer 11	Apr. 5, 1973	Jupiter, Saturn	Passed Jupiter 12/3/1974, Saturn 9/1/1979; discovered an additional ring and 2 moons around Saturn. Operated in outer solar system; transmission ended 9/30/1995.
Mariner 10	Nov. 3, 1973	Venus, Mercury	Passed Venus 2/5/1974, arrived at Mercury 3/29/1974. 1st time gravity of 1 planet (Venus) used to whip spacecraft toward another (Mercury); 1st probe to visit 2 planets; took cloud and wind pattern readings in Venusian atmosphere.

Spacecraft	Launch date[1]	Mission	Remarks
Viking 1	Aug. 20, 1975	Mars	Landed on Mars 7/20/1976; 1st probe to land safely on Mars; performed chemical analysis of soil; functioned 6 years.
Viking 2	Sept. 9, 1975	Mars	Sister probe of *Viking 1*; landed on Mars 9/3/1976; functioned 3 years.
Voyager 2	Aug. 20, 1977	Jupiter, Saturn, Uranus, Neptune	Encountered Jupiter 7/9/1979, Saturn 8/25/1981, Uranus 1/24/1986, Neptune 8/25/1989. Confirmed existence of rings around Neptune; observed Neptune's "great dark spot," which has since dissipated. Entered boundary of solar system 10/2007; as of 3/2012, it was 14.7 bil km from Sun and still returning data to Earth.
Voyager 1	Sept. 5, 1977	Jupiter, Saturn	Encountered Jupiter 3/5/1979; provided evidence of rings around Jupiter; passed near Saturn 11/12/1980; passed *Pioneer 10* to become most distant human-made object 2/17/1998; as of 3/2012, it had reached a distance of 17.9 bil km from Sun and was still returning data to Earth.
Pioneer Venus 1	May 20, 1978	Venus	Entered Venus orbit 12/4/1978; studied atmosphere, magnetic field, weather, and surface; fuel ran out, and probe was destroyed in atmospheric entry, 8/1992.
Pioneer Venus 2 (multiprobe)	Aug. 8, 1978	Venus	Consisted of a "bus" carrying 1 large and 3 small atmospheric probes. All 4 probes entered the Venus atmosphere 12/9/1978, followed by the bus; took readings of Venusian atmosphere; probes impacted on surface.
Magellan	May 4, 1989	Venus	Landed on Venus 8/10/1990; monitored geological activity; mapped more than 99% of planet surface, observed more than 1,600 volcanoes and volcanic features, enabling creation of a 3-D map; showed that about 85% of the surface is covered by volcanic flows; ceased operating 10/11/1994.
Galileo	Oct. 18, 1989	Jupiter	Used Earth's gravity to propel itself towards Jupiter; encountered Venus 2/1990, Jupiter 12/7/1995; encountered moons. Released probe into Jovian atmosphere; intentionally flown into Jupiter 9/21/2003 to prevent accidental contamination of Jupiter's moon Europa.
Mars Global Surveyor	Nov. 7, 1996	Mars	Began orbiting Mars 9/11/1997; began mapping entire surface 3/9/1999; discovered a weak magnetic field on planet; observed Martian moon Phobos; found evidence of liquid water in past 6/22/2000.
Mars Pathfinder	Dec. 4, 1996	Mars	Landed on Mars 7/4/1997; rover *Sojourner* made measurements of climate and soil composition, sending thousands of surface images; ceased operating 9/27/1997.
Cassini-Huygens	Oct. 15, 1997	Saturn	Began orbiting Saturn 6/30/2004; 4-year mission to study planet's atmosphere, rings, and moons; spotted evidence of a subterranean ocean and 300-mi-wide hot spot region on moon Titan; detected an atmosphere on moon Enceladus. *Huygens* probe landed on Titan 1/14/2005; found a muddy surface, possible deposits of water ice, channels carved by liquid methane springs.
Lunar Prospector	Jan. 6, 1998	Moon	Began orbiting Moon 1/11/1998; mapped abundance of 11 elements on Moon's surface; discovered evidence of water at both lunar poles; crashed into crater near Moon's south pole 7/31/1999 to end mission.
Deep Space 1	Oct. 24, 1998	Comet Borrelly	Flew within 1,500 mi of comet; sent back photos showing a 6-mi-long nucleus.
Stardust	Feb. 7, 1999	Comet Wild-2	Reached comet 1/2/2004; gathered dust samples, returned to Earth 1/15/2006.
2001 Mars Odyssey	Apr. 7, 2001	Mars	Reached Mars 10/24/2001; detected evidence of water ice near south pole; primary mission to study climate and geologic history completed 8/2004; began extended mission, aiming to identify minerals on Mars.
Genesis	Aug. 8, 2001	Sun	Orbited Sun, collected particles from solar wind; capsule containing specimens crashed to Earth 9/8/2004; some samples survived.
Mars Express/ Beagle 2 lander	June 3, 2003	Mars	1st European Space Agency probe to another planet; arrived at Mars 12/2003; performed remote sensing including photography in search of subsurface water; *Beagle 2* lander was deployed 12/19/2003, but contact was lost soon after.
Mars Exploration Rovers	June 7 and July 10, 2003	Mars	Rovers *Spirit* and *Opportunity* landed on Mars 1/2004, found further evidence that water existed on surface; *Spirit* took 1st photo of a Martian meteor; survived severe dust storms in 2007. *Opportunity* explored massive Victoria Crater 9/2007-8/2008; sighted larger Endeavor Crater 3/2009.
MESSENGER	Mar. 2, 2004	Mercury	Began returning images of Mercury during initial flyby 1/14/2008; entered orbit 3/17/2011; delivered 100,000th image 5/3/2012.
Deep Impact	Jan. 12, 2005	Comet Tempel 1	Reached Tempel 1; deployed an impact probe that slammed into comet 7/4/2005 with a force roughly equivalent to 5 tons of TNT.
Mars Reconnaissance Orbiter	Aug. 12, 2005	Mars	Reached Mars 3/10/2006 and began taking detailed images of Martian surface; in 3/2008, found salt deposits suggesting ancient water supplies; in 6/2008, found largest known crater in solar system.
New Horizons (Pluto)	Jan. 19, 2006	Pluto, Charon	Flew by Jupiter 7/2007. Due to reach Pluto and Charon in 7/2015; may examine other Kuiper Belt Objects.
Phoenix Mars Lander	Aug. 4, 2007	Mars	Landed on Mars 5/25/2008; examined northern polar region; monitored weather and analyzed minerals; evidence of water ice verified 7/31/2008; lost contact 11/2/2008.
Dawn	Sept. 27, 2007	Asteroid Belt (bet. Jupiter and Mars)	Will compare the evolution of dwarf planet Ceres with Vesta, an asteroid, in an effort to shed light on the formation of the solar system. Departed Vesta 8/2012; expected to arrive at Ceres 2/2015.
Lunar CRater Observation and Sensing Satellite (LCROSS)	June 18, 2009	Moon	Impact into Cabeus crater detected presence of water ice in Moon's surface on 10/9/2009; subsequent analysis found methane, ammonia, hydrogen gas, and large amounts of sodium and mercury.
Mars Science Laboratory Curiosity Rover (Mars Rover)	Nov. 26, 2011	Mars	Landed on Mars 8/6/2012 and began assessing whether Mars is or ever was able to support microbial life and other factors in the planet's potential for habitability.

(1) Coordinated Universal Time.

Notable Proposed U.S. Space Missions in 2012-13

Source: National Aeronautics and Space Administration (NASA)

Planned Launch	Mission	Purpose
Dec. 2012	Tracking and Data Relay Satellite-K (TDRS-K)	This spacecraft is part of the next generation of space-based communications satellites providing tracking, telemetry, command, and high-bandwidth data services.
Feb. 2013	Landsat Data Continuity Mission (LDCM)	This collaboration with the U.S. Geological Service continues a program first launched in 1972. The newest satellite will send back high-resolution images of the Earth's surface for use in climate change research, land-use planning, and disaster response.

General Aviation and Air Taxi Active Aircraft, 2010

Source: Federal Aviation Administration; aircraft not associated with major airlines or the military

Aircraft	Total active	Personal	Business	Corporate	Instructional	Aerial apps.	Aerial observation	Other work	Sight-seeing	Air medical	Other	On-demand operations
Fixed wing.....	176,272	117,015	20,476	9,680	12,685	2,709	3,614	618	311	121	3,203	5,545
Piston........	155,419	114,059	17,572	1,300	12,508	1,439	3,017	427	308	73	2,129	2,421
Turboprop......	9,369	1,771	1,716	1,980	124	1,266	582	178	3	29	195	1,402
Turbojet	11,484	1,185	1,189	6,400	53	3	15	13	0	19	879	1,723
Rotorcraft.......	10,102	1,520	486	565	1,324	519	2,124	73	181	89	216	2,421
Piston........	3,588	1,193	314	16	1,215	195	327	15	117	4	57	87
Turbine........	6,514	327	173	550	109	325	1,798	58	65	85	159	2,334
Other aircraft....	5,684	4,534	73	0	329	0	3	78	550	0	77	39
Gliders........	1,899	1,621	0	0	211	0	3	0	30	0	34	0
Lighter-than-air..	3,785	2,914	73	0	118	0	0	78	520	0	43	39
Experimental....	24,784	22,047	575	160	445	85	164	30	415	22	731	106
Amateur.......	21,270	19,604	411	3	388	0	111	5	400	0	349	0
Exhibition......	2,029	1,716	40	0	32	4	7	9	12	0	207	0
Other	1,485	726	125	157	25	80	46	16	2	22	175	106
Light sport.....	6,528	5,738	55	0	621	0	24	7	0	0	83	0
Total aircraft	223,370	150,854	21,666	10,405	15,404	3,313	5,929	806	1,457	232	4,311	8,112

Note: Columns may not add to totals due to rounding. **Personal**—Flying for personal reasons; **Business**—Individual or group use for business transportation without a paid, professional crew; **Corporate**—Individual or group business transportation with a paid, professional crew (includes fractional ownership); **Instructional**—Flying under the supervision of a flight instructor; **Aerial applications**—Includes agriculture, forestry, public health, fire fighting, and other applications; **Aerial observation**—Includes aerial mapping/photography, patrol, search and rescue, hunting, traffic advisory, ranching, surveillance, oil and mineral exploration, etc.; **Other work use**—Construction work, parachuting, aerial advertising, towing gliders, etc.; **Sightseeing**—Commercial sightseeing; **Air medical services**—Air ambulance services, rescue, human organ transportation, emergency medical services; **Other**—Positioning flights, proficiency flights, training, ferrying, sales demos; **On-demand operations**—On-demand air taxi, air tours, commuter, and air medical services.

Estimated Active Airmen Certificates Held, 2011

Source: Federal Aviation Administration, U.S. Dept. of Transportation

Category	Certificates	Category	Certificates	Category	Certificates
Pilot total	617,128	Sport only	4,066	Parachute Rigger	8,491
Airplane[1]		Rotorcraft (helicopters) only	15,220	Ground Instructor	74,586
Private...........	194,441	Glider only	21,141	Dispatcher..............	21,363
Commercial...........	120,865	Nonpilot total	695,515	Flight Navigator..........	146
Airline transport........	142,511	Mechanic..............	335,431	Flight Attendant..........	167,037
Student	118,657	Repairmen..............	40,802	Flight Engineer	47,659
Recreational only.........	227				

Note: The term airmen includes men and women certified as pilots, mechanics, or other aviation technicians. (1) Includes pilots with an airplane-only certificate as well as those with an airplane and a helicopter and/or glider certificate.

Aircraft Operating Statistics, 2012

Source: Airbus S.A.S., The Boeing Company, Embraer S.A.

Manufacturer and model	Max. # of seats	Typical # of seats	Fuel capacity (gal)	Typical cruising speed (mph)[1]	Max. range (naut. mi)	Max. thrust (thous. lbs)	Manufacturer and model	Max. # of seats	Typical # of seats	Fuel capacity (gal)	Typical cruising speed (mph)[1]	Max. range (naut. mi)	Max. thrust (thous. lbs)
Airbus							**Boeing**						
A318.........	132	107	6,400	630	3,200	24.0	727-200*......	189	148	9,806	605	2,500	17.4
A319	156	124	6,400	630	3,700	27.0	737-600	132	110	6,875	602	3,225	22.7
A320	180	150	6,400	630	3,300	27.0	737-700	149	126	6,875	602	3,440	26.3
A321	220	185	6,350	630	6,200	33.0	737-700C	140	126	6,875	599	3,285	27.3
A330-200......	380	253	36,750	660	7,250	72.0	737-800	189	162	6,875	602	3,115	27.3
A330-300......	440	295	26,765	660	5,850	72.0	737-900	215	180	7,837	599	3,265	27.3
A340-300......	440	295	37,150	660	7,400	34.0	747-100	452	366	48,445	645	6,100	50.1
A340-500.....	375	313	56,870	660	9,000	56.0	747-200/300....	452	366	52,410	645	7,900	54.8
A340-600......	475	380	51,750	660	7,900	60.0	747-400	524	416	57,285	653	7,260	63.3
A380	853	525	84,600	684	8,300	70.0	747-8	467	467	64,055	653	8,000	66.5
Embraer							757-200*......	228	200	11,489	614	3,900	43.5
190	114	98	NA	630	2,400	20.0	757-300*......	280	243	11,466	614	3,395	43.5
195	122	108	NA	630	2,200	20.0	767-200ER	255	181	23,980	614	6,385	62.1
McDonnell-Douglas							767-300ER	350	218	23,980	614	5,990	63.3
							767-400ER	375	245	23,980	614	5,625	63.5
DC-10 series*...	380	250	36,650	600	6,220	24.0	777-200	440	305	31,000	645	5,420	77.0
MD-11*	410	285	NA	NA	7,360	NA	777-200ER	440	301	45,220	645	7,725	93.7
MD-80 series* ..	172	155	5,840	584	2,504	21.0	777-200LR	NA	301	47,890	645	9,395	115.3
MD-90 series* ..	172	153	7,620	584	3,205	28.0	777-300	550	368	45,220	645	6,005	98.0
							777-300ER	NA	365	47,890	645	7,390	115.3
							787-8 Dreamliner	250	210	NA	652	8,200	NA
							787-9 Dreamliner	290	250	NA	652	8,500	NA

* = Aircraft no longer in production. NA = Not available. **Note:** Figures are for most commonly flown passenger models. When models within a series vary, maximums are shown. McDonnell-Douglas merged with Boeing in 1997. (1) Figures shown are converted from Mach speed (speed of sound), which varies depending on altitude and temperature. For comparison purposes, this table uses 768 mph as equivalent to Mach 1.

Milestones in Aviation History

Source: National Aeronautics and Space Administration (NASA), National Air and Space Museum, Air Transport Association of America, National Museum of the U.S. Air Force (USAF), U.S. National Park Service

1903, Dec. 17: Brothers Wilbur and Orville Wright (U.S.) made the first human-carrying, powered flight near Kitty Hawk, NC. Each brother made two flights; the longest, about 852 ft, lasted 59 seconds.

1908, May 14: Charles Furnas (U.S.), worker for Wright brothers, became first American airplane passenger.

1911, Feb.: The Burgess Company and Curtiss, Inc. receive authorization to build Wright planes, becoming the first licensed airplane manufacturer in the U.S.

1911, Sept. 23: First transportation of mail by airplane officially approved by the U.S. Postal Service.

1914, Jan. 1: First scheduled passenger airline service began. A seaplane that landed on water operated between St. Petersburg and Tampa, FL.

1918, Mar. 6: The Curtiss-Sperry "Flying Bomb" (U.S.) made its first successful flight. The first radio-controlled plane led to the development of both autopilot systems and cruise missiles.

1918, May 14: First scheduled airmail service began, between New York and Washington, DC, with intermediate stop in Philadelphia. In 1921, scheduled transcontinental airmail service began between New York City and San Francisco.

1919, June 14-15: Capt. John Alcock (UK) and Lt. Arthur W. Brown (U.S.) completed the first nonstop flight across the Atlantic Ocean. They traveled from Newfoundland, Canada, to Ireland in 16 hours and 12 minutes.

1923, Aug.: Rotating beacons enabled the first night flights in the U.S.

1924, Apr. 6-Sept. 28: Two U.S. Army planes landed in Seattle, completing the first circumnavigation of the globe. They completed the 26,000-mi journey in 371 hours of flying time.

1926, May 12-13: Roald Amundsen (Norway), Umberto Nobile (Italy), Lincoln Ellsworth (U.S.), and Oscar Wisting (Norway) made the first flight over the North Pole, in a dirigible that flew between Spitsbergen, Norway, and Teller, AK. Two weeks earlier, Adm. Richard E. Byrd and Floyd Bennett (both U.S.) claimed to have made the first flight over the Pole (May 9, 1926) in a Fokker F-VII. But when Byrd's diary was released to the public in 1996, some historians began to question whether his plane had reached the Pole.

1927, May 20-21: Charles Lindbergh (U.S.) completed the first solo transatlantic flight in the *Spirit of St. Louis.* "Lucky Lindy" traveled 3,610 mi from New York to Paris in 33 hours, 29 minutes, and 30 seconds.

1929, Aug. 8-29: Hugo Eckener (Germany) piloted the *Graf Zeppelin* around the world in record time: 20,373 mi in 21 days, 5 hours, and 31 minutes.

1929, Nov. 28: Adm. Richard E. Byrd (U.S.) and Bernt Balchen (Norway) became the first to fly to the South Pole and back, in 18 hours and 41 minutes.

1930, May 15: Ellen Church (U.S.) became first flight attendant.

1931, June 23-July 1: Wiley Post and Harold Gatty (both U.S.) broke the speed record for around-the-world flight. They traveled 15,474 mi in 8 days, 15 hours, and 51 minutes in the monoplane *Winnie Mae.*

1931, Oct. 3-5: Clyde Pangborn and Hugh Herndon (both U.S.) completed the first nonstop transpacific flight. They traveled 4,558 mi from Misawa, Japan, to East Wenatchee, WA, in 41 hours and 34 minutes.

1932, May 20-21: Amelia Earhart (U.S.) completed first solo transoceanic flight by a woman. She completed the 2,026-mi journey from Newfoundland, Canada, to Ireland in 14 hours and 56 minutes.

1933, July 15-22: Wiley Post (U.S.) completed the first solo circumnavigation of the globe. His 15,596-mi trip took 7 days, 18 hours, and 49 minutes.

1936, June 25: American Airlines began scheduled passenger service of the first Douglas DC-3 aircraft. The DC-3 was the first aircraft with a kitchen onboard and hence offered the first in-flight hot meal service.

1937, May 6: German *Hindenburg* zeppelin exploded and burst into flames in Lakehurst, NJ, killing 35 of the 97 people aboard (and one on the ground). The airship had made 34 transatlantic flights in 1936.

1938, July 10-13: Howard Hughes (U.S.) and four assistants established a new speed record for circumnavigating the globe: 14,824 mi in 3 days, 9 hours, 17 minutes.

1939, Aug. 27: The German-made Heinkel He 178 made the first successful flight powered by a jet engine.

1947, June 17-30: Pan American Airways began the first scheduled around-the-world passenger flights, from New York or San Francisco.

1947, Oct. 14: Chuck Yeager (U.S.) broke the sound barrier, reaching Mach 1 speed in a Bell X-1 rocket-powered aircraft.

1947, Nov. 2: Howard Hughes (U.S.) piloted the *Spruce Goose* on its maiden and only flight. The largest airplane ever built, it could carry 750 troops or two Sherman tanks.

1949, Mar. 2: James Gallagher (U.S.) piloted the first round-the-world flight to be refueled in midair. The *Lucky Lady* USAF B-50 covered 23,452 mi in 94 hours and 1 minute and was refueled four times.

1950, Sept. 22: Col. David Schilling (USAF) made the first nonstop transatlantic jet flight, covering 3,300 mi in 10 hours and 1 minute.

1952, Aug. 26: The UK bomber Canberra made the first round-trip transatlantic crossing on the same day, from Northern Ireland to Newfoundland, Canada, and back in 7 hours and 59 minutes.

1953, May 18: Jacqueline Cochran (U.S.) became the first woman to fly faster than the speed of sound.

1956, Mar. 10: Britain's Fairey FD-2 aircraft set a world speed record of 1,132 mph.

1956, Nov. 11: Convair B-58 (USAF), the first supersonic bomber, was introduced.

1957, Jan. 15-18: Three USAF B-52 Stratofortresses made the first nonstop global flight by jet planes. They were refueled in flight by KC-97 aerial tankers.

1958, Oct. 24: A Mirage III-A achieved Mach 2 (twice the speed of sound) in level flight, the first European plane to reach that speed.

1962, Nov. 29: Britain and France signed an agreement to jointly develop the Concorde, a supersonic plane that could fly twice as fast as most U.S. jets.

1969, June 5: The Soviet Tupolev Tu-144 became the first passenger airliner to reach Mach 2.

1970, May 26: The Tupolev Tu-144 reached a top speed of about 1,335 mph at 53,475 ft.

1976, Aug. 23: The Concorde began the first scheduled supersonic commercial service.

1977, Aug. 23: The *Gossamer Condor*, built by aeronautical engineer Paul MacCready (U.S.), successfully demonstrated human-powered flight through pedalling, completing a figure-8 course of 1.15 mi.

1979, June 12: The human-powered *Gossamer Albatross*, developed by MacCready, crossed the English Channel in 2 hours and 49 minutes.

1981, July 7: The MacCready-developed *Solar Challenger* became the first solar-powered airplane to cross the English Channel.

1995, Aug. 15-16: The Concorde set a new around-the-world speed record of 31 hours, 27 minutes, and 49 seconds.

1999, Mar. 1-21: Bertrand Piccard (Switz.) and Brian Jones (UK) completed the first around-the-world flight in a hot-air balloon. Their 29,055-mi journey began in Chateau-d'Oex, Switzerland, and ended 19 days, 21 hours, and 55 minutes later in the Egyptian desert.

2001, Aug. 13: Solar-powered, propeller-driven plane *Helios* (NASA) reached 96,863 ft, breaking altitude record for non-rocket-powered plane.

2002, June 19-July 4: Steve Fossett (U.S.) completed the first nonstop solo circumnavigation of globe in a balloon.

2003, Nov. 26: The Concorde flew its final flight.

2005, Mar. 1-3: Steve Fossett (U.S.) achieved the first nonstop solo circumnavigation in an airplane without refueling.

2005, Apr. 27: The Airbus A380, the biggest-ever commercial jet, made its maiden voyage. It was 240 ft long, had a wingspan of 262 ft, and could seat a maximum of 840 passengers. Its first commercial flight was Oct. 25, 2007.

2006, Feb. 8-11: Steve Fossett (U.S.) flew the longest nonstop, non-refueled solo flight (25,766 mi).

2009, Dec. 15: Boeing's 787 Dreamliner, the company's most fuel-efficient plane and the first to be constructed primarily from composite materials, made its maiden voyage, two years after it was originally scheduled.

2011, Feb. 4: Northrop Grumman and the U.S. Navy reported the first successful flight for the X-47B, an unmanned fighter jet that can operate safely from an aircraft carrier.

ASTRONOMY

Edited by Michael J. Kaufman, Dept. of Physics and Astronomy, San Jose State University

Celestial Events Summary, 2013

There are five eclipses in 2013: one annular solar eclipse, one hybrid solar eclipse, one partial lunar eclipse, and two penumbral lunar eclipses. The annular solar eclipse will be visible over a narrow path extending from northern Australia across the South Pacific. The hybrid solar eclipse, which starts as an annular eclipse but transitions into a total eclipse, will be visible across a narrow path extending across much of the Atlantic Ocean through equatorial Africa. 2013 is a poor year for lunar eclipses. Although all three are potentially visible over wide areas of the planet, none are notable; even the partial lunar eclipse will only result in a tiny fraction of the Moon's area being shadowed.

The most likely viewing successes for meteor showers will be the Perseids in Aug. and the Geminids in Dec. Other major showers—the Orionids in Oct. and the Leonids in Nov.—will peak when the Moon is full or just past full, so conditions for these will not be ideal. At the start of the year, Jupiter is high in the West at sunset, while Mars is further west, closer to the setting Sun. Mercury and Venus are low in the East at sunrise, and Saturn is high in the East before sunrise. Venus is a bright morning object through the start of Mar., becoming an evening object from mid-Apr. Jupiter is visible in the evening sky through the beginning of June, then moves to the morning sky from late June through the end of the year. Saturn is up for much of the night from Mar. through July, setting several hours after the Sun in fall, and becoming an early morning object by the end of the year. The best opportunities for seeing Mercury in the morning sky occur in early Apr., early Aug., and late Nov.; the planet will be visible in the evening sky in late Feb., mid-June, and early Oct.

The crescent Moon, with its subdued light, regularly makes pretty pairings with the two brightest planets, Venus and Jupiter. Waxing crescent pairings are visible in the early evening soon after sunset, while waning crescent pairings are visible in the early morning before sunrise. The waning crescent Moon pairs with Venus in each of the months from Jan. through Mar. The waxing crescent Moon pairs with Venus in all of the months from Apr. through Dec. The waxing crescent Moon pairs with Jupiter in the evening in Mar. and Apr., and the waning crescent pairs with Jupiter in July and Aug. The waning crescent Moon joins Mercury, Mars, and Jupiter in the early morning sky Aug. 4. It joins Mars and Jupiter in the early morning skies on July 6 and Sept. 1. The waxing crescent Moon joins Venus and Saturn, as well as a difficult-to-spot Mercury in the evening sky Oct. 7. Venus, Jupiter, and Mercury make a beautiful triplet on the evenings of May 25-28.

Astronomical Positions and Constants

Two celestial bodies are in **conjunction** when they are due north and south of each other, either in **right ascension** (with respect to the north celestial pole) or in **celestial longitude** (with respect to the north ecliptic pole). Celestial bodies in conjunction will rise and set at nearly the same time. For the inner planets—Mercury and Venus—**inferior conjunction** occurs when either planet passes between Earth and the Sun, while **superior conjunction** occurs when either Mercury or Venus is on the far side of the Sun. Celestial bodies are in **opposition** when their right ascensions differ by exactly 12 hours, or when their celestial longitudes differ by 180°. In this case one of the two objects in opposition will rise while the other is setting. **Quadrature** refers to the arrangement where the coordinates of two bodies differ by exactly 90°. These terms may refer to the relative positions of any two bodies as seen from Earth, but one of the bodies is so frequently the Sun that mention of the Sun is omitted in that case.

When objects are in conjunction, the alignment is not perfect, and one is usually passing above or below the other. The geocentric angular separation between the Sun and an object is termed **elongation**. Elongation is limited only for Mercury and Venus; the greatest elongation for each of these bodies is approximately the time for longest observation. **Perihelion** is the point in an object's orbit when it is nearest to the Sun, and **aphelion** is the point farthest from the Sun. **Perigee** is the point in an orbit that is nearest Earth, **apogee** the point that is farthest from Earth. An **occultation** of a planet or a star is an eclipse of it by some other body, usually the Moon. A **transit** of the Sun occurs when Mercury or Venus passes directly between Earth and the Sun, appearing to cross the Sun's disk.

The following were adopted as part of the International Astronomical Union System of Astronomical Constants (1976): **Speed of light**, 299,792.458 km per sec., or about 186,282 statute mi per sec.; **solar parallax**, 8".794148; **astronomical unit** (AU, the mean distance between the Earth and the Sun), 149,597,870 km, or 92,955,807 mi; **constant of nutation**, 9".2025; and **constant of aberration**, 20".49552.

Celestial Events Highlights, 2013

(In Coordinated Universal Time, or UTC, the standard time of the prime meridian.)

January

Mercury is visible low in the SE before sunrise early in the month and low in the SW after sunset at the end of the month.

Venus is visible low in the SE before sunrise all month.

Mars is low in the SW at sunset and sets several hours later.

Jupiter is high in the East at sunset and sets in the early morning.

Saturn rises after midnight and is high in the East at sunrise.

Uranus and **Neptune** are in the SW after sunset and set several hours later.

Jan. 1: Sun, Mercury in Sagittarius; Venus in Ophiuchus, Mars in Capricorn, Jupiter in Taurus, Saturn in Libra, Uranus in Pisces, Neptune in Aquarius, Pluto in Sagittarius all year, Moon passes 5.94° S of Regulus

Jan. 5: Last Quarter Moon, Moon passes 0.60° S of Spica

Jan. 6: Mercury passes 4.66° S of Pluto, Venus enters Sagittarius

Jan. 7: Moon passes 3.76° S of Saturn

Jan. 8: Moon passes 5.91° N of Antares

Jan. 10: Moon passes 2.78° N of Venus

Jan. 11: Moon passes 0.30° N of Pluto, Moon passes 5.86° N of Mercury, New Moon

Jan. 13: Moon passes 6.43° N of Mars

Jan. 14: Moon passes 6.01° N of Neptune

Jan. 17: Moon passes 4.80° N of Uranus

Jan. 18: First Quarter Moon, Mercury in superior conjunction 2.03° S, Mercury enters Capricorn

Jan. 19: Sun enters Capricorn

Jan. 22: Moon passes 0.50° S of Jupiter, Moon passes 4.03° N of Aldebaran

Jan. 26: Moon passes 11.31° S of Pollux

Jan. 27: Full Moon

Jan. 29: Moon passes 5.78° S of Regulus, Mars enters Aquarius

February

Mercury is visible low in the SW after sunset all month.

Venus is visible low in the SE before sunrise all month.

Mars is low in the SW at sunset and sets a few hours later.

Jupiter is high overhead at sunset and sets in the middle of the night.

Saturn rises around midnight and is high in the SW at sunrise.

Uranus sets several hours after the Sun.

Neptune begins the month setting just after the Sun and is lost in the Sun's glare by the end of the month.

Feb. 1: Venus enters Capricorn

Feb. 2: Moon passes 0.33° S of Spica

Feb. 3: Moon passes 3.48° S of Saturn, Last Quarter Moon, Mercury enters Aquarius

Feb. 5: Moon passes 6.12° N of Antares

Feb. 6: Mercury passes 0.46° S of Neptune

Feb. 7: Moon passes 0.49° N of Pluto

Feb. 8: Mercury passes 0.31° N of Mars

Feb. 9: Moon passes 6.02° N of Venus

Feb. 10: New Moon

Feb. 11: Moon passes 5.87° N of Neptune, Moon passes 6.16° N of Mars, Moon passes 5.22° N of Mercury

Feb. 13: Moon passes 4.47° N of Uranus

Feb. 16: Mercury at greatest elongation 18.1° E, Sun enters Aquarius

Feb. 17: First Quarter Moon

Feb. 18: Moon passes 0.90° S of Jupiter, Moon passes 3.78° N of Aldebaran, Mercury enters Pisces

Feb. 21: Sun passes 0.61° N of Neptune

Feb. 22: Moon passes 11.43° S of Pollux

Feb. 23: Venus enters Aquarius

Feb. 24: Mercury passes 4.24° N of Mars

Feb. 25: Moon passes 5.74° S of Regulus, Full Moon

March

Mercury is lost in the Sun's glare at the beginning of the month but visible low in the SE before sunrise late in the month.

Venus is visible in the SE before sunrise early in the month.

Mars is low in the SW after sunset and sets soon after.

Jupiter is high overhead at sunset and sets after midnight.

Saturn rises before midnight and is high in the SW at sunrise.

Uranus is low in the SW at sunset at the start of the month and lost in the Sun's glare by late in the month.

Neptune is visible low in the SE before sunrise.

Mar. 1: Moon passes 0.10° S of Spica

Mar. 2: Moon passes 3.32° S of Saturn

Mar. 3: Uranus enters Cetus

Mar. 4: Moon passes 6.38° N of Antares, Mercury in inferior conjunction 3.67° N, Last Quarter Moon, Mars enters Pisces

Mar. 5: Mercury enters Aquarius

Mar. 6: Mercury passes 5.34° N of Venus, Moon passes 0.74° N of Pluto

Mar. 10: Moon passes 5.87° N of Neptune, Moon passes 2.13° N of Mercury

Mar. 11: Moon passes 6.29° N of Venus, New Moon

Mar. 12: Moon passes 4.82° N of Mars, Sun enters Pisces

Mar. 13: Moon passes 4.22° N of Uranus

Mar. 18: Moon passes 1.48° N of Jupiter, Moon passes 3.53° N of Aldebaran, Venus enters Pisces

Mar. 19: First Quarter Moon

Mar. 20: Equinox

Mar. 21: Moon passes 11.63° S of Pollux, Mars enters Cetus

Mar. 23: Mars enters Pisces

Mar. 24: Moon passes 5.83° S of Regulus

Mar. 27: Full Moon, Venus enters Cetus

Mar. 28: Moon passes 0.01° N of Spica, Venus in superior conjunction 1.33° S

Mar. 29: Sun passes 0.67° N of Uranus, Moon passes 3.36° S of Saturn, Uranus enters Pisces

Mar. 30: Venus enters Pisces

Mar. 31: Moon passes 6.57° N of Antares, Mercury at greatest elongation 27.8° W

April

Mercury is visible low in the SE before sunrise all month.

Venus is low in the West after sunset all month.

Mars is not visible.

Jupiter is high in the West at sunset and sets near midnight.

Saturn rises mid-evening and is visible the rest of the night.

Uranus and **Neptune** are low in the SE at sunrise by the end of the month.

Apr. 3: Moon passes 0.96° N of Pluto, Last Quarter Moon

Apr. 7: Moon passes 5.95° N of Neptune

Apr. 8: Moon passes 7.05° N of Mercury

Apr. 9: Moon passes 4.09° N of Uranus

Apr. 10: New Moon, Moon passes 2.75° N of Mars, Moon passes 3.19° N of Venus

Apr. 12: Mercury enters Pisces

Apr. 14: Moon passes 3.39° N of Aldebaran, Moon passes 2.06° S of Jupiter

Apr. 15: Venus enters Aries

Apr. 17: Mercury enters Cetus

Apr. 18: Sun passes 0.40° N of Mars, Moon passes 11.78° S of Pollux, First Quarter Moon, Mars enters Aries, Sun enters Aries

Apr. 19: Mercury passes 2.03° S of Uranus

Apr. 21: Moon passes 5.93° S of Regulus, Mercury enters Pisces

Apr. 25: Moon passes 0.00° N of Spica, Full Moon, Partial Lunar Eclipse

Apr. 26: Moon passes 3.54° S of Saturn

Apr. 28: Moon passes 6.64° N of Antares, Saturn at opposition

Apr. 30: Moon passes 1.05° N of Pluto

May

Mercury is visible low in the West after sunset at the end of the month.

Venus is low in the W after sunset late in the month.

Mars is low in the NE at sunrise.

Jupiter is in the West at sunset and sets a few hours later.

Saturn is in the SE at sunset and up most of the night.

Uranus and **Neptune** rise a few hours before the Sun.

May 2: Last Quarter Moon, Mercury enters Taurus

May 4: Moon passes 6.02° N of Neptune, Venus enters Taurus

May 7: Moon passes 4.01° N of Uranus, Mercury passes 0.44° S of Mars

May 9: Moon passes 0.43° N of Mars, Moon passes 0.29° N of Mercury

May 10: New Moon, Annular Solar Eclipse

May 11: Moon passes 1.38° S of Venus, Moon passes 3.38° N of Aldebaran, Mercury in superior conjunction 0.08° N

May 12: Moon passes 2.59° S of Jupiter

May 13: Saturn enters Virgo

May 14: Sun enters Taurus

May 15: Moon passes 11.80° S of Pollux

May 18: First Quarter Moon, Moon passes 5.94° S of Regulus

May 21: Mercury passes 7.07° N of Aldebaran

May 22: Moon passes 0.00° N of Spica, Mars enters Taurus

May 23: Moon passes 3.70° S of Saturn

May 25: Full Moon, Mercury passes 1.37° N of Venus, Moon passes 6.63° N of Antares, Penumbral Lunar Eclipse

May 27: Mercury passes 2.37° N of Jupiter, Moon passes 1.01° N of Pluto

May 31: Moon passes 5.98° N of Neptune, Last Quarter Moon, Mercury enters Gemini

June

Mercury and **Venus** are visible low in the West after sunset all month.

Mars is high overhead at sunset and sets around midnight.

Jupiter is low in the West after sunset early in the month and low in the East before sunrise late in the month.

Saturn is in the SE at sunset and sets in the early morning hours.

Uranus and **Neptune** rise in the middle of the night and are high overhead at sunrise.

June 3: Moon passes 3.89° N of Uranus, Venus enters Gemini

June 7: Moon passes 1.79° S of Mars

June 8: Moon passes 3.40° N of Aldebaran, New Moon
June 9: Moon passes 3.07° S of Jupiter
June 10: Moon passes 5.33° S of Venus, Moon passes 5.88° S of Mercury
June 11: Moon passes 11.72° S of Pollux
June 12: Mercury at greatest elongation 24.3° E
June 14: Moon passes 5.82° S of Regulus
June 16: First Quarter Moon
June 18: Moon passes 0.11° N of Spica
June 19: Sun passes 0.23° N of Jupiter, Moon passes 3.65° S of Saturn
June 20: Mercury passes 1.94° S of Venus
June 21: Solstice, Moon passes 6.65° N of Antares, Sun enters Gemini
June 23: Full Moon
June 24: Moon passes 0.95° N of Pluto
June 25: Venus enters Cancer
June 27: Moon passes 5.84° N of Neptune, Jupiter enters Gemini
June 30: Last Quarter Moon, Moon passes 3.68° N of Uranus

July

Mercury is visible low in the NW after sunset early in the month and low in the NE before sunrise by the end of the month.
Venus is visible in the NW after sunset all month.
Mars and **Jupiter** are visible in the NE before sunrise all month.
Saturn is high in the SE at sunset and sets after midnight.
Uranus and **Neptune** rise in the middle of the night and are high overhead at sunrise.

July 2: Pluto at opposition
July 5: Moon passes 3.34° N of Aldebaran
July 6: Moon passes 3.70° S of Mars
July 7: Moon passes 3.54° S of Jupiter
July 8: New Moon, Moon passes 0.10° N of Mercury
July 9: Moon passes 11.64° S of Pollux, Mercury in inferior conjunction 4.76° S
July 10: Moon passes 7.02° S of Venus
July 12: Moon passes 5.64° S of Regulus, Venus enters Leo
July 13: Mars enters Gemini
July 16: First Quarter Moon, Moon passes 0.33° N of Spica
July 17: Moon passes 3.34° S of Saturn
July 19: Moon passes 6.78° N of Antares
July 20: Sun enters Cancer
July 21: Moon passes 0.99° N of Pluto
July 22: Full Moon
July 25: Moon passes 5.68° N of Neptune
July 27: Moon passes 3.44° N of Uranus
July 29: Last Quarter Moon
July 30: Mercury at greatest elongation 19.6° W

August

Mercury is visible low in the East before sunrise the first part of the month.
Venus is low in the West after sunset all month.
Mars and **Jupiter** are visible in the East before sunrise all month.
Saturn is high in the SW at sunset and sets around midnight.
Uranus and **Neptune** rise in the late evening and in the W at sunrise.

Aug. 1: Moon passes 3.17° N of Aldebaran
Aug. 3: Moon passes 4.02° S of Jupiter
Aug. 4: Moon passes 5.22° S of Mars
Aug. 5: Mercury passes 7.31° S of Pollux, Moon passes 11.66° S of Pollux, Moon passes 4.41° S of Mercury
Aug. 6: New Moon
Aug. 7: Mercury enters Cancer
Aug. 8: Moon passes 5.51° S of Regulus
Aug. 10: Moon passes 5.12° S of Venus, Sun enters Leo

Aug. 11: Venus enters Virgo
Aug. 12: Moon passes 0.58° N of Spica
Aug. 13: Moon passes 2.87° S of Saturn, Perseid meteor shower
Aug. 14: First Quarter Moon
Aug. 15: Moon passes 7.00° N of Antares
Aug. 17: Moon passes 1.17° N of Pluto, Mercury enters Leo
Aug. 21: Full Moon, Moon passes 5.61° N of Neptune
Aug. 23: Mercury passes 1.39° N of Regulus
Aug. 24: Moon passes 3.27° N of Uranus, Mercury in superior conjunction 1.76° N, Mars enters Cancer
Aug. 27: Neptune at opposition
Aug. 28: Last Quarter Moon, Moon passes 2.92° N of Aldebaran
Aug. 31: Moon passes 4.49° S of Jupiter

September

Mercury is low in the West after sunset at the end of the month.
Venus is in the West after sunset all month.
Mars and **Jupiter** rise several hours before sunrise and are high in the East at sunrise.
Saturn is in the SW at sunset and sets several hours later.
Uranus and **Neptune** rise around sunset and set near sunrise.

Sept. 1: Moon passes 11.79° S of Pollux, Saturn enters Libra
Sept. 2: Moon passes 6.23° S of Mars
Sept. 4: Moon passes 5.50° S of Regulus
Sept. 5: New Moon, Mercury enters Virgo
Sept. 6: Moon passes 4.71° S of Mercury
Sept. 8: Moon passes 0.77° N of Spica, Moon passes 0.43° S of Venus
Sept. 9: Moon passes 2.36° S of Saturn
Sept. 11: Moon passes 7.23° N of Antares
Sept. 12: First Quarter Moon
Sept. 14: Moon passes 1.43° N of Pluto
Sept. 16: Sun enters Virgo
Sept. 17: Moon passes 5.66° N of Neptune
Sept. 18: Venus enters Libra
Sept. 19: Full Moon
Sept. 20: Moon passes 3.25° N of Uranus
Sept. 22: Equinox
Sept. 24: Mercury passes 0.83° N of Spica
Sept. 25: Moon passes 2.72° N of Aldebaran, Mars enters Leo
Sept. 27: Last Quarter Moon
Sept. 28: Moon passes 4.87° S of Jupiter, Moon passes 11.96° S of Pollux

October

Mercury is low in the SW after sunset early in the month.
Venus is in the SW after sunset all month.
Mars rises in the middle of the night and is high in the East at sunrise.
Jupiter rises around midnight and is high in the West at sunrise.
Saturn is visible low in the SW after sunset and sets soon afterwards.
Uranus and **Neptune** are high in the SE at sunset and set in the early morning.

Oct. 1: Moon passes 6.65° S of Mars, Moon passes 5.59° S of Regulus
Oct. 3: Uranus at opposition
Oct. 5: New Moon, Moon passes 0.84° N of Spica
Oct. 6: Moon passes 2.84° N of Mercury, Mercury enters Libra
Oct. 7: Moon passes 1.93° S of Saturn, Venus enters Scorpius
Oct. 8: Moon passes 4.66° N of Venus
Oct. 9: Moon passes 7.37° N of Antares, Mercury at greatest elongation 25.3° E
Oct. 10: Mercury passes 5.40° S of Saturn

Oct. 11: Moon passes 1.67° N of Pluto, First Quarter Moon

Oct. 15: Moon passes 5.76° N of Neptune, Venus enters Ophiuchus

Oct. 17: Moon passes 3.35° N of Uranus, Venus enters Scorpius

Oct. 18: Full Moon, Penumbral Lunar Eclipse

Oct. 21: Venus enters Ophiuchus

Oct. 22: Moon passes 2.64° N of Aldebaran, Orionid meteor shower

Oct. 25: Moon passes 5.09° S of Jupiter

Oct. 26: Last Quarter Moon, Moon passes 12.05° S of Pollux

Oct. 28: Mercury passes 4.10° S of Saturn

Oct. 29: Moon passes 5.65° S of Regulus

Oct. 30: Moon passes 6.44° S of Mars

Oct. 31: Sun enters Libra

November

Mercury is low in the SE before sunrise late in the month.
Venus is in the SW after sunset all month.
Mars rises after midnight and is high in the East at sunrise.
Jupiter rises late evening and is high in the West at sunrise.
Saturn is visible low in the SE before sunrise late in the month.
Uranus and **Neptune** are high overhead at sunset and set after midnight.

Nov. 1: Venus at greatest elongation 47.1° E, Mercury in inferior conjunction 0.52° S, Venus enters Sagittarius

Nov. 2: Moon passes 0.83° N of Spica, Mercury enters Virgo

Nov. 3: Moon passes 0.02° N of Mercury, New Moon, Moon passes 1.58° S of Saturn, Hybrid Solar Eclipse

Nov. 5: Moon passes 7.39° N of Antares

Nov. 6: Sun passes 2.12° S of Saturn

Nov. 7: Moon passes 8.01° N of Venus, Moon passes 1.80° N of Pluto

Nov. 10: First Quarter Moon

Nov. 11: Moon passes 5.78° N of Neptune

Nov. 14: Moon passes 3.42° N of Uranus

Nov. 17: Full Moon, Leonid meteor shower

Nov. 18: Mercury at greatest elongation 19.5° W, Moon passes 2.66° N of Aldebaran, Mercury enters Libra

Nov. 22: Moon passes 5.10° S of Jupiter, Moon passes 12.00° S of Pollux

Nov. 23: Sun enters Scorpius

Nov. 25: Moon passes 5.59° S of Regulus, Last Quarter Moon, Mars enters Virgo

Nov. 26: Mercury passes 0.33° S of Saturn

Nov. 27: Moon passes 5.69° S of Mars

Nov. 29: Moon passes 0.87° N of Spica, Sun enters Ophiuchus

December

Mercury is low in the SE before sunrise early in the month.
Venus is in the SW after sunset all month.
Mars rises after midnight and is high overhead at sunrise.
Jupiter rises a few hours after sunset and is up the rest of the night.
Saturn is visible in the SE before sunrise all month.
Uranus and **Neptune** are overhead at sunset and in the late evening.

Dec. 1: Moon passes 1.26° S of Saturn, Moon passes 0.43° N of Mercury

Dec. 2: Moon passes 7.37° N of Antares

Dec. 3: New Moon

Dec. 5: Moon passes 1.84° N of Pluto

Dec. 6: Moon passes 7.67° N of Venus, Mercury enters Scorpius

Dec. 8: Moon passes 5.64° N of Neptune

Dec. 9: First Quarter Moon, Mercury enters Ophiuchus

Dec. 11: Mercury passes 4.69° N of Antares, Moon passes 3.33° N of Uranus, Uranus enters Cetus

Dec. 14: Geminid meteor shower

Dec. 16: Moon passes 2.66° N of Aldebaran

Dec. 17: Full Moon

Dec. 18: Sun enters Sagittarius

Dec. 19: Moon passes 4.98° S of Jupiter, Moon passes 11.88° S of Pollux

Dec. 21: Solstice, Mercury enters Sagittarius, Uranus enters Pisces

Dec. 22: Moon passes 5.39° S of Regulus

Dec. 25: Last Quarter Moon

Dec. 26: Moon passes 4.64° S of Mars

Dec. 27: Moon passes 1.05° N of Spica

Dec. 29: Moon passes 0.92° S of Saturn, Mercury in superior conjunction 1.69° S

Dec. 30: Moon passes 7.43° N of Antares

Dec. 31: Mercury passes 4.57° S of Pluto

Meteorites and Meteor Showers

When a chunk of material, ice or rock, plunges into Earth's atmosphere and burns up in a fiery display, the event is a **meteor**. While the chunk of material is still in space, it is a **meteoroid**. If a portion of the material survives passage through the atmosphere and reaches the ground, the remnant on the ground is a **meteorite**.

Meteorites found on Earth are classified into types, depending on their composition: **irons**, those composed chiefly of iron, a small percentage of nickel, and traces of other metals such as cobalt; **stones**, stony meteors consisting of silicates; and **stony irons**, containing varying proportions of both iron and stone.

Serious study of meteorites as non-earth objects began in the 20th century. Scientists use sophisticated chemical analysis, X-rays, and mass spectrography in determining their origin and composition. Although most meteorites are now believed to be fragments of asteroids or comets, geochemical studies have shown that a few Antarctic stones came from the Moon or from Mars, presumably ejected by the explosive impact of asteroids.

The **largest known meteorite**, estimated to weigh about 55 metric tons, is situated at Hoba West near Grootfontein, Namibia. The Manicouagan impact crater in Quebec, Canada, with an estimated diameter of 60 mi, is one of the largest crater structures still visible on the surface of the Earth. Although not visible to the eye, larger impact craters identified include the Vredefort crater in South Africa at 185 mi across and the Sudbury crater in Ontario, Canada,

estimated at 125 mi across. The Bedout impact site off the NW coast of Australia gained attention in 2004 when scientists identified further evidence in support of the idea that it may be linked to the Permian extinction event 250 mil years ago.

Meteor showers vary in strength, but usually the three most visible meteor showers of the year are the **Perseids**, around Aug. 13, the **Orionids**, around Oct. 21, and the **Geminids**, around Dec. 14. These showers feature meteors at the rate of about 60 per hour. Best observing conditions occur with the absence of moonlight, usually when the Moon's phase is between waning crescent Moon and waxing quarter Moon.

For most meteor showers the cometary debris is relatively uniformly scattered along the comet's orbit. However, in the case of the **Leonid** meteor shower, which occurs every year around Nov. 17-18, the cometary debris, from Comet Temple-Tuttle, seems to be bunched up in one stretch. Hence, most years when Earth crosses the orbit of this comet, the meteor shower produced is relatively weak. However, about every 33 years, Earth encounters the bunched-up debris. Sometimes the storm is a disappointment, as it was in 1899 and 1933; at other times it is a roaring success, as in 1833 and 1866. The Leonids stormed again more recently, producing rates of 1,000-3,000 meteors per hour in 2001. Bright Moons can adversely affect viewing of some of the best showers of the year.

Rising and Setting of Planets, 2013

(In Coordinated Universal Time. 0 in the h col. designates 12 AM.)

Venus, 2013

Date		20° N Latitude Rise h m	Set h m	30° N Latitude Rise h m	Set h m	40° N Latitude Rise h m	Set h m	50° N Latitude Rise h m	Set h m	60° N Latitude Rise h m	Set h m
Jan.	1	5 05	16 01	5 25	15 41	5 50	15 16	6 26	14 40	7 28	13 38
	11	5 21	16 15	5 42	15 54	6 08	15 28	6 46	14 50	7 52	13 44
	21	5 35	16 31	5 56	16 10	6 22	15 45	6 58	15 08	8 02	14 04
	31	5 47	16 48	6 06	16 29	6 29	16 05	7 03	15 32	7 59	14 36
Feb.	10	5 55	17 05	6 12	16 49	6 32	16 28	7 00	16 01	7 46	15 15
	20	6 00	17 21	6 13	17 08	6 29	16 53	6 51	16 31	7 26	15 56
Mar.	1	6 03	17 37	6 12	17 27	6 23	17 16	6 39	17 02	7 02	16 38
	12	6 03	17 51	6 08	17 46	6 15	17 40	6 23	17 32	6 35	17 20
	22	6 03	18 04	6 03	18 04	6 04	18 03	6 05	18 02	6 07	18 01
Apr.	1	6 01	18 18	5 58	18 21	5 53	18 26	5 48	18 32	5 38	18 42
	11	6 00	18 32	5 53	18 40	5 43	18 49	5 30	19 03	5 09	19 24
	21	6 01	18 46	5 49	18 58	5 34	19 13	5 14	19 34	4 42	20 07
May	1	6 03	19 01	5 48	19 17	5 28	19 37	5 01	20 05	4 16	20 51
	11	6 09	19 18	5 50	19 37	5 26	20 01	4 52	20 35	3 54	21 34
	21	6 17	19 34	5 56	19 56	5 29	20 23	4 50	21 03	3 39	22 14
	31	6 29	19 50	6 06	20 13	5 37	20 42	4 55	21 25	3 36	22 44
June	10	6 43	20 05	6 20	20 28	5 51	20 57	5 08	21 39	3 49	22 58
	20	6 58	20 16	6 37	20 38	6 09	21 05	5 29	21 45	4 17	22 56
	30	7 14	20 24	6 55	20 44	6 31	21 08	5 56	21 42	4 55	22 41
July	10	7 30	20 29	7 14	20 45	6 53	21 05	6 25	21 33	5 38	22 19
	20	7 44	20 31	7 32	20 43	7 16	20 58	6 55	21 19	6 21	21 52
	30	7 57	20 29	7 49	20 38	7 39	20 48	7 24	21 01	7 02	21 23
Aug.	9	8 09	20 26	8 05	20 30	8 00	20 35	7 53	20 41	7 42	20 51
	19	8 20	20 22	8 20	20 22	8 21	20 21	8 21	20 20	8 22	20 19
	29	8 30	20 18	8 35	20 13	8 41	20 07	8 49	19 59	9 01	19 47
Sept.	8	8 41	20 14	8 50	20 05	9 02	19 53	9 17	19 38	9 40	19 14
	18	8 52	20 11	9 06	19 58	9 22	19 41	9 45	19 18	10 21	18 42
	28	9 04	20 10	9 21	19 52	9 43	19 31	10 13	19 01	11 02	18 11
Oct.	8	9 16	20 11	9 37	19 50	10 03	19 24	10 39	18 47	11 44	17 42
	18	9 27	20 13	9 50	19 50	10 20	19 20	11 03	18 38	12 21	17 19
	28	9 36	20 18	10 01	19 52	10 33	19 21	11 20	18 34	12 50	17 04
Nov.	7	9 42	20 22	10 08	19 56	10 40	19 24	11 28	18 36	13 02	17 02
	17	9 42	20 24	10 07	19 59	10 39	19 27	11 25	18 41	12 54	17 12
	27	9 35	20 21	9 59	19 58	10 28	19 28	11 11	18 46	12 29	17 28
Dec.	7	9 18	20 11	9 40	19 49	10 06	19 23	10 44	18 45	11 51	17 38
	17	8 49	19 48	9 08	19 29	9 31	19 05	10 05	18 32	11 01	17 36
	27	8 03	19 08	8 20	18 51	8 41	18 31	9 10	18 02	9 58	17 14

Mars, 2013

Date		20° N Latitude Rise h m	Set h m	30° N Latitude Rise h m	Set h m	40° N Latitude Rise h m	Set h m	50° N Latitude Rise h m	Set h m	60° N Latitude Rise h m	Set h m
Jan.	1	8 14	19 18	8 32	19 00	8 54	18 37	9 25	18 06	10 17	17 15
	11	8 03	19 14	8 19	18 58	8 39	18 38	9 06	18 11	9 50	17 27
	21	7 51	19 09	8 05	18 56	8 22	18 39	8 44	18 17	9 21	17 41
	31	7 38	19 05	7 50	18 54	8 03	18 40	8 21	18 22	8 50	17 54
Feb.	10	7 25	19 00	7 33	18 51	7 43	18 41	7 57	18 28	8 19	18 06
	20	7 10	18 54	7 16	18 49	7 23	18 42	7 32	18 32	7 47	18 18
Mar.	1	6 55	18 48	6 58	18 45	7 02	18 42	7 07	18 37	7 14	18 30
	12	6 40	18 42	6 40	18 42	6 40	18 42	6 41	18 41	6 41	18 41
	22	6 24	18 35	6 22	18 38	6 19	18 41	6 15	18 45	6 08	18 52
Apr.	1	6 08	18 29	6 03	18 34	5 57	18 40	5 49	18 49	5 35	19 03
	11	5 53	18 22	5 45	18 30	5 36	18 39	5 23	18 52	5 03	19 13
	21	5 37	18 15	5 27	18 25	5 15	18 38	4 58	18 56	4 30	19 23
May	1	5 22	18 09	5 10	18 21	4 55	18 37	4 33	18 58	3 59	19 33
	11	5 08	18 02	4 54	18 17	4 35	18 35	4 10	19 01	3 28	19 43
	21	4 55	17 55	4 38	18 12	4 17	18 33	3 48	19 02	2 59	19 52
	31	4 42	17 48	4 23	18 07	4 00	18 30	3 27	19 03	2 31	20 00
June	10	4 30	17 41	4 10	18 01	3 44	18 26	3 08	19 02	2 05	20 06
	20	4 18	17 33	3 57	17 55	3 30	18 21	2 52	19 00	1 43	20 10
	30	4 07	17 25	3 45	17 47	3 17	18 15	2 37	18 56	1 24	20 09
July	10	3 57	17 16	3 35	17 39	3 06	18 07	2 25	18 49	1 09	20 05
	20	3 47	17 06	3 25	17 29	2 56	17 58	2 15	18 39	0 58	19 55
	30	3 38	16 56	3 15	17 18	2 47	17 46	2 07	18 26	0 52	19 41
Aug.	9	3 28	16 44	3 06	17 05	2 39	17 32	2 00	18 11	0 49	19 22
	19	3 18	16 31	2 57	16 51	2 31	17 17	1 54	17 54	0 49	18 59
	29	3 08	16 16	2 48	16 35	2 24	17 00	1 50	17 34	0 50	18 33
Sept.	8	2 57	16 01	2 39	16 19	2 17	16 41	1 45	17 12	0 52	18 06
	18	2 46	15 44	2 30	16 01	2 09	16 21	1 41	16 49	0 53	17 36
	28	2 34	15 27	2 20	15 41	2 02	15 59	1 36	16 24	0 55	17 05
Oct.	8	2 22	15 08	2 09	15 21	1 53	15 37	1 31	15 58	0 56	16 33
	18	2 09	14 49	1 58	15 00	1 44	15 13	1 26	15 32	0 56	16 01
	28	1 55	14 29	1 46	14 38	1 35	14 49	1 19	15 04	0 55	15 28
Nov.	7	1 41	14 08	1 33	14 15	1 25	14 24	1 12	14 36	0 53	14 55
	17	1 25	13 47	1 20	13 52	1 13	13 58	1 04	14 07	0 50	14 21
	27	1 09	13 24	1 06	13 28	1 01	13 32	0 55	13 38	0 46	13 48
Dec.	7	0 52	13 02	0 51	13 03	0 48	13 06	0 45	13 09	0 40	13 14
	17	0 34	12 38	0 34	12 38	0 34	12 39	0 33	12 39	0 32	12 40
	27	0 15	12 14	0 17	12 12	0 18	12 11	0 20	12 09	0 23	12 06

Jupiter, 2013

Date	20° N Latitude Rise h m	Set h m	30° N Latitude Rise h m	Set h m	40° N Latitude Rise h m	Set h m	50° N Latitude Rise h m	Set h m	60° N Latitude Rise h m	Set h m
Jan. 1	15 04	4 15	14 45	4 34	14 20	4 58	13 46	5 33	12 47	6 32
11	14 21	3 32	14 02	3 51	13 38	4 15	13 04	4 50	12 05	5 49
21	13 40	2 51	13 21	3 10	12 57	3 34	12 23	4 08	11 24	5 07
31	13 00	2 11	12 41	2 30	12 17	2 54	11 43	3 28	10 44	4 27
Feb. 10	12 22	1 32	12 02	1 52	11 38	2 16	11 04	2 50	10 05	3 49
20	11 44	0 55	11 25	1 15	11 01	1 39	10 26	2 13	9 26	3 13
Mar. 1	11 08	0 20	10 49	0 39	10 24	1 04	9 49	1 39	8 49	2 39
12	10 33	23 42	10 13	0 05	9 49	0 30	9 13	1 05	8 12	2 07
22	9 59	23 09	9 39	23 29	9 14	23 54	8 38	0 33	7 35	1 36
Apr. 1	9 26	22 37	9 06	22 57	8 40	23 22	8 04	0 02 / 23 59	7 00	1 06
11	8 54	22 05	8 33	22 26	8 07	22 52	7 31	23 29	6 25	0 37
21	8 22	21 34	8 01	21 55	7 35	22 21	6 58	22 59	5 51	0 08
May 1	7 51	21 04	7 30	21 25	7 04	21 52	6 26	22 30	5 18	23 38
11	7 20	20 34	6 59	20 55	6 32	21 22	5 54	22 01	4 45	23 10
21	6 50	20 05	6 29	20 26	6 02	20 53	5 23	21 32	4 13	22 42
31	6 20	19 35	5 59	19 57	5 32	20 24	4 53	21 03	3 42	22 14
June 10	5 51	19 06	5 29	19 28	5 02	19 55	4 22	20 34	3 11	21 46
20	5 21	18 37	5 00	18 58	4 32	19 26	3 53	20 05	2 41	21 17
30	4 52	18 07	4 30	18 29	4 03	18 57	3 23	19 36	2 11	20 48
July 10	4 22	17 38	4 01	18 00	3 33	18 27	2 54	19 06	1 42	20 18
20	3 53	17 08	3 31	17 30	3 04	17 57	2 24	18 36	1 13	19 48
30	3 23	16 38	3 01	16 59	2 34	17 27	1 55	18 06	0 44	19 17
Aug. 9	2 53	16 07	2 31	16 29	2 04	16 56	1 26	17 35	0 15	18 45
19	2 22	15 36	2 01	15 57	1 34	16 24	0 56	17 03	23 43	18 12
29	1 51	15 05	1 30	15 26	1 04	15 52	0 25	16 30	23 14	17 39
Sept. 8	1 19	14 32	0 59	14 53	0 32	15 19	23 51	15 57	22 44	17 05
18	0 47	13 59	0 26	14 20	0 00 / 23 57	14 46	23 19	15 23	22 13	16 30
28	0 13	13 25	23 50	13 46	23 24	14 11	22 47	14 49	21 41	15 54
Oct. 8	23 35	12 50	23 15	13 10	22 49	13 36	22 12	14 13	21 07	15 18
18	22 59	12 14	22 39	12 34	22 14	13 00	21 37	13 36	20 32	14 41
28	22 22	11 36	22 02	11 57	21 36	12 22	21 00	12 59	19 56	14 03
Nov. 7	21 43	10 58	21 23	11 18	20 58	11 44	20 21	12 20	19 17	13 24
17	21 03	10 18	20 43	10 38	20 17	11 04	19 41	11 40	18 36	12 45
27	20 22	9 37	20 01	9 57	19 36	10 23	18 59	10 59	17 54	12 04
Dec. 7	19 39	8 54	19 18	9 15	18 52	9 41	18 15	10 18	17 09	11 23
17	18 54	8 11	18 34	8 31	18 08	8 57	17 30	9 35	16 23	10 41
27	18 09	7 26	17 49	7 47	17 22	8 14	16 44	8 51	15 37	9 59

Saturn, 2013

Date	20° N Latitude Rise h m	Set h m	30° N Latitude Rise h m	Set h m	40° N Latitude Rise h m	Set h m	50° N Latitude Rise h m	Set h m	60° N Latitude Rise h m	Set h m
Jan. 1	2 04	13 30	2 15	13 20	2 28	13 07	2 45	12 49	3 13	12 22
11	1 28	12 54	1 39	12 43	1 52	12 30	2 10	12 12	2 38	11 44
21	0 51	12 16	1 02	12 05	1 15	11 52	1 33	11 34	2 02	11 05
31	0 13	11 38	0 24	11 27	0 38	11 14	0 56	10 56	1 25	10 27
Feb. 10	23 31	11 00	23 42	10 49	23 56	10 35	0 18	10 17	0 47	9 48
20	22 52	10 21	23 03	10 10	23 16	9 56	23 35	9 38	0 07	9 09
Mar. 1	22 12	9 41	22 23	9 30	22 37	9 17	22 55	8 59	23 23	8 30
12	21 32	9 01	21 42	8 50	21 56	8 37	22 14	8 19	22 42	7 51
22	20 50	8 20	21 01	8 10	21 14	7 57	21 32	7 39	22 00	7 11
Apr. 1	20 09	7 39	20 19	7 29	20 32	7 16	20 49	6 58	21 16	6 31
11	19 26	6 58	19 37	6 47	19 49	6 35	20 06	6 18	20 33	5 51
21	18 44	6 16	18 54	6 06	19 06	5 54	19 23	5 37	19 49	5 11
May 1	18 01	5 34	18 11	5 24	18 23	5 12	18 40	4 56	19 05	4 30
11	17 19	4 52	17 28	4 43	17 40	4 31	17 56	4 15	18 21	3 50
21	16 36	4 11	16 46	4 01	16 57	3 49	17 13	3 34	17 37	3 09
31	15 55	3 29	16 04	3 20	16 15	3 08	16 31	2 53	16 54	2 29
June 10	15 13	2 48	15 22	2 39	15 34	2 28	15 49	2 12	16 12	1 49
20	14 32	2 07	14 41	1 58	14 53	1 47	15 08	1 32	15 31	1 09
30	13 52	1 27	14 01	1 18	14 12	1 07	14 27	0 52	14 51	0 29
July 10	13 13	0 48	13 22	0 39	13 33	0 27	13 48	0 12	14 11	23 45
20	12 34	0 09	12 43	23 55	12 54	23 44	13 09	23 29	13 33	23 05
30	11 56	23 26	12 05	23 17	12 16	23 05	12 32	22 50	12 56	22 26
Aug. 9	11 18	22 48	11 28	22 39	11 39	22 27	11 55	22 11	12 19	21 47
19	10 41	22 11	10 51	22 01	11 03	21 49	11 19	21 33	11 44	21 08
29	10 05	21 34	10 15	21 24	10 27	21 12	10 44	20 55	11 09	20 30
Sept. 8	9 29	20 57	9 40	20 47	9 52	20 34	10 09	20 18	10 35	19 51
18	8 54	20 21	9 05	20 10	9 17	19 58	9 35	19 40	10 02	19 13
28	8 19	19 45	8 30	19 34	8 43	19 21	9 01	19 03	9 29	18 35
Oct. 8	7 45	19 09	7 56	18 58	8 09	18 45	8 28	18 26	8 57	17 57
18	7 10	18 34	7 22	18 22	7 36	18 08	7 55	17 49	8 25	17 19
28	6 36	17 59	6 48	17 47	7 02	17 32	7 22	17 13	7 53	16 42
Nov. 7	6 02	17 23	6 14	17 11	6 29	16 56	6 49	16 36	7 22	16 04
17	5 28	16 48	5 41	16 36	5 56	16 21	6 17	16 00	6 50	15 27
27	4 54	16 13	5 07	16 00	5 22	15 45	5 44	15 23	6 18	14 49
Dec. 7	4 20	15 38	4 33	15 25	4 49	15 09	5 11	14 47	5 45	14 12
17	3 45	15 02	3 58	14 49	4 15	14 33	4 37	14 10	5 13	13 34
27	3 10	14 27	3 24	14 13	3 40	13 56	4 03	13 34	4 40	12 57

Morning and Evening "Stars," 2013

(In Coordinated Universal Time)

	Morning	Evening		Morning	Evening
Jan.	Mercury to Jan. 18 Saturn	Mercury from Jan. 19 Mars Jupiter Uranus Neptune	July	Mercury from July 11 Mars Jupiter Uranus Neptune	Mercury to July 10 Venus Saturn
Feb.	Venus Saturn Neptune from Feb. 21	Mercury Mars Jupiter Uranus Neptune to Feb. 20	Aug.	Mercury to Aug. 24 Mars Jupiter Uranus Neptune to Aug. 27	Mercury from Aug. 25 Venus Saturn Neptune from Aug. 28
Mar.	Mercury from Mar. 5 Venus to Mar. 28 Saturn Uranus from Mar. 30 Neptune	Mercury to Mar. 4 Venus from Mar. 29 Mars Jupiter Uranus to Mar. 29	Sept.	Mars Jupiter Uranus	Mercury Venus Saturn Neptune
Apr.	Mercury Mars from Apr. 18 Saturn Uranus Neptune	Venus Mars to Apr. 17 Jupiter	Oct.	Mars Jupiter Uranus to Sept. 5	Mercury Venus Saturn Uranus from Sept. 6 Neptune
May	Mercury to May 11 Mars Uranus Neptune	Mercury from May 12 Venus Jupiter Saturn	Nov.	Mercury from Nov. 2 Mars Jupiter Saturn from Nov. 6	Mercury to Nov. 1 Venus Saturn to Nov. 5 Uranus Neptune
June	Mars Jupiter from June 20 Uranus Neptune	Mercury Venus Jupiter to June 19 Saturn	Dec.	Mercury to Dec. 29 Mars Jupiter Saturn	Mercury from Dec. 30 Venus Uranus Neptune

Greenwich Sidereal Time for 0h UTC, 2013

UTC = Coordinated Universal Time. Add 12 hours to obtain right ascension of mean sun.

Date	d	h	m	Date	d	h	m	Date	d	h	m	Date	d	h	m
Jan.	1	6	43.2	Apr.	1	12	38.1	July	10	19	12.3	Oct.	8	1	7.2
	11	7	22.7		11	13	17.5		20	19	51.8		18	1	46.6
	21	8	2.1		21	13	56.9		30	20	31.2		28	2	26.0
	31	8	41.5	May	1	14	36.4	Aug.	9	21	10.6	Nov.	7	3	5.4
Feb.	10	9	20.9		11	15	15.8		19	21	50.0		17	3	44.9
	20	10	0.4		21	15	55.2		29	22	29.5		27	4	24.3
Mar.	1	10	39.8		31	16	34.6	Sept.	8	23	8.9	Dec.	7	5	3.7
	12	11	19.2	June	10	17	14.1		18	23	48.3		17	5	43.1
	22	11	58.6		20	17	53.5		28	0	27.7		27	6	22.6
					30	18	32.9								

Largest Telescopes

Astronomers indicate the size of telescopes not by length or magnification but by the diameter of the primary light-gathering component of the system, such as the lens or mirror. This measurement is a direct indication of the telescope's light-gathering power. The bigger the diameter, the fainter the objects that can be detected. The Earth's atmosphere limits the resolution of what can be seen from the ground. That is why the Hubble Space Telescope, which orbits the Earth outside of its atmosphere, can achieve higher resolution with its 2.4-m (7.9-ft) mirror than larger telescopes on Earth.

Refracting (lens) telescopes are currently not made with lens diameters of more than 40 in. Because **reflecting telescopes** can be made less expensively than refracting telescopes, all modern large optical telescopes are made with mirrors. **Radio telescopes** view at wavelengths not visible to optical telescopes or to the human eye. Radio telescopes are larger than optical telescopes because larger diameters are required at longer wavelengths to obtain equivalent resolution. Arrays of telescopes are used to achieve even better resolution through a technique called interferometry. Originally developed for radio telescopes, the technique is now also used with optical and infrared telescopes.

Largest refracting (lens) optical telescope: Yerkes Observatory, 1 m (40 in.), at Williams Bay, WI

Largest reflecting (mirror) optical/infrared telescope: Gran Telescopio Canarias, 10.4 m (34 ft), on La Palma, Canary Islands (segmented mirror)

Largest infrared interferometer: Four 8.2-m (27-ft) telescopes of the Very Large Telescope Interferometer (VLTI) with a 200-m (656-ft) baseline on Cerro Paranal in Chile

Largest fully steerable radio dish: Robert Byrd Green Bank Telescope (GBT), 100 m × 110 m (328 ft × 360 ft), in Green Bank, WV

Largest single radio dish: Arecibo Observatory, 305 m (1,000 ft), in Puerto Rico

Largest radio interferometer: Ten 25-m (82-ft) diameter telescopes of the Very Long Baseline Array (VLBA), dispersed from Hawaii to the Virgin Islands with a resolution equal to a radio dish of 8,600 km (5,000 mi), making it the highest resolution telescope in the solar system

Largest airborne telescope: Stratospheric Observatory for Infrared Astronomy (SOFIA), 2.5-m (8.2-ft) infrared telescope aboard a NASA 747

Constellations

Culturally, constellations are imagined patterns among the stars that, in some cases, have been recognized through millennia. Knowledge of constellations was once necessary in order to function as an astronomer. For today's astronomers, constellations are simply areas of the sky in which objects await observation and interpretation.

Because Western culture has dominated much of modern scientific discourse, equally viable and interesting constellations and celestial traditions of other cultures are not well known outside their regions of origin. Even the patterns with which we are most familiar today have undergone considerable change over the centuries.

Today, **88 constellations** are officially recognized. Although many have ancient origins, some are modern, devised out of unclaimed stars by astronomers a few centuries ago. Unclaimed stars were those too faint or inconveniently placed to be included in the more prominent constellations. Stars in a constellation are not necessarily near each other; they are just located in the same direction on the celestial sphere.

When Western astronomers began to travel to South Africa in the 16th and 17th centuries, they found an unfamiliar sky that showed numerous brilliant stars. Thus, constellations in the Southern Hemisphere are named after technological marvels of the time, as well as some arguably traditional forms, such as Musca, the fly.

Many of the commonly recognized constellations had their origins in ancient Asia Minor. These were adopted by the Greeks and Romans, who translated their names and stories into their own languages, modifying some details in the process. After the declines of those cultures, most such knowledge entered oral tradition or remained hidden in monastic libraries. In the 8th century, Muslims began to spread through the Mediterranean world. Wherever possible, everything was translated into Arabic to be taught in the universities the Muslims established throughout their new-found world.

In the 13th century, Alfonso X of Castile, an avid student of astronomy, had Ptolemy's *Almagest* translated into Latin. It thus became widely available to European scholars. In the process, the constellation names were translated, but the star names were retained in their Arabic forms. Thus the names of many stars—Altair, Alnitak, and Mirfak, among others—have Arabic roots, although linguistic adaptation and the inaccuracies of transliteration have wrought changes.

Until the 1920s, astronomers used curved boundaries for the constellation areas. As these were rather arbitrary, the International Astronomical Union adopted new constellation boundaries that ran due N-S and E-W. These boundaries divide the sky into the 88 constellations, much as the lower 48 states make up the contiguous U.S.

Common names of stars often referred to parts of the traditional figures they represented: Deneb, the tail of the swan, and Betelgeuse, the armpit of the giant. Astronomers may avoid traditional names by labeling stars with Greek letters, generally to denote order of brightness. Thus, the "alpha star" would typically be the brightest star in a constellation. The "of" implies possession, so the genitive (possessive) form of the constellation name is used as in Alpha Orionis, the first star of Orion (Betelgeuse). Astronomers usually use a three-letter abbreviation for the constellation name, as indicated here.

Asterisms are widely recognized patterns of stars. The so-called Big Dipper is a small part of the constellation Ursa Major, the big bear; the Sickle is the traditional head and mane of Leo, the lion; the three stars of the Summer Triangle are each in a different constellation, with Vega in Lyra the lyre, Deneb in Cygnus the swan, and Altair in Aquila the eagle. The northeast star of the Great Square of Pegasus is Alpha Andromedae.

Name	Genitive case	Abbr.	Meaning
Andromeda	Andromedae	And	Chained Maiden
Antlia	Antliae	Ant	Air Pump
Apus	Apodis	Aps	Bird of Paradise
Aquarius	Aquarii	Aqr	Water Bearer
Aquila	Aquilae	Aql	Eagle
Ara	Arae	Ara	Altar
Aries	Arietis	Ari	Ram
Auriga	Aurigae	Aur	Charioteer
Boötes	Boötis	Boo	Herdsmen
Caelum	Caeli	Cae	Chisel
Camelopardalis	Camelopardalis	Cam	Giraffe
Cancer	Cancri	Cnc	Crab
Canes Venatici	Canum Venaticorum	CVn	Hunting Dogs
Canis Major	Canis Majoris	CMa	Greater Dog
Canis Minor	Canis Minoris	CMi	Littler Dog
Capricornus	Capricorni	Cap	Sea-Goat
Carina	Carinae	Car	Keel
Cassiopeia	Cassiopeiae	Cas	Queen
Centaurus	Centauri	Cen	Centaur
Cepheus	Cephei	Cep	King
Cetus	Ceti	Cet	Whale
Chamaeleon	Chamaeleontis	Cha	Chameleon
Circinus	Circini	Cir	Compasses (art)
Columba	Columbae	Col	Dove
Coma Berenices	Comae Berenices	Com	Berenice's Hair
Corona Australis	Coronae Australis	CrA	Southern Crown
Corona Borealis	Coronae Borealis	CrB	Northern Crown
Corvus	Corvi	Crv	Crow
Crater	Crateris	Crt	Cup
Crux	Crucis	Cru	Cross (southern)
Cygnus	Cygni	Cyg	Swan
Delphinus	Delphini	Del	Dolphin
Dorado	Doradus	Dor	Goldfish
Draco	Draconis	Dra	Dragon
Equuleus	Equulei	Equ	Little Horse
Eridanus	Eridani	Eri	River
Fornax	Fornacis	For	Furnace
Gemini	Geminorum	Gem	Twins
Grus	Gruis	Gru	Crane (bird)
Hercules	Herculis	Her	Hercules
Horologium	Horologii	Hor	Clock
Hydra	Hydrae	Hya	Water Snake (female)
Hydrus	Hydri	Hyi	Water Snake (male)
Indus	Indi	Ind	Indian
Lacerta	Lacertae	Lac	Lizard
Leo	Leonis	Leo	Lion
Leo Minor	Leonis Minoris	LMi	Littler Lion
Lepus	Leporis	Lep	Hare
Libra	Librae	Lib	Balance
Lupus	Lupi	Lup	Wolf
Lynx	Lyncis	Lyn	Lynx
Lyra	Lyrae	Lyr	Lyre
Mensa	Mensae	Men	Table Mountain
Microscopium	Microscopii	Mic	Microscope
Monoceros	Monocerotis	Mon	Unicorn
Musca	Muscae	Mus	Fly
Norma	Normae	Nor	Square (rule)
Octans	Octantis	Oct	Octant
Ophiuchus	Ophiuchi	Oph	Serpent Bearer
Orion	Orionis	Ori	Hunter
Pavo	Pavonis	Pav	Peacock
Pegasus	Pegasi	Peg	Flying Horse
Perseus	Persei	Per	Hero
Phoenix	Phoenicis	Phe	Phoenix
Pictor	Pictoris	Pic	Painter
Pisces	Piscium	Psc	Fishes
Piscis Austrinus	Piscis Austrini	PsA	Southern Fish
Puppis	Puppis	Pup	Stern (deck)
Pyxis	Pyxidis	Pyx	Compass (sea)
Reticulum	Reticuli	Ret	Reticle
Sagitta	Sagittae	Sge	Arrow
Sagittarius	Sagittarii	Sgr	Archer
Scorpius	Scorpii	Sco	Scorpion
Sculptor	Sculptoris	Scl	Sculptor
Scutum	Scuti	Sct	Shield
Serpens	Serpentis	Ser	Serpent
Sextans	Sextantis	Sex	Sextant
Taurus	Tauri	Tau	Bull
Telescopium	Telescopii	Tel	Telescope
Triangulum	Trianguli	Tri	Triangle
Triangulum Australe	Trianguli Australis	TrA	Southern Triangle
Tucana	Tucanae	Tuc	Toucan
Ursa Major	Ursae Majoris	UMa	Greater Bear
Ursa Minor	Ursae Minoris	UMi	Littler Bear
Vela	Velorum	Vel	Sail
Virgo	Virginis	Vir	Maiden
Volans	Volantis	Vol	Flying Fish
Vulpecula	Vulpeculae	Vul	Fox

Eclipses, 2013

(In Coordinated Universal Time, or UTC, the standard time of the prime meridian.)

There are five eclipses in 2013: one annular solar eclipse, one hybrid solar eclipse, one partial lunar eclipse, and two penumbral lunar eclipses. The annular solar eclipse will be visible over a narrow path extending from northern Australia across the South Pacific. The hybrid solar eclipse, which starts as an annular eclipse but transitions into a total eclipse, will be visible across a narrow path extending across much of the Atlantic Ocean through equatorial Africa. Although all three lunar eclipses are potentially visible over wide areas of the planet in 2013, none are especially notable; even the partial lunar eclipse will only result in a tiny fraction of the Moon's area being shadowed.

During an annular eclipse of the Sun, the Moon's angular diameter is not large enough to block the entire disk of the Sun, and the Sun appears as a bright ring about the dark disk of the Moon. Penumbral lunar eclipses are unspectacular since the Moon never enters the dark portion of the Earth's shadow. The tables below give the times, in UTC, when the Moon or Sun reaches certain phases of eclipse. In the case of the lunar eclipses, the times are relevant for any observer who can see the Moon. In the case of solar eclipses, the tabulated times refer to when the given event begins or ends from specific points along the eclipse path; as the Moon's shadow sweeps quickly across the Earth, the observed duration of totality depends precisely on the observer's location.

I. Partial Eclipse of the Moon, Apr. 25

This eclipse is potentially visible to observers throughout Africa, Asia, and Europe, but so little of the Moon enters into the Earth's full shadow that the eclipse will barely be noticeable.

Event	Date	h	m
Penumbral eclipse begins	Apr. 25	18	3.7
Partial eclipse begins	25	19	54.1
Greatest eclipse	25	20	8.6
Partial eclipse ends	25	20	21.1
Penumbral eclipse ends	25	22	11.4

II. Annular Eclipse of the Sun, May 10

The eclipse will be visible across a narrow path extending from northern Australia and across the South Pacific, while the partially eclipsed Sun will be visible over much of the Pacific Ocean. The eclipse path crosses the International Date Line; it will be seen in the afternoon of May 10 west of the Date Line and the afternoon of May 9 east of the Date Line.

Event	Date	h	m
Penumbral eclipse begins	May 10	21	25.2
Partial eclipse begins	10	22	30.5
Greatest eclipse	10	0	26.3
Annular eclipse ends	10	2	19.9
Penumbral eclipse ends	10	3	25.3

III. Penumbral Eclipse of the Moon, May 25

During a penumbral lunar eclipse, the Moon dims only slightly, so this eclipse will not be noticeable. In this particular instance, the Moon barely even enters the Earth's penum-bral shadow when visible across a wide area extending from western and southern Africa across North and South America.

Event	Date	h	m
Penumbral eclipse begins	May 25	3	15.3
Greatest eclipse	25	4	11.1
Penumbral eclipse ends	25	4	26.8

IV. Penumbral Eclipse of the Moon, Oct. 18

Although the Moon moves deeper into the Earth's penum-bra during this eclipse, the effect is minor and hardly noticeable. The eclipse occurs when the Moon is visible from Europe, Africa, most of Asia, and the Americas.

Event	Date	h	m
Penumbral eclipse begins	Oct. 18	21	50.6
Greatest eclipse	18	23	51.4
Penumbral eclipse ends	19	1	49.8

V. Hybrid Eclipse of the Sun, Nov. 3

This eclipse begins as an annular eclipse over the western Atlantic Ocean but quickly changes to a total solar eclipse. The path of totality extends across the Atlantic and nearly across Africa near the equator. Partial phases of the eclipse will be visible in Columbia, northern Brazil, and most of Africa.

Event	Date	h	m
Penumbral eclipse begins	Nov. 3	10	4.6
Hybrid eclipse begins	3	11	5.3
Greatest eclipse	3	12	46.5
Hybrid eclipse ends	3	14	27.7
Penumbral eclipse ends	3	15	28.3

Total Solar Eclipses, 2010-20

Total solar eclipses actually take place nearly as often as total lunar eclipses. Total lunar eclipses are visible over at least half of the Earth, while total solar eclipses can be seen only along a very narrow path up to a few hundred miles wide and a few thousand miles long. Observing a total solar eclipse is thus a rarity for most people.

Solar eclipses can be dangerous to observe. This is not because the Sun emits more potent rays, but because the Sun is always dangerous to observe directly, and people are particularly likely to stare at it during a solar eclipse.

Date	Duration[1] m	s	Width (mi)	Path of totality
2010, July 11	5	20	164	Pacific Ocean, southern S America
2012, Nov. 13	4	2	112	N Australia, Pacific Ocean
2013, Nov. 3	1	40	36	Atlantic Ocean, Africa
2015, Mar. 20	2	47	304	N Atlantic Ocean, Arctic Ocean
2016, Mar. 9	4	10	96	Indonesia, Pacific Ocean
2017, Aug. 21	2	40	71	Pacific Ocean, U.S., Atlantic Ocean
2019, July 2	4	33	125	S Pacific Ocean, S America
2020, Dec. 14	2	10	56	S Pacific Ocean, S America, S Atlantic Ocean

(1) Length of time at optimal viewing area.

Total Solar Eclipses in the U.S. in the 21st Century

During the 21st century there will be 8 total solar eclipses visible somewhere in the continental U.S. The first comes after a long gap. The last total solar eclipse was on Feb. 26, 1979, in the northwestern U.S.

Date	Path of totality	Date	Path of totality
Aug. 21, 2017	Oregon to South Carolina	Mar. 30, 2052	Florida to Georgia
Apr. 8, 2024	Mexico to Texas and N through Maine	May 11, 2078	Louisiana to North Carolina
Aug. 23, 2044	Montana to North Dakota	May 1, 2079	New Jersey to the lower edge of New England
Aug. 12, 2045	N California to Florida	Sept. 14, 2099	North Dakota to Virginia

Beginnings of the Universe

One of the dominating astronomical discoveries of the 20th century was that the galaxies of the universe all seem to be moving away from Earth. Doppler redshifts were observed for the spiral nebulae around 1920 even though they were not yet known to be galaxies. By the early 1930s, Edwin Hubble and M. L. Humason had established that the more distant a galaxy, the faster it was receding. It turned out that they are moving away not just from the Earth but from one another—that is, the **universe is expanding**. Scientists conclude that the universe must once, very long ago, have been extremely compact and dense, until an explosion or a similar event caused the matter to spread out. The explosion that gave birth to the universe is called the **Big Bang**.

On the subatomic level, according to this theory, there were vast changes of energy and matter and the way physical laws operated during the first few minutes. After those early minutes the percentages of the basic matter of the universe—hydrogen, helium, and lithium—were set. Everything was so compact and so hot that radiation dominated the early universe and there were no stable, un-ionized atoms. At first, the universe was opaque, in the sense that any energy emitted was quickly absorbed and then re-emitted by free electrons. As the universe expanded, density and temperature continued to drop. A few hundred thousand years after the Big Bang, the temperature dropped far enough that electrons and nuclei could combine to form stable atoms as the universe became transparent. Once that occurred, the radiation that had been trapped was free to escape.

In the 1940s, George Gamov and others predicted that astronomers should be able to see remnants of this escaped radiation. They were starting to search for this background radiation when physicists Arno Penzias and Robert Wilson, using a radio telescope, inadvertently beat them to the punch (the two were later awarded a Nobel Prize).

In 2003, NASA's Wilkinson Microwave Anisotropy Probe made measurements of the temperature of this **cosmic** microwave background radiation to within millionths of a degree. From these measurements, scientists were able to deduce that our universe is 13.7 bil years old and that first-generation stars began to form a mere 200 mil years after the Big Bang.

A related mystery is evidence suggesting hidden matter and hidden energy that cannot be directly observed. This **dark matter** may be composed of gas, large numbers of cool, small objects, or even subatomic particles. The presence of dark matter is indicated by the rotation curves of galaxies and the dynamics of clusters of galaxies. Evidence for **dark energy** is derived from studies of distant Type Ia supernovae in far galaxies indicating that the expansion of the universe is accelerating rather than slowing. The visible matter we see seems to constitute only about 4% of the total mass of the universe while the rest of the mass of the universe is in the form of dark matter (23%) and dark energy (73%). Dark energy is a mysterious force that seems to work on the very fabric of the universe, spreading it apart.

Galaxies

The 20th century might be called the century of the galaxy. By the start of the century, more than 10,000 **nebulae**—cloud-like luminous objects in the sky—had been discovered. Some were correctly identified as star clusters and others as clouds of gas and dust. Those nebulae which were spiral or elliptical in shape were found in regions of the sky far from the glowing band that is our own Milky Way galaxy. Immanuel Kant had written in 1775 that some of these fuzzy objects might be **"island universes"** apart from our own. But the idea remained speculative until 1923-24, when Edwin Hubble discovered the existence of variable stars in some of these nebulae. This provided conclusive evidence that these systems were outside our own island universe, the Milky Way galaxy.

Galaxies range in size from small dwarf elliptical ones, with perhaps 1 mil stars, to spiral galaxies containing 300 bil stars, to giant elliptical galaxies that may be home to more than 10 tril stars. The diameters of galaxies range from 3,000 light-years in dwarf elliptical galaxies to over 500,000 light-years in giant elliptical galaxies. It is estimated that the Milky Way galaxy is about 100,000 light-years in diameter with about 400 bil stars.

Galaxies also congregate into **clusters**. The smallest are poor clusters of only a few dozen galaxies, while the largest rich clusters may contain thousands of galaxies. The Milky Way is part of a poor cluster of about three dozen galaxies called the **Local Group**. The largest member of the Local Group is the Andromeda Galaxy, a spiral galaxy visible to the unaided eye in the constellation of Andromeda on a very dark night away from lights. The Milky Way is the second largest galaxy in this group; most other galaxies in our Local Group are small.

The Solar System

The major planets of the solar system, in order of mean distance from the Sun, are **Mercury**, **Venus**, **Earth**, **Mars**, **Jupiter**, **Saturn**, **Uranus**, and **Neptune**. The dwarf planets in order of average distance from the Sun are **Ceres** (located between Mars and Jupiter), **Pluto**, **Haumea**, **Makemake**, and **Eris**. All planets orbit counterclockwise around the Sun as viewed from above the Earth's North Pole.

Because **Mercury** and **Venus** are nearer to the Sun than is Earth, their motions about the Sun appear from Earth as wide swings first to one side of the Sun then to the other, though both planets move around the Sun in almost circular orbits. When their passage takes them between Earth and the Sun or beyond the Sun as seen from Earth, they cannot be seen. The planets that lie farther from the Sun than does Earth may be seen for longer periods and are invisible only when so located in the sky that they rise and set at about the same time as the Sun—and thus are overwhelmed by the Sun's light.

The giant planets emit their own energy. On occasion, radio emissions from Jupiter exceed even those emitted by the Sun in intensity.

Mercury and Venus, because they are between Earth and the Sun, show phases much as the Moon does. The planets farther from the Sun are always seen as full, although Mars does occasionally present a slightly gibbous phase, like the Moon when it is not quite full.

The planets appear to move rapidly among the stars because they are relatively closer to Earth. The stars are also in motion, some at tremendous speeds, but they are so far away that their motion does not change their apparent positions in the heavens enough to be perceived. The nearest star is about 9,000 times farther away than Neptune. The count for identified **moons** in the solar system orbiting planets and dwarf planets stood at 179 as of Aug. 2012. Several dwarf planet candidates are also known to have moons.

Planet Superlatives			
Largest, most massive planet	Jupiter	Smallest, least massive planet	Mercury
Fastest orbiting planet	Mercury	Slowest orbiting planet	Neptune
Fastest sidereal rotation	Jupiter	Slowest sidereal rotation	Venus
Longest (synodic) day	Mercury	Shortest (synodic) day	Jupiter
Rotational pole closest to ecliptic	Uranus	Hottest planet	Venus
Most moons	Jupiter	No moons	Mercury, Venus
Planet with largest moon	Jupiter	Planet with moon with most eccentric orbit	Neptune
Greatest average density	Earth	Lowest average density	Saturn
Tallest mountain	Mars	Deepest oceans	Jupiter
Strongest magnetic fields	Jupiter	Greatest amount of liquid, surface water	Earth
Most circular orbit	Venus		

Planets and the Sun, by Selected Characteristics

Sun and planets	at unit distance[1] "	Radius— at mean least distance[2] "	in mi mean radius	Volume[3]	Mass[3]	Density[3]	Sidereal period d	h	m	s	Gravity at surface[3]	Reflect-ing power (pct.)	Daytime surface temp. (°F)
Sun	959.50	976.0	432,500	1,304,000	333,000	0.26	25	9	7		28.00		+9,941
Mercury	3.36	6.5	1,516	0.0562	0.0553	0.98	58	15	36		0.38	0.11	845
Venus	8.34	33.0	3,760	0.857	0.815	0.95	243		30[R]		0.91	0.65	867
Earth	8.78	—	3,959	1.000	1.000	1.00		23	56	4.2	1.00	0.37	59
Moon	2.40	986.2	1,079	0.0203	0.0123	0.61	27	7	43	40	0.16	0.12	260
Mars	4.67	12.8	2,106	0.151	0.107	0.71		24	37	22	0.38	0.15	−24
Jupiter	96.40	24.5	43,441	1,321	317.8	0.24		9	55	30	2.53	0.52	−162
Saturn	80.29	10.05	36,184	764	95.16	0.12		10	39	20	1.06	0.47	−218
Uranus	34.97	2.05	15,759	63.1	14.54	0.23		17	14	20[R]	0.90	0.51	−323
Neptune	33.95	1.2	15,301	57.7	17.15	0.30		16	6	40	1.14	0.41	−330

R = Retrograde rotation. (1) Angular radius, in seconds of arc, if object were seen at a distance of 1 astronomical unit. (2) Angular radius, in seconds of arc, when object is closest to Earth. (3) Earth = 1.

Planets: Motion, Distance, and Brightness

Planet	Mean daily motion[1]	Orbital velocity mi per sec.[2]	Sidereal revolution days[3]	Synodic revolution days[4]	Distance from Sun in mil of mi Max.	Min.	Distance from Earth in mil of mi Max.	Min.	Light at[5]— perihelion	aphelion
Mercury	14,732	29.75	87.97	115.9	43.4	28.6	137.9	48	10.56	4.59
Venus	5,768	21.76	224.7	583.9	67.7	66.8	162.2	23.7	1.94	1.89
Earth	3,548	18.50	365.256	—	94.5	91.4	—	—	1.03	0.97
Mars	1,887	15.00	686.98	779.9	154.9	128.4	249.4	33.9	0.52	0.36
Jupiter	299	8.12	4,332.6	398.9	507.4	460.1	602	366	0.041	0.034
Saturn	120	6.02	10,759.2	378.1	941.1	840.4	1,031	743	0.012	0.0098
Uranus	42	4.23	30,685.4	369.7	1,866.4	1,703.4	1,962	1,605	0.0030	0.0025
Neptune	22	3.37	60,189.0	367.5	2,824.5	2,761.7	2,913	2,676	0.0011	0.0011

(1) Average angular motion measured in seconds of arc per day. (2) Speed of revolution around Sun. (3) Number of Earth days to orbit Sun with respect to background stars. (4) Number of Earth days to get back to the same position in its orbit around Sun, relative to Earth. (5) Light at perihelion and aphelion is solar illumination measured in units of mean illumination at Earth.

Planets of the Solar System

Note: AU = astronomical unit (92.96 mil mi, mean distance of Earth from the Sun); **d** = 1 Earth synodic (solar) day (24 hours); **synodic day** = rotation period of a planet measured with respect to the Sun (the "true" day, i.e., the time from midday to midday, or from sunrise to sunrise); **sidereal day** = rotation period of a planet with respect to the stars.

The International Astronomical Union (IAU) on Aug. 24, 2006, at their General Assembly in Prague, Czech Republic, agreed on a new definition for planet, and in the process effectively removed Pluto's planet status. The ruling came after years of debate as to whether Pluto, discovered in 1930, should still be considered the ninth planet in our solar system because of its size, orbit, and other characteristics. New discoveries of other Pluto-like objects in the solar system, such as the 2003 discovery of Eris, a **Kuiper Belt object** (KBO) bigger than Pluto, also contributed to the debate.

Under the IAU's new definition, Mercury, Venus, Earth, Mars, Jupiter, Saturn, Uranus, and Neptune are regarded as "classical" planets. A **planet** is now defined as a celestial body that (a) is in orbit around the Sun, (b) has sufficient mass for its self-gravity to overcome rigid body forces so that it assumes a hydrostatic equilibrium (nearly round) shape, and (c) has cleared the neighborhood around its orbit.

Pluto, Eris, Ceres, Makemake, and Haumea are regarded as dwarf planets, with the status of Pluto's largest moon, Charon, still to be determined. A **dwarf planet** is a celestial body that (a) is in orbit around the Sun, (b) has sufficient mass for its self-gravity to overcome rigid body forces so that it assumes a hydrostatic equilibrium (nearly round) shape, (c) has not cleared the neighborhood around its orbit, and (d) is not a satellite.

The IAU also created a new category, **small solar system bodies**, for all other objects orbiting the Sun, including comets, asteroids, KBOs, and other small objects. It has not yet established a process by which other solar system objects will be classified.

Mercury

Distance from the Sun	
Perihelion	28.6 mil mi
Semi-major axis (mean distance)	36 mil mi (0.387 AU)
Aphelion	43.4 mil mi
Period of revolution around Sun	87.97 d
Orbital eccentricity	0.2056
Orbital inclination	7.00°
Synodic day (midday to midday)	175.94 d
Sidereal day	58.65 d
Rotational inclination	0.01°
Mass (Earth = 1)	0.0553
Mean radius	1,516 mi
Mean density (Earth = 1)	0.984
Natural satellites	0
Average surface temperature	333°F

Mercury, named for the Roman gods' messenger, is the closest planet to the Sun and the smallest in the solar system. Mercury is too much in line with the Sun to be observed against a dark sky; therefore it is always seen during morning or evening twilight. In 2008, the MESSENGER spacecraft made the first flybys of Mercury since the 1970s. Messenger went into orbit about Mercury in Mar. 2011, for a reconnaissance mission; the original one-year science program was extended in 2012. The goals of the mission include mapping, imaging, and measuring the surface composition of Mercury, as well as probing the planet's interior structure and interactions with the Sun.

Among the early discoveries are that at least part of Mercury's metallic core is liquid, that there may be water ice in shadowed craters near the poles, and that the planet's magnetic field is offset from the planet's center.

Orbit and rotation. Mercury moves with great speed around the Sun, averaging about 30 mi per second to complete its orbit, which takes about 88 Earth days. Mercury takes nearly 59 days to rotate on its axis. Because its orbital period is only about 50% longer than its sidereal rotation, the time from one sunrise to the next on Mercury is about 176 days—twice as long as a Mercurial year. Oddly, Mercury has a magnetic field, albeit a very weak one. It has been held that both a fluid core and rapid rotation—neither of which Mercury was believed to have—are necessary for the generation of a planetary magnetic field. Mercury may demonstrate the contrary.

Atmosphere. Mercury's atmosphere is almost nonexistent. What very little it has is composed of 42% oxygen, 29% sodium, 22% hydrogen, 6% helium, 0.5% potassium, and 0.5% other particles. Because of Mercury's lack of atmosphere, the surface during the day may reach a temperature of about 845°F, while the temperature at night may fall as low as −300°F. Earth-based observation has provided evidence of water ice near the poles.

Surface and composition. Mercury's surface is rocky and cratered similar to that of the Earth's moon. The most imposing feature on Mercury, the Caloris Basin, is a huge impact crater more than 800 mi in diameter. Mercury has a huge iron core that takes up about 75% of the planet's radius; it has a higher percentage of iron than any other planet in the solar system.

Venus

Distance from the Sun	
Perihelion	66.8 mil mi
Semi-major axis (mean distance)	67.2 mil mi (0.723 AU)
Aphelion	67.7 mil mi
Period of revolution around Sun	224.7 d
Orbital eccentricity	0.0067
Orbital inclination	3.39°
Synodic day (midday to midday)	116.75 d (retrograde)
Sidereal day	243.02 d (retrograde)
Rotational inclination	177.4°
Mass (Earth = 1)	0.815
Mean radius	3,760 mi
Mean density (Earth = 1)	0.951
Natural satellites	0
Average surface temperature	867°F

Venus, named for the Roman goddess of love, is the second planet out from the Sun. Because Venus is almost the same size as Earth, it is believed that the two planets were formed at the same time by the same general process and from the same mixture of chemical elements. Venus can easily be seen from Earth with the naked eye; it is the third-brightest object in the sky, exceeded only by the Sun and the Moon.

Orbit and rotation. It takes Venus 225 Earth days to complete its orbit around the Sun. Its synodic revolution—the amount of time it takes for Venus to return to the same position relative to Earth and the Sun, which is a result of the combination of its own motion with that of Earth—is 584 days. Because of this, every 19 months Venus is closer to Earth than any other planet. The rotation period of Venus appears to be 243 days clockwise. In other words, its rotation is contrary to the rotation of the other planets and contrary to its own motion around the Sun. This rate and sense of rotation makes for a solar day (sunrise to sunrise) on Venus of 116.8 Earth days. Night lasts 58 days, and day lasts 58 days. Venus has no detectible magnetic field.

Atmosphere. The Venusian atmosphere is very thick and toxic. It is composed primarily of 96.5% carbon dioxide, 3.5% nitrogen, and trace concentrations of sulfur dioxide, argon, water, carbon monoxide, helium, and neon. In addition, it exerts an atmospheric pressure at the surface more than 90 times Earth's normal sea-level pressure. The planet is covered with a dense, white, cloudy atmosphere that conceals whatever is below it. These clouds are believed to contain sulfuric acid, meaning that it rains sulfuric acid on Venus. Due to the thickness of the atmosphere and resulting extreme greenhouse effect, the temperature is essentially the same day and night; the planet has an average surface temperature of about 867°F, making it the hottest planet in the solar system. Winds of about 200 mph in the clouds may account for the transfer of heat into the night side despite the low rotation speed of the planet. However, at the surface, the winds are very slow.

Surface and composition. Radar-produced maps of the planet show large craters, continent-sized highlands, and extensive dry lowlands. No tectonic activity has been found similar to Earth's moving tectonic plates, but a system of global rift zones and numerous broad, low, dome-like structures, called coronae, may have been produced by the upwelling and subsidence of magma from the mantle. Volcanic surface features, such as vast lava plains, fields of small lava domes, and large shield volcanoes, are common. About 1,600 volcanoes and volcanic features appear on the Venusian surface; more than 85% of the surface is covered by volcanic flows. Theia Mons, a huge shield volcano, has a diameter of over 600 mi and a height of over 3.5 mi. (The largest Hawaiian volcano is only about 125 mi in diameter, but rises nearly 5.5 mi from the ocean floor.) Aside from volcanoes, there are highly deformed mountain belts across Venus along with a few meteor-impact craters more than 20 mi wide. Erosion is a very slow process on Venus due to the lack of water. There are indications of some wind movement of dust and sand. The few impact craters on Venus suggest that the surface is generally geologically young—less than 800 mil years old. Despite the fact that probes have landed on Venus, there are very few pictures because the probes couldn't survive the high temperature and atmospheric pressure.

Mars

Distance from the Sun	
Perihelion	128.4 mil mi
Semi-major axis (mean distance)	141.6 mil mi (1.524 AU)
Aphelion	154.9 mil mi
Period of revolution around Sun	686.98 d (1.88 y)
Orbital eccentricity	0.0935
Orbital inclination	1.85°
Synodic day (midday to midday)	24h 39m 35s
Sidereal day	24h 37m 22s
Rotational inclination	25.19°
Mass (Earth = 1)	0.107
Mean radius	2,106 mi
Mean density (Earth = 1)	0.713
Natural satellites	2
Average surface temperature	−81°F

Named for the Roman god of war, the Red Planet has some features much like Earth. Mars has climate, seasons, volcanoes, and possibly once had liquid water flowing across its surface. Mars can easily be seen with the naked eye on most clear nights, which is why it was one of the first planets to be studied by ancient astronomers. Later, when telescopes came into use, many observers claimed that canals made by Martians existed on the planet's surface, which led to speculation as to whether there was intelligent life there. Unmanned probes have since put all those theories to rest; the canals turned out to be topographic patterns and dust storms.

Mars is currently being explored by a number of robotic craft, both on the surface and in orbit. The *Curiosity*/Mars Science Laboratory, an SUV-sized robot, landed on the surface in Aug. 2012. Its mission was to search for evidence of microbial life on the planet.

Orbit and rotation. Although Mars's orbital path is nearly circular, it is somewhat more eccentric than that of most other planets. Mars is more than 26 mil mi farther from the Sun at its most distant point compared to its closest approach. Its orbit and speed in relation to Earth's bring it fairly close to Earth about every two years. Every 15-17 years the close approaches are especially favorable for observation.

Mars rotates in 24 hours and 37 minutes, almost the same period of time as Earth. Mars's mean distance from the Sun is 142 mil mi. Because Mars's axis of rotation is inclined by about 25° from the vertical to the plane of its solar orbit about the Sun, the planet has seasons.

Unlike Earth's global magnetic field, the Martian magnetic field is small, weak, and localized and may be the remnant of a stronger field from the planet's past.

Atmosphere. The Martian atmosphere is composed primarily of 95.32% carbon dioxide, 2.7% nitrogen, 1.6% argon, 0.13% oxygen, 0.08% carbon monoxide, and in very minor quantities, water, hydrogen oxide, and neon. The atmosphere on Mars is very thin. It has an atmospheric pressure between 1% and 2% of Earth's (if Earth's atmosphere were that thin, we would not have enough oxygen to breathe). Because the Martian atmosphere is so thin and because of the planet's weak magnetic field, its surface is bombarded by cosmic radiation about 100 times as intense as on Earth.

Martian weather systems consist mainly of huge dust storms. On the poles, white caps (believed to be both water ice and carbon dioxide ice) grow in winter and shrink in summer. It is mainly the carbon dioxide that comes and goes with the seasons. The water ice is apparently in many layers with dust between them, indicating climatic cycles.

Surface and composition. Mars is an alien world with rust-red sand and pink skies. In the planet's beginning stages when it was much hotter, Mars's surface melted to a sufficient extent to separate into dense and lighter layers. Mars later cooled enough to allow liquid water to possibly flow across its surface. Today, Mars is very dry.

Natural satellites. Mars has two satellites called Phobos and Deimos, each discovered in 1877 by Asaph Hall. (Phobos measures about 11 by 17 mi, and Deimos about 7 by 9 mi.) Deimos, the outer satellite, revolves around the planet in about 31 hours. Phobos, the inner satellite, whips around Mars in a little more than 7 hours, making three trips each Martian day. Since it orbits Mars faster than the planet rotates, Phobos rises in the west and sets in the east, opposite to what other bodies appear to do in the Martian sky. Both moons are irregularly shaped and pitted with numerous craters. Their origins are not known; however, some astronomers consider them to be asteroid-like objects that were captured by Mars very early in its history.

Jupiter

Distance from the Sun	
Perihelion	460.1 mil mi
Semi-major axis (mean distance) 483.8 mil mi (5.204 AU)	
Aphelion	507.4 mil mi
Period of revolution around Sun	11.862 y
Orbital eccentricity	0.0489
Orbital inclination	1.304°
Synodic day (midday to midday)	9h 55m 33s
Sidereal day	9h 55m 30s
Rotational inclination	3.13°
Mass (Earth = 1)	317.8
Mean radius	43,441 mi
Mean density (Earth = 1)	0.24
Natural satellites	66
Average temperature*	−162°F
*i.e., temperature where atmosphere pressure equals 1 Earth atmosphere.	

Jupiter, named for the Roman ruler of the gods, is the largest planet in the solar system (11 times the diameter of Earth). Its mass is more than twice the mass of all the other planets, moons, and asteroids put together. Visible to the naked eye and known to the ancients, it was a focus of the Italian scientist Galileo Galilei, who viewed the planet and its four largest moons through a homemade telescope.

Orbit and rotation. Jupiter is at an average distance of 484 mil mi from the Sun and takes almost 12 Earth years to make a complete revolution. The largest of the planets, Jupiter has an equatorial diameter of 88,846 mi; its polar diameter is more than 5,700 mi shorter. This noticeable oblateness is a result of the liquidity of the planet and its extremely rapid rotation rate—a Jupiter day is less than 10 Earth hours long. For a planet this size, this rotational speed is amazing. A point on Jupiter's equator moves at a speed of 22,000 mph, as compared with 1,000 mph for a point on Earth's equator. Jupiter's magnetic field is by far the strongest of any planet. Electrical activity caused by this field is so strong that it discharges billions of watts into Earth's magnetic field daily.

Atmosphere. Jupiter's atmosphere is primarily composed of 90% molecular hydrogen and 10% helium. Minor constituents include methane, ammonia, hydrogen deuteride, ethane, and water. Jupiter has a turbulent atmosphere characterized by thick clouds, high winds, and huge lightning storms many times larger than those on Earth. The atmospheric temperature varies, but the temperature at the tops of clouds may be about –280°F. The Great Red Spot seen prominently on Jupiter is a huge hurricane-like storm that is three times the diameter of Earth. In 2006, the Hubble Space Telescope detected the appearance of a second, smaller red spot.

Surface and composition. Gas giant planets like Jupiter, Saturn, and Neptune do not have a surface like Earth or any of the other rocky planets. The gases become denser with depth, until they may turn into a slush or slurry. Jupiter has a liquid hydrogen ocean more than 35,000 mi deep. It likely has a rocky core about the size of Earth, but 13 times more massive. There is no sharp interface between the gaseous atmosphere and the hydrogen ocean that accounts for most of Jupiter's volume. At lower depths, under enormous pressure, the liquid hydrogen takes on the properties of a metal. It is likely that this liquid metallic hydrogen is the source for both Jupiter's persistent radio noise and for its improbably strong magnetic field.

Natural satellites. Jupiter has 66 known satellites. Four of the moons (in order of distance from Jupiter), Io, Europa, Ganymede, and Callisto—all discovered by Galileo in 1610—are large and bright and are close in diameter to Earth's moon and Mercury. Because they move so rapidly around Jupiter, their change in position from night to night can be seen from Earth using binoculars.

Io is one of the most intriguing moons because it is the most volcanically active body in the solar system. A gaseous, doughnut-shaped ring, or torus, enveloping Io's orbit around Jupiter may have been formed by material ejected from Io's active volcanoes. (This is not to be confused with Jupiter's rings.) These volcanoes, hotter than Earth's volcanoes, erupt mainly molten sulfur.

Europa may have a 30-mi-deep salty, liquid ocean beneath its icy crust, perhaps a small metallic core, and a very tenuous atmosphere. Ganymede is the biggest moon in the solar system. With a diameter of 3,120 mi, it is bigger than both Mercury and Pluto. Ganymede also has it own magnetic field produced by a molten core perhaps of iron sulfide. Callisto has the oldest, most heavily cratered surface in the solar system, a very thin atmosphere of carbon dioxide, and possibly a subsurface liquid ocean.

The other satellites are much smaller, with four closer to Jupiter than Io, five between Ganymede and Callisto, and the rest farther out. Most of Jupiter's moons revolve around Jupiter clockwise as seen from the north, contrary to the motions of most satellites in the solar system and to the direction of revolution of planets around the Sun. These moons may be captured asteroids.

Rings. Jupiter has a set of rings that cannot be seen from Earth without powerful telescopes. They are composed of small dust grains possibly blasted off the 4 innermost moons by meteoroid impacts.

Saturn

Distance from the Sun	
Perihelion	840.44 mil mi
Semi-major axis (mean distance) 890.8 mil mi (9.582 AU)	
Aphelion	941.07 mil mi
Period of revolution around Sun	29.458 y
Orbital eccentricity	0.0565
Orbital inclination	2.485°
Synodic day (midday to midday)	10h 39m 23s
Sidereal day	10h 39m 22s
Rotational inclination	26.73°
Mass (Earth = 1)	95.159
Mean radius	36,184 mi
Mean density (Earth = 1)	0.125
Natural satellites	62
Average temperature*	−218°F
*i.e., temperature where atmosphere pressure equals 1 Earth atmosphere.	

Saturn, named for the Roman ruler of the Titans, is the sixth planet from the Sun and most distant of the planets visible to the unaided eye. Saturn is second in size to Jupiter, but its mass is much smaller. Saturn is the only planet less dense than water, meaning that Saturn would float if there were a pool of water gigantic enough to hold it.

Orbit and rotation. Saturn's diameter is almost 74,900 mi at the equator, while its polar diameter is more than 7,300 mi shorter. Like Jupiter, its noticeable oblateness is a result of the liquidity of the planet and its extremely rapid rate of rotation; a day is little more than 10 Earth hours long.

Atmosphere. Saturn's atmosphere is composed primarily of 96.3% hydrogen, 3.3% helium, and traces of methane, ammonia, hydrogen deuteride, ethane, and water. Saturn's atmosphere is much like that of Jupiter, except that the temperature at the top of its cloud layer is at least 50°F colder.

Surface and composition. Saturn's atmosphere resembles Jupiter's; it likely has a small dense center surrounded by a deep ocean of hydrogen.

Natural satellites. Saturn has 62 known natural satellites, most of which were not discovered until space probes reached the planet. Saturn's moon Mimas has an impact crater 81 mi across (the moon itself is only 249 mi across). Enceladus has an atmosphere and shows evidence of geysers that spit water ice and vapor. Two tiny moons orbit within the rings, plowing through and making gaps in the rings along their orbits. Pan, the innermost satellite, creates the Encke Gap of Saturn's A-ring. 2005 S1 creates the Keeler Gap. The most intriguing Saturnian moon is Titan. The second-biggest moon in the solar system, Titan is bigger than Mercury. Its atmosphere is similar to Earth's atmosphere of long ago; it is made up of approximately 95% nitrogen with traces of methane. Titan's atmosphere extends about 360 mi into space whereas Earth's atmosphere extends about 37 mi. Photographs from its surface show a muddy terrain, with possible deposits of water ice, channels carved by liquid methane springs, and an interesting boundary between light and dark material on the surface. In 2006, scientists found sand dunes on Titan's surface. The "sand" is believed to be tiny water ice crystals or organic compounds. Surface phenomena such as sand dunes are signs of erosion and wind. Unlike winds on Earth or Mars, Titan's winds are not the result of uneven solar heating on the moon's surface but rather Saturn's gravitational pull (similar to how the Moon acts on the Earth's oceans).

Rings. Saturn's ring system is the planet's most recognizable feature. It begins about 4,000 mi above the visible disk of Saturn lying above its equator and extends about 260,000 mi into space. The diameter of the ring system visible from Earth is about 170,000 mi; the rings are estimated to be about 700 ft thick. The rings are composed of rock and ice and range in size from tiny particles to large chunks of material the size of a bus. There are several divisions in the rings. The 2,920-mi Cassini division, the gap between the A and B rings, is the largest division.

Uranus

Distance from the Sun	
Perihelion	1,703.4 mil mi
Semi-major axis (mean distance) 1,784.8 mil mi (19.201 AU)	
Aphelion	1,866.4 mil mi
Period of revolution around Sun	84.01 y
Orbital eccentricity	0.0457
Orbital inclination	0.772°
Synodic day (midday to midday)	17h 14m 23s (retrograde)
Sidereal day	17h 14m 24s (retrograde)
Rotational inclination	97.77°
Mass (Earth = 1)	14.536
Mean radius	15,759 mi
Mean density (Earth = 1)	0.23
Natural satellites	27
Average temperature*	−323°F
*i.e., temperature where atmosphere pressure equals 1 Earth atmosphere.	

Uranus, discovered by Sir William Herschel in 1781, was the first planet discovered using a telescope. It was named for the father of the Titans in Roman mythology.

Orbit and rotation. Uranus has a diameter of over 31,000 mi and spins once in approximately 17.23 hours, according to flyby magnetic data. One of the most fascinating features of Uranus is how far over it is tipped. Its north pole lies 98° from its orbital plane. Thus, its seasons are extreme. Over its 84-year orbit, when the Sun rises at the north pole, it shines there for about 42 Earth years; then it sets, and the north pole is in darkness for 42 Earth years. In addition to its rotational tilt, Uranus's magnetic field axis is tipped 58.6° from its rotational axis and is displaced about 30% of its radius away from the planet's center.

Atmosphere. The atmosphere is composed primarily of 82.5% hydrogen, 15.2% helium, and 2.3% methane, with small amounts of hydrogen deuteride, ammonia ice, water ice, ammonia hydrosulfide, and methane ice.

Surface and composition. Uranus has no solid surface, and likely no rocky core but rather a mixture of rocks and assorted ices with about 15% hydrogen and some helium.

Natural satellites. Uranus has 27 known moons, which have orbits lying in the plane of the planet's equator. Five moons are relatively large, while 22 are very small and were only discovered with the *Voyager 2* mission or in later observations. Miranda has grooved markings, reminiscent of Jupiter's Ganymede, but often arranged in a chevron pattern. Rifts and channels on Ariel provide evidence of liquid flowing over its surface in the past. Umbriel is extremely dark, prompting some observers to regard its surface as among the oldest in the system. Titania has rifts and fractures, but not the evidence of flow found on Ariel. Oberon's main feature is its surface saturated with craters, unrelieved by other formations.

Rings. In the equatorial plane there is also a complex of 11 rings, 9 of which were discovered in 1978 by observers watching Uranus pass before a star.

Neptune

Distance from the Sun	
Perihelion	2,761.7 mil mi
Semi-major axis (mean distance) 2,793.1 mil mi (30.047 AU)	
Aphelion	2,824.5 mil mi
Period of revolution around Sun	164.79 y
Orbital eccentricity	0.0113
Orbital inclination	1.769°
Synodic day (midday to midday)	16h 6m 37s
Sidereal day	16h 6m 36s
Rotational inclination	28.32°
Mass (Earth = 1)	17.147
Mean radius	15,301 mi
Mean density (Earth = 1)	0.297
Natural satellites	13
Average temperature*	−330°F
*i.e., temperature where atmosphere pressure equals 1 Earth atmosphere.	

Named for the Roman god of the sea, Neptune was the first planet discovered through mathematical calculations and not observation. Its approximate orbit and position were first calculated independently by British astronomer John Couch Adams and French astronomer Urbain Le Verrier in 1845. In 1846, German astronomer Johann Galle first observed Neptune through a telescope.

Orbit and rotation. Neptune orbits the Sun in 164.8 years in a nearly circular orbit. Its magnetic field is considerably asymmetric to the planet's structure, similar to, but not so extreme as, Uranus's magnetic field. Neptune's magnetic field axis is tipped 46.9° from its rotational axis and is displaced more than 55% of its radius away from the planet's center.

Atmosphere. The Neptunian atmosphere is composed primarily of 80% hydrogen, 19% helium, 1.5% methane, and small amounts of hydrogen deuteride, ethane, ammonia ice, water ice, ammonia hydrosulfide, and methane ice. Neptune's atmosphere is quite blue, with quickly changing white clouds often suspended high above an apparent surface. A Great Dark Spot was discovered in 1989 when *Voyager 2* visited the planet, reminiscent of Jupiter's Great Red Spot. Observations with the Hubble Space Telescope have shown that the Great Dark Spot originally seen by *Voyager* has apparently dissipated, but a new dark spot has since appeared. Lightning and auroras have been found on other giant planets, but only the aurora phenomenon has been seen on Neptune. As with the other giant planets, Neptune emits more energy than it receives from the Sun. The excess has been found to be 2.7 times the solar contribution.

Surface and composition. As with the other giant planets, Neptune may have no solid surface or exact diameter. However, a mean value of 30,600 mi may be assigned to a diameter between atmosphere levels where the pressure is about the same as sea level on Earth.

Natural satellites. Largest of Neptune's 13 satellites is Triton. It is the only large moon in a retrograde orbit, which suggests that it was captured rather than having been there from the beginning. Triton's large size, sufficient to raise significant tides on the planet, may one day, billions of years from now, bring Triton close enough to Neptune for Triton to be torn apart. Triton has a tenuous atmosphere of nitrogen with a trace of hydrocarbons and evidence of active geysers injecting material into it. Triton is the coldest object yet measured in the solar system with a surface temperature of −391°F. Only about half of Triton has been observed, but its terrain shows cratering and a strange regional feature described as resembling the skin of a cantaloupe. Nereid has the highest orbital eccentricity (0.75) of any moon. Its long looping orbit suggests that it was also captured. In 2003, two more moons, which orbit farther from their parent planet than any other moons in the solar system, were discovered. The *Voyager 2* probe in 1989 confirmed the existence of six rings around Neptune composed of very fine particles. There may be some clumps in the rings' structure. It is not known whether Neptune's satellites influence the formation or maintenance of the rings.

Dwarf Planets

Ceres

Distance from the Sun	
Perihelion	237 mil mi (2.55 AU)
Semi-major axis (mean distance)	257 mil mi (2.77 AU)
Period of revolution around Sun	4.6 y
Orbital eccentricity	0.0789
Orbital inclination	10.58°
Sidereal day	9.075 h
Mass (Earth = 1)	0.00016
Mean radius	300 mi

Ceres was the first asteroid ever discovered, on Jan. 1, 1801, by the Italian astronomer Guiseppe Piazzi. In the 1800s, it was considered a planet, but as more asteroids were discovered, it lost that designation. In Aug. 2006, it was designated a dwarf planet by the International Astronomical Union.

No probe has ever visited Ceres. NASA's Dawn space probe, launched in Sept. 2007, may become the first. The probe's mission is to Vesta and Ceres, the solar system's two largest asteroids. When Dawn arrives at Ceres in Feb. 2015, months before the New Horizons probe arrives at Pluto, it will be the first mission to study a dwarf planet.

Orbit and rotation. Ceres orbits the Sun in the asteroid belt region between Mars and Jupiter.

Surface and composition. Ceres is in a class of stony meteorites known as carbonaceous chondrites. These are considered to be the oldest materials in the solar system, with a composition reflecting that of the primitive solar nebula. Extremely dark in color, probably because of their hydrocarbon content, they show evidence of having absorbed water of hydration. Thus, unlike the Earth and the Moon, they have never either melted or been reheated since they first formed.

Pluto

Distance from the Sun	
Perihelion	2,756.9 mil mi
Semi-major axis (mean distance)	3,647.2 mil mi
	(39.482 AU)
Aphelion	4,583.2 mil mi
Period of revolution around Sun	247.68 y
Orbital eccentricity	0.2488
Orbital inclination	17.16°
Synodic day (midday to midday)	6d 9h 17m (retrograde)
Sidereal day	6d 9h 18m (retrograde)
Rotational inclination	122.53°
Mass (Earth = 1)	0.0021
Mean radius	742.5 mi
Mean density (Earth = 1)	0.317
Natural satellites	5
Average surface temperature	−369°F

Pluto, named for the Roman god of the underworld, is the second-largest known Kuiper Belt object (KBO) in the solar system. It was first discovered in 1930 by American astronomer Clyde Tombaugh and classified as a planet until 2006, when the International Astronomical Union (IAU) changed its designation to dwarf planet. The New Horizons spacecraft was launched on a voyage to Pluto and beyond in 2006; the spacecraft will make its closest approach to Pluto in July 2015. In 2008, Pluto was designated by the IAU as the prototype for a class of objects called **plutoids**, bodies (a) whose average distance from the Sun is greater than Neptune's; (b) that are large enough that gravity determines their shape; and (c) that have not cleared their orbit of other objects. Haumea, Makemake, and Eris are also Plutoids. At least 10 other Plutoid candidates have been identified through mid-2012.

Orbit and rotation. Pluto's orbit and rotation are highly irregular. Although on average it stays about 3.6 bil mi from the Sun, it may get as close as 2.76 bil mi. And for about 20 years of its orbit, it is closer to the Sun than Neptune. Currently, it is beyond Neptune's orbit.

Atmosphere and surface. Because no probes have visited Pluto, it is difficult for astronomers to accurately take readings of the dwarf planet's atmospheric composition. It is believed that an atmosphere of methane, nitrogen, and carbon monoxide exists when the dwarf planet is closer to the Sun. When Pluto is farther away from the Sun, the atmosphere freezes and becomes part of the surface. Large regions of Pluto are dark, others light; Pluto has spots and perhaps polar caps. There is also evidence of temperature fluctuations on the dwarf planet that may indicate primitive weather. Its core may be rocky with a mantle of water ice surrounding it.

Natural satellites. Pluto has five natural satellites. Charon, the biggest, has a diameter of 737 mi—about half of Pluto's diameter of 1,485 mi. No other planet in the solar system has a moon so close to its size. Discovered in 1978, Charon orbits Pluto at a distance of 12,200 mi and takes 6.39 days to move around the dwarf planet. In this same length of time, Pluto and Charon both rotate once on their axes, meaning that a person standing on Pluto would always see the same face of Charon in the same part of the sky, every day and night. The Pluto-Charon system thus appears to rotate as virtually a rigid body. Both worlds are roughly spherical and have comparable densities. Because of these similarities and their peculiar relationship, there is debate as to whether Charon should one day be designated a dwarf planet.

Two other moons, discovered in 2005 and 2006, were officially named Nix and Hydra. Two moons, discovered in 2011 and 2012, had not been officially named as of Aug. 2012; they are known provisionally as P4 and P5.

Haumea

Distance from the Sun	
Semi-major axis (mean distance)	43.335 AU
Period of revolution around Sun	285 y
Mean radius	420 mi
Orbital eccentricity	0.189
Orbital inclination	28.19°
Mass (Earth = 1)	0.0007
Natural satellites	2

Haumea was discovered in 2004 and was accepted as a dwarf planet by the IAU in 2008.

Orbit and rotation. Haumea has a moderately eccentric orbit and takes about 285 years to go around the Sun.

Surface and composition. Spectra of Haumea indicate the presence of almost pure crystalline water ice. The surface reflects about 60% of the sunlight that reaches it. Haumea has a very oblong shape, twice as long as it is wide.

Natural satellites. Haumea has two natural satellites.

Makemake

Distance from the Sun	
Semi-major axis (mean distance)	45.791 AU
Period of revolution around Sun	310 y
Mean radius	450 mi
Orbital eccentricity	0.159
Orbital inclination	28.96°
Mass (Earth = 1)	0.0007

Makemake was discovered in 2005 and was accepted as a dwarf planet by the IAU in 2008.

Orbit and rotation. Makemake has a moderately eccentric orbit and takes about 310 years to go around the Sun.

Surface and composition. Spectra of Makemake indicate the presence of frozen methane, as well as several organic compounds. The surface is highly reflective and appears similar to that of Pluto.

Eris

Distance from the Sun	
Semi-major axis (mean distance)	67.6681 AU
Period of revolution around Sun	560 y
Mean radius	925 mi
Orbital eccentricity	0.44177
Orbital inclination	44.177°
Natural satellites	1
Mass (Earth = 1)	0.0027

Eris is the largest dwarf planet. Discovered in 2003 by astronomers at the California Institute of Technology, it is the most distant object ever seen in orbit around the Sun.

Orbit and rotation. Eris has a highly elliptical orbit and takes about 560 years to go around the Sun—more than twice the time it takes Pluto. Its inclination is steep, tilted at 44° to the planetary plane. It also has an extremely eccentric orbit. It will be at its closest, actually coming inside part of Pluto's orbit, in about 280 years.

Surface and composition. Eris, with a surface covered in frozen methane, may be similar to Pluto and the Neptunian moon Triton. Observations made by the Hubble Space Telescope show that Eris's surface is almost white and uniform, reflecting 86% of the light that hits it. This makes it the most reflective body in the solar system. The dwarf planet's interior is likely a mixture of rock and ice.

Natural satellites. Eris has one moon, Dysnomia.

Small Solar System Bodies: Asteroids, Comets, Kuiper Belt, and the Oort Cloud

Asteroids

Besides planets and moons, many smaller objects orbit the Sun. In 2006, the International Astronomical Union (IAU) officially designated these objects "small solar system bodies." **Asteroids** or minor planets are found mainly in a belt between the orbits of Mars and Jupiter. Within this belt there may be millions of asteroids of varying sizes. Most asteroids are very small. Ceres, which can be classified both as an asteroid and a dwarf planet, is 588 mi in diameter, about one-quarter the diameter of our moon.

Some of these objects, or asteroids, are gravitationally locked with Jupiter and the Sun so that they have roughly the same orbit as Jupiter but are either 60° ahead or behind the planet. These are the **Trojan asteroids**. Many of the smaller moons of the solar system, especially those in retrograde orbits, may be captured asteroids. Asteroids whose orbits either cross or come close to the Earth's orbit are labeled **Near Earth asteroids** or NEAs. A handful of asteroids have actually been imaged by the Arecibo and Goldstone radio telescopes and by the NEAR Shoemaker space probe. The *Galileo* spacecraft imaged the asteroids Gaspra and Ida (including its moon Dactyl) on its way to Jupiter.

Comets

Comets are small icy bodies that orbit the Sun. When one approaches the Sun, the energy from the Sun boils off material from the comet's icy nucleus, producing an enlarged head (or **coma**), and in many cases an extended tail. Because of that, comets are brighter when near the Sun. For large comets, the head may be 100,000 mi across and the tail more than a million mi long, though both are mainly empty space.

Comets have been known since ancient times; ultimately, British astronomer Edmund Halley (1656-1742) realized that a group of historical reports were just repeated visits of the same object. Comets are the only astronomical objects named after their discoverers. In 1986, the European spacecraft *Giotto* took the first close-up images of a comet's nucleus, specifically of Comet Halley, showing it had a peanut-shaped nucleus whose longest dimension was about 10 mi.

In 1995, U.S. observers Alan Hale (1958-) and Thomas Bopp (1949-) independently discovered a comet that was then beyond the orbit of Jupiter. It is one of the brightest comets of all time. It also holds the record for length of naked-eye visibility—19 months—and is the most photographed comet in history. In July 2009, an amateur astronomer discovered a large impact scar in the upper atmosphere of Jupiter, likely the results of another cometary impact.

Kuiper Belt

The **Kuiper Belt** is a doughnut-shaped region that extends to about 50 AU from the Sun and is thought to be the source of short-period comets such as Comets Halley or Swift-Tuttle. It is filled with icy bodies that are in solar order. The more than 1,000 objects found in this region in recent years are called Kuiper Belt objects (KBOs). It is estimated that there are more than 70,000 objects 60 mi in diameter or larger within the Kuiper Belt. Dwarf planets Pluto and Eris are considered KBOs. There are at least 6 KBOs larger than 300 mi in diameter.

Oort Cloud

The Oort Cloud is a vast spherical shell hypothesized to exist around the Sun. Dutch astronomer Jan Oort (1900-92) proposed its existence as the origin for long-period comets that enter the inner part of the solar system where the planets orbit. Current technology is not sufficient to detect any members of the Oort Cloud other than observed comets whose orbits may reach out as far as 50,000 AU. Recent examples of such long-period comets are Comets Hale-Bopp and Hyakutake.

The Sun

Distance from Earth, mean	92.96 mil mi (1 AU)
Sidereal day	25.38 d
Mass (Earth=1)	332,900
Mean radius	432,200 mi
Mean density (Earth=1)	0.255
Average surface temperature	9,941°F

The Sun is the Earth's primary source of light and heat and its closest star. The biggest object in the solar system, the Sun is 332,900 times more massive than Earth and contains 99.86% of the mass of the entire solar system. On the whole, the Sun is made up of about 92.1% hydrogen and 7.8% helium, with trace amounts of other elements. It has a mass and luminosity greater than that of 90% of the stars in the Milky Way galaxy. Although most of the stars that can be easily seen on a clear night are bigger and brighter than the Sun, its proximity to Earth makes it appear tremendously large and bright. The Sun is 400,000 times as bright as the full moon, and it gives Earth 6 mil times as much light as do all the other stars put together. Because of the great distance between the Sun and Earth, it takes about 499 seconds, or slightly more than 8 minutes, for light from the Sun to reach Earth.

Composition. The Sun has six regions. The first three from the inside out are the core, the radiative zone, and the convective zone. Together they form the interior. The others, which comprise the visible surface, are the photosphere, the chromosphere, and the outermost region, the corona.

The Sun's core is where its heat and energy are produced. Through a series of nuclear fusion reactions, hydrogen nuclei are converted to helium nuclei. Temperatures in the core are theorized to be 28 mil °F. From the core, photons transport the energy outward through the radiative zone. It can take photons several million years to pass through this area. In the convective zone, gases move energy outward at a faster rate. Like a boiling pot, bubbles of gas bring energy to the surface.

The photosphere is the visible surface of the Sun, that is, the light that we see as sunlight. When sunlight is analyzed with a spectroscope, it is found to consist of a continuous spectrum composed of all the colors of the rainbow, crossed by many dark lines. The dark "absorption lines" are produced by gaseous materials in the outer layers of the Sun. More than 60 of the natural terrestrial elements have been identified in the Sun, all in gaseous form because of the Sun's intense heat.

Just above the photosphere is the chromosphere, which is visible to the naked eye only in total solar eclipses, during which it appears to be a pinkish-violet layer with occasional great prominences projecting above its general level. With proper instruments, the chromosphere can be seen or photographed whenever the Sun is visible. Above the chromosphere is the corona, also visible to the naked eye only at times of total eclipse or with instruments that permit the brighter portions of the corona to be seen. The light of the corona surges millions of miles from the Sun; its atoms are all in a state of extreme attenuation and high ionization that indicates temperatures nearly 2 mil °F.

Sunspots. These dark, irregularly shaped regions may reach diameters of thousands of miles. There is an intimate connection between sunspots and the corona. At times of low sunspot activity, the fine streamers of the corona are longer above the Sun's equator than over the polar regions of the Sun; during periods of high sunspot activity, the corona extends fairly evenly outward from all regions of the Sun but to a much greater distance in space. The average life of a sunspot group is two months, but some have lasted for more than a year. Sunspots reach a low point, on average, every 11.3 years, with a peak of activity occurring irregularly between two successive periods of minimal activity. Currently, the number of sunspots is declining. Solar minimum occurred late in 2006.

Solar wind and magnetic field. Magnetic arches, called prominences, may extend tens of thousands of miles into the corona and may release enormous amounts of energy heating the corona. Coronal mass ejections are enormous releases of solar energy. Coronal holes are regions where the corona appears dark in X-rays, and are associated with open magnetic field lines, where the magnetic field lines project out into space instead of back toward the Sun. It is in these regions where the high-speed solar wind originates.

The solar wind carries the Sun's magnetic field, which extends beyond the planets. This is called the interplanetary magnetic field (IMF). Far past Pluto and the Kuiper Belt, the solar wind and the IMF lose their influence. The boundary between them and interstellar space is called the heliopause.

Searching for Extrasolar Planets

During the last 10 years of the 20th century, astronomers began to detect the presence of planets orbiting stars other than the Sun. Except for a few possible instances, they have not seen those objects, but merely inferred their existence by their effect on their parent star. The Sun is a typical star in many respects. With over 200 bil stars in the Milky Way, it seems plausible that many other stars might have planets.

As of summer 2012, astronomers had found a total of 777 planets orbiting some 623 stars. Of those, 417 were at least as massive as Jupiter, which is about 318 times more massive than the Earth. Planets with masses less than Jupiter are now regularly discovered; at the time of this writing, the minimum confirmed mass for an extrasolar planet was about the mass of the Earth.

Using the Doppler effect to detect radial velocity changes in the motions of individual stars, astronomers are more likely to find high-mass planets in close and eccentric orbits around star because that situation produces larger and more noticeable changes.

In addition to the radial velocity method, astronomers are now using an optical gravitational lensing means of detecting extrasolar planets. Using this technique, Southern Hemisphere astronomers found the most distant planet yet detected, about halfway to the center of our own Milky Way galaxy. Astronomers have also found planets by looking for the periodic dimming of starlight as orbiting planets pass in front of their host stars. About 16 planets have been discovered this way.

In 2005, astronomers obtained the first direct photograph of an extrasolar planet. The unnamed planet orbits a star called GQ Lupi, which is a star like our Sun but younger. The planet is about 100 AUs away from its star, and it is estimated to be about twice as massive as Jupiter.

In 2006, astronomers discovered what they call a "super Earth" orbiting a red dwarf star 9,000 light-years away. The planet appears to have about 13 times the mass of Earth and may be composed of rock and ice. Although the planet is similar in structure to the Earth, it is believed to orbit too far from its star for there to be any liquid on the surface. In 2007, astronomers for the first time detected water in the atmosphere of an extrasolar planet.

In Apr. 2009, NASA launched Kepler, the first telescope sensitive enough to detect Earth-sized planets around other stars. Kepler's first released data, in summer 2010, included indications that small planets are more common than large planets, with hints of planets with diameters as small as twice the diameter of Earth. All of the planet candidates to date orbit their stars much closer than Earth orbits the Sun. Kepler will need to observe for several more years to find evidence of Earth-sized planets at comparable distances from their stars. As of this writing, Kepler had identified nearly 3,000 candidate planets, of which 74 have thus far been confirmed.

Earth: Size, Computation of Time, Seasons

Distance from the Sun	
Perihelion	91.4 mil mi
Semi-major axis (mean distance)	93 mil mi (1.0000 AU)
Aphelion	94.5 mil mi
Period of revolution	365.256 d
Orbital eccentricity	0.0167
Orbital inclination	0°
Synodic day (midday to midday)	24h 0m 0s
Sidereal day (rotation period)	23h 56m 4.2s
Rotational inclination	23.45°
Mass (Earth = 1)	1
Mean radius	3,958.8 mi
Mean density (Earth = 1)	1
Natural satellites	1
Average surface temperature	59°F

Earth is the fifth-largest planet and the third from the Sun. Its mass is 5.9736×10^{24} kg. Earth's equatorial diameter is 7,926 mi while its polar diameter is only 7,900 mi.

Size and dimensions. Earth is considered a solid mass, yet it has a large, liquid iron, **magnetic core** with a radius of about 2,160 mi. Surprisingly, it has a solid **inner core** that may be a large iron crystal, with a radius of 760 mi. Around the core is a thick shell, or **mantle**, of dense rock. This mantle is composed of materials rich in iron and magnesium. It is somewhat plastic-like, and under slow steady pressure, it can flow like a liquid. The mantle, in turn, is covered by a thin **crust** forming the solid granite and basalt base of the continents and ocean basins. Over broad areas of Earth's surface, the crust has a thin cover of sedimentary rock such as sandstone, shale, and limestone formed by weathering and by deposits of sands, clays, and plant and animal remains.

The temperature inside the Earth increases about 1°F with every 100 to 200 ft in depth, in the upper 100 km of Earth. It reaches nearly 8,000-9,000°F at the center. The heat is believed to come from radioactivity in rocks, pressures within Earth, and the original heat of formation.

Atmosphere. Earth's atmosphere is a blanket composed of 78% nitrogen, 21% oxygen, and 1% argon. Present in minute quantities are carbon dioxide, hydrogen, neon, helium, krypton, and xenon. Water vapor displaces other gases and varies from nearly zero to about 4% by volume. The atmosphere rests on Earth's surface with a weight equivalent to a layer of water 34 ft deep. For about 300,000 ft upward, the gases remain in the proportions stated. Gravity holds the gases to Earth. The weight of the air compresses it at the bottom so that the greatest density is at Earth's surface. Pressure and density decrease as height increases.

The lowest layer of the atmosphere extending up from the Earth's surface about 7.5 mi is the **troposphere**, which contains 90% of the air. This is also where most weather phenomena occur. The temperature drops with increasing height through this layer. The **stratosphere** extends about 23 mi above the troposphere; the the temperature generally increases with height within this layer. The stratosphere contains **ozone**, which prevents ultraviolet rays from reaching Earth's surface. Since there is very little convection in the stratosphere, jets regularly cruise in the lower parts to provide a smoother ride for passengers.

Above the stratosphere is the **mesosphere**, where the temperature again decreases with height for another 19 mi. Extending above the mesosphere to the outer fringes of the atmosphere is the **thermosphere**, a region where temperature once more increases with height to a value measured in thousands of degrees Fahrenheit. The lower portion of this region, extending from 50 to about 400 mi in altitude, is characterized by high ion density and is thus called the **ionosphere**. Most meteors are in the lower thermosphere or the mesosphere at the time they are observed.

Longitude and latitude. Position on the globe is measured by meridians and parallels. Meridians, which are imaginary lines drawn around Earth through the poles, determine **longitude**. The meridian running through Greenwich, England, is the **prime meridian** of longitude; all others are either E or W. Parallels, which are imaginary circles parallel with the equator, determine **latitude**. The length of a degree of longitude varies as the cosine of the latitude. At the equator a degree of longitude is 69.171 statute mi; this is gradually reduced toward the poles. Value of a longitude degree at the poles is zero.

Latitude is reckoned by the number of degrees N or S of the **equator**, an imaginary circle on Earth's surface everywhere equidistant between the two poles. According to the International Astronomical Union, the length of a degree of latitude is 68.708 statute mi at the equator and varies slightly N and S because of the oblate form of the globe. At the poles, it is 69.403 statute mi.

Definitions of time. Earth rotates on its axis and follows an elliptical orbit around the Sun. The rotation makes the Sun appear to move across the sky from E to W. This rotation determines day and night, and the complete rotation, in relation to the Sun, is called the **apparent or true solar day.** A sundial thus measures **apparent solar time.** This length of time varies, but an average determines a mean solar day of 24 hours.

The mean solar day and **mean solar time** are in universal use for civil purposes. Mean solar time may be obtained from apparent solar time by correcting observations of the Sun for the **equation of time.** Mean solar time may be up to 16 minutes different from apparent solar time.

Sidereal time is the measure of time defined by the diurnal motion of the vernal equinox and is determined from observation of the meridian transits of stars. One complete rotation of Earth relative to the equinox is called the **sidereal day.** The **mean sidereal day** is 23 hours, 56 minutes, 4.2 seconds of mean solar time.

The interval required for Earth to make one absolute revolution around the Sun is a **sidereal year**; it consisted of 365 days, 6 hours, 9 minutes, and 9.5 seconds of mean solar time (approximately 24 hours per day) in 1900 and has been increasing at the rate of 0.0001 second annually.

The **tropical year**, upon which our calendar is based, is the interval between two consecutive returns of the Sun to the vernal equinox. The tropical year consisted of 365 days, 5 hours, 48 minutes, and 46 seconds in 1900. It has been decreasing at the rate of 0.53 second per century. The **calendar year** begins at 12 o'clock midnight precisely, local clock time, on the night of Dec. 31-Jan. 1. The day and the calendar month also begin at midnight by the clock.

On Jan. 1, 1972, the Bureau International des Poids et Mesures in Paris introduced **International Atomic Time** (TAI) as the most precisely determined time scale for astronomical usage. The fundamental unit of TAI in the international system of units is the second, defined as the duration of 9,192,631,770 periods of the radiation corresponding to the transition between two hyperfine levels of the ground state of the cesium-133 atom. **Coordinated Universal Time** (UTC), which serves as the basis for civil timekeeping and is the standard time of the prime meridian, is officially defined by a formula which relates UTC to mean sidereal time in Greenwich, England. (UTC has replaced GMT as the basis for standard time for the world.)

Zones and seasons. The five zones of Earth's surface are the Torrid, lying between the Tropics of Cancer and Capricorn; the N Temperate, between Cancer and the Arctic Circle; the S Temperate, between Capricorn and the Antarctic Circle; and the two Frigid Zones, between the Polar Circles and the Poles.

The inclination, or tilt, of Earth's axis, 23°45′ away from a perpendicular to Earth's orbit of the Sun, determines the seasons. These are commonly marked in the N Temperate Zone, where spring begins at the vernal equinox, summer at the summer solstice, autumn at the autumnal equinox, and winter at the winter solstice. In the S Temperate Zone, the seasons are reversed. Spring begins at the autumnal equinox, summer at the winter solstice and so on.

The points at which the Sun crosses the equator are the **equinoxes**, when day and night are most nearly equal. The points at which the Sun is at a maximum distance from the equator are the **solstices.** Days and nights are then most unequal. However, at the equator, day and night are equal throughout the year.

In June, the North Pole is tilted 23°27′ toward the Sun, and the days in the Northern Hemisphere are longer than the nights, while the days in the Southern Hemisphere are shorter than the nights. In Dec., the North Pole is tilted 23°27′ away from the Sun, and the situation is reversed.

The Seasons in 2013. In 2013, the four seasons begin in the Northern Hemisphere as shown. (Add 1 hour to Eastern Standard Time for Atlantic Time; subtract 1 hour for Central, 2 for Mountain, 3 for Pacific, 4 for Alaska, 5 for Hawaii-Aleutian. Also shown is Coordinated Universal Time.)

Seasons	Date	UTC	EST/EDT
Vernal Equinox (spring)	Mar. 20	11:02	07:02 EDT
Northern Solstice (summer)	June 21	05:04	01:04 EDT
Autumnal Equinox (fall)	Sept. 22	20:44	16:44 EDT
Southern Solstice (winter)	Dec. 21	17:11	12:11 EST

Poles. The geographic (rotation) poles, or points where Earth's axis of rotation cuts the surface, are not absolutely fixed in the body of Earth. The pole of rotation describes an irregular curve about its mean position.

Two periods have been detected in this motion: (1) an annual period due to seasonal changes in barometric pressure, to load of ice and snow on the surface, and to other seasonal phenomena; (2) a period of about 14 months due to the shape and constitution of Earth. In addition, there are small but as yet unpredictable irregularities. The whole motion is so small that the actual pole at any time remains within a circle of 30 or 40 ft in radius centered at the mean position of the pole.

The pole of rotation for the time being is of course the pole having a latitude of 90° and an indeterminate longitude.

Magnetic poles. Although Earth's magnetic field resembles that of an ordinary bar magnet, this magnetic field is probably produced by electric currents in the liquid currents of the Earth's outer core. The **north magnetic pole** of Earth is that region where the magnetic force is downward, and the **south magnetic pole** is that region where the magnetic force is upward. A compass placed at the magnetic poles experiences no directive force in azimuth (i.e., direction).

There are slow changes in the distribution of Earth's magnetic field. This slow temporal change is referred to as the secular change of the main magnetic field, and the magnetic poles shift due to this. The location of the N magnetic pole was first measured in 1831 at Cape Adelaide on the W coast of Boothia Peninsula in Canada's Northwest Territories (about latitude 70°N and longitude 96°W). Since then it has moved over 500 mi. It is now estimated to be at 82.7°N and 114.4°W, NW of Ellef Ringnes Island in northern Canada. Measurement for several decades by Canadian scientists indicates the motion of the pole has accelerated, now averaging about 25 mi per year.

The direction of the horizontal components of the magnetic field at any point is known as magnetic N at that point, and the angle by which it deviates E or W of true N is known as the magnetic declination.

A compass without error points in the direction of magnetic north. (In general, this is not the direction of the true rotational north pole.) If you follow the direction indicated by the N end of the compass, you will go along an irregular curve that eventually reaches the north magnetic pole (though not usually by a great-circle route). However, the action of the compass should not be thought of as due to any influence of the distant pole, but simply as an indication of the distribution of Earth's magnetism at the place of observation.

Rotation. The speed of Earth's rotation about its axis is slightly variable. The variations may be classified as:

(A) **Secular.** Tidal friction acts as a brake on the rotation and causes a slow secular increase in the length of the day, about 1 millisecond per century.

(B) **Irregular.** The speed of rotation may increase for a number of years (about 5 to 10) and then start decreasing. The maximum difference from the mean in the length of the day during a century is about 5 milliseconds. The accumulated difference in time has amounted to approximately 44 seconds since 1900. The cause is probably motion in the interior of Earth.

(C) **Periodic.** Seasonal variations exist with periods of 1 year and 6 months. The cumulative effect is such that each year, Earth is late about 30 milliseconds near June 1 and is ahead about 30 milliseconds near Oct. 1. The maximum seasonal variation in the length of the day is about 0.5 millisecond. It is believed that the principal cause of the annual variation is the seasonal change in the wind patterns of the Northern and Southern Hemispheres. The semiannual variation is due chiefly to tidal action of the Sun, which distorts the shape of Earth slightly.

The Moon

Distance from Earth	
Perigee	225,744 mi
Semi-major axis (mean distance)	238,855 mi
Apogee	251,966 mi
Period of revolution	27.322 d
Synodic orbital period (period of phases)	29.53 d
Orbital eccentricity	0.0549
Orbital inclination	5.145°
Sidereal day (rotation period)	27.322 d
Rotational inclination	6.68°
Mass (Earth = 1)	0.0123
Mean radius	1,079 mi
Mean density (Earth = 1)	0.607
Average surface temperature	–100°F

The Moon is the second-brightest object in the sky (the Sun is the first). Earth's only natural satellite, the Moon is the force behind the rising and falling of tides, and it helps to regulate the Earth's orbit around the Sun. Many probes have been sent to the Moon, and between 1969 and 1972, 12 U.S. astronauts walked on its surface. The Moon is the subject of renewed international interest. In 2007, Japan and China orbited satellites around the Moon, India orbited a spacecraft in fall 2008, and the U.S. sent an orbiter and impactor in 2009. It is expected that several nations, including the U.S. and China, will send humans back to the Moon in the next 15 years. In Sept. 2009, American scientists announced the discovery of a thin layer of water ice near the lunar poles. The LCROSS impactor mission impacted the lunar south polar region in Oct. 2009. The plume of material thrown up in the impact included water plus a variety of other chemical species, indicating that the lunar regolith harbors a rich and active chemistry.

Orbit and rotation. The Moon completes a circuit around Earth in a period that averages 27 days, 7 hours, 43.2 minutes. This is the Moon's sidereal period. Because of the motion of the Moon in common with Earth around the Sun, the mean duration of the lunar month—the period from one new moon to the next new moon—is 29 days, 12 hours, 44.05 minutes. This is the Moon's synodic period.

The mean distance of the Moon from Earth is 238,855 mi, but its orbit about Earth is elliptical, and thus the actual distance varies considerably. The maximum distance from Earth that the Moon may reach is 251,966 mi and the least distance is 225,744 mi.

The Moon rotates on its axis in a period of time that is exactly equal to its sidereal revolution about Earth—27.322 days. Thus the backside, or farside, of the Moon always faces away from Earth. But this does not mean that the backside is always dark. The farside of the Moon gets just as much direct sunlight as the nearside; at new moon phase, the farside of the Moon is fully lit but not visible from Earth.

The Moon's revolution about Earth is irregular because of its elliptical orbit. The Moon's rotation, however, is regular, and this, together with the irregular revolution, produces what is called libration in longitude, which permits an observer on Earth to see first farther around the eastern side and then farther around the western side of the Moon. The Moon's variation north or south of the ecliptic permits one to see farther over first one pole of the Moon and then the other; this is called libration in latitude. These two libration effects permit observers on Earth to see a total of about 60% of the Moon's surface over a period of time.

Atmosphere and surface. The Moon, like the planet Mercury, has no real atmosphere to speak of. What little exists is variable and tenuous. With its long day and night, the daytime temperature can reach 260°F. The coldest nighttime temperature is –280°F. This day-to-night contrast is exceeded only by that on Mercury.

The lunar surface has not changed much since humans began observing it. The side visible from Earth has large craters and vast dark areas called *maria* that were once lava. The farside has almost no maria but is pockmarked with craters.

Recent findings show that up to 300 mil metric tons of water ice may exist in craters at the lunar poles. In its interior, the Moon may have a small core, which supports the idea that most of the Moon's mass was ripped away from the early Earth when a Mars-size object collided with Earth. The hidden side of the Moon was first photographed in 1959 by the Soviet space probe *Lunik III*.

Harvest moon and hunter's moon. The harvest moon, the full Moon nearest the autumnal equinox, ushers in a period of several successive days when the Moon rises soon after sunset. This phenomenon gives farmers in temperate latitudes extra hours of light in which to harvest their crops before the onset of cold weather. The 2013 harvest moon falls on Sept. 19. Harvest moon in the Southern Hemisphere temperate latitudes falls on Mar. 27.

The next full moon after harvest moon is called the hunter's moon; it is accompanied by a similar but less marked phenomenon. In 2013, the hunter's moon occurs on Oct. 18 in the Northern Hemisphere and on Apr. 25 in the Southern Hemisphere.

Moon's Perigee and Apogee, 2013

Perigee is the point in the Moon's orbit where it is closest to the Earth. Apogee is the point where it is farthest.

(In Coordinated Universal Time, the standard time of the prime meridian.)

Perigee

Month	Day	Hour	Month	Day	Hour
Jan.	10	10	July	21	20
Feb.	7	12	Aug.	19	1
Mar.	5	23	Sept.	15	17
Mar.	31	4	Oct.	10	23
Apr.	27	20	Nov.	6	9
May	26	2	Dec.	4	10
June	23	11			

Apogee

Month	Day	Hour	Month	Day	Hour
Jan.	22	11	Aug.	3	9
Feb.	19	7	Aug.	30	24
Mar.	19	3	Sept.	27	18
Apr.	15	22	Oct.	25	14
May	13	14	Nov.	22	10
June	9	22	Dec.	19	24
July	7	1			

Moon Phases, 2013

(In Coordinated Universal Time, the standard time of the prime meridian.)

New Moon				Waxing Quarter				Full Moon				Waning Quarter			
Month	d	h	m	Month	d	h	m	Month	d	h	m	Month	d	h	m
												Jan.	5	3	58
Jan.	11	19	44	Jan.	18	23	45	Jan.	27	4	38	Feb.	3	13	56
Feb.	10	7	20	Feb.	17	20	31	Feb.	25	20	26	Mar.	4	21	53
Mar.	11	19	51	Mar.	19	17	27	Mar.	27	9	27	Apr.	3	4	37
Apr.	10	9	35	Apr.	18	12	31	Apr.	25	19	57	May	2	11	14
May	10	0	28	May	18	4	35	May	25	4	25	May	31	18	58
June	8	15	56	June	16	17	24	June	23	11	32	June	30	4	54
July	8	7	14	July	16	3	18	July	22	18	15	July	29	17	43
Aug.	6	21	51	Aug.	14	10	56	Aug.	21	1	45	Aug.	28	9	35
Sept.	5	11	36	Sept.	12	17	8	Sept.	19	11	13	Sept.	27	3	55
Oct.	5	0	35	Oct.	11	23	2	Oct.	18	23	38	Oct.	26	23	40
Nov.	3	12	50	Nov.	10	5	57	Nov.	17	15	16	Nov.	25	19	28
Dec.	3	0	22	Dec.	9	15	12	Dec.	17	9	28	Dec.	25	13	48

CALENDAR

Western Calendars

The **Julian calendar**, under which all Western nations measured time until 1582 CE, was authorized by Julius Caesar in 46 BCE. It called for a year of 365¼ days, starting in January, with every 4th year being a **leap year** of 366 days. St. Bede, an Anglo-Saxon monk also known as the Venerable Bede, announced in 730 CE that the Julian year was 11 min., 14 sec. too long, a cumulative error of about a day every 128 years, but nothing was done about this for centuries.

By 1582 the accumulated error was estimated at 10 days. In that year, Pope Gregory XIII decreed that the day following Oct. 4, 1582, should be called Oct. 15, thus dropping 10 days and initiating the **Gregorian calendar**.

The Gregorian calendar perpetuated a chronological system devised by the monk Dionysius Exiguus (fl. 6th cent.). His chronology started with the first year following the birth of Jesus Christ, which he inaccurately took to be year 753 in the Roman calendar. Leap years were continued but, to prevent further displacements, centesimal years (years ending in 00) were made common years, not leap years, unless divisible by 400. Under this plan, 1600 and 2000 were leap years; 1700, 1800, and 1900 were not.

The Gregorian calendar was adopted at once by France, Italy, Spain, Portugal, and Luxembourg. Within two years, most German Catholic states, Belgium, and parts of Switzerland and the Netherlands were brought under the new calendar, and Hungary followed in 1587. The rest of the Netherlands, along with Denmark and the German Protestant states, made the change in 1699-1700.

The British government adopted the Gregorian calendar and imposed it on all its possessions, including the American colonies, in 1752, decreeing that the day following Sept. 2, 1752, should be called Sept. 14, a loss of 11 days. All dates preceding were marked OS, for Old Style. In addition, New Year's Day was moved to Jan. 1 from Mar. 25 (under the old reckoning, for example, Mar. 24, 1700, had been followed by Mar. 25, 1701). Thus George Washington's birth date, which was Feb. 11, 1731, OS, became Feb. 22, 1732, NS (New Style). In 1753, Sweden also went Gregorian.

In 1793, the French revolutionary government adopted a calendar of 12 months of 30 days each with 5 extra days in Sept. of each common year and 6 extra days every 4th year. Napoleon reinstated the Gregorian calendar in 1806.

The Gregorian system later spread to non-European regions, replacing traditional calendars at least for official purposes. Japan in 1873, Egypt in 1875, China in 1912, and Turkey in 1925 made the change, usually in conjunction with political upheaval. In China, the republican government began reckoning years from its 1911 founding. After 1949, the People's Republic adopted the Common, or Christian Era, year count, even for the traditional lunar calendar, which it retained. In 1918, the Soviet Union decreed that the day after Jan. 31, 1918, OS, would be Feb. 14, 1918, NS. Greece changed over in 1923. For the first time in history, all major nations had one calendar. The Russian Orthodox church and some other Christian sects retained the Julian calendar.

To convert from the Julian to the Gregorian calendar, add 10 days to dates Oct. 5, 1582, through Feb. 28, 1700; after that date, add 11 days through Feb. 28, 1800; 12 days through Feb. 28, 1900; and 13 days through Feb. 28, 2100.

A **century** consists of 100 consecutive years. The 1st century CE may be said to have run from the years 1 through 100. The 20th century by this reckoning consisted of the years 1901 through 2000 and ended Dec. 31, 2000, as did the 2nd millennium CE. The 21st century thus technically began on Jan. 1, 2001.

For a **Perpetual Calendar**, see pages 382-83.

Gregorian Calendar

Choose the desired year from the table below or from the Perpetual Calendar (for years 1803 to 2080). The number after each year designates which calendar to use for that year, as shown in the Perpetual Calendar. (The Gregorian calendar was inaugurated Oct. 15, 1582. From that date through Dec. 31, 1582, use calendar 6.)

1583-1802

Year	No.	Year	No.	Year	No.	Year	No.	Year	No.	Year	No.	Year	No.	Year	No.	Year	No.	Year	No.	Year	No.
1583	7	1603	4	1623	1	1643	5	1663	2	1683	6	1703	2	1723	6	1743	3	1763	7	1783	4
1584	8	1604	12	1624	9	1644	13	1664	10	1684	14	1704	10	1724	14	1744	11	1764	8	1784	12
1585	3	1605	7	1625	4	1645	1	1665	5	1685	2	1705	5	1725	2	1745	6	1765	3	1785	7
1586	4	1606	1	1626	5	1646	2	1666	6	1686	3	1706	6	1726	3	1746	7	1766	4	1786	1
1587	5	1607	2	1627	6	1647	3	1667	7	1687	4	1707	7	1727	4	1747	1	1767	5	1787	2
1588	13	1608	10	1628	14	1648	11	1668	8	1688	12	1708	8	1728	12	1748	9	1768	13	1788	10
1589	1	1609	5	1629	2	1649	6	1669	3	1689	7	1709	3	1729	7	1749	4	1769	1	1789	5
1590	2	1610	6	1630	3	1650	7	1670	4	1690	1	1710	4	1730	1	1750	5	1770	2	1790	6
1591	3	1611	7	1631	4	1651	1	1671	5	1691	2	1711	5	1731	2	1751	6	1771	3	1791	7
1592	11	1612	8	1632	12	1652	9	1672	13	1692	10	1712	13	1732	10	1752	14	1772	11	1792	8
1593	7	1613	3	1633	7	1653	4	1673	1	1693	5	1713	1	1733	5	1753	2	1773	6	1793	3
1594	7	1614	4	1634	1	1654	5	1674	2	1694	6	1714	2	1734	6	1754	3	1774	7	1794	4
1595	1	1615	5	1635	2	1655	6	1675	3	1695	7	1715	3	1735	7	1755	4	1775	1	1795	5
1596	9	1616	13	1636	10	1656	14	1676	11	1696	8	1716	11	1736	8	1756	12	1776	9	1796	13
1597	1	1617	1	1637	5	1657	2	1677	6	1697	3	1717	6	1737	3	1757	7	1777	4	1797	1
1598	5	1618	2	1638	6	1658	3	1678	7	1698	4	1718	7	1738	4	1758	1	1778	5	1798	2
1599	6	1619	3	1639	7	1659	4	1679	1	1699	5	1719	1	1739	5	1759	2	1779	6	1799	3
1600	14	1620	11	1640	8	1660	12	1680	9	1700	7	1720	9	1740	13	1760	10	1780	14	1800	4
1601	2	1621	6	1641	3	1661	7	1681	4	1701	7	1721	4	1741	1	1761	5	1781	2	1801	5
1602	3	1622	7	1642	4	1662	1	1682	5	1702	1	1722	5	1742	2	1762	6	1782	3	1802	6

The Julian Period

How many days have you lived? To determine this, multiply your age by 365, add the number of days since your last birthday, and account for all leap years. Chances are your calculations will go wrong somewhere. Astronomers, however, find it convenient to express dates and time intervals in days rather than in years, months, and days. This is done by placing events within the Julian period.

The Julian period was devised in 1582 by the French classical scholar Joseph Scaliger (1540-1609), who named it after his father, Julius Caesar Scaliger, not after the Julian calendar as might be supposed.

Scaliger began with a zero hour, or starting time, of noon on Jan. 1, 4713 BCE (on the Julian calendar). This was the most recent time that three major chronological cycles began on the same day: (1) the 28-year solar cycle, after which dates in the Julian calendar (e.g., Feb. 11) return to the same days of the week (e.g., Monday); (2) the 19-year lunar cycle, after which the phases of the moon return to the same dates of the year; and (3) the 15-year indiction cycle, used in ancient Rome to regulate taxes.

It will take 7,980 years to complete the period, the product of the numbers 28, 19, and 15.

Noon (Universal Time) of Jan. 1, 2013, will be Julian Date (JD) 2,456,294; that many days will have passed since the start of the Julian period. The JD at noon of any date in 2013 may be found by adding to that number the day of the year for that date and subtracting one. The day of the year can be obtained from the left half of the "How Far Apart Are Two Dates?" chart on the next page.

Julian Calendar

To find which of the 14 calendars of the Perpetual Calendar (pages 382-83) applies to any year under the Julian system, find the century for the desired year in the 3 leftmost columns below. Locate the desired year from among the 4 top rows. Then read down. The number at the intersection of that row and column is the calendar designation for that year. For some years and countries, the Julian new year did not start Jan. 1; to find the correct Perpetual Calendar for Britain and its possessions, you can generally add one year for dates from Jan. 1to Mar. 24. For example, to look up Feb. 2, 1705, Old Style, use the year 1706.

Year (last 2 digits of desired year)

Century	01	02	03	04	05	06	07	08	09	10	11	12	13	14	15	16	17	18	19	20	21	22	23	24	25	26	27	28
	29	30	31	32	33	34	35	36	37	38	39	40	41	42	43	44	45	46	47	48	49	50	51	52	53	54	55	56
	57	58	59	60	61	62	63	64	65	66	67	68	69	70	71	72	73	74	75	76	77	78	79	80	81	82	83	84
	00	85	86	87	88	89	90	91	92	93	94	95	96	97	98	99												
0 700 1400	12	7	1	2	10	5	6	7	8	3	4	5	13	1	2	3	11	6	7	1	9	4	5	6	14	2	3	4 12
100 800 1500	11	6	7	1	9	4	5	6	14	2	3	4	12	7	1	2	10	5	6	7	8	3	4	5	13	1	2	3 11
200 900 1600	10	5	6	7	8	3	4	5	13	1	2	3	11	6	7	1	9	4	5	6	14	2	3	4	12	7	1	2 10
300 1000 1700	9	4	5	6	14	2	3	4	12	7	1	2	10	5	6	7	8	3	4	5	13	1	2	3	11	6	7	1 9
400 1100 1800	8	3	4	5	13	1	2	3	11	6	7	1	9	4	5	6	14	2	3	4	12	7	1	2	10	5	6	7 8
500 1200 1900	14	2	3	4	12	7	1	2	10	5	6	7	8	3	4	5	13	1	2	3	11	6	7	1	9	4	5	6 14
600 1300 2000	13	1	2	3	11	6	7	1	9	4	5	6	14	2	3	4	12	7	1	2	10	5	6	7	8	3	4	5 13

How Far Apart Are Two Dates?

This table covers a range of two years. To use, find the numbers listed in the tables for each date and subtract the smaller number from the larger. For example, to find the number of days between Mar. 15, 2013, and Sept. 22, 2014, subtract 74 from 630; the result is 556. For leap years, such as 2012, where Feb. 29 intervenes, one day must be added to the result; thus Feb. 4, 2012, and Mar. 13, 2013, were 403 days apart.

First year

Date	Jan.	Feb.	Mar.	Apr.	May	June	July	Aug.	Sept.	Oct.	Nov.	Dec.
1	1	32	60	91	121	152	182	213	244	274	305	335
2	2	33	61	92	122	153	183	214	245	275	306	336
3	3	34	62	93	123	154	184	215	246	276	307	337
4	4	35	63	94	124	155	185	216	247	277	308	338
5	5	36	64	95	125	156	186	217	248	278	309	339
6	6	37	65	96	126	157	187	218	249	279	310	340
7	7	38	66	97	127	158	188	219	250	280	311	341
8	8	39	67	98	128	159	189	220	251	281	312	342
9	9	40	68	99	129	160	190	221	252	282	313	343
10	10	41	69	100	130	161	191	222	253	283	314	344
11	11	42	70	101	131	162	192	223	254	284	315	345
12	12	43	71	102	132	163	193	224	255	285	316	346
13	13	44	72	103	133	164	194	225	256	286	317	347
14	14	45	73	104	134	165	195	226	257	287	318	348
15	15	46	74	105	135	166	196	227	258	288	319	349
16	16	47	75	106	136	167	197	228	259	289	320	350
17	17	48	76	107	137	168	198	229	260	290	321	351
18	18	49	77	108	138	169	199	230	261	291	322	352
19	19	50	78	109	139	170	200	231	262	292	323	353
20	20	51	79	110	140	171	201	232	263	293	324	354
21	21	52	80	111	141	172	202	233	264	294	325	355
22	22	53	81	112	142	173	203	234	265	295	326	356
23	23	54	82	113	143	174	204	235	266	296	327	357
24	24	55	83	114	144	175	205	236	267	297	328	358
25	25	56	84	115	145	176	206	237	268	298	329	359
26	26	57	85	116	146	177	207	238	269	299	330	360
27	27	58	86	117	147	178	208	239	270	300	331	361
28	28	59	87	118	148	179	209	240	271	301	332	362
29	29	—	88	119	149	180	210	241	272	302	333	363
30	30	—	89	120	150	181	211	242	273	303	334	364
31	31	—	90	—	151	—	212	243	—	304	—	365

Second year

Date	Jan.	Feb.	Mar.	Apr.	May	June	July	Aug.	Sept.	Oct.	Nov.	Dec.
1	366	397	425	456	486	517	547	578	609	639	670	700
2	367	398	426	457	487	518	548	579	610	640	671	701
3	368	399	427	458	488	519	549	580	611	641	672	702
4	369	400	428	459	489	520	550	581	612	642	673	703
5	370	401	429	460	490	521	551	582	613	643	674	704
6	371	402	430	461	491	522	552	583	614	644	675	705
7	372	403	431	462	492	523	553	584	615	645	676	706
8	373	404	432	463	493	524	554	585	616	646	677	707
9	374	405	433	464	494	525	555	586	617	647	678	708
10	375	406	434	465	495	526	556	587	618	648	679	709
11	376	407	435	466	496	527	557	588	619	649	680	710
12	377	408	436	467	497	528	558	589	620	650	681	711
13	378	409	437	468	498	529	559	590	621	651	682	712
14	379	410	438	469	499	530	560	591	622	652	683	713
15	380	411	439	470	500	531	561	592	623	653	684	714
16	381	412	440	471	501	532	562	593	624	654	685	715
17	382	413	441	472	502	533	563	594	625	655	686	716
18	383	414	442	473	503	534	564	595	626	656	687	717
19	384	415	443	474	504	535	565	596	627	657	688	718
20	385	416	444	475	505	536	566	597	628	658	689	719
21	386	417	445	476	506	537	567	598	629	659	690	720
22	387	418	446	477	507	538	568	599	630	660	691	721
23	388	419	447	478	508	539	569	600	631	661	692	722
24	389	420	448	479	509	540	570	601	632	662	693	723
25	390	421	449	480	510	541	571	602	633	663	694	724
26	391	422	450	481	511	542	572	603	634	664	695	725
27	392	423	451	482	512	543	573	604	635	665	696	726
28	393	424	452	483	513	544	574	605	636	666	697	727
29	394	—	453	484	514	545	575	606	637	667	698	728
30	395	—	454	485	515	546	576	607	638	668	699	729
31	396	—	455	—	516	—	577	608	—	669	—	730

Signs of the Zodiac

The zodiac is the apparent yearly path of the sun among the stars as viewed from Earth and was divided by the ancients into 12 equal sections or signs, each named for the constellation situated within its limits in ancient times. Astrologers claim that the temperament and destiny of each individual depend on the zodiac sign under which the person was born and the relationships between the planets at that time and throughout the person's life.

Below are the 12 traditional signs and the traditional range of dates pertaining to each:

♈ **Aries** (Ram), March 21-April 19

♉ **Taurus** (Bull), April 20-May 20

♊ **Gemini** (Twins), May 21-June 21

♋ **Cancer** (Crab), June 22-July 22

♌ **Leo** (Lion), July 23-August 22

♍ **Virgo** (Virgin), August 23-September 22

♎ **Libra** (Scales), September 23-October 23

♏ **Scorpio** (Scorpion), October 24-November 21

♐ **Sagittarius** (Archer), November 22-December 21

♑ **Capricorn** (Goat), December 22-January 19

♒ **Aquarius** (Water Bearer), January 20-February 18

♓ **Pisces** (Fishes), February 19-March 20

Calendar for the Year 2013

January

S	M	T	W	T	F	S
		1	2	3	4	5
6	7	8	9	10	11	12
13	14	15	16	17	18	19
20	21	22	23	24	25	26
27	28	29	30	31		

February

S	M	T	W	T	F	S
					1	2
3	4	5	6	7	8	9
10	11	12	13	14	15	16
17	18	19	20	21	22	23
24	25	26	27	28		

March

S	M	T	W	T	F	S
					1	2
3	4	5	6	7	8	9
10	11	12	13	14	15	16
17	18	19	20	21	22	23
24	25	26	27	28	29	30
31						

April

S	M	T	W	T	F	S
	1	2	3	4	5	6
7	8	9	10	11	12	13
14	15	16	17	18	19	20
21	22	23	24	25	26	27
28	29	30				

May

S	M	T	W	T	F	S
			1	2	3	4
5	6	7	8	9	10	11
12	13	14	15	16	17	18
19	20	21	22	23	24	25
26	27	28	29	30	31	

June

S	M	T	W	T	F	S
						1
2	3	4	5	6	7	8
9	10	11	12	13	14	15
16	17	18	19	20	21	22
23	24	25	26	27	28	29
30						

July

S	M	T	W	T	F	S
	1	2	3	4	5	6
7	8	9	10	11	12	13
14	15	16	17	18	19	20
21	22	23	24	25	26	27
28	29	30	31			

August

S	M	T	W	T	F	S
				1	2	3
4	5	6	7	8	9	10
11	12	13	14	15	16	17
18	19	20	21	22	23	24
25	26	27	28	29	30	31

September

S	M	T	W	T	F	S
1	2	3	4	5	6	7
8	9	10	11	12	13	14
15	16	17	18	19	20	21
22	23	24	25	26	27	28
29	30					

October

S	M	T	W	T	F	S
		1	2	3	4	5
6	7	8	9	10	11	12
13	14	15	16	17	18	19
20	21	22	23	24	25	26
27	28	29	30	31		

November

S	M	T	W	T	F	S
					1	2
3	4	5	6	7	8	9
10	11	12	13	14	15	16
17	18	19	20	21	22	23
24	25	26	27	28	29	30

December

S	M	T	W	T	F	S
1	2	3	4	5	6	7
8	9	10	11	12	13	14
15	16	17	18	19	20	21
22	23	24	25	26	27	28
29	30	31				

Federal Holidays and Other Notable Dates, 2013

Some dates may be subject to change.

The dates in **bold** on the calendar above and shown below in *italics* are U.S. federal holidays, designated by the president or Congress and applicable to federal employees and in the District of Columbia. Most U.S. states also observe these holidays, and many states observe others; practices vary from state to state. In most states the secretary of state's office can provide details.

January
1 *New Year's Day;* Rose Bowl; Orange Bowl
2 Sugar Bowl
3 Fiesta Bowl
7 BCS Football Championship Game (Miami, FL)
14-27 Australian Open tennis tournament
21 *Martin Luther King Jr. Day*
26 Australia Day
27 NFL Pro Bowl (Honolulu, HI)
28 Australia Day (observed)

February
2 Groundhog Day
3 Super Bowl XLVII (New Orleans, LA)
9-12 Carnival, Brazil
11-12 Westminster Dog Show
12 Lincoln's Birthday; Mardi Gras
13 Ash Wednesday
14 Valentine's Day
17 NBA All-Star Game (Houston, TX)
18 *Washington's Birthday* (observed), Presidents' Day, or
   Washington-Lincoln Day (3rd Mon. in Feb.)
24 Daytona 500; Academy Awards;
   Purim (Feast of Lots) begins previous night

March
2 Iditarod Trail Sled Dog Race begins
10 Daylight-saving time begins in U.S.
17 St. Patrick's Day
20 First day of spring (Northern Hemisphere)
21 Benito Juárez's Birthday, Mexico
26 Passover, 1st full day
29 Good Friday
31 Easter

April
1 April Fools' Day
6, 8 NCAA men's basketball Final Four (Atlanta, GA)
7, 9 NCAA women's basketball Final Four (New Orleans, LA)
8-14 Masters golf tournament
15 Patriots' Day; Boston Marathon (3rd Mon. in Apr.);
   Tax Day (IRS filing deadline)
22 Earth Day
25 Take Our Daughters and Sons to Work Day
26 Arbor Day, U.S.

May
1 May Day
4 Kentucky Derby
5 Easter (Orthodox);
   Cinco de Mayo (Battle of Puebla Day), Mexico
12 Mother's Day
17 Buddha's Birthday, Korea, Hong Kong
18 Armed Forces Day; Preakness Stakes
20 Victoria Day, Canada
26-June 9 French Open tennis tournament
27 *Memorial Day,* or Decoration Day (last Mon. in May)

June
8 Belmont Stakes
12 Dragon Boat Festival, China
13-16 U.S. Open golf tournament (Ardmore, PA)
14 Flag Day
16 Father's Day
21 First day of summer (Northern Hemisphere)
24-July 7 Wimbledon tennis tournament

July
1 Canada Day, Canada
4 *Independence Day*
7-14 Running of the Bulls (Pamplona, Spain)
9 Ramadan (Islamic month of fasting), 1st full day
14 Bastille Day, France
18-24 British Open golf tournament

August
8-11 PGA Championship (Rochester, NY)

September
2 *Labor Day,* U.S., Canada (1st Mon. in Sept.)
5 Rosh Hashanah (New Year), 1st full day
8 Grandparents' Day, U.S.
14 Yom Kippur (Day of Atonement) begins previous night
16 Independence Day, Mexico
17 Constitution Day and Citizenship Day, U.S.
22 First day of autumn (Northern Hemisphere)

October
3 German Unity Day, Germany
7 U.S. Supreme Court session begins
12 Día de la Raza, Spain, Mexico
14 *Columbus Day* (2nd Mon. in Oct.); Thanksgiving Day, Canada
31 Halloween

November
1 All Saints' Day
3 New York City Marathon; daylight-saving time ends in U.S.
4 Islamic New Year (Muharram 1) begins previous night
5 Guy Fawkes Day, UK;
   Election Day (1st Tues. after 1st Mon. in Nov.)
10 Remembrance Sunday, UK
11 *Veterans Day*; Remembrance Day, Canada
28 *Thanksgiving Day* (4th Thurs. in Nov.)
28-Dec. 5 Hanukkah (Festival of Lights) begins previous night

December
10 Nobel Prizes awarded (winners announced in Oct.)
12 Día de la Virgen de Guadalupe, Mexico
21 First day of winter (Northern Hemisphere)
25 *Christmas Day*
26 Boxing Day, Australia, Canada, New Zealand, UK
26-Jan. 1 Kwanzaa

Chinese Calendar and Asian Festivals

The Chinese calendar, like the Jewish and Islamic calendars (see the Religion chapter), is a lunar calendar. It is divided into 12 months of 29 or 30 days (compensating for the lunar month's mean duration of 29 days, 12 hr., 44.05 min.). This calendar is synchronized with the solar year by the addition of extra months at fixed intervals.

The Chinese calendar runs on a 60-year cycle. The cycles 1876-1935 and 1936-95, with the years grouped under their 12 animal designations, are printed below, along with the first 24 years of the current cycle. This cycle began in 1996 and will last until 2055. Feb. 10, 2013, marks the beginning of the year 4711 in the Chinese calendar and is designated the Year of the Snake. Readers can find the animal name for the year of their birth in the chart below. (Note: The first 3-7 weeks of each Western year belong to the previous Chinese year.)

Both the Western (Gregorian) and traditional lunar calendars are used publicly in China and in North and South Korea, and two New Year's celebrations are held. In Taiwan, overseas Chinese communities, and Vietnam, the lunar calendar is used only to set the dates for traditional festivals, with the Gregorian system in general use.

The 4-day Chinese New Year, the 3-day Vietnamese New Year festival, Tet, and the 3-to-4-day Korean festival, Suhl, begin at the second new moon after the winter solstice. The new moon in East Asia, which is west of the International Date Line, may be a day later than the new moon in the U.S. The festivals may start, therefore, anywhere between Jan. 21 and Feb. 19 of the Gregorian calendar.

Rat	Ox	Tiger	Hare (Rabbit)	Dragon	Snake	Horse	Sheep (Goat)	Monkey	Rooster	Dog	Pig (Boar)
1876	1877	1878	1879	1880	1881	1882	1883	1884	1885	1886	1887
1888	1889	1890	1891	1892	1893	1894	1895	1896	1897	1898	1899
1900	1901	1902	1903	1904	1905	1906	1907	1908	1909	1910	1911
1912	1913	1914	1915	1916	1917	1918	1919	1920	1921	1922	1923
1924	1925	1926	1927	1928	1929	1930	1931	1932	1933	1934	1935
1936	1937	1938	1939	1940	1941	1942	1943	1944	1945	1946	1947
1948	1949	1950	1951	1952	1953	1954	1955	1956	1957	1958	1959
1960	1961	1962	1963	1964	1965	1966	1967	1968	1969	1970	1971
1972	1973	1974	1975	1976	1977	1978	1979	1980	1981	1982	1983
1984	1985	1986	1987	1988	1989	1990	1991	1992	1993	1994	1995
1996	1997	1998	1999	2000	2001	2002	2003	2004	2005	2006	2007
2008	2009	2010	2011	2012	2013	2014	2015	2016	2017	2018	2019

Other Calendars: Year and New Year's Day, 2013

Era	Year	Begins in 2013	Era	Year	Begins in 2013
Byzantine	7522	Sept. 14	Islamic/Muslim (Hijra)	1435	Nov. 4[1]
Chinese (Year of the Snake)	4711	Feb. 10	Japanese (starts at 0 with new emperor)	25	Jan. 1
Diocletian	1730	Sept. 11	Jewish	5774	Sept. 25[1]
Grecian (Seleucidae)	2325	Sept. 14 or Oct. 14	Nabonassar (Babylonian)	2762	Apr. 23
Indian (Saka)	1935	Mar. 22	Roman (Ab Urbe Condita)	2766	Jan. 14

(1) Year begins the previous night.

Chronological Cycles, 2013

Dominical Letter	F	Roman Indiction	6	Solar Cycle	6
Golden Number (Lunar Cycle)	19	Epact	17	Julian Period (year of)	6726

Special Months

There are many thousands of special months, days, and weeks because of anniversaries, official proclamations, and promotional events, both trivial and serious. Here are a few of the special months:

January: Jump Out of Bed Month, National Mentoring Month, National Poverty in America Awareness Month

February: Black History Month, American Heart Month, Library Lovers Month, Youth Leadership Month, Return Shopping Carts to the Supermarket Month

March: Irish-American Heritage Month, Women's History Month, American Red Cross Month, National Frozen Food Month, National Talk With Your Teen About Sex Month

April: National Child Abuse Prevention Month, National Humor Month, Stress Awareness Month, Grange Month

May: Clean Air Month, Get Caught Reading Month, National Barbecue Month, Asian Pacific American Heritage Month, National Inventors Month, National Mental Health Month

June: National Candy Month; Lesbian, Gay, Bisexual, and Transgender Pride Month; Potty Training Awareness Month; National Safety Month

July: Cell Phone Courtesy Month, National Hot Dog Month, Women's Motorcycle Month

August: Black Business Month, Happiness Happens Month, National Immunization Awareness Month, National Toddler Month

September: Library Card Sign-Up Month, National Hispanic Heritage Month (Sept. 15-Oct. 15), National Biscuit Month

October: National Domestic Violence Awareness Month, National Breast Cancer Awareness Month, Diversity Awareness Month, National Popcorn Poppin' Month

November: National AIDS Awareness Month, National American Indian Heritage Month, National Adoption Month, American Diabetes Month, National Peanut Butter Lovers' Month

December: Universal Human Rights Month, National Drunk and Drugged Driving Prevention Month, National Tie Month, National Colorectal Cancer Education and Awareness Month

Wedding Anniversary Gifts

The traditional names for wedding anniversaries go back many years in social usage and have been used to suggest types of appropriate anniversary gifts. Traditional products for gifts are listed here in capital letters, with allowable revisions in parentheses, followed by common modern gifts in each category.

1st	PAPER, clocks	**9th**	POTTERY (CHINA), leather goods	**25th**	SILVER, sterling silver
2nd	COTTON, china	**10th**	TIN, ALUMINUM, diamond	**30th**	PEARL, diamond
3rd	LEATHER, crystal, glass	**11th**	STEEL, fashion jewelry	**35th**	CORAL (JADE), jade
4th	LINEN (SILK), appliances	**12th**	SILK, pearls, colored gems	**40th**	RUBY, ruby
5th	WOOD, silverware	**13th**	LACE, textiles, furs	**45th**	SAPPHIRE, sapphire
6th	IRON, wood objects	**14th**	IVORY, gold jewelry	**50th**	GOLD, gold
7th	WOOL (COPPER), desk sets	**15th**	CRYSTAL, watches	**55th**	EMERALD, emerald
8th	BRONZE, linens, lace	**20th**	CHINA, platinum	**60th**	DIAMOND, diamond

Birthstones

Source: Jewelry Industry Council

Birth month	Ancient birthstone	Modern birthstone	Birth month	Ancient birthstone	Modern birthstone
January	Garnet	Garnet	July	Onyx	Ruby
February	Amethyst	Amethyst	August	Carnelian	Sardonyx or Peridot
March	Jasper	Bloodstone or Aquamarine	September	Chrysolite	Sapphire
April	Sapphire	Diamond	October	Aquamarine	Opal or Tourmaline
May	Agate	Emerald	November	Topaz	Topaz
June	Emerald	Pearl, Moonstone, or Alexandrite	December	Ruby	Turquoise or Zircon

Standard Time and Daylight Saving Time

Source: National Institute of Standards and Technology, U.S. Dept. of Commerce

See also Time Zone map, page 468.

Standard Time

Standard Time is reckoned from the prime meridian of longitude in Greenwich, England. The world is divided into 24 zones, each 15 deg of arc, or one hour in time apart. The Greenwich meridian (0 deg) extends through the center of the initial zone. Zones to the east are numbered from 1 to 12, with the prefix "minus" indicating the number of hours to be subtracted to obtain Greenwich Time. Each zone extends 7.5 deg on either side of its central meridian.

Westward zones are similarly numbered, but prefixed "plus," showing the number of hours that must be added to get Greenwich Time. Although these zones apply generally to sea areas, the standard time maintained in many countries does not coincide with zone time.

The U.S. and possessions are divided into nine standard time zones. Each zone is approximately 15 deg of longitude in width. All places in each zone use, instead of their own local time, the time counted from the transit of the "mean sun" across the standard time meridian that passes near the middle of that zone. These time zones are designated as Atlantic, Eastern, Central, Mountain, Pacific, Alaska, Hawaii-Aleutian, Samoa, and Chamorro (Guam and Northern Mariana Isls.); the time in these zones is reckoned from the 60th, 75th, 90th, 105th, 120th, 135th, 150th, and 165th meridians west of Greenwich and the 150th meridian east of Greenwich. The time zone line wanders to conform to local geographical regions. The time in the various zones in the U.S. and U.S. territories west of Greenwich is earlier than Greenwich Time by 4, 5, 6, 7, 8, 9, 10, and 11 hours, respectively. However, Chamorro crosses the International Date Line and is 10 hours later than Greenwich Time.

24-Hour Time

Twenty-four-hour time is widely used in scientific work throughout the world. In the U.S., it is also used in operations of the armed forces. In Europe, it is frequently used by the transportation networks in preference to the 12-hour AM and PM system. With the 24-hour system, the day begins at midnight, and times are designated 00:00 through 23:59.

International Date Line

The Date Line, approximately coinciding with the 180th meridian, separates the calendar dates. The date must be advanced one day when crossing in a westerly direction and set back one day when crossing in an easterly direction. The Date Line frequently deviates from the 180th meridian because of decisions made by individual nations affected. The line is deflected eastward through the Bering Strait and westward of the Aleutians to prevent separating these areas by date. The line is deflected eastward of the Tonga and New Zealand Islands in the South Pacific for the same reason. In 1995, Kiribati announced that all of its islands east of the Date Line would observe the same date as islands to the west, though most maps and atlases do not depict this as a deviation in the Date Line. The line is established by international custom; there is no international authority prescribing its exact course.

Daylight Saving Time

Daylight-saving time is achieved by advancing the clock one hour. Since 2007, daylight-saving time has begun at 2 AM on the 2nd Sunday in Mar. and has ended at 2 AM on the first Sunday in Nov. **In 2013, daylight-saving time begins at 2 AM on Mar. 10 and ends at 2 AM on Nov. 3.** Prior to 2007, daylight-saving time traditionally ran from the first Sunday in Apr. to the last Sunday in Oct.

Daylight-saving time was first observed in the U.S. during World War I, and then again during World War II. In the intervening years, some states and communities observed daylight-saving time, using whatever beginning and ending dates they chose. In 1966, Congress passed the Uniform Time Act, which provided that any state or territory choosing to observe daylight-saving time must begin and end on the federal dates. Any state could, by law, exempt itself; a 1972 amendment to the act authorized states in more than one time zone to exempt the entire state or one time zone only. Currently, most of Arizona, Hawaii, Puerto Rico, the U.S. Virgin Islands, Guam, and American Samoa do not observe daylight-saving time. On Apr. 2, 2006, all of Indiana observed daylight-saving time for the first time. (The state is divided between two time zones.)

Congress and the secretary of transportation both have authority to change time zone boundaries, which they have done on a number of occasions since 1966. In addition, efforts to conserve energy have prompted various changes in the times that daylight-saving time is observed.

Daylight Saving Time: International Usage

Adjusting clock time so as to gain the added daylight on summer evenings is common throughout the world.

Canada, which extends over 6 time zones, generally observes daylight-saving time during the same period as the U.S. Most provincial governments observe the 4-week extension to daylight-saving time that went into effect in 2007. Most of Saskatchewan remains on standard time year-round. Communities elsewhere in Canada also may exempt themselves from daylight-saving time. Except for the state of Sonora, which shares a border with Arizona, most of Mexico observes daylight-saving time.

Member nations of the European Union (EU) observe a "summer-time period," a version of daylight-saving time, from the last Sunday of Mar. until the last Sunday in Oct.

Russia, which extends geographically over 11 time zones and uses 9, historically has maintained its standard time 1 hour ahead of its zone designation. Additionally, Russian observation of daylight-saving time ended in 2011. Though an hour of time was added in Mar. 2011, clocks were not set back an hour in the fall, meaning that standard time in most of Russia is effectively 2 hours ahead of the zone designation.

China, which extends across 5 time zones, has decreed that the entire country be placed on Greenwich time plus 8 hours. Daylight-saving time is not observed. Japan, which lies within one time zone, also does not modify its legal time during the summer months.

Many countries in the Southern Hemisphere maintain daylight-saving time generally from Oct. to Mar. However, most countries near the equator do not deviate from standard time.

Standard Time Differences: World Cities

The time indicated in the table is fixed by law and is called the legal time or, more generally, standard time. Use of daylight-saving time varies widely. An asterisk (*) indicates morning of the following day. At 12:00 noon, Eastern Standard Time, the standard time (in 24-hour time) in selected cities is as follows:

City	Time		City	Time		City	Time	
Addis Ababa	20	00	Hong Kong	1	00*	Paris	18	00
Amsterdam	18	00	Islamabad	22	00	Prague	18	00
Ankara	19	00	Istanbul	19	00	Quito	12	00
Athens	19	00	Jakarta	0	00*	Rio de Janeiro	14	00
Auckland	5	00*	Jerusalem	19	00	Riyadh	20	00
Baghdad	20	00	Johannesburg	19	00	Rome	18	00
Bangkok	0	00*	Kabul	21	50	St. Petersburg	20	00
Beijing	1	00*	Karachi	22	00	Santiago	13	00
Belfast	17	00	Kathmandu	22	45	São Paulo	14	00
Belgrade	18	00	Kiev	19	00	Sarajevo	18	00
Berlin	18	00	Kolkata (Calcutta)	22	30	Seoul	2	00*
Bogotá	12	00	Lagos	18	00	Shanghai	1	00*
Brussels	18	00	Lima	12	00	Singapore	1	00*
Bucharest	19	00	Lisbon	17	00	Stockholm	18	00
Budapest	18	00	London	17	00	Sydney	3	00*
Buenos Aires	14	00	Madrid	18	00	Taipei	1	00*
Cairo	19	00	Manila	1	00*	Tashkent	22	00
Cape Town	19	00	Mecca	20	00	Tehran	20	30
Caracas	13	00	Melbourne	3	00*	Tel Aviv	19	00
Casablanca	17	00	Montevideo	14	00	Tokyo	2	00*
Copenhagen	18	00	Moscow	20	00	Vienna	18	00
Dhaka	23	00	Mumbai (Bombay)	22	30	Vladivostok	3	00*
Dublin	17	00	Munich	18	00	Warsaw	18	00
Edinburgh	17	00	Nagasaki	2	00*	Wellington	5	00*
Geneva	18	00	Nairobi	20	00	Yangon (Rangoon)	23	30
Helsinki	19	00	New Delhi	22	30	Yokohama	2	00*
Ho Chi Minh City	0	00*	Oslo	18	00	Zurich	18	00

Standard Time Differences: North American Cities

At 12:00 noon, Eastern Standard Time, the standard time in selected North American cities is as follows:

City	Time			City	Time			City	Time		
Akron, OH	12	00	Noon	Fort Wayne, IN[1]	12	00	Noon	Ottawa, ON	12	00	Noon
Albuquerque, NM	10	00	AM	Frankfort, KY	12	00	Noon	*Panama City, Panama	12	00	Noon
Anchorage, AK	8	00	AM	Havana, Cuba	12	00	Noon	Peoria, IL	11	00	AM
Atlanta, GA	12	00	Noon	Helena, MT	10	00	AM	*Phoenix, AZ	10	00	AM
Austin, TX	11	00	AM	*Honolulu, HI	7	00	AM	Pierre, SD	11	00	AM
Baltimore, MD	12	00	Noon	Houston, TX	11	00	AM	Pittsburgh, PA	12	00	Noon
Birmingham, AL	11	00	AM	Indianapolis, IN[1]	12	00	Noon	*Regina, SK	11	00	AM
Bismarck, ND	11	00	AM	Jackson, MS	11	00	AM	Reno, NV	9	00	AM
Boise, ID	10	00	AM	Jacksonville, FL	12	00	Noon	Richmond, VA	12	00	Noon
Boston, MA	12	00	Noon	Juneau, AK	8	00	AM	Rochester, NY	12	00	Noon
Buffalo, NY	12	00	Noon	Kansas City, MO	11	00	AM	Sacramento, CA	9	00	AM
Butte, MT	10	00	AM	*Kingston, Jamaica	12	00	Noon	St. John's, NL	1	30	PM
Calgary, AB	10	00	AM	Knoxville, TN	12	00	Noon	St. Louis, MO	11	00	AM
Charleston, SC	12	00	Noon	Las Vegas, NV	9	00	AM	St. Paul, MN	11	00	AM
Charleston, WV	12	00	Noon	Lexington, KY	12	00	Noon	Salt Lake City, UT	10	00	AM
Charlotte, NC	12	00	Noon	Lincoln, NE	11	00	AM	San Antonio, TX	11	00	AM
Charlottetown, PE	1	00	PM	Little Rock, AR	11	00	AM	San Diego, CA	9	00	AM
Chattanooga, TN	12	00	Noon	Los Angeles, CA	9	00	AM	San Francisco, CA	9	00	AM
Cheyenne, WY	10	00	AM	Louisville, KY	12	00	Noon	San Jose, CA	9	00	AM
Chicago, IL	11	00	AM	Madison, WI	11	00	AM	*San Juan, PR	1	00	PM
Cincinnati, OH	12	00	Noon	Mexico City, Mexico	11	00	AM	Santa Fe, NM	10	00	AM
Cleveland, OH	12	00	Noon	Memphis, TN	11	00	AM	Savannah, GA	12	00	Noon
Colorado Spr., CO	10	00	AM	Miami, FL	12	00	Noon	Seattle, WA	9	00	AM
Columbus, OH	12	00	Noon	Milwaukee, WI	11	00	AM	Shreveport, LA	11	00	AM
Dallas, TX	11	00	AM	Minneapolis, MN	11	00	AM	Sioux Falls, SD	11	00	AM
*Dawson, YT	9	00	AM	Mobile, AL	11	00	AM	Spokane, WA	9	00	AM
Dayton, OH	12	00	Noon	Montréal, QC	12	00	Noon	Tampa, FL	12	00	Noon
Denver, CO	10	00	AM	Nashville, TN	11	00	AM	Toledo, OH	12	00	Noon
Des Moines, IA	11	00	AM	Nassau, Bahamas	12	00	Noon	Topeka, KS	11	00	AM
Detroit, MI	12	00	Noon	New Haven, CT	12	00	Noon	Toronto, ON	12	00	Noon
Duluth, MN	11	00	AM	New Orleans, LA	11	00	AM	*Tucson, AZ	10	00	AM
Edmonton, AB	10	00	AM	New York, NY	12	00	Noon	Tulsa, OK	11	00	AM
El Paso, TX	10	00	AM	Nome, AK	8	00	AM	Vancouver, BC	9	00	AM
Erie, PA	12	00	Noon	Norfolk, VA	12	00	Noon	Washington, DC	12	00	Noon
Evansville, IN[1]	11	00	AM	Oklahoma City, OK	11	00	AM	Wichita, KS	11	00	AM
Fairbanks, AK	8	00	AM	Omaha, NE	11	00	AM	Wilmington, DE	12	00	Noon
Flint, MI	12	00	Noon	Orlando, FL	12	00	Noon	Winnipeg, MB	11	00	AM

Note: This same table can be used for daylight-saving time when it is in effect, but allowance must be made for cities that do not observe it; they are marked with an asterisk (*). Daylight-saving time is one hour later than standard time. (1) While most of Indiana is in the Eastern Time Zone, 12 counties in the southwestern and northwestern parts of the state observe Central Time.

Perpetual Calendar

The number shown for each year indicates which Gregorian calendar to use. For 1583-1802, see "Gregorian Calendar" on page 376. For 1803-20, use numbers for 1983-2000, respectively. The years in the calendar labels are the last and next occurrences of each calendar.

Year	No.	Year	No.	Year	No.	Year	No.
1821	2	1847	6	1873	4	1899	1
1822	3	1848	14	1874	5	1900	2
1823	4	1849	2	1875	6	1901	3
1824	12	1850	3	1876	14	1902	4
1825	7	1851	4	1877	2	1903	5
1826	1	1852	12	1878	3	1904	13
1827	2	1853	7	1879	4	1905	1
1828	10	1854	1	1880	12	1906	2
1829	5	1855	2	1881	7	1907	3
1830	6	1856	10	1882	1	1908	11
1831	7	1857	5	1883	2	1909	6
1832	8	1858	6	1884	10	1910	7
1833	3	1859	7	1885	5	1911	1
1834	4	1860	8	1886	6	1912	9
1835	5	1861	3	1887	7	1913	4
1836	13	1862	4	1888	8	1914	5
1837	1	1863	5	1889	3	1915	6
1838	2	1864	13	1890	4	1916	14
1839	3	1865	1	1891	5	1917	2
1840	11	1866	2	1892	13	1918	3
1841	6	1867	3	1893	1	1919	4
1842	7	1868	11	1894	2	1920	12
1843	1	1869	6	1895	3	1921	7
1844	9	1870	7	1896	11	1922	1
1845	4	1871	1	1897	6	1923	2
1846	5	1872	9	1898	7	1924	10

Year	No.	Year	No.	Year	No.	Year	No.
1925	5	1951	2	1977	7	2003	4
1926	6	1952	10	1978	1	2004	12
1927	7	1953	5	1979	2	2005	7
1928	8	1954	6	1980	10	2006	1
1929	3	1955	7	1981	5	2007	2
1930	4	1956	8	1982	6	2008	10
1931	5	1957	3	1983	7	2009	5
1932	13	1958	4	1984	8	2010	6
1933	1	1959	5	1985	3	2011	7
1934	2	1960	13	1986	4	2012	8
1935	3	1961	1	1987	5	2013	3
1936	11	1962	2	1988	13	2014	4
1937	6	1963	3	1989	1	2015	5
1938	7	1964	11	1990	2	2016	13
1939	1	1965	6	1991	3	2017	1
1940	9	1966	7	1992	11	2018	2
1941	4	1967	1	1993	6	2019	3
1942	5	1968	9	1994	7	2020	11
1943	6	1969	4	1995	1	2021	6
1944	14	1970	5	1996	9	2022	7
1945	2	1971	6	1997	4	2023	1
1946	3	1972	14	1998	5	2024	9
1947	4	1973	2	1999	6	2025	4
1948	12	1974	3	2000	14	2026	5
1949	7	1975	4	2001	2	2027	6
1950	1	1976	12	2002	3	2028	14

Year	No.	Year	No.
2029	2	2055	6
2030	3	2056	14
2031	4	2057	2
2032	12	2058	3
2033	7	2059	4
2034	1	2060	12
2035	2	2061	7
2036	10	2062	1
2037	5	2063	2
2038	6	2064	10
2039	7	2065	5
2040	8	2066	6
2041	3	2067	7
2042	4	2068	8
2043	5	2069	3
2044	13	2070	4
2045	1	2071	5
2046	2	2072	13
2047	3	2073	1
2048	11	2074	2
2049	6	2075	3
2050	7	2076	11
2051	1	2077	6
2052	9	2078	7
2053	4	2079	1
2054	5	2080	9

The page also contains six reference calendar blocks, each labeled with its last/next occurrence years and its calendar number. Each block shows all twelve months (January–December) with columns S M T W T F S.

- **1** — 2006/2017
- **2** — 2007/2018
- **3** — 2013/2019
- **4** — 2003/2014
- **5** — 2009/2015
- **6** — 2010/2021

7 — 2011/2022

8 — 2012/2040

9 — 1996/2024

10 — 2008/2036

11 — 1992/2020

12 — 2004/2032

13 — 1988/2016

14 — 2000/2028

Each block contains twelve monthly calendars: JANUARY, FEBRUARY, MARCH, APRIL, MAY, JUNE, JULY, AUGUST, SEPTEMBER, OCTOBER, NOVEMBER, DECEMBER, with day-of-week columns S M T W T F S.

WEIGHTS AND MEASURES

Source: National Institute of Standards and Technology (NIST), U.S. Dept. of Commerce

International System of Units (SI)

Two systems of weights and measures coexist in the U.S. today: the **U.S. Customary System** and the **International System of Units** (SI, for Système International). SI is a more complete, coherent version of the **metric system**. Throughout U.S. history, the Customary System—parts of which were inherited but are now different from the British Imperial System—has been generally used. Federal and state legislation gave it, through implication, standing as the primary weights and measures system. The metric system, however, is the only system that Congress has ever specifically sanctioned, dating back to an 1866 law. Along with 17 other nations, the U.S. signed the International Metric Convention (a.k.a. the Treaty of the Meter) May 20, 1875, establishing several intergovernmental organizations to oversee and refine SI. The U.S. is represented to these organizations by the Natl. Institute of Standards and Technology (NIST).

Since that time, use of the metric system in the U.S. has slowly increased, particularly in the scientific community, the pharmaceutical industry, and the manufacturing sector—the last motivated by the predominant use of the metric system in international commerce.

On Dec. 23, 1975, Pres. Gerald R. Ford signed the Metric Conversion Act of 1975. It defined the "metric system of measurement" as the SI, as established in 1960 by the General Conference on Weights and Measures and interpreted in the U.S. by the secretary of commerce, who delegated that authority to the director of the NIST. The Trade and Competitiveness Act of 1988 declared the metric system the preferred system of weights and measures for U.S. trade and commerce, but explicitly permitted "the continued use of traditional systems of weights and measures in nonbusiness activities." The Code of Federal Regulations made the use of metric units mandatory for federal agencies in 1991. However, the metric system has still not become the system of choice for most Americans' daily use.

The following are the seven base SI units: **length**—meter; **mass**—kilogram; **time**—second; **electric current**—ampere; **thermodynamic temperature**—kelvin; **amount of substance**—mole; and **luminous intensity**—candela.

Frequently Used Conversions

Boldface indicates exact values. For greater accuracy, use the "multiply by" number in parentheses. For weights, avoirdupois (avdp) weight is the system applied to all goods except medicines, precious metals, and precious stones.

U.S. Customary to Metric

	If you have:	Multiply by:		To get:
Length	inches	25.4		millimeters
	inches	2.54		centimeters
	inches	0.0254		meters
	feet	0.3	(**0.3048**)	meters
	yards	0.9	(**0.9144**)	meters
	miles[1]	1.6	(**1.609344**)	kilometers
Area	sq inches	6.5	(**6.4516**)	sq cm
	sq feet	0.09	(**0.09290304**)	sq meters
	sq yards	0.84	(**0.83612736**)	sq meters
	acres	0.4	(0.4046873)	hectares
	sq miles[1]	2.6	(2.58998811)	sq kilometers
Weight	ounces (avdp)	28	(28.34952)	grams
	pounds (avdp)	454	(**453.59237**)	grams
	pounds (avdp)	0.45	(**0.45359237**)	kilograms
	short tons[2]	0.91	(**0.90718474**)	metric tons
	long tons[3]	1	(1.016047)	metric tons
Liquid	ounces	0.03	(0.02957353)	liters
	cups	0.24	(0.23658824)	liters
	pints	0.47	(0.473176473)	liters
	quarts	0.95	(0.946352946)	liters
	gallons	3.79	(3.785412)	liters

Metric to U.S. Customary

	If you have:	Multiply by:		To get:
Length	millimeters	0.04	(0.03937)	inches
	centimeters	0.4	(0.3937)	inches
	meters	39	(39.37)	inches
	meters	3.3	(3.280840)	feet
	meters	1.1	(1.093613)	yards
	kilometers	0.6	(0.621371)	miles[1]
Area	sq cm	0.16	(0.15500)	sq inches
	sq meters	10.8	(10.76391)	sq feet
	sq meters	1.2	(1.195990)	sq yards
	hectares	2.5	(2.471044)	acres
	sq kilometers	0.39	(0.386102)	sq miles[1]
Weight	grams	0.035	(0.03527396)	ounces (avdp)
	grams	0.002	(0.00220462)	pounds (avdp)
	kilograms	2.2	(2.204623)	pounds (avdp)
	metric tons	1.1	(1.102311)	short tons[2]
	metric tons	0.98	(0.9842065)	long tons[3]
Liquid	liters	33.8	(33.81402)	ounces
	liters	4.2	(4.226752)	cups
	liters	2.1	(2.113376)	pints
	liters	1.1	(1.056688)	quarts
	liters	0.26	(0.264172)	gallons

(1) Survey mile. (2) A short ton is 2,000 pounds. (3) A long ton is 2,240 pounds.

Temperature Conversions

The left-hand column below gives a temperature according to the **Celsius** scale, and the right-hand gives the same temperature according to the **Fahrenheit** scale. The lowest number on each scale is equivalent to absolute zero, the temperature at which all motion within a molecule would stop.

For temperatures not shown: To convert Fahrenheit to Celsius, subtract 32 degrees and divide by 1.8; to convert Celsius to Fahrenheit, multiply by 1.8 and add 32 degrees.

Celsius	Fahrenheit	Celsius	Fahrenheit	Celsius	Fahrenheit	Celsius	Fahrenheit	Celsius	Fahrenheit
−273.15	−459.67	−45.6	−50	−1.1	30	30	86	65.6	150
−250	−418	**−40**	**−40**	0	32	32.2	90	70	158
−200	−328	−34.4	−30	4.4	40	35	95	80	176
−184.4	−300	−30	−22	10	50	**37**	**98.6**	90	194
−156.7	−250	−28.9	−20	15.6	60	37.8	100	93.3	200
−150	−238	−23.3	−10	**20**	**68**	40	104	**100**	**212**
−128.9	−200	−20	−4	21.1	70	43.3	110	121.1	250
−101.1	−150	−17.8	0	23.9	75	48.9	120	148.9	300
−100	−148	−12.2	10	25	77	50	122	150	302
−73.3	−100	−10	14	26.7	80	54.4	130	200	392
−50	−58	−6.7	20	29.4	85	60	140	300	572

Note: Although the term *centigrade* is still frequently used, the International Committee on Weights and Measures and the National Institute of Standards and Technology have recommended since 1948 that this scale be called *Celsius*.

Boiling and Freezing Points

Water boils at 212°F (100°C) at sea level. For every 550 feet above sea level, the boiling point of water is lower by about 1°F. Methyl alcohol boils at 148.5°F. Average human oral temperature is 98.6°F. **Water freezes** at 32°F (0°C).

Mathematical Formulas

The value of π (the Greek letter pi) is approximately 3.14159265 (equal to the ratio of the circumference of a circle to the diameter). The equivalence is typically rounded further to 3.1416 or 3.14.

Calculating Circumference

Circle: Multiply the diameter by π.

Calculating Area

Circle: Multiply the square of the radius (equal to ½ the diameter) by π.

Rectangle: Multiply the length of the base by the height.

Sphere (surface): Multiply the square of the radius by π and multiply by 4.

Square: Square the length of one side.

Trapezoid: Add the 2 parallel sides, multiply by the height, and divide by 2.

Triangle: Multiply the base by the height and divide by 2.

Calculating Volume

Cone: Multiply the square of the radius of the base by π, multiply by the height, and divide by 3.

Cube: Cube the length of one edge.

Cylinder: Multiply the square of the radius of the base by π and multiply by the height.

Pyramid: Multiply the area of the base by the height and divide by 3.

Rectangular prism: Multiply the length by the width by the height.

Sphere: Multiply the cube of the radius by π, multiply by 4, and divide by 3.

Playing Cards and Dice Chances

5-Card Poker Hands

Hand	Number possible	Odds against
Royal flush	4	649,739 to 1
Other straight flush	36	72,192 to 1
Four of a kind	624	4,164 to 1
Full house	3,744	693 to 1
Flush	5,108	508 to 1
Straight	10,200	254 to 1
Three of a kind	54,912	46 to 1
Two pairs	123,552	20 to 1
One pair	1,098,240	4 to 3 (1.37 to 1)
Nothing	1,302,540	1 to 1
Total	**2,598,960**	

Bridge

The odds—against suit distribution in a hand of 4-4-3-2 are about 4 to 1; against 5-4-2-2 about 8 to 1; against 6-4-2-1 about 20 to 1; against 7-4-1-1 about 254 to 1; against 8-4-1-0 about 2,211 to 1; and against 13-0-0-0 about 158,753,389,899 to 1.

Dice
(probabilities on 2 dice)

Total	Odds against (single toss)	Total	Odds against (single toss)
2	35 to 1	8	31 to 5
3	17 to 1	9	8 to 1
4	11 to 1	10	11 to 1
5	8 to 1	11	17 to 1
6	31 to 5	12	35 to 1
7	5 to 1		

Large Numbers

No. of zeros	U.S.	British[1], French, German	No. of zeros	U.S.	British[1], French, German
6	million	million	42	tredecillion	septillion
9	billion	milliard	45	quattuordecillion	1,000 septillion
12	trillion	billion	48	quindecillion	octillion
15	quadrillion	1,000 billion	51	sexdecillion	1,000 octillion
18	quintillion	trillion	54	septendecillion	nonillion
21	sextillion	1,000 trillion	57	octodecillion	1,000 nonillion
24	septillion	quadrillion	60	novemdecillion	decillion
27	octillion	1,000 quadrillion	63	vigintillion	1,000 decillion
30	nonillion	quintillion	100	googol	googol
33	decillion	1,000 quintillion	303	centillion	NA
36	undecillion	sextillion	600	NA	centillion
39	duodecillion	1,000 sextillion	googol	googolplex	googolplex

(1) In recent years, it has become more common in Britain to use U.S. terminology for large numbers.

Prime Numbers to 1,009

A prime number is any positive integer greater than 1 that is divisible only by two positive integers—1 and itself.

	2	3	5	7	11	13	17	19	23
29	31	37	41	43	47	53	59	61	67
71	73	79	83	89	97	101	103	107	109
113	127	131	137	139	149	151	157	163	167
173	179	181	191	193	197	199	211	223	227
229	233	239	241	251	257	263	269	271	277
281	283	293	307	311	313	317	331	337	347
349	353	359	367	373	379	383	389	397	401
409	419	421	431	433	439	443	449	457	461
463	467	479	487	491	499	503	509	521	523
541	547	557	563	569	571	577	587	593	599
601	607	613	617	619	631	641	643	647	653
659	661	673	677	683	691	701	709	719	727
733	739	743	751	757	761	769	773	787	797
809	811	821	823	827	829	839	853	857	859
863	877	881	883	887	907	911	919	929	937
941	947	953	967	971	977	983	991	997	1,009

Common Fractions Converted to Decimals

8ths	16ths	32nds	64ths			8ths	16ths	32nds	64ths			8ths	16ths	32nds	64ths			8ths	16ths	32nds	64ths		
			1	= 0.015625					17	= 0.265625					33	= 0.515625					49	= 0.765625
		1	2	= 0.03125				9	18	= 0.28125				17	34	= 0.53125				25	50	= 0.78125
			3	= 0.046875					19	= 0.296875					35	= 0.546875					51	= 0.796875
	1	2	4	= 0.0625			5	10	20	= 0.3125			9	18	36	= 0.5625			13	26	52	= 0.8125
			5	= 0.078125					21	= 0.328125					37	= 0.578125					53	= 0.828125
		3	6	= 0.09375				11	22	= 0.34375				19	38	= 0.59375				27	54	= 0.84375
			7	= 0.109375					23	= 0.359375					39	= 0.609375					55	= 0.859375
1	2	4	8	= 0.125		3	6	12	24	= 0.375		5	10	20	40	= 0.625		7	14	28	56	= 0.875
			9	= 0.140625					25	= 0.390625					41	= 0.640625					57	= 0.890625
	5	10	= 0.15625				13	26	= 0.40625				21	42	= 0.65625				29	58	= 0.90625
		11	= 0.171875					27	= 0.421875					43	= 0.671875					59	= 0.921875
	3	6	12	= 0.1875			7	14	28	= 0.4375			11	22	44	= 0.6875			15	30	60	= 0.9375
			13	= 0.203125					29	= 0.453125					45	= 0.703125					61	= 0.953125
		7	14	= 0.21875				15	30	= 0.46875				23	46	= 0.71875				31	62	= 0.96875
			15	= 0.234375					31	= 0.484375					47	= 0.734375					63	= 0.984375
2	4	8	16	= 0.25		4	8	16	32	= 0.5		6	12	24	48	= 0.75		8	16	32	64	= 1.0

Roman Numerals

I — 1	IV — 4	VII — 7	X — 10	XX — 20	L — 50	C — 100	D — 500
II — 2	V — 5	VIII — 8	XI — 11	XXX — 30	LX — 60	CC — 200	CM — 900
III — 3	VI — 6	IX — 9	XIX — 19	XL — 40	XC — 90	CD — 400	M — 1,000

Note: The numerals V, X, L, C, D, or M shown with a horizontal line on top denote 1,000 times the original value.

Ancient Measures

Biblical
Cubit..........	= 21.8 inches
Omer..........	= 0.45 peck
	= 3.964 liters
Ephah.........	= 10 omers
Shekel........	= 0.497 ounce
	= 14.1 grams

Greek
Cubit..........	= 18.3 inches
Stadion	= 607.2 or 622 feet
Obolos	= 715.38 milligrams
Drachma.......	= 4.2923 grams
Mina	= 0.9463 pound
Talent	= 60 mina

Roman
Cubit..........	= 17.5 inches
Stadium	= 202 yards
As, libra,	
pondus	= 325.971 grams
	= 0.71864 pound

Metric System Prefixes

The following prefixes, in combination with the basic unit names, provide the multiples and submultiples in the metric system. For example, the unit name *meter*, with the prefix *kilo* added, produces *kilometer*, meaning "1,000 meters."

Prefix	Symbol	Multiples	Equivalent	Prefix	Symbol	Multiples	Equivalent
yotta	Y	10^{24}	septillionfold	deci	d	10^{-1}	tenth part
zetta	Z	10^{21}	sextillionfold	centi	c	10^{-2}	hundredth part
exa	E	10^{18}	quintillionfold	milli	m	10^{-3}	thousandth part
peta	P	10^{15}	quadrillionfold	micro	μ	10^{-6}	millionth part
tera	T	10^{12}	trillionfold	nano	n	10^{-9}	billionth part
giga	G	10^{9}	billionfold	pico	p	10^{-12}	trillionth part
mega	M	10^{6}	millionfold	femto	f	10^{-15}	quadrillionth part
kilo	k	10^{3}	thousandfold	atto	a	10^{-18}	quintillionth part
hecto	h	10^{2}	hundredfold	zepto	z	10^{-21}	sextillionth part
deka	da	10	tenfold	yocto	y	10^{-24}	septillionth part

Weight and Measurement Equivalents

In this table it is necessary to distinguish between the international and the survey foot. The international foot, defined in 1959 as exactly equal to 0.3048 meter, is shorter than the old survey foot by exactly 2 parts in 1 million. The survey foot is still used in the publication of some geodetic surveys within the U.S. In this table, the survey foot is indicated with capital letters, as FEET.

When the name of a unit is enclosed in brackets, e.g., [1 hand], either (1) the unit is not in general current use in the U.S. or (2) the unit is believed to be based on custom and usage rather than on formal definition.

Equivalents involving decimals are, in most instances, rounded to the 3rd decimal place; exact equivalents are so designated.

Lengths

1 angstrom (Å)	= 0.1 nanometer (exactly)
	= 0.0001 micrometer (exactly)
	= 0.0000001 millimeter (exactly)
	= 0.000000004 inch
1 cable's length............	= 120 fathoms (exactly)
	= 720 FEET (exactly)
	= 219 meters
1 centimeter (cm)	= 0.3937 inch
1 chain (ch) (Gunter's or surveyor's)	= 66 FEET (exactly)
	= 20.1168 meters
1 chain (engineer's)	= 30.48 meters (exactly)
	= 100 feet
1 decimeter (dm)	= 3.937 inches
1 degree (geographical)	= 364,566.929 feet
	= 69.047 miles (avg.)
	= 111.123 kilometers (avg.)
of latitude	= 68.708 miles at equator
	= 69.403 miles at poles
of longitude.............	= 69.171 miles at equator

1 dekameter (dam)..........	= 32.808 feet
1 fathom (fath)	= 6 FEET (exactly)
	= 1.8288 meters
1 foot (ft).................	= 12 inches (exactly)
	= 0.3048 meters (exactly)
	= 0.015 chains (surveyor's)
1 furlong (fur)	= 660 FEET (exactly)
	= $^{1}/_{8}$ survey mile (exactly)
	= 201.168 meters
[1 hand (height measure for horses, from ground to top of their shoulders)]	= 4 inches
1 inch (in.)................	= 2.54 centimeters (exactly)
1 kilometer (km)	= 0.621371 mile
	= 3,280.8 feet
1 league (land)	= 3 survey miles (exactly)
	= 4.828 kilometers
1 link (engineer's)	= 1 foot
	= 0.305 meter
1 link (Gunter's or surveyor's)	= 7.92 inches (exactly)
	= 0.201 meter

1 meter (m). . . . . = 39.37 inches
= 1.09361 yards
1 micrometer (μm) . . . . = 0.001 millimeter (exactly)
= 0.00003937 inch
1 mil . . . . = 0.001 inch (exactly)
= 0.0254 millimeter (exactly)
1 mile (mi) (statute or land). . . . = 5,280 FEET (exactly)
= 1.609344 kilometers (exactly)
1 international nautical mile
(nmi). . . . . = 1.852 kilometers (exactly)
= 1.151 miles
= 6,076.1 feet
1 millimeter (mm) . . . . = 0.03937 inch
1 nanometer (nm). . . . . = 0.001 micrometer (exactly)
= 0.00000003937 inch
1 pica (typography). . . . . = 12 points
1 point (pt) (typography) . . . . . = 0.013837 inch (exactly)
= 0.351 millimeter
1 rod (rd), pole, or perch. . . . . = 16½ FEET (exactly)
= 5.029 meters
1 yard (yd) . . . . = 3 feet (exactly)
= 0.9144 meter (exactly)

Areas or Surfaces

1 acre (A) . . . . = 43,560 square FEET (exactly)
= 4,840 square yards
= 0.405 hectare
1 are (a) . . . . = 119.599 square yards
= 0.025 acre
1 bolt (cloth measure):
length . . . . = 100 yards
width . . . . = 45 or 60 inches
1 hectare (ha). . . . . = 2.471 acres
[1 square (building)] . . . . = 100 square feet
1 square centimeter (cm²) . . . = 0.155 square inch
1 square decimeter (dm²). . . . = 15.500 square inches
1 square foot (ft²) . . . . = 929.030 square centimeters
1 square inch (in.²) . . . . = 6.4516 square centimeters
(exactly)
1 square kilometer (km²) . . . . = 247.104 acres
= 0.386102 square mile
1 square meter (m²) . . . . = 1.196 square yards
= 10.764 square feet
1 square mile (mi²) . . . . = 640 acres (exactly)
= 258.999 hectares
1 square millimeter (mm²) . . . = 0.002 square inch
1 square rod (rd²), square
pole, or square perch . . . . . = 25.293 square meters
1 square yard (yd²). . . . . = 0.836127 square meter

Capacities or Volumes

1 barrel (bbl), liquid. . . . . = 31 to 42 gallons*

*There are a variety of "barrels" established by law or usage. For example, federal taxes on fermented liquors are based on a barrel of 31 gallons. Many state laws fix the "barrel for liquids" as 31½ gallons; one state fixes a 36-gallon barrel for cistern measurement. Federal law recognizes a 40-gallon barrel for "proof spirits." By custom, 42 gallons constitute a barrel of crude oil or petroleum products for statistical purposes, and this equivalent is recognized "for liquids" by some states.

1 barrel (bbl), standard for
fruits, vegetables, and other
dry commodities except dry
cranberries . . . . = 7,056 cubic inches
= 105 dry quarts
= 3.281 bushels, struck measure
1 barrel, standard, cranberry . . = 86⁴⁵/₆₄ dry quarts
= 2.709 bushels, struck measure
= 5,826 cubic inches
1 board foot (lumber measure) = a foot-square board 1 inch
thick
1 bushel (U.S.) (struck
measure) . . . . = 2,150.42 cu in. (exactly)
= 35.239 liters
[1 bushel, heaped (U.S.)] . . . . = 2,747.715 cubic inches
= 1.278 bushels,
struck measure**
**Frequently recognized as 1¼ bushels, struck measure.
[1 bushel (bu) (British Imperial)
(struck measure)] . . . . = 1.032 U.S. bushels,
struck measure
= 2,219.36 cubic inches
1 cord (cd) (firewood) . . . . . . = 128 cubic feet (exactly)

1 cubic centimeter (cm³) . . . . = 0.061 cubic inch
1 cubic decimeter (dm³). . . . . = 61.024 cubic inches
1 cubic inch (in³) . . . . = 0.554 fluid ounce
= 4.433 fluid drams
= 16.387 cubic centimeters
1 cubic foot (ft³) . . . . = 7.481 gallons
= 28.317 cubic decimeters
1 cubic meter (m³) . . . . = 1.308 cubic yards
1 cubic yard (yd³). . . . . = 0.765 cubic meter
1 cup, measuring . . . . = 8 fluid ounces (exactly)
= ½ liquid pint (exactly)
1 dekaliter (daL). . . . . = 2.642 gallons
= 1.135 pecks
[1 dram, fluid (fl dr) (British)] . . = 0.961 U.S. fluid dram
= 0.217 cubic inch
= 3.552 milliliters
1 gallon (gal) (U.S.) . . . . = 4 quarts, liquid (exactly)
= 231 cubic inches (exactly)
= 3.785 liters
= 0.833 British gallon
= 128 U.S. fluid ounces (exactly)
[1 gallon (British Imperial)] . . . . = 277.42 cubic inches
= 1.201 U.S. gallons
= 4.546 liters
= 160 British fluid ounces
(exactly)
1 gill (gi) . . . . = 7.219 cubic inches
= 4 fluid ounces (exactly)
= 0.118 liter
1 hectoliter (hL) . . . . = 26.418 gallons
= 2.838 bushels
1 liter (L) (1 cubic decimeter
exactly). . . . . = 1.057 liquid quarts
= 0.908 dry quart
= 61.024 cubic inches
1 milliliter (mL) (1 cu cm
exactly). . . . . = 0.271 fluid dram
= 16.231 minims
= 0.061 cubic inch
1 ounce, liquid (U.S.) . . . . = 1.805 cubic inches
= 29.574 milliliters
= 1.041 British fluid ounces
[1 ounce, fluid (fl oz) (British)] = 0.961 U.S. fluid ounce
= 1.734 cubic inches
= 28.412 milliliters
1 peck (pk) . . . . = 8.810 liters
1 pint (pt), dry. . . . . = 33.600 cubic inches
= 0.551 liter
1 pint, liquid . . . . = 28.875 cubic inches (exactly)
= 0.473 liter
1 quart (qt), dry (U.S.) . . . . . . = 67.201 cubic inches
= 1.101 liters
= 0.969 British quart
1 quart, liquid (U.S.). . . . . = 2 pints, liquid (exactly)
= 4 cups (exactly)
= 57.75 cubic inches (exactly)
= 0.946 liter
= 0.833 British quart
[1 quart (British)] . . . . = 69.354 cubic inches
= 1.032 U.S. dry quarts
= 1.201 U.S. liquid quarts
1 tablespoon (T., Tbs, tbsp.) . . = 3 teaspoons (exactly)
= 4 fluid drams
= ½ fluid ounce (exactly)
1 teaspoon (t., tsp.) . . . . = ⅓ tablespoon (exactly)
= 1⅓ fluid drams***

***The equivalent "1 teaspoon = 1⅓ fluid drams" has been found to correspond more closely with the actual capacities of teaspoons in use than the equivalent "1 teaspoon = 1 fluid dram" given by many dictionaries.

Weights or Masses

1 assay ton* (AT) . . . . = 29.167 grams

*Used in assaying. The assay ton bears the same relation to the milligram that a ton of 2,000 pounds avoirdupois bears to the ounce troy; hence, the weight in milligrams of precious metal obtained from one assay ton of ore gives directly the number of troy ounces to the net ton.

1 carat (c). . . . . = 200 milligrams (exactly)
= 3.086 grains
1 dram avoirdupois (dr avdp). . = 27¹¹/₃₂ (= 27.344) grains
= 1.772 grams
1 gamma (γ) . . . . = 1 microgram (exactly)
1 grain (gr) . . . . = 64.79891 milligrams (exactly)

1 gram (g) . . . . = 15.432 grains
= 0.035 ounce, avoirdupois

1 hundredweight, gross or
long** (gross cwt) . . . . = 112 pounds (exactly)
= 50.802 kilograms

**The gross, or long, ton and hundredweight are used commercially in the U.S. to only a limited extent, usually in restricted industrial fields. These units are the same as the British ton and hundredweight.

1 hundredweight, gross or
short (cwt or net cwt) . . . . . . = 100 pounds (exactly)
= 45.359 kilograms

1 kilogram (kg) . . . . = 2.20462 pounds

1 microgram (µg) . . . . = 0.000001 gram (exactly)

1 milligram (mg) . . . . = 0.015 grain

1 ounce, avoirdupois (oz avdp) = 437.5 grains (exactly)
= 0.911 troy ounce
= 28.3495 grams

1 ounce, troy (oz t) . . . . = 480 grains (exactly)
= 1.097 avoirdupois ounces
= 31.103 grams

1 pennyweight (dwt) . . . . = 1.555 grams

1 pound, avoirdupois (lb avdp) = 7,000 grains (exactly)
= 1.215 troy pounds
= 453.59237 grams (exactly)

1 pound, troy (lb t) . . . . = 5,760 grains (exactly)
= 0.823 pound, avoirdupois
= 373.242 grams

1 stone (st) . . . . = 14 pounds avdp (exactly)
= 6.350 kilograms

1 ton, gross or long. . . . . = 2,240 pounds (exactly)
= 1.12 net tons (exactly)
= 1.016 metric tons

1 ton, metric (t) . . . . = 2,204.623 pounds
= 0.984 gross ton
= 1.102 net tons

1 ton, net or short (sh ton) . . . . = 2,000 pounds (exactly)
= 0.893 gross ton
= 0.907 metric ton

Electrical Units

The **watt** (W) is the unit of power (electrical, mechanical, thermal). Electrical power is given by the product of the voltage and the current.

Energy is sold by the **joule** (J), but in common practice the billing of electrical energy is expressed in terms of the **kilowatt-hour** (kWh), which is 3,600,000 joules or 3.6 megajoules.

The **horsepower** (hp) is a nonmetric unit sometimes used in mechanics. It is equal to 746 watts.

The **ohm** is the unit of electrical resistance and represents the physical property of a conductor that offers a resistance to the flow of electricity, permitting just 1 ampere to flow at 1 volt of pressure.

Measures of Force and Pressure

Dyne (dyn) = force necessary to accelerate a 1-gram mass 1 centimeter per second squared = 0.000072 poundal

Poundal (pdl) = force necessary to accelerate a 1-pound mass 1 foot per second squared = 13,825.5 dynes = 0.138255 newton

Newton (N) = force needed to accelerate a 1-kilogram mass 1 meter per second squared = 100,000 dynes (exactly)

Pascal (pressure) (Pa) = 1 newton per square meter = 0.020885 pound per square foot

Atmosphere (air pressure at sea level) (atm) = 2,116.217 pounds per square foot = 14.6959 pounds per square inch = 1.0332 kilograms per square centimeter = 101,325 newtons per square meter

Spirits Measures

Pony . . . . = 1.0 fluid ounce

Shot . . . . = varies, usu. 1.0-1.5 fluid ounces

Jigger . . . . = 1.5 fluid ounces

Pint (pt) . . . . = 16 fluid ounces
= 0.625 fifth

Fifth . . . . = 25.6 fluid ounces
= 1.6 pints
= 0.8 quart
= 0.757 liter

Quart (qt) . . . . = 32 fluid ounces
= 1.25 fifths

Wine bottle
(standard) . . . . = 0.750 liter
= 25.4 fluid ounces

Magnum . . . . = 1.5 liters

For champagne and brandy:
Jeroboam . . . . = 2 magnums
= 3 liters
= 101 fluid ounces

For champagne:
Rehoboam . . . . = 3 magnums
Methuselah. . . . . = 4 magnums
Salmanazar . . . . = 6 magnums
Balthazar . . . . = 8 magnums
Nebuchadnezzar . . . = 10 magnums

Miscellaneous Measures

Caliber (cal)—the diameter of a gun bore. In the U.S., caliber is traditionally expressed in hundredths of inches, e.g., .22. In Britain, caliber is often expressed in thousandths of inches, e.g., .270. Now it is commonly expressed in millimeters, e.g., the 5.56 mm M16 rifle. Heavier weapons' caliber has long been expressed in millimeters, e.g., the 155 mm howitzer. Naval guns' caliber refers to the barrel length as a multiple of the bore diameter. A 5-inch, 50-caliber naval gun has a 5-inch bore and a barrel length of 250 inches.

Decibel (dB)—a measure of the relative loudness or intensity of sound. A 20-decibel sound is 10 times louder than a 10-decibel sound; 30 decibels is 100 times louder; 40 decibels is 1,000 times louder.

One decibel is the smallest difference between sounds detectable by the human ear. A 125-decibel sound is painful.

10 decibels . . . breathing
20 . . . . rustling leaves
30 . . . . whisper
40 . . . . refrigerator humming
50 . . . . quiet conversation
60 . . . . conversation, laughter
70 . . . . vacuum cleaner
80 . . . . city traffic
90 . . . . subway, lawn mower
100 . . . . chainsaw

Em—a printer's measure designating the square width of any given type size. For example, an em of 10-point type is 10 points. An en is half an em.

Gauge (ga)—a measure of shotgun bore diameter. Gauge numbers originally referred to the number of lead balls just fitting the gun barrel diameter required to make a pound. Thus, a 16-gauge shotgun's bore was smaller than a 12-gauge shotgun's. Today, an international agreement assigns millimeter measures to each gauge.

Gauge	Bore diameter (mm)	Gauge	Bore diameter (mm)
6	23.34	14	17.60
10	19.67	16	16.81
12	18.52	20	15.90

Horsepower (hp)—the power needed to lift 550 pounds 1 foot in 1 second or to lift 33,000 pounds 1 foot in 1 minute. Equivalent to 746 watts or 2,546 British thermal units per hour.

Karat or carat (k or c)—a measure of fineness for gold equal to $\frac{1}{24}$ part of pure gold in an alloy. Thus 24-karat gold is pure; 18-karat gold is ¼ alloy. The carat is also used as a unit of weight for precious stones; it is equal to 200 milligrams or 3.086 grains.

Knot (kn or kt)—a measure of the speed of ships. A knot equals 1 nautical mile per hour.

Quire (qr)—25 sheets of paper of the same size and quality.

Ream (rm)—500 sheets of paper of the same size and quality.

Computer Milestones

1623: German mathematician Wilhelm Schickard developed the 1st mechanical calculator, capable of adding, subtracting, multiplying, and dividing.

1642: French mathematician Blaise Pascal built the 1st of more than 4 dozen copies of an adding and subtracting machine that he invented.

1801: French inventor Joseph Marie Jacquard demonstrated a new control system for looms. He "programmed" the loom, communicating desired weaving operations to the machine via patterns of holes in paper cards.

1833-71: British mathematician and scientist Charles Babbage used the Jacquard punch-card system in his design for a sophisticated, programmable "Analytical Engine" that foreshadowed basic features of today's computers. Babbage's concept was beyond the capabilities of the technology of his time, and the machine remained unfinished at his death in 1871.

1889: American engineer Herman Hollerith patented an electromechanical punch-card tabulating system that facilitated the handling of large amounts of statistical data and quickly found use in censuses in the U.S. and other countries.

1911: Hollerith's Tabulating Machine Company merged with 2 other enterprises to form the Computing-Tabulating-Recording Company, which was renamed the International Business Machines Corporation (IBM) in 1924.

1941: German engineer Konrad Züse completed the Z3, the 1st fully functional digital computer to be controlled by a program; the Z3 was not electronic—it was based on electrical switches called relays.

1942: Iowa State Coll. physicist John Vincent Atanasoff and his assistant Clifford Berry completed a working model of the 1st fully electronic computer using vacuum tubes, which could operate much more quickly than relays; the rudimentary machine was not programmable.

1943: IBM and Harvard professor Howard Aiken completed the 1st large-scale automatic digital computer, the Mark I, a relay-based machine 55 ft long and 8 ft high. British scientists built the Colossus, an electronic computer designed specifically for breaking German codes during World War II.

1946: ENIAC (Electronic Numerical Integrator and Computer), a 30-ton room-sized electronic computer with more than 18,000 vacuum tubes, was completed by physicist John Mauchly and engineer J. Presper Eckert at the Univ. of Pennsylvania for the U.S. Army. ENIAC could be programmed to do different tasks, but cables had to be plugged in and switches had to be set by hand.

1951: Eckert and Mauchly's UNIVAC (Universal Automatic Computer) became the 1st commercially available computer in the U.S. The 1st customer was the Census Bureau. CBS-TV used a UNIVAC in 1952 to predict election results.

1969-71: The powerful Unix operating system was developed at Bell Laboratories; later versions became widely used on large computers and formed the basis for Linux and Macintosh OS X operating systems for personal computers.

1971: Intel released the 4004, the 1st commercial microprocessor (an entire computer processing unit on a chip).

1973: The Alto computer, developed at Xerox's Palo Alto Research Center, became operational, implementing many features of modern commercial personal computers, including a graphical user interface (GUI) featuring windows, icons, and pointers that could be manipulated by a mouse.

1975: The 1st widely marketed personal computer (PC), the MITS Altair 8800, was introduced in kit form, with no keyboard, video display, or printer, for under $400. Microsoft was founded by college dropouts Bill Gates and Paul Allen.

1976: The 1st word-processing program for personal computers, Electric Pencil, was written. Apple Computer Company was founded by Steven Jobs and Stephen Wozniak.

1977: Apple introduced the Apple II; capable of displaying text and graphics in color, the machine enjoyed phenomenal success.

1981: IBM unveiled its Personal Computer (IBM 5150), which used an operating system from Microsoft known as MS-DOS (Disk Operating System).

1984: Apple introduced the 1st Macintosh. The easy-to-use Macintosh came with a proprietary operating system and was the 1st popular computer to have a GUI and a mouse.

1990: Microsoft released Windows 3.0, the 1st workable version of its own GUI.

1991: The Linux operating system was invented for the personal computer by Helsinki Univ. student Linus Torvalds and made available for free.

1996: The Palm Pilot, the 1st widely successful handheld computer and personal information manager, arrived.

1997: The IBM computer Deep Blue beat world chess champion Garry Kasparov in a 6-game match, 2-1, with 3 draws.

2000: Microsoft was found guilty of antitrust violations by a federal district judge. Microsoft settled in 2001 by accepting certain restrictions on its competitive practices and creating an antitrust compliance committee.

2001: Apple introduced the Unix-based operating system OS X for the Macintosh.

2002: The total number of personal computers, including desktop and laptop machines of all types, shipped by manufacturers since 1975 reached 1 bil, according to computer industry research firm Gartner Dataquest.

2004: The European Union found Microsoft guilty of anti-competitive practices and fined the company $613 mil.

2006: Apple began using Intel microprocessors instead of the IBM PowerPC in its Macintosh computers.

2007: Microsoft released Windows Vista, the successor to its 6-year-old Windows XP operating system. Apple introduced the iPhone, a touchscreen-equipped smartphone. Amazon released the Kindle, a proprietary hardware/software system for displaying books electronically.

2008: Google released the Android OS for mobile devices.

2010: Apple released the iPad tablet computer and sold more than 3 mil devices in the first 80 days.

Nations With the Most Personal Computers in Use, 2011

Source: Computer Industry Almanac at www.c-i-a.com for year-end 2011

Rank	Nations	PCs in use (mil)	PCs per 1,000 pop.	% of world total	Rank	Nations	PCs in use (mil)	PCs per 1,000 pop.	% of world total
1.	U.S.	310.64	991.9	19.40%	10.	Italy	44.72	769.6	2.79%
2.	China	195.14	144.0	12.19	11.	South Korea	40.90	838.6	2.55
3.	Japan	98.05	774.0	6.12	12.	Canada	31.30	920.1	1.96
4.	Germany	71.49	869.2	4.47	13.	Mexico	27.37	240.7	1.71
5.	India	57.02	47.5	3.56	14.	Spain	22.80	561.7	1.42
6.	UK	54.52	887.2	3.41	15.	Australia	19.47	893.9	1.22
7.	Russia	53.52	385.6	3.34					
8.	France	53.49	851.3	3.34	**Top 15 countries**		**1,128.57**	**NA**	**70.50**
9.	Brazil	48.14	236.5	3.01	**World**		**1,600.84**	**231.6**	**NA**

NA = Not available.

U.S. Sales of Selected Hardware, 2004-12

Source: Consumer Electronics Association

(factory sales to dealers in millions of dollars and millions of units)

	2004 Sales	2004 Units	2006 Sales	2006 Units	2008 Sales	2008 Units	2010 Sales	2010 Units	2012 Sales	2012 Units
Desktop computers..........	$7,710	10.8	$7,340	10.7	$6,744	10.2	$3,755	7.0	$2,750	5.5
Notebook computers[1]........	10,523	9.2	11,936	13.7	16,668	20.0	12,517	20.1	14,916	21.3
Netbooks[1]..................	—	—	—	—	(2)	(2)	2,322	7.7	1,037	3.8
Tablets[1]...................	—	—	—	—	(2)	(2)	6,708	10.3	29,168	68.5
Smartphones	1,708	4.5	4,781	14.0	11,393	28.6	17,594	54.1	33,661	108.4
Video game consoles........	3,162	—	4,425	—	7,780	—	4,532	21.5	4,109	26.5
Digital video recorders (DVRs) ..	635	3.3	975	5.0	3,237	20.2	2,618	17.0	2,582	16.2
Digital cameras............	4,739	18.9	7,149	32.9	6,813	33.2	6,778	36.5	5,117	24.3
Digital camcorders	1,651	5.6	1,828	5.3	1,885	5.6	1,150	7.2	301	3.0
MP3 players	1,289	7.1	5,559	38.1	5,844	43.7	7,030	39.7	3,807	27.3

— = Not available. (1) U.S. consumer channels. (2) Notebooks, netbooks, and tablets were not separated.

Status of Electronics Sold in the U.S., 1980-2009

Source: U.S. Environmental Protection Agency

(in millions of units)

	Disposed or recycled Units	Disposed or recycled %	In storage Units	In storage %	Still in use Units	Still in use %	Total Units
Computers..............	462	53.9%	71	8.2%	325	37.9%	857
Computer displays........	422	64.6	40	6.2	191	29.2	653
Mobile devices[1]	789	47.5	58	3.5	812	48.9	1,660
Hard copy devices[2]	262	55.6	41	8.8	167	35.5	471
Televisions[3].............	356	46.1	104	13.5	312	40.4	772
Total	**2,291**	**51.9**	**314**	**7.1**	**1,807**	**40.9**	**4,413**

Note: Estimates released in 2011. (1) Cell phones, personal digital assistants, smartphones, and pagers. (2) Printers, scanners, fax machines, digital copiers, and multifunction devices. (3) Monochrome, cathode ray tube, flat-panel, and projection.

Top-Selling Software, 2011-12

Source: The NPD Group/Retail Tracking Service

(Based on unit U.S. sales, July 2011-June 2012; does not include software bundled with computers at point of sale.)

Business
1. MS Office 2010 Home & Student Product Key Card   Microsoft
2. MS Office 2010 Home & Student 3-User .... Microsoft
3. MS Office 2011 Home & Student 3-User .... Microsoft
4. MS Office 2010 Home & Business Product Key Card Microsoft
5. MS Office 2010 Home & Business.............. Microsoft
6. MS Office 2011 Home & Student Product Key Card   Microsoft
7. MS Office 2011 Home & Business.............. Microsoft
8. MS Office 2011 Home & Student................ Microsoft
9. iWork 2009 (M)...........................Apple
10. MS Office 2011 Home & Business 2-User .... Microsoft

Education
1. Learning QuickBooks 2012 (W/M)...................Intuit
2. Mavis Beacon Teaches Typing Deluxe
   25th Anniversary Ed. (W/M) .... Encore
3. JumpStart Advanced Kindergarten 3.0
   (W/M) .... Knowledge Adventure
4. JumpStart Advanced Preschool
   3.0 (W/M) .... Knowledge Adventure
5. JumpStart Advanced 1st Grade
   3.0 (W/M) .... Knowledge Adventure
6. Berlitz Spanish Premier (W/M)........... Nova Development
7. Typing Instructor for Kids Platinum (W/M) .. Individual Software
8. Instant Immersion Spanish Levels
   1, 2, & 3 (W/M) ....Topics Entertainment
9. Rosetta Stone 4.0 TOTALe Spanish Ed. Levels
   1-5 (W/M) .... Rosetta Stone
10. Mavis Beacon Teaches Typing 20.0 Deluxe .... Encore

Finance
1. TurboTax 2011 Deluxe Federal + State + e-File (W/M) ....Intuit
2. TurboTax 2011 Home & Business Federal + State +
   e-File (W/M)................................Intuit
3. TurboTax 2011 Premier Federal + State + e-File (W/M) ....Intuit
4. H&R Block At Home 11 Deluxe + State (W/M)...... H&R Block
5. TurboTax 2011 Deluxe Federal + e-File (W/M).......... Intuit
6. QuickBooks 2012 Pro............................Intuit
7. TurboTax 2011 Basic Federal + e-File (W/M)..........Intuit
8. Quicken 2012 Deluxe...........................Intuit
9. Quicken 2012 Starter...........................Intuit
10. TurboTax 2011 Business Federal + e-File (W/M) ....Intuit

Games
1. Diablo III (W/M) .... Blizzard Entertainment
2. Star Wars: The Old Republic .... Electronic Arts
3. Elder Scrolls V: Skyrim............. Bethesda Game Studios
4. The Sims 3 (W/M) .... Electronic Arts
5. The Sims 3: Pets Expansion Pack (W/M)....... Electronic Arts
6. The Sims 3: Generations Expansion Pack (W/M) Electronic Arts
7. World of Warcraft: Battle Chest (W/M) .. Blizzard Entertainment
8. Starcraft II: Wings of Liberty .... Blizzard Entertainment
9. The Sims 3: Town Life Stuff (W/M) .... Electronic Arts
10. Battlefield 3 Limited Ed. .... Electronic Arts

Imaging/Graphics
1. Adobe Photoshop Elements 10.0 (W/M) .... Adobe
2. Adobe Photoshop Elements 10.0/Premiere Elements
   10.0 Bundle (W/M) .... Adobe
3. Adobe Photoshop Lightroom 3.0 (W/M) .... Adobe
4. Adobe Photoshop Elements 9.0 (W/M) .... Adobe
5. Printmaster 2012 Platinum....................... Encore
6. MS Publisher 2010.......................... Microsoft
7. Photo Explosion 4.0 Deluxe............. Nova Development
8. Corel Paint Shop Pro X4........................... Corel
9. PDF Converter 7.0 Pro.................Nuance Communications
10. Adobe Photoshop CS5 Extended Student & Teacher Ed. Adobe

Operating System
1. Mac OS X 10.6 Snow Leopard Upgrade (M) ....Apple
2. MS Windows 7 Home Premium Upgrade.......... Microsoft
3. MS Windows 7 Home Premium .... Microsoft
4. MS Windows 7 Anytime Pro Upgrade............. Microsoft
5. MS Windows 7 Pro Upgrade .... Microsoft

Personal Productivity
1. VHS to DVD 5.0 Deluxe .... Honest Technology
2. Easy VHS to DVD................................. Roxio
3. MS Streets & Trips .... Microsoft
4. Easy CD & DVD Burning .... Roxio
5. Family Tree Maker 2012 Deluxe.......... Nova Development
6. ResumeMaker Pro 17.0 Deluxe .... Individual Software
7. Roxio Creator 2012 .... Roxio
8. HGTV Home & Landscape Platinum Suite 3.0 Nova Development
9. Nero Burn Express............................ Nero Inc.
10. 123 Copy DVD 2012 Gold .... Bling Software

Note: Software is Windows-only unless otherwise noted; M = Macintosh, W/M = Windows/Mac.

About the Internet

The Internet is a vast and rapidly growing computer network. In 1994, a total of 3 mil people (most of them in the U.S.) made use of it; by the end of 2011 the number of users worldwide exceeded 2.2 bil (Computer Industry Almanac Inc.).

The Internet is not owned or funded by any one institution, organization, or government. It has no CEO and is not a commercial service. Its development is guided by the Internet Society (ISOC), which is composed of volunteers. The ISOC appoints the Internet Architecture Board (IAB), which oversees issues of standards and network resources, among others.

Major Historical Highlights

1969: ARPANET, an experimental 4-computer network, was established by the Advanced Research Projects Agency (ARPA) of the U.S. Defense Dept. Two years later, ARPANET linked about 23 computers ("hosts") at 15 sites, including MIT and Harvard.

1978: The 1st spam, or junk email, was sent over ARPANET.

1983: The set of communications rules (protocol) known as TCP/IP became the main networking protocol of ARPANET. TCP/IP facilitates connection between networks. Its adoption was tantamount to the birth of the Internet. The military portion of ARPANET was moved onto the MILNET.

1986: The U.S. National Science Foundation (NSF) launched NSFNET, the 1st large-scale network using Internet technology.

1988: Internet Relay Chat (IRC) was developed by Finnish student Jarkko Oikarinen, enabling people to communicate via the Internet in "real time."

1988: A "worm" crafted by Cornell Univ. computer science graduate student Robert Morris Jr. infected thousands of computers, shutting many down and causing millions of dollars of damage—the 1st known case of large-scale damage caused by a computer virus spread via the Internet.

1989: The World—the 1st commercial Internet service provider supplying dial-up access—debuted.

1989-90: Tim Berners-Lee invented the World Wide Web. Created as an environment in which scientists at the European Center for Nuclear Research in Switzerland could share information, it gradually evolved into a medium with text, graphics, audio, animation, and video.

1990: ARPANET was disbanded.

1991: The NSFNET was opened to commercial traffic. Berners-Lee introduced the 1st browser, or software for accessing the web.

1993: The U.S. National Center for Supercomputing Applications released versions of Mosaic, the 1st web browser able to present both text and images in a single page.

1994: Netscape Communications released the Netscape Navigator browser.

1995: Microsoft released its Internet Explorer browser. It initially failed to make a dent in Netscape's dominance of the browser market but surpassed it by 1999.

1996: A group of universities launched Internet2, an advanced, high-performance network for the research community and a test bed for development of new capabilities that might find use in the commercial Internet.

1998: Under a contract with the U.S. Dept. of Commerce, the nonprofit Internet Corporation for Assigned Numbers and Names (ICANN) took over the management of assigning domain names and Internet (IP) addresses.

1999: Release of the free Napster file-sharing service enabled users to easily exchange files containing music or other content without regard to copyright restrictions.

2003: Niue, a self-governing Pacific island associated with New Zealand, became the 1st country to offer free nationwide wireless access to the Internet, using Wi-Fi technology.

2004: The Mozilla Foundation released the first official version of the open-source browser Mozilla Firefox.

2006: Websites with rich user interfaces that encourage collective participation and personalization through online applications and scripts, features of Web 2.0, became prevalent.

2007: Apple Inc. releases the iPhone, a touchscreen-equipped smartphone; the company sold 1 mil units within 3 days of its launch.

2010: A U.S. appellate court rules that the FCC cannot regulate an Internet provider's ability to charge tiered rates for different download speeds.

2011: ICANN allows generic top level domains to be almost any word in any alphabet.

Safety and Security on the Internet

Common sense dictates some basic security rules:

- Pick passwords that are difficult to guess, preferably consisting of both letters and numbers and other symbols, if permitted. Avoid using the same password for multiple websites.

- Do not give out your phone number, address, credit card number, or other personal information unless needed for a transaction at a site you trust.

- If you feel someone is being threatening or dangerous, inform your Internet service provider.

- Use protective "firewall," antivirus, and antispyware software to guard your system against attacks by hackers.

- Be careful about opening email and file attachments from unknown correspondents.

- If you have programs that can make use of macros—bits of auxiliary coding that are meant to play a helpful role but can be taken advantage of by viruses—make sure the programs' macro virus protection is turned on. Disable macros if you do not know how to use them.

- Users of so-called **peer-to-peer** (P2P) file-sharing networks or protocols should open up only part of their computer system to sharing, not the entire hard drive.

- When manufacturers provide **patches** to solve security flaws or other problems with operating systems, software, or web browsers, it is usually advisable to install these fixes. If a fix is not available for a serious security problem, you may want to consider switching to an alternative program.

Malware. Software designed to harm a computer system—such as a virus (malicious code carried within a program) or a worm (a self-contained malicious program)—may be transmitted via the Internet, received on a disk, or communicated via email.

Malicious software may install a "back door" on an infected system, giving hackers access; attempt to turn off any antivirus program on the system; or try to log the user's keystrokes.

A **Trojan horse** is computer code concealed within harmless code or data that is capable of taking control and causing damage. It can be used to mount a massive **denial-of-service** attack, which overwhelms targeted computers by inundating them with messages. Infected computers, acting under hacker control without their owners' knowledge, are called **zombies**, and a network of zombie computers that carry out an attack is called a **botnet**.

Spyware. Software that observes your computer activity without your knowledge is often regarded as a type of malware. Spyware programs, which can gain entry to your machine via a Trojan horse, may record your keystrokes and report passwords or other personal information to a hacker. Some can flood your screen with ads.

Phishing. A popular scam is **phishing**—the use of a forged email message purportedly from a respectable organization, such as a bank, to elicit personal data. The email typically contains a hyperlink that leads to a fabricated website resembling the site of the ostensible sender. To avoid falling victim to a phishing scam, do not click on any links in emails sent by companies with whom you do business. If you want to visit a company's website, open your browser and manually enter the site's address.

Spam. Junk email, or **spam**, can be a time-wasting annoyance or worse—spam may offer pornography or products dangerous to health; seek to defraud the recipient; carry a destructive virus; or turn the recipient's machine into a zombie that stores illicit material, takes part in a denial-of-service attack, or distributes spam. Net administrators worry that the flood of spam could cause a breakdown in the flow of Internet traffic.

In 2003, Congress enacted a law that attempted to restrict spam, but it had little effect on the volume of spam received by email accounts.

While filtering software can help reduce the deluge of spam—some email programs include filters—it is not completely accurate. Experts recommend that you be wary of revealing your email address as you surf the web. If possible, do not list your email address on a public website.

Internet Addresses

The fundamental part of an address on the Internet is called the domain. The final part of a domain name, known as the **top-level domain (TLD)**, is its most basic part. For example, .com is the top-level domain of *The World Almanac*'s web address (www.worldalmanac.com).

So-called generic top-level domains (gTLDs), consisting of 3 or more letters, include the following:

Domain	What it is (usually)
.aero	an organization in the air-transport industry
.asia	a legal entity in the Pan-Asia and Asia-Pacific region
.biz	a business
.cat	a site associated with Catalan language and culture
.com	generally a commercial organization, business, or company
.coop	a nonprofit business cooperative, such as a rural electric co-op
.edu	an educational institution
.gov	a nonmilitary U.S. governmental entity, usually federal
.info	an informational site for an individual or organization
.int	an international organization
.jobs	information about employment
.mil	a U.S. military organization
.mobi	a site providing content for mobile devices
.museum	a museum
.name	an individual
.net	suggested for a network administration but actually used by a wide variety of sites
.org	suggested for a nonprofit organization but actually used by a wide variety of sites
.post	postal services
.pro	a professional, such as an accountant, lawyer, or physician
.tel	contact data for a group or individual
.travel	information about travel
.xxx	adult entertainment community

Domain names with 2 letters are generally for countries or regions. The **top-level domain** .us, for instance, is available to persons, organizations, and entities in the U.S. More examples: .eu (European Union), .jp (Japan), .ru (Russia), .uk (United Kingdom).

Internet Lingo

The following abbreviations are sometimes used on the Internet and in email.

BTW	By the way	GOK	God only knows	LOL	Laughing out loud
CBLO	See below	GTG	Got to go	PLS	Please
F2F	Face to face; a personal meeting	HHOK	Ha, ha—only kidding	ROFL	Rolling on the floor laughing
FCOL	For crying out loud	IMHO	In my humble opinion	TAFN	That's all for now
FWIW	For what it's worth	IMO	In my opinion	TTFN	Ta-ta for now

Emoticons, or smileys, are a series of typed characters that resemble a face when looked at sideways and express an emotion. Here are some smileys often encountered on the Internet.

:-)	Smile	:-D	Laugh	:-(	Unhappy	:-b..	Drooling
;-)	Wink	:-*	Kiss	:-o	Surprised	{*}	A hug and a kiss

Nations With the Most Internet Users, 2011

Source: Computer Industry Almanac at www.c-i-a.com for year-end 2011

Rank	Nations	Internet users (mil)	Internet users per 1,000 pop.	% of worldwide users	Rank	Nations	Internet users (mil)	Internet users per 1,000 pop.	% of worldwide users
1.	China	439.62	324.3	19.45%	10.	France	48.63	774.0	2.15%
2.	U.S.	263.33	840.7	11.65	11.	Italy	44.37	763.6	1.96
3.	India	165.68	137.9	7.33	12.	South Korea	40.38	828.0	1.79
4.	Japan	106.85	844.8	4.73	13.	Mexico	33.04	290.5	1.46
5.	Brazil	71.72	352.4	3.17	14.	Spain	29.32	722.4	1.30
6.	Germany	65.72	799.0	2.91	15.	Canada	28.87	848.6	1.28
7.	Russia	55.35	398.8	2.45					
8.	UK	50.37	819.7	2.23		Top 15 total	1,492.78	NA	66.04
9.	Indonesia	49.53	201.6	2.19		World total	2,260.31	327.0	NA

NA = Not available.

Most-Visited World Websites, 2012

Source: comScore Media Metrix

Some websites represent an aggregation of commonly owned domain names; popular domains within a group added in parentheses by World Almanac editors.

Rank	Website	Visitors[1]	Rank	Website	Visitors[1]
1.	Google sites (YouTube; Blogger)	1,150,458	11.	Baidu.com Inc.	261,378
2.	Microsoft sites (Bing; Xbox Live)	848,309	12.	CBS Interactive (CNET; ZDNet)	247,315
3.	Facebook.com	824,321	13.	eBay (PayPal; Half.com; Stubhub)	241,288
4.	Yahoo! sites (Yahoo! Voices; Flickr)	697,068	14.	Vevo	239,669
5.	Wikimedia Foundation sites (Wikipedia)	478,472	15.	Sohu.com Inc.	228,954
6.	Amazon sites (Zappos; Audible; IMDb; LoveFilm)	346,225	16.	BitTorrent Network	228,422
7.	Apple Inc. (iTunes)	298,541	17.	Glam Media (Glam; Brash)	227,776
8.	Federated Media Publishing (Imgur; Boing Boing)	274,230	18.	AOL, Inc. (Moviefone; Patch; Huffington Post)	215,637
9.	Tencent Inc. (QQ)	266,334	19.	Alibaba.com Corp.	209,212
10.	Ask Network	264,504	20.	Viacom Digital	193,418

(1) Number of persons age 15 or older, in thousands, who visited a website from any location at least once in Apr.-June 2012.

U.S. Broadband and Dial-Up Adoption, 2000-12

Source: Pew Internet and American Life Project, Aug. 2012

(% of American adults who access the Internet via broadband or dial-up)

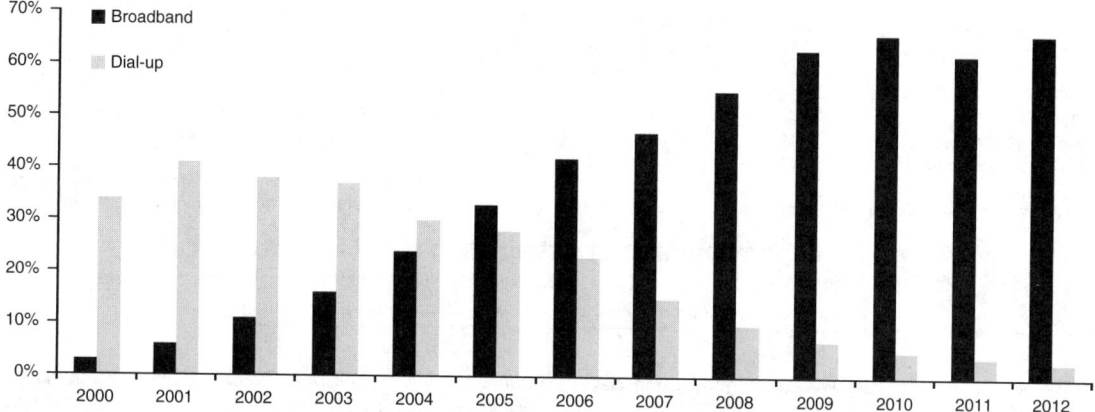

Note: Survey of adults, persons age 18 and older, on which report is based takes place annually in Mar.-June.

U.S. Broadband Internet Access by Selected Characteristics, 2011-12

Source: Pew Internet and American Life Project, Aug. 2012

	% broadband 2011	2012		% broadband 2011	2012		% broadband 2011	2012
All adults	62%	66%	**Race/ethnicity**			**Annual household income**		
Gender			White.	66%	70%	Less than $30,000 . .	41%	46%
Male	65	66	Black.	49	54	$30,000-$49,999 . . .	66	68
Female	60	66	Hispanic	51	51	$50,000-$74,999 . . .	81	85
Age			**Education**			$75,000 or more. . . .	89	87
18-29	76	75	No high school diploma	22	34	**Geography**		
30-49	70	76	High school graduate	52	55	Urban	64	67
50-64	60	62	Some college	73	74	Suburban	65	70
65+.	30	39	College graduate. . . .	85	87	Rural.	55	53

Note: Survey of persons age 18 and older, who had broadband Internet access at home. Respondents were contacted July 25-Aug. 26, 2011, and Mar. 15-Apr. 3, 2012. Interviews were conducted in English and Spanish.

Most-Visited U.S. Websites, 2012

Source: comScore Media Metrix

Some websites represent an aggregation of commonly owned domain names; popular domains within a group as of June 2012 added in parentheses by World Almanac editors.

All U.S. Sites

Rank	Website	Visitors[1]
1.	Google sites (YouTube; Blogger)	189,057
2.	Yahoo! sites (Flickr; Rivals.com)	168,494
3.	Microsoft sites (Bing; Xbox Live)	166,993
4.	Facebook.com (Instagram).	158,843
5.	AOL Inc. (Moviefone; Patch; Huffington Post)	111,706
6.	Amazon sites (Zappos; Audible; IMDb)	100,403
7.	Ask Network (Dictionary; Mindspark; Pronto).	88,546
8.	Wikimedia Foundation sites (Wikipedia).	85,048
9.	Glam Media (Glam; Brash).	82,139
10.	Apple Inc. (iTunes)	80,177

Video Sites

Rank	Website	Visitors[1]
1.	Google sites (YouTube)	154,609
2.	Yahoo! sites	54,273
3.	Vevo	47,980
4.	Facebook.com	45,870
5.	Microsoft sites (Xbox Live)	41,770
6.	Viacom Digital (BET; Comedy Central; MTV).	39,789
7.	AOL Inc.	38,890
8.	NDN	33,192
9.	Amazon sites (IMDb)	29,051
10.	Turner Digital (CNN; SI; Golf; NCAA; PGA)	24,364

Blog Sites

Rank	Website	Visitors[1]
1.	Blogger.	72,266
2.	Federated Media Publishing (Imgur; Boing Boing). .	62,955
3.	Technorati Media	36,332
4.	Gawker Media (Gizmodo; Lifehacker)	16,673
5.	MSN Now	14,394

Social Networking Sites

Rank	Website	Visitors[1]
1.	Facebook	158,843
2.	Twitter.	41,075
3.	LinkedIn	39,563
4.	Myspace	29,332
5.	Tumblr	24,759

Search and Navigation

Rank	Website	Searches (mil)	Searchers[1]	% of searches
1.	Google sites	36,540	192,415	65
2.	Yahoo! sites	8,569	105,836	15
3.	Microsoft sites.	8,421	93,015	15
4.	Ask Network	1,548	71,488	3
5.	AOL Inc.	804	16,205	1

Email

Rank	Website	Visitors[1]
1.	Yahoo! Mail.	84,198
2.	Google Gmail	68,581
3.	Windows Live Hotmail	40,230
4.	AOL Email	24,628
5.	Comcast.net WebMail.	9,213

(1) Number of persons age 2 and older in any U.S. location, in thousands, who visited the website at least once in Apr.-June 2012.

Internet Access in the U.S., 2000-10

Source: 2011 Digital Future Report, USC Annenberg School Center for the Digital Future

	% of Americans accessing Internet[1]						Avg. hours per week spent online[1]					
Type of Internet access	**2000**	**2002**	**2005**	**2008**	**2009**	**2010**	**2000**	**2002**	**2005**	**2008**	**2009**	**2010**
All access	**67%**	**71%**	**79%**	**80%**	**82%**	**82%**	**9.4**	**11.1**	**13.3**	**17.3**	**19.0**	**18.3**
At home	47	59	66	72	71	76	3.3	6.8	7.8	10.1	10.6	12.3
At school[2]	55	63	67	66	66	69	NA	NA	NA	3.6	4.0	5.0
At work[3]	42	40	55	59	59	65	NA	5.5	5.6	8.3	9.0	9.2
By cell phone/mobile devices[4]	NA	5	9	13	17	27	NA	3.6	2.0	1.7	2.5	3.9
By wireless computer[4]	NA	3	7	32	41	NA	NA	5.8	5.7	9.7	10.3	NA

NA = Not available. (1) Internet users age 12 and older who connect from all locations. (2) Percentages are from adult respondents with children in household; hours are for students using a wired PC. (3) Active use. Work outside the home. (4) Via wireless device.

Frequency of Internet Activities in the U.S., 2010

Source: 2011 Digital Future Report, USC Annenberg School Center for the Digital Future

(as % of all Internet users age 12 and older who connect from any location)

Online activity	Daily[1]	Weekly	Monthly	Less often	Never	Online activity	Daily[1]	Weekly	Monthly	Less often	Never
Use email	80%	11%	4%	2%	3%	Watch/download videos	16%	23%	9%	15%	37%
Browse (surf)	57	22	6	7	9	Online banking	15	32	15	7	31
Read news	43	21	10	12	14	Read blogs	13	14	8	18	48
Social networking or video sharing	33	13	6	10	38	Make/receive phone calls	5	5	4	9	77
Find or check a fact	27	32	17	16	8	Pay bills	3	19	32	7	39
Play games..........	23	16	7	15	40	Work on a blog	3	7	3	8	79
Instant message.......	21	11	6	14	48	Buy things...........	1	14	34	35	17
Listen/download music..	19	19	13	19	30	Gamble.............	1	2	2	8	87

(1) One or more times daily.

Informative and Useful Websites

Name	URL	Description
Daily Data		
Federal Register	www.federalregister.gov	Online magazine approach to the government's daily journal. Browse by topic, location, or agency.
Flowing Data	flowingdata.com	Online data visualizations and statistics.
ResourceShelf	www.resourceshelf.com	Running list of newly published databases, reports, and other research aids.
Today's Front Pages	www.newseum.org/todaysfrontpages/	Today's front page from more than 800 newspapers worldwide.
Education and Exhibits		
American Memory	memory.loc.gov	More than 9 mil items from the Library of Congress, including audio, maps, movies, photos, prints, and sheet music.
Europeana	europeana.eu	Network of European cultural organizations linking to more than 20 mil digital items.
Internet Archive	www.archive.org	Digital library of free cultural artifacts and Internet sites.
MIT OpenCourseWare	ocw.mit.edu	Free and open educational course material from the Massachusetts Institute of Technology.
New York Public Library Digital Gallery	digitalgallery.nypl.org	More than 800,000 images digitized from primary sources and printed rarities in the library's collections.
Our Documents	www.ourdocuments.gov	Digitized images and text of 100 milestone documents from America's history.
SmART History	smarthistory.org	Open educational resource on art history.
World Digital Library	www.wdl.org	Collection of significant primary documents from countries around the world.
Statistics		
DATA.gov	www.data.gov	Open access to raw government data files.
FedStats	www.fedstats.gov	Statistics by topic or program from more than 100 federal agencies.
United Nations Statistics Division	unstats.un.org	International data sets and country profiles with demographics and stats on society, industry, and the environment.
U.S. Economy at a Glance	stats.bls.gov/eag/	Quick reference tables on employment and wages from the Bureau of Labor Statistics.
Online Tools		
Kayak	www.kayak.com	One-stop search of multiple travel-booking sites for the lowest fares and price trends.
LibraryThing	www.librarything.com	Track the books you've read, receive suggestions for new books, and compare lists with other readers.
Wolfram Alpha	www.wolframalpha.com	Ready reference through computation of databases maintained by Wolfram Research.
Open Congress	www.opencongress.org	Easily follow Congress and find news about specific members, bills, committees, and issues. Receive updates by RSS feed.
Downloadable Tools		
Google Earth	earth.google.com	Free downloadable interactive world atlas and mapping software.
Stellarium	www.stellarium.org	Free downloadable planetarium that visualizes astronomical phenomena in real time from any point on Earth.

Note: Websites are subject to change. The World Almanac cannot take responsibility for contents.

Worldwide Telecommunications: Market Data, 1990-2011

Source: © International Telecommunication Union

	1990		2000		2005		2009		2010		2011	
	(mil)	(per 100 pop.)	(mil)	(per 100 pop.)	(mil)	(per 100 pop.)	(mil)	(per 100 pop.)	(mil)	(per 100 pop.)	(mil)	(per 100 pop.)
Fixed telephone lines	520	NA	975	15.9	1,253	19.3	1,214	17.8	1,189	17.2	1,204	17.3
Mobile cellular subscriptions	11	NA	739	12.0	2,207	33.9	4,650	68.3	5,373	78.0	5,972	85.7
Internet users	NA	NA	394	6.4	1,023	15.7	1,805	26.5	2,044	29.7	2,265	32.5
Wired broadband subscriptions	NA	NA	NA	NA	220	3.4	472	6.9	527	7.6	589	8.5
Active mobile broadband subscriptions	NA	NA	NA	NA	NA	NA	531	7.8	872	12.6	1,093	15.7

NA = Not available.

World Cell Phone Use by Nation, 2011

Source: © International Telecommunication Union, estimated; top countries ranked by subscriptions

Country	Subscriptions (thous.)	Per 100 pop.	Country	Subscriptions (thous.)	Per 100 pop.
China	986,253.0	73.19	Colombia	46,200.4	98.45
India	893,862.5	72.00	Malaysia	36,661.3	127.04
United States	331,600.0	105.91	Morocco	36,553.9	113.26
Russia.	256,116.6	179.31	Algeria	35,615.9	98.99
Brazil.	242,231.5	123.18	Peru	32,461.4	110.41
Indonesia	236,799.5	97.72	Taiwan	28,861.8	124.07
Japan	129,868.4	102.67	Venezuela.	28,782.0	97.78
Vietnam	127,318.0	143.39	Kenya	26,980.8	64.84
Pakistan	108,894.5	61.61	Canada.	25,858.3	75.28
Germany.	108,700.0	132.30	Tanzania	25,666.5	55.53
Nigeria	95,167.3	58.58	Iraq	25,519.0	78.12
Mexico	94,565.3	82.38	Uzbekistan	25,441.8	91.65
Italy.	92,300.0	151.84	Sudan	25,107.3	56.25
Philippines	87,256.4	91.99	Australia	24,490.0	108.34
Bangladesh.	85,000.0	56.48	Romania	23,400.0	109.16
Egypt.	83,425.1	101.08	Kazakhstan	23,102.7	142.55
United Kingdom	81,612.0	130.75	Chile	22,400.0	129.71
Thailand	78,667.9	113.16	Ghana.	21,165.8	84.78
France.	66,300.0	105.03	Guatemala	20,715.7	140.38
Turkey.	65,321.7	88.70	Netherlands	19,835.0	NA
South Africa	64,000.0	126.83	Sri Lanka	18,319.4	87.05
Iran	56,043.0	74.93	Afghanistan.	17,558.3	54.26
Ukraine.	55,566.9	122.96	Côte d'Ivoire	17,416.4	86.42
Argentina	55,000.0	134.92	Uganda.	16,697.0	48.38
Saudi Arabia	53,705.8	191.24	Congo, Dem. Rep of	15,673.1	23.13
Spain	53,066.8	114.23	Ecuador	15,332.7	104.55
Korea, South.	52,506.8	108.50	World	5,972,000.0	85.70
Poland.	49,200.0	128.46			

U.S. Wireless Industry, 1985-2011

Source: The CTIA Semi-Annual Industry Survey, used with permission of CTIA. As of Dec. of year shown.

Year	Est. total subscribers	Total service revenues (thous.)	Cell phone antennas	Avg. local monthly bill	Avg. local call length (mins.)
1985	340,213	$482,428	913	NA	NA
1987	1,230,855	1,151,519	2,305	$96.83	2.33
1989	3,508,944	3,340,595	4,169	89.30	2.48
1991	7,557,148	5,708,522	7,847	72.74	2.38
1993	16,009,461	10,892,175	12,824	61.49	2.41
1995	33,785,661	19,081,239	22,663	51.00	2.15
1996	44,042,992	23,634,971	30,045	47.70	2.32
1997	55,312,293	27,485,633	51,600	42.78	2.31
1998	69,209,321	33,133,175	65,887	39.43	2.39
1999	86,047,003	40,018,489	81,698	41.24	2.38
2000	109,478,031	52,466,020	104,288	45.27	2.56
2001	128,374,512	65,316,235	127,540	47.37	2.74
2002	140,766,842	76,508,187	139,338	48.40	2.73
2003	158,721,981	87,624,093	162,986	49.91	3.07
2004	182,140,362	102,121,210	175,725	50.64	3.05
2005	207,896,198	113,538,221	183,689	49.98	3.00
2006	233,040,781	125,456,825	195,613	50.56	3.03
2007	255,395,599	138,869,304	213,299	49.79	NA
2008	270,333,881	148,084,170	242,130	50.07	2.27
2009	290,941,191	152,551,854	247,081	48.16	1.81
2010	310,996,629	159,929,648	253,086	47.21	1.79
2011	331,594,848	169,767,314	283,385	47.00	1.78

NA = Not available.

U.S. Sales and Household Penetration of Selected Products, 1985-2012

Source: Consumer Electronics Association

	1985		1990		1995		2000		2005		2012	
Product	Sales (mil)	% of all house-holds	Sales (mil)	% of all house-holds	Sales (mil)	% of all house-holds	Sales (mil)	% of all house-holds	Sales (mil)	% of all house-holds	Sales (mil)	% of all house-holds
Cordless telephones.	$280	11%	$842	28%	$1,141	55%	$1,307	80%	$943	88%	$701	NA
Pagers	NA	NA	118	1	300	11	750	23	525	11	7	NA
Modems/fax modems	10	0	191	2.7	770	16	1,564	55	1,525	70	1,372	70%
Telephone answering devices	325	7	827	35	1,077	57	984	75	1,279	76	577	63
Cellular phones[1]	116	0.1	1,098	5	2,574	29	8,995	60	14,265	NA	39,473	91

NA = Not available. (1) For 2005 and 2012, also includes other wireless communication devices such as PDAs and smartphones. Smartphones were 27% of sales in 2005 and 85% of sales in 2012.

Telephone Area Codes, by Number

As of Nov. 2012.

Code	Location or *service*	Code	Location or *service*	Code	Location or *service*	Code	Location or *service*
201	New Jersey	407	Florida	*611*	*Repair Service*	808	Hawaii
202	District of Columbia	408	California	612	Minnesota	809	Dominican Republic
203	Connecticut	409	Texas	613	Ontario	810	Michigan
204	Manitoba	410	Maryland	614	Ohio	*811*	*Utility location (U.S.);*
205	Alabama	*411*	*Directory Assistance*	615	Tennessee		*health serv. (Canada)*
206	Washington	412	Pennsylvania	616	Michigan	812	Indiana
207	Maine	413	Massachusetts	617	Massachusetts	813	Florida
208	Idaho	414	Wisconsin	618	Illinois	814	Pennsylvania
209	California	415	California	619	California	815	Illinois
210	Texas	416	Ontario	620	Kansas	816	Missouri
211	*Community info.*	417	Missouri	623	Arizona	817	Texas
212	New York	418	Quebec	626	California	818	California
213	California	419	Ohio	630	Illinois	819	Quebec
214	Texas	423	Tennessee	631	New York	828	North Carolina
215	Pennsylvania	424	California	636	Missouri	829	Dominican Republic
216	Ohio	425	Washington	641	Iowa	830	Texas
217	Illinois	430	Texas	646	New York	831	California
218	Minnesota	431	Manitoba	647	Ontario	832	Texas
219	Indiana	432	Texas	649	Turks and Caicos Isls.	843	South Carolina
224	Illinois	434	Virginia	650	California	845	New York
225	Louisiana	435	Utah	651	Minnesota	847	Illinois
226	Ontario	438	Quebec	657	California	848	New Jersey
228	Mississippi	440	Ohio	660	Missouri	849	Dominican Republic
229	Georgia	441	Bermuda	661	California	850	Florida
231	Michigan	442	California	662	Mississippi	*855*	*Toll-Free Service*
234	Ohio	443	Maryland	664	Montserrat	856	New Jersey
239	Florida	450	Quebec	667	Maryland	857	Massachusetts
240	Maryland	456	Inbound intl.	669	California	858	California
242	The Bahamas	458	Oregon	670	N. Mariana Islands	859	Kentucky
246	Barbados	469	Texas	671	Guam	860	Connecticut
248	Michigan	470	Georgia	678	Georgia	862	New Jersey
249	Ontario	473	Grenada	681	West Virginia	863	Florida
250	British Columbia	475	Connecticut	682	Texas	864	South Carolina
251	Alabama	478	Georgia	684	American Samoa	865	Tennessee
252	North Carolina	479	Arkansas	*700*	*Interexchange carriers*	*866*	*Toll-Free Service*
253	Washington	480	Arizona	701	North Dakota	867	Yukon, NW Terr., Nunavut
254	Texas	484	Pennyslvania	702	Nevada	868	Trinidad and Tobago
256	Alabama	*500*	*Personal Comm. Serv.*	703	Virginia	869	St. Kitts and Nevis
260	Indiana	501	Arkansas	704	North Carolina	870	Arkansas
262	Wisconsin	502	Kentucky	705	Ontario	872	Illinois
264	Anguilla	503	Oregon	706	Georgia	873	Quebec
267	Pennsylvania	504	Louisiana	707	California	876	Jamaica
268	Antigua and Barbuda	505	New Mexico	708	Illinois	*877*	*Toll-Free Service*
269	Michigan	506	New Brunswick	709	Newfoundland	878	Pennsylvania
270	Kentucky	507	Minnesota	710	U.S. Government	*880*	*Paid Toll-Free Serv.*
276	Virginia	508	Massachusetts	*711*	*Telecommunications*	*881*	*Paid Toll-Free Serv.*
281	Texas	509	Washington		*Relay Service (TRS)*	*882*	*Paid Toll-Free Serv.*
284	British Virgin Islands	510	California	712	Iowa	*888*	*Toll-Free Service*
289	Ontario	*511*	*Traffic info.*	713	Texas	*900*	*Premium Service*
301	Maryland	512	Texas	714	California	901	Tennessee
302	Delaware	513	Ohio	715	Wisconsin	902	Nova Scotia, Prince Ed. Isl.
303	Colorado	514	Quebec	716	New York	903	Texas
304	West Virginia	515	Iowa	717	Pennsylvania	904	Florida
305	Florida	516	New York	718	New York	905	Ontario
306	Saskatchewan	517	Michigan	719	Colorado	906	Michigan
307	Wyoming	518	New York	720	Colorado	907	Alaska
308	Nebraska	519	Ontario	721	Sint Maarten	908	New Jersey
309	Illinois	520	Arizona	724	Pennsylvania	909	California
310	California	530	California	727	Florida	910	North Carolina
311	*Non-Emergency Access*	*533*	*Personal Comm. Serv.*	731	Tennessee	*911*	*Emergency*
312	Illinois	534	Wisconsin	732	New Jersey	912	Georgia
313	Michigan	539	Oklahoma	734	Michigan	913	Kansas
314	Missouri	540	Virginia	740	Ohio	914	New York
315	New York	541	Oregon	747	California	915	Texas
316	Kansas	*544*	*Personal Comm. Serv.*	754	Florida	916	California
317	Indiana	551	New Jersey	757	Virginia	917	New York
318	Louisiana	559	California	758	St. Lucia	918	Oklahoma
319	Iowa	561	Florida	760	California	919	North Carolina
320	Minnesota	562	California	762	Georgia	920	Wisconsin
321	Florida	563	Iowa	763	Minnesota	925	California
323	California	*566*	*Personal Comm. Serv.*	765	Indiana	928	Arizona
325	Texas	567	Ohio	767	Dominica	929	New York
330	Ohio	570	Pennsylvania	769	Mississippi	931	Tennessee
331	Illinois	571	Virginia	770	Georgia	936	Texas
334	Alabama	573	Missouri	772	Florida	937	Ohio
336	North Carolina	574	Indiana	773	Illinois	938	Alabama
337	Louisiana	575	New Mexico	774	Massachusetts	939	Puerto Rico
339	Massachusetts	579	Quebec	775	Nevada	940	Texas
340	U.S. Virgin Islands	580	Oklahoma	778	British Columbia	941	Florida
343	Ontario	581	Quebec	779	Illinois	947	Michigan
345	Cayman Islands	585	New York	780	Alberta	949	California
347	New York	586	Michigan	781	Massachusetts	951	California
351	Massachusetts	587	Alberta	784	St. Vincent and Gren.	952	Minnesota
352	Florida	*600*	*Canadian Services*	785	Kansas	954	Florida
360	Washington	601	Mississippi	786	Florida	956	Texas
361	Texas	602	Arizona	787	Puerto Rico	970	Colorado
385	Utah	603	New Hampshire	*800*	*Toll-Free Service*	971	Oregon
386	Florida	604	British Columbia	801	Utah	972	Texas
401	Rhode Island	605	South Dakota	802	Vermont	973	New Jersey
402	Nebraska	606	Kentucky	803	South Carolina	978	Massachusetts
403	Alberta	607	New York	804	Virginia	979	Texas
404	Georgia	608	Wisconsin	805	California	980	North Carolina
405	Oklahoma	609	New Jersey	806	Texas	984	North Carolina
406	Montana	610	Pennsylvania	807	Ontario	985	Louisiana
						989	Michigan

POSTAL INFORMATION

Basic U.S. Postal Service

The Postal Reorganization Act, creating a government-owned postal service under the executive branch and replacing the old Post Office Department, was signed into law by Pres. Richard Nixon, Aug. 12, 1970. The service officially came into being on July 1, 1971. The U.S. Postal Service is governed by an 11-person board of governors. Nine of the members are appointed by the president, with Senate approval. These nine choose a postmaster general. The board and the postmaster general choose the 11th member, who serves as deputy postmaster general.

Congress passed the Postal Accountability and Enhancement Act, which overhauled postal service operations for the first time since 1971, on Dec. 8, 2006. New operating provisions included the ability to adjust rates annually, negotiate for contracts, and invest profits in internal improvements. (The Postal Service last received a public service subsidy, i.e., taxpayer dollars, in 1982.)

Historical Postage Rates, 1851-2012

Postage cost for a prepaid, one-ounce letter (the first-class standard after July 1, 1885).

Effective date	Rate	2012 dollars	Effective date	Rate	2012 dollars	Effective date	Rate	2012 dollars
July 1, 1851	$0.06[1]	$1.68	May 16, 1971	$0.08	$0.46	Jan. 1, 1995	$0.32	$0.49
July 1, 1863	0.06	1.13	Mar. 2, 1974	0.10	0.47	Jan. 10, 1999	0.33	0.46
Oct. 1, 1883	0.04	1.00	Dec. 31, 1975	0.13	0.56	Jan. 7, 2001	0.34	0.45
July 1, 1885	0.02	0.52	May 29, 1978	0.15	0.53	June 30, 2002	0.37	0.48
Nov. 2, 1917	0.03[2]	0.54	Mar. 22, 1981	0.18	0.46	Jan. 8, 2006	0.39	0.45
July 1, 1919	0.02[2]	0.27	Nov. 1, 1981	0.20	0.51	May 14, 2007	0.41	0.46
July 6, 1932	0.03	0.51	Feb. 17, 1985	0.22	0.48	May 12, 2008	0.42	0.45
Aug. 1, 1958	0.04	0.32	Apr. 3, 1988	0.25	0.49	May 11, 2009	0.44	0.48
Jan. 7, 1963	0.05	0.38	Feb. 3, 1991	0.29	0.49	June 24, 2012	0.45	0.45
Jan. 7, 1968	0.06	0.40						

(1) For domestic letters traveling under 3,000 miles. (2) The price increased one cent during World War II; Congress restored its prewar rate in 1919.

Status of the U.S. Postal Service, 2001-11

Source: *Postal Facts 2012*, U.S. Postal Service

	2001	2004	2005	2006	2007	2008	2009	2010	2011	% change, 2001-11
Total mail items (bil)	207.5	206.1	211.7	213.1	212.2	202.7	177.0	171.0	168.0	−19.0%
First-class mail items (bil) . . .	103.7	97.9	98.1	97.7	95.9	91.7	83.8	78.2	73.5	−29.1
Stamped mail items (bil)	53.6	47.7	45.9	44.4	42.3	35.4	31.6	28.9	25.8	−51.9
Advertising mail items (bil) . .	89.9	95.6	100.9	102.5	103.5	99.1	82.7	82.5	84.7	−5.8
Annual revenue (bil)	$65.8	$68.9	$69.9	$72.7	$74.7	$74.9	$68.0	$67.1	$65.7	−0.2
Total retail revenue (bil)	$14.8	$15.2	$14.9	$14.5	$14.6	$14.1	$13.1	$12.5	$12.3	−16.9
Total customer visits (bil) . . .	1.4	1.2	1.3	1.3	1.2	1.2	1.1	1.1	0.9	−33.2
Delivery points (mil)	137.7	142.5	144.3	146.2	148.0	149.2	150.0	150.7	151.5	10.0
Total delivery routes	242,600	241,200	243,000	244,700	246,500	244,800	232,900	230,600	228,160	−6.0
Total retail offices	38,123	37,159	37,142	36,826	36,451	36,723	36,496	36,222	35,756	−6.2
Career employees	775,903	707,485	704,716	696,138	684,762	663,238	623,128	583,908	551,570	−28.9

U.S. Domestic Mail Rates

Source: *Price List (Notice 123)*, U.S. Postal Service. Effective June 24, 2012. Rates are for domestic retail customers unless otherwise noted. Domestic rates apply to the U.S., its territories and possessions, and APOs and FPOs.

First-Class Mail

First-Class Mail includes written matter such as letters, postcards, bills, account statements, and any matter sealed or closed against inspection. In most cases, **delivery is in 3 days or less**.

Written matter sealed against inspection costs 45¢ for the first ounce, 20¢ for each additional ounce or fraction thereof, up to 3.5 oz. Postcard postage is 32¢. Large envelopes measuring up to 12 in. by 15 in. (or standard envelopes over 3.5 oz.) cost 90¢ for the first ounce and 20¢ for each additional ounce or fraction thereof. Presort- and automation-compatible mail can qualify for lower rates if certain piece minimums, mailing permits, and other requirements are met.

Express Mail

Express Mail provides guaranteed expedited service for any mailable article (up to 70 lbs and not over 108 in. in combined length and girth). Offers **next day delivery** by noon to most destinations; there is a $12.50 extra charge for Sunday or holiday delivery. Second-day service is available to locations not in the Next Day Delivery Network. Prices start at $12.95 for items weighing up to 8 oz., dependent on distance. All rates include insurance up to $100, shipment receipt, record of delivery at the destination post office, and free tracking.

Express Mail Flat Rate: $18.95, regardless of weight, if matter fits into a designated Postal Service flat-rate envelope.

Pickup On Demand service is available for **$15.30** per stop, regardless of the number of pieces or service used.

Priority Mail

Due to expeditious handling and transportation, Priority Mail is **delivered in 2 days** in most cases. Priority Mail may include any mailable article up to 70 lbs and not over 108 in. in length and girth combined.

Priority Mail Flat Rate: $5.15 or **$5.30**, regardless of weight, if matter fits into designated Postal Service flat-rate envelopes. **$5.35**, **$11.35**, or **$15.45**, regardless of weight (under 70 lbs), if matter fits into special Postal Service flat-rate boxes.

Priority Mail Rates

Weight not over	Zone 1-2	3	4	5	6	7	8
1 lb	$5.20	$5.25	$5.35	$5.50	$5.65	$5.90	$6.30
2	5.30	5.65	6.30	8.05	8.75	9.45	10.40
3	6.05	6.95	8.05	9.70	10.95	11.80	13.85
4	6.85	8.15	9.20	12.85	14.05	15.00	16.70
5	8.10	9.35	10.55	14.55	16.05	17.25	19.25
6	8.95	10.30	11.85	16.20	18.00	19.35	21.75
7	9.50	11.20	12.75	18.05	19.90	21.80	24.45
8	10.20	12.20	14.25	19.60	21.85	24.00	27.40
9	10.85	13.15	15.45	21.25	23.80	26.00	30.50
10	11.60	14.15	16.85	23.00	25.70	28.60	33.20
11	12.40	15.10	18.15	24.80	27.60	31.55	36.45
12	13.25	16.20	19.45	26.60	30.00	34.10	39.15
13	14.10	17.20	20.55	28.15	32.20	35.50	40.55
14	14.90	18.25	21.80	29.90	33.95	37.50	42.55
15	15.55	19.25	23.00	31.65	35.45	38.30	43.75

Parcel Post

Parcel Post applies to packages not mailed as Priority Mail, Express Mail, Media Mail, or Library Mail. (Parcel Select, a separate service, is used for medium-to-large volumes of packages.) Parcel Post is a ground service for nonurgent shipping and oversized packages; delivery depends on distance and takes 2-8 days.

Any package matter may be mailed at Parcel Post rates provided it does not exceed 70 lbs or 130 in. in combined length and girth. Packages over 84 in. and up to 108 in. in combined length and girth and under 20 lbs use the 20-lb "balloon" price. Packages exceeding 108 in. use the oversized price—consult postal worker. Fractions of a pound are counted as a full pound.

Parcel Post Rates

Weight not over	Zone						
	1-2	3	4	5	6	7	8
1 lb	$5.20	$5.25	$5.35	$5.45	$5.55	$5.60	$5.70
2	5.30	5.65	6.16	7.49	7.78	8.13	8.83
3	5.75	6.53	7.37	8.54	9.36	9.87	11.14
4	6.17	7.33	8.10	9.51	10.41	11.10	12.09
5	7.29	8.42	9.18	10.34	11.08	11.74	12.70
6	8.01	9.28	10.13	11.17	11.74	12.38	13.48
7	8.46	9.98	10.66	12.03	12.65	13.39	14.61
8	8.77	10.48	11.03	12.40	13.27	14.13	15.51
9	9.01	10.81	11.43	12.77	13.86	14.85	16.39
10	9.27	11.17	11.80	13.16	14.48	15.62	17.29
11	9.56	11.50	12.19	13.52	15.07	16.34	18.18
12	9.86	11.86	12.53	13.88	15.68	17.08	19.05
13	10.19	12.18	12.92	14.24	16.29	17.85	19.97
14	10.49	12.54	13.30	14.61	16.89	18.57	20.88
15	10.79	12.87	13.66	14.97	17.49	19.33	21.78
Balloon	12.33	14.61	15.48	17.15	20.53	23.06	26.23
Oversized	62.42	65.30	66.60	68.57	91.83	97.79	108.23

Standard Mail

Standard Mail is limited to items less than 16 oz. such as solicitations, newsletters, advertising materials, books, cassettes, and other merchandise. It may not be used for personal correspondence. A minimum volume of 200 pieces or 50 lbs of such items is necessary, and specific bulk mail preparation and sortation requirements apply.

The minimum rate per piece for pieces 3.3 oz. or less is $0.392 for basic nonmachinable letters. Contact a post office for discounts for automation, presorted, carrier route, and destination entry, among others. Separate rates are available for some nonprofit organizations.

Any mailer who uses standard mail is required to pay an annual fee of $190, good for 365 days. Additional standards apply to mailings of nonidentical-weight pieces.

Periodicals

Periodicals include newspapers and magazines.

For the general public, the applicable retail postage is paid for periodicals.

For publishers, rates vary according to the following:
(1) whether item is sent to same county,
(2) percentage of editorial and advertising matter,
(3) whether the publisher is a nonprofit or produces educational material for use in classrooms,
(4) weight,
(5) distance,
(6) level of presort, and
(7) automation compatibility.

Library Mail

Applies to books, printed music, bound academic theses, periodicals, sound recordings, museum materials, and other library materials mailed between schools, colleges, universities, public libraries, museums, veterans' and fraternal organizations, and nonprofit religious, educational, scientific, and labor organizations or associations (or to or from such organizations). Advertising restrictions apply. All packages must be marked "Library Mail" and may not exceed 108 in. in combined length and girth. Contact a post office for further information.

Rates are calculated by weight only. Single-piece rates: $2.35, up to 1 lb; 40¢ for each additional pound or fraction thereof up to 7 lbs; additional pounds thereafter, 38¢.

Media Mail

Applies to books of at least 8 printed pages; 16-mm or narrower-width films; printed music; printed test materials; sound recordings, playscripts, and manuscripts for books; printed educational charts; loose-leaf pages and binders consisting of medical information; and computer-readable media. Advertising restrictions apply. Packages must be marked "Media Mail" and may not exceed 108 in. in combined length and girth. Contact a post office for further information.

Rates are calculated by weight only. Single-piece rates: $2.47, up to 1 lb; 42¢, for each additional pound or fraction thereof up to 7 lbs; additional pounds thereafter, 40¢.

Bound Printed Matter

Applies to advertising, promotional, directory, or editorial material that is bound by permanent fastening and consists of sheets of which at least 90% are imprinted by any process other than handwriting or typewriting. Does not include stationery (or pads of blank forms) or personal correspondence. Packages may not exceed 108 in. in combined length and girth and must be marked "Bound Printed Matter" or "BPM."

Bound Printed Matter Rates
(zone rate for nonpresorted commercial parcels)

Weight not over	Zone						
	1-2	3	4	5	6	7	8
1.0 lb	$2.38	$2.44	$2.50	$2.59	$2.69	$2.75	$2.95
1.5	2.38	2.44	2.50	2.59	2.69	2.75	2.95
2.0	2.48	2.56	2.64	2.76	2.90	2.98	3.24
2.5	2.59	2.69	2.79	2.94	3.11	3.21	3.54
3.0	2.69	2.81	2.93	3.11	3.32	3.44	3.83
3.5	2.80	2.94	3.08	3.29	3.53	3.67	4.13
4.0	2.90	3.06	3.22	3.46	3.74	3.90	4.42
4.5	3.01	3.19	3.37	3.64	3.95	4.13	4.72
5.0	3.11	3.31	3.51	3.81	4.16	4.36	5.01
6.0	3.32	3.56	3.80	4.16	4.58	4.82	5.60
7.0	3.53	3.81	4.09	4.51	5.00	5.28	6.19
8.0	3.74	4.06	4.38	4.86	5.42	5.74	6.78
9.0	3.95	4.31	4.67	5.21	5.84	6.20	7.37
10.0	4.16	4.56	4.96	5.56	6.26	6.66	7.96
11.0	4.37	4.81	5.25	5.91	6.68	7.12	8.55
12.0	4.58	5.06	5.54	6.26	7.10	7.58	9.14
13.0	4.79	5.31	5.83	6.61	7.52	8.04	9.73
14.0	5.00	5.56	6.12	6.96	7.94	8.50	10.32
15.0	5.21	5.81	6.41	7.31	8.36	8.96	10.91

Domestic Mail Special Services

Delivery Confirmation

Applies to First-Class Mail parcels, Priority Mail, and Package Services. Available for purchase at the time of mailing only. Provides mailer with the date and time an article was delivered or date and time of any unsuccessful delivery attempts. Electronic confirmation is available for bar-coded matter.

Confirmation is accessible to retail purchasers on the Internet (www.usps.com) or toll-free by phone at (800) 222-1811.

First-Class Mail parcels fees: retail, 85¢; electronic, free. Priority Mail fees: retail, 75¢; electronic, free. Standard Mail fee: electronic, 19¢.

Change of Address

The USPS will forward mail to another address provided a Change of Address (COA) card has been filed, either in person (free), on www.usps.com ($1 fee), or by phone at (800) ASK-USPS ($1). The COA card, which can be picked up at any post office or printed off the Internet, can also be dropped in any mailbox for free filing.

Special Handling

Provides preferential handling, but not preferential delivery, to the extent practicable in dispatch and transportation. Available for First-Class Mail, Priority Mail, and Package Services for the following surcharge: up to 10 lb, $7.70; over 10 lb, $10.80. Pieces must be marked "Special Handling."

> The USPS introduced the "Forever" stamp Apr. 12, 2007. The Forever stamp initially cost 41¢ and will always be valid as First-Class postage on standard envelopes weighing one ounce or less, even after rates increased. The Forever stamp can be purchased at the current First-Class standard rate (45¢ as of Sept. 2012).

Registered Mail

Provides sender with mailing receipt, and a delivery record is maintained. Only matter prepaid with postage at First-Class Mail or Priority Mail rates may be registered. Stamps or meter stamps must be attached. The face of the article must be at least 5 in. long, 3.5 in. high.

Declared value	Fee
$0.00	$10.95
$0.01 to $100.00	11.75
$100.01 to $500.00	13.50
$500.01 to $1,000.00	14.90
$1,000.01 to $2,000.00	16.30
$2,000.01 to $3,000.00	17.70
$3,000.01 to $4,000.00	19.10
$4,000.01 to $5,000.00	20.50
$5,000.01 to $6,000.00	21.90
$6,000.01 to $7,000.00	23.30
$7,000.01 to $8,000.00	24.70
$8,000.01 to $9,000.00	26.10
$9,000.01 to $10,000.00	27.50
$10,000.01 to $11,000.00	28.90
Each additional $1,000 or fraction thereof	1.40

Note: The mailer is required to declare the value of mail presented for registration. Fee for articles with declared value of more than $0.00 up to $25,000 includes insurance.

Collect on Delivery (C.O.D.)

Fee: $5.90 for up to $50; increases incrementally. Items must be sent as bona fide orders or be in conformity with agreements between senders and addressees. Maximum amount collectible is $1,000. For details, consult a post office.

Certified Mail

Available for any matter having no intrinsic value on which First-Class Mail or Priority Mail postage is paid. A receipt is furnished at the time of mailing, and evidence of delivery is obtained. Basic fee is $2.95 in addition to regular postage. Return receipt and restricted delivery available upon payment of additional fees. No indemnity.

Insured Mail

Applicable to Standard Mail, First-Class Mail, or Priority Mail packages. Matter for sale addressed to prospective purchasers who have not ordered it or authorized its sending cannot be insured. **Note:** For Express Mail, insurance is included up to $100; additional insurance can be purchased for significantly lower fees than those shown here.

Declared value	Insured mail fee[1]
$0.01 to $50.00	$1.85
$50.01 to $100.00	2.35
$100.01 to $200.00	2.90
$200.01 to $300.00	4.85
$300.01 to $400.00	5.95
$400.01 to $500.00	7.05
$500.01 to $600.00	8.15
Each additional $100 or fraction thereof	1.10

(1) In addition to postage. (Maximum liability is $5,000.) See a post office for details on bulk discounts.

International Mail Special Services

Insurance: Available to many countries for loss of or damage to items paid at parcel post rate. Consult a post office for indemnity limits for individual countries.

Priority Mail International Insurance Rates

Limit of indemnity not over	Fee
$50	$2.45
$100	3.60
$200	4.75
$300	5.90
$400	7.05
$500	8.20
$600	9.35
$700	10.50
Each additional $100 or fraction thereof	1.15

Note: Maximum insurance $5,000 ($2,499 in Canada). Varies by country.

International postcards (single): 85¢ to Canada or Mexico; $1.05 to all other countries.

Registration: Available for letter-post items only to most countries. Fee: $11.75.

Return Receipt: Shows to whom and when item is delivered. Fee: $2.35 (must be purchased at time of mailing).

First-Class Mail International: Letter-post items weighing under 1 oz. can be sent airmail for $1.05 to most countries; 85¢ to Canada or Mexico.

International Reply Coupons (IRC): Provide foreign addressees with a prepaid means of responding to communications initiated by a U.S. sender. Each IRC is equivalent to the destination country's minimum postage rate for an unregistered airmail letter. Fee: $2.20 per coupon.

Restricted Delivery: Places restrictions on who receives an item. Available to many countries for registered mail, with some limitations. Fee: $4.55.

State and Territory Postal Abbreviations

The state, territory, and possession abbreviations below are approved by the U.S. Postal Service for use in addresses.

Alabama	AL	Hawaii	HI	Missouri	MO	Pennsylvania	PA
Alaska	AK	Idaho	ID	Montana	MT	Puerto Rico	PR
American Samoa	AS	Illinois	IL	Nebraska	NE	Rhode Island	RI
Arizona	AZ	Indiana	IN	Nevada	NV	South Carolina	SC
Arkansas	AR	Iowa	IA	New Hampshire	NH	South Dakota	SD
California	CA	Kansas	KS	New Jersey	NJ	Tennessee	TN
Colorado	CO	Kentucky	KY	New Mexico	NM	Texas	TX
Connecticut	CT	Louisiana	LA	New York	NY	Utah	UT
Delaware	DE	Maine	ME	North Carolina	NC	Vermont	VT
District of Columbia	DC	Marshall Islands[1]	MH	North Dakota	ND	Virgin Islands	VI
Federated States of Micronesia[1]	FM	Maryland	MD	Northern Mariana Isls.	MP	Virginia	VA
		Massachusetts	MA	Ohio	OH	Washington	WA
Florida	FL	Michigan	MI	Oklahoma	OK	West Virginia	WV
Georgia	GA	Minnesota	MN	Oregon	OR	Wisconsin	WI
Guam	GU	Mississippi	MS	Palau[1]	PW	Wyoming	WY

(1) Although an independent nation, this country is subject to domestic rates and fees.

Canadian Province and Territory Postal Abbreviations

Source: Canada Post

Alberta	AB	Newfoundland and Labrador	NL	Nunavut	NU	Quebec	QC
British Columbia	BC			Ontario	ON	Saskatchewan	SK
Manitoba	MB	Northwest Territories	NT	Prince Edward Island	PE	Yukon	YT
New Brunswick	NB	Nova Scotia	NS				

Social Security Coverage

Source: Social Security Administration; World Almanac research; provisions shown are as under current law, Sept. 2012

Social Security Benefits

Social Security's **Old-Age, Survivors, and Disability Insurance (OASDI)** program benefits are based on a worker's **primary insurance amount (PIA)**, which is related by law to the average indexed monthly earnings (AIME) on which Social Security contributions have been paid. The full PIA is currently payable to a worker retiring at age 66 (varies depending on birth year), and to an entitled disabled worker at any age. Spouses and children of retired or disabled workers and survivors of deceased workers receive set proportions of the PIA subject to a family maximum amount.

The PIA is calculated by applying varying percentages to succeeding parts of the AIME. The formula is adjusted annually to reflect changes in average annual wages.

Increases in Social Security benefits are initiated for Dec. of each year, assuming the Consumer Price Index (CPI) for the 3rd calendar quarter of the year increased relative to the base quarter, which is the 3rd calendar quarter of the year in which an increase last became effective. The size of the benefit increase is determined by the percentage rise of the CPI between the quarters measured.

The **average monthly benefit** payable to all retired workers amounted to $1,229 in Dec. 2011. The average benefit for disabled workers in that month amounted to $1,111.

Maximum Monthly Retired-Worker Benefits Payable for Individuals who Retired at Age 65[1]

Year attaining age 65	Maximum benefit— Payable at retirement	Maximum benefit— Payable effective Dec. 2011
1990	$975	$1,762
1995	1,199	1,826
1996	1,248	1,854
1997	1,326	1,914
1998	1,342	1,897
1999	1,373	1,915
2000	1,435	1,953
2001	1,538	2,022
2002	1,660	2,128
2003	1,721	2,176
2004	1,784	2,209
2005	1,874	2,259
2006	1,961	2,272
2007	1,998	2,240
2008	2,030	2,225
2009	2,172	2,250
2010	2,191	2,270
2011	2,249	2,330
2012	2,310	2,310

(1) Assumes retirement at beginning of year.

Amount of Work Required

To qualify for benefits, the worker generally must have worked a certain length of time in covered employment. Just how long depends on when the worker reaches age 62 or, if earlier, when he or she dies or becomes disabled. A person born after 1929 who dies, becomes disabled, or reaches 62 after 1991 must generally have had at least 10 years of work credit to qualify for benefits.

Contribution and Benefit Base

Calendar year	OASDI[1]	Calendar year	OASDI[1]	Calendar year	OASDI[1]
1994	$60,600	2001	$80,400	2007	$97,500
1995	61,200	2002	84,900	2008	102,000
1996	62,700	2003	87,000	2009	106,800
1997	65,400	2004	87,900	2010	106,800
1998	68,400	2005	90,000	2011	106,800
1999	72,600	2006	94,200	2012	110,100
2000	76,200				

(1) Old-Age, Survivors, and Disability Insurance.

A person is **fully insured** who has 1 quarter of coverage for every year after age 21 is reached (or 1950, if later) up to but not including the year the worker reaches 62, dies, or becomes disabled. In 2012, a person earns 1 quarter of coverage for each $1,130 of annual earnings in covered employment, up to 4 quarters per year.

To receive **disability benefits**, the worker, in addition to being fully insured, must generally have credit for 20 quarters of coverage out of the 40 calendar quarters before he or she became disabled. A disabled blind worker need meet only the fully insured requirement. Persons disabled before age 31 can qualify with a briefer period of coverage. Certain survivor benefits are payable if the deceased worker had 6 quarters of coverage in the 13 quarters preceding death.

Tax Rate Schedule
(percentage of covered earnings)

Year	Total (for employees and employers, each)	OASDI[1]	HI[2]
1979-80	6.13%	5.08%	1.05%
1981	6.65	5.35	1.30
1982-83	6.70	5.40	1.30
1984	7.00	5.70	1.30
1985	7.05	5.70	1.35
1986-87	7.15	5.70	1.45
1988-89	7.51	6.06	1.45
1990 and after[3]	7.65	6.20	1.45

Year	Total (for self-employed)	OASDI[1]	HI[2]
1979-80	8.10%	7.05%	1.05%
1981	9.30	8.00	1.30
1982-83	9.35	8.05	1.30
1984	14.00	11.40	2.60
1985	14.10	11.40	2.70
1986-87	14.30	11.40	2.90
1988-89	15.02	12.12	2.90
1990 and after[3]	15.30	12.40	2.90

(1) Old-Age, Survivors, and Disability Ins. (2) Hospital Ins. (Medicare). (3) Public Law 111-147 exempted most employers from paying the employer share of OASDI payroll tax on wages paid Mar. 19-Dec. 31, 2010, to certain qualified individuals hired after Feb. 3, 2010. PL 111-312 reduced the OASDI payroll tax rate for 2011 by 2 percentage points for employees and for self-employed workers. PL 112-96 extended the 2011 rate reduction through 2012. The laws require that the general fund of the treasury reimburses the OASI and DI Trust Funds for these temporary reductions.

What Aged Workers Receive

A person may receive monthly old-age benefits when he or she has enough work in covered employment and has reached retirement age—age 62 for reduced benefits, the age below for full benefits.

Full-Benefit Retirement Age (FRA) by Birth Year

Year of birth	FRA	Year of birth	FRA
1937 or earlier	65	1955	66 and 2 mos.
1938	65 and 2 mos.	1956	66 and 4 mos.
1939	65 and 4 mos.	1957	66 and 6 mos.
1940	65 and 6 mos.	1958	66 and 8 mos.
1941	65 and 8 mos.	1959	66 and 10 mos.
1942	65 and 10 mos.	1960 or later	67
1943-54	66		

Note: If born on Jan. 1, refer to the previous birth year.

In 2000, the retirement earnings test was eliminated beginning with the month when the beneficiary reaches **full-benefit retirement age (FRA)**. A person at or above FRA no longer has benefits reduced because of earnings. However, in the calendar year a beneficiary reaches FRA, benefits are reduced $1 for every $3 of earnings above the limit allowed by law ($38,880 for 2012) in the months prior to FRA. For years before the beneficiary attains FRA, the reduction is $1 for every $2 of earnings over the exempt amount ($14,640 for 2012).

For workers who reached age 65 between 1982 and 1989, Social Security benefits are raised by 3% for each year for which the worker failed to receive benefits between FRA and 70 (72 before 1984), whether because of earnings from work, because the worker did not apply for benefits, or because the worker declined benefits after entitlement. The **delayed retirement credit** is 1% per year for workers who reached age 65 before 1982. The delayed retirement credit rose to 8% per year for 2008 and years after. The rate for workers who reached age 65 in 1998-99 is 5.5%; 2000-01, 6.0%; 2002-03, 6.5%; 2004-05, 7.0%. For 2006-07, it is 7.5%.

For workers retiring early, benefits are permanently reduced $5/9$ of 1% for each month before the FRA, up to 36 months. If the number of months exceeds 36, then the benefit is further reduced $5/12$ of 1% per month.

For example, when FRA reaches 67, for workers who retire at exactly age 62, there are a total of 60 months of reduction. The reduction for the first 36 months is $5/9$ of 36%, or 20%. The reduction for the remaining 24 months is $5/12$ of 24%, or 10%. Thus, when the FRA reaches 67, the amount of reduction at age 62 will be 30%. The nearer to FRA the worker is when he or she begins collecting a benefit, the larger the monthly benefit will be.

Benefits for Worker's Spouse

The spouse of a worker who is getting Social Security retirement or disability payments may become entitled to an insurance benefit of **one-half of the worker's PIA** if claiming benefits at full retirement age. Reduced spouse's benefits are available at age 62 and are permanently reduced $^{25}/_{36}$ of 1% for each month before FRA, up to 36 months. If the number of months exceeds 36, then the benefit is further reduced $^{5}/_{12}$ of 1% per month. Benefits are also payable to the aged divorced spouse of an insured worker if he or she was married to the worker for at least 10 years. To qualify for divorced spouse benefits, the insured worker does not have to be receiving benefits if the divorce occurred at least 2 years earlier. Benefits received as a spouse are reduced by the amount of one's own PIA.

Benefits for Children of Workers

If a retired or disabled worker has a child under age 18, the child will usually get a benefit equal to **one-half of the worker's unreduced benefit**. So will the worker's spouse, even if under age 62, if he or she is caring for an entitled child of the worker who is under 16 or who became disabled before age 22. However, total benefits paid on a worker's earnings record are subject to a family maximum. Total monthly benefits paid to the family of a worker who retired in 2012 at age 66 and always had the maximum earnings creditable under Social Security cannot exceed $4,429.

When entitled children reach age 18, their benefits generally stop, but a child disabled before age 22 may get a benefit as long as the disability meets the definition in the law. Benefits will be paid until a child attending elementary or secondary school full-time reaches age 19.

Benefits may also be paid to a grandchild or step-grandchild of a worker or of his or her spouse, in special circumstances.

OASDI Beneficiaries

Beneficiaries	May 2005	May 2010	May 2011	May 2012
Total (in thous.)[1]	48,068	53,349	54,790	56,158
Age 65 and over, total..	33,811	36,914	37,584	38,905
Retired workers.....	27,413	30,734	31,488	32,714
Disabled workers ...	112	339	344	453
Survivors/ dependents........	6,286	5,841	5,752	5,738
Under age 65, total ...	14,257	16,435	17,206	17,253
Retired workers.....	2,809	3,314	3,593	3,407
Disabled workers ...	6,239	7,628	8,027	8,254
Survivors/ dependents........	5,209	5,492	5,587	5,592
Total monthly benefits (in mil)	$42,074	$56,966	$59,042	$63,243

(1) Numbers may not add up to totals due to rounding or incomplete enumeration.

What Disabled Workers Receive

A worker who becomes unable to work may be eligible for a monthly disability benefit. Benefits continue until it is determined that the individual is no longer disabled. When a disabled-worker beneficiary reaches FRA (66 years for workers born 1943-54), the disability benefit becomes a retired-worker benefit.

Benefits—generally like those for dependents of retired-worker beneficiaries—may be paid to dependents of disabled beneficiaries. However, the maximum family benefit in disability cases is generally lower than in retirement cases.

Survivor Benefits

If an insured worker should die, one or more types of benefits may be payable to survivors, again subject to a maximum family benefit described above.

1. If claiming benefits at FRA, the **surviving spouse** will receive a benefit equal to 100% of the deceased worker's benefit. Benefits claimed before FRA are reduced for age with a maximum reduction of 28.5% at age 60. However, if the deceased worker claimed benefits before FRA, the surviving spouse's benefits are limited to the reduced amount the worker would be getting if alive, but not less than 82.5% of the worker's PIA. Remarriage after the worker's death ends the surviving spouse's benefit rights. However, if the widow(er) marries, and the marriage later ends, he or she

regains benefit rights. (A marriage after age 60, age 50 if disabled, is deemed not to have occurred for benefit purposes.) Survivor benefits may also be paid to a divorced spouse if the marriage lasted for at least 10 years.

Disabled widows and widowers may under certain circumstances qualify for benefits after attaining age 50 at the rate of 71.5% of the deceased worker's PIA. The widow or widower must have become totally disabled before or within 7 years after the spouse's death or the last month in which he or she received mother's or father's insurance benefits.

2. There is a benefit for each **child under age 18**. The monthly benefit for a child of a deceased worker is $^3/_4$ of the PIA, subject to the family maximum. A child with a disability that began before age 22 may also receive benefits. Also, a child may receive benefits until age 19 if he or she is in full-time attendance at an elementary or secondary school.

3. There is a **mother's or father's benefit** for the widow(er) if children of the worker under age 16 are in his or her care. The benefit is 75% of the PIA (subject to the family maximum), and it continues until the youngest child reaches age 16, at which time payments stop even if the child's benefit continues. Benefits may continue if the widow(er) has a disabled child beneficiary age 16 or over in his or her care.

4. Dependent parents may be eligible for benefits if they have been receiving at least half their support from the worker before his or her death, have reached age 62, and (except in certain circumstances) have not remarried since the worker's death. Each parent gets 75% of the worker's PIA; if only one parent survives, the benefit is 82%, but could be reduced for the family maximum.

5. A lump sum cash payment of **$255** is made when there is a spouse who was living with the worker or a spouse or child eligible for immediate monthly survivor benefits.

Self-Employed Workers

A self-employed person who has **net earnings of $400 or more** in a year must report such earnings for Social Security tax and credit purposes. The person reports net returns from the business. Income from real estate, savings, dividends, loans, pensions, or insurance policies are not included unless it is part of the business.

A self-employed person receives 1 quarter of coverage for each $1,130 (for 2012), up to a maximum of 4 quarters per year.

The nonfarm self-employed have the option of reporting their earnings as $^2/_3$ of their gross income from self-employment. This option can be used only if actual net earnings from self-employment income are less than $1,600 and less than $^2/_3$ of their gross income. The option may be used only 5 times. Also, the self-employed person must have actual net earnings of $400 or more in 2 of the 3 taxable years immediately preceding the year in which he or she uses the option.

When a person has both taxable wages and earnings from self-employment, wages are credited for Social Security purposes first; only as much self-employment income as brings total earnings up to the current taxable maximum becomes subject to the self-employment tax.

Farm Owners and Workers

Self-employed farmers whose gross annual earnings from farming are from **$600 to $2,400** may report $^2/_3$ of their gross earnings instead of net earnings for Social Security purposes. (Farmers whose gross annual earnings are under $600 cannot use the optional method.) Farmers whose gross income is over $2,400 and whose net earnings are less than $1,600 can report $1,600. Cash or crop shares received from a tenant or share farmer count if the owner participated materially in production or management. The self-employed farmer pays contributions at the same rate as other self-employed persons.

Agricultural employees. A worker's earnings from farm work count toward benefits if (1) the employer pays the worker $150 or more in cash during the year; or (2) the employer spends $2,500 or more in the year for agricultural labor. Under these rules, a person gets credit for 1 calendar quarter for each $1,130 in cash pay in 2012.

Foreign farm workers admitted to the U.S. on a temporary basis are not covered.

Household Workers

If an employer pays a household worker (e.g., maid, cook, laundry worker, nurse, babysitter, chauffeur, gardener) who is age 18 or older **$1,800 or more** in wages in 2012, the wages are covered under Social Security. This includes transportation costs paid for in cash. The job need not be regular or full-time.

The employee should get a Social Security card at the Social Security office and show it to the employer. The employer deducts the amount of the employee's Social Security tax from the worker's pay, adds an identical amount as the employer's Social Security tax, and sends the total amount to the federal government.

Medicare Coverage

The Medicare health insurance program provides acute-care coverage for Social Security and Railroad Retirement beneficiaries age 65 and over; workers and spouses age 65 and over with sufficient Medicare-only coverage in federal, state, or local government employment; certain persons entitled to receive Social Security or Railroad Retirement disability benefits; certain disabled persons with Medicare-only coverage through government employment; certain persons with end-stage kidney disease; and certain persons in the vicinity of Libby, MT, with asbestos-related conditions. What follows is a basic description that may not cover all circumstances.

The **basic Medicare plan**, available nationwide, is a fee-for-service arrangement, where the beneficiary may use any provider accepting Medicare; some services are not covered, and there are some out-of-pocket costs.

Hospital insurance (Part A). The basic hospital insurance program pays covered services for hospital and post-hospital care, including:

- All necessary inpatient hospital care for the first 60 days of each benefit period, except for a deductible ($1,156 in 2012). For days 61-90, Medicare pays for services over and above a coinsurance amount ($289 per day in 2012). After 90 days, the beneficiary has 60 lifetime reserve days for which Medicare helps pay. The coinsurance amount for reserve days was $578 in 2012.
- Up to 100 days of care in a skilled-nursing facility in each benefit period. Hospital insurance pays for all covered services for the first 20 days; for days 21-100, the beneficiary pays coinsurance ($144.50 per day in 2012).
- Part-time home health care provided by nurses or other health workers.
- Limited coverage of hospice care for terminally ill.

There is a premium for this insurance in certain—but not most—cases.

Medical insurance (Part B). Eligible elderly and disabled persons can receive benefits under this supplementary program only if they sign up and agree to a monthly premium. As of 2007, the monthly premium is tied to annual income. Individuals with an income of $85,000 or less and couples with an income of $170,000 or less pay $99.90 per person if they sign up upon becoming eligible in 2012. Part B covers certain medical services and supplies, including:

- Physicians' and surgeons' services, as well as some services furnished by other medical professionals.
- Services in an emergency room, outpatient clinic, or ambulatory surgical center.
- Home health care not covered under Part A.
- Laboratory tests, X-rays, and other diagnostic radiology services.
- Certain preventative care services and screening tests.
- Most physical and occupational therapy and speech pathology services.
- Comprehensive outpatient rehabilitation facility services and mental health care in a partial hospitalization psychiatric program, if inpatient care would otherwise be required.
- Radiation therapy, renal (kidney) dialysis and transplants, heart, lung, heart-lung, liver, pancreas, bone marrow, and intestinal transplants.
- Approved durable medical equipment for home use.
- Drugs that are not usually self-administered. Certain services for diabetes.
- Ambulance services when other transportation methods are contraindicated.
- Rural health clinic and health center services, including some telemedicine.

Part B services are generally subject to a deductible ($140 in 2012), coinsurance (generally 20% of the remaining allowed charges with certain exceptions), a deductible for blood, and amounts above the allowed charge if the doctor or supplier is not one who accepts the Medicare-approved rate as payment in full. For outpatient mental health services, coinsurance is phasing down from 50% to 20% of allowed charges over the period 2010-14. For outpatient hospital services, coinsurance varies by service, usually falling between 20% and 50% of allowed charges. There are no deductibles or coinsurance for certain services, such as clinical lab tests, home health agency services (except some durable medical equipment, which is subject to 20% coinsurance), and some preventative care services. Payments for certain physical, speech, and occupational therapy services are subject to certain limits. Dental care, hearing aids, and routine eye care are generally not covered under the basic plan.

To get medical insurance (Part B), persons approaching age 65 may enroll during the Initial Enrollment Period that lasts from 3 months before to 3 months after the 65th birthday, and the month of their birthday. If new enrollees desire coverage to begin in the month they reach age 65, they must enroll in the 3 months before their birthday. Persons who enroll after their first enrollment period may be subject to late-enrollment premiums.

The monthly premium is deducted from the cash benefit for persons receiving Social Security, Railroad Retirement, or Civil Service retirement benefits. Income from the medical premiums and the federal matching payments are put in a Supplementary Medical Insurance Trust Fund, from which benefits and administrative expenses are paid.

Medicare Advantage (Part C) (formerly Medicare+Choice). Persons eligible for Medicare may have the option of getting services through a Medicare-certified health maintenance organization (HMO), preferred provider organization (PPO), provider-sponsored organization (PSO), or other Medicare-certified **managed care** plan. Any such plan must provide at least the same benefits as Parts A and B, except for hospice services. They may provide added benefits (such as vision or hearing coverage) or reduce cost sharing or premiums. Enrollees may be required to use the plan's network of participating providers or pay higher out-of-pocket costs to go outside the network. Also available as options in some areas are Medicare-approved private fee-for-service plans and, for certain beneficiaries, special needs plans.

Prescription Drug Coverage (Part D). Effective Jan. 1, 2006, a Medicare prescription drug plan provides insurance coverage for prescription drugs. Medicare recipients pay a monthly premium (averaging $30 in 2012, depending on the provider) and a portion of drug costs. Enrollment is scheduled to take place Oct. 15-Dec. 7 and is optional. Coverage varies depending on the drug plan selected.

Further details are available on the Internet at www.medicare.gov or by calling 1-800-MEDICARE (1-800-633-4227).

Medicare card. Persons qualifying for hospital insurance under Social Security receive a health insurance card. The card indicates whether the individual has taken out medical insurance protection. It is to be shown to the hospital, skilled-nursing facility, home health agency, doctor, or whoever provides the covered services.

Payments are generally made only in the 50 states, Puerto Rico, U.S. Virgin Isls., Guam, American Samoa, and N. Mariana Isls.

Social Security Financing

Social Security is paid for by a tax on certain earnings (for 2012, on earnings up to $110,100) for **Old Age, Survivors, and Disability Insurance (OASDI)** and on all earnings (no upper limit) for hospital insurance with the **Medicare** program; the taxable earnings base for OASDI is adjusted annually to reflect increases in average wages. The employed worker and his or her employer share Social Security taxes equally.

Employers remit amounts withheld from employee wages for Social Security and income taxes to the Internal Revenue Service; employer Social Security taxes are also payable at the same time. (Self-employed workers pay Social Security taxes when filing their regular income tax forms.) The Social Security taxes (along with revenues arising from partial taxation of the Social Security benefits of certain high-income people) are transferred to the Social Security Trust Funds; they can be used only to pay benefits, the cost of rehabilitation services, and administrative expenses. By law, money not immediately needed for those purposes is invested in obligations of the federal government, which must pay interest on the money borrowed and must repay the principal when the obligations are redeemed or mature.

On Jan. 1, 1974, the **Supplemental Security Income (SSI)** program, established by the Social Security Amendments of 1972, replaced federal grants to states for aid to the needy aged, blind, and disabled in the 50 states and the District of Columbia. The program provides both for federal payments, based on uniform national standards and eligibility requirements, and for state supplementary payments, which vary by state. The Social Security Administration administers the federal payments financed from general funds of the Treasury—and the state supplements as well, if the state elects to have its supplementary program federally administered. States may supplement the federal payment for all recipients and must supplement it for persons otherwise adversely affected by the transition from the former public assistance programs. In May 2012, the number of persons receiving federally administered SSI payments was 8,179,285, and the payments totaled about $4.5 bil.

The **maximum monthly federal SSI payment** for individuals without an eligible spouse and with no other countable income, living in their own household, was $698 in 2012. For couples where both members were eligible, the maximum payment was $1,048.

For further information, contact the Social Security Administration toll-free at 1-800-772-1213 or visit its website at www.socialsecurity.gov.

Examples of Monthly Social Security Benefits Available, 2012

Benefit or beneficiary	For low earnings[1]	For med. earnings[1]	For max. earnings[1,2]
Primary insurance amount (worker retiring at 66 years, 0 months) . .	$961.50	$1,584.40	$2,513.60
Maximum family benefit (worker retiring at 66 years, 0 months).	1,442.30	2,892.00	4,398.80
Maximum family disability benefit (worker disabled at 55; in 2012) . .	1,351.50	2,363.50	3,757.50
Disabled worker (worker disabled at 55):			
Worker alone.	953.60	1,575.70	2,505.00
Worker, spouse, and 1 child	1,349.00	2,361.00	3,757.00
Retired worker claiming benefits at age 62:			
Worker alone[3].	708.00	1,167.00	1,845.00
Worker with spouse claiming benefits at—			
NRA or over[4].	1,180.00	1,945.00	3,075.00
Age 62[3].	1,038.00	1,711.00	2,706.00
Widow or widower claiming benefits at—			
Age 66 or over[4].	961.00	1,584.00	2,513.00
Age 60[4].	691.00	1,139.00	1,807.00
Disabled widow or widower claiming benefits at age 50-59[5]	687.00	1,132.00	1,797.00
1 surviving child[4]	721.00	1,188.00	1,885.00
Widow or widower NRA or over and 1 child[4]	1,442.00	2,772.00	4,398.00
Widowed mother or father and 1 child[4].	1,442.00	2,376.00	3,770.00
Widowed mother or father and 2 children[4]	1,442.00	2,892.00	4,398.00

NRA = Normal retirement age. **Note:** Effective Jan. 2012. (1) Career average earnings: an average of lifetime earnings indexed to the year prior to entitlement (2011 in this case). (2) Assumes work beginning at age 22. (3) Assumes maximum reduction. (4) Assumes worker lived and worked until NRA without receiving reduced benefits. (5) Effective Jan. 1984, disabled widow(er) claiming a benefit at age 50-59 receive a benefit equal to 71.5% of the primary insurance amount.

Social Security Recipients by Age, Sex, Race, and Hispanic Origin, 2011

Source: Social Security Administration

Social Security beneficiaries[1] (thous.)	Total[2]	White	Black	American Indian, Alaska Native	Asian	Hispanic
Total.	44,514	38,495	4,690	584	1,165	3,087
Sex						
Male	19,744	17,184	1,994	266	502	1,367
Female	24,770	21,312	2,696	318	663	1,720
Age						
15-54 years.	4,921	3,746	1,063	115	89	516
55-64 years.	6,416	5,392	839	107	142	517
65-74 years.	17,161	15,018	1,542	208	548	1,147
75 years or older.	16,016	14,339	1,246	154	386	907
Supplemental Security Income recipients[1] (thous.)						
Total.	5,562	3,745	1,506	182	226	868
Sex						
Male	2,360	1,660	576	82	83	366
Female	3,202	2,085	929	100	143	503
Age						
15-54 years.	3,163	2,129	920	117	61	490
55-64 years.	1,330	914	367	41	33	163
65-74 years.	573	371	128	16	64	117
75 years or older.	496	332	90	8	68	99
Average annual benefit in 2010 (dollars)						
Social Security	$12,870	$13,090	$11,336	$11,690	$11,947	$10,629
Supplemental Security Income.	7,129	7,132	7,184	6,569	6,935	7,147

Note: Race categories include people who reported being of that race, alone or in combination with another race. Persons of Hispanic origin may be of any race. (1) Persons 15 or older receiving Social Security benefits or Supplemental Security Income in Mar. 2011. (2) The sum of the individual categories may not add up to totals because of rounding and because the totals include persons who reported being of more than one race.

OASDI Recipients and Monthly Payments, 1940-2011

Source: Social Security Administration

Year	Total recipients	Monthly benefits Total (thous.)	Avg.[1]	Avg. (2011 dollars)[2]	Year	Total recipients	Monthly benefits Total (thous.)	Avg.[1]	Avg. (2011 dollars)[2]
1940	222,488	$4,070	$18.29	$287.26	2000	45,414,794	$34,848,920	$767.35	$1,006.18
1945	1,288,107	23,801	18.48	226.22	2001	45,877,506	36,504,206	795.69	1,015.54
1950	3,477,243	126,857	36.48	333.96	2002	46,444,317	37,854,453	815.05	1,026.30
1955	7,960,616	411,613	51.71	424.92	2003	47,038,486	39,541,528	840.62	1,035.34
1960	14,844,589	936,321	63.07	469.49	2004	47,687,722	41,574,363	871.80	1,046.53
1965	20,866,767	1,516,802	72.69	507.69	2005	48,434,445	44,351,772	915.71	1,061.87
1970	26,228,629	2,628,326	100.21	568.68	2006	49,122,831	46,938,176	955.53	1,073.41
1975	32,085,372	5,727,903	178.52	730.32	2007	49,864,982	49,218,232	987.03	1,078.57
1980	35,618,840	10,694,022	300.23	801.78	2008	50,898,396	53,666,202	1,054.38	1,106.95
1985	37,058,353	15,901,643	429.10	888.81	2009	52,522,819	55,905,731	1,064.41	1,125.06
1990	39,832,125	21,686,763	544.45	934.37	2010	54,032,097	58,048,364	1,074.33	1,112.53
1995	43,387,259	28,148,078	648.76	959.37	2011	55,404,480	62,213,382	1,122.89	1,122.89

OASDI = Old Age, Survivors, and Disability Insurance. **Note:** Disability insurance payments began in 1957. (1) Avg. monthly benefit does not necessarily reflect individual payments to OASDI recipients. (2) Adjusted for inflation.

Social Security Trust Funds

Source: Social Security Administration

Old-Age and Survivors Insurance Trust Fund, 1940-2011

(in millions)

Fiscal year[1]	Total	INCOME Net payroll tax contribs.	Income from taxing benefits	General fund reimburse-ments[2]	Net interest[3]	DISBURSEMENTS Total	Benefit pymts.[4]	Admin. expenses	Transfers to Railroad Retirement program	Net increase in fund[5]	Year-end balance
1940	$592	$550	—	—	$42	$28	$16	$12	—	$564	$1,745
1950	2,367	2,106	—	$4	257	784	727	57	—	1,583	12,893
1960	10,360	9,843	—	—	517	11,073	10,270	202	$600	−713	20,829
1970	31,746	29,955	—	442	1,350	27,321	26,268	474	579	4,425	32,616
1980	100,051	97,608	—	557	1,886	103,228	100,626	1,160	1,442	−3,177	24,566
1990	278,607	260,069	$2,924	1,471	14,143	223,481	218,948	1,564	2,969	55,126	203,445
1995	326,067	289,525	5,114	11	31,417	294,456	288,607	1,797	4,052	31,611	447,946
2000	484,228	418,219	12,476	1	53,532	353,396	347,868	1,990	3,538	130,832	893,003
2005	599,992	502,998	15,332	—	81,662	436,919	430,439	2,900	3,579	163,073	1,615,623
2006	632,157	530,006	15,176	−350	87,324	455,560	449,191	2,911	3,458	176,597	1,792,220
2007	663,376	553,414	16,661	—	93,300	488,553	481,828	3,151	3,575	174,822	1,967,042
2008	692,873	573,750	16,396	—	102,727	509,864	502,973	3,259	3,632	183,009	2,150,052
2009	697,326	571,228	18,967	—	107,131	551,542	544,484	3,369	3,690	145,784	2,295,835
2010	682,448	552,037	21,068	737	108,606	579,907	572,515	3,462	3,930	102,541	2,398,377
2011	692,510	495,031	21,174	68,886	107,419	599,232	591,477	3,645	4,110	93,278	2,491,654

Note: Numbers may not add up to totals due to rounding. (1) Fiscal years 1977 and later consist of the 12 months ending on Sept. 30 of each year. Fiscal years prior to 1977 consisted of the 12 months ending on June 30 of each year. (2) Includes reimbursements from the General Fund of the Treasury to the OASI Trust Fund for certain legislated measures since 1957. (3) Net interest includes net profits or losses on marketable investments. Beginning in 1967, the trust fund paid administrative expenses on an estimated basis, with a final adjustment including interest made in the following fiscal year. Net interest includes these interest adjustments. Beginning in Oct. 1973, figures include relatively small amounts of gifts to the fund. (4) Beginning in 1967, includes payments for vocational rehabilitation services furnished to disabled persons receiving benefits because of their disabilities. Beginning in 1983, net benefit amounts include reimbursements paid from the general fund to the trust fund for unnegotiated benefit checks. (5) Net change in assets during fiscal year, including amounts borrowed or repaid by other funds.

Disability Insurance Trust Fund, 1960-2011

(in millions)

Fiscal year[1]	Total	INCOME Net payroll tax contribs.	Income from taxing benefits	General fund reimburse-ments[2]	Net interest[3]	DISBURSEMENTS Total	Benefit pymts.[4]	Admin. expenses	Transfers to Railroad Retirement program	Net increase in fund[5]	Year-end balance
1960	$1,034	$987	—	—	$47	$533	$528	$32	−$27	$501	$2,167
1970	4,380	4,141	—	$16	223	2,954	2,795	149	10	1,426	5,104
1980	17,376	16,805	—	118	453	15,320	14,998	334	−12	2,056	7,680
1990	28,215	27,154	$158	138	766	25,124	24,327	717	80	3,091	11,455
1995	70,209	67,986	335	—	1,888	41,374	40,234	1,072	68	28,835	35,206
2000	77,023	70,001	756	—	6,266	56,008	54,244	1,608	159	21,014	113,752
2005	96,765	85,418	1,164	—	10,183	86,360	83,721	2,301	338	10,405	193,298
2006	101,571	90,001	1,174	—	10,396	92,932	90,064	2,480	388	8,640	201,938
2007	108,396	93,973	1,351	—	13,072	96,758	93,955	2,357	445	11,638	213,577
2008	109,816	97,432	1,373	8	11,003	107,153	104,222	2,513	418	2,663	216,239
2009	109,681	97,008	1,841	—	10,832	118,144	115,073	2,623	448	−8,462	207,777
2010	105,513	93,739	1,745	125	9,904	126,344	122,935	2,947	462	−20,831	186,946
2011	106,225	84,031	1,878	11,745	8,571	131,489	127,990	3,034	465	−25,264	161,682

Note: Numbers may not add up to totals due to rounding. (1) Fiscal years 1977 and later consist of the 12 months ending on Sept. 30 of each year. Fiscal years prior to 1977 consisted of the 12 months ending on June 30 of each year. (2) Includes reimbursements from the General Fund of the Treasury to the DI Trust Fund for certain legislated measures since 1957. (3) Net interest includes net profits or losses on marketable investments. Beginning in 1967, the trust fund paid administrative expenses on an estimated basis, with a final adjustment including interest made in the following fiscal year. Net interest includes these interest adjustments. The 1970 report describes the accounting for administrative expenses for years prior to 1967. Beginning in July 1974, figures include relatively small amounts of gifts to the fund. (4) Beginning in 1967, includes payments for vocational rehabilitation services furnished to disabled persons receiving benefits because of their disabilities. Beginning in 1983, net benefit amounts include reimbursements paid from the general fund to the trust fund for unnegotiated benefit checks. (5) Net change in assets during fiscal year, including amounts borrowed or repaid by other funds.

Supplementary Medical Insurance Trust Fund (Medicare SMI), 1975-2011
(in millions)

Fiscal year[1]	INCOME					DISBURSEMENTS			Net change	Year-end balance[9]
	Total	Premium from participants[2]	Govt. contribs.[3]	Transfers from states[4]	Interest and other income[5,6]	Total	Benefit pymts.[6,7,8]	Admin. expenses		
1975	$4,322	$1,887	$2,330	—	$106	$4,170	$3,765	$404	$152	$1,424
1980	10,275	2,928	6,932	—	416	10,737	10,144	593	-462	4,532
1990	46,138[10]	11,494[10]	33,210	—	1,434[10]	43,022[10]	41,498	1,524[10]	3,115[10]	14,527[10]
1995	58,169	19,244	36,988	—	1,937	65,213	63,491	1,722	-7,044	13,874
2000	89,239	20,515	65,561	—	3,164	88,992	87,212[11]	1,780	247	45,896
2001	95,336	22,307	69,838	—	3,191	99,452	97,466[11]	1,986	-4,116	41,780
2002	105,705	24,427	78,318	—	2,960	108,825	106,995[11]	1,830	-3,120	38,659
2003	110,194	26,834	80,905	—	2,455	124,055	121,699[11]	2,356	-13,861	24,799
2004	126,805	30,341	94,734	—	1,730	134,490	131,673	2,817	-7,684	17,114
2005	152,505	35,939	115,200	—	1,366	152,735	149,820[12]	2,914	-230	16,885
2006	211,951	44,241[13]	162,601	$3,630	1,478	195,557	192,083[12,13]	3,474	16,394	33,279
2007	237,890	49,666[13]	179,181	6,977	2,065	232,022	228,596[12,13]	3,426	5,867	39,146
2008	244,872	54,158[13]	180,434	7,042	3,238	224,869	221,445[13,14]	3,423	20,003	59,149
2009	262,573	57,709[13]	194,267	7,504	3,093	260,257	256,938[13]	3,318	2,317	61,466
2010	282,734	61,364[13]	213,709	4,493	3,168	272,224	268,710[13]	3,514	10,510	71,976
2011	301,523	64,502[13]	225,178	6,536	5,307	300,672	296,839	3,833	851	72,827

Note: Numbers may not add up to totals because of rounding. (1) Fiscal year 1975 consists of the 12 months ending on June 30, 1975; fiscal years 1980 and later consist of the 12 months ending on Sept. 30 of each year. (2) For Part D, premiums include both amounts withheld from Social Security benefit checks (and certain other federal benefit payments) and amounts paid directly to Part D plans (estimated). (3) For Part B, includes matching payments from the general fund, plus certain interest-adjustment items. For Part D, includes all federal govt. transfers. (4) As of 2006, Medicaid is no longer the primary payer for full-benefit dual eligibles. As of 2006, states pay 90% of estimated costs. (5) "Other income" includes recoveries of amounts reimbursed from the trust fund that are not trust fund obligations and other miscellaneous income. (6) Values after 2005 include additional premiums for Medicare Advantage (MA) plans that are deducted from beneficiaries' Social Security benefit checks, transferred to HI and SMI trust funds, and then to the plans. (7) Includes costs of Peer Review Organizations in 1983-2001 and costs of Quality Review Organizations beginning in 2002. (8) For Part D, includes payments to plans, subsidies to employer-sponsored retiree drug plans, payments to states for low-income eligibility determinations, and Part D drug premiums (the amount collected from beneficiaries and transferred to plans and an estimated amount for premiums paid directly by enrollees to plans. Includes amounts for transitional assistance benefits in 2004-06. (9) The financial status of SMI depends on the trust fund's assets and liabilities. (10) Includes the impact of the Medicare Catastrophic Coverage Act of 1988. (11) Benefit payments less monies transferred from the HI trust fund for home health agency costs. (12) Certain HI hospice costs were misallocated to, and paid from, the Part B account of the SMI trust fund. See also footnote 14. (13) Includes an estimated $1.804 bil (2006), $2.295 bil (2007), $2.970 bil (2008), $3.699 bil (2009), $4.221 bil (2010), and $4.843 bil (2011) for premiums paid directly to Part D plans. (14) Benefit payments were $229.9 bil; amount shown includes -$8.5 bil, which represents a transfer from the general fund of the Treasury to the Part B account of the SMI trust fund for HI hospice costs that were misallocated to, and paid from, the Part B account from May 2005 to Sept. 2007. (The HI trust fund, in turn, transferred $8.5 bil to the general fund.)

Hospital Insurance Trust Fund (Medicare HI), 1975-2011
(in millions)

Fiscal year[1]	INCOME								DISBURSEMENTS			Net change	Year-end balance
	Total	Payroll taxes	Taxation of benefits	Transfers from Railroad Retirement acct.	Rmbrsmt. for uninsured persons	Premiums from voluntary enrollees	Pymts. for military wage credits	Interest and other income[2,3]	Total	Benefit pymts.[3,4]	Admin. expenses[5]		
1975	$12,568	$11,291	—	$132	$481	$6	$48	$609	$10,612	$10,353	$259	$1,956	$9,870
1980	25,415	23,244	—	244	697	17	141	1,072	24,288	23,790	497	1,127	14,490
1990	79,563	70,655	—	367	413	113	107	7,908	66,687	65,912	774	12,876	95,631
1995	114,847	98,053	$3,913	396	462	998	61	10,963	114,883	113,583	1,300	-36	129,520
1996	121,135	106,934	4,069	401	419	1,107	-2,293[6]	10,496	125,317	124,088	1,229	-4,182	125,338
1997	128,548	112,725	3,558	419	481	1,279	70	10,017	137,836	136,175	1,661	-9,287	116,050
1998	138,203	121,913	5,067	419	34	1,320	67	9,382	137,140	135,487[7]	1,653	1,063	117,113
1999	153,015	134,385	6,552	430	652	1,401	71	9,523	131,441	129,463[7]	1,978	21,574	138,687
2000	159,681	137,738	8,787	465	470	1,392	2	10,827	130,284	127,934[7]	2,350	29,397	168,084
2005	196,921	168,954	8,765	445	286	2,303	0	16,168	184,142	181,292[8]	2,850	12,779	277,723
2006	210,309	180,892	10,319	471	408	2,632	0	16,086	184,901	181,815[8]	3,086	25,408	303,130
2007	219,207	187,992	10,593	483	468	2,761	0	16,910	202,827	200,191[8]	2,636	16,380	319,510
2008	229,729	197,195	11,733	526	506	2,913	0	16,856	230,240	227,008[9]	3,231	-511	319,000
2009	228,915	194,102	12,376	524	614	2,817	968[10]	17,514	238,001	234,659	3,343	-9,086	309,914
2010	218,004	183,603	13,760	535	-142	3,314	0	16,933	248,978	245,650	3,328	-30,975	278,939
2011	226,486	192,063	15,143	477	275	3,273	0	15,255	259,628	255,701	3,927	-33,142	245,797

Note: Numbers may not add up to totals because of rounding. (1) Fiscal year 1975 consists of the 12 months ending on June 30, 1975; fiscal years 1980 and later consist of the 12 months ending on Sept. 30 of each year. (2) Other income includes recoveries of amounts reimbursed from the trust fund that are not trust fund obligations, receipts from the fraud and abuse control program, and other small amounts of miscellaneous income. In 2008, includes an adjustment of -$853 mil for interest inadvertently earned as a result of HI hospice costs that were misallocated to, and paid from, the Part B account of the SMI trust fund from May 2005 to Sept. 2007. (3) Values after 2005 include additional premiums for Medicare Advantage (MA) plans that are deducted from beneficiaries' Social Security checks, transferred to the HI and SMI trust funds, and then transferred to the plans. (4) Includes costs of Peer Review Organizations from 1983 through 2001 (beginning with the implementation of the Prospective Payment System on Oct. 1, 1983), and costs of Quality Improvement Organizations beginning in 2002. (5) Includes costs of experiments and demonstration projects. Beginning in 1997, includes fraud and abuse control expenses. (6) Includes the lump-sum general revenue adjustment of -$2.366 bil. (7) Includes monies transferred to the SMI trust fund for home health agency costs. (8) Certain HI hospice costs were misallocated to, and paid from, the Part B account of the SMI trust fund. (9) Benefit payments were $218,525 mil. Amount shown includes a transfer of $8,484 mil to the general fund of the Treasury for HI hospice costs that were misallocated to, and paid from, the Part B account of the SMI trust fund from May 2005 to Sept. 2007. (The general fund, in turn, transferred $8,484 mil to the Part B account.) (10) Includes the lump-sum general revenue adjustment of -$968 mil.

Temporary Assistance for Needy Families (TANF), 2010

Source: Office of Family Assistance, Admin. for Children and Families, U.S. Dept. of Health and Human Services

State/territory	Total federal and state TANF expenditures, 2010[1]	2010 average monthly expenditure per— Family	Recipient	2010 average monthly number of— Families	Recipients	Children
Alabama	$191,087	$750.39	$310.84	21,221	51,228	38,019
Alaska	61,678	1,555.17	558.80	3,305	9,198	6,374
Arizona	350,059	898.33	426.72	32,473	68,362	51,473
Arkansas	232,779	2,269.60	999.14	8,547	19,415	14,019
California	7,238,867	1,047.02	414.03	576,151	1,456,979	1,129,407
Colorado	323,266	2,338.24	901.42	11,521	29,885	22,294
Connecticut	500,225	2,414.02	1,219.05	17,268	34,195	24,332
Delaware	74,570	1,204.53	553.31	5,159	11,231	8,800
Dist. of Columbia	251,234	2,394.07	1,058.29	8,745	19,783	14,266
Florida	900,886	1,288.44	701.91	58,267	106,956	85,739
Georgia	563,258	2,281.88	1,244.55	20,570	37,715	34,106
Guam	NA	NA	NA	1,257	3,757	2,957
Hawaii	377,776	3,490.17	1,247.08	9,020	25,244	17,076
Idaho	34,772	1,673.96	1,094.27	1,731	2,648	2,461
Illinois	1,254,679	4,712.30	2,220.26	22,188	47,092	39,656
Indiana	343,572	790.61	314.73	36,214	90,969	67,255
Iowa	193,662	900.33	354.19	17,925	45,564	30,953
Kansas	206,622	1,180.32	461.48	14,588	37,311	25,167
Kentucky	280,819	774.66	386.73	30,209	60,511	47,170
Louisiana	263,506	2,072.96	953.82	10,593	23,022	19,802
Maine	141,372	1,068.96	457.09	11,021	25,774	17,140
Maryland	563,872	1,915.82	809.57	24,527	58,042	43,031
Massachusetts	1,021,678	1,727.01	903.53	49,299	94,230	63,465
Michigan	1,703,006	2,079.89	803.99	68,233	176,517	127,731
Minnesota	475,283	1,727.15	797.43	22,932	49,668	37,465
Mississippi	105,666	728.21	346.55	12,092	25,409	18,685
Missouri	404,574	943.64	496.00	35,728	67,973	41,389
Montana	47,291	1,050.08	410.60	3,753	9,598	6,690
Nebraska	98,456	1,042.00	431.73	7,874	19,004	15,057
Nevada	108,254	878.48	339.75	10,269	26,552	19,518
New Hampshire	86,261	1,351.72	652.48	5,318	11,017	8,058
New Jersey	1,445,745	3,600.47	1,478.21	33,462	81,503	57,883
New Mexico	237,088	997.99	378.01	19,797	52,266	37,081
New York	5,346,657	3,674.92	1,638.55	121,242	271,920	206,191
North Carolina	563,445	1,918.75	975.07	24,471	48,154	40,239
North Dakota	36,885	1,510.46	592.59	2,035	5,187	3,883
Ohio	1,331,348	1,076.84	470.50	103,029	235,803	170,131
Oklahoma	178,999	1,584.34	599.64	9,415	24,876	20,781
Oregon	391,635	1,204.56	471.38	27,094	69,235	48,349
Pennsylvania	964,229	1,548.72	645.47	51,883	124,487	93,533
Puerto Rico	NA	NA	NA	13,003	34,874	23,531
Rhode Island	148,626	1,664.05	708.96	7,443	17,470	11,989
South Carolina	179,919	811.28	318.88	18,481	47,019	32,518
South Dakota	30,853	795.75	381.18	3,231	6,745	5,703
Tennessee	338,332	459.62	182.78	61,343	154,254	111,349
Texas	908,117	1,480.98	653.15	51,099	115,864	99,874
Utah	131,859	1,654.11	753.50	6,643	14,583	10,702
Vermont	78,080	2,249.10	1,028.07	2,893	6,329	4,480
Virgin Islands	NA	NA	NA	519	1,499	1,062
Virginia	298,535	716.14	319.16	34,739	77,947	56,110
Washington	1,494,308	1,898.75	783.50	65,583	158,936	110,002
West Virginia	198,862	1,701.95	797.68	9,737	20,775	15,714
Wisconsin	523,552	2,011.96	877.27	21,685	49,733	38,943
Wyoming	29,373	7,485.41	3,647.88	327	671	547
Totals by year						
2010 totals	33,255,476	1,500.30	634.89	1,847,152	4,364,979	3,280,150
2009 totals	30,577,765	1,475.65	630.53	1,726,799	4,041,292	3,084,413
2008 totals	28,129,745	1,438.71	620.06	1,629,344	3,780,543	2,911,078
2007 totals	26,921,973	1,321.70	566.92	1,697,432	3,957,330	3,047,043
2006 totals	25,593,809	1,191.88	510.33	1,789,460	4,179,295	3,207,216
2005 totals	25,580,110	1,120.87	474.21	1,901,810	4,495,175	3,428,885
2004 totals	25,821,230	1,094.51	455.63	1,965,960	4,722,588	3,581,448
2003 totals	26,339,994	1,092.22	447.88	2,009,666	4,900,889	3,693,056
2002 totals	25,414,383	1,039.00	417.89	2,038,373	5,067,963	3,791,560
2001 totals	25,667,381	1,024.57	400.86	2,087,646	5,335,891	3,968,499
2000 totals	24,780,711	926.32	353.72	2,229,315	5,838,043	4,303,943
1999 totals	23,114,572	267.99	267.99	2,673,610	7,187,658	NA
1998 totals	22,036,420	208.91	208.91	3,199,700	8,790,149	NA
1997 totals	19,010,190	144.87	144.87	3,936,610	10,935,125	NA

NA = Not available. **Note:** Under 1996 legislation, the Aid to Families with Dependent Children (AFDC) program was converted to this state block-grant program. Covers period from previous Oct. to Sept. of fiscal years shown. (1) In thousands.

Adults Receiving TANF Funds by Employment Status, 2010

Source: Office of Family Assistance, Admin. for Children and Families, U.S. Dept. of Health and Human Services

State/terr.	Adults	Employed	State/terr.	Adults	Employed	State/terr.	Adults	Employed	State/terr.	Adults	Employed
AL	13,209	31.2%	IL	7,436	15.7%	NE	3,947	46.4%	SC	14,501	22.3%
AK	2,824	29.6	IN	23,714	24.5	NV	7,034	41.1	SD	1,042	17.9
AZ	16,889	14.5	IA	14,611	36.8	NH	2,959	24.3	TN	42,905	28.6
AR	5,396	25.8	KS	12,144	31.7	NJ	23,620	10.4	TX	15,990	30.6
CA	327,572	25.1	KY	13,341	22.7	NM	15,185	21.3	UT	3,881	14.9
CO	7,591	23.9	LA	3,220	23.9	NY	65,729	27.4	VT	1,849	20.3
CT	9,863	25.5	ME	8,634	18.2	NC	7,915	17.0	Virgin Isls.	437	3.7
DE	2,431	26.4	MD	15,011	12.9	ND	1,304	41.4	VA	21,837	25.3
DC	5,517	16.9	MA	30,765	8.8	OH	65,672	16.2	WA	48,934	13.2
FL	21,217	10.5	MI	48,786	22.0	OK	4,095	8.3	WV	5,061	14.9
GA	3,609	11.0	MN	12,203	31.1	OR	20,886	6.4	WI	10,790	18.9
Guam	800	3.3	MS	6,724	19.0	PA	30,954	36.8	WY	124	8.9
HA	8,168	39.3	MO	26,584	14.5	Puerto Rico	11,343	2.6	**U.S.**	**1,084,828**	**22.3**
ID	187	9.9	MT	2,908	30.8	RI	5,481	18.0			

NA = Not available. TANF = Temporary Assistance for Needy Families state block-grant program. **Note:** For fiscal year 2010; covers period from Oct. 2009 to Sept. 2010.

TAXES

Federal Income Tax

Source: George W. Smith III, CPA, Managing Partner, George W. Smith & Company, P.C.

Tax Return Facts

Deadlines. The due date for filing 2012 U.S. individual income tax returns is Mon., Apr. 15, 2013. Calendar year-ending U.S. partnership tax returns also are due on Apr. 15, 2013. Corporate calendar year-ending returns are due Fri., Mar. 15, 2013.

E-Filing. On June 10, 2011, the IRS announced that 1 bil individual tax returns had been processed since the electronic filing program began as a pilot project in 1986. For the tax season ending Apr. 17, 2012, 111,325,000 e-filed returns were received by the IRS. This was an increase of 6.1% from 2011.

Refunds. The average refund for 2011 tax returns received by Apr. 17, 2012, was $2,716.

Odds of an Audit. The odds of an audit increase with higher taxpayer income. For taxpayers with incomes of $200,000 or higher, the audit rate is 3.39%. For taxpayers with gross income of $1 mil or more, the rate is 12.5%. If income is lower than $200,000, the audit rate drops to one in 100. In 2011, audits claimed over $55 bil of unpaid taxes.

Tax-Free States. Seven states don't impose state income taxes: Alaska, Florida, Nevada, South Dakota, Texas, Washington, and Wyoming. Two other states, New Hampshire and Tennessee, tax income only if it's from interest or dividends. Residents of these states must still pay federal income taxes.

Highlights of Recent Legislation

Patient Protection and Affordable Care Act and Education Reconciliation Act

Pres. Barack Obama signed into law the Patient Protection and Affordable Care Act Mar. 23, 2010. Shortly thereafter, he signed the Education Reconciliation Act. The bills together created an estimated $437 bil in new tax provisions.

2010 Tax Provisions. Small businesses with up to 25 employees may qualify for a tax credit for the cost of purchased health insurance for their employees.

2013 Tax Provisions. The income threshold for deducting itemized medical expenses increases to 10% for individuals under age 65. For single taxpayers with income over $200,000 or married taxpayers filing jointly with income over $250,000, a 9% Medicare tax will be imposed on earned income over those respective levels. A 3.8% Medicare tax will be imposed on unearned investment income. A 2.3% excise tax will be imposed on the sale of certain medical devices.

2014 Tax Provisions. Individuals who are not covered by Medicare, Medicaid, employer-provided insurance, or other health insurance plans generally will be required to obtain health insurance coverage or pay a penalty when filing tax returns. Various tax credits will increase based upon premiums paid by qualifying small businesses that provide health coverage for their employees. Subsidies and tax credits are available to help lower-income taxpayers pay for coverage.

Tax Relief Acts

In Dec. 2010, Congress temporarily extended the Tax Relief Reconciliation Act of 2001 and the Jobs and Growth Tax Relief Act of 2003 for two additional years, 2011 and 2012. Some of the provisions affected individual income tax rates, capital gains, dividends, and estate taxes. Congress also extended the 2% FICA payroll tax cut for employees through 2012.

Military Tax Relief Bill

Congress unanimously passed the Heroes Earnings Assistance and Relief Tax Act in May 2008. The law includes tax breaks for members of the military, tax-free combat pay, various credits, and retirement provisions.

Combat Pay. For enlisted personnel or warrant officers serving in a combat zone for any part of a month, all pay received for military service that month is not taxable. For officers, tax-free income is capped at the highest enlisted pay level plus any hostile-fire or imminent-danger pay.

Extensions. The deadline for filing tax returns, paying taxes, filing claims for refunds, and taking other actions with the IRS is automatically extended for qualifying members of the military.

IRA Withdrawals. The law makes permanent the ability for military reservists to make penalty-free withdrawals from IRAs when called to active duty.

IRS Rulings and Other Tax Issues

Alimony. Payments to an individual under a written separation agreement constitute alimony for federal tax purposes, even if the agreement is not enforceable under state law.

Auto Damage. Damage to a person's car may be a deductible casualty loss unless it was caused by the person's willful conduct, such as drunken driving.

Bicycling. A maximum $20 per month commuting reimbursement is excludable from income for employees who bicycle between their home and work. Expenses include the purchase of a bicycle, repairs, and storage.

Charitable Giving. Real estate and securities donated to a charity resulting in long-term capital gains is deductible at fair market value. Donations also include tangible personal property such as furniture, books, jewelry, paintings, and cars.

Counseling. Parent(s) of a child with psychological problems may deduct as a medical expense that part of a private school fee directly related to psychological aid given to the child.

Day Camp. The cost of day camps (not overnight) for children may qualify for the child care credit. The child must be under the age of 13, and the expenses must be incurred so the parent(s) can work.

Employee Parking. Reimbursement for parking expenses provided to an employee who commutes caps out at $240 per month. The limit for employees who commute by mass transportation is $125.

Estate Taxes. In general, after the death of an individual, federal estate tax returns need only be filed for 2012 when a decedent's gross estate, plus adjusted taxable gifts and specific exemptions, is more than $5.12 mil.

First Jobs. Graduates may not deduct expenses of seeking their first job. These expenses include auto rental, plane travel, lodging costs, and meals.

Garage Sales. Revenues received from a garage sale usually do not result in taxable income. In most cases, the item that was sold cost more than the revenue received. These losses are considered personal and, therefore, not deductible.

Investment Expenses. Investors may take a miscellaneous deduction on Schedule A, Form 1040, for financial newspapers, reports, and other expenses incurred in managing their investment portfolio. However, investors cannot deduct expenses for attending a convention, seminar, or similar meeting.

Madoff Victims. The IRS approved a theft loss deduction and net operating loss carryback by investors who were victims of the Ponzi scheme perpetrated by Bernard Madoff.

Business Mileage. Beginning Jan. 1, 2012, the standard mileage rate for the use of a car, van, pickup, or panel truck is 55.5 cents per mile for business miles driven. The business portion of parking fees and tolls may be deducted in addition to the mileage.

Personal Mileage. The mileage allowance deduction for moving and medical expenses is 23 cents per mile. The rate used for volunteer work for charitable activities remains at 14 cents per mile. Charitable rates are set by Congress, not the IRS.

Penalties. Penalties and fines paid to a governmental agency or department are not deductible. This includes parking and speeding tickets as well as penalties for late filing of a tax return.

Refunds. Not all taxpayers expecting a refund will necessarily receive one. If an individual owes taxes to the federal government, has failed to pay child support, or has unpaid education loans, the IRS can take the individual's refund to satisfy the debt.

Retirement Accounts. For taxpayers who converted a traditional IRA to a Roth IRA in 2010 and deferred half the tax on the income to 2011, the final 50% is includable on 2012 income tax returns (to be filed in 2013). In a unanimous 2005 decision, the U.S. Supreme Court held that Individual Retirement Accounts (IRAs) are beyond the reach of creditors. This includes IRA assets of taxpayers who have filed for bankruptcy.

Sale of Residence. Married couples filing jointly who have lived in their principal residence for at least two years out of the last five can exclude up to $500,000 of the gain on the sale of their residence. Single taxpayers can exclude up to $250,000.

Same-Sex Marriage. The IRS ruled that it is unlawful for same-sex couples to file federal tax returns under any married status, even if the jurisdiction in which the couple lives recognizes such marriages.

Smoking. Taxpayers can deduct the cost of two types of aids for quitting cigarette smoking as a medical expense: (1) participation in a smoking-cessation program or (2) prescription drugs to alleviate the effects of nicotine withdrawal. Over-the-counter products such as nicotine patches and chewing gum remain nondeductible.

Full-Time Students. For 2012, a taxpayer may not claim a dependency exemption for an individual who qualifies as a full-time student and is over age 23 at the end of the year, unless the student's gross income is less than $3,800.

Student Loans. For taxable years beginning in 2012, the income phase-out range for the $2,500 maximum deduction for interest paid on qualified education loans is $60,000-$75,000 income for single taxpayers and $125,000-$155,000 for married taxpayers filing jointly.

Weekend Business Travel. If a business trip is extended over a weekend to take advantage of reduced airfares, the additional costs of meals, lodging, and other incidental expenses are deductible.

Weight Loss. The IRS allows a medical deduction for costs of certain weight-loss programs. Participation must be for treatment of a physician-diagnosed disease, including obesity. No deduction is allowed for diets that are not prescribed by a physician or for special diet foods.

Working Abroad. Many Americans who live and work abroad are eligible to exclude a certain amount of their pay from U.S. income taxes. The amount of earned income excludable for 2012 is $95,100.

Income Tax Due Dates

Tax Returns. The 2012 U.S. Individual Income Tax Return Form 1040, 1040A, or 1040EZ filing date is Mon., Apr. 15, 2013. Different filing dates may apply for state/local returns and taxes.

Estimated Payments. Due dates for filing individual quarterly federal estimated tax payments, Form 1040-ES: 1st quarter, Mon., Apr. 15, 2013; 2nd quarter, Mon., June 17; 3rd quarter, Mon., Sept. 16; and 4th quarter, Wed., Jan. 15, 2014.

Filing Extensions. Individuals who cannot file their 2012 individual income tax return by the due date, Apr. 15, 2013, may apply for an automatic six-month extension to Tue., Oct. 15, 2013. To qualify for an extension, Form 4868 must be filed no later than the tax return due date. Approximately 9 mil extensions were filed in 2011.

Penalties. The IRS can levy two potential penalties after the filing due date when there is a balance owed. One penalty is for failing to file a timely tax return; the other is for failure to pay the tax when due. In addition, interest will be charged on any unpaid tax balance. There is a $195 late filing penalty for S corporations and partnerships per shareholder or partner each month for up to 12 months when the return is late.

Status of Refunds. Individuals can check on the status of their expected federal refund by calling the IRS at (800) 829-4477 or by checking at www.irs.gov. For security purposes, taxpayers should request that tax refunds be deposited directly into their bank accounts.

Statute of Limitations. Taxpayers who have not yet filed their 2009 federal tax return have until Apr. 15, 2013, to file and claim their refund. After that date any refunds for income tax or withholding tax for 2009, including the refundable earned income tax credit, will be lost.

IRS Contact Information

Website: www.irs.gov
Fax: (703) 368-9694
For Tax Questions: (800) 829-1040
For Forms/Publications: (800) TAX-FORM (829-3676)
For Spanish Forms/Publications: The IRS provides instructions in Spanish at participating libraries. Taxpayers can also view and download tax forms and publications in Spanish directly from www.irs.gov/Spanish. For more information, call (800) TAX-FORM and ask for the free IRS Publication 1SP, *Derechos del Contribuyente*.

For Hearing Impaired: The IRS telephone service for hearing impaired persons is available for taxpayers with access to TDD equipment. The number is (800) 829-4059.

Most Common Income Tax Errors

Periodically, the IRS issues a list of the most commonly made income tax errors.

1. Incorrect or missing Social Security numbers.
2. Incorrect tax entered from tax tables.
3. Mathematical errors or wrong ID numbers listed for tax credits.
4. Entering withholding and estimated tax payments on the wrong line.
5. General math mistakes.

Working With a Tax Preparer

Here are some ideas to keep in mind when using a tax preparer:

- **Choose** wisely. Regulations in effect in 2012 require all paid tax return preparers including attorneys, certified public accountants, and IRS-enrolled agents to have a Preparer Tax Identification Number. Check the preparer's qualifications and history. Ask about service fees in advance.
- **Review** last year's tax return. Make note of any changes since then such as marriage, divorce, number of dependents, retirement, job changes, additional income, new deductions, etc.
- **Organize** your records with income items first, followed by itemized deductions (medical, taxes, interest, and charitable and other miscellaneous deductions), followed by gains, losses, rentals, or other items.
- **Time** spent with your preparer may affect your bill. If you provide disorganized records and deductions, there may be an additional cost to have your tax preparer organize your information.
- **Prepare** a list of questions in advance. Ask about any invoices or bills that you are not sure apply.
- **Alert** your preparer if you're waiting to receive additional information. He or she can begin preparing your tax return and include the missing data later to finalize your return. Amending a return after it is completed may incur additional fees.
- **Review** your tax return before signing it. Ask questions about any item you don't understand. Remember that even though your preparer is required to sign the return, you are responsible for its contents.

Individual Federal Income Tax Rates and Brackets, 2012

Tax rate	Single	Married filing jointly or qualifying widow(er)	Married filing separately	Head of household
10%	$1 to $8,700	$1 to $17,400	$1 to $8,700	$1 to $12,400
15%	$8,701 to $35,350	$17,401 to $70,700	$8,701 to $35,350	$12,401 to $47,350
25%	$35,351 to $85,650	$70,701 to $142,700	$35,351 to $71,350	$47,351 to $122,300
28%	$85,651 to $178,650	$142,701 to $217,450	$71,351 to $108,725	$122,301 to $198,050
33%	$178,651 to $388,350	$217,451 to $388,350	$108,726 to $194,175	$198,051 to $388,350
35%	Over $388,350	Over $388,350	Over $194,175	Over $388,350

Note: The 2012 income tax brackets were only slightly increased from the prior year because of mild inflation during the 12-month period from Sept. 2010 through Aug. 2011. The Tax Relief Act of 2010 extended these tax rates for two more years, through 2012. Each rate increase applies only to taxable income that exceeds the previous bracket. For example, a single person with taxable income of $40,000 would pay 10% on the first $8,700, 15% on the next $26,649 (up to $35,350), and 25% on the next $4,650.

Personal Exemptions, 2012

Dollar Amounts. The personal exemption amount for each taxpayer, spouse, and dependent for 2012 is $3,800, up $100 from 2011. The exemption amount is adjusted each year for cost-of-living increases. The personal exemption of an individual who is a dependent of another taxpayer is zero.

Exemption Phase-Out. The exemption deduction phase-out rule for higher-income taxpayers was eliminated.

Standard Deduction, 2012

The standard deduction is a flat dollar amount that is subtracted from the adjusted gross income of taxpayers who do not itemize their deductions. The dollar amounts were adjusted for inflation.

Single	$5,950
Married filing jointly or qualifying widow(er)	$11,900
Married filing separately	$5,950
Head of household	$8,700

Dependents' Tax Returns. An individual reported as a dependent on another person's 2012 income tax return generally may claim on his or her own tax return only the greater of $950 or the sum of $300 plus earned income not to exceed the regular standard deduction.

Additional Standard Deduction, 2012

Taxpayers in 2012 who do not itemize, are 65 or older, and/or blind may claim an additional standard deduction.

Single or head of household, 65 or older OR blind	$1,450
Single or head of household, 65 or older AND blind	$2,900
Married filing jointly or qualifying widow(er), 65 or older OR blind (per person)	$1,150
Married filing jointly or qualifying widow(er), 65 or older AND blind (per person)	$2,300
Married filing separately, 65 or older OR blind	$1,150
Married filing separately, 65 or older AND blind	$2,300

Savings Plans

401(k) Plan. The maximum amount that an individual under age 50 can contribute to a 401(k) plan for 2012 is $17,000. Individuals age 50 or older can put away an additional $5,500, for a total of $22,500.

Traditional IRA. The maximum tax-deferred Individual Retirement Account (IRA) deduction for a married couple filing jointly is $10,000 ($5,000 for singles). Each spouse can contribute up to $5,000 annually even if one spouse has little or no income. Individuals age 50 or older can fund an additional "catch-up" amount of $1,000. However, there are income limitations and phaseouts. Funds may be deposited into a traditional IRA for 2012 up to Apr. 15, 2013. There is no additional extension of time for 2012 IRAs. Contributions after Apr. 15 will automatically be considered funds deposited for 2013. The owner of a traditional IRA (or a SIMPLE plan, pension, or profit-sharing plan account) must begin receiving distributions by Apr. 1 of the calendar year following the year in which he or she reaches age 70½. Any employee who works beyond 70½ and is not a 5% or more owner of the business can continue to defer profit-sharing and pension plan distributions. There is a 10% penalty for IRA distributions before age 59½. Distributions paid to the beneficiary due to disability or death of the owner are not subject to this penalty, nor are payments used for certain unreimbursed medical expenses, higher-education

expenses, or first-time homebuyer acquisition costs (up to $10,000).

Roth IRA. Contributions paid into a Roth IRA are not tax deductible. Distributions of funds including investment earnings held in the account for five years or longer and distributed after age 59½ are both free of income tax and the 10% early-withdrawal penalty. Withdrawals from the account in less than five years can be subject to tax and a 10% withdrawal penalty regardless of age. There are income limitations on contributions. Children can open a Roth IRA as long as they have earned income from a job up to a maximum of $5,000.

More Information. For more information on IRAs, call the IRS at (800) TAX-FORM (829-3676) for a free copy of Publication 590, *Individual Retirement Arrangements (IRAs)*.

2012 Itemized Deductions

If the total amount of itemized deductions is more than the standard deduction, taxpayers generally should itemize their deductions on Schedule A, Form 1040. The following examples are just a few of the many deductions that may be itemized. Some are subject to income limitations.

Business Expenses. Deductible miscellaneous expenses include unreimbursed employee business expenses such as travel, automobile, telephone, and gifts. However, only 50% of the cost of customer meals and entertainment is deductible.

Charitable Contributions. Individuals may not deduct the value of volunteer work they personally perform for charities.

Gambling. Lottery, slots, Texas Hold-Em poker, craps, bingo, or other gambling expenses are deductible if the taxpayer itemizes on Schedule A. However, expenses are limited to gambling winnings reported on page one, Form 1040. If there are no winnings, the taxpayer cannot deduct expenses on Schedule A.

Interest. Mortgage interest paid on a primary residence or a second home is deductible. However, there are limitations on mortgages in excess of $1 mil. Interest on home equity loans also is deductible, but only covering the first $100,000 of equity debt. Personal credit card interest is not deductible.

Lamaze Class. A mother-to-be may deduct as a medical expense the cost of classes taken for Lamaze breathing and relaxation techniques, stages of labor, and delivery procedures.

Long-Term Care Insurance. Based on various annual limits, long-term care insurance premiums are deductible as medical expenses. For 2012, taxpayers age 71 and older can claim as much as $4,370 per person; ages 61-70, up to $3,500; ages 51-60, up to $1,310; ages 41-50, up to $660; and ages 40 and younger are limited to $350.

Medical Expenses that exceed 7.5% of the taxpayer's adjusted gross income are deductible. Cosmetic surgery for a congenital abnormality, for personal injury from an accident or trauma, or for a disfiguring disease may qualify as a medical deduction.

Medical Traveling. Taxpayers may deduct part of the travel expense to seek health care. Travel can include auto and airfare expenses.

Miscellaneous Deductions. Certain miscellaneous expenses are deductible, but only the amount that exceeds 2% of adjusted gross income. Expenses include investment expenses, union and professional dues, tax preparation fees, safe-deposit box rental fees, and most (but not all) expenses for a job search.

Moving Expenses. Taxpayers who change jobs or are transferred usually can deduct part of their moving expenses, including travel and the cost of moving household goods, but not the cost of meals.

Personal Losses. Casualty and theft losses are deductible subject to a $100 reduction and further reduced 10% for each occurrence. Separate rules apply for federally declared disasters. Unreimbursed automobile accident damage may be a deductible casualty loss.

Taxes. State and local income taxes including real estate taxes are deductible. An auto license fee based on weight, model, year, or horsepower is not deductible. A tax based on the car's value qualifies as a personal property tax deduction.

Tax Credits

A tax deduction reduces a taxpayer's taxable income, whereas tax credits reduce, dollar-for-dollar, the amount of tax owed.

Adoption Credit. The adoption credit for qualified expenses is $12,650 in 2012. The credit limit is per person, not per year; is adjusted annually for inflation; and is non-refundable. The exclusion phases out for taxpayers whose income is between $189,710 and $229,710, when the credit is completely phased out.

American Opportunity Tax Credit. Modifying the Hope credit, this credit provides a partially refundable $2,500 credit to cover each of four years of college. Up to 40% of the credit is refundable, which means that a taxpayer may be able to receive up to $1,000 even if he or she owes no taxes. The credit begins to phase out for higher-income individuals.

Child and Dependent Care Credit. This credit is for expenses for the care of taxpayers' qualifying children under age 13, or for a disabled spouse or dependent, while the taxpayer works or looks for work.

Child Tax Credit. The maximum child tax credit is $1,000 for each qualifying child.

Earned Income Credit. Lower-income workers who maintain a household may be eligible for an Earned Income Credit (EIC). This credit is based on total earned income such as wages, commissions, and tips. Military personnel can include tax-free combat pay in income to compute the credit. There are phaseout rules.

Energy Credits. There are many energy-related credits—from the purchase of an alternative fuel vehicle and the installation of solar/fuel cell property in a residence, to the production of biodiesel or ethanol.

Alternative Minimum Tax

The Alternative Minimum Tax (AMT) was established in 1969 to prevent people with very high incomes from using special tax breaks to pay little or no tax. It hasn't been indexed or adjusted for inflation. Because of changes in the tax law, this tax now affects more and more middle-income taxpayers every year.

Instructions included with tax forms 1040 and 1040A help individuals determine if they are subject to the AMT. Tax Form 6251 is used to figure how much additional tax, if any, is owed.

Estate and Gift Taxes Exclusion

Estate Tax. The Tax Relief Reconciliation Act of 2001 increased the estate tax exclusion from $675,000 in 2001 to $3.5 mil through 2009. The maximum tax rate in 2001, based on the value of an estate, was 55%. The rate was decreased over the years to a maximum 45% in 2009. The estate tax was set to expire in 2010. The Tax Relief Act of 2010 reinstated the estate tax with a 35% flat rate and increased the exemptions to $5 mil in 2011 and $5.12 mil in 2012.

Gifting. U.S. citizens, residents, and nonresident aliens have an annual gift tax exclusion of up to $13,000 per individual to as many individuals as he or she chooses. For married couples the exclusion is twice that amount, $26,000, even if only one spouse does all the gifting.

International Property. All property owned worldwide by American citizens is subject to U.S. estate tax rules and regulations.

Resident Aliens. Aliens residing in the U.S. are subject to the same rules as that of an American citizen.

Tax-Free. The annual $13,000 gift tax does not apply to most charities or for tuition that donors pay directly to schools or medical expenses paid on behalf of donees.

Taxable Social Security Benefits

Earnings Limitations. For 2012, Social Security recipients who have not reached the full retirement age of 66 will lose $1 of their benefits for every $2 of earned income over $14,640. Recipients who reached full retirement age in 2012 will not lose any benefits if they earned $38,880 or less. Recipients will have to pay back some benefits if their income exceeded that amount.

Taxable Benefits. Up to 50% of Social Security benefits may be taxable if the person's total income is more than $25,000 but less than $34,000 for a single individual, head of household, qualifying widow(er), or a married person who is filing separately if spouses lived apart all year; or more than $32,000 but less than $44,000 for married individuals filing jointly. For higher incomes, 85% of Social Security benefits may become taxable.

Tax-Free. If the only income received during the year was Social Security, these benefits are not taxable, and the recipient probably does not have to file a tax return.

Retention of Income Tax Records

How long should a taxpayer keep copies of their tax returns and supporting records? The answer is a combination of judgment and the statutes of limitations. Because federal tax returns generally can be audited for up to three years after filing, or six years if the IRS suspects underreported income, it's wise to keep copies of the income tax return and records at least seven years after a return is filed.

Tax Audits

The IRS audit rate for individual returns filed last year was 1.11%. Most taxpayers have no reason to be concerned about being audited.

Decision to Audit. The IRS audit selection process is not done randomly. It is based on a set of formulas that are designed to spot questionable returns. If the IRS concludes that the taxpayer owes more tax and he or she disagrees with the findings, the taxpayer can meet with a supervisor.

If the taxpayer still does not agree, he or she can appeal to a separate Appeals Office, or take it to the U.S. Tax Court, Federal District Court, or the U.S. Court of Federal Claims.

Tax Court. The U.S. Tax Court is a federal court where taxpayers can dispute tax deficiencies as determined by the Commissioner of Internal Revenue before payment of the disputed amounts. The Tax Court is composed of presidentially appointed members. Many taxpayers choose the Tax Court because they are not required to pay the contested tax up front.

Appeals. For more information about audits, call the IRS at (800) TAX-FORM (829-3676) for its free Publication 556, *Examination of Returns, Appeal Rights, and Claims for Refund.* Or visit www.irs.gov.

Your Rights as a Taxpayer

Congress has enacted "Taxpayer Bill of Rights" legislation and created an Office of the Taxpayer Advocate within the IRS, with authority to order IRS personnel to issue refund checks and meet deadlines for resolving disputes. Taxpayer advocates can be contacted at (877) 777-4778; (800) 829-4059 for TTY/TDD.

For more information, ask for free IRS Publication 1, *Your Rights as a Taxpayer*, by calling (800) TAX-FORM (829-3676).

Reporting Wrongdoing

To confidentially report misconduct, waste, fraud, or abuse by an IRS employee, call the Treasury Inspector General for Tax Administration Hotline at (800) 366-4484.

More IRS Services

To find out what additional services are available, ask for Publication 910, *IRS Guide to Free Tax Services*. This guide contains a list of free tax publications and other information including tax education and assistance programs.

State Government Personal Income Tax Rates, 2012

Source: Reproduced with permission from *CCH State Tax Guide*, published and copyrighted by CCH Inc., a Wolters Kluwer business

Alaska, Florida, Nevada, South Dakota, Texas, Washington, and Wyoming did not have state income taxes and are thus not listed. Tax rates apply in stages—for example, a single person in Arizona making $60,000 in taxable income would pay 2.59% on the first $10,000 of income, 2.88% on the next $15,000, and so on. For further details, see notes at end of table.

Alabama

Single, Head of household, or Married filing separately
- $0 to $500. . . . . 2%
- $501 to $3,000 . . . . 4%
- $3,001 and over 5%

Married filing jointly
- $0 to $1,000 . . . . 2%
- $1,001 to $6,000. . . . . 4%
- $6,001 and over 5%

Arizona[1]

Single or Married filing separately
- $0 to $10,000 . . . . 2.59%
- $10,001 to $25,000. . . . . 2.88%
- $25,001 to $50,000. . . . . 3.36%
- $50,001 to $150,000. . . . 4.24%
- $150,001 and over 4.54%

Married filing jointly or Head of household
- $0 to $20,000 . . . . 2.59%
- $20,001 to $50,000. . . . . 2.88%
- $50,001 to $100,000. . . . 3.36%
- $100,001 to $300,000. . . 4.24%
- $300,001 and over 4.54%

Arkansas[2,3]

Single, Head of household, Married filing jointly, or Married filing separately
- $0 to $3,999 . . . . 1%
- $4,000 to $7,999. . . . . . . 2.5%
- $8,000 to $11,899. . . . . . 3.5%
- $11,900 to $19,899. . . . . 4.5%
- $19,900 to $33,199. . . . . . . 6%
- $33,200 and over 7%

California[1,2]

Single, Married filing separately, or Registered domestic partner filing separately
- $0 to $7,455 . . . . 1%
- $7,456 to $17,676. . . . . 2%
- $17,677 to $27,897. . . . . . . 4%
- $27,898 to $38,726. . . . . . . 6%
- $38,727 to $48,942. . . . . . . 8%
- $48,943 and over 9.3%

Head of household
- $0 to $14,920 . . . . 1%
- $14,921 to $35,351. . . . . . . 2%
- $35,352 to $45,571. . . . . . . 4%
- $45,572 to $56,400. . . . . . . 6%
- $56,401 to $66,618. . . . . . . 8%
- $66,619 and over 9.3%

Married filing jointly, Registered domestic partner filing jointly, or Qualifying widow(er)
- $0 to $14,910 . . . . 1%
- $14,911 to $35,352. . . . . . . 2%
- $35,353 to $55,794. . . . . . . 4%
- $55,795 to $77,452. . . . . . . 6%
- $77,453 to $97,884. . . . . . . 8%
- $97,885 and over 9.3%

Colorado

4.63% of federal taxable income

Connecticut

Single or Married filing separately
- $0 to $10,000 . . . . 3%
- $10,001 to $50,000. . . . . . . 5%
- $50,001 to $100,000. . . . 5.5%
- $100,001 to $200,000. . . . . 6%
- $200,001 to $250,000. . . 6.5%
- $250,001 and over 6.7%

Head of household
- $0 to $16,000 . . . . 3%
- $16,001 to $80,000. . . . . . . 5%
- $80,001 to $160,000. . . . 5.5%
- $160,001 to $320,000. . . . . 6%
- $320,001 to $400,000. . . 6.5%
- $400,001 and over 6.7%

Married filing jointly or Qualifying widow(er)
- $0 to $20,000 . . . . 3%
- $20,001 to $100,000. . . . . 5%
- $100,001 to $200,000. . . 5.5%
- $200,001 to $400,000. . . . 6%
- $400,001 to $500,000. . . 6.5%
- $500,001 and over 6.7%

Delaware

Single, Head of household, Married filing jointly, or Married filing separately
- $0 to $2,000 . . . . 0%
- $2,001 to $5,000. . . . . 2.2%
- $5,001 to $10,000. . . . . . 3.9%
- $10,001 to $20,000. . . . . 4.8%
- $20,001 to $25,000. . . . . 5.2%
- $25,001 to $60,000. . . . . 5.55%
- $60,001 and over 6.95%

District of Columbia

- $0 to $10,000 . . . . 4%
- $10,001 to $40,000. . . . . . 6%
- $40,001 to $350,000. . . . 8.5%
- $350,001 and over 8.950%

Georgia

Single
- $0 to $750. . . . . 1%
- $751 to $2,250 . . . . 2%
- $2,251 to $3,750 . . . . 3%
- $3,751 to $5,250. . . . . 4%
- $5,251 to $7,000 . . . . 5%
- $7,001 and over 6%

Head of household, Married filing jointly, or Qualifying widow(er)
- $0 to $1,000 . . . . 1%
- $1,001 to $3,000. . . . . 2%
- $3,001 to $5,000. . . . . 3%
- $5,001 to $7,000. . . . . 4%
- $7,001 to $10,000. . . . . 5%
- $10,001 and over 6%

Married filing separately
- $0 to $500. . . . . 1%
- $501 to $1,500 . . . . 2%
- $1,501 to $2,500 . . . . 3%
- $2,501 to $3,500 . . . . 4%
- $3,501 to $5,000. . . . . 5%
- $5,001 and over 6%

Hawaii

Single or Married filing separately
- $0 to $2,400 . . . . 1.4%
- $2,401 to $4,800. . . . . 3.2%
- $4,801 to $9,600. . . . . 5.5%
- $9,601 to $14,400. . . . . . . 6.4%
- $14,401 to $19,200. . . . . . 6.8%
- $19,201 to $24,000. . . . . . 7.2%
- $24,001 to $36,000. . . . . . 7.6%
- $36,001 to $48,000. . . . . . 7.9%
- $48,001 to $150,000. . . 8.25%
- $150,001 to $175,000. . . . . 9%
- $175,001 to $200,000. . . . 10%
- $200,001 and over 11%

Head of household
- $0 to $3,600 . . . . 1.4%
- $3,601 to $7,200. . . . . 3.2%
- $7,201 to $14,400. . . . . . . 5.5%
- $14,401 to $21,600. . . . . . 6.4%
- $21,601 to $28,800. . . . . . 6.8%
- $28,801 to $36,000. . . . . . 7.2%
- $36,001 to $54,000. . . . . . 7.6%
- $54,001 to $72,000. . . . . . 7.9%
- $72,001 to $225,000. . . 8.25%
- $225,001 to $262,500 . . . . 9%
- $262,501 to $300,000 . . . 10%
- $300,001 and over 11%

Married filing jointly or Surviving spouse
- $0 to $4,800 . . . . 1.4%
- $4,801 to $9,600. . . . . 3.2%
- $9,601 to $19,200. . . . . . . 5.5%

Idaho[1,2]

Single or Married filing separately
- $0 to $1,379 . . . . 1.6%
- $1,380 to $2,759. . . . . 3.6%
- $2,760 to $4,139. . . . . 4.1%
- $4,140 to $5,519. . . . . 5.1%
- $5,520 to $6,899. . . . . 6.1%
- $6,900 to $10,349. . . . . . . 7.1%
- $10,350 and over 7.4%

Head of household, Married filing jointly, or Surviving spouse
- $0 to $2,759 . . . . 1.6%
- $2,760 to $5,519. . . . . 3.6%
- $5,520 to $8,279. . . . . 4.1%
- $8,280 to $11,039. . . . . . . 5.1%
- $11,040 to $13,799. . . . . . 6.1%
- $13,800 to $20,699. . . . . . 7.1%
- $20,700 and over 7.4%

Illinois

5% of federal AGI with modifications

Indiana

3.4% of AGI

Iowa[2]

- $0 to $1,469 . . . . 0.36%
- $1,470 to $2,938. . . . . 0.72%
- $2,939 to $5,876. . . . . 2.43%
- $5,877 to $13,221. . . . . . . 4.5%
- $13,222 to $22,035. . . . . . 6.12%
- $22,036 to $29,380. . . . . . 6.48%
- $29,381 to $44,070. . . . . . 6.8%
- $44,071 to $66,105. . . . . . 7.92%
- $66,106 and over 8.98%

Kansas

Single, Head of household, or Married filing separately
- $0 to $15,000 . . . . 3.5%
- $15,001 to $30,000. . . . . 6.25%
- $30,001 and over 6.45%

Married filing jointly
- $0 to $30,000 . . . . 3.5%
- $30,001 to $60,000. . . . . 6.25%
- $60,001 and over 6.45%

Kentucky

Single, Head of household, Married filing jointly, or Married filing separately
- $0 to $3,000 . . . . 2%
- $3,001 to $4,000. . . . . 3%
- $4,001 to $5,000. . . . . 4%
- $5,001 to $8,000. . . . . 5%
- $8,001 to $75,000. . . . . . . 5.8%
- $75,001 and over 6%

Louisiana[1]

Single, Head of household, or Married filing separately
- $0 to $12,500 . . . . 2%
- $12,501 to $50,000. . . . . . 4%
- $50,001 and over 6%

Married filing jointly
- $0 to $25,000 . . . . 2%
- $25,001 to $100,000 . . . . . 4%
- $100,001 and over. 6%

Maine[2]

Single or Married filing separately
- $0 to $5,099 . . . . 2%
- $5,100 to $10,149. . . . . . . 4.5%
- $10,150 to $20,349. . . . . . 7%

- $19,201 to $28,800. . . . . 6.4%
- $28,801 to $38,400. . . . . 6.8%
- $38,401 to $48,000. . . . . 7.2%
- $48,001 to $72,000. . . . . 7.6%
- $72,001 to $96,000. . . . . 7.9%
- $96,001 to $300,000. . . 8.25%
- $300,001 to $350,000. . . . 9%
- $350,001 to $400,000. . . 10%
- $400,001 and over 11%

Head of household
- $0 to $7,649 . . . . 2%
- $7,650 to $15,199. . . . . . 4.5%
- $15,200 to $30,499. . . . . . 7%
- $30,500 and over 8.5%

Married filing jointly or Qualifying widow(er)
- $0 to $10,199 . . . . 2%
- $10,200 to $20,349. . . . . 4.5%
- $20,350 to $40,699. . . . . . 7%
- $40,700 and over 8.5%

Maryland

Single, Married filing separately, and Dependent taxpayers
- $0 to $1,000 . . . . 2%
- $1,001 to $2,000. . . . . 3%
- $2,001 to $3,000. . . . . 4%
- $3,001 to $100,000. . . . . 4.75%
- $100,001 to $125,000. . . . . 5%
- $125,001 to $150,000. . . 5.25%
- $150,001 to $250,000. . . 5.5%
- $250,001 and over 5.75%

Head of household, Married filing jointly, or Qualifying widow(er)
- $0 to $1,000 . . . . 2%
- $1,001 to $2,000. . . . . 3%
- $2,001 to $3,000. . . . . 4%
- $3,001 to $150,000. . . . . 4.75%
- $150,001 to $175,000. . . . . 5%
- $175,001 to $225,000. . . 5.25%
- $225,001 to $300,000. . . 5.5%
- $300,001 and over 5.75%

Massachusetts

- Part A income (short-term capital gains). 12.0%
- Part A income (interest and dividends). 5.3%
- Part B income. 5.25%
- Part C income. 5.3%

Michigan

4.25% of taxable income

Minnesota[2]

Single
- $0 to $23,670 . . . . 5.35%
- $23,671 to $77,730. . . . . 7.05%
- $77,731 and over 7.85%

Head of household
- $0 to $29,130 . . . . 5.35%
- $29,131 to $117,060. . . . 7.05%
- $117,061 and over 7.85%

Married filing jointly
- $0 to $34,590 . . . . 5.35%
- $34,591 to $137,430. . . . 7.05%
- $137,431 and over 7.85%

Married filing separately
- $0 to $17,300 . . . . 5.35%
- $17,301 to $68,720. . . . . 7.05%
- $68,721 and over 7.85%

Mississippi

- $0 to $5,000 . . . . 3%
- $5,001 to $10,000. . . . . 4%
- $10,001 and over 5%

Missouri

- $0 to $1,000 . . . . 1.5%
- $1,001 to $2,000. . . . . 2%
- $2,001 to $3,000. . . . . 2.5%
- $3,001 to $4,000. . . . . 3%
- $4,001 to $5,000. . . . . 3.5%
- $5,001 to $6,000. . . . . 4%
- $6,001 to $7,000. . . . . 4.5%
- $7,001 to $8,000. . . . . 5%
- $8,001 to $9,000. . . . . 5.5%
- $9,001 and over 6%

Montana[2,3]

- $0 to $2,700 . . . . 1%
- $2,701 to $4,800. . . . . 2%
- $4,801 to $7,300. . . . . 3%

$7,301 to $9,900. . . . . 4%
$9,901 to $12,700 . . . . 5%
$12,701 to $16,400. . . . . . . 6%
$16,401 and over 6.9%

Nebraska
Single
$0 to $2,400 . . . . 2.56%
$2,401 to $17,500. . . . . . 3.57%
$17,501 to $27,000. . . . . 5.12%
$27,001 and over 6.84%
Head of household
$0 to $4,500 . . . . 2.56%
$4,501 to $28,000. . . . . . 3.57%
$28,001 to $40,000. . . . . 5.12%
$40,001 and over 6.84%
Married filing jointly or
Surviving spouse
$0 to $4,800 . . . . 2.56%
$4,801 to $35,000. . . . . . 3.57%
$35,001 to $54,000. . . . . 5.12%
$54,001 and over 6.84%
Married filing separately
$0 to $2,400 . . . . 2.56%
$2,401 to $17,500. . . . . . 3.57%
$17,501 to $27,000. . . . . 5.12%
$27,001 and over 6.84%

New Hampshire
5% on interest and dividends
only

New Jersey
Single or Married/civil-union
partner filing separately
$0 to $20,000 . . . . 1.4%
$20,001 to $35,000. . . . . 1.75%
$35,001 to $40,000. . . . . . 3.5%
$40,001 to $75,000. . . 5.525%
$75,001 to $500,000. . . . 6.37%
$500,001 and over 8.97%
Head of household, Married/
civil-union couple filing jointly,
or Qualifying widow(er)/Surviving
civil-union partner
$0 to $20,000 . . . . 1.4%
$20,001 to $50,000. . . . . 1.75%
$50,001 to $70,000. . . . . 2.45%
$70,001 to $80,000. . . . . . 3.5%
$80,001 to $150,000. . . 5.525%
$150,001 to $500,000. . . 6.37%
$500,001 and over 8.97%

New Mexico[1]
Single
$0 to $5,500 . . . . 1.7%
$5,501 to $11,000. . . . . . 3.2%
$11,001 to $16,000. . . . . . 4.7%
$16,001 and over 4.9%
Head of household
$0 to $8,000 . . . . 1.7%
$8,001 to $16,000. . . . . . 3.2%
$16,001 to $24,000. . . . . . 4.7%
$24,001 and over 4.9%
Married filing jointly or
Qualifying widow(er)
$0 to $8,000 . . . . 1.7%
$8,001 to $16,000. . . . . . 3.2%
$16,001 to $24,000. . . . . . 4.7%
$24,001 and over 4.9%
Married filing separately
$0 to $4,000 . . . . 1.7%
$4,001 to $8,000. . . . . . . 3.2%
$8,001 to $12,000. . . . . . 4.7%
$12,001 and over 4.9%

New York
Single or Married filing separately
$0 to $8,000 . . . . 4%
$8,001 to $11,000. . . . . . 4.5%
$11,001 to $13,000. . . . 5.25%
$13,001 to $20,000. . . . . 5.9%
$20,001 to $75,000. . . . 6.45%
$75,001 to $200,000. . . . 6.65%
$200,001 to $1,000,000 6.85%
$1,000,001 and over. . . 8.82%
Head of household
$0 to $12,000 . . . . 4%
$12,001 to $16,500. . . . . 4.5%
$16,501 to $19,500. . . . 5.25%
$19,501 to $30,000. . . . . 5.9%
$30,001 to $100,000. . . 6.45%
$100,001 to $250,000. . 6.65%
$250,001 to $1,500,000 6.85%
$1,500,001 and over . . . 8.82%
Married filing jointly or
Qualifying widow(er)
$0 to $16,000 . . . . 4%
$16,001 to $22,000. . . . . 4.5%
$22,001 to $26,000. . . . 5.25%
$26,001 to $40,000. . . . . 5.9%
$40,001 to $150,000. . . 6.45%
$150,001 to $300,000. . 6.65%
$300,001 to $2,000,000 6.85%
$2,000,001 and over. . . 8.82%

North Carolina
Single
$0 to $12,750 . . . . 6%
$12,751 to $60,000. . . . . . 7%
$60,001 and over 7.75%
Head of household
$0 to $17,000 . . . . 6%
$17,001 to $80,000. . . . . . 7%
$80,001 and over 7.75%
Married filing jointly or
Surviving spouse
$0 to $21,250 . . . . 6%
$21,251 to $100,000. . . . . 7%
$100,001 and over 7.75%
Married filing separately
$0 to $10,625 . . . . 6%
$10,626 to $50,000. . . . . . 7%
$50,001 and over 7.75%

North Dakota[2]
Single
$0 to $35,350 . . . . 1.51%
$35,351 to $85,650. . . . 2.82%
$85,651 to $178,650. . . 3.13%
$178,651 to $388,350. . 3.63%
$388,351 and over 3.99%
Head of household
$0 to $47,350. . . . . 1.51%
$47,351 to $122,300. . . 2.82%
$122,301 to $198,050. . 3.13%
$198,051 to $388,350. . 3.63%
$388,351 and over 3.99%
Married filing jointly or
Surviving spouse
$0 to $59,100 . . . . 1.51%
$59,101 to $142,700. . . 2.82%
$142,701 to $217,540. . 3.13%
$217,541 to $388,350. . 3.63%
$388,351 and over 3.99%
Married filing separately
$0 to $29,550 . . . . 1.51%
$29,551 to $71,350. . . . 2.82%
$71,351 to $108,725. . . 3.13%
$108,726 to $194,175. . 3.63%
$194,176 and over 3.99%

Ohio
$0 to $5,200 . . . . 0.587%
$5,201 to $10,400. . . . . 1.174%
$10,401 to $15,650. . . . 2.348%
$15,651 to $20,900. . . . 2.935%
$20,901 to $41,700. . . . 3.521%
$41,701 to $83,350. . . . 4.109%
$83,351 to $104,250. . . 4.695%
$104,251 to $208,500. . 5.451%
$208,501 and over 5.925%

Oklahoma
Single or Married filing separately
$0 to $1,000 . . . . 0.5%
$1,001 to $2,500. . . . . 1%
$2,501 to $3,750. . . . . 2%
$3,751 to $4,900. . . . . 3%
$4,901 to $7,200 . . . . 4%
$7,201 to $8,700 . . . . 5%
$8,701 and over 5.25%
Head of household, Married filing
jointly, or Qualifying widow(er)
$0 to $2,000 . . . . 0.5%
$2,001 to $5,000. . . . . 1%
$5,001 to $7,500. . . . . 2%
$7,501 to $9,800. . . . . 3%
$9,801 to $12,200. . . . . . . 4%
$12,201 to $15,000. . . . . . 5%
$15,001 and over 5.25%

Oregon[2]
Single or Married filing separately
$0 to $2,000 . . . . 5%
$2,001 to $5,000. . . . . 7%
$5,001 to $125,000. . . . . . 9%
$125,001 and over 9.9%
Married filing jointly,
Head of household, or
Qualifying widow(er)
$0 to $4,000 . . . . 5%
$4,001 to $10,000. . . . . . . 7%
$10,001 to $250,000. . . . . 9%
$250,001 and over 9.9%

Pennsylvania
3.07% of taxable compensation,
net profits, net gains from the sale
of property, rent, royalties, income
from estates or trusts, dividends,
interest, and winnings

Rhode Island[2]
Single, Head of household,
Married filing jointly, Surviving
spouse, or Married filing
separately
$0 to $57,150 . . . . 3.75%
$57,151 to $129,900. . . 4.75%
$129,901 and over 5.99%

South Carolina[2]
$0 to $2,800 . . . . 0%
$2,801 to $5,600. . . . . 3%
$5,601 to $8,400. . . . . 4%
$8,401 to $11,200. . . . . . . 5%
$11,201 to $14,000. . . . . . 6%
$14,001 and over 7%

Tennessee
6% upon interest and dividend
income

Utah
5% on state taxable income

Vermont[2]
Single
$0 to $35,350 . . . . 3.55%
$35,351 to $85,650. . . . . 6.8%
$85,651 to $178,650. . . . 7.8%
$178,651 to $388,350. . . . 8.8%
$388,351 and over 8.95%
Head of household
$0 to $47,350 . . . . 3.55%
$47,351 to $122,300. . . . . 6.8%
$122,301 to $198,050. . . . 7.8%
$198,051 to $388,350. . . . 8.8%
$388,351 and over 8.95%
Married filing jointly,
Qualifying widow(er), or
Civil union filing jointly
$0 to $59,050 . . . . 3.55%
$59,051 to $142,700. . . . . 6.8%
$142,701 to $217,450. . . . 7.8%
$217,451 to $388,350. . . . 8.8%
$388,351 and over 8.95%
Married or
Civil union filing separately
$0 to $29,525 . . . . 3.55%
$29,526 to $71,350. . . . . 6.8%
$71,351 to $108,725. . . . 7.8%
$108,726 to $194,175. . . . 8.8%
$194,176 and over 8.95%

Virginia
Single, Head of household,
Married filing jointly, or
Married filing separately
$0 to $3,000 . . . . 2%
$3,001 to $5,000. . . . . 3%
$5,001 to $17,000. . . . . . . 5%
$17,001 and over 5.75%

West Virginia
Single, Head of household,
Married filing jointly, or Widower
with dependent child
$0 to $10,000 . . . . 3%
$10,001 to $25,000. . . . . . 4%
$25,001 to $40,000. . . . . 4.5%
$40,001 to $60,000. . . . . . 6%
$60,001 and over 6.5%
Married filing separately
$0 to $5,000 . . . . 3%
$5,001 to $12,500. . . . . . . 4%
$12,501 to $20,000. . . . . 4.5%
$20,001 to $30,000. . . . . . 6%
$30,001 and over 6.5%

Wisconsin[1,2]
Single or Head of household
$0 to $10,570. . . . . 4.6%
$10,571 to $21,130. . . . 6.15%
$21,131 to $158,500. . . . 6.5%
$158,501 to $232,660 . . 6.75%
$232,661 and over. 7.75%
Married filing jointly
$0 to $14,090. . . . . 4.6%
$14,091 to $28,180. . . . 6.15%
$28,181 to $211,330. . . . 6.5%
$211,331 to $310,210 . . 6.75%
$310,211 and over. 7.75%
Married filing separately
$0 to $7,040. . . . . 4.6%
$7,041 to $14,090 . . . . . 6.15%
$14,091 to $105,660. . . . 6.5%
$105,661 to $155,110 . . 6.75%
$155,111 and over. 7.75%

AMT = Alternative minimum tax; AGI = Adjusted gross income; MFS = Married filing separately. (1) Community property state in which, in general, one-half of the community income is taxable to each spouse. (2) Brackets indexed for inflation annually. (3) 2012 adjusted brackets were not available. Bracketed rates listed are for 2011. **Arkansas:** Married filing separately combined-status couples calculate taxes separately and add the results. **California:** An additional 1% tax is imposed on taxable income in excess of $1 mil. **Colorado:** Individual taxpayers are subject to an AMT equal to the amount by which 3.47% of their Colorado alternative minimum taxable income exceeds their Colorado normal tax. **Connecticut:** Resident estates and trusts are subject to 6.7% rate on all income. **Indiana:** Counties may impose an AGI tax on residents or on nonresidents, or a county option income tax. **Iowa:** An AMT of 6.7% of alternative minimum income is imposed if the minimum tax exceeds the taxpayer's regular income tax liability. **Massachusetts:** Part A income represents either interest and dividends or short-term capital gains. Part B income represents wages, salaries, tips, pensions, state bank interest, partnership income, business income, rents, alimony, winnings, and certain other items of income. Part C income represents gains from the sale of capital assets held for more than one year. **Minnesota:** A 6.4% AMT is imposed. **Montana:** Minimum tax, $1. **Nebraska:** There is an additional tax on taxpayers with federal AGI of more than a certain amount, which is $169,550 ($84,775 for MFS) in 2012. **New Mexico:** Qualified nonresident taxpayers may pay alternative tax of 0.75% of gross receipts from New Mexico sales. **New York:** A supplemental tax is imposed to recapture the tax table benefit. **Ohio:** The brackets listed reflect the annual adjustment for inflation that was made in Aug. 2012. **Vermont:** The tax amount in the schedules is increased by 24% of a taxpayer's federal tax liability for certain items. **Wisconsin:** An economic development surcharge is imposed on individuals with gross receipts of $4 mil or more. The minimum surcharge is $25 or 0.2% of net business income attributable to state sources, up to a maximum of $9,800.

EDUCATION

U.S. Public Schools: Students, Staff, Spending, 1899-2009

Source: National Center for Education Statistics, U.S. Dept. of Education

	1899-1900	1919-20	1939-40	1959-60	1969-70	1979-80	1989-90	1999-2000	2008-09
Population (thous.)									
Total U.S. population[1]	75,995	104,514	131,028	177,830	201,385	225,055	246,819	279,040	304,375
Population 5-17 years of age	21,573	27,571	30,151	43,881	52,386	48,043	44,947	52,811	53,277
Percentage 5-17 years of age. . . .	28.4%	26.4%	23.0%	24.7%	26.0%	21.3%	18.2%	18.9%	17.5%
Enrollment (thous.)									
Elementary and secondary[2]	15,503	21,578	25,434	36,087	45,550	41,651	40,543	46,857	49,266
Pre-kindergarten and grades 1-8	14,984	19,378	18,833	27,602	32,513	28,034	29,152	33,486	34,286
Grades 9-12	519	2,200	6,601	8,485	13,037	13,616	11,390	13,371	14,980
Percentage pop. 5-17 enrolled	71.9%	78.3%	84.4%	82.2%	87.0%	86.7%	90.2%	88.7%	92.5%
Percentage enrolled in high schools	3.3%	10.2%	26.0%	23.5%	28.6%	32.7%	28.1%	28.5%	30.4%
High school grads. (thous.)	62	231	1,143	1,627	2,589	2,748	2,320	2,554	3,005
Instructional staff (thous.)									
Total instructional staff	*	678	912	1,457	2,286	2,406	2,986	3,819	4,275
Teachers, librarians, and other nonsupervisory instructional staff	423	657	875	1,393	2,195	2,300	2,860	3,682	4,155
Revenue and expenditures (mil)									
Total revenue	$220	$970	$2,261	$14,747	$40,267	$96,881	$208,548	$372,944	$593,061
Total expenditures.	215	1,036	2,344	15,613	40,683	95,962	212,770	381,838	610,110
Current expenditures[3,4]	180	861	1,942	12,329	34,218	86,984	188,229	323,889	518,997
Capital outlay	35	154	258	2,662	4,659	6,506	17,781	43,357	65,882
Interest on school debt	*	18	131	490	1,171	1,874	3,776	9,135	16,691
Others	*	3	13	133	636	598	2,983	5,457	8,539
Salaries and pupil cost									
Avg. annual salary of instruct. staff[5]	$325	$871	$1,441	$4,995	$8,626	$15,970	$31,367	$41,807	$54,319
Expenditure per capita total pop. . . .	2.83	9.91	17.89	88	202	426	862	1,368	2,004
Current expenditure per pupil ADA[4,6]	16.67	53.32	88.09	375	816	2,272	4,980	7,394	10,591

* = Data not collected. **Note:** Because of rounding, details may not add up to totals. Prior to 1959-60, data do not include Alaska and Hawaii. (1) Data for 1899-1900 are based on total population from the decennial census. From 1919-20 to 1959-60, population data are total population, including armed forces overseas, as of July 1 preceding the school year. Data for later years are for resident population excluding armed forces overseas. (2) Data for 1899-1960 are school year enrollment; data for later years are fall enrollment. (3) In 1899-1900, includes interest on school debt. (4) Because of changes in the definition of "current expenditures," data for 1959-60 and later years are not entirely comparable with prior years. (5) Data prior to 1959-60 include supervisors, principals, teachers, and nonsupervisory instructional staff. (6) ADA = average daily attendance.

U.S. Public High School Graduation Rates, 2008-09

Source: National Center for Education Statistics, U.S. Dept. of Education

State	Rate	Rank	State	Rate	Rank	State	Rate	Rank	State	Rate	Rank
Alabama	69.9%	43	Illinois	77.7%	21	Montana	82.0%	11	Rhode Island . . .	75.3%	30
Alaska.	72.6	40	Indiana	75.2	33	Nebraska	82.9	10	South Carolina . .	66.0	47
Arizona	72.5	41	Iowa	85.7	5	Nevada	56.3	51	South Dakota . . .	81.7	12
Arkansas	74.0	36	Kansas	80.2	15	New Hampshire	84.3	7	Tennessee	77.4	24
California	71.0	42	Kentucky.	77.6	22	New Jersey	85.3	6	Texas	75.4	28
Colorado.	77.6	22	Louisiana	67.3	46	New Mexico	64.8	48	Utah	79.4	19
Connecticut.	75.4	28	Maine	79.9	17	New York	73.5	39	Vermont	89.6	2
Delaware	73.7	37	Maryland.	80.1	16	North Carolina . .	75.1	35	Virginia	78.4	20
Dist. of Columbia	62.4	49	Massachusetts . .	83.3	8	North Dakota . . .	87.4	3	Washington.	73.7	37
Florida.	68.9	44	Michigan.	75.3	30	Ohio	79.6	18	West Virginia . . .	77.0	26
Georgia.	67.8	45	Minnesota	87.4	3	Oklahoma	77.3	25	Wisconsin	90.7	1
Hawaii.	75.3	30	Mississippi	62.0	50	Oregon	76.5	27	Wyoming.	75.2	33
Idaho.	80.6	13	Missouri	83.1	9	Pennsylvania . . .	80.5	14	**Total U.S.**	**75.5**	

Note: The averaged freshman graduation rate provides an estimate of the percentage of students who receive a regular diploma within four years of entering ninth grade. The rate uses aggregate student enrollment data to estimate the size of an incoming freshman class and aggregate counts of the number of diplomas awarded four years later.

High School Dropouts by Sex, Race, and Ethnicity, 1960-2010

Source: Current Population Survey, Census Bureau, U.S. Dept. of Commerce

Data for Oct. of year shown unless otherwise noted.

Year[1]	Total dropout rate				Male dropout rate				Female dropout rate			
	All races[2]	White	Black	Hispanic	All races[2]	White	Black	Hispanic	All races[2]	White	Black	Hispanic
1960[3]	27.2%	NA	NA	NA	27.8%	NA	NA	NA	26.7%	NA	NA	NA
1970[4]	15.0	13.2%	27.9%	NA	14.2	12.2%	29.4%	NA	15.7	14.1%	26.6%	NA
1975	13.9	11.4	22.9	29.2%	13.3	11.0	23.0	26.7%	14.5	11.8	22.9	31.6%
1980	14.1	11.4	19.1	35.2	15.1	12.3	20.8	37.2	13.1	10.5	17.7	33.2
1985	12.6	10.4	15.2	27.6	13.4	11.1	16.1	29.9	11.8	9.8	14.3	25.2
1990	12.1	9.0	13.2	32.4	12.3	9.3	11.9	34.3	11.8	8.7	14.4	30.3
1995	12.0	8.6	12.1	30.0	12.2	9.0	11.1	30.0	11.7	8.2	12.9	30.0
2000	10.9	6.9	13.1	27.8	12.0	7.0	15.3	31.8	9.9	6.9	11.1	23.5
2001	10.7	7.3	10.9	27.0	12.2	7.9	13.0	31.6	9.3	6.7	9.0	22.1
2002	10.5	6.5	11.3	25.7	11.8	6.7	12.8	29.6	9.2	6.3	9.9	21.2
2003[5]	9.9	6.3	10.9	23.5	11.3	7.1	12.5	26.7	8.4	5.6	9.5	20.1
2004[5]	10.3	6.8	11.8	23.8	11.6	7.1	13.5	28.5	9.0	6.4	10.2	18.5
2005[5]	9.4	6.0	10.4	22.4	10.8	6.6	12.0	26.4	8.0	5.3	9.0	18.1
2006[5]	9.3	5.8	10.7	22.1	10.3	6.4	9.7	25.7	8.3	5.3	11.7	18.1
2007[5]	8.7	5.3	8.4	21.4	9.8	6.0	8.0	24.7	7.7	4.5	8.8	18.0
2008[5]	8.0	4.8	9.9	18.3	8.5	5.4	8.7	19.9	7.5	4.2	11.1	16.7
2009[5]	8.1	5.2	9.3	17.6	9.1	6.3	10.6	19.0	7.0	4.1	8.1	16.1
2010[5]	7.4	5.1	8.0	15.1	8.5	5.9	9.5	17.3	6.3	4.2	6.7	12.8

NA = Not available. **Note:** Table shows "status" dropouts, defined as 16- to 24-year-olds who are not enrolled in school and who have not completed a high school program, regardless of when they left school. People who have received GED credentials are not shown. Excludes persons in prisons or in the military, and other persons not living in households. Race categories exclude persons of Hispanic ethnicity unless otherwise noted. (1) Because of changes in data collection procedures, data for years prior to 1992 may not be comparable to later years. (2) Includes other racial/ethnic categories not separately shown. (3) Based on the Apr. 1960 decennial census. (4) White and black data include persons of Hispanic ethnicity. (5) White and black data exclude persons identifying themselves as being of two or more races.

Overview of U.S. Public Schools, 2010-11

Source: National Center for Education Statistics, U.S. Dept. of Education; National Education Association (NEA)

State	Local school districts	Elementary schools[1,2]	Secondary schools[2,3]	Classroom teachers	Total enrollment	Pupils per teacher	Teacher's avg. pay	Expend. per pupil
Alabama	132	964	423	46,798	741,043	15.8	$47,803	$8,820
Alaska	54	193	85	8,196	129,114	15.8	62,918	16,744*
Arizona	627*	1,361	718	58,305*	1,071,484*	18.4*	47,553*	6,448*
Arkansas	245*	715	392	30,700*	459,419*	15.0*	46,500	11,999*
California	1,042*	6,917	2,608	263,630	6,219,649*	23.6*	67,871	9,313*
Colorado	178	1,273	413	48,478	843,315	17.4	49,228	9,596
Connecticut	195*	838	282	41,464	566,030*	13.7*	69,165	14,989*
Delaware	37*	152	38	8,740*	128,530*	14.7*	57,934*	13,960*
Dist. of Columbia	41*	168	40	5,835*	76,210*	13.1*	66,601*	13,803*
Florida	67*	2,662	657	169,719	2,637,224	15.5	45,732	8,983
Georgia	192	1,784	437	112,094	1,676,412	15.0	52,815	9,847*
Hawaii	1	209	51	10,851	179,122	16.5	55,063	11,659
Idaho	137*	442	227	15,669*	285,236*	18.2*	47,416*	8,101*
Illinois	869*	3,198	1,040	129,289	2,098,145	16.2	64,509	11,946*
Indiana	354	1,415	447	63,266*	1,047,084	16.6*	50,801	10,436
Iowa	359	1,005	423	34,614	495,897	14.3	49,844	9,484
Kansas	289	962	405	34,331	481,467	14.0	46,598	9,505
Kentucky	174	990	428	41,331	658,328	15.9	48,908	9,563
Louisiana	122	981	307	48,894	696,558	14.2	49,006	10,327
Maine	229*	486	150	17,248*	187,401*	10.9*	47,182*	15,032*
Maryland	24	1,119	268	59,330	852,211	14.4	63,960	15,060*
Massachusetts	392	1,355	367	70,217	954,687	13.6	70,752	14,902
Michigan	773*	2,475	1,044	96,663*	1,662,067*	17.2*	63,940*	12,015*
Minnesota	471*	1,276	862	52,524	810,123*	15.4*	53,680	11,905*
Mississippi	152	620	335	32,041	490,526*	15.3*	41,975	8,713*
Missouri	524*	1,581	655	67,385	903,887*	13.4*	45,321	9,422*
Montana	417*	479	349	10,570*	140,533*	13.3*	47,132*	9,973*
Nebraska	251	742	349	26,470	298,083	11.3	47,368	10,433
Nevada	17*	465	137	25,049*	456,844*	18.2*	53,023*	8,089*
New Hampshire	161	378	106	15,622*	193,264*	12.4*	52,792*	13,797*
New Jersey	591*	1,899	551	109,998	1,366,067*	12.4*	66,612	17,717*
New Mexico	89	600	235	21,263	334,465	15.7	46,888	10,415*
New York	695*	3,308	1,090	223,862	2,642,524*	11.8*	72,708	17,750*
North Carolina	115	1,873	526	94,879	1,424,536	15.0	46,605	8,572
North Dakota	182	298	185	8,022	94,729	11.8	44,807	8,631
Ohio	986	2,600	1,021	108,888	1,881,436	17.3	56,715	9,813*
Oklahoma	526	1,240	552	41,326	659,622	16.0	44,343	8,058*
Oregon	196	917	317	27,646	561,331	20.3	56,503	9,899
Pennsylvania	499	2,293	823	125,902	1,763,946*	14.0*	60,760	13,334*
Rhode Island	49*	237	74	11,081*	138,803*	12.5*	60,923*	15,803*
South Carolina	89	900	272	46,247	714,421	15.4	47,050	9,167
South Dakota	152	437	254	9,284	123,629	13.3	39,850	8,997
Tennessee	135	1,290	354	65,008	988,822	15.2	45,891	8,213
Texas	1,228	5,871	2,130	334,946	4,912,385	14.7	48,638	8,751
Utah	41	628	353	26,328	576,245	21.9	47,033*	6,672*
Vermont	286*	238	68	8,901*	85,635*	9.6*	50,141*	17,447*
Virginia	132	1,514	405	105,830*	1,252,529*	11.8*	48,761*	10,832*
Washington	295	1,433	569	53,884	1,041,245	19.3	52,926	9,720
West Virginia	55*	566	132	19,791	282,130	14.3	44,260	11,423*
Wisconsin	424	1,554	596	58,041	872,286	15.0	54,195	11,787*
Wyoming	48	239	101	7,115	88,165	12.4	56,100	15,997
Total U.S.	**15,339***	**67,140**	**24,651**	**3,153,567***	**49,244,844***	**15.6***	**55,623***	**10,770***

* = NEA estimate. (1) Includes primary and middle schools (schools with no grade higher than 8th). (2) 2009-10 estimates. (3) Includes schools with no grade lower than 7th.

Programs for the Disabled, 1995-2011

Source: Office of Special Education and Rehabilitative Services, U.S. Dept. of Education

Number of children and young adults 3 to 21 years old served annually in federally funded educational programs for the disabled; in thousands.

Type of disability	1995 -96	2000 -01	2001 -02	2002 -03	2003 -04	2004 -05	2005 -06	2006 -07	2007 -08	2008 -09	2009 -10	2010 -11
Learning disabilities	2,578	2,868	2,861	2,848	2,831	2,798	2,735	2,665	2,577	2,537	2,498	2,423
Speech impairments.......	1,022	1,409	1,391	1,412	1,441	1,463	1,468	1,475	1,458	1,451	1,449	1,429
Mental retardation.........	571	624	616	602	593	578	556	534	500	488	473	457
Emotional disturbance	437	481	483	485	489	489	477	464	442	421	409	391
Multiple disabilities	93	133	136	138	140	140	141	142	138	132	132	131
Hearing impairments	67	78	78	78	79	79	79	80	79	79	79	79
Orthopedic impairments....	63	83	83	83	77	73	71	69	67	70	66	63
Other health impairments[1] ..	133	303	350	403	464	521	570	611	641	666	698	724
Visual impairments........	25	29	28	29	28	29	29	29	29	29	29	29
Autism..................	28	94	114	137	163	191	223	258	296	338	380	419
Deaf-blindness	1	1	2	2	2	2	2	2	2	2	2	2
Traumatic brain injury	9	16	22	22	23	24	24	25	25	26	25	26
Developmental delay	—	178	242	283	305	332	339	333	358	354	368	381
All disabilities	**5,572**	**6,296**	**6,407**	**6,523**	**6,634**	**6,719**	**6,713**	**6,686**	**6,613**	**6,593**	**6,608**	**6,553**

— = Not available or not reliable data. **Note:** Counts based on reports from states and District of Columbia. Details may not add up to totals because of rounding and/or incomplete enumeration. (1) Includes limited strength, vitality, or alertness due to chronic or acute health problems such as a heart condition, tuberculosis, rheumatic fever, nephritis, asthma, sickle cell anemia, hemophilia, epilepsy, lead poisoning, leukemia, or diabetes.

Students Reporting School Bullying and Cyberbullying, 2008-09
Source: National Center for Education Statistics, U.S. Dept. of Education

Total students	Number of students (thous.)	Percent of students		Number of students (thous.)	Percent of students
Total students	25,217	100.0%	Not cyberbullied	23,642	94.0%
Not bullied	18,151	72.0	Cyberbullied students	1,521	6.0
Bullied students	7,066	28.0	Hurtful information on Internet	502	2.0
Made fun of, called names, or insulted	4,735	18.8	Unwanted contact via email	335	1.3
Subject of rumors	4,149	16.5	Unwanted contact via instant messaging	448	1.8
Threatened with harm	1,442	5.7	Unwanted contact via text messaging	753	3.0
Pushed, shoved, tripped, or spit on	2,266	9.0			
Tried to make do things they did not want to do	916	3.6	Unwanted contact via online gaming	193	0.8
Excluded from activities on purpose	1,190	4.7	Purposeful exclusion from an online community	224	0.9
Property destroyed on purpose	832	3.3			

Note: Includes bullying among students ages 12-18 taking place in the school building, on school property, on a school bus, or going to and from school and cyberbullying anywhere during the school year.

High School Students in a Fight or Bullied on School Property, 2011
Source: *Youth Risk Behavior Surveillance–United States, 2011*, Centers for Disease Control and Prevention

	In a physical fight on school property[1]			Bullied on school property[2]		
Race/ethnicity	Female	Male	Total	Female	Male	Total
White[3]	5.6%	13.8%	9.9%	25.2%	20.7%	22.9%
Black[3]	13.1	19.6	16.4	12.2	11.1	11.7
Hispanic	9.0	19.4	14.4	19.3	16.0	17.6
Grade						
9	10.4	21.7	16.2	27.1	21.5	24.2
10	8.0	17.0	12.8	24.6	20.4	22.4
11	6.0	12.3	9.2	17.5	16.7	17.1
12	6.1	11.4	8.8	17.2	13.4	15.2
Total	7.8	16.0	12.0	22.0	18.2	20.1

(1) One or more times during the 12 months before the survey. (2) During the 12 months before the survey. (3) Non-Hispanic.

High School Students Electronically Bullied or Concerned About Safety, 2011
Source: *Youth Risk Behavior Surveillance—United States, 2011*, Centers for Disease Control and Prevention

	Electronically bullied[1,2]			Did not go to school because of safety concerns[3]		
Race/ethnicity	Female	Male	Total	Female	Male	Total
White[4]	25.9%	11.8%	18.6%	4.7%	4.0%	4.4%
Black[4]	11.0	6.9	8.9	5.3	8.0	6.7
Hispanic	18.0	9.5	13.6	9.6	8.5	9.1
Grade						
9	22.6	8.9	15.5	6.3	5.4	5.8
10	24.2	12.6	18.1	7.1	6.4	6.8
11	19.8	12.4	16.0	5.1	5.3	5.2
12	21.5	8.8	15.0	5.1	5.9	5.5
Total	22.1	10.8	16.2	6.0	5.8	5.9

(1) During the 12 months before the survey. (2) Including being bullied through email, chat rooms, instant messaging, websites, or texting. (3) On at least 1 day during the 30 days before the survey. (4) Non-Hispanic.

Trends in International Mathematics and Science Study (TIMSS), 1995-2007
Source: National Center for Education Statistics, U.S. Dept. of Education

The TIMSS is an international assessment test that was administered to 4th and 8th graders in 1995, 1999 (5th graders only), 2003, and 2007, to measure the degree to which students have learned concepts of mathematics and science. Listed below are the average scaled scores for each country. Scores are reported on a scale of 0 to 1,000, with the scale average set at 500. Student achievement is considered "high" with a score of at least 550; a score of at least 475 is considered "intermediate."

4th Grade	Mathematics 2007	% change, 1995-2007	Science 2007	% change, 1995-2007
Australia	516	22%	527	6%
Austria	505	−25	526	−12
Czech Republic	486	−54	515	−17
England	541	57	542	14
Hong Kong	607	50	554	46
Hungary	510	−12	536	28
Iran	402	15	436	55
Japan	568	1	548	−5
Latvia	537	38	542	56
Netherlands	535	−14	523	−7
New Zealand	492	23	504	−1
Norway	473	−3	477	−27
Scotland	494	1	500	−14
Singapore	599	9	587	63
Slovenia	502	40	518	54
United States	**529**	**11**	**539**	**−3**

8th Grade	Mathematics 2007	% change, 1995-2007	Science 2007	% change, 1995-2007
Australia	496	−13%	NA	NA
Bulgaria	464	−63	515	1%
Colombia	380	47	417	52
Cyprus	465	−2	452	0
Czech Republic	504	−42	539	−16
England	513	16	542	8
Hong Kong	572	4	530	20
Hungary	517	−10	539	2
Iran	403	−15	459	−4
Japan	570	−11	554	−1
Korea, South	597	17	553	7
Lithuania	506	34	519	55
Norway	469	−29	487	−28
Romania	461	−12	462	−9
Russia	512	−12	530	7
Scotland	487	−6	496	−5
Singapore	593	−16	567	−13
Slovenia	501	7	538	24
Sweden	491	−48	511	−42
United States	**508**	**16**	**520**	**7**

Mathematics, Reading, and Science Achievement of U.S. Students, 1998-2011

Source: National Assessment of Educational Progress, National Center for Education Statistics, U.S. Dept. of Education

Percent of public school students who scored at or above basic levels in national tests. Basic level denotes a partial mastery of prerequisite knowledge and skills fundamental for proficient work at each grade.

State	4th Grade Math 2000	4th Grade Math 2011	4th Grade Reading 1998	4th Grade Reading 2011	8th Grade Math 2000	8th Grade Math 2011	8th Grade Reading 1998	8th Grade Reading 2011	Science 2000	Science 2011
AL	55	75	56	68	52	60	67	69	53	54
AK	NA	78	NA	55	NA	74	NA	73	NA	68
AZ	57	77	51	58	62	68	72	71	55	57
AR	55	80	54	63	52	70	68	71	53	62
CA	50	74	48	57	52	61	63	66	38	52
CO	NA	84	69	70	NA	80	77	81	NA	74
CT	76	81	76	73	72	75	81	83	64	69
DE	NA	84	53	72	NA	74	64	76	NA	63
DC	24	59	27	44	23	48	44	51	NA	24
FL	NA	83	53	71	NA	68	67	72	NA	62
GA	57	80	54	66	55	69	68	75	52	63
HI	55	80	45	59	52	68	59	68	40	55
ID	68	83	NA	68	71	78	NA	81	71	75
IL	63	79	NA	66	68	73	NA	77	59	60
IN	77	86	NA	77	76	77	NA	78	66	68
IA	75	86	67	68	NA	77	NA	77	NA	73
KS	76	90	70	71	77	79	81	79	NA	70
KY	59	85	62	72	63	71	74	79	60	71
LA	57	73	44	56	48	63	63	65	44	56
ME	73	87	72	69	76	79	83	80	72	78
MD	60	87	58	75	65	75	70	80	57	64
MA	77	92	70	83	76	85	79	84	70	76
MI	71	78	62	65	70	71	NA	77	68	72
MN	76	88	69	70	80	83	78	81	72	76
MS	45	72	47	55	41	58	62	65	41	47
MO	71	83	61	67	67	73	75	79	66	72
MT	72	87	72	73	80	83	83	85	79	80
NE	65	82	NA	70	74	75	NA	80	52	72
NV	60	79	51	59	58	67	70	69	NA	58
NH	NA	93	75	77	NA	82	NA	84	NA	79
NJ	NA	89	NA	77	NA	82	NA	84	NA	69
NM	50	75	51	53	50	64	71	68	48	58
NY	66	79	62	68	68	70	76	76	NA	62
NC	73	89	58	68	70	75	74	74	54	61
ND	73	89	NA	74	77	84	NA	83	72	82
OH	73	86	NA	72	75	79	NA	80	72	73
OK	67	83	66	63	64	71	80	73	60	63
OR	65	77	58	62	71	71	78	76	68	71
PA	NA	87	NA	73	NA	73	NA	77	NA	66
RI	65	84	64	71	64	74	76	76	58	63
SC	59	79	53	61	55	70	66	72	48	61
SD	NA	86	NA	68	NA	81	NA	82	NA	79
TN	59	76	57	61	53	64	71	70	55	64
TX	76	85	59	65	68	81	74	75	52	67
UT	69	85	62	68	68	73	77	79	67	77
VT	73	88	NA	73	75	70	NA	83	71	80
VA	71	87	62	72	67	78	78	78	61	73
WA	NA	84	64	66	NA	76	77	77	NA	72
WV	65	78	60	61	62	65	75	68	57	64
WI	NA	86	72	77	NA	79	78	79	NA	75
WY	71	87	64	72	70	80	76	82	69	77
U.S.	**64**	**81**	**58**	**66**	**65**	**73**	**71**	**75**	**57**	**65**

NA = Not administered.

Enrollment in U.S. Public and Private Schools, 1899-2021

Source: National Center for Education Statistics, U.S. Dept. of Education

Of all students enrolled at private schools in 2009-10, 80% attended religious schools and 20% attended nonsectarian schools.

School year[1]	Public school[2]	Private school[2]	% private[3]	School year[1]	Public school[2]	Private school[2]	% private[3]
1899-1900	15,503	1,352	8.0%	1979-80	41,651	5,000[4]	10.7%
1909-10	17,814	1,558	8.0	1989-90	40,543	5,599	12.1
1919-20	21,578	1,699	7.3	1999-2000	46,857	6,018	11.4
1929-30	25,678	2,651	9.4	2007-08	49,293	5,910	10.7
1939-40	25,434	2,611	9.3	2008-09	49,265	5,707[4]	10.4
1949-50	25,111	3,380	11.9	2009-10	49,282	5,488	10.0
1959-60	35,182	5,675	13.9	2019-20[5]	52,204	5,234	9.1
1969-70	45,550	5,500[4]	10.8	2020-21[5]	52,666	5,273	9.1

Note: Private includes all nonpublic schools. (1) Fall enrollment. (2) In thousands. Data from fall 1980 onward covers an expanded universe of private schools; comparisons with earlier years should be avoided. (3) Percent of U.S. students enrolled in private schools. (4) Estimated. (5) Projected.

Characteristics of Public Charter Schools and Students, 1999-2010

Source: National Center for Education Statistics, U.S. Dept. of Education

	1999-2000	2001-02	2003-04	2005-06	2007-08	2009-10
Number of charter school students	**339,678**	**571,029**	**789,479**	**1,012,906**	**1,276,731**	**1,611,332**
Sex						
Male	51.1%	50.8%	50.4%	49.9%	49.5%	49.5%
Female	48.9	49.2	49.6	50.1	50.5	50.5
Race/ethnicity						
White	42.5	42.6	41.8	40.5	38.8	37.3
Black	33.5	32.5	31.9	32.1	31.8	30.3
Hispanic	19.6	20.1	21.5	22.4	24.5	26.1
Asian/Pacific Islander	2.8	3.1	3.2	3.6	3.8	3.8
American Indian/Alaska Native	1.5	1.7	1.5	1.4	1.2	1.1
Other[1]	NA	NA	NA	NA	NA	1.4
Number of charter schools	**1,524**	**2,348**	**2,977**	**3,780**	**4,388**	**4,952**
School level						
Elementary	55.7%	51.7%	52.1%	52.9%	54.1%	54.3%
Secondary	24.9	24.6	26.4	28.1	27.5	26.7
Combined	18.9	23.0	21.4	18.8	18.4	18.8
Enrollment size						
Under 300	77.0	73.5	70.9	69.5	65.5	61.3
300-499	12.0	13.7	15.6	16.6	19.4	21.0
500-999	8.7	10.0	10.3	10.9	12.0	14.0
1,000 or more	2.4	2.8	3.2	3.0	3.1	3.7
Locale						
City	NA	NA	52.5	53.4	54.6	54.8
Suburban	NA	NA	22.2	21.9	21.8	21.1
Town	NA	NA	9.6	8.8	8.5	8.0
Rural	NA	NA	15.8	15.8	15.2	16.1

NA = Not available. **Note:** Numbers may not add up to totals due to rounding. Race categories exclude persons of Hispanic ethnicity, who may be of any race. (1) Includes data for states reporting students of two or more races.

Homeschooled Students

Source: National Center for Education Statistics, U.S. Dept. of Education

A total of 1,508,000 U.S. students in grades K-12 were homeschooled in 2007, 84% of them full-time, according to the latest available statistics from the U.S. Dept. of Education.

In a 2007 U.S. Dept. of Education survey of parents who homeschool their children, the reasons given as most important included concern over the school environment, including such factors as safety, drugs, or negative peer pressure (20.5%); desire to provide religious or moral instruction (35.8%); dissatisfaction with academic instruction in schools (17.1%); and a physical or mental health problem or other special need (5.7%). In all, 87.6% cited concern over school environment as one of their reasons, while 83.3% cited religious or moral instruction, and 72.7% cited dissatisfaction with academic instruction.

Characteristic	1999			2007		
	No. of students	Percentage distribution	Home-schooling rate[1]	No. of students	Percentage distribution	Home-schooling rate[1]
Total U.S.	850,000	100.0%	1.7%	1,508,000	100.0%	2.9%
Homeschooled entirely	697,000	82.0	—	1,266,000	84.0	—
Homeschooled and enrolled in school part-time	153,000	18.0	—	242,000	16.0	—
Race/ethnicity[2]						
White........................	640,000	75.3	2.0	1,159,000	76.8	3.9
Black........................	84,000	9.9	1.0	61,000	4.0	0.8
Hispanic	77,000	9.1	1.1	147,000	9.8	1.5
Other........................	49,000	5.8	1.9	141,000	9.3	3.4
Number of children in household						
One child....................	120,000	14.1	1.5	187,000	12.4	2.2
Two children	207,000	24.4	1.0	412,000	27.3	2.0
Three or more children	523,000	61.6	2.4	909,000	60.3	4.1
Household income						
$25,000 or less...............	262,000	30.9	1.6	239,000	15.9	2.1
$25,001-$50,000...............	278,000	32.7	1.8	364,000	24.1	3.4
$50,001-$75,000...............	162,000	19.1	1.9	405,000	26.8	3.9
$75,001 or more	148,000	17.4	1.5	501,000	33.2	2.7
Parents' education						
High school diploma or less	160,000	18.9	0.9	206,000	13.7	1.4
Some college or vocational/technical	287,000	33.7	1.9	549,000	36.4	3.8
Bachelor's degree....................	213,000	25.1	2.6	444,000	29.4	3.9
Graduate/professional degree	190,000	22.3	2.3	309,000	20.5	2.9

(1) Percentage of the total group or subgroup within the general population that is homeschooled. For example, in 1999, 1.1% of all Hispanic students grades K-12 in the U.S. were homeschooled. (2) Hispanic or Latino persons may be of any race. Race categories include non-Hispanic population only.

Revenues for Public Elementary and Secondary Schools by State, 2008-09

Source: National Education Association (NEA); amounts in thousands

State	Total	Federal		State		Local and intermediate	
		Amount	% of tot. rev.	Amount	% of tot. rev.	Amount	% of tot. rev.
Alabama	$7,239,083	$777,591	10.7%	$4,166,018	57.5%	$2,295,475	31.7%
Alaska	2,262,964	314,949	13.9	1,459,658	64.5	488,356	21.6
American Samoa	79,922	68,432	85.6	11,282	14.1	209	0.3
Arizona	9,771,972	1,137,316	11.6	4,594,648	47.0	4,040,008	41.3
Arkansas	4,823,956	556,500	11.5	2,684,309	55.6	1,583,147	32.8
California	70,687,012	9,185,270	13.0	40,605,913	57.4	20,895,829	29.6
Colorado	8,353,849	578,233	6.9	3,670,240	43.9	4,105,376	49.1
Connecticut	9,871,755	440,826	4.5	3,842,177	38.9	5,588,751	56.6
Delaware	1,755,133	142,428	8.1	1,094,909	62.4	517,796	29.5
District of Columbia[1]	1,651,014	175,732	10.6	NA	NA	1,475,283	89.4
Florida	26,322,090	2,694,579	10.2	9,047,588	34.4	14,579,923	55.4
Georgia	18,017,477	1,688,274	9.4	7,780,725	43.2	8,548,478	47.4
Guam	262,823	50,170	19.1	NA	NA	212,652	80.9
Hawaii[1]	2,689,757	392,837	14.6	2,205,032	82.0	91,889	3.4
Idaho	2,243,784	229,156	10.2	1,509,815	67.3	504,812	22.5
Illinois	26,512,711	3,146,741	11.9	7,324,750	27.6	16,041,221	60.5
Indiana	12,569,782	1,432,813	11.4	4,964,928	39.5	6,172,042	49.1
Iowa	5,519,854	443,827	8.0	2,545,360	46.1	2,530,666	45.8
Kansas	5,757,927	453,608	7.9	3,323,346	57.7	1,980,973	34.4
Kentucky	6,641,128	731,351	11.0	3,802,150	57.3	2,107,627	31.7
Louisiana	8,099,981	1,264,057	15.6	3,740,262	46.2	3,095,662	38.2
Maine	2,575,516	245,719	9.5	1,127,032	43.8	1,202,765	46.7
Maryland	13,097,508	694,847	5.3	5,698,735	43.5	6,703,926	51.2
Massachusetts	15,102,480	1,276,250	8.5	6,036,202	40.0	7,790,028	51.6
Michigan	19,585,635	2,253,644	11.5	10,904,987	55.7	6,427,004	32.8
Minnesota	10,542,303	632,057	6.0	6,914,839	65.6	2,995,407	28.4
Mississippi	4,360,702	675,972	15.5	2,334,355	53.5	1,350,375	31.0
Missouri	10,042,753	833,909	8.3	3,425,716	34.1	5,783,128	57.6
Montana	1,595,197	199,017	12.5	774,091	48.5	622,089	39.0
Nebraska	3,455,794	280,666	8.1	1,213,317	35.1	1,961,810	56.8
Nevada	4,450,741	434,484	9.8	1,362,123	30.6	2,654,134	59.6
New Hampshire	2,717,115	147,318	5.4	1,003,249	36.9	1,566,547	57.7
New Jersey	25,283,290	1,040,733	4.1	10,525,550	41.6	13,717,006	54.3
New Mexico	3,820,116	569,047	14.9	2,675,916	70.0	575,152	15.1
New York	55,558,190	3,220,417	5.8	25,346,556	45.6	26,991,217	48.6
North Carolina	13,322,946	1,406,049	10.6	8,401,249	63.1	3,515,648	26.4
North Dakota	1,102,479	161,484	14.6	408,004	37.0	532,990	48.3
Northern Mariana Islands	65,538	30,711	46.9	34,602	52.8	225	0.3
Ohio	22,956,215	1,685,617	7.3	10,917,974	47.6	10,352,625	45.1
Oklahoma	5,729,610	770,745	13.5	3,042,487	53.1	1,916,378	33.4

State	Total	Federal Amount	% of tot. rev.	State Amount	% of tot. rev.	Local and intermediate Amount	% of tot. rev.
Oregon	$6,145,206	$670,547	10.9%	$3,117,303	50.7%	$2,357,357	38.4%
Pennsylvania	25,632,072	1,868,034	7.3	9,920,340	38.7	13,843,699	54.0
Puerto Rico	3,542,658	1,076,147	30.4	2,462,725	69.5	3,787	0.1
Rhode Island	2,232,149	215,514	9.7	817,590	36.6	1,199,044	53.7
South Carolina	7,702,962	762,297	9.9	3,679,907	47.8	3,260,758	42.3
South Dakota	1,241,892	203,354	16.4	410,179	33.0	628,359	50.6
Tennessee	8,283,928	935,135	11.3	3,809,467	46.0	3,539,325	42.7
Texas	46,962,119	5,014,820	10.7	19,973,129	42.5	21,974,171	46.8
Utah	4,542,690	565,022	12.4	2,387,698	52.6	1,589,970	35.0
Vermont	1,571,006	102,785	6.5	1,346,300	85.7	121,922	7.8
Virgin Islands (U.S.)	243,079	40,037	16.5	NA	NA	203,042	83.5
Virginia	14,964,444	914,524	6.1	6,303,648	42.1	7,746,272	51.8
Washington	11,903,510	1,385,449	11.6	7,146,394	60.0	3,371,667	28.3
West Virginia	3,281,385	366,038	11.2	1,938,999	59.1	976,347	29.8
Wisconsin	10,832,105	1,302,449	12.0	4,809,185	44.4	4,720,471	43.6
Wyoming	1,675,896	110,634	6.6	945,167	56.4	620,095	37.0

NA = Not applicable. **Note:** Included as revenue receipts are all appropriations from general funds of federal, state, county, and local governments; receipts from taxes levied for school purposes; income from permanent school funds and endowments; and income from leases of school lands and miscellaneous sources (interest on bank deposits, tuition, gifts, school lunch charges, etc.). (1) District of Columbia and Hawaii have only one school district each; neither is comparable to other states.

Population With Upper Secondary Education in Selected Countries, 2010

Source: Organization for Economic Cooperation and Development

Percentage of the population ages 25-64 that have received at least an upper secondary (senior high school) education.

Country	%	Country	%	Country	%	Country	%	Country	%
Czech Republic	92%	Sweden	87%	Hungary	81%	Australia	73%	Greece	65%
Slovakia	91	Switzerland	86	Norway	81	New Zealand	73	Italy	55
Estonia	89	Germany	86	Korea, South	80	Netherlands	73	Spain	53
United States	89	Slovenia	83	Luxembourg	78	Chile	71	Argentina	42
Poland	89	Finland	83	Denmark	76	France	71	Brazil	41
Canada	88	Austria	82	United Kingdom	75	Belgium	70	Mexico	36
Russia	88	Israel	82	Ireland	73	Iceland	67	Portugal	32

Financial Aid to U.S. Undergraduate Students, 2006-10

Source: National Center for Education Statistics, U.S. Dept. of Education

	No. receiving aid	% receiving aid	Avg. amt. aid received	No. receiving aid	% receiving aid	Avg. amt. aid received
	All institutions			**Public**		
	4-year institutions					
2006-07						
Any student financial aid	1,243,600	75.5%	NA	716,300	75.5%	NA
Grant or scholarship aid	NA	NA	NA	NA	NA	NA
Student loan aid	813,600	49.4	$5,193	415,400	43.8	$4,433
2009-10						
Any student financial aid	1,492,400	85.0	NA	832,600	81.5	NA
Grant or scholarship aid	1,292,100	73.6	9,526	681,400	66.7	6,931
Student loan aid	1,030,000	58.7	7,213	511,000	50.0	6,063
	2-year institutions					
2006-07						
Any student financial aid	522,700	67.1%	NA	380,500	61.4%	NA
Grant or scholarship aid	NA	NA	NA	NA	NA	NA
Student loan aid	241,500	31.0	$4,410	121,300	19.6	$2,877
2009-10						
Any student financial aid	831,300	75.5	NA	550,500	70.3	NA
Grant or scholarship aid	737,300	66.9	4,635	493,800	63.0	4,544
Student loan aid	430,600	39.1	6,536	186,000	23.7	4,627
	Private, nonprofit			**Private, for profit**		
	4-year institutions					
2006-07						
Any student financial aid	400,000	85.3%	NA	127,200	55.4%	NA
Grant or scholarship aid	NA	NA	NA	NA	NA	NA
Student loan aid	278,700	59.4	$5,558	119,500	52.0	$6,989
2009-10						
Any student financial aid	436,300	88.8	NA	223,500	91.8	NA
Grant or scholarship aid	413,700	84.2	16,037	197,000	80.9	4,832
Student loan aid	309,400	63.0	7,466	209,700	86.1	9,641
	2-year institutions					
2006-07						
Any student financial aid	7,200	82.5%	NA	135,000	89.3%	NA
Grant or scholarship aid	NA	NA	NA	NA	NA	NA
Student loan aid	4,700	53.5	$4,715	115,500	76.4	$6,007
2009-10						
Any student financial aid	9,000	89.4	NA	271,800	88.3	NA
Grant or scholarship aid	8,600	84.8	6,762	234,900	76.3	4,749
Student loan aid	5,900	58.6	6,078	238,700	77.5	8,035

NA = Not available. **Note:** Data for full-time, first-time, degree-seeking undergraduate students. Any student financial aid includes students awarded Federal Work-Study, loans to students, or grant or scholarship aid from the federal government, state/local government, the institution, or other sources known to the institution. Grant or scholarship aid includes grants from the federal government, state/local government, and the institution. Student loan aid includes loans from the federal government and other sources, including private sources, and does not include PLUS loans or loans made to anyone other than the student.

Undergraduate Students Taking Distance Education Courses, 2003-08

Source: National Center for Education Statistics, U.S. Dept. of Education

Selected characteristic	2003-04				2007-08			
	Taking any distance education courses		Taking entire program through distance education		Taking any distance education courses		Taking entire program through distance education	
	Number (thous.)	Percent	Number (thous.)	Percent	Number (thous.)	Percent	Number (thous.)	Percent
Total	2,961	15.5%	973	5.1%	4,277	20.4%	769	3.7%
Sex								
Male	1,099	13.6	365	4.5	1,679	18.6	297	3.3
Female	1,862	17.0	609	5.5	2,598	21.8	472	4.0
Age								
15-23 years.	1,283	11.7	353	3.2	1,891	15.1	169	1.4
24-29 years.	592	18.4	213	6.6	938	25.9	192	5.3
30 years or older.	1,086	22.4	408	8.4	1,448	30.1	408	8.5
Attendance status								
Exclusively full-time	1,179	12.7	360	3.9	1,648	16.5	299	3.0
Exclusively part-time.	1,251	18.7	470	7.0	1,839	24.8	373	5.0
Mixed full-time and part-time . .	531	17.3	143	4.7	791	22.3	97	2.7
Work status								
No job.	533	12.4	158	3.7	708	16.1	121	2.8
Regular job only	2,282	17.2	768	5.8	3,259	22.3	607	4.2
Work-study/assistantship only	60	8.8	18	2.6	112	12.9	13	1.5
Both regular job and work-study/assistantship. . . .	86	11.1	29	3.7	198	18.7	27	2.5
Housing status								
On-campus.	194	7.2	48	1.8	263	8.9	13	0.5
Off-campus.	1,851	17.7	634	6.1	2,709	24.0	606	5.4
With parents or relatives.	604	13.2	171	3.7	854	17.1	83	1.7
Attended more than one institution.	312	23.4	120	9.1	452	27.1	66	4.0
Dependency status								
Dependent	1,064	11.1	291	3.0	1,589	14.3	108	1.0
Independent, no dependents, not married	454	15.6	152	5.2	788	24.0	155	4.7
Independent, no dependents, married	269	19.6	101	7.4	356	28.7	83	6.6
Independent, with dependents, not married	522	20.5	180	7.1	712	25.5	197	7.0
Independent, with dependents, married	653	25.1	251	9.6	833	33.0	227	9.0

Note: Distance education courses include live, interactive audio- or video-conferencing; prerecorded instructional videos; webcasts; CD-ROMs or DVDs; or computer-based systems accessed over the Internet. Does not include correspondence courses. Estimates pertain to all postsecondary students who enrolled at any time during the school year at an institution participating in Title IV programs. Includes students attending more than one institution.

Charges at U.S. Institutions of Higher Education, 1969-70 to 2010-11

Source: National Center for Education Statistics, U.S. Dept. of Education

Figures for 1969-70 are average charges for full-time resident degree-credit students; figures for later years are average charges per full-time equivalent student. Room and board are based on full-time students. These figures are enrollment-weighted according to the number of full-time equivalent undergraduates and thus may vary from averages given elsewhere.

Public (in-state)	Tuition and fees			Board rates			Dormitory charges		
	All institutions	2-yr	4-yr	All institutions	2-yr	4-yr	All institutions	2-yr	4-yr
1969-70	$323	$178	NA	$511	$465	NA	$369	$308	NA
1979-80	583	355	$738	867	893	$865	715	574	$725
1989-90	1,356	756	1,780	1,635	1,581	1,638	1,513	962	1,557
1999-2000	2,504	1,348	3,349	2,364	1,834	2,406	2,440	1,549	2,519
2000-01	2,562	1,333	3,501	2,455	1,906	2,499	2,569	1,600	2,654
2001-02	2,700	1,380	3,735	2,598	2,036	2,645	2,723	1,722	2,816
2002-03	2,903	1,483	4,046	2,669	2,164	2,712	2,930	1,954	3,029
2003-04	3,319	1,702	4,587	2,822	2,221	2,876	3,106	2,089	3,212
2004-05	3,629	1,849	5,027	2,931	2,353	2,981	3,304	2,174	3,418
2005-06	3,874	1,935	5,351	3,035	2,306	3,093	3,545	2,251	3,664
2006-07	4,102	2,018	5,666	3,191	2,390	3,253	3,757	2,407	3,878
2007-08	4,291	2,061	5,943	3,331	2,409	3,404	3,952	2,506	4,082
2008-09	4,512	2,136	6,312	3,554	2,769	3,619	4,190	2,664	4,331
2009-10	4,751	2,285	6,695	3,653	2,574	3,754	4,399	2,845	4,565
2010-11	5,076	2,439	7,136	3,848	2,685	3,958	4,640	2,960	4,824
Private									
1969-70	$1,533	$1,034	NA	$561	$546	NA	$436	$413	NA
1979-80	3,130	2,062	$3,225	955	923	$957	827	766	$831
1989-90	8,147	5,196	8,396	1,948	1,811	1,953	1,923	1,663	1,935
1999-2000	14,100	8,225	14,616	2,877	2,753	2,879	3,236	3,067	3,242
2000-01	15,000	9,067	15,470	2,991	2,834	2,993	3,382	3,006	3,392
2001-02	15,742	10,076	16,211	3,104	2,633	3,109	3,567	3,116	3,576
2002-03	16,383	10,651	16,826	3,206	3,870	3,197	3,752	3,232	3,764
2003-04	17,315	11,545	17,763	3,364	4,432	3,354	3,945	3,581	3,952
2004-05	18,154	12,122	18,604	3,485	3,700	3,483	4,178	4,475	4,173
2005-06	18,862	12,450	19,292	3,645	4,781	3,637	4,400	4,173	4,404
2006-07	20,048	12,708	20,517	3,785	3,429	3,788	4,606	4,147	4,613
2007-08	20,972	13,126	21,427	3,992	4,074	3,991	4,804	4,484	4,808
2008-09	21,570	13,562	22,036	4,209	4,627	4,206	5,025	4,537	5,032
2009-10	21,444	14,876	21,908	4,331	4,390	4,331	5,249	5,217	5,249
2010-11	22,186	14,467	22,771	4,434	4,475	4,433	5,406	4,928	5,413

NA = Not available.

Top 20 Colleges and Universities in Endowment Assets, 2011

Source: *2011 NACUBO-Commonfund Study of Endowments*, National Association of College and University Business Officers (NACUBO)

Rank	College/university	Endowment assets[1]	% change, 2010-11	Rank	College/university	Endowment assets[1]	% change, 2010-11
1.	Harvard University	$31,728,080	15.1%	11.	University of Pennsylvania	$6,582,029	16.1%
2.	Yale University	19,374,000	16.3	12.	University of Chicago	6,575,126	18.6
3.	University of Texas System	17,148,649	22.0	13.	University of California	6,342,217	16.6
4.	Princeton University	17,109,508	18.9	14.	University of Notre Dame	6,259,598	19.6
5.	Stanford University	16,502,606	19.1	15.	Duke University	5,747,377	19.2
6.	Massachusetts Institute of Technology	9,712,628	16.8	16.	Emory University	5,400,367	15.0
7.	University of Michigan	7,834,752	19.4	17.	Washington University in St. Louis	5,280,143	18.0
8.	Columbia University	7,789,578	19.5	18.	Cornell University	5,059,406	15.5
9.	Northwestern University	7,182,745	20.8	19.	University of Virginia	4,760,515	28.4
10.	Texas A&M University System & Foundations	6,999,517	22.0	20.	Rice University	4,451,452	17.6

Note: Market value of endowment assets, excluding pledges and working capital, in the fiscal year. (1) In thousands.

U.S. Higher Education Trends: Bachelor's Degrees Conferred

Source: National Center for Education Statistics, U.S. Dept. of Education

(*) figures are projected.

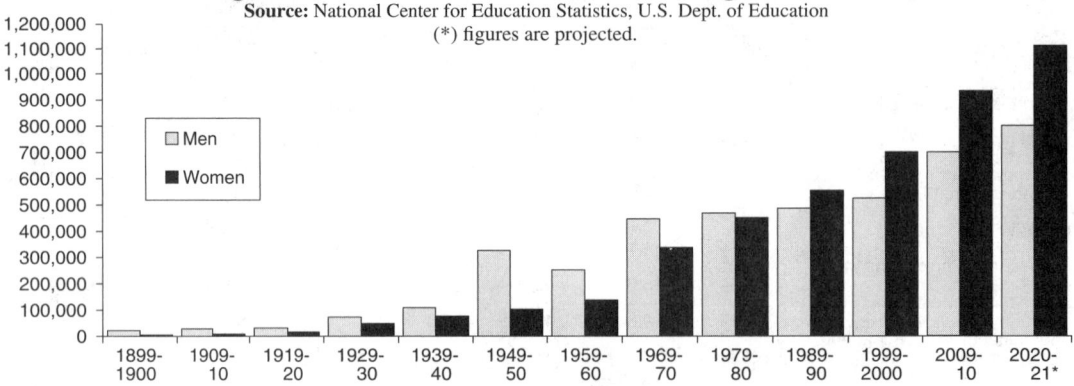

Financial Aid for College and Other Postsecondary Education

As of Aug. 2012. Reviewed by National Assoc. of Student Financial Aid Administrators.

The cost of postsecondary education in the U.S. continues to increase, but financial aid—in the form of **grants** (no repayment needed), **loans**, and/or **work-study** programs—is widely available to help families meet these expenses. Most federal aid is limited to families that demonstrate financial need as determined by standard formulas and is designed to help students attend the college of their choice regardless of their ability to pay. Financial aid personnel at each school can provide information about all aid programs (federal, state, institutional, and private) available to students, steps to apply for them, and deadlines.

All applicants for federal aid must file a Free Application for Federal Student Aid (**FAFSA**), generally as soon as possible after Jan. 1 for the academic year starting the following Sept. Figures provided should match federal income tax forms filed for the previous year. Applicants may also import certain information from their tax forms when they file their taxes online. Many other sources of aid—state governments, employers and unions, civic organizations, and the institutions themselves—also use the FAFSA to determine eligibility for aid. There are also federal programs that pay for postsecondary education in return for service: AmeriCorps (1-800-942-2677), Reserve Officers' Training Corps (1-800-USA-ROTC), the G.I. Bill (1-888-GIBILL-1), and the National Health Service Corps (1-800-221-9393). Additional forms and applications may be required if a student is to be considered for non-federal aid. A student must reapply for aid annually.

A **federal formula**, based on information provided in the FAFSA, takes into account such factors as family income in the preceding calendar year, parental and student assets (excluding the parents' home, farm, or small business), length of time to parents' retirement, and unusual expenses (such as very high medical expenses). Outside scholarships (even non-need-based) are also taken into account in determining eligibility for federal, institutional, and state financial aid programs.

The formula determines a family's **expected family contribution** (EFC), which is divided among the number of family members—excluding parents—in college. The EFC is subtracted from the total cost of attending college for each person (including tuition and fee charges, room and board or allowance for living costs, books and supplies, transportation to and from

school, and other miscellaneous costs). The difference determines financial need and the maximum federal aid for which the family may be eligible. (Some institutions use a separate formula for need-based institutional aid.) Some schools guarantee to meet the full financial need of each admitted student; most do their best to cover a student's financial need using various forms of financial aid but may not be able to because of a lack of funds.

The **aid package** offered by each school may include one or more of the following resources: Federal Pell Grants, for those who demonstrate sufficient financial need; Federal Supplemental Educational Opportunity Grants, for those who still have need after receiving Pell Grants; grants from the school; Federal Work-Study or other work programs; low-interest Perkins loans; and federal subsidized and unsubsidized Stafford loans. Parents of undergraduates may also apply for a Federal PLUS loan. Unsubsidized Stafford loans and all PLUS loans to parents are available to all students regardless of their financial need, but students and parents must still complete the FAFSA to get these loans.

Loans have varying interest rates and other requirements. Repayment of Perkins and Stafford loans does not begin until after graduation; deferments, income-based repayment plans, and loan forgiveness are available on federal loans for students who meet certain requirements. For PLUS loans, parents must pass a credit check and may need to begin repayment of both principal and interest while the student is still in school.

Certain federal income **tax credits and refunds** are also available to families who meet requirements; see the chapter on taxes.

Rules for financial aid are complex and changeable. *Funding Your Education: The Guide to Federal Student Aid*, a comprehensive resource on financial aid from the U.S. Dept. of Education, is available in English and Spanish on the Department's website: studentaid.ed.gov/resources/. The website also has a booklet called *The EFC Formula*.

Further information and FAFSA forms are available from schools or from the Federal Student Aid Information Center, P.O. Box 84, Washington, DC 20044; 1-800-4-FED-AID, Mon.-Fri., 8 AM-10 PM EST. FAFSA forms can be filled out online at fafsa.ed.gov.

Average Salaries of U.S. College Professors, 2011-12

Source: American Association of University Professors

Teaching level		Men			Women		
		Public institution	Private/ independent institution	Religiously affiliated institution	Public institution	Private/ independent institution	Religiously affiliated institution
Doctoral level	Professor	$123,738	$165,378	$135,844	$111,732	$152,787	$124,374
	Associate	85,138	104,981	92,978	79,195	97,123	87,240
	Assistant	74,233	93,061	80,251	68,394	84,368	73,696
Master's level	Professor	90,367	105,754	94,355	86,083	97,701	87,195
	Associate	72,206	79,334	73,634	69,543	75,008	70,227
	Assistant	61,885	66,780	61,443	59,526	63,604	59,480
Baccalaureate level	Professor	85,419	103,056	78,553	82,918	98,734	75,104
	Associate	70,383	75,910	63,560	67,185	74,139	61,811
	Assistant	58,339	62,017	53,424	56,315	60,668	52,896
2-year	Professor	74,713	NA	NA	72,325	NA	NA
	Associate	62,077	NA	NA	60,316	NA	NA
	Assistant	53,611	NA	NA	53,474	NA	NA

NA = Not available.

Average ACT Scores and Characteristics of College-Bound Students, 1990-2012

Source: ACT, Inc. (formerly American College Testing)

(for class graduating in spring of year shown)

Scores[1]	Unit	1990	1995	2000	2005	2006	2007	2008	2009	2010	2011	2012
Composite scores	Points	20.6	20.8	21.0	20.9	21.1	21.2	21.1	21.1	21.0	21.1	21.1
Male	Points	21.0	21.0	21.2	21.1	21.2	21.2	21.2	21.3	21.2	21.2	21.2
Female	Points	20.3	20.7	20.9	20.9	21.0	21.0	21.0	20.9	20.9	21.0	21.0
English score	Points	20.5	20.2	20.5	20.4	20.6	20.7	20.6	20.6	20.5	20.6	20.5
Male	Points	20.1	19.8	20.0	20.0	20.1	20.2	20.1	20.2	20.1	20.2	20.0
Female	Points	20.9	20.6	20.9	20.8	21.0	21.0	21.0	20.9	20.8	20.9	20.9
Math score	Points	19.9	20.2	20.7	20.7	20.8	21.0	21.0	21.0	21.0	21.1	21.1
Male	Points	20.7	20.9	21.4	21.3	21.5	21.6	21.6	21.6	21.6	21.6	21.7
Female	Points	19.3	19.7	20.2	20.2	20.3	20.4	20.4	20.4	20.5	20.6	20.6
Participants												
Total number	(Thous.)	817	945	1,065	1,186	1,206	1,301	1,422	1,480	1,569	1,623	1,666
Male	Percent	46	44	43	44	44	42	44	45	45	46	46
White	Percent	79	80	72	66	63	60	63	64	62	60	59
Black	Percent	9	9	10	12	12	12	13	13	14	14	13
Hispanic[2]	Percent	4	5	5	7	7	7	8	9	10	12	14
Composite scores												
27 or above	Percent	12	13	14	14	14	15	9[3]	12	16	17	17
18 or below	Percent	35	34	32	34	33	32	33	34	35	34	34

(1) Minimum point score, 1; maximum score, 36. Test scores and characteristics of college-bound students are based on the performance of all ACT-tested students who graduated in the spring of a given school year and took the ACT assessment during junior or senior year of high school. (2) Persons of Hispanic origin may be of any race. (3) Composite scores of 28 or above.

Average ACT Composite Scores by State, 2012

Source: ACT, Inc. (formerly American College Testing)

State	Avg. comp. score	% grads taking ACT	State	Avg. comp. score	% grads taking ACT	State	Avg. comp. score	% grads taking ACT
Alabama	20.3	86%	Kentucky	19.8	100%	Ohio	21.8	71%
Alaska	21.2	35	Louisiana	20.3	100	Oklahoma	20.7	80
Arizona	19.7	35	Maine	23.4	9	Oregon	21.4	38
Arkansas	20.3	88	Maryland	22.1	21	Pennsylvania	22.4	18
California	22.1	25	Massachusetts	24.1	23	Rhode Island	22.9	13
Colorado	20.6	100	Michigan	20.1	100	South Carolina	20.2	57
Connecticut	23.8	27	Minnesota	22.8	74	South Dakota	21.8	81
Delaware	22.6	14	Mississippi	18.7	100	Tennessee	19.7	100
District of Columbia	19.7	32	Missouri	21.6	75	Texas	20.8	39
			Montana	22.0	61	Utah	20.7	97
Florida	19.8	70	Nebraska	22.0	78	Vermont	23.0	28
Georgia	20.7	52	Nevada	21.3	34	Virginia	22.4	25
Hawaii	21.3	27	New Hampshire	23.8	19	Washington	22.9	21
Idaho	21.6	67	New Jersey	23.4	20	West Virginia	20.6	68
Illinois	20.9	100	New Mexico	19.9	75	Wisconsin	22.1	71
Indiana	22.3	32	New York	23.3	29	Wyoming	20.3	100
Iowa	22.1	63	North Carolina	21.9	20	**U.S. average**	**21.1**	**52**
Kansas	21.9	81	North Dakota	20.7	100			

Mean SAT Scores of College-Bound Seniors, 1975-2012
Source: The College Board
(recentered scale; for school year ending in year shown)

	1975	1980	1985	1990	1995	2000	2003	2004	2005	2006	2007	2008	2009	2010	2011	2012
Critical reading scores[1]	512	502	509	500	504	505	507	508	508	503	502	502	501	501	497	496
Male	515	506	514	505	505	507	512	512	513	505	504	504	503	503	500	498
Female	509	498	503	496	502	504	503	504	505	502	502	500	498	498	495	493
Math scores..........	498	492	500	501	506	514	519	518	520	518	515	515	515	516	514	514
Male	518	515	522	521	525	533	537	537	538	536	533	533	534	534	531	532
Female	479	473	480	483	490	498	503	501	504	502	499	500	499	500	500	499
Writing scores........	NA	NA	NA	NA	NA	NA	NA	NA	NA	497	494	494	493	492	489	488
Male	NA	NA	NA	NA	NA	NA	NA	NA	NA	491	489	488	486	486	482	481
Female	NA	NA	NA	NA	NA	NA	NA	NA	NA	502	500	501	499	498	496	494

NA = Not applicable. **Note:** In 1995, the College Board recentered the scoring scale for the SAT by reestablishing the original mean score of 500 on the 200-800 scale. Earlier scores have been adjusted to account for this recentering. The writing test was first given in Mar. 2005; however, only the scores of the first graduating class to take the revised test are given. (1) Pre-2006 scores are for the Verbal section.

Mean SAT Scores by State, 1990-2012
Source: The College Board
(for school year ending in year shown; V = Verbal, M = Math, CR = Critical reading, W = Writing)

	1990		2000		2005		2010			2012			% grads
State	V	M	V	M	V	M	CR	M	W	CR	M	W	taking SAT[1]
Alabama	545	534	559	555	567	559	556	550	544	538	531	527	8%
Alaska	514	501	519	515	523	519	518	515	491	512	507	485	54
Arizona	521	520	521	523	526	530	519	525	500	517	525	499	27
Arkansas	545	532	563	554	563	552	566	566	552	565	566	549	4
California	494	508	497	518	504	522	501	516	500	495	512	496	55
Colorado	533	534	534	537	560	560	568	572	555	575	581	562	17
Connecticut	506	496	508	509	517	517	509	514	513	506	512	510	88
Delaware	510	496	502	496	503	502	493	495	481	456	462	444	100
District of Columbia	483	467	494	486	490	478	474	464	466	466	460	456	83
Florida	495	493	498	500	498	498	496	498	479	492	492	476	66
Georgia	478	473	488	486	497	496	488	490	475	488	489	475	81
Hawaii	480	505	488	519	490	516	483	505	470	478	500	467	66
Idaho	542	524	540	541	544	542	543	541	517	547	541	525	20
Illinois	542	547	568	586	594	606	585	600	577	596	615	587	5
Indiana	486	486	498	501	504	508	494	505	477	493	501	476	69
Iowa	584	588	589	600	596	608	603	613	582	603	606	580	3
Kansas	566	563	574	580	585	588	590	595	567	584	594	561	6
Kentucky	548	541	548	550	561	559	575	575	563	579	575	566	6
Louisiana	551	537	562	558	565	562	555	550	547	542	536	529	9
Maine	501	490	504	500	509	505	468	467	454	470	472	452	93
Maryland	506	502	507	509	511	515	501	506	495	497	502	488	74
Massachusetts	503	498	511	513	520	527	512	526	509	513	530	508	89
Michigan	529	534	557	569	568	579	585	605	576	586	603	574	4
Minnesota	552	558	581	594	592	597	594	607	580	592	606	573	7
Mississippi	552	538	562	549	564	554	566	548	552	561	544	551	4
Missouri	548	541	572	577	588	588	593	595	580	589	592	575	5
Montana	540	542	543	546	540	540	538	538	517	536	536	511	28
Nebraska	559	562	560	571	574	579	585	593	568	576	585	562	5
Nevada	511	511	510	517	508	513	496	501	473	491	493	466	49
New Hampshire	518	510	520	519	525	525	520	524	510	521	525	510	75
New Jersey	495	498	498	513	503	517	495	514	497	495	517	499	78
New Mexico	554	546	549	543	558	547	553	549	534	550	546	529	13
New York	489	496	494	506	497	511	484	499	478	483	500	475	90
North Carolina	478	470	492	496	499	511	497	511	477	491	506	472	68
North Dakota	579	578	588	609	590	605	580	594	559	588	610	568	3
Ohio	526	522	533	539	539	543	538	548	522	543	552	525	19
Oklahoma	553	542	563	560	570	563	569	568	547	568	566	546	5
Oregon	515	509	527	527	526	528	523	524	499	521	523	498	57
Pennsylvania	497	490	498	497	501	503	492	501	480	491	501	480	74
Rhode Island	498	488	505	500	503	505	494	495	488	490	491	485	69
South Carolina	475	467	484	482	494	499	484	495	468	481	488	462	73
South Dakota	580	570	587	588	589	589	592	603	571	589	610	570	3
Tennessee	558	544	563	553	572	563	576	571	565	576	570	566	10
Texas	490	489	493	500	493	502	484	505	473	474	499	461	62
Utah	566	555	570	569	566	557	568	559	547	568	566	548	6
Vermont	507	493	513	508	521	517	519	521	506	519	523	505	69
Virginia	501	496	509	500	516	514	512	512	497	510	512	495	72
Washington	513	511	526	528	532	534	524	532	508	519	530	503	58
West Virginia	520	514	526	511	523	511	515	507	500	516	502	497	17
Wisconsin	552	559	584	597	592	599	595	604	579	594	605	577	4
Wyoming	534	538	545	545	544	543	570	567	546	567	579	549	5
National average	**500**	**501**	**505**	**514**	**508**	**520**	**501**	**516**	**492**	**496**	**514**	**488**	

Note: In 1995, the College Board recentered the scoring scale for the SAT by reestablishing the original mean score of 500 on the 200-800 scale. In 2005, the SAT was changed. The verbal portion became critical reading, and a writing test was added. The 2006 graduating class was the first to take the new test. (1) Based on number of high school graduates in 2012, as projected by the Western Interstate Commission for Higher Education, and number of students in the class of 2012 who took the SAT.

Top 100 Libraries in U.S. by Volumes Held, 2010

Source: *ALA Library Fact Sheet Number 22*, American Library Association.

Rank	Institution	Volumes held	Rank	Institution	Volumes held
1.	Library of Congress	34,528,818	51.	Washington Univ.–St. Louis	4,323,958
2.	Boston Public Library[1]	19,090,261	52.	Univ. of Kansas	4,318,644
3.	Harvard Univ.	16,832,952	53.	Brigham Young Univ.	4,292,056
4.	New York Public Library[1]	16,342,365	54.	Cleveland Public Library	4,273,202
5.	Univ. of Illinois–Urbana-Champaign	13,158,748	55.	Brooklyn Public Library	4,233,304
6.	Yale Univ.	12,787,962	56.	Brown Univ.	4,187,257
7.	Univ. of California–Berkeley	11,545,418	57.	Univ. of Southern California	4,180,515
8.	Columbia Univ.	11,189,036	58.	Univ. of California–Davis	4,175,047
9.	Univ. of Michigan	10,778,736	59.	Tulane Univ.	4,155,793
10.	Univ. of Texas–Austin	9,990,941	60.	Louisiana State Univ.	4,128,626
11.	Univ. of Chicago	9,837,021	61.	Univ. of Connecticut	4,096,396
12.	Univ. of California–Los Angeles	9,151,964	62.	King County Library System (WA)	4,044,907
13.	Public Library of Cincinnati and Hamilton County (OH)	8,819,759	63.	State Univ. of New York–Buffalo	4,029,865
14.	Indiana Univ.	8,677,974	64.	Temple Univ.	3,990,379
15.	Stanford Univ.	8,500,000	65.	Univ. of South Carolina	3,963,958
16.	Univ. of Wisconsin–Madison	8,421,198	66.	Univ. of Maryland	3,930,013
17.	Cornell Univ.	8,173,778	67.	Univ. of Kentucky	3,915,579
18.	Princeton Univ.	7,226,744	68.	Univ. of California–San Diego	3,830,802
19.	Univ. of Washington	7,203,156	69.	Univ. of Rochester	3,826,916
20.	Univ. of Minnesota	7,111,311	70.	Hawaii State Public Library System	3,776,405
21.	Detroit Public Library	7,070,433	71.	Johns Hopkins Univ.	3,701,215
22.	Univ. of North Carolina–Chapel Hill	7,012,787	72.	Univ. of Massachusetts–Amherst	3,697,796
23.	County of Los Angeles Public Library	6,795,552	73.	Miami-Dade Public Library System	3,674,651
24.	Queens Borough Public Library (NY)	6,544,609	74.	Univ. of Notre Dame	3,673,092
25.	Los Angeles Public Library	6,459,552	75.	Wayne State Univ.	3,655,805
26.	Univ. of Pennsylvania	6,438,305	76.	Emory Univ.	3,619,813
27.	Duke Univ.	6,174,814	77.	Univ. of Hawaii	3,602,058
28.	Ohio State Univ.	6,161,657	78.	Univ. of Missouri–Columbia	3,561,607
29.	Univ. of Pittsburgh	6,148,036	79.	Univ. of Alabama	3,533,794
30.	Univ. of Arizona	5,998,148	80.	Vanderbilt Univ.	3,531,208
31.	Chicago Public Library	5,790,289	81.	Univ. of Nebraska–Lincoln	3,500,601
32.	Univ. of Oklahoma	5,662,666	82.	Broward County Libraries Division (FL)	3,477,312
33.	Michigan State Univ.	5,609,761	83.	Auburn Univ.	3,472,547
34.	Univ. of Virginia	5,607,915	84.	Oklahoma State Univ.	3,468,428
35.	San Diego Public Library	5,535,415	85.	Georgetown Univ.	3,461,170
36.	Univ. of Iowa	5,490,825	86.	Univ. of Utah	3,441,965
37.	Pennsylvania State Univ.	5,441,121	87.	Univ. of New Mexico	3,430,200
38.	New York Univ.	5,382,424	88.	Mid-Continent Public Library (MO)	3,419,516
39.	Northwestern Univ.	5,047,970	89.	Allen County Public Library (IN)	3,412,830
40.	Free Library of Philadelphia	5,043,943	90.	St. Louis Public Library	3,352,775
41.	Dallas Public Library	4,972,494	91.	Univ. of Miami	3,348,622
42.	Hennepin County Library (MN)	4,961,514	92.	Univ. of Tennessee–Knoxville	3,330,181
43.	Univ. of Georgia	4,810,192	93.	Syracuse Univ.	3,291,384
44.	Rutgers Univ.	4,722,407	94.	Cuyahoga County Public Library (OH)	3,252,456
45.	Univ. of Colorado	4,681,261	95.	Univ. of California–Irvine	3,223,679
46.	Texas A&M Univ.	4,577,498	96.	Buffalo & Erie County Public Library (NY)	3,211,709
47.	Arizona State Univ.	4,497,114	97.	Southern Illinois Univ.–Carbondale	3,203,455
48.	Univ. of Florida	4,414,450	98.	Massachusetts Institute of Technology	3,119,157
49.	Univ. of Cincinnati	4,379,445	99.	Univ. of California–Riverside	3,066,630
50.	North Carolina State Univ.	4,332,899	100.	Houston Public Library	3,061,773

Note: For academic libraries, a volume is a single physical unit of any printed, typewritten, handwritten, mimeographed, or processed work, distinguished from other units by a separate binding, encasement, portfolio, or other clear distinction, which has been cataloged, classified, and made ready for use, and which is typically the unit used to charge circulation transactions. For public libraries, holdings are the number of cataloged items plus paperbacks and videocassettes even if uncataloged. (1) Includes both public library and research library collection numbers.

Number of Public Libraries and Operating Income by State, 2009

Source: Public Libraries Survey, Institute of Museum and Library Services

State	No.[1]	Income[2] (thous.)	State	No.[1]	Income[2] (thous.)	State	No.[1]	Income[2] (thous.)	State	No.[1]	Income[2] (thous.)
AL	210	$96,586	IL	634	$734,146	MT	80	$23,165	RI	48	$49,611
AK	87	36,862	IN	238	322,349	NE	269	48,809	SC	42	118,944
AZ	89	201,318	IA	541	106,478	NV	22	104,814	SD	112	23,266
AR	52	63,687	KS	328	109,953	NH	230	52,177	TN	186	113,554
CA	181	1,342,162	KY	117	152,767	NJ	301	502,489	TX	559	455,930
CO	114	264,930	LA	68	177,905	NM	91	45,650	UT	71	86,951
CT	195	184,380	ME	269	40,355	NY	756	1,243,601	VT	184	21,209
DE	21	29,773	MD	24	273,933	NC	77	209,220	VA	91	281,422
DC	1	46,377	MA	370	265,061	ND	85	13,891	WA	63	338,899
FL	80	622,722	MI	384	439,593	OH	251	673,684	WV	97	34,659
GA	61	210,252	MN	138	206,348	OK	115	98,355	WI	380	219,603
HI	1	33,040	MS	50	48,385	OR	127	178,261	WY	23	31,562
ID	104	45,110	MO	150	225,617	PA	458	346,963	**Total U.S.**	**9,225**	**11,593,779**

(1) Includes central libraries only. (2) Some totals may be underestimated because of nonresponse.

Four-Year Colleges and Universities

Source: Peterson's College Database © 2012 Peterson's Nelnet, LLC. All rights reserved.

Note: These listings **include only accredited degree-granting institutions** in the U.S. and the U.S. territories with a total enrollment of 1,000 or more. Only four-year colleges and universities (which award a bachelor's degree as their highest undergraduate degree) are included. Data reported **only for institutions that provided updated information** on Peterson's Annual Survey of Undergraduate Institutions for the 2011-12 academic year.

All institutions are coeducational except those where the ZIP code is followed directly by a number in parentheses. (1) = men only, (2) = primarily men, (3) = women only, (4) = primarily women.

The **Tuition & fees** column shows the annual tuition and required fees for full-time students, or, where indicated, the tuition and standard fees per unit for part-time students. Where tuition varies according to residence, the figure is given for the most local resident and is coded as follows: (A) = area residents, (S) = state residents; all other figures apply to all students regardless of residence. Where annual expenses are expressed as a lump sum (including full-time tuition, mandatory fees, and room and board), the figure is entered under Tuition & fees and coded (C) = comprehensive fee. **Room & board** is the average cost for one academic year.

Control: 1 = independent (nonprofit), 2 = independent-religious, 3 = proprietary (profit-making), 4 = federal, 5 = state, 6 = commonwealth (Puerto Rico), 7 = territory (U.S. territories), 8 = county, 9 = district, 10 = city, 11 = state and local, 12 = state-related, 13 = private (unspecified). **Degree** means the highest degree offered: B = bachelor's, M = master's, D = doctorate.

Enrollment is the total number of matriculated undergraduate and (if applicable) graduate students.

Faculty is the total number of faculty members teaching undergraduate courses and (if available) graduate courses.

Grad. rate is the percentage of full-time, first-time bachelor's (or equivalent) degree-seeking undergraduate students who obtain their degrees within six years.

NA indicates category is inapplicable, or data is not available from a consistent source.

Name, address	Year founded	Tuition & fees	Room & board	Control, degree	Enroll-ment	Faculty	Grad. rate
Abilene Christian Univ., Abilene, TX 79699-9100	1906	$25,270	$8,316	2-D	4,558	354	59.0%
Abraham Baldwin Agr. Coll., Tifton, GA 31793	1933	$3,496(S)	$7,220	5-B	3,327	162	NA
Acad. of Art Univ., San Francisco, CA 94105-3410	1929	$22,950	NA	3-M	18,273	1,347	29.0
Adams State Coll., Alamosa, CO 81102	1921	$5,627(S)	$7,120	5-M	3,262	174	24.0
Adelphi Univ., Garden City, NY 11530-0701	1896	$28,460	$11,420	1-D	7,922	975	66.0
Adrian Coll., Adrian, MI 49221-2575	1859	$27,440	$8,346	2-M	1,678	176	50.0
Alabama Agr. & Mech. Univ., Huntsville, AL 35811	1875	$8,160(S)	$6,980	5-D	5,814	290	100.0
Alabama State Univ., Montgomery, AL 36101-0271	1867	$7,932(S)	$5,366	5-D	5,429	407	27.0
Albany Coll. of Pharm. & Health Sci., Albany, NY 12208	1881	$26,930	$9,560	1-D	1,641	148	64.0
Albany State Univ., Albany, GA 31705-2717	1903	$5,802(S)	$6,124	5-M	4,663	270	40.0
Albertus Magnus Coll., New Haven, CT 06511-1189	1925	$26,294	$11,088	2-M	2,010	76	62.0
Albion Coll., Albion, MI 49224-1831	1835	$32,662	$9,260	2-B	1,514	155	75.0
Albright Coll., Reading, PA 19612-5234	1856	$33,990	$9,200	2-M	2,411	166	60.0
Alcorn State Univ., Alcorn State, MS 39096-7500	1871	$5,256(S)	$7,592	5-M	4,018	199	33.0
Alfred Univ., Alfred, NY 14802-1205	1836	$27,794	$11,498	1-D	2,393	201	60.0
Allegheny Coll., Meadville, PA 16335	1815	$37,610	$9,540	1-B	2,123	196	80.0
Alliant Intl. Univ., San Diego, CA 92131-1799	1952	$16,870	$7,270	1-D	4,012	670	NA
Alma Coll., Alma, MI 48801-1599	1886	$29,230	$8,840	2-B	1,417	155	67.0
Alvernia Univ., Reading, PA 19607-1799	1958	$27,950	$10,010	2-D	3,011	324	53.0
Alverno Coll., Milwaukee, WI 53234-3922	1887	$21,063	$6,966	2-M	2,605	255	40.0
Amberton Univ., Garland, TX 75041-5595	1971	$5,600	NA	2-M	1,461	40	NA
Amer. InterContinental Univ. Online, Hoffman Estates, IL 60192	1970	$355/credit	NA	3-M	22,424	396	NA
Amer. Intl. Coll., Springfield, MA 01109-3189	1885	$27,902	$11,314	1-D	3,401	323	34.0
Amer. Public Univ. System, Charles Town, WV 25414	1991	$7,500	NA	3-M	50,838	1,805	NA
Amer. Univ., Washington, DC 20016-8001	1893	$39,499	$13,920	2-D	12,724	1,277	77.0
Amer. Univ. of Puerto Rico, Bayamón, PR 00960-2037	1963	$4,865	NA	1-M	1,798	221	NA
Amherst Coll., Amherst, MA 01002-5000	1821	$42,874	$11,200	1-B	1,795	236	94.0
Anderson Univ., Anderson, IN 46012-3495	1917	$25,480	$8,860	2-D	2,611	253	63.0
Anderson Univ., Anderson, SC 29621-4035	1911	$20,910	$7,725	2-D	2,705	242	47.0
Andrews Univ., Berrien Springs, MI 49104	1874	$23,428	$7,374	2-D	3,547	301	63.0
Angelo State Univ., San Angelo, TX 76909	1928	$7,350(S)	$6,812	5-D	7,084	347	31.0
Anna Maria Coll., Paxton, MA 01612	1946	$30,456	$11,405	2-M	1,456	200	46.0
Antioch Univ. Seattle, Seattle, WA 98121-1814	1975	$19,335	NA	1-D	1,080	NA	NA
Appalachian State Univ., Boone, NC 28608	1899	$5,538(S)	$6,810	5-D	17,344	1,180	65.0
Aquinas Coll., Grand Rapids, MI 49506-1799	1886	$25,250	$7,810	2-M	2,327	251	NA
Arcadia Univ., Glenside, PA 19038-3295	1853	$34,150	$11,640	2-D	3,932	479	62.0
Arizona State Univ., Tempe, AZ 85287	1885	$9,720(S)	$11,436	5-D	72,254	2,698	58.0
Arkansas State Univ., State University, AR 72467	1909	$6,934(S)	$6,920	5-D	13,900	654	38.0
Arkansas Tech. Univ., Russellville, AR 72801	1909	$6,258(S)	$5,456	5-M	10,464	496	44.0
Armstrong Atlantic State Univ., Savannah, GA 31419-1997	1935	$5,734(S)	$9,342	5-D	7,493	424	32.0
Art Ctr. Coll. of Design, Pasadena, CA 91103	1930	$33,944	NA	1-M	1,842	372	NA
The Art Inst. of Boston at Lesley Univ., Boston, MA 02215-2598	1912	$28,750	$13,250	1-D	5,564	258	62.0
Asbury Univ., Wilmore, KY 40390-1198	1890	$25,311	$5,792	2-M	1,638	154	70.0
Ashford Univ., Clinton, IA 52733-2967	1918	$16,270	$6,000	3-M	10,568	748	NA
Ashland Univ., Ashland, OH 44805-3702	1878	$28,582	$9,352	2-D	6,491	591	59.0
Ashworth Coll., Norcross, GA 30092	1987	$1,846	NA	3-M	57,650	NA	NA
Assumption Coll., Worcester, MA 01609-1296	1904	$33,805	$10,590	2-M	2,581	222	67.0
Athens State Univ., Athens, AL 35611	1822	$5,340(S)	NA	5-B	3,389	219	NA
Atlantic Coll., Guaynabo, PR 00970	1983	NA	NA	1-M	1,236	NA	NA
Auburn Univ., Auburn, AL 36849	1856	$8,698(S)	$9,992	5-D	25,469	1,358	66.0
Auburn Univ. Montgomery, Montgomery, AL 36124-4023	1967	$231/cr. hr.(S)	$3,970	5-D	5,305	321	33.0
Augsburg Coll., Minneapolis, MN 55454-1351	1869	$30,418	$8,072	2-D	4,073	403	62.0
Augustana Coll., Rock Island, IL 61201-2296	1860	$33,582	$8,784	2-B	2,518	307	76.0
Augustana Coll., Sioux Falls, SD 57197	1860	$26,590	$6,400	2-M	1,871	204	65.0
Augusta State Univ., Augusta, GA 30904-2200	1925	$5,742(S)	$5,550	5-M	7,061	435	21.0
Aurora Univ., Aurora, IL 60506-4892	1893	$19,450	$9,034	1-D	4,355	418	48.0
Austin Coll., Sherman, TX 75090-4400	1849	$32,825	$10,154	2-M	1,353	146	75.0
Austin Peay State Univ., Clarksville, TN 37044	1927	$6,432(S)	$7,014	5-M	10,873	626	35.0
Avila Univ., Kansas City, MO 64145-1698	1916	$24,050	$6,850	2-M	1,818	200	40.0
Azusa Pacific Univ., Azusa, CA 91702-7000	1899	$29,940	$7,221	2-D	9,929	1,102	63.0
Babson Coll., Babson Park, MA 02457-0310	1919	$40,400	$13,330	1-M	3,380	267	90.0
Baker Coll. of Allen Park, Allen Park, MI 48101 (4)	2003	$7,740	NA	1-B	3,954	88	NA
Baker Coll. of Auburn Hills, Auburn Hills, MI 48326-1586	1911	$7,740	NA	1-B	3,803	155	NA
Baker Coll. of Cadillac, Cadillac, MI 49601	1986	$7,740	NA	1-B	1,639	105	NA
Baker Coll. of Clinton Township, Clinton Township, MI 48035-4701	1990	$7,740	NA	1-B	5,712	208	NA
Baker Coll. of Flint, Flint, MI 48507-5508	1911	$7,740	$3,000	1-B	6,329	315	NA
Baker Coll. of Jackson, Jackson, MI 49202	1994	$7,740	NA	1-B	2,730	85	NA
Baker Coll. of Muskegon, Muskegon, MI 49442-3497	1888	$7,740	NA	1-B	4,994	177	NA
Baker Coll. of Owosso, Owosso, MI 48867-4400	1984	$7,740	$3,000	1-B	3,078	144	NA

Name, address	Year founded	Tuition & fees	Room & board	Control, degree	Enroll-ment	Faculty	Grad. rate
Baker Coll. of Port Huron, Port Huron, MI 48060-2597.	1990	$7,740	NA	1-B	1,453	126	NA
Baldwin Wallace Univ., Berea, OH 44017-2088	1845	$26,396	$7,346	2-M	4,177	397	69.0%
Ball State Univ., Muncie, IN 47306-1099	1918	$8,980(S)	$8,714	5-D	22,147	1,145	57.0
Baptist Bible Coll. of Pennsylvania, Clarks Summit, PA 18411-1297	1932	$19,031	$6,950	2-D	1,001	47	36.0
Bard Coll., Annandale-on-Hudson, NY 12504	1860	$43,306	$12,286	1-D	2,302	257	77.0
Barnard Coll., New York, NY 10027-6598 (3)	1889	$42,184	$13,382	1-B	2,445	335	88.0
Barry Univ., Miami Shores, FL 33161-6695	1940	$28,160	$9,030	2-D	8,905	838	NA
Barton Coll., Wilson, NC 27893-7000	1902	$22,982	$7,632	2-M	1,194	108	47.0
Bates Coll., Lewiston, ME 04240-6028.	1855	$55,300(C)	NA	1-B	1,769	189	92.0
Bayamón Central Univ., Bayamón, PR 00960-1725.	1970	$8,200	NA	2-M	1,202	153	NA
Baylor Univ., Waco, TX 76798	1845	$33,716	$9,422	2-D	15,029	1,211	72.0
Bay Path Coll., Longmeadow, MA 01106-2292	1897	$27,045	$10,950	1-M	2,191	236	65.0
Becker Coll., Worcester, MA 01609	1784	$28,490	$10,420	1-B	1,784	177	27.0
Belhaven Univ., Jackson, MS 39202-1789.	1883	$19,200	$6,890	2-M	3,103	173	48.0
Bellarmine Univ., Louisville, KY 40205-0671	1950	$32,140	$9,560	2-D	3,432	363	69.0
Bellevue Univ., Bellevue, NE 68005-3098	1965	$7,700	NA	1-D	10,304	411	37.0
Belmont Abbey Coll., Belmont, NC 28012-1802.	1876	$26,182	$10,403	2-B	1,711	145	37.0
Belmont Univ., Nashville, TN 37212-3757	1951	$26,130	$12,420	2-D	6,365	657	65.0
Beloit Coll., Beloit, WI 53511-5596.	1846	$36,674	$7,502	1-B	1,385	127	76.0
Bemidji State Univ., Bemidji, MN 56601-2699	1919	$7,796(S)	$6,690	5-M	5,360	271	50.0
Benedict Coll., Columbia, SC 29204	1870	$17,188	$7,906	2-B	2,641	NA	NA
Benedictine Coll., Atchison, KS 66002-1499	1859	$21,475	$7,705	2-M	2,069	138	56.0
Benedictine Univ., Lisle, IL 60532-0900	1887	$24,650	$8,060	2-D	7,013	709	52.0
Bentley Univ., Waltham, MA 02452-4705	1917	$38,328	$12,520	1-D	5,565	448	89.0
Berea Coll., Berea, KY 40404.	1855	$910	$5,792	1-B	1,661	158	62.0
Berkeley Coll., Woodland Park, NJ 07424-3353.	1931	$21,750	$6,900	3-B	3,709	NA	NA
Berkeley Coll.–New York City Campus, New York, NY 10017-4604	1936	$21,750	NA	3-B	4,430	NA	NA
Berklee Coll. of Music, Boston, MA 02215-3693	1945	$32,520	$15,830	1-B	4,307	577	53.0
Bernard M. Baruch Coll. of the City Univ. of New York, New York, NY 10010-5585.	1919	$5,610(S)	$10,776	11-M	18,055	1,043	63.0
Berry Coll., Mount Berry, GA 30149-0159	1902	$26,090	$9,158	2-M	2,093	211	57.0
Bethel Coll., Mishawaka, IN 46545-5591	1947	$24,280	$7,280	2-M	2,074	217	60.0
Bethel Univ., St. Paul, MN 55112-6999	1871	$29,460	$8,530	2-D	5,380	308	73.0
Bethel Univ., McKenzie, TN 38201	1842	$13,552	$7,782	2-M	4,295	291	34.0
Beth Medrash Govoha, Lakewood, NJ 08701-2797 (1)	1943	NA	NA	2-M	5,639	NA	NA
Bethune-Cookman Univ., Daytona Beach, FL 32114-3099	1904	$13,990	$8,300	2-M	3,577	230	37.0
Biola Univ., La Mirada, CA 90639-0001	1908	$29,908	$7,570	2-D	6,250	497	66.0
Birmingham-Southern Coll., Birmingham, AL 35254	1856	$29,290	$9,950	2-B	1,305	107	61.0
Black Hills State Univ., Spearfish, SD 57799	1883	$6,951(S)	$5,729	5-M	4,412	NA	28.0
Bloomfield Coll., Bloomfield, NJ 07003-9981	1868	$23,700	$10,600	2-M	2,146	239	32.0
Bloomsburg Univ. of Pennsylvania, Bloomsburg, PA 17815-1301	1839	$8,082(S)	$7,216	5-D	10,159	490	61.0
Bluefield State Coll., Bluefield, WV 24701-2198.	1895	$4,908(S)	NA	5-B	1,929	145	23.0
Bluffton Univ., Bluffton, OH 45817.	1899	$27,426	$9,010	2-M	1,229	112	59.0
Bob Jones Univ., Greenville, SC 29614	1927	$12,480	$5,430	2-D	3,631	291	62.0
Boise State Univ., Boise, ID 83725-0399	1932	$5,566(S)	$6,020	5-D	19,664	1,251	29.0
Boricua Coll., New York, NY 10032-1560.	1974	$9,500	NA	1-M	1,058	133	49.0
Boston Arch. Coll., Boston, MA 02115-2795.	1889	$16,148	NA	1-M	1,091	229	NA
Boston Coll., Chestnut Hill, MA 02467-3800	1863	$42,204	$12,324	2-D	13,906	1,371	91.0
Boston Univ., Boston, MA 02215	1839	$41,420	$12,710	1-D	32,944	2,630	85.0
Bowdoin Coll., Brunswick, ME 04011.	1794	$42,816	$11,654	1-B	1,778	222	92.0
Bowie State Univ., Bowie, MD 20715-9465	1865	$6,347(S)	$8,998	5-M	5,608	410	40.0
Bowling Green State Univ., Bowling Green, OH 43403	1910	$10,044(S)	$7,794	5-D	17,583	1,087	58.0
Bradley Univ., Peoria, IL 61625-0002.	1897	$28,264	$8,700	1-D	5,640	536	73.0
Brandeis Univ., Waltham, MA 02454-9110.	1948	$42,060	$11,894	1-D	5,828	507	NA
Briarcliffe Coll., Bethpage, NY 11714	1966	NA	NA	3-B	1,779	NA	NA
Briar Cliff Univ., Sioux City, IA 51104-0100	1930	$25,642	$7,542	2-M	1,185	106	45.0
Bridgewater Coll., Bridgewater, VA 22812-1599.	1880	$26,750	$10,350	2-B	1,648	141	59.0
Bridgewater State Univ., Bridgewater, MA 02325-0001	1840	$7,552(S)	$10,400	5-M	11,294	733	52.0
Brigham Young Univ., Provo, UT 84602-1001.	1875	$4,710	$7,228	2-D	34,101	1,699	78.0
Brigham Young Univ.–Hawaii, Laie, HI 96762-1294	1955	$4,450	$4,900	2-B	2,555	228	52.0
Brigham Young Univ.–Idaho, Rexburg, ID 83460	1888	$3,660	$4,160	2-B	14,944	NA	NA
Brookline Coll., Phoenix, AZ 85021	1979	$13,750	NA	3-B	1,072	43	NA
Brooklyn Coll. of the City Univ. of New York, Brooklyn, NY 11210-2889	1930	$5,584(S)	NA	11-D	17,094	1,401	43.0
Brooks Inst., Santa Barbara, CA 93101	1945	NA	NA	3-M	1,240	NA	NA
Brown Univ., Providence, RI 02912	1764	$42,230	$10,906	1-D	8,768	977	95.0
Bryan Coll., Dayton, TN 37321-7000	1930	$18,740	$5,454	2-M	1,304	66	55.0
Bryant & Stratton Coll.–Wauwatosa Campus, Wauwatosa, WI 53226	NA	$15,695	NA	3-B	1,264	NA	NA
Bryant Univ., Smithfield, RI 02917	1863	$35,940	$13,240	1-M	3,595	306	77.0
Bryn Mawr Coll., Bryn Mawr, PA 19010-2899	1885	$42,246	$13,340	1-D	1,785	210	87.0
Bucknell Univ., Lewisburg, PA 17837	1846	$45,378	$10,812	1-M	3,635	379	91.0
Buena Vista Univ., Storm Lake, IA 50588.	1891	$27,226	$7,770	2-M	1,002	108	NA
Buffalo State Coll., State Univ. of New York, Buffalo, NY 14222-1095	1867	$6,353(S)	$10,320	5-M	12,204	810	48.0
Butler Univ., Indianapolis, IN 46208-3485	1855	$31,948	$10,600	1-D	4,667	475	73.0
Cabrini Coll., Radnor, PA 19087-3698	1957	$29,000	$11,860	2-M	3,291	302	56.0
Caldwell Coll., Caldwell, NJ 07006-6195	1939	$26,890	$9,440	2-D	2,253	216	58.0
California Baptist Univ., Riverside, CA 92504-3206	1950	$25,768	$8,700	2-M	5,413	460	56.0
California Coll., San Diego, CA 92108	1978	NA	NA	3-B	1,299	NA	NA
California Coll. of the Arts, San Francisco, CA 94107.	1907	$37,310	$7,400	1-M	1,992	571	49.0
California Inst. of Integral Studies, San Francisco, CA 94103.	1968	$15,060	NA	1-D	1,166	NA	NA
California Inst. of Tech., Pasadena, CA 91125-0001	1891	$37,704	$11,676	1-D	2,231	338	87.0
California Inst. of the Arts, Valencia, CA 91355-2340	1961	$38,260	$9,626	1-D	1,454	314	60.0
California Lutheran Univ., Thousand Oaks, CA 91360-2787	1959	$34,360	$11,510	2-D	4,103	373	NA
California Polytechnic State Univ., San Luis Obispo, San Luis Obispo, CA 93407	1901	$7,921(S)	$10,444	5-M	18,762	1,244	76.0
California State Polytechnic Univ., Pomona, Pomona, CA 91768-2557	1938	$6,106(S)	$10,752	5-M	21,107	1,023	51.0
California State Univ.–Bakersfield, Bakersfield, CA 93311	1970	$6,682(S)	$7,808	5-M	8,002	NA	41.0
California State Univ.–Channel Islands, Camarillo, CA 93012	2002	$6,316(S)	$10,200	5-D	3,599	294	NA
California State Univ.–Chico, Chico, CA 95929-0722	1887	NA	$11,138	5-M	15,920	872	62.0
California State Univ.–Dominguez Hills, Carson, CA 90747-0001	1960	$6,593(S)	$10,320	5-M	14,364	743	24.0
California State Univ.–East Bay, Hayward, CA 94542-3000	1957	$6,333(S)	$11,352	5-D	13,160	683	43.0
California State Univ.–Fresno, Fresno, CA 93740-8027	1911	$6,262(S)	$10,550	5-D	21,981	1,089	NA
California State Univ.–Fullerton, Fullerton, CA 92834-9480	1957	$6,128(S)	$10,587	5-D	36,156	1,680	5.0
California State Univ.–Long Beach, Long Beach, CA 90840	1949	$6,738(S)	$11,300	5-D	34,870	1,996	54.0
California State Univ.–Los Angeles, Los Angeles, CA 90032-8530	1947	$6,094(S)	$9,264	5-D	21,284	1,233	37.0
California State Univ.–Monterey Bay, Seaside, CA 93955-8001.	1994	$5,963(S)	$9,152	5-M	5,173	336	38.0
California State Univ.–Northridge, Northridge, CA 91330.	1958	$6,488(S)	$12,276	5-M	35,272	1,833	48.0
California State Univ.–Sacramento, Sacramento, CA 95819	1947	$6,572(S)	$9,628	5-D	28,016	1,400	42.0

Name, address	Year founded	Tuition & fees	Room & board	Control, degree	Enrollment	Faculty	Grad. rate
California State Univ.–San Bernardino, San Bernardino, CA 92407-2397	1965	$6,453(S)	$9,796	5-D	17,250	912	48.0%
California State Univ.–San Marcos, San Marcos, CA 92096-0001	1990	NA	NA	5-M	10,017	569	55.0
California State Univ.–Stanislaus, Turlock, CA 95382	1957	$6,582(S)	$8,553	5-D	9,246	444	49.0
California Univ. of Pennsylvania, California, PA 15419-1394	1852	$9,014(S)	$9,934	5-M	9,483	413	54.0
Calumet Coll. of St. Joseph, Whiting, IN 46394-2195	1951	$14,880	NA	2-M	1,148	50	NA
Calvin Coll., Grand Rapids, MI 49546-4388	1876	$25,565	$8,760	2-B	3,967	384	77.0
Cambridge Coll., Cambridge, MA 02138-5304	1971	$13,280	NA	1-D	3,995	453	NA
Cameron Univ., Lawton, OK 73505-6377	1908	$4,590(S)	$3,754	5-M	6,466	326	19.0
Campbellsville Univ., Campbellsville, KY 42718-2799	1906	$21,600	$7,120	2-M	3,615	309	42.0
Campbell Univ., Buies Creek, NC 27506	1887	$23,720	$8,300	2-D	4,743	305	51.7
Canisius Coll., Buffalo, NY 14208-1098	1870	$30,657	$9,015	2-M	5,148	546	67.0
Capella Univ., Minneapolis, MN 55402	1993	$10,980	NA	3-D	36,375	NA	NA
Capital Univ., Columbus, OH 43209-2394	1830	$30,450	$8,180	2-D	3,550	429	61.0
Cardinal Stritch Univ., Milwaukee, WI 53217-3985	1937	$23,330	$6,850	2-D	4,734	431	NA
Caribbean Univ., Bayamón, PR 00960-0493	1969	$4,465	$8,000	1-M	5,846	424	NA
Carleton Coll., Northfield, MN 55057-4001	1866	$42,942	$11,238	1-B	2,018	243	93.0
Carlos Albizu Univ., Miami Campus, Miami, FL 33172-2209 (4)	1980	$12,048	NA	1-D	1,047	66	68.0
Carlow Univ., Pittsburgh, PA 15213-3165 (4)	1929	$23,504	$9,256	2-D	2,958	280	51.0
Carnegie Mellon Univ., Pittsburgh, PA 15213-3891	1900	$43,812	$11,110	1-D	12,058	991	87.0
Carroll Coll., Helena, MT 59625-0002	1909	$25,198	$7,750	2-B	1,436	143	59.0
Carroll Univ., Waukesha, WI 53186-5593	1846	$25,248	$7,736	2-D	3,385	330	57.0
Carson-Newman Coll., Jefferson City, TN 37760	1851	$22,652	$6,406	2-M	1,970	204	45.0
Carthage Coll., Kenosha, WI 53140	1847	$31,300	$8,600	2-M	2,778	NA	54.0
Case Western Reserve Univ., Cleveland, OH 44106	1826	$39,120	$11,938	1-D	9,636	956	78.0
Castleton State Coll., Castleton, VT 05735	1787	$9,864(S)	$8,786	5-M	2,192	234	52.0
Catawba Coll., Salisbury, NC 28144-2488	1851	$25,160	$8,700	2-M	1,321	106	54.0
The Catholic Univ. of America, Washington, DC 20064	1887	$35,460	$13,824	2-D	6,894	797	68.0
Cazenovia Coll., Cazenovia, NY 13035-1084	1824	$26,736	$11,470	1-B	1,092	129	44.0
Cedar Crest Coll., Allentown, PA 18104-6196 (4)	1867	$30,110	$9,804	2-M	1,620	171	50.0
Cedarville Univ., Cedarville, OH 45314-0601	1887	$25,496	$5,540	2-M	3,299	311	68.0
Centenary Coll., Hackettstown, NJ 07840-2100	1867	$28,890	$9,720	2-M	2,644	222	50.0
Central Coll., Pella, IA 50219	1853	$27,844	$9,136	2-B	1,604	129	63.0
Central Connecticut State Univ., New Britain, CT 06050-4010	1849	$8,055(S)	$9,814	5-D	12,521	968	47.0
Central Methodist Univ., Fayette, MO 65248-1198	1854	$20,130	$6,480	2-M	1,447	110	43.0
Central Michigan Univ., Mount Pleasant, MI 48859	1892	$10,740(S)	$8,212	5-D	28,194	1,137	54.0
Central Penn Coll., Summerdale, PA 17093-0309	1881	$14,991	$6,570	3-B	1,462	133	63.0
Central State Univ., Wilberforce, OH 45384	1887	$5,672(S)	$8,484	5-M	2,503	224	24.0
Central Washington Univ., Ellensburg, WA 98926	1891	$8,946(S)	$9,240	5-M	11,320	589	6.0
Centre Coll., Danville, KY 40422-1394	1819	$42,500(C)	NA	2-B	1,309	141	82.0
Chadron State Coll., Chadron, NE 69337	1911	$5,330(S)	$5,311	5-M	2,649	NA	NA
Chamberlain Coll. of Nursing, Addison, IL 60101-6106	NA	NA	NA	3-B	2,251	100	NA
Chamberlain Coll. of Nursing, St. Louis, MO 63146	1889	$15,600	NA	3-B	7,952	246	NA
Chaminade Univ. of Honolulu, Honolulu, HI 96816-1578	1955	$18,440	$11,100	2-M	2,045	NA	46.0
Champlain Coll., Burlington, VT 05402-0670	1878	$28,400	$12,520	1-M	2,374	324	65.0
Chapman Univ., Orange, CA 92866	1861	$42,084	$12,204	2-D	7,155	748	72.0
Charleston Southern Univ., Charleston, SC 29423-8087	1964	$20,680	$8,000	2-M	3,286	210	39.0
Charter Oak State Coll., New Britain, CT 06053-2142	1973	$236/cr. hr.(S)	NA	5-B	2,241	153	NA
Chatham Univ., Pittsburgh, PA 15232-2826	1869	$31,532	$9,692	1-D	2,220	319	59.0
Chestnut Hill Coll., Philadelphia, PA 19118-2693	1924	$30,095	NA	2-D	2,309	354	44.0
Cheyney Univ. of Pennsylvania, Cheyney, PA 19319	1837	$8,404(S)	$8,910	5-M	1,200	102	25.0
Chicago State Univ., Chicago, IL 60628	1867	$9,062(S)	$8,221	5-D	6,882	499	21.0
Chowan Univ., Murfreesboro, NC 27855	1848	$20,900	$3,680	2-M	1,080	60	NA
Christian Brothers Univ., Memphis, TN 38104-5581	1871	$27,284	$6,140	2-M	1,638	194	52.0
Christopher Newport Univ., Newport News, VA 23606-2998	1960	$10,084(S)	$9,728	5-M	4,990	388	63.0
The Citadel, The Military Coll. of South Carolina, Charleston, SC 29409 (2)	1842	$11,465(S)	$5,979	5-M	3,390	264	72.0
City Coll. of the City Univ. of New York, New York, NY 10031-9198	1847	$5,131(S)	NA	11-D	16,544	1,490	39.0
City Univ. of Seattle, Bellevue, WA 98005	1973	$15,280	NA	1-D	2,302	617	53.0
Claflin Univ., Orangeburg, SC 29115	1869	$14,424	$8,040	2-M	1,961	158	40.0
Claremont McKenna Coll., Claremont, CA 91711	1946	$42,240	$13,700	1-M	1,321	152	91.0
Clarion Univ. of Pennsylvania, Clarion, PA 16214	1867	$8,830(S)	$6,932	5-M	6,988	343	54.0
Clark Atlanta Univ., Atlanta, GA 30314	1865	$18,912	$9,285	2-D	3,843	306	41.0
Clarke Univ., Dubuque, IA 52001-3198	1843	$25,760	$7,740	2-D	1,232	149	60.0
Clarkson Univ., Potsdam, NY 13699	1896	$38,610	$12,534	1-D	3,539	270	75.0
Clark Univ., Worcester, MA 01610-1477	1887	$38,450	$7,320	1-D	3,462	245	80.0
Clayton State Univ., Morrow, GA 30260-0285	1969	$4,926(S)	$8,634	5-M	6,863	380	27.0
Clemson Univ., Clemson, SC 29634	1889	$12,668(S)	$7,228	5-D	19,914	1,122	80.0
Cleveland State Univ., Cleveland, OH 44115	1964	$9,002(S)	$11,848	5-D	17,446	1,032	30.0
Coastal Carolina Univ., Conway, SC 29528-6054	1954	$9,760(S)	$7,700	5-M	9,084	619	46.0
Coe Coll., Cedar Rapids, IA 52402-5092	1851	$34,220	$7,700	2-M	1,378	169	72.0
Colby Coll., Waterville, ME 04901-8840	1813	$53,800(C)	NA	1-B	1,815	200	91.0
Colegio Universitario de San Juan, San Juan, PR 00918	1971	NA	NA	10-B	1,785	NA	NA
Colgate Univ., Hamilton, NY 13346-1386	1819	$42,920	$10,650	1-M	2,964	343	92.0
The Coll. at Brockport, State Univ. of New York, Brockport, NY 14420-2997	1867	$6,508(S)	$10,320	5-M	8,414	595	65.0
Coll. for Creative Stds, Detroit, MI 48202-4034	1926	$32,785	$7,700	1-M	1,391	253	57.0
Coll. of Charleston, Charleston, SC 29424-0001	1770	$9,616(S)	$10,179	5-M	11,649	937	63.0
Coll. of Coastal Georgia, Brunswick, GA 31520	1961	$3,481(S)	$7,475	5-B	3,474	176	NA
The Coll. of Idaho, Caldwell, ID 83605	1891	$22,975	$8,113	1-M	1,041	101	63.0
Coll. of Mount St. Joseph, Cincinnati, OH 45233-1670	1920	$25,100	$7,860	2-D	2,324	247	60.0
Coll. of Mount St. Vincent, Riverdale, NY 10471-1093	1911	$27,810	$10,800	1-M	1,888	213	56.0
The Coll. of New Jersey, Ewing, NJ 08628	1855	$13,887(S)	$10,677	5-M	7,152	754	86.0
The Coll. of New Rochelle, New Rochelle, NY 10805-2308 (4)	1904	$29,100	$10,600	1-M	1,820	217	57.0
Coll. of St. Benedict, Saint Joseph, MN 56374 (3)	1887	$34,308	$8,956	2-B	2,086	198	81.0
Coll. of St. Elizabeth, Morristown, NJ 07960-6989 (4)	1899	$28,221	$11,560	2-D	1,874	222	58.0
Coll. of St. Mary, Omaha, NE 68106 (3)	1923	$25,310	$6,800	2-D	1,063	169	41.0
The Coll. of St. Rose, Albany, NY 12203-1419	1920	$26,622	$10,984	1-M	4,863	NA	63.0
The Coll. of St. Scholastica, Duluth, MN 55811-4199	1912	$29,506	$7,716	2-D	3,898	361	62.0
Coll. of Staten Island of the City Univ. of New York, Staten Island, NY 10314-6600	1955	$5,558(S)	NA	11-D	14,200	1,256	48.0
Coll. of the Holy Cross, Worcester, MA 01610-2395	1843	$43,400	$11,730	2-B	2,905	325	91.0
Coll. of the Ozarks, Point Lookout, MO 65726	1906	$430	$5,900	2-B	1,374	135	62.0
The Coll. of William & Mary, Williamsburg, VA 23187-8795	1693	$13,132(S)	$8,772	5-D	8,200	NA	90.0
The Coll. of Wooster, Wooster, OH 44691-2363	1866	$39,810	$9,590	2-B	2,033	179	75.0
Collins Coll., Tempe, AZ 85281-5206	1978	NA	NA	3-B	1,287	NA	NA
Colorado Christian Univ., Lakewood, CO 80226	1914	$22,960	$9,840	2-M	2,511	NA	NA
The Colorado Coll., Colorado Springs, CO 80903-3294	1874	$40,100	$9,416	1-M	2,043	202	88.0
Colorado Mesa Univ., Grand Junction, CO 81501-3122	1925	$6,548(S)	$8,657	5-D	9,005	531	25.0

Name, address	Year founded	Tuition & fees	Room & board	Control, degree	Enroll- ment	Faculty	Grad. rate
Colorado Sch. of Mines, Golden, CO 80401-1887	1874	$14,454(S)	$8,838	5-D	5,346	337	72.0%
Colorado State Univ., Fort Collins, CO 80523-0015	1870	$8,042(S)	$9,172	5-D	30,450	961	64.0
Colorado State Univ.–Pueblo, Pueblo, CO 81001-4901	1933	$6,269(S)	$8,970	5-M	5,049	418	32.0
Colorado Tech. Univ. Colorado Springs, Colorado Springs, CO 80907-3896	1965	$13,275	NA	3-D	2,359	343	NA
Colorado Tech. Univ. Online, Colorado Springs, CO 80907	NA	NA	NA	3-M	25,797	613	NA
Columbia Centro Universitario, Caguas, PR 00726	1966	$9,435	NA	3-M	1,429	104	14.0
Columbia Coll., Columbia, MO 65216-0002	1851	$17,950	$6,254	2-M	1,224	121	42.0
Columbia Coll., Columbia, SC 29203-5998	1854	$25,050	$6,638	2-D	1,269	135	48.0
Columbia Coll. Chicago, Chicago, IL 60605-1996	1890	$21,750	$11,920	1-M	11,625	2,037	NA
Columbia Intl. Univ., Columbia, SC 29230-3122	1923	$18,380	$6,670	2-D	1,139	53	53.0
Columbia Southern Univ., Orange Beach, AL 36561	1993	$4,895	NA	3-D	22,658	285	35.0
Columbia Univ., New York, NY 10027	1754	$41,160	$10,570	1-D	6,027	1,965	96.0
Columbia Univ., Sch. of General Studies, New York, NY 10027-6939	1754	$43,958	$10,125	1-B	1,499	1,823	NA
Columbus Coll. of Art & Design, Columbus, OH 43215-1758	1879	$27,132	$9,410	1-M	1,445	201	64.0
Columbus State Univ., Columbus, GA 31907-5645	1958	$6,404(S)	$7,560	5-M	8,307	469	31.0
Concordia Coll., Moorhead, MN 56562	1891	$30,860	$7,000	2-M	2,772	257	69.0
Concordia Univ., Irvine, CA 92612-3299	1972	$28,500	$8,760	2-M	3,251	320	51.0
Concordia Univ., Portland, OR 97211-6099	1905	$25,392	$7,040	2-M	1,709	172	54.0
Concordia Univ. Chicago, River Forest, IL 60305-1499	1864	$26,656	$8,580	2-D	5,135	426	60.0
Concordia Univ. Nebraska, Seward, NE 68434-1599	1894	$23,800	$6,440	2-M	2,196	178	55.0
Concordia Univ. St. Paul, St. Paul, MN 55104-5494	1893	$29,700	$7,750	2-M	2,800	331	46.0
Concordia Univ. Texas, Austin, TX 78726	1926	$22,920	$8,460	2-M	2,658	270	35.0
Concordia Univ. Wisconsin, Mequon, WI 53097-2402	1881	$22,995	$8,956	2-D	7,485	277	60.0
Concord Univ., Athens, WV 24712-1000	1872	$5,446(S)	$7,240	5-M	2,937	207	89.0
Connecticut Coll., New London, CT 06320-4196	1911	$43,990	$10,980	1-M	1,903	243	NA
Converse Coll., Spartanburg, SC 29302-0006	1889	$28,276	$8,854	1-M	1,296	88	60.0
Coppin State Univ., Baltimore, MD 21216-3698	1900	$5,732(S)	$8,018	5-M	3,800	312	15.0
Corban Univ., Salem, OR 97301-9392	1935	$25,445	$7,980	2-D	1,123	117	50.0
Cornell Coll., Mount Vernon, IA 52314-1098	1853	$34,705	$7,900	2-B	1,197	90	70.0
Cornell Univ., Ithaca, NY 14853-0001	1865	$41,541	$13,160	1-D	21,131	1,827	93.0
Cornerstone Univ., Grand Rapids, MI 49525-5897	1941	$22,388	$7,314	2-M	2,747	114	43.0
Covenant Coll., Lookout Mountain, GA 30750	1955	$26,226	$7,450	2-M	1,094	93	52.0
Creighton Univ., Omaha, NE 68178-0001	1878	$31,894	$9,238	2-D	7,730	772	77.0
Crown Coll., St. Bonifacius, MN 55375-9001	1916	$22,100	$7,480	2-M	1,198	151	53.0
The Culinary Inst. of America, Hyde Park, NY 12538-1499	1946	$25,560	$8,420	1-B	2,807	184	NA
Cumberland Univ., Lebanon, TN 37087	1842	$19,200	$6,600	1-M	1,375	122	31.0
Curry Coll., Milton, MA 02186-9984	1879	$32,210	$12,285	1-M	2,979	500	48.0
Daemen Coll., Amherst, NY 14226-3592	1947	$22,310	$10,300	1-D	3,005	291	44.0
Dakota State Univ., Madison, SD 57042-1799	1881	$7,621(S)	$5,088	5-D	3,075	129	34.0
Dallas Baptist Univ., Dallas, TX 75211-9299	1965	$19,850	$6,120	2-D	5,545	536	47.0
Dalton State Coll., Dalton, GA 30720	1963	$3,006(S)	$4,750	5-B	5,485	237	20.0
Dartmouth Coll., Hanover, NH 03755	1769	$42,996	$12,369	1-D	6,144	682	95.0
Davenport Univ., Grand Rapids, MI 49512	1866	$12,386	$8,412	1-M	12,401	1,069	NA
Davidson Coll., Davidson, NC 28035	1837	$38,866	$10,857	2-B	1,756	167	92.0
Defiance Coll., Defiance, OH 43512-1610	1850	$25,890	$8,450	2-M	1,083	107	51.0
Delaware State Univ., Dover, DE 19901-2277	1891	$7,886(S)	$10,244	5-D	4,178	357	35.0
Delaware Valley Coll., Doylestown, PA 18901-2697	1896	$31,746	$11,262	1-M	2,253	195	55.0
Delta State Univ., Cleveland, MS 38733-0001	1924	$5,288(S)	$6,026	5-D	4,624	259	32.0
Denison Univ., Granville, OH 43023	1831	$42,280	$10,360	1-B	2,275	223	83.0
DePaul Univ., Chicago, IL 60604-2287	1898	$30,618	$11,335	2-D	25,398	1,908	66.0
DePauw Univ., Greencastle, IN 46135	1837	$36,970	$9,730	2-B	2,352	275	85.0
DeSales Univ., Center Valley, PA 18034-9568	1964	$29,094	$10,130	2-D	3,170	312	69.0
DeVry Coll. of New York, New York, NY 10016-5267	1998	$15,374	NA	3-M	2,129	93	NA
DeVry Univ., Phoenix, AZ 85021-2995	1967	$15,374	NA	3-M	1,596	133	NA
DeVry Univ., Fremont, CA 94555	1998	$15,374	NA	3-M	1,553	231	39.0
DeVry Univ., Long Beach, CA 90806	1984	$15,374	NA	3-M	1,172	101	32.0
DeVry Univ., Pomona, CA 91768-2642	1983	$15,374	NA	3-M	2,969	107	NA
DeVry Univ., Miramar, FL 33027-4150	2002	$15,374	NA	3-M	1,234	77	NA
DeVry Univ., Orlando, FL 32839	2000	$15,374	NA	3-M	1,970	144	NA
DeVry Univ., Decatur, GA 30030-2556	1969	$15,374	NA	3-M	3,156	143	NA
DeVry Univ., Addison, IL 60101-6106	1982	$15,374	NA	3-B	1,508	154	36.0
DeVry Univ., Chicago, IL 60618-5994	1931	$15,374	NA	3-M	2,119	196	NA
DeVry Univ., Naperville, IL 60563-2361	NA	$14,826	NA	3-M	8,828	2,248	NA
DeVry Univ., Tinley Park, IL 60477	2000	$15,374	NA	3-M	1,471	79	39.0
DeVry Univ., Kansas City, MO 64131	1931	$15,374	NA	3-M	1,168	76	NA
DeVry Univ., North Brunswick, NJ 08902-3362	1969	$15,374	NA	3-M	1,796	153	NA
DeVry Univ., Columbus, OH 43209-2705	1952	$15,374	NA	3-M	3,061	102	NA
DeVry Univ., Fort Washington, PA 19034	2002	$15,374	NA	3-M	1,055	124	NA
DeVry Univ., Houston, TX 77041	NA	$15,374	NA	3-M	1,840	184	NA
DeVry Univ., Irving, TX 75063-2439	1969	$15,374	NA	3-M	1,740	98	NA
DeVry Univ. Online, Addison, IL 60101-6106	2000	$15,374	NA	3-M	28,189	3,215	NA
Dickinson Coll., Carlisle, PA 17013-2896	1773	$43,060	$10,800	1-B	2,397	252	84.0
Dickinson State Univ., Dickinson, ND 58601-4896	1918	$5,608(S)	$1,774	5-B	2,668	233	38.0
Dillard Univ., New Orleans, LA 70122-3097	1869	$14,850	$8,686	2-B	1,249	NA	24.0
Dixie State Coll. of Utah, St. George, UT 84770-3876	1911	$3,888(S)	$4,348	5-B	9,044	NA	32.0
Doane Coll., Crete, NE 68333-2430	1872	$23,590	$6,650	2-M	1,066	117	62.0
Dominican Coll., Orangeburg, NY 10962-1210	1952	$22,940	$10,980	1-D	2,058	233	40.0
Dominican Univ., River Forest, IL 60305-1099	1901	$27,730	$8,520	2-D	3,612	394	63.0
Dominican Univ. of California, San Rafael, CA 94901-2298	1890	$37,350	$13,900	2-M	2,278	371	56.0
Dordt Coll., Sioux Center, IA 51250-1697	1955	$24,300	$6,870	2-M	1,405	122	62.0
Dowling Coll., Oakdale, NY 11769-1999	1955	$25,908	$10,850	1-D	4,416	431	36.0
Drake Univ., Des Moines, IA 50311-4516	1881	$29,556	$8,680	1-D	5,384	461	78.0
Drew Univ., Madison, NJ 07940-1493	1867	$41,004	$11,150	2-D	2,632	293	71.0
Drexel Univ., Philadelphia, PA 19104-2875	1891	$36,100	$14,175	1-D	24,860	1,636	68.0
Drury Univ., Springfield, MO 65802	1873	$21,575	$7,780	1-M	2,088	181	64.0
Duke Univ., Durham, NC 27708-0586	1838	$42,033	$11,640	2-D	14,350	1,155	95.0
Duquesne Univ., Pittsburgh, PA 15282-0001	1878	$28,671	$9,806	2-D	9,933	991	75.0
D'Youville Coll., Buffalo, NY 14201-1084	1908	$21,760	$10,000	1-D	2,971	322	63.0
Earlham Coll., Richmond, IN 47374-4095	1847	$38,284	$7,570	2-M	1,193	107	67.0
East Carolina Univ., Greenville, NC 27858-4353	1907	$5,364(S)	$7,950	5-D	27,386	1,463	59.0
East Central Univ., Ada, OK 74820-6899	1909	$4,703(S)	$4,574	5-M	4,851	270	31.0
Eastern Connecticut State Univ., Willimantic, CT 06226-2295	1889	$8,555(S)	$10,256	5-M	5,586	446	49.0
Eastern Illinois Univ., Charleston, IL 61920-3099	1895	$10,534(S)	$8,884	5-M	11,178	741	62.0
Eastern Kentucky Univ., Richmond, KY 40475-3102	1906	$6,960(S)	$7,012	5-D	16,062	1,114	38.0
Eastern Mennonite Univ., Harrisonburg, VA 22802-2462	1917	$26,400	$8,520	2-M	1,521	205	66.0
Eastern Michigan Univ., Ypsilanti, MI 48197	1849	$8,684(S)	$7,896	5-D	23,341	1,299	40.0

Name, address	Year founded	Tuition & fees	Room & board	Control, degree	Enroll- ment	Faculty	Grad. rate
Eastern Nazarene Coll., Quincy, MA 02170	1918	$26,884	$8,300	2-M	1,036	122	52.0%
Eastern New Mexico Univ., Portales, NM 88130	1934	$4,147(S)	$5,830	5-M	5,574	340	24.0
Eastern Oregon Univ., La Grande, OR 97850-2899	1929	$7,046(S)	$8,100	5-M	4,298	128	32.0
Eastern Univ., St. Davids, PA 19087-3696	1952	$25,900	$9,330	2-D	4,331	NA	NA
Eastern Washington Univ., Cheney, WA 99004-2431	1882	$6,604(S)	$7,470	5-D	12,126	647	46.0
East Stroudsburg Univ. of Pennsylvania, East Stroudsburg, PA 18301-2999	1893	$8,351(S)	$6,948	5-M	7,353	319	59.0
East Tennessee State Univ., Johnson City, TN 37614	1911	$6,271(S)	$6,000	5-D	15,250	828	44.0
East Texas Baptist Univ., Marshall, TX 75670-1498	1912	$21,530	$6,145	2-M	1,214	104	43.0
East-West Univ., Chicago, IL 60605-2103	1978	$16,650	NA	1-B	1,170	67	22.0
Eckerd Coll., St. Petersburg, FL 33711	1958	$35,926	$9,846	2-B	1,843	163	63.0
ECPI Coll. of Tech., Virginia Beach, VA 23462	1966	NA	NA	3-B	13,717	1,371	NA
Edgewood Coll., Madison, WI 53711-1997 (4)	1927	$22,850	$8,113	2-D	2,658	304	51.0
Edinboro Univ. of Pennsylvania, Edinboro, PA 16444	1857	$8,359(S)	$8,068	5-M	8,262	396	54.0
EDP Coll. of Puerto Rico, Inc., Hato Rey, PR 00918	1968	$6,120	NA	3-M	1,193	96	13.0
Elizabeth City State Univ., Elizabeth City, NC 27909-7806	1891	$2,348(S)	$5,657	5-M	2,930	241	42.0
Elizabethtown Coll., Elizabethtown, PA 17022-2298	1899	$36,550	$9,050	2-M	2,389	250	78.0
Ellis Univ., Chicago, IL 60606-7204	2008	$452/cr. hr.	NA	3-M	1,950	NA	NA
Elmhurst Coll., Elmhurst, IL 60126-3296	1871	$30,054	$8,524	2-M	3,455	399	70.0
Elmira Coll., Elmira, NY 14901	1855	$36,950	$11,500	1-M	1,634	221	58.0
Elms Coll., Chicopee, MA 01013-2839 (4)	1928	$28,128	$10,202	2-M	1,260	NA	NA
Elon Univ., Elon, NC 27244-2010	1889	$27,881	$9,090	2-D	5,916	522	82.0
Embry-Riddle Aeron Univ.–Daytona, Daytona Beach, FL 32114-3900	1926	$30,720	$9,340	1-D	5,205	365	NA
Embry-Riddle Aeron Univ.–Prescott, Prescott, AZ 86301-3720	1978	$30,420	$9,340	1-M	1,723	127	57.0
Embry-Riddle Aeron Univ.–Worldwide, Daytona Beach, FL 32114-3900	1970	$7,320	NA	1-D	16,244	2,650	NA
Emerson Coll., Boston, MA 02116-4624	1880	$34,198	$13,958	1-D	4,438	438	81.0
Emmanuel Coll., Boston, MA 02115	1919	$32,475	$12,750	2-M	2,509	231	63.0
Emory Univ., Atlanta, GA 30322-1100	1836	$41,164	$11,628	2-D	13,893	1,534	90.0
Emporia State Univ., Emporia, KS 66801-5087	1863	$4,952(S)	$6,380	5-D	5,976	272	44.0
Endicott Coll., Beverly, MA 01915-2096	1939	$27,130	$12,760	1-M	4,453	335	67.0
Eugene Lang Coll. The New Sch. for Liberal Arts, New York, NY 10011-8601	1978	$37,240	$14,910	1-B	1,511	157	56.0
Evangel Univ., Springfield, MO 65802	1955	$18,000	$6,310	2-M	2,168	NA	53.0
Everest Univ., Pompano Beach, FL 33062	1940	$14,328	NA	3-M	1,633	NA	NA
Everest Univ., Tampa, FL 33614-5899	1890	$15,336	NA	3-M	3,430	61	NA
Everest Univ., Tampa, FL 33619	1890	$16,452	NA	3-M	12,695	61	NA
Everglades Univ., Boca Raton, FL 33431	1989	$12,920	NA	1-M	1,039	NA	NA
The Evergreen State Coll., Olympia, WA 98505	1967	$7,486(S)	$9,000	5-M	4,794	247	52.0
Excelsior Coll., Albany, NY 12203-5159	1970	$355/cr. hr.	NA	1-M	33,067	NA	NA
Fairfield Univ., Fairfield, CT 06824-5195	1942	$40,490	$12,210	2-D	4,991	541	81.0
Fairleigh Dickinson Univ., Coll. at Florham, Madison, NJ 07940-1099	1942	$35,002	$11,662	1-M	3,082	394	55.0
Fairleigh Dickinson Univ., Metropolitan Campus, Teaneck, NJ 07666-1914	1942	$32,538	$12,046	1-D	9,107	771	41.3
Fairmont State Univ., Fairmont, WV 26554	1865	$5,326(S)	$7,132	5-M	4,617	317	31.0
Farmingdale State Coll., Farmingdale, NY 11735	1912	$6,434(S)	$11,440	5-B	7,633	569	40.0
Fashion Inst. of Tech., New York, NY 10001-5992 (4)	1944	$5,603(S)	$12,190	11-M	10,223	977	NA
Faulkner Univ., Montgomery, AL 36109-3398	1942	$16,580	$6,650	2-D	3,574	287	35.0
Fayetteville State Univ., Fayetteville, NC 28301-4298	1867	$4,459(S)	$5,500	5-D	5,930	331	31.0
Felician Coll., Lodi, NJ 07644-2117	1942	$29,400	$11,400	2-M	2,341	241	36.0
Ferris State Univ., Big Rapids, MI 49307	1884	$10,440(S)	$9,344	5-D	14,560	775	47.0
Ferrum Coll., Ferrum, VA 24088	1913	$24,945	$8,080	2-B	1,512	123	31.0
Fisher Coll., Boston, MA 02116-1500	1903	$25,778	$13,786	1-B	1,751	155	40.0
Fitchburg State Univ., Fitchburg, MA 01420-2697	1894	$8,300(S)	$8,256	5-M	6,891	274	47.0
Five Towns Coll., Dix Hills, NY 11746-6055	1972	$19,570	$12,660	1-D	1,041	213	NA
Flagler Coll., St. Augustine, FL 32085-1027	1968	$14,510	$7,990	1-B	2,878	223	60.0
Florida Agr. & Mech. Univ., Tallahassee, FL 32307-3200	1887	$5,187(S)	$8,754	5-D	13,204	720	41.0
Florida Atlantic Univ., Boca Raton, FL 33431-0991	1961	$5,330(S)	$10,940	5-D	29,290	1,332	42.0
Florida Gulf Coast Univ., Fort Myers, FL 33965-6565	1991	$5,352(S)	$8,771	5-D	12,671	630	47.0
Florida Hosp. Coll. of Health Sci., Orlando, FL 32803	1913	$10,030	$3,500	1-M	2,207	84	NA
Florida Inst. of Tech., Melbourne, FL 32901-6975	1958	$34,990	$11,820	1-D	8,983	616	56.0
Florida Intl. Univ., Miami, FL 33199	1965	$5,678(S)	$11,330	5-D	44,686	1,941	43.0
Florida Memorial Univ., Miami-Dade, FL 33054	1879	$14,024	$6,112	2-M	1,750	173	33.0
Florida Natl. Coll., Hialeah, FL 33012	1982	$13,170	NA	3-M	2,744	147	NA
Florida Southern Coll., Lakeland, FL 33801-5698	1885	$27,200	$9,100	2-M	2,219	223	55.0
Florida State Univ., Tallahassee, FL 32306	1851	$5,825(S)	$9,412	5-D	41,087	1,624	74.0
Fontbonne Univ., St. Louis, MO 63105-3098	1917	$20,420	$7,780	2-M	2,293	276	43.0
Fordham Univ., New York, NY 10458	1841	$39,235	$14,926	2-D	15,189	1,510	79.0
Fort Hays State Univ., Hays, KS 67601-4099	1902	$135/cr. hr.(S)	$6,625	5-M	12,802	479	NA
Fort Lewis Coll., Durango, CO 81301-3999	1911	$5,592(S)	$8,010	5-B	3,856	229	38.0
Fort Valley State Univ., Fort Valley, GA 31030	1895	$6,030(S)	$7,418	5-D	3,571	202	39.0
Framingham State Univ., Framingham, MA 01701-9101	1839	$7,580(S)	$9,170	5-M	6,415	298	52.0
Franciscan Univ. of Steubenville, Steubenville, OH 43952-1763	1946	$22,180	$7,400	2-M	2,823	223	70.0
Francis Marion Univ., Florence, SC 29502-0547	1970	$8,802(S)	$6,620	5-M	4,187	287	41.0
Franklin & Marshall Coll., Lancaster, PA 17604-3003	1787	$42,570	$11,500	1-B	2,363	268	85.0
Franklin Coll., Franklin, IN 46131	1834	$25,865	$7,650	2-B	1,048	111	60.0
Franklin Pierce Univ., Rindge, NH 03461-0060	1962	$29,450	$10,620	1-D	2,396	316	50.0
Franklin Univ., Columbus, OH 43215-5399	1902	$13,500	NA	1-M	7,465	766	19.0
Freed-Hardeman Univ., Henderson, TN 38340-2399	1869	$17,204	$7,296	2-D	1,992	145	56.0
Fresno Pacific Univ., Fresno, CA 93702-4709	1944	$24,790	$6,440	2-M	2,353	355	60.0
Friends Univ., Wichita, KS 67213	1898	$21,030	$5,966	2-M	2,905	629	27.0
Frostburg State Univ., Frostburg, MD 21532-1099	1898	$7,436(S)	$7,796	5-M	5,429	369	46.0
Full Sail Univ., Winter Park, FL 32792-7437 (2)	1979	NA	NA	3-M	8,921	702	NA
Furman Univ., Greenville, SC 29613	1826	$39,560	$10,192	1-M	3,028	269	87.0
Gallaudet Univ., Washington, DC 20002-3625	1864	$12,806	$10,790	1-D	1,546	185	41.0
Gannon Univ., Erie, PA 16541-0001	1925	$26,526	$10,580	2-D	4,076	356	69.0
Gardner-Webb Univ., Boiling Springs, NC 28017	1905	$23,510	$7,570	2-D	4,705	422	55.0
Geneva Coll., Beaver Falls, PA 15010-3599	1848	$23,330	$8,560	2-M	1,630	178	68.0
George Fox Univ., Newberg, OR 97132-2697	1891	$29,380	$9,050	2-D	3,519	388	62.0
George Mason Univ., Fairfax, VA 22030	1957	$9,066(S)	$8,950	5-D	33,320	2,375	64.0
Georgetown Coll., Georgetown, KY 40324-1696	1829	$29,300	$7,610	2-M	1,818	161	59.0
Georgetown Univ., Washington, DC 20057	1789	$41,393	$12,517	2-D	16,871	1,749	93.0
The George Washington Univ., Washington, DC 20052	1821	$45,780	$10,530	1-D	25,260	2,220	81.0
Georgia Coll. & State Univ., Milledgeville, GA 31061	1889	$8,344(S)	$8,998	5-M	6,636	436	55.0
Georgia Gwinnett Coll., Lawrenceville, GA 60043	2006	$5,290(S)	$9,000	5-B	7,742	489	NA
Georgia Health Sci. Univ., Augusta, GA 30912	1828	$8,908(S)	$2,372	5-D	2,438	824	NA
Georgia Inst. of Tech., Atlanta, GA 30332-0001	1885	$9,652(S)	$8,826	5-D	20,941	1,225	79.0
Georgian Court Univ., Lakewood, NJ 08701-2697 (4)	1908	$27,984	$10,250	2-M	2,555	272	52.0
Georgia Southern Univ., Statesboro, GA 30460	1906	$6,606(S)	$9,020	5-D	20,212	870	47.0
Georgia Southwestern State Univ., Americus, GA 31709-4693	1906	$5,660(S)	$6,344	5-M	3,046	160	30.0
Georgia State Univ., Atlanta, GA 30302-3083	1913	$9,410(S)	$11,390	5-D	32,022	1,633	48.0

Name, address	Year founded	Tuition & fees	Room & board	Control, degree	Enroll-ment	Faculty	Grad. rate
Gettysburg Coll., Gettysburg, PA 17325-1483	1832	$42,610	$10,180	2-B	2,516	292	85.0%
Glenville State Coll., Glenville, WV 26351-1200	1872	$5,352(S)	$7,900	5-B	1,857	112	30.0
Global Univ., Springfield, MO 65804	1948	$3,520	NA	2-D	4,551	633	NA
Globe Univ.–Woodbury, Woodbury, MN 55125	1885	$19,575	NA	3-D	1,542	159	NA
Golden Gate Univ., San Francisco, CA 94105-2968	1901	$15,390	NA	1-D	3,528	489	NA
Goldey-Beacom Coll., Wilmington, DE 19808-1999	1886	$21,120	$5,248	1-M	1,153	54	49.0
Gonzaga Univ., Spokane, WA 99258	1887	$32,222	$8,340	2-D	7,764	720	83.0
Gordon Coll., Wenham, MA 01984-1899	1889	$32,100	$8,840	2-M	1,898	173	74.0
Goucher Coll., Baltimore, MD 21204-2794	1885	$36,553	$10,569	1-M	2,173	212	70.0
Governors State Univ., University Park, IL 60484	1969	$8,936(S)	NA	5-D	5,489	NA	NA
Grace Coll., Winona Lake, IN 46590-1294	1948	$22,546	$7,214	2-D	1,616	85	55.0
Graceland Univ., Lamoni, IA 50140	1895	$22,680	$7,580	2-D	2,318	172	50.0
Grambling State Univ., Grambling, LA 71245	1901	$4,882(S)	$8,498	5-D	5,207	260	29.0
Grand Canyon Univ., Phoenix, AZ 85017-1097	1949	$19,000	$8,100	2-D	NA	NA	NA
Grand Valley State Univ., Allendale, MI 49401-9403	1960	$9,716(S)	$7,774	5-D	24,662	1,631	61.0
Grand View Univ., Des Moines, IA 50316-1599	1896	$21,970	$7,596	2-M	2,229	238	41.0
Granite State Coll., Concord, NH 03301	1972	$6,600(S)	NA	11-M	1,919	169	56.0
Grantham Univ., Kansas City, MO 64153	1951	$7,950	NA	3-M	6,214	183	NA
Greensboro Coll., Greensboro, NC 27401-1875	1838	$25,000	$9,100	2-M	1,264	96	43.0
Greenville Coll., Greenville, IL 62246-0159	1892	$22,198	$7,338	2-M	1,501	161	52.0
Grinnell Coll., Grinnell, IA 50112-1690	1846	$39,810	$9,334	1-B	1,693	206	88.0
Grove City Coll., Grove City, PA 16127-2104	1876	$13,598	$7,410	2-B	2,461	217	82.0
Guilford Coll., Greensboro, NC 27410-4173	1837	$30,430	$8,270	2-B	2,739	214	58.0
Gustavus Adolphus Coll., St. Peter, MN 56082-1498	1862	$35,477	$8,700	2-B	2,471	269	80.0
Gwynedd-Mercy Coll., Gwynedd Valley, PA 19437-0901	1948	$28,340	$9,850	2-M	2,710	272	52.0
Hamilton Coll., Clinton, NY 13323-1296	1812	$42,640	$10,830	1-B	1,864	219	89.0
Hamline Univ., St. Paul, MN 55104-1284	1854	$33,588	$8,700	2-D	4,852	485	68.0
Hampden-Sydney Coll., Hampden-Sydney, VA 23943 (1)	1776	$33,874	$10,632	2-B	1,057	115	66.0
Hampshire Coll., Amherst, MA 01002	1965	$42,900	$11,180	1-B	1,500	160	63.0
Hampton Univ., Hampton, VA 23668	1868	$18,798	$8,370	1-D	5,221	779	55.0
Hannibal-LaGrange Univ., Hannibal, MO 63401-1999	1858	$17,800	$6,570	2-M	1,128	146	50.0
Hanover Coll., Hanover, IN 47243-0108	1827	$28,850	$8,650	2-B	1,068	100	NA
Harding Univ., Searcy, AR 72149-0001	1924	$14,610	$6,030	2-D	7,056	485	63.0
Hardin-Simmons Univ., Abilene, TX 79698-0001	1891	$22,560	$6,630	2-D	2,358	202	47.0
Harris-Stowe State Univ., St. Louis, MO 63103-2136	1857	$5,320(S)	$8,080	5-B	1,886	190	NA
Hartwick Coll., Oneonta, NY 13820-4020	1797	$36,040	$9,625	1-B	1,578	183	55.0
Harvard Univ., Cambridge, MA 02138	1636	$39,851	$12,801	1-D	10,573	1,113	97.0
Hastings Coll., Hastings, NE 68901-7696	1882	$23,734	$6,780	2-M	1,138	123	62.3
Haverford Coll., Haverford, PA 19041-1392	1833	$42,208	$12,842	1-B	1,198	138	93.0
Hawai'i Pacific Univ., Honolulu, HI 96813	1965	$18,600	$12,230	1-M	8,071	642	39.0
Heidelberg Univ., Tiffin, OH 44883-2462	1850	$24,582	$8,974	2-M	1,317	150	57.0
Henderson State Univ., Arkadelphia, AR 71999-0001	1890	$6,714(S)	$5,084	5-M	3,712	242	33.0
Hendrix Coll., Conway, AR 72032-3080	1876	$34,230	$9,714	2-M	1,426	139	73.0
Heritage Univ., Toppenish, WA 98948-9599	1982	$15,480	NA	1-M	1,115	NA	NA
High Point Univ., High Point, NC 27262-3598	1924	$39,800(C)	NA	2-M	4,205	349	61.0
Hilbert Coll., Hamburg, NY 14075-1597	1957	$19,620	$8,570	1-M	1,096	126	43.0
Hillsdale Coll., Hillsdale, MI 49242-1298	1844	$21,930	$8,640	1-B	1,457	163	76.0
Hiram Coll., Hiram, OH 44234-0067	1850	$28,950	$9,460	1-M	1,395	139	69.0
Hobart & William Smith Colls., Geneva, NY 14456-3397	1822	$42,915	$10,852	1-M	2,242	214	75.0
Hodges Univ., Naples, FL 34119	1990	$11,780	NA	1-M	2,441	168	NA
Hofstra Univ., Hempstead, NY 11549	1935	$34,150	$11,940	1-D	11,404	1,114	58.0
Holy Family Univ., Philadelphia, PA 19114	1954	$24,550	$11,750	2-D	3,184	370	61.0
Holy Names Univ., Oakland, CA 94619-1699 (4)	1868	$30,390	$10,260	2-M	1,216	138	31.0
Hood Coll., Frederick, MD 21701-8575	1893	$31,060	$10,390	1-M	2,435	259	68.0
Hope Coll., Holland, MI 49422-9000	1866	$27,810	$8,510	2-B	3,249	316	79.0
Hope Intl. Univ., Fullerton, CA 92831-3138	1928	$25,389	$8,100	2-M	1,365	188	31.0
Houghton Coll., Houghton, NY 14744	1883	$26,094	$7,550	2-M	1,287	135	69.0
Houston Baptist Univ., Houston, TX 77074-3298	1960	$26,795	$6,290	2-M	2,432	211	45.0
Howard Payne Univ., Brownwood, TX 76801-2715	1889	$22,560	$6,382	2-M	1,201	128	45.0
Howard Univ., Washington, DC 20059-0002	1867	$20,371	$9,504	1-D	10,288	1,520	65.0
Humboldt State Univ., Arcata, CA 95521-8299	1913	$7,622(S)	$10,948	5-M	8,046	517	40.0
Hunter Coll. of the City Univ. of New York, New York, NY 10021-5085	1870	$215/credit(S)	NA	11-M	22,822	1,873	45.0
Huntingdon Coll., Montgomery, AL 36106-2148	1854	$21,990	$8,000	2-B	1,123	115	52.0
Huntington Univ., Huntington, IN 46750-1299	1897	$23,780	$7,940	2-M	1,253	113	62.0
Husson Univ., Bangor, ME 04401-2999	1898	$13,980	$7,520	1-D	3,090	309	42.0
Idaho State Univ., Pocatello, ID 83209	1901	$5,796(S)	$5,322	5-D	12,587	846	26.0
Illinois Inst. of Tech., Chicago, IL 60616-3793	1890	$37,664	$10,464	1-D	7,787	714	64.0
Illinois State Univ., Normal, IL 61790-2200	1857	$12,230(S)	$9,090	5-D	21,310	1,205	71.0
Illinois Wesleyan Univ., Bloomington, IL 61702-2900	1850	$36,572	$8,476	1-B	2,090	226	82.0
Immaculata Univ., Immaculata, PA 19345 (4)	1920	$28,850	$11,460	2-D	4,312	408	47.0
Indiana State Univ., Terre Haute, IN 47809	1865	$8,098(S)	$8,262	5-D	11,528	661	44.0
Indiana Tech, Fort Wayne, IN 46803-1297	1930	$24,370	$9,160	1-D	4,912	306	NA
Indiana Univ.–Bloomington, Bloomington, IN 47405-7000	1820	$10,033(S)	$8,144	5-D	43,284	2,297	72.0
Indiana Univ.–East, Richmond, IN 47374-1289	1971	$6,496(S)	NA	5-M	3,725	258	19.0
Indiana Univ.–Kokomo, Kokomo, IN 46904-9003	1945	$6,542(S)	NA	5-M	3,318	187	20.0
Indiana Univ.–Northwest, Gary, IN 46408-1197	1959	$6,627(S)	NA	5-M	6,035	401	23.0
Indiana Univ.–Purdue Univ. Fort Wayne, Fort Wayne, IN 46805-1499	1917	$6,708(S)	$5,900	5-M	14,326	880	25.0
Indiana Univ.–Purdue Univ. Indianapolis, Indianapolis, IN 46202-2896	1969	$8,605(S)	$3,906	5-D	30,530	3,208	33.0
Indiana Univ.–South Bend, South Bend, IN 46634-7111	1922	$6,728(S)	$5,656	5-M	8,385	542	22.0
Indiana Univ.–Southeast, New Albany, IN 47150-6405	1941	$6,575(S)	$6,570	5-M	7,256	487	26.0
Indiana Univ. of Pennsylvania, Indiana, PA 15705-1087	1875	$8,362(S)	$9,782	5-D	15,132	703	54.0
Indiana Wesleyan Univ., Marion, IN 46953-4974	1920	$23,165	$7,511	2-D	3,299	292	70.0
Inter Amer. Univ. of Puerto Rico, Aguadilla Campus, Aguadilla, PR 00605	1957	$5,495	NA	1-M	4,502	231	20.0
Inter Amer. Univ. of Puerto Rico, Arecibo Campus, Arecibo, PR 00614-4050	1957	$4,596	NA	1-M	4,878	298	NA
Inter Amer. Univ. of Puerto Rico, Barranquitas Campus, Barranquitas, PR 00794	1957	NA	NA	1-M	2,418	135	NA
Inter Amer. Univ. of Puerto Rico, Bayamón Campus, Bayamón, PR 00957	1912	$5,616	NA	1-M	5,231	307	24.0
Inter Amer. Univ. of Puerto Rico, Fajardo Campus, Fajardo, PR 00738-7003	1965	$4,338	NA	1-M	2,192	114	NA
Inter Amer. Univ. of Puerto Rico, Guayama Campus, Guayama, PR 00785	1958	$4,558	NA	1-M	2,358	203	26.0
Inter Amer. Univ. of Puerto Rico, Metropolitan Campus, San Juan, PR 00919-1293	1960	$5,106	NA	1-D	10,093	599	25.0
Inter Amer. Univ. of Puerto Rico, Ponce Campus, Mercedita, PR 00715-1602	1962	$4,600	NA	1-M	6,341	347	NA
Inter Amer. Univ. of Puerto Rico, San Germán Campus, San Germán, PR 00683-5008	1912	$5,616	$2,500	1-D	5,621	326	NA
Intl. Acad. of Design & Tech., Chicago, IL 60602-9736	1977	$15,030	NA	3-B	1,832	113	15.0
Iona Coll., New Rochelle, NY 10801-1890	1940	$31,490	$12,488	2-M	4,065	372	57.0
Iowa State Univ. of Sci. & Tech., Ames, IA 50011	1858	$7,726(S)	$7,878	5-D	29,611	1,667	68.0

Name, address	Year founded	Tuition & fees	Room & board	Control, degree	Enroll-ment	Faculty	Grad. rate
Ithaca Coll., Ithaca, NY 14850	1892	$35,252	$12,854	1-D	6,760	701	74.0%
Jackson State Univ., Jackson, MS 39217	1877	$5,504(S)	$6,596	5-D	8,783	525	36.4
Jacksonville State Univ., Jacksonville, AL 36265-1602	1883	$7,650(S)	$5,778	5-D	9,490	484	32.0
Jacksonville Univ., Jacksonville, FL 32211	1934	$27,900	$9,168	1-M	3,715	318	40.0
James Madison Univ., Harrisonburg, VA 22807	1908	$8,448(S)	$8,340	5-D	19,722	1,400	81.0
Jefferson Coll. of Health Sci., Roanoke, VA 24031-3186	1982	$18,810	$4,700	1-M	1,032	128	69.0
John Brown Univ., Siloam Springs, AR 72761-2121	1919	$20,766	$7,562	2-M	2,018	123	66.0
John Carroll Univ., University Heights, OH 44118-4581	1886	$33,180	$9,610	2-M	3,664	353	71.0
John F. Kennedy Univ., Pleasant Hill, CA 94523-4817 (4)	1964	$15,120	NA	1-D	1,580	237	NA
John Jay Coll. of Criminal Justice of the City Univ. of New York, New York, NY 10019-1093	1964	$5,460(S)	NA	11-M	14,788	NA	38.0
The Johns Hopkins Univ., Baltimore, MD 21218-2699	1876	$42,280	$12,962	1-D	7,047	609	92.0
Johnson & Wales Univ., Denver, CO 80220	1993	$25,107	$10,314	1-B	1,532	87	53.0
Johnson & Wales Univ., North Miami, FL 33181	1992	$25,107	$9,261	1-B	2,098	90	51.0
Johnson & Wales Univ., Charlotte, NC 28202	2004	$25,107	$10,314	1-B	2,587	110	62.0
Johnson & Wales Univ., Providence, RI 02903-3703	1914	$25,107	$10,314	1-D	10,974	519	56.0
Johnson C. Smith Univ., Charlotte, NC 28216-5398	1867	$17,368	$6,752	1-B	1,543	144	37.0
Johnson State Coll., Johnson, VT 05656	1828	$9,672(S)	$8,444	5-M	1,884	137	35.0
Judson Univ., Elgin, IL 60123-1498	1963	$27,000	$8,990	2-M	1,124	200	48.4
The Juilliard Sch., New York, NY 10023-6588	1905	$32,180	$12,280	1-D	1,009	307	93.0
Juniata Coll., Huntingdon, PA 16652-2119	1876	$35,780	$9,800	2-B	1,619	147	72.0
Kalamazoo Coll., Kalamazoo, MI 49006-3295	1833	$35,820	$8,079	2-B	1,403	113	83.0
Kansas State Univ., Manhattan, KS 66506	1863	$7,657(S)	$7,198	5-D	23,863	1,154	56.0
Kean Univ., Union, NJ 07083	1855	$10,200(S)	$13,528	5-D	16,187	1,461	49.0
Keene State Coll., Keene, NH 03435	1909	$12,776(S)	$8,762	5-M	5,247	464	57.0
Kendall Coll., Chicago, IL 60201-2899	1934	$22,920	$9,900	3-B	2,545	209	37.0
Kennesaw State Univ., Kennesaw, GA 30144-5591	1963	$6,282(S)	$9,557	5-D	24,175	1,295	41.0
Kent State Univ., Kent, OH 44242-0001	1910	$9,346(S)	$8,830	5-D	27,855	1,592	50.0
Kent State Univ. at Geauga, Burton, OH 44021-9500	1964	$5,288(S)	NA	5-B	2,581	126	33.0
Kent State Univ. at Stark, Canton, OH 44720-7599	1967	$5,288(S)	NA	5-M	4,919	262	24.0
Kentucky State Univ., Frankfort, KY 40601	1886	$6,532(S)	$6,480	12-M	2,746	176	21.0
Kenyon Coll., Gambier, OH 43022-9623	1824	$44,420	$10,340	1-B	1,657	166	87.0
Kettering Univ., Flint, MI 48504 (2)	1919	$33,946	$6,660	1-M	2,079	154	58.0
Keuka Coll., Keuka Park, NY 14478-0098	1890	$25,100	$9,880	2-M	1,919	223	52.0
Keystone Coll., La Plume, PA 18440	1868	$19,620	$9,200	1-B	1,752	260	43.0
King Coll., Bristol, TN 37620-2699	1867	$24,052	$8,180	2-M	2,127	182	42.0
King's Coll., Wilkes-Barre, PA 18711-0801	1946	$27,680	$10,470	2-M	2,621	235	63.0
Knox Coll., Galesburg, IL 61401	1837	$36,492	$7,932	1-B	1,420	130	78.0
Kutztown Univ. of Pennsylvania, Kutztown, PA 19530-0730	1866	$8,359(S)	$8,536	5-M	10,283	461	54.0
Lafayette Coll., Easton, PA 18042-1798	1826	$40,658	$12,362	2-B	2,478	261	88.0
Lake Erie Coll., Painesville, OH 44077-3389	1856	$27,368	$8,336	1-M	1,146	116	49.0
Lake Forest Coll., Lake Forest, IL 60045	1857	$38,300	$9,050	1-M	1,516	161	68.0
Lakeland Coll., Sheboygan, WI 53082-0359	1862	$20,230	$7,360	2-M	3,932	71	42.0
Lake Superior State Univ., Sault Sainte Marie, MI 49783	1946	$9,439(S)	$8,319	5-M	2,806	184	35.0
Lamar Univ., Beaumont, TX 77710	1923	$8,496(S)	$7,682	5-D	14,021	592	30.0
Lander Univ., Greenwood, SC 29649-2099	1872	$9,504(S)	$6,740	5-M	2,614	222	43.8
Lane Coll., Jackson, TN 38301-4598	1882	$8,220	$5,800	2-B	2,002	102	31.0
Langston Univ., Langston, OK 73050	1897	$3,960(S)	$7,502	5-M	2,526	NA	NA
La Roche Coll., Pittsburgh, PA 15237-5898	1963	$23,160	$9,182	2-M	1,419	178	52.0
La Salle Univ., Philadelphia, PA 19141-1199	1863	$35,140	$11,680	2-D	6,685	441	67.0
Lasell Coll., Newton, MA 02466-2709	1851	$27,500	$12,300	1-M	1,750	202	47.0
La Sierra Univ., Riverside, CA 92515	1922	$28,335	$7,350	2-D	2,199	250	35.0
Lawrence Tech. Univ., Southfield, MI 48075-1058	1932	$26,278	$8,306	1-D	4,257	423	39.0
Lawrence Univ., Appleton, WI 54911	1847	$38,481	$7,890	1-B	1,496	201	76.0
Lebanon Valley Coll., Annville, PA 17003-1400	1866	$33,200	$8,800	2-D	2,102	227	73.0
Lee Univ., Cleveland, TN 37320-3450	1918	$12,680	$6,010	2-M	4,411	380	48.0
Lehigh Univ., Bethlehem, PA 18015-3094	1865	$40,960	$10,840	1-D	7,055	681	87.0
Lehman Coll. of the City Univ. of New York, Bronx, NY 10468-1589	1931	$5,508(S)	$8,085	11-M	12,287	912	40.0
Le Moyne Coll., Syracuse, NY 13214	1946	$29,460	$11,320	2-M	3,533	366	72.0
Lenoir-Rhyne Univ., Hickory, NC 28601	1891	$27,718	$9,796	2-M	1,860	178	47.0
Lesley Univ., Cambridge, MA 02138-2790 (4)	1909	$30,420	$13,250	1-D	5,564	258	62.0
LeTourneau Univ., Longview, TX 75607-7001	1946	$24,540	$8,940	2-M	2,950	NA	49.0
Lewis & Clark Coll., Portland, OR 97219-7899	1867	$40,330	$10,358	1-D	3,712	374	75.0
Lewis-Clark State Coll., Lewiston, ID 83501-2698	1893	$5,348(S)	NA	5-B	4,693	249	24.0
Lewis Univ., Romeoville, IL 60446	1932	$24,770	$8,900	2-D	6,394	655	62.0
Liberty Univ., Lynchburg, VA 24502	1971	$19,968	$7,050	2-D	12,577	NA	54.0
Life Univ., Marietta, GA 30060-2903	1974	$11,651	$12,854	1-D	2,609	172	20.0
LIM Coll., New York, NY 10022-5268 (4)	1939	$21,475	$19,875	3-M	1,388	170	60.0
Lincoln Christian Univ., Lincoln, IL 62656-2167	1944	$14,340	$6,679	2-M	1,086	111	50.0
Lincoln Memorial Univ., Harrogate, TN 37752-1901	1897	$17,720	$6,220	1-D	4,550	275	39.0
Lincoln Univ., Jefferson City, MO 65102	1866	$6,478(S)	$8,404	5-M	3,388	244	20.0
Lincoln Univ., Lincoln University, PA 19352	1854	$8,890(S)	$8,404	12-M	2,240	197	39.0
Lindenwood Univ., St. Charles, MO 63301-1695	1827	$14,000	$7,360	2-D	11,480	736	45.0
Lindsey Wilson Coll., Columbia, KY 42728	1903	$21,230	$8,230	2-M	2,600	233	26.0
Linfield Coll., McMinnville, OR 97128-6894	1849	$32,416	$9,090	2-B	1,727	194	72.0
Lipscomb Univ., Nashville, TN 37204-3951	1891	$24,654	$9,224	2-D	4,010	417	63.0
Lock Haven Univ. of Pennsylvania, Lock Haven, PA 17745-2390	1870	$8,239(S)	$7,056	5-M	5,366	250	46.0
Loma Linda Univ., Loma Linda, CA 92350	1905	NA	NA	2-D	4,270	840	NA
Long Island Univ.–Brooklyn Campus, Brooklyn, NY 11201-8423	1926	$29,650	$11,940	1-D	8,633	789	20.0
Long Island Univ.–C. W. Post Campus, Brookville, NY 11548-1300	1954	$31,646	$11,840	1-D	11,287	822	43.0
Longwood Univ., Farmville, VA 23909	1839	$10,530(S)	$8,114	5-M	4,860	300	60.0
Loras Coll., Dubuque, IA 52004-0178	1839	$28,167	$7,825	2-M	1,555	141	58.0
Louisiana Coll., Pineville, LA 71359-0001	1906	$13,280	$4,448	2-M	1,557	115	46.0
Louisiana State Univ. & Agr. & Mech. Coll., Baton Rouge, LA 70803	1860	$6,354(S)	$8,670	5-D	29,718	1,366	62.0
Louisiana State Univ. at Alexandria, Alexandria, LA 71302-9121	1960	$3,817(S)	NA	5-B	2,675	NA	NA
Louisiana State Univ. Health Sci. Ctr., New Orleans, LA 70112-2223	1931	$4,356(S)	$6,396	5-D	2,644	893	NA
Louisiana State Univ. in Shreveport, Shreveport, LA 71115-2399	1965	$4,674(S)	$6,228	5-M	4,562	193	29.0
Louisiana Tech. Univ., Ruston, LA 71272	1894	$5,955(S)	$5,289	5-D	11,264	476	46.0
Lourdes Univ., Sylvania, OH 43560-2898	1958	$16,470	$7,200	2-M	2,538	257	35.0
Loyola Marymount Univ., Los Angeles, CA 90045-2659	1911	$37,605	$14,200	2-D	9,352	1,095	77.0
Loyola Univ. Chicago, Chicago, IL 60660	1870	$34,578	$12,010	2-D	16,040	1,367	70.0
Loyola Univ. Maryland, Baltimore, MD 21210-2699	1852	$42,430	$12,120	2-D	6,080	531	83.0
Loyola Univ. New Orleans, New Orleans, LA 70118-6195	1912	$34,952	$11,629	2-D	5,008	481	NA
Lubbock Christian Univ., Lubbock, TX 79407-2099	1957	$16,870	$6,446	2-M	2,038	179	48.0
Luther Coll., Decorah, IA 52101	1861	$36,100	$6,220	2-B	2,471	257	69.0
Luther Rice Univ., Lithonia, GA 30038-2454	1962	$5,376	NA	2-M	1,047	NA	NA
Lycoming Coll., Williamsport, PA 17701-5192	1812	$32,756	$9,420	2-B	1,369	119	70.0

Name, address	Year founded	Tuition & fees	Room & board	Control, degree	Enroll-ment	Faculty	Grad. rate
Lynchburg Coll., Lynchburg, VA 24501-3199	1903	$30,805	$8,380	2-D	2,828	294	52.0%
Lyndon State Coll., Lyndonville, VT 05851-0919	1911	$9,948(S)	$8,446	5-M	1,436	160	39.0
Lynn Univ., Boca Raton, FL 33431-5598	1962	$32,600	$10,900	1-D	2,102	170	42.0
Macalester Coll., St. Paul, MN 55105-1899	1874	$43,693	$9,726	2-B	2,005	233	87.0
Macon State Coll., Macon, GA 31206	1968	$3,644(S)	$6,750	5-B	5,702	289	NA
Madonna Univ., Livonia, MI 48150-1173	1947	$14,700	$7,430	2-D	4,416	420	49.7
Maharishi Univ. of Mgmt., Fairfield, IA 52557	1971	$26,430	$7,400	1-D	1,134	98	72.0
Malone Univ., Canton, OH 44709	1892	$23,420	$8,090	2-M	2,428	235	58.0
Manchester Coll., North Manchester, IN 46962-1225	1889	$25,970	$9,100	2-M	1,320	103	53.0
Manhattan Coll., Riverdale, NY 10471	1853	$32,775	$12,220	2-M	3,657	401	73.0
Manhattanville Coll., Purchase, NY 10577-2132	1841	$35,370	$14,340	1-D	2,796	340	56.0
Mansfield Univ. of Pennsylvania, Mansfield, PA 16933.	1857	$8,654(S)	$8,078	5-M	3,275	178	54.0
Maranatha Baptist Bible Coll., Watertown, WI 53094	1968	$12,260	$6,290	2-M	1,019	76	51.0
Marian Univ., Indianapolis, IN 46222-1997.	1851	$26,000	$8,084	2-M	2,287	202	50.0
Marian Univ., Fond du Lac, WI 54935-4699	1936	$22,440	$5,900	2-D	2,615	277	52.0
Marietta Coll., Marietta, OH 45750-4000	1835	$29,690	$9,090	1-M	1,615	147	51.0
Marist Coll., Poughkeepsie, NY 12601-1387	1929	$28,800	$12,100	1-M	6,303	611	80.0
Marquette Univ., Milwaukee, WI 53201-1881	1881	$33,244	$10,420	2-D	12,002	1,128	81.0
Marshall Univ., Huntington, WV 25755.	1837	$5,648(S)	$8,710	5-D	13,966	760	46.0
Mars Hill Coll., Mars Hill, NC 28754	1856	$23,318	$8,082	2-M	1,295	135	39.0
Martin Univ., Indianapolis, IN 46218-3867	1977	NA	NA	1-M	1,236	43	13.0
Mary Baldwin Coll., Staunton, VA 24401-3610 (4)	1842	$26,960	$7,790	1-M	1,789	136	47.0
Marygrove Coll., Detroit, MI 48221-2599 (4).	1905	$17,840	$7,600	2-M	2,953	64	34.0
Maryland Inst. Coll. of Art, Baltimore, MD 21217	1826	$39,340	$10,880	1-M	2,139	369	71.0
Marylhurst Univ., Marylhurst, OR 97036-0261 (4)	1893	$18,405	NA	2-M	1,722	263	NA
Marymount Manhattan Coll., New York, NY 10021-4597	1936	$24,708	$14,030	1-B	1,953	318	40.0
Marymount Univ., Arlington, VA 22207-4299	1950	$25,178	$11,000	2-D	3,633	346	57.0
Maryville Coll., Maryville, TN 37804-5907	1819	$30,522	$9,696	2-B	1,078	107	53.0
Maryville Univ. of St. Louis, St. Louis, MO 63141-7299	1872	$22,882	$8,892	1-D	3,846	421	66.0
Marywood Univ., Scranton, PA 18509-1598.	1915	$28,175	$12,520	2-D	3,479	398	63.0
Massachusetts Coll. of Art & Design, Boston, MA 02115-5882	1873	$9,700(S)	$12,150	5-M	2,422	281	68.0
Massachusetts Coll. of Liberal Arts, North Adams, MA 01247-4100	1894	$8,075(S)	$8,658	5-M	1,886	171	53.0
Massachusetts Coll. of Pharm. & Health Sci., Boston, MA 02115-5896.	1823	$26,455	$12,825	1-D	5,334	212	69.0
Massachusetts Inst. of Tech., Cambridge, MA 02139-4307	1861	$40,732	$11,775	1-D	10,894	1,432	93.0
Massachusetts Maritime Academy, Buzzards Bay, MA 02532-1803 (2)	1891	$6,867(S)	$9,700	5-M	1,368	137	66.0
The Master's Coll. & Sem., Santa Clarita, CA 91321-1200	1927	$28,080	$9,010	2-D	1,575	195	60.0
McDaniel Coll., Westminster, MD 21157-4390	1867	$35,800	$7,740	1-M	3,374	356	73.0
McKendree Univ., Lebanon, IL 62254-1299	1828	$24,190	$8,430	2-D	3,308	316	53.0
McMurry Univ., Abilene, TX 79601	1923	$21,870	$7,214	2-B	1,469	119	36.0
McNeese State Univ., Lake Charles, LA 70609	1939	$4,400(S)	$7,198	5-M	8,791	434	35.0
Medaille Coll., Buffalo, NY 14214-2695	1875	$21,598	$10,244	1-M	2,679	277	NA
Medgar Evers Coll. of the City Univ. of New York, Brooklyn, NY 11225-2298.	1969	$5,432(S)	NA	11-B	6,966	498	13.0
Med. Univ. of South Carolina, Charleston, SC 29425	1824	$15,158(S)	NA	5-D	2,679	223	NA
Mercer Univ., Macon, GA 31207-0003	1833	$31,548	$10,408	2-D	6,231	677	61.0
Mercy Coll., Dobbs Ferry, NY 10522-1189	1951	$17,556	$12,184	1-D	11,539	1,047	32.0
Mercy Coll. of Ohio, Toledo, OH 43604 (4)	1993	$10,624	NA	2-B	1,210	159	17.0
Mercyhurst Coll., Erie, PA 16546	1926	$27,657	$11,139	2-M	4,298	339	67.0
Meredith Coll., Raleigh, NC 27607-5298	1891	$27,770	$7,950	1-M	1,980	207	59.0
Merrimack Coll., North Andover, MA 01845-5800	1947	$32,865	$11,350	2-M	2,453	271	69.0
Messiah Coll., Mechanicsburg, PA 17055	1909	$29,460	$8,760	2-M	2,976	288	74.0
Methodist Univ., Fayetteville, NC 28311-1498	1956	$25,625	$9,521	2-M	2,416	213	44.0
Metropolitan Coll. of New York, New York, NY 10013 (4)	1964	$16,720	NA	1-M	1,084	183	40.0
Metropolitan State Coll. of Denver, Denver, CO 80217-3362	1963	$4,834(S)	NA	5-M	23,789	1,414	21.0
Metropolitan State Univ., St. Paul, MN 55106-5000	1971	$6,341(S)	NA	5-D	8,170	NA	NA
Miami Univ., Oxford, OH 45056	1809	$13,213(S)	$10,640	12-D	17,395	1,134	81.0
Miami Univ. Hamilton, Hamilton, OH 45011-3399	1968	$4,632(S)	NA	5-M	4,194	224	NA
Michigan State Univ., East Lansing, MI 48824	1855	$12,203(S)	$8,154	5-D	47,954	2,937	77.0
Michigan Tech. Univ., Houghton, MI 49931	1885	$12,853(S)	$8,648	5-D	7,034	469	65.0
MidAmerica Nazarene Univ., Olathe, KS 66062-1899	1966	$21,500	$7,000	2-M	1,848	264	44.0
Mid-Continent Univ., Mayfield, KY 42066-9007	1949	$13,350	$6,800	2-M	2,472	199	28.0
Middlebury Coll., Middlebury, VT 05753-6002	1800	$53,800(C)	NA	1-D	2,507	323	90.0
Middle Tennessee State Univ., Murfreesboro, TN 37132	1911	$7,018(S)	$8,843	5-D	26,442	NA	NA
Midland Coll., Midland, TX 79705-6399	1969	$2,160(A)	$4,571	11-B	6,067	276	NA
Midway Coll., Midway, KY 40347-1120 (4)	1847	$19,800	$7,640	2-D	1,600	118	38.0
Midwestern State Univ., Wichita Falls, TX 76308	1922	$7,238(S)	$6,350	5-M	6,181	337	35.0
Miles Coll., Fairfield, AL 35064	1905	$10,490	$5,306	2-B	1,738	147	NA
Millersville Univ. of Pennsylvania, Millersville, PA 17551-0302	1855	$8,361(S)	$8,732	5-M	8,725	431	65.0
Milligan Coll., Milligan College, TN 37682	1866	$25,260	$5,650	2-M	1,208	134	65.0
Millikin Univ., Decatur, IL 62522-2084	1901	$28,644	$8,970	2-M	2,341	302	65.0
Mills Coll., Oakland, CA 94613-1000	1852	$40,080	$11,580	1-D	1,548	203	57.0
Milwaukee Sch. of Engr., Milwaukee, WI 53202-3109 (2).	1903	$31,920	$8,028	1-M	2,486	243	57.0
Minnesota Sch. of Bus.–Blaine, Blaine, MN 55449 (4)	1877	$16,760	NA	3-B	1,012	132	NA
Minnesota State Univ. Mankato, Mankato, MN 56001	1868	$7,148(S)	$6,470	5-D	15,616	761	51.0
Minnesota State Univ. Moorhead, Moorhead, MN 56563-0002	1885	$7,378(S)	$6,726	5-D	7,254	462	44.0
Minot State Univ., Minot, ND 58707-0002	1913	$5,762(S)	$5,762	5-M	3,657	304	34.0
Misericordia Univ., Dallas, PA 18612-1098 (4)	1924	$25,990	$10,760	2-D	2,830	316	64.0
Mississippi Coll., Clinton, MS 39058.	1826	$14,430	$6,950	2-D	5,218	457	51.0
Mississippi State Univ., Mississippi State, MS 39762	1878	$5,805(S)	$8,162	5-D	20,424	963	60.0
Mississippi Univ. for Women, Columbus, MS 39701-9998 (4)	1884	$5,120(S)	$5,668	5-M	2,661	202	39.0
Mississippi Valley State Univ., Itta Bena, MS 38941-1400	1946	$5,382(S)	$6,200	5-M	2,452	160	24.0
Missouri Baptist Univ., St. Louis, MO 63141-8660	1964	$20,654	$8,230	2-D	5,186	300	37.0
Missouri Southern State Univ., Joplin, MO 64801-1595.	1937	$5,090(S)	$5,976	5-M	5,591	306	NA
Missouri State Univ., Springfield, MO 65897	1905	$6,598(S)	$6,580	5-D	20,276	1,031	56.0
Missouri Univ. of Sci. & Tech., Rolla, MO 65409 (2)	1870	$9,093(S)	$8,520	5-D	8,522	455	67.0
Missouri Valley Coll., Marshall, MO 65340-3197	1889	$17,780	$6,700	2-B	1,639	90	23.0
Missouri Western State Univ., St. Joseph, MO 64507-2294	1915	$6,041(S)	$6,796	5-M	6,260	383	26.0
Molloy Coll., Rockville Centre, NY 11571-5002	1955	$23,300	$12,880	1-D	4,434	653	63.0
Monmouth Coll., Monmouth, IL 61462-1998	1853	$895/cr. hr.	NA	2-B	1,316	121	56.0
Monmouth Univ., West Long Branch, NJ 07764-1898	1933	$28,000	$10,459	1-D	6,568	603	66.0
Monroe Coll., Bronx, NY 10468-5407.	1933	$11,400	$8,150	3-M	5,068	251	66.0
Monroe Coll., New Rochelle, NY 10801	1983	$11,400	$8,150	3-M	2,222	93	75.0
Montana State Univ., Bozeman, MT 59717	1893	$6,472(S)	$7,840	5-D	14,153	880	51.0
Montana State Univ. Billings, Billings, MT 59101-0298.	1927	$5,470(S)	$5,960	5-M	5,274	343	33.0
Montana State Univ.–Northern, Havre, MT 59501-7751	1929	$5,070(S)	$6,275	5-M	1,273	96	30.0
Montana Tech. of The Univ. of Montana, Butte, MT 59701-8997	1895	$6,420(S)	$7,266	5-M	2,803	212	41.0
Montclair State Univ., Montclair, NJ 07043-1624	1908	$10,646(S)	$11,264	5-D	18,171	1,489	62.0

Name, address	Year founded	Tuition & fees	Room & board	Control, degree	Enroll-ment	Faculty	Grad. rate
Moody Bible Inst., Chicago, IL 60610-3284	1886	$10,008	$8,240	2-M	3,349	211	NA
Moravian Coll., Bethlehem, PA 18018-6650	1742	$33,446	$9,623	2-M	2,003	192	76.0%
Morehead State Univ., Morehead, KY 40351	1922	$6,942(S)	$7,014	5-M	10,968	462	40.0
Morehouse Coll., Atlanta, GA 30314 (1)	1867	$23,792	$12,184	1-B	2,438	214	55.0
Morgan State Univ., Baltimore, MD 21251	1867	$6,928(S)	$8,750	5-D	7,005	558	100.0
Morningside Coll., Sioux City, IA 51106	1894	$24,050	$7,320	2-M	2,047	184	57.0
Morrisville State Coll., Morrisville, NY 13408-0901	1908	$6,472(S)	$9,980	5-B	3,432	261	NA
Mountain State Univ., Beckley, WV 25802-9003	1933	$9,600	$7,030	1-D	4,743	457	10.0
Mount Aloysius Coll., Cresson, PA 16630-1999	1939	$18,750	$8,120	2-M	1,692	180	36.0
Mount Holyoke Coll., South Hadley, MA 01075 (3)	1837	$41,456	$12,140	1-M	2,362	283	85.0
Mount Ida Coll., Newton, MA 02459-3310	1899	$26,929	$12,500	1-M	1,481	189	38.0
Mount Marty Coll., Yankton, SD 57078-3724	1936	$20,656	$5,918	2-M	1,242	59	51.0
Mount Mary Coll., Milwaukee, WI 53222-4597	1913	$23,000	$7,498	2-D	1,738	213	37.0
Mount Mercy Univ., Cedar Rapids, IA 52402-4797	1928	$24,360	$7,470	2-M	1,824	151	60.0
Mount Olive Coll., Mount Olive, NC 28365	1951	$16,300	$6,500	2-B	3,855	183	44.0
Mount St. Mary Coll., Newburgh, NY 12550-3494	1960	$25,340	$12,810	1-M	2,710	276	55.0
Mount St. Mary's Coll., Los Angeles, CA 90049-1599 (4)	1925	$32,894	$10,530	2-D	2,941	359	62.0
Mount St. Mary's Univ., Emmitsburg, MD 21727-7799	1808	$32,954	$11,018	2-M	2,305	181	76.0
Mount Vernon Nazarene Univ., Mount Vernon, OH 43050-9500	1964	$22,890	$6,700	2-M	2,574	241	57.0
Muhlenberg Coll., Allentown, PA 18104-5586	1848	$39,915	$9,505	2-B	2,483	275	86.0
Murray State Univ., Murray, KY 42071	1922	$6,840(S)	$7,638	5-D	10,623	582	52.0
Musicians Inst., Hollywood, CA 90028	1976	$30,420	NA	3-B	1,337	204	NA
Muskingum Univ., New Concord, OH 43762	1837	$21,610	$8,540	2-M	2,099	NA	NA
Naropa Univ., Boulder, CO 80302-6697	1974	$26,390	$8,442	1-M	1,094	175	42.0
Natl. Louis Univ., Chicago, IL 60603	1886	$18,975	NA	1-D	5,737	521	20.0
Natl. Univ., La Jolla, CA 92037-1011	1971	$11,436	NA	1-M	19,281	2,914	38.0
Natl. Univ. Coll., Bayamón, PR 00960	1983	$6,315	NA	13-B	2,703	NA	NA
Nazareth Coll. of Rochester, Rochester, NY 14618-3790	1924	$27,222	$11,144	1-D	3,108	493	74.0
Nebraska Wesleyan Univ., Lincoln, NE 68504-2796	1887	$24,656	$6,672	2-M	2,070	160	65.0
Neumann Univ., Aston, PA 19014-1298	1965	$23,350	$10,644	2-D	3,087	321	55.0
Nevada State Coll. at Henderson, Henderson, NV 89015	2002	$3,563(S)	NA	5-B	2,988	94	17.0
Newberry Coll., Newberry, SC 29108-2197	1856	$23,575	$8,684	2-B	1,110	99	48.0
Newbury Coll., Brookline, MA 02445	1962	$26,600	$12,150	1-B	1,024	111	46.0
New England Coll., Henniker, NH 03242-3293	1946	$30,400	$11,954	1-D	1,668	164	39.0
New England Inst. of Tech., Warwick, RI 02886-2244	1940	$19,980	NA	1-M	2,933	198	NA
New Jersey City Univ., Jersey City, NJ 07305-1597	1927	$236/cr. hr.(S)	NA	5-M	8,328	694	39.0
New Jersey Inst. of Tech., Newark, NJ 07102	1881	$13,974(S)	$10,486	5-D	8,934	654	55.0
Newman Univ., Wichita, KS 67213-2097	1933	$22,298	$6,390	2-M	3,021	264	32.0
New Mexico Highlands Univ., Las Vegas, NM 87701	1893	$3,264(S)	$7,873	5-M	3,781	298	21.0
New Mexico Inst. of Mining & Tech., Socorro, NM 87801	1889	$5,301(S)	$6,108	5-D	2,009	178	47.0
New Mexico State Univ., Las Cruces, NM 88003-8001	1888	$5,827(S)	$6,620	5-D	18,024	975	47.0
New Orleans Baptist Theol. Sem., New Orleans, LA 70126-4858 (2)	1917	NA	NA	2-D	2,036	NA	NA
The New Sch. for General Studies, New York, NY 10011-8603	1919	$24,630	$14,910	1-M	1,958	385	NA
New York City Coll. of Tech. of the City Univ. of New York, Brooklyn, NY 11201-2983	1946	$5,469(S)	NA	11-B	15,961	1,230	23.0
New York Inst. of Tech., Old Westbury, NY 11568-8000	1955	$27,290	$12,674	1-D	8,306	1,260	48.0
New York Univ., New York, NY 10012-1019	1831	$41,606	$15,182	1-D	43,911	6,120	86.0
Niagara Univ., Niagara University, NY 14109	1856	$26,400	$11,000	2-D	4,182	350	65.0
Nicholls State Univ., Thibodaux, LA 70310	1948	$6,024(S)	$8,580	5-M	6,774	262	39.0
Nichols Coll., Dudley, MA 01571-5000	1815	$31,740	$10,700	1-M	1,547	80	38.0
Norfolk State Univ., Norfolk, VA 23504	1935	$6,700(S)	$7,927	5-D	7,063	379	33.0
North Carolina Agr. & Tech. State Univ., Greensboro, NC 27411	1891	$4,678(S)	$7,225	5-D	10,881	674	43.0
North Carolina Central Univ., Durham, NC 27707-3129	1910	$5,689(S)	$9,421	5-D	8,359	608	44.0
North Carolina State Univ., Raleigh, NC 27695	1887	$7,018(S)	$8,536	5-D	34,767	1,881	73.0
North Carolina Wesleyan Coll., Rocky Mount, NC 27804-8677	1956	$26,210	$8,426	2-B	1,402	189	22.0
North Central Coll., Naperville, IL 60566-7063	1861	$29,733	$8,610	2-M	2,989	247	64.0
Northcentral Univ., Prescott Valley, AZ 86314	1996	$9,520	NA	3-D	9,683	633	NA
North Central Univ., Minneapolis, MN 55404-1322	1930	$16,546	$5,610	2-B	1,125	102	37.0
North Dakota State Univ., Fargo, ND 58108	1890	$7,175(S)	$6,722	5-D	14,399	812	53.0
Northeastern Illinois Univ., Chicago, IL 60625-4699	1961	$9,849(S)	NA	5-M	11,746	718	20.0
Northeastern State Univ., Tahlequah, OK 74464-2399	1846	$4,602(S)	$5,220	5-D	9,361	513	26.0
Northeastern Univ., Boston, MA 02115-5096	1898	$38,252	$13,220	1-D	23,706	1,530	77.0
Northern Arizona Univ., Flagstaff, AZ 86011	1899	$8,830(S)	$8,474	5-D	25,364	1,496	52.0
Northern Illinois Univ., De Kalb, IL 60115-2854	1895	$11,025(S)	$10,420	5-D	22,990	1,145	51.0
Northern Kentucky Univ., Highland Heights, KY 41099	1968	$7,584(S)	$7,152	5-D	15,724	1,018	37.0
Northern Michigan Univ., Marquette, MI 49855-5301	1899	$8,414(S)	$8,174	5-M	9,252	496	51.0
Northern State Univ., Aberdeen, SD 57401-7198	1901	$6,951(S)	$6,059	5-M	3,205	90	46.0
North Georgia Coll. & State Univ., Dahlonega, GA 30597	1873	$6,452(S)	$6,550	5-D	6,067	372	49.0
North Greenville Univ., Tigerville, SC 29688-1892	1892	$13,936	$8,164	2-D	2,433	190	47.0
North Park Univ., Chicago, IL 60625-4895	1891	$20,990	$7,870	2-D	2,181	NA	NA
Northwestern Coll., Orange City, IA 51041-1996	1882	$25,740	$7,770	2-B	1,211	134	66.0
Northwestern Coll., St. Paul, MN 55113-1598	1902	$26,960	$8,210	2-M	2,299	198	66.0
Northwestern Oklahoma State Univ., Alva, OK 73717-2799	1897	$4,591(S)	$3,700	5-M	2,294	166	34.0
Northwestern State Univ. of Louisiana, Natchitoches, LA 71497	1884	$4,972(S)	$7,350	5-M	9,191	517	40.0
Northwestern Univ., Evanston, IL 60208	1851	$41,983	$12,780	1-D	18,431	1,153	93.0
Northwest Missouri State Univ., Maryville, MO 64468-6001	1905	$7,435(S)	$8,272	5-M	7,225	324	50.0
Northwest Nazarene Univ., Nampa, ID 83686-5897	1913	$25,090	$6,400	2-M	2,077	110	NA
Northwest Univ., Kirkland, WA 98033	1934	$23,470	$6,884	2-D	1,549	108	51.8
Northwood Univ., Michigan Campus, Midland, MI 48640-2398	1959	$20,996	$8,770	1-M	1,976	131	53.0
Norwich Univ., Northfield, VT 05663 (2)	1819	$31,782	$10,976	1-M	3,348	205	55.0
Notre Dame Coll., South Euclid, OH 44121-4293	1922	$24,652	$8,054	2-M	1,393	118	NA
Notre Dame de Namur Univ., Belmont, CA 94002-1908	1851	$30,522	$11,970	2-M	1,967	202	51.0
Notre Dame of Maryland Univ., Baltimore, MD 21210-2476 (4)	1873	$30,850	$10,150	2-D	2,731	121	60.0
Nova Southeastern Univ., Fort Lauderdale, FL 33314-7796	1964	$24,500	$9,516	1-D	28,457	1,737	43.0
Nyack Coll., Nyack, NY 10960-3698	1882	$22,500	$8,400	2-D	3,263	305	NA
Oakland City Univ., Oakland City, IN 47660-1099	1885	$16,640	$7,700	2-D	2,550	178	60.0
Oakland Univ., Rochester, MI 48309-4401	1957	$9,938(S)	$7,986	5-D	19,379	1,085	40.0
Oakwood Univ., Huntsville, AL 35896	1896	$14,822	$8,303	2-M	1,824	171	46.0
Oberlin Coll., Oberlin, OH 44074	1833	$43,210	$11,550	1-M	2,974	285	86.0
Occidental Coll., Los Angeles, CA 90041-3314	1887	$44,540	$12,450	1-M	2,132	265	84.0
Oglala Lakota Coll., Kyle, SD 57752-0490	1970	NA	NA	11-M	1,000	NA	NA
Oglethorpe Univ., Atlanta, GA 30319-2797	1835	$29,150	$10,440	1-M	1,144	102	48.0
Ohio Dominican Univ., Columbus, OH 43219-2099	1911	$26,790	$9,090	2-M	3,052	170	44.0
Ohio Northern Univ., Ada, OH 45810-1599	1871	$35,678	$10,220	2-D	3,611	308	65.0
The Ohio State Univ., Columbus, OH 43210	1870	$9,735(S)	$9,180	5-D	56,064	4,632	78.0
The Ohio State Univ. at Lima, Lima, OH 45804	1960	$7,329(S)	NA	5-M	1,306	87	45.0

Name, address	Year founded	Tuition & fees	Room & board	Control, degree	Enroll- ment	Faculty	Grad. rate
The Ohio State Univ. at Marion, Marion, OH 43302-5695	1958	$6,903(S)	NA	5-M	1,521	101	37.0%
The Ohio State Univ.–Mansfield Campus, Mansfield, OH 44906-1599	1958	$6,903(S)	$7,589	5-M	1,388	95	39.0
The Ohio State Univ.–Newark Campus, Newark, OH 43055-1797	1957	$6,903(S)	$7,185	5-M	2,677	140	38.0
Ohio Univ., Athens, OH 45701-2979	1804	$9,936(S)	$9,753	5-D	26,201	1,163	65.0
Ohio Univ.–Chillicothe, Chillicothe, OH 45601	1946	$3,060(S)	NA	5-M	2,350	NA	NA
Ohio Univ.–Lancaster, Lancaster, OH 43130-1097	1968	$3,060(S)	NA	5-M	1,728	NA	NA
Ohio Univ.–Southern Campus, Ironton, OH 45638-2214	1956	$2,930(S)	NA	5-M	1,836	NA	NA
Ohio Univ.–Zanesville, Zanesville, OH 43701-2695	1946	$4,728(S)	NA	5-B	2,106	130	NA
Ohio Wesleyan Univ., Delaware, OH 43015	1842	$37,820	$9,784	2-B	1,829	220	61.0
Oklahoma Baptist Univ., Shawnee, OK 74804	1910	$19,756	$6,000	2-M	1,764	163	54.0
Oklahoma Christian Univ., Oklahoma City, OK 73136-1100	1950	$18,800	$6,175	2-M	2,194	207	48.0
Oklahoma City Univ., Oklahoma City, OK 73106-1402	1904	$28,190	$9,170	2-D	3,546	343	60.0
Oklahoma Panhandle State Univ., Goodwell, OK 73939-0430	1909	$5,344(S)	$3,652	5-B	1,387	91	38.0
Oklahoma State Univ., Stillwater, OK 74078	1890	$4,304(S)	$6,680	5-D	24,231	1,300	62.0
Oklahoma Wesleyan Univ., Bartlesville, OK 74006-6299	1909	$21,140	$7,240	2-M	1,178	168	45.0
Old Dominion Univ., Norfolk, VA 23529	1930	$8,144(S)	$8,796	5-D	24,753	1,246	50.0
Olivet Coll., Olivet, MI 49076-9701	1844	$21,118	$7,000	2-M	1,049	NA	NA
Olivet Nazarene Univ., Bourbonnais, IL 60914	1907	$27,590	$6,400	2-M	4,636	NA	NA
Oral Roberts Univ., Tulsa, OK 74171	1963	$20,756	$8,594	2-D	3,259	263	NA
Oregon Health & Sci. Univ., Portland, OR 97239-3098	1974	$18,996(S)	NA	12-D	2,802	2,129	NA
Oregon Inst. of Tech., Klamath Falls, OR 97601-8801	1947	$7,260(S)	$8,145	5-M	3,911	257	45.0
Oregon State Univ., Corvallis, OR 97331	1868	$7,600(S)	$10,464	5-D	23,761	980	60.0
Otis Coll. of Art & Design, Los Angeles, CA 90045-9785	1918	$35,354	NA	1-M	1,209	420	52.0
Otterbein Univ., Westerville, OH 43081	1847	$29,550	$8,252	2-D	2,997	337	62.0
Ouachita Baptist Univ., Arkadelphia, AR 71998-0001	1886	$20,630	$6,040	2-B	1,594	158	62.0
Our Lady of Holy Cross Coll., New Orleans, LA 70131-7399	1916	$9,170	NA	2-M	1,298	NA	NA
Our Lady of the Lake Coll., Baton Rouge, LA 70808 (4)	1990	$8,664	NA	2-M	1,748	183	67.0
Our Lady of the Lake Univ. of San Antonio, San Antonio, TX 78207-4689	1895	$22,756	$7,326	2-D	2,751	249	32.0
Pace Univ., New York, NY 10038	1906	$35,032	$12,110	1-D	12,593	1,279	56.0
Pacific Lutheran Univ., Tacoma, WA 98447	1890	$32,800	$9,620	2-M	3,461	251	66.0
Pacific Oaks Coll., Pasadena, CA 91103 (4)	1945	$22,064	NA	1-M	1,028	125	NA
Pacific Union Coll., Angwin, CA 94508-9707	1882	$26,040	$7,350	2-M	1,530	130	45.0
Pacific Univ., Forest Grove, OR 97116-1797	1849	$33,612	$9,208	1-D	3,293	NA	61.0
Palm Beach Atlantic Univ., West Palm Beach, FL 33416-4708	1968	$24,100	$8,212	2-D	3,663	343	58.0
Palmer Coll. of Chiropractic, Davenport, IA 52803-5287	1897	$186/cr. hr.	NA	1-D	2,310	15	NA
Park Univ., Parkville, MO 64152-3795	1875	$9,340	$6,510	1-M	2,403	168	39.0
Parsons The New Sch. for Design, New York, NY 10011-8878	1896	$37,430	$14,910	1-M	4,746	1,104	71.0
Patten Univ., Oakland, CA 94601-2699	1944	$13,440	$7,380	2-M	1,050	125	37.0
Peirce Coll., Philadelphia, PA 19102-4699 (4)	1865	$15,900	NA	1-B	2,276	158	27.0
Penn State Abington, Abington, PA 19001	1950	$13,102(S)	NA	12-B	3,425	230	44.0
Penn State Altoona, Altoona, PA 16601-3760	1939	$13,636(S)	$8,940	12-B	4,105	299	65.0
Penn State Berks, Reading, PA 19610-6009	1924	$13,636(S)	$9,770	12-B	2,873	217	55.0
Penn State Erie, The Behrend Coll., Erie, PA 16563-0001	1948	$13,636(S)	$8,940	12-M	4,226	302	66.0
Penn State Harrisburg, Middletown, PA 17057-4898	1966	$13,628(S)	$10,210	12-D	4,269	321	63.0
Penn State Univ. Park, University Park, PA 16802-1503	1855	$15,984(S)	$9,420	12-D	45,628	2,880	87.0
Pennsylvania Coll. of Tech., Williamsport, PA 17701-5778	1965	$13,590(S)	$9,766	12-B	5,976	480	NA
Pepperdine Univ., Malibu, CA 90263	1937	$40,752	$11,844	2-D	7,539	695	81.0
Peru State Coll., Peru, NE 68421	1867	$5,371(S)	$5,820	5-M	2,358	109	NA
Pfeiffer Univ., Misenheimer, NC 28109-0960	1885	$21,650	$8,720	2-M	2,019	150	59.0
Philadelphia Biblical Univ., Langhorne, PA 19047-2990	1913	$21,705	$8,525	2-M	1,206	128	63.0
Philadelphia Univ., Philadelphia, PA 19144	1884	$30,446	$9,834	1-D	3,579	499	58.0
Piedmont Coll., Demorest, GA 30535-0010	1897	$19,000	$7,500	2-D	2,825	274	47.0
Pittsburg State Univ., Pittsburg, KS 66762	1903	$5,162(S)	$6,288	5-M	7,275	417	49.0
Pitzer Coll., Claremont, CA 91711-6101	1963	$41,130	$11,950	1-B	1,099	116	81.0
Plymouth State Univ., Plymouth, NH 03264-1595	1871	$11,518(S)	$9,290	5-D	5,903	418	59.0
Point Loma Nazarene Univ., San Diego, CA 92106-2899	1902	$29,510	$9,550	2-M	3,317	NA	73.0
Point Park Univ., Pittsburgh, PA 15222-1984	1960	$23,720	$9,720	1-M	3,920	433	50.0
Point Univ., East Point, GA 30344-1999	1937	$16,226	$5,980	2-B	1,288	114	35.0
Polytechnic Inst. of New York Univ., Brooklyn, NY 11201-2990	1854	$37,882	$10,080	1-D	4,487	369	54.0
Polytechnic Univ. of Puerto Rico, Hato Rey, PR 00919 (2)	1966	$7,263	$11,704	1-M	5,046	265	22.0
Pomona Coll., Claremont, CA 91711	1887	$39,883	$13,227	1-B	1,586	226	95.0
Pontifical Catholic Univ. of Puerto Rico, Ponce, PR 00717-0777	1948	$5,468	$1,300	2-D	7,682	385	39.0
Portland State Univ., Portland, OR 97207-0751	1946	$7,764(S)	$10,368	5-D	28,584	1,581	35.0
Prairie View A&M Univ., Prairie View, TX 77446-0519	1878	$7,402(S)	$7,337	5-D	8,425	457	32.0
Pratt Inst., Brooklyn, NY 11205-3899	1887	$41,092	$10,506	1-M	4,722	1,005	62.0
Presbyterian Coll., Clinton, SC 29325	1880	$31,130	$8,670	2-D	1,359	136	68.0
Prescott Coll., Prescott, AZ 86301	1966	$28,019	$3,400	1-D	1,134	90	29.0
Princeton Univ., Princeton, NJ 08544-1019	1746	$39,515	$12,630	1-D	7,859	1,082	96.1
Providence Coll., Providence, RI 02918	1917	$40,975	$12,140	2-M	4,448	401	85.0
Purchase Coll., State Univ. of New York, Purchase, NY 10577-1400	1967	$6,829(S)	$11,058	5-M	4,268	388	57.0
Purdue Univ., West Lafayette, IN 47907	1869	$10,063(S)	$9,794	5-D	39,637	2,325	69.0
Purdue Univ. Calumet, Hammond, IN 46323-2094	1951	$6,821(S)	$7,515	5-M	9,786	604	26.0
Purdue Univ. North Central, Westville, IN 46391-9542	1967	$7,045(S)	NA	5-M	5,279	282	19.0
Queens Coll. of the City Univ. of New York, Flushing, NY 11367-1597	1937	$5,607(S)	$11,840	11-M	20,993	1,464	52.0
Queens Univ. of Charlotte, Charlotte, NC 28274-0002	1857	$25,396	$9,192	2-M	2,491	258	59.0
Quincy Univ., Quincy, IL 62301-2699	1860	$24,140	$9,420	2-M	1,735	176	50.0
Quinnipiac Univ., Hamden, CT 06518-1940	1929	$38,000	$13,800	1-D	8,352	925	77.0
Radford Univ., Radford, VA 24142	1910	$8,320(S)	$7,589	5-D	9,370	623	56.0
Ramapo Coll. of New Jersey, Mahwah, NJ 07430-1680	1969	$12,758(S)	$10,510	5-M	5,926	481	72.0
Randolph-Macon Coll., Ashland, VA 23005-5505	1830	$31,265	$9,970	2-B	1,257	151	62.0
Reed Coll., Portland, OR 97202-8199	1908	$42,800	$11,050	1-M	1,477	139	79.0
Regent Univ., Virginia Beach, VA 23464-9800	1977	$15,308	$5,900	2-D	5,915	537	NA
Regis Coll., Weston, MA 02493	1927	$31,785	$12,800	2-D	1,883	156	63.0
Regis Univ., Denver, CO 80221-1099	1877	$31,188	$9,530	2-D	11,253	1,093	62.0
Reinhardt Univ., Waleska, GA 30183-2981	1883	$17,840	$6,580	2-M	1,154	157	39.0
Rensselaer Polytechnic Inst., Troy, NY 12180-3590	1824	$42,704	$11,975	1-D	6,914	482	84.0
Rhode Island Coll., Providence, RI 02908-1991	1854	$7,268(S)	$9,256	5-D	9,044	753	44.0
Rhode Island Sch. of Design, Providence, RI 02903-2784	1877	$38,295	$11,310	1-D	2,259	503	90.2
Rhodes Coll., Memphis, TN 38112-1690	1848	$34,580	$8,480	1-M	1,830	205	76.0
Rice Univ., Houston, TX 77251-1892	1912	$37,287	$12,600	1-D	6,224	737	92.0
The Richard Stockton Coll. of New Jersey, Pomona, NJ 08240-0195	1969	$11,963(S)	$10,477	5-D	8,108	601	65.0
Rider Univ., Lawrenceville, NJ 08648-3001	1865	$31,930	$11,810	1-M	5,636	612	63.0
Ringling Coll. of Art & Design, Sarasota, FL 34234-5895	1931	$33,230	$11,290	1-B	1,376	155	66.0
Rivier Univ., Nashua, NH 03060	1933	$25,735	$9,798	2-D	2,289	193	54.0
Roanoke Coll., Salem, VA 24153-3794	1842	$34,846	$11,142	2-B	2,057	216	69.0

Name, address	Year founded	Tuition & fees	Room & board	Control, degree	Enroll-ment	Faculty	Grad. rate
Robert Morris Univ., Moon Township, PA 15108-1189	1921	$23,038	$11,030	1-D	4,984	409	59.0%
Robert Morris Univ. Illinois, Chicago, IL 60605	1913	$22,200	$11,340	1-M	4,218	275	78.0
Roberts Wesleyan Coll., Rochester, NY 14624-1997	1866	$26,324	$9,264	2-M	1,823	255	67.0
Rochester Inst. of Tech., Rochester, NY 14623-5603	1829	$32,037	$10,413	1-D	17,397	1,475	65.0
Rockford Coll., Rockford, IL 61108-2393	1847	$26,350	$7,320	1-M	1,318	157	NA
Rockhurst Univ., Kansas City, MO 64110-2561	1910	$28,440	$7,820	2-D	2,801	233	74.0
Rocky Mountain Coll., Billings, MT 59102-1796	1878	$22,892	$7,122	2-M	1,042	120	49.0
Rogers State Univ., Claremore, OK 74017-3252	1909	$4,777(S)	$6,540	5-B	4,632	268	12.0
Roger Williams Univ., Bristol, RI 02809	1956	$31,618	$13,690	1-D	4,843	541	59.0
Rollins Coll., Winter Park, FL 32789-4499	1885	$38,400	$12,000	1-M	2,475	174	70.0
Roosevelt Univ., Chicago, IL 60605	1945	$25,950	$12,100	1-D	6,620	722	47.0
Rose-Hulman Inst. of Tech., Terre Haute, IN 47803-3999 (2)	1874	$37,947	$10,455	1-M	1,980	177	77.0
Rowan Univ., Glassboro, NJ 08028-1701	1923	$12,018(S)	$10,450	5-D	11,816	1,049	67.0
Rush Univ., Chicago, IL 60612-3832	1969	NA	NA	1-D	1,566	796	NA
Rutgers, The State Univ. of New Jersey, Camden, Camden, NJ 08102-1401	1927	$12,615(S)	$10,226	5-D	6,428	522	61.0
Rutgers, The State Univ. of New Jersey, Newark, Newark, NJ 07102	1892	$12,294(S)	$12,013	5-D	11,804	788	68.0
Rutgers, The State Univ. of New Jersey, New Brunswick, Piscataway, NJ 08854-8097	1766	$12,755(S)	$11,262	5-D	39,950	2,745	77.0
Sacred Heart Univ., Fairfield, CT 06825-1000	1963	$32,724	$12,776	2-D	6,377	570	67.0
Saginaw Valley State Univ., University Center, MI 48710	1963	$8,016(S)	$8,220	5-M	10,790	597	38.0
St. Ambrose Univ., Davenport, IA 52803-2898	1882	$25,970	$9,195	2-D	3,567	401	62.0
St. Anselm Coll., Manchester, NH 03102-1310	1889	$3,150/course	NA	2-B	1,899	205	73.0
St. Augustine Coll., Chicago, IL 60640-3501	1980	$8,400	NA	1-B	1,430	154	NA
St. Augustine's Coll., Raleigh, NC 27610-2298	1867	$17,160	$7,340	2-B	1,506	151	NA
St. Bonaventure Univ., St. Bonaventure, NY 14778-2284	1858	$27,890	$10,042	2-M	2,460	223	63.0
St. Catherine Univ., St. Paul, MN 55105	1905	$31,640	$8,002	2-D	5,227	458	66.0
St. Cloud State Univ., St. Cloud, MN 56301-4498	1869	$7,105(S)	$6,600	5-D	17,231	872	48.0
St. Edward's Univ., Austin, TX 78704	1885	$31,110	$10,044	2-M	5,330	519	68.0
St. Francis Coll., Brooklyn Heights, NY 11201-4398	1884	$18,100	NA	2-M	2,511	243	54.0
St. Francis Univ., Loretto, PA 15940-0600	1847	$29,012	$9,996	2-D	2,398	192	66.0
St. John Fisher Coll., Rochester, NY 14618-3597	1948	$26,260	$10,510	2-D	3,977	423	73.0
St. John's Univ., Collegeville, MN 56321 (1)	1857	$33,606	$8,344	2-M	2,016	180	80.0
St. John's Univ., Queens, NY 11439	1870	$33,875	$14,300	2-D	21,067	1,490	58.0
St. Joseph's Coll., Rensselaer, IN 47978	1889	$27,350	$8,250	2-M	1,100	113	57.0
St. Joseph's Coll., Long Island Campus, Patchogue, NY 11772-2399	1916	$18,425	NA	1-M	4,333	435	66.0
St. Joseph's Coll., New York, Brooklyn, NY 11205-3688	1916	$18,425	NA	1-M	1,504	181	62.0
St. Joseph's Coll. of Maine, Standish, ME 04084	1912	$28,700	$11,000	2-M	3,355	126	50.0
St. Joseph's Univ., Philadelphia, PA 19131-1395	1851	$36,640	$12,206	2-D	9,011	774	76.0
St. Lawrence Univ., Canton, NY 13617-1455	1856	$42,725	$11,005	1-M	2,457	192	80.0
St. Leo Univ., Saint Leo, FL 33574-6665	1889	$18,870	$9,120	2-M	4,779	153	45.0
St. Louis Coll. of Pharm., St. Louis, MO 63110-1088	1864	$23,968	$8,636	1-D	1,260	135	73.0
St. Louis Univ., St. Louis, MO 63103-2097	1818	$33,986	$9,432	2-D	14,073	1,286	71.0
St. Martin's Univ., Lacey, WA 98503	1895	$27,622	$8,458	2-M	1,800	202	48.0
St. Mary-of-the-Woods Coll., Saint Mary-of-the-Woods, IN 47876 (4)	1840	$27,622	$9,334	2-M	1,441	176	55.0
St. Mary's Coll., Notre Dame, IN 46556 (3)	1844	$32,000	$9,800	2-B	1,510	219	79.0
St. Mary's Coll. of California, Moraga, CA 94556	1863	$38,450	$12,840	2-D	4,099	495	61.0
St. Mary's Coll. of Maryland, St. Mary's City, MD 20686-3001	1840	$14,445(S)	$10,915	5-M	1,992	226	79.0
St. Mary's Univ., San Antonio, TX 78228-8507	1852	$23,386	$8,350	2-D	4,188	367	56.0
St. Mary's Univ. of Minnesota, Winona, MN 55987-1399	1912	$28,320	$7,440	2-D	5,688	578	62.0
St. Michael's Coll., Colchester, VT 05439	1904	$37,510	$9,350	2-M	2,455	208	82.0
St. Norbert Coll., De Pere, WI 54115-2099	1898	$29,395	$7,513	2-M	2,225	197	71.0
St. Olaf Coll., Northfield, MN 55057-1098	1874	$38,150	$8,800	2-B	3,179	333	85.0
St. Petersburg Coll., St. Petersburg, FL 33733-3489	1927	$3,088(S)	NA	11-B	31,793	1,731	28.0
St. Peter's Coll., Jersey City, NJ 07306-5997	1872	$29,800	$12,692	2-D	2,986	283	51.0
St. Thomas Aquinas Coll., Sparkill, NY 10976	1952	$23,720	$10,650	1-M	2,025	129	57.0
St. Thomas Univ., Miami Gardens, FL 33054-6459	1961	$23,910	$7,140	2-D	2,472	238	38.0
St. Vincent Coll., Latrobe, PA 15650-2690	1846	$28,428	$8,882	2-M	1,929	195	72.0
St. Xavier Univ., Chicago, IL 60655-3105	1847	$27,060	$9,040	2-M	4,709	431	52.0
Salem Intl. Univ., Salem, WV 26426-0500	1888	$14,100	$6,400	1-M	NA	16	39.4
Salem State Univ., Salem, MA 01970-5353	1854	$7,670(S)	$8,130	5-M	9,646	761	NA
Salisbury Univ., Salisbury, MD 21801-6837	1925	$7,332(S)	$8,586	5-M	8,606	614	67.0
Salve Regina Univ., Newport, RI 02840-4192	1934	$32,800	$11,600	2-D	2,604	241	73.0
Samford Univ., Birmingham, AL 35229	1841	$23,673	$7,775	2-D	4,758	478	70.0
Sam Houston State Univ., Huntsville, TX 77341	1879	$7,328(S)	$7,644	5-D	17,617	843	47.0
Samuel Merritt Univ., Oakland, CA 94609-3108 (4)	1909	$39,719	NA	1-D	1,473	266	89.0
San Diego State Univ., San Diego, CA 92182	1897	$7,076(S)	$13,052	5-D	31,303	1,453	66.0
San Diego State Univ.–Imperial Valley Campus, Calexico, CA 92231	1959	$4,464(S)	$10,388	5-M	1,003	NA	NA
San Francisco State Univ., San Francisco, CA 94132-1722	1899	$6,276(S)	$11,408	5-D	29,541	1,593	46.0
San Jose State Univ., San Jose, CA 95192-0001	1857	$6,840(S)	$10,733	5-M	29,076	1,593	48.0
Santa Clara Univ., Santa Clara, CA 95053	1851	$39,048	$11,997	2-D	8,800	832	85.0
Santa Fe Coll., Gainesville, FL 32606	1966	$2,456(S)	NA	11-B	15,745	829	NA
Sarah Lawrence Coll., Bronxville, NY 10708-5999	1926	$46,924	$9,324	1-M	1,744	311	70.0
Savannah Coll. of Art & Design, Savannah, GA 31402-3146	1978	$31,905	$12,945	1-M	11,063	724	64.0
Savannah State Univ., Savannah, GA 31404	1890	$6,031(S)	$6,604	5-M	4,080	200	35.0
Sch. of the Art Inst. of Chicago, Chicago, IL 60603-3103	1866	$35,950	$9,800	1-M	3,170	597	63.0
Sch. of Visual Arts, New York, NY 10010-3994	1947	$29,550	$15,700	3-M	4,214	929	69.0
Schreiner Univ., Kerrville, TX 78028-5697	1923	$21,640	$10,062	2-M	1,078	117	39.0
Seattle Pacific Univ., Seattle, WA 98119-1997	1891	$32,067	$9,492	2-D	4,167	363	76.0
Seattle Univ., Seattle, WA 98122-1090	1891	$32,700	$9,855	2-D	7,755	719	71.0
Seton Hall Univ., South Orange, NJ 07079-2697	1856	$33,490	$12,412	2-D	9,616	879	63.0
Seton Hill Univ., Greensburg, PA 15601	1883	$29,446	$9,944	2-M	2,137	192	44.0
Sewanee: The Univ. of the South, Sewanee, TN 37383-1000	1857	$34,714	$9,916	2-D	1,557	172	86.0
Shawnee State Univ., Portsmouth, OH 45662-4344	1986	$6,762(S)	$8,494	5-M	4,711	316	21.0
Shaw Univ., Raleigh, NC 27601-2399	1865	$13,228	$7,560	2-M	2,405	227	28.0
Shenandoah Univ., Winchester, VA 22601-5195	1875	$26,940	$8,950	2-D	4,052	428	47.0
Shepherd Univ., Shepherdstown, WV 25443	1871	$5,554(S)	$8,190	5-M	4,393	347	46.0
Shippensburg Univ. of Pennsylvania, Shippensburg, PA 17257-2299	1871	$8,856(S)	$7,620	5-M	8,183	419	60.0
Shorter Univ., Rome, GA 30165	1873	$17,870	$8,600	2-M	1,696	186	43.0
Siena Coll., Loudonville, NY 12211-1462	1937	$28,915	$11,970	2-M	3,342	353	74.0
Siena Heights Univ., Adrian, MI 49221-1796	1919	$21,152	$8,210	2-M	2,630	216	43.0
Silicon Valley Univ., San Jose, CA 95131	1997	$295/unit	NA	3-M	1,090	31	NA
Simmons Coll., Boston, MA 02115	1899	$33,356	$12,906	1-D	4,785	NA	69.0
Simpson Coll., Indianola, IA 50125-1297	1860	$29,529	$7,960	2-M	1,867	190	70.0
Simpson Univ., Redding, CA 96003-8606	1921	$22,400	$7,400	2-M	1,297	128	43.0
Skidmore Coll., Saratoga Springs, NY 12866	1903	$42,380	$11,304	1-M	2,730	339	84.0
Slippery Rock Univ. of Pennsylvania, Slippery Rock, PA 16057-1383	1889	$8,506(S)	$9,150	5-D	8,712	399	59.0

Name, address	Year founded	Tuition & fees	Room & board	Control, degree	Enroll-ment	Faculty	Grad. rate
Smith Coll., Northampton, MA 01063	1871	$40,070	$13,390	1-D	3,162	300	85.0%
Sojourner-Douglass Coll., Baltimore, MD 21205-1814 (4)	1980	$8,750	NA	1-M	1,268	240	22.0
Sonoma State Univ., Rohnert Park, CA 94928-3609	1960	$6,862(S)	$10,961	5-M	8,668	539	53.0
South Carolina State Univ., Orangeburg, SC 29117-0001	1896	$9,258(S)	$9,286	5-D	4,326	279	36.0
South Dakota Sch. of Mines & Tech., Rapid City, SD 57701-3995	1885	$8,820(S)	$5,700	5-D	2,311	153	46.0
South Dakota State Univ., Brookings, SD 57007	1881	$6,887(S)	$5,778	5-D	12,725	692	55.0
Southeastern Baptist Theol. Sem., Wake Forest, NC 27588-1889	1950	$6,358	$1,935	2-M	2,332	85	NA
Southeastern Louisiana Univ., Hammond, LA 70402	1925	$4,634(S)	$6,620	5-D	15,414	630	33.0
Southeastern Oklahoma State Univ., Durant, OK 74701-0609	1909	$4,794(S)	$4,760	5-M	4,127	262	29.0
Southeastern Univ., Lakeland, FL 33801-6099	1935	$17,718	$8,220	2-M	2,546	169	42.0
Southeast Missouri State Univ., Cape Girardeau, MO 63701-4799	1873	$6,555(S)	$7,715	5-M	11,510	582	46.0
Southern Adventist Univ., Collegedale, TN 37315-0370	1892	$18,324	$5,786	2-M	3,053	269	48.0
Southern Arkansas Univ.–Magnolia, Magnolia, AR 71753	1909	$6,786(S)	$4,700	5-M	3,381	218	32.0
Southern Baptist Theol. Sem., Louisville, KY 40280-0004	1858	$8,590	NA	2-D	3,190	NA	NA
Southern Connecticut State Univ., New Haven, CT 06515-1355	1893	$8,248(S)	$10,087	5-D	11,533	1,046	44.0
Southern Illinois Univ. Carbondale, Carbondale, IL 62901-4701	1869	$11,038(S)	$8,648	5-D	19,817	1,054	44.0
Southern Illinois Univ. Edwardsville, Edwardsville, IL 62026-0001	1957	$8,865(S)	$8,051	5-D	14,235	874	52.0
Southern Methodist Univ., Dallas, TX 75275	1911	$41,750	$13,539	2-D	10,982	1,106	75.0
Southern Nazarene Univ., Bethany, OK 73008	1899	$19,794	$7,600	2-M	2,051	189	46.0
Southern New Hampshire Univ., Manchester, NH 03106-1045	1932	$28,050	$10,900	1-D	11,500	870	58.0
Southern Oregon Univ., Ashland, OR 97520	1926	$6,155(S)	$9,918	5-M	6,855	346	NA
Southern Polytechnic State Univ., Marietta, GA 30060-2896	1948	$6,524(S)	$6,892	5-M	5,784	305	34.0
Southern Univ. & Agr. & Mech. Coll., Baton Rouge, LA 70813	1880	$5,126(S)	$5,614	5-D	7,699	546	30.0
Southern Univ. at New Orleans, New Orleans, LA 70126-1009 (4)	1959	$3,906(S)	$7,680	5-M	3,141	102	5.2
Southern Utah Univ., Cedar City, UT 84720-2498	1897	$5,188(S)	$2,086	5-M	7,750	419	38.0
Southern Wesleyan Univ., Central, SC 29630-1020	1906	$20,550	$7,550	2-M	1,883	193	39.0
Southwest Baptist Univ., Bolivar, MO 65613-2597	1878	$18,200	$6,050	2-D	3,633	260	49.0
Southwestern Assemblies of God Univ., Waxahachie, TX 75165-5735	1927	$15,730	$6,426	2-M	2,064	142	39.0
Southwestern Coll., Winfield, KS 67156-2499	1885	$22,756	$6,514	2-M	1,687	113	57.0
Southwestern Oklahoma State Univ., Weatherford, OK 73096-3098	1901	$4,590(S)	$4,360	5-D	5,340	234	30.0
Southwestern Univ., Georgetown, TX 78626	1840	$33,440	$9,680	2-B	1,347	164	72.0
Southwest Florida Coll., Fort Myers, FL 33907	1940	NA	NA	1-B	1,263	NA	NA
Southwest Minnesota State Univ., Marshall, MN 56258	1963	$7,743(S)	$6,944	5-M	6,588	180	39.0
Spalding Univ., Louisville, KY 40203-2188	1814	$19,350	$8,800	2-D	2,432	169	42.0
Spelman Coll., Atlanta, GA 30314-4399 (3)	1881	$23,254	$10,986	1-B	2,170	250	77.0
Spring Arbor Univ., Spring Arbor, MI 49283-9799	1873	$21,520	$7,570	2-M	4,271	143	55.0
Springfield Coll., Springfield, MA 01109-3797	1885	$30,660	$10,280	1-D	5,000	342	NA
Spring Hill Coll., Mobile, AL 36608-1791	1830	$28,060	$10,760	2-M	1,460	135	61.0
Stanford Univ., Stanford, CA 94305-9991	1891	$41,006	$12,291	1-D	19,444	1,452	96.0
State Univ. of New York at Albany, Albany, NY 12222-0001	1844	$7,472(S)	$11,276	5-D	17,142	1,267	65.0
State Univ. of New York at Binghamton, Binghamton, NY 13902-6000	1946	$7,216(S)	$11,810	5-D	14,746	848	78.0
State Univ. of New York at Buffalo, Buffalo, NY 14260	1846	$7,482(S)	$10,728	5-D	28,860	1,676	69.0
State Univ. of New York at Fredonia, Fredonia, NY 14063-1136	1826	$6,688(S)	$10,290	5-M	5,726	482	63.0
State Univ. of New York at New Paltz, New Paltz, NY 12561	1828	$6,458(S)	$9,950	5-M	7,972	650	70.0
State Univ. of New York at Oswego, Oswego, NY 13126	1861	$6,510(S)	$12,310	5-M	8,216	562	63.0
State Univ. of New York at Plattsburgh, Plattsburgh, NY 12901-2681	1889	$6,482(S)	$9,550	5-M	6,350	504	59.0
State Univ. of New York Coll. at Cortland, Cortland, NY 13045	1868	$6,574(S)	$11,060	5-M	7,331	622	67.1
State Univ. of New York Coll. at Geneseo, Geneseo, NY 14454-1401	1871	$6,733(S)	$10,476	5-M	5,683	352	81.0
State Univ. of New York Coll. at Old Westbury, Old Westbury, NY 11568-0210	1965	$6,324(S)	$9,700	5-M	4,459	308	35.0
State Univ. of New York Coll. at Oneonta, Oneonta, NY 13820-4015	1889	$6,596(S)	$10,164	5-M	6,023	483	67.0
State Univ. of New York Coll. at Potsdam, Potsdam, NY 13676	1816	$6,506(S)	$9,830	5-M	4,398	363	58.0
State Univ. of New York Coll. of Agr. & Tech. at Cobleskill, Cobleskill, NY 12043	1916	$7,435(S)	$10,366	5-B	2,619	175	40.0
State Univ. of New York Coll. of Envir. Sci. & Forestry, Syracuse, NY 13210-2779	1911	$6,241(S)	$14,032	5-D	2,346	177	66.0
State Univ. of New York Coll. of Tech. at Canton, Canton, NY 13617	1906	$6,970(S)	$10,952	5-M	3,861	205	51.0
State Univ. of New York Coll. of Tech. at Delhi, Delhi, NY 13753	1913	$6,445(S)	$9,720	5-B	3,430	225	50.0
State Univ. of New York Downstate Med. Ctr., Brooklyn, NY 11203-2098	1858	$5,789(S)	$12,134	5-D	1,694	981	NA
State Univ. of New York Empire State Coll., Saratoga Springs, NY 12866-4391	1971	$5,615(S)	NA	5-M	11,866	1,404	NA
State Univ. of New York Inst. of Tech., Utica, NY 13504-3050	1966	$6,439(S)	$9,600	5-M	2,828	183	NA
State Univ. of New York Maritime Coll., Throggs Neck, NY 10465-4198 (2)	1874	$6,457(S)	$10,090	5-M	1,823	148	51.0
State Univ. of New York Upstate Med. Univ., Syracuse, NY 13210-2334	1950	$5,880(S)	$10,710	5-D	1,787	54	NA
Stephen F. Austin State Univ., Nacogdoches, TX 75962	1923	$7,344(S)	$8,186	5-D	12,903	674	43.0
Stephens Coll., Columbia, MO 65215-0002 (4)	1833	$26,420	$7,170	1-M	1,032	97	51.0
Stetson Univ., DeLand, FL 32723	1883	$36,644	$10,688	1-D	3,877	375	64.0
Stevens Inst. of Tech., Hoboken, NJ 07030	1870	$41,782	$13,340	1-D	5,541	406	79.0
Stevenson Univ., Stevenson, MD 21153	1952	$23,636	$11,422	1-M	4,317	448	62.0
Stillman Coll., Tuscaloosa, AL 35403-9990	1876	$15,665	$7,056	2-B	1,072	61	34.0
Stonehill Coll., Easton, MA 02357	1948	$35,110	$13,310	2-B	2,471	267	81.0
Stony Brook Univ., State Univ. of New York, Stony Brook, NY 11794	1957	$6,580(S)	$10,142	5-D	24,061	1,448	67.0
Stratford Univ., Falls Church, VA 22043	1976	$15,330	$7,000	3-M	1,385	72	NA
Suffolk Univ., Boston, MA 02108-2770	1906	$29,895	$14,624	1-D	9,292	963	55.0
Sullivan Univ., Louisville, KY 40205	1864	$16,700	$6,345	3-D	5,880	340	NA
Sul Ross State Univ., Alpine, TX 79832	1920	$6,060(S)	$6,810	5-M	2,940	175	23.0
Susquehanna Univ., Selinsgrove, PA 17870	1858	$35,860	$9,600	2-B	2,261	252	NA
Swarthmore Coll., Swarthmore, PA 19081-1397	1864	$41,150	$12,100	1-B	1,545	208	95.0
Syracuse Univ., Syracuse, NY 13244	1870	$37,667	$13,254	1-D	20,829	1,559	82.0
Tarleton State Univ., Stephenville, TX 76402	1899	$6,409(S)	$7,474	5-D	9,893	NA	40.0
Taylor Univ., Upland, IN 46989-1001	1846	$27,438	$7,532	2-M	2,422	251	80.0
Temple Univ., Philadelphia, PA 19122-6096	1884	$13,596(S)	$9,886	12-D	36,855	2,894	67.0
Tennessee State Univ., Nashville, TN 37209-1561	1912	$6,088(S)	$5,910	5-M	8,254	603	NA
Tennessee Tech. Univ., Cookeville, TN 38505	1915	$6,406(S)	$7,384	5-D	11,538	640	48.0
Tennessee Wesleyan Coll., Athens, TN 37371-0040	1857	$19,700	$6,480	2-B	1,103	89	50.0
Texas A&M Intl. Univ., Laredo, TX 78041-1900	1969	$6,558(S)	$6,496	5-D	7,037	291	41.0
Texas A&M Univ., College Station, TX 77843	1876	$8,421(S)	$8,200	5-D	49,861	2,501	80.0
Texas A&M Univ. at Galveston, Galveston, TX 77553-1675	1962	$7,464(S)	$7,100	5-M	1,774	170	53.0
Texas A&M Univ.–Commerce, Commerce, TX 75429-3011	1889	$6,283(S)	$7,450	5-D	9,170	843	35.4
Texas A&M Univ.–Corpus Christi, Corpus Christi, TX 78412-5503	1947	$6,968(S)	$9,528	5-D	10,162	547	36.0
Texas A&M Univ.–Kingsville, Kingsville, TX 78363	1925	$6,640(S)	$6,138	5-D	6,823	389	37.0
Texas A&M Univ.–Texarkana, Texarkana, TX 75505-5518	1971	$5,167(S)	NA	5-M	1,653	NA	NA
Texas Christian Univ., Fort Worth, TX 76129-0002	1873	$34,500	$10,650	2-D	9,518	845	74.0
Texas Lutheran Univ., Seguin, TX 78155-5999	1891	$23,930	$6,940	2-B	1,415	126	49.0
Texas Southern Univ., Houston, TX 77004-4584	1947	$7,312(S)	$9,536	5-D	9,730	553	12.0
Texas State Univ.–San Marcos, San Marcos, TX 78666	1899	$8,232(S)	$6,912	5-D	34,087	1,588	56.0
Texas Tech. Univ., Lubbock, TX 79409	1923	$8,765(S)	$8,095	5-D	32,327	1,348	61.0
Texas Wesleyan Univ., Fort Worth, TX 76105-1536	1890	$19,760	$7,180	2-D	3,181	283	33.0

Name, address	Year founded	Tuition & fees	Room & board	Control, degree	Enroll-ment	Faculty	Grad. rate
Texas Woman's Univ., Denton, TX 76201 (4)	1901	$6,960(S)	$6,170	5-D	14,718	391	42.0
Thiel Coll., Greenville, PA 16125-2181	1866	$25,988	$10,120	2-B	1,109	105	39.0
Thomas Edison State Coll., Trenton, NJ 08608-1176	1972	$5,322(S)	NA	5-M	20,251	NA	NA
Thomas Jefferson Univ., Philadelphia, PA 19107	1824	$27,139	NA	1-D	3,326	NA	NA
Thomas More Coll., Crestview Hills, KY 41017-3495	1921	$25,720	$7,030	2-M	1,832	149	52.0%
Thomas Univ., Thomasville, GA 31792-7499	1950	$13,320	$3,550	1-M	1,109	53	NA
Tiffin Univ., Tiffin, OH 44883-2161	1888	$19,890	$9,202	1-M	6,816	446	46.0
Touro Coll., New York, NY 10010	1971	$15,370	$10,400	1-D	17,544	NA	NA
Towson Univ., Towson, MD 21252-0001	1866	$7,906(S)	$9,942	5-D	21,464	1,671	64.0
Transylvania Univ., Lexington, KY 40508-1797	1780	$29,865	$8,750	2-B	1,029	104	70.0
Trevecca Nazarene Univ., Nashville, TN 37210-2877	1901	$20,590	$7,488	2-D	2,478	230	54.0
Trident Univ. Intl., Cypress, CA 90630	1998	$9,440	NA	1-D	5,716	479	NA
Trine Univ., Angola, IN 46703-1764	1884	$26,730	$8,800	1-M	1,778	137	45.0
Trinity Christian Coll., Palos Heights, IL 60463-0929	1959	$22,352	$8,448	2-B	1,470	161	NA
Trinity Coll., Hartford, CT 06106-3100	1823	$45,750	$11,800	1-M	2,440	243	86.0
Trinity Intl. Univ., Deerfield, IL 60015-1284	1897	$23,370	NA	2-D	2,671	82	52.0
Trinity Univ., San Antonio, TX 78212-7200	1869	$33,093	$10,197	2-M	2,635	325	80.0
Trinity Washington Univ., Washington, DC 20017-1094	1897	$20,775	$9,210	2-M	1,630	NA	NA
Troy Univ., Troy, AL 36082	1887	$7,990(S)	$6,534	5-D	29,322	1,477	35.0
Truman State Univ., Kirksville, MO 63501-4221	1867	$7,012(S)	$7,254	5-M	6,101	370	70.0
Tufts Univ., Medford, MA 02155	1852	$42,962	$11,512	1-D	10,777	1,025	90.0
Tulane Univ., New Orleans, LA 70118-5669	1834	$43,434	$11,450	1-D	13,359	1,070	70.0
Tusculum Coll., Greeneville, TN 37743-9997	1794	$20,910	$8,000	2-M	2,128	224	38.0
Tuskegee Univ., Tuskegee, AL 36088	1881	$17,720	$7,950	1-D	3,152	297	NA
Union Coll., Barbourville, KY 40906-1499	1879	$20,800	$6,650	2-M	1,380	107	32.0
Union Coll., Schenectady, NY 12308-2311	1795	$54,273(C)	NA	1-B	2,220	237	86.0
Union Inst. & Univ., Cincinnati, OH 45206-1925	1969	$11,592	NA	1-D	1,650	353	NA
Union Univ., Jackson, TN 38305-3697	1823	$24,030	$8,110	2-D	4,007	242	61.0
United States Air Force Academy, USAF Academy, CO 80840-5025 (2)	1954	$0(C)	NA	4-B	4,413	529	76.0
United States Coast Guard Academy, New London, CT 06320-8100	1876	$0(C)	NA	4-B	1,045	143	NA
United States Merchant Marine Academy, Kings Point, NY 11024-1699	1943	$0(C)	NA	4-M	1,082	NA	NA
United States Military Academy, West Point, NY 10996	1802	$0(C)	NA	4-B	4,624	613	83.0
United States Naval Academy, Annapolis, MD 21402-5000 (2)	1845	$0(C)	NA	4-B	4,576	528	90.0
United Talmudical Sem., Brooklyn, NY 11211 (1)	1949	NA	NA	2-M	1,500	NA	NA
Universidad Adventista de las Antillas, Mayagüez, PR 00681-0118	1957	$5,600	$2,900	2-M	1,235	92	NA
Universidad del Este, Carolina, PR 00984	1949	NA	NA	1-M	13,317	NA	NA
Universidad del Turabo, Gurabo, PR 00778-3030	1972	$19,512	$7,062	1-D	16,605	1,325	13.0
Universidad Metropolitana, San Juan, PR 00928-1150	1980	NA	NA	1-M	12,622	903	23.0
Univ. of Advancing Tech., Tempe, AZ 85283-1042 (2)	1983	$19,500	$11,060	3-M	1,073	60	NA
The Univ. of Akron, Akron, OH 44325	1870	$9,545(S)	$9,586	5-D	27,470	1,756	35.0
The Univ. of Alabama, Tuscaloosa, AL 35487	1831	$8,600(S)	$8,564	5-D	31,647	1,590	66.0
The Univ. of Alabama at Birmingham, Birmingham, AL 35294	1969	$7,740(S)	$9,094	5-D	17,575	943	41.0
The Univ. of Alabama in Huntsville, Huntsville, AL 35899	1950	$8,094(S)	$7,930	5-D	7,629	486	45.0
Univ. of Alaska Anchorage, Anchorage, AK 99508	1954	$5,306(S)	$9,427	5-M	18,898	1,374	NA
Univ. of Alaska Fairbanks, Fairbanks, AK 99775-7520	1917	$6,443(S)	$6,960	5-D	9,818	1,042	31.0
Univ. of Alaska Southeast, Juneau, AK 99801	1972	$5,477(S)	$7,100	5-M	3,458	229	31.0
The Univ. of Arizona, Tucson, AZ 85721	1885	$10,208(S)	$8,540	5-D	39,236	2,021	61.0
Univ. of Arkansas, Fayetteville, AR 72701-1201	1871	$6,834(S)	$8,204	5-D	23,199	1,087	59.0
Univ. of Arkansas at Little Rock, Little Rock, AR 72204-1099	1927	$6,758(S)	$6,056	5-D	13,068	820	25.0
Univ. of Arkansas at Monticello, Monticello, AR 71656	1909	$5,430(S)	$4,610	5-M	3,920	240	24.0
Univ. of Arkansas at Pine Bluff, Pine Bluff, AR 71601-2799	1873	$3,975(S)	$6,148	5-M	3,428	234	24.0
Univ. of Arkansas for Med. Sci., Little Rock, AR 72205-7199	1879	$6,856(S)	$5,900	5-D	2,836	NA	NA
Univ. of Arkansas–Fort Smith, Fort Smith, AR 72913-3649	1928	$5,267(S)	$7,642	11-B	7,606	448	23.0
Univ. of Atlanta, Atlanta, GA 30360	1991	$3,150	NA	1-D	1,410	299	NA
Univ. of Baltimore, Baltimore, MD 21201-5779	1925	$7,330(S)	NA	5-D	6,501	404	NA
Univ. of Bridgeport, Bridgeport, CT 06604	1927	$27,330	$11,700	1-D	4,805	473	27.0
Univ. of California, Berkeley, Berkeley, CA 94720-1500	1868	$12,835(S)	$14,990	5-D	36,142	NA	90.0
Univ. of California, Davis, Davis, CA 95616	1905	$13,860(S)	$12,697	5-D	31,732	1,620	82.0
Univ. of California, Irvine, Irvine, CA 92697	1965	$14,090(S)	$11,611	5-D	27,189	1,923	85.0
Univ. of California, Los Angeles, Los Angeles, CA 90095	1919	$13,910(S)	$13,979	5-D	40,675	2,577	90.0
Univ. of California, Merced, Merced, CA 95343	2005	$10,130(S)	$12,801	5-D	5,198	264	58.0
Univ. of California, Riverside, Riverside, CA 92521-0102	1954	$15,310(S)	$12,100	5-D	20,956	882	70.0
Univ. of California, San Diego, La Jolla, CA 92093	1959	$13,202(S)	$10,383	5-D	26,723	1,144	84.0
Univ. of California, Santa Barbara, Santa Barbara, CA 93106-2014	1909	$13,576(S)	$13,110	5-D	21,685	1,052	80.0
Univ. of California, Santa Cruz, Santa Cruz, CA 95064	1965	NA	$14,871	5-D	17,454	803	73.0
Univ. of Central Arkansas, Conway, AR 72035-0001	1907	$7,183(S)	$5,260	5-D	11,163	715	42.0
Univ. of Central Florida, Orlando, FL 32816	1963	$5,584(S)	$9,063	5-D	58,587	1,834	62.9
Univ. of Central Missouri, Warrensburg, MO 64093	1871	$7,785(S)	$7,094	5-M	11,637	NA	50.0
Univ. of Central Oklahoma, Edmond, OK 73034-5209	1890	$4,718(S)	$8,360	5-M	16,092	860	36.0
Univ. of Charleston, Charleston, WV 25304-1099	1888	$25,000	$8,800	1-D	1,372	NA	52.0
Univ. of Chicago, Chicago, IL 60637-1513	1891	$42,783	$12,633	1-D	14,965	1,701	92.0
Univ. of Cincinnati, Cincinnati, OH 45221	1819	$10,419(S)	$9,780	5-D	33,329	1,201	59.0
Univ. of Colorado at Colorado Springs, Colorado Springs, CO 80933-7150	1965	$7,894(S)	$7,990	5-D	9,882	676	41.0
Univ. of Colorado Boulder, Boulder, CO 80309	1876	$8,511(S)	$10,792	5-D	32,252	2,011	68.0
Univ. of Colorado Denver, Denver, CO 80217-3364	1912	$7,394(S)	$10,090	5-D	24,108	3,158	42.0
Univ. of Connecticut, Storrs, CT 06269	1881	$11,242(S)	$11,380	5-D	25,868	1,363	83.0
Univ. of Dallas, Irving, TX 75062-4736	1955	$31,070	$9,890	2-D	2,725	235	73.0
Univ. of Dayton, Dayton, OH 45469-1300	1850	$31,640	$9,950	2-D	11,045	955	78.0
Univ. of Delaware, Newark, DE 19716	1743	$11,192(S)	$10,470	12-D	20,737	1,485	78.0
Univ. of Denver, Denver, CO 80208	1864	$39,177	$10,818	1-D	11,797	1,299	79.0
Univ. of Detroit Mercy, Detroit, MI 48221	1877	$32,500	$9,090	2-D	5,725	NA	NA
Univ. of Dubuque, Dubuque, IA 52001-5099	1852	$21,620	$7,580	2-D	2,003	166	41.0
Univ. of Evansville, Evansville, IN 47722	1854	$29,416	$9,530	2-D	2,885	230	63.0
The Univ. of Findlay, Findlay, OH 45840-3653	1882	$28,104	$9,074	2-D	4,999	288	53.0
Univ. of Florida, Gainesville, FL 32611	1853	$5,657(S)	$8,800	5-D	49,589	NA	83.7
Univ. of Georgia, Athens, GA 30602	1785	$9,472(S)	$8,708	5-D	34,816	2,187	83.0
Univ. of Great Falls, Great Falls, MT 59405	1932	$19,580	$6,922	2-M	1,075	114	NA
Univ. of Guam, Mangilao, GU 96923	1952	$5,818(S)	$2,270	7-M	3,721	258	23.0
Univ. of Hartford, West Hartford, CT 06117-1599	1877	$32,172	$12,104	1-D	7,025	848	53.0
Univ. of Hawaii at Hilo, Hilo, HI 96720-4091	1970	$5,944(S)	$7,134	5-D	4,139	300	36.0
Univ. of Hawaii at Manoa, Honolulu, HI 96822	1907	$9,404(S)	$10,279	5-D	20,429	1,229	50.0
Univ. of Hawaii–West Oahu, Pearl City, HI 96782-3366	1976	$5,146(S)	NA	5-B	1,662	74	NA
Univ. of Houston, Houston, TX 77204	1927	$9,211(S)	$8,318	5-D	39,820	1,813	46.0
Univ. of Houston–Clear Lake, Houston, TX 77058-1098	1971	$6,508(S)	$8,458	5-D	8,177	458	NA

Name, address	Year founded	Tuition & fees	Room & board	Control, degree	Enroll-ment	Faculty	Grad. rate
Univ. of Houston–Downtown, Houston, TX 77002	1974	$5,716(S)	NA	5-M	12,918	642	15.0%
Univ. of Houston–Victoria, Victoria, TX 77901-4450	1973	$5,828(S)	$6,956	5-M	4,330	208	NA
Univ. of Idaho, Moscow, ID 83844-2282	1889	$5,856(S)	$7,304	5-D	12,312	677	51.0
Univ. of Illinois at Chicago, Chicago, IL 60607-7128.	1946	$12,636(S)	$10,194	5-D	28,091	1,590	53.0
Univ. of Illinois at Springfield, Springfield, IL 62703-5407.	1969	$10,865(S)	$9,870	5-D	5,137	358	61.0
Univ. of Illinois at Urbana-Champaign, Champaign, IL 61820	1867	$14,960(S)	$10,332	5-D	44,407	1,872	82.0
Univ. of Indianapolis, Indianapolis, IN 46227-3697	1902	$23,010	$8,730	2-D	5,417	493	52.0
The Univ. of Iowa, Iowa City, IA 52242-1316	1847	$7,765(S)	$8,750	5-D	29,810	1,613	71.0
The Univ. of Kansas, Lawrence, KS 66045.	1866	$9,222(S)	$7,080	5-D	27,939	1,703	61.0
Univ. of Kentucky, Lexington, KY 40506-0032	1865	$9,128(S)	$9,974	5-D	26,295	1,683	60.0
Univ. of La Verne, La Verne, CA 91750-4443	1891	$33,350	$11,660	1-D	4,692	455	58.0
Univ. of Louisiana at Lafayette, Lafayette, LA 70504.	1898	$4,864(S)	$5,558	5-D	16,885	743	42.0
Univ. of Louisiana at Monroe, Monroe, LA 71209-0001	1931	$5,101(S)	$6,212	5-D	8,583	361	37.0
Univ. of Louisville, Louisville, KY 40292-0001.	1798	$8,930(S)	$7,440	5-D	21,153	1,280	51.0
Univ. of Maine, Orono, ME 04469.	1865	$10,588(S)	$8,644	5-D	11,168	789	60.0
Univ. of Maine at Augusta, Augusta, ME 04330-9410.	1965	$7,448(S)	NA	5-B	4,974	290	20.0
Univ. of Maine at Farmington, Farmington, ME 04938-1990	1863	$9,367(S)	$8,168	5-M	2,269	172	59.0
Univ. of Maine at Fort Kent, Fort Kent, ME 04743-1292	1878	$7,575(S)	$7,400	5-B	1,077	75	35.0
Univ. of Maine at Presque Isle, Presque Isle, ME 04769-2888	1903	$7,435(S)	$7,422	5-B	1,453	103	30.0
Univ. of Mary, Bismarck, ND 58504-9652	1959	$13,568	$5,330	2-D	3,135	257	52.0
Univ. of Mary Hardin-Baylor, Belton, TX 76513.	1845	$23,050	$6,221	2-D	3,137	261	49.0
Univ. of Maryland, Baltimore Cty, Baltimore, MD 21250	1963	$9,467(S)	$9,937	5-D	13,199	740	57.0
Univ. of Maryland, Coll. Park, College Park, MD 20742	1856	$8,655(S)	$9,677	5-D	37,580	2,328	82.0
Univ. of Maryland Eastern Shore, Princess Anne, MD 21853-1299	1886	$8,602(S)	$7,758	5-D	4,509	354	31.0
Univ. of Maryland Univ. Coll., Adelphi, MD 20783.	1947	$6,168(S)	NA	5-D	42,713	2,402	NA
Univ. of Mary Washington, Fredericksburg, VA 22401-5358	1908	$8,800(S)	$8,900	5-M	5,170	377	70.0
Univ. of Massachusetts Amherst, Amherst, MA 01003	1863	$12,612(S)	$10,310	5-D	28,084	1,345	67.0
Univ. of Massachusetts Boston, Boston, MA 02125-3393	1964	$11,407(S)	NA	5-D	15,741	1,088	40.0
Univ. of Massachusetts Dartmouth, North Dartmouth, MA 02747-2300.	1895	$11,135(S)	$9,408	5-D	9,225	636	48.0
Univ. of Massachusetts Lowell, Lowell, MA 01854-2881	1894	$11,122(S)	$9,520	5-D	15,431	NA	50.0
Univ. of Med. & Dent. of New Jersey, Newark, NJ 07107-1709	1970	NA	NA	5-D	1,457	434	NA
Univ. of Memphis, Memphis, TN 38152	1912	$7,390(S)	$8,330	5-D	22,725	1,497	39.0
Univ. of Miami, Coral Gables, FL 33124	1925	$39,654	$11,528	1-D	16,068	1,402	78.0
Univ. of Michigan, Ann Arbor, MI 48109	1817	$13,437(S)	$9,468	5-D	42,716	3,139	90.0
Univ. of Michigan–Dearborn, Dearborn, MI 48128-1491	1959	$10,107(S)	NA	5-D	8,664	539	49.0
Univ. of Michigan–Flint, Flint, MI 48502-1950.	1956	$9,184(S)	$7,287	5-D	8,262	530	37.0
Univ. of Minnesota, Crookston, Crookston, MN 56716-5001	1966	$11,096(S)	$6,764	5-B	2,653	NA	NA
Univ. of Minnesota, Duluth, Duluth, MN 55812-2496	1947	$12,643(S)	$6,614	5-D	11,806	566	55.0
Univ. of Minnesota, Morris, Morris, MN 56267-2134.	1959	$12,091(S)	$7,194	5-B	1,607	153	66.0
Univ. of Minnesota, Twin Cities Campus, Minneapolis, MN 55455-0213	1851	$12,998(S)	$7,834	5-D	52,557	2,700	70.0
Univ. of Mississippi, University, MS 38677	1844	$5,790(S)	$8,390	5-D	18,224	922	60.0
Univ. of Mississippi Med. Ctr., Jackson, MS 39216-4505	1955	NA	NA	5-D	2,092	836	NA
Univ. of Missouri, Columbia, MO 65211	1839	$8,989(S)	$8,643	5-D	33,805	1,438	48.4
Univ. of Missouri–Kansas City, Kansas City, MO 64110-2499	1929	$9,220(S)	$11,428	5-D	15,492	1,185	49.0
Univ. of Missouri–St Louis, St. Louis, MO 63121	1963	$9,038(S)	$8,404	5-D	16,817	889	43.0
Univ. of Mobile, Mobile, AL 36613.	1961	$17,130	$8,076	2-M	1,734	178	43.0
The Univ. of Montana, Missoula, MT 59812-0002	1893	$5,942(S)	$7,060	5-D	14,207	800	42.0
The Univ. of Montana Western, Dillon, MT 59725-3598	1893	$2,942(S)	$5,834	5-B	1,379	91	33.0
Univ. of Montevallo, Montevallo, AL 35115	1896	$8,520(S)	$5,192	5-M	3,067	211	43.0
Univ. of Mount Union, Alliance, OH 44601-3993.	1846	$25,700	$8,150	2-M	2,231	236	65.0
Univ. of Nebraska at Kearney, Kearney, NE 68849-0001	1903	$6,199(S)	$7,558	5-M	7,100	422	52.0
Univ. of Nebraska at Omaha, Omaha, NE 68182.	1908	$7,027(S)	$8,858	5-D	14,712	939	43.0
Univ. of Nebraska–Lincoln, Lincoln, NE 68588.	1869	$7,563(S)	$8,647	5-D	24,593	1,060	67.0
Univ. of Nebraska Med. Ctr., Omaha, NE 68198	1869	$8,424(S)	NA	5-D	3,625	1,232	NA
Univ. of Nevada, Las Vegas, Las Vegas, NV 89154	1957	$6,705(S)	$10,524	5-D	27,378	1,259	40.0
Univ. of Nevada, Reno, Reno, NV 89557	1874	$6,436(S)	$9,518	5-D	18,004	566	53.0
Univ. of New England, Biddeford, ME 04005-9526.	1831	$30,500	$12,020	1-D	5,587	439	56.0
Univ. of New Hampshire, Durham, NH 03824.	1866	$15,250(S)	$9,452	5-D	15,172	1,027	75.0
Univ. of New Haven, West Haven, CT 06516-1916	1920	$31,750	$13,230	1-D	6,385	572	53.0
Univ. of New Mexico, Albuquerque, NM 87131-2039	1889	$5,809(S)	$8,068	5-D	NA	1,481	45.0
Univ. of New Orleans, New Orleans, LA 70148	1958	$5,257(S)	$8,310	5-D	10,903	550	38.0
Univ. of North Alabama, Florence, AL 35632-0001.	1830	$7,518(S)	$5,490	5-M	7,116	332	33.0
The Univ. of North Carolina at Asheville, Asheville, NC 28804-3299	1927	$5,393(S)	$7,302	5-M	3,863	276	61.0
The Univ. of North Carolina at Chapel Hill, Chapel Hill, NC 27599.	1789	$7,009(S)	$9,470	5-D	29,137	1,810	90.0
The Univ. of North Carolina at Charlotte, Charlotte, NC 28223-0001	1946	$5,440(S)	$7,742	5-D	25,277	1,368	53.0
The Univ. of North Carolina at Greensboro, Greensboro, NC 27412-5001.	1891	$5,275(S)	$6,840	5-D	18,478	1,185	53.0
The Univ. of North Carolina at Pembroke, Pembroke, NC 28372-1510	1887	$4,668(S)	$6,830	5-M	6,913	418	38.0
The Univ. of North Carolina Wilmington, Wilmington, NC 28403-3297	1947	$5,671(S)	$7,900	5-D	13,145	964	67.0
Univ. of North Dakota, Grand Forks, ND 58202	1883	$7,092(S)	$6,100	5-D	14,697	703	51.0
Univ. of Northern Colorado, Greeley, CO 80639.	1890	$6,623(S)	$9,750	5-D	12,599	683	46.0
Univ. of Northern Iowa, Cedar Falls, IA 50614	1876	$7,635(S)	$7,597	5-D	13,168	832	67.0
Univ. of North Florida, Jacksonville, FL 32224	1965	$5,449(S)	$8,452	5-D	16,198	816	47.0
Univ. of North Texas, Denton, TX 76203.	1890	$8,736(S)	$6,892	5-D	35,754	1,644	49.0
Univ. of Northwestern Ohio, Lima, OH 45805-1498	1920	NA	NA	1-B	3,848	127	NA
Univ. of Notre Dame, Notre Dame, IN 46556	1842	$41,417	$11,388	2-D	12,004	1,085	96.0
Univ. of Oklahoma, Norman, OK 73019-0390	1890	$7,125(S)	$8,060	5-D	27,138	1,374	68.0
Univ. of Oklahoma Health Sci. Ctr., Oklahoma City, OK 73190	1890	$5,929(S)	NA	5-D	3,624	444	NA
Univ. of Oregon, Eugene, OR 97403	1872	$8,789(S)	$9,801	5-D	24,396	1,445	67.0
Univ. of Pennsylvania, Philadelphia, PA 19104	1740	$43,738	$12,368	1-D	19,919	2,196	96.0
Univ. of Phoenix, Phoenix, AZ 85034-7209	1989	NA	NA	3-D	292,797	11,477	NA
Univ. of Pikeville, Pikeville, KY 41501	1889	$17,050	$6,700	2-D	1,839	105	25.0
Univ. of Pittsburgh, Pittsburgh, PA 15260	1787	$16,132(S)	$9,430	12-D	28,766	2,334	79.0
Univ. of Pittsburgh at Bradford, Bradford, PA 16701-2812	1963	$12,496(S)	$8,140	12-B	1,565	157	54.0
Univ. of Pittsburgh at Greensburg, Greensburg, PA 15601-5860	1963	$12,626(S)	$8,410	12-B	1,846	133	58.0
Univ. of Pittsburgh at Johnstown, Johnstown, PA 15904-2990.	1927	$12,528(S)	$9,132	12-B	2,957	NA	60.0
Univ. of Portland, Portland, OR 97203-5798.	1901	$34,988	$9,966	2-D	3,936	321	77.0
Univ. of Puerto Rico, Aguadilla Univ. Coll., Aguadilla, PR 00604	1972	NA	NA	6-B	3,076	NA	NA
Univ. of Puerto Rico at Arecibo, Arecibo, PR 00613	1967	NA	NA	6-B	4,352	NA	NA
Univ. of Puerto Rico at Bayamón, Bayamón, PR 00959	1971	$2,944(S)	NA	6-B	4,948	246	30.0
Univ. of Puerto Rico at Carolina, Carolina, PR 00984-4800	1974	NA	NA	6-B	4,321	NA	NA
Univ. of Puerto Rico at Humacao, Humacao, PR 00791.	1962	$2,944(S)	$8,280	6-B	3,774	257	45.0
Univ. of Puerto Rico at Ponce, Ponce, PR 00732-7186	1970	$2,819(S)	$8,280	6-B	2,909	178	NA
Univ. of Puerto Rico at Utuado, Utuado, PR 00641-2500.	1979	NA	NA	6-B	1,623	107	NA
Univ. of Puerto Rico, Cayey Univ. Coll., Cayey, PR 00736	1967	$1,848(S)	$8,180	6-B	3,830	164	41.0
Univ. of Puerto Rico, Mayagüez Campus, Mayagüez, PR 00681-9000	1911	$2,746(S)	$8,280	6-D	13,852	NA	NA

Name, address	Year founded	Tuition & fees	Room & board	Control, degree	Enroll- ment	Faculty	Grad. rate
Univ. of Puerto Rico, Med. Sci. Campus, San Juan, PR 00936-5067 (4)	1950	NA	NA	6-D	2,381	NA	NA
Univ. of Puerto Rico, Río Piedras, San Juan, PR 00931-3300	1903	$1,368(S)	$8,280	6-D	18,966	1,084	47.0%
Univ. of Puget Sound, Tacoma, WA 98416	1888	$38,720	$10,020	1-D	2,938	283	73.0
Univ. of Redlands, Redlands, CA 92373-0999	1907	$39,338	$11,924	1-D	4,769	482	63.0
Univ. of Rhode Island, Kingston, RI 02881	1892	$11,366(S)	$10,796	5-D	16,317	1,206	63.0
Univ. of Richmond, Richmond, VA 23173	1830	$44,210	$9,760	1-D	3,555	427	83.0
Univ. of Rio Grande, Rio Grande, OH 45674	1876	$19,520	$8,220	1-M	2,261	150	37.0
Univ. of Rochester, Rochester, NY 14627	1850	$41,826	$12,120	1-D	10,319	NA	NA
Univ. of St. Francis, Joliet, IL 60435-6169	1920	$25,932	$8,462	2-D	2,232	248	63.0
Univ. of St. Francis, Fort Wayne, IN 46808-3994	1890	$24,560	$8,170	2-M	2,464	249	NA
Univ. of St. Joseph, West Hartford, CT 06117-2700	1932	$31,826	$13,598	2-D	2,592	290	56.0
Univ. of St. Mary, Leavenworth, KS 66048-5082	1923	$21,980	$7,250	2-M	1,044	118	42.0
Univ. of St. Thomas, St. Paul, MN 55105-1096	1885	$32,073	$8,628	2-D	10,534	NA	74.0
Univ. of St. Thomas, Houston, TX 77006-4696	1947	$25,300	$7,900	2-D	3,754	333	44.0
Univ. of San Diego, San Diego, CA 92110-2492	1949	$38,578	$11,752	2-D	8,317	845	75.0
Univ. of San Francisco, San Francisco, CA 94117-1080	1855	$37,424	$12,250	2-D	9,494	962	69.0
Univ. of Sci. & Arts of Oklahoma, Chickasha, OK 73018	1908	$5,040(S)	$4,990	5-B	1,033	87	38.0
The Univ. of Scranton, Scranton, PA 18510	1888	$37,456	$12,804	2-D	6,034	494	77.0
Univ. of Sioux Falls, Sioux Falls, SD 57105-1699	1883	$22,850	$6,570	2-M	1,564	140	49.2
Univ. of South Alabama, Mobile, AL 36688-0002	1963	$7,380(S)	$6,270	5-D	14,769	834	39.0
Univ. of South Carolina, Columbia, SC 29208	1801	$10,168(S)	$8,026	5-D	30,721	1,792	70.0
Univ. of South Carolina Aiken, Aiken, SC 29801-6309	1961	$8,750(S)	$6,630	5-M	3,277	241	42.0
Univ. of South Carolina Beaufort, Bluffton, SC 29909	1959	$8,158(S)	$6,530	5-B	1,874	141	20.0
Univ. of South Carolina Upstate, Spartanburg, SC 29303-4999	1967	$9,596(S)	$7,122	5-M	5,493	406	39.0
The Univ. of South Dakota, Vermillion, SD 57069-2390	1862	$7,209(S)	$6,543	5-D	9,970	534	49.0
Univ. of Southern California, Los Angeles, CA 90089	1880	$42,818	$12,078	1-D	38,010	3,123	90.0
Univ. of Southern Indiana, Evansville, IN 47712-3590	1965	$6,032(S)	$7,200	5-D	10,820	660	35.0
Univ. of Southern Maine, Portland, ME 04104-9300	1878	$8,900(S)	$9,666	5-D	9,301	643	33.0
Univ. of Southern Mississippi, Hattiesburg, MS 39406-0001	1910	$5,834(S)	$6,634	5-D	16,604	842	47.0
Univ. of South Florida, Tampa, FL 33620-9951	1956	$5,806(S)	$5,232	5-D	40,027	1,190	NA
Univ. of South Florida–St. Petersburg Campus, St. Petersburg, FL 33701	1965	$5,199(S)	$7,570	5-M	4,391	255	29.0
The Univ. of Tampa, Tampa, FL 33606-1490	1931	$23,976	$8,830	1-M	6,737	564	59.0
The Univ. of Tennessee, Knoxville, TN 37996	1794	$8,396(S)	$8,480	5-D	30,194	1,919	63.0
The Univ. of Tennessee at Chattanooga, Chattanooga, TN 37403-2598	1886	$6,718(S)	$8,250	5-D	11,438	730	38.0
The Univ. of Tennessee at Martin, Martin, TN 38238-1000	1900	$6,718(S)	$5,424	5-M	7,913	562	48.0
The Univ. of Texas at Arlington, Arlington, TX 76019	1895	$8,878(S)	$7,554	5-D	33,439	1,316	42.0
The Univ. of Texas at Austin, Austin, TX 78712-1111	1883	$9,794(S)	$10,422	5-D	51,112	2,964	81.0
The Univ. of Texas at Brownsville, Brownsville, TX 78520-4991	1973	$4,990(S)	$6,376	5-D	17,189	701	16.0
The Univ. of Texas at Dallas, Richardson, TX 75080	1969	$11,168(S)	$8,364	5-D	18,864	877	61.0
The Univ. of Texas at El Paso, El Paso, TX 79968-0001	1913	$6,869(S)	$4,725	5-D	22,640	1,183	35.0
The Univ. of Texas at San Antonio, San Antonio, TX 78249-0617	1969	$8,283(S)	$9,271	5-D	30,968	1,290	26.0
The Univ. of Texas at Tyler, Tyler, TX 75799-0001	1971	$6,592(S)	$8,527	5-D	6,696	380	38.0
The Univ. of Texas Health Sci. Ctr. at Houston, Houston, TX 77225-0036	1972	$306/cr. hr.(S)	NA	5-D	4,600	103	NA
The Univ. of Texas Health Sci. Ctr. at San Antonio, San Antonio, TX 78229-3900	1976	NA	NA	5-D	3,093	NA	NA
The Univ. of Texas Med. Branch, Galveston, TX 77555	1891	$5,740(S)	NA	5-D	2,430	NA	NA
The Univ. of Texas of the Permian Basin, Odessa, TX 79762-0001	1969	$6,302(S)	$6,970	5-M	3,831	182	32.0
The Univ. of Texas–Pan Amer., Edinburg, TX 78539	1927	$5,034(S)	$5,614	5-D	19,034	761	42.0
The Univ. of the Arts, Philadelphia, PA 19102-4944	1870	$33,500	$12,300	1-M	2,246	493	62.0
Univ. of the Cumberlands, Williamsburg, KY 40769-1372	1889	$19,000	$7,000	2-D	3,748	182	43.0
Univ. of the District of Columbia, Washington, DC 20008-1175	1976	$7,000(S)	$6,600	9-M	4,921	312	8.0
Univ. of the Incarnate Word, San Antonio, TX 78209-6397	1881	$22,790	$9,658	2-D	7,782	499	43.0
Univ. of the Pacific, Stockton, CA 95211-0197	1851	$36,290	$11,688	1-D	6,710	812	69.0
Univ. of the Sacred Heart, San Juan, PR 00914-0383	1935	NA	NA	2-M	5,666	367	35.3
Univ. of the Sci. in Philadelphia, Philadelphia, PA 19104-4495	1821	$32,148	$12,564	1-D	2,807	267	65.0
Univ. of the Virgin Islands, Saint Thomas, VI 00802-9990	1962	$4,594(S)	$9,386	7-M	2,733	241	33.0
The Univ. of Toledo, Toledo, OH 43606-3390	1872	$8,788(S)	$9,708	5-D	22,610	1,319	46.0
Univ. of Tulsa, Tulsa, OK 74104-3189	1894	$31,126	$9,514	1-D	4,092	412	68.0
Univ. of Utah, Salt Lake City, UT 84112-1107	1850	$6,763(S)	$6,699	5-D	31,660	1,933	55.0
Univ. of Vermont, Burlington, VT 05405	1791	$14,754(S)	$9,738	5-D	13,478	743	72.0
Univ. of Virginia, Charlottesville, VA 22903	1819	$11,576(S)	$8,866	5-D	24,297	1,296	94.0
The Univ. of Virginia's Coll. at Wise, Wise, VA 24293	1954	$7,721(S)	$8,362	5-B	2,067	175	37.0
Univ. of Washington, Seattle, WA 98195	1861	$8,973(S)	$8,169	5-D	42,428	3,602	80.0
Univ. of Washington, Bothell, Bothell, WA 98011-8246	1990	$10,241(S)	$8,340	5-M	3,759	221	NA
Univ. of Washington, Tacoma, Tacoma, WA 98402-3100	1990	$8,689(S)	$8,949	5-M	3,331	197	NA
The Univ. of West Alabama, Livingston, AL 35470	1835	$6,918(S)	$5,840	5-M	5,258	273	NA
Univ. of West Florida, Pensacola, FL 32514-5750	1963	$5,425(S)	$8,684	5-D	11,982	543	48.0
Univ. of West Georgia, Carrollton, GA 30118	1933	$6,592(S)	$7,168	5-D	11,646	602	38.0
Univ. of Wisconsin–Eau Claire, Eau Claire, WI 54702-4004	1916	$8,025(S)	$5,950	5-D	11,233	529	65.0
Univ. of Wisconsin–Green Bay, Green Bay, WI 54311-7001	1968	$7,282(S)	$7,210	5-M	6,665	344	54.0
Univ. of Wisconsin–La Crosse, La Crosse, WI 54601-3742	1909	$8,329(S)	$5,930	5-D	10,074	551	69.0
Univ. of Wisconsin–Madison, Madison, WI 53706-1380	1848	$9,671(S)	$7,780	5-D	42,441	2,856	83.0
Univ. of Wisconsin–Milwaukee, Milwaukee, WI 53201-0413	1956	$8,681(S)	$11,092	5-D	29,726	NA	43.0
Univ. of Wisconsin–Oshkosh, Oshkosh, WI 54901	1871	$7,067(S)	$6,852	5-M	12,669	608	52.0
Univ. of Wisconsin–Parkside, Kenosha, WI 53141-2000	1968	$6,936(S)	$6,872	5-M	5,160	300	31.0
Univ. of Wisconsin–Platteville, Platteville, WI 53818-3099	1866	$7,119(S)	$6,064	5-M	8,153	243	52.0
Univ. of Wisconsin–River Falls, River Falls, WI 54022	1874	$7,277(S)	$6,574	5-M	6,788	360	54.0
Univ. of Wisconsin–Stevens Point, Stevens Point, WI 54481-3897	1894	$7,152(S)	$5,893	5-D	9,418	453	61.0
Univ. of Wisconsin–Stout, Menomonie, WI 54751	1891	$8,542(S)	$5,844	5-M	9,356	477	53.0
Univ. of Wisconsin–Superior, Superior, WI 54880-4500	1893	$7,536(S)	$5,730	5-M	2,825	223	44.0
Univ. of Wisconsin–Whitewater, Whitewater, WI 53190-1790	1868	$7,195(S)	$5,500	5-M	11,629	529	56.0
Univ. of Wyoming, Laramie, WY 82070	1886	$4,278(S)	$9,084	5-D	12,925	811	53.0
Upper Iowa Univ., Fayette, IA 52142-1857	1857	$24,400	$7,290	1-M	5,713	508	45.0
Urbana Univ., Urbana, OH 43078-2091	1850	$21,566	$8,100	1-M	1,551	120	NA
Ursinus Coll., Collegeville, PA 19426-1000	1869	$41,820	$10,300	1-B	1,742	194	83.0
Ursuline Coll., Pepper Pike, OH 44124-4398 (4)	1871	$24,910	$8,288	2-D	1,488	215	54.0
Utah State Univ., Logan, UT 84322	1888	$5,563(S)	$5,280	5-D	26,757	961	56.0
Utah Valley Univ., Orem, UT 84058-5999	1941	$4,584(S)	NA	5-M	33,395	1,609	24.0
Utica Coll., Utica, NY 13502-4892	1946	$29,996	$11,650	1-D	2,981	363	44.0
Valdosta State Univ., Valdosta, GA 31698	1906	$5,697(S)	$6,850	5-D	13,089	616	43.0
Valley Forge Christian Coll., Phoenixville, PA 19460	1938	$16,250	$7,556	2-M	1,204	77	39.0
Valparaiso Univ., Valparaiso, IN 46383	1859	$31,040	$8,756	2-D	3,964	375	71.0
Vanderbilt Univ., Nashville, TN 37240-1001	1873	$41,332	$13,560	1-D	12,836	1,128	92.0
Vanguard Univ. of Southern California, Costa Mesa, CA 92626-9601	1920	$27,400	$8,430	2-M	2,197	203	55.0
Vassar Coll., Poughkeepsie, NY 12604	1861	$44,705	$10,430	1-M	2,386	323	91.0
Vaughn Coll. of Aeronautics & Tech., Flushing, NY 11369 (2)	1932	$19,500	$11,430	1-M	1,680	162	50.0

Name, address	Year founded	Tuition & fees	Room & board	Control, degree	Enroll-ment	Faculty	Grad. rate
Vermont Tech. Coll., Randolph Center, VT 05061-0500	1866	$11,788(S)	$8,520	5-B	1,607	182	NA
Villanova Univ., Villanova, PA 19085-1699	1842	$41,110	$10,960	2-D	10,661	951	91.0%
Virginia Coll. at Birmingham, Birmingham, AL 35209	1989	NA	NA	3-M	3,826	NA	NA
Virginia Commonwealth Univ., Richmond, VA 23284-9005	1838	$9,517(S)	$8,646	5-D	31,899	3,164	53.0
Virginia Military Inst., Lexington, VA 24450 (2)	1839	$13,184(S)	$7,446	5-B	1,569	180	73.0
Virginia Polytechnic Inst. & State Univ., Blacksburg, VA 24061	1872	$11,078(S)	$6,856	5-D	30,936	1,579	80.0
Virginia State Univ., Petersburg, VA 23806-0001	1882	$7,090(S)	$8,880	5-D	5,890	499	40.0
Virginia Union Univ., Richmond, VA 23220-1170	1865	$14,630	$7,174	2-D	1,710	114	31.0
Virginia Wesleyan Coll., Norfolk, VA 23502-5599	1961	$29,680	$7,988	2-B	1,404	131	48.0
Viterbo Univ., La Crosse, WI 54601-4797	1890	$21,870	$7,180	2-M	3,092	378	47.0
Wagner Coll., Staten Island, NY 10301-4495	1883	$37,440	$11,160	1-M	2,232	261	67.0
Wake Forest Univ., Winston-Salem, NC 27109	1834	$43,200	$11,660	1-D	7,351	639	88.0
Walden Univ., Minneapolis, MN 55401	1970	$12,810	NA	3-D	48,982	2,535	NA
Walla Walla Univ., College Place, WA 99324-1198	1892	$23,970	$5,841	2-M	1,791	207	52.0
Walsh Coll. of Accountancy & Bus. Admin., Troy, MI 48007-7006	1922	$11,770	NA	1-M	3,106	178	NA
Walsh Univ., North Canton, OH 44720-3396	1958	$23,585	$8,640	2-D	2,913	314	56.0
Warner Pacific Coll., Portland, OR 97215-4099	1937	$18,290	$7,260	2-M	1,333	116	53.0
Wartburg Coll., Waverly, IA 50677-0903	1852	$32,740	$8,315	2-B	1,805	171	61.0
Washburn Univ., Topeka, KS 66621	1865	$6,566(S)	$6,059	10-D	7,303	558	41.0
Washington Adventist Univ., Takoma Park, MD 20912	1904	$20,180	$7,600	2-M	1,493	134	26.0
Washington & Jefferson Coll., Washington, PA 15301	1781	$36,420	$9,560	1-B	1,457	160	74.0
Washington & Lee Univ., Lexington, VA 24450-0303	1749	$41,837	$9,130	1-D	2,193	285	91.0
Washington Coll., Chestertown, MD 21620-1197	1782	$38,542	$8,228	1-M	1,557	166	76.0
Washington State Univ., Pullman, WA 99164	1890	$10,798(S)	$9,662	5-D	27,327	1,650	67.0
Washington Univ. in St. Louis, St. Louis, MO 63130-4899	1853	$43,705	$13,580	1-D	13,908	1,089	93.0
Wayland Baptist Univ., Plainview, TX 79072-6998	1908	$14,630	$4,157	2-M	1,725	145	41.0
Waynesburg Univ., Waynesburg, PA 15370-1222	1849	$19,090	$7,930	2-D	2,458	259	58.0
Wayne State Coll., Wayne, NE 68787	1910	$5,318(S)	$5,740	5-M	3,517	215	47.0
Wayne State Univ., Detroit, MI 48202	1868	$9,809(S)	$8,696	5-D	30,765	1,872	26.0
Weber State Univ., Ogden, UT 84408-1001	1889	$4,548(S)	$4,600	5-M	25,301	940	43.0
Webster Univ., St. Louis, MO 63119-3194	1915	$22,340	$9,680	1-D	5,300	904	61.0
Wellesley Coll., Wellesley, MA 02481 (3)	1870	$40,660	$12,590	1-B	2,502	351	92.0
Wentworth Inst. of Tech., Boston, MA 02115-5998	1904	$24,000	$11,300	1-M	3,988	290	61.0
Wesleyan Univ., Middletown, CT 06459	1831	$43,674	$12,032	1-D	3,202	375	92.0
Wesley Coll., Dover, DE 19901-3875	1873	$21,565	$9,940	2-M	1,871	157	40.0
West Chester Univ. of Pennsylvania, West Chester, PA 19383	1871	$8,274(S)	$7,784	5-M	15,100	878	68.0
West Coast Univ., North Hollywood, CA 91606	1909	NA	NA	3-B	1,792	NA	NA
Western Carolina Univ., Cullowhee, NC 28723	1889	$5,925(S)	$7,178	5-D	9,352	614	50.0
Western Connecticut State Univ., Danbury, CT 06810-6885	1903	$8,104(S)	$10,223	5-D	6,407	528	40.0
Western Governors Univ., Salt Lake City, UT 84107	1998	NA	NA	1-M	9,022	NA	NA
Western Illinois Univ., Macomb, IL 61455-1390	1899	$9,981(S)	$8,460	5-D	12,554	731	53.0
Western Intl. Univ., Phoenix, AZ 85021-2718	1978	$12,900	NA	3-M	2,993	369	NA
Western Kentucky Univ., Bowling Green, KY 42101	1906	$8,084(S)	$7,320	5-D	21,036	1,200	50.0
Western Michigan Univ., Kalamazoo, MI 49008	1903	$9,606(S)	$8,249	5-D	25,086	1,437	52.0
Western New England Univ., Springfield, MA 01119	1919	$30,844	$11,732	1-D	3,729	337	61.0
Western New Mexico Univ., Silver City, NM 88062-0680	1893	$4,054(S)	$5,660	5-M	2,697	259	NA
Western Oregon Univ., Monmouth, OR 97361-1394	1856	$8,076(S)	$8,620	5-M	6,217	444	38.0
Western State Coll. of Colorado, Gunnison, CO 81231	1901	$5,473(S)	$8,472	5-M	2,242	174	39.0
Western Washington Univ., Bellingham, WA 98225-5996	1893	$7,756(S)	$9,100	5-M	14,842	730	73.0
Westfield State Univ., Westfield, MA 01086	1838	$7,886(S)	$8,665	5-M	6,092	465	58.0
West Liberty Univ., West Liberty, WV 26074	1837	$5,266(S)	$7,710	5-M	2,789	224	39.0
Westminster Coll., Fulton, MO 65251-1299	1851	$20,570	$7,990	2-B	1,102	95	67.0
Westminster Coll., New Wilmington, PA 16172-0001	1852	$31,410	$9,570	2-M	1,608	163	74.0
Westminster Coll., Salt Lake City, UT 84105-3697	1875	$27,182	$7,584	1-M	3,358	394	66.0
Westmont Coll., Santa Barbara, CA 93108-1099	1937	$35,650	$11,340	2-B	1,378	151	77.0
West Texas A&M Univ., Canyon, TX 79016-0001	1909	$6,790(S)	$5,000	5-D	7,886	367	41.0
West Virginia State Univ., Institute, WV 25112-1000	1891	$4,918(S)	$6,602	5-M	2,827	202	25.0
West Virginia Univ., Morgantown, WV 26506	1867	$5,674(S)	$8,404	5-D	29,617	1,324	59.0
West Virginia Univ. Inst. of Tech., Montgomery, WV 25136	1895	$5,344(S)	$8,130	5-M	1,316	NA	29.0
West Virginia Wesleyan Coll., Buckhannon, WV 26201	1890	$25,804	$7,514	2-M	1,452	171	55.0
Wheaton Coll., Wheaton, IL 60187-5593	1860	$28,960	$8,220	2-D	3,005	272	87.0
Wheaton Coll., Norton, MA 02766	1834	$41,894	$10,670	1-B	1,622	166	77.0
Wheeling Jesuit Univ., Wheeling, WV 26003-6295	1954	$25,640	$5,000	2-D	1,429	154	58.0
Wheelock Coll., Boston, MA 02215-4176 (4)	1888	$30,955	$12,800	1-M	1,308	167	58.0
Whitman Coll., Walla Walla, WA 99362-2083	1859	$42,106	$10,560	1-B	1,596	200	85.0
Whittier Coll., Whittier, CA 90608-0634	1887	$38,670	$11,388	1-D	1,779	153	55.0
Whitworth Univ., Spokane, WA 99251-0001	1890	$34,346	$9,364	2-M	2,506	331	80.0
Wichita State Univ., Wichita, KS 67260	1895	$6,189(S)	$6,350	5-D	15,100	507	43.0
Widener Univ., Chester, PA 19013-5792	1821	$34,762	$11,896	1-D	6,464	681	54.0
Wilkes Univ., Wilkes-Barre, PA 18766-0002	1933	$28,210	$11,698	1-D	5,163	416	58.0
Willamette Univ., Salem, OR 97301-3931	1842	$39,012	$9,350	2-D	2,968	337	77.0
William Carey Univ., Hattiesburg, MS 39401-5499	1906	$10,350	$3,450	2-M	3,248	NA	NA
William Jewell Coll., Liberty, MO 64068-1843	1849	$30,500	$7,790	1-B	1,060	147	63.0
William Paterson Univ. of New Jersey, Wayne, NJ 07470-8420	1855	$11,464(S)	$10,500	5-D	11,440	1,134	47.0
William Penn Univ., Oskaloosa, IA 52577-1799	1873	$23,210	$5,472	2-M	2,071	50	26.0
Williams Coll., Williamstown, MA 01267	1793	$43,190	$11,370	1-M	2,109	320	95.0
William Woods Univ., Fulton, MO 65251-1098	1870	$19,000	$7,500	2-M	2,020	357	50.0
Wilmington Coll., Wilmington, OH 45177	1870	$26,840	$8,870	2-M	1,458	119	52.0
Wilmington Univ., New Castle, DE 19720-6491	1967	$7,586	NA	1-D	10,605	1,116	38.0
Wingate Univ., Wingate, NC 28174-0159	1896	$23,845	$9,320	2-D	2,531	235	53.0
Winona State Univ., Winona, MN 55987	1858	$8,520(S)	$7,540	5-D	8,890	556	54.0
Winston-Salem State Univ., Winston-Salem, NC 27110-0003	1892	$4,584(S)	NA	5-M	6,427	336	37.0
Winthrop Univ., Rock Hill, SC 29733	1886	$12,656(S)	$7,270	5-M	5,913	508	60.0
Wittenberg Univ., Springfield, OH 45501-0720	1845	$38,030	$9,736	2-M	1,910	200	71.0
Wofford Coll., Spartanburg, SC 29303-3663	1854	$33,190	$9,375	2-B	1,536	155	79.0
Woodbury Univ., Burbank, CA 91504-1099	1884	$29,994	$9,920	1-M	1,615	291	53.0
Worcester Polytechnic Inst., Worcester, MA 01609-2280	1865	$41,234	$12,292	1-D	5,778	424	76.0
Worcester State Univ., Worcester, MA 01602-2597	1874	$7,653(S)	$10,400	5-M	6,204	420	47.0
Wright State Univ., Dayton, OH 45435	1964	$8,070(S)	$8,387	5-D	18,304	658	40.0
Xavier Univ., Cincinnati, OH 45207	1831	$31,160	$9,920	2-D	6,945	666	79.0
Xavier Univ. of Louisiana, New Orleans, LA 70125-1098	1925	$18,700	$7,600	2-D	3,399	267	53.0
Yale Univ., New Haven, CT 06520	1701	$40,500	$12,200	1-D	11,875	816	96.0
Yeshiva Univ., New York, NY 10033-3201	1886	$35,200	$10,650	1-D	6,563	1,327	85.0
York Coll. of Pennsylvania, York, PA 17405-7199	1787	$16,520	$9,300	1-D	5,605	557	60.0
York Coll. of the City Univ. of New York, Jamaica, NY 11451-0001	1967	$5,496(S)	NA	11-M	8,242	548	17.0
Youngstown State Univ., Youngstown, OH 44555-0001	1908	$7,451(S)	$7,900	5-D	14,529	1,066	35.0

DIRECTORY

Associations and Organizations

Source: World Almanac research

Selected list, generally by category and first distinctive key word in each title. Listed by acronym when that is the official name. Year established is in parentheses. Entries for religious organizations include addresses and leadership information for 2012.

Academic and Educational

Academies, Natl. (1863): (202) 334-2000; www.nationalacademies.org

African American Life and History, Assn. for the Study of (1915): (202) 238-5910; www.asalh.org

Alpha Delta Kappa (1947): (816) 363-5525; www.alphadeltakappa.org

AMIDEAST (America-Mideast Educational and Training Services, Inc.) (1951): (202) 776-9600; www.amideast.org

Anthropological Assn., American (1902): (703) 528-1902; www.aaanet.org

Archaeological Institute of America (1879): (617) 353-9361; www.archaeological.org

Arts, Americans for the (1960): (202) 371-2830; www.artsusa.org

Arts and Sciences, American Academy of (1780): (617) 576-5000; www.amacad.org

Beta Gamma Sigma Honor Society (1913): (314) 432-5650; www.betagammasigma.org

Beta Sigma Phi Intl. (1931): (816) 444-6800; www.betasigmaphi.org

Biological Sciences, American Institute of (1947): (703) 674-2500; www.aibs.org

College Board (1900): (212) 713-8000; www.collegeboard.org

Colleges and Universities, Assn. of American (1915): (202) 387-3760; www.aacu.org

Community Colleges, American Assn. of (1920): (202) 728-0200; www.aacc.nche.edu

Consumer Interests, American Council on (1953): (727) 493-2131; www.consumerinterests.org

Delta Kappa Gamma Society Intl. (1929): (512) 478-5748; www.deltakappagamma.net

Education, American Council on (1918): (202) 939-9300; www.acenet.edu

Education, Council for Advancement and Support of (1974): (202) 328-2273; www.case.org

Education of Young Children, Natl. Assn. for the (1926): (202) 232-8777; www.naeyc.org

Educators for World Peace, Intl. Assn. of (1973): (256) 534-5501; www.iaewp.org

English-Speaking Union of the U.S. (1920): (212) 818-1200; www.esuus.org

Entomological Society of America (1889): (301) 731-4535; www.entsoc.org

Esperanto-USA (1952): (510) 653-0998; www.esperanto-usa.org

Family Relations, Natl. Council on (1938): (888) 781-9331; www.ncfr.org

Foreign Study, American Institute for (1964): (866) 906-2437; www.aifs.com

Freedom of Information Center (1958): (573) 882-3075; www.nfoic.org/foi-center

French Institute/Alliance Française (1971): (212) 355-6100; www.fiaf.org

Genealogical Society, Natl. (1903): (703) 525-0050; www.ngsgenealogy.org

Genetic Assn., American (1914): (541) 867-0334; www.theaga.org

Geological Society of America (1888): (303) 357-1000; www.geosociety.org

Hemispheric Affairs, Council on (1975): (202) 223-4975; www.coha.org

Industrial and Applied Mathematics, Society for (1952): (215) 382-9800; www.siam.org

Intl. Education, Institute of (1919): (212) 883-8200; www.iie.org

Intl. Educational Exchange, Council on (1947): (207) 553-4000; www.ciee.org

Intl. Law, American Society of (1906): (202) 939-6000; www.asil.org

Irish American Cultural Inst. (1962): (973) 605-1991; www.iaci-usa.org

Law Libraries, American Assn. of (1906): (312) 939-4764; www.aallnet.org

Learned Societies, American Council of (1919): (212) 697-1505; www.acls.org

Libraries Assn., Special (1909): (703) 647-4900; www.sla.org

Linguistic Society of America (1924): (202) 835-1714; www.lsadc.org

Mathematical Society, American (1888): (401) 455-4000; www.ams.org

Mensa, Ltd., American (1960): (817) 607-0060; www.us.mensa.org

Meteorological Society, American (1919): (617) 227-2425; www.ametsoc.org

Metric Assn., Inc., U.S. (1916): (310) 832-3763; www.metric.org

Microbiology, American Society for (1899): (202) 737-3600; www.asm.org

Modern Language Assn. of America (1883): (646) 576-5000; www.mla.org

Museums, American Assn. of (1906): (202) 289-1818; www.aam-us.org

Music Education, Natl. Assn. for (formerly Music Educators Natl. Conference) (1907): (703) 860-4000; musiced.nafme.org

Musicological Society, American (1934): (207) 798-4243; www.ams-net.org

Negro College Fund, United (1944): (800) 331-2244; www.uncf.org

Oriental Society, American (1842): (734) 647-4760; www.umich.edu/~aos/

ORT America (1922): (212) 505-7700; www.ortamerica.org

PEN American Center (1922): (212) 334-1660; www.pen.org

Phi Beta Kappa Society (1776): (202) 265-3808; www.pbk.org

Phi Theta Kappa Honor Society (1918): (800) 946-9995; www.ptk.org

Philological Assn., American (1869): (215) 898-4975; www.apaclassics.org

Philosophical Assn., American (1900): (302) 831-1112; www.apaonline.org

Physics, American Inst. of (1931): (301) 209-3100; www.aip.org

Physiological Society, American (1887): (301) 634-7118; www.the-aps.org

Poetry Society of America (1910): (212) 254-9628; www.poetrysociety.org

Poets, Academy of American (1934): (212) 274-0343; www.poets.org

Political Science, Academy of (1880): (212) 870-2500; www.psqonline.org

Population Connection (1968): (202) 332-2200; www.populationconnection.org

Radio and Television Society Foundation, Intl. (1939): (212) 867-6650; www.irts.org

Reading Assn., Intl. (1956): (302) 731-1600; www.reading.org

Religion, American Academy of (1909): (404) 727-3049; www.aarweb.org

Science Fiction Society, World (1939): www.wsfs.org

Sciences, Natl. Academy of (1863): (202) 334-2000; www.nasonline.org

Sigma Beta Delta (1994): (314) 516-4723; www.sigmabetadelta.org

Sociological Assn., American (1905): (202) 383-9005; www.asanet.org

Tau Beta Pi Assn. (1885): (865) 546-4578; www.tbp.org

Teach For America (1990): (212) 279-2080; www.teachforamerica.org

Theological Schools in the U.S. and Canada, Assn. of (1918): (412) 788-6505; www.ats.edu

Theosophical Society in America (1875): (630) 668-1571; www.theosophical.org

Universities, Assn. of American (1900): (202) 408-7500; www.aau.edu

World Learning (1932): (802) 257-7751; www.worldlearning.org

Animal Welfare and Environment

Animals, American Society for the Prevention of Cruelty to (ASPCA) (1866): (212) 876-7700; www.aspca.org

Animals, People for the Ethical Treatment of (PETA) (1980): (757) 622-7382; www.peta.org

Animal Welfare Institute (1951): (202) 337-2332; www.awionline.org

Appalachian Trail Conservancy (1925): (304) 535-6331; www.appalachiantrail.org

Audubon Society, Natl. (1905): (212) 979-3000; www.audubon.org

Bat Conservation Intl. (1982): (512) 327-9721; www.batcon.org

Cat Fanciers' Assn., Inc., The (1906): (330) 680-4070; www.cfa.org

Conservation Intl. (1987): (703) 341-2400; www.conservation.org

Defenders of Wildlife (1947): (800) 385-9712; www.defenders.org

Ducks Unlimited (1937): (901) 758-3825; www.ducks.org

Foresters, Society of American (1900): (301) 897-8720; www.safnet.org

Forest History Society (1946): (919) 682-9319; www.foresthistory.org

Friends of the Earth (1969): (202) 783-7400; www.foe.org

Garden Club of America (1913): (212) 753-8287; www.gcamerica.org

Garden Clubs, Inc., Natl. (1929): (314) 776-7574; www.gardenclub.org

Geographic Society, Natl. (1888): (813) 979-6845; www.nationalgeographic.com

Green Mountain Club (1910): (802) 244-7037; www.greenmountainclub.org

Greenpeace (1971): (202) 462-1177; www.greenpeaceusa.org

Hiking Society, American (1976): (301) 565-6704; www.americanhiking.org

Horse Council, American (1969): (202) 296-4031; www.horsecouncil.org

Humane Society of the U.S., The (1954): (202) 452-1100; www.humanesociety.org

Natural Resources Defense Council (1970): (212) 727-2700; www.nrdc.org

Nature Conservancy, The (1951): (703) 841-5300; www.nature.org

Ocean Conservancy (1972): (202) 429-5609; www.oceanconservancy.org

Ornithologists' Union, American (1883): (505) 326-1579; www.aou.org

Recreation and Park Assn., Natl. (1965): (800) 626-6772; www.nrpa.org

Recycling Coalition, Inc., Natl. (1978): (202) 618-2107; www.nrcrecycles.org

Rose Society, American (1892): (318) 938-5402; www.ars.org

Save the Redwoods League (1918): (415) 362-2352; www.savetheredwoods.org

Sierra Club (1892): (415) 977-5500; www.sierraclub.org

Water Environment Federation (1928): (800) 666-0206; www.wef.org

Wildflower Center, Lady Bird Johnson (1982): (512) 232-0100; www.wildflower.org

Wildlife Federation, Natl. (1936): (800) 822-9919; www.nwf.org

World Wildlife Fund (1961): (202) 293-4800; www.worldwildlife.org

Children and Social Services

Big Brothers Big Sisters of America (1904): (215) 567-7000; www.bbbs.org

Boy Scouts of America (1910): (972) 580-2000; www.scouting.org

Boys & Girls Clubs of America (1906): (404) 487-5700; www.bgca.org

Camp Fire USA (formerly Camp Fire Boys & Girls) (1910): (816) 285-2010; www.camp-fireusa.org

Children's Aid Society (1913): (205) 251-7148; www.childrensaid.org

Children's Book Council, The (1945): (212) 966-1990; www.cbcbooks.org

Child Welfare League of America (1920): (202) 688-4200; www.cwla.org

Feeding America (formerly America's Second Harvest) (1976): (800) 771-2303; feedingamerica.org

4-H Council, Natl. (1914): (301) 961-2800; www.4-h.org

Future Business Leaders of America-Phi Beta Lambda, Inc. (1942): (800) 325-2946; www.fbla-pbl.org

Future Farmers of America Org., Natl. (1928): (317) 802-6060; www.ffa.org
Gifted Children, Natl. Assn. for (1954): (202) 785-4268; www.nagc.org
Girl Scouts of the USA (1912): (212) 852-8000; www.girlscouts.org
Honor Society, Natl. (1921): (703) 860-0200; www.nhs.us
Junior Achievement, Inc. (1919): (719) 540-8000; www.ja.org
Junior Auxiliaries, Inc., Natl. Assn. of (1941): (662) 332-3000; www.najanet.org
Junior Chamber, U.S. (1914): (636) 681-1857; www.usjaycees.org
Junior Honor Society, Natl. (1929): (703) 860-0200; www.njhs.us
Missing and Exploited Children, Natl. Center for (1984): (703) 224-2150; www.missingkids.com
Pilot Intl. (1921): (478) 477-1208; www.pilotinternational.org
Student Councils, Natl. Assn. of (1931): (703) 860-0200; www.nasc.us

Fraternal

Eagles, Fraternal Order of (1898): (614) 883-2200; www.foe.com
Eastern Star, General Grand Chapter, Order of the (1876): (202) 667-4737; www.easternstar.org
Elks of the USA, Benevolent and Protective Order of (1868): (773) 755-4700; www.elks.org
Freemasonry, Scottish Rite of, Supreme Council, 33°, Northern Masonic Jurisdiction (1813): (781) 862-4410; www.scottishritenmj.org
Freemasonry, Supreme Council, 33°, Scottish Rite of, Southern Jurisdiction (1802): (202) 232-3579; www.srmason-sj.org
Kiwanis Intl. (1915): (317) 875-8755; www.kiwanis.org
Knights of Columbus (1882): (203) 752-4000; www.kofc.org
Knights of Pythias, Order of (1864): (610) 544-3500; www.pythias.org
Lions Clubs Intl. (1917): (630) 571-5466; www.lionsclubs.org
Men, Natl. Coalition for (1977): (888) 223-1280; www.ncfm.org
Moose Intl., Inc. (1888): (630) 859-2000; www.mooseintl.org
Odd Fellows, Independent Order of (1819): (336) 725-5955; www.ioof.org
Rotary Intl. (1905): (847) 866-3000; www.rotary.org
Shriners Intl. (1872): (813) 281-0300; www.shrinersinternational.org
Sons of Italy in America, Order (1905): (202) 547-2900; www.osia.org
Sons of Norway (1895): (612) 827-3611; www.sofn.com
Woodmen of America, Modern (1883): (800) 447-9811; www.modern-woodmen.org

Historical

Civil War Trust (1987): (202) 367-1861; www.civilwar.org
Colonial Dames XVII Century, Natl. Soc. (1915): (202) 293-1700; www.colonialdames17c.org
Daughters of the American Revolution (1890): (202) 628-1776; www.dar.org
Daughters of the Confederacy, United (1894): (804) 355-1636; www.hqudc.org
Historical Assn., American (1884): (202) 544-2422; www.historians.org
Historic Preservation, Natl. Trust for (1949): (202) 588-6000; www.preservationnation.org
Lewis and Clark Trail Heritage Foundation (1969): (406) 454-1234; lewisandclark.org
Mayflower Descendants, General Soc. of (1897): (508) 746-3188; www.themayflowersociety.com
Pilgrims, Natl. Soc. Sons and Daughters of the (1908): www.nssdp.com
Railway Historical Society, Natl. (1935): (215) 557-6606; www.nrhs.org
Sons of the American Revolution, Natl. Soc. (1889): (502) 589-1776; www.sar.org

Sons of Confederate Veterans (1896): (800) 380-1896; www.scv.org
State and Local History, American Assn. for (1940): (615) 320-3203; www.aaslh.org
Supreme Court Historical Society (1974): (202) 543-0400; www.supremecourthistory.org
Theodore Roosevelt Assn. (1920): (516) 921-6319; www.theodoreroosevelt.org
Thoreau Society (1941): (978) 369-5310; www.thoreausociety.org
Titanic Historical Society, Inc. (1963): (413) 543-4770; www.titanichistoricalsociety.org
Victorian Society in America (1966): (215) 636-9872; www.victoriansociety.org

Industrial and Trade

Aerospace Industries Assn. (1919): (703) 358-1000; www.aia-aerospace.org
Better Business Bureaus, Council of (1912): (703) 276-0100; www.bbb.org
Chamber of Commerce of the U.S.A. (1912): (202) 659-6000; www.uschamber.com
Chemistry Council, American (1872): (202) 249-7000; www.americanchemistry.com
Construction Specifications Institute (1948): (800) 689-2900; www.csinet.org
CropLife America (1933): (202) 296-1585; www.croplifeamerica.org
Cryogenic Soc. of America, Inc. (1964): (708) 383-6220; www.cryogenicsociety.org
Electrical Manufacturers Assn., Natl. (1926): (703) 841-3200; www.nema.org
Fire Protection Assn., Natl. (NFPA) (1896): (617) 770-3000; www.nfpa.org
Fisheries Soc., American (1870): (301) 897-8616; www.fisheries.org
Foreign Trade Council, Inc., Natl. (1914): (202) 887-0278; www.nftc.org
Funeral Consumers Alliance (1963): (802) 865-8300; www.funerals.org
Hotel & Lodging Assn., American (1910): (202) 289-3100; www.ahla.com
Insurance Assn., American (1866): (202) 828-7100; www.aiadc.org
Magazine Media, Assn. of (1919): (212) 872-3700; www.magazine.org
Manufacturers, Natl. Assn. of (1895): (202) 637-3000; www.nam.org
Newspaper Assn. of America (1992): (571) 366-1000; www.naa.org
Nuclear Society, American (1954): (708) 352-6611; www.ans.org
Orchestras, League of American (1942): (212) 262-5161; www.symphony.org
Petroleum Institute, American (1919): (202) 682-8000; www.api.org
Printing Industries of America, Inc. (1887): (412) 741-6860; www.printing.org
Publishers, Assn. of American (1970): (202) 347-3375; www.publishers.org
Retail Federation, Natl. (1908): (202) 783-7971; www.nrf.com
Safety Council, Natl. (1913): (630) 285-1121; www.nsc.org
Shipbuilders Council of America (1920): (202) 347-5462; www.shipbuilders.org
Small Business Assn., Natl. (1937): (800) 345-6728; www.nsba.biz
Software and Information Industry Assn. (1999): (202) 289-7442; www.siia.net
Tall Buildings and Urban Habitat, Council on (1969): (312) 567-3307; www.ctbuh.org
Toy Industry Assn., Inc. (1916): (212) 675-1141; www.toyassociation.org
Water Works Assn., American (1881): (303) 794-7711; www.awwa.org
Zoos & Aquariums, Assn. of (1924): (301) 562-0777; www.aza.org

Lifestyle and Travel

AAA (American Automobile Assn.) (1902): (407) 444-7000; www.aaa.com
AARP (formerly American Assn. of Retired Persons) (1958): (888) 687-2277; www.aarp.org
AFS Intercultural Programs USA (1947): (800) 237-4636; www.afsusa.org
Aircraft Owners and Pilots Assn. (1939): (800) 872-2672; www.aopa.org

Appalachian Mountain Club (1876): (617) 523-0636; www.outdoors.org
Boat Owners Assn. of the U.S. (1966): (703) 461-4666; www.boatus.com
Camp Assn., American (1910): (765) 342-8456; www.acacamps.org
Consumer Federation of America (1968): (202) 387-6121; www.consumerfed.org
Consumers Union (1936): (914) 378-2000; www.consumersunion.org
Green America (formerly Co-op America) (1982): (800) 584-7336; www.greenamerica.org
Helicopter Society Intl., American (1943): (703) 684-6777; www.vtol.org
Hostelling Intl. USA (1934): (301) 495-1240; www.hiusa.org
Jewish Community Centers Assn. of North America (1917): (212) 532-4949; www.jcca.org
Motorcyclist Assn., American (1924): (800) 262-5646; www.americanmotorcyclist.com
Nude Recreation, American Assn. for (1931): (800) 879-6833; www.aanr.com
Parents Without Partners, Inc. (1957): (800) 637-7974; www.parentswithoutpartners.org
Planetary Society (1980): (626) 793-5100; www.planetary.org
SCRABBLE® Assn., Natl. (1978): (631) 477-0033; www.scrabble-assoc.com
Sports Car Club of America (1944): (785) 357-7222; www.scca.org
Toastmasters Intl. (1924): (949) 858-8255; www.toastmasters.org
YMCA (Young Men's Christian Assn.) of the USA (1851): (800) 872-9622; www.ymca.net
YWCA (Young Women's Christian Assn.) USA (1858): (202) 467-0801; www.ywca.org

Military and Veterans'

Air Force Assn. (1946): (703) 247-5800; www.afa.org
American Legion (1919): (317) 630-1200; www.legion.org
American Legion Auxiliary (1919): (317) 569-4500; www.alaforveterans.org
AMVETS (American Veterans) (1944): (877) 726-8387; www.amvets.org
Army, Assn. of the United States (1950): (703) 841-4300; www.ausa.org
Blinded Veterans Assn. (1958): (202) 371-8880; www.bva.org
Civil Air Patrol (1941): (877) 227-9142; www.gocivilairpatrol.com
Coast Guard Combat Veterans Assn. (1985): (610) 539-1000; www.coastguardcombatvets.com
Disabled American Veterans (1920): (859) 441-7300; www.dav.org
82nd Airborne Division Assn., Inc. (1944): (910) 223-1182; www.82ndassociation.org
Ex-Prisoners of War, American (1942): (817) 649-2979; www.axpow.org
Fleet Reserve Assn. (1924): (703) 683-1400; www.fra.org
Iraq and Afghanistan Veterans of America (2004): (212) 982-9699; www.iava.org
Jewish War Veterans of the U.S.A. (1896): (202) 265-6280; www.jwv.org
Legion of Valor Museum (1991): (559) 498-0510; www.legionofvalor.com/museum.php
Marine Corps League (1937): (703) 207-9588; www.mcleague.org
Military Officers Assn. of America (1929): (703) 549-2311; www.moaa.org
Military Order of the World Wars (1919): (703) 683-4911; www.militaryorder.net
National Guard Assn. of the U.S. (1878): (202) 789-0031; www.ngaus.org
Naval Institute, U.S. (1873): (410) 268-6110; www.usni.org
Navy League of the United States (1902): (703) 528-1775; www.navyleague.org
Ninety-Nines, Inc. (Intl. Org. of Women Pilots) (1929): (405) 685-7969; www.ninety-nines.org
Non-Commissioned Officers Assn. (1960): (800) 662-2620; www.ncoausa.org
Paralyzed Veterans of America (1946): (800) 424-8200; www.pva.org

POW/MIA Families, Natl. League of (1970): (703) 465-7432; www.pow-miafamilies.org
Purple Heart, Military Order of the (1932): (703) 354-2140; www.purpleheart.org
Reserve Officers Assn. of the U.S. (1922): (202) 479-2200; www.roa.org
Sons of the American Legion (1932): (317) 630-1200; www.legion.org/sons
Tin Can Sailors (Natl. Assn. of Destroyer Veterans) (1976): (508) 677-0515; www.destroyers.org
Uniformed Services, Natl. Assn. for (1968): (703) 750-1342; www.naus.org
USO, Inc. (United Service Org.) (1941): (888) 484-3876; www.uso.org
USS Los Angeles CA-135 Assn. (1977): c/o Jim Osborne, 1314 N. Alden Rd., Muncie, IN 47304; www.uss-la-ca135.org/2la-assoc.htm
USS Missouri Memorial Assn., Inc. (1998): (808) 455-1600; www.ussmissouri.org
Veterans of Foreign Wars (1899): (816) 756-3390; www.vfw.org
Veterans of Foreign Wars, Ladies Auxiliary to the (1914): (816) 561-8655; www.ladiesauxvfw.org
Vietnam Veterans of America (1978): (301) 585-4000; www.vva.org
Women's Army Corps Veterans' Assn. (1946): (256) 820-6824; www.armywomen.org

Political

Abortion Federation, National (1977): (202) 667-5881; www.prochoice.org
Advancement and Support of Education, Council for (1974): (202) 328-2273; www.case.org
American Indians, Natl. Congress of (1944): (202) 466-7767; www.ncai.org
American-Islamic Relations, Council on (1994): (202) 488-8787; www.cair.com
Center for Responsive Politics (1983): (202) 857-0044; www.opensecrets.org
Cities, Natl. League of (1924): (202) 626-3100; www.nlc.org
Civil Liberties Union, American (ACLU) (1920): (212) 549-2500; www.aclu.org
Coffee Party USA (2010): (301) 259-1869; www.coffeepartyusa.com
Common Cause (1970): (202) 833-1200; www.commoncause.org
Concerned Women for America (1979): (202) 488-7000; www.cwfa.org
Congress of Racial Equality (CORE) (1942): (212) 598-4000; www.core-online.org
Crime and Delinquency, Natl. Council on (1907): (800) 306-6223; www.nccdglobal.org
Democratic Natl. Committee (1848): (202) 863-8000; www.democrats.org
Feminists for Life of America (1972): (703) 836-3354; www.feministsforlife.org
Gay & Lesbian Alliance Against Defamation (GLAAD) (1985): (212) 629-3322; www.glaad.org
Gay and Lesbian Task Force, Natl. (1973): (202) 393-5177; www.thetaskforce.org
Governors Assn., Natl. (1908): (202) 624-5300; www.nga.org
Grange of the Order of Patrons of Husbandry, Natl. (1867): (202) 628-3507; www.nationalgrange.org
Gray Panthers (1970): (202) 737-6637; www.graypanthers.org
Greens/Green Party USA (1984): (866) 473-3672; www.greenparty.org
Homeless, Natl. Coalition for the (1984): (202) 462-4822; www.nationalhomeless.org
Japanese American Citizens League (1929): (415) 921-5225; www.jacl.org
Jewish Committee, American (1906): (212) 751-4000; www.ajc.org
John Birch Society (1958): (920) 749-3780; www.jbs.org
Libertarian Party (1971): (202) 333-0008; www.lp.org
Mayors, U.S. Conference of (1932): (202) 293-7330; www.usmayors.org
NAACP (Natl. Assn. for the Advancement of Colored People) (1909): (410) 580-5777; www.naacp.org

National Tea Party Federation (2010): www.thenationalteapartyfederation.com
NRA (National Rifle Assn.) (1871): (800) 672-3888; www.nra.org
Parliamentarians, Natl. Assn. of (1930): (816) 833-3892; www.parliamentarians.org
Reform Party Natl. Committee (1995): (972) 275-9297; www.reformparty.org
Republican Natl. Committee (1856): (202) 863-8500; www.rnc.org
Science, American Assn. for the Advancement of (1848): (202) 326-6400; www.aaas.org
Southern Christian Leadership Conference (1957): (404) 522-1420; sclcnational.org
Southern Poverty Law Center (1971): (334) 956-8200; www.splcenter.org
State Governments, Council of (1933): (859) 244-8000; www.csg.org
Tax Foundation (1937): (202) 464-6200; www.taxfoundation.org
Taxpayers Union, Natl. (1969): (703) 683-5700; www.ntu.org
Tea Party Patriots (2009): www.teapartypatriots.org
Term Limits, U.S. (1992): (703) 383-0907; www.termlimits.org
Urban League, Natl. (1910): (212) 558-5300; www.nul.org
Women, Natl. Organization for (NOW) (1966): (202) 628-8669; www.now.org
Women and Families, Natl. Partnership for (1971): (202) 986-2600; www.nationalpartnership.org
Women's Christian Temperance Union (1874): (847) 864-1397; www.wctu.org
Women Voters of the U.S., League of (1920): (202) 429-1965; www.lwv.org
Zionist Organization of America (1897): (212) 481-1500; www.zoa.org

Religious

African Methodist Episcopal Church (1787): 500 8th Ave. S., Nashville, TN 37203; (615) 254-0911; www.ame-church.com; Gen. Sec., Dr. Clement W. Fugh
African Methodist Episcopal Zion Church (1796): 3225 West Sugar Creek Rd., Charlotte, NC 28269; (704) 599-4630; www.amez.org; Senior Bishop, George W. C. Walker Sr.
American Baptist Churches USA (1907): P.O. Box 851, Valley Forge, PA 19482; (610) 768-2000; www.abc-usa.org; Gen. Sec., A. Roy Medley
Antiochian Orthodox Christian Archdiocese of North America (1895): P.O. Box 5238, Englewood, NJ 07631; (201) 871-1355; www.antiochian.org; Primate, Archbishop, Metropolitan Philip Saliba
Armenian Apostolic Church of America: *Eastern Prelacy* (1958): 138 E. 39th St., New York, NY 10016; (212) 689-7810; www.armenianprelacy.org; Prelate, Archbishop Oshagan Choloyan; *Western Prelacy (1973)*: 6252 Honolulu Ave., La Crescenta, CA 91214; (818) 248-7737; www.westernprelacy.org; Prelate, Archbishop Moushegh Mardirossian
Assemblies of God USA (1914): 1445 N. Boonville Ave., Springfield, MO 65802; (417) 862-2781; www.ag.org; Gen. Supt., George O. Wood
Atheists, American (1963): P.O. Box 158, Cranford, NJ 07016; (908) 276-7300; www.atheists.org; Pres., David P. Silverman
Bahá'ís of the U.S., National Spiritual Assembly of the (1909): 1233 Central St., Evanston, IL 60201; (847) 733-3400; www.bahai.us; Sec., Kenneth E. Bowers
Baptist Bible Fellowship Intl. (1950): 720 E. Kearney St., Springfield, MO 65803; (417) 862-5001; www.bbfi.org; Pres., Linzy Slayden
Baptist Convention, Southern (1845): 901 Commerce St., Nashville, TN 37203; (615) 244-2355; www.sbc.net; Pres. Bryant Wright
Baptist Convention, USA, Inc., National (1886): 1700 Baptist World Center Dr., Nashville, TN 37207; (615) 228-6292; www.nationalbaptist.com; Pres., Dr. Julius R. Scruggs

Baptist Convention of America, Inc., Intl., National (1880): 777 S.R.L. Thornton Freeway, Ste. 210, Dallas, TX 75203; (214) 942-3311; www.nbcainc.com; Pres., Rev. Stephen J. Thurston
Baptist Conventional of America, National Missionary (1880): 6925 Wofford Dr., Dallas, TX 75227; (877) 886-6222; www.nmbca.com; Pres., Dr. C. C. Robertson
Bible Society, American (1816): 1865 Broadway, New York, NY 10023; (212) 408-1200; www.americanbible.org; Pres. and CEO, Dr. Lamar Vest
Biblical Literature, Society of (1880): 825 Houston Mill Rd., Atlanta, GA 30329; (404) 727-3100; www.sbl-site.org
B'nai B'rith Intl. (1843): 2020 K St. NW, 7th Fl., Washington, DC 20006; (202) 857-6600; www.bnaibrith.org
Brethren in Christ Church (c. 1778): 431 Grantham Rd., Grantham, PA 17027; (717) 697-2634; www.bic-church.org; Moderator, Dr. Warren L. Hoffman
Buddhist Churches of America (1899): 1710 Octavia St., San Francisco, CA 94109; (415) 776-5600; www.buddhistchurchesofamerica.com; Pres., Ron Murakami
Catholic Bishops, U.S. Conference of (2001): 3211 4th St. NE, Washington, DC 20017; (202) 541-3000; www.usccb.org; Gen. Sec., Msgr. Ronny E. Jenkins
Christian Church (Disciples of Christ) (1832): Disciples Center, 130 E. Washington St., Indianapolis, IN 46204; (317) 635-3100; www.disciples.org; Gen. Min. and Pres., Rev. Dr. Sharon E. Watkins
Christian Methodist Episcopal Church (1870): 4466 Elvis Presley Blvd., Memphis, TN 38116; (901) 345-0580; www.c-m-e.org; Senior Bishop, Thomas L. Hoyt, Jr.
Church of the Brethren (1708): General Offices, 1451 Dundee Ave., Elgin, IL 60120; (847) 742-5100; www.brethren.org; Gen. Sec., Stanley J. Noffsinger
Church of Christ (1830): P.O. Box 472, Independence, MO 64051; (816) 833-3995; www.churchofchrist-tl.org; Council of Apostles, Sec., Apostle Smith N. Brickhouse
Church of God (Anderson, IN) (1881): Box 2420, Anderson, IN 46018; (765) 642-0256; www.chog.org; Gen. Dir., Dr. Ronald V. Duncan
Church of God (Cleveland, TN) (1886): 2490 Keith St. NW, Cleveland, TN 37320; (423) 472-3361; www.churchofgod.org; Gen. Overseer, Dr. Raymond F. Culpepper
Church of God in Christ (1897): Mason Temple, 930 Mason St., Memphis, TN 38126; (901) 947-9300; www.cogic.org; Presiding Bishop, Bishop Charles E. Blake Sr.
Church of Jesus Christ (1862): 525 6th St., Monongahela, PA 15063; (412) 771-1686; www.thechurchofjesuschrist.org; Pres., Larry Watson
Church of Jesus Christ of Latter-day Saints, The (Mormons) (1830): 50 W. North Temple St., Salt Lake City, UT 84150; (801) 240-2640; www.lds.org; Pres., Thomas S. Monson
Church of the Nazarene (1908): Global Ministry Center, 17001 Prairie Star Pkwy., Lenexa, KS 66220; (913) 577-0500; www.nazarene.org; Gen. Sec., David P. Wilson
Community of Christ (reorganized Church of Jesus Christ of Latter-Day Saints) (1830): Intl. Headquarters, 1001 W. Walnut, Independence, MO 64050; (816) 833-1000; www.cofchrist.org; Pres., Stephen M. Veazey
Community Churches, International Council of (1950): 21116 Washington Pkwy., Frankfort, IL 60423; (815) 464-5690; www.icccusa.org; Exec. Dir., Michael Livingston
Conservative Judaism, United Synagogue of (1913): 820 Second Ave., New York, NY 10017; (212) 533-7800; www.uscj.org; Pres., Richard Skolnik
Converge Worldwide (formerly Baptist General Conference) (1852): 2002 S. Arlington Heights Rd., Arlington

Heights, IL 60005; (800) 323-4215; www.convergeworldwide.org; Pres. and CEO, Jerry Sheveland

Cumberland Presbyterian Church (1810): 8207 Traditional Pl., Cordova, TN 38016; (901) 276-4572; www.cumberland.org; Moderator, Don Tabor

Episcopal Church (1789): 815 Second Ave., New York, NY 10017; (212) 716-6000; www.episcopalchurch.org; Presiding Bishop and Primate, Most Rev. Katharine Jefferts Schori

Evangelical Lutheran Church in America (1988): 8765 W. Higgins Rd., Chicago, IL 60631; (773) 380-2700; www.elca.org; Presiding Bishop, Rev. Mark S. Hanson

First Church of Christ, Scientist, The (1879): 210 Massachusetts Ave., Boston, MA 02115; (617) 450-2000; christianscience.com; Pres., Chet Manchester

Free Methodist Church USA (1860): 770 N. High School Rd., Indianapolis, IN 46214; (317) 244-3660; fmcusa.org; The Board of Bishops

Freedom From Religion Foundation (1978): PO Box 750, Madison, WI 53701; (608) 256-8900; www.ffrf.org

Friends General Conference (1900): 1216 Arch St., #2B, Philadelphia, PA 19107; (215) 561-1700; www.fgcquaker.org; Gen. Sec., Barry Crossno

Gideons Intl. (1899): P.O. Box 140800, Nashville, TN 37214; (615) 564-5000; www.gideons.org

Greek Orthodox Archdiocese of America (1922): 8 E. 79th St., New York, NY 10075; (212) 570-3500; www.goarch.org; Primate, Archbishop Demetrios

Hadassah, the Women's Zionist Organization of America, Inc. (1912): 50 W. 58th St., New York, NY 10019; (888) 303-3640; www.hadassah.org

Interfaith Alliance (1994): 1212 New York Ave. NW, Ste. 1250, Washington, DC 20005; (202) 238-3300; www.interfaithalliance.org; Pres., Rev. Dr. C. Welton Gaddy

Islamic Society of North America: 6555 S. 750 East, Plainfield, IN 46168; (317)

839-8157; www.isna.net; Pres., Mohamed Hagmagid Ali

Jehovah's Witnesses (1931): 25 Columbia Heights, Brooklyn, NY 11201; (718) 560-5000; www.jw.org

Jewish Congress, American (1918): 115 E. 57th St., Ste. 11, New York, NY 10022; (212) 879-4500; www.ajcongress.org; Pres., Richard S. Gordon

Jewish Reconstructionist Federation (1955): Beit Devora, 101 Greenwood Ave., Ste. 430, Jenkintown, PA 19046; (215) 885-5601; www.jrf.org; Pres., Robert Barkin

Jewish Women, Natl. Council of (1893): 475 Riverside Dr., Ste. 1901, New York, NY 10115; (212) 645-4048; www.ncjw.org; Pres., Linda Slucker

Lutheran Church—Missouri Synod (1847): 1333 S. Kirkwood Rd., St. Louis, MO 63122; (800) 248-1930; www.lcms.org; Pres., Rev. Dr. Matthew C. Harrison

Mennonite Church USA (2001): 718 N. Main St., Newton, KS 67114; (316) 283-5100; www.mennoniteusa.org; Exec. Dir., Ervin Stutzman

Moravian Church in North America (1735): www.moravian.org; *Northern Prov.:* 1021 Center St., P.O. Box 1245, Bethlehem, PA 18016; (610) 867-7566; Pres., Betsy Miller; *Southern Prov.:* 459 S. Church St., Winston-Salem, NC 27101; (336) 725-5811; Pres., Rt. Rev. Wayne Burkette

North American Shia Ithnasheri Muslim Communities, Org. of (1986) P.O. Box 29691, Minneapolis, MN 55429; (905) 763-7512; www.nasimco.info; Pres., Gulamabbas Najafi

Orthodox Union (1898): 11 Broadway, New York, NY 10004; (212) 563-4000; www.ou.org; Pres., Dr. Simcha Katz

Pentecostal Assemblies of the World, Inc. (1906): 3939 N. Meadows Dr., Indianapolis, IN 46205; (317) 547-9541; www.pawinc.org; Presiding Bishop, Charles H. Ellis, III

Presbyterian Church (U.S.A.) (1983): 100 Witherspoon St., Louisville, KY 40202; (800) 728-7228; www.pcusa.org; Exec. Dir., Linda Valentine

Progressive National Baptist Convention, Inc. (1961): 601 50th St. NE, Washington, DC 20019; (202) 396-0558; www.pnbc.org; Pres., Dr. Carroll A. Baltimore Sr.

Rabbis, Central Conference of American (1889): 355 Lexington Ave., New York, NY 10017; (212) 972-3636; www.ccarnet.org; Pres., Jonathan Stein

Reform Judaism, Union for (1873): 633 3rd Ave., New York, NY 10017; (212) 650-4000; www.urj.org; Pres., Rabbi Rick Jacobs

Secular Humanism, Council for (1980): P.O. Box 664, Amherst, NY 14226; (716) 636-7571; www.secularhumanism.org; Pres., Ronald A. Lindsay

Separation of Church and State, Americans United for (1947): 1301 K St. NW, Ste. 850E, Washington, DC 20005; (202) 466-3234; www.au.org; Exec. Dir., Rev. Barry W. Lynn

Seventh-day Adventist Church (1863): 12501 Old Columbia Pike, Silver Spring, MD 20904; (301) 680-6000; www.adventist.org; Pres., Ted N. C. Wilson

Unitarian Universalist Assn. of Congregations (1961): 25 Beacon St., Boston, MA 02108; (617) 742-2100; www.uua.org; Pres., Rev. Peter Morales

United Church of Christ (1957): 700 Prospect Ave., Cleveland, OH 44115; (216) 736-2100; www.ucc.org; Pres., Rev. Geoffrey A. Black

United Methodist Church (1968): 100 Maryland Ave. NE, Washington, DC 20002; (202) 488-5600; www.umc.org

United Pentecostal Church Intl. (1945): 8855 Dunn Rd., Hazelwood, MO 63042; (314) 837-7300; www.upci.org; Gen. Supt., David K. Bernard

Wesleyan Church (1843): 13300 Olio Rd., Fishers, IN 46037; (317) 774-7900; www.wesleyan.org; Gen. Sec., Dr. Ronald D. Kelly

Businesses and Corporations

Source: World Almanac research

Listed below are major corporations offering products and services to U.S. consumers, as of June 2012. Alphabetization is by first key word or founder last name. Listings generally include examples of products offered.

Company name (NYSE/Nasdaq symbol, if traded on those markets): Address; Telephone number; Website; Top executive; Business, products, or services.

A&P: see Great Atlantic & Pacific Tea Co., Inc.

Abbott Laboratories (ABT): 100 Abbott Park Rd., Abbott Park, IL 60064; (847) 937-6100; www.abbott.com; Miles D. White; develops, mfr. pharmaceutical, nutritional, diagnostic prods.

ABC: see Disney Co.

adidas Group: Adi-Dassler-Strasse 1, D-91074 Herzogenaurach, Germany; +49 9132-84-0; www.adidas-group.com; Herbert Hainer; apparel and accessories mfr. (Reebok, Rockport, Taylor Golf).

Advance Publications, Inc.: 950 Fingerboard Rd., Staten Island, NY, 10305; (718) 981-1234; www.advance.net; Samuel I. Newhouse Jr.; communications, newspaper and magazine publisher (*Parade*; Condé Nast subsids.: *New Yorker, Vanity Fair, Vogue*).

Aetna, Inc. (AET): 151 Farmington Ave., Hartford, CT 06156; (860) 273-0123; www.aetna.com; Mark T. Bertolini; health care, employee benefits.

Aflac, Inc. (AFL): 1932 Wynnton Rd., Columbus, GA 31999; (706) 323-3431; www.aflac.com; Daniel P. Amos; supplemental health and life insurance.

Alaska Air Group, Inc. (ALK): 19300 International Blvd., Seattle, WA 98188; (206) 392-5040; www.alaskaair.com; William S. Ayer; airline carriers (Alaska Airlines, Horizon Air).

Alberto Culver Co.: see Unilever USA.

Alcatel-Lucent (ALU): 3 av. Octave Gréard, Paris 75007, France; +33 (1) 4076-1010;

www.alcatel-lucent.com; Ben Verwaayen; telecommunications equip., broadband networks.

Alcoa Inc. (AA): 201 Isabella St., Pittsburgh, PA 15212; (412) 553-4545; www.alcoa.com; Klaus Kleinfeld; prod., mfr. of aluminum, aluminum products (aerospace, automotive, industrial materials and components).

Allegheny Technologies Inc. (ATI): 1000 Six PPG Pl., Pittsburgh, PA 15222; (412) 394-2800; www.atimetals.com; Richard J. Harshman; specialty metals mfr. (titanium, alloys).

Allstate Corp. (ALL): 2775 Sanders Rd., Northbrook, IL 60062; (847) 402-5000; www.allstate.com; Thomas J. Wilson; personal property and casualty insurance; financial services.

Altria Group, Inc. (MO): 6601 West Broad St., Richmond, VA 23230; (807) 274-2200; www.altria.com; Michael E. Szymanczyk; largest U.S. tobacco company (Marlboro, Merit, Parliament, Virginia Slims). Acquired UST Inc. smokeless tobacco mfr., 1/6/2009.

Amazon.com, Inc. (AMZN): 410 Terry Ave., Seattle, WA 98109; (206) 266-1000; www.amazon.com; Jeffrey P. Bezos; online retailer of books, music, other consumer and household prods.

American Electric Power Co., Inc. (AEP): 1 Riverside Plz., Columbus, OH 43215; (614) 716-1000; www.aep.com; Michael G. Morris; public utilities.

American Express Co. (AXP): World Financial Ctr., 200 Vesey St., NY, NY 10285; (212) 640-2000; www.americanexpress.com; Kenneth I. Chenault; charge and credit cards, travel-related services.

American Greetings Corp. (AM): 1 American Rd., Cleveland, OH 44144; (216) 252-7300; www.americangreetings.com; Morry Weiss; greeting cards, stationery, party goods, gift items.

American Intl. Group, Inc. (AIG): 70 Pine St., NY, NY 10038; (212) 770-7000; www.aigcorporate.com; Robert H. Benmosche; insurance, financial services. AIG received $182 bil in govt. bailouts, 2008.

American Standard Brands (AS America, Inc.): 1 Centennial Plz., Piscataway, NJ 08855; (800) 442-1902; www.americanstandard-us.com; Donald C. Devine; kitchen and bath prods. Formed from merger of American Standard America, Crane Plumbing, and Eljer, 2/2008.

AMR Corp. (AMR): 4333 Amon Carter Blvd., Ft. Worth, TX 76155; (817) 963-1234; www.aa.com; Thomas W. Horton; one of the world's largest air carriers (American Airlines, American Eagle). Filed for Chap. 11 reorganization, 11/29/2011.

Anheuser-Busch InBev (BUD): Brouwerijplein 1, 3000 Leuven, Belgium; +32 (16) 247111; www.ab-inbev.com; Carlos Brito; world's largest brewer (Budweiser, Bud Light, Michelob, Busch), soft drinks. Anheuser-Busch became wholly owned subsid. of InBev, 11/18/2008; sold subsid.

Busch Entertainment Corp., 2nd largest theme park operator in U.S., 12/1/2009.

Apple Inc. (AAPL): 1 Infinite Loop, Cupertino, CA 95014; (408) 996-1010; www. apple.com; Tim Cook; mfr. of computers (Mac), digital media devices (iPod, iPhone, iPad) and distrib. (iTunes store).

ARAMARK Corp.: 1101 Market St., Philadelphia, PA 19107; (215) 238-3000; www. aramark.com; Eric J. Foss; food/support services to institutions and facilities, uniforms and career apparel.

ArcelorMittal USA, Inc.: 1 South Dearborn, East Chicago, IN 46312; (312) 899-3440; www.arcelormittal.com; Michael G. Rippey; U.S. subsidiary of Arcelor Mittal, world's largest steel co., based in Luxembourg.

Archer Daniels Midland Co. (ADM): 4666 Faries Pkwy., Decatur, IL 62526; (217) 424-5200; www.adm.com; Patricia A. Woertz; agricultural commodities and prods.

Armstrong World Industries, Inc. (AWI): 2500 Columbia Ave., P.O. Box 3001, Lancaster, PA 17604; (717) 397-0611; www.armstrong.com; Matthew J. Espe; mfr. of flooring, ceiling prods., cabinets.

ArvinMeritor, Inc.: see Meritor, Inc.

Ashland Inc. (ASH): 50 E. RiverCenter Blvd., P.O. Box 391, Covington, KY 41012; (859) 815-3333; www.ashland.com; James J. O'Brien; petroleum producer and refiner (Valvoline, plastics), chemicals, road construction. Acquired Hercules, Inc., 11/13/2008.

AT&T Inc. (T): 208 S. Akard St., Dallas, TX 75202; (210) 821-4105; www.att.com; Randall L. Stephenson; telecommunications, global information management.

AutoNation, Inc. (AN): 110 SE 6th St., Ft. Lauderdale, FL 33301; (954) 769-6000; www.autonation.com; Mike Jackson; largest U.S. auto retailer; new and used vehicles; auto parts, maintenance, and repair; auto finance and insurance.

Avon Products, Inc. (AVP): 1345 Ave. of the Americas, NY, NY 10105; (212) 282-5000; www.avon.com; Sheri S. McCoy; cosmetics, fragrances, skin and personal care items; fashion.

Bank of America Corp. (BAC): 100 N. Tryon St., Charlotte, NC 28255; (704) 386-5681; www.bankofamerica.com; Brian T. Moynihan; banking and nonbanking financial services. Acquired Merrill Lynch, 1/1/2009.

Barnes & Noble, Inc. (BKS): 122 Fifth Ave., NY, NY 10011; (212) 633-3300; www. barnesandnobleinc.com; Leonard S. Riggio; leading U.S. bookseller (retail and college), publisher (Sterling Pub. Co.).

Bausch + Lomb Inc.: One Bausch & Lomb Pl., Rochester, NY 14604; (585) 338-6000; www.bausch.com; Brent L. Saunders; vision care prods., pharmaceuticals, surgical equip. Acquired by Warburg Pincus, 10/26/2007.

Baxter International Inc. (BAX): 1 Baxter Pkwy., Deerfield, IL 60015; (847) 948-2000; www.baxter.com; Robert L. Parkinson Jr.; mfr. of health care prods.

Beam Inc. (BEAM): 510 Lake Cook Rd., Deerfield, IL 60015; (847) 948-8888; www. beamglobal.com; Matt Shattock; spirits (Jim Beam, Maker's Mark, Courvoisier, Sauza). Spun off from Fortune Brands, Inc., 10/3/2011.

Bear Stearns Cos. Inc.: see JPMorgan Chase & Co.

Becton, Dickinson & Co. (BDX): 1 Becton Dr., Franklin Lakes, NJ 07417; (201) 847-6800; www.bd.com; Edward J. Ludwig; medical, laboratory, diagnostic prods.

Berkshire Hathaway Inc. (BRK.A): 3555 Farnam St., Ste. 1440, Omaha, NE 68131; (402) 346-1400; www.berkshirehathaway. com; Warren E. Buffett; insurance (GEICO), building materials (Benjamin Moore & Co., Shaw), apparel (Fruit of the Loom), food (Dairy Queen). Merged Burlington Northern Santa Fe Corp. rail transportation co. into Berkshire subsidiary, 2/12/2010.

Bertelsmann AG: Carl-Bertelsmann-Str. 270, 33311 Gütersloh, Germany; +49-5241-80-0; www.bertelsmann.de; Thomas Rabe; intl. media corp., world's largest trade book publisher (Random House: Knopf, Doubleday). Sold stake in Sony BMG to Sony Corp., 10/1/2008.

Best Buy Co., Inc. (BBY): 7601 Penn Ave. S., Richfield, MN 55423; (612) 291-1000; www.bestbuy.com; Mike Mikan; retailer of software, appliances, cellular phones, largest U.S. retailer of consumer electronics.

Blackstone Group LP, The (BX): 345 Park Ave., NY, NY 10154; (212) 583-5000; www. blackstone.com; Stephen A. Schwarzman; asset mgmt., financial services.

Blockbuster Inc.: 3000 N. Redbud Blvd., McKinney, TX 75069; (972) 683-8000; www.blockbuster.com; Michael Kelly; in-home movie and video game rental, purchases. Filed for bankruptcy 9/23/2010; acquired by DISH Network, 4/26/2011.

Boeing Co. (BA): 100 N. Riverside, Chicago, IL 60606; (312) 544-2000; www. boeing.com; W. James McNerney Jr.; world's leading aerospace co., largest mfr. of commercial jet and military aircraft; one of the largest U.S. defense contractors.

Brink's Co., The (BCO): 1801 Bayberry Ct., P.O. Box 18100, Richmond, VA 23226; (804) 289-9600; www.brinkscompany. com; Thomas C. Schievelbein; security (armored transport, money processing, trans. of valuables). Completed spin-off of Home Security Holdings, 10/31/2008.

Bristol-Myers Squibb Co. (BMY): 345 Park Ave., NY, NY 10154; (212) 546-4000; www.bms.com; Lamberto Andreotti; development, mfr., and sale of pharmaceuticals (Plavix, Abilify, Atripla). Acquired ZymoGenetics, Inc., 10/12/2010.

Brown-Forman Corp. (BFB): 850 Dixie Hwy., Louisville, KY 40210; (502) 585-1100; www.brown-forman.com; Paul C. Varga; distilled spirits (Jack Daniel's, Southern Comfort, Finlandia), wine and champagne (Sonoma-Cutrer, Korbel).

Brown Shoe Co., Inc. (BWS): 8300 Maryland Ave., St. Louis, MO 63105; (314) 854-4000; www.brownshoe.com; Diane M. Sullivan; shoe mfr. (Buster Brown, Naturalizer, Dr. Scholl's, AVIA) and retailer (Famous Footwear, shoes.com). Acquired American Sporting Goods Corp., 2/17/2011.

Brunswick Corp. (BC): 1 N. Field Ct., Lake Forest, IL 60045; (847) 735-4700; www. brunswick.com; Dustan E. McCoy; leisure and recreation prods., incl. marine engines and boats; billiards, bowling, and fitness equipment; bowling centers.

Burger King Holdings, Inc.: 5505 Blue Lagoon Dr., Miami, FL 33126; (305) 378-3000; www.bk.com; Bernardo Hees; world's 2nd-largest fast food hamburger restaurant chain. Acquired by 3G Capital 10/19/2010.

Cablevision Systems Corp. (CVC): 1111 Stewart Ave., Bethpage, NY 11714; (516) 803-2300; www.cablevision.com; James L. Dolan; cable and Internet services provider (Optimum); local media and programming; movie theaters (Clearview). Spun off Madison Square Garden, 2/9/2010; spun off AMC Networks, 6/30/2011.

Caesars Entertainment Corp. (CZR): One Caesars Palace Dr., Las Vegas, NV 89109; (702) 407-6000; www.caesars.com; Gary W. Loveman; world's largest provider of branded casino entertainment (Caesars, Harrah's, Horseshoe, World Series of Poker). Changed name from Harrah's Entertainment, Inc., 11/23/2010.

Campbell Soup Co. (CPB): One Campbell Pl., Camden, NJ 08103; (856) 342-4800; www.campbellsoupcompany.com; Denise Morrison; world's largest soup mfr.; sauces (Pace, Prego), V8 juice, Pepperidge Farm prods.

Caterpillar Inc. (CAT): 100 NE Adams St., Peoria, IL 61629; (309) 675-1000; www. caterpillar.com; Douglas R. Oberhelman; world's largest mfr. of construction and mining equip.

CBS Corp. (CBS): 51 W. 52nd St., NY, NY 10019; (212) 975-4321; www. cbscorporation.com; Leslie Moonves; TV networks (CBS, Showtime); TV distribution; radio stations; book publishing (Simon & Schuster); advertising.

CenturyLink, Inc. (CTL): 100 CenturyLink Dr., Monroe, LA 71203; (318) 388-9000; www.centurylink.com; Glen F. Post III; 3rd-largest telecommunications provider in the U.S. Acquired Qwest Communications, 4/1/2011; acquired Savvis, 7/15/2011.

Chevron Corp. (CVX): 6001 Bollinger Canyon Rd., San Ramon, CA 94583; (925) 842-1000; www.chevron.com; John S. Watson; one of the world's largest integrated-energy co. Acquired Atlas Energy, 2/18/2011.

Chiquita Brands International, Inc. (CQB): 250 E. 5th St., Cincinnati, OH 45202; (513) 784-8000; www.chiquita.com; Fernando Aguirre; bananas and other fruits and vegetables.

Church & Dwight Co., Inc. (CHD): 469 N. Harrison St., Princeton, NJ 08543; (609) 683-5900; www.churchdwight.com; James R. Craigie; top world producer of sodium bicarbonate (ARM & HAMMER baking soda); household (OxiClean) and personal care prods. (Arrid, Trojan, First Response).

Cigna Corp. (CI): 900 Cottage Grove Rd., Bloomfield, CT 06002; (860) 226-6000; www.cigna.com; David M. Cordani; health-care, life, and accident insurance provider.

Cintas Corp. (CTAS): 6800 Cintas Blvd., Cincinnati, OH 45262; (513) 459-1200; www.cintas.com; Scott D. Farmer; largest uniform supplier in U.S.

Circuit City Stores, Inc.: see Systemax Inc.

Cisco Systems, Inc. (CSCO): 170 West Tasman Dr., San Jose, CA 95134; (408) 526-4000; www.cisco.com; John T. Chambers; networking and communication products.

Citigroup, Inc. (C): 399 Park Ave., NY, NY 10022; (212) 559-1000; www.citigroup. com; Vikram Pandit; diversified financial services. Announced plans to realign into two business segments (Citicorp and Citi Holdings), 1/16/2009.

Clear Channel Communications, Inc.: 200 E. Basse Rd., San Antonio, TX 78209; (210) 822-2828; www.clearchannel.com; Bob Pittman; largest radio station owner in U.S. (850+ stations); outdoor advertising (billboards, mass transit ads).

Clorox Co. (CLX): 1221 Broadway, Oakland, CA 94612; (510) 271-7000; www.clorox. com; Donald R. Knauss; retail consumer prods. (Clorox, Formula 409, Pine-Sol, S.O.S., Tilex; Scoop Away, Fresh Step cat litters; Kingsford charcoal; Hidden Valley dressing; Glad plastic bags; Brita water systems; Burt's Bees personal care prods.).

Coca-Cola Co. (KO): 1 Coca-Cola Plz., Atlanta, GA 30313; (404) 676-2121; www. coca-cola.com; Muhtar Kent; world's largest beverage co. (Coca-Cola, Sprite, DASANI water), world's largest dist. of juice prods. (Minute Maid).

Colgate-Palmolive Co. (CL): 300 Park Ave., NY, NY 10022; (212) 310-2000; www. colgate.com; Ian M. Cook; soap (Irish Spring), detergent (Palmolive), household cleansers (Ajax), toothpaste (Colgate, Tom's of Maine), pet food (Hill's Science Diet).

Collective Brands, Inc. (PSS): 3231 SE 6th Ave., Topeka, KS 66607; (785) 233-5171; www.collectivebrands.com; Michael J. Massey; shoe mfr./retailer (StrideRite, Payless).

Comcast Corp. (CMCSA): 1 Comcast Ctr., Philadelphia, PA 19103; (215) 286-1700; www.comcast.com; Brian L. Roberts; largest U.S. cable company; broadband cable, Internet, and voice services. Some programming (E!, Golf Channel); controlling stake in NBCUniversal (NBC, Bravo, USA, Telemundo).

Computer Sciences Corp. (CSC): 3170 Fairview Park Dr., Falls Church, VA 22042; (703) 876-1000; www.csc.com; Mike Lawrie; technology services.

ConAgra Foods, Inc. (CAG): 1 ConAgra Dr., Omaha, NE 68102; (402) 240-4000; www.

conagrafoods.com; Gary M. Rodkin; food processor (Chef Boyardee, Healthy Choice frozen dinners, Egg Beaters, Reddi-wip); food service supplier.

ConocoPhillips Co. (COP): 600 N. Dairy Ashford, P.O. Box 2197, Houston, TX 77079; (281) 293-1000; www.conocophillips.com; Ryan M. Lance; oil and gas exploration and prod. company. Spun off refining and marketing segment of co. 5/1/2012, as new independent co., Phillips 66.

Consolidated Edison, Inc. (ED): 4 Irving Pl., NY, NY 10003; (212) 460-4600; www.conedison.com; Kevin Burke; electric, natural gas utilities.

Continental Airlines, Inc.: see United Continental Holdings, Inc.

Corning Inc. (GLW): 1 Riverfront Plz., Corning, NY 14831; (607) 974-9000; www.corning.com; Wendell P. Weeks; mfr. of telecommunications, specialty equipment, fiber optics.

Costco Wholesale Corp. (COST): 999 Lake Dr., Issaquah, WA 98027; (425) 313-8100; www.costco.com; W. Craig Jelinek; largest U.S. chain of wholesale warehouse stores.

Countrywide Financial: see Bank of America Corp.

Crane Co. (CR): 100 First Stamford Pl., Stamford, CT 06902; (203) 363-7300; www.craneco.com; Eric C. Fast; mfr. of fluid control devices, vending machines, aircraft components.

A. T. Cross Co. (ATX): 1 Albion Rd., Lincoln, RI 02865; (401) 333-1200; www.cross.com; David G. Whalen; writing instruments, timepieces, personal accessories.

Crown Holdings, Inc. (CCK): 1 Crown Way, Philadelphia, PA 19154; (215) 698-5100; www.crowncork.com; John W. Conway; leading producer of packaging prods.

CSX Corp. (CSX): 500 Water St., 15th Fl., Jacksonville, FL 32202; (904) 359-3200; www.csx.com; Michael J. Ward; rail freight transport.

CVS Caremark Corp. (CVS): 1 CVS Dr., Woonsocket, RI 02895; (401) 765-1500; www.cvs.com; Larry J. Merlo. Nation's largest drugstore chain; announced acquisition of Longs Drug Stores Corp., 8/12/2008.

Dana Holding Corp. (DAN): 3939 Technology Dr., Maumee, OH 43537; (419) 887-3000; www.dana.com; Roger J. Wood; truck and auto parts, supplies; emerged from Chap. 11 reorganization, 2/1/2008.

Darden Restaurants, Inc. (DRI): 1000 Darden Center Dr., Orlando, FL 32837; (407) 245-4000; www.darden.com; Clarence Otis Jr.; casual-dining restaurants (Red Lobster, Olive Garden).

Dean Foods Co. (DF): 2711 N. Haskell Ave., Ste. 3400, Dallas, TX 75204; (214) 303-3400; www.deanfoods.com; Gregg L. Engles; milk and specialty dairy prods. (LAND O LAKES, Horizon Organic, Silk soy milk, International Delight coffee creamers).

Deere & Co. (DE): One John Deere Pl., Moline, IL 61265; (309) 765-8000; www.deere.com; Samuel R. Allen; one of the world's largest mfrs. of farm equip.; mfr. industrial equip., lawn and garden tractors.

Dell Inc. (DELL): 1 Dell Way, Round Rock, TX 78682; (512) 338-4400; www.dell.com; Michael S. Dell; laptop and desktop computers, network accessories, peripherals, tablets, smartphones.

Delta Air Lines, Inc. (DAL): 1030 Delta Blvd., Atlanta, GA 30320; (404) 715-2600; www.delta.com; Richard H. Anderson; air transportation; merged with Northwest Airlines, 10/29/2008.

Dial Corp.: 15501 N. Dial Blvd., Scottsdale, AZ 85260; (480) 754-3425; www.henkelna.com; Bradley A. Casper; consumer prods. (Dial soap, Purex detergent, Right Guard antiperspirant, Renuzit air fresheners); U.S. subsidiary of Germany's Henkel company.

Diebold, Inc. (DBD): 5995 Mayfair Rd., North Canton, OH 44720; (330) 490-4000;

www.diebold.com; Thomas W. Swidarski; mfr. ATMs, security systems and prods.

Dillard's, Inc. (DDS): 1600 Cantrell Rd., Little Rock, AR 72201; (501) 376-5200; www.dillards.com; William Dillard II; dept. store chain.

Walt Disney Co., The (DIS): 500 S. Buena Vista St., Burbank, CA 91521; (818) 560-1000; disney.go.com; Robert A. Iger; one of the world's largest media conglomerates; motion pictures (Touchstone, Pixar); TV (ABC, ESPN) and radio; publishing; theme parks (Walt Disney World, Disneyland) and resorts. Acquired Marvel Entertainment, 12/31/2009. Announced sale of Miramax Films, 7/29/2010.

Doctor's Associates Inc.: 325 Bic Dr., Milford, CT 06461; (203) 877-4281; www.subway.com; Frederick A. DeLuca; restaurants (Subway).

Dole Food Co., Inc. (DOLE): One Dole Dr., Westlake Village, CA 91362; (818) 879-6600; www.dole.com; David A. DeLorenzo; food prods., fresh fruits, and vegetables. Announced plans to go public through an IPO, 8/14/2009; shares began trading 10/23/2009.

R. R. Donnelley & Sons Co. (RRD): 111 S. Wacker Dr., Chicago, IL 60606; (312) 326-8000; www.rrdonnelley.com; Thomas J. Quinlan III; commercial printing; photos/graphics, translation; printer of *The World Almanac*.

Dow Chemical Co. (DOW): 2030 Dow Ctr., Midland, MI 48674; (989) 636-1000; www.dow.com; Andrew N. Liveris; chemicals, plastics (world's 2nd-largest chemical co.). Acquired Rohm and Haas, 4/1/2009.

Dow Jones & Co., Inc.: see News Corp.

Dr Pepper Snapple Group, Inc. (DPS): 5301 Legacy Dr., Plano, TX 75024; (972) 673-7000; www.drpeppersnapplegroup.com; Larry D. Young; bottler and distributor of nonalcoholic beverages (Dr Pepper, Hawaiian Punch, 7UP, Snapple, Mott's).

Duke Energy Corp. (DUK): 526 S. Church St., Charlotte, NC 28202; (704) 594-6200; www.duke-energy.com; James E. Rogers; utilities, fiber optic networks.

Dun & Bradstreet Corp. (DNB): 103 JFK Pkwy., Short Hills, NJ 07078; (973) 921-5500; www.dnb.com; Sara Mathew; business information, research.

Dupont (E. I. du Pont de Nemours & Co.) (DD): 1007 Market St., Wilmington, DE 19898; (302) 774-1000; www.dupont.com; Ellen J. Kullman; 3rd-largest U.S. chemical co.; petroleum, consumer prods.

Eastman Kodak Co. (EK): 343 State St., Rochester, NY 14650; (585) 724-4000; www.kodak.com; Antonio M. Perez; photo printers, high-speed commercial inkjet presses, workflow software and packaging. Filed for Chap. 11 reorganization, 1/19/2012.

Eaton Corp. (ETN): Eaton Ctr., 1111 Superior Ave., Cleveland, OH 44114; (216) 523-5000; www.eaton.com; Alexander M. Cutler; mfr. vehicle components, controls.

eBay Inc. (EBAY): 2145 Hamilton Ave., San Jose, CA 95125; (408) 376-7400; www.ebay.com; John Donahoe; e-commerce (PayPal, StubHub.com).

Edison Intl. (EIX): 2244 Walnut Grove Ave., Rosemead, CA 91770; (626) 302-2222; www.edison.com; Theodore F. Craver Jr.; electric utilities.

Electronic Arts Inc. (EA): 209 Redwood Shores Pkwy., Redwood City, CA 94065; (650) 628-1500; www.ea.com; John Riccitiello; leading U.S. video game publisher (Madden NFL, Battlefield, The Sims).

Electronic Data Systems: see Hewlett-Packard Co.

Eli Lilly and Co. (LLY): Lilly Corporate Center, Indianapolis, IN 46285; (317) 276-2000; www.lilly.com; John C. Lechleiter; pharmaceutical research, development, and manufacturing (Prozac, Strattera, Cialis).

EMC Corp. (EMC): 176 South St., Hopkinton, MA 01748; (508) 435-1000; www.emc.com; Joseph M. Tucci; data storage/protection.

Emerson Electric Co. (EMR): 8000 W. Florissant Ave., St. Louis, MO 63136; (314)

553-2000; www.emerson.com; David N. Farr; electrical, electronics prods. and systems.

Energizer Holdings, Inc. (ENR): 533 Maryville Univ. Dr., St. Louis, MO 63141; (314) 985-2000; www.energizer.com; Ward M. Klein; batteries, flashlights, personal care prods.

Estée Lauder Cos. Inc. (EL): 767 Fifth Ave., NY, NY 10153; (212) 572-4200; www.elcompanies.com; Fabrizio Freda; cosmetics (Clinique, Bobbi Brown), fragrance, skin care prods.

Exelon Corp. (EXC): 10 S. Dearborn St., 48th Fl., Chicago, IL 60680; (312) 394-7398; www.exeloncorp.com; Christopher M. Crane; electricity generation/distribution; natural gas. Merged with Constellation Energy, 3/12/2012.

Express Scripts Holding Co. (ESRX): 1 Express Way, St. Louis, MO 63121; www.express-scripts.com; George Paz; largest U.S. pharmacy benefits management co. Acquired Medco Health Solutions Inc., 4/2/2012.

ExxonMobil Corp. (XOM): 5959 Las Colinas Blvd., Irving, TX 75039; (972) 444-1000; www.exxonmobil.com; Rex W. Tillerson; world's largest integrated oil co.

Federal Home Loan Mortgage Corp. (Freddie Mac): 8200 Jones Branch Dr., McLean, VA 22102; (703) 903-2000; www.freddiemac.com; Donald H. Layton; residential mortgage provider. Taken over by U.S. government, 9/7/2008.

Federal National Mortgage Assn. (Fannie Mae): 3900 Wisconsin Ave. NW, Washington, DC 20016; (202) 752-7000; www.fanniemae.com; Timothy J. Mayopoulos; largest U.S. provider of residential mortgage loans. Taken over by U.S. government, 9/7/2008.

FedEx Corp. (FDX): 942 S. Shady Grove Rd., Memphis, TN 38120; (901) 818-7500; www.fedex.com; Frederick W. Smith; world's largest express delivery service.

Fifth & Pacific Cos., Inc. (FNP): 1441 Broadway, NY, NY 10018; (212) 354-4900; fifthandpacific.com; William L. McComb; women's apparel (kate spade, Juicy Couture, Lucky Brand Jeans). Sold Liz Claiborne brand to J.C. Penney Co. Inc., 11/2/2011; changed name from Liz Claiborne, Inc., 5/15/2012.

First Data Corp.: 5565 Glenridge Connector NE, Ste. 2000, Atlanta, GA 30342; (404) 890-2000; www.firstdata.com; Jonathan J. Judge; financial transaction processing.

FirstEnergy Corp. (FE): 76 S. Main St., Akron, OH 44308; (800) 736-3402; www.firstenergycorp.com; Anthony J. Alexander; public electricity supplier.

Fluor Corp. (FLR): 6700 Las Colinas Blvd., Irving, TX 75039; (469) 398-7000; www.fluor.com; David T. Seaton; international engineering and construction co.

Foot Locker, Inc. (FL): 112 W. 34th St., NY, NY 10120; (212) 720-3700; www.footlocker-inc.com; Ken C. Hicks; retail athletic stores (Footaction, Foot Locker, Champs Sports).

Ford Motor Co. (F): 1 American Rd., Dearborn, MI 48126; (313) 322-3000; www.ford.com; William C. Ford Jr.; auto mfr.; motor vehicle sales (Ford, Lincoln); one of the largest U.S. auto finance co. (Ford Motor Credit).

Fortune Brands Home and Security, Inc. (FBHS): 520 Lake Cook Rd., Deerfield, IL 60015; (847) 484-4400; www.fbhs.com; Christopher Klein; kitchen & bath cabinetry, plumbing (Moen), windows & doors, security & storage (Master Lock). Spun off from Fortune Brands, Inc., 10/3/2011.

Fox: see News Corp.

Gannett Co., Inc. (GCI): 7950 Jones Branch Dr., McLean, VA 22107; (703) 854-6000; www.gannett.com; Gracia Martore; largest U.S. newspaper publisher (*USA Today*); network and cable TV; employment web site (CareerBuilder).

Gap Inc. (GPS): 2 Folsom St., San Francisco, CA 94105; (650) 952-4400; www.gapinc.com; Glenn K. Murphy; casual apparel retailer (Gap, Banana Republic, Old Navy).

General Dynamics Corp. (GD): 2941 Fairview Park Dr., Ste. 100, Falls Church, VA 22042; (703) 876-3000; www.general dynamics.com; Jay L. Johnson; defense contractor: aerospace, combat systems, marine systems, computing devices.

General Electric Co. (GE): 3135 Easton Tpke., Fairfield, CT 06828; (203) 373-2211; www.ge.com; Jeffrey Immelt; electrical, electronic equip., financial services, radio and TV broadcasting, aircraft engines, power generation, appliances.

General Mills, Inc. (GIS): One General Mills Blvd., Minneapolis, MN 55426; (763) 764-7600; www.generalmills.com; Kendall J. Powell; food mfr. (Betty Crocker, Bisquick, Cheerios, Chex, Green Giant, Häagen-Dazs, Pillsbury, Progresso, Total, Wheaties, Yoplait).

General Motors Co. (GM): 300 Renaissance Ctr., Detroit, MI 48265; (313) 556-5000; www.gm.com; Daniel F. Akerson; world's largest auto mfr. (Chevrolet, Cadillac, Buick, GMC); auto financing (GM Financial); vehicle security (OnStar). General Motors Corp. filed for Chap. 11 reorganization, 6/1/2009; sold its profitable components to a new, smaller company called General Motors Co., 7/10/2009.

Genuine Parts Co. (GPC): 2999 Circle 75 Pkwy., Atlanta, GA 30339; (770) 953-1700; www.genpt.com; Thomas C. Gallagher; distrib. of auto (NAPA), industrial replacement parts.

Goldman Sachs Group, Inc. (GS): 200 West St., 29th Fl., NY, NY 10282; (212) 902-1000; www.goldmansachs.com; Lloyd C. Blankfein; investment banking, asset management, securities services.

Goodyear Tire & Rubber Co. (GT): 1144 E. Market St., Akron, OH 44316; (330) 796-2121; www.goodyear.com; Richard J. Kramer; tires and other auto prods.

Google, Inc. (GOOG): 1600 Amphitheatre Pkwy., Mountain View, CA 94043; (650) 253-0000; www.google.com; Eric E. Schmidt; Internet-related products and services (leading search engine, ad sales; YouTube).

W. R. Grace & Co. (GRA): 7500 Grace Dr., Columbia, MD 21044; (410) 531-4000; www.grace.com; Alfred E. Festa; chemicals, construction prods.

Great Atlantic & Pacific Tea Co., Inc.: 2 Paragon Dr., Montvale, NJ 07645; (201) 573-9700; www.aptea.com; Samuel Martin; supermarkets (A&P, The Food Emporium, Super Fresh, Waldbaum's, Pathmark Emerged from Chap. 11 reorganization, 3/13/2012.

Halliburton Co. (HAL): 3000 N. Sam Houston Pkwy., Houston, TX 77032; (281) 871-4000; www.halliburton.com; David J. Lesar; oil field mgmt., energy services.

Hanesbrands Inc. (HBI): 1000 E. Hanes Mill Rd., Winston-Salem, NC 27105; (336) 519-8080; www.hanesbrands.com; Richard A. Noll; apparel mfr. (Hanes, L'eggs, Champion, Just My Size, Playtex, Wonderbra).

Harley-Davidson, Inc. (HOG): 3700 W. Juneau Ave., Milwaukee, WI 53208; (414) 342-4680; www.harley-davidson.com; Keith E. Wandell; mfr. motorcycles, parts, and accessories.

Hartford Financial Services Group, Inc. (HIG): One Hartford Plz., Hartford, CT 06155; (860) 547-5000; www.thehartford.com; Liam E. McGee; insurance, financial services.

Hasbro, Inc. (HAS): 1027 Newport Ave., Pawtucket, RI 02862; (401) 431-8697; www.hasbro.com; Brian Goldner; toy and game mfr. (Milton Bradley, Playskool, G.I. Joe, Parker Bros., Nerf, Play-Doh).

HCA Holdings, Inc. (HCA): 1 Park Plz., Nashville, TN 37203; (615) 344-9551; www.hcahealthcare.com; Richard M. Bracken; owns and operates hospitals; other diagnostic, surgical, health treatment centers.

H. J. Heinz Co. (HNZ): 1 PPG Pl., Ste. 3100, Pittsburgh, PA 15222; (412) 456-5700; www.heinz.com; William R. Johnson; food mfr. (Ore-Ida, 57 Varieties ketchup, Weight Watchers foods).

Hershey Co., The (HSY): 100 Crystal A Dr., Hershey, PA 17033; (717) 534-4200; www.thehersheycompany.com; John P. Bilbrey; largest North American producer of chocolate prods. (Reese's, Kit Kat, Mounds, Almond Joy, Jolly Rancher, Twizzlers, Milk Duds, Good & Plenty, York).

Hertz Global Holdings, Inc. (HTZ): 225 Brae Blvd., Park Ridge, NJ 07656; (201) 307-2000; www.hertz.com; Mark P. Frissora; car rentals.

Hess Corp. (HES): 1185 Ave. of the Americas, NY, NY 10036; (212) 997-8500; www.hess.com; John B. Hess; integrated oil and gas co.

Hewlett-Packard Co. (HPQ): 3000 Hanover St., Palo Alto, CA 94304; (650) 857-1501; www.hp.com; Meg Whitman; computers, electronic prods. and systems. Acquired Electronic Data Systems, 8/26/2008.

Hillenbrand, Inc. (HI): One Batesville Blvd., Batesville, IN 47006; (812) 934-7000; www.hillenbrandinc.com; Kenneth A. Camp; holder of Batesville Caskets, coffin mfr. Spun off from Hill-Rom Holdings, 4/1/2008.

Hill-Rom Holdings, Inc. (HRC): 1069 State Rte. 46 E., Batesville, IN 47006; (812) 934-7777; www.hill-rom.com; John J. Greisch; mfr. hospital beds, other hospital equip.

Hillshire Brands Co. (HSH): 3500 Lacey Rd., Downers Grove, IL 60515; (630) 598-6000; www.hillshirebrands.com; Sean Connolly; split from Sara Lee, 6/28/2012.

Hilton Worldwide: 7930 Jones Branch Dr., Ste. 1100, McLean, VA 22102; (703) 883-1000; www.hiltonworldwide.com; Christopher J. Nassetta; hotels and resorts (Doubletree, Embassy, Hampton).

Home Depot, Inc. (HD): 2455 Paces Ferry Rd. NW, Atlanta, GA 30339; (770) 433-8211; www.homedepot.com; Francis S. Blake; world's largest home improvement retailer; 5th-largest retailer in the world; home improvement warehouse stores.

Honeywell Intl. Inc. (HON): 101 Columbia Rd., Morristown, NJ 07962; (973) 455-2000; www.honeywell.com; David Cote; industrial and home control systems, aerospace guidance systems.

Hormel Foods Corp. (HRL): 1 Hormel Pl., Austin, MN 55912; (507) 437-5611; www.hormelfoods.com; Jeffrey M. Ettinger; meat processor; pork, turkey, and beef prods. (SPAM, Dinty Moore, Jennie-O).

Hostess Brands: 6031 Connection Dr., Ste. 600, Irving, TX 75039; (972) 532-4500; www.hostessbrands.com; Gregory F. Rayburn; baked goods wholesaler, distributor (Wonder, Hostess, Dolly Madison, Drake's, Home Pride). Files for Chap. 11 reorganization, 1/11/2012.

Houghton Mifflin Harcourt: 222 Berkeley St., Boston, MA 02116; (617) 351-5000; www.hmhco.com; Linda K. Zecher; publisher of textbooks and other educational prods. (Holt McDougal Clarion), trade and reference books. Emerged from Chap. 11 reorganization, 6/22/2012.

H&R Block, Inc. (HRB): 1 H&R Block Way, Kansas City, MO 64105; (816) 854-3000; www.hrblock.com; William C. Cobb; tax return preparation; business and consulting services.

Humana Inc. (HUM): 500 W. Main St., Louisville, KY 40202; (502) 580-1000; www.humana.com; Michael B. McCallister; managed health care service provider, related specialty products.

IAC/InterActiveCorp (IACI): 555 W. 18th St., NY, NY 10011; (212) 314-7300; www.iac.com; Barry Diller; Internet conglomerate (Ask.com, Match.com, Citysearch, Urbanspoon, Vimeo). Split off TV, leisure, and financial holdings into 5 separate cos., 8/21/2008.

Illinois Tool Works Inc. (ITW): 3600 W. Lake Ave., Glenview, IL 60026; (847) 724-7500; www.itw.com; David B. Speer; consumer, industrial tools; food equip. (Hobart), packaging (Zip-Pak).

Ingersoll-Rand plc (IR): 170/175 Lakeview Dr., Airside Business Park, Swords, Dublin, Ireland; 353-1-870-7400; company. ingersollrand.com; Michael W. Lamach; locks and security systems (Schlage, Kryptonite); refrigeration equip. (Thermo King, Hussmann); industrial equip.; air conditioning systems (Trane).

Intel Corp. (INTC): 2200 Mission College Blvd., Santa Clara, CA 95054; (408) 765-8080; www.intel.com; Paul S. Otellini; mfr. semiconductors, microprocessors (Core, Centrino).

International Business Machines Corp. (IBM): One New Orchard Rd., Armonk, NY 10504; (914) 499-1900; www.ibm.com; Virginia M. Rometty; world's largest supplier of advanced information processing technology equip., services.

International Paper Co. (IP): 6400 Poplar Ave., Memphis, TN 38197; (901) 419-7000; www.internationalpaper.com; John V. Faraci Jr.; world's largest paper/forest prods. co.

International Textile Group, Inc.: 804 Green Valley, Greensboro, NC 27408; (336) 379-6220; www.itg-global.com; Joseph L. Gorga; apparel and home textiles/fabrics.

J.C. Penney Co., Inc. (JCP): 6501 Legacy Dr., Plano, TX 75024; (972) 431-1000; www.jcpenney.net; Ron Johnson; dept. store retailer, general merchandise catalog sales.

J. Crew Group, Inc.: 770 Broadway, NY, NY 10003; (212) 209-2500; www.jcrew.com; Millard S. Drexler; retail and mail order apparel and accessories. Acquired by TPG Capital and Leonard Green & Partners, 3/7/2011.

JetBlue Airways Corp. (JBLU): 118-29 Queens Blvd., Forest Hills, NY 11375; (718) 286-7900; www.jetblue.com; David Barger; air transportation.

Jo-Ann Stores, Inc.: 5555 Darrow Rd., Hudson, OH 44236; (330) 656-2600; www.joann.com; Travis Smith; nation's largest specialty fabric and craft stores. Acquired by Leonard Green & Partners, 3/18/2011.

Johnson Controls, Inc. (JCI): 5757 N. Green Bay Ave., Milwaukee, WI 53209; (414) 524-1200; www.johnsoncontrols.com; Stephen A. Roell; equipment and controls for heating, ventilating, AC, refrigeration, and building security; auto interiors, batteries.

Johnson & Johnson (JNJ): 1 Johnson & Johnson Plz., New Brunswick, NJ 08933; (732) 524-0400; www.jnj.com; Alex Gorsky; health care prods. (Band-Aid, Neosporin), pharmaceuticals (Tylenol, Motrin, Sudafed), toiletries (Neutrogena, Aveeno).

S. C. Johnson & Son, Inc.: 1525 Howe St., Racine, WI 53403; (262) 260-2000; www.scjohnson.com; H. Fisk Johnson; cleaning and other household prods. (Johnson's Wax, Windex, Pledge, Fantastik, Raid, OFF!, Shout, Glade, Scrubbing Bubbles, Ziploc bags).

Jones Group, Inc. (JNY): 1411 Broadway, NY, NY 10018; (212) 642-3860; www.jny.com; Wesley R. Card; apparel (Jones New York, Gloria Vanderbilt), shoes (Nine West, Anne Klein); retail and outlet stores.

JPMorgan Chase & Co. (JPM): 270 Park Ave., NY, NY 10017; (212) 270-6000; www.jpmorganchase.com; James Dimon; financial service. Acquired Bear Stearns, 6/2/2008; acquired Washington Mutual, 9/25/2008.

KBR, Inc. (KBR): 601 Jefferson St., Ste. 3400, Houston, TX 77002; (713) 753-3011; www.kbr.com; William P. Utt; engineering, construction mgmt. services.

Kellogg Co. (K): One Kellogg Sq., Battle Creek, MI 49016; (269) 961-2000; www.kelloggcompany.com; John A. Bryant; world's largest mfr. of ready-to-eat cereals, other food prods. (Frosted Flakes, Rice Krispies, Froot Loops, Pop-Tarts, Nutri-Grain, Keebler, Eggo, Pringles). Acquired Pringles from Procter & Gamble, 6/1/2012.

Kelly Services, Inc. (KELYA): 999 W. Big Beaver Rd., Troy, MI 48084; (248) 362-4444; www.kellyservices.com; Carl T. Camden; temporary staffing services.

Kimberly-Clark Corp. (KMB): P.O. Box 619100, Irving, TX 75261; (972) 281-1200; www.kimberly-clark.com; Thomas J. Falk; personal care prods. (Kleenex, Scott, Cottonelle, Huggies, Kotex).

Kinder Morgan, Inc. (KMI): 500 Dallas St., Ste. 1000, Houston, TX 77002; (713) 369-9000; www.kindermorgan.com; Richard D. Kinder; energy trans. and storage. Acquired El Paso Corp., 5/24/2012.

Kmart Corp.: see Sears Holdings Corp.

Koch Industries, Inc.: P.O. Box 2256, Wichita, KS 67201; (316) 828-5500; www.kochind.com; Charles G. Koch; forest prod. mfr.; oil refineries/pipeline; chemicals; pollution-control equipment; ranching.

Kraft Foods Inc. (KFT): 3 Lakes Dr., Northfield, IL 60093; (847) 646-2000; www.kraftfoodscompany.com; Irene B. Rosenfeld; world's second largest food co., largest U.S. food co., including Nabisco (Oreo), Jell-O, Oscar Mayer, Maxwell House, Trident. Spun off Post cereals into Ralcorp Holdings, 8/4/2008. Announced acquisition of Cadbury plc, 2/2/2010. Announced plan to split into 2 public cos., 8/4/2011.

Kroger Co. (KR): 1014 Vine St., Cincinnati, OH 45202; (513) 762-4000; www.thekrogerco.com; David B. Dillon; one of the largest U.S. grocery retailers, convenience stores, mall jewelry stores.

La-Z-Boy Inc. (LZB): 1284 N. Telegraph Rd., Monroe, MI 48162; (734) 242-1444; www.la-z-boy.com; Kurt L. Darrow; reclining chairs, other furniture.

Leggett & Platt, Inc. (LEG): No. 1 Leggett Rd., Carthage, MO 64836; (417) 358-8131; www.leggett.com; David S. Haffner; furniture and its components, industrial materials, automotive seating suspension, control and power train cable systems.

Levi Strauss & Co.: 1155 Battery St., San Francisco, CA 94111; (415) 501-6000; www.levistrauss.com; Charles Bergh; blue jeans, casual sportswear (Dockers).

Lexmark Intl., Inc. (LXK): 740 W. New Circle Rd., Lexington, KY 40550; (859) 232-2000; www.lexmark.com; Paul Rooke; computer printers and peripherals.

Liberty Mutual Holding Co. Inc.: 175 Berkeley St., Boston, MA 02116; (617) 357-9500; www.libertymutual.com; David H. Long; auto, home, and life insurance.

Limited Brands, Inc. (LTD): 3 Limited Pkwy., Columbus, OH 43216; (614) 415-7000; www.limitedbrands.com; Leslie H. Wexner; apparel stores (La Senza, Victoria's Secret, PINK, Henri Bendel), home decor (White Barn Candle Co.), personal care (Bath & Body Works).

Liz Claiborne, Inc.: See J.C. Penney Co., Inc.

L.L. Bean, Inc.: 15 Casco St., Freeport, ME 04033; (207) 552-3028; www.llbean.com; Christopher J. McCormick; catalog and retail outdoor apparel, footwear, gear.

Lockheed Martin Corp. (LMT): 6801 Rockledge Dr., Bethesda, MD 20817; (301) 897-6000; www.lockheedmartin.com; Robert J. Stevens; leading U.S. defense contractor; commercial and military aircraft, electronics, missiles, information tech., and communications.

Loews Corp. (L): 667 Madison Ave., NY, NY 10065; (212) 521-2000; www.loews.com; James S. Tisch; hotels, insurance (CNA Financial), offshore drilling (Diamond).

Longs Drug Stores: see CVS Caremark Corp.

Lorillard, Inc. (LO): 714 Green Valley Rd., Greensboro, NC 27408; (336) 335-7000; www.lorillard.com; Murray S. Kessler; 3rd-largest U.S. cigarette mfr. (Newport, Kent).

Lowe's Cos., Inc. (LOW): 1000 Lowe's Blvd., Mooresville, NC 28117; (704) 758-1000; www.lowes.com; Robert A. Niblock;

building material and home improvement superstores.

Macy's, Inc. (M): 7 W. 7th St., Cincinnati, OH 45202; (513) 579-7000; www.macysinc.com; Terry J. Lundgren; dept. stores (Macy's, Bloomingdale's).

ManpowerGroup (MAN): 100 Manpower Pl., Milwaukee, WI 53212; (414) 961-1000; www.manpowergroup.com; Jeffrey A. Joerres; employment services.

Marathon Oil Corp. (MRO): 5555 San Felipe Rd., Houston, TX 77056; (713) 629-6600; www.marathonoil.com; Clarence P. Cazalot Jr.; integrated oil co. Spun off Marathon Petroleum Corp., 7/1/2011.

Marriott International, Inc. (MAR): 10400 Fernwood Rd., Bethesda, MD 20817; (301) 380-3000; www.marriott.com; J. W. Marriott Jr.; hotels (Renaissance, Courtyard, Fairfield Inn, Ritz-Carlton).

Mars, Inc.: 6885 Elm St., McLean, VA 22101; (703) 821-4900; www.mars.com; Paul S. Michaels; one of the largest food mfrs. in the world, including chocolate (M&M's, Snickers, Dove), food (Uncle Ben's), pet food (Pedigree, Whiskas). Acquired Wm. Wrigley Jr., 10/6/2008.

Masco Corp. (MAS): 21001 Van Born Rd., Taylor, MI 48180; (313) 274-7400; www.masco.com; Timothy Wadhams; mfr. kitchen, bathroom prods. (Delta, Peerless faucets; Merillat cabinets); paints (Behr).

Massachusetts Mutual Life Insurance Co. (MassMutual Financial Group): 1295 State St., Springfield, MA 01111; (413) 744-8411; www.massmutual.com; Roger W. Crandall; financial planning and investment, life insurance.

Mattel, Inc. (MAT): 333 Continental Blvd., El Segundo, CA 90245; (310) 252-2000; www.mattel.com; Bryan Stockton; world's largest toymaker (Barbie, Fisher-Price, Hot Wheels, Matchbox, American Girls).

McClatchy Co. (MNI): 2100 Q St., Sacramento, CA 95816; (916) 321-1855; www.mcclatchy.com; Patrick J. Talamantes; 3rd-largest U.S. newspaper publisher.

McDonald's Corp. (MCD): 2111 McDonald's Dr., Oak Brook, IL 60523; (630) 623-3000; www.mcdonalds.com; Don Thompson; world's largest fast food co.

McGraw-Hill Cos., Inc. (MHP): 1221 Ave. of the Americas, NY, NY 10020; (212) 512-2000; www.mcgraw-hill.com; Harold McGraw III; book, textbook publishing; information and financial services (Standard & Poor's). Sold broadcasting group to E.W. Scripps Co., 12/30/2011.

McKesson Corp. (MCK): 1 Post St., San Francisco, CA 94104; (415) 983-8300; www.mckesson.com; John H. Hammergren; distributor of drugs and toiletries; provides mgmt. software and services.

MeadWestvaco Corp. (MWV): 501 S. 5th St., Richmond, VA 23219; (804) 444-1000; www.meadwestvaco.com; John A. Luke Jr.; packaging, shipping containers, chemicals. Spun off consumer and office products, 5/1/2012.

Medco Health Solutions, Inc.: see Express Scripts Holding Co.

Medtronic, Inc. (MDT): 710 Medtronic Pkwy., Minneapolis, MN 55432; (763) 514-4000; www.medtronic.com; Omar Ishrak; mfr. of implantable biomedical devices.

Merck & Co., Inc. (MRK): 1 Merck Dr., Whitehouse Station, NJ 08889; (908) 423-1000; www.merck.com; Kenneth C. Frazier; pharmaceuticals (Gardasil, Propecia, Singulair, Vytorin, Zocor); consumer health prods. (Claritin, Coppertone, Dr. Scholl's, MiraLAX). Merged with Schering-Plough Corp., 11/3/2009.

Meredith Corp. (MDP): 1716 Locust St., Des Moines, IA 50309; (515) 284-3000; www.meredith.com; Stephen M. Lacy; magazine publishing (*Better Homes and Gardens*, *Ladies' Home Journal*, *Parents*, *Family Circle*, *Every Day With Rachael Ray*, *FamilyFun*), book publishing, broadcasting, online media (allrecipes.com).

Meritor, Inc. (MTOR): 2135 W. Maple Rd., Troy, MI 48084; (248) 435-1000; www.

meritor.com; Charles G. McClure; commercial vehicles systems and components. ArvinMeritor completed divestiture of its light vehicle business, 1/2011; and changed name to Meritor, 3/30/2011.

Merrill Lynch & Co., Inc.: see Bank of America Corp.

MetLife, Inc. (MET): 200 Park Ave., NY, NY 10166; (212) 578-2211; www.metlife.com; Steven A. Kandarian; insurance, financial services. Acquired American Life Insurance Co. (Alico) from American International Group, Inc. (AIG), 11/1/2010.

MGM Resorts Intl. (MGM): 3600 Las Vegas Blvd. S., Las Vegas, NV 89109; (702) 693-7120; www.mgmresorts.com; James J. Murren; hotel-casino operator (Mirage, New York-New York, Luxor, Bellagio, Circus Circus, Monte Carlo).

Microsoft Corp. (MSFT): One Microsoft Way, Redmond, WA 98052; (425) 882-8080; www.microsoft.com; William H. Gates III; world's largest consumer software maker (Windows, Word, Excel); video game consoles (Xbox).

Miller Brewing Co.: see SABMiller plc.

Molson Coors Brewing Co. (TAP): 1225 17th St., Ste. 3200, Denver, CO 80202; (303) 927-2337; www.molsoncoors.com; Peter Swinburn; brewer (Coors, Killian's, Molson, Heineken, Miller). Announced creation of MillerCoors, joint venture with SABMiller, 7/1/2008.

Morgan Stanley (MS): 1585 Broadway, NY, NY 10036; (212) 761-4000; www.morganstanley.com; James P. Gorman; diversified financial services.

Motorola Solutions, Inc. (MSI): 1303 E. Algonquin Rd., Schaumburg, IL 60196; (847) 576-5000; www.motorolasolutions.com; Greg Brown; electronic equipment and components; communication devices. Spun off from Motorola, Inc., 1/4/2011.

National Semiconductor Corp.: see Texas Instruments, Inc.

Nationwide Mutual Insurance Co.: One Nationwide Plz., Columbus, OH 43215; (614) 249-7111; www.nationwide.com; Stephen S. Rasmussen; property/casualty, life insurance; financial services.

Navistar Intl. Corp. (NAV): 2701 Navistar Dr., Lisle, IL 60532; (331) 332-5000; www.navistar.com; Daniel C. Ustian; mfr. heavy-duty trucks, parts, school buses.

NBC Universal: 30 Rockefeller Plaza, NY, NY 10112; (212) 664-4444; www.nbcuni.com; Stephen B. Burke; news/entertainment producer and developer; TV and CATV stations (NBC, Bravo, USA, Telemundo); film production. Owned by Comcast and General Electric.

NCR Corp. (NCR): 3097 Satellite Blvd., Duluth, GA 30096; (937) 445-5000; www.ncr.com; William R. Nuti; mfr. ATMs, retail technology, hardware and software; computer services and supplies.

Nestlé USA, Inc.: 800 N. Brand Blvd., Glendale, CA 91203; (818) 549-6000; www.nestleusa.com; Brad Alford; candy (Baby Ruth, Raisinets), beverages (Nestea, Juicy Juice), food (Buitoni, Coffee-Mate), frozen foods (Stouffer's, Häagen-Dazs, Lean Cuisine), pet foods (Purina, Alpo, Friskies). Subsidiary of Nestlé SA in Switzerland, world's largest food co.

Netflix, Inc. (NFLX): 100 Winchester Cir., Los Gatos, CA 95032; (408) 540-3700; www.netflix.com; Reed Hastings; online DVD rentals; streaming video.

New York Life Insurance Co.: 51 Madison Ave., NY, NY 10010; (212) 576-7000; www.newyorklife.com; Theodore A. Mathas; life insurance, annuities, mutual funds.

New York Times Co. (NYT): 620 8th Ave., NY, NY 10018; (212) 556-1234; www.nytco.com; Arthur O. Sulzberger Jr.; newspapers (*New York Times*, *Boston Globe*).

Newell Rubbermaid Inc. (NWL): 3 Glenlake Pkwy., Atlanta, GA 30328; (770) 418-7000; www.newellrubbermaid.com; Michael B. Polk; housewares (Rubbermaid, Levolor,

Calphalon); hair accessories (Goody); writing utensils (Parker, Sharpie, Paper Mate); hardware and tools (Irwin, Amerock); juvenile prods. (Graco).

News Corp. (NWS): 1211 Ave. of the Americas, NY, NY 10036; (212) 852-7000; www.newscorp.com; K. Rupert Murdoch; global newspaper, magazine, book publishing (HarperCollins; Wall Street Journal); TV and CATV stations (FOX, Fox News Channel, FX); film production; websites (hulu.com). Sold RottenTomatoes.com to Flixter, 1/4/2010; sold MySpace.com to Specific Media Inc., 6/29/2011. Announced plans to split into 2 cos., publishing and entertainment, 6/28/2012.

NIKE, Inc. (NKE): 1 Bowerman Dr., Beaverton, OR 97005; (503) 671-6453; nikeinc.com; Mark G. Parker; world's largest mfr. athletic footwear and apparel.

Nordstrom, Inc. (JWN): 1617 6th Ave., Seattle, WA 98101; (206) 628-2111; www.nordstrom.com; Blake W. Nordstrom; upscale dept. store chain.

Norfolk Southern Corp. (NSC): Three Commercial Pl., Norfolk, VA 23510; (757) 629-2600; www.nscorp.com; Charles W. Moorman; railway operator; freight carrier.

Northrop Grumman Corp. (NOC): 2980 Fairview Park Dr., Falls Church, VA 22042; (703) 280-2900; www.northropgrumman.com; Wes Bush; defense contractor: aircraft, electronics, data systems, information systems, missiles. Spun off shipbuilding sector, 3/31/2011.

Northwest Airlines Corp.: see Delta Air Lines, Inc.

Northwestern Mutual Life Insurance Co.: 720 E. Wisconsin Ave., Milwaukee, WI 53202; (414) 271-1444; www.northwesternmutual.com; John E. Schlifske; life insurance, investment products and services, annuities.

Occidental Petroleum Corp. (OXY): 10889 Wilshire Blvd., Los Angeles, CA 90024; (310) 208-8800; www.oxy.com; Stephen I. Chazen; oil, natural gas, chemicals, plastics.

Office Depot, Inc. (ODP): 6600 N. Military Trl., Boca Raton, FL 33496; (561) 438-4800; www.officedepot.com; Neil R. Austrian; office supply retail stores.

Omnicom Group Inc. (OMC): 437 Madison Ave., NY, NY 10022; (212) 415-3600; www.omnicomgroup.com; John D. Wren; advertising, marketing, interactive/digital media.

Oracle Corp. (ORCL): 500 Oracle Pkwy., Redwood City, CA 94065; (650) 506-7000; www.oracle.com; Lawrence J. Ellison; database and file management software. Acquired BEA Systems, 4/29/2010; acquired Sun Microsystems, 1/27/2010.

Owens Corning (OC): 1 Owens Corning Pkwy., Toledo, OH 43659; (419) 248-8000; www.owenscorning.com; Michael H. Thaman; world leader in insulation, advanced glass, composite materials.

Owens-Illinois, Inc. (OI): 1 Michael Owens Way, Perrysburg, OH 43551; (567) 336-5000; Albert P. L. Stroucken; www.o-i.com; mfr. glass containers.

PepsiCo, Inc. (PEP): 700 Anderson Hill Rd., Purchase, NY 10577; (914) 253-2000; www.pepsico.com; Indra K. Nooyi; soft drinks and other beverages (Pepsi-Cola, Mountain Dew, Gatorade, Tropicana), snacks and cereals (Fritos, Lay's, Ruffles, Quaker). Acquired Pepsi Bottling Group and Pepsi Americas, 3/1/2010, making it largest food and beverage co. in North America.

Pfizer, Inc. (PFE): 235 E. 42nd St., NY, NY 10017; (212) 733-2323; www.pfizer.com; Ian Read; biopharmaceuticals (Celebrex, Lipitor, Viagra, Zoloft); human and animal health care prods. Acquired Wyeth, 10/15/2009.

PG&E Corp. (PCG): One Market, Spear Tower, Ste. 2400, San Francisco, CA 94105; (415) 267-7000; www.pgecorp.com; Anthony F. Earley Jr.; operates Pacific Gas and Electric public utility.

Philip Morris Intl. Inc. (PM): 120 Park Ave., NY, NY 10017; (917) 663-2000; www.pmi.com; Louis C. Camilleri; mfr. and distributor of tobacco. Spun off from parent company Altria Group, 3/28/2008.

Phillips 66 Co. (PSX): P.O. Box 4428, Houston, TX 77210; (281) 293-6600; www.phillips66.com; Greg C. Garland; oil, gas co. Formed when refining and marketing segment of ConocoPhillips was spun off, 5/1/2012.

Pitney Bowes Inc. (PBI): 1 Elmcroft Rd., Stamford, CT 06926; (203) 356-5000; www.pb.com; Murray D. Martin; postage meters and mailing equip.

Plains All American Pipeline, L.P. (PAA): 333 Clay St., Ste. 1600, Houston, TX 77002; (713) 646-4100; www.paalp.com; Greg L. Armstrong; oil and natural gas transportation, storage.

Post Holdings, Inc. (POST): 2503 S. Hanley Rd., St. Louis, MO 63144; (314) 644-7600; www.postfoods.com; William Stiritz; ready-to-eat cereals. Spun off from Ralcorp Holdings, 2/6/2012.

PPG Industries, Inc. (PPG): 1 PPG Pl., Pittsburgh, PA 15272; (412) 434-3131; www.ppg.com; Charles E. Bunch; glass prods., silicas, fiberglass, chemicals, sealants; world's leading supplier of automobile/industrial coatings. Acquired SigmaKalon, 1/2/2008.

Procter & Gamble Co. (PG): 1 Procter & Gamble Plz., Cincinnati, OH 45202; (513) 983-1100; www.pg.com; Bob McDonald; soaps and detergents (Ivory, Cheer, Tide, Mr. Clean); toiletries (Crest, Scope, Head & Shoulders, Old Spice); pharmaceuticals (Pepto-Bismol, Vicks cough medicines); paper prods. (Charmin toilet tissues, Bounty towels), Tampax tampons; disposable diapers (Pampers, Luvs); CoverGirl and Max Factor cosmetics, Clairol hair care; Gillette razors; sold Pringles to Kellogg, 6/1/2012.

Prudential Financial, Inc. (PRU): 751 Broad St., Newark, NJ 07102; (973) 802-6000; www.prudential.com; John R. Strangfeld Jr.; insurance, financial services.

Publix Super Markets Inc.: 3300 Publix Corporate Pkwy., Lakeland, FL 33811; (863) 688-1188; www.publix.com; William Crenshaw; supermarket chain.

PVH Corp. (PVH): 200 Madison Ave., NY, NY 10016; (212) 381-3500; www.pvh.com; Emanuel Chirico; mfr. of apparel, including licensed brands (Calvin Klein, IZOD, Geoffrey Beene, Kenneth Cole, Tommy Hilfiger, Sean John).

Quest Diagnostics Inc. (DGX): 3 Giralda Farms, Madison, NJ 07940; (800) 222-0446; www.questdiagnostics.com; Surya N. Mohapatra; leading clinical laboratory.

RadioShack Corp. (RSH): 300 RadioShack Cir., Fort Worth, TX 76102; (817) 415-3011; www.radioshack.com; James F. Gooch; consumer electronics retailer.

Ralcorp Holdings, Inc. (RAH): 800 Market St., St. Louis, MO 63101; (314) 877-7000; www.ralcorp.com; Kevin J. Hunt; private-label breakfast cereals, snack foods, pasta. Spun off Post Holdings, 2/6/2012.

Ralph Lauren Corp. (RL): 650 Madison Ave., NY, NY 10022; (212) 318-7000; www.ralphlauren.com; Ralph Lauren; men's and women's apparel, home furnishings, fragrances.

Raytheon Co. (RTN): 870 Winter St., Waltham, MA 02451; (781) 522-3000; www.raytheon.com; William Swanson; defense, communications systems.

Reader's Digest Assn., Inc.: 750 Third Ave., NY, NY 10017; (646) 293-6000; www.rda.com; Robert E. Guth; magazine publisher; marketer of books, music, video prods. Emerged from Chap. 11 reorganization, 2/22/2010.

Republic Services, Inc. (RSG): 18500 N. Allied Way, Phoenix, AZ 85054; (480) 627-2700; www.republicservices.com; Donald W. Slager; waste management

co. Merged with Allied Waste Industries, 12/5/2008.

Revlon, Inc. (REV): 237 Park Ave., NY, NY 10017; (212) 527-4000; www.revlon.com; Ronald O. Perelman; cosmetics, skin care.

Reynolds American Inc. (RAI): 401 N. Main St., Winston-Salem, NC 27101; (336) 741-2000; www.reynoldsamerican.com; Daniel M. Delen; 2nd-largest U.S. producer of cigarettes (Winston, Camel, Pall Mall, Kool, Doral).

Rite Aid Corp. (RAD): 30 Hunter Ln., Camp Hill, PA 17011; (717) 761-2633; www.riteaid.com; John T. Standley; 3rd-largest U.S. drugstore chain.

Rock-Tenn Co. (RKT): 504 Thrasher St., Norcross, GA 30071; (770) 448-2193; www.rocktenn.com; James A. Rubright; corrugated and consumer packaging. Acquired Smurfit-Stone Container Corp., 5/27/2011.

Rockwell Automation, Inc. (ROK): 1201 S. 2nd St., Milwaukee, WI 53204; (414) 382-2000; www.rockwellautomation.com; Keith D. Nosbusch; industrial automation co.

Rohm and Haas Co.: see Dow Chemical Co.

Ryder System, Inc. (R): 11690 NW 105th St., Miami, FL 33178; (305) 500-3726; www.ryder.com; Gregory T. Swienton; truck-leasing service.

SABMiller plc: Stanhope Gate, London, W1K 1AF, United Kingdom; + 44 1483 264000; www.sabmiller.com; Graham Mackay; brewing company (Miller, Peroni, Grolsch). Announced creation of Miller-Coors, joint venture with Molson Coors, 7/1/2008. Acquired Foster's Group Ltd., 12/16/2011.

Safeway Inc. (SWY): 5918 Stoneridge Mall Rd., Pleasanton, CA 94588; (925) 467-3000; www.safeway.com; Steven A. Burd; supermarkets.

Sara Lee Corp.: see Hillshire Brands Co.

Schering-Plough Corp.: see Merck & Co., Inc.

Sears Holdings Corp. (SHLD): 3333 Beverly Rd., Hoffman Estates, IL 60179; (847) 286-2500; www.searsholdings.com; Louis J. D'Ambrosio; U.S. retailer.

Shell Oil Co.: 910 Louisiana St., Houston, TX 77002; (713) 241-6161; www.shell.us; Marvin Odum; integrated oil co.; subsidiary of Royal Dutch Shell, world's 2nd-largest oil co.

Sherwin-Williams Co. (SHW): 101 W. Prospect Ave., Cleveland, OH 44115; (216) 566-2000; www.sherwin-williams.com; Christopher M. Connor; paint and varnish producer (Dutch Boy, Krylon, Minwax).

Smithfield Foods, Inc. (SFD): 200 Commerce St., Smithfield, VA 23430; (757) 365-3000; www.smithfieldfoods.com; C. Larry Pope; world's largest producer and processor of pork.

J. M. Smucker Co. (SJM): One Strawberry Ln., Orrville, OH 44667; (330) 682-3000; www.smuckers.com; Timothy P. Smucker; leading producer of fruit spreads, toppings (Magic Shell), peanut butter (Jif), oils (Crisco). Merged with Folgers Coffee Co., 11/6/2008.

Smurfit-Stone Container Corp.: see Rock-Tenn Co.

Sony Corp. of America: 550 Madison Ave., NY, NY 10022; (212) 833-6800; www.sony.com; Howard Stringer; U.S. subsidiary of Japan-based Sony Corp.; electronics, movies, music. Acquired Bertelsmann's stake in Sony BMG and renamed it Sony Music Entertainment, 10/1/2008.

Southwest Airlines Co. (LUV): 2702 Love Field Dr., Dallas, TX 75235; (214) 792-4000; www.southwest.com; Gary C. Kelly; air transportation. Acquired AirTran Holdings, Inc., 5/2/2011.

Sprint Nextel Corp. (S): 6200 Sprint Pkwy., Overland Park, KS 66251; (703) 433-4000; www.sprint.com; Dan Hesse; wireless and long-distance telecommunications.

Stanley Black & Decker, Inc. (SWK): 1000 Stanley Dr., New Britain, CT 06053; (860) 225-5111; www.stanleyblackanddecker.com; John F. Lundgren; one of the top U.S. mfrs. of hand and power tools (DeWalt,

Bostitch), household prods. (Kwikset, Baldwin). The Stanley Works and Black & Decker merged, 3/12/2010.

Staples, Inc. (SPLS): 500 Staples Dr., Framingham, MA 01702; (508) 253-5000; www.staples.com; Ronald L. Sargent; largest U.S. office-supply retailer.

Starbucks Corp. (SBUX): 2401 Utah Ave. S., Seattle, WA 98134; (206) 447-1575; www.starbucks.com; Howard D. Schultz; coffee producer; world's leading specialty coffee retailer.

Starwood Hotels & Resorts Worldwide, Inc. (HOT): 1 StarPoint, Stamford, CT 06902; (203) 964-6000; www.starwoodhotels.com; Frits van Paasschen; hotel and resort co. (Westin, Sheraton, W Hotels).

State Farm Mutual Automobile Ins. Co.: 1 State Farm Plz., Bloomington, IL 61710; (309) 766-2311; www.statefarm.com; Edward B. Rust Jr.; largest U.S. provider of auto/homeowners insurance.

Sun Microsystems, Inc.: see Oracle Corp.

Sunoco, Inc. (SUN): 1735 Market St., Ste. LL, Philadelphia, PA 19103; (215) 977-3000; www.sunocoinc.com; Brian P. MacDonald; energy resources co., gasoline retailer.

SUPERVALU Inc. (SVU): East View Innovation Ctr., 7075 Flying Cloud Dr., Eden Prairie, MN 55344; (952) 828-4000; www.supervalu.com; Craig R. Herkert; food retailer, wholesale distrib. (Acme, Albertsons, Shoppers).

SYSCO Corp. (SYY): 1390 Enclave Pkwy., Houston, TX 77077; (281) 584-1390; www.sysco.com; William J. DeLaney; world's largest food-service distributor.

Systemax Inc. (SYX): 11 Harbor Park Dr., Port Washington, NY 11050; (516) 608-7000; www.systemax.com; Richard Leeds; computers, electronics, industrial prod. retailer. Acquired CompUSA, 1/6/2008; acquired Circuit City, 5/19/2009.

Target Corp. (TGT): 1000 Nicollet Mall, Minneapolis, MN 55403; (612) 304-6073; www.target.com; Gregg W. Steinhafel; 2nd-largest U.S. discount retailer.

Tenneco Inc. (TEN): 500 N. Field Dr., Lake Forest, IL 60045; (847) 482-5000; www.tenneco.com; Gregg M. Sherrill; automotive parts (Monroe, Walker).

Texas Instruments Inc. (TXN): 12500 TI Blvd., Dallas, TX 75266; (972) 995-2011; www.ti.com; Richard K. Templeton; processors, semiconductors, software, handheld calculators. Acquired Natl. Semiconductor Corp., 9/23/2011.

Textron Inc. (TXT): 40 Westminster St., Providence, RI 02903; (401) 421-2800; www.textron.com; Scott C. Donnelly; aircraft (Cessna, Bell), industrial, automotive prods.; financial services.

3M Co. (MMM): 3M Center, St. Paul, MN 55144; (651) 733-1110; www.3m.com; Inge G. Thulin; abrasives, adhesives, electrical, health care, cleaning (Scotch-Brite, O-Cel-O sponges, Scotchgard), printing, consumer prods. (Scotch Tape, Post-it).

TIAA-CREF: 730 Third Ave., NY, NY 10017; (212) 490-9000; www.tiaa-cref.org; Roger W. Ferguson Jr.; financial services provider.

Time Warner Inc. (TWX): One Time Warner Ctr., NY, NY 10019; (212) 484-8000; www.timewarner.com; Jeffrey L. Bewkes; magazine publishing (*Time, Sports Illustrated, Fortune, Money, People*, DC Comics), TV and CATV (Cartoon Network, HBO, CNN, TBS, TNT), motion pictures (Warner Bros.), recordings. AOL and Time Warner completed the largest corporate merger in history in 2001; Time Warner spun off AOL, 12/9/2009.

TJX Cos., Inc. (TJX): 770 Cochituate Rd., Framingham, MA 01701; (508) 390-1000; www.tjx.com; Carol Meyrowitz; world's largest off-price apparel retailer (T.J. Maxx, Marshalls); home furnishing retailer (HomeGoods).

Toro Co. (TTC): 8111 Lyndale Ave. S, Bloomington, MN 55420; (952) 888-8801; www.thetorocompany.com; Michael J. Hoffman; lawn and turf maintenance prods.

(Lawn-Boy), snow removal equip.; irrigation systems.

Toys "R" Us, Inc.: 1 Geoffrey Way, Wayne, NJ 07470; (973) 617-3500; www.toysrus.com; Gerald L. Storch; children's specialty retailer. Acquired FAO Schwarz, 5/28/2009.

Tribune Co.: 435 N. Michigan Ave., Chicago, IL 60611; (312) 222-9100; www.tribune.com; Sam Zell; newspapers (*Los Angeles Times, Chicago Tribune*), broadcasting (incl. WGN and 23 other television and radio stations). Filed for Chap. 11 reorganization, 12/8/2008.

Trinity Industries, Inc. (TRN): 2525 Stemmons Fwy., Dallas, TX 75207; (214) 631-4420; www.trin.net; Timothy R. Wallace; mfr. metal prods., rail and freight equip.

Tyco Intl. Ltd. (TYC): 9 Roszel Rd., Princeton, NJ 08540; (609) 720-4200; www.tyco.com; Edward D. Breen Jr.; security and engineered prods.

Tyson Foods, Inc. (TSN): 2200 Don Tyson Pkwy., Springdale, AR 72762; (479) 290-4000 www.tysonfoods.com; Donnie Smith; fresh and processed poultry; beef and pork prods.

UBS Financial Services Inc.: 1285 Ave. of the Americas, NY, NY 10019; (212) 713-2000; www.ubs.com; Robert J. McCann; financial services; subsidiary of Switzerland's UBS AG.

Unilever USA (UN/UL): 800 Sylvan Ave., Englewood Cliffs, NJ 07632; (201) 894-4000; www.unilever.com; Paul Polman; food (Hellmann's mayonnaise, Knorr soups, Wish-Bone salad dressing, Lipton, Skippy peanut butter, Slim-Fast), hygiene prods. (Dove, Q-tips, Vaseline). Subsidiary of Unilever NV (Neth.) and Unilever plc (UK). Acquired Alberto Culver, 5/10/2011.

Union Pacific Corp. (UNP): 1400 Douglas St., Omaha, NE, 68179; (402) 544-5000; www.up.com; James R. Young; one of the largest railroad freight cos. in U.S.

Unisys Corp. (UIS): 801 Lakeview Dr., Ste. 100, Blue Bell, PA 19422; (215) 986-4011; www.unisys.com; J. Edward Coleman; designs, manuf. computer information systems; IT consulting.

United Continental Holdings, Inc. (UAL): 77 W. Wacker Dr., Chicago IL 60601; (312) 997-8000; www.unitedcontinentalholdings.com; Jeffery A. Smisek; air transportation (United Airlines, Continental Airlines); formed by merger of United Airlines and Continental Airlines, 10/1/2010.

UnitedHealth Group Inc. (UNH): UHG Center, 9900 Bren Rd. E., Minnetonka, MN 55343; (952) 936-1300; www.unitedhealthgroup.com; Stephen J. Hemsley; health insurer.

United Parcel Service, Inc. (UPS): 55 Glenlake Pkwy. NE, Atlanta, GA 30328; (404) 828-6000; www.ups.com; D. Scott Davis; world's largest package delivery co.

United States Steel Corp. (X): 600 Grant St., Pittsburgh, PA 15219; (412) 433-1121; www.ussteel.com; John P. Surma Jr.; steel, tin prods., resource mgmt.

United Technologies Corp. (UTX): One Financial Plz., Hartford, CT 06103; (860) 728-7000; www.utc.com; Louis R. Chênevert; aerospace, industrial prods. and services (Carrier, Otis, Pratt & Whitney, Sikorsky).

US Airways Group, Inc. (LCC): 111 W. Rio Salado Pkwy., Tempe, AZ 85281; (480) 693-0800; www.usairways.com; William Douglas Parker; air transportation.

Verizon Communications Inc. (VZ): 140 West St., NY, NY 10007; (212) 395-1000; www.verizon.com; Lowell C. McAdam; broadband, wireless, wireline services provider.

VF Corp. (VFC): 105 Corporate Center Blvd., Greensboro, NC 27408; (336) 424-6000; www.vfc.com; Eric C. Wiseman; apparel (Lee, Wrangler, North Face, Timberland). Acquired Timberland 9/13/2011.

Viacom Inc. (VIA): 1515 Broadway, NY, NY 10036; (212) 258-6000; www.viacom.com; Philippe P. Dauman; media networks (BET, Comedy Central, MTV, VH1, Nickelodeon); movies (Paramount).

Visteon Corp. (VC): One Village Center Dr., Van Buren Twp., MI 48111; (734) 710-5000; www.visteon.com; Donald J. Stebbins; automotive parts mfr. Emerged from Chap. 11 reorganization, 10/1/2010.

Walgreen Co. (Walgreens) (WAG): 200 Wilmot Rd., Deerfield, IL 60015; (847) 315-2500; www.walgreens.com; Gregory D. Wasson; retail drugstores.

Wal-Mart Stores, Inc. (WMT): 702 SW 8th St., Bentonville, AR 72716; (479) 273-4000; www.walmartstores.com; Michael T. Duke; world's largest retailer; discount stores, membership warehouse clubs (Sam's Club).

Washington Post Co. (WPO): 1150 15th St. NW, Washington, DC 20071; (202) 334-6000; www.washpostco.com; Donald E. Graham; media (newspapers, Slate.com, TV) and education (Kaplan). Sold *Newsweek*, 9/30/2010.

Waste Management, Inc. (WM): 1001 Fannin St., Ste. 4000, Houston, TX 77002; (713) 512-6200; www.wm.com; David P. Steiner; North America's largest waste co., recycler.

WellPoint, Inc. (WLP): 120 Monument Cir., Indianapolis, IN 46204; (317) 532-6000; www.wellpoint.com; Angela F. Braly; U.S. health benefits co.; HMOs and PPOs, an independent licensee of the Blue Cross Blue Shield Assn.

Wells Fargo & Co. (WFC): 420 Montgomery St., San Francisco, CA 94163; (866) 249-3302; www.wellsfargo.com; John G. Stumpf; financial services. Acquired Wachovia, 12/31/2008.

Wendy's Co. (WEN): 1 Dave Thomas Blvd., Dublin, OH 43017; (614) 764-3100; www.aboutwendys.com; Emil J. Brolick; one of the largest fast food restaurant companies in the U.S. Sold Arby's Restaurant Group, Inc., 7/4/2011.

Western Union Co. (WU): 12500 E. Belford Ave., Englewood, CO 80112; (720) 332-1000; www.westernunion.com; Hikmet Ersek; money transfers, payment services.

Weyerhaeuser Co. (WY): 33663 Weyerhaeuser Way S., Federal Way, WA 98063; (253) 924-2345; www.weyerhaeuser.com; Daniel S. Fulton; produces, distributes wood prods.; real estate development.

Whirlpool Corp. (WHR): 2000 N. M-63, Benton Harbor, MI 49022; (269) 923-5000; www.whirlpoolcorp.com; Jeff M. Fettig; mfr. of major home appliances (KitchenAid, Amana, Maytag).

Whole Foods Market, Inc. (WFM): 550 Bowie St., Austin, TX 78703; (512) 477-4455; www.wholefoodsmarket.com; John P. Mackey/Walter Robb; largest U.S. retailer of natural and organic foods.

Winn-Dixie Stores, Inc.: 5050 Edgewood Ct., Jacksonville, FL 32254; (904) 783-5000; www.winndixie.com; Peter Lynch; one of the largest food retailers in U.S. Acquired by BI-LO Holding, 3/12/2012.

Winnebago Industries, Inc. (WGO): 605 W. Crystal Lake Rd., Forest City, IA 50436; (641) 585-3535; www.winnebagoind.com; Randy J. Potts; mfr. of motor homes, or recreational vehicles (RVs).

Wm. Wrigley Jr. Co.: 410 N. Michigan Ave., Chicago, IL 60611; (312) 644-2121; www.wrigley.com; Martin Radvan; mfr. of chewing gum and other confections (Juicy Fruit, Wrigley's, Altoids, Life Savers). Acquired by Mars, Inc., 10/6/2008.

Xerox Corp. (XRX): 45 Glover Ave., P.O. Box 4505, Norwalk, CT 06856; (203) 968-3000; www.xerox.com; Ursula M. Burns; printers, multifunction devices, document publishing technology and support.

Yahoo! Inc. (YHOO): 701 First Ave., Sunnyvale, CA 94089; (408) 349-3300; www.yahoo.com; Ross B. Levinsohn; Internet media company.

Yum! Brands, Inc. (YUM): 1441 Gardiner Ln., Louisville, KY 40213; (502) 874-8300; www.yum.com; David C. Novak; fast food restaurants (Pizza Hut, KFC, Taco Bell). Sold Long John Silver's, 12/5/2011; sold A&W, 12/19/2011.

Labor Unions and Professional Organizations

Source: Bureau of Labor Statistics, U.S. Dept. of Labor; AFL-CIO; World Almanac research

= Member of Change to Win Federation, formed in 2005 by unions disaffiliated from AFL-CIO. * = Independent union or one not otherwise affiliated with Change to Win or AFL-CIO. All other groups listed here are affiliated with AFL-CIO as of 2012. Year established is in parenthesis.

Labor Unions

Air Line Pilots Assn. (ALPA) (1931): 53,000 members, 37 U.S. and Canadian airlines; (703) 689-2270; www.alpa.org

American Federation of Labor and Congress of Industrial Organizations (AFL-CIO) (1955): federation of 56 unions, 12 mil members; (202) 637-5000; www.aflcio.org

Automobile, Aerospace & Agricultural Implement Workers of America, International Union, United (UAW) (1935): 390,000 active (600,000 ret.) members, 750 locals; (313) 926-5000; www.uaw.org

Bakery, Confectionery, Tobacco Workers, and Grain Millers International Union (BCTGM) (1886): 100,000+ members; (301) 933-8600; www.bctgm.org

Bricklayers and Allied Craftworkers, International Union of (BAC) (1865): 100,000 members, 50 locals; (202) 783-3788; www.bacweb.org

***Carpenters and Joiners of America, United Brotherhood of** (UBC) (1881): 500,000 members, 600+ locals; (732) 417-9229; www.carpenters.org

#Change to Win Federation (2005): 4 unions, ex-affiliates of AFL-CIO, 5.5 mil+ members; (202) 721-0660; www.changetowin.org

Communications Workers of America (CWA) (1938): 700,000+ members, 1,200 locals; (202) 434-1100; www.cwa-union.org

***Education Assn., National** (NEA) (1857): 3 mil members, 14,000+ affiliates; (202) 833-4000; www.nea.org

Electrical Workers, International Brotherhood of (IBEW) (1891): 675,000 members, 900 locals; (202) 833-7000; www.ibew.org

Engineers, International Union of Operating (IUOE) (1896): 400,000 members, 123 locals; (202) 429-9100; www.iuoe.org

#Farm Workers of America, United (UFW) (1962): 27,000+ members; (661) 823-6151; www.ufw.org

***Federal Employees, National Federation of** (NFFE; affiliated with IAMAW) (1917): 110,000 members, nearly 200 locals; (202) 216-4420; www.nffe.org

Fire Fighters, International Assn. of (IAFF) (1918): 298,000+ members, 3,100+ locals; (202) 737-8484; www.iaff.org

Flight Attendants, Assn. of (AFA-CWA) (1945): nearly 60,000 members, 21 airlines; merged with Communications Workers of America in 2004; (202) 434-1300; www.afanet.org

#Food and Commercial Workers International Union, United (UFCW) (1979): 1.3 mil members, 500 locals; (202) 223-3111; www.ufcw.org

Glass, Molders, Pottery, Plastics and Allied Workers Intl. Union (GMP) (1842): 51,000 members, 250+ locals; (610) 565-5051; www.gmpiu.org

Government Employees, American Federation of (AFGE) (1932): 600,000 members; 1,100 locals; (202) 737-8700; www.afge.org

#Graphic Communications Conference (GCC/IBT) (1983): 60,000+ members; merged with Teamsters in 2005; (202) 462-1400; www.teamster.org/content/graphics-communications

Iron Workers, Intl. Assn. of Bridge, Structural, Ornamental, and Reinforcing (1896): 120,000 members, 213 locals; (202) 383-4800; www.ironworkers.org

Laborers' International Union of North America (LiUNA) (1903): 500,000 members, 500+ locals; (202) 737-8320; www.liuna.org

Letter Carriers, National Assn. of (NALC) (1889): nearly 300,000 members, 2,500 locals; (202) 393-4695; www.nalc.org

#Locomotive Engineers and Trainmen, Brotherhood of (BLET) (1863): 59,000+ members, 600+ divisions; (216) 241-2630; www.ble-t.org

Longshoremen's Assn., Intl. (ILA) (1892): 65,000+ members, approx. 200 locals; (212) 425-1200; www.ilaunion.org

Machinists and Aerospace Workers, International Assn. of (IAM) (1888): 720,000 members (current and retired), 1,174 locals; affiliated with TCU in 2005; (301) 967-4500; www.goiam.org

#Maintenance of Way Employes, Division of the Intl. Brotherhood of Teamsters; Brotherhood of (BMWED) (1887): 35,000 members, 770 locals; merged with Teamsters in 2004; (248) 662-2660; www.bmwed.org (Note: In honor of tradition, the union maintains the variant spelling of "employes" in its logo.)

Mine Workers of America, United (UMWA) (1890): 110,000 members, 600 locals; (703) 291-2400; www.umwa.org

Musicians of the United States and Canada, American Federation of (AFM) (1896): 90,000+ members, 240+ locals; (212) 869-1330; www.afm.org

Newspaper Guild—Communications Workers of America, The (TNG) (CWA) (1933): 34,000+ members, 90 locals; (202) 434-7177; www.newsguild.org

***Nurses Assn., American** (ANA) (1911): 3.1 mil members, 54 constituent state & territorial assns.; (301) 628-5000; www.nursingworld.org

Office and Professional Employees Intl. Union (OPEIU) (1945): 110,000 members, 200 locals; (800) 346-7348; www.opeiu.org

Painters and Allied Trades, International Union of (IUPAT) (1887): 160,000+ members, 425 locals; (410) 564-5900; www.iupat.org

Plumbing and Pipe Fitting Industry of the U.S. and Canada, United Assn. of Journeymen and Apprentices of the (UA) (1889): 340,000 members, 300+ locals; (410) 269-2000; www.ua.org

***Police, Fraternal Order of** (1915): 325,000+ members, 2,100+ affiliates; (615) 399-0900; www.grandlodgefop.org

Police Assns., International Union of (IUPA) (1979): 80,000 members, 500 locals; (941) 487-2560; www.iupa.org

Postal Workers Union, American (APWU) (1971): 220,000+ U.S.P.S. employees, 2,000 private employees, 1,000+ locals; (202) 842-4200; www.apwu.org

Roofers, Waterproofers and Allied Workers, United Union of (1906): 22,000 members; (202) 463-7663; www.unionroofers.com

***Rural Letter Carriers' Assn., National** (1903): 100,000+ members; 50 state org; (703) 684-5545; www.nrlca.org

***Security, Police, Fire Professionals of America, Intl. Union,** (SPFPA) (1948): 27,000+ members, 200 locals; (586) 772-7250; www.spfpa.org

#Service Employees International Union (SEIU) (1921): 2.1 mil members, 150+ locals; (202) 730-7000; www.seiu.org

Sheet Metal Workers' International Assn. (SMWIA) (1888): 150,000 members, 200 locals; (202) 783-5880; www.smwia.org

State, County, and Municipal Employees, American Federation of (AFSCME) (1932): 1.6 mil members (active and retired), 3,400 locals; (202) 429-1000; www.afscme.org

Steel, Paper and Forestry, Rubber, Manufacturing, Energy, Allied Industrial and Service Workers International Union, United (USW) (2005): 850,000+ members, 1,800+ locals; formed from merger of the unions United Steelworkers of America (USWA) (1936) and Paper, Allied-Industrial, Chemical and Energy Workers (PACE) (1999); (412) 562-2400; www.usw.org

Teachers, American Federation of (AFT) (1916): 1.5 mil members, 3,000+ locals; (202) 879-4400; www.aft.org

#Teamsters, International Brotherhood of (IBT) (1903): 1.4 mil. members, 440 locals; (202) 624-6800; www.teamster.org

Theatrical Stage Employees, Moving Picture Technicians, Artists and Allied Crafts of the U.S., Its Territories, and Canada, Intl. Alliance of (IATSE) (1893): 113,000+ members, 555+ locals; (212) 730-1770; www.iatse-intl.org

Transit Union, Amalgamated (ATU) (1892): 190,000+ members, 268 locals; (202) 537-1645; www.atu.org

Transportation Communications Intl. Union (TCU) (1899): affiliated with IAM in 2005; see Machinists and Aerospace Workers.

Transportation Union, United (UTU) (1969): 125,000 members, 500+ locals; (216) 228-9400; www.utu.org

Transport Workers Union of America (TWU) (1934): 130,000 members, 114 locals; (212) 719-3900; www.twu.org

***Treasury Employees Union, National** (NTEU) (1938): 150,000 represented, 270+ chapters; (202) 572-5500; www.nteu.org

UNITE HERE (UNITE, 1900; HERE, 1891; merged 2004): 265,000 members; (212) 265-7000; www.unitehere.org

#Workers United (affiliated with SEIU) (2009): 150,000 members

***Writers Guild of America, West** (1933): 12,000+ members; (323) 951-4000; www.wga.org

Professional Organizations and Societies

Accountants, American Institute of Certified Public (1887): nearly 377,000 members; (888) 777-7077; www.aicpa.org

ACMP—The Chamber Music Network (1947): 5,400 members; (212) 645-7424; www.acmp.net

Actuaries, Soc. of (1949): 22,000 members; (847) 706-3500; www.soa.org

Administrative Professionals, Intl. Assn. of (1942): 22,000 members; (816) 891-6600; www.iaap-hq.org

Aerospace Medical Assn. (1929): 2,600+ members; (703) 739-2240; www.asma.org

Agricultural and Biological Engineers, American Soc. of (1907): 9,000 members; (269) 429-0300; www.asabe.org

AIGA (formerly American Institute of Graphic Arts) (1914): 22,000+ members; (212) 807-1990; www. aiga.org

Air & Waste Management Assn. (1907): 8,000+ members; (412) 232-3444; www.awma.org

AMSUS—The Society of the Federal Health Agencies (1891): nearly 8,000 members; (301) 897-8800; www.amsus.org

APICS—The Assn. for Operations Management (1957): 43,000+ members; (773) 867-1777; www.apics.org

Architects, American Institute of (1857): nearly 80,000 members; (202) 626-7300; www.aia.org

ASIS Intl. (formerly Amer. Soc. for Industrial Security) (1955): 38,000 members; (703) 519-6200; www.asisonline.org

Astrologers, Inc., American Federation of (1938): 4,000 members; (480) 838-1751; www.astrologers.com

Astronautical Society, American (1954): 1,500 members; (703) 866-0020; www.astronautical.org

Astronomical Society, American (1899): 7,000 members; (202) 328-2010 www.aas.org

Authors Guild, The (1912): 8,000+ members; (212) 563-5904; www.authorsguild.org

Bankers of America, Independent Community (1930): nearly 5,000 members; (202) 659-8111; www.icba.org

Bar Assn., American (1878): nearly 400,000 members; (312) 988-5000; www.abanet.org

Bar Assn., Federal (1920): 15,000+ members; (571) 481-9100; www.fedbar.org

Biochemistry and Molecular Biology, American Society for (1906): 12,000+ members; (240) 283-6600; www.asbmb.org

Broadcasters, Natl. Assn. of (1923): 8,300 members; (202) 429-5300; www.nab.org

Business Women's Assn., American (1949): 40,000 members; (800) 228-0007; www.abwa.org

Cartoonists Society, Natl. (1946): 500+ members; (407) 647-8839; www.reuben.org

Ceramic Society, American (1898): 9,500+ members; (240) 646-7054; www.ceramics.org

Chemical Society, American (1876): 164,000+ members; (202) 872-4600; www.chemistry.org

Chiefs of Police, Intl. Assn. of (1893): 20,000+ members; (703) 836-6767; www.theiacp.org

Chiropractic Assn., American (1963): 15,000 members; (703) 276-8800; www.acatoday.org

Civil Engineers, American Soc. of (1852): 140,000+ members; (703) 295-6300; www.asce.org

College Admission Counseling, Natl. Assn. for (1937): 12,000+ members; (703) 836-2222; www.nacacnet.org

Commercial Law League of America (1895): nearly 3,000 members; (312) 240-1400; www.clla.org

Communication Assn., Natl. (1914): 8,000+ members; (202) 464-4622; www.natcom.org

Composers, Authors & Publishers, American Soc. of (ASCAP) (1914): 435,000+ members; (212) 621-6000; www.ascap.com

Computing Machinery, Assn. for (1947): 100,000+ members; (212) 626-0500; www.acm.org

Computing Professionals, Institute for Certification of (1973): nearly 55,000 members; (847) 299-4227; www.iccp.org

Construction Inspectors, Assn. of (1974): 1,000 members; (760) 327-5284; www.aci-assoc.org

Counseling Assn., American (1952): 50,000+ members; (800) 347-6647; www.counseling.org

Country Music Assn. (1958): 11,000+ members; (615) 244-2840; www.cmaworld.com

Customs Brokers and Forwarders Assn. of America, Inc., Natl. (1897): nearly 870 cos.; (202) 466-0222; www.ncbfaa.org

Dental Assn., American (1859): 156,000+ members; (312) 440-2500; www.ada.org

Directors Guild of America (1936): 14,500+ members; (310) 289-2000; www.dga.org

Electrical and Electronics Engineers, Institute of (1963): 395,000+ members; (732) 981-0060; www.ieee.org

Electronics Technicians, Intl. Soc. of Certified (1980): 50,000+ members; (817) 921-9101; www.iscet.org

Energy Engineers, Assn. of (1977): 16,000+ members; (770) 447-5083; www.aeecenter.org

Engineers, Natl. Society of Professional (1934): 45,000 members; (703) 684-2800; www.nspe.org

Environmental Assessment Association (1972): 3,500 members; (760) 327-5284; www.eaa-assoc.org

Environmental Health Assn., Natl. (1937): 4,500+ members; (303) 756-9090; www.neha.org

Family Physicians, American Academy of (1947): 105,900+; (913) 906-6000; www.aafp.org

Farm Bureau Federation, American (1919): 6.2 mil members; (202) 406-3600; www.fb.org

Farmers Union, Natl. (1902): 250,000 families; (202) 554-1600; www.nfu.org

Financial Professionals, Assn. for (1979): 16,000+ members; (301) 907-2862; www.AFPonline.org

Financial Service Professionals, Soc. of (1928): 15,000 members; (610) 526-2500; www.financialpro.org

Fire Chiefs, Intl. Assn. of (1873): 10,000+ members; (703) 273-0911; www.iafc.org

Fire Protection Engineers, Soc. of (1950): 5,000+ members; (301) 718-2910; www.sfpe.org

Food Technologists, Institute of (1939): 22,000 members; (312) 782-8424; www.ift.org

Forensic Sciences, American Academy of (1948): 6,260 members; (719) 636-1100; www.aafs.org

Funeral Directors Assn., Natl. (1882): 19,000 members; (262) 789-1880; www.nfda.org

General Contractors of America, Associated (1918): nearly 30,000 cos.; (703) 548-3118; www.agc.org

Geographers, Assn. of American (1904): 10,000 members; (202) 234-1450; www.aag.org

Ground Water Assn., Natl. (1948): 12,000+ members; (614) 898-7791; www.ngwa.org

Heating, Refrigerating and Air-Conditioning Engineers, Inc., American Soc. of (1894): 50,000+ members; (404) 636-8400; www.ashrae.org

Home Builders, Natl. Assn. of (1942): 140,000+ members; (202) 266-8200; www.nahb.org

Human Resource Management, Soc. for (SHRM) (1948): 250,000+ members; (703) 548-3440; www.shrm.org

Illustrators, Society of (1901): 1,000 members; (212) 838-2560; www.societyillustrators.org

Industrial Designers Society of America (1965): 3,000+ members; (703) 707-6000; www.idsa.org

Intelligence Officers, Assn. of Former (1975): 24 chap., 5,000+ members; (703) 790-0320; www.afio.com

Interior Designers, American Soc. of (1975): 30,000+ members; (202) 546-3480; www.asid.org

Investigative Pathology, American Soc. for (1900): 1,718 members; (301) 634-7130; www.asip.org

Jail Assn., American (1981): 5,000 members; (301) 790-3930; www.aja.org

Journalists, Society of Professional (1909): 9,000 members; (317) 927-8000; www.spj.org

Journalists and Authors, American Soc. of (1948): 1,300+ members; (212) 997-0947; www.asja.org

Judicature Society, American (1913): 6,000 members; (515) 271-2281; www.ajs.org

Landscape Architects, American Society of (1899): 17,000 members; (202) 898-2444; www.asla.org

Legal Administrators, Assn. of (1971): 10,000+ members; (847) 267-1252; www.alanet.org

Library Assn., American (1876): 61,000+ members; (800) 545-2433; www.ala.org

Lifesaving Assn., U.S. (1964): 11,000 members; (866) 367-8752; www.usla.org

Logistics, Intl. Society of (SOLE) (1966): 3,000+ members; (301) 459-8446; www.sole.org

Magicians, Intl. Brotherhood of (1922): 13,000 members; (636) 724-2400; www.magician.org

Management Accountants, Inst. of (1919): 60,000+ members; (201) 573-9000; www.imanet.org

Management Assn., American (1923): 4,100 cos., 38,000 ind.; (212) 903-7976; www.amanet.org

Marketing Assn., American (1937): 30,000+ members; (312) 542-9000; www.marketingpower.com

Master Brewers Assn. of the Americas (1887): 3,500 members; (651) 454-7250; www.mbaa.com

Material and Process Engineering, Soc. for the Advancement of (1944): 4,500 members; (626) 331-0616; www.sampe.org

Mechanical Engineers, American Soc. of (1880): 120,000+ members; (973) 882-1170; www.asme.org

Medical Assn., American (1847): 250,000 members; (800) 621-8335; www.ama-assn.org

Medical Library Assn. (1898): 4,000+ members; (312) 419-9094; www.mlanet.org

Motion Picture Arts & Sciences, Academy of (1927): 6,000+ members; (310) 247-3000; www.oscars.org

Motion Picture and Television Engineers, Soc. of (1916): 5,000+ members; (914) 761-1100; www.smpte.org

Mystery Writers of America (1945): 3,000+ members; (212) 888-8171; www.mysterywriters.org

NALS...the association for legal professionals (formerly the Natl. Assn. of Legal Secretaries) (1929): 6,000 members; (918) 582-5188; www.nals.org

Notaries, American Society of (1965): approx. 20,000 members; (850) 671-5164; www.notaries.com

Nursing, Natl. League for (1893): 33,000 members, 1,200 institutions; (212) 363-5555; www.nln.org

Operations Management, Assn. for (APICS) (1957): 30,000+ members; (773) 867-1777; www.apics.org

Optometric Assn., American (1898): 36,000 members; (800) 365-2219; www.aoa.org

Organists, American Guild of (1896): 20,000 members; (212) 870-2310; www.agohq.org

Pen Women, Natl. League of American (1897): 2,600+ members; (202) 785-1997; www.nlapw.org

Pharmacists Assn., American (1852): 60,000+ members; (202) 628-4410; www.pharmacist.com

Physical Therapy Assn., American (1921): 80,000+ members; (703) 684-2782; www.apta.org

Plastics Engineers, Society of (1942): nearly 20,000 members; (203) 775-0471; www.4spe.org

Police Assn.—United States Section, Intl. (1962): 10,000 members; (248) 486-7137; www.ipa-usa.org

Population Assn. of America (1930): 3,000 members; (301) 565-6710; www.populationassociation.org

Postmasters of the U.S., Natl. Assn. of (1898): 42,000+ members, 95 clubs; (703) 683-9027; www.napus.org

Press Club, National (1908): 3,500+ members; (202) 662-7500; www.press.org

Professional Ball Players of America, Assn. of (1924): 11,000 members; (714) 528-2012; www.apbpa.org

Professional Beauty Assn. (1904): 12,000+ members; (480) 281-0424; www.probeauty.org

Psychiatric Assn., American (1844): 36,000+ members; (703) 907-7300; www.psychiatry.org

Psychological Assn., American (1892): 137,000+ members; (202) 336-5500; www.apa.org

Public Administration, American Soc. for (1939): 9,000 members; (202) 393-7878; www.aspanet.org

Public Health Assn., American (1872): 50,000+ members; (202) 777-2742; www.apha.org

Public Relations Soc. of America (1947): 21,000+ members; (212) 460-1400; www.prsa.org

Range Management, Society for (1948): 4,000+ members; (303) 986-3309; www.rangelands.org

Real Estate Appraisers, Natl. Assn. of (1966): 5,500 members; (760) 327-5284; www.narea-assoc.org

Rehabilitation Assn., Natl. (1923): 5,500+ members; (703) 836-0850; www.nationalrehab.org

Road & Transportation Builders Assn., American (1902): 5,000+ members; (202) 289-4434; www.artba.org

Safety Engineers, American Soc. of (1911): 34,000+ members; (847) 699-2929; www.asse.org

School Administrators, American Assn. of (1865): 13,000+ members; (703) 528-0700; www.aasa.org

Science Teachers Assn., Natl. (1944): 60,000 members; (703) 243-7100; www.nsta.org

Science Writers, Natl. Assn. of (1955): 2,188 members; (510) 647-9500; www.nasw.org

Screen Actors Guild—American Federation of Television and Radio Artists (2012): 160,000 members; (855) SAG-AGTRA; www.sagaftra.org

Songwriters Guild of America (1931): 5,000+ members; (615) 742-9945; www.songwritersguild.com

Sportscasters Assn., American (1980): 500+ members; (212) 227-8080; www.americansportscastersonline.com

Surgeons, American College of (1913): 78,000 members; (312) 202-5000; www.facs.org

Tax Administrators, Federation of (1937): (202) 624-5890; www.taxadmin.org

Teachers of English, Natl. Council of (1911): 60,000+ members; (217) 328-3870; www.ncte.org

Teachers of English to Speakers of Other Languages, Inc. (1966): 12,000+ members; (703) 836-0774; www.tesol.org

Teachers of French, American Assn. of (1927): nearly 10,000 members; (618) 453-5731; www.frenchteachers.org

Teachers of German, American Assn. of (1926): 5,000 members; (856) 795-5553; www.aatg.org

Teachers of Mathematics, Natl. Council of (1920): nearly 90,000 members; (703) 620-9840; www.nctm.org

Teachers of Spanish and Portuguese, American Assn. of (1917): 11,000 members; (248) 960-2180; www.aatsp.org

Television Arts and Sciences, Natl. Academy of (1955): (212) 586-8424; www.emmyonline.org

Theological Library Assn., American (1946): nearly 1,000 members; (312) 454-5100; www.atla.org

Transportation Engineers, Inst. of (1930): nearly 17,000 members; (202) 785-0060; www.ite.org

Travel Agents, American Soc. of (1931): 12,000 members; (703) 739-2782; www.astanet.com

Underwriters Soc., Chartered Property Casualty (1944): 22,000+ members; (800) 932-2728; www.cpcusociety.org

University Women, American Assn. of (1881): 100,000+ members; (202) 785-7700; www.aauw.org

Veterinary Medical Assn., American (1863): 82,500+ members; (800) 248-2862; www.avma.org

Women in Communications, The Assn. for (1909): 3,000+ members; (703) 370-7436; www.womcom.org

Women Engineers, Society of (1950): 17,000 members; (877) 793-4636; societyofwomenengineers.swe.org

Women in Media, Alliance for (1951): nearly 10,000 members; (703) 506-3290; www.allwomeninmedia.org

Professional Sports Organizations

Source: World Almanac research

Major League Baseball

Office of the Commissioner, 245 Park Ave., 31st Fl., New York, NY 10167; www.mlb.com

American League

Baltimore Orioles (1953): 333 W. Camden St., Baltimore, MD 21201; (410) 685-9800; www.orioles.com

Boston Red Sox (1901): 4 Yawkey Way, Boston, MA 02215; (617) 267-9440; www.redsox.com

Chicago White Sox (1900, as Chicago White Stockings): 333 W. 35th St., Chicago, IL 60616; (312) 674-1000; www.whitesox.com

Cleveland Indians (1901, as Cleveland Blues): 2401 Ontario St., Cleveland, OH 44115; (216) 420-4200; www.indians.com

Detroit Tigers (1901): 2100 Woodward Ave., Detroit, MI 48201; (313) 471-2000; www.tigers.com

Houston Astros (1962, as Houston Colt .45s): 501 Crawford St., Houston, TX 77002; (713) 259-8000; www.astros.com. (The Astros were a National League team, 1962-2012; the franchise was scheduled to join the AL West beginning with the 2013 season.)

Kansas City Royals (1969): One Royal Way, Kansas City, MO 64129; (816) 921-8000; www.royals.com

Los Angeles Angels of Anaheim (1961): 2000 Gene Autry Way, Anaheim, CA 92806; (714) 940-2000; www.angelsbaseball.com

Minnesota Twins (1960): 1 Twins Way, Minneapolis, MN 55403; (612) 659-3400; www.twinsbaseball.com

New York Yankees (1903): One East 161st St., Bronx, NY 10451; (718) 293-4300; www.yankees.com

Oakland Athletics (1901, as Philadelphia Athletics): 7000 Coliseum Way, Oakland, CA 94621; (510) 638-4900; www.oaklandathletics.com

Seattle Mariners (1977): P.O. Box 4100, Seattle, WA 98194; (206) 346-4000; www.mariners.com

Tampa Bay Rays (1995, as Tampa Bay Devil Rays): One Tropicana Dr., St. Petersburg, FL 33705; (727) 825-3137; www.raysbaseball.com

Texas Rangers (1960, as Washington Senators): 1000 Ballpark Way, Arlington, TX 76011; (817) 273-5222; www.texasrangers.com

Toronto Blue Jays (1976): One Blue Jays Way, Ste. 3200, Toronto, ON M5V 1J1, Canada; (416) 341-1000; www.bluejays.com

National League

Arizona Diamondbacks (1998): 401 E. Jefferson St., Phoenix, AZ 85004; (602) 462-6500; www.dbacks.com

Atlanta Braves (1876, as Boston Red Stockings): 755 Hank Aaron Dr., Atlanta, GA 30315; (404) 522-7630; www.braves.com

Chicago Cubs (1876, as Chicago White Stockings): 1060 W. Addison, Chicago, IL 60613; (773) 404-2827; www.cubs.com

Cincinnati Reds (1869, as Cincinnati Red Stockings): 100 Main St., Cincinnati, OH 45202; (513) 765-7000; www.reds.com

Colorado Rockies (1991): 2001 Blake St., Denver, CO 80205; (303) 292-0200; www.coloradorockies.com

Houston Astros see American League.

Los Angeles Dodgers (1890): 1000 Elysian Park Ave., Los Angeles, CA 90012; (323) 224-1500; www.dodgers.com

Miami Marlins (1991, as Florida Marlins): 501 Marlins Way, Miami, FL 33125; (305) 480-1300; www.marlins.com

Milwaukee Brewers (1970): One Brewers Way, Milwaukee, WI 53214; (414) 902-4400; www.brewers.com

New York Mets (1961): Citi Field, Flushing, NY 11368; (718) 507-6387; www.mets.com

Philadelphia Phillies (1883): One Citizens Bank Way, Philadelphia, PA 19148; (215) 463-6000; www.phillies.com

Pittsburgh Pirates (1887, as Pittsburgh Alleghenies): 115 Federal St., Pittsburgh, PA 15212; (412) 323-5000; www.pirates.com

St. Louis Cardinals (1892, as St. Louis Browns): 700 Clark St., St. Louis, MO 63102; (314) 345-9600; www.cardinals.com

San Diego Padres (1969): 100 Park Blvd., San Diego, CA 92101; (619) 795-5000; www.padres.com

San Francisco Giants (1883, as New York Gothams): 24 Willie Mays Plz., San Francisco, CA 94107; (415) 972-2000; www.sfgiants.com

Washington Nationals (1969, as Montréal Expos): 1500 South Capitol St., SE, Washington, DC 20003; (202) 675-6287; www.nationals.com

National Basketball Association

League Office, 645 Fifth Ave., New York, NY 10022; www.nba.com

Atlanta Hawks (1949, as Tri-Cities Blackhawks): 101 Marietta St. NW, Ste. 1900, Atlanta, GA 30303; (866) 715-1500; www.nba.com/hawks/

Boston Celtics (1946): 226 Causeway St., 4th Fl., Boston, MA 02114; (866) 423-5849; www.nba.com/celtics/

Brooklyn Nets (1967, as New Jersey Americans): 15 MetroTech Ctr., 11th Fl., Brooklyn, NY 11201; (718) 933-3000; www.nba.com/nets/

Charlotte Bobcats (2004): 333 E. Trade St., Charlotte, NC 28202; (704) 688-8600; www.nba.com/bobcats/

Chicago Bulls (1966): 1901 W. Madison St., Chicago, IL 60612; (312) 455-4000; www.nba.com/bulls/

Cleveland Cavaliers (1970): One Center Ct., Cleveland, OH 44115; (216) 420-2000; www.nba.com/cavaliers/

Dallas Mavericks (1980): 2909 Taylor St., Dallas, TX 75226; (214) 747-6287; www.nba.com/mavericks/

Denver Nuggets (1967, as Denver Rockets): 1000 Chopper Cir., Denver, CO 80204; (303) 405-1100; www.nba.com/nuggets/

Detroit Pistons (1957): Six Championship Dr., Auburn Hills, MI 48326; (248) 377-0100; www.nba.com/pistons/

Golden State Warriors (1946, as Philadelphia Warriors): 1011 Broadway, Oakland, CA 94605; (510) 986-2200; www.nba.com/warriors/

Houston Rockets (1967, as San Diego Rockets): 1510 Polk St., Houston, TX 77002; (713) 627-3865; www.nba.com/rockets/

Indiana Pacers (1967): 125 S. Pennsylvania St., Indianapolis, IN 46204; (317) 917-2500; www.nba.com/pacers/

Los Angeles Clippers (1970, as Buffalo Braves): 1111 S. Figueroa St., Ste. 1100, Los Angeles, CA 90015; (213) 742-7500; www.nba.com/clippers/

Los Angeles Lakers (1947, as Minneapolis Lakers): 555 N. Nash St., El Segundo, CA 90245; (310) 426-6000; www.nba.com/lakers/

Memphis Grizzlies (1995, as Vancouver Grizzlies): 191 Beale St., Memphis, TN 38103; (901) 888-4667; www.nba.com/grizzlies/

Miami Heat (1988): 601 Biscayne Blvd., Miami, FL 33132; (786) 777-1000; www.nba.com/heat/

Milwaukee Bucks (1968): 1001 N. 4th St., Milwaukee, WI 53203; (414) 227-0500; www.nba.com/bucks/

Minnesota Timberwolves (1989): 600 1st Ave. North, Minneapolis, MN 55403; (612) 673-1600; www.nba.com/timberwolves/

New Orleans Hornets (1988, as Charlotte Hornets): 1250 Poydras St., 19th Fl., New Orleans, LA 70113; (504) 593-4700; www.nba.com/hornets/

New York Knickerbockers (1946): Two Pennsylvania Plz., New York, NY 10121; (212) 465-6471; www.nba.com/knicks/

Oklahoma City Thunder (1967, as Seattle SuperSonics): 2 Leadership Square, 211 N. Robinson Ave., Ste. 300; Oklahoma City, OK 73102; (405) 208-4800; www.nba.com/thunder/

Orlando Magic (1989): 8701 Maitland Summit Blvd., Orlando, FL 32810; (407) 916-2400; www.nba.com/magic/

Philadelphia 76ers (1937, as Syracuse Nationals): 3601 S. Broad St., Philadelphia, PA 19148; (215) 339-7676; www.nba.com/sixers/

Phoenix Suns (1968): 201 E. Jefferson St., Phoenix, AZ 85004; (602) 379-7900; www.nba.com/suns/

Portland Trail Blazers (1970): One Center Ct., Ste. 200, Portland, OR 97227; (503) 234-9291; www.nba.com/blazers/

Sacramento Kings (1945, as Rochester Royals): One Sports Pkwy., Sacramento, CA 95834; (916) 928-0000; www.nba.com/kings/

San Antonio Spurs (1967, as Dallas Chaparrals): One AT&T Center, San Antonio, TX 78219; (210) 444-5000; www.nba.com/spurs/

Toronto Raptors (1995): 40 Bay St., Toronto, ON M5J 2X2, Canada; (416) 366-3865; www.nba.com/raptors/

Utah Jazz (1974, as New Orleans Jazz): 301 W. South Temple, Salt Lake City, UT 84101; (801) 325-2500; www.nba.com/jazz/

Washington Wizards (1961, as Chicago Packers): 601 F St. NW, Washington, DC 20004; (202) 661-5000; www.nba.com/wizards/

National Hockey League

NHL Headquarters, 1185 Ave. of the Americas, 15th Fl., New York, NY 10036; www.nhl.com

Anaheim Ducks (1993): 2695 E. Katella Ave., Anaheim, CA 92806; (877) 945-3946; ducks.nhl.com

Boston Bruins (1924): 100 Legends Way, Boston, MA 02114; (617) 624-1900; bruins.nhl.com

Buffalo Sabres (1970): One Seymour H. Knox III Plz., Buffalo, NY 14203; (716) 855-4100; sabres.nhl.com

Calgary Flames (1980): P.O. Box 1540, Station M, Calgary, AB T2P 3B9, Canada; (403) 777-2177; flames.nhl.com

Carolina Hurricanes (1972, as New England Whalers): 1400 Edwards Mill Rd., Raleigh, NC 27607; (919) 467-7825; hurricanes.nhl.com

Chicago Blackhawks (1926): 1901 W. Madison St., Chicago, IL 60612; (312) 455-7000; blackhawks.nhl.com

Colorado Avalanche (1972, as Quebec Nordiques): 1000 Chopper Cir., Denver, CO 80204; (303) 405-1100; avalanche.nhl.com

Columbus Blue Jackets (2000): 200 W. Nationwide Blvd., Columbus, OH 43215; (614) 246-4625; bluejackets.nhl.com

Dallas Stars (1967, as Minnesota North Stars): 2601 Ave. of the Stars, Frisco, TX 75034; (214) 387-5500; stars.nhl.com

Detroit Red Wings (1926, as Detroit Cougars): 600 Civic Center Dr., Detroit, MI 48226; (313) 983-6606; redwings.nhl.com

Edmonton Oilers (1972, as Alberta Oilers): 11230 - 110 St., Edmonton, AB T5G 3H7, Canada; (780) 414-4000; oilers.nhl.com

Florida Panthers (1993): One Panther Pkwy., Sunrise, FL 33323; (954) 835-7000; panthers.nhl.com

Los Angeles Kings (1967): 1111 S. Figueroa St., Ste. 3100, Los Angeles, CA 90015; (213) 742-7100; kings.nhl.com

Minnesota Wild (2000): 317 Washington St., St. Paul, MN 55102; (651) 602-6000; wild.nhl.com

Montréal Canadiens (1917): 1909, avenue des Canadiens-de-Montréal, Montréal, QC H3C 5L2, Canada; (514) 932-2582; canadiens.nhl.com

Nashville Predators (1998): 501 Broadway, Nashville, TN 37203; (615) 770-2355; predators.nhl.com

New Jersey Devils (1974, as Kansas City Scouts): Prudential Center, 165 Mulberry St., Newark, NJ 07102; (973) 757-6100; devils.nhl.com

New York Islanders (1972): 1255 Hempstead Tpke., Uniondale, NY 11553; (516) 501-6700; islanders.nhl.com

New York Rangers (1926): Two Pennsylvania Plz., New York, NY 10121; (212) 465-6000; rangers.nhl.com

Ottawa Senators (1992): 1000 Palladium Dr., Ottawa, ON K2V 1A5, Canada; (613) 599-0250; senators.nhl.com

Philadelphia Flyers (1967): 3601 S. Broad St., Philadelphia, PA 19148; (215) 336-3600; flyers.nhl.com

Phoenix Coyotes (1979, as Winnipeg Jets): 6751 N. Sunset Blvd. #200, Glendale, AZ 85305; (623) 772-3200; coyotes.nhl.com

Pittsburgh Penguins (1967): 1001 5th Ave., Pittsburgh, PA 15219; (412) 642-1800; penguins.nhl.com

St. Louis Blues (1967): 1401 Clark Ave. at Brett Hull Way, St. Louis, MO 63103; (314) 622-2500; blues.nhl.com

San Jose Sharks (1991): 525 W. Santa Clara St., San Jose, CA 95113; (408) 287-7070; sharks.nhl.com

Tampa Bay Lightning (1992): 401 Channelside Dr., Tampa, FL 33602; (813) 301-6500; lightning.nhl.com

Toronto Maple Leafs (1919, as Toronto St. Pats): 40 Bay St., Ste. 400, Toronto, ON M5J 2X2, Canada; (416) 703-5323; mapleleafs.nhl.com

Vancouver Canucks (1946): 800 Griffiths Way, Vancouver, BC V6B 6G1, Canada; (604) 899-7400; canucks.nhl.com

Washington Capitals (1974): 627 N. Glebe Rd., Ste. 850, Arlington, VA 22203; (202) 266-2200; capitals.nhl.com

Winnipeg Jets (1999, as Atlanta Thrashers): 345 Graham Ave., Winnipeg, MB R3C 5S6, Canada; (204) 987-7825; jets.nhl.com

National Football League

League Office, 345 Park Ave., New York, NY 10017; www.nfl.com

Arizona Cardinals (1898, as Morgan Athletic Club): P.O. Box 888, Phoenix, AZ 85001; (602) 379-0101; www.azcardinals.com

Atlanta Falcons (1965): 4400 Falcon Pkwy., Flowery Branch, GA 30542; (770) 965-3115; www.atlantafalcons.com

Baltimore Ravens (1996): 1101 Russell St., Baltimore, MD 21230; (410) 261-7283; www.baltimoreravens.com

Buffalo Bills (1960): One Bills Dr., Orchard Park, NY 14127; (716) 648-1800; www.buffalobills.com

Carolina Panthers (1993): 800 S. Mint St., Charlotte, NC 28202; (704) 358-7000; www.panthers.com

Chicago Bears (1920, as Decatur Staleys): 1000 Football Dr., Lake Forest, IL 60045; (847) 615-2327; www.chicagobears.com

Cincinnati Bengals (1968): One Paul Brown Stadium, Cincinnati, OH 45202; (513) 621-3550; www.bengals.com

Cleveland Browns (1946): 76 Lou Groza Blvd., Berea, OH 44017; (440) 824-3434; www.clevelandbrowns.com

Dallas Cowboys (1960): 900 E. Randol Mill Rd., Arlington, TX 76011; (817) 892-5000; www.dallascowboys.com

Denver Broncos (1960): 13655 Broncos Pkwy., Englewood, CO 80112; (303) 649-9000; www.denverbroncos.com

Detroit Lions (1934): 222 Republic Dr., Allen Park, MI 48101; (313) 262-2000; www.detroitlions.com

Green Bay Packers (1919): 1265 Lombardi Ave., Green Bay, WI 54304; (920) 569-7500; www.packers.com

Houston Texans (2002): Two Reliant Park, Houston, TX 77054; (832) 667-2002; www.houstontexans.com

Indianapolis Colts (1946, as Baltimore Colts): 7001 W. 56th St., Indianapolis, IN 46254; (317) 297-2658; www.colts.com

Jacksonville Jaguars (1995): One EverBank Field Dr., Jacksonville, FL 32202; (904) 633-2000; www.jaguars.com

Kansas City Chiefs (1960, as Dallas Texans): One Arrowhead Dr., Kansas City, MO 64129; (816) 920-9300; www.kcchiefs.com

Miami Dolphins (1966): 347 Don Shula Dr., Miami Gardens, FL 33056; (305) 943-8000; www.miamidolphins.com

Minnesota Vikings (1961): 9520 Viking Dr., Eden Prairie, MN 55344; (952) 858-6500; www.vikings.com

New England Patriots (1960): One Patriot Pl., Foxboro, MA 02035; (508) 543-8200; www.patriots.com

New Orleans Saints (1967): 5800 Airline Dr., Metairie, LA 70003; (504) 733-0255; www.neworleanssaints.com

New York Giants (1925): MetLife Stadium, E. Rutherford, NJ 07073; (201) 935-8111; www.giants.com

New York Jets (1960, as New York Titans): One Jets Dr., Florham Park, NJ 07932; (800) 469-5387; www.newyorkjets.com

Oakland Raiders (1960): 1220 Harbor Bay Pkwy., Alameda, CA 94502; (510) 864-5000; www.raiders.com

Philadelphia Eagles (1933): One NovaCare Way, Philadelphia, PA 19145; (215) 463-2500; www.philadelphiaeagles.com

Pittsburgh Steelers (1933): 3400 S. Water. St., Pittsburgh, PA 15203; (412) 432-7800; www.steelers.com

St. Louis Rams (1937, as Cleveland Rams): One Rams Way, St. Louis, MO 63045; (314) 982-7267; www.stlouisrams.com

San Diego Chargers (1960, as Los Angeles Chargers): P.O. Box 609609, San Diego, CA 92160; (858) 874-4500; www.chargers.com

San Francisco 49ers (1950): 4949 Centennial Blvd., Santa Clara, CA 95054; (408) 562-4949; www.49ers.com

Seattle Seahawks (1976): 12 Seahawks Way, Renton, WA 98056; (888) 635-4295; www.seahawks.com

Tampa Bay Buccaneers (1976): One Buccaneer Pl., Tampa, FL 33607; (813) 870-2700; www.buccaneers.com

Tennessee Titans (1960, as Houston Oilers): 460 Great Circle Rd., Nashville, TN 37228; (615) 565-4000; www.titansonline.com

Washington Redskins (1937): 21300 Redskin Park Dr., Ashburn, VA 20147; (703) 726-7000; www.redskins.com

Health Organizations

Source: World Almanac research

Entries are roughly alphabetized by the basic condition addressed or organization name. Year established is in parentheses. In addition to these selected sites, there is a vast array of medical information on the Internet. It is important, however, to be certain that the source of information is reliable and accurate. Always check with a physician before embarking on any new health-related undertaking.

Al-Anon Family Groups (1951): (757) 563-1600; www.al-anon.alateen.org

Alcohol and Drug Information, SAMHSA National Clearinghouse: (877) SAMHSA-7 (726-4727); store.samhsa.gov/home

Alcoholics Anonymous (1935): (212) 870-3400; www.aa.org

Alcoholism and Drug Dependence, Inc., National Council on (1944): (212) 269-7797; www.ncadd.org

Aging, National Institute on (1974): (301) 496-1752; www.nia.nih.gov

Aging's Eldercare Locator, Administration on (1991): (800) 677-1116; www.eldercare.gov

AIDSinfo: (800) HIV-0440 (448-0440); www.aidsinfo.nih.gov

AIDS Society, Canadian (1988): (613) 230-3580; www.cdnaids.ca

Allergy, Asthma, and Immunology, American Academy of (1943): (414) 272-6071; www.aaaai.org

ALS Assn. [Lou Gehrig's disease] (1985): (202) 407-8580; www.alsa.org

Alzheimer's Assn. (1979): (312) 335-8700; www.alz.org

Alzheimer Society of Canada (1978): (416) 488-8772; www.alzheimer.ca

Anorexia Nervosa and Associated Disorders, National Assn. of (1976): (630) 577-1333; www.anad.org

Arc of the United States, The [intellectual and developmental disabilities] (1950): (800) 433-5255; www.thearc.org

Arthritis Foundation (1948): (800) 283-7800; www.arthritis.org

Arthritis and Musculoskeletal and Skin Diseases, National Institute of (1986): (877) 226-4267; www.niams.nih.gov

Asthma and Allergy Foundation of America (1953): (800) 727-8462; www.aafa.org

Autism Society (1965): (800) 328-8476; www.autism-society.org

Blind, American Council of the (1961): (202) 467-5081; www.acb.org

Blind, Inc., Guide Dog Foundation for the (1946): (800) 548-4337; www.guidedog.org

Blind, National Federation of the (1940): (410) 659-9314; www.nfb.org

Blind and Physically Handicapped, National Library Service for the (1931): (202) 707-5100; TDD (202) 707-0744; www.loc.gov/nls/

Blindness, Foundation Fighting (1971): (800) 683-5555; www.blindness.org

Blindness America, Prevent (1908): (800) 331-2020; www.preventblindness.org

Brain Tumor Society, National (2008): (800) 770-8287; www.braintumor.org

Breast Cancer Organization, Y-ME National (1978): (800) 221-2141; www.y-me.org

Cancer Institute's Cancer Information Service, National (1975): (800) 422-6237; www.cancer.gov/aboutnci/cis/

Cancer Society, American (1913): (800) 227-2345; www.cancer.org

Cancer Society, Canadian (1938): (416) 961-7223; www.cancer.ca

Centers for Disease Control and Prevention (CDC) (1946): (800) 232-4636; www.cdc.gov

Cerebral Palsy, United (1949): (202) 776-0406; www.ucp.org

CFIDS Assn. of America [chronic fatigue syndrome] (1987): (704) 365-2343; www.cfids.org

Child Abuse and Family Violence, National Council on (1984): (202) 429-6695; www.nccafv.org

Childhelp National Child Abuse Hotline (1959): (800) 4-A-CHILD (422-4453); www.childhelp.org

Children, National Center for Missing and Exploited (1984): (703) 224-2150; www.missingkids.com

Children's Tumor Foundation (1978): (212) 344-6633; www.ctf.org

Chronic Pain Assn., American (1980): (800) 533-3231; www.theacpa.org

Continence, National Assn. for (1982): (843) 377-0900; www.nafc.org

Continence, Simon Foundation for (1983): (800) 237-4666; www.simonfoundation.org

Cooley's Anemia Foundation [thalassemia major] (1954): (800) 522-7222; www.thalassemia.org

Crohn's and Colitis Foundation of America (1967): (800) 932-2423; www.ccfa.org

Crohn's and Colitis Foundation of Canada (1974): (416) 920-5035; www.ccfc.ca

Cystic Fibrosis Foundation (1955): (800) 344-4823 or (301) 951-4422; www.cff.org

Deaf, Natl. Assn. of the (1880): (301) 587-1788, TTY (301) 587-1789; www.nad.org

Depression and Bipolar Support Alliance (1985): (800) 826-3632; www.dbsalliance.org

Diabetes Assn., American (1940): (800) 342-2383; www.diabetes.org

Diabetes Assn., Canadian (1953): (416) 363-3373; www.diabetes.ca

Dial-A-Hearing Screening Test: (800) 222-EARS (322-3277)

Domestic Violence Hotline, National (1996): (800) 799-7233; TTY (800) 787-3224; www.thehotline.org

Down Syndrome Congress, Natl. (1973): (800) 232-6372; www.ndsccenter.org

Down Syndrome Society, National (1979): (800) 221-4602; www.ndss.org

Dyslexia Assn., International (1949): (410) 296-0232; www.interdys.org

Easter Seals [disabilities, special needs] (1919): (800) 221-6827; www.easterseals.com

Endometriosis Assn. (1980): (414) 355-2200; www.endometriosisassn.org

Epilepsy Foundation (1967): (800) 332-1000; www.epilepsyfoundation.org

Fat Acceptance, Natl. Assn. to Advance (1969): (916) 558-6880; www.naafa.org

First Candle [sudden infant death syndrome] (1987): (800) 221-7437; www.sidsalliance.org

FoodSafety.gov—Gateway to Federal Food Safety Information: Food (except for meat, poultry, eggs): (888) 723-3366 (FDA Center for Food Safety and Applied Nutrition); Meat, poultry, eggs: (888) 674-6854 (USDA Meat and Poultry Hotline); Illness or food poisoning: (800) 232-4636 (CDC)

Gamblers Anonymous (1957): (626) 960-3500; www.gamblersanonymous.org

Geriatrics Society, American (1942): (212) 308-1414; www.americangeriatrics.org

Hard of Hearing Assn., Canadian (1982): (613) 526-1584, TTY (613) 526-2692; www.chha.ca

Headache Foundation, National (1970): (888) 643-5552; www.headaches.org

HealthyWomen (1988): (877) 986-9472; www.healthywomen.org

Hearing Society, Intl. (1951): (734) 522-7200; www.ihsinfo.org

Heart Assn., American (1924): (800) 242-8721; www.heart.org/HEARTORG

Hearts, Inc., Mended (1951): (214) 296-9252; www.mendedhearts.org

Hospice Education Institute (1985): (800) 331-1620; www.hospiceworld.org

Hospice International, Children's (1983): (800) 242-4453; www.chionline.org

Hospital Assn., American (1899): (312) 422-3000; www.aha.org

Huntington's Disease Society of America (1967): (800) 345-4372; www.hdsa.org

JDRF (formerly Juvenile Diabetes Research Foundation) (1970): (800) 533-2873; www.jdrf.org

Kidney Foundation, National (1950): (212) 889-2210; www.kidney.org

Kidney Foundation of Canada (1964): (514) 369-4806; www.kidney.ca

Kidney Fund, American (1971): (800) 638-8299; www.kidneyfund.org

Kidney and Urologic Diseases Information Clearinghouse, National: (800) 891-5390; www.kidney.niddk.nih.gov

La Leche League Intl. [breastfeeding] (1957): (800) 525-3243; www.llli.org

Leukemia and Lymphoma Society (1949): (800) 955-4572; www.lls.org

Liver Foundation, American (1976): (212) 668-1000; www.liverfoundation.org

Living Bank [organ donation] (1968): (800) 528-2971; www.livingbank.org

Lung Assn., American (1904): (800) 548-8252; www.lungusa.org

Lung Line (1983): (800) 222-5864; www.nationaljewish.org/about/contact/lung-line/

Lupus Foundation of America, Inc. (1977): (202) 349-1155; www.lupus.org

March of Dimes [babies' health] (1938): (914) 997-4488; www.marchofdimes.com

Marfan Foundation, Natl. (1981): (800) 8-MARFAN (862-7326); www.marfan.org

Mayo Clinic (1889): (507) 284-2511; www.mayoclinic.com

Mental Health, National Institute of (1946): (301) 443-4513, TTY (301) 443-8431; www.nimh.nih.gov

Mental Health America (1909): (800) 969-6642; www.nmha.org

Mental Illness, Natl. Alliance on (1979): (703) 524-7600; www.nami.org

Multiple Sclerosis Society, National (1946): (800) 344-4867; www.nationalmssociety.org

Multiple Sclerosis Society of Canada (1948): (416) 922-6065; www.mssociety.ca

Muscular Dystrophy Assn. (1950): (800) 572-1717; www.mdausa.org

Myeloma Foundation, Intl. (1990): (800) 452-2873; www.myeloma.org

Narcotics Anonymous (1953): (818) 773-9999; www.na.org

National Health Council (1920): (202) 785-3910; www.nationalhealthcouncil.org

National Health Information Center (1979): (800) 336-4797; www.health.gov/NHIC/

National Institutes of Health (NIH) (1887): (301) 496-4000; www.nih.gov

Neurological Disorders and Stroke, Natl. Institute of (1950): (800) 352-9424, TTY (301) 468-5981; www.ninds.nih.gov

Organ Sharing, United Network for (1984): (804) 782-4800; www.unos.org

Osteoporosis Foundation, National (1984): (800) 231-4222; www.nof.org

Overeaters Anonymous (1960): (505) 891-2664; www.oa.org

Parkinson Foundation, National (1957): (800) 327-4545; www.parkinson.org

Parkinson's Disease Foundation (1957): (212) 923-4700; www.pdf.org

Parkinson Society Canada (1965): (416) 227-9700; www.parkinson.ca

Pediatrics, American Academy of (1930): (847) 434-4000; www.aap.org

Phoenix House [substance abuse] (1967): (800) DRUG-HELP (378-4435); www.phoenixhouse.org

Planned Parenthood Federation of America, Inc. (1916): (212) 541-7800; www.plannedparenthood.org

Plastic Surgeons, American Society of (1931): (847) 228-9900; www.plasticsurgery.org

Post-Polio Health International (1960): (314) 534-0475; www.post-polio.org

Psoriasis Foundation, Natl. (1966): (800) 723-9166; www.psoriasis.org

Rare Disorders, Natl. Organization for (1983): (203) 744-0100; www.rarediseases.org

Rehabilitation Information Center, National (1977): (800) 346-2742; TTY (301) 459-5984; www.naric.com

Reye's Syndrome Foundation, Natl. (1974): (800) 233-7393; www.reyessyndrome.org

Runaway Switchboard, National (1971): (773) 880-9860; www.1800runaway.org

Scleroderma Foundation (1989): (800) 722-HOPE (722-4673); www.scleroderma.org

Social Health Assn., American (sexual health information) (1914): (919) 361-8400; www.ashastd.org

Sickle Cell Disease Assn. of America (1971): (800) 421-8453; www.sicklecelldisease.org

Sjögren's Syndrome Foundation (1983): (800) 475-6473; www.sjogrens.org

Speech-Language-Hearing Assn., American (1925): (800) 638-8255, TTY (301) 296-5650; www.asha.org

Spinal Cord Injury Assn., National (1948): (718) 803-3782; www.spinalcord.org

Stroke Assn., National (1984): (800) 787-6537; www.stroke.org

Stuttering Assn., Natl. (1977): (212) 944-4050; www.nsastutter.org

Stuttering Foundation of America (1947): (800) 992-9392; www.stutteringhelp.org

Sudden Infant Death Syndrome Institute, American (1983): (239) 431-5425; www.sids.org

Suicide Prevention Lifeline, National (2004): (800) 273-TALK (273-8255); www.suicidepreventionlifeline.org

Therapy Dogs Intl. (1976): (973) 252-9800; www.tdi-dog.org

Tourette Syndrome Assn. (1972): (718) 224-2999; tsa-usa.org

Tuberous Sclerosis Alliance (1974): (301) 562-9890; www.tsalliance.org

Urological Assn., American (1902): (866) 746-4282; www.auanet.org

Visual Impairments, Natl. Assn. for Parents of Children with (1980): (800) 562-6265; www.napvi.org

Women's Health Network, National (1975): (202) 682-2640; www.nwhn.org

UNITED STATES FACTS

Superlative U.S. Statistics

Source: U.S. Geological Survey, U.S. Dept. of the Interior; U.S. Census Bureau, U.S. Dept. of Commerce; World Almanac research

Superlative Statistics for the 50 States

Total area for 50 states and Washington, DC		3,796,742 sq mi
Land area for 50 states and Washington, DC		3,531,905 sq mi
Water area for 50 states and Washington, DC		264,837 sq mi
Largest state	Alaska	665,384 sq mi
Smallest state	Rhode Island	1,545 sq mi
Largest county (excluding Alaska)	San Bernardino County, CA	20,105 sq mi
Smallest county	Arlington County, VA[1]	26 sq mi
Largest incorporated city (by area, pop. 1,000+)	Sitka, AK	4,812 sq mi
Northernmost city	Barrow, AK	71°17′ N
Northernmost point	Point Barrow, AK	71°23′ N
Southernmost city	Hilo, HI	19°44′ N
Southernmost settlement	Naalehu, HI	19°03′ N
Southernmost point	Ka Lae (South Cape), island of Hawaii	18°55′ N (155°41′ W)
Easternmost city	Eastport, ME	66°59′05′′ W
Easternmost settlement[2]	Attu Station, AK	173°11′ E
Easternmost point[2]	Pochnoi Point, Semisopochnoi Island, AK	179°52′ E
Westernmost city	Adak Station, AK	173°11′ E
Westernmost settlement	Adak Station, AK	173°11′ E
Westernmost point	Amatignak Island, AK	179°09′ W
Highest settlement	Tordal Estates, CO	10,653 ft
Lowest settlement	Bombay Beach, CA	−223 ft
Highest point on Atlantic coast	Cadillac Mountain, Mount Desert Island, ME	1,530 ft
Oldest national park	Yellowstone National Park (1872), WY-MT-ID	2,219,791 acres
Largest national park	Wrangell-St. Elias, AK	8,323,147 acres
Highest waterfall	Yosemite Falls—total in 3 sections	2,425 ft
	(Upper Yosemite Fall, 1,430 ft; Cascades, 675 ft; Lower Yosemite Fall, 320 ft)	
Longest river system	Mississippi-Missouri-Red Rock	3,710 mi
Highest mountain	Mount McKinley (Denali), AK	20,320 ft
Lowest point	Death Valley, CA	−282 ft
Deepest lake	Crater Lake, OR	1,958 ft
Rainiest spot	Mount Waialeale, HI	annual avg. rainfall 424 in.
Largest gorge	Grand Canyon, Colorado River, AZ	277 mi long, 600 ft to 18 mi wide, 1 mi deep
Deepest gorge	Hells Canyon, Snake River, OR-ID	7,900 ft
Largest dam	New Cornelia Tailings, Ten Mile Wash, AZ[3]	274,026,000 cu yds material used
Tallest building	Willis Tower (formerly Sears Tower), Chicago, IL	1,451 ft
Largest building	Boeing Manufacturing Plant, Everett, WA	472,000,000 cu ft; covers 98 acres
Largest office building	Pentagon, Arlington, VA	77,015,000 cu ft; covers 29 acres
Tallest structure	KVLY-TV Tower, Blanchard, ND[4]	2,063 ft
Longest bridge span	Verrazano-Narrows Bridge, New York, NY	4,260 ft
Highest bridge	Royal Gorge Bridge, Cañon City, CO	1,053 ft above water
Deepest well	Bertha Rogers gas well (inactive), Washita County, OK	31,441 ft

Superlative Statistics for the 48 Contiguous States

Total area for 48 states and Washington, DC		3,120,426 sq mi[5]
Land area for 48 states and Washington, DC		2,954,842 sq mi
Water area for 48 states and Washington, DC		165,585 sq mi
Largest state	Texas	268,596 sq mi
Northernmost city	Bellingham, WA	48°46′ N
Northernmost settlement	Angle Inlet, MN	49°21′ N
Northernmost point	Northwest Angle, MN	49°23′ N
Southernmost city	Key West, FL	24°32′ N
Southernmost mainland city	Florida City, FL	25°27′ N
Southernmost point	Ballast Key, FL	24°31′ N
Easternmost settlement	Lubec, ME	66°58′49′′ W
Easternmost point	West Quoddy Head, ME	66°57′ W
Westernmost town	La Push, WA	124°38′ W
Westernmost point	Bodelteh Islands, WA	124°46′ W
Highest mountain	Mount Whitney, CA	14,500 ft

(1) Smallest county by land area is New York County (Manhattan) at 23 sq mi; its total area including water is 34 sq mi. Superlative shown is for smallest total area. (2) Alaska's Aleutian Islands extend into the Eastern Hemisphere (across 180° longitude) and thus technically contain the easternmost point and settlement in the U.S. (3) Privately owned industrial dam composed of tailings, remnants of a mining process. (4) Supported tower. Tallest freestanding tower is Stratosphere Tower, Las Vegas, NV, at 1,149 ft. (5) Components do not add up to total due to rounding.

Additional Statistical Information About the U.S.

The U.S. Census Bureau has published the *Statistical Abstract of the United States* annually since 1878. Because of budget concerns, however, it terminated the collection of data for the publication in 2011. The 2012 *Statistical Abstract* as well as earlier editions can be viewed online at www.census.gov/compendia/statab/. Beginning with the 2013 edition, the *Statistical Abstract* will be co-published by ProQuest and Bernan Press. For more information, visit www.proquest.com.

Highest and Lowest Altitudes in U.S. States and Territories

Source: U.S. Geological Survey, U.S. Dept. of the Interior
(negative sign indicates below sea level)

State/territory	Highest point Name	County	Elev. (ft)	Lowest point Name	County	Elev. (ft)
Alabama	Cheaha Mountain	Cleburne	2,407	Gulf of Mexico		Sea level
Alaska	Mount McKinley/Denali	Denali	20,320	Pacific Ocean		Sea level
American Samoa	Lata Mountain	Tau Island	3,160	Pacific Ocean		Sea level
Arizona	Humphreys Peak	Coconino	12,637	Colorado R.	Yuma	70
Arkansas	Magazine Mountain	Logan	2,753	Ouachita R.	Ashley-Union	55
California	Mount Whitney	Inyo-Tulare	14,500	Death Valley	Inyo	−282
Colorado	Mount Elbert	Lake	14,440	Arikaree R.	Yuma	3,315
Connecticut	S. slope of Mt. Frissell	Litchfield	2,380	Long Island Sound		Sea level
Delaware	Ebright Azimuth	New Castle	448	Atlantic Ocean		Sea level
Dist. of Columbia	Tenleytown	NW quadrant	410	Potomac R.		1
Florida	Britton Hill	Walton	345	Atlantic Ocean		Sea level
Georgia	Brasstown Bald	Towns-Union	4,784	Atlantic Ocean		Sea level
Guam	Mount Lamlam	Agat District	1,332	Pacific Ocean		Sea level
Hawaii	Pu'u Wekiu, Mauna Kea	Hawaii	13,796	Pacific Ocean		Sea level
Idaho	Borah Peak	Custer	12,661	Snake R.	Nez Perce	710
Illinois	Charles Mound	Jo Daviess	1,235	Mississippi R.	Alexander	279
Indiana	Hoosier Hill	Wayne	1,257	Ohio R.	Posey	320
Iowa	Hawkeye Point	Osceola	1,670	Mississippi R.	Lee	480
Kansas	Mount Sunflower	Wallace	4,039	Verdigris R.	Montgomery	679
Kentucky	Black Mountain	Harlan	4,145	Mississippi R.	Fulton	257
Louisiana	Driskill Mountain	Bienville	535	New Orleans	Orleans	−8
Maine	Mount Katahdin	Piscataquis	5,268	Atlantic Ocean		Sea level
Maryland	Hoye Crest	Garrett	3,360	Atlantic Ocean		Sea level
Massachusetts	Mount Greylock	Berkshire	3,491	Atlantic Ocean		Sea level
Michigan	Mount Arvon	Baraga	1,979	Lake Erie		571
Minnesota	Eagle Mountain	Cook	2,301	Lake Superior		601
Mississippi	Woodall Mountain	Tishomingo	806	Gulf of Mexico		Sea level
Missouri	Taum Sauk Mountain	Iron	1,772	St. Francis R.	Dunklin	230
Montana	Granite Peak	Park	12,804	Kootenai R.	Lincoln	1,800
Nebraska	Panorama Point	Kimball	5,424	Missouri R.	Richardson	840
Nevada	Boundary Peak	Esmeralda	13,146	Colorado R.	Clark	479
New Hampshire	Mount Washington	Coos	6,288	Atlantic Ocean		Sea level
New Jersey	High Point	Sussex	1,803	Atlantic Ocean		Sea level
New Mexico	Wheeler Peak	Taos	13,166	Red Bluff Reservoir	Eddy	2,842
New York	Mount Marcy	Essex	5,344	Atlantic Ocean		Sea level
North Carolina	Mount Mitchell	Yancey	6,684	Atlantic Ocean		Sea level
North Dakota	White Butte	Slope	3,506	Red R. of the North	Pembina	750
Ohio	Campbell Hill	Logan	1,550	Ohio R.	Hamilton	455
Oklahoma	Black Mesa	Cimarron	4,973	Little R.	McCurtain	289
Oregon	Mount Hood	Clackamas-Hood R.	11,240	Pacific Ocean		Sea level
Pennsylvania	Mount Davis	Somerset	3,213	Delaware R.	Delaware	Sea level
Puerto Rico	Cerro de Punta	Ponce District	4,390	Atlantic Ocean		Sea level
Rhode Island	Jerimoth Hill	Providence	812	Atlantic Ocean		Sea level
South Carolina	Sassafras Mountain	Pickens	3,560	Atlantic Ocean		Sea level
South Dakota	Harney Peak	Pennington	7,242	Big Stone Lake	Roberts	966
Tennessee	Clingmans Dome	Sevier	6,643	Mississippi R.	Shelby	178
Texas	Guadalupe Peak	Culberson	8,749	Gulf of Mexico		Sea level
Utah	Kings Peak	Duchesne	13,534	Beaver Dam Wash	Washington	2,000
Vermont	Mount Mansfield	Chittenden	4,393	Lake Champlain		95
Virginia	Mount Rogers	Grayson-Smyth	5,729	Atlantic Ocean		Sea level
Virgin Islands	Crown Mountain	St. Thomas Island	1,556	Atlantic Ocean		Sea level
Washington	Mount Rainier	Pierce	14,416	Pacific Ocean		Sea level
West Virginia	Spruce Knob	Pendleton	4,863	Potomac R.	Jefferson	240
Wisconsin	Timms Hill	Price	1,951	Lake Michigan		579
Wyoming	Gannett Peak	Fremont	13,810	Belle Fourche R.	Crook	3,099

U.S. Coastline by State

Source: National Oceanic and Atmospheric Administration, U.S. Dept. of Commerce
(in statute miles; only states with coastline or shoreline are shown)

	Coastline[1]	Shoreline[2]		Coastline[1]	Shoreline[2]
Atlantic Coast	**2,069**	**28,673**	**Gulf Coast**	**1,631**	**17,141**
Connecticut	0	618	Alabama	53	607
Delaware	28	381	Florida	770	5,095
Florida	580	3,331	Louisiana	397	7,721
Georgia	100	2,344	Mississippi	44	359
Maine	228	3,478	Texas	367	3,359
Maryland	31	3,190			
Massachusetts	192	1,519	**Pacific Coast**	**7,623**	**40,298**
New Hampshire	13	131	Alaska	5,580	31,383
New Jersey	130	1,792	California	840	3,427
New York	127	1,850	Hawaii	750	1,052
North Carolina	301	3,375	Oregon	296	1,410
Pennsylvania	0	89	Washington	157	3,026
Rhode Island	40	384			
South Carolina	187	2,876	**Arctic Coast**	**1,060**	**2,521**
Virginia	112	3,315	**United States**	**12,383**	**88,633**

(1) Length of general outline of seacoast. Measurements were made in 1948 with a unit measure of 30 minutes of latitude on charts as near the scale of 1:1,200,000 as possible. Includes coastlines of large sounds and bays. (2) Figures obtained in 1939-40 with a recording instrument on the largest-scale charts and maps then available. Shoreline of outer coast, offshore islands, sounds, bays, rivers, and creeks is included to the head of tidewater or to a point where tidal waters narrow to a width of 100 ft.

States: Capitals, Key Dates, Geographic Data

Source: *Statistical Abstract of the United States*, U.S. Census Bureau, U.S. Dept. of Commerce

The 13 colonies that declared independence from Great Britain and fought the War of Independence (American Revolution) became the 13 original states. They were, in the order in which they ratified the Constitution: Delaware, Pennsylvania, New Jersey, Georgia, Connecticut, Massachusetts, Maryland, South Carolina, New Hampshire, Virginia, New York, North Carolina, and Rhode Island.

State	Settled[1]	Capital	Entered Union Date	Entered Union Order	Extent (mi) Length (approx. mean)	Extent (mi) Width (approx. mean)	Area (sq mi) Land	Area (sq mi) Water	Area (sq mi) Total	Rank in area[2]
AL	1702	Montgomery	Dec. 14, 1819	22	330	190	50,645	1,775	52,420	30
AK	1784	Juneau	Jan. 3, 1959	49	1,480[3]	810	570,641	94,743	665,384	1
AZ	1776	Phoenix	Feb. 14, 1912	48	400	310	113,594	396	113,990	6
AR	1686	Little Rock	June 15, 1836	25	260	240	52,035	1,143	53,179	29
CA	1769	Sacramento	Sept. 9, 1850	31	770	250	155,779	7,916	163,094	3
CO	1858	Denver	Aug. 1, 1876	38	380	280	103,642	452	104,094	8
CT	1634	Hartford	Jan. 9, 1788	5	110	70	4,842	701	5,543	48
DE	1638	Dover	Dec. 7, 1787	1	100	30	1,949	540	2,489	49
DC	NA	NA	NA	NA	NA	NA	61	7	68	51
FL	1565	Tallahassee	Mar. 3, 1845	27	500	160	53,625	12,133	65,758	22
GA	1733	Atlanta	Jan. 2, 1788	4	300	230	57,513	1,912	59,425	24
HI	1820	Honolulu	Aug. 21, 1959	50	NA	NA	6,423	4,509	10,932	43
ID	1842	Boise	July 3, 1890	43	570	300	82,643	926	83,569	14
IL	1720	Springfield	Dec. 3, 1818	21	390	210	55,519	2,395	57,914	25
IN	1733	Indianapolis	Dec. 11, 1816	19	270	140	35,826	593	36,420	38
IA	1788	Des Moines	Dec. 28, 1846	29	310	200	55,857	416	56,273	26
KS	1727	Topeka	Jan. 29, 1861	34	400	210	81,759	520	82,278	15
KY	1774	Frankfort	June 1, 1792	15	380	140	39,486	921	40,408	37
LA	1699	Baton Rouge	Apr. 30, 1812	18	380	130	43,204	9,174	52,378	31
ME	1624	Augusta	Mar. 15, 1820	23	320	190	30,843	4,537	35,380	39
MD	1634	Annapolis	Apr. 28, 1788	7	250	90	9,707	2,699	12,406	42
MA	1620	Boston	Feb. 6, 1788	6	190	50	7,800	2,754	10,554	44
MI	1668	Lansing	Jan. 26, 1837	26	490	240	56,539	40,175	96,714	11
MN	1805	St. Paul	May 11, 1858	32	400	250	79,627	7,309	86,936	12
MS	1699	Jackson	Dec. 10, 1817	20	340	170	46,923	1,509	48,432	32
MO	1735	Jefferson City	Aug. 10, 1821	24	300	240	68,742	965	69,707	21
MT	1809	Helena	Nov. 8, 1889	41	630	280	145,546	1,494	147,040	4
NE	1823	Lincoln	Mar. 1, 1867	37	430	210	76,824	524	77,348	16
NV	1849	Carson City	Oct. 31, 1864	36	490	320	109,781	791	110,572	7
NH	1623	Concord	June 21, 1788	9	190	70	8,953	397	9,349	46
NJ	1660	Trenton	Dec. 18, 1787	3	150	70	7,354	1,368	8,723	47
NM	1610	Santa Fe	Jan. 6, 1912	47	370	343	121,298	292	121,590	5
NY	1614	Albany	July 26, 1788	11	330	283	47,126	7,429	54,555	27
NC	1660	Raleigh	Nov. 21, 1789	12	500	150	48,618	5,201	53,819	28
ND	1812	Bismarck	Nov. 2, 1889	39	340	211	69,001	1,698	70,698	19
OH	1788	Columbus	Mar. 1, 1803	17	220	220	40,861	3,965	44,826	34
OK	1889	Oklahoma City	Nov. 16, 1907	46	400	220	68,595	1,304	69,899	20
OR	1811	Salem	Feb. 14, 1859	33	360	261	95,988	2,391	98,379	9
PA	1682	Harrisburg	Dec. 12, 1787	2	283	160	44,743	1,312	46,054	33
RI	1636	Providence	May 29, 1790	13	40	30	1,034	511	1,545	50
SC	1670	Columbia	May 23, 1788	8	260	200	30,061	1,960	32,020	40
SD	1859	Pierre	Nov. 2, 1889	40	380	210	75,811	1,305	77,116	17
TN	1769	Nashville	June 1, 1796	16	440	120	41,235	909	42,144	36
TX	1682	Austin	Dec. 29, 1845	28	790	660	261,232	7,365	268,596	2
UT	1847	Salt Lake City	Jan. 4, 1896	45	350	270	82,170	2,727	84,897	13
VT	1724	Montpelier	Mar. 4, 1791	14	160	80	9,217	400	9,616	45
VA	1607	Richmond	June 25, 1788	10	430	200	39,490	3,285	42,775	35
WA	1811	Olympia	Nov. 11, 1889	42	360	240	66,456	4,842	71,298	18
WV	1727	Charleston	June 20, 1863	35	240	130	24,038	192	24,230	41
WI	1766	Madison	May 29, 1848	30	310	260	54,158	11,339	65,496	23
WY	1834	Cheyenne	July 10, 1890	44	360	280	97,093	720	97,813	10

NA = Not applicable. **Note:** Land and water areas may not add up to totals because of rounding. (1) First permanent settlement by Europeans. (2) Rank is based on total area as shown. (3) Does not include Aleutian Islands or Alexander Archipelago.

Continental Divide of the U.S.

The Continental Divide of the U.S., also known as the Great Divide, is located at the watershed created by the mountain ranges, or tablelands, of the Rocky Mountains. This watershed separates the waters that drain into the Atlantic Ocean and its marginal seas, such as the Gulf of Mexico, from those waters that drain into the Pacific Ocean. The majority of water flowing east in the U.S. drains into the Gulf of Mexico before reaching the Atlantic. The majority of water flowing west drains either through the Columbia River or through the Colorado River, which flows into the Gulf of California before reaching the Pacific Ocean.

The location and route of the Continental Divide across the U.S. can briefly be described as follows:

Beginning at the U.S.-Mexican boundary, near longitude 108°45′ W, the Divide, in a northerly direction, crosses New Mexico along the W edge of the Rio Grande drainage basin, entering Colorado near longitude 106°41′ W.

From there by a very irregular route north across Colorado along the W summits of the Rio Grande and of the Arkansas, the South Platte, and the North Platte river basins, and across Rocky Mountain National Park, entering Wyoming near longitude 106°52′ W.

From there in a northwesterly direction, forming the W rims of the North Platte, the Big Horn, and the Yellowstone river basins, crossing the SW portion of Yellowstone National Park.

From there in a westerly and then a northerly direction forming the common boundary of Idaho and Montana, to a point on said boundary near longitude 114°00′ W.

From there northeasterly and northwesterly through Montana and Glacier National Park, entering Canada near longitude 114°04′ W.

Chronological List of Territories, With State Admissions to Union

Source: U.S. National Archives and Records Administration

Territory	Date of act creating territory	When act took effect	Date of admission as state	Years as terr.
Northwest Territory[1]	July 13, 1787	No fixed date	Mar. 1, 1803[2]	16
Territory southwest of Ohio River	May 26, 1790	No fixed date	June 1, 1796[3]	6
Mississippi	Apr. 7, 1798	When president acted	Dec. 10, 1817	19
Indiana	May 7, 1800	July 4, 1800	Dec. 11, 1816	16
Orleans	Mar. 26, 1804	Oct. 1, 1804	Apr. 30, 1812[4]	7
Michigan	Jan. 11, 1805	June 30, 1805	Jan. 26, 1837	31
Louisiana-Missouri[5]	Mar. 3, 1805	July 4, 1805	Aug. 10, 1821	16
Illinois	Feb. 3, 1809	Mar. 1, 1809	Dec. 3, 1818	9
Alabama	Mar. 3, 1817	When MS became a state	Dec. 14, 1819	2
Arkansas	Mar. 2, 1819	July 4, 1819	June 15, 1836	17
Florida	Mar. 30, 1822	No fixed date	Mar. 3, 1845	23
Wisconsin	Apr. 20, 1836	July 3, 1836	May 29, 1848	12
Iowa	June 12, 1838	July 3, 1838	Dec. 28, 1846	8
Oregon	Aug. 14, 1848	Date of act	Feb. 14, 1859	10
Minnesota	Mar. 3, 1849	Date of act	May 11, 1858	9
New Mexico	Sept. 9, 1850	On president's proclamation	Jan. 6, 1912	61
Utah	Sept. 9, 1850	Date of act	Jan. 4, 1896	46
Washington	Mar. 2, 1853	Date of act	Nov. 11, 1889	36
Nebraska	May 30, 1854	Date of act	Mar. 1, 1867	12
Kansas	May 30, 1854	Date of act	Jan. 29, 1861	6
Colorado	Feb. 28, 1861	Date of act	Aug. 1, 1876	15
Nevada	Mar. 2, 1861	Date of act	Oct. 31, 1864	3
Dakota	Mar. 2, 1861	Date of act	Nov. 2, 1889	28
Arizona	Feb. 24, 1863	Date of act	Feb. 14, 1912	49
Idaho	Mar. 3, 1863	Date of act	July 3, 1890	27
Montana	May 26, 1864	Date of act	Nov. 8, 1889	25
Wyoming	July 25, 1868	When officers were qualified	July 10, 1890	22
Alaska	May 17, 1884[6]	No fixed date	Jan. 3, 1959	75
Oklahoma	May 2, 1890	Date of act	Nov. 16, 1907	17
Hawaii	Apr. 30, 1900	June 14, 1900	Aug. 21, 1959	59

(1) Included what is now Ohio, Indiana, Illinois, Michigan, Wisconsin, and E Minnesota. (2) Date of admission for Ohio, the first state from NW territory admitted. (3) Admitted as the state of Tennessee. (4) Admitted as the state of Louisiana. (5) The act renaming Louisiana Territory as Missouri Territory (June 4, 1812) became effective Dec. 7, 1812. (6) Act constituted Alaska as a district, though it was often referred to and administered as a territory. The Territory of Alaska was formally organized by an act of Aug. 24, 1912.

U.S. Geographic Centers

Source: U.S. Geological Survey, U.S. Dept. of the Interior

There is no generally accepted definition of a geographic center and no uniform method for determining it. Geographic center is defined here as the center of gravity of the surface of an area, or that point on which an area would balance if it were a plane of uniform thickness.

No government agency has officially established any points marking the geographic center of the U.S., the conterminous U.S. (48 states), or the North American continent. Private citizens erected a monument in Lebanon, KS, marking it as the geographic center of the conterminous U.S.; a cairn in Rugby, ND, asserts that location as the center of the North American continent.

The geographic centers in the following list are approximate. They are indicated by county then city unless otherwise noted.

U.S., including Alaska and Hawaii: W of Castle Rock, Butte County, South Dakota; 44°58′ N, 103°46′ W
Conterminous U.S. (48 states): near Lebanon, Smith County, Kansas; 39°50′ N, 98°35′ W
North American continent: 6 mi W of Balta, Pierce County, North Dakota; 48°10′ N, 100°10′ W
Alabama: Chilton, 12 mi SW of Clanton
Alaska: approx. 60 mi NW of Mt. McKinley (Denali); 63°50′ N, 152° W;
Arizona: Yavapai, 55 mi E-SE of Prescott
Arkansas: Pulaski, 12 mi NW of Little Rock
California: Madera, 38 mi E of Madera
Colorado: Park, 30 mi NW of Pikes Peak
Connecticut: Hartford, at East Berlin
Delaware: Kent, 11 mi S of Dover
District of Columbia: near 4th and L Sts. NW
Florida: Hernando, 12 mi N-NW of Brooksville
Georgia: Twiggs, 18 mi SE of Macon
Hawaii: off Maui; 20°15′ N, 156°20′ W
Idaho: Custer, SW of Challis
Illinois: Logan, 28 mi NE of Springfield
Indiana: Boone, 14 mi N-NW of Indianapolis
Iowa: Story, 5 mi NE of Ames
Kansas: Barton, 15 mi NE of Great Bend
Kentucky: Marion, 3 mi N-NW of Lebanon
Louisiana: Avoyelles, 3 mi SE of Marksville
Maine: Piscataquis, 18 mi N of Dover
Maryland: Prince George's, 4.5 mi NW of Davidsonville
Massachusetts: Worcester, N part of city of Worcester
Michigan: Wexford, 5 mi N-NW of Cadillac
Minnesota: Crow Wing, 10 mi SW of Brainerd
Mississippi: Leake, 9 mi W-NW of Carthage
Missouri: Miller, 20 mi SW of Jefferson City
Montana: Fergus, 11 mi W of Lewistown
Nebraska: Custer, 10 mi NW of Broken Bow
Nevada: Lander, 26 mi SE of Austin
New Hampshire: Belknap, 3 mi E of Ashland
New Jersey: Mercer, 5 mi SE of Trenton
New Mexico: Torrance, 12 mi S-SW of Willard
New York: Madison, 12 mi S of Oneida and 26 mi SW of Utica
North Carolina: Chatham, 10 mi NW of Sanford
North Dakota: Sheridan, 5 mi SW of McClusky
Ohio: Delaware, 25 mi N-NE of Columbus
Oklahoma: Oklahoma, 8 mi N of Oklahoma City
Oregon: Crook, 25 mi S-SE of Prineville
Pennsylvania: Centre, 2.5 mi SW of Bellefonte
Rhode Island: Kent, 1 mi S-SW of Crompton
South Carolina: Richland, 13 mi SE of Columbia
South Dakota: Hughes, 8 mi NE of Pierre
Tennessee: Rutherford, 5 mi NE of Murfreesboro
Texas: McCulloch, 15 mi NE of Brady
Utah: Sanpete, 3 mi N of Manti
Vermont: Washington, 3 mi E of Roxbury
Virginia: Buckingham, 5 mi SW of Buckingham
Washington: Chelan, 10 mi W-SW of Wenatchee
West Virginia: Braxton, 4 mi E of Sutton
Wisconsin: Wood, 9 mi SE of Marshfield
Wyoming: Fremont, 58 mi E-NE of Lander

Lengths of U.S. Boundaries

The length of the N boundary of the conterminous U.S.—the U.S.-Canadian border excluding Alaska—is 3,987 mi according to the U.S. Geological Survey. The length of the Alaskan-Canadian border is 1,538 mi. The U.S.-Mexican border, from the Gulf of Mexico to the Pacific Ocean, is about 1,933 mi per a 1963 boundary agreement.

Origins of the Names of U.S. States

Source: State officials; Smithsonian Institution; Topographic Division, U.S. Geological Survey, U.S. Dept. of the Interior

Alabama: Choctaw word for a Chickasaw tribe. First noted in accounts of Hernando de Soto expedition.

Alaska: Russian version of Aleutian (Eskimo) word *alakshak* for "peninsula," "great lands," or "land that is not an island."

Arizona: Spanish version of Pima Indian word for "little spring place" or Aztec *arizuma*, meaning "silver-bearing."

Arkansas: Algonquin name for Quapaw Indians, meaning "south wind."

California: Bestowed by Spanish conquistadors (possibly Hernán Cortés). It was the name of an imaginary island in the 1510 Spanish novel *Las Sergas de Esplandián*, by Garci Rodríguez de Montalvo. The Spanish first visited *Baja* (Lower) *California* in 1533. The present-day U.S. state was called *Alta* (Upper) *California*.

Colorado: From Spanish for "red," first applied to Colorado River.

Connecticut: From Mohican and other Algonquin words meaning "long river place."

Delaware: Named for Lord De La Warr, early governor of Virginia; first applied to river, then to Indian tribe (Lenni-Lenape).

District of Columbia: For Christopher Columbus, 1791.

Florida: Named by Juan Ponce de León *Pascua Florida*, "Flowery Easter," on Easter Sunday, 1513.

Georgia: Named by colonial administrator James Oglethorpe for King George II of England in 1732.

Hawaii: Possibly derived from *Hawaiki* or *Owhyhee*, Polynesian word for "homeland."

Idaho: Said to be a coined name with the invented meaning "gem of the mountains"; suggested for the Pikes Peak mining territory (Colorado), then applied to the new mining territory of the Pacific Northwest. Another theory suggests *Idaho* may be Kiowa Apache term for the Comanche.

Illinois: French for *Illini* or "land of *Illini*," Algonquin word meaning "men" or "warriors."

Indiana: Means "land of the Indians."

Iowa: Indian word variously translated as "here I rest" or "beautiful land." Named for the Iowa River, which was named for the Iowa Indians.

Kansas: Sioux word for "south wind people."

Kentucky: Indian word variously translated as "dark and bloody ground," "meadowland," and "land of tomorrow."

Louisiana: Part of territory called Louisiana by René-Robert Cavelier Sieur de La Salle for French King Louis XIV.

Maine: From Maine, ancient French province. Also descriptive, referring to the mainland as distinct from coastal islands.

Maryland: For Queen Henrietta Maria, wife of Charles I of England.

Massachusetts: From Indian tribe whose name meant "at or about the Great Hill" in Blue Hills region south of Boston.

Michigan: From Chippewa *mici gama*, meaning "great water," after lake of the same name.

Minnesota: From Dakota Sioux word meaning "cloudy water" or "sky-tinted water" of the Minnesota River.

Mississippi: Probably Chippewa *mici zibi*, meaning "great river" or "gathering-in of all the waters." Also Algonquin word *messipi*.

Missouri: Algonquin Indian term meaning "river of the big canoes."

Montana: Latin or Spanish for "mountainous."

Nebraska: From Omaha or Otos Indian word meaning "broad water" or "flat river," describing the Platte River.

Nevada: Spanish, meaning "snow-clad."

New Hampshire: Named by Capt. John Mason of Plymouth Council, in 1629, for his home county in England.

New Jersey: The Duke of York, in 1664, gave a patent to Lord John Berkeley and Sir George Carteret for *Nova Caesaria*, or New Jersey, after England's Isle of Jersey.

New Mexico: Spaniards in Mexico applied term to land north and west of Rio Grande in the 16th century.

New York: For James, Duke of York and Albany, who received patent for New Netherland from his brother Charles II and sent an expedition to capture it, 1664.

North Carolina: In 1619, Charles I gave patent to Sir Robert Heath for Province of Carolana, from *Carolus*, Latin name for Charles. Charles II granted a new patent to Earl of Clarendon and others. Divided into North and South Carolina, 1710.

North Dakota: Sioux word *Dakota*, meaning "friend" or "ally."

Ohio: Iroquois word for "fine or good river."

Oklahoma: Choctaw word meaning "red man," proposed by Rev. Allen Wright, Choctaw-speaking Indian.

Oregon: Origin unknown. One theory is that the name derives from *wauregan*, meaning "beautiful," term used by Indians in New England.

Pennsylvania: William Penn, Quaker who was made full proprietor of area by King Charles II in 1681, suggested "Sylvania," or "woodland," for his tract. The king's government owed 16,000 pounds to Penn's father, Adm. William Penn, and the land was granted as partial settlement. Charles II added "Penn" to "Sylvania," against the modest proprietor's desires, in honor of the admiral.

Puerto Rico: Spanish for "rich port."

Rhode Island: Origin unknown. One theory notes that Giovanni de Verrazano recorded observing an island about the size of the Greek island of Rhodes in 1524. Another theory is that Dutch explorer Adriaen Block named the state *Roode Eylandt* for its red clay.

South Carolina: See North Carolina.

South Dakota: See North Dakota.

Tennessee: *Tanasi* was the name of Cherokee villages on the Little Tennessee River. From 1784 to 1788, this was the State of Franklin, or Frankland.

Texas: Variant of word used by Caddo and other Indians meaning "friends" or "allies" and applied to them by the Spanish in eastern Texas. Also written *Texias, Tejas, Teysas*.

Utah: From a Navajo word meaning "upper," or "higher up," as applied to Shoshone tribe called Ute. Proposed name *Deseret*, "land of honeybees," from Book of Mormon, was rejected by Congress.

Vermont: From French words *vert* (green) and *mont* (mountain). The Green Mountains were said to have been named by Samuel de Champlain. When the state was formed in 1777, Dr. Thomas Young suggested combining *vert* and *mont*.

Virginia: Named by Sir Walter Raleigh, who outfitted an expedition in 1584, in honor of England's Queen Elizabeth, the Virgin Queen.

Washington: Named after George Washington. When the bill creating the Territory of Columbia was introduced in the 32nd Congress, its name was changed to Washington because of the existence of the District of Columbia.

West Virginia: So named when western counties of Virginia refused to secede from the U.S. in 1863.

Wisconsin: Indian name, spelled *Ouisconsin* or *Mesconsing* by early chroniclers, believed to mean "grassy place" in Chippewa. Congress made it *Wisconsin*.

Wyoming: From Algonquin words for "large prairie place," "at the big plains," or "on the great plain."

Territorial Sea of the U.S.

According to a Dec. 27, 1988, proclamation by Pres. Ronald Reagan, "The territorial sea of the United States henceforth extends to 12 nautical miles from the baselines of the United States determined in accordance with international law. In accordance with international law, as reflected in the applicable provisions of the 1982 United Nations Convention on the Law of the Sea, within the territorial sea of the United States, the ships of all countries enjoy the right of innocent passage and the ships and aircraft of all countries enjoy the right of transit passage through international straits."

Major Accessions of Territory by the U.S.

Source: U.S. Dept. of the Interior; U.S. Census Bureau, U.S. Dept. of Commerce

Not including territories such as the Panama Canal Zone and the Philippines, which are no longer under U.S. jurisdiction. Area figures are for total area and may differ from figures given elsewhere in *The World Almanac*.

Accession	Date	Area (sq mi)	Accession	Date	Area (sq mi)	Accession	Date	Area (sq mi)
Territory in 1790[1]	NA	888,685	Mexican Cession	1848	529,017	Guam[3]	1899	212
Louisiana Purchase	1803	827,192	Gadsden Purchase	1853	29,640	American Samoa[4]	1900	76
Treaty of Florida	1819	72,003	Alaska	1867	586,412	U.S. Virgin Islands	1917	133
Texas	1845	390,143	Hawaii	1898	6,450	Northern Marianas[5]	1986	179
Oregon Territory	1846	285,680	Puerto Rico[2]	1899	3,435			

NA = Not applicable. (1) Includes that part of a drainage basin of Red River of the North, south of 49th parallel, sometimes considered part of Louisiana Purchase. (2) Ceded by Spain in 1898, ratified in 1899, and became the Commonwealth of Puerto Rico by Act of Congress on July 25, 1952. (3) Acquired in 1898; ratified 1899. (4) Acquired in 1899; ratified 1900. (5) Formerly a part of the U.S.-administered Trust Territory of the Pacific Islands; became a U.S. commonwealth Nov. 3, 1986.

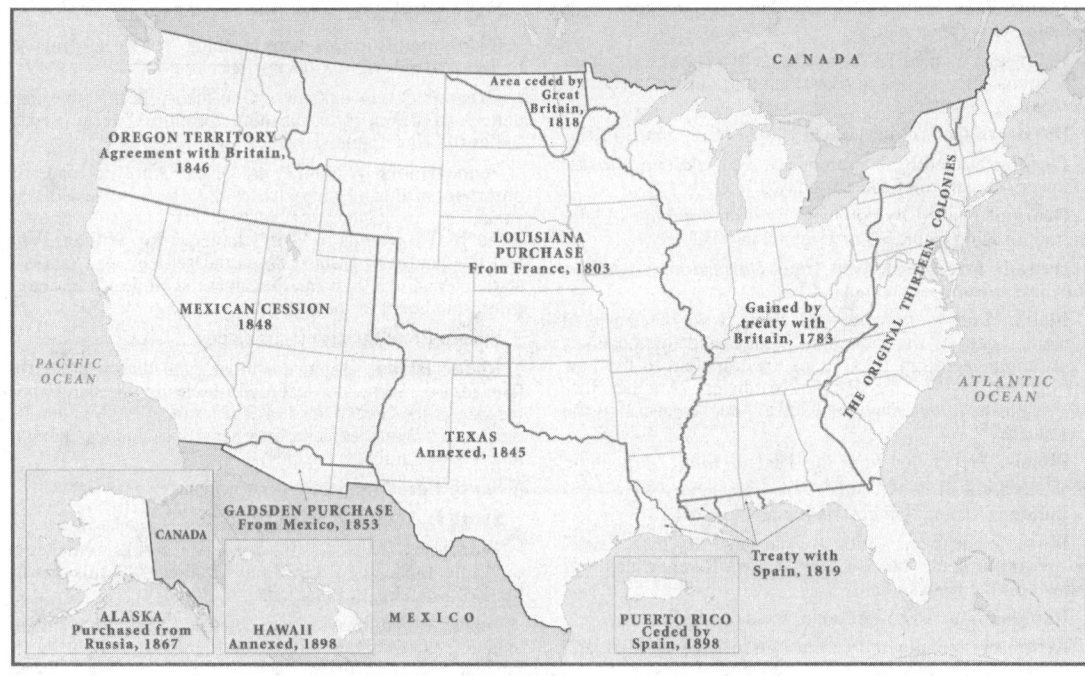

Special Areas Administered by the U.S. Forest Service

Source: U.S. Forest Service, U.S. Dept. of Agriculture; as of Sept. 30, 2011

Areas have been specially designated by Presidential Proclamation or Act of Congress. Figure in Acres column does not include acreage of an area that may lie within a National Forest boundary but is not federally owned or administered by the Forest Service.

NHL = Natl. Historic Landmark; NHS = Natl. Historic Scenic Area; NM = Natl. Monument; NP = Natl. Preserve; NRA = Natl. Recreation Area; NS(A) = Natl. Scenic (Area); NVM = Natl. Volcanic Monument; SRA = Scenic Recreation Area

Area	Location	Estab.	Acres	Area	Location	Estab.	Acres
Admiralty Island NM	AK	1980	974,278	Mount Baker NRA	WA	1984	8,473
Allegheny NRA	PA	1984	24,145	Mount Hood NRA	OR	2009	34,474
Arapaho NRA	CO	1978	32,521	Mount Pleasant NSA	VA	1994	7,580
Bear Creek NSA	VA	2009	5,128	Mount Rogers NRA	VA	1966	118,509
Beech Creek NSA	OK	1988	6,200	Mount St. Helens NVM	WA	1989	112,605
Cascade Head NS Research Area	OR	1974	6,637	Newberry NVM	OR	1990	54,822
Columbia River Gorge NSA	OR-WA	1986	72,814	Opal Creek SRA	OR	1996	12,645
Coosa Bald NSA	GA	1991	7,100	Oregon Dunes NRA	OR	1972	27,232
Ed Jenkins NRA	GA	1991	23,166	Pine Ridge NRA	NE	1986	6,600
Flaming Gorge NRA	UT-WY	1968	189,825	Rattlesnake NRA	MT	1980	59,119
Giant Sequoia NM	CA	2000	327,769	Robert T. Stafford White Rocks NRA	VT	1984	36,152
Grand Island NRA	MI	1990	12,974	Santa Rosa and			
Grey Towers NHL	PA	1963	102	San Jacinto Mountains NM	CA	2000	64,400
Hells Canyon NRA	OR-ID	1975	537,770	Sawtooth NRA	ID	1972	729,428
Indian Nations NS Wildlife Area	OK	1988	39,171	Seng Mountain NSA	VA	2009	5,192
Jemez NRA	NM	1993	44,670	Smith River NRA	CA	1990	305,591
Jewel Cave NM	ND	1908	1,120	Spring Mountains NRA	NV	1993	314,367
Land Between the Lakes NRA	KY-TN	1998	170,310	Spruce Knob-Seneca Rocks NRA	WV	1965	57,232
Misty Fiords NM	AK	1980	2,293,774	Valles Caldera NP	NM	2000	89,716
Mono Basin NSA	CA	1984	128,303	Whiskeytown-Shasta-Trinity NRA	CA	1965	176,367
Moosalamoo NRA	VT	2006	15,170	Winding Stair Mountain NRA	OK	1988	25,890

Most-Visited Sites in the National Park System, 2011

Source: National Park Service, U.S. Dept. of the Interior

Attendance at all areas administered by the National Park Service in 2011 totaled 278,939,216 recreation visits.

Rank	Site (location)	Recreation visits
1.	Blue Ridge Parkway (NC-VA)	15,382,447
2.	Golden Gate Natl. Recreation Area (CA)	14,567,487
3.	Great Smoky Mountains Natl. Park (NC-TN)	9,008,830
4.	Gateway Natl. Recreation Area (NJ-NY)	7,697,727
5.	George Washington Memorial Pkwy. (VA-MD-DC)	7,417,397
6.	Lake Mead Natl. Recreation Area (AZ-NV)	6,396,682
7.	Lincoln Memorial (DC)	5,971,220
8.	Natchez Trace Parkway (MS-AL-TN)	5,765,343
9.	Gulf Islands National Seashore (FL-MS)	5,501,872
10.	Delaware Water Gap Natl. Recreation Area (NJ-PA)	4,986,700
11.	Cape Cod National Seashore (MA)	4,454,771
12.	Grand Canyon National Park (AZ)	4,298,178
13.	San Francisco Maritime Natl. Historical Park (CA)	4,224,897
14.	Vietnam Veterans Memorial (DC)	4,020,127
15.	Castle Clinton National Monument (NY)	3,985,366
16.	Yosemite National Park (CA)	3,951,393
17.	Chesapeake & Ohio Canal Natl. Historical Park (DC-MD-WV)	3,937,504
18.	World War II Memorial (DC)	3,752,172
19.	Statue of Liberty National Monument (NJ-NY)	3,749,982
20.	Independence National Historical Park (PA)	3,572,770

National Parks, Other Areas Administered by National Park Service

As of Dec. 31, 2011, the National Park Service administered about 84,394,246 acres of federal and non-federal land across 397 sites. Date when area was authorized or established by Congress or by presidential proclamation is given in parentheses; any date that follows indicates when a site received its current designation or was transferred to the National Park Service. Figure after the date is gross area acres as of Dec. 31, 2011. Some parks, rivers, trails, and other areas are not listed.

National Parks

Acadia, ME (1916/1929): 47,453. Incl. Mount Desert Isl., half of Isle au Haut, Schoodic Peninsula on mainland. Highest elevation on Eastern seaboard.

American Samoa, AS (1988): 9,000. Paleotropical rain forest, coral reef.

Arches, UT (1929/1971): 76,679. Contains giant red sandstone arches and other products of erosion.

Badlands, SD (1929/1978): 242,756. Reformations and native prairie; animal fossils 23-37 mil years old.

Big Bend, TX (1935): 801,163. Rio Grande, Chisos Mts.

Biscayne, FL (1968/1980): 172,971. Aquatic park encompassing chain of islands south of Miami.

Black Canyon of the Gunnison, CO (1933/1999): 30,750. Has canyon 2,900 ft deep and 40 ft wide at narrowest part.

Bryce Canyon, UT (1923/1928): 35,835. Colorful display of erosion effects.

Canyonlands, UT (1964): 337,598. At junction of Colorado and Green Rivers; extensive evidence of prehistoric peoples.

Capitol Reef, UT (1937/1971): 241,904. 70-mi uplift of sandstone cliffs dissected by high-walled gorges.

Carlsbad Caverns, NM (1923/1930): 46,766. More than 110 limestone caves, incl. Carlsbad Cavern; Chihuahuan Desert.

Channel Islands, CA (1938/1980): 249,561. Sea lion breeding place, nesting seabirds, unique plants.

Congaree, SC (1976/2003): 26,546. Largest intact tract of old-growth bottomland hardwood forest in U.S.

Crater Lake, OR (1902): 183,224. Deepest U.S. lake, in crater of Mt. Mazama, volcano that erupted about 7,700 years ago.

Cuyahoga Valley, OH (1974/2000): 32,832. Along Ohio and Erie Canal system between Akron and Cleveland.

Death Valley, CA-NV (1933/1994): 3,373,063. Large desert. Incl. lowest point in Western Hemisphere and Scotty's Castle.

Denali, AK (1917/1980): 4,740,911. Formerly known as Mt. McKinley; highest mountain in U.S.

Dry Tortugas, FL (1935/1992): 64,701. Ft. Jefferson and seven coral reef and sand islands near Key West.

Everglades, FL (1934): 1,509,154. Largest remaining subtropical wilderness in continental U.S.

Gates of the Arctic, AK (1978/1984): 7,523,897. Vast wilderness in north central region. Limited federal facilities.

Glacier, MT (1910): 1,013,322. Rocky Mt. scenery, numerous glaciers and glacial lakes. Part of Waterton-Glacier Intl. Peace Park established by U.S. and Canada in 1932.

Glacier Bay, AK (1925/1986): 3,223,384. Tidewater glaciers that move down mountainsides and break up into sea.

Grand Canyon, AZ (1893/1919): 1,217,262. Carved by Colorado River.

Grand Teton, WY (1929): 310,044. Most impressive part of Teton Mts.; winter feeding ground of largest American elk herd.

Great Basin, NV (1922/1986): 77,180. Incl. Wheeler Peak, Lexington Arch, Lehman Caves.

Great Sand Dunes, CO (1932/2000): 44,246. North America's tallest dunes.

Great Smoky Mountains, NC-TN (1926/1934): 522,419. Largest Eastern U.S. mountain range; magnificent forests.

Guadalupe Mountains, TX (1966): 86,367. Extensive Permian limestone fossil reef; tremendous earth fault.

Haleakala, HI (1916/1960): 33,265. Dormant volcano on island of Maui with large craters.

Hawaii Volcanoes, HI (1916/1961): 323,431. Contains Kilauea and Mauna Loa, active volcanoes.

Hot Springs, AR (1832/1921): 5,550. Waters from park's 47 hot springs used for bathing and drinking.

Isle Royale, MI (1931): 571,790. Largest island in Lake Superior.

Joshua Tree, CA (1936/1994): 790,636. Desert region incl. Joshua trees, other plant and animal life.

Katmai, AK (1918/1980): 3,674,378. "Valley of Ten Thousand Smokes," scene of 1912 volcanic eruption.

Kenai Fjords, AK (1978/1980): 669,984. Marine mammals, birdlife; Harding Icefield, one of four major icecaps in U.S.

Kings Canyon, CA (1890/1940): 461,901. Mountain wilderness, dominated by Kings River Canyons and High Sierra; giant sequoias.

Kobuk Valley, AK (1978/1980): 1,750,716. Contains geological and recreational sites. Limited federal facilities.

Lake Clark, AK (1978/1980): 2,619,722. Across Cook Inlet from Anchorage; scenic wilderness, fish and wildlife. Limited federal facilities.

Lassen Volcanic, CA (1907/1916): 106,452. Contains Lassen Peak, recently active volcano, and other volcanic phenomena.

Mammoth Cave, KY (1926/1941): 52,830. Longest known cave system in world (more than 390 mi currently surveyed), river 300 ft below surface.

Mesa Verde, CO (1906): 52,485. Most notable and best preserved prehistoric cliff dwellings in U.S.

Mount Rainier, WA (1899): 236,381. Most glaciated peak in contiguous U.S.

North Cascades, WA (1968): 504,781. Mountainous region with many glaciers, lakes.

Olympic, WA (1909/1938): 922,650. Mountain wilderness containing remnant of Pacific Northwest rain forest, active glaciers, shoreline, rare elk.

Petrified Forest, AZ (1906/1962): 221,552. Extensive petrified wood and Indian artifacts. Contains part of Painted Desert.

Redwood, CA (1968): 112,618. 40 mi of Pacific coastline, groves of ancient redwoods and world's tallest trees.

Rocky Mountain, CO (1915): 265,761. On Continental Divide; incl. peaks over 14,000 ft.

Saguaro, AZ (1933/1994): 91,442. Part of Sonoran Desert; incl. giant saguaro cacti, unique to region.

Sequoia, CA (1890): 404,063. Giant sequoia groves; world's largest tree (by volume). Mt. Whitney, highest mountain in conterminous U.S.

Shenandoah, VA (1926): 199,100. Portion of Blue Ridge Mts.; overlooks Shenandoah Valley; Skyline Drive.

Theodore Roosevelt, ND (1947/1978): 70,447. Contains part of Roosevelt's ranch and scenic badlands.

Virgin Islands, VI (1956): 14,737. Covers 75% of St. John Isl. and Hassel Isl.; beaches, Carib Indian petroglyphs, evidence of colonial Danes.

Voyageurs, MN (1971): 218,200. Abundant lakes, forests, wildlife.

Wind Cave, SD (1903): 33,847. Limestone caverns in Black Hills; extensive wildlife incl. bison herd.

Wrangell-St. Elias, AK (1978/1980): 8,323,147. Largest area in park system; most peaks over 16,000 ft. No federal facilities.

Yellowstone, ID-MT-WY (1872): 2,219,791. World's first national park. World's greatest geyser area with about 10,000 geysers, hot springs; falls and canyons of Yellowstone River; grizzly bear, moose, bison.

Yosemite, CA (1890): 761,268. Yosemite Valley, country's highest waterfall, grove of sequoias, mountains.

Zion, UT (1909/1919): 146,597. Unusual shapes, landscapes resulting from erosion and faulting; evidence of past volcanic activity; contains 2,394-ft monolith "Great White Throne."

National Historical Parks

Abraham Lincoln Birthplace, Hodgenville, KY (1916/1959): 345. Memorial building, sinking spring.

Adams, MA (1946/1998): 24. Home of Pres. John Adams, John Quincy Adams, and descendants.

Appomattox Court House, VA (1930/1954): 1,774. Where Confederate Gen. Lee surrendered to Gen. Grant, signaling Civil War's end.

Boston, MA (1974): 43. Incl. Faneuil Hall, Old North Church, Bunker Hill, Paul Revere House.

Cane River Creole, LA (1994): 206. Preserves Creole culture as it developed along the Cane River.

Cedar Creek & Belle Grove, VA (2002): 3,712. Civil War battle site and an antebellum plantation in Shenandoah Valley.

Chaco Culture, NM (1907/1980): 33,960. Ruins of pueblos built by prehistoric peoples incl. Pueblo, Hopi, and Navajo.

Chesapeake & Ohio Canal, MD-DC-WV (1938/1971): 19,612. 184-mi historic canal; DC to Cumberland, MD.

Colonial, VA (1930/1936): 8,677. Incl. most of Jamestown Isl., site of first successful English colony; Yorktown, site of Cornwallis's surrender to George Washington; Colonial Parkway.

Cumberland Gap, KY-TN-VA (1940): 24,547. Mountain pass of Wilderness Road, which carried first great migration of pioneers into America's interior.

Dayton Aviation Heritage, OH (1992): 86. Commemorates area's aviation heritage.

George Rogers Clark, IN (1966): 26. Commemorates American defeat of British in West during Revolution.

Harpers Ferry, MD-VA-WV (1944/1963): 3,661. At confluence of Shenandoah and Potomac Rivers, the site of John Brown's 1859 raid on the Army arsenal.

Hopewell Culture, OH (1923/1992): 1,170. Remains of ceremonial mounds built in the Ohio River Valley, 200 BCE-500 CE.

Independence, PA (1948): 45. Several properties associated with American Revolution and founding of U.S., incl. Independence Hall, Liberty Bell Center.

Jean Lafitte (and Preserve), LA (1907/1978): 23,664. Incl. Chalmette, site of 1815 Battle of New Orleans; French Quarter.

Kalaupapa, HI (1980): 10,779. Molokai's former leper colony.

Kaloko-Honokohau, HI (1978): 1,163. Preserves native culture of Hawaii.

Keweenaw, MI (1992): 1,869. Site of first significant copper mine in U.S.

Klondike Gold Rush, AK-WA (1976): 12,996. Preserves Chilkoot Trail used in 1898 Gold Rush. Museum in Seattle.

Lewis & Clark, OR-WA (1958/2004): 3,410. Lewis and Clark encampment, 1805-06. Incorporates former Fort Clatsop Natl. Mem. Park and OR-WA state parks.

Lowell, MA (1978): 141. Textile mills, canal, 19th-cent. structures; park shows planned city of Industrial Revolution.

Lyndon B. Johnson, TX (1969/1980): 1,570. President's birthplace, boyhood home, ranch.

Marsh-Billings-Rockefeller, VT (1992): 643. Boyhood home of conservationist George Perkins Marsh.

Minute Man, MA (1959): 1,027. Where Minute Men battled British, Apr. 19, 1775. Also contains Nathaniel Hawthorne's home.

Morristown, NJ (1933): 1,711. Site of important military encampments during the American Revolution; Washington's headquarters, 1779-80.

Natchez, MS (1988): 108. Mansions, townhouses, and villas related to history of Natchez.

New Bedford Whaling, MA (1996): 34. Preserves structures and relics associated with the city's 19th-cent. whaling industry.

New Orleans Jazz, LA (1994): 5. Preserves, educates, and interprets jazz as it has evolved in New Orleans.

Nez Perce, ID-MT-OR-WA (1965): 4,561. Illustrates history and culture of Nez Perce, or Nimiipuu, homeland (38 separate sites).

Palo Alto Battlefield, TX (1978): 3,442. Scene of first battle of the Mexican War.

Paterson Great Falls, NJ (2011): 36. Falls helped make city one of U.S.'s earliest industrial centers.

Pecos, NM (1965/1990): 6,703. Ruins of ancient Pueblo of Pecos, archaeological sites, and two associated Spanish colonial missions from 17th and 18th centuries.

Pu'uhonua o Honaunau, HI (1955/1978): 420. Until 1819, a sanctuary for Hawaiians vanquished in battle and for those guilty of crimes or breaking taboos.

Rosie the Riveter/WWII Home Front, CA (2000): 145. Site of shipyard that employed thousands of women during WWII; commemorates women who worked in wartime industries.

Salt River Bay (and Ecological Preserve), St. Croix, VI (1992): 986. Only known site where, in 1493, members of a Columbus party landed on what is now U.S. territory.

San Antonio Missions, TX (1978): 826. Four Spanish missions, 18th-cent. irrigation system.

San Francisco Maritime, CA (1988): 50. Artifacts, photographs, and historic vessels related to development of the Pacific Coast.

San Juan Island, WA (1966): 2,072. Commemorates peaceful relations between U.S., Canada, and Great Britain since the 1872 boundary disputes.

Saratoga, NY (1938): 3,394. Scene of a major 1777 battle that became a turning point in the American Revolution.

Sitka, AK (1910/1972): 112. Scene of last major resistance of Tlingit to the Russians, 1804.

Thomas Edison, West Orange, NJ (1955/1962): 21. Inventor's home and laboratory.

Tumacacori, AZ (1908/1990): 360. Historic Spanish mission building near site first visited by Father Kino in 1691.

Valley Forge, PA (1976): 3,468. Continental Army campsite in 1777-78 winter.

War in the Pacific, GU (1978): 2,037. Seven distinct units illustrating the Pacific theater of WWII. Limited federal facilities.

Women's Rights, NY (1980): 7. Seneca Falls site where Lucretia Mott, Elizabeth Cady Stanton organized movement in 1848.

National Battlefields/Parks/Sites

Antietam, MD (1890/1978): 3,230. Battle here ended first Confederate invasion of North, Sept. 17, 1862.

Big Hole, MT (1910/1963): 1,011. Site of major battle with Nez Perce Indians, Aug. 9-10, 1877.

Brices Cross Roads, MS (1929): 1. Site of Confederate victory, June 10, 1864.

Cowpens, SC (1929/1972): 842. American Revolution battlefield, Jan. 17, 1781.

Fort Donelson, TN-KY (1928/1985): 1,009. Site of first major Union victory, Feb. 14-16, 1862.

Fort Necessity, PA (1931/1961): 903. Site of first battle of French and Indian War, July 3, 1754.

Kennesaw Mountain, GA (1917/1935): 2,853. Site of major battle of Atlanta campaign in Civil War.

Manassas, VA (1940): 5,073. Scene of two Civil War battles, 1861 and 1862.

Monocacy, MD (1934/1976): 1,647. Civil War battle in defense of Washington, DC, fought here, July 9, 1864.

Moores Creek, NC (1926/1980): 88. Commemorates Feb. 27, 1776, battle between Patriots and Loyalists.

Petersburg, VA (1926/1962): 2,740. Scene of Union campaigns, 1864-65.

Richmond, VA (1936): 7,131. Site of battles defending Confederate capital.

River Raisin, MI (2010): 42. Site of major battles of War of 1812.

Stones River, TN (1927/1960): 709. Scene of battle that began federal offensive to trisect Confederacy, Dec. 31, 1862-Jan. 2, 1863.

Tupelo, MS (1929/1961): 1. Site of crucial battle over Union Gen. Sherman's supply line, July 14-15, 1865.

Wilson's Creek, MO (1960/1970): 2,369. Scene of Civil War battle for control of Missouri, Aug. 10, 1861.

National Military Parks

Chickamauga and Chattanooga, GA-TN (1890): 9,036. Where Gen. Sherman and Union armies gained control of TN, 1863.

Fredericksburg and Spotsylvania, VA (1927/1933): 8,382. Sites of several major Civil War battles and campaigns.

Gettysburg, PA (1895/1933): 5,989. Site of decisive Confederate defeat in North, July 1863, and of Gettysburg Address.

Guilford Courthouse, NC (1917/1933): 248. American Revolution battle site.

Horseshoe Bend, AL (1956): 2,040. On Tallapoosa River, where Gen. Andrew Jackson broke power of Upper Creek Indian Confederacy on Mar. 27, 1814.

Kings Mountain, SC (1931/1933): 3,945. Site of American Revolution battle, fought on Oct. 7, 1780.

Pea Ridge, AR (1956): 4,300. Scene of Civil War battle, Mar. 7-8, 1862.

Shiloh, TN-MS (1894/1933): 5,966. Major Civil War battle site; incl. Indian burial mounds.

Vicksburg, MS-LA (1899/1933): 1,806. Union victory gave North control of Mississippi and split Confederate forces.

National Memorials

Arkansas Post, AR (1960): 758. First permanent French settlement in lower Mississippi River valley.

Arlington House, The Robert E. Lee Memorial, VA (1925/1972): 28. Lee's home overlooking the Potomac River.

Chamizal, El Paso, TX (1966/1974): 55. Commemorates 1963 settlement of 99-year border dispute with Mexico.

Coronado, AZ (1941/1952): 4,830. Commemorates first European exploration of the Southwest.

De Soto, FL (1948): 30. Commemorates 16th-cent. Spanish explorations.

Federal Hall, New York, NY (1939/1955): 0.45. First seat of U.S. government under the Constitution.

Flight 93, Shanksville, PA (2002): 2,322. Commemorates passengers and crew of Flight 93, who died thwarting an attack on Sept. 11, 2001. First features of memorial completed and dedicated in 2011.

Fort Caroline, FL (1950): 138. On St. Johns River, overlooks site of former French Huguenot colony.

Franklin Delano Roosevelt Memorial, DC (1982): 8. Statues of Pres. Roosevelt and Eleanor Roosevelt; waterfalls and gardens.

General Grant, NY (1958): 0.76. Tomb of Ulysses Grant and wife.

Hamilton Grange, NY (1962): 1. Home of Alexander Hamilton.

Jefferson National Expansion, MO (1935): 193. Commemorates 19-cent. westward expansion; incl. Gateway Arch.

Johnstown Flood, PA (1964): 178. Commemorates 1889 flood.

Korean War Veterans Memorial, DC (1986): 2. Honors those who served in the Korean War.

Lincoln Boyhood, IN (1962): 200. Site of Lincoln cabin, Lincoln's boyhood home, and grave site of Lincoln's mother.

Lincoln Memorial, DC (1911/1933): 7. Marble statue of 16th president.

Lyndon Baines Johnson Memorial Grove on the Potomac, DC (1973): 17. Overlooks Potomac River; vista of the Capitol.

Martin Luther King Jr., DC (1996): 3. Granite statue of Dr. King close to where he delivered "I Have a Dream" speech.

Mount Rushmore, SD (1925): 1,278. World-famous sculpture of presidents Washington, Jefferson, Lincoln, T. Roosevelt.

Perry's Victory and International Peace Memorial, Put-in-Bay, OH (1936/1972): 25. World's most massive Doric column promotes pursuit of peace through arbitration and disarmament.

Port Chicago Naval Magazine, Danville, CA (2009): 5. Where 1944 munitions ship explosion killed 320 men.

Roger Williams, Providence, RI (1965): 5. Memorial to founder of Rhode Island.

Thaddeus Kosciuszko, Philadelphia, PA (1972): 0.02. Memorial to Polish hero of American Revolution.

Theodore Roosevelt Island, DC (1932/1933): 89. Statue of Roosevelt in wooded island sanctuary.

Thomas Jefferson Memorial, DC (1934): 18. Statue of Jefferson in an inscribed circular, colonnaded structure.

Vietnam Veterans Memorial, DC (1980): 2. Black granite wall inscribed with names of those missing or killed in action in Vietnam War.

Washington Monument, DC (1848/1933): 106. Obelisk honoring the first U.S. president.

World War II Memorial, Natl., DC (1994/2004): 8. Oval plaza with central pool commemorating those who fought and died.

Wright Brothers, NC (1927/1953): 428. Site of first powered flight.

National Historic Sites

Allegheny Portage Railroad, PA (1964): 1,287. Linked Pennsylvania Canal system and the West.

Andersonville, GA (1970): 515. Noted Civil War prisoner-of-war camp.

Andrew Johnson, Greeneville, TN (1935/1963): 17. Two homes and the tailor shop of 17th U.S. president.

Bent's Old Fort, CO (1960): 799. Replica of fort on Sante Fe Trail.

Boston African-American, MA (1980): 0.59. Pre-Civil War black-owned structures.

Brown v. Board of Education, KS (1992): 2. Commemorates landmark 1954 U.S. Supreme Court decision, which ended legal segregation in schools.

Carl Sandburg Home, Flat Rock, NC (1968): 264. Home of Pulitzer Prize-winning poet and biographer.

Carter G. Woodson Home, DC (1976/2006): 0.15. Home of "Father of Black History."

Charles Pinckney, SC (1988): 28. Farm of a principal author and signer of the Constitution.

Christiansted, St. Croix, VI (1952/1961): 27. Commemorates Danish colony.

Clara Barton, Glen Echo, MD (1974): 9. Home of American Red Cross founder.

Edgar Allan Poe, Philadelphia, PA (1978/1980): 0.52. Writer's home.

Eisenhower, Gettysburg, PA (1967): 690. Home of 34th president.

Eleanor Roosevelt, Hyde Park, NY (1977): 181. Former first lady's personal retreat.

Eugene O'Neill, Danville, CA (1976): 13. Home where playwright wrote his final plays, incl. *The Iceman Cometh.*

First Ladies, Canton, OH (2000): 0.46. Home of first lady Ida Sexton McKinley. Library now devoted to America's first ladies.

Ford's Theatre, DC (1866/1970): 0.30. Incl. theater where Lincoln was assassinated, house where he died, and Lincoln Museum.

Fort Bowie, AZ (1964): 999. Focal point of operations against Geronimo and Apaches.

Fort Davis, TX (1961): 474. Frontier outpost in West Texas; established to guard the San Antonio-El Paso Road.

Fort Laramie, WY (1938/1960): 833. Military post on Oregon Trail.

Fort Larned, KS (1964/1966): 718. Military post on Santa Fe Trail.

Fort Point, CA (1970): 29. West Coast fortification; protected San Francisco during and after Civil War.

Fort Raleigh, NC (1941): 513. First attempted English settlement in North America.

Fort Scott, KS (1965/1978): 17. Commemorates U.S. frontier of 1840s and '50s. Was a focal point of black troop activity, training during Civil War.

Fort Smith, AR-OK (1961): 75. One of the earliest U.S. posts in Missouri Territory, active 1817-90.

Fort Union Trading Post, MT-ND (1966): 441. Principal fur-trading post on upper Missouri, 1829-67.

Fort Vancouver, WA-OR (1948/1961): 207. Headquarters for Hudson's Bay Company.

Frederick Douglass, DC (1962/1988): 9. Home of black abolitionist, writer, orator.

Frederick Law Olmsted, MA (1979): 7. Home of city planner, famous for designing Central Park in NYC.

Friendship Hill, PA (1978): 675. Home of Albert Gallatin, Jefferson's and Madison's secretary of treasury.

Golden Spike, UT (1957): 2,735. Commemorates completion of first transcontinental railroad in 1869.

Grant-Kohrs Ranch, MT (1972): 1,618. Ranch house owned by John Grant, 19th-cent. range-cattle pioneer.

Hampton, MD (1948): 62. 18th-cent. Georgian mansion, which in 1790 was largest house in U.S.

Harry S. Truman, MO (1983): 10. Home of 33rd president from 1919 on.

Herbert Hoover, West Branch, IA (1965): 187. Birthplace and boyhood home of 31st president.

Home of Franklin D. Roosevelt, Hyde Park, NY (1944): 836. FDR's birthplace, home, and "summer White House."

Hopewell Furnace, PA (1938/1985): 848. 19th-cent. iron-making village.

Hubbell Trading Post, AZ (1965): 160. Oldest continuously operating trading post in the Southwest; founded in 1878 on Navajo Nation.

James A. Garfield, Mentor, OH (1980): 8. Home of 20th president; site of his front-porch campaign.

Jimmy Carter, Plains, GA (1987): 72. Birthplace and home of 39th president.

John Fitzgerald Kennedy, Brookline, MA (1967): 0.09. Birthplace and childhood home of 35th president.

John Muir, Martinez, CA (1964): 344. Home of Sierra Club cofounder and "Father of the National Park Service."

Knife River Indian Villages, ND (1974): 1,749. Remnants of villages last occupied by Hidatsa and Mandan Indians.

Lincoln Home, Springfield, IL (1971): 12. Lincoln's residence when he was elected 16th president, 1860.

Little Rock Central High School, AR (1998): 27. Commemorates 1957 desegregation during which federal troops were called in to protect nine black students.

Longfellow House–Washington's Headquarters, Cambridge, MA (1972): 2. Poet's home, 1837-82; Washington's headquarters during Boston siege, 1775-76.

Maggie L. Walker, VA (1978): 1. Richmond home of black leader and first female bank president, daughter of former slave.

Manzanar, Lone Pine, CA (1992): 814. Manzanar War Relocation Ctr., a WWII Japanese-American internment camp.

Martin Luther King Jr., Atlanta, GA (1980): 39. Birthplace, grave, church of the civil rights leader.

Martin Van Buren, Kinderhook, NY (1974): 285. Lindenwald, home of 8th president.

Mary McLeod Bethune Council House, DC (1982/1991): 0.07. Commemorates Bethune's leadership in the black women's movement.

Minidoka, ID (2008): 210. WWII Japanese internment center.

Minuteman Missile, SD (1999): 15. Missile launch facilities dating back to Cold War era.

Nicodemus, KS (1996): 5. Only remaining Western town established by African Americans during Reconstruction.

Ninety Six, SC (1976): 1,022. Colonial trading village and site of Gen. Nathanael Greene's siege on Loyalist-held fort in 1781.

Pennsylvania Avenue, DC (1965): 19. Central area between Capitol and White House, encompassing U.S. Navy Memorial, Freedom Plaza, Old Post Office Pavilion, and other sites.

President William Jefferson Clinton Birthplace Home, Hope, AR (2010): 1. Birthplace and early home of 42nd president.

Puukohola Heiau, HI (1972): 86. Ruins of temple built by King Kamehameha, first king of united Hawaiian islands.

Sagamore Hill, Oyster Bay, NY (1962): 83. Home of Pres. Theodore Roosevelt from 1885 until his death in 1919.

Saint-Gaudens, Cornish, NH (1964): 191. Home, studio, and gardens of American sculptor Augustus Saint-Gaudens.

Saint Paul's Church, New York, NY (1943): 6. Site associated with John Peter Zenger's "freedom of press" trial.

Salem Maritime, MA (1938): 9. Major fishing and whaling port famous for 1692 witchcraft trials.

Sand Creek Massacre, CO (2000): 12,583. Site where more than 160 Cheyenne and Arapaho Indians were killed by U.S. soldiers in 1864.

San Juan, PR (1949): 75. 16th-cent. Spanish fortifications.

Saugus Iron Works, MA (1974): 9. Reconstructed 17th-cent. colonial ironworks.

Springfield Armory, MA (1974): 55. Small-arms manufacturing center for nearly 200 years.

Steamtown, PA (1986): 62. Rail yard, roadhouse, repair shops of former Delaware, Lackawanna & Western Railroad.

Theodore Roosevelt Birthplace, New York, NY (1962): 0.11. Reconstructed brownstone where 26th president was born.

Theodore Roosevelt Inaugural, Buffalo, NY (1966): 1. Wilcox House, where 26th president took oath of office, 1901.

Thomas Stone, Port Tobacco, MD (1978): 328. Home of signer of Declaration of Independence.

Tuskegee Airmen, AL (1998): 90. Airfield where pilots of all-black WWII air corps unit received flight training.

Tuskegee Institute, AL (1974): 58. College founded by Booker T. Washington in 1881 for blacks.

Ulysses S. Grant, St. Louis, MO (1989): 10. Home of Grant during pre-Civil War years.

Vanderbilt Mansion, Hyde Park, NY (1940): 212. Mansion of 19th-cent. financier.

Washita Battlefield, OK (1996): 315. Scene of Nov. 27, 1868, battle between Plains tribes and U.S. army.

Weir Farm, Wilton, CT (1990): 74. Home and studio of American impressionist painter J. Alden Weir.

Whitman Mission, WA (1936/1963): 139. Site of Protestant Missionaries to Cayuse Indians during mid-19th cent.

William Howard Taft, Cincinnati, OH (1969): 4. Birthplace and early home of 27th president.

National Monuments

Name	State	Year[1]	Acreage
African Burial Ground	NY	2006	0.35
Agate Fossil Beds	NE	1965	3,058
Alibates Flint Quarries	TX	1965	1,371
Aniakchak[2]	AK	1978	137,176
Aztec Ruins	NM	1923	318
Bandelier	NM	1916	33,677
Booker T. Washington	VA	1956	239
Buck Island Reef	VI	1961	19,015
Cabrillo	CA	1913	160
Canyon de Chelly	AZ	1931	83,840
Cape Krusenstern[3]	AK	1978	649,082
Capulin Volcano	NM	1916	793
Casa Grande Ruins	AZ	1889	473
Castillo de San Marcos	FL	1924	19
Castle Clinton	NY	1946	1
Cedar Breaks	UT	1933	6,155
Chiricahua	AZ	1924	11,985
Colorado	CO	1911	20,534
Craters of the Moon	ID	1924	53,571
Devils Postpile	CA	1911	798
Devils Tower	WY	1906	1,347
Dinosaur	CO-UT	1915	210,283
Effigy Mounds	IA	1949	2,526
El Malpais	NM	1987	114,277
El Morro	NM	1906	1,279
Florissant Fossil Beds	CO	1969	5,998
Fort Frederica	GA	1936	284
Fort Matanzas	FL	1924	300
Fort McHenry (and Historic Shrine)	MD	1925	43
Fort Monroe	VA	2011	325
Fort Pulaski	GA	1924	5,623
Fort Stanwix	NY	1935	16
Fort Sumter	SC	1948	235
Fort Union	NM	1954	721
Fossil Butte	WY	1972	8,198
George Washington Birthplace	VA	1930	662
George Washington Carver	MO	1943	210
Gila Cliff Dwellings	NM	1907	533
Governors Island	NY	2001	23
Grand Portage	MN	1951	710
Hagerman Fossil Beds	ID	1988	4,351
Hohokam Pima[4]	AZ	1972	1,690
Homestead NM of America	NE	1936	211
Hovenweep	CO-UT	1923	785
Jewel Cave	SD	1908	1,274
John Day Fossil Beds	OR	1974	14,061
Lava Beds	CA	1925	46,692
Little Bighorn Battlefield	MT	1879	765
Montezuma Castle	AZ	1906	859
Muir Woods	CA	1908	554
Natural Bridges	UT	1908	7,636
Navajo	AZ	1909	360
Ocmulgee	GA	1934	702
Oregon Caves	OR	1909	488
Organ Pipe Cactus	AZ	1937	330,689
Petroglyph	NM	1990	7,533
Pinnacles	CA	1908	26,606
Pipe Spring	AZ	1923	40
Pipestone	MN	1937	282
Poverty Point[2]	LA	1988	911
Rainbow Bridge[3]	UT	1910	160
Russell Cave	AL	1961	310
Salinas Pueblo Missions	NM	1909	1,071
Scotts Bluff	NE	1919	3,005
Statue of Liberty	NJ-NY	1924	61
Sunset Crater Volcano	AZ	1930	3,040
Timpanogos Cave	UT	1922	250
Tonto	AZ	1907	1,120
Tuzigoot	AZ	1939	812
Virgin Islands Coral Reef	VI	2001	12,708
Walnut Canyon	AZ	1915	3,529
White Sands	NM	1933	143,733
World War II Valor in the Pacific	HI-CA	2008	59
Wupatki	AZ	1924	35,422
Yucca House[2]	CO	1919	34

National Preserves

Name	State	Year[1]	Acreage
Aniakchak	AK	1978	464,118
Bering Land Bridge	AK	1978	2,697,391
Big Cypress	FL	1974	720,567
Big Thicket	TX	1974	106,305
Craters of the Moon	ID	2002	410,733
Denali	AK	1917	4,740,911
Gates of the Arctic	AK	1978	7,523,897
Glacier Bay	AK	1925	58,406
Great Sand Dunes	CO	2000	41,686
Katmai	AK	1918	418,699
Lake Clark	AK	1978	1,410,294
Little River Canyon[3]	AL	1992	15,288

Name	State	Year[1]	Acreage
Mojave	CA	1994	1,538,015
Noatak	AK	1978	6,587,071
Tallgrass Prairie	KS	1996	10,894
Timucuan Ecological and Historic	FL	1988	46,301
Wrangell-St. Elias	AK	1978	4,852,652
Yukon-Charley Rivers[3]	AK	1978	2,526,512

National Seashores

Name	State	Year[1]	Acreage
Assateague Island	MD-VA	1965	41,320
Canaveral	FL	1975	57,662
Cape Cod	MA	1961	43,607
Cape Hatteras	NC	1937	30,351
Cape Lookout	NC	1966	28,243
Cumberland Island	GA	1972	36,347
Fire Island	NY	1964	19,580
Gulf Islands	FL-MS	1971	137,989
Padre Island	TX	1962	130,434
Point Reyes	CA	1962	71,055

National Parkways

Name	State	Year[1]	Acreage
Blue Ridge	NC-VA	1933	95,194
George Washington Memorial	VA-MD-DC	1930	6,922
John D. Rockefeller Jr. Mem.	WY	1972	23,777
Natchez Trace	MS-TN-AL	1938	52,302

National Lakeshores

Name	State	Year[1]	Acreage
Apostle Islands	WI	1970	69,372
Indiana Dunes	IN	1966	15,201
Pictured Rocks	MI	1966	73,236
Sleeping Bear Dunes	MI	1970	71,210

National Reserves

Name	State	Year[1]	Acreage
City of Rocks	ID	1988	14,407
Ebey's Landing Historical	WA	1978	19,333

National Rivers

Name	State	Year[1]	Acreage
Big South Fork (and Rec. Area)	KY-TN	1976	125,310
Buffalo	AR	1972	94,293
Mississippi (and Rec. Area)	MN	1988	53,775
New River Gorge	WV	1978	72,186
Ozark Scenic Riverways	MO	1964	80,785

National Wild and Scenic Rivers

Name	State	Year[1]	Acreage
Alagnak Wild	AK	1980	30,665
Bluestone Scenic[2]	WV	1978	4,310
Delaware (Middle) Scenic	NJ-PA	1978	1,973
Great Egg Harbor Scenic (and Rec.)	NJ	1992	43,311
Missouri Recreational	NE-SD	1991	34,159
Niobrara Scenic	NE	1991	29,101
Obed	TN	1976	5,073
Rio Grande[3]	TX	1978	9,600
Saint Croix Scenic Riverway	MN-WI	1968	67,470
Upper Delaware Scenic (and Rec.)	NY-PA	1978	75,000

National Recreation Areas

Name	State	Year[1]	Acreage
Amistad	TX	1965	58,500
Bighorn Canyon	MT-WY	1966	120,296
Boston Harbor Islands	MA	1996	1,482
Chattahoochee River	GA	1978	9,792
Chickasaw	OK	1902	9,899
Curecanti	CO	1965	43,095
Delaware Water Gap	NJ-PA	1965	66,741
Gateway	NJ-NY	1972	26,607
Gauley River[3]	WV	1988	11,560
Glen Canyon	AZ-UT	1958	1,254,117
Golden Gate	CA	1972	80,002
Lake Chelan	WA	1968	61,949
Lake Mead	AZ-NV	1936	1,495,806
Lake Meredith	TX	1965	44,978
Lake Roosevelt[5]	WA	1946	100,390
Ross Lake	WA	1968	117,575
Santa Monica Mountains[3]	CA	1978	156,670
Whiskeytown-Shasta-Trinity	CA	1965	42,503

Other Designations

Name	State	Year[1]	Acreage
Catoctin Mountain	MD	1954	5,874
Constitution Gardens	DC	1974	39
Fort Washington	MD	1930	341
Greenbelt	MD	1950	1,175
National Capital-East	DC-MD	1933	6,834
National Mall	DC	1933	156
Piscataway	MD	1961	4,626
Prince William Forest	VA	1948	16,084
Rock Creek	DC	1890	1,755
White House	DC	1933	18
Wolf Trap Park for Performing Arts	VA	1966	130

International Historic Site

Name	State	Year[1]	Acreage
Saint Croix Island[3]	ME	1949	6.5

National Scenic Trails[6]

Name	State	Year[1]	Acreage
Appalachian	ME to GA	1968	2,181
Ice Age	WI	1980	635
Natchez Trace	MS-TN-AL	1983	65
North Country	NY to ND	1980	1,903
Potomac Heritage	VA to PA	1983	764

(1) Year first designated. (2) No federal facilities. (3) Limited federal facilities. (4) Not open to the public. (5) Formerly Coulee Dam National Recreation Area. (6) Figure given in right column is length of public trail in miles, not acreage.

AFGHANISTAN ALBANIA ALGERIA ANDORRA ANGOLA

ANTIGUA AND BARBUDA ARGENTINA ARMENIA AUSTRALIA AUSTRIA

AZERBAIJAN THE BAHAMAS BAHRAIN BANGLADESH BARBADOS

BELARUS BELGIUM BELIZE BENIN BHUTAN

BOLIVIA BOSNIA AND HERZEGOVINA BOTSWANA BRAZIL BRUNEI

BULGARIA BURKINA FASO BURUNDI CAMBODIA CAMEROON

CANADA CAPE VERDE CENTRAL AFRICAN REPUBLIC CHAD CHILE

CHINA COLOMBIA COMOROS CONGO, DEM. REP. OF THE CONGO REPUBLIC

COSTA RICA CÔTE D'IVOIRE CROATIA CUBA CYPRUS

CZECH REPUBLIC DENMARK DJIBOUTI DOMINICA DOMINICAN REPUBLIC

ECUADOR EGYPT EL SALVADOR EQUATORIAL GUINEA ERITREA

Note: Flag proportions have been standardized to fit page.

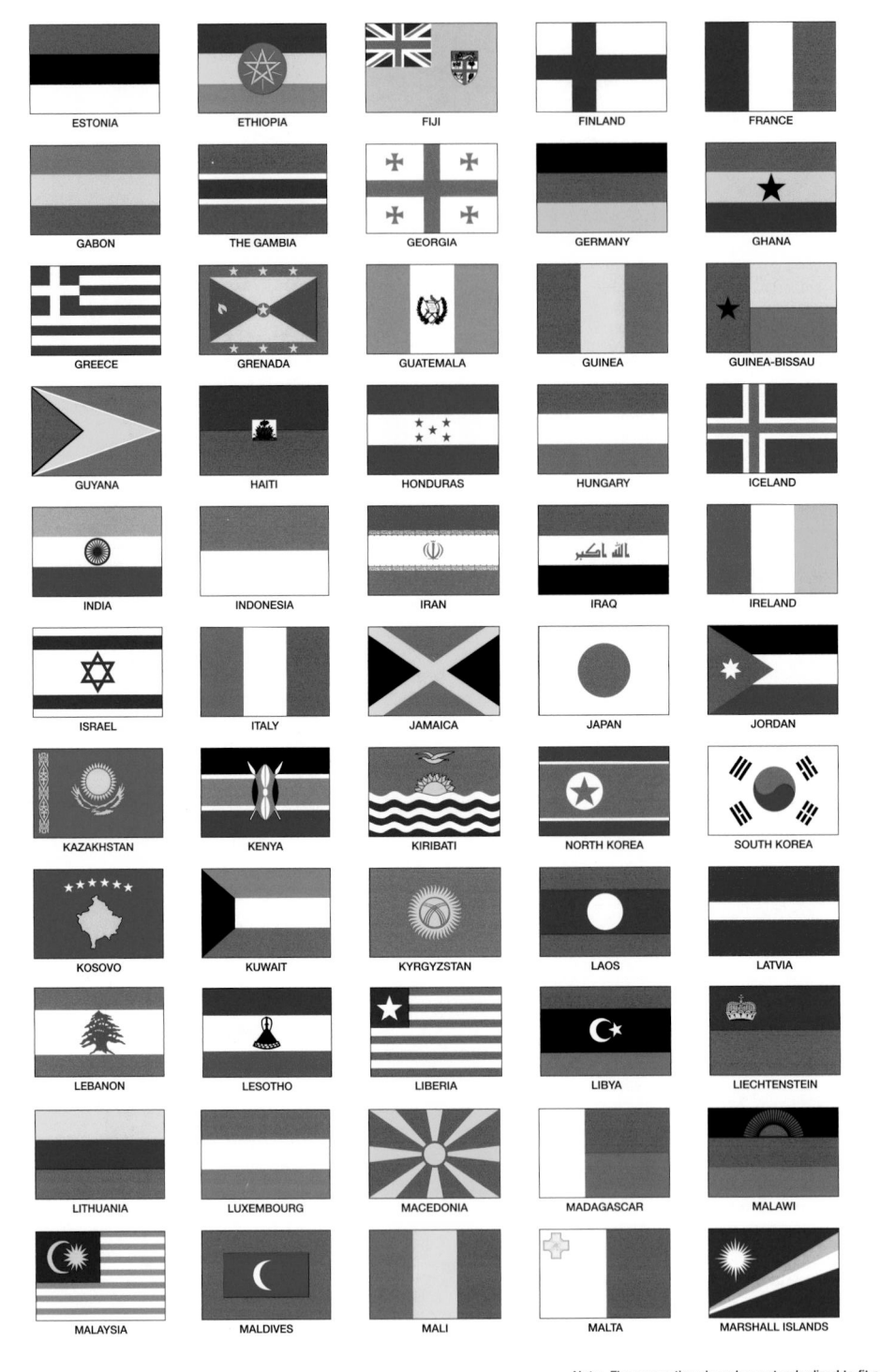

ESTONIA   ETHIOPIA   FIJI   FINLAND   FRANCE

GABON   THE GAMBIA   GEORGIA   GERMANY   GHANA

GREECE   GRENADA   GUATEMALA   GUINEA   GUINEA-BISSAU

GUYANA   HAITI   HONDURAS   HUNGARY   ICELAND

INDIA   INDONESIA   IRAN   IRAQ   IRELAND

ISRAEL   ITALY   JAMAICA   JAPAN   JORDAN

KAZAKHSTAN   KENYA   KIRIBATI   NORTH KOREA   SOUTH KOREA

KOSOVO   KUWAIT   KYRGYZSTAN   LAOS   LATVIA

LEBANON   LESOTHO   LIBERIA   LIBYA   LIECHTENSTEIN

LITHUANIA   LUXEMBOURG   MACEDONIA   MADAGASCAR   MALAWI

MALAYSIA   MALDIVES   MALI   MALTA   MARSHALL ISLANDS

Note: Flag proportions have been standardized to fit page.

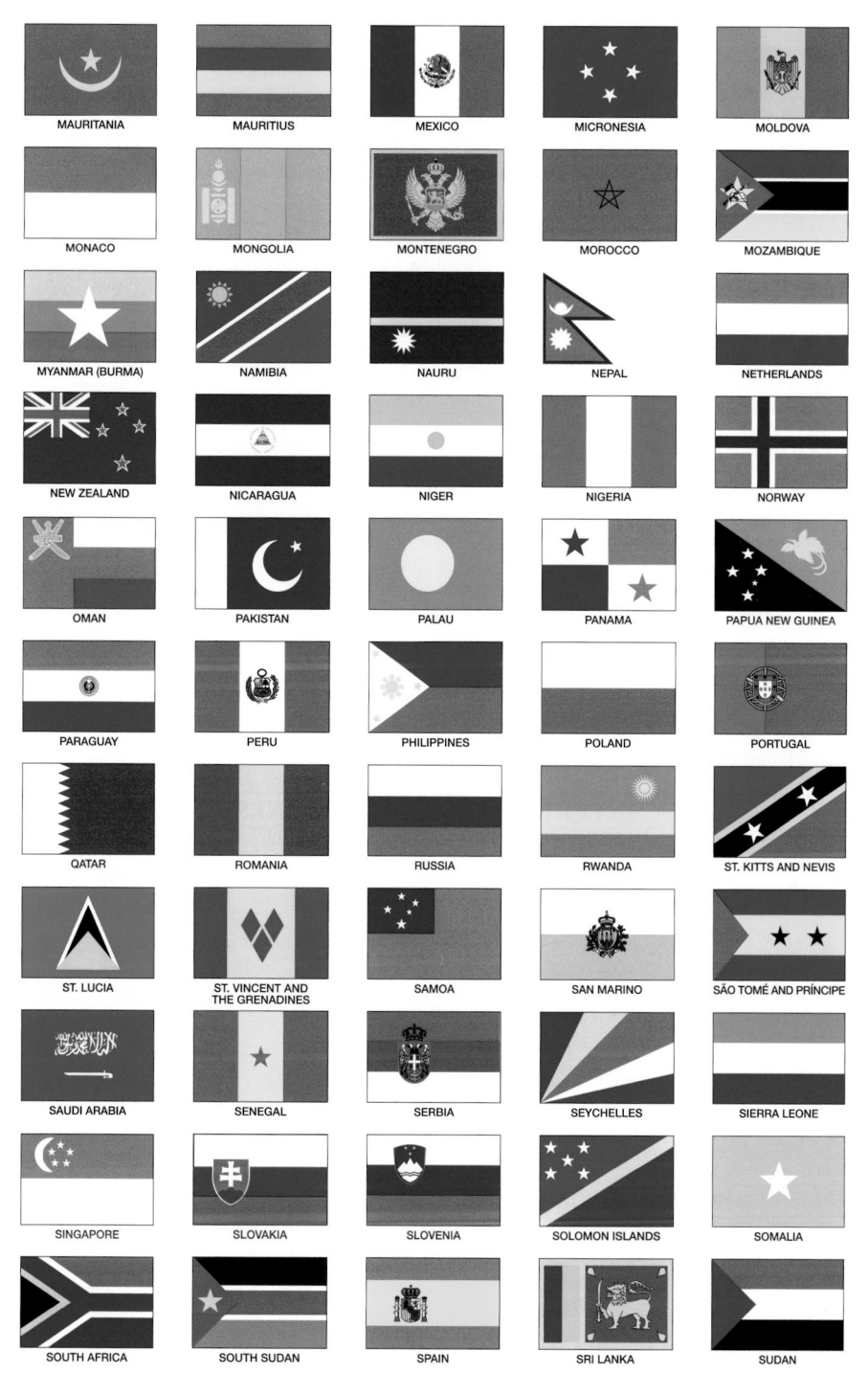

MAURITANIA · MAURITIUS · MEXICO · MICRONESIA · MOLDOVA

MONACO · MONGOLIA · MONTENEGRO · MOROCCO · MOZAMBIQUE

MYANMAR (BURMA) · NAMIBIA · NAURU · NEPAL · NETHERLANDS

NEW ZEALAND · NICARAGUA · NIGER · NIGERIA · NORWAY

OMAN · PAKISTAN · PALAU · PANAMA · PAPUA NEW GUINEA

PARAGUAY · PERU · PHILIPPINES · POLAND · PORTUGAL

QATAR · ROMANIA · RUSSIA · RWANDA · ST. KITTS AND NEVIS

ST. LUCIA · ST. VINCENT AND THE GRENADINES · SAMOA · SAN MARINO · SÃO TOMÉ AND PRÍNCIPE

SAUDI ARABIA · SENEGAL · SERBIA · SEYCHELLES · SIERRA LEONE

SINGAPORE · SLOVAKIA · SLOVENIA · SOLOMON ISLANDS · SOMALIA

SOUTH AFRICA · SOUTH SUDAN · SPAIN · SRI LANKA · SUDAN

Note: Flag proportions have been standardized to fit page.

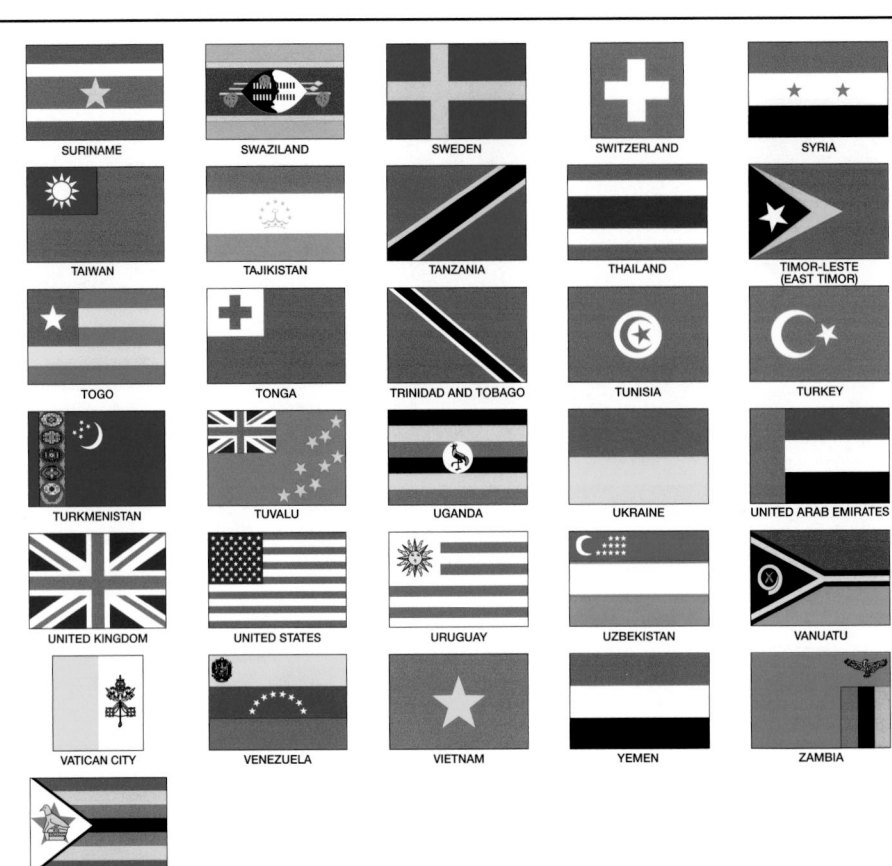

SURINAME	SWAZILAND	SWEDEN	SWITZERLAND	SYRIA
TAIWAN	TAJIKISTAN	TANZANIA	THAILAND	TIMOR-LESTE (EAST TIMOR)
TOGO	TONGA	TRINIDAD AND TOBAGO	TUNISIA	TURKEY
TURKMENISTAN	TUVALU	UGANDA	UKRAINE	UNITED ARAB EMIRATES
UNITED KINGDOM	UNITED STATES	URUGUAY	UZBEKISTAN	VANUATU
VATICAN CITY	VENEZUELA	VIETNAM	YEMEN	ZAMBIA
ZIMBABWE				

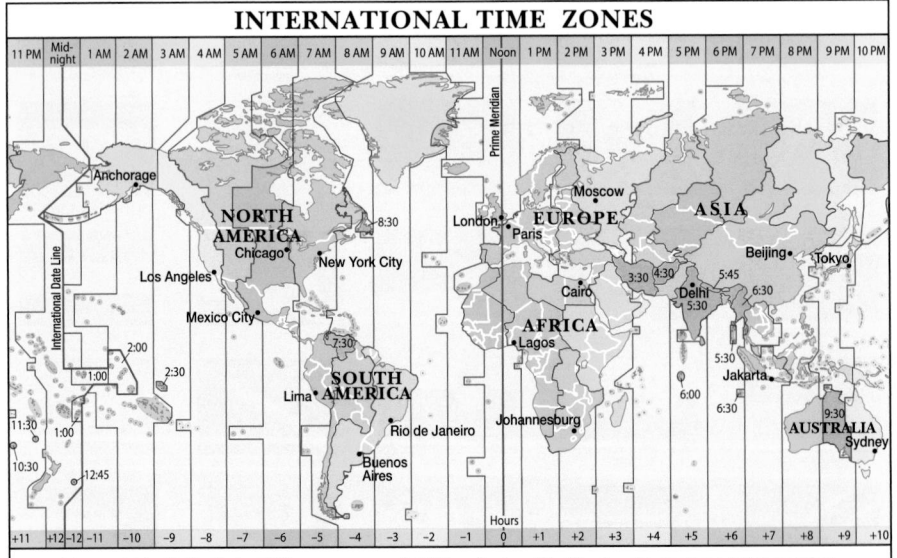

INTERNATIONAL TIME ZONES

The world is divided into 24 time zones, each 15° longitude wide. The longitudinal meridian passing through Greenwich, England, is the starting point, and is called the *prime meridian*. The 12th zone is divided by the 180th meridian (International Date Line). When the line is crossed going west, the date is advanced one day; when crossed going east, the date becomes a day earlier.

Note: Flag proportions have been standardized to fit page.

468

UNITED STATES

ATLANTIC OCEAN

CANADA

MEXICO

Gulf of Mexico

THE BAHAMAS

CUBA

PACIFIC OCEAN

ALASKA....See page 470

Hawai'i

469

EUROPE
NORWAY •Oslo
GREAT BRITAIN

ICELAND •Reykjavík

Greenland Sea

Svalbard (Nor.)

Denmark Strait

Arctic Circle

ARCTIC OCEAN

+ North Pole

Cape Morris Jesup

Cape Columbia
Ellesmere I.
Alert
Eureka
Grise Fiord
Devon I.
Arctic Bay
Resolute
Queen Elizabeth Islands
Melville I.
Banks I.
Victoria I.
Sachs Harbour
Cambridge Bay
Kugluktuk

Beaufort Sea

BROOKS RANGE

Point Barrow
Barrow
Point Hope
Kotzebue
Nome
SEWARD PENINSULA
Alaska
Fairbanks
ALASKA RANGE
Highest point in North America
Mt. McKinley
6194 m (20,320 ft)
Mt. Logan
5959 m (19,551 ft)
Anchorage
Valdez
Kenai
Seward
Mt. Katmai
2047 m (6,716 ft)
Bethel
Kodiak
Kodiak I.

Gulf of Alaska

Chukchi Sea

Bering Strait

Bering Sea

RUSSIA

ASIA

Arctic Circle

GREENLAND
(KALAALLIT NUNAAT)
(Den.)

Ittoqqortoormiit
(Scoresbysund)

Nuuk

Tasiilaq

Cape Farewell

Baffin Bay

Qaanaaq (Thule)
Nord

Baffin Island

Davis Strait

Pangnirtung
Iqaluit

Hudson Strait

UNGAVA PENINSULA
Puvirnituq

Repulse Bay
Southampton I.

Rankin Inlet
Arviat

Hudson Bay

Churchill

Nunavut

CANADA

Great Slave Lake
Yellowknife
Fort Smith
Uranium City
Lake Athabasca
Fort Simpson
Déline
Great Bear Lake
Hay River
Northwest Territories

Inuvik
Fort McPherson
Mackenzie

YUKON PLATEAU
Dawson
Carmacks
Whitehorse
Yukon
Watson Lake

Skagway
Juneau
Sitka
Alexander Archipelago
Ketchikan
Prince Rupert
Kitimat
Queen Charlotte Is.

COAST MOUNTAINS

British Columbia

Dawson Creek
Peace River
Grande Prairie
Prince George
Williams Lake
Mt. Waddington
3994 m (13,104 ft)
Fraser

Alberta
Fort McMurray
Lake Athabasca
La Loche
La Ronge
Saskatchewan
Prince Albert
Saskatoon
Saskatchewan
Regina
Brandon

Flin Flon
Thompson
Manitoba
Lake Winnipeg
Winnipeg

ROCKY

GREAT RANGE

Jasper
Edmonton
Calgary
Great Falls
Williston

Columbia
Spokane
Wash.
Mt. Rainier
4392 m (14,410 ft)
Seattle
Tacoma
Missoula
Vancouver
Victoria
Vancouver I.
Port Hardy

CANADIAN SHIELD

Labrador Sea

Newfoundland and Labrador
St. Anthony
Newfoundland
St. John's
Corner Brook
Cape Breton I.
St. Pierre and Miquelon Is. (Fr.)
Sydney
Charlottetown
P.E.I.
New Brunswick
Fredericton
Saint John
Halifax
Maine

Labrador
Hebron
Schefferville
Labrador City
Happy Valley–Goose Bay
Anticosti I.
Sept-Îles
Chibougamau
Chicoutimi
Quebec
Val-d'Or
Moosonee
James Bay
Belcher Is.
Ontario
Timmins
Thunder Bay
L.

Denmark Strait

470

ATLANTIC OCEAN

Caribbean Sea

PACIFIC OCEAN

CENTRAL AMERICA

HONDURAS
Tegucigalpa
San Salvador
EL SALVADOR
NICARAGUA
Managua
COSTA RICA
San José
PANAMA
Panama City

Aruba (Neth.)
Bonaire (Neth.)
Curaçao (Neth.)
Margarita I.
TRINIDAD AND TOBAGO
Port-of-Spain

VENEZUELA
Maracaibo
Cabimas
Coro
Valencia
Caracas
Barcelona
Maracay
Barquisimeto
Valera
Cúcuta
San Cristóbal
Mérida
Valledupar
Bucaramanga
Ciudad Bolívar
El Tigre
Cumaná
Maturín
San Fernando de Apure
Puerto Ayacucho

COLOMBIA
Barranquilla
Santa Marta
Cartagena
Sincelejo
Montería
Barrancabermeja
Medellín
Manizales
Pereira
Armenia
Ibagué
Cali
Palmira
Popayán
Buenaventura
Pasto
Bogotá
Tunja
Villavicencio
Neiva
Florencia
Nevada del Huila 5364 m (17,598 ft)

GUYANA
Georgetown
New Amsterdam

SURINAME
Paramaribo

French Guiana (Fr.)
Cayenne
Kourou

GUIANA HIGHLANDS
Pico da Neblina 2994 m (9,823 ft)
Boa Vista

ECUADOR
Quito
Ambato
Riobamba
Cuenca
Loja
Guayaquil
Portoviejo
Machala
Tumbes
Talara
Sullana
Piura
Chiclayo
Aguja Point
Cotopaxi 5911 m (19,393 ft)
Chimborazo 6310 m (20,702 ft)
Esmeraldas
Tumaco
Galapagos Islands (Ecuador)
Equator

PERU
Iquitos
Yurimaguas
Trujillo
Chimbote
Cajamarca
Huánuco
Cerro de Pasco
Pucallpa
Huancayo
Ayacucho
Lima
Callao
Ica
Arequipa
Tacna
LA MONTAÑA
Nev. Huascarán 6768 m (22,205 ft)
Nev. Yerupajá 6634 m (21,765 ft)
Leticia
Benjamin Constant
Cruzeiro do Sul

BRAZIL
Belém
Macapá
Santarém
Manaus
Altamira
Marabá
Imperatriz
São Luís
Teresina
Caxias
Floriano
Araguaína
Fortaleza
Parnaíba
Mossoró
Natal
João Pessoa
Recife
Maceió
Aracaju
Campina Grande
Alagoinhas
Salvador
Ilhéus
Jequié
Itabuna
Juazeiro
Petrolina
Feira de Santana
Vitória da Conquista
Montes Claros
Teófilo Otoni
Governador Valadares
Vitória
Juiz de Fora
Volta Redonda
Niterói
Rio de Janeiro
Belo Horizonte
Pico da Bandeira 2890 m (9,482 ft)
Brasília
Goiânia
Uberlândia
Anápolis
Jataí
Rondonópolis
Cuiabá
Campo Grande
Corumbá
São José do Rio Preto
Ribeirão Preto
Bauru
Londrina
Campinas
Sorocaba
São Paulo
Santos
Jundiaí
Curitiba
Ponta Grossa
Presidente Prudente
Dourados
BRAZILIAN HIGHLANDS
MATO GROSSO PLATEAU

BOLIVIA
La Paz
Cochabamba
Santa Cruz
Sucre
Potosí
Oruro
Trinidad
Riberalta
Cobija
Guajará-Mirim
Puerto Maldonado
Cuzco
Puno
Juliaca
ALTIPLANO
Lake Titicaca

PARAGUAY
Asunción
Concepción
Formosa
Pedro Juan Caballero
Coronel Oviedo
Iguaçu
Foz do Iguaçu

ANDES
ATACAMA DESERT
Arica
Iquique
Antofagasta
Calama
San Miguel
San Salvador de Jujuy
Salta
Tarija
Camiri

AMAZON BASIN
SELVAS
GRAN CHACO

LLANOS

SOUTH AMERICA

ANTARCTICA

Rio de Janeiro
Santos
São Paulo
Curitiba
Joinvile
Itajaí
Florianópolis
Caxias do Sul
Lajes
Porto Alegre
Ponta Grossa
Passo Fundo
Foz do Iguaçu
Rio Grande
Santa Maria
Santo Ângelo
Oviedo
Coronel Oviedo
Santa Tomé
Pelotas
Rivera
Encarnación
Posadas
Santo Tomé
Melo
Uruguaiana
Montevideo
URUGUAY
Salto
Paysandú
Minas
Asunción
Formosa
Resistencia
Corrientes
Reconquista
Concordia
Paraná
La Plata
Mar del Plata
Santiago del Estero
Santa Fe
Rosario
Buenos Aires
Avellaneda
Tandil
Catamarca
La Rioja
Córdoba
San Juan
Junín
Azul
Necochea
Salta
Mendoza
San Rafael
Santa Rosa
Punta Alta
ARGENTINA
Cerro Ojos del Salado
6887 m (22,595 ft)
Copiapó
Cerro Bonete
6872 m (22,546 ft)
Cerro Tupungato
6800 m (22,310 ft)
Cerro Aconcagua
6959 m (22,831 ft)
Highest point in South America
San Miguel de Tucumán
CHILE
La Serena
Viña del Mar
Valparaíso
San Bernardo
Santiago
Rancagua
Chillán
San Martín de los Andes
Viedma
Neuquén
San Antonio Oeste
Comodoro Rivadavia
Valdés Peninsula
Cape Tres Puntas
Puerto Deseado
Talcahuano
Concepción
Los Ángeles
Temuco
Valdivia
Osorno
Puerto Montt
Chiloé Island
Los Chonos Archipelago
Taitao Peninsula
San Carlos de Bariloche
Esquel
Trelew
Rawson
Coihaique
Gulf of San Jorge
San Matías Gulf
Lowest point in South America
Bahía Blanca
Tierra Del Fuego
Cape Horn
Strait of Magellan
Punta Arenas
Ushuaia
Río Gallegos
Bahía Grande
Stanley
Falkland Islands
(Islas Malvinas)
(U.K.)
(claimed by Arg.)
South Georgia
(U.K.)
SOUTHERN OCEAN
ANTARCTICA
PARAGUAY
GRAN
PAMPA
PATAGONIA

Tropic of Capricorn

San Ambrosio Island
(Chile)

San Félix Island
(Chile)

Juan Fernández Islands
(Chile)

0   250   500   750 Miles
0   250   500   750   1,000 Kilometers

30°
40°
50°
60°
20°
30°
40°
50°
60°
70°
80°
90°
100°
110°

ANTARCTICA

SOUTHERN OCEAN
ATLANTIC OCEAN
Falkland Is.
(U.K.)
South Orkney Is.
South Shetland Is.
Elephant I.
ANTARCTIC PENINSULA
Adelaide I.
Alexander I.
Weddell Sea
Ronne Ice Shelf
Larsen Ice Shelf
Berkner I.
Filchner Ice Shelf
Cape Norvegia
QUEEN MAUD LAND
NEW SCHWABENLAND
Riiser-Larsen Pen.
Fimbul Ice Shelf
COATS LAND
POLAR PLATEAU
MAC ROBERTSON LAND
AMERICAN HIGHLAND
ENDERBY LAND
EAST ANTARCTICA
WEST ANTARCTICA
ELLSWORTH LAND
ELLSWORTH MTS.
MARIE BYRD LAND
Thurston I.
Siple I.
Bellingshausen Sea
Amundsen Sea
Ross Sea
Roosevelt I.
Ross Ice Shelf
TRANSANTARCTIC MOUNTAINS
South Pole
Amundsen-Scott Station
Vinson Massif
(4,897 m)
(16,066 ft)
WILKES LAND
Shackleton Ice Shelf
West Ice Shelf
Amery Ice Shelf
South Magnetic Pole
Cape Poinsett
Cape Adare
Ross I.
McMurdo Station
Scott I.
Balleny Is.
PACIFIC OCEAN
INDIAN OCEAN
Antarctic Circle
SOUTH AMERICA

0   800 Miles
0   800 Kilometers

0°   20°   40°   60°   80°   100°   120°   140°   160°   180°   160°   140°   120°   100°   80°   60°   40°   20°

EUROPE

GREENLAND
(KALAALLIT NUNAAT)
(Denmark)

ICELAND
Ísafjördur
Keflavík • Akureyri
Reykjavik
Seydhisfjördhur

Arctic Circle

Norwegian Sea

Narvik
Bodø

Namsos

Faroe Islands (Den.)
Torshavn

Molde
Trondheim
Ålesund
Östersund

NORWAY **SWEDEN**
Bergen
Sundsvall

Shetland Islands (U.K.)

Haugesund
Stavanger
Drammen ⊛ Oslo
Skien
Karlstad
Uppsala
Örebro

Orkney Islands
Thurso

Kristiansand
Göteborg
Norrköping
Linköping

Hebrides
Inverness
Jönköping
Växjö

Scotland Aberdeen
Ålborg
Halmstad
Helsingborg
Öland

Glasgow Dundee
Jutland Århus
Got (Sw

*ATLANTIC
OCEAN*

Ayr **Edinburgh**
Esbjerg
Copenhagen ⊛
Malmö
Baltic

Londonderry
Northern Ireland
Belfast **UNITED**
KINGDOM Newcastle
*North
Sea*
DENMARK Odense
Bornholm (Den.)

Galway
IRELAND ⊛ Dublin
Kiel
Lübeck
Rostock
Gdańsk

Limerick
Liverpool
Leeds
Kingston upon Hull
Groningen
Hamburg
Szczecin

Cork
Waterford
Manchester
Sheffield
Bremen
NORTHERN
Bydgoszcz

Birmingham
Coventry
Norwich
Amsterdam
Hannover
Berlin
POLAND

Wales
Swansea
England
NETHERLANDS
Bielefeld
Madgeburg
Poznań

Cardiff
London ⊛
Thames
Rotterdam
Essen
GERMANY
Leipzig
Wrocław

Plymouth
Bristol
The Hague
Antwerp
Cologne
Kassel
Dresden
Walbrzych
Kat

Land's End
Portsmouth
Dover
Brussels
Liege
Bonn
Erfurt
Liberec
Ostrava

Channel Is. (U.K.)
Le Havre
Caen
BELGIUM
Wiesbaden
Chemnitz
Prague
CZECH REP.
Brno

Brest
Rouen
LUXEMBOURG
Frankfurt
Mannheim
Plzen
**C A
SLO**

Rennes
Le Mans
Luxembourg
Saarbrucken
Nürnberg
Regensburg

Nantes
Paris
Seine
Nancy
Stuttgart
Danube
Bratislava

Orleans
Strasbourg
Augsburg
Munich Linz
Vienna

Loire
Dijon
Basel
Zürich
Salzburg
AUSTRIA
Bu

Tours
Bern
Innsbruck
Graz
HUNGA

FRANCE
Limoges
Geneva **LIECHTENSTEIN**
Klagenfurt

SWITZERLAND
A L P S
Pécs

*Bay
of
Biscay*
Clermont-Ferrand
Lyon
Mt. Blanc
Matterhorn
Udine
SLOVENIA
⊛ Zagreb

A Coruña
Saint-Etienne
4810 m (15,781 ft)
4478 m (14,692 ft)
Trieste
Ljubljana
CROATIA

Gijón
Bordeaux
Grenoble
Milan
Verona
Rijeka
Banja

Vigo
Donostia–
San Sebastián
Torino
Venice
Luka
**BOS. &
HERZ.**

Porto
Braga
Santander
Bilbao
Po
Bologna
DINARIC
Split
Sarajevo

Leon
Vitoria-Gasteiz
Pamplona
Toulouse
Parma
**SAN
MARINO**

Duero
Valladolid
Montpellier
Avignon
Genoa
Pisa
Florence
Ancona
MON
KO

Coimbra
IBERIAN
Salamanca
Zaragoza
PYRENEES
Marseille
Nice
Perugia
Tiber
Dubrovnik

PORTUGAL
Pico de Aneto
3404 m
(11,168 ft)
ANDORRA
Toulon
MONACO
*Adriatic
Sea*

Lisbon ⊛
Setubal
Madrid
Corsica (Fr.)
Elba
⊛ **Rome**

Badajoz
Toledo
Barcelona
Ajaccio
VATICAN CITY
ITALY
Foggia

SPAIN
Tarragona
Castellon de la Plana
Naples
Bari

PENINSULA
Cordoba
Valencia
Majorca
Minorca
Sassari
Vesuvius
Salerno
Taranto

*Cape
St. Vincent*
Seville
Alicante
Palma de
Mallorca
*Balearic
Is. (Sp.)*
Sardinia (It.)
1277 m (4,190 ft)

Cádiz
Málaga
Granada
Murcia
Cartagena
*Tyrrhenian
Sea*
*Ionian
Sea*
Cor

*Strait of
Gibraltar*
GIBRALTAR (U.K.)
Almería
Cagliari

Rabat
Algiers
M e d i t e r r a n e a n
Palermo
Messina
Etna
Reggio di
Calabria

Tunis ⊛
3369 m (11,053 ft)
Sicily (It.)
Catania

AFRICA

0 ——— 250 ——— 500 Miles
0 — 250 — 500 — 750 Kilometers

TUNISIA
MALTA ⊛ Valletta
Sea

MOROCCO
ALGERIA

NORTH AMERICA

Chukchi Sea

Bering Strait

Providoniya

Bering Sea

Wrangel I.

Anadyr

New Siberian Islands

East Siberian Sea

Cherskiy

KOLYMA MOUNTAINS

Laptev Sea

Nordvik

Tiksi

Verkhoyansk

VERKHOYANSK RA.

Zyryanka

Susuman

Magadan

KAMCHATKA PEN.

Shiveluch 3283 m (10,771 ft)
Klyuchevskaya 4835 m (15,863 ft)
Karymsky 1536 m (5,039 ft)

Petropavlovsk-Kamchatskiy

CENTRAL

SIBERIAN

PLATEAU

Tura

Kansk

yarsk

Vilyuysk

Yakutsk

Lensk

Aldan

Berkakit

Okhotsk

Sea of Okhotsk

Alaid 2339 m (7,674 ft)

Bodaybo

STANOVOY RANGE

Tynda

Komsomol'sk-na-Amure

Okha

Sakhalin

Sarycheva 1496 m (4,908 ft)

Kuril Is. (Russia)

Bratsk

Ust'-Kut

Tulun

Ulan-Ude

Lake Baykal

VABLONOWY RANGE

Chita

Hailar

Svobodnyy

Blagoveshchensk

Khabarovsk

Yuzhno-Sakhalinsk

Tiatia 1819 m (5,968 ft)

Irkutsk

Darhan Moron

Choybalsan

Ulaanbaatar

GREATER KHINGAN RANGE

Yichun

Qiqihar

Jixi

Ussuriysk

Vladivostok

Hokkaido

Sapporo

Hakodate

MONGOLIA

MONGOLIAN PLATEAU

Bayanhongor

Changchun

Harbin

Jilin

Chongjin

Sea of Japan (East Sea)

Akita

Sendai

Niigata

Honshu

Hohhot

Shenyang

Fushun

N. KOREA

Hamhung

Pyongyang

JAPAN

Tokyo

Yokohama

Mt. Fuji 3776 m (12,388 ft)

Baotou

Beijing

Tianjin

Anshan

Dalian

Incheon

Seoul

Daegu

Busan

S. KOREA

Kyoto

Kobe

Nagoya

Osaka

Hiroshima

Shikoku

GOBI DESERT

Shijiazhuang

Taiyuan

Jinan

Qingdao

Kitakyushu

Fukuoka

Yinchuan

Handan

Xuzhou

Yellow Sea

Kagoshima

Nagasaki

Kyushu

Xining

Lanzhou

Xi'an

Luoyang

Zhengzhou

Huainan

Nanjing

Shanghai

Grand Canal

Ryukyu Is. (Japan)

Qinghai Lake

Hefei

Hangzhou

Huang

Yellow

Okinawa

Naha

CHINA

Wuhan

Jingdezhen

East China Sea

Chengdu

Nanchang

Wenzhou

Chongqing

Zigong

Changsha

Shaoyang

Ganzhou

Fuzhou

Northern Mariana Islands (U.S.)

PACIFIC OCEAN

Gulyang

Guilin

Xiamen

Taipei

Chong (Yangtze)

Liuzhou

Guangzhou

TAIWAN

Tropic of Cancer

Kunming

Nanning

Macao

Hong Kong

Kaohsiung

Myitkyina

Zhanjiang

Haikou

Laoag

Luzon

Philippine Sea

Phongsali

Haiphong

Hanoi

Baguio

PHILIPPINES

Mandalay

Taunggyi

LAOS

Louangphabang

Vientiane

Hainan (China)

Quezon City

PALAU

Nay Pyi Taw

Chiang Mai

Vinh

Hue

Manila

Naga

Samar

Pyay

Yangon THAILAND (Rangoon)

Nakhon Ratchasima

VIETNAM

Mindoro

Panay

Iloilo

Cebu

Tacloban

Leyte

Butuan

Mawlamyine

South China Sea

Dawei

Nakhon Sawan

CAMBODIA

Batdambang

Nha Trang

Negros

Puerto Princesa

Mindanao

Davao

Equator 0°

Bangkok

Phnom Penh

Ho Chi Minh City

Palawan

Sulu Sea

Zamboanga

Kompong Som

Can Tho

Isthmus of Kra

Gulf of Thailand

Kota Kinabalu

Sandakan

Jayapura

Phuket

Hat Yai

Bandar Seri Begawan

Celebes Sea

Ternate

Halmahera

New Guinea

PAPUA NEW GUINEA

Port Moresby

Andaman Sea

George Town

MALAYSIA

Natuna Is.

BRUNEI

Tarakan

Manado

Ceram

Banda Aceh

Kuala Lumpur

Kuching

Gorontalo

Ambon

Medan

Kelang

Pontianak

Samainda

Celebes

MOLUCCAS

Arafura Sea

Sibolga

Singapore

SINGAPORE

Borneo

Balikpapan

Palopo

Banda Sea

Pekanbaru

Sampit

Banjarmasin

Parepare

Baubau

Padang

Jambi

Makassar

Sumatra

Palembang

Java Sea

Dili

TIMOR LESTE

AUSTRALIA

Bengkulu

Bandar Lampung

Jakarta

Semarang

Surabaya

INDONESIA

Ende

Timor

Timor Sea

Bandung

Yogyakarta

Java

Malang

Bali

Mataram

Sumba

Kupang

Banda Lampung

0   500   1,000 Miles
0   500   1,000   1,500 Kilometers

478

AFRICA

Map labels

Bodies of water and geographic features:
INDIAN OCEAN
ATLANTIC OCEAN
Gulf of Guinea
Mozambique Channel
Cape Palmas
Cape Agulhas
Cape of Good Hope
Equator
Tropic of Capricorn

Countries and regions:
SOMALIA
KENYA
UGANDA
RWANDA
BURUNDI
TANZANIA
MOZAMBIQUE
MALAWI
ZAMBIA
ZIMBABWE
BOTSWANA
NAMIBIA
ANGOLA
DEMOCRATIC REPUBLIC OF THE CONGO
REPUBLIC OF THE CONGO
GABON
CAMEROON
EQUATORIAL GUINEA
SÃO TOMÉ AND PRÍNCIPE
SOUTH AFRICA
LESOTHO
SWAZILAND
COMOROS
MADAGASCAR
SEYCHELLES

Highlands/deserts/plateaus:
HIGHLANDS
SERENGETI PLAIN
RIFT VALLEY
CONGO BASIN
KATANGA PLATEAU
KALAHARI DESERT
NAMIB DESERT

Cities:
Beledweyne, Mogadishu, Marka, Baldea, Kismayo, Kismaayo
Marsabit, Eldoret, Nairobi, Nakuru, Kisumu, Machakos, Meru
Kampala, Jinja, Mwanza, Kigali, Bukavu, Bujumbura, Goma, Beni, Isiro, Buta
Mombasa, Tanga, Arusha, Dar es Salaam, Zanzibar, Dodoma, Morogoro, Iringa, Tabora, Kigoma, Songea, Mtwara
Mahajanga, Antsiranana, Antsirabe, Antananarivo, Fianarantsoa, Toamasina, Antsirananan, Toliara, Tolanaro
Moroni, Mayotte (Fr.)
Nacala, Nampula, Quelimane, Blantyre, Chimoio, Beira, Inhambane, Xai-Xai, Maputo
Lilongwe, Chipata, Lusaka, Kabwe, Luanshya, Ndola, Kitwe, Chingola, Lubumbashi, Likasi, Kolwezi, Kabinda, Mwene-Ditu, Kananga, Mbuji-Mayi, Kindu, Kalemie, Kabalo, Kamina
Harare, Mutare, Gweru, Bulawayo, Francistown
Serowe, Gaborone, Mahalapye, Palapye, Mmabatho
Windhoek, Tsumeb, Grootfontein, Lüderitz, Keetmanshoop, Walvis Bay, Swakopmund, Namibe
Luanda, Huambo, Lobito, Benguela, Malanje, Menongue, Lubango, Lobatse
Kinshasa, Mbandaka, Kisangani, Kananga, Kikwit, Bandundu, Tshikapa, Ilebo, Boma, Matadi, Mbanza-Ngungu
Brazzaville, Pointe-Noire, Loubomo, Franceville, Cabinda (Angola)
Libreville, Lambaréné, Port-Gentil
Yaoundé, Douala
Malabo, Bioko, São Tomé, Príncipe, Annobón (Eq. Guinea)
Bangui, Bumba, Ouésso
Aba, Port Harcourt, Takoradi
Pretoria (Tshwane), Johannesburg, Klerksdorp, Welkom, Kimberley, Bloemfontein, Vereeniging, Newcastle, Pietermaritzburg, Maseru, Upington, Springbok, Worcester, Cape Town, Port Elizabeth, East London, Durban, Mbabane, Lobamba, Umtata, Bisho, Middelburg
Mbeya, Mbala
Livingstone, Victoria Falls, Kariba
Ruacana Falls, Augrabies Falls, Boyoma Falls, Stanley Falls

Lakes and rivers:
Lake Turkana, Lake Victoria, Lake Albert, Lake Tanganyika, Lake Nyasa, Lake Mweru, Lake Kariba, Lake Malawi
Congo, Kasai, Zambezi, Limpopo, Orange, Vaal, Cunene, Cuango

Mountains:
Margherita Pk. 5119 m (16,795 ft)
Mt. Kenya 5199 m (17,057 ft)
Kilimanjaro 5896 m (19,344 ft) (Highest point in Africa)
Mt. Meru 4565 m (14,977 ft)

Ascension (U.K.)

Scale

750 Miles
1,000 Kilometers
0 250 500 750
0 250 500

Coordinates

0° 10° 20° 30° 40° 50°
479

AUSTRALIA AND THE PACIFIC

UNITED STATES HISTORY

Chronology of Events

1492 **Christopher Columbus** and crew sighted land Oct. 12 in present-day Bahamas.

1513 **Juan Ponce de León** explored Florida coast.

1524 **Giovanni da Verrazano** led French expedition along coast from Carolina north to Nova Scotia; entered New York Harbor.

1526 San Miguel de Guadalupe, **first European settlement** in what became U.S. territory, was established in the summer off South Carolina coast; abandoned in Oct.

1539 **Hernando de Soto** landed in Florida May 28; crossed Mississippi River, 1541.

1540 **Francisco Vásquez de Coronado** explored Southwest north of Rio Grande. **Hernando de Alarcón** reached Colorado River; **García López de Cárdenas** reached Grand Canyon. Others explored California coast.

1562 **First French colony** in what became U.S. territory founded on Parris Island off South Carolina coast; abandoned, 1564.

1565 **St. Augustine, FL**, oldest continuously occupied European settlement in U.S., founded Sept. 8 by Pedro Menéndez de Avilés. Spain ceded settlement to U.S. in 1821.

1579 **Sir Francis Drake** entered San Francisco Bay and claimed region for Britain.

1585 **First English colony** in America, sponsored by Sir Walter Raleigh, founded on **Roanoke Island**, off North Carolina coast; colony failed.

1587 Second colony attempted on Roanoke Island. Virginia Dare of colony became **first English infant born** in the New World. Settlers of second colony found to have vanished, 1590.

1607 Capt. **John Smith** and 105 cavaliers in 3 ships landed on Virginia coast and started Jamestown, **first permanent English settlement** in New World.

1609 **Henry Hudson**, English explorer of Northwest Passage, employed by Dutch, sailed into New York Harbor in Sept. and up Hudson to Albany. **Samuel de Champlain** explored Lake Champlain, to the north. Spaniards settled **Santa Fe, NM**.

1619 House of Burgesses, **first representative assembly** in New World, elected July 30 at Jamestown, VA. **First black laborers**—indentured servants—in English North American colonies, brought by Dutch to Jamestown in Aug. Chattel slavery legally recognized, 1650.

1620 **Pilgrims**, Puritan separatists, left Plymouth, England, Sept. 16 on *Mayflower*; reached Cape Cod Nov. 19; 103 passengers landed at Plymouth, Dec. 26. **Mayflower Compact**, signed Nov. 11, was agreement to form a self-government. Half of colony died during harsh winter.

1620: Pilgrims and other colonists sign the Mayflower Compact to form a "civil body politic."

1624 Dutch settled in Albany and along Hudson River, establishing the colony of **New Netherland** in May.

1626 Peter Minuit bought **Manhattan** for Dutch West India Co. from Manahatta Indians during summer for goods valued at $24; named island **New Amsterdam**.

1630 Settlement of **Boston** established by Massachusetts colonists led by John Winthrop; Winthrop began *The History of New England*. **William Bradford**, a governor of Plymouth Colony, began his chronicle *History of Plymouth Plantation (1620-1647)*, first published in entirety in 1856.

1634 **Maryland** founded as Catholic colony under charter to Lord Baltimore. Act of Toleration passed 1649 provided for religious tolerance.

1635 Boston Latin School, **oldest public school** in continuous existence in U.S., founded Apr. 23.

1636 Roger Williams founded **Providence, RI**, in June, as a democratically ruled colony with separation of church and state. Charter granted, 1644. **Harvard College** founded; oldest institution of higher learning in U.S.

1640 **First book printed** in America, the so-called *Bay Psalm Book*.

1647 **Liberal constitution** drafted in Rhode Island. First law in America providing for **free compulsory basic education** enacted in Massachusetts.

1660 British Parliament passed first **Navigation Act** Dec. 1, regulating colonial commerce to suit English needs.

1661 Missionary John Eliot's translation of the New Testament into Algonquian became the **first Bible printed** in North America.

1664 British troops Sept. 8 seized New Netherland from Dutch. Charles II granted New Netherland and city of New Amsterdam to brother, Duke of York; both renamed **New York**. Dutch recaptured colony 1673 but ceded it to Britain Nov. 10, 1674.

1670 **Charles Town, SC**, founded by English colonists in Apr.

1673 **Regular mail service** on horseback instituted Jan. 1 between New York and Boston. **Jacques Marquette** and **Louis Jolliet** reached the upper Mississippi and traveled down it.

1674 Future **Salem witch trial** judge Samuel Sewall began renowned diary covering events through 1729.

1676 Bloody **Indian war** in New England ended Aug. 12. King Philip, Wampanoag chief, and Narragansett Indians killed. **Nathaniel Bacon** led planters against autocratic British Gov. Sir William Berkeley, burned Jamestown, VA, Sept. 19. Rebellion collapsed when Bacon died; 23 followers executed.

1678 A book of poetry by **Anne Bradstreet** (first published in Britain) revised and expanded for posthumous publication in Massachusetts. Considered first female poet in American colonies.

1679 Fire destroyed 150 houses in Boston. City imported **first fire engines** from England.

1681 John Bunyan's *The Pilgrim's Progress* published in America; became best seller.

1682 **René-Robert Cavelier, Sieur de La Salle**, claimed lower Mississippi River country for France and called it Louisiana Apr. 9. Had French outposts built in Illinois and Texas, 1684. Killed during mutiny, 1687. Spanish colonists became the **first Europeans to settle Texas**, at site of present-day El Paso.

1683 William Penn signed treaty with Delaware Indians Apr. 23 and made payment for **Pennsylvania** lands. The **first German colonists** in America settled near Philadelphia.

1689 New York's English colonial governor, **Sir Edmund Andros**, resigned after armed uprising in Boston on Apr. 18.

1690 **First colonial newspaper**, *Publick Occurrences*, published by Benjamin Harris but promptly shut down for lack of official permission. Harris also published *New England Primer* for use as elementary school textbook. Large-scale **whaling** operations began in Nantucket, MA.

1692 Hysteria over **witchcraft** began in Salem Village (now Danvers), MA; 19 women and 1 man were executed by special court.

1697 *The Essays* of **Sir Francis Bacon**, first published in England in 1597, was published in America; it became a best seller.

1699 Former privateer Capt. **William Kidd** arrested and sent to England; hanged for piracy, 1701. French settlements made in Mississippi, Louisiana.

1702 Legislation enacted making **Church of England** the established church in Maryland.

1704 Indians attacked **Deerfield**, MA, Feb. 28-29; killed 40, carried off 100. *Boston News Letter*, **first regular newspaper**, started by postmaster John Campbell.

1710 British-colonial troops captured French fort, Port Royal, Nova Scotia, in **Queen Anne's War**, 1702-13. France yielded Nova Scotia by treaty, 1713.

1712 **Slaves revolted** in New York Apr. 6; 21 were executed. Second uprising, 1741; 13 slaves hanged, 13 burned, 71 deported.

1716 **First theater** in colonies opened in Williamsburg, VA.

1726 **Great Awakening**, general revival of evangelical religion, began in colonies.

1731 America's **first circulating library** founded in Philadelphia by Benjamin Franklin.

1732 Benjamin Franklin published the **first** *Poor Richard's Almanack*; published annually until 1757. Georgia, last of 13 colonies, chartered.

1733 **Influenza epidemic** swept through New York City and Philadelphia.

1735 Editor **John Peter Zenger** was acquitted of libel Aug. 5 in New York after criticizing the British governor's conduct in office.

1739 A series of **slave uprisings** put down in South Carolina.

1741 Famous sermon "Sinners in the Hands of an Angry God," delivered July 8 at Enfield, MA, by Jonathan Edwards, one of the most important preachers in the **Great Awakening** religious revival. Danish navigator **Vitus Bering**, commanding Russian expedition, reached Alaska.

1744 **King George's War** pitted British and colonials versus French. Colonials captured Louisbourg, Cape Breton Isl., Nova Scotia, June 17, 1745. Returned to France 1748 by Treaty of Aix-la-Chapelle.

1752 **Benjamin Franklin**, flying kite in thunderstorm, proved lightning is electricity, June 15; invented lightning rod. **Liberty Bell**, cast in England, was delivered to Pennsylvania.

1754 **French and Indian War** began with Ft. Necessity campaign in Pennsylvania. Skirmish May 28, battle at fort July 3-4. British moved Acadian French from Nova Scotia to Louisiana Oct. 8, 1755. British captured Québec Sept. 18, 1759, in battles in which French Gen. Joseph de Montcalm and British Gen. James Wolfe were killed. Peace pact signed Feb. 10, 1763. French lost Canada and Midwest. Delegates from 7 colonies to New York for **Albany Congress**, July 19, approved plan of union by Benjamin Franklin; plan rejected by the colonies.

1757 **First streetlights** appeared in Philadelphia.

1764 **Sugar Act**, Apr. 5, placed duties on lumber, foodstuffs in colonies. First law passed by Parliament to specifically raise revenue from colonies, alleviate French and Indian War debts. British enforced this act, unlike with **Molasses Act** of 1733.

1765 **Stamp Act**, enacted by Parliament Mar. 22, required revenue stamps to help fund royal troops. Nine colonies, at Stamp Act Congress in New York Oct. 7-25, adopted Declaration of Rights. Stamp Act repealed Mar. 17, 1766. **Quartering Act**, requiring colonists to house British troops, went into effect Mar. 24.

1767 **Townshend Acts** levied taxes on glass, lead, paper, paint, and tea. In 1770 all duties except on tea were repealed.

1770 British troops fired Mar. 5 into Boston mob, killed 5 including **Crispus Attucks**, a black man, reportedly leader of group; later called **Boston Massacre**.

1773 East India Co. tea ships turned back at Boston, New York, and Philadelphia in May. Cargo ship burned at Annapolis, Oct. 14; cargo thrown overboard at **Boston Tea Party**, Dec. 16, to protest the tea tax. **First museum** in the colonies was officially established in Charleston, SC; later named the Charleston Museum.

1752: Benjamin Franklin's kite experiment proves that lightning is electricity.

1774 **"Intolerable Acts"** of Parliament curtailed Massachusetts self-rule; barred use of Boston Harbor until dumped tea was paid for. **First Continental Congress** held in Philadelphia Sept. 5-Oct. 26; called for civil disobedience against British. Rhode Island **abolished slavery**.

1775 **Patrick Henry** addressed Virginia convention, Mar. 23, said, "Give me liberty or give me death!" **Paul Revere**, **William Dawes**, and Dr. **Samuel Prescott**, Apr. 18, rode to alert patriots that British were on their way to Concord, MA, to destroy arms. At **Lexington**, MA, Apr. 19, Minutemen lost 8. On return from **Concord**, British suffered 273 casualties. Col. Ethan Allen (joined by Col. Benedict Arnold) captured **Ft. Ticonderoga** in New York, May 10, also Crown Point. Colonials headed for **Bunker Hill** and fortified nearby Breed's Hill, Charlestown, MA. Repulsed British under Gen. William Howe twice before retreating, June 17. Continental Congress June 15 named **George Washington** commander in chief; established a postal system, July 26. Benjamin Franklin became the **first postmaster general**.

1776 **Thomas Paine**'s *Common Sense*, famous pro-independence pamphlet, published Jan. 10; quickly sold some 100,000 copies. France and Spain agreed May 2 to provide arms to U.S. In Continental Congress June 7, Richard Henry Lee (VA) moved "that these united colonies are, and of right ought to be, free and independent states." Resolution adopted July 2. **Declaration of Independence** approved July 4, signed Aug. 2. Col. William Moultrie's batteries at **Charleston, SC**, repulsed British sea attack June 28. Washington lost **Battle of Long Island** Aug. 27; evacuated New York. **Nathan Hale** executed as spy by British Sept. 22. Brig. Gen. Arnold's **Lake Champlain** fleet was defeated at Valcour Oct. 11, but British returned to Canada. Howe failed to destroy Washington's army at White Plains, Oct. 28. Hessians captured Ft. Washington, Manhattan, and 3,000 men, Nov. 16; captured Ft. Lee, NJ, Nov. 20. Washington, in Pennsylvania, recrossed **Delaware River** Dec. 25-26, defeated Hessians at **Battle of Trenton**, NJ, Dec. 26.

1777 Washington defeated Lord Charles Cornwallis at **Princeton**, NJ, Jan. 3. Continental Congress, June 14, authorized an **American flag**, the Stars and Stripes. Maj. Gen. John Burgoyne's force of 8,000 from Canada captured **Ft. Ticonderoga**, NY, July 6. Americans beat back Burgoyne at Bemis Heights, Oct. 7, cut off British escape route. Burgoyne surrendered 5,000 men at Saratoga, NY, Oct. 17. **Articles of Confederation** adopted by Continental Congress, Nov. 15; took effect Mar. 1, 1781.

1776: George Washington's army crosses the Delaware River to defeat Hessian forces in the Battle of Trenton.

1778 **France signed treaty** of aid with U.S. Feb. 6; sent fleet. British evacuated Philadelphia, June 18.

1779 **George Rogers Clark** took Ft. Vincennes in what is now Indiana in Feb. **John Paul Jones** on the *Bonhomme Richard* defeated *Serapis* in British North Sea waters, Sept. 23.

1780 Charleston, SC, fell to the British May 12, but Loyalists were defeated in battle of **Kings Mountain**, NC, Oct. 7 in what Thomas Jefferson called "the turn of the tide of success." **Benedict Arnold** found to be a traitor Sept. 23. Arnold escaped, made brigadier general in British army.

1781 Bank of North America, **first commercial bank**, incorporated May 26. Cornwallis retired to **Yorktown, VA**. Adm. Francois Joseph de Grasse landed 3,000 French and stopped British fleet in **Hampton Roads**, VA. Washington and Jean Baptiste de Rochambeau joined forces, arrived near Williamsburg, Sept. 26. Siege of Cornwallis began, Oct. 6; **Cornwallis surrendered** Oct. 19.

1782 New British cabinet agreed in Mar. to **recognize U.S. independence**. Preliminary agreement signed in Paris, Nov. 30. Use of **scarlet letter A**, sewn on clothing or branded on skin of adulterers, discontinued in New England.

1783 Massachusetts Supreme Court decision in final Quock Walker trial **legally ended slavery**. Newspapers typically published weekly; **first regular daily newspaper**, *Pennsylvania Evening Post*, went on sale in Philadelphia, May 30. Britain, U.S. signed **Paris peace treaty**, Sept. 3, recognizing American independence; Congress ratified it Jan. 14, 1784. Washington ordered army disbanded Nov. 3, bade farewell to his officers at Fraunces Tavern, New York City, Dec. 4.

1784 Thomas Jefferson's proposal to **ban slavery in new territories** after 1802 was narrowly defeated, Mar. 1.

1785 Regular **stagecoach routes** established between Albany, New York City, and Philadelphia.

1786 Delegates from 5 states at Annapolis, MD, Sept. 11-14 asked Congress to call a **constitutional convention**.

1787 **Shays's Rebellion** of debt-ridden farmers in Massachusetts failed, Jan. 25. **Constitutional convention** opened in Philadelphia, May 25, with Washington presiding. Constitution accepted by delegates, Sept. 17. Delaware was first state to ratify it, Dec. 7; Pennsylvania and New Jersey followed. **Northwest Ordinance** adopted July 13 by Continental Congress for Northwest Territory, north of Ohio River, west of New York; made rules for statehood and guaranteed freedom of religion; support for schools, no slavery. *Federalist Papers* first appeared in *NY Independent Journal*.

1788 A large fire in **New Orleans**, then a Spanish territory, destroyed much of the city, Mar. 21. **Constitution adopted** June 21 after being ratified by the requisite ninth state (New Hampshire); also ratified by Georgia, Connecticut, Massachusetts, Maryland, South Carolina, Virginia, and New York throughout the year. **First U.S. senators elected** Sept. 30, from Pennsylvania.

1789 George Washington chosen president by all electors voting (73 eligible, 69 voting, 4 absent); **John Adams**, vice president, got 34 votes. **First Congress** met at Federal Hall, New York City, and declared Constitution in effect, Mar. 4; Washington inaugurated there Apr. 30; **first inaugural ball** held May 7. U.S. **State Dept.** established by Congress July 27. (Thomas Jefferson installed as first secretary of state Feb. 1790.) **War Dept.** created Aug. 7, with Henry Knox as secretary; **Treasury Dept.** created Sept. 2, with Alexander Hamilton to be secretary. **Supreme Court** created by Federal Judiciary Act, Sept. 24; **John Jay** confirmed by Congress as first Supreme Court chief justice, Sept. 26.

1790 **First Supreme Court session** held Feb. 2 in New York City. Congress, Mar. 1, authorized decennial **U.S. census**. Collection of data took 18 months. **Naturalization Act** (2-year residency) passed Mar. 26. John Carroll consecrated as **first American Catholic bishop**, Aug. 15. Congress met in **Philadelphia**, new temporary capital, Dec. 6.

1791 **Bill of Rights**, submitted to states, Sept. 25, 1789, went into effect Dec. 15. First Bank of the United States, **first bank chartered by federal government**, established in Philadelphia.

1792 Coinage Act established **U.S. Mint** in Philadelphia, Apr. 2. Gen. **"Mad" Anthony Wayne** made commander in Ohio-Indiana area, trained American Legion, established string of forts. Routed Indians at Fallen Timbers on Maumee River, Aug. 20, 1794; checked British at Fort Miami, OH, same year. **White House** cornerstone laid Oct. 13.

1793 Washington inaugurated for second term, Mar. 4, having received 132 electoral votes; **John Adams** again became vice president, having received second highest total, 77. Washington declared **U.S. neutrality**, Apr. 22, in war between Britain and France. Eli Whitney invented **cotton gin**, reviving Southern slavery.

1794 **Whiskey Rebellion**, western Pennsylvania farmers protesting liquor tax of 1791, suppressed by federal militia in Sept. **Jay's Treaty**, controversial treaty with Britain negotiated by John Jay, signed Nov. 19, ratified June 24, 1795. This treaty intended to settle long-standing differences between U.S. and Britain.

1795 U.S. bought peace from **Algerian pirates** by paying $1 mil ransom for 115 seamen Sept. 5, followed by annual tributes. Gen. Wayne signed **Treaty of Greenville** with Indians, opening Northwest Territory to settlers. Univ. of North Carolina became **first operating state university**.

1796 **Washington's farewell address** as president delivered Sept. 17. Warned against permanent alliances with foreign powers, big public debt, large military establishment, and devices of "small, artful, enterprising minority."

1797 **John Adams** inaugurated as second president Mar. 4, having received 71 electoral votes; **Thomas Jefferson** became vice president, having received 68. U.S. frigate *United States* launched at Philadelphia, July 10; *Constellation* at Baltimore, Sept. 7; *Constitution* (Old Ironsides) at Boston, Sept. 20.

1798 **Alien and Sedition Acts** passed by Federalists June-July; intended to silence political opposition. **War with France threatened** over French raids on U.S. shipping and rejection of U.S. diplomats. Navy (45 ships) and 365 privateers captured 84 French ships. USS *Constellation* took French warship *Insurgente*, 1799. Napoleon stopped French raids after becoming first consul.

1800 Federal government moved to **Washington, DC**.

1801 **John Marshall** named Supreme Court chief justice, Jan. 20. **Thomas Jefferson**, who had received same number of electoral votes as Aaron Burr in 1800 election, won out over Burr in House vote Feb. 17; Burr named vice president. **Tripoli declared war** June 10 against U.S., which refused added tribute to commerce-raiding Arab corsairs. Land and naval campaigns forced Tripoli to negotiate peace, June 4, 1805. **Oldest U.S. art institution**, Pennsylvania Academy of Fine Arts, founded in Philadelphia.

1802 Congress established U.S. Military Academy at **West Point**, NY.

1803 Supreme Court, in *Marbury v. Madison*, overturned U.S. law for first time, Feb. 24. Napoleon sold all of Louisiana, stretching to Canadian border, to U.S. for $11.25 mil in bonds, plus $3.75 mil indemnities to American citizens with claims against France. U.S. took title Dec. 20. **Louisiana Purchase** doubled U.S. area.

1804 Meriwether Lewis and **William Clark** expedition ordered by Pres. Thomas Jefferson to explore what is now Northwest U.S. Started from St. Louis May 14; ended Sept. 23, 1806, back in St. Louis. Vice Pres. **Aaron Burr** shot Alexander Hamilton in duel July 11 in Weehawken, NJ; Hamilton died next day.

1805 U.S. Marines aided by Arab mercenaries, Apr. 27, captured Tripolitan port of Derna. Major victory in war against **Barbary pirates**; inspiration for "to the shores of Tripoli" in Marines Corps hymn.

1807 Robert Fulton made **first practical steamboat trip**; left New York City Aug. 17 and reached Albany, 150 mi away, in 32 hrs. **Embargo Act** banned all trade with foreign countries, forbidding ships to set sail for foreign ports Dec. 22.

1808 Slave importation outlawed. Some 250,000 slaves were illegally imported 1808-60.

1810 Third U.S. Census found population of 7,239,814. The slave population was put at 1,191,364 and the population of all other non-white free persons at 186,446.

1811 Indiana Territory governor William Henry Harrison defeated Indians led by Tenskwatawa, called the Prophet, in **Battle of Tippecanoe**, Nov. 7. Construction began on **Cumberland Road** in Cumberland, MD; road became important route to West. About 400 **slaves revolted** in Louisiana, killing the son of a plantation owner and marching on New Orleans. The insurrection was suppressed; some 75 slaves killed.

1812 War of 1812 had 3 main causes: Britain seized U.S. ships trading with France; Britain had seized 4,000 naturalized U.S. sailors by 1810; Britain armed Indians, who raided Western border. U.S. stopped trade with Europe 1807 and 1809. Trade with Britain only was stopped 1810. Unaware that Britain had raised blockade against France two days before, **Congress declared war** June 18. British took **Detroit** Aug. 16.

1813 Oliver H. Perry defeated British fleet at **Battle of Lake Erie**, Sept. 10. U.S. won **Battle of the Thames**, Ontario, Oct. 5, but failed in Canadian invasion attempts. York (Toronto) and Buffalo, NY, were burned.

1814 Troops under Andrew Jackson defeated Creek Indians led by Chief Weatherford at Battle of Horseshoe Bend in Alabama, Mar. 29, ending **Creek Indian War**, begun a year earlier. British landed in Maryland in Aug., defeated U.S. force Aug. 24, **burned Capitol and White House**. Maryland militia stopped British advance, Sept. 12. British bombardment of Ft. McHenry, Baltimore, for 25 hrs., Sept. 13-14, failed, inspiring **Francis Scott Key** to write the words to **"The Star-Spangled Banner."** U.S. won naval **Battle of Lake Champlain** Sept. 11. Peace treaty with Great Britain signed at Ghent, Belgium, Dec. 24.

1815 Some 5,300 British, unaware of peace treaty, attacked U.S. entrenchments near **New Orleans**, Jan. 8. British had more than 2,000 casualties; Americans lost 71. U.S. flotilla finally ended attacks by **pirates** from Ottoman states of Algiers, Tunis, Tripoli.

1816 Second Bank of the U.S. chartered Apr. 10. The **American Colonization Society**, which sought to address slavery issue by transporting freed blacks to Africa, formed in Washington, DC, Dec. 1816-Jan. 1817.

1808: Laws outlawing slave importation go into effect, but an estimated 250,000 slaves are illegally imported, 1808-60.

1817 Thomas Hopkins Gallaudet established the **first free public school for the deaf** in Hartford, CT.

1818 Connecticut expanded **suffrage** among white male voters. Massachusetts followed suit in 1820, and New York in 1821, reducing or eliminating property qualifications.

1819 Spain ceded **Florida** to U.S. Feb. 22. American steamship *Savannah* made first part-steam-powered, part-sail-powered **crossing of Atlantic**, traveling from Savannah, GA, to Liverpool, England, in 29 days. **Washington Irving**'s *Sketch Book* became best seller.

1820 First organized immigration of blacks to Africa from U.S. began with 86 free blacks sailing to Sierra Leone in Feb. Henry Clay's **Missouri Compromise** bill passed by Congress, Mar. 3. Slavery was allowed in Missouri but not west of the Mississippi River, north of 36° 30´ (the southern line of Missouri). Compromise repealed 1854.

1821 Emma Willard founded Troy Female Seminary, **first U.S. women's college**. Stephen Austin established **first American community in Texas**, San Felipe de Austin. **James Fenimore Cooper**'s *The Spy*, novel set during American Revolution, published and became a best seller.

1822 Tension between sports and academics surfaced when Yale College Pres. Timothy Dwight banned a **primitive form of football**, setting fines for violators.

1823 Monroe Doctrine, opposing European intervention in the Americas, enunciated by Pres. James Monroe Dec. 2. The **Hudson River School**, painters who focused on the beauties of nature, began to receive public attention.

1824 Pawtucket, RI, **weavers strike**, first such action by women workers. **Slavery abolished** in state of Illinois Aug. 2.

1825 After a deadlocked election, **John Quincy Adams** was elected president by the House, Feb. 9. **Erie Canal** opened; first boat left Buffalo, NY, Oct. 26, reached New York City Nov. 4. John Stevens, of Hoboken, NJ, built and operated **first experimental steam locomotive** in U.S.

1826 Thomas Jefferson and **John Adams** both died July 4. **James Fenimore Cooper**'s *The Last of the Mohicans* published.

1827 Massachusetts became first state to pass a law providing for tax-supported **public high schools**.

1828 Baltimore & Ohio, the **first U.S. passenger railroad**, began operations July 4. South Carolina Dec. 19 declared right of **state nullification of federal laws**, opposing the "Tariff of Abominations." **Noah Webster** published his *American Dictionary of the English Language*.

1829 Andrew Jackson inaugurated as president, Mar. 4.

1830 Famous **debate** Jan. 27 between Sen. **Daniel Webster** (MA) and Robert Hayne (SC), on state right to nullify federal law. **Mormon church** organized by Joseph Smith in Fayette, NY, Apr. 6. Pres. Jackson, May 28, signed **Indian Removal Act**, granting president authority to negotiate treaties whereby Indians living east of Mississippi R. give up lands in exchange for lands in West.

1831 William Lloyd Garrison began **abolitionist newspaper** *The Liberator* Jan. 1. **Nat Turner**, black slave in Virginia, led local slave rebellion, starting Aug. 21; 57 whites killed. Troops called in, 100 slaves killed. Turner captured, tried, and hanged Nov. 11.

1832 Black Hawk War in Illinois and Wisconsin Apr.-Sept. pushed Sauk and Fox Indians west across Mississippi.

1833 American Anti-Slavery Society founded in Philadelphia, Dec. 4. **Oberlin College** became first to adopt coeducation in U.S.

1835 Liberty Bell cracked July 8 while tolling death of Chief Justice John Marshall. **Seminole Indians** in Florida under Osceola began attacks Nov. 1, protesting forced removal. The unpopular war ended Aug. 14, 1842; most of the Indians sent to Oklahoma. **Texas** proclaimed right to secede from Mexico; **Sam Houston** put in command of Texas army, Nov. 2-4. **Gold** discovered on Cherokee land in Georgia. Indians forced to cede lands, Dec. 20, and to cross Mississippi.

1836 Texans besieged at **Alamo** in San Antonio by Mexicans under Antonio López de Santa Anna, Feb. 23-Mar. 6; entire garrison killed. Texas independence had been declared, Mar. 2. At San Jacinto Apr. 21, Sam Houston and Texans defeated Mexicans. Ralph Waldo Emerson published his first work, *Nature*, espousing his philosophy of **transcendentalism**. Marcus Whitman, H. H. Spaulding, and wives reached

1838: Cherokee Indians are marched from their homes in southeast U.S. to present-day Oklahoma on the "Trail of Tears."

Fort Walla Walla on Columbia River, OR, **first white women to cross the Continental Divide**, in the Rocky Mountains.

1838 Cherokee Indians forced to walk **"Trail of Tears"** from southeast U.S. to area in present-day Oklahoma. At least 4,000—nearly one-fifth of Cherokee population—are estimated to have died.

1841 **First emigrant wagon train bound for California**, 47 people, left Independence, MO, May 1, reached California Nov. 4. Edgar Allan Poe published one of the **first American detective stories**, *The Murders in the Rue Morgue*.

1842 **Webster-Ashburton Treaty** signed Aug. 9, fixing U.S.-Canada border in Maine and Minnesota. **First use of anesthetic** (sulfuric ether gas) in an operation performed by Georgia doctor Crawford Long.

1843 More than 1,000 settlers left Independence, MO, for Oregon May 22, arriving in Oct. via **Oregon Trail**.

1844 **First message over first telegraph line** sent May 24 by inventor Samuel F. B. Morse from Washington to Baltimore: "What hath God wrought?"

1845 Congress **overrode a presidential veto for the first time**, Mar. 3, after Pres. John Tyler vetoed a tariff bill. Congress of **Texas** voted for annexation by U.S., July 4; Texas admitted to Union, Dec. 29. **Edgar Allan Poe**'s poem "The Raven" published.

1846 **Mexican War** began after Pres. James K. Polk ordered Gen. Zachary Taylor to seize disputed Texan land settled by Mexicans. After border clash, U.S. declared war May 13; Mexico declared war May 23. About 12,000 U.S. troops took Vera Cruz Mar. 27, 1847, and Mexico City Sept. 14, 1847. Treaty signed Feb. 2, 1848, ended war, and Mexico ceded claims to Texas, California, and other territory. Bear flag of **Republic of California** raised by American settlers at Sonoma, June 14. Treaty with Britain June 15 set **Oregon territory** boundary at 49th parallel (extension of existing line). Expansionists had used slogan "54° 40´ or fight." The term **"manifest destiny,"** coined by journalist in 1845, also came into play. **Mormons**, after violent clashes with settlers over polygamy, left Nauvoo, IL, for West under Brigham Young. They settled July 1847 at Salt Lake City, UT. Elias Howe invented **sewing machine**.

1847 **First adhesive U.S. postage stamps**—Benjamin Franklin 5¢, Washington 10¢—sold July 1. **Henry Wadsworth Longfellow**'s *Evangeline* published.

1848 **Gold discovered** Jan. 24 in California; 80,000 prospectors emigrated in 1849. Lucretia Mott and Elizabeth Cady Stanton led Seneca Falls, NY, **Women's Rights Convention** July 19-20.

1850 Sen. Henry Clay's **Compromise of 1850** admitted California as 31st state Sept. 9, with slavery forbidden; made Utah and New Mexico territories; made **Fugitive Slave Law** harsher; and ended District of Columbia slave trade. **Nathaniel Hawthorne**'s *The Scarlet Letter* published.

1851 **Herman Melville**'s *Moby-Dick* published.

1852 **Harriet Beecher Stowe**'s *Uncle Tom's Cabin* published.

1853 Japan receives Comm. Matthew C. Perry, July 14. He negotiated treaty to **open Japan** to U.S. ships. New York City hosted **first World's Fair** in the U.S., beginning July 14. **Stephen Foster** published "My Old Kentucky Home."

1854 **Republican Party** formed at Ripon, WI, Feb. 28. Opposed Kansas-Nebraska Act, which left issue of slavery to vote of settlers. Act became law May 30. Treaty ratified with Mexico Apr. 25, providing for **Gadsden Purchase** of a strip of land. **Henry David Thoreau**'s *Walden* published.

1855 **First railroad train crossed Mississippi River** on river's first bridge, between Rock Island, IL, and Davenport, IA, Apr. 21. **Walt Whitman**'s *Leaves of Grass* published.

1856 Proslavery group sacked **Lawrence, KS**, May 21; abolitionist John Brown led antislavery contingent against Missourians at Osawatomie, KS, Aug. 30. Antislavery Republican Party's **first presidential nominee**, John C. Frémont, defeated by James Buchanan. Abraham Lincoln made 50 speeches for Frémont. **First U.S. kindergarten** opened in Watertown, WI.

1857 In **Dred Scott** case, which involved determination of constitutionality of already-repealed Missouri Compromise, Supreme Court decided Mar. 6 that slaves did not become free in a free state, and blacks were not and could not be citizens. **Currier & Ives**, firm of American lithographers, issued their first print.

1858 **First Atlantic cable** completed, by Cyrus W. Field Aug. 5. **Lincoln-Douglas debates** in Illinois, Aug. 21-Oct. 15.

1859 Edwin L. Drake drilled the **first commercially productive oil well** near Titusville, PA, Aug. 27. Abolitionist John Brown, with 21 men, seized U.S. armory at **Harpers Ferry**, WV, Oct. 16. U.S. Marines captured raiders, killing several. Brown was hanged for treason Dec. 2.

1860 Shoeworkers in Lynn, MA, went on strike Feb. 22. Within a week, strike spread to include 20,000 shoeworkers throughout New England in country's **largest strike to date**. **First Pony Express** between Sacramento, CA, and St. Joseph, MO, started Apr. 3. Republican **Abraham Lincoln** elected president Nov. 6 in 4-way race.

1861 Seven southern states set up **Confederate States of America** Feb. 8, with **Jefferson Davis** as president. **Civil War** began as Confederates fired on **Ft. Sumter** in Charleston, SC, Apr. 12; they captured it Apr. 14. Pres. Lincoln called for 75,000 volunteers Apr. 15. Lincoln blockaded Southern ports Apr. 19, cutting off vital exports and aid. By May, 11 states had seceded. Confederates repelled Union forces at first **Battle of Bull Run**, July 21. **First transcontinental telegraph line** put in operation.

1862 Union forces were victorious in Western campaigns, took New Orleans May 1. Battles in East were largely inconclusive despite heavy casualties. The **Battle of Antietam**, in western Maryland Sept. 17, was bloodiest one-day battle of war; each side lost more than 2,000 men. **Homestead Act**, which granted free farms to settlers, approved May 20. **Land Grant Act**, which provided for public land sale to benefit agricultural education, approved July 7. It eventually led to establishment of state university systems.

1863 Pres. Lincoln issued **Emancipation Proclamation** Jan. 1, freeing "all slaves in areas still in rebellion." Union forces won major victory at Gettysburg, PA, July 1-3. Confederate forces under siege surrendered **Vicksburg, MS**, to Union forces under Gen. Ulysses S. Grant, July 4; control of Mississippi River in Union hands. About 1,000 were killed or wounded in **draft riots** in New York City; some blacks were hanged by mobs July 13-16. Pres. Lincoln gave his **Gettysburg Address** Nov. 19. Lincoln declared **Thanksgiving** a national holiday.

1864 Gen. **William Tecumseh Sherman** marched through Georgia, taking Atlanta Sept. 1 and Savannah Dec. 22. **Sand Creek massacre** of Cheyenne and Arapaho Indians Nov. 29. Soldiers drove Indians out of village; about 150 killed.

1865 Gen. **Robert E. Lee surrendered** 27,800 Confederate troops to Gen. Grant at Appomattox Court House in VA, Apr. 9. J. E. Johnston surrendered 31,200 to Sherman at Durham Station, NC, Apr. 18. Last rebel troops surrendered May 26. Pres. Lincoln shot Apr. 14 by **John Wilkes Booth** in Ford's Theater, Washington, DC; died the following morning. Vice Pres. **Andrew Johnson** was sworn in as president. Booth was hunted down and fatally wounded, perhaps by his own hand, Apr. 26. Four co-conspirators were hanged July 7. **13th Amendment**, abolishing slavery, ratified Dec. 6.

1866 Congress took control of Southern **Reconstruction**, backed freedmen's rights in legislation vetoed by Pres. Johnson; veto overridden by Congress, Apr. 9. **Ku Klux Klan** formed secretly in South to terrorize blacks who voted. Disbanded 1869-71.

1867 **Alaska** sold to U.S. by Russia for $7.2 mil Mar. 30, through efforts of Sec. of State William H. Seward. Fraternal

1863: Pres. Abraham Lincoln's Gettysburg Address eloquently commemorates the sacrifice of thousands in fewer than 300 words.

society the **Grange** was organized Dec. 4 to protect farmer interests. **Horatio Alger**'s *Ragged Dick* published.

1868 Pres. Johnson dismissed Sec. of War Edwin M. Stanton without Senate approval. **Johnson impeached** by the House Feb. 24 for violation of Tenure of Office Act, though charges were actually made in response to his opposition to congressional Reconstruction. He was acquitted by the Senate Mar.-May. **14th Amendment**, providing for citizenship of all persons born or naturalized in U.S. and subject to the jurisdiction thereof, ratified July 9. **Louisa May Alcott**'s *Little Women* published. *The World Almanac*, a publication of the *New York World* newspaper, appeared for first time.

1869 **Transcontinental railroad** completed; golden spike driven at Promontory Summit, UT, May 10, marking junction of Central Pacific and Union Pacific lines. Attempt to "corner" gold led to financial **"Black Friday"** in New York Sept. 24. **Woman suffrage law** passed in Wyoming Territory Dec. 10. **Knights of Labor** labor union formed in Philadelphia. By 1886, it had 700,000 members nationally.

1870 **15th Amendment**, making race no bar to voting rights, ratified Feb. 8. **First U.S. boardwalk** completed, in Atlantic City, NJ. **U.S. Weather Bureau** founded.

1871 **Great Chicago fire** destroyed city Oct. 8-11. **National Rifle Association (NRA)** founded.

1872 **Amnesty Act** May 22 restored civil rights to citizens of the South, except for 500 Confederate leaders. Congress established Yellowstone, **first national park**. James McNeill Whistler painted famous portrait known informally as **"Whistler's Mother."**

1873 **First U.S. postal card** issued May 1. **Jesse James** and his gang robbed their first passenger train July 21. Banks failed, panic began in Sept. **Depression** lasted 5 years. **"Boss" William Tweed** of New York City was convicted Nov. 19 of stealing public funds. He died in jail in 1878. New York's Bellevue Hospital started **first nursing school**.

1874 **Women's Christian Temperance Union** established in Cleveland. **First public zoo** in U.S. established in Philadelphia.

1875 Congress passed **Civil Rights Act** Mar. 1, giving equal rights to blacks in public accommodations and jury duty. Supreme Court invalidated act in 1883. First **Kentucky Derby** held May 17. First **Jim Crow segregation law** enacted, in Tennessee.

1876 Alexander Graham Bell patented the telephone Mar. 7. Col. **George A. Custer** and 264 soldiers of the 7th Cavalry were killed June 25 in "last stand," **Battle of the Little Bighorn**, MT, in Sioux Indian War. Democrat **Samuel J. Tilden** received majority of popular vote for president over Republican **Rutherford B. Hayes**, Nov. 7, but 22 electoral votes were in dispute. Congress agreed to certify Hayes as winner in Feb. 1877 after Republicans agreed to end federal Reconstruction of South.

1877 **Molly Maguires**—Irish terrorist society in mining areas of Scranton, PA—was broken up by hanging, June 21, of 11 leaders for murders of mine officials and police. Pres. Rutherford B. Hayes sent federal troops to control violent national **railroad strike**, which began in July.

1878 **First commercial telephone exchange** opened, New Haven, CT, Jan. 28. **Thomas A. Edison** founded Edison Electric Light Co. on Oct. 15.

1879 **F. W. Woolworth** opened his first five-and-ten store, in Utica, NY, Feb. 22. French actress **Sarah Bernhardt** made her U.S. debut Nov. 8 at New York City's Booth Theater. Economist and social philosopher **Henry George** published *Progress & Poverty*, advocating single tax on land.

1881 **Clara Barton** founded **American Red Cross** May 21. Pres. **James A. Garfield** shot in Washington, DC, July 2; died Sept. 19. Famous gun battle between the Earp brothers and outlaw rustlers Oct. 26 near the **OK Corral**, Tombstone, AZ. **Booker T. Washington** founded Tuskegee Institute for blacks. **Helen Hunt Jackson**'s *A Century of Dishonor*, about mistreatment of Indians, published.

1882 **Chinese Exclusion Act**, barring immigration of Chinese laborers for 10 years, later made permanent, passed by Congress May 6; prohibited naturalization of Chinese resident aliens.

1883 Civil Service Act, or **Pendleton Act**, passed Jan. 16, created foundations of American civil service system. The **Brooklyn Bridge** opened May 24 as world's longest suspension bridge. Transcontinental **Northern Pacific Railroad** was completed Sept. 8. **Buffalo Bill Cody**'s Wild West Show began its 30-year touring run.

1884 **First long-distance telephone call** completed, Mar. 27, between Boston and New York. Switchback Railway—**first U.S. roller coaster** built as amusement park ride—opened at Coney Island in New York City. **Mark Twain**'s *The Adventures of Huckleberry Finn* published.

1885 **Washington Monument** dedicated Feb. 21.

1886 **Haymarket riot** and bombing, May 4, followed labor battles for 8-hr. work day in Chicago; 7 police and 4 workers died. Eight anarchists found guilty Aug. 20; 4 hanged Nov. 11. **Coca-Cola** first sold, May 8, at Jacob's Pharmacy in Atlanta. Apache Indian **Geronimo** surrendered Sept. 4, ending last major Indian war. **Statue of Liberty** dedicated Oct. 28. **American Federation of Labor** (AFL) formed Dec. 8 by 25 craft unions.

1887 **Interstate Commerce Act** enacted Feb. 4, created Interstate Commerce Commission.

1888 **Great blizzard** struck Eastern U.S. Mar. 11-14, causing about 400 deaths. Ernest Thayer's poem **"Casey at the Bat"** recited for first time in public at New York City theater in May.

1889 U.S. opened 2-mil acre **Oklahoma District** to settlement Apr. 22, initiating land run; "sooner" settlers illegally entered the territory before that date to stake favorable claims. More than 2,200 lives lost in **Johnstown flood** (PA) May 31. **Electric lights** installed at White House.

1890 **Sherman Antitrust Act** passed July 2, began federal effort to curb monopolies. Massacre at **Wounded Knee**, SD, Dec. 29, the last major conflict between Indians and U.S. troops; about 200 Indian men, women, and children and 29 soldiers were killed. **Jacob Riis**'s *How the Other Half Lives*, about city slums, published, instigating reform legislation in New York City. **Emily Dickinson**'s poems published, 4 years after her death.

1891 **Forest Reserve Act**, Mar. 3, let president close public forest land to settlement for establishment of national parks. **Carnegie Hall**, in New York City, opened May 5.

1892 **Ellis Island**, in New York Bay, opened Jan. 1 to receive immigrants; closed 1954. **Homestead strike** (PA) at Carnegie steel mills; 7 guards and 11 strikers and spectators shot to death July 6. James J. Corbett defeated John L. Sullivan Sept. 7 to become **first world heavyweight champion** under Marquess of Queensbury rules.

1893 **Columbian Exposition** world's fair held May-Oct. in Chicago. Financial panic led to 4-year **depression**. **Mormon Temple** dedicated in Salt Lake City, UT.

1894 Thomas A. Edison's **kinetoscope**, for motion pictures (invented 1887), given first public showing Apr. 14. **Jacob S. Coxey** led army of unemployed from the Midwest, reaching Washington, DC, Apr. 30. Coxey arrested May 1 for trespassing on Capitol grounds; his army disbanded. **Pullman strike**

1892: Ellis Island immigration station opens; it would process more than 12 million immigrants before closing in 1954.

began May 11 at railroad car plant in Chicago. Milton Hershey started **Hershey Chocolate Company**.

1895 **"America, the Beautiful"** appeared for first time, in church publication, July 4. **Stephen Crane**'s *The Red Badge of Courage* published.

1896 Supreme Court, in *Plessy v. Ferguson*, May 18, approved racial segregation under the **"separate but equal"** doctrine. **William Jennings Bryan** delivered "Cross of Gold" speech July 9; won Democratic Party nomination. **John Philip Sousa** composed "Stars and Stripes Forever" on Dec. 25.

1897 **Olney-Pauncefote Treaty** with Britain, Jan. 11, gave wide scope to arbitration in settling disputes; never ratified by U.S. John J. McDermott won **first Boston Marathon** Apr. 19. First Klondike gold arrived in San Francisco July 14, helping set off **Klondike gold rush**. **First subway service** in country opens to public in Boston, Sept. 1.

1898 U.S. battleship *Maine* blown up Feb. 15 in Havana, Cuba; 260 killed. U.S. blockaded Cuba Apr. 22 in aid of independence forces. U.S. declared **war on Spain** Apr. 24; destroyed Spanish fleet in Philippines May 1; took Guam June 20. U.S. took **Puerto Rico** July 25-Aug. 12. Spain agreed Dec. 10 to cede Philippines, Puerto Rico, and Guam, and approved independence for Cuba. Annexation of **Hawaii** signed by Pres. William McKinley, July 7.

1899 Filipino insurgents, unable to get recognition of independence from U.S., started guerrilla war Feb. 4. Their leader, Emilio Aguinaldo, captured May 23, 1901. **Philippine insurrection** ended 1902. Killed were 20,000 Filipino troops and some 200,000 civilians, mostly from disease and starvation. Pres. McKinley signed treaty officially ending **Spanish-American War**, Feb. 10. U.S. declared **Open Door Policy** Sept. 6, to make China an open international market. Philosopher **John Dewey**'s *School and Society*, advocating progressive education ("learn by doing"), published. Pianist Scott Joplin's "Maple Leaf Rag" published, popularizing **ragtime music**.

1900 **International Ladies' Garment Workers Union** founded in New York City June 3. Fought sweatshop working conditions. **Carry Nation**, Kansas temperance leader, began raiding saloons with a hatchet. U.S. helped suppress **Boxer Rebellion** in Beijing, China. Eastman Kodak Co. introduced the **Brownie camera**, popularizing picture-taking.

1901 Texas had first significant oil strike at **Spindletop** well near Beaumont, Jan. 10. U.S. withdrew troops from **Cuba** May 20, and Cuba became independent. Pres. **McKinley** shot Sept. 6 in Buffalo, NY, by anarchist Leon Czolgosz; died Sept. 14. Vice Pres. **Theodore Roosevelt** sworn in as youngest-ever president, at age 42 years, 11 months. **Booker T. Washington**'s *Up From Slavery* published.

1902 Permanent **Bureau of the Census** established Mar. 6. **Helen Keller** autobiography appeared in serial form.

1903 Treaty between U.S. and Colombia to have U.S. dig **Panama Canal** signed Jan. 22, rejected by Colombia. Panama declared independence from Colombia with U.S. support Nov. 3; recognized by Pres. Roosevelt Nov. 6. U.S., Panama signed canal treaty Nov. 18. Wisconsin set first **direct primary voting system**, May 23. **Henry Ford** founded Ford Motor Co., June 16. Boston defeated Pittsburgh, 5 games to 3, Oct. 13 in **first modern World Series**. **First successful flight** in heavier-than-air mechanically propelled airplane by **Orville Wright** Dec. 17 near Kitty Hawk, NC, 120 ft in 12 secs. Later flight same day by **Wilbur Wright**, 852 ft in 59 secs. Improved plane patented, 1906. **Iroquois Theater fire** in Chicago killed about 600 out of 1,900 in audience, Dec. 30. Pioneering film *Great Train Robbery* produced.

1904 St. Louis hosted **first Olympics in U.S.**, July 1-Nov. 23. First section of **New York subway** system opened, Oct. 27. **Ida Tarbell** published muckraking *The History of the Standard Oil Company*. **Henry James**'s last major novel, *The Golden Bowl*, published.

1905 **Industrial Workers of the World**, which advocated Marxian theory of class struggle between workers and capitalists, founded in Chicago, June 27. **Rotary**, oldest service club organization in U.S., founded in Chicago.

1906 **San Francisco earthquake** and fire, Apr. 18-19, caused more than 3,000 deaths and $400 mil in damages. **Upton Sinclair**'s *The Jungle*, which exposed working conditions in meat-packing industry, published. Helped spur passage of the **Pure Food and Drug Act** and **Meat Inspection Act** June 30.

1907 Financial panic and **depression** started Mar. 13. Pres. Roosevelt sent **"Great White Fleet"** of 16 U.S. battleships around the world in show of power.

1908 Springfield, IL, torn by **anti-black rioting**, Aug. 14-15. Henry Ford introduced **Model T** car, priced at $850, Oct. 1.

1909 Adm. Robert E. Peary claimed to have reached **North Pole** Apr. 6 on sixth attempt, accompanied by black explorer Matthew Henson and 4 Inuit; may have fallen short. National Conference on the Negro convened May 30, leading to founding of **National Association for the Advancement of Colored People** (NAACP).

1910 **Boy Scouts** of America founded Feb. 8. Former Pres. Roosevelt called for **"new nationalism"** in famous speech in Kansas, Aug. 10.

1911 Building with New York City's **Triangle Shirtwaist Co.** factory caught fire Mar. 25; 146 died. Supreme Court ruled May 15 that **Standard Oil Co.** must be dissolved because it unreasonably restrained trade. **First transcontinental airplane flight** (with numerous stops) by C. P. Rodgers, from New York to Pasadena, CA, Sept. 17-Nov. 5; time in air 82 hrs., 4 mins.

1912 American Girl Guides founded Mar. 12; name changed in 1913 to **Girl Scouts**. U.S. Marines, Aug. 14, sent to **Nicaragua**, which was in default of loans to U.S. and Europe.

1913 **16th Amendment**, authorizing federal income tax, ratified Feb. 3. The **Armory Show** in New York City brought modern art to U.S. for first time, Feb. 17. **17th Amendment**, providing for direct popular election of U.S. senators, ratified Apr. 8. **Federal Reserve System** authorized Dec. 23, in major reform of U.S. banking and finance.

1914 Ford Motor Co. raised basic wage rates from $2.40 for 9-hr. day to $5 for 8-hr. day, Jan. 5, increasing stability in labor force. When U.S. sailors were arrested in Tampico, Mexico, Apr. 9, Atlantic fleet was sent to **Veracruz**, occupied city. Pres. Woodrow Wilson proclaimed **U.S. neutrality** in the European war, Aug. 4. The **Panama Canal** officially opened Aug. 15. The **Clayton Antitrust Act** passed Oct. 15, strengthening federal antimonopoly powers.

1915 **First transcontinental telephone call**, New York to San Francisco, completed Jan. 25 by Alexander Graham Bell and Thomas A. Watson. British ship *Lusitania* sunk May 7 by German submarine; 1,198 passengers died, including 128 Americans. (In notice in morning newspapers the day *Lusitania* set sail, Germany had warned Americans against taking passage on British vessels.) As result of U.S. campaign, Germany issued apology and promise of payments, Oct. 5. U.S. troops landed in **Haiti**, July 28. Haiti became virtual U.S. protectorate under Sept. 16 treaty. Pres. Wilson asked for a military fund increase, Dec. 7. D. W. Griffith's film *The Birth of a Nation* released. William J. Simmons partly inspired by film to revive **Ku Klux Klan**, which peaks in 1920s.

1916 Gen. **John J. Pershing** entered Mexico in Mar. to pursue **Francisco (Pancho) Villa**, who had raided U.S. border areas. Forces withdrew Feb. 5, 1917. **Rural Credits Acts** passed July 17, followed by **Warehouse Act** Aug. 11; both provided financial aid to farmers. Bomb exploded during **San Francisco Preparedness Day parade** July 22, killed 10. Thomas J. Mooney, labor organizer, and Warren K. Billings, shoeworker, convicted 1917; both later pardoned. U.S. bought **Virgin Islands** from Denmark Aug. 4. U.S. established military government in the **Dominican Republic** Nov. 29. Jeannette Rankin (R, MT) elected to House of Representatives, **first female member of Congress.**

1917 Germany, suffering from British blockade, declared almost unrestricted **submarine warfare** Jan. 31. U.S. cut diplomatic ties with Germany Feb. 3 and formally **declared war** Apr. 6. Jones Act, passed Mar. 2, made **Puerto Rico** a U.S. territory, its inhabitants U.S. citizens. **Conscription law** passed May 18. First U.S. troops arrived in Europe June 26.

1918 Pres. Wilson set out his **14 Points** as basis for peace, Jan. 8. More than 1 mil American troops were in Europe by July. Allied counteroffensive launched at Château-Thierry July 18. War ended with signing of **armistice** Nov. 11. **Influenza epidemic** killed an estimated 20 mil worldwide, 548,000 in U.S.

1919 18th Amendment, providing for prohibition of manufacture, sale, or transportation of alcoholic beverages, ratified Jan. 16, to take effect on Jan. 16, 1920. **First transatlantic flight**, by U.S. Navy seaplane, left Rockaway, NY, May 8; stopped at Newfoundland, Azores, Lisbon May 27. **Boston police strike** Sept. 9, earliest strike conducted by government employees. About 250 **foreign-born radicals** deported Dec. 21 to Soviet Union. **Sherwood Anderson**'s *Winesburg, Ohio* published.

1920 In national **Red Scare**, some 2,700 Communists, anarchists, and other radicals were arrested Jan.-May. **League of Women Voters** founded Feb. 14. Senate refused Mar. 19 to ratify **League of Nations Covenant**. Nicola Sacco and **Bartolomeo Vanzetti** accused of killing 2 men in Massachusetts payroll holdup Apr. 15; found guilty 1921. A 7-year campaign for their release failed; both executed Aug. 23, 1927. Verdict repudiated 1977 by proclamation of Massachusetts Gov. Michael Dukakis. **19th Amendment** ratified Aug. 18, giving women the vote. **First regular licensed radio broadcasting** began Aug. 20. **Wall St. bombing** in New York City killed 30, injured 100, did $2 mil damage, Sept. 16. **Sinclair Lewis**'s *Main Street*, **F. Scott Fitzgerald**'s *This Side of Paradise*, and **Edith Wharton**'s *The Age of Innocence* published.

1921 Congress sharply curbed immigration, set **national quota system** May 19. Joint congressional resolution declaring **peace with Germany, Austria, and Hungary** signed July 2 by Pres. Warren G. Harding; treaties were signed in Aug. In so-called **Black Sox scandal**, 8 Chicago White Sox players were banned from baseball Aug. 4 for conspiring with gamblers to throw the 1919 World Series. Limitation of Armaments Conference met in Washington, DC, Nov. 12-Feb. 6, 1922. Major powers agreed to curtail naval construction, outlaw poison gas, restrict submarine attacks on merchant vessels, and respect China's integrity.

1922 During nationwide coal strike, union miners killed some 21 strikebreakers at Herrin, IL, June 21-22, in incident referred to as the **Herrin Massacre**. **T. S. Eliot**'s *The Waste Land* published in London.

1923 First sound-on-film motion picture, *Phonofilm*, shown at Rivoli Theater, New York City, beginning in Apr. Pres. Calvin Coolidge addressed Congress, Dec. 6; **first radio broadcast of president's annual speech.**

1924 Law approved by Congress June 15 made all **Native Americans U.S. citizens**. **Nellie Tayloe Ross** elected governor of Wyoming, and **Miriam (Ma) Ferguson** elected governor of Texas Nov. 9. Ross inaugurated as nation's **first female governor** Jan. 5, 1925. Ferguson installed Jan. 20, 1925. **George Gershwin** wrote "Rhapsody in Blue."

1925 John T. Scopes found guilty of having taught **evolution** in Dayton, TN, high school, fined $100 and costs, July 24. **F. Scott Fitzgerald**'s *The Great Gatsby* published.

1926 Dr. Robert H. Goddard, Mar. 16, demonstrated **first liquid-fuel rocket**. Congress established **Army Air Corps** July 2. **Air Commerce Act** passed Nov. 2, established government agencies for development of airports, radio navigation, and other services. **Ernest Hemingway**'s *The Sun Also Rises* published.

1927 Capt. **Charles A. Lindbergh** left Roosevelt Field, NY, May 20 alone in *Spirit of St. Louis* on first New York-Paris nonstop flight. Reached Le Bourget airfield May 21, 3,610 mi. in 33½ hrs. *The Jazz Singer*, **first feature-length film** in which **spoken dialogue was part of narrative action**, released Oct. 6. *Show Boat*, Jerome Kern and Oscar Hammerstein II's adaptation of Edna Ferber's novel, opened in New York Dec. 27. Considered musical with first serious libretto.

1928 Amelia Earhart became first woman to fly across the Atlantic, June 17. **Herbert Hoover** elected president Nov. 6, defeating New York Gov. Alfred E. Smith, a Catholic.

1929 Gangsters killed 7 rivals in Chicago **St. Valentine's Day massacre** Feb. 14, which won Al Capone control of Chicago's underworld. Stock market crash Oct. 29 marked end of past prosperity as stock prices plummeted. Stock losses for 1929-31 estimated at $50 bil; beginning of **Great Depression**. Albert B. Fall, former interior sec., was convicted of accepting $10,000 bribe in leasing of the **Elk Hills (Teapot Dome)** naval oil reserve; sentenced Nov. 1 to a year in prison and fined. **Thomas Wolfe**'s *Look Homeward, Angel* and **William Faulkner**'s *The Sound and the Fury* published.

1930 London **Naval Reduction Treaty** signed by U.S., Britain, Italy, France, and Japan Apr. 22; in effect Jan. 1, 1931; expired Dec. 31, 1936. **Hawley-Smoot Tariff** signed; rate hikes slash world trade. **Sinclair Lewis** became first American to win a Nobel Prize in literature. **Dashiell Hammett**'s *The Maltese Falcon* published.

1931 Empire State Building opened in New York City May 1, displacing NYC's Chrysler Building as world's tallest. **Al Capone** convicted of tax evasion Oct. 17. **Pearl Buck**'s *The Good Earth* published. **Charlie Chaplin** film *City Lights* released.

1932 Reconstruction Finance Corp. established Jan. 22 to stimulate banking and business. Unemployment at 12 mil. Twenty-month-old **Charles Lindbergh Jr.** kidnapped Mar. 1; found dead May 12. Bruno Hauptmann found guilty Feb. 1935; executed Apr. 3, 1936. Unemployed World War I veterans demanding Congress pay promised bonus early launched **Bonus March** on Washington, DC, May 29. **Franklin D. Roosevelt** elected president for first time in Democratic

1927: Flying the *Spirit of St. Louis*, Charles A. Lindbergh becomes the first pilot ever to make a solo, nonstop, transatlantic flight.

landslide, Nov. 8. Chicago Bears won **first NFL title game** Dec. 18, defeating the Portsmouth (OH) Spartans, 9-0.
1933 Pres. Roosevelt named **Frances Perkins** U.S. sec. of labor; **first woman in U.S. cabinet.** Pres. Roosevelt ordered **all U.S. banks closed** Mar. 6. In a "100 days" special session, Mar. 9-June 16, Congress passed **New Deal**, including measures to regulate banks, distribute funds to the jobless, create jobs, raise agricultural prices, and set wage and production standards for industry. **Gold standard** dropped by U.S. in favor of "modified gold bullion standard"; announced by Pres. Roosevelt Apr. 19, ratified by Congress June 5. **Tennessee Valley Authority (TVA)** created by act of Congress, May 18. **Prohibition** ended in the U.S. as 36th state ratified **21st Amendment** Dec. 5. Pres. Roosevelt foreswore armed intervention in **Western Hemisphere** nations, Dec. 26.
1934 Pres. Roosevelt signed law creating **Securities and Exchange Commission**, June 6. U.S. troops pulled out of **Haiti**, Aug. 6.
1935 Works Progress Administration (WPA) instituted May 6. Rural Electrification Administration created May 11. National Industrial Recovery Act struck down by Supreme Court May 27. **Boulder Dam** (later renamed **Hoover Dam**) completed, May 29. **Social Security Act** passed by Congress Aug. 8-9. Comedian **Will Rogers** and aviator Wiley Post killed Aug. 15 in Alaska plane crash. **Huey Long**, Louisiana senator and national political leader, shot Sept. 8; died Sept. 10. George Gershwin's jazz opera *Porgy and Bess* opened Oct. 10 in New York. **Committee for Industrial Organization** (later Congress of Industrial Organizations) formed to expand industrial unionism Nov. 9.
1936 Jesse Owens won 4 gold medals at the **Berlin Olympics** in Aug. **Baseball Hall of Fame** founded in Cooperstown, NY. **Margaret Mitchell**'s *Gone With the Wind* published.
1937 Airship *Hindenburg* caught fire May 6 as it was landing in Lakehurst, NJ; 36 killed. **Golden Gate Bridge** opened May 27. **Joe Louis** knocked out James J. Braddock to become world heavyweight champ June 22. Aviator **Amelia Earhart** and copilot Fred Noonan disappeared July 2 near Howland Isl., in the Pacific. Pres. Roosevelt proposed judicial reforms that would allow him to appoint additional Supreme Court justices; his **"court-packing" plan** defeated. **Auto, steel labor unions** won first big contracts.
1938 National minimum wage enacted June 25. Orson Welles's radio dramatization of H. G. Wells's *War of the Worlds*, Oct. 30, caused Martian invasion scare. **Seabiscuit** beat War Admiral in match race of the century, at Pimlico track, MD, Nov. 1. Artist Anna Mary Robertson, **"Grandma Moses,"** discovered. **Thornton Wilder**'s *Our Town* produced on Broadway.
1939 Opera singer **Marian Anderson** performed for integrated crowd of 75,000 at Lincoln Memorial Apr. 9 after Daughters of the American Revolution refused to let Anderson sing in DC's Constitution Hall. **New York World's Fair**—theme: "The World of Tomorrow"—opened Apr. 30, closed Oct. 31. Reopened for second season May 11-Oct. 27, 1940. **Lou Gehrig**, seriously ill, said farewell to fans at Yankee Stadium, July 4. Albert Einstein alerted Pres. Roosevelt to **A-bomb possibilities** in Aug. 2 letter. **U.S. declared its neutrality** in European war Sept. 5. Pres. Roosevelt proclaimed limited **national emergency** Sept. 8, unlimited emergency May 27, 1941. Both ended by Pres. Harry Truman, Apr. 28, 1952. Pocket Books, **first paperback publisher** in U.S., established. **John Steinbeck**'s *The Grapes of Wrath* published. Film versions of *Gone With the Wind*—which went on to win a then-record 8 Academy Awards—and *The Wizard of Oz* released.
1940 U.S. OK'd sale of **surplus war material** to Britain June 3; announced transfer of 50 overaged destroyers Sept. 3. **First peacetime military draft** in U.S. history approved, Sept. 14. **Forty-hour work week** went into effect, Oct. 24. Pres. **Roosevelt** elected Nov. 5 to third presidential term. **Carson McCullers**'s *The Heart Is a Lonely Hunter* and **Richard Wright**'s *Native Son* published.
1941 Four Freedoms—freedom of speech and religion, freedom from want and fear—termed essential by Pres. Roosevelt in speech to Congress Jan. 6. **Lend-Lease Act** signed Mar. 11 provided $7 bil in military credits for Britain. Lend-lease for USSR approved in Nov. Pres. Roosevelt signed executive order June 25 barring federal government and war contractors from **racial discrimination**. Order also established Fair Employment Practice Committee. The **Atlantic Charter**, 8-point declaration of principles, issued by Pres. Roosevelt and British Prime Min. Winston Churchill, Aug. 14. Japan attacked **Pearl Harbor**, Hawaii, 7:55 AM Hawaiian time, Dec. 7; 19 ships sunk or damaged, 2,300 dead. Pres. Roosevelt called it "a date which will live in infamy." U.S. declared war on Japan Dec. 8. Germany and Italy declared war on U.S. Dec. 11. U.S. responded with declaration of war later on same day. Japanese invaded **Philippines**, Dec. 22; Wake Island fell, Dec. 23. *Citizen Kane*, directed by Orson Welles, released.
1942 Pres. Roosevelt issued executive order Feb. 19 authorizing relocation of Japanese-Americans. Federal government began forcibly moving 110,000 Japanese-Americans from West Coast to **detention camps**; exclusion lasted 3 years. Japanese troops took **Bataan** peninsula Apr. 8 and **Corregidor** May 6. **Battle of Midway** June 4-7 was Japan's first major defeat. Marines landed on **Guadalcanal** Aug. 7; last Japanese not expelled until Feb. 9, 1943. U.S., Britain invaded **North Africa** Nov. 8. **First nuclear chain reaction** (fission of uranium isotope U-235) produced at Univ. of Chicago under physicists Arthur Compton, Enrico Fermi, others, Dec. 2. The movie *Casablanca*, starring Humphrey Bogart and Ingrid Bergman, released.
1943 *Oklahoma!* opened Mar. 31 on Broadway. Pres. Roosevelt signed June 10 pay-as-you-go income tax bill. Starting July 1, wage and salary earners were subject to **paycheck withholding tax**. **Detroit race riot** June 21 left 34 dead, 700 injured. Six killed in riot in New York City's **Harlem** section Aug. 2. U.S., Britain invaded **Sicily** July 9, Italian **mainland** Sept. 3. Marines in Nov. recaptured the **Gilbert Islands**, captured by Japan in 1941 and 1942.
1944 U.S., Allied forces invaded Europe at Normandy, France, on **"D Day,"** June 6, in greatest amphibious landing in history. **GI Bill of Rights**, providing benefits to veterans, signed by Pres. Roosevelt June 22. Representatives of the U.S. and other major powers met at **Dumbarton Oaks**, Washington, DC, Aug. 21-Oct. 7, to work out formation of postwar world organization that would become the **United Nations**. U.S. forces landed on **Leyte**, Philippines, Oct. 20.

1936: Jesse Owens wins four gold medals at the Olympic Games in Berlin, Germany, but is not acknowledged by German Chancellor Adolf Hitler nor officially by the U.S. government.

1941: The U.S. enters World War II with 12 million women in the workforce and adds more than 6 million to that figure by 1945; 3 million women work in war-related factories.

Pres. **Roosevelt** elected to fourth term as president Nov. 7. **Battle of the Bulge**, failed Nazi counteroffensive, waged Dec. 16 to Jan. 28, 1945.
1945 Yalta Conference met in the Crimea, USSR, Feb. 4-11. Pres. Roosevelt, Prime Min. Churchill, and Soviet leader Joseph Stalin agreed that their 3 countries, plus France, would occupy Germany and that the Soviet Union would enter war against Japan. Marines landed on **Iwo Jima** Feb. 19, won control Mar. 16 after heavy casualties. U.S. forces invaded **Okinawa** Apr. 1, captured it June 21. Pres. **Roosevelt** died in Warm Springs, GA, Apr. 12; Vice Pres. **Harry S. Truman** became president. Germany surrendered May 7; May 8 proclaimed **V-E Day**. **First atomic bomb**, produced at Los Alamos, NM, exploded at Alamogordo, NM, July 16. Bomb dropped on **Hiroshima**, Japan, Aug. 6, killing about 75,000; bomb dropped on **Nagasaki**, Japan, Aug. 9, killing about 40,000. Japan agreed to surrender Aug. 14; formally surrendered Sept. 2. At **Potsdam Conference**, July 17-Aug. 2, leaders of U.S., USSR, and Britain agreed on disarmament of Germany, occupation zones, war crimes trials. **Empire State Building** struck accidentally by Army B-25 bomber, July 28, killing 14. U.S. forces entered **Korea** south of 38th parallel to displace Japanese Sept. 8. Gen. **Douglas MacArthur** took over supervision of Japan Sept. 9.
1946 Steel strike by 750,000 started Jan. 21, settled in 4 weeks. Strike by 400,000 **mine workers** began Apr. 1 (settled May 29); other industries (including rail, maritime) followed. Former Prime Min. Winston Churchill employed the phrase **"Iron Curtain"** in Mar. 5 speech at Westminster College in Fulton, MO. Atomic bomb tested off **Bikini Atoll** in Pacific, July 1. In all, U.S. conducted 23 nuclear tests between 1946 and 1958. **Philippines** given independence by U.S. July 4. Mother Frances Xavier Cabrini **first American to be canonized**, July 7. Dr. Benjamin Spock's *Baby and Child Care* published as **baby boom** began.
1947 Pres. Truman asked Congress for financial and military aid for Greece and Turkey to help combat Communist subversion, Mar. 12; **Truman Doctrine** approved May 15. UN Security Council voted Apr. 2 to place under U.S. trusteeship the **Pacific islands** formerly mandated to Japan. **Jackie Robinson** joined Brooklyn Dodgers Apr. 11, breaking color barrier in major league baseball. The **Marshall Plan** for U.S. aid to European countries proposed by Sec. of State George C. Marshall June 5. Congress authorized some $12 bil in next 4 years. **Taft-Hartley Labor Act** restricting labor union power vetoed by Pres. Truman June 20; Congress overrode

veto. Air Force Capt. **Chuck Yeager** broke sound barrier, Oct. 14, in X-1 rocket plane.
1948 Organization of American States (OAS) founded Apr. 30 by 21 countries. USSR halted all surface traffic into **West Berlin** June 24; in response, U.S. and British troops launched an **airlift**. Soviet blockade halted May 12, 1949; airlift ended Sept. 30. Pres. **Truman** elected Nov. 2, defeating NY Gov. Thomas E. Dewey in historic upset. **Alger Hiss** indicted Dec. 15 for perjury, after denying he had passed secret documents to Whittaker Chambers to go to a Communist spy ring; convicted Jan. 21, 1950. **Kinsey Report** on sexuality in the human male published.
1949 North Atlantic Treaty Organization (**NATO**) established Aug. 24 by U.S., Canada, and 10 Western European nations, agreeing that an armed attack against one would be considered an attack against all. Eleven leaders of U.S. **Communist Party** convicted Oct. 14 of advocating violent overthrow of U.S. government; sentenced to prison. Supreme Court upheld convictions, 1951. Pres. Truman, Oct. 26, signed legislation raising **federal minimum wage** from 40¢ an hour to 75¢. **Arthur Miller**'s *Death of a Salesman* opened on Broadway.
1950 Masked bandits robbed **Brink's, Inc.**, Boston express office, Jan. 17, of $2.8 mil. Case solved 1956; 8 sentenced to life. Pres. Truman authorized production of **H-bomb** Jan. 31. Special Senate committee to investigate organized crime established May 3, chaired by Sen. **Estes Kefauver** (D, TN). North Korean forces **invaded South Korea** June 25. UN asked for troops to restore peace. Pres. Truman ordered Air Force and Navy to Korea June 27. Truman approved ground forces, air strikes against North Korea June 30. U.S. sent 35 military advisers to **South Vietnam** June 27 and agreed to aid anti-Communist government. U.S. forces landed at **Inchon**, South Korea, Sept. 15. UN forces took Pyongyang Oct. 20, reached China border Nov. 20. China sent troops across border Nov. 26. U.S. banned shipments Dec. 8 to **Communist China** and to Asiatic ports trading with it.
Army **seized all railroads** Aug. 27 on Truman's order to prevent general strike; returned to owners in 1952. Charles Schulz's *Peanuts* comic strip first appeared in newspapers, Oct. 2. Two members of **Puerto Rican nationalist movement** tried to kill Pres. Truman Nov. 1. Variety show *Your Show of Shows* debuted on TV. David Riesman's *The Lonely Crowd* published.
1951 22nd Amendment, limiting presidential term of office, ratified Feb. 27. **Julius Rosenberg**; his wife, **Ethel Rosenberg**; and **Morton Sobell** found guilty Mar. 29 of conspiracy to commit wartime espionage. Rosenbergs received death penalty. Sobell sentenced to 30 years; released 1969.
Pres. Truman removed Gen. **Douglas MacArthur** from Korea command Apr. 11 for unauthorized policy statements. **Korea cease-fire** talks began in July; lasted 2 years. Fighting ended July 27, 1953.
Transcontinental TV began Sept. 4 with Pres. Truman's address at Japanese Peace Treaty Conference in San Francisco. **Japanese peace treaty** signed in San Francisco Sept. 8 by U.S., Japan, and 47 other nations. **J. D. Salinger**'s *Catcher in the Rye* published.
1952 Pres. Truman ordered seizure of nation's **steel mills** Apr. 8 to avert strike. Ruled illegal by Supreme Court June 2. **Peace contract** between West Germany, U.S., Great Britain, and France signed May 26. Last racial and ethnic barriers to naturalization removed, June 26-27, with passage of **Immigration and Naturalization Act** of 1952. **Puerto Rico** proclaimed commonwealth July 25, after referendum Mar. 3. Richard Nixon, as vice-pres. candidate, gave **"Checkers" speech**, so called because of sentimental reference to his dog Checkers, Sept. 23. **First hydrogen device explosion** Nov. 1 in Pacific. **Ralph Ellison**'s *Invisible Man* published.
1953 Federal jury in New York convicted 13 **Communist** leaders on conspiracy charges, Jan. 20. **Julius and Ethel Rosenberg** executed in Sing Sing Prison electric chair, Ossining, NY, June 19, for relaying nuclear secrets to Soviet Union. **Korean War armistice** signed July 27. California Gov. **Earl Warren** sworn in Oct. 5 as 14th chief justice of U.S. Supreme Court.
1954 *Nautilus*, **first atomic-powered submarine**, launched at Groton, CT, Jan. 21. Five members of Congress were wounded in the House Mar. 1 by 4 **Puerto Rican independence supporters** who fired at random from a spectators' gallery.

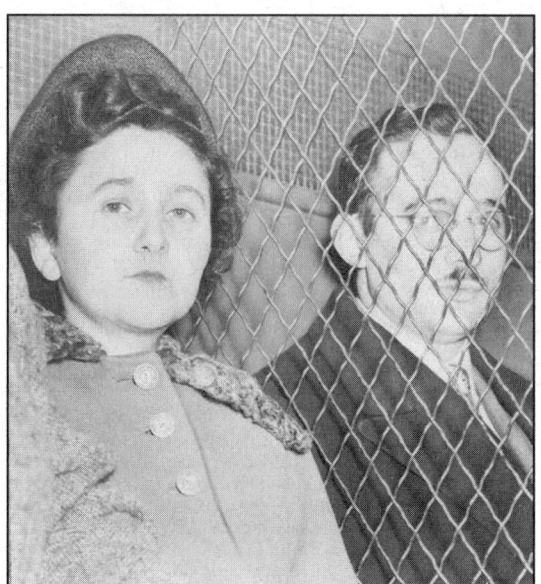

1951: Julius and Ethel Rosenberg are sentenced to death for spying for the Soviet Union amidst heightening Cold War suspicions.

At televised Army-McCarthy hearings, Apr. 22-June 17, before a Senate subcommittee, Army officials accused Sen. **Joseph McCarthy** (R, WI) of seeking preferential treatment for a draftee, and McCarthy accused Army of hindering probe of Communist infiltration into Army. McCarthy was cleared in the hearings, but the Senate later voted to condemn him, 67-22, for abuse of the Senate during hearings and debates.

Supreme Court ruled unanimously May 17 that racial segregation in public schools was unconstitutional, in *Brown v. Board of Education* of Topeka. **Ernest Hemingway** won Nobel Prize in literature for *The Old Man and the Sea*.

1955 U.S. agreed Feb. 12 to help train **South Vietnamese army**. Supreme Court ordered "all deliberate speed" in **integration** of public schools, May 31. A summit meeting of leaders of **Big 4**—U.S., Britain, France, and USSR—took place July 18-23 in Geneva, Switzerland.

Rosa Parks refused Dec. 1 to give her seat to white man on bus in Montgomery, AL. Her arrest, detention, and conviction sparked boycott of bus system, organized by Rev. **Martin Luther King Jr.**, by Montgomery's black community, Dec. 5. Bus segregation ordinance declared unconstitutional by federal court in 1956. Boycott ended Dec. 23 of that year.

America's 2 largest labor organizations merged Dec. 5, creating **AFL-CIO**. Russian-born U.S. citizen **Vladimir Nabokov**'s *Lolita* published.

1956 Massive resistance to Supreme Court **desegregation rulings** was called for Mar. 12 by 101 Southern congressmen. U.S. Supreme Court, Apr. 23, unanimously ruled against **racial segregation** on intrastate buses.

Federal-Aid Highway Act signed June 29, creating **interstate highway system**. **First transatlantic telephone cable** activated Sept. 25. On Oct. 8, in Game 5, Yankee right-hander Don Larsen pitched **only perfect World Series game**. **Eugene O'Neill**'s *Long Day's Journey Into Night* opened Nov. 7 on Broadway.

1957 Congress approved **Civil Rights Act of 1957**, Apr. 29, first such bill since Reconstruction to protect voting rights. Pres. Eisenhower signed act into law Sept. 9; provided for creation of Civil Rights Commission. The U.S. surgeon general July 12 said studies showed "direct link" between cigarette **smoking and lung cancer**.

Arkansas Gov. Orval Faubus (D) called National Guardsmen Sept. 4 to bar 9 black students from entering all-white high school in **Little Rock**. Faubus complied Sept. 21 with federal court order to remove Guardsmen, but local authorities ordered black students to withdraw. Pres. Eisenhower sent troops Sept. 24 to enforce court order. **Jack Kerouac**'s *On the Road* published.

1958 Army launched **first U.S. Earth-orbiting satellite**, *Explorer I*, Jan. 31 from Cape Canaveral, FL; discovered Van Allen radiation belt. U.S. Marines sent to **Lebanon** to protect elected government from threatened overthrow July-Oct. Nuclear sub *Nautilus* made **first undersea crossing of North Pole** Aug. 5. Presidential aide **Sherman Adams** resigned Sept. 22 over scandal involving alleged improper gifts. **First domestic jet airline passenger service** in U.S. opened by National Airlines Dec. 10 between New York and Miami.

1959 Alaska admitted as 49th state, Jan. 3; **Hawaii** admitted as 50th, Aug. 21. Completion of **St. Lawrence Seaway** Apr. 25 allowed passage of oceangoing vessels between Atlantic Ocean and Great Lakes.

Vice Pres. Richard Nixon, on tour of USSR, held **"kitchen debate,"** July 24, with Soviet Prem. Nikita Khrushchev at U.S. exhibit in Moscow. Prem. **Khrushchev** paid unprecedented visit to U.S. Sept. 15-27; made transcontinental tour.

Pres. Eisenhower issued injunction Oct. 12, upheld and made effective by Supreme Court Nov. 7, ending record **116-day steel strike**. In **quiz show scandal**, Columbia Univ. Prof. Charles Van Doren admitted to U.S. House subcommittee Nov. 2 that he had been coached before appearances on NBC-TV's *21* in 1956; he had won $129,000. William Wyler's *Ben-Hur* released; the movie won a record 11 Academy Awards the following year.

1960 Sit-ins began Feb. 1 when 4 black college students in Greensboro, NC, refused to move from a Woolworth lunch counter after being denied service. By Sept. 1961, more than 70,000 students, whites and blacks, had participated in sit-ins. Pres. Eisenhower signed **Civil Rights Act** May 6.

A U.S. **U-2 reconnaissance plane** was shot down in the Soviet Union May 1; pilot Gary Powers captured. The incident led to cancellation of a Paris summit conference. A **birth control pill** approved as safe for first time by Food and Drug Administration May 9. Vice Pres. **Richard Nixon** and Sen. **John F. Kennedy** faced each other Sept. 26 in first in series of televised debates. Kennedy defeated Nixon to win presidency, Nov. 8. U.S. announced Dec. 15 its backing of rightist group in **Laos**, which took power the next day. Alfred Hitchcock film *Psycho* released.

1961 U.S. severed diplomatic and consular relations with Cuba Jan. 3, after disputes over nationalizations of U.S. firms, U.S. military presence at Guantánamo base. U.S.-directed invasion of Cuba's **Bay of Pigs** Apr. 17 by Cuban exiles unsuccessfully attempted to overthrow the regime of Prem. Fidel Castro.

Peace Corps created by executive order, Mar. 1. **23rd Amendment**, giving DC citizens the right to vote in presidential elections, ratified Mar. 29. Comm. Alan B. Shepard Jr. rocketed from Cape Canaveral, FL, in a Mercury capsule May 5, in **first U.S.-crewed suborbital space flight**.

"Freedom Rides" from Washington, DC, across Deep South were launched May 20 to protest segregation in interstate transportation.

1962 Pres. Kennedy said Feb. 14 that U.S. military advisers in **Vietnam** would fire if fired upon. Lt. Col. John H. Glenn Jr. became **first American in orbit** Feb. 20 when he circled the Earth 3 times in the Mercury capsule *Friendship 7*.

In *Baker v. Carr*, Mar. 26, Supreme Court ruled that constitutional challenges to unequal distribution of voters among legislative districts could be resolved by federal courts. **James Meredith** became first black student at Univ. of Mississippi Oct. 1 after 3,000 troops put down riots.

A Soviet **offensive missile buildup** in Cuba was revealed Oct. 22 by Pres. Kennedy, who ordered naval and air quarantine on shipment of offensive military equipment to the island. He and Soviet Prem. Khrushchev agreed Oct. 28 on formula to end crisis. Kennedy announced Nov. 2 that missile bases in Cuba were being dismantled. **Rachel Carson**'s *Silent Spring* launched environmentalist movement.

1963 In *Gideon v. Wainwright*, Mar. 18, Supreme Court ruled that all criminal defendants must have counsel.

March for civil rights began May 2 in Birmingham, AL; led to desegregation accord, which in turn sparked rioting and violence. Univ. of Alabama **desegregated** after Gov. George Wallace stepped aside when confronted by federally deployed National Guard troops June 11. Civil rights leader **Medgar Evers** assassinated June 12. On Aug. 28, 200,000 joined in **March on Washington** in support of black demands for

1963: Lyndon Johnson takes the presidential oath aboard *Air Force One*, hours after Pres. John F. Kennedy was assassinated.

equal rights led by **Rev. Martin Luther King Jr.**; highlight was King's **"I Have a Dream" speech**.

Supreme Court ruled June 17 that laws requiring **recitation of Lord's Prayer or Bible verses** in public schools were unconstitutional. Pres. Kennedy, on Europe trip, addressed huge crowd in **West Berlin**, June 23. Limited **nuclear test-ban treaty** agreed upon July 25 by the U.S., the Soviet Union, and Britain. Four black girls killed in bombing of **16th St. Baptist Church** in Birmingham, AL, Sept. 15.

South Vietnam Pres. **Ngo Dinh Diem** assassinated Nov. 2; U.S. had earlier withdrawn support. Pres. **Kennedy** shot and fatally wounded Nov. 22 as he rode in motorcade through downtown Dallas, TX. Vice Pres. **Lyndon B. Johnson** sworn in as president. **Lee Harvey Oswald** arrested and charged with murder but was himself shot and fatally wounded Nov. 24. Nightclub owner **Jack Ruby** convicted of Oswald's murder; Ruby died in 1967 while awaiting retrial following reversal of his conviction. **Betty Friedan**'s feminist work *The Feminine Mystique* published.

1964 **Panama** suspended relations with U.S. Jan. 9 after riots. U.S. offered Dec. 18 to negotiate new canal treaty. **The Beatles** arrived in U.S. for first time; appeared Feb. 9 on *The Ed Sullivan Show*. Supreme Court ruled Feb. 17 in *Wesberry v. Sanders* that **congressional districts** as near as practicable be equal in population. U.S. reported May 27 it was sending military planes to **Laos**.

Three **civil rights workers** reported missing in Mississippi June 22; bodies found Aug. 4. Eighteen white men tried. On Oct. 20, 1967, an all-white federal jury convicted 7 of conspiracy in the slayings. Omnibus **civil rights bill** signed by Pres. Johnson July 2, banning discrimination in voting, jobs, public accommodations.

Congress Aug. 7 passed **Tonkin Gulf Resolution**, authorizing presidential action in Vietnam, after North Vietnamese boats reportedly attacked 2 U.S. destroyers Aug. 2. Congress approved **War on Poverty** bill Aug. 11, providing for a domestic Peace Corps (VISTA), **Job Corps**, and antipoverty funding. The **Warren Commission** released a report Sept. 27 concluding that Lee Harvey Oswald was solely responsible for the Kennedy assassination. Pres. **Johnson** elected to full term, Nov. 3, defeating Sen. **Barry Goldwater** (R, AZ) in landslide. **Verrazano-Narrows Bridge** opened in New York City, Nov. 21, with world's then-longest suspension span.

1965 In State of the Union address Jan. 4, Pres. Johnson outlined plans for **"Great Society,"** program of civil rights, antipoverty, and health-care legislation. Johnson in Feb. ordered continuous bombing of **North Vietnam** below 20th parallel.

Malcolm X assassinated Feb. 21 at New York City rally. March from **Selma to Montgomery**, AL, Mar. 21-25, by Rev. Martin Luther King Jr. to demand federal protection of blacks' voting rights. Some 14,000 U.S. troops sent to **Dominican Republic** during civil war Apr. 28. All troops withdrawn by next year. Bill establishing **Medicare**, government health insurance program for elderly, signed by Pres. Johnson July 30.

New **Voting Rights Act**, which banned literacy tests and other voter qualification tests, signed Aug. 6. Arrest of black motorist by white police officers precipitated **Watts riot** in predominantly-black Los Angeles neighborhood Aug. 11-16. Riots resulted in 34 deaths and $200 mil in property damage.

National **immigration quota system** abolished Oct. 3. **Electric power failure** blacked out most of northeastern U.S., parts of 2 Canadian provinces the night of Nov. 9-10.

1966 U.S. forces began firing into **Cambodia** May 1. Bombing of **Hanoi** area of North Vietnam by U.S. planes began June 29. By Dec. 31, 385,300 U.S. troops were stationed in South Vietnam, plus 60,000 offshore and 33,000 in Thailand.

Supreme Court ruled June 13, in *Miranda v. Arizona*, that suspects must be read their rights before police questioning. **Medicare** began July 1. In **Univ. of Texas shooting** rampage, 25-year-old student Charles Whitman killed 15 and wounded 31 from tower observation deck on Austin campus, Aug. 1; shot dead by police.

Dept. of Transportation created, Oct. 15. Edward Brooke (R, MA) elected Nov. 8 as first black U.S. senator in 85 years. Robert C. Weaver named secretary of newly created Dept. of Housing and Urban Development, becoming **first black cabinet member**.

1967 Green Bay Packers beat Kansas City Chiefs, 35-10, in **first Super Bowl**, Jan. 15, in Los Angeles. Three astronauts died Jan. 27 in *Apollo 1* fire on ground at Cape Canaveral, FL. **25th Amendment**, providing for presidential succession, ratified Feb. 10. Rep. **Adam Clayton Powell** (D, NY) was denied seat Mar. 1 because of charges he misused government funds. Seated following reelection in 1968 but was fined and stripped of seniority. Pres. Johnson and Soviet Prem. **Aleksei Kosygin** met June 23 and 25 at Glassboro State College in New Jersey; agreed not to let any crisis push them into war.

Riots erupted among residents of predominantly black Newark, NJ, July 12-17; 26 killed, 1,500 injured, more than 1,000 arrested. In **Detroit**, MI, July 23-30, 43 died, 2,000 injured; 5,000 left homeless by rioting, looting, and burning in city's black neighborhoods. **Thurgood Marshall** sworn in Oct. 2 as first black Supreme Court justice. **Antiwar march** on Washington, DC, Oct. 21-22, drew 50,000 participants. Carl B. Stokes (D, Cleveland) and Richard G. Hatcher (D, Gary, IN) elected **first black mayors** of major U.S. cities Nov. 7.

1968 In **"Tet offensive,"** Communist troops attacked several provincial capitals and other major cities, including Saigon, Jan. 30, but suffered heavy casualties. Pres. Johnson **curbed bombing** of North Vietnam Mar. 31. Peace talks began in Paris May 10. All bombing of North halted Oct. 31.

Rev. **Martin Luther King Jr.** assassinated Apr. 4 in Memphis, TN. **James Earl Ray**, an escaped convict, pleaded guilty to slaying, was sentenced to 99 years. Students at **Columbia Univ.**, Apr. 23-24, seized school buildings in protest against school's involvement in military research among other issues. Sen. **Robert F. Kennedy** (D, NY) shot June 5 in Los Angeles after celebrating presidential primary victories, died June 6. **Sirhan Sirhan** convicted of murder, 1969; death sentence commuted to life in prison, 1972.

Vice Pres. Hubert Humphrey nominated for president at **Democratic National Convention** in Chicago, marked by clash between police and antiwar protestors, Aug. 26-29. Republican nominee **Richard Nixon** won presidency, defeating Humphrey in close race Nov. 5.

Apollo 8 **orbited moon** in 5-day mission, Dec. 21-27. North Korea released 82-man crew of the **USS *Pueblo*** Dec. 22, 11 months after seizing the ship in Sea of Japan; one crew member had been killed in battle.

1969 Expanded 4-party **Vietnam peace talks** began Jan. 18. U.S. force peaked at 543,400 in Apr.; withdrawal started July 8. Pres. Nixon set Vietnamization policy Nov. 3. Earl Warren retired upon swearing in **Warren Burger**, June 23, as Supreme Court chief justice. In incident that marked birth of gay rights movement, police clashed with patrons of gay bar, the **Stonewall Inn**, in New York City June 27.

U.S. astronaut **Neil Armstrong**, commander of the *Apollo 11* mission, became the **first person to set foot on the moon**, July 20, followed by astronaut **Edwin "Buzz" Aldrin**. Astronaut **Michael Collins** remained aboard command module.

Woodstock rock music festival near Bethel, NY, drew 300,000-500,000 people, Aug. 15-18. **Anti-Vietnam War**

1968: The assassination of civil rights leader Martin Luther King Jr. in Memphis, TN, is just one of many violent events that defined a tumultuous year.

demonstrations held in cities across the U.S., marking Vietnam Moratorium day, Oct. 15; on Nov. 15, some 250,000 marched in Washington, DC. Massacre of hundreds of civilians by U.S. troops at **My Lai**, South Vietnam, in 1968 reported Nov. 16. **Kurt Vonnegut**'s *Slaughterhouse Five* published. *Sesame Street* launched on public TV.

1970 A federal jury Feb. 18 found the **"Chicago 7"** antiwar activists not guilty of conspiring to incite riots during 1968 Democratic National Convention. However, 5 were convicted of crossing state lines with intent to incite riots.

Three astronauts safely returned to Earth Apr. 17 after oxygen tank on *Apollo 13* ruptured. Lunar landing had been cancelled. Millions of Americans participated in antipollution demonstrations Apr. 22 to mark **first Earth Day**.

U.S. and South Vietnamese forces crossed **Cambodian** borders Apr. 30 to get at enemy bases. Four students killed May 4 at **Kent State Univ.** in Ohio by National Guardsmen during war protest. In protest at **Jackson State Univ.** in Mississippi, 2 killed when police fired on protesters.

First female U.S. generals appointed June 11. **Postal reform** measure signed Aug. 12 created an independent U.S. Postal Service. Pres. Nixon, Dec. 31, signed **clean air bill** calling for development of cleaner auto engine and national air quality standards for 10 major pollutants. Garry Trudeau's *Doonesbury* comic strip launched in 30 papers.

1971 **Charles Manson** and 3 of his cult followers found guilty Jan. 25 of first-degree murder in 1969 slaying of actress Sharon Tate and 6 others. A court-martial jury Mar. 29 convicted Lt. **William Calley** in murder of 22 South Vietnamese at **My Lai** on Mar. 16, 1968. He was sentenced to life in prison Mar. 31, later reduced to 20 years.

Pres. Nixon, Apr. 14, relaxed 20-year **trade embargo with China**. *New York Times* began publishing June 13 classified **Pentagon Papers**, secret Pentagon study on U.S. involvement in Vietnam leaked by Daniel Ellsberg, military analyst consulting for government. Supreme Court June 30 upheld, 6-3, right of the *Times* and *Washington Post* to publish the documents. **26th Amendment**, lowering the minimum voting age to 18 in all elections, ratified June 30. Pres. Nixon, Aug. 15, instituted 90-day **wage and price freeze**.

U.S. bombers initiated massive 5-day strike Dec. 26 in North Vietnam in retaliation for alleged violations of agreements reached prior to 1968 bombing halt.

1972 Pres. Nixon arrived in **Beijing** Feb. 21 for 8-day visit to China, in "journey for peace." Joint communiqué released Feb. 27 called for increased Sino-U.S. contacts. Senate, Mar. 22, approved **Equal Rights Amendment** banning discrimination on basis of sex; sent measure to states for ratification.

North Vietnamese forces launched biggest attacks in 4 years across the demilitarized zone Mar. 30. The U.S. responded Apr. 15 with **resumption of bombing** of Hanoi and Haiphong. Pres. Nixon announced May 8 the mining of North Vietnam ports.

Gov. **George C. Wallace** (D, AL), campaigning for president at Laurel, MD, shopping center May 15, shot and seriously wounded. **Arthur Bremer** convicted Aug. 4, sentenced to 63 years for shooting Wallace and 3 others. In **first visit of U.S. president to Moscow**, Pres. Nixon arrived May 22 for summit talks with Kremlin leaders that culminated in landmark strategic arms pact (**SALT I**). Five men arrested June 17 for breaking into Democratic National Committee offices in **Watergate** office complex in Washington, DC. Supreme Court in *Furman v. Georgia* June 29 ruled **capital punishment** as currently practiced was unconstitutional. **Mark Spitz** won 7 gold medals in world record times at the Munich Olympics in Aug.-Sept.

Last U.S. combat troops left Vietnam Aug. 11. Pres. **Nixon** reelected Nov. 7 in landslide, carrying 49 states to defeat Sen. George McGovern (D, SD). Three astronauts, part of *Apollo 17*, made 6th and last lunar landing on Dec. 11. Full-scale **bombing of North Vietnam** resumed after Paris peace negotiations reached impasse Dec. 18. *The Godfather*, directed by Francis Ford Coppola, is released.

1973 In *Roe v. Wade*, Supreme Court ruled, 7-2, Jan. 22, fetus not a person with constitutional rights and that right to privacy protected woman's decision to have abortion; states may not ban abortions during first 3 months of pregnancy but may regulate, not ban, abortions during second trimester.

Four-party **Vietnam peace pacts** signed in Paris Jan. 27. **End of military draft** announced on same day. Last U.S. troops left Vietnam Mar. 29. North Vietnam released some 590 U.S. prisoners by Apr. 1. Pres. Nixon announced, Apr. 30, resignation of top Nixon aides H. R. Haldeman and John Ehrlichman and firing of White House Counsel **John Dean** as a consequence of the widening **Watergate** scandal. Dean told Senate hearings June 25 that Nixon, his aides, and Justice Dept. had conspired to cover up Watergate facts. The U.S. officially ceased bombing in **Cambodia** at midnight Aug. 14 in accord with June congressional action.

Vice Pres. **Spiro Agnew**, Oct. 10, resigned and pleaded no contest to charge of tax evasion on payments made to him by contractors when he was Maryland governor. **Gerald R. Ford**, Oct. 12, became **first appointed vice president** under 25th Amendment; sworn in Dec. 6. The **"Saturday Night Massacre"** occurred Oct. 20, when Pres. Nixon ordered Attorney Gen. Elliot Richardson to fire Watergate special prosecutor Archibald Cox, who had sought handover of Nixon's subpoenaed **White House tapes**. Richardson refused to comply and resigned; Dep. Attorney Gen. William Ruckelshaus refused and was fired. Solicitor Gen. Robert Bork, as acting attorney gen., then fired Cox. Nixon administration named Leon Jaworski, Nov. 1, to succeed Cox.

Skylab, **first U.S. space station**, launched May 14. **Secretariat** became first Triple Crown winner since **Citation** in 1948 by winning Belmont Stakes June 9 in record time. **Billie Jean King** defeated Bobby Riggs in 3 straight sets in tennis's nationally televised "Battle of the Sexes," Sept. 20. Total **ban on oil exports** to U.S. imposed by Arab oil-producing nations Oct. 19-21 after outbreak of an Arab-Israeli war. Ban was lifted Mar. 18, 1974. Congress overrode Nov. 7 Pres. Nixon's veto of **war powers bill**, which curbed president's power to commit forces to hostilities abroad without congressional approval.

1974 On Apr. 8, **Hank Aaron** of the Atlanta Braves hit his 715th career home run to break Babe Ruth's record.

House Judiciary Committee opened **impeachment** hearings May 9 against Pres. Nixon. John Ehrlichman and 3 **White House "plumbers"** found guilty July 12 of conspiring to violate the civil rights of the psychiatrist of **Pentagon Papers** leaker Daniel Ellsberg by breaking into psychiatrist's office. Supreme Court ruled, 8-0, July 24 that Pres. Nixon had to turn over 64 **audio tapes of White House conversations**. House Judiciary Committee, in televised hearings July 24-30, recommended 3 **articles of impeachment** against Pres. Nixon, involving conspiracy to obstruct justice in Watergate cover-up, abuses of power, and defiance of committee subpoenas.

Knowing he faced certain impeachment, Pres. Nixon announced his **resignation**, Aug. 8, and stepped down the next day. His support in Congress had begun to collapse Aug. 5 after release of tapes appearing to implicate him in Watergate cover-up. Vice Pres. **Ford** sworn in Aug. 9 as 38th U.S. president. Pres. Ford, Aug. 20, nominated **Nelson Rockefeller** to

1974: Pres. Richard Nixon resigns from office and departs the White House.

be vice president; Rockefeller sworn in Dec. 10. Citing need to move on, Pres. Ford, Sept. 8, issued **pardon to Nixon** for any federal crimes he committed while president.

New York Times published article Dec. 22 on CIA engagement in illegal domestic surveillance. Reports of other apparently illegal CIA activities, recorded in **"family jewels"** file kept by the CIA, leaked out over the years.

1975 Former Atty. Gen. John Mitchell and ex-presidential advisers H. R. Haldeman and John Ehrlichman found guilty Jan. 1 of **Watergate cover-up** charges. Mitchell released 1979, last of 25 jailed over scandal to leave prison.

U.S. launched **evacuation from Saigon** of Americans and some South Vietnamese Apr. 29 as Communist forces completed takeover of South Vietnam; **South Vietnamese** government officially surrendered Apr. 30. U.S. merchant ship *Mayaguez* and its crew of 39 seized by Cambodian forces in Gulf of Siam May 12. In rescue operation, U.S. Marines attacked Tang Island, planes bombed air base; Cambodia surrendered ship and crew. Congress voted $405 mil for **South Vietnam refugees** May 16; 140,000 flown to U.S.

Publishing heiress **Patricia (Patty) Hearst**, kidnapped Feb. 5, 1974, by Symbionese Liberation Army (SLA), captured in San Francisco Sept. 18 with other militants. She was convicted Mar. 20, 1976, of bank robbery.

1976 In **right-to-die** case, New Jersey Supreme Court, Mar. 31, allowed comatose Karen Ann Quinlan to be removed from respirator. She survived until 1985 when she died in a nursing home. U.S. Supreme Court reinstated **death penalty**, July 2, subject to conditions.

U.S. celebrated **200th anniversary of independence** July 4 with festivals, parades, and New York City's Operation Sail, gathering of tall ships from around the world. **"Legionnaire's disease"** killed 29 people who attended American Legion convention July 21-24 in Philadelphia.

Two U.S. officers on routine mission near DMZ slain by **North Korean soldiers** Aug. 18; North Korea stated "regret," Aug. 21. *Viking II* set down on Utopia Plains of **Mars** Sept. 3, following successful landing of *Viking I* on Chryse Plains, July 20.

1977 Convicted murderer Gary Gilmore executed by Utah firing squad Jan. 17; **first use of capital punishment** in U.S. since 1967. Pres. Jimmy Carter Jan. 21 pardoned most Vietnam War **draft evaders**.

Natural gas shortage caused by severe winter weather led Congress Feb. 2 to approve emergency gas bill temporarily authorizing reallocation of interstate gas from surplus areas to shortage areas. Pres. Carter signed act Aug. 4 creating new cabinet-level **energy department**.

FBI Dec. 7 released 40,000 pages of previously secret files relating to **Kennedy assassination**. George Lucas's first *Star Wars* film released.

1978 Senate voted Apr. 18 to turn over **Panama Canal** to Panama on Dec. 31, 1999; Mar. 16 vote had given approval to treaty guaranteeing area's neutrality after the year 2000. Californians, June 6, approved **Proposition 13**, state constitutional amendment slashing property taxes.

Supreme Court, June 28, ruled that while race could be a factor in admission to institutions of higher education, **numerical quotas** could not be used.

Egyptian Pres. **Anwar al-Sadat** and Israeli Prem. **Menachem Begin** reached accord on "framework for peace," Sept. 17, after Pres. Carter-mediated talks at Camp David. New York's Chemical Bank Dec. 20 initiated industry-wide move to raise **lending rate** to near-record 11.75%.

1979 Partial meltdown released radioactive material Mar. 28 at nuclear reactor on **Three Mile Island** near Middletown, PA. American Airlines DC-10 **jetliner crashed** May 25 after takeoff from Chicago, killing 275 people.

In speech July 15, Pres. Carter spoke of national "crisis of confidence" and outlined proposed 10-year $140 bil program to reduce **dependence on foreign oil**. Militant followers of **Ayatollah Khomeini** took hostage some 90 people, including 66 Americans, Nov. 4 at **American embassy in Tehran**, Iran. Khomeini demanded return of former Shah Muhammad Reza Pahlavi, who was undergoing medical treatment in New York City, to stand trial.

1980 Pres. Carter announced, Jan. 4, economic sanctions against USSR in retaliation for Soviet invasion of Afghanistan. At Carter's request, U.S. Olympic Committee voted, Apr. 12, against U.S. participation in **Moscow Summer Olympics**. At **Winter Olympics** in Lake Placid, NY, U.S. hockey team defeated Russian team Feb. 22 en route to gold medal in "miracle on ice."

Eight Americans killed and 5 wounded, Apr. 24, in ill-fated attempt to rescue hostages held by Iranian militants. **Mt. St. Helens**, in Washington state, erupted May 18. The blast, with others May 25 and June 12, left 57 dead. In sweeping victory, Nov. 4, **Ronald Reagan** (R) was elected 40th president, defeating incumbent Pres. Carter. Republicans gained control of Senate. Former Beatle **John Lennon** was shot and killed by Mark David Chapman, Dec. 8, in New York City.

1981 Minutes after Reagan's inauguration Jan. 20, 52 **American hostages in Iran** were freed after being held for 444 days. Pres. **Reagan** was shot and seriously wounded, Mar. 30, in Washington, DC; also seriously wounded were a Secret Service agent, a policeman, and Press Sec. **James Brady**. **John W. Hinckley Jr.** arrested, found not guilty by reason of insanity in 1982, and committed to mental institution.

World's **first reusable spacecraft**, space shuttle *Columbia*, sent into space, Apr. 12. It performed its first operational mission in 1982. U.S. Centers for Disease Control, June 5, reported first cases of what became known as **AIDS**.

Members of the Professional **Air Traffic Controllers** Organization, Aug. 3, went on strike. Most defied a back-to-work order and were dismissed by Pres. Reagan Aug. 5 for violating federal law. Pres. Reagan signed into law Aug. 13 **tax-cut legislation**, expected to save taxpayers $750 bil over 5 years, largest tax cut to date. The Senate confirmed, Sept. 21, appointment of **Sandra Day O'Connor** as **first female Supreme Court justice**.

1982 The 13-year-old Justice Dept. lawsuit against **AT&T** was settled Jan. 8. AT&T agreed to give up 22 Bell System companies and was allowed to expand. **Equal Rights Amendment**, sent to states in 1972, defeated when deadline for ratification passed June 30 with only 35 states supporting amendment; 38 were needed for ratification. The economy showed signs of recovery from a **recession** that began in mid-1981, as Dow Jones Industrial Average hit 1,016.93 Oct. 13, its highest level in 18 months.

NFL strike ended Nov. 16 after 57 days when players and team owners settled with $1.6 bil pact. Singer **Michael Jackson**'s album *Thriller*, released Nov. 30, became monumental best-seller. Retired dentist Dr. Barney B. Clark became **first permanent artificial heart recipient**, Dec. 2; he died Mar. 23, 1983. The House, Dec. 16, cited EPA administrator Anne Gorsuch for contempt after she refused to release records relating to enforcement of **Superfund** law.

1981: Pres. Ronald Reagan nominates Sandra Day O'Connor to be the first woman to serve on the U.S. Supreme Court.

1983 Pres. Reagan, Jan. 3, declared Times Beach, MO, a federal disaster area because of toxic **dioxin** in soil, prompting evacuation of residents and town's closure. Harold Washington (D) elected Apr. 12 as **first black mayor of Chicago**. On Apr. 20, Pres. Reagan signed compromise bipartisan bill designed to save **Social Security** from bankruptcy.

Sally Ride became **first American woman to travel in space**, June 18, when space shuttle *Challenger* launched from Cape Canaveral, FL. On Sept. 1, **South Korean passenger jet** in Soviet air space and apparently misidentified was shot down; 269 people, including 61 Americans, killed.

On Oct. 23, 241 U.S. Marines and sailors were killed when TNT-laden **suicide truck bomb** blew up Marine barracks at Beirut International Airport in Lebanon. U.S. troops, with small force from 6 Caribbean nations, invaded **Grenada** Oct. 25. After a few days, Grenadian militia and Cuban "construction workers" were overcome, U.S. citizens were evacuated, and the Marxist regime was deposed.

1984 Seven regional companies took over **local telephone service** from AT&T, Jan. 1. On space shuttle *Challenger*'s fourth trip, launched Feb. 3, two astronauts became **first humans to fly free of a spacecraft**. On May 7, Vietnam War veterans reached out-of-court settlement with 7 chemical companies in class-action suit over the herbicide **Agent Orange**.

Former Vice Pres. **Walter Mondale** won Democratic presidential nomination, June 6. He chose Rep. **Geraldine Ferraro** (D, NY) as vice presidential candidate, first woman to be nominated for position by major political party. Pres. Reagan signed bill July 17 cutting federal transportation aid to states that keep their **drinking age** under 21. Pres. **Reagan** reelected Nov. 6 in Republican landslide, carrying 49 states for record 525 electoral votes. **Bernhard Goetz** shot and wounded 4 allegedly menacing teenage boys on NYC subway train, Dec. 22; later acquitted of major charges but was successfully sued.

1985 Visiting Germany, Pres. Reagan, May 5, laid wreath at Bergen-Belsen Nazi concentration camp site and also at military cemetery at **Bitburg**, where some Nazis were buried. Philadelphia police bombed a rowhouse occupied by **MOVE radical group**, May 13; 11 killed, and fire damaged 2 blocks of houses. On June 14, **terrorists seized TWA jet** after takeoff from Athens, Greece, with 153 passengers and crew. Thirty-nine Americans held hostage for 17 days; 1 U.S. service member killed.

Reversing an Apr. 23 decision to market "new" Coke, the **Coca-Cola Co.** said, July 10, it would resume marketing soda made under its original "Classic" formula. **Live Aid** rock concert broadcast around the world July 13, raised $70 mil for famine relief in Ethiopia.

On Oct. 7, 4 **Palestinian hijackers** seized Italian cruise ship *Achille Lauro* in the Mediterranean for 2 days. One American, Leon Klinghoffer, killed. For first time in 6 years U.S. and Soviet leaders met at **summit in Geneva**, Nov. 19-20. **General Electric** agreed Dec. 11 to buy RCA Corp.

1986 The U.S. officially observed **Martin Luther King Jr. Day** for first time Jan. 20. Space shuttle *Challenger* exploded 73 seconds after liftoff, Jan. 28, killing 6 astronauts and

Teacher in Space Project participant Christa McAuliffe. In 4-day extravaganza in July, the U.S. celebrated 100th birthday of the **Statue of Liberty**.

The Senate confirmed, Sept. 17, Reagan's nomination of **William Rehnquist** as chief justice and **Antonin Scalia** as associate justice of Supreme Court. Congress completed action Oct. 2 overriding a veto to place economic sanctions on **South Africa**. Lebanese newspaper first broke news of **Iran-Contra scandal** Nov. 3, involving secret U.S. sale of arms to Iran and diversion of some of the proceeds to support the Contras, a right-wing, anti-Communist insurgent movement in Nicaragua.

Financier **Ivan Boesky** agreed Nov. 14 to pay $100 mil in fines and illicit profits for **insider trading**. Robert Penn Warren named America's **first poet laureate** by the Library of Congress.

1987 Pres. Reagan produced nation's **first trillion-dollar budget**, Jan. 5. **Dow Jones** closed above 2,000 for first time, Jan. 8. The FDA approved, Mar. 20, AZT—first drug shown to be effective in fight against **AIDS**. Nearly 1.4 mil **illegal aliens** met May 4 deadline for applying for amnesty under new federal policy.

Joint public hearings by Senate and House committees investigating **Iran-Contra affair** opened May 5. Lt. Col. **Oliver North**, former National Security Council staff member, said he had believed all his activities were authorized by his superiors. Hearings ended Aug. 3. Pres. Reagan, Aug. 12, denied knowing of diversion of funds to Contras.

An **Iraqi missile** killed 37 sailors on the USS *Stark* in the Persian Gulf, May 17. Iraq called it an accident. The 200th anniversary of **U.S. Constitution** signing was observed, Sept. 17, in Philadelphia and around the U.S. **Stock market crashed**, Oct. 19, with the Dow Jones plummeting a then-record 508 points to 1,738, ending bull market that began mid-1982. Pres. Reagan and Soviet leader Mikhail Gorbachev Dec. 8, signed **pact to dismantle** all 1,752 U.S. and 859 Soviet missiles with 300- to 3,400-mi range.

1988 In report issued May 16, Surgeon Gen. C. Everett Koop declared **cigarettes addictive**. Congress approved, in June, greatest expansion yet of **Medicare** benefits, to protect the elderly and disabled against "catastrophic" medical costs; act was repealed in Nov. 1989.

A missile, fired from U.S. Navy warship *Vincennes* in the Persian Gulf, mistakenly struck a commercial **Iranian airliner**, July 3, killing all 290 aboard. **George H. W. Bush** (R) elected 41st U.S. president, Nov. 8, decisively defeating Massachusetts Gov. **Michael Dukakis** (D). **Pan Am Flight 103** exploded and crashed, due to terrorist bomb, into town of Lockerbie, Scotland, Dec. 21, killing all 259 people aboard and 11 on the ground. **Drexel Burnham Lambert** agreed, Dec. 21, to plead guilty to insider trading and other violations, and pay penalties of $650 mil. U.S. suffered widespread **drought** conditions, the worst in over 50 years.

1989 Major oil spill occurred when *Exxon Valdez* struck Bligh Reef in Alaska's Prince William Sound, Mar. 24. Oliver North convicted, May 4, on charges related to **Iran-Contra**

1986: The *Challenger* space shuttle explodes 73 seconds after liftoff.

scandal. Conviction thrown out on appeal in 1991 because of his immunized testimony. A measure to rescue **savings and loan industry** signed into law, Aug. 9, by Pres. Bush, launching largest federal rescue to date. Army Gen. **Colin Powell** became **first black chairman of Joint Chiefs of Staff** after being nominated Aug. 10 by Pres. Bush.

Baseball legend **Pete Rose** banned from game for life Aug. 24 for involvement with gamblers. **Hurricane Hugo** swept through the Carolinas Sept. 22, causing at least 86 deaths and $7 bil damage. Just before a World Series game, Oct. 17, an **earthquake** struck the San Francisco Bay area, causing 63 deaths.

L. Douglas Wilder (D) declared governor of Virginia Nov. 27, **first elected black governor** in U.S. history. U.S. troops invaded Panama, Dec. 20, overthrowing the government of **Manuel Noriega**. Noriega, wanted by U.S. authorities on drug charges, surrendered Jan. 3, 1990.

1990 Junk bond financier **Michael Milken** pleaded guilty to fraud-related charges, Apr. 14; agreed to pay $500 mil in restitution and sentenced Nov. 21 to 10 years in prison. Justice **William Brennan** announced, July 20, resignation from U.S. Supreme Court. His replacement, Judge **David Souter**, confirmed Sept. 27. Pres. Bush signed **Americans With Disabilities Act** barring discrimination against, and requiring accommodations for, the disabled, July 26. **Operation Desert Shield** forces left for Saudi Arabia Aug. 7 to defend that country following invasion of **Kuwait** by Iraq, Aug. 2. Pres. Bush Nov. 15 signed into law **Clean Air Act**, strengthened version of Clean Air Act of 1970; focus on urban pollution, cancer-causing emissions from industrial sources.

1991 The U.S. and its allies defeated Iraq in **Persian Gulf War** and liberated Kuwait, which Iraq had invaded. On Jan. 17, the allies launched a devastating air attack. In rapid ground war starting Feb. 24, which lasted just 100 hours, U.S.-led forces killed or captured thousands of Iraqi soldiers and sent the rest into retreat before Pres. Bush ordered cease-fire Feb. 27.

An 8-month **recession** showed signs of having ended in Mar. The **Dow Jones** Industrial Average closed above 3,000 for first time, Apr. 17. Justice **Thurgood Marshall**, first black to sit on U.S. Supreme Court, announced, June 17, plans to retire. House Speaker Tom Foley announced Oct. 3 closure of **House Bank** by end of year after revelations that House members had written numerous bad checks. Senate, voting 52-48 on Oct. 15, confirmed nomination of **Clarence Thomas** to replace Marshall, despite allegations that Thomas had sexually harassed former aide Anita Hill.

1992 Retail giant **R.H. Macy & Co.** filed for bankruptcy, Jan. 27. Major U.S. carrier Trans World Airlines (**TWA**) filed for bankruptcy, Jan. 31. **Riots** swept South Central Los Angeles Apr. 29 after jury acquitted 4 white police officers on all but one count in 1991 videotaped beating of black motorist **Rodney King**. Death toll in L.A. violence was put at 53. **27th Amendment**, regarding congressional pay raises, ratified May 7.

Hurricane Andrew ravaged South Florida and Louisiana Aug. 24-26, causing 65 deaths. White supremacist and fugitive Randall Weaver surrendered Aug. 31 after 11-day **FBI siege** at his **Ruby Ridge**, ID, cabin, during which his wife, son, and a deputy sheriff were killed.

Bill Clinton (D) elected 42nd president, Nov. 3, defeating Pres. Bush (R) and independent Ross Perot. A UN-sanctioned military force, led by U.S. troops, arrived in **Somalia** Dec. 9. Presidents of U.S., Canada, and Mexico Dec. 17 signed **North American Free Trade Agreement** (NAFTA), which took effect Jan. 1, 1994.

1993 A bomb exploded in a parking garage beneath the **World Trade Center** in New York City, Feb. 26, killing 6. Four men found guilty, Mar. 4, 1994. Four federal agents killed, Feb. 28, during unsuccessful raid on **Branch Davidian** compound near **Waco**, TX. A 51-day siege by agents ended Apr. 19 when the compound burned down, leaving more than 70 cult members dead. Eleven cult members acquitted Feb. 26, 1994, of deaths of federal agents.

Janet Reno became **first female attorney general** Mar. 12. Federal jury, Apr. 17, found 2 Los Angeles police officers guilty and 2 not guilty of violating civil rights of motorist **Rodney King** in 1991 videotaped beating.

Defense Sec. Les Aspin, Apr. 28, removed restrictions on aerial **combat roles for women** in the armed forces. In a May 14 plebiscite, voters in **Puerto Rico** supported continu-

ing commonwealth status with U.S. **"Motor-voter" bill** was signed by Pres. Clinton, May 20, easing voting procedures. The **"Great Flood of 1993"** inundated at least 15 mil acres in 9 Midwestern states in summer, leaving about 50 dead and $15 bil in damages as a direct result of flood.

Pres. Clinton, July 2, approved recommendations that 33 major U.S. military bases be closed. On July 19 he announced **"don't ask, don't tell, don't pursue"** policy for homosexuals in the military. Judge **Ruth Bader Ginsburg** sworn in, Aug. 10, as 107th justice and second woman on Supreme Court, replacing retiring Justice Byron White. Pres. Clinton, Aug. 10, signed measure designed to **cut federal budget deficits** by $496 bil over 5 years, through spending cuts and new taxes. **Brady Bill**, a major gun-control measure named after former Reagan press sec. James Brady, who was injured in Reagan assassination attempt, was signed into law by Pres. Clinton Nov. 30.

1994 A predawn **earthquake** in the Los Angeles area, Jan. 17, claimed 61 lives. Pres. Clinton Feb. 3 lifted 19-year ban on U.S. trade with **Vietnam**. Byron De La Beckwith convicted Feb. 5 of 1963 murder of civil rights leader **Medgar Evers**. Longtime CIA officer **Aldrich Ames** and his wife charged, Feb. 21, with spying for Russians. Under plea bargain, he received life in prison, while she drew 63 months.

U.S. troops, Mar. 25, officially ended peacekeeping and humanitarian aid mission in **Somalia**, begun in 1992. Congressional committees, late July, began **Whitewater hearings**. Kenneth Starr named Aug. 5 as independent counsel to probe Whitewater affair. Major league **baseball players** went on strike following Aug. 11 games. World Series canceled; strike ended Apr. 25, 1995. Senate Majority Leader George Mitchell (D, ME), Sept. 26, dropped efforts to pass Pres. Clinton's **health-care reform** package.

Republicans gained control of both House and Senate in Nov. 8 elections after many years of Democratic control. House speaker **Tom Foley** (MA) was among the defeated Democrats.

1995 104th Congress opened Jan. 4. **Newt Gingrich** (R, GA) elected House speaker. A bill to end Congress's exemption from federal labor laws, first in series of measures in Republicans' **"Contract With America,"** cleared Congress Jan. 17; signed into law Jan. 23. Pres. Clinton, Jan. 31, authorized $20 bil loan to **Mexico** to help it avert financial collapse. Last UN peacekeeping troops withdrew from **Somalia** Feb. 28-Mar. 3, with aid of U.S. Marines. In **Haiti**, peacekeeping responsibilities were transferred from U.S. to UN forces Mar. 31, with U.S. providing 2,400 soldiers.

Truck **bomb exploded outside Oklahoma City federal office** building Apr. 19, killing 168 in deadliest terrorist attack up to then on U.S. soil; Timothy McVeigh arrested as key suspect, Apr. 21. U.S. space shuttle *Atlantis* made first in series of dockings with Russian space station *Mir*, June 29-July 4. The U.S. announced July 11 it was reestablishing diplomatic **relations with Vietnam**.

Ten Muslim militants convicted, Oct. 1, in failed **plot to blow up UN Headquarters**, other buildings and assassinate political leaders. Former football star **O. J. Simpson** found not guilty Oct. 3 of June 1994 murders of former wife, Nicole Brown Simpson, and a friend of hers. Hundreds of thousands of black men participated in **Million Man March** and rally in Washington, DC, Oct. 16, organized by Rev. Louis Farrakhan.

Five Americans among 7 killed, Nov. 13, in **bombing** of U.S. military post in **Riyadh, Saudi Arabia**. Budget impasse between Congress and Pres. Clinton led to partial **government shutdown** beginning Nov. 14; operations resumed Nov. 20 under continuing resolutions. After talks outside Dayton, OH, warring parties in **Bosnia and Herzegovina** reached agreement Nov. 21 to end their conflict; treaty signed Dec. 14, after which U.S. peacekeeping troops arrived. A 1973 federal law imposing **55-mph speed limit** repealed Nov. 28.

1996 Senate, Jan. 26, approved, 87-4, Second Strategic Arms Reduction Treaty (**START II**). Congress, Mar. 27-28, approved **line item veto**; struck down by Supreme Court, June 1998.

James and Susan McDougal convicted May 28 of fraud and conspiracy in **Whitewater** case; Arkansas Gov. Jim Guy Tucker (D) convicted on similar charges. The antitax **Freemen** surrendered to federal authorities June 13 after 81-day standoff near Jordan, MT; 4 were convicted, July 1998, of conspiring to defraud banks.

Bomb exploded at **Khobar Towers** military complex near Dhahran, Saudi Arabia, June 25, killing 19 American

1995: The Murrah Federal Building in Oklahoma City is targeted in the deadliest act of domestic terrorism in U.S. history.

service personnel. Homemade pipe bomb exploded July 27 in **Atlanta**, GA, park during **Summer Olympics**; 1 person killed. Extremist Eric Robert Rudolph, arrested in May 2003, pleaded guilty to this and other bombings.

Major **welfare reform bill** signed into law, Aug. 22. U.S. signed **Comprehensive Test Ban Treaty**, Sept. 24, which banned all nuclear weapons tests and explosions; Senate failed to ratify treaty. Pres. **Clinton reelected** to 2nd term, Nov. 5.

1997 **Madeleine Albright** sworn in as sec. of state Jan. 23, becoming first female State Dept. head. Former CIA official Harold Nicholson pleaded guilty, Mar. 3, to **spying for Russia**. Thirty-nine members of **Heaven's Gate** religious cult found dead in Rancho Santa Fe, CA, house Mar. 26, in apparent mass suicide.

Timothy McVeigh convicted of conspiracy and murder, June 2, in 1995 **Oklahoma City** bombing; executed June 2001. Terry Nichols convicted Dec. 23 on related charges. Two Islamic militants convicted, Nov. 12, of key roles in 1993 **bombing of World Trade Center**. The film *Titanic*, released Dec. 14, went on to win 11 Oscars and gross over $600 mil.

1998 Media outlets reported Jan. 21 on evidence of sexual relationship between Pres. Clinton and former White House intern **Monica Lewinsky**. Clinton initially denied affair, but in grand jury testimony and address to the nation, Aug. 17, acknowledged relationship that was "not appropriate." On Sept. 9, independent counsel **Kenneth Starr** sent findings to House of Representatives; Judiciary Committee, Oct. 5, voted 21-16 to recommend full inquiry. House, Dec. 19, approved 2 articles of **impeachment** charging Pres. Clinton with grand jury perjury and obstruction of justice in cover-up.

"Unabomber" **Theodore Kaczynski**, arrested in Montana in 1993, pleaded guilty Jan. 22 to California and New Jersey bombings that killed 3 people; sentenced in May to 4 life terms plus 30 years. Texas, Feb. 3, executed its first female convict in 135 years.

Bombs at U.S. embassies in Nairobi, Kenya, and Dar-es-Salaam, Tanzania, killed at least 257, Aug. 7; U.S. launched retaliatory strikes, Aug. 20, against targets in Afghanistan and Sudan. On Sept. 30, Pres. Clinton announced federal **budget surplus** of $70 bil for fiscal year 1998, the first since 1969.

Pres. Clinton, Nov. 13, settled suit by agreeing to pay $850,000 to **Paula Jones**, who alleged he had made an unwanted sexual advance in 1991. Country's 4 largest **tobacco companies**, in settlement Nov. 23, agreed to pay states and territories $206 bil over 25 years to cover public health costs.

1999 Pres. **Clinton** was acquitted, Feb. 12, at end of Senate impeachment trial. Perjury article failed with 45 votes; obstruction of justice article drew 50-50 vote, with two-thirds vote needed for conviction.

Dr. **Jack Kevorkian** convicted of second-degree murder Mar. 26 in death of terminally ill man. One man pleaded guilty Apr. 5, another convicted Nov. 4, in 1998 kidnapping and beating death of **Matthew Shepard**, an openly gay student at the Univ. of Wyoming.

Eric Harris, 18, and Dylan Klebold, 17, killed 12 fellow students and a teacher Apr. 20 at **Columbine High School** in Littleton, CO, then fatally shot themselves. One NYC police officer pleaded guilty to 6 charges, May 25, another convicted of assault, June 8, in 1997 police-station torture of **Abner Louima**, Haitian immigrant. **John F. Kennedy Jr.** killed in crash of private plane July 16.

2000 Across U.S., midnight celebrations marked changeover to year 2000 on Jan. 1; feared **Y2K** computer glitch caused only minor problems. Vermont Gov. Howard Dean (D) signed legislation Apr. 26 allowing same-sex couples in **civil unions** to gain legal rights. Scientists from U.S. and Britain announced jointly, June 26, that they had determined structure of the **human genome**.

Six-year-old **Elián González** was returned to father in Cuba June 28, 7 months after rescue from boat wreck in which his mother and other refugees drowned. **Tiger Woods** became youngest player, at age 24, to win all 4 of golf's majors, with record score in British Open, July 23.

Food and Drug Administration announced, Sept. 28, approval of **RU-486**, a pill that induces abortions. Seventeen U.S. sailors died Oct. 12 in terrorist bombing of **USS** *Cole*, which was refueling in Aden, Yemen.

On election night, Nov. 7, the winner of **Florida's electoral votes** remained uncertain, leaving national result in doubt for weeks. Florida Supreme Court, Dec. 8, ordered manual recount of certain ballots; on Dec. 12, U.S. Supreme Court reversed that decision, and Vice Pres. **Al Gore** (D), the following day, conceded election to Texas Gov. **George W. Bush** (R).

2001 **AOL-Time Warner merger** completed Jan. 11. FBI agent **Robert Hanssen** arrested Feb. 20, charged with spying for Soviet Union and Russia over 20-year period; under plea bargain, sentenced in 2002 to life in prison. **U.S. Navy spy plane** collided with Chinese fighter plane over South China Sea Apr. 1, killing fighter pilot: 24 U.S. crew members detained in Hainan until U.S. officials expressed apology, Apr. 12.

Sen. **James Jeffords** (R, VT) announced May 24 he was leaving his party, giving Democrats control of Senate. Pres. Bush signed, June 7, $1.35 tril tax-cut package. Bush announced Aug. 9 he would allow federal funding of limited research on existing **stem-cell** lines derived from human embryos.

On morning of **Sept. 11**, 2 hijacked commercial airliners struck **World Trade Center twin towers** in New York City in **worst-ever terrorist attack** on American soil. A 3rd hijacked plane destroyed a portion of the **Pentagon**; a 4th crashed in a field near Shanksville, PA. Some 3,000 people were killed, including about 2,750 at World Trade Center. Five people died and 14 became ill from exposure to **anthrax** through U.S. postal system, Oct. 4-Nov. 21.

U.S. and Britain, Oct. 7, launched air-strike campaign against Afghan-based terrorist organization **al-Qaeda** and Afghanistan's ruling **Taliban** militia. Pres. Bush created **Office of Homeland Security**, Oct. 8, and signed federal **antiterrorism bill**, Oct. 26. **Taliban** surrendered Kabul, Nov. 13, and fled from Kandahar, their stronghold, Dec. 7. Taliban member and U.S. citizen **John Walker Lindh** captured Dec. 2 in Afghanistan; under plea bargain, sentenced in Oct. 2002 to 20 years. U.S. government, Dec. 11, indicted al-Qaeda

2001: The attacks of Sept. 11, 2001, kill more than 2,750 people in New York, including 343 firefighters.

member **Zacarias Moussaoui** as Sept. 11 co-conspirator; he pleaded guilty, sentenced in May 2006 to life in prison. Operation in Afghanistan's **Tora Bora** cave complex, Dec. 12-17, failed to capture al-Qaeda leader **Osama bin Laden**.

Leading energy-trading company **Enron** filed for bankruptcy, Dec. 2. Pres. Bush announced, Dec. 13, U.S. withdrawal from **1972 Antiballistic Missile Treaty**.

2002 Taliban and al-Qaeda fighters captured in Afghanistan flown to U.S. naval base at **Guantánamo Bay** in Cuba, starting Jan. 11. House committee, Jan. 14, released parts of whistle-blowing letter from Enron employee Sherron Watkins to CEO **Kenneth Lay**. Lay resigned Jan. 23; Congress, Jan. 24, began hearings into **Enron bankruptcy**.

In State of the Union address, Jan. 29, Pres. Bush called Iran, Iraq, and North Korea part of **"axis of evil."** By Mar. 6, 1,200 U.S. troops were involved in **Operation Anaconda** against al-Qaeda and Taliban forces in Afghanistan.

Independent prosecutor's report, Mar. 20, found insufficient evidence that Pres. Clinton or Hillary Clinton committed any crime in connection with **Whitewater**. Pres. Bush, Mar. 27, signed into law McCain-Feingold **campaign-finance reform bill** banning unregulated, unrestricted "soft money" donations; part of bill struck down by Supreme Court, June 2007.

Ceremonial last girder removed May 30 from **World Trade Center** site, signaling end of massive clean-up and recovery operation. FBI agent Coleen Rowley testified before congressional committee June 6 that Washington FBI agents had stymied investigative efforts in Minneapolis prior to Sept. 11. **WorldCom** filed for bankruptcy, July 21.

Richard Reid pleaded guilty Oct. 4 to all charges stemming from incident aboard plane in Dec. 2001, when he tried to ignite explosives in his shoes; sentenced Jan. 2003 to life in prison. On Oct. 10-11 the House, 296-133, and Senate, 77-23, gave Bush backing to use military force against **Iraq**. Bush administration revealed Oct. 16 that **North Korea** had acknowledged developing nuclear arms. Bush signed measure, Nov. 25, creating **Dept. of Homeland Security**.

U.S. Roman Catholic bishops, Nov. 13, approved revised, Vatican-vetted policies dealing with priests who **sexually abuse minors**. Cardinal **Bernard Law**, Dec. 13, resigned as archbishop of Boston; he had been accused of covering up sexual abuse by priests. **Trent Lott** (R, MS) bowed out as new Senate majority leader Dec. 20 after remarks apparently supporting segregation.

2003 On Jan. 10-11, Illinois Gov. George Ryan (R) pardoned or **commuted death sentences** of all 171 Illinois death row convicts.

Space shuttle *Columbia* broke apart Feb. 1 during descent toward planned landing; all 7 crew members killed. Report issued Aug. 26 blamed damage sustained during liftoff; also cited "broken safety culture" at NASA. Senate, Mar. 6, approved the **Strategic Offensive Reductions Treaty (Moscow Treaty)** for reducing nuclear stockpiles signed in 2002 by U.S. and Russian leaders.

U.S.-led military offensive aimed at ousting **Saddam Hussein** got underway Mar. 19, when 40 Tomahawk cruise missiles hit targets in Baghdad. U.S. forces Mar. 21 seized oil fields near Basra. On Apr. 3, U.S. Marines crossed Tigris River and moved close to **Baghdad**. By Apr. 9, U.S. forces reported control over much of Baghdad. With collapse of regime, services were disrupted and looting became widespread. Pres. Bush, speaking from aircraft carrier May 1, declared **end of major combat operations in Iraq**; insurgents continued to mount attacks.

Pres. Bush signed bill May 28 providing $330 bil in **tax cuts** over several years. Under settlement in private antitrust suit brought by Netscape (unit of AOL), **Microsoft** agreed May 29 to pay $750 mil. A power failure caused **blackouts** affecting some 50 mil people in Ohio, Michigan, and the Northeast, as well as eastern Canada, on Aug. 14.

The Roman Catholic archdiocese of Boston agreed to pay up to $85 mil in **sex abuse settlement** announced Sept. 9. Californians, Oct. 7, voted to recall Gov. Gray Davis (D) and replace him with actor-turned-politician **Arnold Schwarzenegger** (R). Rev. V. Gene Robinson consecrated Nov. 2 as Episcopal Church's **first openly gay bishop**.

Senate, Nov. 3, approved $87.5 bil for **U.S. military forces in Iraq** and help rebuilding the country. Virginia jury, Nov. 17, found **John Muhammad** guilty in 2002 Washington, DC, area **sniper attacks** that killed 10; sentenced to death. Another Virginia jury found accomplice **Lee Malvo** guilty of murder in the attacks, Dec. 18; sentenced to life in prison without parole. Massachusetts court decided 4-3, Nov. 18, that **gay couples had right to marry** under state constitution.

Pres. Bush signed bill Dec. 8 to overhaul **Medicare**, adding prescription drug benefit and expanding role of private insurance companies. **Saddam Hussein captured** by U.S. forces Dec. 13, in underground hideout southeast of Tikrit.

2004 On Feb. 12, San Francisco began issuing marriage licenses to same-sex couples; process blocked Mar. 11 by state supreme court. Photos showing abuse of **Abu Ghraib prison inmates** in Iraq by American soldiers emerged Apr. 3. **National World War II Memorial** in Washington, DC, opened Apr. 29.

Ronald Reagan, 40th U.S. president, died June 5. U.S.-led coalition formally transferred power to **interim Iraqi government,** June 28. The **9/11 Commission Report**, released July 22, called for restructuring U.S. intelligence operations.

In Boston, July 28-29, Democrats nominated Sen. **John Kerry** (MA) for president and Sen. **John Edwards** (NC) for vice president.

Four hurricanes hit Florida and surrounding states, Aug. 13-Sept. 25; blamed for over 50 deaths and $20 bil in damage in U.S. **Boston Red Sox** won World Series Oct. 27, for first time since 1918.

Pres. Bush reelected Nov. 2. U.S. forces took control of the Iraqi city of **Fallujah** from insurgents, Nov. 14. Pres. Bush signed intelligence reform bill Dec. 17, creating a **director of national intelligence**.

2005 Two U.S. soldiers found guilty, Jan. 14, in **Abu Ghraib prisoner abuses** in Iraq and sentenced to prison terms.

Pres. **Bush inaugurated** for 2nd term, Jan. 20. **Condoleezza Rice** became first black woman sec. of state, Jan. 26. **Alberto**

2005: Hurricane Katrina and subsequent failure of levees cause unprecedented destruction in New Orleans and along the Gulf Coast.

Gonzales became first Hispanic U.S. atty. gen., Feb. 3. **Terri Schiavo**, in a persistent vegetative state since 1990, died Mar. 31, 13 days after feeding tube was removed.

Vanity Fair article revealed May 31 that former FBI official W. Mark Felt was **"Deep Throat"**—key source for *Washington Post* reporters Bob Woodward and Carl Bernstein probing 1972 **Watergate break-in**.

Hurricane Katrina hit Gulf coast, Aug. 29, causing devastation in Louisiana, Mississippi, and Alabama. Breach in a levee on Lake Pontchartrain, Aug. 30, flooded **New Orleans**. Relief efforts widely criticized as insufficient.

Chief Justice **William H. Rehnquist** died Sept. 3. Bush Sept. 5 nominated as successor **John G. Roberts Jr.**; on Sept. 29 he was confirmed by Senate, 78-22, and sworn in as 17th chief justice. White House counsel **Harriet Miers**, nominated Oct. 3 to Supreme Court, withdrew Oct. 27. In her place, Bush, Oct. 31, nominated **Samuel A. Alito Jr.**; confirmed Jan. 31, 2006.

House Majority Leader **Tom DeLay** (R, TX) indicted in Texas Sept. 28 for allegedly conspiring to launder illegal contributions; he stepped down from his leadership post.

New York Times, Dec. 16, reported that Pres. Bush in 2002 had secretly authorized National Security Agency to **eavesdrop without court warrant** on people in U.S. suspected of terrorist activities. Senate, Dec. 21, passed $453 bil defense appropriations bill with **anti-torture amendment**.

2006 Former top Republican lobbyist **Jack Abramoff** pleaded guilty Jan. 3 to bribery and other charges; in plea agreement, promised to cooperate with investigation into his dealings with members of Congress. Former Enron CEO **Jeffrey Skilling** convicted May 25 of fraud, conspiracy, and insider trading related to Enron's 2001 bankruptcy. **Kenneth Lay**, Enron's founder and Skilling's successor as CEO, found guilty same day of fraud and conspiracy; died July 15.

U.S. Supreme Court ruled June 29 that Pres. Bush's system for trying terrorism detainees at **Guantánamo** Bay was unauthorized under federal law and Geneva Conventions. Bush, July 19, issued his **first veto**, rejecting bill to end federal funding constraints on human embryonic **stem cell research**.

British authorities announced Aug. 10 they had foiled terrorist plot to use **liquid explosives** on flights between Britain and U.S.; new security restrictions introduced. In speech Sept. 6 Bush confirmed existence of **secret overseas prisons** for terrorism suspects run by CIA.

Pres. Bush signed bill Oct. 26 authorizing construction of 700-mi fence along **U.S.-Mexico border**; broader immigration bill failed in Congress.

Democrats won control of House and Senate in **midterm congressional elections** Nov. 7. Pres. Bush announced Nov. 8 that Defense Sec. **Donald Rumsfeld**, a focus of criticism over Iraq war, had resigned. **Gerald R. Ford**, 38th U.S. president, died Dec. 26 at age 93.

2007 Rep. Nancy Pelosi (D, CA) chosen Jan. 4 as **first woman Speaker of the House**. Pres. Bush announced Jan. 10 he was sending more than 20,000 additional troops to Iraq, in **troop "surge"** backed by Lt. Gen. **David Petraeus**, new top U.S. commander in Iraq.

Reports of substandard conditions at **Walter Reed Army Medical Center** in Washington, DC, resulted in dismissals of military officials, Mar. 1-2. I. Lewis **"Scooter" Libby**, former chief of staff for Vice Pres. Cheney, found guilty Mar. 6 of perjury and obstructing justice in the investigation into a leak exposing undercover CIA agent Valerie Plame Wilson; Bush commuted his prison sentence.

A senior at **Virginia Tech** killed 27 students and 5 faculty members on Apr. 16 before killing himself. On Apr. 18, Supreme Court upheld, 5-4, a 2003 federal law that banned so-called **partial birth abortions**.

U.S. Senate and House May 24 approved Iraq and Afghanistan **war-funding bill** without timetable for withdrawal of U.S. troops from Iraq; Congress also raised **minimum wage** from $5.15 to $7.25 per hour over 2 years.

Dow Jones closed over 14,000 July 19, just 59 trading days after passing 13,000. Pres. Bush issued an executive order July 20 requiring that **imprisoned terror suspects** receive "the basic necessities of life" and barring cruel, inhuman, or degrading treatment. *Harry Potter and the Deathly Hallows*, final novel in J. K. Rowling's series, released July 21, earning record U.S. sales.

2007: Pres. George W. Bush sends a "surge" of additional U.S. troops to Iraq.

A **Minneapolis highway bridge collapsed** Aug. 1, causing the deaths of 13 people. Congress, Aug. 4, cleared measure allowing **National Security Agency** to monitor communications without court warrants if believed related to terrorism. Barry Bonds tied Major League Baseball's all-time career **home-run record** at 755—set by Hank Aaron—on Aug. 4 in San Diego; hit No. 756 on Aug. 7.

Karl Rove, Bush's chief political strategist, announced Aug. 13 that he was resigning. **José Padilla** convicted of conspiracy in terrorism case, Aug. 16; later sentenced to 17 years, 4 months in prison. Atty. Gen. **Alberto Gonzales**, blamed for alleged firing of U.S. attorneys, announced his resignation Aug. 27.

Congress voted, Nov. 6 and 8, to **overturn veto** by Pres. Bush for first time, on a $23 bil water projects bill. Report by former U.S. Sen. George J. Mitchell, released Dec. 13, presented evidence of **performance-enhancing drug use** by 86 Major League Baseball players.

On Dec. 6 Pres. Bush announced accord among mortgage lenders to freeze interest rates for some and provide refinancing options. Under law signed Dec. 17, New Jersey became the first state to **repeal the death penalty** since Supreme Court reinstated it in 1976. An energy bill mandating an increase in automobile **fuel-economy standards** to 35 mi per gallon by 2030 signed by Pres. Bush Dec. 19.

2008 Sen. **John McCain** (AZ) won New Hampshire primary, Jan. 8; clinched 2008 Republican presidential nomination by early Mar. Among Democrats, Sen. **Barack Obama** (IL) moved ahead of closest rival Sen. **Hillary Clinton** (NY) to clinch nomination in early June.

The Federal Reserve cut key interest rates, Jan. 22 and 30, to aid U.S. economy; $168 bil **economic stimulus** package, signed Feb. 13 by Pres. Bush, provided tax rebates.

In Mar. 18 speech, Sen. Obama discussed America's racial divide and condemned inflammatory rhetoric used by Rev. **Jeremiah Wright**, his former pastor.

Justice Dept., Apr. 1, declassified 2003 legal brief that sanctioned use of extreme methods in questioning detainees linked to al-Qaeda. U.S. Supreme Court ruled June 12 that foreign prisoners at **Guantánamo Bay** could challenge detention by filing writs of **habeas corpus**.

Benedict XVI made his first U.S. papal visit, Apr. 15-20. **Oil prices spiked** above $140 per barrel in June; national average price for gallon of regular gas topped $4.

Sec. of State Condoleezza Rice signed agreements in Czech Republic, July 8, and Poland, Aug. 20, to place components of a U.S. **missile defense system** there (agreements rescinded by U.S., Sept. 17, 2009). Measure signed July 10 by Pres. Bush expanded government power to spy on suspected terrorists. U.S. **military deaths in Iraq** dropped to 13 in July, lowest monthly total since the war began. U.S., Sept. 1, gave Iraqi forces security responsibilities in Anbar province, formerly center of a Sunni insurgency. U.S. air strike in **Afghanistan** village of Azizabad, Aug. 22, killed up to 90 civilians, according to Afghan sources.

Meeting Aug. 25-28 in Denver, CO, Democrats nominated Sen. **Barack Obama** (IL) for president and Sen. **Joe Biden** (DE) for vice president. Meeting Sept. 3 in St. Paul, MN,

Republicans nominated Sen. **John McCain** (AZ) for president and Alaska Gov. **Sarah Palin** for vice president.

With financial system in crisis, federal government Sept. 7 took control of mortgage finance companies **Fannie Mae** and **Freddie Mac**. On Wall Street a week later, investment titan **Merrill Lynch** agreed to sell itself to Bank of America for $50 bil, and **Lehman Brothers** declared bankruptcy, after finding no buyer. The Fed Sept. 16 took control of insurance giant American International Group (**AIG**), giving it a credit line that expanded to $144 bil by Oct. 31.

On Sept. 20, a Treasury Dept. plan was introduced to purchase up to $700 bil of **"toxic" mortgage-backed securities** to restore confidence among investors and banks. Legislation to implement Troubled Assets Relief Program (**TARP**) failed in the House, Sept. 29, sending Dow Jones down 778 points. Revised **"bailout" plan** passed Senate Oct. 1, 74-25, and House Oct. 3, 263-171; gave Treasury immediate access to half of $700 bil in TARP funds, with broad discretion in their use. On Oct. 21 Fed pledged $540 bil as a backup to protect money market funds.

Barack Obama elected, Nov. 4, as **first African American president** in U.S. history, earning 53% of popular vote and 365 of 538 electoral votes. Democrats also increased majorities in House and Senate. California voters approved **Proposition 8**, banning same-sex marriages in the state.

Dow Jones fell 427 points, or 5.1%, Nov. 19, going below 8,000. U.S. government Nov. 23 announced plan to provide $20 bil in cash and up to $306 bil more as backup to protect ailing **Citigroup** from potential mortgage losses; Dow Jones rose 397 points. Pres.-elect Obama Nov. 24 named **Timothy Geithner** to be treasury sec.; he was confirmed Jan. 26, 2009. Dow Jones dropped 680 points Dec. 1 after reports that manufacturing had hit 26-year low and that U.S economy fell into **recession** in Dec. 2007.

Pres.-elect Obama named former rival **Hillary Clinton**, Dec. 1, to be sec. of state (confirmed Jan. 21, 2009). Illinois Gov. **Rod Blagojevich** (D) arrested Dec. 9, accused of seeking to sell Senate seat being vacated by Obama. Asserting innocence, Blagojevich appointed former state Atty. Gen. **Roland Burris** to the Senate seat, Dec. 30. **Bernard Madoff** arrested Dec. 11 on charges he had defrauded investment clients in massive **Ponzi scheme**; sentenced to 150 years in jail in guilty plea, June 2009. Fed, Dec. 16, cut benchmark interest rate to near zero. On Dec. 19, Pres. Bush announced that $17 bil in **TARP funds** would be used to help keep **General Motors** and **Chrysler** afloat.

2009 Illinois Gov. **Rod Blagojevich** (D) impeached Jan. 9, convicted Jan. 29 by state Senate and removed from office. Treasury Dept., Jan. 15, gained access to remaining $350 bil in TARP funds; provided funds to prop up **Bank of America**.

Barack Obama inaugurated Jan. 20 as 44th U.S. president. He issued executive orders Jan. 22 restricting CIA interrogation practices and calling for closing of U.S. military prison at **Guantánamo Bay**, Cuba, within a year (closing blocked by Congress). Treasury Sec. Geithner, Feb. 10, outlined $2 tril program to stabilize banking and ease credit markets with "stress tests" that led to greater capital requirements for some banks. Pres. Obama signed **economic stimulus** bill Feb. 17, providing for $212 bil in tax cuts and $575 bil in new spending; introduced $275 bil program Feb. 18 to help protect homeowners from **foreclosure** and ease terms for refinancing.

Pres. Obama announced, Feb. 17, that U.S. would send 17,000 more troops to **Afghanistan** and said, Feb. 27, that most U.S. troops would be out of Iraq by Aug. 2010. California legislators, ending 15-week deadlock, closed $42 bil budget gap, Feb. 19; revised plan passed July 24.

Treasury Sec. Geithner, Mar. 23, introduced Public-Private Investment Program (PPIP), offering incentives to encourage purchases of **"toxic assets."**

Iowa's Supreme Court Apr. 3 struck down state law barring **same-sex marriage**; measures allowing it were approved in Vermont, Apr. 7; Maine, May 6 (repealed in Nov. 3 referendum); and New Hampshire, June 3.

Justice Dept. Apr. 16 released memos offering legal rationale for CIA interrogation methods that included **waterboarding**. On Aug. 24, Atty. Gen. Eric Holder appointed special prosecutor to investigate **possible detainee abuse**.

Obama administration Apr. 13 eased restrictions on family travel and remittances to **Cuba**. After outbreak of influenza A (H1N1), or **swine flu**, in Mexico and then in U.S., U.S. officials declared public health emergency Apr. 26.

Chrysler LLC filed for bankruptcy protection Apr. 30; auto workers' union retirement health-care fund given 55% stake in reorganized company. Pres. Obama, May 19, tightened **fuel efficiency** standards for vehicles. **General Motors** filed for bankruptcy June 1, under plan providing new federal funds. On June 9, 10 financial firms got permission from U.S. Treasury to return some $68 bil in **TARP funds**.

George Tiller, Kansas doctor who performed **late-term abortions**, murdered May 31; anti-abortion activist was convicted Jan. 2010 and sentenced Mar. 2010 to life in prison.

Speaking June 4 in Egypt, Pres. Obama called for "new beginning" in relations with **Muslim world**. U.S. military completed **withdrawal from Iraq's cities** and towns June 30; some 130,000 U.S. troops remained at bases.

Pres. Obama, June 22, signed measure to regulate content and marketing of tobacco products. Pop superstar **Michael Jackson** died June 25; death attributed to intoxication from a powerful hospital anesthetic. Jackson's personal physician convicted of manslaughter in 2011. Alaska Gov. **Sarah Palin** (R), July 3, announced resignation. Obama and Russian Pres. Dmitri Medvedev, in Russia July 6, agreed on **reducing nuclear arsenals** and allowing U.S. flights to Afghanistan through Russian airspace.

Judge **Sonia Sotomayor** confirmed Aug. 6 for Supreme Court vacancy left by retirement of David Souter; sworn in Aug. 8, she became first Hispanic to join the court.

Short-term federal **"cash for clunkers"** program, for trading in old gas-guzzling vehicles, began July 24; ultimately funded at $3 bil. Sen. Edward M. (Ted) Kennedy (D, MA) died Aug. 25.

Airport shuttle driver Najibullah Zazi arrested Sept. 19 and charged, Sept. 24, with involvement in plot to produce bombs for **terror attacks** in the New York City subway system; he later pleaded guilty.

Government reported Oct. 29 that real GDP grew at 3.5% annual rate in July-Sept., signaling **recession** ended. However, **unemployment** in Oct. passed 10%. Pres. Obama Nov. 6 signed measure extending unemployment benefits and $8,000 tax credit for first-time homebuyers.

Pres. Obama announced Oct. 30 end to U.S. travel and immigration restrictions on people infected with AIDS virus. On Nov. 5, 12 soldiers and a civilian were killed in **mass shooting at Ft. Hood**, TX; Army psychiatrist Maj. Nidal Malik Hasan, shot and captured by police SWAT team, was charged in the shootings.

U.S. House Nov. 7 approved a $1.1 tril **health care reform bill**, 220-215, with only 1 Republican vote in favor; Senate Dec. 24 approved a different $871 bil version, 60-39, with no Republican votes, leaving the final fate of the legislation in limbo. Pres. Obama Dec. 1 announced a surge of 30,000 additional troops to **Afghanistan** so as to peak at 100,000, with drawdown to begin within 18 months. Accepting **Nobel Peace Prize**, Dec. 10 in Oslo, Norway, Obama defended U.S.-led military action in Afghanistan as a "just war."

Tiger Woods Dec. 11 acknowledged infidelity in his marriage and announced he was taking a break from pro golf. Pres. Obama brokered **greenhouse-gas accord**, Dec. 18 in Copenhagen, establishing nonbinding reduction goals.

Detroit-bound airline passengers, Dec. 25, thwarted attempt by Nigerian man to ignite **explosives hidden in his underwear**. On Dec. 30, a Jordanian CIA informant acting as a double agent set off bomb at high-level CIA meeting site near Afghan-Pakistan border, killing himself and 8 others.

2010 In special election Jan. 19 in Massachusetts, state Sen. **Scott Brown** (R) won U.S. Senate seat held by Sen. Edward Kennedy (D) for nearly 47 years; result cost Democrats their filibuster-proof majority. U.S. Supreme Court Jan. 21 held that corporations had a First Amendment right to spend unlimited funds on advertising to influence election outcomes.

The Obama administration Feb. 1 released 10-year spending plan, projecting declining deficits but still-rising public debt. Obama Feb. 18 created bipartisan National Commission on **Fiscal Responsibility and Reform**, headed by former Clinton chief of staff Erskine Bowles (D) and former Sen. Alan Simpson (R, WY).

2010: The _Deepwater Horizon_ rig explodes, spilling oil into the Gulf of Mexico for nearly 3 months.

U.S. and other coalition troops launched major offensive in **Helmand Province**, Afghanistan, Feb. 13, targeting Taliban strongholds.

Measure legalizing **same-sex marriage** in Washington, DC, came into force Mar. 3. Pres. Obama, Mar. 18, signed $18 bil **job-stimulus** measure providing tax cuts and other employer incentives.

Long effort by Democrats to enact **health care reform legislation** succeeded on Mar. 21 when the House voted, 219-212, with no Republican support, to approve bill as passed by Senate in Dec. 2009. The wide-ranging, controversial measure, signed by Pres. Obama on Mar. 23, aimed in part at extending **health insurance** to some 32 mil uninsured over 10 years; the estimated cost was $938 bil.

Community organizing group **ACORN** announced Mar. 22 that it would disband. Explosion in **West Virginia coal mine**, Apr. 5, killed 29. Meeting Apr. 8 in Prague, Pres. Obama and Russian Pres. Dmitri Medvedev signed New Strategic Arms Reduction Treaty, or **New START** (ratified by Senate Dec. 2010; in force Feb. 2011). On Apr. 15, Pres. Obama outlined plans for **NASA** to send manned missions to an asteroid by 2025 and to Mars by the mid-2030s; defended decision to terminate Bush administration program to return astronauts to the moon by 2020.

Toyota agreed Apr. 19 to pay $16.4 mil penalty for failing to disclose gas pedal problems. A gas explosion and fire engulfed _Deepwater Horizon_ drilling platform off Louisiana, killing 11 people on board Apr. 20. About 4.9 mil barrels of **oil spilled into the Gulf** of Mexico over 3 months, damaging Gulf ecology and the regional economy. Federal government, May 27, imposed **moratorium** on deepwater exploratory drilling in the Gulf. After White House meeting June 16, parent company BP agreed to set aside $20 bil fund to compensate persons for losses. Oil flow was stopped July 15.

Arizona Gov. Jan Brewer (R), Apr. 23, signed controversial **immigration measure** which authorized police to arrest anyone reasonably suspected of being an illegal immigrant. Implementation blocked by court challenge. New York City police May 1 dismantled crude **car bomb in Times Square**; quickly traced to suspect who pleaded guilty to terrorism charges.

Pres. Obama May 10 nominated **Elena Kagan** to the U.S. Supreme Court to replace retiring Justice John Paul Stevens; confirmed by Senate, Aug. 5. Long-serving Sen. **Arlen Specter** (D, PA), who had switched parties in 2009, was defeated for nomination in May 18 primary.

Pres. Obama June 23 named Gen. **David Petraeus** as commander of troops in Afghanistan, replacing Gen. Stanley McChrystal, who was forced to resign after publication of disparaging comments he and his staff had made about Obama administration. Ten **Russian agents** were arrested June 27. They were later allowed to return to Russia in exchange for 4 men imprisoned there on charges of spying for the U.S.

Investment giant **Goldman Sachs** agreed July 15 to pay $550 mil to settle case brought by the SEC, alleging it had duped investors. Pres. Obama signed major **financial reform measure**, July 21.

More than 75,000 Afghanistan documents, many of them classified, were published July 25 on website run by **WikiLeaks** and in some news outlets. U.S. had filed charges, July 6, against Pfc. Bradley Manning, arrested May 26 in connection with earlier WikiLeaks releases.

New York City's landmark commission Aug. 3 cleared way for construction of an **Islamic cultural center** near site of former World Trade Center, generating controversy. Plans by a tiny Pentecostal church in Gainesville, FL, to **burn Korans** on Sept. 11 sparked denunciations in U.S. and riots abroad before being called off.

Last U.S. combat unit left Iraq Aug. 19 and Pres. Obama, Aug. 31, declared **U.S. combat mission in Iraq ended**; however, 50,000 troops remained in noncombat units.

Congress passed measures to **aid small businesses** with loans and tax breaks; signed into law Sept. 27. **TARP program** reached 2-year mark Oct. 3, the day its authority to make new commitments expired. Treasury Dept. estimated net cost at $51 bil or less, though this figure was disputed. Taxpayers continued to pay for federal bailout of **Fannie Mae** and **Freddie Mac**.

WikiLeaks released documents covering Iraq conflict Oct. 22. Authorities in UK and UAE Oct. 29 confiscated packages with bombs concealed in printer cartridges, bound for Chicago area.

In Nov. 2 elections **Republicans gained control** of the U.S. House and picked up 6 more seats in the Senate. The Fed Nov. 3 announced plan to buy $600 bil worth of Treasury securities over 8 months as means of stimulating the sluggish economy. Former House Majority Leader **Tom DeLay** (R, TX) convicted of money laundering, Nov. 24. On Dec. 2, U.S. House voted, 333-79, to censure veteran Rep. **Charles Rangel** (D, NY) for ethics violations.

Pres. Obama, Dec. 17, signed $858 bil compromise measure that extended **Bush-era tax cuts** for two years, including tax cuts for the wealthy, while also extending **unemployment** insurance benefits and reducing the Social Security payroll tax rate for one year. **"Don't ask, don't tell"** policy with respect to gays in the military was repealed, Dec. 22.

2011 The 112th Congress convened Jan. 5 with Republicans taking control of the House and Democrats retaining control of Senate; **John Boehner** (R, OH) elected House Speaker. Gunman in Tucson, AZ, Jan. 8, killed 6 people and injured 13 others, including Rep. **Gabrielle Giffords** (D, AZ), making a public appearance.

Rep. **Christopher Lee** (R, NY) resigned Feb. 9 after website Gawker published a flirtatious e-mail exchange between the married congressman and a woman. U.S. Atty. Gen. Eric Holder disclosed Feb. 23 that the Obama administration would no longer defend in court the 1996 **Defense of Marriage Act** (DOMA), which allowed federal government and states to deny recognition to same-sex marriages legal in some states. U.S. Supreme Court Mar. 2 ruled that the anti-gay **Westboro Baptist Church** of Topeka, KS, had right to protest at funeral of a U.S. marine killed in Iraq.

A measure to limit **collective bargaining** by most public sector employees, championed by Wisconsin Gov. **Scott Walker** (R), passed state legislature Mar. 9-10 despite large demonstrations by opponents and a walkout by Senate Democrats.

With federal government shutdown looming, congressional leaders reached agreement Apr. 9 on **omnibus appropriations bill**. Pres. Obama outlined broad economic plan, Apr. 13, to cut $4 tril from projected deficits over 12 years by cutting spending and raising taxes on the wealthy. Two days later, House approved budget resolution based on cost-cutting plan by Rep. Paul Ryan (R, WI). **Ryan plan** would reduce deficits by $4.4 tril over 10 years while cutting spending and taxes; would replace Medicaid with block grants to states and transform Medicare into subsidized private insurance for new recipients. House plan defeated in Senate, May 25.

Former baseball slugger **Barry Bonds** was convicted Apr. 13 of obstructing justice in 2003 for evasive answers to a grand jury investigating use of banned **performance-enhancing drugs**. Sen. **John Ensign** (R, NV) announced Apr. 21 that he would resign his Senate seat, amid an ethics committee probe into alleged financial irregularities

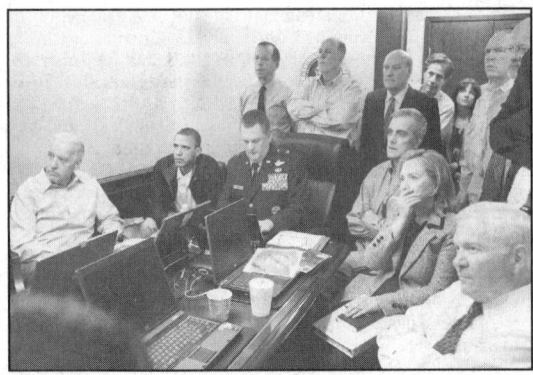

2011: As administration officials monitored the operation from Washington, U.S. forces kill Osama bin Laden, mastermind of the Sept. 11, 2001, terrorist attacks.

connected to an extramarital affair. Pres. Obama Apr. 27 denounced rumors by so-called birthers and released copies of his "long-form" **birth certificate**.

On May 2, in Abbottabad, Pakistan, a CIA-led squadron of U.S. Navy SEALs breached hideout of al-Qaeda leader **Osama bin Laden**, responsible for Sept. 11, 2001, attacks on U.S., and killed him; he was buried at sea the same day.

Early candidates for the 2012 GOP presidential nomination met May 5 for first televised **campaign debate**. Participants included Rep. **Ron Paul** (TX), executive **Herman Cain**, former Minnesota Gov. **Tim Pawlenty**, and former Sen. **Rick Santorum** (PA). Joining in a June 13 debate were former House Speaker **Newt Gingrich** (GA), Rep. **Michele Bachmann** (MN), and former Massachusetts Gov. **Mitt Romney**.

Intl. Monetary Fund chief **Dominique Strauss-Kahn** was arrested in New York City May 14, charged with attempted rape of a hotel maid; he was released from house arrest, July 1, after prosecutors questioned alleged victim's credibility. The single **deadliest U.S. tornado** in more than a half-century hit Joplin, MO, May 22, claiming an estimated 161 lives. A record 758 tornadoes, concentrated in the Southeast, had struck the U.S. during Apr., causing an estimated 363 deaths.

House rejected measure to raise federal **debt ceiling** from $14.3 tril to $16.7 tril without compensating deficit reductions May 31; U.S. faced possible loss of borrowing authority starting Aug. 2. Talks between Obama and House Speaker Boehner on possible "grand bargain" collapsed July 22. Budget control act shaped by Vice Pres. Joe Biden and Senate minority leader Mitch McConnell (R, KY) finally passed by bipartisan votes in Congress, Aug. 1-2. It called for 3-stage rise in the debt ceiling and some $900 bil in spending cuts, with an additional $1.5 tril in cuts to be worked out by supercommittee. Standard & Poor's, Aug. 5, downgraded nation's top-grade AAA **credit rating**.

U.S. stepped up **drone attacks** against jihadists in Yemen after Pres. Ali Abdullah Saleh and others were wounded June 3 in a rocket attack. Accused of having used campaign contributions to conceal an affair and resulting paternity, former Sen. **John Edwards** (D, NC), 2004 Democratic vice-presidential nominee, indicted June 3 for violating campaign finance laws. Rep. **Anthony Weiner** (D, NY) announced resignation June 16, after suggestive photos he had sent via Twitter became public.

Obama administration June 22 announced timetable for drawing down troops in **Afghanistan**, with all combat troops to be out by the end of 2014. U.S. House June 24 voted down measure to authorize military operations in **Libya** but also defeated a measure to sharply restrict them.

Championed by New York Gov. Andrew Cuomo (D), a measure legalizing **same-sex marriage** gained final approval of the state senate June 24. After a deadlocked jury failed to reach a verdict on most counts in Aug. 2010, former Gov. **Rod Blagojevich** (D, IL) was convicted in a retrial on 17 felony corruption charges June 27 and sentenced Dec. 7 to 14 years in prison. **Bank of America**, June 29, agreed to pay $8.5 bil to cover investor losses on mortgage-backed securities issued by its Countrywide Financial unit.

Leon Panetta was confirmed by Senate, replacing Robert Gates as sec. of defense July 1. Gen. **David Petraeus**, commander of troops in Afghanistan, succeeded Panetta as CIA director. On July 5, in a widely publicized case, an Orlando, FL, jury found **Casey Anthony** not guilty of killing 2-year-old daughter, Caylee.

Minnesota Gov. Mark Dayton (D) signed 2-year, $36 bil budget bills July 20, ending a 20-day state **government shutdown** caused by budget deadlock. After 30 years and 135 missions, NASA's **space shuttle** program ended with landing of the *Atlantis*, July 21, at Florida's Kennedy Space Center. Rep. **David Wu** (D, OR) announced resignation July 26, after reports alleged that he had pressured an 18-year-old woman into an unwanted sexual encounter.

Taliban insurgents in Afghanistan shot down U.S. transport helicopter Aug. 6, killing 38 people, including 17 Navy SEAL commandos. Rep. **Michele Bachmann** (MN) won GOP Ames straw poll in Iowa Aug. 13, edging out Rep. Ron Paul (TX). Former Minnesota Gov. **Tim Pawlenty**, who finished a distant third, dropped out of race. **Hurricane Irene** slammed into the Eastern seaboard, Aug. 27-28, causing at least 40 deaths and $15.8 bil in damage in 13 states.

Atty. Gen. Eric Holder announced Aug. 30 the departure of 2 senior Justice Dept. officials who had overseen Operation Fast and Furious, a failed sting operation that had arranged for sale of guns to be smuggled to drug traffickers in Mexico. Pres. Obama, Sept. 8, proposed $447 bil economic **stimulus plan**, to be paid for by limiting tax breaks and raising taxes on high incomes. **Solyndra**, a solar panel manufacturer touted by the Obama administration, filed for bankruptcy Sept. 6 after having received $535 mil in federal loan guarantees.

A diffuse left-wing movement that began Sept. 17 as **Occupy Wall Street** in New York City expanded by Oct. 15 to demonstrations in hundreds of cities in the U.S. and overseas. Violence erupted Oct. 25 in Oakland, CA, when police used force to keep protesters from reestablishing a tent camp in a downtown plaza. **Anwar al-Awlaki**, a U.S. citizen and Muslim cleric linked to terrorist attacks in U.S., was killed Sept. 30 in U.S. drone attack in Yemen.

Jerry Sandusky, a former football coach at **Penn State** Univ., arrested Nov. 5 on charges he had sexually abused young boys; resulting scandal led to firing of longtime head coach **Joe Paterno** and university president Graham Spanier.

U.S. Office of Special Counsel disclosed Nov. 8 that the mortuary at Dover Air Force Base in Delaware had **mishandled remains** of slain military personnel. Justice Dept. announced Nov. 22 that Merck would pay $950 mil and plead guilty to a criminal complaint over marketing of **Vioxx**, linked to increased cardiac and stroke risk. AMR Corp., parent company of **American Airlines**, sought bankruptcy protection Nov. 29. Under pressure from allegations of an extramarital affair, **Herman Cain** announced Dec. 3 that he was suspending his campaign for Republican presidential nomination.

Formalities Dec. 12-15 marked the end of the U.S. military mission in **Iraq**. Last U.S. troop convoy crossed into Kuwait, Dec. 18. Insurgent attacks Dec. 22 killed 69 people in Baghdad; al-Qaeda in Iraq claimed responsibility. Since U.S.-led invasion in Mar. 2003, nearly 4,500 U.S. service members had been killed and another 32,000 wounded. In **Afghanistan**, about 90,000 U.S. troops and 40,000 allied forces remained, supporting Afghan government against insurgents; more than 400 U.S. troops died there in 2011.

Averting new government shutdown, Congress Dec. 16-17 passed $915 bil omnibus measure to fund various federal agencies through 2012 fiscal year. Congress Dec. 23 also approved 2-month extension of a **payroll tax** break, extended benefits for long-term **unemployed**, and continued Medicare reimbursement rates for physicians. A $662 bil military spending bill approved by Congress Dec. 14-15 was signed Dec. 31 by Obama, with signing statement saying the administration would not authorize indefinite military detention of U.S citizens without trial.

Dow Jones Industrial Average closed Dec. 30 up 5.5% for the year; S&P 500 was nearly flat, and Nasdaq Composite Index was down 1.8%.

Patrick Henry's Speech to the Virginia Convention

The following is an excerpt from Patrick Henry's speech to the Virginia Convention, which met at St. John's Church in Richmond, on Mar. 23, 1775, to react to British oppression.

Gentlemen may cry, peace, peace—but there is no peace. The war is actually begun! The next gale that sweeps from the north will bring to our ears the clash of resounding arms! Our brethren are already in the field! Why stand we here idle? What is it that gentlemen wish? What would they have? Is life so dear, or peace so sweet, as to be purchased at the price of chains and slavery? Forbid it, Almighty God! I know not what course others may take; but as for me, give me liberty, or give me death!

Adoption of the Declaration of Independence

On June 7, 1776, Richard Henry Lee, who had issued the first call for a congress of the colonies, introduced in the Continental Congress at Philadelphia a resolution declaring "that these United Colonies are, and of right ought to be, free and independent states, that they are absolved from all allegiance to the British Crown, and that all political connection between them and the state of Great Britain is, and ought to be, totally dissolved."

The resolution, seconded by John Adams on behalf of the Massachusetts delegation, came up again June 11 when a committee of five chaired by Thomas Jefferson (VA) was appointed to express the purpose of the resolution in a declaration of independence. The other four were John Adams, Benjamin Franklin (PA), Robert R. Livingston (NY), and Roger Sherman (CT).

Drafting the Declaration was assigned to Jefferson, who worked on a portable desk of his own construction in a room at Market and 7th St. The committee reported the result on June 28, 1776. The members of the Congress suggested a number of changes, which Jefferson called "deplorable." They did not approve Jefferson's arraignment of the British people and King George III for encouraging and fostering the slave trade, which Jefferson called "an execrable commerce." They eliminated 630 words and added 146, leaving 1,322 words in the final draft. In its final form, capitalization was erratic. Jefferson had written that men were endowed with "inalienable" rights; in the final copy it came out as "unalienable" and has been thus ever since.

The Lee-Adams resolution of independence was adopted by 12 yeas on July 2—the actual date of the act of independence. The Declaration, which explains the act, was adopted July 4.

After the Declaration was adopted, July 4, 1776, it was turned over to printer John Dunlap to be printed on broadsides. The original copy was lost and one of his broadsides was attached to a page in the journal of the Congress. It was read aloud July 8 in Philadelphia, PA; Easton, PA; and Trenton, NJ. On July 9, it was read by order of Gen. George Washington to the troops assembled on the Common in New York City (now City Hall Park).

The Continental Congress of July 19, 1776, adopted the following resolution:

"Resolved, That the Declaration passed on the 4th, be fairly engrossed on parchment with the title and stile of 'The Unanimous Declaration of the thirteen United States of America' and that the same, when engrossed, be signed by every member of Congress."

Not all delegates who signed the engrossed Declaration were present on July 4. Robert Morris (PA), William Williams (CT), and Samuel Chase (MD) signed on Aug. 2; Oliver Wolcott (CT), George Wythe (VA), Richard Henry Lee (VA), and Elbridge Gerry (MA) signed in Aug. and Sept.; Matthew Thornton (NH) joined the Congress Nov. 4 and signed later. Thomas McKean (DE) rejoined Washington's army before signing and said later that he signed in 1781.

Charles Carroll of Carrollton was appointed a delegate by Maryland on July 4, 1776, presented his credentials July 18, and signed the engrossed Declaration on Aug. 2. Born Sept. 19, 1737, he was 95 years old and the last surviving signer when he died Nov. 14, 1832.

Two Pennsylvania delegates who did not support the Declaration July 4, 1776, were replaced. The four New York delegates did not have authority from their state to vote on July 4. On July 9, the New York state convention authorized its delegates to approve the Declaration, and the Congress was so notified on July 15, 1776. The four signed the Declaration on Aug. 2.

Declaration of Independence

The Declaration of Independence was adopted by the Continental Congress in Philadelphia on July 4, 1776. John Hancock was president of the Congress, and Charles Thomson was secretary. A copy of the Declaration, engrossed on parchment, was signed by members of Congress on and after Aug. 2, 1776. On Jan. 18, 1777, Congress ordered that "an authenticated copy, with the names of the members of Congress subscribing the same, be sent to each of the United States, and that they be desired to have the same put on record." Authenticated copies were printed in broadside form in Baltimore, where the Continental Congress was then in session. The following text is that of the original printed by John Dunlap at Philadelphia for the Continental Congress. The original is on display at the National Archives in Washington, DC.

IN CONGRESS, July 4, 1776.
A DECLARATION
By the REPRESENTATIVES of the
UNITED STATES OF AMERICA,
In GENERAL CONGRESS assembled

When in the Course of human Events, it becomes necessary for one People to dissolve the Political Bands which have connected them with another, and to assume among the Powers of the Earth, the separate and equal Station to which the Laws of Nature and of Nature's God entitle them, a decent Respect to the Opinions of Mankind requires that they should declare the causes which impel them to the Separation.

We hold these Truths to be self-evident, that all Men are created equal, that they are endowed by their Creator with certain unalienable Rights, that among these are Life, Liberty, and the Pursuit of Happiness—That to secure these Rights, Governments are instituted among Men, deriving their just Powers from the Consent of the Governed, that whenever any Form of Government becomes destructive of these Ends, it is the Right of the People to alter or to abolish it, and to institute new Government, laying its Foundation on such Principles, and organizing its Powers in such Form, as to them shall seem most likely to effect their Safety and Happiness. Prudence, indeed, will dictate that Governments long established should not be changed for light and transient Causes; and accordingly all Experience hath shewn, that Mankind are more disposed to suffer, while Evils are sufferable, than to right themselves by abolishing the Forms to which they are accustomed. But when a long Train of Abuses and Usurpations, pursuing invariably the same Object, evinces a Design to reduce them under absolute Despotism, it is their Right, it is their Duty, to throw off such Government, and to provide new Guards for their future Security. Such has been the patient Sufferance of these Colonies; and such is now the Necessity which constrains them to alter their former Systems of Government. The History of the present King of Great Britain is a History of repeated Injuries and Usurpations, all having in direct Object the Establishment of an absolute Tyranny over these States. To prove this, let Facts be submitted to a candid World.

He has refused his Assent to Laws, the most wholesome and necessary for the public Good.

He has forbidden his Governors to pass Laws of immediate and pressing Importance, unless suspended in their Operation till his Assent should be obtained; and when so suspended, he has utterly neglected to attend to them.

He has refused to pass other Laws for the Accommodation of large Districts of People, unless those People would relinquish the Right of Representation in the Legislature, a Right inestimable to them, and formidable to Tyrants only.

He has called together Legislative Bodies at Places unusual, uncomfortable, and distant from the Depository of their Public Records, for the sole Purpose of fatiguing them into Compliance with his Measures.

He has dissolved Representative Houses repeatedly, for opposing with manly Firmness his Invasions on the Rights of the People.

He has refused for a long Time, after such Dissolutions, to cause others to be elected; whereby the Legislative Powers, incapable of Annihilation, have returned to the People at large for their exercise; the State remaining in the mean time exposed to all the Dangers of Invasion from without, and Convulsions within.

He has endeavoured to prevent the Population of these States; for that Purpose obstructing the Laws for Naturalization of Foreigners; refusing to pass others to encourage their Migrations hither, and raising the Conditions of new Appropriations of Lands.

He has obstructed the Administration of Justice, by refusing his Assent to Laws for establishing Judiciary Powers.

He has made Judges dependent on his Will alone, for the Tenure of their Offices, and the Amount and payment of their Salaries.

He has erected a Multitude of new Offices, and sent hither Swarms of Officers to harrass our People, and eat out their Substance.

He has kept among us, in Times of Peace, Standing Armies, without the consent of our Legislatures.

He has affected to render the Military independent of, and superior to the Civil Power.

He has combined with others to subject us to a Jurisdiction foreign to our Constitution, and unacknowledged by our Laws; giving his Assent to their Acts of pretended Legislation:

For Quartering large bodies of armed troops among us:

For protecting them, by a mock Trial, from Punishment for any Murders which they should commit on the Inhabitants of these States:

For cutting off our Trade with all Parts of the World:

For imposing Taxes on us without our Consent:

For depriving us, in many Cases, of the Benefits of Trial by Jury:

For transporting us beyond Seas to be tried for pretended Offences:

For abolishing the free System of English Laws in a neighbouring Province, establishing therein an arbitrary Government, and enlarging its Boundaries, so as to render it at once an Example and fit Instrument for introducing the same absolute Rule into these Colonies:

For taking away our Charters, abolishing our most valuable Laws, and altering fundamentally the Forms of our Governments:

For suspending our own Legislatures, and declaring themselves invested with Power to legislate for us in all Cases whatsoever.

He has abdicated Government here, by declaring us out of his Protection and waging War against us.

He has plundered our Seas, ravaged our Coasts, burnt our towns, and destroyed the Lives of our People.

He is, at this Time, transporting large Armies of foreign Mercenaries to complete the works of Death, Desolation, and Tyranny, already begun with circumstances of Cruelty and Perfidy, scarcely paralleled in the most barbarous Ages, and totally unworthy the Head of a civilized Nation.

He has constrained our fellow Citizens taken Captive on the high Seas to bear Arms against their Country, to become the Executioners of their Friends and Brethren, or to fall themselves by their Hands.

He has excited domestic Insurrections amongst us, and has endeavoured to bring on the Inhabitants of our Frontiers, the merciless Indian Savages, whose known Rule of Warfare, is an undistinguished Destruction, of all Ages, Sexes and Conditions.

In every stage of these Oppressions we have Petitioned for Redress in the most humble Terms: Our repeated Petitions have been answered only by repeated Injury. A Prince, whose Character is thus marked by every act which may define a Tyrant, is unfit to be the Ruler of a free People.

Nor have we been wanting in Attentions to our British Brethren. We have warned them from Time to Time of Attempts by their Legislature to extend an unwarrantable Jurisdiction over us. We have reminded them of the Circumstances of our Emigration and Settlement here. We have appealed to their native Justice and Magnanimity, and we have conjured them by the Ties of our common Kindred to disavow these Usurpations, which, would inevitably interrupt our Connections and Correspondence. They too have been deaf to the Voice of Justice and of Consanguinity. We must, therefore, acquiesce in the Necessity, which denounces our Separation, and hold them, as we hold the rest of Mankind, Enemies in War, in Peace, Friends.

We, therefore, the Representatives of the UNITED STATES OF AMERICA, in General Congress, Assembled, appealing to the Supreme Judge of the World for the Rectitude of our Intentions, do, in the Name, and by Authority of the good People of these Colonies, solemnly Publish and Declare, That these United Colonies are, and of Right ought to be, Free and Independent States; that they are absolved from all Allegiance to the British Crown, and that all political Connection between them and the State of Great Britain, is and ought to be totally dissolved; and that as Free and Independent States, they have full Power to levy War, conclude Peace, contract Alliances, establish Commerce, and to do all other Acts and Things which Independent States may of right do. And for the support of this declaration, with a firm Reliance on the Protection of Divine Providence, we mutually pledge to each other our lives, our Fortunes, and our sacred Honor.

JOHN HANCOCK, President

Attest.

CHARLES THOMSON, Secretary.

Signers of the Declaration of Independence

Delegate (state)	Occupation	Birthplace	Born	Died
Adams, John (MA)	Lawyer	Braintree (Quincy), MA	Oct. 30, 1735	July 4, 1826
Adams, Samuel (MA)	Political leader	Boston, MA	Sept. 27, 1722	Oct. 2, 1803
Bartlett, Josiah (NH)	Physician, judge	Amesbury, MA	Nov. 21, 1729	May 19, 1795
Braxton, Carter (VA)	Farmer	Newington Plantation, VA	Sept. 10, 1736	Oct. 10, 1797
Carroll, Charles of Carrollton (MD)	Merchant	Annapolis, MD	Sept. 19, 1737	Nov. 14, 1832
Chase, Samuel (MD)	Judge	Princess Anne, MD	Apr. 17, 1741	June 19, 1811
Clark, Abraham (NJ)	Surveyor	Elizabethtown, NJ	Feb. 15, 1726	Sept. 15, 1794
Clymer, George (PA)	Merchant	Philadelphia, PA	Mar. 16, 1739	Jan. 23, 1813
Ellery, William (RI)	Lawyer	Newport, RI	Dec. 22, 1727	Feb. 15, 1820
Floyd, William (NY)	Soldier	Brookhaven, NY	Dec. 17, 1734	Aug. 4, 1821
Franklin, Benjamin (PA)	Printer, publisher	Boston, MA	Jan. 17, 1706	Apr. 17, 1790
Gerry, Elbridge (MA)	Merchant	Marblehead, MA	July 17, 1744	Nov. 23, 1814
Gwinnett, Button (GA)	Merchant	Gloucester, England	c. 1735	May 19, 1777
Hall, Lyman (GA)	Physician	Wallingford, CT	Apr. 12, 1724	Oct. 19, 1790
Hancock, John (MA)	Merchant	Braintree (Quincy), MA	Jan. 12, 1737	Oct. 8, 1793
Harrison, Benjamin (VA)	Farmer	Charles City County, VA	Apr. 5, 1726	Apr. 24, 1791
Hart, John (NJ)	Farmer	Stonington, CT	c. 1711	May 11, 1779
Hewes, Joseph (NC)	Merchant	Kingston, NJ	Jan. 23, 1730	Nov. 10, 1779
Heyward, Thos. Jr. (SC)	Lawyer, farmer	St. Luke's Parish, SC	July 28, 1746	Mar. 6, 1809
Hooper, William (NC)	Lawyer	Boston, MA	June 17, 1742	Oct. 14, 1790
Hopkins, Stephen (RI)	Judge, educator	Providence, RI	Mar. 7, 1707	July 13, 1785
Hopkinson, Francis (NJ)	Judge, author	Philadelphia, PA	Oct. 2, 1737	May 9, 1791
Huntington, Samuel (CT)	Judge	Windham, CT	July 3, 1731	Jan. 5, 1796
Jefferson, Thomas (VA)	Lawyer	Shadwell, VA	Apr. 13, 1743	July 4, 1826
Lee, Francis Lightfoot (VA)	Farmer	Westmoreland County, VA	Oct. 14, 1734	Jan. 11, 1797
Lee, Richard Henry (VA)	Farmer	Westmoreland County, VA	Jan. 20, 1732	June 19, 1794
Lewis, Francis (NY)	Merchant	Llandaff, Wales	Mar. 21, 1713	Dec. 31, 1802
Livingston, Philip (NY)	Merchant	Albany, NY	Jan. 15, 1716	June 12, 1778
Lynch, Thomas Jr. (SC)	Farmer	Winyah, SC	Aug. 5, 1749	(at sea) 1779
McKean, Thomas (DE)	Lawyer	New London, PA	Mar. 19, 1734	June 24, 1817
Middleton, Arthur (SC)	Farmer	Charleston, SC	June 26, 1742	Jan. 1, 1787
Morris, Lewis (NY)	Farmer	Morrisania (Bronx County), NY	Apr. 8, 1726	Jan. 22, 1798
Morris, Robert (PA)	Merchant	Liverpool, England	Jan. 31, 1734	May 8, 1806
Morton, John (PA)	Judge	Ridley, PA	c. 1724	Apr. 1777
Nelson, Thos. Jr. (VA)	Farmer	Yorktown, VA	Dec. 26, 1738	Jan. 4, 1789
Paca, William (MD)	Judge	Abingdon, MD	Oct. 31, 1740	Oct. 23, 1799
Paine, Robert Treat (MA)	Judge	Boston, MA	Mar. 11, 1731	May 12, 1814
Penn, John (NC)	Lawyer	Caroline County, VA	May 17, 1741	Sept. 14, 1788
Read, George (DE)	Judge	Cecil County, MD	Sept. 18, 1733	Sept. 21, 1798
Rodney, Caesar (DE)	Judge	Dover, DE	Oct. 7, 1728	June 29, 1784
Ross, George (PA)	Judge	New Castle, DE	May 10, 1730	July 14, 1779
Rush, Benjamin (PA)	Physician	Byberry (Philadelphia), PA	Jan. 4, 1746	Apr. 19, 1813
Rutledge, Edward (SC)	Lawyer	Charleston, SC	Nov. 23, 1749	Jan. 23, 1800
Sherman, Roger (CT)	Lawyer	Newton, MA	Apr. 19, 1721	July 23, 1793
Smith, James (PA)	Lawyer	Northern Ireland	c. 1719	July 11, 1806
Stockton, Richard (NJ)	Lawyer	Princeton, NJ	Oct. 1, 1730	Feb. 28, 1781
Stone, Thomas (MD)	Lawyer	Charles County, MD	c. 1743	Oct. 5, 1787
Taylor, George (PA)	Ironmaster	Ireland	c. 1716	Feb. 23, 1781
Thornton, Matthew (NH)	Physician	Ireland	c. 1714	June 24, 1803
Walton, George (GA)	Judge	Cumberland County, VA	c. 1741	Feb. 2, 1804
Whipple, William (NH)	Merchant, judge	Kittery, ME	Jan. 14, 1730	Nov. 28, 1785
Williams, William (CT)	Merchant	Lebanon, CT	Apr. 8, 1731	Aug. 2, 1811
Wilson, James (PA)	Judge	Carskerdo, Scotland	Sept. 14, 1742	Aug. 21, 1798
Witherspoon, John (NJ)	Clergyman, educator	Gifford, Scotland	Feb. 5, 1723	Nov. 15, 1794
Wolcott, Oliver (CT)	Judge	Windsor, CT	Nov. 20, 1726	Dec. 1, 1797
Wythe, George (VA)	Lawyer	Elizabeth City County, VA	c. 1726	June 8, 1806

Origin of the Constitution

The War of Independence was conducted by delegates from the original 13 states, who composed the Congress of the United States of America, known as the Continental Congress. In 1777 the Congress submitted to the legislatures of the states the Articles of Confederation and Perpetual Union, which were ratified by New Hampshire, Massachusetts, Rhode Island, Connecticut, New York, New Jersey, Pennsylvania, Delaware, Virginia, North Carolina, South Carolina, Georgia, and finally, in 1781, Maryland.

The first article read: "The stile of this confederacy shall be the United States of America." This did not signify a sovereign nation, because the states delegated only those powers they could not handle individually, such as to wage war, make treaties, and contract debts for general expenses (e.g., paying the army). Taxes for payment of such debts were levied by the individual states. The president signed himself "President of the United States in Congress assembled," but here the United States were considered in the plural, a cooperating group.

When the war was over, it became evident that a stronger federal union was needed. The Congress left the initiative to the legislatures. Virginia in Jan. 1786 appointed commissioners to meet with representatives of other states; delegates from Virginia, Delaware, New York, New Jersey, and Pennsylvania met at Annapolis. Alexander Hamilton prepared their call asking delegates from all states to meet in Philadelphia in May 1787 "to render the Constitution of the federal government adequate to the exigencies of the union." Congress endorsed the plan on Feb. 21, 1787. Delegates were appointed by all states except Rhode Island.

The convention was called for May 14, 1787, but a quorum was not present until May 25. George Washington was chosen president (presiding officer). The states certified 65 delegates, but 10 did not attend. The work was done by 55, not all of whom were present at all sessions. Of the 55 attending delegates, 39 signed Sept. 17, 1787, some with reservations, and 16 failed to sign. Some historians have said 74 delegates (nine more than the 65 actually certified) were named, and 19 failed to attend. These additional persons refused the appointment, were never delegates, and were never counted as absentees. Washington sent the Constitution to Congress, and that body, Sept. 28, 1787, ordered it sent to the legislatures, "in order to be submitted to a convention of delegates chosen in each state by the people thereof."

The Constitution was ratified by votes of state conventions as follows: Delaware, Dec. 7, 1787, unanimous; Pennsylvania, Dec. 12, 1787, 46 to 23; New Jersey, Dec. 18, 1787, unanimous; Georgia, Jan. 2, 1788, unanimous; Connecticut, Jan. 9, 1788, 128 to 40; Massachusetts, Feb. 6, 1788, 187 to 168; Maryland, Apr. 28, 1788, 63 to 11; South Carolina, May 23, 1788, 149 to 73; New Hampshire, June 21, 1788, 57 to 46; Virginia, June 25, 1788, 89 to 79; New York, July 26, 1788, 30 to 27. Nine states were needed to establish the operation of the Constitution "between the states so ratifying the same," and New Hampshire was the 9th state. The government did not declare the Constitution in effect until the first Wednesday in Mar. 1789, which was Mar. 4. After that, North Carolina ratified it on Nov. 21, 1789, 194 to 77; and Rhode Island, May 29, 1790, 34 to 32. Vermont in convention ratified it on Jan. 10, 1791, and by act of Congress approved on Feb. 18, 1791, was admitted into the Union as the 14th state, Mar. 4, 1791.

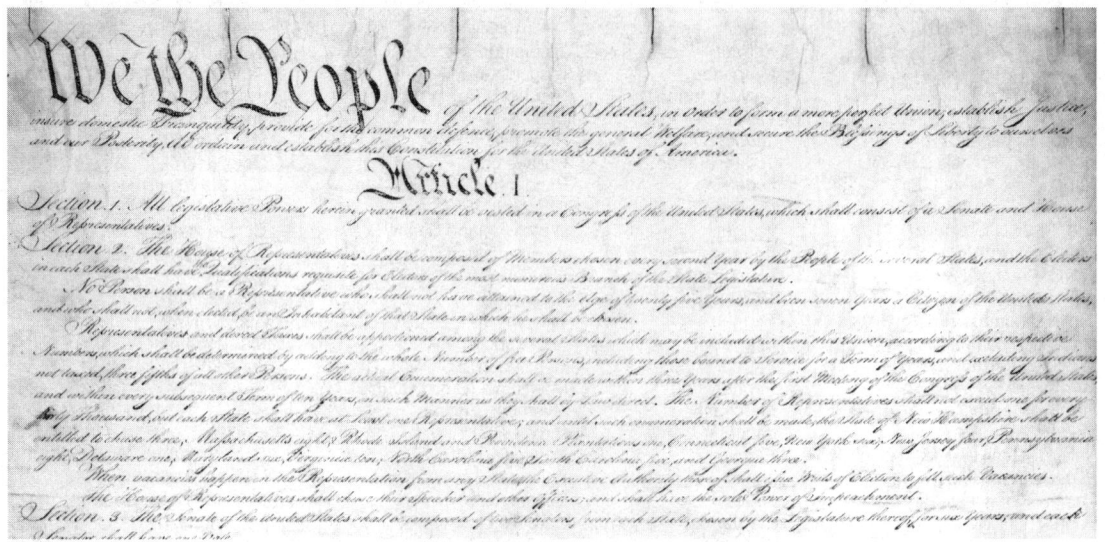

Constitution of the United States

The Original 7 Articles

The text of the Constitution given here (except for Amendment XXVII) is from the pocket-size edition of the Constitution published by the U.S. Government Printing Office as a result of a congressional resolution to print the Constitution in its original form as amended through July 5, 1971. *Text in brackets* indicates that an item has been superseded or amended, or provides background information. **Boldface text** preceding an article, section, or amendment is a brief summary, added by *The World Almanac*.

PREAMBLE

We, the People of the United States, in Order to form a more perfect Union, establish Justice, insure domestic Tranquility, provide for the common defence, promote the general Welfare, and secure the Blessings of Liberty to ourselves and our Posterity, do ordain and establish this Constitution for the United States of America.

ARTICLE I.

Section 1—Legislative powers; in whom vested.

All legislative Powers herein granted shall be vested in a Congress of the United States, which shall consist of a Senate and House of Representatives.

Section 2—House of Representatives, how and by whom chosen. Qualifications of a Representative. Representatives and direct taxes, how apportioned. Enumeration. Vacancies to be filled. Power of choosing officers, and of impeachment.

The House of Representatives shall be composed of Members chosen every second Year by the People of the several States, and the Electors in each State shall have the Qualifications requisite for Electors of the most numerous Branch of the State Legislature.

No Person shall be a Representative who shall not have attained to the Age of twenty five Years, and been seven Years a Citizen of the United States, and who shall not, when elected, be an Inhabitant of that State in which he shall be chosen.

[Representatives and direct taxes shall be apportioned among the several States which may be included within this Union, according to their respective Numbers, which shall be determined by adding to the whole Number of free Persons, including those bound to Service for a Term of Years, and excluding Indians not taxed, three-fifths of all other persons.] [The previous sentence was superseded by Amendment XIV, section 2.] The actual Enumeration shall be made within three Years after the first Meeting of the Congress of the United States, and within every subsequent Term of ten Years, in such Manner as they shall by Law direct. The Number of Representatives shall not exceed one for every thirty Thousand, but each State shall have at Least one Representative; and until such enumeration shall be made, the State of New Hampshire shall be entitled to chuse three, Massachusetts eight, Rhode-Island and Providence Plantations one, Connecticut five, New-York six, New Jersey four, Pennsylvania eight, Delaware one, Maryland six, Virginia ten, North Carolina five, South Carolina five, and Georgia three.

When vacancies happen in the Representation from any State, the Executive Authority thereof shall issue Writs of Election to fill such Vacancies.

The House of Representatives shall chuse their Speaker and other Officers; and shall have the sole Power of Impeachment.

Section 3—Senators, how and by whom chosen. How classified. Qualifications of a Senator. President of the Senate, his right to vote. President pro tem., and other officers of the Senate, how chosen. Power to try impeachments. When President is tried, Chief Justice to preside. Sentence.

The Senate of the United States shall be composed of two Senators from each State, *[chosen by the Legislature thereof] [The preceding five words were superseded by Amendment XVII.]* for six Years; and each Senator shall have one Vote.

Immediately after they shall be assembled in Consequence of the first Election, they shall be divided as equally as may be into three Classes. The Seats of the Senators of the first Class shall be vacated at the Expiration of the second Year, of the second Class at the Expiration of the fourth Year, and of the third Class at the Expiration of the Sixth year, so that one-third may be chosen every second Year; *[and if Vacancies happen by Resignation, or otherwise, during the Recess of the Legislature of any State, the Executive thereof may make temporary Appointments until the next Meeting of the Legislature, which shall then fill such Vacancies.] [The words in brackets were superseded by Amendment XVII.]*

No Person shall be a Senator who shall not have attained to the Age of thirty Years, and been nine Years a Citizen of the United States, and who shall not, when elected, be an Inhabitant of that State for which he shall be chosen.

The Vice President of the United States shall be President of the Senate, but shall have no Vote, unless they be equally divided.

The Senate shall chuse their other Officers, and also a President pro tempore, in the absence of the Vice President, or when he shall exercise the Office of President of the United States.

The Senate shall have the sole Power to try all Impeachments. When sitting for that Purpose, they shall be on Oath or Affirmation. When the President of the United States is tried, the Chief Justice shall preside: And no Person shall be convicted without the Concurrence of two thirds of the Members present.

Judgment in Cases of Impeachment shall not extend further than to removal from Office, and disqualification to hold and enjoy any Office of honor, Trust or Profit under the United States: but the Party convicted shall nevertheless be liable and subject to Indictment, Trial, Judgment and Punishment, according to Law.

Section 4—Times, etc., of holding elections, how prescribed. One session each year.

The Times, Places and Manner of holding Elections for Senators and Representatives, shall be prescribed in each State by the Legislature thereof; but the Congress may at any time by Law make or alter such Regulations, except as to the Place of Chusing Senators.

The Congress shall assemble at least once in every Year, and such Meeting shall be *[on the first Monday in December,] [The words in brackets were superseded by Amendment XX, section 2.]* unless they shall by Law appoint a different Day.

Section 5—Membership, quorum, adjournments, rules. Power to punish or expel. Journal. Time of adjournments, how limited, etc.

Each House shall be the Judge of the Elections, Returns and Qualifications of its own Members, and a Majority of each shall constitute a Quorum to do Business; but a smaller number may adjourn from day to day, and may be authorized to compel the Attendance of absent Members, in such manner, and under such Penalties as each House may provide.

Each House may determine the Rules of its Proceedings, punish its members for disorderly Behavior, and, with the Concurrence of two thirds, expel a Member.

Each House shall keep a Journal of its Proceedings, and from time to time publish the same, excepting such Parts as may in their Judgment require Secrecy; and the Yeas and Nays of the Members of either House on any question shall, at the Desire of one fifth of those Present, be entered on the Journal.

Neither House, during the Session of Congress, shall, without the Consent of the other, adjourn for more than three days, nor to any other Place than that in which the two Houses shall be sitting.

Section 6—Compensation, privileges, disqualifications in certain cases.

The Senators and Representatives shall receive a Compensation for their Services, to be ascertained by Law, and paid out of the Treasury of the United States. They shall in all Cases, except Treason, Felony and Breach of the Peace, be privileged from Arrest during their Attendance at the Session of their respective Houses, and in going to and returning from the same; and for any Speech or Debate in either House, they shall not be questioned in any other Place.

No Senator or Representative shall, during the Time for which he was elected, be appointed to any civil Office under the Authority of the United States, which shall have been created, or the Emoluments whereof shall have been encreased during such time; and no Person holding any Office under the United States, shall be a Member of either House during his Continuance in Office.

Section 7—House to originate all revenue bills. Veto. Bill may be passed by two-thirds of each House, notwithstanding, etc. Bill, not returned in ten days, to become a law. Provisions as to orders, concurrent resolutions, etc.

All bills for raising Revenue shall originate in the House of Representatives; but the Senate may propose or concur with Amendments as on other Bills.

Every Bill which shall have passed the House of Representatives and the Senate, shall, before it become a Law, be presented to the President of the United States; If he approve he shall sign it, but if not he shall return it, with his Objections to that House in which it shall have originated, who shall enter the Objections at large on their Journal, and proceed to reconsider it. If after such Reconsideration two thirds of that House shall agree to pass the Bill, it shall be sent, together with the Objections, to the other House, by which it shall likewise be reconsidered, and if approved by two thirds of that House, it shall become a Law. But in all such Cases the Votes of both Houses shall be determined by Yeas and Nays, and the Names of the Persons voting for and against the Bill shall be entered on the Journal of each House respectively. If any Bill shall not be returned by the President within ten Days (Sundays excepted) after it shall have been presented to him, the Same shall be a Law, in like Manner as if he had signed it, unless the Congress by their Adjournment prevent its Return, in which Case it shall not be a Law.

Every order, Resolution, or Vote to which the Concurrence of the Senate and House of Representatives may be necessary (except on a question of Adjournment) shall be presented to the President of the United States; and before the Same shall take Effect, shall be approved by him, or being disapproved by him, shall be repassed by two thirds of the Senate and House of Representatives, according to the Rules and Limitations prescribed in the Case of a Bill.

Section 8—Powers of Congress.

The Congress shall have Power To lay and collect Taxes, Duties, Imposts and Excises, to pay the Debts and provide for the common Defence and general Welfare of the United States; but all Duties, Imposts and Excises shall be uniform throughout the United States;

To borrow money on the credit of the United States;

To regulate Commerce with foreign Nations, and among the several States, and with the Indian Tribes;

To establish an uniform Rule of Naturalization, and uniform Laws on the subject of Bankruptcies throughout the United States;

To coin Money, regulate the Value thereof, and of foreign Coin, and fix the Standard of Weights and Measures;

To provide for the Punishment of counterfeiting the Securities and current Coin of the United States;

To establish Post Offices and post Roads;

To promote the Progress of Science and useful Arts, by securing for limited Times to Authors and Inventors the exclusive Right to their respective Writings and Discoveries;

To constitute Tribunals inferior to the supreme Court;

To define and punish Piracies and Felonies committed on the high Seas, and Offenses against the Law of Nations;

To declare War, grant Letters of Marque and Reprisal, and make Rules concerning Captures on Land and Water;

To raise and support Armies, but no Appropriation of Money to that Use shall be for a longer Term than two Years;

To provide and maintain a Navy;

To make Rules for the Government and Regulation of the land and naval Forces;

To provide for calling forth the Militia to execute the Laws of the Union, suppress Insurrections and repel Invasions;

To provide for organizing, arming, and disciplining the Militia, and for governing such Part of them as may be employed in the Service of the United States, reserving to the States respectively, the Appointment of the Officers, and the Authority of training the Militia according to the discipline prescribed by Congress;

To exercise exclusive Legislation in all Cases whatsoever, over such District (not exceeding ten Miles square) as may, by Cession of particular States, and the acceptance of Congress, become the Seat of the Government of the United States, and to exercise like Authority over all Places purchased by the Consent of the Legislature of the State in which the Same shall be, for the Erection of Forts, Magazines, Arsenals, dock-Yards, and other needful Buildings;—And

To make all Laws which shall be necessary and proper for carrying into Execution the foregoing Powers, and all other Powers vested by this Constitution in the Government of the United States, or in any Department or Officer thereof.

Section 9—Provision as to migration or importation of certain persons. Habeas corpus, bills of attainder, etc. Taxes, how apportioned. No export duty. No commercial preference. Money, how drawn from Treasury, etc. No titular nobility. Officers not to receive presents, etc.

The Migration or Importation of such Persons as any of the States now existing shall think proper to admit, shall not be prohibited by the Congress prior to the Year one thousand eight hundred and eight, but a tax or duty may be imposed on such Importation, not exceeding ten dollars for each Person.

The privilege of the Writ of Habeas Corpus shall not be suspended, unless when in Cases of Rebellion or Invasion the public Safety may require it.

No Bill of Attainder or ex post facto Law shall be passed.

[No capitation, or other direct, Tax shall be laid, unless in Proportion to the Census or Enumeration herein before directed to be taken.] [Words in brackets modified by Amendment XVI.]

No Tax or Duty shall be laid on Articles exported from any State.

No Preference shall be given by any Regulation of Commerce or Revenue to the Ports of one State over those of another: nor shall Vessels bound to, or from, one State, be obliged to enter, clear, or pay Duties in another.

No Money shall be drawn from the Treasury, but in Consequence of Appropriations made by Law; and a regular Statement and Account of the Receipts and Expenditures of all public Money shall be published from time to time.

No Title of Nobility shall be granted by the United States: and no Person holding any Office of Profit or Trust under them, shall, without the Consent of the Congress, accept of any present, Emolument, Office, or Title, of any kind whatever, from any King, Prince, or foreign State.

Section 10—States prohibited from the exercise of certain powers.

No State shall enter into any Treaty, Alliance, or Confederation; grant Letters of Marque and Reprisal; coin Money; emit Bills of Credit; make any Thing but gold and silver Coin a Tender in Payment of Debts; pass any Bill of Attainder, ex post facto Law, or Law impairing the Obligation of Contracts, or grant any Title of Nobility.

No State shall, without the Consent of the Congress, lay any Imposts or Duties on Imports or Exports, except what may be absolutely necessary for executing its inspection Laws: and the net Produce of all Duties and Imposts, laid by any State on Imports or Exports, shall be for the Use of the Treasury of the United States; and all such Laws shall be subject to the Revision and Control of the Congress.

No State shall, without the Consent of Congress, lay any duty of Tonnage, keep Troops, or Ships of War in time of Peace, enter into any Agreement or Compact with another State, or with a foreign Power, or engage in War, unless actually invaded, or in such imminent Danger as will not admit of delay.

ARTICLE II.

Section 1—President: his term of office. Electors of President; number and how appointed. Electors to vote on same day. Qualification of President. On whom his duties devolve in case of his removal, death, etc. President's compensation. His oath of office.

The executive Power shall be vested in a President of the United States of America. He shall hold his Office during the Term of four Years, and, together with the Vice President, chosen for the same Term, be elected, as follows.

Each State shall appoint, in such Manner as the Legislature thereof may direct, a Number of Electors, equal to the whole Number of Senators and Representatives to which the State may be entitled in the Congress: but no Senator or Representative, or Person holding an Office of Trust or Profit under the United States, shall be appointed an Elector.

[The Electors shall meet in their respective States, and vote by Ballot for two persons, of whom one at least shall not be an Inhabitant of the same State with themselves. And they shall make a List of all the Persons voted for, and of the Number of Votes for each; which List they shall sign and certify, and transmit sealed to the Seat of the Government of the United States, directed to the President of the Senate. The President of the Senate shall, in the Presence of the Senate and House of Representatives, open all the Certificates, and the Votes shall then be counted. The Person having the greatest Number of Votes shall be the President, if such Number be a Majority of the whole Number of Electors appointed; and if there be more than one who have such Majority, and have an equal Number of Votes, then the House of Representatives shall immediately chuse by Ballot one of them for President; and if no Person have a Majority, then from the five highest on the List the said House shall in like Manner chuse the President. But in chusing the President,

the Votes shall be taken by States, the Representation from each State having one Vote; a quorum for this Purpose shall consist of a Member or Members from two thirds of the States, and a Majority of all the States shall be necessary to a Choice. In every Case, after the Choice of the President, the Person having the greatest Number of Votes of the Electors shall be the Vice President. But if there should remain two or more who have equal Votes, the Senate shall chuse from them by Ballot the Vice-President.] [This clause was superseded by Amendment XII.]

The Congress may determine the Time of chusing the Electors, and the Day on which they shall give their Votes; which Day shall be the same throughout the United States.

No person except a natural born Citizen, or a Citizen of the United States, at the time of the Adoption of this Constitution, shall be eligible to the Office of President; neither shall any Person be eligible to that Office who shall not have attained to the Age of thirty-five Years, and been fourteen Years a Resident within the United States. *[For qualification of the Vice President, see Amendment XII.]*

[In Case of the Removal of the President from Office, or of his Death, Resignation, or Inability to discharge the Powers and Duties of the said Office, the same shall devolve on the Vice President, and the Congress may by Law, provide for the Case of Removal, Death, Resignation or Inability, both of the President and Vice President, declaring what Officer shall then act as President, and such Officer shall act accordingly, until the Disability be removed, or a President shall be elected.] [This clause was superseded by Amendments XXV.]

The President shall, at stated Times, receive for his Services, a Compensation, which shall neither be encreased nor diminished during the Period for which he shall have been elected, and he shall not receive within that Period any other Emolument from the United States, or any of them.

Before he enter on the Execution of his Office, he shall take the following Oath or Affirmation:–"I do solemnly swear (or affirm) that I will faithfully execute the Office of President of the United States, and will to the best of my Ability, preserve, protect and defend the Constitution of the United States."

Section 2—President to be Commander-in-Chief. He may require opinions of cabinet officers, etc., may pardon. Treaty-making power. Nomination of certain officers. When President may fill vacancies.

The President shall be Commander in Chief of the Army and Navy of the United States, and of the Militia of the several States, when called into the actual Service of the United States; he may require the Opinion in writing, of the principal Officer in each of the executive Departments, upon any subject relating to the Duties of their respective Offices, and he shall have Power to Grant Reprieves and Pardons for Offenses against the United States, except in Cases of Impeachment.

He shall have Power, by and with the Advice and Consent of the Senate, to make Treaties, provided two-thirds of the Senators present concur; and he shall nominate, and by and with the Advice and Consent of the Senate, shall appoint Ambassadors, other public Ministers and Consuls, Judges of the supreme Court, and all other Officers of the United States, whose Appointments are not herein otherwise provided for, and which shall be established by Law: but the Congress may by Law vest the Appointment of such inferior Officers, as they think proper, in the President alone, in the Courts of Law, or in the Heads of Departments.

The President shall have Power to fill up all Vacancies that may happen during the Recess of the Senate, by granting Commissions which shall expire at the End of their next Session.

Section 3—President shall communicate to Congress. He may convene and adjourn Congress, in case of disagreement, etc. Shall receive ambassadors, execute laws, and commission officers.

He shall from time to time give to the Congress Information of the State of the Union, and recommend to their Consideration such Measures as he shall judge necessary and expedient; he may, on extraordinary Occasions, convene both Houses, or either of them, and in Case of Disagreement between them, with Respect to the Time of Adjournment, he may adjourn them to such Time as he shall think proper; he shall receive Ambassadors and other public Ministers; he shall take Care that the Laws be faithfully executed, and shall Commission all the Officers of the United States.

Section 4—All civil offices forfeited for certain crimes.

The President, Vice President and all civil Officers of the United States, shall be removed from Office on Impeachment for, and Conviction of, Treason, Bribery, or other high Crimes and Misdemeanors.

ARTICLE III.

Section 1—Judicial powers, tenure. Compensation.

The judicial Power of the United States, shall be vested in one supreme Court, and in such inferior Courts as the Congress may from time to time ordain and establish. The Judges, both of the supreme and inferior Courts, shall hold their Offices during good Behaviour, and shall, at stated Times, receive for their Services, a Compensation, which shall not be diminished during their Continuance in Office.

Section 2—Judicial power; to what cases it extends. Original jurisdiction of Supreme Court; appellate jurisdiction. Trial by jury, etc. Trial, where.

The judicial Power shall extend to all Cases, in Law and Equity, arising under this Constitution, the Laws of the United States, and Treaties made, or which shall be made, under their Authority;–to all Cases affecting Ambassadors, other public Ministers and Consuls;–to all Cases of admiralty and maritime Jurisdiction;–to Controversies to which the United States shall be a Party;–to Controversies between two or more States; *[–between a State and Citizens of another State;–]* between Citizens of different States; – between Citizens of the same State claiming Lands under Grants of different States, *[and between a State, or the Citizens thereof, and foreign States, Citizens or Subjects.] [This section is modified by Amendment XI.]*

In all Cases affecting Ambassadors, other public Ministers and Consuls, and those in which a State shall be Party, the supreme Court shall have original Jurisdiction. In all the other Cases before mentioned, the supreme Court shall have appellate Jurisdiction, both as to Law and Fact, with such Exceptions, and under such Regulations as the Congress shall make.

The trial of all Crimes, except in Cases of Impeachment, shall be by Jury; and such Trial shall be held in the State where the said Crimes shall have been committed; but when not committed within any State, the Trial shall be at such Place or Places as the Congress may by Law have directed.

Section 3—Treason Defined. Proof of. Punishment of.

Treason against the United States, shall consist only in levying War against them, or in adhering to their Enemies, giving them Aid and Comfort. No Person shall be convicted of Treason unless on the Testimony of two Witnesses to the same overt Act, or on Confession in open Court.

The Congress shall have Power to declare the Punishment of Treason, but no Attainder of Treason shall work Corruption of Blood, or Forfeiture except during the Life of the Person attainted.

ARTICLE IV.

Section 1—Each State to give credit to the public acts, etc., of every other State.

Full Faith and Credit shall be given in each State to the public Acts, Records, and judicial Proceedings of every other State. And the Congress may by general Laws prescribe the Manner in which such Acts, Records and Proceedings shall be proved, and the Effect thereof.

Section 2—Privileges of citizens of each State. Fugitives from justice to be delivered up. Persons held to service having escaped, to be delivered up.

The Citizens of each State shall be entitled to all Privileges and Immunities of Citizens in the several States.

A Person charged in any State with Treason, Felony, or other Crime, who shall flee from Justice, and be found in another State, shall on demand of the executive Authority of the State from which he fled, be delivered up, to be removed to the State having Jurisdiction of the Crime.

[No Person held to Service or Labour in one State, under the Laws thereof, escaping into another, shall, in Consequence of any Law or Regulation therein, be discharged from such Service or Labour, but shall be delivered up on Claim of the Party to whom such Service or Labour may be due.] [This clause was superseded by Amendment XIII.]

Section 3—Admission of new States. Power of Congress over territory and other property.

New States may be admitted by the Congress into this Union; but no new State shall be formed or erected within the Jurisdiction of any other State; nor any State be formed by the Junction of two or more States, or parts of States, without the Consent of the Legislatures of the States concerned as well as of the Congress.

The Congress shall have Power to dispose of and make all needful Rules and Regulations respecting the Territory or other Property belonging to the United States; and nothing in this Constitution shall be so construed as to Prejudice any Claims of the United States, or of any particular State.

Section 4—Republican form of government guaranteed. Each State to be protected.

The United States shall guarantee to every State in this Union a Republican Form of Government, and shall protect each of them against Invasion; and on Application of the Legislature, or of the Executive (when the Legislature cannot be convened) against domestic Violence.

ARTICLE V.

Constitution: how amended; proviso.

The Congress, whenever two-thirds of both Houses shall deem it necessary, shall propose Amendments to this Constitution, or, on the Application of the Legislatures of two-thirds of the several States, shall call a Convention for proposing Amendments, which, in either Case, shall be valid to all Intents and Purposes, as part of this Constitution, when ratified by the Legislatures of three-fourths of the several States, or by Conventions in three-fourths thereof, as the one or the other Mode of Ratification may be proposed by the Congress: Provided that no Amendment which may be made prior to the Year One thousand eight hundred and eight shall in any Manner affect the first and fourth Clauses in the Ninth Section of the first Article; and that no State, without its Consent, shall be deprived of its equal Suffrage in the Senate.

ARTICLE VI.

Certain debts, etc., declared valid. Supremacy of Constitution, treaties, and laws of the United States. Oath to support Constitution, by whom taken. No religious test.

All Debts contracted and Engagements entered into, before the Adoption of this Constitution, shall be as valid against the United States under this Constitution, as under the Confederation.

This Constitution, and the Laws of the United States which shall be made in Pursuance thereof; and all Treaties made, or which shall be made, under the Authority of the United States, shall be the supreme Law of the Land; and the Judges in every State shall be bound thereby, any Thing in the Constitution or Laws of any State to the Contrary notwithstanding.

The Senators and Representatives before mentioned, and the Members of the several State Legislatures, and all executive and judicial Officers, both of the United States and of the several States, shall be bound by Oath or Affirmation, to support this Constitution; but no religious Test shall ever be required as a Qualification to any Office or public Trust under the United States.

ARTICLE VII.

What ratification shall establish Constitution.

The Ratification of the Conventions of nine States shall be sufficient for the Establishment of this Constitution between the States so ratifying the Same.

Done in Convention by the Unanimous Consent of the States present the Seventeenth Day of September in the Year of our Lord one thousand seven hundred and Eighty seven and of the Independence of the United States of America the Twelfth.

In Witness whereof We have hereunto subscribed our Names.

G⁰. Washington, Presidt and deputy from Virginia

New Hampshire—John Langdon, Nicholas Gilman

Massachusetts—Nathaniel Gorham, Rufus King

Connecticut—Wm. Saml. Johnson, Roger Sherman

New York—Alexander Hamilton

New Jersey—Wil: Livingston, David Brearley, Wm. Paterson, Jona: Dayton

Pennsylvania—B Franklin, Thomas Mifflin, Robt. Morris, Geo. Clymer, Thos. FitzSimons, Jared Ingersoll, James Wilson, Gouv Morris

Delaware—Geo: Read, Gunning Bedford jun, John Dickinson, Richard Bassett, Jaco: Broom

Maryland—James McHenry, Dan of St Thos. Jenifer, Danl Carroll

Virginia—John Blair, James Madison Jr.

North Carolina—Wm. Blount, Rich'd Dobbs Spaight, Hu Williamson

South Carolina—J. Rutledge, Charles Cotesworth Pinckney, Charles Pinckney, Pierce Butler

Georgia—William Few, Abr Baldwin

Attest: William Jackson, Secretary.

The Bill of Rights
In force Dec. 15, 1791

[Congress, at its first session in New York, NY, submitted to the states 12 amendments Sept. 25, 1789, to clarify certain individual and state rights not named in the Constitution. They are generally called the Bill of Rights.

Influential in framing these amendments was the Declaration of Rights of Virginia, written by George Mason (1725-92) in 1776. Mason, a Virginia delegate to the Constitutional Convention, did not sign the Constitution and opposed its ratification on the ground that it did not sufficiently oppose slavery or safeguard individual rights.

In the preamble to the resolution offering the proposed amendments, Congress said: "The conventions of a number of the States having at the time of their adopting the Constitution, expressed a desire, in order to prevent misconstruction or abuse of its powers, that further declaratory and restrictive clauses should be added, and as extending the ground of public confidence in the government will best insure the beneficent ends of its institution, be it resolved," etc.

Ten of these amendments, now commonly known as one to 10 inclusive, but originally three to 12 inclusive, were ratified by the states as follows: New Jersey, Nov. 20, 1789; Maryland, Dec. 19, 1789; North Carolina, Dec. 22, 1789; South Carolina, Jan. 19, 1790; New Hampshire, Jan. 25, 1790; Delaware, Jan. 28, 1790; New York, Feb. 27, 1790; Pennsylvania, Mar. 10, 1790; Rhode Island, June 7, 1790; Vermont, Nov. 3, 1791; Virginia, Dec. 15, 1791; Massachusetts, Mar. 2, 1939; Georgia, Mar. 18, 1939; Connecticut, Apr. 19, 1939. These original 10 ratified amendments follow as Amendments I to X inclusive.

Of the two original proposed amendments that were not ratified promptly by the necessary number of states, the first related to apportionment of Representatives; the second, relating to compensation of members of Congress, was ratified in 1992 and became Amendment 27.]

AMENDMENT I.
Religious establishment prohibited. Freedom of speech, of press, right to assemble and to petition.
Congress shall make no law respecting an establishment of religion, or prohibiting the free exercise thereof; or abridging the freedom of speech, or of the press; or the right of the people peaceably to assemble, and to petition the Government for a redress of grievances.

AMENDMENT II.
Right to keep and bear arms.
A well regulated Militia, being necessary to the security of a free State, the right of the people to keep and bear Arms, shall not be infringed.

AMENDMENT III.
Conditions for quarters for soldiers.
No Soldier shall, in time of peace be quartered in any house, without the consent of the Owner, nor in time of war, but in a manner to be prescribed by law.

AMENDMENT IV.
Protection from unreasonable search and seizure.
The right of the people to be secure in their persons, houses, papers, and effects, against unreasonable searches and seizures, shall not be violated, and no Warrants shall issue, but upon probable cause, supported by Oath or affirmation, and particularly describing the place to be searched, and the persons or things to be seized.

AMENDMENT V.
Provisions concerning prosecution and due process of law. Double jeopardy restriction. Private property not to be taken without compensation.
No person shall be held to answer for a capital, or otherwise infamous crime, unless on a presentment or indictment of a Grand Jury, except in cases arising in the land or naval forces, or in the Militia, when in actual service in time of War or public danger; nor shall any person be subject for the same offence to be twice put in jeopardy of life or limb; nor shall be compelled in any criminal case to be a witness against himself, nor be deprived of life, liberty, or property, without due process of law; nor shall private property be taken for public use, without just compensation.

AMENDMENT VI.
Right to speedy trial, witnesses, etc.
In all criminal prosecutions, the accused shall enjoy the right to a speedy and public trial, by an impartial jury of the State and district wherein the crime shall have been committed, which district shall have been previously ascertained by law, and to be informed of the nature and cause of the accusation; to be confronted with the witnesses against him; to have compulsory process for obtaining witnesses in his favor, and to have the Assistance of Counsel for his defence.

AMENDMENT VII.
Right of trial by jury.
In suits at common law, where the value in controversy shall exceed twenty dollars, the right of trial by jury shall be preserved, and no fact tried by a jury, shall be otherwise reexamined in any Court of the United States, than according to the rules of the common law.

AMENDMENT VIII.
Excessive bail or fines; cruel and unusual punishment.
Excessive bail shall not be required, nor excessive fines imposed, nor cruel and unusual punishments inflicted.

AMENDMENT IX.
Rule of construction of Constitution.
The enumeration in the Constitution, of certain rights, shall not be construed to deny or disparage others retained by the people.

AMENDMENT X.
Rights of States under Constitution.
The powers not delegated to the United States by the Constitution, nor prohibited by it to the States, are reserved to the States respectively, or to the people.

Amendments Since the Bill of Rights

AMENDMENT XI.
Judicial powers construed.
The Judicial power of the United States shall not be construed to extend to any suit in law or equity, commenced or prosecuted against one of the United States by Citizens of another State, or by Citizens or Subjects of any Foreign State.

[This amendment was proposed to the Legislatures of the several States by the Third Congress on March 4, 1794, and was declared to have been ratified in a message from the President to Congress, dated Jan. 8, 1798.]

[It was on Jan. 5, 1798, that Secretary of State Pickering received from 12 of the States authenticated ratifications, and informed President John Adams of that fact.]

[As a result of later research in the Department of State, it is now established that Amendment XI became part of the Constitution on Feb. 7, 1795, for on that date it had been ratified by 12 States as follows.]

[1. New York, Mar. 27, 1794. 2. Rhode Island, Mar. 31, 1794. 3. Connecticut, May 8, 1794. 4. New Hampshire, June 16, 1794. 5. Massachusetts, June 26, 1794. 6. Vermont, between Oct. 9, 1794, and Nov. 9, 1794. 7. Virginia, Nov. 18, 1794. 8. Georgia, Nov. 29, 1794. 9. Kentucky, Dec. 7, 1794. 10. Maryland, Dec. 26, 1794. 11. Delaware, Jan. 23, 1795. 12. North Carolina, Feb. 7, 1795]

[On June 1, 1796, more than a year after Amendment XI had become a part of the Constitution—but before anyone was officially aware of this—Tennessee had been admitted as a State; but not until Oct. 16, 1797, was a certified copy of the resolution of Congress proposing the amendment sent to the Governor of Tennessee, John Sevier, by Secretary of State Pickering, whose office was then at Trenton, New Jersey, because of the epidemic of yellow fever at Philadelphia; it seems, however, that the Legislature of Tennessee took no action on Amendment XI, owing doubtless to the fact that public announcement of its adoption was made soon thereafter.]

[Besides the necessary 12 States, one other, South Carolina, ratified Amendment XI, but this action was not taken until Dec. 4, 1797; the two remaining States, New Jersey and Pennsylvania, failed to ratify.]

AMENDMENT XII.

Manner of choosing President and Vice-President.

[Proposed by Congress Dec. 9, 1803; ratified June 15, 1804.]

The Electors shall meet in their respective states and vote by ballot for President and Vice-President, one of whom, at least, shall not be an inhabitant of the same state with themselves; they shall name in their ballots the person voted for as President, and in distinct ballots the person voted for as Vice-President, and they shall make distinct lists of all persons voted for as President, and of all persons voted for as Vice-President, and of the number of votes for each, which lists they shall sign and certify, and transmit sealed to the seat of the government of the United States, directed to the President of the Senate;—the President of the Senate shall, in presence of the Senate and House of Representatives, open all the certificates and the votes shall then be counted;—The person having the greatest number of votes for President, shall be the President, if such number be a majority of the whole number of Electors appointed; and if no person have such majority, then from the persons having the highest numbers not exceeding three on the list of those voted for as President, the House of Representatives shall choose immediately, by ballot, the President. But in choosing the President, the votes shall be taken by states, the representation from each state having one vote; a quorum for this purpose shall consist of a member or members from two-thirds of the states, and a majority of all the states shall be necessary to a choice. *[And if the House of Representatives shall not choose a President whenever the right of choice shall devolve upon them, before the fourth day of March next following, then the Vice-President shall act as President, as in the case of the death or other constitutional disability of the President.] [The words in brackets were superseded by Amendment XX, section 3.]* The person having the greatest number of votes as Vice-President, shall be the Vice-President, if such number be a majority of the whole number of Electors appointed, and if no person have a majority, then from the two highest numbers on the list, the Senate shall choose the Vice-President; a quorum for the purpose shall consist of two-thirds of the whole number of Senators, and a majority of the whole number shall be necessary to a choice. But no person constitutionally ineligible to the office of President shall be eligible to that of Vice-President of the United States.

THE RECONSTRUCTION AMENDMENTS

[Amendments XIII, XIV, and XV are commonly known as the Reconstruction Amendments, inasmuch as they followed the Civil War, and were drafted by Republicans who were bent on imposing their own policy of reconstruction on the South. Postbellum legislatures there—Mississippi, South Carolina, Georgia, for example—had set up laws which, it was charged, were contrived to perpetuate Negro slavery under other names.]

AMENDMENT XIII.

Slavery abolished.

[Proposed by Congress Jan. 31, 1865; ratified Dec. 6, 1865. The amendment, when first proposed by a resolution in Congress, was passed by the Senate, 38 to 6, on Apr. 8, 1864, but was defeated in the House, 95 to 66 on June 15, 1864. On reconsideration by the House, on Jan. 31, 1865, the resolution passed, 119 to 56. It was approved by President Lincoln on Feb. 1, 1865, although the Supreme Court had decided in 1798 that the President has nothing to do with the proposing of amendments to the Constitution, or their adoption.]

1. Neither slavery nor involuntary servitude, except as a punishment for crime whereof the party shall have been duly convicted, shall exist within the United States, or any place subject to their jurisdiction.

2. Congress shall have power to enforce this article by appropriate legislation.

AMENDMENT XIV.

Citizenship rights not to be abridged.

[The following amendment was proposed to the Legislatures of the several states by the 39th Congress, June 13, 1866, ratified July 9, 1868, and declared to have been ratified in a proclamation by the Secretary of State, July 28, 1868.]

[The 14th amendment was adopted only by virtue of ratification subsequent to earlier rejections. Newly constituted legislatures in both North Carolina and South Carolina (respectively July 4 and 9, 1868), ratified the proposed amendment, although earlier legislatures had rejected the proposal. The Secretary of State issued a proclamation, which, though doubtful as to the effect of attempted withdrawals by Ohio and New Jersey, entertained no doubt as to the validity of the ratification by North and South Carolina. The following day (July 21, 1868), Congress passed a resolution which declared the 14th Amendment to be a part of the Constitution and directed the Secretary of State so to promulgate it. The Secretary waited, however, until the newly constituted Legislature of Georgia had ratified the amendment, subsequent to an earlier rejection, before the promulgation of the ratification of the new amendment.]

1. All persons born or naturalized in the United States, and subject to the jurisdiction thereof, are citizens of the United States and of the State wherein they reside. No State shall make or enforce any law which shall abridge the privileges or immunities of citizens of the United States; nor shall any State deprive any person of life, liberty, or property, without due process of law; nor deny to any person within its jurisdiction the equal protection of the laws.

2. Representatives shall be apportioned among the several States according to their respective numbers, counting the whole number of persons in each State, excluding Indians not taxed. But when the right to vote at any election for the choice of electors for President and Vice-President of the United States, Representatives in Congress, the Executive and Judicial officers of a State, or the members of the Legislature thereof, is denied to any of the male inhabitants of such State, being *[twenty-one] [The words in brackets were changed by Amendment XXVI.]* years of age, and citizens of the United States, or in any way abridged, except

for participation in rebellion, or other crime, the basis of representation therein shall be reduced in the proportion which the number of such male citizens shall bear to the whole number of male citizens twenty-one years of age in such State.

3. No person shall be a Senator or Representative in Congress, or elector of President and Vice-President, or hold any office, civil or military, under the United States, or under any State, who, having previously taken an oath, as a member of Congress, or as an officer of the United States, or as a member of any State legislature, or as an executive or judicial officer of any State, to support the Constitution of the United States, shall have engaged in insurrection or rebellion against the same, or given aid or comfort to the enemies thereof. But Congress may by a vote of two-thirds of each House, remove such disability.

4. The validity of the public debt of the United States, authorized by law, including debts incurred for payment of pensions and bounties for services in suppressing insurrection or rebellion, shall not be questioned. But neither the United States nor any State shall assume or pay any debt or obligation incurred in aid of insurrection or rebellion against the United States, or any claim for the loss or emancipation of any slave; but all such debts, obligations and claims shall be held illegal and void.

5. The Congress shall have power to enforce, by appropriate legislation, the provisions of this article.

AMENDMENT XV.

Race no bar to voting rights.

[The following amendment was proposed to the legislatures of the several States by the 40th Congress, Feb. 26, 1869, and ratified Feb. 3, 1870.]

1. The right of citizens of the United States to vote shall not be denied or abridged by the United States or by any State on account of race, color, or previous condition of servitude–

2. The Congress shall have power to enforce this article by appropriate legislation.

AMENDMENT XVI.

Income taxes authorized.

[Proposed by Congress July 12, 1909; ratified Feb. 3, 1913.]

The Congress shall have power to lay and collect taxes on incomes, from whatever source derived, without apportionment among the several States, and without regard to any census or enumeration.

AMENDMENT XVII.

United States Senators to be elected by direct popular vote.

[Proposed by Congress May 13, 1912; ratified Apr. 8, 1913.]

The Senate of the United States shall be composed of two Senators from each State, elected by the people thereof, for six years; and each Senator shall have one vote. The electors in each State shall have the qualifications requisite for electors of the most numerous branch of the State legislatures.

When vacancies happen in the representation of any State in the Senate, the executive authority of such State shall issue writs of election to fill such vacancies: *Provided,* That the legislature of any State may empower the executive thereof to make temporary appointments until the people fill the vacancies by election as the legislature may direct.

This amendment shall not be so construed as to affect the election or term of any Senator chosen before it becomes valid as part of the Constitution.

AMENDMENT XVIII.

Liquor prohibition amendment.

[Proposed by Congress Dec. 18, 1917; ratified Jan. 16, 1919. Repealed by Amendment XXI, effective Dec. 5, 1933.]

1. After one year from the ratification of this article the manufacture, sale, or transportation of intoxicating liquors within, the importation thereof into, or the exportation thereof from the United States and all territory subject to the jurisdiction thereof for beverage purposes is hereby prohibited.

2. The Congress and the several States shall have concurrent power to enforce this article by appropriate legislation.

3. This article shall be inoperative unless it shall have been ratified as an amendment to the Constitution by the legislatures of the several States as provided in the Constitution, within seven years from the date of the submission hereof to the States by the Congress.

[The total vote in the Senates of the various States was 1,310 for, 237 against—84.6% dry. In the lower houses of the States the vote was 3,782 for, 1,035 against—78.5% dry.

[The amendment ultimately was adopted by all the States except Rhode Island.]

AMENDMENT XIX.

Giving nationwide suffrage to women.

[Proposed by Congress June 4, 1919; ratified Aug. 18, 1920.]

The right of citizens of the United States to vote shall not be denied or abridged by the United States or by any State on account of sex.

Congress shall have power to enforce this Article by appropriate legislation.

AMENDMENT XX.

Terms of President and Vice President to begin on Jan. 20; those of Senators, Representatives, Jan. 3.

[Proposed by Congress Mar. 2, 1932; ratified Jan. 23, 1933.]

1. The terms of the President and Vice President shall end at noon on the 20th day of January, and the terms of Senators and Representatives at noon on the 3d day of January, of the years in which such terms would have ended if this article had not been ratified; and the terms of their successors shall then begin.

2. The Congress shall assemble at least once in every year, and such meeting shall begin at noon on the 3d day of January, unless they shall by law appoint a different day.

3. If, at the time fixed for the beginning of the term of the President, the President elect shall have died, the Vice President elect shall become President. If a President shall not have been chosen before the time fixed for the beginning of his term, or if the President elect shall have failed to qualify, then the Vice President elect shall act as President until a President shall have qualified; and the Congress may by law provide for the case wherein neither a President elect nor a Vice President elect shall have qualified, declaring who shall then act as President, or the manner in which one who is to act shall be selected, and such person shall act accordingly until a President or Vice President shall have qualified.

4. The Congress may by law provide for the case of the death of any of the persons from whom the House of Representatives may choose a President whenever the right of choice shall have devolved upon them, and for the case of the death of any of the persons from whom the Senate may choose a Vice President whenever the right of choice shall have devolved upon them.

5. Sections 1 and 2 shall take effect on the 15th day of October following the ratification of this article. *[Oct. 1933]*

6. This article shall be inoperative unless it shall have been ratified as an amendment to the Constitution by the legislatures of three-fourths of the several States within seven years from the date of its submission.

AMENDMENT XXI.

Repeal of Amendment XVIII.

[Proposed by Congress Feb. 20, 1933; ratified Dec. 5, 1933.]

1. The eighteenth article of amendment to the Constitution of the United States is hereby repealed.

2. The transportation or importation into any State, Territory, or possession of the United States for delivery or use therein of intoxicating liquors, in violation of the laws thereof, is hereby prohibited.

3. This article shall be inoperative unless it shall have been ratified as an amendment to the Constitution by conventions in the several States, as provided in the Constitution, within seven years from the date of the submission hereof to the States by the Congress.

AMENDMENT XXII.

Limiting Presidential terms of office.

[Proposed by Congress Mar. 24, 1947; ratified Feb. 27, 1951.]

1. No person shall be elected to the office of the President more than twice, and no person who has held the office of President, or acted as President, for more than two years of a term to which some other person was elected President shall be elected to the office of the President more than once. But this Article shall not apply to any person holding the office of President when this Article was proposed by the Congress, and shall not prevent any person who may be holding the office of President, or acting as President, during the term within which this Article becomes operative from holding the office of President or acting as President during the remainder of such term.

2. This article shall be inoperative unless it shall have been ratified as an amendment to the Constitution by the legislatures of three-fourths of the several States within seven years from the date of its submission to the States by the Congress.

AMENDMENT XXIII.

Presidential vote for District of Columbia.

[Proposed by Congress June 16, 1960; ratified Mar. 29, 1961.]

1. The District constituting the seat of Government of the United States shall appoint in such manner as the Congress may direct:

A number of electors of President and Vice President equal to the whole number of Senators and Representatives in Congress to which the District would be entitled if it were a State, but in no event more than the least populous State; they shall be in addition to those appointed by the States, but they shall be considered, for the purposes of the election of President and Vice President, to be electors appointed by a State; and they shall meet in the District and perform such duties as provided by the twelfth article of amendment.

2. The Congress shall have power to enforce this article by appropriate legislation.

AMENDMENT XXIV.

Barring poll tax in federal elections.

[Proposed by Congress Sept. 14, 1962; ratified Jan. 23, 1964.]

1. The right of citizens of the United States to vote in any primary or other election for President or Vice President, for electors for President or Vice President, or for Senator or Representative in Congress, shall not be denied or abridged by the United States or any State by reason of failure to pay any poll tax or other tax.

2. The Congress shall have power to enforce this article by appropriate legislation.

AMENDMENT XXV.

Presidential disability and succession.

[Proposed by Congress July 6, 1965; ratified Feb. 10, 1967.]

1. In case of the removal of the President from office or of his death or resignation, the Vice President shall become President.

2. Whenever there is a vacancy in the office of the Vice President, the President shall nominate a Vice President who shall take office upon confirmation by a majority vote of both houses of Congress.

3. Whenever the President transmits to the President pro tempore of the Senate and the Speaker of the House of Representatives his written declaration that he is unable to discharge the powers and duties of his office, and until he transmits to them a written declaration to the contrary, such powers and duties shall be discharged by the Vice President as Acting President.

4. Whenever the Vice President and a majority of either the principal officers of the executive departments or of such other body as Congress may by law provide, transmit to the President pro tempore of the Senate and the Speaker of the House of Representatives their written declaration that the President is unable to discharge the powers and duties of his office, the Vice President shall immediately assume the powers and duties of the office as Acting President.

Thereafter, when the President transmits to the President pro tempore of the Senate and the Speaker of the House of Representatives his written declaration that no inability exists, he shall resume the powers and duties of his office unless the Vice President and a majority of either the principal officers of the executive department or of such other body as Congress may by law provide, transmit within four days to the President pro tempore of the Senate and the Speaker of the House of Representatives their written declaration that the President is unable to discharge the powers and duties of his office. Thereupon Congress shall decide the issue, assembling within forty-eight hours for that purpose if not in session. If the Congress, within twenty-one days after receipt of the latter written declaration, or, if Congress is not in session, within twenty-one days after Congress is required to assemble, determines by two-thirds vote of both Houses that the President is unable to discharge the powers and duties of his office, the Vice President shall continue to discharge the same as Acting President; otherwise, the President shall resume the powers and duties of his office.

AMENDMENT XXVI.

Lowering voting age to 18 years.

[Proposed by Congress Mar. 23, 1971; ratified July 1, 1971.]

1. The right of citizens of the United States, who are eighteen years of age or older, to vote shall not be denied or abridged by the United States or by any State on account of age.

2. The Congress shall have the power to enforce this article by appropriate legislation.

AMENDMENT XXVII.

Congressional pay.

[Proposed by Congress Sept. 25, 1789; ratified May 7, 1992.]

No law, varying the compensation for the services of the Senators and Representatives, shall take effect, until an election of Representatives shall have intervened.

How a Bill Becomes a Law

A senator or representative introduces a bill in Congress by sending it to the clerk of the Senate or the House, who assigns it a number and title. This procedure is termed the first reading. The clerk then refers the bill to the appropriate committee of the Senate or House.

If the committee does not wish to consider the bill, it will table it. Otherwise, the committee holds hearings to listen to opinions and facts offered by members and other interested parties. The committee then debates the bill and may offer amendments. A vote is taken, and if favorable, the bill is sent back to the clerk of the Senate or House.

The clerk reads the bill to the house—the second reading. Members may then debate the bill and suggest amendments.

After debate and any amendments, the bill is given a third reading, simply of the title, and put to a voice or roll-call vote.

If the bill has passed, it goes to the other house, where it may be defeated or passed, with or without amendments. If defeated, the bill dies. If passed with amendments, a conference committee made up of members of both houses works out the differences between the two bills and arrives at a compromise.

After passage of the final version by both houses, the bill is sent to the president. If the president signs it, the bill becomes a law. The president may instead veto the bill by refusing to sign it and sending it back to the house where it originated, with reasons for the veto.

The president's objections are then read and debated, and a roll-call vote is taken. If the bill receives less than a two-thirds majority, it is defeated. If it receives at least two-thirds, it is sent to the other house. If that house also passes it by at least a two-thirds majority, the president's veto is overridden, and the bill becomes a law.

If the president neither signs nor vetoes the bill within 10 days—not including Sundays—it automatically becomes a law even without the president's signature. However, if Congress has adjourned within those 10 days, the bill is automatically killed; this indirect rejection is termed a pocket veto.

Note: Under the Line Item Veto Act, effective Jan. 1, 1997, the president was authorized, under certain circumstances, to veto a bill in part. The legislation was found unconstitutional by the Supreme Court, June 25, 1998.

Confederate States and Secession

The American Civil War (1861-65) grew out of sectional disputes over the continued existence of slavery in the South. Southern legislators contended that the states retained many rights, including the right to own slaves and the right to secede.

The war was not fought by state against state but by one federal regime against another. A Confederate government in Richmond assumed control over the economic, political, and military life of the seceding states, under protest from Georgia and South Carolina.

South Carolina voted unanimously in convention to secede from the Union, repealing its 1788 ratification of the U.S. Constitution on Dec. 20, 1860, to take effect on Dec. 24. Other states seceded in 1861. Their votes in conventions were: Mississippi, Jan. 9, 84-15; Florida, Jan. 10, 62-7; Alabama, Jan. 11, 61-39; Georgia, Jan. 19, 208-89; Louisiana, Jan. 26, 113-17; Texas, Feb. 1, 166-7, ratified by popular vote (34,794 to 11,325) Feb. 23; Virginia, Apr. 17, 88-55, ratified by popular vote (128,884 to 32,134) May 23; Arkansas, May 6,

69-1; Tennessee, May 7, ratified by popular vote (104,019 to 47,238) June 8; North Carolina, unanimous, May 20.

Missouri Unionists stopped secession in conventions Feb. 28 and Mar. 9, 1861. The legislature condemned secession Mar. 7. Under the protection of Confederate troops, secessionist members of the legislature adopted a resolution of secession at Neosho, Oct. 31. The Confederate Congress seated the secessionists' representatives.

Kentucky did not secede, and its government remained Unionist. In a part of the state occupied by Confederate troops, Kentuckians approved secession, and the Confederate Congress admitted their representatives.

The Maryland legislature voted against secession Apr. 27, 1861, 53-13. Delaware did not secede. Western Virginia held conventions at Wheeling, named a pro-Union governor on June 11, 1861, and was admitted to the Union as West Virginia on June 20, 1863. Its constitution provided for gradual abolition of slavery.

Confederate Government

Forty-two delegates from South Carolina, Georgia, Alabama, Mississippi, Louisiana, and Florida met in convention at Montgomery, AL, on Feb. 4, 1861. They adopted a provisional constitution of the Confederate States of America and elected Jefferson Davis (MS) as provisional president and Alexander H. Stephens (GA) as provisional vice president.

A permanent constitution was adopted Mar. 11. It banned African slave trade, but it did not bar interstate commerce in

slaves. On July 20 the Congress moved to Richmond, VA. Davis was elected president in Nov. 1861 and was inaugurated Feb. 22, 1862.

The Congress adopted a flag, consisting of a red field with a white stripe, and a blue jack with a circle of white stars. Later the more popular flag was the red field with blue diagonal crossbars that held 13 white stars, for the 11 states in the Confederacy plus Kentucky and Missouri.

The Gettysburg Address

Delivered by Pres. Abraham Lincoln at Gettysburg, PA, on Nov. 19, 1863.

Fourscore and seven years ago our fathers brought forth on this continent a new nation, conceived in liberty and dedicated to the proposition that all men are created equal.

Now we are engaged in a great civil war, testing whether that nation or any nation so conceived and so dedicated can long endure. We are met on a great battle field of that war. We have come to dedicate a portion of that field, as a final resting-place for those who here gave their lives that this nation might live. It is altogether fitting and proper that we should do this.

But, in a larger sense, we can not dedicate—we can not consecrate—we can not hallow—this ground. The brave men, living and dead, who struggled here, have consecrated

it, far above our poor power to add or detract. The world will little note, nor long remember, what we say here, but it can never forget what they did here. It is for us the living, rather, to be dedicated here to the unfinished work which they who fought here have thus far so nobly advanced. It is rather for us to be here dedicated to the great task remaining before us—that from these honored dead we take increased devotion to that cause for which they gave the last full measure of devotion—that we here highly resolve that these dead shall not have died in vain—that this nation, under God, shall have a new birth of freedom—and that government of the people, by the people, for the people, shall not perish from the earth.

Presidential Oath of Office

The Constitution (Article II) directs that the president-elect shall take the following oath or affirmation to be inaugurated as president: "I do solemnly swear [affirm] that I will faithfully execute the office of President of the United States, and will, to the best of my ability, preserve, protect, and defend the Constitution of the United States."

Custom decrees the addition of the words "So help me God" at the end of the oath when taken by the president-elect, with the left hand on the Bible for the duration of the oath, and the right hand slightly raised.

Presidential Succession

If, by reason of death, resignation, removal from office, inability, or failure to qualify, there is neither a president nor vice president to discharge the powers and duties of the office of president, then the speaker of the House of Representatives shall upon his resignation as speaker and as representative, act as president. The same rule shall apply in the case of the death, resignation, removal from office, or inability of an individual acting as president.

If, at the time when a speaker is to begin the discharge of the powers and duties of the office of president, there is no speaker, or the speaker fails to qualify as acting president, then the president pro tempore of the Senate, upon his resignation as president pro tempore and as senator, shall act as president.

An individual acting as president shall continue to act until the expiration of the then current presidential term, except that (1) if his discharge of the powers and duties of the office is founded in whole or in part in the failure of both the president-elect and the vice president-elect to qualify, then

he shall act only until a president or vice president qualifies, and (2) if his discharge of the powers and duties of the office is founded in whole or in part on the inability of the president or vice president, then he shall act only until the removal of the disability of one of such individuals.

If, by reason of death, resignation, removal from office, or failure to qualify, there is no president pro tempore to act as president, then the officer of the United States who is highest on the following list, and who is not under any disability to discharge the powers and duties of president shall act as president: the secretaries of state, treasury, defense, attorney general, secretaries of interior, agriculture, commerce, labor, health and human services, housing and urban development, transportation, energy, education, veterans affairs, homeland security.

[Legislation approved July 18, 1947; amended Sept. 9, 1965, Oct. 15, 1966, Aug. 4, 1977, Sept. 27, 1979, and Mar. 9, 2006. See also Constitutional Amendment XXV.]

Origin of the United States National Motto

In God We Trust, designated as the U.S. National Motto by Congress in 1956, originated during the Civil War as an inscription for U.S. coins, although it was used by Francis Scott Key in a slightly different form when he wrote "The Star-Spangled Banner" in 1814. On Nov. 13, 1861, when Union morale had been shaken by battlefield defeats, the Rev. M. R. Watkinson, of Ridleyville, PA, wrote to Sec. of the Treasury Salmon P. Chase. "From my heart I have felt our national shame in disowning God as not the least of our present national disasters," the minister wrote,

suggesting "recognition of the Almighty God in some form on our coins." Sec. Chase ordered designs prepared with the inscription *In God We Trust* and backed coinage legislation that authorized use of this slogan. The motto first appeared on some U.S. coins in 1864, and it appeared sporadically on coins until 1938, after which all U.S. coins bear the inscription. A joint resolution passed by the 84th Congress and signed by Pres. Dwight D. Eisenhower July 30, 1956, declared *In God We Trust* the national motto of the United States.

The Great Seal of the U.S.

On July 4, 1776, the Continental Congress appointed a committee consisting of Benjamin Franklin, John Adams, and Thomas Jefferson "to bring in a device for a seal of the United States of America." The designs submitted by this and a subsequent committee were

considered unacceptable. After many delays, a third committee, appointed early in 1782, presented a design prepared by lawyer William Barton. Charles Thomson, the secretary of Congress, suggested certain changes, and Congress finally approved the design on June 20, 1782. The obverse side of the seal shows an American bald eagle. In its mouth is a ribbon bearing the motto *E Pluribus Unum* (out of many, one). In the eagle's talons are 13 arrows of war and an olive branch of peace. The reverse side shows an unfinished pyramid with an eye (Eye of Providence) above it.

The Flag of the U.S.—The Stars and Stripes

The 50-star flag of the United States was raised for the first time officially at 12:01 AM on July 4, 1960, at Ft. McHenry National Monument in Baltimore, MD. The 50th star had been added for Hawaii; a year earlier the 49th, for Alaska. Before that, no star had been added since 1912, when New Mexico and Arizona were admitted to the Union.

The true history of the Stars and Stripes has become so cluttered by myth and tradition that the facts are difficult, and in some cases impossible, to establish. For example, it is not certain who designed the Stars and Stripes, who made the first such flag, or even whether it ever flew during any battle of the American Revolution.

All agree, however, that the Stars and Stripes originated as the result of a resolution offered by the Marine Committee of the Second Continental Congress at Philadelphia and adopted on June 14, 1777. It read:

"Resolved: that the flag of the United States be thirteen stripes, alternate red and white; that the union be thirteen stars, white in a blue field, representing a new constellation."

Congress gave no hint as to the designer of the flag, no instructions as to the arrangement of the stars, and no information on its appropriate uses. Historians have been unable to find the original flag details.

The resolution establishing the flag was not even published until Sept. 2, 1777. Despite repeated requests, Washington did not get the flags until 1783, after the American Revolution was over. And there is no certainty that they were the Stars and Stripes.

Early Flags

Many historians consider the first flag of the U.S. to have been the Grand Union (sometimes called Great Union) flag, although the Continental Congress never officially adopted it. This flag was a modification of the British Meteor flag, which had the red cross of St. George and the white cross of St. Andrew combined in the blue canton. For the Grand Union flag, six horizontal stripes were imposed on the red field, dividing it into 13 alternating red and white stripes. On

Jan. 1, 1776, when the Continental Army came into formal existence, this flag was unfurled on Prospect Hill, Somerville, MA. Washington wrote that "we hoisted the Union Flag in compliment to the United Colonies."

One of several flags about which controversy has raged for years is at Easton, PA. Containing the devices of the national flag in reversed order, this flag has been in the public library at Easton for more than 150 years. Some contend that this flag was actually the first Stars and Stripes, first displayed on July 8, 1776. This flag has 13 red and white stripes in the canton, 13 white stars centered in a blue field.

A flag was hastily improvised from garments by the defenders of Ft. Schuyler at Rome, NY, Aug. 3-22, 1777. Historians believe it was the Grand Union Flag.

The Sons of Liberty had a flag of nine red and white stripes, to signify nine colonies, when they met in New York in 1765 to oppose the Stamp Tax. By 1775, the flag had grown to 13 red and white stripes, with a rattlesnake on it.

At Concord, Apr. 19, 1775, the minutemen from Bedford, MA, are said to have carried a flag having a silver arm with sword on a red field. At Cambridge, MA, the Sons of Liberty used a plain red flag with a green pine tree on it.

In June 1775, Washington went from Philadelphia to Boston to take command of the army, escorted to New York by the Philadelphia Light Horse Troop. It carried a yellow flag that had an elaborate coat of arms—the shield charged with 13 knots, the motto "For These We Strive"—and a canton of 13 blue and silver stripes.

In Feb. 1776, Col. Christopher Gadsden, a member of the Continental Congress, gave the South Carolina Provincial Congress a flag "such as is to be used by the commander-in-chief of the American Navy." It had a yellow field, with a rattlesnake about to strike and the words "Don't Tread on Me."

At the Battle of Bennington, Aug. 16, 1777, patriots used a flag of 7 white and 6 red stripes with a blue canton extending down 9 stripes and showing an arch of 11 white stars over the figure 76 and a star in each of the upper corners. The stars are 7-pointed. This flag is preserved in the historical museum in Bennington, VT.

At the Battle of Cowpens, Jan. 17, 1781, the 3rd Maryland Regiment is said to have carried a flag of 13 red and white stripes, with a blue canton containing 12 stars in a circle around one star.

Who Designed the Flag? No one knows for certain. Francis Hopkinson, designer of a naval flag, declared he had designed the flag and in 1781 asked Congress to reimburse him for his services. Congress did not do so. Dumas Malone of Columbia Univ. wrote: "This talented man . . . designed the American flag."

Who Called the Flag "Old Glory"? The flag is said to have been named Old Glory by William Driver, a sea captain of Salem, MA. One legend has it that when he raised the flag on his brig, the *Charles Doggett*, in 1824, he said: "I name thee Old Glory." But his daughter, who presented the flag to the Smithsonian Institution, said he named it at his 21st birthday celebration on Mar. 17, 1824, when his mother presented the homemade flag to him.

The Betsy Ross Legend. The widely publicized legend that Betsy Ross made the first Stars and Stripes in June 1776, at the request of a committee composed of George Washington, Robert Morris, and George Ross, an uncle, was first made public in 1870, by a grandson of Ross. Historians have been unable to find a historical record of such a meeting or committee.

Adding New Stars

The flag of 1777 was used until 1795. Then, on the admission of Vermont and Kentucky to the Union, Congress passed and Pres. Washington signed an act that after May 1, 1795, the flag should have 15 stripes, alternating red and white, and 15 white stars on a blue field.

When new states were admitted, it became evident that the flag would become burdened with stripes. Congress thereupon ordered that after July 4, 1818, the flag should have 13 stripes, symbolizing the 13 original states; that the union have 20 stars, and that whenever a new state was admitted a new star should be added on the July 4 following admission.

No law designates the permanent arrangement of the stars. However, since 1912, when a new state has been admitted, the new design has been announced by executive order. No star is specifically identified with any state.

Code of Etiquette for Display and Use of the U.S. Flag
Reviewed by National Flag Foundation

Although the Stars and Stripes originated in 1777, it was not until 146 years later that there was a serious attempt to establish a uniform code of etiquette for the U.S. flag. On Feb. 15, 1923, the War Department issued a circular on the rules of flag usage. These rules were adopted almost in their entirety June 14, 1923, by a conference of 68 patriotic organizations in Washington, DC. A joint resolution of Congress June 22, 1942, amended by Public Law 94-344, July 7, 1976, codified "existing rules and customs pertaining to the display and use of the flag." Military branches have their own codes of etiquette regarding the flag; this guide is for civilian purposes.

When to Display the Flag. The flag should be displayed on all days, especially on legal holidays and other special occasions, on official buildings when in use, in or near polling places on election days, and in or near schools when in session. Citizens may fly the flag at any time. It is customary to display it only from sunrise to sunset on buildings and on stationary flagstaffs in the open. It may be displayed at night, however, on special occasions, preferably lighted. The flag now flies over the White House both day and night. It flies over the Senate wing of the Capitol when the Senate is in session and over the House wing when that body is in session. It flies day and night over the east and west fronts of the Capitol, without floodlights at night but receiving illumination from the Capitol Dome. It flies 24 hours a day at several other places, including the Ft. McHenry National Monument in Baltimore, where it inspired Francis Scott Key to write "The Star Spangled Banner." The flag also flies 24 hours a day, properly illuminated, at U.S. Customs ports of entry.

Flying the Flag at Half-Staff. Flying the flag at half-staff, that is, halfway up the staff, is a signal of mourning. The flag should be hoisted to the top of the staff for an instant before being lowered to half-staff. It should be hoisted to the peak again before being lowered for the day.

As provided by presidential proclamation, the flag should fly at half-staff for 30 days from the day of death of a president or former president; for 10 days from the day of death of a vice president, chief justice or retired chief justice of the U.S., or speaker of the House of Representatives; from day of death until burial of an associate justice of the Supreme Court, cabinet member, former vice president, Senate president pro tempore, or majority or minority Senate or House leader; for a U.S. senator, representative, territorial delegate, or the resident commissioner of Puerto Rico, on day of death and the following day within the metropolitan area of the District of Columbia and from day of death until burial within the decedent's state, congressional district, territory or commonwealth; and for the death of the governor of a state, territory, or possession of the U.S., from day of death until burial.

On Memorial Day, the flag should fly at half-staff until noon and then be raised to the peak. The flag should also fly at half-staff on Korean War Veterans Armistice Day (July 27), National Pearl Harbor Remembrance Day (Dec. 7), and Peace Officers Memorial Day (May 15).

How to Fly the Flag. The flag should be hoisted briskly and lowered ceremoniously and should never be allowed to touch the ground or the floor. When the flag is hung over a sidewalk from a rope extending from a building to a pole, the union (the blue field with white stars) should be away from the building. When the flag is hung over the center of a street the union should be to the north in an east-west street and to the east in a north-south street. No other flag may be flown above or, if on the same level, to the right of the U.S. flag, except that at the United Nations Headquarters, the UN flag may be placed above flags of all member nations and other national flags may be flown with equal prominence or honor with the flag of the U.S.

When two flags are placed against a wall with crossed staffs, the U.S. flag should be at right—its own right, and its staff should be in front of the staff of the other flag; when a number of flags are grouped and displayed from staffs, it should be at the center and highest point of the group.

Church and Platform Use. In an auditorium, the flag may be displayed flat, above and behind the speaker. When displayed from a staff in a church or in a public auditorium, the flag should hold the position of superior prominence, in advance of the audience, and in the position of honor at the speaker's right as she or he faces the audience. Any other flag so displayed should be placed on the left of the speaker or to the right of the audience.

When the flag is displayed horizontally or vertically against a wall, the stars should be uppermost and at the observer's left.

When used to cover a casket, the flag should be placed so that the union is at the head and over the left shoulder. It should not be lowered into the grave nor touch the ground.

How to Dispose of Worn Flags. When the flag is in such condition that it is no longer a fitting emblem for display, it should be destroyed in a dignified way, preferably by burning.

When to Salute the Flag. All persons present should face the flag, stand at attention, and salute on the following occasions: (1) when the flag is passing in a parade or in a review, (2) during the ceremony of hoisting or lowering, (3) when the national anthem is played, and (4) during the Pledge of Allegiance. Those present in uniform should render the military salute. Those not in uniform should place the right hand over the heart. A man wearing a hat should remove it with his right hand and hold it to his left shoulder during the salute.

Prohibited Uses of the Flag. The flag should not be dipped to any person or thing. (An exception—customarily, ships salute by dipping their colors.) It should never be displayed with the union down save as a distress signal. It should never be carried flat or horizontally, but always aloft and free.

It should not be displayed on a float, an automobile, or a boat except from a staff. It should never be used as a covering for a ceiling, nor have placed on it any word, design, or drawing. It should never be used as a receptacle for carrying anything. It should not be used to cover a statue or a monument.

The flag should never be used for advertising purposes, nor be embroidered on such articles as cushions or handkerchiefs, printed or otherwise impressed on boxes or anything that is designed for temporary use and discard; or used as a costume or athletic uniform. Advertising signs should not be fastened to its staff or halyard.

The flag should never be used as drapery of any sort, never festooned, drawn back, nor up, in folds, but always allowed to fall free. Bunting of blue, white, and red, always arranged with the blue above and the white in the middle, should be used for covering a speaker's desk, draping the front of a platform, and for decoration in general.

An act of Congress approved on Feb. 8, 1917, provided certain penalties for the desecration, mutilation, or improper use of the flag within the District of Columbia. A 1968 federal law provided penalties of as much as a year's imprisonment or a $1,000 fine or both for publicly burning or otherwise desecrating any U.S. flag. In addition, many states have laws against flag desecration. In 1989, the Supreme Court ruled that no laws could prohibit political protesters from burning the flag. The decision had the effect of declaring unconstitutional the flag desecration laws of 48 states, as well as a similar federal statute, in cases of peaceful political expression.

The Supreme Court, in June 1990, declared that a new federal law making it a crime to burn or deface the American flag violated the free-speech guarantee of the First Amendment. The 5-4 Court decision led to renewed calls in Congress for a constitutional amendment to make it possible to prosecute flag burners. In 2005, the House passed a flag desecration amendment with the requisite two-thirds majority, but the measure failed by one vote to achieve two-thirds majority in the Senate in 2006.

Pledge of Allegiance to the Flag

I pledge allegiance to the flag of the United States of America and to the republic for which it stands, one nation under God, indivisible, with liberty and justice for all.

This, the current official version of the Pledge of Allegiance, developed from the original pledge, which was first published in the Sept. 8, 1892, issue of *Youth's Companion*, a weekly magazine. The original pledge contained the phrase "my flag," which was changed more than 30 years later to "flag of the United States of America." A 1954 act of Congress added the words "under God." (In 2002, the 9th Circuit U.S. Court of Appeals ruled that recitation of the pledge in public schools could not include that phrase. In 2004, however, the U.S. Supreme Court voted to decline to decide the case on a technicality. The lower court's decision was thus overturned.)

The authorship of the pledge was in dispute for many years. *Youth's Companion* stated in 1917 that the original draft was written by James B. Upham, an executive of the magazine who died in 1910. A leaflet circulated by the magazine later named Upham as the originator of the draft "afterwards condensed and perfected by him and his associates of the Companion force."

Francis Bellamy, a former member of *Youth's Companion* editorial staff, publicly claimed authorship of the pledge in 1923. In 1939, the United States Flag Association, acting on the advice of a committee named to study the controversy, upheld the claim of Bellamy, who had died eight years earlier. In 1957 the Library of Congress issued a report attributing the authorship to Bellamy.

History of the National Anthem

"The Star-Spangled Banner" was ordered played by the military and naval services by Pres. Woodrow Wilson in 1916. It was designated the national anthem by Act of Congress, Mar. 3, 1931. The words were written by Francis Scott Key, of Georgetown, MD, during the bombardment of Ft. McHenry in Baltimore MD, Sept. 13-14, 1814. Key was a lawyer, a graduate of St. John's College, Annapolis, MD, and a volunteer in a light artillery company. When a friend, Dr. Beanes, a Maryland physician, was taken aboard Adm. Cockburn's British squadron for interfering with ground troops, Key and J. S. Skinner, carrying a note from Pres. Madison, went to the fleet under a flag of truce on a cartel ship to ask Beanes's release. Cockburn consented, but as the fleet was about to sail up the Patapsco to bombard Ft. McHenry, he detained them, first on HMS *Surprise* and then on a supply ship.

Key witnessed the bombardment from his own vessel. It began at 7 AM, Sept. 13, 1814, and lasted 25 hours. The British fired more than 1,500 shells, each weighing as much as 220 lbs. They were unable to approach closely because the U.S. had sunk 22 vessels. Only four Americans were killed and 24 wounded. A British bomb-ship was disabled.

During the event, Key wrote a stanza on the back of an envelope. The next day at Indian Queen Inn in Baltimore, he wrote out the poem and gave it to his brother-in-law, Judge J. H. Nicholson. Nicholson suggested use of the tune, "Anacreon in Heaven" (attributed to a British composer named John Stafford Smith), and had the poem printed on broadsides, of which two survive. On Sept. 20 it appeared in the *Baltimore American*. Later Key made three copies; one is in the Library of Congress, and one in the Pennsylvania Historical Society. The copy Key wrote on Sept. 14 remained in the Nicholson family for 93 years. In 1907, it was sold to Henry Walters of Baltimore. In 1934, it was bought by Walters Art Gallery in Baltimore for $26,400. In 1953, it was sold to the Maryland Historical Society for the same price.

The flag that Key saw during the bombardment is preserved in the Smithsonian Institution, Washington, DC. It measures 30 by 42 ft and has 15 alternating red and white stripes and 15 stars, for the original 13 states plus Kentucky and Vermont. It was made by Mary Pickersgill. The Star-Spangled Banner Flag House, a museum, occupies her premises, which were restored in 1953.

The Star-Spangled Banner

Note: The second and third verses are commonly omitted as a courtesy to the British.

I

Oh, say can you see by the dawn's early light
What so proudly we hailed at the twilight's last gleaming?
Whose broad stripes and bright stars thru the perilous fight,
O'er the ramparts we watched were so gallantly streaming?
And the rocket's red glare, the bombs bursting in air,
Gave proof through the night that our flag was still there.
Oh, say does that star-spangled banner yet wave
O'er the land of the free and the home of the brave?

II

On the shore, dimly seen through the mists of the deep,
Where the foe's haughty host in dread silence reposes,
What is that which the breeze, o'er the towering steep,
As it fitfully blows, half conceals, half discloses?
Now it catches the gleam of the morning's first beam,
In full glory reflected now shines in the stream:
'Tis the star-spangled banner! Oh long may it wave
O'er the land of the free and the home of the brave!

III

And where is that band who so vauntingly swore
That the havoc of war and the battle's confusion,
A home and a country should leave us no more!
Their blood has washed out their foul footsteps' pollution.
No refuge could save the hireling and slave
From the terror of flight, or the gloom of the grave:
And the star-spangled banner in triumph doth wave
O'er the land of the free and the home of the brave!

IV

Oh! thus be it ever, when freemen shall stand
Between their loved home and the war's desolation!
Blest with victory and peace, may the heav'n rescued land
Praise the Power that hath made and preserved us a nation.
Then conquer we must, when our cause it is just,
And this be our motto: "In God is our trust."
And the star-spangled banner in triumph shall wave
O'er the land of the free and the home of the brave!

History of the Liberty Bell

The Liberty Bell is housed in the Liberty Bell Center, located in Philadelphia's Independence National Historical Park.

The original bell was ordered by Assembly Speaker and Chairman of the State House Superintendents Isaac Norris and was ordered from Thomas Lester, Whitechapel Foundry, London. It reached Philadelphia at the end of Aug. 1752. It bore an inscription from Leviticus 25:10: "PROCLAIM LIBERTY THROUGHOUT ALL THE LAND UNTO ALL THE INHABITANTS THEREOF."

The bell was cracked by a stroke of its clapper in Sept. 1752 while it hung on a truss in the State House yard for testing. Pass & Stow, Philadelphia founders, recast the bell, adding 1½ ounces of copper to a pound of the original "Whitechapel" metal to reduce its high tone and brittleness. The bell then contained too much copper, injuring its tone, so Pass & Stow recast it again, this time successfully.

In June 1753, the bell was hung in the old wooden steeple of the State House. In use while the Continental Congress was in session in the State House, it rang out in defiance of British tax and trade restrictions, and it proclaimed the Boston Tea Party and, on July 8, 1776, the first public reading of the Declaration of Independence.

On Sept. 18, 1777, when the British Army was about to occupy Philadelphia, the Liberty Bell was moved in a baggage train to Allentown, PA, where it was hidden until June 27, 1778. The bell was moved back to Philadelphia after the British left the city.

In July 1781, the wooden steeple became insecure and had to be taken down. The bell was lowered into the brick section of the tower, where it remained until 1828. Between 1828 and 1844, the old State House bell continued to ring during special occasions. According to tradition, it cracked in 1835 as it tolled the death of U.S. Supreme Court Chief Justice John Marshall. It rang for the last time on Feb. 23, 1846. In 1852 it was placed on exhibition in the Declaration Chamber of Independence Hall.

In 1876, when thousands of Americans visited Philadelphia for the Centennial Exposition, the bell was placed in its old wooden support in the tower hallway. In 1877, it was hung from the ceiling of the tower by a chain of 13 links. It was returned again to the Declaration Chamber and in 1896 taken back to the tower hall, where it occupied a glass case. In 1915, the case was removed so that the public might touch it. On Jan. 1, 1976, just after midnight to mark the opening of the Bicentennial Year, the bell was moved to a new glass and steel pavilion behind Independence Hall for easier viewing.

On Oct. 9, 2003, the bell was transferred to its present location, where exhibits and displays explain the history of the bell.

Measurements of the bell: circumference around the lip, 12 ft ½ in.; circumference around the crown, 6 ft 11¼ in.; lip to the crown, 3 ft; height over the crown, 2 ft 3 in.; thickness at lip, 3 in.; thickness at crown, 1¼ in.; weight, 2,080 lbs; length of clapper, 3 ft 2 in.

Statue of Liberty National Monument

Since 1886, the Statue of Liberty, formally known as "Liberty Enlightening the World," has stood as a symbol of freedom in New York harbor. It also commemorates French-American friendship, because it was given by the people of France to the people of the U.S. It was designed by French sculptor Frederic Auguste Bartholdi (1834-1904).

On Washington's Birthday, Feb. 22, 1877, Congress approved the use of a site on Bedloe's Island suggested by Bartholdi. This island of 12 acres had been owned in the 17th cent. by a Walloon colonist named Isaac Bedloe. It was called Bedloe's Island until Aug. 3, 1956, when Pres. Dwight Eisenhower approved a measure changing the name to Liberty Island.

The statue was finished on May 21, 1884, and presented to the U.S. minister to France, Levi Parsons Morton, July 4, 1884, by Ferdinand de Lesseps, head of the Franco-American Union, promoter of the Panama Canal, and builder of the Suez Canal.

On Aug. 5, 1884, the Americans laid the cornerstone for the pedestal, to be built on the foundations of Fort Wood, erected by the government in 1811. The American committee had raised an inadequate $125,000 and *New York World* newspaper owner Joseph Pulitzer appealed Mar. 16, 1885, for general donations. By Aug. 11, 1885, he had raised $100,000. The statue itself arrived dismantled, in 214 packing cases, from Rouen, France, in June 1885. The last rivet of the statue was driven on Oct. 28, 1886, when Pres. Grover Cleveland dedicated the monument.

The Statue of Liberty National Monument was designated as such in 1924. It is administered by the National Park Service. A $2.5-mil building housing the American Museum of Immigration was opened by Pres. Richard Nixon on Sept. 26, 1972, at the base of the statue. It houses a permanent exhibition tracing the history of American immigration.

Four years of restoration work funded and led by the Statue of Liberty-Ellis Island Foundation were completed before the statue's 1986 centennial. Among other repairs, the $87-mil project included replacing the 1,600 wrought iron bands that hold the statue's copper skin to its frame, replacing its torch, and installing an elevator. A four-day "Liberty Weekend" extravaganza of concerts, tall ships, ethnic festivals, and fireworks, July 3-6, 1986, celebrated the 100th anniversary. U.S. Supreme Court Chief Justice Warren E. Burger swore in 5,000 new citizens on Ellis Island, while 20,000 others across the country were sworn in through a satellite telecast. Other ceremonies followed on Oct. 28, 1986, the statue's exact 100th birthday.

After the Sept. 11, 2001, terrorist attacks, Liberty Island was closed to visitors. On Dec. 20, 2001, the secretary of the interior reopened the island after installing airport-type screening facilities at passenger embarkation areas at Battery Park in Manhattan and Liberty State Park in New Jersey.

To open the statue, the federal government needed to increase security throughout the park. In addition to federally funded security upgrades, significant safety improvements were made to meet building codes. Access to the statue was finally restored on Aug. 3, 2004.

Following the 125th anniversary celebration Oct. 28, 2011, the statue was closed for one year. A $27-mil renovation brought the statue up to contemporary safety standards and allowed for increased visitor access. The island was open to visitors during the renovations, and views of the statue were largely unobstructed but visitors could not go inside.

The statue interior was scheduled to reopen Oct. 28, 2012. Visitors require reservations to visit the top of the pedestal or the statue's crown. If the past rules are retained, pedestal tickets to enter any level of the monument will be limited to 3,000 visitors per day, and access to the crown will be limited to 240 people each day. Reservations will be available by visiting www.statuecruises.com or by calling 1-877-LADY-TIX. A limited number of "walk up" reservations may also be available at ferry embarkation areas. Free, ranger-guided tours are available daily. Pedestal pass holders will be able to visit the original torch, taken down during renovation in the 1980s, and the museum. For more information, visit www.nps.gov/stli/ and www.statueofliberty.org.

Statue Statistics

The statue weighs 450,000 lbs, or 225 tons. The copper sheeting weighs 200,000 lbs. There are 167 steps from the land level to the top of the pedestal, 168 steps inside the statue to the head, and 54 rungs on the ladder leading to the arm that holds the torch.

	Ft	In.
Height from base to torch tip	151	1
Foundation of pedestal to torch tip	305	1
Heel to top of head	111	1
Hand, length	16	5
Index finger, length	8	0
Size of fingernail		13x10
Head from chin to cranium	17	3
Head thickness, ear to ear	10	0
Nose, length	4	6
Right arm, length	42	0
Right arm, max. thickness	12	0
Thickness of waist	35	0
Mouth, width	3	0
Tablet, length	23	7
Tablet, width	13	7

Ellis Island

Ellis Island was the gateway to America for over 12 mil immigrants between 1892 and 1924. In the late 18th cent., Samuel Ellis, a New York City merchant, purchased the island and gave it his name. From Ellis, it passed to New York state, and the U.S. government bought it in 1808. On Jan. 1, 1892, the government opened the first federal immigration center in the U.S. there. The 27½-acre site eventually supported more than 35 buildings, including the Main Building with its Great Hall, in which as many as 5,000 people a day were processed.

Closed as an immigration station in 1954, Ellis Island was proclaimed part of the Statue of Liberty National Monument in 1965 by Pres. Lyndon B. Johnson. After a six-year, $170 mil restoration project funded by the Statue of Liberty-Ellis Island Foundation, Ellis Island was reopened as a museum in 1990. Artifacts, historic photographs and documents, oral histories, and ethnic music depicting 400 years of American immigration are housed in the museum. The museum also includes The American Immigrant Wall of Honor (www.wallofhonor.org), which is inscribed with more than 700,000 names that have been placed in tribute. Registrations are still being accepted for inclusion in the memorial.

The American Family Immigration History Center® opened in Apr. 2001. It contains an electronic database of ship passenger arrival information through the Port of New York and Ellis Island from 1892 to 1924. Data on over 25 mil individuals are available, as well as an interactive database which features a Living Family Archive, multimedia presentations on various immigration groups and patterns, reproductions of original ships' passenger manifests, and pictures of over 800 immigrant ships (www.ellisisland.org).

In 1998, the U.S. Supreme Court ruled that nearly 90% of the island (the 24.2 acres that are landfill) lies in New Jersey, while the original 3.3 acres, on which the museum is located, are in New York.

U.S. SUPREME COURT

(as of Sept. 2012)

Justices of the U.S. Supreme Court

The Supreme Court comprises the chief justice of the U.S. and eight associate justices, all appointed for life by the president with advice and consent of the U.S. Senate. Names of chief justices are in **boldface**. Terms of service begin with the year each justice took the judicial oath. Service years are the number of complete years served by a justice. Current salaries: chief justice, $223,500; associate justice, $213,900. The U.S. Supreme Court Building is at 1 First St. NE, Washington, DC 20543. The Court website is www.supremecourt.gov.

Current membership. Chief justice: John G. Roberts Jr.; associate justices in seniority order: Antonin Scalia, Anthony M. Kennedy, Clarence Thomas, Ruth Bader Ginsburg, Stephen G. Breyer, Samuel A. Alito Jr., Sonia Sotomayor, Elena Kagan.

Name, appointed from	Service Term	Yrs.	Born	Died	Name, appointed from	Service Term	Yrs.	Born	Died
John Jay, NY	1789-1795	5	1745	1829	Oliver W. Holmes, MA	1902-1932	29	1841	1935
John Rutledge, SC[1]	1790-1791	1	1739	1800	William R. Day, OH	1903-1922	19	1849	1923
William Cushing, MA	1790-1810*	20	1732	1810	William H. Moody, MA	1906-1910	3	1853	1917
James Wilson, PA	1789-1798	8	1742	1798	Horace H. Lurton, TN	1910-1914	4	1844	1914
John Blair, VA	1790-1795*	5	1732	1800	Charles E. Hughes, NY[1]	1910-1916	5	1862	1948
James Iredell, NC	1790-1799	9	1751	1799	Willis Van Devanter, WY	1911-1937	26	1859	1941
Thomas Johnson, MD	1792-1793	<1	1732	1819	Joseph R. Lamar, GA	1911-1916	5	1857	1916
William Paterson, NJ	1793-1806	13	1745	1806	**Edward D. White**, LA[2]	1910-1921	10	1845	1921
John Rutledge, SC[2,3]	1795	<1	1739	1800	Mahlon Pitney, NJ	1912-1922	10	1858	1924
Samuel Chase, MD	1796-1811	15	1741	1811	James C. McReynolds, TN	1914-1941	26	1862	1946
Oliver Ellsworth, CT	1796-1800	4	1745	1807	Louis D. Brandeis, MA	1916-1939	22	1856	1941
Bushrod Washington, VA	1799-1829*	30	1762	1829	John H. Clarke, OH	1916-1922	5	1857	1945
Alfred Moore, NC	1800-1804	3	1755	1810	**William H. Taft**, CT	1921-1930	8	1857	1930
John Marshall, VA	1801-1835	34	1755	1835	George Sutherland, UT	1922-1938	15	1862	1942
William Johnson, SC	1804-1834	30	1771	1834	Pierce Butler, MN	1923-1939	16	1866	1939
Henry B. Livingston, NY	1807-1823	16	1757	1823	Edward T. Sanford, TN	1923-1930	7	1865	1930
Thomas Todd, KY	1807-1826	18	1765	1826	Harlan F. Stone, NY[1]	1925-1941	16	1872	1946
Gabriel Duvall, MD	1811-1835	23	1752	1844	**Charles E. Hughes**, NY[2]	1930-1941	11	1862	1948
Joseph Story, MA	1812-1845*	33	1779	1845	Owen J. Roberts, PA	1930-1945	15	1875	1955
Smith Thompson, NY	1823-1843	20	1768	1843	Benjamin N. Cardozo, NY	1932-1938	6	1870	1938
Robert Trimble, KY	1826-1828	2	1777	1828	Hugo L. Black, AL	1937-1971	34	1886	1971
John McLean, OH	1830-1861*	31	1785	1861	Stanley F. Reed, KY	1938-1957	19	1884	1980
Henry Baldwin, PA	1830-1844	14	1780	1844	Felix Frankfurter, MA	1939-1962	23	1882	1965
James M. Wayne, GA	1835-1867	32	1790	1867	William O. Douglas, CT	1939-1975	36[4]	1898	1980
Roger B. Taney, MD	1836-1864	28	1777	1864	Frank Murphy, MI	1940-1949	9	1890	1949
Philip P. Barbour, VA	1836-1841	4	1783	1841	**Harlan F. Stone**, NY[2]	1941-1946	4	1872	1946
John Catron, TN	1837-1865	28	1786	1865	James F. Byrnes, SC	1941-1942	1	1879	1972
John McKinley, AL	1838-1852*	14	1780	1852	Robert H. Jackson, NY	1941-1954	13	1892	1954
Peter V. Daniel, VA	1842-1860*	18	1784	1860	Wiley B. Rutledge, IA	1943-1949	6	1894	1949
Samuel Nelson, NY	1845-1872	27	1792	1873	Harold H. Burton, OH	1945-1958	13	1888	1964
Levi Woodbury, NH	1845-1851	5	1789	1851	**Fred M. Vinson**, KY	1946-1953	7	1890	1953
Robert C. Grier, PA	1846-1870	23	1794	1870	Tom C. Clark, TX	1949-1967	17	1899	1977
Benjamin R. Curtis, MA	1851-1857	5	1809	1874	Sherman Minton, IN	1949-1956	7	1890	1965
John A. Campbell, AL	1853-1861*	8	1811	1889	**Earl Warren**, CA	1953-1969	15	1891	1974
Nathan Clifford, ME	1858-1881	23	1803	1881	John Marshall Harlan, NY	1955-1971	16	1899	1971
Noah H. Swayne, OH	1862-1881	18	1804	1884	William J. Brennan Jr., NJ	1956-1990	33	1906	1997
Samuel F. Miller, IA	1862-1890	28	1816	1890	Charles E. Whittaker, MO	1957-1962	5	1901	1973
David Davis, IL	1862-1877	14	1815	1886	Potter Stewart, OH	1958-1981	22	1915	1985
Stephen J. Field, CA	1863-1897	33	1816	1899	Byron R. White, CO	1962-1993	31	1917	2002
Salmon P. Chase, OH	1864-1873	8	1808	1873	Arthur J. Goldberg, IL	1962-1965	2	1908	1990
William Strong, PA	1870-1880	10	1808	1895	Abe Fortas, TN	1965-1969	3	1910	1982
Joseph P. Bradley, NJ	1870-1892	21	1813	1892	Thurgood Marshall, NY	1967-1991	24	1908	1993
Ward Hunt, NY	1873-1882	9	1810	1886	**Warren E. Burger**, VA	1969-1986	17	1907	1995
Morrison R. Waite, OH	1874-1888	14	1816	1888	Harry A. Blackmun, MN	1970-1994	24	1908	1999
John M. Harlan, KY	1877-1911	33	1833	1911	Lewis F. Powell Jr., VA	1972-1987	15	1907	1998
William B. Woods, GA	1881-1887	6	1824	1887	William H. Rehnquist, AZ[1]	1972-1986	14	1924	2005
Stanley Matthews, OH	1881-1889	7	1824	1889	John Paul Stevens, IL	1975-2010	34	1920	
Horace Gray, MA	1882-1902	20	1828	1902	Sandra Day O'Connor, AZ	1981-2006	24	1930	
Samuel Blatchford, NY	1882-1893	11	1820	1893	**William H. Rehnquist**, VA[2]	1986-2005	18	1924	2005
Lucius Q.C. Lamar, MS	1888-1893	5	1825	1893	Antonin Scalia, VA	1986-		1936	
Melville W. Fuller, IL	1888-1910	21	1833	1910	Anthony M. Kennedy, CA	1988-		1936	
David J. Brewer, KS	1890-1910	20	1837	1910	David H. Souter, NH	1990-2009	18	1939	
Henry B. Brown, MI	1891-1906	15	1836	1913	Clarence Thomas, GA	1991-		1948	
George Shiras Jr., PA	1892-1903	10	1832	1924	Ruth Bader Ginsburg, NY	1993-		1933	
Howell E. Jackson, TN	1893-1895	2	1832	1895	Stephen G. Breyer, MA	1994-		1938	
Edward D. White, LA[1]	1894-1910	16	1845	1921	**John G. Roberts Jr.**, MD	2005-		1955	
Rufus W. Peckham, NY	1896-1909	13	1838	1909	Samuel A. Alito Jr., NJ	2006-		1950	
Joseph McKenna, CA	1898-1925	26	1843	1926	Sonia Sotomayor, NY	2009-		1954	
					Elena Kagan, MA	2010-		1960	

*Because of inadequate government record keeping, date of oath is estimated. (1) Later, chief justice, as listed. (2) Formerly associate justice. (3) Named acting chief justice; confirmation rejected by the Senate. (4) Longest term of service.

Selected Landmark Decisions of the U.S. Supreme Court, 1803-2011

1803: *Marbury v. Madison.* The Court ruled that Congress exceeded its power in the Judiciary Act of 1789. The Court thus established its power to review acts of Congress and to declare invalid those it found to be in conflict with the Constitution.

1819: *McCulloch v. Maryland.* The Court ruled that Congress had the authority to charter a national bank, under the Constitution's granting of power to enact all laws "necessary and proper" to responsibilities of government.

1819: *Trustees of Dartmouth College v. Woodward.* The Court ruled that a state could not arbitrarily alter the terms of a college's contract. The Court later used a similar principle to limit the states' ability to interfere with business contracts.

1857: *Dred Scott v. Sandford.* The Court declared unconstitutional the already-repealed Missouri Compromise of 1820 because it deprived a person of property—a slave—without due process of law. The Court also ruled that slaves were not citizens of any state nor of the U.S. The latter part of the decision was overturned by ratification of the 14th Amendment in 1868.

1896: *Plessy v. Ferguson.* The Court ruled that a state law requiring federal railroad trains to provide separate but equal facilities for black and white passengers neither infringed upon federal authority to regulate interstate commerce nor violated the 13th and 14th Amendments. The "separate but equal" doctrine remained effective until the 1954 **Brown v. Board of Education** decision.

1904: *Northern Securities Co. v. U.S.* The Court ruled that a holding company formed solely to eliminate competition between two railroad lines was a combination in restraint of trade, violating the 1890 federal Sherman Antitrust Act.

1908: *Muller v. Oregon.* The Court upheld a state law limiting the working hours of women. (Louis D. Brandeis, counsel for the state, cited evidence from social workers, physicians, and factory inspectors that the number of hours women worked affected their health and morals.)

1911: *Standard Oil Co. of New Jersey v. U.S.* The Court ruled that the Standard Oil Trust must be dissolved because of its unreasonable restraint of trade.

1919: *Schenck v. U.S.* The Court sustained the Espionage Act of 1917, maintaining that freedom of speech and press could be constrained if "the words used... create a clear and present danger."

1925: *Gitlow v. New York.* The Court ruled that the 1st Amendment prohibition against government abridgment of the freedom of speech applied to the states as well as to the federal government. The decision was the first of a number of rulings holding that the 14th Amendment extended the guarantees of the Bill of Rights to state action.

1935: *Schechter Poultry Corp. v. U.S.* The Court ruled that Congress exceeded its authority to delegate legislative powers and to regulate interstate commerce when it enacted the National Industrial Recovery Act (1933), which afforded the U.S. president too much discretionary power.

1951: *Dennis v. U.S.* The Court upheld convictions under the Smith Act of 1940 for invoking Communist theory advocating the forcible overthrow of the government. In **Yates v. U.S.** (1957), the Court moderated this ruling by allowing such advocacy in the abstract, if not connected to action to achieve the goal.

1954: *Brown v. Board of Education of Topeka.* The Court ruled that separate public schools for black and white students were inherently unequal, so state-sanctioned segregation in public schools violated the equal protection guarantee of the 14th Amendment. And in **Bolling v. Sharpe** the same year, the Court ruled that the congressionally mandated segregated public school system in the District of Columbia violated the 5th Amendment's due process guarantee of personal liberty. The Brown ruling also led to abolition of state-sponsored segregation in other public facilities.

1957: *Roth v. U.S.; Alberts v. California.* The Court ruled obscene material was not protected by 1st Amendment guarantees of freedom of speech and press, defining as obscene something "utterly without redeeming social value" in the average person's view. This definition was modified in later decisions, and the "average person" standard was replaced by the "local community" standard in **Miller v. California** (1973).

1961: *Mapp v. Ohio.* The Court ruled that evidence obtained in violation of the 4th Amendment guarantee against unreasonable search and seizure must be excluded from use in state as well as federal trials.

1962: *Baker v. Carr.* The Court held that constitutional challenges to the unequal distribution of voters among legislative districts could be resolved by federal courts.

1962: *Engel v. Vitale.* The Court held that government bodies could not encourage the recitation of a state-composed prayer in public schools, even if nondenominational, because that would be an unconstitutional attempt to establish religion.

1963: *Gideon v. Wainwright.* The Court ruled that defendants in state cases must have access to an attorney even if they could not afford one.

1964: *New York Times Co. v. Sullivan.* The Court ruled that the 1st Amendment protected the press from libel suits for defamatory reports about public officials unless an injured party could prove that a defamatory report was made out of malice or "reckless disregard" for the truth.

1965: *Griswold v. Connecticut.* The Court ruled that a state unconstitutionally interfered with personal privacy in the marriage relationship when it prohibited everyone, including married couples, from using contraceptives.

1966: *Miranda v. Arizona.* The Court ruled that, under the guarantee of due process, suspects in custody, before being questioned, must be informed that they have the right to remain silent, that anything they say may be used against them, and that they have the right to counsel.

1973: *Roe v. Wade; Doe v. Bolton.* The Court ruled that the fetus was not a "person" with constitutional rights and that a right to privacy inherent in the 14th Amendment's due process guarantee of personal liberty protected a woman's decision to have an abortion. During the first trimester of pregnancy, the Court maintained, the decision should be left entirely to a woman and her physician. Some regulation of abortion procedures was allowed in the second trimester and some restriction of abortion in the third.

1974: *U.S. v. Nixon.* The Court ruled that neither the separation of powers nor the need to preserve the confidentiality of presidential communications could alone justify an absolute executive privilege of immunity from judicial demands for evidence to be used in a criminal trial.

1976: *Gregg v. Georgia; Proffitt v. Florida; Jurek v. Texas.* The Court held that death, as a punishment for persons convicted of first-degree murder, was not in and of itself cruel and unusual punishment in violation of the 8th Amendment. But the Court ruled that the sentencing judge and jury must consider the character of the offender and the circumstances of the particular crime.

1978: *Regents of the Univ. of Calif. v. Bakke.* The Court ruled that an admissions program for a state medical school, under which a set number of places were reserved for minorities, violated the 1964 Civil Rights Act, which forbids the exclusion of anyone from a federally funded program based on race. However, the Court ruled that race could be considered as one of a complex of factors.

1986: *Bowers v. Hardwick.* The Court refused to extend any right of privacy to homosexual activity, upholding a Georgia antisodomy law that in effect made such activity a crime. However, the law was struck down by the state supreme court in 1998, and in **Lawrence v. Texas** (2003), the U.S. Supreme Court struck down all state antisodomy laws as violations of liberty prohibited in the 14th Amendment's due process clause. In **Romer v. Evans** (1996), the

Court struck down a Colorado constitutional provision that barred homosexuals from recognition as a protected class, ruling that it violated the 14th Amendment's Equal Protection clause.

1990: *Cruzan v. Missouri*. The Court ruled that a person had the right to refuse life-sustaining medical treatment. However, the Court ruled a state could require evidence that a comatose patient would not have wanted to live before withholding treatment. In two 1997 rulings, ***Washington v. Glucksberg*** and ***Vacco v. Quill*,** the Court ruled that states could ban doctor-assisted suicide.

1995: *U.S. Term Limits, Inc. v. Thornton*. The Court ruled that neither states nor Congress could limit terms of members of Congress because the Constitution reserves to the people the right to choose federal lawmakers.

1995: *Adarand Constructors, Inc. v. Peña*. The Court held that federal programs that classify people by race, unless "narrowly tailored" to accomplish a "compelling governmental interest," may violate the right to equal protection.

1997: *Clinton v. Jones*. Rejecting an appeal by Pres. Clinton in a sexual harassment suit, the Court ruled that a sitting president did not have temporary immunity from a lawsuit for actions outside the realm of official duties.

1997: *City of Boerne v. Flores*. The Court overturned a 1993 law banning enforcement of laws that "substantially burden" religious practice unless there is a "compelling need" to do so. The Court held that the act was an unwarranted intrusion by Congress on states' prerogatives and an infringement of the judiciary's role.

1997: *Reno v. ACLU*. Citing the right to free expression, the Court overturned a provision making it a crime to display or distribute "indecent" or "patently offensive" material on the Internet. The Court ruled, however, in ***NEA v. Finley*** (1998) that "general standards of decency" may be used as a criterion in federal arts funding.

1998: *Clinton v. City of New York*. The Court struck down the Line-Item Veto Act (1996), holding that it unconstitutionally gave the president "the unilateral power to change the text of duly enacted statutes."

1998: *Faragher v. City of Boca Raton*; *Burlington Industries, Inc. v. Ellerth*. The Court issued new guidelines for workplace sexual harassment suits, holding employers responsible for misconduct by supervisory employees. And in ***Oncale v. Sundowner Offshore Services, Inc.*,** the Court ruled that the law against discrimination based on sex applies regardless of whether the harasser and harassed are the same sex.

1999: *Dept. of Commerce v. U.S. House of Representatives*. Upholding a challenge to plans for the 2000 census, the Court prohibited statistical sampling, favored by Democrats, in apportioning seats in the U.S. House. The Court maintained that an actual head count was required.

1999: *Alden v. Maine*; *Florida Prepaid v. College Savings Bank*; *College Savings Bank v. Florida Prepaid*. In a series of rulings, the Court applied the principle of sovereign immunity to shield states in large part from being sued under federal law.

2000: *Boy Scouts of America v. Dale*. The Court ruled that the Boy Scouts could dismiss a troop leader after learning he was gay, holding that the right to freedom of association outweighed a New Jersey antidiscrimination statute.

2000: *Bush v. Gore*. The Court ruled that manual recounts of presidential ballots in the Nov. 2000 election could not proceed because inconsistent evaluation standards in different counties violated the equal protection clause. In effect, the ruling meant existing official results leaving George W. Bush as narrow winner of the election would prevail.

2001: *Good News Club v. Milford Central School*. The justices found that religious and secular organizations were entitled to equal access to public elementary school grounds for after-school meetings.

2002: *Federal Maritime Commission v. South Carolina State Ports Authority*. The Court ruled that the 11th Amendment gave states immunity from private lawsuits involving federal agencies.

2002: *Atkins v. Virginia*. The Court ruled that the execution of mentally retarded felons violated the 8th Amendment ban on cruel and unusual punishment. The Court ruled in ***Roper v. Simmons*** (2005) that executions of convicts who committed their crimes before age 18 were also prohibited on the same grounds.

2002: *Zelman v. Simmons-Harris*. The Court ruled that publicly funded tuition vouchers could be used at religious schools without violating the separation of church and state.

2003: *Grotter v. Bollinger*; *Gratz v. Bollinger*. The Court upheld affirmative action in admission policies at the Univ. of Michigan Law School. However, in a second decision, the Court ruled against a strict point system based on racial and ethnic backgrounds, as used in the university's undergraduate admissions process.

2004: *Tennessee v. Lane*. The Court ruled that disabled individuals could sue states under the Americans with Disabilities Act (1990) for failing to provide adequate access to state courthouses, despite states' usual immunity from private lawsuits in federal court under the 11th Amendment, which the Court ruled on in ***Federal Maritime Commission v. South Carolina State Ports Authority*** (2002).

2004: *Locke v. Davey*. The justices decided that a scholarship program provided by the state of Washington did not violate the right to free exercise of religion in denying aid to students preparing for the clergy.

2004: *Ashcroft v. ACLU*. The Court struck down federal legislation passed in 1998 to restrict online access to pornography by minors, on the basis that the law violated the 1st Amendment right of free speech.

2005: *Kelo v. City of New London*. The Court ruled that local governments could force property owners to sell their land in order to facilitate private development projects deemed to be economically beneficial to the community.

2006: *Garcetti v. Ceballos*. The Court ruled that the 1st Amendment guarantee of free speech did not protect statements made by public employees in the course of their official duties.

2006: *Hamdan v. Rumsfeld*. The Court ruled that Pres. George W. Bush's system for trying terrorism detainees at the U.S. military base in Guantánamo Bay, Cuba, was unauthorized under federal law and the international Geneva Conventions. The Court furthermore ruled in ***Boumediene v. Bush*** (2008) that habeas corpus applied and that detainees had a right to challenge their detention in federal court.

2007: *Gonzales v. Carhart*; *Gonzales v. Planned Parenthood Federation of America*. The Court upheld a 2003 federal law prohibiting the abortion procedure known as intact dilation and extraction, or "partial-birth" abortion.

2007: *Parents Involved in Community Schools v. Seattle School District No. 1*; *Meredith v. Jefferson County Board of Education*. The Court ruled that two school districts could not, to encourage diversity, use "racial classifications in making school assignments."

2008: *District of Columbia v. Heller*. The Court overturned DC's handgun ban, ruling that the 2nd Amendment protected an individual's right to own guns for personal use.

2010: *Citizens United v. Federal Election Commission*. The Court ruled that a federal law barring corporations from using general funds to finance campaign advertisements was unconstitutional. The decision cast doubt on many laws restricting political spending by corporations and unions.

2011: *Snyder v. Phelps*. The justices found that an anti-gay church whose members protested at the funeral of a Marine could not be held liable for intrusion or the emotional distress of the father of the deceased; their protests were protected by the 1st Amendment.

See also Year in Review: Notable Supreme Court Decisions, 2011-12.

PRESODENTS OF THE UNITED STATES

U.S. Presidents

	Name	Politics	Born	Birthplace	Inaug.	Age at inaug.	Died	Age at death
1.	George Washington	Fed.	1732, Feb. 22	VA	1789	57	1799, Dec. 14	67
2.	John Adams	Fed.	1735, Oct. 30	MA	1797	61	1826, July 4	90
3.	Thomas Jefferson	Dem.-Rep.	1743, Apr. 13	VA	1801	57	1826, July 4	83
4.	James Madison	Dem.-Rep.	1751, Mar. 16	VA	1809	57	1836, June 28	85
5.	James Monroe	Dem.-Rep.	1758, Apr. 28	VA	1817	58	1831, July 4	73
6.	John Quincy Adams	Dem.-Rep.	1767, July 11	MA	1825	57	1848, Feb. 23	80
7.	Andrew Jackson	Dem.	1767, Mar. 15	SC	1829	61	1845, June 8	78
8.	Martin Van Buren	Dem.	1782, Dec. 5	NY	1837	54	1862, July 24	79
9.	William Henry Harrison	Whig	1773, Feb. 9	VA	1841	68	1841, Apr. 4	68
10.	John Tyler	Whig	1790, Mar. 29	VA	1841	51	1862, Jan. 18	71
11.	James Knox Polk	Dem.	1795, Nov. 2	NC	1845	49	1849, June 15	53
12.	Zachary Taylor	Whig	1784, Nov. 24	VA	1849	64	1850, July 9	65
13.	Millard Fillmore	Whig	1800, Jan. 7	NY	1850	50	1874, Mar. 8	74
14.	Franklin Pierce	Dem.	1804, Nov. 23	NH	1853	48	1869, Oct. 8	64
15.	James Buchanan	Dem.	1791, Apr. 23	PA	1857	65	1868, June 1	77
16.	Abraham Lincoln	Rep.	1809, Feb. 12	KY	1861	52	1865, Apr. 15	56
17.	Andrew Johnson	(1)	1808, Dec. 29	NC	1865	56	1875, July 31	66
18.	Ulysses S. Grant	Rep.	1822, Apr. 27	OH	1869	46	1885, July 23	63
19.	Rutherford Birchard Hayes	Rep.	1822, Oct. 4	OH	1877	54	1893, Jan. 17	70
20.	James Abram Garfield	Rep.	1831, Nov. 19	OH	1881	49	1881, Sept. 19	49
21.	Chester Alan Arthur	Rep.	1829, Oct. 5	VT	1881	51	1886, Nov. 18	57
22.	Grover Cleveland	Dem.	1837, Mar. 18	NJ	1885	47	1908, June 24	71
23.	Benjamin Harrison	Rep.	1833, Aug. 20	OH	1889	55	1901, Mar. 13	67
24.	Grover Cleveland	Dem.	1837, Mar. 18	NJ	1893	55	1908, June 24	71
25.	William McKinley	Rep.	1843, Jan. 29	OH	1897	54	1901, Sept. 14	58
26.	Theodore Roosevelt	Rep.	1858, Oct. 27	NY	1901	42	1919, Jan. 6	60
27.	William Howard Taft	Rep.	1857, Sept. 15	OH	1909	51	1930, Mar. 8	72
28.	(Thomas) Woodrow Wilson	Dem.	1856, Dec. 28	VA	1913	56	1924, Feb. 3	67
29.	Warren Gamaliel Harding	Rep.	1865, Nov. 2	OH	1921	55	1923, Aug. 2	57
30.	(John) Calvin Coolidge	Rep.	1872, July 4	VT	1923	51	1933, Jan. 5	60
31.	Herbert Clark Hoover	Rep.	1874, Aug. 10	IA	1929	54	1964, Oct. 20	90
32.	Franklin Delano Roosevelt	Dem.	1882, Jan. 30	NY	1933	51	1945, Apr. 12	63
33.	Harry S. Truman	Dem.	1884, May 8	MO	1945	60	1972, Dec. 26	88
34.	Dwight David Eisenhower	Rep.	1890, Oct. 14	TX	1953	62	1969, Mar. 28	78
35.	John Fitzgerald Kennedy	Dem.	1917, May 29	MA	1961	43	1963, Nov. 22	46
36.	Lyndon Baines Johnson	Dem.	1908, Aug. 27	TX	1963	55	1973, Jan. 22	64
37.	Richard Milhous Nixon[2]	Rep.	1913, Jan. 9	CA	1969	56	1994, Apr. 22	81
38.	Gerald Rudolph Ford	Rep.	1913, July 14	NE	1974	61	2006, Dec. 26	93
39.	James Earl (Jimmy) Carter	Dem.	1924, Oct. 1	GA	1977	52		
40.	Ronald Wilson Reagan	Rep.	1911, Feb. 6	IL	1981	69	2004, June 5	93
41.	George Herbert Walker Bush	Rep.	1924, June 12	MA	1989	64		
42.	Wm. Jefferson (Bill) Clinton	Dem.	1946, Aug. 19	AR	1993	46		
43.	George Walker Bush	Rep.	1946, July 6	CT	2001	54		
44.	Barack Hussein Obama	Dem.	1961, Aug. 4	HI	2009	47		

(1) Andrew Johnson, a Democrat, was nominated vice president by Republicans and elected with Lincoln on National Union ticket.
(2) Resigned Aug. 9, 1974.

U.S. Presidents, Vice Presidents, Congresses

President	Service	Vice President	Congresses
1. George Washington	Apr. 30, 1789-Mar. 3, 1797	1. John Adams	1, 2, 3, 4
2. John Adams	Mar. 4, 1797-Mar. 3, 1801	2. Thomas Jefferson	5, 6
3. Thomas Jefferson	Mar. 4, 1801-Mar. 3, 1805	3. Aaron Burr	7, 8
	Mar. 4, 1805-Mar. 3, 1809	4. George Clinton	9, 10
4. James Madison	Mar. 4, 1809-Mar. 3, 1813	George Clinton[1]	11, 12
	Mar. 4, 1813-Mar. 3, 1817	5. Elbridge Gerry[2]	13, 14
5. James Monroe	Mar. 4, 1817-Mar. 3, 1825	6. Daniel D. Tompkins	15, 16, 17, 18
6. John Quincy Adams	Mar. 4, 1825-Mar. 3, 1829	7. John C. Calhoun	19, 20
7. Andrew Jackson	Mar. 4, 1829-Mar. 3, 1833	John C. Calhoun[3]	21, 22
	Mar. 4, 1833-Mar. 3, 1837	8. Martin Van Buren	23, 24
8. Martin Van Buren	Mar. 4, 1837-Mar. 3, 1841	9. Richard M. Johnson	25, 26
9. William Henry Harrison[4]	Mar. 4, 1841-Apr. 4, 1841	10. John Tyler	27
10. John Tyler	Apr. 6, 1841-Mar. 3, 1845	(None)	27, 28
11. James K. Polk	Mar. 4, 1845-Mar. 3, 1849	11. George M. Dallas	29, 30
12. Zachary Taylor[4]	Mar. 5, 1849-July 9, 1850	12. Millard Fillmore	31
13. Millard Fillmore	July 10, 1850-Mar. 3, 1853	(None)	31, 32
14. Franklin Pierce	Mar. 4, 1853-Mar. 3, 1857	13. William R. King[5]	33, 34
15. James Buchanan	Mar. 4, 1857-Mar. 3, 1861	14. John C. Breckinridge	35, 36
16. Abraham Lincoln	Mar. 4, 1861-Mar. 3, 1865	15. Hannibal Hamlin	37, 38
(4)	Mar. 4, 1865-Apr. 15, 1865	16. Andrew Johnson	39
17. Andrew Johnson	Apr. 15, 1865-Mar. 3, 1869	(None)	39, 40
18. Ulysses S. Grant	Mar. 4, 1869-Mar. 3, 1873	17. Schuyler Colfax	41, 42
	Mar. 4, 1873-Mar. 3, 1877	18. Henry Wilson[6]	43, 44
19. Rutherford B. Hayes	Mar. 4, 1877-Mar. 3, 1881	19. William A. Wheeler	45, 46
20. James A. Garfield[4]	Mar. 4, 1881-Sept. 19, 1881	20. Chester A. Arthur	47
21. Chester A. Arthur	Sept. 20, 1881-Mar. 3, 1885	(None)	47, 48
22. Grover Cleveland[7]	Mar. 4, 1885-Mar. 3, 1889	21. Thomas A. Hendricks[8]	49, 50
23. Benjamin Harrison	Mar. 4, 1889-Mar. 3, 1893	22. Levi P. Morton	51, 52
24. Grover Cleveland[7]	Mar. 4, 1893-Mar. 3, 1897	23. Adlai E. Stevenson	53, 54
25. William McKinley	Mar. 4, 1897-Mar. 3, 1901	24. Garret A. Hobart[9]	55, 56
(4)	Mar. 4, 1901-Sept. 14, 1901	25. Theodore Roosevelt	57
26. Theodore Roosevelt	Sept. 14, 1901-Mar. 3, 1905	(None)	57, 58
	Mar. 4, 1905-Mar. 3, 1909	26. Charles W. Fairbanks	59, 60
27. William H. Taft	Mar. 4, 1909-Mar. 3, 1913	27. James S. Sherman[10]	61, 62

President	Service	Vice President	Congresses
28. Woodrow Wilson	Mar. 4, 1913-Mar. 3, 1921	28. Thomas R. Marshall	63, 64, 65, 66
29. Warren G. Harding[4]	Mar. 4, 1921-Aug. 2, 1923	29. Calvin Coolidge	67
30. Calvin Coolidge	Aug. 3, 1923-Mar. 3, 1925	(None)	68
	Mar. 4, 1925-Mar. 3, 1929	30. Charles G. Dawes	69, 70
31. Herbert C. Hoover	Mar. 4, 1929-Mar. 3, 1933	31. Charles Curtis	71, 72
32. Franklin D. Roosevelt[11]	Mar. 4, 1933-Jan. 20, 1941	32. John N. Garner	73, 74, 75, 76, 77
	Jan. 20, 1941-Jan. 20, 1945	33. Henry A. Wallace	77, 78, 79
(4)	Jan. 20, 1945-Apr. 12, 1945	34. Harry S. Truman	79
33. Harry S. Truman	Apr. 12, 1945-Jan. 20, 1949	(None)	79, 80, 81
	Jan. 20, 1949-Jan. 20, 1953	35. Alben W. Barkley	81, 82, 83
34. Dwight D. Eisenhower	Jan. 20, 1953-Jan. 20, 1961	36. Richard M. Nixon	83, 84, 85, 86, 87
35. John F. Kennedy[4]	Jan. 20, 1961-Nov. 22, 1963	37. Lyndon B. Johnson	87, 88
36. Lyndon B. Johnson	Nov. 22, 1963-Jan. 20, 1965	(None)	88, 89
	Jan. 20, 1965-Jan. 20, 1969	38. Hubert H. Humphrey	89, 90, 91
37. Richard M. Nixon	Jan. 20, 1969-Jan. 20, 1973	39. Spiro T. Agnew[12]	91, 92, 93
(13)	Jan. 20, 1973-Aug. 9, 1974	40. Gerald R. Ford[14]	93
38. Gerald R. Ford[15]	Aug. 9, 1974-Jan. 20, 1977	41. Nelson A. Rockefeller[16]	93, 94, 95
39. Jimmy Carter	Jan. 20, 1977-Jan. 20, 1981	42. Walter F. Mondale	95, 96, 97
40. Ronald W. Reagan	Jan. 20, 1981-Jan. 20, 1989	43. George H. W. Bush	97, 98, 99, 100, 101
41. George H. W. Bush	Jan. 20, 1989-Jan. 20, 1993	44. Dan Quayle	101, 102, 103
42. Bill Clinton	Jan. 20, 1993-Jan. 20, 2001	45. Al Gore	103, 104, 105, 106, 107
43. George W. Bush	Jan. 20, 2001-Jan. 20, 2009	46. Dick Cheney	107, 108, 109, 110, 111
44. Barack H. Obama	Jan. 20, 2009-	47. Joe Biden	111, 112

(1) Died Apr. 20, 1812. (2) Died Nov. 23, 1814. (3) Resigned Dec. 28, 1832, to become U.S. senator. (4) Died in office. (5) Died Apr. 18, 1853. (6) Died Nov. 22, 1875. (7) Terms not consecutive. (8) Died Nov. 25, 1885. (9) Died Nov. 21, 1899. (10) Died Oct. 30, 1912. (11) First president to be inaugurated under 20th Amendment, Jan. 20, 1937. (12) Resigned Oct. 10, 1973. (13) Resigned Aug. 9, 1974. (14) First nonelected vice president, chosen under 25th Amendment procedure. (15) First president never elected president or vice president. (16) Second nonelected vice president, chosen under 25th Amendment. Confirmed Dec. 19, 1974.

Vice Presidents of the U.S.

The numerals given vice presidents do not coincide with those given presidents, because some presidents (Tyler, Fillmore, A. Johnson, Arthur) had none, and some had more than one.

Name	Birthplace	Year	Home	Inaug.	Politics	Place of death	Year	Age at death
1. John Adams	Quincy, MA	1735	MA	1789	Fed.	Quincy, MA	1826	90
2. Thomas Jefferson	Shadwell, VA	1743	VA	1797	Dem.-Rep.	Monticello, VA	1826	83
3. Aaron Burr	Newark, NJ	1756	NY	1801	Dem.-Rep.	Staten Island, NY	1836	80
4. George Clinton	Little Britain, NY	1739	NY	1805	Dem.-Rep.	Washington, DC	1812	73
5. Elbridge Gerry	Marblehead, MA	1744	MA	1813	Dem.-Rep.	Washington, DC	1814	70
6. Daniel D. Tompkins	Scarsdale, NY	1774	NY	1817	Dem.-Rep.	Staten Island, NY	1825	51
7. John C. Calhoun[1]	Abbeville, SC	1782	SC	1825	Dem.-Rep.	Washington, DC	1850	68
8. Martin Van Buren	Kinderhook, NY	1782	NY	1833	Dem.	Kinderhook, NY	1862	79
9. Richard M. Johnson[2]	Louisville, KY	1780	KY	1837	Dem.	Frankfort, KY	1850	70
10. John Tyler	Greenway, VA	1790	VA	1841	Whig	Richmond, VA	1862	71
11. George M. Dallas	Philadelphia, PA	1792	PA	1845	Dem.	Philadelphia, PA	1864	72
12. Millard Fillmore	Cayuga Co., NY	1800	NY	1849	Whig	Buffalo, NY	1874	74
13. William R. King	Sampson Co., NC	1786	AL	1853	Dem.	Cahaba, AL	1853	67
14. John C. Breckinridge	Lexington, KY	1821	KY	1857	Dem.	Lexington, KY	1875	54
15. Hannibal Hamlin	Paris, ME	1809	ME	1861	Rep.	Bangor, ME	1891	81
16. Andrew Johnson	Raleigh, NC	1808	TN	1865	(3)	Carter Co., TN	1875	66
17. Schuyler Colfax	New York, NY	1823	IN	1869	Rep.	Mankato, MN	1885	62
18. Henry Wilson	Farmington, NH	1812	MA	1873	Rep.	Washington, DC	1875	63
19. William A. Wheeler	Malone, NY	1819	NY	1877	Rep.	Malone, NY	1887	68
20. Chester A. Arthur	Fairfield, VT	1829	NY	1881	Rep.	New York, NY	1886	57
21. Thomas A. Hendricks	Zanesville, OH	1819	IN	1885	Dem.	Indianapolis, IN	1885	66
22. Levi P. Morton	Shoreham, VT	1824	NY	1889	Rep.	Rhinebeck, NY	1920	96
23. Adlai E. Stevenson[4]	Christian Co., KY	1835	IL	1893	Dem.	Chicago, IL	1914	78
24. Garret A. Hobart	Long Branch, NJ	1844	NJ	1897	Rep.	Paterson, NJ	1899	55
25. Theodore Roosevelt	New York, NY	1858	NY	1901	Rep.	Oyster Bay, NY	1919	60
26. Charles W. Fairbanks	Unionville Centre, OH	1852	IN	1905	Rep.	Indianapolis, IN	1918	66
27. James S. Sherman	Utica, NY	1855	NY	1909	Rep.	Utica, NY	1912	57
28. Thomas R. Marshall	N. Manchester, IN	1854	IN	1913	Dem.	Washington, DC	1925	71
29. Calvin Coolidge	Plymouth Notch, VT	1872	MA	1921	Rep.	Northampton, MA	1933	60
30. Charles G. Dawes	Marietta, OH	1865	IL	1925	Rep.	Evanston, IL	1951	85
31. Charles Curtis	Topeka, KS	1860	KS	1929	Rep.	Washington, DC	1936	76
32. John Nance Garner	Red River Co., TX	1868	TX	1933	Dem.	Uvalde, TX	1967	98
33. Henry A. Wallace	Adair County, IA	1888	IA	1941	Dem.	Danbury, CT	1965	77
34. Harry S. Truman	Lamar, MO	1884	MO	1945	Dem.	Kansas City, MO	1972	88
35. Alben W. Barkley	Graves County, KY	1877	KY	1949	Dem.	Lexington, VA	1956	78
36. Richard M. Nixon	Yorba Linda, CA	1913	CA	1953	Rep.	New York, NY	1994	81
37. Lyndon B. Johnson	Stonewall, TX	1908	TX	1961	Dem.	San Antonio, TX	1973	64
38. Hubert H. Humphrey	Wallace, SD	1911	MN	1965	Dem.	Waverly, MN	1978	66
39. Spiro T. Agnew[5]	Baltimore, MD	1918	MD	1969	Rep.	Berlin, MD	1996	77
40. Gerald R. Ford[6]	Omaha, NE	1913	MI	1973	Rep.	Rancho Mirage, CA	2006	93
41. Nelson A. Rockefeller[7]	Bar Harbor, ME	1908	NY	1974	Rep.	New York, NY	1979	70
42. Walter F. Mondale	Ceylon, MN	1928	MN	1977	Dem.			
43. George H. W. Bush	Milton, MA	1924	TX	1981	Rep.			
44. James Danforth (Dan) Quayle Jr.	Indianapolis, IN	1947	IN	1989	Rep.			
45. Albert A. Gore	Washington, DC	1948	TN	1993	Dem.			
46. Richard B. Cheney	Lincoln, NE	1941	WY	2001	Rep.			
47. Joseph R. Biden Jr.	Scranton, PA	1942	DE	2009	Dem.			

(1) Resigned Dec. 28, 1832, having been elected to the Senate to fill a vacancy. (2) Richard M. Johnson was the only vice president to be chosen by the Senate because of a tied vote in the Electoral College. (3) Andrew Johnson was a Democrat, nominated vice president by Republicans, and elected with Lincoln on the National Union Ticket. (4) Grandfather of Democratic candidate for president in 1952 and 1956. (5) Resigned Oct. 10, 1973. (6) First nonelected vice president, chosen under 25th Amendment procedure. (7) Second nonelected vice president, chosen under 25th Amendment.

Biographies of the Presidents

George Washington (1789-97), 1st president, Federalist, was born on Feb. 22, 1732, in Wakefield on Pope's Creek, Westmoreland Co., VA, the son of Augustine and Mary Ball Washington. He spent his early childhood on a farm near Fredericksburg. His father died when Washington was 11. He studied mathematics and surveying, and at 16, he went to live with his elder half brother, Lawrence, who built and named Mount Vernon in Virginia. Washington surveyed the lands of Thomas Fairfax in the Shenandoah Valley. He accompanied Lawrence to Barbados, West Indies, where he contracted smallpox and was deeply scarred. Lawrence died in 1752, and Washington inherited his property. He valued land, and when he died, he owned 70,000 acres in Virginia and 40,000 acres in what is now West Virginia.

Washington's military service began in 1753, when Lt. Gov. Robert Dinwiddie of Virginia sent him on missions deep into Ohio country. He clashed with the French and had to surrender Fort Necessity on July 3, 1754. He was an aide to the British general Edward Braddock and was at his side when the army was ambushed and defeated (July 9, 1755) on a march to Fort Duquesne. He helped take Fort Duquesne from the French in 1758.

After Washington's marriage to Martha Dandridge Custis, a widow, in 1759, he managed his family estate at Mount Vernon. Although not at first for independence, he opposed the repressive measures of the British crown and took charge of the Virginia troops before war broke out. He was made commander of the newly created Continental Army by the Continental Congress on June 15, 1775.

The American victory was due largely to Washington's leadership. He was resourceful, a disciplinarian, and the one dependable force for unity. Washington favored a federal government. He became chairman of the Constitutional Convention of 1787 and helped get the Constitution ratified. Unanimously elected president by the electoral college, he was inaugurated Apr. 30, 1789, on the balcony of New York's Federal Hall. He was reelected in 1792. Washington made an effort to avoid partisan politics as president.

Refusing to consider a third term, Washington retired to Mount Vernon in Mar. 1797. A ride in snow and rain around his estate led to what present-day doctors believe to have been an attack of acute epiglottitis. Doctors were unsuccessful in treating the inflammation in his throat, and Washington died Dec. 14, 1799.

John Adams (1797-1801), 2nd president, Federalist, was born on Oct. 30, 1735, in Braintree (now Quincy), MA, the son of John and Susanna Boylston Adams. He was a great-grandson of Henry Adams, who came from England in 1636. He graduated from Harvard in 1755, then taught school and studied law. He married Abigail Smith in 1764. In 1765 he argued against taxation without representation before the royal governor. In 1770, he successfully defended in court the British soldiers who fired on civilians in the Boston Massacre. He was a delegate to the Continental Congress and a signer of the Declaration of Independence. In 1778, Congress sent Adams and John Jay to join Benjamin Franklin as diplomatic representatives in Europe. Because he ran second to Washington in electoral college balloting in Feb. 1789, Adams became the nation's first vice president, a post he characterized as highly insignificant; he was reelected in 1792.

In 1796 Adams was chosen president by the electors. His administration was marked by growing conflict with fellow Federalist Alexander Hamilton and with others in his own cabinet who supported Hamilton's strongly anti-French position. Adams avoided full-scale war with France but became unpopular, especially after securing passage of the Alien and Sedition Acts in 1798. His foreign policy contributed significantly to the election of Thomas Jefferson in 1800.

Adams lived for a quarter century after he left office, during which time he wrote extensively. He died July 4, 1826, on the same day as his rival Thomas Jefferson (the 50th anniversary of the Declaration of Independence).

Thomas Jefferson (1801-09), 3rd president, Democratic-Republican, was born on Apr. 13, 1743, in Shadwell in Goochland (now Albemarle) Co., VA, the son of Peter and Jane Randolph Jefferson. His father died when Jefferson was 14, leaving him 2,750 acres and his slaves. Jefferson attended (1760-62) the College of William and Mary, read Greek and Latin classics, and played the violin. In 1769 he was elected to the Virginia House of Burgesses. In 1770 he began building his home, Monticello, and in 1772 he married Martha Wayles Skelton, a wealthy widow. Jefferson helped establish the Virginia Committee of Correspondence. As a member of the 2nd Continental Congress he drafted the Declaration of Independence. He also was a member of the Virginia House of Delegates (1776-79) and was elected governor of Virginia in 1779. Reelected in 1780, he resigned the next year after British troops invaded Virginia. During his term he wrote the statute on religious freedom. After his wife's death in 1782, Jefferson again became a delegate to the Congress, and in 1784 he drafted the report that was the basis for the Ordinances of 1784, 1785, and 1787. He was minister to France from 1785 to 1789, when George Washington appointed him secretary of state.

Jefferson's strong faith in the consent of the governed conflicted with the emphasis on executive control, favored by Sec. of the Treasury Alexander Hamilton, and Jefferson resigned on Dec. 31, 1793. In the 1796 election Jefferson was the Democratic-Republican candidate for president; John Adams won the election, and Jefferson became vice president. In 1800, Jefferson and Aaron Burr received equal electoral college votes; the House of Representatives elected Jefferson president. Jefferson was a strong advocate of westward expansion; major events of his first term were the Louisiana Purchase (1803) and the Lewis and Clark expedition. An important development during his second term was passage of the Embargo Act, barring U.S. ships from setting sail to foreign ports. Jefferson established the Univ. of Virginia and designed its buildings. He died July 4, 1826, on the same day as John Adams (the 50th anniversary of the Declaration of Independence).

Analysis of contemporary accounts, plantation records, and DNA taken from descendants of Jefferson and of Sally Hemings, one of his slaves, has caused many historians to conclude Jefferson fathered one or more of her six children.

James Madison (1809-17), 4th president, Democratic-Republican, was born on Mar. 16, 1751, in Port Conway, King George Co., VA, the son of James and Eleanor Rose Conway Madison. Madison graduated from the College of New Jersey in 1771. He served in the Virginia Constitutional Convention (1776), and, in 1780, became a delegate to the 2nd Continental Congress. He was chief recorder at the Constitutional Convention in 1787 and supported ratification in the *Federalist Papers*, written with Alexander Hamilton and John Jay. In 1789, Madison was elected to the House of Representatives, where he helped frame the Bill of Rights and fought against passage of the Alien and Sedition Acts. In the 1790s, he helped found the Democratic-Republican Party, which ultimately became the Democratic Party. He became Jefferson's secretary of state in 1801.

Madison was elected president in 1808. His first term was marked by tensions with Great Britain, and his conduct of foreign policy was criticized by the Federalists and by his own party. Nevertheless, he was reelected in 1812, the year war was declared on Great Britain. The war that many considered a second American revolution ended with a treaty that did not settle any of the issues. Madison's most important action after the war was demilitarizing the U.S.-Canadian border.

In 1817, Madison retired to his estate, Montpelier, where he served as an elder statesman. He edited his famous papers on the Constitutional Convention and helped found the Univ. of Virginia, of which he became rector in 1826. He died June 28, 1836.

James Monroe (1817-25), 5th president, Democratic-Republican, was born on Apr. 28, 1758, in Westmoreland Co., VA, the son of Spence and Elizabeth Jones Monroe. He entered the College of William and Mary in 1774 but left to serve in the 3rd Virginia Regiment during the American Revolution. After the war, he studied law with Thomas Jefferson. In 1782 he was elected to the Virginia House of Delegates, and he served (1783-86) as a delegate to the Continental Congress. He opposed ratification of the Constitution because it lacked a bill of rights. Monroe was elected to the U.S. Senate in 1790. In 1794, Pres. Washington appointed Monroe minister to France. He served twice as governor of Virginia (1799-1802, 1811). Pres. Jefferson also sent him to France as minister (1803), and from 1803 to 1807, he served as minister to Great Britain.

In 1816 Monroe was elected president; he was reelected in 1820 with all but one electoral college vote. His administration became known as the Era of Good Feeling. He obtained Florida from Spain, settled boundary disputes with Britain over Canada, and eliminated border forts. He supported the antislavery position that led to the Missouri Compromise. His most significant contribution was the Monroe Doctrine, which opposed European intervention in the Western Hemisphere and became a cornerstone of U.S. foreign policy.

Although Monroe retired to Oak Hill, VA, financial problems forced him to sell his property and move to New York City. He died there on July 4, 1831.

John Quincy Adams (1825-29), 6th president, independent Federalist, later Democratic-Republican, was born on July 11, 1767, in Braintree (now Quincy), MA, the son of John and Abigail Adams. His father was the second president. He studied abroad and at Harvard College, from which he graduated in 1787. In 1803, he was elected to the U.S. Senate. President Monroe chose him as his secretary of state in 1817. In this capacity he negotiated the cession of Florida from Spain, supported exclusion of slavery in the Missouri Compromise, and helped formulate the Monroe Doctrine.

After no candidate won an Electoral College majority in 1824, the presidential election was thrown into the House of Representatives; Adams won with support from rival Henry Clay, whom he named secretary of state, fueling accusations of a "corrupt bargain." His expansion of executive powers was strongly opposed, and in the 1828 election he lost to Andrew Jackson. In 1831 he entered the House of Representatives and served 17 years with distinction. He opposed slavery, the annexation of Texas, and the Mexican War. He helped establish the Smithsonian Institution.

Adams suffered a stroke in the House and died in the Speaker's Room on Feb. 23, 1848.

Andrew Jackson (1829-37), 7th president, Democratic-Republican, later a Democrat, was born on Mar. 15, 1767, in the Waxhaw district, on the border of North and South Carolina, the son of Andrew and Elizabeth Hutchinson Jackson. At the age of 13, he joined the militia to fight in the American Revolution and was captured. Orphaned at age 14, Jackson was brought up by a well-to-do uncle. By age 20, he was practicing law, and he later served as prosecuting attorney in Nashville, TN. In 1796 he helped draft the constitution of Tennessee, and for a year he occupied its one seat in the House of Representatives. The next year he served in the U.S. Senate.

In the War of 1812, Jackson crushed the Creek Indians at Horseshoe Bend, AL (1814), and, with a greatly outnumbered army consisting chiefly of backwoods militia members and volunteers, defeated Gen. Edward Pakenham's British troops at the Battle of New Orleans (1815). Nicknamed "Old Hickory" for his toughness, he emerged a national hero.

In 1818 Jackson briefly invaded Spanish Florida to quell Seminoles and outlaws who harassed frontier settlements. He ran for president against John Quincy Adams in 1824, but, although he won the most popular and electoral votes, he did not have a majority. The House of Representatives decided the election and chose Adams. In the 1828 election, however, Jackson defeated Adams, carrying the West and the South.

As president, Jackson introduced what became known as the spoils system—rewarding party members with government posts. A self-professed champion of the common man, he also viewed the Second Bank of the U.S. as a bastion of privilege and made it a major issue in the election of 1832, the first where candidates were chosen at national conventions rather than in congressional caucuses. Defeating Henry Clay, Jackson increasingly diverted funds from the national bank into so-called pet banks run by members of his own party. When South Carolina refused to collect imports under a federal tariff, which it declared null and void, Jackson won passage of legislation confirming his right to use military force to obtain compliance; eventually the tariff rate was reduced and the nullifiers backed down. After leaving office in 1837, he retired to the Hermitage, outside Nashville, where he died on June 8, 1845.

Martin Van Buren (1837-41), 8th president, Democrat, was born on Dec. 5, 1782, in Kinderhook, NY, the son of Abraham and Maria Hoes Van Buren. After attending local schools, he studied law and became a lawyer at the age of 20. A consummate politician, Van Buren began his career in the New York state senate and then served as state attorney general from 1816 to 1819. He was elected to the U.S. Senate in 1821. He helped swing Eastern support to Andrew Jackson in the 1828 election and then served as Jackson's secretary of state from 1829 to 1831. In 1832 he was elected vice president. Known as the "Little Magician," Van Buren was extremely influential in Jackson's administration.

In 1836, Van Buren defeated William Henry Harrison for president and took office as the financial panic of 1837 initiated a nationwide depression. Although he instituted the independent treasury system, his refusal to spend land revenues led to his defeat by William Henry Harrison in 1840. In 1844 he lost the Democratic nomination to James K. Polk. In 1848 he again ran for president on the Free Soil ticket but lost. He died in Kinderhook on July 24, 1862.

William Henry Harrison (1841), 9th president, Whig, who served only 31 days, was born on Feb. 9, 1773, in Berkeley, Charles City Co., VA, the son of Benjamin Harrison—a signer of the Declaration of Independence—and of Elizabeth Bassett Harrison. He attended Hampden-Sydney College. Harrison served as secretary of the Northwest Territory in 1798 and was its delegate to the House of Representatives in 1799. He was the first governor of Indiana Territory and served as superintendent of Indian affairs. With 900 men he put down a Shawnee uprising at Tippecanoe, IN, on Nov. 7, 1811. A generation later, in 1840, he waged a rousing presidential campaign, using the slogan "Tippecanoe and Tyler Too." The Tyler of the slogan was his running mate, John Tyler.

Although born to one of the wealthiest, most prestigious, and most influential families in Virginia, Harrison was elected president with the slogan, "Log Cabin and Hard Cider." He caught pneumonia during his inauguration and died Apr. 4, 1841, after only one month in office.

John Tyler (1841-45), 10th president, independent Whig, was born on Mar. 29, 1790, in Greenway, Charles City Co., VA, the son of John and Mary Armistead Tyler. His father was governor of Virginia (1808-11). Tyler graduated from the College of William and Mary in 1807 and in 1811 was elected to the Virginia legislature. In 1816 he was chosen for the U.S. House of Representatives. He served in the Virginia legislature again from 1823 to 1825, when he was elected governor of Virginia. After a stint in the U.S. Senate (1827-36), he was elected vice president (1840).

When William Henry Harrison died only a month after taking office, Tyler succeeded him. Because he was the first person to occupy the presidency without having been elected to that office, he was referred to as "His Accidency." He gained passage of the Preemption Act of 1841, which gave squatters on government land the right to buy 160 acres at the minimum auction price. His last act as president was to sign a resolution annexing Texas. Tyler accepted renomination in 1844 from some Democrats but withdrew in favor of the official party candidate, James K. Polk. A strong advocate of states' rights, he served briefly in the Confederate House of Representatives before he died in Richmond, VA, on Jan. 18, 1862.

James Knox Polk (1845-49), 11th president, Democrat, was born on Nov. 2, 1795, in Mecklenburg Co., NC, the son of Samuel and Jane Knox Polk. He graduated from the Univ. of North Carolina in 1818 and served in the Tennessee state legislature from 1823 to 1825. He served in the U.S. House of Representatives from 1825 to 1839, the last 4 years as Speaker. He was governor of Tennessee from 1839 to 1841. In 1844, after the Democratic National Convention became deadlocked, it nominated Polk, who became the first "dark horse" candidate for president. He was nominated primarily because he favored annexation of Texas.

As president, Polk reestablished the independent treasury system originated by Van Buren. He was so intent on acquiring California from Mexico that he sent troops to the Mexican border and, when Mexicans attacked, declared that a state of war existed. The Mexican War ended with the annexation of California and much of the Southwest as part of America's "manifest destiny." Polk compromised on the Oregon boundary ("54-40 or fight!") by accepting the 49th parallel and yielding Vancouver Island to the British. Polk died in Nashville, TN, on June 15, 1849, a few months after leaving office.

Zachary Taylor (1849-50), 12th president, Whig, who served only 16 months, was born on Nov. 24, 1784, in Orange Co., VA, the son of Richard and Sarah Strother Taylor. He grew up on his father's plantation near Louisville, KY, where he was educated by private tutors. In 1808 Taylor joined the regular army and was commissioned first lieutenant. He fought in the War of 1812, the Black Hawk War (1832), and the second Seminole War (beginning in 1837). He was called "Old Rough and Ready." In 1846 Pres. Polk sent him with an army to the Rio Grande. When the Mexicans attacked him, Polk declared war. Outnumbered four to one, Taylor defeated Antonio López de Santa Anna at Buena Vista (1847).

A national hero, Taylor received the Whig nomination in 1848 and was elected president, even though he had never bothered to vote. He resumed the spoils system and, though a slaveholder, worked to admit California as a free state. He fell ill, likely from a case of acute gastroenteritis, and died in office on July 9, 1850.

Millard Fillmore (1850-53), 13th president, Whig, was born on Jan. 7, 1800, in Cayuga Co., NY, the son of Nathaniel and Phoebe Millard Fillmore. Although he had little schooling, he became a law clerk at the age of 22 and a year later was admitted to the bar. He was elected to the New York state assembly in 1828 and served until 1831. From 1833 until 1835 and again from 1837 to 1843, he represented his district in the U.S. House of Representatives. He opposed the entrance of Texas as a slave state and voted for a protective tariff. In 1844 he was defeated for governor of New York.

In 1848, he was elected vice president, and he succeeded as president after Taylor's death. Fillmore favored the Compromise of 1850 and signed the Fugitive Slave Law. His policies pleased neither expansionists nor slaveholders, and he was not renominated in 1852. In 1856 he was nominated by the American (Know-Nothing) Party, but despite the support of the Whigs, he was defeated by James Buchanan. He died in Buffalo, NY, on Mar. 8, 1874.

Franklin Pierce (1853-57), 14th president, Democrat, was born on Nov. 23, 1804, in Hillsboro, NH, the son of Benjamin Pierce, Revolutionary War general and governor of New Hampshire, and Anna Kendrick. He graduated from Bowdoin College in 1824 and was admitted to the bar in 1827. He was elected to the New Hampshire state legislature in 1829 and was chosen Speaker in 1831. He went to the U.S. House in 1833 and was elected a U.S. senator in 1837. He enlisted in the Mexican War and became brigadier general under Gen. Winfield Scott.

In 1852 Pierce was nominated as the Democratic presidential candidate on the 49th ballot. He decisively defeated Gen. Scott, his Whig opponent, in the election. Although he was against slavery, Pierce was influenced by proslavery Southerners. He supported the controversial Kansas-Nebraska Act, which left the question of slavery in the new territories of Kansas and Nebraska to popular vote. Pierce signed a reciprocity treaty with Canada and approved the Gadsden Purchase of a border area on a proposed railroad route, from Mexico. Denied renomination, he spent most of his remaining years in Concord, NH, where he died on Oct. 8, 1869.

James Buchanan (1857-61), 15th president, Federalist, later Democrat, was born on Apr. 23, 1791, near Mercersburg, PA, the son of James and Elizabeth Speer Buchanan. He graduated from Dickinson College in 1809 and was admitted to the bar in 1812. He fought in the War of 1812 as a volunteer. He was twice elected to the Pennsylvania general assembly, and in 1821 he entered the U.S. House of Representatives. After briefly serving (1832-33) as minister to Russia, he was elected U.S. senator from Pennsylvania. As Polk's secretary of state (1845-49), he ended the Oregon dispute with Britain and supported the Mexican War and annexation of Texas. As minister to Great Britain, he signed the Ostend Manifesto (1854), declaring a U.S. right to take Cuba by force should efforts to purchase it fail.

Nominated by Democrats, Buchanan was elected president in 1856. On slavery he favored popular sovereignty and choice by state constitutions but did not consistently uphold this position. He denied the right of states to secede but opposed coercion and attempted to keep peace by not provoking secessionists. Buchanan left office having failed to deal decisively with the situation. He died at Wheatland, his estate, near Lancaster, PA, on June 1, 1868.

Abraham Lincoln (1861-65), 16th president, Whig, then Republican, was born on Feb. 12, 1809, in a log cabin on a farm in Hardin (now Larue) Co., KY, the son of Thomas and Nancy Hanks Lincoln. The Lincolns moved to Spencer Co., IN, near Gentryville, when Lincoln was 7. After Lincoln's mother died, his father married Mrs. Sarah Bush Johnston in 1819. In 1830 the family moved to Macon Co., IL.

Defeated in 1832 in a race for the state legislature, Lincoln was elected on the Whig ticket two years later and served in the lower house from 1834 to 1842. In 1837 Lincoln was admitted to the bar and became partner in a Springfield, IL, law office. In 1846, he was elected to Congress, where he attracted attention during a single term for his opposition to the Mexican War and his position on slavery. In 1856 he campaigned for the newly founded Republican Party, and in 1858 he became its senatorial candidate against Stephen A. Douglas. Although he lost the election, Lincoln gained national recognition from his debates with Douglas.

In 1860, Lincoln was nominated for president by the Republican Party on a platform of restricting slavery. He ran against Douglas, a northern Democrat; John C. Breckinridge, a Southern proslavery Democrat; and John Bell, of the Constitutional Union Party. In response to Lincoln's victory, South Carolina seceded from the Union on Dec. 20, 1860, soon followed by six other Southern states.

The Civil War erupted when Fort Sumter, which Lincoln decided to resupply, was attacked by Confederate forces on Apr. 12, 1861. Lincoln called successfully for recruits from the North, and four more Southern states seceded. Hundreds of thousands of Union and Confederate solders were killed or wounded in four years of battle that followed. On Sept. 22, 1862, five days after the Battle of Antietam, Lincoln announced that slaves in territory then in rebellion would be free Jan. 1, 1863, under his Emancipation Proclamation. His speeches, including his Gettysburg and inaugural addresses, are remembered for their eloquence.

Lincoln was reelected, in 1864, over Gen. George B. McClellan, a Democrat. Confederate Gen. Robert E. Lee surrendered on Apr. 9, 1865. On Apr. 14, Lincoln was shot by actor John Wilkes Booth in Ford's Theater, in Washington, DC. He died the next day.

Andrew Johnson (1865-69), 17th president, Democrat, was born on Dec. 29, 1808, in Raleigh, NC, the son of Jacob and Mary McDonough Johnson. He was apprenticed to a tailor as a youth, but ran away after two years and eventually settled in Greeneville, TN, where he was elected councilman and later mayor. In 1835 he was sent to the state general assembly. In 1843 he was elected to the U.S. House of Representatives, where he served for 10 years. Johnson was also governor of Tennessee from 1853 to 1857, when he was elected to the U.S. Senate. Although Johnson had held slaves, he opposed secession and tried to prevent Tennessee from seceding. In Mar. 1862, Lincoln appointed him military governor of occupied Tennessee.

In 1864, in order to balance Lincoln's ticket with a Southern Democrat, the Republicans nominated Johnson for vice president. He was elected vice president with Lincoln and then succeeded to the presidency upon Lincoln's death. Soon afterward, in a controversy with Congress over the president's power over the South, he proclaimed an amnesty to all Confederates, except certain leaders, if they would ratify the 13th Amendment abolishing slavery. States doing so added anti-Negro provisions that enraged Congress, which restored military control over the South. When Johnson removed Sec. of War Edwin M. Stanton, without notifying the Senate, the House impeached him in Feb. 1868. Charging him with thereby having violated the Tenure of Office Act, the House was actually responding to his opposition to harsh congressional Reconstruction, expressed in repeated vetoes. He was acquitted in the Senate by one-vote margins on each of two counts.

Johnson was denied renomination but remained politically active. He was reelected to the Senate in 1874. Johnson died July 31, 1875, at Carter Station, TN.

Ulysses S. Grant (1869-77), 18th president, Republican, was born on Apr. 27, 1822, in Point Pleasant, OH, the son of Jesse R. and Hannah Simpson Grant. The next year the family moved to Georgetown, OH. Grant was named Hiram Ulysses. Upon entering West Point in 1839, he found his name had been put down as Ulysses S. Grant, with his middle name first and his mother's maiden name as his middle name. He eventually adopted it as his true name but maintained the "S" did not stand for anything. Grant graduated in 1843. During the Mexican War, Grant served under both Gen. Zachary Taylor and Gen. Winfield Scott. In 1854, he resigned his commission because of loneliness and drinking problems, and in the following years he engaged in generally unsuccessful farming and business ventures. With the start of the Civil War, he was named colonel and then brigadier general of the Illinois Volunteers. He took Forts Henry and Donelson and fought at Shiloh. His brilliant campaign against Vicksburg and his victory at Chattanooga made him so prominent that Lincoln placed him in command of all Union armies. Grant accepted Lee's surrender at Appomattox Court House on Apr. 9, 1865.

Grant was nominated for president by the Republicans in 1868 and elected over Democrat Horatio Seymour. The 15th Amendment, the amnesty bill, and peaceful settlement of disputes with Great Britain were events of his administration. The Liberal Republicans and Democrats opposed him with Horace Greeley in the 1872 election, but Grant was reelected. His second administration was marked by scandals, including the Crédit Mobilier affair, the Whiskey Ring, in which high-ranked officials conspired to defraud the government of taxes, and the impeachment of his Secretary of War. An attempt by the Stalwarts (Old Guard Republicans) to nominate him in 1880 failed. Left penniless by the 1884 collapse of an investment firm in which he was a partner, he wrote his well-regarded memoirs to provide income for his family while he was suffering from cancer. He died at Mt. McGregor, NY, on July 23, 1885.

Rutherford Birchard Hayes (1877-81), 19th president, Republican, was born on Oct. 4, 1822, in Delaware, OH, the son of Rutherford and Sophia Birchard Hayes. He was reared by his uncle, Sardis Birchard. Hayes graduated from Kenyon College in 1842 and from Harvard Law School in 1845. He practiced law in Lower Sandusky (now Fremont), OH, and was city solicitor of Cincinnati from 1858 to 1861. During the Civil War, he was major of the 23rd Ohio Volunteers. He was wounded several times, and by the end of the war he had risen to the rank of brevet major general. While serving (1865-67) in the U.S. House of Representatives, Hayes supported Reconstruction and Johnson's impeachment. He was twice elected governor of Ohio (1867, 1869). After losing a race for the U.S. House in 1872, he was reelected governor of Ohio in 1875.

In 1876, Hayes was nominated for president and believed he had lost the election to Democrat Samuel J. Tilden. But a few Southern states submitted two sets of electoral votes, and the result was in dispute. An electoral commission, consisting of 8 Republicans and 7 Democrats, awarded all disputed votes to Hayes, allowing him to become president by one electoral vote. Hayes, keeping a promise to Southerners, withdrew troops from areas still occupied in the South, ending the era of Reconstruction. He proposed civil service reforms, alienating those favoring the spoils system, and advocated repeal of the Tenure of Office Act restricting presidential power to dismiss officials. He supported sound money and specie payments.

Hayes died in Fremont, OH, on Jan. 17, 1893.

James Abram Garfield (1881), 20th president, Republican, was born on Nov. 19, 1831, in Orange, Cuyahoga Co., OH, the son of Abram and Eliza Ballou Garfield. His father died in 1833, and he was reared in poverty by his mother. He worked as a canal bargeman, a farmer, and a carpenter. He attended Western Reserve Eclectic Institute and graduated from Williams College in 1856. He returned to Western Reserve to teach and in 1857, at age 25, he became the school's president. In 1859 he was elected to the Ohio legislature. Antislavery and antisecession, he volunteered for military service in the Civil War, becoming colonel of the 42nd Ohio Infantry and brigadier in 1862. He fought at Shiloh, TN, was chief of staff for Gen. William Starke Rosecrans, and was made major general for gallantry at Chickamauga, GA. He entered Congress as a radical Republican in 1863, calling for execution or exile of Confederate leaders, but he moderated his views after the Civil War. On the electoral commission in 1877 he voted for Hayes against Tilden on strict party lines.

Garfield was a senator-elect in 1880 when he became the Republican nominee for president. He was chosen as a compromise over Gen. Grant, James G. Blaine, and John Sherman, and won election despite some bitterness among Grant's supporters. For much of his brief tenure as president, Garfield was concerned with a fight with New York Sen. Roscoe Conkling, who opposed two major appointments made by Garfield. On July 2, 1881, Garfield was shot and seriously wounded by a mentally disturbed office seeker, Charles J. Guiteau, while entering a railroad station in Washington, DC. He died on Sept. 19, 1881, in Elberon, NJ.

Chester Alan Arthur (1881-85), 21st president, Republican, was born on Oct. 5, 1829, in Fairfield, VT, to William and Malvina Stone Arthur. He graduated from Union College in 1848, taught school in Vermont, then studied law and practiced in New York City. In 1853, he argued in a fugitive slave case that slaves transported through New York State were thereby freed. In 1871, he was appointed collector of the Port of New York. Pres. Hayes, an opponent of the spoils system, forced him to resign in 1878. This made the New York machine enemies of Hayes. Arthur and the Stalwarts (Old Guard Republicans) tried to nominate Grant for a third term as president in 1880. When Garfield was nominated, Arthur was nominated for vice president in the interests of harmony.

Upon Garfield's assassination, Arthur became president. Despite his past connections, he signed major civil service reform legislation. Arthur tried to dissuade Congress from enacting the high protective tariff of 1883. He was defeated for renomination in 1884 by James G. Blaine. He died in New York City on Nov. 18, 1886.

Grover Cleveland (1885-89; 1893-97) *(According to a State Dept. ruling, Grover Cleveland should be counted as both the 22nd and the 24th president because his two terms were not consecutive)*, Democrat, was born Stephen Grover Cleveland on Mar. 18, 1837, in Caldwell, NJ, the son of Richard F. and Ann Neal Cleveland. When he was a small boy, his family moved to New York. Prevented by his father's death from attending college, he studied by himself and was admitted to the bar in Buffalo, NY, in 1859. In succession he became assistant district attorney (1863), sheriff (1871), mayor (1881), and governor of New York (1882). He was an independent, honest administrator who hated corruption. Cleveland was nominated for president over Tammany Hall opposition in 1884 and defeated Republican James G. Blaine.

As president, he enlarged the civil service and vetoed many pension raids on the Treasury. In the 1888 election he was defeated by Benjamin Harrison, although his popular vote was larger. Reelected over Harrison in 1892, he faced a money crisis brought about by a lowered gold reserve, circulation of paper, and exorbitant silver purchases under the Sherman Silver Purchase Act. He obtained a repeal of the Sherman Act but was unable to secure effective tariff reform. A severe economic depression and labor troubles racked his administration, but he refused to interfere in business matters and rejected Jacob Coxey's demand for unemployment relief. In 1894, he broke the Pullman strike. Cleveland was not renominated in 1896.

He died in Princeton, NJ, on June 24, 1908.

Benjamin Harrison (1889-93), 23rd president, Republican, was born on Aug. 20, 1833, in North Bend, OH, the son of John Scott and Elizabeth Irwin Harrison. His great-grandfather, Benjamin Harrison, was a signer of the Declaration of Independence; his grandfather, William Henry Harrison, was the ninth president; his father was a member of Congress. He attended school on his father's farm and graduated from Miami Univ. in Oxford, OH, in 1852. He was admitted to the bar in 1854 and practiced in Indianapolis, IN. During the Civil War, he rose to the rank of brevet brigadier general and fought at Kennesaw Mountain, Peachtree Creek, Nashville, and in the Atlanta campaign. He lost the 1876 gubernatorial election in Indiana but succeeded in becoming a U.S. senator in 1881.

In 1888 he defeated Cleveland for president despite receiving fewer popular votes. As president, he expanded the pension list and signed the McKinley high tariff bill, the Sherman Antitrust Act, and the Sherman Silver Purchase Act. During his administration, six states were admitted to the Union. He was defeated for reelection in 1892. He died in Indianapolis, IN, on Mar. 13, 1901.

William McKinley (1897-1901), 25th president, Republican, was born on Jan. 29, 1843, in Niles, OH, the son of William and Nancy Allison McKinley. McKinley briefly attended Allegheny College. When the Civil War broke out in 1861, he enlisted and served for the duration. He rose to captain and in 1865 was made brevet major. After studying law in Albany, NY, he opened a law office in Canton, OH (1867). He served twice in the U.S. House (1877-83; 1885-91) and led the fight there for the McKinley Tariff, passed in 1890; he was not reelected to the House as a result. He served two terms (1892-96) as governor of Ohio.

In 1896 he was elected president as a proponent of a protective tariff and sound money (gold standard) over William Jennings Bryan, the Democrat and a proponent of free silver. McKinley was reluctant to intervene in Cuba, but the loss of the battleship *Maine* at Havana crystallized opinion. He

demanded Spain's withdrawal from Cuba; Spain made some concessions, but Congress announced a state of war as of Apr. 21, 1898. He was reelected in the 1900 campaign, defeating Bryan's anti-imperialist arguments with the promise of a "full dinner pail." McKinley was respected for his conciliatory nature and for his conservative stance on business issues. On Sept. 6, 1901, at the Pan-American Exposition, in Buffalo, NY, he was shot by Leon Czolgosz, an anarchist. He died Sept. 14.

Theodore Roosevelt (1901-09), 26th president, Republican, was born on Oct. 27, 1858, in New York City, the son of Theodore and Martha Bulloch Roosevelt. He was a 5th cousin of Franklin D. Roosevelt and an uncle of Eleanor Roosevelt. Roosevelt graduated from Harvard Univ. in 1880. He attended Columbia Law School briefly but abandoned law to enter politics. He was elected to the New York State Assembly in 1881 and served until 1884. He spent the next two years ranching and hunting in the Dakota Territory. In 1886, he ran unsuccessfully for mayor of New York City. He was civil service commissioner in Washington, DC, from 1889 to 1895. From 1895 to 1897, he served as New York City's police commissioner. He was assistant secretary of the Navy under McKinley. The Spanish-American War made him nationally known. He organized the 1st U.S. Volunteer Cavalry (Rough Riders) and, as lieutenant colonel, led the charge up Kettle Hill in San Juan. Elected New York governor in 1898, he fought the spoils system and achieved taxation of corporation franchises.

Nominated for vice president in 1900, Roosevelt became the nation's youngest president when McKinley was assassinated. He was reelected in 1904. As president he fought corruption of politics by big business, dissolved the Northern Securities Co. and others for violating antitrust laws, intervened in the 1902 coal strike on behalf of the public, obtained the Elkins Law (1903) forbidding rebates to favored corporations, and helped pass the Hepburn Railway Rate Act of 1906 (extending jurisdiction of the Interstate Commerce Commission). He helped obtain passage of the Pure Food and Drug Act (1906) and of employers' liability laws. Roosevelt vigorously organized conservation efforts. He mediated the peace between Japan and Russia in 1905, for which he won the Nobel Peace Prize. He abetted the 1903 revolution in Panama that led to U.S. acquisition of territory for the Panama Canal.

In 1908 Roosevelt obtained the nomination of William H. Taft, who was elected. Feeling that Taft had abandoned his policies, he unsuccessfully sought the nomination in 1912. He then ran on the Progressive "Bull Moose" ticket against Taft and Woodrow Wilson, splitting the Republicans and ensuring Wilson's election. During the campaign he was shot by a mentally deranged man but was not seriously wounded. In 1916, after unsuccessfully seeking the presidential nomination, he supported the Republican candidate, Charles E. Hughes. A strong friend of Britain, he fought for U.S. intervention in World War I.

Roosevelt was a voracious reader and wrote some 40 books, including *The Winning of the West*. He died Jan. 6, 1919, at Sagamore Hill, his home in Oyster Bay, NY.

William Howard Taft (1909-13), 27th president, Republican, and 10th chief justice of the U.S., was born on Sept. 15, 1857, in Cincinnati, OH, the son of Alphonso and Louisa Maria Torrey Taft. His father was secretary of war and attorney general in Grant's cabinet and minister to Austria and Russia under Arthur. Taft graduated from Yale in 1878 and from Cincinnati Law School in 1880. After working as a law reporter for Cincinnati newspapers, he served as assistant prosecuting attorney (1881-82), assistant county solicitor (1885), superior court judge (1887), U.S. solicitor-general (1890), and federal circuit judge (1892). In 1900 he became head of the U.S. Philippines Commission and was the first civil governor of the Philippines (1901-04). In 1904 he served as secretary of war, and in 1906 he was sent to Cuba to help avert a threatened revolution.

Taft was groomed for the presidency by Theodore Roosevelt and elected over William Jennings Bryan in 1908.

Taft vigorously continued Roosevelt's trust-busting, instituted the Dept. of Labor, and drafted the amendments calling for direct election of senators and the income tax. However, his tariff and conservation policies angered progressives. Although renominated in 1912, he was opposed by Roosevelt, who ran on the Progressive Party ticket; the result was Democrat Woodrow Wilson's election.

Taft, with some reservations, supported the League of Nations. After leaving office, he was professor of constitutional law at Yale (1913-21) and chief justice of the U.S. (1921-30). Taft was the only person in U.S. history to have been both president and chief justice. He died in Washington, DC, on Mar. 8, 1930.

(Thomas) Woodrow Wilson (1913-21), 28th president, Democrat, was born on Dec. 28, 1856, in Staunton, VA, the son of Joseph Ruggles and Janet (Jessie) Woodrow Wilson. He grew up in Georgia and South Carolina. He attended Davidson College in North Carolina before graduating from Princeton Univ. in 1879. He studied law at the Univ. of Virginia and political science at Johns Hopkins Univ., where he received his PhD in 1886. He taught at Bryn Mawr (1885-88) and at Wesleyan (1888-90) before joining the faculty at Princeton. He was president of Princeton from 1902 until 1910, when he was elected governor of New Jersey. In 1912 he was nominated for president with the aid of William Jennings Bryan, who sought to block James "Champ" Clark and Tammany Hall. Wilson won because the Republican vote for Taft was split by the Progressives.

As president, Wilson protected American interests in revolutionary Mexico and fought for American rights on the high seas. He oversaw the creation of the Federal Reserve system, cut the tariff, and developed a reputation as a reformer. His sharp warnings to Germany led to the resignation of his secretary of state, Bryan, a pacifist. In 1916 he was reelected by a slim margin with the slogan, "He kept us out of war," although his attempts to mediate in the war failed. After several American ships were sunk by the Germans, he secured a declaration of war against Germany on Apr. 6, 1917.

Wilson outlined his peace program on Jan. 8, 1918, in the Fourteen Points, a state paper that had worldwide influence. He enunciated a doctrine of self-determination for the settlement of territorial disputes. The Germans accepted his terms and an armistice on Nov. 11, 1918.

Wilson went to Paris to help negotiate the peace treaty, the crux of which he considered the League of Nations. The Senate demanded reservations that would not make the U.S. subordinate to the votes of other nations in case of war. Wilson refused and toured the country to get support. After Wilson suffered a severe stroke in Oct. 1919, his wife, Edith Wilson, concealed the extent of his infirmity, controlled access to him, and in effect largely acted in his place.

Wilson was awarded the 1919 Nobel Peace Prize, but the treaty embodying the League of Nations was ultimately rejected by the Senate in 1920. He left the White House in Mar. 1921. He died in Washington, DC, on Feb. 3, 1924.

Warren Gamaliel Harding (1921-23), 29th president, Republican, was born on Nov. 2, 1865, near Corsica (now Blooming Grove), OH, the son of George Tyron and Phoebe Elizabeth Dickerson Harding. He attended Ohio Central College, studied law, and became editor and publisher of a county newspaper. He entered the political arena as state senator (1901-04) and then served as lieutenant governor (1904-06). In 1910 he ran unsuccessfully for governor of Ohio; in 1914 he was elected to the U.S. Senate. In the Senate he voted for antistrike legislation, women's suffrage, and the Volstead Prohibition Enforcement Act over Pres. Wilson's veto. He opposed the League of Nations.

In 1920 he was nominated for president and defeated James M. Cox in the election. The Republicans capitalized on war weariness and fear that Wilson's League of Nations would curtail U.S. sovereignty. Harding stressed a return to "normalcy" and worked for tariff revision and the repeal of excess profits law and high income taxes. In what became known as the Teapot Dome scandal, his secretary of the interior, Albert B. Fall, resigned and was later convicted of accepting bribes in the leasing of government-owned oil reserves to private companies.

As rumors began to circulate about the corruption in his administration, Harding fell ill after a trip to Alaska, and he died suddenly in San Francisco on Aug. 2, 1923.

(John) Calvin Coolidge (1923-29), 30th president, Republican, was born on July 4, 1872, in Plymouth Notch, VT, the son of John Calvin and Victoria J. Moor Coolidge. Coolidge graduated from Amherst College in 1895. He entered Republican state politics and served as mayor of Northampton, MA, as state senator, as lieutenant governor, and, in 1919, as governor. In Sept. 1919, Coolidge attained national prominence by calling out the state guard in the Boston police strike. He declared, "There is no right to strike against the public safety by anybody, anywhere, anytime." This brought his name before the Republican convention of 1920, where he was nominated for vice president.

Coolidge succeeded to the presidency on Harding's death. As president, he opposed the League of Nations and the soldiers' bonus bill, which was passed over his veto. In 1924 he was elected to the presidency by a huge majority. He substantially reduced the national debt. He twice vetoed the McNary-Haugen farm bill, which would have provided relief to financially hard-pressed farmers.

With Republicans eager to renominate him, Coolidge simply announced on Aug. 2, 1927, "I do not choose to run for president in 1928." He died in Northampton, MA, on Jan. 5, 1933.

Herbert Clark Hoover (1929-33), 31st president, Republican, was born on Aug. 10, 1874, in West Branch, IA, the son of Jesse Clark and Hulda Randall Minthorn Hoover. Hoover grew up in Indian Territory (now Oklahoma) and Oregon and graduated from Stanford Univ. with a degree in geology in 1895. He worked briefly with the U.S. Geological Survey and then managed mines in Australia, Asia, Europe, and Africa. While chief engineer of imperial mines in China, he directed food relief for victims of the Boxer Rebellion. He gained a reputation not only as an engineer but as a humanitarian as he directed the American Relief Committee, London (1914-15) and the U.S. Commission for Relief in Belgium (1915-19). He was U.S. Food Administrator (1917-19), American Relief Administrator (1918-23), and in charge of Russian Relief (1918-23). He served as secretary of commerce under both Harding and Coolidge. Some historians believe that he was the most effective secretary of commerce ever to hold that office.

In 1928 Hoover was elected president over Alfred E. Smith. In 1929 the stock market crashed, and the economy collapsed. During the Great Depression, Hoover inaugurated some government assistance programs, but he was opposed to administration of aid through a federal bureaucracy. As the effects of the depression continued, he was defeated in the 1932 election by Franklin D. Roosevelt. Hoover remained active after leaving office. President Truman named him coordinator of the European Food Program (1946) and chairman of the Commission on Organization of the Executive Branch (1947-49); he was later appointed by President Eisenhower to serve in the same role (1953-55).

Hoover died in New York City on Oct. 20, 1964.

Franklin Delano Roosevelt (1933-45), 32nd president, Democrat, was born on Jan. 30, 1882, in Hyde Park, NY, the son of James and Sara Delano Roosevelt. He graduated from Harvard Univ. in 1903. He attended Columbia University Law School without taking a degree and was admitted to the New York State bar in 1907. His political career began when he was elected to the New York State senate in 1910. In 1913 Pres. Wilson appointed him assistant secretary of the navy, a post he held during World War I.

In 1920 Roosevelt ran for vice president with James Cox and was defeated. From 1921 to 1928 he worked in his New York law office and was also vice president of a bank. In Aug. 1921, he was stricken with poliomyelitis, which left his legs paralyzed. As a result of therapy he was able to stand, or walk a few steps, with the aid of leg braces.

Roosevelt served two terms as governor of New York (1929-33). In 1932, Democratic convention delegate W. G. McAdoo, pledged to nominee John N. Garner, threw his votes to Roosevelt, who was nominated for president. The Depression and the promise to repeal Prohibition ensured his election. He asked for emergency powers, proclaimed the New Deal, and put into effect a vast number of administrative changes. Foremost was the use of public funds for relief and public works, resulting in deficit financing. He greatly expanded the federal government's regulation of business and by an excess profits tax and progressive income taxes produced a redistribution of earnings on an unprecedented scale. He also promoted legislation establishing the Social Security system. He was the last president inaugurated on Mar. 4 (1933) and the first inaugurated on Jan. 20 (1937).

Roosevelt was the first president to use radio for "fireside chats." When the Supreme Court nullified some New Deal laws, he sought power to "pack" the Court with additional justices, but Congress refused to give him the authority. He was the first president to break the "no third term" tradition (1940) and was elected to a fourth term in 1944, despite failing health.

Roosevelt was openly hostile to fascist governments before World War II and launched a lend-lease program on behalf of the Allies. With British Prime Min. Winston Churchill he wrote a declaration of principles to be followed after Nazi defeat (the Atlantic Charter of Aug. 14, 1941) and urged the Four Freedoms (freedom of speech, of worship, from want, from fear) Jan. 6, 1941. When Japan attacked Pearl Harbor on Dec. 7, 1941, the U.S. entered the war. Roosevelt guided the nation through the war and conferred with allied heads of state at Casablanca, Morocco (Jan. 1943), Quebec, Canada (Aug. 1943), Tehran, Iran (Nov.-Dec. 1943), Cairo, Egypt (Nov. and Dec. 1943), and Yalta, Ukraine (Feb. 1945).

Roosevelt did not live to see the end of the war. He died of a cerebral hemorrhage in Warm Springs, GA, on Apr. 12, 1945.

Harry S. Truman (1945-53), 33rd president, Democrat, was born on May 8, 1884, in Lamar, MO, the son of John Anderson and Martha Ellen Young Truman. A family disagreement over whether his middle name should be Shipp or Solomon, after his two grandfathers, resulted in his using only the middle initial S.

After graduating from high school (1901) in Independence, MO, he worked in the mailroom of the *Kansas City Star*, as a railroad timekeeper, and as a clerk in Kansas City banks until about 1905. He ran his family's farm from 1906 to 1917, then served in France during World War I. After the war he opened a haberdashery, was a judge on the Jackson Co. Court (1922-24), and attended Kansas City School of Law (1923-25).

Truman was elected to the U.S. Senate in 1934 and reelected in 1940. In 1944, with Roosevelt's backing, he was nominated for vice president and elected. On Roosevelt's death in 1945, Truman became president. In 1948, in a famous upset victory, he defeated Republican Thomas E. Dewey to win a new term.

Truman authorized the first uses of the atomic bomb (Hiroshima and Nagasaki, Aug. 6 and 9, 1945), bringing World War II to a rapid end. He was responsible for what came to be called the Truman Doctrine to aid nations such as Greece and Turkey, threatened by Communist takeover, and his strong commitment to NATO and to the Marshall Plan helped bring the two about. In 1948-49, he broke a Soviet blockade of West Berlin with a massive airlift. When Communist North Korea invaded South Korea (June 1950), he won UN approval for a "police action" and, without prior congressional consent, sent in forces under Gen. Douglas MacArthur. When MacArthur opposed his policy of limited objectives, Truman removed him.

He died in Kansas City, MO, on Dec. 26, 1972.

Dwight David Eisenhower (1953-61), 34th president, Republican, was born on Oct. 14, 1890, in Denison, TX, the son of David Jacob and Ida Elizabeth Stover Eisenhower, as David Dwight Eisenhower. He grew up on a small farm in Abilene, KS, and graduated from West Point in 1915. He was on the staff of Gen. Douglas MacArthur in the Philippines from 1935 to 1939. In 1942, he was made commander of Allied forces landing in North Africa; the next year he was made full general. He became supreme Allied commander in Europe that same year and as such led the Normandy invasion (June 6, 1944). On Dec. 20, 1944, he was given the rank of general of the Army, which was made permanent in 1946.

On May 7, 1945, Eisenhower received the surrender of Germany at Rheims, France. He returned to the U.S. to serve as chief of staff (1945-48). His memoir, *Crusade in Europe* (1948), was a best-seller. In 1948 he became president of Columbia Univ.; in 1950 he became commander of NATO forces.

Eisenhower resigned from the army and was nominated for president by the Republicans in 1952. He defeated Adlai E. Stevenson in the 1952 election and again in 1956. Eisenhower called himself a moderate, favored the "free market system" versus government price and wage controls, kept government out of labor disputes, reorganized the defense establishment, and promoted missile programs. He continued foreign aid, helped negotiate a cease fire truce in the Korean War, endorsed Taiwan and SE Asia defense treaties, backed the UN in condemning the Anglo-French raid on Egypt, and advocated the "open skies" policy of mutual inspection with the USSR. He sent U.S. troops into Little Rock, AR, in Sept. 1957, to enforce school integration.

Eisenhower died on Mar. 28, 1969, in Washington, DC.

John Fitzgerald Kennedy (1961-63), 35th president, Democrat, was born on May 29, 1917, in Brookline, MA, the son of Joseph P. and Rose Fitzgerald Kennedy. He graduated from Harvard Univ. in 1940. While serving in the Navy (1941-45), he commanded a PT (patrol torpedo) boat in the Solomons and won the Navy and Marine Corps Medal. In 1956, while recovering from spinal surgery, he wrote *Profiles in Courage*, which won a Pulitzer Prize in 1957. He served in the House of Representatives from 1947 to 1953 and was elected to the Senate in 1952 and 1958. In 1960, he won the Democratic nomination for president and narrowly defeated Republican Vice Pres. Richard M. Nixon. Kennedy was the youngest president ever elected to the office and the first Catholic.

Despite the image of youth and vigor he conveyed to the public, Kennedy suffered from serious medical problems, including Addison's disease and severe chronic back pain that required him to wear a back brace. The public was not aware of the extent of these problems, or of his frequent sexual liaisons.

In Apr. 1961, the new Kennedy administration suffered a severe setback when an invasion force of anti-Castro Cubans, trained and directed by the CIA, failed to establish a beachhead at the Bay of Pigs in Cuba. But he weathered a major foreign crisis with his successful demand on Oct. 22, 1962, that the Soviet Union dismantle its missile bases in Cuba. Kennedy also defied Soviet attempts to force the Allies out of Berlin. He also established the Peace Corps, spurred space exploration, and won passage of other "New Frontier" legislation. But Congress balked at initiatives such as medical coverage for the aged and aid to education. After some delay he introduced major civil rights legislation, but death intervened before it could be passed.

On Nov. 22, 1963, President Kennedy was assassinated while riding in a motorcade in Dallas, TX. A commission chaired by Chief Justice Earl Warren concluded in Sept. 1964 that the sole assassin had been Lee Harvey Oswald, a former U.S. Marine and an ardent Marxist. Oswald was captured a short time after the assassination and charged with the crime. Two days later, he was shot dead by nightclub owner Jack Ruby while being moved to a county jail.

Lyndon Baines Johnson (1963-69), 36th president, Democrat, was born on Aug. 27, 1908, near Stonewall, TX, the son of Sam Ealy and Rebekah Baines Johnson. He graduated from Southwest Texas State Teachers College in 1930 and attended Georgetown University Law School. He taught public speaking in Houston (1930-31) and then served as secretary to Rep. R. M. Kleberg (1931-35). In 1937 Johnson won an election to fill the vacancy caused by the death of a U.S. representative. In 1938 he was elected to the first of five full terms. During 1941 and 1942 he also served in the Navy in the Pacific, earning a Silver Star for bravery. He was elected U.S. senator in 1948 and reelected in 1954. He became Democratic leader of the Senate in 1953. Johnson had strong support for the Democratic presidential nomination at the 1960 convention, where the nominee, John F. Kennedy, asked him to run for vice president. His campaigning helped overcome religious bias against Kennedy in the South.

Johnson became president when Kennedy was assassinated. He was elected to a full term in 1964. Johnson's domestic program was of considerable importance. He won passage of major civil rights, anti-poverty, aid to education, and health-care (Medicare, Medicaid) legislation—the "Great Society" program. However, his escalation of the war in Vietnam came to overshadow the achievements of his administration. In the face of increasing division in the nation and in his own party over his handling of the war, Johnson declined to seek another term.

Johnson died on Jan. 22, 1973, in San Antonio, TX.

Richard Milhous Nixon (1969-74), 37th president, Republican, was born on Jan. 9, 1913, in Yorba Linda, CA, the son of Francis Anthony and Hannah Milhous Nixon. He graduated from Whittier College in 1934 and from Duke University Law School in 1937. After practicing law in Whittier, CA, and serving briefly in the Office of Price Administration in 1942, he entered the Navy and served in the South Pacific. Nixon was elected to the House of Representatives in 1946 and 1948. He achieved prominence as the House Un-American Activities Committee member who forced the showdown leading to the Alger Hiss perjury conviction. In 1950 he was elected to the Senate.

Nixon was elected vice president in the Eisenhower landslides of 1952 and 1956. He won the Republican nomination for president in 1960 but was narrowly defeated by John F. Kennedy. He ran unsuccessfully for governor of California in 1962. In 1968 he again won the GOP presidential nomination, then defeated Hubert Humphrey for the presidency.

As president, Nixon appointed four Supreme Court justices, including the chief justice, moving the court to the right. As a "new federalist," he sought to shift greater responsibility to state and local governments. At the same time, he championed important federal initiatives, including creation of the Office of Management and Budget and the Environmental Protection Agency. The economy suffered periods of high unemployment and inflation, and he imposed wage and price controls in 1971.

In foreign affairs, Nixon dramatically altered relations with China, which he visited in 1972—the first U.S. president to do so. With adviser Henry Kissinger, he pursued détente with the Soviet Union, signing major arms limitation and other treaties and increasing trade. He began a gradual withdrawal from Vietnam, but U.S. troops remained there through his first term. He ordered an incursion into Cambodia (1970) and the bombing of Hanoi and mining of Haiphong Harbor (1972). Reelected by a large majority in Nov. 1972, he secured a Vietnam cease-fire in Jan. 1973.

Nixon's second term was cut short by scandal, after disclosures relating to a June 1972 burglary of Democratic Party headquarters in the Watergate office complex in DC. The courts and Congress sought tapes of Nixon's office conversations and called for criminal proceedings against former White House aides and for a House inquiry into possible impeachment. Nixon claimed executive privilege, but the Supreme Court ruled against him. In July 1974, the House Judiciary Committee recommended adoption of three impeachment articles charging him with obstruction of justice, abuse of power, and contempt of Congress. On Aug. 5, he released transcripts of conversations that linked him to cover-up activities. He resigned on Aug. 9, becoming the first president ever to do so.

In later years, Nixon emerged as an elder statesman. He died Apr. 22, 1994, in New York City.

Gerald Rudolph Ford (1974-77), 38th president, Republican, was born on July 14, 1913, in Omaha, NE, the son of Leslie and Dorothy Gardner King, and was named Leslie Lynch King Jr. When he was 2, his parents divorced, and he and his mother moved to Grand Rapids, MI. There she met and married Gerald R. Ford, who formally adopted him and gave him his name. Ford graduated from the Univ. of Michigan in 1935 and from Yale Law School in 1941. He began practicing law in Grand Rapids, but in 1942, he joined the Navy and served in the Pacific, leaving the service in 1946 as a lieutenant commander. He entered the House of Representatives in 1949 and spent 25 years in the House, eight of them as Republican leader.

On Oct. 12, 1973, after Vice Pres. Spiro T. Agnew resigned, Pres. Nixon nominated Ford to replace him. It was the first use of the procedures set out in the 25th Amendment. When Nixon resigned, Aug. 9, 1974, because of the Watergate scandal, Ford became president; he was the only president who was never elected either to the presidency or to the vice presidency.

Ford was widely credited with having contributed to rebuilding morale after the Nixon presidency. But he was also criticized by many when, in a controversial move, he pardoned

Nixon for any federal crimes he might have committed as president. Ford vetoed 48 bills in his first 21 months in office, mostly in the interest of fighting high inflation; he was less successful in curbing high unemployment. In foreign policy, Ford continued to pursue détente.

Ford was narrowly defeated in the 1976 election. In 1999, he received the Medal of Freedom. He died Dec. 26, 2006, at home in Rancho Mirage, CA.

James Earl (Jimmy) Carter (1977-81), 39th president, Democrat, was the first president from the Deep South since before the Civil War. He was born on Oct. 1, 1924, in Plains, GA, the son of James and Lillian Gordy Carter. Carter graduated from the U.S. Naval Academy in 1946 and in 1952 entered the Navy's nuclear submarine program as an aide to Capt. (later Adm.) Hyman Rickover. He studied nuclear physics at Union College. Carter's father died in 1953, and he left the Navy to take over the family peanut farming businesses. He served in the Georgia state senate (1963-67) and as governor of Georgia (1971-75). In 1976, Carter won the Democratic nomination and defeated Pres. Gerald R. Ford.

On his first full day in office, Carter pardoned all Vietnam draft evaders. He played a major role in the negotiations leading to the 1979 peace treaty between Israel and Egypt, and he won passage of new treaties with Panama providing for U.S. control of the Panama Canal to end in 2000. Carter was widely criticized, however, for the poor state of the economy and was viewed by some as weak in his handling of foreign policy. In Nov. 1979, Iranian student militants attacked the U.S. embassy in Tehran and held members of the embassy staff hostage. Efforts to obtain release of the hostages were a major preoccupation during the rest of his term. He reacted to the Soviet invasion of Afghanistan by imposing a grain embargo and boycotting the Moscow Olympic Games.

Carter was defeated by Ronald Reagan in the 1980 election. The 52 American hostages in Iran were finally released on inauguration day, 1981, just after Reagan officially became president. After leaving office, Carter played an active role in diplomatic and humanitarian efforts around the world, especially through the Carter Center, which he founded with his wife in 1982. He was awarded the Nobel Peace Prize in 2002.

Ronald Wilson Reagan (1981-89), 40th president, Republican, was born on Feb. 6, 1911, in Tampico, IL, the son of John Edward and Nellie Wilson Reagan. Reagan graduated from Eureka College in 1932, after which he worked as a sports announcer in Des Moines, IA. He began a successful career as a movie actor in 1937. During World War II Reagan served in the Army Air Force, making training films. He was president of the Screen Actors Guild in 1947-52 and in 1959-60. Reagan was elected governor of California in 1966 and reelected in 1970.

In 1980, Reagan gained the Republican presidential nomination and won a landslide victory over Jimmy Carter. He was easily reelected in 1984. Reagan forged a bipartisan coalition in Congress, which led to enactment of his program of large-scale tax cuts, cutbacks in many government programs, and a major defense buildup. He signed a Social Security reform bill designed to provide for the long-term solvency of the system. In 1986, he signed into law a major tax-reform bill. He was shot and seriously wounded in 1981 by John Hinckley, who was tried and found not guilty by reason of insanity.

In 1982, the U.S. joined France and Italy in maintaining a peacekeeping force in Beirut, Lebanon, and the next year Reagan sent a task force to invade Grenada after two Marxist coups on the island. Reagan's opposition to international terrorism led to the U.S. bombing of Libyan military installations in 1986. He strongly supported El Salvador, the Nicaraguan contras, and other anticommunist governments and forces throughout the world. He also held four summit meetings with Soviet leader Mikhail Gorbachev. At the 1987 meeting in Washington, DC, a historic treaty eliminating short- and medium-range missiles from Europe was signed.

In 1986, it was revealed that the U.S. had sold weapons through Israeli brokers to Iran in exchange for the release of U.S. hostages being held in Lebanon and that subsequently some of the money had been illegally diverted to the Nicaraguan contras. The scandal led to the resignation of leading White House aides, but despite several investigations no proof of Reagan's involvement was discovered. As Reagan left office in Jan. 1989, the nation was experiencing its sixth consecutive year of economic prosperity. Over the same period, however, the federal government recorded large budget deficits.

In 1994, in a letter to the American people, Reagan revealed that he was suffering from Alzheimer's disease. He died on June 5, 2004, in Los Angeles, CA, from complications of the disease.

George Herbert Walker Bush (1989-93), 41st president, Republican, was born on June 12, 1924, in Milton, MA, the son of Prescott and Dorothy Walker Bush. He served as a U.S. Navy pilot in World War II. After graduating from Yale Univ. in 1948, he settled in Texas, where, in 1953, he helped found an oil company. After losing a bid for a U.S. Senate seat in 1964, he was elected to the House of Representatives in 1966 and 1968. He lost a second U.S. Senate race in 1970. Subsequently he served as U.S. ambassador to the United Nations (1971-73), headed the U.S. Liaison Office in Beijing (1974-75), and was director of the CIA (1976-77). Following an unsuccessful bid for the 1980 Republican presidential nomination, Bush became Ronald Reagan's running mate, and served as vice president from 1981 to 1989.

In 1988, Bush gained the GOP presidential nomination and defeated Michael Dukakis. Bush took office faced with U.S. budget and trade deficits, and insolvent U.S. savings and loan institutions. He faced a severe budget deficit annually, struggled with military cutbacks, and vetoed abortion-rights legislation. In 1990 he agreed to a budget deficit-reduction plan that included tax hikes, despite a campaign promise to the contrary, angering many conservatives.

Bush supported Soviet reforms, Eastern Europe democratization, and good relations with Beijing. In Dec. 1989, he sent troops to Panama; they overthrew the government and captured military dictator Gen. Manuel Noriega. Bush reacted to Iraq's Aug. 1990 invasion of Kuwait by sending U.S. forces to the Persian Gulf area and assembling a UN-backed coalition, including NATO and Arab League members. After a month-long air war, in Feb. 1991, Allied forces retook Kuwait in a 4-day ground assault. The quick victory, with extremely light casualties on the U.S. side, gave Bush at that time one of the highest presidential approval ratings in history. His popularity plummeted by the end of 1991, however, as the economy slipped into recession. He was defeated by Bill Clinton in the 1992 election.

Bush saw his son George W. inaugurated as the 43rd president in 2001. In 2005 the elder Bush teamed with former Pres. Clinton to raise money for victims of the Indian Ocean tsunami and Hurricane Katrina.

William Jefferson (Bill) Clinton (1993-2001), 42nd president, Democrat, was born Aug. 19, 1946, in Hope, AR, son of William Blythe and Virginia Cassidy Blythe, and was named William Jefferson Blythe IV. Blythe died in an auto accident before his son was born. His widow married Roger Clinton, whose last name Bill Clinton then took. Clinton earned his undergraduate degree from Georgetown Univ. in 1968. While attending Oxford Univ. as a Rhodes scholar, he legally avoided the draft and possible service in Vietnam, according to some critics by misleading his draft board. Clinton worked on George McGovern's 1972 presidential campaign and earned a degree from Yale Law School in 1973. He taught at the Univ. of Arkansas law school until 1976, when he was elected state attorney general. In 1978 he was elected governor, becoming the nation's youngest at the time. Though defeated for reelection in 1980, he was returned to office several times thereafter. He married law school classmate Hillary Rodham in 1975.

Clinton won most of the 1992 presidential primaries, moving his party toward the center as he tried to broaden his appeal; as the Democratic nominee he defeated Pres. George H. W. Bush and independent candidate H. Ross Perot in the Nov. election. In 1993, Clinton won passage of a measure to reduce the federal budget deficit and won congressional approval of the North American Free Trade Agreement. However, his administration's plan for major health care reform legislation died in Congress. After 1994 midterm elections, Clinton faced Republican majorities in both houses of Congress. He followed a centrist course at home, sent troops to Bosnia to help implement a peace settlement, and cultivated relations with Russia and China.

Though accused of improprieties in his involvement in the Whitewater Development Corp., an Arkansas land-development venture, Clinton won reelection with 49% of the vote in 1996. Independent prosecutor Kenneth Starr did not find wrongdoing related to Whitewater, but did report evidence of an affair between Clinton and White House intern Monica Lewinsky. In 1998, Clinton became only the second U.S. president to be impeached by the House of Representatives. He was charged with perjury and obstruction of justice in an attempted cover-up of the affair but was acquitted by the Senate.

In 1999 the United States joined other NATO nations in an aerial bombing campaign that induced Serbia to withdraw troops from Kosovo, where they had been terrorizing ethnic Albanians. In 2000 Clinton became the first president since the Vietnam War to visit Vietnam. On Clinton's last full day in office, the Whitewater investigation ended in a deal; Clinton admitted having given false testimony and agreed to penalties. Clinton remained active in politics, supporting candidates he favored, including his wife, who became a U.S. senator (D, NY), ran unsuccessfully for the 2008 Democratic presidential nomination, then served as Pres. Obama's secretary of state. He took a leadership role in various humanitarian programs and founded an institute to promote practical solutions to global problems.

George Walker Bush (2001-09), 43rd president, Republican, was born on July 6, 1946, in New Haven, CT. He was the oldest of six children born to the 41st president, George Herbert Walker Bush, and the former Barbara Pierce. He became the first son of a former president to occupy the White House since John Quincy Adams took office in 1825.

Bush grew up in Midland and Houston, TX. He attended Andover Prep in Massachusetts and then Yale Univ., graduating in 1968. Eligible for the draft, he fulfilled his military service requirement with the Texas Air National Guard. After earning a master's degree from Harvard Business School, he returned to Midland in 1975 and went into the oil business. Two years later he married Laura Welch, a librarian; they had twin daughters, Barbara and Jenna, in 1981. After aiding his father's winning 1988 presidential campaign, he became managing partner of the Texas Rangers baseball team. He was elected governor of Texas in 1994 and reelected in 1998.

Campaigning as a "compassionate conservative" in 2000, Bush won the Republican presidential nomination and, with running mate Dick Cheney, defeated the Democratic ticket led by Vice Pres. Al Gore, in one of the closest-ever U.S. presidential elections. The result was not settled until a mid-Dec. ruling by the U.S. Supreme Court left Florida's crucial electoral votes in Bush's column.

In May 2001, Bush won passage of a tax cut package projected at $1.35 tril over 10 years. After the Sept. 11, 2001, terrorist attacks on the U.S., he declared a "war against terrorism." By Dec. 2001, the U.S. military, aided by forces from other nations, had deposed Afghanistan's Taliban regime, which was sheltering al-Qaeda terrorists. The new Afghan government, however, was weak and corrupt. In Mar. 2003, the U.S., aided mainly by UK forces, launched an air and ground war against Iraq and deposed its autocratic leader, Saddam Hussein. However, no evidence was found that his regime had developed weapons of mass destruction, the key rationale for the war. A new Iraqi government was formed in June 2004, but insurgent violence and U.S. troop casualties continued.

Bush was reelected in Nov. 2004 with 51% of the popular vote, but his popularity declined in his second term. His push for Social Security reform failed in Congress, and his administration drew criticism for its response to Hurricane Katrina in Aug.-Sept. 2005. He also failed to win passage of a broad immigration reform measure. But the Senate confirmed, in 2005 and 2006, Bush's nominations of a new chief justice and associate justice of the Supreme Court. In 2006, Bush exercised his first veto, preventing legislation to ease restrictions on federal funding for stem cell research.

After Democrats won majorities in House and Senate 2006 midterm elections, Bush accepted the resignation of Defense Sec. Donald Rumsfeld, a target of widespread criticism over the Iraq war. Two months later, he announced a "surge" in U.S. troop strength in Iraq. A sharp drop in casualties ensued, aided also by a shift in alliances, and in late 2008 the administration reached an agreement with Iraq allowing U.S. troops to remain there through but not beyond 2011. But the Taliban was gaining strength in Afghanistan and Pakistan, and the Bush administration was damaged by revelations of prisoner abuse and memos that had given legal sanction to extreme interrogation methods.

The U.S. economy fell into recession in Dec. 2007; Bush and congressional leaders responded with a $168 bil stimulus plan. Problems in home finance and credit markets triggered a deep economic crisis in Sept. The Treasury Dept. announced a bailout of mortgage finance firms Fannie Mae and Freddie Mac. Lehman Bros. filed for bankruptcy, while the Federal Reserve rescued insurance giant AIG with a line of credit reaching $144 bil. A Bush administration-backed plan to buy up to $700 bil in devalued mortgage-related assets, cleared Congress Oct. 3, after a severe stock market plunge bolstered support. The economic crisis added to Bush's unpopularity and contributed to the Nov. 2008 defeat of GOP presidential candidate Sen. John McCain (AZ).

In early 2010 Bush and former Pres. Clinton established a nonprofit organization to raise funds for earthquake relief in Haiti. In Nov. 2010, Bush published a memoir entitled *Decision Points.*

Barack Hussein Obama (2009-), 44th president, Democrat, was born Aug. 4, 1961, in Honolulu, HI. His father, Barack Obama Sr., was a black Kenyan, and his mother, Stanley Ann Dunham, was a white American born in Kansas. By the time Obama was 6, his parents had divorced and his mother had married an Indonesian man and moved to Indonesia. Later returning to Hawaii, Obama lived with his grandparents while attending high school. He received a bachelor's degree (1983) from Columbia Univ., worked from the mid-1980s as a community organizer in impoverished areas of Chicago's South Side, and earned a law degree (1991) from Harvard Univ., where he was president of the law review. He then practiced civil rights law in Chicago and taught at the Univ. of Chicago Law School. In 1992, he married attorney Michelle Robinson (1964-). They have 2 daughters, Malia (1998-) and Natasha (Sasha) (2001-).

Obama won election to the Illinois state senate in 1996 and was twice reelected. He failed to capture the Democratic nomination for a U.S. House seat in 2000, but won nomination for a U.S. Senate seat in a Mar. 2004 primary. Already known to many through his 1995 memoir, *Dreams From My Father: A Story of Race and Inheritance*, he gained national attention with his keynote address at the Democratic National Convention in July 2004. He was easily elected, becoming only the third African American in the Senate since Reconstruction. His second book, *The Audacity of Hope: Thoughts on Reclaiming the American Dream* (2006), was a best-seller.

In early 2007 Obama announced his candidacy for the 2008 Democratic presidential nomination. He stressed his opposition to the Iraq war and expressed determination to bring change to Washington and transcend partisanship. In the primaries of 2008, he pulled ahead of expected front-runner Sen. Hillary Clinton (NY) to clinch the nomination.

In the fall campaign, Republican nominee Sen. John McCain (AZ) portrayed Obama as inexperienced and devoted to higher taxes and big government. Obama and his running mate, Sen. Joe Biden (DE), drew strength from a smooth-running campaign organization and fundraising apparatus, the unpopularity of the Iraq war, and an economic crisis that came to dominate the campaign. Obama won 53% of the popular vote, to become the nation's first African American president.

As president-elect, Obama named a new economic team, including Timothy Geithner for treasury secretary, and chose former rival Hillary Clinton for secretary of state, while retaining Robert Gates as defense secretary. Upon becoming president, he moved to signal a change of direction. For example, he lifted restrictions on federal funding for groups that provide abortion services or counseling abroad and reversed certain Bush-era policies on interrogation of detainees suspected of terrorism. He also mandated that the U.S. military detention facility at Guantánamo Bay be closed within a year, but this plan fell through. He set out to strike a more cooperative and conciliatory tone in foreign relations; on that basis he was honored with the 2009 Nobel Peace Prize.

Obama sought both to wind down U.S. military involvement in Iraq and temporarily step up operations in Afghanistan. In Feb. 2009, he announced that all U.S. combat units would leave Iraq by Aug. 31, 2010; this deadline was met, and remaining troops were withdrawn by the end of 2011, ending the U.S. military presence there. In Dec. 2009, Obama announced the second of two surges in U.S. troop levels to counter insurgency in Afghanistan. Troop strength began winding down in the summer of 2011, with plans to end all combat operations by the end

of 2014. However, the U.S. reached agreement with the Afghan government to maintain a military presence there beyond 2014. Popular uprisings in Arab countries also posed challenges for the Obama administration. In Libya, the U.S. and other NATO countries launched air strikes, with the stated aim of protecting civilians, while also providing guidance to the ultimately successful rebels. But the administration resisted intervening in Egypt's popular revolution or in Syria's bloody civil war. Obama achieved a major success when Osama bin Laden, mastermind of the terrorist attacks of Sept. 11, 2001, was tracked down in Pakistan and killed in a May 2011 operation by U.S. Navy SEALs. In general, the president's foreign policy attracted some opposition from both left and right but remained overshadowed by domestic economic concerns.

In an effort to revive the economy, the administration had won passage, in Feb. 2009, of a $787 bil stimulus package providing for tax cuts and some $575 bil in new spending. The country did technically pull out of recession in third quarter 2009, but economic growth fell short of expectations and unemployment continued to be high. At least partly for this reason, Obama's approval rating, which had started out at around 70%, slid downward.

Democrats lost their filibuster-proof Senate majority after a Jan. 2010 special election in Massachusetts. Obama nevertheless secured passage, in Mar. 2010, of his top priority, a massive health care reform bill; opposed by Republicans as costly and bureaucratic, it aimed in part at extending coverage to millions of uninsured Americans. Obama won confirmation, in 2009 and 2010, of two new Supreme Court justices, and while this did not move the balance of the court in his favor, he later won a big victory when the court in 2012 upheld most provisions of the health care law. In July 2010 the administration won passage of a major financial reform bill.

In Nov. 2010 elections Democrats lost their majority in the House and reduced it in the Senate. Many of the new Republicans were allied with the rising Tea Party movement, committed to shrinking the size of government and fending off tax increases. During the ensuing lame-duck session, Obama reached a controversial compromise with Republicans on an $858 bil spending plan that kept the Bush tax cuts for all income levels for two years while extending unemployment benefits and temporarily reducing the Social Security payroll tax. He also won passage of a measure to repeal the "don't ask, don't tell" policy for gays in the military.

Following the elections, the bipartisan Simpson Bowles commission, formed by the president to recommend deficit reduction measures, released a detailed $4 tril plan, calling for an ambitious, politically provocative mix of entitlement and other spending cuts along with tax reforms. Obama avoided endorsing these proposals, but in an Apr. 2011 speech, after Republicans had issued a detailed, conservatively oriented deficit reduction plan, he outlined a plan with higher taxes on the wealthy and no entitlement cuts.

With the federal government set to run out of funding in Aug. 2011, Republicans in Congress insisted that the U.S. debt ceiling should not be raised without compensating cost savings. After tortuous negotiations, a last-minute compromise to avert default was passed by Congress and signed by Obama. It raised the debt ceiling by up to $2.4 tril. About half of the compensating reductions were left to be determined later by a bipartisan congressional committee. The long gridlock and the terms of the final compromise led Standard & Poor's to downgrade its U.S. credit rating, which shook stock markets. The committee ultimately deadlocked and large automatic funding cuts in domestic programs and defense were scheduled to go into effect in 2013.

Among other actions in 2012, the Obama administration at least temporarily denied authorization for a controversial pipeline to transport oil from Canada through the U.S. Obama became the first sitting president to publicly support same-sex marriages in an interview May 9 and issued an executive order June 15, providing for many undocumented immigrants under 30 to remain and work in the U.S. for a time.

Most attention focused on the upcoming presidential election, in which Obama was running for reelection. Republicans, including the GOP nominee, former Gov. Mitt Romney (MA), blamed him for failure to deal with high unemployment and escalating federal deficits. Obama argued that progress was being made in recovery from an inherited recession, and faulted congressional Republicans for failing to act on measures such as a proposed $447-bil jobs bill. No major action on economic issues was expected before the Nov. 2012 election, after which Congress would face a year-end "fiscal cliff," with tax cuts due to expire and automatic spending cuts set to kick in.

Wives and Children of the Presidents

Name (born-died; married)	State	Sons/ daughters	Name (born-died; married)	State	Sons/ daughters
Martha Dandridge Custis Washington (1731-1802; 1759)	VA	None	Mary Scott Lord Dimmick Harrison (1858-1948; 1896)	PA	0/1
Abigail Smith Adams (1744-1818; 1764)	MA	3/2	Ida Saxton McKinley (1847-1907; 1871)	OH	0/2
Martha Wayles Skelton Jefferson (1748-82; 1772)	VA	1/5	Alice Hathaway Lee Roosevelt (1861-84; 1880)	MA	0/1
Dolley Payne Todd Madison (1768-1849; 1794)	NC	None	Edith Kermit Carow Roosevelt (1861-1948; 1886)	CT	4/1
Elizabeth Kortright Monroe (1768-1830; 1786)	NY	1/2	Helen Herron Taft (1861-1943; 1886)	OH	2/1
Louisa Catherine Johnson Adams (1775-1852; 1797)	MD[1]	3/1	Ellen Louise Axson Wilson (1860-1914; 1885)	GA	0/3
Rachel Donelson Robards Jackson (1767-1828; 1791)	VA	1/0[2]	Edith Bolling Galt Wilson (1872-1961; 1915)	VA	None
Hannah Hoes Van Buren (1783-1819; 1807)	NY	4/0	Florence Kling De Wolfe Harding (1860-1924; 1891)	OH	None
Anna Tuthill Symmes Harrison (1775-1864; 1795)	NJ	6/4	Grace Anna Goodhue Coolidge (1879-1957; 1905)	VT	2/0
Letitia Christian Tyler (1790-1842; 1813)	VA	3/5	Lou Henry Hoover (1875-1944; 1899)	IA	2/0
Julia Gardiner Tyler (1820-89; 1844)	NY	5/2	Anna Eleanor Roosevelt (1884-1962; 1905)	NY	5/1
Sarah Childress Polk (1803-91; 1824)	TN	None	Elizabeth Virginia (Bess) Wallace Truman (1885-1982; 1919)	MO	0/1
Margaret (Peggy) Mackall Smith Taylor (1788-1852; 1810)	MD	1/5	Mamie Geneva Doud Eisenhower (1896-1979; 1916)	IA	2/0
Abigail Powers Fillmore (1798-1853; 1826)	NY	1/1	Jacqueline Lee Bouvier Kennedy (1929-94; 1953)	NY	2/1
Caroline Carmichael McIntosh Fillmore (1813-81; 1858)	NJ	None	Claudia (Lady Bird) Alta Taylor Johnson (1912-2007; 1934)	TX	0/2
Jane Means Appleton Pierce (1806-63; 1834)	NH	3/0	Thelma Catherine Patricia Ryan Nixon (1912-93; 1940)	NV	0/2
Mary Todd Lincoln (1818-82; 1842)	KY	4/0	Elizabeth (Betty) Bloomer Warren Ford (1918-2011; 1948)	IL	3/1
Eliza McCardle Johnson (1810-76; 1827)	TN	3/2	Eleanor Rosalynn Smith Carter (1927- ; 1946)	GA	3/1
Julia Boggs Dent Grant (1826-1902; 1848)	MO	3/1	Anne Frances (Nancy) Robbins Davis Reagan (1921- ; 1952)	NY	1/1[3]
Lucy Ware Webb Hayes (1831-89; 1852)	OH	7/1	Barbara Pierce Bush (1925- ; 1945)	NY	4/2
Lucretia Rudolph Garfield (1832-1918; 1858)	OH	5/2	Hillary Diane Rodham Clinton (1947- ; 1975)	IL	0/1
Ellen Lewis Herndon Arthur (1837-80; 1859)	VA	2/1	Laura Lane Welch Bush (1946- ; 1977)	TX	0/2
Frances Folsom Cleveland (1864-1947; 1886)	NY	2/3	Michelle LaVaughn Robinson Obama (1964- ; 1992)	IL	0/2
Caroline Lavinia Scott Harrison (1832-92; 1853)	OH	1/1			

Note: Pres. Buchanan was unmarried. (1) Born in London, father a MD citizen. (2) Adopted son. (3) Pres. Reagan's first wife, whom he later divorced, was Jane Wyman. They had a daughter who died in infancy, a daughter who lived past infancy, and an adopted son.

First Lady Michelle Obama

Michelle Robinson Obama was born in Chicago, IL, Jan. 17, 1964. She graduated from Princeton Univ., 1985, earned a law degree from Harvard Univ., 1988, and joined Chicago law firm Sidley & Austin. She served as assistant commissioner of planning and development for Chicago, then as founding executive director of the Chicago chapter of Public Allies, an AmeriCorps program. She began working for the Univ. of Chicago in 1996, first as associate dean of student services, then as the Univ. of Chicago Medical Center's vice president of community and external affairs. Michelle and Barack Obama were married in 1992; in 1998, their daughter Malia was born, followed by Natasha (Sasha) in 2001.

As First Lady, Michelle Obama has focused on supporting military families, helping women balance career and family, encouraging national service, and promoting the arts and arts education. She has also launched a major campaign to deal with the problem of childhood obesity in the U.S.

Burial Places of the Presidents

President	Burial place	President	Burial place	President	Burial place
Washington	Mt. Vernon, VA	Pierce	Concord, NH	Wilson	Wash. Natl. Cathedral, DC
J. Adams	Quincy, MA	Buchanan	Lancaster, PA	Harding	Marion, OH
Jefferson	Charlottesville, VA	Lincoln	Springfield, IL	Coolidge	Plymouth Notch, VT
Madison	Montpelier Station, VA	A. Johnson	Greeneville, TN	Hoover	West Branch, IA
Monroe	Richmond, VA	Grant	New York, NY	F. Roosevelt	Hyde Park, NY
J. Q. Adams	Quincy, MA	Hayes	Fremont, OH	Truman	Independence, MO
Jackson	Nashville, TN	Garfield	Cleveland, OH	Eisenhower	Abilene, KS
Van Buren	Kinderhook, NY	Arthur	Albany, NY	Kennedy	Arlington Natl. Cem., VA
W. H. Harrison	North Bend, OH	Cleveland	Princeton, NJ	L. B. Johnson	Stonewall, TX
Tyler	Richmond, VA	B. Harrison	Indianapolis, IN	Nixon	Yorba Linda, CA
Polk	Nashville, TN	McKinley	Canton, OH	Ford	Grand Rapids, MI
Taylor	Louisville, KY	T. Roosevelt	Oyster Bay, NY	Reagan	Simi Valley, CA
Fillmore	Buffalo, NY	Taft	Arlington Natl. Cem., VA		

Presidential Facts

Oldest president: Ronald Reagan, who was 77 when he left office

Youngest president: Theodore Roosevelt, who was 42 when sworn in after McKinley's death

Youngest person elected president: John F. Kennedy, who was 43 when elected in 1960

Tallest president: Abraham Lincoln, who was 6 feet, 4 inches

Shortest president: James Madison, who was 5 feet, 4 inches

Heaviest president: William Howard Taft, who was 332 pounds in 1911

First president to live in the White House: John Adams, who moved there in 1800

First president inaugurated in Washington, DC: Thomas Jefferson, in 1801

First president whose parents were immigrants: Andrew Jackson; his parents immigrated from Ireland in 1765

First president born a U.S. citizen: Martin Van Buren, in Kinderhook, NY, 1782

First president born outside the original colonies: Abraham Lincoln, in Kentucky, 1809

First president born west of the Mississippi: Herbert Hoover, in West Branch, IA, 1874

Most common presidential home state: Virginia, with 8 presidents

First president born in the 20th century: John F. Kennedy, in 1917

First president born in a hospital: Jimmy Carter, in Plains, GA, 1924

First president to be photographed while in office: James K. Polk, in 1849

First president to have a telephone in the White House: Rutherford B. Hayes, in 1879

First president to address the nation on radio: Warren G. Harding, in 1922

First president to appear on TV: Franklin D. Roosevelt, at opening ceremonies for the 1939 World's Fair

First president to give a live, televised news conference: John F. Kennedy, in 1961

First president to hold an Internet chat: Bill Clinton, in 1999

Presidents who lost the popular vote while winning election: John Quincy Adams, in 1824 (elected by the House after general election failed to produce a majority); Rutherford B. Hayes, in 1876; Benjamin Harrison, in 1888; George W. Bush, in 2000. (Popular vote totals before 1824 are unknown.)

Only presidents chosen by the House of Representatives: Thomas Jefferson (1st term) and John Quincy Adams

Only president never elected either president or vice president: Gerald Ford; named vice president when Spiro Agnew resigned (1973), became president when Nixon resigned (1974)

Only left-handed presidents: James Garfield, Herbert Hoover, Harry Truman, Gerald Ford, Ronald Reagan, George H. W. Bush, Bill Clinton, and Barack Obama

Only Catholic president: John F. Kennedy; the most common religious affiliations have been Episcopalian (11) and Presbyterian (7)

Only bachelor presidents: James Buchanan, who never married, and Grover Cleveland, who married Frances Folsom in the White House in 1886

Only divorced president: Ronald Reagan; divorced from Jane Wyman in 1948, married Nancy Davis in 1952

Presidents who died on July 4: John Adams and Thomas Jefferson (both 1826) and James Monroe (1831)

Only president buried in Washington, DC: Woodrow Wilson, who was interred at Washington National Cathedral

Presidential Libraries

Presidential libraries are coordinated by the National Archives and Records Administration (www.archives.gov/presidential-libraries/). Materials for presidents before Herbert Hoover are held by private institutions. Under the Presidential Records Act, presidential records are not available to the public for the first five years following the end of an administration. The George W. Bush Library and Museum was scheduled to open to the public in Apr. 2013; his records will become subject to FOIA requests on Jan. 20, 2014.

Herbert Hoover Library and Museum
210 Parkside Dr.
West Branch, IA 52358
Phone: (319) 643-5301
Email: hoover.library@nara.gov
Website: hoover.archives.gov

Franklin D. Roosevelt Library and Museum
4079 Albany Post Rd.
Hyde Park, NY 12538-1990
Phone: (800) FDR-VISIT
Email: roosevelt.library@nara.gov
Website: www.fdrlibrary.marist.edu

Harry S. Truman Library and Museum
500 West U.S. Hwy. 24
Independence, MO 64050-2481
Phone: (800) 833-1225
Email: truman.library@nara.gov
Website: www.trumanlibrary.org

Dwight D. Eisenhower Library
200 SE 4th St.
Abilene, KS 67410-2900
Phone: (877) RING-IKE
Email: eisenhower.library@nara.gov
Website: eisenhower.archives.gov

John F. Kennedy Library and Museum
Columbia Pt.
Boston, MA 02125-3312
Phone: (866) JFK-1960

Email: kennedy.library@nara.gov
Website: www.jfklibrary.org

Lyndon Baines Johnson Library and Museum
2313 Red River St.
Austin, TX 78705-5737
Phone: (512) 721-0200
Email: johnson.library@nara.gov
Website: www.lbjlib.utexas.edu

Richard Nixon Library and Museum
18001 Yorba Linda Blvd.
Yorba Linda, CA 92886-3903
Phone: (714) 983-9120
Email: nixon@nara.gov
Website: www.nixonarchives.gov
MD Office: Natl. Archives at College Park
8601 Adelphi Rd.
College Park, MD 20740-6001
Phone: (301) 837-3290

Gerald R. Ford Library and Museum
Library: 1000 Beal Ave.
Ann Arbor, MI 48109-2109
Phone: (734) 205-0555
Museum: 303 Pearl St. NW
Grand Rapids, MI 49504-5353
Phone: (616) 254-0400
Email: ford.library@nara.gov
Website: www.fordlibrarymuseum.gov

Jimmy Carter Library and Museum
441 Freedom Pkwy.

Atlanta, GA 30307-1498
Phone: (404) 865-7100
Email: carter.library@nara.gov
Website: www.jimmycarterlibrary.gov

Ronald Reagan Library and Museum
40 Presidential Dr.
Simi Valley, CA 93065-0600
Phone: (800) 410-8354
Email: reagan.library@nara.gov
Website: www.reagan.utexas.edu

George Bush Library and Museum
1000 George Bush Dr. West
College Station, TX 77845
Phone: (979) 691-4000
Email: library.bush@nara.gov
Website: bushlibrary.tamu.edu

William J. Clinton Library and Museum
1200 President Clinton Ave.
Little Rock, AR 72201
Phone: (501) 374-4242
Email: clinton.library@nara.gov
Website: www.clintonlibrary.gov

George W. Bush Presidential Library and Museum
1725 Lakepointe Dr.
Lewisville, TX 75057
Phone: (972) 353-0545
Email: gwbush.library@nara.gov
Website: www.georgewbushlibrary.smu.edu

Presidential Impeachment in U.S. History

The U.S. Constitution provides for impeachment and removal from office of federal officials on grounds of "Treason, Bribery, or other high Crimes and Misdemeanors" (Article II, Sect. 4). Impeachment is the bringing of charges by the House of Representatives. It is followed by a Senate trial; a two-thirds majority vote of Senators present is needed for conviction and removal from office.

In 1868, **Andrew Johnson** became the first president impeached by the House, for his removal of Sec. of War Edwin M. Stanton without first notifying the Senate. He was tried but not convicted. In 1974, impeachment articles against Pres. **Richard Nixon**, in connection with the Watergate scandal, were adopted by the House Judiciary Committee. He resigned Aug. 9, and the House accepted the committee report without taking further action. In 1998, Pres. **Bill Clinton** was impeached by the House in connection with covering up a sexual relationship with former White House intern Monica Lewinsky. He was tried in the Senate in 1999 and acquitted.

PRESIDENTIAL ELECTIONS

Historical election statistics as of Sept. 2012. For information about the 2012 election, see pp. 10-44.

Electoral and Popular Vote, 2004 and 2008

Source: Federal Election Commission

	2008					2004					
	Electoral vote		Popular vote			Electoral vote		Popular vote			
State	Obama	McCain	Obama	McCain	Nader	Kerry	Bush	Kerry	Bush	Nader	State
AL	0	9	813,479	1,266,546	6,788	0	9	693,933	1,176,394	6,701	AL
AK	0	3	123,594	193,841	3,783	0	3	111,025	190,889	5,069	AK
AZ	0	10	1,034,707	1,230,111	11,301	0	10	893,524	1,104,294	2,773	AZ
AR	0	6	422,310	638,017	12,882	0	6	469,953	572,898	6,171	AR
CA	55	0	8,274,473	5,011,781	108,381	55	0	6,745,485	5,509,826	21,213	CA
CO	9	0	1,288,633	1,073,629	13,352	0	9	1,001,732	1,101,255	12,718	CO
CT	7	0	997,772	629,428	19,162	7	0	857,488	693,826	12,969	CT
DE	3	0	255,459	152,374	2,401	3	0	200,152	171,660	2,153	DE
DC	3	0	245,800	17,367	958	3	0	202,970	21,256	1,485	DC
FL	27	0	4,282,074	4,045,624	28,124	0	27	3,583,544	3,964,522	32,971	FL
GA	0	15	1,844,123	2,048,759	1,158	0	15	1,366,149	1,914,254	2,231	GA
HI	4	0	325,871	120,566	3,825	4	0	231,708	194,191	—	HI
ID	0	4	236,440	403,012	7,175	0	4	181,098	409,235	1,115	ID
IL	21	0	3,419,348	2,031,179	30,948	21	0	2,891,550	2,345,946	3,571	IL
IN	11	0	1,374,039	1,345,648	909	0	11	969,011	1,479,438	1,328	IN
IA	7	0	828,940	682,379	8,014	0	7	741,898	751,957	5,973	IA
KS	0	6	514,765	699,655	10,527	0	6	434,993	736,456	9,348	KS
KY	0	8	751,985	1,048,462	15,378	0	8	712,733	1,069,439	8,856	KY
LA	0	9	782,989	1,148,275	6,997	0	9	820,299	1,102,169	7,032	LA
ME	4	0	421,923	295,273	10,636	4	0	396,842	330,201	8,069	ME
MD	10	0	1,629,467	959,862	14,713	10	0	1,334,493	1,024,703	11,854	MD
MA	12	0	1,904,097	1,108,854	28,841	12	0	1,803,800	1,071,109	4,806	MA
MI	17	0	2,872,579	2,048,639	33,085	17	0	2,479,183	2,313,746	24,035	MI
MN	10	0	1,573,354	1,275,409	30,152	9[1]	0	1,445,014	1,346,695	18,683	MN
MS	0	6	554,662	724,597	4,011	0	6	458,094	684,981	3,177	MS
MO	0	11	1,441,911	1,445,814	17,813	0	11	1,259,171	1,455,713	1,294	MO
MT	0	3	231,667	242,763	3,686	0	3	173,710	266,063	6,168	MT
NE[2]	1	4	333,319	452,979	5,406	0	5	254,328	512,814	5,698	NE[2]
NV	5	0	533,736	412,827	6,150	0	5	397,190	418,690	4,838	NV
NH	4	0	384,826	316,534	3,503	4	0	340,511	331,237	4,479	NH
NJ	15	0	2,215,422	1,613,207	21,298	15	0	1,911,430	1,670,003	19,418	NJ
NM	5	0	472,422	346,832	5,327	0	5	370,942	376,930	4,053	NM
NY	31	0	4,804,945	2,752,771	41,249	31	0	4,314,280	2,962,567	99,873	NY
NC	15	0	2,142,651	2,128,474	1,448	0	15	1,525,849	1,961,166	1,805	NC
ND	0	3	141,278	168,601	4,189	0	3	111,052	196,651	3,756	ND
OH	20	0	2,940,044	2,677,820	42,337	0	20	2,741,167	2,859,768	—	OH
OK	0	7	502,496	960,165	—	0	7	503,966	959,792	—	OK
OR	7	0	1,037,291	738,475	18,614	7	0	943,163	866,831	—	OR
PA	21	0	3,276,363	2,655,885	42,977	21	0	2,938,095	2,793,847	2,656	PA
RI	4	0	296,571	165,391	4,829	4	0	259,765	169,046	4,651	RI
SC	0	8	862,449	1,034,896	5,053	0	8	661,699	937,974	5,520	SC
SD	0	3	170,924	203,054	4,267	0	3	149,244	232,584	4,320	SD
TN	0	11	1,087,437	1,479,178	11,560	0	11	1,036,477	1,384,375	8,992	TN
TX	0	34	3,528,633	4,479,328	5,751	0	34	2,832,704	4,526,917	9,159	TX
UT	0	5	327,670	596,030	8,416	0	5	241,199	663,742	11,305	UT
VT	3	0	219,262	98,974	3,339	3	0	184,067	121,180	4,494	VT
VA	13	0	1,959,532	1,725,005	11,483	0	13	1,454,742	1,716,959	2,393	VA
WA	11	0	1,750,848	1,229,216	29,489	11	0	1,510,201	1,304,894	23,283	WA
WV	0	5	303,857	397,466	7,219	0	5	326,541	423,778	4,063	WV
WI	10	0	1,677,211	1,262,393	17,605	10	0	1,489,504	1,478,120	16,390	WI
WY	0	3	82,868	164,958	2,525	0	3	70,776	167,629	2,741	WY
Total	**365**	**173**	**69,498,516**	**59,948,323**	**739,034**	**251[1]**	**286**	**59,028,444**	**62,040,610**	**465,650**	**Total**

— = Not listed on state's ballot. (1) Minnesota has 10 electoral votes. One elector cast a vote for John Ewards [sic] for president, presumably by mistake. All 10 electors voted for John Edwards for vice president. (2) Nebraska is one of two states (the other is Maine) that allows electoral votes to be split between candidates.

Presidential Popular Vote, 2008

Candidate (party)	Vote total	Percent of vote
Barack Obama (Democrat)	69,498,516	52.93%
John McCain (Republican)	59,948,323	45.65
Ralph Nader (Independent/Peace and Freedom)	739,034	0.56
Bob Barr (Libertarian)	523,715	0.40
Chuck Baldwin (Constitution/Reform/ U.S. Taxpayers)	199,750	0.15
Cynthia McKinney (Green/Independent/ Mountain)	161,797	0.12
Alan Keyes (America's Independent)	47,746	0.04
Ron Paul (Constitution/Louisiana Taxpayers)	42,426	0.03
Gloria La Riva (Socialism and Liberation)	6,818	0.01
Brian Moore (Liberty Union/Socialist)	6,538	<0.01
Róger Calero (Socialist Workers)	5,151	<0.01
Richard Duncan (Independent)	3,905	<0.01
James Harris (Socialist Workers)	2,424	<0.01

Candidate (party)	Vote total	Percent of vote
Charles Jay (Boston Tea Party/ Independent)	2,422	<0.01%
John Joseph Polachek (New)	1,149	<0.01
Frank Edward McEnulty (Unaffiliated)	829	<0.01
Jeffrey J. Wamboldt (Independent)	764	<0.01
Thomas Robert Stevens (Objectivist)	755	<0.01
Gene C. Amondson (Prohibition)	653	<0.01
Jeffrey "Jeff" Boss (Vote Here)	639	<0.01
George Phillies (Libertarian)	531	<0.01
Ted Weill (Reform)	481	<0.01
Jonathan E. Allen (HeartQuake '08)	480	<0.01
Bradford Lyttle (U.S. Pacifist)	110	<0.01
Write-In (Miscellaneous)	112,597	0.09
None of These Candidates (Nevada)	6,267	<0.01
Total votes cast	**131,313,820**	
Voting age population, Nov. 2008	225,499,000	
Percentage casting vote for president	58.23%	

Note: Party designations vary from one state to another; party label listed may not necessarily represent a political party organization. Vote totals for the candidates listed above include any write-in votes they received.

The Electoral College

The president and the vice president are the only elective federal officials not chosen by direct vote of the people. They are elected by the members of the Electoral College, an institution provided for in the U.S. Constitution.

On presidential election day, the first Tuesday after the first Monday in Nov. of every fourth year, each state chooses as many electors as it has senators and representatives in Congress. In 1964, for the first time, as provided by the 23rd Amendment to the Constitution, the District of Columbia voted for three electors. Thus, with 100 senators and 435 representatives, there are 538 members of the Electoral College, with a majority of 270 electoral votes needed to elect the president and vice president.

Although political parties were not part of the original plan created by the Founding Fathers, today political parties customarily nominate their lists of electors at their respective state conventions. Some states print names of the candidates for president and vice president at the top of the Nov. ballot; others list only the electors' names. In either case, the electors of the party receiving the highest vote are elected. Two states, Maine and Nebraska, allow for proportional allocation.

The electors meet on the first Monday after the second Wednesday in Dec. in their respective state capitals or in some other place prescribed by state legislatures. By long-established custom, they vote for their party nominees, although this is not required by federal law; some states do require it.

The Constitution requires electors to cast a ballot for at least one person who is not an inhabitant of that elector's home state. This ensures that presidential and vice presidential candidates from the same party will not be from the same state. (In 2000, Republican vice presidential nominee Dick Cheney changed his voter registration to Wyoming, where he grew up and which he'd once represented in Congress, from Gov. George W. Bush's home state of Texas.) Also, an elector cannot be a member of Congress or hold federal office.

Certified and sealed lists of the votes of the electors in each state are sent to the president of the U.S. Senate, who then opens them in the presence of the members of the Senate and House of Representatives in a joint session held in early Jan., and the electoral votes of all the states are then officially counted.

If no candidate for president has a majority, the House of Representatives chooses a president from the top three candidates, with all representatives from each state combining to cast one vote for that state. The House decided the outcome of the 1800 and 1824 presidential elections. If no candidate for vice president has a majority, the Senate chooses from the top two, with the senators voting as individuals. The Senate chose the vice president following the 1836 election.

Under the electoral college system, a candidate who fails to be the top vote getter in the popular vote still may win a majority of electoral votes. This happened in the elections of 1876, 1888, and 2000.

Electoral Votes for President, 2008

Electoral votes based on the 2000 Census were in force beginning with the 2004 elections.

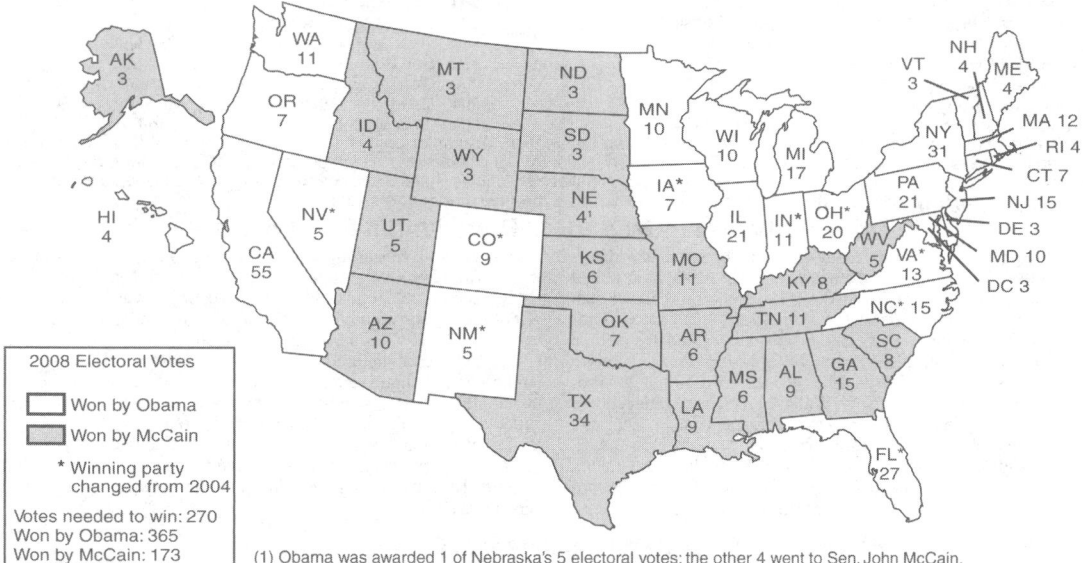

(1) Obama was awarded 1 of Nebraska's 5 electoral votes; the other 4 went to Sen. John McCain.

Voter Turnout in Presidential Elections, 1932-2008

Source: Federal Election Commission; Center for the Study of the American Electorate, American Univ.; *Congressional Quarterly*

Year	Candidates	Voter participation (% of voting-age population)	Year	Candidates	Voter participation (% of voting-age population)
1932	F. D. Roosevelt-Hoover	52.4%	1972	Nixon-McGovern	55.2%[1]
1936	F. D. Roosevelt-Landon	56.0	1976	Carter-Ford	53.5
1940	F. D. Roosevelt-Willkie	58.9	1980	Reagan-Carter	54.0
1944	F. D. Roosevelt-Dewey	56.0	1984	Reagan-Mondale	53.1
1948	Truman-Dewey	51.1	1988	G. H. W. Bush-Dukakis	50.2
1952	Eisenhower-Stevenson	61.6	1992	Clinton-G. H. W. Bush-Perot	55.9
1956	Eisenhower-Stevenson	59.3	1996	Clinton-Dole-Perot	49.0
1960	Kennedy-Nixon	62.8	2000	G. W. Bush-Gore	51.3
1964	L. B. Johnson-Goldwater	61.9	2004	G. W. Bush-Kerry	60.7
1968	Nixon-Humphrey	60.9	2008	Obama-McCain	58.2

(1) The drop in voter participation followed the expansion of eligibility with the enfranchisement of 18- to 20-year-olds.

Major-Party Nominees for President and Vice President, 1856-2008
Asterisk (*) denotes winning ticket.

	Democratic			Republican	
Year	**President**	**Vice President**	**Year**	**President**	**Vice President**
1856	James Buchanan*	John Breckinridge	1856	John Frémont	William Dayton
1860	Stephen A. Douglas[1]	Herschel V. Johnson	1860	Abraham Lincoln*	Hannibal Hamlin
1864	George McClellan	G. H. Pendleton	1864	Abraham Lincoln*	Andrew Johnson
1868	Horatio Seymour	Francis Blair	1868	Ulysses S. Grant*	Schuyler Colfax
1872	Horace Greeley	B. Gratz Brown	1872	Ulysses S. Grant*	Henry Wilson
1876	Samuel J. Tilden	Thomas Hendricks	1876	Rutherford B. Hayes*	William Wheeler
1880	Winfield Hancock	William English	1880	James A. Garfield*	Chester A. Arthur
1884	Grover Cleveland*	Thomas Hendricks	1884	James G. Blaine	John Logan
1888	Grover Cleveland	A. G. Thurman	1888	Benjamin Harrison*	Levi Morton
1892	Grover Cleveland*	Adlai Stevenson	1892	Benjamin Harrison	Whitelaw Reid
1896	William J. Bryan	Arthur Sewall	1896	William McKinley*	Garret Hobart
1900	William J. Bryan	Adlai Stevenson	1900	William McKinley*	Theodore Roosevelt
1904	Alton Parker	Henry Davis	1904	Theodore Roosevelt*	Charles Fairbanks
1908	William J. Bryan	John Kern	1908	William H. Taft*	James Sherman
1912	Woodrow Wilson*	Thomas Marshall	1912	William H. Taft	James Sherman[2]
1916	Woodrow Wilson*	Thomas Marshall	1916	Charles E. Hughes	Charles Fairbanks
1920	James M. Cox	Franklin D. Roosevelt	1920	Warren G. Harding*	Calvin Coolidge
1924	John W. Davis	Charles W. Bryan	1924	Calvin Coolidge*	Charles G. Dawes
1928	Alfred E. Smith	Joseph T. Robinson	1928	Herbert Hoover*	Charles Curtis
1932	Franklin D. Roosevelt*	John N. Garner	1932	Herbert Hoover	Charles Curtis
1936	Franklin D. Roosevelt*	John N. Garner	1936	Alfred M. Landon	Frank Knox
1940	Franklin D. Roosevelt*	Henry A. Wallace	1940	Wendell L. Willkie	Charles McNary
1944	Franklin D. Roosevelt*	Harry S. Truman	1944	Thomas E. Dewey	John W. Bricker
1948	Harry S. Truman*	Alben W. Barkley	1948	Thomas E. Dewey	Earl Warren
1952	Adlai E. Stevenson	John J. Sparkman	1952	Dwight D. Eisenhower*	Richard M. Nixon
1956	Adlai E. Stevenson	Estes Kefauver	1956	Dwight D. Eisenhower*	Richard M. Nixon
1960	John F. Kennedy*	Lyndon B. Johnson	1960	Richard M. Nixon	Henry Cabot Lodge
1964	Lyndon B. Johnson*	Hubert H. Humphrey	1964	Barry M. Goldwater	William E. Miller
1968	Hubert H. Humphrey	Edmund S. Muskie	1968	Richard M. Nixon*	Spiro T. Agnew
1972	George S. McGovern	R. Sargent Shriver Jr.[3]	1972	Richard M. Nixon*	Spiro T. Agnew
1976	Jimmy Carter*	Walter F. Mondale	1976	Gerald R. Ford	Bob Dole
1980	Jimmy Carter	Walter F. Mondale	1980	Ronald Reagan*	George H. W. Bush
1984	Walter F. Mondale	Geraldine Ferraro	1984	Ronald Reagan*	George H. W. Bush
1988	Michael S. Dukakis	Lloyd Bentsen	1988	George H. W. Bush*	Dan Quayle
1992	Bill Clinton*	Al Gore	1992	George H. W. Bush	Dan Quayle
1996	Bill Clinton*	Al Gore	1996	Bob Dole	Jack Kemp
2000	Al Gore	Joseph Lieberman	2000	George W. Bush*	Richard Cheney
2004	John Kerry	John Edwards	2004	George W. Bush*	Richard Cheney
2008	Barack Obama*	Joseph Biden	2008	John McCain	Sarah Palin

(1) Douglas and Johnson were nominated at the Baltimore convention. An earlier convention in Charleston, SC, failed to reach a consensus and resulted in a split in the party. The Southern faction of the Democrats nominated John Breckinridge for president and Joseph Lane for vice president. (2) Died Oct. 30; replaced on ballot by Nicholas Butler. (3) Chosen by Democratic National Committee after Thomas Eagleton withdrew because of controversy over past treatments for depression.

Third-Party and Independent Presidential Candidates

Although many third-party candidates or independents have pursued the presidency, only 10 of these from 1832 to 2000 have polled more than a million votes. In most elections since 1860, fewer than one vote in 20 has been cast for a third-party candidate. Major vote getters among third-party and independent candidates include James B. Weaver (People's Party), 1892; former Pres. Theodore Roosevelt (Progressive Party), 1912; Robert M. La Follette (Progressive Party), 1924; George C. Wallace (American Independent Party), 1968; and H. Ross Perot, as an independent in 1992 and with the Reform Party in 1996. In these six elections, non-major-party candidates combined polled at least 10% of the vote.

Roosevelt outpolled the Republican candidate, William Howard Taft, in 1912, capturing 28% of the popular vote and 88 electoral votes. In 1948, Strom Thurmond was able to capture 39 electoral votes (from five Southern states); however, all third parties received only 5.75% of the popular vote in the election. Twenty years later, George Wallace's popularity in the same region allowed him to get 46 electoral votes and 13.5% of the popular vote.

In 1992 Perot captured 19% of the popular vote. However, he did not win a single state. In 1996, Perot won 8% of the popular vote; all third-party candidates combined won just over 10%. In 2000, Ralph Nader won about 3% of the vote.

Despite the difficulty in winning the presidency, independent and third-party candidates often bring attention to prominent issues. They can also affect the outcome between major-party candidates.

Notable Third Party and Independent Campaigns by Year

Party	Presidential nominee	Year	Issues	Strength in
Anti-Masonic	William Wirt	1832	Against secret societies and oaths	PA, VT
Liberty	James G. Birney	1844	Anti-slavery	North
Free Soil	Martin Van Buren	1848	Anti-slavery	NY, OH
American (Know-Nothing)	Millard Fillmore	1856	Anti-immigrant	Northeast, South
Greenback	Peter Cooper	1876	For "cheap money," labor rights	National
Greenback	James B. Weaver	1880	For "cheap money," labor rights	National
Prohibition	John P. St. John	1884	Anti-liquor	National
People's (Populist)	James B. Weaver	1892	For "cheap money," end of national banks	South, West
Socialist	Eugene V. Debs	1900-12; 1920	For public ownership	National
Progressive (Bull Moose)	Theodore Roosevelt	1912	Against high tariffs	Midwest, West
Progressive	Robert M. La Follette	1924	For farmer and labor rights	Midwest, West
Socialist	Norman Thomas	1928-48	For liberal reforms	National
Union	William Lemke	1936	Anti-New Deal	National
States' Rights (Dixiecrat)	Strom Thurmond	1948	For states' rights	South
Progressive	Henry A. Wallace	1948	Anti-Cold War	NY, CA
American Independent	George C. Wallace	1968	For states' rights	South
American	John G. Schmitz	1972	For "law and order"	West, OH, LA
None (independent)	John B. Anderson	1980	A third choice	National
None (independent)	H. Ross Perot	1992	Federal budget deficit	National
Reform	H. Ross Perot	1996	Deficit; campaign finance	National
Green, independent	Ralph Nader	2000-08	Corporate power; domestic priorities	National

Popular and Electoral Vote for President, 1789-2008

(D) Democrat; (DR) Democratic Republican; (F) Federalist; (LB) Libertarian; (LR) Liberal Republican; (NR) National Republican; (P) People's; (PR) Progressive; (R) Republican; (W) Whig; * = see notes below table.

Year	President elected	Popular	Elec.	Major losing candidate(s)	Popular	Elec.
1789	George Washington (F)	Unknown	69	No opposition	—	—
1792	George Washington (F)	Unknown	132	No opposition	—	—
1796	John Adams (F)	Unknown	71	Thomas Jefferson (DR)	Unknown	68
1800*	Thomas Jefferson (DR)	Unknown	73	Aaron Burr (DR)	Unknown	73
1804	Thomas Jefferson (DR)	Unknown	162	Charles Pinckney (F)	Unknown	14
1808	James Madison (DR)	Unknown	122	Charles Pinckney (F)	Unknown	47
1812	James Madison (DR)	Unknown	128	DeWitt Clinton (F)	Unknown	89
1816	James Monroe (DR)	Unknown	183	Rufus King (F)	Unknown	34
1820	James Monroe (DR)	Unknown	231	John Quincy Adams (DR)	Unknown	1
1824*	John Quincy Adams (DR)	113,122	84	Andrew Jackson (DR)	151,271	99
				Henry Clay (DR)	46,587	37
				William H. Crawford (DR)	44,282	41
1828	Andrew Jackson (D)	642,553	178	John Quincy Adams (NR)	500,897	83
1832	Andrew Jackson (D)	701,780	219	Henry Clay (NR)	484,205	49
1836	Martin Van Buren (D)	764,176	170	William H. Harrison (W)	550,816	73
1840	William H. Harrison (W)	1,275,390	234	Martin Van Buren (D)	1,128,854	60
1844	James K. Polk (D)	1,339,494	170	Henry Clay (W)	1,300,004	105
1848	Zachary Taylor (W)	1,361,393	163	Lewis Cass (D)	1,223,460	127
				Martin Van Buren (Free Soil)	291,501	—
1852	Franklin Pierce (D)	1,607,510	254	Winfield Scott (W)	1,386,942	42
1856	James Buchanan (D)	1,836,072	174	John C. Fremont (R)	1,342,345	114
				Millard Fillmore (W-American)	873,053	8
1860	Abraham Lincoln (R)	1,865,908	180	Stephen A. Douglas (D)	848,019	12
				John C. Breckinridge (D)	845,763	72
				John Bell (Constitutional Union)	589,581	39
1864	Abraham Lincoln (R)	2,218,388	212	George McClellan (D)	1,812,807	21
1868	Ulysses S. Grant (R)	3,013,650	214	Horatio Seymour (D)	2,708,744	80
1872*	Ulysses S. Grant (R)	3,598,235	286	Horace Greeley (D-LR)	2,834,671	—
1876*	Rutherford B. Hayes (R)	4,034,311	185	Samuel J. Tilden (D)	4,288,546	184
1880	James A. Garfield (R)	4,446,158	214	Winfield S. Hancock (D)	4,444,260	155
1884	Grover Cleveland (D)	4,874,621	219	James G. Blaine (R)	4,848,936	182
1888	Benjamin Harrison (R)	5,443,892	233	Grover Cleveland (D)	5,534,488	168
1892	Grover Cleveland (D)	5,551,883	277	Benjamin Harrison (R)	5,179,244	145
				James Weaver (P)	1,027,329	22
1896	William McKinley (R)	7,108,480	271	William J. Bryan (D-P)	6,511,495	176
1900	William McKinley (R)	7,218,039	292	William J. Bryan (D)	6,358,345	155
1904	Theodore Roosevelt (R)	7,626,593	336	Alton B. Parker (D)	5,082,898	140
1908	William H. Taft (R)	7,676,258	321	William J. Bryan (D)	6,406,801	162
1912	Woodrow Wilson (D)	6,293,152	435	Theodore Roosevelt (PR)	4,119,207	88
				William H. Taft (R)	3,483,922	8
1916	Woodrow Wilson (D)	9,126,300	277	Charles E. Hughes (R)	8,546,789	254
1920	Warren G. Harding (R)	16,153,115	404	James M. Cox (D)	9,133,092	127
1924	Calvin Coolidge (R)	15,719,921	382	John W. Davis (D)	8,386,704	136
				Robert M. La Follette (PR)	4,822,856	13
1928	Herbert Hoover (R)	21,437,277	444	Alfred E. Smith (D)	15,007,698	87
1932	Franklin D. Roosevelt (D)	22,829,501	472	Herbert Hoover (R)	15,760,684	59
1936	Franklin D. Roosevelt (D)	27,757,333	523	Alfred Landon (R)	16,684,231	8
1940	Franklin D. Roosevelt (D)	27,313,041	449	Wendell Willkie (R)	22,348,480	82
1944	Franklin D. Roosevelt (D)	25,612,610	432	Thomas E. Dewey (R)	22,117,617	99
1948	Harry S. Truman (D)	24,179,345	303	Thomas E. Dewey (R)	21,991,291	189
				Strom Thurmond (States' Rights)	1,169,021	39
				Henry A. Wallace (PR)	1,157,172	—
1952	Dwight D. Eisenhower (R)	33,936,234	442	Adlai E. Stevenson (D)	27,314,992	89
1956*	Dwight D. Eisenhower (R)	35,590,472	457	Adlai E. Stevenson (D)	26,022,752	73
1960*	John F. Kennedy (D)	34,226,731	303	Richard M. Nixon (R)	34,108,157	219
1964	Lyndon B. Johnson (D)	43,129,566	486	Barry M. Goldwater (R)	27,178,188	52
1968	Richard M. Nixon (R)	31,785,480	301	Hubert H. Humphrey (D)	31,275,166	191
				George C. Wallace (Amer. Indep.)	9,906,473	46
1972*	Richard M. Nixon (R)	47,169,911	520	George S. McGovern (D)	29,170,383	17
1976*	Jimmy Carter (D)	40,830,763	297	Gerald R. Ford (R)	39,147,793	240
1980	Ronald Reagan (R)	43,904,153	489	Jimmy Carter (D)	35,483,883	49
				John B. Anderson (independent)	5,719,437	—
1984	Ronald Reagan (R)	54,455,075	525	Walter F. Mondale (D)	37,577,185	13
1988*	George H. W. Bush (R)	48,886,097	426	Michael S. Dukakis (D)	41,809,074	111
1992	Bill Clinton (D)	44,908,254	370	George H. W. Bush (R)	39,102,343	168
				H. Ross Perot (independent)	19,741,065	—
1996	Bill Clinton (D)	45,590,703	379	Bob Dole (R)	37,816,307	159
				H. Ross Perot (Reform)	7,866,284	—
2000*	George W. Bush (R)	50,459,211	271	Al Gore (D)	51,003,894	266
				Ralph Nader (Green)	2,834,410	—
2004*	George W. Bush (R)	62,040,610	286	John Kerry (D)	59,028,444	251
2008	Barack H. Obama (D)	69,498,459	365	John McCain (R)	59,948,283	173

*1800—Elected by House of Representatives because of tied electoral vote. 1824—Elected by House of Representatives because no candidate polled a majority. By 1824, the Democratic Republicans had become a loose coalition of competing political groups. By 1828, the supporters of Jackson were known as Democrats, and the John Q. Adams and Henry Clay supporters as National Republicans. 1872—Greeley died Nov. 29, 1872. His electoral votes were split among four individuals. 1876—FL, LA, OR, and SC election returns were disputed. Congress in joint session (Mar. 2, 1877) declared Hayes and Wheeler elected president and vice president. 1956—Democrats elected 74 electors, but 1 from AL refused to vote for Stevenson. 1960—Sen. Harry F. Byrd (D, VA) received 15 electoral votes. 1972—John Hospers of CA received 1 vote from an elector of VA. 1976—Ronald Reagan of CA received 1 vote from an elector of WA. 1988—Sen. Lloyd Bentsen (D, TX) received 1 vote from an elector of WV. 2000—One Gore elector from Washington, DC, abstained. Nader was listed as "Independent" on the ballot in some states; he was not on the ballot in all states. 2004—One MN elector voted for VP candidate John Edwards for both president and vice president.

Presidential Election Results by State

Source: Federal Election Commission

Historical election statistics as of Sept. 2012. For information about the 2012 election, see pp. 10-44.

Alabama Vote Since 1952

2008: McCain, R., 1,266,546; Obama, D., 813,479; Nader, Ind., 6,788; Barr, Ind., 4,991; Baldwin, Ind., 4,310.
2004: Bush, R., 1,176,394; Kerry, D., 693,933; Nader, Ind., 6,701; Badnarik, Ind., 3,529; Peroutka, Ind., 1,994.
2000: Bush, R., 941,173; Gore, D., 692,611; Nader, Ind., 18,323; Buchanan, Ind., 6,351; Browne, LB., 5,893; Phillips, Ind., 775; Hagelin, Ind., 447.
1996: Dole, R., 769,044; Clinton, D., 662,165; Perot, RF., 92,149; Browne, LB., 5,290; Phillips, Ind., 2,365; Hagelin, Natural Law, 1,697; Harris, Ind., 516.
1992: Bush, R., 804,283; Clinton, D., 690,080; Perot, Ind., 183,109; Marrou, LB., 5,737; Fulani, New Alliance, 2,161.
1988: Bush, R., 815,576; Dukakis, D., 549,506; Paul, LB., 8,460; Fulani, Ind., 3,311.
1984: Reagan, R., 872,849; Mondale, D., 551,899; Bergland, LB., 9,504.
1980: Reagan, R., 654,192; Carter, D., 636,730; Anderson, Ind., 16,481; Rarick, Amer. Ind., 15,010; Clark, LB., 13,318; Bubar, Statesman, 1,743; Hall, Comm., 1,629; DeBerry, Soc. Workers, 1,303; McReynolds, Soc., 1,006; Commoner, Citizens, 517.
1976: Carter, D., 659,170; Ford, R., 504,070; Maddox, Amer. Ind., 9,198; Bubar, Prohib., 6,669; Hall, Comm., 1,954; MacBride, LB., 1,481.
1972: Nixon, R., 728,701; McGovern, D., 219,108 plus 37,815 Natl. Dem. Party of AL; Schmitz, Conservative, 11,918; Munn, Prohib., 8,551.
1968: Wallace, 3rd party, 691,425; Humphrey, D., 196,579; Nixon, R., 146,923; Munn, Prohib., 4,022.
1964: Goldwater, R., 479,085; D. (electors unpledged), 209,848; scattered, 105.
1960: Kennedy, D., 324,050; Nixon, R., 237,981; Faubus, States' Rights, 4,367; Decker, Prohib., 2,106; King, Afro-Americans, 1,485; scattered, 236.
1956: Stevenson, D., 290,844; Eisenhower, R., 195,694; Ind. electors, 20,323.
1952: Stevenson, D., 275,075; Eisenhower, R., 149,231; Hamblen, Prohib., 1,814.

Alaska Vote Since 1960

2008: McCain, R., 193,841; Obama, D., 123,594; Nader, Ind., 3,783; Baldwin, AK Ind., 1,660; Barr, LB., 1,589.
2004: Bush, R., 190,889; Kerry, D., 111,025; Nader, Populist, 5,069; Peroutka, AK Ind., 2,092; Badnarik, LB., 1,675; Cobb, Green, 1,058.
2000: Bush, R., 167,398; Gore, D., 79,004; Nader, Green, 28,747; Buchanan, RF., 5,192; Browne, LB., 2,636; Hagelin, Natural Law, 919; Phillips, Const., 596.
1996: Dole, R., 122,746; Clinton, D., 80,380; Perot, RF., 26,333; Nader, Green, 7,597; Browne, LB., 2,276; Phillips, U.S. Taxpayers, 925; Hagelin, Natural Law, 729.
1992: Bush, R., 102,000; Clinton, D., 78,294; Perot, Ind., 73,481; Gritz, Populist/America First, 1,379; Marrou, LB., 1,378.
1988: Bush, R., 119,251; Dukakis, D., 72,584; Paul, LB., 5,484; Fulani, New Alliance, 1,024.
1984: Reagan, R., 138,377; Mondale, D., 62,007; Bergland, LB., 6,378.
1980: Reagan, R., 86,112; Carter, D., 41,842; Clark, LB., 18,479; Anderson, Ind., 11,155; write-in, 857.
1976: Ford, R., 71,555; Carter, D., 44,058; MacBride, LB., 6,785.
1972: Nixon, R., 55,349; McGovern, D., 32,967; Schmitz, Amer., 6,903.
1968: Nixon, R., 37,600; Humphrey, D., 35,411; Wallace, 3rd party, 10,024.
1964: Johnson, D., 44,329; Goldwater, R., 22,930.
1960: Nixon, R., 30,953; Kennedy, D., 29,809.

Arizona Vote Since 1952

2008: McCain, R., 1,230,111; Obama, D., 1,034,707; Barr, LB., 12,555; Nader, New Prog., 11,301; McKinney, Green, 3,406.
2004: Bush, R., 1,104,294; Kerry, D., 893,524; Badnarik, LB., 11,856.
2000: Bush, R., 781,652; Gore, D., 685,341; Nader, Green, 45,645; Buchanan, RF., 12,373; Smith, LB., 5,775; Hagelin, Natural Law, 1,120.
1996: Clinton, D., 653,288; Dole, R., 622,073; Perot, RF., 112,072; Browne, LB., 14,358.

1992: Bush, R., 572,086; Clinton, D., 543,050; Perot, Ind., 353,741; Gritz, Populist/America First, 8,141; Marrou, LB., 6,759; Hagelin, Natural Law, 2,267.
1988: Bush, R., 702,541; Dukakis, D., 454,029; Paul, LB., 13,351; Fulani, New Alliance, 1,662.
1984: Reagan, R., 681,416; Mondale, D., 333,854; Bergland, LB., 10,585.
1980: Reagan, R., 529,688; Carter, D., 246,843; Anderson, Ind., 76,952; Clark, LB., 18,784; De Berry, Soc. Workers, 1,100; Commoner, Citizens, 551; Hall, Comm., 25; Griswold, Workers World, 2.
1976: Ford, R., 418,642; Carter, D., 295,602; McCarthy, Ind., 19,229; MacBride, LB., 7,647; Camejo, Soc. Workers, 928; Anderson, Amer., 564; Maddox, Amer. Ind., 85.
1972: Nixon, R., 402,812; McGovern, D., 198,540; Jenness, Soc. Workers, 30,945; Schmitz, Amer. Ind., 21,208.
1968: Nixon, R., 266,721; Humphrey, D., 170,514; Wallace, 3rd party, 46,573; McCarthy, New Party, 2,751; Cleaver, Peace/Freedom, 217; Halstead, Soc. Workers, 85; Blomen, Soc. Labor, 75.
1964: Goldwater, R., 242,535; Johnson, D., 237,753; Hass, Soc. Labor, 482.
1960: Nixon, R., 221,241; Kennedy, D., 176,781; Hass, Soc. Labor, 469.
1956: Eisenhower, R., 176,990; Stevenson, D., 112,880; Andrews, Ind., 303.
1952: Eisenhower, R., 152,042; Stevenson, D., 108,528.

Arkansas Vote Since 1952

2008: McCain, R., 638,017; Obama, D., 422,310; Nader, Ind., 12,882; Barr, LB., 4,776; Baldwin, Const., 4,023; McKinney, Green, 3,470; La Riva, Socialism/Liberation, 1,139.
2004: Bush, R., 572,898; Kerry, D., 469,953; Nader, Populist, 6,171; Badnarik, LB., 2,352; Peroutka, Const., 2,083; Cobb, Green, 1,488.
2000: Bush, R., 472,940; Gore, D., 422,768; Nader, Green, 13,421; Buchanan, RF., 7,358; Browne, LB., 2,781; Phillips, Const., 1,415; Hagelin, Natural Law, 1,098.
1996: Clinton, D., 475,171; Dole, R., 325,416; Perot, RF., 69,884; Nader, Ind., 3,649; Browne, Ind., 3,076; Phillips, Ind., 2,065; Forbes, Ind., 932; Collins, Ind., 823; Masters, Ind., 749; Moorehead, Ind., 747; Hagelin, Ind., 729; Hollis, Ind., 538; Dodge, Ind., 483.
1992: Clinton, D., 505,823; Bush, R., 337,324; Perot, Ind., 99,132; Phillips, U.S. Taxpayers, 1,437; Marrou, LB., 1,261; Fulani, New Alliance, 1,022.
1988: Bush, R., 466,578; Dukakis, D., 349,237; Duke, Populist, 5,146; Paul, LB., 3,297.
1984: Reagan, R., 534,774; Mondale, D., 338,646; Bergland, LB., 2,220.
1980: Reagan, R., 403,164; Carter, D., 398,041; Anderson, Ind., 22,468; Clark, LB., 8,970; Commoner, Citizens, 2,345; Bubar, Statesman, 1,350; Hall, Comm., 1,244.
1976: Carter, D., 498,604; Ford, R., 267,903; McCarthy, Ind., 639; Anderson, Amer. Ind., 389.
1972: Nixon, R., 445,751; McGovern, D., 198,899; Schmitz, Amer. Ind., 3,016.
1968: Wallace, 3rd party, 235,627; Nixon, R., 189,062; Humphrey, D., 184,901.
1964: Johnson, D., 314,197; Goldwater, R., 243,264; Kasper, Natl. States' Rights, 2,965.
1960: Kennedy, D., 215,049; Nixon, R., 184,508; Faubus, Natl. States' Rights, 28,952.
1956: Stevenson, D., 213,277; Eisenhower, R., 186,287; Andrews, Ind., 7,008.
1952: Stevenson, D., 226,300; Eisenhower, R., 177,155; Hamblen, Prohib., 886; MacArthur, Christian Nationalist, 458; Hass, Soc. Labor, 1.

California Vote Since 1952

2008: Obama, D., 8,274,473; McCain, R., 5,011,781; Nader, Peace/Freedom, 108,381; Barr, LB., 67,582; Alan Keyes, Amer. Ind., 40,673; McKinney, Green, 38,774.
2004: Kerry, D., 6,745,485; Bush, R., 5,509,826; Badnarik, LB., 50,165; Cobb, Green, 40,771; Peltier, Peace/Freedom, 27,607; Peroutka, Amer. Ind., 26,645.

2000: Gore, D., 5,861,203; Bush, R., 4,567,429; Nader, Green, 418,707; Browne, LB., 45,520; Buchanan, RF., 44,987; Phillips, Amer. Ind., 17,042; Hagelin, Natural Law, 10,934.
1996: Clinton, D., 5,119,835; Dole, R., 3,828,380; Perot, RF., 697,847; Nader, Green, 237,016; Browne, LB., 73,600; Feinland, Peace/Freedom, 25,332; Phillips, Amer. Ind., 21,202; Hagelin, Natural Law, 15,403.
1992: Clinton, D., 5,121,325; Bush, R., 3,630,575; Perot, Ind., 2,296,006; Marrou, LB., 48,139; Daniels, Ind., 18,597; Phillips, U.S. Taxpayers, 12,711.
1988: Bush, R., 5,054,917; Dukakis, D., 4,702,233; Paul, LB., 70,105; Fulani, Ind., 31,181.
1984: Reagan, R., 5,305,410; Mondale, D., 3,815,947; Bergland, LB., 48,400.
1980: Reagan, R., 4,524,858; Carter, D., 3,083,661; Anderson, Ind., 739,833; Clark, LB., 148,434; Commoner, Ind., 61,063; Smith, Peace/Freedom, 18,116; Rarick, Amer. Ind., 9,856.
1976: Ford, R., 3,882,244; Carter, D., 3,742,284; McCarthy, write-in, 58,412; MacBride, LB., 56,388; Maddox, Amer. Ind., 51,098; Wright, People's, 41,731; Camejo, Soc. Workers, 17,259; Hall, Comm., 12,766; write-in, 4,935.
1972: Nixon, R., 4,602,096; McGovern, D., 3,475,847; Schmitz, Amer. Ind., 232,554; Spock, Peace/Freedom, 55,167; Hospers, LB., 980; Jenness, Soc. Workers, 574; Hall, Comm., 373; Fisher, Soc. Labor, 197; Munn, Prohib., 53; Green, Universal, 21.
1968: Nixon, R., 3,467,664; Humphrey, D., 3,244,318; Wallace, 3rd party, 487,270; Peace/Freedom, 27,707; McCarthy, Alternative, 20,721; Gregory, write-in, 3,230; Blomen, Soc. Labor, 341; Mitchell, Comm., 260; Munn, Prohib., 59; Soeters, Defense, 17.
1964: Johnson, D., 4,171,877; Goldwater, R., 2,879,108; Hass, Soc. Labor, 489; DeBerry, Soc. Workers, 378; Munn, Prohib., 305; Hensley, Universal, 19.
1960: Nixon, R., 3,259,722; Kennedy, D., 3,224,099; Decker, Prohib., 21,706; Hass, Soc. Labor, 1,051.
1956: Eisenhower, R., 3,027,668; Stevenson, D., 2,420,136; Holtwick, Prohib., 11,119; Andrews, Const., 6,087; Hass, Soc. Labor, 300; Hoopes, Soc., 123; Dobbs, Soc. Workers, 96; Smith, Christian Nationalist, 8.
1952: Eisenhower, R., 2,897,310; Stevenson, D., 2,197,548; Hallinan, Prog., 24,106; Hamblen, Prohib., 15,653; MacArthur write-in (Christian Nationalist), 3,326, and write-in (Const.), 178 (total, 3,504); Hass, Soc. Labor, 273; Hoopes, Soc., 206; scattered, 3,249.

Colorado Vote Since 1952

2008: Obama, D., 1,288,633; McCain, R., 1,073,629; Nader, Unaff., 13,352; Barr, LB., 10,898; Baldwin, Const., 6,233; Alan Keyes, Amer. Ind., 3,051; McKinney, Green, 2,822; McEnulty, unaff., 829; Jay, Boston Tea, 598; Allen, HeartQuake '08, 348; Stevens, Objectivist, 336; Moore, Soc. USA, 226; La Riva, Socialism/Liberation, 158; Harris, Soc. Workers, 154; Lyttle, U.S. Pacifist, 110; Amondson, Prohib., 85.
2004: Bush, R., 1,101,255; Kerry, D., 1,001,732; Nader, RF., 12,718; Badnarik, LB., 7,664; Peroutka, Amer. Const., 2,562; Cobb, Green, 1,591; Andress, Ind., 804; Amondson, Concerns of People, 378; Van Auken, Soc. Equal., 329; Harris, Soc. Workers, 241; Brown, Soc., 216; Dodge, Prohib., 140.
2000: Bush, R., 883,748; Gore, D., 738,227; Nader, Green, 91,434; Browne, LB., 12,799; Buchanan, RF., 10,465; Hagelin, RF., 2,240; Phillips, Amer. Const., 1,319; McReynolds, Soc., 712; Harris, Soc. Workers, 216; Dodge, Prohib., 208.
1996: Dole, R., 691,848; Clinton, D., 671,152; Perot, RF., 99,629; Nader, Green, 25,070; Browne, LB., 12,392; Phillips, Amer. Const., 2,813; Collins, Ind., 2,809; Hagelin, Natural Law, 2,547; Hollis, Soc., 669; Moorehead, Workers World, 599; Templin, Amer., 557; Dodge, Prohib., 375; Harris, Soc. Workers, 244.
1992: Clinton, D., 629,681; Bush, R., 562,850; Perot, Ind., 366,010; Marrou, LB., 8,669; Fulani, New Alliance, 1,608.
1988: Bush, R., 728,177; Dukakis, D., 621,453; Paul, LB., 15,482; Dodge, Prohib., 4,604.
1984: Reagan, R., 821,817; Mondale, D., 454,975; Bergland, LB., 11,257.
1980: Reagan, R., 652,264; Carter, D., 367,973; Anderson, Ind., 130,633; Clark, LB., 25,744; Commoner, Citizens, 5,614; Bubar, Statesman, 1,180; Pulley, Soc., 520; Hall, Comm., 487.
1976: Ford, R., 584,367; Carter, D., 460,353; McCarthy, Ind., 26,107; MacBride, LB., 5,330; Bubar, Prohib., 2,882.
1972: Nixon, R., 597,189; McGovern, D., 329,980; Schmitz, Amer., 17,269; Fisher, Soc. Labor, 4,361; Spock, People's, 2,403; Hospers, LB., 1,111; Jenness, Soc. Workers, 555; Munn, Prohib., 467; Hall, Comm., 432.

1968: Nixon, R., 409,345; Humphrey, D., 335,174; Wallace, 3rd party, 60,813; Blomen, Soc. Labor, 3,016; Gregory, New Party, 1,393; Munn, Prohib., 275; Halstead, Soc. Workers, 235.
1964: Johnson, D., 476,024; Goldwater, R., 296,767; DeBerry, Soc. Workers, 2,537; Munn, Prohib., 1,356; Hass, Soc. Labor, 302.
1960: Nixon, R., 402,242; Kennedy, D., 330,629; Hass, Soc. Labor, 2,803; Dobbs, Soc. Workers, 572.
1956: Eisenhower, R., 394,479; Stevenson, D., 263,997; Hass, Soc. Labor, 3,308; Andrews, Ind., 759; Hoopes, Soc., 531.
1952: Eisenhower, R., 379,782; Stevenson, D., 245,504; MacArthur, Const., 2,181; Hallinan, Prog., 1,919; Hoopes, Soc., 365; Hass, Soc. Labor, 352.

Connecticut Vote Since 1952

2008: Obama, D., 997,772; McCain, R., 629,428; Nader, Ind., 19,162.
2004: Kerry, D., 857,488; Bush, R., 693,826; Nader, petitioning cand., 12,969; Cobb, Green, 9,564; Badnarik, LB., 3,367; Peroutka, Concerned Citizens, 1,543.
2000: Gore, D., 816,015; Bush, R., 561,094; Nader, Green, 64,452; Phillips, Concerned Citizens, 9,695; Buchanan, RF., 4,731; Browne, LB., 3,484.
1996: Clinton, D., 735,740; Dole, R., 483,109; Perot, RF., 139,523; Nader, Green, 24,321; Browne, LB., 5,788; Phillips, Concerned Citizens, 2,425; Hagelin, Natural Law, 1,703.
1992: Clinton, D., 682,318; Bush, R., 578,313; Perot, Ind., 348,771; Marrou, LB., 5,391; Fulani, New Alliance, 1,363.
1988: Bush, R., 750,241; Dukakis, D., 676,584; Paul, LB., 14,071; Fulani, New Alliance, 2,491.
1984: Reagan, R., 890,877; Mondale, D., 569,597.
1980: Reagan, R., 677,210; Carter, D., 541,732; Anderson, Ind., 171,807; Clark, LB., 8,570; Commoner, Citizens, 6,130; scattered, 836.
1976: Ford, R., 719,261; Carter, D., 647,895; Maddox, George Wallace Party, 7,101; LaRouche, U.S. Labor, 1,789.
1972: Nixon, R., 810,763; McGovern, D., 555,498; Schmitz, Amer., 17,239; scattered, 777.
1968: Humphrey, D., 621,561; Nixon, R., 556,721; Wallace, 3rd party, 76,650; scattered, 1,300.
1964: Johnson, D., 826,269; Goldwater, R., 390,996; scattered, 1,313.
1960: Kennedy, D., 657,055; Nixon, R., 565,813.
1956: Eisenhower, R., 711,837; Stevenson, D., 405,079; scattered, 205.
1952: Eisenhower, R., 611,012; Stevenson, D., 481,649; Hoopes, Soc., 2,244; Hallinan, Prog., 1,466; Hass, Soc. Labor, 535; write-in, 5.

Delaware Vote Since 1952

2008: Obama, D., 255,459; McCain, R., 152,374; Nader, Ind. (DE), 2,401; Barr, LB., 1,109; Baldwin, Const., 626; McKinney, Green, 385; Calero, Soc. Workers, 58.
2004: Kerry, D., 200,152; Bush, R., 171,660; Nader, Ind., 2,153; Badnarik, LB., 586; Peroutka, Const., 289; Cobb, Green, 250; Brown, Natural Law, 100.
2000: Gore, D., 180,068; Bush, R., 137,288; Nader, Green, 8,307; Buchanan, RF., 777; Browne, LB., 774; Phillips, Const., 208; Hagelin, Natural Law, 107.
1996: Clinton, D., 140,355; Dole, R., 99,062; Perot, RF., 28,719; Browne, LB., 2,052; Phillips, U.S. Taxpayers, 348; Hagelin, Natural Law, 274.
1992: Clinton, D., 126,054; Bush, R., 102,313; Perot, Ind., 59,213; Fulani, New Alliance, 1,105.
1988: Bush, R., 139,639; Dukakis, D., 108,647; Paul, LB., 1,162; Fulani, New Alliance, 443.
1984: Reagan, R., 152,190; Mondale, D., 101,656; Bergland, LB., 268.
1980: Reagan, R., 111,252; Carter, D., 105,754; Anderson, Ind., 16,288; Clark, LB., 1,974; Greaves, Amer., 400.
1976: Carter, D., 122,596; Ford, R., 109,831; McCarthy, nonpartisan, 2,437; Anderson, Amer., 645; LaRouche, U.S. Labor, 136; Bubar, Prohib., 103; Levin, Soc. Labor, 86.
1972: Nixon, R., 140,357; McGovern, D., 92,283; Schmitz, Amer., 2,638; Munn, Prohib., 238.
1968: Nixon, R., 96,714; Humphrey, D., 89,194; Wallace, 3rd party, 28,459.
1964: Johnson, D., 122,704; Goldwater, R., 78,078; Munn, Prohib., 425; Hass, Soc. Labor, 113.
1960: Kennedy, D., 99,590; Nixon, R., 96,373; Faubus, States' Rights, 354; Decker, Prohib., 284; Hass, Soc. Labor, 82.
1956: Eisenhower, R., 98,057; Stevenson, D., 79,421; Oltwick, Prohib., 400; Hass, Soc. Labor, 110.

1952: Eisenhower, R., 90,059; Stevenson, D., 83,315; Hass, Soc. Lab., 242; Hamblen, Prohib., 234; Hallinan, Prog., 155; Hoopes, Soc., 20.

District of Columbia Vote Since 1964

2008: Obama, D., 245,800; McCain, R., 17,367; Nader, Ind., 958; McKinney, Green, 590.

2004: Kerry, D., 202,970; Bush, R., 21,256; Nader, Ind., 1,485; Cobb, DC Statehood Green, 737; Badnarik, LB., 502; Harris, Soc. Workers, 130.

2000: Gore, D., 171,923; Bush, R., 18,073; Nader, Green, 10,576; Browne, LB., 669; Harris, Soc. Workers, 114.

1996: Clinton, D., 158,220; Dole, R., 17,339; Nader, Green, 4,780; Perot, RF., 3,611; Browne, LB., 588; Hagelin, Natural Law, 283; Harris, Soc. Workers, 257.

1992: Clinton, D., 192,619; Bush, R., 20,698; Perot, Ind., 9,681; Fulani, New Alliance, 1,459; Daniels, Ind., 1,186.

1988: Dukakis, D., 159,407; Bush, R., 27,590; Fulani, New Alliance, 2,901; Paul, LB., 554.

1984: Mondale, D., 180,408; Reagan, R., 29,009; Bergland, LB., 279.

1980: Carter, D., 130,231; Reagan, R., 23,313; Anderson, Ind., 16,131; Commoner, Citizens, 1,826; Clark, LB., 1,104; Hall, Comm., 369; DeBerry, Soc. Workers, 173; Griswold, Workers World, 52; write-in, 690.

1976: Carter, D., 137,818; Ford, R., 27,873; Camejo, Soc. Workers, 545; MacBride, LB., 274; Hall, Comm., 219; LaRouche, U.S. Labor, 157.

1972: McGovern, D., 127,627; Nixon, R., 35,226; Reed, Soc. Workers, 316; Hall, Comm., 252.

1968: Humphrey, D., 139,566; Nixon, R., 31,012.

1964: Johnson, D., 169,796; Goldwater, R., 28,801.

Florida Vote Since 1952

2008: Obama, D., 4,282,074; McCain, R., 4,045,624; Nader, Ecology (FL), 28,124; Barr, LB., 17,218; Baldwin, Const., 7,915; McKinney, Green, 2,887; Keyes, Amer. Ind., 2,550; La Riva, Socialism/Liberation, 1,516; Jay, Boston Tea, 795; Harris, Soc. Workers, 533; Stevens, Objectivist, 419; Moore, Soc. USA, 405; Amondson, Prohib., 293.

2004: Bush, R., 3,964,522; Kerry, D., 3,583,544; Nader, RF., 32,971; Badnarik, LB., 11,996; Peroutka, Const., 6,626; Cobb, Green, 3,917; Brown, Soc., 3,502; Harris, Soc. Workers, 2,732.

2000: Bush, R., 2,912,790; Gore, D., 2,912,253; Nader, Green, 97,488; Buchanan, RF., 17,484; Browne, LB., 16,415; Hagelin, Natural Law, 2,281; Moorehead, Workers World, 1,804; Phillips, Const., 1,371; McReynolds, Soc., 622; Harris, Soc. Workers, 562.

1996: Clinton, D., 2,545,968; Dole, R., 2,243,324; Perot, RF., 483,776; Browne, LB., 23,312.

1992: Bush, R., 2,171,781; Clinton, D., 2,071,651; Perot, Ind., 1,052,481; Marrou, LB., 15,068.

1988: Bush, R., 2,616,597; Dukakis, D., 1,655,851; Paul, LB., 19,796, Fulani, New Alliance, 6,655.

1984: Reagan, R., 2,728,775; Mondale, D., 1,448,344.

1980: Reagan, R., 2,046,951; Carter, D., 1,419,475; Anderson, Ind., 189,692; Clark, LB., 30,524; write-in, 285.

1976: Carter, D., 1,636,000; Ford, R., 1,469,531; McCarthy, Ind., 23,643; Anderson, Amer., 21,325.

1972: Nixon, R., 1,857,759; McGovern, D., 718,117; scattered, 7,407.

1968: Nixon, R., 886,804; Humphrey, D., 676,794; Wallace, 3rd party, 624,207.

1964: Johnson, D., 948,540; Goldwater, R., 905,941.

1960: Nixon, R., 795,476; Kennedy, D., 748,700.

1956: Eisenhower, R., 643,849; Stevenson, D., 480,371.

1952: Eisenhower, R., 544,036; Stevenson, D., 444,950; scattered, 351.

Georgia Vote Since 1952

2008: McCain, R., 2,048,759; Obama, D., 1,844,123; Barr, LB., 28,731.

2004: Bush, R., 1,914,254; Kerry, D., 1,366,149; Badnarik, LB., 18,387.

2000: Bush, R., 1,419,720; Gore, D., 1,116,230; Browne, LB., 36,332; Buchanan, Ind., 10,926.

1996: Dole, R., 1,080,843; Clinton, D., 1,053,849; Perot, RF., 146,337; Browne, LB., 17,870.

1992: Clinton, D., 1,008,966; Bush, R., 995,252; Perot, Ind., 309,657; Marrou, LB., 7,110.

1988: Bush, R., 1,081,331; Dukakis, D., 714,792; Paul, LB., 8,435; Fulani, New Alliance, 5,099.

1984: Reagan, R., 1,068,722; Mondale, D., 706,628.

1980: Carter, D., 890,955; Reagan, R., 654,168; Anderson, Ind., 36,055; Clark, LB., 15,627.

1976: Carter, D., 979,409; Ford, R., 483,743; write-in, 4,306.

1972: Nixon, R., 881,496; McGovern, D., 289,529; Schmitz, Amer., 812; scattered, 2,935.

1968: Wallace, 3rd party, 535,550; Nixon, R., 380,111; Humphrey, D., 334,440; write-in, 162.

1964: Goldwater, R., 616,600; Johnson, D., 522,557.

1960: Kennedy, D., 458,638; Nixon, R., 274,472; write-in, 239.

1956: Stevenson, D., 444,388; Eisenhower, R., 222,778; Andrews, write-in, 1,754.

1952: Stevenson, D., 456,823; Eisenhower, R., 198,979; Liberty Party, 1.

Hawaii Vote Since 1960

2008: Obama, D., 325,871; McCain, R., 120,566; Nader, Ind. (HI), 3,825; Barr, LB., 1,314; Baldwin, Const., 1,013; McKinney, Green, 979.

2004: Kerry, D., 231,708; Bush, R., 194,191; Cobb, Green, 1,737; Badnarik, LB., 1,377.

2000: Gore, D., 205,286; Bush, R., 137,845; Nader, Green, 21,623; Browne, LB., 1,477; Buchanan, RF., 1,071; Phillips, Const., 343; Hagelin, Natural Law, 306.

1996: Clinton, D., 205,012; Dole, R., 113,943; Perot, RF., 27,358; Nader, Green, 10,386; Browne, LB., 2,493; Hagelin, Natural Law, 570; Phillips, Taxpayers, 358.

1992: Clinton, D., 179,310; Bush, R., 136,822; Perot, Ind., 53,003; Gritz, Populist/America First, 1,452; Marrou, LB., 1,119.

1988: Dukakis, D., 192,364; Bush, R., 158,625; Paul, LB., 1,999; Fulani, New Alliance, 1,003.

1984: Reagan, R., 184,934; Mondale, D., 147,098; Bergland, LB., 2,167.

1980: Carter, D., 135,879; Reagan, R., 130,112; Anderson, Ind., 32,021; Clark, LB., 3,269; Commoner, Citizens, 1,548; Hall, Comm., 458.

1976: Carter, D., 147,375; Ford, R., 140,003; MacBride, LB., 3,923.

1972: Nixon, R., 168,865; McGovern, D., 101,409.

1968: Humphrey, D., 141,324; Nixon, R., 91,425; Wallace, 3rd party, 3,469.

1964: Johnson, D., 163,249; Goldwater, R., 44,022.

1960: Kennedy, D., 92,410; Nixon, R., 92,295.

Idaho Vote Since 1952

2008: McCain, R., 403,012; Obama, D., 236,440; Nader, Ind., 7,175; Baldwin, Const., 4,747; Barr, LB., 3,658.

2004: Bush, R., 409,235; Kerry, D., 181,098; Badnarik, LB., 3,844; Peroutka, Const., 3,084.

2000: Bush, R., 336,937; Gore, D., 138,637; Buchanan, RF., 7,615; Browne, LB., 3,488; Phillips, Const., 1,469; Hagelin, Natural Law, 1,177.

1996: Dole, R., 256,595; Clinton, D., 165,443; Perot, RF., 62,518; Browne, LB., 3,325; Phillips, U.S. Taxpayers, 2,230; Hagelin, Natural Law, 1,600.

1992: Bush, R., 202,645; Clinton, D., 137,013; Perot, Ind., 130,395; Gritz, Populist/America First, 10,281; Marrou, LB., 1,167.

1988: Bush, R., 253,881; Dukakis, D., 147,272; Paul, LB., 5,313; Fulani, Ind., 2,502.

1984: Reagan, R., 297,523; Mondale, D., 108,510; Bergland, LB., 2,823.

1980: Reagan, R., 290,699; Carter, D., 110,192; Anderson, Ind., 27,058; Clark, LB., 8,425; Rarick, Amer., 1,057.

1976: Ford, R., 204,151; Carter, D., 126,549; Maddox, Amer., 5,935; MacBride, LB., 3,558; LaRouche, U.S. Labor, 739.

1972: Nixon, R., 199,384; McGovern, D., 80,826; Schmitz, Amer., 28,869; Spock, People's, 903.

1968: Nixon, R., 165,369; Humphrey, D., 89,273; Wallace, 3rd party, 36,541.

1964: Johnson, D., 148,920; Goldwater, R., 143,557.

1960: Nixon, R., 161,597; Kennedy, D., 138,853.

1956: Eisenhower, R., 166,979; Stevenson, D., 105,868; Andrews, Ind., 126; write-in, 16.

1952: Eisenhower, R., 180,707; Stevenson, D., 95,081; Hallinan, Prog., 443; write-in, 23.

Illinois Vote Since 1952

2008: Obama, D., 3,419,348; McCain, R., 2,031,179; Nader, Ind., 30,948; Barr, LB., 19,642; McKinney, Green, 11,838; Baldwin, Const., 8,256; Polachek, New Party, 1,149.

2004: Kerry, D., 2,891,550; Bush, R., 2,345,946; Badnarik, LB., 32,442.

2000: Gore, D., 2,589,026; Bush, R., 2,019,421; Nader, Green, 103,759; Buchanan, Ind., 16,106; Browne, LB., 11,623; Hagelin, RF., 2,127.
1996: Clinton, D., 2,341,744; Dole, R., 1,587,021; Perot, RF., 346,408; Browne, LB., 22,548; Phillips, U.S. Taxpayers, 7,606; Hagelin, Natural Law, 4,606.
1992: Clinton, D., 2,453,350; Bush, R., 1,734,096; Perot, Ind., 840,515; Marrou, LB., 9,218; Fulani, New Alliance, 5,267; Gritz, Populist/America First, 3,577; Hagelin, Natural Law, 2,751; Warren, Soc. Workers, 1,361.
1988: Bush, R., 2,310,939; Dukakis, D., 2,215,940; Paul, LB., 14,944; Fulani, Solidarity, 10,276.
1984: Reagan, R., 2,707,103; Mondale, D., 2,086,499; Bergland, LB., 10,086.
1980: Reagan, R., 2,358,049; Carter, D., 1,981,413; Anderson, Ind., 346,754; Clark, LB., 38,939; Commoner, Citizens, 10,692; Hall, Comm., 9,711; Griswold, Workers World, 2,257; DeBerry, Soc. Workers, 1,302; write-in, 604.
1976: Ford, R., 2,364,269; Carter, D., 2,271,295; McCarthy, Ind., 55,939; Hall, Comm., 9,250; MacBride, LB., 8,057; Camejo, Soc. Workers, 3,615; Levin, Soc. Labor, 2,422; LaRouche, U.S. Labor, 2,018; write-in, 1,968.
1972: Nixon, R. 2,788,179; McGovern, D., 1,913,472; Fisher, Soc. Labor, 12,344; Hall, Comm., 4,541; Schmitz, Amer., 2,471; others, 2,229.
1968: Nixon, R., 2,174,774; Humphrey, D., 2,039,814; Wallace, 3rd party, 390,958; Blomen, Soc. Labor, 13,878; write-in, 325.
1964: Johnson, D., 2,796,833; Goldwater, R., 1,905,946; write-in, 62.
1960: Kennedy, D., 2,377,846; Nixon, R., 2,368,988; Hass, Soc. Labor, 10,560; write-in, 15.
1956: Eisenhower, R., 2,623,327; Stevenson, D., 1,775,682; Hass, Soc. Labor, 8,342; write-in, 56.
1952: Eisenhower, R., 2,457,327; Stevenson, D., 2,013,920; Hass, Soc. Labor, 9,363; write-in, 448.

Indiana Vote Since 1952

2008: Obama, D., 1,374,039; McCain, R., 1,345,648; Barr, LB., 29,257.
2004: Bush, R., 1,479,438; Kerry, D., 969,011; Badnarik, LB., 18,058.
2000: Bush, R., 1,245,836; Gore, D., 901,980; Buchanan, Ind., 16,959; Browne, LB., 15,530.
1996: Dole, R., 1,006,693; Clinton, D., 887,424; Perot, RF., 224,299; Browne, LB., 15,632.
1992: Bush, R., 989,375; Clinton, D., 848,420; Perot, Ind., 455,934; Marrou, LB., 7,936; Fulani, New Alliance, 2,583.
1988: Bush, R., 1,297,763; Dukakis, D., 860,643; Fulani, New Alliance, 10,215.
1984: Reagan, R., 1,377,230; Mondale, D., 841,481; Bergland, LB., 6,741.
1980: Reagan, R., 1,255,656; Carter, D., 844,197; Anderson, Ind.,111,639; Clark, LB., 19,627; Commoner, Citizens, 4,852; Greaves, Amer., 4,750; Hall, Comm., 702; DeBerry, Soc., 610.
1976: Ford, R., 1,185,958; Carter, D., 1,014,714; Anderson, Amer., 14,048; Camejo, Soc. Workers, 5,695; LaRouche, U.S. Labor, 1,947.
1972: Nixon, R., 1,405,154; McGovern, D., 708,568; Reed, Soc. Workers, 5,575; Spock, Peace/Freedom, 4,544; Fisher, Soc. Labor, 1,688.
1968: Nixon, R., 1,067,885; Humphrey, D., 806,659; Wallace, 3rd party, 243,108; Munn, Prohib., 4,616; Halstead, Soc. Workers, 1,293; Gregory, write-in, 36.
1964: Johnson, D., 1,170,848; Goldwater, R., 911,118; Munn, Prohib., 8,266; Hass, Soc. Labor, 1,374.
1960: Nixon, R., 1,175,120; Kennedy, D., 952,358; Decker, Prohib., 6,746; Hass, Soc. Labor, 1,136.
1956: Eisenhower, R., 1,182,811; Stevenson, D., 783,908; Holtwick, Prohib., 6,554; Hass, Soc. Labor, 1,334.
1952: Eisenhower, R., 1,136,259; Stevenson, D., 801,530; Hamblen, Prohib., 15,335; Hallinan, Prog., 1,222; Hass, Soc. Labor, 979.

Iowa Vote Since 1952

2008: Obama, D., 828,940; McCain, R., 682,379; Nader, Peace/Freedom, 8,014; Barr, LB., 4,590; Baldwin, Const., 4,445; McKinney, Green, 1,423; Harris, Soc. Workers, 292; Moore, Soc. USA, 182; La Riva, Socialism/Liberation, 121.
2004: Bush, R., 751,957; Kerry, D., 741,898; Nader, petitioning cand., 5,973; Badnarik, LB., 2,992; Peroutka, Const., 1,304; Cobb, Green, 1,141; Harris, Soc. Workers, 373; Van Auken, petitioning cand., 176.

2000: Gore, D., 638,517; Bush, R., 634,373; Nader, Green, 29,374; Buchanan, RF., 5,731; Browne, LB., 3,209; Hagelin, Ind., 2,281; Phillips, Const., 613; Harris, Soc. Workers, 190; McReynolds, Soc., 107.
1996: Clinton, D., 620,258; Dole, R., 492,644; Perot, RF., 105,159; Nader, Green, 6,550; Hagelin, Natural Law, 3,349; Browne, LB., 2,315; Phillips, Taxpayers, 2,229; Harris, Soc. Workers, 331.
1992: Clinton, D., 586,353; Bush, R., 504,891; Perot, Ind., 253,468; Hagelin, Natural Law, 3,079; Gritz, Populist/America First, 1,177; Marrou, LB., 1,076.
1988: Dukakis, D., 670,557; Bush, R., 545,355; LaRouche, Ind., 3,526; Paul, LB., 2,494.
1984: Reagan, R., 703,088; Mondale, D., 605,620; Bergland, LB., 1,844.
1980: Reagan, R., 676,026; Carter, D., 508,672; Anderson, Ind., 115,633; Clark, LB., 13,123; Commoner, Citizens, 2,273; McReynolds, Soc., 534; Hall, Comm., 298; DeBerry, Soc. Workers, 244; Greaves, Amer., 189; Bubar, Statesman, 150; scattered, 519.
1976: Ford, R., 632,863; Carter, D., 619,931; McCarthy, Ind., 20,051; Anderson, Amer., 3,040; MacBride, LB., 1,452.
1972: Nixon, R., 706,207; McGovern, D., 496,206; Schmitz, Amer., 22,056; Jenness, Soc. Workers, 488; Hall, Comm., 272; Green, Universal, 199; Fisher, Soc. Labor, 195; scattered, 321.
1968: Nixon, R., 619,106; Humphrey, D., 476,699; Wallace, 3rd party, 66,422; Halstead, Soc. Workers, 3,377; Cleaver, Peace/Freedom, 1,332; Munn, Prohib., 362; Blomen, Soc. Labor, 241.
1964: Johnson, D., 733,030; Goldwater, R., 449,148; Munn, Prohib., 1,902; Hass, Soc. Labor, 182; DeBerry, Soc. Workers, 159.
1960: Nixon, R., 722,381; Kennedy, D., 550,565; Hass, Soc. Labor, 230; write-in, 634.
1956: Eisenhower, R., 729,187; Stevenson, D., 501,858; Andrews (A.C.P. of IA), 3,202; Hoopes, Soc., 192; Hass, Soc. Labor, 125.
1952: Eisenhower, R., 808,906; Stevenson, D., 451,513; Hallinan, Prog., 5,085; Hamblen, Prohib., 2,882; Hoopes, Soc., 219; Hass, Soc. Labor, 139; scattered, 29.

Kansas Vote Since 1952

2008: McCain, R., 699,655; Obama, D., 514,765; Nader, Ind., 10,527; Barr, LB., 6,706; Baldwin, RF., 4,148.
2004: Bush, R., 736,456; Kerry, D., 434,993; Nader, RF., 9,348; Badnarik, LB., 4,013; Peroutka, Ind., 2,899.
2000: Bush, R., 622,332; Gore, D., 399,276; Nader, Ind., 36,086; Buchanan, RF., 7,370; Browne, LB., 4,525; Hagelin, Ind., 1,373; Phillips, Const., 1,254.
1996: Dole, R., 583,245; Clinton, D., 387,659; Perot, RF., 92,639; Browne, LB., 4,557; Phillips, Ind., 3,519; Hagelin, Ind., 1,655.
1992: Bush, R., 449,951; Clinton, D., 390,434; Perot, Ind., 312,358; Marrou, LB., 4,314.
1988: Bush, R., 554,049; Dukakis, D., 422,636; Paul, Ind., 12,553; Fulani, Ind., 3,806.
1984: Reagan, R., 674,646; Mondale, D., 332,471; Bergland, LB., 3,585.
1980: Reagan, R., 566,812; Carter, D., 326,150; Anderson, Ind., 68,231; Clark, LB., 14,470; Shelton, Amer., 1,555; Hall, Comm., 967; Bubar, Statesman, 821; Rarick, Conservative, 789.
1976: Ford, R., 502,752; Carter, D., 430,421; McCarthy, Ind., 13,185; Anderson, Amer., 4,724; MacBride, LB., 3,242; Maddox, Conservative, 2,118; Bubar, Prohib., 1,403.
1972: Nixon, R., 619,812; McGovern, D., 270,287; Schmitz, Conservative, 21,808; Munn, Prohib., 4,188.
1968: Nixon, R., 478,674; Humphrey, D., 302,996; Wallace, 3rd party, 88,921; Munn, Prohib., 2,192.
1964: Johnson, D., 464,028; Goldwater, R., 386,579; Munn, Prohib., 5,393; Hass, Soc. Labor, 1,901.
1960: Nixon, R., 561,474; Kennedy, D., 363,213; Decker, Prohib., 4,138.
1956: Eisenhower, R., 566,878; Stevenson, D., 296,317; Holtwick, Prohib., 3,048.
1952: Eisenhower, R., 616,302; Stevenson, D., 273,296; Hamblen, Prohib., 6,038; Hoopes, Soc., 530.

Kentucky Vote Since 1952

2008: McCain, R., 1,048,462; Obama, D., 751,985; Nader, Ind., 15,378; Barr, LB., 5,989; Baldwin, Const., 4,694.
2004: Bush, R., 1,069,439; Kerry, D., 712,733; Nader, Ind., 8,856; Badnarik, LB., 2,619; Peroutka, Const., 2,213.

2000: Bush, R., 872,520; Gore, D., 638,923; Nader, Green, 23,118; Buchanan, RF., 4,152; Browne, LB., 2,885; Hagelin, Natural Law, 1,513; Phillips, Const., 915.
1996: Clinton, D., 636,614; Dole, R., 623,283; Perot, RF., 120,396; Browne, LB., 4,009; Phillips, U.S. Taxpayers, 2,204; Hagelin, Natural Law, 1,493.
1992: Clinton, D., 665,104; Bush, R., 617,178; Perot, Ind., 203,944; Marrou, LB., 4,513.
1988: Bush, R., 734,281; Dukakis, D., 580,368; Duke, Populist, 4,494; Paul, LB., 2,118.
1984: Reagan, R., 815,345; Mondale, D., 536,756.
1980: Reagan, R., 635,274; Carter, D., 616,417; Anderson, Ind., 31,127; Clark, LB., 5,531; McCormack, Respect for Life, 4,233; Commoner, Citizens, 1,304; Pulley, Soc., 393; Hall, Comm., 348.
1976: Carter, D., 615,717; Ford, R., 531,852; Anderson, Amer., 8,308; McCarthy, Ind., 6,837; Maddox, Amer. Ind., 2,328; MacBride, LB., 814.
1972: Nixon, R., 676,446; McGovern, D., 371,159; Schmitz, Amer., 17,627; Spock, People's, 1,118; Jenness, Soc. Workers, 685; Hall, Comm., 464.
1968: Nixon, R., 462,411; Humphrey, D., 397,547; Wallace, 3rd party, 193,098; Halstead, Soc. Workers, 2,843.
1964: Johnson, D., 669,659; Goldwater, R., 372,977; Kasper, Natl. States' Rights, 3,469.
1960: Nixon, R., 602,607; Kennedy, D., 521,855.
1956: Eisenhower, R., 572,192; Stevenson, D., 476,453; Byrd, States' Rights, 2,657; Holtwick, Prohib., 2,145; Hass, Soc. Labor, 358.
1952: Stevenson, D., 495,729; Eisenhower, R., 495,029; Hamblen, Prohib., 1,161; Hass, Soc. Labor, 893; Hallinan, Prog., 336.

Louisiana Vote Since 1952

2008: McCain, R., 1,148,275; Obama, D., 782,989; Paul, LA Taxpayers, 9,368; McKinney, Green, 9,187; Nader, Ind., 6,997; Baldwin, Const., 2,581; Harris, Soc. Workers, 735; La Riva, Socialism/Liberation, 354; Amondson, Prohib., 275.
2004: Bush, R., 1,102,169; Kerry, D., 820,299; Nader, Better Life, 7,032; Peroutka, Const., 5,203; Badnarik, LB., 2,781; Brown, Protect Working Fam., 1,795; Amondson, Prohib., 1,566; Cobb, Green, 1,276; Harris, Soc. Workers, 985.
2000: Bush, R., 927,871; Gore, D., 792,344; Nader, Green, 20,473; Buchanan, RF., 14,356; Phillips, Const., 5,483; Browne, LB., 2,951; Harris, Soc. Workers, 1,103; Hagelin, Natural Law, 1,075.
1996: Clinton, D., 927,837; Dole, R., 712,586; Perot, RF., 123,293; Browne, LB., 7,499; Nader, Liberty, Ecology, Community, 4,719; Phillips, U.S. Taxpayers, 3,366; Hagelin, Natural Law, 2,981; Moorehead, Workers World, 1,678.
1992: Clinton, D., 815,971; Bush, R., 733,386; Perot, Ind., 211,478; Gritz, Populist/America First, 18,545; Marrou, LB., 3,155; Daniels, Ind., 1,663; Phillips, U.S. Taxpayers, 1,552; Fulani, New Alliance, 1,434; LaRouche, Ind., 1,136.
1988: Bush, R., 883,702; Dukakis, D., 717,460; Duke, Populist, 18,612; Paul, LB., 4,115.
1984: Reagan, R., 1,037,299; Mondale, D., 651,586; Bergland, LB., 1,876.
1980: Reagan, R., 792,853; Carter, D., 708,453; Anderson, Ind., 26,345; Rarick, Amer. Ind., 10,333; Clark, LB., 8,240; Commoner, Citizens, 1,584; DeBerry, Soc. Work., 783.
1976: Carter, D., 661,365; Ford, R., 587,446; Maddox, Amer., 10,058; Hall, Comm., 7,417; McCarthy, Ind., 6,588; MacBride, LB., 3,325.
1972: Nixon, R., 686,852; McGovern, D., 298,142; Schmitz, Amer., 52,099; Jenness, Soc. Workers, 14,398.
1968: Wallace, 3rd party, 530,300; Humphrey, D., 309,615; Nixon, R., 257,535.
1964: Goldwater, R., 509,225; Johnson, D., 387,068.
1960: Kennedy, D., 407,339; Nixon, R., 230,890; States' Rights (unpledged), 169,572.
1956: Eisenhower, R., 329,047; Stevenson, D., 243,977; Andrews, States' Rights, 44,520.
1952: Stevenson, D., 345,027; Eisenhower, R., 306,925.

Maine Vote Since 1952

2008: Obama, D., 421,923; McCain, R., 295,273; Nader, Ind., 10,636; McKinney, Green, 2,900.
2004: Kerry, D., 396,842; Bush, R., 330,201; Nader, Better Life, 8,069; Cobb, Green, 2,936; Badnarik, LB., 1,965; Peroutka, Const., 735.
2000: Gore, D., 319,951; Bush, R., 286,616; Nader, Green, 37,127; Buchanan, RF., 4,443; Browne, LB., 3,074; Phillips, Const., 579.

1996: Clinton, D., 312,788; Dole, R., 186,378; Perot, RF., 85,970; Nader, Green, 15,279; Browne, LB., 2,996; Phillips, Taxpayers, 1,517; Hagelin, Natural Law, 825.
1992: Clinton, D., 263,420; Perot, Ind., 206,820; Bush, R., 206,504; Marrou, LB., 1,681.
1988: Bush, R., 307,131; Dukakis, D., 243,569; Paul, LB., 2,700; Fulani, New Alliance, 1,405.
1984: Reagan, R., 336,500; Mondale, D., 214,515.
1980: Reagan, R., 238,522; Carter, D., 220,974; Anderson, Ind., 53,327; Clark, LB., 5,119; Commoner, Citizens, 4,394; Hall, Comm., 591; write-in, 84.
1976: Ford, R., 236,320; Carter, D., 232,279; McCarthy, Ind., 10,874; Bubar, Prohib., 3,495.
1972: Nixon, R., 256,458; McGovern, D., 160,584; scattered, 229.
1968: Humphrey, D., 217,312; Nixon, R., 169,254; Wallace, 3rd party, 6,370.
1964: Johnson, D., 262,264; Goldwater, R., 118,701.
1960: Nixon, R., 240,608; Kennedy, D., 181,159.
1956: Eisenhower, R., 249,238; Stevenson, D., 102,468.
1952: Eisenhower, R., 232,353; Stevenson, D., 118,806; Hallinan, Prog., 332; Hass, Soc. Labor, 156; Hoopes, Soc., 138; scattered, 1.

Maryland Vote Since 1952

2008: Obama, D., 1,629,467; McCain, R., 959,862; Nader, MD Ind., 14,713; Barr, LB., 9,842; McKinney, Green, 4,747; Baldwin, RF., 3,760.
2004: Kerry, D., 1,334,493; Bush, R., 1,024,703; Nader, Populist, 11,854; Badnarik, LB., 6,094; Cobb, Green, 3,632; Peroutka, Const., 3,421.
2000: Gore, D., 1,144,008; Bush, R., 813,827; Nader, Green, 53,768; Browne, LB., 5,310; Buchanan, RF., 4,248; Phillips, Const., 918.
1996: Clinton, D., 966,207; Dole, R., 681,530; Perot, RF., 115,812; Browne, LB., 8,765; Phillips, Taxpayers, 3,402; Hagelin, Natural Law, 2,517.
1992: Clinton, D., 988,571; Bush, R., 707,094; Perot, Ind., 281,414; Marrou, LB., 4,715; Fulani, New Alliance, 2,786.
1988: Bush, R., 876,167; Dukakis, D., 826,304; Paul, LB., 6,748; Fulani, New Alliance, 5,115.
1984: Reagan, R., 879,918; Mondale, D., 787,935; Bergland, LB., 5,721.
1980: Carter, D., 726,161; Reagan, R., 680,606; Anderson, Ind., 119,537; Clark, LB., 14,192.
1976: Carter, D., 759,612; Ford, R., 672,661.
1972: Nixon, R., 829,305; McGovern, D., 505,781; Schmitz, Amer., 18,726.
1968: Humphrey, D., 538,310; Nixon, R., 517,995; Wallace, 3rd party, 178,734.
1964: Johnson, D., 730,912; Goldwater, R., 385,495; write-in, 50.
1960: Kennedy, D., 565,800; Nixon, R., 489,538.
1956: Eisenhower, R., 559,738; Stevenson, D., 372,613.
1952: Eisenhower, R., 499,424; Stevenson, D., 395,337; Hallinan, Prog., 7,313.

Massachusetts Vote Since 1952

2008: Obama, D., 1,904,097; McCain, R., 1,108,854; Nader, Ind., 28,841; Barr, LB., 13,189; McKinney, Green, 6,550; Baldwin, RF., 4,971.
2004: Kerry, D., 1,803,800; Bush, R., 1,071,109; Badnarik, LB., 15,022; Cobb, Green, 10,623.
2000: Gore, D., 1,616,487; Bush, R., 878,502; Nader, Green, 173,564; Browne, LB., 16,366; Buchanan, RF., 11,149; Hagelin, Natural Law, 2,884.
1996: Clinton, D., 1,571,509; Dole, R., 718,058; Perot, RF., 227,206; Browne, LB., 20,424; Hagelin, Natural Law, 5,183; Moorehead, Workers World, 3,276.
1992: Clinton, D., 1,318,639; Bush, R., 805,039; Perot, Ind., 630,731; Marrou, LB., 9,021; Fulani, New Alliance, 3,172; Phillips, U.S. Taxpayers, 2,218; Hagelin, Natural Law, 1,812; LaRouche, Ind., 1,027.
1988: Dukakis, D., 1,401,415; Bush, R., 1,194,635; Paul, LB., 24,251; Fulani, New Alliance, 9,561.
1984: Reagan, R., 1,310,936; Mondale, D., 1,239,606.
1980: Reagan, R., 1,057,631; Carter, D., 1,053,802; Anderson, Ind., 382,539; Clark, LB., 22,038; DeBerry, Soc. Workers, 3,735; Commoner, Citizens, 2,056; McReynolds, Soc., 62; Bubar, Statesman, 34; Griswold, Workers World, 19; scattered, 2,382.
1976: Carter, D., 1,429,475; Ford, R., 1,030,276; McCarthy, Ind., 65,637; Camejo, Soc. Workers, 8,138; Anderson, Amer., 7,555; LaRouche, U.S. Labor, 4,922; MacBride, LB., 135.

1972: McGovern, D., 1,332,540; Nixon, R., 1,112,078; Jenness, Soc. Workers, 10,600; Schmitz, Amer., 2,877; Fisher, Soc. Labor, 129; Spock, People's, 101; Hall, Comm., 46; Hospers, LB., 43; scattered, 342.
1968: Humphrey, D., 1,469,218; Nixon, R., 766,844; Wallace, 3rd party, 87,088; Blomen, Soc. Labor, 6,180; Munn, Prohib., 2,369; scattered, 53; blank, 25,394.
1964: Johnson, D., 1,786,422; Goldwater, R., 549,727; Hass, Soc. Labor, 4,755; Munn, Prohib., 3,735; scattered, 159; blank, 48,104.
1960: Kennedy, D., 1,487,174; Nixon, R., 976,750; Hass, Soc. Labor, 3,892; Decker, Prohib., 1,633; others, 31; blank and void, 26,024.
1956: Eisenhower, R., 1,393,197; Stevenson, D., 948,190; Hass, Soc. Labor, 5,573; Holtwick, Prohib., 1,205; others, 341.
1952: Eisenhower, R., 1,292,325; Stevenson, D., 1,083,525; Hallinan, Prog., 4,636; Hass, Soc. Labor, 1,957; Hamblen, Prohib., 886; scattered, 69; blank, 41,150.

Michigan Vote Since 1952

2008: Obama, D., 2,872,579; McCain, R., 2,048,639; Nader, Natural Law, 33,085; Barr, LB., 23,716; Baldwin, U.S. Taxpayers, 14,685; McKinney, Green, 8,892.
2004: Kerry, D., 2,479,183; Bush, R., 2,313,746; Nader, Ind., 24,035; Badnarik, LB., 10,552; Cobb, Green, 5,325; Peroutka, U.S. Taxpayers, 4,980; Brown, Natural Law, 1,431.
2000: Gore, D., 2,170,418; Bush, R., 1,953,139; Nader, Green, 84,165; Browne, LB., 16,711; Phillips, U.S. Taxpayers, 3,791; Hagelin, Natural Law, 2,426.
1996: Clinton, D., 1,989,653; Dole, R., 1,481,212; Perot, RF., 336,670; Browne, LB., 27,670; Hagelin, Natural Law, 4,254; Moorehead, Workers World, 3,153; White, Soc. Equality, 1,554.
1992: Clinton, D., 1,871,182; Bush, R., 1,554,940; Perot, Ind., 824,813; Marrou, LB., 10,175; Phillips, U.S. Taxpayers, 8,263; Hagelin, Natural Law, 2,954.
1988: Bush, R., 1,965,486; Dukakis, D., 1,675,783; Paul, LB., 18,336; Fulani, Ind., 2,513.
1984: Reagan, R., 2,251,571; Mondale, D., 1,529,638; Bergland, LB., 10,055.
1980: Reagan, R., 1,915,225; Carter, D., 1,661,532; Anderson, Ind., 275,223; Clark, LB., 41,597; Commoner, Citizens, 11,930; Hall, Comm., 3,262; Griswold, Workers World, 30; Greaves, Amer., 21; Bubar, Statesman, 9.
1976: Ford, R., 1,893,742; Carter, D., 1,696,714; McCarthy, Ind., 47,905; MacBride, LB., 5,406; Wright, People's, 3,504; Camejo, Soc. Workers, 1,804; LaRouche, U.S. Labor, 1,366; Levin, Soc. Labor, 1,148; scattered, 2,160.
1972: Nixon, R., 1,961,721; McGovern, D., 1,459,435; Schmitz, Amer., 63,321; Fisher, Soc. Labor, 2,437; Jenness, Soc. Workers, 1,603; Hall, Comm., 1,210.
1968: Humphrey, D., 1,593,082; Nixon, R., 1,370,665; Wallace, 3rd party, 331,968; Halstead, Soc. Workers, 4,099; Blomen, Soc. Labor, 1,762; Cleaver, New Politics, 4,585; Munn, Prohib., 60; scattered, 29.
1964: Johnson, D., 2,136,615; Goldwater, R., 1,060,152; DeBerry, Soc. Workers, 3,817; Hass, Soc. Labor, 1,704; Prohib. (no candidate listed), 699; scattered, 145.
1960: Kennedy, D., 1,687,269; Nixon, R., 1,620,428; Dobbs, Soc. Workers, 4,347; Decker, Prohib., 2,029; Daly, Tax Cut, 1,767; Hass, Soc. Labor, 1,718; Ind. Amer. (unpledged), 539.
1956: Eisenhower, R., 1,713,647; Stevenson, D., 1,359,898; Holtwick, Prohib., 6,923.
1952: Eisenhower, R., 1,551,529; Stevenson, D., 1,230,657; Hamblen, Prohib., 10,331; Hallinan, Prog., 3,922; Hass, Soc. Labor, 1,495; Dobbs, Soc. Workers, 655; scattered, 3.

Minnesota Vote Since 1952

2008: Obama, D., 1,573,354; McCain, R., 1,275,409; Nader, Ind., 30,152; Barr, LB., 9,174; Baldwin, Const., 6,787; McKinney, Green, 5,174; Calero, Soc. Workers, 790.
2004: Kerry, D., 1,445,014; Bush, R., 1,346,695; Nader, Better Life, 18,683; Badnarik, LB., 4,639; Cobb, Green, 4,408; Peroutka, Const., 3,074; Harens, other, 2,387; Van Auken, Soc. Equal., 539; Calero, Soc. Workers, 416.
2000: Gore, D., 1,168,266; Bush, R., 1,109,659; Nader, Green, 126,696; Buchanan, RF. MN, 22,166; Browne, LB., 5,282; Phillips, Const., 3,272; Hagelin, RF., 2,294; Harris, Soc. Workers, 1,022.
1996: Clinton, D., 1,120,438; Dole, R., 766,476; Perot, RF., 257,704; Nader, Green, 24,908; Browne, LB., 8,271; Peron, Grass Roots, 4,898; Phillips, U.S. Taxpayers, 3,416; Hagelin, Natural Law, 1,808; Birrenbach, Ind. Grass Roots, 787; Harris, Soc. Workers, 684; White, Soc. Equality, 347.

1992: Clinton, D., 1,020,997; Bush, R., 747,841; Perot, Ind., 562,506; Marrou, LB., 3,373; Gritz, Populist/America First, 3,363; Hagelin, Natural Law, 1,406.
1988: Dukakis, D., 1,109,471; Bush, R., 962,337; McCarthy, Minn. Prog., 5,403; Paul, LB., 5,109.
1984: Mondale, D., 1,036,364; Reagan, R., 1,032,603; Bergland, LB., 2,996.
1980: Carter, D., 954,173; Reagan, R., 873,268; Anderson, Ind., 174,997; Clark, LB., 31,593; Commoner, Citizens, 8,406; Hall, Comm., 1,117; DeBerry, Soc. Workers, 711; Griswold, Workers World, 698; McReynolds, Soc., 536; write-in, 281.
1976: Carter, D., 1,070,440; Ford, R., 819,395; McCarthy, Ind., 35,490; Anderson, Amer., 13,592; Camejo, Soc. Workers, 4,149; MacBride, LB., 3,529; Hall, Comm., 1,092.
1972: Nixon, R., 898,269; McGovern, D., 802,346; Schmitz, Amer., 31,407; Fisher, Soc. Labor, 4,261; Spock, People's, 2,805; Jenness, Soc. Workers, 940; Hall, Comm., 662; scattered, 962.
1968: Humphrey, D., 857,738; Nixon, R., 658,643; Wallace, 3rd party, 68,931; Cleaver, Peace/Freedom, 935; Halstead, Soc. Workers, 808; McCarthy, write-in, 585; Mitchell, Comm., 415; Blomen, Industrial Govt., 285; scattered, 2,613.
1964: Johnson, D., 991,117; Goldwater, R., 559,624; Hass, Industrial Gov., 2,544; DeBerry, Soc. Workers, 1,177.
1960: Kennedy, D., 779,933; Nixon, R., 757,915; Dobbs, Soc. Workers, 3,077; Hass, Industrial Govt. 962.
1956: Eisenhower, R., 719,302; Stevenson, D., 617,525; Hass, Soc. Labor (Indust. Govt.), 2,080; Dobbs, Soc. Workers, 1,098.
1952: Eisenhower, R., 763,211; Stevenson, D., 608,458; Hallinan, Prog., 2,666; Hass, Soc. Labor, 2,383; Hamblen, Prohib., 2,147; Dobbs, Soc. Workers, 618.

Mississippi Vote Since 1952

2008: McCain, R., 724,597; Obama, D., 554,662; Nader, Ind., 4,011; Baldwin, Const., 2,551; Barr, LB., 2,529; McKinney, Green, 1,034; Weill, RF., 481.
2004: Bush, R., 684,981; Kerry, D., 458,094; Nader, RF., 3,177; Badnarik, LB., 1,793; Peroutka, Const., 1,759; Harris, Ind., 1,268; Cobb, Green, 1,073.
2000: Bush, R., 572,844; Gore, D., 404,614; Nader, Ind., 8,122; Phillips, Const., 3,267; Buchanan, RF., 2,265; Browne, LB., 2,009; Harris, Ind., 613; Hagelin, Natural Law, 450.
1996: Dole, R., 439,838; Clinton, D., 394,022; Perot, RF., 52,222; Browne, LB., 2,809; Phillips, U.S. Taxpayers, 2,314; Hagelin, Natural Law, 1,447; Collins, Ind., 1,205.
1992: Bush, R., 487,793; Clinton, D., 400,258; Perot, Ind., 85,626; Fulani, New Alliance, 2,625; Marrou, LB., 2,154; Phillips, U.S. Taxpayers, 1,652; Hagelin, Natural Law, 1,140.
1988: Bush, R., 557,890; Dukakis, D., 363,921; Duke, Ind., 4,232; Paul, LB., 3,329.
1984: Reagan, R., 582,377; Mondale, D., 352,192; Bergland, LB., 2,336.
1980: Reagan, R., 441,089; Carter, D., 429,281; Anderson, Ind., 12,036; Clark, LB., 5,465; Griswold, Workers World, 2,402; Pulley, Soc. Workers, 2,347.
1976: Carter, D., 381,309; Ford, R., 366,846; Anderson, Amer., 6,678; McCarthy, Ind., 4,074; Maddox, Ind., 4,049; Camejo, Soc. Workers, 2,805; MacBride, LB., 2,609.
1972: Nixon, R., 505,125; McGovern, D., 126,782; Schmitz, Amer., 11,598; Jenness, Soc. Workers, 2,458.
1968: Wallace, 3rd party, 415,349; Humphrey, D., 150,644; Nixon, R., 88,516.
1964: Goldwater, R., 356,528; Johnson, D., 52,618.
1960: D. (electors unpledged), 116,248; Kennedy, D., 108,362; Nixon, R., 73,561. *Mississippi's victorious slate of 8 unpledged Democratic electors cast their votes for Sen. Harry F. Byrd (D, VA).
1956: Stevenson, D., 144,498; Eisenhower, R., 56,372 and Black and Tan Grand Old Party, 4,313 (total, 60,685); Byrd, Ind., 42,966.
1952: Stevenson, D., 172,566; Eisenhower, Ind., vote pledged to R. candidate, 112,966.

Missouri Vote Since 1952

2008: McCain, R., 1,445,814; Obama, D., 1,441,911; Nader, Ind., 17,813; Barr, LB., 11,386; Baldwin, Const., 8,201.
2004: Bush, R., 1,455,713; Kerry, D., 1,259,171; Badnarik, LB., 9,831; Peroutka, Const., 5,355.
2000: Bush, R., 1,189,924; Gore, D., 1,111,138; Nader, Green, 38,515; Buchanan, RF., 9,818; Browne, LB., 7,436; Phillips, Const., 1,957; Hagelin, Natural Law, 1,104.
1996: Clinton, D., 1,025,935; Dole, R., 890,016; Perot, RF., 217,188; Phillips, U.S. Taxpayers, 11,521; Browne, LB., 10,522; Hagelin, Natural Law, 2,287.

1992: Clinton, D., 1,053,873; Bush, R., 811,159; Perot, Ind., 518,741; Marrou, LB., 7,497.
1988: Bush, R., 1,084,953; Dukakis, D., 1,001,619; Fulani, New Alliance, 6,656; Paul, write-in, 434.
1984: Reagan, R., 1,274,188; Mondale, D., 848,583.
1980: Reagan, R., 1,074,181; Carter, D., 931,182; Anderson, Ind., 77,920; Clark, LB., 14,422; DeBerry, Soc. Workers, 1,515; Commoner, Citizens, 573; write-in, 31.
1976: Carter, D., 999,163; Ford, R., 928,808; McCarthy, Ind., 24,329.
1972: Nixon, R., 1,154,058; McGovern, D., 698,531.
1968: Nixon, R., 811,932; Humphrey, D., 791,444; Wallace, 3rd party, 206,126.
1964: Johnson, D., 1,164,344; Goldwater, R., 653,535.
1960: Kennedy, D., 972,201; Nixon, R., 962,221.
1956: Stevenson, D., 918,273; Eisenhower, R., 914,299.
1952: Eisenhower, R., 959,429; Stevenson, D., 929,830; Hallinan, Prog., 987; Hamblen, Prohib., 885; MacArthur, Christian Nationalist, 302; America First, 233; Hoopes, Soc., 227; Hass, Soc. Labor, 169.

Montana Vote Since 1952

2008: McCain, R., 242,763; Obama, D., **231,667**; Paul, Const., 10,638; Nader, Ind., 3,686; Barr, LB., 1,355.
2004: Bush, R., 266,063; Kerry, D., 173,710; Nader, Ind., 6,168; Peroutka, Const., 1,764; Badnarik, LB., 1,733; Cobb, Green, 996.
2000: Bush, R., 240,178; Gore, D., 137,126; Nader, Green, 24,437; Buchanan, RF., 5,697; Browne, LB., 1,718; Phillips, Const., 1,155; Hagelin, Natural Law, 675.
1996: Dole, R., 179,652; Clinton, D., 167,922; Perot, RF., 55,229; Browne, LB., 2,526; Hagelin, Natural Law, 1,754.
1992: Clinton, D., 154,507; Bush, R., 144,207; Perot, Ind., 107,225; Gritz, Populist/America First, 3,658.
1988: Bush, R., 190,412; Dukakis, D., 168,936; Paul, LB., 5,047; Fulani, New Alliance, 1,279.
1984: Reagan, R., 232,450; Mondale, D., 146,742; Bergland, LB., 5,185.
1980: Reagan, R., 206,814; Carter, D., 118,032; Anderson, Ind., 29,281; Clark, LB., 9,825.
1976: Ford, R., 173,703; Carter, D., 149,259; Anderson, Amer., 5,772.
1972: Nixon, R., 183,976; McGovern, D., 120,197; Schmitz, Amer., 13,430.
1968: Nixon, R., 138,835; Humphrey, D., 114,117; Wallace, 3rd party, 20,015; Munn, Prohib., 510; Caton, New RF., 470; Halstead, Soc. Workers, 457.
1964: Johnson, D., 164,246; Goldwater, R., 113,032; Kasper, Natl. States' Rights, 519; Munn, Prohib., 499; DeBerry, Soc. Workers, 332.
1960: Nixon, R., 141,841; Kennedy, D., 134,891; Decker, Prohib., 456; Dobbs, Soc. Workers, 391.
1956: Eisenhower, R., 154,933; Stevenson, D., 116,238.
1952: Eisenhower, R., 157,394; Stevenson, D., 106,213; Hallinan, Prog., 723; Hamblen, Prohib., 548; Hoopes, Soc., 159.

Nebraska Vote Since 1952

2008: McCain, R., 452,979; Obama, D., 333,319; Nader, petitioning cand., 5,406; Baldwin, Nebraska, 2,972; Barr, LB., 2,740; McKinney, Green, 1,028.
2004: Bush, R., 512,814; Kerry, D., 254,328; Nader, petitioning cand., 5,698; Badnarik, LB., 2,041; Peroutka, Nebraska, 1,314; Cobb, Green, 978; Calero, petitioning cand., 82.
2000: Bush, R., 433,862; Gore, D., 231,780; Nader, Green, 24,540; Buchanan, Ind., 3,646; Browne, LB., 2,245; Hagelin, Natural Law, 478; Phillips, Ind., 468.
1996: Dole, R., 363,467; Clinton, D., 236,761; Perot, RF., 71,278; Browne, LB., 2,792; Phillips, Ind., 1,928; Hagelin, Natural Law, 1,189.
1992: Bush, R., 343,678; Clinton, D., 216,864; Perot, Ind., 174,104; Marrou, LB., 1,340.
1988: Bush, R., 397,956; Dukakis, D., 259,235; Paul, LB., 2,534; Fulani, New Alliance, 1,740.
1984: Reagan, R., 459,135; Mondale, D., 187,475; Bergland, LB., 2,075.
1980: Reagan, R., 419,214; Carter, D., 166,424; Anderson, Ind., 44,854; Clark, LB., 9,041.
1976: Ford, R., 359,219; Carter, D., 233,287; McCarthy, Ind., 9,383; Maddox, Amer. Ind., 3,378; MacBride, LB., 1,476.
1972: Nixon, R., 406,298; McGovern, D., 169,991; scattered, 817.
1968: Nixon, R., 321,163; Humphrey, D., 170,784; Wallace, 3rd party, 44,904.

1964: Johnson, D., 307,307; Goldwater, R., 276,847.
1960: Nixon, R., 380,553; Kennedy, D., 232,542.
1956: Eisenhower, R., 378,108; Stevenson, D., 199,029.
1952: Eisenhower, R., 421,603; Stevenson, D., 188,057.

Nevada Vote Since 1952

2008: Obama, D., 533,736; McCain, R., 412,827; None of These Candidates, 6,267; Nader, Ind., 6,150; Barr, LB., 4,263; Baldwin, Const., 3,194; McKinney, Green, 1,411.
2004: Bush, R., 418,690; Kerry, D., 397,190; Nader, Ind., 4,838; None of These Candidates, 3,688; Badnarik, LB., 3,176; Peroutka, Ind. Amer., 1,152; Cobb, Green, 853.
2000: Bush, R., 301,575; Gore, D., 279,978; Nader, Green, 15,008; Buchanan, Citizens First, 4,747; None of These Candidates, 3,315; Browne, LB., 3,311; Phillips, Ind. Amer., 621; Hagelin, Natural Law, 415.
1996: Clinton, D., 203,974; Dole, R., 199,244; Perot, RF., 43,986; None of These Candidates, 5,608; Nader, Green, 4,730; Browne, LB., 4,460; Phillips, Ind. Amer., 1,732; Hagelin, Natural Law, 545.
1992: Clinton, D., 189,148; Bush, R., 175,828; Perot, Ind., 132,580; Gritz, Populist/America First, 2,892; Marrou, LB., 1,835.
1988: Bush, R., 206,040; Dukakis, D., 132,738; Paul, LB., 3,520; Fulani, New Alliance, 835.
1984: Reagan, R., 188,770; Mondale, D., 91,655; Bergland, LB., 2,292.
1980: Reagan, R., 155,017; Carter, D., 66,666; Anderson, Ind., 17,651; Clark, LB., 4,358.
1976: Ford, R., 101,273; Carter, D., 92,479; MacBride, LB., 1,519; Maddox, Amer. Ind., 1,497; scattered, 5,108.
1972: Nixon, R., 115,750; McGovern, D., 66,016.
1968: Nixon, R., 73,188; Humphrey, D., 60,598; Wallace, 3rd party, 20,432.
1964: Johnson, D., 79,339; Goldwater, R., 56,094.
1960: Kennedy, D., 54,880; Nixon, R., 52,387.
1956: Eisenhower, R., 56,049; Stevenson, D., 40,640.
1952: Eisenhower, R., 50,502; Stevenson, D., 31,688.

New Hampshire Vote Since 1952

2008: Obama, D., 384,826; McCain, R., 316,534; Nader, Ind., 3,503; Barr, LB., 2,217; Phillies, LB., 531.
2004: Kerry, D., 340,511; Bush, R., 331,237; Nader, Ind., 4,479.
2000: Bush, R., 273,559; Gore, D., 266,348; Nader, Green, 22,198; Browne, LB., 2,757; Buchanan, Independence, 2,615; Phillips, Const., 328.
1996: Clinton, D., 246,166; Dole, R., 196,486; Perot, RF., 48,387; Browne, LB., 4,214; Phillips, Taxpayers, 1,344.
1992: Clinton, D., 209,040; Bush, R., 202,484; Perot, Ind., 121,337; Marrou, LB., 3,548.
1988: Bush, R., 281,537; Dukakis, D., 163,696; Paul, LB., 4,502; Fulani, New Alliance, 790.
1984: Reagan, R., 267,051; Mondale, D., 120,377; Bergland, LB., 735.
1980: Reagan, R., 221,705; Carter, D., 108,864; Anderson, Ind., 49,693; Clark, LB., 2,067; Commoner, Citizens, 1,325; Hall, Comm., 129; Griswold, Workers World, 76; DeBerry, Soc. Workers, 72; scattered, 68.
1976: Ford, R., 185,935; Carter, D., 147,645; McCarthy, Ind., 4,095; MacBride, LB., 936; Reagan, write-in, 388; LaRouche, U.S. Labor, 186; Camejo, Soc. Workers, 161; Levin, Soc. Labor, 66; scattered, 215.
1972: Nixon, R., 213,724; McGovern, D., 116,435; Schmitz, Amer., 3,386; Jenness, Soc. Workers, 368; scattered, 142.
1968: Nixon, R., 154,903; Humphrey, D., 130,589; Wallace, 3rd party, 11,173; New Party, 421; Halstead, Soc. Workers, 104.
1964: Johnson, D., 182,065; Goldwater, R., 104,029.
1960: Nixon, R., 157,989; Kennedy, D., 137,772.
1956: Eisenhower, R., 176,519; Stevenson, D., 90,364; Andrews, Const., 111.
1952: Eisenhower, R., 166,287; Stevenson, D., 106,663.

New Jersey Vote Since 1952

2008: Obama, D., 2,215,422; McCain, R., 1,613,207; Nader, Ind., 21,298; Barr, Ind., 8,441; Baldwin, Ind., 3,956; McKinney, Ind., 3,636; Moore, Ind., 699; Boss, Ind., 639; Calero, Ind., 523; La Riva, Ind., 416.
2004: Kerry, D., 1,911,430; Bush, R., 1,670,003; Nader, Ind., 19,418; Badnarik, Ind., 4,514; Peroutka, Ind., 2,750; Cobb, Ind., 1,807; Brown, Ind., 664; Van Auken, Ind., 575; Calero, Ind., 530.

2000: Gore, D., 1,788,850; Bush, R., 1,284,173; Nader, Ind., 94,554; Buchanan, Ind., 6,989; Browne, Ind., 6,312; Hagelin, Ind., 2,215; McReynolds, Ind., 1,880; Phillips, Ind., 1,409; Harris, Ind., 844.
1996: Clinton, D., 1,652,361; Dole, R., 1,103,099; Perot, RF., 262,134; Nader, Green, 32,465; Browne, LB., 14,763; Hagelin, Natural Law, 3,887; Phillips, U.S. Taxpayers, 3,440; Harris, Soc. Workers, 1,837; Moorehead, Workers World, 1,337; White, Soc. Equality, 537.
1992: Clinton, D., 1,436,206; Bush, R., 1,356,865; Perot, Ind., 521,829; Marrou, LB., 6,822; Fulani, New Alliance, 3,513; Phillips, U.S. Taxpayers, 2,670; LaRouche, Ind., 2,095; Warren, Soc. Workers, 2,011; Daniels, Ind., 1,996; Gritz, Populist/America First, 1,867; Hagelin, Natural Law, 1,353.
1988: Bush, R., 1,740,604; Dukakis, D., 1,317,541; Lewin, Peace/ Freedom, 9,953; Paul, LB., 8,421.
1984: Reagan, R., 1,933,630; Mondale, D., 1,261,323; Bergland, LB., 6,416.
1980: Reagan, R., 1,546,557; Carter, D., 1,147,364; Anderson, Ind., 234,632; Clark, LB., 20,652; Commoner, Citizens, 8,203; McCormack, Right to Life, 3,927; Lynen, Middle Class, 3,694; Hall, Comm., 2,555; Pulley, Soc. Workers, 2,198; McReynolds, Soc., 1,973; Gahres, Down With Lawyers, 1,718; Griswold, Workers World, 1,288; Wendelken, Ind., 923.
1976: Ford, R., 1,509,688; Carter, D., 1,444,653; McCarthy, Ind., 32,717; MacBride, LB., 9,449; Maddox, Amer., 7,716; Levin, Soc. Labor, 3,686; Hall, Comm., 1,662; LaRouche, U.S. Labor, 1,650; Camejo, Soc. Workers, 1,184; Wright, People's, 1,044; Bubar, Prohib., 554; Zeidler, Soc., 469.
1972: Nixon, R., 1,845,502; McGovern, D., 1,102,211; Schmitz, Amer., 34,378; Spock, People's, 5,355; Fisher, Soc. Labor, 4,544; Jenness, Soc. Workers, 2,233; Mahalchik, Amer. First, 1,743; Hall, Comm., 1,263.
1968: Nixon, R., 1,325,467; Humphrey, D., 1,264,206; Wallace, 3rd party, 262,187; Halstead, Soc. Workers, 8,667; Gregory, Peace/Freedom, 8,084; Blomen, Soc. Labor, 6,784.
1964: Johnson, D., 1,867,671; Goldwater, R., 963,843; DeBerry, Soc. Workers, 8,181; Hass, Soc. Labor, 7,075.
1960: Kennedy, D., 1,385,415; Nixon, R., 1,363,324; Dobbs, Soc. Workers, 11,402; Lee, Conservative, 8,708; Hass, Soc. Labor, 4,262.
1956: Eisenhower, R., 1,606,942; Stevenson D., 850,337; Holtwick, Prohib., 9,147; Hass, Soc. Labor, 6,736; Andrews, Conservative, 5,317; Dobbs, Soc. Workers, 4,004; Krajewski, Amer. Third Party, 1,829.
1952: Eisenhower, R., 1,373,613; Stevenson, D., 1,015,902; Hoopes, Soc., 8,593; Hass, Soc. Labor, 5,815; Hallinan, Prog., 5,589; Krajewski, Poor Man's, 4,203; Dobbs, Soc. Workers, 3,850; Hamblen, Prohib., 989.

New Mexico Vote Since 1952

2008: Obama, D., 472,422; McCain, R., 346,832; Nader, Ind., 5,327; Barr, LB., 2,428; Baldwin, Const., 1,597; McKinney, Green, 1,552.
2004: Bush, R., 376,930; Kerry, D., 370,942; Nader, Ind., 4,053; Badnarik, LB., 2,382; Cobb, Green, 1,226; Peroutka, Const., 771.
2000: Gore, D., 286,783; Bush, R., 286,417; Nader, Green, 21,251; Browne, LB., 2,058; Buchanan, RF., 1,392; Hagelin, Natural Law, 361; Phillips, Const., 343.
1996: Clinton, D., 273,495; Dole, R., 232,751; Perot, RF., 32,257; Nader, Green, 13,218; Browne, LB., 2,996; Phillips, Taxpayers, 713; Hagelin, Natural Law, 644.
1992: Clinton, D., 261,617; Bush, R., 212,824; Perot, Ind., 91,895; Marrou, LB., 1,615.
1988: Bush, R., 270,341; Dukakis, D., 244,497; Paul, LB., 3,268; Fulani, New Alliance, 2,237.
1984: Reagan, R., 307,101; Mondale, D., 201,769; Bergland, LB., 4,459.
1980: Reagan, R., 250,779; Carter, D., 167,826; Anderson, Ind., 29,459; Clark, LB., 4,365; Commoner, Citizens, 2,202; Bubar, Statesman, 1,281; Pulley, Soc. Workers, 325.
1976: Ford, R., 211,419; Carter, D., 201,148; Camejo, Soc. Workers, 2,462; MacBride, LB., 1,110; Zeidler, Soc., 240; Bubar, Prohib., 211.
1972: Nixon, R., 235,606; McGovern, D., 141,084; Schmitz, Amer., 8,767; Jenness, Soc. Workers, 474.
1968: Nixon, R., 169,692; Humphrey, D., 130,081; Wallace, 3rd party, 25,737; Chavez, 1,519; Halstead, Soc. Workers, 252.
1964: Johnson, D., 194,017; Goldwater, R., 131,838; Hass, Soc. Labor, 1,217; Munn, Prohib., 543.
1960: Kennedy, D., 156,027; Nixon, R., 153,733; Decker, Prohib., 777; Hass, Soc. Labor, 570.

1956: Eisenhower, R., 146,788; Stevenson, D., 106,098; Holtwick, Prohib., 607; Andrews, Ind., 364; Hass, Soc. Labor, 69.
1952: Eisenhower, R., 132,170; Stevenson, D., 105,661; Hamblen, Prohib., 297; Hallinan, Ind. Prog., 225; MacArthur, Christian Nationalist, 220; Hass, Soc. Labor, 35.

New York Vote Since 1952

2008: Obama, D., 4,804,945; McCain, R., 2,752,771; Nader, Populist, 41,249; Barr, LB., 19,596; McKinney, Green, 12,801; Calero, Soc. Workers, 3,615; La Riva, Socialism/Liberation, 1,639.
2004: Kerry, D., 4,314,280; Bush, R., 2,962,567; Nader, Ind., 99,873; Badnarik, LB., 11,607; Calero, Soc. Workers, 2,405.
2000: Gore, D., 4,112,965; Bush, R., 2,405,570; Nader, Green, 244,360; Buchanan, RF., 31,554; Hagelin, Independence, 24,369; Browne, LB., 7,664; Harris, Soc. Workers, 1,790; Phillips, Const., 1,503.
1996: Clinton, D., 3,756,177; Dole, R., 1,933,492; Perot, RF., 503,458; Nader, Green, 75,956; Phillips, Right to Life, 23,580; Browne, LB., 12,220; Hagelin, Natural Law, 5,011; Moorehead, Workers World, 3,473; Harris, Soc. Workers, 2,762.
1992: Clinton, D., 3,444,450; Bush, R., 2,346,649; Perot, Ind., 1,090,721; Warren, Soc. Workers, 15,472; Marrou, LB., 13,451; Fulani, New Alliance, 11,318; Hagelin, Natural Law, 4,420.
1988: Dukakis, D., 3,347,882; Bush, R., 3,081,871; Marra, Right to Life, 20,497; Fulani, New Alliance, 15,845.
1984: Reagan, R., 3,664,763; Mondale, D., 3,119,609; Bergland, LB., 11,949.
1980: Reagan, R., 2,893,831; Carter, D., 2,728,372; Anderson, Liberal, 467,801; Clark, LB., 52,648; McCormack, Right to Life, 24,159; Commoner, Citizens, 23,186; Hall, Comm., 7,414; DeBerry, Soc. Workers, 2,068; Griswold, Workers World, 1,416; scattered, 1,064.
1976: Carter, D., 3,389,558; Ford, R., 3,100,791; MacBride, LB., 12,197; Hall, Comm., 10,270; Camejo, Soc. Workers, 6,996; LaRouche, U.S. Labor, 5,413; blank, void, or scattered, 143,037.
1972: Nixon, R., 3,824,642; McGovern, D., 2,767,956 and Liberal, 183,128 (total, 2,951,084); Reed, Soc. Workers, 7,797; Fisher, Soc. Labor, 4,530; Hall, Comm., 5,641; blank, void, and scattered, 161,641.
1968: Humphrey, D., 3,378,470; Nixon, R., 3,007,932; Wallace, 3rd party, 358,864; Gregory, Peace/Freedom, 24,517; Halstead, Soc. Workers, 11,851; Blomen, Soc. Labor, 8,432; blank, void, and scattered, 171,624.
1964: Johnson, D., 4,913,156; Goldwater, R., 2,243,559; Hass, Soc. Labor, 6,085; DeBerry, Soc. Workers, 3,215; scattered, 188; blank and void, 151,383.
1960: Kennedy, D., 3,423,909 and Liberal, 406,176 (total, 3,830,085); Nixon, R., 3,446,419; Dobbs, Soc. Workers, 14,319; scattered, 256; blank and void, 88,896.
1956: Eisenhower, R., 4,340,340; Stevenson, D., 2,458,212 and Liberal, 292,557 (total, 2,750,769); Andrews, write-in, 1,027; Werdel, 492; Hass, 150; Hoopes, 82; others, 476.
1952: Eisenhower, R., 3,952,815; Stevenson, D., 2,687,890 and Liberal, 416,711 (total, 3,104,601); Hallinan, Amer. Labor, 64,211; Hoopes, Soc., 2,664; Dobbs, Soc. Workers, 2,212; Hass, Industrial Govt., 1,560; scattered, 178; blank and void, 87,813.

North Carolina Vote Since 1952

2008: Obama, D., 2,142,651; McCain, R., 2,128,474; Barr, LB., 25,722.
2004: Bush, R., 1,961,166; Kerry, D., 1,525,849; Badnarik, LB., 11,731.
2000: Bush, R., 1,631,163; Gore, D., 1,257,692; Browne, LB., 13,891; Buchanan, RF., 8,874.
1996: Dole, R., 1,225,938; Clinton, D., 1,107,849; Perot, RF., 168,059; Browne, LB., 8,740; Hagelin, Natural Law, 2,771.
1992: Bush, R., 1,134,661; Clinton, D., 1,114,042; Perot, Ind., 357,864; Marrou, LB., 5,171.
1988: Bush, R., 1,237,258; Dukakis, D., 890,167; Fulani, New Alliance, 5,682; Paul, write-in, 1,263.
1984: Reagan, R., 1,346,481; Mondale, D., 824,287; Bergland, LB., 3,794.
1980: Reagan, R., 915,018; Carter, D., 875,635; Anderson, Ind., 52,800; Clark, LB., 9,677; Commoner, Citizens, 2,287; DeBerry, Soc. Workers, 416.
1976: Carter, D., 927,365; Ford, R., 741,960; Anderson, Amer., 5,607; MacBride, LB., 2,219; LaRouche, U.S. Labor, 755.
1972: Nixon, R., 1,054,889; McGovern, D., 438,705; Schmitz, Amer., 25,018.

1968: Nixon, R., 627,192; Wallace, 3rd party, 496,188; Humphrey, D., 464,113.
1964: Johnson, D., 800,139; Goldwater, R., 624,844.
1960: Kennedy, D., 713,136; Nixon, R., 655,420.
1956: Stevenson, D., 590,530; Eisenhower, R., 575,062.
1952: Stevenson, D., 652,803; Eisenhower, R., 558,107.

North Dakota Vote Since 1952

2008: McCain, R., 168,601; Obama, D., 141,278; Nader, Ind., 4,189; Barr, LB., 1,354; Baldwin, Const., 1,199.
2004: Bush, R., 196,651; Kerry, D., 111,052; Nader, Ind., 3,756; Badnarik, LB., 851; Peroutka, Const., 514.
2000: Bush, R., 174,852; Gore, D., 95,284; Nader, Ind., 9,486; Buchanan, RF., 7,288; Browne, Ind., 660; Phillips, Const., 373; Hagelin, Ind., 313.
1996: Dole, R., 125,050; Clinton, D., 106,905; Perot, RF., 32,515; Browne, LB., 847; Phillips, Ind., 745; Hagelin, Natural Law, 349.
1992: Bush, R., 136,244; Clinton, D., 99,168; Perot, Ind., 71,084.
1988: Bush, R., 166,559; Dukakis, D., 127,739; Paul, LB., 1,315; LaRouche, Natl. Econ. Recovery, 905.
1984: Reagan, R., 200,336; Mondale, D., 104,429; Bergland, LB., 703.
1980: Reagan, R., 193,695; Carter, D., 79,189; Anderson, Ind., 23,640; Clark, LB., 3,743; Commoner, LB., 429; McLain, Natl. People's League, 296; Greaves, Amer., 235; Hall, Comm., 93; DeBerry, Soc. Workers, 89; McReynolds, Soc., 82; Bubar, Statesman, 54.
1976: Ford, R., 153,470; Carter, D., 136,078; Anderson, Amer., 3,698; McCarthy, Ind., 2,952; Maddox, Amer. Ind., 269; MacBride, LB., 256; scattered, 371.
1972: Nixon, R., 174,109; McGovern, D., 100,384; Schmitz, Amer., 5,646; Jenness, Soc. Workers, 288; Hall, Comm., 87.
1968: Nixon, R., 138,669; Humphrey, D., 94,769; Wallace, 3rd party, 14,244; Halstead, Soc. Workers, 128; Munn, Prohib., 38; Troxell, Ind., 34.
1964: Johnson, D., 149,784; Goldwater, R., 108,207; DeBerry, Soc. Workers, 224; Munn, Prohib., 174.
1960: Nixon, R., 154,310; Kennedy, D., 123,963; Dobbs, Soc. Workers, 158.
1956: Eisenhower, R., 156,766; Stevenson, D., 96,742; Andrews, Amer., 483.
1952: Eisenhower, R., 191,712; Stevenson, D., 76,694; MacArthur, Christian Nationalist, 1,075; Hallinan, Prog., 344; Hamblen, Prohib., 302.

Ohio Vote Since 1952

2008: Obama, D., 2,940,044; McCain, R., 2,677,820; Nader, Ind., 42,337; Barr, LB., 19,917; Baldwin, Const., 12,565; McKinney, Green, 8,518; Duncan, Ind., 3,905; Moore, Soc., 2,735.
2004: Bush, R., 2,859,768; Kerry, D., 2,741,167; Badnarik, nonpartisan, 14,676; Peroutka, nonpartisan, 939.
2000: Bush, R., 2,351,209; Gore, D., 2,186,190; Nader, Ind., 117,857; Buchanan, Ind., 26,724; Browne, LB., 13,475; Hagelin, Natural Law, 6,169; Phillips, Ind., 3,823.
1996: Clinton, D., 2,148,222; Dole, R., 1,859,883; Perot, RF., 483,207; Browne, Ind., 12,851; Moorehead, Ind., 10,813; Hagelin, Natural Law, 9,120; Phillips, Ind., 7,361.
1992: Clinton, D., 1,984,942; Bush, R., 1,894,310; Perot, Ind., 1,036,426; Marrou, LB., 7,252; Fulani, New Alliance, 6,413; Gritz, Populist/America First, 4,699; Hagelin, Natural Law, 3,437; LaRouche, Ind., 2,446.
1988: Bush, R., 2,416,549; Dukakis, D., 1,939,629; Fulani, Ind., 12,017; Paul, Ind., 11,926.
1984: Reagan, R., 2,678,559; Mondale, D., 1,825,440; Bergland, LB., 5,886.
1980: Reagan, R., 2,206,545; Carter, D., 1,752,414; Anderson, Ind., 254,472; Clark, LB., 49,033; Commoner, Citizens, 8,564; Hall, Comm., 4,729; Congress, Ind., 4,029; Griswold, Workers World, 3,790; Bubar, Statesman, 27.
1976: Carter, D., 2,011,621; Ford, R., 2,000,505; McCarthy, Ind., 58,258; Maddox, Amer. Ind., 15,529; MacBride, LB., 8,961; Hall, Comm., 7,817; Camejo, Soc. Workers, 4,717; LaRouche, U.S. Labor, 4,335; scattered, 130.
1972: Nixon, R., 2,441,827; McGovern, D., 1,558,889; Schmitz, Amer., 80,067; Fisher, Soc. Labor, 7,107; Hall, Comm., 6,437; Wallace, Ind., 460.
1968: Nixon, R., 1,791,014; Humphrey, D., 1,700,586; Wallace, 3rd party, 467,495; Gregory, 372; Blomen, Soc. Labor, 120; Halstead, Soc. Workers, 69; Mitchell, Comm., 23; Munn, Prohib., 19.
1964: Johnson, D., 2,498,331; Goldwater, R., 1,470,865.

1960: Nixon, R., 2,217,611; Kennedy, D., 1,944,248.
1956: Eisenhower, R., 2,262,610; Stevenson, D., 1,439,655.
1952: Eisenhower, R., 2,100,391; Stevenson, D., 1,600,367.

Oklahoma Vote Since 1952

2008: McCain, R., 960,165; Obama, D., 502,496.
2004: Bush, R., 959,792; Kerry, D., 503,966.
2000: Bush, R., 744,337; Gore, D., 474,276; Buchanan, RF., 9,014; Browne, LB., 6,602.
1996: Dole, R., 582,315; Clinton, D., 488,105; Perot, RF., 130,788; Browne, LB., 5,505.
1992: Bush, R., 592,929; Clinton, D., 473,066; Perot, Ind., 319,878; Marrou, LB., 4,486.
1988: Bush, R., 678,367; Dukakis, D., 483,423; Paul, LB., 6,261; Fulani, New Alliance, 2,985.
1984: Reagan, R., 861,530; Mondale, D., 385,080; Bergland, LB., 9,066.
1980: Reagan, R., 695,570; Carter, D., 402,026; Anderson, Ind., 38,284; Clark, LB., 13,828.
1976: Ford, R., 545,708; Carter, D., 532,442; McCarthy, Ind., 14,101.
1972: Nixon, R., 759,025; McGovern, D., 247,147; Schmitz, Amer., 23,728.
1968: Nixon, R., 449,697; Humphrey, D., 301,658; Wallace, 3rd party, 191,731.
1964: Johnson, D., 519,834; Goldwater, R., 412,665.
1960: Nixon, R., 533,039; Kennedy, D., 370,111.
1956: Eisenhower, R., 473,769; Stevenson, D., 385,581.
1952: Eisenhower, R., 518,045; Stevenson, D., 430,939.

Oregon Vote Since 1952

2008: Obama, D., 1,037,291; McCain, R., 738,475; Nader, Peace Party of OR, 18,614; Baldwin, Const., 7,693; Barr, LB., 7,635; McKinney, Pacific Green, 4,543.
2004: Kerry, D., 943,163; Bush, R., 866,831; Badnarik, LB., 7,260; Cobb, Pacific Green, 5,315; Peroutka, Const., 5,257.
2000: Gore, D., 720,342; Bush, R., 713,577; Nader, Green, 77,357; Browne, LB., 7,447; Buchanan, Ind., 7,063; Hagelin, RF., 2,574; Phillips, Const., 2,189.
1996: Clinton, D., 649,641; Dole, R., 538,152; Perot, RF., 121,221; Nader, Pacific, 49,415; Browne, LB., 8,903; Phillips, Taxpayers, 3,379; Hagelin, Natural Law, 2,798; Hollis, Soc., 1,922.
1992: Clinton, D., 621,314; Bush, R., 475,757; Perot, Ind., 354,091; Marrou, LB., 4,277; Fulani, New Alliance, 3,030.
1988: Dukakis, D., 616,206; Bush, R., 560,126; Paul, LB., 14,811; Fulani, Ind., 6,487.
1984: Reagan, R., 658,700; Mondale, D., 536,479.
1980: Reagan, R., 571,044; Carter, D., 456,890; Anderson, Ind., 112,389; Clark, LB., 25,838; Commoner, Citizens, 13,642; scattered, 1,713.
1976: Ford, R., 492,120; Carter, D., 490,407; McCarthy, Ind., 40,207; write-in, 7,142.
1972: Nixon, R., 486,686; McGovern, D., 392,760; Schmitz, Amer., 46,211; write-in, 2,289.
1968: Nixon, R., 408,433; Humphrey, D., 358,866; Wallace, 3rd party, 49,683; write-ins: McCarthy, 1,496; N. Rockefeller, 69; others, 1,075.
1964: Johnson, D., 501,017; Goldwater, R., 282,779; write-in, 2,509.
1960: Nixon, R., 408,060; Kennedy, D., 367,402.
1956: Eisenhower, R., 406,393; Stevenson, D., 329,204.
1952: Eisenhower, R., 420,815; Stevenson, D., 270,579; Hallinan, Ind., 3,665.

Pennsylvania Vote Since 1952

2008: Obama, D., 3,276,363; McCain, R., 2,655,885; Nader, Ind., 42,977; Barr, LB., 19,912.
2004: Kerry, D., 2,938,095; Bush, R., 2,793,847; Badnarik, LB., 21,185; Cobb, Green, 6,319; Peroutka, Const., 6,318.
2000: Gore, D., 2,485,967; Bush, R., 2,281,127; Nader, Green, 103,392; Buchanan, RF., 16,023; Phillips, Const., 14,428; Browne, LB., 11,248.
1996: Clinton, D., 2,215,819; Dole, R., 1,801,169; Perot, RF., 430,984; Browne, LB., 28,000; Phillips, Const., 19,552; Hagelin, Natural Law, 5,783.
1992: Clinton, D., 2,239,164; Bush, R., 1,791,841; Perot, Ind., 902,667; Marrou, LB., 21,477; Fulani, New Alliance, 4,661.
1988: Bush, R., 2,300,087; Dukakis, D., 2,194,944; McCarthy, Consumer, 19,158; Paul, LB., 12,051.

1984: Reagan, R., 2,584,323; Mondale, D., 2,228,131; Bergland, LB., 6,982.
1980: Reagan, R., 2,261,872; Carter, D., 1,937,540; Anderson, Ind., 292,921; Clark, LB., 33,263; DeBerry, Soc. Workers, 20,291; Commoner, Consumer, 10,430; Hall, Comm., 5,184.
1976: Carter, D., 2,328,677; Ford, R., 2,205,604; McCarthy, Ind., 50,584; Maddox, Const., 25,344; Camejo, Soc. Workers, 3,009; LaRouche, U.S. Labor, 2,744; Hall, Comm., 1,891; others, 2,934.
1972: Nixon, R., 2,714,521; McGovern, D., 1,796,951; Schmitz, Amer., 70,593; Jenness, Soc. Workers, 4,639; Hall, Comm., 2,686; others, 2,715.
1968: Humphrey, D., 2,259,405; Nixon, R., 2,090,017; Wallace, 3rd party, 378,582; Gregory, Peace/Freedom, 7,821; Blomen, Soc. Labor, 4,977; Halstead, Soc. Workers, 4,862; others, 2,264.
1964: Johnson, D., 3,130,954; Goldwater, R., 1,673,657; DeBerry, Soc. Workers, 10,456; Hass, Soc. Labor, 5,092; scattered, 2,531.
1960: Kennedy, D., 2,556,282; Nixon, R., 2,439,956; Hass, Soc. Labor, 7,185; Dobbs, Soc. Workers, 2,678; scattered, 440.
1956: Eisenhower, R., 2,585,252; Stevenson, D., 1,981,769; Hass, Soc. Labor, 7,447; Dobbs, Militant Workers, 2,035.
1952: Eisenhower, R., 2,415,789; Stevenson, D., 2,146,269; Hamblen, Prohib., 8,771; Hallinan, Prog., 4,200; Hoopes, Soc., 2,684; Dobbs, Militant Workers, 1,502; Hass, Industrial Govt., 1,347; scattered, 155.

Rhode Island Vote Since 1952

2008: Obama, D., 296,571; McCain, R., 165,391; Nader, Ind., 4,829; Barr, LB., 1,382; McKinney, Green, 797; Baldwin, Const., 675; La Riva, Socialism/Liberation, 122.
2004: Kerry, D., 259,765; Bush, R., 169,046; Nader, RF., 4,651; Cobb, Green, 1,333; Badnarik, LB., 907; Peroutka, Const., 339; Parker, Workers World, 253.
2000: Gore, D., 249,508; Bush, R., 130,555; Nader, Ind., 25,052; Buchanan, RF., 2,273; Browne, Ind., 742; Hagelin, Ind., 271; Moorehead, Ind., 199; Phillips, Ind., 97; McReynolds, Ind., 52; Harris, Ind., 34.
1996: Clinton, D., 233,050; Dole, R., 104,683; Perot, RF., 43,723; Nader, Green, 6,040; Browne, LB., 1,109; Phillips, U.S. Taxpayers, 1,021; Hagelin, Natural Law, 435; Moorehead, Workers World, 186.
1992: Clinton, D., 213,299; Bush, R., 131,601; Perot, Ind., 105,045; Fulani, New Alliance, 1,878.
1988: Dukakis, D., 225,123; Bush, R., 177,761; Paul, LB., 825; Fulani, New Alliance, 280.
1984: Reagan, R., 212,080; Mondale, D., 197,106; Bergland, LB., 277.
1980: Carter, D., 198,342; Reagan, R., 154,793; Anderson, Ind., 59,819; Clark, LB., 2,458; Hall, Comm., 218; McReynolds, Soc., 170; DeBerry, Soc. Workers, 90; Griswold, Workers World, 77.
1976: Carter, D., 227,636; Ford, R., 181,249; MacBride, LB., 715; Camejo, Soc. Workers, 462; Hall, Comm., 334; Levin, Soc. Labor, 188.
1972: Nixon, R., 220,383; McGovern, D., 194,645; Jenness, Soc. Workers, 729.
1968: Humphrey, D., 246,518; Nixon, R., 122,359; Wallace, 3rd party, 15,678; Halstead, Soc. Workers, 383.
1964: Johnson, D., 315,463; Goldwater, R., 74,615.
1960: Kennedy, D., 258,032; Nixon, R., 147,502.
1956: Eisenhower, R., 225,819; Stevenson, D., 161,790.
1952: Eisenhower, R., 210,935; Stevenson, D., 203,293; Hallinan, Prog., 187; Hass, Soc. Labor, 83.

South Carolina Vote Since 1952

2008: McCain, R., 1,034,896; Obama, D., 862,449; Barr, LB., 7,283; Baldwin, Const., 6,827; Nader, petitioning cand., 5,053; McKinney, Green, 4,461.
2004: Bush, R., 937,974; Kerry, D., 661,699; Nader, Ind., 5,520; Peroutka, Const., 5,317; Badnarik, LB., 3,608; Brown, United Citizens, 2,124; Cobb, Green, 1,488.
2000: Bush, R., 786,892; Gore, D., 566,039; Nader, United Citizens, 20,279; Browne, LB., 4,898; Buchanan, RF., 3,309; Phillips, Const., 1,682; Hagelin, Natural Law, 943.
1996: Dole, R., 573,458; Clinton, D., 506,283; Perot, RF./Patriot, 64,386; Browne, LB., 4,271; Phillips, U.S. Taxpayers, 2,043; Hagelin, Natural Law, 1,248.
1992: Bush, R., 577,507; Clinton, D., 479,514; Perot, Ind., 138,872; Marrou, LB., 2,719; Phillips, U.S. Taxpayers, 2,680; Fulani, New Alliance, 1,235.

1988: Bush, R., 606,443; Dukakis, D., 370,554; Paul, LB., 4,935; Fulani, United Citizens, 4,077.
1984: Reagan, R., 615,539; Mondale, D., 344,459; Bergland, LB., 4,359.
1980: Reagan, R., 439,277; Carter, D., 428,220; Anderson, Ind., 13,868; Clark, LB., 4,807; Rarick, Amer. Ind., 2,086.
1976: Carter, D., 450,807; Ford, R., 346,149; Anderson, Amer., 2,996; Maddox, Amer. Ind., 1,950; write-in, 681.
1972: Nixon, R., 477,044; McGovern, D., 184,559; Schmitz, Amer., 10,075; United Citizens, 2,265; write-in, 17.
1968: Nixon, R., 254,062; Wallace, 3rd party, 215,430; Humphrey, D., 197,486.
1964: Goldwater, R., 309,048; Johnson, D., 215,700; write-ins: Wallace, 5; Nixon, 1; Powell, 1; Thurmond, 1.
1960: Kennedy, D., 198,129; Nixon, R., 188,558; write-in, 1.
1956: Stevenson, D., 136,372; Byrd, Ind., 88,509; Eisenhower, R., 75,700; Andrews, Ind., 2.
1952: Stevenson, D., 173,004. *Under state law votes cast for 2 Eisenhower slates of electors could not be combined. Eisenhower, Ind., 158,289 and R., 9,793 (total, 168,082); Hamblen, Prohib., 1.

South Dakota Vote Since 1952

2008: McCain, R., 203,054; Obama, D., 170,924; Nader, Ind., 4,267; Baldwin, Const., 1,895; Barr, Ind., 1,835.
2004: Bush, R., 232,584; Kerry, D., 149,244; Nader, Ind., 4,320; Peroutka, Const., 1,103; Badnarik, LB., 964.
2000: Bush, R., 190,700; Gore, D., 118,804; Buchanan, RF., 3,322; Phillips, Ind., 1,781; Browne, LB., 1,662.
1996: Dole, R., 150,543; Clinton, D., 139,333; Perot, RF., 31,250; Browne, LB., 1,472; Phillips, Taxpayers, 912; Hagelin, Natural Law, 316.
1992: Bush, R., 136,718; Clinton, D., 124,888; Perot, Ind., 73,295.
1988: Bush, R., 165,415; Dukakis, D., 145,560; Paul, LB., 1,060; Fulani, New Alliance, 730.
1984: Reagan, R., 200,267; Mondale, D., 116,113.
1980: Reagan, R., 198,343; Carter, D., 103,855; Anderson, Ind., 21,431; Clark, LB., 3,824; Pulley, Soc. Workers, 250.
1976: Ford, R., 151,505; Carter, D., 147,068; MacBride, LB., 1,619; Hall, Comm., 318; Camejo, Soc. Workers, 168.
1972: Nixon, R., 166,476; McGovern, D., 139,945; Jenness, Soc. Workers, 994.
1968: Nixon, R., 149,841; Humphrey, D., 118,023; Wallace, 3rd party, 13,400.
1964: Johnson, D., 163,010; Goldwater, R., 130,108.
1960: Nixon, R., 178,417; Kennedy, D., 128,070.
1956: Eisenhower, R., 171,569; Stevenson, D., 122,288.
1952: Eisenhower, R., 203,857; Stevenson, D., 90,426.

Tennessee Vote Since 1952

2008: McCain, R., 1,479,178; Obama, D., 1,087,437; Nader, Ind., 11,560; Barr, Ind., 8,547; Baldwin, Ind., 8,191; McKinney, Ind., 2,499; Moore, Ind., 1,326; Jay, Ind., 1,011.
2004: Bush, R., 1,384,375; Kerry, D., 1,036,477; Nader, Ind., 8,992; Badnarik, Ind., 4,866; Peroutka, Ind., 2,570.
2000: Bush, R., 1,061,949; Gore, D., 981,720; Nader, Green, 19,781; Browne, LB., 4,284; Buchanan, RF., 4,250; Brown, Ind., 1,606; Phillips, Ind., 1,015; Hagelin, RF., 613; Venson, Ind., 535.
1996: Clinton, D., 909,146; Dole, R., 863,530; Perot, RF., 105,918; Nader, Ind., 6,427; Browne, Ind., 5,020; Phillips, Ind., 1,818; Collins, Ind., 688; Hagelin, Ind., 636; Michael, Ind., 408; Dodge, Ind., 324.
1992: Clinton, D., 933,521; Bush, R., 841,300; Perot, Ind., 199,968; Marrou, LB., 1,847.
1988: Bush, R., 947,233; Dukakis, D., 679,794; Paul, Ind., 2,041; Duke, Ind., 1,807.
1984: Reagan, R., 990,212; Mondale, D., 711,714; Bergland, LB., 3,072.
1980: Reagan, R., 787,761; Carter, D., 783,051; Anderson, Ind., 35,991; Clark, Ind., 7,116; Commoner, Citizens, 1,112; Bubar, Statesman, 521; McReynolds, Soc., 519; Hall, Comm., 503; DeBerry, Soc. Workers, 490; Griswold, Workers World, 400; write-in, 152.
1976: Carter, D., 825,879; Ford, R., 633,969; Anderson, Amer., 5,769; McCarthy, Ind., 5,004; Maddox, Amer. Ind., 2,303; MacBride, LB., 1,375; Hall, Comm., 547; LaRouche, U.S. Labor, 512; Bubar, Prohib., 442; Miller, Ind., 316; write-in, 230.
1972: Nixon, R., 813,147; McGovern, D., 357,293; Schmitz, Amer., 30,373; write-in, 369.

1968: Nixon, R., 472,592; Wallace, 3rd party, 424,792; Humphrey, D., 351,233.
1964: Johnson, D., 635,047; Goldwater, R., 508,965; write-in, 34.
1960: Nixon, R., 556,577; Kennedy, D., 481,453; Faubus, States' Rights, 11,304; Decker, Prohib., 2,458.
1956: Eisenhower, R., 462,288; Stevenson, D., 456,507; Andrews, Ind., 19,820; Holtwick, Prohib., 789.
1952: Eisenhower, R., 446,147; Stevenson, D., 443,710; Hamblen, Prohib., 1,432; Hallinan, Prog., 885; MacArthur, Christian Nationalist, 379.

Texas Vote Since 1952

2008: McCain, R., 4,479,328; Obama, D., 3,528,633 Barr, LB., 56,116.
2004: Bush, R., 4,526,917; Kerry, D., 2,832,704; Badnarik, LB., 38,787.
2000: Bush, R., 3,799,639; Gore, D., 2,433,746; Nader, Green, 137,994; Browne, LB., 23,160; Buchanan, Ind., 12,394.
1996: Dole, R., 2,736,167; Clinton, D., 2,459,683; Perot, RF., 378,537; Browne, LB., 20,256; Phillips, U.S. Taxpayers, 7,472; Hagelin, Natural Law, 4,422.
1992: Bush, R., 2,496,071; Clinton, D., 2,281,815; Perot, Ind., 1,354,781; Marrou, LB., 19,699.
1988: Bush, R., 3,036,829; Dukakis, D., 2,352,748; Paul, LB., 30,355; Fulani, New Alliance, 7,208.
1984: Reagan, R., 3,433,428; Mondale, D., 1,949,276.
1980: Reagan, R., 2,510,705; Carter, D., 1,881,147; Anderson, Ind., 111,613; Clark, LB., 37,643; write-in, 528.
1976: Carter, D., 2,082,319; Ford, R., 1,953,300; McCarthy, Ind., 20,118; Anderson, Amer., 11,442; Camejo, Soc. Workers, 1,723; write-in, 2,982.
1972: Nixon, R., 2,298,896; McGovern, D., 1,154,289; Jenness, Soc. Workers, 8,664; Schmitz, Amer., 6,039; others, 3,393.
1968: Humphrey, D., 1,266,804; Nixon, R., 1,227,844; Wallace, 3rd party, 584,269; write-in, 489.
1964: Johnson, D., 1,663,185; Goldwater, R., 958,566; Lightburn, Const., 5,060.
1960: Kennedy, D., 1,167,932; Nixon, R., 1,121,699; Sullivan, Const., 18,169; Decker, Prohib., 3,870; write-in, 15.
1956: Eisenhower, R., 1,080,619; Stevenson, D., 859,958; Andrews, Ind., 14,591.
1952: Eisenhower, R., 1,102,878; Stevenson, D., 969,228; Hamblen, Prohib., 1,983; MacArthur, Christian Nationalist, 833; MacArthur, Const., 730; Hallinan, Prog., 294.

Utah Vote Since 1952

2008: McCain, R., 596,030; Obama, D., 327,670; Baldwin, Const., 12,012; Nader, unaff., 8,416; Barr, LB., 6,966; McKinney, unaff., 982; La Riva, unaff., 262.
2004: Bush, R., 663,742; Kerry, D., 241,199; Nader, Ind., 11,305; Peroutka, Const., 6,841; Badnarik, LB., 3,375; Jay, Pers. Choice, 946; Harris, Soc. Workers, 393.
2000: Bush, R., 515,096; Gore, D., 203,053; Nader, Green, 35,850; Buchanan, RF., 9,319; Browne, LB., 3,616; Phillips, Ind. Amer., 2,709; Hagelin, Natural Law, 763; Harris, Soc. Workers, 186; Youngkeit, Ind., 161.
1996: Dole, R., 361,911; Clinton, D., 221,633; Perot, RF., 66,461; Nader, Green, 4,615; Browne, LB., 4,129; Phillips, Taxpayers, 2,601; Templin, Ind. Amer., 1,290; Crane, Ind., 1,101; Hagelin, Natural Law, 1,085; Moorehead, Workers World, 298; Harris, Soc. Workers, 235; Dodge, Prohib., 111.
1992: Bush, R., 322,632; Perot, Ind., 203,400; Clinton, D., 183,429; Gritz, Populist/America First, 28,602; Marrou, LB., 1,900; Hagelin, Natural Law, 1,319; LaRouche, Ind., 1,089.
1988: Bush, R., 428,442; Dukakis, D., 207,352; Paul, LB., 7,473; Dennis, Amer., 2,158.
1984: Reagan, R., 469,105; Mondale, D., 155,369; Bergland, LB., 2,447.
1980: Reagan, R., 439,687; Carter, D., 124,266; Anderson, Ind., 30,284; Clark, LB., 7,226; Commoner, Citizens, 1,009; Greaves, Amer., 965; Rarick, Amer. Ind., 522; Hall, Comm., 139; DeBerry, Soc. Workers, 124.
1976: Ford, R., 337,908; Carter, D., 182,110; Anderson, Amer., 13,304; McCarthy, Ind., 3,907; MacBride, LB., 2,438; Maddox, Amer. Ind., 1,162; Camejo, Soc. Workers, 268; Hall, Comm., 121.
1972: Nixon, R., 323,643; McGovern, D., 126,284; Schmitz, Amer., 28,549.
1968: Nixon, R., 238,728; Humphrey, D., 156,665; Wallace, 3rd party, 26,906; Peace/Freedom, 180; Halstead, Soc. Workers, 89.
1964: Johnson, D., 219,628; Goldwater, R., 181,785.

1960: Nixon, R., 205,361; Kennedy, D., 169,248; Dobbs, Soc. Workers, 100.
1956: Eisenhower, R., 215,631; Stevenson, D., 118,364.
1952: Eisenhower, R., 194,190; Stevenson, D., 135,364.

Vermont Vote Since 1952

2008: Obama, D., 219,262; McCain, R., 98,974; Nader, Ind., 3,339; Barr, LB., 1,067; Baldwin, Const., 500; Calero, Soc. Workers, 150; La Riva, Socialism/Liberation, 149; Moore, Liberty Union, 141.
2004: Kerry, D., 184,067; Bush, R., 121,180; Nader, Ind., 4,494; Badnarik, LB., 1,102; Parker, Liberty Union, 265; Calero, Soc. Workers, 244.
2000: Gore, D., 149,022; Bush, R., 119,775; Nader, Green, 20,374; Buchanan, RF., 2,192; Lane, Grass Roots, 1,044; Browne, LB., 784; Hagelin, Natural Law, 219; McReynolds, Liberty Union, 161; Phillips, Const., 153; Harris, Soc. Workers, 70.
1996: Clinton, D., 137,894; Dole, R., 80,352; Perot, RF., 31,024; Nader, Green, 5,585; Browne, LB., 1,183; Hagelin, Natural Law, 498; Peron, Grass Roots, 480; Phillips, Taxpayers, 382; Hollis, Liberty Union, 292; Harris, Soc. Workers, 199.
1992: Clinton, D., 133,590; Bush, R., 88,122; Perot, Ind., 65,985.
1988: Bush, R., 124,331; Dukakis, D., 115,775; Paul, LB., 1,000; LaRouche, Ind., 275.
1984: Reagan, R., 135,865; Mondale, D., 95,730; Bergland, LB., 1,002.
1980: Reagan, R., 94,598; Carter, D., 81,891; Anderson, Ind., 31,760; Commoner, Citizens, 2,316; Clark, LB., 1,900; McReynolds, Liberty Union, 136; Hall, Comm., 118; DeBerry, Soc. Workers, 75; scattered, 413.
1976: Ford, R., 100,387; Carter, D., 77,798 and Ind. Vermonters, 991 (total, 79,789); McCarthy, Ind., 4,001; Camejo, Soc. Workers, 430; LaRouche, U.S. Labor, 196; scattered, 99.
1972: Nixon, R., 117,149; McGovern, D., 68,174; Spock, Liberty Union, 1,010; Jenness, Soc. Workers, 296; scattered, 318.
1968: Nixon, R., 85,142; Humphrey, D., 70,255; Wallace, 3rd party, 5,104; Gregory, New Party, 579; Halstead, Soc. Workers, 295.
1964: Johnson, D., 107,674; Goldwater, R., 54,868.
1960: Nixon, R., 98,131; Kennedy, D., 69,186.
1956: Eisenhower, R., 110,390; Stevenson, D., 42,549; scattered, 39.
1952: Eisenhower, R., 109,717; Stevenson, D., 43,355; Hallinan, Prog., 282; Hoopes, Soc., 185.

Virginia Vote Since 1952

2008: Obama, D., 1,959,532; McCain, R., 1,725,005; Nader, Ind., 11,483; Barr, LB., 11,067; Baldwin, Ind. Green, 7,474; McKinney, Green, 2,344.
2004: Bush, R., 1,716,959; Kerry, D., 1,454,742; Badnarik, LB., 11,032; Peroutka, Const., 10,161.
2000: Bush, R., 1,437,490; Gore, D., 1,217,290; Nader, Green, 59,398; Browne, LB., 15,198; Buchanan, RF., 5,455; Phillips, Const., 1,809.
1996: Dole, R., 1,138,350; Clinton, D., 1,091,060; Perot, RF., 159,861; Phillips, Taxpayers, 13,687; Browne, LB., 9,174; Hagelin, Natural Law, 4,510.
1992: Bush, R., 1,150,517; Clinton, D., 1,038,650; Perot, Ind., 348,639; LaRouche, Ind., 11,937; Marrou, LB., 5,730; Fulani, New Alliance, 3,192.
1988: Bush, R., 1,309,162; Dukakis, D., 859,799; Fulani, Ind., 14,312; Paul, LB., 8,336.
1984: Reagan, R., 1,337,078; Mondale, D., 796,250.
1980: Reagan, R., 989,609; Carter, D., 752,174; Anderson, Ind., 95,418; Commoner, Citizens, 14,024; Clark, LB., 12,821; DeBerry, Soc. Workers, 1,986.
1976: Ford, R., 836,554; Carter, D., 813,896; Camejo, Soc. Workers, 17,802; Anderson, Amer., 16,686; LaRouche, U.S. Labor, 7,508; MacBride, LB., 4,648.
1972: Nixon, R., 988,493; McGovern, D., 438,887; Schmitz, Amer., 19,721; Fisher, Soc. Labor, 9,918.
1968: Nixon, R., 590,319; Humphrey, D., 442,387; Wallace, 3rd party, 320,272; Blomen, Soc. Labor, 4,671; Gregory, Peace/Freedom, 1,680; Munn, Prohib., 601. *10,561 votes for Wallace were omitted in the count.
1964: Johnson, D., 558,038; Goldwater, R., 481,334; Hass, Soc. Labor, 2,895.
1960: Nixon, R., 404,521; Kennedy, D., 362,327; Coiner, Conservative, 4,204; Hass, Soc. Labor, 397.
1956: Eisenhower, R., 386,459; Stevenson, D., 267,760; Andrews, States' Rights, 42,964; Hoopes, Soc. Democrat, 444; Hass, Soc. Labor, 351.

1952: Eisenhower, R., 349,037; Stevenson, D., 268,677; Hass, Soc. Labor, 1,160; Hoopes, Soc. Democrat, 504; Hallinan, Prog., 311.

Washington Vote Since 1952

2008: Obama, D., 1,750,848; McCain, R., 1,229,216; Nader, Ind., 29,489; Barr, LB., 12,728; Baldwin, Const., 9,432; McKinney, Green, 3,819; La Riva, Socialism/Liberation, 705; Harris, Soc. Workers, 641.

2004: Kerry, D., 1,510,201; Bush, R., 1,304,894; Nader, Ind., 23,283; Badnarik, LB., 11,955; Peroutka, Const., 3,922; Cobb, Green, 2,974; Parker, Workers World, 1,077; Harris, Soc. Workers, 547; Van Auken, Soc. Equal., 231.

2000: Gore, D., 1,247,652; Bush, R., 1,108,864; Nader, Green, 103,002; Browne, LB., 13,135; Buchanan, Freedom, 7,171; Hagelin, Natural Law, 2,927; Phillips, Const., 1,989; Moorehead, Workers World, 1,729; McReynolds, Soc., 660; Harris, Soc. Workers, 304.

1996: Clinton, D., 1,123,323; Dole, R., 840,712; Perot, RF., 201,003; Nader, Ind., 60,322; Browne, LB., 12,522; Hagelin, Natural Law, 6,076; Phillips, U.S. Taxpayers, 4,578; Collins, Ind., 2,374; Moorehead, Workers World, 2,189; Harris, Soc. Workers, 738.

1992: Clinton, D., 993,037; Bush, R., 731,234; Perot, Ind., 541,780; Marrou, LB., 7,533; Gritz, Populist/America First, 4,854; Hagelin, Natural Law, 2,456; Phillips, U.S. Taxpayers, 2,354; Fulani, New Alliance, 1,776; Daniels, Ind., 1,171.

1988: Dukakis, D., 933,516; Bush, R., 903,835; Paul, LB., 17,240; LaRouche, Ind., 4,412.

1984: Reagan, R., 1,051,670; Mondale, D., 798,352; Bergland, LB., 8,844.

1980: Reagan, R., 865,244; Carter, D., 650,193; Anderson, Ind., 185,073; Clark, LB., 29,213; Commoner, Citizens, 9,403; DeBerry, Soc. Workers, 1,137; McReynolds, Soc., 956; Hall, Comm., 834; Griswold, Workers World, 341.

1976: Ford, R., 777,732; Carter, D., 717,323; McCarthy, Ind., 36,986; Maddox, Amer. Ind., 8,585; Anderson, Amer., 5,046; MacBride, LB., 5,042; Wright, People's, 1,124; Camejo, Soc. Workers, 905; LaRouche, U.S. Labor, 903; Hall, Comm., 817; Levin, Soc. Labor, 713; Zeidler, Soc., 358.

1972: Nixon, R., 837,135; McGovern, D., 568,334; Schmitz, Amer., 58,906; Spock, Ind., 2,644; Hospers, LB., 1,537; Fisher, Soc. Labor, 1,102; Jenness, Soc. Workers, 623; Hall, Comm., 566.

1968: Humphrey, D., 616,037; Nixon, R., 588,510; Wallace, 3rd party, 96,990; Cleaver, Peace/Freedom, 1,609; Blomen, Soc. Labor, 488; Mitchell, Free Ballot, 377; Halstead, Soc. Workers, 270.

1964: Johnson, D., 779,699; Goldwater, R., 470,366; Hass, Soc. Labor, 7,772; DeBerry, Freedom Soc., 537.

1960: Nixon, R., 629,273; Kennedy, D., 599,298; Hass, Soc. Labor, 10,895; Curtis, Const., 1,401; Dobbs, Soc. Workers, 705.

1956: Eisenhower, R., 620,430; Stevenson, D., 523,002; Hass, Soc. Labor, 7,457.

1952: Eisenhower, R., 599,107; Stevenson, D., 492,845; MacArthur, Christian Nationalist, 7,290; Hallinan, Prog., 2,460; Hass, Soc. Labor, 633; Hoopes, Soc., 254; Dobbs, Soc. Workers, 119.

West Virginia Vote Since 1952

2008: McCain, R., 397,466; Obama, D., 303,857; Nader, unaff., 7,219; Baldwin, Const., 2,465; McKinney, Mountain, 2,355.

2004: Bush, R., 423,778; Kerry, D., 326,541; Nader, Ind., 4,063; Badnarik, LB., 1,405.

2000: Bush, R., 336,475; Gore, D., 295,497; Nader, Green, 10,680; Buchanan, RF., 3,169; Browne, LB., 1,912; Hagelin, Natural Law, 367.

1996: Clinton, D., 327,812; Dole, R., 233,946; Perot, RF., 71,639; Browne, LB., 3,062.

1992: Clinton, D., 331,001; Bush, R., 241,974; Perot, Ind., 108,829; Marrou, LB., 1,873.

1988: Dukakis, D., 341,016; Bush, R., 310,065; Fulani, New Alliance, 2,230.

1984: Reagan, R., 405,483; Mondale, D., 328,125.

1980: Carter, D., 367,462; Reagan, R., 334,206; Anderson, Ind., 31,691; Clark, LB., 4,356.

1976: Carter, D., 435,864; Ford, R., 314,726.

1972: Nixon, R., 484,964; McGovern, D., 277,435.

1968: Humphrey, D., 374,091; Nixon, R., 307,555; Wallace, 3rd party, 72,560.

1964: Johnson, D., 538,087; Goldwater, R., 253,953.

1960: Kennedy, D., 441,786; Nixon, R., 395,995.

1956: Eisenhower, R., 449,297; Stevenson, D., 381,534.

1952: Stevenson, D., 453,578; Eisenhower, R., 419,970.

Wisconsin Vote Since 1952

2008: Obama, D., 1,677,211; McCain, R., 1,262,393; Nader, Ind., 17,605; Barr, LB., 8,858; Baldwin, Ind., 5,072; McKinney, Green, 4,216; Wamboldt, Ind., 764; Moore, Ind., 540; La Riva, Ind., 237.

2004: Kerry, D., 1,489,504; Bush, R., 1,478,120; Nader, Ind., 16,390; Badnarik, LB., 6,464; Cobb, Green, 2,661; Brown, Ind., 471; Harris, Ind., 411.

2000: Gore, D., 1,242,987; Bush, R., 1,237,279; Nader, Green, 94,070; Buchanan, RF., 11,446; Browne, LB., 6,640; Phillips, Const., 2,042; Moorehead, Workers World, 1,063; Hagelin, RF., 878; Harris, Soc. Workers, 306.

1996: Clinton, D., 1,071,971; Dole, R., 845,029; Perot, RF., 227,339; Nader, Green, 28,723; Phillips, U.S. Taxpayers, 8,811; Browne, LB., 7,929; Hagelin, Natural Law, 1,379; Moorehead, Workers World, 1,333; Hollis, Soc., 848; Harris, Soc. Workers, 483.

1992: Clinton, D., 1,041,066; Bush, R., 930,855; Perot, Ind., 544,479; Marrou, LB., 2,877; Gritz, Populist/America First, 2,311; Daniels, Ind., 1,883; Phillips, U.S. Taxpayers, 1,772; Hagelin, Natural Law, 1,070.

1988: Dukakis, D., 1,126,794; Bush, R., 1,047,499; Paul, LB., 5,157; Duke, Populist, 3,056.

1984: Reagan, R., 1,198,584; Mondale, D., 995,740; Bergland, LB., 4,883.

1980: Reagan, R., 1,088,845; Carter, D., 981,584; Anderson, Ind., 160,657; Clark, LB., 29,135; Commoner, Citizens, 7,767; Rarick, Const., 1,519; McReynolds, Soc., 808; Hall, Comm., 772; Griswold, Workers World, 414; DeBerry, Soc. Workers, 383; scattered, 1,337.

1976: Carter, D., 1,040,232; Ford, R., 1,004,987; McCarthy, Ind., 34,943; Maddox, Amer. Ind., 8,552; Zeidler, Soc., 4,298; MacBride, LB., 3,814; Camejo, Soc. Workers, 1,691; Wright, People's, 943; Hall, Comm., 749; LaRouche, U.S. Labor, 738; Levin, Soc. Labor, 389; scattered, 2,839.

1972: Nixon, R., 989,430; McGovern, D., 810,174; Schmitz, Amer., 47,525; Spock, Ind., 2,701; Fisher, Soc. Labor, 998; Hall, Comm., 663; Reed, Ind., 506; scattered, 893.

1968: Nixon, R., 809,997; Humphrey, D., 748,804; Wallace, 3rd party, 127,835; Blomen, Soc. Labor, 1,338; Halstead, Soc. Workers, 1,222; scattered, 2,342.

1964: Johnson, D., 1,050,424; Goldwater, R., 638,495; DeBerry, Soc. Workers, 1,692; Hass, Soc. Labor, 1,204.

1960: Nixon, R., 895,175; Kennedy, D., 830,805; Dobbs, Soc. Workers, 1,792; Hass, Soc. Labor, 1,310.

1956: Eisenhower, R., 954,844; Stevenson, D., 586,768; Andrews, Ind., 6,918; Hoopes, Soc., 754; Hass, Soc. Labor, 710; Dobbs, Soc. Workers, 564.

1952: Eisenhower, R., 979,744; Stevenson, D., 622,175; Hallinan, Ind., 2,174; Dobbs, Ind., 1,350; Hoopes, Ind., 1,157; Hass, Ind., 770.

Wyoming Vote Since 1952

2008: McCain, R., 164,958; Obama, D., 82,868; Nader, Ind., 2,525; Barr, LB., 1,594; Baldwin, Ind., 1,192.

2004: Bush, R., 167,629; Kerry, D., 70,776; Nader, Ind., 2,741; Badnarik, LB., 1,171; Peroutka, Ind., 631.

2000: Bush, R., 147,947; Gore, D., 60,481; Buchanan, RF., 2,724; Browne, LB., 1,443; Phillips, Ind., 720; Hagelin, Natural Law, 411.

1996: Dole, R., 105,388; Clinton, D., 77,934; Perot, RF., 25,928; Browne, LB., 1,739; Hagelin, Natural Law, 582.

1992: Bush, R., 79,347; Clinton, D., 68,160; Perot, Ind., 51,263.

1988: Bush, R., 106,867; Dukakis, D., 67,113; Paul, LB., 2,026; Fulani, New Alliance, 545.

1984: Reagan, R., 133,241; Mondale, D., 53,370; Bergland, LB., 2,357.

1980: Reagan, R., 110,700; Carter, D., 49,427; Anderson, Ind., 12,072; Clark, LB., 4,514.

1976: Ford, R., 92,717; Carter, D., 62,239; McCarthy, Ind., 624; Reagan, Ind., 307; Anderson, Amer., 290; MacBride, LB., 89; Brown, Ind., 47; Maddox, Amer. Ind., 30.

1972: Nixon, R., 100,464; McGovern, D., 44,358; Schmitz, Amer., 748.

1968: Nixon, R., 70,927; Humphrey, D., 45,173; Wallace, 3rd party, 11,105.

1964: Johnson, D., 80,718; Goldwater, R., 61,998.

1960: Nixon, R., 77,451; Kennedy, D., 63,331.

1956: Eisenhower, R., 74,573; Stevenson, D., 49,554.

1952: Eisenhower, R., 81,047; Stevenson, D., 47,934; Hamblen, Prohib., 194; Hoopes, Soc., 40; Haas, Soc. Labor, 36.

UNITED STATES GOVERNMENT

EXECUTIVE BRANCH	LEGISLATIVE BRANCH	JUDICIAL BRANCH
President	**CONGRESS**	**Supreme Court of the United States**
Vice President	**Senate/House of Representatives**	Courts of Appeals
Executive Office of the President	Architect of the Capitol	District Courts
Council of Economic Advisers	U.S. Botanic Garden	Territorial Courts
Council on Environmental Quality	Government Accountability Office	Court of International Trade
Executive Residence	Government Printing Office	Bankruptcy Courts
National Security Council	Library of Congress	Court of Federal Claims
Office of Administration	Congressional Budget Office	Tax Court
Office of Management and Budget	Medicare Payment Advisory Commission	Court of Appeals for the Armed Forces
Office of National Drug Control Policy	Stennis Center for Public Service	Court of Appeals for Veterans Claims
Office of Science and Technology Policy		Administrative Office of the Courts
Office of the U.S. Trade Representative		Federal Judicial Center
Office of the Vice President		Sentencing Commission
White House Office*		Judicial Panel on Multidistrict Litigation

*Includes Domestic Policy Council, National Security Advisor, National Economic Council, Office of Cabinet Affairs, Office of the Chief of Staff, Office of Communications, Office of Digital Strategy, Office of the First Lady, Office of Legislative Affairs, Office of Management and Administration, Oval Office Operations, Office of Presidential Personnel, Office of Public Engagement and Intergovernmental Affairs, Office of Scheduling and Advance, Office of the Staff Secretary, and Office of the White House Counsel.

The Obama Administration

As of Aug. 2012; mailing addresses are for Washington, DC, except where otherwise noted.
Terms of office of the president and vice president: Jan. 20, 2009 to Jan. 20, 2013.

President: By law, Pres. Barack H. Obama received an annual salary of $400,000 (taxable) and an annual expense allowance of $50,000 (nontaxable) for costs resulting from official duties. In addition, up to $100,000 a year may be spent on travel expenses and $19,000 on official entertainment (both nontaxable). This does not include amounts available for expenditures within the Executive Office of the President, including $3,850,000 for necessary expenses for the White House and amounts for travel and entertainment.
Website: www.whitehouse.gov/administration/president-obama
Vice President: By law, Vice Pres. Joseph R. Biden received an annual salary of $230,700 (taxable) and an annual expense allowance of $20,000 for costs resulting from official duties, plus $90,000 for official entertainment expenses (nontaxable).
Website: www.whitehouse.gov/administration/vice-president-biden

Cabinet Department Heads

(Salary: $199,700 per year)

Secretary of State: Hillary Rodham Clinton
Secretary of the Treasury: Timothy F. Geithner
Secretary of Defense: Leon E. Panetta
Attorney General (Dept. of Justice): Eric H. Holder Jr.
Secretary of the Interior: Kenneth L. Salazar
Secretary of Agriculture: Thomas J. Vilsack
Secretary of Commerce: Rebecca M. Blank, acting
Secretary of Labor: Hilda L. Solis
Secretary of Health and Human Services: Kathleen Sebelius
Secretary of Housing and Urban Development: Shaun L.S. Donovan
Secretary of Transportation: Raymond L. LaHood
Secretary of Energy: Steven Chu
Secretary of Education: Arne Duncan
Secretary of Veterans Affairs: Eric K. Shinseki
Secretary of Homeland Security: Janet A. Napolitano

Executive Agencies

Council of Economic Advisers: Alan B. Krueger, chair; www.whitehouse.gov/administration/eop/cea/
Council on Environ. Quality: Nancy Sutley, chair; www.whitehouse.gov/administration/eop/ceq/
Office of Administration: Beth Jones, dir.; www.whitehouse.gov/administration/eop/oa/
Office of Management and Budget: Jeffrey Zients, acting dir.; www.whitehouse.gov/omb/
Office of Natl. Drug Control Policy: R. Gil Kerlikowske, dir.; www.whitehouse.gov/ondcp/
Office of Science and Technology Policy: John Holdren, dir.; www.whitehouse.gov/administration/eop/ostp/
Office of the U.S. Trade Representative: Amb. Ronald Kirk; www.ustr.gov

White House Staff

1600 Pennsylvania Ave. NW, 20500;
www.whitehouse.gov

Counselor to the President: Peter M. Rouse
Physician to the President: Jeffrey C. Kuhlman
Director, National Intelligence: James R. Clapper
Assistants to the President:
  Chief of Staff: Jacob J. Lew
  Deputy Chief of Staff for Operations: Alyssa Mastromonaco
  Deputy Chief of Staff for Planning: Mark B. Childress
  Deputy Chief of Staff for Policy: Nancy-Ann DeParle
  Cabinet Secretary: Christopher P. Lu
  Counsel to the President: Kathryn H. Ruemmler
  White House Press Secretary: Jay Carney
  Deputy National Security Advisor: Denis R. McDonough
  Deputy National Security Advisor for Intl. Economics: Michael B. Froman
  Director of Communications: Howard D. Pfeiffer
  Domestic Policy Advisor and Director of the Domestic Policy Council: Cecilia Muñoz
  Economic Policy and Director of the National Economic Council: Gene B. Sperling
  Homeland Security and Counterterrorism: John O. Brennan
  Director of Legislative Affairs: Robert L. Nabors
  Manufacturing Policy: Jason S. Miller
  National Security Advisor: Thomas E. Donilon
  Director of Speechwriting: Jonathan E. Favreau
Senior Advisors: Valerie B. Jarrett, David Plouffe
Chief of Staff to the Vice President: Bruce Reed
White House Social Secretary: Jeremy M. Bernard
Chief of Staff to the First Lady: Christina M. Tchen
Press Secretary to the First Lady: Hannah M. August

Cabinet-Level Departments

Department of State

2201 C St. NW, 20520; www.state.gov

Conducts U.S. foreign policy. The Foreign Service protects American citizens and interests through embassies in some 180 countries under eight geographic bureaus. Maintains contact with foreign governments, negotiates agreements and treaties, and supports U.S. foreign trade. Promotes democracy, international security, human rights—including issues related to AIDS, human trafficking, war crimes, and migration—and arms and narcotics control. Represents the nation in international organizations. Issues passports to U.S. citizens and visas to foreigners. **Budget** (includes State Dept. and other international programs): $45.2 bil (2011); $56.0 bil (est. 2012); $59.5 bil (est. 2013).

- Intl. Boundary and Water Commission (4171 North Mesa, Ste. C-100, El Paso, TX 79902); www.ibwc.gov
- Intl. Information Programs (2201 C St. NW, SA-5, Rm. 5B17, 20520); www.state.gov/r/iip/
- Intl. Narcotics and Law Enforcement Affairs (2201 C St. NW, Rm. 7333 HST, 20520); www.state.gov/j/inl/
- Intl. Organization Affairs (2201 C St. NW, Rm. 6323, 20520); www.state.gov/p/io/
- Population, Refugees, and Migration (2201 C St. NW, HST, Rm. 5805, 20520); www.state.gov/j/prm/
- U.S. Global AIDS Coordinator (2201 C St. NW, SA-29, Ste. 200, 20520); www.state.gov/s/gac/

Department of the Treasury

1500 Pennsylvania Ave. NW, 20220; www.treasury.gov

Responsible for the fiscal affairs of the U.S. Serves as the government's financial agent; collects, borrows, and disburses funds for the federal government. Monitors the nation's financial infrastructure and economic development; recommends domestic and international financial, monetary, economic, trade, and tax policies. Manufactures currency and coins. Carries out monetary and tax law enforcement activities, sanctions, embargoes, and fights illicit finance—counterfeiting, money laundering, narcotics trafficking, terrorist financing. **Budget:** $104.9 bil (2011); $162.2 bil (est. 2012); $110.3 bil (est. 2013).

- Alcohol and Tobacco Tax and Trade Bureau (1310 G St. NW, Box 12, 20005); www.ttb.gov
- Bureau of Engraving and Printing (14th and C Sts. SW, 20228); www.moneyfactory.gov
- Bureau of the Public Debt (200 3rd St., Parkersburg, WV 26106); www.publicdebt.treas.gov
- Financial Crimes Enforcement Network (P.O. Box 39, Vienna, VA 22183); www.fincen.gov
- Financial Management Service (401 14th St. SW, 20227); www.fms.treas.gov
- Internal Revenue Service (1111 Constitution Ave. NW, 20224); www.irs.gov
- U.S. Mint (801 9th St. NW, 20220); www.usmint.gov

Department of Defense

1400 Defense Pentagon, 20301; www.defense.gov

Directs and controls the armed forces and assists the president in protecting the nation's security. Military departments of the Army, Navy, and Air Force are each separately organized under its own secretary but all function under the command of the Secretary of Defense. They conduct military operations as unified commands. The chairman of the Joint Chiefs of Staff is the principal military adviser to the President. Undersecretaries supervise acquisition, technology, and logistics; intelligence; personnel and readiness; and policy. **Budget:** $678.0 bil (2011); $688.3 bil (est. 2012); $672.9 bil (est. 2013).

- Def. Advanced Research Projects Agency (675 N. Randolph St., Arlington, VA 22203); www.darpa.mil
- Def. Intelligence Agency (200 MacDill Blvd., 20340); www.dia.mil
- Def. Security Cooperation Agency (2800 Defense Pentagon, 20301); www.dsca.osd.mil
- Missile Def. Agency (5700 18th St., Bldg. 245, Fort Belvoir, VA 22060-5573); www.mda.mil
- Natl. Geospatial-Intelligence Agency (7500 GEOINT Dr., Springfield, VA 22150); www.nga.mil
- Natl. Security Agency/Central Security Service (Ft. Meade, MD 20755); www.nsa.gov

Department of Justice

950 Pennsylvania Ave. NW, 20530; www.justice.gov

Provides means for the enforcement of federal laws and investigating violations thereof; furnishes legal counsel in cases involving the federal government and interprets laws relating to the activities of other federal departments; supervises federal penal institutions. The Attorney General and Office of Legal Counsel render legal advice, upon request, to the president and department heads. The Solicitor General conducts all suits brought before the U.S. Supreme Court in which the federal government is concerned. The Civil Division represents the U.S. government in many civil or criminal matters. The 94 U.S. Attorneys are the principal litigators in the U.S. and its territories. Divisions for suits regarding antitrust laws, civil rights, civil and criminal statutes, natural resources and the environment, national security, and taxes. **Budget:** $30.5 bil (2011); $34.6 bil (est. 2012); $36.5 bil (est. 2013).

- Bureau of Alcohol, Tobacco, Firearms, and Explosives (99 New York Ave. NE, Rm. 5S 144, 20226); www.atf.gov
- Bureau of Prisons (320 First St. NW, 20534); www.bop.gov
- Drug Enforcement Admin. (AES, 8701 Morrissette Dr., Springfield, VA 22152); www.dea.gov
- Executive Office for Immigration Review (5107 Leesburg Pike, Falls Church, VA 22041); www.justice.gov/eoir/
- Federal Bureau of Investigation (935 Pennsylvania Ave. NW, 20535); www.fbi.gov
- INTERPOL Washington (U.S. Natl. Central Bureau) (20530); www.justice.gov/interpol-washington/
- U.S. Marshals Service (2604 Jefferson Davis Hwy., Alexandria, VA 22301-1025); www.usmarshals.gov
- U.S. Parole Commission (90 K St. NE, 3rd Fl., 20530); www.justice.gov/uspc/

Department of the Interior

1849 C St. NW, 20240; www.doi.gov

Custodian of natural resources. Has the responsibility of protecting and conserving the country's land, water, minerals, fish, and wildlife; of promoting the wise use of all these natural resources; of maintaining national parks and recreation areas; and of preserving historic places. It also provides for the welfare of American Indian reservation communities and of inhabitants of island territories under U.S. administration. **Budget:** $13.7 bil (2011); $11.3 bil (est. 2012); $13.5 bil (est. 2013).

- Bureau of Indian Affairs (1849 C Street NW, 20240); www.bia.gov
- Bureau of Land Management (1849 C St. NW, 20240); www.blm.gov
- Bureau of Ocean Energy Management (1849 C St. NW, 20240); www.boem.gov
- Bureau of Reclamation (1849 C St. NW, 20240); www.usbr.gov
- Bureau of Safety and Environmental Enforcement (1849 C St. NW, 20240); www.bsee.gov
- National Park Service (1849 C St. NW, 20240); www.nps.gov
- Office of Surface Mining (1951 Constitution Ave. NW, 20240); www.osmre.gov
- U.S. Fish and Wildlife Service (1849 C St. NW, 20240); www.fws.gov
- U.S. Geological Survey (12201 Sunrise Valley Dr., Reston, VA 20192); www.usgs.gov

Department of Agriculture

1400 Independence Ave. SW, 20250; www.usda.gov

Provides leadership on food, agriculture, and natural resources; supports scientific research and education for agriculture, nutrition, and food safety. Develops nutrition assistance programs, promotes healthy eating, supplies food stamps, grades and inspects the commercial supply of food. Responsible for the health of the land through sustainable management and conservation, manages public lands in national forests and grasslands; safeguards against invasive pests and diseases; ensures the health and care of animals and plants. Oversees assistance and conservation programs for farmers and ranchers and programs to improve the rural economy and quality of life. Facilitates domestic and international marketing of U.S. agricultural products. **Budget:** $139.4 bil (2011); $150.7 bil (est. 2012); $154.5 bil (est. 2013).

- Agricultural Research Service (1400 Independence Ave. SW, 20250); www.ars.usda.gov
- Economic Research Service (1400 Independence Ave. SW, Mail Stop 1800, 20250); www.ers.usda.gov
- Food and Nutrition Service (3101 Park Center Dr., Alexandria, VA 22302); www.fns.usda.gov
- Food Safety and Inspection Service (1400 Independence Ave. SW, 20250); www.fsis.usda.gov
- Foreign Agricultural Service (1400 Independence Ave. SW, 20250); www.fas.usda.gov
- Forest Service (1400 Independence Ave. SW, 20250); www.fs.fed.us
- Natl. Agricultural Statistics Service (1400 Independence Ave. SW, 20250); www.nass.usda.gov
- Natural Resources Conservation Service (1400 Independence Ave. SW, 20250); www.nrcs.usda.gov

Department of Commerce

1401 Constitution Ave. NW, 20230; www.commerce.gov

Fosters, serves, and promotes the nation's economic development and technological advancement; supports the comprehension and use of the physical environment and its oceanic life; assists states, communities, and individuals with economic progress; promotes trade abroad and ensures an effective export control and treaty compliance system. Issues trademarks and patents, maintains measurement standards, and manages the federal telecommunications spectrum. Collects, analyzes, and distributes statistics regarding the nation and the economy through the Bureaus of the Census and Economic Analysis. The NOAA explores, monitors, and conserves oceans and coasts, tracks weather and other environmental data. **Budget:** $9.9 bil (2011); $11.3 bil (est. 2012); $9.0 bil (est. 2013).

- Bureau of the Census (4600 Silver Hill Rd., 20233); www.census.gov
- Bureau of Economic Analysis (1441 L St. NW, 20230); www.bea.gov
- Minority Business Development Agency (1401 Constitution Ave. NW, 20230); www.mbda.gov
- Natl. Institute of Standards and Technology (100 Bureau Dr., Stop 1070, Gaithersburg, MD 20899); www.nist.gov
- Natl. Oceanic and Atmospheric Admin. (1401 Constitution Ave. NW, Rm. 5128, 20230); www.noaa.gov
- Natl. Technical Information Service (5301 Shawnee Rd., Alexandria, VA 22312); www.ntis.gov
- Natl. Telecommunications and Information Admin. (1401 Constitution Ave. NW, 20230); www.ntia.doc.gov

Department of Labor

200 Constitution Ave. NW, 20210; www.dol.gov

Administers federal labor laws to foster, promote, and develop the welfare of job seekers, wage earners, and retirees of the U.S., to improve working conditions, and to advance opportunities for profitable employment. Administers standards for wages and overtime pay, safety and health conditions, workers' compensation. Tracks changes in employment, prices, and other national economic measurements. Regulates pension and welfare benefit plans, the hiring and employment of migrant and seasonal workers, and requirements pertaining to the mining, construction, and transportation industries. Monitors labor unions and their funds. **Budget:** $133.2 bil (2011); $127.1 bil (est. 2012); $101.7 bil (est. 2013).

- Bureau of Labor Statistics (2 Massachusetts Ave. NE, 20212); www.bls.gov
- Employment and Training Admin. (200 Constitution Ave. NW, 20210); www.doleta.gov
- Mine Safety and Health Admin. (1100 Wilson Blvd., 21st Fl., Arlington, VA 22209); www.msha.gov
- Occupational Safety and Health Admin. (200 Constitution Ave. NW, 20210); www.osha.gov
- Office of Federal Contract Compliance Programs (200 Constitution Ave. NW, 20210); www.dol.gov/ofccp/
- Office of Labor-Management Standards (200 Constitution Ave. NW, 20210); www.dol.gov/olms/
- Office of Workers' Compensation Programs (200 Constitution Ave. NW, 20210); www.dol.gov/owcp/
- Wage and Hour Div. (200 Constitution Ave. NW, 20210); www.dol.gov/whd/

Department of Health and Human Services

200 Independence Ave. SW, 20201; www.hhs.gov

Administers a wide range of programs in the fields of health care and social services that affect nearly all Americans. Medicare and Medicaid provide health care insurance for one in four Americans. The HRSA improves health care services for people who are uninsured, isolated, or medically vulnerable; also oversees organ, tissue, and blood cell donations. The FDA assures the safety of food, drugs, cosmetics, biological products, and medical devices. The CDC monitors and safeguards against disease outbreaks. The NIH supports research projects nationwide and 27 health institutes and centers. The Surgeon General is the nation's chief health educator and leads the U.S. Public Health Service Commissioned Corps. **Budget:** $891.3 bil (2011); $871.9 bil (est. 2012); $940.9 bil (est. 2013).

- Agency for Healthcare Research and Quality (540 Gaither Rd., Rockville, MD 20850); www.ahrq.gov
- Centers for Disease Control and Prevention (1600 Clifton Rd., Atlanta, GA 30333); www.cdc.gov
- Centers for Medicare and Medicaid Services (7500 Security Blvd., Baltimore, MD 21244); www.cms.gov
- Food and Drug Admin. (10903 New Hampshire Ave., Silver Spring, MD 20993); www.fda.gov
- Health Resources and Services Admin. (5600 Fishers Ln., Rockville, MD 20857); www.hrsa.gov
- Natl. Institutes of Health (9000 Rockville Pike, Bethesda, MD 20892); www.nih.gov
- Office of the Surgeon General (Tower Bldg., Plaza Level 1, Rm. 100, 1101 Woonton Pkwy., Rockville, MD 20852); www.surgeongeneral.gov

Department of Housing and Urban Development

451 7th St. SW, 20410; www.hud.gov

Responsible for housing needs and the improvement and development of urban areas. Supports affordable housing, provides grants for community development and redevelopment. Enforces fair and safe housing standards. Provides funds to assist homeless individuals and families with emergency and transitional shelters. The FHA provides mortgage insurance on loans made by approved lenders. **Budget:** $57.0 bil (2011); $56.8 bil (est. 2012); $46.3 bil (est. 2013).

- Fannie Mae (Federal Natl. Mortgage Association) (3900 Wisconsin Ave. NW, 20016); www.fanniemae.com
- Federal Housing Admin. (451 7th St. SW, 20410); www.fha.gov
- Freddie Mac (Federal Home Loan Mortgage Corporation) (8200 Jones Branch Dr., McLean, VA 22102); www.freddiemac.com
- Ginnie Mae (Government Natl. Mortgage Association) (451 7th St. SW, Rm. B-133, 20410); www.ginniemae.gov

Note: Fannie Mae and Freddie Mac are government-sponsored enterprises (GSEs).

Department of Transportation

1200 New Jersey Ave. SE, 20590; www.dot.gov

Promotes and develops rapid, safe, efficient, and convenient transportation in the U.S.; monitors and administers assistance to transportation industries; negotiates and implements international transportation agreements. Manages airspace, commercial space transportation, and the movement of hazardous materials. Resolves railroad rate and service disputes and reviews proposed railroad mergers. Analyzes and shares research and statistics to develop and improve transportation through RITA. Develops and enforces regulations on the nation's pipeline transportation system. The Maritime Administration maintains a fleet of cargo ships in reserve for war or national emergencies and commissions officers of the merchant marines. Operates the U.S. portion of the St. Lawrence Seaway between Montreal and Lake Erie. **Budget:** $77.3 bil (2011); $84.1 bil (est. 2012); $98.5 bil (est. 2013).

- Federal Aviation Admin. (800 Independence Ave. SW, 20591); www.faa.gov
- Federal Highway Admin. (1200 New Jersey Ave. SE, 20590); www.fhwa.dot.gov
- Federal Railroad Admin. (1200 New Jersey Ave. SE, 20590); www.fra.dot.gov
- Federal Transit Admin. (East Bldg., 1200 New Jersey Ave. SE, 20590); www.fta.dot.gov
- Maritime Admin. (1200 New Jersey Ave. SE, 20590); www.marad.dot.gov
- Natl. Highway Traffic Safety Admin. (West Bldg., 1200 New Jersey Ave. SE, 20590); www.nhtsa.gov
- Research and Innovative Technology Admin. (1200 New Jersey Ave. SE, 20590); www.rita.dot.gov

Department of Energy

1000 Independence Ave. SW, 20585; www.energy.gov

Secures the nation's energy and promotes scientific and technological innovation. Oversees the national energy supply and electric grid. Investigates and promotes clean and reliable energy. Manages and cleans up nuclear and other radioactive material, including nuclear weapons. The OSTI supports much of America's scientific research through program offices, education initiatives, national laboratories, and technology centers. Four power administrations sell hydroelectric power across the west and southeast. **Budget:** $32.7 bil (2011); $40.6 bil (est. 2012); $35.0 bil (est. 2013).

- Energy Information Admin. (1000 Independence Ave. SW, 20585); www.eia.gov
- Federal Energy Regulatory Commission (888 1st St. NE, 20426); www.ferc.gov (independent regulatory agency)
- Natl. Nuclear Security Admin. (1000 Independence Ave. SW, 20585); www.nnsa.energy.gov
- Office of Scientific and Technical Information (P.O. Box 62, Oak Ridge, TN 37831); www.osti.gov

Department of Education

400 Maryland Ave. SW, 20202; www.ed.gov

Works with state agencies and local systems to ensure equal access to all levels of education and seeks to improve the quality of that education through federal support, research programs, and information sharing. Oversees a variety of financial aid distributed through competition, financial needs, or by a set formula. Sets policy goals and initiatives like No Child Left Behind. Conducts research and gathers educational information to disseminate to educators and the general public. **Budget:** $68.3 bil (2011); $68.1 bil (est. 2012); $69.9 bil (est. 2013).

Department of Veterans Affairs

810 Vermont Ave. NW, 20420; www.va.gov

Supports veterans and their families with nationwide programs for health care, financial assistance, and burial benefits. Compensates for disabilities incurred during wartime and provides pensions for veterans with low incomes, education assistance, loan guaranty, and life insurance. Manages America's largest medical education and health professions training program as well as hospitals, clinics, nursing homes, veterans centers, rehabilitation treatment, readjustment counseling, and home-care programs. Also funds medical research pertaining to veterans issues. Manages 131 national cemeteries, provides headstones and markers. **Budget:** $126.9 bil (2011); $129.1 bil (est. 2012); $139.7 bil (est. 2013).

Department of Homeland Security

20528 (requires no street address); www.dhs.gov

Provides a unified core for the vast national network of organizations and institutions involved in efforts to secure the U.S., its borders, infrastructure, and major events. Provides funding, intelligence, and training for law enforcement and disaster relief.

Leads and coordinates response teams to natural and human-created disasters. Directs security for borders, customs, and transportation. Identifies threats, administers the National Terrorism Advisory System. **Budget:** $45.8 bil (2011); $60.5 bil (est. 2012); $55.4 bil (est. 2013).

- Fed. Emergency Management Agency (500 C St. SW, 20472); www.fema.gov
- Immigration and Customs Enforcement (500 12th St. SW, 20536); www.ice.gov
- Transportation Security Admin. (601 S. 12th St., Arlington, VA 20598); www.tsa.gov

- U.S. Citizenship and Immigration Services (20 Massachusetts Ave. NW, 20001); www.uscis.gov
- U.S. Coast Guard (2100 2nd St. SW, 20593); www.uscg.mil
- U.S. Customs and Border Protection (1300 Pennsylvania Ave. NW, 20229); www.cbp.gov
- U.S. Fire Admin. (16825 S. Seton Ave., Emmitsburg, MD 21727); www.usfa.dhs.gov
- U.S. Secret Service (245 Murray Dr., Bldg. 410, 20223); www.secretservice.gov

Other Notable U.S. Government Agencies

Source: *The U.S. Government Manual*; National Archives and Records Administration; World Almanac research
All addresses are for Washington, DC, unless otherwise noted; as of Aug. 2012.

African Development Foundation: Lloyd O. Pierson, pres. and CEO (1400 I St. NW, Ste. 1000, 20005); www.adf.gov

AMTRAK (Natl. Railroad Passenger Corporation): Joseph H. Boardman, pres. and CEO (60 Mass. Ave. NE, 20002); www.amtrak.com

Broadcasting Board of Governors: chair vacant (330 Independence Ave. SW, 20237); www.bbg.gov

Central Intelligence Agency: David Petraeus, dir. (20505); www.cia.gov

Commodity Futures Trading Commission: Gary Gensler, chair (3 Lafayette Ctr., 1155 21st St. NW, 20581); www.cftc.gov

Consumer Financial Protection Bureau: Rich Cordray, dir. (P.O. Box 4503, Iowa City, IA 52244); www.consumerfinance.gov

Consumer Product Safety Commission: Inez Tenenbaum, chair (4330 East-West Hwy., Bethesda, MD 20814); www.cpsc.gov

Corporation for Natl. and Community Service: Wendy Spencer, CEO (1201 New York Ave. NW, 20525); www.nationalservice.gov

Court Services and Offender Supervision Agency for the District of Columbia: Nancy M. Ware, dir. (633 Indiana Ave. NW, 20004); www.csosa.gov

Defense Nuclear Facilities Safety Board: Peter S. Winokur, chair (625 Indiana Ave. NW, Ste. 700, 20004); www.dnfsb.gov

Election Assistance Commission: chair vacant (1201 New York Ave. NW, Ste. 300, 20005); www.eac.gov

Environmental Protection Agency: Lisa P. Jackson, administrator (Cabinet rank) (Ariel Rios Bldg., 1200 Pennsylvania Ave. NW, 20004); www.epa.gov

Equal Employment Opportunity Commission: Jacqueline A. Berrien, chair (131 M St. NE, 20507); www.eeoc.gov

Export-Import Bank of the U.S.: Fred P. Hochberg, pres. and chair (811 Vermont Ave. NW, 20571); www.exim.gov

Farm Credit Admin.: Leland A. Strom, chair and CEO (1501 Farm Credit Dr., McLean, VA 22102); www.fca.gov

Federal Communications Commission: Julius Genachowski, chair (445 12th St. SW, 20554); www.fcc.gov

Federal Deposit Insurance Corporation: Martin J. Gruenberg, acting chair (550 17th St. NW, 20429); www.fdic.gov

Federal Election Commission: Caroline C. Hunter, chair (999 E St. NW, 20463); www.fec.gov

Federal Housing Finance Agency: Edward DeMarco, act. dir. (400 7th St. SW, 20024); www.fhfa.gov

Federal Labor Relations Authority: Carol Waller Pope, chair (1400 K St. NW, 20424); www.flra.gov

Federal Maritime Commission: Richard A. Lidinsky Jr., chair (800 N. Capitol St. NW, 20573); www.fmc.gov

Federal Mediation and Conciliation Service: George H. Cohen, dir. (2100 K St. NW, 20427); www.fmcs.gov

Federal Mine Safety and Health Review Commission: Mary Lucille Jordan, chair (601 New Jersey Ave. NW, Ste. 9500, 20001); www.fmshrc.gov

Federal Reserve System: Ben S. Bernanke, chair (20th St. and Constitution Ave. NW, 20551); www.federalreserve.gov

Federal Retirement Thrift Investment Board: Michael D. Kennedy, chair (77 K. St. NE, 20002); www.frtib.gov

Federal Trade Commission: Jon Leibowitz, chair (600 Pennsylvania Ave. NW, 20580); www.ftc.gov

General Services Admin.: Daniel M. Tangherlini, administrator (One Constitution Sq., 1275 1st St. NE, 20417); www.gsa.gov

Institute of Museum and Library Services: Susan Hildreth, dir. (1800 M St. NW, 9th Fl., 20036); www.imls.gov

Inter-American Foundation: Robert N. Kaplan, pres. (1331 Pennsylvania Ave. NW, Ste. 1200N, 20004); www.iaf.gov

Merit Systems Protection Board: Susan Tsui Grundmann, chair (1615 M St. NW, 20419); www.mspb.gov

National Aeronautics and Space Admin.: Charles F. Bolden Jr., administrator (Suite 5K39, 20546); www.nasa.gov

National Archives and Records Admin.: David S. Ferriero, archivist (8601 Adelphi Rd., College Park, MD 20740); www.archives.gov

National Capital Planning Commission: L. Preston Bryant Jr., chair (401 9th St. NW, N. Lobby, Ste. 500, 20004); www.ncpc.gov

National Council on Disability: Jonathan M. Young, chair (1331 F St. NW, Ste. 850, 20004); www.ncd.gov

National Credit Union Admin.: Debbie Matz, chair (1775 Duke St., Alexandria, VA 22314); www.ncua.gov

National Endowment for the Arts: Rocco Landesman, chair (1100 Pennsylvania Ave. NW, 20506); www.arts.gov

National Endowment for the Humanities: Jim Leach, chair (1100 Pennsylvania Ave. NW, 20506); www.neh.gov

National Indian Gaming Commission: Tracie Stevens, chair (1441 L St. NW, Ste. 9100, 20005); www.nigc.gov

National Labor Relations Board: Mark G. Pearce, chair (1099 14th St. NW, 20570); www.nlrb.gov

National Mediation Board: Linda Puchala, chair (1301 K St. NW, Ste. 250 East, 20005); www.nmb.gov

National Science Foundation: Subra Suresh, dir. (4201 Wilson Blvd., Arlington, VA 22230); www.nsf.gov

National Transportation Safety Board: Deborah A.P. Hersman, chair (490 L'Enfant Plaza SW, 20594); www.ntsb.gov

Nuclear Regulatory Commission: Allison M. Macfarlane, chair (20555); www.nrc.gov

Nuclear Waste Technical Review Board: B. John Garrick, chair (2300 Clarendon Blvd., Ste. 1300, Arlington, VA 22201); www.nwtrb.gov

Occupational Safety and Health Review Commission: Thomasina V. Rogers, chair (1120 20th St. NW, 9th Fl., 20036); www.oshrc.gov

Office of Government Ethics: dir. vacant (1201 New York Ave. NW, Ste. 500, 20005); www.oge.gov

Office of Personnel Management: John Berry, dir. (1900 E St. NW, 20415); www.opm.gov

Office of Special Counsel: Carolyn Lerner, spec. counsel (1730 M St. NW, Ste. 218, 20036); www.osc.gov

Overseas Private Investment Corporation: Elizabeth L. Littlefield, pres. and CEO (1100 New York Ave. NW, 20527); www.opic.gov

Peace Corps: Aaron S. Williams, dir. (1111 20th St. NW, 20526); www.peacecorps.gov

Pension Benefit Guaranty Corporation: Joshua Gotbaum, dir. (1200 K St. NW, 20005); www.pbgc.gov

Postal Regulatory Commission: Ruth Y. Goldway, chair (901 New York Ave. NW, Ste. 200, 20268); www.prc.gov

Railroad Retirement Board: Michael S. Schwartz, chair (844 N. Rush St., Chicago, IL 60611); www.rrb.gov

Securities and Exchange Commission: Mary L. Schapiro, chair (100 F St. NE, 20549); www.sec.gov

Selective Service System: Lawrence G. Romo, dir. (Natl. Headquarters, Arlington, VA 22209); www.sss.gov

Small Business Admin.: Karen G. Mills, administrator (409 3rd St. SW, Ste. 7800, 20416); www.sba.gov

Social Security Admin.: Michael J. Astrue, comm. (6401 Security Blvd., Baltimore, MD 21235); www.ssa.gov

Tennessee Valley Authority: Tom Kilgore, CEO and pres. (400 W. Summit Hill Dr., Knoxville, TN 37902); www.tva.gov

U.S. Agency for International Development: Rajiv Shah, administrator (Ronald Reagan Building, 1300 Pennsylvania Ave. NW, 20523); www.usaid.gov

U.S. Commission on Civil Rights: Martin R. Castro, chair (624 9th St. NW, 20425); www.usccr.gov

U.S. International Trade Commission: Irving A. Williamson, chair (500 E St. SW, 20436); www.usitc.gov

U.S. Postal Service: Patrick R. Donahoe, postmaster general and CEO (475 L'Enfant Plaza SW, 20260); www.usps.com

U.S. Trade and Development Agency: Leocadia I. Zak, dir. (1000 Wilson Blvd., Ste. 1600, Arlington, VA 22209); www.ustda.gov

The U.S. Cabinet and Its Role

The heads of major executive departments of the federal government constitute the Cabinet. This institution, not provided for in the U.S. Constitution, developed as an advisory body out of the desire of presidents to consult on policy matters. Aside from its advisory role, the Cabinet as a body has no formal function and wields no executive authority. Individual members exercise authority as heads of their departments, reporting to the president. The Cabinet meets at times set by the president.

In addition to the heads of federal departments as listed below, the Cabinet commonly includes other officials designated by the president as being of Cabinet rank.

The officials so designated by Pres. Barack Obama include Vice Pres. Joseph R. Biden, White House Chief of Staff Jacob J. Lew, Environmental Protection Agency Administrator Lisa P. Jackson, Office of Management and Budget Acting Director Jeffrey Zients, U.S. Trade Representative Ambassador Ronald Kirk, U.S. Ambassador to the United Nations Susan Rice, Council of Economic Advisers Chair Alan B. Krueger, and Small Business Administration Administrator Karen G. Mills.

Members of Pres. Obama's Cabinet listed in this chapter are as of Oct. 2012. Commerce Sec. John Bryson resigned June 21, 2012, and was not formally replaced; Deputy Sec. Rebecca M. Blank assumed the role of acting secretary.

Secretaries of State

The Department of Foreign Affairs was created by act of Congress on July 27, 1789, and the name changed to Department of State on Sept. 15, 1789.

President	Secretary	Home	Sworn in
Washington	Thomas Jefferson	VA	1789
	Edmund J. Randolph	VA	1794
	Timothy Pickering	PA	1795
Adams, J.	Timothy Pickering	PA	1797
	John Marshall	VA	1800
Jefferson	James Madison	VA	1801
Madison	Robert Smith	MD	1809
	James Monroe	VA	1811
Monroe	John Quincy Adams	MA	1817
Adams, J. Q.	Henry Clay	KY	1825
Jackson	Martin Van Buren	NY	1829
	Edward Livingston	LA	1831
	Louis McLane	DE	1833
	John Forsyth	GA	1834
Van Buren	John Forsyth	GA	1837
Harrison, W. H.	Daniel Webster	MA	1841
Tyler	Daniel Webster	MA	1841
	Abel P. Upshur	VA	1843
	John C. Calhoun	SC	1844
Polk	John C. Calhoun	SC	1845
	James Buchanan	PA	1845
Taylor	James Buchanan	PA	1849
	John M. Clayton	DE	1849
Fillmore	John M. Clayton	DE	1850
	Daniel Webster	MA	1850
	Edward Everett	MA	1852
Pierce	William L. Marcy	NY	1853
Buchanan	William L. Marcy	NY	1857
	Lewis Cass	MI	1857
	Jeremiah S. Black	PA	1860
Lincoln	Jeremiah S. Black	PA	1861
	William H. Seward	NY	1861
Johnson, A.	William H. Seward	NY	1865
Grant	Elihu B. Washburne	IL	1869
	Hamilton Fish	NY	1869
Hayes	Hamilton Fish	NY	1877
	William M. Evarts	NY	1877
Garfield	William M. Evarts	NY	1881
	James G. Blaine	ME	1881
Arthur	James G. Blaine	ME	1881
	F. T. Frelinghuysen	NJ	1881
Cleveland	F. T. Frelinghuysen	NJ	1885
	Thomas F. Bayard	DE	1885
Harrison, B.	Thomas F. Bayard	DE	1889
	James G. Blaine	ME	1889
	John W. Foster	IN	1892
Cleveland	Walter Q. Gresham	IN	1893
	Richard Olney	MA	1895
McKinley	Richard Olney	MA	1897
	John Sherman	OH	1897
	William R. Day	OH	1898
	John M. Hay	DC	1898
Roosevelt, T.	John M. Hay	DC	1901
	Elihu Root	NY	1905
	Robert Bacon	NY	1909
Taft	Robert Bacon	NY	1909
	Philander C. Knox	PA	1909
Wilson	Philander C. Knox	PA	1913
	William J. Bryan	NE	1913
	Robert Lansing	NY	1915
	Bainbridge Colby	NY	1920

President	Secretary	Home	Sworn in
Harding	Charles E. Hughes	NY	1921
Coolidge	Charles E. Hughes	NY	1923
	Frank B. Kellogg	MN	1925
Hoover	Frank B. Kellogg	MN	1929
	Henry L. Stimson	NY	1929
Roosevelt, F. D.	Cordell Hull	TN	1933
	Edward R. Stettinius Jr.	VA	1944
Truman	Edward R. Stettinius Jr.	VA	1945
	James F. Byrnes	SC	1945
	George C. Marshall	PA	1947
	Dean G. Acheson	CT	1949
Eisenhower	John Foster Dulles	NY	1953
	Christian A. Herter	MA	1959
Kennedy	D. Dean Rusk	NY	1961
Johnson, L. B.	D. Dean Rusk	NY	1963
Nixon	William P. Rogers	NY	1969
	Henry A. Kissinger	DC	1973
Ford	Henry A. Kissinger	DC	1974
Carter	Cyrus R. Vance	NY	1977
	Edmund S. Muskie	ME	1980
Reagan	Alexander M. Haig Jr.	CT	1981
	George P. Shultz	CA	1982
Bush, G. H. W.	James A. Baker III	TX	1989
	Lawrence S. Eagleburger	MI	1992
Clinton	Warren M. Christopher	CA	1993
	Madeleine K. Albright	DC	1997
Bush, G. W.	Colin L. Powell	NY	2001
	Condoleezza Rice	AL	2005
Obama	Hillary Rodham Clinton	NY	2009

Secretaries of the Treasury

The Treasury Department was organized by act of Congress on Sept. 2, 1789.

President	Secretary	Home	Sworn in
Washington	Alexander Hamilton	NY	1789
	Oliver Wolcott Jr.	CT	1795
Adams, J.	Oliver Wolcott Jr.	CT	1797
	Samuel Dexter	MA	1801
Jefferson	Samuel Dexter	MA	1801
	Albert Gallatin	PA	1801
Madison	Albert Gallatin	PA	1809
	George W. Campbell	TN	1814
	Alexander J. Dallas	PA	1814
	William H. Crawford	GA	1816
Monroe	William H. Crawford	GA	1817
Adams, J. Q.	Richard Rush	PA	1825
Jackson	Samuel D. Ingham	PA	1829
	Louis McLane	DE	1831
	William J. Duane	PA	1833
	Roger B. Taney	MD	1833
	Levi Woodbury	NH	1834
Van Buren	Levi Woodbury	NH	1837
Harrison, W. H.	Thomas Ewing	OH	1841
Tyler	Thomas Ewing	OH	1841
	Walter Forward	PA	1841
	John C. Spencer	NY	1843
	George M. Bibb	KY	1844
Polk	Robert J. Walker	MS	1845
Taylor	William M. Meredith	PA	1849
Fillmore	Thomas Corwin	OH	1850
Pierce	James Guthrie	KY	1853
Buchanan	Howell Cobb	GA	1857
	Phillip F. Thomas	MD	1860
	John A. Dix	NY	1861

President	Secretary	Home	Sworn in
Lincoln	Salmon P. Chase	OH	1861
	William P. Fessenden	ME	1864
	Hugh McCulloch	IN	1865
Johnson, A.	Hugh McCulloch	IN	1865
Grant	George S. Boutwell	MA	1869
	William A. Richardson	MA	1873
	Benjamin H. Bristow	KY	1874
	Lot M. Morrill	ME	1876
Hayes	John Sherman	OH	1877
Garfield	William Windom	MN	1881
Arthur	Charles J. Folger	NY	1881
	Walter Q. Gresham	IN	1884
	Hugh McCulloch	IN	1884
Cleveland	Daniel Manning	NY	1885
	Charles S. Fairchild	NY	1887
Harrison, B.	William Windom	MN	1889
	Charles Foster	OH	1891
Cleveland	John G. Carlisle	KY	1893
McKinley	Lyman J. Gage	IL	1897
Roosevelt, T.	Lyman J. Gage	IL	1901
	Leslie M. Shaw	IA	1902
	George B. Cortelyou	NY	1907
Taft	Franklin MacVeagh	IL	1909
Wilson	William G. McAdoo	NY	1913
	Carter Glass	VA	1918
	David F. Houston	MO	1920
Harding	Andrew W. Mellon	PA	1921
Coolidge	Andrew W. Mellon	PA	1923
Hoover	Andrew W. Mellon	PA	1929
	Ogden L. Mills	NY	1932
Roosevelt, F. D.	William H. Woodin	NY	1933
	Henry Morgenthau Jr.	NY	1934
Truman	Fred M. Vinson	KY	1945
	John W. Snyder	MO	1946
Eisenhower	George M. Humphrey	OH	1953
	Robert B. Anderson	CT	1957
Kennedy	C. Douglas Dillon	NJ	1961
Johnson, L. B.	C. Douglas Dillon	NJ	1963
	Henry H. Fowler	VA	1965
	Joseph W. Barr	IN	1968
Nixon	David M. Kennedy	IL	1969
	John B. Connally	TX	1971
	George P. Shultz	IL	1972
	William E. Simon	NJ	1974
Ford	William E. Simon	NJ	1974
Carter	W. Michael Blumenthal	MI	1977
	G. William Miller	RI	1979
Reagan	Donald T. Regan	NY	1981
	James A. Baker III	TX	1985
	Nicholas F. Brady	NJ	1988
Bush, G. H. W.	Nicholas F. Brady	NJ	1989
Clinton	Lloyd M. Bentsen	TX	1993
	Robert E. Rubin	NY	1995
	Lawrence H. Summers	CT	1999
Bush, G. W.	Paul H. O'Neill	MO	2001
	John W. Snow	OH	2003
	Henry M. Paulson Jr.	FL	2006
Obama	Timothy F. Geithner	NY	2009

Secretaries of Defense

The Department of Defense, originally designated the National Military Establishment, was created on Sept. 18, 1947. It is headed by the secretary of defense, who is a member of the president's Cabinet. The departments of the Army, of the Navy, and of the Air Force function within the Defense Department. Since 1947, the secretaries of those departments have not been members of the president's Cabinet.

President	Secretary	Home	Sworn in
Truman	James V. Forrestal	NY	1947
	Louis A. Johnson	WV	1949
	George C. Marshall	PA	1950
	Robert A. Lovett	NY	1951
Eisenhower	Charles E. Wilson	MI	1953
	Neil H. McElroy	OH	1957
	Thomas S. Gates Jr.	PA	1959
Kennedy	Robert S. McNamara	MI	1961
Johnson, L. B.	Robert S. McNamara	MI	1963
	Clark M. Clifford	MD	1968
Nixon	Melvin R. Laird	WI	1969
	Elliot L. Richardson	MA	1973
	James R. Schlesinger	VA	1973
Ford	James R. Schlesinger	VA	1974
	Donald H. Rumsfeld	IL	1975
Carter	Harold Brown	CA	1977
Reagan	Caspar W. Weinberger	CA	1981
	Frank C. Carlucci	PA	1987
Bush, G. H. W.	Richard B. Cheney	WY	1989
Clinton	Les Aspin	WI	1993
	William J. Perry	CA	1994
	William S. Cohen	ME	1997
Bush, G. W.	Donald H. Rumsfeld	IL	2001
	Robert M. Gates	TX	2006
Obama	Robert M. Gates	TX	2009
	Leon E. Panetta	CA	2011

Secretaries of War

The War Department (which included jurisdiction over the Navy until 1798) was created by act of Congress on Aug. 7, 1789. Gen. Henry Knox was commissioned secretary of war under that act on Sept. 12, 1789.

President	Secretary	Home	Sworn in
Washington	Henry Knox	MA	1789
	Timothy Pickering	PA	1795
	James McHenry	MD	1796
Adams, J.	James McHenry	MD	1797
	Samuel Dexter	MA	1800
Jefferson	Henry Dearborn	MA	1801
Madison	William Eustis	MA	1809
	John Armstrong	NY	1813
	James Monroe	VA	1814
	William H. Crawford	GA	1815
Monroe	John C. Calhoun	SC	1817
Adams, J. Q.	James Barbour	VA	1825
	Peter B. Porter	NY	1828
Jackson	John H. Eaton	TN	1829
	Lewis Cass	MI	1831
	Benjamin F. Butler	NY	1837
Van Buren	Joel R. Poinsett	SC	1837
Harrison, W. H.	John Bell	TN	1841
Tyler	John Bell	TN	1841
	John C. Spencer	NY	1841
	James M. Porter	PA	1843
	William Wilkins	PA	1844
Polk	William L. Marcy	NY	1845
Taylor	George W. Crawford	GA	1849
Fillmore	Charles M. Conrad	LA	1850
Pierce	Jefferson Davis	MS	1853
Buchanan	John B. Floyd	VA	1857
	Joseph Holt	KY	1861
Lincoln	Simon Cameron	PA	1861
	Edwin M. Stanton	PA	1862
Johnson, A.	Edwin M. Stanton	PA	1865
	John M. Schofield	IL	1868
Grant	John A. Rawlins	IL	1869
	William T. Sherman	OH	1869
	William W. Belknap	IA	1869
	Alphonso Taft	OH	1876
	James D. Cameron	PA	1876
Hayes	George W. McCrary	IA	1877
	Alexander Ramsey	MN	1879
Garfield	Robert T. Lincoln	IL	1881
Arthur	Robert T. Lincoln	IL	1881
Cleveland	William C. Endicott	MA	1885
Harrison, B.	Redfield Proctor	VT	1889
	Stephen B. Elkins	WV	1891
Cleveland	Daniel S. Lamont	NY	1893
McKinley	Russell A. Alger	MI	1897
	Elihu Root	NY	1899
Roosevelt, T.	Elihu Root	NY	1901
	William H. Taft	OH	1904
	Luke E. Wright	TN	1908
Taft	Jacob M. Dickinson	TN	1909
	Henry L. Stimson	NY	1911
Wilson	Lindley M. Garrison	NJ	1913
	Newton D. Baker	OH	1916
Harding	John W. Weeks	MA	1921
Coolidge	John W. Weeks	MA	1923
	Dwight F. Davis	MO	1925
Hoover	James W. Good	IL	1929
	Patrick J. Hurley	OK	1929
Roosevelt, F. D.	George H. Dern	UT	1933
	Harry H. Woodring	KS	1937
	Henry L. Stimson	NY	1940
Truman	Robert P. Patterson	NY	1945
	Kenneth C. Royall[1]	NC	1947

(1) Last member of the Cabinet with this title. The War Department became the Department of the Army, a branch of the Department of Defense, in 1947.

Secretaries of the Navy

The Navy Department was created by act of Congress on Apr. 30, 1798. The Marine Corps is part of this department.

President	Secretary	Home	Sworn in
Adams, J.	Benjamin Stoddert	MD	1798
Jefferson	Benjamin Stoddert	MD	1801
	Robert Smith	MD	1801
Madison	Paul Hamilton	SC	1809
	William Jones	PA	1813
	Benjamin W. Crowninshield	MA	1814
Monroe	Benjamin W. Crowninshield	MA	1817
	Smith Thompson	NY	1818
	Samuel L. Southard	NJ	1823
Adams, J. Q.	Samuel L. Southard	NJ	1825
Jackson	John Branch	NC	1829
	Levi Woodbury	NH	1831
	Mahlon Dickerson	NJ	1834
Van Buren	Mahlon Dickerson	NJ	1837
	James K. Paulding	NY	1838
Harrison, W. H.	George E. Badger	NC	1841
Tyler	George E. Badger	NC	1841
	Abel P. Upshur	VA	1841
	David Henshaw	MA	1843
	Thomas W. Gilmer	VA	1844
	John Y. Mason	VA	1844
Polk	George Bancroft	MA	1845
	John Y. Mason	VA	1846
Taylor	William B. Preston	VA	1849
Fillmore	William A. Graham	NC	1850
	John P. Kennedy	MD	1852
Pierce	James C. Dobbin	NC	1853
Buchanan	Isaac Toucey	CT	1857
Lincoln	Gideon Welles	CT	1861
Johnson, A.	Gideon Welles	CT	1865
Grant	Adolph E. Borie	PA	1869
	George M. Robeson	NJ	1869
Hayes	Richard W. Thompson	IN	1877
	Nathan Goff Jr.	WV	1881
Garfield	William H. Hunt	LA	1881
Arthur	William E. Chandler	NH	1882
Cleveland	William C. Whitney	NY	1885
Harrison, B.	Benjamin F. Tracy	NY	1889
Cleveland	Hilary A. Herbert	AL	1893
McKinley	John D. Long	MA	1897
Roosevelt, T.	John D. Long	MA	1901
	William H. Moody	MA	1902
	Paul Morton	IL	1904
	Charles J. Bonaparte	MD	1905
	Victor H. Metcalf	CA	1906
	Truman H. Newberry	MI	1908
Taft	George von L. Meyer	MA	1909
Wilson	Josephus Daniels	NC	1913
Harding	Edwin Denby	MI	1921
Coolidge	Edwin Denby	MI	1923
	Curtis D. Wilbur	CA	1924
Hoover	Charles Francis Adams	MA	1929
Roosevelt, F. D.	Claude A. Swanson	VA	1933
	Charles Edison	NJ	1940
	Frank Knox	IL	1940
	James V. Forrestal	NY	1944
Truman	James V. Forrestal[1]	NY	1945

(1) Last member of Cabinet with this title. The Navy Department became a branch of the Department of Defense when the latter was created on Sept. 18, 1947.

Attorneys General

The Office of Attorney General was established by act of Congress on Sept. 24, 1789. It officially reached Cabinet rank in Mar. 1792, when the first attorney general, Edmund Randolph, attended his initial Cabinet meeting. The Department of Justice, headed by the attorney general, was created June 22, 1870.

President	Attorney General	Home	Sworn in
Washington	Edmund J. Randolph	VA	1789
	William Bradford	PA	1794
	Charles Lee	VA	1795
Adams, J.	Charles Lee	VA	1797
Jefferson	Levi Lincoln	MA	1801
	John Breckenridge	KY	1805
	Caesar A. Rodney	DE	1807
Madison	Caesar A. Rodney	DE	1807
	William Pinkney	MD	1811
	Richard Rush	PA	1814
Monroe	Richard Rush	PA	1817
	William Wirt	VA	1817
Adams, J. Q.	William Wirt	VA	1825
Jackson	John M. Berrien	GA	1829
	Roger B. Taney	MD	1831
	Benjamin F. Butler	NY	1833
Van Buren	Benjamin F. Butler	NY	1837
	Felix Grundy	TN	1838
	Henry D. Gilpin	PA	1840
Harrison, W. H.	John J. Crittenden	KY	1841
Tyler	John J. Crittenden	KY	1841
	Hugh S. Legaré	SC	1841
	John Nelson	MD	1843
Polk	John Y. Mason	VA	1845
	Nathan Clifford	ME	1846
	Isaac Toucey	CT	1848
Taylor	Reverdy Johnson	MD	1849
Fillmore	John J. Crittenden	KY	1850
Pierce	Caleb Cushing	MA	1853
Buchanan	Jeremiah S. Black	PA	1857
	Edwin M. Stanton	PA	1860
Lincoln	Edward Bates	MO	1861
	James Speed	KY	1864
Johnson, A.	James Speed	KY	1865
	Henry Stanbery	OH	1866
	William M. Evarts	NY	1868
Grant	Ebenezer R. Hoar	MA	1869
	Amos T. Akerman	GA	1870
	George H. Williams	OR	1871
	Edwards Pierrepont	NY	1875
	Alphonso Taft	OH	1876
Hayes	Charles Devens	MA	1877
Garfield	I. Wayne MacVeagh	PA	1881
Arthur	Benjamin H. Brewster	PA	1882
Cleveland	Augustus H. Garland	AR	1885
Harrison, B.	William H. H. Miller	IN	1889
Cleveland	Richard Olney	MA	1893
	Judson Harmon	OH	1895
McKinley	Joseph McKenna	CA	1897
	John W. Griggs	NJ	1898
	Philander C. Knox	PA	1901
Roosevelt, T.	Philander C. Knox	PA	1901
	William H. Moody	MA	1904
	Charles J. Bonaparte	MD	1906
Taft	George W. Wickersham	NY	1909
Wilson	James C. McReynolds	TN	1913
	Thomas W. Gregory	TX	1914
	A. Mitchell Palmer	PA	1919
Harding	Harry M. Daugherty	OH	1921
Coolidge	Harry M. Daugherty	OH	1923
	Harlan F. Stone	NY	1924
	John G. Sargent	VT	1925
Hoover	William D. Mitchell	MN	1929
Roosevelt, F. D.	Homer S. Cummings	CT	1933
	Frank Murphy	MI	1939
	Robert H. Jackson	NY	1940
	Francis Biddle	PA	1941
Truman	Thomas C. Clark	TX	1945
	J. Howard McGrath	RI	1949
	James P. McGranery	PA	1952
Eisenhower	Herbert Brownell Jr.	NY	1953
	William P. Rogers	MD	1957
Kennedy	Robert F. Kennedy	MA	1961
Johnson, L. B.	Robert F. Kennedy	MA	1963
	Nicholas Katzenbach	IL	1964
	W. Ramsey Clark	TX	1967
Nixon	John N. Mitchell	NY	1969
	Richard G. Kleindienst	AZ	1972
	Elliot L. Richardson	MA	1973
	William B. Saxbe	OH	1974
Ford	William B. Saxbe	OH	1974
	Edward H. Levi	IL	1975

President	Attorney General	Home	Sworn in
Carter	Griffin B. Bell	GA	1977
	Benjamin R. Civiletti	MD	1979
Reagan	William French Smith	CA	1981
	Edwin Meese III	CA	1985
	Richard L. Thornburgh	PA	1988
Bush, G. H. W.	Richard L. Thornburgh	PA	1989
	William P. Barr	NY	1991
Clinton	Janet Reno	FL	1993
Bush, G. W.	John Ashcroft	MO	2001
	Alberto R. Gonzales	TX	2005
	Michael B. Mukasey	NY	2007
Obama	Eric H. Holder Jr.	DC	2009

Secretaries of the Interior

The Department of the Interior was created by act of Congress on Mar. 3, 1849.

President	Secretary	Home	Sworn in
Taylor	Thomas Ewing	OH	1849
Fillmore	Thomas M. T. McKennan	PA	1850
	Alex H. H. Stuart	VA	1850
Pierce	Robert McClelland	MI	1853
Buchanan	Jacob Thompson	MS	1857
Lincoln	Caleb B. Smith	IN	1861
	John P. Usher	IN	1863
Johnson, A.	John P. Usher	IN	1865
	James Harlan	IA	1865
	Orville H. Browning	IL	1866
Grant	Jacob D. Cox	OH	1869
	Columbus Delano	OH	1870
	Zachariah Chandler	MI	1875
Hayes	Carl Schurz	MO	1877
Garfield	Samuel J. Kirkwood	IA	1881
Arthur	Henry M. Teller	CO	1882
Cleveland	Lucius Q. C. Lamar	MS	1885
	William F. Vilas	WI	1888
Harrison, B.	John W. Noble	MO	1889
Cleveland	M. Hoke Smith	GA	1893
	David R. Francis	MO	1896
McKinley	Cornelius N. Bliss	NY	1897
	Ethan A. Hitchcock	MO	1898
Roosevelt, T.	Ethan A. Hitchcock	MO	1901
	James R. Garfield	OH	1907
Taft	Richard A. Ballinger	WA	1909
	Walter L. Fisher	IL	1911
Wilson	Franklin K. Lane	CA	1913
	John B. Payne	IL	1920
Harding	Albert B. Fall	NM	1921
	Hubert Work	CO	1923
Coolidge	Hubert Work	CO	1923
	Roy O. West	IL	1929
Hoover	Ray Lyman Wilbur	CA	1929
Roosevelt, F. D.	Harold L. Ickes	IL	1933
Truman	Harold L. Ickes	IL	1945
	Julius A. Krug	WI	1946
	Oscar L. Chapman	CO	1949
Eisenhower	Douglas McKay	OR	1953
	Fred A. Seaton	NE	1956
Kennedy	Stewart L. Udall	AZ	1961
Johnson, L. B.	Stewart L. Udall	AZ	1963
Nixon	Walter J. Hickel	AK	1969
	Rogers C. B. Morton	MD	1971
Ford	Rogers C. B. Morton	MD	1971
	Stanley K. Hathaway	WY	1975
	Thomas S. Kleppe	ND	1975
Carter	Cecil D. Andrus	ID	1977
Reagan	James G. Watt	CO	1981
	William P. Clark	CA	1983
	Donald P. Hodel	OR	1985
Bush, G. H. W.	Manuel Lujan	NM	1989
Clinton	Bruce Babbitt	AZ	1993
Bush, G. W.	Gale Norton	CO	2001
	Dirk Kempthorne	ID	2006
Obama	Kenneth L. Salazar	CO	2009

Secretaries of Agriculture

The Department of Agriculture was created by act of Congress on May 15, 1862. On Feb. 8, 1889, its commissioner was renamed secretary of agriculture and became a member of the Cabinet.

President	Secretary	Home	Sworn in
Cleveland	Norman J. Colman	MO	1889
Harrison, B.	Jeremiah M. Rusk	WI	1889
Cleveland	J. Sterling Morton	NE	1893
McKinley	James Wilson	IA	1897
Roosevelt, T.	James Wilson	IA	1901
Taft	James Wilson	IA	1909
Wilson	David F. Houston	MO	1913
	Edwin T. Meredith	IA	1920
Harding	Henry C. Wallace	IA	1921
Coolidge	Henry C. Wallace	IA	1923
	Howard M. Gore	WV	1924
	William M. Jardine	KS	1925
Hoover	Arthur M. Hyde	MO	1929
Roosevelt, F. D.	Henry A. Wallace	IA	1933
	Claude R. Wickard	IN	1940
Truman	Clinton P. Anderson	NM	1945
Truman	Charles F. Brannan	CO	1948
Eisenhower	Ezra Taft Benson	UT	1953
Kennedy	Orville L. Freeman	MN	1961
Johnson, L. B.	Orville L. Freeman	MN	1963
Nixon	Clifford M. Hardin	IN	1969
	Earl L. Butz	IN	1971
Ford	Earl L. Butz	IN	1974
	John A. Knebel	VA	1976
Carter	Bob Bergland	MN	1977
Reagan	John R. Block	IL	1981
	Richard E. Lyng	CA	1986
Bush, G. H. W.	Clayton K. Yeutter	NE	1989
	Edward Madigan	IL	1991
Clinton	Mike Espy	MS	1993
	Dan Glickman	KS	1995
Bush, G. W.	Ann M. Veneman	CA	2001
	Mike Johanns	NE	2005
	Ed Schafer	ND	2008
Obama	Thomas J. Vilsack	IA	2009

Secretaries of Commerce and Labor

The Department of Commerce and Labor, created by Congress on Feb. 14, 1903, was divided by Congress Mar. 4, 1913, into two separate departments. The secretary of each was made a Cabinet member.

President	Secretary	Home	Sworn in
Roosevelt, T.	George B. Cortelyou	NY	1903
	Victor H. Metcalf	CA	1904
	Oscar S. Straus	NY	1906
Taft	Charles Nagel	MO	1909

Secretaries of Labor

President	Secretary	Home	Sworn in
Wilson	William B. Wilson	PA	1913
Harding	James J. Davis	PA	1921
Coolidge	James J. Davis	PA	1923
Hoover	James J. Davis	PA	1929
	William N. Doak	VA	1930
Roosevelt, F. D.	Frances Perkins	NY	1933
Truman	L. B. Schwellenbach	WA	1945
	Maurice J. Tobin	MA	1949
Eisenhower	Martin P. Durkin	IL	1953
	James P. Mitchell	NJ	1953
Kennedy	Arthur J. Goldberg	IL	1961
	W. Willard Wirtz	IL	1962
Johnson, L. B.	W. Willard Wirtz	IL	1963
Nixon	George P. Shultz	IL	1969
	James D. Hodgson	CA	1970
	Peter J. Brennan	NY	1973
Ford	Peter J. Brennan	NY	1974
	John T. Dunlop	CA	1975
	W. J. Usery Jr.	GA	1976
Carter	F. Ray Marshall	TX	1977
Reagan	Raymond J. Donovan	NJ	1981
	William E. Brock	TN	1985
	Ann D. McLaughlin	DC	1987
Bush, G. H. W.	Elizabeth H. Dole	NC	1989
	Lynn Martin	IL	1991
Clinton	Robert B. Reich	MA	1993
	Alexis M. Herman	AL	1997
Bush, G. W.	Elaine L. Chao	KY	2001
Obama	Hilda L. Solis	CA	2009

Secretaries of Commerce

President	Secretary	Home	Sworn in
Wilson	William C. Redfield	NY	1913
	Joshua W. Alexander	MO	1919
Harding	Herbert C. Hoover	CA	1921
Coolidge	Herbert C. Hoover	CA	1923
	William F. Whiting	MA	1928
Hoover	Robert P. Lamont	IL	1929
	Roy D. Chapin	MI	1932
Roosevelt, F. D.	Daniel C. Roper	SC	1933
	Harry L. Hopkins	NY	1939
	Jesse H. Jones	TX	1940
	Henry A. Wallace	IA	1945
Truman	Henry A. Wallace	IA	1945
	W. Averell Harriman	NY	1947
	Charles W. Sawyer	OH	1948
Eisenhower	Sinclair Weeks	MA	1953
	Lewis L. Strauss	NY	1958
	Frederick H. Mueller	MI	1959
Kennedy	Luther H. Hodges	NC	1961
Johnson, L. B.	Luther H. Hodges	NC	1963
	John T. Connor	NJ	1965
	Alex B. Trowbridge	NJ	1967
	Cyrus R. Smith	NY	1968
Nixon	Maurice H. Stans	MN	1969
	Peter G. Peterson	IL	1972
	Frederick B. Dent	SC	1973
Ford	Frederick B. Dent	SC	1974
	Rogers C. B. Morton	MD	1975
	Elliot L. Richardson	MA	1975
Carter	Juanita M. Kreps	NC	1977
	Philip M. Klutznick	IL	1979
Reagan	Malcolm Baldrige	CT	1981
	C. William Verity Jr.	OH	1987
Bush, G. H. W.	Robert A. Mosbacher	TX	1989
	Barbara H. Franklin	PA	1992
Clinton	Ronald H. Brown	DC	1993
	Mickey Kantor	CA	1996
	William M. Daley	IL	1997
	Norman Y. Mineta	CA	2000
Bush, G. W.	Donald L. Evans	TX	2001
	Carlos M. Gutierrez	MI	2005
Obama	Gary F. Locke	WA	2009
	John Bryson	CA	2011

Secretaries of Housing and Urban Development

The Department of Housing and Urban Development was created by act of Congress on Sept. 9, 1965.

President	Secretary	Home	Sworn in
Johnson, L. B.	Robert C. Weaver	WA	1966
	Robert C. Wood	MA	1969
Nixon	George W. Romney	MI	1969
	James T. Lynn	OH	1973
Ford	James T. Lynn	OH	1974
	Carla Anderson Hills	CA	1975
Carter	Patricia Roberts Harris	DC	1977
	Moon Landrieu	LA	1979
Reagan	Samuel R. Pierce Jr.	NY	1981
Bush, G. H. W.	Jack F. Kemp	NY	1989
Clinton	Henry G. Cisneros	TX	1993
	Andrew M. Cuomo	NY	1997
Bush, G. W.	Mel Martinez	FL	2001
	Alphonso Jackson	TX	2004
	Steve Preston	VA	2008
Obama	Shaun L. S. Donovan	NY	2009

Secretaries of Transportation

The Department of Transportation was created by act of Congress on Oct. 15, 1966.

President	Secretary	Home	Sworn in
Johnson, L. B.	Alan S. Boyd	FL	1966
Nixon	John A. Volpe	MA	1969
	Claude S. Brinegar	CA	1973
Ford	Claude S. Brinegar	CA	1974
	William T. Coleman Jr.	PA	1975
Carter	Brock Adams	WA	1977
	Neil E. Goldschmidt	OR	1979
Reagan	Andrew L. Lewis Jr.	PA	1981
	Elizabeth H. Dole	NC	1983
	James H. Burnley	NC	1987
Bush, G. H. W.	Samuel K. Skinner	IL	1989
	Andrew H. Card Jr.	MA	1992
Clinton	Federico F. Peña	CO	1993
	Rodney E. Slater	AR	1997
Bush, G. W.	Norman Y. Mineta	CA	2001
	Mary E. Peters	AZ	2006
Obama	Raymond L. LaHood	IL	2009

Secretaries of Energy

The Department of Energy was created by federal law on Aug. 4, 1977.

President	Secretary	Home	Sworn in
Carter	James R. Schlesinger	VA	1977
	Charles W. Duncan Jr.	WY	1979
Reagan	James B. Edwards	SC	1981
	Donald P. Hodel	OR	1982
	John S. Herrington	CA	1985
Bush, G. H. W.	James D. Watkins	CA	1989
Clinton	Hazel R. O'Leary	MN	1993
	Federico F. Peña	CO	1997
	Bill Richardson	NM	1998
Bush, G. W.	Spencer Abraham	MI	2001
	Samuel W. Bodman	MA	2005
Obama	Steven Chu	CA	2009

Secretaries of Health, Education, and Welfare

The Department of Health, Education, and Welfare was created by Congress on Apr. 11, 1953. On Sept. 27, 1979, Congress approved creation of a separate Department of Education. The existing department was renamed the Department of Health and Human Services.

President	Secretary	Home	Sworn in
Eisenhower	Oveta Culp Hobby	TX	1953
	Marion B. Folsom	NY	1955
	Arthur S. Flemming	OH	1958
Kennedy	Abraham A. Ribicoff	CT	1961
	Anthony J. Celebrezze	OH	1962
Johnson, L. B.	Anthony J. Celebrezze	OH	1963
	John W. Gardner	NY	1965
	Wilbur J. Cohen	MI	1968
Nixon	Robert H. Finch	CA	1969
	Elliot L. Richardson	MA	1970
	Caspar W. Weinberger	CA	1973
Ford	Caspar W. Weinberger	CA	1974
	Forrest D. Mathews	AL	1975
Carter	Joseph A. Califano Jr.	DC	1977
	Patricia Roberts Harris	DC	1979

Secretaries of Health and Human Services

President	Secretary	Home	Sworn in
Carter	Patricia Roberts Harris	DC	1979
Reagan	Richard S. Schweiker	PA	1981
	Margaret M. Heckler	MA	1983
Reagan	Otis R. Bowen	IN	1985
Bush, G. H. W.	Louis W. Sullivan	GA	1989
Clinton	Donna E. Shalala	WI	1993
Bush, G. W.	Tommy Thompson	WI	2001
	Michael O. Leavitt	UT	2005
Obama	Kathleen Sebelius	KS	2009

Secretaries of Education

President	Secretary	Home	Sworn in
Carter	Shirley Hufstedler	CA	1979
Reagan	Terrel H. Bell	UT	1981
	William J. Bennett	NY	1985
	Lauro F. Cavazos	TX	1988
Bush, G. H. W.	Lauro F. Cavazos	TX	1989
	Lamar Alexander	TN	1991
Clinton	Richard W. Riley	SC	1993
Bush, G. W.	Roderick R. Paige	TX	2001
	Margaret Spellings	TX	2005
Obama	Arne Duncan	IL	2009

Secretaries of Veterans Affairs

The Department of Veterans Affairs was created on Oct. 25, 1988, when Pres. Ronald Reagan signed a bill that made the Veterans Administration into a Cabinet department, effective Mar. 15, 1989.

President	Secretary	Home	Sworn in
Bush, G. H. W.	Edward J. Derwinski	IL	1989
Clinton	Jesse Brown	IL	1993
	Togo D. West Jr.	NC	1998
Bush, G. W.	Anthony J. Principi	CA	2001
	R. James Nicholson	CO	2005
	James B. Peake	MO	2007
Obama	Eric K. Shinseki	VA	2009

Secretaries of Homeland Security

The Department of Homeland Security was created by act of Congress on Nov. 25, 2002.

President	Secretary	Home	Sworn in
Bush, G. W.	Thomas Ridge	PA	2003
	Michael Chertoff	DC	2005
Obama	Janet Napolitano	AZ	2009

CONGRESS

As of Oct. 2012.

Floor Leaders in the U.S. Senate, 1920-2012

Majority leaders				Minority leaders			
Name	Party	State	Tenure	Name	Party	State	Tenure
Charles Curtis[1]	Rep.	KS	1925-1929	Oscar W. Underwood[2]	Dem.	AL	1920-1923
James E. Watson	Rep.	IN	1929-1933	Joseph T. Robinson	Dem.	AR	1923-1933
Joseph T. Robinson	Dem.	AR	1933-1937	Charles L. McNary	Rep.	OR	1933-1944
Alben W. Barkley	Dem.	KY	1937-1947	Wallace H. White	Rep.	ME	1944-1947
Wallace H. White	Rep.	ME	1947-1949	Alben W. Barkley	Dem.	KY	1947-1949
Scott W. Lucas	Dem.	IL	1949-1951	Kenneth S. Wherry	Rep.	NE	1949-1951
Ernest W. McFarland	Dem.	AZ	1951-1953	Henry Styles Bridges	Rep.	NH	1952-1953
Robert A. Taft	Rep.	OH	1953	Lyndon B. Johnson	Dem.	TX	1953-1955
William F. Knowland	Rep.	CA	1953-1955	William F. Knowland	Rep.	CA	1955-1959
Lyndon B. Johnson	Dem.	TX	1955-1961	Everett M. Dirksen	Rep.	IL	1959-1969
Mike Mansfield	Dem.	MT	1961-1977	Hugh D. Scott	Rep.	PA	1969-1977
Robert C. Byrd	Dem.	WV	1977-1981	Howard H. Baker Jr.	Rep.	TN	1977-1981
Howard H. Baker Jr.	Rep.	TN	1981-1985	Robert C. Byrd	Dem.	WV	1981-1987
Robert J. Dole	Rep.	KS	1985-1987	Robert J. Dole	Rep.	KS	1987-1995
Robert C. Byrd	Dem.	WV	1987-1989	Thomas A. Daschle	Dem.	SD	1995-2001[3]
George J. Mitchell	Dem.	ME	1989-1995	Trent Lott	Rep.	MS	2001-2002[3,4]
Robert J. Dole	Rep.	KS	1995-1996	Thomas A. Daschle	Dem.	SD	2003-2005[5]
Trent Lott	Rep.	MS	1996-2001[3]	Harry M. Reid	Dem.	NV	2005-2007[5]
Thomas A. Daschle	Dem.	SD	2001-2003[3]	Mitch McConnell	Rep.	KY	2007[6]-
William Frist	Rep.	TN	2003-2007[4,6]				
Harry M. Reid	Dem.	NV	2007-				

Note: The offices of party (majority and minority) leaders in the Senate did not evolve until the 20th century. (1) First Republican to be formally designated floor leader. Henry Cabot Lodge (MA) served as unofficial party leader prior to Curtis's election. (2) First Democrat to be designated floor leader. (3) Democrats held the majority Jan. 3, 2001, until Dick Cheney (R) was installed as vice pres., Jan. 20. Republicans subsequently lost the majority when Jim Jeffords (VT) switched from Republican to Independent, June 6, 2001. (4) Trent Lott resigned from Republican leadership Dec. 20, 2002. William Frist was elected Republican leader Dec. 23, 2002, and began service Jan. 7, 2003, as majority leader. (5) Thomas A. Daschle was defeated in the 2004 election and retired from the Senate Jan. 3, 2005; Democratic Whip Harry M. Reid was elected minority leader for the 109th Congress. (6) William Frist retired from the Senate Jan. 3, 2007. Republican whip Mitch McConnell was elected Republican leader for the 110th Congress.

Speakers of the U.S. House of Representatives, 1789-2012

Name	Party	State	Tenure	Name	Party	State	Tenure
Frederick A. C. Muhlenberg	Federalist	PA	1789-1791	Michael C. Kerr	Dem.	IN	1875-1876
Jonathan Trumbull	Federalist	CT	1791-1793	Samuel J. Randall	Dem.	PA	1876-1881
Frederick A. C. Muhlenberg	Federalist	PA	1793-1795	J. Warren Keifer	Rep.	OH	1881-1883
Jonathan Dayton	Federalist	NJ	1795-1799	John G. Carlisle	Dem.	KY	1883-1889
Theodore Sedgwick	Federalist	MA	1799-1801	Thomas B. Reed	Rep.	ME	1889-1891
Nathaniel Macon	Dem.-Rep.	NC	1801-1807	Charles F. Crisp	Dem.	GA	1891-1895
Joseph B. Varnum	Dem.-Rep.	MA	1807-1811	Thomas B. Reed	Rep.	ME	1895-1899
Henry Clay	Dem.-Rep.	KY	1811-1814	David B. Henderson	Rep.	IA	1899-1903
Langdon Cheves	Dem.-Rep.	SC	1814-1815	Joseph G. Cannon	Rep.	IL	1903-1911
Henry Clay	Dem.-Rep.	KY	1815-1820	Champ Clark	Dem.	MO	1911-1919
John W. Taylor	Dem.-Rep.	NY	1820-1821	Frederick H. Gillett	Rep.	MA	1919-1925
Philip P. Barbour	Dem.-Rep.	VA	1821-1823	Nicholas Longworth	Rep.	OH	1925-1931
Henry Clay	Dem.-Rep.	KY	1823-1825	John N. Garner	Dem.	TX	1931-1933
John W. Taylor	Dem.	NY	1825-1827	Henry T. Rainey	Dem.	IL	1933-1934
Andrew Stevenson	Dem.	VA	1827-1834	Joseph W. Byrns	Dem.	TN	1935-1936
John Bell	Dem.	TN	1834-1835	William B. Bankhead	Dem.	AL	1936-1940
James K. Polk	Dem.	TN	1835-1839	Sam Rayburn	Dem.	TX	1940-1947
Robert M. T. Hunter	Dem.	VA	1839-1841	Joseph W. Martin Jr.	Rep.	MA	1947-1949
John White	Whig	KY	1841-1843	Sam Rayburn	Dem.	TX	1949-1953
John W. Jones	Dem.	VA	1843-1845	Joseph W. Martin Jr.	Rep.	MA	1953-1955
John W. Davis	Dem.	IN	1845-1847	Sam Rayburn	Dem.	TX	1955-1961
Robert C. Winthrop	Whig	MA	1847-1849	John W. McCormack	Dem.	MA	1962-1971
Howell Cobb	Dem.	GA	1849-1851	Carl B. Albert	Dem.	OK	1971-1977
Linn Boyd	Dem.	KY	1851-1855	Thomas P. O'Neill Jr.	Dem.	MA	1977-1987
Nathaniel P. Banks	American	MA	1856-1857	James C. Wright Jr.	Dem.	TX	1987-1989
James L. Orr	Dem.	SC	1857-1859	Thomas S. Foley	Dem.	WA	1989-1995
William Pennington	Rep.	NJ	1860-1861	Newt Gingrich	Rep.	GA	1995-1999
Galusha A. Grow	Rep.	PA	1861-1863	J. Dennis Hastert	Rep.	IL	1999-2007
Schuyler Colfax	Rep.	IN	1863-1869	Nancy Pelosi	Dem.	CA	2007-2011
Theodore M. Pomeroy	Rep.	NY	1869	John Boehner	Rep.	OH	2011-
James G. Blaine	Rep.	ME	1869-1875				

Political Divisions of the U.S. Senate and House of Representatives, 1901-2012

Source: Office of the Clerk, U.S. House of Representatives; Congressional Research Service, Library of Congress

All figures reflect immediate post-election party breakdown except where noted; **boldface** denotes party in majority immediately after election.

		SENATE					HOUSE OF REPRESENTATIVES				
Congress	Years	Total members	Dem.	Rep.	Other parties	Vacant	Total members	Dem.	Rep.	Other parties	Vacant
57th	1901-1903	90	32	**56**	2		357	151	**200**	6	
58th	1903-1905	90	33	**57**			386	176	**207**	3	
59th	1905-1907	90	32	**58**			386	135	**251**		
60th	1907-1909	92	31	**61**			391	167	**223**	1	
61st	1909-1911	92	32	**60**			391	172	**219**		
62nd	1911-1913	96	44	**52**			394	**230**	162	2	
63rd	1913-1915	96	**51**	44	1		435	**291**	134	10	
64th	1915-1917	96	**56**	40			435	**230**	196	9	
65th	1917-1919	96	**54**	42			435	214[1]	215	6	
66th	1919-1921	96	47	**49**			435	192	**240**	2	1
67th	1921-1923	96	37	**59**			435	131	**302**	2	
68th	1923-1925	96	42	**53**	1		435	207	**225**	3	
69th	1925-1927	96	41	**54**	1		435	183	**247**	5	
70th	1927-1929	96	46	**48**	1	1	435	194	**238**	3	
71st	1929-1931	96	39	**56**	1		435	164	**270**	1	
72nd	1931-1933	96	47	**48**	1		435	216[2]	218	1	

		SENATE				HOUSE OF REPRESENTATIVES				
Congress	Years	Total members	Dem.	Rep.	Other parties	Vacant	Total members	Dem.	Rep.	Other parties	Vacant
73rd	1933-1935	96	59	36	1		435	313	117	5	
74th	1935-1937	96	69	25	2		435	322	103	10	
75th	1937-1939	96	76	16	4		435	334	88	13	
76th	1939-1941	96	69	23	4		435	262	169	4	
77th	1941-1943	96	66	28	2		435	267	162	6	
78th	1943-1945	96	57	38	1		435	222	209	4	
79th	1945-1947	96	57	38	1		435	242	191	2	
80th	1947-1949	96	45	51			435	188	246	1	
81st	1949-1951	96	54	42			435	263	171	1	
82nd	1951-1953	96	49	47			435	235	199	1	
83rd	1953-1955	96	47	48	1		435	213	221	1	
84th	1955-1957	96	48	47	1		435	232	203		
85th	1957-1959	96	49	47			435	234	201		
86th	1959-1961	100	65	35			437[3,4]	283	153	1	
87th	1961-1963	100	64	36			437	263	174		
88th	1963-1965	100	66	34			435	259	176		
89th	1965-1967	100	68	32			435	295	140		
90th	1967-1969	100	64	36			435	247	187		1
91st	1969-1971	100	57	43			435	243	192		
92nd	1971-1973	100	54	44	2		435	255	180		
93rd	1973-1975	100	56	42	2		435	242	192	1	
94th	1975-1977	100	60	38	2		435	291	144		
95th	1977-1979	100	61	38	1		435	292	143		
96th	1979-1981	100	58	41	1		435	277	158		
97th	1981-1983	100	46	53	1		435	242	192	1	
98th	1983-1985	100	46	54			435	269	166		
99th	1985-1987	100	47	53			435	253	182		
100th	1987-1989	100	55	45			435	258	177		
101st	1989-1991	100	55	45			435	260	175		
102nd	1991-1993	100	56	44			435	267	167	1	
103rd	1993-1995	100	57	43			435	258	176	1	
104th	1995-1997	100	48	52			435	204	230	1	
105th	1997-1999	100	45	55			435	206	228	1	
106th	1999-2001	100	45	55			435	211	223	1	
107th	2001-2003	100	50	50[5]			435	212	221	2	
108th	2003-2005	100	48	51	1		435	204	229	1	1
109th	2005-2007	100	44	55	1		435	202	232	1	
110th	2007-2009	100	49	49	2[6]		435	233	202		
111th	2009-2011	100	57[7]	41	2[6]		435	257	178		
112th	2011-	100	51	47	2[6]		435	193	242		

(1) Democrats organized the House with help of other parties. (2) Democrats organized the House because of Republican deaths. (3) Proclamation declaring Alaska a state issued Jan. 3, 1959. (4) Proclamation declaring Hawaii a state issued Aug. 21, 1959. (5) While the Senate was split 50-50, control was held by whichever party had an incumbent vice president. Republican Sen. Jim Jeffords (VT) changed his party designation to Independent on June 6, 2001, switching control of the Senate to Democrats. (6) Both Independent senators chose to caucus with the Democrats. (7) Sen. Al Franken (D, MN) was not seated until July 7, 2009.

Congressional Bills Vetoed, 1789-2012

Source: Virtual Reference Desk, U.S. Senate

President	Regular vetoes	Pocket vetoes	Total vetoes	Vetoes overridden	President	Regular vetoes	Pocket vetoes	Total vetoes	Vetoes overridden
Washington	2	—	2	—	B. Harrison	19	25	44	1
J. Adams	—	—	—	—	Cleveland[2]	42	128	170	5
Jefferson	—	—	—	—	McKinley	6	36	42	—
Madison	5	2	7	—	T. Roosevelt	42	40	82	1
Monroe	1	—	1	—	Taft	30	9	39	1
J. Q. Adams	—	—	—	—	Wilson	33	11	44	6
Jackson	5	7	12	—	Harding	5	1	6	—
Van Buren	—	1	1	—	Coolidge	20	30	50	4
W. H. Harrison	—	—	—	—	Hoover	21	16	37	3
Tyler	6	4	10	1	F. D. Roosevelt	372	263	635	9
Polk	2	1	3	—	Truman	180	70	250	12
Taylor	—	—	—	—	Eisenhower	73	108	181	2
Fillmore	—	—	—	—	Kennedy	12	9	21	—
Pierce	9	—	9	5	L. Johnson	16	14	30	—
Buchanan	4	3	7	—	Nixon	26	17	43	7
Lincoln	2	5	7	—	Ford	48	18	66	12
A. Johnson	21	8	29	15	Carter	13	18	31	2
Grant	45	48	93	4	Reagan	39	39	78	9
Hayes	12	1	13	1	G. H. W. Bush[3]	29	15	44	1
Garfield	—	—	—	—	Clinton[4]	36	1	37	2
Arthur	4	8	12	1	G. W. Bush	12	—	12	4
Cleveland[1]	304	110	414	2	Obama	2	—	2	—
					Total[3,4]	1,498	1,066	2,564	110

— = 0. (1) First term only. (2) Second term only. (3) Excluded from the figures are two bills that Pres. Bush claimed to be vetoed but Congress considered enacted into law because the president failed to return them to Congress during a recess period. (4) Does not include line-item vetoes, which were ruled unconstitutional by the U.S. Supreme Court on June 25, 1998.

Librarians of Congress, 1802-2012

Source: Library of Congress

Librarian	Tenure	Appointed by	Librarian	Tenure	Appointed by
John J. Beckley	1802-1807	Jefferson	Herbert Putnam	1899-1939	McKinley
Patrick Magruder	1807-1815	Jefferson	Archibald MacLeish	1939-1944	F. D. Roosevelt
George Watterston	1815-1829	Madison	Luther H. Evans	1945-1953	Truman
John Silva Meehan	1829-1861	Jackson	L. Quincy Mumford	1954-1974	Eisenhower
John G. Stephenson	1861-1864	Lincoln	Daniel J. Boorstin	1975-1987	Ford
Ainsworth Rand Spofford	1864-1897	Lincoln	James H. Billington	1987-	Reagan
John Russell Young	1897-1899	McKinley			

Sources: Population: Decennial Censuses and Population Estimates Program, U.S. Census Bureau, U.S. Dept. of Commerce; population as of July 1, 2011, unless otherwise noted. Pop. density is for land area only. **Racial distribution** categories are abbreviated here; their full forms are white, black or African American, Asian, American Indian and Alaska Native, Native Hawaiian and Other Pacific Islander, two or more races. **Hispanic** or Latino persons may be of any race. Categories under racial distribution may not add up to 100% due to rounding. **Area:** Geography Division, U.S. Census Bureau, U.S. Dept. of Commerce. **Acres forested:** U.S. Forest Service, U.S. Dept. of Agriculture; source year may vary. **Chief airports:** Federal Aviation Admin., U.S. Dept. of Transportation. Chief airports had 500,000+ boardings in 2011. All **Economy** data as of 2011 unless otherwise noted. **Chief manuf. goods:** Manufacturing and Construction Division, U.S. Census Bureau, U.S. Dept. of Commerce. **Chief crops** and **Livestock:** Agriculture Dept., Natl. Agricultural Statistics Service, U.S. Dept. of Agriculture. Cattle/calves and sheep/lambs as of Jan. 2012; hogs/pigs as of June 2012. Many states do not disclose broiler or hog/pig data. **Broadband:** Industry Analysis and Tech. Division, Fed. Communications Commission. Broadband Internet has minimum speeds of at least 768 Kbps downstream and 200 Kbps upstream; figure given is a percentage of total Internet connections. **Nonfuel minerals:** Office of Mineral Information, U.S. Dept. of Interior; preliminary data. Some states exclude small amounts to avoid disclosing proprietary data. **Commercial fishing:** Natl. Marine Fisheries Service, U.S. Dept. of Commerce; for 2010. **Gross state product** and **Per cap. pers. income:** Bureau of Economic Analysis, U.S. Dept. of Commerce; income data are preliminary. **Sales tax:** Federation of Tax Administrators; as of Jan. 1, 2012. **Employment distrib.** and **Unemployment:** Bureau of Labor Statistics, U.S. Dept. of Labor; distribution is for non-farm jobs as of June 2012. **New private housing:** Residential Construction Division, U.S. Census Bureau, U.S. Dept. of Commerce. **Commercial banks** and **Savings institutions:** Federal Deposit Insurance Corp.; FDIC-insured institutions only. **Lottery figures:** North American Assn. of State and Provincial Lotteries. Data may be unaudited and in some cases were gathered by third party. Some states reported rounded sums; others reported exact figures. **Federal employees:** Office of Personnel Mgmt., U.S. Dept. of Labor; as of Mar. 2012. **Energy:** Energy Information Admin., U.S. Dept. of Energy; average per capita monthly electricity consumption and cost for residential customers in 2010. Other information from sources in individual states.

Famous persons lists may include non-natives associated with the state as well as persons born there. **Websites** are subject to change and are not endorsed by *The World Almanac*.

Alabama (AL)
Heart of Dixie, Camellia State

People. Population: 4,802,740; rank: 23. **Pop. change** (2000–11): 8.0%. **Pop. density:** 94.8 per sq mi. **Racial distribution:** 70.1% white; 26.5% black; 1.2% Asian; 0.7% Amer. Ind.; 0.1% Pac. Isl.; 2 or more races, 1.4%. **Hispanic pop.:** 4.0%.

Geography. Total area: 52,420 sq mi; rank: 30. **Land area:** 50,645 sq mi; rank: 28. **Acres forested:** 22.9 mil. **Location:** East South Central state extending N-S from Tenn. to the Gulf of Mexico; E of the Mississippi R. **Climate:** long, hot summers; mild winters; generally abundant rain. **Topography:** coastal plains, including Prairie Black Belt, give way to hills, broken terrain; highest elevation, 2,407 ft. **Capital:** Montgomery. **Chief airports:** Birmingham, Huntsville.

Economy. Chief industries: chemicals, electronics, apparel, primary metals, lumber and wood products, food processing, fabricated metals, automotive tires, oil and gas exploration. **Chief manuf. goods:** poultry processing, paper & paperboard, iron & steel, petroleum, automotive tires, aerospace, aluminum, auto body & parts. **Chief crops:** cotton, greenhouse & nursery, hay, peanuts, corn, soybeans. **Livestock:** 15.36 mil chickens (excl. broilers), 1.02 bil broilers, 1.21 mil cattle/calves. **Broadband Internet:** 70.9%. **Nonfuel minerals:** $964 mil; stone (crushed), cement (portland), lime, sand and gravel (construction), clays (common). **Commercial fishing:** $27.7 mil. **Chief port:** Mobile. **Gross state product:** $173.1 bil. **Sales tax:** 4.0%. **Employment distrib.:** 19.9% govt.; 19.4% trade/trans./util.; 12.8% mfg.; 11.7% ed./health; 11.5% prof./bus. serv.; 9.5% leisure/hosp.; 5.0% finance; 4.6% constr./mining/log.; 1.2% info.; 4.4% other serv. **Unemployment:** 9.0%. **Per cap. pers. income:** $34,650. **New private housing:** 11,667 units/$1.7 bil. **Commercial banks:** 162; deposits: $83.1 bil. **Savings institutions:** 11; deposits: $1.1 bil.

Federal govt. Fed. civ. employees: 41,827; **avg. salary:** $76,332. **Notable fed. facilities:** Redstone Arsenal; Ft. Rucker; Marshall Space Flight Ctr.; Anniston Army Depot; Maxwell-Gunter AFB; Army Corps of Engineers, Mobile District.

Energy. Monthly electricity use: 1,384 kWh, $147.69.

State data. Motto: Audemus Jura Nostra Defendere (We dare defend our rights). **Flower:** Camellia. **Bird:** Northern flicker (yellowhammer is local nickname). **Tree:** Southern longleaf pine. **Song:** "Alabama." **Entered union:** Dec. 14, 1819; rank: 22nd. **State fair:** at Pelham, late Aug.-early Sept.

History. Alabama was inhabited by the Creek, Cherokee, Chickasaw, Alabama, and Choctaw peoples when Spanish explorers arrived in the early 1500s. The French made the first permanent settlement at Ft. Louis, 1702, and founded Mobile, 1711. France later gave up the entire region to England under the Treaty of Paris, 1763. Spanish forces took control of the Mobile Bay area, 1780, and it remained under Spanish control until seized by U.S. troops, 1813. Most of present-day Alabama was held by the Creeks until Gen. Andrew Jackson broke their power, 1814. When Alabama became a state, 1819, black slaves made up about $\frac{1}{3}$ of the population. The Indian Removal Act of 1830 forced most remaining Creeks west. The state seceded, 1861, and the Confederate states were organized Feb. 4, at Montgomery, the first capital. The state was readmitted, 1868. Birmingham, founded 1871, became a center for iron- and steel-making. The Montgomery bus boycott, 1955, sparked by Rosa Parks, helped launch the civil rights movement. Other confrontations occurred at Birmingham, 1963, and Selma, 1965. The leading political figure from the 1960s through the '80s, 4-term gov. George Wallace, started as a segregationist but later won with black support. Growth in the auto industry boosted the state economy as the 21st cent. began. A string of tornadoes in western Alabama in Apr. 2011 killed at least 248. Jefferson County, which includes the city of Birmingham, filed for the most expensive municipal bankruptcy in history in Nov. 2011 due to more than $3.1 bil in sewer-system debt.

Tourist attractions. First White House of the Confederacy, Civil Rights Memorial, Alabama Shakespeare Festival, in Montgomery; Ivy Green (Helen Keller's birthplace), Tuscumbia; Civil Rights Museum, statue of Vulcan, in Birmingham; Carver Museum, Tuskegee; W. C. Handy Home, Museum, & Library, Florence; Alabama Space and Rocket Ctr., Huntsville; Moundville State Monument; Pike Pioneer Museum, Troy; USS *Alabama* Memorial Park, Mobile; Russell Cave Natl. Monument, near Bridgeport: a detailed record of occupancy by humans from about 10,000 BCE to 1650 CE.

Famous Alabamians. Hank Aaron, Tallulah Bankhead, Hugo L. Black, Paul "Bear" Bryant, George Washington Carver, Nat King Cole, William C. Handy, Polly Holliday, Bo Jackson, Helen Keller, Coretta Scott King, Harper Lee, Joe Louis, Willie Mays, John Hunt Morgan, Jim Nabors, Jesse Owens, Condoleezza Rice, George Wallace, Booker T. Washington, Hank Williams.

Tourist information. Alabama Tourism Department, 401 Adams Ave., Ste. 126, P.O. Box 4927, Montgomery, AL 36103; 1-800-ALABAMA, (334) 242-4169; www.alabama.travel

Website. www.alabama.gov

Alaska (AK)
The Last Frontier (unofficial)

People. Population: 722,718; rank: 47. **Pop. change** (2000–11): 15.3%. **Pop. density:** 1.3 per sq mi. **Racial distribution:** 67.9% white; 3.6% black; 5.6% Asian; 14.9% Amer. Ind.; 1.1% Pac. Isl.; 2 or more races, 7.0%. **Hispanic pop.:** 5.8%.

Geography. Total area: 665,384 sq mi; rank: 1. **Land area:** 570,641 sq mi; rank: 1. **Acres forested:** 15.3 mil. **Location:** NW corner of North America, bordered on E by Canada. **Climate:** SE, SW, and central regions, moist and mild; far N extremely dry. Extended summer days, winter nights throughout. **Topography:** includes Pacific and Arctic mountain systems, central plateau, and Arctic slope. Mt. McKinley,

20,320 ft, is the highest point in N. America. **Capital:** Juneau. **Chief airport:** Anchorage.

Economy. Chief industries: petroleum, tourism, fishing, mining, forestry, transportation, aerospace. **Chief manuf. goods:** petroleum, seafood. **Chief crops:** greenhouse products, barley, oats, hay, potatoes, carrots. **Livestock:** 13,000 cattle/calves. **Broadband Internet:** 84.2%. **Nonfuel minerals:** $3.8 bil; zinc, gold, silver, lead, sand and gravel (construction). **Commercial fishing:** $1.6 bil. **Chief ports:** Anchorage, Dutch Harbor, Kodiak, Juneau, Sitka, Valdez. **Gross state product:** $51.4 bil. **Sales tax:** none. **Employment distrib.:** 25.6% govt.; 19.9% trade/trans./util.; 3.0% mfg.; 14.1% ed./health; 8.6% prof./bus. serv.; 10.1% leisure/hosp.; 4.5% finance; 9.0% constr./mining/log.; 1.9% info.; 3.4% other serv. **Unemployment:** 7.6%. **Per cap. pers. income:** $45,529. **New private housing:** 877 units/$204.0 mil. **Commercial banks:** 6; deposits: $8.9 bil. **Savings institutions:** 2; deposits: $390 mil.

Federal govt. Fed. civ. employees: 12,903; **avg. salary:** $75,486. **Notable fed. facilities:** Joint Base Elmendorf-Richardson; Ft. Wainwright; Eilson AFB; Ft. Greely.

Energy. Monthly electricity use: 641 kWh, $104.29.

State data. Motto: North to the future. **Flower:** Forget-me-not. **Bird:** Willow ptarmigan. **Tree:** Sitka spruce. **Song:** "Alaska's Flag." **Entered union:** Jan. 3, 1959; rank: 49th. **State fair** at Palmer, late Aug.-early Sept.

History. Early inhabitants included the Tlingit-Haida and Athabascan peoples. Ancestors of the Aleut and Inuit (Eskimo) probably arrived from Siberia between 10,000 and 6,000 years ago. Vitus Bering, a Dane sailing for Russia, was the first European to land in Alaska, 1741. Russians, pursuing the fur trade, established a permanent settlement on Kodiak Island, 1784. Sec. of State William H. Seward bought Alaska from Russia for $7.2 mil in 1867, a deal some called "Seward's Folly." Discovery of gold in the Klondike region of Canada's Yukon Territory, 1896, triggered an Alaskan gold rush. Alaska became a territory, 1912, and a state, 1959. A huge oil find at Prudhoe Bay, 1968, led to construction of the Trans-Alaska Pipeline, 1974-77. The *Exxon Valdez* supertanker ran aground, 1989, spilling about 11 mil gallons of crude oil; the cleanup cost more than $2.2 bil. Repeated attempts by Congress members to allow oil and gas drilling in the Arctic National Wildlife Refuge have failed.

Tourist attractions. Inside Passage; Portage Glacier; Mendenhall Glacier; Ketchikan Totems; Glacier Bay Natl. Park and Preserve; Denali Natl. Park, one of N. America's great wildlife sanctuaries, surrounding Mt. McKinley, N. America's highest peak; Mt. Roberts Tramway, Juneau; Pribilof Islands fur seal rookeries; restored St. Michael's Russian Orthodox Cathedral, Sitka; White Pass & Yukon Route railroad; Skagway; Katmai Natl. Park & Preserve.

Famous Alaskans. Tom Bodett, Susan Butcher, Ernest Gruening, Jewel (Kilcher), Gov. Tony Knowles, Sydney Laurence, Sarah Palin, Libby Riddles, Jefferson "Soapy" Smith.

Tourist information. Alaska Travel Industry Association, 2600 Cordova St., Ste. 201, Anchorage, AK 99503; 1-800-327-9372; www.travelalaska.com

Website. www.alaska.gov

Arizona (AZ)
Grand Canyon State

People. Population: 6,482,505; rank: 16. **Pop. change** (2000-11): 26.3%. **Pop. density:** 57.1 per sq mi. **Racial distribution:** 84.6% white; 4.5% black; 3.0% Asian; 5.2% Amer. Ind.; 0.3% Pac. Isl.; 2 or more races, 2.5%. **Hispanic pop.:** 30.1%.

Geography. Total area: 113,990 sq mi; rank: 6. **Land area:** 113,594 sq mi; rank: 6. **Acres forested:** 18.7 mil. **Location:** southwestern U.S. **Climate:** clear and dry in the southern regions and northern plateau; high central areas have heavy winter snows. **Topography:** Colorado plateau in the N, containing the Grand Canyon; Mexican Highlands running diagonally NW to SE; Sonoran Desert in the SW. **Capital:** Phoenix. **Chief airports:** Mesa, Phoenix, Tucson.

Economy. Chief industries: manufacturing, construction, tourism, mining, agriculture. **Chief manuf. goods:** aerospace, semiconductors, navigational instruments, cement, plastics, structural metals, dairy, printing, furniture. **Chief crops:** cotton, grapes, apples, lettuce, hay, potatoes, sorghum, barley, corn,

wheat. **Livestock:** 920,000 cattle/calves, 140,000 sheep/lambs. **Broadband Internet:** 69.8%. **Nonfuel minerals:** $8.3 bil; copper, molybdenum concentrates, sand and gravel (construction), silver, cement (portland). **Gross state product:** $258.4 bil. **Sales tax:** 6.6%. **Employment distrib.:** 16.8% govt.; 19.6% trade/trans./util.; 6.2% mfg.; 14.8% ed./health; 14.3% prof./bus. serv.; 11.0% leisure/hosp.; 6.9% finance; 5.4% constr./mining/log.; 1.5% info.; 3.6% other serv. **Unemployment:** 9.5%. **Per cap. pers. income:** $35,875. **New private housing:** 13,007 units/$2.6 bil. **Commercial banks:** 66; deposits: $80.8 bil. **Savings institutions:** 9; deposits: $3.9 bil. **Lottery:** total sales: $583.5 mil; profit: $146.3 mil.

Federal govt. Fed. civ. employees: 42,100; **avg. salary:** $64,986. **Notable fed. facilities:** Luke AFB, Davis-Monthan AFB; Ft. Huachuca; Yuma Proving Ground.

Energy. Monthly electricity use: 1,059 kWh, $116.09.

State data. Motto: Ditat Deus (God enriches). **Flower:** Blossom of the saguaro cactus. **Bird:** Cactus wren. **Tree:** Paloverde. **Song:** "Arizona." **Entered union:** Feb. 14, 1912; rank: 48th. **State fair** at Phoenix, Oct.-early Nov.

History. Paleo-Indians hunted large game in the area at least 12,000 years ago. Anasazi, Mogollon, and Hohokam civilizations lived there c. 300 BCE-1300 CE; Navajo and Apache came c. 15th cent. Marcos de Niza, a Franciscan, and Estevanico, a black former slave, explored, 1539; Spanish explorer Francisco Vásquez de Coronado visited, 1540. Eusebio Francisco Kino, a Jesuit missionary, taught Indians 1692-1711, and left missions. Tubac, a Spanish fort, became the first European settlement, 1752. Spain ceded Arizona to Mexico, 1821. The U.S. took over, 1848, after the Mexican War. The area below the Gila R. came from Mexico in the Gadsden Purchase, 1853. Arizona became a territory, 1863. Apache wars ended with Geronimo's surrender, 1886. Arizona became a state, 1912, and grew rapidly after 1960 with a fourfold rise in population over the next 4 decades. Barry Goldwater was a leading conservative voice in the U.S. Senate (1953-65, 1969-87). The border with Mexico is a major gateway for illegal immigration to the U.S. In 2012, the U.S. Supreme Court struck down most provisions of a 2010 state immigration law that allowed police to make warrantless arrests of those reasonably suspected of having immigrated illegally, but left the provision requiring police to check the immigration status of those stopped or arrested for any other reason.

Tourist attractions. Grand Canyon; Painted Desert; Petrified Forest Natl. Park; Canyon de Chelly; Meteor Crater; London Bridge, Lake Havasu City; Biosphere 2, Oracle; Navajo Natl. Monument.

Famous Arizonans. Bruce Babbitt, Cochise, Alice Cooper, Geronimo, Barry Goldwater, Zane Grey, Carl Hayden, George W. P. Hunt, Helen Jacobs, Bil Keane, Percival Lowell, John McCain, William H. Pickering, John J. Rhodes, Morris Udall, Stewart Udall, Frank Lloyd Wright.

Tourist information. Arizona Office of Tourism, 1110 W. Washington St., Ste. 155, Phoenix, AZ 85007; 1-866-275-5816; www.arizonaguide.com

Website. www.az.gov

Arkansas (AR)
Natural State, Razorback State

People. Population: 2,937,979; rank: 32. **Pop. change** (2000-11): 9.9%. **Pop. density:** 56.5 per sq mi. **Racial distribution:** 80.1% white; 15.6% black; 1.3% Asian; 0.9% Amer. Ind.; 0.2% Pac. Isl.; 2 or more races, 1.8%. **Hispanic pop.:** 6.6%.

Geography. Total area: 55,179 sq mi; rank: 29. **Land area:** 52,035 sq mi; rank: 27. **Acres forested:** 18.7 mil. **Location:** West South Central state. **Climate:** long, hot summers, mild winters; generally abundant rainfall. **Topography:** eastern delta and prairie, southern lowland forests, and the northwestern highlands, which include the Ozark Plateaus. **Capital:** Little Rock. **Chief airports:** Bentonville, Little Rock.

Economy. Chief industries: manufacturing, agriculture, tourism, forestry. **Chief manuf. goods:** poultry processing, motor vehicles & parts, iron & steel, paper & paperboard, plastics, preserved fruits & vegetables, aerospace, rubber. **Chief crops:** rice, soybeans, cotton, hay, wheat, corn, sorghum, tomatoes, peaches, watermelons, pecans, blueberries, grapes. **Livestock:** 19.93 mil chickens (excl. broilers), 1.03 bil broilers, 1.67 mil cattle/calves. **Broadband Internet:** 76.6%.

Nonfuel minerals: $771 mil; bromine, stone (crushed), cement (portland), sand and gravel (construction), lime. **Chief port:** Helena. **Gross state product:** $105.8 bil. **Sales tax:** 6.0%. **Employment distrib.:** 19.2% govt.; 20.0% trade/trans./util.; 13.3% mfg.; 14.6% ed./health; 10.0% prof./bus. serv.; 9.0% leisure/hosp.; 4.0% finance; 4.8% constr./mining/log.; 1.2% info.; 3.8% other serv. **Unemployment:** 8.0%. **Per cap. pers. income:** $34,014. **New private housing:** 6,800 units/$861.5 mil. **Commercial banks:** 139; deposits: $51 bil. **Savings institutions:** 6; deposits: $966 mil. **Lottery:** total sales: $464.0 mil; profit: $94.2 mil.

Federal govt. Fed. civ. employees: 14,206; **avg. salary:** $63,693. **Notable fed. facilities:** Little Rock AFB; Pine Bluff Arsenal; Natl. Ctr. for Toxicological Research, Jefferson.

Energy. Monthly electricity use: 1,211 kWh, $107.28.

State data. Motto: Regnat Populus (The people rule). **Flower:** Apple blossom. **Bird:** Mockingbird. **Tree:** Pine. **Song:** "Arkansas." **Entered union:** June 15, 1836; rank: 25th. **State fair** at Little Rock, mid-Oct.

History. Quapaw, Caddo, Osage, Cherokee, and Choctaw peoples lived in the area at the time of European contact. The first European explorers were de Soto, 1541; Marquette and Jolliet, 1673; and La Salle, 1682. French fur trader Henri de Tonty founded the first settlement, 1686, at Arkansas Post. In 1762, the area was ceded by France to Spain, then given back, 1800, and was part of the Louisiana Purchase, 1803. It was made a territory, 1819, and entered the Union as a slave state, 1836. Arkansas seceded in 1861, after the Civil War began; it was readmitted, 1868. Pres. Eisenhower sent federal troops, 1957, to keep Gov. Orval Faubus from blocking racial integration at Central High School in Little Rock. Wal-Mart, now the world's leading retailer, opened its first store in Rogers, 1962. Elected 5 times as governor, Bill Clinton later served 2 terms in the White House (1993-2001). His presidential library opened, 2004, in Little Rock.

Tourist attractions. Hot Springs Natl. Park (water ranging 95°F-147°F); Eureka Springs; Ozark Folk Ctr., Blanchard Caverns, near Mountain View; Crater of Diamonds (only U.S. diamond mine) near Murfreesboro; Toltec Mounds Archeological State Park, Little Rock; Buffalo Natl. River; Mid-America Museum, Hot Springs; Pea Ridge Natl. Military Park; Tanyard Springs, Morrilton; Wiederkehr Wine Village.

Famous Arkansans. Daisy Bates, Dee Brown, Paul "Bear" Bryant, Glen Campbell, Johnny Cash, Hattie Caraway, Wesley Clark, Bill Clinton, "Dizzy" Dean, Orval Faubus, James W. Fulbright, John Grisham, John H. Johnson, Douglas MacArthur, John L. McClellan, James S. McDonnell, Scottie Pippen, Dick Powell, Brooks Robinson, Billy Bob Thornton, Winthrop Rockefeller, Mary Steenburgen, Edward Durell Stone, Sam Walton, Archibald Yell.

Tourist information. Arkansas Dept. of Parks & Tourism, 1 Capitol Mall, Little Rock, AR 72201; 1-800-NATURAL; www.arkansas.com

Website. www.portal.arkansas.gov

California (CA)
Golden State

People. Population: 37,691,912; rank: 1. **Pop. change** (2000-11): 11.3%. **Pop. density:** 242.0 per sq mi. **Racial distribution:** 74.0% white; 6.6% black; 13.6% Asian; 1.7% Amer. Ind.; 0.5% Pac. Isl.; 2 or more races, 3.6%. **Hispanic pop.:** 38.1%.

Geography. Total area: 163,695 sq mi; rank: 3. **Land area:** 155,779 sq mi; rank: 3. **Acres forested:** 18.8 mil. **Location:** western coast of U.S. **Climate:** moderate temperatures and rainfall along the coast; extremes in the interior. **Topography:** long mountainous coastline; central valley; Sierra Nevada on the E; desert basins of the southern interior; rugged mountains of the N. **Capital:** Sacramento. **Chief airports:** Burbank, Fresno, Long Beach, Los Angeles, Oakland, Ontario, Palm Springs, Sacramento, San Diego, San Francisco, San Jose, Santa Ana.

Economy. Chief industries: agriculture, tourism, apparel, electronics, telecommunications, entertainment. **Chief manuf. goods:** petroleum, aerospace, precision instruments, semiconductors, telecom. & broadcasting equip., pharmaceutical, wineries, plastics, medical equip., preserved fruits & vegetables, printing, dairy, cut & sew apparel, motor vehicles. **Chief crops:** grapes, nursery products, almonds, lettuce, hay, strawberries, floriculture, tomatoes, cotton, oranges, pistachios,

walnuts, broccoli, carrots, rice, peaches, lemons. **Livestock:** 24.69 mil chickens (excl. broilers), 5.35 mil cattle/calves, 570,000 sheep/lambs. **Broadband Internet:** 74.2%. **Nonfuel minerals:** $2.9 bil; boron minerals, sand and gravel (construction), cement (portland), gold, stone (crushed). **Commercial fishing:** $176.2 mil. **Chief ports:** Long Beach, Los Angeles, San Diego, Port Hueneme, Richmond, Oakland, San Francisco, Stockton. **Gross state product:** $1.96 tril. **Sales tax:** 7.25%. **Employment distrib.:** 16.9% govt.; 18.7% trade/trans./util.; 8.7% mfg.; 13.2% ed./health; 15.4% prof./bus. serv.; 11.0% leisure/hosp.; 5.4% finance; 4.1% constr./mining/log.; 3.1% info.; 3.4% other serv. **Unemployment:** 11.7%. **Per cap. pers. income:** $44,481. **New private housing:** 45,471 units/$9.6 bil. **Commercial banks:** 280; deposits: $853.1 bil. **Savings institutions:** 29; deposits: $31.6 bil. **Lottery:** total sales: $3.4 bil; profit: $1.1 bil.

Federal govt. Fed. civ. employees: 169,550; **avg. salary:** $76,302. **Notable fed. facilities:** USMC Camp Pendleton; Naval Base Coronado; Marine Corps Air Ground Combat Ctr., 29 Palms; Marine Corps Air Station Miramar; Travis AFB; Naval Research Lab., Monterey; Lawrence Livermore Natl. Lab; Lawrence Berkeley Natl. Lab; NASA Jet Propulsion Lab; Edwards AFB (NASA Dryden Flight Research Ctr., AF Flight Test Ctr.); San Francisco Mint.

Energy. Monthly electricity use: 562 kWh, $82.85.

State data. Motto: Eureka (I have found it). **Flower:** Golden poppy. **Bird:** California valley quail. **Tree:** California redwood. **Song:** "I Love You, California." **Entered union:** Sept. 9, 1850; rank: 31st. **State fair** at Sacramento, mid-late July.

History. Early inhabitants included more than 100 different Native American tribes with multiple dialects. The first European explorers were Juan Rodríguez Cabrillo, 1542, and Sir Francis Drake, 1579. The first settlement was the Spanish Alta California mission at San Diego, 1769, first in a string founded by Franciscan Father Junípero Serra. California became a province of independent Mexico, 1821. U.S. traders and settlers arrived in the 19th cent. and staged the Bear Flag revolt, 1846, in protest against Mexican rule; later that year U.S. forces occupied California. At the end of the Mexican War, Mexico ceded the territory to the U.S., 1848; that same year gold was discovered, and the famed gold rush began. California became a state, 1850. An economic downturn in the 1870s spurred riots against Chinese immigrants, who had come as laborers in the boom years. An earthquake and related fires devastated San Francisco, 1906. During World War II, Japanese Americans, many of them U.S. citizens, were held in detention camps, 1942-45. Ronald Reagan, a former movie actor, became state governor (1967-75) and U.S. president (1981-89). A budget crisis, 2003, resulted in the recall of Gov. Gray Davis and the election of another actor, Arnold Schwarzenegger. Led by Hollywood in entertainment and Silicon Valley in high-tech, the state's economy dwarfs that of most nations. Still, billion-dollar budget deficits have been a perennial problem.

Tourist attractions. The *Queen Mary*, Aquarium of the Pacific, Long Beach; Palomar Mountain; Disneyland, Anaheim; Getty Center, Universal Studios, in Los Angeles; Tournament of Roses and Rose Bowl, Pasadena; Golden State Museum, Sacramento; San Diego Zoo; Yosemite Valley; Lassen and Sequoia-Kings Canyon natl. parks; Lake Tahoe; Mojave and Colorado Deserts; San Francisco Bay; Napa Valley; Monterey Peninsula; oldest living things on Earth believed to be a stand of bristlecone pines in the Inyo Natl. Forest, est. 4,700 years old; Redwood Natl. and State Parks.

Famous Californians. Edmund G. (Pat) Brown, Jerry Brown, Luther Burbank, Julia Child, Ted Danson, Cameron Diaz, Leonardo DiCaprio, Joe DiMaggio, Dianne Feinstein, John C. Fremont, Tom Hanks, Bret Harte, William Randolph Hearst, Helen Hunt, Jack Kemp, Monica Lewinsky, Jack London, George Lucas, Mark McGwire, Marilyn Monroe, John Muir, Richard M. Nixon, George S. Patton Jr., Gregory Peck, Nancy Pelosi, Ronald Reagan, Sally K. Ride, William Saroyan, Father Junípero Serra, O. J. Simpson, Kevin Spacey, Leland Stanford, John Steinbeck, Arnold Schwarzenegger, Shirley Temple, Earl Warren, Ted Williams, Serena Williams, Venus Williams, Tiger Woods.

Tourist information. California Tourism, P.O. Box 1499, Sacramento, CA 95812-1499; 1-877-225-4367; www.visitcalifornia.com

Website. www.ca.gov

Colorado (CO)
Centennial State

People. Population: 5,116,796; rank: 22. **Pop. change** (2000-11): 19.0%. **Pop. density:** 49.4 per sq mi. **Racial distribution:** 88.3% white; 4.3% black; 2.9% Asian; 1.6% Amer. Ind.; 0.2% Pac. Isl.; 2 or more races, 2.7%. **Hispanic pop.:** 20.9%.

Geography. Total area: 104,094 sq mi; rank: 8. **Land area:** 103,642 sq mi; rank: 8. **Acres forested:** 23.0 mil. **Location:** W central U.S. **Climate:** low relative humidity, abundant sunshine, wide daily/seasonal temperature ranges; alpine conditions in the high mountains. **Topography:** eastern dry high plains; hilly to mountainous central plateau; western Rocky Mts. of high ranges, with broad valleys, deep, narrow canyons. **Capital:** Denver. **Chief airports:** Colorado Springs, Denver.

Economy. Chief industries: manufacturing, construction, government, tourism, agriculture, aerospace, electronics equipment. **Chief manuf. goods:** animal slaughtering, beer, petroleum, pharmaceuticals, aerospace, medical equip., precision instruments, printing, semiconductors. **Chief crops:** hay, corn, potatoes, wheat, onions, dry edible beans, sunflowers, sugar beets, barley, proso millet, cabbage, peaches, lettuce, apples, cantaloupes. **Livestock:** 5.64 mil chickens (excl. broilers), 2.75 mil cattle/calves, 460,000 sheep/lambs, 150,000 hogs/pigs. **Broadband Internet:** 75.2%. **Nonfuel minerals:** $1.9 bil; molybdenum concentrates, gold, sand and gravel (construction), cement (portland), stone (crushed). **Gross state product:** $264.3 bil. **Sales tax:** 2.9%. **Employment distrib.:** 17.6% govt.; 17.7% trade/trans./util.; 5.8% mfg.; 12.2% ed./health; 15.3% prof./bus. serv.; 11.7% leisure/hosp.; 6.3% finance; 6.4% constr./mining/log.; 3.0% info.; 4.1% other serv. **Unemployment:** 8.3%. **Per cap. pers. income:** $44,088. **New private housing:** 13,502 units/$2.9 bil. **Commercial banks:** 145; deposits: $94.4 bil. **Savings institutions:** 15; deposits: $2 bil. **Lottery:** total sales: $518.9 mil; profit $113.4 mil.

Federal govt. Fed. civ. employees: 40,170; **avg. salary:** $75,915. **Notable fed. facilities:** U.S. Air Force Academy; Peterson AFB; Denver Mint; Ft. Carson; Natl. Renewable Energy Laboratory; Transportation Tech. Ctr.; Cheyenne Mtn. Operations Ctr. (NORAD); Denver Federal Ctr.; Natl. Ctr. for Atmospheric Research; Natl. Inst. of Standards & Tech., Boulder; Natl. Wildlife Research Ctr.; NOAA Environmental Tech. Lab.

Energy. Monthly electricity use: 709 kWh, $78.22.

State data. Motto: Nil Sine Numine (Nothing without Providence). **Flower:** Rocky Mountain columbine. **Bird:** Lark bunting. **Tree:** Colorado blue spruce. **Songs:** "Where the Columbines Grow"; "Rocky Mountain High." **Entered union:** Aug. 1, 1876; rank 38th. **State fair** at Pueblo, mid-Aug.-early Sept.

History. Paleo-Indians hunted big game in the area at least 11,000 years ago. Anasazi cliff dwellers flourished around Mesa Verde until about 1300 CE; other Native Americans were the Ute, Pueblo, Cheyenne, and Arapaho. The region was claimed by Spain, but passed to France, 1800. The U.S. acquired eastern Colorado in the Louisiana Purchase, 1803. Lt. Zebulon M. Pike explored the area, 1806, sighting the peak that bears his name. After the Mexican War, 1846-48, U.S. immigrants settled in the east, former Mexicans in the south. Gold was discovered in 1858, causing a population boom. Congress created Colorado Territory, 1861. Conflict between newcomers and displaced Native Americans led to the Sand Creek Massacre, 1864, in which U.S. soldiers and settlers killed some 150 Cheyenne and Arapaho. Most Native Americans were later removed to Oklahoma Territory. The 1870s brought statehood, 1876, and rich silver finds that turned Leadville into a boomtown. Federal military and civilian employment in Colorado surged in the 1940s and '50s; since then, tourism and high-tech industries have fueled the economy. The state's Hispanic population grew from 5.8% in 1980 to 20.7% in 2010.

Tourist attractions. Rocky Mountain and Black Canyon of the Gunnison natl. parks; Aspen Ski Resort; Garden of the Gods, Colorado Springs; Great Sand Dunes, Dinosaur, and Colorado natl. monuments; Pikes Peak and Mt. Evans highways; Mesa Verde Natl. Park (ancient Anasazi Indian cliff dwellings); Grand Mesa Natl. Forest; mining towns of Central City, Silverton, Cripple Creek; Burlington's Old Town; Bent's Fort, near La Junta; Georgetown Loop Historic Mining Railroad Park, Cumbres and Toltec Scenic Railroad; limited stakes gaming in Central City, Blackhawk, Cripple Creek, Ignacio, and Towaoe.

Famous Coloradans. Tim Allen, Frederick Bonfils, Henry Brown, Molly Brown, William N. Byers, M. Scott Carpenter, Lon Chaney, Jack Dempsey, Mamie Eisenhower, Douglas Fairbanks, Barney Ford, Scott Hamilton, John Kerry, Chief Ourey, "Baby Doe" Tabor, Lowell Thomas, Byron R. White, Paul Whiteman.

Tourist information. Colorado Tourism Office, 1625 Broadway, Ste. 1700, Denver, CO 80202; 1-800-COLORADO; www.colorado.com

Website. www.colorado.gov

Connecticut (CT)
Constitution State, Nutmeg State

People. Population: 3,580,709; rank: 29. **Pop. change** (2000-11): 5.1%. **Pop. density:** 739.5 per sq mi. **Racial distribution:** 82.3% white; 11.1% black; 4.0% Asian; 0.5% Amer. Ind.; 0.1% Pac. Isl.; 2 or more races, 2.0%. **Hispanic pop.:** 13.8%.

Geography. Total area: 5,543 sq mi; rank: 48. **Land area:** 4,842 sq mi; rank: 48. **Acres forested:** 1.7 mil. **Location:** New England state in NE corner of the U.S. **Climate:** moderate; winters avg. slightly below freezing; warm, humid summers. **Topography:** western upland, the Berkshires, in the NW, highest elevations; narrow central lowland N-S; hilly eastern upland drained by rivers. **Capital:** Hartford. **Chief airport:** Windsor Locks.

Economy. Chief industries: manufacturing, retail trade, government, services, finances, insurance, real estate. **Chief manuf. goods:** aerospace, chemicals, fabricated metals, precision instruments, toiletries, medical equip., printing, plastics. **Chief crops:** nursery stock, Christmas trees, mushrooms, sweet corn, apples, tobacco, hay. **Livestock:** 2.96 mil chickens (excl. broilers), 49,000 cattle/calves. **Broadband Internet:** 74.1%. **Nonfuel minerals:** $125 mil; stone (crushed), sand and gravel (construction), clays (common), stone (dimension), gemstones (natural). **Commercial fishing:** $18.1 mil. **Chief ports:** New Haven, Bridgeport, New London. **Gross state product:** $230.0 bil. **Sales tax:** 6.35%. **Employment distrib.:** 14.7% govt.; 18.1% trade/trans./util.; 10.1% mfg.; 19.8% ed./health; 12.0% prof./bus. serv.; 8.6% leisure/hosp.; 8.1% finance; 3.1% constr./mining/log.; 1.9% info.; 3.6% other serv. **Unemployment:** 8.8%. **Per cap. pers. income:** $56,889. **New private housing:** 3,173 units/$679.2 mil. **Commercial banks:** 35; deposits: $68.8 bil. **Savings institutions:** 35; deposits: $32.8 bil. **Lottery:** total sales: $1.0 bil; profit: $289.3 mil.

Federal govt. Fed. civ. employees: 8,847; **avg. salary:** $77,555. **Notable fed. facilities:** U.S. Coast Guard Academy; Navy Sub Base New London.

Energy. Monthly electricity use: 750 kWh, $144.40.

State data. Motto: Qui Transtulit Sustinet (He who transplanted still sustains). **Flower:** Mountain laurel. **Bird:** American robin. **Tree:** White oak. **Song:** "Yankee Doodle." **Fifth** of the 13 original states to ratify the Constitution, Jan. 9, 1788. **State fair:** no official state fair; district and local fairs, largest at Durham, late Sept.

History. At the time of European contact, inhabitants of the area were Algonquian peoples, including the Mohegan and Pequot. Dutch explorer Adriaen Block was the first European visitor, 1614. By 1634, settlers from Plymouth Bay had started colonies along the Connecticut R.; in 1637 they defeated the Pequots. The Colony of Connecticut was chartered by England, 1662, adding New Haven, 1665. A Patriot stronghold in the American Revolution, the state actively supported the antislavery movement and the Union cause in the Civil War. The state economy prospered in the 20th cent. from insurance- and defense-related industries. *Nautilus*, the first nuclear-powered submarine, was launched at Groton, 1954. Connecticut Sen. Joseph Lieberman was the Democratic nominee for vice president in 2000. American Indian casinos, starting with Foxwoods in 1992, were an economic boon to the state, but tourism revenues declined sharply with the recession that began in late 2007.

Tourist attractions. Mark Twain House, Hartford; Yale Univ.'s Art Gallery, Peabody Museum, in New Haven; Mystic Seaport, Marine Life Aquarium; P. T. Barnum Museum, Bridgeport; Gillette Castle, Hadlyme; USS *Nautilus* Memorial, Groton (1st nuclear-powered submarine); Mashantucket Pequot Museum & Research Ctr., Foxwoods Resort & Casino, Ledyard; Mohegan Sun, Uncasville; Lake Compounce, Bristol.

Famous "Nutmeggers." Ethan Allen, Phineas T. Barnum, G. W. Bush, Samuel Colt, Jonathan Edwards, Nathan Hale, Katharine Hepburn, Isaac Hull, Robert Mitchum, J. Pierpont Morgan, Ralph Nader, Israel Putnam, Wallace Stevens, Harriet Beecher Stowe, Mark Twain, Noah Webster, Eli Whitney.

Tourist information. Connecticut Commission on Culture and Tourism, One Constitution Plz., 2nd Fl., Hartford, CT 06103; 1-888-CTVISIT, (860) 256-2800; www.ctvisit.com

Website. www.ct.gov

Delaware (DE)
First State, Diamond State

People. Population: 907,135; rank: 45. **Pop. change** (2000-11): 15.8%. **Pop. density:** 465.5 per sq mi. **Racial distribution:** 71.7% white; 21.9% black; 3.4% Asian; 0.7% Amer. Ind.; 0.1% Pac. Isl.; 2 or more races, 2.3%. **Hispanic pop.:** 8.4%.

Geography. Total area: 2,489 sq mi; rank: 49. **Land area:** 1,949 sq mi; rank: 50. **Acres forested:** 0.3 mil. **Location:** Delmarva Peninsula on the Atlantic coastal plain. **Climate:** moderate. **Topography:** Piedmont plateau to the N, sloping to a near sea-level plain. **Capital:** Dover.

Economy. Chief industries: chemicals, agriculture, finance, poultry, shellfish, tourism, auto assembly, food processing, transportation equipment. **Chief manuf. goods:** pharmaceuticals, poultry processing, soap & cleaning compounds, precision instruments, basic chemicals, plastics. **Chief crops:** soybeans, corn, greenhouse & nursery, wheat, potatoes, barley, hay, watermelons, lima beans, green peas, pumpkins, mushrooms, cabbage. **Livestock:** 217.8 mil broilers, 19,000 cattle/calves. **Broadband Internet:** 69.8%. **Nonfuel minerals:** $7.4 mil; magnesium compounds, stone (crushed), sand and gravel (construction), gemstones (natural). **Commercial fishing:** $7.8 mil. **Chief port:** Wilmington. **Gross state product:** $65.8 bil. **Sales tax:** none. **Employment distrib.:** 15.3% govt.; 18.1% trade/trans./util.; 6.0% mfg.; 16.3% ed./health; 12.9% prof./bus. serv.; 10.7% leisure/hosp.; 10.2% finance; 4.4% constr./mining/log.; 1.3% info.; 4.6% other serv. **Unemployment:** 7.3%. **Per cap. pers. income:** $41,635. **New private housing:** 2,954 units/$370.2 mil. **Commercial banks:** 32; deposits: $233.6 bil. **Savings institutions:** 9; deposits: $89.8 bil. **Lottery:** total sales: $710.6 mil; profit: $287 mil.

Federal govt. Fed. civ. employees: 3,406; **avg. salary:** $67,784. **Notable fed. facilities:** Dover AFB; Bombay Hook National Wildlife Refuge.

Energy. Monthly electricity use: 1,001 kWh, $138.24.

State data. Motto: Liberty and independence. **Flower:** Peach blossom. **Bird:** Blue hen chicken. **Tree:** American holly. **Song:** "Our Delaware." **First** of original 13 states to ratify the Constitution, Dec. 7, 1787. **State fair** at Harrington, mid-late July.

History. The Lenni Lenape (Delaware) people lived in the region at the time of European contact. Henry Hudson located the Delaware R., 1609, and in 1610, English explorer Samuel Argall entered Delaware Bay, naming the area after Virginia's governor, Lord De La Warr. Dutch, Swedish, and Finnish settlers were followed by the British, who took control in 1664. After 1682, Delaware became part of Pennsylvania, and in 1704 it was granted its own assembly. It adopted a constitution as the state of Delaware, 1776, and was first to ratify the federal Constitution, 1787. Although it remained in the Union during the Civil War, Delaware retained slavery until the 13th Amendment abolished it in 1865. The DuPont company, founded as a gunpowder mill in 1802, became an industrial giant in the 20th cent. making nylon, Teflon, and other synthetics. Pro-business laws drew many out-of-state firms to incorporate in Delaware. In 2000, Ruth Ann Minner was elected Delaware's first woman governor.

Tourist attractions. Ft. Christina Monument, site of founding of New Sweden, Holy Trinity (Old Swedes) Church, erected 1698, the oldest Protestant church in the U.S. still in use, in Wilmington; Hagley Museum, Winterthur Museum and Gardens, near Wilmington; New Castle historic district; John Dickinson "Penman of the Revolution" home, Dover; Rehoboth Beach; Dover Downs Intl. Speedway.

Famous Delawareans. Thomas F. Bayard, Joseph Biden, Henry Seidel Canby, E. I. du Pont, John P. Marquand, Howard Pyle, Caesar Rodney.

Tourist information. Delaware Tourism Office, 99 Kings Hwy., Dover, DE 19901; 1-866-2VISITDE; www.visitdelaware.com

Website. www.delaware.gov

Florida (FL)
Sunshine State

People. Population: 19,057,542; rank: 4. **Pop. change** (2000-11): 19.2%. **Pop. density:** 355.4 per sq mi. **Racial distribution:** 78.5% white; 16.5% black; 2.6% Asian; 0.5% Amer. Ind.; 0.1% Pac. Isl.; 2 or more races, 1.8%. **Hispanic pop.:** 22.9%.

Geography. Total area: 65,758 sq mi; rank: 22. **Land area:** 53,625 sq mi; rank: 26. **Acres forested:** 17.3 mil. **Location:** peninsula jutting southward 500 mi between the Atlantic and the Gulf of Mexico. **Climate:** subtropical N of Bradenton-Lake Okeechobee-Vero Beach line; tropical S of line. **Topography:** land is flat or rolling; highest point is 345 ft in the NW. **Capital:** Tallahassee. **Chief airports:** Fort Lauderdale, Fort Myers, Jacksonville, Miami, Orlando, Pensacola, Sanford, Sarasota, Tampa, West Palm Beach.

Economy. Chief industries: tourism, agriculture, manufacturing, construction, services, international trade. **Chief manuf. goods:** navigational instruments, medical equip., cement, broadcasting equip., beverages, phosphatic fertilizer, preserved fruits & vegetables, structural metal, printing. **Chief crops:** greenhouse & nursery, oranges, sugarcane, tomatoes, green peppers, grapefruit, strawberries, snap beans, sweet corn, potatoes, cucumbers, tangerines. **Livestock:** 11.86 mil chickens (excl. broilers), 61.8 mil broilers, 1.71 mil cattle/calves. **Broadband Internet:** 82.0%. **Nonfuel minerals:** $3.3 bil; phosphate rock, stone (crushed), cement (portland), sand and gravel (construction), zirconium concentrates. **Commercial fishing:** $188.7 mil. **Chief ports:** Pensacola, Tampa, Port Manatee, Miami, Port Everglades, Jacksonville, Canaveral. **Gross state product:** $754.3 bil. **Sales tax:** 6.0%. **Employment distrib.:** 14.9% govt.; 20.5% trade/trans./util.; 4.3% mfg.; 15.3% ed./health; 14.7% prof./bus. serv.; 13.3% leisure/hosp.; 6.7% finance; 4.4% constr./mining/log.; 1.8% info.; 4.1% other serv. **Unemployment:** 10.5%. **Per cap. pers. income:** $39,563. **New private housing:** 42,360 units/$8.8 bil. **Commercial banks:** 275; deposits: $371 bil. **Savings institutions:** 38; deposits: $40.1 bil. **Lottery:** total sales: $4.0 bil; profit: $1.2 bil.

Federal govt. Fed. civ. employees: 89,673; **avg. salary:** $70,715. **Notable fed. facilities:** John F. Kennedy Space Ctr.; Eglin AFB; MacDill AFB; Hurlburt Field; Pensacola NAS; Jacksonville NAS; Mayport Naval Sta.

Energy. Monthly electricity use: 1,194 kWh, $136.61.

State data. Motto: In God we trust. **Flower:** Orange blossom. **Bird:** Mockingbird. **Tree:** Sabal palmetto palm. **Song:** "Old Folks at Home." **Entered union:** Mar. 3, 1845; rank: 27th. **State fair** at Tampa, early-mid Feb.

History. Florida has been inhabited for at least 12,000 years. Timucua, Apalachee, and Calusa peoples were living in the region when the earliest Europeans came; later the Seminole migrated from Georgia to Florida, becoming dominant there in the early 18th cent. The first European to see Florida was Ponce de León, 1513. France established a colony, Ft. Caroline, on the St. Johns R., 1564. Spain settled St. Augustine, 1565, and Spanish troops massacred most of the French. Britain's Sir Francis Drake burned St. Augustine, 1586. In 1763, Spain ceded Florida to Great Britain, which held the area 20 years before returning it to Spain. Florida was ceded to the U.S. in the Adams-Onís Treaty, 1819. The Seminole War, 1835-42, resulted in removal of most Native Americans to Indian Territory. Florida joined the Union in 1845, seceded in 1861, and was readmitted in 1868. In the late 19th cent., hotel and railroad builder Henry M. Flagler laid the foundations of the tourism industry. The state experienced phenomenal population growth in the 20th cent., especially after 1950. The first U.S. astronaut was launched into space from Cape Canaveral, 1961. Walt Disney World opened near Orlando, 1971. Hurricane Andrew slammed S. Florida, 1992, causing at least $25 bil in property damage. A dispute over Florida's presidential vote in 2000 was decided by the U.S. Supreme Court decision and resulted in George W. Bush's electoral college victory; his brother Jeb was state governor

1999-2007. Four hurricanes hit the state in 2004, causing more than $40 bil in damages.

Tourist attractions. Miami Beach; Castillo de San Marcos, St. Augustine (oldest permanent European settlement in U.S.); Walt Disney World Resort, Sea World, Universal Studios, near Orlando; Kennedy Space Ctr. and U.S. Astronaut Hall of Fame; Everglades Natl. Park; Ringling Museums of Art & the Circus, in Sarasota; Cypress Gardens, Winter Haven; Busch Gardens, Tampa; Florida Caverns State Park, near Mariana; Church St. Station, Orlando; Silver Springs, Ocala.

Famous Floridians. Edna Buchanan, Jeb Bush, Marjory Stoneman Douglas, Henry M. Flagler, Carl Hiaasen, Zora Neale Hurston, James Weldon Johnson, MacKinlay Kantor, John D. MacDonald, Chief Osceola, Claude Pepper, Henry B. Plant, A. Philip Randolph, Marjorie Kinnan Rawlings, Janet Reno, Joseph W. Stilwell, Charles P. Summerall, Ben Vereen.

Tourist information. Visit Florida, 2540 W. Executive Center Cir., Ste. 200, Tallahassee, FL 32301; 1-888-7FLA-USA; www.visitflorida.com

Website. www.myflorida.com

Georgia (GA)
Empire State of the South, Peach State

People. Population: 9,815,210; rank: 9. **Pop. change** (2000-11): 19.9%. **Pop. density:** 170.7 per sq mi. **Racial distribution:** 63.2% white; 31.0% black; 3.4% Asian; 0.5% Amer. Ind.; 0.1% Pac. Isl.; 2 or more races, 1.8%. **Hispanic pop.:** 9.1%.

Geography. Total area: 59,425 sq mi; rank: 24. **Land area:** 57,513 sq mi; rank: 21. **Acres forested:** 24.8 mil. **Location:** South Atlantic state. **Climate:** maritime tropical air masses dominate in summer; polar air masses in winter; E central area drier. **Topography:** most southerly of the Blue Ridge Mts. cover NE and N central; central Piedmont extends to the fall line of rivers; coastal plain levels to the coast flatlands. **Capital:** Atlanta. **Chief airports:** Atlanta, Savannah.

Economy. Chief industries: services, manufacturing, retail trade. **Chief manuf. goods:** carpet & rugs, animal slaughtering & processing, motor vehicles & parts, plastics, aircrafts, paper, chemicals, food. **Chief crops:** cotton, greenhouse & nursery, peanuts, pecans, corn, tomatoes, cucumbers, onions, watermelons, tobacco, squash, blueberries, hay, cabbage, soybeans, peaches, snap beans, wheat. **Livestock:** 24.7 mil chickens (excl. broilers), 1.38 bil broilers, 1.02 mil cattle/calves. **Broadband Internet:** 74.3%. **Nonfuel minerals:** $1.4 bil; clays (kaolin), stone (crushed), clays (fuller's earth), cement (portland), sand and gravel (construction). **Commercial fishing:** $13.7 mil. **Chief ports:** Savannah, Brunswick. **Gross state product:** $418.9 bil. **Sales tax:** 4.0%. **Employment distrib.:** 17.0% govt.; 21.3% trade/trans./util.; 9.0% mfg.; 12.9% ed./health; 14.5% prof./bus. serv.; 9.9% leisure/hosp.; 5.3% finance; 3.8% constr./mining/log.; 2.4% info.; 3.9% other serv. **Unemployment:** 9.8%. **Per cap. pers. income:** $36,104. **New private housing:** 18,493 units/$2.8 bil. **Commercial banks:** 267; deposits: $177.5 bil. **Savings institutions:** 25; deposits: $5.4 bil. **Lottery:** total sales: $3.6 bil; profit: $846.1 mil.

Federal govt. Fed. civ. employees: 79,909; **avg. salary:** $70,934. **Notable fed. facilities:** Ft. Benning; Ft. Stewart; Fed. Law Enforcement Training Ctr., Robins AFB; Ft. Gordon; Kings Bay Naval Base; Moody AFB; Centers for Disease Control; Marine Corps Logistics Base.

Energy. Monthly electricity use: 1,265 kWh, $127.41.

State data. Motto: Wisdom, justice, and moderation. **Flower:** Cherokee rose. **Bird:** Brown thrasher. **Tree:** Live oak. **Song:** "Georgia on My Mind." **Fourth** of the 13 original states to ratify the Constitution, Jan. 2, 1788. **State fair** at Macon, late Apr.-early May.

History. Creek and Cherokee peoples were living in the region when Spaniards founded Santa Catalina mission, 1566, on Saint Catherines Island. Gen. James Oglethorpe established a colony at Savannah, 1733, for the poor and religiously persecuted. Oglethorpe defeated a Spanish army from Florida at Bloody Marsh, 1742. Georgia was a battleground in the American Revolution, with the British finally evacuating Savannah in 1782. When Georgia entered the Union, 1788, its plantation economy relied on slaves for rice and cotton growing. The Cherokee were removed to Indian Territory, 1838-39, and thousands died on the long march, known as the Trail of Tears. By 1860 the number of slaves exceeded 462,000 (44% of the total population). Georgia seceded from the Union, 1861, and was invaded by Union forces, 1864, under Gen. William T. Sherman, who took Atlanta, Sept. 2, and proceeded on his famous "march to the sea," ending in Dec., in Savannah. Georgia was readmitted, 1870. Born 1929 in Atlanta, Martin Luther King Jr., made the city his base during the civil rights struggles of the 1960s. Atlanta became the leading city of the "New South," world headquarters of Coca-Cola and CNN, and host of the 1996 Summer Olympic Games. Hispanics are a rapidly growing economic and political force in the state.

Tourist attractions. State Capitol, Stone Mt. Park, Six Flags Over Georgia, Kennesaw Mt. Natl. Battlefield Park, Martin Luther King Jr. Natl. Historic Site, Underground Atlanta, Jimmy Carter Library & Museum, all Atlanta; Chickamauga and Chattanooga Natl. Military Park, near Dalton; Chattahoochee Natl. Forest; Helen alpine village; Dahlonega, site of America's first gold rush; Brasstown Bald Mt.; Lake Lanier; Franklin D. Roosevelt's Little White House, Warm Springs; Callaway Gardens, Pine Mt.; Andersonville Natl. Historic Site; Okefenokee Swamp, near Waycross; Jekyll, St. Simons, Cumberland islands; Savannah historic riverfront district.

Famous Georgians. Kim Basinger, Griffin Bell, James Bowie, James Brown, Erskine Caldwell, Jimmy Carter, Ray Charles, Lucius D. Clay, Ty Cobb, James Dickey, John C. Fremont, Newt Gingrich, Joel Chandler Harris, "Doc" Holliday, Holly Hunter, Alan Jackson, Jasper Johns, Martin Luther King Jr., Gladys Knight, Sidney Lanier, Little Richard, Juliette Gordon Low, Margaret Mitchell, Sam Nunn, Flannery O'Connor, Otis Redding, Burt Reynolds, Julia Roberts, Jackie Robinson, Clarence Thomas, Travis Tritt, Ted Turner, Carl Vinson, Alice Walker, Herschel Walker, Joseph Wheeler, Joanne Woodward, Trisha Yearwood, Andrew Young.

Tourist information. Dept. of Economic Development, 75 Fifth St., NW, Ste. 1200, Atlanta, GA 30308; 1-800-VISITGA; www.exploregeorgia.org

Website. www.georgia.gov

Hawai'i (HI)
Aloha State

People. Population: 1,374,810; rank: 40. **Pop. change** (2000-11): 13.5%. **Pop. density:** 214.1 per sq mi. **Racial distribution:** 26.0% white; 2.0% black; 38.5% Asian; 0.4% Amer. Ind.; 10.1% Pac. Isl.; 2 or more races, 22.9%. **Hispanic pop.:** 9.2%.

Geography. Total area: 10,932 sq mi; rank: 43. **Land area:** 6,423 sq mi; rank: 47. **Acres forested:** 1.7 mil. **Location:** Hawaiian Islands lie in the North Pacific, 2,397 mi SW from San Francisco. **Climate:** subtropical, with wide variations in rainfall; Waialeale, on Kaua'i, wettest spot in U.S. (annual rainfall 460 in.) **Topography:** islands are tops of a chain of submerged volcanic mountains; active volcanoes: Mauna Loa, Kilauea. **Capital:** Honolulu. **Chief airports:** Hilo, Honolulu, Kahului, Kailua Kona, Lihue.

Economy. Chief industries: tourism, defense, sugar, pineapples. **Chief manuf. goods:** concrete, printing, baked goods, sugar, preserved fruits & vegetables, apparel. **Chief crops:** flowers & nursery, pineapples, seed crops, sugarcane, macadamia nuts, coffee, algae, papayas, tomatoes, bananas, basil, ginger. **Livestock:** 366,000 chickens (excl. broilers), 140,000 cattle/calves. **Broadband Internet:** 82.8%. **Nonfuel minerals:** $94.8 mil; stone (crushed), sand and gravel (construction), gemstones (natural). **Commercial fishing:** $84.0 mil. **Chief ports:** Honolulu, Hilo, Barbers Point, Kahului. **Gross state product:** $67.0 bil. **Sales tax:** 4.0%. **Employment distrib.:** 21.2% govt.; 18.8% trade/trans./util.; 2.1% mfg.; 12.6% ed./health; 12.4% prof./bus. serv.; 18.0% leisure/hosp.; 4.6% finance; 4.6% constr./mining/log.; 1.4% info.; 4.2% other serv. **Unemployment:** 6.7%. **Per cap. pers. income:** $43,053. **New private housing:** 2,743 units/$653.9 mil. **Commercial banks:** 8; deposits: $24.6 bil. **Savings institutions:** 3; deposits: $5.6 bil.

Federal govt. Fed. civ. employees: 25,626; **avg. salary:** $70,900. **Notable fed. facilities:** Joint Base Pearl Harbor-Hickam; Schofield Barracks; Marine Corps Base Hawaii

Kaneohe Bay; Tripler Army Med. Ctr.; Ft. Shafter; Wheeler Army Airfield; Prince Kuhio Federal Bldg.

Energy. Monthly electricity use: 601 kWh, $168.86.

State data. Motto: Ua mau ke ea o ka aina i ka pono (The life of the land is perpetuated in righteousness). **Flower:** Yellow hibiscus. **Bird:** Hawaiian goose. **Tree:** Kukui (candlenut). **Song:** "Hawai'i Pono'i" (Hawai'i's Own). **Entered union:** Aug. 21, 1959; rank: 50th. **State fair** at Honolulu, late May-June.

History. Polynesians from islands 2,000 mi to the S settled the Hawaiian Islands, probably 300-600 CE. The first European visitor was British captain James Cook, 1778. King Kamehameha I united the islands by 1810. Christian missionaries arrived, 1819, bringing Western culture. Under the reign, 1825-54, of King Kamehameha III, a constitution, legislature, and public school system were instituted. Sugar production began, 1835, and it became the dominant industry. Queen Liliuokalani was deposed, 1893, and a republic was established, 1894, headed by Sanford B. Dole. Annexation by the U.S. came in 1898. The Japanese attack on Pearl Harbor, Dec. 7, 1941, brought the U.S. into World War II. Hawai'i attained statehood, 1959. Hurricane Iniki pounded Kaua'i, 1992, causing about $1 bil in damage. In 2006, Pres. George W. Bush designated the Northwestern Hawaiian Islands Natl. Monument, a marine area of 140,000 sq mi.

Tourist attractions. Hawaii Volcanoes, Haleakala natl. parks; Natl. Memorial Cemetery of the Pacific, Waikiki Beach, Diamond Head, in Honolulu; USS *Arizona* Memorial, Pearl Harbor; Hanauma Bay; Polynesian Cultural Ctr., Laie; Nu'uanu Pali; Waimea Canyon; Wailoa and Wailuku River state parks.

Famous Islanders. Bernice Pauahi Bishop, Tia Carrere, Father Damien de Veuster, Don Ho, Duke Kahanamoku, King Kamehameha, Brook Mahealani Lee, Daniel K. Inouye, Jason Scott Lee, Queen Liliuokalani, Bette Midler, Barack Obama, Ellison Onizuka.

Tourist information. Hawaii Visitors and Conventions Bureau, 2270 Kalakaua Ave., Ste. 801, Honolulu, HI 96815; 1-800-GOHAWAII; www.gohawaii.com

Website. www.ehawaii.gov

Idaho (ID)
Gem State

People. Population: 1,584,985; rank: 39. **Pop. change** (2000-11): 22.5%. **Pop. density:** 19.2 per sq mi. **Racial distribution:** 93.9% white; 0.8% black; 1.3% Asian; 1.7% Amer. Ind.; 0.2% Pac. Isl.; 2 or more races, 2.1%. **Hispanic pop.:** 11.5%.

Geography. Total area: 83,569 sq mi; rank: 14. **Land area:** 82,643 sq mi; rank: 11. **Acres forested:** 21.4 mil. **Location:** northwestern Mountain state bordering on British Columbia. **Climate:** tempered by Pacific westerly winds; drier, cooler, continental climate in SE; altitude an important factor. **Topography:** Snake R. plains in the S; central region of mountains, canyons, gorges (Hells Canyon, 7,900 ft, deepest in N. America); subalpine northern region. **Capital:** Boise. **Chief airport:** Boise.

Economy. Chief industries: manufacturing, agriculture, tourism, lumber, mining, electronics. **Chief manuf. goods:** computers & electronics, preserved fruits & vegetables, cheese, lumber. **Chief crops:** potatoes, wheat, hay, sugar beets, barley, greenhouse & nursery, onions, dry beans, corn, mint, apples, hops, peaches, lentils, peas, cherries, plums & prunes, oats. **Livestock:** 2.22 mil cattle/calves, 240,000 sheep/lambs. **Broadband Internet:** 64.9%. **Nonfuel minerals:** $1.3 bil; molybdenum concentrates, phosphate rock, silver, sand and gravel (construction), lead. **Chief port:** Lewiston. **Gross state product:** $57.9 bil. **Sales tax:** 6.0%. **Employment distrib.:** 19.1% govt.; 20.3% trade/trans./util.; 9.2% mfg.; 14.4% ed./health; 12.3% prof./bus. serv.; 9.7% leisure/hosp.; 4.5% finance; 5.5% constr./mining/log.; 1.6% info.; 3.5% other serv. **Unemployment:** 8.7%. **Per cap. pers. income:** $33,326. **New private housing:** 3,815 units/$732.8 mil. **Commercial banks:** 33; deposits: $17.9 bil. **Savings institutions:** 2; deposits: $975 mil. **Lottery:** total sales: $147.2 mil; profit: $37 mil.

Federal govt. Fed. civ. employees: 8,779; **avg. salary:** $64,814. **Notable fed. facilities:** Idaho Natl. Lab; Mountain Home AFB.

Energy. Monthly electricity use: 1,020 kWh, $81.46.

State data. Motto: Esto Perpetua (It is perpetual). **Flower:** Syringa. **Bird:** Mountain bluebird. **Tree:** White pine. **Song:** "Here We Have Idaho." **Entered union:** July 3, 1890; rank: 43rd. **State fair** at Boise, late Aug.; at Blackfoot, early Sept.

History. Paleo-Indian hunters roamed the land over 13,000 years ago; later inhabitants included Shoshone, Northern Paiute, Bannock, and Nez Percé peoples. Meriwether Lewis and William Clark Expedition took place, 1804-06. Next came fur traders, 1809-34, and missionaries, 1830s-50s. Mormons made their first permanent settlement at Franklin, 1860. Idaho's gold rush began the same year and brought thousands of permanent settlers. A series of Indian wars followed, including a remarkable campaign by Chief Joseph and the Nez Percé that ended with his surrender in Montana, 1877. Idaho became a territory, 1863, and a state, 1890. In the 20th cent., it emerged as a leader in potato, lumber, and silver output. The Sun Valley ski resort opened in 1936, boosting tourism. Startup of Lewiston's river port, 1975, opened Idaho to oceangoing trade. Fueled by high-tech job growth, the state's population jumped 19.5% in 2000-09.

Tourist attractions. Hells Canyon, deepest gorge in N. America; World Ctr. for Birds of Prey, Boise; Craters of the Moon Natl. Monument; Sun Valley, Sawtooth Mts.; Shoshone Falls; Lava Hot Springs; Lake Pend Oreille; Lake Coeur d'Alene; Sawtooth Natl. Recreation Area, Redfish Lake; River of No Return Wilderness Area.

Famous Idahoans. William E. Borah, Frank Church, Lou Dobbs, Fred T. Dubois, Chief Joseph, Harmon Killebrew, Ezra Pound, Sacagawea, Picabo Street, Lana Turner.

Tourist information. Idaho Division of Tourism Development, 700 W. State St., P.O. Box 83720, Boise, ID 83720; 1-800-VISITID; www.visitid.org

Website. www.state.id.us

Illinois (IL)
Prairie State

People. Population: 12,869,257; rank: 5. **Pop. change** (2000-11): 3.6%. **Pop. density:** 231.8 per sq mi. **Racial distribution:** 78.0% white; 14.8% black; 4.8% Asian; 0.6% Amer. Ind.; 0.1% Pac. Isl.; 2 or more races, 1.7%. **Hispanic pop.:** 16.2%.

Geography. Total area: 57,914 sq mi; rank: 25. **Land area:** 55,519 sq mi; rank: 24. **Acres forested:** 4.8 mil. **Location:** East North Central state; western, southern, and eastern boundaries formed by Mississippi, Ohio, and Wabash Rivers, respectively. **Climate:** temperate; typically cold, snowy winters, hot summers. **Topography:** prairie and fertile plains throughout; open hills in the southern region. **Capital:** Springfield. **Chief airports:** Chicago (2).

Economy. Chief industries: services, manufacturing, travel, wholesale and retail trade, finance, insurance, real estate, construction, health care, agriculture. **Chief manuf. goods:** food, petroleum, plastics, chemicals, agricultural machinery, pharmaceuticals, motor vehicles, printing. **Chief crops:** corn, soybeans, hay, wheat, greenhouse & nursery, apples, peaches, sorghum. **Livestock:** 4.66 mil chickens (excl. broilers), 1.07 mil cattle/calves, 57,000 sheep/lambs, 500,000 hogs/pigs. **Broadband Internet:** 78.4%. **Nonfuel minerals:** $894 mil; stone (crushed), sand and gravel (industrial), sand and gravel (construction), cement (portland), tripoli. **Chief port:** Chicago. **Gross state product:** $670.7 bil. **Sales tax:** 6.25%. **Employment distrib.:** 14.7% govt.; 19.9% trade/ trans./util.; 10.3% mfg.; 14.9% ed./health; 14.9% prof./bus. serv.; 9.4% leisure/hosp.; 6.4% finance; 3.5% constr./mining/ log.; 1.7% info.; 4.3% other serv. **Unemployment:** 9.8%. **Per cap. pers. income:** $44,140. **New private housing:** 11,809 units/$2.1 bil. **Commercial banks:** 558; deposits: $346.5 bil. **Savings institutions:** 86; deposits: $23.6 bil. **Lottery:** total sales: $2.3 bil; profit: $690 mil.

Federal govt. Fed. civ. employees: 49,696; **avg. salary:** $76,540. **Notable fed. facilities:** Great Lakes Naval Station; Fermi Natl. Accelerator Lab; Argonne Natl. Lab; Scott AFB; Rock Island Arsenal.

Energy. Monthly electricity use: 799 kWh, $92.03.

State data. Motto: State sovereignty, national union. **Flower:** Native violet. **Bird:** Cardinal. **Tree:** White oak. **Song:** "Illinois." **Entered union:** Dec. 3, 1818; rank: 21st. **State fair** at Springfield, mid-Aug.; DuQuoin, late Aug.-Sept.

History. The region has been inhabited for at least 10,000 years; seminomadic Algonquian peoples, including the Peoria, Illinois, Kaskaskia, and Tamaroa, lived there at the time of European contact. Fur traders were the first Europeans in Illinois, followed shortly by Louis Jolliet and Jacques Marquette, 1673, and René-Robert Cavelier, sieur de La Salle, 1680, who built a fort near present-day Peoria. French priests established the first permanent settlements at Cahokia, near present-day St. Louis, 1699, and Kaskaskia, 1703. France ceded the area to Britain, 1763, and in 1778, American Gen. George Rogers Clark took Kaskaskia from the British without a shot. Illinois became a separate territory, 1809, and a state, 1818. Defeat of Native American tribes in the Black Hawk War, 1832, and canal, rail, and road construction brought rapid change. Mormon settlers at Nauvoo, 1839, met with hostility, and a Carthage mob killed Mormon leader Joseph Smith and his brother, 1844. The Great Chicago Fire, 1871, destroyed the city's downtown. Illinois became a center for the labor movement, leading to bitter conflicts such as the Haymarket riot, 1886, and Pullman strike, 1894. Social reformer Jane Addams founded Hull House, 1889, to aid immigrants and the poor. During 1900-70, as manufacturing expanded, many African Americans arrived from the southern U.S. Chicago police violently suppressed antiwar protests at the 1968 Democratic National Convention. Dennis Hastert was the longest serving Republican Speaker of the House, 1999-2007. Barack Obama, elected in 2004, was only the fifth African American to serve in the U.S. Senate; he became the 44th U.S. president in 2009. Political corruption and criminality have plagued the state for decades; since 1960, five former governors have been charged with criminal offenses.

Tourist attractions. Chicago museums and parks; Illinois State Museum, Abraham Lincoln Presidential Library and Museum, in Springfield; Cahokia Mounds, Collinsville; Starved Rock State Park; Crab Orchard Wildlife Refuge; Mormon settlement at Nauvoo; Fts. Kaskaskia, Chartres, Massac (parks); Shawnee Natl. Forest; Dickson Mounds Museum, Lewistown.

Famous Illinoisans. Jane Addams, John Ashcroft, Saul Bellow, Jack Benny, Ray Bradbury, Gwendolyn Brooks, William Jennings Bryan, St. Frances Xavier Cabrini, Hillary Rodham Clinton, Clarence Darrow, John Deere, Stephen A. Douglas, James T. Farrell, George W. Ferris, Marshall Field, Betty Friedan, Benny Goodman, Ulysses S. Grant, Dennis Hastert, Ernest Hemingway, Charlton Heston, Wild Bill Hickok, Henry J. Hyde, Abraham Lincoln, Vachel Lindsay, Edgar Lee Masters, Oscar Mayer, Cyrus McCormick, Ronald Reagan, Donald Rumsfeld, Carl Sandburg, Adlai Stevenson, James Watson, Frank Lloyd Wright, Philip Wrigley.

Tourist information. Illinois Bureau of Tourism, 100 W. Randolph St., Ste. 3-400, Chicago, IL 60601; 1-800-2CONNECT; www.enjoyillinois.com
Website. www.illinois.gov

Mt. Vernon, Jeffersonville. **Gross state product:** $278.1 bil. **Sales tax:** 7.0%. **Employment distrib.:** 14.8% govt.; 19.0% trade/trans./util.; 16.7% mfg.; 14.9% ed./health; 10.2% prof./ bus. serv.; 10.3% leisure/hosp.; 4.5% finance; 4.6% constr./ mining/log.; 1.2% info.; 3.7% other serv. **Unemployment:** 9.0%. **Per cap. pers. income:** $35,550. **New private housing:** 12,618 units/$2.0 bil. **Commercial banks:** 139; deposits: $90.3 bil. **Savings institutions:** 48; deposits: $9.2 bil. **Lottery:** total sales: $791.4 mil; profit: $188.2 mil.

Federal govt. Fed. civ. employees: 24,233; **avg. salary:** $67,630. **Notable fed. facilities:** Nav. Surface Warfare Ctr., Crane Div.; Grissom Air Reserve Base.

Energy. Monthly electricity use: 1,065 kWh, $101.79.

State data. Motto: Crossroads of America. **Flower:** Peony. **Bird:** Cardinal. **Tree:** Tulip poplar. **Song:** "On the Banks of the Wabash, Far Away." **Entered union:** Dec. 11, 1816; rank: 19th. **State fair** at Indianapolis, early-to-mid-Aug.

History. When the Europeans arrived, Miami, Potawatomi, Kickapoo, Piankashaw, Wea, and Shawnee peoples inhabited the region. René-Robert Cavelier, sieur de La Salle visited the present South Bend area, 1679 and 1681. The first French fort was built near present-day Lafayette, 1717. A French trading post was established, 1731-32, at Vincennes. France ceded the area to Britain, 1763. During the American Revolution, American Gen. George Rogers Clark captured Vincennes, 1778, and defeated British forces, 1779. Indiana became a territory, 1800, and a state, 1816. The Miami were beaten, 1794, at Fallen Timbers, and Gen. William H. Harrison defeated Tecumseh's Indian confederation, 1811, at Tippecanoe. Manufacturing grew rapidly after the Civil War. U.S. Steel founded Gary, 1906. An automotive test track was the site of the first Indianapolis 500 race, 1911. The auto industry remains key to the state economy; in 2008, Honda opened a $550-mil plant near Greensburg. Heavy rain in June 2008 flooded southwest and central Indiana.

Tourist attractions. Lincoln Log Cabin Historic Site, near Charleston; George Rogers Clark Park, Vincennes; Wyandotte Caves; Tippecanoe Battlefield Park, near Lafayette; Benjamin Harrison home, Indianapolis 500 raceway and museum, in Indianapolis; Indiana Dunes, Chesterton; Natl. College Football Hall of Fame, South Bend; Hoosier Natl. Forest.

Famous "Hoosiers." Larry Bird, Ambrose Burnside, Hoagy Carmichael, Jim Davis, James Dean, Eugene V. Debs, Theodore Dreiser, Paul Dresser, Jeff Gordon, Benjamin Harrison, Gil Hodges, Michael Jackson, David Letterman, Carole Lombard, John Mellencamp, Jane Pauley, Cole Porter, Gene Stratton Porter, Ernie Pyle, Dan Quayle, James Whitcomb Riley, Oscar Robertson, Red Skelton, Booth Tarkington, Kurt Vonnegut, Lew Wallace, Wendell L. Willkie, Wilbur Wright.

Tourist information. Indiana Office of Tourism Development, 1 North Capital, Ste. 600, Indianapolis, IN 46204; 1-800-677-9800; www.visitindiana.com
Website. www.in.gov

Indiana (IN)
Hoosier State

People. Population: 6,516,922; rank: 15. **Pop. change** (2000-11): 7.2%. **Pop. density:** 181.9 per sq mi. **Racial distribution:** 86.8% white; 9.4% black; 1.7% Asian; 0.4% Amer. Ind.; 0.1% Pac. Isl.; 2 or more races, 1.7%. **Hispanic pop.:** 6.2%.

Geography. Total area: 36,420 sq mi; rank: 38. **Land area:** 35,826 sq mi; rank: 38. **Acres forested:** 4.8 mil. **Location:** East North Central state; Lake Michigan on N border. **Climate:** 4 distinct seasons with a temperate climate. **Topography:** hilly southern region; fertile rolling plains of central region; flat, heavily glaciated N; dunes along Lake Michigan shore. **Capital:** Indianapolis. **Chief airport:** Indianapolis.

Economy. Chief industries: manufacturing, services, agriculture, government, wholesale and retail trade, transportation and public utilities. **Chief manuf. goods:** motor vehicles & parts, iron & steel mills, pharmaceuticals, petroleum, plastics, medical equip., printing. **Chief crops:** corn, soybeans, greenhouse & nursery, wheat, hay, tomatoes, watermelons, apples. **Livestock:** 31.14 mil chickens (excl. broilers), 860,000 cattle/calves, 55,000 sheep/lambs, 280,000 hogs/pigs. **Broadband Internet:** 71.4%. **Nonfuel minerals:** $772 mil; stone (crushed), cement (portland), sand and gravel (construction), lime, cement (masonry). **Chief ports:** Burns Harbor-Portage,

Iowa (IA)
Hawkeye State

People. Population: 3,062,309; rank: 30. **Pop. change** (2000-11): 4.6%. **Pop. density:** 54.8 per sq mi. **Racial distribution:** 93.0% white; 3.1% black; 1.9% Asian; 0.5% Amer. Ind.; 0.1% Pac. Isl.; 2 or more races, 1.5%. **Hispanic pop.:** 5.2%.

Geography. Total area: 56,273 sq mi; rank: 26. **Land area:** 55,857 sq mi; rank: 23. **Acres forested:** 3.0 mil. **Location:** West North Central state bordered by Mississippi R. on the E and Missouri R. on the W. **Climate:** humid, continental. **Topography:** watershed from NW to SE; soil especially rich and land level in the N central counties. **Capital:** Des Moines. **Chief airport:** Des Moines.

Economy. Chief industries: agriculture, communications, construction, finance, insurance, trade, services, manufacturing. **Chief manuf. goods:** machinery, vegetable oils, animal slaughtering & processing, laundry equip., plastics, motor vehicles & parts. **Chief crops:** corn, soybeans, hay, greenhouse & nursery, oats. **Livestock:** 66.32 mil chickens (excl. broilers), 3.9 mil cattle/calves, 195,000 sheep/lambs, 1.02 mil hogs/pigs. **Broadband Internet:** 70.1%. **Nonfuel minerals:** $565 mil; stone (crushed), cement (portland), sand and gravel (construction), sand and gravel (industrial), lime. **Gross state product:** $149.0 bil. **Sales tax:** 6.0%. **Employment distrib.:** 16.9% govt.; 20.0% trade/trans./util.; 14.4% mfg.; 14.4% ed./health; 8.1% prof./bus. serv.; 9.0% leisure/hosp.; 6.7% finance; 4.8% constr./mining/log.; 1.9% info.; 3.9% other serv. **Unemployment:** 5.9%. **Per cap. pers. income:** $40,470. **New private housing:** 7,526 units/$1.2 bil. **Commercial banks:** 357; deposits: $66.1 bil. **Savings institutions:** 14; deposits: $3.9 bil. **Lottery:** total sales: $271.4 mil; profit: $68.1 mil.

Federal govt. Fed. civ. employees: 9,113; **avg. salary:** $64,092. **Notable fed. facilities:** Ames Lab; Natl. Animal Disease Ctr.

Energy. Monthly electricity use: 913 kWh, $95.19.

State data. Motto: Our liberties we prize, and our rights we will maintain. **Flower:** Wild rose. **Bird:** Eastern goldfinch. **Tree:** Oak. **Song:** "The Song of Iowa." **Entered union:** Dec. 28, 1846; rank: 29th. **State fair** at Des Moines, mid-Aug.

History. Early inhabitants were Mound Builders who dwelt on Iowa's fertile plains. Later, Iowa and Yankton Sioux lived in the area. The first Europeans, Jacques Marquette and Louis Jolliet, gave France its claim to the area, 1673. In 1762, France ceded the region to Spain, but Napoleon took it back, 1800. It became part of the U.S. through the Louisiana Purchase, 1803. Native American Sauk and Fox tribes moved into the area but relinquished their land in defeat, after the 1832 uprising led by Sauk chieftain Black Hawk. Iowa became a territory in 1838, and entered as a free state, 1846, strongly supporting the Union. Fertile land lured farmers from eastern states, 1850-1900 and the population rose rapidly. Growth slowed in the 20th cent., as farming became mechanized. Surging demand for ethanol fuel from Iowa corn contributed more than $2.6 bil to the state economy in 2005. Severe flooding in eastern Iowa in June 2008 caused billions of dollars in damages and forced the evacuation of thousands of residents.

Tourist attractions. Herbert Hoover birthplace and library, West Branch; Effigy Mounds Natl. Monument, prehistoric Indian burial site, Marquette; Amana Colonies; Grant Wood's paintings and memorabilia, Davenport Municipal Art Gallery; Living History Farms, Des Moines; Adventureland, Prairie Meadows horse racing, in Altoona; Boone and Scenic Valley Railroad; Greyhound Parks, in Dubuque and Council Bluffs; riverboat cruises and casino gambling, Mississippi and Missouri Rivers; Iowa Great Lakes, Okoboji.

Famous Iowans. Tom Arnold, Johnny Carson, Marquis Childs, Buffalo Bill Cody, Mamie Dowd Eisenhower, Bob Feller, George Gallup, Susan Glaspell, James Norman Hall, Harry Hansen, Herbert Hoover, Ann Landers, Glenn Miller, Lillian Russell, Billy Sunday, James A. Van Allen, Abigail Van Buren, Carl Van Vechten, Henry Wallace, John Wayne, Meredith Willson, Grant Wood.

Tourist information. Iowa Tourism Office, Iowa Dept. of Economic Development, 200 E. Grand Ave., Des Moines, IA 50309; 1-888-472-6035; www.traveliowa.com

Website. www.iowa.gov

Kansas (KS)
Sunflower State

People. Population: 2,871,238; rank: 33. **Pop. change** (2000-11): 6.8%. **Pop. density:** 35.1 per sq mi. **Racial distribution:** 87.4% white; 6.1% black; 2.5% Asian; 1.2% Amer. Ind.; 0.1% Pac. Isl.; 2 or more races, 2.7%. **Hispanic pop.:** 10.8%.

Geography. Total area: 82,278 sq mi; rank: 15. **Land area:** 81,759 sq mi; rank: 13. **Acres forested:** 2.5 mil. **Location:** West North Central state, with Missouri R. on E. **Climate:** temperate but continental, with great extremes between summer and winter. **Topography:** hilly Osage Plains in the E; central region level prairie and hills; high plains in the W. **Capital:** Topeka. **Chief airport:** Wichita.

Economy. Chief industries: manufacturing, finance, insurance, real estate, services. **Chief manuf. goods:** animal slaughtering, aerospace, petroleum, plastics, machinery, navigational instruments, printing. **Chief crops:** wheat, corn, soybeans, hay, sorghum, sunflowers, cotton, potatoes. **Livestock:** 6.1 mil cattle/calves, 70,000 sheep/lambs, 170,000 hogs/pigs. **Broadband Internet:** 74.6%. **Nonfuel minerals:** $1.2 bil; helium (Grade-A), salt, cement (portland), stone (crushed), helium (crude). **Chief port:** Kansas City. **Gross**

state product: $130.9 bil. **Sales tax:** 6.3%. **Employment distrib.:** 19.4% govt.; 18.6% trade/trans./util.; 12.1% mfg.; 13.8% ed./health; 11.5% prof./bus. serv.; 8.8% leisure/hosp.; 5.4% finance; 4.6% constr./mining/log.; 2.0% info.; 3.8% other serv. **Unemployment:** 6.7%. **Per cap. pers. income:** $40,481. **New private housing:** 5,386 units/$860.7 mil. **Commercial banks:** 343; deposits: $54.4 bil. **Savings institutions:** 16; deposits: $6.7 bil. **Lottery:** total sales: $232.4 mil; profit: $70 mil.

Federal govt. Fed. civ. employees: 17,851; **avg. salary:** $65,677. **Notable fed. facilities:** Ft. Riley; Leavenworth Fed. Pen.; McConnell AFB; Colmery-O'Neal VA Medical Ctr.

Energy. Monthly electricity use: 985 kWh, $98.73.

State data. Motto: Ad Astra per Aspera (To the stars through difficulties). **Flower:** Native sunflower. **Bird:** Western meadowlark. **Tree:** Cottonwood. **Song:** "Home on the Range." **Entered union:** Jan. 29, 1861; rank: 34th. **State fair** at Hutchinson, begins Fri. after Labor Day.

History. Wichita, Pawnee, Kansa, and Osage peoples lived in the area when Francisco de Coronado explored it in 1541. These Native Americans—hunters who also farmed—were joined on the Plains by the nomadic Cheyenne, Arapaho, Comanche, and Kiowa about 1800. France claimed the region, 1682, ceded its claim to Spain, 1762, then regained control, 1800, before selling it to the U.S. in the Louisiana Purchase, 1803. After 1830, thousands of Native Americans were removed from more eastern states to Kansas. Organized as a territory, 1854, the area witnessed violent clashes between pro- and antislavery settlers and became known as "Bleeding Kansas." It entered the Union as a free state, 1861. After the Civil War, rail construction and huge cattle drives from Texas turned Abilene and Dodge City into cowboy capitals. Russian Mennonite immigrants brought a new strain of winter wheat, 1874, transforming Kansas agriculture. Carry Nation launched her anti-saloon crusade in the 1890s. Part of the "Dust Bowl," the state experienced drought and depression in the 1930s. Topeka was the focus of the famous *Brown v. Board of Education* decision, 1954, that led to desegregation of U.S. public schools. Bob Dole represented Kansas in the U.S. Senate (1969-96) but failed in several efforts to win higher office.

Tourist attractions. Eisenhower Center, Abilene; Natl. Agricultural Ctr. and Hall of Fame, Bonner Springs; Dodge City-Boot Hill; Old Cowtown Museum, Wichita; Ft. Scott and Ft. Larned, restored 1800s cavalry forts; Kansas Cosmosphere and Space Ctr., Hutchinson; Woodlands Racetrack, Kansas City; U.S. Cavalry Museum, Ft. Riley; Heartland Park Raceway, Topeka.

Famous Kansans. Kirstie Alley, Roscoe "Fatty" Arbuckle, Ed Asner, Gwendolyn Brooks, John Brown, George Washington Carver, Wilt Chamberlain, Walter P. Chrysler, Glenn Cunningham, John Stuart Curry, Robert Dole, Amelia Earhart, Wyatt Earp, Dwight D. Eisenhower, Ron Evans, Maurice Greene, Wild Bill Hickok, Cyrus Holliday, Dennis Hopper, William Inge, Don Johnson, Walter Johnson, Nancy Landon Kassebaum, Buster Keaton, Emmett Kelly, Alf Landon, Edgar Lee Masters, Hattie McDaniel, Oscar Micheaux, Carry Nation, Georgia Neese-Gray, Charlie Parker, Gordon Parks, Jim Ryun, Barry Sanders, Vivian Vance, William Allen White, Jess Willard.

Tourist information. Kansas Dept. of Commerce, Travel and Tourism Div., 1000 SW Jackson St., Ste. 100, Topeka, KS 66612; (785) 296-2009; www.travelks.com

Website. www.kansas.gov

Kentucky (KY)
Bluegrass State

People. Population: 4,369,356; rank: 26. **Pop. change** (2000-11): 8.1%. **Pop. density:** 110.7 per sq mi. **Racial distribution:** 88.9% white; 8.0% black; 1.2% Asian; 0.3% Amer. Ind.; 0.1% Pac. Isl.; 2 or more races, 1.6%. **Hispanic pop.:** 3.2%.

Geography. Total area: 40,408 sq mi; rank: 37. **Land area:** 39,486 sq mi; rank: 37. **Acres forested:** 12.5 mil. **Location:** East South Central state, bordered on N by Illinois, Indiana, Ohio; on E by West Virginia and Virginia; on S by Tennessee; on W by Missouri. **Climate:** moderate, with plentiful rainfall. **Topography:** mountainous in E; rounded hills of the Knobs in the N; Bluegrass, heart of state; wooded rocky hillsides of the Pennyroyal; Western Coal Field; the fertile Purchase in the SW. **Capital:** Frankfort. **Chief airports:** Greater Cincinnati, Lexington, Louisville.

Economy. Chief industries: manufacturing, services, finance, insurance and real estate, retail trade, public utilities. **Chief manuf. goods:** motor vehicles & parts, aluminum, basic chemicals, plastics, iron & steel, rubber, printing. **Chief crops:** hay, corn, soybeans, tobacco, wheat. **Livestock:** 6.42 mil chickens (excl. broilers), 310 mil broilers, 2.15 mil cattle/calves, 40,000 sheep/lambs. **Broadband Internet:** 80.7%. **Nonfuel minerals:** $836 mil; stone (crushed), lime, cement (portland), sand and gravel (construction), clays (common). **Chief ports:** Louisville, Hickman-Fulton County. **Gross state product:** $164.8 bil. **Sales tax:** 6.0%. **Employment distrib.:** 18.0% govt.; 20.0% trade/trans./util.; 11.9% mfg.; 14.1% ed./health; 11.1% prof./bus. serv.; 10.0% leisure/hosp.; 4.6% finance; 4.9% constr./mining/log.; 1.5% info.; 3.9% other serv. **Unemployment:** 9.5%. **Per cap. pers. income:** $33,667. **New private housing:** 7,782 units/$915.1 mil. **Commercial banks:** 202; deposits: $66.8 bil. **Savings institutions:** 22; deposits: $2.2 bil. **Lottery:** total sales: $772.3 mil; profit: $212.3 mil.

Federal govt. Fed. civ. employees: 26,750; **avg. salary:** $60,246. **Notable fed. facilities:** U.S. Bullion Depository, Ft. Knox; Ft. Campbell; Fed. Medical Ctr., Lexington; Army Corps of Engineers, Louisville District.

Energy. Monthly electricity use: 1,258 kWh, $107.77.

State data. Motto: United we stand, divided we fall. **Flower:** Goldenrod. **Bird:** Cardinal. **Tree:** Tulip poplar. **Song:** "My Old Kentucky Home." **Entered union:** June 1, 1792; rank: 15th. **State fair** at Louisville, mid-Aug.

History. Paleo-Indians first arrived about 14,000 years ago. Much later, Shawnee, Wyandot, Delaware, and Cherokee peoples also used the area mostly for hunting. Explored by Thomas Walker and Christopher Gist, 1750-51, Kentucky was the first area W of the Alleghenies settled by American pioneers. The first permanent settlement was Harrodsburg, 1774. Daniel Boone blazed the Wilderness Trail through the Cumberland Gap and founded Ft. Boonesborough, 1775. Clashes with Native Americans were frequent, 1774-94. Virginia dropped its claims to the region, and Kentucky became a state, 1792. Tobacco growing, horse breeding, coal mining, and bourbon whiskey making were major industries in the 19th cent. A slave state, Kentucky tried to stay neutral in the Civil War, but then opted for the Union; many Kentuckians sided with the Confederacy. The U.S. gold depository at Ft. Knox opened, 1937. Prior to the 2008 economic downturn, auto manufacturing had grown in recent decades. An ice storm in southwestern Kentucky in Jan. 2009 killed 14 and caused severe power outages.

Tourist attractions. Churchill Downs (Kentucky Derby), Louisville; Land Between the Lakes Natl. Recreation Area, lakes Kentucky and Barkley; Mammoth Cave Natl. Park; Lake Cumberland; Lincoln's birthplace, Hodgenville; My Old Kentucky Home State Park, Bardstown; Cumberland Gap Natl. Historical Park, Middlesboro; Kentucky Horse Park, Lexington; Shaker Village, Pleasant Hill.

Famous Kentuckians. Muhammad Ali, John James Audubon, Alben W. Barkley, Daniel Boone, Louis D. Brandeis, John C. Breckinridge, Kit Carson, Albert B. "Happy" Chandler, Henry Clay, Jefferson Davis, D. W. Griffith, "Casey" Jones, Abraham Lincoln, Mary Todd Lincoln, Thomas Hunt Morgan, Carry Nation, Col. Harland Sanders, Diane Sawyer, Adlai Stevenson, Jesse Stuart, Zachary Taylor, Hunter S. Thompson, Robert Penn Warren, Whitney Young Jr.

Tourist information. Kentucky Dept. of Travel, Capital Plaza Tower, 22nd Fl., 500 Mero St., Frankfort, KY 40601; 1-800-225-8747; www.kentuckytourism.com

Website. www.kentucky.gov

Louisiana (LA)

Pelican State

People. Population: 4,574,836; rank: 25. **Pop. change** (2000-11): 2.4%. **Pop. density:** 105.9 per sq mi. **Racial distribution:** 63.8% white; 32.4% black; 1.6% Asian; 0.7% Amer. Ind.; 0.1% Pac. Isl.; 2 or more races, 1.4%. **Hispanic pop.:** 4.4%.

Geography. Total area: 52,378 sq mi; rank: 31. **Land area:** 43,204 sq mi; rank: 33. **Acres forested:** 14.5 mil. **Location:** West South Central state on the Gulf Coast. **Climate:** subtropical, affected by continental weather patterns. **Topography:** lowlands of marshes and Mississippi R. flood plain; Red R. Valley lowlands; upland hills in the Florida Parishes; avg. elevation, 100 ft. **Capital:** Baton Rouge. **Chief airport:** Metairie.

Economy. Chief industries: wholesale and retail trade, tourism, manufacturing, construction, transportation, communication, public utilities, finance, insurance, real estate, mining. **Chief manuf. goods:** petroleum, chemicals, plastics material & resin, pesticides & fertilizers, cleaning prods., paper & paperboard, ships, structural metals. **Chief crops:** sugarcane, cotton, rice, soybeans, corn, sweet potatoes. **Livestock:** 2.69 mil chickens (excl. broilers), 790,000 cattle/calves. **Broadband Internet:** 79.6%. **Nonfuel minerals:** $498 mil; salt, sand and gravel (construction), stone (crushed), sand and gravel (industrial), lime. **Commercial fishing:** $247.8 mil. **Chief ports:** New Orleans, Baton Rouge, Lake Charles, Port of S. Louisiana (La Place), Shreveport, Plaquemine, St. Bernard, Alexandria. **Gross state product:** $247.7 bil. **Sales tax:** 4.0%. **Employment distrib.:** 18.6% govt.; 19.4% trade/trans./util.; 7.2% mfg.; 14.9% ed./health; 10.3% prof./bus. serv.; 10.9% leisure/hosp.; 5.1% finance; 9.2% constr./mining/log.; 1.3% info.; 3.3% other serv. **Unemployment:** 7.3%. **Per cap. pers. income:** $38,578. **New private housing:** 21,173 units/$1.9 bil. **Commercial banks:** 137; deposits: $82.4 bil. **Savings institutions:** 23; deposits: $4.5 bil. **Lottery:** total sales: $383.6 mil; profit: $136.4 mil.

Federal govt. Fed. civ. employees: 21,134; **avg. salary:** $66,399. **Notable federal facilities:** Ft. Polk (Joint Readiness Training Ctr.); Barksdale AFB; Strategic Petroleum Reserve, Michoud Assembly Facility, USDA Southern Regional Research Ctr., Army Corps of Engineers, all New Orleans; New Orleans NAS JRB.

Energy. Monthly electricity use: 1,380 kWh, $123.96.

State data. Motto: Union, justice, and confidence. **Flower:** Magnolia. **Bird:** Eastern brown pelican. **Tree:** Cypress. **Song:** "Give Me Louisiana." **Entered union:** Apr. 30, 1812; rank: 18th. **State fair** at Shreveport; late Oct.-early Nov.

History. Caddo, Tunica, Choctaw, Chitimacha, and Chawash peoples lived in the region at the time of European contact. Spanish explorers in the early 16th cent. reached the mouth of the Mississippi. René-Robert Cavelier, sieur de La Salle, 1682, claimed the region for France. Early French and Spanish settlers were the ancestors of Louisiana Creoles. Cajuns descended from the Acadians, French settlers expelled by the British from Nova Scotia, Canada, in 1755. France ceded the Louisiana region to Spain, 1762, took it back, 1800, and sold it to the U.S., 1803, in the Louisiana Purchase. Admitted as a state in 1812, Louisiana witnessed the Battle of New Orleans, 1815. Cotton and sugar plantations relied on black slaves, who made up 47% of the population in 1860, on the eve of the Civil War. Louisiana seceded, 1861, and was readmitted, 1868. Jazz was born in New Orleans in the early 20th cent. As governor (1928-32), Huey Long pushed populist programs. Many tropical storms and floods have battered Louisiana, including Hurricane Katrina and subsequent flooding, 2005, which devastated New Orleans. The offshore oil and gas industry developed after World War II. An oil rig explosion off the state's Gulf coast spilled millions of barrels of oil into the gulf, damaging coastal wetlands and many of the state's marine-dependent industries in 2010.

Tourist attractions. French Quarter and other New Orleans attractions; Jean Lafitte Natl. Hist. Park, Chalmette; Longfellow-Evangeline State Hist. Site, St. Martinville; Kent Plantation House, Alexandria; Hodges Gardens, Natchitoches; USS *Kidd* Memorial, Baton Rouge.

Famous Louisianans. Louis Armstrong, Pierre Beauregard, Judah P. Benjamin, Braxton Bragg, Kate Chopin, Johnnie Cochran, Harry Connick Jr., Ellen DeGeneres, Fats Domino, Lillian Hellman, Grace King, Elmore Leonard, Bob Livingston, Huey Long, Eli Manning, Peyton Manning, Wynton Marsalis, Leonidas K. Polk, Anne Rice, Henry Miller Shreve, Britney Spears, Edward D. White Jr.

Tourist information. Louisiana Office of Tourism, P.O. Box 94291, Baton Rouge, LA 70804-9291; 1-800-677-4082; www.louisianatravel.com

Website. www.louisiana.gov

Maine (ME)
Pine Tree State

People. Population: 1,328,188; rank: 41. **Pop. change (2000-11):** 4.2%. **Pop. density:** 43.1 per sq mi. **Racial distribution:** 95.4% white; 1.3% black; 1.1% Asian; 0.7% Amer. Ind.; <0.05% Pac. Isl.; 2 or more races, 1.5%. **Hispanic pop.:** 1.4%.

Geography. Total area: 35,380 sq mi; rank: 39. **Land area:** 30,843 sq mi; rank: 39. **Acres forested:** 17.7 mil. **Location:** New England state at northeastern tip of U.S. **Climate:** Southern interior and coastal, influenced by air masses from the S and W; northern clime harsher, avg. over 100 in. snow in winter. **Topography:** Appalachian Mts. extend through state; western borders have rugged terrain; long sand beaches on southern coast; northern coast mainly rocky promontories, peninsulas, fjords. **Capital:** Augusta. **Chief airport:** Portland.

Economy. Chief industries: manufacturing, agriculture, fishing, services, trade, government, finance, insurance, real estate, construction. **Chief manuf. goods:** paper, ships & boats, cardboard, frozen/canned fruits & vegetables, plastics, baked goods. **Chief crops:** potatoes, greenhouse & nursery, wild blueberries, apples, hay, maple syrup. **Livestock:** 3.57 mil chickens (excl. broilers), 86,000 cattle/calves. **Broadband Internet:** 76.9%. **Nonfuel minerals:** $94.2 mil; sand and gravel (construction), cement (portland), stone (crushed), stone (dimension), cement (masonry). **Commercial fishing:** $377.8 mil. **Chief ports:** Searsport, Portland, Eastport. **Gross state product:** $51.6 bil. **Sales tax:** 5.0%. **Employment distrib.:** 17.5% govt.; 19.6% trade/trans./util.; 8.4% mfg.; 20.7% ed./health; 9.6% prof./bus. serv.; 9.8% leisure/hosp.; 5.3% finance; 4.5% constr./mining/log.; 1.3% info.; 3.3% other serv. **Unemployment:** 7.5%. **Per cap. pers. income:** $37,973. **New private housing:** 2,744 units/$435.7 mil. **Commercial banks:** 12; deposits: $21.1 bil. **Savings institutions:** 21; deposits: $9.6 bil. **Lottery:** total sales: $216.4 mil; profit: $49.5 mil.

Federal govt. Fed. civ. employees: 11,063; **avg. salary:** $65,241. **Notable fed. facilities:** Portsmouth Naval Shipyard.

Energy. Monthly electricity use: 521 kWh, $81.83.

State data. Motto: Dirigo (I direct). **Flower:** White pine cone and tassel. **Bird:** Black-capped chickadee. **Tree:** Eastern white pine. **Song:** "State of Maine Song." **Entered union:** Mar. 15, 1820; rank: 23rd. **State fair** at Bangor, late July-early Aug.; at Skowhegan, mid-Aug.

History. Paleo-Indians arrived about 11,500 years ago. Maine was inhabited by Algonquian peoples including the Abnaki, Penobscot, and Passamaquoddy at the time of European contact. French settled, 1604, at the St. Croix R., English, c. 1607, on the Kennebec; both settlements failed. A royal charter, 1691, made Maine part of Massachusetts. Maine broke off, 1819, and became a separate state, 1820. Drawing on vast forest resources, the pulp and paper industry developed after the Civil War. Bath Iron Works began building U.S. Navy vessels and other ships in the 1890s. Mail-order and retail giant L.L. Bean was founded, 1912. Women have fared well in state politics: Margaret Chase Smith became the first woman to serve in both houses of Congress (House, 1940-49; Senate, 1949-73), and Olympia Snowe and Susan Collins have represented Maine in the Senate since the mid-1990s (Snowe in 2012 announced plans to retire in Jan. 2013, the end of her current term).

Tourist attractions. Acadia Natl. Park, Bar Harbor, on Mt. Desert Island; Old Orchard Beach; Portland's Old Port; Kennebunkport; Common Ground Country Fair, Unity; Portland Head Light; Baxter State Park; Freeport/L.L. Bean.

Famous "Down Easters." Leon Leonwood (L. L.) Bean, James G. Blaine, Cyrus H. K. Curtis, Hannibal Hamlin, Sarah Jewett, Stephen King, Henry Wadsworth Longfellow, Sir Hiram and Hudson Maxim, Edna St. Vincent Millay, George Mitchell, Edmund Muskie, Judd Nelson, Edwin Arlington Robinson, Joan Benoit Samuelson, Liv Tyler, Kate Douglas Wiggin, Ben Ames Williams.

Tourist information. Maine Office of Tourism, 59 State House Station, Augusta, ME 04333; 1-888-624-6345; www.visitmaine.com
Website. www.maine.gov

Maryland (MD)
Old Line State, Free State

People. Population: 5,828,289; rank: 19. **Pop. change (2000-11):** 10.0%. **Pop. density:** 600.4 per sq mi. **Racial distribution:** 61.1% white; 30.0% black; 5.8% Asian; 0.5% Amer. Ind.; 0.1% Pac. Isl.; 2 or more races, 2.5%. **Hispanic pop.:** 8.4%.

Geography. Total area: 12,406 sq mi; rank: 42. **Land area:** 9,707 sq mi; rank: 42. **Acres forested:** 2.5 mil. **Location:** South Atlantic state stretching from the ocean to the Allegheny Mts. **Climate:** continental in the W; humid subtropical in the E. **Topography:** Eastern Shore of coastal plain and Maryland Main of coastal plain, Piedmont Plateau, and the Blue Ridge, separated by the Chesapeake Bay. **Capital:** Annapolis. **Chief airport:** Glen Burnie.

Economy. Chief industries: manufacturing, biotechnology and information technology, services, tourism. **Chief manuf. goods:** navigational instruments, pharmaceutical & medicine, broadcasting equip., plastics, printing, milk & ice cream. **Chief crops:** greenhouse & nursery, corn, soybeans, wheat, hay, tomatoes, watermelons, barley, potatoes, apples. **Livestock:** 2.54 mil chickens (excl. broilers), 311 mil broilers, 200,000 cattle/calves. **Broadband Internet:** 71.1%. **Nonfuel minerals:** $276 mil; stone (crushed), cement (portland), sand and gravel (construction), cement (masonry), stone (dimension). **Commercial fishing:** $104.9 mil. **Chief port:** Baltimore. **Gross state product:** $301.1 bil. **Sales tax:** 6.0%. **Employment distrib.:** 19.9% govt.; 17.1% trade/trans./util.; 4.3% mfg.; 16.4% ed./health; 15.6% prof./bus. serv.; 9.3% leisure/hosp.; 5.5% finance; 5.7% constr./mining/log.; 1.7% info.; 4.5% other serv. **Unemployment:** 7.0%. **Per cap. pers. income:** $51,038. **New private housing:** 13,481 units/$2.2 bil. **Commercial banks:** 87; deposits: $108.2 bil. **Savings institutions:** 43; deposits: $7.7 bil. **Lottery:** total sales: $1.8 bil; profit: $576.6 mil.

Federal govt. Fed. civ. employees: 135,877; **avg. salary:** $94,985. **Notable fed. facilities:** U.S. Naval Academy; Natl. Agriculture Res. Ctr.; Ft. Meade; Aberdeen Proving Ground; Andrews AFB; Naval Air Sys. Command; Goddard Space Flight Ctr.; Natl. Inst. of Health; Natl. Inst. of Standards & Technology; Food & Drug Admin.; Bureau of the Census; Natl. Naval Med. Ctr., Bethesda; Natl. Marine Fisheries Serv.; Natl. Oceanic and Atmospheric Admin.

Energy. Monthly electricity use: 1,096 kWh, $156.94.

State data. Motto: Fatti Maschii, Parole Femine (Manly deeds, womanly words). **Flower:** Black-eyed Susan. **Bird:** Baltimore oriole. **Tree:** White oak. **Song:** "Maryland, My Maryland." **Seventh** of the original 13 states to ratify the U.S. Constitution, Apr. 28, 1788. **State fair** at Timonium, late Aug.-early Sept.

History. Europeans encountered Algonquian-speaking Nanticoke and Piscataway and Iroquois-speaking Susquehannock when they first visited the area. Italian navigator Verrazano reached the Chesapeake region in the early 16th cent. English Capt. John Smith explored and mapped the area, 1608. William Claiborne set up a trading post on Kent Island in Chesapeake Bay, 1631. King Charles I granted land to Cecilius Calvert, Lord Baltimore, 1632; Calvert's brother Leonard, with about 200 settlers, founded St. Marys, 1634. During the Revolutionary War, Baltimore (1776-77) and Annapolis (1783-84) served as temporary capitals of the U.S. In the War of 1812, when a British fleet tried to take Ft. McHenry, Marylander Francis Scott Key wrote "The Star-Spangled Banner," 1814. Born into slavery at Tuckahoe in 1818, Frederick Douglass became a leading abolitionist. Although a slaveholding state, Maryland stayed in the Union during the Civil War and was the site of the battle of Antietam, 1862. Gov. Spiro Agnew elected U.S. vice pres. 1968, 1972; pleaded no contest to tax evasion and resigned 1973. Israeli and Egyptian leaders reached a historic peace accord at the Camp David presidential retreat, 1978. A major effort is under way to clean up pollution in the Chesapeake Bay watershed.

Tourist attractions. Laurel Park (Maryland Million); Ocean City; restored Ft. McHenry—near which Francis Scott Key wrote "The Star-Spangled Banner," Pimlico track (The Preakness), Edgar Allan Poe house, Camden Yards, Natl. Aquarium, Harborplace, all Baltimore; Antietam Battlefield, near Hagerstown; South Mountain Battlefield; U.S. Naval Academy, Maryland State House (oldest still in legislative use in the U.S.), Annapolis; Natl. Cryptologic Museum, Ft. Meade.

Famous Marylanders. John Astin, Benjamin Banneker, Tom Clancy, Jonathan Demme, Francis Scott Key, H. L. Mencken, Kweisi Mfume, Ogden Nash, Charles Willson Peale, William Pinkney, Edgar Allan Poe, Cal Ripken Jr., Babe Ruth, Upton Sinclair, Roger B. Taney, John Waters, Montel Williams.

Tourist information. Maryland Office of Tourism Development, 401 E. Pratt St., 14th Fl., Baltimore, MD 21202; 1-866-639-3526; www.visitmaryland.org

Website. www.maryland.gov

Massachusetts (MA)
Bay State, Old Colony

People. Population: 6,587,536; rank: 14. **Pop. change** (2000-11): 3.8%. **Pop. density:** 844.5 per sq mi. **Racial distribution:** 84.1% white; 7.8% black; 5.6% Asian; 0.5% Amer. Ind.; 0.1% Pac. Isl.; 2 or more races, 2.0%. **Hispanic pop.:** 9.9%.

Geography. Total area: 10,554 sq mi; rank: 44. **Land area:** 7,800 sq mi; rank: 45. **Acres forested:** 3.0 mil. **Location:** New England state along Atlantic seaboard. **Climate:** temperate, with colder and drier clime in western region. **Topography:** jagged indented coast from Rhode Island around Cape Cod; flat land yields to stony upland pastures near central region and gentle hilly country in W; except in W, land is rocky, sandy, and not fertile. **Capital:** Boston. **Chief airport:** Boston.

Economy. Chief industries: services, trade, manufacturing. **Chief manuf. goods:** electronics & instruments, pharmaceuticals, telecom. & broadcasting equip., plastics, medical equip., printing. **Chief crops:** greenhouse & nursery, cranberries, tomatoes, sweet corn, apples, hay, tobacco. **Livestock:** 142,000 chickens (excl. broilers), 41,000 cattle/calves. **Broadband Internet:** 73.0%. **Nonfuel minerals:** $196 mil; stone (crushed), sand and gravel (construction), stone (dimension), lime, clays (common). **Commercial fishing:** $478.6 mil. **Chief ports:** Boston, Fall River. **Gross state product:** $391.8 bil. **Sales tax:** 6.25%. **Employment distrib.:** 13.6% govt.; 17.1% trade/trans./util.; 7.8% mfg.; 20.7% ed./health; 15.3% prof./bus. serv.; 9.8% leisure/hosp.; 6.2% finance; 3.3% constr./mining/log.; 2.6% info.; 3.7% other serv. **Unemployment:** 7.4%. **Per cap. pers. income:** $53,621. **New private housing:** 7,725 units/$1.8 bil. **Commercial banks:** 52; deposits: $152.2 bil. **Savings institutions:** 135; deposits: $79.1 bil. **Lottery:** total sales: $4.4 bil; profit: $887.9 mil.

Federal govt. Fed. civ. employees: 28,974; **avg. salary:** $77,989. **Notable fed. facilities:** Thomas P. O'Neill Jr. Fed. Bldg.; J.W. McCormack Bldg.; JFK Fed. Bldg.; Hanscom AFB; Natick Army Soldier Systems Ctr.

Energy. Monthly electricity use: 667 kWh, $97.34.

State data. Motto: Ense Petit Placidam Sub Libertate Quietem (By the sword we seek peace, but peace only under liberty). **Flower:** Mayflower. **Bird:** Black-capped chickadee. **Tree:** American elm. **Song:** "All Hail to Massachusetts." **Sixth** of the original 13 states to ratify Constitution, Feb. 6, 1788. **State fair** at West Springfield, mid-late Sept.

History. Early inhabitants were Algonquian peoples: Nauset, Wampanoag, Massachuset, Pennacook, Nipmuc, and Pocumtuc. Pilgrims settled in Plymouth, 1620, giving thanks for their survival with the first Thanksgiving Day, 1621. About 20,000 new settlers arrived, 1630-40. Colonist-Native American relations deteriorated, leading to King Philip's War, 1675-76, which the colonists won. Witch trials at Salem, 1692, led to the execution of 20 people. Demonstrations against British restrictions set off the Boston Massacre, 1770, and the Boston Tea Party, 1773. The first bloodshed of American Revolution was at Lexington, 1775. After statehood, Massachusetts prospered from shipbuilding, seafaring, and the making of textiles, shoes, and metal goods, while artists, writers, and social reformers flourished. The controversial Sacco-Vanzetti case, 1920-27, ended with the execution of two Italian immigrants on murder and robbery charges. After World War II, old industries declined, knowledge-intensive enterprises thrived, and the Kennedys became a dominant political family. The state's highest court ruled, 2003, that same-sex couples could legally marry.

Tourist attractions. Provincetown arts colony; Cape Cod; Plymouth Rock, Plimoth Plantation, Mayflower II, all Plymouth; Freedom Trail, Museum of Fine Arts, New England Aquarium, and other Boston attractions; Tanglewood, Hancock Shaker Village, Berkshire Scenic Railway Museum,

Norman Rockwell Museum, and other Berkshires attractions; Salem; Old Sturbridge Village; Old Deerfield Historic District; Walden Pond, Concord; Naismith Memorial Basketball Hall of Fame, Springfield.

Famous "Bay Staters." John Adams, John Quincy Adams, Samuel Adams, Louisa May Alcott, Horatio Alger, Susan B. Anthony, Crispus Attucks, Clara Barton, Alexander Graham Bell, Stephen Breyer, George H. W. Bush, John Cheever, E. E. Cummings, Emily Dickinson, Charles Eliot, Ralph Waldo Emerson, William Lloyd Garrison, Edward Everett Hale, John Hancock, Nathaniel Hawthorne, Oliver Wendell Holmes, Winslow Homer, Elias Howe, John F. Kennedy, John Kerry, Jack Kerouac, Jack Lemmon, James Russell Lowell, Cotton Mather, Samuel F. B. Morse, Edgar Allan Poe, Paul Revere, Norman Rockwell, Dr. Seuss (Theodor Seuss Geisel), Henry David Thoreau, Barbara Walters, James McNeil Whistler, John Greenleaf Whittier.

Tourist information. Massachusetts Office of Travel & Tourism, 10 Park Plz., Ste. 4510, Boston, MA 02116; 1-800-227-MASS; www.massvacation.com

Website. www.mass.gov

Michigan (MI)
Great Lakes State, Wolverine State

People. Population: 9,876,187; rank: 8. **Pop. change** (2000-11): -0.6%. **Pop. density:** 174.7 per sq mi. **Racial distribution:** 80.2% white; 14.3% black; 2.5% Asian; 0.7% Amer. Ind.; <0.05% Pac. Isl.; 2 or more races, 2.1%. **Hispanic pop.:** 4.5%.

Geography. Total area: 96,714 sq mi; rank: 11. **Land area:** 56,539 sq mi; rank: 22. **Acres forested:** 20.1 mil. **Location:** East North Central state bordering on 4 of the 5 Great Lakes, divided into an Upper and Lower Peninsula by the Straits of Mackinac, which link lakes Michigan and Huron. **Climate:** well-defined seasons tempered by the Great Lakes. **Topography:** low rolling hills give way to northern tableland of hilly belts in Lower Peninsula; Upper Peninsula is level in the E, with swampy areas; western region is higher and more rugged. **Capital:** Lansing. **Chief airports:** Detroit, Grand Rapids.

Economy. Chief industries: manufacturing, services, tourism, agriculture, forestry/lumber. **Chief manuf. goods:** motor vehicles & parts, plastics, metalworking machinery, non-wood office furniture, fabricated metals. **Chief crops:** greenhouse & nursery, soybeans, corn, wheat, sugar beets, apples, blueberries, potatoes, dry beans, cherries, hay, cucumbers, tomatoes, grapes. **Livestock:** 12.98 mil chickens (excl. broilers), 1.11 mil cattle/calves, 79,000 sheep/lambs, 110,000 hogs/pigs. **Broadband Internet:** 71.6%. **Nonfuel minerals:** $2.5 bil; iron ore (usable shipped), cement (portland), sand and gravel (construction), salt, stone (crushed). **Commercial fishing:** $9.8 mil. **Chief ports:** Detroit, Escanaba, Calcite, Port Inland, Muskegon, Port Huron. **Gross state product:** $385.2 bil. **Sales tax:** 6.0%. **Employment distrib.:** 15.3% govt.; 18.0% trade/trans./util.; 13.0% mfg.; 15.7% ed./health; 14.5% prof./bus. serv.; 9.7% leisure/hosp.; 5.0% finance; 3.3% constr./mining/log.; 1.3% info.; 4.2% other serv. **Unemployment:** 10.3%. **Per cap. pers. income:** $36,533. **New private housing:** 9,341 units/$1.7 bil. **Commercial banks:** 140; deposits: $147.3 bil. **Savings institutions:** 20; deposits: $10.4 bil. **Lottery:** total sales: $2.3 bil; profit: $727.0 mil.

Federal govt. Fed. civ. employees: 30,073; **avg. salary:** $75,355. **Notable fed. facilities:** Detroit Arsenal (Army TACOM Life Cycle Mgmt.); Def. Logistics Info. Service; Selfridge Army Garrison; Hart-Dole-Inouye Fed. Ctr.

Energy. Monthly electricity use: 681 kWh, $84.82.

State data. Motto: Si Quaeris Peninsulam Amoenam, Circumspice (If you seek a pleasant peninsula, look about you). **Flower:** Apple blossom. **Bird:** Robin. **Tree:** White pine. **Song:** "Michigan, My Michigan." **Entered union:** Jan. 26, 1837; rank: 26th. **State fair** at Novi, late Aug.-early Sept.

History. Hunting and fishing peoples lived in the region as early as 11,000 years ago. Ojibwa, Ottawa, Miami, Potawatomi, and Huron inhabited the area at the time of European contact. French fur traders and missionaries arrived in the 17th cent. and established a settlement at Sault Ste. Marie, 1668. British took over, 1763, and crushed a Native American uprising led by Ottawa chieftain Pontiac. Treaty of Paris ceded the area to U.S., 1783, but British remained until 1796. Michigan was organized as a territory, 1805. The British seized Ft. Mackinac and Detroit, 1812, but the U.S. regained control, 1814. The opening of the Erie Canal, 1825, and new land laws and Native American cessions led the way for a flood of settlers. Strongly antislavery, Michigan became a state, 1837, and supplied 90,000 soldiers to the Union army in the Civil War. In the 20th cent., automobile manufacturing was the backbone of the economy. Henry Ford launched the Model T car, 1908; the United Auto Workers union was founded, 1935. Motown music flourished in Detroit in the 1960s, but riots in 1967 dealt the city a heavy blow. As the auto industry faltered, Michigan lost more than 20% of its automotive-related jobs between 2002 and 2007. In 2009, the federal government loaned billions of dollars to GM and Chrysler to keep them solvent.

Tourist attractions. Henry Ford Museum/Greenfield Village, Dearborn; Frederick Meijer Gardens and Sculpture Park, Grand Rapids; Tahquamenon (*Hiawatha*) Falls; De Zwaan windmill and Tulip Festival, Holland; "Soo Locks," St. Mary's Falls Ship Canal, Sault Ste. Marie; Air Zoo, Kalamazoo; Mackinac Island; Museum of African-American History, Motown Historical Museum, Detroit.

Famous Michiganders. Ralph Bunche, Francis Ford Coppola, Paul de Kruif, Thomas Edison, Edna Ferber, Gerald R. Ford, Henry Ford, Aretha Franklin, Edgar Guest, Lee Iacocca, Robert Ingersoll, Magic Johnson, Casey Kasem, Will Kellogg, Ring Lardner, Elmore Leonard, Charles Lindbergh, Joe Louis, Madonna, Malcolm X, Terry McMillan, Michael Moore, Pontiac, Gilda Radner, Mitt Romney, Diana Ross, Glenn Seaborg, Tom Selleck, Sinbad (David Adkins), John Smoltz, Lily Tomlin, Stewart Edward White, Serena Williams.

Tourist information. Michigan Economic Development Corp., 300 N. Washington Sqs., Lansing, MI 48913; 1-888-784-7328; www.michigan.org

Website. www.michigan.gov

Minnesota (MN)
North Star State, Gopher State

People. Population: 5,344,861; rank: 21. **Pop. change** (2000-11): 8.6%. **Pop. density:** 67.1 per sq mi. **Racial distribution:** 86.9% white; 5.4% black; 4.2% Asian; 1.3% Amer. Ind.; 0.1% Pac. Isl.; 2 or more races, 2.2%. **Hispanic pop.:** 4.9%.

Geography. Total area: 86,936 sq mi; rank: 12. **Land area:** 79,627 sq mi; rank: 14. **Acres forested:** 17.4 mil. **Location:** West North Central state bounded on the E by Wisconsin and Lake Superior, on the N by Canada, on the W by the Dakotas, and on the S by Iowa. **Climate:** northern part of state lies in the moist Great Lakes storm belt; the western border lies at the edge of the semi-arid Great Plains. **Topography:** central hill and lake region covering approx. half the state; to the NE, rocky ridges and deep lakes; to the NW, flat plain; to the S, rolling plains and deep river valleys. **Capital:** St. Paul. **Chief airport:** Minneapolis.

Economy. Chief industries: agribusiness, forest products, mining, manufacturing, tourism. **Chief manuf. goods:** petroleum & asphalt, computers & electronics, milk & cheese, printing, animal slaughtering, paper & prod., medical equip. **Chief crops:** corn, soybeans, hay, sugar beets, wheat, potatoes, greenhouse & nursery, dry edible beans, green peas, sunflowers. **Livestock:** 13.11 mil chickens (excl. broilers), 41.6 mil broilers, 2.36 mil cattle/calves, 150,000 sheep/lambs, 560,000 hogs/pigs. **Broadband Internet:** 73.9%. **Nonfuel minerals** (2010 prelim.): $5.1 bil; iron ore (usable shipped), sand and gravel (construction), sand and gravel (industrial), stone (crushed), lime. **Commercial fishing:** $228,000. **Chief ports:** Two Harbors, Silver Bay, Duluth, St. Paul. **Gross state product:** $281.7 bil. **Sales tax:** 6.875%. **Employment distrib.:** 15.2% govt.; 18.2% trade/trans./util.; 11.2% mfg.; 17.7% ed./health; 12.4% prof./bus. serv.; 8.7% leisure/hosp.; 6.5% finance; 3.8% constr./mining/log.; 1.9% info.; 4.3% other serv. **Unemployment:** 6.4%. **Per cap. pers. income:** $44,672. **New private housing:** 8,890 units/$1.8 bil. **Commercial banks:** 402; deposits: $141 bil. **Savings institutions:** 36; deposits: $9.4 bil. **Lottery:** total sales: $504.4 mil; profit: $121.9 mil.

Federal govt. Fed. civ. employees: 18,043; **avg. salary:** $71,739. **Notable fed. facilities:** Bishop Henry Whipple Fed. Bldg.; Minneapolis-St Paul Air Reserve Station.

Energy. Monthly electricity use: 814 kWh, $86.19.

State data. Motto: L'Etoile du Nord (The star of the north). **Flower:** Pink and white lady's-slipper. **Bird:** Common loon. **Tree:** Red pine. **Song:** "Hail! Minnesota." **Entered union:** May 11, 1858; rank: 32nd. **State fair** at St. Paul, late Aug.-early Sept.

History. Inhabited for at least 10,000 years, the region was home to Dakota Sioux when Europeans arrived. French fur traders Pierre Esprit Radisson and Médard Chouart, sieur des Groseilliers, explored in the mid-17th cent. In 1679, Daniel Greysolon, sieur Duluth, claimed the entire region for France. Ojibwa arrived in the 18th cent. and warred with the Sioux for over 100 years. Britain took the area east of the Mississippi, 1763. The U.S. took over that portion after the American Revolution and gained the western area, 1803, in the Louisiana Purchase. The U.S. built Ft. St. Anthony (now Ft. Snelling), 1819, and bought Native American lands, 1837, spurring an influx of settlers from the east. Minnesota became a territory, 1849, and a state, 1858. Sioux staged a bloody uprising, the Battle of Wood Lake, 1862, and were driven from the state. Railroad construction after the Civil War spurred the growth of the grain, timber, and iron mining industries. Opening of the St. Lawrence Seaway, 1959, aided the port of Duluth. Elected as a reformer, former wrestler Jesse Ventura served as governor, 1999-2003. Two-term Sen. Paul Wellstone, one of a long line of liberal Minnesota Democrats, died when his campaign plane crashed, 2002. The I-35W Mississippi River Bridge in Minneapolis collapsed, 2007, killing 13.

Tourist attractions. Minneapolis Institute of Arts, Walker Art Center, Minneapolis Sculpture Garden, Minnehaha Falls (*Hiawatha*), Guthrie Theater, all Minneapolis; Ordway Theater, Winter Carnival, in St. Paul; Voyageurs Natl. Park; Mayo Clinic, Rochester; North Shore (of Lake Superior).

Famous Minnesotans. Warren Burger, Ethan and Joel Coen, William O. Douglas, Bob Dylan, F. Scott Fitzgerald, Al Franken, Judy Garland, Cass Gilbert, Hubert Humphrey, Garrison Keillor, Sister Elizabeth Kenny, Jessica Lange, Sinclair Lewis, Paul Manship, Roger Maris, E. G. Marshall, William and Charles Mayo, Eugene McCarthy, Walter F. Mondale, Prince (Rodgers Nelson), Charles Schulz, Harold Stassen, Thorstein Veblen, Jesse Ventura, Paul Wellstone.

Tourist information. Explore Minnesota Tourism, Metro Square, 121 7th Pl. E., Ste. 100, St. Paul, MN 55101; 1-888-TOURISM; www.exploreminnesota.com

Website. www.state.mn.us

Mississippi (MS)
Magnolia State

People. Population: 2,978,512; rank: 31. **Pop. change** (2000-11): 4.7%. **Pop. density:** 63.5 per sq mi. **Racial distribution:** 60.0% white; 37.3% black; 0.9% Asian; 0.6% Amer. Ind.; 0.1% Pac. Isl.; 2 or more races, 1.1%. **Hispanic pop.:** 2.9%.

Geography. Total area: 48,432 sq mi; rank: 32. **Land area:** 46,923 sq mi; rank: 31. **Acres forested:** 19.5 mil. **Location:** East South Central state bordered on the W by the Mississippi R. and on the S by the Gulf of Mexico. **Climate:** semi-tropical, with abundant rainfall and long growing season. **Topography:** low, fertile delta between the Yazoo and Mississippi Rivers; loess bluffs stretching around delta border; sandy gulf coastal terraces followed by piney woods and prairie; rugged, high sandy hills in extreme NE followed by Black Prairie Belt, Pontotoc Ridge, and flatwoods into the N central highlands. **Capital:** Jackson. **Chief airport:** Jackson.

Economy. Chief industries: warehousing & distribution, services, manufacturing, government, wholesale and retail trade. **Chief manuf. goods:** petroleum, upholstered furniture, poultry processing, motor vehicle parts, plastics, ships & boats, chemicals. **Chief crops:** cotton, soybeans, rice, hay, corn, sweet potatoes. **Livestock:** 9.68 mil chickens (excl. broilers), 784 mil broilers, 950,000 cattle/calves. **Broadband Internet:** 62.8%. **Nonfuel minerals:** $195 mil; sand and gravel (construction), stone (crushed), clays (fuller's earth), clays (ball), clays (bentonite). **Commercial fishing:** $21.9 mil. **Chief ports:** Pascagoula, Vicksburg, Gulfport, Biloxi, Greenville. **Gross state product:** $97.8 bil. **Sales tax:** 7.0%. **Employment distrib.:** 22.7% govt.; 19.6% trade/trans./util.; 12.5% mfg.; 12.4% ed./health; 8.4% prof./bus. serv.; 10.9% leisure/hosp.; 4.1% finance; 5.0% constr./mining/log.; 1.1%

info.; 3.2% other serv. **Unemployment:** 10.7%. **Per cap. pers. income:** $32,176. **New private housing:** 5,273 units/$724.1 mil. **Commercial banks:** 99; deposits: $46.1 bil. **Savings institutions:** 5; deposits: $484 mil.

Federal govt. Fed. civ. employees: 18,919; **avg. salary:** $65,608. **Notable fed. facilities:** Keesler AFB; Meridian NAS; Columbus AFB; NASA Stennis Space Ctr.; Army Corps of Eng. Waterways Experiment Sta.; Naval Constr. Battalion Ctr., Gulfport.

Energy. Monthly electricity use: 1,345 kWh, $132.76.

State data. Motto: Virtute et Armis (By valor and arms). **Flower:** Magnolia. **Bird:** Mockingbird. **Tree:** Magnolia. **Song:** "Go, Mississippi!" **Entered union:** Dec. 10, 1817; rank: 20th. **State fair** at Jackson, begins first Wed. in Oct.

History. Choctaw, Chickasaw, and Natchez peoples were living in the region at the time of European contact. The Span- iard Hernando de Soto explored the area, 1540-41. La Salle traced the Mississippi R. from Illinois to its mouth and claimed the entire Mississippi Valley for France, 1682. The first settlement was the French Ft. Maurepas, 1699, on Biloxi Bay. The region was ceded to Britain, 1763, and claimed by Spain, 1779-98, then became a U.S. territory, 1798, and a state, 1817. Slavery spread along with cotton plantations, and slaves made up 55% of the population, 1860. Mississippi seceded, 1861. In the Civil War, Union forces captured Vicksburg, 1863, and caused extensive damage elsewhere. Mississippi reentered the Union, 1870. For the next 100 years, resistance to desegregation and violence against blacks made the state a battleground for the African American civil rights movement. Hurricanes Camille, 1969, and Katrina, 2005, caused substantial damage to the Gulf Coast. Since the early 1990s, casino gambling has boosted the economy, but the state's poverty rate remained the highest in the nation in 2010.

Tourist attractions. Vicksburg Natl. Military Park and Cemetery, other Civil War sites; Hattiesburg; Natchez Trace; Indian mounds; Antebellum homes; pilgrimages in Natchez and some 25 other cities; Elvis Presley Birthplace and Museum, Tupelo; Smith Robertson Museum, Mynelle Gardens, in Jackson; Mardi Gras, Shrimp Festival, in Biloxi; Gulf Islands Natl. Seashore.

Famous Mississippians. Margaret Walker Alexander, Dana Andrews, Jimmy Buffett, Bo Diddley, William Faulkner, Brett Favre, Shelby Foote, Morgan Freeman, John Grisham, Fannie Lou Hamer, Jim Henson, Faith Hill, John Lee Hooker, Robert Johnson, James Earl Jones, B. B. King, L. Q. C. Lamar, Trent Lott, Gerald McRaney, Willie Morris, Walter Payton, Elvis Presley, Leontyne Price, Charley Pride, LeAnn Rimes, Muddy Waters, Eudora Welty, Tennessee Williams, Oprah Winfrey, Johnny Winter, Richard Wright, Tammy Wynette.

Tourist information. Mississippi Division of Tourism. P.O. Box 849, Jackson, MS 39205; 1-866-SEE-MISS; www.visitmississippi.org

Website. www.ms.gov

Missouri (MO)
Show Me State

People. Population: 6,010,688; rank: 18. **Pop. change** (2000-11): 7.4%. **Pop. density:** 87.4 per sq mi. **Racial distribution:** 84% white; 11.7% black; 1.7% Asian; 0.5% Amer. Ind.; 0.1% Pac. Isl.; 2 or more races, 1.9%. **Hispanic pop.** : 3.7%.

Geography. Total area: 69,707 sq mi; rank: 21. **Land area:** 68,742 sq mi; rank: 18. **Acres forested:** 15.5 mil. **Location:** West North Central state near the geographic center of the conterminous U.S.; bordered on the E by the Mississippi R., on the NW by the Missouri R. **Climate:** continental, susceptible to cold Canadian air, moist, warm gulf air, and drier SW air. **Topography:** rolling hills, open, fertile plains, and well-watered prairie N of the Missouri R.; S of the river land is rough and hilly with deep, narrow valleys; alluvial plain in the SE; low elevation in the W. **Capital:** Jefferson City. **Chief airports:** Kansas City, St. Louis.

Economy. Chief industries: agriculture, manufacturing, aerospace, tourism. **Chief manuf. goods:** motor vehicles & parts, aerospace, pharmaceuticals, plastics, soap, animal slaughtering & processing, printing. **Chief crops:** soybeans, corn, hay, cotton & cottonseed, wheat, rice, sorghum.

Livestock: 10.53 mil chickens (excl. broilers), 285.2 mil broilers, 3.9 mil cattle/calves, 83,000 sheep/lambs, 365,000 pigs/hogs. **Broadband Internet:** 80.4%. **Nonfuel minerals:** $2.2 bil; cement (portland), stone (crushed), lead, lime, sand and gravel (construction). **Gross state product:** $249.5 bil. **Sales tax:** 4.225%. **Employment distrib.:** 16.7% govt.; 19.0% trade/trans./util.; 9.4% mfg.; 15.8% ed./health; 12.8% prof./bus. serv.; 10.2% leisure/hosp.; 5.9% finance; 3.8% constr./mining/log.; 2.2% info.; 4.2% other serv. **Unemployment:** 8.6%. **Per cap. pers. income:** $38,248. **New private housing:** 9,242 units/$1.4 bil. **Commercial banks:** 348; deposits: $118.2 bil. **Savings institutions:** 34; deposits: $13.3 bil. **Lottery:** total sales: $1.0 bil; profit: $259.4 mil.

Federal govt. Fed. civ. employees: 39,138; **avg. salary:** $62,851. **Notable fed. facilities:** Federal Reserve banks; Ft. Leonard Wood; Jefferson Barracks Natl. Cem.; Natl. Personnel Records Ctr.; Whiteman AFB.

Energy. Monthly electricity use: 1,153 kWh, $104.66.

State data. Motto: Salus Populi Suprema Lex Esto (Let the welfare of the people be the supreme law). **Flower:** Hawthorn. **Bird:** Bluebird. **Tree:** Dogwood. **Song:** "Missouri Waltz." **Entered union:** Aug. 10, 1821; rank: 24th. **State fair** at Sedalia, mid-Aug.; at Bethany, late Aug.-early Sept.

History. In the 17th cent., when French explorers arrived, Algonquian Sauk, Fox, and Illinois and Siouan Osage, Missouri, Iowa, and Kansa peoples were living in the region; few remained by the 1830s. French hunters and lead miners made the first settlement c. 1735, at Ste. Genevieve. The territory was ceded to Spain by the French, 1762, then returned to France, 1800, and acquired by the U.S. in the Louisiana Purchase, 1803. Powerful earthquakes rocked New Madrid, 1811-12. Missouri became a territory, 1812, and entered the Union as a slave state, 1821. St. Louis became the gateway for pioneers heading West. Though Missouri stayed with the Union, pro- and antislavery forces battled there during the Civil War. In the late 19th cent. railroad building and the cattle trade made Kansas City a boomtown. The most notable Missourian of the 20th cent., Harry S. Truman, was U.S. president, 1945-53. The state, a political bellwether, voted for the winner in every presidential election from 1960 to 2004. In May 2011, a tornado in Joplin killed about 162.

Tourist attractions. Silver Dollar City, Branson; Mark Twain Area, Hannibal; Pony Express Museum, St. Joseph; Harry S. Truman Library, Independence; Gateway Arch, St. Louis; Worlds of Fun, Kansas City; Lake of the Ozarks; Churchill Mem., Fulton; State Capitol, Jefferson City.

Famous Missourians. Maya Angelou, Robert Altman, Burt Bacharach, Josephine Baker, Scott Bakula, Thomas Hart Benton, Tom Berenger, Yogi Berra, Chuck Berry, George Caleb Bingham, Daniel Boone, Omar Bradley, William Burroughs, Kate Capshaw, Dale Carnegie, George Washington Carver, Bob Costas, Walter Cronkite, Walt Disney, T. S. Eliot, Richard Gephardt, John Goodman, Betty Grable, Edwin Hubble, Jesse James, Rush Limbaugh, Marianne Moore, Reinhold Niebuhr, J. C. Penney, John J. Pershing, Brad Pitt, Joseph Pulitzer, Ginger Rogers, Bess Truman, Harry S. Truman, Kathleen Turner, Tina Turner, Mark Twain, Dick Van Dyke, Tennessee Williams, Lanford Wilson, Shelley Winters, Jane Wyman.

Tourist information. Missouri Division of Tourism. P.O. Box 1055, Jefferson City, MO 65102; 1-800-519-2100; www.visitmo.com

Website. www.mo.gov

Montana (MT)
Treasure State

People. Population: 998,199; rank: 44. **Pop. change** (2000-11): 10.6%. **Pop. density:** 6.9 per sq mi. **Racial distribution:** 89.9% white; 0.5% black; 0.7% Asian; 6.4% Amer. Ind.; 0.1% Pac. Isl.; 2 or more races, 2.4%. **Hispanic pop.:** 3.1%.

Geography. Total area: 147,040 sq mi; rank: 4. **Land area:** 145,546 sq mi; rank: 4. **Acres forested:** 25.6 mil. **Location:** Mountain state bounded on the E by the Dakotas, on the S by Wyoming, on the SSW by Idaho, and on the N by Canada. **Climate:** colder, continental climate with low humidity. **Topography:** Rocky Mts. in western third of the state; eastern two-thirds gently rolling northern Great Plains. **Capital:** Helena.

Economy. Chief industries: agriculture, timber, mining, tourism, oil and gas. **Chief manuf. goods:** sawmills, softwood veneer & plywood, petroleum. **Chief crops:** wheat, barley, hay, sugar beets, potatoes, dry beans, flaxseed, cherries, corn, oats. **Livestock:** 545,000 chickens (excl. broilers), 2.5 mil cattle/calves, 225,000 sheep/lambs. **Broadband Internet:** 55.5%. **Nonfuel minerals:** $1.4 bil; copper, palladium metal, molybdenum concentrates, platinum metal, gold. **Gross state product:** $38.0 bil. **Sales tax:** none. **Employment distrib.:** 20.6% govt.; 19.9% trade/trans./util.; 3.9% mfg.; 15.0% ed./health; 9.9% prof./bus. serv.; 12.7% leisure/hosp.; 4.8% finance; 7.7% constr./mining/log.; 1.7% info.; 3.9% other serv. **Unemployment:** 6.8%. **Per cap. pers. income:** $36,573. **New private housing:** 1,914 units/$285.9 mil. **Commercial banks:** 76; deposits: $17.7 bil. **Savings institutions:** 3; deposits: $286 mil. **Lottery:** total sales: $46.0 mil; profit: $10.6 mil.

Federal govt. Fed. civ. employees: 10,439; **avg. salary:** $62,606. **Notable fed. facilities:** Malmstrom AFB and missile silos; Ft. Peck, Hungry Horse, Libby, Yellowtail, and other dams.

Energy. Monthly electricity use: 845 kWh, $77.37.

State data. Motto: Oro y Plata (Gold and silver). **Flower:** Bitterroot. **Bird:** Western meadowlark. **Tree:** Ponderosa pine. **Song:** "Montana." **Entered union:** Nov. 8, 1889; rank: 41st. **State fair** at Great Falls, late July-early Aug.

History. Paleo-Indian hunters reached the area over 12,000 years ago. Cheyenne, Blackfoot, Crow, Assiniboin, Salish (Flatheads), Kootenai, and Kalispel peoples lived in the region before Europeans arrived. French explorers visited the region, 1742. The U.S. acquired the area partly through the Louisiana Purchase, 1803, partly through the Lewis and Clark Expedition, 1804-06. Fur traders and missionaries established posts in the early 19th cent. Gold was discovered on Grasshopper Creek, 1862, and Montana Territory was established, 1864. Indian uprisings reached their peak with the defeat of Gen. George Custer at the Battle of Little Bighorn, 1876. Chief Joseph and the Nez Percé tribe surrendered here, 1877, after a long trek across the state. Mining activity and the coming of the Northern Pacific Railway, 1883, brought population growth. Montana became a state, 1889. Copper wealth from the Butte pits resulted in the turn of the century "War of Copper Kings" as feuding factions contended for "the richest hill on earth." During the first half of the 20th cent., the Anaconda Copper firm wielded enormous political influence. Jeannette Rankin, a suffragist and pacifist, was the first woman elected to Congress, 1916. Mike Mansfield served 34 years in Congress and was Senate Democratic leader, 1961-77. An 18-year hunt for notorious "Unabomber" Theodore Kaczynski ended with his arrest, 1996, at his cabin near Lincoln.

Tourist attractions. Glacier Natl. Park; Yellowstone Natl. Park; Museum of the Rockies, Bozeman; Museum of the Plains Indian, Blackfeet Reservation, near Browning; Little Bighorn Battlefield Natl. Monument and Custer Natl. Cemetery; Flathead Lake; Helena; Lewis and Clark Caverns State Park, near Whitehall; Lewis and Clark Interpretive Ctr., Great Falls.

Famous Montanans. Dana Carvey, Gary Cooper, Marcus Daly, Chet Huntley, Will James, Myrna Loy, David Lynch, Mike Mansfield, Brent Musburger, Jeannette Rankin, Charles M. Russell, Lester Thurow.

Tourist information. Travel Montana, Dept. of Commerce, 301 S. Park Ave., P.O. Box 200533, Helena, MT 59601; 1-800-VISITMT; www.visitmt.org

Website. www.mt.gov

Nebraska (NE)
Cornhusker State

People. Population: 1,842,641; rank: 38. **Pop. change (2000-11):** 7.7%. **Pop. density:** 24.0 per sq mi. **Racial distribution:** 90.1% white; 4.7% black; 1.9% Asian; 1.3% Amer. Ind.; 0.1% Pac. Isl.; 2 or more races, 1.8%. **Hispanic pop.:** 9.5%.

Geography. Total area: 77,348 sq mi; rank: 16. **Land area:** 76,824 sq mi; rank: 15. **Acres forested:** 1.6 mil. **Location:** West North Central state with the Missouri R. for a border on NE and E. **Climate:** continental semi-arid. **Topography:** till plains of the central lowland in the eastern third rising to the

Great Plains and hill country of the N central and NW. **Capital:** Lincoln. **Chief airport:** Omaha.

Economy. Chief industries: agriculture, manufacturing. **Chief manuf. goods:** animal slaughtering, grain & oilseed, farm machinery, medical equip., motor vehicle parts, printing, structural metals. **Chief crops:** corn, sorghum, soybeans, hay, wheat, dry beans, oats, potatoes, sugar beets. **Livestock:** 11.29 mil chickens (excl. broilers), 6.45 mil cattle/calves, 77,000 sheep/lambs, 385,000 hogs/pigs. **Broadband Internet:** 59.7%. **Nonfuel minerals:** $259 mil; sand and gravel (construction), cement (portland), stone (crushed), sand and gravel (industrial), lime. **Gross state product:** $94.2 bil. **Sales tax:** 5.5%. **Employment distrib.:** 17.9% govt.; 20.5% trade/trans./util.; 9.7% mfg.; 14.5% ed./health; 10.9% prof./bus. serv.; 9.0% leisure/hosp.; 7.1% finance; 4.8% constr./mining/log.; 1.7% info.; 3.8% other serv. **Unemployment:** 4.4%. **Per cap. pers. income:** $41,584. **New private housing:** 5,203 units/$726.3 mil. **Commercial banks:** 222; deposits: $44.3 bil. **Savings institutions:** 12; deposits: $3.6 bil. **Lottery:** total sales: $131.9 mil; profit: $32.6 mil.

Federal govt. Fed. civ. employees: 11,035; **avg. salary:** $66,762. **Notable fed. facilities:** Offutt AFB.

Energy. Monthly electricity use: 1,051 kWh, $93.97.

State data. Motto: Equality before the law. **Flower:** Goldenrod. **Bird:** Western meadowlark. **Tree:** Cottonwood. **Song:** "Beautiful Nebraska." **Entered union:** Mar. 1, 1867; rank: 37th. **State fair** at Grand Island, late Aug.-early Sept.

History. When Europeans arrived, Pawnee, Ponca, Omaha, and Oto peoples lived in the region. Spanish and French explorers and fur traders visited the area prior to its acquisition in the Louisiana Purchase, 1803. Meriwether Lewis and William Clark passed through, 1804-06. The first permanent settlement was Bellevue, near Omaha, 1823. The 1834 Indian Intercourse Act declared Nebraska Indian country and excluded white settlement, but conflicts with settlers eventually forced Native Americans to move to reservations. Nebraska became a territory, 1854, and a state, 1867. Many Civil War veterans settled under free land terms of the 1862 Homestead Act; as agriculture grew, struggles followed between homesteaders and ranchers. Since the mid-1930s, Nebraska has been the only state with a unicameral legislature. A leader in agribusiness, Nebraska has also become a major telemarketing center. The "Oracle of Omaha," investor Warren Buffett, one of the world's wealthiest men, announced in 2006 he would give most of his $44 bil fortune to charity.

Tourist attractions. State Museum (Elephant Hall), State Capitol, in Lincoln; Stuhr Museum of the Prairie Pioneer, Grand Island; Museum of the Fur Trade, Chadron; Boys Town, Henry Doorly Zoo, Joslyn Art Museum, Omaha; Ashfall Fossil Beds, Strategic Air and Space Museum, Ashland; Arbor Lodge State Park, Nebraska City; Buffalo Bill Ranch State Hist. Park, North Platte; Pioneer Village, Minden; Oregon Trail landmarks; Scotts Bluff Natl. Monument; Chimney Rock Natl. Historic Site; Ft. Robinson; Hastings Museum of Natural and Cultural Hist.

Famous Nebraskans. Grover Cleveland Alexander, Fred Astaire, Marlon Brando, Charles W. Bryan, William Jenningsy Bryan, Warren Buffett, Johnny Carson, Willa Cather, Dick Cavett, Dick Cheney, William F. "Buffalo Bill" Cody, Loren Eiseley, Rev. Edward J. Flanagan, Henry Fonda, Gerald R. Ford, Bob Gibson, Rollin Kirby, Harold Lloyd, Malcolm X, J. Sterling Morton, John Neihardt, Nick Nolte, George Norris, Tom Osborne, John J. Pershing, Roscoe Pound, Chief Red Cloud, Mari Sandoz, Robert Taylor, Darryl F. Zanuck.

Tourist information. Nebraska Division of Travel and Tourism, 301 Centennial Mall S., Lincoln, NE 68508; 1-888-444-1867; www.visitnebraska.gov

Website. www.nebraska.gov

Nevada (NV)
Sagebrush State, Battle Born State, Silver State

People. Population: 2,723,322; rank: 35. **Pop. change (2000-11):** 36.3%. **Pop. density:** 24.8 per sq mi. **Racial distribution:** 77.7% white; 8.6% black; 7.7% Asian; 1.6% Amer. Ind.; 0.7% Pac. Isl.; 2 or more races, 3.7%. **Hispanic pop.:** 27.1%.

Geography. Total area: 110,572 sq mi; rank: 7. **Land area:** 109,781 sq mi; rank: 7. **Acres forested:** 11.2 mil. **Location:**

Mountain state bordered on N by Oregon and Idaho, on E by Utah and Arizona, on SE by Arizona, and on SW and W by California. **Climate:** semi-arid and arid. **Topography:** rugged N-S mountain ranges; highest elevation, Boundary Peak, 13,140 ft; southern area is within the Mojave Desert; lowest elevation, Colorado R. at southern tip of state, 479 ft. **Capital:** Carson City. **Chief airports:** Las Vegas, Reno.

Economy. Chief industries: gaming, tourism, mining, manufacturing, government, retailing, warehousing, trucking. **Chief manuf. goods:** gaming machines, cement & concrete, plastics, printing, architectural & structural metals, electricity instruments. **Chief crops:** hay, onions, potatoes, alfalfa, wheat, garlic, mint, barley. **Livestock:** 470,000 cattle/calves, 70,000 sheep/lambs. **Broadband Internet:** 80.9%. **Nonfuel minerals:** $10.4 bil; gold, copper, silver, lime, sand and gravel (construction). **Gross state product:** $130.4 bil. **Sales tax:** 6.85%. **Employment distrib.:** 13.2% govt.; 18.7% trade/trans./util.; 3.3% mfg.; 9.4% ed./health; 12.5% prof./bus. serv.; 28.6% leisure/hosp.; 4.5% finance; 5.7% constr./mining/log.; 1.2% info.; 3.0% other serv. **Unemployment:** 13.5%. **Per cap. pers. income:** $38,173. **New private housing:** 6,163 units/$789.4 mil. **Commercial banks:** 39; deposits: $207.4 bil. **Savings institutions:** 10; deposits: $51.6 bil.

Federal govt. Fed. civ. employees: 11,967; **avg. salary:** $65,970. **Notable fed. facilities:** Nevada Test Site; Hawthorne Army Depot; Creech AFB; Nellis AFB & Range Complex; Fallon NAS; Natl. Wild Horse & Burro Ctr. at Palomino Valley.

Energy. Monthly electricity use: 914 kWh, $113.03.

State data. Motto: All for our country. **Flower:** Sagebrush. **Bird:** Mountain bluebird. **Trees:** Single-leaf piñon and bristlecone pine. **Song:** "Home Means Nevada." **Entered union:** Oct. 31, 1864; rank: 36th. **State fair** at Reno, late Aug.

History. Shoshone, Paiute, Bannock, and Washoe peoples lived in the area at the time of European contact. Nevada was first explored by Spaniards, 1776. In the 1820s, fur traders Peter Skene Ogden and Jedediah Smith separately explored the area. It was acquired by the U.S., 1848, at the end of the Mexican War. A trading post at Mormon Station, now Genoa, was established, 1850. Discovery of the Comstock Lode, rich in gold and silver, 1859, spurred a population boom. Nevada became a territory, 1861, and a state, 1864. Hoover Dam was built, 1931-36. With gambling legal since 1931, a surge in resort casino construction after World War II turned Las Vegas into one of the nation's most popular tourist destinations. An influx of Hispanics and Asians, attracted by service-industry and construction jobs, helped make Nevada the fastest-growing state in the U.S. during 1990-2005, and again in 2007. The recession in recent years has had an equally powerful effect. Nevada had the highest state unemployment and home foreclosure rates in 2011.

Tourist attractions. Legalized gambling at Lake Tahoe, Reno, Las Vegas, Laughlin, Elko County, and elsewhere; Hoover Dam; Lake Mead; Great Basin Natl. Park; Valley of Fire State Park; Virginia City; Red Rock Canyon Natl. Conservation Area; Liberace Museum, The Strip, Fremont St., Atomic Testing Museum, Pinball Hall of Fame, all Las Vegas; Lamoille Canyon; Pyramid Lake; Lost City Museum, Overton; Skiing near Lake Tahoe.

Famous Nevadans. Andre Agassi, Walter Van Tilburg Clark, George Ferris, Sarah Winnemucca Hopkins, Paul Laxalt, Dat So La Lee, John William Mackay, Anne Martin, Pat McCarran, Key Pittman, William Morris Stewart.

Tourist information. Commission on Tourism, 401 N. Carson St., Carson City, NV 89701; 1-800-NEVADA8; www.travelnevada.com

Website. www.nv.gov

New Hampshire (NH)
Granite State

People. Population: 1,318,194; rank: 42. **Pop. change** (2000-11): 6.7%. **Pop. density:** 147.2 per sq mi. **Racial distribution:** 94.6% white; 1.3% black; 2.3% Asian; 0.3% Amer. Ind.; <0.05% Pac. Isl.; 2 or more races, 1.5%. **Hispanic pop.:** 2.9%.

Geography. Total area: 9,349 sq mi; rank: 46. **Land area:** 8,953 sq mi; rank: 44. **Acres forested:** 4.8 mil. **Location:** New England state bounded on S by Massachusetts, on W

by Vermont, on N and NW by Canada, on E by Maine and the Atlantic Ocean. **Climate:** highly varied, due to its nearness to high mountains and ocean. **Topography:** low, rolling coast followed by countless hills and mountains rising out of a central plateau. **Capital:** Concord. **Chief airport:** Manchester.

Economy. Chief industries: tourism, manufacturing, agriculture, trade, mining. **Chief manuf. goods:** navigational instruments, circuit boards, electrical equip., fabricated metal, machinery, medical equip., plastics. **Chief crops:** greenhouse & nursery, apples, sweet corn, hay, Christmas trees, berries, maple syrup. **Livestock:** 35,000 cattle/calves. **Broadband Internet:** 65.1%. **Nonfuel minerals:** $78.7 mil; sand and gravel (construction), stone (crushed), stone (dimension), gemstones (natural). **Commercial fishing:** $20.7 mil. **Chief port:** Portsmouth. **Gross state product:** $63.6 bil. **Sales tax:** none. **Employment distrib.:** 15.1% govt.; 20.9% trade/trans./util.; 10.5% mfg.; 18.1% ed./health; 10.4% prof./bus. serv.; 10.3% leisure/hosp.; 5.4% finance; 3.7% constr./mining/log.; 1.8% info.; 3.7% other serv. **Unemployment:** 5.4%. **Per cap. pers. income:** $45,787. **New private housing:** 2,346 units/$432.3 mil. **Commercial banks:** 16; deposits: $19.6 bil. **Savings institutions:** 24; deposits: $7.5 bil. **Lottery:** total sales: $228.4 mil; profit: $62.2 mil.

Federal govt. Fed. civ. employees: 4,474; **avg. salary:** $82,553. **Notable fed. facilities:** Army Cold Regions Res. & Engineering Lab.

Energy. Monthly electricity use: 626 kWh, $102.11.

State data. Motto: Live free or die. **Flower:** Purple lilac. **Bird:** Purple finch. **Tree:** White birch. **Song:** "Old New Hampshire." **Ninth** of the original 13 states to ratify the Constitution, June 21, 1788. **State fair:** Hopkinton State Fair at Contoocook, late Aug.-early Sept.

History. The area has been inhabited for about 10,000 years. Algonquian-speaking peoples, including the Pennacook, lived in the region when the Europeans arrived. The first explorers to visit the area were England's Martin Pring, 1603, and France's Samuel de Champlain, 1605. The first settlement was Odiorne's Point (now port of Rye), 1623. Before the American Revolution, New Hampshire residents raided a British fort at Portsmouth, 1774, and drove the royal governor out, 1775. New Hampshire became the first colony to adopt its own constitution, 1776. After statehood, 1788, New Hampshire became a textile manufacturing center. The mill towns declined in the first half of the 20th cent., but tourism and high-tech industries, lured by low taxes, have revived the economy since the 1960s. A state law requires it to hold the first primary of the presidential campaign season.

Tourist attractions. Mt. Washington, highest peak in Northeast; Lake Winnipesaukee; Crawford, Franconia, Pinkham notches, Flume Gorge, Canon Mt. aerial tramway, all White Mt. region; Strawbery Banke Historic District, Portsmouth; Canterbury Shaker Village; Saint-Gaudens, Natl. Historic Site, Cornish; Mt. Monadnock.

Famous New Hampshirites. Salmon P. Chase, Ralph Adams Cram, Mary Baker Eddy, Daniel Chester French, Robert Frost, Horace Greeley, Sarah Buell Hale, Franklin Pierce, Augustus Saint-Gaudens, Adam Sandler, Alan Shepard, David H. Souter, Daniel Webster.

Tourist information. Division of Travel & Tourism Development, 172 Pembroke Rd., P.O. Box 1856; Concord, NH 03302; 1-800-FUNINNH; www.visitnh.gov

Website. www.nh.gov

New Jersey (NJ)
Garden State

People. Population: 8,821,155; rank: 11. **Pop. change** (2000-11): 4.8%. **Pop. density:** 1,199.5 per sq mi. **Racial distribution:** 74.1% white; 14.6% black; 8.7% Asian; 0.6% Amer. Ind.; 0.1% Pac. Isl.; 2 or more races, 1.9%. **Hispanic pop.:** 18.1%.

Geography. Total area: 8,723 sq mi; rank: 47. **Land area:** 7,354 sq mi; rank: 46. **Acres forested:** 2.0 mil. **Location:** Middle Atlantic state bounded on N and E by New York and Atlantic Ocean, on S and W by Delaware and Pennsylvania. **Climate:** moderate, with marked difference between NW and SE extremities. **Topography:** Appalachian Valley in the NW also has highest elevation, High Pt., 1,801 ft; Appalachian Highlands, flat-topped NE-SW mountain ranges; Piedmont

Plateau, low plains broken by high ridges (Palisades) rising 400-500 ft; Coastal Plain, covering three-fifths of state in SE, rises from sea level to gentle slopes. **Capital:** Trenton. **Chief airports:** Atlantic City, Newark.

Economy. Chief industries: pharmaceuticals, telecommunications, biotechnology, printing & publishing. **Chief manuf. goods:** petroleum, pharmaceuticals, toiletries, chemicals, plastics, printing, navigational instruments, medical equip., paper prod. **Chief crops:** greenhouse & nursery, blueberries, peaches, corn, hay, tomatoes, bell peppers, cranberries, soybeans, apples. **Livestock:** 31,000 cattle/calves. **Broadband Internet:** 70.0%. **Nonfuel minerals:** $221 mil; stone (crushed), sand and gravel (construction), sand and gravel (industrial), greensand marl, peat. **Commercial fishing:** $178.1 mil. **Chief ports:** Newark-Elizabeth, Camden. **Gross state product:** $487.0 bil. **Sales tax:** 7.0%. **Employment distrib.:** 16.1% govt.; 21.0% trade/trans./util.; 6.4% mfg.; 16.2% ed./health; 15.6% prof./bus. serv.; 9.0% leisure/hosp.; 6.4% finance; 3.2% constr./mining/log.; 1.7% info.; 4.4% other serv. **Unemployment:** 9.3%. **Per cap. pers. income:** $53,181. **New private housing:** 12,952 units/$2.0 bil. **Commercial banks:** 96; deposits: $181 bil. **Savings institutions:** 72; deposits: $74.4 bil. **Lottery:** total sales: $2.6 bil; profit: $930 mil.

Federal govt. Fed. civ. employees: 26,263; **avg. salary:** $82,241. **Notable fed. facilities:** Joint Base McGuire-Dix-Lakehurst; Picatinny Arsenal; FAA William J. Hughes Technical Ctr.

Energy. Monthly electricity use: 731 kWh, $121.13.

State data. Motto: Liberty and prosperity. **Flower:** Purple violet. **Bird:** Eastern goldfinch. **Tree:** Red oak. **Third** of the original 13 states to ratify the Constitution, Dec. 18, 1787. **State fair** at Augusta, early-mid Aug.

History. The Lenni Lenape (Delaware) peoples lived in the region and had mostly peaceful relations with European colonists, who arrived after the explorers Giovanni da Verrazano, 1524, and Henry Hudson, 1609. The first permanent European settlement was Dutch, at Bergen (now Jersey City), 1660. When the British took New Netherland, 1664, the area between the Delaware and Hudson Rivers was given to Lord John Berkeley and Sir George Carteret. During the American Revolution, New Jersey was the scene of many major battles, including Trenton, 1776; Princeton, 1777; and Monmouth, 1778. New Jersey was the third state to ratify the Constitution, 1787, and the first to approve the Bill of Rights, 1789. In a duel at Weehawken, 1804, Vice Pres. Aaron Burr fatally shot Alexander Hamilton. Canal and railroad building stimulated the growth of cities and industries in the 19th cent. The 20th cent. arrival of large numbers of African Americans, Italians, Irish, European Jews, Puerto Ricans, South Asians, and other groups made New Jersey one of the most diverse states in the U.S. Construction of resort casinos in Atlantic City from the late 1970s revitalized tourism. Gov. James McGreevey resigned, 2004, after acknowledging an extramarital affair with a man identified as his former homeland security adviser.

Tourist attractions. 127 mi of beaches, boardwalks at Atlantic City (with gambling), Seaside Heights, Ocean City, Wildwood; Grover Cleveland birthplace, Caldwell; Cape May Historic District; Edison Natl. Historic Site, W. Orange; Six Flags Great Adventure, Jackson; Liberty State Park, Liberty Science Ctr., Jersey City; Pine Barrens wilderness area; Princeton Univ.; Revolutionary War sites; Adventure Aquarium, Battleship *New Jersey*, Walt Whitman house, Camden.

Famous New Jerseyans. Jason Alexander, Samuel Alito, Count Basie, Judy Blume, Jon Bon Jovi, Bill Bradley, Aaron Burr, Grover Cleveland, James Fenimore Cooper, Stephen Crane, Danny DeVito, Thomas Edison, Albert Einstein, James Gandolfini, Allen Ginsberg, Alexander Hamilton, Ed Harris, Whitney Houston, Buster Keaton, Joyce Kilmer, Norman Mailer, Jack Nicholson, Thomas Paine, Dorothy Parker, Joe Pesci, Molly Pitcher, Paul Robeson, Philip Roth, Antonin Scalia, Wally Schirra, H. Norman Schwarzkopf, Frank Sinatra, Bruce Springsteen, Martha Stewart, Meryl Streep, Dave Thomas, John Travolta, Walt Whitman, William Carlos Williams, Woodrow Wilson.

Tourist information. Dept. of State, Division of Travel and Tourism, P.O. Box 460, Trenton, NJ 08625; 1-800-VISITNJ; www.visitnj.org

Website. www.state.nj.us

New Mexico (NM)
Land of Enchantment

People. Population: 2,082,224; rank: 36. **Pop. change** (2000-11): 14.5%. **Pop. density:** 17.2 per sq mi. **Racial distribution:** 83.4% white; 2.5% black; 1.6% Asian; 10.1% Amer. Ind.; 0.2% Pac. Isl.; 2 or more races, 2.3%. **Hispanic pop.:** 46.7%.

Geography. Total area: 121,590 sq mi; rank: 5. **Land area:** 121,298 sq mi; rank: 5. **Acres forested:** 16.7 mil. **Location:** southwestern state bounded by Colorado on the N, Oklahoma, Texas, and Mexico on the E and S, and Arizona on the W. **Climate:** dry, with temperatures rising or falling 5°F with every 1,000 ft elevation. **Topography:** eastern third, Great Plains; central third, Rocky Mts. (85% of the state is over 4,000-ft elevation); western third, high plateau. **Capital:** Santa Fe. **Chief airport:** Albuquerque.

Economy. Chief industries: government, services, trade. **Chief manuf. goods:** semiconductors, medical equip., navigational/measuring/medical/control instruments, aircraft, chemicals, jewelry. **Chief crops:** hay, pecans, corn, greenhouse & nursery, chiles, onions, cotton, wheat, peanuts. **Livestock:** 1.39 mil cattle/calves, 100,000 sheep/lambs. **Broadband Internet:** 66.4%. **Nonfuel minerals:** $1.3 bil; copper, potash, sand and gravel (construction), stone (crushed), salt. **Gross state product:** $79.4 bil. **Sales tax:** 5.125%. **Employment distrib.:** 24.3% govt.; 16.5% trade/trans./util.; 3.7% mfg.; 15.7% ed./health; 11.9% prof./bus. serv.; 10.8% leisure/hosp.; 4.0% finance; 8.1% constr./mining/log.; 1.7% info.; 3.3% other serv. **Unemployment:** 7.4%. **Per cap. pers. income:** $34,575. **New private housing:** 4,067 units/$677.7 mil. **Commercial banks:** 56; deposits: $24.7 bil. **Savings institutions:** 9; deposits: $1.5 bil. **Lottery:** total sales: $135.5 mil; profit: $41.3 mil.

Federal govt. Fed. civ. employees: 26,327; **avg. salary:** $68,196. **Notable fed. facilities:** Kirtland, Cannon, Holloman AFB; Los Alamos Natl. Lab; White Sands Missile Range; Natl. Solar Observatory; Natl. Radio Astronomy Observatory; Sandia Natl. Labs.

Energy. Monthly electricity use: 659 kWh, $69.35.

State data. Motto: Crescit Eundo (It grows as it goes). **Flower:** Yucca. **Bird:** Roadrunner. **Tree:** Piñon. **Songs:** "O, Fair New Mexico"; "Asi Es Nuevo Mexico." **Entered union:** Jan. 6, 1912; rank: 47th. **State fair** at Albuquerque, mid-Sept.; at Las Cruces, early Oct.; at Roswell, early Oct.

History. Inhabited for more than 10,000 years, the region was home to Sandia, Clovis, Folsom, Mogollon, and Anasazi cultures, followed by the Pueblo people, Anasazi descendants; later, nomadic Navajo and Apache came. Franciscan Marcos de Niza and a former black slave, Estevanico, explored the area, 1539, seeking gold; Coronado followed, 1540. First settlements were near San Juan Pueblo, 1598, and at Santa Fe, 1610. Settlers alternately traded and fought with the Apache, Comanche, and Navajo. Trade on the Santa Fe Trail to Missouri started, 1821. After the Mexican War began, 1846, Gen. Stephen Kearny took Santa Fe without firing a shot, and declared New Mexico part of the U.S. All Hispanic New Mexicans and Pueblo became U.S. citizens by terms of the 1848 treaty ending the war. New Mexico became a territory, 1850, but did not attain statehood until 1912. Pancho Villa raided Columbus, 1916, and U.S. troops were sent to the area. The world's first atomic bomb was exploded at a test site near Alamogordo, 1945. An underground nuclear waste depository opened near Carlsbad, 1999. Spaceport America, a state-owned commercial spaceport, hosted its first test launch in 2006 and expected to complete construction in 2013.

Tourist attractions. Carlsbad Caverns Natl. Park, with world's largest natural underground chamber; Santa Fe, oldest capital in U.S.; White Sands Natl. Monument, world's largest gypsum deposit; Chaco Culture Natl. Hist. Park; Acoma Pueblo, "sky city" built atop a 357-ft mesa; Taos Art Colony and Ski Valley; Ute Lake State Park; Shiprock; Roswell.

Famous New Mexicans. Ben Abruzzo, Maxie Anderson, Jeff Bezos, Billy (the Kid) Bonney, Kit Carson, Bob Foster, Peter Hurd, Tony Hillerman, Archbishop Jean Baptiste Lamy, Nancy Lopez, Bill Mauldin, Georgia O'Keeffe, Bill Richardson, Kim Stanley, Al Unser, Bobby Unser, Lew Wallace.

Tourist information. New Mexico Dept. of Tourism, 491 Old Santa Fe Trl., Santa Fe, NM 87501; 1-800-733-6396; www.newmexico.org

Website. www.newmexico.gov

New York (NY)
Empire State

People. Population: 19,465,197; rank: 3. **Pop. change** (2000-11): 2.6%. **Pop. density:** 413.0 per sq mi. **Racial distribution:** 71.5% white; 17.5% black; 7.8% Asian; 1.0% Amer. Ind.; 0.1% Pac. Isl.; 2 or more races, 2.2%. **Hispanic pop.:** 18.0%.

Geography. Total area: 54,555 sq mi; rank: 27. **Land area:** 47,126 sq mi; rank: 30. **Acres forested:** 18.9 mil. **Location:** Middle Atlantic state, bordered by the New England states, Atlantic Ocean, New Jersey and Pennsylvania, Lakes Ontario and Erie, and Canada. **Climate:** variable; the SE region moderated by the ocean. **Topography:** highest and most rugged mountains in the NE Adirondack upland; St. Lawrence-Champlain lowlands extend from Lake Ontario NE along the Canadian border; Hudson-Mohawk lowland follows the flows of the rivers N and W, 10-30 mi wide; Atlantic coastal plain in the SE; Appalachian Highlands, covering half the state westward from the Hudson Valley, include the Catskill Mts., Finger Lakes; plateau of Erie-Ontario lowlands. **Capital:** Albany. **Chief airports:** Albany, Buffalo, Islip, New York (2), Rochester, Syracuse, White Plains.

Economy. Chief industries: manufacturing, finance, communications, tourism, transportation, services. **Chief manuf. goods:** pharmaceuticals, photographic chemicals, electronics, automotive parts, toiletries, printing, plastics, apparel. **Chief crops:** greenhouse & nursery, apples, corn, hay, cabbage, onions, soybeans, potatoes, snap beans, grapes, squash, pumpkins, tomatoes, wheat, cucumbers, green peas. **Livestock:** 5.65 mil chickens (excl. broilers), 1.41 mil cattle/calves, 62,000 sheep/lambs. **Broadband Internet:** 72.9%. **Nonfuel minerals:** $1.1 bil; stone (crushed), salt, sand and gravel (construction), cement (portland), clays (common). **Commercial fishing:** $34.0 mil. **Chief ports:** New York, Buffalo, Albany. **Gross state product:** $1.16 tril. **Sales tax:** 4.0%. **Employment distrib.:** 17.0% govt.; 17.0% trade/trans./util.; 5.2% mfg.; 20.1% ed./health; 13.4% prof./bus. serv.; 9.0% leisure/hosp.; 7.9% finance; 3.4% constr./mining/log.; 2.9% info.; 4.2% other serv. **Unemployment:** 8.2%. **Per cap. pers. income:** $50,545. **New private housing:** 22,575 units/$3.4 bil. **Commercial banks:** 158; deposits: $891.2 bil. **Savings institutions:** 73; deposits: $80.8 bil. **Lottery:** total sales: $7.9 bil; profit: $3.0 bil.

Federal govt. Fed. civ. employees: 67,342; **avg. salary:** $74,323. **Notable fed. facilities:** Ft. Drum; West Point Military Academy; Merchant Marine Academy; NY Fed. Reserve; Griffis AFB (Research Lab), Rome; U.S. Army Watervliet Arsenal; Brookhaven Natl. Lab.; U.S. Mission to the United Nations.

Energy. Monthly electricity use: 610 kWh, $114.39.

State data. Motto: Excelsior (Ever upward). **Flower:** Rose. **Bird:** Bluebird. **Tree:** Sugar maple. **Song:** "I Love New York." **Eleventh** of the original 13 states to ratify the Constitution, July 26, 1788. **State fair** at Syracuse, late Aug.-early Sept.

History. When Europeans arrived, Algonquians including the Mahican, Wappinger, and Lenni Lenape inhabited the region, as did the Iroquoian Mohawk, Oneida, Onondaga, Cayuga, and Seneca tribes, who established the League of the Five Nations. Giovanni da Verrazano entered New York harbor, 1524. In 1609, Henry Hudson visited the river later named for him, and Samuel de Champlain explored the lake that now bears his name. The first permanent settlement was Dutch, near present-day Albany, 1624. New Amsterdam was settled, 1626, at the southern tip of Manhattan island. A British fleet seized New Netherland, 1664. Key battles of the American Revolution included Saratoga, 1777. In the 19th cent., New York City emerged as one of the world's great metropolitan areas, a center for trade, finance, and arts, and a haven for millions of immigrants. Completion of Erie Canal, 1825, established the state as a gateway to the West. The first women's rights convention was held in Seneca Falls, 1848. Although the state backed the Union in the Civil War, an 1863 military draft triggered 3 days of riots in New York City. Industry declined in the 20th cent., and California and Texas passed New York

in population. Attica was the scene of a bloody prison revolt, 1971. Two jet aircraft hijacked by terrorists on Sept. 11, 2001, destroyed the World Trade Center in lower Manhattan. Gov. Eliot Spitzer resigned in Mar. 2008 after 14-months in office; he was alleged to have patronized a prostitution ring.

Tourist attractions. New York City; Adirondack and Catskill Mts.; Finger Lakes; Great Lakes; Thousand Islands; Niagara Falls; Saratoga Springs; Philipsburg Manor, Sunnyside (Washington Irving's home), Dutch Church of Sleepy Hollow, near Tarrytown; Corning Museum of Glass; Fenimore House, Natl. Baseball Hall of Fame and Museum, Cooperstown; Ft. Ticonderoga; Empire State Plaza, Albany; Lake Placid; Franklin D. Roosevelt Natl. Historic Site, Hyde Park; Long Island beaches; Theodore Roosevelt estate, Sagamore Hill, Oyster Bay; Turning Stone Casino.

Famous New Yorkers. Woody Allen, Susan B. Anthony, James Baldwin, Lucille Ball, Ann Bancroft, L. Frank Baum, Milton Berle, Humphrey Bogart, Barbara Boxer, Mel Brooks, Benjamin Cardozo, De Witt Clinton, Peter Cooper, Aaron Copland, Tom Cruise, Robert De Niro, George Eastman, Millard Fillmore, Lou Gehrig, George and Ira Gershwin, Ruth Bader Ginsburg, Rudolph Giuliani, Jackie Gleason, Stephen Jay Gould, Julia Ward Howe, Charles Evans Hughes, Washington Irving, Henry and William James, John Jay, Michael Jordan, Edward Koch, Fiorello LaGuardia, Herman Melville, Arthur Miller, J. Pierpont Morgan Jr., Eddie Murphy, Joyce Carol Oates, Carroll O'Connor, Rosie O'Donnell, Eugene O'Neill, Jerry Orbach, George Pataki, Colin Powell, Nancy Reagan, John D. Rockefeller, Nelson Rockefeller, John Roberts, Richard Rodgers, Ray Romano, Eleanor Roosevelt, Franklin D. Roosevelt, Theodore Roosevelt, Tim Russert, J. D. Salinger, Caroline Kennedy Schlossberg, Jerry Seinfeld, Al Sharpton, Paul Simon, Alfred E. Smith, Elizabeth Cady Stanton, Barbra Streisand, Donald Trump, William (Boss) Tweed, Martin Van Buren, Luther Vandross, Gore Vidal, Denzel Washington, Edith Wharton, Walt Whitman.

Tourist information. Empire State Development, Travel Information Center, 30 South Pearl St., Albany, NY 12245; 1-800-CALLNYS; www.iloveny.com

Website. www.state.ny.us

North Carolina (NC)
Tar Heel State, Old North State

People. Population: 9,656,401; rank: 10. **Pop. change** (2000-11): 20.0%. **Pop. density:** 198.6 per sq mi. **Racial distribution:** 72.1% white; 22% black; 2.3% Asian; 1.5% Amer. Ind.; 0.1% Pac. Isl.; 2 or more races, 1.9%. **Hispanic pop.:** 8.6%.

Geography. Total area: 53,819 sq mi; rank: 28. **Land area:** 48,618 sq mi; rank: 29. **Acres forested:** 18.6 mil. **Location:** South Atlantic state bounded by Virginia, South Carolina, Georgia, Tennessee, and the Atlantic Ocean. **Climate:** subtropical in SE, medium-continental in mountain region; tempered by the Gulf Stream and the mountains in W. **Topography:** coastal plain and tidewater, two-fifths of state, extending to the fall line of the rivers; Piedmont Plateau, another two-fifths, of gentle to rugged hills; southern Appalachian Mts. contains the Blue Ridge and Great Smoky Mts. **Capital:** Raleigh. **Chief airports:** Charlotte, Greensboro, Raleigh.

Economy. Chief industries: manufacturing, agriculture, tourism. **Chief manuf. goods:** transportation, tobacco, pharmaceuticals, toiletries, plastics, animal slaughtering & processing, household furniture, fabric & apparel. **Chief crops:** greenhouse & nursery, tobacco, cotton, soybeans, corn, Christmas trees, sweet potatoes, wheat, peanuts, blueberries, cucumbers, tomatoes, hay, potatoes. **Livestock:** 19.36 mil chickens (excl. broilers), 786.9 mil broilers, 810,000 cattle/calves, 26,000 sheep/lambs, 870,000 hogs/pigs. **Broadband Internet:** 68.5%. **Nonfuel minerals:** $883 mil; stone (crushed), phosphate rock, sand and gravel (construction), sand and gravel (industrial), stone (dimension). **Commercial fishing:** $79.8 mil. **Chief ports:** Morehead City, Wilmington. **Gross state product:** $439.9 bil. **Sales tax:** 4.75%. **Employment distrib.:** 18.1% govt.; 18.5% trade/trans./util.; 11.0% mfg.; 14.0% ed./health; 13.0% prof./bus. serv.; 10.3% leisure/hosp.; 5.2% finance; 4.5% constr./mining/log.; 1.7% info.; 3.9% other serv. **Unemployment:** 10.5%. **Per cap. pers. income:** $36,164. **New private housing:** 32,804 units/$5.1 bil. **Commercial banks:** 96; deposits: $277.1 bil.

Savings institutions: 32; deposits: $7.1 bil. **Lottery:** total sales: $1.5 bil; profit: $436.2 mil.

Federal govt. Fed. civ. employees: 44,864; **avg. salary:** $67,042. **Notable fed. facilities:** Ft. Bragg; Camp LeJeune Marine Base, Marine Corps Air Station Cherry Point; NOAA Natl. Climatic Data Ctr.; Natl. Inst. of Environmental Health Sciences, EPA Research and Dev. Labs, all in Research Triangle Park.

Energy. Monthly electricity use: 1,238 kWh, $125.20.

State data. Motto: Esse Quam Videri (To be rather than to seem). **Flower:** Dogwood. **Bird:** Cardinal. **Tree:** Pine. **Song:** "The Old North State." **Twelfth** of the original 13 states to ratify the Constitution, Nov. 21, 1789. **State fair** at Raleigh, mid-Oct.; at Fletcher, mid-Sept.

History. Algonquian, Siouan, and Iroquoian peoples lived in the region at the time of European contact. Sir Walter Raleigh tried to found a colony, 1584-87; the "Lost Colony" on Roanoke Island, 1587, disappeared without a trace. Permanent settlers came from Virginia in the mid-17th cent. The province's congress was the first to vote for independence, 1776. In the Revolutionary War, Gen. Charles Cornwallis's forces were defeated at Kings Mountain, 1780, and forced out after Guilford Courthouse, 1781. The state ratified the Constitution, 1789, only after Congress passed the Bill of Rights. North Carolina, where one-third of the population was slaves, seceded from the Union, 1861, and provided more troops to the Confederacy than any other state; it was readmitted, 1868. The Wright brothers made the first powered airplane flight at Kitty Hawk, 1903. Sit-ins at segregated Greensboro lunch counters, 1960, drew national attention to the civil rights movement. Long reliant on tobacco, textiles, and wood products, North Carolina has prospered since the 1960s from advanced technologies in the Raleigh-Durham-Chapel Hill area and banking in Charlotte. The hurricane-prone state was hit hard by Hazel, 1954, Fran, 1996, and Floyd, 1999.

Tourist attractions. Cape Hatteras and Cape Lookout natl. seashores; Great Smoky Mts.; Guilford Courthouse and Moore's Creek parks; 66 American Revolution battle sites; Bennett Place (where last Confederate army surrendered), near Durham; Ft. Raleigh, Roanoke Island; Wright Brothers Natl. Mem., Kitty Hawk; Battleship *North Carolina*, Wilmington; NC Zoo, Asheboro; NC Symphony, Exploris, NC museums of Art, Natural Sciences, History, in Raleigh; Carl Sandburg Home, Hendersonville; Biltmore House and Gardens, Asheville.

Famous North Carolinians. David Brinkley, Shirley Caesar, John Coltrane, Rick Dees, Elizabeth Hanford Dole, John Edwards, Ava Gardner, Richard J. Gatling, Billy Graham, Andy Griffith, O. Henry, Andrew Jackson, Andrew Johnson, Michael Jordan, Wm. Rufus King, Charles Kuralt, Meadowlark Lemon, Dolley Madison, Thelonious Monk, Edward R. Murrow, Arnold Palmer, Richard Petty, James K. Polk, Charlie Rose, Carl Sandburg, Enos Slaughter, Dean Smith, James Taylor, Thomas Wolfe.

Tourist information. North Carolina Division of Tourism, Film and Sports Development, 4324 Mail Service Ctr., Raleigh, NC 27699; 1-800-VISIT-NC; (919) 733-8372; www.visitnc.com

Website. www.nc.gov

Chief manuf. goods: machinery, wood prods., motor vehicles & parts, furniture, processed foods. **Chief crops:** wheat, soybeans, corn, sugar beets, barley, dry beans, sunflowers, canola, potatoes, flaxseed, hay, dry peas, lentils, oats. **Livestock:** 1.69 mil cattle/calves, 73,000 sheep/lambs. **Broadband Internet:** 63.2%. **Nonfuel minerals:** $98.4 mil; sand and gravel (construction), lime, stone (crushed), clays (common), sand and gravel (industrial). **Gross state product:** $40.3 bil. **Sales tax:** 5.0%. **Employment distrib.:** 19.3% govt.; 22.0% trade/trans./util.; 5.9% mfg.; 13.9% ed./health; 7.9% prof./bus. serv.; 8.6% leisure/hosp.; 5.2% finance; 11.6% constr./mining/log.; 1.8% info.; 3.8% other serv. **Unemployment:** 3.5%. **Per cap. pers. income:** $45,747. **New private housing:** 6,201 units/$783.6 mil. **Commercial banks:** 98; deposits: $17.9 bil. **Savings institutions:** 2; deposits: $1.2 bil. **Lottery:** total sales: $23.0 mil; profit: $5.9 mil.

Federal govt. Fed. civ. employees: 6,469; **avg. salary:** $62,412. **Notable fed. facilities:** Minot AFB; Grand Forks AFB; Northern Prairie Wildlife Res. Ctr.; Garrison Dam Natl. Fish Hatchery; Grand Forks Human Nutrition Res. Ctr.

Energy. Monthly electricity use: 1,121 kWh, $91.16.

State data. Motto: Liberty and union, now and forever, one and inseparable. **Flower:** Wild prairie rose. **Bird:** Western meadowlark. **Tree:** American elm. **Song:** "North Dakota Hymn." **Entered union:** Nov. 2, 1889; rank: 39th. **State fair** at Minot, late July.

History. Paleo-Indian peoples hunted in the area at least 11,000 years ago. At the time of European contact, the Ojibwa, Yanktonai and Teton Sioux, Mandan, Arikara, and Hidatsa peoples lived in the region. Pierre de Varennes, sieur de La Vérendrye, was the first French fur trader in the area, 1738, followed by the English at the end of the 18th cent. Lewis and Clark built Ft. Mandan, near present-day Washburn, 1804-05, and wintered there. The first permanent settlement was at Pembina, 1812. Missouri River steamboats reached the area, 1832. Dakota Territory was organized, 1861. The first railroad arrived, 1872. The "bonanza farm" craze of the 1870s-80s led to statehood, 1889. The Nonpartisan League, a farmers' group favoring state ownership of industries, helped elect Lynn Frazier as governor, 1916, but he and others were ousted in a recall vote, 1921. The predominantly agricultural state has one of the nation's lowest unemployment rates, mostly due to surging oil production since late-2008 in the state's Bakken formation.

Tourist attractions. North Dakota Heritage Ctr., Bisarck; Bonanzaville, Fargo; Ft. Union Trading Post Natl. Historic Site; Lake Sakakawea; Intl. Peace Garden; Theodore Roosevelt Natl. Park, including Elkhorn Ranch, Badlands; Ft. Abraham Lincoln State Park and Museum, near Mandan; Dakota Dinosaur Museum, Dickinson; Knife River Indian Villages-Natl. Hist. Site.

Famous North Dakotans. Maxwell Anderson, Angie Dickinson, John Bernard Flannagan, Phil Jackson, Louis L'Amour, Peggy Lee, Eric Sevareid, Ann Sothern, Vilhjalmur Stefansson, Lawrence Welk.

Tourist information. North Dakota Tourism Division, Century Center, 1600 E. Century Ave., Ste. 2, P.O. Box 2057, Bismarck, ND 58502; 1-800-435-5663; www.ndtourism.com

Website. www.nd.gov

North Dakota (ND)
Peace Garden State

People. Population: 683,932; rank: 48. **Pop. change** (2000-11): 6.5%. **Pop. density:** 9.9 per sq mi. **Racial distribution:** 90.4% white; 1.3% black; 1.1% Asian; 5.5% Amer. Ind.; 0.1% Pac. Isl.; 2 or more races, 1.7%. **Hispanic pop.:** 2.2%.

Geography. Total area: 70,698 sq mi; rank: 19. **Land area:** 69,001 sq mi; rank: 17. **Acres forested:** 0.8 mil. **Location:** West North Central state, situated exactly in the middle of North America, bounded on the N by Canada, on the E by Minnesota, on the S by South Dakota, on the W by Montana. **Climate:** continental, with a wide range of temperature and moderate rainfall. **Topography:** Central Lowland in the E comprises the flat Red River Valley and the Rolling Drift Prairie; Missouri Plateau of the Great Plains on the W. **Capital:** Bismarck.

Economy. Chief industries: agriculture, mining, tourism, manufacturing, telecommunications, energy, food processing.

Ohio (OH)
Buckeye State

People. Population: 11,544,951; rank: 7. **Pop. change** (2000-11): 1.7%. **Pop. density:** 282.5 per sq mi. **Racial distribution:** 83.6% white; 12.4% black; 1.7% Asian; 0.3% Amer. Ind.; <0.05% Pac. Isl.; 2 or more races, 1.9%. **Hispanic pop.:** 3.2%.

Geography. Total area: 44,826 sq mi; rank: 34. **Land area:** 40,861 sq mi; rank: 35. **Acres forested:** 8.0 mil. **Location:** East North Central state bounded on the N by Michigan and Lake Erie; on the E and S by Pennsylvania, West Virginia, and Kentucky; on the W by Indiana. **Climate:** temperate but variable; weather subject to much precipitation. **Topography:** generally rolling plain; Allegheny plateau in E; Lake Erie plains extend southward; central plains in the W. **Capital:** Columbus. **Chief airports:** Akron, Cleveland, Columbus, Dayton.

Economy. Chief industries: manufacturing, trade, services. **Chief manuf. goods:** motor vehicles & parts, petroleum, plastics & rubber, iron & steel, aircraft, machinery, fabricated metal, printing. **Chief crops:** corn, soybeans, hay, wheat, grapes, potatoes, tomatoes, apples, strawberries, tobacco. **Livestock:** 35.98 mil chickens (excl. broilers), 59.6 mil broilers, 1.28 mil cattle/calves, 126,000 sheep/lambs, 170,000 hogs/pigs. **Broadband Internet:** 63.9%. **Nonfuel minerals:** $1.2 bil; stone (crushed), salt, sand and gravel (construction), lime, cement (portland). **Commercial fishing:** $4.0 mil. **Chief ports:** Cincinnati, Toledo, Conneaut, Cleveland, Ashtabula. **Gross state product:** $484.0 bil. **Sales tax:** 5.5%. **Employment distrib.:** 15.1% govt.; 18.8% trade/trans./util.; 12.6% mfg.; 16.8% ed./health; 12.6% prof./bus. serv.; 9.5% leisure/hosp.; 5.4% finance; 3.7% constr./mining/log.; 1.5% info.; 4.1% other serv. **Unemployment:** 8.6%. **Per cap. pers. income:** $37,791. **New private housing:** 13,762 units/$2.3 bil. **Commercial banks:** 167; deposits: $201.5 bil. **Savings institutions:** 96; deposits: $31.9 bil. **Lottery:** total sales: $2.6 bil; profit: $738.8 mil.

Federal govt. Fed. civ. employees: 52,590; **avg. salary:** $75,701. **Notable fed. facilities:** Wright-Patterson AFB; Defense Supply Ctr., Columbus; NASA Glenn Research Ctr.; Lima Army Tank Plant.

Energy. Monthly electricity use: 931 kWh, $105.33.

State data. Motto: With God, all things are possible. **Flower:** Scarlet carnation. **Bird:** Cardinal. **Tree:** Buckeye. **Song:** "Beautiful Ohio." **Entered union:** Mar. 1, 1803; rank: 17th. **State fair** at Columbus, late July-early Aug.

History. Paleo-Indians hunted in the area about 11,000 years ago; the Adena and Hopewell cultures followed. Wyandot, Delaware, Miami, and Shawnee peoples sparsely occupied the area when the first Europeans arrived. René-Robert Cavelier, sieur de La Salle visited the region, 1669. France claimed it, 1682, but ceded it to Britain, 1763. After the American Revolution, Ohio became part of the Northwest Territory, 1787. The first permanent settlement was at Marietta, 1788. Cincinnati was also founded, 1788; Cleveland, 1796. Indian warfare abated with the Treaty of Greenville, 1795. Ohio became a state, 1803. In the War of 1812, Oliver Hazard Perry's victory on Lake Erie and William Henry Harrison's invasion of Canada, 1813, ended British incursions. Columbus, founded 1812, became the state capital, 1816. Before the Civil War, Ohioans aided the Underground Railroad, helping runaway slaves. Agricultural for much of the 19th cent., the state became an industrial powerhouse in the 20th. Manufacturing jobs dropped by 24%, 1998-2007. No Republican has ever won the presidency without carrying Ohio, and the state's 20 electoral votes proved crucial to Pres. George W. Bush in 2004.

Tourist attractions. Mound City Group, Hopewell Culture Natl. Hist. Park; Neil Armstrong Air and Space Museum, Wapakoneta; Air Force Museum, Dayton; Pro Football Hall of Fame, Canton; King's Island amusement park, Mason; Lake Erie Islands, Cedar Point amusement park, in Sandusky; birthplaces, homes of, and memorials to U.S. Pres. W. H. Harrison, Grant, Garfield, Hayes, B. Harrison, McKinley, Harding, Taft; Amish Region, Tuscarawas/Holmes counties; German Village, Columbus; Jack Nicklaus' Golf Ctr., Mason; Bob Evans Farm, Rio Grande; Rock and Roll Hall of Fame and Museum, Cleveland.

Famous Ohioans. Sherwood Anderson, Neil Armstrong, George Bellows, Halle Berry, Ambrose Bierce, Erma Bombeck, Drew Carey, Hart Crane, George Custer, Clarence Darrow, Paul Laurence Dunbar, Thomas Edison, Clark Gable, John Glenn, Zane Grey, Bob Hope, William Dean Howells, Toni Morrison, Jack Nicklaus, Jesse Owens, Jack Paar, Pontiac, Eddie Rickenbacker, John D. Rockefeller Sr. and Jr., Roy Rogers, Pete Rose, Arthur Schlesinger Jr., Gen. William Sherman, Steven Spielberg, Gloria Steinem, Harriet Beecher Stowe, Charles Taft, Robert A. Taft, William H. Taft, Tecumseh, James Thurber, Ted Turner, Orville and Wilbur Wright.

Tourist information. Division of Travel and Tourism, P.O. Box 1001, Columbus, OH 43216; 1-800-BUCKEYE; www.discoverohio.com

Website. www.ohio.gov

Oklahoma (OK)

Sooner State

People. Population: 3,791,508; rank: 28. **Pop. change** (2000-11): 9.9%. **Pop. density:** 55.3 per sq mi. **Racial distribution:** 75.8% white; 7.7% black; 1.8% Asian; 8.9% Amer. Ind.; 0.1% Pac. Isl.; 2 or more races, 5.7%. **Hispanic pop.:** 9.2%.

Geography. Total area: 69,899 sq mi; rank: 20. **Land area:** 68,595 sq mi; rank: 19. **Acres forested:** 12.6 mil. **Location:** West South Central state bounded on the N by Colorado and Kansas; on the E by Missouri and Arkansas; on the S and W by Texas and New Mexico. **Climate:** temperate; southern humid belt merging with colder northern continental; humid eastern and dry western zones. **Topography:** high plains predominate in the W, hills and small mountains in the E; the E central region is dominated by the Arkansas R. Basin, and the Red R. Plains, in the S. **Capital:** Oklahoma City. **Chief airports:** Oklahoma City, Tulsa.

Economy. Chief industries: manufacturing, mineral and energy exploration and production, agriculture, services. **Chief manuf. goods:** animal slaughtering & processing, petroleum, plastics & rubber, fabricated metals, machinery, motor vehicles & parts. **Chief crops:** wheat, greenhouse & nursery, hay, cotton, corn, soybeans, pecans, sorghum, peanuts. **Livestock:** 4.26 mil chickens (excl. broilers), 214.7 mil broilers, 4.5 mil cattle/calves, 70,000 sheep/lambs, 410,000 hogs/pigs. **Broadband Internet:** 86.9%. **Nonfuel minerals:** $749 mil; stone (crushed), cement (portland), sand and gravel (construction), sand and gravel (industrial), iodine. **Chief port:** Catoosa. **Gross state product:** $155.0 bil. **Sales tax:** 4.5%. **Employment distrib.:** 21.7% govt.; 18.3% trade/trans./util.; 8.6% mfg.; 13.0% ed./health; 11.3% prof./bus. serv.; 9.1% leisure/hosp.; 5.1% finance; 7.8% constr./mining/log.; 1.5% info.; 3.8% other serv. **Unemployment:** 6.2%. **Per cap. pers. income:** $37,277. **New private housing:** 8,782 units/$1.3 bil. **Commercial banks:** 251; deposits: $65.1 bil. **Savings institutions:** 6; deposits: $6.1 bil. **Lottery:** total sales: $198.2 mil; profit: $69.4 mil.

Federal govt. Fed. civ. employees: 39,341; **avg. salary:** $64,247. **Notable fed. facilities:** Tinker AFB; FAA Mike Monroney Aeronautical Ctr.; Ft. Sill; Altus AFB; McAlester Army Ammunition Plant; Vance AFB; Natl. Severe Storms Lab.

Energy. Monthly electricity use: 1,189 kWh, $108.61.

State data. Motto: Labor Omnia Vincit (Labor conquers all things). **Flower:** Mistletoe. **Bird:** Scissor-tailed flycatcher. **Tree:** Redbud. **Song:** "Oklahoma!" **Entered union:** Nov. 16, 1907; rank: 46th. **State fair** at Oklahoma City, mid-Sept.; at Tulsa, 4th Thurs. after Labor Day-2nd Sun. of Oct.

History. Few Native Americans inhabited the region when the Spanish explorer Coronado arrived, 1541; in the 16th and 17th cent., French traders visited. Part of the Louisiana Purchase, 1803, Oklahoma was known as Indian Country and, from 1834, Indian Territory. It became home to the "Five Civilized Tribes"—Cherokee, Choctaw, Chickasaw, Creek, and Seminole—after the forced removal of Indians from the eastern U.S., 1828-46. The land was also used by Comanche, Osage, and other Plains Indians. As white settlers pressed west, land was opened for homesteading by "runs" and lottery. The first run was in 1889; the most famous run, 1893, was to the Cherokee Outlet. Oklahoma became a state, 1907. In the early 20th cent., oil finds brought wealth to the Tulsa area; the Greenwood section of the city, then known as the "Negro Wall Street," was devastated by a white mob, 1921. Depression and drought drove many "Okies" from the Dust Bowl to California in the 1930s. A truck bomb in Oklahoma City, 1995, destroyed a federal office building, killing 168 people; Timothy McVeigh was executed for the crime, 2001.

Tourist attractions. Cherokee Heritage Ctr., Tahlequah; Oklahoma City Natl. Memorial; Natl. Cowboy Hall of Fame, Remington Park Race Track, White Water Bay and Frontier City theme parks, in Oklahoma City; Will Rogers Memorial, Claremore; Ft. Gibson; Ouachita Natl. Forest; Philbrook Museum of Art, Gilcrease Museum, in Tulsa; Tulsa's art deco district; Wichita Mts. Wildlife Refuge; Woolaroc Museum and Wildlife Preserve, Bartlesville; Sequoyah's Home Site, Sallisaw.

Famous Oklahomans. Troy Aikman, Carl Albert, Gene Autry, Johnny Bench, William "Hopalong Cassidy" Boyd, Garth Brooks, Lon Chaney, L. Gordon Cooper, Walter Cronkite, Jerome "Dizzy" Dean, Ralph Ellison, John Hope Franklin, James Garner, Geronimo, Woody Guthrie, Paul Harvey, Ron Howard, Gen. Patrick J. Hurley, Ben Johnson, Jeane Kirkpatrick, Louis L'Amour, Shannon Lucid, Mickey

Mantle, Reba McEntire, Wiley Post, Tony Randall, Oral Roberts, Will Rogers, Sam Snead, Barry Switzer, Maria Tallchief, Jim Thorpe, J. C. Watts Jr.

Tourist information. Travel and Tourism Division, 120 N. Robinson, 6th Fl., P.O. Box 52002, Oklahoma City, OK 73152-2002; 1-800-652-6552; www.travelok.com

Website. www.ok.gov

Oregon (OR)
Beaver State

People. Population: 3,871,859; rank: 27. **Pop. change** (2000-11): 13.2%. **Pop. density:** 40.3 per sq mi. **Racial distribution:** 88.6% white; 2.0% black; 3.9% Asian; 1.8% Amer. Ind.; 0.4% Pac. Isl.; 2 or more races, 3.4%. **Hispanic pop.:** 12.0%.

Geography. Total area: 98,379 sq mi; rank: 9. **Land area:** 95,988 sq mi; rank: 10. **Acres forested:** 30.0 mil. **Location:** Pacific state, bounded on N by Washington; on E by Idaho; on S by Nevada and California; on W by the Pacific. **Climate:** coastal mild and humid climate; continental dryness and extreme temperatures in the interior. **Topography:** Coast Range of rugged mountains; fertile Willamette R. Valley to E and S; Cascade Mt. Range of volcanic peaks E of the valley; plateau E of Cascades, remaining two-thirds of state. **Capital:** Salem. **Chief airport:** Portland.

Economy. Chief industries: manufacturing, services, trade, finance, insurance, real estate, government, construction. **Chief manuf. goods:** wood prods., frozen produce, printing, computers & electronics, transportation equip., industrial machinery. **Chief crops:** greenhouse & nursery, grass seed, hay, wheat, potatoes, Christmas trees, onions, pears, hazelnuts, corn, grapes, cherries, blackberries, blueberries, peppermint, snap beans, apples, hops. **Livestock:** 2.94 mil chickens (excl. broilers), 1.3 mil cattle/calves, 200,000 sheep/lambs. **Broadband Internet:** 77.3%. **Nonfuel minerals:** $297 mil; stone (crushed), sand and gravel (construction), cement (portland), diatomite, perlite (crude). **Commercial fishing:** $104.7 mil. **Chief ports:** Portland, Coos Bay. **Gross state product:** $194.8 bil. **Sales tax:** none. **Employment distrib.:** 18.4% govt.; 19.3% trade/trans./util.; 10.1% mfg.; 14.5% ed./health; 11.4% prof./bus. serv.; 10.3% leisure/hosp.; 5.6% finance; 4.6% constr./mining/log.; 2.0% info.; 3.7% other serv. **Unemployment:** 9.5%. **Per cap. pers. income:** $37,909. **New private housing:** 7,663 units/$1.4 bil. **Commercial banks:** 51; deposits: $58.3 bil. **Savings institutions:** 8; deposits: $2.2 bil. **Lottery:** total sales: $2.8 bil; profit: $559.9 mil.

Federal govt. Fed. civ. employees: 20,285; **avg. salary:** $69,960. **Notable fed. facilities:** Bonneville Power Admin.

Energy. Monthly electricity use: 964 kWh, $85.52.

State data. Motto: She flies with her own wings. **Flower:** Oregon grape. **Bird:** Western meadowlark. **Tree:** Douglas fir. **Song:** "Oregon, My Oregon." **Entered union:** Feb. 14, 1859; rank: 33rd. **State fair** at Salem, 11 days ending with Labor Day.

History. More than 100 Native American tribes inhabited the area at the time of European contact, including the Chinook, Yakima, Cayuse, Modoc, and Nez Percé. Capt. Robert Gray sighted and sailed into the Columbia R., 1792. Lewis and Clark, traveling overland, wintered at its mouth, 1805-06. Fur traders sent by John Jacob Astor established the Astoria trading post in the Columbia River region, 1811. Settlers arrived in the Willamette Valley, 1834. In 1843, the first large wave of settlers arrived via the Oregon Trail. Oregon became a territory, 1848, and a state, 1859. Early in the 20th cent., the "Oregon System"—political reforms that included initiative, referendum, recall, direct primary, and woman suffrage—was adopted. Originally dominated by forest products, the economy diversified after World War II, with high-tech firms clustering in the "Silicon Forest" area around Portland. Oregonians were the first in the U.S. to pass measures allowing physician-assisted suicide for terminally ill patients, 1994, and establishing an all-mail voting system, 1998.

Tourist attractions. John Day Fossil Beds Natl. Monument; Columbia River Gorge; Timberline Lodge, Mt. Hood Natl. Forest; Crater Lake Natl. Park; Oregon Dunes Natl. Recreation Area; Ft. Clatsop Natl. Memorial; Oregon Caves Natl. Monument; Oregon Museum of Science and Industry,

Portland; Shakespeare Festival, Ashland; High Desert Museum, Bend; Multnomah Falls; Diamond Lake; "Spruce Goose," Evergreen Aviation Museum, McMinnville.

Famous Oregonians. Ernest Bloch, Bill Bowerman, Ernest Haycox, Chief Joseph, Ken Kesey, Phil Knight, Ursula K. Le Guin, Edwin Markham, Tom McCall, Dr. John McLoughlin, Joaquin Miller, Bob Packwood, Linus Pauling, Steve Prefontaine, John Reed, Alberto Salazar, Mary Decker Slaney, William Simon U'Ren.

Tourist information. Travel Oregon, 670 Hawthorne SE, Ste. 240, Salem, OR 97301; 1-800-547-7842; www.traveloregon.com

Website. www.oregon.gov

Pennsylvania (PA)
Keystone State

People. Population: 12,742,886; rank: 6. **Pop. change** (2000-11): 3.8%. **Pop. density:** 284.8 per sq mi. **Racial distribution:** 83.8% white; 11.3% black; 2.9% Asian; 0.3% Amer. Ind.; 0.1% Pac. Isl.; 2 or more races, 1.6%. **Hispanic pop.:** 5.9%.

Geography. Total area: 46,054 sq mi; rank: 33. **Land area:** 44,743 sq mi; rank: 32. **Acres forested:** 16.7 mil. **Location:** Middle Atlantic state, bordered on the E by the Delaware R.; on the S by the Mason-Dixon Line; on the W by West Virginia and Ohio; on the N/NE by Lake Erie and New York. **Climate:** continental with wide fluctuations in seasonal temperatures. **Topography:** Allegheny Mts. run SW-NE, with Piedmont and Coast Plain in the SE triangle; Allegheny Front a diagonal spine across the state's center; N and W rugged plateau falls to Lake Erie Lowland. **Capital:** Harrisburg. **Chief airports:** Harrisburg, Philadelphia, Pittsburgh.

Economy. Chief industries: agribusiness, advanced manufacturing, health care, travel & tourism, depository institutions, biotechnology, printing & publishing, research & consulting, trucking & warehousing, transportation by air, engineering & management, legal services. **Chief manuf. goods:** petroleum, pharmaceuticals, plastics, iron & steel, printing, paper & paperboard, confectionery & snacks, animal slaughtering & processing. **Chief crops:** greenhouse & nursery, mushrooms, corn, hay, soybeans, apples, tomatoes, wheat, grapes, peaches, potatoes, strawberries, tobacco. **Livestock:** 28.89 mil chickens (excl. broilers), 155.6 mil broilers, 1.61 mil cattle/calves, 89,000 sheep/lambs, 100,000 hogs/pigs. **Broadband Internet:** 72.5%. **Nonfuel minerals:** $1.6 bil; stone (crushed), cement (portland), lime, sand and gravel (construction), cement (masonry). **Commercial fishing:** $192,000. **Chief ports:** Philadelphia, Pittsburgh. **Gross state product:** $578.8 bil. **Sales tax:** 6.0%. **Employment distrib.:** 13.0% govt.; 19.2% trade/trans./util.; 9.9% mfg.; 20.1% ed./health; 12.5% prof./bus. serv.; 9.4% leisure/hosp.; 5.4% finance; 4.5% constr./mining/log.; 1.6% info.; 4.4% other serv. **Unemployment:** 7.9%. **Per cap. pers. income:** $42,478. **New private housing:** 14,967 units/$2.5 bil. **Commercial banks:** 161; deposits: $231.7 bil. **Savings institutions:** 88; deposits: $68.5 bil. **Lottery:** total sales: $3.2 bil; profit: $960.6 mil.

Federal govt. Fed. civ. employees: 68,164; **avg. salary:** $69,054. **Notable fed. facilities:** Army War College, Carlisle Barracks; NAVSUP Weapon Systems Support, Mechanicsburg; Philadelphia Mint, Defense Supply Ctr., Naval Surface Warfare Ctr., in Phila.; Defense Distribution Ctr. Susquehanna, New Cumberland; Tobyhanna Army Depot; Letterkenny Army Depot.

Energy. Monthly electricity use: 878 kWh, $111.50.

State data. Motto: Virtue, liberty, and independence. **Flower:** Mountain laurel. **Bird:** Ruffed grouse. **Tree:** Hemlock. **Song:** "Pennsylvania." **Second** of the original 13 states to ratify the Constitution, Dec. 12, 1787. **State fair:** no official state fair; county and community fairs, Mar.-Oct.

History. When Europeans came, Algonquian-speaking Lenni Lenape (Delaware) and Shawnee and the Iroquoian Susquehannocks, Erie, and Seneca occupied the region. Swedish explorers made the first permanent settlement, 1643, on Tinicum Island. The Dutch seized the settlement, 1655, but lost it to the British, 1664. The region was given by Charles II to William Penn, 1681. Philadelphia ("brotherly love") was the capital of the colonies during most of the American Revolution, and of the U.S., 1790-1800; the Declaration of Independence, 1776, and Constitution, 1787, were signed here. Philadelphia was taken by the British, 1777; George Washington's troops encamped at Valley Forge in the bitter winter of 1777-78. Slavery was abolished, 1780. Union victory at the Battle of Gettysburg, July 1-3, 1863, marked a turning point in the Civil War. A dam collapse at Johnstown, 1889, killed at least 2,200 people. From the late 19th to the mid-20th cent., Pittsburgh prospered from coal and steel; later, heavy industry declined, but the city revived as a hub of finance, health care, and research. The Three Mile Island nuclear plant near Harrisburg had a near-meltdown, 1979. One of 4 hijacked planes on Sept. 11, 2001, crashed near Shanksville; a national memorial was designated on the site in 2002.

Tourist attractions. Independence Natl. Historic Park; Franklin Institute Science Museum, Philadelphia Museum of Art, in Philadelphia; Valley Forge Natl. Historic Park; Gettysburg Natl. Military Park; Pennsylvania Dutch Country; Hershey; Duquesne Incline, Carnegie Institute, Heinz Hall, in Pittsburgh; Pocono Mts.; Pennsylvania's Grand Canyon, Tioga County; Allegheny Natl. Forest; Laurel Highlands; Presque Isle State Park; Fallingwater, Mill Run; Johnstown; Steamtown, Scranton; U.S. Brig *Niagara*, Erie; Oil Heritage Region, Northwest PA.

Famous Pennsylvanians. Marian Anderson, Maxwell Anderson, George Blanda, James Buchanan, Andrew Carnegie, Rachel Carson, Perry Como, Bill Cosby, Thomas Eakins, Stephen Foster, Benjamin Franklin, Robert Fulton, Martha Graham, Milton Hershey, Gene Kelly, Grace Kelly (Princess Grace of Monaco), Dan Marino, George C. Marshall, Chris Matthews, John J. McCloy, Margaret Mead, Andrew W. Mellon, Joe Montana, Stan Musial, Joe Namath, John O'Hara, Arnold Palmer, Robert E. Peary, Mike Piazza, Tom Ridge, Mary Roberts Rinehart, Fred Rogers, Betsy Ross, Will Smith, Jimmy Stewart, Jim Thorpe, Johnny Unitas, John Updike, Honus Wagner, Andy Warhol, Benjamin West.

Tourist information. Pennsylvania Tourism Office, Department of Community and Economic Development, Commonwealth Keystone Building, 4th Fl., 400 North St., Harrisburg, PA 17120-0225; 1-800-VISITPA; www.visitpa.com

Website. www.pa.gov

Rhode Island (RI)
Little Rhody, Ocean State

People. Population: 1,051,302; rank: 43. **Pop. change** (2000-11): 0.3%. **Pop. density:** 1,016.9 per sq mi. **Racial distribution:** 86.3% white; 7.2% black; 3.1% Asian; 0.9% Amer. Ind.; 0.2% Pac. Isl.; 2 or more races, 2.4%. **Hispanic pop.:** 12.8%.

Geography. Total area: 1,545 sq mi; rank: 50. **Land area:** 1,034 sq mi; rank: 50. **Acres forested:** 0.4 mil. **Location:** New England state. **Climate:** invigorating and changeable. **Topography:** eastern lowlands of Narragansett Basin; western uplands of flat and rolling hills. **Capital:** Providence. **Chief airport:** Warwick.

Economy. Chief industries: services, manufacturing. **Chief manuf. goods:** plastics, fabricated metals, electrical equip., jewelry. **Chief crops:** greenhouse & nursery, sweet corn, berries, potatoes, apples, hay. **Livestock:** 4,500 cattle/calves. **Broadband Internet:** 75.2%. **Nonfuel minerals:** $27.7 mil; stone (crushed), sand and gravel (construction), sand and gravel (industrial), gemstones (natural). **Commercial fishing:** $62.7 mil. **Chief ports:** Providence, Davisville, Newport. **Gross state product:** $50.1 bil. **Sales tax:** 7.0%. **Employment distrib.:** 13.3% govt.; 15.7% trade/trans./util.; 8.8% mfg.; 22.7% ed./health; 11.7% prof./bus. serv.; 10.8% leisure/hosp.; 6.6% finance; 3.5% constr./mining/log.; 2.3% info.; 4.6% other serv. **Unemployment:** 11.3%. **Per cap. pers. income:** $43,992. **New private housing:** 700 units/$129.3 mil. **Commercial banks:** 12; deposits: $38.9 bil. **Savings institutions:** 14; deposits: $4.8 bil. **Lottery:** total sales: $3.1 bil; profit: $354.9 mil.

Federal govt. Fed. civ. employees 7,311; **avg. salary:** $84,180. **Notable fed. facilities:** Naval War College; Naval Undersea Warfare Ctr.; EPA Atlantic Ecology Div. Lab.

Energy. Monthly electricity use: 603 kWh, $96.08.

State data. Motto: Hope. **Flower:** Violet. **Bird:** Rhode Island red chicken. **Tree:** Red maple. **Song:** "Rhode Island." **Thirteenth** of original 13 states to ratify the Constitution,

May 29, 1790. **State fair:** none; largest fair at Richmond, mid-Aug.

History. When Europeans arrived, Narragansett, Niantic, Nipmuc, and Wampanoag peoples lived in the region. Verrazano visited the area, 1524. The first permanent settlement was founded at Providence, 1636, by Roger Williams, who was exiled from the Massachusetts Bay Colony; Anne Hutchinson, also exiled, settled Portsmouth, 1638. Quaker and Jewish immigrants seeking freedom of worship began arriving, 1650s-60s. The colonists broke the power of the Narragansett in the Great Swamp Fight, 1675, the decisive battle in King Philip's War. The colony was the first to formally renounce all allegiance to King George III, May 4, 1776. Initially opposed to joining the Union, Rhode Island was the last of the 13 colonies to ratify the Constitution, 1790. Trade, textiles, and metal goods dominated the economy in the 19th cent., and Newport became a fashionable resort after the Civil War. The U.S. Navy was the state's largest civilian employer, 1945-73, until the destroyer force was relocated from Newport. A nightclub fire in West Warwick killed 100 people in 2003.

Tourist attractions. Newport mansions; yachting races, including Newport to Bermuda; Block Island; Touro Synagogue (oldest in U.S.) Newport; First Baptist Church in America, Providence; Slater Mill Historic Site, Pawtucket; Gilbert Stuart birthplace, Saunderstown.

Famous Rhode Islanders. Ambrose Burnside, George M. Cohan, Nelson Eddy, Jabez Gorham, Nathanael Greene, Christopher and Oliver La Farge, John McLaughlin, Matthew C. and Oliver Hazard Perry, Gilbert Stuart.

Tourist information. Rhode Island Tourism Division, 315 Iron Horse Way, Ste. 101, Providence, RI 02908; 1-800-556-2484; www.visitrhodeisland.com

Website. www.ri.gov

South Carolina (SC)
Palmetto State

People. Population: 4,679,230; rank: 24. **Pop. change** (2000-11): 16.6%. **Pop. density:** 155.7 per sq mi. **Racial distribution:** 68.4% white; 28.1% black; 1.4% Asian; 0.5% Amer. Ind.; 0.1% Pac. Isl.; 2 or more races, 1.5%. **Hispanic pop.:** 5.3%.

Geography. Total area: 32,020 sq mi; rank: 40. **Land area:** 30,061 sq mi; rank: 40. **Acres forested:** 13.1 mil. **Location:** South Atlantic state, bordered by North Carolina on the N; Georgia on the SW and W; the Atlantic Ocean on the E, SE, and S. **Climate:** humid subtropical. **Topography:** Blue Ridge province in NW has highest peaks; piedmont lies between the mountains and the fall line; coastal plain covers two-thirds of the state. **Capital:** Columbia. **Chief airports:** Charleston, Greer, Myrtle Beach.

Economy. Chief industries: tourism, agriculture, manufacturing. **Chief manuf. goods:** chemicals & synthetics, motor vehicles & parts, plastics, paper & paper prods., turbines, rubber, textiles. **Chief crops:** greenhouse & nursery, tobacco, soybeans, cotton, corn, peaches, wheat, tomatoes, peanuts. **Livestock:** 5.83 mil chickens (excl. broilers), 223.4 mil broilers, 370,000 cattle/calves. **Broadband Internet:** 66.0%. **Nonfuel minerals:** $502 mil; cement (portland), stone (crushed), sand and gravel (construction), cement (masonry), sand and gravel (industrial). **Commercial fishing:** $21.2 mil. **Chief ports:** Charleston, Georgetown. **Gross state product:** $165.8 bil. **Sales tax:** 6.0%. **Employment distrib.:** 18.5% govt.; 19.1% trade/trans./util.; 11.8% mfg.; 11.8% ed./health; 12.6% prof./bus. serv.; 11.7% leisure/hosp.; 5.1% finance; 4.2% constr./mining/log.; 1.4% info.; 3.7% other serv. **Unemployment:** 10.3%. **Per cap. pers. income:** $33,673. **New private housing:** 15,542 units/$2.8 bil. **Commercial banks:** 83; deposits: $62.7 bil. **Savings institutions:** 23; deposits: $5.2 bil. **Lottery:** total sales: $1.0 bil; profit: $271.1 mil.

Federal govt. Fed. civ. employees: 22,219; **avg. salary:** $66,179. **Notable fed. facilities:** Ft. Jackson; Joint Base Charleston; Marine Corps Recruit Depot Parris Island; Shaw AFB; USMC Air Station Beaufort; Savannah River Site.

Energy. Monthly electricity use: 1,310 kWh, $137.59.

State data. Motto: Dum Spiro Spero (While I breathe, I hope). **Flower:** Yellow jessamine. **Bird:** Carolina wren. **Tree:** Palmetto. **Song:** "Carolina." **Eighth** of the original 13 states to ratify the Constitution, May 23, 1788. **State fair** at Columbia, mid-Oct.; at Aiken, mid-late Oct.

History. When Europeans arrived, Cherokee, Catawba, and Muskogean peoples lived in the area. Spanish and French came in the 16th cent. The first English colonists settled near the Ashley R., 1670, and moved to the site of present-day Charleston, 1680. The colonists seized the government, 1775, and the royal governor fled. The British took Charleston, 1780, but were defeated at Kings Mountain that same year, and at Cowpens, 1781. In the 1830s, South Carolinians, angered by federal protective tariffs, adopted the Nullification Doctrine, holding that a state can void an act of Congress. Plantation agriculture relied on slave labor to cultivate rice and cotton; slaves made up 57% of the population in 1860, when South Carolina was the first state to secede from the Union. Confederate troops fired on and forced the surrender of U.S. troops at Ft. Sumter, in Charleston Harbor, 1861, launching the Civil War. The state was readmitted to the Union, 1868. Strom Thurmond, who ran for president as a segregationist in 1948, later served 48 years in the U.S. Senate (1955-2003). Formerly dependent on textiles, the state has attracted new industries by courting foreign investment.

Tourist attractions. Historic Charleston, Charleston Museum (est. 1773, oldest in U.S.); Ft. Sumter Natl. Monument, in Charleston Harbor; Middleton Place, Magnolia Plantation, Cypress Gardens, Drayton Hall, all near Charleston; other gardens at Brookgreen, Edisto, Glencairn; Myrtle Beach; Hilton Head Island; Revolutionary War battle sites; Andrew Jackson State Park; SC State Museum, Riverbanks Zoo Columbia.

Famous South Carolinians. Charles Bolden, James F. Byrnes, John C. Calhoun, Joe Frazier, DuBose Heyward, Ernest F. Hollings, Andrew Jackson, Jesse Jackson, "Shoeless" Joe Jackson, James Longstreet, Francis Marion, Andie McDowell, Ronald McNair, Charles Pinckney, John Rutledge, Thomas Sumter, Strom Thurmond, John B. Watson.

Tourist information. SC Dept. of Parks, Recreation, & Tourism, 1205 Pendleton St., Columbia, SC 29201; 1-866-224-9339; (803) 734-1700; www.discoversouthcarolina.com

Website. www.sc.gov

South Dakota (SD)
Coyote State, Mount Rushmore State

People. Population: 824,082; rank: 46. **Pop. change** (2000-11): 9.2%. **Pop. density:** 10.9 per sq mi. **Racial distribution:** 86.6% white; 1.4% black; 1.0% Asian; 8.9% Amer. Ind.; 0.1% Pac. Isl.; 2 or more races, 2.0%. **Hispanic pop.:** 2.9%.

Geography. Total area: 77,116 sq mi; rank: 17. **Land area:** 75,811 sq mi; rank: 16. **Acres forested:** 1.9 mil. **Location:** West North Central state bounded on the N by North Dakota; on the E by Minnesota and Iowa; on the S by Nebraska; on the W by Wyoming and Montana. **Climate:** characterized by extremes of temperature, persistent winds, low precipitation and humidity. **Topography:** Prairie Plains in the E; rolling hills of the Great Plains in the W; the Black Hills, rising 3,500 ft, in the SW corner. **Capital:** Pierre.

Economy. Chief industries: agriculture, services, manufacturing. **Chief manuf. goods:** animal slaughtering, machinery, semiconductors, surgical appliances. **Chief crops:** corn, soybeans, wheat, hay, sunflowers, sorghum, oats, barley. **Livestock:** 2.77 mil chickens (excl. broilers), 3.65 mil cattle/calves, 285,000 sheep/lambs, 180,000 hogs/pigs. **Broadband Internet:** 66.7%. **Nonfuel minerals:** $320 mil; sand and gravel (construction), gold, cement (portland), stone (crushed), lime. **Gross state product:** $40.1 bil. **Sales tax:** 4.0%. **Employment distrib.:** 19.2% govt.; 20.1% trade/trans./util.; 9.7% mfg.; 16.2% ed./health; 7.1% prof./bus. serv.; 10.3% leisure/hosp.; 6.8% finance; 5.3% constr./mining/log.; 1.5% info.; 3.7% other serv. **Unemployment:** 4.7%. **Per cap. pers. income:** $41,590. **New private housing:** 2,813 units/$391.9 mil. **Commercial banks:** 86; deposits: $83 bil. **Savings institutions:** 6; deposits: $1.9 bil. **Lottery:** total sales: $630.5 mil; profit: $105.2 mil.

Federal govt. Fed. civ. employees: 8,556; **avg. salary:** $60,409. **Notable fed. facilities:** Ellsworth AFB.

Energy. Monthly electricity use: 1,041 kWh, $93.40.

State data. Motto: Under God, the people rule. **Flower:** Pasqueflower. **Bird:** Chinese ring-necked pheasant. **Tree:**

Black Hills spruce. **Song:** "Hail, South Dakota." **Entered union:** Nov. 2, 1889; rank: 40th. **State fair** at Huron, late Aug.-early Sept.

History. Paleo-Indians hunted in the region at least 11,500 years ago. At the time of first European contact, Mandan, Hidatsa, Arikara, and Sioux lived in the area. The French Vérendrye brothers explored the region, 1742-43. The U.S. acquired the territory in the Louisiana Purchase, 1803, and Meriwether Lewis and William Clark passed through, 1804-06. In 1817 a trading post opened at what would become Ft. Pierre. Dakota Territory was established, 1861. Gold was discovered, 1874, in the Black Hills on Sioux land; the "Great Dakota Boom" began in 1879. South Dakota became a state, 1889. The massacre of Native American families at Wounded Knee, 1890, ended Sioux resistance; 83 years later, armed supporters of the American Indian Movement, a Native American rights group, occupied the area, leading to a 70-day standoff. Major economic activities include agribusiness and, since the 1980s, credit card services. Republicans scored a key election victory, 2004, with the defeat of 3-term U.S. Sen. Tom Daschle, a national Democratic leader.

Tourist attractions. Black Hills; Mt. Rushmore; Needles Highway; Harney Peak, tallest E of Rockies; Deadwood, 1876 Gold Rush town; Custer State Park; Jewel Cave Natl. Monument; Badlands Natl. Park "moonscape"; "Great Lakes of S. Dakota"; Ft. Sisseton; Great Plains Zoo and Museum, Sioux Falls; Corn Palace, Mitchell; Wind Cave Natl. Park; Crazy Horse Memorial, mountain carving in progress.

Famous South Dakotans. Sparky Anderson, Black Elk, Bob Barker, Tom Brokaw, Crazy Horse, Thomas Daschle, Myron Floren, Mary Hart, Cheryl Ladd, Dr. Ernest O. Lawrence, George McGovern, Billy Mills, Allen Neuharth, Pat O'Brien, Sitting Bull.

Tourist information. Department of Tourism and State Development, Capitol Lake Plaza, 711 E. Wells Ave., c/o 500 E. Capitol Ave., Pierre, SD 57501; 1-800-SDAKOTA; www.travelsd.com

Website. www.sd.gov

Tennessee (TN)
Volunteer State

People. Population: 6,403,353; rank: 17. **Pop. change** (2000-11): 12.6%. **Pop. density:** 155.3 per sq mi. **Racial distribution:** 79.5% white; 16.9% black; 1.5% Asian; 0.4% Amer. Ind.; 0.1% Pac. Isl.; 2 or more races, 1.6%. **Hispanic pop.:** 4.7%.

Geography. Total area: 42,144 sq mi; rank: 36. **Land area:** 41,235 sq mi; rank: 34. **Acres forested:** 13.9 mil. **Location:** East South Central state bounded on the N by Kentucky and Virginia; on the E by North Carolina; on the S by Georgia, Alabama, and Mississippi; on the W by Arkansas and Missouri. **Climate:** humid continental to the N; humid subtropical to the S. **Topography:** rugged country in the E; the Great Smoky Mts. of the Unakas; low ridges of the Appalachian Valley; the flat Cumberland Plateau; slightly rolling terrain and knobs of the Interior Low Plateau, the largest region; Eastern Gulf Coastal Plain to the W, laced with streams; Mississippi Alluvial Plain, a narrow strip of swamp and flood plain in the extreme W. **Capital:** Nashville. **Chief airports:** Alcoa, Memphis, Nashville.

Economy. Chief industries: manufacturing, trade, services, tourism, finance, insurance, real estate. **Chief manuf. goods:** motor vehicles & parts, computers & electronics, food, chemicals, plastics, printing, appliances, aluminum. **Chief crops:** greenhouse & nursery, soybeans, cotton, corn, tobacco, hay, tomatoes, wheat. **Livestock:** 2.58 mil chickens (excl. broilers), 190.3 mil broilers, 1.97 mil cattle/calves, 35,000 sheep/lambs. **Broadband Internet:** 67.6%. **Nonfuel minerals:** $848 mil; stone (crushed), zinc, cement (portland), sand and gravel (construction), sand and gravel (industrial). **Chief ports:** Memphis, Nashville, Chattanooga. **Gross state product:** $266.5 bil. **Sales tax:** 7.0%. **Employment distrib.:** 16.5% govt.; 20.7% trade/trans./util.; 11.6% mfg.; 14.4% ed./health; 12.0% prof./bus. serv.; 10.2% leisure/hosp.; 5.0% finance; 4.3% constr./mining/log.; 1.6% info.; 3.8% other serv. **Unemployment:** 9.2%. **Per cap. pers. income:** $36,533. **New private housing:** 14,977 units/$2.4 bil. **Commercial banks:** 212; deposits: $112.3 bil. **Savings**

institutions: 18; deposits: $4.4 bil. **Lottery:** total sales: $1.2 bil; profit: $293.5 mil.

Federal govt. Fed. civ. employees 28,498; **avg. salary:** $66,283. **Notable fed. facilities:** Tennessee Valley Authority; Oak Ridge Natl. Lab; Arnold Engineering Development Ctr.; Ft. Campbell; NSA Mid-South, Millington.

Energy. Monthly electricity use: 1,393 kWh, $128.58.

State data. Motto: Agriculture and commerce. **Flower:** Iris. **Bird:** Mockingbird. **Tree:** Tulip poplar. **Songs:** "My Homeland, Tennessee"; "When It's Iris Time in Tennessee"; "My Tennessee"; "Tennessee Waltz"; "Rocky Top"; "Smoky Mountain Rain." **Entered union:** June 1, 1796; rank: 16th. **State fair** at Nashville, early-mid Sept.; at Jackson, mid-Sept.

History. Inhabited for at least 20,000 years, the region was home to Creek and Yuchi peoples when the first Europeans arrived; the Cherokee moved into the region in the early 18th cent. Spanish explorers visited the area, 1540. English traders crossed the Great Smoky Mtns. from the east, while France's Marquette and Jolliet sailed down the Mississippi on the west, 1673. The first permanent settlement was of Virginians on the Watauga R., 1769. After the American Revolution, in which Tennesseans fought in eastern campaigns, the region became a territory, 1790, and a state, 1796. Slavery was widespread in western Tennessee, where cotton was the main crop, but much less common in the east. The state seceded, 1861, and saw many Civil War engagements; some 187,000 Tennesseans fought for the Confederacy and 51,000 for the Union. Tennessee was readmitted in 1866, the only former Confederate state not to have a postwar military government. The famous Scopes trial, 1925, questioned the teaching of evolution in public schools. In the 1930s, the Tennessee Valley Authority, a federal program, brought electric power to rural areas. Nashville became the capital of country music, while Memphis fostered the blues and, with Elvis Presley in the 1950s, rock 'n' roll. Martin Luther King Jr. was assassinated in Memphis, 1968. Since the 1970s, auto plants have become major employers, as has Federal Express. Al Gore Jr., U.S. vice pres. (1993-2001), lost his 2000 presidential bid partly because he failed to carry his home state of Tennessee. Record amounts of rainfall flooded parts of Tennessee, including Nashville, in May 2010.

Tourist attractions. Reelfoot Lake; Lookout Mountain, Tennessee Aquarium, Chattanooga; Fall Creek Falls; Great Smoky Mts. Natl. Park; Lost Sea, Sweetwater; Cherokee Natl. Forest; Cumberland Gap Natl. Park; Andrew Jackson's home, the Hermitage, near Nashville; homes of Pres. Polk and Andrew Johnson; American Museum of Science and Energy, Oak Ridge; Parthenon, Grand Old Opry, Opryland USA, Nashville; Dollywood theme park, Pigeon Forge; Graceland, home of Elvis Presley, Memphis; Alex Haley Home and Museum, Henning; Casey Jones Village, Jackson.

Famous Tennesseans. Roy Acuff, Davy Crockett, David Farragut, Ernie Ford, Aretha Franklin, Morgan Freeman, Bill Frist, Al Gore Jr., Alex Haley, William C. Handy, Sam Houston, Cordell Hull, Andrew Jackson, Andrew Johnson, Casey Jones, Estes Kefauver, Grace Moore, Dolly Parton, Minnie Pearl, James Polk, Elvis Presley, Dinah Shore, Bessie Smith, Fred Thompson, Hank Williams Jr., Alvin York.

Tourist information. Dept. of Tourist Development, Wm. Snodgrass/Tennessee Tower, 312 Rosa L. Parks Ave., 25th Fl., Nashville, TN 37243; 1-800-462-8366; www.tnvacation.com

Website. www.tn.gov

Texas (TX)
Lone Star State

People. Population: 25,674,681; rank: 2. **Pop. change** (2000-11): 23.1%. **Pop. density:** 98.3 per sq mi. **Racial distribution:** 80.9% white; 12.2% black; 4.0% Asian; 1.0% Amer. Ind.; 0.1% Pac. Isl.; 2 or more races, 1.7%. **Hispanic pop.:** 38.1%.

Geography. Total area: 268,596 sq mi; rank: 2. **Land area:** 261,232 sq mi; rank: 2. **Acres forested:** 12.0 mil. **Location:** southwestern state, bounded on the SE by the Gulf of Mexico; on the SW by Mexico, separated by the Rio Grande; surrounding states are Louisiana, Arkansas, Oklahoma, New Mexico. **Climate:** extremely varied; driest region is the Trans-Pecos; wettest is the NE. **Topography:** Gulf Coast Plain in the S and SE; North Central Plains slope upward with some hills; the

Great Plains extend over the Panhandle, are broken by low mountains; the Trans-Pecos is the southern extension of the Rockies. **Capital:** Austin. **Chief airports:** Austin, Dallas, El Paso, Ft. Worth, Houston (2), Lubbock, San Antonio.

Economy. Chief industries: manufacturing, trade, oil and gas extraction, services. **Chief manuf. goods:** petroleum, chemicals & resins, computers & electronics, animal slaughtering & processing, plastics, aerospace. **Chief crops:** cotton, greenhouse & nursery, corn, wheat, sorghum, hay, peanuts, onions, rice, pecans, grapefruit. **Livestock:** 23.61 mil chickens (excl. broilers), 630.5 mil broilers, 11.9 mil cattle/calves, 650,000 sheep/lambs, 100,000 hogs/pigs. **Broadband Internet:** 81.7%. **Nonfuel minerals:** $2.8 bil; cement (portland), stone (crushed), sand and gravel (construction), salt, sand and gravel (industrial). **Commercial fishing:** $204.5 mil. **Chief ports:** Houston, Galveston, Brownsville, Beaumont, Port Arthur, Corpus Christi, Texas City, Freeport. **Gross state product:** $1.31 tril. **Sales tax:** 6.25%. **Employment distrib.:** 16.7% govt.; 19.8% trade/trans./util.; 7.9% mfg.; 13.5% ed./health; 12.7% prof./bus. serv.; 10.3% leisure/hosp.; 6.0% finance; 7.7% constr./mining/log.; 1.8% info.; 3.5% other serv. **Unemployment:** 7.9%. **Per cap. pers. income:** $39,593. **New private housing:** 97,450 units/$14.7 bil. **Commercial banks:** 606; deposits: $486 bil. **Savings institutions:** 57; deposits: $57.8 bil. **Lottery:** total sales: $3.8 bil; profit: $982.0 mil.

Federal govt. Fed. civ. employees: 143,838; **avg. salary:** $69,168. **Notable fed. facilities:** Ft. Hood; Ft. Bliss; Sheppard, Dyess, Goodfellow AF Bases; Joint Base San Antonio; NASA Johnson Space Ctr.; Naval Air Training School, Corpus Christi NAS; Red River Army Depot; Ft. Worth Western Currency Facility.

Energy. Monthly electricity use: 1,199 kWh, $138.99.

State data. Motto: Friendship. **Flower:** Bluebonnet. **Bird:** Mockingbird. **Tree:** Pecan. **Song:** "Texas, Our Texas." **Entered union:** Dec. 29, 1845; rank: 28th. **State fair** at Dallas, late Sept.-mid-Oct.; at Beaumont, late Mar.-early Apr.; at Belton, late Aug.-early Sept.; at Denton, mid-Aug.; at Tyler, late Sept.

History. Humans have lived in the region for at least 12,000 years. Coahuiltecan, Karankawa, Caddo, Jumano, and Tonkawa peoples were in the area when the first Europeans came; later, Apache, Comanche, Cherokee, and Wichita arrived. Early Spanish explorers included Alonso Álvarez de Pineda, who sailed along the Texas coast, 1519; Cabeza de Vaca, shipwrecked near Galveston along with the former slave Estevanico, 1528; and Coronado, who crossed the Panhandle, 1541. Spaniards made the first settlement at Ysleta, near El Paso, 1682. Americans moved into the land early in the 19th cent. Mexico, of which Texas was a part, won independence from Spain, 1821. Texas rebelled, 1836, losing to Santa Anna at the Alamo, but winning decisively under Sam Houston at San Jacinto. With Houston as president, 1836-38 and 1841-44, the Republic of Texas functioned as a nation until admitted to the Union. With a slave population of 30%, Texas seceded, 1861; mostly unscathed by the Civil War, it was readmitted, 1870. In 1900 a powerful hurricane lashed Galveston, killing at least 8,000. Cotton and cattle were dominant until 1901, when the Spindletop gusher, near Beaumont, launched the petroleum and petrochemical industries. By 2000, the state population ranked second in the U.S. With wealth and population came political power, notably in the presidencies of Lyndon B. Johnson (1963-69), George H. W. Bush (1989-93), and George W. Bush (2001-09). Texas was plagued with drought conditions and wildfires starting in late 2010, with almost 4 mil acres burned and close to 3,000 homes destroyed in the 2011 fire season.

Tourist attractions. Padre Island Natl. Seashore; Big Bend, Guadalupe Mts. natl. parks; Ft. Davis; Six Flags Over Texas, Arlington SeaWorld, Six Flags Fiesta Texas, The Alamo, San Antonio Missions Natl. Hist. Park, all San Antonio; Cowgirl Hall of Fame, Kimball Art Museum, Ft. Worth; Lyndon B. Johnson Natl. Historical Park, Johnson City; Lyndon B. Johnson Library and Museum, Austin; Texas State Aquarium, Corpus Christi; George Bush Library, College Station.

Famous Texans. Lance Armstrong, Stephen F. Austin, Lloyd Bentsen, James Bowie, Carol Burnett, George H. W. Bush, George W. Bush, Joan Crawford, J. Frank Dobie, Dwight D. Eisenhower, Morgan Fairchild, Farrah Fawcett, Sam Houston, Howard Hughes, Kay Bailey Hutchison, Molly Ivins, Lyndon

B. Johnson, Tommy Lee Jones, Janis Joplin, Barbara Jordan, Mary Martin, Chester Nimitz, Sandra Day O'Connor, H. Ross Perot, Katherine Anne Porter, Dan Rather, Sam Rayburn, Ann Richards, Sissy Spacek, Kenneth Starr, George Strait.

Tourist information. Texas Tourism, P.O. Box 141009, Austin, TX 78714; (512) 486-5876; 1-800-452-9292; www.traveltex.com

Website. www.texas.gov

Utah (UT)
Beehive State

People. Population: 2,817,222; rank: 34. **Pop. change** (2000-11): 26.2%. **Pop. density:** 34.3 per sq mi. **Racial distribution:** 91.9% white; 1.3% black; 2.2% Asian; 1.5% Amer. Ind.; 1.0% Pac. Isl.; 2 or more races, 2.2%. **Hispanic pop.:** 13.2%.

Geography. Total area: 84,897 sq mi; rank: 13. **Land area:** 82,170 sq mi; rank: 12. **Acres forested:** 18.3 mil. **Location:** Middle Rocky Mountain state; its southeastern corner touches Colorado, New Mexico, and Arizona, and is the only spot in the U.S. where 4 states join. **Climate:** arid; ranging from warm desert in SW to alpine in NE. **Topography:** high Colorado plateau is cut by brilliantly colored canyons of the SE; broad, flat, desert-like Great Basin of the W; the Great Salt Lake and Bonneville Salt Flats to the NW; Middle Rockies in the NE run E-W; valleys and plateaus of the Wasatch Front. **Capital:** Salt Lake City. **Chief airport:** Salt Lake City.

Economy. Chief industries: services, trade, manufacturing, government, transportation, utilities. **Chief manuf. goods:** food, petroleum, nonferrous metal, motor vehicles & parts, aerospace, sporting goods, fabricated metal, computers & electronics. **Chief crops:** hay, greenhouse & nursery, wheat, cherries, onions, apples, barley, peaches, corn. **Livestock:** 4.28 mil chickens (excl. broilers), 800,000 cattle/calves, 305,000 sheep/lambs, 80,000 hogs/pigs. **Broadband Internet:** 77.1%. **Nonfuel minerals:** $4.6 bil; copper, molybdenum concentrates, gold, potash, magnesium metal. **Gross state product:** $124.5 bil. **Sales tax:** 5.95%. **Employment distrib.:** 18.2% govt.; 19.3% trade/trans./util.; 9.6% mfg.; 12.8% ed./health; 13.6% prof./bus. serv.; 9.0% leisure/hosp.; 5.8% finance; 6.4% constr./mining/log.; 2.5% info.; 2.8% other serv. **Unemployment:** 6.7%. **Per cap. pers. income:** $33,790. **New private housing:** 9,983 units/$1.8 bil. **Commercial banks:** 64; deposits: $257 bil. **Savings institutions:** 7; deposits: $36.7 bil.

Federal govt. Fed. civ. employees: 30,027; **avg. salary:** $63,248. **Notable fed. facilities:** Hill AFB; Tooele Army Depot; Army Dugway Proving Ground.

Energy. Monthly electricity use: 786 kWh, $68.43.

State data. Motto: Industry. **Flower:** Sego lily. **Bird:** (California) sea gull. **Tree:** Blue spruce. **Song:** "Utah, This Is the Place." **Entered union:** Jan. 4, 1896; rank: 45th. **State fair** at Salt Lake City, early Sept.

History. Ute, Gosiute, Southern Paiute, and Navajo peoples lived in the region at the time of European contact. Spanish Franciscans visited the area, 1776; American fur traders followed. Permanent settlement began with the arrival of the Latter-day Saints, or Mormons, 1847; they made the arid land bloom and created a prosperous economy. Organized in 1849, the State of Deseret asked admission to the Union; instead, Congress established Utah Territory, 1850, and Brigham Young was appointed governor. The Union Pacific and Central Pacific railroads met near Promontory Point, May 10, 1869, creating the first transcontinental railroad. Statehood was not achieved until 1896, after a long controversy over the Mormon practices of economic isolationism and polygamy (the church renounced the latter in 1890). The 20th cent. brought expansion in mining, defense-related industries, and, more recently, information technologies. More than two-thirds of Utahans are Mormons; the church has its world headquarters in Salt Lake City. Utah experienced 60% population growth, 1990-2010, and has the highest birthrate and lowest median age of any state in the U.S.

Tourist attractions. Temple Square, Mormon Church headquarters, in Salt Lake City; Great Salt Lake; Zion, Canyonlands, Bryce Canyon, Arches, and Capitol Reef natl. parks; Dinosaur, Rainbow Bridge, Timpanogos Cave, and Natural Bridges natl. monuments; Lake Powell; Flaming Gorge Natl. Recreation Area.

Famous Utahans. Maude Adams, Ezra Taft Benson, John Moses Browning, Mariner Eccles, Philo Farnsworth, James Fletcher, David M. Kennedy, J. Willard Marriott, Merlin Olsen, Osmond family, Ivy Baker Priest, George Romney, Roseanne, Wallace Stegner, Brigham Young, Loretta Young.

Tourist information. Utah Office of Tourism, Council Hall/Capitol Hill, 300 N. State St., Salt Lake City, UT 84114; 1-800-200-1160; www.utah.com

Website. www.utah.gov

Vermont (VT)
Green Mountain State

People. Population: 626,431; rank: 49. **Pop. change** (2000-11): 2.9%. **Pop. density:** 68.0 per sq mi. **Racial distribution:** 95.5% white; 1.1% black; 1.4% Asian; 0.4% Amer. Ind.; <0.05% Pac. Isl.; 2 or more races, 1.7%. **Hispanic pop.:** 1.6%.

Geography. Total area: 9,616 sq mi; rank: 45. **Land area:** 9,217 sq mi; rank: 43. **Acres forested:** 4.6 mil. **Location:** northern New England state. **Climate:** temperate, with considerable temperature extremes; heavy snowfall in mountains. **Topography:** Green Mts. N-S backbone 20-36 mi wide; avg. altitude 1,000 ft. **Capital:** Montpelier. **Chief airport:** Burlington.

Economy. Chief industries: manufacturing, tourism, agriculture, trade, finance, insurance, real estate, government. **Chief manuf. goods:** dairy, plastics, printing, wood furniture, sporting goods, metalworking machinery. **Chief crops:** greenhouse & nursery, hay, maple syrup, apples, berries, sweet corn. **Livestock:** 236,000 chickens (excl. broilers), 260,000 cattle/calves. **Broadband Internet:** 71.7%. **Nonfuel minerals:** $123 mil; stone (crushed), sand and gravel (construction), stone (dimension), talc (crude), gemstones (natural). **Gross state product:** $25.9 bil. **Sales tax:** 6.0%. **Employment distrib.:** 18.3% govt.; 18.8% trade/trans./util.; 10.3% mfg.; 20.0% ed./health; 9.0% prof./bus. serv.; 9.7% leisure/hosp.; 4.0% finance; 4.9% constr./mining/log.; 1.6% info.; 3.3% other serv. **Unemployment:** 5.6%. **Per cap. pers. income:** $41,832. **New private housing:** 1,299 units/$221.3 mil. **Commercial banks:** 13; deposits: $6.4 bil. **Savings institutions:** 10; deposits: $4.5 bil. **Lottery:** total sales: $95.5 mil; profit: $21.4 mil.

Federal govt. Fed. civ. employees: 4,637; **avg. salary:** $68,914. **Notable fed. facilities:** Law Enforcement Support Ctr.

Energy. Monthly electricity use: 576 kWh, $89.71.

State data. Motto: Freedom and unity. **Flower:** Red clover. **Bird:** Hermit thrush. **Tree:** Sugar maple. **Song:** "These Green Mountains." **Entered union:** Mar. 4, 1791; rank: 14th. **State fair** at Rutland, early Sept.

History. Inhabited for 10,000 years or more, the region attracted Abenaki and Mahican peoples before Europeans arrived. Champlain explored the lake that now bears his name, 1609. The first European settlement was on Isle la Motte, in Lake Champlain, 1666. During the American Revolution, Ethan Allen and the Green Mountain Boys captured Ft. Ticonderoga (NY), 1775. Under a constitution that provided for public schools and abolished slavery, settlers declared a republic, 1777. Vermont joined the Union, 1791. Agriculture dominated in the 19th cent. Still mainly rural, the state expanded tourism and manufacturing after World War II, and IBM became the largest private employer. Vermont was the first state to recognize same-sex civil unions (2000) and to enact equal same-sex marriage rights via legislation (2009).

Tourist attractions. Shelburne Museum; Rock of Ages Quarry, Graniteville; Vermont Marble Museum, Proctor; Bennington Battle Monument; Pres. Calvin Coolidge homestead, Plymouth; Maple Grove Maple Museum, St. Johnsbury; Ben & Jerry's Factory, N. Waterbury.

Famous Vermonters. Ethan Allen, Chester A. Arthur, Calvin Coolidge, Howard Dean, John Deere, George Dewey, John Dewey, Stephen A. Douglas, Dorothy Canfield Fisher, James Fisk, James Jeffords, Rudy Vallee.

Tourist information. Vermont Dept. of Tourism and Marketing, Natl. Life Building, 6th Fl., Montpelier, VT 05620; (802) 828-3237; 1-800-VERMONT; www.vermontvacation.com

Website. www.vermont.gov

Virginia (VA)
Old Dominion

People. Population: 8,096,604; rank: 12. **Pop. change** (2000-11): 14.4%. **Pop. density:** 205.0 per sq mi. **Racial distribution:** 71.3% white; 19.8% black; 5.8% Asian; 0.5% Amer. Ind.; 0.1% Pac. Isl.; 2 or more races, 2.5%. **Hispanic pop.:** 8.2%.

Geography. Total area: 42,775 sq mi; rank: 35. **Land area:** 39,490 sq mi; rank: 36. **Acres forested:** 15.9 mil. **Location:** South Atlantic state bounded by the Atlantic Ocean on the E and surrounded by North Carolina, Tennessee, Kentucky, West Virginia, and Maryland. **Climate:** mild and equable. **Topography:** mountain and valley region in the W, including the Blue Ridge Mts.; rolling Piedmont Plateau; tidewater, or coastal plain, including the eastern shore. **Capital:** Richmond. **Chief airports:** Arlington, Dulles, Highland Springs, Newport News, Norfolk.

Economy. Chief industries: services, trade, government, manufacturing, tourism, agriculture. **Chief manuf. goods:** beverages & tobacco, transportation equip., animal slaughtering & processing, plastics, textiles, paper & paper prods., printing, pharmaceuticals, furniture, chemicals. **Chief crops:** greenhouse & nursery, soybeans, tomatoes, corn, tobacco, hay, cotton, apples, wheat, peanuts, potatoes. **Livestock:** 4.22 mil chickens (excl. broilers), 243.8 mil broilers, 1.49 mil cattle/calves, 84,000 sheep/lambs. **Broadband Internet:** 68.7%. **Nonfuel minerals:** $1.0 bil; stone (crushed), zirconium concentrates, cement (portland), lime, sand and gravel (construction). **Commercial fishing:** $183.9 mil. **Chief ports:** Norfolk Harbor, Newport News, Richmond, Hopewell. **Gross state product:** $428.9 bil. **Sales tax:** 5.0%. **Employment distrib.:** 19.3% govt.; 17.0% trade/trans./util.; 6.1% mfg.; 12.9% ed./health; 17.9% prof./bus. serv.; 9.7% leisure/hosp.; 5.1% finance; 5.1% constr./mining/log.; 1.9% info.; 5.1% other serv. **Unemployment:** 6.2%. **Per cap. pers. income:** $45,920. **New private housing:** 23,297 units/$3.4 bil. **Commercial banks:** 138; deposits: $192.7 bil. **Savings institutions:** 13; deposits: $35.3 bil. **Lottery:** total sales: $1.5 bil; profit: $444.2 mil.

Federal govt. Fed. civ. employees: 146,392; **avg. salary:** $86,002. **Notable fed. facilities:** Pentagon; Norfolk Naval Sta., Shipyard, and other Hampton Roads military bases; Ft. Belvoir; Joint Base Langley-Eustis; NASA Langley Res. Ctr.; CIA George Bush Ctr. for Intelligence, Langley; Quantico USMC Base, FBI Academy; Dahlgren Nav. Surface Warfare Ctr. & Lab; USDA Food and Nutrition Serv.; U.S. Geological Survey Natl. Ctr.

Energy. Monthly electricity use: 1,239 kWh, $129.43.

State data. Motto: Sic Semper Tyrannis (Thus always to tyrants). **Flower:** Dogwood. **Bird:** Cardinal. **Tree:** Dogwood. **Song emeritus:** "Carry Me Back to Old Virginia." **Tenth** of the original 13 states to ratify the Constitution, June 25, 1788. **State fair** at Doswell, late Sept.-early Oct.

History. Cherokee and Susquehanna peoples and the Algonquians of the Powhatan Confederacy were in the region when Europeans arrived. English settlers founded Jamestown, 1607. Virginians were indispensable to the founding of the American republic, and 4 of the first 5 U.S. presidents—Washington, Jefferson, Madison, and Monroe—came from there. The conclusive battle of the American Revolution took place at Yorktown, 1781. The state profited from tobacco, cotton, and the slave trade; in 1860, slaves made up nearly one-third of the population. Virginia seceded from the Union, 1861, and Richmond became the capital of the Confederacy, but western counties, loyal to the Union, split off to become West Virginia, 1863. The war ended with Robert E. Lee's surrender to Ulysses S. Grant at Appomattox, 1865, and Virginia was readmitted to the Union, 1870. In the 20th cent., expansion of federal civilian jobs and military facilities transformed the economy. State officials pledged "massive resistance" to racial integration in the mid-1950s, but eventually accommodated. In 1989, L. Douglas Wilder became the first elected black governor in U.S. history. On Sept. 11, 2001, terrorist hijackers crashed a jet into U.S. defense headquarters at the Pentagon, in Arlington.

Tourist attractions. Colonial Williamsburg; Busch Gardens Williamsburg; Wolf Trap Farm, near Vienna; Arlington Natl. Cemetery; Mt. Vernon, home of George Washington; Jamestown Settlement; Yorktown; Jefferson's Monticello, Charlottesville; Robert E. Lee's birthplace, Stratford Hall, and grave, Lexington; Appomattox; Shenandoah Natl. Park; Blue Ridge Parkway; Virginia Beach; Kings Dominion, near Richmond.

Famous Virginians. Richard E. Byrd, James B. Cabell, Henry Clay, Katie Couric, Jubal Early, Jerry Falwell, William Henry Harrison, Patrick Henry, A. P. Hill, Thomas Jefferson, Joseph E. Johnston, Robert E. Lee, Meriwether Lewis and William Clark, James Madison, John Marshall, George Mason, James Monroe, George Pickett, Pocahontas, Edgar Allan Poe, John Randolph, Walter Reed, Rev. Pat Robertson, John Smith, J. E. B. Stuart, William Styron, Zachary Taylor, John Tyler, Maggie Walker, Booker T. Washington, George Washington, L. Douglas Wilder, Woodrow Wilson.

Tourist Information. Virginia Tourism Corp., 901 E. Byrd St., Richmond, VA 23219; 1-800-VISITVA; www.virginia.org **Website.** www.virginia.gov

Washington (WA)
Evergreen State

People. Population: 6,830,038; rank: 13. **Pop. change** (2000-11): 15.9%. **Pop. density:** 102.8 per sq mi. **Racial distribution:** 82.0% white; 3.8% black; 7.5% Asian; 1.8% Amer. Ind.; 0.7% Pac. Isl.; 2 or more races, 4.3%. **Hispanic pop.:** 11.6%.

Geography. Total area: 71,298 sq mi; rank: 18. **Land area:** 66,456 sq mi; rank: 20. **Acres forested:** 22.4 mil. **Location:** Pacific state bordered by Canada on the N, Idaho on the E, Oregon on the S, and the Pacific Ocean on the W. **Climate:** mild, dominated by the Pacific Ocean and protected by the Cascades. **Topography:** Olympic Mts. on NW peninsula; open land along coast to Columbia R.; flat terrain of Puget Sound Lowland; Cascade Mts. region's high peaks to the E; Columbia Basin in central portion; highlands to the NE; mountains to the SE. **Capital:** Olympia. **Chief airports:** Bellingham, Seattle, Spokane.

Economy. Chief industries: advanced technology, aerospace, biotechnology, intl. trade, forestry, tourism, recycling, agriculture & food processing. **Chief manuf. goods:** aerospace, petroleum, food, paper, milled lumber, plastics, structural metals, computers & electronics. **Chief crops:** apples, potatoes, wheat, hay, cherries, greenhouse & nursery, forest products, pears, grapes, onions, hops, sweet corn, Christmas trees, mint, raspberries. **Livestock:** 7.98 mil chickens (excl. broilers), 1.11 mil cattle/calves, 52,000 sheep/lambs. **Broadband Internet:** 76.9%. **Nonfuel minerals:** $727 mil; gold, sand and gravel (construction), stone (crushed), cement (portland), diatomite. **Commercial fishing:** $255.3 mil. **Chief ports:** Seattle, Tacoma, Vancouver, Kelso-Longview, Anacortes. **Gross state product:** $355.1 bil. **Sales tax:** 6.5%. **Employment distrib.:** 19.1% govt.; 18.6% trade/trans./util.; 9.7% mfg.; 13.7% ed./health; 12.0% prof./bus. serv.; 9.8% leisure/hosp.; 4.8% finance; 5.0% constr./mining/log.; 3.6% info.; 3.7% other serv. **Unemployment:** 9.2%. **Per cap. pers. income:** $44,294. **New private housing:** 20,864 units/$4.0 bil. **Commercial banks:** 86; deposits: $97.3 bil. **Savings institutions:** 19; deposits: $12 bil. **Lottery:** total sales: $510.5 mil; profit: $150.1 mil.

Federal govt. Fed. civ. employees: 57,178; **avg. salary:** $72,187. **Notable fed. facilities:** Bonneville Power Admin.; Lewis-McChord Joint Base; Fairchild AFB; DOE Hanford Nuclear Site; Naval Base Kitsap (Bremerton and Bangor); Whidbey Island NAS; Pacific Northwest Natl. Lab.

Energy. Monthly electricity use: 1,030 kWh, $82.75.

State data. Motto: Alki (By and by). **Flower:** Western rhododendron. **Bird:** Willow goldfinch. **Tree:** Western hemlock. **Song:** "Washington, My Home." **Entered union:** Nov. 11, 1889; rank: 42nd. **State fairs:** at Monroe, late Aug-early Sept.; at Yakima, late Sept.

History. People of the Clovis culture lived in the region 11,000 years ago. At the time of European contact, Native Americans in the area included Nez Percé, Spokane, Yakima, Cayuse, Okanogan, Walla Walla, and Colville peoples in the interior, and Nooksak, Chinook, Nisqually, Clallam, Makah, Quinault, and Puyallup peoples along the coast. Spain's Bruno de Hezeta sailed the coast, 1775. In 1792, British naval officer George Vancouver mapped the Puget Sound area, and

American Capt. Robert Gray sailed up the Columbia R. Fur traders and missionaries arrived in the first half of the 19th cent. Final agreement on the border of Washington and Canada was made with Britain, 1846. Completion in 1883 of a transcontinental rail link between Puget Sound and the eastern U.S. aided immigration, and Washington became a state in 1889. In the 20th cent., cheap hydroelectric power spurred growth in the aluminum and aircraft industries. Founded in 1975, Microsoft became a computer software giant. Mt. St. Helens erupted, 1980. With grunge music, Starbucks coffee, and Amazon.com, Seattle became a national trendsetter in the 1990s. Violent street protests disrupted a World Trade Organization meeting there in 1999. Gary Locke, in office 1997-2005, was the first U.S. governor of Chinese ancestry.

Tourist attractions. Seattle Center, Space Needle, waterfront, Museum of Flight, Underground Tour, Seattle; Mt. Rainier, Olympic, and North Cascades natl. parks; Mt. St. Helens; Puget Sound; San Juan Islands; Grand Coulee Dam; Columbia R. Gorge Natl. Scenic Area; Spokane's Riverfront Park.

Famous Washingtonians. Raymond Carver, Kurt Cobain, Bing Crosby, William O. Douglas, Bill Gates, Jimi Hendrix, Henry M. Jackson, Gary Larson, Mary McCarthy, Robert Motherwell, Edward R. Murrow, Theodore Roethke, Ann Rule, Hilary Swank, Julia Sweeney, Adam West, Marcus Whitman, Minoru Yamasaki.

Tourist information. WA State Tourism Office, 128 10th Ave. SW, P.O. Box 42525, Olympia, WA 98504; 1-866-964-8913; www.experiencewa.com

Website. access.wa.gov

West Virginia (WV)
Mountain State

People. Population: 1,855,364; rank: 37. **Pop. change** (2000-11): 2.6%. **Pop. density:** 77.2 per sq mi. **Racial distribution:** 94.1% white; 3.5% black; 0.7% Asian; 0.2% Amer. Ind.; <0.05% Pac. Isl.; 2 or more races, 1.4%. **Hispanic pop.:** 1.3%.

Geography. Total area: 24,230 sq mi; rank: 41. **Land area:** 24,038 sq mi; rank: 41. **Acres forested:** 12.2 mil. **Location:** South Atlantic state bounded on the N by Ohio, Pennsylvania, Maryland; on the S and W by Virginia, Kentucky, Ohio; on the E by Maryland and Virginia. **Climate:** humid continental climate except for marine modification in the lower panhandle. **Topography:** ranging from hilly to mountainous; Allegheny Plateau in the W, covers two-thirds of the state; mountains here are the highest in the state, over 4,000 ft. **Capital:** Charleston.

Economy. Chief industries: manufacturing, services, mining, tourism. **Chief manuf. goods:** chemicals, aluminum, motor vehicle parts, lumber & plywood, primary & fabricated metals. **Chief crops:** hay, apples, corn, peaches, soybeans, tobacco, wheat. **Livestock:** 1.45 mil chickens (excl. broilers), 85.4 mil broilers, 390,000 cattle/calves, 33,000 sheep/lambs. **Broadband Internet:** 84.6%. **Nonfuel minerals:** $350 mil; cement (portland), stone (crushed), lime, sand and gravel (industrial), cement (masonry). **Chief port:** Huntington. **Gross state product:** $66.8 bil. **Sales tax:** 6.0%. **Employment distrib.:** 20.5% govt.; 17.5% trade/trans./util.; 6.3% mfg.; 16.5% ed./health; 8.3% prof./bus. serv.; 9.9% leisure/hosp.; 3.6% finance; 8.8% constr./mining/log.; 1.4% info.; 7.2% other serv. **Unemployment:** 8.0%. **Per cap. pers. income:** $33,513. **New private housing:** 2,220 units/$306.4 mil. **Commercial banks:** 77; deposits: $28.3 bil. **Savings institutions:** 6; deposits: $865 mil. **Lottery:** total sales: $1.4 bil; profit: $558.1 mil.

Federal govt. Fed. civ. employees: 16,021; **avg. salary:** $69,197. **Notable fed. facilities:** Natl. Radio Astronomy Observatory, Green Bank; Bureau of Public Debt Bldg.; Alderson Fed. Prison Camp; FBI Criminal Justice Information Services.

Energy. Monthly electricity use: 1,195 kWh, $105.05.

State data. Motto: Montani Semper Liberi (Mountaineers are always free). **Flower:** Big rhododendron. **Bird:** Cardinal. **Tree:** Sugar maple. **Songs:** "The West Virginia Hills"; "This Is My West Virginia"; "West Virginia, My Home, Sweet Home."

Entered union: June 20, 1863; rank: 35th. **State fair** at Lewisburg, mid-Aug.

History. Sparsely inhabited at the time of European contact, the area was primarily Native American hunting grounds. British explorers Thomas Batts and Robert Fallam reached the New R., 1671. Coal, discovered in 1742, was mined extensively by the mid-19th cent. White settlement led to conflicts with Native Americans, including a major battle in which settlers defeated an Indian confederacy at Point Pleasant, 1774. The region joined the Union as part of Virginia, 1788. Longstanding tensions between the E and W parts of the state came to a head in 1861, when Virginia seceded. Delegates of W counties, meeting at Wheeling, repudiated the act and created a new state, Kanawha, later renamed West Virginia, which was admitted to the Union in 1863. Poverty has been a problem for much of the state's subsequent history. West Virginia continued to rank low in per capita personal income, despite billions of dollars in federal contracts brought to the state by 9-term U.S. Sen. Robert Byrd, who passed away in 2010. Coal mining, though dangerous, continues to be a major industry; nearly 30 miners were killed in a mine explosion in 2010.

Tourist attractions. Harpers Ferry Natl. Historic Park; Clay Center and Avampato Discovery Museum, Charleston; White Sulphur Springs (The Greenbrier) and Berkeley Springs mineral water spas; New River Gorge Natl. River; Beckley Exhibition Coal Mine; Monongahela Natl. Forest; Fenton Glass, Williamstown; Blenko Glass, Milton; Sternwheel Regatta, Charleston; Mountain State Forest Festival, Elkins; skiing at Canaan Valley, Snowshoe, Timberline, Winterplace; Mountain State Art & Craft Festival, Ripley; Oglebay Resort, Wheeling; white-water rafting on New and Gauley Rivers.

Famous West Virginians. Newton D. Baker, Pearl Buck, Robert Byrd, John W. Davis, Thomas "Stonewall" Jackson, Don Knotts, Dwight Whitney Morrow, Michael Owens, Mary Lou Retton, Walter Reuther, Cyrus Vance, Jerry West, Charles "Chuck" Yeager.

Tourist information. West Virginia Division of Tourism, Capitol Complex, Bldg. 6, Rm. 525, Charleston, WV 25305; 1-800-CALLWVA; www.wvtourism.com

Website. www.wv.gov

Wisconsin (WI)
Badger State

People. Population: 5,711,767; rank: 20. **Pop. change** (2000-11): 6.5%. **Pop. density:** 105.5 per sq mi. **Racial distribution:** 88.4% white; 6.5% black; 2.4% Asian; 1.1% Amer. Ind.; <0.05% Pac. Isl.; 2 or more races, 1.6%. **Hispanic pop.:** 6.1%.

Geography. Total area: 65,496 sq mi; rank: 23. **Land area:** 54,158 sq mi; rank: 25. **Acres forested:** 17.0 mil. **Location:** East North Central state, bounded on the N by Lake Superior and Upper Michigan; on the E by Lake Michigan; on the S by Illinois; on the W by the St. Croix and Mississippi Rivers. **Climate:** long, cold winters and short, warm summers tempered by the Great Lakes. **Topography:** narrow Lake Superior Lowland plain met by Northern Highland, which slopes gently to the sandy crescent Central Plain; Western Upland in the SW; 3 broad parallel limestone ridges running N-S are separated by wide and shallow lowlands in the SE. **Capital:** Madison. **Chief airports:** Madison, Milwaukee.

Economy. Chief industries: services, manufacturing, trade, government, agriculture, tourism. **Chief manuf. goods:** transportation, dairy, animal slaughtering & processing, paper, printing, plastics, computers & electronics. **Chief crops:** corn, greenhouse & nursery, soybeans, potatoes, cranberries, hay, wheat, snap beans, apples, peas. **Livestock:** 6.03 mil chickens (excl. broilers), 46.5 mil broilers, 3.4 mil cattle/calves, 84,000 sheep/lambs. **Broadband Internet:** 77.7%. **Nonfuel minerals:** $599 mil; sand and gravel (construction), sand and gravel (industrial), stone (crushed), lime, stone (dimension). **Commercial fishing:** $3.7 mil. **Chief ports:** Superior, Milwaukee, Green Bay. **Gross state product:** $254.8 bil. **Sales tax:** 5.0%. **Employment distrib.:** 15.3% govt.; 18.5% trade/trans./util.; 16.2% mfg.; 15.2% ed./health; 10.3% prof./bus. serv.; 9.0% leisure/hosp.; 5.7% finance; 3.2% constr./mining/

log.; 1.7% info.; 5.0% other serv. **Unemployment:** 7.5%. **Per cap. pers. income:** $40,073. **New private housing:** 9,939 units/$1.6 bil. **Commercial banks:** 259; deposits: $114.6 bil. **Savings institutions:** 37; deposits: $14 bil. **Lottery:** total sales: $502.7 mil; profit: $143.7 mil.

Federal govt. Fed. civ. employees: 16,009; **avg. salary:** $66,023. **Notable fed. facilities:** Ft. McCoy; USDA Forest Products Lab.

Energy. Monthly electricity use: 716 kWh, $90.59.

State data. Motto: Forward. **Flower:** Wood violet. **Bird:** Robin. **Tree:** Sugar maple. **Song:** "On, Wisconsin!" **Entered union:** May 29, 1848; rank: 30th. **State fair** at West Allis, early Aug.

History. At the time of European contact, Ojibwa, Menominee, Winnebago, Kickapoo, Sauk, Fox, and Potawatomi peoples inhabited the area. French explorer Jean Nicolet reached Green Bay, 1634; French missionaries and fur traders followed. The British took over, 1763. The U.S. won the land after the American Revolution but did not wield control until forts were established at Green Bay and Prairie du Chien, 1816. Native Americans rebelled against the seizure of tribal lands in the Black Hawk War, 1832, but were defeated and relocated to reservations. Wisconsin became a territory, 1836, and a state, 1848. Some 96,000 soldiers served the Union cause during the Civil War. Many immigrants arrived from Germany, Poland, and Scandinavia. Wisconsin agriculture focused on dairy; Milwaukee became a manufacturing center. As governor, 1901-06, Robert La Follette pushed Progressive reforms such as direct primary voting and consumer protection laws. An era of "McCarthyism" ended when anti-Communist crusader Sen. Joseph McCarthy (WI) was censured by the U.S. Senate, 1954. After weeks of protests in Madison, the Republican-controlled state legislature passed controversial measures in 2011 to restrict collective bargaining by some 170,000 public-sector employees.

Tourist attractions. Old Wade House and Carriage Museum, Greenbush; Villa Louis, Prairie du Chien; Circus World Museum, Baraboo; Wisconsin Dells; Old World Wisconsin, Eagle; Door County peninsula; Chequamegon and Nicolet natl. forests; Lake Winnebago; House on the Rock, Dodgeville; Monona Terrace, Madison.

Famous Wisconsinites. Don Ameche, Carrie Chapman Catt, Willem Dafoe, Edna Ferber, Hamlin Garland, King Camp Gillette, Harry Houdini, Robert La Follette, Alfred Lunt, Pat O'Brien, Georgia O'Keeffe, William H. Rehnquist, John Ringling, Donald K. "Deke" Slayton, Spencer Tracy, Thorstein Veblen, Orson Welles, Laura Ingalls Wilder, Thornton Wilder, Frank Lloyd Wright.

Tourist information. Wisconsin Dept. of Tourism, 201 W. Washington Ave., P.O. Box 8690, Madison, WI 53708; 1-800-432-TRIP; www.travelwisconsin.com

Website. www.wisconsin.gov

Wyoming (WY)

Equality State, Cowboy State

People. Population: 568,158; rank: 51. **Pop. change** (2000-11): 15.1%. **Pop. density:** 5.9 per sq mi. **Racial distribution:** 93.5% white; 1.1% black; 0.9% Asian; 2.6% Amer. Ind.; 0.1% Pac. Isl.; 2 or more races, 1.8%. **Hispanic pop.:** 9.1%.

Geography. Total area: 97,813 sq mi; rank: 10. **Land area:** 97,093 sq mi; rank: 9. **Acres forested:** 11.4 mil. **Location:** Mountain state lying in the high western plateaus of the Great Plains. **Climate:** semi-desert conditions throughout; true desert in the Big Horn and Great Divide basins. **Topography:** eastern Great Plains rise to the foothills of the Rocky Mts.; the Continental Divide crosses the state from the NW to the SE. **Capital:** Cheyenne.

Economy. Chief industries: mineral extraction, oil, natural gas, tourism and recreation, agriculture. **Chief manuf. goods:** petroleum, chemicals, fabricated metal, beet sugar, lumber. **Chief crops:** hay, sugar beets, barley, dry beans, wheat, corn, greenhouse & nursery, oats. **Livestock:** 13,000 chickens (excl. broilers), 1.36 mil cattle/calves, 370,000

sheep/lambs. **Broadband Internet:** 57.6%. **Nonfuel minerals:** $2.0 bil; soda ash, clays (bentonite), helium (Grade-A), sand and gravel (construction), cement (portland). **Gross state product:** $37.6 bil. **Sales tax:** 4.0%. **Employment distrib.:** 26.2% govt.; 18.3% trade/trans./util.; 3.1% mfg.; 9.3% ed./health; 6.2% prof./bus. serv.; 11.4% leisure/hosp.; 3.7% finance; 16.4% constr./mining/log.; 1.3% info.; 4.1% other serv. **Unemployment:** 6.0%. **Per cap. pers. income:** $47,301. **New private housing:** 2,114 units/$425.2 mil. **Commercial banks:** 44; deposits: $11.9 bil. **Savings institutions:** 3; deposits: $480 mil.

Federal govt. Fed. civ. employees: 5,807; **avg. salary:** $60,813. **Notable fed. facilities:** Warren AFB.

Energy. Monthly electricity use: 883 kWh, $77.43.

State data. Motto: Equal rights. **Flower:** Indian paintbrush. **Bird:** Western meadowlark. **Tree:** Plains cottonwood. **Song:** "Wyoming." **Entered union:** July 10, 1890; rank: 44th. **State fair** at Douglas, mid-Aug.

History. Inhabited for at least 12,000 years, the region supported Shoshone, Crow, Cheyenne, Oglala Sioux, and Arapaho peoples when Europeans arrived. France's Vérendrye brothers were the first Europeans to see the region, 1742-43. John Colter, an American, traversed the Yellowstone area, 1807-08. Trappers and fur traders followed in the 1820s. Forts Laramie and Bridger became important stops on trails to the West Coast. Population grew after the Union Pacific crossed the state, 1867-68. Wyoming became a territory, 1868, and the first to extend full voting rights to women, 1869. Statehood was attained, 1890. Disputes between large landowners and small ranchers culminated in the Johnson County Cattle War, 1892; federal troops were called in to restore order. Nellie Tayloe Ross was the first woman governor to take office in the U.S., 1925. Wyoming, the least populous state, has relied on the energy, tourism, and ranching industries in recent decades. Dick Cheney, Wyoming's representative in the U.S. House, 1979-89, served as U.S. vice pres. (2001-09).

Tourist attractions. Yellowstone Natl. Park, the first U.S. national park, est. 1872; Grand Teton Natl. Park; Natl. Elk Refuge; Devils Tower Natl. Monument; Ft. Laramie Natl. Hist. Site and nearby pioneer trail ruts; Buffalo Bill Historical Ctr., Cody; Cheyenne Frontier Days.

Famous Wyomingites. James Bridger, William F. "Buffalo Bill" Cody, Curt Gowdy, Esther Hobart Morris, Jackson Pollock, Nellie Tayloe Ross.

Tourist information. Wyoming Travel and Tourism, 1520 Etchepare Cir., Cheyenne, WY 82007; 1-800-225-5996; www.wyomingtourism.org

Website. www.wyoming.gov

District of Columbia (DC)

People. Population: 617,996; rank: 50. **Pop. change** (2000-11): 8.0%. **Pop. density:** 10,123.0 per sq mi. **Racial distribution:** 42.4% white; 50.7% black; 3.7% Asian; 0.6% Amer. Ind.; 0.1% Pac. Isl.; 2 or more races, 2.5%. **Hispanic pop.:** 9.5%.

Geography. Total area: 68 sq mi; rank: 51. **Land area:** 61 sq mi; rank: 51. **Location:** at the confluence of the Potomac and Anacostia Rivers, flanked by Maryland on the N, E, and SE and by Virginia on the SW. **Climate:** hot humid summers, mild winters. **Topography:** low hills rise toward the N away from the Potomac R. and slope to the S; highest elevation, 410 ft, lowest Potomac R., 1 ft.

Economy. Chief industries: government, legal, publishing, medical, service, tourism. **Broadband Internet:** 69.0%. **Gross state product:** $107.6 bil. **Sales tax:** 6.0%. **Employment distrib.:** 33.2% govt.; 3.7% trade/trans./util.; 0.2% mfg.; 16.1% ed./health; 20.5% prof./bus. serv.; 9.0% leisure/hosp.; 3.7% finance; 1.8% constr./mining/log.; 2.5% info.; 9.4% other serv. **Unemployment:** 10.2%. **Per cap. pers. income:** $73,105. **New private housing:** 4,612 units/$609.4 mil. **Commercial banks:** 27; deposits: $31.4 bil. **Savings institutions:** 5; deposits: $231 mil. **Lottery:** total sales: $245 mil; profit: $63 mil.

Federal govt. Fed. civ. employees: 164,348; **avg. salary:** $104,644.

Energy. Monthly electricity use: 778 kWh, $108.93.

District data. Motto: Justitia omnibus (Justice for all). **Flower:** American beauty rose. **Tree:** Scarlet oak. **Bird:** Wood thrush.

History. The District of Columbia, coextensive with the city of Washington, is the seat of the U.S. federal government. It lies on the west central edge of Maryland on the Potomac R., opposite Virginia. The Piscataway, an Algonquian-speaking people, were living in the region when Europeans arrived in the 17th cent. Proposals for a "federal town" for the deliberations of the Continental Congress were made in 1783. Authorized by Congress, 1790, Pres. George Washington chose the Potomac site and persuaded landowners to sell their holdings to the government. Its area was originally 100 sq mi taken from the sovereignty of Maryland and Virginia. Virginia's portion south of the Potomac was given back to that state in 1846.

Pres. Washington chose Pierre Charles L'Enfant, a Frenchman, to plan the capital. Surveyor Andrew Ellicott finished the official map and design of the city, assisted by Benjamin Banneker, a black architect and astronomer. Washington laid the cornerstone of the north wing of the Capitol building, 1793, and Pres. John Adams moved to the new national capital, 1800. The City of Washington was incorporated, 1802. British troops invaded, 1814, setting fire to the Capitol, the President's House (as the White House was then called), and other buildings. Pres. Abraham Lincoln ended slavery in the district, 1862. Many African Americans arrived after the Civil War, but racial segregation remained legal until the mid-20th cent. After federal government expansion spurred population growth, 1930-50, an exodus to the suburbs shrank the city's population, 1950-2005.

The 23rd Amendment (1961) granted residents the right to vote for president and vice president. Congress, which has legislative authority over the District under the Constitution, approved legislation in 1970 giving the District one delegate to the House of Representatives, who could vote in committee but not on the floor. Voters approved, 1974, a congressionally drafted charter giving them the right to elect their own mayor and city council. The district won the right to levy taxes, but Congress retained power to veto council actions and approve the city budget. Security measures were dramatically increased after terrorists attacked the U.S. on Sept. 11, 2001. After a 34-year absence, major league baseball returned to the city in 2005.

Tourist attractions. See Attractions in Washington, DC, Capital of the U.S.

Famous Washingtonians. Edward Albee, Frederick Douglass, John Foster Dulles, Duke Ellington, Katherine Graham, Goldie Hawn, J. Edgar Hoover, Pete Sampras, John Philip Sousa.

Tourist information. Destination DC, 901 7th St. NW, 4th Fl., Washington, DC, 20001-3719; 1-800-422-8644; www.washington.org

Website. www.dc.gov

OUTLYING U.S. AREAS

American Samoa (AS)

People. Population (2012): 54,947. **Pop. change** (2000-12): –4.1%. **Pop. density:** 713.6 per sq mi. **Racial distrib.** (2000): 91.6% Pac. Isl.; 2.8% Asian; 1.1% white; 2 or more races, 4.2%. **Languages:** Samoan, English, Tongan.

Geography. Total area: 77 sq mi. **Land area:** 77 sq mi. **Location:** most southerly of all lands under U.S. sovereign, about 2,300 mi SW of Honolulu. It is an unincorporated territory consisting of 7 small islands of the Samoan group: **Tutuila** (52.59 sq mi), **Aunu'u** (0.59 sq mi); Manu'a group: **Ta'u** (17.57 sq mi), **Olosega** (2.03 sq mi), **Ofu** (2.83 sq mi), and the atolls **Rose** (0.03 sq mi) and **Swains** (1.38 sq mi). **Climate:** marine tropical, avg. temp 82°F with little seasonal variation; avg. annual rainfall about 36 in. **Topography:** volcanic islands, rugged peaks, and limited coastal plains. About 70% of the land is bush and mountains. **Capital:** Pago Pago on Tutuila. **Airport:** Pago Pago.

Economy. Chief industries: tuna fishing and processing, trade, services, tourism. **Chief crops:** giant taro, taro, yams, coconuts, breadfruits, bananas, papayas. **Livestock** (2008): 35,709 chickens; 16,904 hogs/pigs. **Nonfuel minerals:** crushed stone, trap rock. **Commercial fishing** (2008): $9.7 mil. **Unemployment** (2007): 29.8%. **Gross domestic product** (2009): $703.0 mil. **Commercial banks:** 2; deposits: $193.0 mil.

Energy. Electricity production (2008): 190 mil kWh.

Fed. civ. employees (Mar. 2012): 114; **avg. salary:** $54,067.

Misc. data. Motto: Samoa Muamua le Atua (In Samoa, God is first). **Flower:** Paogo (Ula-fala). **Plant:** Ava. **Song:** "Amerika Samoa."

History. A tripartite agreement between Great Britain, Germany, and the U.S. in 1899 gave the U.S. sovereignty over the eastern islands of the Samoan group; these islands became American Samoa. Local chiefs ceded Tutuila and Aunu'u to the U.S. in 1900, and the Manu'a group and Rose Island in 1904; Swains Island was annexed in 1925. Samoa (Western), comprising the larger islands of the Samoan group, was a New Zealand mandate and UN Trusteeship until it became independent Jan. 1, 1962 (now called Samoa).

From 1900 to 1951, American Samoa was under the jurisdiction of the U.S. Navy. Since 1951, it has been under the Interior Dept. On Jan. 3, 1978, the first popularly elected Samoan governor and lieutenant governor were inaugurated. Previously, the governor was appointed by the Sec. of the Interior. American Samoa has a bicameral legislature and elects a delegate to the U.S. House of Representatives who has a voice but no vote, except in committees.

Five of the 7 islands are volcanoes. Scientists discovered a rapidly growing volcano, Vailulu'u, between Ta'u and Rose in 1975.

The tuna canning industry has been the backbone of the economy since the 1950s, but one of the two canneries closed in 2009. An 8.1 magnitude earthquake in Sept. 2009 triggered a tsunami that severely damaged Tutuila.

American Samoans are of Polynesian origin. They are nationals of the U.S. As of 2000, 91,029 lived in the U.S., including 16,166 in Hawaii, 37,498 in California, and 8,049 in Washington.

Tourist attractions. Rose Atoll; Vaitogi coast; Natl. Park of American Samoa; tropical rainforest.

Tourist information. Office of Tourism, Dept. of Commerce, American Samoa Govt., P.O. Box 1147, Pago Pago, AS 96799; (684) 699-9411; www.amsamoatourism.com

Website. www.americansamoa.gov

Guam (GU)

People. Population (2012): 154,805. **Pop change** (2000-12): 3.3%. **Pop. density:** 754.3 per sq mi. **Racial/ethnic distrib.** (2010 est.): 41.0% Chamorro; 30.6% Filipino; 11.7% other Pac. Isl.; 3.2% white. **Languages:** English, Chamorro, Philippine/other Pacific Island languages.

Geography. Total area: 212 sq mi. **Land area:** 212 sq mi. **Location:** largest and southernmost of the Mariana Islands in the West Pacific, 3,700 mi W of Hawaii. **Climate:** tropical, with temperatures from 70° to 90° F; rainy July to Nov., avg. annual rainfall, about 80-100 in. **Topography:** coralline limestone plateau in the N; southern chain of low volcanic mountains sloping gently to the W, more steeply to coastal cliffs on the E; general elevation, 500 ft; highest point, Mt. Lamlam, 1,334 ft. **Capital:** Hagåtña. **Chief airport:** Tamuning.

Economy. Chief industries: U.S. military, tourism, construction, shipping, concrete products, printing & publishing. **Chief manuf. goods:** textiles, foods. **Chief crops:** watermelons, cucumbers, eggplant, long beans, bananas, corn. **Livestock** (2007): 112 cattle; 635 hogs/pigs; 124 goats; 533 chickens. **Nonfuel minerals** (2008): $3.8 mil; crushed stone. **Commercial fishing** (2008): $499,095. **Chief port:** Apra Harbor. **Gross domestic product** (2009): $4.0 bil. **Employment distrib.** (Dec. 2008): 33.3% trade/trans; 26.7% serv.; 24.8% govt.; 10.6% constr.; 2.8% mfg.; 0.6% agric. **Unemployment** (2009): 9.3%. **Per capita income** (2010): $12,864.

Commercial banks: 6; deposits: $1.8 bil. Savings institutions: 1; deposits: $80 mil.

Energy. Electricity production (2008): 1.8 bil kWh.

Federal govt. Fed. employees (Mar. 2012): 2,896; avg. salary: $58,544. Notable fed. facilities: Andersen AFB.

Misc. data. Motto: Where America's day begins. Flower: Puti Tai Nobio (Bougainvillea). Bird: Ko'ko (Guam rail). Tree: Ifit (Intsia bijuga). Song: "Stand Ye Guamanians."

History. Guam was probably settled by voyagers from the Indonesian-Philippine archipelago by 3rd cent. BCE. Pottery, rice cultivation, and megalithic technology show strong East Asian cultural influence. Centralized, village clan-based communities engaged in agriculture and offshore fishing. The estimated population by the early 16th cent. was 50,000-75,000. Ferdinand Magellan arrived in the Marianas Mar. 6, 1521. They were colonized in 1668 by Spanish missionaries, who named them the Mariana Islands in honor of Maria Anna, queen of Spain. When Spain ceded Guam to the U.S., it sold the other Marianas to Germany. Japan obtained a League of Nations mandate over the German islands in 1919; in Dec. 1941 it seized Guam, which was retaken by the U.S. in July-Aug. 1944.

Guam is a self-governing organized unincorporated U.S. territory. The Organic Act of 1950 provided for a governor, elected to a 4-year term, and a 21-member unicameral legislature, elected biennially by the residents, who are American citizens. In 1970, the first governor was elected. In 1972, a U.S. law gave Guam one delegate to the U.S. House of Representatives who has a voice but no vote, except in committees.

Guam's quest to change its status to a U.S. commonwealth began in the late 1970s. The Guam Commission on Self-Determination, created in 1984, developed a draft Commonwealth Act. In 1993, legislation proposing a change of status was submitted to the U.S. Congress. In 1994, the U.S. Congress passed legislation transferring 3,200 acres of land on Guam from federal to local control. The U.S. plans to move 8,000 Marines stationed in Okinawa, Japan, to Guam by 2014.

Tourist attractions. Tropical climate, oceanic marine environment; Tarzan Falls; Plaza de España; beaches; water sports; duty-free port shopping.

Tourist information. Guam Visitors Bureau, 401 Pale San Vitores Rd., Tumon, Guam 96913; (671) 646-5278; www.visitguam.org

Website. www.guam.gov

Commonwealth of the Northern Mariana Islands (MP)

People. Population (2012): 51,395; Pop. change (2000-10): −25.8%. Pop. density: 279.0 per sq mi. Racial/ethnic distrib. (2000): 56.3% Asian; 36.3% Pac. Isl.; 1.8% white; 0.8% other; 2 or more races/ethnicities, 4.8%. Languages: Philippine languages, Chinese, Chamorro, English.

Geography. Total area: 184.2 sq mi. Land area: 184.2 sq mi. Location: between Guam and the Tropic of Cancer, the 14 islands of the Northern Marianas form a 300-mi long archipelago. The indigenous population is concentrated on the 3 largest of the 6 inhabited islands: Saipan, the seat of government and commerce, Rota, and Tinian. Climate: tropical, with avg. temperature around 82°F, moderated by NE trade winds; avg. annual rainfall, 80-100 in. Topography: Limestone S islands with even terraces and coral reefs; volcanic N isles. Capital: Saipan. Airport: Saipan.

Economy. Chief industries: banking, construction, fishing, mining, tourism, apparel mfg., retail. Chief manuf. goods: apparel, stone, clay and glass prods. Chief crops: bananas, cucumbers, sweet potatoes, taro, watermelons. Livestock (2007): 1,395 cattle; 1,483 hogs/pigs; 9,700 chickens. Commercial fishing (2008): $751,388. Chief port: Saipan. Gross domestic product (2009): $716.0 mil. Fed. employees (2005): 124. Unemployment (2005): 8.0%. Commercial banks: 3; deposits: $430.0 mil. Savings institutions: 1; deposits: $6 mil.

Energy. Electricity production (2009): 60,600 kWh.

Federal govt. Fed. employees (Mar. 2011): 190; avg. salary: $52,298.

Misc. data. Flower: Plumeria. Bird: Mariana fruit-dove. Tree: Flame tree. Song: "Gi Talo Gi Halom Tasi" (In the middle of the sea).

History. The people of the Northern Marianas are predominantly of Chamorro cultural extraction, although Carolinians and immigrants from other areas of E. Asia and Micronesia have also settled in the islands. English is among the several languages commonly spoken.

The German-controlled Northern Marianas were placed under Japanese control by a League of Nations mandate after World War I. The U.S. captured the islands during World War II. From July 18, 1947, the U.S. had administered the Northern Marianas under a trusteeship agreement with the UN Security Council. In 1975, the residents voted to become a U.S. commonwealth.

The Northern Mariana Islands has been self-governing since 1978, when a constitution drafted and adopted by the people became effective and a popularly elected bicameral legislature (2-year term), with offices of governor (4-year term) and lieut. governor, was inaugurated. Pres. Ronald Reagan proclaimed the Northern Marianas a commonwealth, 1986, and the UN formally ended its trusteeship, 1990. In 2008, U.S. law gave the islands one delegate to the U.S. House of Representatives who has a voice but no vote, except in committees.

Under the 1976 Commonwealth Covenant with the U.S., the islands are exempt from federal immigration and import laws, and minimum wage is lower than on the mainland. The garment-making industry, which has since boomed, has drawn accusations of sweatshop conditions from some critics. Legislation passed in 2007 will raise the minimum wage to the federal rate by 2015.

Tourist attractions. WWII sites; House of Taga; beaches, water sports; resorts; gambling.

Tourist information. Marianas Visitors Authority, P.O. Box 500861, Saipan, MP 96950; (670) 664-3200; www.mymarianas.com

Website. www.gov.mp

Commonwealth of Puerto Rico (PR)
(Estado Libre Asociado de Puerto Rico)

People. Population (2012): 3,690,923 (about 4.6 mil additional Puerto Ricans reside in the mainland U.S.); Pop. change (2000-12): −3.1%. Pop. density: 1,078.0 per sq mi. Racial distribution: 75.8% white; 12.4% black; 0.2% Asian; 0.5% Amer. Ind.; <0.05% Pac. Isl.; 2 or more races, 3.3%. Hispanic pop.: 99.0%. Languages: Spanish and English are joint official languages.

Geography. Total area: 5,325 sq mi. Land area: 3,424 sq mi. Location: island lying between the Atlantic to the N and the Caribbean to the S; it is easternmost of the West Indies group called the Greater Antilles, of which Cuba, Hispaniola, and Jamaica are the larger islands. Climate: mild, with a mean temperature of 77°F. Topography: mountainous throughout three-fourths of its rectangular area, surrounded by a broken coastal plain; highest peak, Cerro de Punto, 4,390 ft. Capital: San Juan. Chief airport: San Juan.

Economy. Chief industries: manufacturing, service, tourism. Chief manuf. goods: pharmaceuticals, medical equip., electronics, apparel, food products. Chief crops: pumpkins, coffee, watermelons, plantains, yams, oranges. Livestock (2007): 490,817 cattle; 11,137 sheep; 69,892 hogs/pigs; 5.1 mil broilers; 1.4 mil chickens. Broadband Internet: 78.4%. Nonfuel minerals (est. 2008): $164 mil; crushed stone, lime, salt, portland cement, clays (common). Commercial fishing (2008): $3.8 mil. Chief ports: San Juan, Ponce, Mayaguez. Gross domestic product (est. 2010): $93.5 bil. Employment distrib.: 29% govt.; 17.5% trade/trans./util.; 8.9% mfg.; 13% ed./health; 11.1% prof./bus. serv.; 7.9% leisure/hosp.; 4.8% finance; 3.7% constr./mining/log.; 2.1% other serv. Unemployment (2012): 14.2%. Per capita pers. income (est. 2009): $14,905. Commercial banks: 9;

deposits: $50.1 bil. **Lottery** (2009): total sales: $421.2 mil; profit: $146.9 mil.

Federal govt. Fed. civ. employees (Mar. 2012): 11,208; **avg. salary:** $63,192. **Notable fed. facilities:** PR Natl. Guard Training Area at Camp Santiago; Ft. Buchanan; Intl. Inst. of Tropical Forestry; Vieques Natl. Wildlife Refuge; USGS Caribbean Water Science Ctr.

Energy. Electricity production (2009): 22.7 bil kWh.

Misc. data. Motto: Joannes Est Nomen Eius (John is his name). **Flower:** Maga. **Bird:** Reinita. **Tree:** Ceiba. **Anthem:** La Borinqueña.

History. Puerto Rico (or Borinquen, after the original Arawak Indian name, Boriquen) was visited by Christopher Columbus on his second voyage, Nov. 19, 1493. In 1508, the Spanish arrived.

Sugarcane was introduced, 1515, and slaves were imported 3 years later. Gold mining petered out, 1570. Spaniards fought off a series of British and Dutch attacks; slavery was abolished, 1873. Under the treaty of Paris, Puerto Rico was ceded to the U.S. after the Spanish-American War, 1898. In 1952 the people voted in favor of Commonwealth status.

The Commonwealth of Puerto Rico is a self-governing part of the U.S. with a primarily Hispanic culture. The island's citizens have virtually the same control over their internal affairs as do the 50 states of the U.S. However, they do not vote in national general elections, only in national primaries.

Puerto Rico is represented in the U.S. House of Representatives by a Resident Commissioner who has a voice but no vote, except in committees.

No federal income tax is collected from residents on income earned from local sources in Puerto Rico. Nevertheless, as part of the U.S. legal system, Puerto Rico is subject to the provisions of the U.S. Constitution; most federal laws apply as they do in the 50 states.

Puerto Rico's famous "Operation Bootstrap," begun in the late 1940s, succeeded in changing the island from the "Poorhouse of the Caribbean" to an area with the highest per capita income in Latin America. This program encouraged manufacturing and development of the tourist trade by selective tax exemption, low-interest loans, and other incentives. Despite the marked success of Puerto Rico's development efforts over an extended period of time, per capita income in Puerto Rico is low in comparison to that of the 50 states.

In plebiscites held in 1967, 1993, and 1998, voters chose to retain Commonwealth status. Protests mounted in the late-1990s over the U.S. Navy's use of Vieques Island for live ammunition training; official military exercises there were terminated, 2003.

Tourist attractions. Ponce Museum of Art; Forts El Morro and San Cristóbal; Old Walled City of San Juan; Arecibo Observatory; Cordillera Central and state parks; El Yunque Rain Forest; San Juan Cathedral; Porta Coeli Chapel and Museum of Religious Art, Interamerican Univ., San Germán; Condado Convention Ctr.; Casa Blanca, Ponce de León family home, Puerto Rican Family Museum of 16th and 17th centuries, and Fine Arts Center, all in San Juan.

Cultural facilities and events. Festival Casals classical music concerts, mid-June; Puerto Rico Symphony Orchestra at Music Conservatory; Botanical Garden and Museum of Anthropology, Art, and History at the Univ. of Puerto Rico; Institute of Puerto Rican Culture, at the Dominican Convent.

Famous Puerto Ricans. Julia de Burgos, Marta Casals Istomin, Pablo Casals, José Celso Barbosa, Orlando Cepeda, Roberto Clemente, José de Diego, José Feliciano, Doña Felisa Rincón de Gautier, Luis A. Ferré, José Ferrer, Commodore Diégo E. Hernández, Miguel Hernández Agosto, Rafael Hernández (El Jibarito), Rafael Hernández Colón, Raúl Juliá, René Marqués, Ricky Martin, Concha Meléndez, Rita Moreno, Luis Muñoz Marín, Luis Palés Matos, Adm. Horacio Rivero.

Tourist information. The Puerto Rico Tourism Company, La Princesa Bldg. #2, Paseo La Princesa, Old San Juan, PR 00902; (800) 866-7827; www.seepuertorico.com
Website. www.gobierno.pr (in Spanish)

Virgin Islands (VI)
St. John, St. Croix, St. Thomas

People. Population (2012): 105,275. **Pop. change** (2000-12): –3.1%. **Pop. density:** 779.8 per sq mi. **Racial distrib.** (2000): 76.2% black; 13.1% white; 1.1% Asian; 6.1% other races; 2 or more races, 3.5%. **Languages:** English (official), Spanish, Creole.

Geography. Total area: 136 sq mi. **Land area:** 135 sq mi. **Location:** 3 larger and 50 smaller islands and cays in the S and W of the V.I. group (British V.I. colony to the N and E), which is situated 70 mi E of Puerto Rico, located W of the Anegada Passage, a major channel connecting the Atlantic Ocean and the Caribbean Sea. **Climate:** subtropical; the sun tempered by gentle trade winds; humidity is low; avg. temperature, 78°F. **Topography:** St. Thomas is mainly a ridge of hills running E-W, and has little tillable land; St. Croix rises abruptly in the N but slopes to the S to flatlands and lagoons; St. John has steep, lofty hills and valleys with little level tillable land. **Capital:** Charlotte Amalie on St. Thomas. **Chief airport:** Charlotte Amalie.

Economy. Chief industries: retail, petroleum, tourism, prof. consulting. **Chief manuf. goods:** rum, stone, glass & clay products, electronics, textiles. **Chief crops:** cucumbers, coconuts, mangoes, tomatoes, bananas. **Livestock** (2007): 776 cattle; 2,981 sheep; 2,331 goats; 1,125 hogs/pigs; 699 chickens. **Broadband Internet:** 74.4%. **Nonfuel minerals:** crushed stone, limestone, traprock. **Commercial fishing** (2008): $8.8 mil. **Chief port:** Charlotte Amalie. **Gross domestic product** (2009): $4.2 bil. **Employment distrib.:** 27.8% govt.; 20.6% trade/trans./util.; 3.1% mfg.; 6.2% ed./health; 8.9% prof./bus. serv.; 18.2% leisure/hosp.; 5.7% finance; 4.8% constr./mining/log.; 1.9% info.; 2.9% other serv. **Unemployment** (June 2011): 9.4%. **Commercial banks:** 4; deposits: $1.8 bil.

Energy. Electricity production (2008 est.): 843.6 mil kWh.

Federal govt. Fed. civ. employees: 695; **avg. salary:** $59,598.

Misc. data. Motto: United in pride and hope. **Flower:** Yellow cedar. **Bird:** Yellow breast. **Song:** "Virgin Islands March."

History. The islands were visited by Columbus in 1493. Spanish forces, 1555, defeated the Caribes and claimed the territory; by 1596 the native population was annihilated. First permanent settlement in the U.S. territory, 1672, by the Danes; U.S. purchased the islands, 1917, for defense purposes.

The Virgin Islands has a republican form of government, headed by a governor and lieut. governor elected, since 1970, by popular vote for 4-year terms. There is a 15-member unicameral legislature, elected by popular vote for a 2-year term. Residents of the V.I. have been U.S. citizens since 1927. Since 1973 they have elected a delegate to the U.S. House of Representatives, who has a voice but no vote, except in committees.

Tourist attractions. Magens Bay, St. Thomas; duty-free shopping; Virgin Islands Natl. Park; beaches, Indian relics, and evidence of colonial Danes.

Tourist information. USVI Division of Tourism, P.O. Box 6400, St. Thomas 00804; 1-800-372-USVI; www.visitusvi.com
Website. ltg.gov.vi

Other Islands

Navassa lies between Haiti and Jamaica, 100 mi S of Guantanamo Bay, Cuba, in the Caribbean; it covers 1,147 acres, and is uninhabited. Claimed 1857, USCG lighthouse built 1917, now inoperative. Natl. Wildlife Refuge since 1999. Administered by the Dept. of Interior.

The 3 coral islands of **Wake Atoll—Wake, Wilkes,** and **Peale**—lie in the Pacific Ocean on a direct route from Hawaii to Hong Kong, about 2,300 mi W of Honolulu and 1,500 mi NE of Guam. The group is 4.5 mi long, 1.5 mi wide. Land area totals 2.5 sq mi. The U.S. annexed Wake Atoll Jan. 17, 1899. Japan occupied Wake 1941-45. Designated a National Historic Landmark in 1985. Wake is owned by the U.S. Air Force, administered by the Dept. of Interior, but used by the Army as a missile launch facility. The population consists of military personnel and contractors. Most infrastructure damaged by super typhoon Ioke in 2006.

The following mostly uninhabited islands are part of the **Pacific/Remote Islands National Wildlife Refuge Complex**, along with Wake Atoll, administered by the Dept. of Interior: **Midway Atoll**, acquired in 1867, has 3 main islands—Sand, Spit, and Eastern—1,250 mi WNW of Honolulu, with an area of about 1,500 acres. Naval activity ended in 1997. Has the world's largest colony of Laysan albatross. **Johnston Atoll**, 800 mi WSW of Honolulu, is 2 natural and 2 artificial islands across 107 sq mi administered by the Navy. Johnston was a nuclear test site in 1958, 1962; the Army disposed of chemical weapons 1990-2000. Cleanup ended in 2005. **Kingman Reef** is a barren, coral atoll 932 mi S of Hawaii, annexed 1922. **Palmyra Atoll** is 54 islets over 753 sq mi, 1,052 mi S of Hawaii; annexed with Hawaii in 1898. Part privately owned by the Nature Conservancy. **Jarvis Island** covers 1,086 acres, 1,300 mi S of Honolulu near the equator. West of Jarvis are **Howland and Baker Islands**, 36 mi apart and about 1,600 mi SW of Honolulu.

Attractions in Washington, DC, Capital of the U.S.

Most attractions are free. All times are subject to change. For more details call the Washington, DC, Convention and Visitors Association at 1-800-422-8644, or visit www.washington.org

Bureau of Engraving and Printing

The **Bureau of Engraving and Printing** of the U.S. Treasury Dept. is the headquarters for the making of U.S. paper money. Public tours are offered Mon.-Fri., 9 AM-2 PM (7 PM in summer), except on federal holidays. 14th and C Sts. SW; (866) 874-2330. **Website:** www.moneyfactory.gov

Capitol

The **United States Capitol** was originally designed by Dr. William Thornton, an amateur architect, who submitted a plan in 1793 that won him $500 and a city lot. Three other architects designed or supervised the construction of the Capitol before its completion.

The present cast iron dome at its greatest exterior height measures 135 ft, 5 in. and is topped by the bronze Statue of Freedom, which stands 19½ ft and weighs 14,985 lbs. On its base are the words *E Pluribus Unum* (Out of Many, One).

The Capitol is open to the public Mon.-Sat., 8:30 AM-4:30 PM. It is closed Jan. 1, Inauguration Day, Thanksgiving Day, and Dec. 25.

To observe debate while Congress is in session, those living in the U.S. May obtain tickets from their U.S. representative or senator. Visitors from other countries May obtain passes at the Capitol. Between Constitution & Independence Aves., at Pennsylvania Ave.; (202) 225-6827. **Website:** www.visitthecapital.gov

Federal Bureau of Investigation

The **Federal Bureau of Investigation** does not currently offer tours of its headquarters. Visitors to the city may learn about the FBI through exhibits at the Newseum, the National Crime and Punishment Museum, and the International Spy Museum. J. Edgar Hoover Bldg., Pennsylvania Ave., between 9th and 10th Sts. NW; (202) 324-3447. **Website:** www.fbi.gov

Folger Shakespeare Library

The **Folger Shakespeare Library**, on Capitol Hill, is a research institution holding rare books and manuscripts of the Renaissance period and the largest collection of Shakespearean materials in the world. Exhibit may be visited Mon.-Sat., 10 AM-5 PM and Sun. 12 PM-5 PM except federal holidays. Building and garden tours are available to groups and the public. 201 E. Capitol St. SE; (202) 544-4600. **Website:** www.folger.edu

Holocaust Memorial Museum

The **U.S. Holocaust Memorial Museum** opened on Apr. 21, 1993. The museum documents the events of the Holocaust through permanent and temporary displays, interactive videos, and special lectures. The permanent exhibition is not recommended for children under age 11.

The museum is open daily, 10 AM-5:20 PM, except Yom Kippur and Dec. 25; extended hrs. Mon.-Thurs. (10 AM-6:20 PM) from Apr.-June. Admission is free. Tickets are needed only for the permanent exhibition, Mar. through Aug. A limited number of free tickets are available at the door; advance tickets May be ordered for a small fee at 1-800-400-9373. 100 Raoul Wallenberg Pl. SW; (202) 488-0400. **Website:** www.ushmm.org

Jefferson Memorial

Dedicated Apr. 13, 1943, the **Thomas Jefferson Memorial** stands on the south shore of the Tidal Basin in West Potomac Park. It is a circular stone structure that combines architectural elements of the dome of the Pantheon in Rome and the rotunda designed by Jefferson for the Univ. of Virginia.

The memorial is open daily, 24 hrs., staffed 9:30 AM-11:30 PM. Ohio Dr. SW & E. Basin Dr. SW; (202) 426-6841. **Website:** www.nps.gov/thje

John F. Kennedy Center

The **John F. Kennedy Center for the Performing Arts** opened Sept. 8, 1971. Designed by Edward Durell Stone, it includes an opera house, a concert hall, several theaters, 2 restaurants, and a library. Free tours are available Mon.-Fri., 10 AM-5 PM and Sat. & Sun., 10 AM-1 PM. 2700 F St. NW; (202) 467-4600; (800) 444-1324. **Website:** www.kennedycenter.org

Korean War Veterans Memorial

Dedicated on July 27, 1995, the **Korean War Veterans Memorial** honors Americans who served in the war. Situated at the west end of the Mall, the triangular-shaped stone and steel memorial features a multiservice formation of 19 combat-ready troops clad in ponchos with the wind at their back. A granite wall, with images of men and women who served, juts into the Pool of Remembrance.

The memorial is open daily, 24 hrs., staffed 9:30 AM-11:30 PM. French Dr. SW across from Lincoln Memorial; (202) 426-6841. **Website:** www.nps.gov/kowa

Library of Congress

Established by and for Congress in 1800, the **Library of Congress** extends its services to other government agencies and libraries, scholars, and the general public. It contains more than 134 mil items in some 460 languages.

Most exhibit halls are open to the public Mon.-Fri., 8:30 AM-9:30 PM; Sat., 8:30 AM-5 PM. Thomas Jefferson Building (Great Hall and Exhibitions) is open Mon.-Sat., 8:30 AM-4:30 PM. A few areas are open on most federal holidays; all are closed Jan. 1, Thanksgiving, and Dec. 25. 101 Independence Ave. SE; (202) 707-8000. **Website:** www.loc.gov

Lincoln Memorial

Designed by Henry Bacon, the **Lincoln Memorial** in West Potomac Park is a large marble hall enclosing a statue of Abraham Lincoln seated on an armchair. The memorial was dedicated May 30, 1922. The statue was designed by Daniel Chester French and sculpted by French and the Piccirilli brothers. The text of the Gettysburg Address is in the south chamber; that of Lincoln's Second Inaugural speech is in the north chamber. Each is engraved on a stone tablet.

The memorial is open daily, 24 hrs., staffed 9:30 AM-11:30 PM, and is wheelchair-accessible. W. Potomac Park at 23rd St. NW; (202) 426-6841. **Website:** www.nps.gov/linc

National Archives and Records

Original copies of the Declaration of Independence, the Constitution, and the Bill of Rights are on display in the **National Archives** Exhibition Hall. The National Archives also holds other valuable U.S. government records and historic maps, photographs, and manuscripts. Central Research and Microfilm Research Rooms are also available to the public for genealogical research.

Exhibition Hall open daily 10 AM-5:30 PM (later in spring and summer). 7th St. and Pennsylvania Ave. NW; (202) 357- 5000. **Website:** www.archives.gov

National Gallery of Art

The **National Gallery of Art** was established by Congress, Mar. 24, 1937, and opened Mar. 17, 1941. The original West Building was designed by John Russell Pope. The East Building, opened in 1978, was designed by I. M. Pei. Open daily, Mon.-Sat. 10 AM-5 PM, Sun. 11 AM-6 PM. Closed Jan. 1 and Dec. 25. 4th St. and Constitution Ave NW; (202) 737-4215. **Website:** www.nga.gov

Franklin Delano Roosevelt Memorial

Opened May 2, 1997, the **FDR Memorial** features 9 bronze sculptural ensembles depicting FDR, Eleanor Roosevelt, and events from the Great Depression and World War II. This 7.5-acre memorial is located near the Tidal Basin in a park-like setting and is wheelchair accessible.

Grounds, staffed daily, 9:30 AM-11:30 PM, except Dec. 25. 1850 W. Basin Dr. SW; (202) 426-6841. **Website:** www.nps.gov/fdrm

Smithsonian Institution

The **Smithsonian Institution**, established in 1846, is the world's largest museum complex. It holds some 137 mil artifacts and specimens in its trust. There are 15 museums and the National Zoo in the DC area. The **Smithsonian Information Center** is located in "the Castle" on the Mall. Also on the Mall are the **National Museum of American History**, the **National Museum of Natural History**, the **National Air and Space Museum**, the **National Museum of the American Indian**, the **Hirshhorn Museum and Sculpture Garden**, the **Arthur M. Sackler & Freer Galleries of Art**, the **National Museum of African Art**, and the **Arts and Industries Building** (currently closed for renovation). Located nearby are the **National Postal Museum**, the **National Museum of American Art**, the **National Portrait Gallery**, and the **Renwick Gallery**. Farther away is the **Anacostia Museum**. The **Air and Space Museum's Udvar-Hazy Center** is near Dulles Airport in Virginia.

Most museums are open daily, except Dec. 25, 10 AM-5:30 PM (later in summer); (202) 633-1000. **Website:** www.si.edu

Vietnam Veterans Memorial

Originally dedicated Nov. 13, 1982, the **Vietnam Veterans Memorial** recognizes the men and women who served in the armed forces in the Vietnam War. The names of more than 58,000 Americans who lost their lives or remain missing are inscribed on a V-shaped black-granite wall, designed by Maya Ying Lin.

Since 1982, 2 additions have been made to the Memorial. The 1st, dedicated on Nov. 11, 1984, is the Frederick Hart sculpture *Three Servicemen*. On Nov. 11, 1993, the Vietnam Women's Memorial, designed by Glenna Goodacre, was dedicated, honoring the more than 11,500 women who served in Vietnam.

The memorial is open daily, 24 hrs., staffed 9:30 AM-11:30 PM. Constitution Ave. and Bacon Dr. NW; (202) 426-6841. **Website:** www.nps.gov/vive

Washington Monument

The **Washington Monument**, dedicated in 1885, is a tapering shaft, or obelisk, of white marble, 555 ft, 5⅛ in. in height and 55 ft, 1½ in. square at base. Eight small windows, 2 on each side, are located at the 500-ft level.

(As of Sept. 30, 2012, the monument was still closed to the public while damages caused during a Aug. 23, 2011, earthquake, were assessed.) Normally open daily, 9 am-5 pm (later in summer), except July 4 and Dec. 25. Free timed passes are available; advance passes are available for a small fee. 15th St. and Constitution Ave. NW; (202) 426-6841. **Website:** www.nps.gov/wamo

White House

The **White House**, the President's residence, stands on 18 acres on the south side of Pennsylvania Ave., between the Treasury and the old Executive Office Building. The walls are of sandstone, quarried at Aquia Creek, VA. The building was first made white with lime-based whitewash in 1798, but the name did not become official until 1901.

The White House is normally open for free self-guided tours of 10 or more Tues.-Thurs., 7:30-11 AM; Fri., 7:30 AM-noon; Sat., 7:30 AM-1 PM. (Tour requests must be made at least 21 days in advance through your member of Congress.) Only the public rooms on the ground floor and state floor May be visited. 1600 Pennsylvania Ave. The White House Visitor Center at 1450 Pennsylvania Ave. is open daily 7:30 AM-4 PM; (202) 456-7041. **Website:** www.whitehouse.gov

National World War II Memorial

The **National WWII Memorial** is dedicated to the approx. 16 mil veterans who served and the more than 400,000 who died in the war. It rests on 7.4 acres of land at the east end of the reflecting pool on the Mall. The memorial opened on Apr. 29, 2004, and was dedicated on May 29.

At the north and south entrances are 43-ft archways, representing the Atlantic and Pacific theaters. Inside the grounds is a large, oval plaza with a wall of 4,000 gold stars; each represents 100 American deaths. Fifty-six pillars ringing the center represent the states, territories, and District of Columbia. There is also a garden enclosed by a stone wall, the Circle of Remembrance.

The memorial is wheelchair-accessible and open daily, 24 hrs., staffed 9:30 AM-11:30 PM. Located on 17th St. between Constitution and Independence Aves.; (202) 426-6841. **Website:** www.nps.gov/nwwm

Attractions Near Washington, DC

Arlington National Cemetery

Arlington National Cemetery, on the former Custis-Lee estate in Arlington, VA, is the site of the **Tomb of the Unknowns** and is the final resting place of Pres. W. H. Taft and Pres. John F. Kennedy and his wife, Jacqueline Bouvier Kennedy Onassis. An eternal flame burns over the site of Kennedy's grave. Many other famous Americans are buried at Arlington, as well as more than 300,000 U.S. military personnel, from every major war.

North of the National Cemetery stands the **U.S. Marine Corps War Memorial**, also known as Iwo Jima. The memorial is a bronze statue of the raising of the U.S. flag on Mt. Suribachi, Feb. 23, 1945, during World War II, executed by Felix de Weldon from the photograph by Joe Rosenthal.

On the southern side of the Memorial Bridge, near the cemetery entrance, a memorial honoring the women in the military was dedicated Oct. 18, 1997. The **Women in Military Service for America Memorial** is a semicircular retaining wall 226 ft long with a central niche 30 ft high.

Open daily, 8 AM-5 PM (8 AM-7 PM, Apr.-Sept.), Arlington, VA; (703) 607-8000; (877) 907-8585. **Website:** www.arlingtoncemetery.org

Mount Vernon

Mount Vernon, George Washington's estate, is on the south bank of the Potomac R., 16 mi from Washington, DC, in northern Virginia. The present house is believed to be an enlargement of one built by Augustine Washington in 1735. His son Lawrence renamed the estate after British Navy Adm. Edward Vernon. George Washington, Lawrence's half brother, inherited it in 1761. The estate has been restored to its 18th-cent. appearance and includes many original furnishings. Washington and his wife, Martha, are buried on the grounds.

Open 365 days, Apr.-Aug. 8 AM-5 PM; Mar., Sept.-Oct. 9 AM-5 PM; Nov.-Feb. 9 AM-4 PM; (703) 780-2000; (800) 429-1520. Admission: adults $15, seniors (62+) $14, children (6-11) $7, age 5 and under free. **Website:** www.mountvernon.org

The Pentagon

The **Pentagon**, headquarters of the Dept. of Defense, is the largest office building in the U.S. It houses more than 23,000 employees in offices occupying 3,705,793 sq ft. The building was severely damaged when struck by a plane Sept. 11, 2001.

Tours available by reservation only. General public must use the Pentagon website or contact their member of Congress to request a tour. Non U.S. citizens must contact their national embassy. Arlington, VA (I-395 S to Boundary Channel Dr. exit); (703) 697-1776. **Website:** www.pentagon.afis.osd.mil

100 MOST POPULOUS U.S. CITIES

Sources: Population: Decennial Census and Population Estimates Program, U.S. Census Bureau, U.S. Dept. of Commerce. Population is as of July 1, 2011; population rank is indicated within parentheses. **Pop. density** specifies the number of persons per square mile (sq mi). Unless otherwise noted, **all other figures** are estimates for 2006-10 from the American Community Survey, U.S. Census Bureau. **Racial distribution** categories are abbreviated here; their full forms are white, black or African American, Asian, American Indian and Alaska Native, Native Hawaiian and Other Pacific Islander, some other race, two or more races. **Hispanic** or Latino persons may be of any race. **Language** includes those spoken at home; languages other than Spanish spoken by less than 5% of the population over age 5 are omitted. **Employment:** Bureau of Labor Statistics, U.S. Dept. of Labor, for 2011. **Per capita income:** Bureau of Economic Analysis, U.S. Dept. of Commerce; figures apply to MSA for 2010. **Educational attainment** is the percentage of persons ages 25 and up who have graduated high school and those with a bachelor's degree or higher. **Avg. commute** is the time it takes for workers 16 years and over to travel from home to work. "Drive" includes only those who drive to work alone. Forms of transport used by less than 10% are omitted. **Avg. home:** National Association of Realtors®. Figures represent median 2011 sales price of existing single-family homes in the metropolitan area; data not available for all cities. **Avg. rent** is the median gross rent per month. **Mayor** (or other city leader) and **website:** World Almanac research as of mid-2012; subject to change.

Included here are the 100 most populous U.S. cities, according to U.S. Census Bureau estimates released in June 2012. Most data are for the city proper; some, where noted, apply to the Metropolitan Statistical Area (MSA). Inc. = incorporated; est. = established; HS = high school diploma.

Albuquerque, New Mexico

Population: 552,804 (32). **Pop. density:** 2,945. **Pop. change (2000-11):** 23.2%. **Area:** 187.7 sq mi. **Racial distribution:** 68.6% white; 3.2% black; 2.8% Asian; 4.5% Amer. Ind.; <0.05% Pac. Isl.; 17.2% other; 2+ races 3.8%. **Hispanic pop.:** 45.4%. **Foreign born:** 10.9%. **U.S. citizens:** 92.7%. **Language:** 70.1% English only; 24.4% Spanish.
Employment: 236,833 employed; 7.2% unemployed. **Per capita income:** $34,482; change (2009-10): 1.1%. **Below poverty level:** 11.8%; 15.7% of families. **Educational attainment:** 87.1% HS; 32.2% bachelor's. **Avg. commute:** 21.2 min. 78.4% drive; 11.1% carpool. **Housing units:** 234,891; 92.5% occupied. **Home ownership:** 61.5%. **Avg. home:** $167,900; change (2009-11): −7.0%. **Avg. rent:** $712.
Mayor: Richard J. Berry, nonpartisan
History: Founded 1706 by the Spanish; inc. 1890.
Website: www.cabq.gov

Anaheim, California

Population: 341,361 (54). **Pop. density:** 6,850. **Pop. change (2000-11):** 4.1%. **Area:** 49.8 sq mi. **Racial distribution:** 60.4% white; 2.6% black; 14.8% Asian; 0.4% Amer. Ind.; 0.4% Pac. Isl.; 18.7% other; 2+ races 2.7%. **Hispanic pop.:** 51.8%. **Foreign born:** 38.3%. **U.S. citizens:** 76.8%. **Language:** 40.0% English only; 43.5% Spanish.
Employment: 156,549 employed; 11.1% unemployed. **Per capita income:** $43,688; change (2009-10): 3.2%. **Below poverty level:** 11.3%; 13.7% of families. **Educational attainment:** 73.7% HS; 23.1% bachelor's. **Avg. commute:** 26.6 min. 74.5% drive; 14.1% carpool. **Housing units:** 105,050; 94.5% occupied. **Home ownership:** 49.1%. **Avg. home:** $307,700; change (2009-11): −7.9%. **Avg. rent:** $1,262.
Mayor: Tom Tait, nonpartisan
History: Founded 1857; inc. 1870. Home of Disneyland, the Anaheim Ducks, and the Los Angeles Angels.
Website: www.anaheim.net

Anchorage, Alaska

Population: 295,570 (65). **Pop. density:** 173. **Pop. change (2000-11):** 13.6%. **Area:** 1,704.7 sq mi. **Racial distribution:** 67.9% white; 5.4% black; 7.3% Asian; 6.5% Amer. Ind.; 1.8% Pac. Isl.; 1.9% other; 2+ races 9.3%. **Hispanic pop.:** 7.4%. **Foreign born:** 9.2%. **U.S. citizens:** 95.7%. **Language:** 83.7% English only; 4.5% Spanish.
Employment: 147,604 employed; 6.1% unemployed. **Per capita income:** $47,039; change (2009-10): 2.1%. **Below poverty level:** 5.8%; 7.9% of families. **Educational attainment:** 91.9% HS; 33.0% bachelor's. **Avg. commute:** 18.2 min. 75.9% drive; 13.2% carpool. **Housing units:** 112,166; 93.0% occupied. **Home ownership:** 61.7%. **Avg. rent:** $1,009.
Mayor: Dan Sullivan, Republican
History: Founded 1914 as a construction camp for railroad; HQ of Alaska Defense Command, WWII. Severely damaged in earthquake, 1964. Current population center of Alaska.
Website: www.muni.org

Arlington, Texas

Population: 373,698 (50). **Pop. density:** 3,897. **Pop. change (2000-11):** 12.2%. **Area:** 95.9 sq mi. **Racial distribution:** 62.4% white; 18.9% black; 6.9% Asian; 0.5% Amer. Ind.; 0.1% Pac. Isl.; 8.8% other; 2+ races 2.4%. **Hispanic pop.:** 26.6%. **Foreign born:** 19.6%. **U.S. citizens:** 86.8%. **Language:** 69.1% English only; 21.4% Spanish.
Employment: 186,451 employed; 7.6% unemployed. **Per capita income:** $41,282; change (2009-10): 2.6%. **Below poverty level:** 11.1%; 14.3% of families. **Educational attainment:** 84.6% HS; 28.7% bachelor's. **Avg. commute:** 25.7 min. 81.0% drive; 12.2% carpool. **Housing units:** 145,194; 90.7% occupied. **Home ownership:** 58.0%. **Avg. home:** $148,900; change (2009-11): 6.0%. **Avg. rent:** $814.
Mayor: Robert N. Cluck, nonpartisan
History: Settled in 1840s; inc. 1884.
Website: www.arlingtontx.gov

Atlanta, Georgia

Population: 432,427 (40). **Pop. density:** 3,248. **Pop. change (2000-11):** 3.8%. **Area:** 133.2 sq mi. **Racial distribution:** 38.2% white; 54.3% black; 3.3% Asian; 0.2% Amer. Ind.; <0.05% Pac. Isl.; 2.3% other; 2+ races 1.6%. **Hispanic pop.:** 4.8%. **Foreign born:** 7.8%. **U.S. citizens:** 94.5%. **Language:** 89.4% English only; 5.2% Spanish.
Employment: 166,268 employed; 12.1% unemployed. **Per capita income:** $38,321; change (2009-10): 1.7%. **Below poverty level:** 19.2%; 22.6% of families. **Educational attainment:** 86.2% HS; 45.0% bachelor's. **Avg. commute:** 25.8 min. 66.6% drive; 12.7% public trans. **Housing units:** 224,908; 79.3% occupied. **Home ownership:** 47.9%. **Avg. home:** $98,600; change (2009-11): −20.2%. **Avg. rent:** $884.
Mayor: Kasim Reed, nonpartisan
History: Founded as Terminus 1837; renamed Atlanta 1845; inc. 1847. Played major role in Civil War; became permanent state capital 1877. Birthplace of civil rights movement. Host to 1996 Centennial Olympic Games.
Website: www.atlantaga.gov

Aurora, Colorado

Population: 332,354 (56). **Pop. density:** 2,148. **Pop. change (2000-11):** 20.2%. **Area:** 154.7 sq mi. **Racial distribution:** 66.9% white; 15.2% black; 4.8% Asian; 1.2% Amer. Ind.; 0.3% Pac. Isl.; 7.8% other; 2+ races 3.8%. **Hispanic pop.:** 28.1%. **Foreign born:** 20.6%. **U.S. citizens:** 84.7%. **Language:** 69.3% English only; 21.4% Spanish.
Employment: 161,671 employed; 9.0% unemployed. **Per capita income:** $46,871; change (2009-10): 2.1%. **Below poverty level:** 13.6%; 16.7% of families. **Educational attainment:** 84.7% HS; 25.4% bachelor's. **Avg. commute:** 27.9 min. 76.6% drive; 11.7% carpool. **Housing units:** 131,334; 91.9% occupied. **Home ownership:** 62.1%. **Avg. home:** $231,400; change (2009-11): 5.2%. **Avg. rent:** $853.
Mayor: Steve Hogan, nonpartisan
History: Founded 1891; originally called Fletcher; renamed Aurora 1907; inc. 1929. Early growth stimulated by presence of military bases; fast-growing trade, technology, and med. science center.
Website: www.auroragov.org

Austin, Texas

Population: 820,611 (13). **Pop. density:** 2,755. **Pop. change (2000-11):** 25.0%. **Area:** 297.9 sq mi. **Racial distribution:** 66.4% white; 8.4% black; 6.0% Asian; 0.4% Amer. Ind.; 0.1% Pac. Isl.; 16.4% other; 2+ races 2.2%. **Hispanic pop.:** 35.0%. **Foreign born:** 19.5%. **U.S. citizens:** 84.9%. **Language:** 66.0% English only; 26.3% Spanish.
Employment: 420,678 employed; 6.2% unemployed. **Per capita income:** $38,736; change (2009-10): 2.9%. **Below poverty level:** 12.8%; 18.4% of families. **Educational attainment:** 85.1% HS; 44.1% bachelor's. **Avg. commute:** 22.7 min. 71.8% drive; 11.7% carpool. **Housing units:** 345,283; 91.6% occupied. **Home ownership:** 45.8%. **Avg. home:** $193,100; change (2009-11): 3.0%. **Avg. rent:** $882.
Mayor: Lee Leffingwell, nonpartisan
History: First permanent settlement 1835; capital of Rep. of Texas 1839; named after Stephen Austin; inc. 1840.
Website: www.austintexas.gov

Bakersfield, California

Population: 352,428 (52). **Pop. density:** 2,479. **Pop. change (2000-11):** 42.7%. **Area:** 142.2 sq mi. **Racial distribution:** 59.8% white; 8.2% black; 5.4% Asian; 0.9% Amer. Ind.; 0.1% Pac. Isl.; 20.9% other; 2+ races 4.7%. **Hispanic pop.:** 43.8%. **Foreign born:** 18.2%. **U.S. citizens:** 88.8%. **Language:** 63.6% English only; 30.3% Spanish.
Employment: 142,575 employed; 10.5% unemployed. **Per capita income:** $29,609; change (2009-10): 4.4%. **Below poverty level:** 13.9%; 17.3% of families. **Educational attainment:** 78.1% HS; 19.9% bachelor's. **Avg. commute:** 22.1 min. 78.9% drive; 14.4% carpool. **Housing units:** 114,587; 92.2% occupied. **Home ownership:** 60.4%. **Avg. rent:** $906.
Mayor: Harvey L. Hall, nonpartisan
History: Named after Col. Thomas Baker, an early settler; inc. 1898.
Website: www.bakersfieldcity.us

Baltimore, Maryland

Population: 619,493 (24). **Pop. density:** 7,653. **Pop. change (2000-11):** −4.9%. **Area:** 80.9 sq mi. **Racial distribution:** 30.0% white; 64.3% black; 2.3% Asian; 0.4% Amer. Ind.; <0.05% Pac. Isl.; 1.1% other; 2+ races 1.9%. **Hispanic pop.:** 3.7%. **Foreign born:** 7.0%. **U.S. citizens:** 95.7%. **Language:** 90.9% English only; 3.7% Spanish.
Employment: 246,957 employed; 10.5% unemployed. **Per capita income:** $49,129; change (2009-10): 3.2%. **Below poverty level:** 16.5%; 21.3% of families. **Educational attainment:** 77.4% HS; 25.2% bachelor's. **Avg. commute:** 29.2 min. 59.1% drive; 18.5% public trans.; 11.0% carpool. **Housing units:** 296,615; 80.4% occupied. **Home ownership:** 49.8%. **Avg. home:** $230,000; change (2009-11): −8.4%. **Avg. rent:** $859.
Mayor: Stephanie C. Rawlings-Blake, Democrat
History: Founded by Maryland legislature 1729; inc. 1797. War of 1812 British artillery barrage of Ft. McHenry (1814) inspired Francis Scott Key to write "Star-Spangled Banner." Birthplace of America's railroads 1828; rebuilt after fire 1904. Site of National Aquarium.
Website: www.baltimorecity.gov

Baton Rouge, Louisiana

Population: 230,139 (88). **Pop. density:** 2,991. **Pop. change (2000-11):** 1.0%. **Area:** 76.9 sq mi. **Racial distribution:** 40.1% white; 54.5% black; 3.1% Asian; 0.2% Amer. Ind.; <0.05% Pac. Isl.; 0.7% other; 2+ races 1.3%. **Hispanic pop.:** 3.1%. **Foreign born:** 4.9%. **U.S. citizens:** 96.9%. **Language:** 91.8% English only; 3.0% Spanish.
Employment: 98,893 employed; 8.4% unemployed. **Per capita income:** $37,254; change (2009-10): 1.0%. **Below poverty level:** 18.1%; 25.5% of families. **Educational attainment:** 84.2% HS; 32.0% bachelor's. **Avg. commute:** 20.7 min. 78.2% drive; 11.9% carpool. **Housing units:** 99,943; 88.6% occupied. **Home ownership:** 51.3%. **Avg. home:** $163,400; change (2009-11): 0.2%. **Avg. rent:** $733.
Mayor-President: Melvin "Kip" Holden, Democrat
History: Claimed by Spain at time of Louisiana Purchase 1803; est. independence by rebellion 1810; inc. as town 1817. Became state capital 1849; Union-held most of Civil War.
Website: www.brgov.com

Birmingham, Alabama

Population: 212,413 (98). **Pop. density:** 1,454. **Pop. change (2000-11):** −12.5%. **Area:** 146.1 sq mi. **Racial distribution:** 22.9% white; 73.9% black; 1.0% Asian; 0.2% Amer. Ind.; <0.05% Pac. Isl.; 1.4% other; 2+ races 0.6%. **Hispanic pop.:** 3.2%. **Foreign born:** 3.6%. **U.S. citizens:** 97.1%. **Language:** 94.9% English only; 3.3% Spanish.
Employment: 81,128 employed; 10.9% unemployed. **Per capita income:** $38,734; change (2009-10): 2.2%. **Below poverty level:** 21.2%; 26.4% of families. **Educational attainment:** 82.4% HS; 21.3% bachelor's. **Avg. commute:** 22.0 min. 78.7% drive; 14.2% carpool. **Housing units:** 111,375; 81.1% occupied. **Home ownership:** 52.1%. **Avg. home:** $139,800; change (2009-11): −4.3%. **Avg. rent:** $683.
Mayor: William A. Bell, nonpartisan
History: Settled 1871 at the intersection of two major railroads, within proximity of elements needed for iron and steel production.
Website: www.birminghamal.gov

Boston, Massachusetts

Population: 625,087 (21). **Pop. density:** 12,948. **Pop. change (2000-11):** 6.1%. **Area:** 48.3 sq mi. **Racial distribution:** 53.9% white; 25.0% black; 9.0% Asian; 0.4% Amer. Ind.; 0.1% Pac. Isl.; 8.3% other; 2+ races 3.5%. **Hispanic pop.:** 16.7%. **Foreign born:** 27.2%. **U.S. citizens:** 84.9%. **Language:** 64.5% English only; 15.0% Spanish.
Employment: 293,063 employed; 7.1% unemployed. **Per capita income:** $55,431; change (2009-10): 3.0%. **Below poverty level:** 15.9%; 21.2% of families. **Educational attainment:** 84.3% HS; 42.5% bachelor's. **Avg. commute:** 28.4 min. 38.7% drive; 32.9% public trans.; 14.9% walk. **Housing units:** 270,470; 90.9% occupied. **Home ownership:** 34.9%. **Avg. home:** $346,200; change (2009-11): 4.1%. **Avg. rent:** $1,199.
Mayor: Thomas M. Menino, Democrat
History: Settled 1630 by John Winthrop; capital of Mass. Bay Colony. Figured strongly in American Revolution, earning distinction as the "Cradle of Liberty"; inc. 1822.
Website: www.cityofboston.gov

Buffalo, New York

Population: 261,025 (72). **Pop. density:** 6,464. **Pop. change (2000-11):** −10.8%. **Area:** 40.4 sq mi. **Racial distribution:** 51.8% white; 38.4% black; 2.5% Asian; 0.6% Amer. Ind.; <0.05% Pac. Isl.; 3.7% other; 2+ races 2.8%. **Hispanic pop.:** 9.1%. **Foreign born:** 7.0%. **U.S. citizens:** 96.2%. **Language:** 86.3% English only; 6.8% Spanish.
Employment: 103,073 employed; 10.4% unemployed. **Per capita income:** $38,271; change (2009-10): 3.5%. **Below poverty level:** 25.2%; 29.6% of families. **Educational attainment:** 80.6% HS; 21.7% bachelor's. **Avg. commute:** 20.2 min. 66.3% drive; 13.2% public trans.; 10.0% carpool. **Housing units:** 139,171; 81.1% occupied. **Home ownership:** 43.3%. **Avg. home:** $119,200; change (2009-11): 4.9%. **Avg. rent:** $646.
Mayor: Byron W. Brown, Democrat
History: Settled 1780 by Seneca Indians; raided twice by British in War of 1812. Served as western terminus for Erie Canal; became a center for trade and manufacturing; inc. 1832. A last stop on the Underground Railroad. Key point for Canada-U.S. political, trade, and social relations.
Website: www.ci.buffalo.ny.us

Chandler, Arizona

Population: 240,101 (81). **Pop. density:** 3,728. **Pop. change (2000-11):** 36.0%. **Area:** 64.4 sq mi. **Racial distribution:** 79.1% white; 4.7% black; 7.7% Asian; 1.2% Amer. Ind.; 0.1% Pac. Isl.; 3.9% other; 2+ races 3.3%. **Hispanic pop.:** 21.9%. **Foreign born:** 13.7%. **U.S. citizens:** 92.4%. **Language:** 78.1% English only; 12.9% Spanish.
Employment: 122,763 employed; 7.1% unemployed. **Per capita income:** $36,047; change (2009-10): 1.3%. **Below poverty level:** 5.1%; 7.3% of families. **Educational attainment:** 92.2% HS; 39.4% bachelor's. **Avg. commute:** 25.1 min. 78.7% drive; 11.3% carpool. **Housing units:** 93,081; 91.3% occupied. **Home ownership:** 67.0%. **Avg. home:** $115,500; change (2009-11): −15.7%. **Avg. rent:** $1,034.
Mayor: Jay Tibshraeny, nonpartisan
History: Formed 1912; population doubled in 1990s as "the high-tech oasis of the Silicon Desert."
Website: www.chandleraz.gov

Charlotte, North Carolina

Population: 751,087 (17). **Pop. density:** 2,523. **Pop. change (2000-11):** 38.9%. **Area:** 297.7 sq mi. **Racial distribution:** 53.3% white; 34.5% black; 4.8% Asian; 0.4% Amer. Ind.; 0.1% Pac. Isl.; 4.8% other; 2+ races 2.1%. **Hispanic pop.:** 12.3%. **Foreign born:** 14.6%. **U.S. citizens:** 89.4%. **Language:** 81.2% English only; 11.0% Spanish.
Employment: 341,982 employed; 9.2% unemployed. **Per capita income:** $38,895; change (2009-10): 3.5%. **Below poverty level:** 10.4%; 13.9% of families. **Educational attainment:** 87.4% HS; 39.1% bachelor's. **Avg. commute:** 24.3 min. 76.3% drive; 12.4% carpool. **Housing units:** 311,891; 90.4% occupied. **Home ownership:** 59.3%. **Avg. rent:** $823.
Mayor: Anthony R. Foxx, Democrat
History: Settled by Scotch-Irish immigrants 1740s; inc. 1768 and named after Queen Charlotte, wife of English King George III. Scene of first major U.S. gold discovery 1799.
Website: www.charmeck.org

Chesapeake, Virginia

Population: 225,050 (91). **Pop. density:** 660. **Pop. change (2000-11):** 13.0%. **Area:** 340.8 sq mi. **Racial distribution:** 63.2% white; 29.9% black; 2.8% Asian; 0.5% Amer. Ind.; <0.05% Pac. Isl.; 1.4% other; 2+ races 2.2%. **Hispanic pop.:** 3.9%. **Foreign born:** 4.4%. **U.S. citizens:** 98.1%. **Language:** 93.3% English only; 3.0% Spanish.
Employment: 111,771 employed; 6.5% unemployed. **Per capita income:** $40,234; change (2009-10): 2.3%. **Below poverty level:** 5.2%; 6.8% of families. **Educational attainment:** 89.3% HS; 27.9% bachelor's. **Avg. commute:** 24.1 min. 85.8% drive. **Housing units:** 82,132; 95.9% occupied. **Home ownership:** 74.9%. **Avg. home:** $182,900; change (2009-11): −12.9%. **Avg. rent:** $1,005.
Mayor: Alan P. Krasnoff, Independent
History: Region settled in 1620s with first English colonies on banks of Elizabeth R. Home to Great Dismal Swamp Canal, first envisioned by George Washington in 1763. Battle of Great Bridge fought here Dec. 1775; inc. 1963.
Website: www.cityofchesapeake.net

Chicago, Illinois

Population: 2,707,120 (3). **Pop. density:** 11,892. **Pop. change (2000-11):** –6.5%. **Area:** 227.6 sq mi. **Racial distribution:** 42.7% white; 34.0% black; 5.4% Asian; 0.2% Amer. Ind.; <0.05% Pac. Isl.; 16.0% other; 2+ races 1.6%. **Hispanic pop.:** 27.9%. **Foreign born:** 21.1%. **U.S. citizens:** 87.4%. **Language:** 64.7% English only; 24.2% Spanish.
Employment: 1,116,216 employed; 11.3% unemployed. **Per capita income:** $44,344; change (2009-10): 2.3%. **Below poverty level:** 17.2%; 20.9% of families. **Educational attainment:** 79.4% HS; 32.2% bachelor's. **Avg. commute:** 33.6 min. 50.9% drive; 26.6% public trans.; 10.0% carpool. **Housing units:** 1,197,741; 86.2% occupied. **Home ownership:** 47.8%. **Avg. home:** $176,500; change (2009-11): –11.4%. **Avg. rent:** $885.
Mayor: Rahm Emanuel, nonpartisan
History: Site acquired from Indians 1795; significant white settlement began with completion of Erie Canal 1825; chartered as city 1837. Boomed with arrival of railroads and canal to Mississippi R.; one-third of city destroyed by fire 1871. Major grain and livestock market.
Website: www.cityofchicago.org

Chula Vista, California

Population: 247,535 (76). **Pop. density:** 4,988. **Pop. change (2000-11):** 42.6%. **Area:** 49.6 sq mi. **Racial distribution:** 62.6% white; 4.8% black; 14.3% Asian; 0.6% Amer. Ind.; 0.7% Pac. Isl.; 12.7% other; 2+ races 4.3%. **Hispanic pop.:** 55.9%. **Foreign born:** 30.8%. **U.S. citizens:** 85.9%. **Language:** 42.9% English only; 46.0% Spanish; 6.5% Tagalog.
Employment: 82,373 employed; 11.6% unemployed. **Per capita income:** $45,627; change (2009-10): 2.7%. **Below poverty level:** 8.0%; 9.6% of families. **Educational attainment:** 81.5% HS; 26.4% bachelor's. **Avg. commute:** 26.8 min. 78.2% drive; 11.7% carpool. **Housing units:** 80,281; 89.5% occupied. **Home ownership:** 60.3%. **Avg. home:** $370,300; change (2009-11): 3.0%. **Avg. rent:** $1,201.
Mayor: Cheryl Cox, nonpartisan
History: Visited by Spanish in 1542; became part of Spanish land grant in 1795; brought into the U.S. during the Mexican War in 1847; inc. 1911. WWII brought aircraft industry and growth.
Website: www.chulavistaca.gov

Cincinnati, Ohio

Population: 296,223 (64). **Pop. density:** 3,801. **Pop. change (2000-11):** –10.6%. **Area:** 77.9 sq mi. **Racial distribution:** 50.7% white; 44.0% black; 1.7% Asian; 0.2% Amer. Ind.; <0.05% Pac. Isl.; 0.9% other; 2+ races 2.4%. **Hispanic pop.:** 2.7%. **Foreign born:** 4.5%. **U.S. citizens:** 97.1%. **Language:** 93.2% English only; 2.9% Spanish.
Employment: 130,288 employed; 9.4% unemployed. **Per capita income:** $39,673; change (2009-10): 2.9%. **Below poverty level:** 22.0%; 27.2% of families. **Educational attainment:** 83.6% HS; 30.8% bachelor's. **Avg. commute:** 21.9 min. 71.1% drive. **Housing units:** 167,515; 79.2% occupied. **Home ownership:** 41.2%. **Avg. home:** $122,300; change (2009-11): –2.8%. **Avg. rent:** $593.
Mayor: Mark Mallory, nonpartisan
History: Founded 1788; named after the Society of Cincinnati, an organization of Revolutionary War officers; chartered as village 1802; inc. 1819.
Website: www.cincinnati-oh.gov

Cleveland, Ohio

Population: 393,806 (47). **Pop. density:** 5,068. **Pop. change (2000-11):** –17.7%. **Area:** 77.7 sq mi. **Racial distribution:** 40.2% white; 53.1% black; 1.7% Asian; 0.3% Amer. Ind.; <0.05% Pac. Isl.; 2.5% other; 2+ races 2.2%. **Hispanic pop.:** 9.2%. **Foreign born:** 4.6%. **U.S. citizens:** 97.6%. **Language:** 88.4% English only; 7.1% Spanish.
Employment: 150,814 employed; 10.3% unemployed. **Per capita income:** $40,509; change (2009-10): 3.8%. **Below poverty level:** 26.4%; 31.2% of families. **Educational attainment:** 75.7% HS; 13.1% bachelor's. **Avg. commute:** 24.0 min. 69.5% drive; 12.0% public trans.; 10.0% carpool. **Housing units:** 216,561; 78.7% occupied. **Home ownership:** 47.1%. **Avg. home:** $105,100; change (2009-11): –1.6%. **Avg. rent:** $628.
Mayor: Frank G. Jackson, nonpartisan
History: Surveyed in 1796; given recognition as village 1815; inc. 1836; annexed Ohio City 1854.
Website: www.city.cleveland.oh.us

Colorado Springs, Colorado

Population: 426,388 (41). **Pop. density:** 2,192. **Pop. change (2000-11):** 18.1%. **Area:** 194.5 sq mi. **Racial distribution:** 80.0% white; 6.3% black; 2.7% Asian; 0.9% Amer. Ind.; 0.2% Pac. Isl.; 4.9% other; 2+ races 5.0%. **Hispanic pop.:** 15.5%. **Foreign born:** 8.0%. **U.S. citizens:** 95.4%. **Language:** 87.6% English only; 7.4% Spanish.
Employment: 189,105 employed; 9.1% unemployed. **Per capita income:** $38,405; change (2009-10): 2.5%. **Below** poverty level: 8.6%; 11.8% of families. **Educational attainment:** 91.9% HS; 35.9% bachelor's. **Avg. commute:** 20.8 min. 79.2% drive; 10.2% carpool. **Housing units:** 177,677; 91.3% occupied. **Home ownership:** 62.3%. **Avg. home:** $187,200; change (2009-11): –1.4%. **Avg. rent:** $781.
Mayor: Steve Bach, nonpartisan
History: Founded 1871 at the foot of Pike's Peak; inc. 1872.
Website: www.springsgov.com

Columbus, Ohio

Population: 797,434 (15). **Pop. density:** 3,672. **Pop. change (2000-11):** 12.1%. **Area:** 217.2 sq mi. **Racial distribution:** 63.4% white; 27.8% black; 4.1% Asian; 0.2% Amer. Ind.; <0.05% Pac. Isl.; 1.6% other; 2+ races 2.8%. **Hispanic pop.:** 5.1%. **Foreign born:** 10.1%. **U.S. citizens:** 93.1%. **Language:** 87.4% English only; 4.3% Spanish.
Employment: 389,766 employed; 7.6% unemployed. **Per capita income:** $38,205; change (2009-10): 2.2%. **Below poverty level:** 15.8%; 21.4% of families. **Educational attainment:** 87.3% HS; 31.9% bachelor's. **Avg. commute:** 20.8 min. 80.8% drive. **Housing units:** 370,489; 86.0% occupied. **Home ownership:** 49.5%. **Avg. home:** $123,900; change (2009-11): –8.2%. **Avg. rent:** $753.
Mayor: Michael B. Coleman, Democrat
History: First settlement 1797; laid out as new state capital 1812 with current name; inc. 1834.
Website: www.columbus.gov

Corpus Christi, Texas

Population: 307,953 (60). **Pop. density:** 1,917. **Pop. change (2000-11):** 11.0%. **Area:** 160.6 sq mi. **Racial distribution:** 81.8% white; 4.4% black; 1.7% Asian; 0.4% Amer. Ind.; <0.05% Pac. Isl.; 9.6% other; 2+ races 2.1%. **Hispanic pop.:** 58.7%. **Foreign born:** 7.6%. **U.S. citizens:** 95.4%. **Language:** 60.8% English only; 36.7% Spanish.
Employment: 148,439 employed; 7.3% unemployed. **Per capita income:** $36,091; change (2009-10): 5.2%. **Below poverty level:** 14.8%; 18.8% of families. **Educational attainment:** 79.3% HS; 20.6% bachelor's. **Avg. commute:** 18.9 min. 79.0% drive; 11.7% carpool. **Housing units:** 122,352; 89.2% occupied. **Home ownership:** 60.2%. **Avg. home:** $134,200; change (2009-11): –0.1%. **Avg. rent:** $796.
Mayor: Joe Adame, nonpartisan
History: Settled 1839; inc. 1852. One of the largest U.S. ports.
Website: www.cctexas.com

Dallas, Texas

Population: 1,223,229 (9). **Pop. density:** 3,592. **Pop. change (2000-11):** 2.9%. **Area:** 340.5 sq mi. **Racial distribution:** 54.4% white; 24.6% black; 2.8% Asian; 0.4% Amer. Ind.; <0.05% Pac. Isl.; 16.1% other; 2+ races 1.8%. **Hispanic pop.:** 41.6%. **Foreign born:** 24.9%. **U.S. citizens:** 80.2%. **Language:** 58.3% English only; 37.1% Spanish.
Employment: 527,684 employed; 8.5% unemployed. **Per capita income:** $41,242; change (2009-10): 2.6%. **Below poverty level:** 18.9%; 22.3% of families. **Educational attainment:** 72.9% HS; 28.6% bachelor's. **Avg. commute:** 25.0 min. 76.5% drive; 12.4% carpool. **Housing units:** 515,414; 87.2% occupied. **Home ownership:** 45.8%. **Avg. home:** $148,900; change (2009-11): 6.0%. **Avg. rent:** $789.
Mayor: Mike Rawlings, nonpartisan
History: First settled 1841; platted 1846; inc. 1871. Developed as financial and commercial center of Southwest; headquarters of regional Federal Reserve Bank; major center for distribution and high-tech manufacturing.
Website: www.dallascityhall.com

Denver, Colorado

Population: 619,968 (23). **Pop. density:** 4,052. **Pop. change (2000-11):** 11.8%. **Area:** 153.0 sq mi. **Racial distribution:** 72.9% white; 10.3% black; 3.3% Asian; 1.1% Amer. Ind.; 0.1% Pac. Isl.; 9.3% other; 2+ races 2.9%. **Hispanic pop.:** 32.1%. **Foreign born:** 16.6%. **U.S. citizens:** 88.1%. **Language:** 72.3% English only; 21.4% Spanish.
Employment: 292,806 employed; 9.1% unemployed. **Per capita income:** $46,871; change (2009-10): 2.1%. **Below poverty level:** 14.8%; 19.2% of families. **Educational attainment:** 84.0% HS; 40.1% bachelor's. **Avg. commute:** 24.6 min. 69.3% drive; 10.1% carpool. **Housing units:** 281,296; 90.4% occupied. **Home ownership:** 52.5%. **Avg. home:** $231,400; change (2009-11): 5.2%. **Avg. rent:** $798.
Mayor: Michael Hancock, nonpartisan
History: Settled 1858 by gold prospectors and miners; inc. 1861; became territorial capital 1867. Growth spurred by gold and silver boom. Became financial, industrial, cultural center of Rocky Mt. region.
Website: www.denvergov.org

Detroit, Michigan

Population: 706,585 (18). **Pop. density:** 5,093. **Pop. change (2000-11):** –25.7%. **Area:** 138.8 sq mi. **Racial distribution:** 10.6% white; 82.7% black; 1.2% Asian; 0.3% Amer. Ind.; <0.05% Pac. Isl.; 3.4% other; 2+ races 1.7%. **Hispanic pop.:** 6.4%. **Foreign born:** 5.1%. **U.S. citizens:** 96.5%. **Language:** 90.8% English only; 5.8% Spanish.
Employment: 279,291 employed; 19.9% unemployed. **Per capita income:** $38,017; change (2009-10): 3.3%. **Below poverty level:** 29.4%; 34.5% of families. **Educational attainment:** 76.8% HS; 11.8% bachelor's. **Avg. commute:** 26.2 min. 72.8% drive; 11.5% carpool. **Housing units:** 365,058; 74.2% occupied. **Home ownership:** 54.5%. **Avg. home:** $53,800. **Avg. rent:** $747.
Mayor: Dave Bing, nonpartisan
History: Founded by French 1701; controlled by British 1760; acquired by U.S. 1796. Destroyed by fire 1805; fought over during War of 1812; inc. 1815; capital of state 1837-47. Auto manufacturing began 1890.
Website: www.detroitmi.gov

Durham, North Carolina

Population: 233,252 (84). **Pop. density:** 2,172. **Pop. change (2000-11):** 24.7%. **Area:** 107.4 sq mi. **Racial distribution:** 42.4% white; 40.3% black; 5.0% Asian; 0.1% Amer. Ind.; <0.05% Pac. Isl.; 9.3% other; 2+ races 2.8%. **Hispanic pop.:** 13.2%. **Foreign born:** 14.7%. **U.S. citizens:** 88.5%. **Language:** 80.0% English only; 12.5% Spanish.
Employment: 108,853 employed; 7.9% unemployed. **Per capita income:** $40,597; change (2009-10): 1.3%. **Below poverty level:** 12.4%; 17.9% of families. **Educational attainment:** 85.9% HS; 45.6% bachelor's. **Avg. commute:** 21.3 min. 74.1% drive; 14.0% carpool. **Housing units:** 101,761; 89.1% occupied. **Home ownership:** 51.3%. **Avg. rent:** $786.
Mayor: William V. Bell, nonpartisan
History: Inc. 1869. Trinity College moved to Durham in 1892, renamed Duke Univ. in 1924.
Website: durhamnc.gov

El Paso, Texas

Population: 665,568 (19). **Pop. density:** 2,608. **Pop. change (2000-11):** 18.1%. **Area:** 255.2 sq mi. **Racial distribution:** 78.2% white; 3.2% black; 1.2% Asian; 0.5% Amer. Ind.; 0.1% Pac. Isl.; 14.5% other; 2+ races 2.3%. **Hispanic pop.:** 80.3%. **Foreign born:** 25.8%. **U.S. citizens:** 85.3%. **Language:** 27.0% English only; 70.7% Spanish.
Employment: 247,754 employed; 9.5% unemployed. **Per capita income:** $28,698; change (2009-10): 5.2%. **Below poverty level:** 21.0%; 24.1% of families. **Educational attainment:** 73.6% HS; 21.3% bachelor's. **Avg. commute:** 21.8 min. 80.3% drive; 10.8% carpool. **Housing units:** 223,836; 92.2% occupied. **Home ownership:** 61.3%. **Avg. home:** $134,300; change (2009-11): 1.3%. **Avg. rent:** $620.
Mayor: John Cook, nonpartisan
History: First settled 1598; inc. 1873. Arrival of railroad, 1881, boosted city's population and industries.
Website: www.elpasotexas.gov

Fort Wayne, Indiana

Population: 255,824 (74). **Pop. density:** 2,313. **Pop. change (2000-11):** 24.4%. **Area:** 110.6 sq mi. **Racial distribution:** 75.3% white; 15.3% black; 2.8% Asian; 0.3% Amer. Ind.; <0.05% Pac. Isl.; 3.3% other; 2+ races 3.0%. **Hispanic pop.:** 7.5%. **Foreign born:** 6.5%. **U.S. citizens:** 95.9%. **Language:** 90.4% English only; 5.4% Spanish.
Employment: 113,668 employed; 9.6% unemployed. **Per capita income:** $33,698; change (2009-10): 2.2%. **Below poverty level:** 11.4%; 15.0% of families. **Educational attainment:** 87.7% HS; 25.5% bachelor's. **Avg. commute:** 19.6 min. 85.8% drive. **Housing units:** 115,024; 88.1% occupied. **Home ownership:** 64.5%. **Avg. home:** $95,400; change (2009-11): 1.5%. **Avg. rent:** $623.
Mayor: Tom Henry, Democrat
History: French fort 1680; U.S. fort 1794; settled by 1832; inc. 1840 prior to Wabash-Erie Canal completion in 1843.
Website: www.cityoffortwayne.org

Fort Worth, Texas

Population: 758,738 (16). **Pop. density:** 2,233. **Pop. change (2000-11):** 41.9%. **Area:** 339.8 sq mi. **Racial distribution:** 62.6% white; 18.6% black; 3.4% Asian; 0.6% Amer. Ind.; 0.1% Pac. Isl.; 12.7% other; 2+ races 2.0%. **Hispanic pop.:** 33.2%. **Foreign born:** 17.4%. **U.S. citizens:** 87.3%. **Language:** 68.1% English only; 27.2% Spanish.
Employment: 322,341 employed; 8.0% unemployed. **Per capita income:** $41,282; change (2009-10): 2.6%. **Below poverty level:** 13.5%; 17.0% of families. **Educational attainment:** 78.6% HS; 25.7% bachelor's. **Avg. commute:** 25.5 min. 80.5% drive; 11.7% carpool. **Housing units:** 282,500; 89.1% occupied.

Home ownership: 60.3%. **Avg. home:** $148,900; change (2009-11): 6.0%. **Avg. rent:** $803.
Mayor: Betsy Price, nonpartisan
History: Established as military post 1849; inc. 1873; oil discovered 1917.
Website: fortworthtexas.gov

Fremont, California

Population: 216,916 (95). **Pop. density:** 2,800. **Pop. change (2000-11):** 6.6%. **Area:** 77.5 sq mi. **Racial distribution:** 34.9% white; 3.3% black; 49.2% Asian; 0.4% Amer. Ind.; 0.8% Pac. Isl.; 6.8% other; 2+ races 4.6%. **Hispanic pop.:** 14.1%. **Foreign born:** 43.1%. **U.S. citizens:** 80.9%. **Language:** 43.5% English only; 9.6% Spanish; 16.3% Chinese; 5.7% Hindi.
Employment: 101,068 employed; 7.5% unemployed. **Per capita income:** $59,295; change (2009-10): 3.0%. **Below poverty level:** 3.4%; 5.2% of families. **Educational attainment:** 91.1% HS; 50.1% bachelor's. **Avg. commute:** 29.0 min. 75.4% drive; 10.7% carpool. **Housing units:** 74,218; 92.9% occupied. **Home ownership:** 64.8%. **Avg. home:** $483,400; change (2009-11): –2.0%. **Avg. rent:** $1,456.
Mayor: Gus Morrison, nonpartisan
History: Area first settled by Spanish 1769; inc. 1956 with consolidation of five communities.
Website: www.fremont.gov

Fresno, California

Population: 501,362 (34). **Pop. density:** 4,478. **Pop. change (2000-11):** 17.2%. **Area:** 112.0 sq mi. **Racial distribution:** 54.2% white; 7.7% black; 12.4% Asian; 0.9% Amer. Ind.; 0.1% Pac. Isl.; 20.3% other; 2+ races 4.3%. **Hispanic pop.:** 45.7%. **Foreign born:** 20.9%. **U.S. citizens:** 86.4%. **Language:** 57.6% English only; 29.0% Spanish.
Employment: 195,782 employed; 15.6% unemployed. **Per capita income:** $30,905; change (2009-10): 2.5%. **Below poverty level:** 19.9%; 24.9% of families. **Educational attainment:** 74.7% HS; 20.5% bachelor's. **Avg. commute:** 20.8 min. 77.0% drive; 12.2% carpool. **Housing units:** 169,066; 92.4% occupied. **Home ownership:** 49.5%. **Avg. rent:** $832.
Mayor: Ashley Swearengin, nonpartisan
History: Founded 1872; inc. 1885.
Website: www.fresno.gov

Garland, Texas

Population: 231,517 (86). **Pop. density:** 4,056. **Pop. change (2000-11):** 7.3%. **Area:** 57.1 sq mi. **Racial distribution:** 50.1% white; 14.2% black; 9.8% Asian; 0.4% Amer. Ind.; 0.1% Pac. Isl.; 21.0% other; 2+ races 4.5%. **Hispanic pop.:** 36.0%. **Foreign born:** 27.4%. **U.S. citizens:** 81.2%. **Language:** 56.3% English only; 31.7% Spanish.
Employment: 106,155 employed; 8.1% unemployed. **Per capita income:** $41,282; change (2009-10): 2.6%. **Below poverty level:** 10.6%; 13.4% of families. **Educational attainment:** 75.6% HS; 21.7% bachelor's. **Avg. commute:** 27.8 min. 78.5% drive; 13.9% carpool. **Housing units:** 78,349; 92.6% occupied. **Home ownership:** 65.5%. **Avg. home:** $148,900; change (2009-11): 6.0%. **Avg. rent:** $890.
Mayor: Ronald Jones, nonpartisan
History: Settled 1850s; inc. 1891.
Website: www.garlandtx.gov

Gilbert, Arizona

Population: 211,951 (99). **Pop. density:** 3,119. **Pop. change (2000-11):** 93.2%. **Area:** 68.0 sq mi. **Racial distribution:** 81.8% white; 4.1% black; 5.5% Asian; 0.7% Amer. Ind.; 0.4% Pac. Isl.; 4.3% other; 2+ races 3.2%. **Hispanic pop.:** 13.2%. **Foreign born:** 8.8%. **U.S. citizens:** 95.8%. **Language:** 84.9% English only; 7.8% Spanish.
Employment: 106,597 employed; 6.4% unemployed. **Per capita income:** $36,047; change (2009-10): 1.3%. **Below poverty level:** 4.4%; 5.5% of families. **Educational attainment:** 95.4% HS; 38.8% bachelor's. **Avg. commute:** 27.4 min. 79.3% drive; 12.3% carpool. **Housing units:** 69,322; 92.8% occupied. **Home ownership:** 76.0%. **Avg. home:** $115,500; change (2009-11): –15.7%. **Avg. rent:** $1,231.
Mayor: John Lewis, nonpartisan
History: Est. 1891; inc. 1920.
Website: www.gilbertaz.gov

Glendale, Arizona

Population: 230,482 (87). **Pop. density:** 3,843. **Pop. change (2000-11):** 5.3%. **Area:** 60.0 sq mi. **Racial distribution:** 75.9% white; 5.9% black; 3.7% Asian; 1.6% Amer. Ind.; 0.1% Pac. Isl.; 9.6% other; 2+ races 3.2%. **Hispanic pop.:** 34.5%. **Foreign born:** 16.4%. **U.S. citizens:** 88.7%. **Language:** 69.7% English only; 23.6% Spanish.
Employment: 106,242 employed; 8.9% unemployed. **Per capita income:** $36,047; change (2009-10): 1.3%. **Below poverty level:** 13.1%; 16.6% of families. **Educational attainment:** 82.7% HS; 21.0% bachelor's. **Avg. commute:** 26.3 min. 74.7%

drive; 15.2% carpool. **Housing units:** 89,931; 89.2% occupied. **Home ownership:** 61.8%. **Avg. home:** $115,500; change (2009-11): −15.7%. **Avg. rent:** $832.
Mayor: Elaine M. Scruggs, nonpartisan
History: Est. 1892; inc. 1910.
Website: www.glendaleaz.com

Greensboro, North Carolina

Population: 273,425 (69). **Pop. density:** 2,161. **Pop. change (2000-11):** 22.1%. **Area:** 126.5 sq mi. **Racial distribution:** 51.4% white; 38.9% black; 4.1% Asian; 0.5% Amer. Ind.; 0.1% Pac. Isl.; 3.2% other; 2+ races 1.8%. **Hispanic pop.:** 7.0%. **Foreign born:** 10.2%. **U.S. citizens:** 93.0%. **Language:** 86.7% English only; 6.7% Spanish.
Employment: 124,378 employed; 10.2% unemployed. **Per capita income:** $34,296; change (2009-10): 2.0%. **Below poverty level:** 12.7%; 18.1% of families. **Educational attainment:** 87.1% HS; 35.4% bachelor's. **Avg. commute:** 19.7 min. 81.9% drive. **Housing units:** 122,124; 88.2% occupied. **Home ownership:** 55.2%. **Avg. home:** $123,800; change (2009-11): −6.8%. **Avg. rent:** $717.
Mayor: Robbie Perkins, nonpartisan
History: Settled 1749; site of Revolutionary War conflict 1781 between Generals Nathanael Greene and Lord Charles Cornwallis; inc. 1807. Origin of civil rights sit-in movement.
Website: www.greensboro-nc.gov

Henderson, Nevada

Population: 260,068 (73). **Pop. density:** 2,414. **Pop. change (2000-11):** 48.3%. **Area:** 107.7 sq mi. **Racial distribution:** 78.9% white; 5.3% black; 7.2% Asian; 0.5% Amer. Ind.; 0.6% Pac. Isl.; 3.9% other; 2+ races 3.5%. **Hispanic pop.:** 13.9%. **Foreign born:** 11.8%. **U.S. citizens:** 95.4%. **Language:** 83.8% English only; 7.8% Spanish.
Employment: 124,335 employed; 12.9% unemployed. **Per capita income:** $35,723; change (2009-10): 0.7%. **Below poverty level:** 4.9%; 7.3% of families. **Educational attainment:** 92.0% HS; 29.2% bachelor's. **Avg. commute:** 22.9 min. 82.7% drive. **Housing units:** 110,962; 88.5% occupied. **Home ownership:** 67.6%. **Avg. home:** $124,700; change (2009-11): −12.7%. **Avg. rent:** $1,188.
Mayor: Andy A. Hafen, nonpartisan
History: Early growth spurred by WWII magnesium mining; inc. 1953.
Website: www.cityofhenderson.com

Hialeah, Florida

Population: 229,969 (89). **Pop. density:** 10,721. **Pop. change (2000-11):** 1.6%. **Area:** 21.5 sq mi. **Racial distribution:** 92.2% white; 2.4% black; 0.3% Asian; <0.05% Amer. Ind.; <0.05% Pac. Isl.; 4.0% other; 2+ races 1.0%. **Hispanic pop.:** 95.6%. **Foreign born:** 73.2%. **U.S. citizens:** 59.1%. **Language:** 5.8% English only; 93.8% Spanish.
Employment: 89,482 employed; 14.1% unemployed. **Per capita income:** $41,769; change (2009-10): 1.7%. **Below poverty level:** 17.0%; 20.1% of families. **Educational attainment:** 66.7% HS; 13.5% bachelor's. **Avg. commute:** 24.9 min. 77.9% drive. **Housing units:** 78,047; 94.6% occupied. **Home ownership:** 52.2%. **Avg. home:** $181,100; change (2009-11): −14.3%. **Avg. rent:** $937.
Mayor: Carlos Hernandez, nonpartisan
History: Founded 1917; inc. 1925. Industrial and residential city NW of Miami; site of Hialeah Park Racetrack.
Website: www.hialeahfl.gov

Honolulu, Hawaii

Population: 340,936 (55). **Pop. density:** 5,633. **Pop. change (2000-11):** 9.0%. **Area:** 60.5 sq mi. **Racial distribution:** 18.1% white; 1.5% black; 56.7% Asian; 0.2% Amer. Ind.; 7.5% Pac. Isl.; 0.7% other; 2+ races 15.4%. **Hispanic pop.:** 4.7%. **Foreign born:** 28.4%. **U.S. citizens:** 86.6%. **Language:** 62.2% English only; 1.5% Spanish; 7.2% Chinese; 7.2% Japanese; 5.5% Tagalog; 8.0% other Pac. Isl. languages.
Employment: 434,211 employed; 5.7% unemployed. **Per capita income:** $45,216; change (2009-10): 2.4%. **Below poverty level:** 7.3%; 11.3% of families. **Educational attainment:** 87.6% HS; 33.3% bachelor's. **Avg. commute:** 22.2 min. 56.8% drive; 14.1% carpool; 12.6% public trans. **Housing units:** 143,452; 88.0% occupied. **Home ownership:** 45.8%. **Avg. home:** $597,000; change (2009-11): 0.1%. **Avg. rent:** $1,135.
Mayor: Peter Carlisle, nonpartisan
History: Europeans entered harbor 1778; declared capital of kingdom by King Kamehameha III 1850. Pearl Harbor naval base attacked by Japanese Dec. 7, 1941.
Website: www.honolulu.gov

Houston, Texas

Population: 2,145,146 (4). **Pop. density:** 3,578. **Pop. change (2000-11):** 9.8%. **Area:** 599.6 sq mi. **Racial distribution:** 54.8% white; 24.4% black; 5.9% Asian; 0.4% Amer. Ind.; 0.1% Pac. Isl.;

13.2% other; 2+ races 1.3%. **Hispanic pop.:** 42.4%. **Foreign born:** 28.3%. **U.S. citizens:** 79.3%. **Language:** 54.7% English only; 37.2% Spanish.
Employment: 931,857 employed; 8.2% unemployed. **Per capita income:** $44,001; change (2009-10): 2.8%. **Below poverty level:** 17.6%; 21.0% of families. **Educational attainment:** 74.0% HS; 28.2% bachelor's. **Avg. commute:** 26.0 min. 74.2% drive; 13.5% carpool. **Housing units:** 889,489; 86.0% occupied. **Home ownership:** 46.6%. **Avg. home:** $155,700; change (2009-11): 1.7%. **Avg. rent:** $793.
Mayor: Annise D. Parker, Democrat
History: Founded 1836; inc. 1837; capital of Rep. of Texas 1837-39. Developed rapidly after completion of channel to Gulf of Mexico 1914. World center of oil, natural gas technology.
Website: www.houstontx.gov

Indianapolis, Indiana

Population: 827,609 (12). **Pop. density:** 2,290. **Pop. change (2000-11):** 4.5%. **Area:** 361.4 sq mi. **Racial distribution:** 64.3% white; 27.1% black; 2.0% Asian; 0.2% Amer. Ind.; <0.05% Pac. Isl.; 3.9% other; 2+ races 2.5%. **Hispanic pop.:** 8.4%. **Foreign born:** 8.1%. **U.S. citizens:** 94.0%. **Language:** 88.5% English only; 7.7% Spanish.
Employment: 380,724 employed; 9.4% unemployed. **Per capita income:** $38,796; change (2009-10): 2.1%. **Below poverty level:** 14.0%; 17.9% of families. **Educational attainment:** 83.7% HS; 27.3% bachelor's. **Avg. commute:** 22.2 min. 81.9% drive; 10.1% carpool. **Housing units:** 379,532; 85.5% occupied. **Home ownership:** 58.1%. **Avg. home:** $123,900; change (2009-11): 8.5%. **Avg. rent:** $716.
Mayor: Gregory A. Ballard, Republican
History: Settled 1820; became state capital 1825.
Website: www.indy.gov

Irvine, California

Population: 215,529 (96). **Pop. density:** 3,260. **Pop. change (2000-11):** 50.6%. **Area:** 66.1 sq mi. **Racial distribution:** 54.0% white; 1.9% black; 38.0% Asian; 0.3% Amer. Ind.; 0.3% Pac. Isl.; 2.2% other; 2+ races 3.4%. **Hispanic pop.:** 9.0%. **Foreign born:** 34.1%. **U.S. citizens:** 84.8%. **Language:** 57.8% English only; 5.6% Spanish; 9.4% Chinese; 6.4% Korean.
Employment: 77,840 employed; 6.5% unemployed. **Per capita income:** $43,688; change (2009-10): 3.2%. **Below poverty level:** 4.9%; 10.2% of families. **Educational attainment:** 96.4% HS; 65.5% bachelor's. **Avg. commute:** 22.3 min. 77.1% drive. **Housing units:** 76,184; 94.1% occupied. **Home ownership:** 53.2%. **Avg. home:** $307,700; change (2009-11): −7.9%. **Avg. rent:** $1,788.
Mayor: Sukhee Kang, nonpartisan
History: Univ. of CA–Irvine campus announced 1959; planned city developed around campus 1960s; inc. 1971.
Website: www.cityofirvine.org

Irving, Texas

Population: 220,702 (93). **Pop. density:** 3,293. **Pop. change (2000-11):** 15.2%. **Area:** 67.0 sq mi. **Racial distribution:** 61.1% white; 11.9% black; 13.1% Asian; 0.7% Amer. Ind.; 0.1% Pac. Isl.; 11.2% other; 2+ races 1.9%. **Hispanic pop.:** 40.6%. **Foreign born:** 32.8%. **U.S. citizens:** 75.7%. **Language:** 50.6% English only; 34.9% Spanish.
Employment: 112,129 employed; 7.2% unemployed. **Per capita income:** $41,282; change (2009-10): 2.6%. **Below poverty level:** 13.8%; 16.4% of families. **Educational attainment:** 78.3% HS; 32.6% bachelor's. **Avg. commute:** 22.0 min. 78.3% drive; 13.4% carpool. **Housing units:** 90,079; 89.5% occupied. **Home ownership:** 39.6%. **Avg. home:** $148,900; change (2009-11): 6.0%. **Avg. rent:** $847.
Mayor: Beth Van Duyne, nonpartisan
History: Founded 1903; inc. 1914; remained small until 1950s.
Website: www.ci.irving.tx.us

Jacksonville, Florida

Population: 827,908 (11). **Pop. density:** 1,108. **Pop. change (2000-11):** 12.5%. **Area:** 747.0 sq mi. **Racial distribution:** 60.8% white; 30.5% black; 4.1% Asian; 0.3% Amer. Ind.; 0.1% Pac. Isl.; 1.9% other; 2+ races 2.4%. **Hispanic pop.:** 7.2%. **Foreign born:** 9.2%. **U.S. citizens:** 95.4%. **Language:** 87.1% English only; 5.8% Spanish.
Employment: 376,764 employed; 10.4% unemployed. **Per capita income:** $39,550; change (2009-10): 3.0%. **Below poverty level:** 10.5%; 14.3% of families. **Educational attainment:** 86.9% HS; 24.0% bachelor's. **Avg. commute:** 23.4 min. 80.5% drive; 11.4% carpool. **Housing units:** 361,128; 86.1% occupied. **Home ownership:** 63.2%. **Avg. home:** $123,600; change (2009-11): −15.3%. **Avg. rent:** $872.
Mayor: Alvin Brown, Democrat
History: Settled 1816 as Cowford; renamed after Andrew Jackson 1822; inc. 1832; rechartered 1851. Scene of conflicts in Seminole and Civil Wars.
Website: www.coj.net

Jersey City, New Jersey

Population: 250,323 (75). **Pop. density:** 16,921. **Pop. change (2000-11):** 4.3%. **Area:** 14.8 sq mi. **Racial distribution:** 34.2% white; 26.8% black; 22.4% Asian; 0.4% Amer. Ind.; <0.05% Pac. Isl.; 13.8% other; 2+ races 2.3%. **Hispanic pop.:** 28.1%. **Foreign born:** 38.2%. **U.S. citizens:** 78.9%. **Language:** 48.0% English only; 24.4% Spanish; 5.7% Tagalog.
Employment: 104,855 employed; 10.8% unemployed. **Per capita income:** $54,365; change (2009-10): 3.7%. **Below poverty level:** 15.1%; 17.5% of families. **Educational attainment:** 83.1% HS; 39.6% bachelor's. **Avg. commute:** 34.0 min. 45.9% public trans.; 34.1% drive. **Housing units:** 106,937; 87.0% occupied. **Home ownership:** 32.2%. **Avg. home:** $378,500; change (2009-11): –0.8%. **Avg. rent:** $1,082.
Mayor: Jerramiah Healy, nonpartisan
History: Site bought from Indians 1630; chartered as town by British 1668; scene of Revolutionary War conflict 1779; chartered under present name 1838. Important station on Underground Railroad.
Website: www.cityofjerseycity.com

Kansas City, Missouri

Population: 463,202 (37). **Pop. density:** 1,471. **Pop. change (2000-11):** 4.9%. **Area:** 315.0 sq mi. **Racial distribution:** 60.5% white; 29.9% black; 2.3% Asian; 0.5% Amer. Ind.; 0.2% Pac. Isl.; 3.5% other; 2+ races 3.1%. **Hispanic pop.:** 9.7%. **Foreign born:** 7.5%. **U.S. citizens:** 95.3%. **Language:** 88.4% English only; 7.1% Spanish.
Employment: 210,698 employed; 9.2% unemployed. **Per capita income:** $41,557; change (2009-10): 1.2%. **Below poverty level:** 13.7%; 18.1% of families. **Educational attainment:** 86.4% HS; 29.6% bachelor's. **Avg. commute:** 21.2 min. 80.5% drive. **Housing units:** 224,317; 85.9% occupied. **Home ownership:** 58.2%. **Avg. home:** $133,200; change (2009-11): –5.3%. **Avg. rent:** $721.
Mayor: Sly James, nonpartisan
History: Settled by 1838 at confluence of Missouri and Kansas Rivers; inc. 1850.
Website: www.kcmo.org

Laredo, Texas

Population: 241,935 (80). **Pop. density:** 2,721. **Pop. change (2000-11):** 37.0%. **Area:** 88.9 sq mi. **Racial distribution:** 84.0% white; 0.4% black; 0.7% Asian; 0.3% Amer. Ind.; <0.05% Pac. Isl.; 13.4% other; 2+ races 1.2%. **Hispanic pop.:** 95.3%. **Foreign born:** 29.2%. **U.S. citizens:** 79.2%. **Language:** 7.6% English only; 91.6% Spanish.
Employment: 88,304 employed; 7.7% unemployed. **Per capita income:** $23,680; change (2009-10): 5.3%. **Below poverty level:** 24.8%; 29.2% of families. **Educational attainment:** 63.8% HS; 17.3% bachelor's. **Avg. commute:** 20.4 min. 77.5% drive. 14.1% carpool. **Housing units:** 66,773; 91.7% occupied. **Home ownership:** 63.8%. **Avg. rent:** $693.
Mayor: Raul G. Salinas, nonpartisan
History: Founded by Spanish colonists in 1755; part of U.S. from 1848. Fast growth fueled by immigration. Principal port of entry into Mexico.
Website: www.cityoflaredo.com

Las Vegas, Nevada

Population: 589,317 (31). **Pop. density:** 4,339. **Pop. change (2000-11):** 23.2%. **Area:** 135.8 sq mi. **Racial distribution:** 70.2% white; 10.8% black; 6.1% Asian; 0.6% Amer. Ind.; 0.5% Pac. Isl.; 7.6% other; 2+ races 4.1%. **Hispanic pop.:** 30.9%. **Foreign born:** 22.3%. **U.S. citizens:** 85.2%. **Language:** 66.9% English only; 24.8% Spanish.
Employment: 248,022 employed; 14.2% unemployed. **Per capita income:** $35,723; change (2009-10): 0.7%. **Below poverty level:** 9.7%; 13.1% of families. **Educational attainment:** 81.6% HS; 21.1% bachelor's. **Avg. commute:** 25.3 min. 76.9% drive; 11.9% carpool. **Housing units:** 243,741; 87.0% occupied. **Home ownership:** 57.7%. **Avg. home:** $124,700; change (2009-11): –12.7%. **Avg. rent:** $999.
Mayor: Carolyn G. Goodman, nonpartisan
History: Occupied by Mormons 1855-57; bought by railroad 1903; city of Las Vegas inc. 1911. Gambling legalized 1931.
Website: www.lasvegasnevada.gov

Lexington, Kentucky

Population: 301,569 (62). **Pop. density:** 1,063. **Pop. change (2000-11):** 15.8%. **Area:** 283.6 sq mi. **Racial distribution:** 77.2% white; 14.3% black; 3.3% Asian; 0.2% Amer. Ind.; 0.1% Pac. Isl.; 2.9% other; 2+ races 2.1%. **Hispanic pop.:** 6.2%. **Foreign born:** 8.5%. **U.S. citizens:** 93.7%. **Language:** 89.4% English only; 5.6% Spanish.
Employment: 141,601 employed; 7.4% unemployed. **Per capita income:** $36,015; change (2009-10): 0.5%. **Below poverty level:** 11.1%; 17.4% of families. **Educational attainment:** 88.3% HS; 39.1% bachelor's. **Avg. commute:** 19.7 min. 80.2% drive; 10.5% carpool. **Housing units:** 132,874; 91.0% occupied. **Home ownership:** 56.9%. **Avg. home:** $138,600; change (2009-11): –2.0%. **Avg. rent:** $693.

Mayor: Jim Gray, nonpartisan
History: Site bought and named in 1775 after site of the Revolutionary War's opening battle at Lexington, MA; settled 1779; chartered 1782; inc. 1832.
Website: www.lexingtonky.gov

Lincoln, Nebraska

Population: 262,341 (71). **Pop. density:** 2,944. **Pop. change (2000-11):** 16.3%. **Area:** 89.1 sq mi. **Racial distribution:** 88.3% white; 3.6% black; 3.8% Asian; 0.7% Amer. Ind.; 0.1% Pac. Isl.; 1.2% other; 2+ races 2.3%. **Hispanic pop.:** 5.8%. **Foreign born:** 7.4%. **U.S. citizens:** 95.6%. **Language:** 88.9% English only; 4.3% Spanish.
Employment: 142,335 employed; 3.9% unemployed. **Per capita income:** $37,599; change (2009-10): 1.9%. **Below poverty level:** 8.5%; 14.9% of families. **Educational attainment:** 92.7% HS; 35.1% bachelor's. **Avg. commute:** 17.3 min. 80.7% drive. **Housing units:** 108,939; 93.7% occupied. **Home ownership:** 59.4%. **Avg. home:** $133,000; change (2009-11): –0.2%. **Avg. rent:** $667.
Mayor: Chris Beutler, nonpartisan
History: Originally called Lancaster; chosen state capital 1867, renamed after Abraham Lincoln; inc. 1869.
Website: lincoln.ne.gov

Long Beach, California

Population: 465,576 (36). **Pop. density:** 9,257. **Pop. change (2000-11):** 0.9%. **Area:** 50.3 sq mi. **Racial distribution:** 47.8% white; 13.2% black; 13.3% Asian; 0.5% Amer. Ind.; 0.9% Pac. Isl.; 19.4% other; 2+ races 4.8%. **Hispanic pop.:** 40.3%. **Foreign born:** 27.4%. **U.S. citizens:** 83.7%. **Language:** 54.1% English only; 32.6% Spanish.
Employment: 206,873 employed; 13.5% unemployed. **Per capita income:** $43,688; change (2009-10): 3.2%. **Below poverty level:** 15.4%; 19.1% of families. **Educational attainment:** 78.5% HS; 28.0% bachelor's. **Avg. commute:** 27.9 min. 72.0% drive; 11.8% carpool. **Housing units:** 175,732; 92.1% occupied. **Home ownership:** 42.3%. **Avg. home:** $307,700; change (2009-11): –7.9%. **Avg. rent:** $1,033.
Mayor: Bob Foster, nonpartisan
History: Settled as early as 1784 by Spanish; by 1884, present site developed on harbor; inc. 1888. Oil discovered 1921.
Website: www.longbeach.gov

Los Angeles, California

Population: 3,819,702 (2). **Pop. density:** 8,150. **Pop. change (2000-11):** 3.4%. **Area:** 468.7 sq mi. **Racial distribution:** 50.6% white; 9.7% black; 11.4% Asian; 0.5% Amer. Ind.; 0.2% Pac. Isl.; 24.7% other; 2+ races 2.9%. **Hispanic pop.:** 48.1%. **Foreign born:** 39.6%. **U.S. citizens:** 76.1%. **Language:** 40.3% English only; 43.1% Spanish.
Employment: 1,669,752 employed; 13.6% unemployed. **Per capita income:** $43,688; change (2009-10): 3.2%. **Below poverty level:** 16.0%; 19.5% of families. **Educational attainment:** 73.7% HS; 30.2% bachelor's. **Avg. commute:** 29.1 min. 67.3% drive; 11.0% public trans.; 10.8% carpool. **Housing units:** 1,408,765; 93.3% occupied. **Home ownership:** 38.9%. **Avg. home:** $307,700; change (2009-11): –7.9%. **Avg. rent:** $1,077.
Mayor: Antonio Villaraigosa, nonpartisan
History: Founded by Spanish 1781; captured by U.S. 1846; inc. 1850; grew rapidly after coming of railroads, 1876 and 1885. Hollywood is a district of Los Angeles.
Website: www.lacity.org

Louisville, Kentucky

Population: 602,011 (27). **Pop. density:** 1,851. **Pop. change (2000-11):** 134.9%. **Area:** 325.2 sq mi. **Racial distribution:** 72.2% white; 22.5% black; 2.0% Asian; 0.2% Amer. Ind.; <0.05% Pac. Isl.; 1.1% other; 2+ races 2.1%. **Hispanic pop.:** 4.0%. **Foreign born:** 5.7%. **U.S. citizens:** 96.2%. **Language:** 92.5% English only; 3.5% Spanish.
Employment: 327,926 employed; 10.0% unemployed. **Per capita income:** $36,992; change (2009-10): 1.1%. **Below poverty level:** 13.6%; 17.3% of families. **Educational attainment:** 85.5% HS; 25.3% bachelor's. **Avg. commute:** 21.8 min. 80.5% drive. **Housing units:** 269,195; 89.0% occupied. **Home ownership:** 63.5%. **Avg. home:** $130,400; change (2009-11): –0.5%. **Avg. rent:** $647.
Mayor: Greg Fischer, Democrat
History: Settled 1778; named for Louis XVI of France; inc. 1828. Base for Union forces in Civil War.
Website: www.louisvilleky.gov

Lubbock, Texas

Population: 233,740 (83). **Pop. density:** 1,909. **Pop. change (2000-11):** 17.1%. **Area:** 122.4 sq mi. **Racial distribution:** 77.6% white; 8.0% black; 2.4% Asian; 0.6% Amer. Ind.; 0.1% Pac. Isl.; 8.8% other; 2+ races 2.6%. **Hispanic pop.:** 31.2%. **Foreign born:** 5.6%. **U.S. citizens:** 96.4%. **Language:** 77.8% English only; 19.1% Spanish.
Employment: 113,174 employed; 6.1% unemployed. **Per capita income:** $33,818; change (2009-10): 3.7%. **Below**

poverty level: 13.2%; 20.4% of families. Educational attainment: 84.1% HS; 29.5% bachelor's. Avg. commute: 15.5 min. 81.9% drive; 10.5% carpool. Housing units: 95,561; 90.1% occupied. Home ownership: 56.3%. Avg. rent: $737.
Mayor: Glen Robertson, nonpartisan
History: Settled 1879; laid out 1891; inc. 1909 through merger of two towns.
Website: www.ci.lubbock.tx.us

Madison, Wisconsin
Population: 236,901 (82). Pop. density: 3,085. Pop. change (2000-11): 13.9%. Area: 76.8 sq mi. Racial distribution: 80.7% white; 7.6% black; 7.0% Asian; 0.4% Amer. Ind.; <0.05% Pac. Isl.; 1.5% other; 2+ races 2.8%. Hispanic pop.: 6.3%. Foreign born: 10.2%. U.S. citizens: 93.1%. Language: 85.2% English only; 5.4% Spanish.
Employment: 137,667 employed; 4.9% unemployed. Per capita income: $44,337; change (2009-10): 3.0%. Below poverty level: 8.1%; 17.9% of families. Educational attainment: 94.1% HS; 52.2% bachelor's. Avg. commute: 18.7 min. 64.1% drive. Housing units: 107,523; 91.3% occupied. Home ownership: 52.2%. Avg. home: $213,200; change (2009-11): 0.4%. Avg. rent: $847.
Mayor: Paul R. Soglin, nonpartisan
History: Settled 1832; selected as site for state capital, named after James Madison, 1836; chartered 1856.
Website: www.cityofmadison.com

Memphis, Tennessee
Population: 652,050 (20). Pop. density: 2,070. Pop. change (2000-11): 0.3%. Area: 315.1 sq mi. Racial distribution: 31.3% white; 62.6% black; 1.6% Asian; 0.2% Amer. Ind.; <0.05% Pac. Isl.; 2.9% other; 2+ races 1.5%. Hispanic pop.: 5.7%. Foreign born: 6.1%. U.S. citizens: 95.4%. Language: 91.4% English only; 5.7% Spanish.
Employment: 262,363 employed; 11.1% unemployed. Per capita income: $37,569; change (2009-10): 3.3%. Below poverty level: 20.7%; 25.4% of families. Educational attainment: 81.2% HS; 22.5% bachelor's. Avg. commute: 21.5 min. 78.7% drive; 12.9% carpool. Housing units: 296,018; 83.3% occupied. Home ownership: 53.7%. Avg. home: $112,300; change (2009-11): -5.8%. Avg. rent: $758.
Mayor: A. C. Wharton, nonpartisan
History: French, Spanish, and U.S. forts by 1797; settled by 1819; inc. as town 1826, as city 1840; surrendered charter to state 1879 after yellow fever epidemics; rechartered as city 1893.
Website: www.cityofmemphis.org

Mesa, Arizona
Population: 446,518 (38). Pop. density: 3,272. Pop. change (2000-11): 12.7%. Area: 136.5 sq mi. Racial distribution: 84.0% white; 2.8% black; 2.1% Asian; 2.3% Amer. Ind.; 0.2% Pac. Isl.; 6.0% other; 2+ races 2.6%. Hispanic pop.: 25.2%. Foreign born: 14.0%. U.S. citizens: 89.4%. Language: 77.9% English only; 18.4% Spanish.
Employment: 203,836 employed; 8.3% unemployed. Per capita income: $36,047; change (2009-10): 1.3%. Below poverty level: 8.6%; 11.9% of families. Educational attainment: 86.1% HS; 23.5% bachelor's. Avg. commute: 25.4 min. 74.8% drive; 15.1% carpool. Housing units: 193,984; 85.5% occupied. Home ownership: 65.6%. Avg. home: $115,500; change (2009-11): -15.7%. Avg. rent: $856.
Mayor: Scott Smith, nonpartisan
History: Founded by Mormons 1878; inc. 1883. Population boomed fivefold 1960-80.
Website: www.mesaaz.gov

Miami, Florida
Population: 408,750 (44). Pop. density: 11,395. Pop. change (2000-11): 12.8%. Area: 35.9 sq mi. Racial distribution: 72.8% white; 21.2% black; 0.9% Asian; 0.1% Amer. Ind.; <0.05% Pac. Isl.; 3.9% other; 2+ races 1.2%. Hispanic pop.: 70.4%. Foreign born: 58.1%. U.S. citizens: 65.8%. Language: 22.7% English only; 70.2% Spanish.
Employment: 157,052 employed; 12.4% unemployed. Per capita income: $41,769; change (2009-10): 1.7%. Below poverty level: 22.2%; 27.3% of families. Educational attainment: 67.4% HS; 22.2% bachelor's. Avg. commute: 27.3 min. 69.8% drive; 11.7% public trans. Housing units: 182,071; 81.9% occupied. Home ownership: 35.6%. Avg. home: $181,100; change (2009-11): -14.3%. Avg. rent: $875.
Mayor: Tomás Regalado, nonpartisan
History: Site of fort 1836; settlement began 1870; inc. 1896. Modern city developed into financial and recreation center; land speculation in 1920s added to city's growth, as did Cuban, Central and South American, and Haitian immigration since 1960.
Website: www.miamigov.com

Milwaukee, Wisconsin
Population: 597,867 (28). Pop. density: 6,220. Pop. change (2000-11): 0.1%. Area: 96.1 sq mi. Racial distribution: 46.6% white; 39.4% black; 3.5% Asian; 0.7% Amer. Ind.; 0.1% Pac. Isl.;

7.0% other; 2+ races 2.8%. Hispanic pop.: 16.4%. Foreign born: 9.7%. U.S. citizens: 93.3%. Language: 81.0% English only; 13.5% Spanish.
Employment: 242,677 employed; 10.8% unemployed. Per capita income: $42,853; change (2009-10): 2.1%. Below poverty level: 21.7%; 26.3% of families. Educational attainment: 80.4% HS; 21.0% bachelor's. Avg. commute: 21.6 min. 71.1% drive; 11.9% carpool. Housing units: 257,580; 89.4% occupied. Home ownership: 46.4%. Avg. home: $185,200; change (2009-11): -4.2%. Avg. rent: $736.
Mayor: Tom Barrett, Democrat
History: Indian trading post by 1674; settlement began 1835; inc. 1848. Famous beer industry.
Website: city.milwaukee.gov

Minneapolis, Minnesota
Population: 387,753 (48). Pop. density: 7,184. Pop. change (2000-11): 1.3%. Area: 54.0 sq mi. Racial distribution: 68.2% white; 18.2% black; 5.6% Asian; 1.7% Amer. Ind.; <0.05% Pac. Isl.; 2.9% other; 2+ races 3.4%. Hispanic pop.: 9.2%. Foreign born: 15.1%. U.S. citizens: 90.4%. Language: 80.4% English only; 8.1% Spanish.
Employment: 201,601 employed; 6.3% unemployed. Per capita income: $46,819; change (2009-10): 3.4%. Below poverty level: 16.4%; 22.7% of families. Educational attainment: 87.9% HS; 43.6% bachelor's. Avg. commute: 22.1 min. 61.6% drive; 13.9% public trans. Housing units: 183,320; 91.2% occupied. Home ownership: 50.8%. Avg. home: $154,700; change (2009-11): -12.9%. Avg. rent: $774.
Mayor: R. T. Rybak, Democrat
History: Site visited by French missionary Louis Hennepin 1680; included in area of military reservations 1819; inc. 1867.
Website: www.ci.minneapolis.mn.us

Nashville, Tennessee
Population: 609,644 (26). Pop. density: 1,283. Pop. change (2000-11): 7.0%. Area: 475.1 sq mi. Racial distribution: 63.2% white; 28.7% black; 3.2% Asian; 0.3% Amer. Ind.; <0.05% Pac. Isl.; 3.1% other; 2+ races 1.6%. Hispanic pop.: 9.2%. Foreign born: 11.7%. U.S. citizens: 91.5%. Language: 85.0% English only; 8.1% Spanish.
Employment: 305,630 employed; 8.2% unemployed. Per capita income: $40,138; change (2009-10): 3.9%. Below poverty level: 13.7%; 17.8% of families. Educational attainment: 84.8% HS; 33.4% bachelor's. Avg. commute: 23.2 min. 80.4% drive; 10.0% carpool. Housing units: 269,280; 90.1% occupied. Home ownership: 57.0%. Avg. home: $151,900; change (2009-11): 2.7%. Avg. rent: $773.
Mayor: Karl Dean, nonpartisan
History: Settled 1779; first chartered 1806; became permanent state capital 1843. Home of Grand Ole Opry.
Website: www.nashville.gov

Newark, New Jersey
Population: 277,540 (68). Pop. density: 11,475. Pop. change (2000-11): 1.5%. Area: 24.2 sq mi. Racial distribution: 25.9% white; 52.7% black; 1.5% Asian; 0.5% Amer. Ind.; <0.05% Pac. Isl.; 13.9% other; 2+ races 5.5%. Hispanic pop.: 32.6%. Foreign born: 26.0%. U.S. citizens: 82.8%. Language: 55.6% English only; 30.3% Spanish.
Employment: 91,494 employed; 15.2% unemployed. Per capita income: $54,365; change (2009-10): 3.7%. Below poverty level: 22.0%; 25.0% of families. Educational attainment: 68.1% HS; 12.3% bachelor's. Avg. commute: 30.4 min. 48.6% drive; 24.8% public trans.; 14.9% carpool. Housing units: 109,716; 84.4% occupied. Home ownership: 25.3%. Avg. home: $378,500; change (2009-11): -0.8%. Avg. rent: $902.
Mayor: Cory A. Booker, nonpartisan
History: Settled by Puritans 1666; used as supply base by Washington 1776; inc. as town 1833, as city 1836.
Website: www.ci.newark.nj.us

New Orleans, Louisiana
Population: 360,740 (51). Pop. density: 2,129. Pop. change (2000-11): -25.6%. Area: 169.4 sq mi. Racial distribution: 33.8% white; 59.9% black; 3.0% Asian; 0.1% Amer. Ind.; 0.1% Pac. Isl.; 1.5% other; 2+ races 1.4%. Hispanic pop.: 5.1%. Foreign born: 6.0%. U.S. citizens: 96.6%. Language: 90.3% English only; 4.8% Spanish.
Employment: 133,177 employed; 8.8% unemployed. Per capita income: $42,485; change (2009-10): 2.1%. Below poverty level: 19.0%; 24.4% of families. Educational attainment: 83.4% HS; 31.6% bachelor's. Avg. commute: 23.1 min. 68.0% drive; 12.6% carpool. Housing units: 160,937; 72.5% occupied. Home ownership: 49.3%. Avg. home: $153,000; change (2009-11): -4.4%. Avg. rent: $899.
Mayor: Mitchell J. Landrieu, Democrat
History: Founded by French 1718; became major seaport on Mississippi R.; acquired by U.S. as part of Louisiana Purchase 1803; inc. 1805. Americans defeated British forces at Battle of New Orleans in 1815.
Website: www.nola.gov

New York, New York

Population: 8,244,910 (1). **Pop. density:** 27,243. **Pop. change (2000-11):** 3.0%. **Area:** 302.6 sq mi. **Racial distribution:** 44.2% white; 25.2% black; 12.6% Asian; 0.4% Amer. Ind.; <0.05% Pac. Isl.; 15.2% other; 2+ races 2.4%. **Hispanic pop.:** 28.2%. **Foreign born:** 36.8%. **U.S. citizens:** 82.1%. **Language:** 51.7% English only; 24.6% Spanish; 5.4% Chinese.
Employment: 3,592,166 employed; 9.0% unemployed. **Per capita income:** $54,365; change (2009-10): 3.7%. **Below poverty level:** 16.2%; 19.1% of families. **Educational attainment:** 79.0% HS; 33.3% bachelor's. **Avg. commute:** 39.2 min. 55.2% public trans.; 23.0% drive; 10.2% walk. **Housing units:** 3,343,424; 91.1% occupied. **Home ownership:** 33.0%. **Avg. home:** $378,500; change (2009-11): –0.8%. **Avg. rent:** $1,071.
Mayor: Michael R. Bloomberg, Republican
History: Trading post est. 1624; British took control from Dutch 1664, named city New York. Briefly U.S. capital; under new charter, 1898, city expanded to include five boroughs: Bronx, Brooklyn, Queens, and Staten Island, as well as Manhattan. Sept. 11, 2001, terrorist attacks destroyed World Trade Center, killed more than 2,750.
Website: www.nyc.gov

Norfolk, Virginia

Population: 242,628 (79). **Pop. density:** 4,483. **Pop. change (2000-11):** 3.5%. **Area:** 54.1 sq mi. **Racial distribution:** 48.1% white; 43.8% black; 3.3% Asian; 0.4% Amer. Ind.; 0.2% Pac. Isl.; 1.8% other; 2+ races 2.4%. **Hispanic pop.:** 6.2%. **Foreign born:** 6.8%. **U.S. citizens:** 96.1%. **Language:** 90.5% English only; 4.6% Spanish.
Employment: 98,291 employed; 8.4% unemployed. **Per capita income:** $40,234; change (2009-10): 2.3%. **Below poverty level:** 13.5%; 16.5% of families. **Educational attainment:** 83.9% HS; 23.7% bachelor's. **Avg. commute:** 21.5 min. 69.2% drive; 12.0% carpool. **Housing units:** 94,995; 89.5% occupied. **Home ownership:** 46.6%. **Avg. home:** $182,900; change (2009-11): –12.9%. **Avg. rent:** $845.
Mayor: Paul D. Fraim, nonpartisan
History: Founded 1682; burned by colonists to prevent capture by British during Revolutionary War; rebuilt and inc. as town 1805, as city 1845. Site of world's largest naval base; major East Coast commercial port and cruise terminal.
Website: www.norfolk.gov

North Las Vegas, Nevada

Population: 219,020 (94). **Pop. density:** 2,161. **Pop. change (2000-11):** 89.6%. **Area:** 101.3 sq mi. **Racial distribution:** 59.8% white; 20.2% black; 6.7% Asian; 0.5% Amer. Ind.; 0.7% Pac. Isl.; 8.1% other; 2+ races 4.0%. **Hispanic pop.:** 37.2%. **Foreign born:** 23.3%. **U.S. citizens:** 83.9%. **Language:** 62.2% English only; 31.0% Spanish.
Employment: 81,507 employed; 16.3% unemployed. **Per capita income:** $35,723; change (2009-10): 0.7%. **Below poverty level:** 9.4%; 12.2% of families. **Educational attainment:** 76.6% HS; 15.4% bachelor's. **Avg. commute:** 27.8 min. 80.4% drive; 12.9% carpool. **Housing units:** 70,638; 87.7% occupied. **Home ownership:** 63.4%. **Avg. home:** $124,700; change (2009-11): –12.7%. **Avg. rent:** $1,140.
Mayor: Shari L. Buck, nonpartisan
History: Inc. 1946.
Website: www.cityofnorthlasvegas.com

Oakland, California

Population: 395,817 (46). **Pop. density:** 7,095. **Pop. change (2000-11):** –0.9%. **Area:** 55.8 sq mi. **Racial distribution:** 37.7% white; 28.4% black; 15.9% Asian; 0.7% Amer. Ind.; 0.5% Pac. Isl.; 12.5% other; 2+ races 4.3%. **Hispanic pop.:** 25.2%. **Foreign born:** 28.4%. **U.S. citizens:** 83.0%. **Language:** 59.8% English only; 22.2% Spanish; 7.5% Chinese.
Employment: 171,822 employed; 15.6% unemployed. **Per capita income:** $59,295; change (2009-10): 3.0%. **Below poverty level:** 15.7%; 18.7% of families. **Educational attainment:** 78.9% HS; 36.3% bachelor's. **Avg. commute:** 27.5 min. 57.2% drive; 16.7% public trans.; 10.7% carpool. **Housing units:** 173,851; 89.1% occupied. **Home ownership:** 42.4%. **Avg. home:** $483,400; change (2009-11): –2.0%. **Avg. rent:** $1,000.
Mayor: Jean Quan, nonpartisan
History: Area settled by Spanish 1820; inc. 1854.
Website: www.oaklandnet.com

Oklahoma City, Oklahoma

Population: 591,967 (30). **Pop. density:** 976. **Pop. change (2000-11):** 17.0%. **Area:** 606.4 sq mi. **Racial distribution:** 66.1% white; 14.4% black; 3.9% Asian; 3.2% Amer. Ind.; 0.1% Pac. Isl.; 5.4% other; 2+ races 6.9%. **Hispanic pop.:** 16.2%. **Foreign born:** 11.5%. **U.S. citizens:** 91.9%. **Language:** 82.2% English only; 12.7% Spanish.
Employment: 249,688 employed; 5.7% unemployed. **Per capita income:** $37,533; change (2009-10): 3.4%. **Below poverty level:** 12.6%; 16.6% of families. **Educational attainment:** 84.4% HS; 27.0% bachelor's. **Avg. commute:** 20.0 min. 81.6%

drive; 11.9% carpool. **Housing units:** 254,233; 87.6% occupied. **Home ownership:** 61.4%. **Avg. home:** $141,600; change (2009-11): 0.8%. **Avg. rent:** $669.
Mayor: Mick Cornett, nonpartisan
History: Settled during land rush in Midwest 1889; inc. 1890; became state capital 1910. Oil discovered 1928. Bomb in 1995 destroyed federal office bldg., killed 168 people.
Website: www.okc.gov

Omaha, Nebraska

Population: 415,068 (43). **Pop. density:** 3,266. **Pop. change (2000-11):** 6.4%. **Area:** 127.1 sq mi. **Racial distribution:** 76.1% white; 13.1% black; 2.1% Asian; 0.6% Amer. Ind.; 0.1% Pac. Isl.; 4.9% other; 2+ races 3.1%. **Hispanic pop.:** 12.0%. **Foreign born:** 9.1%. **U.S. citizens:** 93.6%. **Language:** 86.6% English only; 9.3% Spanish.
Employment: 204,670 employed; 5.1% unemployed. **Per capita income:** $42,115; change (2009-10): 1.0%. **Below poverty level:** 11.2%; 15.3% of families. **Educational attainment:** 88.3% HS; 32.4% bachelor's. **Avg. commute:** 17.8 min. 80.0% drive; 11.5% carpool. **Housing units:** 178,046; 91.6% occupied. **Home ownership:** 60.1%. **Avg. home:** $135,700; change (2009-11): 1.5%. **Avg. rent:** $712.
Mayor: Jim Suttle, nonpartisan
History: Founded 1854; inc. 1857. Large food-processing, telecommunications, information-processing center.
Website: www.cityofomaha.org

Orlando, Florida

Population: 243,195 (78). **Pop. density:** 2,375. **Pop. change (2000-11):** 30.8%. **Area:** 102.4 sq mi. **Racial distribution:** 57.7% white; 28.0% black; 3.3% Asian; 0.4% Amer. Ind.; <0.05% Pac. Isl.; 8.3% other; 2+ races 2.2%. **Hispanic pop.:** 23.4%. **Foreign born:** 18.6%. **U.S. citizens:** 88.0%. **Language:** 68.7% English only; 20.3% Spanish.
Employment: 120,506 employed; 10.2% unemployed. **Per capita income:** $34,368; change (2009-10): 2.1%. **Below poverty level:** 12.6%; 16.6% of families. **Educational attainment:** 86.6% HS; 32.3% bachelor's. **Avg. commute:** 24.3 min. 78.0% drive; 10.4% carpool. **Housing units:** 118,027; 82.7% occupied. **Home ownership:** 40.2%. **Avg. home:** $124,900; change (2009-11): –15.3%. **Avg. rent:** $971.
Mayor: Buddy Dyer, nonpartisan
History: Ft. Gatlin built just south of present-day Orlando in 1838; name changed from Jernigan to Orlando 1856; inc. 1875. Walt Disney World opened in 1971.
Website: www.cityoforlando.net

Philadelphia, Pennsylvania

Population: 1,536,471 (5). **Pop. density:** 11,458. **Pop. change (2000-11):** 1.2%. **Area:** 134.1 sq mi. **Racial distribution:** 41.4% white; 44.0% black; 6.2% Asian; 0.3% Amer. Ind.; <0.05% Pac. Isl.; 6.1% other; 2+ races 2.0%. **Hispanic pop.:** 11.6%. **Foreign born:** 11.5%. **U.S. citizens:** 93.9%. **Language:** 79.1% English only; 9.7% Spanish.
Employment: 573,813 employed; 10.8% unemployed. **Per capita income:** $47,194; change (2009-10): 2.9%. **Below poverty level:** 20.0%; 25.1% of families. **Educational attainment:** 79.4% HS; 22.2% bachelor's. **Avg. commute:** 31.5 min. 50.7% drive; 26.2% public trans. **Housing units:** 668,944; 85.9% occupied. **Home ownership:** 55.3%. **Avg. home:** $210,100; change (2009-11): –2.7%. **Avg. rent:** $819.
Mayor: Michael A. Nutter, Democrat
History: First settled by Swedes 1638; Swedes surrendered to Dutch 1654; settled by English and Scottish Quakers 1678; named Philadelphia 1682; chartered 1701. Continental Congresses convened 1774, 1775; Declaration of Independence signed here 1776; national capital 1790-1800; state capital 1683-1799.
Website: www.phila.gov

Phoenix, Arizona

Population: 1,469,471 (6). **Pop. density:** 2,844. **Pop. change (2000-11):** 11.2%. **Area:** 516.7 sq mi. **Racial distribution:** 77.5% white; 6.2% black; 2.9% Asian; 1.8% Amer. Ind.; 0.2% Pac. Isl.; 9.2% other; 2+ races 2.3%. **Hispanic pop.:** 40.0%. **Foreign born:** 21.7%. **U.S. citizens:** 83.5%. **Language:** 63.1% English only; 31.0% Spanish.
Employment: 662,583 employed; 8.9% unemployed. **Per capita income:** $36,047; change (2009-10): 1.3%. **Below poverty level:** 14.7%; 19.1% of families. **Educational attainment:** 79.8% HS; 25.5% bachelor's. **Avg. commute:** 24.8 min. 74.0% drive; 13.8% carpool. **Housing units:** 593,221; 86.9% occupied. **Home ownership:** 59.6%. **Avg. home:** $115,500; change (2009-11): –15.7%. **Avg. rent:** $847.
Mayor: Greg Stanton, nonpartisan
History: Founded 1867; inc. 1881; became territorial capital 1889.
Website: www.phoenix.gov

Pittsburgh, Pennsylvania

Population: 307,484 (61). **Pop. density:** 5,554. **Pop. change (2000-11):** –8.1%. **Area:** 55.4 sq mi. **Racial distribution:** 66.5%

white; 25.8% black; 4.1% Asian; 0.1% Amer. Ind.; 0.1% Pac. Isl.; 0.7% other; 2+ races 2.7%. **Hispanic pop.:** 2.3%. **Foreign born:** 6.9%. **U.S. citizens:** 95.7%. **Language:** 90.2% English only; 2.1% Spanish.
Employment: 140,823 employed; 7.6% unemployed. **Per capita income:** $42,688; change (2009-10): 3.5%. **Below poverty level:** 14.8%; 21.9% of families. **Educational attainment:** 88.3% HS; 33.8% bachelor's. **Avg. commute:** 22.7 min. 53.6% drive; 19.5% public trans.; 11.8% walk; 10.2% carpool. **Housing units:** 160,743; 84.0% occupied. **Home ownership:** 51.3%. **Avg. rent:** $700.
Mayor: Luke Ravenstahl, Democrat
History: Settled around Ft. Pitt 1758; inc. 1816. Became an inland port; by Civil War, already a center for iron production.
Website: www.pghgov.com

Plano, Texas

Population: 269,776 (70). **Pop. density:** 3,769. **Pop. change (2000-11):** 21.5%. **Area:** 71.6 sq mi. **Racial distribution:** 72.0% white; 6.9% black; 16.2% Asian; 0.5% Amer. Ind.; 0.1% Pac. Isl.; 2.5% other; 2+ races 1.9%. **Hispanic pop.:** 14.9%. **Foreign born:** 23.0%. **U.S. citizens:** 86.8%. **Language:** 68.6% English only; 12.4% Spanish.
Employment: 136,366 employed; 6.9% unemployed. **Per capita income:** $41,282; change (2009-10): 2.6%. **Below poverty level:** 4.8%; 6.7% of families. **Educational attainment:** 92.9% HS; 54.0% bachelor's. **Avg. commute:** 25.8 min. 82.1% drive. **Housing units:** 101,532; 94.0% occupied. **Home ownership:** 66.5%. **Avg. home:** $148,900; change (2009-11): 6.0%. **Avg. rent:** $981.
Mayor: Phil Dyer, nonpartisan
History: Settled 1846; inc. 1873.
Website: www.plano.gov

Portland, Oregon

Population: 593,820 (29). **Pop. density:** 4,451. **Pop. change (2000-11):** 12.2%. **Area:** 133.4 sq mi. **Racial distribution:** 77.5% white; 6.4% black; 7.1% Asian; 1.2% Amer. Ind.; 0.6% Pac. Isl.; 3.1% other; 2+ races 4.1%. **Hispanic pop.:** 8.8%. **Foreign born:** 13.4%. **U.S. citizens:** 92.0%. **Language:** 81.4% English only; 7.0% Spanish.
Employment: 298,764 employed; 8.4% unemployed. **Per capita income:** $39,843; change (2009-10): 2.2%. **Below poverty level:** 11.3%; 16.3% of families. **Educational attainment:** 89.5% HS; 41.1% bachelor's. **Avg. commute:** 23.9 min. 60.4% drive; 12.0% public trans. **Housing units:** 262,616; 93.2% occupied. **Home ownership:** 55.2%. **Avg. home:** $219,500; change (2009-11): -10.1%. **Avg. rent:** $813.
Mayor: Sam Adams, nonpartisan
History: Settled by pioneers 1845; developed as trading center, aided by California Gold Rush of 1849; city chartered 1851.
Website: www.portlandonline.com

Raleigh, North Carolina

Population: 416,468 (42). **Pop. density:** 2,914. **Pop. change (2000-11):** 50.8%. **Area:** 142.9 sq mi. **Racial distribution:** 59.0% white; 29.5% black; 4.4% Asian; 0.3% Amer. Ind.; <0.05% Pac. Isl.; 5.3% other; 2+ races 1.5%. **Hispanic pop.:** 10.7%. **Foreign born:** 14.5%. **U.S. citizens:** 89.6%. **Language:** 82.3% English only; 9.8% Spanish.
Employment: 198,157 employed; 7.6% unemployed. **Per capita income:** $39,479; change (2009-10): 1.9%. **Below poverty level:** 10.1%; 14.6% of families. **Educational attainment:** 90.4% HS; 46.6% bachelor's. **Avg. commute:** 22.0 min. 78.8% drive; 10.6% carpool. **Housing units:** 171,888; 90.0% occupied. **Home ownership:** 54.4%. **Avg. rent:** $828.
Mayor: Nancy McFarlane, nonpartisan
History: Named after Sir Walter Raleigh; site chosen for state capital 1788; laid out 1792; inc. 1795. Occupied by Union Gen. William Sherman 1865.
Website: www.raleighnc.gov

Reno, Nevada

Population: 227,511 (90). **Pop. density:** 2,209. **Pop. change (2000-11):** 26.1%. **Area:** 103.0 sq mi. **Racial distribution:** 78.2% white; 3.1% black; 6.2% Asian; 1.0% Amer. Ind.; 0.7% Pac. Isl.; 7.5% other; 2+ races 3.3%. **Hispanic pop.:** 22.9%. **Foreign born:** 17.5%. **U.S. citizens:** 89.1%. **Language:** 75.6% English only; 17.4% Spanish.
Employment: 103,155 employed; 13.0% unemployed. **Per capita income:** $42,066; change (2009-10): 1.6%. **Below poverty level:** 11.3%; 16.3% of families. **Educational attainment:** 85.2% HS; 28.5% bachelor's. **Avg. commute:** 18.6 min. 75.6% drive; 10.6% carpool. **Housing units:** 99,329; 89.8% occupied. **Home ownership:** 49.0%. **Avg. home:** $158,000; change (2009-11): -18.5%. **Avg. rent:** $872.
Mayor: Robert Cashell, nonpartisan
History: Founded 1857; originally named Lakes Crossing; name changed to Reno, after a Union Civil War general, 1868, with arrival of transcontinental railroad.
Website: www.reno.gov

Riverside, California

Population: 310,651 (59). **Pop. density:** 3,829. **Pop. change (2000-11):** 21.7%. **Area:** 81.1 sq mi. **Racial distribution:** 62.1% white; 6.5% black; 6.8% Asian; 0.7% Amer. Ind.; 0.4% Pac. Isl.; 19.0% other; 2+ races 4.4%. **Hispanic pop.:** 48.7%. **Foreign born:** 24.6%. **U.S. citizens:** 84.3%. **Language:** 56.8% English only; 35.6% Spanish.
Employment: 142,397 employed; 13.7% unemployed. **Per capita income:** $29,409; change (2009-10): 1.3%. **Below poverty level:** 10.1%; 14.9% of families. **Educational attainment:** 77.6% HS; 22.0% bachelor's. **Avg. commute:** 28.8 min. 75.5% drive; 13.7% carpool. **Housing units:** 99,041; 91.7% occupied. **Home ownership:** 58.6%. **Avg. home:** $172,300; change (2009-11): 1.5%. **Avg. rent:** $1,092.
Mayor: Ronald O. Loveridge, nonpartisan
History: Founded 1870; inc. 1886. Known for its citrus industry; home of the parent navel orange tree, historic Mission Inn resort.
Website: www.riversideca.gov

Rochester, New York

Population: 210,855 (100). **Pop. density:** 5,893. **Pop. change (2000-11):** -4.1%. **Area:** 35.8 sq mi. **Racial distribution:** 47.0% white; 40.8% black; 2.9% Asian; 0.4% Amer. Ind.; <0.05% Pac. Isl.; 5.4% other; 2+ races 3.5%. **Hispanic pop.:** 15.2%. **Foreign born:** 8.2%. **U.S. citizens:** 95.8%. **Language:** 82.9% English only; 10.9% Spanish.
Employment: 83,619 employed; 10.4% unemployed. **Per capita income:** $39,919; change (2009-10): 3.6%. **Below poverty level:** 25.8%; 30.4% of families. **Educational attainment:** 78.2% HS; 24.1% bachelor's. **Avg. commute:** 18.4 min. 70.3% drive. **Housing units:** 102,651; 83.4% occupied. **Home ownership:** 41.7%. **Avg. home:** $119,700; change (2009-11): 2.8%. **Avg. rent:** $714.
Mayor: Thomas S. Richards, Democrat
History: First permanent settlement 1812; inc. as village 1817, as city 1834; developed as Erie Canal town.
Website: www.cityofrochester.gov

Sacramento, California

Population: 472,178 (35). **Pop. density:** 4,822. **Pop. change (2000-11):** 16.0%. **Area:** 97.9 sq mi. **Racial distribution:** 49.5% white; 14.0% black; 18.5% Asian; 1.1% Amer. Ind.; 1.4% Pac. Isl.; 9.5% other; 2+ races 6.0%. **Hispanic pop.:** 25.4%. **Foreign born:** 22.2%. **U.S. citizens:** 88.2%. **Language:** 63.4% English only; 17.2% Spanish.
Employment: 184,573 employed; 14.1% unemployed. **Per capita income:** $39,987; change (2009-10): 1.6%. **Below poverty level:** 12.8%; 17.3% of families. **Educational attainment:** 81.4% HS; 29.6% bachelor's. **Avg. commute:** 23.8 min. 72.5% drive; 13.8% carpool. **Housing units:** 191,000; 91.1% occupied. **Home ownership:** 50.6%. **Avg. home:** $167,100; change (2009-11): -7.4%. **Avg. rent:** $959.
Mayor: Kevin Johnson, nonpartisan
History: Settled 1839; important trading center during California Gold Rush in 1840s; became state capital 1854.
Website: www.cityofsacramento.org

St. Louis, Missouri

Population: 318,069 (58). **Pop. density:** 5,138. **Pop. change (2000-11):** -8.7%. **Area:** 61.9 sq mi. **Racial distribution:** 44.1% white; 49.8% black; 2.7% Asian; 0.2% Amer. Ind.; <0.05% Pac. Isl.; 0.7% other; 2+ races 2.4%. **Hispanic pop.:** 3.3%. **Foreign born:** 6.7%. **U.S. citizens:** 95.7%. **Language:** 91.1% English only; 2.9% Spanish.
Employment: 128,480 employed; 11.7% unemployed. **Per capita income:** $41,528; change (2009-10): 2.2%. **Below poverty level:** 21.4%; 26.0% of families. **Educational attainment:** 80.6% HS; 26.9% bachelor's. **Avg. commute:** 24.4 min. 70.1% drive; 10.9% carpool; 10.6% public trans. **Housing units:** 176,319; 79.7% occupied. **Home ownership:** 47.2%. **Avg. home:** $121,800; change (2009-11): -4.2%. **Avg. rent:** $658.
Mayor: Francis Slay, Democrat
History: Founded 1764 as fur trading post by French; acquired by U.S. 1803; chartered as city 1822; became independent city 1876. Lies on Mississippi R., near confluence with Missouri R.
Website: www.stlouis-mo.gov

St. Paul, Minnesota

Population: 288,448 (66). **Pop. density:** 5,549. **Pop. change (2000-11):** 0.5%. **Area:** 52.0 sq mi. **Racial distribution:** 62.8% white; 14.9% black; 14.5% Asian; 1.0% Amer. Ind.; 0.1% Pac. Isl.; 2.7% other; 2+ races 4.0%. **Hispanic pop.:** 9.6%. **Foreign born:** 16.9%. **U.S. citizens:** 90.0%. **Language:** 74.3% English only; 7.4% Spanish; 9.0% Hmong.
Employment: 136,564 employed; 7.0% unemployed. **Per capita income:** $46,819; change (2009-10): 3.4%. **Below poverty level:** 16.4%; 22.0% of families. **Educational attainment:** 86.6% HS; 37.3% bachelor's. **Avg. commute:** 21.7 min. 68.6% drive; 11.2% carpool. **Housing units:** 121,265; 92.0% occupied. **Home ownership:** 53.8%. **Avg. home:** $154,700; change (2009-11): -12.9%. **Avg. rent:** $756.
Mayor: Chris Coleman, nonpartisan

History: Founded in early 1840s as Pig's Eye Landing; became capital of Minnesota territory 1849; chartered as St. Paul 1854.
Website: www.stpaul.gov

St. Petersburg, Florida

Population: 244,997 (77). **Pop. density:** 3,968. **Pop. change (2000-11):** –1.3%. **Area:** 61.7 sq mi. **Racial distribution:** 69.3% white; 23.8% black; 3.5% Asian; 0.2% Amer. Ind.; <0.05% Pac. Isl.; 1.1% other; 2+ races 2.0%. **Hispanic pop.:** 6.2%. **Foreign born:** 10.3%. **U.S. citizens:** 95.0%. **Language:** 88.5% English only; 4.3% Spanish.
Employment: 108,681 employed; 10.6% unemployed. **Per capita income:** $37,003; change (2009-10): 2.1%. **Below poverty level:** 9.7%; 14.3% of families. **Educational attainment:** 87.2% HS; 27.8% bachelor's. **Avg. commute:** 22.0 min. 80.6% drive. **Housing units:** 129,721; 82.3% occupied. **Home ownership:** 64.7%. **Avg. home:** $127,800; change (2009-11): –9.2%. **Avg. rent:** $874.
Mayor: Bill Foster, nonpartisan
History: Founded 1888; inc. 1903. Site of Salvador Dali Museum.
Website: www.stpete.org

San Antonio, Texas

Population: 1,359,758 (7). **Pop. density:** 2,950. **Pop. change (2000-11):** 18.8%. **Area:** 460.9 sq mi. **Racial distribution:** 71.1% white; 6.8% black; 2.3% Asian; 0.7% Amer. Ind.; 0.1% Pac. Isl.; 16.6% other; 2+ races 2.5%. **Hispanic pop.:** 62.5%. **Foreign born:** 13.7%. **U.S. citizens:** 91.4%. **Language:** 53.2% English only; 43.3% Spanish.
Employment: 574,457 employed; 7.4% unemployed. **Per capita income:** $34,969; change (2009-10): 3.3%. **Below poverty level:** 15.0%; 18.9% of families. **Educational attainment:** 79.5% HS; 23.7% bachelor's. **Avg. commute:** 23.4 min. 78.8% drive; 11.4% carpool. **Housing units:** 512,439; 90.0% occupied. **Home ownership:** 58.6%. **Avg. home:** $152,500; change (2009-11): 2.1%. **Avg. rent:** $748.
Mayor: Julián Castro, nonpartisan
History: First Spanish garrison 1718; Battle of the Alamo 1836; city subsequently captured by Texans; inc. 1837; first town meeting in Texas took place here in 1845.
Website: www.sanantonio.gov

San Bernardino, California

Population: 213,012 (97). **Pop. density:** 3,598. **Pop. change (2000-11):** 14.9%. **Area:** 59.2 sq mi. **Racial distribution:** 46.5% white; 16.1% black; 4.3% Asian; 0.8% Amer. Ind.; 0.3% Pac. Isl.; 28.3% other; 2+ races 3.8%. **Hispanic pop.:** 58.1%. **Foreign born:** 23.8%. **U.S. citizens:** 84.0%. **Language:** 53.3% English only; 41.4% Spanish.
Employment: 70,134 employed; 17.6% unemployed. **Per capita income:** $29,409; change (2009-10): 1.3%. **Below poverty level:** 21.9%; 27.4% of families. **Educational attainment:** 66.7% HS; 12.1% bachelor's. **Avg. commute:** 26.8 min. 75.3% drive; 14.5% carpool. **Housing units:** 66,611; 91.5% occupied. **Home ownership:** 51.9%. **Avg. home:** $172,300; change (2009-11): 1.5%. **Avg. rent:** $905.
Mayor: Patrick J. Morris, nonpartisan
History: Named by Spanish Franciscan missionaries 1810; major Mormon settlement in the 1850s, though Mormons were later recalled to Utah; inc. 1854. Population grew in 1860s when gold was discovered nearby; later became a transportation hub.
Website: www.ci.san-bernardino.ca.us

San Diego, California

Population: 1,326,179 (8). **Pop. density:** 4,078. **Pop. change (2000-11):** 8.4%. **Area:** 325.2 sq mi. **Racial distribution:** 65.9% white; 6.7% black; 15.7% Asian; 0.6% Amer. Ind.; 0.6% Pac. Isl.; 6.4% other; 2+ races 4.1%. **Hispanic pop.:** 27.9%. **Foreign born:** 25.9%. **U.S. citizens:** 86.7%. **Language:** 61.2% English only; 22.2% Spanish.
Employment: 636,638 employed; 10.0% unemployed. **Per capita income:** $45,627; change (2009-10): 2.7%. **Below poverty level:** 9.5%; 14.1% of families. **Educational attainment:** 86.4% HS; 40.8% bachelor's. **Avg. commute:** 22.4 min. 75.1% drive. **Housing units:** 514,841; 92.2% occupied. **Home ownership:** 49.5%. **Avg. home:** $370,300; change (2009-11): 3.0%. **Avg. rent:** $1,259.
Mayor: Jerry Sanders, nonpartisan
History: Claimed by Spanish 1542; first mission est. 1769; scene of conflict during Mexican-American War 1846; inc. 1850.
Website: www.sandiego.gov

San Francisco, California

Population: 812,826 (14). **Pop. density:** 17,341. **Pop. change (2000-11):** 4.6%. **Area:** 46.9 sq mi. **Racial distribution:** 51.6% white; 6.2% black; 33.5% Asian; 0.5% Amer. Ind.; 0.4% Pac. Isl.; 4.2% other; 2+ races 3.6%. **Hispanic pop.:** 14.7%. **Foreign born:** 35.6%. **U.S. citizens:** 86.4%. **Language:** 54.6% English only; 11.7% Spanish; 18.6% Chinese.

Employment: 422,719 employed; 8.6% unemployed. **Per capita income:** $59,295; change (2009-10): 3.0%. **Below poverty level:** 7.2%; 11.9% of families. **Educational attainment:** 85.7% HS; 51.2% bachelor's. **Avg. commute:** 29.4 min. 38.1% drive; 32.6% public trans. **Housing units:** 372,560; 90.2% occupied. **Home ownership:** 37.5%. **Avg. home:** $483,400; change (2009-11): –2.0%. **Avg. rent:** $1,328.
Mayor: Edwin M. Lee, nonpartisan
History: Nearby Farallon Islands sighted by Spanish 1542; city settled by 1776; claimed by U.S. 1846. Became major city during California Gold Rush of 1849; inc. 1850. Devastated by earthquake 1906.
Website: www.sfgov.org

San Jose, California

Population: 967,487 (10). **Pop. density:** 5,481. **Pop. change (2000-11):** 8.1%. **Area:** 176.5 sq mi. **Racial distribution:** 47.1% white; 3.0% black; 31.8% Asian; 0.7% Amer. Ind.; 0.4% Pac. Isl.; 13.1% other; 2+ races 3.9%. **Hispanic pop.:** 32.6%. **Foreign born:** 38.6%. **U.S. citizens:** 81.2%. **Language:** 44.6% English only; 23.9% Spanish; 9.8% Vietnamese; 6.3% Chinese.
Employment: 420,078 employed; 10.8% unemployed. **Per capita income:** $57,338; change (2009-10): 6.3%. **Below poverty level:** 7.9%; 10.8% of families. **Educational attainment:** 82.4% HS; 36.6% bachelor's. **Avg. commute:** 25.2 min. 77.6% drive; 11.0% carpool. **Housing units:** 313,944; 95.6% occupied. **Home ownership:** 60.2%. **Avg. home:** $570,000; change (2009-11): 7.5%. **Avg. rent:** $1,339.
Mayor: Chuck Reed, nonpartisan
History: Founded by Spanish, 1777, between San Francisco and Monterey; state capital 1849-51; inc. 1850.
Website: www.sanjoseca.gov

Santa Ana, California

Population: 329,427 (57). **Pop. density:** 12,080. **Pop. change (2000-11):** –2.5%. **Area:** 27.3 sq mi. **Racial distribution:** 43.8% white; 1.3% black; 10.1% Asian; 0.5% Amer. Ind.; 0.4% Pac. Isl.; 42.5% other; 2+ races 1.5%. **Hispanic pop.:** 78.1%. **Foreign born:** 49.4%. **U.S. citizens:** 65.0%. **Language:** 17.4% English only; 72.2% Spanish; 7.0% Vietnamese.
Employment: 139,837 employed; 13.7% unemployed. **Per capita income:** $43,688; change (2009-10): 3.2%. **Below poverty level:** 15.2%; 17.9% of families. **Educational attainment:** 51.4% HS; 12.0% bachelor's. **Avg. commute:** 24.9 min. 67.3% drive; 19.9% carpool. **Housing units:** 77,796; 95.6% occupied. **Home ownership:** 49.2%. **Avg. home:** $307,700; change (2009-11): –7.9%. **Avg. rent:** $1,231.
Mayor: Miguel Pulido, nonpartisan
History: Founded 1769; inc. 1869.
Website: www.ci.santa-ana.ca.us

Scottsdale, Arizona

Population: 221,020 (92). **Pop. density:** 1,202. **Pop. change (2000-11):** 9.0%. **Area:** 183.9 sq mi. **Racial distribution:** 91.1% white; 1.6% black; 3.4% Asian; 0.8% Amer. Ind.; 0.1% Pac. Isl.; 1.8% other; 2+ races 1.3%. **Hispanic pop.:** 8.7%. **Foreign born:** 10.7%. **U.S. citizens:** 94.3%. **Language:** 86.4% English only; 6.7% Spanish.
Employment: 110,984 employed; 6.8% unemployed. **Per capita income:** $36,047; change (2009-10): 1.3%. **Below poverty level:** 4.0%; 6.9% of families. **Educational attainment:** 95.6% HS; 51.9% bachelor's. **Avg. commute:** 22.7 min. 78.1% drive. **Housing units:** 124,528; 80.8% occupied. **Home ownership:** 71.5%. **Avg. home:** $115,500; change (2009-11): –15.7%. **Avg. rent:** $1,100.
Mayor: W. J. Lane, nonpartisan
History: Founded 1888 by Army Chaplain Winfield Scott; inc. 1951; slogan "West's Most Western Town" adopted same year.
Website: www.scottsdaleaz.gov

Seattle, Washington

Population: 620,778 (22). **Pop. density:** 7,395. **Pop. change (2000-11):** 10.2%. **Area:** 83.9 sq mi. **Racial distribution:** 70.5% white; 7.8% black; 13.7% Asian; 0.9% Amer. Ind.; 0.6% Pac. Isl.; 2.0% other; 2+ races 4.5%. **Hispanic pop.:** 6.1%. **Foreign born:** 17.3%. **U.S. citizens:** 91.6%. **Language:** 78.7% English only; 4.5% Spanish.
Employment: 341,245 employed; 7.5% unemployed. **Per capita income:** $49,115; change (2009-10): 1.5%. **Below poverty level:** 6.8%; 12.7% of families. **Educational attainment:** 92.4% HS; 55.1% bachelor's. **Avg. commute:** 24.9 min. 53.2% drive; 18.8% public trans. **Housing units:** 302,465; 92.7% occupied. **Home ownership:** 48.9%. **Avg. home:** $285,000; change (2009-11): –6.9%. **Avg. rent:** $958.
Mayor: Mike McGinn, nonpartisan
History: Settled 1851; inc. 1869. Suffered severe fire 1889; played prominent role during Klondike Gold Rush beginning in 1897; growth followed opening of Panama Canal 1914. Center of aircraft industry during WWII.
Website: www.seattle.gov

Stockton, California

Population: 296,357 (63). **Pop. density:** 4,806. **Pop. change (2000-11):** 21.6%. **Area:** 61.7 sq mi. **Racial distribution:** 46.2% white; 12.0% black; 21.8% Asian; 1.1% Amer. Ind.; 0.5% Pac. Isl.; 12.3% other; 2+ races 6.0%. **Hispanic pop.:** 38.8%. **Foreign born:** 27.1%. **U.S. citizens:** 84.6%. **Language:** 55.3% English only; 25.6% Spanish.
Employment: 100,575 employed; 20.2% unemployed. **Per capita income:** $30,732; change (2009-10): 2.0%. **Below poverty level:** 15.9%; 19.8% of families. **Educational attainment:** 73.7% HS; 17.7% bachelor's. **Avg. commute:** 27.0 min. 74.2% drive; 17.3% carpool. **Housing units:** 99,376; 90.9% occupied. **Home ownership:** 54.3%. **Avg. rent:** $917.
Mayor: Ann Johnston, nonpartisan
History: Site purchased 1842; settled 1849; inc. 1850. Chief distribution point for agric. products of San Joaquin Valley.
Website: www.stocktongov.com

Tampa, Florida

Population: 346,037 (53). **Pop. density:** 3,051. **Pop. change (2000-11):** 14.0%. **Area:** 113.4 sq mi. **Racial distribution:** 65.0% white; 26.1% black; 3.2% Asian; 0.7% Amer. Ind.; 0.1% Pac. Isl.; 2.6% other; 2+ races 2.3%. **Hispanic pop.:** 23.1%. **Foreign born:** 14.8%. **U.S. citizens:** 91.5%. **Language:** 74.9% English only; 19.0% Spanish.
Employment: 140,730 employed; 11.2% unemployed. **Per capita income:** $37,003; change (2009-10): 2.1%. **Below poverty level:** 15.6%; 19.5% of families. **Educational attainment:** 83.6% HS; 31.2% bachelor's. **Avg. commute:** 22.6 min. 77.4% drive. **Housing units:** 155,446; 85.7% occupied. **Home ownership:** 55.1%. **Avg. home:** $127,800; change (2009-11): -9.2%. **Avg. rent:** $874.
Mayor: Bob Buckhorn, nonpartisan
History: U.S. army fort on site 1824; inc. 1851. Ybor City, Tampa's Latin Quarter, a Natl. Historical Landmark District.
Website: www.tampagov.net

Toledo, Ohio

Population: 286,038 (67). **Pop. density:** 3,545. **Pop. change (2000-11):** -8.8%. **Area:** 80.7 sq mi. **Racial distribution:** 66.5% white; 26.9% black; 1.2% Asian; 0.4% Amer. Ind.; <0.05% Pac. Isl.; 2.0% other; 2+ races 3.0%. **Hispanic pop.:** 6.8%. **Foreign born:** 3.5%. **U.S. citizens:** 98.1%. **Language:** 93.5% English only; 3.1% Spanish.
Employment: 118,754 employed; 10.4% unemployed. **Per capita income:** $34,481; change (2009-10): 2.0%. **Below poverty level:** 19.3%; 23.8% of families. **Educational attainment:** 84.5% HS; 17.6% bachelor's. **Avg. commute:** 19.2 min. 82.1% drive. **Housing units:** 140,034; 86.0% occupied. **Home ownership:** 58.0%. **Avg. home:** $75,700; change (2009-11): -9.2%. **Avg. rent:** $617.
Mayor: Mike Bell, nonpartisan
History: Site of Ft. Industry 1794; Battle of Ft. Meigs 1812; figured in Toledo War 1835-36 between OH and MI over borders; inc. 1837.
Website: toledo.oh.gov

Tucson, Arizona

Population: 525,796 (33). **Pop. density:** 2,319. **Pop. change (2000-11):** 8.0%. **Area:** 226.7 sq mi. **Racial distribution:** 72.1% white; 4.6% black; 2.8% Asian; 2.7% Amer. Ind.; 0.2% Pac. Isl.; 14.3% other; 2+ races 3.4%. **Hispanic pop.:** 40.4%. **Foreign born:** 16.0%. **U.S. citizens:** 89.5%. **Language:** 66.2% English only; 28.8% Spanish.
Employment: 228,560 employed; 9.2% unemployed. **Per capita income:** $34,987; change (2009-10): 2.0%. **Below poverty level:** 15.2%; 21.3% of families. **Educational attainment:** 83.7% HS; 25.1% bachelor's. **Avg. commute:** 21.5 min. 72.8% drive; 11.5% carpool. **Housing units:** 233,002; 89.0% occupied. **Home ownership:** 52.9%. **Avg. home:** $134,500; change (2009-11): -22.0%. **Avg. rent:** $690.
Mayor: Jonathan Rothschild, Democrat
History: Settled 1775 by Spanish as a presidio; acquired by U.S. in Gadsden Purchase 1853; inc. 1877.
Website: www.tucsonaz.gov

Tulsa, Oklahoma

Population: 396,466 (45). **Pop. density:** 2,015. **Pop. change (2000-11):** 0.9%. **Area:** 196.8 sq mi. **Racial distribution:** 62.7% white; 15.5% black; 2.2% Asian; 4.3% Amer. Ind.; 0.1% Pac. Isl.; 4.3% other; 2+ races 6.2%. **Hispanic pop.:** 12.9%. **Foreign born:** 9.3%. **U.S. citizens:** 93.2%. **Language:** 86.3% English only; 9.9% Spanish.
Employment: 173,748 employed; 6.5% unemployed. **Per capita income:** $38,894; change (2009-10): 3.1%. **Below poverty level:** 15.2%; 19.3% of families. **Educational attainment:** 86.4% HS; 29.4% bachelor's. **Avg. commute:** 17.9 min. 79.7%

drive; 11.9% carpool. **Housing units:** 185,574; 88.9% occupied. **Home ownership:** 54.4%. **Avg. home:** $129,500; change (2009-11): -0.5%. **Avg. rent:** $676.
Mayor: Dewey F. Bartlett Jr., Republican
History: Settled in 1836 by Creek Indians; modern town founded 1882; inc. 1898; oil discovered early 20th century. Emerging telecommunications hub.
Website: www.cityoftulsa.org

Virginia Beach, Virginia

Population: 442,707 (39). **Pop. density:** 1,778. **Pop. change (2000-11):** 4.1%. **Area:** 249.0 sq mi. **Racial distribution:** 69.4% white; 19.2% black; 6.0% Asian; 0.2% Amer. Ind.; 0.1% Pac. Isl.; 1.2% other; 2+ races 3.8%. **Hispanic pop.:** 6.2%. **Foreign born:** 8.9%. **U.S. citizens:** 96.3%. **Language:** 88.3% English only; 4.2% Spanish.
Employment: 217,179 employed; 6.0% unemployed. **Per capita income:** $40,234; change (2009-10): 2.3%. **Below poverty level:** 4.8%; 6.8% of families. **Educational attainment:** 92.5% HS; 31.9% bachelor's. **Avg. commute:** 22.7 min. 82.0% drive. **Housing units:** 176,199; 93.0% occupied. **Home ownership:** 66.5%. **Avg. home:** $182,900; change (2009-11): -12.9%. **Avg. rent:** $1,143.
Mayor: William D. Sessoms Jr., nonpartisan
History: Area founded by Capt. John Smith 1607; formed by merger with Princess Anne Co. 1963.
Website: www.vbgov.com

Washington, District of Columbia

Population: 617,996 (25). **Pop. density:** 10,123. **Pop. change (2000-11):** 8.0%. **Area:** 61.0 sq mi. **Racial distribution:** 38.1% white; 52.9% black; 3.5% Asian; 0.3% Amer. Ind.; 0.1% Pac. Isl.; 3.4% other; 2+ races 1.8%. **Hispanic pop.:** 8.8%. **Foreign born:** 13.0%. **U.S. citizens:** 91.7%. **Language:** 85.4% English only; 7.3% Spanish.
Employment: 309,060 employed; 10.2% unemployed. **Per capita income:** $57,343; change (2009-10): 2.5%. **Below poverty level:** 14.5%; 18.5% of families. **Educational attainment:** 86.5% HS; 49.2% bachelor's. **Avg. commute:** 29.3 min. 37.6% public trans.; 35.9% drive; 11.9% walk. **Housing units:** 293,492; 87.7% occupied. **Home ownership:** 43.5%. **Avg. home:** $325,400; change (2009-11): 5.4%. **Avg. rent:** $1,063.
Mayor: Vincent C. Gray, Democrat
History: U.S. capital; site on Potomac R. chosen by George Washington 1790 on land ceded from VA and MD (portion S of Potomac returned to VA 1846). Congress first met 1800; inc. 1802; sacked by British, War of 1812. 125 killed during Sept. 11, 2001, terrorist attack on the Pentagon.
Website: dc.gov

Wichita, Kansas

Population: 384,445 (49). **Pop. density:** 2,413. **Pop. change (2000-11):** 11.7%. **Area:** 159.3 sq mi. **Racial distribution:** 73.0% white; 11.1% black; 4.7% Asian; 1.0% Amer. Ind.; 0.1% Pac. Isl.; 5.7% other; 2+ races 4.5%. **Hispanic pop.:** 13.9%. **Foreign born:** 9.2%. **U.S. citizens:** 94.4%. **Language:** 84.8% English only; 9.7% Spanish.
Employment: 171,872 employed; 8.9% unemployed. **Per capita income:** $37,221; change (2009-10): 1.3%. **Below poverty level:** 11.8%; 15.6% of families. **Educational attainment:** 86.3% HS; 27.6% bachelor's. **Avg. commute:** 17.5 min. 84.1% drive. **Housing units:** 166,470; 90.3% occupied. **Home ownership:** 63.1%. **Avg. home:** $115,600; change (2009-11): -2.6%. **Avg. rent:** $629.
Mayor: Carl Brewer, nonpartisan
History: Founded 1864; inc. 1871. Established itself as aircraft manufacturing hub between WWI and WWII.
Website: www.wichita.gov

Winston-Salem, North Carolina

Population: 232,385 (85). **Pop. density:** 1,755. **Pop. change (2000-11):** 25.1%. **Area:** 132.4 sq mi. **Racial distribution:** 52.1% white; 35.1% black; 2.1% Asian; 0.2% Amer. Ind.; 0.1% Pac. Isl.; 8.7% other; 2+ races 1.7%. **Hispanic pop.:** 13.5%. **Foreign born:** 10.8%. **U.S. citizens:** 91.5%. **Language:** 83.6% English only; 12.6% Spanish.
Employment: 100,611 employed; 9.5% unemployed. **Per capita income:** $35,526; change (2009-10): 2.2%. **Below poverty level:** 15.3%; 19.3% of families. **Educational attainment:** 85.5% HS; 31.8% bachelor's. **Avg. commute:** 19.3 min. 82.3% drive. **Housing units:** 102,882; 86.8% occupied. **Home ownership:** 58.4%. **Avg. rent:** $662.
Mayor: Allen Joines, Democrat
History: Salem founded 1766; Winston founded 1849; became Winston-Salem 1913. The Reynolds Building, completed 1929, used as model for Empire State Building (designed by same architects).
Website: www.cityofws.org

Census Origins and Methods

A census is conducted in the U.S. every 10 years. The primary purpose is to apportion seats in the House of Representatives. Census data is also used to determine the boundaries of state legislative districts.

The first U.S. census, mandated by Article 1, Section 2 of the Constitution, was conducted in 1790, a little more than a year after George Washington became president. It counted the numbers of free white males ages 16 and over (as a measure of available workers or military personnel), free white males under 16, free white females, all other free persons, and slaves. The data was collected over 18 months, at a cost of about $1 million in today's dollars. The 1790 census counted a total of 3.9 million people, resulting in an increase of 41 seats (from 65 to 106) in the House of Representatives.

As the nation grew, so did the scope of the census. The first inquiries on manufacturing were made in 1810. Questions on "the pursuits, industry, education, and resources of the country" were added to the 1840 census. The 1880 and 1890 censuses had many more questions so that it took a full 10 years to publish the results. Because of those delays, Congress limited the 1900 census to questions on population, manufacturing, agriculture, and mortality. Many of the dropped topics reappeared in later censuses.

Today, the secretary of commerce and the Census Bureau are directed by law to take censuses of population, housing, agriculture, irrigation, manufacturing, mineral industries, other businesses (wholesale trade, retail trade, and services), construction, transportation, and governments at stated intervals. They also conduct smaller-scale surveys on behalf of other federal agencies.

U.S. marshals supervised the first nine censuses and reported to the president (1790), to the secretary of state (1800-40), or to the secretary of the interior (1850-70). There was no continuity in personnel from one census to the next. In 1902, Congress authorized a permanent Census Office within the Interior Department. In 1903, the agency was transferred to the new Department of Commerce and Labor. When the department split in 1913, the Bureau of the Census went with the Commerce Department.

The Census Bureau began using statistical sampling techniques in the 1940s, the first modern computer in the 1950s, and enumeration by mail in the 1960s. It introduced these innovations so that it could publish data sooner, at a lower cost, and with less burden on the public. For the 2010 Census, the Census Bureau mailed questionnaires to most housing units in the country. Follow-up interviews at nonresponding households were conducted using handheld computers rather than paper and pencil.

The 2010 Census asked just 10 questions, making its questionnaire one of the shortest in Census history. In previous censuses, about five in six households received a short form; one in six households answered a long-form questionnaire, which asked about details such as ancestry, marital status, and occupation. The American Community Survey (ACS) replaced the need in 2010 for a long-form questionnaire. Implemented nationwide in 2005, the ACS is conducted yearly on a random sample of the population. It gathers demographic, economic, and housing information on communities across the country.

U.S. Population by State and Region, 2000, 2011

Source: Population Estimates Program, Decennial Census, U.S. Census Bureau, U.S. Dept. of Commerce
(ranked by 2011 resident population)

Rank	State	2011[1]	2000[2]	% change, 2000-11	Rank	State	2011[1]	2000[2]	% change, 2000-11
1.	California	37,691,912	33,871,648	11.3%	29.	Connecticut	3,580,709	3,405,565	5.1%
2.	Texas	25,674,681	20,851,820	23.1	30.	Iowa	3,062,309	2,926,324	4.6
3.	New York	19,465,197	18,976,457	2.6	31.	Mississippi	2,978,512	2,844,658	4.7
4.	Florida	19,057,542	15,982,378	19.2	32.	Arkansas	2,937,979	2,673,400	9.9
5.	Illinois	12,869,257	12,419,293	3.6	33.	Kansas	2,871,238	2,688,418	6.8
6.	Pennsylvania	12,742,886	12,281,054	3.8	34.	Utah	2,817,222	2,233,169	26.2
7.	Ohio	11,544,951	11,353,140	1.7	35.	Nevada	2,723,322	1,998,257	36.3
8.	Michigan	9,876,187	9,938,444	−0.6	36.	New Mexico	2,082,224	1,819,046	14.5
9.	Georgia	9,815,210	8,186,453	19.9	37.	West Virginia	1,855,364	1,808,344	2.6
10.	North Carolina	9,656,401	8,049,313	20.0	38.	Nebraska	1,842,641	1,711,263	7.7
11.	New Jersey	8,821,155	8,414,350	4.8	39.	Idaho	1,584,985	1,293,953	22.5
12.	Virginia	8,096,604	7,078,515	14.4	40.	Hawaii	1,374,810	1,211,537	13.5
13.	Washington	6,830,038	5,894,121	15.9	41.	Maine	1,328,188	1,274,923	4.2
14.	Massachusetts	6,587,536	6,349,097	3.8	42.	New Hampshire	1,318,194	1,235,786	6.7
15.	Indiana	6,516,922	6,080,485	7.2	43.	Rhode Island	1,051,302	1,048,319	0.3
16.	Arizona	6,482,505	5,130,632	26.3	44.	Montana	998,199	902,195	10.6
17.	Tennessee	6,403,353	5,689,283	12.6	45.	Delaware	907,135	783,600	15.8
18.	Missouri	6,010,688	5,595,211	7.4	46.	South Dakota	824,082	754,844	9.2
19.	Maryland	5,828,289	5,296,486	10.0	47.	Alaska	722,718	626,932	15.3
20.	Wisconsin	5,711,767	5,363,675	6.5	48.	North Dakota	683,932	642,200	6.5
21.	Minnesota	5,344,861	4,919,479	8.6	49.	Vermont	626,431	608,827	2.9
22.	Colorado	5,116,796	4,301,261	19.0	50.	District of Columbia	617,996	572,059	8.0
23.	Alabama	4,802,740	4,447,100	8.0	51.	Wyoming	568,158	493,782	15.1
24.	South Carolina	4,679,230	4,012,012	16.6		**United States**	**311,591,917**	**281,421,906**	**10.7**
25.	Louisiana	4,574,836	4,468,976	2.4		Northeast[3]	55,521,598	53,594,378	3.6
26.	Kentucky	4,369,356	4,041,769	8.1		Midwest[4]	67,158,835	64,392,776	4.3
27.	Oregon	3,871,859	3,421,399	13.2		South[5]	116,046,736	100,236,820	15.8
28.	Oklahoma	3,791,508	3,450,654	9.9		West[6]	72,864,748	63,197,932	15.3

Note: The U.S. resident population consists of individuals whose "usual place of residence" is in one of the 50 states or DC. It excludes overseas U.S. military personnel and civilian U.S. citizens living abroad. (1) Population estimates are for July 1. (2) Population figures are for Apr. 1 of decennial census year. (3) Incl. the states of the New England division (Connecticut, Maine, Massachusetts, New Hampshire, Rhode Island, Vermont) and Middle Atlantic division (New Jersey, New York, Pennsylvania). (4) Incl. the states of the East North Central division (Illinois, Indiana, Michigan, Ohio, Wisconsin) and West North Central division (Iowa, Kansas, Minnesota, Missouri, Nebraska, North Dakota, South Dakota). (5) Incl. the states of the South Atlantic division (Delaware, DC, Florida, Georgia, Maryland, North Carolina, South Carolina, Virginia, West Virginia), East South Central division (Alabama, Kentucky, Mississippi, Tennessee), and West South Central division (Arkansas, Louisiana, Oklahoma, Texas). (6) Incl. the states of the Mountain division (Arizona, Colorado, Idaho, Montana, Nevada, New Mexico, Utah, Wyoming) and Pacific division (Alaska, California, Hawaii, Oregon, Washington).

U.S. Population by Official

Source: Decennial Censuses, U.S. Census Bureau, (population figures for 1790-1860

State	1790	1800	1810	1820	1830	1840	1850	1860	1870	1880	1890	1900	1910	1920
AL[1]	...	1	9	128	310	591	772	964	996,992	1,262,505	1,513,401	1,828,697	2,138,093	2,348,174
AK	...	...	...	...	...	...	...	...	...	33,426	32,052	63,592	64,356	55,036
AZ[2]	...	...	...	...	...	...	...	...	9,658	40,440	88,243	122,931	204,354	334,162
AR	...	...	1	14	30	98	210	435	484,471	802,525	1,128,211	1,311,564	1,574,449	1,752,204
CA	...	...	...	...	...	...	93	380	560,247	864,694	1,213,398	1,485,053	2,377,549	3,426,861
CO[2]	...	...	...	...	...	...	...	34	39,864	194,327	413,249	539,700	799,024	939,629
CT	238	251	262	275	298	310	371	460	537,454	622,700	746,258	908,420	1,114,756	1,380,631
DE	59	64	73	73	77	78	92	112	125,015	146,608	168,493	184,735	202,322	223,003
DC	...	8	16	23	30	34	52	75	131,700	177,624	230,392	278,718	331,069	437,571
FL	...	...	...	...	35	54	87	140	187,748	269,493	391,422	528,542	752,619	968,470
GA	83	163	252	341	517	69	906	1,057	1,184,109	1,542,180	1,837,353	2,216,331	2,609,121	2,895,832
HI	...	...	...	...	...	...	...	...	...	...	...	154,001	191,909	255,912
ID[3]	...	...	...	...	...	...	...	...	14,999	32,610	88,548	161,772	325,594	431,866
IL	...	...	12	55	157	476	851	1,712	2,539,891	3,077,871	3,826,352	4,821,550	5,638,591	6,485,280
IN	...	6	25	147	343	686	988	1,350	1,680,637	1,978,301	2,192,404	2,516,462	2,700,876	2,930,390
IA	...	...	...	...	...	43	192	675	1,194,020	1,624,615	1,912,297	2,231,853	2,224,771	2,404,021
KS	...	...	...	...	...	...	...	107	364,399	996,096	1,428,108	1,470,495	1,690,949	1,769,257
KY	74	221	407	564	688	780	982	1,156	1,321,011	1,648,690	1,858,635	2,147,174	2,289,905	2,416,630
LA	...	...	77	153	216	352	518	708	726,915	939,946	1,118,588	1,381,625	1,656,388	1,798,509
ME[4]	97	152	229	298	399	502	583	628	626,915	648,936	661,086	694,466	742,371	768,014
MD	320	342	381	407	447	470	583	687	780,894	934,943	1,042,390	1,188,044	1,295,346	1,449,661
MA[4]	379	423	472	523	610	738	995	1,231	1,457,351	1,783,085	2,238,947	2,805,346	3,366,416	3,852,356
MI	...	...	5	9	32	212	398	749	1,184,059	1,636,937	2,093,890	2,420,982	2,810,173	3,668,412
MN	...	...	...	...	...	...	6	172	439,706	780,773	1,310,283	1,751,394	2,075,708	2,387,125
MS[1]	...	8	31	75	137	376	607	791	827,922	1,131,597	1,289,600	1,551,270	1,797,114	1,790,618
MO	...	...	20	67	140	384	682	1,182	1,721,295	2,168,380	2,679,185	3,106,665	3,293,335	3,404,055
MT[3]	...	...	...	...	...	...	...	...	20,595	39,159	142,924	243,329	376,053	548,889
NE	...	...	...	...	...	...	...	29	122,993	452,402	1,062,656	1,066,300	1,192,214	1,296,372
NV[2]	...	...	...	...	...	...	...	7	42,491	62,266	47,355	42,335	81,875	77,407
NH	142	184	214	244	269	285	318	326	318,300	346,991	376,530	411,588	430,572	443,083
NJ	184	211	246	278	321	373	490	672	906,096	1,131,116	1,444,933	1,883,669	2,537,167	3,155,900
NM[2]	...	...	...	...	...	...	62	94	91,874	119,565	160,282	195,310	327,301	360,350
NY	340	589	959	1,373	1,919	2,429	3,097	3,881	4,382,759	5,082,871	6,003,174	7,268,894	9,113,614	10,385,227
NC	394	478	556	639	736	753	869	993	1,071,361	1,399,750	1,617,949	1,893,810	2,206,287	2,559,123
ND[5]	...	...	...	...	...	...	...	...	2,405	36,909	190,983	319,146	577,056	646,872
OH	...	45	231	581	938	1,519	1,980	2,340	2,665,260	3,198,062	3,672,329	4,157,545	4,767,121	5,759,394
OK	...	...	...	...	...	...	...	...	...	...	258,657	790,391	1,657,155	2,028,283
OR[6]	...	...	...	...	...	...	12	52	90,923	174,768	317,704	413,536	672,765	783,389
PA	434	602	810	1,049	1,348	1,724	2,312	2,906	3,521,951	4,282,891	5,258,113	6,302,115	7,665,111	8,720,017
RI	69	69	77	83	97	109	148	175	217,353	276,531	345,506	428,556	542,610	604,397
SC	249	346	415	503	581	594	669	704	705,606	995,577	1,151,149	1,340,316	1,515,400	1,683,724
SD[5]	...	...	...	...	...	...	...	5	11,776	98,268	348,600	401,570	583,888	636,547
TN	36	106	262	423	682	829	1,003	1,110	1,258,520	1,542,359	1,767,518	2,020,616	2,184,789	2,337,885
TX	...	...	...	...	...	...	213	604	818,579	1,591,749	2,235,527	3,048,710	3,896,542	4,663,228
UT	...	...	...	...	...	...	11	40	86,786	143,963	210,779	276,749	373,351	449,396
VT	85	154	218	236	281	292	314	315	330,551	332,286	332,422	343,641	355,956	352,428
VA[7]	692	808	878	938	1,044	1,025	1,120	1,220	1,225,163	1,512,565	1,655,980	1,854,184	2,061,612	2,309,187
WA[3,6]	...	...	...	...	...	...	1	12	23,955	75,116	357,232	518,103	1,141,990	1,356,621
WV[7]	56	79	105	137	177	225	302	377	442,014	618,457	762,794	958,800	1,221,119	1,463,701
WI	...	...	...	...	...	31	305	776	1,054,670	1,315,497	1,693,330	2,069,042	2,333,860	2,632,067
WY[3]	...	...	...	...	...	...	...	...	9,118	20,789	62,555	92,531	145,965	194,402
U.S.[8]	3,929	5,308	7,240	9,638	12,866	17,063	23,192	31,443	38,558,371	50,189,209	62,979,766	76,212,168	92,228,531	106,021,568

Note: Unless otherwise noted, pop. shown is for a state's present-day area. Excl. overseas U.S. military personnel and civilian U.S. citizens living abroad. (1) 1800-10 figures for MS are for those areas of Mississippi Territory now part of present-day AL and MS. (2) 1850 figure for NM incl. parts of New Mexico Territory now part of present-day AZ, NM, CO, and NV; 1860 figure incl. parts taken in formation of Arizona Territory in 1863. (3) 1860 figure for WA incl. pop. in present-day ID and parts of MT and WY. (4) 1790-1810 figures for MA do not incl. district taken to form state of ME in 1820. (5) 1860 figure is for Dakota Territory, which comprised present-day ND and SD; 1870-80 figures are for parts of territory that became the two states in 1889. (6) Parts of Oregon Territory went to Washington Territory in 1853 and 1859. 1850 pop. in those areas are listed under WA, not OR. (7) 1790-1860 figures for VA do not incl. areas taken in creation of WV in 1863. (8) 1830-40 totals incl. persons (5,318 in 1830; 6,100 in 1840) on public ships in service of the U.S. not credited to any state.

Estimated Population of American Colonies, 1630-1780

Source: U.S. Census Bureau, U.S. Dept. of Commerce (numbers in thousands)

Colony	1630	1650	1670	1690	1700	1720	1740	1750	1770	1780
Total	4.6	50.4	111.9	210.4	250.9	466.2	905.6	1,170.8	2,148.1	2,780.4
Maine (counties)[1]	0.4	1.0							31.3	49.1
New Hampshire[2]	0.5	1.3	1.8	4.2	5.0	9.4	23.3	27.5	62.4	87.8
Vermont[3]	...	...	...	...	...	...	...	...	10.0	47.6
Plymouth and Massachusetts[1,2,4]	0.9	15.6	35.3	56.9	55.9	91.0	151.6	188.0	235.3	268.6
Rhode Island[2]	...	0.8	2.2	4.2	5.9	11.7	25.3	33.2	58.2	52.9
Connecticut[2]	...	4.1	12.6	21.6	26.0	58.8	89.6	111.3	183.9	206.7
New York[2]	0.4	4.1	5.8	13.9	19.1	36.9	63.7	76.7	162.9	210.5
New Jersey[2]	...	...	1.0	8.0	14.0	29.8	51.4	71.4	117.4	139.6
Pennsylvania[2]	...	...	...	11.4	18.0	31.0	85.6	119.7	240.1	327.3
Delaware[2]	...	0.2	0.7	1.5	2.5	5.4	19.9	28.7	35.5	45.4
Maryland[2]	...	4.5	13.2	24.0	29.6	66.1	116.1	141.1	202.6	245.5
Virginia[2]	2.5	18.7	35.3	53.0	58.6	87.8	180.4	231.0	447.0	538.0
North Carolina[2]	...	...	3.9	7.6	10.7	21.3	51.8	73.0	197.2	270.1
South Carolina[2]	...	...	0.2	3.9	5.7	17.0	45.0	64.0	124.2	180.0
Georgia[2]	...	...	...	...	...	...	...	2.0	23.4	56.1
Kentucky[5]	...	...	...	...	...	...	...	...	15.7	45.0
Tennessee[6]	...	...	...	...	...	...	...	...	1.0	10.0

(1) For 1660-1750, the pop. of ME counties are included with MA. ME was annexed by MA in the 1650s but became a separate state in 1820. (2) One of the original 13 states. (3) Admitted as state 1791. (4) Plymouth became part of Prov. of Massachusetts in 1691. (5) Admitted as state 1792. (6) Admitted as state 1796.

Census, 1790-2010
U.S. Dept. of Commerce
only are in thousands)

1930	1940	1950	1960	1970	1980	1990	2000	2010	State
2,646,248	2,832,961	3,061,743	3,266,740	3,444,165	3,893,888	4,040,587	4,447,100	4,779,736	AL
59,278	72,524	128,643	226,167	300,382	401,851	550,043	626,932	710,231	AK
435,573	499,261	749,587	1,302,161	1,770,900	2,718,215	3,665,228	5,130,632	6,392,017	AZ
1,854,482	1,949,387	1,909,511	1,786,272	1,923,295	2,286,435	2,350,725	2,673,400	2,915,918	AR
5,677,251	6,907,387	10,586,223	15,717,204	19,953,134	23,667,902	29,760,021	33,871,648	37,253,956	CA
1,035,791	1,123,296	1,325,089	1,753,947	2,207,259	2,889,964	3,294,394	4,301,261	5,029,196	CO
1,606,903	1,709,242	2,007,280	2,535,234	3,031,709	3,107,576	3,287,116	3,405,565	3,574,097	CT
238,380	266,505	318,085	446,292	548,104	594,338	666,168	783,600	897,934	DE
486,869	663,091	802,178	763,956	756,510	638,333	606,900	572,059	601,723	DC
1,468,211	1,897,414	2,771,305	4,951,560	6,789,443	9,746,324	12,937,926	15,982,378	18,801,310	FL
2,908,506	3,123,723	3,444,578	3,943,116	4,589,575	5,463,105	6,478,216	8,186,453	9,687,653	GA
368,336	422,330	499,794	632,772	768,561	964,691	1,108,229	1,211,537	1,360,301	HI
445,032	524,873	588,637	667,191	712,567	943,935	1,006,749	1,293,953	1,567,582	ID
7,630,654	7,897,241	8,712,176	10,081,158	11,113,976	11,426,518	11,430,602	12,419,293	12,830,632	IL
3,238,503	3,427,796	3,934,224	4,662,498	5,193,669	5,490,224	5,544,159	6,080,485	6,483,802	IN
2,470,939	2,538,268	2,621,073	2,757,537	2,824,376	2,913,808	2,776,755	2,926,324	3,046,355	IA
1,880,999	1,801,028	1,905,299	2,178,611	2,246,578	2,363,679	2,477,574	2,688,418	2,853,118	KS
2,614,589	2,845,627	2,944,806	3,038,156	3,218,706	3,660,777	3,685,296	4,041,769	4,339,367	KY
2,101,593	2,363,880	2,683,516	3,257,022	3,641,306	4,205,900	4,219,973	4,468,976	4,533,372	LA
797,423	847,226	913,774	969,265	992,048	1,124,660	1,227,928	1,274,923	1,328,361	ME
1,631,526	1,821,244	2,343,001	3,100,689	3,922,399	4,216,975	4,781,468	5,296,486	5,773,552	MD
4,249,614	4,316,721	4,690,514	5,148,578	5,689,170	5,737,037	6,016,425	6,349,097	6,547,629	MA
4,842,325	5,256,106	6,371,766	7,823,194	8,875,083	9,262,078	9,295,297	9,938,444	9,883,640	MI
2,563,953	2,792,300	2,982,483	3,413,864	3,804,971	4,075,970	4,375,099	4,919,479	5,303,925	MN
2,009,821	2,183,796	2,178,914	2,178,141	2,216,912	2,520,638	2,573,216	2,844,658	2,967,297	MS
3,629,367	3,784,664	3,954,653	4,319,813	4,676,501	4,916,686	5,117,073	5,595,211	5,988,927	MO
537,606	559,456	591,024	674,767	694,409	786,690	799,065	902,195	989,415	MT
1,377,963	1,315,834	1,325,510	1,411,330	1,483,493	1,569,825	1,578,385	1,711,263	1,826,341	NE
91,058	110,247	160,083	285,278	488,738	800,493	1,201,833	1,998,257	2,700,551	NV
465,293	491,524	533,242	606,921	737,681	920,610	1,109,252	1,235,786	1,316,470	NH
4,041,334	4,160,165	4,835,329	6,066,782	7,168,164	7,364,823	7,730,188	8,414,350	8,791,894	NJ
423,317	531,818	681,187	951,023	1,016,000	1,302,894	1,515,069	1,819,046	2,059,179	NM
12,588,066	13,479,142	14,830,192	16,782,304	18,236,967	17,558,072	17,990,455	18,976,457	19,378,102	NY
3,170,276	3,571,623	4,061,929	4,556,155	5,082,059	5,881,766	6,628,637	8,049,313	9,535,483	NC
680,845	641,935	619,636	632,446	617,761	652,717	638,800	642,200	672,591	ND
6,646,697	6,907,612	7,946,627	9,706,397	10,652,017	10,797,630	10,847,115	11,353,140	11,536,504	OH
2,396,040	2,336,434	2,233,351	2,328,284	2,559,229	3,025,290	3,145,585	3,450,654	3,751,351	OK
953,786	1,089,684	1,521,341	1,768,687	2,091,385	2,633,105	2,842,321	3,421,399	3,831,074	OR
9,631,350	9,900,180	10,498,012	11,319,366	11,793,909	11,863,895	11,881,643	12,281,054	12,702,379	PA
687,497	713,346	791,896	859,488	949,723	947,154	1,003,464	1,048,319	1,052,567	RI
1,738,765	1,899,804	2,117,027	2,382,594	2,590,516	3,121,820	3,486,703	4,012,012	4,625,364	SC
692,849	642,961	652,740	680,514	665,507	690,768	696,004	754,844	814,180	SD
2,616,556	2,915,841	3,291,718	3,567,089	3,923,687	4,591,120	4,877,185	5,689,283	6,346,105	TN
5,824,715	6,414,824	7,711,194	9,579,671	11,196,730	14,229,191	16,986,510	20,851,820	25,145,561	TX
507,847	550,310	688,862	890,627	1,059,273	1,461,037	1,722,850	2,233,169	2,763,885	UT
359,611	359,231	377,747	389,881	444,330	511,456	562,758	608,827	625,741	VT
2,421,851	2,677,773	3,318,680	3,966,949	4,648,494	5,346,818	6,187,358	7,078,515	8,001,024	VA
1,563,396	1,736,191	2,378,963	2,853,214	3,409,169	4,132,156	4,866,692	5,894,121	6,724,540	WA
1,729,205	1,901,974	2,005,552	1,860,421	1,744,237	1,949,644	1,793,477	1,808,344	1,852,994	WV
2,939,006	3,137,587	3,434,575	3,951,777	4,417,731	4,705,767	4,891,769	5,363,675	5,686,986	WI
225,565	250,742	290,529	330,066	332,416	469,557	453,588	493,782	563,626	WY
123,202,660	132,164,569	151,325,798	179,323,175	203,211,926	226,545,805	248,709,873	281,421,906	308,745,538	U.S.

U.S. Center of Population, 1790-2010
Source: Decennial Censuses, Geography Division, U.S. Census Bureau, U.S. Dept. of Commerce

The country's **center of population (mean)** is considered here to be the center of population gravity, or that point upon which the U.S. would balance if it were a rigid, weightless plane and the population distributed thereon, with each individual assuming an equal weight and exerting an influence on a central point proportional to his or her distance from that point.

Census year	N Lat °	'	''	W Long °	'	''	Approximate location
1790	39	16	30	76	11	12	Kent Co., MD, 23 miles east of Baltimore
1800	39	16	6	76	56	30	Howard Co., MD, 18 miles west of Baltimore
1810	39	11	30	77	37	12	Loudoun Co., VA, 40 miles northwest by west of Washington, DC
1820[1]	39	5	42	78	33	0	Hardy Co., WV, 16 miles east of Moorefield
1830[1]	38	57	54	79	16	54	Grant Co., WV, 19 miles west-southwest of Moorefield
1840[1]	39	2	0	80	18	0	Upshur Co., WV, 16 miles south of Clarksburg
1850[1]	38	59	0	81	19	0	Wirt Co., WV, 23 miles southeast of Parkersburg
1860	39	0	24	82	48	48	Pike Co., OH, 20 miles south by east of Chillicothe
1870	39	12	0	83	35	42	Highland Co., OH, 48 miles east by north of Cincinnati
1880	39	4	8	84	39	40	Boone Co., KY, 8 miles west by south of Cincinnati, OH
1890	39	11	56	85	32	53	Decatur Co., IN, 20 miles east of Columbus
1900	39	9	36	85	48	54	Bartholomew Co., IN, 6 miles southeast of Columbus
1910	39	10	12	86	32	20	Monroe Co., IN, in the city of Bloomington
1920	39	10	21	86	43	15	Owen Co., IN, 8 miles south-southeast of Spencer
1930	39	3	45	87	8	6	Greene Co., IN, 3 miles northeast of Linton
1940	38	56	54	87	22	35	Sullivan Co., IN, 2 miles southeast by east of Carlisle
1950	38	50	21	88	9	33	Richland Co., IL, 8 miles north-northwest of Olney
1950[2]	38	48	15	88	22	8	Clay Co., IL, 3 miles northeast of Louisville
1960[2]	38	35	58	89	12	35	Clinton Co., IL, 6½ miles northwest of Centralia
1970[2]	38	27	47	89	42	22	St. Clair Co., IL, 5 miles east-southeast of Mascoutah
1980[2]	38	8	13	90	34	26	Jefferson Co., MO, ¼ mile west of DeSoto
1990[2]	37	52	20	91	12	55	Crawford Co., MO, 9.7 miles southeast of Steelville
2000[2]	37	41	49	91	48	34	Phelps Co., MO, 2.8 miles east of Edgar Springs
2010[2]	37	31	3	92	10	23	Texas Co., MO, 2.7 miles northeast of Plato

(1) West Virginia was set off from Virginia on Dec. 31, 1862, and admitted as a state on June 20, 1863. (2) Incl. Alaska and Hawaii.

Density of U.S. Population by State, 1930-2010

Source: Decennial Censuses, U.S. Census Bureau, U.S. Dept. of Commerce

(per square mile, land area only)

State	1930	1950	1970	1990	2010	State	1930	1950	1970	1990	2010
AL.......	52.3	60.5	68.0	79.8	94.4	MT	3.7	4.1	4.8	5.5	6.8
AK.......	0.1	0.2	0.5	1.0	1.2	NE.......	17.9	17.3	19.3	20.5	23.8
AZ.......	3.8	6.6	15.6	32.3	56.3	NV.......	0.8	1.5	4.5	10.9	24.6
AR.......	35.6	36.7	37.0	45.2	56.0	NH	52.0	59.6	82.4	123.9	147.0
CA.......	36.4	68.0	128.1	191.0	239.1	NJ.......	549.5	657.5	974.7	1,051.1	1,195.5
CO	10.0	12.8	21.3	31.8	48.5	NM	3.5	5.6	8.4	12.5	17.0
CT.......	331.8	414.5	626.1	678.5	738.1	NY.......	267.1	314.7	387.0	381.7	411.2
DE.......	122.3	163.2	281.3	341.9	460.8	NC	65.2	83.5	104.5	136.3	196.1
DC 7,975.1		13,140.3	12,392.0	9,941.3	9,856.5	ND	9.9	9.0	9.0	9.3	9.7
FL.......	27.4	51.7	126.6	241.3	350.6	OH	162.7	194.5	260.7	265.5	282.3
GA	50.6	59.9	79.8	112.6	168.4	OK	34.9	32.6	37.3	45.9	54.7
HI	57.3	77.8	119.7	172.6	211.8	OR	9.9	15.8	21.8	29.6	39.9
ID	5.4	7.1	8.6	12.2	19.0	PA.......	215.3	234.6	263.6	265.6	283.9
IL.......	137.4	156.9	200.2	205.9	231.1	RI	665.0	766.0	915.8	970.6	1,018.1
IN	90.4	109.8	145.0	154.8	181.0	SC.......	57.8	70.4	86.2	116.0	153.9
IA	44.2	46.9	50.6	49.7	54.5	SD.......	9.1	8.6	8.8	9.2	10.7
KS.......	23.0	23.3	27.5	30.3	34.9	TN.......	63.5	79.8	95.2	118.3	153.9
KY.......	66.2	74.6	81.5	93.3	109.9	TX.......	22.3	29.5	42.9	65.0	96.3
LA.......	48.6	62.1	84.3	97.7	104.9	UT.......	6.2	8.4	12.9	21.0	33.6
ME	25.9	29.6	32.2	39.8	43.1	VT.......	39.0	41.0	48.2	61.1	67.9
MD	168.1	241.4	404.1	492.6	594.8	VA	61.3	84.0	117.7	156.7	202.6
MA	544.8	601.3	729.4	771.3	839.4	WA	23.5	35.8	51.3	73.2	101.2
MI.......	85.6	112.7	157.0	164.4	174.8	WV	71.9	83.4	72.6	74.6	77.1
MN	32.2	37.5	47.8	54.9	66.6	WI.......	54.3	63.4	81.6	90.3	105.0
MS	42.8	46.4	47.2	54.8	63.2	WY	2.3	3.0	3.4	4.7	5.8
MO	52.8	57.5	68.0	74.4	87.1	**U.S.**	**34.7**	**42.6**	**57.5**	**70.4**	**87.4**

Note: For the sake of comparison, the densities of Alaska and Hawaii in 1930 and 1950 are included though they were not yet states.

U.S. Area and Population, 1790-2010

Source: Decennial Censuses, U.S. Census Bureau, U.S. Dept. of Commerce

Census date	AREA (square miles)			RESIDENT POPULATION			
					Per sq mi of	Increase over preceding census	
	Total area[1]	Land area	Water area[1]	Number	land	Number	%
1790 (Aug. 2)	891,364	864,746	24,065	3,929,214	4.5	—	—
1800 (Aug. 4)	891,364	864,746	24,065	5,308,483	6.1	1,379,269	35.1%
1810 (Aug. 6)	1,722,685	1,681,828	34,175	7,239,881	4.3	1,931,398	36.4
1820 (Aug. 7)	1,792,552	1,749,462	38,544	9,638,453	5.5	2,398,572	33.1
1830 (June 1)	1,792,552	1,749,462	38,544	12,866,020	7.4	3,227,567	33.5
1840 (June 1)	1,792,552	1,749,462	38,544	17,069,453	9.8	4,203,433	32.7
1850 (June 1)	2,991,655	2,940,042	52,705	23,191,876	7.9	6,122,423	35.9
1860 (June 1)	3,021,295	2,969,640	52,747	31,443,321	10.6	8,251,445	35.6
1870 (June 1)	3,612,299	3,540,705	68,082	39,818,449	11.2	8,375,128	26.6
1880 (June 1)	3,612,299	3,540,705	68,082	50,189,209	14.2	10,370,760	26.0
1890 (June 1)	3,612,299	3,540,705	68,082	62,979,766	17.8	12,790,557	25.5
1900 (June 1)	3,618,770	3,547,314	67,901	76,212,168	21.5	13,232,402	21.0
1910 (Apr. 15)	3,618,770	3,547,045	68,170	92,228,496	26.0	16,016,328	21.0
1920 (Jan. 1)	3,618,770	3,546,931	68,284	106,021,537	29.9	13,793,041	15.0
1930 (Apr. 1)	3,618,770	3,554,608	60,607	123,202,624	34.7	17,181,087	16.2
1940 (Apr. 1)	3,618,770	3,554,608	60,607	132,164,569	37.2	8,961,945	7.3
1950 (Apr. 1)	3,618,770	3,552,206	63,005	151,325,798	42.6	19,161,229	14.5
1960 (Apr. 1)	3,618,770	3,540,911	74,212	179,323,175	50.6	27,997,377	18.5
1970 (Apr. 1)	3,618,770	3,536,855	78,444	203,302,031	57.5	23,978,856	13.4
1980 (Apr. 1)	3,618,770	3,539,289	79,481	226,542,199	64.0	23,240,168	11.4
1990 (Apr. 1)	3,717,796	3,536,278	181,518	248,718,302	70.3	22,176,103	9.8
2000 (Apr. 1)	3,794,083	3,537,438	256,645	281,424,603	79.6	32,706,301	13.1
2010 (Apr. 1)	3,796,742	3,531,905	264,837	308,745,538	87.4	27,320,935	9.7

Note: Percent changes are computed on the basis of change in population since the preceding census date, so the period covered is not always exactly 10 years. Population density figures given for various years represent the area within the boundaries of the U.S. under its jurisdiction on the date in question including, in some cases, considerable areas not organized or settled and not actually covered by the census. Area data beginning in 1870 include Alaska; from 1900 on, data include Hawaii. Population figures may reflect corrections made to initial tabulated census counts. (1) Figures for 1790-1980 cover inland water only. Figures for 1990 include inland, coastal, and Great Lakes water. Figures for 2000-10 include additional territorial water.

U.S. Congressional Apportionment by Census Year, 1850-2010
Source: Decennial Censuses, U.S. Census Bureau, U.S. Dept. of Commerce

The U.S. Constitution, in Article 1, Section 2, mandates that the population be counted every 10 years so that the number of representatives can be apportioned among the states. Every state is entitled to at least one House seat. The size of a state's resident population, both citizens and noncitizens, determines if it may send additional representatives to Congress. A congressional apportionment has been made after every decennial census except for that of 1920. Prior to 1870, slaves were counted as being only $\frac{3}{5}$ of a person in the apportionment population. Apportionments made before the 20th century also excluded some Native Americans and armed forces personnel and federal civilian employees stationed overseas. District of Columbia residents remain excluded.

Under the provisions of a law that went into effect Nov. 15, 1941, representatives are apportioned by the method of equal proportions. In the application of this method, the apportionment is made so that the average number of people each House member represents has the least possible variation between states.

The first House of Representatives, in 1789, had 65 members as provided by the Constitution. The largest numbers were from Virginia (10), Massachusetts (8), and Pennsylvania (8). As the nation's population grew, the number of representatives was increased, but a 1911 act fixed the total membership of the House at 435. (Alaska and Hawaii each gained one House seat when they became states, temporarily raising the total to 437 representatives until after the 1960 census was conducted.)

State	2010	2000	1990	1970	1950	1900	1850	State	2010	2000	1990	1970	1950	1900	1850
AL	7	7	7	7	9	9	7	NE	3	3	3	3	4	6	NA
AK	1	1	1	1	1	NA	NA	NV	4	3	2	1	1	1	NA
AZ	9	8	6	4	2	NA	NA	NH	2	2	2	2	2	2	3
AR	4	4	4	4	6	7	2	NJ	12	13	13	15	14	10	5
CA	53	53	52	43	30	8	2	NM	3	3	3	2	2	NA	NA
CO	7	7	6	5	4	3	NA	NY	27	29	31	39	43	37	33
CT	5	5	6	6	6	5	4	NC	13	13	12	11	12	10	8
DE	1	1	1	1	1	1	1	ND	1	1	1	1	2	2	NA
FL	27	25	23	15	8	3	1	OH	16	18	19	23	23	21	21
GA	14	13	11	10	10	11	8	OK	5	5	6	6	6	5	NA
HI	2	2	2	2	1	NA	NA	OR	5	5	5	4	4	2	1
ID	2	2	2	2	2	1	NA	PA	18	19	21	25	30	32	25
IL	18	19	20	24	25	25	9	RI	2	2	2	2	2	2	2
IN	9	9	10	11	11	13	11	SC	7	6	6	6	6	7	6
IA	4	5	5	6	8	11	2	SD	1	1	1	2	2	2	NA
KS	4	4	4	5	6	8	NA	TN	9	9	9	8	9	10	10
KY	6	6	6	7	8	11	10	TX	36	32	30	24	22	16	2
LA	6	7	7	8	8	7	4	UT	4	3	3	2	2	1	NA
ME	2	2	2	2	3	4	6	VT	1	1	1	1	1	2	3
MD	8	8	8	8	7	6	6	VA	11	11	11	10	10	10	13
MA	9	10	10	12	14	14	11	WA	10	9	9	7	7	3	NA
MI	14	15	16	19	18	12	4	WV	3	3	3	4	6	5	NA
MN	8	8	8	8	9	9	2	WI	8	8	9	9	10	11	3
MS	4	4	5	5	6	8	5	WY	1	1	1	1	1	1	NA
MO	8	9	9	10	11	16	7								
MT	1	1	1	2	2	1	NA	**Total**	**435**	**435**	**435**	**435**	**437**	**391**	**237**

NA = Not applicable.

U.S. Slave and "Free Colored" Population, 1790, 1820, 1860
Source: Decennial Censuses, U.S. Census Bureau, U.S. Dept. of Commerce

	1790 census			1820 census			1860 census		
	Slaves	% slaves	Free colored	Slaves	% slaves	Free colored	Slaves	% slaves	Free colored
Northern states[1]	**40,370**	**2.1%**	**33,016**	**18,001**	**0.3%**	**92,351**	**18**	**0%**	**225,224**
Connecticut	2,759	1.2	2,801	97	0	7,844	0	0	8,627
New Jersey	11,423	6.2	2,762	7,557	2.7	12,460	18	0	25,318
New York	21,324	6.3	4,654	10,088	0.7	29,279	0	0	49,005
Pennsylvania	3,737	0.9	6,537	211	0	30,202	0	0	56,949
Border/disputed states	**123,753**	**27.4**	**12,056**	**248,860**	**22.4**	**55,794**	**429,403**	**20.6**	**118,652**
Delaware	8,887	15.0	3,899	4,509	6.2	12,958	1,798	1.6	19,829
Kansas	—	—	—	—	—	—	2	0	625
Kentucky	11,830	16.2	114	126,732	22.5	2,759	225,483	19.5	10,684
Maryland	103,036	32.2	8,043	107,397	26.4	39,730	87,189	12.7	83,942
Missouri	—	—	—	10,222	15.4	347	114,931	9.7	3,572
Southern states	**533,774**	**35.4**	**20,301**	**1,263,780**	**37.8**	**74,381**	**3,521,110**	**34.3**	**132,760**
Alabama	—	—	—	41,879	32.7	571	435,080	45.1	2,690
Arkansas	—	—	—	1,617	11.3	59	111,115	25.5	144
Florida	—	—	—	—	—	—	61,745	44.0	932
Georgia	29,264	35.5	398	149,654	43.9	1,763	462,198	43.7	3,500
Louisiana	—	—	—	69,064	45.2	10,476	331,726	46.9	18,647
Mississippi	—	—	—	32,814	43.5	458	436,631	55.2	773
North Carolina	100,572	25.5	4,975	205,017	32.1	14,612	331,059	33.4	30,463
South Carolina	107,094	43.0	1,801	258,475	51.4	6,826	402,406	57.2	9,914
Tennessee	3,417	9.5	361	80,107	18.9	2,727	275,719	24.8	7,300
Texas	—	—	—	—	—	—	182,566	30.2	355
Virginia	293,427	39.2	12,766	425,153	39.9	36,889	490,865	30.7	58,042
Total territories[2]	**—**	**—**	**—**	**6,377**	**19.3**	**4,048**	**3,229**	**1.1**	**11,434**
Total states and territories	**697,897**	**17.8**	**59,466**	**1,538,125**	**16.0**	**233,504**	**3,953,760**	**12.6**	**488,070**

Note: "Free colored" was an official Census Bureau designation in these decades. Pop. figures shown here include both blacks and those of mixed-race background. (1) Some states had negligible slave pops. that are not listed separately but are included in regional totals (relevant census years in parentheses): California (1860), Illinois (1820, 1860), Indiana (1820, 1860), Iowa (1860), Maine (1820, 1860), Massachusetts (1790, 1820, 1860), Michigan (1860), Minnesota (1860), New Hampshire (1790, 1820, 1860), Ohio (1820, 1860), Oregon (1860), Rhode Island (1790, 1820, 1860), Vermont (1820, 1860), and Wisconsin (1860). (2) Incl. Colorado (1860), Dakota (1860), District of Columbia (1820, 1860), Nebraska (1860), Nevada (1860), New Mexico (1860), Utah (1860), and Washington (1860).

Largest U.S. Metropolitan Areas by Population, 1990-2011

Source: Population Estimates Program, Decennial Censuses, U.S. Census Bureau, U.S. Dept. of Commerce
(ranked by 2011 population; 2011 estimates are as of July 1 while 1990 and 2000 figures are for Apr. 1 of decennial census year)

Metropolitan Statistical Areas (MSAs) are defined, or delineated geographically, for federal statistical use by the Office of Management and Budget (OMB) with technical assistance from the Census Bureau. The standards used to define metropolitan areas are revised before each decennial census. Following a decennial census and between decennial census years, population estimates are used to update area boundaries.

An MSA consists of at least one urbanized area of 50,000 or more inhabitants, plus an adjacent area closely integrated socially and economically with the core as measured by commuting ties. About 83.8% of the total U.S. population resided in an MSA in 2011. That represents an increase of about 28% from 1990. The most recent definitions, issued by the OMB in Dec. 2009, designates 366 MSAs in the U.S. The OMB will release new definitions, based on standards published in 2010, in 2013.

Rank	Metropolitan Statistical Area (MSA)	Population 2011	Population 2000	Population 1990	Percent change 2000-11	Percent change 1990-2011
1.	New York-Northern New Jersey-Long Island, NY-NJ-PA	19,015,900	18,323,002	16,846,046	3.8%	12.9%
2.	Los Angeles-Long Beach-Santa Ana, CA	12,944,801	12,365,627	11,273,720	4.7	14.8
3.	Chicago-Joliet-Naperville, IL-IN-WI	9,504,753	9,098,316	8,182,076	4.5	16.2
4.	Dallas-Fort Worth-Arlington, TX	6,526,548	5,161,544	3,989,294	26.4	63.6
5.	Houston-Sugar Land-Baytown, TX	6,086,538	4,715,407	3,767,335	29.1	61.6
6.	Philadelphia-Camden-Wilmington, PA-NJ-DE-MD	5,992,414	5,687,147	5,435,468	5.4	10.2
7.	Washington-Arlington-Alexandria, DC-VA-MD-WV	5,703,948	4,796,183	4,122,914	18.9	38.3
8.	Miami-Fort Lauderdale-Pompano Beach, FL	5,670,125	5,007,564	4,056,100	13.2	39.8
9.	Atlanta-Sandy Springs-Marietta, GA	5,359,205	4,247,981	3,069,425	26.2	74.6
10.	Boston-Cambridge-Quincy, MA-NH	4,591,112	4,391,344	4,133,895	4.5	11.1
11.	San Francisco-Oakland-Fremont, CA	4,391,037	4,123,740	3,686,592	6.5	19.1
12.	Riverside-San Bernardino-Ontario, CA	4,304,997	3,254,821	2,588,793	32.3	66.3
13.	Detroit-Warren-Livonia, MI	4,285,832	4,452,557	4,248,699	−3.7	0.9
14.	Phoenix-Mesa-Glendale, AZ	4,263,236	3,251,876	2,238,480	31.1	90.5
15.	Seattle-Tacoma-Bellevue, WA	3,500,026	3,043,878	2,559,164	15.0	36.8
16.	Minneapolis-St. Paul-Bloomington, MN-WI	3,318,486	2,968,806	2,538,834	11.8	30.7
17.	San Diego-Carlsbad-San Marcos, CA	3,140,069	2,813,833	2,498,016	11.6	25.7
18.	Tampa-St. Petersburg-Clearwater, FL	2,824,724	2,395,997	2,067,959	17.9	36.6
19.	St. Louis, MO-IL	2,817,355	2,698,687	2,580,897	4.4	9.2
20.	Baltimore-Towson, MD	2,729,110	2,552,994	2,382,172	6.9	14.6
21.	Denver-Aurora-Broomfield, CO	2,599,504	2,179,240	1,666,883	19.3	55.9
22.	Pittsburgh, PA	2,359,746	2,431,087	2,468,289	−2.9	−4.4
23.	Portland-Vancouver-Hillsboro, OR-WA	2,262,605	1,927,881	1,523,741	17.4	48.5
24.	San Antonio-New Braunfels, TX	2,194,927	1,711,703	1,407,745	28.2	55.9
25.	Sacramento–Arden-Arcade–Roseville, CA	2,176,235	1,796,857	1,481,102	21.1	46.9
26.	Orlando-Kissimmee-Sanford, FL	2,171,360	1,644,561	1,224,852	32.0	77.3
27.	Cincinnati-Middletown, OH-KY-IN	2,138,038	2,009,632	1,844,917	6.4	15.9
28.	Cleveland-Elyria-Mentor, OH	2,068,283	2,148,143	2,102,248	−3.7	−1.6
29.	Kansas City, MO-KS	2,052,676	1,836,038	1,636,528	11.8	25.4
30.	Las Vegas-Paradise, NV	1,969,975	1,375,765	741,459	43.2	165.7
31.	San Jose-Sunnyvale-Santa Clara, CA	1,865,450	1,735,819	1,534,274	7.5	21.6
32.	Columbus, OH	1,858,464	1,612,694	1,405,168	15.2	32.3
33.	Charlotte-Gastonia-Rock Hill, NC-SC	1,795,472	1,330,448	1,024,643	35.0	75.2
34.	Austin-Round Rock-San Marcos, TX	1,783,519	1,249,763	846,227	42.7	110.8
35.	Indianapolis-Carmel, IN	1,778,568	1,525,104	1,294,217	16.6	37.4
36.	Virginia Beach-Norfolk-Newport News, VA-NC	1,679,894	1,576,370	1,449,389	6.6	15.9
37.	Nashville-Davidson–Murfreesboro–Franklin, TN	1,617,142	1,311,789	1,048,216	23.3	54.3
38.	Providence-New Bedford-Fall River, RI-MA	1,600,224	1,582,997	1,509,789	1.1	6.0
39.	Milwaukee-Waukesha-West Allis, WI	1,562,216	1,500,741	1,432,149	4.1	9.1
40.	Jacksonville, FL	1,360,251	1,122,750	925,213	21.2	47.0
41.	Memphis, TN-MS-AR	1,325,605	1,205,204	1,067,263	10.0	24.2
42.	Louisville-Jefferson County, KY-IN	1,294,849	1,161,975	1,055,973	11.4	22.6
43.	Oklahoma City, OK	1,278,053	1,095,421	971,042	16.7	31.6
44.	Richmond, VA	1,269,380	1,096,957	949,244	15.7	33.7
45.	Hartford-West Hartford-East Hartford, CT	1,213,255	1,148,618	1,123,678	5.6	8.0
46.	New Orleans-Metairie-Kenner, LA	1,191,089	1,316,510	1,264,391	−9.5	−5.8
47.	Raleigh-Cary, NC	1,163,515	797,071	541,100	46.0	115.0
48.	Salt Lake City, UT	1,145,905	968,858	768,075	18.3	49.2
49.	Buffalo-Niagara Falls, NY	1,134,039	1,170,111	1,189,288	−3.1	−4.6
50.	Birmingham-Hoover, AL	1,132,264	1,052,238	956,844	7.6	18.3
51.	Rochester, NY	1,055,278	1,037,831	1,002,410	1.7	5.3
52.	Tucson, AZ	989,569	843,746	666,880	17.3	48.4
53.	Honolulu, HI	963,607	876,156	836,231	10.0	15.2
54.	Tulsa, OK	946,962	859,532	761,019	10.2	24.4
55.	Fresno, CA	942,904	799,407	667,490	18.0	41.3
56.	Bridgeport-Stamford-Norwalk, CT	925,899	882,567	827,645	4.9	11.9
57.	Albuquerque, NM	898,642	729,649	599,416	23.2	49.9
58.	Omaha-Council Bluffs, NE-IA	877,110	767,041	685,797	14.3	27.9
59.	Albany-Schenectady-Troy, NY	871,478	825,875	809,443	5.5	7.7
60.	New Haven-Milford, CT	861,113	824,008	804,219	4.5	7.1
61.	Bakersfield-Delano, CA	851,710	661,645	543,477	28.7	56.7
62.	Dayton, OH	845,388	848,153	843,835	−0.3	0.2
63.	Oxnard-Thousand Oaks-Ventura, CA	831,771	753,197	669,016	10.4	24.3
64.	Allentown-Bethlehem-Easton, PA-NJ	824,916	740,395	686,688	11.4	20.1
65.	El Paso, TX	820,790	679,622	591,610	20.8	38.7
66.	Baton Rouge, LA	808,242	705,973	623,853	14.5	29.6
67.	Worcester, MA	801,227	750,963	709,705	6.7	12.9
68.	McAllen-Edinburg-Mission, TX	797,810	569,463	383,545	40.1	108.0
69.	Grand Rapids-Wyoming, MI	779,604	740,482	645,914	5.3	20.7
70.	Columbia, SC	777,116	647,158	548,335	20.1	41.7

Largest U.S. Cities by Population, 1850-2011

Source: Population Estimates Program, Decennial Censuses, U.S. Census Bureau, U.S. Dept. of Commerce
(ranked by 2011 population)

Rank City	2011	2000	1990	1980	1970	1950	1900	1850
1. New York, NY	8,244,910	8,008,278	7,322,564	7,071,639	7,895,563	7,891,957	3,437,202	696,115
2. Los Angeles, CA	3,819,702	3,694,820	3,485,398	2,968,528	2,811,801	1,970,358	102,479	1,610
3. Chicago, IL	2,707,120	2,896,016	2,783,726	3,005,072	3,369,357	3,620,962	1,698,575	29,963
4. Houston, TX	2,145,146	1,953,631	1,630,553	1,595,138	1,233,535	596,163	44,633	2,396
5. Philadelphia, PA	1,536,471	1,517,550	1,585,577	1,688,210	1,949,996	2,071,605	1,293,697	121,376
6. Phoenix, AZ	1,469,471	1,321,045	983,403	789,704	584,303	106,818	5,544	...
7. San Antonio, TX	1,359,758	1,144,646	935,933	785,940	654,153	408,442	53,321	3,488
8. San Diego, CA	1,326,179	1,223,400	1,110,549	875,538	697,471	334,387	17,700	...
9. Dallas, TX	1,223,229	1,188,580	1,006,877	904,599	844,401	434,462	42,638	...
10. San Jose, CA	967,487	894,943	782,248	629,400	459,913	95,280	21,500	...
11. Jacksonville, FL	827,908	735,617	635,230	540,920	504,265	204,517	28,429	1,045
12. Indianapolis, IN[1]	827,609	781,870	741,952	700,807	736,856	427,173	169,164	8,091
13. Austin, TX	820,611	656,562	465,622	345,890	253,539	132,459	22,258	629
14. San Francisco, CA	812,826	776,733	723,959	678,974	715,674	775,357	342,782	34,776
15. Columbus, OH	797,434	711,470	632,910	565,021	540,025	375,901	125,560	17,882
16. Fort Worth, TX	758,738	534,694	447,619	385,164	393,455	278,778	26,688	...
17. Charlotte, NC	751,087	540,828	395,934	315,474	241,420	134,042	18,091	1,065
18. Detroit, MI	706,585	951,270	1,027,974	1,203,368	1,514,063	1,849,568	285,704	21,019
19. El Paso, TX	665,568	563,662	515,342	425,259	322,261	130,485	15,906	...
20. Memphis, TN	652,050	650,100	610,337	646,174	623,988	396,000	102,320	8,841
21. Boston, MA	625,087	589,141	574,283	562,994	641,071	801,444	560,892	136,881
22. Seattle, WA	620,778	563,374	516,259	493,846	530,831	467,591	80,671	...
23. Denver, CO	619,968	554,636	467,610	492,686	514,678	415,786	133,859	...
24. Baltimore, MD	619,493	651,154	736,014	786,741	905,787	949,708	508,957	169,054
25. Washington, DC	617,996	572,059	606,900	638,432	756,668	802,178	278,718	40,001
26. Nashville-Davidson, TN[1]	609,644	545,524	510,784	455,651	426,029	174,307	80,865	10,165
27. Louisville-Jefferson Co., KY[1]	602,011	256,231	269,063	298,694	361,706	369,129	204,731	43,194
28. Milwaukee, WI	597,867	596,974	628,088	636,297	717,372	637,392	285,315	20,061
29. Portland, OR	593,820	529,121	437,319	368,148	379,967	373,628	90,426	...
30. Oklahoma City, OK	591,967	506,132	444,719	404,014	368,164	243,504	10,037	...
31. Las Vegas, NV	589,317	478,434	258,295	164,674	125,787	24,624	...	...
32. Albuquerque, NM	552,804	448,607	384,736	332,920	244,501	96,815	6,238	...
33. Tucson, AZ	525,796	486,699	405,390	330,537	262,933	45,454	7,531	...
34. Fresno, CA	501,362	427,652	354,202	217,491	165,655	91,669	12,470	...
35. Sacramento, CA	472,178	407,018	369,365	275,741	257,105	137,572	29,282	6,820
36. Long Beach, CA	465,576	461,522	429,433	361,498	358,879	250,767	2,252	...
37. Kansas City, MO	463,202	441,545	435,146	448,028	507,330	456,622	163,752	...
38. Mesa, AZ	446,518	396,375	288,091	152,404	63,049	16,790	722	...
39. Virginia Beach, VA	442,707	425,257	393,069	262,199	172,106	5,390	...	...
40. Atlanta, GA	432,427	416,474	394,017	425,022	495,039	331,314	89,872	2,572
41. Colorado Springs, CO	426,388	360,890	281,140	215,105	135,517	45,472	21,085	...
42. Raleigh, NC	416,468	276,093	207,951	150,255	122,830	65,679	13,643	4,518
43. Omaha, NE	415,068	390,007	335,795	313,939	346,929	251,117	102,555	...
44. Miami, FL	408,750	362,470	358,548	346,681	334,859	249,276	1,681	...
45. Tulsa, OK	396,466	393,049	367,302	360,919	330,350	182,740	1,390	...
46. Oakland, CA	395,817	399,484	372,242	339,337	361,561	384,575	66,960	...
47. Cleveland, OH	393,806	478,403	505,616	573,822	750,879	914,808	381,768	17,034
48. Minneapolis, MN	387,753	382,618	368,383	370,951	434,400	521,718	202,718	...
49. Wichita, KS	384,445	344,284	304,011	279,838	276,554	168,279	24,671	...
50. Arlington, TX	373,698	332,969	261,721	160,113	90,229	7,692	1,079	...
51. New Orleans, LA	360,740	484,674	496,938	557,927	593,471	570,445	287,104	116,375
52. Bakersfield, CA	352,428	247,057	174,820	105,611	69,515	34,784	4,836	...
53. Tampa, FL	346,037	303,447	280,015	271,577	277,714	124,681	15,839	...
54. Anaheim, CA	341,361	328,014	266,406	219,494	166,408	14,556	1,456	...
55. Honolulu, HI[2]	340,936	371,657	365,272	365,048	324,871	248,034	39,306	...
56. Aurora, CO	332,354	276,393	222,103	158,588	74,974	11,421	202	...
57. Santa Ana, CA	329,427	337,977	293,742	204,023	155,710	45,533	4,933	...
58. St. Louis, MO	318,069	348,189	396,685	452,801	622,236	856,796	575,238	77,860
59. Riverside, CA	310,651	255,166	226,505	170,591	140,089	46,764	7,973	...
60. Corpus Christi, TX	307,953	277,454	257,453	232,134	204,525	108,287	4,703	...
61. Pittsburgh, PA	307,484	334,563	369,879	423,959	520,089	676,806	321,616	46,601
62. Lexington-Fayette, KY	301,569	260,512	225,366	204,165	108,137	55,534	26,369	8,159
63. Stockton, CA	296,357	243,771	210,943	148,283	109,963	70,853	17,506	...
64. Cincinnati, OH	296,223	331,285	364,040	385,409	453,514	503,998	325,902	115,435
65. Anchorage, AK	295,570	260,283	226,338	174,431	48,081	11,254	...	...
66. St. Paul, MN	288,448	287,151	272,235	270,230	309,866	311,349	163,065	1,112
67. Toledo, OH	286,038	313,619	332,943	354,635	383,062	303,616	131,822	3,829
68. Newark, NJ	277,540	273,546	275,221	329,248	381,930	438,776	246,070	38,894
69. Greensboro, NC	273,425	223,891	183,521	155,642	144,076	74,389	10,035	...
70. Plano, TX	269,776	222,030	128,713	72,331	17,872	2,126	1,304	...
71. Lincoln, NE	262,341	225,581	191,972	171,932	149,518	98,884	40,169	...
72. Buffalo, NY	261,025	292,648	328,123	357,870	462,768	580,132	352,387	42,261
73. Henderson, NV	260,068	175,381	64,942	23,376	16,400	5,717	...	...
74. Fort Wayne, IN	255,824	205,727	173,072	172,391	178,269	133,607	45,115	4,282
75. Jersey City, NJ	250,323	240,055	228,537	223,532	260,350	299,017	206,433	6,856
76. Chula Vista, CA	247,535	173,556	135,163	83,927	67,901	31,339	...	...
77. St. Petersburg, FL	244,997	248,232	238,629	238,647	216,159	96,738	1,575	...
78. Orlando, FL	243,195	185,951	164,693	128,394	99,006	52,367	2,481	...
79. Norfolk, VA	242,628	234,403	261,229	266,979	307,951	213,513	46,624	14,326
80. Laredo, TX	241,935	176,576	122,899	91,449	69,024	51,910	13,429	...

Rank City	2011	2000	1990	1980	1970	1950	1900	1850
81. Chandler, AZ	240,101	176,581	89,862	29,673	13,763	3,799	...	...
82. Madison, WI	236,901	208,054	191,262	170,616	171,809	96,056	19,164	1,525
83. Lubbock, TX	233,740	199,564	186,206	174,361	149,101	71,747	...	...
84. Durham, NC	233,252	187,035	136,611	100,831	95,438	71,311	6,679	...
85. Winston-Salem, NC	232,385	185,776	143,485	131,885	133,683	87,811	13,650	...
86. Garland, TX	231,517	215,768	180,650	138,857	81,437	10,571	819	...
87. Glendale, AZ	230,482	218,812	148,134	96,988	36,228	8,179	...	...
88. Baton Rouge, LA	230,139	227,818	219,531	220,394	165,921	125,629	11,269	3,905
89. Hialeah, FL	229,969	226,419	188,004	145,254	102,452	19,676	...	...
90. Reno, NV	227,511	180,480	134,230	100,756	72,863	32,497	4,500	...
91. Chesapeake, VA	225,050	199,184	151,976	114,486	89,580	...	...	...
92. Scottsdale, AZ	221,020	202,705	130,069	88,364	67,823	2,032	...	...
93. Irving, TX	220,702	191,615	155,037	109,943	97,260	2,621	...	...
94. North Las Vegas, NV	219,020	115,488	47,707	42,739	46,067		...	...
95. Fremont, CA	216,916	203,413	173,339	131,945	100,869		...	...
96. Irvine, CA	215,529	143,072	110,330	62,134	...		...	...
97. San Bernardino, CA	213,012	185,401	164,164	117,490	104,251	63,058	6,150	...
98. Birmingham, AL	212,413	242,820	265,968	284,413	300,910	326,037	38,415	...
99. Gilbert, AZ	211,951	109,697	29,188	5,717	1,971	...	...	...
100. Rochester, NY	210,855	219,773	231,636	241,741	295,011	332,488	162,608	36,403

Note: Estimates for 2011 are as of July 1. Population figures for 1950-2010 are for Apr. 1; 1850 and 1900 are for June 1. Cities are incorporated places unless otherwise noted. (1) Consolidated city. Population figures are for the primary incorporated place only, i.e., exclude the populations of semi-independent incorporated places within the consolidated city. For years predating consolidation, city population figures are shown. (2) Census designated place (CDP). Although not incorporated, CDPs are recognized as statistical equivalents by the Census Bureau.

Largest U.S. Counties by Population, 2000, 2011

Source: Population Estimates Program, Decennial Census, U.S. Census Bureau, U.S. Dept. of Commerce
(ranked by 2011 population; 2011 estimates are as of July 1 while 2000 figures are for Apr. 1)

Rank County	2011	2000	% change	Rank County	2011	2000	% change
1. Los Angeles Co., CA .	9,889,056	9,519,338	3.9%	16. Santa Clara Co., CA..	1,809,378	1,682,585	7.5%
2. Cook Co., IL	5,217,080	5,376,741	-3.0	17. Wayne Co., MI	1,802,096	2,061,162	-12.6
3. Harris Co., TX.......	4,180,894	3,400,578	22.9	18. Broward Co., FL.....	1,780,172	1,623,018	9.7
4. Maricopa Co., AZ	3,880,244	3,072,149	26.3	19. Bexar Co., TX.......	1,756,153	1,392,931	26.1
5. San Diego Co., CA...	3,140,069	2,813,833	11.6	20. New York Co., NY ...	1,601,948	1,537,195	4.2
6. Orange Co., CA	3,055,745	2,846,289	7.4	21. Philadelphia Co., PA..	1,536,471	1,517,550	1.2
7. Miami-Dade Co., FL..	2,554,766	2,253,362	13.4	22. Alameda Co., CA	1,529,875	1,443,741	6.0
8. Kings Co., NY.......	2,532,645	2,465,326	2.7	23. Middlesex Co., MA...	1,518,171	1,465,396	3.6
9. Dallas Co., TX	2,416,014	2,218,899	8.9	24. Suffolk Co., NY......	1,498,816	1,419,369	5.6
10. Queens Co., NY.....	2,247,848	2,229,379	0.8	25. Sacramento Co., CA..	1,436,105	1,223,499	17.4
11. Riverside Co., CA...	2,239,620	1,545,387	44.9	26. Bronx Co., NY.......	1,392,002	1,332,650	4.5
12. San Bernardino Co., CA.............	2,065,377	1,709,434	20.8	27. Nassau Co., NY	1,344,436	1,334,544	0.7
13. Clark Co., NV	1,969,975	1,375,765	43.2	28. Palm Beach Co., FL..	1,335,187	1,131,184	18.0
14. King Co., WA	1,969,722	1,737,034	13.4	29. Cuyahoga Co., OH...	1,270,294	1,393,978	-8.9
15. Tarrant Co., TX......	1,849,815	1,446,219	27.9	30. Hillsborough Co., FL..	1,267,775	998,948	26.9

Note: The 10 smallest counties by 2011 population (with % change in 2000-11): (1) Kalawao Co., HI (pop. 90; -38.8%); (2) Loving Co., TX (94; 40.3%); (3) King Co., TX (255; -28.4%); (4) Kenedy Co., TX (437; 5.6%); (5) Arthur Co., NE (469; 5.6%); (6) Blaine Co., NE (473; -18.9%); (7) Petroleum Co., MT (491; -0.4%); (8) McPherson Co., NE (552; 3.6%); (9) Loup Co., NE (610; -14.3%); (10) Borden Co., TX (626; -14.1%).

Mobility of U.S. Population by Selected Characteristics, 2010-11

Source: Annual Social and Economic Supplement, Current Population Survey (CPS), U.S. Census Bureau, U.S. Dept. of Commerce
(numbers in thousands)

	Total movers	Same county	Location of new residence — Diff. county, same state	Diff. state	Abroad		Total movers	Same county	Location of new residence — Diff. county, same state	Diff. state	Abroad
Age						**Marital status**[1]					
1 to 14 years..........	8,259	5,724	1,322	1,034	179	Married, spouse present	8,844	5,356	1,559	1,527	402
1 to 17 years..........	9,465	6,591	1,494	1,162	216	Married, spouse absent	687	400	87	126	74
18 years and older	25,608	16,734	4,419	3,615	841	Widowed.............	745	512	120	98	15
25 years and older	19,366	12,557	3,302	2,859	649	Divorced.............	3,108	2,020	619	444	23
65 years and older	1,233	729	209	246	51	Separated............	1,123	813	182	103	26
85 years and older	169	129	24	17	—	Never married........	12,309	8,499	2,023	1,448	338
Income[1]						**Educational attainment**[2]					
Without income........	4,214	2,780	609	493	331	Not a h.s. graduate	2,764	1,984	397	265	119
Under $5,000 or loss ...	2,437	1,558	419	357	105	High school graduate ...	5,543	3,836	900	711	97
$5,000 to $9,999.	2,901	1,952	490	386	73	Some college or associate degree	5,365	3,509	982	744	129
$10,000 to $19,999.....	4,899	3,413	776	620	89	Bachelor's degree......	3,836	2,286	707	663	179
$20,000 to $29,999.....	3,777	2,539	659	499	82	Prof. or grad. degree	1,859	942	314	477	126
$30,000 to $39,999.....	2,600	1,702	485	373	40	**Tenure**					
$40,000 to $59,999.....	2,991	1,887	579	453	71	In owner-occupied unit ..	9,724	5,975	1,965	1,520	264
$60,000 to $74,999.....	1,125	709	204	189	23	In renter-occupied unit[3]..	25,351	17,350	3,947	3,259	795
$75,000 to $99,999.....	898	506	186	187	20	**Total movers**	35,075	23,325	5,912	4,779	1,058
$100,000 and over	972	553	184	189	46						

— = Zero or rounds to zero. **Note:** Total movers consists of persons ages 1 and older who moved to a new residence in the 12 months preceding the administering of the survey. Figures may not add up to totals due to rounding. (1) Ages 15 and older. (2) Ages 25 and older. (3) Includes units occupied without payment of cash rent.

U.S. Foreign-Born Population

Source: Annual Social and Economic Supplements, Current Population Surveys (CPS), U.S. Census Bureau, U.S. Dept. of Commerce

Percentage of Population That Is Foreign-Born, 1900-2010

Foreign-Born Population by Region of Birth, 1995-2010
(numbers in thousands)

Region	2010[1] No.	2010[1] %	2000	1995
Asia	10,126	26.9%	7,246	6,121
Under 18	760	27.7	657	767
Europe	4,509	12.0	4,355	3,937
Under 18	270	9.8	250	232
Latin America	20,419	54.3	14,477	11,777
Under 18	1,453	52.9	1,684	1,481
Other[2]	2,551	6.8	2,301	2,658
Under 18	265	9.6	245	275
All regions	**37,606**	**100.0**	**28,379**	**24,493**
Under 18	**2,748**	**100.0**	**2,837**	**2,726**

(1) Figures as a percentage of total foreign-born population or of all foreign-born under 18 years of age. (2) Including those born at sea.

U.S. Foreign-Born Population: Top Countries of Origin, 1880-2011

Source: American Community Survey (ACS), Decennial Censuses, U.S. Census Bureau, U.S. Dept. of Commerce
(numbers in thousands; percentage is of all foreign-born)

1880 Country	No.	%	1920 Country	No.	%	1960 Country	No.	%	2000 Country	No.	%	2011[4] Country	No.	%
Germany	1,967	29.4	Germany	1,686	12.1	Italy	1,257	12.9	Mexico	9,177	29.5	Mexico	11,673	28.9
Ireland	1,855	27.8	Italy	1,610	11.6	Germany	990	10.2	China[2]	1,519	4.9	China[2]	2,231	5.5
UK	918	13.7	U.S.S.R.	1,400	10.1	Canada	953	9.8	Philippines	1,369	4.4	India	1,857	4.6
Canada	717	10.7	Poland	1,140	8.2	UK	765	7.9	India	1,023	3.3	Philippines	1,814	4.5
Sweden	194	2.9	Canada	1,138	8.2	Poland	748	7.7	Vietnam	988	3.2	El Salvador	1,265	3.1
Norway	182	2.7	UK	1,135	8.2	U.S.S.R.	691	7.1	Cuba	873	2.8	Vietnam	1,259	3.1
France	107	1.6	Ireland	1,037	7.5	Mexico	576	5.9	Korea[3]	864	2.8	Cuba	1,095	2.7
China[1]	104	1.6	Sweden	626	4.5	Ireland	339	3.5	Canada	821	2.6	Korea[3]	1,083	2.7
Switzerland	89	1.3	Austria	576	4.1	Austria	305	3.1	El Salvador	817	2.6	Dominican Republic	897	2.2
Czech.	85	1.3	Mexico	486	3.5	Hungary	245	2.5	Germany	707	2.3	Guatemala	851	2.1
Total	**6,680**	**100.0**	**Total**	**13,921**	**100.0**	**Total**	**9,738**	**100.0**	**Total**	**31,108**	**100.0**	**Total**	**40,378**	**100.0**

(1) Includes Taiwan. (2) Includes Hong Kong and Taiwan. (3) Includes North and South Korea. (4) Data based on sample and subject to sampling variability.

Language Spoken at Home by the U.S. Population, 2011

Source: American Community Survey (ACS), U.S. Census Bureau, U.S. Dept. of Commerce
(number of speakers ages 5 and older, by major language group)

Language	Number (thous.)	% of total U.S. pop.	% English inability[1]	Language	Number (thous.)	% of total U.S. pop.	% English inability[1]
Total population	291,524.1	100.00%	8.7%	Urdu	373.9	0.13%	30.0%
Speak only English	230,947.1	79.22	NA	Other Indic languages	815.3	0.28	39.4
Speak another language	60,577.0	20.78	41.8	Other Indo-European langs.	449.6	0.15	34.9
Spanish				Asian and Pacific Island languages			
Spanish or Spanish Creole	37,579.8	12.89	43.7	Chinese	2,882.5	0.99	55.7
Other Indo-European languages				Japanese	436.1	0.15	42.5
French (incl. Patois, Cajun)	1,301.4	0.45	20.4	Korean	1,141.3	0.39	55.5
French Creole	754.0	0.26	43.2	Mon-Khmer, Cambodian	212.5	0.07	52.9
Italian	723.6	0.25	26.5	Hmong	211.2	0.07	43.3
Portuguese or Portuguese Creole	673.6	0.23	38.2	Thai	163.3	0.06	56.6
German	1,083.6	0.37	17.1	Laotian	140.9	0.05	49.1
Yiddish	161.0	0.06	31.6	Vietnamese	1,419.5	0.49	60.2
Other West Germanic langs.	290.5	0.10	22.4	Other Asian languages	855.3	0.29	30.7
Scandinavian languages	135.0	0.05	9.4	Tagalog	1,594.4	0.55	32.8
Greek	304.9	0.10	24.7	Other Pacific Island langs.	428.5	0.15	38.4
Russian	905.8	0.31	47.7	All other languages			
Polish	607.5	0.21	40.0	Navajo	169.4	0.06	21.2
Serbo-Croatian	269.6	0.09	38.3	Other Native North American languages	195.4	0.07	14.6
Other Slavic languages	336.1	0.12	37.9	Hungarian	93.1	0.03	29.0
Armenian	246.9	0.08	46.2	Arabic	951.7	0.33	36.7
Persian	407.6	0.14	37.3	Hebrew	216.3	0.07	15.3
Gujarati	358.4	0.12	36.2	African languages	884.7	0.30	31.9
Hindi	649.0	0.22	23.0	Other and unspecified langs.	153.8	0.05	43.7

NA = Not applicable or available. **Note:** Data based on sample and subject to sampling variability. (1) Speakers of other languages were asked how well they spoke English. Respondents who indicated that they spoke English less than very well are given as a percentage of their population. (For example, 26.5% of respondents who use Italian at home do not speak English very well.)

Persons Granted Legal Permanent Resident Status by State of Residence, 2011
Source: Office of Immigration Statistics, U.S. Dept. of Homeland Security
(ranked by fiscal year 2011 number)

State/territory	Number	State/territory	Number	State/territory	Number	State/territory	Number
Total	1,062,040	Michigan	18,347	Kentucky	5,403	New Hampshire	2,478
California	210,591	North Carolina	17,571	Kansas	5,086	Delaware	2,355
New York	148,426	Ohio	13,857	Iowa	4,624	Alaska	1,799
Florida	109,229	Colorado	13,547	Nebraska	4,535	Mississippi	1,666
Texas	94,481	Connecticut	12,577	Oklahoma	4,503	Maine	1,467
New Jersey	55,547	Minnesota	12,389	Louisiana	4,226	South Dakota	1,337
Illinois	38,325	Nevada	10,449	South Carolina	4,216	Guam	1,313
Massachusetts	32,236	Tennessee	8,279	Alabama	4,063	North Dakota	948
Virginia	27,767	Indiana	8,262	New Mexico	3,767	Vermont	943
Georgia	27,015	Oregon	7,694	Rhode Island	3,681	West Virginia	830
Maryland	25,778	Hawaii	7,296	Puerto Rico	3,288	Montana	511
Pennsylvania	25,397	Missouri	7,048	Arkansas	2,874	Wyoming	420
Washington	23,789	Utah	6,426	District of Columbia	2,724	Other[1]	1,480
Arizona	20,333	Wisconsin	6,245	Idaho	2,602		

Note: Applicants for legal permanent resident (LPR) status, or "green cards," may already live in the U.S. Applicants include refugees and asylees, temporary workers, foreign students, family members of U.S. citizens, and undocumented immigrants. Applicants from outside the U.S. enter on a visa and are granted LPR status upon admittance. (1) Includes U.S. territories and armed forces posts.

Persons Granted Legal Permanent Resident Status by Top Areas of Residence, 2011
Source: Office of Immigration Statistics, U.S. Dept. of Homeland Security
(ranked by fiscal year 2011 number)

Core Based Statistical Area (CBSA)[1]	Number	% of total	Core Based Statistical Area (CBSA)[1]	Number	% of total
Total	1,062,040	100.0%	Austin-Round Rock-San Marcos, TX	6,068	0.6%
New York-Northern New Jersey-Long Island, NY-NJ-PA	183,681	17.3	El Paso, TX	5,640	0.5
			Honolulu, HI	5,550	0.5
Los Angeles-Long Beach-Santa Ana, CA	86,161	8.1	San Antonio-New Braunfels, TX	5,422	0.5
Miami-Fort Lauderdale-Pompano Beach, FL	71,775	6.8	Charlotte-Gastonia-Rock Hill, NC-SC	5,010	0.5
Washington-Arlington-Alexandria, DC-VA-MD-WV	39,365	3.7	Columbus, OH	4,955	0.5
Chicago-Joliet-Naperville, IL-IN-WI	35,039	3.3	Providence-New Bedford-Fall River, RI-MA	4,675	0.4
San Francisco-Oakland-Fremont, CA	32,433	3.1	Bridgeport-Stamford-Norwalk, CT	4,651	0.4
Houston-Sugar Land-Baytown, TX	31,136	2.9	Salt Lake City, UT	4,360	0.4
Dallas-Fort Worth-Arlington, TX	28,090	2.6	Nashville-Davidson—Murfreesboro–Franklin, TN	4,149	0.4
Boston-Cambridge-Quincy, MA-NH	25,909	2.4	Kansas City, MO-KS	4,104	0.4
Atlanta-Sandy Springs-Marietta, GA	22,035	2.1	Hartford-West Hartford-East Hartford, CT	4,090	0.4
San Diego-Carlsbad-San Marcos, CA	21,556	2.0	Indianapolis-Carmel, IN	3,900	0.4
Philadelphia-Camden-Wilmington, PA-NJ-DE-MD	18,925	1.8	Raleigh-Cary, NC	3,793	0.4
San Jose-Sunnyvale-Santa Clara, CA	18,554	1.7	St. Louis, MO-IL	3,553	0.3
Seattle-Tacoma-Bellevue, WA	17,823	1.7	Jacksonville, FL	3,453	0.3
Riverside-San Bernardino-Ontario, CA	14,885	1.4	McAllen-Edinburg-Mission, TX	3,409	0.3
Phoenix-Mesa-Glendale, AZ	14,013	1.3	Worcester, MA	3,312	0.3
Detroit-Warren-Livonia, MI	12,198	1.1	Tucson, AZ	3,277	0.3
Orlando-Kissimmee-Sanford, FL	10,204	1.0	Oxnard-Thousand Oaks-Ventura, CA	3,112	0.3
Minneapolis-St. Paul-Bloomington, MN-WI	10,175	1.0	Fresno, CA	3,073	0.3
Denver-Aurora-Broomfield, CO	9,189	0.9	San Juan-Caguas-Guaynabo, PR	2,940	0.3
Tampa-St. Petersburg-Clearwater, FL	8,996	0.8	Stockton, CA	2,900	0.3
Las Vegas-Paradise, NV	8,719	0.8	Milwaukee-Waukesha-West Allis, WI	2,885	0.3
Sacramento—Arden-Arcade–Roseville, CA	8,469	0.8	Cleveland-Elyria-Mentor, OH	2,883	0.3
Baltimore-Towson, MD	8,229	0.8	Other CBSAs	203,441	19.2
Portland-Vancouver-Hillsboro, OR-WA	6,469	0.6	Non-CBSA or unknown	13,407	1.3

Note: Applicants for legal permanent resident (LPR) status, or "green cards," may already live in the U.S. Applicants include refugees and asylees, temporary workers, foreign students, family members of U.S. citizens, and undocumented immigrants. Applicants from outside the U.S. enter on a visa and are granted LPR status upon admittance. (1) CBSAs refer collectively to metropolitan and micropolitan statistical areas. These areas are defined for federal statistical use by the U.S. Office of Management and Budget with technical assistance from the U.S. Census Bureau.

Unauthorized Immigrant Population in the U.S., 2000, 2011
Source: Office of Immigration Statistics, U.S. Dept. of Homeland Security
(ranked by 2011 est. population; figures are for Jan. of given year)

Country of Birth	Est. population 2011	Est. population 2000	% change, 2000-11	State of Residence	Est. population 2011	Est. population 2000	% change, 2000-11
Country	2011	2000	2000-11	State	2011	2000	2000-11
All countries	11,510,000	8,460,000	36%	All states	11,510,000	8,460,000	36%
Mexico	6,800,000	4,680,000	45	California	2,830,000	2,510,000	12
El Salvador	660,000	430,000	55	Texas	1,790,000	1,090,000	64
Guatemala	520,000	290,000	82	Florida	740,000	800,000	−8
Honduras	380,000	160,000	132	New York	630,000	540,000	18
China	280,000	190,000	43	Illinois	550,000	440,000	26
Philippines	270,000	200,000	35	Georgia	440,000	220,000	95
India	240,000	120,000	94	New Jersey	420,000	350,000	19
Korea[1]	230,000	180,000	31	North Carolina	400,000	260,000	53
Ecuador	210,000	110,000	83	Arizona	360,000	330,000	9
Vietnam	170,000	160,000	10	Washington	260,000	170,000	51
Other countries	1,750,000	1,940,000	−10	Other states	3,100,000	1,750,000	77

Note: Unauthorized immigrant population estimates are made using the "residual" method. The estimated size of the legally resident foreign-born population (i.e., legal permanent residents, asylees, refugees, and nonimmigrants) is subtracted from the estimated size of the total foreign-born population. Numbers may not add up to totals because of rounding. (1) Includes North and South Korea.

U.S. Population by Age, Sex, and Household, 2011

Source: American Community Survey (ACS), U.S. Census Bureau, U.S. Dept. of Commerce

	Number	% of tot.		Number	% of tot.
Total population[1]	311,591,919	100.0%	Sex		
Age			Male	153,267,861	49.2%
Under 5 years	20,067,828	6.4	Female	158,324,058	50.8
5 to 14 years	41,131,310	13.2	**Total households[2]**	**114,991,725**	**100.0%**
15 to 17 years[1]	12,711,563	4.1	Family households	76,084,006	66.2
15 to 44 years	126,289,167	40.5	2-person household	32,882,461	28.6
18 years and over	237,681,218	76.3	3-person household	17,225,354	15.0
Male	115,448,178	37.1	4-person household	14,710,713	12.8
Female	122,233,040	39.2	5-or-more person household	11,265,478	9.8
18 to 24 years	31,209,548	10.0	Married-couple family	55,519,648	48.3
25 to 34 years	41,540,346	13.3	Female HH, no husband present	15,107,217	13.1
35 to 44 years	40,827,710	13.1	Male HH, no wife present	5,457,141	4.7
45 to 54 years	44,653,387	14.3	Nonfamily households (total HHs)	38,907,719	33.8
55 to 64 years	38,065,201	12.2	HH living alone	31,886,794	27.7
65 years and over	41,385,026	13.3	HH 65 years and over	11,112,330	9.7
75 years and over	18,895,797	6.1	2-person household	5,752,709	5.0
85 years and over	5,698,445	1.8	3-or-more person household	1,268,216	1.1
Median age (years)	37.3	NA	Average household size	2.64	NA

NA = Not applicable. HH = Householder, or person in whose name a home is owned or rented. **Note:** Data based on sample and subject to sampling variability. (1) Includes population living in group quarters (institutional and noninstitutional, e.g., correctional facilities, university housing). (2) Number of households, not number of household members. Group quarters are not considered households.

Elderly U.S. Population, 1900-2050

Source: Decennial Censuses, Population Projections Program, U.S. Census Bureau, U.S. Dept. of Commerce
(numbers in thousands)

	65 and over		85 and over			65 and over		85 and over	
		% tot.		% tot.			% tot.		% tot.
Year	Number	pop.	Number	pop.	Year	Number	pop.	Number	pop.
1900[1]	3,080	4.1%	122	0.2%	2010	40,268	13.0%	5,493	1.8%
1920[1]	4,933	4.7	210	0.2	2015	46,837	14.4	6,292	1.9
1940[1]	9,019	6.8	365	0.3	2020	54,804	16.1	6,597	1.9
1960	16,560	9.2	929	0.5	2030	72,092	19.3	8,745	2.3
1980	25,549	11.3	2,240	1.0	2040	81,238	20.0	14,198	3.5
2000	34,992	12.4	4,240	1.5	2050	88,547	20.2	19,041	4.3

Note: 1900 figures are for June 1; 1920 figures are for Jan. 1; and 1940-2010 figures are for Apr. 1. 2015-50 projections are for July 1. (1) Excludes Alaska and Hawaii.

U.S. Population Projections by Age, 2015-50

Source: Population Projections Program, U.S. Census Bureau, U.S. Dept. of Commerce
(numbers in thousands)

	2015		2020		2030		2040		2050	
Age	No.	% distrib.	No.	% distrib.	No.	% distrib.	No.	% distrib.	No.	% distrib.
Total	325,540	100.0%	341,387	100.0%	373,504	100.0%	405,655	100.0%	439,010	100.0%
Under 5 years	22,076	6.8	22,846	6.7	24,161	6.5	26,117	6.4	28,148	6.4
5-14 years	43,365	13.3	45,303	13.3	48,799	13.1	51,998	12.8	56,370	12.8
15-24 years	43,551	13.4	44,353	13.0	48,914	13.1	52,909	13.0	56,593	12.9
25-34 years	44,499	13.7	46,061	13.5	47,020	12.6	51,847	12.8	56,165	12.8
35-44 years	41,301	12.7	43,664	12.8	48,223	12.9	49,545	12.2	54,696	12.5
45-54 years	43,368	13.3	41,354	12.1	44,030	11.8	48,784	12.0	50,378	11.5
55-64 years	40,543	12.5	43,003	12.6	40,266	10.8	43,216	10.7	48,111	11.0
65 years and over	46,837	14.4	54,804	16.1	72,092	19.3	81,238	20.0	88,547	20.2
85 years and over	6,292	1.9	6,597	1.9	8,745	2.3	14,198	3.5	19,041	4.3

Note: Projections are for July 1 of given year. They are based on assumptions about future births, deaths, and net international migration. Numbers exclude overseas U.S. military personnel and civilian U.S. citizens living abroad.

Disability Status of U.S. Population by Age, 2011

Source: American Community Survey (ACS), U.S. Census Bureau, U.S. Dept. of Commerce
(numbers in thousands)

Disability type	Number	% of pop.	Disability type	Number	% of pop.
Total population	**306,561**	**100.0%**	**Total population (5 and over)**	**286,496**	**100.0%**
With a disability[1]	37,188	12.1	With a cognitive difficulty[2]	14,079	4.9
Under 5 years	166	0.1	5 to 17 years	2,096	0.7
Under 18 years	2,947	1.0	18 to 64 years	8,198	2.9
18 to 64 years	19,583	6.4	65 years and over	3,784	1.3
65 years and over	14,659	4.8	With an ambulatory difficulty[3]	19,893	6.9
With a hearing difficulty	10,475	3.4	5 to 17 years	351	0.1
Under 5 years	117	0.0	18 to 64 years	10,072	3.5
Under 18 years	456	0.1	65 years and over	9,470	3.3
18 to 64 years	3,989	1.3	With a self-care difficulty[4]	7,682	2.7
65 years and over	6,030	2.0	5 to 17 years	504	0.2
With a vision difficulty	6,623	2.2	18 to 64 years	3,628	1.3
Under 5 years	98	0.0	65 years and over	3,550	1.2
Under 18 years	518	0.2			
18 to 64 years	3,377	1.1	**Total population (18 and over)**	**232,786**	**100.0%**
65 years and over	2,728	0.9	With an independent living difficulty[5]	13,438	5.8
			18 to 64 years	6,946	3.0
			65 years and over	6,492	2.8

Note: Data based on sample and subject to sampling variability. Does not include military personnel and population in civilian institutions (i.e., facilities in which the population is under formal supervision or custody). (1) Defined by the Census Bureau as the "restriction in participation that results from a lack of fit between the individual's functional limitations and the characteristics of the physical and social environment." (2) Concentrating, remembering, or making decisions. (3) Walking or climbing stairs. (4) Dressing or bathing. (5) Doing errands alone, such as visiting a doctor's office or shopping.

Marital Status of the U.S. Population, 1960-2011

Source: Annual Social and Economic Supplements, Current Population Surveys (CPS), U.S. Census Bureau, U.S. Dept. of Commerce
(numbers in millions)

Marital status	Both sexes				Male				Female			
	2011	2000	1980	1960	2011	2000	1980	1960	2011	2000	1980	1960
Total	243.9	213.8	171.9	124.9	118.8	103.1	81.9	60.3	125.0	110.7	89.9	64.6
Married[1]	129.4	120.2	104.8	84.4	64.4	59.7	51.8	41.8	65.0	60.5	53.0	42.6
Never married	75.8	60.0	44.5	27.5	40.8	32.3	24.2	15.3	35.0	27.8	20.2	12.3
Divorced	24.4	19.9	9.9	2.8	10.7	8.6	3.9	1.1	13.8	11.3	6.0	1.7
Widowed	14.2	13.7	12.7	10.2	2.9	2.6	2.0	2.1	11.3	11.1	10.8	8.1
% of total or subset pops.												
Married[1]	53.1%	56.2%	61.0%	67.6%	54.2%	57.9%	63.2%	69.3%	52.0%	54.7%	58.9%	65.9%
Never married	31.1	28.1	25.9	22.0	34.4	31.3	29.6	25.3	28.0	25.1	22.5	19.0
Divorced	10.0	9.3	5.8	2.3	9.0	8.3	4.8	1.8	11.0	10.2	6.6	2.6
Widowed	5.8	6.4	7.4	8.1	2.5	2.5	2.4	3.5	9.0	10.0	12.0	12.5

Note: Total population for 1980, 2000, and 2011 is persons ages 15 and older and for 1960, persons ages 14 and older. Data is based on sample of occupied households. Figures may not add up to totals due to rounding. (1) Comprises subcategories Married, spouse present; Married, spouse absent; and Separated.

Living Arrangements of Children in the U.S. by Parental Presence, 1970-2011

Source: Annual Social and Economic Supplements, Current Population Surveys (CPS), U.S. Census Bureau, U.S. Dept. of Commerce

Race and Hispanic origin/year	No. of children (thous.)	Both parents[3]	% of children (within selected population at left) living with—						
			Total[4]	Mother only—				Father only	Neither parent
				Married spouse absent	Divorced	Widowed	Never married		
All children									
2011	74,630	69%	24%	1%	7%	1%	11%	4%	4%
White alone[1]									
1970	58,791	90	8	3	3	2	Z	1	2
1980	52,242	83	14	4	7	2	1	2	2
1990	51,390	79	16	4	8	1	3	3	2
2000	56,455	75	17	NA	NA	NA	NA	4	3
2011	56,319	75	19	1	7	1	7	4	3
Black alone[1]									
1970	9,422	59	30	16	5	4	4	2	10
1980	9,375	42	44	16	11	4	13	28	12
1990	10,018	38	51	12	10	2	27	4	8
2000	11,412	38	49	NA	NA	NA	NA	4	9
2011	11,155	38	51	3	9	1	33	3	8
Hispanic[2]									
1970	4,006	78	NA	NA	NA	NA	NA	NA	NA
1980	5,459	75	20	8	6	2	4	2	4
1990	7,174	67	27	10	7	2	8	3	3
2000	11,613	65	25	NA	NA	NA	NA	4	5
2011	17,418	67	26	2	6	1	13	3	4

NA = Not available. Z = Less than 1%. **Note:** Children are defined as all persons under 18 years of age excluding those who are a family reference person or spouse or those living in group quarters. Data based on sample of occupied households. (1) One race only, not in combination with another race. (2) May be of any race. (3) Includes married and unmarried couples. (4) Includes children whose mothers are separated, a subcategory not shown in detail here.

Children in the U.S. by Parental Presence, 2011

Source: Annual Social and Economic Supplement, Current Population Survey (CPS), U.S. Census Bureau, U.S. Dept. of Commerce
(numbers in thousands)

	Number	% of total		Number	% of total
Total children	74,630	100.0%	Living with 1 parent	20,264	27.2%
			Mother only	17,636	23.6
Living with 2 parents	51,456	68.9	Biological mother	17,310	23.2
Married parents	48,516	65.0	Father only	2,628	3.5
Unmarried parents	2,940	3.9	Biological father	2,500	3.4
Biological mother and father	46,405	62.2	Living with no parents	2,910	3.9
Married parents	43,828	58.7	Grandparents only	1,648	2.2
Biological mother and stepfather	3,075	4.1	Other relatives only	604	0.8
Biological father and stepmother	835	1.1	Nonrelatives only	514	0.7
Biological mother and adoptive father	174	0.2	Other arrangement	144	0.2
Biological father and adoptive mother	30	0.0	Living with at least 1 biological parent	70,330	94.2
Adoptive mother and father	697	0.9	Living with at least 1 stepparent	4,353	5.8
Other[1]	241	0.3	Living with at least 1 adoptive parent	1,173	1.6

Note: Children are defined as all persons under 18 years of age excluding those who are a family reference person or spouse or those living in group quarters. Data based on sample of occupied households. (1) Includes children living with one adoptive parent and one stepparent, or two stepparents.

Unmarried-Partner Households in the U.S. by Sex of Partners, 2011

Source: American Community Survey (ACS), U.S. Census Bureau, U.S. Dept. of Commerce

Household	Number	% of total	% of cat.	Household	Number	% of total	% of cat.
Total households	114,991,725	100.0%	—	Female HH, female partner	321,177	0.3%	4.8%
Unmarried-partner households	6,715,374	5.8	100.0%	Male HH, male partner	284,295	0.2	4.2
Male HH, female partner	3,074,955	2.7	45.8	All other households	108,276,351	94.2	100.0
Female HH, male partner	3,034,947	2.6	45.2				

HH = Householder, or person in whose name a home is owned or rented. **Note:** Data based on sample and subject to sampling variability. Households do not include people living in group quarters (institutional and noninstitutional, e.g., correctional facilities, university housing).

U.S. Population by Sex, Race, Residence, and Median Age, 1790-2011

Source: Decennial Censuses, U.S. Census Bureau, U.S. Dept. of Commerce

(numbers in thousands, unless otherwise noted)

| | SEX | | RACE[2] | | | | RESIDENCE | | MEDIAN AGE (years) | | |
| | | | | Black | | | | | | | |
	Male	Female	White	Number	% tot. pop	Other	Urban[3]	Rural	All races	White[2]	Black[2]
Conterminous U.S.[1]											
1790 (Aug. 2)	NA	NA	3,172	757	19.3%	NA	202	3,728	NA	NA	NA
1810 (Aug. 6)	NA	NA	5,862	1,378	19.0	NA	525	6,714	NA	16.0	NA
1820 (Aug. 7)	4,897	4,742	7,867	1,772	18.4	NA	693	8,945	16.7	16.6	17.2
1840 (June 1)	8,689	8,381	14,196	2,874	16.8	NA	1,845	15,218	17.8	17.9	17.6
1860 (June 1)	16,085	15,358	26,923	4,442	14.1	79	6,217	25,227	19.4	19.7	17.5
1870 (June 1)	19,494	19,065	33,589	4,880	12.7	89	9,902	28,656	20.2	20.4	18.5
1880 (June 1)	25,519	24,637	43,403	6,581	13.1	172	14,130	36,059	20.9	21.4	18.0
1890 (June 1)	32,237	30,711	55,101	7,489	11.9	358	22,106	40,874	22.0	22.5	17.8
1900 (June 1)	38,816	37,178	66,809	8,834	11.6	351	30,215	45,997	22.9	23.4	19.4
1920 (Jan. 1)	53,900	51,810	94,821	10,463	9.9	427	54,253	51,768	25.3	25.5	22.3
1930 (Apr. 1).	62,137	60,638	110,287	11,891	9.7	597	69,161	54,042	26.5	26.9	23.5
1940 (Apr. 1).	66,062	65,608	118,215	12,866	9.8	589	74,705	57,459	29.0	29.5	25.3
United States											
1950 (Apr. 1).	74,833	75,864	135,150	15,045	10.0	713	96,847	54,479	30.2	30.8	26.1
1960 (Apr. 1).	88,331	90,992	158,832	18,872	10.5	1,620	125,269	54,054	29.5	30.3	23.5
1970 (Apr. 1).	98,926	104,309	178,098	22,581	11.1	2,557	149,647	53,565	28.1	28.9	22.4
1980 (Apr. 1).	110,053	116,493	194,713	26,683	11.8	5,150	167,051	59,495	30.0	30.9	24.9
1990 (Apr. 1).	121,284	127,507	208,741	30,517	12.3	9,533	187,053	61,656	32.8	33.7	27.9
2000 (Apr. 1).	138,056	143,368	195,577	35,705	12.7	13,716	222,361	59,061	35.3	38.6	30.0
2010 (Apr. 1).	151,781	156,964	196,818	37,686	12.2	18,147	249,253	59,492	37.2	42.0	32.4

NA = Not available. (1) Excludes Alaska and Hawaii. (2) New race categories were introduced in the 2000 census. Race data for 2000 and on are for one race alone, not in combination with one or more other races. "White" does not include people who reported being of Hispanic origin. "Other" comprises Asians, Native Hawaiians and other Pacific Islanders, and American Indians and Alaska Natives. Because of these changes, race data from 2000 on are not comparable to figures from previous years. (3) The Census Bureau's definition of "urban" has changed over time. Figures for 2000 and 2010 include residents of so-called urban areas (50,000 or more inhabitants) and urban clusters (at least 2,500 but fewer than 50,000 inhabitants).

U.S. Population by Race and Hispanic Origin, 2000-10

Source: Decennial Censuses, U.S. Census Bureau, U.S. Dept. of Commerce

| | 2010 census | | 2000 census | | % change, 2000-10[2] | |
	One race alone	One or more races[1]	One race alone	One or more races[1]	One race alone	One or more races
Total population	299,736,465	308,745,538	274,595,678	281,421,906	9.2%	9.7%
Race						
White	223,553,265	231,040,398	211,460,626	216,930,975	5.7	6.5
Black or African American	38,929,319	42,020,743	34,658,190	36,419,434	12.3	15.4
American Indian and Alaska Native . . .	2,932,248	5,220,579	2,475,956	4,119,301	18.4	26.7
Asian	14,674,252	17,320,856	10,242,998	11,898,828	43.3	45.6
Native Hawaiian and other Pac. Isl. . . .	540,013	1,225,195	398,835	874,414	35.4	40.1
Some other race	19,107,368	21,748,084	15,359,073	18,521,486	24.4	17.4
Hispanic origin and race						
Hispanic or Latino, any race	47,435,002	50,477,594	33,081,736	35,305,818	43.4	43.0
Not Hispanic or Latino	252,301,463	258,267,944	241,513,942	246,116,088	4.5	4.9
White	196,817,552	201,856,108	194,552,774	198,177,900	1.2	1.9
Black or African American	37,685,848	40,123,525	33,947,837	35,383,751	11.0	13.4
American Indian and Alaska Native . .	2,247,098	4,029,675	2,068,883	3,444,700	8.6	17.0
Asian	14,465,124	16,722,710	10,123,169	11,579,494	42.9	44.4
Native Hawaiian and other Pac. Isl.	481,576	1,014,888	353,509	748,149	36.2	35.7
Some other race	604,265	1,033,866	467,770	1,770,645	29.2	−41.6

(1) Alone or in combination with one or more of the other races listed. Numbers may not add up to totals because of individuals reporting more than one race. (2) Columns 5 and 6 provide, respectively, a minimum-maximum range for the percent change in the population of each race.

U.S. Population by Ancestry Reported, 2011

Source: American Community Survey (ACS), U.S. Census Bureau, U.S. Dept. of Commerce
(numbers in thousands; ranked by number)

Ancestry	Number	% of total	Ancestry	Number	% of total	Ancestry	Number	% of total
Total population	311,592	100.0%	Dutch	4,440	1.4%	French Canadian	1,972	0.6%
German.............	47,384	15.2	Norwegian	4,399	1.4	Welsh	1,773	0.6
Irish...............	34,521	11.1	Swedish	4,002	1.3	Arab[4].............	1,769	0.6
English	25,696	8.2	European	3,651	1.2	Czech	1,508	0.5
American	24,145	7.7	Scotch-Irish[1].......	3,144	1.0	Other groups not listed		
Italian	17,446	5.6	Russian............	2,995	1.0	here	141,698	45.5
Polish	9,448	3.0	Sub-Saharan African[2]..	2,928	0.9	Unclassified or not		
French (excl. Basque)	8,596	2.8	West Indian (excl.			reported	36,325	11.7
Scottish............	5,413	1.7	Hispanic groups)[3]...	2,716	0.9			

Note: Data based on sample and subject to sampling variability. Because respondents could self-identify with more than one ancestry, numbers do not add up to total. (1) People who reported Irish-Scotch ancestry are classified under "Other groups." (2) Incl. Cape Verdean, Ethiopian, Ghanian, Kenyan, Liberian, Nigerian, Senegalese, Sierra Leonean, Somalian, South African, Sudanese, Ugandan, Zimbabwean, African, and other sub-Saharan African. (3) Incl. Bahamian, Barbadian, Belizean, Bermudan, British West Indian, Dutch West Indian, Haitian, Jamaican, Trinidadian and Tobagonian, U.S. Virgin Islander, West Indian, and other West Indian. (4) Incl. Egyptian, Iraqi, Jordanian, Lebanese, Moroccan, Palestinian, Syrian, Arab, and other Arab.

U.S. Race and Minority Group Populations by Age, 2011

Source: American Community Survey (ACS), U.S. Census Bureau, U.S. Dept. of Commerce

Race and origin/age	Number	% of race	Race and origin/age	Number	% of race
White (not Hispanic or Latino)	**197,084,523**	**100.0%**	**Native Hawaiian and other**		
Under 5 years.................	10,095,189	5.1	**Pacific Islander**	**506,017**	**100.0%**
Under 18 years...............	39,182,562	19.9	Under 5 years.................	37,737	7.5
18 to 64 years...............	125,006,951	63.4	Under 18 years...............	145,989	28.9
65 years and over.............	32,895,010	16.7	18 to 64 years...............	329,608	65.1
85 years and over.............	4,786,431	2.4	65 years and over.............	30,420	6.0
Black or African American	**39,189,528**	**100.0**	85 years and over.............	2,032	0.4
Under 5 years.................	2,834,920	7.2	**Some other race**	**14,768,156**	**100.0**
Under 18 years...............	10,578,299	27.0	Under 5 years.................	1,365,078	9.2
18 to 64 years...............	25,043,616	63.9	Under 18 years...............	4,701,465	31.8
65 years and over.............	3,567,613	9.1	18 to 64 years...............	9,449,857	64.0
85 years and over.............	410,886	1.0	65 years and over.............	616,834	4.2
Asian	**15,020,419**	**100.0**	85 years and over.............	55,698	0.4
Under 5 years.................	872,052	5.8	**Two or more races**	**8,721,818**	**100.0**
Under 18 years...............	3,249,674	21.6	Under 5 years.................	1,358,659	15.6
18 to 64 years...............	10,276,025	68.4	Under 18 years...............	4,110,923	47.1
65 years and over.............	1,494,720	10.0	18 to 64 years...............	4,208,353	48.3
85 years and over.............	155,829	1.0	65 years and over.............	402,542	4.6
American Indian and Alaska Native	**2,547,006**	**100.0**	85 years and over.............	39,481	0.5
Under 5 years.................	195,908	7.7	**Hispanic or Latino**	**51,939,916**	**100.0**
Under 18 years...............	735,186	28.9	Under 5 years.................	5,157,437	9.9
18 to 64 years...............	1,613,654	63.4	Under 18 years...............	17,407,003	33.5
65 years and over.............	198,166	7.8	18 to 64 years...............	31,589,081	60.8
85 years and over.............	15,681	0.6	65 years and over.............	2,943,832	5.7
			85 years and over.............	301,782	0.6

Note: Data based on sample and subject to sampling variability. Categories are for one race alone, not in combination with any other race, unless otherwise noted.

Educational Attainment of the U.S. Population, 2011

Source: American Community Survey (ACS), U.S. Census Bureau, U.S. Dept. of Commerce
(numbers in thousands; population 25 years of age and over)

Race and origin/highest ed. level completed	Number	% of group	Race and origin/highest ed. level completed	Number	% of group
White (not Hispanic or Latino)	**140,304**	**100.0%**	**Native Hawaiian and other Pacific**		
Less than high school diploma.........	12,525	8.9	**Islander**	**290**	**100.0%**
High school graduate[1]	40,826	29.1	Less than high school diploma.........	43	14.9
Some college or associate's degree	42,262	30.1	High school graduate[1]	105	36.1
Bachelor's degree or higher	44,692	31.9	Some college or associate's degree	100	34.5
Black or African American	**23,898**	**100.0**	Bachelor's degree or higher	42	14.5
Less than high school diploma.........	4,194	17.5	**Some other race**	**8,153**	**100.0**
High school graduate[1]	7,537	31.5	Less than high school diploma.........	3,466	42.5
Some college or associate's degree	7,767	32.5	High school graduate[1]	2,281	28.0
Bachelor's degree or higher	4,401	18.4	Some college or associate's degree	1,638	20.1
Asian	**10,242**	**100.0**	Bachelor's degree or higher	768	9.4
Less than high school diploma.........	1,522	14.9	**Two or more races**	**3,542**	**100.0**
High school graduate[1]	1,603	15.6	Less than high school diploma.........	544	15.4
Some college or associate's degree	1,995	19.5	High school graduate[1]	860	24.3
Bachelor's degree or higher	5,123	50.0	Some college or associate's degree	1,210	34.2
American Indian and Alaska Native	**1,502**	**100.0**	Bachelor's degree or higher	927	26.2
Less than high school diploma.........	317	21.1	**Hispanic or Latino (any race)**	**28,158**	**100.0**
High school graduate[1]	472	31.4	Less than high school diploma.........	10,364	36.8
Some college or associate's degree	514	34.2	High school graduate[1]	7,625	27.1
Bachelor's degree or higher	200	13.3	Some college or associate's degree	6,445	22.9
			Bachelor's degree or higher	3,724	13.2

Note: Data based on sample and subject to sampling variability. Categories are for one race alone, not in combination with any other race, unless otherwise noted. (1) Incl. equivalency.

U.S. Population Growth by Race and Hispanic Origin, 1970-2030[1]
Source: Decennial Censuses, Population Projections Program, U.S. Census Bureau, U.S. Dept. of Commerce
(numbers in millions)

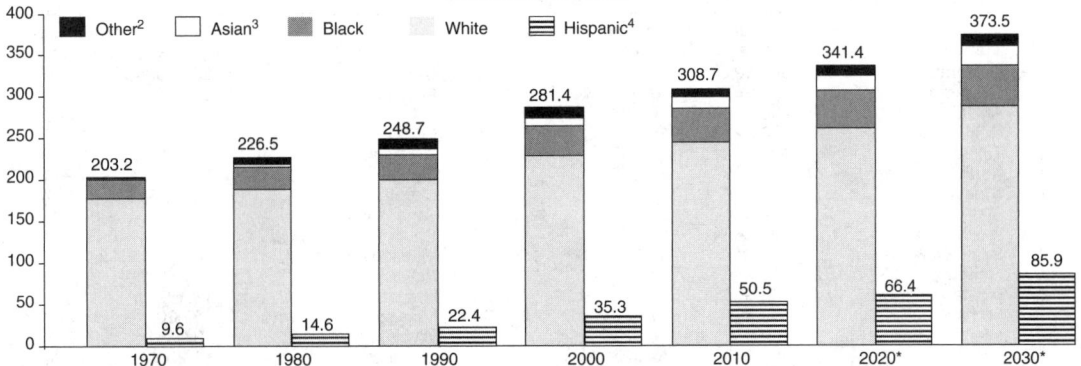

*Projected. (1) Because of changes in census questions and methods, data on race and Hispanic origin are not wholly comparable over time. (2) Includes American Indians and Alaska Natives, and other races. For 2000 and on, this category also includes Native Hawaiians and other Pacific Islanders as well as persons reporting two or more races. (3) Figures for 1970-90 include Pacific Islanders. (4) May be of any race.

U.S. Race and Minority Group Percentages by State, 2010
Source: Decennial Census, U.S. Census Bureau, U.S. Dept. of Commerce
(percentage of area's total population)

State	White	Black or African American	Asian	American Indian and Alaska Native	Native Hawaiian and other Pacific Islander	Some other race	Two or more races[1] (%)	Hispanic or Latino, any race (%)
Alabama	67.0%	26.0%	1.1%	0.5%	0.04%	0.08%	1.3%	3.9%
Alaska	64.1	3.1	5.3	14.4	1.02	0.16	6.4	5.5
Arizona	57.8	3.7	2.7	4.0	0.17	0.13	1.8	29.6
Arkansas	74.5	15.3	1.2	0.7	0.19	0.07	1.6	6.4
California	40.1	5.8	12.8	0.4	0.35	0.23	2.6	37.6
Colorado	70.0	3.8	2.7	0.6	0.11	0.15	2.0	20.7
Connecticut	71.2	9.4	3.8	0.2	0.03	0.34	1.7	13.4
Delaware	65.3	20.8	3.2	0.3	0.03	0.17	2.0	8.2
District of Columbia	34.8	50.0	3.5	0.2	0.04	0.24	2.1	9.1
Florida	57.9	15.2	2.4	0.3	0.05	0.26	1.5	22.5
Georgia	55.9	30.0	3.2	0.2	0.05	0.20	1.6	8.8
Hawaii	22.7	1.5	37.7	0.2	9.43	0.14	19.4	8.9
Idaho	84.0	0.6	1.2	1.1	0.14	0.10	1.7	11.2
Illinois	63.7	14.3	4.5	0.1	0.02	0.12	1.4	15.8
Indiana	81.5	9.0	1.6	0.2	0.03	0.13	1.5	6.0
Iowa	88.7	2.9	1.7	0.3	0.06	0.07	1.4	5.0
Kansas	78.2	5.7	2.3	0.8	0.07	0.10	2.3	10.5
Kentucky	86.3	7.7	1.1	0.2	0.05	0.11	1.5	3.1
Louisiana	60.3	31.8	1.5	0.6	0.03	0.15	1.3	4.2
Maine	94.4	1.1	1.0	0.6	0.02	0.08	1.4	1.3
Maryland	54.7	29.0	5.5	0.2	0.04	0.21	2.2	8.2
Massachusetts	76.1	6.0	5.3	0.2	0.02	0.94	1.9	9.6
Michigan	76.6	14.0	2.4	0.6	0.02	0.10	1.9	4.4
Minnesota	83.1	5.1	4.0	1.0	0.04	0.11	1.9	4.7
Mississippi	58.0	36.9	0.9	0.5	0.03	0.06	0.9	2.7
Missouri	81.0	11.5	1.6	0.4	0.10	0.09	1.8	3.5
Montana	87.8	0.4	0.6	6.1	0.06	0.05	2.2	2.9
Nebraska	82.1	4.4	1.7	0.8	0.05	0.12	1.6	9.2
Nevada	54.1	7.7	7.1	0.9	0.57	0.18	2.9	26.5
New Hampshire	92.3	1.0	2.1	0.2	0.02	0.14	1.4	2.8
New Jersey	59.3	12.8	8.2	0.1	0.02	0.31	1.5	17.7
New Mexico	40.5	1.7	1.3	8.5	0.06	0.18	1.4	46.3
New York	58.3	14.4	7.3	0.3	0.03	0.42	1.7	17.6
North Carolina	65.3	21.2	2.2	1.1	0.06	0.16	1.6	8.4
North Dakota	88.9	1.1	1.0	5.3	0.04	0.05	1.5	2.0
Ohio	81.1	12.0	1.7	0.2	0.03	0.13	1.8	3.1
Oklahoma	68.7	7.3	1.7	8.2	0.11	0.08	5.1	8.9
Oregon	78.5	1.7	3.6	1.1	0.33	0.14	2.9	11.7
Pennsylvania	79.5	10.4	2.7	0.1	0.02	0.13	1.4	5.7
Rhode Island	76.4	4.9	2.8	0.4	0.03	0.84	2.2	12.4
South Carolina	64.1	27.7	1.3	0.4	0.05	0.12	1.4	5.1
South Dakota	84.7	1.2	0.9	8.5	0.04	0.06	1.8	2.7
Tennessee	75.6	16.5	1.4	0.3	0.04	0.10	1.4	4.6
Texas	45.3	11.5	3.8	0.3	0.07	0.14	1.3	37.6
Utah	80.4	0.9	2.0	1.0	0.87	0.13	1.8	13.0
Vermont	94.3	0.9	1.3	0.3	0.02	0.09	1.6	1.5
Virginia	64.8	19.0	5.5	0.3	0.06	0.19	2.3	7.9
Washington	72.5	3.4	7.1	1.3	0.58	0.18	3.7	11.2
West Virginia	93.2	3.4	0.7	0.2	0.02	0.06	1.3	1.2
Wisconsin	83.3	6.2	2.3	0.9	0.03	0.07	1.4	5.9
Wyoming	85.9	0.8	0.8	2.1	0.06	0.08	1.5	8.9
United States	**63.7**	**12.2**	**4.7**	**0.7**	**0.16**	**0.20**	**1.9**	**16.3**

Note: Column headers "One race alone[1] (%)" span White, Black or African American, Asian, American Indian and Alaska Native, Native Hawaiian and other Pacific Islander, and Some other race columns.

(1) Not Hispanic or Latino.

American Indian and Alaska Native Population by State, 2010

Source: Decennial Census, U.S. Census Bureau, U.S. Dept. of Commerce
(ranked by one race alone)

Rank	State	One race alone[1]	More than one race[2]	Rank	State	One race alone[1]	More than one race[2]
1.	California	362,801	360,424	27.	Kansas	28,150	30,980
2.	Oklahoma	321,687	161,073	28.	Missouri	27,376	45,000
3.	Arizona	296,529	56,857	29.	Pennsylvania	26,843	54,249
4.	New Mexico	193,222	26,290	30.	Ohio	25,292	64,832
5.	Texas	170,972	144,292	31.	Arkansas	22,248	25,340
6.	North Carolina	122,110	61,972	32.	Idaho	21,441	14,944
7.	New York	106,906	114,152	33.	Maryland	20,420	38,237
8.	Alaska	104,871	33,441	34.	Tennessee	19,994	34,880
9.	Washington	103,869	95,129	35.	South Carolina	19,524	22,647
10.	South Dakota	71,817	10,256	36.	Massachusetts	18,850	31,855
11.	Florida	71,458	91,104	37.	Indiana	18,462	31,276
12.	Montana	62,555	16,046	38.	Nebraska	18,427	11,389
13.	Michigan	62,007	77,088	39.	Mississippi	15,030	10,880
14.	Minnesota	60,916	40,984	40.	Wyoming	13,336	5,260
15.	Colorado	56,010	51,822	41.	Connecticut	11,256	19,884
16.	Wisconsin	54,526	31,702	42.	Iowa	11,084	13,427
17.	Oregon	53,203	56,020	43.	Kentucky	10,120	21,235
18.	Illinois	43,963	57,488	44.	Maine	8,568	9,914
19.	North Dakota	36,591	6,405	45.	Rhode Island	6,058	8,336
20.	Utah	32,927	17,137	46.	Delaware	4,181	5,718
21.	Georgia	32,151	51,873	47.	Hawaii	4,164	29,306
22.	Nevada	32,062	23,883	48.	West Virginia	3,787	9,527
23.	Louisiana	30,579	24,500	49.	New Hampshire	3,150	7,374
24.	Virginia	29,225	51,699	50.	Vermont	2,207	5,172
25.	New Jersey	29,026	41,690	51.	District of Columbia	2,079	4,442
26.	Alabama	28,218	28,900		**United States**	**2,932,248**	**2,288,331**

(1) Respondents who self-identified as American Indian and Alaska Native (AIAN) alone. (2) Respondents who self-identified as AIAN in combination with one or more other races.

American Indian and Alaska Native Population by Selected Tribal Groupings, 2010

Source: Decennial Census, U.S. Census Bureau, U.S. Dept. of Commerce
(ranked by American Indian and Alaska Native [AIAN] alone, one tribal grouping alone)

Tribal grouping	AIAN alone — One tribal grouping alone[1]	AIAN alone — One or more tribal groupings[2]	AIAN alone or in combination — One or more tribal groupings[3]	Tribal grouping	AIAN alone — One tribal grouping alone[1]	AIAN alone — One or more tribal groupings[2]	AIAN alone or in combination — One or more tribal groupings[3]
Total	2,879,638	2,932,248	5,220,579	Crow	10,332	10,860	15,203
AIAN tribes, not specified	693,709	693,709	1,545,963	Kiowa	9,437	10,355	13,787
American Indian tribes, specified	**1,935,363**	**2,032,133**	**3,397,251**	Paiute	9,340	10,205	13,767
Navajo	286,731	295,016	332,129	Osage	8,938	10,063	18,576
Cherokee	284,247	300,463	819,105	Yakama	8,786	9,096	11,527
Mexican Amer. Ind.	121,221	123,550	175,494	Menominee	8,374	8,627	11,133
Chippewa	112,757	115,402	170,742	Houma	8,169	8,240	10,768
Sioux	112,176	116,477	170,110	Colville	8,114	8,314	10,549
Choctaw	103,910	110,308	195,764	Arapaho	8,014	8,402	10,861
Apache	63,193	69,694	111,810	Shoshone	7,852	8,462	13,002
Lumbee	62,306	62,957	73,691	Delaware	7,843	8,215	18,264
Pueblo	49,695	52,026	62,540	Yuman	7,727	8,278	10,089
Creek	48,352	52,948	88,332	Ute	7,435	8,220	11,491
Iroquois	40,570	42,461	81,002	Ottawa	7,272	8,048	13,033
Chickasaw	27,973	30,206	52,278	Canadian and French Amer. Ind.	6,433	7,051	14,822
Blackfeet	27,279	31,798	105,304	Cree	2,211	2,950	7,983
Pima	22,040	23,205	26,655	All other tribes	270,141	282,747	429,629
Yaqui	21,679	23,195	32,595	Amer. Ind. tribes, not specified	131,943	132,060	234,320
S. Amer. Ind.	20,901	21,380	47,233	**Alaska Native tribes, specified**	**98,892**	**103,086**	**138,850**
Potawatomi	20,412	20,874	33,771	Yup'ik	28,927	29,618	33,889
Tohono O'Odham	19,522	20,247	23,478	Inupiat[4]	24,859	25,736	33,360
Central Amer. Ind.	15,882	16,454	27,844	Alaskan Athabascan	15,623	16,427	22,484
Puget Sound Salish	14,320	14,535	20,260	Tlingit-Haida	15,256	16,115	26,080
Seminole	14,080	16,448	31,971	Aleut	11,920	12,643	19,282
Spanish Amer. Ind.	13,460	13,758	19,951	Tsimshian	2,307	2,547	3,755
Hopi	12,580	14,634	18,327	AK Native tribes, not specified	19,731	19,904	29,933
Comanche	12,284	13,471	23,330				
Cheyenne	11,375	12,493	19,051				

Note: This table measures the number of responses, not respondents. Respondents who self-identified with multiple tribal groupings are counted more than once. A tribal grouping refers to combined individual tribes (e.g., Fort Sill Apache and San Carlos Apache as Apache or King Salmon Tribe and Native Village of Kanatak as Aleut). (1) For example, Navajo or Alaskan Athabascan. (2) As in footnote 1 or in combination with other tribal groupings (e.g., Yakama and Aleut). (3) As in footnotes 1 or 2 or in combination with another race (e.g., Apache, Navajo, and white; or Inupiat, white, and black). (4) Eskimo in previous censuses.

Populations, ZIP, and Area Codes for U.S. Places of 10,000 or More

Source: Decennial Censuses and Population Estimates Program, U.S. Census Bureau, U.S. Dept. of Commerce; NeuStar Inc.

The following is a list of places of 10,000 or more inhabitants in 2011 according to the U.S. Census Bureau's Population Estimates Program and the results of the 2010 census. Also given are 2000 census populations, if available.

Census designated places (CDPs) are marked with a (c). CDP boundaries are defined by the Census Bureau and may change over time. Unless an exception is noted, CDP populations are 2000 and 2010 decennial census results; the Census Bureau does not include CDPs in its estimates program. This list includes **places that are incorporated** under the laws of their respective states as cities, boroughs, towns, and villages. **Townships are not included.** This list also includes, in *italics*, **minor civil divisions (MCDs)** for Connecticut, Maine, Massachusetts, New Hampshire, Rhode Island, and Vermont. MCDs are not incorporated and not recognized as CDPs, but are often the primary political or administrative divisions of a county.

An asterisk (*) denotes that the ZIP code given is for general delivery; named streets and/or P.O. boxes within the community may use a different one; consult www.usps.com. Telephone **area codes** are given in parentheses. New phone numbers may be assigned a different area code from that of existing phone numbers in the area. These areas of overlay are noted. When two or more area codes are listed for one place, consult local operators for assistance. Area codes based on latest information as of Sept. 2012. For a listing in numerical order of specific area codes in the U.S., Canada, and the Caribbean, see Computers and Telecommunications chapter, page 396.

For some places listed, no area code and/or ZIP code is available. — = Not available.

Alabama

Area code (938) overlays area code (256).

ZIP	Place	Area code	2000 population	2011 estimate
*35007	Alabaster	(205)	22,619	30,799
*35950	Albertville	(256)	17,247	21,421
*35010	Alexander City	(256)	15,008	14,876
*36201	Anniston	(256)	24,276	22,959
*35611	Athens	(256)	18,967	22,590
*36502	Atmore	(251)	7,676	10,147
*36830	Auburn	(334)	42,987	54,566
*35020	Bessemer	(205)	29,672	27,475
*35201	Birmingham	(205)	242,820	212,413
35040	Calera	(205)	3,158	11,791
*35215	Center Point	(205)	—	16,942
35043	Chelsea	(205)	2,949	10,332
*35055	Cullman	(256)	13,995	14,799
36526	Daphne	(251)	16,581	22,109
*35601	Decatur	(256.)	53,929	55,902
*36301	Dothan	(334)	57,737	66,010
*36330	Enterprise	(334)	21,178	26,863
*36027	Eufaula	(334)	13,908	12,954
35064	Fairfield	(205)	12,381	11,124
*36532	Fairhope	(251)	12,480	15,703
*35630	Florence	(256)	36,264	39,354
*36535	Foley	(251)	7,590	14,989
35214	Forestdale (c)	(205)	10,509	10,162
*35967	Fort Payne	(256)	12,938	14,162
*35901	Gadsden	(256)	38,978	36,813
35071	Gardendale	(205)	11,626	13,904
35640	Hartselle	(256)	12,019	14,322
*35080	Helena	(205)	10,296	17,008
*35209	Homewood	(205)	25,043	25,183
*35244	Hoover	(205)	62,742	82,003
*35023	Hueytown	(205)	15,364	16,116
*35801	Huntsville	(256)	158,216	182,956
35210	Irondale	(205)	9,813	12,357
36265	Jacksonville	(256)	8,404	12,482
*35501	Jasper	(205)	14,052	14,308
35094	Leeds	(205)	10,455	11,797
*35758	Madison	(256)	29,329	43,685
36054	Millbrook	(334)	10,386	14,809
*36601	Mobile	(251)	198,915	194,914
*36104	Montgomery	(334)	201,568	208,182
35004	Moody	(205)	8,053	11,841
*35223	Mountain Brook	(205)	20,604	20,429
*35661	Muscle Shoals	(256)	11,924	13,175
*35476	Northport	(205)	19,435	23,647
*36801	Opelika	(334)	23,498	27,092
36203	Oxford	(256)	14,592	21,221
*36360	Ozark	(334)	15,119	14,848
35124	Pelham	(205)	14,369	21,669
*35125	Pell City	(205)	9,565	12,812
*36867	Phenix City	(334)	28,265	33,804
35127	Pleasant Grove	(205)	9,983	10,117
*36067	Prattville	(334)	24,303	34,387
36610	Prichard	(251)	28,633	22,637
36206	Saks (c)	(256)	10,698	10,744
36571	Saraland	(251)	12,288	13,416
*35768	Scottsboro	(256)	14,762	14,796
*36701	Selma	(334)	20,512	20,529
*35150	Sylacauga	(256)	12,616	12,678
*35160	Talladega	(256)	15,143	15,568
36619	Tillman's Corner (c)	(251)	15,685	17,398
*36081	Troy	(334)	13,935	18,025
35173	Trussville	(205)	12,924	19,948
*35401	Tuscaloosa	(205)	77,906	91,605
*35216	Vestavia Hills	(205)	24,476	34,058

Alaska (907)

ZIP	Place	2000 population	2011 estimate
*99501	Anchorage	260,283	295,570
99711	Badger (c)	—	19,482
*99708	College (c)	11,402	12,964
*99701	Fairbanks	30,224	32,036
*99801	Juneau	30,711	32,164
99654	Knik-Fairview (c)	7,049	14,923

Arizona

ZIP	Place	Area code	2000 population	2011 estimate
85086	Anthem (c)	(623)	—	21,700
*85120	Apache Junction	(480)	31,814	36,587
85123	Arizona City (c)	(520)	4,385	10,475
*85323	Avondale	(623)	35,883	77,518
*85326	Buckeye	(623)	6,537	51,649
*86442	Bullhead City	(928)	33,769	39,842
86322	Camp Verde	(928)	9,451	10,914
*85122	Casa Grande	(520)	25,224	49,591
85704	Casas Adobes (c)	(520)	54,011	66,795
85718	Catalina Foothills (c)	(520)	53,794	50,796
*85225	Chandler	(480)	176,581	240,101
86323	Chino Valley	(928)	7,835	10,862
85128	Coolidge	(520)	7,786	12,074
86326	Cottonwood	(928)	9,179	11,311
*85607	Douglas	(520)	14,312	17,551
85746	Drexel Heights (c)	(520)	23,849	27,749
85335	El Mirage	(623)	7,609	32,332
85131	Eloy	(520)	10,375	16,964
*86004	Flagstaff	(928)	52,894	65,914
85132	Florence	(520)	17,054	25,517
85705	Flowing Wells (c)	(520)	15,050	16,419
*86427	Fort Mohave (c)	(928)	—	14,364
85367	Fortuna Foothills (c)	(928)	20,478	26,265
*85268	Fountain Hills	(480)	20,235	22,865
*85299	Gilbert	(480)	109,697	211,951
*85302	Glendale	(623)	218,812	230,482
85118	Gold Canyon (c)	(480)	—	10,159
*85338	Goodyear	(623)	18,911	66,309
*85622	Green Valley (c)	(520)	17,283	21,391
*86401	Kingman	(928)	20,069	28,279
*86403	Lake Havasu City	(928)	41,938	52,935
*85653	Marana	(520)	13,556	35,232
*85139	Maricopa	(520)	—	44,396
*85201	Mesa	(480)	396,375	446,518
86401	New Kingman-Butler (c)	(928)	14,810	12,134
*85087	New River (c)	(623)	10,740	14,952
*85621	Nogales	(520)	20,878	20,948
*85737	Oro Valley	(520)	29,700	41,335
85253	Paradise Valley	(480)	13,664	13,035
*85541	Payson	(928)	13,620	15,171
*85345	Peoria	(623)	108,364	156,637
*85034	Phoenix	(480)/(602)/(623)	1,321,045	1,469,471
*86301	Prescott	(928)	33,938	39,984
*86314	Prescott Valley	(928)	23,535	38,982
*85142	Queen Creek	(480)	4,316	26,805
85648	Rio Rico (c)	(520)	—	18,962
*85629	Sahuarita	(520)	3,242	25,458
85349	San Luis	(928)	15,322	27,864
*85142	San Tan Valley (c)	(480)	—	81,321
*85251	Scottsdale	(480)	202,705	221,020
*86336	Sedona	(928)	10,192	10,063
*85901	Show Low	(928)	7,695	10,657
*85635	Sierra Vista	(520)	37,775	46,109
85650	Sierra Vista Southeast (c)	(520)	14,348	14,797
85350	Somerton	(928)	7,266	14,528
*85351	Sun City (c)	(623)	38,309	37,499
*85375	Sun City West (c)	(623)	26,344	24,535
85248	Sun Lakes (c)	(480)	11,936	13,975
*85374	Surprise	(623)	30,848	119,489
85749	Tanque Verde (c)	(520)	16,195	16,901
*85282	Tempe	(480)	158,625	164,268
*85726	Tucson	(520)	486,699	525,796
85735	Tucson Estates (c)	(520)	9,755	12,192
85641	Vail (c)	(520)	2,484	10,208
86326	Verde Village[1] (c)	(928)	10,610	11,605
*85364	Yuma	(928)	77,515	94,536

(1) Formerly Cottonwood-Verde Village CDP.

Arkansas

ZIP	Place	Area code	2000 population	2011 estimate
*71923	Arkadelphia	(870)	10,912	10,658
*72501	Batesville	(870)	9,445	10,305
*72714	Bella Vista	(479)	—	27,207
*72015	Benton	(501)	21,906	31,367
72712	Bentonville	(479)	19,730	36,295

ZIP	Place	Area code	2000 population	2011 estimate
*72315	Blytheville	(870)	18,272	15,447
*72022	Bryant	(501)	9,764	17,064
72023	Cabot	(501)	15,261	24,120
*71701	Camden	(870)	13,154	12,072
*72032	Conway	(501)	43,167	60,470
*71730	El Dorado	(870)	21,530	18,789
*72701	Fayetteville	(479)	58,047	75,102
*72335	Forrest City	(870)	14,774	15,237
*72901	Fort Smith	(479)	80,268	87,152
*72601	Harrison	(870)	12,152	12,994
72342	Helena-West Helena	(870)	—	12,106
*71801	Hope	(870)	10,616	10,065
*71901	Hot Springs	(501)	35,750	35,587
*72076	Jacksonville	(501)	29,916	28,624
*72401	Jonesboro	(870)	55,515	68,547
*72201	Little Rock	(501)	183,133	195,314
*71753	Magnolia	(870)	10,858	11,510
*72104	Malvern	(501)	9,021	10,307
72364	Marion	(870)	8,901	12,253
*72113	Maumelle	(501)	10,557	17,325
*72653	Mountain Home	(870)	11,012	12,454
*72114	North Little Rock	(501)	60,433	62,886
*72450	Paragould	(870)	22,017	26,501
*71601	Pine Bluff	(870)	55,085	48,339
*72756	Rogers	(479)	38,829	57,539
*72801	Russellville	(479)	23,682	28,160
*72143	Searcy	(501)	18,928	23,151
*72120	Sherwood	(501)	21,511	29,801
72761	Siloam Springs	(479)	10,843	15,438
*72764	Springdale	(479)	45,798	71,397
71854	Texarkana	(870)	26,448	30,117
*72956	Van Buren	(479)	18,986	22,790
*72301	West Memphis	(870)	27,666	26,054

California

Area code (442) overlays area code (760). Area code (669) overlays area code (408). Area code (707) overlays area code (714). Area code (747) overlays area code (818).

ZIP	Place	Area code	2000 population	2011 estimate
92301	Adelanto	(760)	18,130	32,221
*91376	Agoura Hills	(818)	20,537	20,477
*94501	Alameda	(510)	72,259	74,774
94507	Alamo (c)	(925)	15,626	14,570
94706	Albany	(510)	16,444	18,786
*91802	Alhambra	(626)	85,804	83,693
92656	Aliso Viejo	(949)	—	48,549
*91901	Alpine (c) (San Diego Co.)	(619)	13,143	14,236
*91003	Altadena (c)	(626)	42,610	42,777
95127	Alum Rock (c)	(408)	13,479	15,536
94589	American Canyon	(707)	9,774	19,690
*92803	Anaheim	(714)	328,014	341,361
95843	Antelope (c)	(916)	—	45,770
*94509	Antioch	(925)	90,532	104,044
*92307	Apple Valley	(760)	54,239	70,172
*91006	Arcadia	(626)	53,054	56,769
*95521	Arcata	(707)	16,651	17,248
95825	Arden-Arcade (c)	(916)	96,025	92,186
*93420	Arroyo Grande	(805)	15,851	17,407
*90701	Artesia	(562)	16,380	16,639
93203	Arvin	(661)	12,956	19,579
94577	Ashland (c)	(510)	20,793	21,925
*93422	Atascadero	(805)	26,411	28,560
95301	Atwater	(209)	23,113	28,626
*95603	Auburn	(530)	12,462	13,660
93204	Avenal	(559)	14,674	15,560
91746	Avocado Heights (c)	(626)	15,148	15,411
91702	Azusa	(626)	44,712	46,678
*93302	Bakersfield	(661)	247,057	352,428
91706	Baldwin Park	(626)	75,837	75,940
92220	Banning	(951)	23,562	30,260
*92312	Barstow	(760)	21,119	22,975
94565	Bay Point (c)	(925)	21,534	21,349
92223	Beaumont	(951)	11,384	37,722
*90201	Bell	(323)	36,664	35,731
*90202	Bell Gardens	(213)/(323)/(562)	44,054	77,170
*90706	Bellflower	(562)	72,878	42,376
94002	Belmont	(650)	25,123	26,147
94510	Benicia	(707)	26,865	27,207
*94704	Berkeley	(510)	102,743	113,905
*90210	Beverly Hills	(213)/(310)/(323)	33,784	34,358
*92314	Big Bear City (c)	(909)	—	12,304
92316	Bloomington (c)	(951)	19,318	23,851
*92225	Blythe	(760)	12,155	21,127
*91902	Bonita (c)	(619)	12,401	12,538
92021	Bostonia (c)	(619)	15,169	15,379
92227	Brawley	(760)	22,052	25,335
*92822	Brea	(562)/(714)	35,410	39,883
*94513	Brentwood	(925)	23,302	52,326
*90622	Buena Park	(714)	78,282	81,747
*91510	Burbank (Los Angeles Co.)	(818)	100,316	104,092
*94010	Burlingame	(650)	28,158	29,157
*91372	Calabasas	(818)	20,033	23,227
*92231	Calexico	(760)	27,109	39,164

ZIP	Place	Area code	2000 population	2011 estimate
*93504	California City	(760)	8,385	14,327
*93010	Camarillo	(805)	57,077	65,895
95682	Cameron Park (c)	(530)	14,549	18,228
92058	Camp Pendleton South (c)	(760)	8,854	10,616
*95008	Campbell	(408)	38,138	39,968
92587	Canyon Lake	(951)	9,952	10,805
*92008	Carlsbad	(760)	78,247	106,888
*95608	Carmichael (c)	(916)	49,742	61,762
*93013	Carpinteria	(805)	14,194	13,135
*90745	Carson	(310)	89,730	92,376
92077	Casa de Oro-Mt. Helix (c)	(619)	18,874	18,762
*91384	Castaic (c)	(661)	—	19,015
*94546	Castro Valley (c)	(510)	57,292	61,388
*92235	Cathedral City	(760)	42,647	52,381
95307	Ceres	(209)	34,609	45,743
90703	Cerritos	(562)	51,488	49,398
94541	Cherryland (c)	(510)	13,837	14,728
*95926	Chico	(530)	59,954	86,290
*91708	Chino	(909)	67,168	79,059
91709	Chino Hills	(909)	66,787	75,928
93610	Chowchilla	(559)	11,127	19,044
*91910	Chula Vista	(619)	173,556	247,535
91702	Citrus (c)	(626)	10,581	10,866
*95621	Citrus Heights	(916)	85,071	84,330
91711	Claremont	(909)	33,998	35,143
94517	Clayton	(925)	10,762	11,076
95422	Clearlake	(707)	13,142	15,170
*93612	Clovis	(559)	68,468	96,929
92236	Coachella	(760)	22,724	41,648
93210	Coalinga	(559)	11,668	13,543
*92324	Colton	(909)	47,662	52,940
90040	Commerce	(323)	12,568	12,915
*90221	Compton	(310)	93,493	97,156
*94520	Concord	(925)	121,780	124,055
*93212	Corcoran	(559)	14,458	24,888
92877	Corona	(951)	124,966	155,896
*92118	Coronado	(619)	24,100	19,167
*92628	Costa Mesa	(714)/(949)	108,724	111,600
92679	Coto de Caza (c)	(949)	13,057	14,866
*91722	Covina	(626)	46,837	48,142
92325	Crestline (c)	(909)	10,218	10,770
90201	Cudahy	(323)	24,208	23,979
*90230	Culver City	(310)	38,816	39,165
*95014	Cupertino	(408)	50,546	59,220
90630	Cypress	(714)	46,229	48,526
*94015	Daly City	(415)/(650)	103,621	102,362
*92629	Dana Point	(949)	35,110	33,858
*94526	Danville	(925)	41,715	42,725
*95616	Davis	(530)	60,308	66,016
90250	Del Aire (c)	(310)/(323)	9,012	10,001
*93215	Delano	(661)	38,824	53,819
95315	Delhi (c)	(209)	8,022	10,755
*92240	Desert Hot Springs	(760)	16,582	27,672
91765	Diamond Bar	(909)	56,287	55,951
93618	Dinuba	(559)	16,844	21,797
*94514	Discovery Bay (c)	(925)	8,981	13,352
95620	Dixon	(707)	16,103	18,536
90239	Downey	(562)	107,323	112,584
*91009	Duarte	(626)	21,486	21,474
94568	Dublin	(925)	29,973	46,572
92343	East Hemet (c)	(951)	14,823	17,418
90022	East Los Angeles (c)	(323)	124,283	126,496
94303	East Palo Alto	(650)	29,506	28,502
90221	East Rancho Dominguez (c)	(310)/(323)	—	15,135
91775	East San Gabriel (c)	(626)	14,512	14,874
*91752	Eastvale	(909)/(951)	—	54,930
*92020	El Cajon	(619)	94,869	100,928
*92244	El Centro	(760)	37,835	43,242
94530	El Cerrito	(510)	23,171	23,934
95762	El Dorado Hills (c)	(916)	18,016	42,108
*91734	El Monte	(626)	115,965	114,296
*93446	El Paso de Robles (Paso Robles)	(805)	24,297	30,065
90245	El Segundo	(310)	16,033	16,775
*94803	El Sobrante (Contra Costa Co.)	(510)	12,260	12,669
92503	El Sobrante (Riverside Co.)	(714)/(909)	—	12,670
*95624	Elk Grove	(916)	—	154,908
*94608	Emeryville	(510)	6,882	10,214
*92024	Encinitas	(760)	58,014	60,400
*92025	Escondido	(760)	133,559	146,032
*95501	Eureka	(707)	26,128	27,217
93221	Exeter	(559)	9,168	10,499
94533	Fairfield	(707)	96,178	106,126
95628	Fair Oaks (c)	(916)	28,008	30,912
94541	Fairview (c)	(510)	9,470	10,000
*92028	Fallbrook (c)	(760)	29,100	30,534
93223	Farmersville	(559)	8,737	10,760
*93015	Fillmore	(805)	13,643	15,157
90001	Florence-Graham (c)	(323)	60,197	63,387
95828	Florin (c)	(916)	27,653	47,513
*95630	Folsom	(916)	51,884	73,001
*92334	Fontana	(909)	128,929	199,028

ZIP	Place	Area code	2000 population	2011 estimate	ZIP	Place	Area code	2000 population	2011 estimate
95841	Foothill Farms (c)	(916)	17,426	33,121	*90086	Los Angeles	(213)/(310)/(323)		
95540	Fortuna	(707)	10,497	11,939			/(818)	3,694,820	3,819,702
94404	Foster City	(650)	28,803	30,943	93635	Los Banos	(209)	25,869	36,558
*92728	Fountain Valley	(714)	54,978	56,153	*95030	Los Gatos	(408)	28,592	29,884
*94537	Fremont	(510)	203,413	216,916	*93402	Los Osos (c)	(805)	—	14,276
92563	French Valley (c)	(951)	—	23,067	90262	Lynwood	(213)/(310)/(323)	69,845	70,257
*93706	Fresno	(559)	427,652	501,362	*93638	Madera	(559)	43,207	62,219
*92834	Fullerton	(714)	126,003	137,183	95954	Magalia (c)	(530)	10,569	11,310
95632	Galt	(209)	19,472	23,941	*90265	Malibu	(310)	12,575	12,736
95215	Garden Acres (c)	(209)	9,747	10,648	*90266	Manhattan Beach	(310)	33,852	35,391
*92842	Garden Grove	(714)	165,196	173,470	*95336	Manteca	(209)	49,258	68,254
*90247	Gardena	(310)	57,746	59,253	93933	Marina	(831)	25,101	20,041
*95020	Gilroy	(408)	41,464	49,582	94553	Martinez	(925)	35,866	36,392
92509	Glen Avon (c)	(951)	14,853	20,199	95901	Marysville	(530)	12,268	12,141
*91209	Glendale	(818)	194,973	193,111	90270	Maywood	(323)	28,083	27,594
*91741	Glendora	(626)	49,415	50,435	93250	McFarland	(661)	9,618	12,890
*93116	Goleta	(805)	—	30,105	95521	McKinleyville (c)	(707)	13,599	15,177
92324	Grand Terrace	(951)	11,626	12,220	93640	Mendota	(559)	7,890	11,166
95746	Granite Bay (c)	(916)	19,388	20,402	*92586	Menifee	(951)	—	79,312
*95945	Grass Valley	(530)	10,922	12,840	*94025	Menlo Park	(650)	30,785	32,412
93927	Greenfield	(831)	12,583	16,611	*95340	Merced	(209)	63,893	80,232
93433	Grover Beach	(805)	13,067	13,275	*94941	Mill Valley	(415)	13,600	14,051
91745	Hacienda Heights (c)	(626)	53,122	54,038	94030	Millbrae	(650)	20,718	21,793
94019	Half Moon Bay	(650)	11,842	11,464	*95035	Milpitas	(408)	62,698	67,804
*93230	Hanford	(559)	41,686	54,284	91752	Mira Loma (c)	(951)	17,617	21,930
90716	Hawaiian Gardens	(562)	14,779	14,360	*92690	Mission Viejo	(949)	93,102	94,721
*90250	Hawthorne	(310)/(323)	84,112	84,905	*95350	Modesto	(209)	188,856	202,751
*94544	Hayward	(510)	140,030	146,069	*91017	Monrovia	(626)	36,929	36,857
95448	Healdsburg	(707)	10,722	11,353	91763	Montclair	(909)	33,049	37,211
92546	Hemet	(951)	58,812	80,467	90640	Montebello	(323)	62,150	62,954
94547	Hercules	(510)	19,488	24,455	*93940	Monterey	(831)	29,674	28,246
90254	Hermosa Beach	(310)	18,566	19,648	*91754	Monterey Park	(323)/(626)/(818)	60,051	60,707
*92340	Hesperia	(760)	62,582	91,534	*93021	Moorpark	(805)	31,415	34,779
92346	Highland	(909)	44,605	53,903	*94556	Moraga	(925)	16,290	16,250
94010	Hillsborough	(650)	10,825	10,958	*92552	Moreno Valley	(951)	142,381	197,838
*95023	Hollister	(831)	34,413	35,437	*95037	Morgan Hill	(408)	33,556	38,477
92879	Home Gardens (c)	(909)	9,461	11,570	*93442	Morro Bay	(805)	10,350	10,327
*92647	Huntington Beach	(714)	189,594	192,888	*94041	Mountain View	(650)	70,708	75,235
90255	Huntington Park	(323)	61,348	58,536	*92564	Murrieta	(951)	44,282	105,857
92251	Imperial	(760)	7,560	14,987	92407	Muscoy (c)	(909)	8,919	10,644
*91932	Imperial Beach	(619)	26,992	26,708	*94558	Napa	(707)	72,585	77,867
*92201	Indio	(760)	49,116	77,780	*91950	National City	(619)	54,260	59,369
*90301	Inglewood	(310)/(323)	112,580	110,464	94560	Newark	(510)	42,471	43,139
*92619	Irvine	(714)/(949)	143,072	215,529	95360	Newman	(209)	7,093	10,306
93117	Isla Vista (c)	(805)	18,344	23,096	*92658	Newport Beach	(949)	70,032	86,484
93630	Kerman	(559)	8,551	13,727	93444	Nipomo (c)	(805)	12,626	16,714
93930	King City	(831)	11,094	13,093	91760	Norco	(951)	24,157	27,594
93631	Kingsburg	(559)	9,199	11,537	95603	North Auburn (c)	(530)	11,847	13,022
*91011	La Cañada Flintridge	(818)	20,318	20,395	94025	North Fair Oaks (c)	(650)	15,440	14,687
*91214	La Crescenta-Montrose (c)	(818)	18,532	19,653	95660	North Highlands (c)	(916)	44,187	42,694
*90631	La Habra	(562)/(949)	58,974	61,164	92705	North Tustin (c)	(714)/(949)	—	24,917
*91941	La Mesa	(619)	54,749	57,907	*90650	Norwalk	(562)	103,298	106,309
*90638	La Mirada	(562)/(714)	46,783	48,859	*94947	Novato	(415)	47,630	52,456
90623	La Palma	(562)/(714)	15,408	15,807	*91377	Oak Park (c)	(805)/(818)	2,320	13,811
91977	La Presa (c)	(619)	32,721	34,169	95361	Oakdale	(209)	15,503	20,838
*91747	La Puente	(626)	41,063	40,107	*94617	Oakland	(510)	399,484	395,817
*92253	La Quinta	(760)	23,694	38,335	94561	Oakley	(925)	25,619	36,014
95401	La Riviera (c)	(916)	10,273	10,802	*92056	Oceanside	(760)	161,029	169,569
91750	La Verne	(909)	31,638	31,285	93308	Oildale (c)	(661)	27,885	32,684
92694	Ladera Ranch (c)	(949)	—	22,980	95961	Olivehurst (c)	(530)	11,061	13,656
94549	Lafayette	(925)	23,908	24,285	*91761	Ontario	(909)	158,007	166,390
*92652	Laguna Beach	(949)	23,727	23,069	*92863	Orange	(714)	128,821	138,409
*92654	Laguna Hills	(949)	31,178	30,804	95662	Orangevale (c)	(916)	26,705	33,960
*92607	Laguna Niguel	(949)	61,891	63,940	*93457	Orcutt (c)	(805)	28,830	28,905
*92654	Laguna Woods	(949)	16,507	16,438	94563	Orinda	(925)	17,599	17,932
92352	Lake Arrowhead (c)	(909)	8,934	12,424	*95965	Oroville	(530)	13,004	15,563
*92531	Lake Elsinore	(951)	28,928	53,417	*93030	Oxnard	(805)	170,358	199,943
92630	Lake Forest	(949)	58,707	78,439	93950	Pacific Grove	(831)	15,522	15,295
*93535	Lake Los Angeles (c)	(661)	11,523	12,328	94044	Pacifica	(650)	38,390	37,691
92530	Lakeland Village (c)	(909)/(951)	5,626	11,541	*92260	Palm Desert	(760)	41,155	49,561
92040	Lakeside (c)	(619)	19,560	20,648	*92262	Palm Springs	(760)	42,807	45,573
*90714	Lakewood	(562)	79,345	80,634	*93590	Palmdale	(661)	116,670	153,867
93241	Lamont (c)	(661)	13,296	15,120	*94303	Palo Alto	(650)	58,598	65,412
*93539	Lancaster	(661)	118,718	157,693	*90274	Palos Verdes Estates	(310)	13,340	13,535
*94939	Larkspur	(415)	12,014	12,054	*95969	Paradise	(530)	26,408	26,249
95330	Lathrop	(209)	10,445	18,316	90723	Paramount	(562)	55,266	54,492
*90260	Lawndale	(310)	31,711	33,006	95823	Parkway (c)	(916)	—	14,670
*91945	Lemon Grove	(619)	24,918	25,694	93648	Parlier	(559)	11,145	14,692
95824	Lemon Hill (c)	(916)	—	13,729	*91109	Pasadena	(323)/(626)/(818)	133,936	138,101
93245	Lemoore	(559)	19,712	24,675		Paso Robles. See El Paso de Robles			
90304	Lennox (c)	(310)	22,950	22,753	95363	Patterson	(209)	11,606	20,578
95648	Lincoln	(916)	11,205	43,970	92509	Pedley (c)	(951)	11,207	12,672
95901	Linda (c)	(530)	13,474	17,773	*92572	Perris	(951)	36,189	69,967
93247	Lindsay	(559)	10,297	11,957	*94952	Petaluma	(707)	54,548	58,453
95062	Live Oak (c)				*92371	Phelan (c)	(760)	—	14,304
	(Santa Cruz Co.)	(831)	16,628	17,158	*90660	Pico Rivera	(562)	63,428	63,400
*94550	Livermore	(925)	73,345	82,039	*94611	Piedmont	(510)	10,952	10,809
95334	Livingston	(209)	10,473	13,271	94564	Pinole	(510)	19,039	18,691
*95240	Lodi	(209)	56,999	63,133	94565	Pittsburg	(925)	56,769	64,294
92354	Loma Linda	(951)	18,681	23,600	*92871	Placentia	(714)	46,488	51,302
90717	Lomita	(310)	20,046	20,402	*95667	Placerville	(530)	9,610	10,383
*93436	Lompoc	(805)	41,103	42,724	94523	Pleasant Hill	(925)	32,837	33,689
*90801	Long Beach	(310)/(562)	461,522	465,576	*94566	Pleasanton	(925)	63,654	71,215
*90720	Los Alamitos	(562)/(949)	11,536	11,620	*91769	Pomona	(909)	149,473	150,119
*94022	Los Altos	(650)	27,693	29,431	*93041	Port Hueneme	(805)	21,845	21,939

ZIP	Place	Area code	2000 population	2011 estimate
*93257	Porterville	(559)	39,615	55,023
*92064	Poway	(858)	48,044	48,518
93907	Prunedale (c)	(831)	16,432	17,560
*93536	Quartz Hill (c)	(661)	9,890	10,912
92065	Ramona (c)	(760)	15,691	20,292
*95670	Rancho Cordova	(916)	—	65,606
*91729	Rancho Cucamonga	(909)	127,743	167,721
92270	Rancho Mirage	(760)	13,249	17,615
90275	Rancho Palos Verdes	(310)	41,145	41,946
91941	Rancho San Diego (c)	(619)	20,155	21,208
92688	Rancho Santa Margarita	(949)	47,214	48,587
96080	Red Bluff	(530)	13,147	14,105
*96049	Redding	(530)	80,865	90,138
*92373	Redlands	(909)	63,591	69,752
*90277	Redondo Beach	(310)	63,261	67,233
*94063	Redwood City	(650)	75,402	77,745
93654	Reedley	(559)	20,756	24,520
*92377	Rialto	(909)	91,873	100,662
*94802	Richmond	(510)	99,216	105,380
*93556	Ridgecrest	(760)	24,927	28,013
95673	Rio Linda (c)	(916)	10,466	15,106
95366	Ripon	(209)	10,146	14,527
95367	Riverbank	(209)	15,826	22,858
*92502	Riverside	(951)	255,166	310,651
*95677	Rocklin	(916)	36,330	58,324
*94928	Rohnert Park	(707)	42,236	41,333
93560	Rosamond (c)	(661)	14,349	18,150
93314	Rosedale (c)	(661)	8,445	14,058
*91770	Rosemead	(626)	53,505	54,154
95826	Rosemont (c)	(916)	22,904	22,681
*95678	Roseville	(916)	79,921	121,767
90720	Rossmoor (c)	(714)	10,298	10,244
91748	Rowland Heights (c)	(626)	48,553	48,993
*92519	Rubidoux (c)	(951)	29,180	34,280
*95814	Sacramento	(916)	407,018	472,178
95368	Salida (c)	(209)	12,560	13,722
*93907	Salinas	(831)	151,060	152,994
*94960	San Anselmo	(415)	12,378	12,468
*92401	San Bernardino	(909)	185,401	213,012
*94066	San Bruno	(650)	40,165	41,616
*93001	San Buenaventura (Ventura)	(805)	100,916	107,514
*94070	San Carlos	(650)	27,718	28,755
*92674	San Clemente	(949)	49,936	64,491
*92138	San Diego	(619)/(858)	1,223,400	1,326,179
92065	San Diego Country Estates (c)	(760)	9,262	10,109
91773	San Dimas	(909)	34,980	33,611
*91341	San Fernando	(818)	23,564	23,818
*94142	San Francisco	(415)	776,733	812,826
*91778	San Gabriel	(626)	39,804	40,005
*92581	San Jacinto	(951)	23,779	45,218
*95113	San Jose	(408)	894,943	967,487
*92690	San Juan Capistrano	(949)	33,826	35,123
*94577	San Leandro	(510)	79,452	86,071
94580	San Lorenzo (c)	(510)	21,898	23,452
*93401	San Luis Obispo	(805)	44,174	45,525
*92069	San Marcos	(760)	54,977	85,022
*91108	San Marino	(626)	12,945	13,241
*94402	San Mateo	(650)	92,482	98,391
94806	San Pablo	(510)	30,215	29,609
*94915	San Rafael	(415)	56,063	58,313
94583	San Ramon	(925)	44,722	73,333
93657	Sanger	(559)	18,931	24,599
*92711	Santa Ana	(714)/(949)	337,977	329,427
*93102	Santa Barbara	(805)	92,325	89,045
*95050	Santa Clara	(408)	102,361	118,263
*91380	Santa Clarita	(661)	151,088	177,601
*95060	Santa Cruz	(831)	54,593	60,342
90720	Santa Fe Springs	(562)	17,438	16,340
*93454	Santa Maria	(805)	77,423	100,277
*90401	Santa Monica	(310)	84,084	90,377
*93060	Santa Paula	(805)	28,598	29,624
*95402	Santa Rosa	(707)	147,595	169,292
*92071	Santee	(619)	52,975	54,197
*95070	Saratoga	(408)	29,843	30,401
*95066	Scotts Valley	(831)	11,385	11,667
90740	Seal Beach	(562)	24,157	24,536
93955	Seaside	(831)	31,696	33,576
93662	Selma	(559)	19,444	23,535
*93263	Shafter	(661)	12,736	17,231
*96019	Shasta Lake	(916)	9,008	10,195
*91025	Sierra Madre	(626)	10,578	10,996
*90806	Signal Hill	(562)	9,333	11,095
*93065	Simi Valley	(805)	111,351	125,522
92075	Solana Beach	(858)	12,979	13,060
93960	Soledad	(831)	11,263	26,012
*95476	Sonoma	(707)	9,128	10,741
91733	South El Monte	(626)	21,144	20,264
90280	South Gate	(323)/(562)	96,375	95,084
*96151	South Lake Tahoe	(530)	23,609	21,388
*91030	S. Pasadena	(213)/(323)/(626)/(818)	24,292	25,806
*94080	South San Francisco	(650)	60,552	64,409
91744	South San Jose Hills (c)	(626)	20,218	20,551
90605	South Whittier (c)	(562)	55,193	57,156

ZIP	Place	Area code	2000 population	2011 estimate
*91977	Spring Valley (c)	(619)	26,663	28,205
*94309	Stanford (c)	(650)	13,315	13,809
90680	Stanton	(714)	37,403	38,765
*95208	Stockton	(209)	243,771	296,357
*94585	Suisun City	(707)	26,118	28,330
93543	Sun Village (c)	(661)	—	11,565
*94086	Sunnyvale	(408)	131,760	142,287
*96130	Susanville	(530)	13,541	17,685
94941	Tamalpais-Homestead Valley (c)	(415)	10,691	10,735
*93581	Tehachapi	(661)	10,957	14,630
*92589	Temecula	(951)	57,716	102,464
92883	Temescal Valley (c)	(951)	—	22,535
91780	Temple City	(626)	33,377	35,816
*91359	Thousand Oaks	(805)	117,005	127,984
*90503	Torrance	(310)	137,946	146,493
95376	Tracy	(209)	56,929	84,266
*96161	Truckee	(916)	13,864	16,154
*93274	Tulare	(559)	43,994	60,289
*95380	Turlock	(209)	55,810	69,089
*92781	Tustin	(714)/(949)	67,504	76,689
*92277	Twentynine Palms	(760)	14,764	25,377
*95482	Ukiah	(707)	15,497	16,023
94587	Union City	(510)	66,869	70,436
*91785	Upland	(909)	68,393	74,837
*95687	Vacaville	(707)	88,625	93,088
91744	Valinda (c)	(626)	21,776	22,822
92343	Valle Vista (c)	(951)	10,488	14,578
*94590	Vallejo	(707)	116,760	116,829
	Ventura. See San Buenaventura			
*92393	Victorville	(760)	64,029	117,597
90043	View Park-Windsor Hills (c)	(310)	10,958	11,075
91722	Vincent (c)	(925)	15,097	15,922
95829	Vineyard (c)	(916)	10,109	24,836
*93291	Visalia	(559)	91,565	126,432
*92083	Vista	(760)	89,857	95,204
*91788	Walnut	(626)	30,004	29,386
*94596	Walnut Creek	(925)	64,296	65,211
90255	Walnut Park (c)	(213)	16,180	15,966
93280	Wasco	(661)	21,263	25,930
*95076	Watsonville	(831)	44,265	51,586
90502	West Carson (c)	(310)	21,138	21,699
*91790	West Covina	(626)	105,080	106,870
90069	West Hollywood	(310)/(323)	35,716	34,650
91746	West Puente Valley (c)	(626)	22,589	22,636
*95691	West Sacramento	(916)	31,615	49,045
*90606	West Whittier-Los Nietos (c)	(562)	24,164	25,540
*92685	Westminster	(714)	88,207	91,064
90047	Westmont (c)	(323)	31,623	31,853
*90605	Whittier	(562)	83,680	85,943
92595	Wildomar	(951)	14,064	32,922
90222	Willowbrook (c)	(323)	34,138	35,983
95492	Windsor	(707)	22,744	27,042
92040	Winter Gardens (c)	(619)	19,771	20,631
95388	Winton (c)	(209)	8,832	10,613
92504	Woodcrest (c)	(909)/(951)	8,342	14,347
*95695	Woodland	(530)	49,151	55,806
*92885	Yorba Linda	(714)	58,918	65,215
*95991	Yuba City	(530)	36,758	65,050
92399	Yucaipa	(909)	41,207	52,139
*92286	Yucca Valley	(760)	16,865	21,009

Colorado

Area code (720) overlays area code (303).

ZIP	Place	Area code	2000 population	2011 estimate
*80004	Arvada	(303)	102,153	107,541
*80017	Aurora	(303)	276,393	332,354
80221	Berkley (c)	(970)	10,743	11,207
*80908	Black Forest (c)	(719)	8,143	13,116
*80302	Boulder	(303)	94,673	98,889
*80601	Brighton	(303)	20,905	34,069
*80020	Broomfield	(303)	38,272	57,352
*81212	Cañon City	(719)	15,431	16,499
80108	Castle Pines North	(303)	—	10,602
*80104	Castle Rock	(303)	20,224	49,355
*80015	Centennial	(303)	—	102,603
80111	Cherry Creek (c)	(303)	—	11,120
81222	Cimarron Hills (c)	(719)	15,194	16,161
81520	Clifton (c)	(970)	17,345	19,889
*80903	Colorado Springs	(719)	360,890	426,388
80120	Columbine (c)	(303)	24,095	24,280
80022	Commerce City	(303)	20,991	46,941
80304	Dakota Ridge (c)	(303)	—	32,005
*80202	Denver	(303)	554,636	619,968
*81301	Durango	(970)	13,922	17,069
81632	Edwards (c)	(970)	8,257	10,266
*80110	Englewood	(303)	31,727	30,930
80516	Erie	(303)	6,291	18,505
80620	Evans	(970)	9,514	18,974
80221	Federal Heights	(303)	12,065	11,724
*80520	Firestone	(303)	1,908	10,385

ZIP	Place	Area code	2000 population	2011 estimate
80913	Fort Carson (c)	(719)	10,566	13,813
*80525	Fort Collins	(970)	118,652	146,762
*80701	Fort Morgan	(970)	11,034	11,428
80817	Fountain	(719)	15,197	26,475
*81521	Fruita	(970)	6,478	12,677
*80401	Golden	(303)	17,159	19,035
*81501	Grand Junction	(970)	41,986	58,704
*80631	Greeley	(970)	76,930	94,962
*80111	Greenwood Village	(303)	11,035	14,237
80163	Highlands Ranch (c)	(303)	70,931	96,713
80534	Johnstown	(970)	3,827	10,119
80127	Ken Caryl (c)	(303)	30,887	32,438
80026	Lafayette	(303)	23,197	24,865
*80226	Lakewood	(303)	144,126	144,406
*80126	Littleton	(303)	40,340	42,639
*80124	Lone Tree	(303)	4,873	11,331
*80501	Longmont	(303)	71,093	87,712
80027	Louisville	(303)	18,937	18,684
*80538	Loveland	(970)	50,608	68,203
*81401	Montrose	(970)	12,344	19,011
*80233	Northglenn	(303)	31,575	36,588
*80134	Parker	(303)	23,558	46,363
*81003	Pueblo	(719)	102,121	107,577
81007	Pueblo West (c)	(719)	16,899	29,637
80911	Security-Widefield (c)	(719)	29,845	32,882
*80221	Sherrelwood (c)	(303)	17,657	18,287
*80477	Steamboat Springs	(970)	9,815	11,951
80751	Sterling	(970)	11,360	14,725
80027	Superior	(303)	9,011	12,692
80134	The Pinery (c)	(303)	7,253	10,517
*80229	Thornton	(303)	82,384	121,435
80229	Welby (c)	(303)	12,973	14,846
*80030	Westminster	(303)	100,940	107,967
*80033	Wheat Ridge	(303)	32,913	30,465
*80550	Windsor	(970)	9,896	19,066

Connecticut

Area code (475) overlays area code (203). See introductory note.

ZIP	Place	Area code	2000 population	2011 estimate
06401	Ansonia	(203)	18,554	19,219
06001	Avon	(860)	15,832	18,113
06037	Berlin	(860)	18,215	19,881
06801	Bethel	(203)	18,067	18,771
06002	Bloomfield	(860)	19,587	20,502
06405	Branford	(203)	28,683	27,980
*06602	Bridgeport	(203)	139,529	145,638
*06010	Bristol	(860)	60,062	60,525
*06804	Brookfield	(203)	15,664	16,617
06019	Canton	(860)	8,840	10,300
*06410	Cheshire	(203)	28,543	29,216
06413	Clinton	(860)	13,094	13,290
*06415	Colchester	(860)	14,551	16,034
06238	Coventry	(860)	11,504	12,418
06416	Cromwell	(860)	12,871	14,037
*06810	Danbury	(203)	74,848	81,671
06820	Darien	(203)	19,607	20,942
06418	Derby	(203)	12,391	12,882
*06424	East Hampton	(860)	13,352	12,989
*06108	East Hartford	(860)	49,575	51,293
*06512	East Haven	(203)	28,189	29,209
06333	East Lyme	(860)	18,118	19,124
*06088	East Windsor	(860)	9,818	11,170
06029	Ellington	(860)	12,921	15,582
*06082	Enfield	(860)	45,212	44,686
*06825	Fairfield	(203)	57,340	59,961
*06032	Farmington	(860)	23,641	25,361
06033	Glastonbury	(860)	31,876	34,454
*06035	Granby	(860)	10,347	11,291
*06830	Greenwich	(203)	61,101	61,782
06351	Griswold	(860)	10,807	11,925
*06340	Groton	(860)	10,010	10,369
06340	Groton	(860)	39,907	40,038
06437	Guilford	(203)	21,398	22,340
*06514	Hamden	(203)	56,913	60,868
*06101	Hartford	(860)	121,578	124,867
*06239	Killingly	(860)	16,472	17,330
06339	Ledyard	(860)	14,687	15,019
06443	Madison	(203)	17,858	18,239
*06040	Manchester	(860)	54,740	58,287
*06250	Mansfield	(860)	20,720	26,524
*06450	Meriden	(203)	58,244	60,770
06457	Middletown	(860)	43,167	47,749
*06460	Milford	(203)	50,594	51,189
06461	Milford	(203)	52,305	52,675
06468	Monroe	(203)	19,247	19,675
06353	Montville	(860)	18,546	19,533
06770	Naugatuck	(203)	30,989	31,810
*06050	New Britain	(860)	71,538	73,261
*06840	New Canaan	(203)	19,395	19,938
06812	New Fairfield	(203)	13,953	14,020
*06511	New Haven	(203)	123,626	129,585
06320	New London	(860)	25,671	27,569
06776	New Milford	(860)	27,121	27,972
*06101	Newington	(860)	29,306	30,586
06470	Newtown	(203)	25,031	27,829
06471	North Branford	(203)	13,906	14,383

ZIP	Place	Area code	2000 population	2011 estimate
06473	North Haven	(203)	23,035	24,054
*06856	Norwalk	(203)	82,951	86,460
06360	Norwich	(860)	36,117	40,408
06475	Old Saybrook	(860)	10,367	10,265
06477	Orange	(203)	13,233	13,933
06478	Oxford	(203)	9,821	12,662
06374	Plainfield	(860)	14,619	15,369
06062	Plainville	(860)	17,328	17,730
06782	Plymouth	(860)	11,634	12,169
06877	Ridgefield	(203)	23,643	24,885
06067	Rocky Hill	(860)	17,966	19,723
*06484	Seymour	(203)	15,454	16,514
06484	Shelton	(203)	38,101	39,954
*06070	Simsbury	(860)	23,234	23,528
06071	Somers	(860)	10,417	11,433
*06074	South Windsor	(860)	24,412	25,729
06488	Southbury	(203)	18,567	19,873
06489	Southington	(860)	39,728	43,103
*06075	Stafford	(860)	11,307	12,072
*06904	Stamford	(203)	117,083	123,868
06378	Stonington	(860)	17,906	18,506
*06268	Storrs (c)	(860)	10,996	15,344
*06602	Stratford	(203)	49,976	51,901
*06078	Suffield	(860)	13,552	15,747
06084	Tolland	(860)	13,146	15,031
*06790	Torrington	(860)	35,202	36,167
06611	Trumbull	(203)	34,243	36,376
06066	Vernon	(860)	28,063	29,139
*06492	Wallingford	(203)	43,026	45,062
06492	Wallingford Center (c)	(203)	17,509	18,209
*06702	Waterbury	(203)	107,271	110,189
*06385	Waterford	(860)	19,152	19,477
06795	Watertown	(860)	21,661	22,377
*06101	West Hartford	(860)	63,589	63,317
06516	West Haven	(203)	52,360	55,477
06883	Weston	(203)	10,037	10,281
*06880	Westport	(203)	25,749	26,656
*06101	Wethersfield	(860)	26,271	26,690
06226	Willimantic (c)	(860)	15,823	17,737
06897	Wilton	(203)	17,633	18,242
*06094	Winchester	(860)	10,664	11,175
*06280	Windham	(860)	22,857	25,214
*06095	Windsor	(860)	28,237	29,067
06096	Windsor Locks	(860)	12,043	12,507
*06716	Wolcott	(203)	15,215	16,652

Delaware (302)

ZIP	Place	2000 population	2011 estimate
19701	Bear (c)	17,593	19,371
19713	Brookside (c)	14,806	14,353
*19901	Dover	32,135	36,560
19702	Glasgow (c)	12,840	14,303
19707	Hockessin (c)	12,902	13,527
19709	Middletown	6,161	18,995
*19711	Newark	28,547	31,618
19808	Pike Creek Valley (c)	—	11,217
19977	Smyrna	5,679	10,180
*19899	Wilmington	72,664	71,305

District of Columbia (202)

ZIP	Place	2000 population	2011 estimate
*20090	Washington	572,059	617,996

Florida

Area code (321) overlays area code (407). Area code (754) overlays area code (954). Area code (786) overlays area code (305).

ZIP	Place	Area code	2000 population	2011 estimate
*32828	Alafaya (c)	(407)	—	78,113
*32714	Altamonte Springs	(407)	41,200	41,727
33572	Apollo Beach (c)	(813)	7,444	14,055
*32712	Apopka	(407)	26,642	42,467
*32233	Atlantic Beach	(904)	13,368	12,751
33823	Auburndale	(863)	11,032	13,675
*33160	Aventura	(305)	25,267	36,610
32807	Azalea Park (c)	(407)	11,073	12,556
*33830	Bartow	(863)	15,340	17,501
34667	Bayonet Point (c)	(727)	23,577	23,467
33507	Bayshore Gardens (c)	(941)	17,350	16,323
*33756	Bellair-Meadowbrook Terrace (c)	(904)	16,53	13,343
33430	Belle Glade	(561)	14,906	17,667
*34420	Belleview (c)	(352)	21,201	23,355
*33509	Bloomingdale (c)	(813)	19,839	22,711
*33431	Boca Raton	(561)	74,764	85,329
*34135	Bonita Springs	(239)	32,797	44,816
*33436	Boynton Beach	(561)	60,389	68,996
*34206	Bradenton	(941)	49,504	50,193
*33509	Brandon (c)	(813)	77,895	103,483
32503	Brent (c)	(850)	22,257	21,804
33142	Brownsville (c)	(305)	14,393	15,313
34743	Buenaventura Lakes (c)	(407)	—	26,079

ZIP	Place	Area code	2000 population	2011 estimate	ZIP	Place	Area code	2000 population	2011 estimate
32404	Callaway	(850)	14,233	14,493	33193	Kendall West (c)	(305)	38,034	36,154
*33920	Cape Coral	(239)	102,286	157,476	33149	Key Biscayne	(305)	10,507	12,637
*33618	Carrollwood (c)	(813)	—	33,365	33037	Key Largo (c)	(305)	11,886	10,433
*32707	Casselberry	(407)	22,629	26,387	*33040	Key West.	(305)	25,478	24,909
33558	Cheval (c)	(813)	7,602	10,702	33556	Keystone (c)	(813)	14,627	24,039
33624	Citrus Park (c)	(813)	20,226	24,252	*34744	Kissimmee	(407)	47,814	61,346
*33758	Clearwater	(727)	108,787	107,784	*32159	Lady Lake	(352)	11,828	14,111
*34711	Clermont.	(352)	9,333	29,126	34786	Lake Butler (c)	(407)	7,062	15,400
*32922	Cocoa	(321)	16,412	17,147	*32055	Lake City.	(386)	9,980	12,026
*32931	Cocoa Beach	(321)	12,482	11,235	33612	Lake Magdalene (c)	(813)	28,755	28,509
*33097	Coconut Creek	(954)	43,566	53,915	*32746	Lake Mary.	(407)	11,458	13,900
32809	Conway (c)	(407)	14,394	13,467	*33853	Lake Wales	(863)	10,194	14,399
*33328	Cooper City.	(954)	27,939	29,076	*33461	Lake Worth	(561)	35,133	35,306
*33114	Coral Gables.	(305)	42,249	47,783	*33804	Lakeland.	(863)	78,452	98,589
*33075	Coral Springs	(954)	117,549	123,338	33801	Lakeland Highlands (c).	(863)	12,557	11,056
33157	Coral Terrace (c)	(305)	24,380	24,376	32073	Lakeside (c)	(904)	30,927	30,943
33015	Country Club (c)	(305)	36,310	47,105	34951	Lakewood Park (c)	(772)	10,458	11,323
33196	Country Walk (c)	(305)	10,653	15,997	*34639	Land O'Lakes (c)	(813)	20,971	31,996
*32536	Crestview	(850)	14,766	21,284	*33465	Lantana	(561)	9,437	10,543
33189	Cutler Bay.	(305)	—	41,236	*33770	Largo	(727)	69,371	77,723
33919	Cypress Lake (c).	(239)	12,072	11,846	*33313	Lauderdale Lakes	(954)	31,705	33,191
*33004	Dania Beach	(954)	—	30,183	*33313	Lauderhill	(954)	57,585	68,117
*33329	Davie.	(954)	75,720	93,674	33714	Lealman (c).	(727)	—	19,879
*32114	Daytona Beach	(386)	64,112	61,028	*34748	Leesburg.	(352)	15,956	20,390
*32713	DeBary	(386)	15,559	19,324	*33936	Lehigh Acres (c)	(239)	33,430	86,784
*33441	Deerfield Beach	(954)	64,583	76,389	*33033	Leisure City (c)	(305)	22,152	22,655
*32720	DeLand	(386)	20,904	27,041	*33074	Lighthouse Point	(954)	10,767	10,536
*33444	Delray Beach	(561)	60,020	61,209	32810	Lockhart (c)	(407)	12,944	13,060
*32783	Deltona	(407)	69,543	85,219	*32750	Longwood	(407)	13,745	13,732
*32541	Destin	(850)	11,119	12,489	*33549	Lutz (c)	(813)	17,081	19,344
32836	Doctor Phillips (c)	(407)	9,548	10,981	32444	Lynn Haven.	(850)	12,451	18,607
*33178	Doral.	(305)	—	46,789	*32751	Maitland	(407)	12,019	16,076
*34698	Dunedin	(727)	35,691	35,354	33550	Mango (c)	(813)	8,842	11,313
33610	East Lake (c)	(813)	29,394	30,962	*34145	Marco Island	(239)	—	16,756
33619	East Lake-Orient Park (c) . .	(813)	5,703	22,753	*33093	Margate.	(954)	53,909	54,270
32583	East Milton (c).	(850)	—	11,074	32824	Meadow Woods (c).	(407)	11,286	25,558
*32132	Edgewater.	(386)	18,668	20,761	*32901	Melbourne	(321)	71,382	76,095
33614	Egypt Lake-Leto (c)	(813)	32,782	35,282	*32953	Merritt Island (c)	(321)	36,090	34,743
34680	Elfers (c)	(727)	13,161	13,986	*33101	Miami	(305)	362,470	408,750
*34295	Englewood (c)	(941)	16,196	14,863	*33152	Miami Beach.	(305)	87,933	89,840
32534	Ensley (c)	(850)	18,752	20,602	33023	Miami Gardens	(305)	—	109,680
*33928	Estero (c)	(239)	9,503	22,612	*33014	Miami Lakes	(305)	—	30,057
*32726	Eustis	(352)	15,106	18,805	33138	Miami Shores	(305)	10,380	10,720
32804	Fairview Shores (c).	(305)	13,898	10,239	*33266	Miami Springs.	(305)	13,712	14,129
*32034	Fernandina Beach	(904)	10,549	11,624	*32068	Middleburg (c).	(904)	10,338	13,008
32514	Ferry Pass (c)	(850)	27,176	28,921	32563	Midway (c)	(850)	—	16,115
33547	Fish Hawk (c)	(813)	1,991	14,087	*33023	Miramar	(954)	72,739	124,302
32003	Fleming Island (c).	(904)	—	27,126	*32757	Mount Dora.	(352)	9,418	12,534
*33034	Florida City.	(305)	7,843	11,511	32526	Myrtle Grove (c)	(850)	17,211	15,870
32960	Florida Ridge (c).	(772)	15,217	18,164	*34102	Naples	(239)	20,976	19,939
32714	Forest City (c).	(407)	12,612	13,854	32566	Navarre (c)	(850)	—	31,378
*33310	Fort Lauderdale	(954)	152,397	168,528	*34653	New Port Richey.	(727)	16,117	14,961
*33902	Fort Myers	(239)	48,208	63,512	34653	New Port Richey East (c) . . .	(727)	9,916	10,036
*34981	Fort Pierce	(772)	37,516	41,993	*32168	New Smyrna Beach	(386)	20,048	22,481
*32548	Fort Walton Beach	(850)	19,973	19,793	*32578	Niceville	(850)	11,684	12,941
33172	Fountainbleau (c)	(305)	59,549	59,764	*33918	North Fort Myers (c)	(239)	40,214	39,407
34747	Four Corners (c)	(863)	—	26,116	*33068	North Lauderdale	(954)	32,264	41,782
*32259	Fruit Cove (c)	(904)	16,077	29,362	*33261	North Miami	(305)	59,880	60,143
34232	Fruitville (c).	(941)	12,741	13,224	*33160	North Miami Beach	(305)	40,786	42,504
*32602	Gainesville	(352)	95,447	125,326	*33408	North Palm Beach	(561)	12,064	12,153
33534	Gibsonton (c)	(813)	8,752	14,234	*34287	North Port.	(941)	22,797	57,780
33138	Gladeview (c)	(954)	14,468	11,535	33624	Northdale (c).	(813)	—	22,079
33143	Glenvar Heights (c).	(305)	16,243	16,898	33860	Oak Ridge (c)	(407)	22,349	22,685
34116	Golden Gate (c)	(239)	20,951	23,961	*33307	Oakland Park	(305)	30,966	42,126
33055	Golden Glades (c)	(305)	32,623	33,145	32065	Oakleaf Plantation (c)	(904)	—	20,315
32733	Goldenrod (c)	(407)	12,871	12,039	*34478	Ocala	(352)	45,943	56,517
32560	Gonzalez (c)	(850)	11,365	13,273	34761	Ocoee.	(407)	24,391	36,320
33170	Goulds (c).	(305)	7,453	10,103	*33163	Ojus (c).	(305)	16,642	18,036
*33454	Greenacres.	(561)	27,569	38,009	34677	Oldsmar	(813)	11,910	13,618
33581	Gulf Gate Estates (c)	(941)	11,647	10,911	*33265	Olympia Heights (c)	(305)	13,452	13,488
*33737	Gulfport.	(727)	12,527	12,041	*33054	Opa-Locka	(305)	14,951	15,579
*33844	Haines City	(863)	13,174	20,807	*32763	Orange City	(386)	6,604	10,724
*33009	Hallandale Beach . . . (305)/(954)		—	37,800	*32802	Orlando.	(407)	185,951	243,195
*33010	Hialeah	(305)	226,419	229,969	*32174	Ormond Beach	(386)	36,301	38,153
*33016	Hialeah Gardens	(305)	19,297	22,257	*32765	Oviedo	(407)	26,316	33,528
33846	Highland City (c)	(863)	2,051	10,834	32571	Pace (c)	(850)	7,393	20,039
*33455	Hobe Sound (c)	(772)	11,376	11,521	*32177	Palatka	(386)	10,033	10,514
*34690	Holiday (c)	(727)	21,904	22,403	*32905	Palm Bay	(321)	79,413	103,227
*32125	Holly Hill	(386)	12,119	11,663	*33408	Palm Beach Gardens	(561)	35,058	49,010
*33022	Hollywood	(954)	139,357	143,357	*34990	Palm City (c)	(772)	20,097	23,120
*33030	Homestead.	(305)	31,909	61,940	*32135	Palm Coast	(386)	32,732	76,499
34447	Homosassa Springs (c) . .	(352)	12,458	13,791	*34683	Palm Harbor (c)	(727)	59,248	57,439
34787	Horizon West (c).	(352)	—	14,000	*33801	Palm River-Clair Mel (c) . . .	(813)	17,589	21,024
*34667	Hudson (c)	(727)	12,765	12,158	*33406	Palm Springs	(561)	11,699	19,195
32837	Hunters Creek (c)	(407)	9,369	14,321	32082	Palm Valley (c)	(904)	19,860	20,019
*34142	Immokalee (c).	(239)	19,763	24,154	*34221	Palmetto	(941)	12,571	12,774
33908	Iona (c)	(239)	11,756	15,369	33157	Palmetto Bay.	(305)	—	23,964
33162	Ives Estates (c)	(305)	17,586	19,525	33157	Palmetto Estates (c)	(305)	13,675	13,535
*32203	Jacksonville	(904)	735,617	827,908	*32401	Panama City	(850)	36,417	36,686
*32250	Jacksonville Beach	(904)	20,990	21,523	*32417	Panama City Beach	(850)	7,671	12,092
33568	Jasmine Estates (c)	(727)	18,213	18,989	*33067	Parkland	(954)	13,835	24,404
*34957	Jensen Beach (c)	(772)	11,100	11,707	*33029	Pembroke Pines	(954)	137,427	157,594
*33458	Jupiter.	(561)	39,328	55,911	*32502	Pensacola.	(850)	56,255	52,197
33478	Jupiter Farms (c).	(561)	—	11,994	*32809	Pine Castle (c)	(407)	8,803	10,805
33183	Kendale Lakes (c).	(305)	56,901	56,148	32858	Pine Hills (c)	(407)	41,764	60,076
*33256	Kendall (c)	(305)	75,226	75,371	33156	Pinecrest.	(305)	19,055	18,657

ZIP	Place	Area code	2000 population	2011 estimate
*33781	Pinellas Park	(727)	45,658	49,150
33168	Pinewood (c)	(305)	16,523	16,520
*33566	Plant City	(813)	29,915	35,817
*33318	Plantation	(954)	82,934	86,524
*34758	Poinciana (c)	(407)	13,647	53,193
*33060	Pompano Beach	(954)	78,191	101,617
*33952	Port Charlotte	(941)	46,451	54,392
*32129	Port Orange	(904)	45,823	56,529
32927	Port St. John (c)	(321)	12,112	12,267
*34981	Port St. Lucie	(772)	88,769	166,149
34992	Port Salerno (c)	(772)	10,141	10,091
*33032	Princeton (c)	(305)	10,090	22,038
*33950	Punta Gorda	(941)	14,344	16,697
33177	Richmond West (c)	(305)	28,082	31,973
*33569	Riverview (c)	(813)	12,035	71,050
*33419	Riviera Beach	(561)	29,884	32,861
*32955	Rockledge	(321)	20,170	24,935
*33411	Royal Palm Beach	(561)	21,523	34,533
*33570	Ruskin (c)	(813)	8,321	17,208
*34695	Safety Harbor	(727)	17,203	16,901
*32084	Saint Augustine	(904)	11,592	13,336
*34769	Saint Cloud	(407)	20,074	36,163
*33733	Saint Petersburg	(727)	248,232	244,997
33912	San Carlos Park (c)	(239)	16,317	16,824
*32771	Sanford	(407)	38,291	53,926
*34230	Sarasota	(941)	52,715	52,341
33577	Sarasota Springs (c)	(941)	15,875	14,395
32937	Satellite Beach	(321)	9,577	10,113
*32958	Sebastian	(772)	16,181	22,067
*33870	Sebring	(863)	9,667	10,474
*33770	Seminole	(813)	10,890	17,250
34610	Shady Hills (c)	(727)	7,798	11,523
33505	South Bradenton (c)	(941)	21,587	22,178
32121	South Daytona	(386)	13,177	12,258
*33243	South Miami	(305)	10,741	11,932
33157	South Miami Heights (c)	(305)	33,522	35,696
33595	South Venice (c)	(941)	13,539	13,949
32824	Southchase (c)	(407)	4,633	15,921
*34604	Spring Hill (c)	(352)	69,078	98,621
*34994	Stuart	(772)	14,633	15,718
*33573	Sun City Center (c)	(813)	—	19,258
33160	Sunny Isles Beach	(305)	—	21,327
*33325	Sunrise	(954)	85,779	85,995
*33283	Sunset (c)	(305)	17,150	16,389
33144	Sweetwater (c)	(305)	—	20,424
*32301	Tallahassee	(850)	150,624	182,965
*33320	Tamarac	(954)	55,588	61,542
33144	Tamiami (c)	(305)	54,788	55,271
*33601	Tampa	(813)	303,447	346,037
*34689	Tarpon Springs	(727)	21,003	23,507
32778	Tavares	(352)	9,700	14,133
*33687	Temple Terrace	(813)	20,918	25,314
33412	The Acreage (c)	(561)	—	38,704
33186	The Crossings (c)	(305)	23,557	22,758
33196	The Hammocks (c)	(305)	47,379	51,003
*32162	The Villages (c)	(352)	8,333	51,442
33592	Thonotosassa (c)	(813)	6,091	13,014
33186	Three Lakes (c)	(305)	6,955	15,047
*32780	Titusville	(321)	40,670	43,777
32615	Town 'n' Country (c)	(813)	72,523	78,442
34655	Trinity (c)	(813)	4,279	10,907
33613	University (c) (Hillsborough Co.)	(813)	—	41,163
32826	University (c) (Orange Co.)	(407)	—	31,084
33165	University Park (c)	(305)	26,538	26,995
32401	Upper Grand Lagoon (c)	(850)	10,889	13,963
*33594	Valrico (c)	(813)	6,582	35,545
*34285	Venice	(941)	17,764	20,897
*32960	Vero Beach	(772)	17,705	15,318
32960	Vero Beach South (c)	(772)	20,362	23,092
32955	Viera East (c)	(321)	—	10,757
33901	Villas (c)	(239)	11,346	11,569
32507	Warrington (c)	(850)	15,207	14,531
32779	Wekiwa Springs (c)	(407)	23,169	21,998
*33414	Wellington (c)	(561)	38,216	57,163
33714	West Lealman (c)	(727)	—	15,651
33138	West Little River (c)	(305)	32,498	34,699
*32912	West Melbourne	(321)	9,824	18,362
*33416	West Palm Beach	(561)	82,103	101,043
33023	West Park (c)	(954)	—	14,417
32505	West Pensacola (c)	(850)	21,939	21,339
33626	Westchase (c)	(813)	11,116	21,747
33165	Westchester (c)	(305)	30,271	29,862
*33326	Weston	(954)	49,286	66,544
33165	Westwood Lakes (c)	(305)	12,005	11,838
*33305	Wilton Manors	(954)	12,697	11,843
*34787	Winter Garden	(407)	14,351	35,287
*33880	Winter Haven	(863)	26,487	34,291
*32789	Winter Park	(407)	24,090	28,398
*32707	Winter Springs	(407)	31,666	33,468
32092	World Golf Village (c)	(904)	—	12,310
32547	Wright (c)	(850)	21,697	23,127
*32097	Yulee (c)	(904)	8,392	11,491
*33540	Zephyrhills	(813)	10,833	13,337

Georgia

Area codes (470) and (678) overlay area code (770). Area code (762) overlays area code (706).

ZIP	Place	Area code	2000 population	2011 estimate
*30101	Acworth	(770)	13,422	20,711
*31706	Albany	(229)	76,939	77,683
*30004	Alpharetta	(770)	34,854	59,397
*31709	Americus	(229)	17,013	16,809
*30603	Athens-Clarke County	(706)	100,266	116,084
*30301	Atlanta	(404)	416,474	432,427
*30903	Augusta-Richmond County	(706)	195,182	196,494
*39818	Bainbridge	(229)	11,722	12,629
30032	Belvedere Park (c)	(404)	18,945	15,152
*31520	Brunswick	(912)	15,600	15,525
*30518	Buford	(404)	10,668	12,525
*30701	Calhoun	(706)	10,667	15,773
30032	Candler-McAfee (c)	(404)	28,294	23,025
*30114	Canton	(770)	7,709	23,380
*30117	Carrollton	(770)	19,843	24,512
*30120	Cartersville	(770)	15,925	19,782
*30341	Chamblee	(770)	9,552	15,675
30337	College Park	(404)	20,382	14,360
*31908	Columbus	(706)	—	194,107
*30013	Conyers	(404)	10,689	15,292
*31015	Cordele	(229)	11,608	11,277
*30014	Covington	(770)	11,547	13,226
31805	Cusseta-Chattahoochee County	(706)	—	11,749
*30132	Dallas	(770)	5,056	11,638
*30720	Dalton	(706)	27,912	33,313
*30030	Decatur	(404)	18,147	19,555
*31533	Douglas	(912)	10,639	11,542
*30134	Douglasville	(404)	20,065	31,173
30333	Druid Hills (c)	(404)	12,741	14,568
*31021	Dublin	(478)	15,857	16,044
*30096	Duluth	(404)	22,122	27,258
*30338	Dunwoody	(770)	—	46,809
30364	East Point	(404)	39,595	34,784
30809	Evans (c)	(706)	17,727	29,011
30213	Fairburn	(770)	5,464	13,363
*30214	Fayetteville	(404)	11,148	16,124
*30297	Forest Park	(404)	21,447	18,616
*30501	Gainesville	(770)	25,578	34,422
31754	Georgetown (c)	(912)	10,599	11,823
*30223	Griffin	(770)	23,451	23,628
30813	Grovetown	(706)	6,089	11,589
*31313	Hinesville	(912)	30,392	34,519
*31546	Jesup	(912)	9,279	10,278
30097	Johns Creek	(770)	—	79,192
*30144	Kennesaw	(404)	21,675	30,196
31548	Kingsland	(912)	10,506	15,913
*30240	LaGrange	(706)	25,998	29,902
*30045	Lawrenceville	(404)	22,397	29,247
*30047	Lilburn	(404)	11,307	11,951
30122	Lithia Springs (c)	(770)	—	15,491
30052	Loganville	(770)	5,435	10,601
30126	Mableton (c)	(404)	29,733	37,115
*31201	Macon	(478)	97,255	91,856
*30060	Marietta	(404)	58,748	57,357
30907	Martinez (c)	(706)	27,749	35,795
30253	McDonough	(770)	8,493	22,446
*31061	Milledgeville	(478)	18,757	17,499
*30004	Milton	(770)	—	33,711
*30655	Monroe	(770)	11,407	13,359
*31768	Moultrie	(229)	14,387	14,160
30087	Mountain Park (c)	(404)	11,753	11,554
*30263	Newnan	(770)	16,242	33,725
30319	North Atlanta (c)	(404)	38,579	40,456
30033	North Decatur (c)	(404)	15,270	16,698
30033	North Druid Hills (c)	(404)	18,852	18,947
*30269	Peachtree City	(404)	31,580	34,757
31069	Perry	(478)	9,602	14,215
31322	Pooler	(912)	6,239	19,640
30127	Powder Springs	(404)	12,481	14,133
30074	Redan (c)	(404)	33,841	33,015
*30274	Riverdale	(404)	12,478	15,251
*30161	Rome	(706)	34,980	36,181
*30077	Roswell	(404)	79,334	91,168
31558	Saint Marys	(912)	13,761	17,099
31522	Saint Simons (c)	(912)	13,381	12,743
30358	Sandy Springs	(404)	—	96,856
*31402	Savannah	(912)	131,510	139,491
30079	Scottdale (c)	(404)	9,803	10,631
*30080	Smyrna	(404)	40,999	51,982
*30078	Snellville	(404)	15,351	18,686
*30458	Statesboro	(912)	22,698	29,399
30281	Stockbridge	(404)	9,853	26,071
30518	Sugar Hill	(404)	11,399	18,980
30024	Suwanee	(770)	8,725	15,734
*31792	Thomasville	(229)	18,162	18,407
*31794	Tifton	(229)	15,060	16,869
*30084	Tucker (c)	(404)	26,532	27,581
30291	Union City	(404)	11,621	20,079
*31603	Valdosta	(229)	43,724	56,019
*30474	Vidalia	(912)	10,491	10,551
30180	Villa Rica	(770)	4,134	14,047

ZIP	Place	Area code	2000 population	2011 estimate
*31088	Warner Robins	(478)	48,804	68,500
*31501	Waycross	(912)	15,333	14,718
31410	Wilmington Island (c)	(912)	14,213	15,138
30680	Winder	(770)	10,201	14,209
*30188	Woodstock	(770)	10,050	24,346

Hawaii (808)

ZIP	Place	2000 population	2011 estimate
96821	East Honolulu (c)	—	49,914
96706	Ewa Beach (c)	14,650	14,955
96706	Ewa Gentry (c)	4,939	22,690
96701	Halawa (c)	13,891	14,014
96749	Hawaiian Paradise Park (c)	7,051	11,404
*96720	Hilo (c)	40,759	43,263
*96820	Honolulu, urban (c).	371,657	340,936[1]
*96732	Kahului (c)	20,146	26,337
96740	Kailua (c) (Hawaii Co.)	9,870	11,975
96734	Kailua (c) (Honolulu Co.)	36,513	38,635
96744	Kaneohe (c)	34,970	34,597
96746	Kapaa (c)	9,472	10,699
*96707	Kapolei (c)	—	15,186
96753	Kihei (c)	16,749	20,881
96706	Makakilo (c)	13,156	18,248
96789	Mililani Mauka (c)	—	21,039
96789	Mililani Town (c)	28,608	27,629
96792	Nanakuli (c)	10,814	12,666
96782	Pearl City (c).	30,976	47,698
96797	Royal Kunia (c)	—	14,525
96857	Schofield Barracks (c).	14,428	16,370
*96786	Wahiawa (c)	16,151	17,821
96792	Waianae (c)	10,506	13,177
96793	Wailuku (c)	12,296	15,313
96701	Waimalu (c).	29,371	13,730
96797	Waipahu (c)	33,108	38,216
96797	Waipio (c)	11,672	11,674

(1) 2011 estimate for Urban Honolulu, a census-designated place. All other CDP populations are from the 2010 decennial census.

Idaho (208)

ZIP	Place	2000 population	2011 estimate
*83401	Ammon	6,187	14,019
83221	Blackfoot.	10,419	11,987
*83707	Boise.	185,787	210,145
83318	Burley	9,316	10,447
*83605	Caldwell	25,967	46,905
83202	Chubbuck	9,700	14,067
*83814	Coeur d'Alene.	34,514	44,962
83616	Eagle	11,085	20,347
*83714	Garden City	10,624	11,217
83835	Hayden	9,159	13,550
*83402	Idaho Falls	50,730	57,646
83338	Jerome	7,780	11,040
*83634	Kuna	5,382	15,548
83501	Lewiston	30,904	32,119
*83642	Meridian	34,919	76,750
*83843	Moscow	21,291	24,080
*83647	Mountain Home	11,143	13,841
*83653	Nampa	51,867	82,755
*83201	Pocatello.	51,466	54,810
*83854	Post Falls	17,247	28,104
*83440	Rexburg	17,257	25,705
*83301	Twin Falls	34,469	44,564

Illinois

Area code (224) overlays area code (847). Area code (331) overlays area code (630). Area code (779) overlays area code (815). Area code (872) overlays area code (312).

ZIP	Place	Area code	2000 population	2011 estimate
60101	Addison.	(630)	35,914	37,198
*60102	Algonquin	(847)	23,276	30,145
60803	Alsip	(708)	19,725	19,362
62002	Alton	(618)	30,496	27,781
60002	Antioch	(847)	8,788	14,488
*60005	Arlington Heights	(847)	76,031	75,428
*60505	Aurora	(630)	142,990	199,672
*60010	Barrington.	(847)	10,168	10,371
*60103	Bartlett.	(630)	36,706	41,458
*60510	Batavia	(630)	23,866	26,298
*60083	Beach Park	(847)	10,072	13,695
*62220	Belleville	(618)	41,410	44,515
60104	Bellwood.	(708)	20,535	19,156
61008	Belvidere	(815)	20,820	25,680
*60106	Bensenville	(630)	20,703	18,478
60402	Berwyn	(708)	54,016	56,906
*60108	Bloomingdale	(630)	21,675	22,167
*61701	Bloomington	(309)	64,808	77,071
*60406	Blue Island	(708)	23,463	23,809
*60440	Bolingbrook.	(630)	56,321	73,802
60914	Bourbonnais	(815)	15,256	18,669
60915	Bradley	(815)	12,784	15,932

ZIP	Place	Area code	2000 population	2011 estimate
60455	Bridgeview	(708)	15,335	16,519
60513	Brookfield	(708)	19,085	19,061
60089	Buffalo Grove	(847)	42,909	41,668
60459	Burbank	(708)	27,902	29,051
60527	Burr Ridge	(630)	10,408	10,624
62206	Cahokia	(618)	16,391	15,251
60409	Calumet City.	(708)	39,071	37,204
*60119	Campton Hills . . . . (630)/(847)		—	11,239
61520	Canton	(309)	15,288	14,666
*62901	Carbondale.	(618)	20,681	25,960
*60188	Carol Stream.	(630)	40,438	39,989
60110	Carpentersville	(847)	30,586	38,062
60013	Cary	(847)	15,531	18,281
62801	Centralia	(618)	14,136	13,021
*61821	Champaign	(217)	67,518	81,291
60410	Channahon.	(815)	7,344	12,619
61920	Charleston	(217)	21,039	21,852
62629	Chatham.	(217)	8,583	11,614
*60607	Chicago . . . . (312)/(773)		2,896,016	2,707,120
*60411	Chicago Heights	(708)	32,776	30,408
60415	Chicago Ridge	(708)	14,127	14,366
60804	Cicero	(708)	85,616	84,261
62234	Collinsville.	(618)	24,707	25,513
60478	Country Club Hills	(708)	16,169	16,615
60435	Crest Hill	(815)	13,329	20,943
60445	Crestwood	(708)	11,251	10,997
*60014	Crystal Lake	(815)	38,000	40,766
*61832	Danville	(217)	33,904	32,982
*60561	Darien.	(630)	22,860	22,241
*62525	Decatur.	(217)	81,860	76,096
60015	Deerfield	(847)	18,420	18,296
60115	DeKalb	(815)	39,018	43,702
*60018	Des Plaines	(847)	58,720	58,617
61021	Dixon	(815)	15,941	15,511
60419	Dolton	(708)	25,614	23,253
*60515	Downers Grove.	(630)	48,724	48,163
61244	East Moline.	(309)	20,333	21,303
*61611	East Peoria	(309)	22,638	23,448
*62201	East St. Louis	(618)	31,542	27,027
*62025	Edwardsville	(618)	21,491	24,220
62401	Effingham	(217)	12,384	12,339
*60120	Elgin	(847)	94,487	109,104
*60009	Elk Grove Village	(847)	34,727	33,272
60126	Elmhurst	(630)	42,762	44,439
60707	Elmwood Park	(708)	25,405	24,993
*60201	Evanston.	(847)	74,239	74,785
60805	Evergreen Park	(708)	20,821	19,940
*62208	Fairview Heights	(618)	15,034	17,091
*60130	Forest Park	(708)	15,688	14,228
60020	Fox Lake	(847)	9,178	10,620
60423	Frankfort	(815)	10,391	17,886
*60131	Franklin Park	(847)	19,434	18,415
61032	Freeport	(815)	26,443	25,559
60030	Gages Lake (c)	(847)	10,415	10,198
*61401	Galesburg.	(309)	33,706	32,193
60134	Geneva.	(630)	19,515	21,707
62034	Glen Carbon	(618)	10,425	12,893
*60137	Glen Ellyn	(630)	26,999	27,648
*60139	Glendale Heights	(630)	31,765	34,445
*60025	Glenview	(847)	41,847	44,888
62035	Godfrey.	(618)	16,286	17,952
62040	Granite City.	(618)	31,301	29,758
60030	Grayslake	(847)	18,506	21,042
60031	Gurnee	(847)	28,834	31,424
60133	Hanover Park	(630)	38,278	38,187
*60426	Harvey	(708)	30,000	25,392
60429	Hazel Crest.	(708)	14,816	14,162
62948	Herrin	(618)	11,298	12,570
*60457	Hickory Hills	(708)	13,926	14,108
*60035	Highland Park	(847)	31,365	29,882
*60521	Hinsdale	(630)	17,349	16,923
*60195	Hoffman Estates	(847)	49,495	52,124
*60491	Homer Glen	(708)	—	24,365
*60430	Homewood	(708)	19,543	19,406
60142	Huntley	(847)	5,730	24,358
*62650	Jacksonville	(217)	18,940	19,445
*60436	Joliet.	(815)	106,221	148,402
60458	Justice	(708)	12,193	12,982
60901	Kankakee	(815)	27,491	27,596
61443	Kewanee	(309)	12,944	12,876
60525	La Grange.	(708)	15,608	15,617
60526	La Grange Park	(708)	13,295	13,636
60045	Lake Forest	(847)	20,059	19,448
*60102	Lake in the Hills	(847)	23,152	28,980
*60047	Lake Zurich	(847)	18,104	19,709
60438	Lansing	(708)	28,332	28,458
*60439	Lemont	(630)	13,098	16,076
*60048	Libertyville	(847)	20,742	20,395
62656	Lincoln	(217)	15,369	14,419
*60645	Lincolnwood	(847)	12,359	12,646
60046	Lindenhurst	(847)	12,539	14,522
60532	Lisle	(630)	21,182	22,539
*60441	Lockport	(815)	15,191	24,987
60148	Lombard	(630)	42,322	43,462
*61130	Loves Park	(815)	20,044	23,904
60534	Lyons	(708)	10,255	10,775
*61115	Machesney Park	(815)	20,759	23,392

ZIP	Place	Area code	2000 population	2011 estimate
61455	Macomb	(309)	18,558	19,280
62959	Marion	(618)	16,035	17,260
*60426	Markham	(708)	12,620	12,562
*60443	Matteson	(708)	12,928	19,093
61938	Mattoon	(217)	18,291	18,570
*60153	Maywood	(708)	26,987	24,196
*60050	McHenry	(815)	21,501	27,010
*60160	Melrose Park	(708)	23,171	25,524
60445	Midlothian	(708)	14,315	14,884
60447	Minooka	(815)	3,971	10,958
60448	Mokena	(708)	14,583	18,854
*61265	Moline	(309)	43,768	43,489
60538	Montgomery	(630)	5,471	18,688
60450	Morris	(815)	11,928	13,654
61550	Morton	(309)	15,198	16,300
60053	Morton Grove	(847)	22,451	23,373
60056	Mount Prospect	(847)	56,265	54,403
62864	Mount Vernon	(618)	16,269	15,236
60060	Mundelein	(847)	30,935	31,186
*60540	Naperville	(630)	128,358	142,773
60451	New Lenox	(815)	17,771	24,538
60714	Niles	(847)	30,068	29,931
*61761	Normal	(309)	45,386	52,772
*60634	Norridge	(708)	14,582	14,635
60542	North Aurora	(630)	10,585	16,922
*60064	North Chicago	(847)	35,918	32,682
*60062	Northbrook	(708)	33,435	33,311
60164	Northlake	(708)	11,878	12,375
62269	O'Fallon	(618)	21,910	28,359
60452	Oak Forest	(708)	28,051	28,084
*60303	Oak Lawn	(708)	55,245	56,937
*60303	Oak Park	(708)	52,524	52,104
*60462	Orland Park	(708)	51,077	57,016
60543	Oswego	(630)	13,326	30,856
61350	Ottawa	(815)	18,307	18,699
*60067	Palatine	(847)	65,479	68,858
60463	Palos Heights	(708)	11,260	12,567
60465	Palos Hills	(708)	17,665	17,561
60466	Park Forest	(708)	23,462	22,075
60068	Park Ridge	(847)	37,775	37,642
*61554	Pekin	(309)	33,857	34,160
*61601	Peoria	(309)	112,936	115,234
61354	Peru	(815)	9,835	10,257
*60544	Plainfield	(815)	13,038	39,840
60545	Plano	(630)	5,633	11,035
61764	Pontiac	(815)	11,864	11,911
60070	Prospect Heights	(847)	17,081	16,327
*62301	Quincy	(217)	40,366	40,665
61866	Rantoul	(217)	12,857	12,984
60471	Richton Park	(708)	12,533	13,705
60305	River Forest	(708)	11,635	11,219
60171	River Grove	(708)	10,668	10,272
60827	Riverdale	(708)	15,055	13,609
*61201	Rock Island	(309)	39,684	39,020
*61125	Rockford	(815)	150,115	152,222
60008	Rolling Meadows	(847)	24,604	24,205
*60446	Romeoville	(815)	21,153	39,912
61073	Roscoe	(815)	6,244	10,738
60172	Roselle	(630)	23,115	22,912
60073	Round Lake	(847)	5,842	18,365
60073	Round Lake Beach	(847)	25,859	28,289
*60174	Saint Charles	(630)	27,896	33,286
60411	Sauk Village	(708)	10,411	10,553
*60194	Schaumburg	(847)	75,386	74,550
*60176	Schiller Park	(847)	11,850	11,844
*62269	Shiloh	(618)	7,643	12,693
*60436	Shorewood	(815)	7,686	15,708
*60077	Skokie	(847)	63,348	65,066
60177	South Elgin	(847)	16,100	22,198
60473	South Holland	(708)	22,147	22,123
*62703	Springfield	(217)	111,454	117,076
61081	Sterling	(815)	15,451	15,410
60107	Streamwood	(630)	36,407	40,031
61364	Streator	(815)	14,190	13,659
60501	Summit	(708)	10,637	11,104
*62221	Swansea	(618)	10,579	13,440
60178	Sycamore	(815)	12,020	17,446
62568	Taylorville	(217)	11,427	11,268
60477	Tinley Park	(708)	48,401	56,965
*61801	Urbana	(217)	36,395	41,518
60061	Vernon Hills	(847)	20,120	25,211
60181	Villa Park	(630)	22,075	22,057
60555	Warrenville	(630)	13,363	13,232
61571	Washington	(309)	10,841	15,165
60084	Wauconda	(847)	9,448	13,656
*60085	Waukegan	(847)	87,901	89,426
*60185	West Chicago	(630)	23,469	27,273
60154	Westchester	(708)	16,824	16,790
60558	Western Springs	(708)	12,493	13,033
60559	Westmont	(630)	24,554	24,855
*60187	Wheaton	(630)	55,416	53,238
60090	Wheeling	(847)	34,496	37,812
60091	Wilmette	(847)	27,651	27,206
60093	Winnetka	(847)	12,419	12,241
*60191	Wood Dale	(630)	13,535	13,865
62095	Wood River	(618)	11,296	10,625
60517	Woodridge	(630)	30,934	33,200
60098	Woodstock	(815)	20,151	24,785
60482	Worth	(708)	11,047	10,835
60560	Yorkville	(630)	6,189	17,198
60099	Zion	(847)	22,866	24,508

Indiana

ZIP	Place	Area code	2000 population	2011 estimate
*46011	Anderson	(765)	59,734	55,957
46706	Auburn	(260)	12,074	12,802
46123	Avon	(317)	6,248	12,667
47421	Bedford	(812)	13,768	13,424
46107	Beech Grove	(317)	14,880	14,319
*47408	Bloomington	(812)	69,291	81,381
46112	Brownsburg	(317)	14,520	21,661
*46032	Carmel	(317)	37,733	81,564
46303	Cedar Lake	(219)	9,279	11,549
46304	Chesterton	(219)	10,488	13,163
*47129	Clarksville	(812)	21,400	21,988
*47201	Columbus	(812)	39,059	44,677
47331	Connersville	(765)	15,411	13,487
*47933	Crawfordsville	(765)	15,243	16,042
*46307	Crown Point	(219)	19,806	27,803
*46311	Dyer	(219)	13,895	16,376
46312	East Chicago	(219)	32,414	29,671
*46515	Elkhart	(574)	51,874	51,320
*47708	Evansville	(812)	121,582	117,825
*46038	Fishers	(317)	37,835	79,127
*46802	Fort Wayne	(260)	205,727	255,824
*46041	Frankfort	(765)	16,662	16,365
46131	Franklin	(317)	19,463	24,040
*46401	Gary	(219)	102,746	80,221
*46526	Goshen	(574)	29,383	31,934
46530	Granger (c)	(574)	28,284	30,465
46135	Greencastle	(765)	9,880	10,316
46140	Greenfield	(317)	14,600	20,754
47240	Greensburg	(812)	10,260	11,581
*46142	Greenwood	(317)	36,037	51,584
46319	Griffith	(219)	17,334	16,877
*46320	Hammond	(219)	83,048	80,757
*46322	Highland	(219)	23,546	23,705
46342	Hobart	(219)	25,363	29,031
46750	Huntington	(260)	17,450	17,431
*46206	Indianapolis	(317)	781,870	827,609
*47546	Jasper	(812)	12,100	15,146
*47130	Jeffersonville	(812)	27,362	45,497
*46902	Kokomo	(765)	46,113	45,494
*46350	La Porte	(219)	21,621	22,033
*47901	Lafayette	(765)	56,397	67,947
46405	Lake Station	(219)	13,948	12,560
46226	Lawrence	(317)	38,915	46,408
46052	Lebanon	(765)	14,222	16,022
*46947	Logansport	(574)	19,684	18,330
47250	Madison	(812)	12,004	11,902
*46952	Marion	(765)	31,320	29,838
46151	Martinsville	(765)	11,698	11,923
*46401	Merrillville	(219)	30,560	35,215
*46360	Michigan City	(219)	32,900	31,452
*46544	Mishawaka	(574)	46,557	48,212
*47302	Muncie	(765)	67,430	70,080
46321	Munster	(219)	21,511	23,583
*47150	New Albany	(812)	37,603	36,570
47362	New Castle	(765)	17,780	18,038
46774	New Haven	(260)	12,406	14,921
*46060	Noblesville	(317)	28,590	53,515
*46970	Peru	(765)	12,994	11,320
46168	Plainfield	(317)	18,396	28,076
46563	Plymouth	(574)	9,840	10,032
46368	Portage	(219)	33,496	37,097
47907	Purdue University (c)	(765)	—	12,183
*47374	Richmond	(765)	39,124	36,670
46373	Saint John	(219)	8,382	14,839
46375	Schererville	(219)	24,851	29,215
47274	Seymour	(812)	18,101	18,283
46176	Shelbyville	(765)	17,951	19,149
*46624	South Bend	(574)	107,789	101,081
46224	Speedway	(317)	12,881	11,917
*47808	Terre Haute	(812)	59,614	60,961
*46383	Valparaiso	(219)	27,428	31,942
47591	Vincennes	(812)	18,701	18,449
46992	Wabash	(260)	11,743	10,573
*46580	Warsaw	(574)	12,415	13,557
47501	Washington	(812)	11,380	11,612
*46580	West Lafayette	(765)	28,778	29,921
46074	Westfield	(317)	9,293	30,971
46077	Zionsville	(317)	8,775	23,668

Iowa

ZIP	Place	Area code	2000 population	2011 estimate
50009	Altoona	(515)	10,345	14,773
*50010	Ames	(515)	50,731	59,042
*50021	Ankeny	(515)	27,117	46,302
52722	Bettendorf	(563)	31,275	33,599
*50036	Boone	(515)	12,803	12,635

ZIP	Place	Area code	2000 population	2011 estimate
52601	Burlington	(319)	26,839	25,564
51401	Carroll	(712)	10,106	10,126
*50613	Cedar Falls	(319)	36,145	39,387
*52401	Cedar Rapids	(319)	120,758	127,905
*52732	Clinton	(563)	27,772	26,830
50325	Clive	(515)	12,855	15,858
52241	Coralville	(319)	15,123	19,219
*51501	Council Bluffs	(712)	58,268	62,466
*52802	Davenport	(563)	98,359	100,802
*50318	Des Moines	(515)	198,682	206,599
*52001	Dubuque	(563)	57,686	58,234
50501	Fort Dodge	(515)	25,136	24,981
52627	Fort Madison	(319)	10,715	10,980
50125	Indianola	(515)	12,998	14,932
*52240	Iowa City	(319)	62,220	68,947
50131	Johnston	(515)	8,649	17,552
52632	Keokuk	(319)	11,427	10,706
52302	Marion	(319)	26,294	35,212
50158	Marshalltown	(641)	26,009	27,775
*50401	Mason City	(641)	29,172	27,944
52761	Muscatine	(563)	22,697	22,924
50208	Newton	(641)	15,579	15,130
52317	North Liberty	(319)	5,367	13,608
52577	Oskaloosa	(641)	10,938	11,538
52501	Ottumwa	(641)	24,998	24,881
50219	Pella	(641)	9,832	10,360
*51101	Sioux City	(712)	85,013	82,967
51301	Spencer	(712)	11,317	11,181
50588	Storm Lake	(712)	10,076	10,674
*50322	Urbandale	(515)	29,072	40,311
*50701	Waterloo	(319)	68,747	68,653
50263	Waukee	(515)	5,126	14,484
*50265	West Des Moines	(515)	46,403	57,909

Kansas

ZIP	Place	Area code	2000 population	2011 estimate
67002	Andover	(316)	6,698	11,779
67005	Arkansas City	(620)	11,963	12,401
66002	Atchison	(913)	10,232	10,943
67337	Coffeyville	(620)	11,021	10,137
67037	Derby	(316)	17,807	22,279
*67801	Dodge City	(620)	25,176	27,921
67042	El Dorado	(316)	12,057	13,008
66801	Emporia	(620)	26,760	24,971
*67846	Garden City	(620)	28,451	26,880
*66030	Gardner	(913)	9,396	19,433
67530	Great Bend	(620)	15,345	16,092
*67601	Hays	(785)	20,013	20,717
67060	Haysville	(316)	8,502	10,883
*67501	Hutchinson	(620)	40,787	42,142
*66441	Junction City	(785)	18,886	24,015
*66102	Kansas City	(913)	146,866	146,453
66043	Lansing	(913)	9,199	11,385
*66044	Lawrence	(785)	80,098	88,727
*66048	Leavenworth	(913)	35,420	35,675
*66209	Leawood	(913)	27,656	32,389
*66214	Lenexa	(913)	40,238	48,972
*67901	Liberal	(620)	19,666	20,861
*66502	Manhattan	(785)	44,831	53,678
67460	McPherson	(620)	13,770	13,182
*66202	Merriam	(913)	11,008	11,180
*67114	Newton	(316)	17,190	19,230
*66061	Olathe	(913)	92,962	127,907
66067	Ottawa	(785)	11,921	12,620
*66204	Overland Park	(913)	149,080	176,185
67357	Parsons	(620)	11,514	10,454
*66762	Pittsburg	(620)	19,243	20,276
*66208	Prairie Village	(913)	22,072	21,795
*67401	Salina	(785)	45,679	47,910
*66203	Shawnee	(913)	47,996	63,219
*66601	Topeka	(785)	122,377	128,188
*67202	Wichita	(316)	344,284	384,445
67156	Winfield	(620)	12,206	12,288

Kentucky

ZIP	Place	Area code	2000 population	2011 estimate
*41101	Ashland	(606)	21,981	21,652
40004	Bardstown	(502)	10,374	11,839
*40403	Berea	(859)	9,851	13,763
42101	Bowling Green	(270)	49,296	58,894
41005	Burlington (c)	(859)	10,779	15,926
41011	Covington	(859)	43,370	40,811
40422	Danville	(859)	15,477	16,273
*42701	Elizabethtown	(270)	22,542	29,044
41018	Erlanger	(859)	16,676	18,161
*41042	Florence	(859)	23,551	30,687
42223	Fort Campbell North (c)	(270)	14,338	13,685
40121	Fort Knox (c)	(270)	12,377	10,124
41075	Fort Thomas	(859)	16,495	16,436
*40601	Frankfort	(502)	27,741	25,583
40324	Georgetown	(502)	18,080	29,690
*42141	Glasgow	(270)	13,019	14,059
*42420	Henderson	(270)	27,373	28,853

ZIP	Place	Area code	2000 population	2011 estimate
*42240	Hopkinsville	(270)	30,089	31,419
41051	Independence	(859)	14,982	24,864
*40269	Jeffersontown	(502)	26,633	26,806
*40342	Lawrenceburg	(502)	9,014	10,615
*40507	Lexington-Fayette	(859)	260,512	301,569
*40232	Louisville-Jefferson Co. (balance)	(502)	(1)	602,011
*40252	Lyndon	(502)	9,369	11,088
42431	Madisonville	(270)	19,307	19,587
42066	Mayfield	(270)	10,349	10,129
40965	Middlesborough	(606)	10,384	10,332
42071	Murray	(270)	14,950	17,893
*41071	Newport	(859)	17,048	15,373
*40356	Nicholasville	(859)	19,680	28,294
*42301	Owensboro	(270)	54,067	57,605
*42003	Paducah	(270)	26,307	25,135
*40160	Radcliff	(502)	21,961	22,092
*40475	Richmond	(859)	27,152	31,809
*40207	Saint Matthews	(502)	15,852	17,606
*40066	Shelbyville	(502)	10,085	14,389
40165	Shepherdsville	(502)	8,334	11,343
40256	Shively	(502)	15,157	15,383
*42501	Somerset	(606)	11,352	11,296
*40391	Winchester	(859)	16,724	18,328

(1) Louisville merged with Jefferson County in 2003.

Louisiana

ZIP	Place	Area code	2000 population	2011 estimate
*70510	Abbeville	(337)	11,887	12,316
*71301	Alexandria	(318)	46,342	48,164
70714	Baker	(225)	13,793	13,935
71220	Bastrop	(318)	12,988	11,214
*70821	Baton Rouge	(225)	227,818	230,139
70360	Bayou Blue (c)	(985)	—	12,352
*70364	Bayou Cane (c)	(985)	17,046	19,355
*70037	Belle Chase (c)	(504)	9,848	12,679
*70427	Bogalusa	(985)	13,365	12,224
*71111	Bossier City	(318)	56,461	62,745
70818	Central	(225)	—	26,946
*70043	Chalmette (c)	(504)	32,069	16,751
70433	Claiborne (c)	(985)	9,830	11,507
*70526	Crowley	(337)	14,225	13,309
*70726	Denham Springs	(225)	8,757	10,390
70634	DeRidder	(337)	9,808	10,711
70047	Destrehan (c)	(985)	11,260	11,535
70072	Estelle (c)	(504)	15,880	16,377
70535	Eunice	(337)	11,499	10,419
*70810	Gardere (c)	(225)	8,992	10,580
*70053	Gretna	(504)	17,423	17,739
*70401	Hammond	(985)	17,639	20,235
*70058	Harvey (c)	(504)	22,226	20,348
*70360	Houma	(985)	32,393	33,745
70121	Jefferson (c)	(504)	11,843	11,193
70546	Jennings	(337)	10,986	10,415
*70062	Kenner	(504)	70,517	66,715
*70501	Lafayette	(337)	110,257	122,130
*70601	Lake Charles	(337)	71,757	72,475
*70068	Laplace (c)	(985)	27,684	29,872
70070	Luling (c)	(985)	11,512	12,119
*70471	Mandeville	(985)	10,489	11,708
*70072	Marrero (c)	(504)	36,165	33,141
*70009	Metairie (c)	(504)	146,136	138,481
*71055	Minden	(318)	13,027	13,106
*71207	Monroe	(318)	53,107	49,183
*70380	Morgan City	(985)	12,703	12,303
70611	Moss Bluff (c)	(337)	10,535	11,557
*71457	Natchitoches	(318)	17,865	18,270
*70560	New Iberia	(337)	32,623	30,683
*70140	New Orleans	(504)	484,674	360,740
*70570	Opelousas	(337)	22,860	16,668
*71360	Pineville	(318)	13,829	14,634
70394	Raceland (c)	(985)	10,224	10,193
70123	River Ridge (c)	(504)	14,588	13,494
*71270	Ruston	(318)	20,546	21,916
70817	Shenandoah (c)	(318)	17,070	18,399
*71102	Shreveport	(318)	200,145	200,975
*70458	Slidell	(985)	25,695	27,419
*70663	Sulphur	(337)	20,512	20,549
70056	Terrytown (c)	(504)	25,430	23,319
*70301	Thibodaux	(985)	14,431	14,615
70056	Timberlane (c)	(504)	11,405	10,243
70094	Waggaman (c)	(504)	9,435	10,015
*71291	West Monroe	(318)	13,250	13,172
*70058	Woodmere (c)	(504)	13,058	12,080
*70791	Zachary	(225)	11,275	15,003

Maine (207)

See introductory note.

ZIP	Place	2000 population	2011 estimate
*04210	Auburn	23,203	22,985
*04330	Augusta	18,560	19,103
*04401	Bangor	31,473	33,011
*04005	Biddeford	20,942	21,386
04011	Brunswick	21,172	20,328

ZIP	Place	2000 population	2011 estimate
04011	Brunswick (c)	14,816	15,175
04105	Falmouth	10,310	11,213
04038	Gorham	14,141	16,420
04043	Kennebunk	10,476	10,856
*04240	Lewiston	35,690	36,491
*04473	Orono	9,112	10,356
*04101	Portland	64,249	66,363
04072	Saco	16,822	18,581
04073	Sanford	20,806	20,909
*04074	Scarborough	16,970	18,968
*04106	South Portland	23,324	25,068
*04901	Waterville	15,605	15,697
*04092	Westbrook	16,142	17,540
*04062	Windham	14,904	17,041
03909	York	12,854	12,598

Maryland

Area code (240) overlays area code (301). Area codes (443) and (667) overlay area code (410).

ZIP	Place	Area code	2000 population	2011 estimate
21001	Aberdeen	(410)	13,842	15,063
20607	Accokeek (c)	(301)	7,349	10,573
*20783	Adelphi (c)	(301)	14,998	15,086
*21401	Annapolis	(410)	35,838	38,880
21403	Annapolis Neck (c)	(410)	—	10,950
21227	Arbutus (c)	(410)	20,116	20,483
*21012	Arnold (c)	(410)	23,422	23,106
*20916	Aspen Hill (c)	(301)	50,228	48,759
21220	Ballenger Creek (c)	(410)	13,518	18,274
*21203	Baltimore	(410)	651,154	619,493
*21014	Bel Air	(410)	10,080	10,187
21050	Bel Air North (c)	(410)	25,798	30,568
21014	Bel Air South (c)	(410)	39,711	47,709
*20705	Beltsville (c)	(301)	15,690	16,772
20603	Bennsville (c)	(301)	7,325	11,923
*20814	Bethesda (c)	(301)	55,277	60,858
*20715	Bowie	(301)	50,269	55,232
21225	Brooklyn Park (c)	(410)	10,938	14,373
20705	Calverton (c)	(301)	12,610	17,724
21613	Cambridge	(410)	10,911	12,335
*20748	Camp Springs (c)	(301)	17,968	19,096
21234	Carney (c)	(410)	28,264	29,941
*21228	Catonsville (c)	(410)	39,820	41,567
20657	Chesapeake Ranch Estates (c)	(301)	—	10,519
20782	Chillum (c)	(301)	34,252	33,513
20735	Clinton (c)	(301)	26,064	35,970
20904	Cloverly (c)	(301)	7,835	15,126
21030	Cockeysville (c)	(410)	19,388	20,776
*20914	Colesville (c)	(301)	19,810	14,647
*20740	College Park	(301)	24,657	30,587
*21045	Columbia (c)	(410)	88,254	99,615
21114	Crofton (c)	(410)	20,091	27,348
*21502	Cumberland	(301)	21,518	20,739
20872	Damascus (c)	(301)	11,430	15,257
21222	Dundalk (c)	(410)	62,306	63,597
20737	East Riverdale (c)	(301)	14,961	15,509
*21601	Easton	(410)	11,708	16,047
21040	Edgewood (c)	(410)	23,378	25,562
21784	Eldersburg (c)	(410)	27,741	30,531
21075	Elkridge (c)	(410)	22,042	15,593
*21921	Elkton (c)	(410)	11,893	15,531
*21043	Ellicott City (c)	(410)	56,397	65,834
21221	Essex (c)	(410)	39,078	39,262
20904	Fairland (c)	(301)	21,738	23,681
21061	Ferndale (c)	(410)	16,056	16,746
*20747	Forestville (c)	(301)	12,707	12,353
*20744	Fort Washington (c)	(301)	23,845	23,717
*21701	Frederick	(301)	52,767	66,169
*20877	Gaithersburg	(301)	52,613	61,045
*20874	Germantown (c)	(301)	55,419	86,395
20745	Glassmanor (c)	(301)	—	17,295
*21061	Glen Burnie (c)	(410)	38,922	67,639
20906	Glenmont (c)	(301)	—	13,529
20769	Glenn Dale (c)	(301)	12,609	13,466
*20770	Greenbelt (c)	(301)	21,456	23,281
*21740	Hagerstown	(301)	36,687	39,890
21740	Halfway (c)	(301)	10,065	10,701
21078	Havre de Grace	(410)	11,331	13,040
20748	Hillcrest Heights (c)	(301)	16,359	16,469
*20780	Hyattsville	(301)	14,733	17,718
21043	Ilchester (c)	(410)	—	23,476
21085	Joppatowne (c)	(410)	11,391	12,616
20902	Kemp Mill (c)	(301)	9,956	12,564
*20772	Kettering (c)	(301)	11,008	12,790
*21122	Lake Shore (c)	(410)	13,065	19,477
20785	Landover (c)	(301)	—	23,078
*20787	Langley Park (c)	(301)	16,214	18,755
20706	Lanham (c)	(301)	—	10,157
*20774	Largo (c)	(301)	8,408	10,709
*20707	Laurel (c)	(301)	19,960	25,346
20653	Lexington Park (c)	(410)	11,021	11,626
21090	Linthicum (c)	(410)	7,539	10,324
21207	Lochearn (c)	(410)	25,269	25,333

ZIP	Place	Area code	2000 population	2011 estimate
20724	Maryland City (c)	(301)	6,814	16,093
21093	Mays Chapel (c)	(410)	11,427	11,420
21220	Middle River (c)	(410)	23,958	25,191
21207	Milford Mill (c)	(410)	26,527	29,042
*20886	Montgomery Village (c)	(301)	38,051	32,032
20784	New Carrollton	(301)	12,589	12,248
*20815	North Bethesda (c)	(301)	38,610	43,828
20878	North Potomac (c)	(301)	23,044	24,410
21811	Ocean Pines (c)	(410)	10,496	11,710
21113	Odenton (c)	(410)	20,534	37,132
*20832	Olney (c)	(301)	31,438	33,844
21206	Overlea (c)	(410)	12,148	12,275
21117	Owings Mills (c)	(410)	20,193	30,622
*20745	Oxon Hill (c)	(301)	—	17,722
21234	Parkville (c)	(410)	31,118	30,734
21401	Parole (c)	(410)	14,031	15,922
*21122	Pasadena (c)	(410)	12,093	24,287
21128	Perry Hall (c)	(410)	28,705	28,474
*21282	Pikesville (c)	(410)	29,123	30,764
*20850	Potomac (c)	(301)	44,822	44,965
21133	Randallstown (c)	(301)	30,870	32,430
20855	Redland (c)	(301)	16,998	17,242
*21136	Reisterstown (c)	(410)	22,438	25,968
*21122	Riviera Beach (c)	(410)	12,695	12,677
*20850	Rockville	(301)	47,388	62,334
20772	Rosaryville (c)	(301)	12,322	10,697
21237	Rosedale (c)	(410)	19,199	19,257
21221	Rossville (c)	(410)	11,515	15,147
*21801	Salisbury	(410)	23,743	30,484
*20706	Seabrook (c)	(301)	—	17,287
21144	Severn (c)	(410)	35,076	44,231
21146	Severna Park (c)	(410)	28,507	37,634
*20907	Silver Spring (c)	(301)	76,540	71,452
20707	South Laurel (c)	(301)	20,479	26,112
*20746	Suitland (c)	(301)	—	25,825
21842	Summerfield (c)	(410)	—	10,898
*20913	Takoma Park	(301)	17,299	17,021
*21204	Towson (c)	(410)	51,793	55,197
20854	Travilah (c)	(301)	7,442	12,159
*20602	Waldorf (c)	(301)	22,312	67,752
20743	Walker Mill (c)	(301)	11,104	11,302
*21157	Westminster	(410)	16,731	18,606
*20902	Wheaton (c)	(301)	—	48,284
20903	White Oak (c)	(301)	20,973	17,403
21207	Woodlawn (c) (Baltimore Co.)	(410)	36,079	37,879

Massachusetts

Area code (339) overlays area code (781). Area code (351) overlays area code (978). Area code (774) overlays area code (508). Area code (857) overlays area code (617). See introductory note.

ZIP	Place	Area code	2000 population	2011 estimate
02351	Abington	(781)	14,605	16,072
*01720	Acton	(978)	20,331	22,152
*02743	Acushnet	(508)	10,161	10,316
01001	Agawam	(413)	28,144	28,455
01913	Amesbury	(978)	16,450	16,411
*01002	Amherst	(413)	34,874	37,776
*01002	Amherst Center (c)	(413)	17,050	19,065
*01810	Andover	(978)	31,247	33,455
*02205	Arlington	(781)	42,389	43,290
01721	Ashland	(508)	14,674	16,767
*01331	Athol	(978)	11,299	11,624
02703	Attleboro	(508)	42,068	43,645
01501	Auburn	(508)	15,901	16,244
*02630	Barnstable	(508)	—	45,167
*01730	Bedford	(781)	12,595	13,455
01007	Belchertown	(413)	12,968	14,621
02019	Bellingham	(508)	15,314	16,447
*02478	Belmont	(781)	24,194	24,987
01915	Beverly	(978)	39,862	39,796
*01821	Billerica	(978)	38,981	40,654
*02205	Boston	(617)	589,141	625,087
*02532	Bourne	(508)	18,721	19,745
*02185	Braintree	(781)	33,828	35,990
*02324	Bridgewater	(508)	25,185	26,686
*02303	Brockton	(508)	94,304	94,316
*02446	Brookline	(617)	57,107	59,132
*01803	Burlington	(781)	22,876	24,755
*02139	Cambridge	(617)	101,355	106,038
02021	Canton	(781)	20,775	21,710
*02330	Carver	(508)	11,163	11,573
01507	Charlton	(508)	11,263	13,026
01824	Chelmsford	(978)	33,858	34,156
02150	Chelsea	(617)	35,080	35,649
*01020	Chicopee	(413)	54,653	55,333
01510	Clinton	(978)	13,435	13,653
01742	Concord	(978)	16,993	17,836
01923	Danvers	(978)	25,212	26,696
*02714	Dartmouth	(508)	30,666	34,065
*02026	Dedham	(781)	23,464	24,895
02638	Dennis	(508)	15,973	14,199
01826	Dracut	(978)	28,562	29,767

ZIP	Place	Area code	2000 population	2011 estimate
01571	Dudley	(508)	10,036	11,426
*02332	Duxbury	(781)	14,248	15,141
02333	East Bridgewater	(508)	12,974	13,866
*01028	East Longmeadow	(413)	14,100	15,731
01027	Easthampton	(413)	15,994	16,023
*02334	Easton	(508)	22,299	23,136
02149	Everett	(617)	38,037	42,101
02719	Fairhaven	(508)	16,159	15,892
*02722	Fall River	(508)	91,938	88,962
*02540	Falmouth	(508)	32,660	31,514
01420	Fitchburg	(978)	39,102	40,449
02035	Foxborough	(508)	16,246	16,983
*01701	Framingham	(508)	66,910	68,991
02038	Franklin	(508)	29,560	31,851
*01440	Gardner	(978)	20,770	20,293
*01930	Gloucester	(978)	30,273	29,014
01519	Grafton	(508)	14,894	17,827
*01301	Greenfield	(413)	18,168	17,511
*01450	Groton	(978)	9,547	10,755
*02339	Hanover	(781)	13,164	13,954
*02341	Hanson	(781)	9,495	10,266
02645	Harwich	(508)	12,386	12,236
*01830	Haverhill	(978)	58,969	61,351
*02043	Hingham	(781)	19,882	22,277
02343	Holbrook	(781)	10,785	10,866
01520	Holden	(508)	15,621	17,407
01746	Holliston	(508)	13,801	13,689
*01040	Holyoke	(413)	39,838	39,905
01748	Hopkinton	(508)	13,346	15,080
01749	Hudson	(978)	18,113	19,264
01749	Hudson (c)	(978)	14,388	14,907
02045	Hull	(781)	11,050	10,349
01938	Ipswich	(978)	12,987	13,279
02364	Kingston	(781)	11,780	12,696
02347	Lakeville	(508)	9,821	10,659
*01842	Lawrence	(978)	72,043	76,976
01524	Leicester	(508)	10,471	11,008
01453	Leominster	(978)	41,303	40,898
*02420	Lexington	(781)	30,355	31,718
*01028	Longmeadow	(413)	15,633	15,795
*01853	Lowell	(978)	105,167	107,584
01056	Ludlow	(413)	21,209	21,116
*01462	Lunenburg	(978)	9,401	10,122
*01901	Lynn	(781)	89,050	91,040
01940	Lynnfield	(781)	11,542	11,687
02148	Malden	(781)	56,340	60,071
*02048	Mansfield	(508)	22,414	23,212
01945	Marblehead	(781)	20,377	19,964
01752	Marlborough	(508)	36,255	38,895
*02050	Marshfield	(781)	24,324	25,271
02649	Mashpee	(508)	12,946	13,998
01754	Maynard	(978)	10,433	10,212
02052	Medfield	(508)	12,273	12,108
*02155	Medford	(781)	55,765	56,738
02053	Medway	(508)	12,448	12,842
02176	Melrose	(781)	27,134	27,263
01844	Methuen	(978)	43,789	47,627
*02346	Middleborough	(508)	19,941	23,241
01757	Milford	(508)	26,799	28,096
01757	Milford (c)	(508)	24,230	25,055
*01527	Millbury	(508)	12,784	13,307
02186	Milton	(617)	26,062	27,182
*02584	Nantucket	(508)	9,520	10,142
01760	Natick	(508)	32,170	33,349
*02494	Needham	(781)	28,911	29,083
*02740	New Bedford	(508)	93,768	95,183
01950	Newburyport	(978)	17,189	17,552
*02456	Newton	(617)	83,829	85,945
02056	Norfolk	(508)	10,460	11,290
01247	North Adams	(413)	14,681	13,632
01845	North Andover	(978)	27,202	28,571
*02760	North Attleborough	(508)	27,143	28,745
*01864	North Reading	(978)	13,837	15,048
*01060	Northampton	(413)	28,978	28,501
01532	Northborough	(508)	14,013	14,203
01534	Northbridge	(508)	13,182	15,761
*02766	Norton	(508)	18,036	19,052
02061	Norwell	(781)	9,765	10,562
02062	Norwood	(781)	28,587	28,801
*01540	Oxford	(508)	13,352	13,758
01069	Palmer	(413)	12,497	12,149
*01960	Peabody	(978)	48,129	51,653
*02359	Pembroke	(781)	16,927	17,934
01463	Pepperell	(978)	11,142	11,616
*01201	Pittsfield	(413)	45,793	44,472
*02360	Plymouth	(508)	51,701	56,767
*02169	Quincy	(617)	88,025	92,909
02368	Randolph	(781)	30,963	32,336
*02767	Raynham	(508)	11,739	13,399
01867	Reading	(781)	23,708	25,001
02769	Rehoboth	(508)	10,172	11,621
02151	Revere	(781)	47,283	52,459
02370	Rockland	(781)	17,670	17,583
*01970	Salem	(978)	40,407	41,654
*02563	Sandwich	(508)	20,136	20,664
01906	Saugus	(781)	26,078	26,836

ZIP	Place	Area code	2000 population	2011 estimate
*02066	Scituate	(781)	17,863	18,233
02771	Seekonk	(508)	13,425	13,740
02067	Sharon	(781)	17,408	17,734
*01545	Shrewsbury	(508)	31,640	35,730
*02725	Somerset	(508)	18,234	18,187
*02143	Somerville	(617)	77,478	76,519
01075	South Hadley	(413)	17,196	17,486
01550	Southbridge	(508)	17,214	16,775
01562	Spencer	(508)	11,691	11,728
*01101	Springfield	(413)	152,082	153,155
02180	Stoneham	(781)	22,219	21,659
02072	Stoughton	(781)	27,149	27,150
01776	Sudbury	(978)	16,841	17,843
01907	Swampscott	(781)	14,412	13,896
02777	Swansea	(508)	15,901	15,884
*02780	Taunton	(508)	55,976	55,940
01876	Tewksbury	(978)	28,851	29,258
01879	Tyngsborough	(978)	11,081	11,411
01569	Uxbridge	(508)	11,156	13,503
01880	Wakefield	(781)	24,804	25,191
02081	Walpole	(508)	22,824	24,234
*02451	Waltham	(781)	59,226	61,181
02571	Wareham	(508)	20,335	21,941
*02471	Watertown	(781)	32,986	32,248
01778	Wayland	(508)	13,100	13,131
01570	Webster	(508)	16,415	16,824
01570	Webster (c)	(508)	11,600	11,412
*02457	Wellesley	(781)	26,613	28,152
*01089	West Springfield	(413)	27,899	28,410
*01581	Westborough	(508)	17,997	18,333
*01085	Westfield	(413)	40,072	41,119
01886	Westford	(978)	20,754	22,181
02493	Weston	(781)	11,469	11,371
02790	Westport	(508)	14,183	15,550
02090	Westwood	(781)	14,117	14,721
*02188	Weymouth	(781)	53,988	54,116
02382	Whitman	(781)	13,882	14,569
01095	Wilbraham	(413)	13,473	14,229
01887	Wilmington	(978)	21,363	22,557
01475	Winchendon	(978)	9,611	10,335
01890	Winchester	(781)	20,810	21,594
02152	Winthrop	(617)	18,303	17,737
*01801	Woburn	(781)	37,258	38,520
*01613	Worcester	(508)	172,648	181,631
*02093	Wrentham	(508)	10,554	11,027
*02675	Yarmouth	(508)	24,807	23,779

Michigan

Area code (947) overlays area code (248).

ZIP	Place	Area code	2000 population	2011 estimate
49221	Adrian	(517)	21,574	21,045
*48101	Allen Park	(313)	29,376	27,921
49401	Allendale (c)	(616)	11,555	17,579
49707	Alpena	(989)	11,304	10,410
*48106	Ann Arbor	(734)	114,024	114,925
*48321	Auburn Hills	(248)	19,837	21,543
*49016	Battle Creek	(269)	53,364	52,093
*48707	Bay City	(989)	36,817	34,717
48505	Beecher (c)	(810)	12,793	10,232
*49022	Benton Harbor	(269)	11,182	10,047
48072	Berkley	(248)	15,531	15,067
48025	Beverly Hills	(248)	10,437	10,333
49307	Big Rapids	(231)	10,849	10,695
*48012	Birmingham	(248)	19,291	20,235
*48509	Burton	(810)	30,308	29,736
49601	Cadillac	(231)	10,000	10,349
*48017	Clawson	(248)	12,732	11,900
49036	Coldwater	(517)	12,697	10,931
49321	Comstock Park (c)	(616)	10,674	10,088
49508	Cutlerville (c)	(616)	15,114	14,370
*48120	Dearborn	(313)	97,775	97,144
*48127	Dearborn Heights	(313)	58,264	57,186
*48231	Detroit	(313)	951,270	706,585
*49506	East Grand Rapids	(616)	10,764	10,799
*48826	East Lansing	(517)	46,525	48,666
48021	Eastpointe	(586)	34,077	32,487
49829	Escanaba	(906)	13,140	12,627
*48333	Farmington	(248)	10,423	10,438
*48333	Farmington Hills	(248)	82,111	80,258
48430	Fenton	(810)	10,582	11,654
48220	Ferndale	(248)	22,105	20,030
*48501	Flint	(810)	124,943	101,558
49506	Forest Hills (c)	(616)	20,942	25,867
48026	Fraser	(586)	15,297	14,501
*48135	Garden City	(734)	30,047	27,408
49417	Grand Haven	(616)	11,168	10,511
*49501	Grand Rapids	(616)	197,800	189,815
*49418	Grandville	(616)	16,263	15,527
48230	Grosse Pointe Park	(313)	12,443	11,436
48230	Grosse Pointe Woods	(313)	17,080	15,969
*48212	Hamtramck	(313)	22,976	22,198
48225	Harper Woods	(313)	14,254	14,092
48840	Haslett (c)	(517)	11,283	19,220
48030	Hazel Park	(248)	18,963	16,530
48203	Highland Park	(313)	16,746	11,664

ZIP	Place	Area code	2000 population	2011 estimate
*49423	Holland	(616)	35,048	33,270
48842	Holt (c)	(517)	11,315	23,973
48141	Inkster	(313)/(734)	30,115	25,111
48846	Ionia	(616)	10,569	11,402
*49204	Jackson	(517)	36,316	33,425
*49428	Jenison (c)	(616)	17,211	16,538
*49001	Kalamazoo	(269)	77,145	74,743
*49518	Kentwood	(616)	45,255	49,184
*48901	Lansing	(517)	119,128	114,605
48146	Lincoln Park	(313)	40,008	37,752
*48150	Livonia	(734)	100,545	95,958
48071	Madison Heights	(248)	31,101	29,887
49855	Marquette	(906)	19,661	21,524
48122	Melvindale	(313)	10,735	10,604
*48640	Midland	(989)	41,685	42,075
*48161	Monroe	(734)	22,076	20,672
*48046	Mount Clemens	(586)	17,312	16,334
*48804	Mount Pleasant	(989)	25,946	26,111
*49440	Muskegon	(231)	40,105	38,225
49444	Muskegon Heights	(231)	12,049	10,798
*48047	New Baltimore	(586)	7,405	12,100
*49120	Niles	(269)	12,204	11,609
49505	Northview (c)	(616)	14,730	14,541
*49441	Norton Shores	(231)	22,527	23,867
*48376	Novi	(248)	47,386	55,583
48237	Oak Park	(248)	29,793	29,511
*48805	Okemos (c)	(517)	20,216	21,369
*48867	Owosso	(989)	15,713	15,024
*48343	Pontiac	(248)	66,337	59,887
*48061	Port Huron	(810)	32,338	29,928
*49081	Portage	(269)	44,897	46,624
*48192	Riverview	(734)	13,272	12,362
*48308	Rochester	(248)	10,467	12,793
*48306	Rochester Hills	(248)	68,825	71,452
48174	Romulus	(313)/(734)	22,979	23,745
48066	Roseville	(586)	48,129	47,366
*48068	Royal Oak	(248)	60,062	57,607
*48605	Saginaw	(989)	61,799	51,230
*48080	Saint Clair Shores	(313)	63,096	59,798
*49783	Sault Sainte Marie	(906)	16,542	14,253
48178	South Lyon	(248)	10,036	11,400
*48037	Southfield	(248)	78,296	72,201
48195	Southgate	(734)	30,136	29,739
*48311	Sterling Heights	(586)	124,471	129,880
49091	Sturgis	(269)	11,285	10,967
48180	Taylor	(313)/(734)	65,868	62,489
*49684	Traverse City	(231)	14,532	14,894
48183	Trenton	(734)	19,584	18,662
*48099	Troy	(248)	80,959	81,508
49534	Walker	(616)	21,842	23,766
*48090	Warren	(586)	138,247	134,243
48917	Waverly (c)	(517)	16,194	23,925
48184	Wayne	(734)	19,051	17,414
*48185	Westland	(313)/(734)	86,602	83,239
48393	Wixom	(248)	13,263	13,587
48183	Woodhaven	(734)	12,530	12,743
*48192	Wyandotte	(734)	28,006	25,618
*49509	Wyoming	(616)	69,368	72,833
*48197	Ypsilanti	(734)	22,362	19,596

Minnesota

ZIP	Place	Area code	2000 population	2011 estimate
56007	Albert Lea	(507)	18,356	17,967
56308	Alexandria	(320)	8,820	11,121
*55304	Andover	(763)	26,588	30,811
*55303	Anoka	(612)	18,076	17,256
55124	Apple Valley	(952)	45,527	49,509
55912	Austin	(507)	23,314	24,834
*56601	Bemidji	(218)	11,917	13,657
55309	Big Lake	(763)	6,063	10,157
*55014	Blaine	(651)	44,942	57,584
*55420	Bloomington	(952)	85,172	84,057
*56401	Brainerd	(218)	13,178	13,646
*55429	Brooklyn Center	(763)	29,172	30,529
*55443	Brooklyn Park	(763)	67,388	76,853
55313	Buffalo	(763)	10,097	15,665
*55337	Burnsville	(651)	60,220	60,828
55316	Champlin	(763)	22,193	23,418
55317	Chanhassen	(952)	20,321	23,358
55318	Chaska	(952)	17,449	24,189
55720	Cloquet	(218)	11,201	12,148
55421	Columbia Heights	(612)	18,520	19,632
*55433	Coon Rapids	(763)	61,607	61,904
55016	Cottage Grove	(651)	30,582	35,052
*55428	Crystal	(763)	22,698	22,463
*55806	Duluth	(218)	86,918	86,277
*55121	Eagan	(651)	63,557	64,765
*55005	East Bethel	(763)	10,941	11,707
*55344	Eden Prairie	(612)	54,901	61,657
*55424	Edina	(952)	47,425	48,620
55330	Elk River	(763)	16,447	23,186
*56031	Fairmont	(507)	10,889	10,589
55021	Faribault	(507)	20,818	23,450
55024	Farmington	(651)	12,365	21,267
*56537	Fergus Falls	(218)	13,471	13,125
55025	Forest Lake	(651)	6,798	18,619
*55432	Fridley	(763)	27,449	27,398
*55427	Golden Valley	(763)	20,281	20,655
*55744	Grand Rapids	(218)	7,764	10,862
*55304	Ham Lake	(763)	12,710	15,402
55033	Hastings	(651)	18,204	22,359
*55746	Hibbing	(218)	17,071	16,364
*55343	Hopkins	(952)	17,145	17,837
55038	Hugo	(651)	6,363	13,509
55350	Hutchinson	(320)	13,080	14,093
*55076	Inver Grove Heights	(651)	29,751	34,175
*55044	Lakeville	(952)	43,128	56,443
*55014	Lino Lakes	(651)	16,791	20,348
*56001	Mankato	(507)	32,427	39,528
*55311	Maple Grove	(763)	50,365	62,440
*55109	Maplewood	(651)	34,947	38,472
56258	Marshall	(507)	12,735	13,700
*55118	Mendota Heights	(651)	11,434	11,168
*55440	Minneapolis	(612)	382,618	387,753
*55345	Minnetonka	(952)	51,301	50,435
*55362	Monticello	(763)	7,868	12,935
*56560	Moorhead	(218)	32,177	38,566
55112	Mounds View	(763)	12,738	12,305
55112	New Brighton	(651)	22,206	21,715
*54427	New Hope	(763)	20,873	20,616
56073	New Ulm	(507)	13,594	13,440
55056	North Branch	(651)	8,023	10,131
*56002	North Mankato	(507)	11,798	13,437
55109	North Saint Paul	(651)	11,929	11,601
55057	Northfield	(507)	17,147	20,084
*55128	Oakdale	(651)	26,653	27,743
*55330	Otsego	(763)	6,389	13,761
55060	Owatonna	(507)	22,434	25,570
*55446	Plymouth	(763)	65,894	71,561
*55372	Prior Lake	(952)	15,917	23,261
55303	Ramsey	(763)	18,510	23,835
55066	Red Wing	(651)	16,116	16,472
55423	Richfield	(612)	34,439	35,724
55422	Robbinsdale	(763)	14,123	14,148
*55901	Rochester	(507)	85,806	107,890
55068	Rosemount	(651)	14,619	22,064
*55113	Roseville	(651)	33,690	34,058
*56301	Saint Cloud	(320)	59,107	66,169
*55426	Saint Louis Park	(952)	44,126	45,882
55376	Saint Michael	(763)	9,099	16,630
*55101	Saint Paul	(651)	287,151	288,448
56082	Saint Peter	(507)	9,747	11,223
56377	Sartell	(320)	9,641	15,954
56379	Sauk Rapids	(320)	10,213	12,846
55378	Savage	(952)	21,115	27,459
*55379	Shakopee	(612)	20,568	37,814
55126	Shoreview	(651)	25,924	25,350
*55075	South Saint Paul	(651)	20,167	20,335
*55082	Stillwater	(651)	15,143	18,464
*55127	Vadnais Heights	(651)	13,069	12,453
*55387	Waconia	(952)	6,814	10,883
*55118	West Saint Paul	(651)	19,405	19,708
*55110	White Bear Lake	(651)	24,325	24,087
56201	Willmar	(320)	18,351	19,582
*55987	Winona	(507)	27,069	27,554
*55125	Woodbury	(651)	46,463	62,787
56187	Worthington	(507)	11,283	12,776

Mississippi

Area code (769) overlays area code (601).

ZIP	Place	Area code	2000 population	2011 estimate
*39530	Biloxi	(228)	50,644	44,940
*39042	Brandon	(601)	16,436	22,032
*39601	Brookhaven	(601)	9,861	12,520
39272	Byram	(601)	—	11,628
39046	Canton	(601)	12,911	13,421
*38614	Clarksdale	(662)	20,645	17,799
*38732	Cleveland	(662)	13,841	12,202
*39056	Clinton	(601)	23,347	25,518
*39701	Columbus	(662)	25,944	23,599
*38834	Corinth	(662)	14,054	14,572
39553	Gautier	(228)	11,681	18,603
*38701	Greenville	(662)	41,633	33,908
*38930	Greenwood	(662)	18,425	14,978
*38901	Grenada	(662)	14,879	12,973
*39501	Gulfport	(228)	71,127	69,220
*39401	Hattiesburg	(601)	44,779	46,626
38632	Hernando	(662)	6,812	14,333
38637	Horn Lake	(662)	14,099	26,519
*38751	Indianola	(662)	12,066	10,618
*39205	Jackson	(601)	184,256	175,561
*39440	Laurel	(601)	18,393	18,625
39560	Long Beach	(228)	17,320	15,110
*39110	Madison	(601)	14,692	24,595
*39648	McComb	(601)	13,337	12,790
*39302	Meridian	(601)	39,968	41,258
*39563	Moss Point	(228)	15,851	13,726
*39120	Natchez	(601)	18,464	15,672

ZIP	Place	Area code	2000 population	2011 estimate
*39564	Ocean Springs	(228)	17,225	17,472
38654	Olive Branch	(662)	21,054	34,068
38655	Oxford	(662)	11,756	19,393
*39567	Pascagoula	(228)	26,200	22,429
*39288	Pearl	(601)	21,961	25,475
39465	Petal	(601)	7,579	10,587
39466	Picayune	(601)	10,535	10,854
*39157	Ridgeland	(601)	20,173	24,488
*38671	Southaven	(662)	28,977	49,831
*39759	Starkville	(662)	21,869	23,926
*38801	Tupelo	(662)	34,211	35,059
*39180	Vicksburg	(601)	26,407	23,649
39773	West Point	(662)	12,145	11,221
39194	Yazoo City	(662)	14,550	11,323

Missouri

ZIP	Place	Area code	2000 population	2011 estimate
63123	Affton (c)	(314)	20,535	20,307
63010	Arnold	(636)	19,965	20,881
*63011	Ballwin	(636)	31,283	30,397
63137	Bellefontaine Neighbors . .	(314)	11,271	10,857
64012	Belton	(816)	21,730	23,251
*64015	Blue Springs	(816)	48,080	52,749
*65613	Bolivar	(417)	9,143	10,334
*65616	Branson	(417)	6,050	10,739
*63044	Bridgeton	(314)	15,550	11,547
*63701	Cape Girardeau	(573)	35,349	38,402
64836	Carthage	(417)	12,668	14,502
*63017	Chesterfield	(636)	46,802	47,471
*63105	Clayton	(314)	12,825	15,936
*65201	Columbia	(573)	84,531	110,438
*63128	Concord (c)	(314)	16,689	16,421
63126	Crestwood	(314)	11,863	11,909
63141	Creve Coeur	(314)	16,500	17,829
*63366	Dardenne Prairie	(636)	4,384	11,646
63025	Eureka	(636)	7,676	10,187
64024	Excelsior Springs	(816)	10,847	11,234
63640	Farmington	(573)	13,924	16,286
*63135	Ferguson	(314)	22,406	21,198
63028	Festus	(636)	9,660	11,643
*63033	Florissant	(314)	50,497	52,145
65473	Fort Leonard Wood (c) . . .	(573)	13,666	15,061
65251	Fulton	(573)	12,128	12,809
*64118	Gladstone	(816)	26,365	25,784
64029	Grain Valley	(816)	5,160	12,898
64030	Grandview	(816)	24,881	24,555
63401	Hannibal	(573)	17,757	17,880
64701	Harrisonville	(816)	8,946	10,076
*63042	Hazelwood	(314)	26,206	25,695
*64050	Independence	(816)	113,288	117,213
63755	Jackson	(573)	11,947	13,938
*65101	Jefferson City	(573)	39,636	43,332
63136	Jennings	(314)	15,469	14,707
*64801	Joplin	(417)	45,504	50,559
*64108	Kansas City	(816)	441,545	463,202
63857	Kennett	(573)	11,260	10,939
63501	Kirksville	(660)	16,988	17,469
63122	Kirkwood	(314)	27,324	27,534
63367	Lake Saint Louis	(636)	10,169	14,736
65536	Lebanon	(417)	12,155	14,500
*64063	Lee's Summit	(816)	70,700	91,668
63125	Lemay (c)	(314)	17,215	16,645
*64068	Liberty	(816)	26,232	29,557
*63011	Manchester	(636)	19,161	18,090
65340	Marshall	(660)	12,433	13,013
63043	Maryland Heights	(314)	25,756	27,466
64468	Maryville	(816)	10,581	12,016
63129	Mehlville (c)	(314)	28,822	28,380
65265	Mexico	(573)	11,320	11,561
65270	Moberly	(660)	11,945	13,940
*64850	Neosho	(417)	10,505	11,894
65714	Nixa	(417)	12,124	19,303
63366	O'Fallon	(636)	46,169	80,519
63129	Oakville (c)	(314)	35,309	36,143
63034	Old Jamestown (c)	(314)	—	19,184
63114	Overland	(314)	16,838	16,059
65721	Ozark	(417)	9,665	18,082
*63901	Poplar Bluff	(573)	16,651	17,135
64083	Raymore	(816)	11,146	19,318
*64133	Raytown	(816)	30,388	29,622
65738	Republic	(417)	8,438	14,864
*65401	Rolla	(573)	16,367	19,506
63074	Saint Ann	(314)	13,607	13,016
*63301	Saint Charles	(636)	60,321	66,598
*64501	Saint Joseph	(816)	73,990	77,185
*63166	Saint Louis	(314)	348,189	318,069
*63376	Saint Peters	(636)	51,381	53,264
*65301	Sedalia	(660)	20,339	21,376
63801	Sikeston	(573)	16,992	16,288
63138	Spanish Lake (c)	(314)	21,337	19,650
*65801	Springfield	(417)	151,580	160,660
63011	Town and Country	(314)	10,894	10,813
63379	Troy	(314)	6,737	10,641
63084	Union	(636)	7,757	10,258

ZIP	Place	Area code	2000 population	2011 estimate
63130	University City	(314)	37,428	35,362
64093	Warrensburg	(660)	16,340	19,110
63090	Washington	(636)	13,243	14,045
64870	Webb City	(417)	9,812	11,095
63119	Webster Groves	(314)	23,230	22,989
63385	Wentzville	(636)	6,896	29,451
*65775	West Plains	(417)	10,866	12,063
*63011	Wildwood	(314)	32,884	35,509

Montana (406)

ZIP	Place	2000 population	2011 estimate
*59101	Billings	89,847	105,636
*59718	Bozeman	27,509	38,025
*59701	Butte-Silver Bow	33,892	33,704
*59401	Great Falls	56,690	58,950
*59601	Helena	25,780	28,592
*59901	Kalispell	14,223	20,008
*59801	Missoula	57,053	67,290

Nebraska

Area code (531) overlays area code (402).

ZIP	Place	Area code	2000 population	2011 estimate
68310	Beatrice	(402)	12,496	12,302
*68108	Bellevue	(402)	44,382	51,319
68108	Chalco (c)	(402)	10,736	10,994
*68601	Columbus	(402)	20,971	22,381
*68025	Fremont	(402)	25,174	26,456
*68802	Grand Island	(308)	42,940	49,239
*68901	Hastings	(402)	24,064	24,788
*68847	Kearney	(308)	27,431	31,174
68128	La Vista	(402)	11,699	16,129
68850	Lexington	(308)	10,011	10,257
*68501	Lincoln	(402)	225,581	262,341
*68701	Norfolk	(402)	23,516	24,248
*69101	North Platte	(308)	23,878	24,634
*68005	Omaha	(402)	390,007	415,068
*68046	Papillion	(402)	16,363	19,331
*69361	Scottsbluff	(308)	14,732	15,069
68776	South Sioux City	(402)	11,925	13,293

Nevada

ZIP	Place	Area code	2000 population	2011 estimate
*89005	Boulder City	(702)	14,966	15,166
*89701	Carson City	(775)	52,457	55,439
*89801	Elko	(775)	16,708	18,546
89139	Enterprise (c)	(702)	14,676	108,481
89408	Fernley	(775)	—	19,327
89410	Gardnerville Ranchos (c)	(775)	11,054	11,312
*89015	Henderson	(702)	175,381	260,068
*89125	Las Vegas	(702)	478,434	589,317
*89024	Mesquite	(702)	9,389	15,423
*89030	North Las Vegas	(702)	115,488	219,020
*89041	Pahrump (c)	(775)	24,631	36,441
89109	Paradise (c)	(702)	186,070	223,167
*89501	Reno	(775)	180,480	227,511
89441	Spanish Springs (c)	(775)	9,018	15,064
*89431	Sparks	(775)	66,346	91,195
89815	Spring Creek (c)	(775)	10,548	12,361
89147	Spring Valley (c)	(702)	117,390	178,395
89135	Summerlin South (c)	(702)	3,735	24,085
89433	Sun Valley (c)	(775)	19,461	19,299
89110	Sunrise Manor (c)	(702)	156,120	189,372
89122	Whitney (c)	(702)	18,273	38,585
89101	Winchester (c)	(702)	26,958	27,978

New Hampshire (603)
See introductory note.

ZIP	Place	2000 population	2011 estimate
03031	Amherst	10,769	11,229
03110	Bedford	18,274	21,256
03743	Claremont	13,151	13,268
*03301	Concord	40,687	42,733
*03818	Conway	8,604	10,077
03038	Derry	34,021	33,220
03038	Derry (c)	22,661	22,015
*03820	Dover	26,884	30,168
03824	Durham	12,664	14,684
03824	Durham (c)	12,904	10,345
03833	Exeter	14,058	14,353
03045	Goffstown	16,929	17,689
*03842	Hampton	14,937	15,480
03755	Hanover	10,850	11,243
03106	Hooksett	11,721	13,463
03051	Hudson	22,928	24,527
*03431	Keene	22,563	23,354
*03246	Laconia	16,411	15,986
*03766	Lebanon	12,568	13,120
03053	Londonderry	23,236	24,211
03053	Londonderry (c)	11,417	11,037
*03103	Manchester	107,006	109,830
03054	Merrimack	25,119	25,557
03055	Milford	13,535	15,152
*03060	Nashua	86,605	86,704

ZIP	Place	2000 population	2011 estimate
03076	Pelham	10,914	12,929
*03801	Portsmouth	20,784	20,848
03077	Raymond	9,674	10,171
*03867	Rochester	28,461	29,935
03079	Salem	28,112	28,871
03878	Somersworth	11,477	11,839
03087	Windham	10,709	13,638

New Jersey

Area code (551) overlays area code (201). Area code (848) overlays area code (732). Area code (862) overlays area code (973).

ZIP	Place	Area code	2000 population	2011 estimate
07712	Asbury Park	(732)	16,930	16,132
*08401	Atlantic City	(609)	40,517	39,527
07001	Avenel (c)	(732)	17,552	17,011
07002	Bayonne	(201)	61,842	63,722
08722	Beachwood	(732)	10,375	11,099
*08031	Bellmawr	(856)	11,262	11,572
07621	Bergenfield	(201)	26,247	26,939
07922	Berkeley Heights (c)	(908)	13,407	13,183
08805	Bound Brook	(732)	10,155	10,449
08807	Bradley Gardens (c)	(908)	—	14,206
08302	Bridgeton	(856)	22,771	25,254
08015	Browns Mills (c)	(609)	11,257	11,223
*08101	Camden	(856)	79,904	77,283
07008	Carteret	(732)	20,709	22,970
08002	Cherry Hill Mall (c)	(856)	13,238	14,171
07010	Cliffside Park	(201)	23,007	23,750
*07015	Clifton	(973)	78,672	84,269
08108	Collingswood	(856)	14,326	13,914
07067	Colonia (c)	(732)	17,811	17,795
*07801	Dover	(973)	18,188	18,257
07628	Dumont	(201)	17,503	17,595
*07019	East Orange	(973)	69,824	64,365
*07724	Eatontown	(732)	14,008	12,722
08043	Echelon (c)	(856)	10,440	10,743
07020	Edgewater	(201)	7,677	11,590
*07207	Elizabeth	(908)	120,568	125,660
*07407	Elmwood Park	(201)	18,925	19,531
*07631	Englewood	(201)	26,203	27,325
07410	Fair Lawn	(201)/(973)	31,637	32,669
07022	Fairview (Bergen Co.)	(201)	13,255	13,925
07932	Florham Park	(973)	8,857	11,751
08863	Fords (c)	(732)	15,032	15,187
07024	Fort Lee	(201)	35,461	35,579
07417	Franklin Lakes	(201)	10,422	10,660
07728	Freehold	(732)	10,976	12,063
07026	Garfield	(973)	29,786	30,687
08028	Glassboro	(856)	19,068	18,626
07452	Glen Rock	(201)	11,546	11,677
*08030	Gloucester City	(856)	11,484	11,445
08053	Greentree (c)	(856)	11,536	11,367
07093	Guttenberg	(201)	10,807	11,299
*07602	Hackensack	(201)	42,677	43,285
08033	Haddonfield	(856)	11,659	11,582
08690	Hamilton Square (c)	(609)	—	12,784
08037	Hammonton	(609)	12,604	14,779
07029	Harrison	(973)	14,424	13,773
07604	Hasbrouck Heights	(201)	11,662	11,919
*07506	Hawthorne	(973)	18,218	18,821
08904	Highland Park	(732)	13,999	14,060
*07642	Hillsdale	(201)	10,087	10,286
07030	Hoboken	(201)	38,577	50,545
08753	Holiday City-Berkeley (c)	(732)	13,884	12,831
07843	Hopatcong	(973)	15,888	15,070
08830	Iselin (c)	(732)	16,698	18,695
*07303	Jersey City	(201)	240,055	250,323
07734	Keansburg	(732)	10,732	10,116
*07032	Kearny	(201)/(973)	40,513	41,108
07405	Kinnelon	(973)	9,365	10,304
08701	Lakewood (c)	(732)	36,065	53,805
07035	Lincoln Park	(973)	10,930	10,576
07036	Linden	(732)/(908)	39,394	40,725
08021	Lindenwold	(856)	17,414	17,598
07643	Little Ferry	(201)	10,800	10,696
07644	Lodi	(201)/(973)	23,971	24,295
07740	Long Branch	(732)	31,340	30,751
07940	Madison	(973)	16,530	15,924
08835	Manville	(908)	10,343	10,392
08053	Marlton (c)	(856)	10,260	10,133
08619	Mercerville (c)	(609)	—	13,230
08840	Metuchen	(732)	12,840	13,648
08846	Middlesex	(732)	13,717	13,710
08332	Millville	(856)	26,847	28,511
08057	Moorestown-Lenola (c)	(856)	13,860	14,217
*07960	Morristown	(973)	18,544	18,510
*08901	New Brunswick	(732)	48,573	55,444
07646	New Milford	(201)	16,400	16,448
07974	New Providence	(908)	11,907	12,238
*07102	Newark	(973)	273,546	277,540
07031	North Arlington	(201)	15,181	15,494
*07060	North Plainfield	(908)	21,103	22,035
07436	Oakland	(201)	12,466	12,836
*08050	Ocean Acres (c)	(609)	13,155	16,142
08226	Ocean City	(609)	15,378	11,619

ZIP	Place	Area code	2000 population	2011 estimate
08857	Old Bridge (c)	(732)	22,833	23,753
07650	Palisades Park	(201)	17,073	19,752
*07652	Paramus	(201)	25,737	26,507
07055	Passaic	(973)	67,861	69,893
*07510	Paterson	(973)	149,222	146,427
08070	Pennsville (c)	(856)	11,667	11,888
*08861	Perth Amboy	(732)	47,303	51,093
08865	Phillipsburg	(908)	15,166	14,900
08021	Pine Hill	(856)	10,880	10,223
*07061	Plainfield	(908)	47,829	50,085
*08232	Pleasantville	(609)	19,012	20,234
08742	Point Pleasant	(732)	19,306	18,481
07442	Pompton Lakes	(973)	10,640	11,114
*08540	Princeton	(609)	14,203	12,131
08536	Princeton Meadows (c)	(609)	13,436	13,834
07065	Rahway	(732)	26,500	27,500
07446	Ramsey	(201)	14,351	14,567
*07701	Red Bank	(732)	11,844	12,218
07657	Ridgefield	(201)	10,830	11,104
07660	Ridgefield Park	(201)	12,873	12,812
*07451	Ridgewood	(201)/(973)	24,936	25,120
07456	Ringwood	(973)	12,396	12,246
07661	River Edge	(201)	10,946	11,414
07751	Robertsville (c)	(732)	—	11,297
07203	Roselle	(908)	21,274	21,205
07204	Roselle Park	(908)	13,281	13,372
07070	Rutherford	(201)	18,110	18,118
*08872	Sayreville	(732)	40,377	42,940
*07094	Secaucus	(201)	15,931	16,436
07078	Short Hills (c)	(973)	—	13,165
08244	Somers Point	(609)	11,614	10,787
*08873	Somerset (c)	(732)	23,040	22,083
08876	Somerville	(908)	12,423	12,150
07080	South Plainfield	(732)/(908)	21,810	23,513
*08882	South River	(732)	15,322	16,097
08003	Springdale (c)	(856)	14,409	14,518
*07901	Summit	(908)	21,131	21,578
07670	Tenafly	(201)	13,806	14,582
*07724	Tinton Falls	(732)	15,053	17,911
*08753	Toms River (c)	(732)	86,327	88,791
*07512	Totowa	(973)	9,892	10,821
*08650	Trenton	(609)	85,403	84,899
*07087	Union City	(201)	67,088	67,187
07043	Upper Montclair (c)	(973)	—	11,565
08406	Ventnor City	(609)	12,910	10,641
*08360	Vineland	(856)	56,271	60,952
07057	Wallington	(201)/(973)	11,583	11,409
07465	Wanaque	(201)/(973)	10,266	11,133
07728	West Freehold (c)	(732)/(908)	12,498	13,613
07093	West New York	(201)	45,768	50,260
*07091	Westfield	(732)/(908)	29,644	30,487
*07675	Westwood	(201)	10,999	10,979
08094	Williamstown (c)	(609)/(856)	11,812	15,567
07095	Woodbridge (c)	(732)/(908)	18,309	19,265
*08096	Woodbury	(856)	10,307	10,201
*07424	Woodland Park	(973)	—	11,837

New Mexico

ZIP	Place	Area code	2000 population	2011 estimate
*88310	Alamogordo	(575)	35,582	31,327
*87101	Albuquerque	(505)	448,607	552,804
*88210	Artesia	(575)	10,692	11,371
*88220	Carlsbad	(575)	25,625	26,296
*88021	Chaparral (c)	(505)	6,117	14,631
*88101	Clovis	(575)	32,667	38,776
*88030	Deming	(575)	14,116	14,963
*87532	Espanola	(505)	9,688	10,313
*87401	Farmington	(505)	37,844	45,256
*87301	Gallup	(505)	20,209	22,329
*88240	Hobbs	(575)	28,657	34,488
*88001	Las Cruces	(575)	74,267	99,665
*87701	Las Vegas	(505)	14,565	13,656
87544	Los Alamos (c)	(505)	11,909	12,019
87031	Los Lunas	(505)	10,034	14,933
*88260	Lovington	(575)	9,471	11,128
87107	North Valley (c)	(505)	11,923	11,333
*88130	Portales	(575)	11,131	12,641
*87124	Rio Rancho	(505)	51,765	89,320
*88201	Roswell	(575)	45,293	48,546
*87501	Santa Fe	(505)	62,203	68,642
*88061	Silver City	(575)	10,545	10,269
87105	South Valley (c)	(505)	39,060	40,976
*88063	Sunland Park	(575)	13,309	14,407

New York

Area codes (347) and (929) overlay area code (718). Area codes (646) and (917) overlay area code (212).

ZIP	Place	Area code	2000 population	2011 estimate
*12201	Albany	(518)	95,658	97,660
12010	Amsterdam	(518)	18,355	18,507
*13021	Auburn	(315)	28,574	27,590
11702	Babylon	(631)	12,615	12,211
11510	Baldwin (c)	(516)	23,455	24,033

ZIP	Place	Area code	2000 population	2011 estimate
*14020	Batavia	(585)	16,256	15,444
11706	Bay Shore (c)	(631)	23,852	26,337
12508	Beacon	(845)	13,808	15,565
11710	Bellmore (c)	(516)	16,441	16,218
11714	Bethpage (c)	(516)	16,543	16,429
*13902	Binghamton	(607)	47,380	46,996
11716	Bohemia (c)	(631)	9,871	10,180
11717	Brentwood (c)	(631)	53,917	60,664
14610	Brighton (c)	(585)	35,584	36,609
*14240	Buffalo	(716)	292,648	261,025
*14424	Canandaigua	(585)	11,264	10,604
11720	Centereach (c)	(631)	27,285	31,578
11722	Central Islip (c)	(516)	31,950	34,450
14225	Cheektowaga (c)	(716)	79,988	75,178
12047	Cohoes	(518)	15,521	16,133
11725	Commack (c)	(631)	36,367	36,124
11726	Copiague (c)	(631)	21,922	22,993
11727	Coram (c)	(631)	34,923	39,113
*14830	Corning	(607)	10,842	11,187
13045	Cortland	(607)	18,740	19,212
11729	Deer Park (c)	(631)	28,316	27,745
14043	Depew	(716)	16,629	15,285
11746	Dix Hills (c)	(631)	26,024	26,892
10522	Dobbs Ferry	(914)	10,622	10,949
*14048	Dunkirk	(716)	13,131	12,511
11730	East Islip (c)	(631)	14,078	14,475
11758	East Massapequa (c)	(516)	19,565	19,069
11554	East Meadow (c)	(516)	37,461	38,132
11731	East Northport (c)	(631)	20,845	20,217
11772	East Patchogue (c)	(631)	20,824	22,469
10709	Eastchester (c)	(914)	18,564	19,554
14226	Eggertsville (c)	(716)		15,019
*14901	Elmira	(607)	30,940	29,204
11003	Elmont (c)	(516)	32,657	33,198
11731	Elwood (c)	(631)	10,916	11,177
*13760	Endicott	(607)	13,038	13,285
13762	Endwell (c)	(607)	11,706	11,446
13219	Fairmount (c)	(315)	10,795	10,224
*11001	Floral Park	(516)	15,967	15,924
13603	Fort Drum (c)	(315)	12,123	12,955
11768	Fort Salonga (c)	(631)	9,634	10,008
11010	Franklin Square (c)	(516)	29,342	29,320
14063	Fredonia	(716)	10,706	11,194
11520	Freeport	(516)	43,783	43,016
13069	Fulton	(315)	11,855	11,906
*11530	Garden City	(516)	21,672	22,450
14456	Geneva	(315)	13,617	13,324
11542	Glen Cove	(516)	26,622	27,063
12801	Glens Falls	(518)	14,354	14,728
12078	Gloversville	(518)	15,413	15,621
*11022	Great Neck	(516)	9,538	10,026
14616	Greece (c)	(585)	14,614	14,519
11740	Greenlawn (c)	(631)	13,286	13,742
11946	Hampton Bays (c)	(631)	12,236	13,603
10528	Harrison	(914)	24,154	27,645
*11788	Hauppauge (c)	(631)	20,100	20,882
10927	Haverstraw	(845)	10,117	12,040
*11551	Hempstead	(516)	56,554	54,088
*11802	Hicksville (c)	(516)	41,260	41,547
11741	Holbrook (c)	(631)	27,512	27,195
11742	Holtsville (c)	(631)	17,006	19,714
11743	Huntington (c)	(631)	18,403	18,046
11746	Huntington Station (c)	(631)	29,910	33,029
14617	Irondequoit (c)	(585)	52,354	51,692
11751	Islip (c)	(631)	20,575	18,689
*14850	Ithaca	(607)	29,287	30,054
*14702	Jamestown	(716)	31,730	31,020
10535	Jefferson Valley-Yorktown (c)	(914)	14,891	14,142
11753	Jericho (c)	(516)	13,045	13,567
13790	Johnson City	(607)	15,535	15,053
*14217	Kenmore	(716)	16,426	15,405
11754	Kings Park (c)	(631)	16,146	—
*12401	Kingston	(845)	23,456	23,887
10950	Kiryas Joel	(845)	13,138	20,291
14218	Lackawanna	(716)	19,064	18,121
11755	Lake Grove	(631)	10,250	11,205
11779	Lake Ronkonkoma (c)	(631)	19,701	20,155
*14086	Lancaster	(716)	11,188	10,339
11756	Levittown (c)	(516)	53,067	51,881
11757	Lindenhurst	(631)	27,819	27,354
*14094	Lockport	(716)	22,279	21,119
11561	Long Beach	(516)	35,462	33,395
11563	Lynbrook	(516)	19,911	19,499
10543	Mamaroneck	(914)	18,752	19,067
11949	Manorville (c)	(631)	11,131	14,314
11758	Massapequa (c)	(516)	22,652	21,685
11762	Massapequa Park	(516)	17,499	17,071
13662	Massena	(315)	11,209	10,910
11950	Mastic (c)	(631)	15,436	15,481
11951	Mastic Beach (c)	(631)	11,543	12,930
11763	Medford (c)	(631)	21,985	24,142
11747	Melville (c)	(631)	14,533	18,985
11566	Merrick (c)	(516)	22,764	22,097
11953	Middle Island (c)	(631)	9,702	10,483
*10940	Middletown	(845)	25,388	28,243
11764	Miller Place (c)	(631)	10,580	12,339
11501	Mineola	(516)	19,234	18,869

ZIP	Place	Area code	2000 population	2011 estimate
10952	Monsey (c)	(845)	14,504	18,412
10549	Mount Kisco	(914)	9,983	10,957
11766	Mount Sinai (c)	(631)	8,734	12,118
*10551	Mount Vernon	(914)	68,381	67,780
10954	Nanuet (c)	(845)	16,707	17,882
11767	Nesconset (c)	(631)	11,992	13,387
11590	New Cassel (c)	(516)	13,298	14,059
10956	New City (c)	(845)	34,038	33,559
*10802	New Rochelle	(914)	72,182	77,606
*10001	New York . . . . (212)/	(718)	8,008,278	8,244,910
*12550	Newburgh	(845)	28,259	29,026
*14302	Niagara Falls	(716)	55,593	50,086
11701	North Amityville (c)	(631)	16,572	17,862
11703	North Babylon (c)	(631)	17,877	17,509
11706	North Bay Shore (c)	(631)	14,992	18,944
11710	North Bellmore (c)	(516)	20,079	19,941
11757	North Lindenhurst (c)	(631)	11,767	11,652
11758	North Massapequa (c)	(516)	19,152	17,886
11566	North Merrick (c)	(516)	11,844	12,272
11040	North New Hyde Park (c)	(516)	14,542	14,899
14120	North Tonawanda	(716)	33,262	31,501
11580	North Valley Stream (c)	(516)	15,789	16,628
11793	North Wantagh (c)	(516)	12,156	11,960
11572	Oceanside (c)	(516)	32,733	32,109
13669	Ogdensburg	(315)	12,364	11,104
14760	Olean . . . . (585)/	(716)	15,347	14,363
13421	Oneida	(315)	10,987	11,387
13820	Oneonta	(607)	13,292	13,843
10562	Ossining	(914)	24,010	25,230
13126	Oswego	(315)	17,954	18,158
11772	Patchogue	(631)	11,919	11,843
10965	Pearl River (c)	(845)	15,553	15,876
10566	Peekskill	(914)	22,441	23,755
11803	Plainview (c)	(516)	25,637	26,217
*12901	Plattsburgh	(518)	18,816	19,949
10573	Port Chester	(914)	27,867	29,178
11050	Port Washington (c)	(516)	15,215	15,846
*12601	Poughkeepsie	(845)	29,871	32,790
11961	Ridge (c)	(631)	13,380	13,336
11901	Riverhead (c)	(631)	10,513	13,299
*14692	Rochester	(585)	219,773	210,855
*11571	Rockville Centre	(516)	24,568	24,111
11778	Rocky Point (c)	(631)	10,185	14,014
*13440	Rome	(315)	34,950	33,660
11779	Ronkonkoma (c)	(631)	20,029	19,082
11575	Roosevelt (c)	(516)	15,854	16,258
12303	Rotterdam (c)	(518)	20,536	20,652
10580	Rye	(914)	14,955	15,834
11780	Saint James (c)	(631)	13,268	13,338
13454	Salisbury (c)	(315)	12,341	12,093
12866	Saratoga Springs	(518)	26,186	26,727
11782	Sayville (c)	(631)	16,735	16,853
10583	Scarsdale	(914)	17,823	17,293
*12301	Schenectady	(518)	61,821	66,273
11783	Seaford (c)	(516)	15,791	15,294
11784	Selden (c)	(631)	21,861	19,851
11733	Setauket-East Setauket (c)	(631)	15,931	15,477
11967	Shirley (c)	(631)	25,395	27,854
11787	Smithtown (c)	(631)	26,901	26,470
11735	South Farmingdale (c)	(516)	15,061	14,486
10977	Spring Valley	(845)	25,464	31,701
*11790	Stony Brook (c)	(631)	13,727	13,740
10980	Stony Point (c)	(845)	11,744	12,147
*10901	Suffern	(845)	11,006	10,843
11791	Syosset (c)	(516)	18,544	18,829
*13220	Syracuse	(315)	147,306	145,151
10591	Tarrytown	(914)	11,090	11,354
11776	Terryville (c)	(631)	10,589	11,849
*14150	Tonawanda	(716)	16,136	15,112
*12180	Troy	(518)	49,170	50,120
11553	Uniondale (c)	(516)	23,011	24,759
*13504	Utica	(315)	60,651	62,110
*11582	Valley Stream	(516)	36,368	37,651
11793	Wantagh (c)	(516)	18,971	18,871
*13601	Watertown	(315)	26,705	27,423
12189	Watervliet	(518)	10,207	10,230
*11704	West Babylon (c)	(631)	43,452	43,213
10993	West Haverstraw	(845)	10,295	10,230
11552	West Hempstead (c)	(516)	18,713	18,862
11795	West Islip (c)	(631)	28,907	28,335
14224	West Seneca (c)	(716)	45,943	44,711
*11590	Westbury	(516)	14,263	15,203
*10602	White Plains	(914)	53,077	57,258
11797	Woodbury (c)	(516)	—	10,747
11598	Woodmere (c)	(516)	16,447	17,121
11798	Wyandanch (c)	(631)	10,546	11,647
*10702	Yonkers	(914)	196,086	197,399

North Carolina

Area code (980) overlays area code (704). Area code (984) overlays area code (919).

ZIP	Place	Area code	2000 population	2011 estimate
28315	Albemarle	(910)	15,680	15,913
*27502	Apex	(919)	20,212	38,702
27263	Archdale	(336)	9,014	11,466
*27203	Asheboro	(336)	21,672	25,284

ZIP	Place	Area code	2000 population	2011 estimate
*28802	Asheville	(828)	68,889	84,458
28012	Belmont	(704)	8,705	10,119
*28607	Boone	(828)	13,472	17,189
*27215	Burlington	(336)	44,917	50,925
27510	Carrboro	(919)	16,782	19,890
*27511	Cary	(919)	94,536	139,633
*27514	Chapel Hill	(919)	48,715	58,011
*28204	Charlotte	(704)	540,828	751,087
*27520	Clayton	(919)	6,973	16,472
27012	Clemmons	(336)	13,827	18,858
*28025	Concord	(704)	55,977	80,597
28031	Cornelius	(704)	11,969	25,547
*28036	Davidson	(704)	7,139	11,188
*27701	Durham	(919)	187,035	233,252
*27288	Eden	(336)	15,908	15,475
*27909	Elizabeth City	(252)	17,188	18,698
*28302	Fayetteville	(910)	121,015	203,945
27526	Fuquay-Varina	(919)	7,898	18,528
27529	Garner	(919)	17,757	26,589
*28052	Gastonia	(704)	66,277	72,068
*27530	Goldsboro	(919)	39,043	36,743
27253	Graham	(336)	12,833	14,357
*27420	Greensboro	(336)	223,891	273,425
*27834	Greenville	(252)	60,476	86,017
28075	Harrisburg	(704)	4,493	11,751
*28532	Havelock	(252)	22,442	20,966
*27536	Henderson	(252)	16,095	15,330
*28739	Hendersonville	(828)	10,420	13,277
*28603	Hickory	(828)	37,222	39,965
*27260	High Point	(336)	85,839	105,753
27540	Holly Springs	(919)	9,192	25,468
28348	Hope Mills	(910)	11,237	15,441
*28070	Huntersville	(704)	24,960	48,048
28079	Indian Trail	(704)	11,905	34,223
*28540	Jacksonville	(910)	66,715	70,801
*28081	Kannapolis	(704)	36,910	43,242
*27284	Kernersville	(336)	17,126	23,411
28086	Kings Mountain	(704)	9,693	10,246
*28502	Kinston	(252)	23,688	21,622
*27545	Knightdale	(919)	5,958	11,776
*28352	Laurinburg	(910)	15,874	15,831
28451	Leland	(910)	1,938	14,006
*28645	Lenoir	(828)	16,793	18,091
27023	Lewisville	(336)	8,826	12,798
*27292	Lexington	(336)	19,953	18,912
*28092	Lincolnton	(704)	9,965	10,570
*28358	Lumberton	(910)	20,795	21,753
*28105	Matthews	(704)	22,127	27,936
27302	Mebane	(919)	7,284	11,562
28227	Mint Hill	(704)	14,922	23,341
*28110	Monroe	(704)	26,228	33,475
*28115	Mooresville	(704)	18,823	33,073
*28655	Morganton	(828)	17,310	16,917
27560	Morrisville	(919)	5,208	19,184
*27030	Mount Airy	(336)	8,484	10,398
28120	Mount Holly	(704)	9,618	13,719
28411	Murraysville (c)	(910)	7,279	14,215
*28562	New Bern	(252)	23,128	29,899
*28658	Newton	(828)	12,560	12,953
*28374	Pinehurst	(910)	9,706	14,861
28399	Piney Green (c)	(910)	11,658	13,293
*27611	Raleigh	(919)	276,093	416,468
*27320	Reidsville	(336)	14,485	14,473
*27870	Roanoke Rapids	(252)	16,957	15,601
*27801	Rocky Mount	(252)	55,893	57,433
*28144	Salisbury	(704)	26,462	33,586
*27330	Sanford	(919)	23,220	28,518
*28150	Shelby	(704)	19,477	20,202
27577	Smithfield	(919)	11,510	11,194
*28387	Southern Pines	(910)	10,918	12,487
*28390	Spring Lake	(910)	8,098	12,164
28104	Stallings	(704)	3,189	14,123
*28677	Statesville	(704)	23,320	24,798
27358	Summerfield	(336)	7,018	10,381
*27886	Tarboro	(252)	11,138	11,315
*27360	Thomasville	(336)	19,788	26,729
*27587	Wake Forest	(919)	12,588	31,073
28173	Waxhaw	(704)	2,625	10,067
*28402	Wilmington	(910)	75,838	108,297
*27893	Wilson	(252)	44,405	49,297
*27102	Winston-Salem	(336)	185,776	232,385

North Dakota (701)

ZIP	Place	2000 population	2011 estimate
*58501	Bismarck	55,532	62,665
*58601	Dickinson	16,010	18,499
*58102	Fargo	90,599	107,349
*58201	Grand Forks	49,321	52,631
*58401	Jamestown	15,527	15,400
58554	Mandan	16,718	18,507
*58701	Minot	36,567	42,485
58078	West Fargo	14,940	26,291
*58801	Williston	12,512	16,006

Ohio

Area code (234) overlays area code (330). Area code (567) overlays area code (419).

ZIP	Place	Area code	2000 population	2011 estimate
*44309	Akron	(330)	217,074	198,402
44601	Alliance	(330)	23,253	22,294
44001	Amherst	(440)	11,797	12,031
44805	Ashland	(419)	21,249	20,367
*44004	Ashtabula	(440)	20,962	19,096
45701	Athens	(740)	21,342	23,835
44202	Aurora	(330)	13,556	15,568
44515	Austintown (c)	(330)	31,627	29,677
44011	Avon	(440)	11,446	21,210
44012	Avon Lake	(440)	18,145	22,602
44203	Barberton	(330)	27,899	26,455
44140	Bay Village	(440)	16,087	15,528
44122	Beachwood	(216)	12,186	11,867
45434	Beavercreek	(937)	37,984	45,566
44146	Bedford	(216)/(440)	14,214	12,972
*44146	Bedford Heights	(216)/(440)	11,375	10,666
43311	Bellefontaine	(937)	13,069	13,322
44017	Berea	(440)	18,970	18,960
43209	Bexley	(614)	13,203	13,221
*45242	Blue Ash	(513)	12,513	12,083
44513	Boardman (c)	(330)	37,215	35,376
*43402	Bowling Green	(419)	29,636	30,221
44141	Brecksville	(440)	13,382	13,555
45211	Bridgetown (c)	(513)	—	14,407
44147	Broadview Heights	(440)	15,967	19,247
44142	Brook Park	(216)/(440)	21,218	19,063
44144	Brooklyn	(216)	11,586	11,082
44212	Brunswick	(330)	33,388	34,441
44820	Bucyrus	(419)	13,224	12,253
*43725	Cambridge	(740)	11,520	10,593
*44711	Canton	(330)	80,806	72,919
*45822	Celina	(419)	10,303	10,406
*45458	Centerville (Montgomery Co.)	(937)	23,024	24,109
45601	Chillicothe	(740)	21,796	21,955
*45202	Cincinnati	(513)	331,285	296,223
43113	Circleville	(740)	13,485	13,389
45315	Clayton	(937)	13,347	13,269
*44101	Cleveland	(216)	478,403	393,806
*44118	Cleveland Heights	(216)	49,958	45,764
*43216	Columbus	(614)	711,470	797,434
44030	Conneaut	(440)	12,485	12,824
43812	Coshocton	(740)	11,682	11,231
*44222	Cuyahoga Falls	(330)	49,374	49,473
*45401	Dayton	(937)	166,179	142,148
43512	Defiance	(419)	16,465	16,622
43015	Delaware	(740)	25,243	35,541
*45247	Dent (c)	(513)	7,612	10,497
44622	Dover	(330)	12,210	12,816
*43016	Dublin	(614)/(740)	31,392	42,346
*44112	East Cleveland	(216)	27,217	17,705
43920	East Liverpool	(330)	13,089	11,199
*44095	Eastlake	(440)	20,255	18,565
*44035	Elyria	(440)	55,953	54,581
*45322	Englewood	(937)	12,235	13,527
*44117	Euclid	(216)	52,717	48,541
45324	Fairborn	(937)	32,052	32,620
*45011	Fairfield	(513)	42,097	42,730
44126	Fairview Park	(440)	17,572	16,694
*45839	Findlay	(419)	38,967	41,351
45224	Finneytown (c)	(513)	13,492	12,741
45240	Forest Park	(513)	19,463	18,673
45230	Forestville (c)	(513)	10,978	10,532
44830	Fostoria	(419)	13,931	13,411
45005	Franklin	(513)	11,396	11,896
43420	Fremont	(419)	17,375	16,677
43230	Gahanna	(614)	32,636	33,694
44833	Galion	(419)	11,341	10,416
*44125	Garfield Heights	(216)	30,734	28,625
44232	Green	(330)	22,817	25,604
45331	Greenville	(937)	13,294	13,189
43123	Grove City	(614)	27,075	36,052
*45011	Hamilton	(513)	60,690	62,795
43056	Heath	(740)	8,527	10,357
43026	Hilliard	(614)/(740)	24,230	28,816
45424	Huber Heights	(937)	38,212	38,278
*44236	Hudson	(330)	22,439	22,182
45638	Ironton	(740)	11,211	11,135
*44240	Kent	(330)	27,906	28,935
*45429	Kettering	(937)	57,502	56,427
44107	Lakewood	(216)	56,646	51,724
43130	Lancaster	(740)	35,335	39,026
45036	Lebanon	(513)	16,962	20,242
*45802	Lima	(419)	40,081	38,693
*44052	Lorain	(440)	68,652	64,152
*45140	Loveland	(513)	11,677	12,082
44124	Lyndhurst	(216)/(440)	15,279	13,893
*44056	Macedonia	(330)	9,224	11,147
*45248	Mack (c)	(513)	—	11,585

ZIP	Place	Area code	2000 population	2011 estimate
*44901	Mansfield	(419)	49,346	47,483
44137	Maple Heights	(216)	26,156	22,959
45750	Marietta	(740)	14,515	14,080
*43302	Marion	(740)	35,318	36,689
*43040	Marysville	(937)	15,942	22,288
45040	Mason	(513)	22,016	31,039
*44646	Massillon	(330)	31,325	32,106
43537	Maumee	(419)	15,237	14,227
44124	Mayfield Heights	(440)	19,386	19,005
*44256	Medina	(330)	25,139	26,822
*44060	Mentor	(440)	50,278	47,126
*45343	Miamisburg	(937)	19,489	20,274
44130	Middleburg Heights	(216)/(440)	15,542	15,825
*45042	Middletown	(513)	51,605	48,962
45211	Monfort Heights (c)	(513)	—	11,948
*45050	Monroe	(513)	7,133	12,509
45242	Montgomery	(513)	10,163	10,225
43050	Mount Vernon	(740)	14,375	17,087
44657	New Franklin	(330)	2,191	14,175
44663	New Philadelphia	(330)	17,056	17,273
*43055	Newark	(740)	46,279	47,790
44446	Niles	(330)	20,932	19,168
*44720	North Canton	(330)	16,369	17,465
44070	North Olmsted	(440)	34,113	32,463
*44039	North Ridgeville	(440)	22,338	29,492
44133	North Royalton	(440)	28,648	30,206
45239	Northbrook (c)	(513)	11,076	10,668
44203	Norton	(330)	11,523	12,040
44857	Norwalk	(419)	16,238	16,997
*45212	Norwood	(513)	21,675	19,159
*43616	Oregon	(419)	19,355	20,206
45056	Oxford	(513)	21,943	21,444
44077	Painesville	(440)	17,503	19,549
*44129	Parma	(216)/(440)	85,655	80,968
44130	Parma Heights	(216)/(440)	21,659	20,558
43062	Pataskala	(740)	10,249	15,031
*43551	Perrysburg	(419)	16,945	20,772
43147	Pickerington	(614)/(740)	9,792	18,408
45356	Piqua	(937)	20,738	20,592
*45662	Portsmouth	(740)	20,909	20,171
43065	Powell	(614)	6,247	11,777
44266	Ravenna	(330)	11,771	11,739
*45215	Reading	(513)	11,292	10,359
43068	Reynoldsburg	(614)/(740)	32,069	36,293
44143	Richmond Heights	(216)/(440)	10,944	10,465
45431	Riverside	(937)	23,545	25,319
44116	Rocky River	(440)	20,735	20,056
44460	Salem	(330)	12,197	12,270
*44870	Sandusky	(419)	27,844	25,682
44131	Seven Hills	(216)/(440)	12,080	11,719
*44122	Shaker Heights	(216)	29,405	28,226
*45241	Sharonville	(513)	13,804	13,544
*45365	Sidney	(937)	20,211	21,178
44139	Solon	(440)	21,802	23,166
*44121	South Euclid	(216)	23,537	22,126
45066	Springboro	(513)	12,380	17,588
45246	Springdale	(513)	10,563	11,195
*45501	Springfield	(937)	65,358	60,333
*43952	Steubenville	(740)	19,015	18,440
44224	Stow	(330)	32,139	34,711
44241	Streetsboro	(330)	12,311	16,050
*44136	Strongsville	(440)	43,858	44,400
44471	Struthers	(330)	11,756	10,640
43560	Sylvania	(419)	18,670	18,886
44278	Tallmadge	(330)	16,390	17,473
44883	Tiffin	(419)	18,135	17,879
*43601	Toledo	(419)	313,619	286,038
45067	Trenton	(513)	8,746	11,931
*45426	Trotwood	(937)	27,420	24,542
*45373	Troy	(937)	21,999	25,143
44087	Twinsburg	(330)	17,006	18,727
*44122	University Heights	(216)	14,146	13,445
*43221	Upper Arlington	(614)	33,686	34,223
43078	Urbana	(937)	11,613	11,707
45891	Van Wert	(419)	10,690	10,793
45377	Vandalia	(937)	14,603	15,317
*44089	Vermilion	(440)	10,927	10,569
*44281	Wadsworth	(330)	18,437	21,683
*44481	Warren	(330)	46,832	41,358
*44122	Warrensville Heights	(216)	15,109	13,437
43160	Washington Court House	(740)	—	14,169
*45449	West Carrollton	(937)	13,818	13,204
*43081	Westerville	(614)	35,318	36,665
44145	Westlake	(440)	31,719	32,479
45239	White Oak (c)	(513)	13,277	19,167
43213	Whitehall	(614)	19,201	18,306
44092	Wickliffe	(440)	13,484	12,742
*44094	Willoughby	(440)	22,621	22,252
*44095	Willowick	(440)	14,361	14,161
45177	Wilmington	(937)	11,921	12,488
44691	Wooster	(330)	24,811	26,139
43085	Worthington	(614)	14,125	13,755
45385	Xenia	(937)	24,164	25,925
*44501	Youngstown	(330)	82,026	66,571
*43701	Zanesville	(740)	25,586	25,531

Oklahoma

Area code (539) overlays area code (918).

ZIP	Place	Area code	2000 population	2011 estimate
*74820	Ada	(580)	15,691	16,942
*73521	Altus	(580)	21,447	19,814
*73401	Ardmore	(580)	23,711	24,553
*74003	Bartlesville	(918)	34,748	36,099
73008	Bethany	(405)	20,307	19,406
74008	Bixby	(918)	13,336	21,137
*74012	Broken Arrow	(918)	74,859	100,073
*73018	Chickasha	(405)	15,850	16,210
73020	Choctaw	(405)	9,377	11,364
*74017	Claremore	(918)	15,873	18,745
*73115	Del City	(405)	22,128	21,746
*73533	Duncan	(580)	22,505	23,507
*74701	Durant	(580)	13,549	16,097
*73034	Edmond	(405)	68,315	82,963
73036	El Reno	(405)	16,212	17,268
*73644	Elk City	(580)	10,510	11,789
*73701	Enid	(580)	47,045	49,451
*74033	Glenpool	(918)	8,123	10,938
73044	Guthrie	(405)	9,925	10,345
73942	Guymon	(580)	10,472	11,823
74037	Jenks	(918)	9,557	17,130
*73501	Lawton	(580)	92,757	98,177
*74501	McAlester	(918)	17,783	18,306
*74354	Miami	(918)	13,704	13,577
*73140	Midwest City	(405)	54,088	55,427
*73153	Moore	(405)	41,138	56,315
*74401	Muskogee	(918)	38,310	39,231
73064	Mustang	(405)	13,156	18,002
*73069	Norman	(405)	95,694	113,273
*73125	Oklahoma City	(405)	506,132	591,967
74447	Okmulgee	(918)	13,022	12,283
*74055	Owasso	(918)	18,502	29,854
*74601	Ponca City	(580)	25,919	25,168
74063	Sand Springs	(918)	17,451	19,140
*74066	Sapulpa	(918)	19,166	20,691
*74801	Shawnee	(405)	28,692	30,212
*74074	Stillwater	(405)	39,065	46,048
*74464	Tahlequah	(918)	14,458	16,021
*74103	Tulsa	(918)	393,049	396,466
*73112	Warr Acres	(405)	9,735	10,238
73096	Weatherford	(580)	9,859	10,939
*73801	Woodward	(580)	11,853	11,944
*73099	Yukon	(405)	21,043	23,491

Oregon

Area code (458) overlays area code (541). Area code (971) overlays area code (503).

ZIP	Place	Area code	2000 population	2011 estimate
*97321	Albany	(541)	40,852	50,724
*97006	Aloha (c)	(503)	41,741	49,425
97601	Altamont (c)	(541)	19,603	19,257
97520	Ashland	(541)	19,522	20,232
*97005	Beaverton	(503)	76,129	91,625
*97701	Bend	(541)	52,029	77,905
97229	Bethany (c)	(503)	—	20,646
97013	Canby	(503)	12,790	16,007
97291	Cedar Mill (c)	(503)	12,597	14,546
97502	Central Point	(541)	12,493	17,308
97420	Coos Bay	(541)	15,374	15,903
97113	Cornelius	(503)	9,652	12,107
*97333	Corvallis	(541)	49,322	54,674
97338	Dallas	(503)	12,459	14,698
*97009	Damascus	(503)	—	10,656
*97440	Eugene	(541)	137,893	156,929
97116	Forest Grove	(503)	17,708	21,488
97301	Four Corners (c)	(503)	13,922	15,947
97027	Gladstone	(503)	11,438	11,626
*97526	Grants Pass	(541)	23,003	34,646
*97030	Gresham	(503)	90,205	107,439
*97015	Happy Valley	(503)	4,519	14,061
97303	Hayesville (c)	(503)	18,222	19,936
97838	Hermiston	(541)	13,154	16,939
*97123	Hillsboro	(503)	70,186	93,455
97307	Keizer	(503)	32,203	36,898
*97601	Klamath Falls	(541)	19,462	20,820
*97850	La Grande	(541)	12,327	13,102
*97034	Lake Oswego	(503)	35,278	37,046
97355	Lebanon	(541)	12,950	15,711
97741	McMinnville	(541)	26,499	32,451
*97501	Medford	(541)	63,154	75,501
*97269	Milwaukie	(503)	20,490	20,518
97132	Newberg	(503)	18,064	22,244
97268	Oak Grove (c)	(503)	12,808	16,629
97006	Oak Hills (c)	(503)	9,050	11,333
97267	Oatfield (c)	(503)	15,750	13,415
97914	Ontario	(541)	10,985	11,268
97045	Oregon City	(503)	25,754	32,211
97801	Pendleton	(541)	16,354	16,784
*97208	Portland	(503)	529,121	593,820
97756	Redmond	(541)	13,481	26,646

ZIP	Place	Area code	2000 population	2011 estimate
97470	Roseburg	(541)	20,017	21,155
97051	Saint Helens	(503)	10,019	12,905
*97309	Salem	(503)	136,924	156,244
97140	Sherwood	(503)	11,791	18,567
*97477	Springfield	(541)	52,864	59,695
97058	The Dalles[1]	(541)	12,156	13,631
*97281	Tigard	(503)	41,223	49,011
97060	Troutdale	(503)	13,777	16,244
97062	Tualatin	(503)	22,791	26,558
97068	West Linn	(503)	22,261	25,392
97070	Wilsonville	(503)	13,991	19,715
97071	Woodburn	(503)	20,100	24,358

(1) Listed as City of The Dalles in 2000 Census.

Pennsylvania

Area code (267) overlays area code (215). Area code (484) overlays area code (610). Area code (878) overlays area code (412).

ZIP	Place	Area code	2000 population	2011 estimate
*18105	Allentown	(610)	106,632	119,141
15101	Allison Park (c)	(412)/(724)	—	21,552
*16603	Altoona	(814)	49,523	46,329
19003	Ardmore (c)	(610)	12,616	12,455
15234	Baldwin	(412)	19,999	19,809
18603	Berwick	(570)	10,774	10,463
15102	Bethel Park	(412)	33,556	32,381
*18016	Bethlehem	(610)	71,329	75,266
*17815	Bloomsburg	(570)	12,375	15,111
19008	Broomall (c)	(610)	11,046	10,789
*16001	Butler	(724)	15,121	13,831
*17013	Carlisle	(717)	17,970	19,072
15108	Carnot-Moon (c)	(412)	10,637	11,372
17201	Chambersburg	(717)	17,862	20,425
*19013	Chester	(610)	36,854	34,184
19320	Coatesville	(610)	10,838	13,216
17109	Colonial Park (c)	(717)	13,259	13,229
17512	Columbia	(717)	10,311	10,484
19023	Darby	(610)	10,299	10,694
19026	Drexel Hill (c)	(610)	29,364	28,043
*18512	Dunmore	(570)	14,018	14,400
*18042	Easton	(610)	26,263	26,995
17022	Elizabethtown	(717)	11,887	11,628
*18049	Emmaus	(610)	11,313	11,321
17522	Ephrata	(717)	13,213	13,505
*16501	Erie	(814)	103,717	101,807
16063	Fernway (c)	(724)	12,188	12,414
15237	Franklin Park	(412)	11,364	13,499
18052	Fullerton (c)	(610)	14,268	14,925
*15601	Greensburg	(724)	15,889	14,865
*17331	Hanover	(717)	14,535	15,348
*17105	Harrisburg	(717)	48,950	49,673
*18201	Hazleton	(570)	23,329	25,317
16148	Hermitage	(724)	16,157	16,133
17033	Hershey (c)	(717)	12,771	14,257
19044	Horsham (c)	(215)	14,779	14,842
*15701	Indiana	(724)	14,895	14,620
15025	Jefferson Hills	(412)	9,666	10,641
*15907	Johnstown	(814)	23,906	20,814
19406	King of Prussia (c)	(610)	18,511	19,936
18704	Kingston	(570)	13,855	13,170
*17604	Lancaster	(717)	56,348	60,058
19446	Lansdale	(215)	16,071	16,366
19050	Lansdowne	(610)	11,044	10,627
*17042	Lebanon	(717)	24,461	25,620
*19055	Levittown (c)	(215)	53,966	52,983
15068	Lower Burrell	(724)	12,608	11,739
*15134	McKeesport	(412)	24,040	19,772
*16335	Meadville	(814)	13,685	13,616
*15146	Monroeville	(412)/(724)	29,349	28,445
18936	Montgomeryville (c)	(215)	12,031	12,624
18707	Mountain Top (c)	(570)	15,269	10,982
15120	Munhall	(412)	12,264	11,430
*15668	Murraysville	(412)/(724)	18,872	20,040
18634	Nanticoke	(570)	10,955	10,456
*16108	New Castle	(724)	26,309	23,128
*15068	New Kensington	(724)	14,701	13,091
*19403	Norristown	(610)	31,282	34,528
16301	Oil City	(814)	11,504	10,499
*19104	Philadelphia	(215)	1,517,550	1,536,471
*19460	Phoenixville	(610)	14,788	16,585
*15233	Pittsburgh	(412)	334,563	307,484
15239	Plum	(412)	26,940	27,183
*19464	Pottstown	(610)	21,859	22,510
17901	Pottsville	(570)	15,549	14,249
*19612	Reading	(610)	81,207	88,414
15857	Saint Marys	(814)	14,502	12,991
*18505	Scranton	(570)	76,415	75,995
*16146	Sharon	(724)	16,328	13,963
17404	Shiloh (c)	(717)	10,192	11,218
15129	South Park Twp. (c)	(814)	14,340	13,416
*16804	State College	(814)	38,420	42,499
15401	Uniontown	(724)	12,422	10,334
15241	Upper Saint Clair (c)	(412)	20,053	19,229
15301	Washington (Wash. Co.)	(724)	15,268	13,691
*17268	Waynesboro	(717)	9,614	10,653

ZIP	Place	Area code	2000 population	2011 estimate
17315	Weigelstown (c)	(717)	10,117	12,875
*19380	West Chester	(610)	17,861	19,248
*15122	West Mifflin	(412)	22,464	20,356
18052	Whitehall (Allegheny Co.)	(412)	14,444	13,973
*18703	Wilkes-Barre	(570)	43,123	41,465
15221	Wilkinsburg	(412)	19,196	15,964
*17701	Williamsport	(570)	30,706	29,534
19090	Willow Grove (c)	(215)	16,234	15,726
19610	Wyomissing	(610)	8,587	10,479
19050	Yeadon	(610)	11,762	11,449
*17405	York	(717)	40,862	43,884

Rhode Island (401)
See introductory note.

ZIP	Place	2000 population	2011 estimate
02806	Barrington	16,819	16,284
02809	Bristol	22,469	22,922
02830	Burrillville	15,796	15,956
02863	Central Falls	18,928	19,379
02816	Coventry	33,668	34,884
*02905	Cranston	79,269	80,392
02864	Cumberland	31,840	33,507
02818	East Greenwich	12,948	13,098
02914	East Providence	48,688	47,039
02919	Johnston	28,195	28,771
02865	Lincoln	20,898	21,108
02842	Middletown	17,334	16,111
02882	Narragansett	16,361	15,814
02840	Newport	26,475	24,619
02843	Newport East (c)	11,463	11,769
02852	North Kingstown	26,326	26,396
02908	North Providence	32,411	32,079
02896	North Smithfield	10,618	11,968
*02860	Pawtucket	72,958	71,153
02871	Portsmouth	17,149	17,348
*02904	Providence	173,618	178,053
02857	Scituate	10,324	10,330
02917	Smithfield	20,613	21,432
02879	South Kingstown	27,921	30,553
02878	Tiverton	15,260	15,743
02864	Valley Falls (c)	11,599	11,547
02885	Warren	11,360	10,594
*02886	Warwick	85,808	82,361
02893	West Warwick	29,581	29,080
02891	Westerly	22,966	22,708
02891	Westerly (c)	17,682	17,936
02895	Woonsocket	43,224	41,188

South Carolina

ZIP	Place	Area code	2000 population	2011 estimate
*29801	Aiken	(803)	25,337	29,627
*29621	Anderson	(864)	25,514	26,871
*29906	Beaufort	(843)	12,950	12,534
29611	Berea (c)	(864)	14,158	14,295
*29910	Bluffton	(843)	1,275	12,734
29033	Cayce	(803)	12,150	12,743
*29402	Charleston	(843)	96,650	122,689
*29631	Clemson	(864)	11,939	13,946
*29201	Columbia	(803)	116,278	130,591
*29526	Conway	(843)	11,788	17,513
29204	Dentsville (c)	(803)	13,009	14,062
*29640	Easley	(864)	17,754	20,058
*29681	Five Forks (c)	(864)	8,064	14,140
*29501	Florence	(843)	30,248	37,326
29206	Forest Acres	(803)	10,558	10,496
*29715	Fort Mill	(803)	7,587	11,027
*29341	Gaffney	(864)	12,968	12,456
29605	Gantt (c)	(864)	13,962	14,229
29445	Goose Creek	(843)	29,208	37,035
*29602	Greenville	(864)	56,002	60,379
*29646	Greenwood	(864)	22,071	23,342
*29650	Greer	(864)	16,843	26,002
*29406	Hanahan	(843)	12,937	18,579
*29928	Hilton Head Island	(843)	33,862	37,675
29063	Irmo	(803)	11,039	11,283
29456	Ladson (c)	(843)	13,264	13,790
*29072	Lexington	(803)	9,793	18,179
29662	Mauldin	(864)	15,224	23,408
*29645	Mount Pleasant	(843)	47,609	69,357
*29575	Myrtle Beach	(803)	22,759	27,820
29108	Newberry	(803)	10,580	10,332
*29841	North Augusta	(803)	17,574	21,435
*29410	North Charleston	(843)	79,641	99,727
*29582	North Myrtle Beach	(843)	10,974	14,118
29073	Oak Grove (c)	(803)	8,183	10,291
*29115	Orangeburg	(803)	12,765	13,885
29611	Parker (c)	(864)	10,760	11,443
29935	Port Royal	(843)	3,950	10,790
29020	Red Hill (c)	(843)	10,509	13,223
*29730	Rock Hill	(803)	49,765	67,423
29417	Saint Andrews (c)	(843)	21,814	20,493
29210	Seven Oaks (c)	(803)	15,755	15,144
*29681	Simpsonville	(864)	14,352	18,652

ZIP	Place	Area code	2000 population	2011 estimate
29577	Socastee (c)	(843)	14,295	19,952
*29306	Spartanburg	(864)	39,673	37,334
*29483	Summerville	(843)	27,752	44,783
*29150	Sumter	(803)	39,643	40,526
*29687	Taylors (c)	(864)	20,125	21,617
29607	Wade Hampton (c)	(864)	20,458	20,622
*29169	West Columbia	(803)	13,064	15,463

South Dakota (605)

ZIP	Place	2000 population	2011 estimate
*57401	Aberdeen	24,658	26,297
*57006	Brookings	18,504	22,228
*57350	Huron	11,893	12,706
57301	Mitchell	14,558	15,368
57501	Pierre	13,876	13,860
*57701	Rapid City	59,607	69,200
*57101	Sioux Falls	123,975	156,592
*57783	Spearfish	8,606	10,585
57069	Vermillion	9,765	10,706
57201	Watertown	20,237	21,658
*57078	Yankton	13,528	14,564

Tennessee

ZIP	Place	Area code	2000 population	2011 estimate
38002	Arlington	(901)	2,569	11,610
*37303	Athens	(423)	13,220	13,520
*38184	Bartlett	(901)	40,543	55,055
*37027	Brentwood	(615)	23,445	38,144
*37621	Bristol	(423)	24,821	26,803
38012	Brownsville	(731)	10,748	10,117
*37401	Chattanooga	(423)	155,554	170,136
*37040	Clarksville	(931)	103,455	136,231
*37311	Cleveland	(423)	37,192	41,723
*38017	Collierville	(901)	31,872	44,324
*38401	Columbia	(931)	33,055	34,915
*38501	Cookeville	(931)	23,923	30,692
*38555	Crossville	(931)	8,981	10,903
*37055	Dickson	(615)	12,244	14,659
*38024	Dyersburg	(731)	17,452	17,082
37412	East Ridge	(423)	20,640	21,259
*37643	Elizabethton	(423)	13,372	14,123
*37922	Farragut	(865)	17,720	20,904
*37064	Franklin	(615)	41,842	64,317
37066	Gallatin	(615)	23,230	30,838
*38138	Germantown	(901)	37,348	39,161
*37072	Goodlettsville	(615)	13,780	16,176
*37743	Greeneville	(423)	15,198	15,170
*37075	Hendersonville	(615)	40,620	52,349
*38301	Jackson	(731)	59,643	65,187
*37601	Johnson City	(423)	55,469	63,815
*37662	Kingsport	(423)	44,905	49,232
*37950	Knoxville	(865)	173,890	180,761
*37086	La Vergne	(615)	18,687	33,389
38002	Lakeland	(901)	6,862	12,533
38464	Lawrenceburg	(931)	10,796	10,489
*37087	Lebanon	(615)	20,235	26,770
37091	Lewisburg	(931)	10,413	11,195
37355	Manchester	(931)	8,294	10,142
38237	Martin	(731)	10,515	11,461
37801	Maryville	(865)	23,120	27,646
*37110	McMinnville	(931)	12,749	13,633
*38101	Memphis	(901)	650,100	652,050
37343	Middle Valley (c)	(423)	11,854	12,684
*38053	Millington	(901)	10,433	10,257
*37813	Morristown	(423)	24,965	29,374
*37122	Mount Juliet	(615)	12,366	24,219
*37130	Murfreesboro	(615)	68,816	111,327
*37202	Nashville-Davidson	(615)	545,524	609,644
*37830	Oak Ridge	(865)	27,387	29,351
38242	Paris	(731)	9,763	10,162
37148	Portland	(615)	8,458	11,704
37415	Red Bank	(423)	12,418	11,808
*37862	Sevierville	(865)	11,757	15,037
*37160	Shelbyville	(931)	16,105	20,536
37167	Smyrna	(615)	25,569	40,946
*37379	Soddy-Daisy	(423)	11,530	12,883
37174	Spring Hill	(931)	7,715	29,735
37172	Springfield	(615)	14,329	16,639
*37388	Tullahoma	(931)	17,994	18,725
*38261	Union City	(731)	10,876	10,888
37188	White House	(615)	7,220	10,419

Texas

Area codes (281) and (832) overlay area code (713). Area code (430) overlays area code (903). Area code (682) overlays area code (817). Area codes (972) and (469) overlay area code (214).

ZIP	Place	Area code	2000 population	2011 estimate
*79604	Abilene	(325)	115,930	118,117
75001	Addison	(214)	14,166	13,323
78516	Alamo	(956)	14,760	18,895

ZIP	Place	Area code	2000 population	2011 estimate
77039	Aldine (c)	(713)	13,979	15,869
*78332	Alice	(361)	19,010	19,337
*75002	Allen	(214)	43,554	87,473
78574	Alton	(956)	4,384	13,969
*77511	Alvin	(713)	21,413	24,774
*79105	Amarillo	(806)	173,627	193,675
79714	Andrews	(432)	9,652	11,578
*77515	Angleton	(979)	18,130	19,280
*76004	Arlington	(817)	332,969	373,698
77346	Atascocita (c)	(281)	35,757	65,844
*75751	Athens	(903)	11,297	12,755
*78712	Austin	(512)	656,562	820,611
*76020	Azle	(817)	9,600	11,170
75180	Balch Springs	(214)	19,375	24,211
*77414	Bay City	(979)	18,667	17,663
*77520	Baytown	(713)	66,430	73,322
*77707	Beaumont	(409)	113,866	118,548
*76021	Bedford	(817)	47,152	48,043
*78102	Beeville	(361)	13,129	12,985
*77401	Bellaire	(713)	15,642	17,223
*76705	Bellmead	(254)	9,214	10,061
76513	Belton	(254)	14,623	18,486
*76126	Benbrook	(817)	20,208	21,715
*79720	Big Spring	(432)	25,233	27,364
*78006	Boerne	(830)	6,178	10,884
75418	Bonham	(903)	9,990	10,136
*79007	Borger	(806)	14,302	13,240
*77833	Brenham	(979)	13,507	15,752
*78520	Brownsville	(956)	139,722	178,430
*76801	Brownwood	(325)	18,813	19,329
78717	Brushy Creek (c)	(903)	15,371	21,764
*77801	Bryan	(979)	65,660	77,321
76354	Burkburnett	(940)	10,927	10,740
*76028	Burleson	(817)	20,976	37,217
*79015	Canyon	(806)	12,875	13,570
78130	Canyon Lake (c)	(830)	16,870	21,262
*75006	Carrollton	(214)	109,576	122,640
*75104	Cedar Hill	(214)	32,093	45,945
*78613	Cedar Park	(512)	26,049	51,283
77530	Channelview (c)	(713)	29,685	38,289
78108	Cibolo	(210)	3,035	15,853
*77450	Cinco Ranch (c)	(281)	11,196	18,274
*76031	Cleburne	(817)	26,005	29,681
77015	Cloverleaf (c)	(713)	23,508	22,942
*77531	Clute	(979)	10,424	11,459
*77840	College Station	(979)	67,890	95,142
76034	Colleyville	(817)	19,636	23,328
*77301	Conroe	(936)	36,811	58,973
78109	Converse	(210)	11,508	18,643
*75019	Coppell	(214)	35,958	39,462
76522	Copperas Cove	(254)	29,592	32,522
*76205	Corinth	(940)	11,325	20,662
*78469	Corpus Christi	(361)	277,454	307,953
*75110	Corsicana	(903)	24,485	23,926
76036	Crowley	(817)	7,467	13,131
*75221	Dallas	(214)	1,188,580	1,223,229
77536	Deer Park	(713)	28,520	32,706
*78840	Del Rio	(830)	33,867	35,766
*75020	Denison	(903)	22,773	22,784
*76201	Denton	(940)	80,537	117,187
*75115	DeSoto	(214)	37,646	50,045
77539	Dickinson	(281)	17,093	18,967
78537	Donna	(956)	14,768	16,274
79029	Dumas	(806)	13,747	14,725
*75138	Duncanville	(214)	36,081	39,310
*78852	Eagle Pass	(830)	22,413	26,807
*78539	Edinburg	(956)	48,465	79,147
77437	El Campo	(979)	10,945	11,612
*79910	El Paso	(915)	563,662	665,568
*75119	Ennis	(214)	16,045	18,901
*76039	Euless	(817)	46,005	52,443
*75381	Farmers Branch	(214)	27,508	29,200
*75022	Flower Mound	(214)	50,702	67,019
76119	Forest Hill	(817)	12,949	12,636
75126	Forney	(214)	5,588	14,950
76544	Fort Hood (c)	(254)	33,711	—
*76161	Fort Worth	(817)	534,694	758,738
77498	Four Corners (c)	(281)	2,954	12,382
78624	Fredericksburg	(830)	8,911	10,643
*77541	Freeport	(979)	12,708	12,317
77545	Fresno (c)	(281)	6,603	19,069
*77546	Friendswood	(281)	29,037	36,420
*75034	Frisco	(214)	33,714	121,387
*76240	Gainesville	(940)	15,538	15,984
77547	Galena Park	(713)	10,592	11,123
*77550	Galveston	(409)	57,247	48,444
*75040	Garland	(214)	215,768	231,517
*76528	Gatesville	(254)	15,591	15,985
*78626	Georgetown	(512)	28,339	49,562
75154	Glenn Heights	(214)	7,224	11,511
*75051	Grand Prairie	(214)	127,427	179,100
*76051	Grapevine	(817)	42,059	47,385
77479	Greatwood (c)	(281)	6,640	11,538
*75401	Greenville	(903)	23,960	25,676
77619	Groves	(409)	15,733	16,181
*76117	Haltom City	(817)	39,018	43,374
*76548	Harker Heights	(254)	17,308	27,136

ZIP	Place	Area code	2000 population	2011 estimate
*78550	Harlingen	(956)	57,564	66,122
*75652	Henderson	(903)	11,273	13,812
79045	Hereford	(806)	14,597	15,546
76643	Hewitt	(254)	11,085	13,767
78557	Hidalgo	(956)	7,322	11,533
75067	Highland Village	(214)	12,173	15,602
*79927	Horizon City	(915)	5,233	17,161
*77052	Houston	(713)	1,953,631	2,145,146
*77338	Humble	(713)	14,579	15,453
*77340	Huntsville	(936)	35,078	38,664
*76053	Hurst	(817)	36,273	38,184
78634	Hutto	(512)	1,250	15,404
*75015	Irving	(214)	191,615	220,702
77029	Jacinto City	(281)	10,320	10,780
75766	Jacksonville	(903)	13,868	14,637
78729	Jollyville (c)	(512)	15,813	16,151
*77449	Katy	(713)	11,775	14,426
*76248	Keller	(817)	27,345	40,530
*78028	Kerrville	(830)	20,425	22,423
*75662	Kilgore	(903)	11,301	13,110
*76540	Killeen	(254)	86,911	130,018
*78363	Kingsville	(361)	25,575	26,322
78640	Kyle	(512)	5,314	29,293
78572	La Homa (c)	(956)	10,433	11,985
77568	La Marque	(409)	13,682	14,732
*77571	La Porte	(713)	31,880	34,537
77566	Lake Jackson	(979)	26,386	27,451
*78734	Lakeway	(512)	8,002	11,830
*75146	Lancaster	(214)	25,894	37,097
*78041	Laredo	(956)	176,576	241,935
*77573	League City	(281)	45,444	84,856
*78641	Leander	(512)	7,596	27,827
*78268	Leon Valley	(210)	9,239	10,402
*79336	Levelland	(806)	12,866	13,517
*75067	Lewisville	(214)	77,737	98,737
75068	Little Elm	(214)	3,646	26,844
*78233	Live Oak	(210)	9,156	13,455
78644	Lockhart	(512)	11,615	12,821
*75606	Longview	(903)	73,344	81,336
*79408	Lubbock	(806)	199,564	233,740
*75901	Lufkin	(936)	32,709	35,425
77657	Lumberton	(409)	8,731	12,077
76063	Mansfield	(817)	28,031	57,627
*75670	Marshall	(903)	23,935	23,753
*78501	McAllen	(956)	106,414	133,742
*75070	McKinney	(214)	54,369	136,067
78570	Mercedes	(956)	13,649	16,175
*75149	Mesquite	(214)	124,523	142,674
*79701	Midland	(432)	94,996	113,931
76065	Midlothian	(214)	7,480	18,417
*76067	Mineral Wells	(940)	16,946	16,793
*78572	Mission	(956)	45,408	79,368
77083	Mission Bend (c)	(713)	30,831	36,501
*77489	Missouri City	(713)	52,913	69,774
*75455	Mount Pleasant	(903)	13,935	15,706
*75094	Murphy	(214)	3,099	18,387
*75961	Nacogdoches	(936)	29,914	33,405
77627	Nederland	(409)	17,422	17,587
*78130	New Braunfels	(830)	36,494	59,590
77479	New Territory (c)	(281)	13,861	15,186
*76161	North Richland Hills	(817)	55,635	64,780
*79761	Odessa	(432)	90,943	102,106
*77630	Orange	(409)	18,643	18,744
*75801	Palestine	(903)	17,598	18,657
*79065	Pampa	(806)	17,887	18,180
*75460	Paris	(903)	25,898	25,314
*77501	Pasadena	(713)	141,674	152,281
*77581	Pearland	(713)	37,640	93,305
78721	Pecan Grove (c)	(254)	13,551	15,963
*78660	Pflugerville	(512)	16,335	48,753
78577	Pharr	(956)	46,660	72,513
*79072	Plainview	(806)	22,336	22,343
*75074	Plano	(214)	222,030	269,776
*77640	Port Arthur	(409)	57,755	53,937
77979	Port Lavaca	(361)	12,035	12,282
77651	Port Neches	(409)	13,601	13,070
78374	Portland	(361)	14,827	15,080
*78560	Raymondville	(965)	9,733	11,259
*75154	Red Oak	(972)	4,301	10,995
76140	Rendon (c)	(817)	9,022	12,552
*75080	Richardson	(214)	91,802	101,742
*77469	Richmond	(713)	11,081	12,067
78582	Rio Grande City	(956)	11,923	13,966
76701	Robinson	(254)	7,845	10,680
78380	Robstown	(361)	12,727	11,590
*75087	Rockwall	(214)	17,976	39,028
77471	Rosenberg	(713)	24,043	31,754
*78681	Round Rock	(512)	61,136	104,664
*75088	Rowlett	(214)	44,503	57,463
75048	Sachse	(214)	9,751	20,860
*76179	Saginaw	(817)	12,374	20,258
*76902	San Angelo	(325)	88,439	94,544
*78265	San Antonio	(210)	1,144,646	1,359,758
78586	San Benito	(956)	23,444	24,729
79849	San Elizario (c)	(915)	11,046	13,603
78589	San Juan	(956)	26,229	34,872
*78666	San Marcos	(512)	34,733	46,685
*77510	Santa Fe	(409)	9,548	12,411
*78154	Schertz	(210)	18,694	32,478
77586	Seabrook	(281)	9,443	12,212
77159	Seagoville	(214)	10,823	15,094
*78155	Seguin	(830)	22,011	25,943
*75090	Sherman	(903)	35,082	38,690
77459	Sienna Plantation (c)	(281)	1,896	13,721
*79549	Snyder	(325)	10,783	11,200
79927	Socorro	(915)	27,152	32,834
77587	South Houston	(713)	15,833	17,354
76092	Southlake	(817)	21,519	27,189
*77733	Spring (c)	(713)	36,385	54,298
*77477	Stafford	(713)	15,681	18,348
*76401	Stephenville	(254)	14,921	17,253
*77478	Sugar Land	(713)	63,328	81,700
*75482	Sulphur Springs	(903)	14,551	15,541
79556	Sweetwater	(325)	11,415	10,943
76574	Taylor	(512)	13,575	16,000
*76501	Temple	(254)	54,514	67,188
*75160	Terrell	(214)	13,606	16,112
*75501	Texarkana	(903)	34,782	36,501
*77590	Texas City	(409)	41,521	45,763
*75056	The Colony	(214)	26,531	37,653
77387	The Woodlands (c)	(713)	55,649	93,847
78260	Timberwood Park (c)	(830)	5,889	13,447
*77375	Tomball	(713)	9,089	10,979
*75702	Tyler	(903)	83,650	98,564
*78148	Universal City	(830)	14,849	18,987
75205	University Park	(214)	23,324	23,490
*78801	Uvalde	(830)	14,929	15,828
*76384	Vernon	(940)	11,660	10,897
*77901	Victoria	(361)	60,603	63,131
*77662	Vidor	(409)	11,440	10,812
*76702	Waco	(254)	113,726	126,697
76148	Watauga	(817)	21,908	24,030
*75165	Waxahachie	(214)	21,426	30,223
*76086	Weatherford	(817)	19,000	25,557
77598	Webster	(281)	9,083	10,621
78728	Wells Branch (c)	(512)	11,271	12,120
*78596	Weslaco	(956)	26,935	36,721
79764	West Odessa (c)	(432)	17,799	22,707
77005	West University Place	(713)	14,211	15,109
76108	White Settlement	(817)	14,831	16,469
*76307	Wichita Falls	(940)	104,197	103,931
75098	Wylie	(214)	15,132	43,001

Utah

Area code (385) overlays area code (801).

ZIP	Place	Area code	2000 population	2011 estimate
84003	American Fork	(801)	21,941	26,982
*84010	Bountiful	(801)	41,301	43,303
84302	Brigham City	(435)	17,411	18,012
*84720	Cedar City	(435)	20,527	29,213
84014	Centerville	(801)	14,585	15,596
*84015	Clearfield	(801)	25,974	30,618
84015	Clinton	(801)	12,585	20,783
84121	Cottonwood Heights	(801)	—	34,068
84020	Draper	(801)	25,220	43,019
84043	Eagle Mountain	(801)	2,157	22,008
84025	Farmington	(801)	12,081	18,585
*84032	Heber City	(435)	7,291	11,795
84065	Herriman	(801)	1,523	22,201
84003	Highland	(801)	8,172	15,953
*84117	Holladay	(801)	14,561	26,971
84737	Hurricane	(435)	8,250	14,094
84037	Kaysville	(801)	20,351	27,778
84118	Kearns (c)	(801)	33,659	35,731
*84041	Layton	(801)	58,474	68,495
84043	Lehi	(801)	19,028	48,717
84042	Lindon	(801)	8,363	10,348
*84321	Logan	(435)	42,670	49,010
84044	Magna (c)	(801)	22,770	26,505
84047	Midvale	(801)	27,029	28,434
84109	Millcreek (c)	(801)	30,377	62,139
*84157	Murray	(801)	34,024	47,632
*84404	North Ogden	(801)	15,026	17,600
84054	North Salt Lake	(801)	8,749	16,607
*84401	Ogden	(801)	77,226	83,949
*84057	Orem	(801)	84,324	90,727
84651	Payson	(801)	12,716	18,798
84062	Pleasant Grove	(801)	23,468	34,435
*84601	Provo	(801)	105,166	115,321
84065	Riverton	(801)	25,011	39,489
*84067	Roy	(801)	32,885	37,395
*84770	Saint George	(435)	49,663	74,770
*84101	Salt Lake City	(801)	181,743	189,899
*84070	Sandy	(801)	88,418	89,200
84043	Saratoga Springs	(801)	1,003	18,299
84095	South Jordan	(801)	29,437	51,377
84403	South Ogden	(801)	14,377	16,760
84165	South Salt Lake	(801)	22,038	24,016
84660	Spanish Fork	(801)	20,246	35,659
84663	Springville	(801)	20,424	30,281

ZIP	Place	Area code	2000 population	2011 estimate
84075	Syracuse..............	(801)	9,398	24,756
84118	Taylorsville	(801)	57,439	59,767
84074	Tooele................	(435)	22,502	32,206
84780	Washington...........	(435)	8,186	19,249
84401	West Haven	(801)	3,976	10,415
*84084	West Jordan	(801)	68,336	105,675
*84170	West Valley City	(801)	108,896	131,942

Vermont (802)
See introductory note.

ZIP	Place	2000 population	2011 estimate
05201	*Bennington*...............	15,737	15,702
*05301	*Brattleboro*	12,005	11,978
*05401	*Burlington*	38,889	42,645
*05446	*Colchester*	16,986	17,165
*05451	*Essex*	18,626	19,713
05468	*Milton*	9,479	10,418
*05701	*Rutland*...................	17,292	16,399
*05403	South Burlington.............	15,814	18,017

Virginia
Area code (571) overlays area code (703).

ZIP	Place	Area code	2000 population	2011 estimate
*22313	Alexandria.............	(703)	128,283	144,301
22003	Annandale (c)	(703)	54,994	41,008
*22210	Arlington.............	(703)	189,453	207,627
*22041	Bailey's Crossroads (c)...	(703)	23,166	23,643
*24060	Blacksburg	(540)	39,573	42,600
23235	Bon Air (c).............	(804)	16,213	16,366
23112	Brandermill (c)	(804)	—	13,173
*24203	Bristol................	(276)	17,367	17,750
20148	Broadlands (c)	(703)	—	12,313
20111	Buckhall (c)............	(703)	—	16,293
20109	Bull Run (c)............	(703)	11,337	14,983
*22015	Burke (c)..............	(703)	57,737	41,055
22015	Burke Centre (c)........	(703)	—	17,326
24069	Cascades (c)	(434)	—	11,912
24018	Cave Spring (c)........	(540)	24,941	24,922
*20120	Centreville (c)	(703)	48,661	71,135
*20151	Chantilly (c)............	(703)	41,041	23,039
*22906	Charlottesville.........	(434)	45,049	43,511
22026	Cherry Hill (c)	(703)	—	16,000
*23320	Chesapeake	(757)	199,184	225,050
*23831	Chester (c)............	(804)	17,890	20,987
*24073	Christiansburg	(540)	16,947	21,030
23834	Colonial Heights	(804)	16,897	17,440
20165	Countryside (c)	(703)	—	10,072
*22701	Culpeper.............	(540)	9,664	16,662
22193	Dale City (c)	(703)	55,971	65,969
*24541	Danville..............	(434)	48,411	42,852
20170	Dranesville (c).........	(703)	—	11,921
23222	East Highland Park (c)...	(804)	12,488	14,796
*22030	Fairfax...............	(703)	21,498	22,549
22039	Fairfax Station (c)	(703)	—	12,030
22033	Fair Oaks (c)	(703)	—	30,223
*22046	Falls Church	(703)	10,377	12,751
22308	Fort Hunt (c)	(703)	12,923	16,045
22310	Franconia (c)	(703)	31,907	18,245
20171	Franklin Farm (c)	(703)	—	19,288
*22404	Fredericksburg	(540)	19,279	25,691
22630	Front Royal	(540)	13,589	14,558
*20155	Gainesville (c)..........	(703)	4,382	11,441
*23060	Glen Allen (c)	(804)	12,562	14,774
22066	Great Falls (c).........	(703)	8,549	15,427
22306	Groveton (c)	(703)	21,296	14,598
*23670	Hampton.............	(757)	146,437	136,401
*22801	Harrisonburg..........	(540)	40,468	49,973
*20170	Herndon	(703)	21,655	23,705
23075	Highland Springs (c)....	(804)	15,137	15,711
24019	Hollins (c).............	(540)	14,309	14,673
23860	Hopewell.............	(804)	22,354	22,580
22303	Huntington (c)..........	(703)	8,325	11,267
22306	Hybla Valley (c)........	(703)	16,721	15,801
22043	Idylwood (c)...........	(703)	16,005	17,288
22038	Kings Park West (c)	(703)	—	13,390
22315	Kingstowne (c)	(703)	—	15,556
22191	Lake Ridge (c)	(540)	30,404	41,058
23228	Lakeside (c)	(804)	11,157	11,849
20176	Lansdowne (c)	(703)	—	11,253
23060	Laurel (c)	(804)	14,875	16,713
*20175	Leesburg (c)	(703)	28,311	44,400
22312	Lincolnia (c)	(703)	15,788	22,855
20136	Linton Hall (c)	(703)	8,620	35,725
*22079	Lorton (c)	(703)	17,786	18,610
20165	Lowes Island (c)	(703)	—	10,756
*24506	Lynchburg............	(434)	65,269	76,504
24572	Madison Heights (c)	(434)	11,584	11,285
*20110	Manassas............	(703)	35,135	39,300
20113	Manassas Park........	(703)	10,290	15,332
23235	Manchester (c)........	(804)	—	10,804
*24112	Martinsville	(276)	15,416	13,559
22191	Marumsco (c)	(703)	—	35,036
*22101	McLean (c)	(703)	38,929	48,115

ZIP	Place	Area code	2000 population	2011 estimate
20171	McNair (c).............	(703)	—	17,513
23234	Meadowbrook (c)	(804)	—	18,312
*23111	Mechanicsville (c)......	(804)	30,464	36,348
*22116	Merrifield (c)	(703)	11,170	15,212
22026	Montclair (c)...........	(703)	15,728	19,570
22121	Mount Vernon (c)	(703)	28,582	12,416
22191	Neabsco (c)...........	(703)	—	12,068
22122	Newington (c)..........	(703)	19,784	12,943
22153	Newington Forest (c)	(703)	—	12,442
*23607	Newport News	(757)	180,150	179,611
*23501	Norfolk..............	(757)	234,403	242,628
22124	Oakton (c).............	(703)	29,348	34,166
*23804	Petersburg	(804)	33,740	32,326
23662	Poquoson	(757)	11,566	12,000
*23707	Portsmouth...........	(757)	100,565	95,684
*24111	Radford	(540)	15,859	16,414
*20190	Reston (c).............	(703)	56,407	58,404
*23232	Richmond............	(804)	197,790	205,533
*24022	Roanoke	(540)	94,911	96,714
24281	Rose Hill (c) (Fairfax Co.)	(276)	15,058	20,226
*24153	Salem	(540)	24,747	24,961
23233	Short Pump (c)	(804)	182	24,729
20152	South Riding (c)	(703)	—	24,256
*22150	Springfield (c)	(703)	30,417	30,484
*24402	Staunton.............	(540)	23,853	23,769
*20164	Sterling (c)	(703)	—	27,822
20109	Sudley (c).............	(703)	7,719	16,203
*23434	Suffolk...............	(757)	63,677	84,930
20164	Sugarland Run (c)	(703)	—	11,799
24502	Timberlake (c).........	(434)	10,683	12,183
23229	Tuckahoe (c)	(804)	43,242	44,990
22101	Tysons Corner (c)......	(703)	18,540	19,627
*22180	Vienna	(703)	14,453	15,964
*23450	Virginia Beach	(757)	425,257	442,707
23888	Wakefield (c)	(757)	1,038	11,275
22980	Waynesboro	(540)	19,520	21,311
22042	West Falls Church (c) ...	(703)	—	29,207
22152	West Springfield (c)	(703)	28,378	22,460
*23185	Williamsburg	(757)	11,998	14,444
*22601	Winchester	(540)	23,585	26,587
24592	Wolf Trap (c)..........	(703)	14,001	16,131
24381	Woodlawn (c) (Fairfax Co.)	(276)	—	20,804

Washington

ZIP	Place	Area code	2000 population	2011 estimate
98520	Aberdeen	(360)	16,461	16,835
*98221	Anacortes	(360)	14,557	15,941
98223	Arlington	(360)	11,713	18,154
98335	Artondale (c)..........	(253)	8,630	12,653
*98002	Auburn	(253)	40,314	71,517
98110	Bainbridge Island	(206)	20,308	23,262
98604	Battle Ground	(360)	9,296	17,893
*98009	Bellevue	(425)	109,569	124,798
*98225	Bellingham	(360)	67,171	81,862
*98390	Bonney Lake..........	(360)	9,687	17,579
*98011	Bothell	(425)	30,150	34,055
98036	Bothell West (c)	(425)	—	16,607
*98337	Bremerton............	(360)	37,259	39,051
98178	Bryn Mawr-Skyway (c) ...	(206)	13,977	15,645
*98166	Burien...............	(206)	31,881	33,977
98607	Camas	(360)	12,534	19,712
98531	Centralia	(360)	14,742	16,432
99004	Cheney..............	(509)	8,832	10,643
98072	Cottage Lake (c)	(206)	24,330	22,494
98042	Covington	(253)	13,783	17,929
*98198	Des Moines...........	(206)	29,267	30,258
98031	East Hill-Meridian (c)	(253)/(425)	29,308	29,878
98056	East Renton Highlands (c)	(425)	13,264	11,140
98802	East Wenatchee	(509)	5,757	13,375
98204	Eastmont (c)...........	(425)	—	20,101
*98020	Edmonds	(425)	39,515	40,215
98387	Elk Plain (c)	(253)	15,697	14,205
*98926	Ellensburg	(509)	15,414	18,468
98022	Enumclaw	(360)	11,116	11,086
*98201	Everett	(425)	91,488	104,295
98058	Fairwood (c) (King Co.) ...	(253)/(425)	—	19,102
*98002	Federal Way	(253)	83,259	91,085
98248	Ferndale	(360)	8,758	11,564
98597	Five Corners (c)	(360)	12,207	18,159
98433	Fort Lewis (c)	(253)	19,089	11,046
98375	Frederickson (c)	(253)	5,758	18,719
98338	Graham (c)	(253)	8,739	23,491
98930	Grandview	(509)	8,377	11,039
98665	Hazel Dell (c)	(360)	—	19,435
98011	Inglewood-Finn Hill (c) ...	(425)	22,661	22,707
*98027	Issaquah	(425)	11,212	31,037
98626	Kelso................	(360)	11,895	11,934
98028	Kenmore	(425)	18,678	20,870
*99336	Kennewick	(509)	54,693	76,224
*98031	Kent	(253)/(425)	79,524	120,916
98033	Kingsgate (c)	(425)	12,222	13,065
*98033	Kirkland	(425)	45,054	49,755
98029	Klahanie (c)	(425)	—	10,674
*98509	Lacey	(360)	31,226	43,117

ZIP	Place	Area code	2000 population	2011 estimate
98155	Lake Forest Park	(206)	13,142	12,849
98042	Lake Morton-Berrydale (c)	(253)/(425)	9,659	10,160
98258	Lake Stevens	(425)	6,361	28,431
98391	Lake Tapps (c)	(253)	—	11,859
98002	Lakeland North (c)	(253)	15,085	12,942
98002	Lakeland South (c)	(253)	11,436	11,574
*98498	Lakewood	(253)	58,211	58,839
98632	Longview	(360)	34,660	36,672
98264	Lynden	(360)	9,020	12,104
*98046	Lynnwood	(425)	33,847	36,291
98290	Maltby (c) .... (360)/(425)		8,267	10,830
98038	Maple Valley	(425)	14,209	23,139
98012	Martha Lake (c)	(425)	12,633	15,473
*98270	Marysville	(360)	25,315	60,785
98040	Mercer Island	(206)	22,036	23,154
*98082	Mill Creek	(425)	11,525	18,480
98012	Mill Creek East (c)	(425)	—	15,709
98272	Monroe...............	(360)	13,795	17,493
98837	Moses Lake	(509)	14,953	20,858
*98273	Mount Vernon	(360)	26,232	32,070
98043	Mountlake Terrace	(425)	20,362	20,165
98275	Mukilteo	(425)	18,019	20,514
*98059	Newcastle...........	(425)	7,737	10,588
98037	North Lynnwood (c)	(425)	—	16,574
*98277	Oak Harbor	(360)	19,795	22,239
*98501	Olympia	(360)	42,514	47,266
98662	Orchards (c)	(360)	17,852	19,556
98444	Parkland (c)	(253)	24,053	35,803
*99301	Pasco	(509)	32,066	63,186
*98362	Port Angeles..........	(360)	18,397	19,154
*98366	Port Orchard	(360)	7,693	11,333
98390	Prairie Ridge (c)	(360)	11,688	11,446
*99163	Pullman	(509)	24,675	29,913
*98371	Puyallup	(253)	33,011	37,454
*98052	Redmond	(425)	45,256	55,228
*98058	Renton	(425)	50,052	92,812
*99352	Richland	(509)	38,708	49,571
98686	Salmon Creek (c)	(360)	16,767	19,686
*98074	Sammamish	(425)	34,104	46,700
*98148	SeaTac	(206)	25,496	27,430
*98101	Seattle .... (206)/(425)		563,374	620,778
98284	Sedro-Woolley	(360)	8,658	10,712
*98133	Shoreline	(206)	53,025	54,044
98208	Silver Firs (c). ... (206)/(425)		—	20,891
*98315	Silverdale (c)........	(360)	15,816	19,204
*98065	Snoqualmie..........	(425)	1,613	10,884
98373	South Hill (c)	(253)	31,623	52,431
98387	Spanaway (c)	(253)	21,588	27,227
*99210	Spokane	(509)	195,629	210,103
*99211	Spokane Valley	(509)	—	90,279
98944	Sunnyside...........	(509)	13,905	16,113
*98402	Tacoma	(253)	193,556	200,678
*98138	Tukwila	(206)	17,181	19,486
*98501	Tumwater	(360)	12,698	17,671
98053	Union Hill-Novelty Hill (c)	(425)	11,265	18,805
98467	University Place	(253)	29,933	31,511
*98661	Vancouver...........	(360)	143,560	164,759
*98013	Vashon (c)	(206)	10,123	10,624
99362	Walla Walla..........	(509)	29,686	32,148
98671	Washougal	(360)	8,595	14,357
*98801	Wenatchee	(509)	27,856	32,373
*99353	West Richland	(509)	8,385	12,184
98166	White Center (c)	(206)	20,975	13,495
*98072	Woodinville...........	(425)	9,194	11,157
*98903	Yakima	(509)	71,845	92,512

West Virginia (304)
Area code (681) overlays area code (304).

ZIP	Place	2000 population	2011 estimate
*25801	Beckley.....................	17,254	17,675
24701	Bluefield...................	11,451	10,482
*25301	Charleston	53,421	51,177
*26301	Clarksburg	16,743	16,649
*26554	Fairmont...................	19,097	18,764
*25704	Huntington	51,475	49,253
*25401	Martinsburg................	14,972	17,487
*26505	Morgantown................	26,809	30,293
*26101	Parkersburg	33,099	31,557
25177	Saint Albans...............	11,567	11,001
*25303	South Charleston	13,390	13,396
25569	Teays Valley (c)............	12,704	13,175
*26105	Vienna....................	10,861	10,770
26062	Weirton....................	20,411	19,651
26003	Wheeling..................	31,419	28,355

Wisconsin
Area code (534) overlays area code (715).

ZIP	Place	Area code	2000 population	2011 estimate
54301	Allouez	(920)	15,443	14,126
*54911	Appleton	(920)	70,087	73,243
*54304	Ashwaubenon..........	(920)	17,634	17,160

ZIP	Place	Area code	2000 population	2011 estimate
53913	Baraboo	(608)	10,711	12,107
53916	Beaver Dam	(920)	15,169	16,194
54311	Bellevue	(920)	—	14,742
*53511	Beloit................	(608)	35,775	36,913
*53045	Brookfield	(262)	38,649	38,001
*53209	Brown Deer	(414)	12,170	12,061
53105	Burlington	(262)	9,936	10,463
53108	Caledonia	(262)	—	24,701
53012	Cedarburg............	(262)	10,908	11,436
*54729	Chippewa Falls	(715)	12,925	13,738
53110	Cudahy..............	(414)	18,429	18,359
54115	De Pere..............	(920)	20,559	24,060
*54703	Eau Claire............	(715)	61,704	66,623
53121	Elkhorn..............	(262)	7,305	10,118
*53711	Fitchburg.............	(608)	20,501	25,665
*54935	Fond du Lac	(920)	42,203	43,208
53538	Fort Atkinson	(920)	11,621	12,407
53132	Franklin.............	(414)	29,494	35,620
53022	Germantown..........	(262)	18,260	19,823
*53209	Glendale	(414)	13,367	12,935
53024	Grafton	(262)	10,312	11,481
*54303	Green Bay	(920)	102,313	105,809
53129	Greendale............	(414)	14,405	14,117
*53220	Greenfield............	(414)	35,476	36,903
53027	Hartford.............	(262)	10,905	14,277
*54303	Howard..............	(920)	13,546	17,602
*54016	Hudson..............	(715)	8,775	12,815
*53545	Janesville............	(608)	59,498	63,479
54130	Kaukauna	(920)	12,983	15,561
*53140	Kenosha.............	(262)	90,352	99,738
*54601	La Crosse............	(608)	51,818	51,719
54140	Little Chute	(920)	10,476	10,514
*53714	Madison	(608)	208,054	236,901
*54220	Manitowoc.	(920)	34,053	33,545
54143	Marinette............	(715)	11,749	10,943
*54449	Marshfield	(715)	18,800	19,129
54952	Menasha.............	(920)	16,331	17,442
*53051	Menomonee Falls	(262)	32,647	35,704
54751	Menomonie	(715)	14,937	16,301
*53097	Mequon..............	(262)	21,823	23,178
53562	Middleton	(608)	15,770	17,729
*53201	Milwaukee............	(414)	596,974	597,867
53566	Monroe..............	(608)	10,843	10,841
53406	Mount Pleasant........	(262)	—	26,195
53150	Muskego.............	(414)	21,397	24,187
*54956	Neenah..............	(920)	24,507	25,615
*53186	New Berlin	(262)	38,220	39,669
53154	Oak Creek............	(414)	28,456	34,626
53066	Oconomowoc	(262)	12,382	15,792
54650	Onalaska	(608)	14,839	17,899
*54901	Oshkosh	(920)	62,916	66,344
53072	Pewaukee (city)	(262)	11,783	13,224
53818	Platteville	(608)	9,989	11,226
*53158	Pleasant Prairie	(262)	16,136	19,822
54467	Plover	(715)	10,520	12,135
53074	Port Washington	(262)	10,467	11,272
53901	Portage..............	(608)	9,728	10,336
*53401	Racine	(262)	81,855	78,853
*53076	Richfield	(262)	—	11,342
54022	River Falls	(715)	12,560	14,889
*53081	Sheboygan	(920)	50,792	49,135
53211	Shorewood	(414)	13,763	13,228
53172	South Milwaukee	(414)	21,256	21,262
*54481	Stevens Point	(715)	24,551	26,741
53589	Stoughton	(608)	12,354	12,817
*54173	Suamico	(920)	—	11,481
*53590	Sun Prairie	(608)	20,369	29,849
54880	Superior	(715)	27,368	27,211
53089	Sussex	(262)	8,828	10,542
*54241	Two Rivers	(920)	12,639	11,644
53593	Verona	(608)	7,052	10,796
*53094	Watertown............	(920)	21,598	23,895
*53186	Waukesha	(262)	64,825	70,867
53597	Waunakee	(608)	8,995	12,295
53963	Waupun	(920)	10,718	11,350
*54403	Wausau	(715)	38,426	39,213
*53213	Wauwatosa...........	(414)	47,271	46,629
*53214	West Allis	(414)	61,254	60,714
*53095	West Bend	(262)	28,152	31,195
*54476	Weston..............	(715)	12,079	14,904
*53217	Whitefish Bay	(414)	14,163	14,182
53190	Whitewater	(262)	13,437	14,769
*54494	Wisconsin Rapids.......	(715)	18,435	18,377

Wyoming (307)

ZIP	Place	2000 population	2011 estimate
*82609	Casper	49,644	55,988
*82009	Cheyenne	53,011	60,096
*82930	Evanston	11,507	12,282
*82716	Gillette...................	19,646	29,389
*82935	Green River	11,808	12,622
*82072	Laramie..................	27,204	31,312
82501	Riverton	9,310	10,867
*82901	Rock Springs	18,708	23,229
82801	Sheridan..................	15,804	17,517

WORLD HISTORY

Chronology of World History

Note: In this section, the notation BCE (before the common era) is applied to years dating to the traditional BC (before Christ) era, and CE (common era) is applied to AD (anno domini) dates. This notation is now preferred in scientific and academic publications. The traditional Gregorian Calendar system and its dates and years are unaltered except by these labels.

Other abbreviations used in this chapter include the following: KYA = thousand years ago, MYA = million years ago, c. = circa, fl. = flourished, r. = ruled, b. = born, d. = died.

Prehistory: Our Ancestors Emerge

Reviewed by Peter N. Stearns, Provost and Professor, George Mason Univ., June 2012

Evidence of the origins of *Homo sapiens sapiens*, the genus, species, and subspecies to which all living humans belong, comes from a small but increasing number of fossils, from genetic and anatomical studies, and from interpretation of the geological and archaeological records. The latest evidence suggests that humans evolved from apelike primate ancestors that lived in eastern and central Africa 7-5 million years ago (MYA). Although all humans living today are members of a single species, the fossil record confirms that our ancestors coexisted with a number of similar species throughout our evolutionary history. Current theories trace the first hominin[1] (upright, bipedal, humanlike primate) to Africa, where several distinct genera appeared 6-4 MYA. They lived in a variety of environments throughout most of the continent, including swampy forest margins, woodlands, and open savannas (usually near lakes or springs). In addition to *Australopithecus afarensis*—better known as "Lucy," a 3.2 MYA Ethiopian specimen found in 1974—these earliest hominins include such recent discoveries as *Sahelanthropus* (c. 6.5 MYA, from Chad), *Ardipithecus* (c. 5 MYA Kenya), *Kenyanthropus* (c. 3.5 MYA, Kenya), and *Orrorin* (c. 5 MYA, Kenya). Later, between 4 and 3 MYA, these earliest hominins gave rise to at least two groups of savanna/lake-edge adapted "man-apes." Called australopithecines, they are divided into "gracile" and "robust" lineages, both containing a number of species. The robust australopithecines were characterized by enormous molar and premolar teeth; they probably went extinct around 1 MYA or slightly thereafter. Although it is uncertain from which australopithecine species humans descended, the most likely species are usually assigned to the gracile lineage.

Our genus, *Homo*, arose 3-2 MYA, when hominins began to produce primitive stone tools. The oldest tools are dated to c. 2.5 MYA from the Kada Gona site, in Ethiopia, and were used for scraping and cutting meat, sinew, and wood. It is not known whether these early hominins had the ability to speak, but they were social animals, lived in groups of 12-20 individuals, aggregated and dispersed seasonally, had campsites, and subsisted by gathering plants and small animals and by scavenging other kills. A closer ancestor, *Homo ergaster*, appeared in E Africa around 1.9 MYA and was the first to leave the continent, spreading throughout Eurasia by c. 1.8 MYA. *H. ergaster* is sometimes grouped with *H. erectus*, a species first identified in the 1890s on the island of Java. It was capable of hunting large and medium-sized hoofed animals, such as antelopes and horses, learned to make and control fire—by c. 500 thousand years ago (KYA) in Europe, possibly earlier in Africa—and almost certainly had primitive language skills.

After about 350 KYA, Europe provides a particularly rich set of fossil evidence usually assigned to *H. erectus*. By a near-universal consensus, this species gave rise to the Neanderthals, who appeared c. 200 KYA. Neanderthals were humanlike in most respects: they could speak, were proficient hunters of large game, had sophisticated tools and weapons and a developed social organization, and were well adapted to the harsh climates of Ice Age Europe. Recent advances in molecular biology support the theory that Neanderthals were a distinct population or species that in some places coexisted but evidently did not interbreed with early modern humans (also called Crô-Magnons). *H. antecessor*, a new species (c. 870 KYA) identified at the Trinchera Dolina site in north-central Spain, might help clarify the relationship between the earliest representatives of *Homo* in western Europe, and the Neanderthals. A similar situation may have occurred in E Asia, where more primitive *Homo* species coexisted with early modern humans after c. 40 KYA, and possibly as recently as 18 KYA, on the island of Flores, in Indonesia.

Genetic evidence indicates that the first *Homo sapiens* originated in E Africa between 200 and 100 KYA. The oldest modern human fossils date to c. 160 KYA and were found at the Herto site in Ethiopia's Middle Awash Valley. The species quickly spread, displacing, extinguishing, outcompeting, and/or genetically swamping the archaic humans it encountered. Modern humans were living in Israel by c. 100 KYA, and in Romania by c. 35 KYA. Migration from Asia to Australia took place as early as 60 KYA. First confirmation for the crossing from Asia to the Americas by the Bering land bridge dates to the end of the last Ice Age, at 14 KYA. However, genetic data suggests that small, isolated groups of hunter-gatherers arrived in the Americas up to 10,000 years earlier, settling in both continents. Their arrival was rapidly followed by the extinction of the indigenous Pleistocene megafauna (e.g., mammoths, mastodons), due either to overexploitation by humans, an extraterrestrial impact c. 12,900 years ago, or a combination of both.

As human cognitive capacities slowly expanded over the Pleistocene (1.7-0.01 MYA), a variety of behavioral modes—in toolmaking, diet, shelter, social arrangements, and spiritual expression—arose as humans adapted to different geographic and climatic zones. By about 13,000 years ago, sites from all over the world show seasonal migration patterns and efficient exploitation of a wide range of plant and animal foods, some of which were eventually domesticated.

The ability to make fire at will enormously expanded the human food niche. Fire-making possibly began as early as 1 MYA in Africa and is clearly documented throughout Eurasia after c. 500 KYA. Hearths were found in northern Israel by c. 750 KYA, and by 465 KYA in southwestern France. Fire-hardened wooden throwing spears about 3 m long were fashioned by big-game hunters 400 KYA at the Schoeningen lignite mine in Germany. Scraping tools, dated after 750 KYA in Europe, N Africa, the Middle East, and Central Asia, suggest the preparation of hides for clothing. The oldest relatively unambiguous evidence of personal adornment—perforated shell beads—dates to c. 120 KYA at Skhul Cave on Mount Carmel in Israel. Although they were probably invented much earlier, impressions in burnt clay from the Czech Republic document the ability to weave cloth baskets and nets by 28 KYA. By the time Australia was settled, human ancestors had learned to navigate in boats over considerable distances in open water. The earliest-known bone tools were fashioned some 90 KYA at Semliki, in the Congo basin, by fishermen who crafted sophisticated bone harpoons to catch giant catfish.

About 60 KYA, the earliest immigrants to Australia carved and painted designs on rocks. Although the painted caves of Cosquer and Chauvet in southern France have (contested) radiocarbon dates of c. 32 KYA, painting, engraving and bodily decoration flourished in Europe 15 KYA, along with stone and ivory sculpture. More than 200 western European caves show remarkable examples of naturalistic wall painting. A few musical instruments—bone flutes with precisely bored holes—have been found in sites dated after 40 KYA. Over the course of the Upper Pleistocene (c. 130-12 KYA), the number of people who survived to become grandparents slowly increased. With more adults available to provide child care, humans began to develop more complex, multigenerational social systems.

Cave paintings in Lascaux, France, discovered in 1940, have been carbon-dated to 11,000 to 30,000 years before the present.

The reach of social memory increased accordingly. Shortly after 12 KYA, among widely separated foraging communities in both hemispheres, a series of dramatic technological and social changes occurred, marking the Neolithic, or New Stone, Age. As the world climate became drier and warmer, population/resource imbalances ensued, creating the conditions that selected for increased human interference in the life cycles of certain plants and animals. This interference ultimately resulted in the appearance of domestication economies, initially in the northern Middle East. Domesticated plants and animals encouraged population growth and the appearance of permanent settlements, which in turn reduced birth spacing and spurred more population growth. Agricultural economies increasingly replaced hunting and gathering. Reliance upon domesticated plants and animals, coupled with technological advances like pottery-making, precipitated a dramatic increase in world population and social complexity. Genetic research suggests that mutations related to traits currently found in some human populations, such as Europeans' unusually light skin pigmentation and ability to process lactose, arose after c. 12 KYA.

Sites in the Americas, SE Europe, and the Middle East show roughly contemporaneous (12-6 KYA) evidence of Neolithic domestication economies; similar evidence of E and S Asian, W European, and sub-Saharan African Neolithic adaptations dates to 10-7 KYA. From W Asian sources, farming and the herding of sheep and goats spread rapidly throughout the Mediterranean Basin, perhaps in as short a time interval as 100-200 years. The variety of crops—wheat, barley, rice, maize, squash, beans, and tubers—and a mix of other characteristics suggest that this adaptation occurred independently in as many as 12 or 13 places in both hemispheres. Evidence for fermented beverages likewise coincides with the early Neolithic settled farming lifestyle. Northern Chinese farmers concocted a wine-like drink from rice, honey, and fruit between 9,000 and 8,000 years ago. In highland W Asia, in what is today Iran, vintners were fermenting grapes and making wine by c. 7400 KYA. The plants and animals associated with the Neolithic Revolution provided the basis for all subsequent social and cultural evolution worldwide.

(1) Although "hominid" was standard usage several decades ago, "hominin" is now more commonly used in reference to human ancestors because of new developments in the interpretation of primate evolution.

Earliest Civilizations: 4000-1000 BCE

Mesopotamia. If history began with writing, the first chapter opened in Mesopotamia, the Tigris-Euphrates river valley. The Sumerians used clay tablets with pictographs to keep records after 4000 BCE. A **cuneiform** (wedge-shaped) script evolved by 3000 BCE as a full syllabic alphabet. Neighboring peoples adapted the script for their own use.

Sumerian life centered, from 4000 BCE, on large cities (Eridu, Ur, Uruk, Nippur, Kish, and Lagash) organized around temples and priestly bureaucracies, with surrounding plains watered by vast irrigation works and worked with traction plows. Sailboats, wheeled vehicles, potter's wheels, and kilns were used. Copper was smelted and tempered from c. 4000 BCE; bronze was produced not long after. Ores, as well as precious stones and metals, were obtained through long-distance ship and caravan trade. Iron was used from c. 2000 BCE. Improved ironworking, developed partly by the Hittites, became widespread by 1200 BCE.

Sumerian political primacy passed among cities and their kingly dynasties. Semitic-speaking peoples, with cultures derived from the Sumerian, founded a succession of dynasties that ruled in Mesopotamia and neighboring areas for most of 1,800 years. Among them were the **Akkadians** (first under Sargon I, c. 2350 BCE), the Amorites (whose laws, codified by **Hammurabi**, c. 1792-1750 BCE, have biblical parallels), and the Assyrians, with interludes of rule by the Hittites, Kassites, and Mitanni.

Mesopotamian learning, preserved in vast libraries, was practically oriented. Scribes maintained lists of astronomical phenomena, plants, animals, and stones. Medical texts listed ailments and herbal cures. The Sumerians worshipped anthropomorphic gods representing natural forces. Sacrifices were made at **ziggurats**, or huge stepped temples.

The Syria-Palestine area, site of some of the earliest urban remains (Jericho, 7000 BCE) and of the recently uncovered **Ebla** civilization (fl. 2500 BCE), experienced Egyptian cultural and political influence along with Mesopotamian. The **Phoenician** coast was an active commercial center. A phonetic alphabet was invented here before 1600 BCE. It became the ancestor of many other alphabets.

Egypt. Agricultural villages along the Nile R. were united by around 3300 BCE into two kingdoms, Upper and Lower Egypt. They were unified (c. 3100 BCE) under the pharaoh Menes. A bureaucracy supervised construction of canals and monuments (**pyramids** starting 2700 BCE). Control over Nubia to the S was asserted from 2600 BCE. Brilliant **Old Kingdom** period achievements in architecture, sculpture, and painting reached their height during the 3rd and 4th dynasties. **Hieroglyphic writing** appeared by 3200 BCE, recording a sophisticated literature that included religious writings, philosophy, history, and science. An ordered hierarchy of gods, including totemistic animal elements, was served by a powerful priesthood in Memphis. The pharaoh was identified with the falcon god Horus. Other trends included belief in an afterlife and short-lived quasi-monotheistic reforms introduced by the pharaoh **Akhenaton** (c. 1379-1362 BCE), who was married to Nefertiti.

After a period of dominance by Semitic Hyksos from Asia (c. 1700-1550 BCE), the **New Kingdom** established an empire in Syria. Egypt became increasingly embroiled in Asiatic wars and diplomacy. Conquered by Persia in 525 BCE, it eventually faded away as an independent culture.

India. An urban civilization with an as-yet undeciphered writing system stretched across the Indus Valley and along the Arabian Sea c. 3000-1500 BCE. Major sites are Harappa and **Mohenjo-Daro** in Pakistan, well-planned geometric cities with underground sewers and vast granaries. The entire region may have been ruled as a single state. Bronze was used, and arts and crafts were well developed. Religious life apparently took the form of fertility cults. Indus civilization was in decline before the arrival of **Aryan** migrants who arrived from the NW, speaking an Indo-European language. Led by a warrior aristocracy whose legendary deeds are in the **Rig Veda**, the Aryans spread E and S, bringing their sky gods, priestly (Brahman) ritual, and the beginnings of the caste system. Local customs and beliefs were assimilated by the conquerors.

Europe. On Crete, the Bronze Age **Minoan civilization** emerged c. 2500 BCE. A prosperous economy and richly decorative art was supported by seaborne commerce. Mycenae and other cities in mainland Greece and Asia Minor (e.g., **Troy**) preserved elements of the culture until c. 1200 BCE. Cretan Linear A script (c. 2000-1700 BCE) remains undeciphered; Linear B script (c. 1300-1200 BCE) records an early Greek dialect. The possible connection between Mycenaean monumental stonework and the megalithic monuments of W Europe, Iberia, and Malta (c. 4000-1500 BCE) is unclear.

China. Proto-Chinese neolithic cultures had long covered N and SE China when the first large political state was organized in the N by the **Shang dynasty** (c. 1523 BCE). Shang kings

The Great Sphinx of Giza is believed to have been built during Egypt's 4th dynasty (c. 2575-2465 BCE).

called themselves Sons of Heaven, and they presided over a cult of human and animal sacrifice to ancestors and nature gods. The Chou dynasty, starting c. 1027 BCE, expanded the area of the Sons of Heaven's dominion, but feudal states exercised most temporal power. A writing system with 2,000 characters was already in use under the Shang, with **pictographs** later supplemented by phonetic characters. Many of its principles and symbols, despite changes in spoken Chinese, were preserved in later writing systems. Technical advances allowed urban specialists to create fine ceramic and jade products, and bronze casting after 1500 BCE was the most advanced in the world. Bronze artifacts discovered in N Thailand date from 3600 BCE, hundreds of years before similar Middle Eastern finds.

Americas. Olmecs settled (1500 BCE) on the Gulf coast of Mexico and developed the first known civilization in the W Hemisphere. Temple cities and huge stone sculptures date from 1200 BCE. A rudimentary calendar and writing system existed. Olmec religion—centered on a jaguar god—and art forms influenced later Mesoamerican cultures.

Formation of Classical Societies: 1000-400 BCE

Greece. After a period of decline during the Dorian Greek invasions (1200-1000 BCE), the Aegean area developed a unique civilization. Drawing on Mycenaean traditions, Mesopotamian learning (weights and measures, lunisolar calendar, astronomy, musical scales), the Phoenician alphabet (modified for Greek), and Egyptian art, **Greek city-states** saw a rich elaboration of intellectual life. The two great epic poems attributed to **Homer**, the *Iliad* and the *Odyssey*, were probably composed around the 8th cent. BCE. Long-range commerce was aided by metal coinage (introduced by the Lydians in Asia Minor before 700 BCE). Colonies were founded around the Mediterranean (Cumae in Italy in 760 BCE; Massalia in France c. 600 BCE) and Black Sea shores.

Philosophy, starting with Ionian speculation on the nature of matter (Thales, c. 634-546 BCE), continued by other "Pre-Socratics" (e.g., Heraclitus, c. 535-415 BCE; Parmenides, b. c. 515 BCE), reached a high point in Athens in the rationalist idealism of **Plato** (c. 428-347 BCE), a disciple of **Socrates** (c. 469-399 BCE; executed for alleged impiety), and in **Aristotle** (384-322 BCE), a pioneer in many fields, from natural sciences to logic, ethics, and metaphysics. The **arts** were highly valued. Architecture culminated in the **Parthenon** (438 BCE) by Phidias (fl. 490-430 BCE). Poetry (Sappho, c. 610-580 BCE; Pindar, c. 518-438 BCE) and **drama** (Aeschylus, 525-456 BCE; Sophocles, c. 496-406 BCE; Euripides, c. 484-406 BCE) thrived. Male beauty and strength, a chief artistic theme, were celebrated at the national games at Olympia.

Ruled by local tyrants or **oligarchies**, the Greeks were not politically united but managed to resist inclusion in the Persian Empire. Persian king Darius was defeated at Marathon (490 BCE), his son Xerxes at Salamis (480 BCE), and the Persian army at Plataea (479 BCE). Democracy sprouted in Athens as statesman Pericles (495-429 BCE) sought participation in government from all citizens. Local warfare was common; the **Peloponnesian Wars** (431-404 BCE) ended in Sparta's victory over Athens. Greek political power subsequently waned, but Greek cultural forms spread far and wide.

Hebrews. Nomadic Hebrew tribes entered Canaan before 1200 BCE, settling among other Semitic peoples speaking the same language. They brought from the desert a **monotheistic** faith said to have been revealed to Abraham in Canaan c. 1800 BCE and Moses at Mt. Sinai c. 1250 BCE, after the Hebrews' escape from bondage in Egypt. David (r. 1000-961 BCE) and Solomon (r. 961-922 BCE) united them in a kingdom that briefly dominated the area. **Phoenicians** to the N founded Mediterranean colonies (Carthage, c. 814 BCE) and sailed into the Atlantic.

A temple in Jerusalem became the national religious center, with sacrifices performed by a hereditary priesthood. Polytheistic influences, especially of the fertility cult of Baal, were opposed by **prophets** (Elijah, Amos, Isaiah).

Divided into **two kingdoms** after Solomon, the Hebrews were unable to resist the revived Assyrian empire, which conquered Israel, the N kingdom, in 722 BCE. Judah, the S kingdom, was conquered in 586 BCE by the Babylonians under Nebuchadnezzar II. With the fixing of most of the biblical canon by the mid-4th cent. BCE and the emergence of rabbis, Judaism successfully survived the loss of Hebrew autonomy. A Jewish kingdom was revived under the Hasmoneans (168-42 BCE).

China. During the **Eastern Zhou** dynasty (770-256 BCE), Chinese culture spread E to the sea and S to the Yangtze R. Large feudal states on the periphery of the empire contended for preeminence but continued to recognize the Son of Heaven (king), who retained a purely ritual role enriched with courtly music and dance. In the Age of Warring States (403-221 BCE), when the first sections of the **Great Wall** were built, the Ch'in state in the W gained supremacy and finally united all of China.

Iron tools entered China c. 500 BCE. Casting techniques were advanced, aiding agriculture. Peasants owned their land and owed civil and military service to nobles. China's cities grew in number and size; barter remained the chief trade medium.

Intellectual ferment among noble scribes and officials produced a classical age of Chinese literature and philosophy. **Confucius** (551-479 BCE) urged a restoration of a supposedly harmonious social order of the past through proper conduct in accordance with one's station and through filial and ceremonial piety. The *Analects* attributed to him are revered throughout E Asia.

Among other thinkers, **Mencius** (d. 289 BCE) added the view that the Mandate of Heaven can be removed from an unjust dynasty. The Legalists sought to curb the supposed natural wickedness of people through new institutions and harsh laws. The Naturalists emphasized the balance of opposites—yin, yang—in the world. **Daoists** sought mystical knowledge through meditation and disengagement.

India. The political and cultural center of India shifted from the Indus to the Ganges River Valley. Buddhism, Jainism, and mystical revisions of orthodox Vedism all developed c. 500-300 BCE. The *Upanishads*, last part of the *Veda*, urged escape from the cycle of rebirth into the physical world. Vedism remained the preserve of the Brahman caste.

In contrast, **Buddhism**, founded by Siddhartha Gautama (c. 563-c. 483 BCE)—Buddha ("Enlightened One")—appealed to merchants in the urban centers and took hold at first (and most lastingly) on the geographic fringes of Indian civilization. The classic Indian epics were composed in this era: the *Ramayana* perhaps c. 300 BCE, the *Mahabharata* over a period starting around 400 BCE.

N India was divided into a large number of monarchies and aristocratic republics, probably derived from tribal groupings, when the Magadha kingdom was formed in Bihar c. 542 BCE. It soon became the dominant power. The **Maurya** dynasty, founded by Chandragupta c. 321 BCE, expanded the kingdom, uniting most of N India in a centralized bureaucratic empire. The third Mauryan king, **Asoka** (reigned c. 274-236 BCE), conquered most of the subcontinent. He converted to Buddhism,

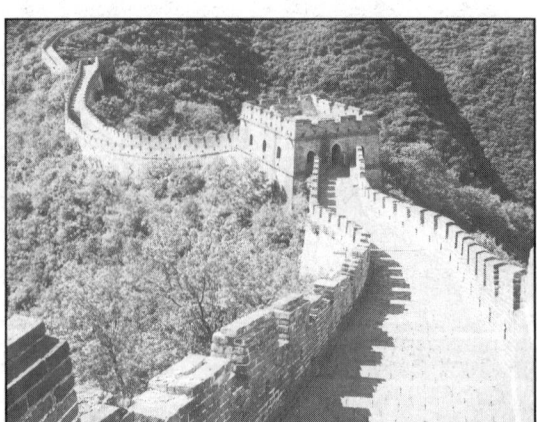

China's Great Wall, first built during the Age of Warring States (403-221 BCE), was rebuilt, extended, and modified over thousands of years to protect China from invaders.

inscribed its tenets on pillars throughout India, and downplayed the caste system.

Before its final decline in India, Buddhism developed into a popular worship of heavenly Bodhisattvas ("enlightened beings"), and it produced a refined architecture (the Great Stupa [shrine] at Sanchi, 100 CE) and sculpture (Gandhara reliefs, 1-400 CE).

Persia. Aryan peoples (Persians, Medes) dominated the area of present Iran by the beginning of the 1st millennium BCE. The prophet **Zoroaster** (b. c. 628 BCE) introduced a dualistic religion in which the forces of good (Ahura Mazda, "Lord of Wisdom") and evil (Ahriman) battle for dominance; individuals are judged by their actions and earn damnation or salvation. Zoroaster's

hymns (*Gathas*) are included in the *Avesta*, the Zoroastrian scriptures. A version of this faith became the established religion of the Persian Empire.

Africa. Nubia, periodically occupied by Egypt since about 2600 BCE, ruled Egypt c. 750-661 BCE and survived as an independent Egyptianized kingdom (**Kush**; capital Meroe) for 1,000 years. The Iron Age Nok culture flourished c. 500 BCE-200 CE on the Benue Plateau of **Nigeria**.

Americas. The Chavin culture controlled N Peru c. 900 BCE to 200 BCE. Its ceremonial centers, featuring the jaguar god, survived long after. Its architecture, ceramics, and textiles had influenced other Peruvian cultures. **Mayan civilization** began to develop in Central America as early as 1500 BCE.

Great Empires Unite the Classical World: 400 BCE-400 CE

Persia and the Mediterranean. Cyrus, ruler of a small kingdom in Persia from 559 BCE, united the Persians and Medes within 10 years and conquered Asia Minor and Babylonia in another 10. His son Cambyses, followed by **Darius** (r. 522-486 BCE), added vast lands to the E and N as far as the Indus Valley and Central Asia, as well as Egypt and Thrace. The whole empire was ruled by an international bureaucracy and army, with Persians holding the chief positions. The resources and styles of all the subject civilizations were exploited to create a rich syncretic art.

The kingdom of Macedon, which under Philip II dominated the Greek world and Egypt, was passed on to Philip's son **Alexander** in 336 BCE. Within 13 years, Alexander had conquered all the Persian dominions. Imbued by his tutor Aristotle with Greek ideals, Alexander encouraged colonization, and Greek-style cities were founded. After his death in 323 BCE, wars of succession divided the empire into three significant dynasties—the **Antigonids** in Asia Minor and Macedon, the **Ptolemies** in Egypt, and the **Seleucids** in Mesopotamia. In the ensuing 300 years (the **Hellenistic Era**), a cosmopolitan Greek-oriented culture permeated the ancient world from W Europe to the borders of India, absorbing native elites everywhere.

Hellenistic philosophy stressed the private individual's search for happiness. The Cynics followed Diogenes (c. 372-287 BCE), who stressed self-sufficiency and restriction of desires and expressed contempt for luxury and social convention. Zeno (c. 335-c. 263 BCE) and the **Stoics** exalted reason, identified it with virtue, and counseled an ascetic disregard for misfortune. The **Epicureans** tried to build lives of moderate pleasure without political or emotional involvement. Hellenistic arts imitated life realistically, especially in sculpture and literature (comedies of Menander, 342-292 BCE).

The sciences thrived, especially at Alexandria, where the Ptolemies financed a great library and museum. Fields of study included mathematics (**Euclid**'s geometry, c. 300 BCE); astronomy (heliocentric theory of Aristarchus, 310-230 BCE; Julian calendar, 45 BCE; **Ptolemy**'s *Almagest*, c. 150 CE); geography (world map of Eratosthenes, 276-194 BCE); hydraulics (**Archimedes**, 287-212 BCE); medicine (Galen, 130-200 CE); and chemistry. Inventors refined uses for siphons, valves, gears, springs, screws, levers, cams, and pulleys.

A restored Persian empire under the **Parthians** (northern Iranian tribesmen) controlled the eastern Hellenistic world from 250 BCE to 229 CE. The Parthians and the succeeding **Sassanian dynasty** (c. 224-651 CE) fought with Rome periodically. The Sassanians revived Zoroastrianism as a state religion and patronized a nationalistic artistic and scholarly renaissance.

Rome. The city of Rome was founded, according to legend, by Romulus in 753 BCE. Through military expansion and colonization, and by granting citizenship to leading members of conquered tribes, the city annexed all of Italy S of the Po R. in the 100-year period before 268 BCE. The Latin and other Italic tribes were annexed first, followed by the **Etruscans** (founders of a great civilization N of Rome) and Greek colonies in the S. With a large standing army and reserve forces of several hundred thousand, Rome was able to defeat **Carthage** in the three **Punic Wars** (264-241 BCE, 218-201 BCE, 149-146 BCE), despite the invasion of Italy by **Hannibal** (218 BCE), thus gaining Sicily and territory in Spain and N Africa.

Rome exploited local disputes to conquer Greece and Asia Minor in the 2nd cent. BCE and Egypt in the 1st (after the defeat and suicide of **Antony and Cleopatra**, 30 BCE). The Mediterranean civilized world, up to the disputed Parthian border, was now Roman and remained so for 500 years. Less civilized regions were added to the Empire: Gaul (conquered by **Julius Caesar**, 58-51 BCE), Britain (43 CE), and Dacia NE of the Danube (107 CE).

The original aristocratic republican government, with democratic features added in the 5th and 4th cent. BCE, deteriorated under the pressures of empire and class conflict (**Gracchus** brothers, social reformers, murdered in 133 BCE and 121 BCE; slave revolts in 135 BCE and 73 BCE). After a series of civil wars (Marius vs. Sulla, 88-82 BCE; Caesar vs. **Pompey**, 49-45 BCE; triumvirate vs. Caesar's assassins, 44-43 BCE; Antony vs. Octavian, 32-30 BCE), the empire came under the rule of a deified monarch (first emperor, **Augustus**, 27 BCE-14 CE).

Provincials (nearly all granted citizenship by Caracalla, 212 CE) came to dominate the army and civil service. Traditional **Roman law**, systematized and interpreted by independent jurists, and local self-rule in provincial cities were supplanted by a vast tax-collecting bureaucracy in the 3rd and 4th cent. The legal rights of women, children, and slaves were strengthened.

Roman innovations in **civil engineering** included water mills, windmills, and rotary mills and the use of cement that hardened under water. Monumental architecture (baths, theaters, temples) relied on the arch and the dome. A network of roads (some still standing) stretched 53,000 mi, passing through mountain tunnels as long as 3.5 mi. Aqueducts brought water to cities; underground sewers removed waste.

Roman art and literature were derivative of Greek models. Innovations were made in sculpture (naturalistic busts, equestrian statues), decorative wall painting (as at Pompeii), satire (**Juvenal**, 60-127 CE), history (**Tacitus**, 56-120 CE), and prose romance (**Petronius**, d. 66 CE). Gladiatorial contests dominated public amusements, which were supported by the state.

India. The **Gupta** monarchs reunited N India c. 320 CE. Their peaceful and prosperous reign saw a revival of Hindu religious thought and Brahman power. The old Vedic traditions were combined with devotion to many indigenous deities (who were seen as manifestations of Vedic gods). Caste lines were reinforced, and Buddhist practices gradually disappeared or were integrated with **Hindu** traditions. The art (often erotic), architecture, and literature of the period, patronized by

Tutored by Aristotle and imbued with Greek ideals, Alexander the Great (356-323 BCE) conquered the Persian Empire and is considered one of the greatest military leaders of all-time.

the Gupta court, are considered among India's finest achievements (Kalidasa, poet and dramatist, fl. c. 400 CE). Mathematical innovations included the use of zero and decimal numbers. Invasions by White Huns from the NW led to the empire's destruction c. 550 CE. Rich cultures also developed in S India during this period. Emotional Tamil religious poetry contributed to the Hindu revival. The Pallava kingdom controlled much of S India c. 350-880 CE and helped to spread Indian civilization to SE Asia.

China. The Ch'in ruler Shih Huang Ti (r. 221-210 BCE), known as the First Emperor, centralized political authority; standardized the written language, laws, weights, measures, and coinage; and conducted a census. But he tried to destroy most philosophical texts. The **Han** dynasty (202 BCE-220 CE) instituted the Mandarin bureaucracy, which lasted 2,000 years. Local officials were selected by examination in Confucian classics and trained at the imperial university and provincial schools.

The invention of **paper** facilitated this bureaucratic system. Agriculture was promoted, but peasants bore most of the tax burden. Irrigation was improved, water clocks and sundials were used, astronomy and mathematics thrived, and landscape painting was perfected.

With the expansion S and W (to nearly the present borders of today's China), trade was opened with India, SE Asia, and the Middle East over sea and caravan routes. Indian missionaries brought Mahayana Buddhism to China by the 1st cent. CE and spawned a variety of sects. Daoism was revived and merged with popular superstitions. **Daoist and Buddhist monasteries** and convents multiplied in the turbulent centuries after the collapse of the Han dynasty in 220 CE.

Monotheism Spreads: 1-750 CE

Roman Empire. Polytheism was practiced in the Roman Empire, and religions indigenous to particular Middle Eastern nations became international. Roman citizens worshiped **Isis** of Egypt, **Mithras** of Persia, **Demeter** of Greece, and the great mother **Cybele** of Phrygia. Their cults centered on mysteries (secret ceremonies) and the promise of an afterlife, symbolized by the death and rebirth of the god. The Jews of the empire preserved their monotheistic religion, Judaism, the world's oldest (c. 1300 BCE) continuous religion. Its teachings are contained in the Bible (the Old Testament). 1st-cent. CE Judaism embraced several sects, including the **Sadducees**, mostly drawn from the Temple priesthood, who were culturally Hellenized; the **Pharisees**, who upheld the full range of traditional customs and practices as of equal weight to literal scriptural law and elaborated synagogue worship; and the **Essenes**, an ascetic, millenarian sect. Messianic fervor led to repeated, unsuccessful rebellions against Rome (66-70, 135 CE). As a result, the Temple in Jerusalem was destroyed and the population decimated; this event marked the beginning of the Diaspora (living in exile). To preserve the faith, codification of law was begun at the academy of Yavneh. The work continued for some 500 years in Palestine and in Babylonia, ending in the final redaction (c. 600) of the **Talmud**, a huge collection of legal and moral debates, rulings, liturgy, biblical exegesis, and legendary materials.

Christianity. Emerging as a distinct sect by the second half of the 1st cent. CE, Christianity is based on the teachings of **Jesus**, whom believers considered the Savior (Messiah or Christ) and son of God. Missionary activities of the Apostles and such early leaders as **Paul of Tarsus** spread the faith. Intermittent persecution, as in Rome under Nero in 64 CE, on grounds of suspected disloyalty, failed to disrupt Christian communities. Each congregation, generally urban and of plebeian character, was tightly organized under a leader (bishop), elders (presbyters or priests), and assistants (deacons). The four **Gospels** (accounts of the life and teachings of Jesus) and the Acts of the Apostles were written down in the late 1st and early 2nd cent. and circulated along with letters of Paul and other Christian leaders. An authoritative canon of these writings was not fixed until the 4th cent.

A school for priests was established at Alexandria in the 2nd cent. Its teachers (**Origen**, c. 182-251) helped define doctrine and promote the faith in Greek-style philosophical works. Neoplatonism underwent Christian coloration in the writings of Church Fathers such as **Augustine** (354-430). Christian hermits began to associate in monasteries, first in Egypt (St. Pachomius, c. 290-345), then in other E lands, then in the W (**St. Benedict's rule**, 529). Devotion to saints, especially Mary, mother of Jesus, spread. Under **Constantine** (r. 306-37), Christianity became in effect the established religion of the Empire. Pagan temples were expropriated, state funds were used to build churches and support the hierarchy, and laws were adjusted in accordance with Christian ideas. Pagan worship was banned by the end of the 4th cent., and severe restrictions were placed on Judaism.

The newly established church was rocked by doctrinal disputes, often exacerbated by regional rivalries. Chief heresies (as defined by church councils, backed by imperial authority) were **Arianism**, which denied the divinity of Jesus; **Monophysitism**, denying the human nature of Christ; **Donatism**, which regarded as invalid any sacraments administered by sinful clergy; and **Pelagianism**, which denied the necessity of unmerited divine aid (grace) for salvation.

Islam. The earliest Arab civilization emerged by the end of the 2nd millennium BCE in the watered highlands of Yemen. Seaborne and caravan trade in frankincense and myrrh connected the area with the Nile and Fertile Crescent. The Minaean, Sabean (Sheba), and Himyarite states successively held sway. By Muhammad's time (7th cent. CE), the region was a province of Sassanian Persia. In the N, the Nabataean kingdom at Petra and the kingdom of Palmyra were Aramaicized, Romanized, and finally absorbed, as neighboring Judea had been, into the Roman Empire. Nomads shared the central region with a few trading towns and oases. Wars between tribes and raids on communities were common and were celebrated in a poetic tradition that by the 6th cent. helped establish a classic literary Arabic.

About 610, **Muhammad**, a 40-year-old Arab man of Mecca, emerged as a prophet. He proclaimed a revelation from the one true God, calling on contemporaries to abandon idolatry and restore the faith of Abraham. He introduced his religion as **Islam**, meaning "submission" to the one God, Allah, as a continuation of the biblical faith of Abraham, Moses, and Jesus, all respected as prophets in this system. His teachings, recorded

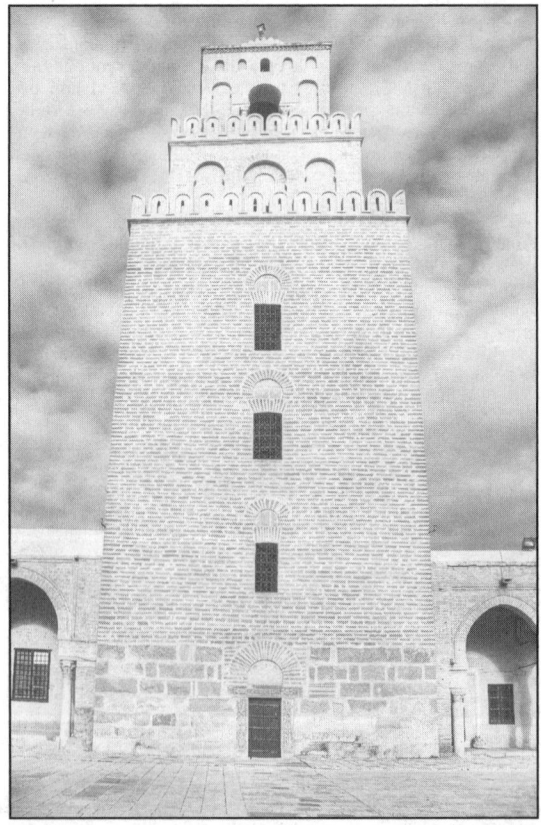

The now-typical use of a minaret as the location for the Muslim call to prayer began at the Mosque of Uqba, or Great Mosque of Kairouan, built from 670 CE in present-day Tunisia.

in the **Koran** (*al-Qur'an* in Arabic), in many ways were inclusive of Abrahamic monotheistic ideas known to the Jews and Christians in Arabia. A key aspect of the Abrahamic connection was insistence on justice in society, which led to severe opposition among the aristocrats in Mecca. As conditions worsened for Muhammad and his followers, he decided in 622 to make a *hegira* (flight) to Medina, 200 mi to the N. This event marks the beginning of the Muslim lunar calendar. Hostilities between Mecca and Medina increased, and in 629 Muhammad conquered Mecca. By the time he died in 632, nearly all the Arabian peninsula accepted his political and religious leadership.

After his death the majority of Muslims (later known as **Sunni** Muslims) recognized the leadership of the **caliph** (successor) Abu Bakr (632-34), followed by Umar (634-44), Uthman (644-56), and Ali (656-60). A minority, the **Shiites**, insisted instead on the leadership of Ali, Muhammad's cousin and son-in-law. By 644, **Muslim rule** over Arabia was confirmed. Muslim armies had threatened the Byzantine and Persian empires, which were weakened by wars and disaffection among subject peoples (including Coptic and Syriac Christians opposed to the Byzantine Orthodox establishment). Syria, Palestine, Egypt, Iraq, and Persia fell to Muslim armies. The new administration assimilated existing systems in the region; hence the conquered peoples participated in running the empire.

The Koran recognized the so-called Peoples of the Book, i.e., Christians, Jews, and Zoroastrians, as tolerated monotheists, and Muslim policy was relatively tolerant to minorities living as "protected" peoples. An expanded tax system, based on conquests of the Persian and Byzantine empires, provided revenue to organize campaigns against neighboring non-Muslim regions.

Under the **Umayyads** (661-750) and **Abbasids** (750-1256), territorial expansion led Muslim armies across N Africa and into Spain (711). Muslim armies in the W were stopped at Tours, France, in 732 by the Frankish ruler **Charles Martel**. Asia Minor, the Indus Valley, and Transoxiana were conquered in the E. The conversion of conquered peoples to Islam was gradual. In many places the official Arabic language supplanted the local tongues. But in the eastern regions the Arab rulers and their armies adopted Persian cultures and language as part of their Muslim identity.

Disputes over succession and pious opposition to injustices in society led to a number of oppositional movements, which led to the factionalization of Muslim community. The **Shiites** supported leadership candidates descended from Muhammad, believing them to be carriers of some kind of divine authority. The **Kharijites** supported an egalitarian system derived from the Koran, opposing and even engaging in battle against those who did not agree with them.

New Peoples Enter World History: 400-900 CE

Barbarian invasions and fall of Rome. Germanic tribes infiltrated S and E from their Baltic homeland during the 1st millennium BCE, reaching S Germany by 100 BCE and the Black Sea by 214 CE. Organized into large federated tribes under elected kings, most resisted Roman domination and raided the empire in times of civil war (Goths took Dacia in 214, raided Thrace in 251-69). Germanic troops and commanders dominated the Roman armies by the end of the 4th cent. **Huns**, invaders from Asia, entered Europe in 372, driving more Germans into the empire. Emperor Valens allowed Visigoths to cross the Danube in 376. Huns under Attila (d. 453) raided Gaul, Italy, and the Balkans.

The western empire, weakened by overtaxation and social stagnation, was overrun in the 5th cent. Gaul was effectively lost in 406-07, Spain in 409, Britain in 410, and Africa in 429-39. Rome was sacked in 410 by Visigoths under Alaric and in 455 by Vandals. The **last western emperor**, Romulus Augustulus, was deposed in 476 by the Germanic chief Odovacar.

Celts. Celtic cultures, which in pre-Roman times covered most of W Europe, were confined almost entirely to the British Isles after the Germanic invasions. **St. Patrick** completed (c. 457-92) the conversion of Ireland and a strong monastic tradition took hold. Irish monastic missionaries in Scotland, England, and on the continent (Columba, c. 521-97; Columbanus, c. 543-615) helped restore Christianity after the Germanic invasions. **Monasteries** became centers of classic and Christian learning and presided over the recording of a Christianized Celtic mythology, elaborated by secular writers and bards. An intricate decorative art style developed, especially in book illumination (Lindisfarne Gospels, c. 700; Book of Kells, 8th cent.).

Successor states. The Visigothic kingdom in Spain (from 419) and much of France (to 507) saw continuation of Roman administration, language, and law (Breviary of Alaric, 506) until its destruction by the Muslims (711). The Vandal kingdom in Africa (from 429) was conquered by the Byzantines in 533. Italy was ruled successively by an Ostrogothic kingdom under Byzantine suzerainty (489-554), direct Byzantine government, and German Lombards (568-774). The Lombards divided the peninsula with the Byzantines and papacy under the dynamic reformer **Pope Gregory the Great** (590-604) and successors.

King Clovis (r. 481-511) united the Franks on both sides of the Rhine, and after his conversion to Christianity, defeated the Arian heretics, Burgundians (after 500), and Visigoths (507) with the support of native clergy and the papacy. Under the **Merovingian** kings, a feudal system emerged: power was fragmented among hierarchies of military landowners. Social stratification, which in late Roman times had acquired legal, hereditary sanction, was reinforced.

The Carolingians (747-987) expanded the kingdom and restored central power. **Charlemagne** (r. 768-814) conquered nearly all the Germanic lands, including Lombard Italy. He was crowned emperor by Pope Leo III in Rome in 800. A centuries-long decline in commerce and arts was reversed under Charlemagne's patronage. He welcomed Jews to his kingdom, which became a center of Jewish learning (Rashi, 1040-1105). He sponsored the Carolingian Renaissance of learning under the Anglo-Latin scholar Alcuin (c. 732-804), who reformed church liturgy.

Byzantine Empire. Under **Diocletian** (r. 284-305) the Roman empire had been divided into two parts to facilitate administration and defense. **Constantine** founded (330) **Constantinople** (at old Byzantium) as a fully Christian city. Commerce and taxation financed a sumptuous, orientalized court, a class of hereditary bureaucratic families, and magnificent urban construction (Hagia Sophia, 532-37). The city's fortifications and naval innovations repelled assaults by Goths, Huns, Slavs, Bulgars, Avars, Arabs, and Scandinavians. Greek replaced Latin as the official language by c. 700. **Byzantine art**, a solemn, sacral, and stylized variation of late classical styles (mosaics at the Church of San Vitale, Ravenna, Italy, 526-48), was a starting point for medieval art in E and W Europe.

Justinian (r. 527-65) briefly reconquered parts of Spain, N Africa, and Italy, codified **Roman law** (Codex Justinianus [529]) was medieval Europe's chief legal text, closed the Platonic Academy at Athens, and ordered all pagans to convert. Lombards in Italy and Arabs in Africa retook most of his conquests. The Isaurian dynasty from Anatolia (from 717) and the Macedonian dynasty (867-1054) restored military and commercial power. The Iconoclast controversy (726-843) over the permissibility of images helped alienate the Eastern Church from the papacy.

Abbasid Empire. Baghdad (established 762), became seat of the **Abbasid dynasty** (established 750), while Umayyads continued to rule in Spain. A brilliant cosmopolitan civilization emerged, inaugurating a Muslim-Arab golden age. Arabic was the lingua franca of the empire; intellectual sources from Persian, Sanskrit, Greek, and Syriac were rendered into Arabic. Christians and Jews equally participated in this translation movement, which also involved interaction between Jewish legal thought and Islamic law, as much as between Christian theology and Muslim scholasticism. Persian-style court life, with art and music, flourished at the court of **Harun al-Rashid** (786-809), celebrated in the masterpiece known to English readers as *The Arabian Nights*. The sciences, medicine, and mathematics were pursued at Baghdad, Cordova, and Cairo (c. 969). The culmination of this intellectual synthesis in Islamic civilization came with the scientific and philosophical works of **Avicenna** (Ibn Sina, 980-1037), **Averroes** (Ibn Rushd, 1126-98), and **Maimonides** (1135-1204), a Jew who wrote in Arabic. This intellectual tradition was translated into Latin and opened a new period in Christian thought.

The decentralization of the **Abbasid** empire, from 874, led to the establishment of various Muslim dynasties under different ethnic groups. Persians, Berbers, and Turks ruled different regions, retaining connection with the Abbasid caliph at the religious level. The Abbasid period also saw various religious

The pyramid of Kukulkan (El Castillo) at Chichen Itza is one of the preeminent existing examples of Mayan architecture in present-day Mexico.

movements against the orthodox position held by governing authorities. This situation in Muslim religion led to the establishment of different legal, theological, and mystical schools of thought. The most influential mass movement was **Sufism**, which aimed at the reaching out of the average individual in quest of a spiritual path. Al-Ghazali (1058-1111) is credited with reconciling personal Sufism with orthodox Sunni tradition.

Africa. Immigrants from Saba in S Arabia helped set up the **Axum** kingdom in Ethiopia in the 1st cent. (their language, Ge'ez, is preserved by the Ethiopian Church). In the 3rd cent., when the kingdom became Christianized, it defeated Kushite Meroe and expanded its influence into Yemen. Axum was the center of a vast ivory trade and controlled the Red Sea coast until c. 1100. Arab conquest in Egypt cut Axum's political and economic ties with Byzantium.

The Iron Age entered W Africa by the end of the 1st millennium BCE. **Ghana**, the first known sub-Saharan state, ruled in the upper Senegal-Niger region c. 400-1240, controlling the trade of gold from mines in the S to trans-Sahara caravan routes to the N. The **Bantu** peoples, probably of W African origin, began to spread E and S perhaps 2,000 years ago, displacing the Pygmies and Bushmen of central and S Africa during a 1,500-year period.

Japan. The advanced Neolithic Yayoi period, when irrigation, rice farming, and iron and bronze casting techniques were introduced from China or Korea, persisted to c. 400 CE. The myriad Japanese states were then united by the **Yamato** clan, under an emperor who acted as chief priest of the animistic Shinto cult. Japanese political and military intervention by the 6th cent. in Korea, then under strong Chinese influence, quickened a Chinese cultural invasion of Japan, bringing Buddhism, the Chinese language (which long remained a literary and governmental medium), Chinese ideographs, and Buddhist styles in painting, sculpture, literature, and architecture (7th cent., Horyuji temple at Nara). The Taika Reforms (646) tried unsuccessfully to centralize Japan according to Chinese bureaucratic and Buddhist philosophical values.

A nativist reaction against the Buddhist **Nara** period (710-94) ushered in the **Heian** period (794-1185) centered at the new capital, Kyoto. Japanese elegance and simplicity modified Chinese styles in architecture, scroll painting, and literature; the writing system was also simplified. The courtly novel *Tale of Genji* (1010-20) testifies to the enhanced role of women in medieval Japanese literature and culture.

Southeast Asia. The historic peoples of SE Asia began arriving some 2,500 years ago from China and Tibet, displacing scattered aborigines. Their agriculture relied on rice and yams. Indian cultural influences were strongest; literacy and Hindu and Buddhist ideas followed the S India-China trade route. From the S tip of Indochina, the kingdom of **Funan** (1st-7th cent.) traded as far W as Persia. It was absorbed by Chenla, itself conquered by the **Khmer Empire** (600-1300). The Khmers, under Hindu god-kings (Suryavarman II, 1113-c. 1150), built the monumental Angkor Wat temple center for the royal phallic cult. The **Nam-Viet** kingdom in Annam, dominated by China and Chinese culture for 1,000 years, emerged in the 10th cent., growing at the expense of the Khmers, who also lost ground in the NW to the new, highly organized **Thai** kingdom. On Sumatra, the **Srivijaya** Empire controlled vital sea lanes (7th-10th cent.). A Buddhist dynasty, the Sailendras, ruled central **Java** (8th-9th cent.), building at Borobudur one of the largest stupas (dome-shaped Buddhist shrine) in the world.

China. The Sui dynasty (581-618) ushered in a period of commercial, artistic, and scientific achievement in China, which continued under the **Tang** dynasty (618-906). Inventions like the magnetic compass, gunpowder, the abacus, and printing were introduced or perfected. Medical innovations included cataract surgery. The state, from its cosmopolitan capital, Chang-an, supervised foreign trade, which exchanged Chinese silks, porcelains, and art for spices and ivory over Central Asian caravan routes and sea routes reaching Africa. A golden age of poetry bequeathed valuable works to later generations (Tu Fu, 712-70; Li Po, 701-62). Landscape painting flourished.

Commercial and industrial expansion continued under the **Northern Sung** dynasty (960-1126), facilitated by paper money and credit notes. But commerce never achieved full respectability; government monopolies expropriated successful merchants. The population, long stable at 50 million, doubled in 200 years with the introduction of early-ripening rice and the double harvest. In art, native Chinese styles were revived.

Americas. From 300 to 600, a Native American empire stretched from the Valley of Mexico to Guatemala, centering on the huge city **Teotihuacán** (founded 100 BCE). To the S, in Guatemala, a high **Mayan** civilization developed (150-900) around hundreds of rural ceremonial centers. The Mayans improved on Olmec writing and the calendar and pursued astronomy and mathematics. In South America, a widespread pre-Inca culture grew from **Tiahuanacu**, Bolivia, near Lake Titicaca (Gateway of the Sun doorway, c. 700).

Christian Europe Regroups and Expands: 900-1300

Scandinavia. Pagan Danish and Norse (Viking) adventurers, traders, and pirates raided the coasts of the British Isles (Dublin, c. 831), France, and even the Mediterranean for over 200 years beginning in the late 8th cent. Inland settlement in the W was limited to Great Britain (King Canute, 994-1035) and Normandy, settled (911) under Rollo, as a fief of France. Vikings also reached Iceland (874), Greenland (c. 986), and North America (**Leif Ericson** and others, c. 1000). Norse traders (**Varangians**) developed Russian river commerce from the 8th to the 11th cent. and helped set up a state at Kiev in the late 9th cent. Conversion to Christianity occurred in the 10th cent., reaching Sweden 100 years later. In the 11th cent. Norman bands conquered S Italy and Sicily, and Duke **William of Normandy** conquered (1066) England, bringing feudal government and the French language, essential elements in later English civilization.

Central and East Europe. Slavs began to expand from about 150 CE in all directions in Europe. By the 7th cent. they reached as far S as the Adriatic and Aegean seas. In the Balkan Peninsula they dislocated Romanized local populations or assimilated newcomers (Bulgarians, a Turkic people). The first **Slavic states** were Moravia (628) in Central Europe and

the Bulgarian state (680) in the Balkans. Byzantine missions of St. Methodius and Cyril (whose Greek-based cyrillic alphabet is still used by some S and E Slavs) converted (863) Moravia.

The Eastern Slavs, part-civilized under the overlordship of the Turkish-Jewish **Khazar** trading empire (7th-10th cent.), gravitated toward Constantinople by the 9th cent. The **Kievan** state adopted (989) Eastern Christianity under Prince Vladimir. King Boleslav I (992-1025) began **Poland**'s long history of conquest. The Magyars (**Hungarians**), in present-day Hungary since 896, accepted (1001) Latin Christianity.

Germany. The German kingdom that emerged after the breakup of Charlemagne's W Empire remained a confederation of largely autonomous states. Otto I, a Saxon who was king from 936, established the **Holy Roman Empire**—a union of Germany and N Italy—in alliance with Pope John XII, who crowned (962) him emperor; he defeated (955) the Magyars. Imperial power was greatest under the **Hohenstaufens** (1138-1254), despite the growing opposition of the papacy, which ruled central Italy, and the Lombard League cities. Frederick II (1194-1250) improved administration and patronized the arts. After his death, German influence was removed from Italy.

Christian Spain. From its N mountain redoubts, Christian rule slowly migrated S through the 11th cent., when Muslim unity collapsed. After the capture (1085) of **Toledo**, the kingdoms of Portugal, Castile, and Aragon undertook repeated crusades of reconquest, finally completed in 1492. Elements of Islamic civilization persisted in recaptured areas, influencing all Western Europe.

Crusades. Pope Urban II called for a crusade (1095) to restore Asia Minor to Byzantium and the Holy Land to Christendom. This first crusade captured Jerusalem and led to the foundation of four Frankish states in the Levant. The defeat inflicted upon crusaders at the Battle of Hattin (1187) by **Saladin** (c. 1137-93), the Kurdish ruler of Egypt and Syria, effectively negated territorial gains. Many crusades followed until 1291. The 4th crusade sacked Constantinople (1204). Other crusades were launched against Christian heretics (Albigensian Crusade, 1229), pagans, and enemies of the papacy.

Economy. The agricultural base of European life benefited from improvements in **plow design** (c. 1000) and by the draining of lowlands and clearing of forests, leading to a rural population increase. Towns grew in N Italy, Flanders, and N Germany (Hanseatic League). Improvements in **loom design** permitted factory textile production. **Guilds** dominated urban trades from the 12th cent. Banking (centered in Italy, 12th-15th cent.) facilitated long-distance trade.

Christianity. The split between the Eastern and Western churches was formalized in 1054. Western and Central Europe was divided into 500 bishoprics under one united hierarchy, but conflicts between secular and church authorities were frequent (German **Investiture Controversy**, 1075-1122). Clerical power was first strengthened through the international monastic reform begun at Cluny in 910. Popular religious enthusiasm often expressed itself in heretical movements (Waldensians from 1173), but was channeled by the **Dominican** (1215) and **Franciscan** (1223) friars into the religious mainstream.

Arts. Romanesque architecture (9th to mid-12th cent.) expanded on late Roman models, using the rounded arch and massed stone to support enlarged basilicas. Painting and sculpture followed Byzantine models. The literature of **chivalry** was exemplified by the epic (*Chanson de Roland*, c. 1100) and by courtly love poems of the troubadours of Provence and minnesingers of Germany. **Gothic** architecture emerged in France (choir of St. Denis, c. 1140) and spread along with French cultural influence. Rib vaulting and pointed arches were used to combine soaring heights with delicacy, and they freed walls for display of stained glass. Exteriors were covered with painted relief sculpture and embellished with elaborate architectural detail.

Learning. Law, medicine, and philosophy were advanced at independent **universities** (Bologna, Paris, 12th cent.), originally corporations of students and masters. Twelfth-cent. translations of Greek classics, especially by Aristotle, encouraged an analytic approach. Scholastic philosophy, from Anselm (1033-1109) to **Aquinas** (1225-74), attempted to understand revelation through reason.

Apogee of Central Asian Power and the Spread of Islam: 1250-1500

Turks. Turkic peoples, of Central Asian ancestry, were a military threat to the Byzantine and Persian Empires from the 6th cent. After several waves of invasions, during which most of the Turks adopted Islam, the **Seljuk Turks** took (1055) Baghdad. They ruled Persia, Iraq, and, after 1071, Asia Minor, where massive numbers of Turks settled. The empire was divided in the 12th cent. into smaller states ruled by Seljuks, Kurds, and Mamluks (a military caste of former Turk, Kurd, and Circassian slaves), which governed Egypt and the Middle East until the Ottoman era (c. 1290-1922).

Osman I (r. c. 1290-1326) and succeeding sultans united Anatolian Turkish warriors in a militaristic state that waged holy war against Byzantium and Balkan Christians. Most of the Balkans had been subdued and Anatolia united when Constantinople fell (1453). By the mid-16th cent., Hungary, the Middle East, and N Africa had been conquered. The Turkish advance was stopped at Vienna (1529) and at the naval battle of Lepanto (1571) by Spain, Venice, and the papacy.

The **Ottoman state** was governed in accordance with orthodox Muslim law. Greek, Armenian, and Jewish communities were segregated and were ruled by religious leaders responsible for taxation; they dominated trade. Many state offices and most army ranks were filled by slaves, in part through a system of child conscription among Christians.

India. Mahmud of Ghazni (971-1030) led repeated Turkish raids into N India. Turkish power was consolidated in 1206 with the start of the **Sultanate at Delhi**. Centralization of state power under the early Delhi sultans went far beyond traditional Indian practice. Muslim rule of much of the subcontinent lasted until the British conquest 600 years later, though Hinduism remained the majority religion.

Mongols. Genghis Khan (c. 1167-1227) first united the feuding Mongol tribes and built their armies into an effective offensive force around a core of highly mobile cavalry. He and his immediate successors created the largest land empire in history; by 1279 it stretched from the E coast of Asia to the Danube and from the Siberian steppes to the Arabian Sea. East-West trade and contacts were facilitated (Marco Polo, c. 1254-1324). The western Mongols were Islamized by 1295; successor states soon lost their Mongol character by assimilation. They were briefly reunited under the Turk Tamerlane (1336-1405).

Kublai Khan ruled China from his new capital Beijing (established c. 1264). Naval campaigns against Japan (1274, 1281) and Java (1293) were defeated, the latter by the Hindu-Buddhist maritime kingdom of Majapahit. The **Yuan** dynasty used Mongols and other foreigners (including Europeans) in official posts and tolerated the return of Nestorian Christianity (suppressed 841-45) and the spread of Islam in the S and W. A native reaction expelled the Mongols in 1367-68.

Russia. The Kievan state in Russia, weakened by the decline of Byzantium and the rise of the Catholic Polish-Lithuanian state, was overrun (1238-40) by the Mongols. Only the northern trading republic of Novgorod remained independent. The grand dukes of Moscow emerged as leaders of a coalition of princes that eventually (by 1481) defeated the Mongols. After the fall of Constantinople in 1453, the **Tsars** (Caesars) at Moscow (from Ivan III, r. 1462-1505) set up an independent Russian Orthodox Church. Commerce failed to revive. The isolated Russian state remained agrarian with the peasant class falling into serfdom.

Persia. A revival of Persian literature, making use of the Arab alphabet and literary forms, began in the 10th cent. (epic of Firdausi, 935-1020). An art revival, influenced by Chinese styles introduced after the Mongols came to power in Iran, began in the 13th cent. Persian cultural and political forms, and often the Persian language, were used for centuries by Turkish and Mongol elites from the Balkans to India. Persian mystics from Rumi (1207-73) to Jami (1414-92) promoted **Sufism** in their poetry.

Africa. Two militant Islamic Berber dynasties emerged from the Sahara to carve out empires from the Sahel to central Spain—the **Almoravids** (c. 1050-1140) and the fanatical **Almohads** (c. 1125-1269). The Ghanaian empire was replaced in the upper Niger by Mali (c. 1230-1340), whose Muslim rulers imported Egyptians to help make **Timbuktu** a center of commerce (in gold, leather, and slaves) and learning. The Songhay empire (to 1590) replaced Mali. To the S, forest kingdoms produced refined artworks (Ife terra cotta, **Benin** bronzes).

Other **Muslim states** in Nigeria (Hausas) and Chad originated in the 11th cent. and continued in some form until the 19th-cent. European conquest. Less-developed Bantu kingdoms existed across central Africa.

Some 40 Muslim Arab-Persian trading colonies and city-states were established all along the E African coast from the 10th cent. (Kilwa, Mogadishu). The interchange with Bantu peoples produced the **Swahili** language and culture. Gold, palm oil, and slaves were brought from the interior, stimulating the growth of the Monamatapa kingdom of the Zambezi (15th cent.). The Christian Ethiopian empire (from 13th cent.) continued the traditions of Axum.

Southeast Asia. Islam was introduced into Malaya and the Indonesian islands by Arab, Persian, and Indian traders. Coastal Muslim cities and states (starting before 1300) soon dominated the interior. Chief among these was the **Malacca** state (c. 1400-1511), on the Malay peninsula.

Arts and Statecraft Thrive in Europe; New Asian Empires Rise: 1350-1600

Italy. Distinctive Italian achievements in literature and fine arts during the late Middle Ages (**Dante**, 1265-1321; Giotto, 1276-1337) led to the vigorous new styles of the Renaissance (14th-16th cent.). Patronized by the rulers of the quarreling petty states of Italy (**Medicis** in Florence and the papacy, c. 1400-1737), the plastic arts perfected realistic techniques, including **perspective** (Masaccio, 1401-28; Leonardo **da Vinci**, 1452-1519). Classical motifs were used in architecture, and increased talent and expense were put into secular buildings. The Florentine dialect was refined as a national literary language (**Petrarch**, 1304-74). Greek refugees from the E strengthened the respect of humanist scholars for the classic sources. Soon an international movement aided by the spread of **printing** (Gutenberg, c. 1397-1468), **humanism** was optimistic about the power of human reason (Erasmus of Rotterdam, 1466-1536, **More**'s *Utopia*, 1516) and valued individual effort in the arts and in politics (**Machiavelli**, 1469-1527).

France. The French monarchy, strengthened in its repeated struggles with powerful nobles (Burgundy, Flanders, Aquitaine) by alliances with the growing commercial towns, consolidated bureaucratic control under Philip IV (r. 1285-1314) and extended French influence into Germany and Italy (popes at Avignon, France, 1309-1417). The **Hundred Years War** (1337-1453) ended English dynastic claims in France (battles of Crécy, 1346, and Poitiers, 1356; Joan of Arc executed, 1431). A French Renaissance, dating from royal invasions (1494, 1499) of Italy, was encouraged at the court of Francis I (r. 1515-47), who centralized taxation and law. French vernacular literature consciously asserted its independence (La Pléiade, 1549).

England. The evolution of England's political institutions began with the **Magna Carta** (1215), by which King John guaranteed the privileges of nobles and church against the monarchy and assured jury trial. After the **Wars of the Roses** (1455-85), the **Tudor** dynasty reasserted royal prerogatives (Henry VIII, r. 1509-47), but the trend toward independent departments and ministerial government also continued. English trade (wool exports from c. 1340) was protected by the nation's growing maritime power (**Spanish Armada** destroyed, 1588).

English replaced French and Latin in the late 14th cent. in law and literature (**Chaucer**, c. 1340-1400), and English translation of the Bible began (Wycliffe, 1380s). **Elizabeth I** (r. 1558-1603) presided over a confident flowering of poetry (Spenser, 1552-99), drama (**Shakespeare**, 1564-1616), and music.

German Empire. From among a welter of minor feudal states, church lands, and independent cities, the **Habsburgs** assembled a far-flung territorial domain, based in Austria from 1276. Family members held the title of Holy Roman Emperor from 1438 to the Empire's dissolution in 1806 but failed to centralize its domains, leaving Germany disunited for centuries. Resistance to Turkish expansion brought Hungary under Austrian control from the 16th cent. The Netherlands, Luxembourg, and Burgundy were added in 1477, curbing French expansion.

The Flemish painting tradition of naturalism, technical proficiency, and bourgeois subject matter began in the 15th cent. (Jan **van Eyck**, c. 1390-1441), the earliest northern manifestation of the Renaissance. Albrecht **Dürer** (1471-1528) typified the merging of late Gothic and Italian trends in 16th-cent. German art. Imposing civic architecture flourished in the prosperous commercial cities.

Black Death. The bubonic plague reached Europe from the E in 1348, killing up to half the population by 1350 (and recurring periodically in most areas until the early 18th cent.) Labor scarcity forced wages to rise and brought greater freedom to the peasantry, making possible **peasant uprisings** (Jacquerie in France, 1358; Wat Tyler's rebellion in England, 1381).

Spain. Despite the unification of Castile and Aragon in 1479, the two countries retained separate governments, and the nobility, especially in Aragon and Catalonia, retained many privileges. Spanish lands in Italy (Naples, Sicily) and the Netherlands entangled the country in European wars through the mid-17th cent., while explorers, traders, and conquerors built up a Spanish empire in the Americas and the Philippines.

From the late 15th cent., a **golden age** of literature and art produced works of social satire (plays of Lope de Vega, 1562-1635; **Cervantes**, 1547-1616), as well as spiritual intensity (**El Greco**, 1541-1614; **Velázquez**, 1599-1660).

Explorations. Organized European maritime exploration began, seeking to evade the Venice-Ottoman monopoly of eastern trade and to promote Christianity. A key goal was to satisfy a growing taste for Asian goods. Beginning in 1418, expeditions from Portugal explored the W coast of Africa, until Vasco da Gama rounded the Cape of Good Hope in 1497 and reached India. A Portuguese trading empire was consolidated by the seizure of Goa (1510) and Malacca (1551). Japan was reached in 1542. The voyages of Christopher **Columbus** (1492-1504) uncovered a world new to Europeans, which Spain hastened to subdue. Navigation schools in Spain and Portugal, the development of large sailing ships (carracks) mounted with cannons, and the invention (c. 1475) of the rifle aided European penetration.

Mughals and Safavids. E of the Ottoman Empire, two Muslim dynasties ruled unchallenged in the 16th and 17th cent. The Mughal dynasty of India, founded by Persianized Turkish invaders from the NW under Babur, dates from their 1526 conquest of the Delhi Sultanate. The dynasty ruled most of India for more than 200 years, surviving nominally until 1857. **Akbar** (r. 1556-1605) consolidated administration at his glorious court, where the Urdu language (Persian-influenced Hindi) developed. Trade relations with Europe increased. Under Shah Jahan (1629-58), a secularized art fusing Hindu and Muslim elements flourished in miniature painting and in architecture (**Taj Mahal**). Sikhism (founded c. 1519) combined elements of both faiths. Suppression of Hindus and Shiite Muslims in S India in the late 17th cent. weakened the empire.

Intense devotion to the Shiite sect characterized the Safavids (1502-1736) of Persia and led to hostilities with the Sunni Ottomans for more than a century. The prosperity and the strength of the empire are evidenced by the mosques at its capital city, **Isfahan**. The Safavids enhanced Iranian national consciousness.

China. The **Ming** emperors (1368-1644), the last native dynasty in China, wielded strong personal power. European trade (Portuguese monopoly through **Macao** from 1557) was strictly controlled. Jesuit scholars and scientists (Matteo Ricci, 1552-1610) introduced some Western science; their writings familiarized the West with China. The arts thrived, especially in the areas

Queen Elizabeth I, who ruled England for more than 40 years (1558-1603), presided over the age in which Shakespeare, Spenser, and Marlowe flourished.

of painting and ceramics. Chinese manufacturing boomed, bringing in new profits from world trade.

Japan. After the decline of the first hereditary *shogunate* (chief generalship) at **Kamakura** (1185-1333), fragmentation of power accelerated, as did the consequent social mobility. Under Kamakura and the Ashikaga shogunate (1338-1573), the *daimyos* (lords) and *samurai* (warriors) grew more powerful and promoted a martial ideology. Japanese pirates and traders plied the China coast. Popular Buddhist movements included the nationalist Nichiren sect (from c. 1250) and **Zen** (brought from China, 1191), which stressed meditation and a disciplined aesthetic (tea ceremony, gardening, martial arts, *No* drama).

Change and Expansion in Europe: 1500-1700

Reformation. Theological debate and protests against real and perceived clerical corruption existed in the medieval Christian world, expressed by such dissenters as John **Wycliffe** (c. 1320-84) and his followers (the Lollards) in England, and Huss (burned as a heretic, 1415) in Bohemia.

Martin **Luther** (1483-1546) preached that faith alone, without the mediation of clergy or good works, leads to salvation. He attacked the authority of the pope, rejected priestly celibacy, and recommended individual study of the Bible (which he translated into German c. 1525). His 95 Theses (1517) led to his excommunication (1521). John **Calvin** (1509-64) said that God's elect were predestined for salvation and all others for damnation; good conduct and success were signs of election. Calvin in Geneva and John **Knox** (1505-72) in Scotland established theocratic states.

Henry VIII asserted English national authority and secular power by breaking away (1534) from the Catholic Church, creating what would become the Anglican Church. Monastic property was confiscated, and some Protestant doctrines given official sanction.

Religious wars. A century and a half of religious wars began with a S German peasant uprising (1524), repressed with Luther's support. Radical sects—democratic, pacifist, millenarian—arose (Anabaptists ruled Münster, 1534-35) and were suppressed violently. Civil war in France from 1562 between **Huguenots** (Protestant nobles and merchants) and Catholics ended with the 1598 **Edict of Nantes**, tolerating Protestants (revoked 1685). Habsburg attempts to restore Catholicism in Germany were resisted in 25 years of fighting. The 1555 Peace of Augsburg guarantee of religious independence to local princes and cities was confirmed only after the **Thirty Years' War** (1618-48), when much of Germany was devastated by local and foreign armies (Sweden, France).

A Catholic Reformation, or **Counter-Reformation**, met the Protestant challenge, defining an official theology at the Council of Trent (1545-63). The **Jesuit** order (Society of Jesus), founded in 1534 by Ignatius Loyola (1491-1556), helped reconvert large areas of Poland, Hungary, and S Germany and sent missionaries to the New World, India, and S China. The **Inquisition** suppressed heresy in Catholic countries. A revival of religious fervor appeared in devotional literature (Teresa of Avila, 1515-82) and in grandiose **Baroque** art (Bernini, 1598-1680).

Scientific Revolution. The late nominalist thinkers (Ockham, c. 1300-49) of Paris and Oxford challenged Aristotelian orthodoxy, allowing for a freer scientific approach. At the same time, metaphysical values, such as the Neoplatonic faith in an orderly, mathematical cosmos, still motivated and directed inquiry. Nicolaus **Copernicus** (1473-1543) promoted the heliocentric theory, which was confirmed when Johannes **Kepler** (1571-1630) discovered the mathematical laws describing the elliptical orbits of the planets. The traditional Christian-Aristotelian belief that the heavens and the Earth were fundamentally different collapsed when **Galileo Galilei** (1564-1642) discovered moving sunspots, irregular moon topography, and moons around Jupiter, but he faced religious opposition (Galileo's retraction, 1633). He and Sir Isaac **Newton** (1642-1727) developed a mechanics that unified cosmic and earthly phenomena. Newton and Gottfried von **Leibniz** (1646-1716) invented calculus. René **Descartes** (1596-1650), best known for his influential philosophy, also invented analytic geometry.

An explosion of **observational science** included the discovery of blood circulation (Harvey, 1578-1657) and microscopic life (Leeuwenhoek, 1632-1723) and advances in anatomy (Vesalius, 1514-64, dissected corpses) and chemistry (Boyle, 1627-91). Scientific research institutes were founded in Florence (1657), London (**Royal Society**, 1660), and Paris (1666). Inventions proliferated (Savery's steam engine, 1696).

Arts. Mannerist trends of the High Renaissance (**Michelangelo**, 1475-1564) exploited virtuosity, grace, novelty, and exotic subjects and poses. The notion of artistic genius was promoted. Private connoisseurs entered the art market. These trends were elaborated in the 17th cent. **Baroque** era on a grander scale. Dynamic movement in painting and sculpture was emphasized by sharp lighting effects, rich materials (colored marble, gilt), and realistic details. Curved facades, broken lines, rich detail, and ceiling decoration characterized Baroque architecture. Monarchs, princes, and prelates, usually Catholic, used Baroque art to enhance and embellish their authority, as in royal portraits (Velázquez, 1599-1660; Van Dyck, 1599-1641).

National styles emerged. In France, a taste for rectilinear order and serenity (Poussin, 1594-1665), linked to the new rational philosophy, was expressed in classical forms. The influence of **classical values** in French literature (tragedies of **Racine**, 1639-99) gave rise to the "battle of the Ancients and Moderns." New forms included the essay (**Montaigne**, 1533-92) and novel (*Princesse de Clèves*, La Fayette, 1678).

Dutch painting of the 17th cent. was unique in its wide social distribution. The Flemish tradition of undemonstrative realism reached its peak in **Rembrandt** (1606-69) and Jan Vermeer (1632-75).

Economy. European economic expansion, known as the **commercial revolution**, was stimulated by new trade with the East, by New World gold and silver, and by a doubling of population (50 million in 1450, 100 million in 1600). **New business and financial techniques** were developed and refined, such as joint-stock companies, insurance, and letters of credit and exchange. The Bank of Amsterdam (1609) and the Bank of England (1694) broke the old monopoly of private banking families. The rise of a business mentality was typified by the spread of clock towers in cities in the 14th cent. By the mid-15th cent., portable clocks were available; the first watch was invented in 1502.

By 1650, most governments had adopted the **mercantile system**, in which they sought to amass metallic wealth by protecting merchants' foreign and colonial trade monopolies. The rise in prices and the new coin-based economy undermined craft guild and feudal manorial systems. Expanding industries (clothweaving, mining) benefited from technical advances. Coal began to replace wood as the chief fuel; it was used to fuel new 16th-cent. blast furnaces making cast iron.

New World. The **Aztecs** united much of the Mesoamerican area in a militarist empire by 1519 from their capital, Tenochtitlán (pop. 300,000), which was the center of a cult requiring ritual human sacrifice. Most of the civilized areas of South

Nicolaus Copernicus's theory of heliocentricity (1533) was later proven by Johannes Kepler, but the concept of a moving Earth was too outlandish for many 16th-century thinkers.

America were ruled by the centralized Inca Empire (1476-1534), stretching 2,000 mi from Ecuador to NW Argentina. Lavish and sophisticated traditions in pottery, weaving, sculpture, and architecture were maintained in both regions.

These empires, beset by revolts, fell in two short campaigns to gold-seeking Spanish forces based in the Antilles and Panama. Hernán **Cortés** took Mexico (1519-21); Francisco **Pizarro**, Peru (1532-35). From these centers, land and sea expeditions claimed most of North and South America for Spain. The indigenous high cultures did not survive the impact of **Christian missionaries** and the new upper class of whites. Although the Spanish administration intermittently concerned itself with their welfare, the population was devastated by European diseases and remained impoverished at most levels. New World silver and such native products as potatoes, tobacco, corn, peanuts, chocolate, and rubber exercised a major economic influence on Europe.

Brazil, which the Portuguese reached in 1500 and settled after 1530, and the Caribbean colonies of several European nations developed a plantation economy where sugarcane, tobacco, cotton, coffee, rice, indigo, and lumber were grown by slaves. From the early 16th to late 19th cent., 10 million Africans were transported to **slavery** in the Americas and Caribbean islands.

Netherlands. The urban, Calvinist N provinces of the Netherlands rebelled (1568) against Habsburg Spain and founded an oligarchic mercantile republic. Their control of the Baltic grain market enabled them to exploit Mediterranean food shortages. Religious refugees—French and Belgian Protestants, Iberian Jews—added to the commercial talent pool. After Spain absorbed Portugal (1580), the Dutch seized Portuguese possessions and created a vast commercial empire ultimately centered in parts of the Caribbean and in Indonesia. The Dutch also challenged or supplanted Portuguese traders in China and Japan. Revolution in 1640 restored Portuguese independence.

England. Anglicanism became firmly established under **Elizabeth I** after a brief Catholic interlude under "Bloody Mary" (1553-58). But religious and political conflicts led to a rebellion (1642) by Parliament. Forces of the Roundheads (Puritans) defeated the Cavaliers (Royalists); Charles I was beheaded (1649). The new Commonwealth was ruled as a military dictatorship by Oliver **Cromwell**, who also brutally crushed (1649-51) an Irish rebellion. Conflicts within the Puritan camp (democratic Levelers defeated, 1649) aided the Stuart restoration (1660), but Parliament was strengthened and the peaceful **"Glorious Revolution"** (1688) advanced political and religious liberties (writings of **Locke**, 1632-1704). British privateers

(Drake, 1540-96) challenged Spanish control of the New World and penetrated Asian trade routes (Madras taken, 1639). North American colonies (Jamestown, 1607; Plymouth, 1620) provided an outlet for private enterprise and religious dissenters from Europe. The British East India company gained growing sway in 18th-cent. India, as Mughal power declined.

France. Emerging from the religious civil wars in 1628, France regained military and commercial great power status (under the ministries of **Richelieu**, Mazarin, and Colbert). Under **Louis XIV** (r. 1643-1715), royal absolutism triumphed over nobles and local *parlements* (defeat of Fronde, 1648-53). Durable colonies were founded in Canada (1608), the Caribbean (1626), and India (1674).

Sweden. Sweden seceded from the Scandinavian Union in 1523. The thinly populated agrarian state (with copper, iron, and timber exports) was united by the Vasa kings, whose conquests by the mid-17th cent. made Sweden the dominant Baltic power. The empire collapsed in the Great Northern War (1700-21).

Poland. After the union with Lithuania in 1447, Poland ruled vast territories from the Baltic to the Black Sea, resisting German and Turkish incursions. Catholic nobles failed to gain the loyalty of their Orthodox Christian subjects in the E; commerce and trades were practiced by German and Jewish immigrants. The bloody 1648-49 Cossack uprising began the kingdom's dismemberment.

Russia. Growing authority of the tsars continued with advancing serfdom. Around 1700, **Peter the Great** imported new Western styles and technologies. Steady territorial expansion created a vast territory touching China, the Ottoman Empire and east-central Europe.

China. A new dynasty, the **Manchus**, invaded from the NE, seized power in 1644, and expanded Chinese control to its greatest extent in Central and SE Asia. Trade and diplomatic contact with Europe grew, carefully controlled by China. New crops (sweet potato, maize, peanut) allowed economic and population growth (pop. 300 million, in 1800). Traditional arts and literature were pursued with increased sophistication (*Dream of the Red Chamber*, novel, mid-18th cent.).

Japan. Tokugawa Ieyasu, shogun from 1603, finally unified and pacified feudal Japan. Hereditary nobles (daimyos and samurai) monopolized government office and the professions. An urban merchant class grew, literacy spread, and a cultural renaissance occurred (**haiku**, a verse innovation of the poet Basho, 1644-94). Fear of European domination led to persecution of Christian converts from 1597 and to substantial isolation from outside contact from 1640.

Philosophy, Industry, and Revolution: 1700-1800

Science and reason. Greater faith in reason and empirical observation, instead of tradition and religious beliefs, espoused since the Renaissance (Francis Bacon, 1561-1626), was bolstered by scientific discoveries. René **Descartes** (1596-1650) used a rationalistic approach modeled on geometry and introspection to discover "self-evident" truths as a foundation of knowledge. Sir Isaac **Newton** emphasized induction from experimental observation. Baruch de **Spinoza** (1632-77), who called for political and intellectual freedom, developed a systematic rationalistic philosophy in his classic work *Ethics*.

French philosophers assumed leadership of the **Enlightenment** in the 18th cent. Montesquieu (1689-1755) used British history to support his notions of limited government. **Voltaire**'s (1694-1778) diaries and novels of exotic travel illustrated the intellectual trends toward secular ethics and relativism. Jean-Jacques **Rousseau**'s (1712-78) radical concepts of the **social contract** and of the inherent goodness of the common man gave impetus to antimonarchical republicanism. The *Encyclopedia* (1751-72, edited by Diderot and d'Alembert), designed as a monument to reason, was largely devoted to practical technology.

In England, ideals of liberty were connected with empiricist philosophy and science in the followers of John **Locke**. But British empiricism, especially as developed by the skeptical David **Hume** (1711-76), radically reduced the role of reason in philosophy, as did the evolutionary approach to law and politics of Edmund Burke (1729-97) and the utilitarian ethics of Jeremy Bentham (1748-1832). Adam Smith (1723-90) and other economists called for a rationalization of economic activity

by removing artificial barriers to a supposedly natural free exchange of goods known as **laissez-faire**.

German writers participated in the new philosophical trends popularized by Christian von Wolff (1679-1754). Immanuel **Kant**'s (1724-1804) transcendental idealism, unifying an empirical epistemology with a priori moral and logical concepts, directed German thought away from skepticism. Italian contributions included work on electricity (Galvani, 1737-98; Volta, 1745-1827), the pioneer historiography of Vico (1668-1744), and writings on penal reform (Beccaria, 1738-94). Benjamin Franklin (1706-90) was celebrated in Europe for his varied achievements.

The growth of the **press** (*Spectator*, 1711-12) and the wide distribution of sentimental **novels** attested to the increase of a large bourgeois public.

Arts. Rococo art, characterized by extravagant decorative effects, asymmetries copied from organic models, and artificial pastoral subjects, was favored by the continental aristocracy for most of the century (Watteau, 1684-1721) and had musical analogies in the ornamentational polyphony of late Baroque. The **Neoclassical** art after 1750, associated with the new scientific archaeology, was more streamlined and was infused with the supposed moral and geometric rectitude of the Roman Republic (David, 1748-1825). In England, **town planning** on a grand scale began.

Industrial Revolution in England. Agricultural improvements, such as the sowing drill (1701) and livestock breeding, were implemented on the large fields provided by enclosure

The invention of the spinning jenny (1764) revolutionized the cotton industry in the late 18th century, allowing women and children to be put to work in large factories.

of common lands by private owners. Profits from agriculture and from colonial and foreign trade (1800 volume, £54 million) were channeled through hundreds of banks and the **Stock Exchange** (est. 1773) into new industrial processes.

The Newcomen steam pump (1712) aided coal mining. Coal fueled the new efficient steam engines patented by James Watt in 1769, and coke-smelting produced cheap, sturdy iron for machinery by the 1730s. The **flying shuttle** (1733) and **spinning jenny** (c. 1764) were used in the large new cotton textile factories, where women and children were much of the workforce. Goods were transported cheaply over **canals** (2,000 mi; built 1760-1800). By the early 19th cent., industrialization spread in Western Europe and North America.

American Revolution. The British colonies in North America attracted a mass immigration of religious dissenters and poor people throughout the 17th and 18th cent., coming from the British Isles, Germany, the Netherlands, and other countries including imported African slaves. The population reached 3 million non-natives by the 1770s. The indigenous population was greatly reduced by European diseases and by wars with the various colonies. British attempts to control colonial trade and to tax the colonists to pay for the costs of colonial administration and defense clashed with local self-government and eventually provoked the colonies to a successful rebellion.

Central and East Europe. The monarchs of the three states that dominated E Europe—Austria, Prussia, and Russia—expanded royal power and centralized institutions in their kingdoms, which were enlarged by the division (1772-95) of Poland.

Under **Frederick II** (called the Great) (r. 1740-86) Prussia, with its efficient modern army, doubled in size. State monopolies and tariff protection fostered industry, and some legal reforms were introduced. Austria's heterogeneous realms were unified under **Maria Theresa** (r. 1740-80) and **Joseph II** (r. 1780-90). Reforms in education, law, and religion were enacted, and the

Austrian serfs were freed (1781). With its defeat in the Seven Years' War in 1763, Austria failed to regain Silesia, which had been seized by Prussia, but it was compensated by expansion to the E and S (Hungary, Slavonia, 1699; Galicia, 1772).

Russia, whose borders continued to expand, adopted some Western bureaucratic and economic policies under **Peter I** (r. 1682-1725) and **Catherine II** (r. 1762-96). Trade and cultural contacts with the West multiplied from the new Baltic Sea capital, **St. Petersburg** (est. 1703).

French Revolution. The growing French middle class lacked political power and resented aristocratic tax privileges, especially in light of the successful American Revolution. Peasants lacked adequate land and were burdened with feudal obligations to nobles. War with Britain led to the loss of French Canada and drained the treasury, finally forcing the king to call the **Estates-General** in 1789 for the first time since 1614, in an atmosphere of food riots (poor crop in 1788).

Aristocratic resistance to absolutism was soon overshadowed by the reformist Third Estate (middle class), which proclaimed itself the **National Constituent Assembly** June 17 and took the "Tennis Court oath" on June 20 to secure a constitution. The storming of the **Bastille** on July 14, 1789, by Parisian artisans was followed by looting and the seizure of aristocratic property throughout France. Assembly reforms included abolition of class and regional privileges, a Declaration of Rights, suffrage by taxpayers (75% of male population), and the **Civil Constitution of the Clergy** providing for election and loyalty oaths for priests. A republic was declared Sept. 22, 1792, in spite of royalist pressure from Austria and Prussia, which had declared war in Apr. (joined by Britain the next year). Louis XVI was beheaded Jan. 21, 1793, and Queen Marie Antoinette was beheaded Oct. 16, 1793.

Royalist uprisings in La Vendée and military reverses led to institution of a **reign of terror** in which tens of thousands of opponents of the Revolution and criminals were executed. Radical reforms in the **Convention** period (Sept. 1793-Oct. 1795) included the abolition of colonial slavery, economic measures to aid the poor, support of public education, and a short-lived de-Christianization.

Division among radicals (execution of Hebert, Danton, and Robespierre, 1794) aided the ascendancy of a moderate **Directory**, which consolidated military victories. **Napoleon Bonaparte** (1769-1821), a popular young general, exploited political divisions and participated in a coup Nov. 9, 1799, making himself first consul (dictator).

India. Sikh and Hindu rebels (Rajputs, Marathas) and Afghans destroyed the power of the Mughals during the 18th cent. After France's defeat (1763) in the Seven Years' War, Britain was the primary European trade power in India. Its control of inland **Bengal** and **Bihar** was recognized (1765) by the Mughal shah, who granted the **British East India Co.** (under Clive, 1725-74) the right to collect land revenue there. Despite objections from Parliament (1784 India Act), the company's involvement in local wars and politics led to repeated acquisitions of new territory. The company exported Indian textiles, sugar, and indigo, but industry was discouraged to promote British imports.

Nationalism Gathers Momentum: 1800-40

French ideals and empire spread. Inspired by the ideals of the French Revolution, and supported by the expanding French armies, new republican regimes arose near France: the **Batavian** Republic in the Netherlands (1795-1806), the **Helvetic** Republic in Switzerland (1798-1803), the **Cisalpine** Republic in N Italy (1797-1805), the **Ligurian** Republic in Genoa (1797-1805), and the **Parthenopean** Republic in S Italy (1799). A Roman Republic existed briefly in 1798 after Pope Pius VI was arrested by French troops. In Italy and Germany, new nationalist sentiments were stimulated both in imitation of and in reaction to developments in France (anti-French and anti-Jacobin peasant uprisings in Italy, 1796-99).

From 1804, when Napoleon declared himself emperor, to 1812, a succession of military victories (Austerlitz, 1805; Jena, 1806) extended his control over most of Europe through puppet states (**Confederation of the Rhine** united W German states for the first time and **Grand Duchy of Warsaw** revived Polish national hopes), expansion of the empire, and alliances.

Among the lasting reforms initiated under Napoleon's absolutist reign were establishment of the Bank of France, centralization of tax collection, codification of law along Roman models (Code Napoléon), and reform and extension of secondary and university education. In an 1801 concordat, the papacy recognized the effective autonomy of the French Catholic Church.

Napoleon's continental successes were offset by a British victory under Adm. Horatio Nelson in the **Battle of Trafalgar** (1805). Some 400,000 French soldiers were killed in the Napoleonic Wars, along with about 600,000 foreign troops.

Last gasp of old regimes. The disastrous 1812 invasion of Russia exposed Napoleon's overextension. After Napoleon's 1814 exile at Elba, his armies were defeated (1815) at **Waterloo** by British and Prussian troops.

At the **Congress of Vienna**, the monarchs and princes of Europe redrew their boundaries, to the advantage of Prussia (in

Saxony and the Ruhr), Austria (in Illyria and Venetia), and Russia (in Poland and Finland). British conquest of Dutch and French colonies (S Africa, Ceylon, Mauritius) was recognized. France, under the restored Bourbons, retained its expanded 1792 borders. The settlement brought 50 years of international peace to Europe.

But the Congress was unable to check the advance of liberal ideals and of nationalism among the smaller European nations. The 1825 **Decembrist uprising** by liberal officers in Russia was easily suppressed. But an independence movement in **Greece**, stirred by commercial prosperity and a cultural revival, succeeded in expelling Ottoman rule by 1831, with the aid of Britain, France, and Russia.

A constitutional monarchy was secured in France by the **1830 Revolution**; Louis Philippe became king. The revolutionary contagion spread to **Belgium**, which gained its independence (1830) from the Dutch monarchy, to **Poland**, whose rebellion was defeated (1830-31) by Russia, and to Germany.

Romanticism. A new style in intellectual and artistic life replaced Neoclassicism and Rococo after the mid-18th cent. By the early 19th cent., Romanticism prevailed in Europe.

Rousseau had begun the reaction against rationalism; in education (*Émile*, 1762) he stressed subjective spontaneity over regularized instruction. German writers (Lessing, 1729-81; Herder, 1744-1803) favorably compared the German folk song to classical forms and began a cult of Shakespeare, whose passion and "natural" wisdom was a model for the romantic *Sturm und Drang* (Storm and Stress) movement. **Goethe**'s *Sorrows of Young Werther* (1774) set the model for the tragic, passionate genius.

A new interest in **Gothic architecture** in England after 1760 (Walpole, 1717-97) spread through Europe, associated with an aesthetic Christian and mystic revival (**Blake**, 1757-1827). Celtic, Norse, and German mythology and folk tales were revived or imitated (Grimm's Fairy Tales, 1812-22). The medieval revival (Scott's *Ivanhoe*, 1819) led to a new interest in history, stressing national differences and organic growth (**Carlyle**, 1795-1881; Michelet, 1798-1874), corresponding to theories of natural evolution (Lamarck's *Philosophie Zoologique*, 1809; Lyell's *Geology*, 1830-33). A reaction against classicism characterized the English **romantic poets** (beginning with **Wordsworth**, 1770-1850). Revolution and war fed an emphasis on freedom and conflict, expressed by both poets (**Byron**, 1788-1824; **Hugo**, 1802-85) and philosophers (**Hegel**, 1770-1831).

Wild gardens replaced the formal French variety, and painters favored rural, stormy, and mountainous landscapes (**Turner**, 1775-1851; **Constable**, 1776-1837). Clothing became freer, with wigs, hoops, and ruffles discarded. Originality and genius were expected in the life and work of inspired artists (Murger's *Scenes From Bohemian Life*, 1847-49). Exotic locales and themes (as in Gothic horror stories) were used in art and literature (Delacroix, 1798-1863; **Poe**, 1809-49). Music exhibited the new dramatic style and a breakdown of classical forms (**Beethoven**, 1770-1827). The use of folk melodies and modes aided the growth of distinct national traditions (Glinka in Russia, 1804-57).

Latin America. Francois **Toussaint L'Ouverture** led a successful slave revolt in Haiti, which subsequently became the first Caribbean state to achieve independence (1804). The mainland Spanish colonies won their independence (1810-24) under such leaders as Simón **Bolívar** (1783-1830). Brazil became an independent empire (1822) under the Portuguese prince regent. A new class of military officers divided power with large landholders and the church.

United States. Territory under U.S. control nearly doubled in size with the **Louisiana Purchase** (1803). Heavy immigration and exploitation of ample natural resources fueled rapid economic growth. The spread of the franchise, public education, and anti-slavery sentiment were signs of a widespread democratic ethic.

China. Failure to keep pace with Western arms technology exposed China to greater European influence and hampered efforts to bar imports of opium, which had damaged Chinese society and drained wealth overseas. In the **Opium War** (1839-42), Britain forced China to expand trade opportunities and to cede Hong Kong.

New Complexities: Reforms and Imperialism: 1840-80

Idea of progress. As a result of the cumulative scientific, economic, and political changes of the preceding eras, the idea took hold among literate people in the West that continuing growth and improvement constituted the usual state of human and natural life.

Charles **Darwin**'s statement of the **theory of evolution** and survival of the fittest (*On the Origin of Species*, 1859), defended by intellectuals and scientists against theological objections, was taken as confirmation that progress was the natural direction of life. The controversy helped define popular ideas of the dedicated scientist and of science's increasing control over the world (Foucault's demonstration of Earth's rotation, 1851; **Pasteur**'s germ theory, 1861).

Liberals following Ricardo (1772-1823) in their faith that unrestrained competition would bring continuous economic expansion sought to adjust political life to new social realities and believed that unregulated competition of ideas would yield truth (**Mill**, 1806-73). In England, successive reform bills (1832, 1867, 1884) gave representation to the new industrial towns and extended the franchise to the middle and lower classes and to Catholics, Dissenters, and Jews. On both sides of the Atlantic, reformists tried to improve conditions for the mentally ill (**Dix**, 1802-87), women (Anthony, 1820-1906), and prisoners. Slavery was barred in the British Empire (1833), the U.S. (1865), and Brazil (1888).

Socialist theories based on ideas of human perfectibility or progress were widely disseminated. Utopian socialists such as Saint-Simon (1760-1825) envisaged an orderly, just society directed by a technocratic elite. A model factory town, New Lanark, Scotland, was set up by utopian Robert Owen (1771-1858), and communal experiments were tried in the U.S. (Brook Farm, MA, 1841-47). Bakunin's (1814-76) anarchism represented the opposite extreme of total freedom. Karl **Marx** (1818-83) posited the inevitable triumph of socialism in industrial countries through a dialectical process of class conflict. Effective development of oceanic steamship lines (Cunard Lines, 1840s) and the opening of the **Suez Canal** accelerated shipping and commerce. Telegraph lines (Australia-Europe, 1871) sped communication. International organizations included the General (later Universal) Postal Union (1874) and conferences to limit epidemics like cholera. The initial **Geneva Convention** (1864) regulated treatment of prisoners of war.

Spread of industry. The technical processes and managerial innovations of the English industrial revolution spread to Europe (especially Germany) and the U.S., causing an explosion of industrial production, demand for raw materials, and competition for markets. Inventors, both trained and self-taught, provided means for larger-scale production (Bessemer steel, 1856; sewing machine, 1846). Many inventions were shown at the universal prosperity-themed 1851 London Great Exhibition at the **Crystal Palace**.

Local specialization and long-distance trade were aided by a revolution in transportation and communication. Railroads were first introduced in the 1820s in England and the U.S. Over 150,000 mi of track had been laid worldwide by 1880, with another 100,000 mi laid in the next decade. Steamships were improved (*Savannah* crossed Atlantic, 1819). The **telegraph**, perfected by 1844 (Morse), connected the Old and New Worlds by cable in 1866 and quickened the pace of international commerce and politics. The first commercial **telephone** exchange went into operation in the U.S. in 1878.

The new class of industrial workers, uprooted from their rural homes, lacked job security and suffered from dangerous overcrowding at work and at home. Many responded by organizing **trade unions** (legalized in England, 1824; France, 1884). The U.S. Knights of Labor had 700,000 members by 1886. The First International (1864-76) tried to unite workers worldwide around a Marxist program. The quasi-Socialist Paris Commune uprising (1871) was violently suppressed. Acts to reduce child labor and regulate conditions were passed (1833-50 in England). Social security measures were introduced by the Bismarck regime (1883-89) in Germany.

Revolutions of 1848. Among the causes of the continent-wide revolutions were an international collapse of credit and resulting unemployment, bad harvests in 1845-47, and a cholera epidemic. The new urban proletariat and expanding bourgeoisie demanded greater political roles. Republics were proclaimed in France, Rome, and Venice. Nationalist

Charles Darwin's *On the Origin of Species* (1859) was based on his travels more than 20 years earlier on the British survey ship HMS *Beagle*.

feelings reached fever pitch in the Habsburg empire, as Hungary declared independence under Kossuth, a Slav Congress demanded equality, and Piedmont tried to drive Austria from Lombardy. A national liberal assembly at Frankfurt called for German unification.

But riots fueled bourgeois fear of socialism (**Marx** and **Engels**, *Communist Manifesto*, 1848), and peasants remained conservative. The old establishment—the Papacy, the Habsburgs with the help of the Czarist Russian army—was able to rout the revolutionaries by 1849. The French Republic succumbed to a renewed monarchy by 1852 (Emperor Napoleon III).

Great nations unified. Using the "blood and iron" tactics of Bismarck from 1862, Prussia controlled N Germany by 1867 (war with Denmark, 1864; Austria, 1866). After defeating France in 1870 (annexation of Alsace-Lorraine), it won the allegiance of S German states. A new **German Empire** was proclaimed (1871). **Italy**, inspired by Giuseppe Mazzini (1805-72) and Giuseppe Garibaldi (1807-82), was unified by the reformed Piedmont kingdom through uprisings, plebiscites, and war.

The **United States** its area expanded after the 1846-48 Mexican War, defeated (1861-65) a secession attempt by Southern states in the **Civil War**. Canadian provinces were united in an autonomous **Dominion of Canada** (1867). Control in **India** was removed from the East India Co. and centralized under British administration after the 1857-58 Sepoy rebellion, laying the groundwork for the modern Indian state. Queen Victoria was named Empress of India (1876).

Europe dominates Asia. The Ottoman Empire began to weaken in the face of Balkan nationalisms and European imperial incursions in N Africa (**Suez Canal**, 1869). The Ottomans had lost control of most of both regions by 1882. Russia completed its expansion S by 1884 (despite the temporary setback of the **Crimean War** with Turkey, Britain, and France, 1853-56), taking Turkestan, all the Caucasus, and Chinese areas in the E and sponsoring Balkan Slavs against the Turks. A succession of reformist and reactionary regimes presided over a slow modernization (serfs freed, 1861). Persian independence suffered as Russia and British India competed for influence.

China was forced to sign a series of unequal treaties with European powers and Japan. Overpopulation and an inefficient dynasty brought misery and caused rebellions (Taiping, Muslims) leaving tens of millions dead. **Japan** was forced by the U.S. (Commodore Perry's visits, 1853-54) and Europe to end its isolation. The Meiji restoration (1868) gave power to a Westernizing oligarchy, abolishing feudalism and expanding education. Intensified empire-building gave Burma to Britain (1824-85) and Indochina to France (1862-95). Christian missionary activity followed imperial and trade expansion in Asia.

The Arts. The official **Beaux Arts** school in Paris set an international style of imposing public buildings (Paris Opera, 1861-74; Vienna Opera, 1861-69) and uplifting statues (Bartholdi's Statue of Liberty, 1884). Realist painting, influenced by photography (Daguerre, 1837), appealed to a new mass audience with social or historical narrative (Wilkie, 1785-1841; Poynter, 1836-1919) or with serious religious, moral, or social messages (pre-Raphaelites, Millet's *Angelus*, 1858), often drawn from ordinary life. The **Impressionists** (Monet, 1840-1926; Pissarro, 1830-1903; Renoir, 1841-1919) rejected the formalism, sentimentality, and precise techniques of academic art in favor of a spontaneous, undetailed rendering of the world through careful representation of the effect of natural light on objects. They were strongly influenced by Asian and African styles.

Realistic **novelists** presented the full panorama of social classes and personalities but retained sentimentality and moral judgment (**Dickens**, 1812-70; **Eliot**, 1819-80; **Tolstoy**, 1828-1910; **Balzac**, 1799-1850).

Veneer of Stability: 1880-1900

Imperialism triumphant. The vast **African** interior, visited by European explorers (Barth, 1821-65; Livingstone, 1813-73), was conquered by the European powers in rapid, competitive thrusts from their coastal bases after 1880, mostly for domestic political and international strategic reasons. W African Muslim kingdoms (Fulani), Arab slave traders (Zanzibar), and Bantu military confederations (Zulu) were alike subdued. Only Christian Ethiopia (defeat of Italy, 1896) and Liberia resisted successfully. France (W Africa) and Britain ("Cape to Cairo," **Boer War**, 1899-1902) were the major beneficiaries. The ideology of "the white man's burden" (Kipling, *Barrack Room Ballads*, 1892) justified the conquests, which in fact reflected Europe's weapons superiority.

W European foreign capital investment soared to nearly $40 billion by 1914, but most was in E Europe (France, Germany), the Americas (Britain), and Europe's colonies. The foundation of the modern interdependent world economy was laid, with cartels dominating raw material trade. Global developments included a new agreement on international patents (1883), the modern Olympics (1896), and the global spread of department stores.

An industrious world. Industrial and technological proficiency characterized the two new great powers—Germany and the U.S. Coal and iron deposits enabled Germany to reach second- or third-place status in iron, steel, and shipbuilding by the 1900s. German electrical and chemical industries were world leaders. The U.S. post-Civil War boom (interrupted by financial panics—1884, 1893, 1896) was shaped by massive immigration from S and E Europe from 1880, government subsidy of railroads, and huge private monopolies (Standard Oil, 1870; U.S. Steel, 1901). The **Spanish-American War**, 1898 (Philippine Insurrection, 1899-1902), and the **Open Door policy** in China (1899) made the U.S. a world power.

England led in **urbanization**, with London the world capital of finance, insurance, and shipping. Sewer systems (Paris, 1850s), electric subways (London, 1890), parks, and bargain department stores helped improve living standards for most of the urban population of the industrial world. Birth rates declined in the West while infant mortality rates plunged (demographic transition, 1880-1920).

Upheavals in Asia. Asian reaction to European economic, military, and religious incursions took the form of imitation of Western techniques and adoption of Western ideas of progress and freedom. The Chinese "self-strengthening" movement of the 1860s and 1870s included rail, port, and arsenal improvements and metal and textile mills. Reformers such as **K'ang Yu-wei** (1858-1927) won liberalizing reforms in 1898, right after the European and Japanese "scramble for concessions."

A universal education system in Japan and importation of foreign industrial, scientific, and military experts aided Japan's rapid modernization after 1868, under the authoritarian Meiji regime. Japan's victory in the **Sino-Japanese War** (1894-95) put Formosa and Korea in its power. Industrialization began in earnest by 1890.

In India, the British alliance with the remaining princely states masked reform sentiment among the Westernized urban elite; higher education had been conducted largely in English for 50 years. The **Indian National Congress**, founded in 1885, demanded a larger government role for Indians.

Fin-de-siècle sophistication. **Naturalist** writers pushed realism to its extreme limits, adopting a quasi-scientific attitude and writing about formerly taboo subjects such as sex, crime, extreme poverty, and corruption (Flaubert, 1821-80; Zola, 1840-1902; Hardy, 1840-1928). Unseen or repressed psychological motivations were explored in the clinical and theoretical works of Sigmund **Freud** (1856-1939) and in works of fiction (**Dostoyevsky**, 1821-81; James, 1843-1916; Schnitzler, 1862-1931).

A contempt for bourgeois life or a desire to shock a complacent audience was shared by the French **symbolist** poets (Verlaine, 1844-96; Rimbaud, 1854-91), by neopagan English writers (Swinburne, 1837-1909), by continental dramatists (**Ibsen**, 1828-1906), and by satirists (**Wilde**, 1854-1900). The German philosopher Friedrich **Nietzsche** (1844-1900) was influential in his elitism and pessimism.

Postimpressionist art neglected long-cherished conventions of representation (**Cézanne**, 1839-1906) and showed a willingness to learn from primitive and non-European art (**Gauguin**, 1848-1903; Japanese prints).

Racism. Gobineau (1816-82) gave a pseudobiological foundation to modern racist theories, which spread in Europe in the latter 19th cent., along with **Social Darwinism**, the belief that societies are and should be organized as a struggle for survival of the fittest. The medieval period was interpreted as an era of natural Germanic rule (Chamberlain, 1855-1927), and notions of racial superiority were associated with German national aspirations (Treitschke, 1834-96). **Anti-Semitism**, with a new racist rationale, became a significant political force in Germany (Anti-Semitic Petition, 1880), Austria (Lueger, 1844-1910), and France (**Dreyfus affair**, 1894-1906).

Imperialism's High Point: 1900-09

Alliances. While the peace of Europe (and its dependencies) continued to hold (1907 **Hague Conference** extended the rules of war and international arbitration procedures), imperial rivalries, protectionist trade practices (in Germany and France), and the escalating arms race (British *Dreadnought* battleship launched; Germany widens Kiel canal, 1906) exacerbated minor disputes (German-French Moroccan "crises," 1905, 1911).

Security was sought through balance-of-power alliances: **Triple Alliance** (Germany, Austria-Hungary, Italy; renewed in 1902 and 1907); Anglo-Japanese Alliance (1902), Franco-Russian Alliance (1899), **Entente Cordiale** (Britain, France, 1904), Anglo-Russian Treaty (1907), German-Ottoman friendship. Global developments included the establishment of an International Court in The Hague, the first transatlantic radio transmission (1901), and the creation of the first international association for European football (1904).

Ottomans decline. The Ottoman government was unable to resist further loss of territory, and earlier reform efforts gave way to greater authoritarianism. Nearly all European lands were lost in 1912 to Serbia, Greece, Montenegro, and Bulgaria. Italy took Libya and the Dodecanese islands the same year. Britain took Kuwait (1899) and the Sinai (1906). The **Young Turk** revolution in 1908 forced the sultan to restore a constitution, and it introduced some social reform and secularization.

British Empire. British trade and cultural influence remained dominant in the empire, but constitutional reforms presaged its eventual dissolution. The colonies of **Australia** were united in 1901 under a self-governing commonwealth. **New Zealand** acquired dominion status in 1907. The old Boer republics joined Cape Colony and Natal in the self-governing Union of **South Africa** in 1910.

The 1909 Indian Councils Act enhanced the role of elected province legislatures in **India**. The Muslim League (founded 1906) sought separate communal representation.

East Asia. Japan exploited its growing industrial power to expand its empire. Victory in the 1904-05 war against Russia (naval battle of Tsushima, 1905) assured Japan's domination of **Korea** (annexed 1910) and Manchuria (Port Arthur taken, 1905).

In China, central authority began to crumble (empress died, 1908). Reforms (Confucian exam system ended 1905, modernization of the army, building of railroads) were inadequate, and secret societies of reformers and nationalists, inspired by the Westernized **Sun Yat-sen** (1866-1925), fomented periodic uprisings in the S.

Siam, whose independence had been guaranteed by Britain and France in 1896, was split into spheres of influence by those countries in 1907.

Russia. The population of the Russian Empire approached 150 million in 1900. Reforms in education, in law, and in local institutions (*zemstvos*) and an industrial boom starting in the 1880s (oil, railroads) created the beginnings of a modern society, despite the autocratic tsarist regime. Liberals (1903 Union of Liberation), Socialists (Social Democrats founded 1898, Bolsheviks split off 1903), and populists (Social Revolutionaries founded 1901) were periodically repressed, and national minorities were persecuted (anti-Jewish pogroms, 1903, 1905-06).

An industrial crisis after 1900 and harvest failures aggravated poverty among urban workers, and the 1904-05 defeat by Japan (which checked Russia's Asian expansion) sparked

the **Revolution of 1905-06**. A **Duma** (parliament) was created under Tsar Nicholas II. Agricultural reform (under Stolypin, prime minister, 1906-11) created a large class of land-owning peasants (*kulaks*).

The world shrinks. Developments in transportation and communication and mass population movements helped create an awareness of an interdependent world. Early **automobiles** (Daimler, Benz, 1885) were experimental or were designed as luxuries. Assembly-line mass production (Ford Motor Co., 1903) made the invention practical, and by 1910 nearly 500,000 motor vehicles were registered in the U.S. alone. **Heavier-than-air flights** began in 1903 in the U.S. (Wright brothers' *Flyer*), preceded by glider, balloon, and model plane advances in several countries. Trade was advanced by improvements in **ship design** (gyrocompass, 1910), speed (*Lusitania* crossed Atlantic in five days, 1907), and reach (Panama Canal begun, 1904).

The first transatlantic **radio** telegraphic transmission occurred in 1901, six years after Marconi discovered radio. Radio transmission of human speech had been made in 1900. Telegraphic transmission of photos was achieved in 1904, lending immediacy to news reports. **Phonographs**, popularized by Caruso's recordings (starting 1902), made for quick

Italian tenor Enrico Caruso was one of the first acclaimed singers to make phonograph records (1902); he became universally famous by means of the new medium.

international spread of musical styles (ragtime). **Motion pictures**, perfected in the 1890s (Dickson, Lumière brothers), became a popular and artistic medium after 1900; newsreels appeared in 1909.

Emigration from crowded European centers soared in the decade: 9 million migrated to the U.S., and millions more went to Siberia, Canada, Argentina, Australia, South Africa, and Algeria. Some 70 million Europeans emigrated in the century before 1914. Several million Chinese, Indians, and Japanese migrated to SE Asia, where their urban skills often enabled them to take a predominant economic role.

Social reform. The social and economic problems of the poor were kept in the public eye by realist fiction writers (Dreiser's *Sister Carrie*, 1900; Gorky's *Lower Depths*, 1902; Sinclair's *The Jungle*, 1906), journalists (U.S. **muckrakers**— Steffens, Tarbell), and artists (Ashcan school). Frequent labor strikes and occasional assassinations by anarchists or radicals (Empress Elizabeth of Austria, 1898; King Umberto I of Italy, 1900; U.S. Pres. McKinley, 1901; Russian Interior Min. Plehve, 1904; Portugal's King Carlos, 1908) added to social tension and fear of revolution. Feminist agitators for the vote surfaced in several countries.

But democratic reformism responded in part. In Germany, Bernstein's (1850-1932) **revisionist Marxism**, downgrading revolution, was accepted by the powerful Social Democrats and trade unions. The British Fabian Society (the Webbs, Shaw) and the Labour Party (founded 1906) worked for reforms such as social security and union rights (1906), while woman suffragists grew more militant. U.S. **progressives** fought big business (Pure Food and Drug Act, 1906). In France, the 10-hour work day (1904) and separation of church and state (1905) were reform victories, as was universal suffrage in Austria (1907).

Arts. An unprecedented period of experimentation, centered in France, produced several **new painting styles**: Fauvism exploited bold color areas (Matisse, *Woman With Hat*, 1905); expressionism reflected powerful inner emotions (Brücke group, 1905); Cubism combined several views of an object on one flat surface (Picasso, *Demoiselles*, 1906-07); futurism tried to depict speed and motion (Italian Futurist Manifesto, 1910). **Architects** explored new uses of steel structures, with facades either neoclassical (Adler and Sullivan in U.S.), curvilinear Art Nouveau (Gaudi's Casa Mila, 1905-10), or functionally streamlined (Wright's Robie House, 1909).

Music and dance shared the experimental spirit. Ruth St. Denis (1877-1968) and Isadora Duncan (1878-1927) pioneered modern dance, while Sergei Diaghilev in Paris revitalized classic ballet from 1909. Composers explored atonal music (Debussy, 1862-1918) and dissonance (Schoenberg, 1874-1951) or revolutionized classical forms (Stravinsky, 1882-1971), often showing jazz or folk music influences.

War and Revolution: 1910-19

War threatens. Germany under Wilhelm II sought a political and imperial role consonant with its industrial strength, challenging Britain's world supremacy and threatening France, which was still resenting the loss (1871) of Alsace-Lorraine. Austria wanted to curb an expanded Serbia (after 1912) and the threat it posed to its own Slav lands. Russia feared Austrian and German political and economic aims in the Balkans and Turkey.

An accelerated arms race resulted from these circumstances. The German standing army rose to more than 2 million men by 1914. Russia and France had more than a million each, and Austria and the British Empire nearly a million each. Dozens of enormous battleships were built by the powers after 1906.

The **assassination of Austrian Archduke Franz Ferdinand** by a Serbian nationalist, June 28, 1914, was the trigger for war. The system of alliances made the conflict Europe-wide; Germany's invasion of Belgium to outflank France forced Britain to enter the war. Patriotic fervor was nearly unanimous among all classes in most countries.

World War I. German forces were stopped in France in one month. The rival armies dug **trench networks**. Artillery and improved machine guns prevented either side from any lasting advance despite repeated assaults (600,000 dead at **Verdun**, Feb.-July 1916). Poison gas, used by Germany in 1915, proved ineffective. The entrance of more than 1 million U.S. troops tipped the balance after mid-1917, forcing Germany to sue for peace the next year. The formal armistice was signed on Nov. 11, 1918, and the German emperor abdicated.

In the E, the Russian armies were thrown back (battle of **Tannenberg**, Aug. 20, 1914), and the war grew unpopular in Russia. An allied attempt to relieve Russia through Turkey failed (**Gallipoli**, 1915). The **Russian Revolution** (1917) abolished the monarchy. The new Bolshevik regime signed the capitulatory Brest-Litovsk peace in Mar. 1918. Italy entered the war on the allied side in May 1915 but was pushed back by Oct. 1917. A renewed offensive with Allied aid in Oct.-Nov. 1918 forced Austria to surrender.

The British Navy successfully blockaded Germany, which responded with submarine U-boat attacks; **unrestricted submarine warfare** against neutrals after Jan. 1917 helped bring the U.S. into the war. Other battlefields included Palestine and Mesopotamia, both of which Britain wrested from the Turks in 1917, and the African and Pacific colonies of Germany, most of which fell to Britain, France, Australia, Japan, and South Africa.

Settlement. At the **Paris Peace Conference** (Jan.-June 1919), concluded by the **Treaty of Versailles**, and in subsequent negotiations and local wars (Russian-Polish War, 1920), the **map of Europe** was redrawn with a nod to U.S. Pres. Woodrow Wilson's principle of self-determination. Austria and Hungary were separated, and much of their land was given to Yugoslavia (formerly Serbia), Romania, Italy, and the newly independent Poland and Czechoslovakia. Germany lost territory in the W, N, and E, while Finland and the Baltic states were detached from Russia. The Ottoman Empire ended (1922) and most of its Arab lands went to British-sponsored Arab states or to direct French and British rule. Belgium's sovereignty was recognized.

From 1916, the civilian populations and economies of both sides were mobilized to an unprecedented degree. Hardships intensified among fighting nations in 1917 (French mutiny crushed in May). More than 10 million soldiers died in the war.

A huge **reparations** burden and partial demilitarization were imposed on Germany. Pres. Wilson obtained approval for a League of Nations, but the U.S. Senate refused to allow the U.S. to join.

Russian revolution. Military defeats and high casualties caused a contagious lack of confidence in Tsar Nicholas, who was forced to abdicate Mar. 1917. A liberal provisional government failed to end the war, and massive desertions, riots, and fighting between factions followed. A moderate socialist government under Aleksandr Kerensky was overthrown (Nov. 1917) in a violent coup by the **Bolsheviks** in Petrograd under **Lenin**, who later disbanded the elected Constituent Assembly.

Both sides in World War I developed elaborate networks of dug-in trenches from which to fight.

The Bolsheviks brutally suppressed all opposition and ended the war with Germany in Mar. 1918. **Civil war** broke out in the summer between the Red Army (the Bolsheviks and their supporters), and monarchists, anarchists, minority nationalities (Ukrainians, Georgians, Poles), and others. Small U.S., British, French, and Japanese units also opposed the Bolsheviks (1918-19; Japan in Vladivostok to 1922). The civil war, anarchy, and pogroms devastated the country until the 1920 Red Army victory. The **Communist Party** leadership retained absolute power.

Other European revolutions. An unpopular monarchy in **Portugal** was overthrown in 1910. The new republic took severe anticlerical measures in 1911.

After a century of Home Rule agitation, during which **Ireland** was devastated by famine (1 million dead, 1846-47) and emigration, republican militants staged an unsuccessful uprising in Dublin during **Easter 1916**. The execution of the leaders and mass arrests by the British won popular support for the rebels. The **Irish Free State**, comprising all but the six northern counties, achieved dominion status in 1922.

In the aftermath of the world war, radical revolutions were attempted in Germany (**Spartacist** uprising, Jan. 1919), **Hungary** (Kun regime, 1919), and elsewhere. All were suppressed or failed for lack of support.

Chinese revolution. The Manchu Dynasty was overthrown and a republic proclaimed in Oct. 1911. First Pres. Sun Yat-sen resigned in favor of strongman Yuan Shih-k'ai. Sun organized the parliamentarian **Kuomintang** party.

Students launched protests on May 4, 1919, against League of Nations concessions in China to Japan. Nationalist, liberal, and socialist ideas and political groups spread. The **Communist Party** was founded in 1921. A Communist regime took power in Mongolia with Soviet support in 1921.

India restive. Indian objections to British rule erupted in nationalist riots as well as in the nonviolent tactics of Mahatma **Gandhi** (1869-1948). Nearly 400 unarmed demonstrators were shot at **Amritsar** in Apr. 1919. Britain approved limited self-rule that year.

Mexican revolution. Under the long Diaz dictatorship (1877-1911) the economy advanced, but Indian and mestizo lands were confiscated, and concessions to foreigners (mostly U.S.) damaged the middle class. A **revolution in 1910** led to civil wars and U.S. intervention (1914, 1916-17). Land reform and a more democratic constitution (1917) were achieved.

Sciences. Scientific specialization prevailed by the 20th cent. Advances in knowledge and technological aptitude increased with the geometric rise in the number of practitioners. Physicists challenged common-sense views of causality, observation, and a mechanistic universe, putting science further beyond popular grasp (**Einstein**'s general theory of relativity, 1916; Bohr's quantum mechanics, 1913; Heisenberg's uncertainty principle, 1927).

Aftermath of War: 1920-29

U.S. Easy credit, technological ingenuity, and war-related industrial decline in Europe caused a long economic boom, in which ownership of new products—**autos, phones, radios**—became more democratized. **Prosperity**, an increase in women workers, women's suffrage (19th Amendment ratified, 1920), and drastic change in fashion (**flappers**, mannish bob for women, clean-shaven men) created a wide perception of social change, despite prohibition of alcoholic beverages (1919-33). Union membership and strikes increased. Fear of radicals led to Palmer raids (1919-20) and the Sacco-Vanzetti case (1921-27).

Europe sorts itself out. Germany's liberal **Weimar constitution** (1919) could not guarantee a stable government in the face of rightist violence (Rathenau assassinated, 1922) and Communist refusal to cooperate with Socialists. Reparations and Allied occupation of the Rhineland caused staggering inflation that destroyed middle-class savings, but economic expansion resumed after mid-decade, aided by U.S. loans. A sophisticated, **innovative culture** developed in architecture and design (Bauhaus, 1919-28), film (Lang, *M*, 1931), painting (Grosz), music (Weill, *Threepenny Opera*, 1928), theater (Brecht, *A Man's a Man*, 1926), criticism (Benjamin), philosophy (Jung), and fashion. This culture was considered decadent and socially disruptive by rightists.

England elected its first Labour governments (Jan. 1924, June 1929). A 10-day general strike in support of coal miners failed in May 1926. In **Italy**, strikes, political chaos, and violence by small Fascist bands culminated in the Oct. 1922 Fascist March on Rome, which established **Mussolini**'s dictatorship. Strikes were outlawed (1926), and Italian influence was pressed in the Balkans (Albania made a protectorate, 1926). A conservative dictatorship was also established in **Portugal** in a 1926 military coup.

Czechoslovakia, the only stable democracy to emerge from the war in Central or E Europe, faced opposition from Germans (in the Sudetenland), Ruthenians, and some Slovaks. As the industrial heartland of the old Habsburg empire, it remained fairly prosperous. With French backing, it formed the Little Entente with Yugoslavia (1920) and **Romania** (1921) to block Austrian or Hungarian irredentism. Croats and Slovenes in **Yugoslavia** demanded a federal state until King Alexander I proclaimed (1929) a royal dictatorship. Poland faced internal nationality problems as well (Germans, Ukrainians, Jews); Pilsudski ruled as dictator from 1926. The Baltic states were threatened by traditionally dominant ethnic Germans and by Soviet-supported Communists.

An economic collapse and famine in **Russia** (1921-22) claimed 5 million lives. The New Economic Policy (1921) allowed land ownership by peasants and some private commerce and industry. **Stalin** was absolute ruler within four years of Lenin's death (1924). He inaugurated a brutal collectivization program (1929-32) and used foreign Communist parties for Soviet state advantage. Industrialization advanced rapidly.

Internationalism. Revulsion against World War I led to pacifist agitation, to the Kellogg-Briand Pact renouncing aggressive war (1928), and to **naval disarmament** pacts (Washington, 1922; London, 1930). But the League of Nations was able to arbitrate only minor disputes (Greece-Bulgaria, 1925). A number of countries pulled back from global contacts, as with American isolationism and Russia's separation from international capitalism.

Middle East. Mustafa Kemal (**Ataturk**) led **Turkish** nationalists in resisting Italian, French, and Greek military advances (1919-23). The sultanate was abolished (1922), and elaborate reforms were passed, including secularization of law and adoption of the Latin alphabet. Ethnic conflict led to persecution of **Armenians** (more than 1 million dead in 1915, 1 million expelled), Greeks (forced Greek-Turk population exchange, 1923), and Kurds (1925 uprising).

With evacuation of the Turks from **Arab** lands, the puritanical Wahabi dynasty of E Arabia conquered (1919-25) what is now Saudi Arabia. British, French, and Arab dynastic and nationalist maneuvering resulted in the creation of two more Arab monarchies in 1921—Iraq and Transjordan (both under British control)—and two French mandates—Syria and Lebanon. Jewish immigration into British-mandated **Palestine**, inspired by the Zionist movement, was resisted by Arabs, at times violently (1921, 1929 massacres).

Reza Khan ruled **Persia** after his 1921 coup (shah from 1925), centralized control, and created the trappings of a modern secular state.

In 1922, English archaeologist Howard Carter discovered the tomb of the boy pharaoh **Tutankhamen** in the Valley of the Kings in Egypt.

China. The Kuomintang under **Chiang Kai-shek** (1887-1975) subdued the warlords by 1928. The Communists were brutally suppressed after their alliance with the Kuomintang was broken in 1927. Relative peace thereafter allowed for industrial and financial improvements, with some Russian, British, and U.S. cooperation.

Arts. Nearly all bounds of subject matter, style, and attitude were broken in the arts of the period. **Abstract** art first took inspiration from natural forms or narrative themes (Kandinsky from 1911) and then worked free of any representational aims (Malevich's suprematism, 1915-19; Mondrian's geometric style from 1917). The **Dada** movement (from 1916) mocked artistic pretension with absurd collages and constructions. Paradox, illusion, and psychological taboos were exploited by **surrealists** by the late 1920s (Dali, Magritte).

Architectural schools celebrated industrial values, whether vigorous abstract constructivism (Tatlin, *Monument to the Third International*, 1919) or the machined, streamlined **Bauhaus** style, which was extended to many design fields (Helvetica typeface).

Prose writers explored revolutionary narrative modes related to dreams (Kafka's *Trial*, 1925), internal monologue (Joyce's *Ulysses*, 1922), and word play (Stein's *Making of Americans*, 1925). Poets and novelists wrote of modern alienation (Eliot's *Waste Land*, 1922) and aimlessness ("The Lost Generation").

Rise of Totalitarians: 1930-39

Depression. A worldwide financial panic and economic depression began with the Oct. 1929 U.S. stock market crash and the May 1931 failure of the Austrian Credit-Anstalt. A credit crunch caused international bankruptcies and **unemployment**: 12 million jobless by 1932 in the U.S., 5.6 million in Germany, 2.7 million in England. Governments responded with **tariff restrictions** (Smoot-Hawley Act, 1930; Ottawa Imperial Conference, 1932), which dried up world trade. Government public works programs were vitiated by deflationary budget balancing.

Germany. Years of agitation by violent extremists were brought to a head by the Depression. Nazi leader Adolf Hitler was named chancellor in Jan. 1933 and given dictatorial power by the Reichstag in Mar. Opposition parties were disbanded, strikes banned, and all aspects of economic, cultural, and religious life were brought under central government and Nazi party control and manipulated by sophisticated propaganda. Severe persecution of Jews began (**Nuremberg Laws**, Sept. 1935). Many Jews, political opponents, and others were sent to concentration camps (Dachau, 1933), where thousands died or were killed. Public works, renewed conscription (1935), arms production, and a four-year plan (1936) all but ended unemployment.

Hitler's expansionism started with reincorporation of the Saar (1935), occupation of the **Rhineland** (Mar. 1936), and annexation of Austria (Mar. 1938). At **Munich** (Sept. 1938) Britain and France attempted to appease Hitler and avoid war by successfully encouraging Czechoslovakia's surrender of the Sudetenland territory.

Russia. Rapid industrialization was achieved through successive **five-year plans** starting in 1928, using severe labor discipline and mass forced labor. Industry was financed by exploitation of agriculture, which was almost totally collectivized by the early 1930s (*kolkhoz* [collective farm]; *sovkhoz* [state farm], often in newly worked lands). Millions perished in a series of manufactured disasters: extermination (1929-34) of kulaks (peasant landowners), severe famine (1932-33), party purges and show trials (Great Purge, 1936-38), suppression of nationalities, and poor conditions in labor camps. Purges also increased Stalin's power in the Communist party.

Spain. An industrial revolution during World War I created an urban proletariat, which was attracted to socialism and anarchism; Catalan nationalists challenged central authority. The five years after King Alfonso left Spain in Apr. 1931 were dominated by tension between intermittent leftist and anticlerical governments and clericals, monarchists, and other rightists. Anarchist and Communist rebellions were crushed, but a July 1936 extreme right rebellion led by Gen. Francisco **Franco** and aided by Nazi Germany and Fascist Italy succeeded after a three-year **civil war** (more than 1 million dead in battles and atrocities). The war polarized international public opinion.

Italy. Despite propaganda for the ideal of the Corporate State, few domestic reforms were attempted. An entente with Hungary and Austria (Mar. 1934), a pact with Germany and Japan (Nov. 1937), and intervention by 50,000-75,000 troops in Spain (1936-39) sealed Italy's identification with the fascist bloc (anti-Semitic laws after Mar. 1938). Ethiopia was conquered (1935-36) and Albania annexed (Jan. 1939) in conscious imitation of ancient Rome.

Eastern Europe. Repressive regimes fought for power against an active opposition (liberals, socialists, Communists, peasants, Nazis). Minority groups and Jews were restricted within national boundaries that did not coincide with ethnic population patterns. In the destruction of **Czechoslovakia**, Hungary occupied S Slovakia (Nov. 1938) and Ruthenia (Mar. 1939), and a pro-Nazi regime took power in the rest of Slovakia. Other boundary disputes (e.g., Poland-Lithuania, Yugoslavia-Bulgaria, and Romania-Hungary) doomed attempts to build joint fronts against Germany or Russia. Economic depression was severe.

East Asia. After a period of liberalism in **Japan**, nativist militarists dominated the government with peasant support. Manchuria was seized (Sept. 1931-Feb. 1932), and a puppet state was set up (Manchukuo). Adjacent Jehol (Inner Mongolia) was occupied in 1933. **China** proper was invaded in July 1937; large areas were conquered by Oct. 1938. Hundreds of thousands of rapes, murders, and other atrocities were attributed to the Japanese.

Communist forces left Kuomintang-besieged strongholds in the S of China in a Long March (1934-35) to the N. The Kuomintang-Communist civil war was suspended in Jan. 1937 in the face of threatening Japan.

Democracies. The Roosevelt Administration, in office Mar. 1933, embarked on an extensive program of **New Deal** social reform and economic stimulation, including protection for labor unions (heavy industries organized), Social Security, public works, wage-and-hour laws, and assistance to farmers. Isolationist sentiment (1937 Neutrality Act) prevented U.S. intervention in Europe, but military expenditures were increased in 1939.

French political instability and polarization prevented resolution of economic and international security questions. The **Popular Front** government under Leon Blum (June 1936-Apr. 1938) passed social reforms (40-hour work week) and raised arms spending. National coalition governments, which ruled Britain from Aug. 1931, brought economic recovery but failed to define a consistent international policy until Chamberlain's government (from May 1937), which practiced **appeasement** of Germany and Italy.

India. Twenty years of agitation for autonomy and then for independence (Gandhi's **salt march**, 1930) achieved some constitutional reform (extended provincial powers, 1935) despite Muslim-Hindu strife. Social issues assumed prominence with

Italy's Benito Mussolini and Germany's Adolf Hitler affirmed their full political and military alliance with the Pact of Steel (1939).

peasant uprisings (1921), strikes (1928), Gandhi's efforts for untouchables (1932 "fast unto death"), and social and agrarian reform by the provinces after 1937.

Arts. The streamlined, geometric design motifs of Art Deco (from 1925) prevailed through the 1930s. **Abstract art** flourished (Moore sculptures from 1931) alongside a new **realism** related to social and political concerns (Socialist Realism, the official Soviet style from 1934; Mexican muralist Rivera, 1886-1957; and Orozco, 1883-1949), which were also expressed in fiction and poetry (Steinbeck's *Grapes of Wrath*, 1939; Sandburg's *The People, Yes*, 1936). Modern architecture (International Style, 1932) was unchallenged in its use of artificial materials (concrete, glass), lack of decoration, and monumentality (Rockefeller Center, 1929-40). Larger-than-life U.S.-made films captured a worldwide audience *(Gone With the Wind, The Wizard of Oz*, both 1939).

War, Hot and Cold: 1940-49

War in Asia-Pacific. Japan occupied Indochina in Sept. 1940, dominated Thailand in Dec. 1941, and attacked Hawaii (**Pearl Harbor**), the Philippines, Hong Kong, and Malaya on Dec. 7, 1941 (precipitating U.S. entrance into the war). Indonesia was attacked in Jan. 1942, and Burma was conquered in Mar. 1942. The Battle of **Midway** (June 1942) turned back the Japanese advance. "Island-hopping" battles (**Guadalcanal**, Aug. 1942-Jan. 1943; **Leyte Gulf**, Oct. 1944; **Iwo Jima**, Feb.-Mar. 1945; **Okinawa**, Apr. 1945) and massive bombing raids on Japan from June 1944 wore out Japanese defenses. U.S. atom bombs, dropped Aug. 6 and 9 on **Hiroshima** and **Nagasaki**, forced Japan to agree, on Aug. 14, to surrender; formal surrender was on Sept. 2, 1945.

War in Europe. The Nazi-Soviet nonaggression pact (Aug. 1939) freed Germany to attack Poland (Sept. 1939). Britain and France, which had guaranteed Polish independence, declared war on Germany. Russia seized E Poland (Sept. 1939), attacked Finland (Nov. 1939), and took the Baltic states (July 1940). Mobile German forces staged *blitzkrieg* attacks during Apr.-June 1940, conquering neutral Denmark, Norway, and the Low Countries and defeating France; 350,000 British and French troops were evacuated at **Dunkirk**, France (May). The **Battle of Britain** (June-Dec. 1940) denied Germany air superiority. German-Italian campaigns won the Balkans by Apr. 1941. Three million Axis troops **invaded Russia** in June 1941, marching through Ukraine to the Caucasus, and through White Russia and the Baltic republics to Moscow and Leningrad.

Russian winter counterthrusts (1941-42 and 1942-43) stopped the German advance (**Stalingrad**, Sept. 1942-Feb. 1943). Sustaining great casualties, the Russians drove the Axis from all E Europe and the Balkans in the next two years. Invasions of N Africa (Nov. 1942), Italy (Sept. 1943), and **Normandy** (launched on D-Day, June 6, 1944) brought U.S.,

British, Free French, and allied troops to Germany by spring 1945. In Feb. 1945, the three Allied leaders, Winston **Churchill** (Britain), Joseph **Stalin** (USSR), and Franklin D. **Roosevelt** (U.S.), met in Yalta to discuss strategy and resolve political issues, including the postwar Allied occupation of Germany. Germany surrendered May 7, 1945.

Atrocities. The war brought 20th-cent. cruelty to its peak. The Nazi regime systematically killed an estimated 5-6 million Jews, including some 3 million who died in death camps, (e.g., **Auschwitz**). Gypsies, political opponents, people with mental or physical disabilities, and others deemed undesirable were also murdered by the Nazis, as were vast numbers of Slavs.

German bombs killed 70,000 British civilians. More than 100,000 Chinese civilians were killed by Japanese forces in the capture and occupation of Nanking. Severe retaliation by the Soviet army, E European partisans, Free French, and others took a heavy toll. U.S. and British bombing of Germany killed hundreds of thousands, as did U.S. bombing of Japan (80,000-200,000 at Hiroshima alone). Some 45 million people died in the war.

Settlement. The **United Nations** charter was signed in San Francisco on June 26, 1945, by 50 nations. The International Tribunal at **Nuremberg** convicted 22 German leaders for war crimes in Sept. 1946; 23 Japanese leaders were convicted in Nov. 1948. Postwar border changes included large gains in territory for the USSR, losses for Germany, a shift to the W in Polish borders, and minor losses for Italy. Communist regimes, supported by Soviet troops, took power in most of E Europe, including Soviet-occupied Germany (GDR, aka East Germany, proclaimed Oct. 1949). Japan lost all overseas lands. Global developments involved establishing new economic coordinating bodies like the International Monetary Fund (1944) and the Universal Declaration of Human Rights (1948).

Recovery. Basic political and social changes were imposed on Japan and W Germany by the Western allies (Japan constitution adopted, Nov. 1946; W German basic law, May 1949). U.S. **Marshall Plan** aid ($12 billion, 1947-51) spurred W European economic recovery after a period of severe inflation and strikes in Europe and the U.S. The British Labour Party introduced a national health service and nationalized basic industries in 1946.

Cold War. Western fears of further Soviet advances (Cominform formed in Oct. 1947; Czechoslovakia coup, Feb. 1948; Berlin blockade, Apr. 1948-Sept. 1949) led to the formation of **NATO**. Civil War in Greece and Soviet pressure on Turkey led to U.S. aid under the **Truman Doctrine** (Mar. 1947). Other anti-Communist security pacts included the Organization of American States (Apr. 1948) and the SE Asia Treaty Organization (Sept. 1954). A new wave of **Soviet purges** and repression intensified in the last years of Stalin's rule, extending to E Europe (Slansky trial in Czechoslovakia, 1951). Only Yugoslavia resisted Soviet control (expelled by Cominform, June 1948; U.S. aid, June 1949).

China, Korea. Communist forces emerged from World War II strengthened by the Soviet takeover of industrial Manchuria. In four years of fighting, the Kuomintang was driven from the mainland; the People's Republic of China was proclaimed Oct. 1, 1949. Korea was divided by USSR and U.S. occupation forces. Separate republics were proclaimed in the two zones in Aug.-Sept. 1948.

India. India and Pakistan became independent dominions on Aug. 15, 1947. Millions of Hindu and Muslim refugees were created by the partition. Riots (1946-47) took hundreds

World War II came to an end soon after atomic bombs devastated Hiroshima and Nagasaki, Japan (1945).

Mao Zedong became chief of state when the People's Republic of China was proclaimed in 1949.

of thousands of lives. Mahatma **Gandhi** was assassinated in Jan. 1948. Burma became completely independent in Jan. 1948; Ceylon took dominion status in Feb.

Middle East. The UN approved partition of Palestine into Jewish and Arab states. **Israel** was proclaimed a state, May 14, 1948. Arabs rejected partition, but failed to defeat Israel in war (May 1948-July 1949). Immigration from Europe and the Middle East swelled Israel's Jewish population. British and French forces left Lebanon and Syria in 1946. Transjordan occupied most of Arab Palestine.

Southeast Asia. Communists and others fought against restoration of French rule in **Indochina** from 1946; a non-Communist government was recognized by France in Mar. 1949, but fighting continued. Both Indonesia and the Philippines became independent; the former in 1949 after four years of war with Netherlands, the latter in 1946. Philippine economic and military ties with the U.S. remained strong; a Communist-led peasant rising was checked in 1948.

Arts. New York became the center of the world art market; **abstract expressionism** was the chief mode (Pollock from 1943, de Kooning from 1947). Literature and philosophy explored **existentialism** (Camus's *The Stranger*, 1942; Sartre's *Being and Nothingness*, 1943). Non-Western attempts to revive or create regional styles (Senghor's Négritude, Mishima's novels) were responses to global cultural influences. Radio and phonograph records spread American popular music (swing, bebop) around the world.

The Cold War Decade: 1950-59

Decolonization. The relatively peaceful decline of European political and military power in Asia and Africa accelerated in the 1950s. Nearly all of **N Africa** was freed by 1956, but France fought a bitter war to retain Algeria, with its large European minority, until 1962. **Ghana**, independent in 1957, led a parade of new black African nations (more than two dozen by 1962), which altered the political character of the UN. Ethnic disputes often exploded in the new nations after decolonization (UN troops in Cyprus, 1964; **Nigerian civil war**, 1967-70). Leaders of the new states, mostly sharing socialist ideologies, tried to create an Afro-Asian bloc (Bandung Conference, 1955), but Western economic influence and U.S. political ties remained strong (Baghdad Pact, 1955).

Trade. World trade volume soared, in an atmosphere of monetary stability assured by international accords (**Bretton Woods**, 1944). In Europe, economic integration advanced (**European Economic Community**, 1957; European Free Trade Association, 1960). Comecon (1949) coordinated the economies of Soviet-bloc countries. Global Developments included transcontinental jet travel (first South Africa to Britain flight, 1952; introduction of term "jet lag," 1965) and the increasing spread of English in global business, sports and transportation.

U.S. Economic growth produced an abundance of consumer goods (9.3 million motor vehicles sold, 1955). Suburban housing changed life patterns for middle and working classes (Levittown, NY, 1947-51). Pres. Dwight **Eisenhower**'s landslide election victories (1952, 1956) reflected consensus politics. A system of alliances and military bases bolstered U.S. influence on all continents. Trade and payments surpluses were balanced by overseas investments and foreign aid ($50 billion, 1950-59).

USSR. In the "thaw" after Stalin's death in 1953, relations with the West improved (evacuation of Vienna, Geneva summit conference, both 1955). Repression of scientific and cultural life eased, and many prisoners were freed culminating in **de-Stalinization** (1956). **Nikita Khrushchev**'s leadership aimed at consumer goods growth, but farm production lagged, despite the virgin lands program (from 1954). Soviet crushing of the 1956 Hungarian revolution, the 1960 U-2 spy plane episode, and other incidents renewed E-W tension and domestic curbs.

Eastern Europe. Resentment of Russian domination and Stalinist repression combined with nationalist, economic, and religious factors to produce periodic violence. E Berlin workers rioted (1953), Polish workers rioted in Poznan (June 1956), and a broad-based **revolution** broke out in **Hungary** (Oct. 1956). All were suppressed by Soviet force or threats (at least 7,000 dead

in Hungary), but Poland was allowed to restore private ownership of farms, and a degree of personal and economic freedom returned to Hungary. Yugoslavia experimented with worker self-management and a market economy.

Korea. The 1945 division of Korea along the 38th parallel left industry in the N, which was organized into a militant regime and armed by the USSR. The S was politically disunited. More than 60,000 N Korean troops invaded the S on June 25, 1950. The U.S., backed by the UN Security Council, sent troops. **UN troops** reached the Chinese border in Nov. Some 200,000 Chinese troops crossed the Yalu R. and drove back UN forces. By spring 1951, battle lines had become stabilized near the original 38th parallel border, but heavy fighting continued. Finally, an armistice was signed on July 27, 1953. U.S. troops remained in the S, and U.S. economic and military aid continued. The war stimulated rapid economic recovery in Japan.

China. Starting in 1952, industry, agriculture, and social institutions were forcibly collectivized. In a massive purge, as many as several million people were executed as Kuomintang supporters or as class and political enemies. The **Great Leap Forward** (1958-60) unsuccessfully tried to force the pace of development by substituting labor for investment.

Indochina. Ho Chi Minh's forces, aided by the USSR and the new Chinese Communist government, fought French and pro-French Vietnamese forces to a standstill and captured the strategic **Dien Bien Phu** camp in May 1954. The Geneva Agreements divided Vietnam in half pending elections (never held) and recognized Laos and Cambodia as independent. The U.S. aided the anti-Communist Republic of Vietnam in the S.

Middle East. Arab revolutions placed leftist, militantly nationalist regimes in power in Egypt (1952) and Iraq (1958). But Arab unity attempts failed (United Arab Republic joined Egypt, Syria, Yemen, 1958-61). Arab refusal to recognize Israel (Arab League economic blockade began Sept. 1951) led to a permanent **state of war**, with repeated incidents (Gaza, 1955). Israel occupied Sinai, and Britain and France took (Oct. 1956) the Suez Canal, but were replaced by the UN Emergency Force. The Mossadegh government in Iran nationalized (May 1951) the British-owned oil industry in May, but was overthrown (Aug. 1953) in a U.S.-aided coup.

Latin America. Argentinian dictator Juan **Perón**, in office 1946, crushed opposition and enforced land reform, some nationalization, welfare state measures, and curbs on the Roman Catholic Church. A Sept. 1955 coup deposed Perón. The 1952 revolution in Bolivia brought land reform, nationalization of tin mines, and improvement in the status of Native Americans, who nevertheless remained poor. The Batista regime in Cuba was overthrown (Jan. 1959) by Fidel **Castro**, who imposed a Communist dictatorship, aligned Cuba with the USSR and improved education and health care. A U.S.-backed anti-Castro invasion (**Bay of Pigs**, Apr. 1961) was crushed. Self-government advanced in the British Caribbean.

Technology. Large outlays on research and development in the U.S. and the USSR focused on military applications (H-bomb in U.S., 1952; USSR, 1953; Britain, 1957; intercontinental missiles, late 1950s). Soviet launching of the **Sputnik** satellite (Oct. 4, 1957) spurred increases in U.S. science education funds (National Defense Education Act).

Literature and film. Alienation from social and literary conventions reached an extreme in the theater of the absurd (Beckett's *Waiting for Godot*, 1952), the "new novel" (Robbe-Grillet's *Voyeur*, 1955), and avant-garde film (Antonioni's *L'Avventura*, 1960). U.S. beatniks (Kerouac's *On the Road*, 1957) and others rejected the supposed conformism of Americans (Riesman's *The Lonely Crowd*, 1950).

Rising Expectations and New Protests: 1960-69

Global economy. The longest sustained economic boom on record spanned almost the entire decade in the capitalist world; the closely watched GNP figure doubled (1960-70) in the U.S., fueled by Vietnam War-related budget deficits. The **General Agreement on Tariffs and Trade** (1967) stimulated W European prosperity, which spread to peripheral areas (Spain, Italy, E Germany). Japan became a top economic power. Foreign investment aided the industrialization of Brazil. There were limited Soviet economic reform attempts. Outside the Soviet zone the global economy was marked by the growing role of multi-national corporations (3,000 in 1914; 6,000 by 1970). International Non-Government Organizations also multiplied rapidly (Amnesty International, 1961). The United Nations began sponsoring international "Years of Women" (1964).

Reform and radicalization. Pres. John F. **Kennedy**, inaugurated 1961, emphasized youthful idealism and vigor; his assassination Nov. 22, 1963, was a national trauma. A series of political and social reform movements took root in the U.S. and other countries. Blacks demonstrated nonviolently and with partial success against segregation and poverty (1963 March on Washington; 1964 **Civil Rights Act**), but some urban areas erupted in extensive riots (Watts, 1965; Detroit, 1967; **Martin Luther King** assassination, Apr. 4, 1968). New concern for the poor (Harrington's *Other America*, 1963) helped lead to Pres. Lyndon Johnson's **"Great Society"** programs (Medicare, Water Quality Act, Higher Education Act, all 1965). Concern for the **environment** surged (Carson's *Silent Spring*, 1962).

Feminism revived as a cultural and political movement (Friedan's *Feminine Mystique*, 1963; National Organization for Women founded 1966), and a movement for homosexual rights emerged (Stonewall riot in NYC, 1969). Pope John XXIII called the **Second Vatican Council** (1962-65), which liberalized Roman Catholic liturgy and some other aspects of Catholicism.

Opposition to U.S. involvement in Vietnam, especially among university students (**Moratorium** protest, Nov. 1969), turned violent (Weatherman Chicago riots, Oct. 1969). **New Left** and Marxist theories became popular, and membership in radical groups (Students for a Democratic Society, Black Panthers) increased. Maoist groups, especially in Europe, called for total transformation of society. In France, students sparked a nationwide strike affecting 10 million workers in May-June 1968, but an electoral reaction barred revolutionary change.

China. China's revolutionary militancy under **Mao** Zedong caused disputes with the USSR under "revisionist" Khrushchev, starting in 1960. The two powers exchanged fire in 1969 border disputes. China used force to capture (1962) areas disputed with India. The **"Great Proletarian Cultural Revolution"** tried to impose a utopian egalitarian program in China and spread revolution abroad; political struggle, often violent, convulsed China in 1965-68.

Indochina. Communist-led guerrillas aided by N Vietnam fought from 1960 against the S Vietnam government of Ngo Dinh Diem (killed 1963). The U.S. military role increased after the 1964 **Tonkin Gulf** incident. U.S. forces there peaked at 543,400 in Apr. 1969. Massive numbers of N Vietnamese troops also fought. Laotian and Cambodian neutrality were threatened by Communist insurgencies, with N Vietnamese aid, and U.S. intrigues.

Developing world. A bloc of authoritarian leftist regimes among the newly independent nations emerged in political opposition to the U.S.-led Western alliance and came to dominate the conference of nonaligned nations (Belgrade, 1961; Cairo, 1964; Lusaka, 1970). Soviet political ties and military bases established in Cuba, Egypt, Algeria, Guinea, and other countries whose leaders were regarded as revolutionary heroes by opposition groups in pro-Western or colonial countries. Some leaders were ousted in coups by pro-Western groups—Congo's Patrice Lumumba (killed 1961), Ghana's Kwame Nkrumah (exiled 1966), and Indonesia's Sukarno (effectively ousted in 1965 after a Communist coup failed).

Middle East. Arab-Israeli tension erupted into a brief war June 1967. Israel emerged from the war as a major regional power. Military shipments before and after the war increased Soviet influence in much of the Arab world. Most Arab states broke U.S. diplomatic ties, while Communist countries cut their ties to Israel. Intra-Arab disputes continued: Egypt and Saudi Arabia supported rival factions in a bloody Yemen civil war 1962-70; Lebanese troops fought Palestinian commandos 1969.

East Europe. To stop the large-scale exodus of citizens, E German authorities built (Aug. 1961) a **fortified wall across Berlin**. Soviet sway in the Balkans was weakened by Albania's support of China (USSR broke ties in Dec. 1961) and Romania's assertion (1964) of industrial and foreign policy autonomy. Liberalization (spring 1968) in Czechoslovakia was crushed with massive force by troops of five Warsaw Pact countries. W German treaties (1970) with the USSR and Poland facilitated the transfer of German technology and confirmed postwar boundaries.

Arts and styles. The boundary between fine and popular arts was blurred to some extent by Pop Art (Warhol) and rock musicals (*Hair*, 1968). Informality and exaggeration prevailed in fashion (beards, miniskirts). A nonpolitical "counterculture" developed, rejecting traditional bourgeois life goals and personal habits, and use of marijuana and hallucinogens spread (**Woodstock** festival, Aug. 1969). Indian influence was felt in religion (Ram Dass) and fashion, and **The Beatles**, who brought unprecedented sophistication to rock music, became for many a symbol of the decade.

Science. Achievements in space (**humans on the moon**, July 1969) and electronics (lasers, integrated circuits) encouraged a faith in scientific solutions to problems in agriculture ("green revolution"), medicine (heart transplants, 1967), and other areas. Harmful technology, it was believed, could be controlled (1963 Limited Test Ban Treaty, 1968 Nuclear Nonproliferation Treaty).

American astronauts walked on the moon (1969) just a dozen years after the Soviet Union launched the first human-made satellite into orbit.

New Global Balances and Religious Revivals: 1970-79

U.S.: Caution and neoconservatism. A relatively sluggish economy, energy shortages, and environmental problems contributed to a **"limits of growth"** philosophy. Suspicion of science and technology killed or delayed major projects (supersonic transport dropped, 1971) and was fed by the Three Mile Island nuclear reactor accident (Mar. 1979).

There were signs of growing mistrust of government and less support for new policies. School busing and racial quotas were opposed (Bakke decision, June 1978); the Equal Rights Amendment for women languished; civil rights legislation aimed at protecting homosexuals was opposed (Dade County referendum, June 1977).

Completion of Communist forces' takeover of **South Vietnam** (evacuation of U.S. civilians, Apr. 1975), revelations of Central Intelligence Agency misdeeds (Rockefeller Commission report, June 1975), and **Watergate** scandals (Nixon resigned in Aug. 1974) reduced faith in U.S. moral and material capacity to influence world affairs. Revelations of Soviet crimes (Solzhenitsyn's *Gulag Archipelago*, 1974) and Soviet intervention in Africa helped foster a revival of anti-Communist sentiment.

Economy sluggish. The 1960s boom faltered in the 1970s; a severe recession in the U.S. and Europe (1974-75) followed a huge oil price hike (Dec. 1973). Monetary instability (U.S. cut ties to gold in Aug. 1971), the decline of the dollar, and protectionist moves by industrial countries (1977-78) threatened trade. Business investment and spending for research declined. Severe inflation plagued many countries (25% in Britain, 1975; 18% in U.S., 1979).

China readjusts. After the 1976 deaths of Mao Zedong and Zhou Enlai, struggle for the leadership succession was won by pragmatists. A nationwide purge of orthodox Maoists was carried out, and the **Gang of Four**, led by Mao's widow, Chiang Ching, was arrested. The new leaders freed more than 100,000 political prisoners and reduced public adulation of Mao. Political and trade ties were expanded with Japan, Europe, and the U.S. in the late 1970s, as relations worsened with the USSR, Cuba, and Vietnam (four-week invasion by China, 1979). Ideological guidelines in industry, science, education, and the armed forces, which the ruling faction said had caused chaos and decline, were reversed (bonuses to workers, Dec. 1977; exams for college entrance, Oct. 1977). Severe restrictions on cultural expression were eased.

Europe. European unity moves (EEC-EFTA trade accord, 1972) faltered as economic problems appeared (Britain floated pound, 1972; France floated franc, 1974). Germany and Switzerland curbed guest workers from S Europe. Greece and Turkey quarreled over Cyprus and Aegean oil rights.

All non-Communist Europe was under democratic rule after free elections (June 1976) in **Spain** seven months after the death of Franco. The conservative, colonialist regime in **Portugal** was overthrown in Apr. 1974. In **Greece** the seven-year military dictatorship yielded power in 1974. N Europe, though ruled mostly by Socialists, became more conservative. The **British** Labour government imposed (1975) wage curbs and suspended nationalization schemes. Terrorism in **Germany** (1972 Munich Olympics killings) led to laws curbing some civil liberties. **French** "new philosophers" rejected leftist ideologies, and the Socialist-Communist coalition lost a 1978 election bid.

Religion and politics. The improvement in **Muslim** countries' political fortunes by the 1950s (with the exception of Central Asia under Soviet and Chinese rule) and the growth of Arab oil wealth were followed by a resurgence of traditional religious fervor. Libyan dictator Muammar al-Qaddafi mixed Islamic laws with socialism. The illegal Muslim Brotherhood in **Egypt** was accused of violence, while extreme groups bombed (1977) theaters to protest Western and secular values.

In **Turkey**, the National Salvation Party was the first Islamic group to share (1974) power since secularization in the 1920s. In **Iran**, Ayatollah Ruhollah **Khomeini** led a revolution that deposed the secular shah (Jan. 1979) and created an Islamic republic. Religiously motivated Muslims took part in an insurrection in Saudi Arabia that briefly seized (1979) the Grand Mosque in Mecca. Muslim puritan opposition to **Pakistan** Pres. Zulfikar Ali-Bhutto helped lead to his overthrow in July 1977. Muslim solidarity, however, could not prevent Pakistan's eastern province (**Bangladesh**) from declaring (Dec. 1971) independence after a bloody civil war.

Muslim and Hindu resentment of coerced sterilization in **India** helped defeat the Indira Gandhi government, which was replaced (Mar. 1977) by a coalition including religious Hindu parties. Muslims in the S **Philippines**, aided by Libya, rebelled against central rule from 1973. The Buddhist Soka Gakkai movement launched (1964) the Komeito party in **Japan**, which became a major opposition party in 1972 and 1976 elections.

Evangelical Protestant groups grew in the U.S. A revival of interest in Orthodox Christianity occurred among **Russian** intellectuals (Solzhenitsyn). The secularist **Israeli** Labor party, after decades of rule, was ousted in 1977 by conservatives led by Menachem Begin; religious militants founded settlements on the disputed West Bank, part of biblically promised Israel. Reform Judaism in U.S. revived many previously discarded traditional practices.

Religious wars raged intermittently in **Northern Ireland** (Catholic vs. Protestant, 1969-97) and **Lebanon** (Christian vs. Muslim, 1975-90), while religious militancy complicated the Israel-Arab dispute (1973 Israel-Arab war). The Camp David Accords in 1978, negotiated by Egyptian Pres. Anwar al-Sadat, Israeli Prime Min. Menachem Begin, and U.S. Pres. Jimmy Carter, facilitated the landmark 1979 **Egypt-Israel peace treaty**, but increased militancy on the West Bank impeded further progress.

Latin America. Repressive conservative regimes strengthened their hold, with a violent coup against the elected (Sept. 1973) Allende government in **Chile**, military coup in **Argentina** (1976), and coups against reformist regimes in **Bolivia** (1971, 1979) and **Peru** (1976). In Central America, increasing liberal and leftist militancy led to the ouster (1979) of the Somoza regime of **Nicaragua** and to civil conflict in **El Salvador**.

Indochina. Communist victories in Vietnam, Cambodia, and Laos by May 1975 led to new turmoil. The **Pol Pot regime** ordered millions to resettle in rural areas, in a program of forced labor and terrorism that cost more than 1 million lives (1975-79) and caused hundreds of thousands to flee. The Vietnamese invasion of Cambodia (1979) swelled the refugee population and contributed to widespread starvation.

Russian expansion. Soviet influence, checked in some countries (troops ousted by Egypt, 1972), was projected farther afield, often with the use of Cuban troops (Angola, 1975-89; Ethiopia, 1977-88) and aided by a growing navy, a merchant fleet, and international banking ability. Détente with the West— 1972 Berlin pact, 1972 strategic arms pact (**SALT**)—gave way to a more antagonistic relationship in the late 1970s, exacerbated by the Soviet invasion (1979) of **Afghanistan**.

Africa. The last remaining European colonies were granted independence (**Spanish Sahara**, 1976; **Djibouti**, 1977), and, after 10 years of civil war, a black government took over (1979) in Zimbabwe (Rhodesia); white domination remained in **South Africa**. European involvement in local wars (Russia in **Angola**, **Ethiopia**; France in **Chad**, **Zaire**, **Mauritania**) and the use of tens of thousands of Cuban troops were denounced by some African leaders. Ethnic or tribal clashes made Africa a locus of sustained warfare during the late 1970s.

Arts. Traditional modes of painting, architecture, and music received increased popular and critical attention in the 1970s. These more conservative styles coexisted with modernist works in an atmosphere of increased variety and tolerance.

The Vietnam War, in which an estimated 2 million Vietnamese and 50,000 Americans died, also engulfed Laos and Cambodia.

End of the Cold War and Demand for Democracy: 1980-89

Global developments. International contacts accelerated thanks to new openness in China (1978) and Russia (1985); global consumerism was symbolized by the rapid spread of McDonald's restaurants (Japan, 1971; Russia, 1990).

USSR, Eastern Europe. The late 1980s saw the remaking of the Soviet state and the beginning of the disintegration of the Soviet empire. After the deaths of Gen. Sec. Leonid **Brezhnev** (1982) and two successors, the harsh treatment of dissent and restriction of emigration, and the Soviet invasion (Dec. 1979) of Afghanistan, Gen. Sec. Mikhail **Gorbachev** (in office 1985-91) promoted *glasnost* and *perestroika*—economic, political, and social reform. Supported by the Communist Party (July 1988), he signed (Dec. 1987) the INF disarmament treaty. Military withdrawal from Afghanistan was completed in Feb. 1989, and the Soviet people chose (Mar. 1989) part of the new Congress of People's Deputies from competing candidates. By decade's end the **Cold War** appeared to be fading away.

In **Poland**, Solidarity, the labor union founded (1980) by Lech Walesa, was outlawed in 1982 and then legalized in 1988, after years of unrest. Poland's first free election since the Communist takeover brought **Solidarity** victory (June 1989); Tadeusz Mazowiecki, a Walesa adviser, became (Aug. 1989) prime minister in a government with the Communists. In the fall of 1989 the failure of Marxist economies in **Hungary**, **East Germany**, **Czechoslovakia**, **Bulgaria**, and **Romania** brought the collapse of the Communist monopoly and a demand for democracy. In a historic step, the **Berlin Wall** was opened in Nov. 1989.

U.S. The **"Reagan Years"** (1981-88) featured new economic policies via budget and tax cuts, deregulation, "junk bond" financing, leveraged buyouts, and mergers. However, there was a stock market crash (Oct. 1987), and federal budget deficits and the trade deficit increased. Foreign policy showed a **strong anti-Communist stance**, via increased defense spending, aid to anti-Communists in Central America, invasion of Cuba-threatened Grenada, and championing of the "Star Wars" missile defense program. Four Reagan-Gorbachev summits (1985-88) climaxed in the INF treaty (1987), as the Cold War began to wind down. The **Iran Contra affair** (Oliver North's testimony, July 1987) was a major political scandal. In 1988, Vice Pres. George H. W. Bush was elected to succeed Ronald Reagan as president.

Middle East. The Middle East remained militarily unstable, with sharp divisions along economic, political, racial, and religious lines. In **Iran**, the Islamic revolution of 1979 created a strong anti-U.S. stance (hostage crisis, Nov. 1979-

Jan. 1981). In Sept. 1980, **Iraq** repudiated its border agreement with Iran and began major hostilities that led to an eight-year war in which hundreds of thousands were killed.

Libya's support for international terrorism induced the U.S. to close (May 1981) its diplomatic mission there and embargo (Mar. 1982) Libyan oil. The U.S. accused Libyan leader Muammar al-Qaddafi of aiding (Dec. 1985) terrorists. Following attack on a West Berlin disco frequented by U.S. military, U.S. bombed targets in Libya (Apr. 1986).

Israel affirmed (July 1980) all Jerusalem as its capital, destroyed (June 1981) an Iraqi atomic reactor, and invaded Lebanon, citing terrorism from the Palestine Liberation Organization; PLO withdrew after cease-fire. A **Palestinian uprising** began (Dec. 1987) in Israeli-occupied Gaza and spread to the West Bank; troops responded with force, killing 300 by the end of 1988, with 6,000 more in detention camps. Israeli withdrawal from **Lebanon** began in Feb. 1985 and ended in June 1985, as Lebanon continued to be torn by military and political conflict. Artillery duels (Mar.-Apr. 1989) between Christian East Beirut and Muslim West Beirut left 200 dead and 700 wounded.

Latin America. In **Nicaragua**, the leftist Sandinista National Liberation Front, in power after the 1979 civil war, faced problems as a result of Nicaragua's military aid to leftist guerrillas in El Salvador and U.S. backing of antigovernment contras. The CIA admitted (1984) having directed the mining of Nicaraguan ports, and the U.S. sent humanitarian (1985) and military (1986) aid. Profits from **secret arms sales** to Iran were found (1987) diverted to contras. Cease-fire talks between the Sandinista government and contras came in 1988, and elections were held in Nicaragua in Feb. 1990.

In **El Salvador**, a military coup (Oct. 1979) failed to halt extremist terrorism. Archbishop Oscar Romero was assassinated in Mar. 1980; from Jan. to June some 4,000 civilians were killed in the civil unrest. In 1984, newly elected Pres. José Napoleon Duarte worked to stem human rights abuses, but violence continued.

In **Chile**, Gen. Augusto Pinochet yielded the presidency after a democratic election (Dec. 1989), but remained as head of the army. He had ruled the country since 1973, imposing harsh measures against leftists and dissidents.

Africa. The 1980s saw continuing economc decline in virtually all African countries, a result of accelerating desertification, the world economic recession, heavy indebtedness to overseas creditors, rapid population growth, and political instability. Some 60 million Africans faced prolonged hunger in 1981. Much of Africa had one of the worst **droughts** ever in 1983, and by year's end, one-third of the population, or about 150 million, were near **famine**. Live Aid, a marathon rock concert, was presented in July 1985, and the U.S. and Western nations sent aid in Sept. 1985. Wars in Ethiopia and Sudan and military strife in several other nations continued. **HIV/AIDS** took a heavy toll.

Anti-apartheid sentiment gathered force in **South Africa** as demonstrations and violent police response grew. White voters approved (Nov. 1983) the first constitution to give "Coloureds" (people of mixed-race background) and Asians a voice, while still excluding blacks (70% of the population). The U.S. imposed economic sanctions in Aug. 1985, and 11 Western nations followed in Sept. 1985. Pres. P. W. **Botha** was succeeded by F. W. **de Klerk**, in Sept. 1989, who promised "evolutionary" change via negotiation with the black population.

Asia and the Pacific. Benazir **Bhutto** became the first woman to lead a majority-Muslim nation as prime minister of **Pakistan** (Dec. 1988). The "people power" revolt in the **Philippines** ousted Ferdinand **Marcos** (Feb. 1986) after two decades as president; replaced by Corazon **Aquino.**

During the 1980s **China**'s Communist government and paramount leader **Deng Xiaoping** pursued far-reaching changes, expanding commercial and technical ties to the industrialized world and increasing the role of market forces in stimulating urban development. Apr. 1989 brought new demands for political reforms; student demonstrators camped out in **Tiananmen Square**, Beijing, in a massive peaceful protest. Some 100,000 students and workers marched, and at least 20 other cities saw protests. In response, martial law was imposed; army troops crushed the demonstration in and around Tiananmen Square on June 3-4, with death toll estimates of 500-7,000, up to 10,000 dissidents arrested, 31 people tried and executed. The conciliatory Communist Party

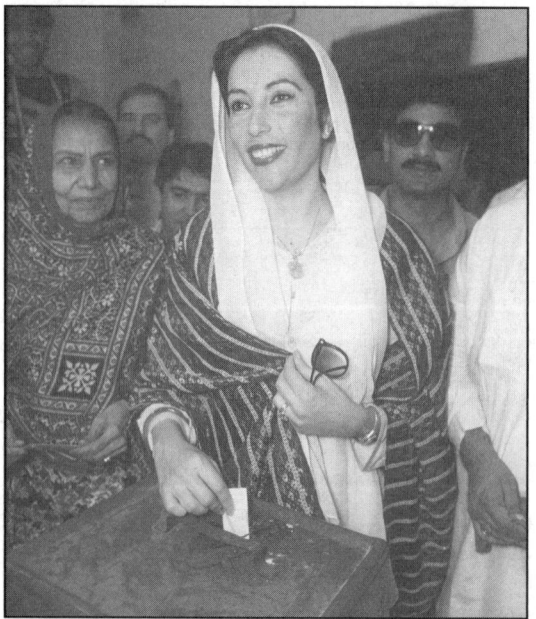

Benazir Bhutto became Pakistan's first woman prime minister (1988) and the first woman ever elected to lead a Muslim nation.

chief was ousted; the Politburo adopted (July 1989) reforms against official corruption.

Japan's relations with other nations, especially the U.S., were dominated by **trade imbalances** favoring Japan. Western Europe and the U.S. accused Japan of restrictive trade policies.

Europe. With the addition of Greece, Portugal, and Spain, the European Community became a common market of more than 300 million people. Margaret **Thatcher** became the first British prime minister in the 20th cent. to win a third consecutive term (1987). **France** elected (1981) its first socialist president, François **Mitterrand**, who was reelected in 1988. Elections in 1983 brought **Italy** its first socialist premier, Bettino **Craxi**.

International terrorism. With the 1979 **overthrow of the shah** of Iran and with instablity in the Middle East, terrorism became a prominent tactic. In 1979-81, Iranian militants held 52 **U.S. hostages in Iran** for 444 days; in 1983 a TNT-laden suicide terrorist blew up U.S. Marine headquarters in Beirut, killing 241 Americans, and a truck bomb blew up a French paratroop barracks, killing 58. The *Achille Lauro* cruise ship was hijacked in 1985, and an American passenger killed; the U.S. subsequently intercepted the Egyptian plane flying the terrorists to safety. Incidents rose to 700 in 1985, and to 1,000 in 1988. **Assassinated leaders** included Egypt's Pres. Anwar al-**Sadat** (1981), India's Prime Min. Indira **Gandhi** (1984), and Lebanese Premier Rashid **Karami** (1987).

New Regional Tensions in the Post-Cold War World: 1990-99

Global developments. Nations in the 1990s made post-Cold War adjustments; a growing awareness of globalization developed with further spread of democracy. International contacts accelerated with the growth of the Internet (1990). Efforts to deal with global environmental change intensified with tentative agreements in Kyoto, Japan (1997). A milestone protest against global economic trends burst forth in a World Bank meeting in Seattle (1999).

Soviet Empire breakup. The breakup of the Soviet Union into 15 independent states began with declarations of independence by the Baltic republics of **Lithuania**, **Latvia**, and **Estonia** during an abortive coup against Mikhail **Gorbachev** (Aug. 1991). Other republics soon took the same step. In Dec. 1991, **Russia**, **Ukraine**, and **Belarus** declared the Soviet Union dead; Gorbachev resigned, and the Soviet Parliament went out of existence. The Warsaw Pact and the Council for Mutual Economic Assistance (Comecon) were disbanded. Most of the former Soviet republics joined in a loose confederation called the **Commonwealth of Independent States**. Russia's people suffered severe economic hardship as the nation, under Pres. Boris **Yeltsin**, moved to reboot the economy under a free market system. In Oct. 1993, **anti-Yeltsin forces** occupied the Parliament building and were ousted by the army.

The Muslim republic of **Chechnya** declared independence from the rest of Russia, but this was met with an invasion by Russian troops (Dec. 1994). A cease-fire took hold in 1996, and the Russians withdrew. In 1999 Russia forcibly suppressed Muslim insurgents in Dagestan and entered Chechnya, again fighting separatist rebels there. Yeltsin resigned Dec. 31, 1999, to be replaced by Vladimir **Putin** (elected in his own right, Mar. 2000).

Europe. Yugoslavia broke apart, and hostilities ensued along ethnic and religious lines. **Croatia**, **Slovenia**, and **Macedonia** declared independence (1991), followed by **Bosnia-Herzegovina** (1992). **Serbia** and **Montenegro** remained as the republic of Yugoslavia. Bitter fighting followed, especially in Bosnia, where Serbs reportedly engaged in **"ethnic cleansing"** of the Muslim population; a peace plan (Dayton accord, 1995), brokered by the U.S., was signed by **Bosnia**, **Serbia**, and **Croatia**, with **NATO** responsible for policing its implementation. In spring 1999, NATO conducted a bombing campaign aimed at stopping Yugoslavia from its campaign to drive out ethnic Albanians from the **Kosovo** region; a peace accord was reached in June under which NATO peacekeeping troops entered Kosovo.

The **two Germanys were reunited** after 45 years (Oct. 1990). The union was greeted with jubilation, but economic stresses followed. West German chancellor Helmut **Kohl**, a Christian Democrat, lost power after 16 years, in Sept. 1998 elections; Gerhard **Schröder**, a Social Democrat, took over. Czechoslovakia broke apart peacefully (Jan. 1993), becoming the **Czech Republic** and **Slovakia**. In **Poland**, Lech **Walesa** was elected president (Dec. 1991) but was defeated in his bid for a second term (Nov. 1995).

NATO approved the **Partnership for Peace** Program (Jan. 1994) coordinating the defense of E and Central European countries; Russia joined the program later that year. NATO signed a pact with **Russia** (1997) providing for NATO expansion into the former Soviet-bloc countries; a similar treaty was set up with **Ukraine**. The **Czech Republic, Hungary**, and **Poland** became members in Jan. 1999. Efforts toward European unity continued with adoption of a single market (Jan. 1993) and conversion of the European Community to the **European Union** as the Maestricht Treaty took effect (Nov. 1993). Agreement was reached for 11 EU members to participate in Economic and Monetary Union, adopting a common currency (**euro**) in Jan. 1999.

An intraparty revolt forced Margaret **Thatcher** out as prime minister of **Great Britain**, to be succeeded by John **Major** (Nov. 1990); seven years later, Labour was returned to power under Tony **Blair** (May 1997). The divorce of Prince **Charles and Diana**, followed by the death of Diana in a car accident (Aug. 1997), made headlines around the world. Talks on peace in **Northern Ireland** that included participation of Sinn Fein, political arm of the IRA, led to a peace plan, approved in an all-Ireland vote (May 1998). In Dec. 1999, Northern Ireland was granted home rule. In **Scotland** voters overwhelmingly approved establishment of a regional legislature (1997), and in **Wales** voters narrowly approved establishment of a local assembly (1997). In a historic innovation, the Church of England ordained women as priests (1994).

Middle East. In Aug. 1990, **Iraq**'s Saddam Hussein ordered troops to invade **Kuwait**. The UN approved military action (Nov. 1990), and an international military force led by the U.S. bombed Iraq (Jan. 1991) and launched a land attack, crushing the invasion (Feb. 1991). Iraq accepted the terms of a cease-fire (Apr. 1991) and U.S. troops withdrew, but "no-fly" zones were set up over some regions to protect Kurds and Shiite Muslims. The **UN** imposed **sanctions** on Iraq for failure to abide by the cease-fire. Iraq's reported failure to cooperate with UN inspectors seeking to eliminate **"weapons of mass destruction"** led to air strikes by the U.S. and Britain (1998, 2001).

The last Western hostages were freed in **Lebanon**, June 1992. **Israel** and the **PLO** signed a peace accord (Sept. 1993) providing for Palestinian self-government in the West Bank and Gaza Strip. Prime Min. Yitzhak **Rabin** and Foreign Min. Shimon **Peres** of Israel and Yasir **Arafat** of the PLO received the Nobel Peace Prize for their efforts (1994). Six Arab nations relaxed boycott against Israel (1994), and Israel and **Jordan** signed a peace treaty (Oct. 1994). Rabin was assassinated (Nov. 1995) by an Israeli opponent of the peace process. Benjamin **Netanyahu** became prime minister (May 1996). Arafat was elected to the presidency of the Palestinian Authority (Jan. 1996). A Labour government under Ehud **Barak** took power after Israel's May 1999 elections.

Asia and the Pacific. Hong Kong was returned to **China** (July 1997) after 156 years as a British colony, and **Macao** reverted to Chinese sovereignty (Dec. 1999) after over 400 years of Portuguese rule. Both were to retain their legal and economic systems for 50 years. **Jiang** Zemin, general secretary of the Chinese Communist Party, assumed the additional post of president of China (Mar. 1993) and emerged as the key leader after the death of leader **Deng** Xiaoping (Feb. 1997). China released from prison—and exiled—some well-known dissidents but continued to earn criticism for widespread **human rights abuses**. In Nov. 1999 the U.S. and China signed a landmark pact normalizing trade relations. China's annual economic growth approached and even eclipsed 10% during the decade.

After years of prosperity, **Thailand, Indonesia**, and **South Korea** in 1997 began to suffer economic reverses that had a worldwide ripple effect. These countries received billion-dollar IMF bailout packages. In **Indonesia**, protests over mismanagement led to the resignation of Pres. Suharto (May 1998) after 32 years of nearly autocratic rule. Abdurraham Wahid was elected (Oct. 1999) in the country's first fully democratic elections. In a referendum (Aug. 1999), **East Timor** voted overwhelmingly for independence from Indonesia; pro-Indonesian militias then rampaged through the territory, but a multinational **peacekeeping force** was allowed to help restore order (Sept. 1999). In South Korea, former dissident **Kim** Dae-jung was elected president (Dec. 1997).

In Japan members of a religious cult released the nerve gas sarin on five **Tokyo subway** cars, killing 12 people and injuring more than 5,500 (Mar. 1995). Tamil rebels continued their armed conflict in **Sri Lanka**. In **Afghanistan** the **Taliban**, an extreme Islamic fundamentalist group, gained control of Kabul (Sept. 1996) and, eventually, most of the country. In **North Korea**, longtime dictator **Kim Il Sung** died (July 1994), to be succeeded by his son, **Kim Jong Il**. In the same year the country signed an agreement with the U.S. setting a timetable for North Korea to eliminate its **nuclear program**. The country also suffered a severe drought, and widespread starvation was feared.

India was beset by riots following destruction of a mosque by Hindu militants (Dec. 1992); Indian army troops repeatedly clashed with pro-independence demonstrators in the disputed Muslim region of **Kashmir**, exacerbating relations with **Pakistan**. Uneasy relations between India and Pakistan reached a new level when both nations conducted nuclear tests in 1998. Conflict in Pakistan between government and the military led to a bloodless coup (Oct. 1999).

Africa. South Africa's Pres. F. W. **de Klerk** released dissident Nelson **Mandela** from prison (Feb. 1990) after 27 years, and lifted a ban on the black nationalist African National Congress. The white minority government repealed apartheid laws (1990, 1991). Mandela was elected president (Apr. 1994), and a new nonracial constitution became law (Dec. 1996). In **Nigeria**, Gen. Olusegun Obasanjo was elected president (Feb. 1999), to become the country's first civilian leader in 15 years. The decades-long rule of **Mobutu** Sese Seko in **Zaire** came to an end (May 1997) at the hands of rebel forces led by Laurent **Kabila**; an ailing Mobutu fled the country and soon after died. Kabila changed the country's name back to **Democratic Republic of the Congo**; conditions remained unstable.

After the presidents of **Burundi** and **Rwanda** were killed in an airplane crash (Apr. 1994), violence erupted in Rwanda between Hutu and Tutsi factions; hundreds of thousands were slain in genocidal fashion. The conflict spread to refugee camps in neighboring Zaire and Burundi. Factional fighting also erupted in **Somalia** (Jan. 1991). The UN sent a U.S.-led **peacekeeping force**, but it was unsuccessful in restoring order. Some soldiers of the peacekeeping force were killed, including 23 Pakistanis (June 1993) and 18 U.S. Rangers (Oct. 1993). The UN ended its mission (Mar. 1995) with no durable government in place. **Liberia** endured factional fighting that lasted almost five years and claimed over 150,000 lives; a cease-fire was concluded in Aug. 1995. The World Health Organization reported (1995) that Africa accounted for 70% of **AIDS** cases worldwide.

A 16-year civil war appeared to end in **Angola** (May 1991) when the government signed a peace accord with the rebel UNITA faction. But despite the inauguration of a national unity government (Apr. 1997), insurgents continued to fight. **Namibia** officially became independent in Mar. 1990 after almost 20 years under UN trusteeship. In **Algeria**, the army cancelled a second round of parliamentary elections (Jan. 1992) after the Islamic party won a first round. Ensuing violence by **Islamic fundamentalists** claimed thousands of lives; a peace plan was worked out in 1999.

North America. The North American Free Trade Agreement (NAFTA), liberalizing trade between the U.S., Canada, and Mexico, went into effect Jan. 1, 1994. In **Canada**, the Progressive Conservative Party suffered a crushing defeat in general elections (Oct. 1993), and liberal Jean **Chrétien** became prime minister. The map of Canada was altered in Apr. 1999 to create a new territory, **Nunavut**, out of an area that had been part of Northwest Territories.

In the **U.S.**'s 1992 presidential election, Bill **Clinton** (D) defeated Pres. George H. W. Bush (R), but Republicans gained control of Congress in 1994 midterm elections. Clinton won reelection in 1996; despite scandals, the administration remained popular, aided by economic prosperity. Clinton proposed (Feb. 1998) the first balanced federal budget in nearly 30 years. In Dec. 1998 Clinton was **impeached** by the U.S. House on charges related to the Monica Lewinsky scandal; he was acquitted by the Senate in Feb. 1999.

In **Mexico**, Ernesto Zedillo of the ruling PRI party was elected president (July 1994) after the party's first candidate was assassinated. The country soon faced a crisis affecting the value of the peso, but recovered with the help of a bailout package from the U.S. A peasant revolt spearheaded by the **Zapatista National Liberation Army** erupted in the state of Chiapas (Jan. 1994) and was suppressed.

Central America and the Caribbean. In **Haiti**, Jean-Bertrand **Aristide** was elected president (Dec. 1990) but was ousted in a military coup after nine months. A delegation headed by former U.S. Pres. Jimmy Carter arranged (Sept. 1994) for the junta to step aside for Aristide, who served until 1996. In **Nicaragua**, Violeta Chamorro defeated Daniel **Ortega** in the presidential election (Feb. 1990), thus ousting the Sandinistas. In **Panama**, U.S. troops invaded and overthrew the government of Manuel **Noriega** (Dec. 1989). Noriega was captured Jan. 1990; convicted and jailed on drug-related charges in U.S. in 1992, and in France in 2010. On Dec. 31, 1999, Panama assumed full control of the **Panama Canal**, in accord with a treaty with the U.S. In **El Salvador** (1992) and **Guatemala** (1996) the governments signed agreements with rebel factions.

South America. Alberto **Fujimori** was elected president of **Peru** in June 1990 and, despite his suppression of the constitution (1992), was reelected in 1995. Peru succeeded in capturing (Sept. 1992) the leader of the Shining Path guerrilla movement. Leftist guerrillas took hostages at an ambassador's residence in Lima (Dec. 1996); one hostage was killed during a government assault rescuing the rest (Apr. 1997). Peronist Pres. Carlos Saúl **Menem** served as **Argentina**'s president for much of the decade (elected 1989, reelected 1995), imposing economic austerity.

Former Chilean Pres. Augusto **Pinochet** continued to head the army until Mar. 1998; he was arrested in London (Oct. 1998) on human rights charges but judged unfit for trial and returned to Chile (Mar. 2000). In **Brazil**, Fernando Henrique **Cardoso** was elected president (Oct. 1994) and reelected in 1998 despite an economic slump; the IMF announced a $42 billion aid package (Nov. 1998). In **Venezuela** two coup attempts were thwarted (1992); coup leader Hugo **Chavez**, a leftist populist, was elected president in Dec. 1998.

Terrorism. The U.S. was a prominent target of terrorism linked to Middle Eastern sources. A bomb exploded in a garage beneath New York City's **World Trade Center**, killing six people (Feb. 1993). Bombs set off outside **U.S. embassies** in Kenya and Tanzania killed over 220 people (Aug. 1998); the U.S. retaliated with missiles fired at alleged terrorist-linked sites in Afghanistan and Sudan. In the U.S.'s deadliest instance of domestic terrorism, 168 people were killed in the bombing of a federal building in **Oklahoma City**, OK (Apr. 1995).

Science and technology. The powerful **Hubble Space Telescope** was launched in Apr. 1990. U.S. space shuttle *Atlantis* docked with the orbiting Russian space station *Mir* (June 1995) in first of several joint missions. In Nov. 1998 the first component for a new **International Space Station** was launched into space from Kazakhstan.

Scottish scientist Ian Wilmut announced (Feb. 1997) the **cloning** of a sheep, nicknamed Dolly—the first mammal successfully cloned from a cell from an adult animal.

Tim Berners-Lee launched the first **World Wide Web** server (1990). User-friendly graphical browsers (Mosaic, 1993; Netscape, 1994) and affordable Internet service providers followed, expanding the reach of the **Internet**.

F. W. de Klerk and Nelson Mandela shared the Nobel Peace Prize in 1993 for negotiating the South African transition to nonracial democracy.

Globalization and Global Realignments: 2000-11

Terrorism and crime. The first decade of the new century saw new levels of international terrorism. Soon after the century opened, in Oct. 2000, 17 American sailors were killed aboard the **USS *Cole*** in Aden, **Yemen**, when a small boat exploded alongside it in a terrorist attack. But terrorism reached a new level on **Sept. 11, 2001**, when hijackers crashed two jetliners into the twin towers of the **World Trade Center** in New York City and another into the **Pentagon** outside Washington, DC, with a fourth crashing in a Pennsylvania field. The attacks, which destroyed both towers and damaged the Pentagon, killed about 3,000 people. Saudi exile Osama **bin Laden** and his **al-Qaeda** terrorist network, based in **Afghanistan** and backed by the Taliban government there, emerged as responsible. American forces raided bin Laden's compound in Abbottabad, Pakistan, and killed the al-Qaeda leader (May 2011).

Among many other incidents generally tied to Islamic radicals, a car bomb on the Indonesian island of **Bali** (Oct. 2002) killed about 200. **Commuter trains** were bombed in **Madrid**, Spain, killing 191 (Mar. 2004); elections held a week later ousted Spain's premier. **Subway** trains and a bus were bombed in **London** (July 2005); 56 people died in all. Eight explosions killed 207 on **commuter trains** in **Mumbai**, India (July 2006); also in Mumbai (Nov. 2008), terrorists launched coordinated attacks on sites frequented by foreigners, killing some 170. Bombs in Kampala, **Uganda**, killed over 70 people gathered to watch **World Cup soccer** final (July 2010). **Chechen** separatist guerrillas were implicated in an attack on a Moscow movie theater (Oct. 2002; over 100 hostages died), bombings in Moscow's subways (Feb. 2004, Mar. 2010; about 100 killed in all), explosions on two Russian planes (Aug. 2004; 89 died), and the takeover of a school in Beslan (Aug.-Sept. 2004; over 330 died).

Other attacks were reportedly foiled, as in Aug. 2006, when British authorities announced having thwarted a plot to detonate **liquid explosives** on transatlantic flights. In Dec. 2009 a Nigerian man—reportedly aided by al-Qaeda in Yemen—attempted to ignite explosives in his underwear, on a Detroit-bound international flight; the incident raised security questions. In Norway, an anti-Muslim right-wing extremist killed 77 people in two incidents, July 2011, including a car bombing in Oslo and a shooting spree at a summer camp.

Global economic crisis. Rapid economic growth in China, Brazil, India, and other countries, along with more sluggish rates in traditional economic powers, signaled global rebalancing. Leadership of efforts at international economic coordination expanded to include rising economies (Group of 20, 2008). A global recession, beginning in late 2007, gathered steam, and a financial meltdown, beginning in Sept. 2008, sent shock waves through industrialized and developing countries alike. Soaring food and **fuel prices** led to unrest in some areas, including an attempted general strike in **Egypt** and riots in **Haiti** (Apr. 2008). Housing values fell, unemployment rose, and governments faced rising budget deficits. Among many ripple effects around the world, **Iceland**'s banking system collapsed (Oct. 2008), rescued by loans and austerity measures. **Dubai**'s state-controlled investment company Dubai World could not meet payments on $59 bil debt; bailed out (Dec. 2009) by a loan from Abu Dhabi. Spending cuts, pension reforms, tax hikes, and other **austerity** measures spurred wide-scale protests in several European countries. The **European Union**, with help from the IMF, provided loan packages to bail out **Greece** (May 2010) and **Ireland** (Nov. 2010). Greece received another bailout pledge from eurozone leaders (July 2011), but the deal was resisted by some EU members and the Greek public in opposition to the related austerity measures.

War in Iraq and Afghanistan. The U.S., with Great Britain, launched an invasion of **Iraq** (Mar. 2003), aimed at ousting the regime of Saddam **Hussein**. Troops took control of Baghdad and other cities, and U.S. Pres. George W. **Bush** declared major combat ended by May 1, but insurgents caused continuing casualties. Searches for **weapons of mass destruction**, cited as major grounds for the invasion, yielded no results. Interim government installed, June 2004. Saddam Hussein was captured by U.S. troops (Dec. 2003) and tried

by Iraqi authorities for crimes against humanity; he was convicted and executed (Dec. 2006).

Photographic evidence that U.S. soldiers at **Abu Ghraib** prison in Iraq abused detainees arose in Apr. 2004. Despite threats by insurgents, Iraqis turned out in large numbers to vote in **elections** for a transitional assembly (Jan. 2005), democratic constitution (Oct. 2005), and parliament (Dec. 2005); negotiations produced a Shiite coalition government under Nouri **al-Maliki** (May 2006). With sectarian and **insurgent violence** intensifying, Bush announced (Jan. 2007) a **"surge"** of additional U.S. troops; military and civilian casualties declined sharply from mid-2007 onward, aided by a cease-fire with Shiite militias and shift in Sunni clan support for al-Qaeda. Under U.S. Pres. Barack **Obama**, last combat unit withdrew from Iraq, Aug. 2010, and the U.S. military mission formally ended, Dec. 2011. Since the U.S.-led invasion in Mar. 2003, nearly 4,500 U.S. service members had been killed and another 32,000 wounded; tens of thousands of Iraqi civilians and combatants had also lost their lives in the conflict, which had cost more than $800 bil.

In **Afghanistan**, a U.S.-led military coalition ousted the **Taliban**, and a transitional government was installed (Dec. 2001), but Taliban insurgency continued, with heavy military and civilian casualties. NATO assumed control of multinational forces in Aug. 2003. Afghans elected Hamid **Karzai** (Nov. 2004) as head of what proved to be a weak central government. The next presidential election (Aug. 2009) was marked by widespread **vote-rigging**; Karzai was reelected after his main opponent withdrew from a runoff, citing transparency issues. In 2007-10, Taliban and other Islamist militants stepped up activities, often operating from safe havens inside **Pakistan**. The U.S. increased its troop strength in Afghanistan (2009), and stepped up activities of unmanned aerial vehicles (drones). Pres. Barack Obama outlined plans to withdraw all U.S. forces by the end of 2014 (June 2011).

Asia. Gen. Pervez **Musharraf**, brought to power in a 1999 coup, assumed **Pakistan**'s presidency in June 2001 and retained office through elections denounced by protesters. In the wake of the terrorist attacks of Sept. 11, 2001, Pakistan pledged cooperation fighting **Taliban** and **al-Qaeda** militants; attacks by militants and counterattacks by Pakistani forces caused heavy casualties over succeeding years. **Pakistan** and **India** restored ties (May 2003) and declared a cease-fire in disputed territory (Nov. 2003), but relations remained tense. An attack on a convoy carrying former Pakistani Prime Min. Benazir **Bhutto** (Oct. 2007) killed about 140 people; she was later assassinated (Dec. 2007) at a political rally. But her party won in parliamentary elections (Feb. 2008), and her widower, Asif Ali **Zardari**, was elected president (Sept. 2008). In May 2009, after a cease-fire broke down, the government launched a major offensive against Taliban insurgents in the Swat Valley. Monsoon rains and **floods** (July-Aug. 2010) inundated nearly one-fifth of the country, leaving millions homeless.

Iran was censured (Dec. 2003) by the UN Intl. Atomic Energy Agency for covering up aspects of its **nuclear weapons** program, which it claimed was for peaceful purposes. Iran continued to enrich uranium in defiance of IAEA deadlines and tested missiles said to be capable of reaching Israel. Pres. Mahmoud **Ahmadinejad** was declared the landslide winner in June 2009 elections widely perceived to have been rigged. **Protests** by hundreds of thousands were crushed by police and Basij paramilitaries; many were injured, some killed, and dissidents were tried en masse (Aug. 2009).

Protests in **Kyrgyzstan** (Mar. 2005) against election fraud brought down Pres. Askar Akayev (in a **"tulip revolution"**), leading to the election of Kumanbek Bakiyev. He was ousted in turn (Apr. 2010), after clashes between protesters and security forces left at least 85 people dead. In June 2010, despite ethnic violence (up to 2,000 killed), a referendum was held and new constitution approved.

South Korean Pres. Kim Dae-jung and **North Korean** ruler Kim Jong Il held a summit meeting and agreed to seek peace and reunification (June 2000), but tensions rose after North Korea admitted conducting a covert **nuclear weapons** development program (Oct. 2002). North Korea withdrew (Jan. 2003) from the Nuclear Nonproliferation Treaty.

One of the deadliest natural disasters in recorded history, a 2004 tsunami killed more than 200,000 people in 11 countries.

Multination talks were held in Beijing; North Korea agreed (Feb. 2007) to end its nuclear program in exchange for an aid package, but subsequently reneged, conducting tests in Apr.-May 2009. An explosion tied to North Korea sank a South Korean Navy ship in the Yellow Sea (Mar. 2010), killing 46 sailors. North Korean dictator Kim Jong Il died (Dec. 2011) and was succeeded by his youngest son, Kim Jong Un.

A massive tsunami in the Indian Ocean (Dec. 2004) devastated parts of Indonesia, Thailand, India, Sri Lanka, and other Asian and African nations, leaving some 200,000 dead. An earthquake struck the disputed territory of Kashmir and parts of Pakistan and India (Oct. 2005); nearly 80,000 were killed. With the retirement of **China**'s Pres. Jiang Zemin, **Hu** Jintao was named Communist party chief (Nov. 2002) and president (Mar. 2003). China's rapidly expanding economy took a hit with several product recall scandals (pet food, Mar. 2007; toys, Aug.-Sept. 2007; infant formula, Sept. 2008). An **earthquake** killed nearly 70,000 in Sichuan province (May 2008). In **Japan**, the Liberal Democrats, in virtually uninterrupted power since the 1950s, were dispatched in parliamentary elections (Aug. 2009). A devastating earthquake and tsunami struck Japan, killing more than 16,000; a nuclear plant overwhelmed by seawater had meltdowns at three of six nuclear reactors, raising radiation fears.

Myanmar's military junta cracked down on hundreds of thousands of antigovernment protesters (Sept. 2007). More than 80,000 people were killed in a **cyclone** in Myanmar (May 2008); the regime thwarted aid agencies. **Sri Lanka** government forces launched a stepped-up offensive in 2008 against **Tamil guerrillas**, leading them to declare an end (May 2009) to a rebellion that since 1983 had claimed at least 80,000 lives. The military carried out a bloodless coup in **Thailand** (Sept. 2006), ousting Prem. Thaksin Shinawatra; civilian rule was restored after Dec. 2007 elections. "Red Shirt" Thaksin supporters stormed the Parliament building and occupied a fortified compound in Bangkok (Apr. 2010); more than 50 were killed in clashes with security forces (May 2010). A UN-sponsored **Cambodia war crimes** tribunal issued its first verdict, July 2010, convicting a former prison warden for mass tortures and killings under Khmer Rouge rule in the 1970s.

Under a Labor government led by Prime Min. Kevin Rudd, **Australia** ended its combat mission in Iraq (July 2008); Rudd

was displaced (June 2010) by his deputy, Julia **Gillard**, who became Australia's first female prime minister.

Middle East. The peace process languished as violence between Israelis and Palestinians escalated, with **suicide bombings** by Palestinians and retaliation by Israeli armed forces. Israel launched a major West Bank offensive (Mar. 2002), and withdrew in early May but, after another wave of suicide bombings, reoccupied much of the West Bank. The U.S., Russia, UN, and EU initiated (Apr. 2003) a **"road map"** plan for peace negotiations, but little progress was made. After Palestinian leader Yasir Arafat's death (Nov. 2004), Mahmoud Abbas was elected in his place. Israeli Prime Min. Ariel **Sharon** decided in 2005 to pull troops and settlers out of the **Gaza Strip**, angering his own party's right wing. He formed a new party and, after being disabled by a stroke (Jan. 2006), was succeeded by an ally, Ehud **Olmert**, who led a coalition government following elections (Apr. 2006). The militant Palestinian party **Hamas** won a parliamentary majority over the long-ruling **Fatah** party (Jan. 2006).

Israel launched attacks on **Lebanon** (July 2006) in response to a raid into N Israel by Lebanon-based **Hezbollah** guerrillas; a cease-fire was declared a month later. In reaction to Hamas rocket and mortar attacks, Israel launched an offensive in the **Gaza Strip** (Dec. 2008), which killed an estimated 1,300 Palestinians. Olmert resigned as prime minister (effective Sept. 2008) amid corruption inquiries, and Feb. 2009 elections led to a coalition government headed by former Prime Min. Benjamin **Netanyahu**, a conservative. Palestinian Authority Pres. Mahmoud Abbas officially applied for full UN membership for an independent Palestinian state, Sept. 2011, but the move was strongly opposed by Israel and the U.S.

Europe. By early 2002 the **euro** was the common currency in 12 EU nations. The EU admitted 10 E European nations (May 2004); 2 more joined in Jan. 2007. A treaty to establish a new **EU constitution** was defeated (May-June 2005) by voters in France and the Netherlands. But a modified plan, known as the **Treaty of Lisbon**, came into force in Dec. 2009 after Irish voters approved it (Oct. 2009).

In Oct. 2000, Yugoslav strongman Slobodan **Milosevic** yielded power to Vojislav **Kostunica**, who had declared himself president after a disputed election. Milosevic surrendered to Serbian authorities; he went on trial (Feb. 2002) for **war crimes** allegedly committed during 1990s ethnic conflicts in the Balkans but died (Mar. 2006) before a verdict was reached. Former Bosnian Serb leader Radovan Karadzic was also arraigned on war crimes charges (July 2008). **Kosovo** unilaterally declared independence (Feb. 2008).

Germany elected its first East German and first female chancellor (Nov. 2005) in Angela **Merkel**, a Christian Democrat. **Rioting** shook France's immigrant communities in 300 cities and towns (Nov. 2005). A Danish newspaper's publication of cartoon **caricatures of Muhammad** sparked violent worldwide protests by Muslims (Jan.-Feb. 2006). **Polish** Pres. Lech **Kaczynski** and 95 others were killed in a plane crash (Apr. 2010).

British Prime Min. Tony **Blair** won reelection twice (2001, 2005), becoming the first-ever Labour prime minister to earn three straight terms. He stepped down in June 2007, to be succeeded by fellow Labourite Gordon **Brown**. But Conservatives were returned to power in a coalition government under David **Cameron** (May 2010). **France** underwent a leadership change with the election (May 2007) of conservative Nicolas **Sarkozy** as president. France rejoined NATO's military command (Apr. 2009) under Sarkozy after a break of more than 40 years. French legislation banning face-hiding **veils** in public won final passage, Sept. 2010, yielding criticism.

Vladimir **Putin**, in power in Russia since 1999, was constitutionally barred from a new term as president in 2008; his protégé, Dmitri **Medvedev**, was elected (May 2008) and named Putin prime minister. Amid accusations of official corruption and voter fraud, Putin won a third term as president, Mar. 2012. Russia and U.S. signed **New START** arms control accord (Apr. 2010). In **Ukraine**, a tainted presidential runoff election (Nov. 2004) led to the country's "orange revolution" and a recount that gave power to nationalist Viktor **Yushchenko**. But his pro-Russian opponent, Viktor **Yanukovich**, captured back the presidency in Feb. 2010.

Governments transitioning amidst Arab Spring upheavals included Egypt, Libya, and Tunisia (2011).

Africa. Ethiopia and Eritrea signed a **peace treaty** (Dec. 2000). Laurent **Kabila**, president of the **Dem. Rep. of the Congo**, was shot to death (Jan. 2001). Liberian Pres. Charles **Taylor** went into exile (Aug. 2003) as part of a deal to end a 14-year-old civil war; other accords were reached aimed at ending civil wars in **Angola** (Apr. 2002) and **Côte d'Ivoire** (Jan. 2003). **Libya** agreed (Dec. 2003) to abandon programs pursuing weapons of mass destruction.

A peace agreement in **Dem. Rep. of the Congo** (Apr. 2003) did not end violence there; the nation agreed to work with Rwanda to disarm Hutu rebels (Nov. 2007). In **Sudan** a power-sharing accord between the Muslim-led government and rebels from the Christian south was signed, Jan. 2005, giving the south limited autonomy, with a referendum on independence held in 2011. Southern Sudanese voted overwhelmingly in favor of secession and became the independent nation of South Sudan (July 2011). Rebellion in the **Darfur** area of western Sudan led to large-scale violence. Arab militias (**janjaweed**), reportedly backed by the government, were accused of displacing over 2 million people in acts bordering on **genocide**, and by Sept. 2009 more than 300,000 people had been killed. The International Criminal Court issued an arrest warrant for Sudanese Pres. Omar Hassan Ahmad al-**Bashir**, for war crimes (Mar. 2009), but he remained in power, winning reelection (Apr. 2010) when his main opponent dropped out citing fraud.

Zimbabwean Pres. Robert **Mugabe** pulled his country out of the Commonwealth (Dec. 2003) after the group reaffirmed suspension of **Zimbabwe** for alleged voter fraud. Violence sparked in **Kenya** (Jan. 2008) and Zimbabwe (Apr. 2008) after disputed elections. As Mugabe continued in power in Zimbabwe, unemployment there topped 90% and hyperinflation left the currency virtually worthless. **Guinea-Bissau**'s defense chief and then its president were assassinated in turn by rival groups (Mar. 2009); **Niger**'s president was ousted in a coup (Feb. 2010).

Arab Spring. Economic inequality, religious tensions, and government corruption and repression fueled a wave of discontent that challenged entrenched Arab regimes from the NW Africa to the Persian Gulf. Mass protests forced the ouster of Tunisian Pres. Zine al-Abidine Ben Ali, (Jan. 2011) and Egyptian Pres. Hosni Mubarak (Feb. 2011). With NATO military backing, insurgents overthrew Libyan dictator Muammar al-Qaddafi, who was killed (Oct. 2011). Syrian Pres. Bashar al-Assad launched a ferocious offensive against antigovernment protesters.

Americas and the Caribbean. The long-supreme **Institutional Revolutionary Party** lost power in **Mexico** with the election of two successive presidents from a center-right party, Vicente **Fox** and Felipe **Calderón** (July 2000, 2006). Calderón launched a crackdown on drug trafficking (Dec. 2006); from then through the end of 2010, more than 30,000 people were killed in violence fueled by warring **drug cartels.** In **Peru**, Pres. Alberto **Fujimori** stepped down during his third term (Nov. 2000) amid scandal and did not seek reelection.

In Jan. 2001, Republican George W. **Bush** was inaugurated as **U.S. president**, after one of the closest elections in U.S. history; he was reelected in Nov. 2004. Democrats claimed the White House with the Nov. 2008 election of Barack **Obama**, the first-ever black U.S. president.

In **Brazil**, reformist candidate Luis Inácio Lula **da Silva** won a runoff (Oct. 2002) to become president; his chosen successor, Dilma **Rousseff**, was elected in 2010. **Chile** was ruled by Socialist governments under Ricardo Lagos Escobar (from 2000) and Michelle **Bachelet** (from 2006), followed by conservative Sebastián **Piñera** (2010). Over 500 Chileans were killed in a Feb. 2010 earthquake. All 33 **men trapped in a mine** in N Chile were successfully rescued (Oct. 2010) after almost 10 weeks underground.

In **Venezuela**, Pres. Hugo **Chávez** regained power after a 48-hour coup (Dec. 2002) and consolidated it, in part through a referendum (Feb. 2009) that gave him new authority and eliminated presidential term limits. In **Bolivia**, Evo **Morales**, another leftist populist, won election as president (Dec. 2005) and passage of a new constitution (Jan. 2009) that gave the federal government control over resources and gave new rights to indigenous peoples. In **Honduras**, leftist opposition leader Manuel **Zelaya** was elected president (Nov. 2005) but was ousted by the military (June 2009) after he had sought constitutional changes; Porfirio (Pepe) **Lobo**, a conservative landowner, was elected (Nov. 2009) to succeed him.

Argentina was beset by economic problems; its **default** on IMF loans led (Sept. 2003) to a massive debt-refinancing agreement, but the money was repaid. **Haiti** was wracked by antigovernment protests, leading to the resignation of Jean-Bertrand **Aristide** in Feb. 2004; a UN peacekeeping mission was brought in. Haiti was struck by **tropical storms**, including Hurricane Jeanne (Sept. 2004; over 3,000 killed), and by a devastating **earthquake** (Jan. 2010) that killed more than 200,000.

For the first time in 12 years, the Liberal Party handed control of **Canada**'s government to the Conservative Party, led by Prime Min. Stephen **Harper** (Jan. 2006). After 47 years in office, Cuban Pres. Fidel **Castro** ceded administrative powers to his brother, Raúl Castro to undergo surgery (July 2006); he formally resigned in Feb. 2008.

Religion. Pope **John Paul II** died, Apr. 2005, after 26 years in the papacy; German cardinal Joseph Ratzinger was elected as his successor, taking the name **Benedict XVI**. During the decade, reports of **sexual abuse** by Catholic priests going back generations, and evidence of inaction by church officials, made news in the U.S., Ireland, Belgium, Brazil, Germany, the Netherlands, and elsewhere. The Vatican (July 2010) issued revised rules for handling sexual abuse allegations.

Science and technology. The U.S. **space shuttle** *Columbia* broke up on reentering Earth's atmosphere (Feb. 2003), killing all seven crew members. NASA space shuttle program resumed with the July 2005 launch of *Discovery*. The Phoenix *Mars Lander* verified the presence of water ice on **Mars** (June 2008).

China, Oct. 2010, unveiled the Tianhe-1A **supercomputer**, said to be the world's fastest. **Internet** penetration and access to technology expanded exponentially, as more than one-fifth of the world's population had regular web access by the decade's end. Online commerce, social networking (Facebook, 2004; Twitter, 2006), and file-sharing services became commonplace. **WikiLeaks**, a controversial organization formed in 2007, began disseminating secret government documents related to the Iraq and Afghanistan wars (Apr., July 2010).

Environment and health. The **Kyoto Protocol** took effect for 141 ratifying nations, Feb. 2005, requiring industrialized nations to achieve targeted reductions by 2012 in emissions of **greenhouse gases** linked to global warming. At a conference in Copenhagen (Dec. 2009), nations agreed only on nonbinding targets beyond 2012. A NASA report (Jan. 2010) found that 2000-09 had the **warmest average global temperatures** since modern records began in the 1880s.

The 13th International **AIDS Conference**, held in Durban, South Africa (July 2000), focused on ways of controlling AIDS in developing countries. Worldwide AIDS estimates were revised downward (Nov. 2007); they now showed new infections had peaked in the late 1990s. An epidemic of **swine flu**, or influenza A (H1N1), broke out in Mexico (Apr. 2009) and spread around the globe; World Health Organization estimated over 18,000 deaths by pandemic's conclusion (Aug. 2010).

HISTORICAL FIGURES

Note: Information accurate as of Sept. 2012.

Ancient Greeks and Romans

Greeks

Aeschines, orator, 389-314 BCE
Aeschylus, dramatist, 525-456 BCE
Aesop, fableist, c. 620-c. 560 BCE
Alcibiades, politician, 450-404 BCE
Anacreon, poet, c. 582-c. 485 BCE
Anaxagoras, philosopher, c. 500-428 BCE
Anaximander, philosopher, 611-546 BCE
Anaximenes, philosopher, c. 570-500 BCE
Antiphon, speechwriter, c. 480-411 BCE
Apollonius, mathematician, c. 265-170 BCE
Archimedes, mathematician, 287-212 BCE
Aristophanes, dramatist, c. 448-380 BCE
Aristotle, philosopher, 384-322 BCE
Athenaeus, scholar, fl. c. 200
Callicrates, architect, fl. 5th cent. BCE
Callimachus, poet, c. 305-240 BCE
Cratinus, comic dramatist, 520-421 BCE
Democritus, philosopher, c. 460-370 BCE
Demosthenes, orator, 384-322 BCE
Diodorus, historian, fl. 20 BCE
Diogenes, philosopher, 372-c. 287 BCE
Dionysius, historian, d. c. 7 BCE
Empedocles, philosopher, c. 490-430 BCE
Epicharmus, dramatist, c. 530-440 BCE
Epictetus, philosopher, c. 55-c. 135
Epicurus, philosopher, 341-270 BCE
Eratosthenes, scientist, 276-194 BCE
Euclid, mathematician, fl. c. 300 BCE
Euripides, dramatist, c. 484-406 BCE
Galen, physician, 129-216
Heraclitus, philosopher, c. 540-c. 475 BCE
Herodotus, historian, c. 484-420 BCE

Hesiod, poet, 8th cent. BCE
Hippocrates, physician, c. 460-377 BCE
Homer, poet, fl. c. 8th cent. BCE
Isocrates, orator, 436-338 BCE
Menander, dramatist, 342-292 BCE
Parmenides, philosopher, b. c. 515 BCE
Pericles, statesman, c. 495-429 BCE
Phidias, sculptor, c. 500-435 BCE
Pindar, poet, c. 518-c. 438 BCE
Plato, philosopher, c. 428-347 BCE
Plutarch, biographer, c. 46-120
Polybius, historian, c. 200-c. 118 BCE
Praxiteles, sculptor, 400-330 BCE
Pythagoras, phil., math., c. 580-c. 500 BCE
Sappho, poet, c. 610-c. 580 BCE
Simonides, poet, 556-c. 468 BCE
Socrates, philosopher, 469-399 BCE
Solon, statesman, 640-560 BCE
Sophocles, dramatist, c. 496-406 BCE
Strabo, geographer, c. 63 BCE-24 CE
Thales, philosopher, c. 634-546 BCE
Themistocles, politician, c. 524-c. 460 BCE
Theocritus, poet, c. 310-250 BCE
Theophrastus, phil., c. 372-c. 287 BCE
Thucydides, historian, fl. 5th cent. BCE
Timon, philosopher, c. 320-c. 230 BCE
Xenophon, historian, c. 434-c. 355 BCE
Zeno, philosopher, c. 335-c. 263 BCE

Romans

Ammianus, historian, c. 330-395
Apuleius, satirist, c. 124-c. 170
Boethius, scholar, c. 480-524
Caesar, Julius, leader, 100-44 BCE

Catiline, politician, c. 108-62 BCE
Cato (Elder), statesman, 234-149 BCE
Catullus, poet, c. 84-54 BCE
Cicero, orator, 106-43 BCE
Claudian, poet, c. 370-c. 404
Ennius, poet, 239-170 BCE
Gellius, author, c. 130-c. 165
Horace, poet, 65-8 BCE
Juvenal, satirist, 60-127
Livy, historian, 59 BCE-17 CE
Lucan, poet, 39-65
Lucilius, poet, c. 180-c.102 BCE
Lucretius, poet, c. 99-c. 55 BCE
Martial, epigrammatist, c. 38-c. 103
Nepos, historian, c. 100-c. 25 BCE
Ovid, poet, 43 BCE-17 CE
Persius, satirist, 34-62
Plautus, dramatist, c. 254-c. 184 BCE
Pliny the Elder, scholar, 23-79
Pliny the Younger, author, 62-113
Quintilian, rhetorician, c. 35-c. 97
Sallust, historian, 86-34 BCE
Seneca, philosopher, 4 BCE-65 CE
Silius, poet, c. 25-101
Statius, poet, c. 45-c. 96
Suetonius, biographer, c. 69-c. 122
Tacitus, historian, 56-120
Terence, dramatist, 195/185-c. 159 BCE
Tibullus, poet, c. 55-c. 19 BCE
Vergil, poet, 70-19 BCE
Vitruvius, architect, fl. 1st cent. BCE

Roman Rulers

From Romulus to the end of the Empire in the West. Rulers in the East sat in Constantinople and, for a brief period, in Nicaea, until the capture of Constantinople by the Turks in 1453, when Byzantium was succeeded by the Ottoman Empire.

The Kingdom

BCE
753 Romulus (Quirinus)
715 Numa Pompilius
673 Tullus Hostilius
641 Ancus Marcius
616 L. Tarquinius Priscus
579 Servius Tullius
534 L. Tarquinius Superbus

The Republic

509 Consulate established
509 Quaestorship instituted
498 Dictatorship introduced
494 Plebeian Tribunate created
494 Plebeian Aedileship created
444 Consular Tribunate organized
435 Censorship instituted
366 Praetorship established
366 Curule Aedileship created
362 Military Tribunate elected
326 Proconsulate introduced
311 Naval Duumvirate elected
217 Dictatorship of Fabius Maximus
133 Tribunate of Tiberius Gracchus
123 Tribunate of Gaius Gracchus
82 Dictatorship of Sulla
60 First Triumvirate formed
(Caesar, Pompeius, Crassus)
47 Dictatorship of Caesar
43 Second Triumvirate formed
(Octavianus, Antonius, Lepidus)

The Empire

27 Augustus (Octavian)
CE
14 Tiberius I
37 Caligula
41 Claudius I
54 Nero
68 Galba
69 Otho, Vitellius
69 Vespasianus

79 Titus
81 Domitianus
96 Nerva
98 Trajanus
117 Hadrianus
138 Antoninus Pius
161 Marcus Aurelius and Lucius Verus
169 Marcus Aurelius (alone)
180 Commodus
193 Pertinax; Julianus I
193 Septimius Severus
211 Caracalla and Geta
212 Caracalla (alone)
217 Macrinus
218 Elagabalus (Heliogabalus)
222 Alexander Severus
235 Maximinus I (the Thracian)
238 Gordianus I and Gordianus II;
Pupienus and Balbinus
238 Gordianus III
244 Philippus (the Arabian)
249 Decius
251 Gallus and Volusianus
253 Aemilianus
253 Valerianus and Gallienus
258 Gallienus (alone)
268 Claudius Gothicus
270 Quintillus
270 Aurelianus
275 Tacitus
276 Florianus
276 Probus
282 Carus
283 Carinus and Numerianus
286 Diocletianus and Maximianus
305 Galerius and Constantius I
306 Galerius, Maximinus II, Severus I
307 Galerius, Maximinus II,
Constantinus I, Licinius, Maxentius
311 Maximinus II, Constantinus I,
Licinius, Maxentius
314 Maximinus II, Constantinus I, Licinius
314 Constantinus I and Licinius
324 Constantinus I (the Great)

337 Constantinus II, Constans I,
Constantius II
340 Constantius II and Constans I
350 Constantius II (alone)
361 Julianus II (the Apostate)
363 Jovianus

West (Rome) and East (Constantinople)

364 Valentinianus I (West),
Valens (East)
367 Valentinianus I with Gratianus
(West), Valens (East)
375 Gratianus with Valentinianus II
(West), Valens (East)
378 Gratianus with Valentinianus II
(West), Theodosius I (East)
383 Valentinianus II (West),
Theodosius I (East)
394 Theodosius I (the Great)
395 Honorius (West), Arcadius (East)
408 Honorius (West),
Theodosius II (East)
423 Valentinianus III (West),
Theodosius II (East)
450 Valentinianus III (West),
Marcianus (East)
455 Maximus (West), Avitus (West);
Marcianus (East)
456 Avitus (West), Marcianus (East)
457 Majorianus (West), Leo I (East)
461 Severus II (West), Leo I (East)
467 Anthemius (West), Leo I (East)
472 Olybrius (West), Leo I (East)
473 Glycerius (West), Leo I (East)
474 Julius Nepos (West), Leo II (East)
475 Romulus Augustulus (West),
Zeno (East)
476 End of Empire in West with
deposing of Romulus Augustulus by
Germanic chief Odovacar, who
proclaimed self king. Odovacar
murdered by King Theodoric of
Ostrogoths, 493

Rulers of England and Great Britain

Reign began	Name	Age at death[1]
	England: Saxons and Danes	
829	Egbert, king of Wessex, won allegiance of all English	NA
839	Ethelwulf, son of Egbert, king of Wessex, Sussex, Kent, Essex	NA
858	Ethelbald, eldest son of Ethelwulf, displaced father in Wessex.	NA
860	Ethelbert, 2nd son of Ethelwulf, united Kent and Wessex.	NA
866	Ethelred I, 3rd son of Ethelwulf, king of Wessex, fought Danes	NA
871	Alfred (the Great), 4th son of Ethelwulf, defeated Danes, fortified London.	52
899	Edward (the Elder), son of Alfred, united English, claimed Scotland	55
924	Athelstan (the Glorious), eldest son of Edward, king of Mercia, Wessex	45
940	Edmund, 3rd son of Edward, king of Wessex, Mercia.	25
946	Edred, 4th son of Edward	32
955	Edwy (the Fair), eldest son of Edmund, king of Wessex.	18
959	Edgar (the Peaceful), 2nd son of Edmund, ruled all English.	32
975	Edward (the Martyr), eldest son of Edgar, murdered by stepmother.	17
978; 1014[2]	Ethelred II (the Unready), 2nd son of Edgar, married Emma of Normandy.	48
1016	Edmund II (Ironside), son of Ethelred II, king of London	27
1016	Canute (the Dane), son of Sweyn, who conquered English territory; gave Wessex to Edmund II; married Emma, Ethelred II's widow.	40
1035	Harold I (Harefoot), illegitimate son of Canute	NA
1040	Hardecanute, son of Canute by Emma, also king of Denmark	24
1042	Edward (the Confessor), son of Ethelred II, canonized 1161	62
1066	Harold II, Edward's brother-in-law, last Saxon king.	44
	England: House of Normandy	
1066	William I (the Conqueror), son of Duke Robert I of Normandy, defeated Harold II at Hastings	60
1087	William II (Rufus), 3rd son of William I, killed by arrow while hunting in possible assassination.	43
1100	Henry I (Beauclerc), youngest son of William I	67
	England: House of Blois	
1135	Stephen, son of Adela, daughter of William I, and Count of Blois.	50
	England: House of Plantagenet	
1154	Henry II, son of Geoffrey Plantagenet (Angevin) by Matilda, daughter of Henry I.	56
1189	Richard I (Coeur de Lion), son of Henry II, crusader.	42
1199	John (Lackland), son of Henry II, approved Magna Carta, 1215.	50
1216	Henry III, son of John, acceded at 9, under regency until 1227	65
1272	Edward I (Longshanks), son of Henry III	68
1307	Edward II, son of Edward I, deposed by Parliament	43
1327	Edward III (of Windsor), son of Edward II	65
1377	Richard II, grandson of Edward III, deposed	33
	England: House of Lancaster	
1399	Henry IV (of Bolingbroke), son of John of Gaunt, duke of Lancaster, son of Edward III	47
1413	Henry V, son of Henry IV, victor over French at Agincourt	34
1422; 1470	Henry VI, son of Henry V, overthrown by Edward IV in 1461 but was returned to throne in 1470. Deposed, died in Tower of London, 1471	49
	England: House of York	
1461; 1471	Edward IV, great-great-grandson of Edward III, son of duke of York. Acclaimed king by Parliament, 1461. Driven into exile in 1470 but regained throne, 1471	40
1483	Edward V, son of Edward IV, murdered in Tower of London	13
1483	Richard III, brother of Edward IV, fell in battle at Bosworth Field against Henry Tudor	32
	England: House of Tudor	
1485	Henry VII, son of Edmund Tudor, earl of Richmond, whose father had married Henry V's widow. Descended from Edward III through mother, Margaret Beaufort, via John of Gaunt. Married Elizabeth of York, eldest daughter of Edward IV, to unite Lancaster and York	53
1509	Henry VIII, 2nd son of Henry VII, by Elizabeth	56
1547	Edward VI, son of Henry VIII, by Jane Seymour, his 3rd queen. Ruled under regents, was forced to name Lady Jane Grey his successor. Council of State proclaimed her queen, July 10, 1553. Mary Tudor won Council, was proclaimed queen, July 19. Mary had Jane beheaded for treason, 1554.	16
1553	Mary I, daughter of Henry VIII, by his 1st wife, Catherine of Aragon.	43
1558	Elizabeth I, daughter of Henry VIII, by his 2nd wife, Anne Boleyn	69
	Great Britain: House of Stuart	
1603	James I (James VI of Scotland), son of Mary, Queen of Scots. First to call self king of Great Britain; this became official with Act of Union, 1707.	59
1625	Charles I, only surviving son of James I.	48
	Great Britain: Commonwealth	
1649	Declared upon execution of Charles I	
	Great Britain: Protectorate	
1653	Oliver Cromwell, served on Council of State, executive body of Commonwealth, following overthrow of monarchy. Named Lord Protector upon creation of Protectorate by 1653 Instrument of Government	59
1658	Richard Cromwell, 3rd son of Oliver Cromwell. Resigned as Lord Protector amid civil war, 1659.	86
	Great Britain: House of Stuart (restored)	
1660	Charles II, eldest son of Charles I, Restoration put him back on throne, died without issue	55
1685	James II, 2nd son of Charles I, deposed 1688.	68
1689	William III, son of William, Prince of Orange, by Mary, daughter of Charles I. Offered joint rule of throne with wife by Parliament	51
1689	Mary II, eldest daughter of James II and wife of William III, died 1694	33
1702	Anne, 2nd daughter of James II, sister-in-law of William III, assumed throne on William's death	49
	Great Britain: House of Hanover	
1714	George I, son of Elector of Hanover by Sophia, granddaughter of James I	67
1727	George II, only son of George I, married Caroline of Brandenburg.	77
1760	George III, grandson of George II, married Charlotte of Mecklenburg	81
1820	George IV, eldest son of George III, prince regent from Feb. 1811	67
1830	William IV, 3rd son of George III, married Adelaide of Saxe-Meiningen.	71
1837	Victoria, daughter of Edward, 4th son of George III; married Prince Albert of Saxe-Coburg and Gotha, 1840	81
	Great Britain: House of Saxe-Coburg and Gotha	
1901	Edward VII, eldest son of Victoria, married Alexandra, Princess of Denmark.	68

Reign began	Great Britain: House of Windsor[3]	Age at death[1]
1910	George V, 2nd son of Edward VII, married Princess Mary of Teck	70
1936	Edward VIII, eldest son of George V, acceded Jan. 20, abdicated Dec. 11..	77
1936	George VI, 2nd son of George V, married Lady Elizabeth Bowes-Lyon	56
1952	Elizabeth II, elder daughter of George VI, acceded Feb. 6	

NA = Age/birth date not certain. (1) Except where noted, year of death is year of accession of succeeding ruler. (2) King Sweyn I of Denmark invaded England in 1013 and declared himself king. Ethelred II reclaimed the throne upon Sweyn's death in 1014. (3) Name adopted by proclamation of George V, July 17, 1917.

Rulers of Scotland

Reign began	Name	Reign began	Name
846	Kenneth I MacAlpin, first Scot to rule both Scots and Picts	1306	Robert I (the Bruce), victor at Bannockburn, 1314. Treaty with England and secured throne, 1328
1005	Malcolm II Mackenneth	1329	David II, only son of Robert
1034	Duncan I, first general ruler	1371	Robert II (the Steward), grandson of Robert, son of
1040	Macbeth, seized kingdom, slain by Malcolm III MacDuncan		Walter, steward of Scotland. First of Stuart line
1057	Malcolm III MacDuncan (Canmore), eldest son of Duncan I	1390	Robert III, son of Robert II
		1406	James I, son of Robert III
1093	Donald Bane, younger brother of Malcolm III	1437	James II, son of James I
1094	Duncan II, eldest son of Malcolm III by first wife	1460	James III, eldest son of James II
1095	Donald Bane (restored)	1488	James IV, eldest son of James III
1097	Edgar, 4th son of Malcolm III and Queen Margaret	1513	James V, eldest son of James IV
1107	Alexander I, brother of Edgar	1542	Mary (Queen of Scots), daughter of James V, became
1124	David I, brother of Edgar		queen before she was 1 week old. Married Francis II,
1153	Malcolm IV (the Maiden), grandson of David I		son of King Henry II of France, 1558. Francis died,
1165	William (the Lion), brother of Malcolm IV		1560. Married her cousin, Henry Stewart, Lord Darnley,
1214	Alexander II, son of William		1565. Married James Hepburn, Earl of Bothwell, 1567.
1249	Alexander III, son of Alexander II		Imprisoned by Elizabeth I, 1568; beheaded, 1587
1286	Margaret (Maid of Norway), granddaughter of Alexander III; died 1290 at age 8. (Interregnum, 1290-92)	1567	James VI, son of Mary and Lord Darnley, became James I, king of England on Elizabeth's death, 1603.
1292	John Balliol, proclaimed king of Scotland by Edward I of England. (Interregnum, 1296-1306[1])		Legislative union of Scotland and England not official until Act of Union, 1707

(1) Edward I decreed annexation of Scotland to England, 1296. William Wallace led resistance, 1297-1305.

Prime Ministers of Great Britain

Designations in parentheses describe each government.

Cl = Coalition; C = Conservative; La = Labour; Li = Liberal; P = Peelite; T = Tory; W = Whig

Entered office	Name	Entered office	Name	Entered office	Name
1721	Sir Robert Walpole (W)[1]	1830	Earl Grey (W)	1915	Herbert H. Asquith (Cl)
1742	Earl of Wilmington (W)	1834	Viscount Melbourne (W)	1916	David Lloyd George (Cl)
1743	Henry Pelham (W)	1834	Sir Robert Peel (C)	1922	Andrew Bonar Law (C)
1754	Duke of Newcastle (W)	1835	Viscount Melbourne (W)	1923	Stanley Baldwin (C)
1756	Duke of Devonshire (W)	1841	Sir Robert Peel (C)	1924	James Ramsay MacDonald (La)
1757	Duke of Newcastle (W)	1846	Lord (later Earl) John Russell (W)	1924	Stanley Baldwin (C)
1762	Earl of Bute (T)	1852	Earl of Derby (C)	1929	James Ramsay MacDonald (La)
1763	George Grenville (W)	1852	Earl of Aberdeen (P)	1931	James Ramsay MacDonald (Cl)
1765	Marquess of Rockingham (W)	1855	Viscount Palmerston (Li)	1935	Stanley Baldwin (Cl)
1766	William Pitt the Elder (Earl of Chatham) (W)	1858	Earl of Derby (C)	1937	Neville Chamberlain (Cl)
		1859	Viscount Palmerston (Li)	1940	Winston Churchill (Cl)
1768	Duke of Grafton (W)	1865	Earl Russell (Li)	1945	Winston Churchill (Cl)
1770	Frederick North (Lord North) (T)	1866	Earl of Derby (C)	1945	Clement Attlee (La)
1782	Marquess of Rockingham (W)	1868	Benjamin Disraeli (C)	1951	Sir Winston Churchill (C)
1782	Earl of Shelburne (W)	1868	William E. Gladstone (Li)	1955	Sir Anthony Eden (C)
1783	Duke of Portland (Cl)	1874	Benjamin Disraeli (C)	1957	Harold Macmillan (C)
1783	William Pitt the Younger (T)	1880	William E. Gladstone (Li)	1963	Sir Alec Douglas-Home (C)
1801	Henry Addington (T)	1885	Marquess of Salisbury (C)	1964	Harold Wilson (La)
1804	William Pitt the Younger (T)	1886	William E. Gladstone (Li)	1970	Edward Heath (C)
1806	William Wyndham Grenville, Baron Grenville (W)	1886	Marquess of Salisbury (C)	1974	Harold Wilson (La)
		1892	William E. Gladstone (Li)	1976	James Callaghan (La)
1807	Duke of Portland (T)	1894	Earl of Rosebery (Li)	1979	Margaret Thatcher (C)
1809	Spencer Perceval (T)	1895	Marquess of Salisbury (C)	1990	John Major (C)
1812	Earl of Liverpool (T)	1902	Arthur J. Balfour (C)	1997	Tony Blair (La)
1827	George Canning (T)	1905	Sir Henry Campbell-Bannerman (Li)	2007	Gordon Brown (La)
1827	Viscount Goderich (T)			2010	David Cameron (Cl)
1828	Duke of Wellington (T)	1908	Herbert H. Asquith (Li)		

Note: The Conservative Party was formed in 1834, an outgrowth of the Tory party. (1) Walpole is commonly regarded as the first prime minister of Britain, though the title was not commonly used then and did not become official until 1905.

Prime Ministers of Canada

The prime minister is head of the party that commands support of a majority of the House of Commons, dominant chamber of Canada's bicameral Parliament. Prime minister's political party is in parentheses.

C = Conservative; Li = Liberal; PC = Progressive Conservative; U = Unionist

Entered office	Name	Entered office	Name	Entered office	Name
1867	Sir John A. Macdonald (C)	1920	Arthur Meighen (U)	1968	Pierre Elliott Trudeau (Li)
1873	Alexander Mackenzie (Li)	1921	W. L. Mackenzie King (Li)	1979	Joe Clark (PC)
1878	Sir John A. Macdonald (C)	1926[3]	Arthur Meighen (C)	1980	Pierre Elliott Trudeau (Li)
1891	Sir John J. C. Abbott (C)	1926	W. L. Mackenzie King (Li)	1984[4]	John Napier Turner (Li)
1892	Sir John S. D. Thompson (C)	1930	Richard Bedford Bennett (C)	1984	Brian Mulroney (PC)
1894	Sir Mackenzie Bowell (C)	1935	W. L. Mackenzie King (Li)	1993[5]	Kim Campbell (PC)
1896[1]	Sir Charles Tupper (C)	1948	Louis St. Laurent (Li)	1993	Jean Chrétien (Li)
1896	Sir Wilfrid Laurier (Li)	1957	John G. Diefenbaker (PC)	2003	Paul Martin (Li)
1911	Sir Robert Laird Borden (C/U)[2]	1963	Lester Bowles Pearson (Li)	2006	Stephen Harper (C)

(1) May-July. (2) Conservative 1911-17, Unionist 1917-20. (3) June-Sept. (4) June-Sept. (5) June-Oct.

Rulers of France: Kings, Queens, Presidents

Caesar to Charlemagne

Julius Caesar subdued the Gauls, native tribes of Gaul (France), 58 to 51 BCE. The Romans ruled 500 years. The Franks, a Teutonic tribe, reached the Somme from the east c. 250 CE. By the 5th century the Merovingian Franks ousted the Romans. In 451, with the help of Visigoths, Burgundians, and others, they defeated Attila and the Huns at Châlons-sur-Marne.

Childeric I became leader of the Merovingians, 458. His son Clovis I (Chlodwig, Ludwig, Louis), crowned 481, founded the dynasty. After defeating the Alemanni (Germans), 496, he was baptized a Christian and made Paris his capital. His line ruled until Childeric III was deposed, 751.

The West Merovingians were called Neustrians, the eastern Austrasians. Pepin of Herstal (687-714), major domus (head of the palace) of Austrasia, took over Neustria as dux (leader) of the Franks. Pepin's son, Charles, called Martel (the Hammer), defeated the Saracens at Tours-Poitiers, 732; was succeeded by his son, Pepin the Short, 741, who deposed Childeric III and ruled as king until 768.

His son, Charlemagne, or Charles the Great (742-814), became king of the Franks, 768, with his brother Carloman, who died 771. Charlemagne ruled France, Germany, parts of Italy, Spain, and Austria, and enforced Christianity. Crowned Emperor of the Romans by Pope Leo III in St. Peter's, Rome, Dec. 25, 800. Succeeded by son, Louis I (the Pious), 814. At death, 840, Louis left empire to sons Lothair (Roman emperor), Pepin I (king of Aquitaine), Louis II (of Germany), and Charles the Bald (France). They quarreled and, by the Treaty of Verdun, 843, divided the empire.

The date preceding each entry is year of accession.

The Carolingians

843 Charles I (the Bald), Roman emperor, 875
877 Louis II (the Stammerer), son
879 Louis III (d. 882) and Carloman, brothers
885 Charles II (the Fat), Roman emperor, 881
888 Eudes (Odo), elected by nobles
898 Charles III (the Simple), son of Louis II, defeated by Robert
922 Robert, brother of Eudes, killed in war
923 Rudolph (Raoul), duke of Burgundy
936 Louis IV, son of Charles III
954 Lothair, son, aged 13, defeated by Capet
986 Louis V (the Sluggard), left no heirs

The Capets

987 Hugh Capet, son of Hugh the Great
996 Robert II (the Pious), son
1031 Henry I, son
1060 Philip I (the Fair), son
1108 Louis VI (the Fat), son
1137 Louis VII (the Younger), son
1180 Philip II (Augustus), son, crowned at Reims
1223 Louis VIII (the Lion), son
1226 Louis IX, son, arbitrated disputes with English King Henry III; led crusades, 1248 (captured in Egypt, 1250) and 1270, when he died of plague in Tunis. Canonized as St. Louis, 1297
1270 Philip III (the Hardy), son
1285 Philip IV (the Fair), son, king at 17
1314 Louis X (the Headstrong), son. His posthumous son, John I, lived and reigned only 5 days.
1316 Philip V (the Tall), brother of Louis X
1322 Charles IV (the Fair), brother of Louis X

House of Valois

1328 Philip VI (of Valois), grandson of Philip III
1350 John II (the Good), son, retired to England
1364 Charles V (the Wise), son
1380 Charles VI (the Beloved), son
1422 Charles VII (the Victorious), son. In 1429, Joan of Arc (Jeanne d'Arc) defeated English at Orleans and Patay and had Charles crowned at Reims, July 17. Joan was captured May 24, 1430, and executed May 30, 1431, at Rouen for heresy. Charles ordered her rehabilitation, effected 1455.
1461 Louis XI (the Cruel), son, civil reformer
1483 Charles VIII (the Affable), son
1498 Louis XII, great-grandson of Charles V
1515 Francis I, of Angouleme, nephew, son-in-law. Fought 4 major wars, was patron of the arts
1547 Henry II, son, killed at joust. Husband of Catherine de Médicis (1519-89) and lover of Diane de Poitiers (1499-1566). Catherine was daughter of Lorenzo de Medici. By marriage to Henry II, she became the mother of Francis II, Charles IX, Henry III, and Queen Margaret (Reine Margot), wife of Henry IV (of Navarre).

1559 Francis II, son. Betrothed in 1548 at age 4 to Mary, Queen of Scots, aged 6; they were married 1558. Francis died 1560, aged 16. Mary returned to rule Scotland, 1561.
1560 Charles IX, brother
1574 Henry III, brother, assassinated

House of Bourbon

1589 Henry IV (of Navarre), grandson of Queen Margaret of Navarre. Made enemies when he gave tolerance to Protestants by Edict of Nantes, 1598. Married Margaret of Valois, daughter of Henry II and Catherine de Médicis; was divorced. In 1600, he married Marie de Médicis. She became regent upon Henry's assassination, 1610-17, for her son, Louis XIII; she was exiled by Richelieu, 1631.
1610 Louis XIII (the Just), son, married Anne of Austria. His chief minister (1622-42), Cardinal Richelieu, determined his policies.
1643 Louis XIV (the Sun King), son; was king 72 years. Until 1661, Anne of Austria was regent, with Cardinal Mazarin as chief minister; after that, Louis reigned absolutely. Known for his lavish court and patronage of the arts, he exhausted a prosperous country in wars for thrones and territory.
1715 Louis XV (the Beloved), great-grandson. Married a Polish princess, lost Canada to the English. His favorite mistresses, Mme. de Pompadou and Mme. Du Barry, influenced policies. Mme. Pompadour's saying "Après moi, le déluge" (After me, the deluge) often incorrectly attributed to Louis XV
1774 Louis XVI, grandson, married Marie Antoinette, daughter of Empress Maria Therese of Austria. King and queen beheaded by Revolution, 1793. Their son, called Louis XVII, died in prison, never ruled

First Republic

1792 National Convention of the French Revolution
1795 Directory, under Barras and others
1799 Consulate, Napoleon Bonaparte, first consul. Elected consul for life, 1802

First Empire

1804 Napoleon I (Napoleon Bonaparte), emperor. Josephine (de Beauharnais), empress, 1804-09; Marie Louise, empress, 1810-14. Her son, Francois (1811-32), titular king of Rome, later duke de Reichstadt and Napoleon II, never ruled. Napoleon abdicated 1814; died in exile, 1821.

House of Bourbon (restored)

1814 Louis XVIII, brother of Louis XVI, king
1824 Charles X, brother, reactionary, deposed by the July Revolution, 1830

House of Orleans

1830 Louis-Philippe (the Citizen King)

Second Republic

1848 Louis Napoleon Bonaparte, nephew of Napoleon I, president

Second Empire

1852 Napoleon III (Louis Napoleon Bonaparte), emperor; Eugenie (de Montijo), empress. Lost Franco-Prussian war, deposed 1870. Son, Prince Imperial (1856-79), died in Zulu War. Eugenie died 1920.

Third Republic: Presidents

1871 Thiers, Louis Adolphe (1797-1877)
1873 MacMahon, Marshal Patrice M. de (1808-93)
1879 Grevy, Paul J. (1807-91)
1887 Sadi-Carnot, M. (1837-94), assassinated
1894 Casimir-Perier, Jean P. P. (1847-1907)
1895 Faure, François Felix (1841-99)
1899 Loubet, Emile (1838-1929)
1906 Fallieres, C. Armand (1841-1931)
1913 Poincare, Raymond (1860-1934)
1920 Deschanel, Paul (1856-1922)
1920 Millerand, Alexandre (1859-1943)
1924 Doumergue, Gaston (1863-1937)
1931 Doumer, Paul (1857-1932), assassinated
1932 Lebrun, Albert (1871-1950), resigned 1940
1940 Vichy govt. under German armistice: Henri Philippe Petain (1856-1951), chief of state, 1940-44. Provisional govt. after liberation: Charles de Gaulle (1890-1970), Oct. 1944-Jan. 21, 1946; Felix Gouin (1884-1977), Jan. 23, 1946; Georges Bidault (1899-1983), June 24, 1946

Fourth Republic: Presidents

1947 Auriol, Vincent (1884-1966)
1954 Coty, Rene (1882-1962)

Fifth Republic: Presidents

1959 De Gaulle, Charles Andre J. M. (1890-1970)
1969 Pompidou, Georges (1911-74)
1974 Giscard d'Estaing, Valéry (1926-)
1981 Mitterrand, François (1916-96)
1995 Chirac, Jacques (1932-)
2007 Sarkozy, Nicolas (1955-)
2012 Hollande, François (1954-)

Rulers of Middle Europe; Rise and Fall of Dynasties; Rulers of Germany

Carolingian Dynasty

Charles (the Great), or Charlemagne, ruled France, Italy, and Middle Europe; established Ostmark (later Austria). Crowned Roman emperor by pope in Rome, 800 CE; died 814.

Louis I (Ludwig) (the Pious), son, crowned by Charlemagne 814; died 840.

Louis II (the German), son, succeeded to East Francia (Germany) 843-76.

Charles (the Fat), son, inherited East Francia and West Francia (France) 876. Reunited empire, crowned emperor by pope, 881; deposed 887.

Arnulf, nephew, 887-99, partition of empire.

Louis (the Child), 899-911, last direct descendant of Charlemagne.

Conrad I, duke of Franconia, first elected German king, 911-18. Founded House of Franconia.

Saxon Dynasty; First Reich

Henry I (the Fowler), duke of Saxony, 919-36.

Otto I (the Great), son, 936-73, crowned Holy Roman Emperor by pope, 962.

Otto II, son, 973-83, failed to oust Greeks and Arabs from Sicily.

Otto III, son, 983-1002, crowned emperor at 16.

Henry II (the Saint), great-grandson of Otto the Great, duke of Bavaria, 1002-24.

House of Franconia

Conrad II, 1024-39, elected king of Germany.

Henry III (the Black), son, 1039-56, deposed three popes, annexed Burgundy.

Henry IV, son, 1056-1106, regency by his mother, Agnes of Poitou. Banned by Pope Gregory VII, he did penance at Canossa.

Henry V, son, 1106-25, last of Salian Dynasty.

Lothair, duke of Saxony, 1125-37. Crowned emperor in Rome, 1134.

House of Hohenstaufen

Conrad III, duke of Swabia, 1138-52, in 2nd Crusade.

Frederick I (Barbarossa), nephew, 1152-90.

Henry VI, 1190-96, took lower Italy from Normans. Son became king of Sicily.

Philip of Swabia, brother, 1197-1208.

Otto IV, House of Welf, 1198-1215, deposed.

Frederick II, son of Henry VI, 1215-50, king of Sicily; crowned king of Jerusalem in 5th Crusade.

Conrad IV, son, 1250-54, lost lower Italy to Charles of Anjou.

Conradin, son, 1252-68, king of Jerusalem and Sicily, beheaded. Last Hohenstaufen.

(Interregnum, 1254-73. Rise of the Electors.)

Transition

Rudolph I, of Hapsburg, 1273-91, defeated King Ottocar II of Bohemia. Bequeathed duchy of Austria to son Albert.

Adolph of Nassau, 1292-98, killed in war with Albert of Austria.

Albert I, eldest son of Rudolph I, king of Germany, 1298-1308.

Henry VII, of Luxemburg, 1308-13, crowned emperor in Rome; seized Bohemia, 1310.

Louis IV, of Bavaria (Wittelsbach), 1314-47. Also elected was Frederick of Austria, 1314-30 (Hapsburg). Abolition of papal sanction for election of Holy Roman Emperor.

Charles IV, of Luxemburg, grandson of Henry VII, 1347-78, German emperor and king of Bohemia, Lombardy, Burgundy; took Mark of Brandenburg.

Wenceslaus, 1378-1400, deposed.

Rupert, duke of Palatine, 1400-10.

Sigismund, 1411-37.

Hungary

Stephen I, House of Arpad, 997-1038. Crowned king, 1000; converted Magyars; canonized 1083. After several centuries of feuds Charles Robert of Anjou became Charles I, 1308-42.

Louis I (the Great), son, 1342-82, joint ruler of Poland with Casimir III, 1370. Defeated Turks.

Mary, daughter, 1382-95, ruled with husband, Sigismund of Luxemburg, 1387-1437, also king of Bohemia. As brother of Wenceslaus he succeeded Rupert as Holy Roman Emperor, 1410.

Albert, son-in-law of Sigismund, 1438-39, also Roman emperor as Albert II (see under **Hapsburg**).

Ulaszlo I, of Poland, 1440-44.

Ladislaus V, posthumous son of Albert II, 1444-57. Janos Hunyadi acted as governor under young king, 1446-52; fought Turks, Czechs.

Matthias I (Corvinus), son of Hunyadi, 1458-90. Shared rule of Bohemia; captured Vienna, 1485. Annexed Austria, Styria, Carinthia.

Ulaszlo II, king of Bohemia, 1490-1516.

Louis II, son, aged 10, 1516-26. Wars with Suleiman, Turk. In 1527, Hungary split between Ferdinand I, Archduke of Austria, brother-in-law of Louis II, and John Zapolya of Transylvania. After Turkish invasion, 1547, Hungary split between Ferdinand, Prince John Sigismund (Transylvania), and the Turks.

House of Hapsburg

Albert V, of Austria, Hapsburg, crowned king of Hungary, Jan. 1438; Roman emperor, Mar. 1438, as Albert II; died 1439.

Frederick III, cousin, 1440-93, fought Turks.

Maximilian I, son, 1493-1519; assumed title of Holy Roman Emperor (German), 1493.

Charles V, grandson, 1519-56. King of Spain with mother co-regent; crowned Roman emperor at Aix, 1520. Confronted Luther at Worms; attempted church reform and religious conciliation; abdicated 1556.

Ferdinand I, king of Bohemia, 1526; of Hungary, 1527; disputed. German king, 1531. Crowned Roman emperor on abdication of brother Charles V, 1556.

Maximilian II, son, 1564-76.

Rudolph II, son, 1576-1612.

Matthias, brother, 1612-19, king of Bohemia and Hungary.

Ferdinand II, of Styria, king of Bohemia, 1617; of Hungary, 1618; Roman emperor, 1619. Bohemian Protestants deposed him, elected Frederick V of Palatine, starting Thirty Years War.

Ferdinand III, son, king of Hungary, 1625, Bohemia, 1627; Roman emperor, 1637. Peace of Westphalia, 1648, ended war.

Leopold I, son, 1658-1705.

Joseph I, son, 1705-11.

Charles VI, brother, 1711-40.

Maria Theresa, daughter, 1740-80, archduchess of Austria, queen of Hungary and Bohemia. Ousted pretender, Charles VII; crowned 1742. In 1745, obtained election of her husband Francis I as Roman emperor and co-regent (d. 1765). Fought Seven Years' War with Frederick II of Prussia. Mother of Marie Antoinette.

Joseph II, son, 1765-90, Roman emperor, reformer. Powers restricted by Empress Maria Theresa until her death, 1780. First partition of Poland.

Leopold II, brother, 1790-92.

Francis II, son, 1792-1835. Fought Napoleon. Proclaimed first hereditary emperor of Austria, 1804. Forced to abdicate as Roman, 1806; last use of title.

Ferdinand I, son, 1835-48, abdicated during revolution.

Austro-Hungarian Monarchy

Francis Joseph I, nephew, 1848-1916, emperor of Austria, king of Hungary. Dual monarchy of Austria-Hungary formed, 1867. After assassination of heir, Archduke Francis Ferdinand, June 28, 1914, Austrian diplomacy precipitated World War I.

Charles I, grand-nephew, 1916-18, last emperor of Austria and king of Hungary. Abdicated Nov. 11-13, 1918; died 1922.

Rulers of Prussia

Nucleus of Prussia was the Mark of Brandenburg. First margrave Albert the Bear (Albrecht), 1134-70. First Hohenzollern margrave was Frederick, burgrave of Nuremberg, 1417-40.

Frederick William (the Great Elector), 1640-88.

Frederick III, son, 1688-1713, crowned King Frederick of Prussia, 1701.

Frederick William I, son, 1713-40.

Frederick II (the Great), son, 1740-86, annexed Silesia, part of Austria.

Frederick William II, nephew, 1786-97.

Frederick William III, son, 1797-1840; Napoleonic wars.

Frederick William IV, son, 1840-61. Uprising of 1848 and first parliament and constitution.

Second and Third Reich

William I, brother, 1861-88. Annexation of Schleswig and Hanover; Franco-Prussian war, 1870-71. Proclamation of German Reich, Jan. 18, 1871, at Versailles; William, German emperor (Deutscher Kaiser); Bismarck, chancellor.

Frederick III, son, 1888.

William II, son, 1888-1918, led Germany in World War I. Abdicated as German emperor and king of Prussia, Nov. 9, 1918. Died in exile in Netherlands, June 4, 1941. Minor rulers of Bavaria, Saxony, Wurttemberg also abdicated.

Germany proclaimed republic at Weimar, July 1, 1919. Presidents included Frederick Ebert, 1919-25; Paul von Hindenburg-Beneckendorff, 1925, reelected 1932, died Aug. 2, 1934. Adolf Hitler, chancellor, chosen successor as Leader-Chancellor (Führer-Reichskanzler) of Third Reich. Annexed Austria, Mar. 1938. Precipitated World War II, 1939-45. Committed suicide Apr. 30, 1945.

Germany After 1945

Following World War II, Germany was split between democratic West and Soviet-dominated East. West German chancellors: Konrad Adenauer, 1949-63; Ludwig Erhard, 1963-66; Kurt Georg Kiesinger, 1966-69; Willy Brandt, 1969-74; Helmut Schmidt, 1974-82; Helmut Kohl, 1982-90. East German Communist party leaders: Walter Ulbricht, 1946-71; Erich Honecker, 1971-89; Egon Krenz, 1989-90.

Germany reunited Oct. 3, 1990. Post-reunification chancellors: Helmut Kohl, 1990-98; Gerhard Schröder, 1998-2005; Angela Merkel, 2005- .

Rulers of Poland

House of Piasts

Mieszko I, 963-92; Poland Christianized 966. Expansion under three Boleslavs: Boleslav I, son, 992-1025, crowned king 1024; Boleslav II, great-grandson, 1058-79, exiled after killing bishop Stanislav, who became chief patron saint of Poland; Boleslav III, nephew, 1106-38, divided Poland among four sons, eldest suzerain.

Feudal division, 1138-1306. Founding in Prussia of military order Teutonic Knights, 1226. Invasion by Tartars/Mongols, 1226.

Vladislav I, 1306-33, reunited most Polish territories; crowned king 1320. Casimir III (the Great), son, 1333-70, developed economy, cultural life, foreign policy.

House of Anjou

Louis I, nephew, 1370-82, was also Louis I of Hungary.

Jadwiga, daughter, 1384-99, married Jagiello, grand duke of Lithuania, 1386.

House of Jagiellonians

Vladislav II, 1386-1434. Christianized Lithuania; founded personal union between Poland and Lithuania. Defeated Teutonic Knights at Grunwald, 1410.

Vladislav III, son, 1434-44, simultaneously king of Hungary. Fought Turks; killed 1444 in Battle of Varna.

Casimir IV, brother, 1446-92, competed with Hapsburgs; put son Vladislav on throne of Bohemia, later also of Hungary (Ulaszlo II).

Sigismund I, son, 1506-48, patronized science and arts; his and son's reign "Golden Age."

Sigismund II, son, 1548-72, established 1569 real union of Poland and Lithuania (lasted until 1795).

Elective Kings

Polish nobles in 1572 proclaimed Poland a republic headed by king to be elected by whole nobility.

Stephen Batory, 1576-86, duke of Transylvania, married Ann, sister of Sigismund II August. Fought Russians.

Sigismund III Vasa, nephew of Sigismund II, 1587-1632. 1592-98 also king of Sweden. Generals fought Russians, Turks.

Vladislav II Vasa, son, 1632-48. Fought Russians.

John II Casimir Vasa, brother, 1648-68 (abdicated). Fought Cossacks, Swedish (the "Deluge"), Russians, Turks, Tatars.

John III Sobieski, 1674-96. Won Vienna from besieging Turks, 1683.

Stanislav II, 1764-95, last king. Encouraged reforms; first modern constitution in Europe, 1791. Poland partitioned among Russia (1772), Prussia (1793), Austria (1795). Unsuccessful insurrection against foreign invasion, 1794, under Thaddeus Kosciusko, American-Polish general.

1795-1918: Poland Under Foreign Rule

Grand Duchy of Warsaw created by Napoleon I, Frederick August of Saxony grand duke, 1807-15.

Congress of Vienna proclaimed part of Poland kingdom in personal union with Russia, 1815.

Polish uprisings against Russia (1830, 1863) and Austria (1846, 1848) all repressed.

1918-39: Second Republic

Head of State Jozef Pilsudski, 1918-22. Presidents: Gabriel Narutowicz, 1922, assassinated; Stanislav Wojciechowski, 1922-26, abdicated after Pilsudski's coup d'état; Ignacy Moscicki, 1926-39, ruled (with Pilsudski until his death, 1935) as virtual dictator.

1939-45: Poland Under Foreign Occupation

Nazi and Soviet invasion, Sept. 1939. Polish government-in-exile first in France, then in England. Vladislav Raczkiewicz, president; Gen. Vladislav Sikorski, then Stanislav Mikolajczyk, prime ministers. Soviet-sponsored Polish Committee of National Liberation proclaimed at Lublin, July 1944, transformed into government Jan. 1, 1945.

Poland After 1945

Communist party ruled in Poland until Aug. 1989, when democratic Solidarity party, led by Lech Walesa, gained control of government. Walesa was elected president in 1990, but lost the office to former communist Aleksander Kwasniewski in 1995.

He was succeeded by Lech Kaczynski, 2005, who died in a plane crash in 2010. Bronislaw Komorowski was inaugurated Aug. 6, 2010, for a 5-year term. (Komorowski and Grzegorz Schetyna served as acting presidents, respectively, before Komorowski was inaugurated.) Donald Tusk was sworn in as prime minister in Nov. 2007, taking over from Jaroslaw Kaczynski, the then-president's identical twin.

Rulers of Denmark, Sweden, Norway

Denmark

Earliest rulers invaded Britain. King Canute, who ruled in London 1016-35, was most famous. The Valdemars furnished kings until the 15th century. In 1282, the Danes won the first national assembly, Danehof, from King Erik V.

Most redoubtable medieval character was Margaret (b. 1353), daughter of Valdemar IV, married at 10 to King Haakon VI of Norway. In 1376, she had her first infant son, Olaf, made king of Denmark. After his death, 1387, she was regent of Denmark and Norway. In 1388, Sweden accepted her as sovereign. In 1389, she made her grand-nephew, Duke Erik of Pomerania, titular king of Denmark, Sweden, and Norway, with herself as regent. In 1397, she effected the Union of Kalmar of the three kingdoms and had Erik VII crowned. In 1439, the three kingdoms deposed him and elected, 1440, Christopher of Bavaria king (Christopher III). On his death, 1448, the union broke up.

Succeeding rulers were unable to enforce their claims as rulers of Sweden until 1520, when Christian II conquered Sweden. He was thrown out 1522, and in 1523, Gustavus Vasa united Sweden. Denmark continued to dominate Norway until the Napoleonic wars when Frederick VI, 1808-39, joined the Napoleonic cause after Britain destroyed the Danish fleet, 1807. In 1814, he was forced to cede Norway to Sweden and Helgoland to Britain, receiving Lauenburg. Succession: Christian VIII, 1839; Frederick VII, 1848; Christian IX, 1863; Frederick VIII, 1906; Christian X, 1912; Frederick IX, 1947; Margrethe II, 1972.

Sweden

Early kings ruled at Uppsala but did not dominate the country. Sverker, c. 1130-c. 1156, united the Swedes and Goths. In 1435, Sweden obtained the Riksdag, or parliament. After the Union of Kalmar, 1397, the Danes either ruled or harried the country until Christian II of Denmark conquered it anew, 1520. This led to a rising under Gustavus Vasa, who ruled Sweden, 1523-60, and established an independent kingdom. Charles IX, 1599-1611, crowned 1604, conquered Moscow. Gustavus II Adolphus, 1611-32, was called the

Lion of the North. Later rulers: Christina, 1632; Charles X Gustavus, 1654; Charles XI, 1660; Charles XII (invader of Russia and Poland, defeated at Poltava, June 28, 1709), 1697; Ulrika Eleanora, sister, elected queen, 1718; Frederick I (of Hesse), her husband, 1720; Adolphus Frederick, 1751; Gustavus III, 1771; Gustavus IV Adolphus, 1792; Charles XIII, 1809. (Union with Norway began 1814.) Charles XIV John (born Jean Bernadotte, made prince of Pontecorvo by Napoleon, elected 1810 to succeed Charles XIII, 1818). Charles XIV John founded the present dynasty, the House of Bernadotte: Oscar I, 1844; Charles XV, 1859; Oscar II, 1872; Gustavus V, 1907; Gustav VI Adolf, 1950; Carl XVI Gustaf, 1973.

Norway

Overcoming many rivals, Harald Haarfager, 872-930, conquered Norway, Orkneys, and Shetlands. Olaf I, great-grandson, 995-1000, brought Christianity into Norway, Iceland, and Greenland. In 1035, Magnus the Good also became king of Denmark. Haakon V, 1299-1319, had married his daughter to Erik of Sweden. Their son, Magnus, became ruler of Norway and Sweden at 6. His son, Haakon VI, married Margaret of Denmark; their son Olaf IV became king of Norway and Denmark, followed by Margaret's regency and the Union of Kalmar, 1397.

In 1450, Norway became subservient to Denmark. Christian IV, 1588-1648, founded Christiania, now Oslo. After Napoleonic wars, when Denmark ceded Norway to Sweden, a strong nationalist movement forced recognition of Norway as an independent kingdom united with Sweden under the Swedish kings, 1814-1905. In 1905, the union was dissolved, and Prince Charles of Denmark became Haakon VII (d. 1957). Succession: Olav V, son, died 1991; Harald V, son.

Rulers of the Netherlands and Belgium

The Netherlands (Holland)

William Frederick, Prince of Orange, led a revolt against French rule, 1813; crowned king, 1815. Belgium seceded Oct. 4, 1830, after a revolt. The secession was ratified by the two kingdoms by treaty, Apr. 19, 1839.

Succession: William II, son, 1840; William III, son, 1849; Wilhelmina, daughter of William III and Princess Emma of Waldeck, 1890; Wilhelmina abdicated, Sept. 4, 1948, in favor of daughter, Juliana. Juliana abdicated, Apr. 30, 1980, in favor of daughter, Beatrix.

Belgium

A national congress elected Prince Leopold of Saxe-Coburg as king. He took the throne July 21, 1831, as Leopold I.

Succession: Leopold II, son, 1865; Albert I, nephew, 1909; Leopold III, son, 1934; Prince Charles, regent 1944; Leopold returned 1950, yielded powers to son Baudouin, prince royal, Aug. 6, 1950, before abdicating July 16, 1951. Baudouin I took throne July 17, 1951; died July 31, 1993. Succeeded by Albert II, brother.

Rulers of Modern Italy

After the fall of Napoleon in 1814, the Congress of Vienna, 1815, restored Italy as a political patchwork, comprising the Kingdom of Naples and Sicily, the Papal States, and smaller units. Piedmont and Genoa were awarded to Sardinia, ruled by King Victor Emmanuel I of Savoy.

United Italy emerged under the leadership of Camillo, Count di Cavour (1810-61), Sardinian prime minister. Agitation was led by Giuseppe Mazzini (1805-72) and Giuseppe Garibaldi (1807-82), soldier. Victor Emmanuel I abdicated 1821. After a brief regency for a brother, Charles Albert was king, 1831-49; abdicated upon defeat by the Austrians at Novara. Succeeded by Victor Emmanuel II, 1849-61.

In 1859, France forced Austria to cede Lombardy to Sardinia, which gave rights to Savoy and Nice to France. In 1860, Garibaldi led 1,000 volunteers in a campaign, took Sicily, and expelled the king of Naples. In 1860, the House of Savoy annexed Tuscany, Parma, Modena, Romagna, the Two Sicilys, the Marches, and Umbria. Victor Emmanuel assumed the title of king of Italy at Turin Mar. 17, 1861.

In 1866, Victor Emmanuel allied with Prussia in the Austro-Prussian War, and with Prussia's victory, received Venetia. On Sept. 20, 1870, his troops under Gen. Raffaele Cadorna entered Rome and took over the Papal States, ending the temporal power of the Roman Catholic Church.

Succession: Umberto I, 1878, assassinated 1900; Victor Emmanuel III, 1900, abdicated 1946, died 1947; Humbert II, 1946, ruled a month. In 1921, Benito Mussolini (1883-1945) formed the Fascist party; he became prime minister Oct. 31, 1922. He entered World War II as an ally of Hitler. He was deposed July 25, 1943.

At a plebiscite June 2, 1946, Italy voted for a republic; Premier Alcide de Gasperi became chief of state June 13, 1946. On June 28, 1946, the Constituent Assembly elected Liberal Enrico de Nicola, provisional president. Successive presidents: Luigi Einaudi, elected May 11, 1948; Giovanni Gronchi, Apr. 29, 1955; Antonio Segni, May 6, 1962; Giuseppe Saragat, Dec. 28, 1964; Giovanni Leone, Dec. 29, 1971; Alessandro Pertini, July 9, 1978; Francesco Cossiga, July 3, 1985; Oscar Luigi Scalfaro, May 28, 1992; Carlo Azeglio Ciampi, May 18, 1999; Giorgio Napolitano, May 15, 2006.

Rulers of Spain

From 8th to 11th centuries, Spain was dominated by the Moors (Arabs and Berbers). The Christian reconquest established small kingdoms (Asturias, Aragon, Castile, Catalonia, Leon, Navarre, and Valencia). In 1474, Isabella (1451-1504), became Queen of Castile and Leon. Her husband, Ferdinand (1452-1516), inherited Aragon, 1479, with Catalonia, Valencia, and the Balearic Islands, became Ferdinand V of Castile. By Isabella's request Pope Sixtus IV established the Inquisition, 1478. Last Moorish kingdom, Granada, fell 1492. Columbus opened New World of colonies, 1492. Isabella was succeeded by daughter, Juana (the Mad), but Ferdinand ruled until his death.

Charles I (b. 1500), son of Juana, grandson of Ferdinand and Isabella, and of Maximilian I of Hapsburg, succeeded later as Holy Roman Emperor, Charles V, 1520; abdicated 1556. Philip II, son, 1556-98, inherited only Spanish throne; conquered Portugal, fought Turks, sent Armada against England. Married to Mary I of England, 1554-58. Succession: Philip III, 1598-1621; Philip IV, 1621-65; Charles II, 1665-1700, left Spain to Philip of Anjou, grandson of Louis XIV, who as Philip V, 1700-46, founded Bourbon dynasty; Ferdinand VI, 1746-59; Charles III, 1759-88; Charles IV, 1788-1808, abdicated.

Napoleon now dominated politics and made his brother Joseph king of Spain, 1808, but the Spanish ousted him in 1813. Ferdinand VII, 1808, 1814-33, lost American colonies (except Cuba, Puerto Rico); succeeded by Isabella II, daughter, aged 3, with wife Maria Christina of Naples regent until 1843. Isabella deposed by revolution, 1868. Amadeo of Savoy elected king by the Cortes (parliament), 1870; abdicated 1873. First republic, 1873-74. Alfonso XII, son of Isabella, 1875-85. Alfonso XIII, his posthumous son, with his mother, Queen Maria Christina, regent. Spanish-American War, 1898; Spain lost Cuba, gave up Puerto Rico, Philippines, Sulu Isls., Marianas. Alfonso took throne, 1902, aged 16; married British Princess Victoria Eugenia of Battenberg, 1906. Dictatorship of Primo de Rivera, 1923-30, precipitated revolution of 1931; Alfonso agreed to leave without formal abdication. Monarchy abolished; the second republic established with socialist backing. Niceto Alcala Zamora was president until 1936, when Manuel Azaña was chosen.

In July 1936, the army in Morocco revolted against the government and Gen. Francisco Franco led the troops into Spain. The revolution succeeded by Feb. 1939, when Azaña resigned. Franco became chief of state, with provisions that if he was incapacitated, the Regency Council by two-thirds vote could propose a king to the Cortes, which needed to have a two-thirds majority to elect him.

Alfonso XIII died in Rome, 1941, aged 54. His property and citizenship had been restored.

A law restoring the monarchy was approved in a 1947 referendum. Prince Juan Carlos (b. 1938), grandson of Alfonso XIII, was designated by Franco and the Cortes in 1969 as future king and chief of state. Franco died in office, Nov. 20, 1975; Juan Carlos I proclaimed king, Nov. 22.

Rulers of Russia; Leaders of the USSR and Russian Federation

First ruler to consolidate Slavic tribes was Rurik, leader of the Russians who established himself at Novgorod, 862 CE. He and his immediate successors had Scandinavian affiliations. They moved to Kiev after 972 and ruled as dukes of Kiev. In 988, Vladimir was converted and adopted the Byzantine Greek Orthodox service, later modified by Slav influences. Important as organizer and lawgiver was Yaroslav, 1019-54, whose daughters married kings of Norway, Hungary, and France. His grandson, Vladimir II (Monomakh), 1113-25, was progenitor of several rulers, but in 1169, Andrew Bogolubski overthrew Kiev and began the line known as grand dukes of Vladimir.

Of the grand dukes of Vladimir, Alexander Nevsky, 1246-63, had a son, Daniel, first to be called duke of Muscovy (Moscow), 1263-1303. His successors became grand dukes of Muscovy. After Dmitri III Donskoi defeated the Tatars in 1380, they also became grand dukes of all Russia. Tatar independence and considerable territorial expansion were achieved under Ivan III, 1462-1505.

Tsars of Muscovy: Ivan III was referred to in church ritual as tsar. He married Sofia, niece of the last Byzantine emperor. Succession: Basil III, died in 1533 when son Ivan was only 3. Ivan IV (the Terrible), crowned 1547 as Tsar of all the Russias, ruled until 1584. Feodor I, son, 1584-98, whose rule was weak; Boris Godunov had control. The dynasty died, and after years of tribal strife and intervention by Polish and Swedish armies, the Russians united under 17-year-old Michael Romanov, distantly related to Ivan IV's first wife. He ruled 1613-45, establishing the Romanov line. Fourth ruler after Michael was Peter I.

Tsars, or emperors, of Russia (Romanovs): Peter I (the Great), 1682-1725, took title of emperor in 1721. Succession: Catherine, his widow, 1725; Peter II, his grandson, 1727; Anne, Duchess of Courland, daughter of Peter the Great's brother, Tsar Ivan V, 1730; Ivan VI, great-grandson of Ivan V, 1740; while still a child, kept in prison and murdered, 1764; Elizabeth, daughter of Peter I, 1741; Peter III, grandson of Peter I, 1761, deposed 1762 for his consort, Catherine II (the Great), former princess of Anhalt Zerbst (Germany); Paul I, son, 1796, killed 1801; Alexander I, son, 1801, defeated Napoleon; Nicholas I, brother, 1825; Alexander II, son, 1855, assassinated 1881 by terrorists; Alexander III, son, 1881. Nicholas II, son, 1894-1917, last tsar of Russia, was forced to abdicate by the March 1917 Revolution that followed losses to Germany in WWI. The tsar, empress, tsarevich (crown prince), and tsar's four daughters were murdered by the Bolsheviks in Yekaterinburg, July 16, 1918.

Provisional government: premiers, Prince Georgi Lvov, followed by Alexander Kerensky, 1917.

Union of Soviet Socialist Republics

Bolshevik Revolution, Nov. 7, 1917, removed Kerensky from power; council of People's Commissars formed. Lenin (Vladimir Ilyich Ulyanov) became premier, died Jan. 21, 1924. Aleksei Rykov (executed 1938) and V. M. Molotov held the office, but actual ruler was Joseph Stalin (Joseph Vissarionovich Dzhugashvili), general secretary of the Central Committee of the Communist Party. Stalin became president of the Council of Ministers (premier) May 7, 1941; died Mar. 5, 1953. Succeeded by Georgi M. Malenkov as head of the Council and premier. Malenkov also briefly served as first secretary of Central Committee before giving up position to Nikita S. Khrushchev. Malenkov resigned Feb. 8, 1955, became deputy premier, was dropped July 3, 1957. Marshal Nikolai A. Bulganin became premier Feb. 8, 1955, was demoted, and Khrushchev became premier Mar. 27, 1958.

Khrushchev was ousted Oct. 14-15, 1964, replaced by Leonid I. Brezhnev as first secretary of the party and by Aleksei N. Kosygin as premier. On June 16, 1977, Brezhnev also took office as president. He died Nov. 10, 1982; two days later, the Central Committee elected former KGB head Yuri V. Andropov president. Andropov died Feb. 9, 1984. On Feb. 13, Konstantin U. Chernenko chosen by Central Committee as its general secretary. Chernenko died Mar. 10, 1985. Mar. 11, he was succeeded as general secretary by Mikhail Gorbachev, who replaced Andrei Gromyko as president on Oct. 1, 1988. Gorbachev resigned Dec. 25, 1991, and the Soviet Union officially disbanded the next day. Each of the 15 former Soviet constituent republics became independent.

Post-Soviet Russia

Boris Yeltsin was sworn in July 10, 1991, as Russia's first elected president. With the Dec. 1991 dissolution of the Soviet Union, Russia (officially Russian Federation) became a founding member of the Commonwealth of Independent States. On Dec. 31, 1999, Yeltsin stepped down as president; he named Vladimir Putin his interim successor. Putin won a presidential election Mar. 26, 2000, and was reelected Mar. 14, 2004. Because Russia's constitution limits presidents to two terms of rule, Putin had to relinquish his office in 2008. His successor, Dmitry Medvedev, was sworn in May 7, 2008. A day later, Medvedev's nomination of Putin as prime minister was confirmed. Putin returned to the presidency in 2012.

Leaders in the South American Wars of Liberation

Sebastián Francisco de Miranda (1750-1816), José de San Martín (1778-1850), and Simón Bolívar (1783-1830) led early 19th-century struggles of South American nations to free themselves from Spain. All three, and their contemporaries, operated in periods of factional strife.

Miranda, a Venezuelan who had served with the French in the American Revolution and commanded parts of the French Revolutionary armies in the Netherlands, attempted to start a revolt in Venezuela in 1806 but failed. In 1810, with British and American backing, he returned and was briefly dictator, until the British withdrew their support. In 1812, he was overcome by royalists in Venezuela and taken prisoner. He died in a Spanish prison.

San Martín was born in Argentina and during 1789-1811, served in campaigns of the Spanish armies in Europe and Africa. He first joined the independence movement in Argentina in 1812. In 1817, he invaded Chile with 4,000 men over the mountain passes. He and Gen. Bernardo O'Higgins (1778-1842) defeated the Spaniards at Chacabuco, 1817. O'Higgins was named Liberator and became first director of Chile, 1817-23. In 1821, San Martín occupied Lima and Callao, Peru, and became protector of Peru.

Bolívar was born in Venezuela, the son of an aristocratic family. He first served under Miranda in 1812. In 1813, he captured Caracas, where he was named Liberator. Forced out the following year by civil strife, he led a campaign that captured Bogota in 1814. In 1817, he was again in control of Venezuela and was named dictator. He organized Nueva Granada with the help of Gen. Francisco de Paula Santander (1792-1840). By joining Nueva Granada, Venezuela, and the area that is now Panama and Ecuador, the republic of Colombia was formed, with Bolívar as president. After numerous setbacks, he decisively defeated the Spaniards in the Second Battle of Carabobo, Venezuela, June 24, 1821.

In May 1822, Gen. Antonio Jose de Sucre, Bolívar's lieutenant, took Quito. Bolívar went to Guayaquil to confer with San Martín, who resigned as protector of Peru. With a new army of Colombians and Peruvians, Bolívar defeated the Spaniards in a battle at Junin in 1824 and cleared Peru.

De Sucre organized Charcas (Upper Peru) as Republica Bolívar (now Bolivia) and acted as president in place of Bolívar, who wrote its constitution. De Sucre defeated the Spanish faction of Peru at Ayacucho, Dec. 19, 1824.

Continued civil strife finally caused the Colombian federation to break apart. Santander turned against Bolívar, but the latter defeated and banished him. In 1828, Bolívar gave up the presidency he had held precariously for 14 years. He died from tuberculosis Dec. 17, 1830. He is buried in the national pantheon in Caracas.

Governments of China

Where dynastic dates overlap, the rulers or events referred to appeared in different areas of China.

Years in power	Government
c. 1994-c. 1766 BCE	Hsia dynasty, first hereditary Chinese dynasty
c. 1766-c. 1027 BCE	Shang dynasty
c. 1027-770 BCE	Western Chou dynasty, capital near present-day Xi'an
770-256 BCE	Eastern Chou dynasty, new capital established at Luoyang
403-221 BCE	Period of the Warring States
221-206 BCE	Ch'in dynasty, quasi-feudal states unified for first time; name of China derived from this dynasty
206 BCE-9 CE	Earlier, or Western Han dynasty, founded by rebel leader Liu Pang; zenith of power under Emperor Wu Ti, 140-87 BCE, Chinese state expanded
9-23	Hsin dynasty, established by courtier Wang Mang, who deposed infant emperor for whom he had been acting as regent
25-220	Later, or Eastern Han dynasty
220-265[1]	Wei dynasty, established by son of Han general Ts'ao Ts'ao
221-263[1]	Shu Han dynasty in SW China
222-280[1]	Wu dynasty in SE China
265-317	Western Chin dynasty, established by Ssu-ma Yen, Wei dynasty general
317-420	Eastern Chin dynasty, established by prince of Ssu-ma family
420-589	Southern dynasties, four short-lived dynasties with capital at Chien-k'ang (present-day Nanjing)
589-618	Sui dynasty, reunified China; first emperor was Yang Chien, military servant who usurped throne of non-Chinese Northern Chou, 581
618-906	T'ang dynasty, founded by Li Yuan, who led rebellion against the Sui. Early rulers included former imperial concubine Empress Wu, 683-705; Hsuan Tsung, 712-56
907-960	Five Dynasties, period of disunion with short-lived dynasties in N China, 10 independent states mostly in S China
907-1125	Liao dynasty, of Khitan Mongols, capital at Yen-ching (present-day Beijing)
960-1126	Northern Sung dynasty, established by military leader Chao K'uang-yin, capital at Kaifeng
1122-1234	Chin dynasty, of Juchen people of Manchuria; drove Sung out of N China
1127-1279	Southern Sung dynasty, capital at Lin-an (present-day Hangzhou)
1279-1368	Yuan dynasty, of Mongols; Kublai Khan, grandson of Genghis Khan, high point of Mongol power
1368-1644	Ming dynasty, founded by rebel leader Chu Yuan-chang, former Buddhist monk. Country again under Chinese rule, capital in present-day Nanjing, then Beijing after defeat of Mongolian tribes
1644-1912	Manchu, or Ch'ing dynasty, under Manchu rule with capital at Chiang-ning (present-day Nanjing). Power of Chinese empire reached highest point in its 2,000-year history. Last imperial dynasty; Hsuan T'ung, or Pu Yi, last emperor. Sun Yat-sen led revolution, 1911. Republic of China formed, 1912
1912-1949	Rep. of China, Gen. Yüan Shih-k'ai elected first president. Power passed to provincial warlords with Yüan's death, 1916. Gen. Chiang Kai-shek sought to reunify China under Kuomintang (Nationalist party) rule, 1926; Kuomintang established new national government at Nanjing, 1928. War with Japan, then civil war, led to Nationalist authority collapse, Communist declaration of People's Rep. of China, 1949

(1) Also known as the period of the Three Kingdoms because of warfare between the Wei, Shu Han, and Wu dynasties.

Leaders of People's Republic of China Since 1949

Name	Title/position, years in power
Mao Zedong	Chairman, 1949-59; Chinese Communist Party (CPC) Chairman, 1949-76
Zhou Enlai	Premier, 1949-76; foreign minister, 1949-76
Deng Xiaoping	Deputy Premier, 1952-66, 1973-76; "paramount leader," 1977-97
Liu Shaoqi	Chairman, 1959-68
Hua Guofeng	Premier, 1976-80; CPC Chairman, 1976-81
Hu Yaobang	CPC General Secretary, 1980-87; CPC Chairman 1981-82
Zhao Ziyang	Premier, 1980-87; CPC General Secretary, 1987-89
Li Xiannian	President, 1983-88
Yang Shangkun	President, 1988-93
Li Peng	Premier, 1988-98
Jiang Zemin	CPC General Secretary, 1989-2002; President, 1993-2003
Zhu Rongji	Premier, 1998-2003
Hu Jintao	CPC General Secretary, 2002- ; President, 2003-
Wen Jiabao	Premier, 2003-

Historical Periods of Japan

Years in power	Period	Founding event
c. 300-592	Yamato	Conquest of Yamato plain, c. 300 CE
592-710	Asuka	Accession of Empress Suiko, 592
710-794	Nara	Heijo (Nara) completed, 710; capital moved to Nagaoka, 784
794-1185	Heian	Heian (Kyoto) completed, 794
858-1160	Fujiwara	Fujiwara-no-Yoshifusa became regent, 858
1160-1185	Taira	Taira-no-Kiyomoro assumed control, 1160; Minamoto-no-Yoritomo victor over Taira, 1185
1192-1333	Kamakura	Yoritomo became shogun, 1192
1334-1392	Namboku	Emperor Godaigo restored, 1334; established Southern Court at Yoshino, 1336
1392-1573	Muromachi	Unification of Southern and Northern Courts, 1392
1467-1600	Sengoku	Onin war began, 1467
1573-1603	Momoyama	Oda Nobunaga entered Kyoto, 1568, deposed last Ashikaga shogun, 1573. Tokugawa Ieyasu victor at Sekigahara, 1600
1603-1867	Edo	Ieyasu became shogun, 1603
1868-1912	Meiji	Emperor Mutsuhito (Meiji) ascended throne, 1867; Meiji Restoration and Charter Oath, 1868
1912-1926	Taisho	Accession of Emperor Yoshihito, 1912
1926-1989	Showa	Accession of Emperor Hirohito, 1926
1989-	Heisei	Accession of Emperor Akihito, 1989

WORLD EXPLORATION AND GEOGRAPHY
Early Explorers of the Western Hemisphere
Reviewed by G. A. Clark, Ph.D., Aug. 2008

In light of recent discoveries, theories about how and when the first people arrived in the Western Hemisphere are being reconsidered. Genetic evidence suggests that beginning around 14,000 years before the present (BP), the earliest immigrants crossed a 1,000-km wide land bridge between Siberia and Alaska in small groups and spread rapidly south through the Americas, arriving at S America's southern tip by c. 10,700 BP. Kennewick Man, found in 1996 in Washington's Columbia River Gorge, dates to 9,600-9,200 BP, and Luzia, dating to 11,500 BP from Brazil, are examples of these early arrivals. Modern Native Americans appear to be descended from peoples indigenous to N and central Asia who arrived in subsequent waves of migration. A growing body of genetic, skeletal, and linguistic evidence documents their migration throughout the Americas.

Archaeologists have confirmed evidence of habitation by 12,900 BP at sites located on the shores of ancient lakes at an elevation of 17,400 ft in Chile's Atacama Desert. There is also growing support for the settlement of Chile's Monte Verde site, dated to c. 12,500 BP, and eight other 13th-millennium sites in Brazil, Chile, and Argentina. One theory on their migration holds that a glacier covered much of N America from c. 20,000 to 13,000 BP, so those who settled in S America might have traveled there in small boats skirting the pack ice along the W coast, or spread from N to S America through an "ice-free corridor" in what today is western Canada. Other theories hold that they arrived before continental glaciation blocked migration from the north, or migrated from Iberia in skin boats. Controversial skeletal evidence from a burial at Santana do Riacho in Brazil (9,460 BP) suggests that some of the early immigrants who came via the land bridge from Siberia may have originated in Africa.

Long before Europeans arrived, the Americas were—for the most part—populated by hunter-gatherers and small-scale horticulturalists. In a few areas (SE U.S., Mesoamerica, coastal Peru and Chile), complex chiefdoms and state-level societies had appeared. Irrigation canals dating to 4,700 BP provide evidence for the origins of large-scale agriculture along the western slopes of Peru's Andes Mountains. The earliest known state in the Americas occupied a 700-sq-mi area spanning four river valleys in coastal Peru between 3,500 and 500 BP.

The Norse (Vikings sailing out of Iceland and Greenland), led by Leif Ericson, are usually credited with having been the first Europeans to reach America, with at least five voyages occurring about 1000 CE to areas they called Helluland, Markland, and Vinland—possibly what are known today as Baffin Island, Labrador, and either Newfoundland or somewhere farther south in New England. L'Anse aux Meadows, on the northern tip of Newfoundland, is the only documented settlement, with evidence of a small village with a church dating to c. 1000 CE. The Norse tried to import farming and herding economies, but these efforts failed after a few centuries, and Greenland and Newfoundland were abandoned by Europeans.

Sustained contact between the hemispheres began with the first voyage of Christopher Columbus (born Cristoforo Colombo, c. 1451, near Genoa, Italy). Columbus made four voyages to the New World while sailing for the Spanish monarchs Ferdinand II and Isabella. He left Palos, Spain, Aug. 3, 1492, with 88 men and landed at San Salvador (Watling Islands, Bahamas), Oct. 12, 1492. His fleet included three vessels, the *Niña*, *Pinta*, and *Santa María*. He also visited Cuba, Hispaniola, and many smaller Caribbean islands, then populated by the now-extinct Taino Indians. A second expedition left Cadíz, Spain, Sept. 25, 1493, with 17 ships and 1,400 men, reaching the island of Dominica, in the Lesser Antilles, on Nov. 3, 1493. His third voyage took him from Sanlucar, Spain (May 30, 1498, with six ships), to the island of Trinidad and to the adjacent coast of S America, where he made landfall at the mouth of the Orinoco River. A fourth voyage departed Cadíz on May 9, 1502, and reached the E coast of Mexico, Honduras, Panama, and what he christened Santiago (the present-day island of Jamaica). Columbus died in Valladolid, Spain, on May 20, 1506, still convinced he had reached Asia by sailing west.

In N America, John and Sebastian Cabot, Italian explorers sailing for the English crown, reached Newfoundland and possibly Nova Scotia in 1497. John's second voyage (1498), seeking the fabled Northwest Passage, a new trade route to Asia, resulted in the loss of his entire fleet. For most of the 16th cent., exploration of the New World was dominated by the empires of Spain and Portugal.

In 1497 and 1499, Amerigo Vespucci (for whom the Americas are named), an Italian explorer sailing for Spain, passed along the N and E coasts of S America. He was the first to argue that these lands were previously unknown and not part of Asia.

Other early explorations are listed below.

Year	Explorer	Nationality (sponsor, if different)	Area reached or explored
1497-98	Vasco da Gama	Portuguese	Cape of Good Hope (Africa), India
1499	Alonso de Ojeda	Spanish	N South American coast, Venezuela
1500, Feb.	Vicente Yañez Pinzon	Spanish	S American coast, Amazon R.
1500, Apr.	Pedro Álvarez Cabral	Portuguese	Brazil
1501	Rodrigo de Bastidas	Spanish	Central America
1513	Vasco Núñez de Balboa	Spanish	Panama, Pacific Ocean
1513	Juan Ponce de León	Spanish	Florida, Yucatán Peninsula
1515	Juan de Solis	Spanish	Río de la Plata
1519	Alonso de Pineda	Spanish	Mouth of Mississippi R.
1519	Hernán Cortés	Spanish	Mexico
1519-20	Ferdinand Magellan	Portuguese (Spanish)	Straits of Magellan, Tierra del Fuego
1524	Giovanni da Verrazano	Italian (French)	Atlantic coast, incl. New York Harbor
1528	Álvar Núñez Cabeza de Vaca	Spanish	Texas coast and interior
1532	Francisco Pizarro	Spanish	Peru
1534	Jacques Cartier	French	Canada, Gulf of St. Lawrence
1536	Pedro de Mendoza	Spanish	Buenos Aires
1539	Francisco de Ulloa	Spanish	California coast
1539-41	Hernando de Soto	Spanish	Mississippi R., near Memphis, TN
1539	Marcos de Niza	Italian (Spanish)	SW United States
1540	Francisco de Coronado	Spanish	SW United States
1540	Hernando de Alarcón	Spanish	Colorado R.
1540	Garcia Lopez de Cárdenas	Spanish	Colorado, Grand Canyon
1541	Francisco de Orellana	Spanish	Amazon R.
1542	Juan Rodriguez Cabrillo	Portuguese (Spanish)	W Mexico, San Diego Harbor
1565	Pedro Menéndez de Avilés	Spanish	St. Augustine, FL
1576	Sir Martin Frobisher	English	Frobisher Bay, Canada
1577-80	Sir Francis Drake	English	California coast
1582	Antonio de Espejo	Spanish	SW U.S. (New Mexico)
1584	Philip Amadas and Arthur Barlowe (for Raleigh)	English	Virginia
1585-87	Sir Walter Raleigh's men	English	Roanoke Isl., NC
1595	Sir Walter Raleigh	English	Orinoco R.
1603-09	Samuel de Champlain	French	Canadian interior, Lake Champlain
1607	Capt. John Smith	English	Atlantic coast
1609-10	Henry Hudson	English (Dutch)	Hudson R., Hudson Bay
1634	Jean Nicolet	French	Lake Michigan, Wisconsin
1673	Jacques Marquette and Louis Jolliet	French	Mississippi R., S to Arkansas
1682	René-Robert Cavelier, sieur de La Salle	French	Mississippi R., S to Gulf of Mexico
1727-29	Vitus Bering	Danish (Russian)	Bering Strait, Alaska
1789	Sir Alexander Mackenzie	Canadian	NW Canada
1804-06	Meriwether Lewis and William Clark	American	Missouri R., Rocky Mts., Columbia R.

Arctic Exploration

Early Explorers

1587: John Davis (Eng.). Davis Strait to Sanderson's Hope, 72°12′N.

1596: Willem Barents and Jacob van Heemskerck (Dutch). Discovered Bear Isl., touched NW tip of Spitsbergen, 79° 49′N, rounded Novaya Zemlya, wintered at Ice Haven.

1607: Henry Hudson (Eng.). North along Greenland's E coast to Cape Hold-with-Hope, 73°30′, then north of Spitsbergen to 80° 23′. Explored Hudson's Touches (Jan Mayen).

1616: William Baffin and Robert Bylot (Eng.). Baffin Bay to Smith Sound.

1728: Vitus Bering (Dan./Russ.). Sailed through strait (Bering) proving Asia and America are separate.

1733-40: Great Northern Expedition (Russ.). Surveyed Siberian Arctic coast.

1741: Vitus Bering (Dan./Russ.). Sighted Alaska, named Mount St. Elias. His lieutenant, Chirikof, explored coast.

1771: Samuel Hearne (Brit., Hudson's Bay Co.). Overland from Prince of Wales Fort (Churchill) on Hudson Bay to mouth of Coppermine R.

1778: James Cook (Brit.). Through Bering Strait to Icy Cape, AK, and North Cape, Siberia.

1789: Alexander Mackenzie (Scot., North West Co.). Montreal to mouth of Mackenzie R.

1806: William Scoresby (Brit.). North of Spitsbergen to 81°30′.

1820-23: Ferdinand von Wrangel (Russ.). Surveyed Siberian Arctic coast. His exploration joined James Cook's at North Cape, confirming separation of the continents.

1878-79: (Nils) Adolf Erik Nordenskjöld (Swed.). 1st to navigate the Northeast Passage—an ocean route connecting Europe's North Sea, along the Arctic coast of Asia and through the Bering Sea, to the Pacific Ocean.

1881: The U.S. steamer *Jeannette*, led by Lt. Cmdr. George W. DeLong, was trapped in ice and crushed, June. DeLong and 11 others died; 12 survived.

1888: Fridtjof Nansen (Nor.) crossed Greenland icecap.

1893-96: Nansen in *Fram* drifted from New Siberian Isls. to Spitsbergen; tried polar dash in 1895, reached Franz Josef Land, 86°14′N.

1897: Salomon A. Andrée (Swed.) and 2 others started in balloon from Spitsbergen, July 11, to drift across pole to U.S., and disappeared. Aug. 6, 1930, their bodies were found on White Isl., 82°57′N, 29°52′E.

1903-06: Roald Amundsen (Nor.). 1st to sail whole length of the Northwest Passage—an ocean route linking the Atlantic Ocean to the Pacific via Canada's marine waterways.

North Pole Exploration

Robert E. Peary explored Greenland's coast, 1891-92; tried for North Pole, 1893. In 1900 he reached northern limit of Greenland and 83°50′N; in 1902 he reached 84°17′N; in 1906 he went from Ellesmere Isl. to 87°06′N. He sailed in the *Roosevelt*, July 1908, to winter off Cape Sheridan, Grant Land. The dash for the North Pole began Mar. 1 from Cape Columbia, Ellesmere Isl. Peary reportedly reached the pole, 90°N, Apr. 6, 1909; however, later research suggests he may have fallen short of his goal by c. 30-60 mi. The first surface expedition independently confirmed to have reached the North Pole was that of Ralph Plaisted in 1968 (see below).

Peary had several support groups carrying supplies until the last group turned back at 87°47′N. Peary, Matthew Henson, and 4 Eskimos proceeded with dog teams and sleds. They were said to have crossed the pole several times, then built an igloo there and remained 36 hrs. Started south, Apr. 7 at 4 PM, for Cape Columbia.

1914: Donald MacMillan (U.S.). Northwest, 200 mi, from Axel Heiberg Isl. to seek Peary's Crocker Land.

1915-17: Vilhjalmur Stefansson (Can.). Discovered Borden, Brock, Meighen, and Lougheed Isls.

1918-20: Roald Amundsen (Nor.). Sailed Northeast Passage.

1925: Amundsen and Lincoln Ellsworth (U.S.) reached 87°44′N in attempt to fly to North Pole from Spitsbergen.

1926: Richard E. Byrd and Floyd Bennett (U.S.) reputedly flew over North Pole, May 9. (Claim to have reached the pole is in dispute.)

1926: Amundsen, Ellsworth, and Umberto Nobile (Ital.) flew from Spitsbergen over North Pole May 12, to Teller, AK, in dirigible *Norge*.

1928: Nobile crossed North Pole in airship, May 24; crashed, May 25. Amundsen died attempting rescue.

North Pole Exploration Records

1958: On Aug. 3, submarine USS *Nautilus*, under Cmdr. William R. Anderson, crossed the North Pole beneath the ice.

1960: In Aug., the nuclear-powered U.S. submarine *Seadragon* (Cmdr. George P. Steele II) made the 1st E-W underwater transit through the Northwest Passage. Traveling mostly submerged, it made the 850-mi trek from Baffin Bay to the Beaufort Sea in 6 days.

1968: On Apr. 19, Ralph Plaisted (U.S.) and 3 amateur explorers on snowmobiles became the 1st independently confirmed surface expedition to reach the North Pole.

1977: On Aug. 16, the Soviet nuclear icebreaker *Arktika* became the 1st surface ship to reach the North Pole.

1978: On Apr. 30, Naomi Uemura (Jpn.) became the 1st person to reach the North Pole alone, traveling by dog sled in a 54-day, 600-mi trek over the frozen Arctic.

1982: In Apr., Sir Ranulph Fiennes and Charles Burton, Brit. explorers, reached the North Pole and became the 1st to circle the Earth from pole to pole. They had reached the South Pole 16 months earlier. The 52,000-mi trek took 3 years, involved 23 people, and cost an estimated $18 mil.

1986: On May 2, 6 explorers reached the North Pole assisted only by dogs. They became the 1st to reach the pole without aerial logistics support since at least 1909. The explorers—Amer. Will Steger, Paul Schurke, Ann Bancroft, and Geoff Carroll and Can. Brent Boddy and Richard Weber—completed the 500-mi journey in 56 days.

1995: On June 15, Weber and Mikhail Malakhov (Russ.) became the 1st pair to make it to the North Pole and back without any mechanical assistance. The 940-mi trip, made entirely on skis, took 121 days.

2003: On May 20, Pen Hadow (Brit.) became the 1st to reach the North Pole from Canada, solo and without resupply. The 377-mi journey across the ice took 64 days.

2006: On Apr. 16, Prince Albert II of Monaco became the 1st royal to reach the North Pole.

Antarctic Exploration

Antarctica has been approached since 1773-75, when Capt. James Cook (Brit.) reached 71°10′S. Many sea and landmarks bear names of early explorers. Fabian von Bellingshausen (Russ.) discovered Peter I and Alexander I Isls., 1819-21. Nathaniel Palmer (U.S.) traveled throughout Palmer Peninsula, 60°W, 1820, without realizing that this was a continent. Capt. John Davis (U.S.) made the 1st known landing on the continent on Feb. 7, 1821. Later, in 1823, James Weddell (Brit.) found Weddell Sea, 74°15′S, the southernmost point that had been reached.

First to announce existence of the continent of Antarctica was Charles Wilkes (U.S.), who followed the coast for 1,500 mi, 1840. Adelie Coast, 140°E, was found by Dumont d'Urville (Fr.), 1840. Ross Ice Shelf was found by James Clark Ross (Brit.), 1841-42.

1895: Leonard Kristensen (Nor.) landed a party on the coast of Victoria Land. They were the 1st ashore on the main continental mass. C. E. Borchgrevink, a member of that party, returned in 1899 with a Brit. expedition, 1st to winter on Antarctica.

1902-04: Robert Falcon Scott (Brit.) explored Edward VII Peninsula to 82°17′S, 146°33′E from McMurdo Sound.

1908-09: Ernest Shackleton (Brit.). 1st to use Manchurian ponies in Antarctic sledging. He reached 88°23′S, discovering a route onto the plateau by way of the Beardmore Glacier and pioneering the way to the pole.

1911: Roald Amundsen (Nor.) with 4 men and dog teams reached the South Pole, Dec. 14.

1912: Scott reached the pole from Ross Isl., Jan. 18, with 4 companions. None of Scott's party survived. Their bodies and expedition notes were found, Nov. 12.

1928: Sir George Hubert Wilkins (Austral.). 1st to use an airplane over Antarctica.

1929: Richard E. Byrd (U.S.) established Little America on Bay of Whales. On 1,600-mi airplane flight begun Nov. 28, he crossed South Pole, Nov. 29, with 3 others.

1934-35: Byrd led 2nd expedition to Little America, explored 450,000 sq mi, wintered alone at 80°08′S.

1934-37: John Rymill (Austral.) led British Graham Land Expedition; discovered Palmer Peninsula is part of mainland.

1935: Lincoln Ellsworth (U.S.) flew south along E Coast of Palmer Peninsula, then crossed continent to Little America, making 4 landings.

1939-41: U.S. Navy planes discovered about 150,000 sq mi of new land.

1940: Byrd charted most of coast between Ross Sea and Palmer Peninsula.

1946-47: U.S. Navy undertook Operation Highjump, commanded by Byrd, included 13 ships and 4,000 men. Airplanes photomapped coastline and penetrated beyond pole.

1946-48: Ronne Antarctic Research Expedition Cmdr. Finn Ronne, USNR, determined the Antarctic to be only one continent with no strait between Weddell Sea and Ross Sea; explored 250,000 sq mi of land by flights to 79°S.

1955-57: U.S. Navy's Operation Deep Freeze led by Adm. Byrd. Supporting U.S. scientific efforts for the International Geophysical Year (IGY), the operation established 5 coastal stations fronting the Indian, Pacific, and Atlantic Oceans and 3 interior stations; explored more than 1 mil sq mi in Wilkes Land.

1957-58: During the IGY, July 1957 through Dec. 1958, scientists from 12 countries conducted Antarctic research at a network of some 60 stations on Antarctica.

Dr. Vivian E. Fuchs (Brit.) led a 12-person Trans-Antarctic Expedition on the 1st land crossing of Antarctica. Starting from the Weddell Sea, they reached Scott Station, Mar. 2, 1958, after traveling 2,158 mi in 99 days.

1958: A group of 5 U.S. scientists led by seismologist Edward C. Thiel, moving by tractor from Ellsworth Station on Weddell Sea, identified a huge mountain range 5,000 ft above the ice sheet and 9,000 ft above sea level. The range,

originally seen by a Navy plane, was named Dufek Massif, for Rear Adm. George Dufek.

1959: Argentina, Australia, Belgium, Chile, France, Japan, New Zealand, Norway, South Africa, USSR, UK, and U.S. signed a treaty suspending territorial claims for 30 years and reserving the continent south of 60°S for research.

1961-62: Scientists discovered the Bentley Trench, running from Ross Ice Shelf into Marie Byrd Land, near the end of the Ellsworth Mts., toward the Weddell Sea.

1962: U.S. nuclear power plant went online at McMurdo Sound; operated until 1972.

1963: On Feb. 22, a U.S. plane made the region's longest nonstop flight from McMurdo Station south past the pole to Shackleton Mts., southeast to the "Area of Inaccessibility," and back to McMurdo Station, covering 3,600 mi in 10 hrs.

1964: New Zealanders mapped the mountain area from Cape Adare west some 400 mi to Pennell Glacier.

1985: Researcher Igor A. Zotikov (Russ.) discovered sediments in the Ross Ice Shelf that seem to support the continental drift theory. Ocean Drilling Project finds that the ice sheets of E Antarctica are 37 mil years old.

1989: Victoria Murden and Shirley Metz became both the 1st women and the 1st Americans to reach the South Pole overland when they arrived with 9 others on Jan. 17, 1989.

1991: 24 nations approved a protocol to the 1959 Antarctica Treaty, Oct. 4. New conservation provisions, including banning oil and other mineral exploration for 50 years.

1994: On Dec. 25, after 50-day trek, Liv Arnesen (Nor.) became 1st woman to ski alone and unaided to the South Pole.

1995: On Dec. 22, Borge Ousland (Nor.) reached the South Pole on skis, becoming 1st to reach both N and S Poles solo.

1996-97: Ousland became 1st to traverse Antarctica alone; reached South Pole Dec. 19, 1996. Traveled 1,675 mi in 64 days, ending Jan. 18, 1997.

2000-01: On Feb. 11, Ann Bancroft (U.S.) and Arnesen became 1st women to ski unaided across Antarctica. The 1,717-mi journey took 94 days.

2008: On Dec. 26, Christian Eide, Rune Midtgaard, Morten Andvig, and Mads Agerup (all Nor.) reached the South Pole unaided in a record 24 days, 8 hrs., 50 mins.

Volcanoes

Source: *Volcanoes of the World*, Geoscience Press; Global Volcanism Program, Smithsonian Institution

Roughly 540 volcanoes are known to have erupted during historical times. Nearly 75% of these historically active volcanoes lie along the so-called **Ring of Fire**, running along the W coast of the Americas from the southern tip of Chile to Alaska, down the E coast of Asia from Kamchatka to Indonesia, and continuing from New Guinea to New Zealand. The Ring of Fire marks the boundary between the tectonic plates underlying the Pacific Ocean and those of the surrounding continents. Other active regions occur along rift zones, where plates pull apart, as in Iceland, or where molten material moves up from the mantle over local hot spots, as in Hawaii. The vast majority of the Earth's volcanism occurs at submarine rift zones. For more information on volcanoes, see the Smithsonian Institution's global volcanism website at www.volcano.si.edu.

Notable Volcanic Eruptions

Approximately 7,000 years ago, Mazama, a 9,900-ft volcano in southern Oregon, erupted violently, ejecting large amounts of ash and pumice and voluminous pyroclastic flows. The ash spread over the entire northwestern U.S. and as far away as Saskatchewan, Canada. During the eruption, the top of the mountain collapsed, leaving a caldera 6 mi across and about a half mile deep, which filled with rainwater to form what is now called Crater Lake.

In 79 CE, Vesuvio, or Vesuvius, a 4,190-ft volcano overlooking Naples Bay, became active after several centuries of apparent inactivity. On Aug. 24 of that year, a heated mud and ash flow swept down the mountain, engulfing the cities of Pompeii, Herculaneum, and Stabiae with debris more than 60 ft deep. About 10% of the population of the three towns were killed.

In 1883, an eruption similar to the Mazama eruption occurred on the island of Krakatau. At least 2,000 people died in pyroclastic flows on Aug. 26. The next day, the 2,640-ft peak of the volcano collapsed to 1,000 ft below sea level, sinking most of the island and killing over 3,000. The collapse generated a tsunami that killed more than 31,000 people in Java and Sumatra and eventually reached England. Ash from the eruption colored sunsets around the world for two years. A similar, more powerful eruption had taken place 68 years earlier at Mt. Tambora on the Indonesian island of Sumbawa.

Date	Volcano	Deaths (est.)	Date	Volcano	Deaths (est.)
Aug. 24, 79 CE	Mt. Vesuvius, Italy	16,000	May 8, 1902	Mt. Pelée, Martinique	28,000
1586	Kelut, Java, Indon.	10,000	Jan. 30, 1911	Mt. Taal, Phil.	1,400
Dec. 15, 1631	Mt. Vesuvius, Italy	4,000	May 19, 1919	Mt. Kelut, Java, Indon.	5,000
Aug. 12, 1772	Mt. Papandayan, Java, Indon.	3,000	Jan. 17-21, 1951	Mt. Lamington, New Guinea	3,000
June 8, 1783	Laki, Iceland	9,350	May 18, 1980	Mt. St. Helens, U.S.	57
May 21, 1792	Mt. Unzen, Japan	14,500	Mar. 28, 1982	El Chichon, Mexico	1,880
Apr. 10-12, 1815	Mt. Tambora, Sumbawa, Indon.	92,000[1]	Nov. 13, 1985	Nevado del Ruiz, Colombia	23,000
Aug. 26-28, 1883	Krakatau, Indon.	36,000	Aug. 21, 1986	Lake Nyos, Cameroon	1,700
Apr. 24, 1902	Santa María, Guatemala	1,000[2]	June 15, 1991	Mt. Pinatubo, Luzon, Phil.	800[3]

(1) Of these, 10,000 were directly related to the eruption; an additional 82,000 were the result of starvation and disease brought on by the event. (2) An additional 3,000 deaths due to a malaria outbreak are sometimes attributed to the eruption. (3) Of these, about 500 were associated with post-eruption lahars (volcanic mudflows), in addition to the 300 deaths caused directly by the eruption.

Notable Active Volcanoes

Active volcanoes display a wide range of activity. In this table, the year given indicates when a volcano last displayed eruptive activity, as of June 2012. An eruption may involve explosive ejection of fragmental material, escape of liquid lava, or both. Volcanoes are listed by height, which does not reflect eruptive magnitude; submarine volcanoes are not included.

Volcano (latest eruption)	Location	Height (ft)
Africa		
Mt. Cameroon (2000)	Cameroon	13,435
Nyiragongo (2011)	Congo	11,384
Nyamuragira (2010)	Congo	10,033
Mt. Oku [Lake Nyos] (1986)	Cameroon	9,878
Ol Doinyo Lengai (2010)	Tanzania	9,718
Fogo (1995)	Cape Verde Isls.	9,281
Piton de la Fournaise (2010)	Réunion Isl., Indian O.	8,635
Karthala (2007)	Comoros	7,746
Nabro (2011)	Eritrea	7,277
Antarctica		
Erebus (2011)	Ross Isl.	12,447
Deception Island (1970)	S. Shetland Isl.	1,890
Asia and Oceania		
Kliuchevskoi (2011)	Kamchatka, Russia	15,863
Kerinci (2009)	Sumatra, Indon.	12,467
Fuji (1708)	Honshu, Japan	12,388
Rinjani (2010)	Lesser Sunda Isl., Indon.	12,224
Tolbachik (1976)	Kamchatka, Russia	12,080
Semeru (2011)	Java, Indon.	12,060
Slamet (2009)	Java, Indon.	11,247
Raung (2008)	Java, Indon.	10,932
Shiveluch (2012)	Kamchatka, Russia	10,771
On-take (1980)	Honshu, Japan	10,049
Merapi (2011)	Java, Indon.	9,737
Marapi (2011)	Sumatra, Indon.	9,485
Bezymianny (2011)	Kamchatka, Russia	9,455
Peuet Sague (2000)	Sumatra, Indon.	9,190
Ruapehu (2007)	New Zealand	9,176
Heard (2008)	Indian Ocean	9,006
Changbaishan (1903)	China-Korea	9,003
Asama (2009)	Honshu, Japan	8,425
Dieng (2009)	Java, Indon.	8,415
Mayon (2010)	Luzon, Phil.	8,077
Sinabung (2010)	Sumatra, Indon.	8,071
Kanlaon (2006)	Negros Isl., Phil.	7,989
Niigata-Yake-yama (1998)	Honshu, Japan	7,874
Kizimen (2011)	Kamchatka, Russia	7,795
Alaid (1996)	Kuril Isls., Russia	7,674
Ulawun (2011)	Papua New Guinea	7,657
Tengger Caldera (2011)	Java, Indon.	7,641
Chokai (1974)	Honshu, Japan	7,326
Galunggung (1984)	Java, Indon.	7,113
Azuma (1977)	Honshu, Japan	6,676
Tongariro (Ngauruhoe) (1977)	New Zealand	6,489
Sangeang Api (1988)	Lesser Sunda Isl., Indon.	6,394
Nasu (1963)	Honshu, Japan	6,283
Karkar (1979)	Papua New Guinea	6,033
Gorely (2010)	Kamchatka, Russia	6,001
Bandai (1888)	Honshu, Japan	5,968
Tiatia (2010)	Kuril Isls., Russia	5,968
Manam (2012)	Papua New Guinea	5,928
Kuju (1996)	Kyushu, Japan	5,876
Karangetang (Api Siau) (2011)	Sangihe Isls., Indon.	5,853
Soputan (2011)	Sulawesi, Indon.	5,853
Bagana (2011)	Papua New Guinea	5,741
Kelut (2008)	Java, Indon.	5,679
Adatara (1996)	Honshu, Japan	5,636
Gamalama (2003)	Halmahera, Indon.	5,627
Kirishima (2011)	Kyushu, Japan	5,577
Gamkonora (2007)	Halmahera, Indon.	5,364
Aso (2011)	Kyushu, Japan	5,223
Lokon-Empung (2011)	Sulawesi, Indon.	5,184
Bulusan (2011)	Luzon, Phil.	5,134
Karymsky (2012)	Kamchatka, Russia	5,039
Unzen (1996)	Kyushu, Japan	4,921
Akan (2008)	Hokkaido, Japan	4,918
Aoba (2011)	Vanuatu	4,908
Sarychev Peak (2009)	Kuril Isls., Russia	4,908
Pinatubo (1993)	Luzon, Phil.	4,875
Lopevi (2008)	Vanuatu	4,636
Akita-Yake-yama (1997)	Honshu, Japan	4,482
Dukono (2012)	Halmahera, Indon.	4,380
Ambrym (2011)	Vanuatu	4,377
Langila (2010)	Papua New Guinea	4,363
Ibu (2011)	Halmahera, Indon.	4,347
Awu (2004)	Sangihe Isls., Indon.	4,331
Akademia Nauk (1996)	Kamchatka, Russia	3,871
Ekarma (2010)	Kuril Isls., Russia	3,839
Ebeko (2010)	Kuril Isls., Russia	3,793
Komaga-take (2000)	Hokkaido, Japan	3,711
Sakura-jima (2012)	Kyushu, Japan	3,665
Tinakula (2011)	Solomon Isls.	2,792
Miyake-jima (2010)	Izu Isls., Japan	2,674
Krakatau (2011)	Indonesia	2,667
Suwanose-jima (2012)	Ryukyu Isls., Japan	2,621
Gaua (2010)	Vanuatu	2,615
Oshima (1990)	Izu Isls., Japan	2,507

Volcano (latest eruption)	Location	Height (ft)
Central America and Caribbean		
Tacaná (1986)	Guatemala	13,320
Acatenango (1972)	Guatemala	13,044
Santa María (2011)	Guatemala	12,375
Fuego (2012)	Guatemala	12,346
Irazú (1994)	Costa Rica	11,260
Turrialba (2011)	Costa Rica	10,958
Poás (2011)	Costa Rica	8,884
Pacaya (2010)	Guatemala	8,373
Santa Ana (2005)	El Salvador	7,812
San Miguel (2002)	El Salvador	6,988
Rincón de la Vieja (1998)	Costa Rica	6,286
San Cristóbal (2011)	Nicaragua	5,725
Concepción (2011)	Nicaragua	5,577
Arenal (2010)	Costa Rica	5,479
Soufrière Guadeloupe (1977)	Guadeloupe Isl. (France)	4,813
Pelée (1932)	Martinique (France)	4,583
Momotombo (1905)	Nicaragua	4,255
Soufrière St. Vincent (1979)	St. Vincent	4,003
Telica (2011)	Nicaragua	3,481
Soufrière Hills (2011)	Montserrat (UK)	3,002
North America		
Pico de Orizaba (1846)	Mexico	18,619
Popocatépetl (2012)	Mexico	17,802
Rainier (1894)	Washington	14,409
Shasta (1786)	California	14,163
Wrangell (2002)	Alaska	14,163
Colima (2011)	Mexico	12,631
Lassen Peak (1917)	California	10,456
Redoubt (2009)	Alaska	10,197
Iliamna (1876)	Alaska	10,016
Shishaldin (2004)	Aleutian Isls., AK	9,373
St. Helens (2008)	Washington	8,363
Pavlof (2007)	Alaska	8,264
Veniaminof (2008)	Alaska	8,225
Katmai (1912)	Alaska	6,716
Makushin (1995)	Aleutian Isls., AK	5,905
Great Sitkin (1974)	Aleutian Isls., AK	5,709
Cleveland (2012)	Aleutian Isls., AK	5,676
Gareloi (1989)	Aleutian Isls., AK	5,161
Korovin (Atka complex) (2007)	Aleutian Isls., AK	5,029
Akutan (1992)	Aleutian Isls., AK	4,275
Augustine (2006)	Alaska	4,108
Kiska (1990)	Aleutian Isls., AK	4,003
El Chichón (1982)	Mexico	3,773
Okmok (2008)	Aleutian Isls., AK	3,520
South America		
Llullaillaco (1877)	Argentina-Chile	22,109
Guallatiri (1960)	Chile	19,918
Tupungatito (1987)	Argentina-Chile	19,685
Cotopaxi (1940)	Ecuador	19,393
El Misti (1985)	Peru	19,101
Láscar (2007)	Chile	18,346
Nevado del Huila (2011)	Colombia	17,598
Nevado del Ruiz (1991)	Colombia	17,457
Sangay (2011)	Ecuador	17,159
Irruputuncu (1995)	Chile-Bolivia	16,939
Tungurahua (2012)	Ecuador	16,479
Guagua Pichincha (2009)	Ecuador	15,695
Puracé (1977)	Colombia	15,256
Galeras (2010)	Colombia	14,029
Planchón-Peteroa (2011)	Chile	13,474
Reventador (2011)	Ecuador	11,686
Llaima (2009)	Chile	10,253
Villarrica (2011)	Chile	9,340
Puyehue-Cordón Caulle (2011)	Chile	7,336
Cerro Hudson (1991)	Chile	6,250
Europe		
Etna (2011)	Italy	10,925
Vesuvius (1944)	Italy	4,203
Stromboli (2011)	Italy	3,031
Santorini (1950)	Greece	1,204
Mid-Atlantic		
Jan Mayen (1985)	N Atlantic O., Norway	7,470
Grímsvötn (2011)	Iceland	5,659
Eyjafjallajökull (2010)	Iceland	5,466
Katla (2011)	Iceland	4,961
Hekla (2000)	Iceland	4,892
Mid-Pacific		
Mauna Loa (1984)	Hawaii, HI	13,681
Haleakala (1750)	Maui, HI	10,023
Kilauea (2012)	Hawaii, HI	4,009

Mountains
North America

Source: U.S. Geological Survey, U.S. Dept. of the Interior. Survey dates and elevation sources may differ.

Peak, state/prov., country	Height (ft)	Peak, state/prov., country	Height (ft)	Peak, state/prov., country	Height (ft)
McKinley (Denali), AK	20,320	Alverstone, AK-YT, U.S.-Can.	14,500	Belford, CO	14,204
Logan, Yukon, Canada	19,551	Whitney, CA	14,500	Princeton, CO	14,204
Pico de Orizaba, Mexico	18,619	University Peak, AK	14,470	Crestone Needle, CO	14,203
St. Elias, AK-YT, U.S.-Can.	18,008	Elbert, CO	14,440	Yale, CO	14,203
Popocatépetl, Mexico	17,802	Massive, CO	14,428	Bross, CO	14,179
Foraker, AK	17,400	Harvard, CO	14,427	Kit Carson, CO	14,171
Iztaccíhuatl, Mexico	17,343	Rainier, WA	14,416	El Diente Peak, CO	14,165
Lucania, YT, Canada	17,147	Williamson, CA	14,376	Point Success, WA	14,164
King, YT, Canada	16,971	La Plata Peak, CO	14,368	Shasta, CA	14,163
Steele, YT, Canada	16,644	Blanca Peak, CO	14,351	Wrangell, AK	14,163
Bona, AK	16,500	Uncompahgre Peak, CO	14,315	Maroon Peak, CO	14,163
Blackburn, AK	16,390	Crestone Peak, CO	14,300	Tabeguache, CO	14,162
Sanford, AK	16,237	Lincoln, CO	14,293	Oxford, CO	14,160
Vancouver, AK-YT, U.S.-Can.	15,979	Antero, CO	14,276	Sill, CA	14,159
South Buttress, AK	15,885	Grays Peak, CO	14,276	Sneffels, CO	14,156
Wood, Yukon, Canada	15,885	Torreys Peak, CO	14,273	Democrat, CO	14,155
Churchill, AK	15,638	Castle Peak, CO	14,272	Capitol Peak, CO	14,137
Fairweather, AK-BC, U.S.-Can.	15,300	Quandary Peak, CO	14,272	Liberty Cap, WA	14,118
Xinantecatl (Toluca), Mexico	15,016	Evans, CO	14,270	Pikes Peak, CO	14,111
Hubbard, AK-YT, U.S.-Can.	14,950	Longs Peak, CO	14,260	Snowmass, CO	14,098
Bear, AK	14,831	McArthur, YT, Can.	14,253	Russell, CA	14,094
Walsh, YT, Canada	14,780	White Mountain Peak, CA	14,252	Eolus, CO	14,089
East Buttress, AK	14,730	Wilson, CO	14,252	Windom, CO	14,088
Matlalcueyetl, Mexico	14,636	North Palisade, CA	14,248	Columbia, CO	14,080
Hunter, AK	14,573	Cameron, CO	14,245	Missouri, CO	14,074
Browne Tower, AK	14,530	Shavano, CO	14,236	Augusta, AK	14,070

The highest point in the West Indies is Pico Duarte (10,417 ft), in the Dominican Republic.

Other Notable U.S. Mountains

Peak, state	Height (ft)	Peak, state	Height (ft)	Peak, state	Height (ft)
Gannett Peak, WY	13,810	Adams, WA	12,281	Clingmans Dome, NC-TN	6,643
Grand Teton, WY	13,775	San Gorgonio, CA	11,503	Washington, NH	6,289
Kings, UT	13,534	Hood, OR	11,240	Rogers, VA	5,729
Cloud, WY	13,171	Lassen, CA	10,461	Marcy, NY	5,344
Wheeler, NM	13,166	Granite, CA	10,325	Katahdin, ME	5,269
Boundary, NV	13,146	Guadalupe, TX	8,751	Spruce Knob, WV	4,863
Granite, MT	12,804	Olympus, WA	7,973	Mansfield, VT	4,393
Borah, ID	12,661	Harney, SD	7,244	Black Mountain, KY	4,145
Humphreys, AZ	12,637	Mitchell, NC	6,683		

South America

Peak, country	Height (ft)	Peak, country	Height (ft)	Peak, country	Height (ft)
Aconcagua, Argentina	22,831	Coropuna, Peru	21,083	Solo, Argentina	20,492
Ojos del Salado, Arg.-Chile	22,595	Laudo, Argentina	20,997	Polleras, Argentina	20,456
Bonete, Argentina	22,546	Ancohuma, Bolivia	20,958	Pular, Chile	20,423
Tupungato, Argentina-Chile	22,310	Ausangate, Peru	20,945	Chani, Argentina	20,341
Pissis, Argentina	22,241	Toro, Argentina-Chile	20,932	Aucanquilcha, Chile	20,295
Mercedario, Argentina	22,211	Illampu, Bolivia	20,873	Juncal, Argentina-Chile	20,276
Huascaran, Peru	22,205	Tres Cruces, Argentina-Chile	20,853	Negro, Argentina	20,184
Llullaillaco, Argentina-Chile	22,109	Huandoy, Peru	20,852	Quela, Argentina	20,128
El Libertador, Argentina	22,047	Parinacota, Bolivia-Chile	20,768	Condoriri, Bolivia	20,095
Cachi, Argentina	22,047	Tortolas, Argentina-Chile	20,745	Palermo, Argentina	20,079
Yerupajá, Peru	21,765	Ampato, Peru	20,702	Solimana, Peru	20,068
Incahuasi, Argentina-Chile	21,720	Chimborazo, Ecuador	20,702	San Juan, Argentina-Chile	20,049
Galan, Argentina	21,654	El Condor, Argentina	20,669	Sierra Nevada, Argentina-Chile	20,023
El Muerto, Argentina-Chile	21,457	Salcantay, Peru	20,574	Antofalla, Argentina	20,013
Sajama, Bolivia	21,391	Huancarhuas, Peru	20,531	Marmolejo, Argentina-Chile	20,013
Nacimiento, Argentina	21,302	Famatina, Argentina	20,505	Chachani, Peru	19,931
Illimani, Bolivia	21,201	Pumasillo, Peru	20,492		

Africa

Peak, country	Height (ft)	Peak, country	Height (ft)	Peak, country	Height (ft)
Kilimanjaro, Tanzania	19,341	Meru, Tanzania	14,977	Guna, Ethiopia	13,881
Kenya, Kenya	17,057	Karisimbi, Congo-Rwanda	14,787	Gughe, Ethiopia	13,780
Margherita Pk., Uganda-Congo	16,763	Elgon, Kenya-Uganda	14,178	Toubkal, Morocco	13,661
Ras Dashan, Ethiopia	15,158	Batu, Ethiopia	14,131	Cameroon, Cameroon	13,435

Australia, New Zealand, SE Asian Islands

Peak, country	Height (ft)	Peak, country	Height (ft)	Peak, country	Height (ft)
Jaya, New Guinea	16,500	Wilhelm, New Guinea	14,793	Cook, New Zealand	12,349
Trikora, New Guinea	15,585	Kinabalu, Malaysia	13,455	Semeru, Java, Indonesia	12,060
Mandala, New Guinea	15,420	Kerinci, Sumatra, Indon.	12,467	Kosciusko, Australia	7,310

Height of Mount Everest

Mt. Everest, the world's highest mountain, was considered 29,002 ft when Edmund Hillary and Tenzing Norgay became the first climbers to scale it, in 1953. That triangulation figure had been accepted since 1850. In 1954, the Surveyor General of the Republic of India set the height at 29,028 ft, plus or minus 10 ft because of snow; the figure was also accepted by the National Geographic Society.

In 1999, a team of climbers sponsored by Boston's Museum of Science and the National Geographic Society measured the height at the summit using satellite-based technology. The new measurement, of 29,035 ft, was accepted by the National Geographic Society and other authorities, including the U.S. National Imagery and Mapping Agency.

As of the end of 2011, in the nearly 60 years since Hillary and Tenzing's achievement, some 3,448 individuals have reached the summit of Everest. About 223 have died in the attempt. Climbers typically ascend Everest on its north (Tibet) or south face (Nepal).

Europe

Peak, country	Height (ft)	Peak, country	Height (ft)	Peak, country	Height (ft)
Alps		Dent D'Herens, Switzerland	13,686	Schalihorn, Switzerland	13,040
Mont Blanc, France-Italy	15,781	Breithorn, It.-Switzerland	13,665	Scerscen, Switzerland	13,028
Monte Rosa (highest peak		Bishorn, Switzerland	13,645	Eiger, Switzerland	13,025
of group), Switzerland	15,203	Jungfrau, Switzerland	13,642	Jagerhorn, Switzerland	13,024
Dom, Switzerland	14,911	Ecrins, France	13,461	Rottalhorn, Switzerland	13,022
Liskamm, It.-Switzerland	14,852	Monch, Switzerland	13,448		
Weisshorn, Switzerland	14,780	Pollux, Switzerland	13,422	**Pyrenees**	
Taschhorn, Switzerland	14,733	Schreckhorn, Switzerland	13,379	Aneto, Spain	11,168
Matterhorn, It.-Switzerland	14,692	Ober Gabelhorn, Switzerland	13,330	Posets, Spain	11,073
Dent Blanche, Switzerland	14,293	Gran Paradiso, Italy	13,323	Perdido, Spain	11,007
Nadelhorn, Switzerland	14,196	Bernina, It.-Switzerland	13,284	Vignemale, France-Spain	10,820
Grand Combin, Switzerland	14,154	Fiescherhorn, Switzerland	13,283	Long, Spain	10,479
Lenzpitze, Switzerland	14,088	Grunhorn, Switzerland	13,266	Estats, Spain	10,304
Finsteraarhorn, Switzerland	14,022	Lauteraarhorn, Switzerland	13,261	Montcalm, Spain	10,105
Castor, Switzerland	13,865	Durrenhorn, Switzerland	13,238		
Zinalrothorn, Switzerland	13,849	Allalinhorn, Switzerland	13,213	**Caucasus (Europe-Asia)**	
Hohberghom, Switzerland	13,842	Weissmies, Switzerland	13,199	Elbrus, Russia	18,510
Alphubel, Switzerland	13,799	Lagginhorn, Switzerland	13,156	Shkhara, Georgia	17,064
Rimpfischhom, Switzerland	13,776	Zupo, Switzerland	13,120	Dykh Tau, Russia	17,054
Aletschorn, Switzerland	13,763	Fletschhorn, Switzerland	13,110	Kashtan Tau, Russia	16,877
Strahlhorn, Switzerland	13,747	Adlerhorn, Switzerland	13,081	Janqi, Georgia	16,565
		Gletscherhorn, Switzerland	13,068	Kazbek, Georgia	16,558

Asia (Mainland)

Peak, country/region	Height (ft)	Peak, country/region	Height (ft)	Peak, country/region	Height (ft)
Everest, Nepal-Tibet	29,035	Kungur, Xinjiang, China	25,325	Gauri Sankar, Nepal-Tibet	23,440
K2 (Godwin Austen), Kashmir	28,250	Tirich Mir, Pakistan	25,230	Badrinath, India	23,420
Kanchenjunga, India-Nepal	28,208	Makalu II, Nepal-Tibet	25,120	Nunkun, Kashmir	23,410
Lhotse I (Everest), Nepal-Tibet	27,923	Minya Konka, China	24,900	Lenin Peak, Tajikistan	23,406
Makalu I, Nepal-Tibet	27,824	Kula Gangri, Bhutan-Tibet	24,784	Pyramid, India-Nepal	23,400
Lhotse II (Everest), Nepal-Tibet	27,560	Changtzu (Everest), Nepal-Tibet	24,780	Api, Nepal	23,399
Dhaulagiri, Nepal	26,810	Muz Tagh Ata, Xinjiang, China	24,757	Pauhunri, India-Tibet	23,385
Manaslu I, Nepal	26,760	Skyang Kangri, Kashmir	24,750	Trisul, India	23,360
Cho Oyu, Nepal-Tibet	26,750	Ismail Semani Peak, Tajikistan	24,590	Kangto, India-Tibet	23,260
Nanga Parbat, Kashmir	26,660	Jongsang Peak,		Nyenchhe Thanglha, Tibet	23,255
Annapurna I, Nepal	26,504	India-Nepal-China	24,472	Trisuli, India	23,210
Gasherbrum, Kashmir	26,470	Jengish Chokusu, Xinjiang,		Pumori, Nepal-Tibet	23,190
Broad, Kashmir	26,400	China-Kyrgyzstan	24,406	Dunagiri, India	23,184
Gosainthan Nepal-Tibet	26,287	Sia Kangri, Kashmir	24,350	Lombo Kangra, Tibet	23,165
Annapurna II, Nepal	26,041	Haramosh Peak, Pakistan	24,270	Saipal, Nepal	23,100
Gyachung Kang, Nepal-Tibet	25,910	Istoro Nal, Pakistan	24,240	Macha Pucchare, Nepal	22,958
Disteghil Sar, Kashmir	25,868	Kirat Chuli, India-Nepal	24,165	Numbar, Nepal	22,817
Himalchuli, Nepal	25,801	Chomo Lhari, Bhutan-Tibet	24,040	Kanjiroba, Nepal	22,580
Nuptse (Everest), Nepal-Tibet	25,726	Chamlang, Nepal	24,012	Ama Dablam, Nepal	22,350
Masherbrum, Kashmir	25,660	Kabru, India-Nepal	24,002	Cho Polu, Nepal	22,093
Nanda Devi, India	25,645	Alung Gangri, Tibet	24,000	Lingtren, Nepal-Tibet	21,972
Rakaposhi, Kashmir	25,550	Baltoro Kangri, Kashmir	23,990	Khumbutse, Nepal-Tibet	21,785
Kamet, India-Tibet	25,447	Mussu Shan, Xinjiang, China	23,890	Hlako Gangri, Tibet	21,266
Namcha Barwa, Tibet	25,445	Mana, India	23,860	Mt. Grosvenor, China	21,190
Gurla Mandhata, Tibet	25,355	Baruntse, Nepal	23,688	Thagchhab Gangri, Tibet	20,970
Ulugh Muz Tagh, Xinjiang,		Nepal Peak, India-Nepal	23,500	Damavand, Iran	18,406
China-Tibet	25,340	Amne Machin, China	23,490	Ararat, Turkey	16,854

Antarctica

Peak	Height (ft)	Peak	Height (ft)	Peak	Height (ft)
Vinson Massif	16,066	Miller	13,650	Falla	12,549
Tyree	15,919	Long Gables	13,620	Rucker	12,520
Shinn	15,750	Dickerson	13,517	Goldthwait	12,510
Gardner	15,375	Giovinetto	13,412	Morris	12,500
Epperly	15,100	Wade	13,400	Erebus	12,450
Kirkpatrick	14,855	Fisher	13,386	Campbell	12,434
Elizabeth	14,698	Fridtjof Nansen	13,350	Don Pedro Christophersen	12,355
Markham	14,290	Wexler	13,202	Lysaght	12,326
Bell	14,117	Lister	13,200	Huggins	12,247
Mackellar	14,098	Shear	13,100	Sabine	12,200
Anderson	13,957	Odishaw	13,008	Astor	12,175
Bentley	13,934	Donaldson	12,894	Mohl	12,172
Kaplan	13,878	Ray	12,808	Frankes	12,064
Andrew Jackson	13,750	Sellery	12,779	Jones	12,040
Sidley	13,720	Waterman	12,730	Gjelsvik	12,008
Ostenso	13,710	Anne	12,703	Coman	12,000
Minto	13,668	Press	12,566		

Notable Islands and Their Areas

Figures are for total areas in square miles. Boldface figure in parentheses shows rank among the world's 10 largest individual islands. Because some islands have not been surveyed accurately, some areas shown are estimates. Some "islands" listed are island groups. Only the largest islands in a group are listed individually. Only islands over 10 sq mi in area are listed.

Antarctica

Adelaide	1,400
Alexander	16,700
Berkner	18,500
Roosevelt	2,900

Arctic Ocean

Akimski, Nunavut (NU), Can.	1,159
Amund Ringnes, NU, Can.	2,029
Axel Heiberg, NU, Can.	16,671
Baffin, NU, Can. **(5)**	195,928
Banks, Northwest Terr. (NT), Can.	27,038
Bathurst, NU, Can.	6,194
Bolshevik, Russia	4,368
Bolshoy Lyakhovsky, Russia	1,776
Borden, NT-NU, Can.	1,079
Bylot, NU, Can.	4,273
Coats, NU, Can.	2,123
Cornwallis, NU, Can.	2,701
Devon, NU, Can.	21,331
Disko, Greenland, Denmark	3,312
Ellef Ringnes, NU, Can.	4,361
Ellesmere, NU, Can. **(10)**	75,767
Faddayevskiy, Russia	1,930
Franz Josef Land, Russia	8,000
Iturup (Etorofu), Russia	2,596
King William, NU, Can.	5,062
Komsomolets, Russia	3,477
Kotelny Russia	4,504
Mackenzie King, NT, Can.	1,949
Mansel, NU, Can.	1,228
Melville, NT-NU, Can.	16,274
Milne Land, Greenland, Den.	1,400
New Siberian Isls., Russia	14,500
Novaya Zemlya, Russia (2 isls.)	31,730
Oktyabrskoy, Russia.	5,471
Prince Charles, NT, Can.	3,676
Prince Patrick, NT, Can.	6,119
Prince of Wales, NU, Can.	12,872
Somerset, NU, Can.	9,570
Southampton, NU, Can.	15,913
Svalbard, Norway (tot. group).	23,957
Nordaustlandet	5,410
Spitsbergen	15,060
Traill, Greenland, Denmark	1,300
Victoria, NT-NU, Can. **(9)**	83,897
Wrangel, Russia	2,800

Atlantic Ocean

Anticosti, QC, Can.	3,068
Ascension, UK	34
Azores, Portugal (tot. group)	868
Faial	67
San Miguel	291
Bahama Isls. (tot. group)	5,382
Andros	2,300
Bermuda Isls., UK (tot. group)	21
Bioko Isl., Equatorial Guinea	785
Block Island, RI, U.S.	21
Canary Isls., Spain (tot. group)	2,807
Fuerteventura	688
Gran Canaria	592
Tenerife	795
Cape Breton, NS, Can.	3,981
Cape Verde Isls.	1,557
Caviana, Pará, Brazil	1,918
Channel Isls., UK (tot. group)	75
Guernsey	24
Jersey	45
Falkland Isls., UK (tot. group)	4,700
East Falkland	2,550
West Falkland	1,750
Faroe Isls., Denmark	540
Great Britain, UK **(8)**	88,407
Greenland, Denmark **(1)**	840,000
Gurupá, Pará, Brazil	1,878
Hebrides, Scotland, UK	2,744
Iceland	39,699
Ireland (tot. group)	32,589
Irish Republic	27,137
Northern Ireland, UK.	5,452
Isle of Man, UK	221
Isle of Wight, England, UK	147
Long Island, NY, U.S.	1,320
Madeira Islands, Portugal	306

Atlantic Ocean (cont.)

Marajo, Brazil	15,444
Martha's Vineyard, MA, U.S.	89
Mount Desert, ME, U.S.	104
Nantucket, MA, U.S.	45
Newfoundland, Canada	42,031
Orkney Isls., Scotland, UK	390
Prince Edward, Canada	2,185
St. Helena, UK	160
Shetland Isls., Scotland, UK.	587
Skye, Scotland, UK.	670
South Georgia, UK	1,450
Tierra del Fuego, Chile-Arg.	18,800
Tristan da Cunha, UK.	40

Baltic Sea

Aland Isls., Finland	590
Bornholm, Denmark	227
Gotland, Sweden	1,159

Caribbean Sea

Antigua	108
Aruba, Netherlands.	75
Barbados	166
Cuba.	42,804
Isle of Youth	926
Cayman Isls., UK	100
Curaçao, Netherlands.	171
Dominica	290
Guadeloupe, France.	687
Hispaniola (Haiti and Dominican Rep.)	29,389
Jamaica	4,244
Martinique, France	436
Puerto Rico, U.S.	3,339
Tobago	116
Trinidad.	1,864
Virgin Isls., UK	59
Virgin Isls., U.S.	134

East Indies

Bali, Indonesia	2,171
Bangka, Indonesia	4,375
Borneo, Indonesia-Malaysia-Brunei **(3)**	280,100
Bougainville, Papua New Guinea	3,880
Buru, Indonesia	3,670
Celebes, Indonesia.	69,000
Flores, Indonesia	5,500
Halmahera, Indonesia	6,865
Java (Jawa), Indonesia.	48,900
Madura, Indonesia	2,113
Moluccas, Indonesia.	32,307
New Britain, Papua New Guinea	14,093
New Guinea, Indon.-PNG **(2)**	306,000
New Ireland, PNG.	3,707
Seram, Indonesia	6,621
Sumatra, Indonesia **(6)**	165,000
Sumba, Indonesia.	4,306
Sumbawa, Indonesia	5,965
Timor, Indon.–Timor-Leste	13,094
Yos Sudarsa, Indonesia	4,500

Indian Ocean

Andaman Isls., India	2,500
Kerguelen, France	2,247
Madagascar **(4)**	226,658
Mauritius.	720
Pemba, Tanzania	380
Réunion, France.	970
Seychelles	176
Sri Lanka	25,332
Zanzibar, Tanzania.	640

Mediterranean Sea

Balearic Isls., Spain	1,927
Corfu, Greece	229
Corsica, France	3,369
Crete, Greece.	3,189
Cyprus	3,572
Elba, Italy	86
Euboea, Greece	1,411
Malta.	95
Rhodes, Greece	540
Sardinia, Italy	9,301
Sicily, Italy.	9,926

Pacific Ocean

Admiralty, AK, U.S.	1,709
Aleutian Isls., AK, U.S. (tot. group)	6,912
Adak	275
Amchitka.	116
Attu	350
Kanaga	142
Kiska.	106
Tanaga	195
Umnak	686
Unalaska.	1,051
Unimak	1,571
Baranof, AK, U.S.	1,636
Chichagof, AK, U.S.	2,062
Chiloe, Chile	3,241
Christmas, Kiribati	94
Diomede (Big), Russia	11
Easter Isl., Chile	69
Fiji (tot. group)	7,056
Vanua Levu	2,242
Viti Levu	4,109
Galapagos Isls., Ecuador	3,043
Graham Isl., BC, Can.	2,456
Guadalcanal, Solomon Isls.	2,180
Guam, U.S.	210
Hainan, China.	13,000
Hawaiian Isls., HI, U.S. (tot. group)	6,428
Hawaii	4,028
Oahu.	600
Hong Kong, China	31
Hoste, Chile	1,590
Japan (tot. group)	145,914
Hokkaido.	30,144
Honshu **(7)**	87,805
Kyushu	14,114
Okinawa	459
Shikoku.	7,049
Kangaroo, South Australia	1,680
Kodiak, AK, U.S.	3,485
Kupreanof, AK, U.S.	1,084
Marquesas Isls., France	492
Marshall Isls.	70
Melville, N Terr., Australia	2,240
Micronesia	271
New Caledonia, France	6,530
New Zealand (tot. group)	103,363
Chatham Isls.	373
North.	43,911
South	58,084
Stewart	649
North Mariana Isls., U.S.	179
Nunivak, AK, U.S.	1,600
Palau	188
Philippines (tot. group)	115,831
Leyte	2,787
Luzon	40,680
Mindanao	36,775
Mindoro.	3,690
Negros	4,907
Palawan	4,554
Panay	4,446
Samar.	5,050
Prince of Wales, AK, U.S.	2,770
Revillagigedo, AK, U.S.	1,134
Riesco, Chile	1,973
St. Lawrence, AK, U.S.	1,780
Sakhalin, Russia.	29,500
Samoa Isls. (tot. group)	1,177
American Samoa, U.S.	77
Savaii, Samoa	659
Tutuila, U.S.	55
Upolu, Samoa.	432
Santa Catalina, CA, U.S.	75
Santa Ines, Chile	1,407
Tahiti, France	402
Taiwan (tot. group)	13,892
Jinmen Dao (Quemoy)	56
Tasmania, Australia	26,178
Tonga Isls.	290
Vancouver Isl., BC, Can.	12,079
Vanuatu	4,707
Wellington, Chile	2,549

Persian Gulf

Bahrain	217

Notable Deserts of the World

Deserts are defined as regions of the Earth receiving less than 10 in. of precipitation annually, usually in combination with an evaporation rate exceeding precipitation.

In addition to areas listed below, the continent of Antarctica, with an area of about 5.4 mil sq mi (roughly doubled by ice in winter), is generally considered a desert. Annual precipitation averages 8 in. along the coast and far less in the deep interior; however, there is little evaporation.

Arabian (Eastern), 86,000 sq mi in Egypt between the Nile R. and Red Sea, extending southward into Sudan
Atacama, 600-mi-long area rich in nitrate and copper deposits in N Chile
Chihuahuan, 140,000 sq mi in TX, NM, AZ, and Mexico
Dasht-e Kavir, approx. 500 mi long by 200 mi wide in N-central Iran
Dasht-e Lut, approx. 300 mi long by 200 mi wide in S-central Iran
Death Valley, 3,300 sq mi in CA and NV
Gibson, 120,000 sq mi in the interior of W Australia
Gobi, 500,000 sq mi in Mongolia and China
Great Sandy, 150,000 sq mi in W Australia
Great Victoria, 150,000 sq mi in SW Australia
Kalahari, 275,000 sq mi in southern Africa
Kara Kum, 115,000 sq mi in Turkmenistan
Kyzyl Kum, 115,000 sq mi in Kazakhstan and Uzbekistan
Libyan, 425,000 sq mi in the Sahara, extending from Libya through SW Egypt into Sudan

Mojave, 15,000 sq mi in southern CA
Namib, long narrow area (varies 30-100 mi wide) extending 800 mi along SW coast of Africa
Nubian, 157,000 sq mi in the Sahara in NE Sudan
Painted Desert, section of high plateau in northern AZ extending 200 mi SE from Grand Canyon
Patagonia, 300,000 sq mi in S Argentina
Rub al-Khali (Empty Quarter), 225,000 sq mi in the S Arabian Peninsula
Sahara, 3,500,000 sq mi in N Africa, extending west to the Atlantic. Largest desert in the world
Sonoran, 70,000 sq mi in southwestern AZ and southeastern CA extending into NW Mexico
Syrian, 100,000-sq-mi area extending over much of N Saudi Arabia, E Jordan, S Syria, and W Iraq
Taklamakan, 140,000 sq mi in Xinjiang Prov., China
Thar (Great Indian), 100,000-sq-mi area extending 400 mi along India-Pakistan border

Areas and Average Depths of Oceans, Seas, and Gulfs

Geographers and mapmakers recognize at least four major bodies of water: the Pacific, Atlantic, Indian, and Arctic Oceans. The Atlantic and Pacific Oceans are considered divided at the equator into the N and S Atlantic and the N and S Pacific. The Arctic Ocean is the name for waters north of the continental landmasses in the region of the Arctic Circle. The International Hydrographic Organization delimited a fifth world ocean in 2000. The Southern Ocean extends from the coast of Antarctica north to 60° S latitude, encompassing portions of the Atlantic, Indian, and Pacific Oceans.

Body of water	Area (sq mi)	Avg. depth (ft)	Body of water	Area (sq mi)	Avg. depth (ft)
Pacific Ocean	60,060,869	14,040	Sea of Japan	391,100	5,468
Atlantic Ocean	29,637,962	11,810	Hudson Bay	281,900	305
Indian Ocean	26,469,609	12,800	East China Sea	256,600	620
Southern Ocean	7,848,295	14,450	Andaman Sea	218,100	3,667
Arctic Ocean	5,427,050	4,300	Black Sea	196,100	3,906
South China Sea	1,148,500	4,802	Red Sea	174,900	1,764
Caribbean Sea	971,400	8,448	North Sea	164,900	308
Mediterranean Sea	969,100	4,926	Baltic Sea	147,500	180
Bering Sea	873,000	4,893	Yellow Sea	113,500	121
Gulf of Mexico	582,100	5,297	Persian Gulf	88,800	328
Sea of Okhotsk	537,500	3,192	Gulf of California	59,100	2,375

Principal Ocean Depths

Source: National Geospatial-Intelligence Agency, U.S. Dept. of Defense

Body of water	Location (lat.)	(long.)	Depth (meters)	(fathoms)	(feet)
Pacific Ocean					
Marianas Trench	11°22′ N	142°36′ E	10,924	5,973	35,840
Tonga Trench	23°16′ S	174°44′ W	10,800	5,906	35,433
Philippine Trench	10°38′ N	126°36′ E	10,057	5,499	32,995
Kermadec Trench	31°53′ S	177°21′ W	10,047	5,494	32,963
Bonin Trench	24°30′ N	143°24′ E	9,994	5,464	32,788
Kuril Trench	44°15′ N	150°34′ E	9,750	5,331	31,988
Izu Trench	31°05′ N	142°10′ E	9,695	5,301	31,808
New Britain Trench	06°19′ S	153°45′ E	8,940	4,888	29,331
Yap Trench	08°33′ N	138°02′ E	8,527	4,663	27,976
Japan Trench	36°08′ N	142°43′ E	8,412	4,600	27,599
Peru-Chile Trench	23°18′ S	71°14′ W	8,064	4,409	26,457
Palau Trench	07°52′ N	134°56′ E	8,054	4,404	26,424
Aleutian Trench	50°51′ N	177°11′ E	7,679	4,199	25,194
New Hebrides Trench	20°36′ S	168°37′ E	7,570	4,139	24,836
North Ryukyu Trench	24°00′ N	126°48′ E	7,181	3,927	23,560
Middle America Trench	14°02′ N	93°39′ W	6,662	3,643	21,857
Atlantic Ocean					
Puerto Rico Trench	19°55′ N	65°27′ W	8,605	4,705	28,232
South Sandwich Trench	55°42′ S	25°56′ W	8,325	4,552	27,313
Romanche Gap	0°13′ S	18°26′ W	7,728	4,226	25,354
Cayman Trench	19°12′ N	80°00′ W	7,535	4,120	24,721
Brazil Basin	09°10′ S	23°02′ W	6,119	3,346	20,076
Indian Ocean					
Java Trench	10°19′ S	109°58′ E	7,125	3,896	23,376
Ob' Trench	09°45′ S	67°18′ E	6,874	3,759	22,553
Diamantina Trench	35°50′ S	105°14′ E	6,602	3,610	21,660
Vema Trench	09°08′ S	67°15′ E	6,402	3,501	21,004
Agulhas Basin	45°20′ S	26°50′ E	6,195	3,387	20,325
Arctic Ocean					
Eurasia Basin	82°23′ N	19°31′ E	5,450	2,980	17,881
Mediterranean Sea					
Ionian Basin	36°32′ N	21°06′ E	5,150	2,816	16,896

Note: Greater depths have been reported in some areas but have not been officially confirmed by research vessels.

Major World Rivers

North American rivers are listed in a separate table.

River	Source or upper limit of length	Outflow	Length (mi)
Africa			
Chari	Bamingui-Bangoran region, Central African Republic	Lake Chad	650
Congo	Junction of Lualaba and Luava Rivers, Congo	Atlantic Ocean	2,720
Cubango (fmr. Okavango)	Central Angola	Okavango Delta	1,000
Gambia	Fouta Djallon Guinea	Atlantic Ocean	700
Kasai	Central Angola	Congo River	1,100
Limpopo	Junction of Marico and Ngotwane Rivers, South Africa	Indian Ocean	1,100
Lualaba	SE Congo	Congo River	1,100
Niger	Fouta Djallon, Guinea	Gulf of Guinea	2,600
Nile	Luvironza River, Burundi	Mediterranean Sea	4,160
Orange	Maluti mountains, N Lesotho	Atlantic Ocean	1,300
Sénégal	Junction of Bafing and Bakoy Rivers, Mali	Atlantic Ocean	1,000
Ubangi	Junction of Uele and Bomu Rivers, Congo	Congo River	700
Zambezi	NW Zambia	Indian Ocean	1,700
Asia			
Amu Darya	Junction of Wakhsh and Panj Rivers, Tajikistan	Aral Sea	1,660
Amur	Junction of Shilka and Argun Rivers, China-Russia	Tartar Strait	1,780
Angara	Lake Baykal, Russia	Yenisei River	1,150
Ayeyarwady (fmr. Irrawaddy)	Junction of Mali and Nmai Rivers, Myanmar	Andaman Sea	1,000
Brahmaputra	Kailas Range, Himalayas, SW Tibet	Bay of Bengal	1,800
Chang-Jiang	Tibetan Plateau, SW Qinghai, China	East China Sea	3,450
Euphrates	Junction of Kara (Sarasu) and Murat Rivers, Turkey	Shatt al-Arab	1,700
Ganges	Gangotri glacier, Himalayas, India	Bay of Bengal	1,560
Godavari	W Ghats, Maharashtra, India	Bay of Bengal	900
Hsi (see Xi He)			
Huang-He	Kunlun Mountains, Qinghai, China	Yellow Sea	3,000
Indus	Kailas Range, Himalayas, Tibet	Arabian Sea	1,900
Irtysh	Kazakhstan-Russia	Ob River	2,650
Jordan	Junction of Dan, Banias, and Hazbani streams, Israel	Dead Sea	200
Kolyma	Kolyma and Cherskogo Ranges Russia	Arctic Ocean	1,500
Krishna	W Ghats, Maharashtra, India	Bay of Bengal	800
Kura	NE Turkey	Caspian Sea	950
Lena	W Baikal Range, Russia	Laptev Sea	2,648
Mekong	E Tibetan Plateau, China	South China Sea	2,700
Narmada	Madhya Pradesh, India	Arabian Sea	775
Ob	Junction of Biya and Katun Rivers, Russia	Gulf of Ob	2,300
Salween	E Tibet, China	Gulf of Martaban	1,750
Songhua Jiang	Changbai Mountains, Jilin, China	Amur River	1,150
Sungari (see Songhua Jiang)			
Sutlej	Kailas Range, Himalayas, Tibet	Indus River	900
Syr	Junction of Naryn and Kara Darya Rivers, Uzbekistan	Aral Sea	1,380
Tarim	Junction of Kashi and Yarkant Rivers, China	Lop Nor	1,300
Tigris	Taurus Mountains, Turkey	Shatt al-Arab	1,150
Xi He	E Yunnan, China	South China Sea	1,250
Yamuna	Uttarakhand, India	Ganges River	850
Yangtze (see Chang-Jiang)			
Yellow (see Huang-He)			
Yenisei	Kyzyl, Tuva Republic, Russia	Kara Sea	2,500
Australia			
Darling	E Highlands, NE New South Wales/SE Queensland	Murray River	1,702
Murray	Australian Alps, SE New South Wales	Southern Ocean	1,609
Murrumbidgee	Australian Alps, SE New South Wales	Murray River	1,050
Europe			
Buh, Southern	NW of Khmel'nyts'kyy, Ukraine	Black Sea	532
Buh, Western	ENE of Zolochiv, Ukraine	Wisla River	500
Danube	Brege and Brigach Rivers, Black Forest, SW Germany	Black Sea	1,770
Dnieper	W of Sychevka, Smolensk, Russia	Black Sea	1,420
Dniester	Carpathian Mountains, Ukraine	Black Sea	850
Don	SE of Tula, Russia	Sea of Azov	1,200
Drava	Carnic Alps, N Italy	Danube River	450
Dvina, North	Near Veliki Ustyug, Vologda, Russia	White Sea	465
Dvina, West	Valdai Hills, Russia	Gulf of Riga	635
Ebro	Cantabrian Mountains, N Spain	Mediterranean Sea	575
Elbe	Giant Mountains, NW Czech Republic	North Sea	725
Garonne	Central Pyrenees, Spain	Bay of Biscay	402
Kama	Ural Mountains, N of Kuliga, Russia	Volga River	1,260
Loire	Mt. Gerbier-de-Jonc, Vivrais Mountains, France	Atlantic Ocean	630
Marne	Langres Plateau, NE France	Seine River	325
Meuse	Langres Plateau, NE France	North Sea	560
Oder	Sudetes Mountains, NE Czech Republic	Baltic Sea	562
Oka	S of Orël, Russia	Volga River	925
Pechora	N Ural Mountains, Russia	Barents Sea	1,120
Po	Cottian Alps, Piedmont, NW Italy	Adriatic Sea	405
Rhine	Swiss Alps	North Sea	820

River	Source or upper limit of length	Outflow	Length (mi)
Rhône	Rhône glacier, NE Valais, Switzerland	Mediterranean Sea	505
Seine	Langres Plateau, N Burgundy, France	English Channel	480
Shannon	Near Cuilcagh Mountain, NW Cavan County, Ireland	Atlantic Ocean	240
Tagus	E of Madrid, Spain	Atlantic Ocean	585
Thames	4 headstreams in the Cotswold Hills, Gloucestershire, England	North Sea	210
Tiber	Etruscan Apennines, Italy	Tyrrhenian Sea	251
Tisza	N of Rakhiv, W Ukraine	Danube River	700
Ural	S Ural Mountains, NE Bashkortostan, Russia	Caspian Sea	1,580
Volga	Valdai Hills, Smolensk, Russia	Caspian Sea	2,290
Weser	Junction of Fulda and Werra Rivers, Germany	North Sea	273
Wisla	W Beskid range, Carpathian Mountains, SW Poland	Gulf of Gdansk	665

South America

River	Source or upper limit of length	Outflow	Length (mi)
Amazon	Junction of Ucayali and Marañón Rivers, Andes Mountains, Peru	Atlantic Ocean	3,900
Araguaía	Serra des Araras, Goiás-Mato Grosso, Brazil	Tocantins River	1,100
Beni	Cordillera Real, La Paz, Bolivia	Madeira River	1,000
Caquetá-Japura	Andes Mountains, SW Colombia	Amazon River	1,750
Juruá	Cerros de Canchyuaya, E Peru	Amazon River	1,500
Madeira	Junction of Beni and Mamoré Rivers, Bolivia	Amazon River	2,100
Magdalena	Cordillera Central, SW Colombia	Caribbean Sea	1,000
Negro	SE Colombia	Amazon River	1,400
Orinoco	Near Mt. Delgado Chalbaud, Guiana Highlands, S Venezuela	Atlantic Ocean	1,600
Paraguay	Central Mato Grosso highlands, Brazil	Paraná River	1,584
Paraná	Junction of Paranaíba and Rio Grande Rivers, SE Brazil	Rio de la Plata	2,485
Pilcomayo	E of Lake Poopó, Bolivia	Paraguay River	1,000
Purus	Andes Mountains, E Peru	Amazon River	2,100
Putumayo	Andes Mountains, S Colombia	Amazon River	1,000
Rio de la Plata	Estuary of Paraná and Uruguay Rivers, Argentina-Uruguay	Atlantic Ocean	170
São Francisco	Serra de Canastra, SW Minas Gerais, Brazil	Atlantic Ocean	1,800
Tocantins	South-central Goiás, Brazil	Para River	1,640
Ucayali	Junction of Apurímac and Urubamba Rivers, E Peru	Marañón River	1,000
Uruguay	S Brazil	Rio de la Plata	1,000
Xingu	Central Mato Grosso, Brazil	Amazon River	1,230

Major Rivers in North America

River	Source or upper limit of length	Outflow	Length (mi)
Alabama	Gilmer County, GA	Mobile River	729
Albany	Lake St. Joseph, ON, Can.	James Bay	610
Allegheny	Potter County, PA	Ohio River	325
Altamaha-Ocmulgee	Junction of Yellow and South Rivers, Newton Co., GA	Atlantic Ocean	392
Apalachicola-Chattahoochee	Towns County, GA	Gulf of Mexico	524
Arkansas	Lake County, CO	Mississippi River	1,459
Assiniboine	E Saskatchewan, Can.	Red River	450
Attawapiskat	Attawapiskat, ON, Can.	James Bay	465
Back (NT)	Contwoyto Lake, NT, Can.	Chantrey Inlet, Arctic Ocean	605
Big Black	Webster County, MS	Mississippi River	330
Brazos	Junction of Salt and Double Mountain Forks, Stonewall Co., TX	Gulf of Mexico	950
Canadian	Las Animas County, CO	Arkansas River	906
Cedar (IA)	Dodge County, MN	Iowa River	329
Cheyenne	Junction of Antelope Creek and Dry Fork, Converse Co., WY	Missouri River	290
Churchill, Labrador	Lake Ashuanipi, NL, Can.	Atlantic Ocean	532
Churchill, Manitoba	Methy Lake, SK, Can.	Hudson Bay	1,000
Cimarron	Colfax County, NM	Arkansas River	600
Colorado (AZ)	Rocky Mountain Natl. Park, CO (90 mi in Mexico)	Gulf of California	1,450
Colorado (TX)	W Texas	Matagorda Bay	862
Columbia	Columbia Lake, BC, Can.	Pacific Ocean, bet. OR and WA	1,243
Columbia, Upper	Columbia Lake, BC, Can.	Mouth of Snake River	890
Connecticut	Third Connecticut Lake, NH	Long Island Sound, CT	407
Coppermine	Lac de Gras, NT, Can.	Coronation Gulf, Arctic Ocean	525
Cumberland	Letcher County, KY	Ohio River	720
Delaware	Schoharie County, NY	Liston Point, Delaware Bay	390
Fraser	Near Mount Robson (on Continental Divide)	Strait of Georgia	850
Gila	Catron County, NM	Colorado River	649
Green (UT-WY)	Junction of Wells and Trail Creeks, Sublette County, WY	Colorado River	730
Hudson	Henderson Lake, Essex County, NY	Upper New York Bay	306
Illinois	St. Joseph County, IN	Mississippi River	420
James (ND-SD)	Wells County, ND	Missouri River	710
James (VA)	Junction of Jackson and Cowpasture Rivers, Botetourt Co., VA	Hampton Roads	340
Kanawha-New	Junction of North and South Forks of New River, NC	Ohio River	352
Kentucky	Junction of North and Middle Forks, Lee County, KY	Ohio River	259
Klamath	Lake Ewauna, Klamath Falls, OR	Pacific Ocean	250

River	Source or upper limit of length	Outflow	Length (mi)
Kootenay	Kootenay Lake, BC, Can.	Columbia River	485
Koyukuk	Endicott Mountains, AK	Yukon River	470
Kuskokwim	Alaska Range	Kuskokwim Bay	724
Liard	Southern Yukon, AK	Mackenzie River	693
Little Missouri	Crook County, WY	Missouri River	560
Mackenzie	Great Slave Lake, NT, Can.	Arctic Ocean	1,060
Milk	Junction of North and South Forks, AB, Can.	Missouri River	625
Minnesota	Big Stone Lake, MN	Mississippi River	332
Mississippi	Lake Itasca, MN	Gulf of Mexico	2,340
Mississippi-Missouri-Red Rock	Source of Red Rock, Beaverhead County, MT	Gulf of Mexico	3,710
Missouri	Junction of Jefferson, Madison, and Gallatin Rivers, Gallatin County, MT	Mississippi River	2,315
Missouri-Red Rock	Source of Red Rock, Beaverhead County, MT	Mississippi River	2,540
Mobile-Alabama-Coosa	Gilmer County, GA	Mobile Bay	774
Nelson	Lake Winnipeg, MB, Can.	Hudson Bay	410
Neosho	Morris County, KS	Arkansas River, OK	460
Niobrara	Niobrara County, WY	Missouri River, NE	431
North Canadian	Union County, NM	Canadian River, OK	800
North Platte	Junction of Grizzly and Little Grizzly Creeks, Jackson Co., CO	Platte River, NE	618
Ohio	Junction of Allegheny and Monongahela Rivers, Pittsburgh, PA	Mississippi River	981
Ohio-Allegheny	Potter County, PA	Mississippi River	1,310
Osage	East-central Kansas	Missouri River	500
Ottawa	Lake Capimitchigama, QC, Can.	St. Lawrence River	790
Ouachita	Polk County, AR	Black River	605
Peace	Junction of Finlay and Parsnip Rivers, BC, Can.	Slave River	1,210
Pearl	Neshoba County, MS	Gulf of Mexico	411
Pecos	Mora County, NM	Rio Grande	926
Pee Dee-Yadkin	Watauga County, NC	Winyah Bay	435
Pend Oreille-Clark Fork	Near Butte, MT	Columbia River	531
Platte	Junction of North and South Platte Rivers, NE.	Missouri River	310
Porcupine	Ogilvie Mountains, AK	Yukon River, AK	569
Potomac	Garrett County, MD	Chesapeake Bay	383
Powder	Junction of South and Middle Forks, WY	Yellowstone River	375
Red (OK-TX-LA)	Curry County, NM.	Mississippi River	1,290
Red River of the North	Junction of Otter Tail and Bois de Sioux Rivers, Wilkin Co., MN	Lake Winnipeg	545
Republican	Junction of North Fork and Arikaree Rivers, NE.	Kansas River	445
Rio Grande	San Juan County, CO.	Gulf of Mexico	1,900
Roanoke	Junction of North and South Forks, Montgomery Co., VA	Albemarle Sound	380
Rock (IL-WI)	Dodge County, WI	Mississippi River	300
Sabine	Junction of South and Caddo Forks, Hunt Co., TX	Sabine Lake	380
Sacramento	Siskiyou County, CA.	Suisun Bay	377
St. Francis	Iron County, MO	Mississippi River	425
St. John	NW Maine	Bay of Fundy	418
St. Lawrence	Lake Ontario, ON-NY	Gulf of St. Lawrence, Atlantic Ocean	800
Saguenay	Lake St. John, QC, Can.	St. Lawrence River	434
Salmon (ID)	Custer County, ID	Snake River	420
San Joaquin	Junction of South and Middle Forks, Madera Co., CA	Suisun Bay	350
San Juan	Silver Lake, Archuleta County, CO.	Colorado River	360
Santee-Wateree-Catawba	McDowell County, NC	Atlantic Ocean	538
Saskatchewan, North	Rocky Mountains, AB, Can.	Saskatchewan R.	800
Saskatchewan, South	Rocky Mountains, AB, Can.	Saskatchewan R.	865
Savannah	Junction of Seneca and Tugaloo Rivers, Anderson Co., SC	Atlantic Ocean, GA-SC	314
Severn (ON)	Sandy Lake, ON, Can.	Hudson Bay	610
Smoky Hill	Cheyenne County, CO	Kansas River, KS	540
Snake	Teton County, WY	Columbia River, WA	1,038
South Platte	Junction of South and Middle Forks, Park County, CO	Platte River	424
Susitna	Alaska Range	Cook Inlet	313
Susquehanna	Huyden Creek, Otsego County, NY	Chesapeake Bay	447
Tallahatchie	Tippah County, MS.	Yazoo River	301
Tanana	Wrangell Mountains, AK	Yukon River	659
Tennessee	Junction of French Broad and Holston Rivers, TN	Ohio River	652
Tennessee-French Broad	Courthouse Creek, Transylvania County, NC	Ohio River	886
Tombigbee	Prentiss County, MS.	Mobile River	525
Trinity	N of Dallas, TX	Galveston Bay	360
Wabash	Darke County, OH	Ohio River	512
Washita	Hemphill County, TX.	Red River, OK	500
White (AR-MO)	Madison County, AR.	Mississippi River	722
Willamette	Douglas County, OR.	Columbia River	309
Wind-Bighorn	Junction of Wind and Little Wind Rivers, Fremont Co., WY (source of Wind R. is Togwotee Pass, Teton Co., WY)	Yellowstone River	338
Wisconsin	Lac Vieux Desert, Vilas County, WI	Mississippi River	430
Yellowstone	Park County, WY	Missouri River	682
Yukon	McNeil River, YT, Can.	Bering Sea	1,979

Major Natural Lakes of the World

Source: Geological Survey, U.S. Dept. of the Interior; GeoAccess Division, Natural Resources Canada

A lake is generally defined as a body of water surrounded by land. By this definition some bodies of water that are called seas, such as the Caspian Sea and the Aral Sea, are really lakes. In the following table, the word "lake" is omitted when it is part of the name.

Name	Continent	Area (sq mi)	Length (mi)	Maximum depth (ft)	Elevation (ft)
Caspian Sea[1]	Asia-Europe	143,244	760	3,363	−92
Superior	North America	31,700	350	1,330	600
Victoria	Africa	26,828	250	270	3,720
Huron	North America	23,000	206	750	579
Michigan	North America	22,300	307	923	579
Aral Sea[1]	Asia	13,000[2]	260	180	125
Tanganyika	Africa	12,700	420	4,823	2,534
Baykal	Asia	12,162	395	5,315	1,493
Great Bear	North America	12,096	192	1,463	512
Nyasa (Malawi)	Africa	11,150	360	2,280	1,550
Great Slave	North America	11,031	298	2,015	513
Erie	North America	9,910	241	210	570
Winnipeg	North America	9,417	266	200	713
Ontario	North America	7,340	193	802	245
Balkhash[1]	Asia	7,115	376	85	1,115
Ladoga	Europe	6,835	124	738	13
Maracaibo	South America	5,217	133	115	sea level
Onega	Europe	3,710	145	328	108
Eyre[1]	Australia	3,600[3]	90	4	−52
Titicaca	South America	3,200	122	922	12,500
Nicaragua	North America	3,100	102	230	102
Athabasca	North America	3,064	208	407	700
Reindeer	North America	2,568	143	720	1,106
Tonle Sap	Asia	2,500[3]	70	45	NA
Turkana (Rudolf)	Africa	2,473	154	240	1,230
Issyk Kul[1]	Asia	2,355	115	2,303	5,279
Torrens[1]	Australia	2,230[3]	130	(3)	92
Vanern	Europe	2,156	91	328	144
Nettilling	North America	2,140	67	(3)	95
Winnipegosis	North America	2,075	141	38	830
Albert	Africa	2,075	100	168	2,030
Nipigon	North America	1,872	72	540	1,050
Gairdner[1]	Australia	1,840[3]	90	(3)	112
Urmia[1]	Asia	1,815	90	49	4,180
Manitoba	North America	1,799	140	21	813
Chad	Africa	500+[4]	175	24	787

NA = Not available. (1) Salt lake. (2) The diversion of feeder rivers since the 1960s has devastated the Aral—once the world's fourth-largest lake (26,000 sq mi). By 2000, the Aral had effectively become three lakes, with the total area shown. (3) Subject to great seasonal variation. (4) Once fourth-largest lake in Africa (about 10,000 sq mi in the 1960s), Chad had shrunk to around 5% of its original size as of 2006 as a result of irrigation and long-term drought.

The Great Lakes

Source: National Ocean Service, National Oceanic and Atmospheric Administration, U.S. Dept. of Commerce

The Great Lakes form the world's **largest freshwater body** (in surface area) and with their connecting waterways are the largest inland water transportation unit. Draining the north-central basin of the U.S., they enable shipping to get to the Atlantic via their outlet, the St. Lawrence R; the Gulf of Mexico can be reached via the Illinois Waterway, between Lake Michigan and the Mississippi R. A third outlet connects with the Hudson R. and then the Atlantic via the New York State Barge Canal System. Illinois Waterway and NYS Barge Canal System traffic is limited to recreational boating and small shipping vessels.

Only Lake Michigan is wholly in the U.S.; the other lakes are shared with Canada. Ships move from the shores of Lake Superior to Whitefish Bay in the east, then through the Soo Locks in Sault Ste. Marie, MI, onto St. Mary's R. and into Lake Huron. To reach the Port of Indiana-Burns Harbor and South Chicago, IL, ships travel west from Lake Huron to Lake Michigan through the Straits of Mackinac. Low water datum is based on the International Great Lakes Datum (1985), with Rimouski, Quebec, as the reference zero point. The distance between Duluth, MN, and Lake Ontario's east end is 1,156 mi.

	Superior	Michigan	Huron	Erie	Ontario
Length (mi)	350	307	206	241	193
Breadth (mi)	160	118	183	57	53
Deepest soundings (ft)	1,333	923	750	210	802
Volume of water (cu mi)	2,935	1,180	850	116	393
Area (sq mi) water surface—U.S.	20,600	22,300	9,100	4,980	3,460
Canada	11,100	NA	13,900	4,930	3,880
Area (sq mi) entire drainage basin—U.S.	16,900	45,600	16,200	18,000	15,200
Canada	32,400	NA	35,500	4,720	12,100
Total area (sq mi), U.S. and Canada	**81,000**	**67,900**	**74,700**	**32,630**	**34,850**
Low water datum above mean water level at Rimouski, Quebec, avg. level (ft)	601.10	577.50	577.50	569.20	243.30
Latitude, N	46°25′	41°37′	43°00′	41°23′	43°11′
	49°00′	46°06′	46°17′	42°52′	44°15′
Longitude, W	84°22′	84°45′	79°43′	78°51′	76°03′
	92°06′	88°02′	84°45′	83°29′	79°53′
National boundary line (mi)	282.8	NA	260.8	251.5	174.6
U.S. shoreline (mainland only) (mi)	863	1,400	580	431	300

NA = Not applicable.

Notable Waterfalls

Source: National Geographic Society

The Earth has thousands of waterfalls, some of considerable magnitude. Their magnitude is determined not only by height but also by volume of flow, steadiness of flow, crest width, whether the water drops sheerly or over a sloping surface, and whether it descends in one leap or in a succession of leaps. A series of low falls flowing over a considerable distance is known as a cascade. Waterfalls are highly variable and few authoritative figures exist. For more information and some alternative measurements, see the World Waterfall Database at www.worldwaterfalldatabase.com.

Estimated mean annual flow (ft³/sec) of major waterfalls: Niagara, 212,200; Paulo Afonso, 100,000; Urubupunga, 97,000; Iguazu, 61,000; Patos-Maribondo, 53,000; Victoria, 35,400; and Kaieteur, 23,400.

Height is total drop in feet in one or more leaps. If river name is not shown, it is the same as the waterfall. # = more than one leap; * = diminishes greatly seasonally; ** = reduces to a trickle or is dry for part of each year; R. = river; (C) = cascade.

Name, location	Height (ft)
Africa	
Angola	
Ruacana, Cunene R.	406
Lesotho	
Maletsunyane*	630
South Africa	
Augrabies, Orange R.*	480
Tugela#.	2,800
Tanzania-Zambia	
Kalambo*	704
Zimbabwe-Zambia	
Victoria, Zambezi R.*	343
Asia and Oceania	
Australia	
New South Wales	
Wentworth	614
Wollomombi	722
Queensland	
Tully**	984
Wallaman, Stony Creek#	1,137
India	
Sivasamudram	320
Jog, Sharavati R.*	830
Japan	
Kegon, Lake Chuzenji*	350
New Zealand	
Helena	722
Sutherland, Arthur R.#	1,904
Europe	
Austria	
Gastein#	487
Krimml#	1,246
France	
Gavarnie*	1,385
Great Britain	
Scotland	
Glomach	370
Wales	
Pistyll Rhaeadr	240
Italy	
Toce (C)	470

Name, location	Height (ft)
Norway	
Mardalsfossen#**	2,154
Skykje**	984
Vetti, Morka-Koldedola R.	900
Sweden	
Handol#	345
Switzerland	
Giessbach (C).	984
Reichenbach#.	820
Staubbach	984
Trümmelbach#	1,312
North America	
Canada	
Alberta	
Panther, Nigel Creek	600
British Columbia	
Della#	1,444
Takakkaw, Daly Glacier#	833
Quebec	
Montmorency	276
Canada-United States	
Niagara (American)	194
Niagara (Horseshoe)	187
United States	
Alabama	
Noccalula Falls	90
California	
Feather*	640
Yosemite National Park	
Bridalveil*	620
Illilouette*	370
Nevada, Merced R.*	594
Ribbon**	1,612
Silver Strand, Meadow Brook**	574
Vernal, Merced R.*	317
Yosemite#**	2,425
Colorado	
Seven Falls, S. Cheyenne Creek#	300
Hawaii	
Akaka, Kolekole Stream	420
Idaho	
Shoshone, Snake R.**	212

Name, location	Height (ft)
Kentucky	
Cumberland	68
Maryland	
Great, Potomac R. (C)*	76
Minnesota	
Minnehaha**	53
New Jersey	
Great, Passaic R.	70
New York	
Taughannock*	215
Oregon	
Multnomah#	850
Tennessee	
Fall Creek	256
Washington	
Sluiskin, Paradise R.	300
Snoqualmie**	268
Wisconsin	
Big Manitou, Black R. (C)*	165
Wyoming	
Tower	132
Yellowstone (upper)*	109
Yellowstone (lower)*	308
South America	
Argentina-Brazil	
Iguazú	269
Brazil	
Cachoeira da Fumaça*	1,312
Paulo Afonso, São Francisco R.	275
Colombia	
Tequendama, Bogota R.*	482
Ecuador	
Agoyan, Pastaza R.*	200
Guyana	
Kaieteur, Potaro R.	741
King George VI, Kamarang R.	1,600
Marina, Ipobe R.#	500
Venezuela	
Angel#*	3,212
Cuquenan	2,000

Latitude, Longitude, and Altitude of U.S. and Canadian Cities

Source: U.S. geographic positions, U.S. altitudes provided by Geological Survey, U.S. Dept. of the Interior.
Canadian geographic positions and altitudes provided by Natural Resources Canada.

City, state/province	Lat. N °	'	''	Long. W °	'	''	Elev. (ft)
Abilene, TX	32	26	55	99	43	58	1,718
Akron, OH	41	4	53	81	31	9	1,050
Albany, NY	42	39	9	73	45	24	20
Albuquerque, NM	35	5	4	106	39	2	4,955
Alert, NU	82	30	0	62	22	0	100
Allentown, PA	40	36	30	75	29	26	350
Amarillo, TX	35	13	19	101	49	51	3,685
Anchorage, AK	61	13	5	149	54	1	101
Ann Arbor, MI	42	16	15	83	43	35	880
Asheville, NC	35	36	3	82	33	15	2,134
Ashland, KY	38	28	42	82	38	17	558
Atlanta, GA	33	44	56	84	23	17	1,050
Atlantic City, NJ	39	21	51	74	25	24	8
Augusta, GA	33	28	15	81	58	30	414
Augusta, ME	44	18	38	69	46	48	45
Austin, TX	30	16	1	97	44	34	501
Bakersfield, CA	35	22	24	119	1	4	408
Baltimore, MD	39	17	25	76	36	45	100
Bangor, ME	44	48	4	68	46	42	158
Baton Rouge, LA	30	27	2	91	9	16	53
Battle Creek, MI	42	19	16	85	10	47	820
Bay City, MI	43	35	40	83	53	20	595
Beaumont, TX	30	5	9	94	6	6	20

City, state/province	Lat. N °	'	''	Long. W °	'	''	Elev. (ft)
Belleville, ON	44	14	0	77	21	0	320
Bellingham, WA	48	45	35	122	29	13	100
Berkeley, CA	37	52	18	122	16	18	150
Billings, MT	45	47	0	108	30	0	3,124
Biloxi, MS	30	23	45	88	53	7	25
Binghamton, NY	42	5	55	75	55	6	865
Birmingham, AL	33	31	14	86	48	9	600
Bismarck, ND	46	48	30	100	47	0	1,700
Bloomington, IL	40	29	3	88	59	37	829
Boise, ID	43	36	49	116	12	9	2,730
Boston, MA	42	21	30	71	3	37	20
Bowling Green, KY	36	59	25	86	26	37	510
Brandon, MB	49	54	35	99	57	03	1,343
Brantford, ON	43	08	0	80	16	0	815
Brattleboro, VT	42	51	3	72	33	30	240
Bridgeport, CT	41	10	1	73	12	19	10
Brockton, MA	42	5	0	71	1	8	112
Buffalo, NY	42	53	11	78	52	43	585
Burlington, ON	43	23	10	79	50	15	640
Burlington, VT	44	28	33	73	12	45	113
Butte, MT	46	0	14	112	32	2	5,549
Calgary, AB	51	03	0	114	05	0	3,557
Cambridge, MA	42	22	30	71	6	22	30

City, state/province	Lat. N °	'	''	Long. W °	'	''	Elev. (ft)
Canton, OH	40	47	56	81	22	43	1,100
Carson City, NV	39	9	50	119	45	59	4,730
Cedar Rapids, IA	42	0	30	91	38	38	730
Central Islip, NY	40	47	26	73	12	8	88
Champaign, IL	40	6	59	88	14	36	740
Charleston, SC	32	46	35	79	55	52	118
Charleston, WV	38	20	59	81	37	58	606
Charlotte, NC	35	13	37	80	50	36	850
Charlottetown, PE	46	14	25	63	08	05	160
Chattanooga, TN	35	2	44	85	18	35	685
Cheyenne, WY	41	8	24	104	49	11	6,067
Chicago, IL	41	51	0	87	39	0	596
Churchill, MB	58	43	30	94	07	0	94
Cincinnati, OH	39	9	43	84	27	25	683
Cleveland, OH	41	29	58	81	41	44	690
Colorado Springs, CO	38	50	2	104	49	15	6,008
Columbia, MO	38	57	6	92	20	2	758
Columbia, SC	34	0	2	81	2	6	314
Columbus, GA	32	27	39	84	59	16	300
Columbus, OH	39	57	40	82	59	56	800
Concord, NH	43	12	29	71	32	17	288
Corpus Christi, TX	27	48	1	97	23	46	35
Dallas, TX	32	47	0	96	48	0	463
Dawson, YT	64	03	45	139	25	50	1,214
Dayton, OH	39	45	32	84	11	30	750
Daytona Beach, FL	29	12	38	81	1	23	10
Decatur, IL	39	50	25	88	57	17	670
Denver, CO	39	44	21	104	59	3	5,260
Des Moines, IA	41	36	2	93	36	32	803
Detroit, MI	42	19	53	83	2	45	585
Dodge City, KS	37	45	10	100	1	0	2,550
Dubuque, IA	42	30	2	90	39	52	620
Duluth, MN	46	47	0	92	6	23	610
Durham, NC	35	59	38	78	53	56	394
Eau Claire, WI	44	48	41	91	29	54	850
Edmonton, AB	53	33	0	113	28	0	2,200
Elizabeth, NJ	40	39	50	74	12	40	38
El Paso, TX	31	45	31	106	29	11	3,695
Enid, OK	36	23	44	97	52	41	1,246
Erie, PA	42	7	45	80	5	7	650
Eugene, OR	44	3	8	123	5	8	419
Eureka, CA	40	48	8	124	9	45	44
Evansville, IN	37	58	29	87	33	21	388
Fairbanks, AK	64	50	16	147	42	59	440
Fall River, MA	41	42	5	71	9	20	200
Fargo, ND	46	52	38	96	47	22	900
Flagstaff, AZ	35	11	53	111	39	2	6,900
Flint, MI	43	0	45	83	41	15	750
Ft. Smith, AR	35	23	9	94	23	54	446
Ft. Wayne, IN	41	7	50	85	7	44	781
Ft. Worth, TX	32	43	31	97	19	14	670
Fredericton, NB	45	56	43	66	40	0	67
Fresno, CA	36	44	52	119	46	17	296
Gadsden, AL	34	0	51	86	0	24	554
Gainesville, FL	29	39	5	82	19	30	183
Gallup, NM	35	31	41	108	44	31	6,508
Galveston, TX	29	18	4	94	47	51	10
Gary, IN	41	35	36	87	20	47	600
Grand Junction, CO	39	3	50	108	33	0	4,597
Grand Rapids, MI	42	57	48	85	40	5	610
Great Falls, MT	47	30	1	111	18	0	3,334
Green Bay, WI	44	31	9	88	1	11	594
Greensboro, NC	36	4	21	79	47	32	770
Greenville, SC	34	51	9	82	23	39	966
Guelph, ON	43	33	0	80	15	0	1,100
Gulfport, MS	30	22	2	89	5	34	25
Halifax, NS	44	52	0	63	43	0	477
Hamilton, OH	39	23	58	84	33	41	600
Hamilton, ON	43	14	0	79	57	0	780
Harrisburg, PA	40	16	25	76	53	5	320
Hartford, CT	41	45	44	72	41	8	40
Helena, MT	46	35	34	112	2	7	4,090
Hilo, HI	19	43	47	155	5	24	38
Honolulu, HI	21	18	25	157	51	30	18
Houston, TX	29	45	47	95	21	47	40
Huntsville, AL	34	43	49	86	35	10	641
Indianapolis, IN	39	46	6	86	9	29	717
Iowa City, IA	41	39	40	91	31	48	685
Jackson, MI	42	14	45	84	24	5	940
Jackson, MS	32	17	55	90	11	5	294
Jacksonville, FL	30	19	55	81	39	21	12
Jersey City, NJ	40	43	41	74	4	41	83
Johnstown, PA	40	19	36	78	55	20	1200
Joplin, MO	37	5	3	94	30	47	990
Juneau, AK	58	18	7	134	25	11	50
Kalamazoo, MI	42	17	30	85	35	14	755
Kansas City, KS	39	6	51	94	37	38	750
Kansas City, MO	39	5	59	94	34	42	740

City, state/province	Lat. N °	'	''	Long. W °	'	''	Elev. (ft)
Kenosha, WI	42	35	5	87	49	16	610
Key West, FL	24	33	19	81	46	58	8
Kingston, ON	44	18	0	76	28	0	305
Kitchener, ON	43	27	0	80	29	0	1,040
Knoxville, TN	35	57	38	83	55	15	889
Lafayette, IN	40	25	0	86	52	31	567
Lancaster, PA	40	2	16	76	18	21	368
Lansing, MI	42	43	57	84	33	20	830
Laredo, TX	27	30	22	99	30	26	414
Las Vegas, NV	36	10	30	115	8	11	2,000
Lawrence, MA	42	42	25	71	9	49	50
Lethbridge, AB	49	42	0	112	49	0	3,047
Lexington, KY	37	59	19	84	28	40	955
Lihue, HI	21	58	52	159	22	16	206
Lima, OH	40	44	33	84	6	19	875
Lincoln, NE	40	48	0	96	40	0	1,150
Little Rock, AR	34	44	47	92	17	22	350
London, ON	42	59	0	81	14	0	875
Los Angeles, CA	34	3	8	118	14	34	330
Louisville, KY	38	15	15	85	45	34	462
Lowell, MA	42	38	0	71	19	0	102
Lubbock, TX	33	34	40	101	51	17	3,195
Macon, GA	32	50	26	83	37	57	400
Madison, WI	43	4	23	89	24	4	863
Manchester, NH	42	59	44	71	27	19	175
Marshall, TX	32	32	41	94	22	2	410
Medicine Hat, AB	50	03	0	110	40	0	2,352
Memphis, TN	35	8	58	90	2	56	254
Meriden, CT	41	32	17	72	48	27	190
Miami, FL	25	46	26	80	11	38	11
Milwaukee, WI	43	2	20	87	54	23	634
Minneapolis, MN	44	58	48	93	15	49	815
Minot, ND	48	13	57	101	17	45	1,555
Mobile, AL	30	41	39	88	2	35	16
Moncton, NB	46	06	57	64	48	11	232
Montgomery, AL	32	22	0	86	18	0	250
Montpelier, VT	44	15	36	72	34	33	525
Montréal, QC	45	31	0	73	39	0	221
Moose Jaw, SK	50	24	0	105	32	0	1,892
Muncie, IN	40	11	36	85	23	11	952
Nashville, TN	36	9	57	86	47	4	440
Natchez, MS	31	33	37	91	24	11	230
Newark, NJ	40	44	8	74	10	22	95
New Britain, CT	41	39	40	72	46	48	200
New Haven, CT	41	18	29	72	55	43	40
New Orleans, LA	29	57	16	90	4	30	11
New York, NY	40	42	51	74	0	23	55
Niagara Falls, ON	43	06	0	79	04	0	589
Nome, AK	64	30	4	165	24	23	25
Norfolk, VA	36	50	48	76	17	8	10
North Bay, ON	46	19	0	79	28	0	1,200
Oakland, CA	37	48	16	122	16	11	42
Ogden, UT	41	13	23	111	58	23	4,299
Oklahoma City, OK	35	28	3	97	30	58	1,195
Omaha, NE	41	15	31	95	56	15	1,040
Orlando, FL	28	32	17	81	22	46	106
Ottawa, ON	45	16	0	75	45	0	382
Paducah, KY	37	5	0	88	36	0	345
Pasadena, CA	34	8	52	118	8	37	865
Paterson, NJ	40	55	0	74	10	20	70
Pensacola, FL	30	25	16	87	13	1	32
Peoria, IL	40	41	37	89	35	20	470
Peterborough, ON	44	18	0	78	19	0	628
Philadelphia, PA	39	57	8	75	9	51	40
Phoenix, AZ	33	26	54	112	4	24	1,090
Pierre, SD	44	22	6	100	21	2	1,484
Pittsburgh, PA	40	26	26	79	59	46	770
Pittsfield, MA	42	27	0	73	14	45	1,039
Pocatello, ID	42	52	17	112	26	41	4,464
Pt. Arthur, TX	29	53	55	93	55	43	10
Portland, ME	43	39	41	70	15	21	25
Portland, OR	45	31	25	122	40	30	50
Portsmouth, NH	43	4	18	70	45	47	21
Portsmouth, VA	36	50	7	76	17	55	10
Prince Rupert, BC	54	19	0	130	19	0	116
Providence, RI	41	49	26	71	24	48	80
Provo, UT	40	14	2	111	39	28	4,549
Pueblo, CO	38	15	16	104	36	31	4,662
Québec City, QC	46	49	0	71	13	0	244
Racine, WI	42	43	34	87	46	58	630
Raleigh, NC	35	46	19	78	38	20	350
Rapid City, SD	44	4	50	103	13	50	3,247
Reading, PA	40	20	8	75	55	38	266
Regina, SK	50	27	0	104	37	0	1,894

City, state/province	Lat. N °	′	″	Long. W °	′	″	Elev. (ft)
Reno, NV	39	31	47	119	48	46	4,498
Richmond, VA	37	33	13	77	27	38	190
Roanoke, VA	37	16	15	79	56	30	940
Rochester, MN	44	1	18	92	28	11	990
Rochester, NY	43	9	17	77	36	57	515
Rockford, IL	42	16	16	89	5	38	715
Sacramento, CA	38	34	54	121	29	36	20
Saginaw, MI	43	25	10	83	57	3	595
St. Catharines, ON	43	10	0	79	15	0	321
St. Cloud, MN	45	33	39	94	9	44	1,040
St. John, NB	45	15	33	66	02	20	357
St. John's, NL	47	34	0	52	44	0	461
St. Joseph, MO	39	46	7	94	50	47	850
St. Louis, MO	38	37	38	90	11	52	455
St. Paul, MN	44	56	40	93	5	35	780
St. Petersburg, FL	27	46	14	82	40	46	44
Salem, OR	44	56	35	123	2	2	154
Salina, KS	38	50	25	97	36	40	1,225
Salt Lake City, UT	40	45	39	111	53	25	4,266
San Antonio, TX	29	25	26	98	29	36	650
San Bernardino, CA	34	6	30	117	17	20	1,200
San Diego, CA	32	42	55	117	9	23	40
San Francisco, CA	37	46	30	122	25	6	63
San Jose, CA	37	20	22	121	53	38	87
San Juan, PR	18	28	6	66	6	22	8
Santa Barbara, CA	34	25	15	119	41	50	50
Santa Cruz, CA	36	58	27	122	1	47	20
Santa Fe, NM	35	41	13	105	56	14	6,989
Sarasota, FL	27	20	10	82	31	51	27
Saskatoon, SK	52	07	0	106	38	0	1,653
Sault Ste. Marie, ON	46	31	0	84	20	0	630
Savannah, GA	32	5	0	81	6	0	42
Schenectady, NY	42	48	51	73	56	24	245
Seattle, WA	47	36	23	122	19	51	350
Sheboygan, WI	43	45	3	87	42	52	630
Sherbrooke, QC	45	24	0	71	54	0	792
Sheridan, WY	44	47	50	106	57	20	3,742
Shreveport, LA	32	31	30	93	45	0	209
Sioux City, IA	42	30	0	96	24	0	1,117
Sioux Falls, SD	43	32	48	96	43	48	1,442
South Bend, IN	41	41	0	86	15	0	725
Spartanburg, SC	34	56	58	81	55	56	816
Spokane, WA	47	39	32	117	25	30	2,000
Springfield, IL	39	48	6	89	38	37	610
Springfield, MA	42	6	5	72	35	25	70
Springfield, MO	37	12	55	93	17	53	1,300
Springfield, OH	39	55	27	83	48	32	1,000
Stamford, CT	41	3	12	73	32	21	35
Steubenville, OH	40	22	11	80	38	3	1,060
Stockton, CA	37	57	28	121	17	23	15
Sudbury, ON	46	31	0	80	54	0	1,140
Superior, WI	46	43	15	92	6	14	642
Sydney, NS	46	09	0	60	11	0	203
Syracuse, NY	43	2	53	76	8	52	400
Tacoma, WA	47	15	11	122	26	35	380
Tallahassee, FL	30	26	17	84	16	51	188
Tampa, FL	27	56	50	82	27	31	48
Terre Haute, IN	39	28	0	87	24	50	501
Texarkana, TX	33	25	30	94	2	51	324
Thunder Bay, ON	48	24	0	89	19	0	653
Timmins, ON	48	28	0	81	20	0	967
Toledo, OH	41	39	50	83	33	19	615
Topeka, KS	39	2	54	95	40	40	1,000
Toronto, ON	43	37	39	79	23	46	251
Trenton, NJ	40	13	1	74	44	36	54
Trois-Rivières, QC	46	21	0	72	33	0	198
Troy, NY	42	43	42	73	41	32	35
Tucson, AZ	32	13	18	110	55	33	2,390
Tulsa, OK	36	9	14	95	59	33	804
Urbana, IL	40	6	38	88	12	26	725
Utica, NY	43	6	3	75	13	59	415
Vancouver, BC	49	15	0	123	7	0	14
Victoria, BC	48	26	0	123	22	0	63
Waco, TX	31	32	57	97	8	47	405
Walla Walla, WA	46	3	53	118	20	31	1,000
Washington, DC	38	53	42	77	2	12	25
Waterloo, IA	42	29	34	92	20	34	850
West Palm Beach, FL	26	42	54	80	3	13	21
Wheeling, WV	40	3	50	80	43	16	672
Whitehorse, YT	60	43	0	135	03	0	2,305
White Plains, NY	41	2	2	73	45	48	220
Wichita, KS	37	41	32	97	20	14	1,305
Wilkes-Barre, PA	41	14	45	75	52	54	550
Wilmington, DE	39	44	45	75	32	49	100
Wilmington, NC	34	13	32	77	56	42	50
Windsor, ON	42	18	0	83	01	0	622
Winnipeg, MB	49	54	39	97	14	36	783
Winston-Salem, NC	36	5	59	80	14	40	912
Worcester, MA	42	15	45	71	48	10	480
Yakima, WA	46	36	8	120	30	17	1,066
Yellowknife, NT	62	27	20	114	21	0	675
Youngstown, OH	41	5	59	80	38	59	861
Yuma, AZ	32	43	31	114	37	25	160
Zanesville, OH	39	56	25	82	0	48	710

Latitude and Longitude of World Cities

Source: National Imagery Mapping Agency, U.S. Dept. of Defense

City, country	Lat. °	′	Long. °	′
Athens, Greece	37	59 N	23	44 E
Bangkok, Thailand	13	45 N	100	31 E
Beijing, China	39	56 N	116	24 E
Berlin, Germany	52	31 N	13	25 E
Bogotá, Colombia	04	36 N	74	05 W
Buenos Aires, Argentina	34	36 S	58	28 W
Cairo, Egypt	30	03 N	31	15 E
Jakarta, Indonesia	06	10 S	106	48 E
Jerusalem, Israel	31	46 N	35	14 E
Johannesburg, South Africa	26	12 S	28	05 E
Kathmandu, Nepal	27	43 N	85	19 E
Kiev, Ukraine	50	26 N	30	31 E
London, UK (Greenwich)	51	30 N	00	00
Manila, Philippines	14	35 N	121	00 E
Mexico City, Mexico	19	24 N	99	09 W
Moscow, Russia	55	45 N	37	35 E
Mumbai (Bombay), India	18	58 N	72	50 E
New Delhi, India	28	36 N	77	12 E
Panama City, Panama	08	58 N	79	32 W
Paris, France	48	52 N	02	20 E
Quito, Ecuador	00	13 S	78	30 W
Rio de Janeiro, Brazil	22	43 S	43	13 W
Rome, Italy	41	53 N	12	30 E
Santiago, Chile	33	27 S	70	40 W
Seoul, South Korea	37	34 N	127	00 E
Sydney, Australia	33	53 S	151	12 E
Tehran, Iran	35	40 N	51	26 E
Tokyo, Japan	35	42 N	139	46 E
Warsaw, Poland	52	15 N	21	00 E
Wellington, New Zealand	41	18 S	174	47 E

Highest and Lowest Continental Altitudes

Source: National Geographic Society

Continent	Highest point	Elev. (ft)	Continent	Lowest point	Ft below sea level
Asia	Mount Everest, Nepal-Tibet	29,035	Antarctica	Bentley Subglacial Trench	8,333[1]
South America	Mount Aconcagua, Argentina	22,834	Asia	Dead Sea, Israel-Jordan	1,348
North America	Mount McKinley, Alaska	20,320	Africa	Lake Assal, Djibouti	512
Africa	Kilimanjaro, Tanzania	19,341	North America	Death Valley, California	282
Europe	Mount Elbrus, Russia	18,510	South America	Valdes Peninsula, Argentina	131
Antarctica	Vinson Massif	16,066	Europe	Caspian Sea, Russia, Azerbaijan	92
Australia	Mount Kosciusko, New South Wales	7,310	Australia	Lake Eyre, South Australia	52

(1) Estimated level of the continental floor. Lower points that have yet to be discovered may exist beneath the ice.

Memberships of Religious Groups in the U.S.

Source: *2013 Yearbook of American & Canadian Churches*, © National Council of Churches in the U.S.A., except where indicated. Figures are the latest available and generally are based on reports made by officials of each group. Figures from other sources may vary. Reporting practices vary from one denomination to another. Many groups keep careful records; others only estimate. Not all groups report annually. Membership figures, for the most part, are inclusive and do not refer solely to full communicants or confirmed members. Groups reporting fewer than 5,000 members or providing no data in recent years are not included.

Religious group (houses of worship)	Members
Adventist Churches	
Advent Christian Ch. (294)	23,629
Seventh-day Adventist Ch. (4,916)	1,060,386
Agnostics	41,889,421[1]
American Evangelical Christian Chs. (192)	17,400
Anglo-Lutheran Catholic Church (19)	11,100
Apostolic Catholic Ch. (29)	7,414
Apostolic Catholic Orthodox Ch. (8)	8,500
Apostolic Christian Churches of America (93)	12,850
Apostolic Episcopal Church (200)	12,000
Apostolic Orthodox Catholic Ch. of N.A. (25)	15,900
Atheists	1,309,897[1]
Baha'i Faith	512,864[1]
Baptist Churches	
Alliance of Baptists (127)	65,000
American Baptist Assn. (1,600)	100,000
American Baptist Chs. in the U.S.A. (5,366)	1,308,054
Baptist Bible Fellowship Intl. (4,000)	110,000
Baptist Missionary Assn. of America (1,272)	137,909
Conservative Baptist Assn. of America (1,200)	200,000
Converge Worldwide (fmr. Baptist Gen. Conf.) (1,100)	16,000
Free Will Baptists, National Assn. of (2,369)	185,798
General Baptists, General Assn. of (1,154)	61,040
Natl. Baptist Convention, U.S.A., Inc. (10,358)	5,197,512
Natl. Baptist Convention of America, Inc.	3,500,000
Natl. Missionary Baptist Conv. of America (280)	449,000[1]
Natl. Primitive Baptist Conv., Inc. (1,565)	600,000[1]
North American Baptist Conference (272)	47,150
Progressive Natl. Baptist Convention, Inc. (1,500)	1,010,000
Regular Baptist Chs., General Assn. of (1,321)	132,700
Separate Baptists in Christ (90)	10,700[1]
Seventh Day Baptist General Conf., USA/Canada (97)	6,300
Southern Baptist Convention (45,727)	16,136,044
Berean Fellowship of Chs. (56)	12,000
Brethren (German Baptists)	
Brethren Ch. (Ashland, OH) (112)	10,227
Church of the Brethren (1,043)	120,041
Buddhists	3,955,046[1]
Calvary Chapel	10,000
Chinese Folk Religionists	108,634[1]
Christian Brethren (Plymouth Brethren) (1,145)	86,000
Christian Church (Disciples of Christ) (3,624)	639,551
Christian Churches and Churches of Christ (5,007)	1,174,000[1]
Christian Congregation, Inc. (1,496)	122,181
Christian and Missionary Alliance (2,042)	436,428
Church of Christ	8,000
Church of Christ (Holiness) U.S.A. (148)	11,468
Church of Christ, Scientist (2,206)	848,000[1]
Church of the Living God (170)	42,000
Church of the Nazarene (5,058)	649,836
Church of the United Brethren in Christ, USA (193)	21,000
Churches of Christ (13,000)	1,639,495
Churches of Christ in Christian Union (230)	11,234
Churches of God	
Church of God (Anderson, IN) (2,187)	249,521
Church of God (Seventh Day; Gen. Conf.), Denver, CO (233)	14,000
Church of God, Mountain Assembly, Inc. (3,390)	7,000
Church of God by Faith, Inc. (149)	35,000
Church of God of Prophecy (1,860)	89,674
Churches of God (Gen. Conf.) (332)	32,560
Community Churches, Intl. Council of (148)	68,300
Congregational Christian Chs., Natl. Assn. of (400)	67,200[1]
Conservative Congregational Christian Conf. (298)	42,296
Eastern Orthodox Churches	
American Carpatho-Russian Orthodox Greek Catholic Ch. (79)	12,660
Antiochian Orthodox Christian Archdiocese of North America (256)	430,000
Armenian Apostolic Ch., Dioceses of America (81)	65,000
Armenian Apostolic Ch. of America (38)	350,000
Coptic Orthodox Ch. (100)	300,000
Greek Orthodox Archdiocese of America (560)	1,500,000
Malankara Orthodox Syrian Ch., Diocese of America (80)	30,000
Mar Thoma Syrian Ch. of India (80)	50,000
Orthodox Ch. in America (750)	131,000
Patriarchal Parishes of the Russian Orthodox Ch. in the U.S.A. (31)	17,000
Russian Orthodox Ch. Outside of Russia (190)	480,000
Serbian Orthodox Ch. in the U.S.A. and Canada (68)	67,000
Syriac-Greek Antiochian Orthodox Catholic Ch. (160)	17,108
Syrian (Syriac) Orthodox Ch. of Antioch (32)	32,500
Ukrainian Orthodox Ch. of the U.S.A. (118)	50,000
Episcopal Church (6,794)	1,951,907
Ethnic religionists	1,084,637[1]
Evangelical Church Alliance	300,000
Evangelical Congregational Church (141)	17,577
Evangelical Covenant Church (783)	114,283
Evangelical Free Church of America (1,475)	356,000
Fellowship of Grace Brethren Churches (260)	36,000[1]
Friends	
Evangelical Friends Intl.–N. Amer. Region (284)	38,428
Friends General Conference (832)	32,000
Friends United Meeting (600)	36,302
Philadelphia Yearly Meeting of the Religious Society of Friends (103)	11,511
Religious Society of Friends (Conservative) (1,200)	104,000
Full Gospel Fellowship of Churches and Ministers Intl. (1,273)	432,632
General Church of the New Jerusalem (37)	7,052
Grace Gospel Fellowship (120)	20,000[1]
Hindus	1,444,775[1]
International Evangelical Church (100)	50,000[1]
Jains	85,356[1]
Jehovah's Witnesses (13,021)	1,184,249
Jews	6-6.4 mil[2]
Jewish Reconstructionist Federation (100)	(2)
Union of Orthodox Jewish Congregations of America (1,500)	(2)
Union for Reform Judaism (1,000)	(2)
United Synagogue of Conservative Judaism (850)	(2)
Latter-Day Saints (Mormons)	
Ch. of Jesus Christ of Latter-day Saints (13,601)	6,157,238
Community of Christ (935)	178,328
Liberal Catholic Church–Province of the United States of America (21)	5,800
Lutheran Churches	
American Assn. of Lutheran Chs. (70)	16,000
Apostolic Lutheran Ch. of America (56)	7,300[1]
Ch. of the Lutheran Brethren of America (105)	13,099
Ch. of the Lutheran Confession (87)	8,390
Evangelical Lutheran Ch. in America (9,995)	4,274,855
Evangelical Lutheran Synod (132)	19,394
Free Lutheran Congregations, Assn. of (280)	44,473
Independent Evangelical Lutheran Chs., Assn. of (45)	7,760
Latvian Evangelical Lutheran Ch. in America (60)	10,950
Lutheran Ch.–Missouri Synod (LCMS) (6,158)	2,278,586
Wisconsin Evangelical Lutheran Synod (1,287)	385,321
Mennonite Churches	
Beachy Amish Mennonite Chs. (201)	11,611
Brethren in Christ Church (222)	46,300[1]
Ch. of God in Christ, Mennonite (150)	14,804
Fellowship of Evangelical Chs. (46)	7,754
Hutterian Brethren (150)	17,000[1]
Mennonite Brethren Chs., Gen. Conf. of (464)	111,000[1]
Mennonite Ch. USA (920)	104,684
Old Order Amish Mennonite Ch. (950)	115,000[1]
Old Order (Wisler) Mennonite Ch. (47)	7,100
Methodist Churches	
African Methodist Episcopal Ch. (4,100)	2,500,000
African Methodist Episcopal Zion Ch. (3,393)	1,400,000
Christian Methodist Episcopal Ch. (3,500)	850,000
Evangelical Methodist Ch. (108)	7,348
Free Methodist Ch. U.S.A. (1,051)	75,020
Southern Methodist Ch. (101)	6,000
United Methodist Ch. (33,583)	7,679,850
Wesleyan Ch. (1,715)	139,330
Metropolitan Community Churches, Universal Fellowship of (115)	15,666

Religious group (houses of worship)	Members	Religious group (houses of worship)	Members
Missionary Church (431)	38,206	Cumberland Presbyterian Ch. (657)	72,167
Moravian Church in America (84)	20,220	Evangelical Presbyterian Ch. (207)	89,190
Muslims	4,106,065[1]	Korean Presbyterian Ch. Abroad (302)	55,000
New Apostolic Church of North America, Natl.		Orthodox Presbyterian Ch. (269)	29,842
Org. of the (303)	39,532	Presbyterian Ch. (U.S.A.) (10,560)	2,675,873
New religionists	1,624,154[1]	Presbyterian Ch. in America (1,737)	341,482
Old Catholic Orthodox Ch. (11)	11,470	Reformed Presbyterian Ch. of North America	6,799
Pentecostal Churches		Reformed Catholic Ch. (100)	57,000
Apostolic Faith Mission Ch. of God (16)	6,880	Reformed Churches	
Assemblies of God (12,457)	3,030,944	Christian Reformed Ch. in North America (808)	180,502
Bible Fellowship Ch. (65)	7,627	Netherlands Reformed Congregations (27)	10,493
Ch. of God (Cleveland, TN) (6,481)	1,074,047	Protestant Reformed Chs. in America (31)	7,806
Ch. of God in Christ (15,300)	5,499,875[1]	Reformed Ch. in America (886)	246,024
Ch. of God of Prophecy (1,860)	89,674	United Church of Christ (5,227)	1,058,423
Congregational Holiness Ch. (225)	25,000	Reformed Episcopal Church (149)	15,573
Elim Assemblies Fellowship (240)	41,400[1]	Roman Catholic Church (18,199)	68,202,492
Intl. Ch. of the Foursquare Gospel (1,875)	353,995	Romanian Orthodox Church in America (32)	9,700
Intl. Pentecostal Holiness Ch. (2,024)	330,054	Romanian Orthodox Episcopate of America (64)	10,635
Open Bible Churches (275)	45,000	Salvation Army (1,232)	413,961
Pentecostal Assemblies of the World, Inc. (2,550)	1,800,000	Shintoists	62,688[1]
Pentecostal Ch. of God (1,134)	98,579	Sikhs	279,346[1]
Pentecostal Chs. of Christ (45)	5,000	Spiritists	225,213[1]
Pentecostal Free Will Baptist Ch., Inc. (200)	20,000[1]	Taoists (or Daoists)	12,415[1]
United House of Prayer (161)	1,632,000[1]	Vineyard USA (554)	181,474
United Pentecostal Ch. Intl. (4,358)	646,304	Unitarian Universalist Assn. of Congregations	
Polish National Catholic Ch. of America (126)	60,000	(1,048)	221,367
Presbyterian Churches		United Evangelical Churches (294)	78,800[1]
Associate Reformed Presbyterian Ch. (General		Zoroastrians	17,636[1]
Synod) (293)	39,639		

(1) Source: World Christian Database. (2) About 35% of Jews classify themselves as Reform, 26% as Conservative, 10% as Orthodox, 2% as Reconstructionist, the rest as "just Jewish." Source: Ira M. Sheskin and Arnold Dashefsky, "Jewish Population of the United States, 2012," in Arnold Dashevsky and Ira M. Sheskin (editors), *The American Jewish Year Book* (2012) (Dordrecht: Springer).

World Adherents of Religions by Continental Area, 2011

Source: *2012 Encyclopædia Britannica Book of the Year*. All figures are midyear estimates.

Religion (no. of countries)	Africa	Asia	Europe	Latin America	Northern America	Oceania	World
Baha'is (222)	2,197,000	3,477,000	144,000	913,000	573,000	113,000	7,417,000
Buddhists (151)	258,000	459,625,000	1,796,000	767,000	4,503,000	597,000	467,546,000
Chinese folk religionists (120)	134,000	466,791,000	442,000	191,000	789,000	104,000	468,451,000
Christians (232)	498,856,000	354,835,000	588,538,000	552,147,000	275,032,100	28,684,900	2,298,093,000
Roman Catholics (232)	182,564,000	140,001,000	277,858,000	488,414,000	86,540,000	8,981,000	1,184,358,000
Protestants (229)	143,411,000	88,298,000	67,683,000	59,437,000	59,426,000	7,810,000	426,065,000
Independents (221)	104,528,000	133,656,000	10,619,000	40,101,000	58,334,000	1,273,000	348,511,000
Orthodox (137)	44,990,000	18,173,000	203,104,000	1,060,000	7,493,000	988,000	275,808,000
Anglicans (162)	52,140,000	865,000	26,434,000	870,000	2,780,000	4,836,000	87,925,000
Marginal (217)	4,086,000	3,183,000	4,110,000	11,491,000	11,965,000	676,000	35,511,000
Unaffiliated (227)	24,688,000	4,070,000	25,610,000	6,178,000	50,888,000	4,648,000	116,082,000
Doubly affiliated (181)	*57,551,000*	*33,411,000*	*26,880,000*	*55,404,000*	*2,393,900*	*527,100*	*176,167,000*
Confucianists (16)	20,200	6,384,000	15,700	490	0	50,100	6,470,490
Ethnic religionists (146)	107,886,000	154,712,000	1,168,000	3,884,000	1,226,000	376,000	269,252,000
Hindus (127)	2,973,000	952,725,000	1,044,000	790,000	1,866,000	543,000	959,941,000
Jains (19)	96,600	5,162,000	19,100	1,400	101,000	3,300	5,383,400
Jews (140)	133,000	6,167,000	1,923,000	970,000	5,563,000	119,000	14,875,000
Muslims (211)	426,923,400	1,084,836,900	40,910,000	1,611,000	5,561,000	549,000	1,560,391,300
New religionists (119)	117,000	59,132,000	366,000	1,756,000	1,724,000	106,000	63,201,000
Shintoists (8)	0	2,693,000	0	7,900	63,000	0	2,763,900
Sikhs (55)	75,000	23,032,000	507,000	7,200	613,000	50,800	24,285,000
Spiritists (57)	2,800	2,100	144,000	13,413,000	245,000	8,000	13,814,900
Taoists (6)	0	8,469,000	0	0	12,500	4,600	8,486,100
Zoroastrians (27)	1,000	168,000	5,700	0	21,200	2,600	198,500
Other religionists (79)	85,000	225,000	275,000	120,000	690,000	12,000	1,407,000
Nonreligious/agnostic (231)	5,590,000	503,509,000	86,551,500	17,111,010	46,952,200	5,355,700	665,069,410
Atheists (221)	575,000	115,503,000	15,450,000	2,939,000	2,028,000	496,000	136,991,000

Note: Continental areas. Following current UN demographic terminology, which divides the world into the 6 major areas shown. "Asia" is defined here to include the former Soviet Central Asian states, while "Europe" includes all of Russia, extending to the Pacific coast. **Countries.** Figures in parentheses indicate the number of sovereign and nonsovereign countries where the religion or type of belief has a statistically significant following. **Adherents.** As defined in the 1948 Universal Declaration of Human Rights, a person's religion is self-declared. Totals here are enumerated following methodology of the *World Christian Encyclopedia*, 2nd ed. (2001), and *World Christian Trends* (2001), using recent censuses, polls, literature, and other data. Figures may conflict with estimates elsewhere. **Buddhists.** 56% Mahayana, 38% Theravada (Hinayana), 6% Tantrayana (Lamaism). **Chinese folk religionists.** Followers of traditional Chinese religion; may involve worship of local deities, ancestor veneration, Confucian ethics, universism, divination, and Buddhist or Taoist elements, among other beliefs and practices. **Christians.** Followers of Jesus Christ. Unaffiliated Christians profess Christian beliefs but are not on specific church rolls; Independents consider themselves post-denominational and thus independent from organized Christianity. Marginal Christians belong to churches that profess Christianity but regard themselves as on the margins of the mainstream, including Unitarians, Mormons, Jehovah's Witnesses, and Christian Science adherents. Doubly-affiliated Christians are baptized members of two denominations. **Confucianists.** Non-Chinese followers of Confucius and Confucianism, mostly Koreans in Korea. **Ethnic religionists.** Followers of local, tribal, animistic, or shamanistic religions, generally belonging to a single ethnic group. **Hindus.** 68% Vaishnavites, 27% Shaivites, 2% neo-Hindus and reform Hindus. **Jews.** Adherents of Judaism. **Muslims.** 84% Sunni Muslims, 14% Shia Muslims (Shiites), 2% other schools. **New religionists.** Followers of Asian 20th-cent. New Religions, New Religious movements, radical new crisis religions, and non-Christian syncretistic mass religions. **Other religionists.** Including various small religions, quasi-religions, parareligions, religious or mystic systems, religious or semireligious brotherhoods, and the like.

Episcopal Church Liturgical Colors and Calendar, 2012-16

The most common liturgical colors in the Episcopal Church are: **White**—Christmas Day through First Sunday after Epiphany; Maundy Thursday (as an alternative to crimson at the Eucharist); from the Vigil of Easter to the Day of Pentecost (Whitsunday); Trinity Sunday; Feasts of the Lord (except Holy Cross Day); the Confession of St. Peter; the Conversion of St. Paul; St. Joseph; St. Mary Magdalene; St. Mary the Virgin; St. Michael and All Angels; All Saints' Day; St. John the Evangelist; memorials of other saints who were not martyred; Independence Day and Thanksgiving Day; weddings and funerals. **Red**—the Day of Pentecost; Holy Cross Day; feasts of apostles and evangelists (except those previously mentioned); feasts and memorials of martyrs (including Holy Innocents' Day). **Violet**—Advent and Lent. **Crimson** or oxblood (dark red)—Holy Week. **Green**—the seasons after Epiphany and after Pentecost. **Black**—optional alternative for funerals and Good Friday.

The days of fasting are Ash Wednesday and Good Friday. Other days of special devotion (penitence) include the 40 days of Lent. Ember Days are days of prayer for the church's ministry. They fall on the Wednesday, Friday, and Saturday after the first Sunday in Lent, the Day of Pentecost, Holy Cross Day, and Dec. 13. Rogation Days, the three days before Ascension Day, are days of prayer for God's blessing on the crops, on commerce and industry, and for conservation of the Earth's resources.

Holy Days and other variables	2012	2013	2014	2015	2016
Golden Number	18	19	1	2	3
Sunday Letter	AG	F	E	D	C/B
Sundays after Epiphany	7	5	8	6	5
Ash Wednesday	Feb. 22	Feb. 13	Mar. 5	Feb. 18	Feb. 10
First Sunday in Lent	Feb. 26	Feb. 17	Mar. 9	Feb. 22	Feb. 14
Passion/Palm Sunday	Apr. 1	Mar. 24	Apr. 13	Mar. 29	Mar. 20
Good Friday	Apr. 6	Mar. 29	Apr. 18	Apr. 3	Mar. 25
Easter Day	Apr. 8	Mar. 31	Apr. 20	Apr. 5	Mar. 27
Ascension Day	May 17	May 9	May 29	May 14	May 5
The Day of Pentecost	May 27	May 19	June 8	May 24	May 15
Trinity Sunday	June 3	May 26	June 15	May 31	May 22
Numbered Proper of 2 Pentecost	#5	#4	#7	#5	#4
First Sunday of Advent	Dec. 2	Dec. 1	Nov. 30	Nov. 29	Nov. 27

Greek Orthodox Movable Ecclesiastical Dates, 2012-16

Feast days and fasting days are determined annually on the basis of the date of Holy Pascha (Easter). This ecclesiastical cycle begins with the first day of the Triodion and ends with the Sunday of All Saints, a total of 18 weeks.

Holy Days and observances	2012	2013	2014	2015	2016
Triodion begins	Feb. 5	Feb. 24	Feb. 9	Feb. 1	Feb. 21
1st Saturday of Souls	Feb. 18	Mar. 9	Feb. 22	Feb. 14	Mar. 5
Meat Fare	Feb. 19	Mar. 10	Feb. 23	Feb. 15	Mar. 6
2nd Saturday of Souls	Feb. 25	Mar. 16	Mar. 1	Feb. 21	Mar. 12
Lent begins	Feb. 27	Mar. 18	Mar. 3	Feb. 23	Mar. 14
St. Theodore—3rd Saturday of Souls	Mar. 3	Mar. 23	Mar. 8	Feb. 28	Mar. 19
Sunday of Orthodoxy	Mar. 4	Mar. 24	Mar. 9	Mar. 1	Mar. 20
Saturday of Lazarus	Apr. 7	Apr. 27	Apr. 12	Apr. 4	Apr. 23
Palm Sunday	Apr. 8	Apr. 28	Apr. 13	Apr. 5	Apr. 24
Holy (Good) Friday	Apr. 13	May 3	Apr. 18	Apr. 10	Apr. 29
Western Easter	Apr. 8	Mar. 31	Apr. 20	Apr. 5	Mar. 27
Orthodox Easter	Apr. 15	May 5	Apr. 20	Apr. 12	May 1
Ascension	May 24	June 13	May 29	May 21	June 9
Saturday of Souls	June 2	June 22	June 7	May 30	June 18
Pentecost	June 3	June 23	June 8	May 31	June 19
All Saints	June 10	June 30	June 15	June 7	June 26
Fast of Holy Apostles (first day)	June 11	—	June 16	June 8	June 27

Important Islamic Holy Days, 1433-1437 AH (late 2011-16)

The Islamic calendar is a strict lunar calendar reckoned from the year of the Hijra (Anno Hegirae, or AH)—Muhammad's flight from Mecca to Medina, in 622 CE. Each year consists of 12 lunar months of 29 or 30 days beginning and ending with each new moon's visible crescent. Common years have 354 days; leap years have 355 days. Some Muslim countries employ a conventionalized calendar with the leap day added to the last month, Dhûl Hijjah, but for religious purposes the leap date is taken into account by tracking each new moon sighting. Holy days begin at sunset on the day previous to the day cited. The actual dates of holy days may also vary slightly from what is cited below, depending on the locality and the times of actual moon sightings as determined by different authorities.

Day (date)	(1433) 2011-12	(1434) 2012-13	(1435) 2013-14	(1436) 2014-15	(1437) 2015-16
New Year's Day (Muharram 1)	Nov. 26, 2011	Nov. 15, 2012	Nov. 4, 2013	Oct. 25 2014	Oct. 14, 2015
Ashura (Muharram 10)	Dec. 5, 2011	Nov. 24, 2012	Nov. 13, 2013	Nov. 3, 2014	Oct. 23, 2015
Mawlid (Rabi'l 12)	Feb. 4, 2012	Jan. 24, 2013	Jan. 13, 2014	Jan. 3, 2015	Dec. 23, 2015
Ramadan begins (Ramadan 1)	July 20, 2012	July 9, 2013	June 28, 2014	June 18, 2015	June 6, 2016
Eid al-Fitr (Shawwal 1)	Aug. 19, 2012	Aug. 8, 2013	July 29, 2014	July 17, 2015	July 7, 2016
Eid al-Adha (Dhûl-Hijjah 10)	Oct. 26, 2012	Oct. 15, 2013	Oct. 4, 2014	Sept. 23, 2015	Sept. 11, 2016

Jewish Holy Days, Festivals, and Fasts, 5771-5775 (late 2011-16)

The Jewish calendar consists of 12 lunar months, alternating between 29 and 30 days. It is lunisolar, and adjusts for the solar cycle by adding an extra month (Adar II) in the 3rd, 6th, 8th, 11th, 14th, 17th, and 19th years of a 19-year cycle. The calendar starts on the day of Creation, reckoned in the 2nd-3rd cent. BCE as Tishrei 1, 3,761 years before the common era.

The religious calendar begins with the month Nisan, from which all other months are counted, and the civil calendar with Tishrei. The months are 1) Nisan; 2) Iyar; 3) Sivan; 4) Tammuz; 5) Av (also Abh); 6) Elul; 7) Tishrei; 8) Cheshvan (also Marcheshvan); 9) Kislev; 10) Tevet (also Tebeth); 11) Shevat (also Shebhat); 12) Adar; 12a) Adar Sheni (II), added in leap years. The names are Aramaic versions of the Babylonian months, adopted during the Jews' exile in Babylon in the 4th cent. BCE. Rosh Hashanah, the New Year, begins on Tishrei 1 (Sept.-Oct.). Yom Kippur is the holiest day of the year. All holidays listed below begin at sunset on the previous day, except where noted, and end at sundown on the last day shown.

Holiday	Date on Jewish cal.	(5772) 2011-12		(5773) 2012-13		(5774) 2013-14		(5775) 2014-15		(5776) 2015-16	
Rosh Hashanah (New Year)	Tishrei 1	Sept. 29	Thu.	Sept. 17	Mon.	Sept. 5	Thu.	Sept. 25	Thu.	Sept. 14	Mon.
	Tishrei 2	Sept. 30	Fri.	Sept. 18	Tue.	Sept. 6	Fri.	Sept. 26	Fri.	Sept. 15	Tue.
Fast of Gedalya[1]	Tishrei 3	Oct. 2	Sun.*	Sept. 19	Wed.	Sept. 8	Sun.*	Sept. 28	Sun.*	Sept. 16	Wed.
Yom Kippur (Day of Atonement). .	Tishrei 10	Oct. 8	Sat.	Sept. 26	Wed.	Sept. 14	Sat.	Oct. 4	Sat.	Sept. 23	Wed.
Sukkot.	Tishrei 15	Oct. 13	Thu.	Oct. 1	Mon.	Sept. 19	Thu.	Oct. 9	Thu.	Sept. 28	Mon.
	Tishrei 21	Oct. 19	Wed.	Oct. 7	Sun.	Sept. 25	Wed.	Oct. 15	Wed.	Oct. 4	Sun.
Shemini Atzeret	Tishrei 22	Oct. 20	Thu.	Oct. 8	Mon.	Sept. 26	Thu.	Oct. 16	Thu.	Oct. 5	Mon.
Simchat Torah	Tishrei 23	Oct. 21	Fri.	Oct. 9	Tue.	Sept. 27	Fri.	Oct. 17	Fri.	Oct. 6	Tue.
Hanukkah	Kislev 25	Dec. 21	Wed.	Dec. 9	Sun.	Nov. 28	Thu.	Dec. 17	Wed.	Dec. 7	Mon.
	Tevet 2 or 3	Dec. 28	Wed.	Dec. 16	Sun.	Dec. 5	Thu.	Dec. 24	Wed.	Dec. 14	Mon.
Fast of the 10th of Tevet[1]	Tevet 10	Jan. 5	Thu.	Dec. 23	Sun.	Dec. 13	Fri.	Jan. 1	Thu.	Dec. 22	Tue.
Tu B'Shevat	Shevat 15	Feb. 8	Wed.	Jan. 26	Sat.	Jan. 16	Thu.	Feb. 4	Wed.	Jan. 25	Mon.
Ta'anis Esther (Fast of Esther)[1] . .	Adar 13	Mar. 7	Wed.	Feb. 21	Thu.*	Mar. 13	Thu.*	Mar. 4	Wed.	Mar. 23	Wed.
Purim	Adar 14	Mar. 8	Thu.	Feb. 24	Sun.	Mar. 16	Sun.	Mar. 5	Thu.	Mar. 24	Thu.
Pesach (Passover)	Nisan 15	Apr. 7	Sat.	Mar. 26	Tue.	Apr. 15	Tue.	Apr. 4	Sat.	Apr. 23	Sat.
	Nisan 22	Apr. 14	Sat.	Apr. 2	Tue.	Apr. 22	Tue.	Apr. 11	Sat.	Apr. 30	Sat.
Lag B'Omer	Iyar 18	May 10	Thu.	Apr. 28	Sun.	May 18	Sun.	May 7	Thu.	May 26	Thu.
Shavuot (Pentecost)	Sivan 6	May 27	Sun.	May 15	Wed.	June 4	Wed.	May 24	Sun.	June 12	Sun.
	Sivan 7	May 28	Mon.	May 16	Thu.	June 5	Thu.	May 25	Mon.	June 13	Mon.
Fast of the 17th Day of Tammuz[1]	Tammuz 17	July 8	Sun.*	June 25	Tue.	July 15	Tue.	July 5	Sun.*	July 24	Sun.*
Fast of the 9th Day of Av	Av 9	July 29	Sun.*	July 16	Tue.	Aug. 5	Tue.	July 26	Sun.*	Aug. 14	Sun.*

*Date changed to avoid Sabbath. (1) "Minor fasts" begin at dawn.

Ash Wednesday and Easter Sunday (Western Churches), 1901-2100

Year	Ash Wed.	Easter Sunday	Year	Ash Wed.	Easter Sunday	Year	Ash Wed.	Easter Sunday	Year	Ash Wed.	Easter Sunday	Year	Ash Wed.	Easter Sunday
1901	Feb. 20	Apr. 7	1941	Feb. 26	Apr. 13	1981	Mar. 4	Apr. 19	2021	Feb. 17	Apr. 4	2061	Feb. 23	Apr. 10
1902	Feb. 12	Mar. 30	1942	Feb. 18	Apr. 5	1982	Feb. 24	Apr. 11	2022	Mar. 2	Apr. 17	2062	Mar. 8	Mar. 26
1903	Feb. 25	Apr. 12	1943	Mar. 10	Apr. 25	1983	Feb. 16	Apr. 3	2023	Feb. 22	Apr. 9	2063	Feb. 28	Apr. 15
1904	Feb. 17	Apr. 3	1944	Feb. 23	Apr. 9	1984	Mar. 7	Apr. 22	2024	Feb. 14	Mar. 31	2064	Feb. 20	Apr. 6
1905	Mar. 8	Apr. 23	1945	Feb. 14	Apr. 1	1985	Feb. 20	Apr. 7	2025	Mar. 5	Apr. 20	2065	Feb. 11	Mar. 29
1906	Feb. 28	Apr. 15	1946	Mar. 6	Apr. 21	1986	Feb. 12	Mar. 30	2026	Feb. 18	Apr. 5	2066	Feb. 24	Apr. 11
1907	Feb. 13	Mar. 31	1947	Feb. 19	Apr. 6	1987	Mar. 4	Apr. 19	2027	Feb. 10	Mar. 28	2067	Feb. 16	Apr. 3
1908	Mar. 4	Apr. 19	1948	Feb. 11	Mar. 28	1988	Feb. 17	Apr. 3	2028	Mar. 1	Apr. 16	2068	Mar. 7	Apr. 22
1909	Feb. 24	Apr. 11	1949	Mar. 2	Apr. 17	1989	Feb. 8	Mar. 26	2029	Feb. 14	Apr. 1	2069	Feb. 27	Apr. 14
1910	Feb. 9	Mar. 27	1950	Feb. 22	Apr. 9	1990	Feb. 28	Apr. 15	2030	Mar. 6	Apr. 21	2070	Feb. 12	Mar. 30
1911	Feb. 1	Apr. 16	1951	Feb. 7	Mar. 25	1991	Feb. 13	Mar. 31	2031	Feb. 26	Apr. 13	2071	Mar. 4	Apr. 19
1912	Feb. 21	Apr. 7	1952	Feb. 27	Apr. 13	1992	Mar. 4	Apr. 19	2032	Feb. 11	Mar. 28	2072	Feb. 24	Apr. 10
1913	Feb. 5	Mar. 23	1953	Feb. 18	Apr. 5	1993	Feb. 24	Apr. 11	2033	Mar. 2	Apr. 17	2073	Feb. 8	Mar. 26
1914	Feb. 25	Apr. 12	1954	Mar. 3	Apr. 18	1994	Feb. 16	Apr. 3	2034	Feb. 22	Apr. 9	2074	Feb. 28	Apr. 15
1915	Feb. 17	Apr. 4	1955	Feb. 23	Apr. 10	1995	Mar. 1	Apr. 16	2035	Feb. 7	Mar. 25	2075	Feb. 20	Apr. 7
1916	Mar. 8	Apr. 23	1956	Feb. 15	Apr. 1	1996	Feb. 21	Apr. 7	2036	Feb. 27	Apr. 13	2076	Mar. 4	Apr. 19
1917	Feb. 21	Apr. 8	1957	Mar. 6	Apr. 21	1997	Feb. 12	Mar. 30	2037	Feb. 18	Apr. 5	2077	Feb. 24	Apr. 11
1918	Feb. 13	Mar. 31	1958	Feb. 19	Apr. 6	1998	Feb. 25	Apr. 12	2038	Mar. 10	Apr. 25	2078	Feb. 16	Apr. 3
1919	Mar. 5	Apr. 20	1959	Feb. 11	Mar. 29	1999	Feb. 17	Apr. 4	2039	Feb. 23	Apr. 10	2079	Mar. 8	Apr. 23
1920	Feb. 18	Apr. 4	1960	Mar. 2	Apr. 17	2000	Mar. 8	Apr. 23	2040	Feb. 15	Apr. 1	2080	Feb. 21	Apr. 7
1921	Feb. 9	Mar. 27	1961	Feb. 15	Apr. 2	2001	Feb. 28	Apr. 15	2041	Mar. 6	Apr. 21	2081	Feb. 12	Mar. 30
1922	Mar. 1	Apr. 16	1962	Mar. 7	Apr. 22	2002	Feb. 13	Mar. 31	2042	Feb. 19	Apr. 6	2082	Mar. 4	Apr. 19
1923	Feb. 14	Apr. 1	1963	Feb. 27	Apr. 14	2003	Mar. 5	Apr. 20	2043	Feb. 11	Mar. 29	2083	Feb. 17	Apr. 4
1924	Mar. 5	Apr. 20	1964	Feb. 12	Mar. 29	2004	Feb. 25	Apr. 11	2044	Mar. 2	Apr. 17	2084	Feb. 9	Mar. 26
1925	Feb. 25	Apr. 12	1965	Mar. 3	Apr. 18	2005	Feb. 9	Mar. 27	2045	Feb. 22	Apr. 9	2085	Feb. 28	Apr. 15
1926	Feb. 17	Apr. 4	1966	Feb. 23	Apr. 10	2006	Mar. 1	Apr. 16	2046	Feb. 7	Mar. 25	2086	Feb. 13	Mar. 31
1927	Mar. 2	Apr. 17	1967	Feb. 8	Mar. 26	2007	Feb. 21	Apr. 8	2047	Feb. 27	Apr. 14	2087	Mar. 5	Apr. 20
1928	Feb. 22	Apr. 8	1968	Feb. 28	Apr. 14	2008	Feb. 6	Mar. 23	2048	Feb. 19	Apr. 5	2088	Feb. 25	Apr. 11
1929	Feb. 13	Mar. 31	1969	Feb. 19	Apr. 6	2009	Feb. 25	Apr. 12	2049	Mar. 3	Apr. 18	2089	Feb. 16	Apr. 3
1930	Mar. 5	Apr. 20	1970	Feb. 11	Mar. 29	2010	Feb. 17	Apr. 4	2050	Feb. 23	Apr. 10	2090	Mar. 1	Apr. 16
1931	Feb. 18	Apr. 5	1971	Feb. 24	Apr. 11	2011	Mar. 9	Apr. 24	2051	Feb. 15	Apr. 2	2091	Feb. 21	Apr. 8
1932	Feb. 10	Mar. 27	1972	Feb. 16	Apr. 2	2012	Feb. 22	Apr. 8	2052	Mar. 6	Apr. 21	2092	Feb. 13	Mar. 30
1933	Mar. 1	Apr. 16	1973	Mar. 7	Apr. 22	2013	Feb. 13	Mar. 31	2053	Feb. 19	Apr. 6	2093	Feb. 25	Apr. 12
1934	Feb. 14	Apr. 1	1974	Feb. 27	Apr. 14	2014	Mar. 5	Apr. 20	2054	Feb. 11	Mar. 29	2094	Feb. 17	Apr. 4
1935	Mar. 6	Apr. 21	1975	Feb. 12	Mar. 30	2015	Feb. 18	Apr. 5	2055	Mar. 3	Apr. 18	2095	Mar. 9	Apr. 24
1936	Feb. 26	Apr. 12	1976	Mar. 3	Apr. 18	2016	Feb. 10	Mar. 27	2056	Feb. 16	Apr. 2	2096	Feb. 29	Apr. 15
1937	Feb. 10	Mar. 28	1977	Feb. 23	Apr. 10	2017	Mar. 1	Apr. 16	2057	Mar. 7	Apr. 22	2097	Feb. 13	Mar. 31
1938	Mar. 2	Apr. 17	1978	Feb. 8	Mar. 26	2018	Feb. 14	Apr. 1	2058	Feb. 27	Apr. 14	2098	Mar. 5	Apr. 20
1939	Feb. 22	Apr. 9	1979	Feb. 28	Apr. 15	2019	Mar. 6	Apr. 21	2059	Feb. 12	Mar. 30	2099	Feb. 25	Apr. 12
1940	Feb. 7	Mar. 24	1980	Feb. 20	Apr. 6	2020	Feb. 26	Apr. 12	2060	Mar. 3	Apr. 18	2100	Feb. 10	Mar. 28

Roman Catholic Hierarchy
Source: U.S. Catholic Conference; Holy See Press

Supreme Pontiff

At the head of the Roman Catholic Church is the supreme pontiff, Pope Benedict XVI, Joseph Ratzinger, born in Marktl am Inn, in Bavaria, Germany, on Apr. 16, 1927. He was ordained as a priest on June 29, 1951, named archbishop of Munich and Feising in Mar. 1977, and elevated to cardinal three months later. In 1981, he was appointed prefect of the Congregation for the Doctrine of the Faith, and he was confirmed as dean of the College of Cardinals on Nov. 30, 2002. He was elected pope by the College of Cardinals on Apr. 19, 2005.

Chronological List of Popes
Source: Annuario Pontificio

The Roman Catholic Church named the Apostle Peter as founder of the church in Rome and the first pope. He arrived there c. 42 CE, was martyred there c. 67, and was ultimately canonized as a saint. The pope's temporal title is Sovereign of the State of Vatican City. The pope's spiritual titles are Bishop of Rome, Vicar of Jesus Christ, Successor of St. Peter, Prince of the Apostles, Supreme Pontiff of the Universal Church, Patriarch of the West, Primate of Italy, Archbishop and Metropolitan of the Roman Province.

Table lists year of accession of each pope. *Asterisks denote antipopes, who were were illegitimate claimants to the papal throne.

Year	Pope	Year	Pope	Year	Pope	Year	Pope	Year	Pope
	St. Peter	526	St. Felix IV (III)	872	John VIII	1100	Theodoric*	1417	Martin V
67	St. Linus	530	Boniface II	882	Marinus I	1102	Albert*	1431	Eugene IV
76	St. Anacletus	530	Dioscorus*	884	St. Adrian III	1105	Sylvester IV*	1439	Felix V*
	or Cletus	533	John II	885	Stephen V (VI)	1118	Gelasius II	1447	Nicholas V
88	St. Clement I	535	St. Agapitus I	891	Formosus	1118	Gregory VIII*	1455	Callistus III
97	St. Evaristus	536	St. Silverius, Martyr	896	Boniface VI	1119	Callistus II	1458	Pius II
105	St. Alexander I	537	Vigilius	896	Stephen VI (VII)	1124	Honorius II	1464	Paul II
115	St. Sixtus I	556	Pelagius I	897	Romanus	1124	Celestine II*	1471	Sixtus IV
125	St. Telesphorus	561	John III	897	Theodore II	1130	Innocent II	1484	Innocent VIII
136	St. Hyginus	575	Benedict I	898	John IX	1130	Anacletus II*	1492	Alexander VI
140	St. Pius I	579	Pelagius II	900	Benedict IV	1138	Victor IV*	1503	Pius III
155	St. Anicetus	590	St. Gregory I	903	Leo V	1143	Celestine II	1503	Julius II
166	St. Soter	604	Sabinian	903	Christopher*	1144	Lucius II	1513	Leo X
175	St. Eleutherius	607	Boniface III	904	Sergius III	1145	Bl. Eugene III	1522	Adrian VI
189	St. Victor I	608	St. Boniface IV	911	Anastasius III	1153	Anastasius IV	1523	Clement VII
199	St. Zephyrinus	615	St. Deusdedit	913	Landus	1154	Adrian IV	1534	Paul III
217	St. Callistus I		or Adeodatus	914	John X	1159	Alexander III	1550	Julius III
217	St. Hippolytus*	619	Boniface V	928	Leo VI	1159	Victor IV*	1555	Marcellus II
222	St. Urban I	625	Honorius I	928	Stephen VII (VIII)	1164	Paschal III*	1555	Paul IV
230	St. Pontian	640	Severinus	931	John XI	1168	Callistus III*	1559	Pius IV
235	St. Anterus	640	John IV	936	Leo VII	1179	Innocent III*	1566	St. Pius V
236	St. Fabian	642	Theodore I	939	Stephen VIII (IX)	1181	Lucius III	1572	Gregory XIII
251	St. Cornelius	649	St. Martin I, Martyr	942	Marinus II	1185	Urban III	1585	Sixtus V
251	Novatian*	654	St. Eugene I	946	Agapitus II	1187	Clement III	1590	Urban VII
253	St. Lucius I	657	St. Vitalian	955	John XII	1187	Gregory VIII	1590	Gregory XIV
254	St. Stephen I	672	Adeodatus II	963	Leo VIII	1191	Celestine III	1591	Innocent IX
257	St. Sixtus II	676	Donus	964	Benedict V	1198	Innocent III	1592	Clement VIII
259	St. Dionysius	678	St. Agatho	965	John XIII	1216	Honorius III	1605	Leo XI
269	St. Felix I	682	St. Leo II	973	Benedict VI	1227	Gregory IX	1605	Paul V
275	St. Eutychian	684	St. Benedict II	974	Boniface VII*	1241	Celestine IV	1621	Gregory XV
283	St. Caius	685	John V	974	Benedict VII	1243	Innocent IV	1623	Urban VIII
296	St. Marcellinus	686	Conon	983	John XIV	1254	Alexander IV	1644	Innocent X
308	St. Marcellus I	687	Theodore*	985	John XV	1261	Urban IV	1655	Alexander VII
309	St. Eusebius	687	Paschal*	996	Gregory V	1265	Clement IV	1667	Clement IX
311	St. Melchiades	687	St. Sergius I	997	John XVI*	1271	Bl. Gregory X	1670	Clement X
314	St. Sylvester I	701	John VI	999	Sylvester II	1276	Bl. Innocent V	1676	Bl. Innocent XI
336	St. Marcus	705	John VII	1003	John XVII	1276	Adrian V	1689	Alexander VIII
337	St. Julius I	708	Sisinnius	1004	John XVIII	1276	John XXI	1691	Innocent XII
352	Liberius	708	Constantine	1009	Sergius IV	1277	Nicholas III	1700	Clement XI
355	Felix II*	715	St. Gregory II	1012	Benedict VIII	1281	Martin IV	1721	Innocent XIII
366	St. Damasus I	731	St. Gregory III	1012	Gregory*	1285	Honorius IV	1724	Benedict XIII
366	Ursinus*	741	St. Zachary	1024	John XIX	1288	Nicholas IV	1730	Clement XII
384	St. Siricius	752	Stephen II (III)[1]	1032	Benedict IX	1294	St. Celestine V	1740	Benedict XIV
399	St. Anastasius I	757	St. Paul I	1045	Sylvester III	1294	Boniface VIII	1758	Clement XIII
401	St. Innocent I	767	Constantine*	1045	Benedict IX	1303	Bl. Benedict XI	1769	Clement XIV
417	St. Zosimus	768	Philip*	1045	Gregory VI	1305	Clement V	1775	Pius VI
418	St. Boniface I	768	Stephen III (IV)	1046	Clement II	1316	John XXII	1800	Pius VII
418	Eulalius*	772	Adrian I	1047	Benedict IX	1328	Nicholas V*	1823	Leo XII
422	St. Celestine I	795	St. Leo III	1048	Damasus II	1334	Benedict XII	1829	Pius VIII
432	St. Sixtus III	816	Stephen IV (V)	1049	St. Leo IX	1342	Clement VI	1831	Gregory XVI
440	St. Leo I	817	St. Paschal I	1055	Victor II	1352	Innocent VI	1846	Pius IX
461	St. Hilary	824	Eugene II	1057	Stephen IX (X)	1362	Bl. Urban V	1878	Leo XIII
468	St. Simplicius	827	Valentine	1058	Benedict X*	1370	Gregory XI	1903	St. Pius X
483	St. Felix III (II)	827	Gregory IV	1059	Nicholas II	1378	Urban VI	1914	Benedict XV
492	St. Gelasius I	844	John*	1061	Alexander II	1378	Clement VII*	1922	Pius XI
496	Anastasius II	844	Sergius II	1061	Honorius II*	1389	Boniface IX	1939	Pius XII
498	St. Symmachus	847	St. Leo IV	1073	St. Gregory VII	1394	Benedict XIII*	1958	John XXIII
498	Lawrence* (501-	855	Benedict III	1080	Clement III*	1404	Innocent VII	1963	Paul VI
	505)	855	Anastasius*	1086	Bl. Victor III	1406	Gregory XII	1978	John Paul I
514	St. Hormisdas	858	St. Nicholas I	1088	Bl. Urban II	1409	Alexander V*	1978	John Paul II
523	St. John I, Martyr	867	Adrian II	1099	Paschal II	1410	John XXIII*	2005	Benedict XVI

Bl. = Blessed (1) After St. Zachary, a Roman priest named Stephen was elected, who died before assuming the papacy. Another Stephen was then elected to succeed Zachary as Stephen II. He is sometimes listed as Stephen III.

College of Cardinals

Members of the Sacred College of Cardinals are chosen by the pope to be his chief assistants and advisers in the administration of the church. Among their duties is the election of the pope.

In its present form, the College of Cardinals dates from the 12th century. The first cardinals, from about the 6th century, were deacons and priests of the leading churches of Rome and were bishops of neighboring dioceses. The title of cardinal was limited to members of the college in 1567. The number of cardinals was set at 70 in 1586 by Pope Sixtus V. From 1959 Pope John XXIII began to increase the number; however, the number eligible to participate in papal elections was limited to 120. Previous limitations were set aside by Pope John Paul II when he created new cardinals. In 1918, the Code of Canon Law specified that all cardinals must be priests. Pope John XXIII in 1962 established a rule that all cardinals must be bishops, though exceptions could be made. In 1971, Pope Paul VI decreed that at age 80, cardinals must retire from curial departments and offices and from participation in papal elections.

As of Sept. 2012, there were 206 cardinals from 66 countries, of whom 118, from 49 countries, remained eligible to vote.

North American Cardinals

Name	Office	Born	Named cardinal
William W. Baum[1]	Archbishop emeritus of Washington, DC	1926	1976
Raymond L. Burke	Prefect, Supreme Tribunal of the Apostolic Signature	1948	2010
Thomas C. Collins	Archbishop of Toronto, ON, Canada	1947	2012
Daniel N. DiNardo	Archbishop of Galveston-Houston	1949	2007
Timothy M. Dolan	Archbishop of New York	1950	2012
Edward M. Egan[1]	Archbishop emeritus of New York	1932	2001
Francis E. George	Archbishop of Chicago	1937	1998
William Henry Keeler[1]	Archbishop emeritus of Baltimore	1931	1994
Bernard F. Law[1]	Archbishop emeritus of Boston	1931	1985
William Levada	Archbishop emeritus of San Francisco	1936	2006
Javier Lozano Barragán	Pres. emeritus, Pontifical Council for Health Care Workers	1933	2003
Roger Mahony	Archbishop emeritus of Los Angeles	1936	1991
Adam Joseph Maida[1]	Archbishop emeritus of Detroit	1930	1994
Theodore McCarrick[1]	Archbishop emeritus of Washington, DC	1930	2001
Edwin F. O'Brien	Grand Master of the Knights of the Holy Sepulcher	1939	2012
Sean O'Malley	Archbishop of Boston	1944	2006
Marc Ouellet	Prefect, Congregation for Bishops	1944	2003
Justin F. Rigali	Archbishop emeritus of Philadelphia	1935	2003
Norberto Rivera Carrera	Archbishop of Mexico City	1942	1998
José Francisco Robles Ortega	Archbishop of Guadalajara, Mexico	1949	2007
Juan Sandoval Íñiguez	Archbishop emeritus of Guadalajara, Mexico	1933	1994
James F. Stafford[1]	Archbishop emeritus of Denver	1932	1998
Edmund C. Szoka[1]	Archbishop emeritus of Detroit	1927	1988
Jean-Claude Turcotte	Archbishop emeritus of Montréal, QC, Canada	1936	1994
Donald W. Wuerl	Archbishop of Washington, DC	1940	2010

(1) Ineligible to take part in papal elections (as of Sept. 2012).

The Ten Commandments

In the Hebrew Bible (Old Testament) the Ten Commandments (also called the Decalogue, from the Greek meaning "ten words") were revealed by God to Moses on Mt. Sinai. They form the covenant between God and the Israelites and the moral code that is the basis for the Jewish and Christian religions. The Ten Commandments appear in two places in the Old Testament—Exodus 20:1-17 and Deuteronomy 5:6-21.

Most Protestant, Anglican, and Orthodox Christians follow Jewish tradition, as here, which considers the introduction ("I am the Lord …") the first commandment and makes the prohibition against idolatry the second. Roman Catholic and Lutheran traditions combine I and II and split the last commandment into two that separately prohibit coveting of a neighbor's wife and of a neighbor's goods. This arrangement alters the numbering of the other commandments by one.

Following is the text as it appears in Exodus 20:1-17, in the King James version of the Bible [Roman numerals added]:

And God spake all these words, saying,

I. I *am* the LORD thy God, which have brought thee out of the land of Egypt, out of the house of bondage. Thou shalt have no other gods before me.

II. Thou shalt not make unto thee any graven image, or any likeness of *any thing* that *is* in heaven above, or that *is* in the earth beneath, or that *is* in the water under the earth. Thou shalt not bow down thyself to them, nor serve them: for I the LORD thy God *am* a jealous God, visiting the iniquity of the fathers upon the children unto the third and fourth *generation* of them that hate me; and shewing mercy unto thousands of them that love me, and keep my commandments.

III. Thou shalt not take the name of the LORD thy God in vain: for the LORD will not hold him guiltless that taketh his name in vain.

IV. Remember the sabbath day, to keep it holy. Six days shalt thou labour, and do all thy work: but the seventh day *is* the sabbath of the LORD thy God: *in it* thou shalt not do any work, thou, nor thy son, nor thy daughter, thy manservant, nor thy maidservant, nor thy cattle, nor thy stranger that *is* within thy gates: for *in* six days the LORD made heaven and earth, the sea, and all that in them *is*, and rested the seventh day: wherefore the LORD blessed the sabbath day, and hallowed it.

V. Honour thy father and thy mother: that thy days may be long upon the land which the LORD thy God giveth thee.

VI. Thou shalt not kill.

VII. Thou shalt not commit adultery.

VIII. Thou shalt not steal.

IX. Thou shalt not bear false witness against thy neighbour.

X. Thou shalt not covet thy neighbour's house, thou shalt not covet thy neighbour's wife, nor his manservant, nor his maidservant, nor his ox, nor his ass, nor any thing that *is* thy neighbour's.

Major Christian Denominations:

Brackets indicate some features that tend to

Denomination	Origins	Organization	Authority	Special rites
Baptists	In radical Reformation, objections to infant baptism, demands for church and state separation; John Smyth, English Separatist, in 1609; Roger Williams, 1638, Providence, RI.	Congregational; each local church is autonomous.	Scripture; some Baptists, particularly in the South, interpret the Bible literally.	[Baptism, usually early teen years and after, by total immersion]; Lord's Supper.
Church of Christ (Disciples)	Among evangelical Presbyterians in KY (1804) and PA (1809), in distress over Protestant factionalism and decline of fervor; organized in 1832.	Congregational.	["Where the Scriptures speak, we speak; where the Scriptures are silent, we are silent."]	Adult baptism; Lord's Supper (weekly).
Episcopalians	Henry VIII separated English Catholic Church from Rome, 1534, for political reasons; Protestant Episcopal Church in U.S. founded in 1789.	[Diocesan bishops, in apostolic succession, are elected by parish representatives; the national Church is headed by General Convention and Presiding Bishop; part of the Anglican Communion.]	Scripture as interpreted by tradition, especially 39 Articles (1563); tri-annual convention of bishops, priests, and lay people.	Infant baptism, Eucharist, and other sacraments; sacrament taken to be symbolic, but as having real spiritual effect.
Jehovah's Witnesses	Founded in 1870 in PA by Charles Taze Russell; incorporated as Watch Tower Bible and Tract Society of PA, 1884; name Jehovah's Witnesses adopted in 1931.	A governing body located in NY coordinates worldwide activities; each congregation cared for by a body of elders; each Witness considered a minister.	The Bible.	Baptism by immersion; annual Lord's Meal ceremony.
Latter-day Saints (Mormons)	In a vision of the Father and the Son reported by Joseph Smith (1820s) in NY; Smith also reported receiving new scripture on golden tablets: the Book of Mormon.	Theocratic; 1st Presidency (church president, two counselors), 12 Apostles preside over international church; local congregations headed by lay priesthood leaders.	Revelation to living prophet (church president). The Bible, Book of Mormon, and other revelations to Smith and his successors.	Baptism at age 8; laying on of hands (which confers the gift of the Holy Ghost); Lord's Supper; temple rites: baptism for the dead, marriage for eternity, others.
Lutherans	Begun by Martin Luther in Wittenberg, Germany, in 1517; objection to Catholic doctrine of salvation and sale of indulgences; break complete, 1519.	Varies from congregational to episcopal; in U.S., a combination of regional synods and congregational polities is most common.	Scripture alone; the Book of Concord (1580), which includes the three Ecumenical Creeds, is subscribed to as a correct exposition of Scripture.	Infant baptism; Lord's Supper; Christ's true body and blood present "in, with, and under the bread and wine."
Methodists	Rev. John Wesley began movement in 1738, within Church of England; first U.S. denomination, Baltimore (1784).	Conference and superintendent system; [in United Methodist Church, general superintendents are bishops— not a priestly order, only an office—who are elected for life].	Scripture as interpreted by tradition, reason, and experience.	Baptism of infants or adults; Lord's Supper commanded; other rites: marriage, ordination, solemnization of personal commitments.
Orthodox	Developed in original Christian proselytizing; broke with Rome in 1054 after centuries of doctrinal disputes and diverging traditions.	Synods of bishops in autonomous, usually national, churches elect a patriarch, archbishop, or metropolitan; these men, as a group, are the heads of the church.	Scripture, tradition, and the first seven church councils up to Nicaea II in 787; bishops in council have authority in doctrine and policy.	Seven sacraments: infant baptism and anointing, Eucharist, ordination, penance, marriage, and anointing of the sick.
Pentecostal	In Topeka, KS (1901) and Los Angeles (1906), in reaction to perceived loss of evangelical fervor among Methodists and others.	Originally a movement, not a formal organization, Pentecostalism now has a variety of organized forms and continues also as a movement.	Scripture; individual charismatic leaders, the teachings of the Holy Spirit.	[Spirit baptism, especially as shown in "speaking in tongues"; healing and sometimes exorcism]; adult baptism; Lord's Supper.
Presbyterians	In 16th-cent. Calvinist reformation; differed with Lutherans over sacraments, church government; John Knox founded Scotch Presbyterian church about 1560.	[Highly structured representational system of ministers and lay persons (presbyters) in local, regional, and national bodies (synods).]	Scripture.	Infant baptism; Lord's Supper; bread and wine symbolize Christ's spiritual presence.
Roman Catholics	Traditionally, founded by Jesus who named St. Peter the first vicar; developed in early Christian proselytizing, especially after the conversion of imperial Rome in the 4th cent.	[Hierarchy with supreme power vested in pope elected by cardinals]; councils of bishops advise on matters of doctrine and policy.	[The pope, when speaking for the whole church in matters of faith and morals; and tradition (which is expressed in church councils and in part contained in Scripture).]	Mass; seven sacraments: baptism, reconciliation, Eucharist, confirmation, marriage, ordination, and anointing of the sick (unction).
United Church of Christ	[By ecumenical union, in 1957, of Congregationalists and Evangelical and Reformed, representing both Calvinist and Lutheran traditions.]	Congregational; a General Synod, representative of all congregations, sets general policy.	Scripture.	Infant baptism; Lord's Supper.

How Do They Differ?

distinguish a denomination sharply from others.

Practice	Ethics	Doctrine	Other	Denom-ination
Worship style varies from staid to evangelistic; extensive missionary activity.	Usually opposed to alcohol and tobacco; some tendency toward a perfectionist ethical standard.	[No creed; true church is of believers only, who are all equal.]	Believing no authority can stand between the believer and God, the Baptists are strong supporters of church and state separation.	**Baptists**
Tries to avoid any rite not considered part of the 1st-cent. church; some congregations may reject instrumental music.	Some tendency toward perfectionism; increasing interest in social action programs.	Simple New Testament faith; avoids any elaboration not firmly based on Scripture.	Highly tolerant in doctrinal and religious matters; strongly supportive of scholarly education.	**Church of Christ (Disciples)**
Formal, based on *Book of Common Prayer*, updated 1979; services range from austerely simple to highly liturgical.	Tolerant, sometimes permissive; some social action programs.	Scripture; the "historic creeds," which include the Apostles, Nicene, and Athanasian, and the *Book of Common Prayer*; ranges from Anglo-Catholic to low church, with Calvinist influences.	Strongly ecumenical, holding talks with many branches of Christendom.	**Episco-palians**
Meetings are held in Kingdom Halls and members' homes for study and worship; [extensive door-to-door visitations].	High moral code; stress on marital fidelity and family values; avoidance of tobacco and blood transfusions.	[God, by his first creation, Christ, will soon destroy all wickedness; 144,000 faithful ones will rule in heaven with Christ over others on a paradise earth.]	Total allegiance proclaimed only to God's kingdom or heavenly government by Christ; main periodical, *The Watchtower*, is printed in 195 languages.	**Jehovah's Witnesses**
Simple service with prayers, hymns, sermon; private temple ceremonies may be more elaborate.	Temperance; strict moral code; [tithing]; a strong work ethic with communal self-reliance; [strong missionary activity]; family emphasis.	Jesus Christ is the Son of God, the Eternal Father. Jesus' atonement saves all humans; those who are obedient to God's laws may become joint-heirs with Christ in God's kingdom.	Mormons believe theirs is the true church of Jesus Christ, restored by God through Joseph Smith. Official name: The Church of Jesus Christ of Latter-day Saints.	**Latter-day Saints (Mormons)**
Relatively simple, formal liturgy with emphasis on the sermon.	Generally conserva-tive in personal and social ethics; doctrine of "two kingdoms" (worldly and holy) supports conserva-tism in secular affairs.	Salvation by grace alone through faith; Lutheranism has made major contributions to Protestant theology.	Though still somewhat divided along ethnic lines (German, Swedish, etc.), main divisions are between fundamentalists and liberals.	**Lutherans**
Worship style varies widely by denomination, local church, geography.	Originally pietist and perfectionist; always strong social activist elements.	No distinctive theological development; 25 articles abridged from Church of England's 39, not binding.	In 1968, The United Methodist Church was formed by the union of The Methodist Church and The Evangelical United Brethren Church.	**Methodists**
Elaborate liturgy, usually in the vernacular, though extremely traditional; the liturgy is the essence of Orthodoxy; veneration of icons.	Tolerant; little stress on social action; divorce, remarriage permitted in some cases; bishops are celibate; priests need not be.	Emphasis on Christ's resurrection, rather than crucifixion; the Holy Spirit proceeds from God the Father only.	Orthodox Church in America originally under Patriarch of Moscow, was granted autonomy in 1970; Greek Orthodox do not recognize this autonomy.	**Orthodox**
Loosely structured service with rousing hymns and sermons, culminating in spirit baptism.	Usually, emphasis on perfectionism, with varying degrees of tolerance.	Simple traditional beliefs, usually Protestant, with emphasis on the immediate presence of God in the Holy Spirit.	Once confined to lower-class "holy rollers," Pentecostalism now appears in mainline churches and has established middle-class congregations.	**Pentecostal**
A simple, sober service in which the sermon is central.	Traditionally, a tendency toward strictness, with firm church- and self-discipline; otherwise tolerant.	Emphasizes the sovereignty and justice of God; no longer dogmatic.	Although traces of belief in predestination (that God has foreordained salvation for the "elect") remain, this idea is no longer a central element in Presbyterianism.	**Presby-terians**
Relatively elaborate ritual centered on the Mass; also rosary recitation, novenas, etc.	Traditionally strict but increasingly tolerant in practice; divorce and remarriage not accepted, but annul-ments sometimes granted; celibate clergy, except in Eastern rite.	Highly elaborated; salva-tion by merit gained through grace; dogmatic; special veneration of Mary, the mother of Jesus.	Relatively rapid change followed Vatican Council II; Mass now in vernacular; more stress on social action, tolerance, ecumenism.	**Roman Catholics**
Usually simple service with emphasis on the sermon.	Tolerant; some social action emphasis.	Standard Protestant; "Statement of Faith" (1959) is not binding.	Two main churches in the 1957 union represented earlier unions with small groups of almost every Protestant denomination.	**United Church of Christ**

Books of the Bible

Old Testament—Standard Protestant List				New Testament List		
Genesis	I Kings	Ecclesiastes	Obadiah	Matthew	Ephesians	Hebrews
Exodus	II Kings	Song of Solomon	Jonah	Mark	Philippians	James
Leviticus	I Chronicles	Isaiah	Micah	Luke	Colossians	I Peter
Numbers	II Chronicles	Jeremiah	Nahum	John	I Thessalonians	II Peter
Deuteronomy	Ezra	Lamentations	Habakkuk	Acts	II Thessalonians	I John
Joshua	Nehemiah	Ezekiel	Zephaniah	Romans	I Timothy	II John
Judges	Esther	Daniel	Haggai	I Corinthians	II Timothy	III John
Ruth	Job	Hosea	Zechariah	II Corinthians	Titus	Jude
I Samuel	Psalms	Joel	Malachi	Galatians	Philemon	Revelation
II Samuel	Proverbs	Amos				

The standard Protestant Old Testament consists of the same 39 books as in the Bible of Judaism, but the latter is organized differently. The Old Testament used by Roman Catholics has 7 additional "deuterocanonical" books, plus some additional parts of books. The 7 are **Tobit, Judith, Wisdom, Sirach (Ecclesiasticus), Baruch, I Maccabees,** and **II Maccabees**. Both Catholic and Protestant versions of the New Testament have 27 books, with the same names.

Figures in the Hebrew Bible (Old Testament)

Aaron: First of Hebrew high priests; brother of Moses and Miriam.

Abel: Second son of Adam and Eve; slain by Cain.

Abraham: Founder of monotheism; patriarch; also called Abram.

Adam: First human according to Genesis.

Amos: Herdsman; prophesized against social injustice and oppression of the poor.

Bathsheba: Seduced by King David; mother of King Solomon.

Cain: First son of Adam and Eve; killed his brother Abel.

Cyrus: Persian ruler; sent Jews home from exile.

Daniel: Cast into lion's den for violating decree of King Darius; saved.

David: Israel's greatest king; shepherd, warrior, musician, psalmist.

Deborah: Prophet and judge; ruled over Israel.

Elijah: Great prophet; was victorious over the priests of the Phoenician god, Baal.

Elisha: Prophet; successor to Elijah.

Esther: Jewish wife of the king of Persia; saved Jews from annihilation.

Eve: First woman according to Genesis.

Ezekiel: Visionary; prophesized hope to exiled Jews in Babylon.

Ezra: Great Jewish leader; rededicated worship and Torah law after exile.

Goliath: Giant Philistine warrior; slain by David.

Hannah: Childless; promised child to God; mother to the prophet Samuel.

Hosea: Enacted prophecy; asked God's forgiveness for Israel's unfaithfulness.

Isaac: Son of Abraham and Sarah; saved from sacrificial altar.

Isaiah: Highly educated prophet; avoided war with Assyria; Israel destroyed; Jerusalem survived.

Jacob: Son of Isaac; father of the Twelve Tribes; renamed "Israel" by angel.

Jeremiah: Confronted leaders; urged surrender to Babylon.

Jezebel: Phoenician queen of King Ahab; had Israelite prophets killed.

Job: "Blameless" man; allowed by God to lose family, health, and possessions, in a test of his faith.

Jonah: Swallowed by a great fish; prophesied destruction of Nineveh, averted when the people repented.

Jonathan: Son of King Saul; friend of David.

Joseph: Favorite of Jacob; interpreted Pharaoh's dreams; brought Hebrews to Egypt.

Joshua: Successor of Moses; led Hebrews into Canaan.

Josiah: Reformist king; repaired Temple; restored worship; reintroduced Passover.

Leah: Matriarch; older sister of Rachel; Jacob's wife.

Micah: Prophet; predicted the end of war and beginning of peace.

Miriam: Prophet and great leader of the Hebrews; sister to Moses and Aaron.

Moses: Most important Hebrew prophet; leader of the Israelites; received the Torah.

Nathan: Prophet; confronted King David over his seduction of Bathsheba.

Nebuchadnezzar: Babylonian king; destroyed Jerusalem.

Nehemiah: Led Jews back to Jerusalem from Babylonian exile.

Noah: Man of great faith who, according to Genesis, saved his family and two of every living thing on Earth from a great flood.

Rachel: Matriarch; younger sister of Leah; Jacob's wife; Joseph's mother.

Rebecca: Matriarch; wife of Isaac; mother of Jacob.

Ruth: Moabite convert; ancestor of David.

Samson: Judge and military leader of Israel; possessed superhuman strength.

Samuel: Prophet; anointed Saul king of Israel and later anointed David to succeed him.

Sarah: First matriarch of Israel; wife of Abraham; mother of Isaac.

Saul: First king of Israel; father of Jonathan.

Solomon: King of Israel at its zenith; known for great wisdom.

Zechariah: Prophet; encouraged rebuilding of Temple destroyed by Babylonians.

Figures in the New Testament

Andrew: One of the Twelve Apostles; brother of Peter and former fisherman; one of the earlier disciples.

Barabbas: Imprisoned with Jesus; set free by Pilate on Passover.

Barnabas: Disciple of Jesus; closely connected with Paul.

Bartholomew: A lesser-known member of the Twelve Apostles; cheerful and prayed often.

Cornelius: A Roman convert; defended by Peter, allowing Gentiles to become Christians.

Elizabeth: Mother of John the Baptist; relation of the Virgin Mary.

Gabriel: Archangel; appeared to the Virgin Mary to announce that she was to give birth to the messiah.

Herod: Two Herods appear in the New Testament: Herod the Great ordered the death of children around the time of Jesus's birth; his son, Herod, imprisoned John the Baptist and later had him beheaded.

James: One of the Twelve; brother of John the apostle.

Jesus: Central figure of the Gospels; believed to be the Messiah and son of God; crucified by the Romans.

John (Apostle): Beloved disciple of Jesus; one of the Twelve; possible author of fourth Gospel; brother of James.

John (Baptist): Known as John the Baptist; important prophet and forerunner to Jesus; relation of the Virgin Mary.

Joseph: Husband of the Virgin Mary; descendant of King David.

Judas Iscariot: Betrayer of Jesus; prominent member of the Apostles; committed suicide.

Judas Thaddeus: One of the Twelve; also called Jude to distinguish him from Judas Iscariot.

Lazarus: Brother of the disciples Martha and Mary of Bethany; raised from the dead at their request; possibly the same Lazarus who appears in Jesus's parable of the rich man.

Luke: Traditional author of the Gospel of Luke; possibly a follower of Paul.

Mark: Traditional author of the Gospel of Mark; possibly a disciple of Peter.

Mary, the mother of Jesus: Traditionally believed to be a virgin who conceived without sin; wife of Joseph.

Mary Magdalene: Important female disciple of Jesus; witness to his death and resurrection.

Matthew: One of the Twelve; possible author of the Gospel of Matthew; former tax collector.

Matthias: Often included on lists of the Twelve Apostles as the apostle who replaced Judas Iscariot after his betrayal.

Paul (Saul): Writer of nearly a quarter of the New Testament; a former persecutor of Christians, converted after a vision; played a significant role in spreading Christianity.

Peter: Considered the foremost of the Twelve Apostles; traditionally the first pope and "rock" of the Christian church; author of epistles; also called Simon and Simon Peter.

Philip: One of the Twelve; considered pragmatic and sensible.

Pilate, Pontius: A Roman prefect; played large role in the trial and crucifixion of Jesus.

Simon: One of the Twelve; known as "the Zealot" to distinguish from Simon Peter.

Stephen: Fervently preached that Jesus was the Messiah; stoned to death by angry mob, including Saul; important figure in Saul's conversion.

Thomas: One of the Twelve; known as "Doubting Thomas" because he did not believe Jesus was risen until he could touch him.

Timothy: A disciple closely connected with Paul; recipient of epistles.

Zacharias: Father of John the Baptist; husband of Elizabeth; struck dumb when he doubted his barren wife could become pregnant.

Major Non-Christian Religions

Source: Baha'i reviewed by the Baha'i Community Relations Center; Islam reviewed by Natana Delong-Bas, Lecturer in Islamic Studies, Boston Coll.; Hinduism and Judaism reviewed by Anthony Padovano, PhD, STD, Prof. of Literature & Relig. Studies, Ramapo College, NJ, Adj. Prof. of Theol., Fordham Univ.; Sikhism reviewed by The Sikh Coalition of New York, NY.

Islam

Founded: Muhammad received his first revelation in 610 CE.

Founder: Muhammad (c. 570-632 CE), the Prophet.

Sacred texts: Two texts constitute the Muslim sacred canon, the *Qur'an* (Koran) and the *Hadith*. The Koran provides the foundation for Islamic religion and culture. It is regarded as the final, perfect, and complete word of God as revealed to Muhammad over the course of his life. Received by Muhammad in the Arabic language, it is memorized in Arabic by adherents regardless of their native language. It is divided into 114 chapters of unequal length, the shortest containing only 3 verses, and the longest containing 306 verses. The Koran is the ultimate source of everything Islamic, from metaphysics to theology to sacred history, to ethics and law, to art. The Hadith, which describes Muhammad's actions, attitudes, and teachings, complements the Koran. Due to its long history of oral transmission, the Hadith's lessons are seen as somewhat vulnerable to human error. It does not contain God's unadulterated voice as does the Koran but functions as a powerful spiritual and behavioral code nonetheless.

Organization: Muhammad was both the last prophet and a statesman. Muslim leaders have often assumed both civil and moral functions within Islamic states. Within the larger community, there are cultural and national groups, held together by a common religious law, the *Sharia*. Muslims believe that God is the ultimate lawgiver and that human beings cannot devise laws that oppose divine laws. Still, the Sharia is approached differently in different parts of the Islamic world. Over the centuries, Sunnis have developed four major schools of law: the Hanafi, the Shafi'i, the Hanbali, and the Maliki schools. The Ja'fari school is the most important and well-known Shiite school. Before the 20th century, religious scholars known as the *ulama* held much legal power. Judges (*qadis*) and law-interpreters (*muftis*) are people learned in religious law who lead congregational prayers in mosques and perform other religious duties.

Practice: Five duties (of both men and women), known as the Pillars of Islam, are regarded as cardinal in Islam and as central to the life of the Islamic community. In accordance with Islam's absolute commitment to monotheism, the first duty is the profession of faith (the *Shahadah*): "There is no God but Allah and Muhammad is His Prophet." A Muslim must profess this belief publicly at least once in his or her lifetime; it defines the membership of an individual in the Islamic community. The second duty is that of five daily prayers organized in intervals throughout the day: sunrise, early afternoon, late afternoon, immediately after sunset, and before midnight. During prayer, Muslims face the Kaaba, a small, cube-shaped structure in the courtyard of al-Haram (the "inviolate place"), at the Grand Mosque of Mecca. All five prayers in Islam are congregational and are to be offered in a mosque, but they may be offered individually if one cannot be present with a congregation. Congregational prayer is required only at the early afternoon prayer on Friday for men. The third cardinal duty of a Muslim is to pay alms, or *zakat*, which should be 2.5% of one's total wealth. This was originally the tax levied by Muhammad on the wealthy members of the community, primarily to help the poor. Only when zakat has been paid is the rest of a Muslim's property considered purified and legitimate. The fourth duty is the fast of the lunar month of Ramadan. During the fasting month, one must abstain from eating, drinking, smoking, impure thoughts, and sexual intercourse from dawn until sunset, and feed at least one poor person, if able. The fifth duty is the pilgrimage to the Kaaba, which a Muslim must undertake, with exceptions for poverty and ill health, at least once during his or her lifetime.

Divisions: There are two major groups: the majority Sunni (84% of the worldwide Muslim population) and the minority Shiites (14%). Sects first appeared in Islam at the time of Muhammad's death. The group that came to be known as Sunni accepted Abu Bakr, an early convert, as his successor (caliph), while a smaller number, which became the Shi'a, believed that Ali ibn Abi Talib, the son-in-law and first cousin of the prophet, should have become his successor (Imam). Imams are believed to interpret the Koran infallibly. **Shiites** fall into three major branches: Fivers, Seveners, and Twelvers, reflecting the number of Imams they recognize. Twelvers believe that the 12th Imam has lived an invisible existence since 874, and will return as the Mahdi (a messiah figure) who will usher in a 1,000-year reign of peace and justice. **Sufism** (mystical dimension of Islam) emphasizes personal relation to God and obedience informed by love of God; it is prevalent among both Sunni and Shiites.

Location: W Africa to Philippines, across a band including E Africa, Central Asia and W China, India, Malaysia, Indonesia. Islam has several million adherents in North America and about 30 mil in Europe.

Beliefs: Strictly monotheistic. God is creator of the universe, omnipotent, omniscient, just, forgiving, and merciful. God revealed the Koran to Muhammad to guide humanity to truth and justice. Those who sincerely "submit" (literal meaning of "Islam") to God attain salvation.

World's Largest Muslim Populations, 2010
Source: Pew Research Center

Rank	Country	Muslim population	% of country pop.
1.	Indonesia	204,847,000	88.1%
2.	Pakistan	178,097,000	96.4
3.	India	177,286,000	14.6
4.	Bangladesh	148,607,000	90.4
5.	Egypt	80,024,000	94.7
6.	Nigeria	75,728,000	47.9
7.	Iran	74,819,000	99.6
8.	Turkey	74,660,000	98.6
9.	Algeria	34,780,000	98.2
10.	Morocco	32,381,000	99.9
11.	Iraq	31,108,000	98.9
12.	Sudan	30,855,000	71.4
13.	Afghanistan	29,047,000	99.8
14.	Ethiopia	28,721,000	33.8
15.	Uzbekistan	26,833,000	96.5
16.	Saudi Arabia	25,493,000	97.1
17.	Yemen	24,023,000	99.0
18.	China	23,308,000	1.8
19.	Syria	20,895,000	92.8
20.	Malaysia	17,139,000	61.4

Baha'i

Founded: Mid-19th century.

Founder: Mirza Husayn-Ali Nuri (1817-92), later known as Baha'u'llah (Arabic for "Glory of God").

Sacred texts: The writings of Baha'u'llah and of his herald the Bab (Siyyid Ali-Muhammad, 1819-50). The primary text is *Kitab-i-Aqdas* (Most Holy Book).

Organization: The Baha'i administrative system consists of elected nine-member councils at the local, national, and international levels. There are also more than 180 National Spiritual Assemblies and an elected, international governing body known as the Universal House of Justice.

Practice: Prayer, meditation, and fasting are key components of the Baha'i Faith. Work performed in a spirit of service to humanity is considered an important form of worship. The Baha'i Faith has no clergy and minimal ritual and congregational worship.

Divisions: In a religion in which unity is perhaps the central spiritual value, the Baha'i Faith has avoided separating into sects with differentiated theologies and practices.

Location: Worldwide, with practitioners in 236 countries.

Beliefs: God has progressively revealed His will and purpose through a series of Divine manifestations including Jesus, Buddha, Muhammad, Zoroaster, and Baha'u'llah. Baha'u'llah's teachings include the oneness of humanity, the equality of men and women, the harmony of science and religion, the abandonment of all forms of prejudice, and the elimination of extremes of poverty and wealth.

Buddhism

Founded: About 525 BCE, reportedly near Benares, India.

Founder: Gautama Siddhartha (c. 563-483 BCE), the Buddha, who achieved enlightenment through intense meditation.

Sacred texts: The *Tripitaka*, a collection of the Buddha's teachings, rules of monastic life, and philosophical commentaries on the teachings; also a vast body of Buddhist teachings and commentaries, many of which are called *sutras*.

Organization: The basic institution is the *sangha*, or monastic order, through which traditions are passed down. Monastic life tends to be democratic and antiauthoritarian.

Practice: Varies widely according to the sect, and ranges from austere meditation to magical chanting and elaborate temple rites. Many practices, such as exorcism of devils, reflect pre-Buddhist beliefs.

Divisions: A variety of sects grouped into three primary branches: Theravada, which emphasizes the importance of pure thought and deed; Mahayana (includes Zen and Soka-gakkai), which ranges from philosophical schools to belief in the saving grace of higher beings or ritual practices and to practical meditative disciplines; and Vajrayana, or Tantrism, a combination of belief in ritual magic and sophisticated philosophy.

Location: Mainly in Asia, from Sri Lanka to Japan.

Beliefs: Life is suffering, and there is no ultimate reality behind it. The cycle of birth and rebirth continues because of desire and attachment to the unreal "self." Meditation and deeds will end the cycle and achieve Nirvana (nothingness, enlightenment).

Hinduism

Founded: About 1500 BCE by Aryans who migrated to India, where their Vedic religion intermixed with the practices and beliefs of the native peoples.

Sacred texts: The *Veda*, including the *Upanishads*, a collection of rituals and commentaries; a vast number of epic stories about gods, heroes, and saints, including the *Bhagavadgita*, a part of the *Mahabharata*, and the *Ramayana*.

Organization: None, strictly speaking. Generally, rituals should be performed or assisted by Brahmins, the priestly caste, but in practice, simpler rituals can be performed by anyone. Brahmins are the final judges of ritual purity, the vital element in Hindu life. Temples and religious organizations are usually presided over by Brahmins.

Practice: Primarily passage rites (e.g., initiation, marriage, death) and daily devotions. Of the public rites, the *puja*, a ceremonial dinner for a god, is the most common.

Divisions: There is no concept of orthodoxy in Hinduism, which presents a variety of sects. The three major living traditions are those devoted to the gods Vishnu and Shiva and to the goddess Shakti. Numerous folk beliefs and practices, often in amalgamation with the above groups, exist side by side with philosophical schools.

Location: Mainly India, Nepal, Malaysia, Guyana, Suriname, and Sri Lanka.

Beliefs: There is only one divine principle; the many gods are only aspects of that unity. Life in all its forms is an aspect of the divine, but it appears as a separation from the divine, a meaningless cycle of birth and rebirth (*samsara*)

determined by the purity or impurity of past deeds (*karma*). To improve one's karma or escape samsara by pure acts, thought, and/or devotion is the aim of every Hindu.

Judaism

Founded: About 2000 BCE.

Founder: Abraham is regarded as the founding patriarch.

Sacred texts: The five books of Moses (the Torah), the basic source of teachings.

Organization: Originally theocratic, Judaism has evolved into a congregational polity. The basic institution is the local synagogue or temple, operated by the congregation and led by a rabbi of their choice. Chief rabbis in France and Great Britain have authority only over those who accept it; in Israel, the two chief rabbis have civil authority in family law.

Practice: Among traditional practitioners, almost all areas of life are governed by strict discipline. Sabbath and holidays are marked by observances, and attendance at public worship is considered especially important. Chief annual observances are Passover, celebrating liberation of the Israelites from Egypt and marked by the Seder meal in homes, and the 10 days from Rosh Hashanah (New Year) to Yom Kippur (Day of Atonement), a period of penitence.

Divisions: Judaism is an unbroken spectrum from ultra-conservative to ultraliberal, largely reflecting different points of view regarding the binding character of the prohibitions and duties—particularly the dietary and Sabbath observations—traditionally prescribed for the daily life of the Jew.

Location: Mainly in Israel and the U.S.

Beliefs: Strictly monotheistic. God is the creator and ruler of the universe. God established a particular relationship with the Hebrew people: by obeying a divine law God gave them, they would be a special witness to God's mercy and justice. Judaism stresses ethical behavior (and, among the traditional, careful ritual obedience) as true worship of God.

Sikhism

Founded: Late 15th century in South Asia.

Founder: Guru Nanak Dev ji, Sikhism's first Guru.

Sacred texts: The *Guru Granth Sahib* was compiled by the Sikh Gurus and contains their experiences of the Divine. It also contains writing by other saintly figures of different faiths.

Organization: Each Sikh must make her or his own spiritual journey and not depend on clergy. Congregational prayer led by both men and women takes place in local *Gurudwaras*. Harmandir Sahib in Amritsar, Punjab (northern India), is the central place of worship.

Practice: Prayers are required in the morning, evening, and before sleeping. The most important mode of congregational prayer is the singing of hymns from the Guru Granth Sahib. The "Five Ks" are five articles of faith required of all Sikhs: *Kes* (uncut hair), *Kangha* (comb), *Kara* (steel bracelet), *Kirpan* (sword), and *Kaccha* (short pants).

Divisions: The last living Guru, Guru Gobind Singh (1666-1708) crystallized the practices and beliefs of the faith and determined that no future living Guru was needed. Today the religion is guided by joint sovereignty of Guru Granth and Guru Panth. Guru Granth is the Sikh scripture, as the spiritual manifestation of the Guru, while the Guru Panth is the collectivity of all initiated Sikhs worldwide, as the physical manifestation of the Guru.

Location: Many Sikhs have Punjabi backgrounds. The Punjab region was divided between India and Pakistan with the end of British rule.

Beliefs: Sikhism preaches a message of devotion, remembrance of God at all times, truthful living, equality between all human beings, and social justice, while emphatically denouncing superstitions and blind rituals. Sikhism is a monotheistic religion based on revelation.

LANGUAGE

New Words in English

The following words and definitions were provided by Merriam-Webster Inc., publishers of *Merriam-Webster's Collegiate Dictionary, Eleventh Edition*, released in 2003. The words are among those that the Merriam-Webster editors decided had achieved enough currency in English to be added to the latest (2012) printing of the dictionary.

after-party: a party for invited guests that follows a main party or event

aha moment: a moment of sudden realization, inspiration, insight, recognition, or comprehension

alcopop: a flavored beverage containing usually 4-6% alcohol

boomerang child: a young adult who returns to live at his or her family home, especially for financial reasons

brain cramp: an instance of temporary mental confusion resulting in an error or lapse in judgment

bucket list: a list of things that one has not done before but wants to do before dying

cloud computing: the practice of storing regularly used computer data on multiple servers that can be accessed through the Internet

craft beer: a specialty beer produced in limited quantities

earworm: a song or melody that keeps repeating in one's mind

energy drink: a usually carbonated beverage that typically contains caffeine and other ingredients (as taurine and ginseng) intended to increase the drinker's energy

e-reader: a handheld electronic device designed to be used for reading e-books [books in electronic, or digital, formats] and similar material

first responder: a person (as a police officer or an EMT) who is among those responsible for going immediately to the scene of an accident or emergency to provide assistance

flexitarian: one whose normally meatless diet occasionally includes meat or fish

game changer: a newly introduced element or factor that changes an existing situation or activity in a significant way

gastropub: a pub, bar, or tavern that offers meals of high quality

geocaching: a game in which players are given the geographical coordinates of a cache of items which they search for with a GPS device

helicopter parent: a parent who is overly involved in the life of his or her child

life coach: an advisor who helps people make decisions, set and reach goals, or deal with problems

man cave: a room or space (as in a basement) designed according to the taste of the man of the house to be used as his personal area for hobbies or leisure activities

mash-up: something created by combining elements from two or more sources

m-commerce: business transactions conducted by using a mobile electronic device (as a cell phone)

multiverse: a theoretical reality that includes a possibly infinite number of universes

obesogenic: promoting excessive weight gain: producing obesity

person of interest: a person who is believed to be possibly involved in a crime but has not been charged or arrested

plus-size: extra large—used of clothing or sometimes of a person

sexting: the sending of sexually explicit messages or images by cell phone

shovel-ready: ready for the start of work—used of a construction project or site

systemic risk: the risk that the failure of one financial institution (as a bank) could cause other interconnected institutions to fail and harm the economy as a whole

tentpole: a big-budget movie whose earnings are expected to compensate the studio for its less profitable movies

tipping point: the critical point in a situation, process, or system beyond which a significant and often unstoppable effect or change takes place

underwater: having, relating to, or being a mortgage loan for which more is owed than the property securing the loan is worth

Words About Words

allegory: extended use of symbols, in the form of characters, animals, or events, that represent ideas or themes. Ex.: John Bunyan, *Pilgrim's Progress*

alliteration: repetition of same, initial consonant sounds of two or more words in sequence or in short intervals. Ex.: "I have stood still and stopped the sound of feet." —Robert Frost, "Acquainted With the Night"

antithesis: an expression in which contrasting ideas are intentionally juxtaposed, usually in parallel structure. Ex.: "The world will little note, nor long remember, what we say here, but it can never forget what they did here." —Abraham Lincoln, Gettysburg Address

assonance: repetition of same or similar vowel sounds in words located near each other. Ex.: "Green as a dream, and deep as death." —Rupert Brooke, "The Old Vicarage, Grantchester"

back-formation: creation of a word from an existing word, whose forms seem to suggest that the previously existing word derived from the newer word. Ex.: The verb "edit" is a back-formation of the word "editor."

cliché: a saying or expression that has been used so often it has lost its effect. Ex.: work like a dog

euphemism: a mild, indirect expression used instead of a plainer one that might be harsh, unpleasant, or offensive. Ex.: restroom instead of toilet; pass away, or pass, instead of die

hyperbole: exaggeration for emphasis or effect. Ex.: "And fired the shot heard round the world." —Ralph Waldo Emerson, "Concord Hymn"

irony: deliberate use of an expression in which the literal or surface meaning is contrary to a hidden intended, often opposite meaning that can be inferred. Ex.: "Yet Brutus says he was ambitious; / And Brutus is an honorable man." —William Shakespeare, *Julius Caesar*

litotes: intentional understatement made by negating the opposite of what is meant. Ex.: This was no small matter.

metaphor: a stated equivalence between two dissimilar things or a reference to one thing rather than another, so as to imply a comparison. Ex.: "Life is a tale told by an idiot, full of sound and fury, signifying nothing." —Shakespeare, *Macbeth*

metonymy: substitution of one word for another that it suggests. Ex.: The pen is mightier than the sword.

onomatopoeia: words that imitate the sounds they describe. Ex.: buzz, murmur

oxymoron: juxtaposition of contradictory words. Ex.: deafening silence

paradox: a statement that is phrased to seem contradictory, odd, or opposed to common sense or expectation, while being presented as true. Ex.: "What a pity that youth must be wasted on the young." —George Bernard Shaw

personification: treatment of objects or abstractions as if they were persons. Ex.: "Because I could not stop for Death— / He kindly stopped for me." —Emily Dickinson, "Because I Could Not Stop for Death"

simile: a comparison between two dissimilar things using the words "like" or "as." Ex.: "My love is like a red, red rose" —Robert Burns, "A Red, Red Rose"

spoonerism: play on words in which the initial sounds of two or more words are transposed, creating different phrases whose meanings when compared can be humorous. Ex.: blushing crow instead of crushing blow

synecdoche: a form of metonymy; the use of a part for the whole, or the whole for the part. Ex.: All hands on deck!

tautology: useless, often unwitting repetition of the same idea in different wording. Ex.: close proximity. In logic, a proposition that would be self-contradictory to deny. Ex.: All bachelors are male.

National Spelling Bee

The annual Scripps National Spelling Bee competition, conducted by The E.W. Scripps Company and other newspapers since 1941, was instituted by *The Courier-Journal* of Louisville, KY, in 1925. Students under 16 who are not beyond the 8th grade are eligible to compete at the local level for a chance to advance to the national competition in Washington, DC. The 2012 winner was Snigdha Nandipati, of San Diego, CA. Second place went to Stuti Mishra of West Melbourne, FL, and third place to Arvind Mahankali of Bayside Hills, NY.

Here are the last words given and spelled correctly at the National Spelling Bee in recent years.

Year	Word	Year	Word	Year	Word	Year	Word	Year	Word
1978	deification	1985	milieu	1992	lyceum	1999	logorrhea	2006	Ursprache
1979	maculature	1986	odontalgia	1993	kamikaze	2000	demarche	2007	serrefine
1980	elucubrate	1987	staphylococci	1994	antediluvian	2001	succedaneum	2008	guerdon
1981	sarcophagus	1988	elegiacal	1995	xanthosis	2002	prospicience	2009	Laodicean
1982	psoriasis	1989	spoliator	1996	vivisepulture	2003	pococurante	2010	stromuhr
1983	Purim	1990	fibranne	1997	euonym	2004	autochthonous	2011	cymotrichous
1984	luge	1991	antipyretic	1998	chiaroscurist	2005	appoggiatura	2012	guetapens

Commonly Misspelled English Words

accidentally	cemetery	eligible	innocuous	miniature	permissible	separate
accommodate	changeable	embarrass	inoculate	miscellaneous	perseverance	sheriff
accumulate	collectible	environment	irresistible	Mississippi	personnel	sincerely
acknowledgment	commitment	existence	jewelry	misspelled	potatoes	supersede
acquainted	committee	fascinating	judgment	mnemonic	prescient	temperament
acquire	connoisseur	February	laboratory	mysterious	privilege	temperature
a lot	conscience	fluorescent	leisure	necessary	propaganda	transferred
already	conscious	forty	license	noticeable	questionnaire	truly
amateur	convenience	gauge	liaison	occasionally	receipt	twelfth
appearance	deceive	government	lieutenant	occurrence	receive	vaccinate
appropriate	defendant	grammar	lightning	omitted	recommend	vacillate
assimilate	definitely	harass	liquefy	opportunity	rhythm	vacuum
bureau	desirable	humorous	maintenance	parallel	ridiculous	vicious
business	desperate	incidentally	marriage	patience	sacrilegious	Wednesday
calendar	deterrent	independent	medieval	performance	seize	weird
Caribbean	eighth	indispensable	millennium	permanent	sergeant	wholly

Foreign Words and Phrases

(A = Arabic; F = French; Ger = German; Gr = Greek; I = Italian; J = Japanese; L = Latin; R = Russian; S = Spanish; Y = Yiddish)

ad hoc (L; ad-HOK): for the end or purpose at hand; impromptu
ad hominem (L; ad-HOH-mee-nem): argument that criticizes an opponent, often unfairly, rather than addressing an issue directly
al fresco (I; ahl-FRAYS-koh): outdoors
anime (J: A-nuh-may): Japanese-style animation
antebellum (L; AHN-teh-BEL-lum): pre-war
aperçu(s) (F; ah-per-SOO): first perception or insight; outline
au courant (F; oh-koo-RAHN): up-to-date, fashionable
belles lettres (F; bel-LET-truh): writing aspiring to artistic merit
bête noire (F; bet-NWAHR): a thing or person viewed with particular dislike or fear
bildungsroman (Ger; BIL-doongs-roh-mahn): novel embodying coming-of-age story
bodega (S; boh-DAY-gah): grocery store
bonhomie (F; bon-noh-MEE): friendliness
bon vivant (F; bon-vee-VAHN): a person with refined tastes, especially for food and drink
bourgeois (F; boo-ZHWAH): middle-class; materialistic
carte blanche (F; kahrt-BLANSH): full discretionary power
casus belli (L; KAH-soos-BEL-lee): reason for going to war
cause célèbre (F; kawz-suh-LEB): a notorious incident
cognoscenti (I; kahn-yuh-SHEN-tee): experts; connoisseurs
comme il faut (F; cum-eel-FOH): proper; as it should be
contretemps (F; kon-truh-TAHN): awkward situation
coup de grâce (F; kooh-duh-GRAHS): the decisive final blow
cum laude/magna cum laude/summa cum laude (L; kuhm-LOU-day; MAG-na ... ; SOO-ma ...): with praise or honor/with great praise or honor/with the highest praise or honor
de facto (L; day-FAK-toh): in fact, if not by law
de jure (L; dee-JOOR-ee, day-YOOR-ay): by right or by law
de rigueur (F; duh-ree-GUR): required by convention or etiquette
détente (F; day-TAHNT): an easing of strained relations
deus ex machina (L; DAY-uhs-eks-MAH-keh-nah): person/event that provides a solution unexpectedly or suddenly, espec. (in literature) a contrived solution to a plot
doppelgänger (G; DAH-pul-gang-ur): a double or ghostly counterpart of a person
double entendre (F; DOO-blahn-TAHN-druh): expression with a double meaning, one meaning of which is often risqué
éminence grise (F; ay-meh-nahns-GREEZ): one who wields power behind the scenes
ennui (F; ah-NOOEE): boredom; world-weariness; annoyance
e pluribus unum (L; eh-PLOO-ree-boos-OO-noom): out of many, one (U.S. motto)
ersatz (Ger; EHR-zats): artificial; being a (usually inferior) substitute
ex post facto (L; eks-pohst-FAK-toh): retroactive(ly)
fait accompli (F; fayt-uh-kom-PLEE): an accomplished fact
fatwa (A; FAHT-wah): in Islam, a legal or religious decree
faux pas (F; foh-PAH): false step; breach of etiquette
habeas corpus (L; HAY-bee-ahs-KOR-pus): an order for a prisoner to be brought to court to challenge his or her detention
hoi polloi (Gr; hoy-puh-LOY): the masses
impresario (I; im-prah-SAH-ri-oh): manager, promoter, or sponsor of a musical or theatrical program or company
imprimatur (L; im-prah-MAH-toor): approval or official permission to print, espec. by the Roman Catholic church

in loco parentis (L; in-LOH-koh-puh-REN-tis): in place of parent
in medias res (L; in-MAY-dee-oos-rays): into the middle of things
intelligentsia (R; in-te-luh-JEN-see-uh): elite social class made up of intellectuals and educated people
ipso facto (L; ip-soh-FAK-toh): by that fact itself
je ne sais quoi (F; zhuh-nuh-say-KWAH): literally, "I don't know what"; the little something that eludes description
jihad (A; jih-HAHD): Islamic holy war; struggle in devotion to Islam
joie de vivre (F; zhwah-duh-VEEV-ruh): zest for life
leitmotif (Ger; lyt-moh-TEEF): the central theme or idea, particularly in art and literature
mano a mano (S; MAH-noh-ah-MAH-noh): hand to hand; in direct combat
mea culpa (L; MAY-uh-CUL-puh): through my fault
mensch (Y; MENTSCH): an upright, noble, admirable person
modus operandi (L; MOH-duhs-op-uh-RAN-dee): method of operation
mujahideen (A; moo-jah-ha-DEEN): Islamic holy warrior
noblesse oblige (F; noh-BLES-oh-BLEEZH): the obligation of nobility to help the less fortunate
nolo contendere (L; NOH-loh-kohn-TEN-duh-ree): a plea of no contest to charges, without admitting guilt
non compos mentis (L; non-KOM-puhs-MEN-tis): not of sound mind
non sequitur (L; non-SEH-kwi-tour): a conclusion that does not logically follow from what preceded it
nouveau riche (F; noo-voh-REESH): a newly rich person, espec. one who spends money conspicuously
ombudsman (Swedish; AHM-budz-muhn): person who receives, investigates, and settles complaints
par excellence (F; par-ek-seh-LANS): best of all; incomparable
parvenu (F; par-vuh-NOO): upstart
persona non grata (L; per-SOH-nah-non-GRAH-tah): unwelcome person
pièce de résistance (F; pee-es-duh-ray-ZEES-tonz): the outstanding item in a series or group
prima facie (L; pry-muh-FAY-shee-ee; pry-muh-FAY-shuh): true at first glance; presumptively valid
pro bono (L; proh-BOH-noh): (work) donated for the public good
quid pro quo (L; kwid-proh-KWOH): something given or received for something else
raison d'être (F; RAY-zohnn-DET-ruh): reason for being
savoir faire (F; sav-wahr-FAIR): dexterity in social affairs
schadenfreude (Ger; SHAH-duhn-froy-deh): joy at another's misfortune
semper fidelis (L; SEM-puhr-fee-DAY-lis): always faithful
sobriquet (F; SOH-bri-kay): nickname or informal descriptive name for someone
sotto voce (I; sah-toh-VOH-chee): in a low voice
sui generis (L; soo-ee-JEN-er-is): unique; one of a kind
terra firma (L; TER-uh-FUR-muh): solid ground
troika (R; TROY-kuh): group of three, espec. a ruling group
verboten (G; ver-BOH-ten): forbidden
vis-à-vis (F; vee-zuh-VEE): compared with; with regard to
voir dire (F; vwar-DEER): examination by lawyers or judge to determine the suitability of a witness or a prospective juror
zeitgeist (Ger; ZITE-gyste): the general intellectual, moral, and cultural climate of an era

Names for Animal Young

calf: cattle, elephant, hippo, camel, others	**filly:** horse, zebra (female)	**parr, smolt, grilse:** salmon
cheeper: grouse, partridge, quail	**fingerling, fry:** fish generally	**piglet, shoat, farrow, suckling:** pig
chick: chicken, penguin, other birds	**fledgling, nestling:** birds generally	**polliwog, tadpole:** frog
cockerel: rooster	**foal:** horse, zebra, others	**poult:** turkey
codling, sprag: codfish	**gosling:** goose	**puggle:** echidna
colt: horse, zebra (male)	**heifer:** cow	**pullet:** hen
cria: llama, alpaca	**hoglet:** hedgehog	**pup:** dog, fox, seal, rat, others
cub: lion, bear, shark, fox, others	**joey:** kangaroo, opossum, wombat	**spat:** oyster, other bivalves
cygnet: swan	**kid:** goat	**spiderling:** spider
duckling: duck	**kit:** beaver, rabbit, ferret, wolverine, others	**spike, blinker, tinker:** mackerel
elver: eel	**kitten:** cat, other small mammals	**squab:** pigeon
ephyra: jellyfish	**lamb:** sheep	**whelp:** dog, tiger, other carnivorous mammals
eyas: hawk, others	**larva:** frog, sea urchin, insects generally	**yearling:** cattle, sheep, horse, others
fawn: deer, antelope		

Names for Animal Collectives

alligators: congregation
ants: army, colony, swarm
apes: shrewdness, troop
bats: colony
bears: sleuth, sloth
bees: colony, swarm, hive, grist
birds: flight, volery
boars/swine: singular, sounder
buffalo: gang, obstinacy
butterflies: flutter
buzzards: wake
camels: caravan, flock, train
cats: clowder, cluster, glaring, pounce
cattle: drove
cheetahs: coalition
clams, oysters: bed
cockroaches: intrusion
cranes: sedge, siege
crocodiles: bask, nest, float
crows: murder, horde
dolphins: pod
doves: dule, pitying
ducks: brace, team
eagles: convocation, aerie
ferrets: business
finches: charm

fish: school, shoal
flamingos: stand, flamboyance
foxes: skulk
geese: flock, gaggle, skein
giraffes: corps, herd, tower
goats: tribe, trip
gorillas: band, whoop
grasshoppers: cloud
hares: down, husk, trip
hawks: cast, kettle
hedgehogs: array, prickle
hippopotamuses: bloat
horses: pair, team
hounds: cry, mute, pack
hyenas: cackle
iguanas: mess
jellyfish: smack
kangaroos: mob, troop
larks: exaltation
leopards: leap
lions: pride
locusts: plague, swarm
moles: labor
monkeys: troop
mules: barren, span
nightingales: watch

otters: romp
owls: parliament
oxen: yoke
peacocks: muster
pheasants: nest, nide, bouquet
ponies: string
raccoons: gaze
ravens: unkindness
rhinoceroses: crash
seals: pod
sheep: flock, drove, hurtle
snakes: nest
squirrels: dray, scurry
starlings: flock, murmuration
swans: bevy
tigers: streak
toads: knot
trout: hover
turkeys: rafter
turtles: bale
vultures: committee
whales: gam, herd, pod
woodchucks: fall
woodpeckers: descent
zebras: herd, zeal

Some Common Abbreviations and Acronyms

Acronyms are pronounceable words formed from first letters (or syllables) of other words. Some abbreviations below (e.g., AIDS, NATO) are thus acronyms. Some acronyms are words coined as abbreviations and written in lowercase (e.g., sonar, yuppie). Acronyms do not have periods; usage for other abbreviations varies, but periods have become less common. Capitalization usage may vary from what is shown here. Some acronyms may have other, typically less common, meanings not given here. Italicized words preceding parenthetical definitions below are Latin unless otherwise noted. See also Computers and Telecommunications, Weights and Measures, and other chapters.

AA: Alcoholics Anonymous; Associate in Arts; administrative assistant
ABA: American Bar Association
AC: alternating current; air-conditioning
ACLU: American Civil Liberties Union
AD: *anno Domini* (in the year of the Lord)
ADD: attention deficit disorder
AFL-CIO: American Federation of Labor and Congress of Industrial Organizations
AFSCME: American Federation of State, County, and Municipal Employees
AI: artificial intelligence
AIDS: acquired immune deficiency syndrome
ALA: American Library Association
a.m. or **AM:** *ante meridiem* (before noon)
APO: army post office
APR: annual percentage rate
ARM: adjustable rate mortgage
ASCAP: American Society of Composers, Authors, and Publishers
ASCII: American Standard Code for Information Interchange
ATM: automated teller machine
Ave.: Avenue
AWOL: absent without leave
BA: Bachelor of Arts
bbl: barrel(s)
BC: before Christ
BCE: before the Common Era; before the Christian Era
bpd: barrels per day
BS: Bachelor of Science
Btu: British thermal unit(s)
bu: bushel(s)
BYOB: bring your own bottle
C: Celsius, centigrade
c: *circa* (about); copyright
CAT: computerized axial tomography
CD: compact disc
CDC: Centers for Disease Control and Prevention; Community Development Corporation
CE: Common Era; Christian Era
CEO: chief executive officer
cf.: *confer* (compare)
CFO: chief financial officer
CIA: Central Intelligence Agency
CIF: cost, insurance, and freight

COD: cash (or collect) on delivery
COL or **Col.:** Colonel
COLA: cost of living adjustment
COO: chief operating officer
CPA: certified public accountant
CPI: consumer price index
CPL or **Cpl.:** Corporal
CPR: cardiopulmonary resuscitation
CPU: central processing unit
CST: central standard time
CV: curriculum vitae
DA: district attorney
DC: direct current
DD: Doctor of Divinity
DDS: Doctor of Dental Surgery
DEA: Drug Enforcement Agency
DHS: Department of Homeland Security
DMD: Doctor of Dental Medicine
DMZ: demilitarized zone
DNA: deoxyribonucleic acid
DNR: do not resuscitate
DOA: dead on arrival
DOB: date of birth
dpi: dots per inch
DPT: diphtheria, pertussis, tetanus
DUI: driving under the influence
DVD: digital video disc
DVM: Doctor of Veterinary Medicine
DWI: driving while intoxicated
ed.: edited; edition; editor
EEG: electroencephalogram
e.g.: *exempli gratia* (for example)
EKG: electrocardiogram
EOE: equal opportunity employer
EP: extended play
EPA: Environmental Protection Agency
ERA: Equal Rights Amendment; earned run average
ESL: English as a second language
ESP: extrasensory perception
Esq.: Esquire
EST: eastern standard time
et al.: *et alii* (and others)
etc.: *et cetera* (and so forth)
EU: European Union
F: Fahrenheit
Fannie Mae: Federal National Mortgage Association
FAQ: frequently asked questions
FBI: Federal Bureau of Investigation

FDA: Food and Drug Administration
FDIC: Federal Deposit Insurance Corporation
FEMA: Federal Emergency Management Agency
ff.: and those following
FICA: Federal Insurance Contributions Act (Social Security)
fl.: *floruit* (flourished), used for historical figures when life dates uncertain
Freddie Mac: Federal Home Loan Mortgage Corporation
FTP: file transfer protocol
FY: fiscal year
FYI: for your information
GATT: General Agreement on Tariffs and Trade
GB: gigabyte(s)
GDP: gross domestic product
GED: general equivalency diploma; General Educational Development (Tests)
GMT: Greenwich mean time
GOP: Grand Old Party (Republican Party)
GPS: Global Positioning System
GUI: graphical user interface
hazmat: HAZardous MATerial
HDTV: high-definition television
HIV: human immunodeficiency virus
HMO: health maintenance organization
HMS: His/Her Majesty's Ship (UK)
Hon.: the Honorable
HOV: high-occupancy vehicle
HRH: Her (His) Royal Highness (UK)
HTML: hypertext markup language
HTTP: hypertext transfer protocol
HUD: Department of Housing and Urban Development
HVAC: heating, ventilating, and air-conditioning
Hz: hertz
ibid: *ibidem* (in the same place)
ICU: intensive care unit
i.e.: *id est* (that is)
IM: instant messaging
IMF: International Monetary Fund
INS: Immigration and Naturalization Service
IPO: initial public offering
IQ: intelligence quotient
IRA: individual retirement account; Irish Republican Army

IRS: Internal Revenue Service
ISBN: International Standard Book Number
ISP: Internet service provider
IVF: in vitro fertilization
JD: *Juris Doctor* (Doctor of Law)
k: karat
K: kelvin
kWh: kilowatt-hour(s)
laser: Light Amplification by Stimulated Emission of Radiation
LGBT: lesbian, gay, bisexual, and transgender
LLP: limited liability partnership
loc. cit.: *loco citato* (in the place cited)
LSAT: Law School Admission Test
LT or **Lt.:** Lieutenant
MA: Master of Arts
MB: megabyte(s)
MBA: Master of Business Administration
MCAT: Medical College Admission Test
MD: *Medicinae Doctor* (Doctor of Medicine)
MIA: missing in action
modem: MOdulator-DEModulator
MP: member of Parliament (UK)
mph: miles per hour
MRI: magnetic resonance imaging
ms, mss: manuscript(s)
MS: Master of Science; multiple sclerosis
MSG: monosodium glutamate
MST: mountain standard time
MVP: most valuable player
NA: not applicable; not available
NAACP: National Association for the Advancement of Colored People
NAFTA: North American Free Trade Agreement
NASA: National Aeronautics and Space Administration
NATO: North Atlantic Treaty Organization
NB or **n.b.:** *nota bene* (note carefully)
NCAA: National Collegiate Athletic Association
NEA: National Education Association

NIH: National Institutes of Health
NOW: National Organization for Women
NPR: National Public Radio
NRA: National Rifle Association
obs.: obsolete
OED: Oxford English Dictionary
OMB: Office of Management and Budget
op: *opus* (work)
OPEC: Organization of Petroleum Exporting Countries
OTC: over-the-counter
p, pp: page(s)
PA: public address
PAC: political action committee
PC: personal computer; politically correct
PDA: Personal Digital Assistant
PhD: *Philosophiae Doctor* (doctor of philosophy)
PIN: personal identification number
p.m. or **PM:** *post meridiem* (after noon)
PPO: preferred provider organization, a type of healthcare provider network
PS: *post scriptum* (postscript)
PST: Pacific standard time
pt: part(s); pint(s); point(s)
PVT or **Pvt.:** Private
QC: Queen's Council (UK)
QED: *quod erat demonstrandum* (which was to be demonstrated)
q.v.: *quod vide* (which see)
radar: RAdio Detecting And Ranging
RAM: random access memory
RCMP: Royal Canadian Mounted Police
REM: rapid eye movement
Rev.: Reverend
rev.: revised; reviewed
RIP: *requiescat in pace* (may he/she rest in peace)
RN: Registered Nurse
RNA: ribonucleic acid
ROM: read only memory
ROTC: Reserve Officers' Training Corps
rpm: revolutions per minute

RSVP: *répondez s'il vous plaît* (Fr.) (please reply)
SARS: severe acute respiratory syndrome
SASE: self-addressed stamped envelope
SEC: Securities and Exchange Commission
SETI: Search for Extraterrestrial Intelligence
SGT or **Sgt.:** Sergeant
SIDS: sudden infant death syndrome
SJ: Society of Jesus (Jesuits)
sonar: SOund NAvigation and Ranging
SPCA: Society for the Prevention of Cruelty to Animals
SSI: Supplementary Security Income
St.: Saint; Street
TB: tuberculosis; terabyte(s)
TBA: to be announced
TBD: to be determined
TEFL: teaching English as a foreign language
UFO: unidentified flying object
UPC: Universal Product Code
URL: Universal Resource Locator
USDA: United States Department of Agriculture
USS: United States ship
UTC: coordinated universal time
var.: variant
VAT: value-added tax
VCR: videocassette recorder
viz: *videlicet* (namely)
VP: vice president
W: watt(s)
WHO: World Health Organization
WMD: weapon of mass destruction
WPM: words per minute
WWW: World Wide Web
YMCA: Young Men's Christian Association
YWCA: Young Women's Christian Association
YTD: year to date
yuppie: young urban professional
ZIP: zone improvement plan (U.S. Postal Service)

Eponyms
(words named for people)

boycott: to avoid trade or dealings with, as a protest; after Charles C. Boycott, an English land agent in County Mayo, Ireland, ostracized in 1880 for refusing to reduce rents
derby: a stiff felt hat with a dome-shaped crown and narrow rolled brim; after Edward Stanley, 12th Earl of Derby, who in 1780 founded the Derby horse race, to which these hats are worn
derrick: a type of crane consisting of a boom connected to the base of an upright mast; after Derrick, early 17th-cent. English hangman who used a gallows that operated via cables and pulleys
draconian: harsh or severe; after Draco, statesman who codified the laws in Athens in 621 BCE
gerrymander: to draw an election district in such a way as to favor a political party; after Elbridge Gerry, who created (1812) just such an election district (shaped like a salamander) during his governorship of Massachusetts
guillotine: a machine for beheading; after Joseph Guillotin, French physician who proposed its use in 1789 as more humane than hanging
Luddite: one who opposes new technology; from Ned Ludd, leader of a group of textile workers in England who destroyed machinery in the early 1800s

maudlin: excessively sentimental; from scriptural figure Mary Magdalene, who is often shown weeping in depictions
milquetoast: a timid, unassertive person; after Caspar Milquetoast, comic strip character created by American Harold Tucker Webster in 1924
Pollyanna: an overly optimistic person; based on the title character of a 1913 novel by American writer Eleanor Porter
salmonella: group of bacteria that can cause infections when contaminated food or water is consumed; named after Daniel Elmer Salmon, American veterinarian and public health official
sandwich: two or more slices of bread with a filling in-between; after John Montagu, 4th Earl of Sandwich (1718-92), who supposedly ate these at the gaming table
shrapnel: originally, a projectile with lead balls designed to inflict maximum damage in explosions, later pieces of shell casings; from Henry Shrapnel (1761-1842), British artillery officer who designed the projectile
silhouette: an outline image; from Étienne de Silhouette (1709-67), a stingy French finance minister
Zamboni: an ice resurfacing machine; after American inventor Frank Zamboni, who owned an ice skating rink

Palindromes and Anagrams

A **palindrome** is a sequence of letters (or other symbols) that reads the same backward and forward. Words such as *radar* and *racecar* are familiar palindromes, as are names such as Hannah, and phrases such as "Madam, I'm Adam" and "A man, a plan, a canal, Panama!" Certain dates, such as 11/02/2011, can also be considered palindromes.

An **anagram** is a word or word sequence made by rearranging all the letters of another word or word sequence. Websites can be consulted that generate large numbers of anagrams for a given expression ("world almanac" has over 2,500 anagrams), but most, even if technically made up of words, make little sense. The best anagrams not only make some sense but fit the subject in a clever or amusing way. Ex.: stipend = spend it!; archaeologists = goal is to search; Elvis Aaron Presley = Seen alive? Sorry, pal; The Leaning Tower of Pisa = I spot one giant flaw here.

Top 10 First Names of Americans by Decade or Year of Birth

Source: U.S. Social Security Administration

BOYS

1880-1889	John, William, Charles, George, James, Frank, Joseph, Harry, Henry, Edward
1890-1899	John, William, George, James, Charles, Joseph, Frank, Robert, Harry, Henry
1900-1909	John, William, James, George, Joseph, Charles, Robert, Frank, Edward, Henry
1910-1919	John, William, James, Robert, Joseph, Charles, George, Edward, Frank, Walter
1920-1929	John, Robert, James, William, Charles, George, Joseph, Richard, Edward, Donald
1930-1939	Robert, James, John, William, Richard, Charles, Donald, George, Thomas, Joseph
1940-1949	James, Robert, John, William, Richard, David, Charles, Thomas, Michael, Ronald
1950-1959	Michael, James, Robert, John, David, William, Steven, Richard, Thomas, Mark
1960-1969	Michael, John, David, James, Robert, Mark, Steven, William, Jeffrey, Richard
1970-1979	Michael, Christopher, Jason, David, James, John, Brian, Robert, Steven, William
1980-1989	Michael, Christopher, Matthew, Joshua, David, Daniel, James, John, Robert, Brian
1990-1999	Michael, Christopher, Matthew, Joshua, Nicholas, Jacob, Andrew, Daniel, Brandon, Tyler
2000-2009	Jacob, Michael, Joshua, Matthew, Daniel, Christopher, Andrew, Ethan, Joseph, William
2011	Jacob, Mason, William, Jayden, Noah, Michael, Ethan, Alexander, Aiden, Daniel

GIRLS

1880-1889	Mary, Anna, Elizabeth, Catherine, Margaret, Emma, Bertha, Minnie, Florence, Clara
1890-1899	Mary, Anna, Margaret, Helen, Catherine, Elizabeth, Florence, Ruth, Rose, Ethel
1900-1909	Mary, Helen, Margaret, Anna, Ruth, Catherine, Elizabeth, Dorothy, Marie, Mildred
1910-1919	Mary, Helen, Dorothy, Margaret, Ruth, Catherine, Mildred, Anna, Elizabeth, Frances
1920-1929	Mary, Dorothy, Betty, Helen, Margaret, Ruth, Virginia, Catherine, Doris, Frances
1930-1939	Mary, Betty, Barbara, Shirley, Patricia, Dorothy, Joan, Margaret, Carol, Nancy
1940-1949	Mary, Linda, Barbara, Patricia, Carol, Sandra, Nancy, Sharon, Judith, Susan
1950-1959	Deborah, Mary, Linda, Patricia, Susan, Barbara, Karen, Nancy, Donna, Catherine
1960-1969	Lisa, Deborah, Mary, Karen, Michelle, Susan, Kimberly, Lori, Teresa, Linda
1970-1979	Jennifer, Michelle, Amy, Melissa, Kimberly, Lisa, Angela, Heather, Kelly, Sarah
1980-1989	Jessica, Jennifer, Ashley, Sarah, Amanda, Stephanie, Nicole, Melissa, Katherine, Megan
1990-1999	Ashley, Jessica, Sarah, Brittany, Emily, Kaitlyn, Samantha, Megan, Brianna, Katherine
2000-2009	Emily, Madison, Emma, Olivia, Hannah, Abigail, Isabella, Samantha, Elizabeth, Ashley
2011	Sophia, Isabella, Emma, Olivia, Ava, Emily, Abigail, Madison, Mia, Chloe

Origins of Popular American Given Names

Source: World Almanac research

Some names are commonly used for either sex but are listed here under the more traditionally associated sex.

Boys

Alexander: Gr. *Alexandros*, "defender of man"

Andrew: Gr. *andreios*, "manly"

Anthony: Roman *Antonius*, possibly from Gr. *anthos*, "flower"

Benjamin: Heb. *Binyamin*, "son of the right hand"

Brandon: Eng. place name, "gorse-covered hill"

Brian: Irish, perhaps Celtic *Brigonos*, "high" or "noble"

Charles: Ger. *ceorl*, "free man"

Christopher: Gr. *Khristophoros*, "bearing Christ [in one's heart]"

Daniel: Heb. "God is my judge"

David: Heb. *Dodavehu*, perhaps "darling"

Edward: Old Eng. *Eadweard*, "wealth-guard"

Elijah: Heb. "the Lord is my God"

Ethan: Heb. "solid, firm"

Frank: Ger. "Frenchman"

George: Gr. *georgos*, "soil tiller, farmer"

Henry: Ger. *Haimric*, "home-power"

Jack: nickname for or variant of John

Jackson: Eng. "son of Jack"

Jacob: Heb. *Yaakov*, "God protects" or "supplanter"

James: Late Lat. *Iacomus*, form of Jacob

Jason: Gr. *Iason*, "healer"

Jayden: prob. from Jay (short form for many *J* names) and Hayden (Old Eng. "little hollow")

Jeffrey: Norman Fr., from Ger. *Gaufrid*, "land-peace," or *Gisfrid*, "pledge-peace"

John: Heb. *Yohanan*, "God is gracious"

Jonathan: Heb. "God has given"

José: Heb. and Aramaic *Yose*, variant of Joseph

Joseph: Heb. *Yosef*, "[God] shall add"

Joshua: Heb. *Yoshua*, "God saves"

Liam: Gaelic form of William

Logan: Gaelic "little hollow"

Mark: Lat. *Marcus*, perhaps from Mars, Roman god of war

Mason: Fr. "stone worker," related to Old Eng. "work"

Matthew: Heb. *Mattathia*, "gift of God"

Michael: Heb. "who could ever be like God?"

Nathan: Heb. "God has given"; modern short form of Nathaniel or Jonathan

Nicholas: Gr. *Nikolaos*, "victory-people"

Noah: Heb. "rest"

Patrick: Lat. *Patricius*, "belonging to the noble class"

Richard: Ger. "power-hardy"

Robert: Ger. *Hrodberht*, "fame-bright"

Ryan: prob. from Irish surname, Gaelic "king"

Samuel: Heb. *Shemuel*, "God heard"

Sean: Gaelic form of John

Steven: Gr. *stephanos*, "crown" or "garland"

Thomas: Aramaic "twin"

Tyler: Old Eng. *tigeler*, "tile layer"

William: Ger. *Wilhelm*, "will-helmet"

Girls

Abigail: Heb. "my father is joy"

Addison: Eng. "son of Adam"

Alexandra, Sandra: fem. forms of Alexander

Alexis: Gr. "helper" or "defender"

Alyssa: variant of Alicia (Eng., Span.) or Alice (Eng., Fr.); may mean "noble"

Amanda: 17th-cent. invention from Lat. "lovable"

Amy: Old Fr. *Amee*, "beloved"

Andrea: fem. form of Andrew

Angela: Gr. *angelos*, "messenger [of God]"

Anna: Lat., Gr. form of Hannah; variants include Ann (Eng.), Ana (Span.), Anne (Eng., Fr., Ger.)

Ashley: Eng. place name, "ash grove"

Aubrey: Fr., orig. from Ger. *Alberic*, "king of elves"

Ava: prob. modern form of Eva, Lat. form of Heb. *Eve*, "to breathe"

Avery: Eng., common place name; may also mean "elf counsel" or "elf ruler"

Barbara: Gr. *barbarus*, "foreign"

Brianna: modern fem. form of Brian

Brittany: place name, Fr. province settled by Britons

Carol: form of Charles

Chloe: Gr. "young shoot," "blooming"

Claire, Clara: Lat. *clarus*, "famous"

Deborah: Heb. "bee"

Donna: Ital. "lady"

Dorothy: Gr. *Dorothea*, "gift of God"

Elizabeth: Heb. *Elisheba*, perhaps "God is my oath" or "God is good fortune"

Ella: prob. variant or nickname for Eleanor or Ellen

Emily: Roman *Aemilia*, possibly from Lat. *aemulus*, "rival"

Emma: Ger. *ermen*, "whole" or "entire"

Frances: fem. form of Francis, "a Frenchman"

Grace: Lat. *gratia*, "grace, blessing"

Hailey: Eng. place name, "hay clearing"

Hannah: Heb. "He has favored me"

Heather: Middle Eng. *hathir*, "heather"

Helen: Gr. *Helene*, possibly "sunbeam"

Isabella, Isabel: Lat., Sp. variant of Elizabeth

Jennifer: Cornish form of Welsh *Gwenhwyfar*, "fair-smooth"

Jessica: Shakesp. invention, prob. fem. form of Jesse, Heb. "God exists"
Judith: Heb. "Jewish woman"
Julia: fem. form of Julius, Roman family name, or Lat. "youthful"
Kaitlyn: American spelling of Caitlin, the Irish form of Katherine
Karen: Danish form of Katherine
Katherine: Egyptian *Aikaterine*, later modified to resemble Gr. *katharos*, "pure"
Kelly: Irish Gaelic *Ceallagh*, perhaps "churchgoer" or "bright-headed"
Kimberly: Eng. place name, "Cyneburgh's clearing"
Laura: Lat. *laurus*, "laurel"
Linda: Sp. "pretty" or Ger. "tender"
Lily: for the flower, suggesting purity, innocence

Lisa: nickname for Elizabeth
Madison: Middle Eng. surname, "son of Madeline or Maud"
Margaret: Gr. *margaron*, "pearl"
Maria, Marie, Mary: Lat., Fr., Eng. forms for Heb. *Maryam*, perhaps "seeress" or "wished-for child"
Megan: Welsh form of Margaret
Melissa: Gr. "bee"
Mia: Nordic or Ital., short for Maria and other names
Michelle: Fr. fem. form of Michael
Nancy: medieval Eng. nickname for Agnes (Gr. *hagnos*, "holy"), later also for Ann
Natalie: Fr., from Lat. *natalia*, "birthday [of Christ]"
Nicole: Fr. fem. form of Nicholas
Olivia: Lat. *oliva*, "olive tree"

Patricia: Lat. fem. form of Patrick
Rachel: Heb. "ewe"
Rose, Rosa: for the flower, suggesting beauty
Ruth: Heb., perhaps "companion"
Samantha: colonial American invention, prob. combining Sam from Samuel with -*antha* from Gr. *anthos*, "flower"
Sarah: Heb. "princess"
Sharon: Biblical place name, Heb. "plain"
Sophia: Gr. "wisdom"
Stephanie: Fr. fem. form of Steven
Susan: Eng. form of Heb. *Shoshana*, "lily"
Teresa: Sp., perhaps "woman from Therasia"
Victoria: fem. form of Victor, from Lat. *vincere*, "to conquer"

American Manual Alphabet

In the American Manual Alphabet, each letter of the alphabet is represented by a position of the fingers. This system was originally developed in France by Charles-Michel de l'Épée in the 1700s. Laurent Clerc and Thomas Gallaudet further refined it into the American Manual Alphabet.

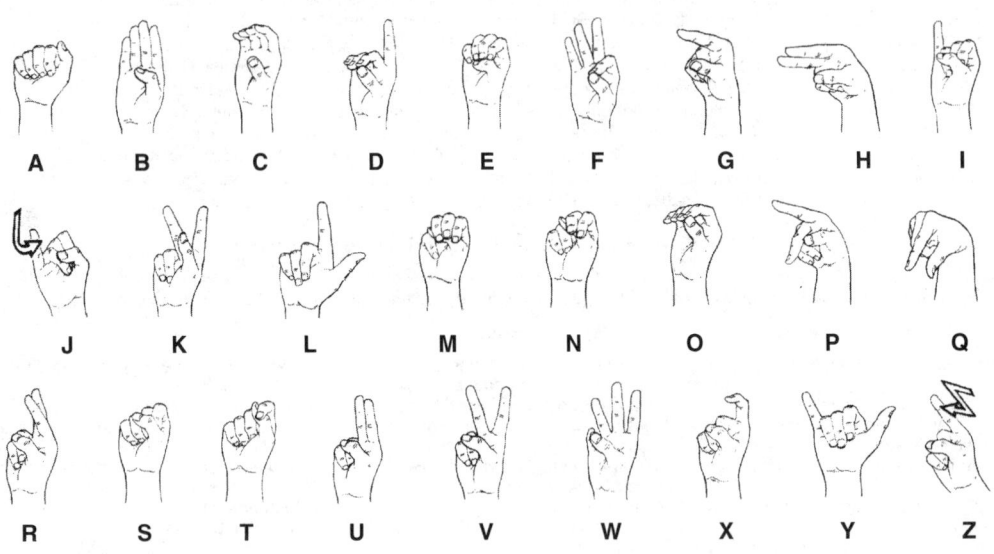

A   B   C   D   E   F   G   H   I

J   K   L   M   N   O   P   Q

R   S   T   U   V   W   X   Y   Z

Words and Expressions in Common Languages

English	Arabic	Chinese[1]	French	German	Hebrew	Russian	Spanish
Hello/hi	Salam	Ni hao	Bonjour	Hallo	Shalom	Privet (informal)	Hola
Good morning	Sabah el kheer	Zao shang hao	Bonjour	Guten Morgen	Boker tov	Dobraye utra	Buenos dias
Good night	Tosbeho 'ala khair	Wan an	Bonne nuit	Gute Nacht	Layla tov	Spakoynay noci	Buenas noches
Good-bye	Ma'a salama	Zai jian	Au revoir	Auf wiedersehen	Lehitraot	Da svidan'ya	Adiós
Please	Men fadlek	Qing	S'il vous plaît	Bitte	Bevakasha	Pazhalusta	Por favor
Thank you very much	Shokran jazeelan	Xie xie	Merci beaucoup	Danke schön	Toda raba	Spasiba	Muchas gracias
You're welcome	Al' afw	Huan ying	De rien/pas de quoi	Keine Ursache	Bevakasha	Pazhalusta	De nada
How are you?	Kaifa haloka?	Ni hao?	Comment allez-vous?	Wie geht's dir/ihnen?	Ma shelomkha?	Kak dela?	Cómo estás?
I'm fine	Ana bekhair	Hen hao	Je vais bien	Mir geht's gut	Tov	Harasho	Estoy bien
I'm sorry	Aasef	Bao qian	Je suis désolé	Entschuldigung	Ani mamash mitstaer	Prastite	Lo siento
Excuse me	Alma'derah	Bao qian	Pardon	Darf ich mal vorbei?	Seliha	Izvinite	Perdone
yes	na'am	shi [it is so]	oui	ja	ken	da	si
no	laa	bu [not]	non	nein	lo	nyet	no
one	wahed	yi	un	eins	ehad	adin	uno
two	ithnaan	er	deux	zwei	shenayim	dva	dos
three	thalatha	san	trois	drei	shelosha	tri	tres
four	arba'a	si	quatre	vier	arbaa	chityri	cuatro
five	khamsa	wu	cinq	fünf	hamisha	p'at	cinco

Note: Actual form or usage of some words and expressions may vary depending on dialect, grammar, or circumstances. Transliterations for languages not in Latin alphabet vary. (1) Mandarin.

Pen Names

Woody Allen	Allen Stewart Konigsberg
Maya Angelou	Marguerite Johnson
Richard Bachman	Stephen King
Currer, Ellis, and Acton Bell	Charlotte, Emily, and Anne Brontë
Nellie Bly	Elizabeth Jane Cochrane Seaman
John le Carré	David John Moore Cornwell
Lewis Carroll	Charles Lutwidge Dodgson
Colette	Sidonie Gabrielle Colette
George Eliot	Mary Ann or Marian Evans
Maksim Gorky	Aleksey Maksimovich Peshkov
O. Henry	William Sydney Porter
Hergé	Georges Rémi
E. L. James	Erika Leonard
P. D. James	Phyllis Dorothy James White
Ann Landers	Esther Pauline Lederer
André Maurois	Émile Herzog
Molière	Jean Baptiste Poquelin
Toni Morrison	Chloe Anthony Wofford
Pablo Neruda	Neftalí Ricardo Reyes Basoalto
Frank O'Connor	Michael Donovan
George Orwell	Eric Arthur Blair
Ellery Queen	Frederic Dannay and Manfred B. Lee
Ayn Rand	Alice Rosenbaum
Anne Rice	Howard Allen O'Brien
Nora Roberts/J. D. Robb	Eleanor Marie Robertson
Saki	Hector Hugh Munro
George Sand	Amandine Lucie Aurore Dupin
Dr. Seuss	Theodor Seuss Geisel
Lemony Snicket	Daniel Handler
Stendhal	Marie-Henri Beyle
Mark Twain	Samuel Clemens
Voltaire	François Marie Arouet

The Principal Languages of the World

Source: Database of *Ethnologue: Languages of the World, 16th Edition.* www.ethnologue.com. M. Paul Lewis, editor. Copyright © 2009, SIL International. Used by permission.

The following tables count only first language (or mother tongue) speakers. All figures are estimates.

Languages/Language Groups Spoken by the Most People

This table combines macrolanguages and individual languages, e.g., the Chinese and Arabic macrolanguages combine all the individual varieties listed in the table below. Ranked by millions of speakers.

Language	Speakers (mil)	Language	Speakers (mil)	Language	Speakers (mil)
Chinese	1,213	Russian	144	French	68
Spanish	329	Japanese	122	Marathi	68
English	328	German	90	Korean	66
Arabic	221	Javanese	85	Tamil	66
Hindi	182	Lahnda	78	Italian	62
Bengali	181	Telugu	70	Urdu	61
Portuguese	178	Vietnamese	69		

Individual Languages Spoken by at Least 2 Million People

Languages listed by hub country (country of origin), not necessarily where the most speakers reside (e.g., Portugal is the hub country of Portuguese, but more Portuguese speakers live in Brazil). Number of speakers is worldwide total for each language.

Hub	Language	Countries	Speakers (mil)
Afghanistan	Farsi, Eastern	3	8
	Hazaragi	4	2
Albania	Albanian, Tosk	10	3
Algeria	Arabic, Algerian Spoken	6	22
	Kabyle	3	3
Angola	Umbundu	2	4
	Kimbundu	1	3
Armenia	Armenian	30	6
Austria	Bavarian	4	13
Azerbaijan	Azerbaijani, North	10	7
Bangladesh	Bengali	10	181
	Rangpuri	2	15
	Chittagonian	1	13
	Sylheti	10	10
Belarus	Belarusan	16	9
Belgium	Vlaams	5	6
Bolivia	Quechua, South Bolivian	2	4
	Aymara, Central	4	2
Bosnia and Herzegovina	Bosnian	4	2
Botswana	Tswana	4	5
Brazil	Hunsrik	5	3
Bulgaria	Bulgarian	16	9
Burkina Faso	Mòoré	7	5
Burundi	Rundi	4	5
Cambodia	Khmer, Central	7	14
Cameroon	Beti	1	2
China	Chinese, Mandarin	20	845
	Chinese, Wu	2	77
	Chinese, Yue	20	56
	Chinese, Min Nan	10	47
	Chinese, Jinyu	1	45
	Chinese, Xiang	2	36
	Chinese, Hakka	17	30
	Chinese, Gan	1	21
	Chinese, Min Bei	2	10
	Chinese, Min Dong	7	9
	Uighur	15	9
	Chinese, Huizhou	1	5
	Mongolian, Peripheral	2	3
	Chinese, Min Zhong	1	3
	Bouyei	4	3
China (cont'd)	Chinese, Pu-Xian	3	3
	Nuosu	1	2
Congo, Dem. Rep.	Luba-Kasai	1	6
	Koongo	3	5
	Kituba	1	4
	Lingala	3	2
Côte d'Ivoire	Baoulé	1	2
Croatia	Croatian	14	6
Czech Republic	Czech	12	9
Denmark	Danish	8	6
Egypt	Arabic, Egyptian Spoken	10	54
	Arabic, Sa'idi Spoken	1	19
Ethiopia	Amharic	6	18
	Oromo, West Central	2	9
	Tigrigna	6	6
	Oromo, Eastern	1	5
	Oromo, Borana-Arsi-Guji	3	4
	Sidamo	1	3
	Sebat Bet Gurage	1	2
Finland	Finnish	7	5
France	French	60	68
	Occitan	4	2
Georgia	Georgian	13	4
Germany	German, Standard	43	90
	Mainfränkisch	1	5
	Saxon, Upper	1	2
Ghana	Abron	2	23
	Akan	1	8
	Éwé	2	3
Greece	Greek	38	13
Guinea	Pular	6	3
	Maninkakan, Eastern	3	2
Haiti	Haitian	10	8
Hungary	Hungarian	14	13
India	Hindi	20	182
	Telugu	10	70
	Marathi	5	68
	Tamil	17	66
	Gujarati	20	47
	Bhojpuri	3	39
	Awadhi	2	38
	Malayalam	11	36

Hub	Language	Countries	Speakers (mil)
India (cont'd).....	Kannada.............	3	35
	Maithili.............	2	35
	Oriya..............	2	32
	Panjabi, Eastern.........	12	28
	Assamese.............	4	17
	Chhattisgarhi...........	1	15
	Haryanvi............	1	13
	Magahi.............	1	13
	Deccan.............	1	13
	Degaru.............	1	13
	Malvi..............	1	10
	Kanauji.............	1	10
	Dhundari............	1	9
	Bagheli.............	2	8
	Varhadi-Nagpuri.........	1	7
	Santali.............	4	6
	Lambadi............	1	6
	Kashmiri............	4	6
	Marwari............	3	6
	Mewati.............	1	5
	Hadothi............	1	5
	Konkani............	2	4
	Merwari............	1	4
	Mina..............	1	4
	Konkani, Goan..........	3	4
	Godwari............	1	3
	Shekhawati...........	1	3
	Garhwali............	1	3
	Indian Sign Language.....	3	3
	Kumaoni............	1	2
	Dogri.............	1	2
	Bagri..............	2	2
	Kurux.............	3	2
	Mewari............	1	2
Indonesia........	Javanese............	5	85
	Sunda.............	1	34
	Indonesian...........	6	23
	Madura.............	2	14
	Minangkabau..........	1	6
	Musi..............	1	4
	Aceh..............	1	4
	Banjar.............	2	4
	Bugis.............	2	4
	Bali..............	1	3
	Betawi.............	1	3
	Malay, Central.........	1	2
	Sasak.............	1	2
	Batak Toba...........	1	2
Iran.............	Farsi, Western.........	27	24
	Azerbaijani, South.......	8	13
	Domari.............	14	4
	Gilaki..............	1	3
	Mazanderani..........	1	3
	Kurdish, Southern.......	2	3
Iraq.............	Arabic, Mesopotamian Spoken............	5	15
	Arabic, North Mesopotamian Spoken..	4	6
	Kurdish, Central.........	2	4
	Arabic, Gulf Spoken......	10	4
Israel...........	Hebrew.............	8	5
Italy.............	Italian.............	34	62
	Lombard............	3	9
	Napoletano-Calabrese....	1	7
	Venetian............	4	6
	Sicilian............	1	5
	Piemontese...........	3	3
	Emiliano-Romagnolo.....	2	2
Jamaica.........	Jamaican Creole English..	7	3
Japan...........	Japanese............	25	122
Jordan...........	Arabic, South Levantine Spoken............	9	6
Kazakhstan......	Kazakh.............	14	8
Kenya...........	Gikuyu.............	1	7
	Dholuo.............	2	4
	Kamba.............	1	4
	Ekegusii............	2	2
Korea, South.....	Korean.............	33	66
Kyrgyzstan.......	Kyrgyz.............	9	3
Laos...........	Lao...............	7	3
Lesotho.........	Sotho, Southern........	4	6
Libya..........	Arabic, Libyan Spoken....	3	4
Lithuania........	Lithuanian...........	19	3
Macedonia.......	Macedonian..........	9	2
Madagascar.....	Malagasy, Plateau......	4	8
Malawi.........	Nyanja.............	6	9
Malaysia........	Malay.............	7	9
	Malay, Kedah..........	2	3

Hub	Language	Countries	Speakers (mil)
Mali...........	Bamanankan.........	7	3
Mauritania......	Hassaniyya..........	8	3
Mongolia.......	Mongolian, Halh.......	5	2
Morocco........	Arabic, Moroccan Spoken	10	21
	Tamazight, Central Atlas...	3	3
	Tachelhit............	3	3
Mozambique.....	Makhuwa...........	1	3
	Ndau..............	2	2
Myanmar (Burma)..	Burmese............	5	32
	Shan..............	3	3
Nepal..........	Nepali.............	5	14
Netherlands......	Dutch..............	12	22
Niger...........	Zarma.............	4	2
Nigeria.........	Hausa.............	13	25
	Yoruba............	6	19
	Igbo..............	1	18
	Kanuri, Central.........	6	3
	Tiv...............	2	2
Norway.........	Norwegian...........	1	5
Pakistan........	Panjabi, Western.......	7	63
	Urdu..............	23	61
	Sindhi.............	8	21
	Seraiki.............	3	14
	Pashto, Northern.......	7	10
	Pashto, Central.........	1	8
	Balochi, Southern.......	4	3
	Pashto, Southern.......	6	3
	Brahui.............	4	2
Paraguay.......	Guaraní, Paraguayan.....	2	5
Philippines......	Filipino.............	1	25
	Tagalog............	8	24
	Cebuano............	2	16
	Ilocano............	2	7
	Hiligaynon...........	2	6
	Waray-Waray.........	1	3
	Bicolano, Central.......	1	3
Poland.........	Polish.............	23	40
Portugal........	Portuguese..........	37	178
Romania........	Romanian...........	20	23
Russia..........	Russian............	33	144
	Tatar.............	19	7
Rwanda........	Rwanda............	4	8
Saudi Arabia.....	Arabic, Najdi Spoken.....	7	10
	Arabic, Hijazi Spoken....	2	6
Senegal........	Wolof.............	6	4
	Pulaar.............	6	4
Serbia.........	Serbian............	22	7
	Albanian, Gheg........	9	4
Slovakia........	Slovak.............	12	5
Somalia.........	Somali.............	13	14
South Africa.....	Zulu..............	6	10
	Xhosa.............	3	8
	Afrikaans...........	12	5
	Sotho, Northern........	2	4
	Tsonga............	4	4
Spain..........	Spanish............	44	329
	Catalan-Valencian-Balear	18	12
	Galician............	2	3
Sri Lanka.......	Sinhala............	8	16
Sudan.........	Arabic, Sudanese Spoken	6	17
Swaziland.......	Swati.............	4	2
Sweden........	Swedish...........	8	8
Switzerland......	German, Swiss........	5	6
Syria..........	Arabic, North Levantine Spoken............	16	14
Tajikistan.......	Tajiki.............	8	4
Tanzania.......	Sukuma...........	1	5
Thailand........	Thai..............	5	20
	Thai, Northeastern......	1	15
	Thai, Northern.........	2	6
	Thai, Southern........	1	5
Tunisia........	Arabic, Tunisian Spoken...	5	9
Turkey.........	Turkish............	36	51
	Kurdish, Northern.......	32	9
Turkmenistan.....	Turkmen...........	14	7
Uganda.........	Ganda.............	1	4
	Nyankore...........	1	2
	Soga..............	1	2
Ukraine........	Ukrainian...........	27	37
United Kingdom...	English............	112	328
Uzbekistan......	Uzbek, Northern.......	12	19
Vietnam........	Vietnamese..........	23	69
Yemen.........	Arabic, Sanaani Spoken...	1	8
	Arabic, Ta'izzi-Adeni Spoken............	8	7
Zambia........	Bemba............	4	4
Zimbabwe.......	Shona............	5	11

BUILDINGS, BRIDGES, AND TUNNELS

100 Tallest Buildings in the World

Source: Phorio, phorio.com; Council on Tall Buildings and Urban Habitat, Illinois Inst. of Technology, www.ctbuh.org

Structures under construction and topped out architecturally are denoted by an asterisk (*). Year in parentheses is date of completion or projected completion. Only buildings that are completed or under construction and topped out as of Sept. 2012 are included here. Height is generally measured from the lowest significant open-air pedestrian entrance to the architectural top, including penthouses, spires, and other decorative features that are an integral part of the design. Stories generally counted from street level.

Building	Ht. (ft)	Stories
Burj Khalifa, Dubai, United Arab Emirates (2010)	2,720	163
*Makkah Royal Clock Tower Hotel, Makkah, Saudi Arabia (2012)	1,972	120
Taipei 101, Taipei, Taiwan (2004)	1,667	101
Shanghai World Financial Center, Shanghai, China (2008)	1,614	101
International Commerce Centre, Hong Kong, China (2010)	1,588	108
Petronas Tower I, Kuala Lumpur, Malaysia (1998)	1,483	88
Petronas Tower II, Kuala Lumpur, Malaysia (1998)	1,483	88
Zifeng Tower, Nanjing, China (2010)	1,476	66
Willis Tower, Chicago, IL, U.S. (1974)	1,451	108
KK100 Development, Shenzhen, China (2011)	1,449	100
Guangzhou International Finance Center, Guangzhou, China (2010)	1,439	103
Trump Intl. Hotel & Tower, Chicago, IL, U.S. (2009)	1,389	98
Jin Mao Building, Shanghai, China (1999)	1,380	88
Princess Tower, Dubai, UAE (2012)	1,358	101
Al Hamra Firdous Tower, Kuwait City, Kuwait (2011)	1,354	77
Two Intl. Finance Centre, Hong Kong, China (2003)	1,352	88
23 Marina, Dubai, UAE (2012)	1,289	90
CITIC Plaza, Guangzhou, China (1997)	1,280	80
Shun Hing Square, Shenzhen, China (1996)	1,260	69
The Domain, Abu Dhabi, UAE (2013)	1,251	88
Empire State Building, New York, NY, U.S. (1931)	1,250	102
Elite Residence, Dubai, UAE (2012)	1,248	87
Central Plaza, Hong Kong, China (1992)	1,227	78
Bank of China Tower, Hong Kong, China (1990)	1,205	72
Bank of America Tower, New York, NY, U.S. (2009)	1,200	55
Almas Tower, Dubai, UAE (2008)	1,181	68
The Pinnacle, Guangzhou, China (2012)	1,181	60
*Emirates Park Towers Hotel & Spa 1, Dubai, UAE (2012)	1,165	77
*Emirates Park Towers Hotel & Spa 2, Dubai, UAE (2013)	1,165	77
Emirates Tower One, Dubai, UAE (2000)	1,163	54
Tuntex Sky Tower, Kaohsiung, Taiwan (1998)	1,140	85
Aon Center, Chicago, IL, U.S. (1973)	1,136	83
The Center, Hong Kong, China (1998)	1,135	73
John Hancock Center, Chicago, IL, U.S. (1969)	1,128	100
*Mercury City Tower, Moscow, Russia (2013)	1,112	75
Tianjin World Financial Center, Tianjin, China (2011)	1,106	76
The Torch, Dubai, UAE (2011)	1,105	79
Keangnam Hanoi Landmark Tower, Hanoi, Vietnam (2011)	1,103	70
Shanghai Shimao Intl. Plaza, Shanghai, China (2006)	1,094	60
Rose Rayhaan by Rotana, Dubai, UAE (2007)	1,093	71
*Modern Media Center, Changzhou, China (2013)	1,089	57
Minsheng Bank Building, Wuhan, China (2008)	1,087	68
*Ryugyong Hotel, Pyongyang, North Korea (2012)	1,083	105
China World Tower, Beijing, China (2010)	1,083	74
Longxi International Hotel, Jiangyin, China (2011)	1,076	74
*Al Yaqoub Tower, Dubai, UAE (2012)	1,076	69
The Index, Dubai, UAE (2010)	1,070	80
*The Landmark, Abu Dhabi, UAE (2012)	1,063	72
*Deji Plaza Phase 2, Nanjing, China (2013)	1,063	62
Q1, Gold Coast, Australia (2005)	1,058	78
Wenzhou Trade Center, Wenzhou, China (2011)	1,056	68
Burj Al Arab Hotel, Dubai, UAE (1999)	1,053	60
Nina Tower, Hong Kong, China (2007)	1,046	80
Chrysler Building, New York, NY, U.S. (1930)	1,046	77
New York Times Tower, New York, NY, U.S. (2007)	1,046	52
HHHR Tower, Dubai, UAE (2010)	1,042	72
Bank of America Plaza, Atlanta, GA, U.S. (1992)	1,039	55
*Moi Center Tower A, Shenyang, China (2013)	1,020	75
US Bank Tower, Los Angeles, CA, U.S. (1990)	1,018	73
Ocean Heights, Dubai, UAE (2010)	1,017	83
Menara Telekom, Kuala Lumpur, Malaysia (2001)	1,017	59
Pearl River Tower, Guangzhou, China (2012)	1,016	71
Emirates Tower Two, Dubai, UAE (2000)	1,014	56
Franklin Center-North Tower, Chicago, IL, U.S. (1989)	1,007	60
*Infinity Tower, Dubai, UAE (2013)	1,005	76
*One57, New York, NY, U.S. (2013)	1,005	75
*East Pacific Center Tower A, Shenzhen, China (2013)	1,004	85
*The Shard, London, United Kingdom (2013)	1,004	73
Etihad Towers T2, Abu Dhabi, UAE (2011)	1,002	80
JPMorganChase Tower, Houston, TX, U.S. (1982)	1,002	75
NE Asia Trade Tower, New Songdo City, Incheon, South Korea (2011)	1,001	68
Baiyoke Tower II, Bangkok, Thailand (1997)	997	85
*Wuxi Maoye City-Marriott Hotel, Wuxi, China (2013)	997	68
Two Prudential Plaza, Chicago, IL, U.S. (1990)	995	64
Leatop Plaza, Guangzhou, China (2011)	993	64
Wells Fargo Plaza, Houston, TX, U.S. (1983)	992	71
Kingdom Centre, Riyadh, Saudi Arabia (2002)	992	41
The Address, Dubai, UAE (2008)	991	63
*Gate of the Orient, Suzhou, China (2013)	990	68
Capital City Moscow Tower, Moscow, Russia (2010)	990	76
Doosan Haeundae Zenith Tower A, Busan, South Korea (2011)	984	80
*Abeno Harukas, Osaka, Japan (2014)	984	62
Arraya Tower, Kuwait City, Kuwait (2009)	984	60
Aspire Tower, Doha, Qatar (2007)	984	36
One Island East Centre, Hong Kong, China (2008)	979	69
First Bank Tower, Toronto, ON, Canada (1975)	978	72
*Four World Trade Center, New York, NY, U.S. (2013)	977	64
Eureka Tower, Melbourne, Australia (2006)	975	91
Comcast Center, Philadelphia, PA, U.S. (2008)	974	57
Landmark Tower, Yokohama, Japan (1993)	972	73
Emirates Crown, Dubai, UAE (2008)	971	63
Khalid Al Attar Tower 2, Dubai, UAE (2011)	965	66
Trump Ocean Club Intl. Hotel & Tower, Panama City, Panama (2011)	961	68
311 South Wacker Drive, Chicago, IL, U.S. (1990)	961	65
Sky Tower, Abu Dhabi, UAE (2011)	959	74
Haeundae I'Park Marina Tower 2, Busan, South Korea (2011)	958	72
SEG Plaza, Shenzhen, China (2000)	957	71
70 Pine Street, New York, NY, U.S. (1932)	952	67
*Global Trade Plaza, Dongguan, China (2012)	948	68
Key Tower, Cleveland, OH, U.S. (1991)	947	57

Tallest Free-Standing Towers in the World

Source: Phorio, phorio.com; Council on Tall Buildings and Urban Habitat, Illinois Inst. of Technology, www.ctbuh.org

Year is date of completion or projected completion. As of Sept. 2012.

Tower	Ht. (ft)	Year
Tokyo Sky Tree, Tokyo, Japan	2,080	2012
Canton Tower, Guangzhou, China	1,969	2010
CN Tower, Toronto, ON, Canada	1,815	1976
Ostankino Tower, Moscow, Russia	1,772	1967
Oriental Pearl Television Tower, Shanghai, China	1,535	1995
Milad Tower, Tehran, Iran	1,427	2008
Manara Kuala Lumpur, Kuala Lumpur, Malaysia	1,379	1996
Tianjin Radio & TV Tower, Tianjin, China	1,362	1991
Henan Province Radio & Television Emission Tower, Zhengzhou, China	1,273	2010
Central Radio & TV Tower, Beijing, China	1,268	1992
Kiev TV Tower, Kiev, Ukraine	1,263	1974
Tashkent Tower, Tashkent, Uzbekistan	1,230	1985
Liberation Tower, Kuwait City, Kuwait	1,220	1996
Alma-Ata Tower, Almaty, Kazakhstan	1,217	1982
TV Tower, Riga, Latvia	1,208	1987
Berliner Fernsehturm, Berlin, Germany	1,207	1969
Stratosphere Tower, Las Vegas, NV, U.S.	1,149	1996
West Pearl Tower, Chengdu, China	1,112	2004
Macau Tower, Macau, China	1,109	2001
Europaturm, Frankfurt, Germany	1,106	1979

Tall Buildings in Selected North American Cities

Source: Phorio, phorio.com; Council on Tall Buildings and Urban Habitat, Illinois Inst. of Technology, www.ctbuh.org

List includes freestanding towers and other structures that do not have stories and are not technically considered buildings. Structures still under construction as of Sept. 2012 are denoted by an asterisk (*). Year in parentheses is date of completion or projected completion. Height is generally measured from the lowest significant open-air pedestrian entrance to the architectural top, including penthouses, spires, and other decorative features that are an integral part of the design. Stories generally counted from street level. NA = Not applicable.

Building/structure	Ht. (ft)	Stories
Atlanta, GA		
Bank of America Plaza (incl. spire), 600 Peachtree St. NE (1992)	1,039	55
SunTrust Plaza, 303 Peachtree St. NE (1993)[1]	867	60
One Atlantic Center, 1201 W. Peachtree (1987)	820	50
191 Peachtree Tower (1991)	770	50
Westin Peachtree Plaza, 210 Peachtree St. NW (1976)[2]	723	73
Georgia Pacific Tower, 133 Peachtree St. NE (1981)	697	51
Promenade II (incl. spire), 1230 Peachtree St. NE (1989)	691	40
AT&T Building, 675 W. Peachtree St. (1980)	677	47
Sovereign, 3344 Peachtree (2008)	665	48
1180 Peachtree (2006)	657	41
GLG Grand/Four Seasons Hotel, 75 14th St. NE (1992)	609	53
The Mansion on Peachtree, 3376 Peachtree Rd. NE (2008)	580	42
Atlantic, 270 17th St. NW (2009)	577	46
State of Georgia Bldg., 2 Peachtree St. NW (1967)[3]	556	44
Marriott Marquis, 265 Peachtree Center Ave. NE (1985)	554	52
Viewpoint, 855 Peachtree St. NE (2008)	501	36

(1) 902 ft incl. antenna. (2) 883 ft incl. antenna. (3) 599 ft incl. antenna.

Building/structure	Ht. (ft)	Stories
Austin, TX		
Austonian, 200 Congress Ave. (2010)	683	56
360 Condominiums (incl. spire), 360 Nueces St. (2008)	581	45
Frost Bank Tower, 401 N. Congress Ave. (2004)	516	33
Boston, MA		
Hancock Place, 200 Clarendon St. (1976)	790	62
Prudential Tower, 800 Boylston St. (1964)[1]	750	52
Federal Reserve Bldg., 600 Atlantic Ave. (1978)	604	32
BNY Mellon Center at One Boston Place, 201 Washington St. (1970)	602	41
One International Place, 100 Oliver St. (1987)	600	46
100 Federal St. (1971)	591	37
One Financial Center, 10 Dewey Sq. (1984)	590	46
111 Huntington Ave. (2002)	564	36
Two International Place (1993)	538	35
One Post Office Square (1981)	525	40
1 Federal St. (1975)	520	38
Exchange Place, 53 State St. (1984)	510	39
Sixty State Street (1977)	509	38
1 Beacon St. (1972)	507	36
State Street Financial Center (incl. spire), 1 Lincoln St. (2003)	503	36
28 State St. (1970)	500	40

(1) 836 ft incl. antenna.

Building/structure	Ht. (ft)	Stories
Calgary, AB, Canada		
The Bow, 500 Centre St. (2012)	774	58
Petro Canada Centre West Tower, 150 6th Ave. SW (1984)	705	53
Eighth Avenue Place East Tower, 8th Ave. and 5th St. SW (2011)	696	49
Bankers Hall East Tower, 855 2nd St. SW (1989)	645	50
Bankers Hall West Tower, 888 3rd St. SW (2000)	645	50
Calgary Tower, 101 9th Ave. SW (1967)	626	NA
Centennial Place 1 (incl. spire), 520 3rd Ave. SW (2010)	599	40
TransCanada Tower, 450 1st St. SW (2001)	581	38
Canterra Tower, 400 3rd Ave. SW (1988)	580	46
Jamieson Place (incl. spires), 302 4th Ave. SW (2009)	568	38
First Canadian Centre, 350 7th Ave. SW (1982)	547	41
Western Canadian Place-North Tower, 707 6th St. SW (1983)	538	41
Canada Trust, Calgary Eatons Centre, 421 7th Ave. SW (1991)	530	40
Scotia Square, 700 2nd St. SW (1976)	509	41
Nexen Building, 801 7th Ave. SW (1982)	500	37
Charlotte, NC		
Bank of America Corporate Center, 100 N. Tryon St. (1992)	871	60
Duke Energy Center, 534 S. Tryon St. (2010)	786	48

Building/structure	Ht. (ft)	Stories
The Vue, 400 W. 5th St. (2010)	677	50
Hearst Tower, 214 N. Tryon St. (2002)	659	47
One Wells Fargo Center, 301 S. College St. (1988)	588	42
Bank of America Plaza, 101 S. Tryon St. (1974)	503	40
Chicago, IL		
Willis Tower, 233 S. Wacker Dr. (1974)[1]	1,451	108
Trump International Hotel & Tower (incl. spire), 401 N. Wabash Ave. (2009)	1,389	98
Aon Center, 200 E. Randolph St. (1973)	1,136	83
John Hancock Center, 875 N. Michigan Ave. (1969)[2]	1,128	100
Franklin Center-North Tower (incl. spires), 227 W. Monroe St. (1989)	1,007	60
Two Prudential Plaza (incl. spire), 180 N. Stetson Ave. (1990)	995	64
311 S. Wacker Drive (1990)	961	65
900 N. Michigan Ave. (1989)	871	66
Aqua, 225 N. Columbus Dr. (2009)	859	86
Water Tower Place, 845 N. Michigan Ave. (1976)	859	74
Chase Tower, 21 S. Clark St. (1969)	850	60
Park Tower, 800 N. Michigan Ave. (2000)	844	68
The Legacy at Millennium Park, 21-39 S. Wabash (2010)	818	73
300 N. LaSalle (2009)	785	60
3 First National Plaza, 70 W. Madison St. (1981)	767	57
Chicago Title and Trust Center, 161 N. Clark St. (1992)	756	50
Blue Cross Headquarters, 300 E. Randolph St. (2010)	744	54
One Museum Park, 1215 S. Prairie Ave. (2009)	726	62
Olympia Centre, 737 N. Michigan Ave. (1986)	725	63
330 N. Wabash Ave. (1973)	695	52
Elysian, 940 N. Rush St. (2009)	686	60
111 S. Wacker Dr. (2005)	681	51
181 W. Madison St. (1990)	680	50
Hyatt Center, 71 S. Wacker Dr. (2005)	679	48
One Magnificent Mile, 980 N. Michigan Ave. (1983)	673	57
340 on the Park, 340 W. Randolph St. (2007)	672	64
United Building, 77 W. Wacker Dr. (1992)	668	49
UBS Tower, 1 N. Wacker Dr. (2001)	652	50
Daley Center, 55 W. Washington St. (1965)	648	32
55 E. Erie St. (2004)	647	56
Lake Point Tower, 505 N. Lake Shore Dr. (1968)	645	70
River East Center, 350 E. Illinois St. (2001)	644	58
Grand Plaza I (incl. spire), 540 N. State St. (2003)	641	57
155 N. Wacker Dr. (2009)	638	45
Leo Burnett Building, 35 W. Wacker Dr. (1989)	635	46
The Heritage at Millennium Park, 125 N. Wabash Ave. (2005)	631	57
NBC Tower (incl. spire), 455 N. Cityfront Plaza Dr. (1989)	627	37
353 North Clark (2009)	623	44
Millennium Centre, 33 W. Ontario St. (2003)	610	58
Chicago Place, 700 N. Michigan Ave. (1991)	608	49
Board of Trade (incl. statue), 141 W. Jackson Blvd. (1930)	605	44
CNA Plaza, 325 S. Wabash St. (1972)	601	44
One Prudential Plaza, 130 E. Randolph St. (1955)[3]	601	41
Heller International Tower, 500 W. Monroe St. (1992)	600	45
One Madison Plaza, 200 W. Madison St. (1982)	599	44
One Museum Park West, 201 E. Roosevelt Rd. (2010)	595	54
1000 Lake Shore Plaza (1964)	590	55
The Clare at Water Tower, 55 E. Pearson St. (2008)	589	52
Citigroup Center, 500 W. Madison St. (1987)	588	42
The Park Monroe, 65 E. Monroe St. (1972)	583	49
Smurfit-Stone Building, 150 N. Michigan Ave. (1983)	582	41
North Pier Apartments, 474 N. Lake Shore Dr. (1990)	581	61
Citadel Center, 131 S. Dearborn St. (2003)	580	39
The Fordham, 25 E. Superior St. (2003)	574	52
190 S. LaSalle St. (1987)	573	40
One S. Dearborn (2005)	571	39
Onterie Center, 446 E. Ontario St. (1986)	570	58

Building/structure	Ht. (ft)	Stories
Chicago Temple, 77 W. Washington St. (1924)	568	23
Palmolive Building (incl. beacon), 919 N. Michigan Ave. (1929)	565	37
Marina City I, 300 N. State St. (1964)	562	61
Marina City II, 301 N. Dearborn St. (1964)	562	61
Huron Plaza Apartments, 30 E. Huron St. (1983)	560	56
Boeing International Headquarters, 100 N. Riverside Plz. (1990)	560	36
The Parkshore, 195 N. Harbor Dr. (1991)	556	56
North Harbor Tower, 175 N. Harbor Dr. (1988)	556	55
Civic Opera Building, 20 N. Wacker Dr. (1929)	555	45
Streeter Place, 351 E. Ohio St. (2009)	554	55
Newberry Plaza, 1000 N. State St. (1974)	553	53
Michigan Plaza South, 205 N. Michigan Ave. (1985)	553	46
30 N. LaSalle St. (1975)	553	44
Pittsfield Building, 55 E. Washington St. (1927)	551	38
Harbor Point, 155 N. Harbor Dr. (1975)	550	54
One S. Wacker Dr. (1982)	550	40
Kluczynski Federal Building, 230 S. Dearborn St. (1975)	545	45
Park Millennium, 222 N. Columbus Dr. (2002)	544	57
*AMLI River North, 401 N. Clark St. (2013)	543	49
Franklin Center-South Tower, 125 S. Franklin St. (1992)	538	35
The Pinnacle, 21 E. Huron St. (2004)	535	48
LaSalle National Bank, 135 S. LaSalle St. (1934)	535	45
Park Place Tower, 655 W. Irving Park Rd. (1971)	531	56
One N. LaSalle St. (1930)	530	48
The Elysees, 111 E. Chestnut St. (1973)	529	56
River Plaza, 405 N. Wabash Ave. (1977)	524	56
35 E. Wacker Dr. (1927)	523	40
Unitrin Building, 1 E. Wacker Dr. (1962)	522	41
Mather Tower, 75 E. Wacker Dr. (1928)	521	41
Chicago Mercantile Exchange, 10 S. Wacker Dr. (1987)	520	40
Chicago Mercantile Exchange, 30 S. Wacker Dr. (1983)	520	40
The Columbian, 1180 S. Michigan Ave. (2008)	517	47
191 N. Wacker Dr. (2002)	516	37
401 E. Ontario St. (1990)	515	51
One Financial Place, 440 S. LaSalle St. (1985)	515	39
The Streeter, 345 E. Ohio St. (2006)	514	50
Park Tower Condominiums, 5415 N. Sheridan Rd. (1973)	513	54
600 North Lake Shore Drive-South Tower (2009)	513	47
LaSalle-Wacker Building, 221 N. LaSalle St. (1930)	512	41
Harris Bank III, 115 S. LaSalle St. (1974)	510	38
321 N. Clark St. (1987)	510	35
215 West, 215 W. Washington St. (2010)	509	50
400 E. Ohio St. (1982)	505	50
Carbide & Carbon Bldg., 230 N. Michigan Ave. (1929)	503	37
One Superior Place, 1 W. Superior St. (1999)	502	52
120 N. LaSalle St. (1992)	501	39
10 S. LaSalle St. (1986)	501	37
The Tides, 360 E. South Water St. (2008)	500	51
200 S. Wacker Dr. (1981)	500	41

(1) 1,729 ft incl. antenna. (2) 1,499 ft incl. antenna. (3) 912 ft incl. antenna.

Cleveland, OH

Building/structure	Ht. (ft)	Stories
Key Tower (incl. spire), 127 Public Sq. (1991)	947	57
Terminal Tower, 50 Public Sq. (1928)[1]	708	52
200 Public Sq. (1985)	658	46
Tower at Erieview, 1301 E. 9th St. (1964)	529	40

(1) 771 ft incl. flagpole.

Columbus, OH

Building/structure	Ht. (ft)	Stories
James A. Rhodes State Office Tower, 30 E. Broad St. (1973)	624	41
Leveque-Lincoln Tower, 50 W. Broad St. (1927)	555	47
William Green Building, 30 W. Spring St. (1990)	530	33
Huntington Center, 41 S. High St. (1983)	512	37
Vern Riffe State Office Tower, 77 S. High St. (1988)	503	33

Dallas, TX

Building/structure	Ht. (ft)	Stories
Bank of America Plaza, 901 Main St. (1985)	921	72
Renaissance Tower (incl. spire), 1201 Elm St. (1974)	886	56
Comerica Bank Tower, 1717 Main St. (1987)	787	60
JP Morgan Chase Tower, 2200 Ross Ave. (1987)	738	55
Fountain Place, 1445 Ross Ave. (1986)	720	58
Trammel Crow Center, 2001 Ross Ave. (1984)	686	50
1700 Pacific Ave. (1983)	655	50
Thanksgiving Tower, 1600 Pacific Ave. (1982)	645	50
Energy Plaza, 1601 Bryan St. (1983)	629	49

Building/structure	Ht. (ft)	Stories
Elm Place, 1401 Elm St. (1965)	628	52
Gables Republic Tower (incl. spire), 300 N. Ervay (1954)	602	36
Republic Center Tower II, 325 N. St. Paul (1964)	598	50
One AT&T Plaza, 208 S. Akard St. (1984)	580	37
One Lincoln Plaza, 500 N. Akard St. (1984)	579	45
*Museum Tower, 2112 Flora St. (2013)	560	42
Cityplace Center East, 2711 N. Haskell Ave. (1989)	560	42
Reunion Tower, 300 Reunion Blvd. (1976)	560	NA
Sheraton Dallas Hotel Center Tower, 400 Olive St. (1959)	550	42
Mercantile Building (incl. spire), 1700 Main St. (1943)	523	31
Bryan Tower, 2001 Bryan St. (1973)	512	40

Denver, CO

Building/structure	Ht. (ft)	Stories
Republic Plaza, 330 17th St. (1984)	714	56
1801 California Street (1982)	709	52
Wells Fargo Center, 1700 Lincoln Ave. (1983)	698	50
Four Seasons Hotel and Private Residences, 1111 14th St. (2010)	639	45
1999 Broadway (1985)	544	43
707 17th St. (1981)	522	42
555 17th St. (1978)	507	40

Detroit, MI

Building/structure	Ht. (ft)	Stories
Marriott Hotel, Renaissance Center I (1977)[1]	727	70
One Detroit Center, 500 Woodward Ave. (1991)	619	43
Penobscot Building, 633 Griswold St. (1928)[2]	565	47
Renaissance Center 100 Tower (1976)	508	39
Renaissance Center 200 Tower (1976)	508	39
Renaissance Center 300 Tower (1976)	508	39
Renaissance Center 400 Tower (1976)	508	39

(1) 755 ft incl. antenna. (2) 665 ft incl. antenna.

Fort Worth, TX

Building/structure	Ht. (ft)	Stories
Burnett Plaza, 801 Cherry St. (1983)	567	40
D.R. Horton Tower, 301 Commerce St. (1984)	547	38
Carter Burgess Plaza, 777 Main St. (1982)	525	40

Hartford, CT

Building/structure	Ht. (ft)	Stories
City Place I, 185 Asylum St. (1980)	535	38
Travelers Tower, 26 Grove St. (1919)	527	24
Goodwin Square, 225 Asylum St. (1990)	522	30

Houston, TX

Building/structure	Ht. (ft)	Stories
JPMorganChase Tower, 600 Travis St. (1982)	1,002	75
Wells Fargo Plaza, 1000 Louisiana St. (1983)	992	71
Williams Tower, 2800 Post Oak Blvd. (1982)	901	64
Bank of America Center, 700 Louisiana St. (1983)	780	56
Texaco Heritage Plaza, 1111 Bagby St. (1987)	762	53
Enterprise Plaza, 1100 Louisiana St. (1980)[1]	756	55
Centerpoint Energy Plaza, 1111 Louisiana St. (1996)	741	47
Continental Center I, 1600 Smith St. (1984)	732	55
Fulbright Tower, 1301 McKinney St. (1982)	725	52
One Shell Plaza, 900 Louisiana St. (1970)[2]	714	50
1400 Smith St. (1983)	691	50
3 Allen Center, 333 Clay St. (1980)	685	50
LyondellBassell Tower, 1221 McKinney St. (1978)	678	47
First City Tower, 1001 Fannin St. (1984)	662	47
BG Group Place, 811 Main St. (2011)	632	46
San Felipe Plaza, 5847 San Felipe Blvd. (1984)	625	45
ExxonMobil Building, 800 Bell Ave. (1962)	606	44
1500 Louisiana St. (2002)	600	40
America General Center, 2929 Allen Pkwy. (1983)	590	42
Two Houston Center, 909 Fannin St. (1974)	579	40
San Jacinto Column, La Porte	570	NA
Marathon Oil Tower, 5555 San Felipe Blvd. (1983)	562	41
Wedge International Tower, 1415 Louisiana St. (1983)	550	44
KBR Tower, 601 Jefferson St. (1973)	550	40
Pennzoil Place I, 700 Milam St. (1976)	523	36
Pennzoil Place II, 700 Louisiana St. (1976)	523	36
Devon Energy Center, 1200 Smith St. (1978)	521	36
RRI Energy Plaza, 1000 Main St. (2003)	518	36
Total Plaza, 1201 Louisiana St. (1971)	518	35
The Huntington, 2121 Kirby Dr. (1982)	503	34
El Paso Energy Bldg, 1001 Louisiana St. (1962)	502	33
One Park Place, 1500 McKinney St. (2009)	501	37
Memorial Hermann Tower, 929 Gessner Rd. (2009)	500	35

(1) 782 ft incl. antenna. (2) 999 ft incl. antenna.

Indianapolis, IN

Building/structure	Ht. (ft)	Stories
Chase Tower, 111 Monument Cir. (1990)[1]	701	49
One America Tower, 200 N. Illinois St. (1982)	533	38
One Indiana Square, 200 N. Delaware St. (1970)	504	36

(1) 811 ft incl. antenna.

Building/structure	Ht. (ft)	Stories
Jersey City, NJ		
30 Hudson St. (2004)	781	42
101 Hudson St. (1992)	548	42
Trump Plaza I, 88 Morgan St. (2008)	532	55
Newport Tower, 525 Washington Blvd. (1990)	531	37
Exchange Place Center, 10 Exchange Pl. (incl. spire) (1990)	516	32
Hudson Green East Tower, 77 Hudson St. (2009)	509	48
Hudson Green West Tower, 77 Hudson St. (2010)	501	48
Las Vegas, NV		
Stratosphere Tower, 2000 Las Vegas Blvd. S. (1996)	1,149	NA
*Fontainebleau Resort Hotel, 2755 Las Vegas Blvd. S. (2013)	735	63
The Palazzo, 3339 Las Vegas Blvd. S. (2007)	642	53
Encore at Wynn Las Vegas, 3145 Las Vegas Blvd. S. (2008)	631	52
Trump International Hotel and Tower 1, 3128 Las Vegas Blvd. S. (2008)	622	64
Wynn Las Vegas, 3145 Las Vegas Blvd. S. (2005)	613	45
Cosmopolitan Casino Spa Tower, Las Vegas Blvd. and Harmon Ave. (2010)	603	52
Cosmopolitan Beach Resort Tower, Las Vegas Blvd. and Harmon Ave. (2010)	603	50
Aria Resort and Casino (2009)	600	60
Planet Hollywood Towers, 3667 Las Vegas Blvd. S. (2009)	597	50
VDARA, 2551 W. Harmon Ave. (2009)	556	55
Eiffel Tower, Paris Hotel and Casino, 3645 Las Vegas Blvd. S. (1998)	540	NA
Mandarin Oriental Hotel Las Vegas, 3750 Las Vegas Blvd. S. (2009)	539	47
New York, New York Hotel and Casino, 3790 Las Vegas Blvd. S. (1997)	529	48
Palms Place, 4321 W. Flamingo Rd. (2008)	518	50
Bellagio Hotel and Casino, 3600 Las Vegas Blvd. S. (1998)	508	36
Sky Las Vegas, 2780 Las Vegas Blvd. S. (2007)	500	45
Los Angeles, CA		
US Bank Tower, 633 W. 5th St. (1990)	1,018	73
Aon Center, 707 Wilshire Blvd. (1974)	858	62
Two California Plaza, 350 S. Grand Ave. (1992)	750	52
Gas Company Tower, 555 W. 5th St. (1991)	749	52
Bank of America Plaza, 333 S. Hope St. (1975)	735	55
777 Tower, 777 S. Figueroa St. (1991)	725	53
Wells Fargo Tower, 333 S. Grand Ave. (1983)	723	54
Figueroa at Wilshire, 601 S. Figueroa St. (1989)	717	52
City National Tower, 555 S. Flower St. (1971)	699	52
Paul Hastings Tower, 515 S. Flower St. (1971)	699	52
L.A. Live Hotel and Condominiums, 900 W. Olympic Blvd. (2010)	667	54
Citigroup Center, 444 S. Flower St. (1979)	625	48
611 Place, 611 W. 6th St. (1967)	620	42
KPMG Tower, 355 S. Grand Ave. (1984)	606	45
One California Plaza, 300 S. Grand Ave. (1985)	578	42
Century Plaza Tower 1, 2029 Century Park East (1973)	571	44
Century Plaza Tower 2, 2049 Century Park East (1973)	571	44
Ernst & Young, LLP Plaza, 725 S. Figueroa St. (1986)	534	41
AIG-SunAmerica Center, 1999 Ave. of the Stars (1989)	533	39
TCW Tower, 865 S. Figueroa St. (1990)	517	37
Union Bank Plaza, 445 S. Figueroa St. (1968)	516	40
10 Universal City Plaza (1984)	506	36
Mexico City, Mexico		
*Torre Reforma, Paseo de la Reforma 483 (2015)	800	57
Torre Mayor, Paseo de la Reforma 505 (2003)	738	55
*Torre BBVA Bancomer, Paseo de la Reforma 506 (2014)	738	50
Torre Ejecutiva Pemex, Marina Nacional 329 Col. Huasteca (1984)	693	51
Torre Altus, Paseo de los Laureles 416 (1999)	640	44
Torre Latino Americana (incl. spire), Eje Central Lazaro Cardenas 2 (1956)	597	45
World Trade Center, Montecito 38 Col. Napoles (1972)	565	50
*Siroco Elite Residences, Av. Santa Fe 482 (2013)	561	43
*Torre Punta Reforma, Paseo de la Reforma 180 (2014)	558	37
Arcos Torre I, Paseo de los Tamarindos 400 (1997)	529	35
Arcos Torre II, Paseo de los Tamarindos 400 (2008)	529	35

Building/structure	Ht. (ft)	Stories
Miami, FL		
Four Seasons Hotel & Tower, 1441 Brickell Ave. (2003)	789	64
Wachovia Financial Center, 200 S. Biscayne Blvd. (1983)	764	55
900 Biscayne Bay, 900 Biscayne Blvd. (2008)	712	65
Marquis, 1100 Biscayne Blvd. (2009)	679	63
Met 2 Office Tower, 200 SE 3rd St. (2010)	655	47
Mint at Riverfront, 90 SW 3rd St. (2009)	631	55
Infinity at Brickell, 60 W. 13th St. (2008)	630	52
Miami Tower, 100 SE 2nd St. (1987)	625	47
Marinablue, 888 Biscayne Blvd. (2007)	615	57
Plaza on Brickell Tower I, 901 Brickell Ave. (2007)	610	56
Icon Brickell North Tower, 495 Brickell Ave. (2008)	586	58
Icon Brickell South Tower, 495 Brickell Ave. (2008)	586	58
Ten Museum Park, 1040 Biscayne Blvd. (2007)	585	50
Paramount at Edgewater Square, 2066 N. Bayshore Dr. (2009)	555	47
50 Biscayne Blvd. (2007)	554	55
Quantum on the Bay South Tower, 1900 N. Bayshore Dr. (2008)	554	51
Opera Tower, 1750 N. Bayshore Dr. (2007)	543	56
Everglades on the Bay North Tower, 244 Biscayne Blvd. (2008)	538	49
Everglades on the Bay South Tower, 244 Biscayne Blvd. (2008)	538	49
Quantum on the Bay North Tower, 1900 N. Bayshore Dr. (2008)	536	44
Jade at Brickell Bay, 1331 Brickell Bay Dr. (2004)	528	49
Plaza on Brickell Tower II, 901 Brickell Ave. (2007)	525	48
Santa Maria, 1643 Brickell Ave. (1997)	520	51
The Ivy, 90-95 SW 3rd St. (2008)	512	45
Stephen P. Clark Center, 111 NW 1st St. (1985)	510	28
Met 2 Marriott Marquis, 200 SE 3rd St. (2010)	502	41
Wind, 330 S. Miami Ave. (2008)	501	41
1450 BRICKELL (2010)	500	34
Minneapolis, MN		
IDS Tower, 80 8th St. South (1973)[1]	792	55
Capella Tower, 225 South Sixth (1992)	776	56
Wells Fargo Center, 90 S. 7th St. (1988)	775	56
33 South Sixth Street (1983)	668	52
Campbell Mithun Tower, 222 S. 9th St. (1985)	582	42
US Bank Plaza I, 200 S. 6th St. (1981)	561	40
RBC Plaza, 60 S. 6th St. (1992)	539	40
Fifth Street Towers II, 150 S. 5th St. (1988)	504	36
(1) 910 ft incl. antenna.		
Monterrey, Mexico		
*Pabellon M (2015)	682	47
Dataflux Tower, San Pedro Garza Garcia (2000)	597	43
Centro de Gobierno Plaza Civica (2010)	591	36
Torre Helicon, San Pedro Garza Garcia (2012)	512	33
Montreal, QC, Canada		
1250 Boulevard Rene Levesque (incl. spire) (1992)	743	47
1000 Rue de la Gauchetiere (1992)	673	51
Tour de la Bourse, 800 Place Victoria (1964)	624	47
1 Place Villa Marie (1962)	616	43
La Tour CIBC, 1155 Rene Levesque Blvd. (1962)[1]	604	45
Montreal Tower (1987)	574	NA
Tour McGill College, 1501 McGill College (1992)	519	38
(1) 740 ft incl. antenna.		
New Orleans, LA		
One Shell Square, 701 Poydras St. (1972)	697	51
CapitalOne Center, 201 St. Charles Ave. (1985)	645	53
Plaza Tower, 1001 Howard Ave. (1969)	531	45
Energy Centre, 1100 Poydras St. (1984)	530	39
New York, NY		
*One World Trade Center (incl. spire) (2014)	1,776	104
*432 Park Avenue (2016)	1,398	89
Empire State Building, 350 5th Ave. (1931)[1]	1,250	102
Bank of America (incl. spire), One Bryant Park (2009)	1,200	55
Chrysler Building (incl. spire), 405 Lexington Ave. (1930)	1,046	77
New York Times Tower (incl. spire), 620 8th Ave. (2007)	1,046	52
*One57, 157 W. 57th St. (2013)	1,005	75
*Four World Trade Center, 150 Greenwich St. (2013)	977	64
American International Building (incl. spire), 70 Pine St. (1932)	952	67
The Trump Building, 40 Wall St. (1930)	927	71
Citigroup Center, 153 E. 53rd St. (1977)	915	59
New York by Gehry at Eight Spruce Street (2011)	870	76
Trump World Tower, 845 UN Plz. (2001)	861	72
GE Building, 30 Rockefeller Center (1933)	850	70

Building/structure	Ht. (ft)	Stories
Cityspire Center, 150 W. 56th St. (1989)	814	75
One Chase Manhattan Plaza (1960)	813	60
4 Times Square (1999)[2]	809	48
MetLife Building, 200 Park Ave. (1963)	808	59
Bloomberg Tower, 731 Lexington Ave. (2005)[3]	806	54
Woolworth Building, 233 Broadway (1913)	792	57
1 Worldwide Plaza, 935 8th Ave. (1989)	778	47
Carnegie Hall Tower, 152 W. 57th St. (1991)	757	60
383 Madison Ave. (2001)	755	47
*Courtyard and Residence Inn Manhattan/ Central Park, 1715 Broadway (2013)	753	68
AXA Center, 787 7th Ave. (1985)	752	51
One Penn Plaza, 250 W. 34th St. (1972)	750	57
1251 Ave. of the Americas (1971)	750	54
Time Warner Center North Tower, 10 Columbus Cir. (2004)	749	55
Time Warner Center South Tower, 10 Columbus Cir. (2004)	749	55
Goldman Sachs HQ, 200 Murray St. (2010)	749	44
60 Wall Street (1989)	745	55
One Astor Plaza, 1515 Broadway (1970)	745	54
1 Liberty Plaza, 165 Broadway (1973)	743	54
7 World Trade Center (2006)	743	49
20 Exchange Place (1931)	741	57
Three World Financial Center, 200 Vesey St. (1986)	739	51
1540 Broadway (incl. spire) (1990)	732	42
Times Square Tower, 1459 Broadway (2004)	726	47
Metropolitan Tower, 142 W. 57th St. (1985)	716	68
JPMorganChase World Headquarters, 270 Park Ave. (1960)	707	52
General Motors Building, 767 5th Ave. (1968)	705	50
Metropolitan Life Tower, 1 Madison Ave. (1909)	700	50
500 5th Ave. (1931)	697	60
Americas Tower, 1177 Ave. of the Americas (1992)	692	48
Solow Building, 9 W. 57th St. (1974)	689	49
HSBC Bank Building, 140 Broadway (1967)	688	52
55 Water St. (1972)	687	53
277 Park Ave. (1963)	687	50
1585 Broadway (1989)	685	42
Random House/Park Imperial, 1739 Broadway (2003)	684	52
Four Seasons Hotel, 57 E. 57th St. (1993)	682	52
McGraw Hill, 1221 Ave. of the Americas (1972)	674	51
Barclay Tower, 10 Barclay St. (2007)	673	56
Lincoln Building, 60 E. 42nd St. (1930)	673	53
Citicorp, 1 Court Sq., Queens (1990)	673	50
Paramount Plaza, 1633 Broadway (1970)	670	48
Trump Tower, 725 5th Ave. (1982)	664	58
Bank of New York Building, 1 Wall St. (1932)	654	50
Silver Towers East, 600 W. 42nd St. (2009)	653	58
Silver Towers West, 600 W. 42nd St. (2009)	653	58
599 Lexington Ave. (1986)	653	51
712 5th Ave. (1990)	650	53
Chanin Building, 122 E. 42nd St. (1929)	649	56
245 Park Ave. (1967)	648	47
Sony Building, 550 Madison Ave. (1983)	647	37
Two World Financial Center, 225 Liberty St. (1986)	645	44
570 Lexington Ave. (1931)	642	50
1 New York Plaza, 1 Water St. (1969)	640	50
1 MiMA Tower, 440 W. 42nd St. (2011)	638	63
1 Dag Hammarskjold Plaza, 885 2nd Ave. (1972)	637	48
345 Park Ave. (1968)	634	44
400 5th Ave. (2010)	632	58
Mercantile Building, 10 E. 40th St. (1929)	632	48
W New York Downtown Hotel & Residences, 123 Washington St. (2010)	631	57
Grace Plaza, 1114 Ave. of the Americas (1972)	630	50
Home Insurance Plaza, 59 Maiden Ln. (1966)	630	44
1095 Avenue of the Americas (1970)	630	40
101 Park Ave. (1982)	629	49
Central Park Place, 301 W. 57th St. (1988)	628	56
888 7th Ave. (1971)	628	45
Burlington House, 1345 Ave. of the Americas (1969)	625	50
Waldorf Astoria, 301 Park Ave. (1931)	625	47
Olympic Tower, 645 5th Ave. (1976)	620	51
425 Fifth Avenue (2003)	618	55
One Madison Park, 20 E. 23rd St. (2010)	621	51
The Epic, 125 W. 31st St. (2007)	615	58
919 3rd Ave. (1970)	615	47
Tower 49, 12 E. 49th St. (1985)	615	44
750 7th Ave. (incl. spire) (1989)	615	35
New York Life, 51 Madison Ave. (1928)	615	33
Eventi, 851 6th Ave. (2010)	614	46

Building/structure	Ht. (ft)	Stories
Credit Lyonnais Building, 1301 Ave. of the Americas (1964)	609	46
The Orion, 350 W. 42nd St. (2006)	604	58
590 Madison Ave. (1983)	603	41
*250 W. 55th St. (2013)	602	40
Eleven Times Square, 644 8th Ave. (2011)	601	40
1166 Avenue of the Americas (1974)	600	44
*160 W. 62nd St. (2014)	598	54
Hearst Magazine Tower, 959 8th Ave. (2006)	597	46
3 Lincoln Center, 160 W. 66th St. (1993)	595	60
Trump Palace, 200 E. 69th St. (1991)	594	54
Celanese Building, 1211 Ave. of the Americas (1973)	592	45
The London NYC, 151 W. 54th St. (1990)	590	54
*388 Bridge St., Brooklyn (2014)	590	51
Thurgood Marshall U.S. Courthouse, 505 Pearl St. (1936)	590	37
The Millenium Hilton Hotel, 55 Church St. (1992)	588	58
Sky House, 11 E. 29th St. (2008)	588	55
Museum Tower Apartments, 21 W. 53rd St. (1985)	588	52
Time-Life Building, 1271 Ave. of the Americas (1959)	587	48
Jacob K. Javits Federal Bldg., 26 Federal Plz. (1967)	587	41
W Times Square, 1567 Broadway (2000)	584	53
Trump International Hotel & Tower, 15 Columbus Cir. (1970)	583	44
Stevens Tower, 1185 Ave. of the Americas (1971)	580	42
Municipal Building, 1 Centre St. (1914)	580	34
520 Madison Ave. (1981)	577	43
One World Financial Center, 200 Liberty St. (1985)	577	37
Merchandise Mart, 41 Madison Ave. (1973)	576	42
Park Avenue Plaza, 55 E. 52nd St. (1981)	575	44
Lehman Building, 745 7th Ave. (2001)	575	38
One Financial Square, 33 Old Slip (1987)	575	37
Marriott Marquis Times Square, 1531 Broadway (1985)	574	50
299 Park Ave. (1967)	574	42
5 Times Square, 590 7th Ave. (2002)	574	40
Socony Mobil Building, 150 E. 42nd St. (1956)	572	42
1290 Ave. of the Americas (1963)	571	43
780 3rd Ave. (1983)	570	49
600 3rd Ave. (1971)	570	42
450 Lexington Ave. (1991)	568	38
Paramount Tower, 240 E. 39th St. (1998)	567	51
230 Park Ave. (1928)	565	35
New York Palace Hotel, 455 Madison Ave. (1980)	563	51
Continental Bank Building, 30 Broad St. (1932)	562	48
Park Avenue Tower, 65 E. 55th St. (1986)	561	36
Nelson Tower, 450 7th Ave. (1931)	560	46
Sherry-Netherland, 781 5th Ave. (1927)	560	40
623 5th Ave. (1990)	560	36
South Park Tower, 124 W. 60th St. (1986)	558	51
100 UN Plaza, 327 E. 48th St. (1986)	557	52
Continental Can, 633 3rd Ave. (1962)	557	39
3 Park Ave. (1975)	556	42
Continental Center, 180 Maiden Ln. (1983)	555	41
Sperry & Hutchinson Bldg., 330 Madison Ave. (1964)	555	41
Reuters Building, 3 Times Sq. (2001)[4]	555	30
Tower 111, 885 6th Ave. (2011)	554	48
The Belvedere, 10 E. 29th St. (1999)	554	48
Inmont Building, 1133 Ave. of the Americas (1970)	552	45
Downtown by Philippe Starck, 15 Broad St. (1927)	551	42
*Hyatt Times Square, 135 W. 45th St. (2013)	550	53
Biltmore Tower, 267 W. 47th St. (2003)	550	51
Unisys Building, 605 3rd Ave. (1963)	550	44
2 Grand Central Tower, 140 E. 45th St. (1982)	550	43
The Tower at 15 Central Park West (2008)	550	35
AT&T Long Lines Building, 33 Thomas St. (1974)	550	29
Bankers Trust, 33 E. 48th St. (1971)	547	41
The Corinthian, 330 E. 38th St. (1988)	546	55
Transportation Building, 225 Broadway (1928)	546	44
Millennium Tower, 101 W. 67th St. (1995)	545	54
Equitable Building, 120 Broadway (1915)	545	36
The Galleria, 117 E. 57th St. (1975)	544	56
2 Gold St. (2005)	543	51
220 Riverside Boulevard at Trump Place (2003)	542	49
17 State St. (1988)	542	41
Grand Central Plaza, 622 3rd Ave. (1973)	542	38
New York Telephone, 375 Pearl St. (1976)	540	42
1285 Ave. of the Americas (1960)	540	42
Ritz Tower, 109 E. 57th St. (1925)	540	41
14 Wall (1912)	540	29
Tribeca Tower, 105 Duane St. (1990)	537	53

Building/structure	Ht. (ft)	Stories
Lefcourt Colonial Building, 295 Madison Ave. (1929)	537	45
300 Madison Ave. (2003)	535	35
1700 Broadway (1969)	533	41
Westin Hotel New York, 43rd St. and 8th Ave. (2002)	532	45
515 Park Ave. (1999)	532	43
DuMont Building, 515 Madison Ave. (1931)	532	42
The Brooklyner, 111 Lawrence St., Brooklyn (2010)	531	52
The Metropolis, 150 E. 44th St. (2001)	528	50
William Beaver House, 15 William St. (2010)	528	47
North American Plywood, 800 3rd Ave. (1972)	526	41
Hotel Pierre, 2 E. 61st St. (1928)	525	44
767 3rd Ave. (1980)	525	39
Citibank, 399 Park Ave. (1961)	524	41
Random House, 825 3rd Ave. (1969)	522	40
Atelier, 625 W. 42nd St. (2007)	521	46
26 Broadway (1924)	520	31
Newsweek Building, 444 Madison Ave. (1931)	518	42
Architects and Designers Building, 964 Third Ave. (1969)	518	39
The Downtown Club, 19 West St. (1930)	518	39
785 8th Ave. (2009)	517	42
High Point Condominium, 250 E. 40th St. (1988)	516	49
House of Seagram, 375 Park Ave. (1958)	516	38
Sterling Drug Building, 90 Park Ave. (1964)	515	41
Millennium Towers North, 512 7th Ave. (1930)	513	44
1214 Fifth Ave. (2012)	513	42
Bank of New York, 48 Wall St. (1927)	513	31
The Belaire, 524 E. 72nd St. (1988)	512	50
One Hanson Place, Brooklyn (1929)	512	42
1407 Broadway Realty Corp. (1950)	512	41
International, Rockefeller Center, 630 5th Ave. (1935)	512	41
ITT-American, 437 Madison Ave. (1967)	512	40
Continental Building, 1450 Broadway (1931)	511	42
1155 Ave. of the Americas (1984)	511	40
Liberty Plaza, 10 Liberty St. (2004)	510	45
810 7th Ave. (1970)	506	41
The Sheffield Apartments, 325 W. 56th St. (1978)	505	50
2 UN Plaza (1981)	505	39
1 UN Plaza (1975)	505	39
United Nations Secretariat Building, 405 E. 42nd St. (1950)	505	39
2 New York Plaza, 125 Broad St. (1970)	504	40
Johns-Manville Building, 22 E. 40th St. (1931)	503	43
60 Broad St. (1962)	503	39
Lefcourt National Building, 521 5th Ave. (1928)	503	37
1325 Ave. of the Americas (1989)	502	35
Sheraton Centre, 811 7th Ave. (1962)	501	51
World Apparel Center, 1411 Broadway (1969)	501	39
Bristol Plaza, 200 E. 65th St. (1987)	500	50
One Columbus Place Tower I, 400 W. 59th St. (1999)	500	49
One Columbus Place Tower II, 400 W. 59th St. (1999)	500	49
Four World Financial Center, 250 Vesey St. (1986)	500	34

(1) 1,455 ft incl. antenna. (2) 1,118 ft incl. antenna. (3) 941 ft incl. antenna. (4) 659 ft incl. antenna.

Philadelphia, PA

Building/structure	Ht. (ft)	Stories
Comcast Center, 1701 JFK Blvd. (2008)	974	57
One Liberty Place (incl. spire), 1650 Market St. (1987)	945	61
Two Liberty Place (incl. spire), 1601 Chestnut St. (1989)	848	58
Mellon Bank Center, 1735 Market St. (1990)	792	54
Three Logan, 1717 Arch St. (1991)	725	53
G. Fred DiBona Jr. Building, 1901 Market St. (1990)	625	45
Commerce Square #2, 2001 Market St. (1992)	572	40
Commerce Square #1, 2005 Market St. (1990)	572	40
City Hall (incl. statue) (1901)	548	7
Residences at Ritz-Carlton, 1416 S. Penn Sq. (2009)	518	46
1818 Market St. (1974)	500	40

(1) 748 ft incl. antenna.

Pittsburgh, PA

Building/structure	Ht. (ft)	Stories
US Steel Tower, 600 Grant St. (1970)	841	64
One Mellon Bank Center, 500 Grant St. (1983)	725	54
One PPG Place (1984)	635	40
Fifth Avenue Place, 120 5th Ave. (1987)	616	32
One Oxford Centre, 301 Grant St. (1982)	615	46
Gulf Tower, 707 Grant St. (1932)	582	44

Building/structure	Ht. (ft)	Stories
University of Pittsburgh Cathedral of Learning, 4200 5th Ave. (1936)	535	42
3 Mellon Bank Center, 525 Wm. Penn Way (1951)	520	41
K & L Gates Center, 210 6th Ave. (1968)	511	39

Portland, OR

Building/structure	Ht. (ft)	Stories
Wells Fargo Center, 1300 SW 5th Ave. (1973)	546	40
U.S. Bancorp Tower, 111 SW 5th Ave. (1983)	536	42
Koin Plaza, 222 SW Columbia St. (1984)	509	31

St. Louis, MO

Building/structure	Ht. (ft)	Stories
Gateway Arch (1965)	630	NA
Metropolitan Square Tower, 211 N. Broadway (1988)	593	42
AT&T Center, 900 Pine St. (1984)	588	44
Thomas F. Eagleton Federal Courthouse, 111 S. 10th St. (2000)	557	29

San Francisco, CA

Building/structure	Ht. (ft)	Stories
Sutro Tower (1972)	977	NA
Transamerica Pyramid, 600 Montgomery St. (1972)	853	48
555 California St. (1969)	779	52
345 California Center (1986)	695	48
Millennium Tower, 301 Mission St. (2009)	645	58
One Ricon Hill South Tower, 425 First St. (2008)	605	54
101 California St. (1982)	600	48
50 Fremont Center (1985)	600	43
Chevron Tower, 575 Market St. (1975)	573	40
Four Embarcadero Center, 55 Clay St. (1984)	570	45
One Embarcadero Center, 355 Clay St. (1970)	569	45
44 Montgomery St. (1967)	565	43
Spear Tower, 1 Market St. (1976)	565	42
One Sansome Street (1984)	550	43
Shaklee Terrace Building, 444 Market St. (1982)	537	38
First Market Tower, 525 Market St. (1972)	529	38
McKesson Plaza, 1 Post St. (1969)	529	38
425 Market St. (1973)	524	38
Telsis Tower, 1 Montgomery St. (1982)	500	38

Seattle, WA

Building/structure	Ht. (ft)	Stories
Columbia Center, 701 5th Ave. (1985)	933	76
1201 Third Avenue Tower, 1201 3rd Ave. (1988)	772	55
Two Union Square, 601 Union St. (1989)	740	56
Seattle Municipal Tower, 700 5th Ave. (1990)	722	57
Safeco Plaza, 1001 4th Ave. (1969)	630	50
City Centre, 1420 5th Ave. (1989)	606	44
Space Needle, 203 6th Ave. (1962)	605	NA
Russell Investments Center, 1301 2nd Ave. (2006)	598	42
Wells Fargo Center, 999 3rd Ave. (1983)	574	47
Bank of America Fifth Avenue Plaza, 800 Fifth Ave. (1981)	543	42
901 5th Ave. (1973)	536	41
Rainier Tower, 1301 5th Ave. (1977)	514	31
Fourth & Madison Building, 915 4th Ave. (2003)	512	40
1918 8th Ave. (2009)	500	36

Sunny Isles Beach, FL

Building/structure	Ht. (ft)	Stories
Jade on the Beach Condominiums, 17001 Collins Ave. (2008)	574	51
Trump Royale, 18201 Collins Ave. (2008)	551	43
Trump Palace, 18101 Collins Ave. (2005)	551	43
Aqualina Ocean Residences, 17875 Collins Ave. (2004)	550	51
Jade Ocean, 17121 Collins Ave. (2009)	543	51

Tampa, FL

Building/structure	Ht. (ft)	Stories
Regions Building, 100 N. Tampa St. (1992)	579	42
Bank of America Plaza, 101 E. Kennedy Blvd. (1986)	577	42
One Tampa City Center, 201 N. Franklin St. (1981)	537	39
SunTrust Financial Center, 401 E. Jackson St. (1992)	525	36

Toronto, ON, Canada

Building/structure	Ht. (ft)	Stories
CN Tower, 310 Front St. West (1976)	1,815	NA
First Bank Tower, 100 King St. West (1975)[1]	978	72
Trump International Hotel & Tower (incl. spire), 325 Bay St. (2012)	908	59
Scotia Tower, 40 King's St. West (1989)	902	68
*Aura at College Park, 388 Yonge St. (2014)	892	78
Brookfield Place (incl. spire), 161 Bay St. (1990)	856	53
Commerce Court West, 199 Bay St. (1973)[2]	784	57
*Number One Bloor, 1 Bloor St. East (2015)	780	70
*Ice Condos at York Centre 2, 16 York St. (2015)	768	67
TD Centre-Toronto Dominion Bank Tower, 66 Wellington St. West (1967)	730	56
Bay-Adelaide Center West Tower, 335 Bay St. (2010)	704	52

Building/structure	Ht. (ft)	Stories
*Living Shangri-La Toronto, 180 University Ave. (2012)	702	65
Ritz-Carlton Hotel and Residences, 185 Wellington St. West (2011)	687	54
BCE Place, Bay-Wellington Tower, 181 Bay St. (1991)	679	49
*L Tower, 1 Front St. (2012)	673	57
*Ice Condos at York Centre 1, 16 York St. (2013)	669	57
*Four Seasons Private Residences West, 48 Yorkville Ave. (2012)	623	55
RBC Centre, 155 Wellington St. West (2009)	607	42
*U Condominiums II, 50 St. Joseph St. (2014)	604	55
TD Centre-Royal Trust Tower, 77 King St. West (1969)	600	46
Maple Leaf Square North Tower, 65 Bremner Blvd. (2010)	595	54
1 King West (2005)	578	51
Success Tower 2, 33 Bay St. (2010)	569	55
Royal Bank Plaza-South Tower, 200 Bay St. (1976)	567	41
Maple Leaf Square South Tower, 55 Bremner Blvd. (2010)	562	50
*Hullmark Centre I, 4789 Yonge St. (2014)	551	45
44 Charles St. West (1974)	545	51
Quantum 2, 2195 Yonge St. (2008)	541	51
Residences @ College Park I, 763 Bay St. (2006)	535	51
*Burano, 832 Bay St. (2012)	535	50
Success Tower 1, 18 Harbour St. (2011)	531	52
*X2, 580 Jarvis St. (2014)	529	44
*Southcore Financial Centre Delta Hotel (2014)	524	47
The Uptown, 35 Balmuto St. (2011)	518	48
*Theatre Park, 224 King St. West (2014)	515	47
Festival Tower, 330 King St. West (2011)	514	42
*Three Hundred, 300 Front St. West (2013)	512	52
*U Condominiums I, 50 St. Joseph St. (2014)	505	45
TD Centre, 79 Wellington St. West (1985)	504	39
35 Mariner (2005)	503	49
*Westlake Village 1 (2014)	503	48
Montage, 20 Fort York Blvd. (2009)	502	48

(1) 1,116 ft incl. antenna. (2) 942 ft incl. antenna.

Tulsa, OK

Building/structure	Ht. (ft)	Stories
BOK Tower, 1 E. 2nd St. (1975)	667	52
Cityplex Central Tower, 2448 E. 81st St. (1979)	648	60
First Place Tower, 15 E. 5th St. (1973)	516	40
Mid-Continent Tower, 401 S. Boston St. (1984)	513	36

Vancouver, BC, Canada

Building/structure	Ht. (ft)	Stories
Shangri-La Vancouver, 1120 W. Georgia St. (2009)	659	59
*The Ritz-Carlton, 1133 W. Georgia (2014)	616	58
*Hotel Georgia, 667 Howe St. (2012)	520	50

Other Tall Buildings in North America

Building/structure	City	Ht. (ft)	Stories
Devon Energy Tower (2012)	Oklahoma City, OK	844	52
RSA Battle House Tower (incl. spire) (2007)	Mobile, AL	745	35
Revel Hotel (2012)	Atlantic City, NJ	718	53

Building/structure	City	Ht. (ft)	Stories
Hotel Riu Plaza Guadalajara (2011)	Guadalajara, Mex.	705	44
Great American Tower at Queen City Square (2011)	Cincinnati, OH	665	40
The Tower at First National Center (2002)	Omaha, NE	634	45
801 Grand (1991)	Des Moines, IA	630	44
One Kansas City Place (incl. spire) (1988)	Kansas City, MO	623	42
Tower of the Americas (1968)	San Antonio, TX	622	NA
Bank of America Tower (1990)	Jacksonville, FL	617	42
AT&T Building (1994)	Nashville TN	617	33
U.S. Bank Center (1973)	Milwaukee, WI.	601	42
Town Pavilion (1986)	Kansas City, MO.	591	38
Erastus Corning II Tower (1973)	Albany, NY	589	44
Niagara Falls Hilton Phase 2 (2009)	Niagara Falls, ON, Can.	581	58
Absolute World 56 (2012)	Mississauga, ON, Can.	576	56
Carew Tower (1931)	Cincinnati, OH	574	49
Concourse Corporate Center V (incl. spire) (1988)	Sandy Springs, GA	570	34
Torre Aura Altitude (2008)	Zapopan, Mex.	563	44
Blue Diamond Tower (2000)	Miami Beach, FL.	559	44
Green Diamond Tower (2000)	Miami Beach, FL.	559	44
Washington Monument (1884)	Washington, DC	555	NA
Concourse Corporate Center VI (incl. spire) (1991)	Sandy Springs, GA	553	34
100 E. Wisconsin Ave. (1989)	Milwaukee, WI.	549	37
AEGON Center (1992)	Louisville, KY	549	35
Metropolitan Tower (1986)	Little Rock, AK	546	40
Marriott Rivercenter (incl. spires) (1988)	San Antonio, TX	546	38
RBC Plaza (incl. spire) (2008)	Raleigh, NC	538	32
Modis Tower (1975)	Jacksonville, FL	535	37
Legg Mason Building (1973)	Baltimore, MD.	529	40
One HSBC Center (1970)	Buffalo, NY	529	38
Vehicle Assembly Building (1965)	Cape Canaveral, FL	526	40
Harrah's Waterfront Tower (2008)	Atlantic City, NJ	525	44
Skylon (1965)	Niagara Falls, ON, Can.	520	NA
Absolute World 50 (2012)	Mississauga, ON, Can.	518	50
*Sovereign (2014)	Burnaby, BC, Can.	511	45
Bank of America (1924)	Baltimore, MD.	509	37
The Westin Virginia Beach Town Center and Residences (2007)	Virginia Beach, VA	508	38
The Beach Club Tower 2 (2006)	Hallandale Beach, FL	505	50
One American Plaza (1991)	San Diego, CA	500	34
Chase Tower (1971)	Oklahoma City, OK	500	36

Notable North American Bridges

Source: World Almanac research; Office of Bridge Technology, Federal Highway Administration, U.S. Dept. of Transportation
Asterisk (*) designates a bridge that carries railroads only. All other bridges carry roads or roads and rail unless otherwise noted. Year is date of completion or projected completion. Span of bridge is the distance between its main supports. As of mid-2012.

Suspension

Year	Bridge	Location	Main span (ft)
1964	Verrazano-Narrows	New York, NY	4,260
1937	Golden Gate	San Francisco Bay, CA	4,200
1957	Mackinac	Straits of Mackinac, MI	3,800
1931	George Washington	New York, NY-Fort Lee, NJ	3,500
2007	Tacoma Narrows (new)	Tacoma, WA	2,800
1950	Tacoma Narrows	Tacoma, WA	2,800
2003	Al Zampa Memorial (new Carquinez)	Carquinez Strait, CA	2,388
1936	San Francisco-Oakland Bay (West Span)[1]	San Francisco-Yerba Buena Isl., CA	2,310
1939	Bronx-Whitestone	East R., New York, NY	2,300
1970	Pierre Laporte	Quebec City, QC, Can.	2,190
1951/1968	Delaware Mem. (twin)	Pennsville, NJ-New Castle, DE	2,150
1957	Walt Whitman	Philadelphia, PA	2,000
1929	Ambassador	Detroit, MI-Windsor, ON, Canada	1,850
1961	Throgs Neck	New York, NY	1,801
1926	Benjamin Franklin	Phila., PA-Camden, NJ.	1,750
1924	Bear Mountain	Hudson R., Peekskill, NY	1,632
1969	Claiborne Pell/Newport	Narragansett Bay, RI	1,600

Year	Bridge	Location	Main span (ft)
1952/73	William Preston Lane Jr. Memorial (twin)	Sandy Point, MD.	1,600
1903	Williamsburg	East R., New York, NY	1,600
1883	Brooklyn	East R., New York, NY	1,596
1938	Lions Gate	Vancouver, BC, Canada	1,550
1963	Vincent Thomas	L.A. Harbor, CA	1,500
1930	Mid-Hudson	Poughkeepsie, NY	1,495
1909	Manhattan	East R., New York, NY	1,470
1955	Angus L. Macdonald	Halifax, NS, Canada	1,447
1970	A. Murray MacKay	Halifax, NS, Canada	1,400
1936	Triborough (Harlem R. Lift/Bronx Crossing/ East R. Suspension)	East R., New York, NY	1,380
2013	San Francisco-Oakland Bay (SAS Span)[2]	San Francisco Bay, CA.	1,263

Cantilever

Year	Bridge	Location	Main span (ft)
1917	Quebec	Quebec City, QC, Can.	1,800
1974	Commodore Barry	Chester, PA-Bridgeport, NJ	1,644
1958/88	Crescent City Connection (twin)	Mississippi R., New Orleans, LA	1,575

Year	Bridge	Location	Main span (ft)
1995	Veterans Memorial	Mississippi R., Gramercy, LA	1,460
1936	San Francisco-Oakland Bay (East Span)[2]	Yerba Buena Isl.-Oakland, CA	1,400
1968	Baton Rouge	Mississippi R., LA	1,235
1955	Tappan Zee (I-287)	Hudson R., Tarrytown, NY	1,212
1930	Lewis and Clark	Longview, WA-Rainier, OR	1,200
1909	Queensboro	East R., New York, NY	1,182
1958	Carquinez Strait (eastbound)	San Francisco Bay, CA	1,100
1930	Jacques Cartier	Montreal, QC, Canada	1,097
1968	Isaiah D. Hart	Jacksonville, FL	1,088
1956	Richmond-San Rafael (twin)	San Francisco Bay, CA	1,070
1963/80	Newburgh-Beacon (twin)	Hudson R., NY	1,000
1950	Martin Luther King Jr.	St. Louis, MO	963
1975	Caruthersville	Mississippi R., MO-TN	920
1988	Carl D. Perkins (U.S. 23)	Ohio R., Scioto Co., OH-KY	900
1981	William S. Ritchie	Ohio R., Ravenswood, WV	900
1977	Saint Marys	Saint Marys, WV-OH	900
1969	Silver Memorial, Ohio R.[3]	Pt. Pleasant, WV-OH	900

Simple Truss

Year	Bridge	Location	Main span (ft)
1977	Jennings Randolph	Chester, WV-E. Liverpool, OH	745
1929	Irvin S. Cobb (U.S. 45)	Ohio R., Brookport, IL-Paducah, KY	716
1923	*Mears Mem., Tanana R.	Nenana, AK	700
1967	Williamstown-Marietta (I-77)	Ohio R., WV-OH	650
1917	*MacArthur	E. St. Louis, IL-St. Louis, MO	647
1992	Discovery	Missouri R., MO	625
1958	*Castleton	Hudson R., NY	598
1938	Easton-Phillipsburg	Delaware R., PA	550
1930	Swindell	Pittsburgh, PA	545
1951	Rankin	Pittsburgh, PA	525
1906	Donora-Webster	Donora-Webster, PA	515

Steel Truss

Year	Bridge	Location	Main span (ft)
1990	Glade Creek	Beckley, WV	784
1973	U.S. 190, Atchafalaya R.	Krotz Springs, LA	780
1971	I-95, Piscataqua R.	Portsmouth, NH-Kittery, ME	756
1972	LA 1, Atchafalaya R.	Simmesport, LA	720
1957	Robert O. Norris (VA 3)	Middlesex Co., VA	648
1933	Long-Allen (LA 182)	Morgan City, LA	608
1968	Reedy Point	Delaware City, DE	600
1960	Summit	Summit, DE	600
1910	McKinley, Mississippi R.	St. Louis, MO-Venice, IL	517
1972	Norbert F. Beckey	Mississippi R., Muscatine, IA-IL	512
1897	Newport and Cincinnati/ Purple People[4]	Ohio R., KY-OH	510

Continuous Truss

Year	Bridge	Location	Main span (ft)
1966	Astoria	Columbia R., OR-WA	1,232
1976	Francis Scott Key	Baltimore, MD	1,200
1981	Ravenswood	Ohio R., Ravenswood, WV	902
1995	Taylor-Southgate, Ohio R.	Cincinnati, OH-Newport, KY	850
1943	Julien Dubuque (U.S. 20)	Mississippi R., IA-IL	845
1966	Charles Braga	Fall River, MA	840
1956	Earle C. Clements (KY 56) (twin)	Ohio R., IL-KY	825
1953	John E. Mathews	Jacksonville, FL	810
1992	Cooper R.	Charleston, SC	800
1957	Kingston-Rhinecliff	Hudson R., NY	800
1950	Maurice J. Tobin	Boston, MA	800
1940	Gov. Nice Mem., Potomac R.	Newburg, MD-Dahlgren, VA	800
1986	Rochester-Monaca	Rochester-Monaca, PA	780
1917	*Sciotoville RR (twin)	Sciotoville, OH-KY	775
1981	Sewickley	Sewickley, PA	750
1974	Carroll C. Cropper (I-275)	Ohio R., IN-KY	750
1940	Glover Cary	Ohio R., Owensboro, KY-IN	750
1984	13th Street	Ohio R., Ashland, KY-OH	740
1959	Monaca-E. Rochester	Monaca-E. Rochester, PA	730
1976	Betsy Ross	Philadelphia, PA	729
1929	Milton-Madison (U.S. 421)	Ohio R., KY-IN	727
1967	Matthew E. Welsh	Ohio R., Mauckport, IN-KY	725
1962	U.S. 41 Twin, Ohio R.	Evansville, IN-Henderson, KY	720
1994	Robert C. Byrd	Huntington, WV	720
1970	Vanport	Vanport, PA	715
1962	Champlain	Montreal, QC, Canada	707
1973	Girard Point	Philadelphia, PA	700
1963	John F. Kennedy (I-65)	Ohio R., Louisville, KY-Jeffersonville, IN	700

Year	Bridge	Location	Main span (ft)
1956	DE R.-PA Turnpike	Delaware R., NJ-PA	682
1949	George C. Platt Memorial	Philadelphia, PA	680
1938	Rainbow	Port Arthur-Orange, TX	680

Continuous Box/Plate Girder

Year	Bridge	Location	Main span (ft)
2010	Kanawha R. (I-64)	S. Charleston-Dunbar, WV	760
1977	LA 27, Intracoastal Canal	Gibbstown, LA	750
1976	LA 82, Intracoastal Canal	Forked Isl., LA	750
1967	San Mateo-Hayward	San Francisco Bay, CA	750
1969	San Diego-Coronado (twin)	San Diego Bay, CA	660
1967	B. F. Dickmann (Poplar St.)	Mississippi R., St. Louis, MO-IL	647
1992/94	Acosta (twin)	Jacksonville, FL	630
1973	Loop 610/Sidney Sherman	Houston, TX	630
1981	Douglas	Juneau, AK	620
1981	Glenn Jackson (I-205)	Columbia R., OR-WA	600

Cable-Stayed

Year	Bridge	Location	Main span (ft)
2012	Baluarte Bicentennial	Mexico	1,706
2011	John James Audubon	Pointe Coupee-West Feliciana, LA	1,583
2005	Arthur Ravenel Jr.	Charleston, SC	1,546
1986	Alex Fraser	Vancouver, BC, Can.	1,526
2014	New Mississippi R. (I-70)	St. Louis, MO-IL	1,500
2010	U.S. 82, Mississippi R.	Greenville, MS-Lake Village, AR	1,378
1994	Clark	Alton, IL-MO	1,360
1989	Dames Point	Jacksonville, FL	1,300
2003	Sidney Lanier	Brunswick, GA	1,250
1995	Fred Hartman	Houston Ship Channel, Baytown, TX	1,250
2007	Veterans' Glass City Skyway	Maumee R., Toledo, OH	1,225
1983	Hale Boggs Memorial	Luling, LA	1,222
2002	William Natcher, Ohio R.	Owensboro, KY-IN	1,200
1987	Sunshine Skyway	Tampa Bay, FL	1,200
2012	Margaret Hunt Hill	Trinity R., Dallas, TX	1,197
1988	Tampico	Panuco R., Mexico	1,181
2006	Penobscot Narrows	Bucksport, ME	1,161
2003	Bill Emerson Memorial	Cape Girardeau, MO-IL	1,150
1988	Skybridge[5]	Vancouver, BC, Canada	1,115
1991	Talmadge Memorial	Savannah, GA	1,100
2000	Maysville (Wm. H. Harsha)	Savannah, GA	1,050

Steel Arch

Year	Bridge	Location	Main span (ft)
1977	New River Gorge	Fayetteville, WV	1,700
1931	Bayonne (Kill Van Kull)	Bayonne, NJ-New York, NY	1,675
1973	Fremont	Portland, OR	1,255
1964	Port Mann	Vancouver, BC, Can.	1,200
1967	Laviolette	Trois-Rivières, QC, Can.	1,100
1990	Roosevelt Lake	Roosevelt Lake, AZ	1,080
1959	Glen Canyon	Page, AZ	1,028
1962	Lewiston-Queenston	NY-ON, Can.	1,001
1976	Perrine	Twin Falls, ID	993
1916	*Hell Gate	East R., New York, NY	978
1941	Rainbow	Niagara Falls, NY-ON, Can.	950
1997	Second Blue Water	Port Huron, MI-ON, Can.	922
1977	Moundsville	Ohio R., WV	912
1983/90	Jefferson Barracks (I-255) (twin)	Mississippi R., IL-MO	910
1973	Hernando DeSoto (I-40) (twin)	Mississippi R., AR-TN	900
2008	Blennerhassett (U.S. 50)	Parkersburg, WV-OH	878
1936	Henry Hudson	Harlem R., New York, NY	840
1966	Bob Cummings Lincoln Trail	Ohio R., IN-KY	825
1978	I-57, Mississippi R.	Cairo, IL	821
1980	I-65, Mobile R.	Mobile, AL	800
1961	Sherman Minton (I-64)	New Albany, IN-Louisville, KY	800
1978	I-470, Ohio R.	Wheeling, WV	780
1932	West End	Pittsburgh, PA	780
1995	Navajo	Marble Canyon, AZ	726
1959	Thaddeus Kosciusko (twin)	Mohawk R., Albany, NY	600
1936	Yaquina Bay	Newport, OR	600
1917	Detroit-Superior High Level	Cuyahoga R., Cleveland, OH	591
2004	Gateway Boulevard	Nashville, TN	545
1874	Eads, Mississippi R.	St. Louis, MO-IL	520

Concrete Arch

Year	Bridge	Location	Main span (ft)
2010	Mike O'Callaghan-Pat Tillman Mem. (U.S. 93)	Colorado R., AZ-NV	1,060
1994	Natchez Trace Parkway	Franklin, TN	582
1993	Lake Street	Minneapolis-St. Paul, MN	556
1971	Fred Redmon (twin)	Selah, WA	549
1968	Cowlitz R.	Mossyrock, WA	520

Segmental Concrete

Year	Bridge	Location	Main span (ft)
1997	Confederation[6]	Prince Edward Isl.-NB, Can.	820
1978	Shubenacadie R.	S. Maitland, NS, Can.	790
1982	Jesse H. Jones Mem.	Houston, TX	750
1992	Jamestown-Verrazano	Narragansett Bay, RI	674
2002	Vietnam Veterans Memorial	James R., Richmond, VA	672
1986	Umatilla	Columbia R., OR-WA	660
2007	Benicia-Martinez (new)	Carquinez Strait, CA	659
1978	Stanislaus R.	Parrots Ferry, CA	640
1981	Juneau-Douglas	Gastineau Channel, AK	620
2010	Allegheny R. (I-76) (twin)	Nr. Oakmont, PA	532
1991	Veterans Mem. Centennial	Coeur d'Alene, ID	520
2008	I-35W St. Anthony Falls	Minneapolis, MN	504

Twin Concrete Trestle[7]

Year	Bridge	Location	Main span (ft)
1956/69	Lake Pontchartrain Causeway[8]	Metairie-Mandeville, LA	126,034
1979	Manchac Swamp	Manchac, LA.	120,384
1972	Atchafalaya Basin (I-10).	Baton Rouge, LA	93,984

Movable Bridges
Vertical Lift

Year	Bridge	Location	Main span (ft)
1959	*Arthur Kill	New York, NY-Elizabeth, NJ	558
1965	Pennsylvania Railroad	Kirkwood-Mt. Pleas., DE	548
1935	*Cape Cod Canal	Buzzards Bay, MA	544
1896	*Delair	Pennsauken, NJ-Phila., PA	542
1937	Marine Pkwy. Gil Hodges Mem.	Jamaica Bay, New York, NY	540
1931	Burlington-Bristol	Delaware R., NJ-PA	540
1958	Columbia R. Interstate (I-5)	Portland, OR-Vancouver, WA	531
1908	*Willamette R.	Portland, OR.	521

Year	Bridge	Location	Main span (ft)
1968	Second Narrows	Vancouver, BC, Canada	493
1911	*Armour-Swift-Burlington	Missouri R., Kansas City, MO	428
1945	*Harry S Truman	Kansas City, MO.	427
1955	Roosevelt Island	East R., New York, NY	418
1980	U.S. 17, James R.	Isle of Wight Co., VA	415
1932	*M-K-T RR	Missouri R., MO	414
1969	Cape Fear Memorial	Wilmington, NC.	408
1930	Aerial Lift.	Duluth, MN	386

Bascule

Year	Bridge	Location	Main span (ft)
2006/08	Woodrow Wilson (twin)	Potomac R., VA-MD	366
1940	Charles Berry Memorial	Lorain, OH	333
1917	Market St./Chief John Ross.	Chattanooga, TN	306
2003	*SW 2nd Avenue	Miami, FL	302
1956/96	1st Ave. S., Duwamish R. (twin)	Seattle, WA.	300

Swing

Year	Bridge	Location	Main span (ft)
1927	Santa Fe, Mississippi R.	Ft. Madison, IA	525
1952	George P. Coleman Mem.	Yorktown, VA	500
1991	SW Spokane St.	Seattle, WA.	480
1899	*C.M.&N. RR	Chicago, IL	474
1913	Rt. 82, Connecticut R.	E. Haddam, CT.	465
1914	*Coos Bay RR	Coos Bay, OR.	458

Floating Pontoon[9]

Year	Bridge	Location	Main span (ft)
1963	Evergreen Pt. (SR 520)	Seattle, WA.	7,578
1961	Hood Canal (SR 104)	Kitsap Co.-Jefferson Co., WA	7,450
1993	Lacey V. Murrow (I-90)	Seattle, WA.	6,561
1989	Homer M. Hadley (I-90)	Seattle, WA.	5,736

Other Notable North American Bridges[7]

Year	Bridge	Type	Location	Length (ft)
1982	Seven Mile (Overseas Hwy, U.S. 1)	Segmental concrete	Florida Keys	35,867
2002	Croatan Sound	Continuous post-tensioned girder.	Manteo, NC	27,000
1962	International	Arch truss	Sault Ste. Marie, MI-ON, Canada	9,278
1987	Powder Point	Tropical hardwood	Duxbury, MA	2,200
1901	Hartland[10]	Covered	St. John R., Hartland, NB, Canada	1,282

(1) Two complete bridges end-to-end, each with a main span of 2,310 ft, which share an anchor point in the middle of San Francisco Bay. (2) The East Span cantilever bridge will be demolished upon completion of and rerouting of traffic onto replacement structures, including the Self-Anchored Suspension (SAS) Span, which will be the world's longest single-tower, self-anchored suspension bridge. (3) Replaced Silver Bridge, the collapse of which in 1967 led to the creation of National Bridge Inspection Standards in the U.S. (4) Rehabilitated and reopened to pedestrians only in 2003. (5) World's longest cable-stayed bridge carrying mass transit only. (6) World's longest bridge crossing ice-covered water, with total length of 8 mi. (7) Length listed is total length of bridge. (8) World's second-longest bridge over water, behind China's Jiaozhou Bay Bridge (26.3 mi.). (9) Length listed is length of bridge's floating section. (10) World's longest covered bridge.

Oldest U.S. Bridges in Continuous Use

Built in 1697, the stone-arch Frankford Ave. Bridge (U.S. 13) crosses Pennypack Creek in Philadelphia, PA. It consists of three spans and has a total length of 154 ft. The bridge was constructed as part of the King's Road, which eventually connected Philadelphia to New York.

The oldest covered bridge, completed in 1829, is the double-span, 256-ft-long Bath-Haverhill Bridge, which spans the Ammonoosuc River between the towns of Bath and Haverhill, NH. The bridge was bypassed in 1999. It has since reopened to pedestrian traffic only.

Notable World Bridges

Source: World Almanac research; Laboratory of Bridge Engineering, Aalto Univ. School of Science and Technology
Year is date of completion or projected completion. Span of bridge is the distance between its main supports. As of mid-2012.

Suspension

Year	Bridge	Location	Main span (ft)
1998	Akashi Kaikyo	Japan	6,532
2009	Xihoumen	China	5,413
1998	Storebælt (Great Belt, East Bridge)	Denmark	5,328
2012	Yi Sun-sin	South Korea	5,069
2005	Runyang Yangtze R. (south)	China	4,888
2012	Nanjing Fourth Yangtze R.	China	4,652
1981	Humber	England	4,626
1999	Jiangyin Yangtze R.	China	4,544
1997	Tsing Ma.	China	4,518
2013	Hardanger.	Norway	4,298
2007	Yangluo Yangtze R.	China	4,199
1997	Höga Kusten	Sweden	3,970
2012	Aizhai	China	3,858
2014	Ulsan Grand	South Korea	3,773
2008	Huangpu	China	3,635
1988	Minami Bisan-Seto	Japan	3,609
1988	Fatih Sultan Mehmet (Bosphorus II)	Turkey	3,576
2010	Baling R.	China	3,570
2012	Taizhou Yangtze R.[1]	China	3,543
1973	Bosphorus	Turkey	3,524
1999	Kurushima III	Japan	3,379
1999	Kurushima II	Japan	3,346
1966	Ponte 25 de Abril, Tagus R.	Portugal	3,323
1964	Forth Road	Scotland	3,300

(1) Two consecutive main spans of 3,543 ft each.

Steel Arch

Year	Bridge	Location	Main span (ft)
2009	Chongqing Chaotianmen Yangtze R.	China	1,811
2003	Lupu	China	1,804
1932	Sydney Harbour	Australia	1,650
2005	Wushan Yangtze R.	China	1,614
2015	Chenab (rail)[1]	India	1,575
2007	Xinguang	China	1,404
2007	Caiyuanba	China	1,378
2008	Airport	Japan	1,247
2000	Yajisha	China	1,181
1962	Bridge of the Americas	Panama	1,128
1967	Zdakov	Czech Republic	1,083
1961	Runcorn-Widnes	England	1,082
1935	Birchenough	Zimbabwe	1,080

(1) When completed, it will be the world's highest arch bridge.

Year	Bridge	Location	Main span (ft)
	Concrete Arch		
1997	Wanxian	China	1,378
1980	Krk I	Croatia	1,280
1995	Jiangjiehe	China	1,083
1996	Yongjiang	China	1,024
1964	Gladesville	Australia	1,000
1965	Amizade	Brazil-Paraguay	951
2003	Infant Dom Henrique	Portugal	919
1984	Bloukrans	South Africa	892
1963	Arrábida	Portugal	886
1943	Sandö	Sweden	866
	Cantilever		
1890	Forth Rail[1]	Scotland	1,710
1974	Minato	Japan	1,673
1943	Howrah	India	1,500

(1) Two spans of 1,710 ft each.

Year	Bridge	Location	Main span (ft)
	Continuous Box/Plate Girder		
2006	Shibanpo	China	1,083
1998	Stolmasundet	Norway	988
1998	Raftsundet	Norway	978
1974	Pres. Costa e Silva (Rio-Niterói)	Brazil	984
1978	Neckar Valley Viaduct, Weitingen	Germany	863
1956	Branko's	Serbia	856
1966	Zoobrücke	Germany	850
	Cable-Stayed		
2012	Russky Island	Russia	3,622
2008	Sutong Yangtze R.	China	3,570
2009	Stonecutters	China	3,340
2009	Edong	China	3,038
1999	Tatara	Japan	2,920
1995	Pont de Normandie	France	2,808
2010	Jingyue Yangtze R.	China	2,677

Year	Bridge	Location	Main span (ft)
2009	Second Incheon	South Korea	2,625
2009	Shanghai Yangtze R.	China	2,395
2009	Minpu	China	2,323
2005	Third Nanjing Yangtze R.	China	2,126
2001	Second Nanjing Yangtze R.	China	2,060
2000	Third Wuhan Yangtze R. (Baishazhou)	China	2,028
2002	Qingzhou Minjiang R.	China	1,985
1993	Yangpu	China	1,975
1998	Meiko Chuo	Japan	1,936
1997	Xupu	China	1,936
2004	Rion-Antirion	Greece	1,837
1991	Skarnsundet	Norway	1,739
1999	Shantou Queshi	China	1,699
1995	Tsurumi Tsubasa	Japan	1,673
2008	Tianxingzhou Yangtze R.	China	1,654
2002	Jingsha	China	1,640
2000	Øresund	Denmark-Sweden	1,608
1991	Ikuchi	Japan	1,608
1994	Higashi Kobe	Japan	1,591
2011	Geo Geum	South Korea	1,575
1998	Zhanjiang	China	1,575
1997	Ting Kau	China	1,558
1999	Seohae Grand	South Korea	1,542
1989	Yokohama Bay	Japan	1,509
	Other Notable World Bridges[1]		
2011	Danyang-Kunshan Grand[2]	China	538,000
2011	Qingdao Jiaozhou Bay[3]	China	139,000
2007	Hangzhou Bay	China	118,000
1978	Demerara Harbour (floating)	Guyana	6,074
1994	Nordhordland (floating)	Norway	4,088

(1) Length listed is total length of bridge. (2) World's longest bridge. Carries Beijing-Shanghai high-speed rail. (3) World's longest transoceanic bridge.

World's Longest Railway Tunnels

Source: World Almanac research

Year is date of completion or projected completion. As of mid-2012.

Year	Tunnel	Location	Operating railway	Length (mi)
2016	Gotthard Base (twin)	Switzerland-Italy	Swiss Federal Railways (SBB)	35.4
1988	Seikan	Japan	Japan Railways Group	33.5
1994	English Channel (twin)	UK-France	Eurotunnel	31.1
2007	Lötschberg Base (twin)	Switzerland	BLS Lötschbergbahn AG	21.0
2007	Guadarrama (twin)	Spain	Renfe	17.6
2009	Taihang (twin)	China	China's Ministry of Railways	17.3
2005	Hakkoda	Japan	Japan Railways Group	16.4
2002	Iwate-Ichinohe	Japan	Japan Railways Group	16.0
2012-13	Pajares (twin)	Spain	Renfe	15.5
2014	Iiyama	Japan	Japan Railways Group	13.8
1982	Daishimizu	Japan	Japan Railways Group	13.8
2006	Wushaoling (twin)	China	China's Ministry of Railways	12.5
1906/22	Simplon No. 1 and 2	Switzerland-Italy	BLS Lötschbergbahn AG	12.3
1999	Vereina	Switzerland	Rhätische Bahn (RhB)	11.8
2007	High Speed 1 (CTRL, or Channel Tunnel Rail Link) (twin)	UK-France	London & Continental Railways (LCR)	11.8
1975	Shin-Kanmon (twin)	Japan	Japan Railways Group	11.6
1934	Apennine	Italy	Ferrovie dello Stato (FS)	11.5
2002	Qinling (twin)	China	China's Ministry of Railways	11.5
2006	Vaglia	Italy	Ferrovie dello Stato (FS)	10.4
2014	West Qinling (twin)	China	China's Ministry of Railways	10.3
1972	Rokko	Japan	Japan Railways Group	10.1
1982	Furka Base	Switzerland	Matterhorn Gotthard Railway	9.6
1982	Haruna	Japan	Japan Railways Group	9.6
2019	Ceneri Base (twin)	Switzerland	Swiss Federal Railways (SBB)	9.6

Underwater Vehicular Tunnels in North America

Source: World Almanac research

(more than 5,000 ft in length; year is date of completion)

Year	Name	Location	Waterway	Length (ft)
1950	Brooklyn Battery (twin)	New York, NY	East River	9,117
1927	Holland (twin)	New York, NY-Jersey City, NJ	Hudson River	8,558/8,371
1937/45/57	Lincoln (center/north/south tubes)	New York, NY-Weehawken, NJ	Hudson River	8,216/7,482/8,006
1985	Fort McHenry (twin)	Baltimore, MD	Patapsco River	7,920
1957/76	Hampton Roads (twin)	Hampton, VA	Hampton Roads	7,479
1957	Baltimore Harbor (twin)	Baltimore, MD	Baltimore Harbor	7,392
1940	Queens Midtown (twin)	New York, NY	East River	6,414
1934	Sumner	Boston, MA	Boston Harbor	5,653
1964	Thimble Shoal	Northampton Co., VA	Chesapeake Bay	5,552
1964	Chesapeake Channel	Northampton Co., VA	Chesapeake Bay	5,237
1930	Detroit-Windsor	Detroit, MI-Windsor, ON, Canada	Detroit River	5,160
1961	Callahan	Boston, MA	Boston Harbor	5,070

Land Vehicular Tunnels in the U.S.

Source: World Almanac research; Federal Highway Administration, U.S. Dept. of Transportation
(3,200 ft or more in length; as of mid-2012)

Name	Location	Length (ft)	Name	Location	Length (ft)
Anton Anderson Memorial[1]	Whittier, AK	13,300	Lehigh (twin)	PA Turnpike, NE Extension	4,461
Edwin Johnson Memorial (eastbound)	I-70, Clear Creek Co., CO	8,960	Cumberland Gap (twin)	U.S. 25E, KY-TN	4,600
Eisenhower Mem. (westbound)	I-70, Summit Co., CO	8,939	Blue Mountain (twin)	PA Turnpike	4,339
Ted Williams[2]	MA Turnpike, Boston, MA	8,448	Wawona	Yosemite Natl. Pk., CA	4,233
Thomas P. O'Neill Jr.	I-93, Boston, MA	7,920	Big Walker Mountain (twin)	Bland Co., VA	4,229
Allegheny (twin)	PA Turnpike	6,070	Squirrel Hill	Pittsburgh, PA	4,225
Liberty (twin)	Pittsburgh, PA	5,920	Hanging Lake (twin)	Glenwood Canyon, CO	4,000
Zion-Mount Carmel	Zion Natl. Park, UT	5,808	Caldecott (3 tubes)[3]	Oakland, CA	3,771/3,610/3,610
East River Mountain (twin)	I-77, Rocky Gap, VA-Bluefield, WV	5,412	Fort Pitt (twin)	Pittsburgh, PA	3,614
			Mount Baker	Seattle, WA	3,456
Tuscarora Mountain (twin)	PA Turnpike	5,326	Dingess	Mingo Co., WV	3,400
Tetsuo Harano (twin)	H-3 Freeway, HI	5,165	Mall	Washington, DC	3,400
Kittatinny Mountain (twin)	PA Turnpike	4,727	Cody	U.S. 14, 16, 20; WY	3,200

(1) Vehicles and trains take turns using the tunnel's one lane. (2) Total length of tunnel is 8,448 ft, 3,960 ft of which is underwater. (3) Construction began in 2010 on a fourth tube that will be 3,389 ft in length. The projected completion date is 2013-14.

Major U.S. Dams and Reservoirs

Source: 2010 National Inventory of Dams, U.S. Army Corps of Engineers

Highest U.S. Dams

Rank	Dam	River	State	Type	Height Feet	Height Meters	Year completed
1.	Oroville	Feather	California	E	770	235	1968
2.	Hoover	Colorado	Nevada	A-G	730	221	1935
3.	Dworshak	N. Fork Clearwater	Idaho	G	717	219	1973
4.	Glen Canyon	Colorado	Arizona	A	710	216	1963
5.	New Bullards Bar	North Yuba	California	A	645	197	1970
6.	New Melones	Stanislaus	California	E-R	625	191	1979
7.	Mossyrock	Cowlitz	Washington	A	606	185	1968
8.	Shasta	Sacramento	California	G	602	183	1945
9.	Don Pedro	Tuolumne	California	E	568	173	1971
10.	Hungry Horse	S. Fork Flathead	Montana	A	564	172	1952

A = Arch; E = Embankment, earthfill; R = Embankment, rockfill; G = Gravity. **Note:** The height of a dam is the distance between the lowest point on its crest and the original streambed. Tailings and other mining dams (i.e., dams built from the waste generated by mining operations) are not included in this list.

Largest U.S. Embankment Dams

Rank	Dam	River	State	Volume Cubic yards (thousands)	Volume Cubic meters (thousands)	Year completed
1.	Fort Peck	Missouri	Montana	125,628	96,049	1957
2.	Diamond Valley Lake	Domenigoni Valley Creek	California	110,551	84,523	2000
3.	Oahe	Missouri	South Dakota	92,000	70,339	1966
4.	Oroville	Feather	California	80,000	61,164	1968
5.	B. F. Sisk	San Luis Creek	California	77,664	59,378	1967
6.	Garrison	Missouri	North Dakota	66,500	50,843	1953
7.	Scotts Flat	Deer Creek	California	66,300	50,690	1948
8.	Cochiti	Rio Grande	New Mexico	65,000	49,696	1975
9.	Herbert Hoover	North New River Canal	Florida	54,700	41,821	1965
10.	Fort Randall	Missouri	South Dakota	50,200	38,381	1954

Note: An embankment dam is any dam constructed with material that has been excavated, including earth, rocks, and mining or other industrial waste. (In contrast, a gravity dam, arch dam, or buttress dam is generally made out of concrete or masonry.) The majority of the world's dams are embankment dams. All dams in this list are earthfill, or formed primarily out of layers of compacted earth.

Largest-Capacity U.S. Reservoirs

Rank	Dam	Reservoir	State	Max. reservoir capacity Acre feet (thousands)	Max. reservoir capacity Cubic meters (thousands)	Year completed
1.	Hoover	Lake Mead	Nevada	30,237	37,296,790	1935
2.	Glen Canyon	Lake Powell	Arizona	29,875	36,850,270	1963
3.	Garrison	Lake Sakakawea	North Dakota	24,500	30,220,305	1953
4.	Oahe	Lake Oahe	South Dakota	23,600	29,110,172	1966
5.	Fort Peck	Fort Peck Lake	Montana	19,100	23,559,503	1957
6.	Grand Coulee	Lake Roosevelt	Washington	9,562	11,794,553	1941
7.	Herbert Hoover	Lake Okeechobee	Florida	8,519	10,508,032	1965
8.	Sam Rayburn	Sam Rayburn Lake	Texas	6,520	8,042,302	1965
9.	Wright Patman	Wright Patman Lake	Texas	6,505	8,023,799	1954
10.	Fort Randall	Lake Francis Case	South Dakota	6,300	7,770,936	1954

Note: A reservoir is a body of water created by a dam for storage. This water may serve a single or multiple purposes, such as irrigation, flood reduction, and electricity generation.

Major Dams and Reservoirs of the World

Source: World Register of Dams, Intl. Commission on Large Dams (ICOLD)
Asterisk (*) designates structure is planned or under construction as of mid-2012.

World's Highest Dams

Rank	Dam	Country	Height above lowest formation Meters	Feet
1.	*Rogun	Tajikistan	335	1,099
2.	*Bakhtiyari	Iran	315	1,033
3.	Jinping	China	305	1,001
4.	Nurek	Tajikistan	300	984
5.	Xiaowan (Yunnan Gorge)	China	292	958
6.	Grand Dixence	Switzerland	285	935
7.	Xiluodu	China	278	912
8.	Inguri	Georgia	272	892
9.	Vajont	Italy	262	860
10.	Chicoasén	Mexico	261	856
11.	Alvaro Obregon	Mexico	260	853
	Tehri	India	260	853
13.	Mauvoisin	Switzerland	250	820
	Laxiwa	China	250	820
15.	Deriner	Turkey	249	817

World's Largest Embankment Dams

Rank	Dam	Country	Volume cubic meters (thousands)
1.	Tarbela	Pakistan	129,200
2.	Fort Peck	U.S.	96,049
3.	Diamond Valley Lake	U.S.	84,523
4.	Yacyreta	Argentina/Paraguay	81,000
5.	Tucurui	Brazil	80,865
6.	Ataturk	Turkey	84,500
7.	*Rogun	Tajikistan	75,500
8.	Guri	Venezuela	70,000
9.	Parambikulam	India	69,165
10.	High Island West	China	67,000
11.	Gardiner	Canada	65,440
12.	Mangla	Pakistan	64,991
13.	Afsluitdijk	Netherlands	63,400
14.	Oroville	U.S.	61,164
15.	B. F. Sisk	U.S.	59,378

World's Largest-Capacity Reservoirs

Rank	Dam	Country	Max. capacity cubic meters (millions)
1.	Kariba	Zimbabwe/Zambia	180,600
2.	Bratsk	Russia	169,000
3.	High Aswan	Egypt	162,000
4.	Kpong	Ghana	150,000
	Akosombo (Lake Volta)	Ghana	150,000
6.	Daniel-Johnson	Canada	141,851
7.	W. A. C. Bennett	Canada	74,300
8.	Krasnoyarsk	Russia	73,300
9.	Zeya	Russia	68,400
10.	Lajeado	Brazil	64,530
11.	Robert-Bourassa (La Grande 2)	Canada	61,715
12.	La Grande 3	Canada	60,020
13.	Ust-Ilim	Russia	59,300
14.	*Boguchany	Russia	58,200
15.	Kuibyshev	Russia	58,000

World's Largest-Capacity Hydro Plants

Rank	Dam	Country	Rated capacity planned (MW)
1.	San Xia (Three Gorges Dam)	China	18,200
2.	Wangjiahe	China	12,630
3.	Xiluodu	China	12,600
	Itaipu	Brazil/Paraguay	12,600
5.	Guri (Raúl Leoni)	Venezuela	10,000
6.	Tucuruí	Brazil	8,370
7.	Grand Coulee	U.S.	6,809
8.	Sayano-Shushenskaya	Russia	6,400
	Qilinguan	China	6,400
10.	Krasnoyarsk	Russia	6,000
	Xiangjiaba	China	6,000
12.	Robert-Bourassa	Canada	5,616
13.	Longtan (Guangxi, Tian'e)	China	5,400
14.	Fengyan	China	5,200
15.	Bratsk	Russia	4,500

Timeline of Selected Architectural Styles and Structures

Asterisk (*) denotes part of a UNESCO World Heritage site.

Style and period	Location; characteristics; significant examples
Mesopotamian c. 3500-539 BCE	City-states of Sumer, Akkad, Babylon, Assyria (modern-day Iraq). Mud-brick rectangular temples on oval platforms with simple corbel vaults, later ziggurats. Painted terra-cotta mosaics and murals; carved reliefs on columns and walls. **Ziggurat of Nanna**, Ur (Muqayyar, Iraq), ordered by Ur-Nammu, c. 2100 BCE **Anu Ziggurat and White Temple**, Uruk (Warka, Iraq), c. 3000 BCE
Egyptian c. 3000-30 BCE	Along Nile R. Mud-brick and limestone tombs and massive, geometric pyramids, post-and-lintel construction. Highly decorative with colorful hieroglyphics, carvings, columns, obelisks, paintings, and sculpture. ***Stepped Pyramid of Pharaoh Zoser** (Saqqara), by Imhotep, c. 2737-2717 BCE ***Great Pyramid of Khufu** (Giza), c. 2250 BCE ***Great Temple of Amon-Ra** (Karnak), c. 1530-300 BCE ***Mortuary Temple of Queen Hatshepsut**, Deir el Bahari (Thebes), by Senenmut, c. 1479-1458 BCE
Three Dynasties c. 2100-221 BCE	China. Single-level mud-brick or mud-smeared timber structures on earthen platforms with thatched roofs. Later, bracketed wooden-framed structures with brick-tiled floors, roofs with overhanging eaves. **City of Erlitou** (Yanshi, China), c. 1900-1500 BCE
Minoan c. 1800-1450 BCE	Crete. Palaces, tombs in monumental style adapted from Mesopotamia and Egypt. Multilevel stone palaces with large central court, no fortifications. Walls made of doors (*polythyron*); stone porticoes and lintels; wooden ceilings and columns; beehive-shaped tombs (*tholi*). **Palace at Knossos** (Heraklion, Crete, Greece), c. 1700 BCE
Mycenaean c. 1600-1100 BCE	Greece. Adapted Minoan style, with large stone masonry, huge walls, and fortified citadels with complex palaces (*megaron*). ***Treasury of Atreus** (Mycenae, Greece), c. 1250 BCE
Olmec c. 1200-400 BCE	Mexico Gulf Coast. Many religious structures, including stone temple-pyramids centered in cities; also large stone sculptures and mosaic pavement with natural and animistic themes. **Great Pyramid** (La Venta, Mexico), c. 800-400 BCE
Mayan c. 900 BCE-900 CE	Central America. Religious structures with plaster-surfaced stone temple-pyramids with stairs containing tombs. Decorative animistic and geometric relief sculptures, lintels, and stone monuments with hieroglyphics. ***Pyramid of the Magician** (Uxmal, Mexico), c. 700-910 CE **North Acropolis** (Tikal, Guatemala), c. 200 BCE

Style and period	Location; characteristics; significant examples
Greek c. 750-323 BCE	Greek peninsula, Asia Minor, North Africa, western Mediterranean. Religious, civic buildings in monumental style, inspired by Egypt, based on strict rules of form and human proportion; many ornamental details. Marble and limestone structures (including rectangular temples) with pediment, colonnaded porticos in diverse regional styles, defined by "orders" of architecture like Ionic, Doric, Corinthian. Most early buildings with timber supports; solid stone in later temples. 　　***Parthenon, Acropolis** (Athens, Greece), by Ictinus and Callicrates, 447-436 BCE 　　***Temple of Zeus** (Olympia, Greece), by Libon of Elis, mid-5th cent. BCE 　　**Mausoleum of Halicarnassus** (Bodrum, Turkey), by Pythis, c. 353 BCE (destroyed) 　　***Temple of Apollo Epicurius** (Bassae, Greece), by Ictinus, c. 420 BCE
Achaemenid c. 550-334 BCE	Persian Empire (Eastern Mediterranean to Indus R.). Palatial complexes influenced by cultures absorbed by the empire; limestone and mud brick complexes on raised stone terraces with ornamental stairways, rectangular pillared audience halls with porticoes and corner towers; pleasure gardens (*bâgh*) as focal point of architecture. 　　***Pasargadae** (Iran), founded by Cyrus II, after 547 BCE 　　***Persepolis** (Iran), founded by Darius I, around 518 BCE
Roman c. 500 BCE-400 CE	Roman Empire. Civic and religious structures with grandiose limestone brick and concrete construction in systematic, practical layout. Adapted Greek orders in many structures, including circular temples and large covered halls (basilica), but emphasized movement with rounded arches and domes, geometric vaults. 　　***Pantheon** (Rome, Italy), ordered by Emperor Hadrian, 118-128 CE 　　***Colosseum** (Rome, Italy), ordered by Emperor Vespasian, 70-82 CE 　　***Roman Forum** (Rome, Italy), 500s BCE-608 CE
Qin and Han c. 221 BCE-220 CE	China. Massive public works, palaces, tombs, and planned cities; systematic layout and design determined by divination techniques (geomancy). Multistoried timber palace complexes with gardens, courtyards laid along a long hall with a south-north axis for weather; decorative roof with overhanging eaves. 　　***The Great Wall** (China), ordered by Qin Shi Huang, 220 BCE-c. 1600 CE 　　***Mausoleum of the First Qin Emperor** (Xianyang [Xi'an], China), c. 210 BCE
Sassanian 226-651 CE	Iran. Mud-brick, mortared rubble, and stone palaces on platforms. Tall, vaulted entry chambers with one open side (*iwans*). Three-aisled hall chambers covered with rudimentary barrel vaults. Parabolic domes abandoned for square courtyards in later Sassanian period. 　　**Palace of Ardashir I** (Firuzabad, Iran), c. 224 　　**Taq-i Kisra** [Arch of Khosrau] (Ctesiphon, Iraq), c. 260 or c. 550
Byzantine 330-1453	Byzantine Empire, Italy, Russia. Religious structures with masonry construction based on Roman architecture, many salvaged pieces. Centralized cross-in-square layout, with large central dome supported by vaults. Highly decorative, with iconographic frescoes, glass mosaics. 　　***Hagia Sophia** (Istanbul, Turkey), by Anthemius and Isidorous, 532-37 　　***St. Mark's Basilica** (Venice, Italy), ordered by Domenico Contarini, 1063-94
Sui and Tang 581-906	China. Includes influences from other cultures; geomancy used to enhance harmony and social status. Rectangular, multistory modular timber structures with interlinking corridors; single-eaved roofs with exposed beams. 　　**Daming Palace** (Xi'an, China), 634 (destroyed) 　　***Hall of the Great Buddha**, Foguang Temple (Mount Wutai), ordered rebuilt by Xuan Zhong, 857
Early Islamic (Umayyad) 692-c. 1000	Syria, Middle East, North Africa, southern Spain. Mosques in adapted Sassanian style. Austere exteriors; simple columned halls with minarets and mihrab, walled courtyards and gardens, onion domes. Highly decorative interiors with patterned marble, mosaics. 　　**Dome of the Rock** [Qubbat al-Sakhra] (Jerusalem), ordered by Abd al-Malik, 692 　　***Great Mosque of Córdoba** (Spain), ordered by Abd al-Rahman I, 784-86
Khmer c. 880-1200s	Indochina. Hindu or Buddhist temple complexes, including brick, later sandstone beehive-shaped shrines with arches atop terraced temple "mountains" symbolizing Mount Meru, Hindu and Buddhist "Mountain of the Gods." Concentric layout of structures mimics the cosmos, relating religious narrative in carved reliefs. 　　***Angkor Wat** (Cambodia), ordered by Suryavarman II, 12th cent.
Romanesque (Norman) c. 900s-1100s	Western Europe. Churches and monasteries in localized Roman style; many reused material from Roman structures. Austere, heavy, simple masonry construction with thick walls, concealed buttresses, small windows, barrel arches, and vaults. Churches like Roman basilica with arched central nave, lower side aisles, apse, transept formed Latin cross. Monumental art and ornaments with Christian narrative throughout, especially on façade and portals. 　　***Durham Cathedral** (England, UK), ordered by Bishop William de Saint-Calais, 1093-1133 　　***Cathedral, Baptistery, and "Leaning" Tower** (Pisa, Italy), by various architects, begun in 1063, tower not completed until 1372
Gothic c. 1100s-1500s	France, Europe. Cathedrals meant to inspire spirituality with design like Roman basilica: pointed arches and spires that reach toward heavens, skeletal masonry, revealed structure like flying buttresses, ribbed vaults to allow better lighting, large stained-glass windows. 　　**Abbey Church of Saint-Denis** (France), ordered by Abbot Suger, 1136-47 　　***Cathedral of Notre-Dame** (Paris, France), ordered by Bishop Maurice de Sully, 1163-1351 　　***Chartres Cathedral** (France), 1194-1260 　　***Cologne Cathedral** (Cologne, Germany), ordered by Archbishop Konrad von Hochstaden, 1248-1880 　　***St. Vitus Cathedral** (Prague, Czech Republic), by Matthias of Arras, later Peter Parler, 1344-1929
Yüan and Ming 1279-1644	China. Mongol-influenced timber and some brick structures influenced by geomancy. Emphasized monumental mass in low-lying, sprawling structures with simple rectangular pavilions, great halls, elaborate wooden latticework, carved and painted details. 　　***Forbidden City** (Beijing, China), ordered by Emperor Yung Lo, 1406-20
Renaissance 1420s-1520s	Italy. The rebirth or rediscovery of ancient Roman design, grounded in a scholarly approach to architecture. Followed rules of proportion in perspective and symmetry, classical orders, and simple but perfected geometric forms; emphasis on human scale. 　　***Pazzi Chapel** (Florence, Italy), by Filippo Brunelleschi, 1429-61 　　***Palazzo Medici-Riccardi** (Florence, Italy), by Michelozzo di Bartolomeo, 1444-60 　　***Tempietto San Pietro** (Rome, Italy), by Donato Bramante, 1502-10 　　**Villa Almerico Capra "La Rotonda"** (near Vicenza, Italy), by Andrea Palladio, later Vincenzo Scamozzi, 1566-1610

Style and period	Location; characteristics; significant examples
Mughal 1526-1858	India. Monumental palaces and mosques blending Hindu and Islamic architecture. Sandstone with marble inlay; highly decorative, with semiprecious stones, vegetal and Koranic motifs. Formulaic four-part pleasure gardens (*charbâgh*), exemplified by grounds of Taj Mahal. ***Humayun Tomb** (Delhi, India), by Sayyid Muhammad, 1562-72 ***Taj Mahal** (Agra, India), ordered by Emperor Shah Jahan, 1631-48
Baroque 1630s-1700s	Italy, later Western Europe. Elaborate and theatrical religious and civic structures, focused on dramatic overall effect. Complex geometric shapes and elaborate sculptures meant to be viewed from many angles. **St. Carlo alle Quattro Fontane** (Rome, Italy), by Francesco Borromini, 1638-41 ***Palace of Versailles** (Versailles, France), royal hunting lodge (built 1631-34) expanded under Louis XIV, 1661-1710 **Church of San Lorenzo** (Turin, Italy), by Guarino Guarini, 1666-79 **Church of St. John of Nepomuk "Asamkirche"** (Munich, Germany), by Cosmas Damian and Egid Quirin Asam, 1733-46
Rococo 1690s-1700s	Europe. Mostly interior, simplified but still fanciful Baroque designs; ornate with natural motifs, gold trim, light and creamy colors, asymmetrical designs, and unusual materials. ***Sanssouci Palace** (Potsdam, Germany), by Georg Wenzeslaus von Knobelsdorff, 1745-47
Neoclassicism 1750-1830	Europe, Americas. Civic, commercial, and religious structures; chaste, non-decorative designs in reaction to Baroque excess. Grounded in Enlightenment-era principles and simple, strict adherence to classic (Greek, Roman, Renaissance) forms and details. Palladian style in England, Federal style in U.S. **Chiswick House** (Chiswick, England, UK), by Richard Boyle, 1725-29 ***Monticello** (Charlottesville, VA), by Thomas Jefferson, 1768-1809
Neo-Gothic 1837-1900s	Britain and U.S. Civic, commercial, and religious structures utilizing Gothic forms in new commercial enterprises like railway stations and hotels. Traditional masonry façade disguised modern structural material like iron and glass. ***Westminster Palace** (London, England, UK), by Charles Barry and A.W.N. Pugin, 1840-47 **Hotel fronting St. Pancras Railway Station** (London, England, UK), by George Gilbert Scott, 1865-71
Arts and Crafts 1850s-1930s	England and U.S. Residential structures made of brick and other indigenous materials with pastoral and traditional elements like gabled roofs. Conceived as a reaction against homogenization of style following the Industrial Revolution. **Red House** (Bexley Heath, England, UK), by Philip Webb, 1859 **Tigbourne Court** (Surrey, England, UK), by Edwin Lutyens, 1898
Beaux-Arts 1870s-1930s	France, U.S. Grandiose, highly decorative style, using a mix of classical forms taught at the École des Beaux-Arts (School of Fine Arts) in Paris: columns, wall projections, elaborate rooftops, high-relief decoration. **Boston Public Library** (Boston, MA), by McKim, Mead, and White, 1888-95 **Grand Central Terminal** (New York, NY), Reed & Stem and Warren & Wetmore, 1903-13
Art Nouveau 1884-1905	Europe (esp. Brussels, Belgium, France). Civic and residential structures using industrial products like metal and glass to mimic natural forms; airy, fluid, and ornate. **Hôtel Tassel** (Brussels, Belgium), by Victor Horta, 1892-93 **Entrances to Métro (subway)** (Paris, France), by Hector Guimard, 1900
Prairie 1893-1917	U.S. Mostly residences, some civic buildings in adapted Arts and Crafts style. Inspired by American Midwest and small-town values. Frank Lloyd Wright most notable architect of the style. Buildings centered on chimney, with overhanging eaves and horizontal emphasis, long bands of windows. **Robie House** (Chicago, IL), by Frank Lloyd Wright, 1908-10 **National Farmer's Bank** (Owatonna, MN), by Louis Sullivan, 1906-08
Futurism 1913-14	Italy. Purely theoretical style that produced no actual structures. Emphasized concrete, glass, and steel construction; pure geometric forms and straight lines; and exposed structure and utilities. **La Citta Nuova** (sketches), by Antonio Sant'Elia, 1913
Constructivism 1914-20s	Russia, Europe. Public buildings based on socialist philosophies. Purely utilitarian industrial design, modern materials. **Rusakov Club** (Moscow, Russia), by Konstantin Melnikov, 1927-28
De Stijl 1917-31	Netherlands. Building and fixtures designed as a complete, sculpture-like piece of art; emphasis on primary colors, simple but asymmetrical geometry. Name is Dutch for "The Style." **Schröder House** (Utrecht, Netherlands), by Gerrit Thomas Rietveld, 1923-24
Bauhaus 1919-33	Weimar Republic Germany. Art and design school founded by Walter Gropius with philosophy that the machine is the modern medium. Concrete, glass, and steel construction that united industrial crafts and fine arts with simple geometric forms and colors. **Bauhaus** (Dessau, Germany), by Walter Gropius, 1925-26
International Style 1920s-70s	Asia, Europe, North America. Reinforced concrete and steel structures, mostly commercial buildings with some residences and civic structures. Post-and-slab construction meant walls no longer supported weight so façades could be continuous strip (ribbon) glass "curtain-walls" with modular interiors. Emphasis on simple forms; glass, marble, and stainless steel; minimal decoration. **Philadelphia Savings Fund Society Building** (Philadelphia, PA), by George Howe and William Lescaze, 1926-32 **Villa Savoye** (Poissy, France), by Le Corbusier, 1928-31 **Seagram Building** (New York, NY), by Ludwig Mies Van Der Rohe with Philip Johnson, 1954-58
Art Deco 1925-30s	Europe, U.S. Traditional, symmetric, elegant construction like Beaux-Arts whimsically mixed with modern styles like geometric forms and steel or chrome features. **Chrysler Building** (New York, NY), by William van Alen, 1928-30 **Empire State Building** (New York, NY), by Shreve, Lamb, & Harmon, 1930-31
Postmodernism 1970s-present	Asia, Europe, North America. Playful reaction against generic, mainstream "orthodox modern architecture," according to Robert Venturi. Token references to traditional architectural elements like pediments or gables on houses; aim to present, Venturi wrote, "old clichés in new settings." **Vanna Venturi House** (Philadelphia, PA), by Robert Venturi, 1962 **Public Service Building** (Portland, OR), by Michael Graves, 1980-83

INTERNATIONAL STATISTICS

World Population Growth

Although the population of the world in ancient times can only be very roughly estimated, there were perhaps 50 mil people in the world in 1000 BCE. The United Nations (UN) Population Division estimates a figure of 300 mil for 1 CE. This diagram shows estimated population growth since then.

While figures for other centuries vary, sources agree that the world's population began growing more rapidly in the 18th and 19th centuries and increased at an even greater rate in the 20th century. According to the UN, the total population reached 1 bil in 1804; rose to 2 bil 123 years later, in 1927; to 3 bil 33 years after that, in 1960; to 4 bil in 1974; to 5 bil in 1987; and to 6 bil in 1999. The U.S. Census Bureau put the world population in mid-2012 at about 7.02 bil.

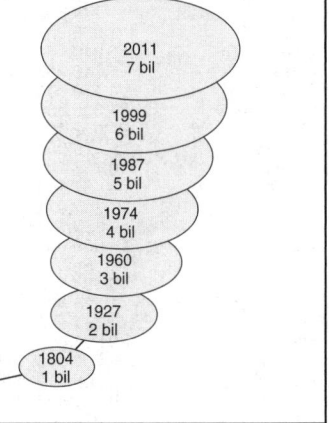

Area and Population of the World by Continent/Region

Source: International Data Base, International Programs Center, U.S. Census Bureau, U.S. Dept. of Commerce; *The World Factbook*, Central Intelligence Agency (CIA)

Composition of geographical (continental) regions are as defined by the United Nations. Land area figures are from *The World Factbook*. Figures may not add up to totals due to rounding.

Continent/region	Land area (sq km)	Land area (sq mi)	% of Earth's land	Population (midyear) 1950	1975	2000	2012	% of world total, 2012	2025[1]
Asia.........	31,119,378	12,015,259	21.3	1,437,565,483	2,413,261,390	3,693,908,399	4,223,612,969	60.2	4,713,703,396
Africa.......	29,771,296	11,494,762	20.4	229,058,740	416,194,561	803,586,680	1,073,487,254	15.3	1,429,328,419
Europe[2]......	22,168,368	8,559,255	15.2	547,140,324	678,635,710	730,597,984	740,028,188	10.5	742,526,332
Northern America.....	20,407,482	7,879,373	14.0	165,945,185	238,783,486	313,388,332	348,280,154	5.0	389,046,607
Latin America and the Caribbean...	20,104,280	7,762,306	13.8	165,442,794	320,629,690	517,908,376	596,305,336	8.5	668,600,120
Oceania	8,490,744	3,278,295	5.8	12,476,128	21,114,852	30,420,890	35,830,063	0.5	41,266,804
Antarctica[3]	14,000,000	5,405,430	9.6	NA	NA	NA	NA	NA	NA
World	146,061,548	56,394,679	100.0	2,557,628,654	4,088,619,689	6,089,810,661	7,017,543,964	100.0	7,984,471,678

NA = Not applicable. (1) Projected. (2) Includes all of Russia. (3) Antarctica has no indigenous inhabitants; researchers stay for various periods of time.

Current Population and Projections for Countries and Other Areas

Source: International Data Base, International Programs Center, U.S. Census Bureau, U.S. Dept. of Commerce; *The World Factbook*, Central Intelligence Agency (CIA)

(midyear figures)

Country/area	2012	2025	2050
Afghanistan	30,419,928	41,117,073	63,795,418
Albania	3,002,859	3,104,932	2,824,012
Algeria	37,367,226	45,841,317	55,444,735
American Samoa	54,947	53,316	49,308
Andorra	85,082	85,112	74,765
Angola	18,056,072	25,673,282	45,888,061
Anguilla	15,423	19,749	26,980
Antigua and Barbuda	89,018	103,830	122,930
Argentina	42,192,494	47,164,630	53,511,279
Armenia	2,970,495	3,044,164	2,943,441
Aruba	107,635	126,130	150,730
Australia	22,015,576	25,053,669	29,012,740
Austria	8,219,743	8,189,560	7,520,950
Azerbaijan	9,493,600	10,533,598	11,209,644
Bahamas, The	316,182	349,116	371,219
Bahrain	1,248,348	1,579,899	1,847,072
Bangladesh	161,083,804	197,673,655	250,155,274
Barbados	287,733	297,015	282,041
Belarus	9,643,566	9,325,020	8,339,664
Belgium	10,438,353	10,453,261	9,882,599
Belize	327,719	411,007	543,690
Benin	9,598,787	13,564,964	22,118,545
Bermuda	69,080	72,851	69,874
Bhutan	716,896	820,143	951,873
Bolivia	10,290,003	12,463,434	16,003,638
Bosnia and Herzegovina	3,879,296	3,787,402	3,216,039
Botswana	2,098,018	2,425,114	2,871,345
Brazil	199,321,413	218,259,140	232,304,177
Brunei	408,786	498,756	638,157
Bulgaria	7,037,935	6,257,716	4,651,477
Burkina Faso	17,275,115	25,384,628	47,429,509
Burundi	10,557,259	15,464,910	27,148,888
Cambodia	14,952,665	18,037,946	22,338,891
Cameroon	20,129,878	25,522,447	34,908,839
Canada	34,300,083	37,558,781	41,135,648
Cape Verde	523,568	619,168	741,842
Cayman Islands	52,560	67,661	91,118
Central African Republic	5,057,208	6,637,613	10,338,863
Chad	10,975,648	13,914,726	20,473,601
Chile	17,067,369	18,764,737	19,688,474
China[1]	1,343,239,923	1,394,638,699	1,303,723,332
Colombia	45,239,079	51,194,904	56,227,630
Comoros	737,284	905,545	1,169,893
Congo, Dem. Rep. of	73,599,190	99,162,003	144,805,434
Congo Republic	4,366,266	6,161,500	9,598,623
Cook Islands	10,777	7,621	5,460
Costa Rica	4,636,348	5,353,218	6,065,989
Côte d'Ivoire	21,952,093	NA	NA
Croatia	4,480,043	4,374,007	3,864,201
Cuba	11,075,244	10,784,894	9,161,479
Curaçao	145,834	153,501	150,128
Cyprus	1,138,071	1,329,908	1,392,078
Czech Republic	10,177,300	9,844,275	8,540,221
Denmark	5,543,453	5,697,913	5,575,147
Djibouti	774,389	1,016,919	1,395,810
Dominica	73,126	74,374	64,772
Dominican Republic	10,088,598	11,702,846	13,690,264
Ecuador	15,223,680	17,867,616	21,102,550
Egypt	83,688,164	103,742,157	137,872,522
El Salvador	6,090,646	6,288,430	6,181,181
Equatorial Guinea	685,991	935,553	1,428,139
Eritrea	6,086,495	7,987,458	11,381,250
Estonia	1,274,709	1,149,245	861,913
Ethiopia	91,195,675	131,260,566	228,066,276
Faroe Islands	49,483	53,200	57,112
Fiji	890,057	956,003	1,013,636
Finland	5,262,930	5,251,272	4,819,615
France	65,630,692	68,860,292	69,484,481

Country/area	2012	2025	2050
French Polynesia	274,512	305,484	324,712
Gabon	1,608,321	2,063,339	3,229,741
Gambia, The	1,840,454	2,369,298	3,210,223
Gaza Strip	1,710,257	2,350,255	3,392,849
Georgia	4,570,934	4,341,061	3,784,724
Germany	81,305,856	79,226,209	71,541,906
Ghana	24,652,402	32,610,058	52,415,526
Gibraltar	29,034	29,753	28,423
Greece	10,767,827	10,670,697	10,035,935
Greenland	57,695	57,174	49,356
Grenada	109,011	114,741	114,205
Guam	159,914	176,770	201,610
Guatemala	14,099,032	17,564,073	22,995,434
Guernsey	65,345	67,710	66,521
Guinea	10,884,958	15,240,839	26,407,254
Guinea-Bissau	1,628,603	2,061,262	2,894,545
Guyana	741,908	786,286	888,494
Haiti	9,801,664	11,252,370	13,352,710
Honduras	8,296,693	10,143,828	12,948,839
Hong Kong	7,153,519	7,354,531	6,172,725
Hungary	9,958,453	9,615,020	8,489,811
Iceland	313,183	337,632	350,922
India	1,205,073,612	1,396,046,308	1,656,553,632
Indonesia	248,645,008	276,746,433	300,183,166
Iran	78,868,711	90,481,226	100,044,564
Iraq	31,129,225	40,387,147	56,316,329
Ireland	4,722,028	5,417,947	6,333,836
Isle of Man	85,421	92,606	92,840
Israel	7,590,758	8,984,285	10,828,462
Italy	61,261,254	62,591,055	61,415,852
Jamaica	2,889,187	3,151,611	3,554,571
Japan	127,368,088	123,385,521	107,209,536
Jersey	94,949	104,140	107,581
Jordan	6,508,887	7,945,150	11,243,177
Kazakhstan	17,522,010	19,809,426	22,237,156
Kenya	43,013,341	53,196,255	70,755,460
Kiribati	101,998	117,779	139,738
Korea, North	24,589,122	26,242,210	26,969,396
Korea, South	48,860,500	49,372,307	43,368,983
Kosovo	1,836,529	1,999,461	2,222,619
Kuwait	2,646,314	3,169,497	3,863,453
Kyrgyzstan	5,496,737	6,218,713	7,063,351
Laos	6,586,266	7,971,675	10,068,995
Latvia	2,191,580	1,992,516	1,544,073
Lebanon	4,140,289	4,307,087	4,155,101
Lesotho	1,930,493	1,970,540	1,920,225
Liberia	3,887,886	5,283,774	8,192,118
Libya	5,613,380	7,374,566	8,970,664
Liechtenstein	36,713	40,505	43,610
Lithuania	3,525,761	3,355,985	2,787,516
Luxembourg	509,074	586,296	720,603
Macao	578,025	630,434	620,184
Macedonia	2,082,370	2,119,511	1,990,728
Madagascar	22,005,222	30,182,920	45,807,534
Malawi	16,323,044	22,859,677	37,406,745
Malaysia	29,179,952	34,683,300	42,928,546
Maldives	394,451	388,681	444,429
Mali	15,494,466	22,533,811	38,395,414
Malta	409,836	421,239	395,639
Marshall Islands	68,480	83,203	103,092
Mauritania	3,359,185	4,425,089	6,536,272
Mauritius	1,313,095	1,412,384	1,441,100
Mexico	114,975,406	130,198,692	147,907,650
Micronesia	106,487	98,948	74,483
Moldova	3,656,843	3,176,863	2,261,208
Monaco	30,510	31,706	29,810
Mongolia	3,179,997	3,725,352	4,340,496
Montenegro	657,394	635,537	577,654
Montserrat	5,164	5,529	5,707
Morocco	32,309,239	36,484,418	42,026,448
Mozambique	23,515,934	32,306,018	58,998,457
Myanmar (Burma)	54,584,650	61,747,758	70,673,160
Namibia	2,165,828	2,283,845	2,149,815
Nauru	9,378	10,008	11,995
Nepal	29,890,686	36,622,606	45,984,605
Netherlands	16,730,632	17,572,113	17,906,594
New Caledonia	260,166	307,452	370,511
New Zealand	4,327,944	4,775,930	5,198,992
Nicaragua	5,727,707	6,493,913	7,233,620
Niger	16,344,687	24,618,828	44,221,854
Nigeria	170,123,740	234,362,895	402,425,535
Northern Mariana Islands	51,395	61,985	77,842
Norway	4,707,270	4,916,787	4,966,385
Oman	3,090,150	3,981,057	5,401,957
Pakistan	190,291,129	228,385,138	290,847,790

Country/area	2012	2025	2050
Palau	21,032	22,102	22,894
Panama	3,510,045	4,117,882	4,859,334
Papua New Guinea	6,310,129	7,823,210	10,110,027
Paraguay	6,541,591	7,602,853	8,840,105
Peru	29,549,517	33,283,408	36,943,693
Philippines	103,775,002	128,921,424	171,964,187
Poland	38,415,284	37,349,696	32,084,570
Portugal	10,781,459	10,806,202	9,933,334
Puerto Rico	3,690,923	3,388,348	2,342,328
Qatar	1,951,591	2,562,764	2,558,854
Romania	21,848,504	20,872,127	18,060,354
Russia	142,517,670	140,139,049	129,908,086
Rwanda	11,689,696	16,080,729	27,506,207
Saint Barthélemy	7,332	7,056	6,527
Saint Helena	7,728	7,888	7,296
Saint Kitts and Nevis	50,726	55,405	56,362
Saint Lucia	162,178	168,519	162,356
Saint Martin	30,959	33,048	34,601
Saint Pierre and Miquelon	5,831	5,030	3,516
Saint Vincent and the Grenadines	103,537	100,409	93,507
Samoa	194,320	210,369	245,010
San Marino	32,140	35,203	35,178
São Tomé and Príncipe	183,176	227,395	309,457
Saudi Arabia	26,534,504	31,877,311	40,250,628
Senegal	12,969,606	17,580,816	27,244,158
Serbia	7,276,604	6,845,638	5,869,146
Seychelles	90,024	98,843	100,391
Sierra Leone	5,485,998	7,500,140	13,593,862
Singapore	5,353,494	6,732,999	8,609,518
Sint Maarten	39,088	46,560	53,001
Slovakia	5,483,088	5,458,581	4,943,616
Slovenia	1,996,617	1,907,560	1,596,947
Solomon Islands	584,578	747,001	1,015,731
Somalia	10,085,638	13,274,251	22,626,120
South Africa	48,810,427	48,714,478	49,400,628
South Sudan	10,625,176	16,615,122	26,843,710
Spain	47,042,984	51,415,437	52,490,040
Sri Lanka	21,481,334	23,563,343	25,166,733
Sudan	34,206,710	42,733,103	59,129,521
Suriname	560,157	636,782	717,936
Swaziland	1,386,914	1,585,439	1,834,151
Sweden	9,103,788	9,315,507	9,084,788
Switzerland	7,925,517	8,665,531	9,539,097
Syria	22,530,746	26,536,400	33,657,629
Taiwan	23,234,936	23,642,264	20,834,040
Tajikistan	7,768,385	9,510,130	12,132,365
Tanzania	46,912,768	66,904,889	118,586,412
Thailand	67,091,089	70,643,689	69,611,256
Timor-Leste	1,143,667	1,539,173	2,191,749
Togo	6,961,049	9,741,450	16,583,950
Tonga	106,146	104,648	78,995
Trinidad and Tobago	1,226,383	1,183,838	1,023,741
Tunisia	10,732,900	11,849,537	12,180,271
Turkey	79,749,461	90,498,016	100,955,188
Turkmenistan	5,054,828	5,800,391	6,607,083
Turks and Caicos Islands	46,335	61,293	84,240
Tuvalu	10,619	11,819	13,423
Uganda	33,640,833	50,692,201	93,476,229
Ukraine	44,854,065	41,037,583	33,573,842
United Arab Emirates	5,314,317	7,063,346	8,018,904
United Kingdom	63,047,162	67,243,723	71,153,797
United States	313,847,465	351,352,771	422,554,384
Uruguay	3,316,328	3,431,610	3,495,238
Uzbekistan	28,394,180	31,823,964	35,116,374
Vanuatu	256,155	323,464	432,658
Vatican City	836	NA	NA
Venezuela	28,047,938	33,188,608	40,255,592
Vietnam	91,519,289	102,458,828	111,173,583
Virgin Islands, British	31,148	41,324	59,618
Virgin Islands, U.S.	105,275	95,902	68,933
Wallis and Futuna	15,453	16,023	15,598
West Bank	2,622,544	3,328,248	4,376,251
Western Sahara	522,928	735,697	1,173,350
Yemen	24,771,809	32,650,107	45,780,651
Zambia	13,817,479	20,104,997	38,992,619
Zimbabwe	12,619,600	17,370,260	25,198,196
World[2]	7,017,544,800	7,984,471,678	9,383,147,855

NA = Not available. (1) Not including the populations of Hong Kong and Macao, listed separately in this table. (2) Total projected populations do not include countries for which populations are not available.

Population of the World's Largest Urban Areas

Source: *World Population Prospects* and *World Urbanization Prospects*, Dept. of Economic and Social Affairs, UN Population Division

Population figures are midyear estimates for urban agglomerations, i.e., whole metropolitan areas comprising an urban center and surrounding settlements of lower density. The UN releases an update every two years. Population counts for 2025 are projections. Data may differ from figures elsewhere in *The World Almanac*.

(ranked by mid-2011 population)

Rank	Urban area, country	Population (thous.)				Rate of change (%)			Pop. of urban area as % of country's
		1975	2000	2011	2025	1975-2000	2000-11	2011-25	2011 pop.
1.	Tokyo, Japan	26,614.7	34,449.9	37,217.4	38,661.4	29.4%	8.0%	3.9%	29.2%
2.	Delhi, India	4,426.0	15,732.3	22,653.6	32,935.0	255.5	44.0	45.4	1.9
3.	Mexico City, Mexico	10,689.7	18,021.6	20,445.8	24,580.9	68.6	13.5	20.2	18.0
4.	New York-Newark, NY-NJ, U.S.	15,880.3	17,845.9	20,351.7	23,572.2	12.4	14.0	15.8	6.5
5.	Shanghai, China	5,626.6	13,959.0	20,207.6	28,403.9	148.1	44.8	40.6	1.5
6.	São Paulo, Brazil	9,614.0	17,099.2	19,924.5	23,174.7	77.9	16.5	16.3	10.1
7.	Mumbai (Bombay), India	7,082.0	16,366.8	19,743.6	26,556.9	131.1	20.6	34.5	1.7
8.	Beijing, China	4,827.9	10,162.4	15,594.4	22,632.8	110.5	53.5	45.1	1.2
9.	Dhaka, Bangladesh	2,221.1	10,284.9	15,390.9	22,906.3	363.1	49.6	48.8	9.7
10.	Kolkata (Calcutta), India	7,887.8	13,058.1	14,402.3	18,711.0	65.5	10.3	29.9	1.2
11.	Karachi, Pakistan	3,989.2	10,031.1	13,876.3	20,190.3	151.5	38.3	45.5	7.4
12.	Buenos Aires, Argentina	8,744.6	11,847.0	13,527.8	15,524.2	35.5	14.2	14.8	32.4
13.	Los Angeles-Long Beach-Santa Ana, CA, U.S.	8,925.5	11,813.5	13,395.0	15,687.0	32.4	13.4	17.1	4.3
14.	Rio de Janeiro, Brazil	7,557.4	10,802.8	11,959.7	13,621.3	42.9	10.7	13.9	6.1
15.	Manila, Philippines	4,999.3	9,958.3	11,861.6	16,277.7	99.2	19.1	37.2	11.6

National Rankings by Population, Area, Population Density, 2012

Source: International Data Base, International Programs Center, U.S. Census Bureau, U.S. Dept. of Commerce; *The World Factbook*, Central Intelligence Agency (CIA)

Population figures are for midyear. The world had an estimated population of 7.02 bil in mid-2012. China was the most populous nation, with nearly one-fifth of the world total. A country's land area does not include its inland water. Rankings by total area may differ. Refer to the Nations chapter for a country's total area. Population density is calculated using land area.

Largest Populations

Rank	Country	Population
1.	China[1]	1,343,239,923
2.	India	1,205,073,612
3.	United States	313,847,465
4.	Indonesia	248,645,008
5.	Brazil	199,321,413
6.	Pakistan	190,291,129
7.	Nigeria	170,123,740
8.	Bangladesh	161,083,804
9.	Russia	142,517,670
10.	Japan	127,368,088

Smallest Populations

Rank	Country	Population
1.	Vatican City	836
2.	Nauru	9,378
3.	Tuvalu	10,619
4.	Palau	21,032
5.	Monaco	30,510
6.	San Marino	32,140
7.	Liechtenstein	36,713
8.	Saint Kitts and Nevis	50,726
9.	Marshall Islands	68,480
10.	Dominica	73,126

Largest Land Areas

Rank	Country	Area (sq mi)	Area (sq km)
1.	Russia	6,323,482	16,377,742
2.	China	3,694,959	9,569,901
3.	United States	3,531,905	9,147,593
4.	Canada	3,511,023	9,093,507
5.	Brazil	3,266,199	8,459,417
6.	Australia	2,966,153	7,682,300
7.	India	1,147,956	2,973,193
8.	Argentina	1,056,642	2,736,690
9.	Kazakhstan	1,042,360	2,699,700
10.	Algeria	919,595	2,381,741

Smallest Land Areas

Rank	Country	Area (sq mi)	Area (sq km)
1.	Vatican City	0.17	0.44
2.	Monaco	0.77	2
3.	Nauru	8.1	21
4.	Tuvalu	10	26
5.	San Marino	24	61
6.	Liechtenstein	62	160
7.	Marshall Islands	70	181
8.	Saint Kitts and Nevis	101	261
9.	Maldives	115	298
10.	Malta	122	316

Most Densely Populated

Rank	Country	Persons per sq mi	Persons per sq km
1.	Monaco	39,510.3	15,255.0
2.	Singapore	20,182.7	7,792.6
3.	Vatican City	4,921.0	1,900.0
4.	Bahrain	4,254.2	1,642.6
5.	Maldives	3,428.3	1,323.7
6.	Malta	3,359.1	1,296.9
7.	Bangladesh	3,205.1	1,237.5
8.	Taiwan	1,865.4	720.2
9.	Barbados	1,733.1	669.1
10.	Mauritius	1,675.3	646.8

Most Sparsely Populated

Rank	Country	Persons per sq mi	Persons per sq km
1.	Mongolia	5.3	2.0
2.	Namibia	6.8	2.6
3.	Australia	7.4	2.9
4.	Iceland	8.1	3.1
5.	Libya	8.3	3.2
6.	Mauritania	8.4	3.3
7.	Suriname	9.3	3.6
8.	Botswana	9.6	3.7
9.	Guyana	9.8	3.8
10.	Canada	9.8	3.8

(1) Does not include mid-2012 population of Hong Kong (7,153,519) and Macao (578,025).

Countries Ranked by Gross Domestic Product and Per Capita GDP, 2011

Source: *The World Factbook*, Central Intelligence Agency (CIA)

Estimates of gross domestic product (GDP)—the value of all final goods and services that a country produced in a year—were made based on purchasing power parity exchange rates. Per capita GDP is calculated using the estimated population size as of July 1 in a given year. Data may differ from estimates made by the U.S. Bureau of Economic Analysis. GDP figures are 2011 estimates unless otherwise noted.

GDP (in mil)		Per capita GDP	
Highest	**Lowest**	**Highest**	**Lowest**
1. U.S. $152,900,000	1. Tuvalu $375	1. Liechtenstein[3] $141,100	1. Congo, Dem. Rep. of $400
2. China[1] 114,400,000	2. Nauru[2] 600	2. Qatar 104,300	2. Zimbabwe 500
3. India 45,150,000	3. Marshall Islands[3] 1,335	3. Luxembourg 81,100	Liberia 500
4. Japan 44,970,000	4. Palau[3,4] 1,640	4. Singapore 60,500	4. Somalia[6] 600
5. Germany 31,390,000	5. Micronesia[3,5] 2,381	5. Norway 54,200	Burundi 600
6. Russia 24,140,000	6. São Tomé and Príncipe 3,839	6. Brunei 50,000	6. Eritrea 700
7. Brazil 23,240,000	7. Kiribati 6,067	7. U.S. 49,000	7. Central African Republic 800
8. UK 22,900,000	8. Tonga 7,728	8. United Arab Emirates 48,800	Niger 800
9. France 22,460,000	9. Comoros 8,477	9. Switzerland 43,900	9. Togo 900
10. Italy 18,710,000	10. St. Kitts and Nevis . . . 8,862	10. Netherlands 42,700	Sierra Leone 900
11. Mexico 16,830,000	11. Dominica 9,895	11. Austria 42,400	Malawi 900
12. Korea, South 15,740,000	12. Samoa 11,040	12. Kuwait 42,200	Madagascar 900
13. Spain 14,320,000	13. San Marino 11,360	13. Canada 41,100	13. Afghanistan 1,000
14. Canada 14,140,000	14. Vanuatu 12,190	14. Sweden 40,900	14. Mali 1,100
15. Indonesia . . . 11,390,000	15. St. Vincent and the Grenadines 12,750	15. Australia 40,800	Guinea 1,100
16. Turkey 10,870,000	16. Grenada 14,680	16. Ireland 40,100	Mozambique 1,100
17. Iran 10,030,000	17. Antigua and Barbuda 15,950	17. Iceland 38,500	Ethiopia 1,100
18. Australia 9,262,000	18. Solomon Islands 17,470	18. Germany 38,400	18. Comoros 1,200
19. Taiwan 8,873,000	19. Liberia 17,920	19. Taiwan 38,200	Guinea-Bissau . . 1,200
20. Poland 7,815,000	20. Guinea-Bissau 19,500	Belgium 38,200	20. Uganda 1,300

(1) Does not include Hong Kong, which had an estimated GDP of $355.6 bil in 2011, or Macao, with an estimated GDP of $18.5 bil in 2009. (2) 2005 est. (3) 2008 est. (4) Incl. U.S. subsidy. (5) Supplemented by grant aid, averaging perhaps $100 mil annually. (6) 2010 est.

Gold Reserves of Selected Central Banks and Governments, 1975-2011

Source: *International Financial Statistics*, International Monetary Fund (IMF)

(in mil fine troy ounces)

Year end	All countries[1]	Canada	China[2]	France	Germany[3]	India	Italy	Japan	Nether-lands	Russia	Switzer-land	UK	U.S.
1975	1,188.0	22.0	NA	100.9	117.6	7.0	82.5	21.1	54.3	NA	83.2	21.0	274.7
1980	1,152.2	21.0	12.8	81.9	95.2	8.6	66.7	24.2	43.9	NA	83.3	18.8	264.3
1985	1,147.4	20.1	12.7	81.9	95.2	9.4	66.7	24.2	43.9	NA	83.3	19.0	262.7
1990	1,144.2	14.8	12.7	81.9	95.2	10.7	66.7	24.2	43.9	NA	83.3	18.9	261.9
1995	1,115.3	3.4	12.7	81.9	95.2	12.8	66.7	24.2	34.8	9.4	83.3	18.4	261.7
2000	1,062.9	1.2	12.7	97.2	111.5	11.5	78.8	24.5	29.3	12.4	77.8	15.7	261.6
2002	1,042.1	0.6	19.3	97.2	110.8	11.5	78.8	24.6	27.4	12.5	61.6	10.1	262.0
2003	1,024.1	0.1	19.3	97.2	110.6	11.5	78.8	24.6	25.0	12.5	52.5	10.1	261.5
2004	1,007.7	0.1	19.3	96.0	110.4	11.5	78.8	24.6	25.0	12.4	43.5	10.0	261.6
2005	988.4	0.1	19.3	90.9	110.2	11.5	78.8	24.6	22.3	12.4	41.5	10.0	261.6
2006	976.7	0.1	19.3	87.4	110.0	11.5	78.8	24.6	20.6	12.9	41.5	10.0	261.5
2007	960.5	0.1	19.3	83.7	109.9	11.5	78.8	24.6	20.0	14.5	36.8	10.0	261.5
2008	960.4	0.1	19.3	80.1	109.7	11.5	78.8	24.6	19.7	16.7	33.4	10.0	261.5
2009	977.1	0.1	33.9	78.3	109.5	17.9	78.8	24.6	19.7	20.9	33.4	10.0	261.5
2010	981.7	0.1	33.9	78.3	109.3	17.9	78.8	24.6	19.7	25.4	33.4	10.0	261.5
2011	964.1	0.1	33.9	78.3	109.2	17.9	78.8	24.6	19.7	28.4	33.4	10.0	261.5

NA = Not available. (1) Covers IMF members with reported gold holdings. (2) Figures are for mainland China only and do not include Hong Kong (0.07 mil oz t in 2011) or Macao. (3) West Germany prior to 1991.

Consumer Price Changes in Selected Countries, 1975-2011

Source: *International Financial Statistics*, International Monetary Fund (IMF)

(annual average % change)

Country	1975-80	1980-85	1995-96	1996-97	1997-98	1998-99	1999-2000	2000-01	2004-05	2006-07	2008-09	2009-10	2010-11
Canada	8.7%	7.4%	1.6%	1.6%	1.0%	1.7%	2.7%	2.3%	2.2%	2.1%	0.3%	1.8%	2.9%
China[1]	NA	NA	8.3	2.8	−0.9	−1.4	0.3	0.5	1.8	4.8	−0.7	3.3	5.4
France	10.5	9.6	2.0	1.2	0.7	0.5	1.7	1.6	1.8	1.5	0.1	1.5	2.1
Germany[2]	4.1	3.9	1.5	1.8	1.0	0.6	1.5	2.0	2.0	2.1	0.3	1.1	2.3
Italy	16.3	13.7	4.0	2.0	2.0	1.7	2.5	2.8	2.0	1.8	0.8	1.5	2.7
Japan	6.5	2.7	0.1	1.7	0.6	−0.3	−0.7	−0.7	−0.3	0.1	−1.4	−0.7	−0.3
Spain	18.6	12.2	3.6	2.0	1.8	2.3	3.4	3.6	3.4	2.8	−0.4	1.9	3.2
Sweden	10.5	9.0	0.5	0.5	−0.1	0.5	0.9	2.4	0.5	2.2	−0.3	1.2	3.0
Switzerland	2.3	4.3	0.8	0.5	0.1	0.7	1.5	1.0	1.2	0.7	−0.5	0.7	0.2
United Kingdom	14.4	7.2	2.4	3.1	3.4	1.6	2.9	1.8	2.8	4.3	−0.6	3.3	4.5
United States	8.9	5.5	3.0	2.3	1.6	2.2	3.4	2.8	3.4	2.9	−0.4	1.6	3.2

NA = Not available. (1) Figures are for mainland China only and do not include Hong Kong (5.3% in 2010-11) or Macao (5.8% in 2010-11). (2) West Germany prior to 1991.

Hourly Compensation Costs in Manufacturing in Selected Countries, 1996-2010

Source: Division of International Labor Comparisons, U.S. Bureau of Labor Statistics, U.S. Dept. of Labor

For all workers in manufacturing, including part-time and temporary employees. Compensation costs include direct pay (pay for time worked and directly-paid benefits), employer social insurance expenditures, and labor-related taxes.

(in U.S. dollars)

Country	1996	1999	2002	2005	2008	2010	Country	1996	1999	2002	2005	2008	2010
Argentina	7.32	7.98	2.98	5.46	9.96	12.66	Korea, South	9.69	8.75	10.37	15.13	16.50	16.62
Australia	19.35	18.32	17.66	28.82	36.94	40.60	Mexico	3.05	4.02	5.59	5.61	6.47	6.23
Austria	28.51	25.25	23.85	33.33	44.28	41.07	Netherlands	NA	23.60	24.21	34.63	43.68	40.92
Belgium	32.93	28.93	27.94	41.27	54.23	50.70	New Zealand	12.43	10.40	10.10	16.56	19.35	20.57
Brazil	7.15	4.21	3.08	5.02	8.44	10.08	Norway	NA	26.71	30.34	42.03	56.92	57.53
Canada	18.96	18.15	18.33	26.68	32.52	35.67	Philippines	1.35	1.05	1.02	1.20	1.77	1.90
Czech Republic	3.41	3.48	4.60	7.28	12.19	11.50	Poland	NA	3.36	3.98	5.47	9.38	8.01
Denmark	NA	25.13	25.17	35.95	46.92	45.48	Portugal	7.04	6.52	6.61	9.40	12.42	11.72
Estonia	NA	NA	3.11	5.51	10.56	9.47	Singapore	11.93	11.01	12.14	13.25	18.87	19.10
Finland	25.00	22.07	22.61	33.63	43.83	42.30	Slovakia	2.75	2.61	3.25	5.83	10.73	10.72
France	27.84	24.30	23.31	33.30	43.29	40.55	Spain	15.44	13.88	13.81	20.69	27.68	26.60
Germany	33.20	27.56	27.63	38.01	47.51	43.76	Sweden	27.10	24.77	24.55	35.34	44.37	43.81
Greece	12.58	11.26	11.07	15.14	22.96	22.19	Switzerland	35.02	29.19	31.19	40.20	49.38	53.20
Hungary	3.11	3.09	4.19	6.71	9.78	8.40	Taiwan	7.10	6.79	6.83	7.93	8.68	8.36
Ireland	17.29	17.11	19.02	28.35	38.37	36.30	United Kingdom	16.80	21.10	22.11	29.74	34.22	29.44
Israel	11.54	12.09	12.57	14.06	19.51	20.12	United States	22.47	24.02	27.37	30.14	32.78	34.74
Italy	20.92	18.64	18.53	27.60	34.94	33.41	OECD countries[1]	NA	16.90	17.24	23.49	28.68	29.09
Japan	23.93	23.88	21.75	25.56	27.80	31.99							

NA = Not available. **Note:** Comparable data for China and India were not available. (1) Australia, Canada, Israel, Japan, South Korea, Mexico, New Zealand, U.S., and all European countries covered in this table are Organisation for Economic Co-operation and Development (OECD) countries.

Unemployment Rates in Selected Countries, 1970-2011

Source: Division of International Labor Comparisons, U.S. Bureau of Labor Statistics, U.S. Dept. of Labor

Year	U.S.	Australia	Canada	France	Germany[1]	Italy	Japan	Netherlands	Sweden	UK
1970	4.9%	1.7%	5.7%	2.5%	0.5%	3.2%	1.2%	NA	1.5%	NA
1975	8.5	4.9	6.9	3.6	3.4	3.4	1.9	5.1%	1.6	4.5%
1980	7.1	6.1	7.3	5.6	2.8	4.4	2.0	6.0	2.0	6.9
1985	7.2	8.3	10.1	9.0	7.2	6.0	2.5	9.6	2.8	11.4
1990	5.6	6.9	7.7	8.0	5.0	7.0	2.0	7.6	1.8	7.1
1995	5.6	8.5	8.6	10.2	8.2	11.3	2.9	7.1	9.1	8.7
1996	5.4	8.5	8.8	10.7	9.0	11.3	3.1	6.6	9.9	8.1
1997	4.9	8.5	8.4	10.8	9.9	11.3	3.1	5.6	10.1	7.0
1998	4.5	7.7	7.7	10.4	9.3	11.4	3.8	4.4	8.4	6.3
1999	4.2	6.9	7.0	10.1	8.5	11.0	4.2	3.5	7.1	6.0
2000	4.0	6.3	6.1	8.6	7.8	10.1	4.4	3.1	5.8	5.5
2001	4.7	6.8	6.5	7.8	7.9	9.1	4.5	2.5	5.0	5.1
2002	5.8	6.4	7.0	8.0	8.6	8.6	4.9	3.1	5.1	5.2
2003	6.0	5.9	6.9	8.6	9.3	8.5	4.6	4.1	5.8	5.0
2004	5.5	5.4	6.4	9.0	10.3	8.1	4.2	5.0	6.6	4.8
2005	5.1	5.0	6.0	9.0	11.2	7.8	3.8	5.3	7.7	4.9
2006	4.6	4.8	5.5	8.9	10.3	6.9	3.6	4.3	7.0	5.5
2007	4.6	4.4	5.2	8.1	8.7	6.2	3.6	3.6	6.1	5.4
2008	5.8	4.3	5.3	7.5	7.6	6.8	3.7	3.1	6.1	5.7
2009	9.3	5.6	7.3	9.2	7.8	7.9	4.8	3.8	8.3	7.7
2010	9.6	5.2	7.1	9.5	7.1	8.5	4.8	4.6	8.3	7.9
2011	8.9	5.1	6.5	9.4	6.0	8.5	4.2	4.5	7.5	8.1

NA = Not available. **Note:** Unemployment rates are for the civilian working-age population. Data from other countries have been adjusted to U.S. concepts so that comparisons can be made. Because of changes in survey methodology, some data may not be fully comparable over time. (1) For former West Germany only through 1990; data after 1991 are for unified Germany.

Tax Payments in Selected Countries, 2011

Source: *Taxing Wages*, Organisation for Economic Co-operation and Development (OECD)

Excluding taxes not listed here, such as sales tax. Rates apply to a single person without children at an average earnings level.

(as % of gross wage earnings in U.S. dollars with equal purchasing power; ranked by size of total payment)

Country	Total payment[1]	Income tax	Soc. sec. contribs.	Gross wage earnings	Country	Total payment[1]	Income tax	Soc. sec. contribs.	Gross wage earnings
Belgium	42.2%	28.2%	14.0%	$49,351	Portugal	24.5%	13.5%	11.0%	$27,836
Germany	39.9	19.0	20.9	54,950	Czech Republic	23.0	12.0	11.0	20,868
Denmark	38.7	28.0	10.7	48,994	Slovakia	22.9	9.5	13.4	18,589
Hungary	35.0	17.5	17.5	20,202	United States	22.8	17.2	5.6	46,800
Austria	33.4	15.3	18.1	46,210	Canada	22.7	15.5	7.3	37,549
Slovenia	33.4	11.3	22.1	27,577	Australia	22.3	22.3	0.0	44,853
Netherlands	31.4	16.0	15.4	55,165	Spain	21.9	15.6	6.4	35,528
Italy	30.8	21.3	9.5	36,360	Japan	21.0	7.6	13.4	44,738
Finland	29.8	22.7	7.2	43,798	Estonia	19.6	16.8	2.8	18,639
Norway	29.3	21.5	7.8	50,644	Ireland	18.9	14.9	4.0	39,225
Iceland	28.3	27.8	0.5	40,507	Israel	16.1	8.4	7.7	32,098
Luxembourg	28.1	15.0	13.1	53,480	Switzerland	16.1	10.0	6.2	51,738
France	28.0	14.3	13.7	41,361	New Zealand	15.9	15.9	0.0	32,426
Turkey	27.4	12.4	15.0	21,736	Korea, South	12.3	4.3	8.1	43,943
United Kingdom	25.1	15.6	9.5	52,013	Chile	7.0	0.0	7.0	14,530
Sweden	24.8	17.8	7.0	42,118	Mexico	6.3	4.9	1.4	11,035
Poland	24.6	6.8	17.8	20,567	**Total OECD**	**24.8**	**14.8**	**10.0**	**36,696**

(1) Figures may not add up to totals due to rounding.

Refugees and People in a Refugee-Like Situation, 2011

Source: *UNHCR Global Trends*, United Nations High Commissioner for Refugees (UNHCR)

Refugees are persons who are recognized under the 1951 UN Convention and 1967 Protocol Relating to the Status of Refugees, the 1969 OAU (Org. of African Unity) Refugee Convention, in accordance with the UNHCR Statute, or persons granted or receiving similar protection. Persons outside of their country or territory of origin who face protection risks similar to those of refugees—but whose refugee status has not been ascertained—are described as being in a refugee-like situation.

Only countries hosting 50,000 or more refugees and people in a refugee-like situation are shown. Only countries of origin with 5,000 or more refugees and people in a refugee-like situation are shown, in decreasing order. As of year-end.

Place of asylum	Origin of most refugees (excl. asylum seekers with pending cases)	Number
Africa		**2,693,358**
Cameroon	Central African Republic, Chad	100,373
Chad	Sudan, Central African Republic	366,494
Congo, Dem. Rep. of	Angola, Rwanda, Burundi	152,749
Congo Republic	Dem. Rep. of the Congo, Rwanda	141,232
Ethiopia	Somalia, Eritrea, Sudan	288,844
Kenya	Somalia, Ethiopia, Sudan, Dem. Rep. of the Congo	566,487
Liberia	Côte d'Ivoire	128,293
Rwanda	Dem. Rep. of the Congo	55,325
South Africa	Somalia, Dem. Rep. of the Congo, Angola	57,899
South Sudan	Sudan, Dem. Rep. of the Congo	105,023
Sudan	Eritrea, Chad	139,415
Tanzania	Burundi, Dem. Rep. of the Congo	131,243
Uganda	Dem. Rep. of the Congo, Sudan, Somalia, Rwanda, Burundi	139,448
Americas		**807,430**
Canada	Colombia, China, Sri Lanka, Pakistan, India, Mexico	164,883
Ecuador	Colombia	123,436
United States	China, Haiti, Colombia, Ethiopia, Cameroon, Russia, India, Venezuela, Armenia, Albania, Iraq, Indonesia	264,763
Venezuela	Colombia	202,022
Asia and Pacific		**3,607,211**
Bangladesh	Myanmar	229,669
China (incl. HK, Macao)	Vietnam	301,018
India	China, Sri Lanka, Afghanistan, Myanmar	185,118
Malaysia	Myanmar	86,680
Nepal	Bhutan, Tibetan	72,654
Pakistan	Afghanistan	1,702,700
Thailand	Myanmar	89,253
Europe		**1,557,493**
France	Sri Lanka, Cambodia, Dem. Rep. of the Congo, Serbia-Kosovo, Turkey, Russia, Vietnam, Laos	210,207
Germany	Serbia-Kosovo, Turkey, Iraq, Russia, Afghanistan, Vietnam, Bosnia and Herzegovina, Iran, Ukraine, Sri Lanka, Lebanon, Syria, Pakistan, Azerbaijan, Macedonia, Dem. Rep. of the Congo, stateless[1]	571,685
Italy	Eritrea, Somalia	58,060
Netherlands	Iraq, Somalia, Afghanistan	74,598
Serbia-Kosovo	Croatia, Bosnia and Herzegovina	70,707
Sweden	Iraq, Somalia, Afghanistan, Serbia-Kosovo, Eritrea	86,615
Switzerland	Eritrea	50,416
United Kingdom	Somalia, Iraq, Zimbabwe, Afghanistan, Iran, Eritrea, Turkey, Sri Lanka	193,510
Middle East and North Africa		**1,739,314**
Algeria	Western Sahara	94,148
Egypt	Palestinian[2], Sudan, Somalia, Iraq	95,087
Iran	Afghanistan, Iraq	886,468
Jordan	Iraq	451,009
Syria	Iraq	755,445
Yemen	Somalia	214,740
TOTAL		**10,404,806**

(1) Persons not considered nationals by any state under the operation of its laws. (2) Palestinians under the UNHCR mandate only.

Internally Displaced Persons, 2011

Source: Internal Displacement Monitoring Centre, Norwegian Refugee Council

Internally displaced persons (IDPs) are people who have been forced to flee due to armed conflict or human rights violations but who have not crossed into another country. As such, they are not protected by international refugee law and legally remain under the protection of their home country. Estimates are latest available and may comprise only registered IDPs or those displaced from a certain area of a country.

Country	Number	Country	Number	Country	Number
Afghanistan	448,000+	India	506,000+	Peru	150,000
Armenia	<8,400	Indonesia	<180,000	Philippines	46,000+
Azerbaijan	<599,000	Iraq	2.3 mil-2.6 mil	Russia	8,500+
Bosnia and Herzegovina	113,000	Kenya	250,000	Senegal	10,000-40,000
Burundi	78,800	Kosovo	18,000	Serbia[2]	225,000
Central African Republic	105,000	Kyrgyzstan	67,000	Somalia	1.5 mil
Chad	126,000	Lebanon	47,000+	Sri Lanka	125,000
Colombia[1]	3.9 mil-5.5 mil	Libya	74,000	Sudan	2.2 mil+
Congo, Dem. Rep. of	1.7 mil	Mali	158,857+	Syria	589,000+
Congo	<7,800	Mexico	160,000	Turkey	954,000-1.2 mil
Côte d'Ivoire	247,000+	Myanmar (Burma)	458,000+	Uganda	30,000
Croatia	2,059	Nepal	50,000	Uzbekistan	3,400
Cyprus	<208,000	Occupied Palestinian		Yemen[3]	463,500+
Eritrea	10,000	Territory	160,000	**Total**	**26.4 mil**
Georgia	<274,000	Pakistan	900,000+		

Note: The number of IDPs in the following countries was undetermined: Algeria, Angola, Bangladesh, Ethiopia, Guatemala, Israel, Laos, Liberia, Macedonia, Niger, Nigeria, Rwanda, South Sudan, Thailand, Timor-Leste, Togo, Turkmenistan, and Zimbabwe. (1) Low end of range cumulative since 2000; high end since 1985. (2) Incl. an est. 36,000-41,000 Roma. (3) Political unrest and counterinsurgency operations displaced more than 170,000 in 2011.

Estimated HIV Infection and Reported AIDS Cases, 2011

Source: Joint United Nations Programme on HIV/AIDS (UNAIDS)

In 2011, about 2.5 mil people were newly infected with HIV, a lower number than in previous years. Changes in behavior among young adults, intravenous drug users, and other at-risk populations have contributed to that decline, as has increased access to HIV prevention services. About 34.2 mil people worldwide—more than ever before—were living with HIV/AIDS in 2011. Approximately 3.4 mil (9.9%) were children under 15 years of age. (Of those, 91% lived in sub-Saharan Africa.) Fifty-four percent of all who are eligible for antiretroviral therapy are receiving it. The number of AIDS-related deaths fell in 2011, to 1.7 mil. Tuberculosis is still the leading cause of death among those living with HIV/AIDS.

Worldwide in 2011, $16.8 bil was spent on the HIV/AIDS epidemic. UNAIDS estimates that between $22 bil and $24 bil would be needed yearly if it is to meet targets it has set for 2015, including the elimination of new infections in children. As of July 2012, 45 countries and territories still restricted the right of those living with HIV/AIDS to enter or stay.

Current and New HIV/AIDS Cases and Deaths by Region, 2011

Region	Number living with HIV/AIDS	Percent of world total[1]	New HIV infections	AIDS-related deaths
Sub-Saharan Africa	23,500,000	68.7%	1,700,000	1,200,000
South and South-East Asia	4,200,000	12.3	280,000	270,000
Eastern Europe and Central Asia	1,500,000	4.4	160,000	90,000
Latin America	1,400,000	4.1	84,000	57,000
North America	1,400,000	4.1	58,000	20,000
Western and Central Europe	860,000	2.5	30,000	9,300
East Asia	830,000	2.4	87,000	60,000
Middle East and North Africa	330,000	1.0	36,000	25,000
Caribbean	230,000	0.7	12,000	10,000
Oceania	53,000	0.2	2,600	1,300
World[2]	**34,200,000**	**100.0**	**2,200,000**	**1,700,000**

(1) Population within a region living with HIV/AIDS as a percentage of population worldwide living with HIV/AIDS. (2) Figures may not add up to totals because of rounding.

Infectious Disease, Sanitation, and Water Quality

Source: *Global Burden of Disease* and *World Health Statistics* publications, World Health Organization (WHO); United Nations Children's Fund (UNICEF)

One of the United Nations' Millennium Development Goals (MDGs) is "halving the proportion of the population without sustainable access to safe drinking water" by 2015. In 2012, WHO and UNICEF announced that the goal was met in 2010, when 89% of the world's population had access to improved drinking-water sources. But the MDG goal for access to improved sanitation has yet to be reached. As of 2010, about 37% of people worldwide, or 2.5 bil, did not have access to improved sanitation. The population in unserved areas are at increased risk of contracting a variety of infectious and parasitic diseases such as diarrhea, malaria, and hepatitis A.

Listed below are nations with the highest death rates from infectious and parasitic diseases in 2008 and the lowest access to improved sanitation and water in 2010. Rankings and death rates for G8 countries and China are included for comparison. With the exception of China and Russia, these nations have near-universal (99% or greater) access to improved sanitation and water. In 2010, 64% of China's population had access to improved sanitation, and 91% had access to improved drinking-water sources. In Russia, the figures were 70% and 97%, respectively.

Deaths from Infectious and Parasitic Diseases, 2008
(per 100,000 population; ranked by deaths from infectious and parasitic diseases)

Rank	Country	Infectious and parasitic diseases	Tuberculosis	Diarrheal diseases	All causes
1.	Zimbabwe	931.4	50.6	36.3	1,467.5
2.	Lesotho	793.3	29.4	41.7	1,558.8
3.	Chad	787.3	66.8	210.9	1,716.9
4.	Swaziland	770.4	32.5	48.6	1,504.4
5.	Central African Republic	754.9	46.2	113.5	1,670.5
6.	Sierra Leone	733.7	128.5	156.0	1,502.3
7.	South Africa	727.6	39.3	71.6	1,344.7
8.	Malawi	719.3	23.7	101.5	1,626.7
9.	Mozambique	697.0	39.5	82.2	1,558.7
10.	Congo, Dem. Rep. of	687.4	78.8	187.5	1,606.8
91.	Russia	53.3	18.0	0.3	1,473.7
123.	China	23.4	11.8	1.4	715.7
124.	United States	22.9	0.2	2.3	817.5
130.	Japan	20.8	3.1	1.8	892.5
136.	France	18.8	1.1	2.2	841.8
144.	Germany	16.0	0.5	1.7	1,009.1
149.	Italy	14.0	0.7	0.3	975.7
151.	United Kingdom	13.4	0.7	5.0	960.2
154.	Canada	12.8	0.3	3.2	704.3

Lowest Access to Improved Sanitation Facilities, 2010

Sanitation facilities are considered improved if they are private and not shared with other households, incl. sewer or septic system connections, ventilated improved pit latrines, and composting toilets.

Rank	Country	% of pop. with access
1.	Niger	9%
2.	Tanzania	10
3.	Benin	13
	Chad	13
	Sierra Leone	13
	Togo	13
7.	Eritrea (2008)	14
	Ghana	14
9.	Madagascar	15
10.	Burkina Faso	17
	Haiti	17

Lowest Access to Improved Drinking-Water Sources, 2010

Improved drinking-water sources, which protect from outside contamination, incl. household connections, public taps or stand-pipes, dug wells, and rainwater collection.

Rank	Country	% of pop. with access
1.	Somalia	29%
2.	Papua New Guinea	40
3.	Ethiopia	44
4.	Congo, Dem. Rep. of	45
5.	Madagascar	46
6.	Mozambique	47
7.	Niger	49
8.	Afghanistan	50
	Mauritania	50
10.	Angola	51
	Chad	51
	Equatorial Guinea (2005)	51

Foreign Development Aid Donors, 2010-11

Source: Development Assistance Committee (DAC), Organisation for Economic Co-operation and Development (OECD)

Listed below is the amount of official development assistance (ODA)—in the form of grants or loans—each DAC member country disbursed in a given year to developing countries. The numbers are net disbursements, or amounts disbursed less repayments on earlier loans. Both bilateral ODA (made directly to an aid recipient) and multilateral ODA (made to an agency like the World Bank) are included. Countries are ranked by the size of their ODA in 2011 as a percentage of their gross national income (GNI). 2011 figures are preliminary.

Rank	Donor	ODA as % of GNI 2011	ODA as % of GNI 2010	ODA in mil of current U.S. dollars 2011	ODA in mil of current U.S. dollars 2010	Rank	Donor	ODA as % of GNI 2011	ODA as % of GNI 2010	ODA in mil of current U.S. dollars 2011	ODA in mil of current U.S. dollars 2010
1.	Sweden.......	1.02%	0.97%	$5,606.24	$4,533.49	14.	Canada......	0.31%	0.34%	$5,291.48	$5,208.57
2.	Norway.......	1.00	1.10	4,935.90	4,579.57	15.	Portugal......	0.29	0.29	668.82	648.96
3.	Luxembourg...	0.99	1.05	413.39	402.69	16.	Spain........	0.29	0.43	4,264.17	5,949.46
4.	Denmark......	0.86	0.91	2,980.54	2,871.24	17.	New Zealand..	0.28	0.26	429.06	342.22
5.	Netherlands...	0.75	0.81	6,324.15	6,357.31	18.	Austria.......	0.27	0.32	1,106.89	1,208.42
6.	United Kingdom	0.56	0.57	13,739.02	13,052.97	19.	United States..	0.20	0.21	30,744.52	30,353.16
7.	Belgium.......	0.53	0.64	2,799.85	3,003.93	20.	Italy.........	0.19	0.15	4,240.89	2,996.39
8.	Finland.......	0.52	0.55	1,408.98	1,332.95	21.	Japan........	0.18	0.20	10,604.41	11,020.98
9.	Ireland........	0.52	0.52	904.08	895.15	22.	Korea, South...	0.12	0.12	1,321.32	1,173.79
10.	France.......	0.46	0.50	12,993.89	12,915.10	23.	Greece.......	0.11	0.17	330.74	507.72
11.	Switzerland....	0.46	0.40	3,085.56	2,299.95		Total DAC.....	0.31	0.32	133,525.89	128,465.48
12.	Germany......	0.40	0.39	14,533.36	12,985.36		Total G7[1].....	0.27	0.28	92,147.57	88,532.53
13.	Australia......	0.35	0.32	4,798.63	3,826.10		EU institutions	NA	NA	12,626.96	12,679.15

NA = Not applicable/available. (1) Canada, France, Germany, Italy, Japan, the UK, and the U.S.

Recipients of U.S. Official Development Assistance, 2009-10

Source: Development Assistance Committee (DAC), Organisation for Economic Co-operation and Development (OECD)

(net disbursements of total ODA in mil of current U.S. dollars; ranked by 2010 figures)

Rank	Country	2010	2009	Rank	Country	2010	2009
1.	Afghanistan................	$2,893.40	$2,979.93	11.	Nigeria..................	$445.90	$354.03
2.	Iraq......................	1,622.91	2,346.31	12.	Colombia................	423.98	652.34
3.	Pakistan..................	1,196.76	613.04	13.	Uganda..................	378.13	366.88
4.	Haiti.....................	1,106.85	319.56	14.	Jordan...................	371.62	394.61
5.	Ethiopia..................	875.34	726.04	15.	Mozambique..............	277.91	255.61
6.	Sudan...................	726.35	954.64	16.	Congo, Dem. Rep. of........	277.85	238.69
7.	West Bank and Gaza Strip....	720.75	844.31	17.	Zambia..................	225.12	231.86
8.	Kenya...................	565.92	590.21	18.	Ghana...................	208.05	150.54
9.	South Africa..............	529.53	523.74	19.	Kosovo..................	100.97	207.44
10.	Tanzania.................	457.41	283.65	20.	Mexico..................	205.60	129.43
					All developing countries....	26,586.41	25,173.65

Nuclear Powers of the World

As of Aug. 2012, eight countries were acknowledged nuclear powers: the **UK, France, China, India, Pakistan, Russia, North Korea,** and the **U.S. Israel** was suspected of having an arsenal. **Iran** was suspected of developing nuclear weapons. More than 40 nations have the knowledge or technology to produce nuclear weapons. All—except Israel, India, and Pakistan—have signed the Nuclear Non-Proliferation Treaty (NPT). North Korea announced its withdrawal Jan. 10, 2003, following its expulsion of Intl. Atomic Energy Agency (IAEA) inspectors in Dec. 2002.

North Korea conducted its first-ever nuclear test Oct. 9, 2006. After a new round of talks, it agreed to a deal in Feb. 2007: in exchange for closing its main nuclear facility and taking steps toward disabling its nuclear weapons program, the country would receive economic aid and diplomatic recognition. In July, IAEA inspectors confirmed the shutdown of the Yongbyon nuclear facility. But the next round of talks, in Dec. 2008, ended in deadlock. North Korea conducted a second nuclear test May 25, 2009. As of Aug. 2012, the Bulletin of the Atomic Scientists believes the country may have enough plutonium for four to eight nuclear bombs.

Despite UN sanctions dating back to Dec. 2006, Iran has refused to suspend its activities in the enrichment of uranium. Iran argued that as an NPT signatory, it had a right to pursue the peaceful application of nuclear technology. The IAEA maintained that Iran has withheld information on the extent of its nuclear activities.

In Sept. 2009, the U.S., France, and Britain accused Iran of building a secret uranium enrichment facility near the city of Qom. Iran acknowledged the existence of the facility as a backup to its main enrichment site, at Natanz. Enrichment at the new facility, called Fordow, began in Jan. 2012. A computer malware program targeting Iran's nuclear program came to public attention in 2010. The Stuxnet worm may have disrupted operations at Iran's nuclear facility by infecting centrifuge hardware. The worm was reportedly created in a joint U.S.-Israeli operation. Since then, researchers have discovered at least two other malicious software programs, named Duqu and Flame, which appeared to collect data from computers in Iran.

Several countries abandoned their nuclear ambitions. **South Africa** announced in 1993 that it had built seven fission weapons (one was under construction) but had dismantled all of them. In the 1980s, **Argentina** and **Brazil** had active nuclear weapons programs but abandoned them by mutual treaty.

Estimated Numbers of Nuclear Weapons by Country, 1945-2012

Source: *Bulletin of the Atomic Scientists*; Carnegie Endowment for International Peace; Federation of American Scientists (FAS); Natural Resources Defense Council (NRDC); Nuclear Threat Initiative (NTI); Stockholm International Peace Research Institute (SIPRI)

Year	United States	USSR/Russia	United Kingdom	France	China	Israel[1]	India	Pakistan	Total
1945................	6	—	—	—	—	—	—	—	6
1950................	369	5	—	—	—	—	—	—	374
1960................	20,434	1,605	30	—	—	—	—	—	22,069
1970................	26,662	11,643	280	36	75	8	—	—	38,696
1980................	24,304	30,062	350	250	280	31	—	—	55,246
1990................	21,004	37,000	300	505	430	53	—	—	59,239
1995................	12,144	27,000	300	500	400	63	—	—	40,344
2000................	10,577	21,000	185	470	400	72	—	—	32,632
2010................	9,400	12,300	225	300	240	60-80	60-80	70-90	22,400
2012................	8,000	10,000	225	300	240	80	80-100	90-110	19,000

(1) Israel is widely presumed to have a nuclear stockpile although it has never confirmed nor denied its nuclear status.

Nuclear Arms Treaties and Negotiations: A Historical Overview

Aug. 5, 1963: Partial (Limited) Test Ban Treaty signed by U.S., USSR, and Britain, went into effect Oct. 10, 1963. Prohibits parties from testing or participating in the testing of nuclear weapons in the atmosphere, in outer space, and under water.

July 1, 1968: Nuclear Nonproliferation Treaty (NPT) opened to signatures, went into effect Mar. 5, 1970. With the U.S., USSR, and Great Britain as major signers, the treaty limits the spread of nuclear material for military purposes by agreement not to help non-nuclear nations get or make nuclear weapons.

On May 11, 1995, at an NPT review conference, parties to the treaty voted to extend it indefinitely. As of Aug. 2012, 190 countries were party to the treaty, not including North Korea, which withdrew in 2003. Israel, India, and Pakistan were not signatories.

May 26, 1972: The **Strategic Arms Limitation Talks (SALT I)** led to the signing of two agreements by the U.S. and USSR: the **Treaty on the Limitation of Anti-Ballistic Missile Systems** (or **ABM Treaty**) and an interim agreement. These treaties cap the numbers of intercontinental ballistic missile (ICBM) launchers and submarine-launched ballistic missile (SLBM) launchers.

July 3, 1974: Treaty on the Limitation of Underground Nuclear Weapon Tests (or **Threshold Test Ban Treaty**) signed by the U.S. and USSR. Limits underground testing of nuclear weapons to yields of 150 kilotons or less. On May 28, 1976, U.S. and Russia signed the **Peaceful Nuclear Explosions Treaty**, governing explosions outside weapons test sites. Both treaties entered into force Dec. 11, 1990.

June 18, 1979: Strategic Offensive Arms Limitation Treaty (or **SALT II**) signed by the U.S. and USSR. Limited each side to 2,400 missile launchers and heavy bombers; ceiling to apply until Jan. 1, 1985. Treaty also set a sub-ceiling of 1,320 ICBMs and SLBMs with multiple warheads on each side. Following Dec. 1979 Soviet invasion of Afghanistan, Pres. Jimmy Carter withdrew SALT II from Senate consideration for ratification.

Dec. 8, 1987: Intermediate-Range Nuclear Forces (INF) Treaty signed by the U.S. and USSR. Eliminates all U.S. and Soviet intermediate- and shorter-range nuclear missiles from Europe and Asia. Entered into force June 1, 1988.

July 31, 1991: Strategic Arms Reduction Treaty (START I) signed by the USSR and U.S., to reduce strategic offensive arms by about 30% in three phases over seven years. This was the first treaty to mandate reductions by the superpowers.

With the Soviet Union breakup in Dec. 1991, four former republics became independent nations with strategic nuclear weapons: Russia, Ukraine, Kazakhstan, and Belarus. Under the **Lisbon Protocol** of May 1992, Ukraine, Kazakhstan, and Belarus agreed to accede to the NPT as non-nuclear-weapon states, to destroy or transfer their nuclear weapons to Russia, and to ratify START I. START I expired on Dec. 5, 2009.

Jan. 3, 1993: START II signed by the U.S. and Russia, ratified by the two countries on Jan. 26, 1996, and Apr. 14, 2000, respectively. Called for reductions in their long-range nuclear arsenals. Both sides withdrew from the treaty before it went into force.

Sept. 24, 1996: Comprehensive Nuclear-Test-Ban Treaty (CTBT) signed by the U.S. and Russia. The CTBT bans all nuclear explosions. It is intended to prevent the nuclear powers from developing more advanced weapons while limiting the ability of other states to acquire such devices. As of Aug. 2012, the CTBT had been signed by 183 nations. It had been ratified by 157, including France, Russia, and the UK but neither the U.S. nor China. It will enter into force only after ratification by all Annex 2 states—the 44 states with nuclear technology capabilities at the time of the treaty's final negotiations. Only 36 have done so.

Dec. 13, 2001: The U.S. announced its intention to withdraw from the **ABM Treaty** in 180 days, arguing that it hindered the government in protecting itself from "future terrorist or rogue state missile attacks." Russia responded by withdrawing from **START II**, stating that U.S. withdrawal from the ABM Treaty effectively invalidated START II.

May 24, 2002: Strategic Offensive Reductions Treaty (SORT or **Moscow Treaty)** signed by the U.S. and Russia, entered into force June 1, 2003. Committed both countries to cutting nuclear arsenals to 1,700-2,200 warheads each, down from about 6,000, by Dec. 31, 2012. SORT terminated upon entry into force of the New START Treaty.

Apr. 8, 2010: New START Treaty signed by the U.S. and Russia and entered into force on Feb. 5, 2011. It limits each country's arsenal of deployed strategic nuclear warheads to 1,550.

Major International Organizations

African Union (AU), inaugurated July 9, 2002, in Durban, South Africa, following disbanding of the Organization of African Unity. All of Africa's countries, with the exception of Morocco, make up its 54 members. (Morocco had left the OAU after it admitted Western Sahara [Sahrawi Arab Dem. Rep.], a territory claimed by Morocco.) The AU is focused on achieving greater socioeconomic integration and unity among its member states. The AU's founding document authorized the organization to intervene to stop genocide, war crimes, or human rights abuses within individual member nations. **Headquarters:** Addis Ababa, Ethiopia. **Website:** www.au.int

Asia-Pacific Economic Cooperation (APEC), founded Nov. 1989 as a forum to further cooperation on trade and investment between nations of the region and the rest of the world. Its 21 members are Australia, Brunei, Canada, Chile, China, Hong Kong, Indonesia, Japan, Malaysia, Mexico, New Zealand, Papua New Guinea, Peru, Philippines, Russia, Singapore, South Korea, Taiwan, Thailand, the U.S., and Vietnam. **Headquarters:** Singapore. **Website:** www.apec.org

Association of Southeast Asian Nations (ASEAN), formed Aug. 8, 1967, to promote economic, social, and cultural cooperation and development among states of the Southeast Asian region. Its members are Brunei, Cambodia, Indonesia, Laos, Malaysia, Myanmar, Philippines, Singapore, Thailand, and Vietnam. **Headquarters:** Jakarta, Indonesia. **Website:** www.asean.org

Caribbean Community and Common Market (CARICOM), established Aug. 1, 1973. Its aim is to increase cooperation in economics, health, education, culture, science and technology, and tax administration, as well as the coordination of foreign policy. Its 15 members are Antigua and Barbuda, The Bahamas, Barbados, Belize, Dominica, Grenada, Guyana, Haiti, Jamaica, Montserrat, St. Kitts and Nevis, St. Lucia, St. Vincent and the Grenadines, Suriname, and Trinidad and Tobago. Anguilla, Bermuda, British Virgin Islands, Cayman Islands, and Turks and Caicos Islands are associate members. **Headquarters:** Georgetown, Guyana. **Website:** www.caricom.org

The Commonwealth, originally called the British Commonwealth of Nations, then the Commonwealth of Nations, is an association of nations and dependencies that were part of the former British Empire. The British monarch is the symbolic head of the Commonwealth.

There are 54 independent nations in the Commonwealth. Regular members include the UK and 15 other nations recognizing the British monarch, represented by a governor-general, as their head of state, and member countries in good standing with their own heads of state. Zimbabwe was suspended in Mar. 2002, following election and land redistribution controversies; it withdrew from the Commonwealth in 2003. In Sept. 2009, Fiji's military regime was suspended. **Headquarters:** London, UK. **Website:** www.thecommonwealth.org

Commonwealth of Independent States (CIS), an alliance established in Dec. 1991, made up of former Soviet constituent republics. Its members are Armenia, Azerbaijan, Belarus, Kazakhstan, Kyrgyzstan, Moldova, Russia, Tajikistan, Turkmenistan, Ukraine, and Uzbekistan. Georgia withdrew from the organization in Aug. 2009 following fighting with Russia over disputed territory. Policy is set through coordinating bodies such as the Council of the Heads of States and Council of the Heads of Governments. **Headquarters:** Minsk, Belarus. **Website:** www.cis.minsk.by or www.cisstat.com/eng/

European Free Trade Association (EFTA), created May 3, 1960, to promote expansion of free trade. Members entered into free trade agreements with the EU in 1972-73. In 1992, EFTA and EU agreed to create a single market—with free flow of goods, services, capital, and labor—among nations of the two organizations. Its members are Iceland, Liechtenstein, Norway, and Switzerland. **Headquarters:** Geneva, Switzerland. **Website:** www.efta.int

European Union (EU), known as the European Community (EC) until 1994, comprises three organizations with common membership: the European Economic Community (EEC, or Common Market), the European Coal and Steel Community, and the European Atomic Energy Community (Euratom). A merger of the three communities' executives went into effect in 1967. As of Aug. 2012, there were 27 EU members: the 12 original members (Belgium, Denmark, France, Germany, Greece, Ireland, Italy, Luxembourg, Netherlands, Portugal, Spain, and UK), three that entered Jan. 1, 1995 (Austria, Finland, Sweden), 10 that joined on May 1, 2004 (Cyprus, Czech Republic, Estonia, Hungary, Latvia, Lithuania, Malta, Poland, Slovakia, Slovenia), and two that joined Jan. 1, 2007 (Bulgaria, Romania). Croatia was set to become an EU member on July 1, 2013. Iceland, Macedonia, Montenegro, Serbia, and Turkey were candidate countries. Some 70 nations in Africa, the Caribbean, and the Pacific are affiliated under the Lomé Convention. **Headquarters:** Brussels, Belgium. **Website:** europa.eu

The EU aims to integrate the economies, coordinate social developments, and bring about political union of the member states. Effective Dec. 31, 1992, there are no restrictions on the movement of goods, services, capital, workers, and tourists within the EU. There are also common agricultural, fisheries, and nuclear research policies.

Leaders of the member nations (12 at the time) met Dec. 9-11, 1991, in Maastricht, the Netherlands, and signed a treaty. The Maastricht treaty, which went into effect in 1993, committed the organization to launching a common currency; establishing common foreign policies; and taking a leading role in social policy among other issues. The European Central Bank was established in 1998. In 1999, 11 of the then-15 EU countries began using the euro. By 2002, national currencies in those 11 countries and Greece were removed from circulation and replaced with the euro as the only currency of legal tender. EU peacekeeping forces replaced NATO troops in Macedonia, Mar. 31, 2003, the first such mission for the organization. A Treaty Establishing a Constitution for Europe was signed in 2004 by EU members but was never ratified.

Group of Eight (G-8), established Sept. 22, 1985; forum of seven major industrial democracies (Canada, France, Germany, Italy, Japan, the UK, and U.S.) and (later) Russia, which meet periodically to discuss economic and other issues. At its annual summit in 1998, the name was changed to G-8 from G-7. The presidency rotates yearly among members.

International Criminal Police Organization (INTERPOL), created 1923 as the International Criminal Police Commission before changing its name in 1956, is the world's largest international police organization. There were 190 member nations as of Aug. 2012. **Headquarters:** Lyon, France. **Website:** www.interpol.int

League of Arab States (Arab League), created Mar. 22, 1945. The League promotes economic, social, political, and military cooperation, mediates disputes, and represents Arab states in certain international negotiations. Its members are Algeria, Bahrain, Comoros, Djibouti, Egypt, Iraq, Jordan, Kuwait, Lebanon, Libya, Mauritania, Morocco, Oman, Palestine (considered an independent state by the League), Qatar, Saudi Arabia, Somalia, Sudan, Syria, Tunisia, United Arab Emirates, and Yemen. **Headquarters:** Cairo, Egypt.

North Atlantic Treaty Organization (NATO), created by treaty (signed Apr. 4, 1949; in effect Aug. 24, 1949). Its 28 members as of Aug. 2012 are Albania, Belgium, Bulgaria, Canada, Croatia, Czech Republic, Denmark, Estonia, France, Germany, Greece, Hungary, Iceland, Italy, Latvia, Lithuania, Luxembourg, Netherlands, Norway, Poland, Portugal, Romania, Slovakia, Slovenia, Spain, Turkey, UK, and U.S. Several of these states are former Warsaw Pact Eastern European nations.

Members have agreed to settle disputes by peaceful means, to develop their capacity to resist armed attack, to regard an attack on one as an attack on all, and to take necessary action to repel an attack under Article 51 of the UN Charter. **Headquarters:** Brussels, Belgium. **Website:** www.nato.int

The NATO structure consists of the North Atlantic Council (NAC), the Defense Planning Committee, the Military Committee (realigned in June 2003 and consisting of two commands: Allied Command Operations and Allied Command Transformation), the Nuclear Planning Group, and the Canada-U.S. Regional Planning Group. France detached itself from the military command structure in 1966.

With the end of the Cold War in the early 1990s, members put greater stress on political action and on creating a rapid deployment force to react to local crises. By the mid-1990s, 27 nations, including Russia and other former Soviet republics, had joined with NATO in the so-called Partnership for Peace (PfP; drafted Dec. 1993), which provided for limited joint military exercises and peacekeeping missions. NATO has proceeded gradually toward extending full membership to former Eastern bloc nations. Three former Warsaw Pact members, Hungary, Poland, and the Czech Republic, formally became members in 1999. NATO and Russia signed a cooperation pact in 2002, forming a NATO-Russia Council; NATO that same year invited seven former Eastern-bloc nations to join the alliance.

A NATO-led multinational force was deployed to help keep the peace in Bosnia and Herzegovina in 1995. In 1999, another force was deployed in Kosovo. Following the Sept. 2001 terrorist attacks on the U.S., the NATO Council agreed to invoke for the first time Article 5 of the treaty, which stipulates mutual defense of alliance members. NATO assumed control of the International Security Assistance Force in Afghanistan (ISAF), Aug. 2003, marking the first time NATO led a mission outside Europe.

Organization of American States (OAS), formed in Bogotá, Colombia, Apr. 30, 1948. It has a Permanent Council, Inter-American Council for Integral Development, Juridical Committee, and Commission on Human Rights. A general assembly meets annually.

Its 35 members are Antigua and Barbuda, Argentina, The Bahamas, Barbados, Belize, Bolivia, Brazil, Canada, Chile, Colombia, Costa Rica, Cuba, Dominica, Dominican Republic, Ecuador, El Salvador, Grenada, Guatemala, Guyana, Haiti, Honduras, Jamaica, Mexico, Nicaragua, Panama, Paraguay, Peru, St. Kitts and Nevis, St. Lucia, St. Vincent and the Grenadines, Suriname, Trinidad and Tobago, U.S., Uruguay, and Venezuela. **Headquarters:** Washington, DC. **Website:** www.oas.org

Organization for Economic Cooperation and Development (OECD), established Dec. 14, 1960, to promote the economic and social welfare of all its member countries and to stimulate efforts on behalf of developing nations. Its 34 members are Australia, Austria, Belgium, Canada, Chile, Czech Republic, Denmark, Estonia, Finland, France, Germany, Greece, Hungary, Iceland, Ireland, Israel, Italy, Japan, Luxembourg, Mexico, Netherlands, New Zealand, Norway, Poland, Portugal, Slovakia, Slovenia, South Korea, Spain, Sweden, Switzerland, Turkey, UK, and the U.S. **Headquarters:** Paris, France. **Website:** www.oecd.org

Organization of Petroleum Exporting Countries (OPEC), created Sept. 14, 1960, by Iran, Iraq, Kuwait, Saudi Arabia, and Venezuela. This group made up of most but not all the major petroleum exporting nations seeks to stabilize the oil market and set world oil prices by controlling production. In addition to the founding countries, members include Algeria, Angola, Ecuador, Indonesia (suspended membership starting in Jan. 2009), Libya, Nigeria, Qatar, and United Arab Emirates. Gabon is a former member. **Headquarters:** Vienna, Austria. **Website:** www.opec.org

Organization for Security and Cooperation in Europe (OSCE), established in 1972 as the Conference on Security and Cooperation in Europe; current name adopted 1995. The group, formed by NATO and Warsaw Pact members, seeks improved East-West relations through a commitment to nonaggression and human rights, and cooperation in economics, science and technology, cultural exchange, and environmental protection. There were 56 member states as of Aug. 2012, making it the world's largest regional security organization. **Headquarters:** Vienna, Austria. **Website:** www.osce.org

United Nations

The 67th regular session of the United Nations General Assembly opened Sept. 18, 2012, attended by world leaders and other delegates from 193 nations. The UN headquarters is in New York, NY, between First Ave. and Roosevelt Dr. and E. 42nd St. and E. 48th St.

Proposals to establish an organization for maintenance of world peace led to the convening of the United Nations Conference on International Organization in San Francisco, Apr. 25-June 26, 1945, where the UN charter was drawn. It was signed June 26 by 50 nations and by Poland, one of the original 51 members, on Oct. 15, 1945. It went into effect Oct. 24, 1945, upon ratification by the permanent members of the Security Council and a majority of the other signatories.

Purposes. To maintain international peace and security; to develop friendly relations among nations; to achieve international cooperation in solving economic, social, cultural, and humanitarian problems and in promoting respect for human rights and basic freedoms; to be a center for harmonizing the actions of nations in attaining these common ends.

Visitors to the UN. The UN headquarters is open to the public every day except New Year's Day, President's Day, Good Friday, Memorial Day, Independence Day, Eid al-Fitr, Labor Day, Eid al-Adha, Thanksgiving, and Christmas. The headquarters may also close on short notice when meetings of heads of state and government are held.

Guided tours and audio tours are conducted weekdays from 9:45 AM to 4:45 PM. Groups of 20 or more require reservations, which can be made by emailing unitg@un.org or calling (212) 963-4440. Smaller groups that wish to have a private tour can make reservations for a fee. For safety reasons, children under 5 are not admitted on tours.

United Nations Secretaries General

Took office	Secretary, nation	Took office	Secretary, nation
1946	Trygve Lie, Norway	1982	Javier Pérez de Cuéllar, Peru
1953	Dag Hammarskjöld, Sweden	1992	Boutros Boutros-Ghali, Egypt
1961	U Thant, Burma (Myanmar)	1997	Kofi Annan, Ghana
1972	Kurt Waldheim, Austria	2007	Ban Ki-moon, South Korea

Six Main Organs of the United Nations

The United Nations consists of six principal organs, 15 agencies, and many programs and other bodies. The six principal organs are the General Assembly, the Security Council, the Secretariat, the Economic and Social Council, the International Court of Justice, and the Trusteeship Council.

General Assembly. The General Assembly is composed of representatives of all the member nations. Each nation is entitled to one vote. The General Assembly meets in regular annual sessions and in special session when convoked at the request of the Security Council or a majority of UN members. On important questions a two-thirds majority of members present and voting is required; on other questions a simple majority is sufficient.

The General Assembly must approve the UN budget and apportion expenses among members. A member in arrears can lose its vote if the amount of arrears equals or exceeds the amount of the contributions due for the preceding two full years. **Website:** www.un.org/en/ga/

Security Council. The Security Council consists of 15 members, five with permanent seats. The remaining 10 are elected for two-year terms by the General Assembly.

The permanent members of the Council are China, France, Russia, United Kingdom, and the United States. Nonpermanent members with terms expiring Dec. 31, 2012, are Colombia, Germany, India, Portugal, and South Africa; those with terms expiring Dec. 31, 2013, are Azerbaijan, Guatemala, Morocco, Pakistan, and Togo.

The Security Council has the primary responsibility within the UN for maintaining international peace and security. The Council may investigate any dispute that threatens international peace and security.

Any UN member may participate in Council discussions at its invitation. Decisions on procedural questions are made by an affirmative vote of nine members. On all other matters the affirmative vote of nine members must include the concurring votes of all permanent members (giving them veto power).

The Security Council directs the various peacekeeping forces deployed throughout the world. **Website:** www.un.org/Docs/sc/

Secretariat. The Secretariat is responsible for the UN's day-to-day operations. It is headed by the secretary-general, who is the chief administrative officer of the UN. This person is appointed by the General Assembly, on the recommendation of the Security Council, for a five-year, renewable term. The secretary-general reports to the General Assembly and may bring to the attention of the Security Council any matter that threatens international peace. As of mid-2011, the Secretariat had an international staff of 43,747. **Website:** www.un.org/en/mainbodies/secretariat/

Economic and Social Council. The Economic and Social Council consists of 54 members elected by the General Assembly to overlapping three-year terms. The council is responsible for economic, social, and environmental matters. It meets with academics, non-governmental organizations, and private-sector representatives throughout the year. A month-long substantive session takes place each July. These sessions are alternately held in New York and Geneva, Switzerland. **Website:** www.un.org/ecosoc/

International Court of Justice (World Court). The International Court of Justice is the principal judicial organ of the UN. The Court has jurisdiction over cases that UN members or parties to the court's statute submit to it. In addition to rendering judgments, the Court gives advisory opinions.

The court's 15 judges are elected to nine-year terms by the General Assembly and the Security Council. No two judges come from the same nation, and they represent the world's principal legal systems. Once elected, the judges no longer act as representatives of a government. The Court remains permanently in session, except during vacations. All questions are decided by a majority. The International Court of Justice sits in The Hague, Netherlands. **Website:** www.icj-cij.org

Trusteeship Council. The Trusteeship Council, made up of the five permanent Security Council members, supervised the administration of UN trust territories. All 11 trust territories have since attained their right to self-determination. The Council formally suspended its work on Nov. 1, 1994, with Palau's independence. **Website:** www.un.org/en/mainbodies/trusteeship/

The text of the **UN Charter** is online at www.un.org/en/documents/charter/index.shtml.

Selected Specialized and Related Agencies

These specialized and related agencies are autonomous, with their own memberships and organs. They have a functional relationship or working agreement with the UN (headquarters) except for UNICEF and UNHCR, which report directly to the General Assembly and the Economic and Social Council. The location in parentheses is the primary office or headquarters; other locations may vary.

Food and Agriculture Org. (FAO) helps countries modernize farms, forests, and fisheries; improves food distribution; and raises levels of nutrition. (Rome, Italy) **Website:** www.fao.org

International Atomic Energy Agency (IAEA) aims to promote safe, peaceful uses of atomic energy. (Vienna, Austria) **Website:** www.iaea.org

International Civil Aviation Org. (ICAO) promotes international civil aviation standards and regulations. (Montréal, Quebec, Canada) **Website:** www.icao.int

International Fund for Agricultural Development (IFAD) seeks to alleviate poverty in rural areas of developing countries. (Rome, Italy) **Website:** www.ifad.org

International Labor Org. (ILO) aims to promote decent and productive employment practices, the improvement of labor conditions, social security, and vocational training. (Geneva, Switzerland) **Website:** www.ilo.org

International Maritime Org. (IMO) aims to promote cooperation on technical matters affecting international shipping. (London, England, UK) **Website:** www.imo.org

International Monetary Fund (IMF) aims to promote international monetary cooperation, currency stabilization, and the expansion of international trade. (Washington, DC) **Website:** www.imf.org

International Telecommunication Union (ITU) regulates all aspects of global communication, including setting standards for radio, telegraph, telephone, and space radio-communications, and allocating radio frequencies. (Geneva, Switzerland) Website: www.itu.int

Office of the High Commissioner for Human Rights (OHCHR) seeks to uphold human rights standards by monitoring areas of concern, investigating abuses, and working with government institutions to improve conditions. (Geneva, Switzerland) Website: www.ohchr.org

Office of the United Nations High Commissioner for Refugees (UNHCR) provides essential assistance for refugees. (Geneva, Switzerland) Website: www.unhcr.org

United Nations Children's Fund (UNICEF) provides financial aid and development assistance to programs for children and mothers in developing countries. (New York, NY) Website: www.unicef.org

United Nations Educational, Scientific, and Cultural Org. (UNESCO) aims to promote collaboration among nations through education, science, and culture. (Paris, France) Website: www.unesco.org

United Nations Industrial Development Org. (UNIDO) helps developing and transitional nations pursue sustainable industrial development while promoting international industrial cooperation. (Vienna, Austria) Website: www.unido.org

Universal Postal Union (UPU) aims to perfect postal services and promote international collaboration. (Berne, Switzerland) Website: www.upu.int

World Bank Group encompasses two development institutions and three affiliates focused on worldwide poverty reduction. The International Bank for Reconstruction and Development (IBRD) provides loans and technical assistance for projects in developing member countries and encourages co-financing for projects from other sources. The International Development Assn. (IDA) provides funds for development projects on concessionary terms to poorer developing member countries. The International Finance Corp. (IFC) promotes private-sector growth in developing member countries; encourages the development of local capital markets; and stimulates the international flow of private capital. The Multilateral Investment Guarantee Agency (MIGA) promotes investment in developing countries; guarantees investments to protect investors from noncommercial risks, such as nationalization; and advises governments on attracting private investment. The International Center for Settlement of Investment Disputes (ICSID) provides conciliation and arbitration services for disputes between foreign investors and host governments that arise out of an investment. (Washington, DC) Website: www.worldbank.org

World Health Org. (WHO) aims for the attainment of the highest possible level of health. (Geneva, Switzerland) Website: www.who.int

World Intellectual Property Org. (WIPO) seeks to protect, through international cooperation, literary, industrial, scientific, and artistic works. (Geneva, Switzerland) Website: www.wipo.int

World Meteorological Org. (WMO) aims to coordinate and improve world meteorological work. (Geneva, Switzerland) Website: www.wmo.int

World Tourism Org. (UNWTO) promotes responsible, sustainable, and universally accessible tourism with the aim of fostering economic development and international understanding. (Madrid, Spain) Website: www.unwto.org

World Trade Org. (WTO) administers trade agreements and treaties between nations, examines members' trade regimes, keeps track of trade measures and statistics, and attempts to settle disputes. (Geneva, Switzerland) Website: www.wto.org

Ongoing UN Peacekeeping Missions, 2012

Source: Dept. of Peacekeeping Operations (DPKO) and Dept. of Field Support (DFS), United Nations Secretariat

Unless otherwise noted, numbers are for peacekeeping operations only, as of July 31, 2012. Year given in graphic is the year each mission started. Graphic does not show the UN Supervision Mission in Syria (UNSMIS), which came to an end on Aug. 19, 2012, four months after it was established, because of violence in the country. UNSMIS data are included in the numbers below.

Uniformed personnel (troops, police, military observers)	96,537	Total personnel serving in 17 DPKO-led peace operations	119,154
Countries contributing uniformed personnel	119	Peacekeeping operations since 1948	67
Civilian personnel (as of June 30, 2012):		Total fatalities in peace operations since 1948	3,017
International	5,534	Est. total cost of operations, 1948 to June 30, 2010	$69 bil
Local	12,636		

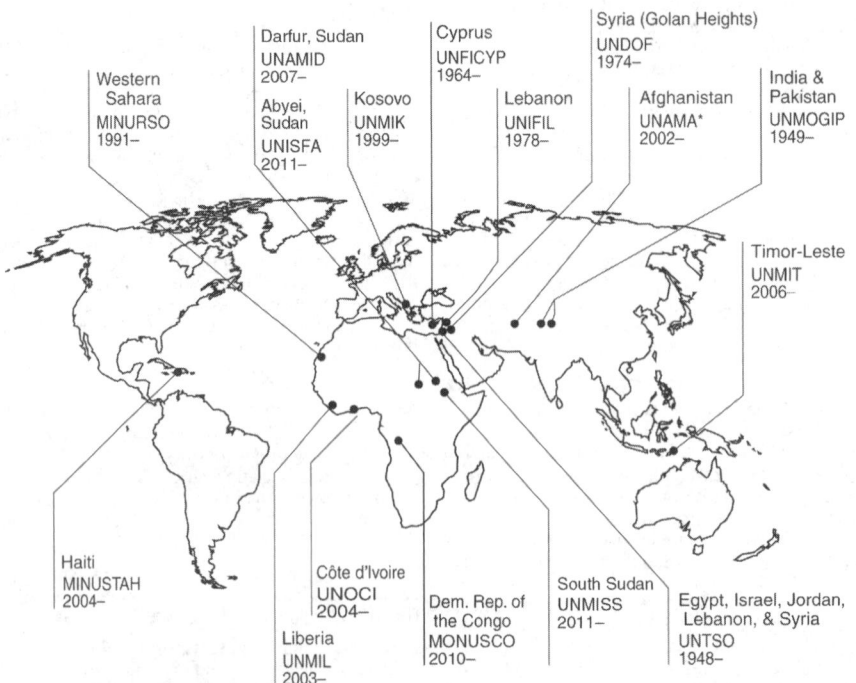

Darfur, Sudan
UNAMID
2007–

Cyprus
UNFICYP
1964–

Syria (Golan Heights)
UNDOF
1974–

Western Sahara
MINURSO
1991–

Abyei, Sudan
UNISFA
2011–

Kosovo
UNMIK
1999–

Lebanon
UNIFIL
1978–

Afghanistan
UNAMA*
2002–

India & Pakistan
UNMOGIP
1949–

Timor-Leste
UNMIT
2006–

Haiti
MINUSTAH
2004–

Côte d'Ivoire
UNOCI
2004–

Liberia
UNMIL
2003–

Dem. Rep. of the Congo
MONUSCO
2010–

South Sudan
UNMISS
2011–

Egypt, Israel, Jordan, Lebanon, & Syria
UNTSO
1948–

*Political mission directed and supported by the Dept. of Peacekeeping Operations.

Roster of the United Nations

Listed below are the 193 members of the United Nations, with the years in which they were admitted (as of Aug. 2012). Vatican City, Kosovo, and China (Taiwan)[1] are not members. Taiwan's repeated bids for UN membership have so far been unsuccessful. Vatican City is a permanent observer.

Member	Year	Member	Year	Member	Year	Member	Year
Afghanistan	1946	Dominica	1978	Libya	1955	Saint Vincent and the	
Albania	1955	Dominican Republic	1945	Liechtenstein	1990	Grenadines	1980
Algeria	1962	Ecuador	1945	Lithuania	1991	Samoa	1976
Andorra	1993	Egypt[4]	1945	Luxembourg	1945	San Marino	1992
Angola	1976	El Salvador	1945	Macedonia[2,7]	1993	São Tomé and Príncipe	1975
Antigua and Barbuda	1981	Equatorial Guinea	1968	Madagascar	1960	Saudi Arabia	1945
Argentina	1945	Eritrea	1993	Malawi	1964	Senegal	1960
Armenia	1992	Estonia	1991	Malaysia[8]	1957	Serbia[2,9]	2000
Australia	1945	Ethiopia	1945	Maldives	1965	Seychelles	1976
Austria	1955	Fiji	1970	Mali	1960	Sierra Leone	1961
Azerbaijan	1992	Finland	1955	Malta	1964	Singapore[8]	1965
Bahamas, The	1973	France	1945	Marshall Islands	1991	Slovakia[3]	1993
Bahrain	1971	Gabon	1960	Mauritania	1961	Slovenia[2]	1992
Bangladesh	1974	Gambia, The	1965	Mauritius	1968	Solomon Islands	1978
Barbados	1966	Georgia	1992	Mexico	1945	Somalia	1960
Belarus	1945	Germany[5]	1973	Micronesia	1991	South Africa[11]	1945
Belgium	1945	Ghana	1957	Moldova	1992	South Sudan[12]	2011
Belize	1981	Greece	1945	Monaco	1993	Spain	1955
Benin	1960	Grenada	1974	Mongolia	1961	Sri Lanka	1955
Bhutan	1971	Guatemala	1945	Montenegro[2,9]	2006	Sudan[12]	1956
Bolivia	1945	Guinea	1958	Morocco	1956	Suriname	1975
Bosnia and		Guinea-Bissau	1974	Mozambique	1975	Swaziland	1968
Herzegovina[2]	1992	Guyana	1966	Myanmar (Burma)	1948	Sweden	1946
Botswana	1966	Haiti	1945	Namibia	1990	Switzerland	2002
Brazil	1945	Honduras	1945	Nauru	1999	Syria[3]	1945
Brunei	1984	Hungary	1955	Nepal	1955	Tajikistan	1992
Bulgaria	1955	Iceland	1946	Netherlands	1945	Tanzania[13]	1961
Burkina Faso	1960	India	1945	New Zealand	1945	Thailand	1946
Burundi	1962	Indonesia[6]	1950	Nicaragua	1945	Timor-Leste	2002
Cambodia	1955	Iran	1945	Niger	1960	Togo	1960
Cameroon	1960	Iraq	1945	Nigeria	1960	Tonga	1999
Canada	1945	Ireland	1955	Norway	1945	Trinidad and Tobago	1962
Cape Verde	1975	Israel	1949	Oman	1971	Tunisia	1956
Central African Rep.	1960	Italy	1955	Pakistan	1947	Turkey	1945
Chad	1960	Jamaica	1962	Palau	1994	Turkmenistan	1992
Chile	1945	Japan	1956	Panama	1945	Tuvalu	2000
China[1]	1945	Jordan	1955	Papua New Guinea	1975	Uganda	1962
Colombia	1945	Kazakhstan	1992	Paraguay	1945	Ukraine	1945
Comoros	1975	Kenya	1963	Peru	1945	United Arab Emirates	1971
Congo, Dem. Rep. of	1960	Kiribati	1999	Philippines	1945	United Kingdom	1945
Congo Republic	1960	Korea, North	1991	Poland	1945	United States	1945
Costa Rica	1945	Korea, South	1991	Portugal	1955	Uruguay	1945
Côte d'Ivoire	1960	Kuwait	1963	Qatar	1971	Uzbekistan	1992
Croatia[2]	1992	Kyrgyzstan	1992	Romania	1955	Vanuatu	1981
Cuba	1945	Laos	1955	Russia[10]	1945	Venezuela	1945
Cyprus	1960	Latvia	1991	Rwanda	1962	Vietnam	1977
Czech Republic[3]	1993	Lebanon	1945	Saint Kitts and Nevis	1983	Yemen[14]	1947
Denmark	1945	Lesotho	1966	Saint Lucia	1979	Zambia	1964
Djibouti	1977	Liberia	1945			Zimbabwe	1980

(1) The General Assembly (GA) voted in 1971 to expel the Chinese government in Taiwan and admit the government in Beijing. (2) The Socialist Federal Republic of Yugoslavia was an original UN member. After four of its six republics (Bosnia and Herzegovina, Croatia, Macedonia, and Slovenia) declared independence in 1991-92, the two remaining republics, Montenegro and Serbia, reconstituted as the Federal Republic of Yugoslavia. They sought to take over the former Yugoslavia's UN seat in 1992 but were expelled a few months later by GA vote. The Federal Republic of Yugoslavia was granted membership in 2000. In 2003, the country changed its name to Serbia and Montenegro. (3) Czechoslovakia, an original UN member from 1945 to 1992, was succeeded by both the Czech Republic and Slovakia in 1993. (4) Egypt and Syria were original UN members. In 1958, Egypt and Syria established the United Arab Republic and continued under a single UN membership. In 1961, Syria resumed separate membership following independence. (5) The Federal Republic of Germany and the German Democratic Republic became UN members in 1973. In 1990, the two formed one sovereign state. (6) Withdrew from the UN in 1965; rejoined in 1966. (7) Provisionally referred to as The Former Yugoslav Republic of Macedonia within the UN pending settlement of Greece's objection to its constitutional name. (8) The Federation of Malaya joined the UN in 1957. In 1963, it changed its name to Malaysia following the accession of Singapore, Sabah, and Sarawak. Singapore became an independent UN member in 1965. (9) After Montenegro declared independence in 2006, the Republic of Serbia continued Serbia and Montenegro's UN membership. Montenegro was admitted to the UN as the Republic of Montenegro the same month. (10) The USSR was an original UN member. After the USSR's dissolution in 1991, Russia informed the UN it would continue the Soviet Union's membership in the Security Council and all other UN organs with the support of the Commonwealth of Independent States (comprising most of the former Soviet republics). (11) Readmitted in 1994. Its delegation had been suspended from participation in 1974 because of apartheid. (12) The Republic of South Sudan seceded from the Republic of the Sudan in 2011 and was admitted to the UN the same year. (13) Tanganyika was a UN member from 1961 and Zanzibar from 1963. The two countries united in 1964 to form the United Republic of Tanganyika and Zanzibar, which continued a single UN membership. It later changed its name to the United Republic of Tanzania. (14) The Yemen Arab Republic was admitted in 1947; the People's Democratic Republic of Yemen in 1967. In 1990, the two nations formed the Republic of Yemen.

U.S. Representatives to the United Nations, 1946-2012

The U.S. Representative to the United Nations is the chief of the U.S. Mission to the United Nations in New York and holds the rank and status of Ambassador Extraordinary and Plenipotentiary (A.E.P.). Year given is the year each took office.

Year	Representative	Year	Representative	Year	Representative	Year	Representative
1946	Edward R. Stettinius Jr.	1968	James Russell Wiggins	1985	Vernon A. Walters	2001	John D. Negroponte
1946	Herschel V. Johnson (act.)	1969	Charles W. Yost	1989	Thomas R. Pickering	2004	John C. Danforth
1947	Warren R. Austin	1971	George H. W. Bush	1992	Edward J. Perkins	2005	Anne W. Patterson (act.)
1953	Henry Cabot Lodge Jr.	1973	John A. Scali	1993	Madeleine K. Albright		
1960	James J. Wadsworth	1975	Daniel P. Moynihan	1997	Bill Richardson	2005	John R. Bolton
1961	Adlai E. Stevenson	1976	William W. Scranton	1998	A. Peter Burleigh (act.)	2006	Alejandro D. Wolff (act.)
1965	Arthur J. Goldberg	1977	Andrew Young	1999	Richard C. Holbrooke	2007	Zalmay M. Khalilzad
1968	George W. Ball	1979	Donald McHenry	2001	James B. Cunningham (act.)	2009	Susan E. Rice
		1981	Jeane J. Kirkpatrick				

International Criminal Court

The International Criminal Court (ICC) was created when 120 nations signed the Rome Statute on July 17, 1998. Its mission is to try individuals accused of genocide, war crimes, or other crimes against humanity, which was undertaken in the past by temporary tribunals. The statute came into force on July 1, 2002. As of Sept. 2012, 121 nations were state parties to the Rome Statute of the ICC. China, Russia, and the U.S. have not yet joined.

The ICC, unlike the World Court, is not part of the UN. It is an independent international agency with its own administration and budget, which is made up of funds from member states and voluntary contributions by other institutions, international groups, individuals, and corporations. It consists of 18 judges elected by member nations. An absolute majority of these 18 judges elect three from among themselves to serve as president, first vice president, and second vice president in three-year, renewable terms. A Registry handles the nonjudicial aspects of administration. The Office of the Prosecutor reviews, investigates, and, prosecutes cases referred to it by a state or by the UN Security Council.

As of Aug. 2012, the ICC prosecutor was investigating situations in the Dem. Rep. of the Congo; Uganda; Darfur, Sudan; Central African Republic; Kenya; and Côte d'Ivoire. The UN Security Council, on Feb. 26, 2011, decided to refer the situation in Libya since Feb. 15 to the ICC prosecutor. On Mar. 14, 2012, the court issued its first-ever conviction when it found the warlord Thomas Lubanga Dyilo guilty of war crimes for his use of child soldiers in the Dem. Rep. of the Congo.

Though jurisdiction is limited to member nations, the ICC is a court of last resort. It may also initiate cases involving non-member nations if it deems the country's authorities have not taken steps to investigate or prosecute a case. The ICC is based in The Hague, Netherlands, though it may sit elsewhere. **Website:** icc-cpi.int

Geneva Conventions

The Geneva Conventions are four international treaties governing the protection of civilians in times of war, the treatment of prisoners of war, and the care of the wounded and sick in the armed forces. The first convention, covering the sick and wounded in war, was concluded in Geneva, Switzerland, in 1864, at a conference convened by the Swiss government at the urging of the International Committee of the Red Cross. The convention was amended and expanded in 1906. In 1929, two more conventions covering the wounded and prisoners of war were signed. Outrage at the treatment of prisoners and civilians during WWII by some belligerents, notably Germany and Japan, prompted the conclusion, on Aug. 12, 1949, of four new conventions. Three of these restated and strengthened the previous conventions. The fourth codified general principles of international law governing the treatment of civilians in wartime.

The 1949 convention for civilians provided for special safeguards for wounded persons, children under 15 years of age, pregnant women, and the elderly. Discrimination on racial, religious, national, or political grounds was forbidden. Torture, collective punishment, reprisals, unwarranted destruction of property, and forced use of civilians for an occupier's armed forces were also prohibited. Also included was a pledge for the humane treatment, adequate feeding, and delivery of supplies to prisoners. They were not to be forced to disclose more than minimal information. Two additional protocols were adopted in June 1977 dealing with the protection of victims, especially civilians, in international and non-international armed conflicts. (A third protocol, adopted in 2005, created the Red Crystal emblem for use along with the Red Cross and Red Crescent.)

Most countries have formally accepted all or most of the humanitarian conventions as binding. As of July 2012, all 195 countries of the world had signed onto the 1949 Conventions. However, there is no permanent international machinery in place to enforce these treaties.

Genocide

Source: Convention on the Prevention and Punishment of the Crime of Genocide, United Nations Treaty Series 277; Rome Statute of the International Criminal Court

The term "genocide" (which combines Greek and Latin roots to mean "murder of a race") was coined by Polish-Jewish lawyer Raphael Lemkin in 1944 to describe the intentional destruction or attempted destruction of a national, ethnic, racial, or religious group, whether in wartime or peacetime. Genocide is defined as killing members of a group, causing serious bodily harm to members of a group, or otherwise attempting to bring about a group's destruction, including efforts to prevent births or transfer children away from a group. Although the legal definition of genocide does not extend to political groups, the term is often used colloquially to refer to large-scale political violence.

The prohibition against genocide is part of customary international law and is codified in the Convention on the Prevention and Punishment of the Crime of Genocide entered into force on Jan. 12, 1951. As of mid-2012, 142 nations, including the U.S., are parties to it. Genocide is also prohibited by the domestic laws of many nations.

The first modern trials for genocide were conducted by the Allies after WWII. Although the charter of the Nuremberg Tribunal, the international court set up to try Nazi war criminals, did not use the term genocide, its definition of "crimes against humanity" included persecution on racial or religious grounds. More recently, the UN Security Council created ad hoc tribunals to try those responsible for genocide and other serious crimes in the former Yugoslavia and in Rwanda. The International Criminal Court (ICC) also has jurisdiction to try perpetrators of genocide. In Mar. 2005, the Security Council referred the situation in Darfur, Sudan, to the ICC prosecutor. The ICC has since issued two arrest warrants for Sudanese Pres. Omar Hassan al-Bashir on multiple counts of genocide, crimes against humanity, and war crimes.

Examples of Genocides Since 1900

Year	Event	Location	Est. deaths
1915	Extermination of Armenians by the Young Turks	Turkey/Ottoman Empire	1,000,000+
1930s	Intentional infliction of famine on Ukraine	Soviet Union (Ukraine)	6,000,000-7,000,000
1933-45	Attempted destruction of European Jewry (Holocaust)	Europe	6,000,000
1975-79	Khmer Rouge campaign of extermination under Pol Pot[1]	Cambodia	1,500,000-2,000,000
1981-83	Army and paramilitary killings of indigenous Mayan during civil war	Guatemala	200,000+
1988	Anfal Campaign (named by the Iraqi government) against Iraqi Kurds	Iraq	100,000-200,000
1992-95	Ethnic killings during the breakup of Yugoslavia, chiefly Serbs against Bosnian Muslims	Bosnia-Herzegovina, Serbia, Croatia	200,000
1994	Hutu massacre of Tutsis	Rwanda	800,000
2003-present	Rebel group and government-backed Arab militia attacks on non-Arab southern tribes, black population[2]	Darfur region, Sudan	200,000-400,000

Note: Estimates based on historical evidence. The legal definition of "genocide" does not include politically motivated mass killings. Therefore, instances of mass violence against political or class enemies, such as Josef Stalin's purges in the 1930s, which killed some 20 mil Soviets, and Mao Zedong's Cultural Revolution, which killed several mil Chinese, are not included. (1) The mass killings during Cambodia's Khmer Rouge regime are often spoken of as genocide, though many of the murders were politically or class motivated. (2) In 2005, a UN commission concluded that although the "international offenses ... that have been committed in Darfur may be no less serious and heinous than genocide," it did not term the situation there a genocide.

NATIONS OF THE WORLD

As of mid-2012, there were **196 nations** in the world. This number includes three nations that are not members of the United Nations—Kosovo, Taiwan, and Vatican City (the Holy See). Certain regions and territories can be found under the entry for their governing nation.

Sources: FAOSTAT, Economic and Social Development Dept. and Fisheries and Aquaculture Dept., Food and Agric. Org. of the UN (FAO); *Global Report: UNAIDS Report on the Global AIDS Epidemic*, Joint UN Programme on HIV/AIDS (UNAIDS) and World Health Org. (WHO); Intl. Civil Aviation Org. (ICAO); Intl. Data Base, U.S. Census Bureau; *International Energy Annual*, Energy Information Admin. (EIA), U.S. Dept. of Energy; *International Financial Statistics*, Intl. Monetary Fund (IMF); ITU World Telecommunication/ICT Indicators Database, Intl. Telecommunication Union (ITU); *The Military Balance*, Intl. Inst. for Strategic Studies; *Oil & Gas Journal*, PennWell Corp.; *Statistical Yearbook*, UN Statistics Div.; UN Educational, Scientific, and Cultural Org. (UNESCO); *UNWTO World Tourism Barometer* © World Tourism Org. (UNWTO); U.S. Dept. of State; Ward's Automotive Group, a div. of Penton Media Inc.; The World Bank; *The World Factbook*, Central Intelligence Agency (CIA); *World Population Prospects* and *World Urbanization Prospects*, Dept. of Economic and Social Affairs, UN Population Div.

Note: Because of rounding or incomplete enumeration, percentages may not add up to 100%. FY = Fiscal year. NA = Not available/applicable. **Population, age distrib.**, and **pop. density** figures are mid-2012 est., unless otherwise noted. Percent of total pop. living in **urban** areas, as defined by each country, are mid-2011 ests. **Principal languages** are ranked with most widely spoken language listed first. Pop. of **capitals** and **cities (urban aggl.)** are mid-2011 ests. **Defense budget** and **active troops** figures are from mid-2011 unless otherwise noted. Selected **industries** are ranked by descending value of annual output. **Chief crops** are listed in descending order of importance. **Crude oil reserves** are as of Jan. 1, 2012, unless otherwise noted; countries without this entry lack reserves. **Arable land** is given as percentage of country's land area. **Livestock** and **fish catch** are for 2010. Fish catch incl. captured aquatic species as well as the harvest from farming. **Electricity prod.** indicate net, not gross, generated in 2009 unless otherwise noted. **Labor force** percentages are latest available. **GDP** data, for 2011 unless otherwise noted, are based on purchasing power parity calculations. **Per capita GDP** is calculated using a country's est. pop. size as of July 1 of given year. Value of **imports** and **exports** are from 2011 unless otherwise noted. Trade partners, listed in descending order of importance with percentages of total dollar value, are latest available. **Tourism** figures are latest available receipts from intl. tourism. **Budget** figures are 2011 expenditures unless otherwise noted. They are calculated on an exchange rate basis, not purchasing power parity terms. **Total reserves less gold** and **gold** are from 2011 unless otherwise noted. **CPI change**, or consumer price index change, measures the percent change in the CPI between 2010 and 2011 unless otherwise noted. The total length of a country's railway network is listed under **Railways**. **Motor vehicle** statistics, for cars and comm. vehicles, are latest available. **Civil aviation** measures the number of passengers carried a certain distance on scheduled flights operated by airlines registered in a country; they are the latest available. The number of **airports** with paved, usable runways are as of 2012 unless otherwise noted. **TV sets** (in both businesses and households), **radios** (receivers used for broadcast to the public), and **daily newspaper circ.** figures are latest available. Number of fixed **telephone lines** and percentage of pop. accessing the **Internet**, regardless of device used, are for 2011 unless otherwise noted. **Life expect.** is at birth for persons born in 2012. **Natural inc.** measures the difference between the numbers of **births** and **deaths** in 2012. **Infant mortality** measures the probability of a child dying between birth and exact age 1 in 2012. **HIV rate** is est. number of 15- to 49-year-olds living with HIV in 2009, out of a country's pop. of persons 15-49 in 2009. **Education** figures and **literacy** rates are latest available. Literacy measures the percent of pop. aged 15 and older able to read and write simple statements; some countries define as literate those who have completed a certain amount of schooling. **Embassy** addresses are for Wash., DC, area code (202), unless otherwise noted.

See pages 465-80 for full-color maps and flags of all nations.

Afghanistan
Islamic Republic of Afghanistan

People: Population: 30,419,928. **Age distrib.:** <15: 43.2%; 65+: 2.5%. **Pop. density:** 120.8 per sq mi, 46.6 per sq km. **Urban:** 23.5%. **Ethnic groups:** Pashtun 42%, Tajik 27%, Hazara 9%, Uzbek 9%, Aimak 4%, Turkmen 3%, Baloch 2%. **Principal languages:** Afghan Persian or Dari (official), Pashto (official), Turkic langs. (Uzbek, Turkmen), 30 minor langs. (Balochi, Pashai). **Chief religions:** Sunni Muslim 80%, Shia Muslim 19%.

Geography: Total area: 251,827 sq mi, 652,230 sq km; **Land area:** 251,827 sq mi, 652,230 sq km. **Location:** In SW Asia, NW of the Indian subcontinent. **Neighbors:** Pakistan on E, S; Iran on W; Turkmenistan, Tajikistan, Uzbekistan on N. The NE tip touches China. **Topography:** The country is landlocked and mountainous, much of it over 4,000 ft above sea level. The Hindu Kush Mts. tower 16,000 ft above Kabul and reach a height of 25,000 ft to the E. Trade with Pakistan flows through the 35-mi-long Khyber Pass. The climate is dry, with extreme temperatures, and there are large desert regions. **Capital:** Kabul, 3,096,910.

Government: Type: Islamic republic. **Head of state and gov.:** Pres. Hamid Karzai; b. Dec. 24, 1957; in office: June 19, 2002. **Local divisions:** 32 provinces. **Defense budget:** $635 mil. **Active troops:** 170,700.

Economy: Industries: small-scale prod. of textiles, soap, furniture, shoes, fertilizer, apparel, food prods. **Chief crops:** opium, wheat, fruits, nuts. **Natural resources:** nat. gas, petroleum, coal, copper, chromite, talc, barites, sulfur, lead, zinc, iron ore, salt, prec. and semiprec. stones. **Arable land:** 11.9%. **Livestock:** cattle: 5.7 mil; chickens: 12.9 mil; goats: 6.8 mil; sheep: 13.3 mil. **Fish catch:** 1,000 metric tons. **Electricity prod.:** 913 mil kWh. **Labor force:** agric. 78.6%, industry 5.7%, services 15.7%.

Finance: Monetary unit: Afghani (AFN) (Sept. 2012: 48.41 = $1 U.S.). **GDP:** $30.1 bil; **per capita GDP:** $1,000; **GDP growth:** 5.7%. **Imports** (2010): $9.2 bil; U.S. 31.4%, Pakistan 20.8%, Russia 8.4%, India 5.6%, Germany 4.1%. **Exports** (2010): $2.6 bil (not incl. illicit exports or reexports); Pakistan 31.4%, India 28.8%, Tajikistan 8.3%, Russia 5.2%, Bangladesh 4.7%. **Tourism:** NA. **Budget:** $3.3 bil. **Total reserves less gold:** $5.3 bil. **Gold:** 703,005 oz t.

Transport: Motor vehicles: 27.5 vehicles per 1,000 pop. **Civil aviation:** 23 airports. **Chief ports:** Kheyrabad, Shir Khan. **Communications: TV sets:** 80 per 1,000 pop. **Radios:** 129 per 1,000 pop. **Telephone lines:** 0.04 per 100 pop. **Internet:** 5%.

Health: Life expect.: 48.5 male; 51.1 female. **Births:** 39.3 (per 1,000 pop.). **Deaths:** 14.6 (per 1,000 pop.). **Natural inc.:** 2.47% **Infant mortality:** 121.6 (per 1,000 live births). **HIV rate:** NA.

Education: Compulsory: ages 7-15. **Literacy:** 18.2%.

Major intl. organizations: UN (FAO, IBRD, ILO, IMF, WHO), WTO (observer).

Embassy: 2341 Wyoming Ave. NW 20008; 483-6410.
Website: www.president.gov.af

Afghanistan, occupying a favored invasion route since antiquity, has been variously known as Ariana or Bactria (in ancient times) and Khorasan (in the Middle Ages). Foreign empires alternated rule with local emirs and kings until the 18th cent., when a unified kingdom was established. In 1973, a military coup ushered in a republic.

Pro-Soviet leftists took power in a bloody 1978 coup and concluded an economic and military treaty with the USSR. In Dec. 1979 the USSR began a massive airlift into Kabul and backed a new coup, leading to the installation of a more pro-Soviet leader. Soviet forces fanned out over Afghanistan and waged a protracted guerrilla war with Muslim rebels, in which some 15,000 Soviet troops reportedly died.

A UN-mediated agreement was signed Apr. 14, 1988, providing for withdrawal of Soviet troops, a neutral Afghan state, and repatriation of refugees. Afghan rebels rejected the pact. The Soviets completed their troop withdrawal Feb. 15, 1989; fighting between Afghan rebels and government forces ensued. Communist Pres. Najibullah resigned Apr. 16, 1992, as competing guerrilla forces advanced on Kabul. The rebels achieved power Apr. 28, ending 14 years of Soviet-backed regimes. More than 2 mil Afghans had been killed and 6 mil had left the country since 1979.

Clashes between moderates and Islamic fundamentalist forces followed the rebel victory. Burhanuddin Rabbani, a guerrilla leader, became president June 28, 1992, but fierce fighting continued around Kabul and elsewhere. The Taliban, an insurgent Islamic radical faction, captured Kabul in Sept. 1996. The Taliban executed Najibullah and empowered Islamic religious police to enforce strict Islamic codes of dress and behavior. Rabbani and other ousted leaders fled to the north.

Victories in the northern cities of Mazar-e Sharif, Aug. 8, 1998, and Taloqan, Aug. 8-11, gave the Taliban control over more than 90% of the country. On Aug. 20, U.S. cruise missiles struck southeast of Kabul, hitting facilities the U.S. said were terrorist training camps run by Osama bin Laden. The UN imposed sanctions Nov. 14, 1999, when Afghanistan refused to turn over bin Laden to the U.S. for prosecution; a UN ban on military aid to the Taliban took effect Jan. 19, 2001.

After the Sept. 11, 2001, attacks on the World Trade Center and Pentagon, the U.S., blaming bin Laden, demanded that the Taliban surrender him and shut down his al-Qaeda terrorist network. When the Taliban refused, the U.S., with British assistance, began bombing Afghanistan Oct. 7, as part of Operation Enduring Freedom.

Supported by the U.S., the opposition Northern Alliance recaptured Mazar-e Sharif Nov. 9 and took Kabul 4 days later; Taliban forces abandoned Kandahar, their last stronghold, to southern tribesmen Dec. 7. A power-sharing agreement signed by 4 anti-Taliban factions, including the Northern Alliance, provided for an interim government headed by Hamid Karzai, a Pashtun tribal leader. The UN authorized a multinational security force Dec. 20, 2001.

Meeting June 13, 2002, in Kabul, a traditional council (*loya jirga*) chose Karzai to head a new transitional government. The U.S.

announced the end of major combat operations in Afghanistan, May 1, 2003, but resistance continued. NATO officially assumed control of peacekeeping forces (ISAF) Aug. 11. A new constitution took effect Jan. 26, 2004.

The most intense fighting in more than 4 years erupted Mar. 2006 with a new wave of suicide bombings, rocket and mortar attacks, and other strikes by Taliban insurgents against military and civilian targets. Erosion of government authority led to an increase in opium growing; the Taliban, local warlords, and some Karzai associates were accused of profiting from the drug trade. A record poppy crop of 8,200 metric tons in 2007 made Afghanistan the source of 93% of the world's illicit opium; drought, blight, and local suppression efforts cut estimated output to 3,600 metric tons by 2010.

Operating from sanctuaries across the border in Pakistan, Islamist suicide bombers and Taliban insurgents stepped up their activities, 2007-11. Violence escalated in the run-up to the presidential election Aug. 20, 2009; on that day, Taliban attacks, intended to suppress turnout, killed at least 30 people. Preliminary results released Sept. 8 showed Karzai above 50% of the vote, but a UN-backed commission overseeing the tally ordered a recount, citing "clear and convincing evidence of fraud" at numerous polling stations; a runoff election scheduled for Nov. 7 was canceled when Karzai's lone opponent dropped out of the race. Karzai was sworn in for a second term Nov. 19, despite growing U.S. doubts about his ability to prosecute the war and root out corruption. Weak turnout, allegations of vote-buying, and Taliban attacks marred parliamentary elections Sept. 18, 2010. After a decade-long manhunt, U.S. commandos killed bin Laden shortly after midnight May 2, 2011, in Abbottabad, Pakistan. Insurgents retaliated Aug. 6 by shooting down a Chinook transport helicopter, killing 30 Americans (including 22 Navy SEALs) and 8 Afghans. Other violence included the killing July 12 of Ahmed Wali Karzai, the powerful half-brother of Pres. Karzai; a truck bombing Sept. 11 in Wardak Province that killed 5 Afghan civilians and wounded 77 NATO soldiers; attacks Sept. 13 on the U.S. embassy, NATO headquarters, and other targets in Kabul; and the assassination Sept. 20 of former Pres. Rabbani, a leader in government-backed peace talks with the Taliban.

Between Jan. 2009 and June 2011, the number of U.S. troops in Afghanistan rose from about 36,000 to 99,000, while the number of allied foreign forces under ISAF increased from nearly 32,000 to more than 42,000. The U.S. June 22, 2011, outlined a timetable for ending the war. 10,000 U.S. troops left by the end of 2011 and another 23,000 were scheduled to pull out Sept. 2012; the combined total of 33,000 roughly equals the "surge" in U.S. troops that Pres. Obama announced in Dec. 2009. Other coalition partners including the UK and France also began troop pullouts. All U.S. forces are scheduled to be withdrawn by the end of 2014.

Intensification of hostilities between coalition forces and insurgents increased casualties. Coalition military fatalities rose from 295 in 2008 to 521 in 2009, 711 in 2010, 566 in 2011, and 318 in Jan.-Aug. 2012; of more than 3,174 coalition military deaths since Operation Enduring Freedom began in Oct. 2001, more than 2,100 were from the U.S., 427 from the UK, and nearly 160 from Canada. According to the UN, 1,145 Afghan civilians were killed and 1,954 wounded during the first 6 months of 2012; the combined total was 15% lower than the corresponding period in 2011. By July 18, 2012, the U.S. Congress had appropriated about $548 bil for the Afghanistan war and related military activities. "Green-on-blue" attacks, or Afghan security forces attacks on coalition troops, increased to 14% of coalition casualties in 2012, up from 6% in 2011, 3% in 2010, 2% in 2009 and less than 1% in 2008.

Albania
Republic of Albania

People: Population: 3,002,859. **Age distrib.:** <15: 20.6%; 65+: 10.6%. **Pop. density:** 283.9 per sq mi, 109.6 per sq km. **Urban:** 53.4%. **Ethnic groups:** Albanian 95%, Greek 3%. **Principal languages:** Albanian (official; derived from Tosk dialect), Greek. **Chief religions:** Muslim 70%, Albanian Orthodox 20%, Roman Catholic 10%.

Geography: Total area: 11,100 sq mi, 28,748 sq km; **Land area:** 10,578 sq mi, 27,398 sq km. **Location:** SE Europe, on SE coast of Adriatic Sea. **Neighbors:** Greece on S; Montenegro, Kosovo, Serbia on N; Macedonia on E. **Topography:** Apart from a narrow coastal plain, Albania consists of hills and mountains covered with scrub forest, cut by small E-W rivers. **Capital:** Tirana, 419,215.

Government: Type: Republic. **Head of state:** Pres. Bamir Topi; b. Apr. 24, 1957; in office: July 24, 2007. **Head of gov.:** Prime Min. Sali Berisha; b. Oct. 15, 1944; in office: Sept. 11, 2005. **Local divisions:** 12 counties divided into 36 districts. **Defense budget:** $136 mil. **Active troops:** 14,245.

Economy: Industries: food proc., textiles and clothing, lumber. **Chief crops:** wheat, corn, potatoes, vegetables, fruits, sugar beets, grapes. **Natural resources:** petroleum, nat. gas, coal, bauxite, chromite, copper, iron ore, nickel, salt, timber, hydropower. **Crude oil reserves:** 199.1 mil bbls. **Arable land:** 22.3%. **Livestock:** cattle: 493,000; chickens: 5.2 mil; goats: 775,000; pigs: 164,000; sheep: 1.8 mil. **Fish catch:** 8,649 metric tons. **Electricity prod.:** 5.2 bil kWh. **Labor force:** agric. 47.8%, industry 23%, services 29.2%.

Finance: Monetary unit: Lek (ALL) (Sept. 2012: 110.11 = $1 U.S.). **GDP:** $25.2 bil (country has an informal and unreported sector that may be as large as 50% of official GDP); **per capita GDP:** $7,800; **GDP growth:** 2%. **Imports:** $5.1 bil; Italy 34.8%, Greece 12.9%, China 6.2%, Turkey 6%, Germany 4.6%. **Exports:** $2 bil; Italy 48.8%, China 8.4%, Turkey 6.7%, Greece 5.6%, Spain 5.4%, India 4.9%. **Tourism:** $1.6 bil. **Budget:** $3.7 bil. **Total reserves less gold:** $2.4 bil. **Gold:** 50,607 oz t. **CPI change:** 3.5%.

Transport: Railways: 211 mi. **Civil aviation:** 105.6 mil pass.-mi; 4 airports. **Chief ports:** Durres, Sarande, Shengjin, Vlore.

Communications: TV sets: 190 per 1,000 pop. **Radios:** 585 per 1,000 pop. **Telephone lines:** 10.5 per 100 pop. **Daily newspaper circ.:** 24.4 per 1,000 pop. **Internet:** 49%.

Health: Life expect.: 75.0 male; 80.5 female. **Births:** 12.4 (per 1,000 pop.). **Deaths:** 6.3 (per 1,000 pop.). **Natural inc.:** 0.61% **Infant mortality:** 14.1 (per 1,000 live births). **HIV rate:** NA.

Major intl. organizations: UN (FAO, IBRD, ILO, IMF, IMO, WHO), NATO, OSCE, WTO.

Education: Compulsory: ages 6-13. **Literacy:** 95.9%.

Embassy: 2100 S St. NW 20008; 223-4942.

Website: www.km.gov.al

Ancient Illyria was conquered by Romans, Slavs, and Turks (15th cent.); the Turks Islamized the population. Independent Albania was proclaimed in 1912; the republic was formed in 1920. King Zog I ruled 1925-39, until Italy invaded.

Communist partisans took over in 1944, allied Albania with the USSR, but broke with the USSR in 1960 over de-Stalinization. Later, China provided billions of dollars in assistance, but cut off aid in 1978 when Albania attacked its policies. Large-scale purges of officials occurred during the 1970s.

Enver Hoxha, the nation's ruler for four decades, died Apr. 11, 1985. The new regime introduced some liberalization, including measures in 1990 providing for freedom to travel abroad. Efforts were begun to improve ties with the outside world.

Albania's former Communists were routed in elections Mar. 1992, amid economic collapse and social unrest. Sali Berisha was elected as the first non-Communist president since WWII. Berisha's party claimed a landslide victory in disputed parliamentary elections, May 26 and June 2, 1996. Public protests over the collapse of fraudulent investment schemes in Jan. 1997 led to armed rebellion. The UN Security Council, Mar. 28, authorized a 7,000-member force to restore order. Socialists and their allies won parliamentary elections, June 29 and July 6, and international peacekeepers pulled out by Aug. 11.

During NATO's air war against Yugoslavia, Mar.-June 1999, Albania hosted some 465,000 Kosovar refugees. A pro-Berisha coalition victory in July 3, 2005, elections ended eight years of Socialist rule. Albania became a full member of NATO Apr. 1, 2009; the nation formally applied for EU membership Apr. 28. Following parliamentary elections June 28, 2009, Berisha remained prime minister. Albania's candidacy for membership in the EU was delayed after parliament refused, Aug. 7, 2012, to curb immunity from prosecution of lawmakers and other government officials.

Algeria
People's Democratic Republic of Algeria

People: Population: 37,367,226. **Age distrib.:** <15: 27.8%; 65+: 5%. **Pop. density:** 40.6 per sq mi, 15.7 per sq km. **Urban:** 73%. **Ethnic groups:** Arab-Berber 99%. **Principal languages:** Arabic (official), French, Berber dialects. **Chief religions:** Sunni Muslim (official) 99%, Christian and Jewish 1%.

Geography: Total area: 919,595 sq mi, 2,381,741 sq km; **Land area:** 919,595 sq mi, 2,381,741 sq km. **Location:** In NW Africa, from Medit. Sea into Sahara Desert. **Neighbors:** Morocco, Western Sahara on W; Mauritania, Mali, Niger on S; Libya, Tunisia on E. **Topography:** The Tell, located on the coast, comprises fertile plains 50-100 mi wide, with a moderate climate and adequate rain. Two major chains of Atlas Mts., running roughly E-W and reaching 7,000 ft, enclose a dry plateau region. Below lies the Sahara, mostly desert with major mineral resources. **Capital:** Algiers, 2,915,650. **Cities (urban aggl.):** Oran, 783,020.

Government: Type: Republic. **Head of state:** Pres. Abdelaziz Bouteflika; b. Mar. 2, 1937; in office: Apr. 27, 1999. **Head of gov.:** Prime Min. Ahmed Ouyahia; b. July 2, 1952; in office: June 23, 2008. **Local divisions:** 48 provinces. **Defense budget:** $8.61 bil. **Active troops:** 130,000.

Economy: Industries: petroleum, nat. gas, light industries, mining, electrical, petrochemical, food proc. **Chief crops:** wheat, barley, oats, grapes, olives, citrus, fruits. **Natural resources:** petroleum, nat. gas, iron ore, phosphates, uranium, lead, zinc. **Crude oil reserves:** 12.2 bil bbls. **Arable land:** 3.1%. **Livestock:** cattle: 1.7 mil; chickens: 125 mil; goats: 3.9 mil; pigs: 5,700; sheep: 20 mil. **Fish catch:** 95,366 metric tons. **Electricity prod.** 40.2 bil kWh. **Labor force:** agric. 14%, industry 13.4%, constr. and public works 10%, trade 14.6%, govt. 32%, other 16%.

Finance: Monetary unit: Dinar (DZD) (Sept. 2012: 80.70 = $1 U.S.). **GDP:** $267 bil; **per capita GDP:** $7,400; **GDP growth:** 2.5%. **Imports:** $44.2 bil; France 18.5%, China 10.4%, Italy 9.5%, Spain 8%, Germany 4.5%. **Exports:** $72.7 bil; U.S. 23.3%, Spain 12.2%, Canada 9.5%, France 9.5%, Brazil 5.4%, Netherlands 5.4%,

Germany 4.3%, Italy 4.1%. **Tourism:** $219 mil. **Budget:** $78.6 bil. **Total reserves less gold:** $182.8 bil. **Gold:** 5.6 mil oz t. **CPI change:** 4.5%.

Transport: Railways: 2,469 mi. **Motor vehicles:** 112.6 vehicles per 1,000 pop. **Civil aviation:** 2.4 bil pass.-mi; 60 airports. **Chief ports:** Algiers, Annaba, Oran.

Communications: TV sets: 190 per 1,000 pop. **Radios:** 229 per 1,000 pop. **Telephone lines:** 8.5 per 100 pop. **Internet:** 14%.

Health: Life expect.: 74.8 male; 77.2 female. **Births:** 24.4 (per 1,000 pop.). **Deaths:** 4.3 (per 1,000 pop.). **Natural inc.:** 2.01% **Infant mortality:** 23.4 (per 1,000 live births). **HIV rate:** 0.1%.

Education: Compulsory: ages 6-16. **Literacy:** 72.6%.

Major intl. organizations: UN (FAO, IBRD, ILO, IMF, IMO, WHO), AL, AU, OPEC, WTO (observer).

Embassy: 2118 Kalorama Rd. NW 20008; 265-2800.

Website: www.premier-ministre.gov.dz or www.algeria-us.org

Earliest known inhabitants were ancestors of Berbers, followed by Phoenicians, Romans, Vandals, and, finally, Arabs. Turkey ruled 1518-1830, when France took control. Large-scale European immigration followed. Arab nationalists launched a guerrilla war, 1954, that more than 400,000 French troops were unable to suppress. After French Pres. Charles de Gaulle came to power, 1958, colonial rule ended, nearly all Europeans left, and Algeria declared independence July 5, 1962. Ahmed Ben Bella ruled until 1965, when an army coup installed Col. Houari Boumedienne, a former guerrilla leader who held power until his death in 1978.

Hundreds died in antigovernment riots protesting economic hardship, Oct. 1988. In 1989, voters approved a new constitution, which cleared the way for a multiparty system. The government canceled the Jan. 1992 elections and banned all nonreligious activities at Algeria's 10,000 mosques. Pres. Mohammed Boudiaf was assassinated June 29, 1992. Over the next 7 years, Muslim fundamentalists staged attacks on high-ranking officials, security forces, foreigners, and others; pro-government death squads also were active.

Liamine Zeroual won the Nov. 16, 1995, presidential election. A new constitution banning Islamic political parties and increasing the president's powers passed in a referendum on Nov. 28, 1996. Abdelaziz Bouteflika, who became president after a flawed Apr. 15, 1999, election, made peace with rebels and won approval for an amnesty plan in a referendum, Sept. 16. Some 100 people died and thousands were injured in violent protests Apr.-June 2001, chiefly by Algeria's Berber minority. Bouteflika was reelected Apr. 8, 2004; opponents charged fraud.

An earthquake in northern Algeria, May 21, 2003, claimed over 2,200 lives. Under a reconciliation plan approved by referendum Sept. 29, 2005, the government in Mar. 2006 began freeing Islamists jailed for their role in the 1990s civil war, which left up to 200,000 people dead and 8,000 "disappeared."

Radical Islamists bombed 2 police stations Oct. 30, 2006, and 7 police stations Feb. 13, 2007. A group known as al-Qaeda in the Islamic Maghreb (AQIM) carried out suicide bombings Apr. 11 at the Government Palace and a police station in Algiers, killing 33 people; more than 50 died in suicide bombings at Batna, Sept. 6, and Dellys, Sept. 8. Car bombs Dec. 11, 2007, killed 17 UN staff members and at least 20 others in Algiers. A surge in AQIM violence in Aug. 2008 left more than 100 people dead.

Parliament, Nov. 12, 2008, amended the constitution to abolish presidential term limits, clearing the way for Bouteflika to run for a 3rd term. He claimed more than 90% of the vote in an Apr. 9, 2009, election denounced as fraudulent by opposition parties. During "Arab Spring" uprisings in early 2011, Bouteflika's government suppressed street protests in Algiers, Feb. 12, and used oil revenues to raise salaries of teachers, police, and other discontented civil servants. The country's governing party, the National Liberation Front, strengthened its hold on power in May 10, 2012, parliamentary elections that opposition groups called fraudulent.

Andorra
Principality of Andorra

People: Population: 85,082. **Age distrib.:** <15: 15.6%; 65+: 13.3%. **Pop. density:** 470.9 per sq mi, 181.8 per sq km. **Urban:** 87.3%. **Ethnic groups:** Spanish 43%, Andorran 33%, Portuguese 11%, French 7%. **Principal languages:** Catalan (official), French, Castilian, Portuguese. **Chief religion:** Roman Catholic (predominant).

Geography: Total area: 181 sq mi, 468 sq km; **Land area:** 181 sq mi, 468 sq km. **Location:** SW Europe, in Pyrenees Mts. **Neighbors:** Spain on S, France on N. **Topography:** High mountains and narrow valleys cover the country. **Capital:** Andorra la Vella, 23,497.

Government: Type: Parliamentary co-principality. **Heads of state:** President of France and Bishop of Urgel (Spain), as co-princes. **Head of gov.:** Antoni Martí Petit; b. 1963; in office: May 12, 2011. **Local divisions:** 7 parishes. **Defense budget:** NA. **Active troops:** No regular military forces. Defense is responsibility of France and Spain.

Economy: Industries: tourism (skiing), cattle raising, timber, banking, tobacco, furniture. **Chief crops:** rye, wheat, barley, oats, vegetables. **Natural resources:** hydropower, mineral water, timber, iron ore, lead. **Arable land:** 2.1%. **Labor force:** agric. 0.4%, industry 4.7%, services 94.9%.

Finance: Monetary unit: Euro (EUR) (Sept. 2012: 0.79 = $1 U.S.). **GDP:** $3.2 bil; **per capita GDP:** $37,200; **GDP growth:** –1.8%. **Imports** (2009): $1.5 bil. **Exports** (2009): $64 mil. **Tourism:** NA. **Budget** (2009): $868.4 mil.

Transport: NA

Communications: TV sets: 440 per 1,000 pop. **Radios:** 243 per 1,000 pop. **Telephone lines:** 44.6 per 100 pop. **Internet:** 81%.

Health: Life expect.: 80.4 male; 84.7 female. **Births:** 9.3 (per 1,000 pop.). **Deaths:** 6.5 (per 1,000 pop.). **Natural inc.:** 0.27% **Infant mortality:** 3.8 (per 1,000 live births). **HIV rate:** NA.

Education: Compulsory: ages 6-16. **Literacy:** 100%.

Major intl. organizations: UN (FAO, WHO), OSCE, WTO (observer).

Embassy: 2 UN Plaza, 27th Fl., New York, NY 10017; (212) 750-8064.

Website: www.andorra.ad

France and the bishop of Urgel held joint sovereignty over Andorra from 1278 to 1993. Voters chose to adopt a parliamentary system Mar. 14, 1993, although co-princes remain heads of state. Tourism, especially skiing, is the economic mainstay. Andorra attracts more than 9 mil visitors annually. For years, Andorra served as a tax haven, but it began reforms in 2008 and was removed from the list of uncooperative tax havens, May 27, 2009, and added South Korea, Apr. 30, 2012; Poland, June 15, 2012; and Italy, July 25, 2012; to the list of countries with which it has Tax Information Exchange treaties.

Angola
Republic of Angola

People: Population: 18,056,072. **Age distrib.:** <15: 43.9%; 65+: 2.9%. **Pop. density:** 37.5 per sq mi, 14.5 per sq km. **Urban:** 59.2%. **Ethnic groups:** Ovimbundu 37%, Kimbundu 25%, Bakongo 13%, mestico (mixed European and native African) 2%, European 1%. **Principal languages:** Portuguese (official), Bantu, other African langs. **Chief religions:** indigenous beliefs 47%, Roman Catholic 38%, Protestant 15%.

Geography: Total area: 481,354 sq mi, 1,246,700 sq km; **Land area:** 481,354 sq mi, 1,246,700 sq km. **Location:** In SW Africa on Atlantic coast. **Neighbors:** Namibia on S, Zambia on E, Congo-Kinshasa on N; Cabinda, an enclave separated from rest of country by short Atlantic coast of Congo-Kinshasa, borders Congo-Brazzaville. **Topography:** Mostly plateau elevated 3,000-5,000 ft above sea level, rising from a narrow coastal strip. There is also a temperate highland area in the west-central region, a desert in S, and a tropical rain forest covering Cabinda. **Capital:** Luanda, 5,067,530. **Cities (urban aggl.):** Huambo, 1,097,970.

Government: Type: Republic. **Head of state and gov.:** Pres. José Eduardo dos Santos; b. Aug. 28, 1942; in office: Sept. 20, 1979. **Local divisions:** 18 provinces. **Defense budget:** $3.63 bil. **Active troops:** 107,000.

Economy: Industries: petroleum, mining, cement, metal prods., fish and food proc. **Chief crops:** bananas, sugarcane, coffee, sisal, corn, cotton, manioc, tobacco. **Natural resources:** petroleum, diamonds, iron ore, phosphates, copper, feldspar, gold, bauxite, uranium. **Crude oil reserves:** 9.5 bil bbls. **Arable land:** 3.2%. **Livestock:** cattle: 5.2 mil; chickens: 7.2 mil; goats: 2.6 mil; pigs: 791,000; sheep: 355,000. **Fish catch:** 260,210 metric tons. **Electricity prod.:** 4.1 bil kWh. **Labor force:** agric. 85%, industry and services 15%.

Finance: Monetary unit: Kwanza (AOA) (Sept. 2012: 95.14 = $1 U.S.). **GDP:** $117.2 bil; **per capita GDP:** $6,000; **GDP growth:** 3.4%. **Imports:** $21.7 bil; Portugal 20.4%, China 17.7%, U.S. 9.5%, Brazil 6.8%, South Africa 6.1%, France 5%, India 4.4%. **Exports:** $65.7 bil; China 37.7%, U.S. 21%, India 9.5%, Canada 4.1%. **Tourism:** $719 mil. **Budget:** $35.3 bil. **Total reserves less gold:** $28.8 bil. **CPI change:** 13.5%.

Transport: Railways: 1,717 mi. **Motor vehicles:** 9.2 vehicles per 1,000 pop. **Civil aviation:** 422.5 mil pass.-mi; 30 airports. **Chief ports:** Cabinda, Lobito, Luanda, Namibe.

Communications: TV sets: 140 per 1,000 pop. **Radios:** 81 per 1,000 pop. **Telephone lines:** 1.6 per 100 pop. **Daily newspaper circ.:** 2.2 per 1,000 pop. **Internet:** 14.8%.

Health: Life expect.: 53.5 male; 55.7 female. **Births:** 39.4 (per 1,000 pop.). **Deaths:** 12.1 (per 1,000 pop.). **Natural inc.:** 2.73% **Infant mortality:** 83.5 (per 1,000 live births). **HIV rate:** 2%.

Education: Compulsory: ages 6-11. **Literacy:** 70.1%.

Major intl. organizations: UN (FAO, IBRD, ILO, IMF, WHO), AU, OPEC, WTO.

Embassy: 2100-2108 16th St. NW 20009; 785-1156.

Website: www.governo.gov.ao or www.angola.org

From the early centuries CE to 1500, Bantu tribes penetrated most of the region. Portuguese came in 1583, allied with the Bakongo kingdom in the north, and developed the slave trade. Large-scale colonization began in the 20th cent., when 400,000 Portuguese immigrated.

A guerrilla war, 1961-75, ended when Portugal granted independence. Fighting then erupted among three rival rebel groups—the National Front, based in Zaire (now Dem. Rep. of the Congo); the Soviet-backed Popular Movement for the Liberation of Angola (MPLA); and the National Union for the Total Independence of Angola (UNITA), aided by the U.S. and South Africa.

Cuban troops and Soviet aid helped the MPLA win control of most of the country by 1976, although fighting continued through the 1980s. The MPLA government and UNITA signed a peace accord May 1, 1991.

Elections were held, Sept. 1992, but fighting again broke out, as UNITA rejected the results. UNITA signed a new peace treaty with the government, Nov. 20, 1994, but the rebels were slow to demobilize. The UN Security Council voted, Aug. 28, 1997, to impose sanctions on UNITA. The UN ended its mission in Angola, Mar. 1999, as the civil war continued.

The UN estimated that the war with UNITA had claimed some 1 mil lives and left another 2.5 mil people homeless by mid-2001. Government troops killed the Rebel leader Jonas Savimbi Feb. 22, 2002. UNITA agreed to a truce Apr. 4, 2002, ending the 27-year-long civil war but not fighting between government forces and separatists in oil-rich Cabinda; rebels there agreed to a cease-fire July 2006.

With proven petroleum reserves estimated at more than 9 bil barrels, Angola is among Africa's leading oil producers. Due to mismanagement and corruption up to $4.2 bil in oil revenues went missing, 1997-2002. The ruling MPLA claimed victory in voting Sept. 2008, in Angola's first parliamentary elections in 16 years. Parliament approved Jan. 21, 2010, a new constitution augmenting the power of MPLA leader José Eduardo dos Santos, Angola's president since 1979. The MPLA won flawed elections, Aug 31, 2012, giving dos Santos another 5-year term.

Antigua and Barbuda

People: Population: 89,018. **Age distrib.:** <15: 25.2%; 65+: 7%. **Pop. density:** 520.4 per sq mi, 201.1 per sq km. **Urban:** 29.8%. **Ethnic groups:** black 91%, mixed 4%, white 2%. **Principal languages:** English (official), local dialects. **Chief religions:** Protestant 76% (Anglican 26%, Seventh-Day Adventist 12%, Pentecostal 11%, Moravian 11%, Methodist 8%, Baptist 5%, Church of God 5%), Roman Catholic 10%, other Christian 5%.

Geography: Total area: 171 sq mi, 443 sq km; **Land area:** 171 sq mi, 443 sq km. **Location:** E Caribbean. **Neighbors:** St. Kitts and Nevis to W, Guadeloupe (Fr.) to S. **Topography:** These are mostly low-lying and limestone coral islands. Antigua is mostly hilly with an indented coast; Barbuda is a flat island with a large lagoon on W. **Capital:** St. John's, 26,720.

Government: Type: Constitutional monarchy with British-style parliament. **Head of state:** Queen Elizabeth II; represented by Gov.-Gen. Dame Louise Agnetha Lake-Tack; b. July 26, 1944; in office: July 17, 2007. **Head of gov.:** Prime Min. Baldwin Spencer; b. Oct. 8, 1948; in office: Mar. 24, 2004. **Local divisions:** 6 parishes, 2 dependencies. **Defense budget:** $6 mil. **Active troops:** 170.

Economy: Industries: tourism, constr., light mfg. **Chief crops:** cotton, fruits, vegetables, bananas, coconuts. **Natural resources:** negligible. **Arable land:** 18.2%. **Livestock:** cattle: 14,600; chickens: 150,000; goats: 37,000; pigs: 3,000; sheep: 22,000. **Fish catch:** 2,293 metric tons. **Electricity prod.:** 115 mil kWh. **Labor force:** agric. 7%, industry 11%, services 82%.

Finance: Monetary unit: East Caribbean Dollar (XCD) (Sept. 2012: 2.70 = $1 U.S.). **GDP:** $1.6 bil; **per capita GDP:** $18,200; **GDP growth:** −0.5%. **Imports:** $437.4 mil. **Exports:** $40.3 mil. **Tourism:** $313 mil. **Budget** (2009): $293.4 mil. **Total reserves less gold:** $147.9 mil. **CPI change:** 3.5%.

Transport: Civil aviation: 76.4 mil pass.-mi; 2 airports. **Chief port:** Saint John's.

Communications: TV sets: 465 per 1,000 pop. **Radios:** 497 per 1,000 pop. **Telephone lines:** 39.6 per 100 pop. **Internet:** 82%.

Health: Life expect.: 73.7 male; 77.8 female. **Births:** 16.2 (per 1,000 pop.). **Deaths:** 5.7 (per 1,000 pop.). **Natural inc.:** 1.05%. **Infant mortality:** 14.2 (per 1,000 live births). **HIV rate:** NA. **Education:** Compulsory: ages 5-15. **Literacy:** 99%.

Major intl. organizations: UN (FAO, IBRD, ILO, IMF, WHO), Caricom, the Commonwealth, OAS, OECS, WTO.

Embassy: 3216 New Mexico Ave. NW 20016; 362-5122.

Website: www.ab.gov.ag

Columbus landed on Antigua in 1493. The British colonized it in 1632. The British associated state of Antigua achieved independence as Antigua and Barbuda on Nov. 1, 1981. Tourism, which accounts for more than 25% of GDP, was hit hard by the worldwide recession in 2008-10. The economy also suffered after Robert Allen Stanford, a Texas businessman, was charged by U.S. authorities Feb. 17, 2009, with employing his Antigua-based Stanford Intl. Bank to conduct a fraudulent $7 bil investment scheme. He was convicted Mar. 6, 2012.

Argentina
Argentine Republic

People: Population: 42,192,494. **Age distrib.:** <15: 25.2%; 65+: 11.1%. **Pop. density:** 39.9 per sq mi, 15.4 per sq km. **Urban:** 92.5%. **Ethnic groups:** white (mostly Spanish and Italian) 97%; mestizo (mixed white and Amerindian), Amerindian, other nonwhite groups 3%. **Principal languages:** Spanish (official), Italian, English, German, French. **Chief religions:** nominally Roman Catholic 92%, Protestant 2%, Jewish 2%.

Geography: Total area: 1,073,518 sq mi, 2,780,400 sq km; **Land area:** 1,056,642 sq mi, 2,736,690 sq km. **Location:** Occupies most of southern S. America. **Neighbors:** Chile on W; Bolivia, Paraguay on N; Brazil, Uruguay on NE. **Topography:** Mountains in W are the Andean, Central, Misiones, and Southern ranges. Aconcagua is the highest peak in the Western Hemisphere, alt. 22,834 ft. E of the Andes are heavily wooded plains, called the Gran Chaco in N, and the fertile, treeless Pampas in the central region. Patagonia, in S, is bleak and arid. Rio de la Plata, an estuary in NE, 170 by 140 mi, is mostly freshwater, from 2,485-mi Parana and 1,000-mi Uruguay rivers. **Capital:** Buenos Aires, 13,527,800. **Cities (urban aggl.):** Córdoba, 1,555,927; Rosario, 1,283,314.

Government: Type: Republic. **Head of state and gov.:** Pres. Cristina Fernández de Kirchner; b. Feb. 19, 1953; in office: Dec. 10, 2007. **Local divisions:** 23 provinces, 1 federal district. **Defense budget:** $3.1 bil. **Active troops:** 73,100.

Economy: Industries: food proc., motor vehicles, consumer durables, textiles, chemicals and petrochemicals. **Chief crops:** sunflower seeds, lemons, soybeans, grapes, corn. **Natural resources:** lead, zinc, tin, copper, iron ore, manganese, petroleum, uranium. **Crude oil reserves:** 2.5 bil bbls. **Arable land:** 11.3%. **Livestock:** cattle: 48.9 mil; chickens: 96 mil; goats: 4.3 mil; pigs: 2.3 mil; sheep: 15.8 mil. **Fish catch:** 814,414 metric tons. **Electricity prod.:** 116 bil kWh. **Labor force:** agric. 5%, industry 23%, services 72%.

Finance: Monetary unit: Peso (ARS) (Sept. 2012: 4.65 = $1 U.S.). **GDP:** $725.6 bil; **per capita GDP:** $17,700; **GDP growth:** 8.9%. **Imports:** $70.7 bil; Brazil 33.2%, U.S. 14.4%, China 12.4%, Germany 4.7%. **Exports:** $84.3 bil; Brazil 21.8%, China 7.6%, Chile 5.6%, U.S. 5.5%. **Tourism:** $5.4 bil. **Budget:** $113.3 bil. **Total reserves less gold:** $43.2 bil. **Gold:** 1.98 mil oz t. **CPI change:** 9.5%.

Transport: Railways: 22,970 mi. **Motor vehicles:** 218.9 vehicles per 1,000 pop. **Civil aviation:** 7.3 bil pass.-mi; 159 airports. **Chief ports:** Bahia Blanca, Buenos Aires, La Plata, Punta Colorado.

Communications: TV sets: 325 per 1,000 pop. **Radios:** 681 per 1,000 pop. **Telephone lines:** 24.9 per 100 pop. **Daily newspaper circ.:** 35.5 per 1,000 pop. **Internet:** 47.7%.

Health: Life expect.: 73.9 male; 80.5 female. **Births:** 17.3 (per 1,000 pop.). **Deaths:** 7.4 (per 1,000 pop.). **Natural inc.:** 1.00%. **Infant mortality:** 10.5 (per 1,000 live births). **HIV rate:** 0.5%. **Education:** Compulsory: ages 5-17. **Literacy:** 97.8%.

Major intl. organizations: UN (FAO, IBRD, ILO, IMF, WHO), OAS, WTO.

Embassy: 1600 New Hampshire Ave. NW 20009; 238-6401. **Website:** www.argentina.ar

Nomadic Indians roamed the Pampas when Spaniards arrived, 1515-16, led by Juan Diaz de Solis. Nearly all the Indians were killed by the late 19th cent. The colonists won independence, 1816, and a long period of disorder ended in a strong centralized government.

Large-scale Italian, German, and Spanish immigration in the decades after 1880 spurred modernization. Social reforms were enacted in the 1920s, but military coups prevailed, 1930-46, until Gen. Juan Perón was elected president.

Perón, with his wife, Eva Duarte (d. 1952), introduced labor reforms but suppressed speech and press freedoms, closed religious schools, and ran the country into debt. A 1955 coup exiled Perón. A series of military and civilian regimes followed. Perón returned in 1973 and was again elected president. He died 10 months later. His wife Isabel, who had been elected vice president, succeeded him, becoming the first woman head of state in the Western Hemisphere.

A military junta ousted Mrs. Perón in 1976 amid charges of corruption. Under a continuing state of siege, the army conducted a "dirty war" against guerrillas and leftists. An estimated 30,000 people "disappeared."

Argentine troops seized control of the British-held Falkland Islands (Islas Malvinas) on Apr. 2, 1982. The British imposed an air and sea blockade around the Falklands. Fighting began May 1. British troops landed on East Falkland May 21. Argentine troops surrendered, June 14.

Democratic rule returned in 1983. On Dec. 9, 1985, 5 former junta members were found guilty of murder and human rights abuses during the "dirty war" period.

Buenos Aires Mayor Fernando de la Rúa won the presidential election Oct. 24, 1999. A prolonged recession and a debt of more than $130 bil left Argentina facing an economic crisis in 2001, which austerity measures and IMF aid failed to remedy. After widespread rioting and looting Dec. 19, de la Rúa resigned.

A 2-week period of protests and political upheavals abated when Congress, Jan. 1, 2002, chose a Peronist, Eduardo Alberto Duhalde, to finish de la Rúa's term. Further economic decline and renewed protests led Duhalde, July 2, to schedule an early presidential election for Mar. 2003; another Peronist, Néstor Kirchner, took office May 25, 2003. Kirchner moved to end corruption and human rights abuses among the military and police. A new IMF aid deal, approved Sept. 10, 2003, rescued Argentina from default.

The supreme court, June 14, 2005, overturned amnesty laws that had barred prosecution for "dirty war" crimes committed while the military ruled Argentina. Economic growth, 2004-05, allowed Argentina to repay its $9.57 bil debt to the IMF, Jan. 3, 2006.

After Pres. Kirchner declined to seek a second term, his wife, Cristina Fernández de Kirchner, ran as the Peronist candidate and was elected president Oct. 28, 2007. Responding to mass protests by farmers, Argentina's senate voted July 17, 2008, to block Kirchner's proposed tax increase on agricultural exports. A candidate slate led by Néstor Kirchner was defeated in legislative elections June 28, 2009, and the Peronists lost control of both houses of congress. Argentina July 2010 became the first Latin American country to extend full marriage rights to same-sex couples.

Néstor Kirchner died Oct. 27, 2010. Cristina Fernández de Kirchner was reelected Oct. 23, 2011. She is the first woman to win reelection in Latin America.

Armenia
Republic of Armenia

People: Population: 2,970,495. **Age distrib.:** <15: 17.4%; 65+: 9.9%. **Pop. density:** 272.8 per sq mi, 105.3 per sq km. **Urban:** 64.1%. **Ethnic groups:** Armenian (official) 98%, Yezidi (Kurd) 1%. **Principal languages:** Armenian (official), Yezidi, Russian. **Chief religions:** Armenian Apostolic 95%, other Christian 4%, Yezidi 1%.

Geography: Total area: 11,484 sq mi, 29,743 sq km; **Land area:** 10,889 sq mi, 28,203 sq km. **Location:** SW Asia. **Neighbors:** Georgia on N, Azerbaijan on E, Iran on S, Turkey on W. **Topography:** Mountainous with many peaks above 10,000 ft. **Capital:** Yerevan, 1,116,380.

Government: Type: Republic. **Head of state:** Pres. Serzh Sargsyan; b. June 30, 1954; in office: Apr. 9, 2008. **Head of gov.:** Prime Min. Tigran Sargsyan; b. Jan. 29, 1960; in office; Apr. 9, 2008. **Local divisions:** 10 provinces, 1 city. **Defense budget:** $395 mil. **Active troops:** 48,834.

Economy: Industries: diamond proc., machine tools, forging-pressing machines, elec. motors, tires, knitted wear. **Chief crops:** fruits (espec. grapes), vegetables. **Natural resources:** gold, copper, molybdenum, zinc, bauxite. **Arable land:** 16.1%. **Livestock:** cattle: 570,633; chickens: 3.9 mil; goats: 29,687; pigs: 112,608; sheep: 511,029. **Fish catch:** 5,617 metric tons. **Electricity prod.:** 5.5 bil kWh. **Labor force:** agric. 44.2%, industry 16.8%, services 39%.

Finance: Monetary unit: Dram (AMD) (Sept. 2012: 410.45 = $1 U.S.). **GDP:** $18.2 bil; **per capita GDP:** $5,500; **GDP growth:** 4.4%. **Imports:** $3.5 bil; Russia 20%, China 8.1%, Ukraine 6.8%, Iran 6.5%, Germany 5.9%, Italy 4.7%. **Exports:** $1.3 bil; Russia 15.4%, Germany 13.9%, Iran 9.8%, Bulgaria 9.3%, Netherlands 7.8%, U.S. 7.6%, Spain 7.6%, Canada 5.7%, Belgium 5.5%, Georgia 4.6%. **Tourism:** $445 mil. **Budget:** $2.6 bil. **Total reserves less gold:** $1.9 bil. **CPI change:** 7.7%.

Transport: Railways: 540 mi. **Civil aviation:** 667.4 mil pass.-mi; 10 airports.

Communications: TV sets: 293 per 1,000 pop. **Radios:** 270 per 1,000 pop. **Telephone lines:** 18.6 per 100 pop. **Daily newspaper circ.:** 7.6 per 1,000 pop. **Internet** (2009): 15.3%.

Health: Life expect.: 69.9 male; 77.6 female. **Births:** 12.9 (per 1,000 pop.). **Deaths:** 8.5 (per 1,000 pop.). **Natural inc.:** 0.44% **Infant mortality:** 18.2 (per 1,000 live births). **HIV rate:** 0.1%.

Education: Compulsory: ages 6-15. **Literacy:** 99.6%.

Major intl. organizations: UN (FAO, IBRD, ILO, IMF, WHO), CIS, OSCE, WTO.

Embassy: 2225 R St. NW 20008; 319-1976.

Website: www.gov.am

Ancient Armenia extended into parts of what are now Turkey and Iran. Present-day Armenia was set up as a Soviet republic Apr. 2, 1921. It joined Georgian and Azerbaijan SSRs Mar. 12, 1922, to form the Transcaucasian SFSR, which became part of the USSR Dec. 30, 1922. Armenia became a constituent republic of the USSR Dec. 5, 1936. An earthquake struck Armenia Dec. 7, 1988; approximately 25,000 were killed.

Armenia declared independence Sept. 23, 1991, and became an independent state when the USSR disbanded Dec. 26, 1991. Both mostly Christian Armenia and mostly Muslim Azerbaijan claimed Nagorno-Karabakh, an enclave in Azerbaijan that has an ethnic Armenian majority; it seceded from Azerbaijan in 1988. A 1992-94 war that cost 30,000 lives ended in a cease-fire with Armenian forces in control of the enclave. Voters in the breakaway region approved a pro-independence constitution Dec. 10, 2006, but the referendum was rejected by the EU and OSCE.

Voters approved, July 5, 1995, a new constitution increasing presidential powers. Pres. Levon Ter-Petrosian won reelection Sept. 22, 1996, amid claims of fraud; he resigned Feb. 3, 1998, in a conflict over Nagorno-Karabakh. Robert Kocharian, a nationalist born in the disputed region, won the presidency Mar. 30, 1998. Gunmen stormed Parliament Oct. 27, 1999, killing Prime Min. Vazgen Sarkissian and 7 others. Kocharian won a second term Mar. 5, 2003, in a runoff vote viewed as flawed by opposition groups and Western observers.

Prime Min. Andranik Margaryan died of a heart attack Mar. 25, 2007, and was replaced by Def. Min. Serzh Sargsyan. He defeated Ter-Petrosian in a Feb. 19, 2008, presidential election criticized as flawed; opposition protests in Yerevan were forcibly suppressed Mar. 1, and a 20-day state of emergency followed. Sargsyan took office Apr. 9, 2008.

Seeking to bridge long-standing bitterness over the killing of more than 1 mil Armenians by Ottoman Turks in 1915-18, Armenian and Turkish negotiators signed a treaty Oct. 10, 2009, intended to normalize relations between their two countries; renewed friction with Turkey led Armenia to halt ratification of the treaty Apr. 22, 2010. Sargsyan's party won May 6, 2012, parliamentary elections that the OSCE called "open and peaceful" in spite of lingering shortcomings.

Australia
Commonwealth of Australia

People: Population: 22,015,576. **Age distrib.:** <15: 18.2%; 65+: 14.4%. **Pop. density:** 7.4 per sq mi, 2.9 per sq km. **Urban:** 89.2%. **Ethnic groups:** white 92%, Asian 7%, aboriginal and other 1%. **Principal languages:** English, Chinese, Italian, Greek, Arabic, Vietnamese. **Chief religions:** Protestant 27% (Anglican 19%, Uniting Church 6%, Presbyterian and Reformed 3%), Catholic 26%, Eastern Orthodox 3%, other Christian 8%, Buddhist 2%, Muslim 2%, none 19%.

Geography: Total area: 2,988,902 sq mi, 7,741,220 sq km; **Land area:** 2,966,153 sq mi, 7,682,300 sq km. **Location:** SE of Asia, Indian O. is W and S, Pacific O. (Coral, Tasman seas) is E; they meet N of Australia in Timor and Arafura seas. Tasmania lies 150 mi S of Victoria state, across Bass Strait. **Neighbors:** Nearest are Indonesia, Papua New Guinea on N; Solomons, Fiji, and New Zealand on E. **Topography:** An island continent. The Great Dividing Range along the E coast has Mt. Kosciusko, 7,310 ft. The W plateau rises to 2,000 ft, with arid areas in the Great Sandy and Great Victoria deserts. The NW part of Western Australia and Northern Terr. are arid and hot. The NE has heavy rainfall and Cape York Peninsula has jungles. **Capital:** Canberra, 398,757. **Cities (urban aggl.):** Sydney, 4,543,205; Melbourne, 3,961,205; Brisbane, 2,038,565; Perth, 1,649,209; Adelaide, 1,198,271.

Government: Type: Democratic, federal state system. **Head of state:** Queen Elizabeth II, represented by Gov.-Gen. Quentin Bryce; b. Dec. 23, 1942; in office: Sept. 5, 2008. **Head of gov.:** Prime Min. Julia Gillard; b. Sept. 29, 1961; in office: June 24, 2010. **Local divisions:** 6 states, 2 territories. **Defense budget:** $27.7 bil. **Active troops:** 56,552.

Economy: Industries: mining, industrial and transp. equip., food proc., chemicals, steel. **Chief crops:** wheat, barley, sugarcane, fruits. **Natural resources:** bauxite, coal, iron ore, copper, tin, gold, silver, uranium, nickel, tungsten, rare earth elements, mineral sands, lead, zinc, diamonds, nat. gas, petroleum. **Crude oil reserves:** 1.4 bil bbls. **Other resources:** Wool (world's leading producer), beef. **Arable land:** 6.1%. **Livestock:** cattle: 26.7 mil; chickens: 83 mil; goats: 4.5 mil; pigs: 2.3 mil; sheep: 68.1 mil. **Fish catch:** 243,126 metric tons. **Electricity prod.** (2010): 241.5 bil kWh. **Labor force:** agric. 3.6%, industry 21.1%, services 75%.

Finance: Monetary unit: Dollar (AUD) (Sept. 2012: 0.98 = $1 U.S.). **GDP:** $926.2 bil; **per capita GDP:** $40,800; **GDP growth:** 2%. **Imports:** $243.4 bil; China 18.5%, U.S. 11.4%, Japan 7.9%, Singapore 6.3%, Germany 4.7%. **Exports:** $272.1 bil; China 27.4%, Japan 19.2%, South Korea 8.9%, India 5.8%. **Tourism:** $31.4 bil. **Budget:** $521.8 bil. **Total reserves less gold:** $42.8 bil. **Gold:** 2.6 mil oz t. **CPI change:** 3.4%.

Transport: Railways: 23,889 mi. **Motor vehicles:** 705.6 vehicles per 1,000 pop. **Civil aviation:** 62.5 bil pass.-mi; 333 airports. **Chief ports:** Brisbane, Darwin, Fremantle, Geelong, Gladstone, Melbourne, Newcastle, Sydney.

Communications: TV sets: 659 per 1,000 pop. **Radios:** 1,885 per 1,000 pop. **Telephone lines:** 46.6 per 100 pop. **Daily newspaper circ.:** 155.1 per 1,000 pop. **Internet:** 79%.

Health: Life expect.: 79.5 male; 84.5 female. **Births:** 12.3 (per 1,000 pop.). **Deaths:** 6.9 (per 1,000 pop.). **Natural inc.:** 0.53% **Infant mortality:** 4.6 (per 1,000 live births). **HIV rate:** 0.1%.

Education: Compulsory: ages 5-15. **Literacy:** 99%.

Major intl. organizations: UN and all of its specialized agencies, APEC, the Commonwealth, OECD, WTO.

Embassy: 1601 Massachusetts Ave. NW 20036; 797-3000.

Website: www.australia.gov.au

Australia harbors many plant and animal species not found elsewhere, including kangaroos, koalas, platypuses, dingoes (wild dogs), Tasmanian devils (raccoon-like marsupials), wombats (bear-like marsupials), and barking and frilled lizards.

Capt. James Cook explored the eastern coast in 1770, when the continent was inhabited by a variety of indigenous peoples. The first European settlers, beginning in 1788, were mostly convicts, soldiers, and government officials. By 1830, Britain had claimed the entire continent, and the immigration of free settlers accelerated. The Commonwealth was proclaimed Jan. 1, 1901. Northern Terr. was granted limited self-rule July 1, 1978.

State/territory, capital	Area (sq mi)	Population (Dec. 2010 est.)
New South Wales, Sydney	309,500	7,247,700
Victoria, Melbourne	87,500	5,574,500
Queensland, Brisbane	666,990	4,513,000
Western Australia, Perth	975,100	2,387,200
South Australia, Adelaide	379,900	1,645,000
Tasmania, Hobart	26,200	511,700
Australian Capital Terr., Canberra	900	370,700
Northern Terr., Darwin	519,800	232,400

Racially discriminatory immigration policies ended in 1973, after 3 mil Europeans (half British) had entered since 1945. Indigenous peoples, 90% of them aborigines, number more than 500,000; in the Northern Territory they account for about 28% of the population and hold about 46% of the land. They remain economically disadvantaged.

Australia is among the top exporters of beef, lamb, wool, and wheat. Major mineral deposits have been developed, largely for export. Industrialization has been completed.

The Labor Party won a majority in Feb. 1983 general elections and was reelected in 1984, 1987, 1990, and 1993. Conservatives swept into power in Mar. 2, 1996 after an election that focused mainly on economic issues. Incumbent Prime Min. John Howard retained power in the 1998, 2001, and 2004 elections.

Australia led an international peacekeeping force into Timor in Sept. 1999. In a referendum Nov. 6, voters rejected a proposal that would have made Australia a republic.

Australian troops fought in U.S.-led military operations in Afghanistan (2001) and Iraq (2003). Some 2,000 Australian peacekeepers began arriving in the Solomon Isls., July 24, 2003; nearly all were withdrawn by mid-2005. In race riots in Sydney suburbs, Dec. 11-12, 2005, thousands of white youths assaulted people of Middle Eastern ancestry, who then retaliated. Australian troops were dispatched, 2006, to suppress disorder in the Solomon Isl. in Apr. and Timor in May. As of mid-2012, about 3,300 Australian troops were serving overseas, including 1,550 in Afghanistan and 390 in Timor.

Pledging to pull combat troops out of Iraq and to ratify the Kyoto Protocol against global warming, Kevin Rudd led the Labor Party to victory in parliamentary elections Nov. 24, 2007. Quentin Bryce, the nation's first female governor-general, was sworn in Sept. 5, 2008. "Black Saturday" bushfires Feb. 7 in Victoria State claimed 173 lives.

After a series of policy missteps eroded his popularity and alienated his Labor supporters, Rudd was forced out June 24, 2010, by his deputy, Julia Gillard, who became Australia's first female prime minister. Inconclusive parliamentary elections Aug. 21 led to the formation of a minority government headed by Gillard. Downpours from Cyclone Tasha and other storms flooded Queensland in late Dec. 2010 and early Jan. 2011, with three-fourths of the state declared a disaster zone. By late Jan. the flood death toll had reached 35. A carbon tax that will cost companies AUD $23 ($24 USD) for each ton of carbon they produce came into effect July 1, 2012.

Australian External Territories

Norfolk Isl., area 14 sq mi, pop. (2012 est.) 2,182, was taken over, 1914. The soil is very fertile, suitable for citrus, bananas, and coffee. Many of the inhabitants are descendants of the *Bounty* mutineers, moved to Norfolk 1856 from Pitcairn Isl. Australia offered the island limited home rule in 1978. **Website:** www.info.gov.nf

Coral Sea Isls. territory, area less than 1.2 sq mi, is administered from Norfolk Isl.

Ashmore and Cartier Isls., area 1.9 sq mi, in the Indian O., came under Australian authority 1934 and are administered as part of Northern Territory. **Heard Isl. and McDonald Isls.**, area 159 sq mi, are administered by the Dept. of Science.

Cocos (Keeling) Isls., 27 small coral islands in the Indian O. 1,750 mi NW of Australia. Pop. (2010 est.) 596; area 5 sq mi. The residents voted to become part of Australia, Apr. 1984.

Christmas Isl., area 52 sq mi, pop (2010 est.) 1,496; 230 mi S of Java, was transferred to Britain in 1958. It has phosphate deposits.

Australian Antarctic Territory was claimed by Australia in 1933, including 2,362,000 sq mi of territory S of 60th parallel S lat. and between 160th-45th meridians E long. It does not include Adelie Coast.

Austria
Republic of Austria

People: Population: 8,219,743. **Age distrib.:** <15: 13.9%; 65+: 18.5%. **Pop. density:** 258.2 per sq mi, 99.7 per sq km. **Urban:** 67.7%. **Ethnic groups:** Austrian 91%, fmr. Yugoslav (incl. Croatian, Slovene, Serb, Bosniak) 4%, Turk 2%. **Principal languages:** German (official), Turkish, Serbian, Croatian (official in Burgenland). **Chief religions:** Roman Catholic 74%, Protestant 5%, Muslim 4%, none 12%.

Geography: Total area: 32,383 sq mi, 83,871 sq km; **Land area:** 31,832 sq mi, 82,445 sq km. **Location:** In S Central Europe. **Neighbors:** Switzerland, Liechtenstein on W; Germany, Czech Rep. on N; Slovakia, Hungary on E; Slovenia, Italy on S. **Topography:** Austria is primarily mountainous, with the Alps and foothills covering the western and southern provinces. The eastern provinces and Vienna are located in the Danube River Basin. **Capital:** Vienna, 1,720,170.

Government: Type: Federal republic. **Head of state:** Pres. Heinz Fischer; b. Oct. 9, 1938; in office: July 8, 2004. **Head of gov.:** Chancellor Werner Faymann; b. May 4, 1960; in office: Dec. 2, 2008. **Local divisions:** 9 bundeslaender (states). **Defense budget:** $2.88 bil. **Active troops:** 25,758.

Economy: Industries: constr., machinery, vehicles and parts, food, metals, chemicals, lumber and wood proc., paper and paperboard, communications equip., tourism. **Chief crops:** grains,

potatoes, wine, fruits. **Natural resources:** oil, coal, lignite, timber, iron ore, copper, zinc, antimony, magnesite, tungsten, graphite, salt, hydropower. **Crude oil reserves:** 50 mil bbls. **Arable land:** 16.6%. **Livestock:** cattle: 2 mil; chickens: 15.5 mil; goats: 68,188; pigs: 3.1 mil; sheep: 344,709. **Fish catch:** 2,517 metric tons. **Electricity prod.** (2010): 64 bil kWh. **Labor force:** agric. 5.5%, industry 27.5%, services 67%.

Finance: Monetary unit: Euro (EUR) (Sept. 2012: 0.79 = $1 U.S.). **GDP:** $356.5 bil; **per capita GDP:** $42,400; **GDP growth:** 3.1%. **Imports:** $183.3 bil; Germany 42.8%, Italy 6.8%, Switzerland 5.6%, Netherlands 4.1%. **Exports:** $173.6 bil; Germany 32.2%, Italy 7.8%, Switzerland 4.4%, France 4.2%. **Tourism:** $19.9 bil. **Budget:** $216.6 bil. **Total reserves less gold:** $11 bil. **Gold:** 9 mil oz t. **CPI change:** 3.3%.

Transport: Railways: 3,976 mi. **Motor vehicles:** 579.5 vehicles per 1,000 pop. **Civil aviation:** 9.2 bil pass.-mi; 24 airports. **Chief ports:** Enns, Krems, Linz, Vienna.

Communications: TV sets: 656 per 1,000 pop. **Radios:** 752 per 1,000 pop. **Telephone lines:** 40.3 per 100 pop. **Daily newspaper circ.:** 311.4 per 1,000 pop. **Internet:** 79.8%.

Health: Life expect.: 77.0 male; 83.0 female. **Births:** 8.7 (per 1,000 pop.). **Deaths:** 10.2 (per 1,000 pop.). **Natural inc.:** −0.15% **Infant mortality:** 4.3 (per 1,000 live births). **HIV rate:** 0.3%.

Education: Compulsory: ages 6-14. **Literacy:** 98%.

Major intl. organizations: UN and all of its specialized agencies, EU, OECD, OSCE, WTO.

Embassy: 3524 International Ct. NW 20008; 895-6700.
Website: www.austria.gv.at

Rome conquered Austrian lands from Celtic tribes around 15 BC. In 788 the territory was incorporated into Charlemagne's empire. By 1300, the House of Hapsburg had gained control; they added vast territories in all parts of Europe to their realm in the next few hundred years.

Austrian dominance of Germany was undermined in the 18th cent. and ended by Prussia by 1866. But the Congress of Vienna, 1815, confirmed Austrian control of a large empire in southeast Europe consisting of Germans, Hungarians, Slavs, Italians, and others. The dual Austro-Hungarian monarchy was established in 1867, giving autonomy to Hungary and almost 50 years of peace.

World War I, started after the June 28, 1914, assassination of Archduke Franz Ferdinand, the Hapsburg heir, by a Serbian nationalist, destroyed the empire. By 1918 Austria was reduced to a small republic, with the borders it has today.

Nazi Germany, ruled by the Austrian-born Adolf Hitler, annexed Austria Mar. 13, 1938. The republic was reestablished in 1945, under Allied occupation. Full independence and neutrality were restored in 1955. Austria joined the EU Jan. 1, 1995.

The rise of the right-wing, anti-immigrant Austrian Freedom Party challenged the dominance of the Austrian Social Democratic Party in the late 1990s. When Freedom Party members joined the cabinet, Feb. 4, 2000, the EU imposed political sanctions on Austria for 7 months. Social Democrats won the parliamentary elections of Oct. 1, 2006; they held onto their plurality in elections Sept. 28, 2008, although far-right parties made gains. One of the stronger economies in the eurozone, Austria's unemployment rate was 4.5%, the zone's lowest, as of Aug. 2012.

Azerbaijan
Republic of Azerbaijan

People: Population: 9,493,600. **Age distrib.:** <15: 22.7%; 65+: 6.3%. **Pop. density:** 297.6 per sq mi, 114.9 per sq km. **Urban:** 53.6%. **Ethnic groups:** Azeri 91%, Dagestani 2%, Russian 2%, Armenian 2%. **Principal languages:** Azerbaijani (Azeri) (official), Lezgi, Russian, Armenian. **Chief religions:** Muslim 93%, Russian Orthodox 3%, Armenian Orthodox 2%.

Geography: Total area: 33,436 sq mi, 86,600 sq km; **Land area:** 31,903 sq mi, 82,629 sq km. **Location:** SW Asia. **Neighbors:** Russia, Georgia on N; Iran on S; Armenia on W; Caspian Sea on E. **Topography:** The Great Caucasus Mts. in N, Karabakh Upland in W border the Kur-Abas lowland; climate is arid except in the subtropical SE. **Capital:** Baku, 2,122,900.

Government: Type: Republic. **Head of state:** Pres. Ilham Aliyev; b. Dec. 24, 1961; in office: Oct. 31, 2003. **Head of gov.:** Prime Min. Artur Rasizade; b. Feb. 26, 1935; in office: Nov. 4, 2003. **Local division:** 59 rayons, 11 cities, 1 autonomous republic. **Defense budget:** $1.68 bil. **Active troops:** 66,940.

Economy: Industries: petroleum and nat. gas, petroleum prods., oil field equip.; steel, iron ore; cement. **Chief crops:** cotton, grain, rice, grapes. **Natural resources:** petroleum, nat. gas, iron ore, nonferrous metals, bauxite. **Crude oil reserves:** 7 bil bbls. **Arable land:** 22.7%. **Livestock:** cattle: 2.4 mil; chickens: 22.4 mil; goats: 620,644; pigs: 6,342; sheep: 7.9 mil. **Fish catch:** 2,081 metric tons. **Electricity prod.:** 17.9 bil kWh. **Labor force:** agric. 38.3%, industry 12.1%, services 49.6%.

Finance: Monetary unit: New Manat (AZN) (Sept. 2012: 0.78 = $1 U.S.). **GDP:** $94.3 bil; **per capita GDP:** $10,300; **GDP growth:** 0.1%. **Imports:** $10.2 bil; Turkey 18.1%, Russia 15.5%, China 7.8%, Germany 7.2%, UK 6.1%, Ukraine 4.6%, Italy 4.2%. **Exports:** $34.5 bil; Italy 32.4%, France 13.2%, U.S. 7.5%, Germany 6.2%,

Indonesia 5.4%, Czech Republic 5.3%. **Tourism:** $1.3 bil. **Budget:** $19.5 bil. **Total reserves less gold:** $10.3 bil. **CPI change:** 7.9%.

Transport: Railways: 1,813 mi. **Motor vehicles:** 110 vehicles per 1,000 pop. **Civil aviation:** 791.6 mil pass.-mi; 30 airports. **Chief port:** Baku.

Communications: TV sets: 216 per 1,000 pop. **Radios:** 214 per 1,000 pop. **Telephone lines:** 18.1 per 100 pop. **Daily newspaper circ.:** 16.1 per 1,000 pop. **Internet:** 50%.

Health: Life expect.: 68.4 male; 74.7 female. **Births:** 17.3 (per 1,000 pop.). **Deaths:** 7.1 (per 1,000 pop.). **Natural inc.:** 1.02% **Infant mortality:** 28.8 (per 1,000 live births). **HIV rate:** 0.1%.

Education: Compulsory: ages 6-17. **Literacy:** 99.8%.

Major intl. organizations: UN (FAO, IBRD, ILO, IMF, WHO), CIS, OSCE, WTO (observer).

Embassy: 2741 34th St. NW 20008; 337-3500.

Website: www.president.az

Azerbaijan was home to Scythian tribes and part of the Roman Empire. Overrun by Turks in the 11th cent. and conquered by Russia in 1806 and 1813, it joined the USSR Dec. 30, 1922, and became a constituent republic in 1936. Azerbaijan gained independence when the Soviet Union disbanded Dec. 26, 1991.

Nagorno-Karabakh, an enclave with a majority population of ethnic Armenians, seceded from Azerbaijan in 1988, triggering a war between mostly Muslim Azerbaijan and mostly Christian Armenia, 1992-94, in which 30,000 lives were lost (see Armenia).

Voters approved a new constitution expanding presidential powers, Nov. 12, 1995. Pres. Haydar Aliyev, a pro-Russian former Communist, was reelected Oct. 11, 1998, but international monitors called the vote seriously flawed.

The dying Pres. Aliyev named his son Ilham prime minister Aug. 4, 2003. The younger Aliyev won the Oct. 15, 2003, presidential election. International observers called the vote fraudulent. He responded to violent protests Oct. 16 by arresting hundreds of opposition leaders and their supporters. Serious abuses also marred parliamentary elections, Nov. 6, 2005, won by parties loyal to Aliyev. The opening May 25, 2005, of the Baku-Tbilisi-Ceyhan pipeline, providing an outlet for Azerbaijan's vast Caspian oil reserves, transformed the nation's economy.

Pres. Ilham Aliyev won a second term Oct. 15, 2008, but main opposition parties boycotted the election. A constitutional amendment abolishing presidential term limits was approved by referendum Mar. 18, 2009. Azerbaijan holds strategic importance as a transit point for U.S. troops and supplies bound for Afghanistan and won a seat for 2012-13 on the UN Security Council, Jan. 1, 2012.

The Bahamas
Commonwealth of The Bahamas

People: Population: 316,182. **Age distrib.:** <15: 24%; 65+: 6.5%. **Pop. density:** 81.8 per sq mi, 31.6 per sq km. **Urban:** 84.3%. **Ethnic groups:** black 85%, white 12%, Asian and Hispanic 3%. **Principal languages:** English (official), Creole (among Haitian immigrants). **Chief religions:** Protestant 68% (Baptist 35%, Anglican 15%, Pentecostal 8%, Church of God 5%, Methodist 4%), Roman Catholic 14%, other Christian 15%.

Geography: Total area: 5,359 sq mi, 13,880 sq km; **Land area:** 3,865 sq mi, 10,010 sq km. **Location:** In Atlantic O., E of Florida. **Neighbors:** Nearest are U.S. on W, Cuba on S. **Topography:** Nearly 700 islands (29 inhabited) and over 2,000 islets in the W Atlantic O. extend 760 mi NW to SE. **Capital:** Nassau, 254,000.

Government: Type: Parliamentary democracy. **Head of state:** Queen Elizabeth II, represented by Gov.-Gen. Sir Arthur Foulkes; b. May 11, 1928; in office: Apr. 14, 2010. **Head of gov.:** Prime Min. Hubert Alexander Ingraham; b. Aug. 4, 1947; in office: May 4, 2007. **Local divisions:** 21 districts. **Defense budget:** $51 mil. **Active troops:** 860.

Economy: Industries: tourism, banking, cement, oil transshipment, salt, rum. **Chief crops:** citrus, vegetables. **Natural resources:** salt, aragonite, timber. **Arable land:** 0.8%. **Livestock:** cattle: 750; chickens: 3 mil; goats: 14,500; pigs: 5,000; sheep: 6,500. **Fish catch:** 11,772 metric tons. **Electricity prod.** 1.9 bil kWh. **Labor force:** agric. 5%, industry 5%, tourism 50%, other services 40%.

Finance: Monetary unit: Dollar (BSD) (Sept. 2012: 1.00 = $1 U.S.). **GDP:** $10.9 bil; **per capita GDP:** $31,400; **GDP growth:** 2%. **Imports:** $2.9 bil; U.S. 25.9%, India 18.8%, South Korea 14.4%, Venezuela 9.6%, Singapore 7.8%, China 4.2%. **Exports:** $709.7 mil; Singapore 26.8%, U.S. 25.6%, Dominican Republic 11.2%, Ecuador 8.1%, Mexico 4.9%, Switzerland 4.9%. **Tourism:** $2.1 bil. **Budget** (FY11/12 est.): $1.7 bil. **Total reserves less gold:** $1.1 bil. **CPI change:** 3.2%.

Transport: Motor vehicles: 397.7 vehicles per 1,000 pop. **Civil aviation:** 171.5 mil pass.-mi; 22 airports. **Chief ports:** Freeport, Nassau.

Communications: TV sets: 248 per 1,000 pop. **Radios:** 746 per 1,000 pop. **Telephone lines:** 38.3 per 100 pop. **Internet:** 65%.

Health: Life expect.: 69.0 male; 73.9 female. **Births:** 16.0 (per 1,000 pop.). **Deaths:** 6.9 (per 1,000 pop.). **Natural inc.:** 0.90% **Infant mortality:** 13.1 (per 1,000 live births). **HIV rate:** 3.1%.

Education: Compulsory: ages 5-15. **Literacy:** NA.

Major intl. organizations: UN (FAO, IBRD, ILO, IMF, WHO), Caricom, the Commonwealth, OAS, WTO (observer).

Embassy: 2220 Massachusetts Ave. NW 20008; 319-2660.

Website: www.bahamas.gov.bs

Christopher Columbus first set foot in the New World on San Salvador (Watling Isl.) in 1492, when Arawak Indians inhabited the islands. British settlement began in 1647; the islands became a British colony in 1783. Internal self-government was granted in 1964; full independence within the Commonwealth was attained July 10, 1973. International banking and investment management have become major industries alongside tourism.

Bahrain
Kingdom of Bahrain

People: Population: 1,248,348. **Age distrib.:** <15: 20.2%; 65+: 2.6%. **Pop. density:** 4,254.2 per sq mi, 1,642.6 per sq km. **Urban:** 88.7%. **Ethnic groups:** Bahraini 62%, non-Bahraini 38%. **Principal languages:** Arabic (official), English, Farsi, Urdu. **Chief religions:** Muslim (Shia and Sunni) 81%, Christian 9%.

Geography: Total area: 293 sq mi, 760 sq km; **Land area:** 293 sq mi, 760 sq km. **Location:** SW Asia, in Persian Gulf. **Neighbors:** Nearest are Saudi Arabia on W, Qatar on E. **Topography:** Bahrain Island, and several adjacent, smaller islands, are flat, hot, and humid, with little rain. **Capital:** Manama, 261,782.

Government: Type: Constitutional monarchy. **Head of state:** King Hamad bin Isa al-Khalifa; b. Jan. 28, 1950; in office: as emir Mar. 6, 1999; as king Feb. 14, 2002. **Head of gov.:** Prime Min. Khalifa bin Sulman al-Khalifa; b. Nov. 24, 1936; in office: Jan. 19, 1970. **Local divisions:** 12 municipalities. **Defense budget:** $873 mil. **Active troops:** 8,200.

Economy: Industries: petroleum proc. and refining, aluminum smelting, iron pelletization, fertilizers, Islamic and offshore banking. **Chief crops:** fruits, vegetables. **Natural resources:** oil, nat. gas, fish, pearls. **Crude oil reserves:** 124.6 mil bbls. **Arable land:** 1.7%. **Livestock:** cattle: 10,000; chickens: 530,000; goats: 19,000; sheep: 40,000. **Fish catch:** 13,493 metric tons. **Electricity prod.:** 11.3 bil kWh. **Labor force:** agric. 1%, industry 79%, services 20%.

Finance: Monetary unit: Dinar (BHD) (Sept. 2012: 0.38 = $1 U.S.). **GDP:** $31.5 bil; **per capita GDP:** $27,900; **GDP growth:** 1.8%. **Imports:** $12.1 bil; Saudi Arabia 27.5%, U.S. 10.2%, India 7.9%, China 7.4%, Brazil 5.8%, Germany 4.7%. **Exports:** $19.9 bil; Saudi Arabia 3.3%, UAE 2.2%, Japan 2%, India 1.9%. **Tourism:** $1.4 bil. **Budget:** $8.4 bil. **Total reserves less gold:** $4.5 bil. **Gold:** 150,000 oz t. **CPI change:** –0.4%.

Transport: Motor vehicles: 400.3 vehicles per 1,000 pop. **Civil aviation:** 8.7 bil pass.-mi; 4 airports. **Chief ports:** Mina Salman, Sitrah.

Communications: TV sets: 414 per 1,000 pop. **Radios:** 544 per 1,000 pop. **Telephone lines:** 20.9 per 100 pop. **Internet:** 77%.

Health: Life expect.: 76.2 male; 80.5 female. **Births:** 14.4 (per 1,000 pop.). **Deaths:** 2.6 (per 1,000 pop.). **Natural inc.:** 1.18% **Infant mortality:** 10.2 (per 1,000 live births). **HIV rate:** NA.

Education: Compulsory: ages 6-14. **Literacy:** 91.9%.

Major intl. organizations: UN (FAO, IBRD, ILO, IMF, WHO), AL, WTO.

Embassy: 3502 International Dr. NW 20008; 342-1111.

Website: www.bahrain.bh

Long ruled by the Khalifa family, Bahrain was a British protectorate from 1861 to Aug. 15, 1971, when it regained independence.

Pearls, shrimp, fruits, and vegetables were the mainstays of the economy until oil was discovered in 1932. Crude oil production has declined since the 1970s, but natural gas output has grown and international banking has thrived. Shiite dissidents have clashed with the Sunni-led government since 1996.

Emir Hamad bin Isa al-Khalifa proclaimed himself king Feb. 14, 2002. Local elections in May 2002 marked the first time Bahraini women were allowed to vote and run for office. The first female judge was appointed June 6, 2006. The monarchy suppressed "Arab Spring" mass demonstrations Feb.-Mar. 2011; to bolster security, a Gulf Cooperation Council force of 1,600, led by Saudi Arabia, entered Bahrain Mar. 14, and the government recruited hundreds of additional former soldiers and police from Pakistan. Protests, however, continued in 2012.

Bangladesh
People's Republic of Bangladesh

People: Population: 161,083,804. **Age distrib.:** <15: 33.6%; 65+: 4.8%. **Pop. density:** 3,205.1 per sq mi, 1,237.5 per sq km. **Urban:** 28.4%. **Principal languages:** Bangla, or Bengali (official), English. **Chief religions:** Muslim 89.5%, Hindu 9.6%.

Geography: Total area: 55,598 sq mi, 143,998 sq km; **Land area:** 50,258 sq mi, 130,168 sq km. **Location:** In S Asia, on N bend of Bay of Bengal. **Neighbors:** India nearly surrounds country on W, N, E; Myanmar on SE. **Topography:** The country is mostly a low plain cut by the Ganges and Brahmaputra rivers and their delta. The land is alluvial and marshy along the coast, with hills only in the extreme SE and NE. A tropical monsoon climate prevails, among the rainiest in the world. **Capital:** Dhaka, 15,390,900. **Cities (urban aggl.):** Chittagong, 5,239,095; Khulna, 1,780,566.

Government: Type: Parliamentary democracy. **Head of state:** Pres. Zillur Rahman; b. Mar. 9, 1929; in office: Feb. 12, 2009. **Head**

of gov.: Prime Min. Sheikh Hasina; b. Sept. 28, 1947; in office: Jan. 6, 2009. **Local divisions:** 6 divisions. **Defense budget:** $1.25 bil. **Active troops:** 157,053.

Economy: Industries: jute, cotton, garments, paper, leather, fertilizer, iron and steel, cement, petroleum prods., tobacco, drugs and pharmaceuticals. **Chief crops:** rice, jute, tea, wheat, sugarcane, potatoes, tobacco, pulses, oilseeds, spices. **Natural resources:** nat. gas, timber, coal. **Crude oil reserves:** 28 mil bbls. **Arable land:** 58.1%. **Livestock:** cattle: 23.1 mil; chickens: 228 mil; goats: 50 mil; sheep: 1.8 mil. **Fish catch:** 3.04 mil metric tons. **Electricity prod.:** 35.7 bil kWh. **Labor force:** agric. 45%, industry 30%, services 25%.

Finance: Monetary unit: Taka (BDT) (Sept. 2012: 81.80 = $1 U.S.). **GDP:** $285.8 bil; **per capita GDP:** $1,700; **GDP growth:** 6.1%. **Imports:** $31.8 bil; China 18.2%, India 13.5%, Malaysia 4.9%. **Exports:** $23.9 bil; U.S. 19.7%, Germany 16.1%, UK 9.5%, France 7.2%, Italy 4.3%, Netherlands 4.3%, Spain 4.3%, Canada 4%. **Tourism:** $81 mil. **Budget:** $17.2 bil. **Total reserves less gold:** $8.5 bil. **Gold:** 434,500 oz t. **CPI change:** 10.7%.

Transport: Railways: 1,629 mi. **Motor vehicles:** 0.7 vehicles per 1,000 pop. **Civil aviation:** 2.7 bil pass.-mi; 16 airports. **Chief ports:** Chittagong, Mongla Port.

Communications: TV sets: 106 per 1,000 pop. **Radios:** 64 per 1,000 pop. **Telephone lines:** 1.1 per 100 pop. **Internet:** 5%.

Health: Life expect.: 68.2 male; 72.0 female. **Births:** 22.5 (per 1,000 pop.). **Deaths:** 5.7 (per 1,000 pop.). **Natural inc.:** 1.68% **Infant mortality:** 49.0 (per 1,000 live births). **HIV rate:** <0.1%.

Education: Compulsory: ages 6-10. **Literacy:** 56.8%.

Major intl. organizations: UN (FAO, IBRD, ILO, IMF, WHO), the Commonwealth, WTO.

Embassy: 3510 International Dr. NW 20008; 244-0183.

Website: www.bangladesh.gov.bd

Muslim invaders conquered the formerly Hindu area in the 12th cent. British rule lasted from the 18th cent. to 1947, when East Bengal became part of Pakistan.

Opposing domination by West Pakistan, the Awami League, based in the East, won control of the National Assembly in 1971. Assembly sessions were postponed; riots broke out. Pakistani troops attacked, Mar. 25; Bangladesh independence was proclaimed the next day. In the ensuing civil war, 1 mil died and 10 mil fled to India.

War between India and Pakistan broke out Dec. 3, 1971. Pakistan surrendered in the East on Dec. 16. Mujibur Rahman, known as Sheikh Mujib, became prime minister; he was killed in a coup Aug. 15, 1975.

Army rivals killed Pres. Ziaur Rahman in an unsuccessful coup attempt, May 30, 1981. Vice Pres. Abdus Sattar assumed the presidency but was ousted in a coup led by army chief of staff Gen. H. M. Ershad, Mar. 1982. Ershad declared Bangladesh an Islamic Republic in 1988; a parliamentary system of government was adopted in 1991. A cyclone struck Apr. 1991, killing over 131,000 people.

Political turmoil led to the resignation, Mar. 30, 1996, of Prime Min. Khaleda Zia, the widow of Ziaur Rahman. Sheikh Mujib's daughter, known as Sheikh Hasina, led the country after the June 12, 1996 election. Floods in July-Sept. 1998 inundated most of the country, killed over 1,400 people (many through disease), and stranded at least 30 mil.

Khaleda Zia returned to power following parliamentary elections, Oct. 1, 2001. Floods July-Aug. 2004 caused at least 950 deaths. Militant Islamists set off more than 400 small bombs in over 50 cities and towns, Aug. 17, 2005, killing three. Another wave of jihadist bombings killed 22, Nov. 29-Dec. 8, 2005. A Bangladeshi economist, Muhammad Yunus, won the 2006 Nobel Peace Prize for using very small loans (microcredit) to help alleviate the nation's severe poverty.

Escalating political violence led Pres. Iajuddin Ahmed to declare a state of emergency Jan. 11, 2007. A military-backed caretaker government filed criminal charges against Khaleda Zia and Sheikh Hasina, but failed to force the two former prime ministers into exile. Cyclone Sidr struck Nov. 15, 2007, damaging more than 1.5 mil homes and leaving about 3,400 dead.

The Awami League triumphed in parliamentary elections Dec. 29, 2008, and Sheikh Hasina was sworn in as prime minister Jan. 6, 2009, ending two years of emergency rule. A mutiny Feb. 25-26, 2009, at the Dhaka headquarters of the Bangladesh Rifles, a border force, left 74 people dead. A fire that raged through a crowded residential area of Dhaka June 3, 2010, killed at least 117. The UN Intl. Tribunal for the Law of the Sea (ITLOS) ruled in favor of Bangladesh in its maritime dispute with Myanmar Mar. 14, 2012, granting its claim to 200 nautical mi in the oil-rich Bay of Bengal and beyond.

Barbados

People: Population: 287,733. **Age distrib.:** <15: 18.8%; 65+: 10%. **Pop. density:** 1,733.1 per sq mi, 669.1 per sq km. **Urban:** 44.4%. **Ethnic groups:** black 93%, white 3%, mixed 3%, East Indian 1%. **Principal language:** English. **Chief religions:** Protestant 63%, Roman Catholic 4%, other Christian 7%.

Geography: Total area: 166 sq mi, 430 sq km; **Land area:** 166 sq mi, 430 sq km. **Location:** In Atlantic O., farthest E of West Indies. **Neighbors:** Nearest are St. Lucia and St. Vincent and the Grenadines to the W. **Topography:** The island lies alone in the Atlantic almost completely surrounded by coral reefs. Highest point is Mt. Hillaby, 1,115 ft. **Capital:** Bridgetown, 121,657.

Government: Type: Parliamentary democracy. **Head of state:** Queen Elizabeth II, represented by Gov.-Gen. Sir Clifford Husbands; b. Aug. 5, 1926; in office: June 1, 1996. **Head of gov.:** Prime Min. Freundel Stuart; b. Apr. 27, 1951; in office: Oct. 23, 2010. **Local divisions:** 11 parishes and Bridgetown. **Defense budget:** $28 mil. **Active troops:** 610.

Economy: Industries: tourism, sugar, light mfg., component assembly for export. **Chief crops:** sugarcane, vegetables, cotton. **Natural resources:** petroleum, fish, nat. gas. **Crude oil reserves:** 2.3 mil bbls. **Other resources:** Fish. **Arable land:** 37.2%. **Livestock:** cattle: 10,700; chickens: 3.6 mil; goats: 5,200; pigs: 21,000; sheep: 11,500. **Fish catch:** 3,271 metric tons. **Electricity prod.** (2010): 1.04 bil kWh. **Labor force:** agric. 10%, industry 15%, services 75%.

Finance: Monetary unit: Dollar (BBD) (Sept. 2012: 2.00 = $1 U.S.). **GDP:** $6.6 bil; **per capita GDP:** $23,700; **GDP growth:** 0.5%. **Imports:** $1.6 bil; Russia 26.6%, Trinidad and Tobago 24.8%, U.S. 18.6%, China 6.1%. **Exports:** $447.3 mil; Trinidad and Tobago 18.7%, France 10.6%, U.S. 9.6%, St. Lucia 8.7%, St. Vincent and the Grenadines 5.4%, Venezuela 4.8%, Antigua and Barbuda 4.4%, St. Kitts and Nevis 4.2%. **Tourism:** $974 mil. **Budget:** $1.4 bil. **Total reserves less gold:** $812.6 mil. **CPI change:** 9.4%.

Transport: Motor vehicles: 342.6 vehicles per 1,000 pop. **Civil aviation:** 1 airport. **Chief port:** Bridgetown.

Communications: TV sets: 291 per 1,000 pop. **Radios:** 287 per 1,000 pop. **Telephone lines:** 51.4 per 100 pop. **Internet:** 71.8%.

Health: Life expect.: 72.3 male; 76.8 female. **Births:** 12.2 (per 1,000 pop.). **Deaths:** 8.4 (per 1,000 pop.). **Natural inc.:** 0.38% **Infant mortality:** 11.6 (per 1,000 live births). **HIV rate:** 1.4%.

Education: Compulsory: ages 5-15. **Literacy:** NA.

Major intl. organizations: UN (FAO, IBRD, ILO, IMF, WHO), Caricom, the Commonwealth, OAS, WTO.

Embassy: 2144 Wyoming Ave. NW 20008; 939-9200.

Website: www.barbados.gov.bb

Barbados was probably named by Portuguese sailors in reference to bearded fig trees. An English ship visited in 1605, and British settled on the uninhabited island in 1627. Slaves worked the sugar plantations until slavery was abolished in 1834. Self-rule came gradually, with full independence proclaimed Nov. 30, 1966. When Prime Min. David Thompson died Oct. 23, 2010, he was succeeded by his deputy, Freundel Stuart. Tourism and manufacturing surpassed the sugar trade in economic importance in the 1990s. The country signed an Economic and Technical Agreement with China Aug. 24, 2012, to strengthen the growing ties between the two countries.

Belarus
Republic of Belarus

People: Population: 9,643,566. **Age distrib.:** <15: 15%; 65+: 13.9%. **Pop. density:** 123.1 per sq mi, 47.5 per sq km. **Urban:** 75%. **Ethnic groups:** Belarusian 81%, Russian 11%, Polish 4%, Ukrainian 2%. **Principal languages:** Belarusian (official), Russian (official). **Chief religions:** Eastern Orthodox 80%, other (incl. Roman Catholic, Protestant, Jewish, Muslim) 20%.

Geography: Total area: 80,155 sq mi, 207,600 sq km; **Land area:** 78,340 sq mi, 202,900 sq km. **Location:** E Europe. **Neighbors:** Poland on W; Latvia, Lithuania on N; Russia on E; Ukraine on S. **Topography:** Belarus is a landlocked country consisting mostly of hilly lowland with significant marsh areas in S. **Capital:** Minsk, 1,861,320.

Government: Type: Republic. **Head of state:** Pres. Aleksandr Lukashenko; b. Aug. 30, 1954; in office: July 20,1994. **Head of gov.:** Prime Min. Mikhail Myasnikovich; b. May 6, 1950; in office: Dec. 28, 2010. **Local divisions:** 6 oblasts and 1 municipality. **Defense budget:** $470 mil. **Active troops:** 72,940.

Economy: Industries: machine tools, tractors, trucks, earthmovers, motorcycles. **Chief crops:** grain, potatoes, vegetables, sugar beets, flax. **Natural resources:** timber, peat, oil, nat. gas, granite, dolomitic limestone, marl, chalk, sand, gravel, clay. **Crude oil reserves:** 198 mil bbls. **Arable land:** 27.3%. **Livestock:** cattle: 4.2 mil; chickens: 34.1 mil; goats: 75,000; pigs: 3.8 mil; sheep: 52,400. **Fish catch:** 17,162 metric tons. **Electricity prod.:** 28.6 bil kWh. **Labor force:** agric. 9.4%, industry 45.9%, services 44.7%.

Finance: Monetary unit: Ruble (BYR) (Sept. 2012: 8,442.02 = $1 U.S.). **GDP:** $143.6 bil; **per capita GDP:** $15,200; **GDP growth:** 5.3%. **Imports:** $42.2 bil; Russia 45.8%, Germany 6.5%, Ukraine 5.7%, China 4.5%. **Exports:** $39.6 bil; Russia 31%, Netherlands 12.6%, Ukraine 11.4%, Latvia 7.2%, Germany 4.7%, Brazil 4.3%. **Tourism:** $459 mil. **Budget:** $22.3 bil. **Total reserves less gold:** $6.01 bil. **Gold:** 1.2 mil oz t. **CPI change:** 53.2%.

Transport: Railways: 3,441 mi. **Motor vehicles:** 256.3 vehicles per 1,000 pop. **Civil aviation:** 272.2 mil pass.-mi; 34 airports. **Chief port:** Mazyr.

Communications: TV sets: 386 per 1,000 pop. **Radios:** 340 per 1,000 pop. **Telephone lines:** 44 per 100 pop. **Daily newspaper circ.:** 81.3 per 1,000 pop. **Internet:** 39.6%.

Health: Life expect.: 65.8 male; 77.5 female. **Births:** 11.1 (per 1,000 pop.). **Deaths:** 13.9 (per 1,000 pop.). **Natural inc.:** −0.28% **Infant mortality:** 3.7 (per 1,000 live births). **HIV rate:** 0.3%.

Education: Compulsory: ages 6-14. **Literacy:** 99.6%.

Major intl. organizations: UN (FAO, IBRD, ILO, IMF, WHO), CIS, OSCE, WTO (observer). **Embassy:** 1619 New Hampshire Ave. NW 20009; 986-1604. **Website:** www.president.gov.by

Belarus became a constituent republic of the USSR in 1922, although Poland controlled the western region. Overrun by German armies in 1941, Belarus was recaptured by Soviet troops in 1944. Following WWII, Belarus increased in area through Soviet annexation of part of NE Poland. Belarus declared independence Aug. 25, 1991, and became independent when the Soviet Union disbanded Dec. 26, 1991.

A new constitution was adopted, Mar. 15, 1994, after which Aleksandr Lukashenko was elected president. Russia and Belarus signed a pact, Apr. 2, 1996, linking their political and economic systems. An authoritarian constitution enacted in Nov. gave Pres. Lukashenko vast new powers. Since then, Lukashenko and his supporters have retained power in elections criticized as seriously flawed by Western observers.

The IMF agreed Jan. 2009 to extend $2.5 bil in credits to help Belarus weather the global economic downturn. A dispute over natural gas deliveries from Russia was resolved June 24, 2010, after Belarus settled its $200 mil energy debt. Belarus agreed July 5 to form a customs union with Russia and Kazakhstan. Lukashenko crushed protests that followed the Dec. 19, 2010 presidential election in which he claimed nearly 80% of the vote; the U.S. and EU imposed sanctions on Lukashenko and other Belarus officials Jan. 31, 2011.

Belgium
Kingdom of Belgium

People: Population: 10,438,353. **Age distrib.:** <15: 15.8%; 65+: 18.4%. **Pop. density:** 892.9 per sq mi, 344.8 per sq km. **Urban:** 97.5%. **Ethnic groups:** Fleming 58%, Walloon 31%, mixed or other 11%. **Principal languages:** Dutch, French, German (all official). **Chief religions:** Roman Catholic 75%, other (incl. Protestant) 25%.

Geography: Total area: 11,787 sq mi, 30,528 sq km; **Land area:** 11,690 sq mi, 30,278 sq km. **Location:** In W Europe, on North Sea. **Neighbors:** France on W and S, Luxembourg on SE, Germany on E, Netherlands on N. **Topography:** Mostly flat, the country is trisected by the Scheldt and Meuse, major commercial rivers. The land becomes hilly and forested in the SE (Ardennes) region. **Capital:** Brussels, 1,948,880 (figure is for urban aggl.). **Cities (urban aggl.):** Antwerp, 959,474.

Government: Type: Parliamentary democracy under a constitutional monarch. **Head of state:** King Albert II; b. June 6, 1934; in office: Aug. 9, 1993. **Head of gov.:** Prime Min. Elio Di Rupo; b. July 18, 1951; in office: Dec. 6, 2011. **Local divisions:** 10 provinces and Brussels. **Defense budget:** $3.88 bil. **Active troops:** 34,336.

Economy: Industries: engineering and metal prods., motor vehicle assembly, transp. equip., scientific instruments, processed food and beverages, chemicals, metals, textiles, glass, petroleum. **Chief crops:** sugar beets, vegetables, fruits, grain, tobacco. **Natural resources:** constr. materials, silica sand, carbonates. **Arable land:** 27.7%. **Livestock:** cattle: 2.6 mil; chickens: 34.4 mil; goats: 22,000; pigs: 6.4 mil; sheep: 120,000. **Fish catch:** 22,957 metric tons. **Electricity prod.** (2010): 89.3 bil kWh. **Labor force:** agric. 2%, industry 25%, services 73%.

Finance: Monetary unit: Euro (EUR) (Sept. 2012: 0.79 = $1 U.S.). **GDP:** $418.6 bil; **per capita GDP:** $38,200; **GDP growth:** 1.9%. **Imports:** $355.1 bil; Netherlands 19.9%, Germany 14.8%, France 10.7%, UK 6%, U.S. 5.3%, Ireland 4.5%, China 4.2%. **Exports:** $344.9 bil; Germany 18.7%, France 16.9%, Netherlands 12.5%, UK 7.2%, Italy 4.6%, U.S. 4.5%. **Tourism:** $11.3 bil. **Budget:** $271.2 bil. **Total reserves less gold:** $17.9 bil. **Gold:** 7.3 mil oz t. **CPI change:** 3.5%.

Transport: Railways: 2,009 mi. **Motor vehicles:** 571.6 vehicles per 1,000 pop. **Civil aviation:** 4.4 bil pass.-mi; 27 airports. **Chief ports:** Antwerp (one of the world's busiest), Gent, Liege, Zeebrugge. **Communications: TV sets:** 585 per 1,000 pop. **Radios:** 791 per 1,000 pop. **Telephone lines:** 43.1 per 100 pop. **Daily newspaper circ.:** 164.7 per 1,000 pop. **Internet:** 78%.

Health: Life expect.: 76.5 male; 83.0 female. **Births:** 10.0 (per 1,000 pop.). **Deaths:** 10.6 (per 1,000 pop.). **Natural inc.:** −0.06%. **Infant mortality:** 4.3 (per 1,000 live births). **HIV rate:** 0.2%. **Education:** Compulsory: ages 6-18. **Literacy:** 99%.

Major intl. organizations: UN and all of its specialized agencies, EU, NATO, OECD, OSCE, WTO. **Embassy:** 3330 Garfield St. NW 20008; 333-6900. **Website:** www.belgium.be

Belgium derives its name from the Belgae, the first recorded inhabitants, probably Celts. The land was ruled for 1800 years by conquerors, including Rome, the Franks, Burgundy, Spain, Austria, and France. After 1815, Belgium was made a part of the Netherlands but became an independent constitutional monarchy in 1830.

Belgian neutrality was violated by Germany in both world wars. King Leopold III surrendered to Germany, May 28, 1940. After the war, he was forced by political pressure to abdicate in favor of his son, King Baudouin. Baudouin was succeeded by his brother, Albert II, Aug. 9, 1993.

The Flemings of northern Belgium speak Dutch, while French is the language of the Walloons in the south. The language difference has been a perennial source of controversy between the 2 groups. Parliament has passed measures aimed at transferring power from the central government to 3 regions—Wallonia, Flanders, and Brussels. Constitutional changes in 1993 made Belgium a federal state.

After elections June 10, 2007, rivalries between Flemings and Walloons led to a 9-month political stalemate. Controversy over the sale of troubled bank Fortis NV to BNP Paribas of France led to the resignation of Prime Min. Yves Leterme, Dec. 19, 2008, and his replacement by former Budget Min. Herman Van Rompuy. Leterme returned to office after Van Rompuy was chosen Nov. 19, 2009, to become president of the EU. Elections June 13, 2010, led to a prolonged political deadlock that ended when Elio Di Rupo became prime min., Dec. 6, 2011.

Belize

People: Population: 327,719. **Age distrib.:** <15: 36.3%; 65+: 3.6%. **Pop. density:** 37.2 per sq mi, 14.4 per sq km. **Urban:** 44.7%. **Ethnic groups:** mestizo 49%, Creole 25%, Maya 11%, Garifuna 6%. **Principal languages:** Spanish, Creole, Mayan dialects, English (official), Garifuna (Carib), German. **Chief religions:** Roman Catholic 39%, Pentacostal 8%, Seventh Day Adventist 5%, Anglican 5%, Mennonite 4%, Baptist 4%, Methodist 3%, Nazarene 3%, Jehovah's Witnesses 2%, none 15%.

Geography: Total area: 8,867 sq mi, 22,966 sq km; **Land area:** 8,805 sq mi, 22,806 sq km. **Location:** Eastern coast of Central America. **Neighbors:** Mexico on N, Guatemala on W and S. **Topography:** Belize has swampy lowlands in N, Maya Mts. in S, coral reefs and cays near coast. Climate is tropical. **Capital:** Belmopan, 14,472.

Government: Type: Parliamentary democracy. **Head of state:** Queen Elizabeth II, represented by Gov.-Gen. Sir Colville Young; b. Nov. 20, 1932; in office: Nov. 17, 1993. **Head of gov.:** Prime Min. Dean Barrow; b. Mar. 2, 1951; in office: Feb. 8, 2008. **Local divisions:** 6 districts. **Defense budget:** $15.5 mil. **Active troops:** 1,050.

Economy: Industries: garment prod., food proc., tourism, constr., oil. **Chief crops:** bananas, cacao, citrus, sugar. **Natural resources:** timber, fish, hydropower. **Crude oil reserves:** 6.7 mil bbls. Arable land: 3.1%. **Livestock:** cattle: 95,000; chickens: 1.5 mil; goats: 180; pigs: 17,038; sheep: 13,018. **Fish catch:** 119,003 metric tons. **Electricity prod.:** 307 mil kWh. **Labor force:** agric. 10.2%, industry 18.1%, services 71.7%.

Finance: Monetary unit: Dollar (BZD) (Sept. 2012: 1.97 = $1 U.S.). **GDP:** $2.8 bil; **per capita GDP:** $8,400; **GDP growth:** 2.5%. **Imports:** $773.9 mil; U.S. 38.5%, Mexico 10.5%, Cuba 9.2%, Guatemala 5.5%, China 5.1%, Trinidad and Tobago 4.1%. **Exports:** $603.3 mil; U.S. 37.7%, UK 16.4%, Costa Rica 9.9%, Nigeria 4.3%. **Tourism:** $264 mil. **Budget:** $450 mil. **Total reserves less gold:** $237.1 mil. **CPI change:** −2.5%.

Transport: Motor vehicles: 93.3 vehicles per 1,000 pop. **Civil aviation:** 6 airports. **Chief ports:** Belize City, Big Creek. **Communications: TV sets:** 445 per 1,000 pop. **Radios:** 590 per 1,000 pop. **Telephone lines:** 9.1 per 100 pop. **Internet** (2010): 14%.

Health: Life expect.: 66.6 male; 70.0 female. **Births:** 26.0 (per 1,000 pop.). **Deaths:** 5.9 (per 1,000 pop.). **Natural inc.:** 2.01%. **Infant mortality:** 21.4 (per 1,000 live births). **HIV rate:** 2.3%. **Education:** Compulsory: ages 5-14. **Literacy:** 70.3%.

Major intl. organizations: UN (FAO, IBRD, ILO, IMF, WHO), Caricom, the Commonwealth, OAS, WTO. **Embassy:** 2535 Massachusetts Ave. NW 20008; 332-9636. **Website:** www.belize.gov.bz

Belize (formerly British Honduras) was Britain's last colony on the American mainland; independence was achieved Sept. 21, 1981. Relations with neighboring Guatemala, which claims the southern half of Belize and its islands as its own territory, have improved in recent years. Belize has become a center for drug trafficking between Colombia and the U.S.

Benin
Republic of Benin

People: Population: 9,598,787. **Age distrib.:** <15: 44.4%; 65+: 2.7%. **Pop. density:** 224.7 per sq mi, 86.8 per sq km. **Urban:** 44.9%. **Ethnic groups:** Fon & related 39%, Adja & related 15%, Yoruba & related 12%, Bariba & related 9%, Peulh & related 7%, Ottamari & related 6%, Yoa-Lokpa & related 4%, Dendi & related 3%. **Principal languages:** French (official), Fon, Yoruba, tribal languages. **Chief religions:** Catholic 27%, Muslim 24%, Vodoun 17%, Protestant 10%.

Geography: Total area: 43,484 sq mi, 112,622 sq km; **Land area:** 42,711 sq mi, 110,622 sq km. **Location:** In W Africa on Gulf of Guinea. **Neighbors:** Togo on W; Burkina Faso, Niger on N; Nigeria on E. **Topography:** Most of Benin is flat and covered with dense vegetation. The coast is hot, humid, and rainy. **Capital:** Porto-Novo (constitutional), 314,496; Cotonou (seat), 923,923.

Government: Type: Republic. **Head of state:** Pres. Boni Yayi; b. July 1, 1952; in office: Apr. 6, 2006. **Head of gov.:** Prime Min. Pascal Koupaki; b. 1951; in office: May 28, 2011. **Local divisions:** 12 departments. **Defense budget:** $73 mil. **Active troops:** 4,750.

Economy: Industries: textiles, food proc., constr. materials, cement. **Chief crops:** cotton, corn, cassava, yams, beans. **Natural resources:** oil, limestone, marble, timber. **Crude oil reserves:** 8 mil bbls. **Arable land:** 22.1%. **Livestock:** cattle: 2 mil; chickens: 16.6 mil; goats: 1.6 mil; pigs: 368,000; sheep: 808,000. **Fish catch:** 40,252 metric tons. **Electricity prod.:** 120 mil kWh. **Labor force:** NA.

Finance: Monetary unit: CFA BCEAO Franc (XOF) (Sept. 2012: 519.73 = $1 U.S.). **GDP:** $14.9 bil; **per capita GDP:** $1,500; **GDP growth:** 3.1%. **Imports:** $2.2 bil; China 31.3%, France 12.3%, UK 7.6%, U.S. 6.8%, India 5.8%, Netherlands 4.6%, Belgium 4.3%. **Exports:** $1.8 bil; India 30.8%, China 20.2%, Indonesia 6.9%, Niger 4.9%, Singapore 4.5%, Nigeria 4.3%. **Tourism:** $133 mil. **Budget:** $1.7 bil. **Total reserves less gold:** $887.4 mil. **CPI change:** 2.7%.

Transport: Railways: 272 mi. **Motor vehicles:** 3.3 vehicles per 1,000 pop. **Civil aviation:** 80.8 mil pass.-mi; 1 airport. **Chief port:** Cotonou.

Communications: TV sets: 45 per 1,000 pop. **Radios:** 323 per 1,000 pop. **Telephone lines:** 1.7 per 100 pop. **Daily newspaper circ.:** 0.4 per 1,000 pop. **Internet:** 3.5%.

Health: Life expect.: 59.0 male; 61.6 female. **Births:** 37.6 (per 1,000 pop.). **Deaths:** 8.8 (per 1,000 pop.). **Natural inc.:** 2.88% **Infant mortality:** 60.0 (per 1,000 live births). **HIV rate:** 1.2%.

Education: Compulsory: ages 6-11. **Literacy:** 42.4%.

Major intl. organizations: UN (FAO, IBRD, ILO, IMF, WHO), AU, WTO.

Embassy: 2124 Kalorama Rd. NW 20008; 232-6656.

Website: www.gouv.bz

The Kingdom of Abomey, rising to power in wars with neighboring kingdoms in the 17th cent., came under French domination in the late 19th cent., and was incorporated into French West Africa by 1904. Under the name Dahomey, the country gained independence Aug. 1, 1960; it became Benin in 1975. In the fifth coup since independence Col. Ahmed Kerekou took power in 1972; two years later he declared a socialist state with a "Marxist-Leninist" philosophy. In Dec. 1989, Kerekou announced Marxism-Leninism would no longer be the state ideology.

In Mar. 1991, Kerekou lost Benin's first free presidential election in 30 years to Nicéphore Soglo. Kerekou defeated Soglo in Mar. 1996 to reclaim the presidency. He won reelection in a runoff Mar. 22, 2001. Boni Yayi, an economist, won a presidential runoff vote, Mar. 19, 2006. Benin, which in 2006 signed a 5-year, $307 mil aid deal with the U.S., received a visit from Pres. George W. Bush Feb. 16, 2008. More than 100,000 people reportedly lost their savings when a fraudulent investment scheme linked to high government officials collapsed in mid-2010. Pres. Yayi won reelection to a second 5-year term Mar. 13, 2011. Pope Benedict XVI arrived in Benin, Nov. 18, 2011, for a 3-day visit.

Bhutan
Kingdom of Bhutan

People: Population: 716,896. **Age distrib.:** <15: 28.4%; 65+: 5.8%. **Pop. density:** 48.4 per sq mi, 18.7 per sq km. **Urban:** 35.6%. **Ethnic groups:** Bhote 50%, ethnic Nepalese 35%, indigenous or migrant tribes 15%. **Principal languages:** Sharchhopka, Dzongkha (official), Lhotshamkha. **Chief religions:** Lamaistic Buddhist 75%, Indian- and Nepalese-influenced Hinduism 25%.

Geography: Total area: 14,824 sq mi, 38,394 sq km; **Land area:** 14,824 sq mi, 38,394 sq km. **Location:** S Asia, in eastern Himalayan Mts. **Neighbors:** India on W (Sikkim) and S, China on N. **Topography:** Bhutan is comprised of very high mountains in the N, fertile valleys in the center, and thick forests in the Duar Plain in the S. **Capital:** Thimphu, 99,337.

Government: Type: Constitutional monarchy. **Head of state:** King Jigme Khesar Namgyal Wangchuk; b. Feb. 21, 1980; in office: Dec. 14, 2006. **Head of gov.:** Prime Min. Jigmi Y. Thinley; b. Sept. 9, 1952; in office: Apr. 9, 2008. **Local divisions:** 18 districts. **Defense budget/active troops:** NA.

Economy: Industries: cement, wood prods., processed fruits, alcoholic beverages, calcium carbide, tourism. **Chief crops:** rice, corn, root crops, citrus, foodgrains. **Natural resources:** timber, hydropower, gypsum, calcium carbonate. **Arable land:** 2.0%. **Livestock:** cattle: 309,277; chickens: 349,000; goats: 43,134; pigs: 19,711; sheep: 12,699. **Fish catch:** 206 metric tons. **Electricity prod.:** 6.8 bil kWh. **Labor force:** agric. 43.7%, industry 39.1%, services 17.2%.

Finance: Monetary unit: Ngultrum (BTN) (Sept. 2012: 55.91 = $1 U.S.). **GDP:** $4.3 bil; **per capita GDP:** $6,200; **GDP growth:** 5.9%. **Imports** (2010): $843.3 mil. **Exports** (2010): $544.5 mil. **Tourism:** $48 mil. **Budget:** $730.7 mil (nearly three-fifths financed by India's govt.). **Total reserves less gold:** $789.6 mil. **CPI change:** 31.1%.

Transport: Civil aviation: 44.7 mil pass.-mi; 1 airport.

Communications: TV sets: 12 per 1,000 pop. **Radios:** 118 per 1,000 pop. **Telephone lines:** 3.7 per 100 pop. **Internet:** 21%.

Health: Life expect.: 67.0 male; 68.8 female. **Births:** 18.8 (per 1,000 pop.). **Deaths:** 7.0 (per 1,000 pop.). **Natural inc.:** 1.18%. **Infant mortality:** 42.2 (per 1,000 live births). **HIV rate:** 0.2%.

Education: Compulsory ages: NA. **Literacy:** 52.8%.

Major intl. organizations: UN (FAO, IBRD, IMF, WHO), WTO (observer).

Permanent UN mission: 763 United Nations Plz., New York, NY 10017; (212) 490-9660.

Website: www.bhutan.gov.bt

The region came under Tibetan rule in the 16th cent. British influence grew in the 19th cent. A Buddhist monarchy was set up in 1907. After a 1910 treaty, Britain guided Bhutan's external affairs, while the country remained internally self-governing. Upon independence the treaty was revised, 1949, to allow India to assume Britain's role.

Isolated for much of its history, Bhutan has taken steps toward modernization. King Jigme Singye Wangchuk, in power since 1972, stepped down Dec. 14, 2006, in favor of his son, Jigme Khesar Namgyal Wangchuk. Multiparty parliamentary elections took place Mar. 24, 2008, and a new constitution was ratified July 18, making Bhutan a democratic constitutional monarchy. Namgay Peldon became the first woman elected governor in the Mar. 2008 election, and Tashi Chhozom became the first woman appointed to the country's supreme court Aug. 3, 2012.

Bolivia
Plurinational State of Bolivia

People: Population: 10,290,003. **Age distrib.:** <15: 34.2%; 65+: 4.7%. **Pop. density:** 24.6 per sq mi, 9.5 per sq km. **Urban:** 66.8%. **Ethnic groups:** Quechua 30%, mestizo (mixed white and Amerindian) 30%, Aymara 25%, white 15%. **Principal languages:** Spanish, Quechua, Aymara (all official). **Chief religions:** Roman Catholic 95%, Protestant (Evangelical Methodist) 5%.

Geography: Total area: 424,164 sq mi, 1,098,581 sq km; **Land area:** 418,265 sq mi, 1,083,301 sq km. **Location:** In W central South America, in the Andes Mts. (one of 2 landlocked countries in South America). **Neighbors:** Peru and Chile on W, Argentina and Paraguay on S, Brazil on E and N. **Topography:** The great central plateau, at an altitude of 12,000 ft, over 500 mi long, lies between two great cordilleras having 3 of the highest peaks in South America. Lake Titicaca, on Peruvian border, is highest lake in world on which steamboats ply (12,506 ft). The E central region has semitropical forests; the llanos, or Amazon-Chaco lowlands are in E. **Capital:** La Paz (admin.), 1,714,530; Sucre (constitutional), 306,597. **Cities (urban aggl.):** Santa Cruz, 1,719,346.

Government: Type: Republic. **Head of state and gov.:** Pres. Juan Evo Morales Ayma; b. Oct. 26, 1959; in office: Jan. 22, 2006. **Local divisions:** 9 departments. **Defense budget:** $357 mil. **Active troops:** 46,100.

Economy: Industries: mining, smelting, petroleum, food and beverages, tobacco, handicrafts, clothing. **Chief crops:** soybeans, coffee, coca, cotton, corn, sugarcane, rice, potatoes. **Natural resources:** tin, nat. gas, petroleum, zinc, tungsten, antimony, silver, iron, lead, gold, timber, hydropower. **Crude oil reserves:** 209.8 mil bbls. **Other resources:** Timber. **Arable land:** 3.4%. **Livestock:** cattle: 8.2 mil; chickens: 198.4 mil; goats: 2.2 mil; pigs: 2.6 mil; sheep: 8.7 mil. **Fish catch:** 7,802 metric tons. **Electricity prod.:** 5.9 bil kWh. **Labor force:** agric. 32%, industry 20%, services 48%.

Finance: Monetary unit: Boliviano (BOB) (Sept. 2012: 7.00 = $1 U.S.). **GDP:** $51.6 bil; **per capita GDP:** $4,900; **GDP growth:** 5.1%. **Imports:** $7.6 bil; Chile 23.6%, Brazil 23%, Argentina 10.4%, U.S. 10.1%, Peru 6.9%, China 5.9%. **Exports:** $8.4 bil; Brazil 41.8%, U.S. 12.2%, South Korea 6.4%, Peru 5.7%, Argentina 5.2%, Japan 4.6%. **Tourism:** $310 mil. **Budget:** $10.7 bil. **Total reserves less gold:** $9.9 bil. **Gold:** 1.4 mil oz t. **CPI change:** 9.8%.

Transport: Railways: 2,269 mi. **Motor vehicles:** 53.7 vehicles per 1,000 pop. **Civil aviation:** 1.2 bil pass.-mi; 21 airports. **Chief port:** Puerto Aguirre.

Communications: TV sets: 155 per 1,000 pop. **Radios:** 672 per 1,000 pop. **Telephone lines:** 8.7 per 100 pop. **Internet:** 30%.

Health: Life expect.: 65.2 male; 70.8 female. **Births:** 24.2 (per 1,000 pop.). **Deaths:** 6.8 (per 1,000 pop.). **Natural inc.:** 1.75% **Infant mortality:** 40.9 (per 1,000 live births). **HIV rate:** 0.2%.

Education: Compulsory: ages 6-13. **Literacy:** 91.2%.

Major intl. organizations: UN (FAO, IBRD, ILO, IMF, WHO), OAS, WTO.

Embassy: 3014 Massachusetts Ave. NW 20008; 483-4410.

Website: www.bolivia.gob.bo

The Incas conquered the region's earlier Indian inhabitants in the 13th cent. Spanish rule began in the 1530s and lasted until Aug. 6, 1825. The country is named after Simon Bolivar, independence fighter.

In a series of wars, Bolivia lost its Pacific coast to Chile, the oil-bearing Chaco to Paraguay, and rubber-growing areas to Brazil, 1879-1935.

Economic unrest, especially among militant mine workers, has led to continuing political instability. A reformist government under Victor Paz Estenssoro, 1951-64, nationalized tin mines and attempted to improve conditions for the Indian majority but was overthrown by a military junta. A series of coups and countercoups continued until constitutional government was restored in 1982.

U.S. pressure on the government to reduce the country's coca output, the raw material for cocaine, has led to clashes between police and coca growers and increased anti-U.S. feeling among Bolivians. Gen. Hugo Banzer Suárez, who ruled as a dictator, 1971-78, later governed as president, 1997-2001.

After an inconclusive presidential election June 30, 2002, Congress Aug. 4 chose Gonzalo Sánchez de Lozada, a U.S.-educated mining executive, as head of state. He quit Oct. 17, 2003, after indigenous Bolivians staged a month of antigovernment protests in which over 70 people died. His successor, Vice Pres. Carlos D. Mesa Gisbert, was embroiled in controversies over energy policy.

Juan Evo Morales Ayma, a leftist and coca-farmer advocate, won the presidential election, Dec. 18, 2005. He nationalized the hydrocarbon sector, launched a land-redistribution program to benefit poor farmers, and tightened ties with Venezuela and Cuba; he faced resistance and demands for autonomy from leaders of Bolivia's relatively prosperous lowland provinces. Voters, Jan. 25, 2009, approved a new constitution strengthening the rights of Bolivia's indigenous majority and increasing federal control over the country's natural resources. In national elections Dec. 6, Pres. Morales won a second term, and his Movement Toward Socialism consolidated its hold over Bolivia's legislature. Morales's popularity has waned, in part because of his support for a Brazilian-funded highway project that will connect Bolivia to Brazil and to the Pacific Ocean but disturb indigenous lands. The arrival of 1,000 indigenous protestors in La Paz Oct. 19, 2011, led to the project's postponement.

Bosnia and Herzegovina

People: Population: 3,879,296. **Age distrib.:** <15: 14.4%; 65+: 12.7%. **Pop. density:** 196.3 per sq mi, 75.8 per sq km. **Urban:** 48.3%. **Ethnic groups:** Bosniak 48%, Serb 37%, Croat 14%. **Principal languages:** Bosnian, Croatian (both official); Serbian. **Chief religions:** Muslim 40%, Orthodox 31%, Roman Catholic 15%.

Geography: Total area: 19,767 sq mi, 51,197 sq km; **Land area:** 19,763 sq mi, 51,187 sq km. **Location:** On Balkan Peninsula in SE Europe. **Neighbors:** Serbia, Montenegro on E and SE, Croatia on N and W. **Topography:** Hilly with some mountains. About 36% of the land is forested. **Capital:** Sarajevo, 389,042.

Government: Type: Federal republic. **Heads of state:** Collective presidency with rotating leadership. **Head of gov.:** Prime Min. Nikola Spiric; b. Sept. 4, 1956; in office: Jan. 11, 2007. **Local divisions:** Muslim-Croat Federation, divided into 10 cantons; Serbian-led region (Republika Srpska); internationally supervised Brcko district. **Defense budget:** $248 mil. **Active troops:** 10,577.

Economy: Industries: steel, coal, mining, vehicle assembly, textiles, tobacco prods., wooden furniture, ammunition, domestic appliances, oil refining. **Chief crops:** wheat, corn, fruits, vegetables. **Natural resources:** coal, iron ore, bauxite, copper, lead, zinc, chromite, cobalt, manganese, nickel, clay, gypsum, salt, sand, timber, hydropower. **Arable land:** 19.5%. **Livestock:** cattle: 462,368; chickens: 19.7 mil; goats: 63,250; pigs: 590,431; sheep: 1.05 mil. **Fish catch:** 9,625 metric tons. **Electricity prod.:** 15 bil kWh. **Labor force:** agric. 20.5%, industry 32.6%, services 47%.

Finance: Monetary unit: Convertible Marka (BAM) (Sept. 2012: 1.55 = $1 U.S.). **GDP:** $32 bil; **per capita GDP:** $8,200; **GDP growth:** 1.7%. **Imports:** $11.1 bil; Croatia 20%, Germany 13.3%, Slovenia 13.1%, Italy 9.7%, Russia 7.7%, Austria 6.2%, Hungary 4.8%. **Exports:** $6 bil; Slovenia 18.3%, Croatia 15.1%, Italy 14.8%, Germany 13.9%, Austria 12.4%. **Tourism:** $628 mil. **Budget:** $9 bil. **Total reserves less gold:** $4.1 bil. **Gold:** 64,000 oz t.

Transport: Railways: 373 mi. **Civil aviation:** 69 mil pass.-mi; 7 airports. **Chief ports:** Bosanski Samac, Brcko.

Communications: TV sets: 282 per 1,000 pop. **Radios:** 251 per 1,000 pop. **Telephone lines:** 25.5 per 100 pop. **Internet:** 60%.

Health: Life expect.: 72.9 male; 79.1 female. **Births:** 8.9 (per 1,000 pop.). **Deaths:** 9.4 (per 1,000 pop.). **Natural inc.:** –0.05%. **Infant mortality:** 6.1 (per 1,000 live births). **HIV rate:** NA.

Education: Compulsory: ages 6-15. **Literacy:** 97.9%.

Major intl. organizations: UN (FAO, IBRD, ILO, IMF, WHO), OSCE, WTO (observer).

Embassy: 2109 E St. NW 20037; 337-1500.

Website: www.fbihvlada.org.ba

Bosnia was ruled by Croatian kings c. 958 CE, and by Hungary 1000-1200. It became organized c. 1200 and later took control of Herzegovina. The kingdom disintegrated after 1391, with the southern part becoming the independent duchy Herzegovina. It was conquered by Turks in 1463 and made a Turkish province. The area was placed under control of Austria-Hungary in 1878 and made part of the province of Bosnia and Herzegovina, which was formally annexed to Austria-Hungary, 1908. Bosnia became a province of Yugoslavia in 1918. It was reunited with Herzegovina as a federated republic in the 1946 Yugoslav constitution.

Bosnia and Herzegovina declared sovereignty Oct. 15, 1991. A referendum for independence was passed Feb. 29, 1992. Ethnic Serbs' opposition to the referendum spurred violent clashes and bombings. The U.S. and EU recognized the republic Apr. 7. Fierce three-way fighting continued between Bosnia's Serbs, Muslims, and Croats. Serb forces massacred thousands of Bosnian Muslims and engaged in ethnic cleansing, expelling Muslims and other non-Serbs from areas under Bosnian Serb control. The capital, Sarajevo, was surrounded and besieged by Bosnian Serb forces. Muslims and Croats in Bosnia began a cease-fire Feb. 23, 1994, and signed an accord, Mar. 18, to create a Muslim-Croat confederation in Bosnia. However, by mid-1994, Bosnian Serbs controlled over 70% of the country.

As fighting continued in 1995, the balance of power shifted toward the Muslim-Croat alliance. Massive NATO air strikes at Bosnian Serb targets beginning Aug. 30 triggered a new round of peace talks, and the siege of Sarajevo was lifted Sept. 15. The new talks produced an agreement to create autonomous regions within Bosnia, with the Serb region (Republika Srpska) constituting 49% of the country. A Croat-Muslim offensive in Sept. recaptured significant territory, leaving Bosnian Serbs in control of approximately half that percentage.

A peace agreement initialed in Dayton, Ohio, Nov. 21, 1995, was signed in Paris, Dec. 14, by leaders of Bosnia, Croatia, and Serbia. Some 60,000 NATO troops (about 20,000 from the U.S.) moved in to police the accord. Meanwhile, a UN tribunal began bringing charges against suspected war criminals. Elections were held Sept. 14, 1996, for a 3-person collective presidency, for seats in a federal parliament, and for regional offices. In Dec. a revamped NATO "stabilization force" (SFOR) of over 30,000 members (more than 8,000 from the U.S.) received an 18-month mandate, which was later extended.

The UN tribunal found Radislav Krstic, a Bosnian Serb general, guilty Aug. 2, 2001, in connection with the genocide of thousands of Muslims at Srebrenica in 1995. A European Union peacekeeping force (EUFOR), with 7,000 members, assumed responsibility from SFOR, Dec. 2, 2004. Accused of complicity in the Sarajevo and Srebrenica atrocities, former Bosnian Serb leader Radovan Karadzic was arrested in Serbia, July 21, 2008, and handed over to the UN tribunal at The Hague, Netherlands. He was charged with 10 counts of genocide, war crimes, and crimes against humanity; the prosecution rested its case in May and Karadzic was set to begin his defense Oct. 16, 2012. Also extradited to The Hague was Ratko Mladic, the former Bosnian Serb military commander accused of directing the Srebrenica massacre, who was arrested in Serbia May 26, 2011. He faced 11 counts of war crimes and crimes against humanity, two of them for genocide, in a trial that began May 16, 2012. It was immediately suspended but resumed July 9. As the security situation in Bosnia improved, EUFOR strength dropped to about 1,600 troops as of Aug. 2012.

Botswana
Republic of Botswana

People: Population: 2,098,018. **Age distrib.:** <15: 33.5%; 65+: 3.9%. **Pop. density:** 9.6 per sq mi, 3.7 per sq km. **Urban:** 61.7%. **Ethnic groups:** Tswana or Setswana 79%, Kalanga 11%, Basarwa 3%, other (incl. Kgalagadi and white) 7%. **Principal languages:** Setswana, Kalanga, Sekgalagadi, English (official). **Chief religions:** Christian 72%, Badimo 6%, none 21%.

Geography: Total area: 224,607 sq mi, 581,730 sq km; **Land area:** 218,816 sq mi, 566,730 sq km. **Location:** In southern Africa. **Neighbors:** Namibia on N and W, South Africa on S, Zimbabwe on NE; Botswana claims border with Zambia on N. **Topography:** The Kalahari Desert, supporting nomadic Bushmen and wildlife, spreads over SW; there are swamplands and farming areas in N, and rolling plains in E where livestock are grazed. **Capital:** Gaborone, 201,709.

Government: Type: Parliamentary republic. **Head of state and gov.:** Pres. Seretse Khama Ian Khama; b. Feb. 27, 1953; in office: Apr. 1, 2008. **Local divisions:** 10 districts, 4 town councils. **Defense budget:** $539 mil. **Active troops:** 9,000.

Economy: Industries: diamonds, copper, nickel, salt, soda ash, potash, coal, iron ore, silver. **Chief crops:** sorghum, maize, millet, beans, sunflowers, groundnuts. **Natural resources:** diamonds, copper, nickel, salt, soda ash, potash, coal, iron ore, silver. **Arable land:** 0.4%. **Livestock:** cattle: 2.6 mil; chickens: 5.1 mil; goats: 2.1 mil; pigs: 12,950; sheep: 152,650. **Fish catch:** 60 metric tons. **Electricity prod.:** 417 mil kWh. **Labor force:** NA.

Finance: Monetary unit: Pula (BWP) (Sept. 2012: 7.77 = $1 U.S.). **GDP:** $30.1 bil; **per capita GDP:** $16,200; **GDP growth:** 4.6%. **Imports:** $6.2 bil. **Exports:** $6 bil. **Tourism:** $218 mil. **Budget:** $6.2 bil. **Total reserves less gold:** $8.1 bil. **CPI change:** 8.9%.

Transport: Railways: 552 mi. **Motor vehicles:** 123.3 vehicles per 1,000 pop. **Civil aviation:** 70.2 mil pass.-mi; 10 airports.

Communications: TV sets: 44 per 1,000 pop. **Radios:** 734 per 1,000 pop. **Telephone lines:** 7.4 per 100 pop. **Daily newspaper circ.:** 41.5 per 1,000 pop. **Internet:** 7%.

Health: Life expect.: 56.9 male; 54.5 female. **Births:** 22.0 (per 1,000 pop.). **Deaths:** 12.0 (per 1,000 pop.). **Natural inc.:** 1.00%. **Infant mortality:** 10.5 (per 1,000 live births). **HIV rate:** 24.8%.

Education: Compulsory: ages 6-15. **Literacy:** 84.5%.

Major intl. organizations: UN (FAO, IBRD, ILO, IMF, WHO), AU, the Commonwealth, WTO.

Embassy: 1531-1533 New Hampshire Ave. NW 20036; 244-4990.

Website: www.gov.bw

First inhabited by Bushmen, then Bantus, the region became the British protectorate of Bechuanaland in 1886. The country became fully independent Sept. 30, 1966, as Botswana. Cattle raising and mining (diamonds, copper, nickel) have contributed to economic growth. According to the UN, nearly 25% of the adult population has HIV/AIDS. Pres. Festus Mogae transferred power Apr. 1, 2008, to Seretse Khama Ian Khama, son of Botswana's independence leader and first president (1966-80), Sir Seretse Khama. In power since independence, the Botswana Democratic Party dominated national elections Oct. 16, 2009, and Ian Khama was sworn in for a full term Oct. 20. De Beers, the world's largest diamond producer, moved its diamond-sorting operations from London to Botswana in 2012.

Brazil
Federative Republic of Brazil

People: Population: 199,321,413. **Age distrib.:** <15: 24.7%; 65+: 7.1%. **Pop. density:** 61 per sq mi, 23.6 per sq km. **Urban:** 84.6%. **Ethnic groups:** white 54%, mixed white & black) 39%, black 6%. **Principal languages:** Portuguese (official), Spanish, minor Amerindian langs. **Chief religions:** Roman Catholic (nominal) 74%, Protestant 15%, Spiritualist 1%, none 7%.

Geography: Total area: 3,287,612 sq mi, 8,514,877 sq km; **Land area:** 3,266,199 sq mi, 8,459,417 sq km. **Location:** Occupies E half of South America. **Neighbors:** French Guiana, Suriname, Guyana, Venezuela on N; Colombia, Peru, Bolivia, Paraguay, on W; Argentina, Uruguay on S. **Topography:** Brazil's Atlantic coastline stretches 4,603 mi. In N is the heavily wooded Amazon basin covering half the country. Its network of rivers is navigable for 15,814 mi. The Amazon itself flows 2,093 mi in Brazil, all navigable. The NE region is semiarid scrubland, heavily settled and poor. The S central region, favored by climate and resources, has almost half of the population, produces 75% of farm goods and 80% of industrial output. The narrow coastal belt includes most of the major cities. Almost the entire country has a tropical or semitropical climate. **Capital:** Brasília, 3,813,010. **Cities (urban aggl.):** São Paulo, 19,924,458; Rio de Janeiro, 11,959,725; Belo Horizonte, 5,487,376.

Government: Type: Federal republic. **Head of state and gov.:** Pres. Dilma Rousseff; b. Dec. 14, 1947; in office: Jan. 1, 2011. **Local divisions:** 26 states, 1 federal district (Brasília). **Defense budget:** $36.6 bil. **Active troops:** 318,480.

Economy: Industries: textiles, shoes, chemicals, cement, lumber, iron ore, tin, steel, aircraft, motor vehicles and parts. **Chief crops:** coffee, soybeans, wheat, rice, corn, sugarcane, cocoa, citrus. **Natural resources:** bauxite, gold, iron ore, manganese, nickel, phosphates, platinum, tin, rare earth elements, uranium, petroleum hydropower, timber. **Crude oil reserves:** 14 bil bbls. **Arable land:** 7.2%. **Livestock:** cattle: 209.5 mil; chickens: 1.2 bil; goats: 9.3 mil; pigs: 39 mil; sheep: 17.4 mil. **Fish catch:** 1.3 mil metric tons. **Electricity prod.:** (2010): 489.5 bil kWh. **Labor force:** agric. 20%, industry 14%, services 66%.

Finance: Monetary unit: Real (BRL) (Sept. 2012: 2.04 = $1 U.S.). **GDP:** $2.3 tril; **per capita GDP:** $11,900; **GDP growth:** 2.7%. **Imports:** $219.6 bil; U.S. 15.1%, China 14.5%, Argentina 7.5%, Germany 6.7%, South Korea 4.5%. **Exports:** $256 bil; China 17.3%, U.S. 10.1%, Argentina 8.9%, Netherlands 5.3%. **Tourism:** $6.6 bil. **Budget:** $901 bil. **Total reserves less gold:** $350.4 bil. **Gold:** 1.1 mil oz t. **CPI change:** 6.6%.

Transport: Railways: 17,733 mi. **Motor vehicles:** 149.2 vehicles per 1,000 pop. **Civil aviation:** 46 bil pass.-mi; 713 airports. **Chief ports:** Ilha Grande, Paranagua, Rio Grande, Santos, São Sebastião, Tubarão.

Communications: TV sets: 279 per 1,000 pop. **Radios:** 255 per 1,000 pop. **Telephone lines:** 21.9 per 100 pop. **Daily newspaper circ.:** 35.5 per 1,000 pop. **Internet:** 45%.

Health: Life expect.: 69.2 male; 76.5 female. **Births:** 15.2 (per 1,000 pop.). **Deaths:** 6.5 (per 1,000 pop.). **Natural inc.:** 0.88% **Infant mortality:** 20.5 (per 1,000 live births). **HIV rate:** NA.

Education: Compulsory: ages 6-14. **Literacy:** 90.3%.

Major intl. organizations: UN and most of its specialized agencies, OAS, WTO.

Embassy: 3006 Massachusetts Ave. NW 20008; 238-2700. **Website:** www.brasil.gov.br

Pedro Alvares Cabral, a Portuguese navigator, is generally credited as the first European to reach Brazil, in 1500. The country was thinly settled by various Indian tribes. Only a few survive today, mostly in the Amazon basin.

In the next centuries, Portuguese colonists gradually pushed inland, bringing along large numbers of African slaves. (Slavery was not abolished until 1888.) The King of Portugal, fleeing before Napoleon's army, moved the seat of government to Brazil in 1808. Brazil thereupon became a kingdom under Dom Joao VI. After Joao VI returned to Portugal, his son Pedro proclaimed Brazil's independence, Sept. 7, 1822, and was crowned emperor. The second emperor, Dom Pedro II, was deposed in 1889, and a republic proclaimed, called the United States of Brazil. It was renamed the Federative Republic of Brazil in 1967.

A military junta took control in 1930; Getulio Vargas assumed dictatorial power. The military forced him out in 1945. A democratic regime prevailed 1945-64, during which time the capital was moved from Rio de Janeiro to Brasília. Military-backed governments ruled Brazil for the next 20 years. Censorship was imposed, and the opposition was suppressed.

Brazil became the leading industrial power of Latin America by the 1970s, while agricultural output soared. By the 1990s, Brazil had one of the world's largest economies; income was poorly distributed, however, and more than one in four Brazilians survived on less than $1 a day. Despite protective environmental legislation, development has destroyed much of the Amazon ecosystem.

Democratic presidential elections were held in 1985, bringing civilian rule back. Fernando Collor de Mello was elected president, Dec. 1989. In Sept. 1992, Collor was impeached for corruption. He resigned on Dec. 29 as his trial was beginning, and Itamar Franco, who had been acting president, was sworn in as president. Fernando Henrique Cardoso won Oct. 3, 1994, elections. Reelected Oct. 4, 1998, he guided Brazil through a series of financial crises.

A new civil code guaranteeing legal equality for women was enacted Aug. 15, 2001. The IMF approved a $30 bil loan to Brazil Aug. 7, 2002; by then, Brazil's debt exceeded $260 bil. Luiz Inácio Lula da Silva, a union leader and reformer, won a presidential runoff, Oct. 27, 2002. Brazil's space program, although suffering a setback when a rocket exploded on its launchpad Aug. 22, 2003, killing 21 people, launched its first rocket into space Oct. 23, 2004.

A top aide to Pres. Lula resigned June 16, 2005, amid allegations the ruling party bribed legislators for votes; despite this and other scandals, Lula won a second presidential term, Oct. 29, 2006. The nation reported huge new offshore oil finds in 2007-08. Lula's former chief of staff, Dilma Rousseff, won a runoff election Oct. 31, 2010 and took office as Brazil's first woman president Jan. 1, 2011. Brazilian police raided Rocinha, Rio de Janeiro's largest slum, Nov. 13, 2011, as part of an effort to bring law to the entire city as it prepared to host the soccer World Cup in 2014 and the Olympic Games in 2016.

Brunei
Brunei Darussalam

People: Population: 408,786. **Age distrib.:** <15: 25%; 65+: 3.7%. **Pop. density:** 201.1 per sq mi, 77.6 per sq km. **Urban:** 76%. **Ethnic groups:** Malay 66%, Chinese 11%, indigenous 3%. **Principal languages:** Malay (official), English, Chinese. **Chief religions:** Muslim (official) 67%, Buddhist 13%, Christian 10%, other (incl. indigenous beliefs) 10%.

Geography: Total area: 2,226 sq mi, 5,765 sq km; **Land area:** 2,033 sq mi, 5,265 sq km. **Location:** In SE Asia, on the N coast of the island of Borneo; it is surrounded on its landward side by the Malaysian state of Sarawak. **Topography:** Brunei has a narrow coastal plain, with mountains in E, hilly lowlands in W. There are swamps in W and NE. Climate is tropical. **Capital:** Bandar Seri Begawan, 16,381.

Government: Type: Independent sultanate. **Head of state and gov.:** Sultan Sir Muda Hassanal Bolkiah Mu'izzadin Waddaulah; b. July 15, 1946; in office: Jan. 1, 1984 (sultan since Oct. 5, 1967). **Local divisions:** 4 districts. **Defense budget:** $406 mil. **Active troops:** 7,000.

Economy: Industries: petroleum, petroleum refining, liquefied nat. gas, constr. **Chief crops:** rice, vegetables, fruits. **Natural resources:** petroleum, nat. gas, timber. **Crude oil reserves:** 1.1 bil bbls. **Arable land:** 0.6%. **Livestock:** cattle: 852; chickens: 14.9 mil; goats: 6,806; pigs: 1,300; sheep: 3,800. **Fish catch:** 2,772 metric tons. **Electricity prod.:** 3.4 bil kWh. **Labor force:** agric. 4.2%, industry 62.8%, services 33%.

Finance: Monetary unit: Dollar (BND) (Sept. 2012: 1.25 = $1 U.S.). **GDP:** $21.2 bil; **per capita GDP:** $50,000; **GDP growth:** 1.9%. **Imports** (2008): $2.6 bil; Singapore 33.2%, China 15.5%, South Korea 12.2%, Malaysia 10.7%, Germany 9.6%. **Exports** (2008): $10.7 bil; Japan 45.6%, South Korea 16.5%, Australia 11.8%, Indonesia 8.4%, India 4.8%, China 4.6%. **Tourism:** $254 mil. **Budget:** $5.8 bil. **Total reserves less gold:** $2.5 bil. **Gold:** 63,287 oz t.

Transport: Motor vehicles: 279.6 vehicles per 1,000 pop. **Civil aviation:** 2.1 bil pass.-mi; 1 airport. **Chief ports:** Lumut, Muara, Seria.

Communications: TV sets: 629 per 1,000 pop. **Radios:** 300 per 1,000 pop. **Telephone lines:** 19.7 per 100 pop. **Daily newspaper circ.:** 68.4 per 1,000 pop. **Internet:** 56%.

Health: Life expect.: 74.1 male; 78.8 female. **Births:** 17.7 (per 1,000 pop.). **Deaths:** 3.4 (per 1,000 pop.). **Natural inc.:** 1.44% **Infant mortality:** 11.2 (per 1,000 live births). **HIV rate:** NA.

Education: Compulsory: ages 6-14. **Literacy:** 95.2%.

Major intl. organizations: UN and some of its specialized agencies, APEC, ASEAN, the Commonwealth, WTO.

Embassy: 3520 International Ct. NW 20008; 237-1838. **Website:** www.gov.bn

The Sultanate of Brunei was a powerful state in the early 16th cent., with authority over all of the island of Borneo as well as parts of the Sulu Islands and the Philippines. In 1888, a treaty placed the state under the protection of Great Britain.

Brunei became a fully sovereign and independent state on Jan. 1, 1984. Much of the country's oil wealth has been squandered by members of the royal family. Brunei broke with its traditions and fielded female athletes for the first time at the 2012 Summer Olympic Games.

Bulgaria
Republic of Bulgaria

People: Population: 7,037,935. **Age distrib.:** <15: 14%; 65+: 18.6%. **Pop. density:** 168 per sq mi, 64.9 per sq km. **Urban:** 73.1%. **Ethnic groups:** Bulgarian 84%, Turk 9%, Roma 5%, other (incl. Macedonian, Armenian, Tatar, Circassian) 2%. **Principal languages:** Bulgarian (official), Turkish, Roma. **Chief religions:**

Eastern Orthodox 60%, Sunni Muslim 7%, other (incl. Catholic, Protestant, Armenian Apostolic Orthodox, Judaism) 2%, none 4%.

Geography: Total area: 42,811 sq mi, 110,879 sq km; **Land area:** 41,888 sq mi, 108,489 sq km. **Location:** SE Europe, in E Balkan Peninsula on Black Sea. **Neighbors:** Romania on N; Serbia, Macedonia on W; Greece, Turkey on S. **Topography:** The Stara Planina (Balkan) Mts. stretch E-W across the center of the country, with the Danubian plain on N, the Rhodope Mts. on SW, and Thracian Plain on SE. **Capital:** Sofia, 1,173,770.

Government: Type: Republic. **Head of state:** Pres. Rosen Plevneliev; b. May 14, 1964; in office: Jan. 22, 2012. **Head of gov.:** Prime Min. Boyko Borisov; b. June 13, 1959; in office: July 27, 2009. **Local divisions:** 28 provinces. **Defense budget:** $725 mil. **Active troops:** 31,315.

Economy: Industries: utilities, food, beverages, tobacco, machinery and equip. **Chief crops:** vegetables, fruits, tobacco, wine grapes, wheat, barley, sunflowers, sugar beets. **Natural resources:** bauxite, copper, lead, zinc, coal, timber. **Crude oil reserves:** 15 mil bbls. **Arable land:** 28.9%. **Livestock:** cattle: 563,000; chickens: 16 mil; goats: 360,822; pigs: 729,798; sheep: 1.4 mil. **Fish catch:** 18,690 metric tons. **Electricity prod.:** 40 bil kWh. **Labor force:** agric. 7.1%, industry 35.2%, services 57.7%.

Finance: Monetary unit: Lev (BGN) (Sept. 2012: 1.55 = $1 U.S.). **GDP:** $102.3 bil; **per capita GDP:** $13,800; **GDP growth:** 1.7%. **Imports:** $30.9 bil; Russia 18%, Germany 11%, Italy 7.3%, Romania 7%, Greece 5.7%, Turkey 4.6%, Spain 4.3%, Ukraine 4%. **Exports:** $28.1 bil; Germany 12.2%, Romania 9.8%, Italy 8.5%, Turkey 8.2%, Greece 7%, Belgium 5.1%, France 4.3%. **Tourism:** $3.97 bil. **Budget:** $19.2 bil. **Total reserves less gold:** $15.3 bil. **Gold:** 1.3 mil oz t. **CPI change:** 4.2%.

Transport: Railways: 2,579 mi. **Motor vehicles:** 454.1 vehicles per 1,000 pop. **Civil aviation:** 775.5 mil pass.-mi; 124 airports. **Chief ports:** Burgas, Varna.

Communications: TV sets: 429 per 1,000 pop. **Radios:** 553 per 1,000 pop. **Telephone lines:** 31 per 100 pop. **Daily newspaper circ.:** 79 per 1,000 pop. **Internet:** 51%.

Health: Life expect.: 70.2 male; 77.7 female. **Births:** 9.2 (per 1,000 pop.). **Deaths:** 14.3 (per 1,000 pop.). **Natural inc.:** −0.51%. **Infant mortality:** 16.1 (per 1,000 live births). **HIV rate:** 0.1%.

Education: Compulsory: ages 7-14. **Literacy:** 98.4%.

Major intl. organizations: UN (FAO, IBRD, ILO, IMF, WHO), EU, NATO, OSCE, WTO.

Embassy: 1621 22nd St. NW 20008; 387-0174.

Website: www.government.bg

Bulgaria was settled by Slavs in the 6th cent. Turkic Bulgars arrived in the 7th cent., merged with the Slavs, became Christians by the 9th cent., and set up powerful empires in the 10th and 12th centuries. Ottomans took over in 1396 and ruled for nearly 500 years.

An 1876 revolt led to an independent kingdom in 1908. Bulgaria expanded after the first Balkan War but lost its Aegean coastline in WWI, when it sided with Germany. Bulgaria joined the Axis in WWII but withdrew in 1944. Communists took power with Soviet aid; the monarchy was abolished Sept. 8, 1946.

On Nov. 10, 1989, Communist Party leader and head of state Todor Zhivkov, who had held power for 35 years, resigned. In Jan. 1990, Parliament voted to revoke the constitutionally guaranteed dominant role of the Communist Party. A new constitution took effect July 13, 1991.

Bulgaria's deteriorating economy provoked nationwide strikes and demonstrations in Jan. 1997. The Union of Democratic Forces (UDF), an anti-Communist group, won national elections on Apr. 19. The UDF lost June 17, 2001, elections to the party of the former king, Simeon II. Socialist opposition leader Georgi Parvanov won a presidential runoff vote Nov. 18, 2001; he was reelected Oct. 29, 2006.

Bulgaria became a full member of NATO, Apr. 2, 2004, and entered the European Union, Jan. 1, 2007. Boyko Borisov became prime minister after his center-right party won parliamentary elections July 5, 2009. A suicide bomber blew up a bus carrying Israeli tourists, July 18, 2012, leaving five Israelis and the Bulgarian bus driver dead. Israel blamed Iran for the attack.

Burkina Faso

People: Population: 17,275,115. **Age distrib.:** <15: 45.7%; 65+: 2.5%. **Pop. density:** 163.4 per sq mi, 63.1 per sq km. **Urban:** 26.5%. **Ethnic groups:** Mossi 40%+, other (incl. Gurunsi, Senufo, Lobi, Bobo, Mande, Fulani) approx. 60%. **Principal languages:** French (official), native African Sudanic-family langs. **Chief religions:** Muslim 61%, Catholic 19%, animist 15%, Protestant 4%.

Geography: Total area: 105,869 sq mi, 274,200 sq km; **Land area:** 105,715 sq mi, 273,800 sq km. **Location:** In W Africa, S of the Sahara. **Neighbors:** Mali on NW; Niger on NE; Benin, Togo, Ghana, Côte d'Ivoire on S. **Topography:** Landlocked Burkina Faso is in the savanna region of W Africa. The N is arid, hot, and thinly populated. **Capital:** Ouagadougou, 2,052,530.

Government: Type: Republic. **Head of state:** Pres. Blaise Compaoré; b. Feb. 3, 1951; in office: Oct. 15, 1987. **Head of gov.:** Prime Min. Luc Adolphe Tiao; b. June 4, 1954; in office: Apr. 18, 2011. **Local divisions:** 45 provinces. **Defense budget** (2010): $124 mil. **Active troops:** 11,200.

Economy: Industries: cotton lint, beverages, agric. proc., soap, cigarettes, textiles, gold. **Chief crops:** cotton, peanuts, shea nuts, sesame, sorghum, millet. **Natural resources:** manganese, limestone, marble, gold, phosphates, pumice, salt. **Arable land:** 21.6%. **Livestock:** cattle: 8.4 mil; chickens: 39 mil; goats: 12.3 mil; pigs: 2.2 mil; sheep: 8.2 mil. **Fish catch:** 14,890 metric tons. **Electricity prod.:** 664 mil kWh. **Labor force:** agric. 90%, industry and services 10%.

Finance: Monetary unit: CFA BCEAO Franc (XOF) (Sept. 2012: 519.73 = $1 U.S.). **GDP:** $22.3 bil; **per capita GDP:** $1,500; **GDP growth:** 5.6%. **Imports:** $2.3 bil; Côte d'Ivoire 16.4%, France 14.9%, Ghana 4.9%, Togo 4.6%, Belgium 4.1%. **Exports:** $2.2 bil; China 22%, Turkey 17.7%, Singapore 8.8%, Indonesia 7%, Thailand 5.2%. **Tourism:** $72 mil. **Budget:** $2.6 bil. **Total reserves less gold:** $957 mil. **CPI change:** 2.8%.

Transport: Railways: 386 mi. **Motor vehicles:** 10.2 vehicles per 1,000 pop. **Civil aviation:** 25.5 mil pass.-mi; 2 airports.

Communications: TV sets: 19 per 1,000 pop. **Radios:** 111 per 1,000 pop. **Telephone lines:** 0.8 per 100 pop. **Internet:** 3%.

Health: Life expect.: 52.1 male; 56.1 female. **Births:** 43.2 (per 1,000 pop.). **Deaths:** 12.5 (per 1,000 pop.). **Natural inc.:** 3.07% **Infant mortality:** 79.8 (per 1,000 live births). **HIV rate:** 1.2%

Education: Compulsory: ages 6-16. **Literacy:** 28.7%.

Major intl. organizations: UN and many of its specialized agencies, AU, WTO.

Embassy: 2340 Massachusetts Ave. NW 20008; 332-5577.

Website: www.gouvernement.gov.bf or burkina-usa.org

The Mossi people entered Burkina Faso in the 11th to 13th cents. Their kingdoms ruled until they were defeated by the Mali and Songhai empires.

French control came by 1896, but Upper Volta (renamed Burkina Faso on Aug. 4, 1984) was not established as a separate territory until 1947. Independence came Aug. 5, 1960, and a pro-French government was elected. The military seized power in 1980. A 1987 coup established the current regime, which instituted a multiparty system in the early 1990s. Pres. Blaise Compaoré won reelection, Nov. 13, 2005. The country, among the world's poorest, depends heavily on foreign aid. Compaoré revamped his cabinet after antigovernment protests Mar.-Apr. 2011 by soldiers, students, merchants, and police. A severe drought threatened the nation with extreme food insecurity, the World Food Programme warned Aug. 8, 2012.

Burma
See Myanmar.

Burundi
Republic of Burundi

People: Population: 10,557,259. **Age distrib.:** <15: 45.8%; 65+: 2.5%. **Pop. density:** 1,064.8 per sq mi, 411.1 per sq km. **Urban:** 10.9%. **Ethnic groups:** Hutu (Bantu) 85%, Tutsi (Hamitic) 14%, Twa (Pygmy) 1%. **Principal languages:** Kirundi, French (both official); Swahili. **Chief religions:** Christian 67% (Roman Catholic 62%, Protestant 5%), indigenous beliefs 23%, Muslim 10%.

Geography: Total area: 10,745 sq mi, 27,830 sq km; **Land area:** 9,915 sq mi, 25,680 sq km. **Location:** In central Africa. **Neighbors:** Rwanda on N, Dem. Rep. of the Congo (formerly Zaire) on W, Tanzania on E and S. **Topography:** Much of the country is grassy highland, with mountains reaching 8,900 ft. The southernmost source of the White Nile is located in Burundi. Lake Tanganyika is the second deepest lake in the world. **Capital:** Bujumbura, 604,732.

Government: Type: Republic. **Head of state and gov.:** Pres. Pierre Nkurunziza; b. Dec. 18, 1963; in office: Aug. 26, 2005. **Local divisions:** 16 provinces. **Defense budget:** $64 mil. **Active troops:** 20,000.

Economy: Industries: light consumer goods, assembly of imported components, public works constr., food proc. **Chief crops:** coffee, cotton, tea, corn, sorghum, sweet potatoes, bananas, manioc. **Natural resources:** nickel, uranium, rare earth oxides, peat, cobalt, copper, platinum, vanadium, hydropower. **Arable land:** 35.0%. **Livestock:** cattle: 596,412; chickens: 5.1 mil; goats: 2.2 mil; pigs: 244,791; sheep: 295,739. **Fish catch:** 17,750 metric tons. **Electricity prod.:** 127 mil kWh. **Labor force:** agric. 93.6%, industry 2.3%, services 4.1%.

Finance: Monetary unit: Franc (BIF) (Sept. 2012: 1,428.08 = $1 U.S.). **GDP:** $5.3 bil; **per capita GDP:** $600; **GDP growth:** 4.2%. **Imports:** $533.3 mil; Saudi Arabia 16.8%, Belgium 8.2%, China 7.5%, Uganda 7.4%, Kenya 6.5%, Zambia 6.4%, U.S. 6.2%, France 5%. **Exports:** $99.5 mil; Germany 15.7%, China 10.5%, Sweden 9.5%, Belgium 9%, Pakistan 7.4%, U.S. 7.4%, France 4.3%. **Tourism:** $2 mil. **Budget:** $526.9 mil. **Total reserves less gold:** $294 mil. **Gold:** 961 oz t. **CPI change:** 9.7%.

Transport: Motor vehicles: 5.9 vehicles per 1,000 pop. **Civil aviation:** 1 airport. **Chief port:** Bujumbura.

Communications: TV sets: 36 per 1,000 pop. **Radios:** 166 per 1,000 pop. **Telephone lines** (2010): 0.4 per 100 pop. **Internet:** 1.1%.

Health: Life expect.: 57.5 male; 61.0 female. **Births:** 40.6 (per 1,000 pop.). **Deaths:** 9.4 (per 1,000 pop.). **Natural inc.:** 3.12% **Infant mortality:** 60.3 (per 1,000 live births). **HIV rate:** 3.3%.

Education: Compulsory: ages 7-12. **Literacy:** 67.2%.

Major intl. organizations: UN (FAO, IBRD, ILO, IMF, WHO), AU, WTO.

Embassy: 2233 Wisconsin Ave. NW, Ste. 212, 20007; 342-2574.

Website: www.burundi-gov.bi or www.burundiembassy-usa.org

The pygmy Twa were the first inhabitants, followed by Bantu Hutus, who were conquered in the 16th cent. by the Tutsi (Watusi), probably from Ethiopia. Germany gained control in 1899. Belgium took over in 1916, successively exercising a League of Nations mandate and UN trusteeship over Ruanda-Urundi (now the two countries of Rwanda and Burundi). Burundi became independent July 1, 1962.

An unsuccessful Hutu rebellion in 1972-73 left 10,000 Tutsi and 150,000 Hutu dead. Over 100,000 Hutu fled to Tanzania and Zaire (now Congo). In the 1980s, Burundi's Tutsi-dominated regime pledged itself to ethnic reconciliation and democratic reform. In the nation's first democratic presidential election, June 1993, a Hutu, Melchior Ndadaye, was elected. He was killed in an attempted coup, Oct. 21, 1993. At least 150,000 Burundians died in ethnic conflict during the next three years. Pres. Cyprien Ntaryamira, elected Jan. 1994, was killed with the president of Rwanda in a mysterious plane crash, Apr. 6. The incident sparked massive carnage in Rwanda; violence in Burundi, initially far more limited, intensified in 1995. Ethnic strife continued after a military coup, July 25, 1996. Former South African Pres. Nelson Mandela mediated peace talks from Dec. 1999; most warring groups signed a draft peace treaty in Arusha, Tanzania, Aug. 28, 2000. Coup attempts were suppressed Apr. 18 and July 23, 2001. A power-sharing government headed by Pierre Buyoya was sworn in Nov. 1, 2001, but clashes with rebels continued.

Domitien Ndayizeye, a Hutu, became president Apr. 30, 2003. The UN Security Council authorized, May 21, 2004, a 5,650-member peacekeeping force (ONUB) for Burundi. Approval of a power-sharing constitution by referendum, Feb. 28, 2005, paved the way for local and parliamentary elections. Pierre Nkurunziza, former leader of a Hutu rebel group, became president Aug. 26, 2005. ONUB was succeeded, Jan. 1, 2007, by the UN Integrated Office in Burundi (BINUB). Under a reconciliation accord reached Dec. 4, 2008, remaining Hutu rebels began to demobilize. Candidates opposing Nkurunziza dropped out of the June 28, 2010, presidential election, claiming the vote was rigged. The government was accused of ordering extrajudicial killings, 2010-11. A probe into the allegations, criticized for its limited scope, concluded, Aug. 23, 2012, the allegations were untrue.

Cambodia
Kingdom of Cambodia

People: Population: 14,952,665. **Age distrib.:** <15: 31.9%; 65+: 3.8%. **Pop. density:** 219.4 per sq mi, 84.7 per sq km. **Urban:** 20%. **Ethnic groups:** Khmer 90%, Vietnamese 5%, Chinese 1%. **Principal languages:** Khmer (official), French, English. **Chief religions:** Buddhist (official) 96%, Muslim 2%.

Geography: Total area: 69,898 sq mi, 181,035 sq km; **Land area:** 68,153 sq mi, 176,515 sq km. **Location:** SE Asia, on Indochina Peninsula. **Neighbors:** Thailand on W and N, Laos on NE, Vietnam on E. **Topography:** The central area, formed by the Mekong R. basin and Tonle Sap lake, is level. Hills and mountains are in SE, a long escarpment separates the country from Thailand on NW. 76% of the area is forested. **Capital:** Phnom Penh, 1,549,760.

Government: Type: Constitutional monarchy. **Head of state:** King Norodom Sihamoni; b. May 14, 1953; in office: Oct. 14, 2004. **Head of gov.:** Prime Min. Samdech Hun Sen; b. Aug. 5, 1952; in office: Nov. 30, 1998. **Local divisions:** 20 provinces and 4 municipalities. **Defense budget:** $298 mil. **Active troops:** 124,300.

Economy: Industries: tourism, garments, constr., rice milling, fishing, wood and wood prods., rubber, cement, gem mining, textiles. **Chief crops:** rice, rubber, corn, vegetables, cashews, tapioca. **Natural resources:** oil and gas, timber, gems, iron ore, manganese, phosphates, hydropower potential. **Arable land:** 22.1%. **Livestock:** cattle: 3.5 mil; chickens: 17.4 mil; pigs: 2.1 mil. **Fish catch:** 550,094 metric tons. **Electricity prod.:** 1.1 bil kWh. **Labor force:** agric. 57.6%, industry 15.9%, services 26.5%.

Finance: Monetary unit: Riel (KHR) (Sept. 2012: 4,059.04 = $1 U.S.). **GDP:** $33.9 bil; **per capita GDP:** $2,200; **GDP growth:** 6.1%. **Imports:** $7 bil; Thailand 29.6%, China 23.9%, Singapore 9.4%, Hong Kong 7.2%, Vietnam 5.1%, South Korea 4.6%. **Exports:** $5.4 bil; U.S. 41.5%, Canada 8.6%, Germany 8.2%, UK 7.9%, Japan 4.6%. **Tourism:** $1.7 bil. **Budget:** $2.7 bil. **Total reserves less gold:** $3.4 bil. **Gold:** 399,800 oz t. **CPI change:** 5.5%.

Transport: Railways: 429 mi (under restoration). **Civil aviation:** 157.2 mil pass.-mi; 6 airports. **Chief ports:** Phnom Penh, Kampong Saom.

Communications: TV sets: 8 per 1,000 pop. **Radios:** 112 per 1,000 pop. **Telephone lines:** 3.7 per 100 pop. **Internet:** 3.1%.

Health: Life expect.: 60.7 male; 65.5 female. **Births:** 25.2 (per 1,000 pop.). **Deaths:** 8.0 (per 1,000 pop.). **Natural inc.:** 1.72% **Infant mortality:** 54.1 (per 1,000 live births). **HIV rate:** 0.5%.

Education: Compulsory ages: NA. **Literacy:** 73.9%.

Major intl. organizations: UN (FAO, IBRD, ILO, IMF, WHO), ASEAN, WTO.

Embassy: 4530 16th St. NW 20011; 726-7742.

Website: www.cambodia.gov.kh

Early kingdoms dating from that of Funan in the 1st cent. CE culminated in the great Khmer empire that flourished from the 9th cent. to the 13th, encompassing present-day Thailand, Cambodia, Laos, and southern Vietnam. The peripheral areas were lost to invading Siamese and Vietnamese. France established a protectorate in 1863. Independence came in 1953.

Prince Norodom Sihanouk, king 1941-55 and head of state from 1960, tried to maintain neutrality during the Vietnam War. The U.S. bombed Cambodia, 1969-73, targeting suspected border sanctuaries of Vietnamese insurgents.

In 1970, pro-U.S. Prem. Lon Nol seized power, demanded removal of 40,000 North Vietnamese troops, and abolished the monarchy. Sihanouk formed a government-in-exile in Beijing, and open war began between the government and Communist Khmer Rouge guerrillas. The U.S. provided heavy military and economic aid.

Khmer Rouge forces captured Phnom Penh Apr. 17, 1975. Cities were depopulated and their residents executed or condemned to forced labor. An estimated 1.7 mil people died in "killing fields" or from other hardships under Khmer Rouge rule, 1975-79.

Severe border fighting broke out with Vietnam in 1978 and developed into a full-fledged Vietnamese invasion. Formation of a Vietnamese-backed government was announced, Jan. 8, 1979, one day after the capture of Phnom Penh. Thousands of refugees fled to Thailand; widespread starvation was reported. Vietnamese troops remained in Cambodia during the 1980s, meeting resistance from Khmer Rouge guerrillas, especially along the Thai border. Vietnam withdrew nearly all its troops by Sept. 1989.

Following UN-sponsored elections in Cambodia that ended May 28, 1993, the 2 leading parties agreed to share power in an interim government. On Sept. 21, the National Assembly adopted a constitution reestablishing a monarchy. It took effect Sept. 24, with Sihanouk as king. The Khmer Rouge boycotted the elections and opposed the new government. The insurgency had weakened and splintered by 1996.

Co-Prime Min. Hun Sen staged a coup July 5, 1997, ousting his rival, Prince Norodom Ranariddh. Pol Pot, the Khmer Rouge leader during the late 1970s, was denounced by his former comrades at a show trial, July 25, 1997, and sentenced to house arrest; he died Apr. 15, 1998. Sihanouk abdicated because of poor health and was succeeded, Oct. 14, 2004, by his son Norodom Sihamoni.

Arrested in 1999, former Khmer Rouge military chief Ta Mok died July 21, 2006, before being tried for genocide and crimes against humanity. Hun Sen's party retained power through a series of flawed elections; the most recent, on July 27, 2008, was a notable improvement over previous votes, according to international observers. On July 26, 2010, a UN-backed war crimes tribunal convicted a former prison warden known as Duch for overseeing the killing and torture of more than 14,000 inmates under Khmer Rouge rule. The tribunal Sept. 16, 2010, announced the indictment of former Pres. Khieu Samphan (arrested 2007) and 3 other senior Khmer Rouge leaders. A panic and stampede on a crowded Phnom Penh bridge Nov. 22, 2010, killed 353 people. Investigations of former Khmer Rouge leaders continued. Cambodia attempted to prevent a Swiss judge, Laurent Kasper-Ansermet, from joining the tribunal when he showed an interest in investigating Prime Min. Hun Sen, a former Khmer Rouge member. U.S. prosecutor Mark Harmon was appointed to replace Kasper-Ansermet July 31, 2012.

Cameroon
Republic of Cameroon

People: Population: 20,129,878. **Age distrib.:** <15: 40.3%; 65+: 3.4%. **Pop. density:** 110.3 per sq mi, 42.6 per sq km. **Urban:** 52.1%. **Ethnic groups:** Cameroon Highlanders 31%, Equatorial Bantu 19%, Kirdi 11%, Fulani 10%, NW Bantu 8%, E Nigritic 7%, other African 13%. **Principal languages:** 24 major African lang. groups; English, French (both official). **Chief religions:** indigenous beliefs 40%, Christian 40%, Muslim 20%.

Geography: Total area: 183,568 sq mi, 475,440 sq km; **Land area:** 182,514 sq mi, 472,710 sq km. **Location:** Between W and central Africa. **Neighbors:** Nigeria on NW; Chad, Central African Republic on E; Congo, Gabon, Equatorial Guinea on S. **Topography:** A low coastal plain with rain forests is in S; plateaus in center lead to forested mountains in W, including Mt. Cameroon, 13,435 ft; grasslands in N lead to marshes around Lake Chad. **Capital:** Yaoundé, 2,431,680. **Cities (urban aggl.):** Douala, 2,449,071.

Government: Type: Republic. **Head of state:** Pres. Paul Biya; b. Feb. 13, 1933; in office: Nov. 6, 1982. **Head of gov.:** Prime Min. Philemon Yang; b. June 14, 1947; in office: June 30, 2009. **Local divisions:** 10 provinces. **Defense budget:** $344 mil. **Active troops:** 14,200.

Economy: Industries: petroleum prod. and refining, aluminum prod., food proc., light consumer goods, textiles, lumber. **Chief crops:** coffee, cocoa, cotton, rubber, bananas, oilseed, grains, root starches. **Natural resources:** petroleum, bauxite, iron ore, timber, hydropower. **Crude oil reserves:** 200 mil bbls. **Arable land:** 12.6%. **Livestock:** cattle: 5.7 mil; chickens: 45 mil; goats: 4.5 mil; pigs: 1.7 mil; sheep: 3.9 mil. **Fish catch:** 140,835 metric tons. **Electricity prod.:** 5.6 bil kWh. **Labor force:** agric. 70%, industry 13%, services 17%.

Finance: Monetary unit: CFA BEAC Franc (XAF) (Sept. 2012: 519.73 = $1 U.S.). **GDP:** $47.9 bil; **per capita GDP:** $2,300; **GDP growth:** 4.1%. **Imports:** $6.1 bil; China 16.9%, France 16.8%, Nigeria 12.4%, Belgium 5.3%, Italy 4.3%, U.S. 4.3%. **Exports:** $5.5 bil; Spain 13.3%, China 11.4%, Netherlands 9.7%, Italy 8.8%, India 6.6%, France 6.4%, U.S. 5.9%, Germany 4.8%, Belgium 4%. **Tourism:** $159 mil. **Budget:** $5.3 bil. **Total reserves less gold:** $3.2 bil. **Gold** (2008): 29,954 oz t. **CPI change:** 2.9%.

Transport: Railways: 613 mi. **Motor vehicles:** 14.8 vehicles per 1,000 pop. **Civil aviation:** 577.9 mil pass.-mi; 11 airports. **Chief ports:** Douala, Limboh Terminal.

Communications: TV sets: 51 per 1,000 pop. **Radios:** 131 per 1,000 pop. **Telephone lines:** 3.3 per 100 pop. **Internet:** 5%.

Health: Life expect.: 53.8 male; 55.6 female. **Births:** 32.5 (per 1,000 pop.). **Deaths:** 11.7 (per 1,000 pop.). **Natural inc.:** 2.08%. **Infant mortality:** 59.7 (per 1,000 live births). **HIV rate:** 5.3%.

Education: Compulsory: ages 6-11. **Literacy:** 70.7%.

Major intl. organizations: UN (FAO, IBRD, ILO, IMF, WHO), AU, the Commonwealth, WTO.

Embassy: 2349 Massachusetts Ave. NW 20008; 265-8790.

Website: www.spm.gov.cm

Portuguese sailors were the first Europeans to reach Cameroon, in the 15th cent. The European and American slave trade was very active in the area. German control lasted from 1884 to 1916, when France and Britain divided the territory, later receiving League of Nations mandates and UN trusteeships. French Cameroon became independent Jan. 1, 1960; one part of British Cameroon joined Nigeria in 1961, the other part joined Cameroon. Stability allowed for development of roads, railways, agriculture, and petroleum production.

Pres. Paul Biya has retained power since 1982 in a series of elections that were boycotted by opposition parties or disputed as fraudulent. Rising food and fuel costs and discontent with Biya's continued rule sparked antigovernment riots Feb. 23-29, 2008. The legislature, controlled by Biya loyalists, voted Apr. 10, 2008, to abolish presidential term limits introduced in 1996.

Canada

People: Population: 34,300,083. **Age distrib.:** <15: 15.6%; 65+: 16.4%. **Pop. density:** 9.8 per sq mi, 3.8 per sq km. **Urban:** 80.7%. **Ethnic groups:** British Isles origin 28%, French origin 23%, other European 15%, Amerindian 2%, other (mostly Asian, African, Arab) 6%, mixed background 26%. **Principal languages:** English, French (both official). **Chief religions:** Roman Catholic 43%, Protestant 23%, other Christian 4%, Muslim 2%, none 16%.

Geography: Total area: 3,855,103 sq mi, 9,984,670 sq km; **Land area:** 3,511,023 sq mi, 9,093,507 sq km. The largest country in land size in the Western Hemisphere. **Topography:** Canada stretches 3,426 mi from east to west and extends southward from the North Pole to the U.S. border. Its seacoast includes 36,356 mi of mainland and 115,133 mi of islands, including the Arctic islands almost from Greenland to near the Alaskan border. **Climate:** While generally temperate, varies from freezing winter cold to blistering summer heat. **Capital:** Ottawa, 1,207,510 (figure is for Ottawa-Gatineau). **Cities (urban aggl.):** Toronto, 5,572,647; Montréal, 3,855,934; Vancouver, 2,267,301; Calgary, 1,216,477; Edmonton, 1,141,658; Québec City, 755,377.

Government: Type: Confederation with parliamentary democracy. **Head of state:** Queen Elizabeth II, represented by Gov.-Gen. David Johnston; b. June 28, 1941; in office: Oct. 1, 2010. **Head of gov.:** Prime Min. Stephen Harper; b. Apr. 30, 1959; in office: Feb. 6, 2006. **Local divisions:** 10 provinces, 3 territories. **Defense budget:** $21.5 bil. **Active troops:** 65,700.

Economy: Industries: transp. equip., chemicals, minerals, food prods., wood and paper prods., fish prods., petroleum and nat. gas. **Chief crops:** wheat, barley, oilseed, tobacco, fruits, vegetables. **Natural resources:** iron ore, nickel, zinc, copper, gold, lead, rare earth elements, molybdenum, potash, diamonds, silver, fish, timber, wildlife, coal, petroleum, nat. gas, hydropower. **Crude oil reserves:** 173.6 bil bbls. **Arable land:** 5.0%. **Livestock:** cattle: 13 mil; chickens: 165 mil; goats: 30,000; pigs: 11.8 mil; sheep: 803,000. **Fish catch:**

1.1 mil metric tons. **Electricity prod.** (2010): 580.6 bil kWh. **Labor force:** agric. 2%, mfg. 13%, constr. 6%, services 76%, other 3%.

Finance: Monetary unit: Dollar (CAD) (Sept. 2012: 0.99 = $1 U.S.). **GDP:** $1.4 tril; **per capita GDP:** $41,100; **GDP growth:** 2.5%. **Imports:** $461 bil; U.S. 49.5%, China 10.8%, Mexico 5.5%. **Exports:** $462.4 bil; U.S. 73.7%, UK 4.2%. **Tourism:** $16.9 bil. **Budget:** $747.8 bil. **Total reserves less gold:** $65.7 bil. **Gold:** 109,000 oz t. **CPI change:** 2.9%.

Transport: Railways: 28,926 mi. **Motor vehicles:** 620.9 vehicles per 1,000 pop. **Civil aviation:** 66.7 bil pass.-mi; 522 airports. **Chief ports:** Fraser River, Halifax, Hamilton, Montréal, Port-Cartier, Québec City, Saint John (New Brunswick), Sept-Isles, Vancouver.

Communications: TV sets: 731 per 1,000 pop. **Radios:** 1,052 per 1,000 pop. **Telephone lines:** 47.9 per 100 pop. **Daily newspaper circ:** 174.6 per 1,000 pop. **Internet:** 83%.

Health: Life expect.: 78.9 male; 84.2 female. **Births:** 10.3 (per 1,000 pop.). **Deaths:** 8.1 (per 1,000 pop.). **Natural inc.:** 0.22%. **Infant mortality:** 4.9 (per 1,000 live births). **HIV rate:** 0.2%.

Education: Compulsory: ages 6-16. **Literacy:** 99%.

Major intl. organizations: UN and all of its specialized agencies, APEC, the Commonwealth, NAFTA, NATO, OAS, OECD, OSCE, WTO.

Embassy: 501 Pennsylvania Ave. NW 20001; 682-1740.

Website: www.canada.gc.ca

French explorer Jacques Cartier, who reached the Gulf of St. Lawrence in 1534, is generally regarded as Canada's founder. But English seaman John Cabot sighted Newfoundland in 1497, and Vikings are believed to have reached the Atlantic coast centuries before either explorer. The French pioneered Canadian settlement, establishing Quebec City (1608) and Montréal (1642) and declaring New France a colony in 1663.

Britain acquired Acadia (later Nova Scotia) in 1717 and defeated French forces in Canada to gain control of Quebec (1759) and the rest of New France in 1763. The French, through the Quebec Act of 1774, retained rights to their own language, religion, and civil law. The British presence in Canada increased during the American Revolution when many colonials, calling themselves United Empire Loyalists, moved north to Canada. Fur traders and explorers led Canadians westward across the continent. Sir Alexander Mackenzie reached the Pacific in 1793 and scrawled on a rock, "From Canada by land."

In Upper and Lower Canada (later called Ontario and Quebec) and in the Maritimes, legislative assemblies appeared in the 18th cent. and reformers called for responsible government. The War of 1812, a conflict between Great Britain and the U.S. fought mainly in Upper Canada that ended in a stalemate in 1814, intervened.

In 1837 political agitation for more democratic government culminated in rebellions in Upper and Lower Canada. Britain sent Lord Durham to investigate; he recommended union of the 2 parts into one colony called Canada in 1839. The union lasted until Confederation, July 1, 1867, when proclamation of the British North America Act (now known as the Constitution Act, 1867) launched the Dominion of Canada, consisting of Ontario, Quebec, and the former colonies of Nova Scotia and New Brunswick.

Since 1840 the Canadian colonies had held the right to internal self-government. The British North America Act, which was the basis for the country's written constitution, established a federal system of government modeled on the British parliament and cabinet structure under the crown. Canada was proclaimed a self-governing Dominion within the British Empire in 1931. With the ratification of the Constitution Act, 1982, Canada obtained the right to amend its constitution, thereby severing its last legislative link with Britain.

Failure in 1990 of the so-called Meech Lake Accord, 1987, which would have assured constitutional protection for Quebec's efforts to preserve its French language and culture, sparked a separatist revival in Quebec. Subsequently, the Charlottetown agreement called for constitutional changes, such as recognition of Quebec as a "distinct society" within the Canadian confederation. It was defeated by a national referendum Oct. 26, 1992.

Canada's Provinces and Territories

Provinces/territories	Joined confed.	Area (sq mi)	Population (Apr. 2011 est.)	Capital	Premier	Party	In office
Alberta	1905	255,287	3,645,257	Edmonton	Ed Stelmach	Prog. Cons.	2006
British Columbia	1871	365,948	4,400,057	Victoria	Christy Clark	Liberal	2011
Manitoba	1870	250,947	1,208,268	Winnipeg	Greg Selinger	New Democratic	2009
New Brunswick	1867	28,355	751,171	Fredericton	David Alward	Prog. Cons.	2010
Newfoundland and Labrador	1949	156,649	514,536	St. John's	Kathy Dunderdale	Prog. Cons.	2010
Nova Scotia	1867	21,425	921,727	Halifax	Darrell Dexter	New Democratic	2009
Ontario	1867	412,581	12,851,821	Toronto	Dalton McGuinty	Liberal	2003
Prince Edward Island	1873	2,185	140,204	Charlottetown	Robert Ghiz	Liberal	2007
Quebec	1867	594,860	7,903,001	Québec	Jean Charest	Liberal	2003
Saskatchewan	1905	251,866	1,033,381	Regina	Brad Wall	Saskatchewan	2007
Northwest Territories[1]	1871	503,951	41,462	Yellowknife	Floyd Roland	nonpartisan	2007
Nunavut[1]	1999[2]	818,959	31,906	Iqaluit	Eva Aariak	nonpartisan	2008
Yukon[1]	1898	186,661	33,897	Whitehorse	Darrell Pasloski	Yukon	2011

(1) Territories also have federally appointed commissioners to represent federal interests. (2) Territory created in 1999 from eastern portion of Northwest Territories.

Canada became the first nation to ratify the North American Free Trade Agreement among Canada, Mexico, and the U.S., June 23, 1993. It went into effect Jan. 1, 1994. In a Quebec referendum held Oct. 30, 1995, proponents of secession lost. On Jan. 7, 1998, the government apologized to indigenous peoples for 150 years of mistreatment and pledged to set up a "healing fund." Canada's highest court ruled, Aug. 20, that Quebec cannot secede unilaterally, even if a majority of the province approves. Nunavut ("Our Land"), carved from Northwest Territories as a homeland for the Inuit, was established Apr. 1, 1999.

Victory by the Liberals in national elections Nov. 27, 2000, made Jean Chrétien the first Canadian prime min. in over 50 years to head a third successive majority government. Canada sent troops and warships to aid the U.S.-led coalition in Afghanistan beginning Oct. 2001; 157 Canadian troops had been killed in Afghanistan by the time Canada's combat mission ended July 7, 2011.

Chrétien retired Dec. 12, 2003, and Paul Martin became prime minister. Weakened by a scandal involving improper payments to Quebec firms for sponsorship of cultural and sporting events, the Liberals won only 135 of 308 seats in parliamentary elections June 28, 2004. Martin became head of a minority government. Parliament enacted a bill, July 19, 2005, making same-sex marriage (already permitted in 8 of 10 provinces) legal throughout the country. Michaëlle Jean, a Haitian-born TV journalist, was installed Sept. 27 as Canada's first black governor-general.

Twelve years of Liberal Party rule ended when Conservatives won 124 seats to the Liberals' 103 in parliamentary elections, Jan. 23, 2006. Conservative leader Stephen Harper took office Feb. 6 as head of a minority government. Police and intelligence officials in the Toronto area, June 2-3, 2006, arrested and charged 17 people with plotting terrorist attacks in Canada. The supreme court, Feb. 23, 2007, unanimously struck down a law under which foreign-born terrorism suspects had been indefinitely detained without charge.

Prime Min. Harper remained the head of a minority government after early elections Oct. 14, 2008, as Conservatives increased their plurality to 143 seats. Canada hosted the Winter Olympics Feb. 12-28, 2010, in Vancouver, BC, and the G-8 and G-20 summit meetings June 25-27, 2010, in Ontario. A vote of no-confidence Mar. 25, 2011, led to federal elections May 2 in which Harper's Conservatives gained a parliamentary majority of 166 seats. The New Democratic Party with 103 seats became the official opposition, as the Liberals only had 34 seats. The importance of oil to Canada's economy was brought to the fore in the tight-budget years that came with the world's economic crisis after 2008. While the technology for extracting oil from tar sands, large deposits of which are found in Alberta, have improved, the lack of a pipeline to Alberta has obliged Canada producers to sell their oil at discounted prices, thereby losing an estimated $5.8 bil in the first six months of 2012 and diminishing much needed tax revenue.

Cape Verde
Republic of Cape Verde

People: Population: 523,568. **Age distrib.:** <15: 31.9%; 65+: 5.3%. **Pop. density:** 336.2 per sq mi, 129.8 per sq km. **Urban:** 62.6%. **Ethnic groups:** Creole (mulatto) 71%, African 28%, European 1%. **Principal languages:** Portuguese (official), Crioulo (blend of Portuguese and W African words). **Chief religions:** Roman Catholic (infused with indigenous beliefs), Protestant (mostly Church of the Nazarene).

Geography: Total area: 1,557 sq mi, 4,033 sq km; **Land area:** 1,557 sq mi, 4,033 sq km. **Location:** In Atlantic O., off W tip of Africa. **Neighbors:** Nearest are Mauritania, Senegal to E. **Topography:** Cape Verde Islands are 15 in number, volcanic in origin (active crater on Fogo). The landscape is eroded and stark, with vegetation mostly in interior valleys. **Capital:** Praia, 132,029.

Government: Type: Republic. **Head of state:** Pres. Jorge Carlos Fonseca; b. Oct. 20, 1950; in office: Sept. 9, 2011. **Head of gov.:** Prime Min. José Maria Neves; b. Mar. 28, 1960; in office: Feb. 1, 2001. **Local divisions:** 17 districts. **Defense budget:** $9 mil. **Active troops:** 1,200.

Economy: Industries: food and beverages, fish proc., shoes and garments, salt mining, ship repair. **Chief crops:** bananas, corn, beans, sweet potatoes, sugarcane, coffee, peanuts. **Natural resources:** salt, basalt rock, limestone, kaolin, fish, clay, gypsum. **Arable land:** 14.9%. **Livestock:** cattle: 46,000; chickens: 640,000; goats: 231,400; pigs: 238,600; sheep: 20,370. **Fish catch:** 19,500 metric tons. **Electricity prod.:** 277 mil kWh. **Labor force:** NA.

Finance: Monetary unit: Escudo (CVE) (Sept. 2012: 87.53 = $1 U.S.). **GDP:** $2.1 bil; **per capita GDP:** $4,000; **GDP growth:** 5%. **Imports:** $980.5 mil; Portugal 37%, Netherlands 25.4%, Spain 7%, Italy 5.2%, China 5.2%. **Exports:** $191.4 mil; Spain 65.9%, Portugal 18.9%. **Tourism:** $369 mil. **Budget:** $743.8 mil. **Total reserves less gold:** $338.6 mil. **CPI change:** 4.5%.

Transport: Civil aviation: 755.6 mil pass.-mi; 9 airports. **Chief port:** Porto Grande.

Communications: TV sets: 128 per 1,000 pop. **Radios:** 176 per 1,000 pop. **Telephone lines:** 14.9 per 100 pop. **Internet:** 32%.

Health: Life expect.: 68.8 male; 73.3 female. **Births:** 21.2 (per 1,000 pop.). **Deaths:** 6.3 (per 1,000 pop.). **Natural inc.:** 1.49% **Infant mortality:** 26.0 (per 1,000 live births). **HIV rate:** NA.

Education: Compulsory: ages 6-11. **Literacy:** 84.3%.

Major intl. organizations: UN (FAO, IBRD, ILO, IMF, WHO), AU, WTO.

Embassy: 3415 Massachusetts Ave. NW 20007; 965-6820.

Website: www.governo.cv

The first Portuguese colonists landed in 1462; African slaves were brought soon after, and most Cape Verdeans descend from both groups. Cape Verde independence came July 5, 1975. Antonio Mascarenhas Monteiro won the nation's first free presidential election Feb. 17, 1991; he was reelected without opposition 5 years later. When Pres. Pedro Pires retired after serving two 5-year terms, 2001-11, Jorge Carlos Fonseca won a presidential runoff election Aug. 21, 2011. Remittances from Cape Verdean emigrants are a major source of income.

Central African Republic

People: Population: 5,057,208. **Age distrib.:** <15: 40.9%; 65+: 3.7%. **Pop. density:** 21 per sq mi, 8.1 per sq km. **Urban:** 39.1%. **Ethnic groups:** Baya 33%, Banda 27%, Mandjia 13%, Sara 10%, Mboum 7%, M'Baka 4%, Yakoma 4%. **Principal languages:** French (official), Sangho (lingua franca and national), tribal langs. **Chief religions:** indigenous beliefs 35%, Protestant 25%, Roman Catholic 25%, Muslim 15%.

Geography: Total area: 240,535 sq mi, 622,984 sq km; **Land area:** 240,535 sq mi, 622,984 sq km. **Location:** In central Africa. **Neighbors:** Chad on N, Cameroon on W, Congo-Brazzaville and Congo-Kinshasa (formerly Zaire) on S, Sudan on E. **Topography:** Mostly rolling plateau, average altitude 2,000 ft, with rivers draining S to the Congo and N to Lake Chad. Open, well-watered savanna covers most of the area, with an arid area in NE, and tropical rain forest in SW. **Capital:** Bangui, 740,062.

Government: Type: Republic. **Head of state:** Pres. François Bozizé; b. Oct. 14, 1946; in office: Mar. 15, 2003. **Head of gov.:** Prime Min. Faustin Archange Touadéra; b. Apr. 21, 1957; in office: Jan. 22, 2008. **Local divisions:** 14 prefectures, 2 economic prefectures, 1 commune. **Defense budget** (2010): $51 mil. **Active troops:** 2,150.

Economy: Industries: gold and diamond mining, logging, brewing, textiles, footwear, bicycle and motorcycle assembly. **Chief crops:** timber, cotton, coffee, tobacco, manioc, yams, millet, corn, bananas. **Natural resources:** diamonds, uranium, timber, gold, oil, hydropower. **Arable land:** 3.1%. **Livestock:** cattle: 3.9 mil; chickens: 6.4 mil; goats: 4.9 mil; pigs: 1.1 mil; sheep: 388,000. **Fish catch:** 35,170 metric tons. **Electricity prod.:** 160 mil kWh. **Labor force:** NA.

Finance: Monetary unit: CFA BEAC Franc (XAF) (Sept. 2012: 519.73 = $1 U.S.). **GDP:** $3.7 bil; **per capita GDP:** $800; **GDP growth:** 3.1%. **Imports:** $380.1 mil; South Korea 45.6%, Netherlands 8.8%, France 7.1%, Cameroon 5.1%. **Exports:** $169.2 mil; Belgium 29.1%, China 16.4%, Morocco 7.6%, Dem. Rep. of the Congo 7.6%, France 6.8%, Indonesia 6%. **Tourism:** $6 mil. **Budget:** $401 mil. **Total reserves less gold:** $154.5 mil. **Gold** (2008): 11,126 oz t. **CPI change:** 0.1%.

Transport: Motor vehicles: 0.9 vehicles per 1,000 pop. **Civil aviation:** 2 airports. **Chief ports:** Bangui, Nola, Nzinga, Salo.

Communications: TV sets: 10 per 1,000 pop. **Radios:** 111 per 1,000 pop. **Telephone lines:** 0.05 per 100 pop. **Internet:** 2.2%.

Health: Life expect.: 49.2 male; 51.8 female. **Births:** 36.1 (per 1,000 pop.). **Deaths:** 14.7 (per 1,000 pop.). **Natural inc.:** 2.14% **Infant mortality:** 97.2 (per 1,000 live births). **HIV rate:** 4.7%.

Education: Compulsory: ages 6-11. **Literacy:** 56.0%.

Major intl. organizations: UN (FAO, IBRD, ILO, IMF, WHO), AU, WTO.

Embassy: 1618 22nd St. NW 20008; 483-7800.

Website: www.state.gov/p/af/ci/car/

Various Bantu peoples migrated through the region for centuries before French control was asserted in the late 19th cent., when the region was named Ubangi-Shari. Complete independence was attained Aug. 13, 1960.

Pres. Jean-Bedel Bokassa, who seized power in a 1965 military coup, proclaimed himself constitutional emperor of the renamed Central African Empire Dec. 1976. Bokassa's rule was characterized by ruthless authoritarianism and human rights violations. He was ousted in a bloodless coup aided by the French government, Sept. 20, 1979. In 1981, Gen. André Kolingba became head of state in another bloodless coup. Multiparty legislative and presidential elections were held Oct. 1992 but were canceled by the government when Kolingba was losing. New elections, held in Aug. and Sept. 1993, led to the replacement of Kolingba with civilian rule under Pres. Ange-Félix Patassé.

France sent in troops to suppress army mutinies in 1996 and 1997. After thwarting several coup attempts, Patassé was ousted Mar. 15, 2003, by rebels under former army chief François Bozizé. Bozizé won a presidential runoff election May 8, 2005, but insurgent activity by Patassé loyalists and others continued in the north. A national peace conference, Dec. 8-20, 2008, paved the way for the installation of a unity government Jan. 19, 2009. Pres. Bozizé won reelection Jan. 23, 2011.

Chad
Republic of Chad

People: Population: 10,975,648. **Age distrib.:** <15: 45.6%; 65+: 2.9%. **Pop. density:** 22.6 per sq mi, 8.7 per sq km. **Urban:** 21.8%. **Ethnic groups:** Sara 28%, Arab 12%, Mayo-Kebbi 12%, Kanem-Bornou 9%, Ouaddai 9%, Hadjarai 7%, Tandjile 7%, Gorane 6%, Fitri-Batha 5%. **Principal languages:** French, Arabic (both official); Sara; 120+ langs. and dialects. **Chief religions:** Muslim 53%, Catholic 20%, Protestant 14%, animist 7%, atheist 3%.

Geography: Total area: 495,755, sq mi, 1,284,000 sq km; **Land area:** 486,180 sq mi, 1,259,200 sq km. **Location:** In central N Africa. **Neighbors:** Libya on N; Niger, Nigeria, Cameroon on W; Central African Republic on S; Sudan on E. **Topography:** Wooded savanna, steppe, and desert in the S; part of the Sahara in the N. Southern rivers flow N to Lake Chad, surrounded by marshland. **Capital:** N'Djaména, 1,078,640.

Government: Type: Republic. **Head of state:** Pres. Idriss Déby Itno; b. 1952; in office: Dec. 4, 1990. **Head of gov.:** Prime Min. Emmanuel Nadingar; b. 1951; in office: Mar. 5, 2010. **Local divisions:** 14 prefectures. **Defense budget** (2010): $126 mil. **Active troops:** 25,350.

Economy: Industries: oil, cotton textiles, meatpacking, brewing, sodium carbonate, soap, cigarettes, constr. materials. **Chief crops:** cotton, sorghum, millet, peanuts, rice, potatoes, manioc. **Natural resources:** petroleum, uranium, natron, kaolin, fish. **Crude oil reserves:** 1.5 bil bbls. **Arable land:** 3.4%. **Livestock:** cattle: 7.4 mil; chickens: 5.6 mil; goats: 6.8 mil; pigs: 30,400; sheep: 3 mil. **Fish catch:** 40,000 metric tons. **Electricity prod.:** 95 mil kWh. **Labor force:** agric. 80% (subsistence farming, herding, fishing), industry and services 20%.

Finance: Monetary unit: CFA BEAC Franc (XAF) (Sept. 2012: 519.73 = $1 U.S.). **GDP:** $19.8 bil; **per capita GDP:** $1,900; **GDP growth:** 1.6%. **Imports:** $3.5 bil; Cameroon 16.9%, France 15.7%, China 10.7%, Finland 6.5%, Sweden 6%, Saudi Arabia 5%, Belgium 4.4%. **Exports:** $4.1 bil; U.S. 83.2%, China 6.8%, France 5.6%. **Tourism:** NA. **Budget:** $3.5 bil. **Total reserves less gold:** $951.1 mil. **Gold** (2008): 11,126 oz t. **CPI change:** –4.9%.

Transport: Civil aviation: 9 airports.

Communications: TV sets: 9 per 1,000 pop. **Radios:** 103 per 1,000 pop. **Telephone lines:** 0.3 per 100 pop. **Internet:** 1.9%.

Health: Life expect.: 47.6 male; 49.8 female. **Births:** 38.7 (per 1,000 pop.). **Deaths:** 15.2 (per 1,000 pop.). **Natural inc.:** 2.35% **Infant mortality:** 93.6 (per 1,000 live births). **HIV rate:** 3.4%.

Education: Compulsory: ages 6-15. **Literacy:** 34.5%.

Major intl. organizations: UN (FAO, IBRD, ILO, IMF, WHO), AU, WTO.

Embassy: 2002 R St. NW 20009; 462-4009.

Website: www.dgmp.gouv.td or www.state.gov/p/af/ci/cd/

Chad was the site of Paleolithic and Neolithic cultures before the Sahara Desert formed. A succession of kingdoms and Arab slave traders dominated Chad until France took control around 1900. Independence came Aug. 11, 1960. Northern Muslim rebels have fought animist and Christian southern government and French troops from 1966, despite numerous cease-fires and peace pacts.

Rebel forces, led by Hissène Habré, captured the capital and forced Pres. Goukouni Oueddei to flee the country in June 1982. In Dec. 1990, a Libyan-supported insurgent group, the Patriotic Salvation Movement, overthrew Habré. After approval of a new constitution Mar. 1996, Chad's first multiparty presidential election was held in June and July.

Oil began flowing July 15, 2003, through a 665-mi pipeline that allows landlocked Chad to export via Cameroon. Pres. Idriss Déby Itno won a third term, May 3, 2006, in an election boycotted by major opposition groups. Violence along the Sudan border escalated during the year, as Sudanese *janjaweed* militias and Chadian rebels attacked civilians, and Darfur rebels preyed on refugee camps. Between 140 and 700 civilians died in N'Djaména, Feb. 2-5, 2008, as more than 2,000 Chadian rebels stormed the capital and clashed with government troops in a failed coup attempt.

On Jan. 15, 2010, Chad and Sudan signed an accord aimed at normalizing relations and suppressing cross-border activities by rebel groups. Established in 2007, a UN peacekeeping force (MINURCAT) completed its mandate Dec. 31, 2010. In early 2011, camps in E Chad housed some 262,900 refugees, most from Darfur, and camps in S Chad held about 73,500 refugees, most from the Central African Republic; more than 157,000 Chadians were internally displaced. Pres. Deby won reelection Apr. 25, 2011, in a vote boycotted as fraudulent by major opposition groups.

Chile
Republic of Chile

People: Population: 17,067,369. **Age distrib.:** <15: 21.4%; 65+: 9.4%. **Pop. density:** 59.4 per sq mi, 22.9 per sq km. **Urban:** 89.2%. **Ethnic groups:** white and white-Amerindian 95%, Mapuche 4%. **Principal languages:** Spanish (official), Mapudungun, German, English. **Chief religions:** Roman Catholic 70%, Evangelical 15%, Jehovah's Witnesses 1%, other Christian 1%, none 8%.

Geography: Total area: 291,933 sq mi, 756,102 sq km; **Land area:** 287,187 sq mi, 743,812 sq km. **Location:** Occupies western coast of S South America. **Neighbors:** Peru on N, Bolivia on NE, Argentina on E. **Topography:** Andes Mts. on E border incl. some of the world's highest peaks; on W is 2,650-mi Pacific coast. Width varies 100-250 mi. In N is Atacama Desert, in center are agricultural regions, in S, forests and grazing lands. **Capital:** Santiago, 6,034,480. **Cities (urban aggl.):** Valparaíso, 882,954.

Government: Type: Republic. **Head of state and gov.:** Pres. Sebastián Piñera Echenique; b. Dec. 1, 1949; in office: Mar. 11, 2010. **Local divisions:** 13 regions. **Defense budget:** $4.2 bil. **Active troops:** 59,059.

Economy: Industries: copper, lithium, other minerals, foodstuffs, fish proc., iron, steel, wood and wood prods., transp. equip., cement, textiles. **Chief crops:** grapes, apples, pears, onions, wheat, corn, oats, peaches, garlic, asparagus, beans. **Natural resources:** copper, timber, iron ore, nitrates, prec. metals, molybdenum, hydropower. **Crude oil reserves:** 150 mil bbls. **Arable land:** 1.7%. **Livestock:** cattle: 3.9 mil; chickens: 47.5 mil; goats: 750,000; pigs: 2.7 mil; sheep: 3.6 mil. **Fish catch:** 3.8 mil metric tons. **Electricity prod.** (2010): 59.8 bil kWh. **Labor force:** agric. 13.2%, industry 23%, services 63.9%.

Finance: Monetary unit: Peso (CLP) (Sept. 2012: 481.61 = $1 U.S.). **GDP:** $303.5 bil; **per capita GDP:** $17,400; **GDP growth:** 5.9%. **Imports:** $70.9 bil; U.S. 20.9%, China 17.9%, Brazil 8.8%, Argentina 6.7%, Japan 4.2%. **Exports:** $81.7 bil; China 22.4%, U.S. 11.3%, Japan 11%, Brazil 5.5%, South Korea 5.4%, Netherlands 4.7%. **Tourism:** $1.8 bil. **Budget:** $51.8 bil. **Total reserves less gold:** $41.9 bil. **Gold:** 7,900 oz t. **CPI change:** 3.3%.

Transport: Railways: 4,401 mi. **Motor vehicles:** 170.7 vehicles per 1,000 pop. **Civil aviation:** 10.9 bil pass.-mi; 88 airports. **Chief ports:** Coronel, Huasco, Lirquen, Puerto Ventanas, San Antonio, San Vicente, Valparaíso.

Communications: TV sets: 313 per 1,000 pop. **Radios:** 783 per 1,000 pop. **Telephone lines:** 19.5 per 100 pop. **Daily newspaper circ:** 50.6 per 1,000 pop. **Internet:** 53.9%.

Health: Life expect.: 75.1 male; 81.3 female. **Births:** 14.3 (per 1,000 pop.). **Deaths:** 5.8 (per 1,000 pop.). **Natural inc.:** 0.85% **Infant mortality:** 7.4 (per 1,000 live births). **HIV rate:** 0.4%.

Education: Compulsory: ages 6-17. **Literacy:** 98.6%.

Major intl. organizations: UN and all of its specialized agencies, APEC, OAS, OECD, WTO.

Embassy: 1732 Massachusetts Ave. NW 20036; 785-1746.

Website: www.gob.cl

Northern Chile was under Inca rule before the Spanish conquest, 1536-40. The southern Araucanian Indians resisted until the late 19th cent. Independence was gained 1810-18, under José de San Martin and Bernardo O'Higgins; the latter, as supreme director 1817-23, sought social and economic reforms until deposed. Chile defeated Peru and Bolivia in 1836-39 and 1879-84, gaining mineral-rich northern land.

In 1970, Salvador Allende Gossens, a Marxist, became president with a narrow plurality of the popular vote. His government improved conditions for the poor, but property seizures by left-wing extremists, poorly planned socialist economic programs, and a destabilization campaign backed by the U.S. led to political and financial chaos. A military junta seized power Sept. 11, 1973. With the presidential palace under attack, Allende refused to surrender; police said he killed himself. (A new autopsy, disclosed July 19, 2011, confirmed the original police account.) The junta, headed by Gen. Augusto Pinochet Ugarte, implemented plans to privatize the economy and "exterminate Marxism." Repression continued into the 1980s.

In Dec. 1989 voters elected a civilian president, although Pinochet continued to head the army until Mar. 10, 1998. In Mar. 1994 a Chilean human rights group estimated that human rights violations had claimed more than 3,100 lives during Pinochet's rule. Efforts to prosecute him failed when courts in Britain and Chile declared him mentally unfit to stand trial.

Ricardo Lagos Escobar, Chile's first Socialist president since the 1973 coup, took office Mar. 11, 2000. Chile and the U.S. signed a free trade accord June 6, 2003. Verónica Michelle Bachelet Jeria, also a Socialist, won a runoff election Jan. 15, 2006, and took office Mar. 11 as Chile's first woman president. Pinochet died Dec. 10, 2006.

Billionaire businessman Sebastián Piñera Echenique, a conservative, won a presidential runoff election Jan. 17, 2010, and took office Mar. 11. In the interim, a powerful earthquake Feb. 27, 2010, off the coast of central Chile killed at least 521 people and caused up to $30 bil in property damage. Chile successfully rescued 33 miners trapped for 10 weeks 2,300 feet underground after a cave-in at the San José gold and copper mine Aug. 5, 2010. A prison fire Dec. 8 in Santiago killed at least 81 inmates. Chile's economy was growing at a 6.6% annual rate in mid-2011, but lagging wages sparked labor protests against the Piñera government that continued into 2012 and spread to the student population. Piñera proposed sweeping tax reform, Apr. 25, 2012, that would raise corporate and reduce individual taxes.

Tierra del Fuego is the largest (18,800 sq mi) island in the archipelago of the same name at the southern tip of S. America, an area of majestic mountains, tortuous channels, and high winds. It was visited 1520 by Magellan and named Land of Fire because of its many Indian bonfires. Part of the island is in Chile, part in Argentina. Punta Arenas, on a mainland peninsula, is a center of sheep raising and the world's southernmost city (pop. [2012 census] 131,067); Puerto Williams is the southernmost settlement.

China
People's Republic of China

(Statistical data do not include Hong Kong or Macao.)

People: Population: 1,343,239,923. **Age distrib.:** <15: 17.4%; 65+: 9.1%. **Pop. density:** 363.5 per sq mi, 140.4 per sq km. **Urban:** 50.6%. Hong Kong and Macao). **Ethnic groups:** Han Chinese 92%; Zhuang, Manchu, Hui, Miao, Uighur, Tujia, Yi, Mongol, Tibetan, Buyi, Dong, Yao, Korean, other nationalities 9%. **Principal languages:** Standard Chinese or Mandarin (Putonghua, based on Beijing dialect), Yue (Cantonese), Wu (Shanghainese), Minbei (Fuzhou), Minnan (Hokkien-Taiwanese), Xiang, Gan, Hakka dialects, minority langs. **Chief religions:** officially atheist; Daoist (Taoist), Buddhist, Christian, Muslim.

Geography: Total area: 3,705,407 sq mi, 9,596,961 sq km; **Land area:** 3,694,959 sq mi, 9,569,901 sq km. **Location:** Occupies most of the habitable mainland of E Asia. **Neighbors:** Mongolia on N; Russia on NE and NW; Afghanistan, Pakistan, Tajikistan, Kyrgyzstan, Kazakhstan on W; India, Nepal, Bhutan, Myanmar, Laos, Vietnam on S; North Korea on NE. **Topography:** Two-thirds of the vast territory is mountainous or desert; only one-tenth is cultivated. Rolling topography rises to high elevations in the N in the Daxinganlingshanmai separating Manchuria and Mongolia; the Tien Shan in Xinjiang; the Himalayan and Kunlunshanmai in the SW and in Tibet. Length is 1,860 mi from N to S, width E to W is more than 2,000 mi. The eastern half of China is one of the world's best-watered lands. Three great river systems, the Chang (Yangtze), Huang (Yellow), and Xi, provide water for vast farmlands. **Capital:** Beijing, 15,594,400. **Cities (urban aggl.):** Shanghai, 20,207,612; Guangzhou, Guangdong, 10,848,502; Shenzhen, 10,629,684; Chongqing, 9,977,035; Wuhan, 9,157,680; Tianjin, 8,744,365; Dongguan, Guangdong, 7,280,345; Chengdu, 6,670,149; Foshan, 6,485,510; Nanjing, Jiangsu, 5,866,243; Haerbin, 5,687,339; Shenyang, 5,567,968; Hangzhou, 5,448,263.

Government: Type: Communist Party-led state. **Head of state:** Pres. Hu Jintao; b. Dec. 1942; in office: Mar. 15, 2003 (also gen. sec. of Communist Party since Nov. 15, 2002). **Head of gov.:** Premier Wen Jiabao; b. Sept. 1942; in office: Mar. 16, 2003. **Local divisions:** 22 provinces (not including Taiwan), 5 autonomous regions, and 4 municipalities, plus the special administrative regions of Hong Kong (as of July 1, 1997) and Macao (as of Dec. 20, 1999). **Defense budget:** $89.8 bil. **Active troops:** 2,285,000.

Economy: Industries: world leader in gross value of industrial output; mining and ore proc., iron, steel, aluminum, other metals, coal; machine building; armaments; textiles and apparel; petroleum; cement; chemicals; fertilizers; consumer prods; food proc.; transp. equip.; telecomm. equip. **Chief crops:** world leader in gross value of agric. output; rice, wheat, potatoes, corn, peanuts, tea, millet, barley, apples, cotton, oilseed. **Natural resources:** coal, iron ore, petroleum, nat. gas, mercury, tin, tungsten, antimony, manganese, molybdenum, vanadium, magnetite, aluminum, lead, zinc, rare earth elements, uranium, hydropower potential (world's largest). **Crude oil reserves:** 20.4 bil bbls. **Arable land:** 11.8%. **Livestock:** cattle: 83.8 mil; chickens: 4.8 bil; goats: 150.7 mil; pigs: 476.3 mil; sheep: 134 mil. **Fish catch:** 63.5 mil metric tons. **Electricity prod.** (2010): 4 tril kWh. **Labor force:** agric. 36.7%, industry 28.7%, services 34.6%.

Finance: Monetary unit: Yuan Renminbi (CNY) (Sept. 2012: 6.35 = $1 U.S.). **GDP:** $11.4 tril; **per capita GDP:** $8,500; **GDP growth:** 9.2%. **Imports:** $1.7 tril; Japan 11.2%, South Korea 9.3%, U.S. 6.8%, Germany 5.3%, Australia 4.6%. **Exports:** $1.9 tril; U.S. 17.1%, Hong Kong 14.1%, Japan 7.8%, South Korea 4.4%, Germany 4%. **Tourism:** $48.5 bil. **Budget:** $1.7 tril. **Total reserves less gold:** $3.2 tril. **Gold:** 33.9 mil oz t. **CPI change:** 5.4%.

Transport: Railways: 53,438 mi. **Motor vehicles:** 46.2 vehicles per 1,000 pop. **Civil aviation:** 205.2 bil pass.-mi (incl. data for Hong Kong and Macao); 452 airports. **Chief ports:** Dalian, Guangzhou, Ningbo, Qingdao, Qinhuangdao, Shanghai, Shenzhen, Tianjin.

Communications: TV sets: 380 per 1,000 pop. **Radios:** 336 per 1,000 pop. **Telephone lines:** 21.2 per 100 pop. **Daily newspaper circ.:** 74.1 per 1,000 pop. **Internet:** 38.3%.

Health: Life expect.: 72.8 male; 77.1 female. **Births:** 12.3 (per 1,000 pop.). **Deaths:** 7.2 (per 1,000 pop.). **Natural inc.:** 0.51% **Infant mortality:** 15.6 (per 1,000 live births). **HIV rate:** 0.1%.

Education: Compulsory: ages 6-14. **Literacy:** 94.3%.

Major intl. organizations: UN (FAO, IBRD, ILO, IMF, WHO), APEC, WTO.

Embassy: 2300 Connecticut Ave. NW 20008; 328-2500.
Website: www.gov.cn

Remains of various humanlike creatures who lived as early as several hundred thousand years ago have been found in many parts of China. Neolithic agricultural settlements dotted the Huang (Yellow) R. basin from about 5000 BCE. Their language, religion, and art were the sources of later Chinese civilization.

Bronze metallurgy reached a peak and Chinese pictographic writing, similar to today's, was in use in the more developed culture of the Shang Dynasty (c. 1500 BCE-c. 1000 BCE), which ruled much of North China.

A succession of dynasties and interdynastic warring kingdoms ruled China for the next 3,000 years. They expanded Chinese political and cultural domination to the south and west, and developed a technologically and culturally advanced society. Rule by foreigners (Mongols in the Yuan Dynasty, 1271-1368, and Manchus in the Ch'ing Dynasty, 1644-1911) did not alter the underlying culture.

A period of relative stagnation left China vulnerable to internal and external pressures in the 19th cent. Rebellions left tens of millions dead, and Russia, Japan, Britain, and other powers exercised political and economic control in large parts of the country. China became a republic Jan. 1, 1912, following the Wuchang Uprising inspired by Dr. Sun Yat-sen, founder of the Kuomintang (Nationalist) party. By 1928, the Kuomintang, led by Chiang Kai-shek, succeeded in nominal reunification of China. About the same time, a bloody purge of Communists from the ranks of the Kuomintang fomented hostilities.

For over 50 years, 1894-1945, China was involved in conflicts with Japan. In 1895, China ceded Korea, Taiwan, and other areas. On Sept. 18, 1931, Japan seized the Northeastern Provinces (Manchuria) and set up a puppet state called Manchukuo. Taking advantage of Chinese dissension, Japan invaded China proper July 7, 1937. On Nov. 20 the retreating Nationalist government moved its capital to Chongqing (Chungking) from Nanking (Nanjing), which Japanese troops then ravaged Dec. 13.

From 1939 the Sino-Japanese War (1937-45) became part of the broader world conflict. After its defeat in World War II, Japan gave up all seized land. Within China, conflicts involving the Kuomintang, Communists, and other factions resumed. China came under the domination of Communist armies, 1949-50. The Kuomintang government fled to Taiwan, Dec. 8, 1949.

The People's Republic of China was proclaimed in Beijing (Peking) Oct. 1, 1949, under Mao Zedong. China and the USSR signed a 30-year treaty of "friendship, alliance, and mutual assistance," Feb. 15, 1950. The U.S. refused recognition of the new regime. On Nov. 26, 1950, the People's Republic sent armies into Korea against U.S. troops and forced a stalemate in the Korean War.

After an initial period of consolidation, 1949-52, industry, agriculture, and social and economic institutions were molded according to Maoist ideals. However, frequent drastic changes in policy and violent factionalism interfered with economic development. In 1957, Mao admitted an estimated 800,000 people had been executed 1949-54; opponents claimed much higher figures.

The Great Leap Forward, 1958-60, tried to force the pace of economic development through intensive labor on huge new rural communes, and through emphasis on ideological purity. The program caused resistance and was largely abandoned.

By the 1960s, relations with the USSR deteriorated, with disagreements on borders, ideology, and leadership of world Communism. The USSR canceled aid accords, and China, with Albania, launched anti-Soviet propaganda drives.

The Great Proletarian Cultural Revolution, 1965, was an attempt to oppose pragmatism and bureaucratic power and instruct a new generation in revolutionary principles. Massive purges took place. A program of forcibly relocating millions of urban teenagers into the countryside was launched. By 1968 the movement had run its course; many purged officials returned to office in subsequent years, and reforms that had placed ideology above expertise were gradually weakened.

On Oct. 25, 1971, the UN General Assembly ousted the Taiwan government from the UN and seated the People's Republic in its place. The U.S. had supported the mainland's admission but opposed Taiwan's expulsion.

U.S. Pres. Richard Nixon visited China Feb. 21-28, 1972, on invitation from Premier Zhou Enlai, ending years of antipathy between the two nations. China and the U.S. opened liaison offices in each other's capitals, May-June 1973. The U.S., Dec. 15, 1978, formally recognized the People's Republic of China as the sole legal government of China; diplomatic relations between the two nations were established, Jan. 1, 1979.

Mao died Sept. 9, 1976. By 1978, Vice Premier Deng Xiaoping had consolidated power, succeeding Mao as "paramount leader" of China. The new ruling group modified Maoist policies in education, culture, and industry, and sought better ties with non-Communist countries. By the mid-1980s, China had enacted far-reaching economic reforms, deemphasizing centralized planning and incorporating market-oriented incentives.

Some 100,000 students and workers staged a march in Beijing to demand political reforms, May 4, 1989. As the unrest spread, martial law was imposed, May 20. Troops entered Beijing, June 3-4, and crushed the pro-democracy protests, as tanks and armored personnel carriers rolled through Tiananmen Square. It is estimated that 5,000 died, 10,000 were injured, and hundreds of students and workers were arrested.

Deng Xiaoping died Feb. 19, 1997, leaving Jiang Zemin in control as president. Hong Kong reverted to Chinese sovereignty July 1, 1997 (see below). Portugal returned Macao to China Dec. 20, 1999.

Hu Jintao was named Communist Party general secretary at the 16th party congress, Nov. 15, 2002, and elected president by the 10th National People's Congress, Mar. 15, 2003. With the successful launch and recovery, Oct. 15-16, 2003, of the *Shenzhou 5* spacecraft, China became the third nation (after the U.S. and USSR) to send a man into space.

China's industries, exports, and demand for oil have all increased rapidly since the 1980s. Reports in 2007 that China had exported hazardous pet products, toothpaste, tires, and toys resulted in the execution, July 10, of Zheng Xiaoyu, the former head of China's food and drug safety agency, for bribe taking and dereliction of duty.

The National People's Congress Mar. 15-16, 2008, reelected Pres. Hu Jintao and Premier Wen Jiabao. A powerful earthquake rocked Sichuan Province May 12, leaving 69,226 people dead and 17,923 missing. China reportedly spent $43 bil preparing for the Summer Olympics, held in Beijing Aug. 8-24, 2008. In a new quality-control scandal, China's health ministry reported Sept. 22 that nearly 53,000 babies had been sickened by contaminated milk powder; on Dec. 1, 2008, the estimate was raised to 300,000.

Western computer security experts Jan.-Feb. 2010 blamed hackers at two Chinese schools for Internet attacks on Google and at least 30 other firms. An earthquake Apr. 14 killed at least 2,200 people in NW China. The government reacted angrily when the Nobel Peace Prize was awarded Oct. 8 to Liu Xiaobo, a human rights activist who had received an 11-year prison sentence in Dec. 2009.

China has invested heavily in environmental technologies, especially wind and solar power, but illegal mining and ore processing remain major public-health hazards. Rapid growth during 2009-10 made China the world's second-largest economy, ranking behind the U.S. but ahead of Japan. A report made public June 2011 by China's central bank alleged that corrupt officials had smuggled more than $120 bil out of the country from the mid-1990s to 2008. China's economy slowed in the first 8 months of 2012 as instability in the world markets caused a decrease in exports. China is the largest holder of U.S. debt, with about $1.16 tril in U.S. obligations as of mid-2012.

Autonomous Regions

Guangxi Zhuang is in SE China, bounded on the N by Guizhou and Hunan provinces, E and S by Guangdong, on the SW by Vietnam, and on the W by Yunnan. It produces rice in the river valleys and has valuable forest products. Pop. (2010): 46,026,629.

Inner Mongolia was organized by the People's Republic in 1947. Its boundaries have undergone frequent changes, reaching its greatest extent in 1956 (and restored in 1979), with an area of 454,600 sq mi, allegedly in order to dilute the minority Mongol population. Chinese settlers outnumber the Mongols more than 10 to 1. Pop. (2010): 24,706,321. Capital: Hohhot.

Ningxia Hui, in north central China, is about 60,000 sq mi. Pop. (2010): 6,301,350. Capital: Yinchuan. The climate is mostly semiarid, with desert areas in the N. The Huang He (Yellow R.) flows across the N, furnishing water for irrigation. Coal is mined in the E. The majority of the population is Han, and the Hui (Chinese Muslims) constitute about one-third of the population. The region experienced a significant population boom, 1950-80, which has now stabilized.

Xinjiang Uighur, in Central Asia, is 635,900 sq mi, pop. (2010): 21,813,334 (75% Uighurs, a Turkic Muslim group, with a heavy Han Chinese increase in recent years). Capital: Urumqi. It is China's richest region in strategic minerals. China has moved to crack down on Uighur separatists, whom Beijing regards as terrorists. A protest march July 5, 2009, by Uighurs in Urumqi led to violent clashes with Han Chinese; at least 197 people (mostly Han) were killed in the riots. Renewed unrest including protests by Han in early Sept. led to the dismissal of the city's top Communist official.

Tibet, 471,700 sq mi, is a thinly populated region of high plateaus and massive mountains, the Himalayas on the S, the Kunluns on the N. High passes connect with India and Nepal; roads lead into China proper. Capital: Lhasa. Average altitude is 15,000 ft. Jiachan, 15,870 ft, is believed to be the highest inhabited town on earth. Agriculture is primitive. Pop. (2010): 3,002,166 (of whom about 500,000 are Chinese). Another 4 mil Tibetans form the majority of the population of vast adjacent areas that have long been incorporated into China.

China ruled all of Tibet from the 18th cent. Independence came in 1911, but China reasserted control in 1951, and a Communist government was installed in 1953. Serfdom was abolished, but all land remained collectivized.

A Tibetan uprising within China in 1956 spread to Lhasa in 1959. The rebellion was crushed by Chinese troops, and Buddhism was almost totally suppressed. The Dalai Lama and 100,000 Tibetans fled to India.

Efforts by Chinese authorities to halt peaceful demonstrations by Tibetan monks led to anti-Chinese riots in Lhasa, Mar. 14, 2008; the Chinese government sent troops into Tibet to crush dissent, sparking international protests.

Hong Kong

Hong Kong (Xianggang), located at the mouth of the Zhu Jiang (Pearl R.) in SE China, 90 mi S of Canton (Guangzhou), was a British dependency from 1842 until July 1, 1997, when it became a Special Administrative Region of China. Its nucleus is Hong Kong Isl., 31 sq mi, occupied by the British in 1841 and formally ceded to them in 1842, on which is located the seat of government. Opposite is Kowloon Peninsula, 3 sq mi, and Stonecutters Isl., added to the territory in 1860. An additional 355 sq mi known as the New Territories, a mainland area and islands, were leased from China, 1898,

for 99 years. Area 426 sq mi, 1,104 sq km (total); 407 sq mi, 1,054 sq km (land); pop. (2012 est.) 7,153,519. **Website:** www.gov.hk

Hong Kong is a major center for trade and banking. Per capita GDP, $45,900 (2010 est.), is among the highest in the world. Principal industries are textiles and apparel; also tourism, electronics, shipbuilding, iron and steel, fishing, cement, and small manufactures. Hong Kong's spinning mills are among the best in the world. Outside of the public sector, the labor force is engaged in the following sectors: wholesale and retail trade, restaurants, and hotels 42.9%; financing, insurance, and real estate 21.4%; community and social services 19.7%; manufacturing 6.1%; and construction 1.9%.

Hong Kong harbor was long an important British naval station and one of the world's great transshipment ports. The colony was often a place of refuge for exiles from mainland China. It was occupied by Japan during WWII.

From 1949 to 1962 Hong Kong absorbed more than a million refugees fleeing Communist China. Starting in the 1950s, cheap labor led to a boom in light manufacturing, while liberal tax policies attracted foreign investment; Hong Kong became one of the wealthiest, most productive areas in the Far East.

With the end of the 99-year lease on the New Territories drawing near, Britain and China signed an agreement, Dec. 19, 1984, under which all of Hong Kong was to be returned to China in 1997; under this agreement Hong Kong was to be allowed to keep its capitalist system for 50 years. Following the transfer of government, Hong Kong retained its street names and its currency, the Hong Kong dollar, but without the queen's picture. Official languages remained Chinese (Cantonese dialect) and English.

Hundreds of thousands of Hong Kong residents turned out July 1, 2003, to protest a proposed anti-subversion law; the bill was withdrawn Sept. 5. Another mass march, July 1, 2004, protested Beijing's refusal to allow greater freedom. Pro-democracy candidates won a majority of the popular vote in elections, Sept. 12, but failed to gain control of the Legislative Council. After Hong Kong's chief executive, Tung Chee-hwa resigned Mar. 10, 2005, Donald Tsang served the remaining two years of Tung's term; he won a full 5-year term Mar. 25, 2007, but left office tarnished by a scandal that involved receiving preferential treatment and favors from wealthy businessmen. Leung Chun-ying, whose close ties to China became an issue during the campaign, was elected Mar. 25, 2012 and took office July 1.

Macao

Macao, area of 11 sq mi, 28 sq km, is an enclave, a peninsula and two small islands, at the mouth of the Xi (Pearl) R. in China. It was established as a Portuguese trading colony in 1557. In 1849, Portugal claimed sovereignty over the territory; this claim was accepted by China in an 1887 treaty. Portugal granted broad autonomy in 1976. Under a 1987 agreement, Macao reverted to China Dec. 20, 1999. As in the case of Hong Kong, the Chinese government guaranteed Macao it would not interfere in its way of life and capitalist system for a period of 50 years. Tourism is the fastest-growing economic sector; revenues from casinos and other gambling activities exceeded $23 bil in 2010. The labor force is occupied in the following areas: gambling 14.2%, restaurants and hotels 13.6%, wholesale and retail trade 12.6%, construction 9.3%, public sector 6.6%, transport and communications 5.2%, manufacturing 4.9%, and financial services 2.1%. Pop. (2012 est.): 578,025. **Website:** www.gov.mo

Colombia
Republic of Colombia

People: Population: 45,239,079. **Age distrib.:** <15: 26.2%; 65+: 6.3%. **Pop. density:** 112.8 per sq mi, 43.6 per sq km. **Urban:** 75.3%. **Ethnic groups:** mestizo 58%, white 20%, mulatto 14%, black 4%, mixed black-Amerindian 3%, Amerindian 1%. **Principal language:** Spanish (official). **Chief religion:** Roman Catholic 90%.

Geography: Total area: 439,736 sq mi, 1,138,910 sq km; **Land area:** 401,044 sq mi, 1,038,700 sq km. **Location:** At the NW corner of South America. **Neighbors:** Panama on NW, Ecuador and Peru on S, Brazil and Venezuela on E. **Topography:** Three ranges of Andes—Western, Central, and Eastern Cordilleras—run through the country from N to S. The eastern range consists mostly of high tablelands, densely populated. The Magdalena R. rises in the Andes, flows N to Caribbean, through a rich alluvial plain. Sparsely settled plains in E are drained by Orinoco and Amazon systems. **Capital:** Bogotá, 8,743,500. **Cities (urban aggl.):** Medellín, 3,693,676; Cali, 2,452,560; Barranquilla, 1,899,609; Bucaramanga, 1,119,622.

Government: Type: Republic. **Head of state and gov.:** Pres. Juan Manuel Santos Calderón; b. Aug. 10, 1951; in office: Aug. 7, 2010. **Local divisions:** 32 departments, capital district of Bogotá. **Defense budget:** $5.57 bil. **Active troops:** 283,004.

Economy: Industries: textiles, food proc., oil, clothing and footwear, beverages, chemicals, cement. **Chief crops:** coffee, cut flowers, bananas, rice, tobacco, corn, sugarcane, cocoa beans, oilseed, vegetables. **Natural resources:** petroleum, nat. gas, coal, iron ore, nickel, gold, copper, emeralds, hydropower. **Crude oil reserves:** 2 bil bbls. **Arable land:** 1.6%. **Livestock:** cattle: 27.8 mil; chickens: 157 mil; goats: 1.2 mil; pigs: 1.9 mil; sheep: 3.4 mil. **Fish catch:** 159,396 metric tons. **Electricity prod.** (2010) 56.3 bil kWh. **Labor force:** agric. 18%, industry 13%, services 68%.

Finance: Monetary unit: Peso (COP) (Sept. 2012: 1,825.02 = $1 U.S.). **GDP:** $478 bil; **per capita GDP:** $10,400; **GDP growth:** 5.9%. **Imports:** $54.7 bil; U.S. 25%, China 15%, Mexico 11%, Brazil 5%, Germany 4.1%. **Exports:** $56.2 bil; U.S. 38%, EU 15%, China 3.5%, Ecuador 3.4%. **Tourism:** $2.2 bil. **Budget:** $97.8 bil. **Total reserves less gold:** $31.4 bil. **Gold:** 332,800 oz t. **CPI change:** 3.4%.

Transport: Railways: 543 mi. **Motor vehicles:** 37.6 vehicles per 1,000 pop. **Civil aviation:** 9 bil pass.-mi; 121 airports. **Chief ports:** Barranquilla, Buenaventura, Cartagena, Puerto Bolivar, Santa Marta, Turbo.

Communications: TV sets: 291 per 1,000 pop. **Radios:** 543 per 1,000 pop. **Telephone lines:** 15.2 per 100 pop. **Daily newspaper circ.:** 22.7 per 1,000 pop. **Internet:** 40.4%.

Health: Life expect.: 71.6 male; 78.2 female. **Births:** 17.2 (per 1,000 pop.). **Deaths:** 5.3 (per 1,000 pop.). **Natural inc.:** 1.19% **Infant mortality:** 15.9 (per 1,000 live births). **HIV rate:** 0.5%.

Education: Compulsory: ages 5-14. **Literacy:** 93.4%.

Major intl. organizations: UN (FAO, IBRD, ILO, IMF, WHO), OAS, WTO.

Embassy: 2118 Leroy Pl. NW 20008; 387-8338.

Website: wsp.presidencia.gov.co

Spain subdued the local Indian kingdoms (Funza, Tunja) by the 1530s and ruled Colombia and neighboring areas as New Granada for 300 years. Independence was won by 1819. Venezuela and Ecuador broke away in 1829-30, and Panama withdrew in 1903.

Colombia is plagued by rural and urban violence. "La Violencia" of 1948-58 claimed 200,000 lives; since 1989, political killings, kidnappings, and "disappearances" have victimized many thousands of civilians, and the internally displaced population has been estimated at up to 3 mil or more. Attempts at land and social reform and progress in industrialization have not reduced massive social problems. Government activity against local drug traffickers has sparked retaliation killings of politicians and judges.

Right-wing paramilitaries launched a campaign Dec. 22, 2000, against suspected left-wing guerrillas. A hardliner, álvaro Uribe Vélez, whose father had been killed by leftist rebels in 1983, won a presidential election May 26, 2002. A wave of guerrilla violence as he took office led Uribe to declare a "state of unrest" Aug. 12. Police powers were increased Sept. 10 as part of a new government offensive. The constitution was amended, Nov. 30, 2004, to allow the president to seek a second consecutive term; Uribe easily won reelection May 28, 2006. Key political figures, including major allies of Uribe, were arrested in 2007 on charges of colluding with paramilitary death squads. Guerrilla strength has waned in recent years. Peace talks were scheduled to begin in Oct. 2012.

Former Def. Min. Juan Manuel Santos Calderón, a conservative ally of Uribe, won a presidential runoff election June 20, 2010, and took office Aug. 7.

Since 2000, the U.S. has provided more than $8 bil to Colombia, mostly to combat the drug trade. Cocaine production, according to U.S. figures disputed by the UN, has fallen 72% since 2001.

Comoros
Union of the Comoros

People: Population: 737,284. **Age distrib.:** <15: 42.2%; 65+: 3.7%. **Pop. density:** 854.4 per sq mi, 329.9 per sq km. **Urban:** 28%. **Ethnic groups:** Antalote, Cafre, Makoa, Oimatsaha, Sakalava. **Principal languages:** Arabic, French (both official); Shikomoro (blend of Swahili and Arabic). **Chief religions:** Sunni Muslim 98%, Roman Catholic 2%.

Geography: Total area: 863 sq mi, 2,235 sq km; **Land area:** 863 sq mi, 2,235 sq km. **Location:** 3 islands—Grande Comore (Njazidja), Anjouan (Nzwani), and Moheli (Mwali)—in the Mozambique Channel between NW Madagascar and SE Africa. **Neighbors:** Nearest are Mozambique on W, Madagascar on E. **Topography:** The islands are of volcanic origin, with an active volcano on Grande Comore. **Capital:** Moroni, 53,819.

Government: Type: Republic. **Head of state and gov.:** Pres. Ikililou Dhoinine; b. Aug. 14, 1962; in office: May 26, 2011. **Local divisions:** 3 main islands with 4 municipalities. **Defense budget/ active troops:** NA.

Economy: Industries: fishing, tourism, perfume distillation. **Chief crops:** vanilla, cloves, ylang-ylang, copra, coconuts, bananas, cassava. Natural resources: negligible. **Arable land:** 43.0%. **Livestock:** cattle: 50,000; chickens: 520,000; goats: 118,000; sheep: 23,000. **Fish catch:** 52,261 metric tons. **Electricity prod.:** 52 mil kWh. **Labor force:** agric. 80%, industry and services 20%.

Finance: Monetary unit: Franc (KMF) (Sept. 2012: 389.80 = $1 U.S.). **GDP:** $847.7 mil; **per capita GDP:** $1,200; **GDP growth:** 2.2%. **Imports:** $219.9 mil; Pakistan 16.2%, France 15.8%, UAE 11.3%, Turkey 7.3%, Kenya 5.5%, India 4.6%, South Africa 4.2%. **Exports:** $18.5 mil; Singapore 36%, Turkey 23.7%, France 10.5%, Netherlands 7.9%. **Tourism:** $32 mil. **Budget:** $139.6 mil. **Total reserves less gold:** $155.2 mil. **Gold:** 579 oz t. **CPI change:** 0.9%.

Transport: Civil aviation: 4 airports. **Chief ports:** Mayotte, Mutsamudu.

Communications: TV sets: 31 per 1,000 pop. **Radios:** 159 per 1,000 pop. **Telephone lines:** 3.1 per 100 pop. **Internet:** 5.5%.

Health: Life expect.: 60.5 male; 65.0 female. **Births:** 31.5 (per 1,000 pop.). **Deaths:** 8.2 (per 1,000 pop.). **Natural inc.:** 2.33% **Infant mortality:** 69.0 (per 1,000 live births). **HIV rate:** 0.1%.

Education: Compulsory: ages 6-13. **Literacy:** 74.9%.

Major intl. organizations: UN (FAO, IBRD, ILO, IMF, WHO), AL, AU, WTO (observer).

Permanent UN Mission: 866 United Nations Plz., Ste. 418, New York, NY 10017; (212) 750-1637.

Website: www.beit-salam.km

The islands were controlled by Muslim sultans until the French acquired them 1841-1909. They became a French overseas territory in 1947. A 1974 referendum favored independence, with only the Christian island of Mayotte preferring association with France. The French National Assembly decided to allow each of the islands to decide its own fate. The Comore Chamber of Deputies declared independence July 6, 1975, with Ahmed Abdallah as president. In a referendum in 1976, Mayotte voted to remain French.

A leftist regime that seized power from Abdallah in 1975 was deposed in a pro-French 1978 coup in which he regained the presidency. In Nov. 1989, Pres. Abdallah was assassinated; soon after, a multiparty system was instituted. A Sept. 1995 military coup, assisted by French mercenaries, ousted Pres. Said Mohamed Djohar. French troops invaded, Oct. 4, and forced coup leaders to surrender.

Anjouan and Moheli seceded from the Comoros in 1997. Unrest on Grande Comore culminated in a military coup, Apr. 30, 1999. Anjouans endorsed secession in a disputed vote Jan. 23, 2000. A constitution adopted in a referendum Dec. 23, 2001, that went into effect the following year reunited Anjouan and Moheli with Grande Comore, granting each a semi-autonomous status with their own presidents.

Irregularities marred the Apr. 14, 2002, presidential runoff election, won by Azali Assoumani, who led the 1999 coup. Elections for national and island assemblies took place Mar.-Apr. 2004. Ahmed Abdallah Mohamed Sambi won a presidential runoff vote, May 14, 2006. Each of the three islands elected its own president in 2002 and 2007. Col. Mohamed Bacar, who refused to relinquish power after the central government ruled his 2007 election illegal, fled when Comorian and African Union troops took control of the island, Mar. 25-26, 2008.

Sambi's Vice Pres. Ikililou Dhoinine won a presidential runoff election Dec. 26, 2010.

Congo
Democratic Republic of the Congo

(Congo, officially Democratic Republic of the Congo, is also known as Congo-Kinshasa. It should not be confused with Republic of the Congo, commonly called Congo Republic, and also known as Congo-Brazzaville.)

People: Population: 73,599,190. **Age distrib.:** <15: 43.9%; 65+: 2.6%. **Pop. density:** 84.1 per sq mi, 32.5 per sq km. **Urban:** 34.3%. **Ethnic groups:** 200+ groups, majority Bantu. Four largest tribes (Mongo, Luba, Kongo [all Bantu], Mangbetu-Azande [Hamitic]) 45%. **Principal languages:** French (official), Lingala (lingua franca), Kingwana (Kiswahili or Swahili dialect), Kikongo, Tshiluba. **Chief religions:** Roman Catholic 50%, Protestant 20%, Kimbanguist 10%, Muslim 10%, other (incl. syncretic sects, indigenous beliefs) 10%.

Geography: Total area: 905,355 sq mi, 2,344,858 sq km; **Land area:** 875,312 sq mi, 2,267,048 sq km. **Location:** In central Africa. **Neighbors:** Congo Republic on W; Central African Republic, Sudan on N; Uganda, Rwanda, Burundi, Tanzania on E; Zambia, Angola on S. **Topography:** Congo includes the bulk of the Congo R. basin. The vast central region is a low-lying plateau covered by rain forest. Mountainous terraces in the W, savannas in the S and SE, grasslands toward the N, and the high Ruwenzori Mts. on the E surround the central region. A short strip of territory borders the Atlantic O. **Capital:** Kinshasa, 8,797,730. **Cities (urban aggl.):** Lubumbashi, 1,556,368; Mbuji-Mayi, 1,503,585.

Government: Type: Republic. **Head of state:** Pres. Joseph Kabila; b. June 24, 1971; in office: Jan. 26, 2001. **Head of gov.:** Prime Min. Adolphe Muzito; b. 1957; in office: Oct. 10, 2008. **Local divisions:** 10 provinces, 1 city. **Defense budget:** $214 mil. **Active troops:** 159,000.

Economy: Industries: mining, mineral proc., consumer prods., metal prods., processed foods and beverages, timber, cement. **Chief crops:** coffee, sugar, palm oil, rubber, tea, cotton, cocoa, quinine, cassava, manioc, bananas, plantains, peanuts, root crops, corn, fruits. **Natural resources:** cobalt, copper, niobium, tantalum, petroleum, diamonds, gold, silver, zinc, manganese, tin, uranium, coal, hydropower, timber. **Crude oil reserves:** 180 mil bbls. **Arable land:** 3.0%. **Livestock:** cattle: 755,000; chickens: 20.5 mil; goats: 4.2 mil; pigs: 967,000; sheep: 905,000. **Fish catch:** 238,970 metric tons. **Electricity prod.:** 7.8 bil kWh. **Labor force:** NA.

Finance: Monetary unit: Franc (CDF) (Sept. 2012: 908.04 = $1 U.S.). **GDP:** $25.6 bil; **per capita GDP:** $400; **GDP growth:** 6.9%. **Imports:** $9 bil; China 17.1%, South Africa 11%, Belgium 9%, Zambia 7.5%, Zimbabwe 6.1%, Kenya 5.1%, France 5%. **Exports:** $10.9 bil; China 48%, Zambia 21.2%, U.S. 9.4%, Belgium 5.4%. **Tourism:** NA. **Budget:** $5.9 bil. **Total reserves less gold:** $1.3 bil. **CPI change (2007-08):** 17.3%.

Transport: Railways: 2,490 mi. **Motor vehicles:** 23.9 vehicles per 1,000 pop. **Civil aviation:** 26 airports. **Chief ports:** Boma, Bukavu, Bumba, Goma, Kinshasa, Kisangani, Matadi, Mbandaka.

Communications: TV sets: 5 per 1,000 pop. **Radios:** 379 per 1,000 pop. **Telephone lines:** 0.06 per 100 pop. **Internet:** 1.2%.

Health: Life expect.: 54.3 male; 57.2 female. **Births:** 37.1 (per 1,000 pop.). **Deaths:** 10.8 (per 1,000 pop.). **Natural inc.:** 2.63% **Infant mortality:** 76.6 (per 1,000 live births). **HIV rate:** NA.

Education: Compulsory: ages 6-11. **Literacy:** 66.8%.

Major intl. organizations: UN and most of its specialized agencies, AU, WTO.

Embassy: 1726 M St. NW 20036; 234-7690.

Website: www.presidentrdc.cd

The earliest inhabitants of Congo may have been the pygmies, followed by Bantus from the east and Nilotic tribes from the north. The large Bantu Bakongo kingdom ruled much of Congo and Angola when Portuguese explorers visited in the 15th cent.

Leopold II, king of the Belgians, formed an international group to exploit the Congo region in 1876. In 1877 Henry M. Stanley explored the Congo, and in 1878 the king's group sent him back to organize the region and win over the indigenous leaders. The Conference of Berlin, 1884-85, established the Congo Free State with Leopold as king and chief owner. Exploitation of Congolese laborers on rubber plantations caused international criticism and led to the granting of a colonial charter, 1908; the colony became known as the Belgian Congo. Millions of Congolese died under brutal European rule between 1880 and 1920.

Belgian and Congolese leaders agreed Jan. 27, 1960, that Congo would become independent in June. In the first general elections, May 31, Patrice Lumumba's party won a plurality in the National Assembly. The Republic of the Congo was proclaimed June 30. Europeans and others fled widespread violence. The UN Security Council, Aug. 9, called on Belgium to withdraw its troops and sent a UN contingent. Lumumba was dismissed as premier Sept. 5, 1960, and was murdered Jan. 17, 1961. The last UN troops left the Congo June 30, 1964.

In late 1965 Gen. Joseph D. Mobutu was named president. He later changed his name to Mobutu Sese Seko and ruled as a dictator. The country became the Democratic Republic of the Congo (1966) and the Republic of Zaire (1971). Under Mobutu, economic decline and government corruption plagued Zaire. He retained power despite mounting international pressure and internal opposition.

During 1994, Zaire was inundated with refugees from the massive ethnic bloodshed in Rwanda. Ethnic violence spread to eastern Zaire in 1996. In Oct. militant Hutus, who dominated in the refugee camps, fought against rebels (mostly Tutsis) in Zaire, precipitating intervention by government troops. As a result of the fighting, Rwandan refugees abandoned the camps; hundreds of thousands returned to Rwanda, while hundreds of thousands more were dispersed throughout eastern Zaire. The rebels, led by Gen. Laurent Kabila—a former Marxist and longtime opponent of Mobutu—began to move west across Zaire. On May 17, 1997, Kabila's troops entered Kinshasa and Mobutu went into exile. The country again became the Democratic Republic of the Congo. Mobutu died Sept. 7 in Rabat, Morocco.

Kabila, who ruled by decree, alienated UN officials, international aid donors, and former allies. Rebels assisted by Rwanda and Uganda threatened Kinshasa in Aug. 1998 but were turned back with help from Angola, Namibia, and Zimbabwe. Rebel groups agreed to a cease-fire, Aug. 31, 1999, but the truce was widely violated. Kabila was assassinated Jan. 16, 2001, and was succeeded by his son Joseph.

The overall death toll from the civil war and related causes was estimated at 3.3 mil through Nov. 2002. By then, Rwanda and Uganda had agreed to pull out their remaining troops. A power-sharing accord signed Apr. 2, 2003, led to the installation of a new Congolese government in July. A new constitution won legislative approval May 13, 2005. A UN peacekeeping force (MONUC), established in 1999, remained in the country to oversee elections, held July 30-31, 2006, the nation's first multiparty vote since 1960. Kabila defeated former rebel leader Jean-Pierre Bemba in a presidential runoff election, Oct. 29, 2006.

Hundreds reportedly died in Kinshasa, Mar. 22-23, 2007, in clashes between security forces and a militia loyal to Bemba, who fled to Europe; he was arrested in Belgium May 24, 2008, on war crimes charges; his trial was ongoing at The Hague in 2012. A peace deal with militia groups in eastern Congo, including one led by Tutsi rebel Gen. Laurent Nkunda, was signed Jan. 23, 2008, but Nkunda launched a new offensive Aug. 28; Rwandan authorities arrested him Jan. 22, 2009.

Visiting eastern Congo Aug. 11, 2009, U.S. Sec. of State Hillary Clinton announced a $17 mil program to curb sexual violence in the region. The UN reported that more than 8,000 Congolese women were raped in 2009. A study published in the *American Journal of Public Health* in June 2011 estimated that more than 1,000 women were raped in Congo every day. The difficulty of ending sexual violence has been exacerbated by the inadequate size of the judiciary, which had only 4,000 magistrates as of Aug. 2012, a ratio of approximately 1 to 20,000.

In the first verdict issued by the Intl. Criminal Court since its establishment in 2002, Congolese warlord Thomas Lubanga Dyilo was convicted Mar. 14, 2012, of war crimes for conscripting child soldiers during the country's civil war.

The MONUC peacekeeping mission, reconstituted and renamed MONUSCO as of July 1, 2010, included about 17,000 military personnel in mid-2012.

Congo Republic
Republic of the Congo

(Congo Republic, officially Republic of the Congo, is also known as Congo-Brazzaville. It should not be confused with Democratic Republic of the Congo [formerly Zaire], now commonly called Congo, and also known as Congo-Kinshasa.)

People: Population: 4,366,266. **Age distrib.:** <15: 45.3%; 65+: 2.8%. **Pop. density:** 33.1 per sq mi, 12.8 per sq km. **Urban:** 63.7%. **Ethnic groups:** Kongo 48%, Sangha 20%, Teke 17%, M'Bochi 12%, Europeans and other 3%. **Principal languages:** French (official); Lingala, Monokutuba (lingua francas); many local languages & dialects (Kikongo most widespread). **Chief religions:** Christian 50%, animist 48%, Muslim 2%.

Geography: Total area: 132,047 sq mi, 342,000 sq km; **Land area:** 131,854 sq mi, 341,500 sq km. **Location:** In W central Africa. **Neighbors:** Gabon and Cameroon on W, Central African Republic on N, Dem. Rep. of the Congo on E, Angola on SW. **Topography:** Much of the Congo is covered by thick forests. A coastal plain leads to the fertile Niari Valley. The center is a plateau; the Congo R. basin consists of flood plains in the lower and savanna in the upper portion. **Capital:** Brazzaville, 1,610,760.

Government: Type: Republic. **Head of state and gov.:** Pres. Denis Sassou-Nguesso; b. 1943; in office: Oct. 25, 1997. **Local divisions:** 10 regions, 6 communes. **Defense budget** (2010): $214 mil. **Active troops:** 10,000.

Economy: Industries: petroleum extraction, cement, lumber, brewing, sugar, palm oil. **Chief crops:** cassava, sugar, rice, corn, peanuts, vegetables, coffee, cocoa. **Natural resources:** petroleum, timber, potash, lead, zinc, uranium, copper, phosphates, gold, magnesium, nat. gas, hydropower. **Crude oil reserves:** 1.6 bil bbls. **Arable land:** 1.5%. **Livestock:** cattle: 330,000; chickens: 2.6 mil; goats: 320,000; pigs: 70,000; sheep: 120,000. **Fish catch:** 65,244 metric tons. **Electricity prod.:** 502 mil kWh. **Labor force:** NA.

Finance: Monetary unit: CFA BEAC Franc (XAF) (Sept. 2012: 519.73 = $1 U.S.). **GDP:** $18.5 bil; **per capita GDP:** $4,600; **GDP growth:** 4.5%. **Imports:** $4.9 bil; France 17.3%, China 12.6%, India 9.5%, Italy 7.5%, Brazil 7.3%, U.S. 5.8%. **Exports:** $12.4 bil; China 37.9%, U.S. 20%, Australia 6.2%, France 6%, Spain 4.8%, Italy 4.3%, Netherlands 4.3%. **Tourism:** NA. **Budget:** $3.5 bil. **Total reserves less gold:** $5.6 bil. **Gold** (2008): 11,126 oz t. **CPI change:** 1.9%.

Transport: Railways: 551 mi. **Motor vehicles:** 15.7 vehicles per 1,000 pop. **Civil aviation:** 19.3 mil pass.-mi; 7 airports. **Chief ports:** Brazzaville, Djeno, Impfondo, Ouesso, Oyo, Pointe-Noire.

Communications: TV sets: 50 per 1,000 pop. **Radios:** 107 per 1,000 pop. **Telephone lines:** 0.2 per 100 pop. **Internet:** 5.6%.

Health: Life expect.: 54.0 male; 56.6 female. **Births:** 40.1 (per 1,000 pop.). **Deaths:** 11.3 (per 1,000 pop.). **Natural inc.:** 2.88% **Infant mortality:** 74.2 (per 1,000 live births). **HIV rate:** 3.4%.

Education: Compulsory: ages 6-15. **Literacy:** NA.

Major intl. organizations: UN (FAO, IBRD, ILO, IMF, WHO), AU, WTO.

Embassy: 4891 Colorado Ave. NW 20011; 726-5500.

Website: www.presidence.cg

The Loango Kingdom flourished in the 15th cent., as did the Anzico Kingdom of the Batekes; by the late 17th cent. they had weakened. By 1885, France established control of the region, then called the Middle Congo. Republic of the Congo gained independence Aug. 15, 1960.

After a 1963 coup sparked by trade unions, the country adopted a Marxist-Leninist stance, with the USSR and China vying for influence. France remained a dominant trade partner and source of technical assistance, however, and French-owned private enterprise retained a major economic role. In 1970, the country was renamed People's Republic of the Congo. Since the 1980s, oil has come to dominate the economy.

In 1990, Marxism was renounced and opposition parties were legalized. In 1991 the country's name was changed back to Republic of the Congo, and a new constitution was approved. A democratically elected government came into office in 1992. Factional fighting broke out in Brazzaville, June 5, 1997, and intensified during the summer, devastating the capital. Troops loyal to former Marxist dictator Denis Sassou-Nguesso took control of the city Oct. 15, 1997; he claimed lopsided victories in the presidential elections of Mar. 10, 2002, and July 12, 2009. His party won an absolute majority in the country's National Assembly, Aug. 5, 2012.

Costa Rica
Republic of Costa Rica

People: Population: 4,636,348. **Age distrib.:** <15: 24.2%; 65+: 6.6%. **Pop. density:** 235.2 per sq mi, 90.8 per sq km. **Urban:** 64.7%. **Ethnic groups:** white (incl. mestizo) 94%, black 3%, Amerindian 1%, Chinese 1%. **Principal languages:** Spanish (official), English. **Chief religions:** Roman Catholic 76%, Evangelical 14%, Jehovah's Witnesses 1%, none 3%.

Geography: Total area: 19,730 sq mi, 51,100 sq km; **Land area:** 19,714 sq mi, 51,060 sq km. **Location:** In Central America. **Neighbors:** Nicaragua on N, Panama on S. **Topography:** Lowlands by the Caribbean are tropical. The interior plateau, with an altitude of about 4,000 ft, is temperate. **Capital:** San José, 1,515,140.

Government: Type: Republic. **Head of state and gov.:** Pres. Laura Chinchilla Miranda; b. Mar. 28, 1959; in office: May 8, 2010. **Local divisions:** 7 provinces. **Defense budget:** $311 mil. **Active troops:** No regular military forces. 9,800 paramilitary only.

Economy: Industries: microprocessors, food proc., medical equip., textiles and clothing, constr. materials, fertilizer, plastic prods. **Chief crops:** bananas, pineapples, coffee, melons, ornamental plants, sugar, corn, rice, beans, potatoes. **Natural resources:** hydropower. **Arable land:** 3.9%. **Livestock:** cattle: 1.3 mil; chickens: 22 mil; goats: 5,000; pigs: 440,000; sheep: 2,700. **Fish catch:** 48,560 metric tons. **Electricity prod.:** 9.1 bil kWh. **Labor force:** agric. 14%, industry 22%, services 64%.

Finance: Monetary unit: Colon (CRC) (Sept. 2012: 499.31 = $1 U.S.). **GDP:** $55.7 bil; **per capita GDP:** $12,100; **GDP growth:** 4.2%. **Imports:** $15.5 bil; U.S. 43.3%, Mexico 6.4%, China 6.2%, Japan 6%. **Exports:** $10.4 bil; U.S. 33.9%, China 12.6%, Netherlands 12.1%, UK 10.7%. **Tourism:** $2.2 bil. **Budget:** $8.1 bil. **Total reserves less gold:** $4.8 bil. **Gold:** 1,755 oz t. **CPI change:** 4.9%.

Transport: Railways: 173 mi (not in current use). **Motor vehicles:** 168.5 vehicles per 1,000 pop. **Civil aviation:** 1.4 bil pass.-mi; 41 airports. **Chief ports:** Caldera, Puerto Limon.

Communications: TV sets: 250 per 1,000 pop. **Radios:** 222 per 1,000 pop. **Telephone lines:** 31.5 per 100 pop. **Daily newspaper circ.:** 64.7 per 1,000 pop. **Internet:** 42.1%.

Health: Life expect.: 75.3 male; 80.7 female. **Births:** 16.4 (per 1,000 pop.). **Deaths:** 4.4 (per 1,000 pop.). **Natural inc.:** 1.20%. **Infant mortality:** 9.2 (per 1,000 live births). **HIV rate:** 0.3%.

Education: Compulsory: ages 5-14. **Literacy:** 96.2%.

Major intl. organizations: UN (FAO, IBRD, ILO, IMF, WHO), OAS, WTO.

Embassy: 2114 S St. NW 20008; 234-2945.

Website: www.gobiernofacil.go.cr

Guaymi Indians inhabited the area when Spaniards arrived, 1502. Independence came in 1821. Costa Rica seceded from the Central American Federation in 1838. Since the civil war of 1948-49, there has been little violent social conflict, and free political institutions have been preserved.

Costa Rica, though still a largely agricultural country, has achieved a relatively high standard of living, and land ownership is widespread. Tourism is growing rapidly. Nobel Peace Prize-winner Óscar Arias Sánchez, president 1986-90, won a second term in a close election, Feb. 5, 2006. An election victory Feb. 7, 2010, made ruling party candidate Laura Chinchilla Miranda the nation's first female president.

Côte d'Ivoire
Republic of Côte d'Ivoire

People: Population: 21,952,093. **Age distrib.:** <15: 39.3%; 65+: 3.1%. **Pop. density:** 178.8 per sq mi, 69 per sq km. **Urban:** 51.3%. **Ethnic groups:** Akan 42%, Voltaiques or Gur 18%, N Mandes 17%, Krous 11%, S Mandes 10%. **Principal languages:** French (official), 60 native dialects (Dioula most widely spoken). **Chief religions:** Muslim 39%, Christian 33%, indigenous 12%, none 17%.

Geography: Total area: 124,504 sq mi, 322,463 sq km; **Land area:** 122,782 sq mi, 318,003 sq km. **Location:** On S coast of W Africa. **Neighbors:** Liberia, Guinea on W; Mali, Burkina Faso on N; Ghana on E. **Topography:** Forests cover the W half of the country, and range from a coastal strip halfway to the N on the E. A sparse inland plain leads to low mountains in NW. **Capital:** Yamoussoukro (official), 966,394; Abidjan (admin.), 4,287,820.

Government: Type: Republic. **Head of state:** Pres. Alassane Ouattara; b. Jan. 1, 1942; in office: Apr. 11, 2011 (sworn in Dec. 4, 2010). **Head of gov.:** Prime Min. Guillaume Soro; b. May 8, 1972; in office: Apr. 4, 2007. **Local divisions:** 58 departments. **Defense budget:** $318 mil. **Active troops:** 40,000 (target).

Economy: Industries: foodstuffs, beverages, wood prods., oil refining, truck and bus assembly, textiles, fertilizer. **Chief crops:** coffee, cocoa beans, bananas, palm kernels, corn, rice, manioc, sweet potatoes, sugar, cotton, rubber. **Natural resources:** petroleum, nat. gas, diamonds, manganese, iron ore, cobalt, bauxite, copper, gold. **Crude oil reserves:** 100 mil bbls. **Arable land:** 8.8%. **Livestock:** cattle: 1.6 mil; chickens: 45.1 mil; goats: 1.3 mil; pigs: 348,590; sheep: 1.7 mil. **Fish catch:** 73,512 metric tons. **Electricity prod.:** 5.5 bil kWh. **Labor force:** agric. 68%.

Finance: Monetary unit: CFA BCEAO Franc (XOF) (Sept. 2012: 519.73 = $1 U.S.). **GDP:** $36.5 bil; **per capita GDP:** $1,600; **GDP growth:** –4.7%. **Imports:** $7.9 bil; Nigeria 35.6%, France 9.9%, China 5.6%, Colombia 5.4%. **Exports:** $11.4 bil; Netherlands 11.6%, U.S. 11.5%, Germany 7.3%, Nigeria 6%, Canada 6%, France 5.9%, South Africa 5.4%. **Tourism:** $201 mil. **Budget:** $6.3 bil. **Total reserves less gold:** $4.3 bil. **CPI change:** 4.9%.

Transport: Railways: 410 mi. **Motor vehicles:** 5.5 vehicles per 1,000 pop. **Civil aviation:** 7 airports. **Chief ports:** Abidjan, Espoir, San-Pédro.

Communications: TV sets: 44 per 1,000 pop. **Radios:** 138 per 1,000 pop. **Telephone lines:** 1.3 per 100 pop. **Internet:** 2.2%.

Health: Life expect.: 56.2 male; 58.3 female. **Births:** 30.4 (per 1,000 pop.). **Deaths:** 10.0 (per 1,000 pop.). **Natural inc.:** 2.04% **Infant mortality:** 63.2 (per 1,000 live births). **HIV rate:** 3.4%.

Education: Compulsory: ages 6-15. **Literacy:** 56.2%.

Major intl. organizations: UN and all of its specialized agencies, AU, WTO.

Embassy: 3421 Massachusetts Ave. NW 20007; 797-0300.

Website: www.gouv.ci

A French protectorate from 1842, Côte d'Ivoire became independent in 1960. The name was officially changed from Ivory Coast, Oct. 1985. The country is a leading producer of coffee and cocoa beans.

Students and workers protested, Feb. 1990, demanding the ouster of longtime Pres. Félix Houphouët-Boigny. Côte d'Ivoire held its first multiparty presidential election Oct. 1990, which Houphouët-Boigny won. He died Dec. 7, 1993. The National Assembly named a successor, Henri Konan Bédié, who was reelected Oct. 22, 1995; he was ousted in a military coup Dec. 24, 1999. The coup leader, Robert Guéi, lost a presidential vote Oct. 22, 2000, but claimed victory anyway. After mass protests, he fled, and Laurent Gbagbo became president. Guéi was killed in Abidjan Sept. 19, 2002.

Agreement on power sharing was reached in Mar. 2003, and Gbagbo and former rebel leaders declared an end to the war July 5. The country remained divided, however. Rebels held the north and government forces controlled the south. Under a new accord reached Mar. 4, 2007, rebel leader Guillaume Soro became prime min. Apr. 4.

Both Gbagbo and his main challenger, former Prime Min. Alassane Ouattara, claimed victory after a presidential runoff election Nov. 28, 2010. Gbagbo clung to power, although the UN, U.S., France, and the Economic Community of West African States recognized Ouattara as the legitimate winner. A violent power struggle followed, claiming an estimated 1,500 lives and displacing at least 1 mil people. With support from French and UN forces, Ouattara loyalists captured Gbagbo in Abidjan, Apr. 11, 2011. Human Rights Watch reported June 2 that after taking power, Ouattara's troops killed at least 149 suspected Gbagbo supporters. A UN peacekeeping mission (UNOCI), authorized since 2004, had more than 9,300 military personnel in Côte d'Ivoire in mid-2012.

Croatia
Republic of Croatia

People: Population: 4,480,043. **Age distrib.:** <15: 14.8%; 65+: 17.1%. **Pop. density:** 207.3 per sq mi, 80 per sq km. **Urban:** 57.8%. **Ethnic groups:** Croat 90%, Serb 5%, other (incl. Bosniak, Hungarian, Slovene, Czech, Roma) 6%. **Principal languages:** Croatian (official). **Chief religions:** Roman Catholic 88%, Orthodox 4%, Muslim 1%, none 5%.

Geography: Total area: 21,851 sq mi, 56,594 sq km; **Land area:** 21,612 sq mi, 55,974 sq km. **Location:** SE Europe, on the Balkan Peninsula. **Neighbors:** Slovenia, Hungary on N; Bosnia and Herzegovina, Serbia, Montenegro on E. **Topography:** Flat plains in NE; highlands, low mts. along Adriatic coast. **Capital:** Zagreb, 686,439.

Government: Type: Parliamentary democracy. **Head of state:** Pres. Ivo Josipovic; b. Aug. 28, 1957; in office: Feb. 18, 2010. **Head of gov.:** Prime Min. Jadranka Kosor; b. July 1, 1953; in office: July 6, 2009. **Local divisions:** 20 counties and Zagreb. **Defense budget:** $935 mil. **Active troops:** 18,600.

Economy: Industries: chemicals and plastics, machine tools, fabricated metal, electronics. **Chief crops:** wheat, corn, sugar beets, sunflower seeds, barley, alfalfa, clover, olives. **Natural resources:** oil, coal, bauxite, iron ore, calcium, gypsum, nat. asphalt, silica, mica, clays, salt, hydropower. **Crude oil reserves:** 71 mil bbls. **Arable land:** 15.5%. **Livestock:** cattle: 444,000; chickens: 5 mil; goats: 75,000; pigs: 1.2 mil; sheep: 630,000. **Fish catch:** 66,857 metric tons. **Electricity prod.:** 12 bil kWh. **Labor force:** agric. 5%, industry 31.3%, services 63.6%.

Finance: Monetary unit: Kuna (HRK) (Sept. 2012: 5.91 = $1 U.S.). **GDP:** $81.4 bil; **per capita GDP:** $18,400; **GDP growth:** 0%. **Imports:** $20.4 bil; Italy 16.2%, Germany 12.8%, China 7.2%, Russia 7.2%, Slovenia 6.4%, Austria 4.4%. **Exports:** $12.3 bil; Italy 16.6%, Bosnia and Herzegovina 12.7%, Germany 10.4%, Slovenia 8.2%, Austria 5.8%, Luxembourg 4.5%. **Tourism:** $9.2 bil. **Budget:** $26.3 bil. **Total reserves less gold:** $14.5 bil. **CPI change:** 2.3%.

Transport: Railways: 1,691 mi. **Motor vehicles:** 379.2 vehicles per 1,000 pop. **Civil aviation:** 715.2 mil pass.-mi; 24 airports. **Chief ports:** Omisalj, Ploce, Rijeka, Sibenik, Split, Vukovar.

Communications: TV sets: 550 per 1,000 pop. **Radios:** 327 per 1,000 pop. **Telephone lines:** 40.1 per 100 pop. **Internet:** 70.7%.

Health: Life expect.: 72.4 male; 79.8 female. **Births:** 9.6 (per 1,000 pop.). **Deaths:** 12.0 (per 1,000 pop.). **Natural inc.:** –0.24% **Infant mortality:** 6.1 (per 1,000 live births). **HIV rate:** <0.1%.

Education: Compulsory: ages 7-14. **Literacy:** 98.8%.

Major intl. organizations: UN (FAO, IBRD, ILO, IMF, WHO), NATO, OSCE, WTO.

Embassy: 2343 Massachusetts Ave. NW 20008; 588-5899.

Website: www.vlada.hr

From the 7th cent. the area was inhabited by Croats, a south Slavic people. It was formed into a kingdom under Tomislav in 924, and joined with Hungary in 1102. The Croats became westernized and separated from Slavs under Austro-Hungarian influence. Croatia united with other Yugoslav areas to proclaim the Kingdom of Serbs, Croats, and Slovenes in 1918. A nominally independent state between 1941 and 1945, it became a constituent republic of Yugoslavia in the 1946 constitution.

On June 25, 1991, Croatia declared independence from Yugoslavia. Fighting began between ethnic Serbs and Croats. The Serbs gained control of about 30% of Croatian territory, but Croatian troops recaptured most of the Serb-held territory Aug. 1995. Pres. Franjo Tudjman signed a peace accord with leaders of Bosnia and Serbia in Paris, Dec. 14. The last Serb-held enclave, E Slavonia, returned to Croatian control Jan. 15, 1998. Indicted in 2001 and arrested in 2005, former Croatian Gen. Ante Gotovina was convicted by a UN tribunal Apr. 15, 2011, and sentenced to 24 years in prison for war crimes committed in the mid-1990s. Stipe Mesic, a moderate, won a presidential runoff election Feb. 7, 2000, and was reelected Jan. 16, 2005. Croatia became a full NATO member Apr. 1, 2009. Law professor and composer Ivo Josipovic, the nominee of the Social Democratic Party, won a presidential runoff election Jan. 10, 2010, and took office Feb. 18. The EU signed, Dec. 9, 2011, an accession treaty with Croatia, which is expected to become an EU member July 2013.

Cuba
Republic of Cuba

People: Population: 11,075,244. **Age distrib.:** <15: 17%; 65+: 12%. **Pop. density:** 261.2 per sq mi, 100.8 per sq km. **Urban:** 75.2%. **Ethnic groups:** white 65%, mulatto & mestizo 25%, black 10%. **Principal language:** Spanish (official). **Chief religion:** Roman Catholic (nominally, prior to Castro assuming power) 85%.

Geography: Total area: 42,803 sq mi, 110,860 sq km; **Land area:** 42,402 sq mi, 109,820 sq km. **Location:** In Caribbean, westernmost of West Indies. **Neighbors:** Bahamas, U.S. to N; Mexico to W; Jamaica to S; Haiti to E. **Topography:** Coastline is about 2,500 mi. The N coast is steep and rocky, the S coast low and marshy. Low hills and fertile valleys cover more than half the country. Sierra Maestra, in E, is the highest of 3 mountain ranges. **Capital:** Havana, 2,116,470.

Government: Type: Communist state. **Head of state and gov.:** Pres. Raúl Castro Ruz; b. June 3, 1931; in office: Feb. 24, 2008 (acting from July 31, 2006). **Local divisions:** 14 provinces, 1 special municipality. **Defense budget:** NA. **Active troops:** 49,000.

Economy: Industries: sugar, petroleum, tobacco, constr., nickel, steel, cement, agric. machinery, pharmaceuticals. **Chief crops:** sugar, tobacco, citrus, coffee, rice, potatoes, beans. **Natural resources:** cobalt, nickel, iron ore, chromium, copper, salt, timber, silica, petroleum. **Crude oil reserves:** 124 mil bbls. **Arable land:** 34.3%. **Livestock:** cattle: 4 mil; chickens: 31 mil; goats: 938,100; pigs: 1.6 mil; sheep: 2.4 mil. **Fish catch:** 55,418 metric tons. **Electricity prod.:** (2010): 16.9 bil kWh. **Labor force:** agric. 20%, industry 19.4%, services 60.6%.

Finance: Monetary unit: Peso (CUP) (Sept. 2012: 26.50 = $1 U.S.). **GDP** (2010 est.): $114.1 bil; **per capita GDP** (2010 est.): $9,900; **GDP growth** (2010): 1.5%. **Imports:** $13.3 bil; Venezuela 37.6%, China 9.9%, Spain 8.5%, Brazil 5.2%, Canada 4.4%. **Exports:** $6.3 bil; China 24.9%, Canada 21.6%, Venezuela 7.2%, Netherlands 7.1%, Spain 6.5%. **Tourism:** $2.2 bil. **Budget:** $46.2 bil.

Transport: Railways: 5,343 mi. **Motor vehicles:** 38.4 vehicles per 1,000 pop. **Civil aviation:** 1.5 bil pass.-mi; 65 airports. **Chief ports:** Cienfuegos, Guantánamo, Havana, Mariel, Matanzas, Santiago de Cuba.

Communications: TV sets: 213 per 1,000 pop. **Radios:** 276 per 1,000 pop. **Telephone lines:** 10.6 per 100 pop. **Daily newspaper circ.:** 64.7 per 1,000 pop. **Internet:** 23.2%.

Health: Life expect.: 75.6 male; 80.3 female. **Births:** 10.0 (per 1,000 pop.). **Deaths:** 7.5 (per 1,000 pop.). **Natural inc.:** 0.24% **Infant mortality:** 4.8 (per 1,000 live births). **HIV rate:** 0.1%.

Education: Compulsory: ages 6-14. **Literacy:** 99.8%.

Major intl. organizations: UN (FAO, ILO, WHO), WTO. Cuba is an OAS member state, but its current govt. has been excluded from formal participation since 1962.

Cuban Interests Section: 2630 16th St. NW 20009; 797-8518. **Website:** www.cubagob.cu

Some 50,000 indigenous people lived in Cuba when Columbus reached it in 1492. Its name derives from the Indian Cubanacan. Except for British occupation of Havana, 1762-63, Cuba remained Spanish until 1898. A slave-based sugar plantation economy developed from the 18th cent. Sugar remains a leading export.

A 10-year uprising ended in 1878 with guarantees of rights by Spain, which Spain failed to deliver. A full-scale liberation movement under Jose Martí began Feb. 24, 1895.

The Spanish-American War began Apr. 1898, after the sinking of the USS *Maine* in Havana harbor. Spain, which lost the war, gave up all claims to Cuba. U.S. troops withdrew in 1902, but under 1903 and 1934 agreements, the U.S. continued to lease a site at Guantánamo Bay in the southeast as a naval base. U.S. and other foreign investors acquired a dominant role in the economy. In 1952,

former Pres. Fulgencio Batista seized control and established a dictatorship, which grew increasingly harsh and corrupt. Fidel Castro assembled a rebel band in 1956; guerrilla fighting intensified in 1958. Batista fled Jan. 1, 1959, and in the resulting political vacuum, Castro took power, becoming premier Feb. 16.

The government began a program of sweeping economic and social changes, without restoring promised liberties. Opponents were imprisoned, and some were executed. Some 700,000 Cubans emigrated in the first years after the Castro takeover, mostly to the U.S. By 1960 all banks and industrial companies had been nationalized, including over $1 bil worth of U.S.-owned properties, mostly without compensation.

In 1961, some 1,400 Cubans, trained and backed by the U.S. Central Intelligence Agency, unsuccessfully tried to overthrow the regime. In the fall of 1962, the U.S. learned the USSR had brought nuclear missiles to Cuba. On Oct. 22, Pres. John F. Kennedy ordered a naval blockade and demanded that the missiles be withdrawn. The crisis ended Oct. 28 when Soviet Prem. Nikita S. Khrushchev agreed to pull out the missiles; the U.S. ended the blockade, pledged not to invade Cuba, and removed its missiles from Turkey.

In 1977, Cuba and the U.S. signed agreements to exchange diplomats, without restoring full ties, and to regulate offshore fishing. In 1978 and 1980, the U.S. agreed to accept political prisoners released by Cuba, some of whom were criminals and mental patients. A 1987 agreement provided for 20,000 Cubans to emigrate to the U.S. each year; Cuba agreed to take back some 2,500 jailed in the U.S. since 1980. Cuba's support for left-wing regimes and liberation movements in Central America, Africa, and the Caribbean contributed to poor relations with the U.S.

Cuba's economy, hobbled by U.S. sanctions and dependent on aid from other Communist countries, was shaken by the collapse of the Communist bloc in the late 1980s. Stiffer trade sanctions enacted by the U.S. in 1992 made things worse. Antigovernment demonstrations in Aug. 1994 prompted Castro to loosen emigration restrictions. A new U.S.-Cuba accord in Sept. ended the exodus of "boat people" after more than 30,000 had left Cuba. In another policy shift, the U.S. announced May 2, 1995, it would admit 20,000 Cuban refugees held at Guantánamo but would send further boat people back to Cuba.

The U.S. imposed additional sanctions after Cuba, Feb. 24, 1996, shot down 2 aircraft operated by anti-Castro exiles. Cuba blamed exile groups for bombings at Havana tourist hotels, July-Sept. 1997. Pope John Paul II visited Cuba, Jan. 21-25, 1998.

On July 31, 2006, the ailing Fidel Castro yielded power to his 75-year-old brother Raúl, who served as acting president until formally succeeding Fidel Feb. 24, 2008.

The U.S. in 2009 eased restrictions on remittances and family travel to the island but retained its trade embargo with Cuba. The Cuban government announced plans Sept. 13, 2010, to restructure the economy by cutting more than 500,000 workers from the public payroll. A Communist Party conference, Apr. 16-19, 2011, confirmed Raúl Castro as first secretary and approved economic reforms including an expansion of private property rights. Pope Benedict XVI visited Cuba, March 26-28, 2012.

The U.S., Jan. 11, 2002, began using its naval base at Guantánamo Bay to detain prisoners captured in Afghanistan. The indefinite detention and aggressive interrogation of the prisoners at Guantánamo were criticized by human rights groups. Pres. Obama signed, Jan. 22, 2009, an executive order calling for the closure of the Guantánamo detention center within a year; as of Aug. 2012, however, 168 detainees were still held there.

Cyprus
Republic of Cyprus

People: Population: 1,138,071. **Age distrib.:** <15: 15.9%; 65+: 10.7%. **Pop. density:** 319 per sq mi, 123.2 per sq km. **Urban:** 70.5%. **Ethnic groups:** Greek 77%, Turkish 18%. **Principal languages:** Greek, Turkish (both official); English. **Chief religions:** Greek Orthodox 78%, Muslim 18%, other (incl. Maronite, Armenian Apostolic) 4%.

Geography: Total area: 3,572 sq mi, 9,251 sq km; **Land area:** 3,568 sq mi, 9,241 sq km. **Location:** In eastern Mediterranean Sea, off Turkish coast. **Neighbors:** Nearest are Turkey on N, Syria and Lebanon on E. **Topography:** Two mountain ranges run E-W, separated by a wide, fertile plain. **Capital:** Nicosia (Lefkosia), 252,570.

Government: Type: Republic. **Head of state and gov.:** Pres. Dimitris Christofias; b. Aug. 29, 1946; in office; Feb. 28, 2008. **Local divisions:** 6 districts. **Defense budget:** $512 mil. **Active troops:** 12,000.

Economy: Industries: tourism, food and beverage proc., cement and gypsum prod., ship repair and refurb., textiles, light chemicals, metal prods. **Chief crops:** citrus, vegetables, barley, grapes, olives, vegetables. **Natural resources:** copper, pyrites, asbestos, gypsum, timber, salt, marble, clay earth pigment. **Arable land:** 9.4%. **Livestock:** cattle: 55,522; chickens: 3 mil; goats: 208,571; pigs: 463,932; sheep: 226,641. **Fish catch:** 5,536 metric tons. **Electricity prod.:** 4.9 bil kWh. **Labor force:** agric. 8.5%, industry 20.5%, services 71%.

Finance: Monetary unit: Euro (EUR) (Sept. 2012: 0.79 = $1 U.S.). **GDP:** $24 bil; **per capita GDP:** $29,400; **GDP growth:** 0.5%.

Imports: $8 bil; Greece 21.5%, Israel 10.4%, UK 9.2%, Italy 8.3%, Germany 8.1%, France 5.7%, China 4.8%, Netherlands 4.6%. **Exports:** $2.2 bil; Greece 26.2%, UK 10.2%, Germany 5.6%. **Tourism:** $2.5 bil. **Budget:** $12 bil. **Total reserves less gold:** $504.3 mil. **Gold:** 446,000 oz t. **CPI change:** 3.3%.

Transport: Motor vehicles: 562.2 vehicles per 1,000 pop. **Civil aviation:** 2.6 bil pass.-mi; 13 airports. **Chief ports:** Larnaca, Limassol (under govt. control); Famagusta (admin. by Turkish Cypriots).

Communications: TV sets: 358 per 1,000 pop. **Radios:** 505 per 1,000 pop. **Telephone lines:** 36.3 per 100 pop. **Internet:** 57.7%.

Health: Life expect.: 75.2 male; 80.9 female. **Births:** 11.4 (per 1,000 pop.). **Deaths:** 6.5 (per 1,000 pop.). **Natural inc.:** 0.50%. **Infant mortality:** 9.1 (per 1,000 live births). **HIV rate:** NA.

Education: Compulsory: ages 6-14. **Literacy:** 98.3%.

Major intl. organizations: UN (FAO, IBRD, ILO, IMF, WHO), the Commonwealth, EU, OSCE, WTO.

Embassy: 2211 R St. NW 20008; 462-5772.

Website: www.cyprus.gov.cy

The Ottoman Empire held Cyprus, 1571-1878, until it yielded control over the island to Britain. Agitation for *enosis* (union) with Greece increased after WWII, with the Turkish minority opposed, and led to violence in 1955-56. In 1959, Britain, Greece, Turkey, and Cypriot leaders approved a plan for an independent republic, with constitutional guarantees for the Turkish minority and permanent division of offices on an ethnic basis.

Archbishop Makarios III, formerly the leader of the *enosis* movement, was elected president, and full independence became final Aug. 16, 1960. Communal strife led the UN to send a peacekeeping force (UNFICYP) in 1964; its mandate has been repeatedly renewed.

The Cypriot National Guard, led by officers from the army of Greece, seized the government July 15, 1974. On July 20, Turkey invaded the island; Greece mobilized its forces but did not intervene. By Aug. 16, Turkish forces had occupied the northeastern 40% of the island.

Turkish Cyprus opened its border with Greek Cyprus Apr. 23, 2003, for the first time since partition. In separate referendums Apr. 24, 2004, 65% of Turkish Cypriot voters accepted a UN-sponsored reunification plan, but 76% of Greek Cypriots rejected it. Still divided, Cyprus became a full member of the EU on May 1. Dimitris Christofias won a runoff election Feb. 24, 2008, becoming the country's first Communist president. A blast July 11, 2011, at a naval base in southern Cyprus killed 13 people; also in mid-2011, exposure to Greece's troubled economy raised doubts about Cyprus's own credit rating, which the U.S. ratings agency Fitch downgraded to "junk status," June 25, 2012.

Turkish Republic of Northern Cyprus

A declaration of independence was announced by Turkish-Cypriot leader Rauf Denktash, Nov. 15, 1983. The state is not internationally recognized, but has trade relations with some countries. Denktash was succeeded as president by Mehmet Ali Talat (2005-10) and Dervis Eroglu, who unseated Talat in the Apr. 18, 2010, election. Area of TRNC: 1,295 sq mi; pop. (2010): 287,856, nearly all Turkish. Capital: Nicosia (Lefkosia).

Czech Republic

People: Population: 10,177,300. **Age distrib.:** <15: 13.4%; 65+: 17%. **Pop. density:** 341.2 per sq mi, 131.8 per sq km. **Urban:** 73.4%. **Ethnic groups:** Czech 90%, Moravian 4%, Slovak 2%. **Principal languages:** Czech, Slovak. **Chief religions:** Roman Catholic 27%, Protestant 2%, unaffiliated 59%.

Geography: Total area: 30,451 sq mi, 78,867 sq km; **Land area:** 29,825 sq mi, 77,247 sq km. **Location:** In E central Europe. **Neighbors:** Poland on N, Germany on N and W, Austria on S, Slovakia on E and SE. **Topography:** Bohemia, in W, is a plateau surrounded by mountains; Moravia is hilly. **Capital:** Prague, 1,275,550.

Government: Type: Republic. **Head of state:** Pres. Vaclav Klaus; b. June 19, 1941; in office: Mar. 7, 2003. **Head of gov.:** Prime Min. Petr Necas; b. Nov. 19, 1964; in office: June 28, 2010. **Local divisions:** 13 regions and Prague. **Defense budget:** $2.52 bil. **Active troops:** 25,421.

Economy: Industries: motor vehicles, metallurgy, machinery and equip., glass, armaments. **Chief crops:** wheat, potatoes, sugar beets, hops, fruits. **Natural resources:** coal, kaolin, clay, graphite, timber. **Crude oil reserves:** 15 mil bbls. **Arable land:** 41.2%. **Livestock:** cattle: 1.3 mil; chickens: 24.3 mil; goats: 22,486; pigs: 1.9 mil; sheep: 205,923. **Fish catch:** 24,410 metric tons. **Electricity prod.** (2010): 80.4 bil kWh. **Labor force:** agric 3.1%, industry 38.6%, services 58.3%.

Finance: Monetary unit: Koruna (CZK) (Sept. 2012: 19.63 = $1 U.S.). **GDP:** $288.6 bil; **per capita GDP:** $27,400; **GDP growth:** 1.7%. **Imports:** $133.2 bil; Germany 29.7%, China 7.6%, Poland 7.1%, Slovakia 7%, Netherlands 5.7%, Russia 4.8%, Austria 4.4%. **Exports:** $138.5 bil; Germany 32.4%, Slovakia 9%, Poland 6.3%, France 5.5%, Austria 4.6%, UK 4.6%, Italy 4.2%. **Tourism:** $7.6 bil. **Budget:** $59.4 bil. **Total reserves less gold:** $39.7 bil. **Gold:** 400,326 oz t. **CPI change:** 1.9%.

Transport: Railways: 5,884 mi. **Motor vehicles:** 503.3 vehicles per 1,000 pop. **Civil aviation:** 3.9 bil pass.-mi; 41 airports. **Chief ports:** Decin, Prague, Usti nad Labem.

Communications: TV sets: 457 per 1,000 pop. **Radios:** 802 per 1,000 pop. **Telephone lines:** 20.9 per 100 pop. **Daily newspaper circ.:** 182.5 per 1,000 pop. **Internet:** 73%.

Health: Life expect.: 74.1 male; 80.8 female. **Births:** 8.6 (per 1,000 pop.). **Deaths:** 10.9 (per 1,000 pop.). **Natural inc.:** –0.23% **Infant mortality:** 3.7 (per 1,000 live births). **HIV rate:** <0.1%.

Education: Compulsory: ages 6-15. **Literacy:** 99%.

Major intl. organizations: UN (FAO, IBRD, ILO, IMF, WHO), EU, NATO, OECD, OSCE, WTO.

Embassy: 3900 Spring of Freedom St. NW 20008; 274-9100.

Website: www.czech.cz

Bohemia and Moravia were part of the Great Moravian Empire in the 9th cent. and later became part of the Holy Roman Empire. Under the kings of Bohemia, Prague in the 14th cent. was the cultural center of Central Europe. Bohemia and Hungary became part of Austria-Hungary.

In 1914-18 Thomas G. Masaryk and Eduard Benes formed a provisional government with the support of Slovak leaders including Milan Stefanik. They proclaimed the Republic of Czechoslovakia Oct. 28, 1918.

Czechoslovakia

By 1938 Nazi Germany had worked up disaffection among German-speaking citizens in Sudetenland and demanded its cession. British Prime Min. Neville Chamberlain, with the acquiescence of France, signed with Hitler at Munich, Sept. 30, 1938, an agreement to the cession, with a guarantee of peace by Hitler and Mussolini. Germany occupied Sudetenland Oct. 1-2.

Hitler on Mar. 15, 1939, dissolved Czechoslovakia, made protectorates of Bohemia and Moravia, and supported the autonomy of Slovakia, proclaimed independent Mar. 14, 1939.

Soviet troops with some Czechoslovak contingents entered eastern Czechoslovakia in 1944 and reached Prague in May 1945; Benes returned as president. In May 1946 elections, the Communist Party won 38% of the votes. In Feb. 1948, the Communists seized power in advance of scheduled elections. The country was renamed the Czechoslovak Socialist Republic. A harsh Stalinist period followed; all opposition was suppressed.

In Jan. 1968 a liberalization movement spread through Czechoslovakia. Antonin Novotny, long the Stalinist ruler, was deposed as party leader, and the Slovak Alexander Dubcek, who supported democratic reforms, succeeded him. In July, the USSR and 4 Warsaw Pact nations demanded an end to liberalization. On Aug. 20, the Soviet, Polish, East German, Hungarian, and Bulgarian armies invaded Czechoslovakia. Despite demonstrations and riots by students and workers, press censorship was imposed and liberal leaders were ousted. On Apr. 17, 1969, Dubcek resigned as leader of the Communist Party and was succeeded by Gustav Husak. Censorship was tightened, and the Communist Party expelled a third of its members.

More than 700 leading Czechoslovak intellectuals and former party leaders signed a human rights manifesto in 1977, called Charter 77, prompting a renewed crackdown by the regime.

The police crushed the largest antigovernment protests since 1968, when tens of thousands of demonstrators took to the streets of Prague, Nov. 17, 1989. As protesters demanded free elections, the Communist Party leadership resigned Nov. 24; millions went on strike Nov. 27.

On Dec. 10, 1989, the first cabinet in 41 years without a Communist majority took power; Vaclav Havel, playwright and human rights campaigner, was chosen president, Dec. 29. In Mar. 1990 the country was officially renamed the Czech and Slovak Federal Republic. A Slovak-led coalition blocked Havel's bid to win reelection July 3, 1992.

Slovakia declared sovereignty, July 17, 1992. Czech and Slovak leaders agreed, July 23, on a plan for a peaceful division of Czechoslovakia into two independent states.

Czech Republic

Czechoslovakia split into two separate states—the Czech Republic and Slovakia—on Jan. 1, 1993. Havel was elected president of the Czech Republic on Jan. 26. The country became a full member of NATO on Mar. 12, 1999.

Vaclav Klaus was chosen Feb. 28, 2003, to replace the retiring Havel. After Czech voters June 13-14, 2003, endorsed joining the EU, the nation became a full EU member May 1, 2004. Inconclusive parliamentary elections, June 2-3, 2006, led to a political deadlock, after which a minority center-right government took office Sept. 4, 2006. Center-right parties made a strong showing in parliamentary elections May 28-29, 2010.

Denmark
Kingdom of Denmark

People: Population: 5,543,453. **Age distrib.:** <15: 17.4%; 65+: 17.6%. **Pop. density:** 338.3 per sq mi, 130.6 per sq km. **Urban:** 86.9%. **Ethnic groups:** Scandinavian, Inuit, Faroese, German, Turkish, Iranian, Somali. **Principal languages:** Danish, Faroese, Greenlandic, English (predominant second language). **Chief religions:** Evangelical Lutheran (official) 95%, other Christian (incl. Protestant, Roman Catholic) 3%, Muslim 2%.

Geography: Total area: 16,639 sq mi, 43,094 sq km; **Land area:** 16,384 sq mi, 42,434 sq km. **Location:** In N Europe, separating North and Baltic seas. **Neighbors:** Germany on S, Norway on NW, Sweden on NE. **Topography:** Consists of the Jutland Peninsula and about 500 islands, 100 inhabited. Land is flat or gently rolling and is almost all in productive use. **Capital:** Copenhagen, 1,206,020.

Government: Type: Constitutional monarchy. **Head of state:** Queen Margrethe II; b. Apr. 16, 1940; in office: Jan. 14, 1972. **Head of gov.:** Prime Min. Helle Thorning-Schmidt; b. Dec. 14, 1966; in office: Oct. 3, 2011. **Local divisions:** 5 regions. **Defense budget:** $4.9 bil. **Active troops:** 18,628.

Economy: Industries: iron, steel, nonferrous metals, chemicals, food proc., machinery and transp. equip., textiles and clothing, electronics, constr., furniture and other wood prods. **Chief crops:** barley, wheat, potatoes, sugar beets. **Natural resources:** petroleum, nat. gas, fish, salt, limestone, chalk, stone, gravel and sand. **Crude oil reserves:** 900 mil bbls. **Arable land:** 57.3%. **Livestock:** cattle: 1.6 mil; chickens: 14.1 mil; pigs: 13.2 mil; sheep: 159,626. **Fish catch:** 867,523 metric tons. **Electricity prod.:** (2010): 36.4 bil kWh. **Labor force:** agric. 2.6%, industry 20.3%, services 77.1%.

Finance: Monetary unit: Krone (DKK) (Sept. 2012: 5.90 = $1 U.S.). **GDP:** $209.2 bil; **per capita GDP:** $37,600; **GDP growth:** 1.1%. **Imports:** $102.1 bil; Germany 20.8%, Sweden 13.6%, Netherlands 7.1%, UK 6.3%, China 6.3%, Norway 5.8%. **Exports:** $111.7 bil; Germany 16.9%, Sweden 13.2%, UK 9.9%, Norway 5.7%, U.S. 5.5%, Netherlands 4.9%, France 4.4%. **Tourism:** $6.2 bil. **Budget:** $127.5 bil. **Total reserves less gold:** $81.7 bil. **Gold:** 2.1 mil oz t. **CPI change:** 2.8%.

Transport: Railways: 1,657 mi. **Motor vehicles:** 480.4 vehicles per 1,000 pop. **Civil aviation:** 5.5 bil pass.-mi; 28 airports. **Chief ports:** Aalborg, Aarhus, Copenhagen, Ensted, Esbjerg, Fredericia, Kalundborg.

Communications: TV sets: 975 per 1,000 pop. **Radios:** 1,399 per 1,000 pop. **Telephone lines:** 45.1 per 100 pop. **Daily newspaper circ.:** 352.8 per 1,000 pop. **Internet:** 90%.

Health: Life expect.: 76.4 male; 81.3 female. **Births:** 10.2 (per 1,000 pop.). **Deaths:** 10.2 (per 1,000 pop.). **Natural inc.:** 0% **Infant mortality:** 4.2 (per 1,000 live births). **HIV rate:** 0.2%.

Education: Compulsory: ages 7-16. **Literacy:** 99%.

Major intl. organizations: UN and all of its specialized agencies, EU, NATO, OECD, OSCE, WTO.

Embassy: 3200 Whitehaven St. NW 20008; 234-4300.

Website: www.denmark.dk

Danes formed a large component of the Viking raiders in the early Middle Ages. The Danish kingdom was a major power until the 17th cent., when it lost its land in southern Sweden. Norway was separated in 1815, and Schleswig-Holstein in 1864. Northern Schleswig was returned in 1920. Denmark was occupied by Nazi Germany, Apr. 1940-May 1945, but Danes helped more than 7,200 Jews escape to safety in Sweden, Sept. 1943.

Voters ratified the Maastricht Treaty, the basic document of the European Union, in May 1993, after rejecting it in 1992. On Sept. 28, 2000, Danes voted not to join the euro currency zone.

The Danish newspaper *Jyllands-Posten* published, Sept. 30, 2005, cartoon images of the prophet Muhammad, offensive to Muslims; the caricatures, republished elsewhere, triggered violent protests and a boycott of Danish products in Islamic countries in early 2006. Raids by Danish police broke up alleged Islamist bomb plots Sept. 2006 and Sept. 2007. A car bomb blast linked to al-Qaeda killed 8 people outside Denmark's embassy in Islamabad, Pakistan, June 2, 2008.

Ten years of center-right government ended Sept. 15, 2011, as a left-wing coalition won parliamentary elections. Helle Thorning-Schmidt, a Social Democrat, became Denmark's first female prime minister Oct. 3. A bill granting marriage rights to same-sex couples was voted into law, June 7, 2012.

The **Faroe Islands** in the North Atlantic, about 300 mi NW of the Shetlands, and 850 mi from Denmark proper, 18 inhabited, have an area of 540 sq mi and pop. (2012 est.) of 49,483. They are an administrative division of Denmark, self-governing in most matters. Torshavn is the capital. Fish is a primary export (292,519 metric tons in 2006). **Website:** www.us.fo

Greenland (Kalaallit Nunaat)

Greenland, a huge island between the North Atlantic and the Polar Sea, is separated from the North American continent by Davis Strait and Baffin Bay. Its total area is 836,330 sq mi, 2,166,086 sq km, 81% of which is ice-capped. Most of the island is a lofty plateau 9,000 to 10,000 ft in altitude. The average thickness of the cap is 1,000 ft. Scientists point to accelerated melting of Greenland's ice sheet in recent years as evidence of global warming. The population (2012 est.) is 57,695. Under the 1953 Danish constitution the colony became an integral part of the realm with representatives in the Folketing (Danish legislature). The Danish parliament, 1978, approved home rule for Greenland, effective May 1, 1979. With home rule, Greenlandic place names came into official use. The technically correct name for Greenland is now Kalaallit Nunaat; the official name for its capital is Nuuk, rather than Godthab.

Fish is the principal export (120,725 metric tons in 2006). Other natural resources include coal, iron ore, lead, zinc, molybdenum, diamonds, gold, and platinum. **Website:** www.nanoq.gl

Djibouti
Republic of Djibouti

People: Population: 774,389. **Age distrib.:** <15: 34.3%; 65+: 3.4%. **Pop. density:** 86.5 per sq mi, 33.4 per sq km. **Urban:** 77.1%. **Ethnic groups:** Somali 60%, Afar 35%, other (incl. French, Arab, Ethiopian, Italian) 5%. **Principal languages:** French, Arabic (both official); Somali; Afar. **Chief religions:** Muslim 94%, Christian 6%.

Geography: Total area: 8,958 sq mi, 23,200 sq km; **Land area:** 8,950 sq mi, 23,180 sq km. **Location:** On E coast of Africa, separated from Arabian Peninsula by strategically vital strait of Bab el-Mandeb. **Neighbors:** Ethiopia on W and SW, Eritrea on NW, Somalia on SE. **Topography:** The territory, divided into a low coastal plain, mountains behind, and an interior plateau, is arid, sandy, and desolate. Climate is generally hot and dry. **Capital:** Djibouti, 495,804.

Government: Type: Republic. **Head of state:** Pres. Ismail Omar Guelleh; b. Nov. 27, 1947; in office: May 8, 1999. **Head of gov.:** Prime Min. Dileita Mohamed Dileita; b. Mar. 12, 1958; in office: Mar. 7, 2001. **Local divisions:** 5 districts. **Defense budget** (2010): $10 mil. **Active troops:** 10,450.

Economy: Industries: constr., agric. proc. **Chief crops:** fruits, vegetables. **Natural resources:** potential geothermal power, gold, clay, granite, limestone, marble, salt, diatomite, gypsum, pumice, petroleum. **Arable land:** 0.1%. **Livestock:** cattle: 297,000; goats: 512,000; sheep: 466,000. **Fish catch:** 1,058 metric tons. **Electricity prod.:** 350 mil kWh. **Labor force:** NA.

Finance: Monetary unit: Franc (DJF) (Sept. 2012: 180.02 = $1 U.S.). **GDP:** $2.3 bil; **per capita GDP:** $2,700; **GDP growth:** 4.5%. **Imports:** $413.7 mil; Saudi Arabia 18.1%, China 16.6%, India 14%, Indonesia 6.1%, Malaysia 5.3%, U.S. 4.3%, Pakistan 4.2%. **Exports:** $96.3 mil; Somalia 77.2%, Egypt 8.6%. **Tourism:** $18 mil. **Budget:** $473.8 mil. **Total reserves less gold:** $244.1 mil. **CPI change:** 4.4%.

Transport: Railways: 62 mi (part of Addis Ababa-Djibouti railway, under joint control with Ethiopia, but largely inoperable). **Civil aviation:** 3 airports. **Chief port:** Djibouti.

Communications: TV sets: 67 per 1,000 pop. **Radios:** 93 per 1,000 pop. **Telephone lines:** 2 per 100 pop. **Internet:** 7%.

Health: Life expect.: 59.2 male; 64.1 female. **Births:** 24.9 (per 1,000 pop.). **Deaths:** 8.1 (per 1,000 pop.). **Natural inc.:** 1.68% **Infant mortality:** 53.3 (per 1,000 live births). **HIV rate:** 2.5%.

Education: Compulsory: ages 6-16. **Literacy:** NA.

Major intl. organizations: UN (FAO, IBRD, ILO, IMF, WHO), AL, AU, WTO.

Embassy: 1156 15th St. NW, Ste. 515, 20005; 331-0270.

Website: www.presidence.dj

France gained control of the territory in stages between 1862 and 1900. As French Somaliland it became an overseas territory of France in 1945; in 1967 it was renamed the French Territory of the Afars and the Issas.

Ethiopia and Somalia have renounced their claims to the area, but each has accused the other of trying to gain control. There were clashes between Afars (ethnically related to Ethiopians) and Issas (related to Somalis) in 1976. Immigrants from both countries continued to enter Djibouti until independence, which came June 27, 1977.

French aid along with assistance from Arab countries, is the mainstay of the economy. A peace accord Dec. 1994 ended a 3-year-long uprising by Afar rebels. Drought 2007-11 devastated crops and livestock. An estimated 3,000 French and 2,200 U.S. military personnel are based in Djibouti. Protests associated with the "Arab Spring" broke out in late Jan. 2011. They demanded the resignation of Pres. Ismail Omar Guelleh. Authorities clamped down on the protests, and Guelleh won a third term in an election Apr. 8, 2011, boycotted by the main opposition.

Dominica
Commonwealth of Dominica

People: Population: 73,126. **Age distrib.:** <15: 22.6%; 65+: 10.3%. **Pop. density:** 252.2 per sq mi, 97.4 per sq km. **Urban:** 67.1%. **Ethnic groups:** black 87%, mixed 9%, Carib Amerindian 3%. **Principal languages:** English (official), French patois. **Chief religions:** Roman Catholic 61%, Protestant 21% (Seventh-Day Adventist 6%, Pentecostal 6%, Baptist 4%, Methodist 4%, Church of God 1%), Jehovah's Witnesses 1%, none 6%.

Geography: Total area: 290 sq mi, 751 sq km; **Land area:** 290 sq mi, 751 sq km. **Location:** In E Caribbean, most northerly Windward Isl. **Neighbors:** Guadeloupe to N, Martinique to S. **Topography:** Mountainous, a central ridge running from N to S, terminating in cliffs; volcanic in origin, with numerous thermal springs; rich deep topsoil on leeward side, red tropical clay on windward coast. **Capital:** Roseau, 13,562.

Government: Type: Parliamentary democracy. **Head of state:** Pres. Nicholas Liverpool; b. Sept. 9, 1934; in office: Oct. 2, 2003. **Head of gov.:** Prime Min. Roosevelt Skerrit; b. June 8, 1972; in office: Jan. 8, 2004. **Local divisions:** 10 parishes. **Defense budget:** NA. **Active troops:** No regular military forces.

Economy: Industries: soap, coconut oil, tourism, copra, furniture, cement blocks, shoes. **Chief crops:** bananas, citrus, mangoes, root crops, coconuts, cocoa. **Natural resources:** timber, hydropower. **Arable land:** 8.0%. **Livestock:** cattle: 13,500; chickens: 190,000; goats: 9,700; pigs: 5,000; sheep: 7,600. **Fish catch:** 735 metric tons. **Electricity prod.:** 86 mil kWh. **Labor force:** agric. 40%, industry 32%, services 28%.

Finance: Monetary unit: East Caribbean Dollar (XCD) (Sept. 2012: 2.70 = $1 U.S.). **GDP:** $989.5 mil; **per capita GDP:** $14,000; **GDP growth:** 0.5%. **Imports:** $207.1 mil; Japan 34.3%, U.S. 15.7%, Trinidad and Tobago 14%, China 5.7%, Singapore 5.5%. **Exports:** $40.4 mil; Japan 45.8%, Antigua and Barbuda 8.2%, Jamaica 7.3%, Guyana 7%, Trinidad and Tobago 4.5%. **Tourism:** $80 mil. **Budget:** $111.1 mil. **Total reserves less gold:** $81.1 mil. **CPI change:** 2.8%.

Transport: Civil aviation: 2 airports. **Chief ports:** Portsmouth, Roseau.

Communications: TV sets: 230 per 1,000 pop. **Radios:** 602 per 1,000 pop. **Telephone lines** (2010): 22.9 per 100 pop. **Daily newspaper circ.:** 39.1 per 1,000 pop. **Internet:** 51.3%.

Health: Life expect.: 73.2 male; 79.3 female. **Births:** 15.6 (per 1,000 pop.). **Deaths:** 8.0 (per 1,000 pop.). **Natural inc.:** 0.76% **Infant mortality:** 12.4 (per 1,000 live births). **HIV rate:** NA.

Education: Compulsory: ages 5-15. **Literacy:** NA.

Major intl. organizations: UN (FAO, IBRD, ILO, IMF, WHO), Caricom, the Commonwealth, OAS, OECS, WTO.

Embassy: 3216 New Mexico Ave. NW 20016; 364-6781.

Website: www.dominica.gov.dm

A British colony since 1805, Dominica was granted self-government in 1967. Independence was achieved Nov. 3, 1978.

Hurricane David struck, Aug. 30, 1979, devastating the island and destroying the banana plantations, Dominica's economic mainstay. Coups were attempted in 1980 and 1981.

Dominica participated in the 1983 U.S.-led invasion of nearby Grenada. Prime Min. Pierre Charles, 49, died of a heart attack Jan. 6, 2004, and was succeeded by Roosevelt Skerrit.

Dominican Republic

People: Population: 10,088,598. **Age distrib.:** <15: 29%; 65+: 6.7%. **Pop. density:** 540.8 per sq mi, 208.8 per sq km. **Urban:** 69.7%. **Ethnic groups:** mixed 73%, white 16%, black 11%. **Principal language:** Spanish (official). **Chief religion:** Roman Catholic 95%.

Geography: Total area: 18,792 sq mi, 48,670 sq km; **Land area:** 18,656 sq mi, 48,320 sq km. **Location:** In W Indies, eastern isl. of Hispaniola with Haiti. **Neighbors:** Haiti to W, Puerto Rico (U.S.) to E. **Topography:** The Cordillera Central range crosses center of the country, rising to over 10,000 ft, highest in the Caribbean. The Cibao Valley to N is major agricultural area. **Capital:** Santo Domingo, 2,190,990.

Government: Type: Republic. **Head of state and gov.:** Pres. Danila Medina Sánchez; b. Nov. 10, 1951; in office: Aug. 16, 2012. **Local divisions:** 29 provinces and national district. **Defense budget:** $229 mil. **Active troops:** 24,500.

Economy: Industries: tourism, sugar proc., mining, textiles, cement, tobacco. **Chief crops:** sugarcane, coffee, cotton, cocoa, tobacco, rice, beans, potatoes, corn, bananas. **Natural resources:** nickel, bauxite, gold, silver. **Arable land:** 16.6%. **Livestock:** cattle: 2.8 mil; chickens: 100.5 mil; goats: 225,000; pigs: 630,000; sheep: 240,000. **Fish catch:** 15,470 metric tons. **Electricity prod.** (2010): 12.3 bil kWh. **Labor force:** agric. 14.6%, industry 22.3%, services 63.1%.

Finance: Monetary unit: Peso (DOP) (Sept. 2012: 39.10 = $1 U.S.). **GDP:** $94.6 bil; **per capita GDP:** $9,400; **GDP growth:** 4.5%. **Imports:** $17.4 bil; U.S. 43.4%, Venezuela 7.1%, Mexico 6%, China 5.7%. **Exports:** $8.5 bil; U.S. 49.3%, Haiti 16.9%. **Tourism:** $4.4 bil. **Budget:** $9.5 bil. **Total reserves less gold:** $4.1 bil. **Gold:** 18,296 oz t. **CPI change:** 8.5%.

Transport: Railways: 88 mi. **Motor vehicles:** 131.5 vehicles per 1,000 pop. **Civil aviation:** 16 airports. **Chief ports:** Puerto Haina, Puerto Plata, Santo Domingo.

Communications: TV sets: 219 per 1,000 pop. **Radios:** 185 per 1,000 pop. **Telephone lines:** 10.4 per 100 pop. **Daily newspaper circ.:** 39.1 per 1,000 pop. **Internet:** 35.5%.

Health: Life expect.: 75.3 male; 79.7 female. **Births:** 19.4 (per 1,000 pop.). **Deaths:** 4.4 (per 1,000 pop.). **Natural inc.:** 1.50% **Infant mortality:** 21.3 (per 1,000 live births). **HIV rate:** 0.9%.

Education: Compulsory: ages 5-17. **Literacy:** 89.5%.

Major intl. organizations: UN (FAO, IBRD, ILO, IMF, WHO), OAS, WTO.

Embassy: 1715 22nd St. NW 20008; 332-6280.

Website: www.presidencia.gov.do

Carib and Arawak Indians inhabited the island of Hispaniola when Columbus landed in 1492. The city of Santo Domingo, founded 1496, is the oldest European settlement in the hemisphere.

France took over the western third of the island in 1697 and Santo Domingo, in 1795. Haitian leader Toussaint L'Ouverture seized it, 1801. Spain returned intermittently 1803-21, as several native republics came and went. Haiti ruled again, 1822-44; Spanish occupation occurred 1861-63. U.S. Marines occupied the country 1916-24.

In 1930, Gen. Rafael Leonidas Trujillo Molina was elected president. The brutal Trujillo era ended with his assassination in 1961. Pres. Joaquín Balaguer, appointed by Trujillo in 1960, resigned under pressure in 1962.

Juan Bosch, elected president in the first free elections in 38 years, was overthrown in 1963. On Apr. 24, 1965, Bosch's followers and others, including a few Communists, launched a revolt. Four days later U.S. Marines intervened against pro-Bosch forces. Five South American countries later sent token units as a peacekeeping force. A provisional government supervised a June 1966 election in which Balaguer was returned to office for most of the next 28 years, but his May 1994 reelection was widely denounced as fraudulent. He cut short his term and on June 30, 1996, Leonel Fernández Reyna was elected.

Hurricane Georges struck Sept. 22, 1998, claiming more than 200 lives. The leftist candidate, Hipólito Mejía, won a presidential vote May 16, 2000. With the nation reeling from a banking scandal and soaring inflation, Fernández defeated Mejía in a May 16, 2004, election. Floods and mudslides in late May killed about 395 people. A fight between rival prison gangs led to a fire, Mar. 7, 2005, in which 136 inmates died. Torrential rains from Tropical Storm Noel, Oct. 28-31, 2007, claimed at least 87 lives. Fernández was reelected May 16, 2008. Danilo Medina Sánchez, Fernández's ally, was elected May 20, 2012, and sworn into office Aug 16.

East Timor
See **Timor-Leste.**

Ecuador
Republic of Ecuador

People: Population: 15,223,680. **Age distrib.:** <15: 29.5%; 65+: 6.6%. **Pop. density:** 142.4 per sq mi, 55 per sq km. **Urban:** 67.5%. **Ethnic groups:** mestizo (mixed Amerindian & white) 65%, Amerindian 25%, Spanish & others 7%, black 3%. **Principal languages:** Spanish (official), Amerindian languages (espec. Quechua). **Chief religion:** Roman Catholic 95%.

Geography: Total area: 109,484 sq mi, 283,561 sq km; **Land area:** 106,889 sq mi, 276,841 sq km. **Location:** In NW S. America, on Pacific coast, astride the equator. **Neighbors:** Colombia on N, Peru on E and S. **Topography:** Two ranges of Andes run N and S, splitting country into 3 zones: hot, humid lowlands on coast; temperate highlands between ranges; and rainy, tropical lowlands to E. **Capital:** Quito, 1,622,390. **Cities (urban aggl.):** Guayaquil, 2,286,682.

Government: Type: Republic. **Head of state and gov.:** Pres. Rafael Correa; b. Apr. 6, 1963; in office: Jan. 15, 2007. **Local divisions:** 22 provinces. **Defense budget:** $1.51 bil. **Active troops:** 58,483.

Economy: Industries: petroleum, food proc., textiles, wood prods., chemicals. **Chief crops:** bananas, coffee, cocoa, rice, potatoes, manioc, plantains, sugarcane. **Natural resources:** petroleum, fish, timber, hydropower. **Crude oil reserves:** 7.2 bil bbls. **Arable land:** 4.8%. **Livestock:** cattle: 5.3 mil; chickens: 152.9 mil; goats: 134,825; pigs: 1.5 mil; sheep: 1.9 mil. **Fish catch:** 663,633 metric tons. **Electricity prod.:** 16.7 bil kWh. **Labor force:** agric. 27.6%, industry 18.8%, services 53.6%.

Finance: Monetary unit: U.S. Dollar (USD). **GDP:** $129.1 bil; **per capita GDP:** $8,600; **GDP growth:** 7.8%. **Imports:** $23.2 bil; U.S. 27.9%, China 10.3%, Colombia 9.2%, Panama 4.6%, Peru 4.6%, Brazil 4.3%, South Korea 4.1%. **Exports:** $22.3 bil; U.S. 38.3%, Panama 10.1%, Peru 6.3%, Venezuela 5.3%, Chile 5%, Russia 4.6%. **Tourism:** $837 mil. **Budget:** $22.3 bil. **Total reserves less gold:** $1.7 bil. **Gold:** 845,000 oz t. **CPI change:** 4.5%.

Transport: Railways: 600 mi. **Motor vehicles:** 52.8 vehicles per 1,000 pop. **Civil aviation:** 2.5 bil pass.-mi; 101 airports. **Chief ports:** Esmeraldas, Guayaquil, Manta, Puerto Bolivar.

Communications: TV sets: 261 per 1,000 pop. **Radios:** 517 per 1,000 pop. **Telephone lines:** 15.1 per 100 pop. **Internet:** 31.4%.

Health: Life expect.: 73.0 male; 79.0 female. **Births:** 19.6 (per 1,000 pop.). **Deaths:** 5.0 (per 1,000 pop.). **Natural inc.:** 1.46% **Infant mortality:** 19.1 (per 1,000 live births). **HIV rate:** 0.4%.

Education: Compulsory: ages 5-17. **Literacy:** 91.9%.

Major intl. organizations: UN (FAO, IBRD, ILO, IMF, WHO), OAS, OPEC, WTO.

Embassy: 2535 15th St. NW 20009; 234-7200.

Website: www.presidencia.gob.ec

The region, which was the northern Inca empire, was conquered by Spain in 1533. Liberation forces defeated the Spanish May 24, 1822, near Quito. Ecuador became part of the Great Colombia Republic but seceded, May 13, 1830.

Ecuadoran indigenous peoples, demanding greater rights, staged protests in the 1990s. A border war with Peru flared Jan. 26-Mar. 1, 1995. Vice Pres. Alberto Dahik resigned and fled Ecuador, Oct. 11, 1995, to avoid arrest on corruption charges. Elected president in a runoff, July 7, 1996, Abdalá Bucaram—a populist known as El Loco, or "The Crazy One"—imposed stiff price increases and other austerity measures. His rising unpopularity and erratic behavior led the National Congress, Feb. 6, 1997, to dismiss him for "mental incapacity."

Jamil Mahuad Witt won a presidential runoff election July 12, 1998. In Sept. 1998 and Mar. 1999 he imposed emergency measures to cope with a continuing economic crisis. Opposed by Indian groups and military leaders, he was ousted Jan. 21, 2000, and succeeded by Vice Pres. Gustavo Noboa Bejarano. Noboa went ahead with a plan introduced by Mahuad to replace the sucre with the U.S. dollar as Ecuador's currency. Lucio Gutiérrez Borbúa, a leader in the 2000 coup, won a presidential runoff Nov. 24, 2002. Noboa, under investigation for financial mismanagement, went into exile Aug. 23, 2003.

Gutiérrez imposed economic austerity measures, purged opponents from the supreme court, Dec. 2004, and then dissolved the court, Apr. 15, 2005. With street protests rising, Congress ousted Gutiérrez Apr. 20, and Vice Pres. Alfredo Palacio González became president. The U.S. suspended free-trade talks after Ecuador, May 15, 2006, took over oil assets belonging to U.S.-based Occidental Petroleum.

Rafael Correa, a left-wing economist, won a presidential runoff vote Nov. 26, 2006. After a power struggle with the National Congress, Correa won voter approval, Apr. 15, 2007, to convene an assembly to rewrite the constitution. The revised constitution won overwhelming approval in a national referendum Sept. 28, 2008. Early in his term, when oil revenues were high, he boosted development spending and aid to poor families; later, as oil prices dropped, he restricted imports to prevent an outflow of dollars and, in Dec. 2008, allowed Ecuador to default on part of its $10 bil foreign debt.

Correa, who won reelection Apr. 26, 2009, pressured foreign oil companies in 2010 to renegotiate contracts to increase the government's share of mineral revenues. A confrontation Sept. 30, 2010 between Correa and rebellious police officers led to a shootout between government troops and police: 5 people were killed and at least 38 wounded. An Ecuadoran judge Feb. 14, 2011, ordered Chevron (which had absorbed Texaco in 2001) to pay $9.5 bil to clean up oil pollution from Texaco operations in Ecuador, 1965-92; the plaintiffs and defendants disputed the ruling. In 2012, Ecuador granted asylum, Aug. 16, to Julian Assange, the founder of WikiLeaks. Assange had been in Ecuador's embassy since June 19, avoiding extradition to Sweden from Britain.

The **Galápagos Islands**, pop. (2008 est.) 30,000, about 600 mi to the W, are the home of huge tortoises and other unusual animals. The oil tanker *Jessica* ran aground Jan. 16, 2001, off San Cristóbal Isl., spilling some 185,000 gallons of fuel.

Egypt
Arab Republic of Egypt

People: Population: 83,688,164. **Age distrib.:** <15: 32.5%; 65+: 4.7%. **Pop. density:** 217.7 per sq mi, 84.1 per sq km. **Urban:** 43.5%. **Ethnic groups:** Egyptian 99.6%. **Principal languages:** Arabic (official), English and French widely understood by educated classes. **Chief religions:** Muslim (mostly Sunni) 90%, Coptic 9%.

Geography: Total area: 386,662 sq mi, 1,001,450 sq km; **Land area:** 384,345 sq mi, 995,450 sq km. **Location:** NE corner of Africa. **Neighbors:** Libya on W; Sudan on S; Israel, Gaza Strip on E. **Topography:** Almost entirely desolate and barren, with hills and mountains in E and along Nile. The Nile Valley, where most of the people live, stretches 550 mi. **Capital:** Cairo, 11,169,000. **Cities (urban aggl.):** Alexandria, 4,494,482.

Government: Type: In transition. **Head of state:** Pres. Mohammed Morsi; b. Aug. 20, 1951; in office: June 30, 2012. **Head of gov.:** Prime Min. Hisham Qandil; b. 1962; in office: July 24, 2012. **Local divisions:** 26 governorates. **Defense budget:** $4.2 bil. **Active troops:** 438,500.

Economy: Industries: textiles, food proc., tourism, chemicals, pharmaceuticals, hydrocarbons, constr., cement, metals, light manufactures. **Chief crops:** cotton, rice, corn, wheat, beans, fruits, vegetables. **Natural resources:** petroleum, nat. gas, iron ore, phosphates, manganese, limestone, gypsum, talc, asbestos, lead, rare earth elements, zinc. **Crude oil reserves:** 4.4 bil bbls. **Arable land:** 2.9%. **Livestock:** cattle: 4.5 mil; chickens: 100 mil; goats: 4.2 mil; pigs: 12,000; sheep: 5.7 mil. **Fish catch:** 1.3 mil metric tons. **Electricity prod.** (2010): 136.6 bil kWh. **Labor force:** agric. 32%, industry 17%, services 51%.

Finance: Monetary unit: Pound (EGP) (Sept. 2012: 6.10 = $1 U.S.). **GDP:** $525.6 bil; **per capita GDP:** $6,600; **GDP growth:** 1.8%. **Imports:** $54 bil; China 11.5%, U.S. 9.8%, Italy 5.6%, Germany 4.9%, Turkey 4.4%, Brazil 4.1%. **Exports:** $27.9 bil; Italy 8.8%, Germany 5.5%, U.S. 5.5%, India 5.2%, Saudi Arabia 5.1%, Spain 4.7%, France 4.5%. **Tourism:** $8.7 bil. **Budget:** $67.7 bil. **Total reserves less gold:** $14.9 bil. **Gold:** 2.4 mil oz t. **CPI change:** 10.1%.

Transport: Railways: 3,158 mi. **Motor vehicles:** 43.5 vehicles per 1,000 pop. **Civil aviation:** 9.2 bil pass.-mi; 72 airports. **Chief ports:** Alexandria, Ayn Sukhnah, Damietta, El Dekheila, Port Said, Sidi Kurayr, Suez.

Communications: TV sets: 243 per 1,000 pop. **Radios:** 242 per 1,000 pop. **Telephone lines:** 10.6 per 100 pop. **Internet:** 35.6%.

Health: Life expect.: 70.3 male; 75.7 female. **Births:** 24.2 (per 1,000 pop.). **Deaths:** 4.8 (per 1,000 pop.). **Natural inc.:** 1.94%. **Infant mortality:** 24.2 (per 1,000 live births). **HIV rate:** <0.1%.

Education: Compulsory: ages 6-14. **Literacy:** 72%.

Major intl. organizations: UN (FAO, IBRD, ILO, IMF, WHO), AL, AU, WTO.
Embassy: 3521 International Ct. NW 20008; 895-5400.
Website: www.egypt.gov.eg

Archaeological records of ancient Egyptian civilization date back to 4000 BCE. A unified kingdom arose around 3200 BCE and extended its way south into Nubia and as far north as Syria. A high culture of rulers and priests was built on an economic base of serfdom, fertile soil, and annual flooding of the Nile.

Imperial decline facilitated conquest by Asian invaders (Hyksos, Assyrians). The last native dynasty fell in 341 BCE to the Persians, who were in turn replaced by Greeks (Alexander and the Ptolemies), Romans, Byzantines, and Arabs, who introduced Islam and the Arabic language. The ancient Egyptian language is preserved only in Coptic Christian liturgy.

Egypt was ruled as part of larger Islamic empires for many centuries. Britain intervened in Egypt in 1882 and ruled the country as a protectorate, 1914-22. A 1936 treaty strengthened Egyptian autonomy, but Britain retained bases in Egypt and a condominium over the Sudan. When the state of Israel was proclaimed in 1948, Egypt joined other Arab nations invading Israel and was defeated. In 1951 Egypt abrogated the 1936 treaty; the Sudan became independent in 1956.

An uprising on July 23, 1952, overthrew King Farouk and established a republic. Lt. Col. Gamal Abdel Nasser rose to power, becoming premier in 1954 and president in 1956. Nasser soon emerged as the most influential leader in the Arab world; within Egypt, he pushed construction of the Aswan High Dam, completed in 1970.

After guerrilla raids across its border, Israel invaded Egypt's Sinai Peninsula, Oct. 29, 1956. Egypt rejected a cease-fire demand by Britain and France; on Oct. 31 the 2 nations dropped bombs and on Nov. 5-6 landed forces. Egypt and Israel accepted a UN cease-fire; fighting ended Nov. 7. Subsequently, a UN Emergency Force guarded the border. Full-scale war with Israel broke out again, June 5, 1967; before it ended under a UN cease-fire June 10, Israel had captured Gaza and the Sinai Peninsula and taken control of the E bank of the Suez Canal.

Nasser died Sept. 28, 1970, and was replaced by Vice Pres. Anwar Sadat. In a surprise attack Oct. 6, 1973, Egyptian forces crossed the Suez Canal into the Sinai. (At the same time, Syrian forces attacked Israelis on the Golan Heights.) A USSR military airlift supplied Egypt; the U.S. responded with an airlift to Israel. Israel counterattacked, crossed the canal, and surrounded Suez City. A UN cease-fire took effect Oct. 24. Under an agreement signed Jan. 18, 1974, Israeli forces withdrew from the canal's W bank; limited numbers of Egyptian forces occupied a strip along the E bank. A second accord was signed in 1975, with Israel yielding Sinai oil fields.

Pres. Sadat's surprise visit to Jerusalem, Nov. 1977, opened the prospect of peace with Israel. On Mar. 26, 1979, Egypt and Israel signed a formal peace treaty, ending 30 years of war and establishing diplomatic relations. On Oct. 6, 1981, Muslim extremists within the army assassinated Pres. Sadat, who was succeeded by Hosni Mubarak. Israel returned control of the Sinai to Egypt in Apr. 1982.

Egyptian security forces battled Islamist violence in the 1990s and after. Pres. Mubarak escaped assassination in Ethiopia, June 26, 1995; Egypt blamed Sudan for the attack. On Nov. 17, 1997, near Luxor, Muslim extremists killed 58 foreign tourists and 4 Egyptians. Mubarak won a 4th presidential term Sept. 26, 1999. Bombs Oct. 7, 2004, in and near Taba (a Sinai tourist site popular with Israelis) killed at least 35 people. Another 88 people were killed in bombings July 23, 2005, at Sharm el Sheikh, a Red Sea resort city.

Pressured by the U.S., Mubarak allowed opposition candidates in the Sept. 7, 2005, presidential election, which he easily won. Suicide bombings at the Sinai resort town of Dahab, Apr. 24, 2006, killed at least 18 people; security forces May 9 killed Nasser Khamis al-Mallahi, leader of the group blamed for the Taba, Sharm el Sheikh, and Dahab attacks. Constitutional amendments expanding presidential powers and barring religiously-based political parties were approved Mar. 26, 2007, in a referendum criticized as fraudulent by opposition groups and human rights observers.

Following 18 days of mass protests in which at least 846 people died in clashes between "Arab Spring" dissidents and Mubarak loyalists, Mubarak surrendered power Feb. 11, 2011, to the Supreme Council of the Armed Forces. While Islamists and pro-democracy secularists contended for influence, the transitional military regime prepared for elections and charged Mubarak and his associates with corruption and abuse of power. Mubarak was convicted June 2, 2012, and sentenced to life in prison; six other officials, as well as Mubarak's sons, were acquitted. The Islamist candidate Mohammed Morsi was declared winner of the presidential election, June 24, 2012. Egypt continued to adhere to the 1979 peace treaty with Israel, but improved ties with Hamas in Gaza and deployed troops to Sinai Aug. 9, 2012, in breach of the treaty, to crack down on Islamist militants.

The **Suez Canal**, 103 mi long, links the Mediterranean and Red Seas. It was built by a French corporation 1859-69, but Britain obtained controlling interest in 1875. The last British troops were removed June 13, 1956. On July 26, Egypt nationalized the canal.

El Salvador
Republic of El Salvador

People: Population: 6,090,646. **Age distrib.:** <15: 29.7%; 65+: 6.6%. **Pop. density:** 761.3 per sq mi, 293.9 per sq km. **Urban:** 64.8%. **Ethnic groups:** mestizo 90%, white 9%, Amerindian 1%. **Principal languages:** Spanish (official), Nahua. **Chief religions:** Roman Catholic 57%, Protestant 21%, Jehovah's Witnesses 2%, none 17%.

Geography: Total area: 8,124 sq mi, 21,041 sq km; **Land area:** 8,000 sq mi, 20,721 sq km. **Location:** In Central America. **Neighbors:** Guatemala on W, Honduras on N. **Topography:** A hot Pacific coastal plain in S rises to a cooler plateau and valley region, densely populated. The N is mountainous, including many volcanoes. **Capital:** San Salvador, 1,604,650.

Government: Type: Republic. **Head of state and gov.:** Pres. Mauricio Funes; b. Oct. 18, 1959; in office: June 1, 2009. **Local divisions:** 14 departments. **Defense budget:** $138 mil. **Active troops:** 15,500.

Economy: Industries: food proc., beverages, petroleum, chemicals, fertilizer, textiles, furniture, light metals. **Chief crops:** coffee, sugar, corn, rice, beans, oilseed, cotton, sorghum. **Natural resources:** hydropower, geothermal power, petroleum. **Arable land:** 32.7%. **Livestock:** cattle: 1.4 mil; chickens: 13.5 mil; goats: 15,000; pigs: 422,792; sheep: 5,100. **Fish catch:** 40,500 metric tons. **Electricity prod.:** 5.7 bil kWh. **Labor force:** agric. 21%, industry 20%, services 58%.

Finance: Monetary unit: Colon (SVC) (Sept. 2012: 8.75 = $1 U.S.). This exchange rate has been fixed since 2001, when U.S. dollars went into circulation in El Salvador. **GDP:** $45.2 bil; **per capita GDP:** $7,600; **GDP growth:** 1.4%. **Imports:** $9.8 bil; U.S. 39.4%, Guatemala 9.9%, Mexico 9%, China 5.2%. **Exports:** $5.3 bil; U.S. 44.6%, Guatemala 13.2%, Honduras 9.8%, Nicaragua 5.1%, Germany 4.1%. **Tourism:** $415 mil. **Budget:** $5.3 bil. **Total reserves less gold:** $2.2 bil. **Gold:** 233,100 oz t. **CPI change:** 5.1%.

Transport: Railways: 176 mi (inoperable because of disuse and costs). **Motor vehicles:** 33.1 vehicles per 1,000 pop. **Civil aviation:** 2.2 bil pass.-mi; 5 airports. **Chief ports:** Acajutla, Puerto Cutuco.

Communications: TV sets: 227 per 1,000 pop. **Radios:** 477 per 1,000 pop. **Telephone lines:** 15.3 per 100 pop. **Daily newspaper circ.:** 38 per 1,000 pop. **Internet:** 17.7%.

Health: Life expect.: 70.4 male; 77.1 female. **Births:** 17.4 (per 1,000 pop.). **Deaths:** 5.6 (per 1,000 pop.). **Natural inc.:** 1.18%. **Infant mortality:** 19.7 (per 1,000 live births). **HIV rate:** 0.8%.

Education: Compulsory: ages 4-15. **Literacy:** 84.5%.

Major intl. organizations: UN (FAO, IBRD, ILO, IMF, WHO), OAS, WTO.

Embassy: 1400 16th St. NW, Ste. 100, 20036; 265-9671.

Website: www.presidencia.gob.sv

El Salvador became independent of Spain in 1821, and of the Central American Federation in 1839. A fight with Honduras in 1969 over the presence of 300,000 Salvadoran workers left 2,000 dead.

A military coup overthrew the government of Pres. Carlos Humberto Romero in 1979, but the ruling military-civilian junta failed to quell a rebellion by leftist insurgents, armed by Cuba and Nicaragua. Extreme right-wing death squads organized to eliminate suspected leftists killed thousands in the 1980s. The Reagan administration staunchly supported the government with military aid.

After taking the lives of some 75,000 people (with thousands more "disappeared"), the 12-year civil war ended Jan. 16, 1992, as the government and leftist rebels signed a formal peace treaty. Rightist legislators in the National Assembly passed a sweeping amnesty Mar. 20, 1993, for civil war atrocities.

Members of the right-wing ARENA party held the presidency from 1989 to 2009. Mauricio Funes, a leftist, won the Mar. 15, 2009, presidential election and took office June 1. The right-wing Nationalist Republican Alliance won a majority of congressional seats in Mar. 11, 2012, elections. Remittances from Salvadorans working in the U.S. are a major source of income.

Equatorial Guinea
Republic of Equatorial Guinea

People: Population: 685,991. **Age distrib.:** <15: 41.3%; 65+: 4.1%. **Pop. density:** 63.3 per sq mi, 24.5 per sq km. **Urban:** 39.5%. **Ethnic groups:** Fang 86%, Bubi 7%, Mdowe 4%, Annobon 2%, Bujeba 1%. **Principal languages:** Spanish, French (both official); Fang; Bubi. **Chief religions:** nominally Christian and predominantly Roman Catholic, pagan practices.

Geography: Total area: 10,831 sq mi, 28,051 sq km; **Land area:** 10,831 sq mi, 28,051 sq km. **Location:** Bioko Isl. off W Africa coast in Gulf of Guinea, and Rio Muni, mainland enclave. **Neighbors:** Gabon on S, Cameroon on E and N. **Topography:** Bioko Isl. consists of 2 volcanic mountains and connecting valley. Rio Muni, with over 90% of the area, has coastal plain and low hills beyond. **Capital:** Malabo, 136,971.

Government: Type: Republic. **Head of state:** Pres. Teodoro Obiang Nguema Mbasogo; b. June 5, 1942; in office: Aug. 3, 1979. **Head of gov.:** Prime Min. Vicente Ehate Tomi; b. 1968; in office: May 22, 2012. **Local divisions:** 7 provinces. **Defense budget:** NA. **Active troops:** 1,320.

Economy: Industries: petroleum, nat. gas, sawmilling. **Chief crops:** coffee, cocoa, rice, yams, cassava, bananas, palm oil nuts. **Natural resources:** petroleum, nat. gas, timber, gold, bauxite, diamonds, tantalum, sand and gravel, clay. **Crude oil reserves:** 1.1 bil bbls. **Arable land:** 4.7%. **Livestock:** cattle: 5,200; chickens: 340,000; goats: 9,200; pigs: 6,400; sheep: 39,000. **Fish catch:** 7,391 metric tons. **Electricity prod.:** 97 mil kWh. **Labor force:** NA.

Finance: Monetary unit: CFA BEAC Franc (XAF) (Sept. 2012: 519.73 = $1 U.S.). **GDP:** $26.5 bil; **per capita GDP:** $19,600 (pop. figures uncertain; per capita GDP might be significantly lower); per capita GDP might be significantly lower); **GDP growth:** 7.1%. **Imports:** $7.3 bil; Spain 16.7%, U.S. 12.8%, France 12.1%, China 12%, Italy 6.6%, Côte d'Ivoire 5.8%, Morocco 4.7%. **Exports:** $15.6 bil; Spain 14.6%, China 13%, Italy 10.8%, Japan 10.5%, U.S. 9.5%, Netherlands 7.5%, Canada 5.5%, Brazil 5%, France 4.7%, South Korea 4.1%. **Tourism:** NA. **Budget:** $8.5 bil. **Total reserves less gold:** $3.1 bil. **CPI change:** 6.9%.

Transport: Civil aviation: 6 airports. **Chief ports:** Bata, Luba, Malabo.

Communications: TV sets: 116 per 1,000 pop. **Radios:** 431 per 1,000 pop. **Telephone lines** (2010): 1.9 per 100 pop. **Internet** (2010): 6%.

Health: Life expect.: 61.8 male; 63.8 female. **Births:** 34.9 (per 1,000 pop.). **Deaths:** 8.8 (per 1,000 pop.). **Natural inc.:** 2.61% **Infant mortality:** 75.2 (per 1,000 live births). **HIV rate:** 5%.

Education: Compulsory: ages 7-12. **Literacy:** 93.9%.

Major intl. organizations: UN (FAO, IBRD, ILO, IMF, WHO), AU, WTO (observer).

Embassy: 2020 16th St. NW 20009; 518-5700.

Website: www.state.gov/p/af/ci/ek/

Fernando Po (now Bioko) Island was reached by Portugal in the late 15th cent. and ceded to Spain in 1778. Independence came Oct. 12, 1968. Riots occurred in 1969 over disputes between the island and the more backward Rio Muni province on the mainland.

Masie Nguema Biyogo, a mainlander, became president for life in 1972. His reign, among the most brutal in Africa, left the nation bankrupt; most of the nation's 7,000 Europeans emigrated. He was ousted in a military coup, Aug. 1979. Teodoro Obiang Nguema Mbasogo, leader of the coup, became president and installed his family members in key government posts. Multiparty presidential elections, held in 1996, 2002, and 2009, were seriously flawed. Oil sales, especially to the U.S., have boomed in recent years. Foreign investment in the oil sector has been extensive, but poverty remains widespread. Human Rights Watch (HRW) reported in 2012 that the Obiang regime regularly tortures and arbitrarily detains" suspected dissidents. A referendum on constitutional reforms was overwhelmingly approved Nov. 13, 2011, but HRW reported voter fraud and intimidation.

Eritrea
State of Eritrea

People: Population: 6,086,495. **Age distrib.:** <15: 41.7%; 65+: 3.7%. **Pop. density:** 156.1 per sq mi, 60.3 per sq km. **Urban:** 21.3%. **Ethnic groups:** Tigrinya 55%, Tigre 30%, Saho 4%, Kunama 2%, Rashaida 2%, Bilen 2%, other (Afar, Beni Amir, Nera) 5%. **Principal languages:** Tigrinya, Arabic, English (all official); Tigre; Kunama; Afar; other Cushitic langs. **Chief religions:** Muslim, Coptic Christian, Roman Catholic, Protestant.

Geography: Total area: 45,406 sq mi, 117,600 sq km; **Land area:** 38,996 sq mi, 101,000 sq km. **Location:** In E Africa, on SW coast of Red Sea. **Neighbors:** Ethiopia on S, Djibouti on SE, Sudan on W. **Topography:** Includes many islands of the Dahlak Archipelago, low coastal plains in S, mountain range with peaks to 9,000 ft in N. **Capital:** Asmara, 711,605.

Government: Type: In transition. **Head of state and gov.:** Pres. Isaias Afwerki; b. Feb. 2, 1946; in office: May 24, 1993. **Local divisions:** 8 provinces. **Defense budget:** NA. **Active troops:** 201,750.

Economy: Industries: food proc., beverages, clothing and textiles, light mfg. **Chief crops:** sorghum, lentils, vegetables, corn, cotton, tobacco, sisal. **Natural resources:** gold, potash, zinc, copper, salt, poss. oil and nat. gas, fish. **Arable land:** 6.8%. **Livestock:** cattle: 2.1 mil; chickens: 1.3 mil; goats: 1.8 mil; sheep: 2.3 mil. **Fish catch:** 3,286 metric tons. **Electricity prod.:** 277 mil kWh. **Labor force:** agric. 80%, industry and services 20%.

Finance: Monetary unit: Nakfa (ERN) (Sept. 2012: 15.08 = $1 U.S.). **GDP:** $4.1 bil; **per capita GDP:** $700; **GDP growth:** 8.7%. **Imports:** $900 mil; Saudi Arabia 15.7%, Egypt 11.9%, China 11.1%, India 8.9%, Germany 7.2%, Italy 7.2%, South Africa 6.5%, Brazil 5.9%, South Korea 4.3%. **Exports:** $415.4 mil; Italy 30.5%, Sudan 24%, Saudi Arabia 8.8%, China 8.5%, UK 5.7%, Egypt 4.8%. **Tourism:** NA. **Budget:** $1.02 bil. **Total reserves less gold:** $114.8 mil.

Transport: Railways: 190 mi. **Civil aviation:** 4 airports. **Chief ports:** Assab, Massawa.

Communications: TV sets: 67 per 1,000 pop. **Radios:** 458 per 1,000 pop. **Telephone lines:** 1.1 per 100 pop. **Internet:** 6.2%.

Health: Life expect.: 60.7 male; 65.1 female. **Births:** 32.1 (per 1,000 pop.). **Deaths:** 7.9 (per 1,000 pop.). **Natural inc.:** 2.42% **Infant mortality:** 40.3 (per 1,000 live births). **HIV rate:** 0.8%.

Education: Compulsory: ages 7-14. **Literacy:** 67.8%.

Major intl. organizations: UN (FAO, IBRD, ILO, IMF, WHO), AU. **Embassy:** 1708 New Hampshire Ave. NW 20009; 319-1991. **Website:** www.shabait.com

Eritrea was part of the Ethiopian kingdom of Aksum. It was an Italian colony from 1890 to 1941, when it was captured by the British. Following a period of British and UN supervision, Eritrea was awarded to Ethiopia as part of a federation in 1952. Ethiopia annexed Eritrea as a province in 1962. A 31-year struggle for independence followed, ending when Eritrea formally declared itself an independent nation May 24, 1993. A constitution was ratified in 1997 but not implemented.

A border war with Ethiopia that erupted in June 1998 intensified in May 2000, as Ethiopian troops plunged into western Eritrea; a cease-fire signed June 18 provided for a UN peacekeeping force (UNMEE) to patrol a buffer zone on Eritrean territory. A peace treaty was signed Dec. 12, 2000.

A UN report in July 2007 accused Eritrea of aiding an Islamic insurgency in Somalia. Citing Eritrean obstruction of UNMEE activities, the UN Security Council ended the peacekeeping mission July 31, 2008. Many thousands have fled repressive conditions in Eritrea, including all 12 players from the national soccer team, who defected to Kenya during a Dec. 2009 tournament. The Eritrean government is suspected of plotting a failed attack against an African Union summit conference Jan. 30-31, 2011, in Addis Ababa, Ethiopia. Four Eritrean athletes sought asylum in the UK during the 2012 Summer Olympics in London.

Estonia
Republic of Estonia

People: Population: 1,274,709. **Age distrib.:** <15: 15.3%; 65+: 18%. **Pop. density:** 77.9 per sq mi, 30.1 per sq km. **Urban:** 69.5%. **Ethnic groups:** Estonian 69%, Russian 26%, Ukrainian 2%, Belarusian 1%, Finn 1%. **Principal languages:** Estonian (official), Russian. **Chief religions:** Evangelical Lutheran 14%, Orthodox 13%, unaffiliated 34%, none 6%.

Geography: Total area: 17,463 sq mi, 45,228 sq km; **Land area:** 16,366 sq mi, 42,388 sq km. **Location:** E Europe, bordering Baltic Sea and Gulf of Finland. **Neighbors:** Russia on E, Latvia on S. **Topography:** Marshy lowland with numerous lakes and swamps; about 40% forested. Elongated hills show evidence of former glaciation. More than 800 islands on Baltic coast. **Capital:** Tallinn, 400,308.

Government: Type: Republic. **Head of state:** Pres. Toomas Hendrik Ilves; b. Dec. 26, 1953; in office: Oct. 9, 2006. **Head of gov.:** Prime Min. Andrus Ansip; b. Oct. 1, 1956; in office: Apr. 13, 2005. **Local divisions:** 15 counties. **Defense budget:** $393 mil. **Active troops:** 5,750.

Economy: Industries: engineering, electronics, wood and wood prods., textiles, information technology, telecom. **Chief crops:** grain, potatoes, vegetables. **Natural resources:** oil shale, peat, rare earth elements, phosphorite, clay, limestone, sand, dolomite, sea mud. **Arable land:** 14.1%. **Livestock:** cattle: 234,700; chickens: 1.8 mil; goats: 3,900; pigs: 365,100; sheep: 76,500. **Fish catch:** 96,322 metric tons. **Electricity prod.:** (2010): 12.9 bil kWh. **Labor force:** agric. 4.2%, industry 20.2%, services 75.6%.

Finance: Monetary unit: Euro (EUR) (Sept. 2012: 0.79 = $1 U.S.). **GDP:** $27.7 bil; **per capita GDP:** $20,600; **GDP growth:** 7.6%. **Imports:** $17.1 bil; Finland 13.4%, Latvia 11.6%, Sweden 11.3%, Germany 10.9%, Lithuania 8.7%, Poland 7.2%, China 4.7%. **Exports:** $16.8 bil; Sweden 17%, Finland 16.3%, Russia 11.9%, Latvia 8.6%, Germany 4.9%, Lithuania 4.9%. **Tourism:** $1.2 bil. **Budget:** $8.6 bil. **Total reserves less gold:** $194.9 mil. **Gold:** 8,000 oz t. **CPI change:** 4.98%.

Transport: Railways: 743 mi. **Civil aviation:** 223.1 mil pass.-mi; 13 airports. **Chief ports:** Kuivastu, Kunda, Muuga, Sillamae, Tallinn. **Communications: TV sets:** 511 per 1,000 pop. **Radios:** 1,200 per 1,000 pop. **Telephone lines:** 35.1 per 100 pop. **Daily newspaper circ.:** 190.6 per 1,000 pop. **Internet:** 76.5%.

Health: Life expect.: 68.3 male; 79.2 female. **Births:** 10.4 (per 1,000 pop.). **Deaths:** 13.6 (per 1,000 pop.). **Natural inc.:** −0.32%. **Infant mortality:** 6.9 (per 1,000 live births). **HIV rate:** 1.2%.

Education: Compulsory: ages 7-15. **Literacy:** 99.8%.

Major intl. organizations: UN (FAO, IBRD, ILO, IMF, WHO), EU, NATO, OECD, OSCE, WTO. **Embassy:** 2131 Massachusetts Ave. NW 20008; 588-0101. **Website:** www.eesti.ee

Estonia, a province of imperial Russia before World War I, was independent between World Wars I and II. The USSR conquered it in 1940 and incorporated it as the Estonian SSR. During an abortive Soviet coup, Estonia, Aug. 20, 1991, declared immediate full independence, which the Soviet Union recognized Sept. 1991. The first free elections in over 50 years were held Sept. 20, 1992. The last occupying Russian troops departed Aug. 31, 1994.

Estonia became a full member of the EU and NATO in 2004. The government accused Russia of orchestrating a cyber attack against Estonia's computer network in Apr.-May 2007. A former high-ranking defense official, Herman Simm, was convicted of treason Feb. 25, 2009, for passing Estonian and NATO security secrets to Russia. Estonia adopted the euro Jan. 1, 2011.

Ethiopia
Federal Democratic Republic of Ethiopia

People: Population: 91,195,675. **Age distrib.:** <15: 44.6%; 65+: 2.8%. **Pop. density:** 236.2 per sq mi, 91.2 per sq km. **Urban:** 17%. **Ethnic groups:** Oromo 35%, Amara 27%, Somalie 6%, Tigraway 6%, Sidama 4%, Guragie 3%, Welaita 2%, Hadiya 2%, Affar 2%, Gamo 2%, Gedeo 1%. **Principal languages:** Amarigna (Amharic) (official); Oromigna, Tigrigna (both official regional); Somaligna; Guaragigna; Sidamigna; Hadiyigna; English (official; major foreign lang. taught in schools); Arabic (official). **Chief religions:** Orthodox 44%, Muslim 34%, Protestant 19%, traditional 3%.

Geography: Total area: 426,373 sq mi, 1,104,300 sq km; **Land area:** 386,102 sq mi, 1,000,000 sq km. **Location:** In E Africa. **Neighbors:** Sudan on W; Kenya on S; Somalia, Djibouti on E; Eritrea on N. **Topography:** A high central plateau, 6,000-10,000 ft high, rises to higher mountains near the Great Rift Valley, cutting in from SW. Blue Nile and other rivers cross the plateau, which descends to plains on both W and SE. **Capital:** Addis Ababa, 2,979,100.

Government: Type: Federal republic. **Head of state:** Pres. Girma Wolde Giorgis; b. Dec. 1924; in office: Oct. 8, 2001. **Head of gov.:** Prime Min. Hailemariam Desalegn; b. July 19, 1965; in office: Aug. 21, 2012. **Local divisions:** 9 states, 2 charted cities. **Defense budget:** $257 mil. **Active troops:** 138,000.

Economy: Industries: food proc., beverages, textiles, leather, chemicals, metals proc., cement. **Chief crops:** cereals, pulses, coffee, oilseed, cotton, sugarcane, potatoes, qat, cut flowers. **Natural resources:** gold, platinum, copper, potash, nat. gas, hydropower. **Crude oil reserves:** 430,000 bbls. **Arable land:** 13.9%. **Livestock:** cattle: 53.4 mil; chickens: 49.3 mil; goats: 22.8 mil; pigs: 29,000; sheep: 25.5 mil. **Fish catch:** 18,083 metric tons. **Electricity prod.:** 4 bil kWh. **Labor force:** agric. 85%, industry 5%, services 10%.

Finance: Monetary unit: Birr (ETB) (Sept. 2012: 17.92 = $1 U.S.). **GDP:** $96.1 bil; **per capita GDP:** $1,100; **GDP growth:** 7.5%. **Imports:** $8.3 bil; Saudi Arabia 10.2%, China 10.2%, U.S. 7.8%. **Exports:** $2.8 bil; Germany 13.7%, China 11.8%, Belgium 7.5%, Saudi Arabia 6.5%, U.S. 6%, Italy 4.9%, Sudan 4.1%. **Tourism:** $522 mil. **Budget:** $6 bil. **Total reserves less gold** (2009): $1.8 bil. **CPI change:** 33.2%.

Transport: Railways: 423 mi (part of Addis Ababa-Djibouti railway, under joint control with Djibouti, but largely inoperable). **Motor vehicles:** 1.6 vehicles per 1,000 pop. **Civil aviation:** 6.1 bil pass.-mi; 17 airports. **Chief port:** None. A landlocked country, Ethiopia uses ports in Djibouti and Somalia. **Communications: TV sets:** 7 per 1,000 pop. **Radios:** 171 per 1,000 pop. **Telephone lines:** 1 user per 100 pop. **Daily newspaper circ.:** 4.6 per 1,000 pop. **Internet:** 1.1%.

Health: Life expect.: 57.0 male; 61.5 female. **Births:** 38.5 (per 1,000 pop.). **Deaths:** 9.3 (per 1,000 pop.). **Natural inc.:** 2.92% **Infant mortality:** 60.9 (per 1,000 live births). **HIV rate:** NA.

Education: Compulsory ages: NA. **Literacy:** 39%.

Major intl. organizations: UN (FAO, IBRD, ILO, IMF, WHO), AU, WTO (observer). **Embassy:** 3506 International Dr. NW 20008; 364-1200. **Website:** www.ethiopia.gov.et

Ethiopian culture was influenced by Egypt and Greece. Italy invaded the region in 1880, but it maintained its independence until the Italian invasion of 1936. British forces freed the country in 1941.

A series of droughts in the 1970s killed hundreds of thousands. An army mutiny, strikes, and student demonstrations led to the dethronement, Sept. 12, 1974, of Ethiopia's last emperor, Haile Selassie I, ending his 58-year reign; he died a prisoner of the ruling junta, known as the Dergue, Aug. 1975. The junta dissolved parliament, abolished the monarchy, established a socialist state, redistributed land, curbed the influence of the Coptic Church, and violently suppressed opposition.

The regime, torn by bloody coups, faced uprisings by tribal and political groups aided in part by Sudan and Somalia. Ties with the U.S., once a major ally, deteriorated, while cooperation accords were signed with the USSR in 1977. In 1978, Soviet advisers and Cuban troops helped defeat Somali forces. Ethiopia and Somalia signed a peace agreement in 1988.

A worldwide relief effort began in 1984, as an extended drought precipitated famine; up to 1 mil people died as a result.

The Ethiopian People's Revolutionary Democratic Front (EPRDF), an umbrella group of 6 rebel armies, launched a major push against government forces, Feb. 1991. In May, Pres. Mengistu Haile Mariam resigned, finding refuge in Zimbabwe. The EPRDF set up a transitional government. Ethiopia's first multiparty general elections were held in 1995.

Eritrea, a province on the Red Sea, declared its independence May 24, 1993. Fighting along the border with Eritrea, which erupted in June 1998, intensified in May 2000, as Ethiopian forces entered Eritrean territory; a cease-fire was signed June 18 and a peace treaty Dec. 12. The war displaced 350,000 Ethiopians and cost the country nearly $3 bil.

The ruling EPRDF won parliamentary elections May 15, 2005, but opposition parties made big gains. Police opened fire on anti-government protesters in Addis Ababa, June 8, killing at least

36; the government arrested some 3,000 dissidents. Police suppression of further protests in the capital, Nov. 1-4, left at least 46 dead. As part of a crackdown on Oromo Liberation Front rebels, the government rounded up thousands of Oromo, Nov. 2005-Jan. 2006. In July 2006, Ethiopia sent troops into Somalia in response to advances by Islamist militias there. Tried in absentia, former Pres. Mengistu was convicted of genocide Dec. 12, 2006. Drought and other food supply disruptions led Ethiopia June 2008 to appeal for $325 mil in emergency aid; the nation requested $175 mil in additional food aid Oct. 2009. Ethiopia pulled its troops out of Somalia Jan. 2009. The EPRDF dominated parliamentary elections May 23, 2010, though the opposition contested the results, accusing the EPRDF of voter fraud. As of June 2012, Ethiopia housed 195,000 refugees fleeing violence and famine in Somalia. Prime Min. Meles Zenawi died Aug. 21, 2012; the EPRDF's Hailemariam Desalegn became acting prime min.

Fiji
Republic of Fiji

People: Population: 890,057. **Age distrib.:** <15: 28.6%; 65+: 5.4%. **Pop. density:** 126.1 per sq mi, 48.7 per sq km. **Urban:** 52.2%. **Ethnic groups:** Fijian (predominantly Melanesian with Polynesian) 57%, Indian 38%, Rotuman 1%, other (European, other Pacific Islanders, Chinese) 4%. **Principal languages:** English, Fijian (both official); Hindustani. **Chief religions:** Protestant 55% (Methodist 35%, Assembly of God 6%, Seventh-Day Adventist 4%), Hindu 28%, Roman Catholic 9%, Muslim 6%.

Geography: Total area: 7,056 sq mi, 18,274 sq km; **Land area:** 7,056 sq mi, 18,274 sq km. **Location:** In western S Pacific O. **Neighbors:** Nearest are Vanuatu to W, Tonga to E. **Topography:** 322 isls. (106 inhabited), many mountainous, with tropical forests and large fertile areas. Viti Levu, the largest isl., has over half the total land area. **Capital:** Suva, 177,316.

Government: Type: In transition. **Head of state:** Pres. Ratu Epeli Nailatikau; b. July 5, 1941; in office: Nov. 5, 2009 (acting from July 30). **Head of gov.:** Interim Prime Min. Vorege (Frank) Bainimarama; b. Apr. 27, 1954; in office: Jan. 5, 2007. **Local divisions:** 4 divisions comprising 14 provinces and 1 dependency. **Defense budget:** $66 mil. **Active troops:** 3,500.

Economy: Industries: tourism, sugar, clothing, copra, gold, silver, lumber. **Chief crops:** sugarcane, coconuts, cassava, rice, sweet potatoes, bananas. **Natural resources:** timber, fish, gold, copper, offshore oil potential, hydropower. **Arable land:** 8.8%. **Livestock:** cattle: 312,000; chickens: 3.5 mil; goats: 255,000; pigs: 145,000; sheep: 6,200. **Fish catch:** 42,274 metric tons. **Electricity prod.** (2010): 869.1 mil kWh. **Labor force:** agric. 70%, industry and services 30%.

Finance: Monetary unit: Dollar (FJD) (Sept. 2012: 1.81 = $1 U.S.). **GDP:** $4.2 bil; **per capita GDP:** $4,700; **GDP growth:** 2%. **Imports:** $1.8 bil; Singapore 34.1%, Australia 16.3%, New Zealand 14.1%, China 8.9%. **Exports:** $901.5 mil; Australia 14.3%, U.S. 11%, Japan 6.3%, UK 5.9%, Samoa 5.8%, Tonga 5.1%. **Tourism:** $523 mil. **Budget:** $1.1 bil. **Total reserves less gold:** $832.2 mil. **Gold:** 800 oz t. **CPI change:** 8.5%.

Transport: Railways: 371 mi. **Motor vehicles:** 166.7 vehicles per 1,000 pop. **Civil aviation:** 2.2 bil pass.-mi; 4 airports. **Chief ports:** Lautoka, Levuka, Suva.

Communications: TV sets: 117 per 1,000 pop. **Radios:** 678 per 1,000 pop. **Telephone lines:** 15 per 100 pop. **Daily newspaper circ.:** 53.5 per 1,000 pop. **Internet:** 28%.

Health: Life expect.: 69.0 male; 74.3 female. **Births:** 20.7 (per 1,000 pop.). **Deaths:** 5.9 (per 1,000 pop.). **Natural inc.:** 1.48% **Infant mortality:** 10.7 (per 1,000 live births). **HIV rate:** 0.1%.

Education: Compulsory: ages 6-15. **Literacy:** NA.

Major intl. organizations: UN (FAO, IBRD, ILO, IMF, WHO), WTO.

Embassy: 2000 M St. NW, Ste. 710, 20036; 466-8320.

Website: www.fiji.gov.fj

A British colony since 1874, Fiji became independent Oct. 10, 1970. Cultural differences between the Indian community (descendants of contract laborers brought to the islands in the 19th cent.) and indigenous Fijians have led to political polarization. More than 100,000 Indians have left Fiji since the mid-1980s.

Military coups have been frequent in recent decades. Fiji's first Indian prime minister, Mahendra Chaudhry, took office May 19, 1999. He and other government officials were taken captive May 19, 2000, by indigenous Fijian gunmen led by George Speight. The hostage crisis culminated in a military takeover, May 29, led by Frank Bainimarama. Release of the last remaining hostages in July 2000 coincided with the installation of an interim military-backed government. Speight was later tried for treason; he was sentenced to life in prison, Feb. 18, 2002. Prime Min. Laisenia Qarase headed an elected civilian government, 2001-06. He retained his office in parliamentary voting, May 6-13, 2006, but was ousted in a military coup Dec. 5, and Bainimarama took office as interim prime minister. After a court ruled Apr. 9, 2009, that the 2006 coup was illegal, Pres. Ratu Josefa Iloilo abrogated the constitution, dissolved the judiciary, and reappointed Interim Prime Min. Bainimarama. In July, Bainimarama promised a new constitution by 2013 and legislative elections by 2014; he also named Vice Pres. Ratu Epeli Nailatikau

to replace the retiring Pres. Iloilo, who died Feb. 6, 2011. In a move applauded by neighbors Australia and New Zealand, Bainimarama announced Jan. 1, 2012, that the state of emergency in place since 2009, which banned public meetings and imposed other limits on civil liberties, would be lifted Jan. 7. However, on Jan 5 he announced new, albeit less severe, civil liberty regulations.

Finland
Republic of Finland

People: Population: 5,262,930. **Age distrib.:** <15: 15.9%; 65+: 18.5%. **Pop. density:** 44.9 per sq mi, 17.3 per sq km. **Urban:** 83.7%. **Ethnic groups:** Finn 93%, Swede 6%, Russian 1%. **Principal languages:** Finnish, Swedish (both official). **Chief religions:** Lutheran Church of Finland 83%, Orthodox Church 1%, none 15%.

Geography: Total area: 130,559 sq mi, 338,145 sq km; **Land area:** 117,304 sq mi, 303,815 sq km. **Location:** In N Europe. **Neighbors:** Norway on N, Sweden on W, Russia on E. **Topography:** South and central are generally flat areas with low hills and many lakes. The N has mountainous areas, 3,000-4,000 ft above sea level. **Capital:** Helsinki, 1,133,780.

Government: Type: Constitutional republic. **Head of state:** Pres. Sauli Ninisto; b. Aug. 24, 1948; in office: Mar. 1, 2012. **Head of gov.:** Prime Min. Jyrki Katainen; b. Oct. 14, 1971; in office: June 22, 2011. **Local divisions:** 6 laanit (provinces). **Defense budget:** $3.43 bil. **Active troops:** 22,100.

Economy: Industries: metals and metal prods., electronics, machinery and scientific instruments, shipbuilding, pulp and paper, foodstuffs, chemicals, textiles, clothing. **Chief crops:** barley, wheat, sugar beets, potatoes. **Natural resources:** timber, iron ore, copper, lead, zinc, chromite, nickel, gold, silver, limestone. **Arable land:** 7.4%. **Livestock:** cattle: 925,808; chickens: 4.6 mil; goats: 4,890; pigs: 1.4 mil; sheep: 125,673. **Fish catch:** 170,929 metric tons. **Electricity prod.** (2010): 76.2 bil kWh. **Labor force:** agric. and forestry 4.4%; industry 15.5%; constr. 7.1%; commerce 21.3%; finance, insurance, and business services 13.3%; transp. and communications 9.9%; public services 28.5%.

Finance: Monetary unit: Euro (EUR) (Sept. 2012: 0.79 = $1 U.S.). **GDP:** $198.2 bil; **per capita GDP:** $36,700; **GDP growth:** 2.9%. **Imports:** $80.4 bil; Russia 18%, Sweden 14.1%, Germany 13.9%, Netherlands 7.8%, China 4.3%. **Exports:** $78.8 bil; Sweden 12.1%, Germany 10.2%, Russia 9.5%, Netherlands 6.9%, UK 5.3%, U.S. 5.1%, China 4.8%. **Tourism:** $3.6 bil. **Budget:** $137.6 bil (central govt. budget). **Total reserves less gold:** $7.9 bil. **Gold:** 1.6 mil oz t. **CPI change:** 3.5%.

Transport: Railways: 3,678 mi. **Motor vehicles:** 611.6 vehicles per 1,000 pop. **Civil aviation:** 10.2 bil pass.-mi; 75 airports. **Chief ports:** Helsinki, Kotka, Naantali, Porvoo, Raahe, Rauma.

Communications: TV sets: 679 per 1,000 pop. **Radios:** 1,623 per 1,000 pop. **Telephone lines:** 20.1 per 100 pop. **Daily newspaper circ.:** 431.1 per 1,000 pop. **Internet:** 89.4%.

Health: Life expect.: 75.9 male; 83.0 female. **Births:** 10.4 (per 1,000 pop.). **Deaths:** 10.3 (per 1,000 pop.). **Natural inc.:** 0% **Infant mortality:** 3.4 (per 1,000 live births). **HIV rate:** 0.1%.

Education: Compulsory: ages 7-16. **Literacy:** 100%.

Major intl. organizations: UN (FAO, IBRD, ILO, IMF, WHO), EU, OECD, OSCE, WTO.

Embassy: 3301 Massachusetts Ave. NW 20008; 298-5800.

Website: www.government.fi

The early Finns probably migrated from the Ural area at about the beginning of the Christian era. Swedish settlers brought the country into Sweden, 1154 to 1809, when Finland became an autonomous grand duchy of the Russian Empire. Russian exactions created a strong national spirit; on Dec. 6, 1917, Finland declared its independence, and in 1919 it became a republic.

On Nov. 30, 1939, the Soviet Union invaded, and the Finns were forced to cede 16,173 sq mi of territory. After World War II, further cessions were exacted. In 1948, Finland signed a treaty of mutual assistance with the USSR; Finland and Russia nullified this treaty with a new pact in Jan. 1992.

Following approval by Finnish voters in an advisory referendum Oct. 16, 1994, Finland entered the EU Jan. 1, 1995. Pres. Tarja Halonen won a second 6-year term, Jan. 29, 2006. Former Pres. Martti Ahtisaari was awarded the Nobel Peace Prize, Oct. 10, 2008, for his efforts in mediating international conflicts. Following parliamentary elections Apr. 17, 2011, Jyrki Katainen, leader of the conservative National Coalition Party, became prime minister. The conservative Sauli Niinistö won the presidential election Feb. 5, 2012, and assumed office Mar. 1.

Aland, or Ahvenanmaa, constituting an autonomous province, is a group of small islands, 590 sq mi, in the Gulf of Bothnia, 25 mi from Sweden, 15 mi from Finland. Mariehamn is the chief port.

France
French Republic

People: Population: 65,630,692. **Age distrib.:** <15: 18.7%; 65+: 17.5%. **Pop. density:** 265.4 per sq mi, 102.5 per sq km. **Urban:** 85.8%. **Ethnic groups:** Celtic and Latin with Teutonic, Slavic, N African, Indochinese, Basque minorities. **Principal languages:** French (official); rapidly declining regional dialects (Provençal, Breton, Alsatian, Corsican, Catalan, Basque, Flemish). **Chief religions:** Roman Catholic 83%-88%, Muslim 5%-10%, Protestant 2%, Jewish 1%.

Geography: Total area: 248,573 sq mi, 643,801 sq km; **Land area:** 247,270 sq mi, 640,427 sq km. **Location:** In W Europe, between Atlantic O. and Medit. Sea. **Neighbors:** Spain, Andorra, Monaco on S; Italy, Switzerland, Germany on E; Luxembourg, Belgium on N. **Topography:** A wide plain covers more than half of the country, in N and W, drained to W by Seine, Loire, Garonne rivers. The Massif Central is a mountainous plateau in center. In E are Alps (Mt. Blanc is tallest in W Europe, 15,771 ft), the lower Jura range, and forested Vosges. The Rhone flows from Lake Geneva to Mediterranean. Pyrenees are in SW, on border with Spain. **Capital:** Paris, 10,620,100. **Cities (urban aggl.):** Marseille-Aix-en-Provence, 1,488,596; Lyon, 1,487,507; Lille, 1,042,382.

Government: Type: Republic. **Head of state:** Pres. François Hollande; b. Aug. 12, 1954; in office: May 15, 2012. **Head of gov.:** Prime Min. François Fillon; b. Mar. 4, 1954; in office: May 17, 2007. **Local divisions:** 22 administrative regions containing 96 departments. **Defense budget:** $58.8 bil. **Active troops:** 238,591.

Economy: Industries: machinery, chemicals, automobiles, metallurgy, aircraft, electronics, textiles, food proc., tourism. **Chief crops:** wheat, cereals, sugar beets, potatoes, wine grapes. **Natural resources:** coal, iron ore, bauxite, zinc, uranium, antimony, arsenic, potash, feldspar, fluorspar, gypsum, timber, fish. **Crude oil reserves:** 90 mil bbls. **Other resources:** Timber, dairy. **Arable land:** 33.5%. **Livestock:** cattle: 19.6 mil; chickens: 124.2 mil; goats: 1.3 mil; pigs: 14.5 mil; sheep: 8 mil. **Fish catch:** 674,404 metric tons. **Electricity prod.** (2010): 539 bil kWh. **Labor force:** agric. 3.8%, industry 24.3%, services 71.8%.

Finance: Monetary unit: Euro (EUR) (Sept. 2012: 0.79 = $1 U.S.). **GDP:** $2.2 tril; **per capita GDP:** $35,600; **GDP growth:** 1.7%. **Imports:** $688.5 bil; Germany 19.1%, Belgium 11.3%, Italy 7.7%, Netherlands 7.5%, Spain 6.6%, UK 5.1%, China 4.8%. **Exports:** $587.1 bil; Germany 16.7%, Italy 8.3%, Spain 7.4%, Belgium 7.4%, UK 6.7%, U.S. 5%, Netherlands 4.3%. **Tourism:** $53.8 bil. **Budget:** $1.5 tril. **Total reserves less gold:** $48.6 bil. **Gold:** 78.3 mil oz t. **CPI change:** 2.1%.

Transport: Railways: 18,417 mi. **Motor vehicles:** 581.2 vehicles per 1,000 pop. **Civil aviation:** 94.6 bil pass.-mi (incl. airlines based in territories and dependencies); 297 airports. **Chief ports:** Calais, Dunkerque, Le Havre, Marseille, Nantes, Paris, Rouen.

Communications: TV sets: 661 per 1,000 pop. **Radios:** 943 per 1,000 pop. **Telephone lines:** 55.9 per 100 pop. **Daily newspaper circ.:** 163.5 per 1,000 pop. **Internet:** 79.6%.

Health: Life expect.: 78.4 male; 84.7 female. **Births:** 12.7 (per 1,000 pop.). **Deaths:** 8.9 (per 1,000 pop.). **Natural inc.:** 0.39% **Infant mortality:** 3.4 (per 1,000 live births). **HIV rate:** 0.4%.

Education: Compulsory: ages 6-16. **Literacy:** 99%.

Major intl. organizations: UN and most of its specialized agencies, EU, NATO, OECD, OSCE, WTO.

Embassy: 4101 Reservoir Rd. NW 20007; 944-6195.

Website: www.gouvernement.fr

Celtic Gaul was conquered by Julius Caesar 58-51 BCE; Romans ruled for 500 years. Under Charlemagne, Frankish rule extended over much of Europe. After his death France emerged as one of the successor kingdoms.

The monarchy was overthrown in the French Revolution (1789-93) and succeeded by the First Republic, followed by the First Empire under Napoleon (1804-15), a monarchy (1814-48), the Second Republic (1848-52), the Second Empire (1852-70), the Third Republic (1871-1946), the Fourth Republic (1946-58), and the Fifth Republic (1958 to present).

France suffered severe losses in manpower and wealth in WWI, when it was invaded by Germany. By the Treaty of Versailles, France exacted return of Alsace and Lorraine, provinces seized by Germany in 1871. Germany invaded France again in May 1940, and signed an armistice with a government based in Vichy. After France was liberated by the Allies in Sept. 1944, Gen. Charles de Gaulle became head of the provisional government, serving until 1946. De Gaulle again became premier in 1958, during a crisis over Algeria, and obtained voter approval for a new constitution, ushering in the Fifth Republic. He then became president.

France withdrew from Indochina in 1954 and from Morocco and Tunisia in 1956. Most of its remaining African territories, including Algeria, were freed 1958-62.

In May 1968, rebellious students in Paris and other centers rioted, battled police, and were joined by workers who launched nationwide strikes. The government awarded pay increases to the strikers May 26. De Gaulle resigned from office in Apr. 1969, after losing a nationwide referendum on constitutional reform. Georges Pompidou was elected to succeed him. After Pompidou's death, in 1974, Valery Giscard d'Estaing was elected president; he continued the basically conservative policies of his predecessors.

On May 10, 1981, France elected François Mitterrand, a Socialist, president. Under Mitterrand the government nationalized 5 major industries and most private banks. After 1986, however, when rightists won a narrow victory in the National Assembly, Mitterrand chose conservative Jacques Chirac as premier. A 2-year period of "cohabitation" ensued, and France pursued a privatization program, selling many state-owned companies. After Mitterrand was elected to a second 7-year term in 1988, he appointed a Socialist as premier. The center-right won a large majority in 1993 legislative elections, ushering in another period of "cohabitation" with a conservative premier.

Chirac won the presidency in a runoff election May 7, 1995. He cut government spending to meet budgetary goals for the introduction of a common European currency, the euro. With unemployment at nearly 13%, legislative elections completed June 1, 1997, produced a decisive victory for the leftist parties. The result was a new period of "cohabitation," this time between a conservative president and a Socialist prime minister, Lionel Jospin.

French voters, disaffected by government scandals, shocked the political establishment in presidential voting Apr. 21, 2002, by giving Jean-Marie Le Pen, leader of the far-right National Front, a second place finish. Chirac easily won the May 5 runoff, and his center-right allies won parliamentary elections June 9 and 16. Parliament gave final approval, Mar. 3, 2004, to a law barring the wearing of Islamic head scarves and other religious symbols in public schools.

Displeased with sluggish economic growth, high unemployment, and budget cuts in entitlement programs, voters rejected, May 29, 2005, a proposed EU constitution supported by the Chirac government. A state of emergency was declared Nov. 8 after 12 days of riots that began in Paris and spread to some 300 French cities and towns; rioters were mainly young immigrants from N and W Africa. After a wave of mass protests and strikes, Chirac agreed, Apr. 10, 2006, to rescind a law that made it easier for employers to fire inexperienced young workers.

The conservative Nicolas Sarkozy won a presidential runoff election May 6, 2007. The French bank Société Générale disclosed Jan. 24, 2008, that it had lost more than $7 bil because of a rogue trader, who was sentenced to 3 years in prison and ordered to pay restitution Oct. 5, 2010.

Sarkozy responded to the global recession, Dec. 4, 2008, with a $33 bil economic stimulus plan focused on infrastructure development; measures announced Feb. 18, 2009, following labor protests, added $3.3 bil in aid for lower-income people. A French court Jan. 28, 2010, acquitted former Prime Min. Dominique de Villepin of conspiring to smear Sarkozy during the campaign. Sarkozy's policy of shutting Roma (Gypsy) encampments and expelling thousands of Roma to Romania and Bulgaria drew public rebukes from EU allies, Sept. 2010.

France, a founding member of NATO, formally returned to the alliance's military command structure Apr. 2009 after 43 years. In Sept 2012, France had about 3,3000 troops deployed with NATO forces in Afghanistan. France participated in military operations that removed Pres. Laurent Gbagbo from power in Côte d'Ivoire, Apr. 11, 2011, and ousted Libyan leader Muammar al-Qaddafi, Aug. 23, 2011.

Former Pres. Chirac was convicted Dec. 15, 2011, of corruption charges stemming from his tenure (1977-95) as mayor of Paris. With France's economy still struggling, the socialist François Hollande won a presidential runoff over incumbent Sarkozy May 6, 2012; he took office May 15. The Socialist Party also won an absolute majority in parliamentary elections June 17.

The island of **Corsica**, in the Mediterranean W of Italy and N of Sardinia, is a territorial collectivity and region of France comprising 2 departments. It elects a total of 2 senators and 3 deputies to the French Parliament. Area: 3,369 sq mi; pop. (2006 census): 294,118. The capital is Ajaccio, birthplace of Napoleon I. Violence by Corsican separatist groups has hurt tourism, a leading industry on the island. Corsicans rejected, 51%-49%, a limited autonomy plan in a referendum July 6, 2003.

Overseas Departments

French Guiana is on the NE coast of South America with Suriname on the W and Brazil on the E and S. Its area is 35,135 sq mi (total); 34,421 sq mi (land); pop. (2011 est.) 237,200. Guiana sends one senator and 2 deputies to the French Parliament. Guiana is administered by a prefect and has a Council General of 16 elected members; capital is Cayenne.

The famous penal colony, Devil's Island, was phased out between 1938 and 1951. The European Space Agency maintains a satellite-launching center (established by France in 1964) in the city of Kourou.

Immense forests of rich timber cover 88% of the land. Fishing (especially shrimp), forestry, and gold mining are the most important industries. Natural resources include petroleum, kaolin, niobium, tantalum, and clay.

Guadeloupe, in the West Indies' Leeward Islands, consists of 2 large islands, Basse-Terre and Grande-Terre, separated by the Salt River, plus Marie Galante and the Saintes group to the S and, to the N, Desirade. A French possession since 1635, the department is represented in the French Parliament; administration consists of a prefect (governor) as well as an elected general and regional councils. St. Barthelemy and over half of Sint Martin (the Netherlands' portion is called St. Maarten), both formerly part of Guadeloupe, voted for secession in 2003 and became separate overseas territorial collectivities in 2007.

Area of the islands is 525 sq mi; pop. (2011 est., incl. St. Barthelemy and St. Martin) 463,000, mainly descendants of slaves; capital is Basse-Terre on Basse-Terre Island. The land is fertile; sugar, rum, and bananas are exported. Tourism is an important industry.

Martinique, the northernmost of the Windward Islands, in the West Indies, has been a possession since 1635, and a department since Mar. 1946. It is represented in the French Parliament by 2 senators and 4 deputies. The island was the birthplace of Napoleon's first wife, Empress Josephine.

It has an area of 425 sq mi (total); 409 sq mi (land); pop. (2008 est.) 407,000, mostly descendants of slaves. The capital is Fort-de-France, pop. (2006): 90,347. It is a popular tourist stop. The chief exports are rum, bananas, and petroleum products. **Website:** www.region-martinique.mq

Mayotte, claimed by Comoros and administered by France, voted in 1976 to become a territorial collectivity of France. An island NW of Madagascar, area is 144 sq mi, pop. (2010 est.) 231,139. The capital is Mamoudzou. In a Mar. 29, 2009, referendum, 95% of voters endorsed a plan under which Mayotte became an overseas department of France as of Mar. 31, 2011.

Réunion is a volcanic island in the Indian O. about 420 mi E of Madagascar, and has belonged to France since 1665. Area, 972 sq mi (total); 968 sq mi (land); pop. (2011 est.) 839,500, 30% of French extraction. Capital: Saint-Denis. The chief export is sugar. It elects 5 deputies, 3 senators to the French Parliament. **Website:** www.wereunion.re

Overseas Territorial Collectivities

French Polynesia, comprises 130 islands widely scattered among 5 archipelagos in the S Pacific; administered by a Council of Ministers (headed by a president). Territorial Assembly and the Council have headquarters at Papeete, on Tahiti, one of the Society Islands (which include the Windward Isls. and Leeward Isls.). Two deputies and a senator are elected to the French Parliament.

Other groups are the Marquesas Islands; the Tuamotu Archipelago; the Gambier Islands; and the Austral, or Tubuai, Islands.

Total area of the islands administered from Tahiti is 1,609 sq mi (total); 1,478 sq mi (land); pop. (2011 est.) 291,000, more than half on Tahiti. Tahiti is mountainous with a productive coastline bearing coconuts, citrus, pineapples, and vanilla. Cultured pearls are also produced.

Tahiti was visited by Capt. James Cook in 1769 and by Capt. Bligh in the *Bounty*, 1788-89. Its beauty impressed Herman Melville, Paul Gauguin, and Charles Darwin. A coalition favoring independence for French Polynesia within 20 years gained control of the territorial assembly after elections May 23, 2004.

St. Pierre and Miquelon became a territorial collectivity in 1985. It consists of 2 groups of rocky islands near the SW coast of Newfoundland, inhabited by fishermen. Fish products are the chief export. The St. Pierre group has an area of 10 sq mi; Miquelon, 83 sq mi. Total pop. (2011 est.) 5,888. Capital: Saint-Pierre. Both Mayotte and St. Pierre and Miquelon elect a deputy and a senator to the French Parliament.

St. Barthelemy and **St. Martin** became overseas territorial collectivities in 2007, with total pop. (2012 est.) of 7,332 and 30,959, respectively.

The territorial collectivity of **Wallis and Futuna** comprises 2 island groups in the SW Pacific S of Tuvalu, N of Fiji, and W of Western Samoa; became an overseas territory July 29, 1961. The islands have a total area of 55 sq mi and pop. (2012 est.) of 15,453. Alofi, attached to Futuna, is uninhabited. Capital: Mata-Utu. Chief products are copra, yams, taro roots, bananas, and coconuts. A senator and a deputy are elected to the French Parliament.

Overseas Territory and Special Collectivity

The territory of the **French Southern and Antarctic Lands** comprises Adelie Land, on Antarctica, and island groups in the Indian O. Area: 2,991 sq mi (total); 2,960 sq mi (land).

Adelie, reached 1840, has a 185-mi coastline and tapers 1,240 mi inland to the S Pole. (The U.S. does not recognize national claims in Antarctica.) It has a research station. There are 2 glaciers: Ninnis, 22 mi wide, 99 mi long, and Mentz, 11 mi by 140 mi.

The Indian O. groups are as follows: Kerguelen Archipelago, visited 1772, consists of one large and 300 small islands. The chief is 87 mi long, 74 mi wide, and has Mt. Ross, 6,429 ft tall. Principal research station is Port-aux-Français. Seals often weigh two tons; there are blue whales, coal, peat, semiprecious stones. Crozet Archipelago, reached 1772, covers 136 sq mi. Eastern Island rises to 6,560 ft. Saint Paul, in southern Indian O., has warm springs with earth at places heating to 120° to 390°F. Amsterdam is nearby; both produce cod and rock lobster. Military garrisons and meteorological stations are located on the Scattered Isls.

The special collectivity of **New Caledonia** and Dependencies is a group of islands in the Pacific O. about 1,115 mi E of Australia and approx. the same distance NW of New Zealand. Dependencies are the Loyalty Isls., Isle of Pines, Belep Archipelago, and Huon Isls.

The largest island, New Caledonia, is 6,530 sq mi. Total area of the territory is 7,172 sq mi (total); 7,056 sq mi (land); pop. (2012 est.) 260,166. The group was acquired by France in 1853.

The territory is administered by a High Commissioner. There is a popularly elected Territorial Congress. Two deputies and a senator are elected to the French Parliament. Capital: Noumea.

Mining is the chief industry. New Caledonia is one of the world's largest nickel producers. Chrome, iron, cobalt, manganese, silver, gold, lead, and copper are also found. Agric. products include yams, sweet potatoes, potatoes, manioc, corn, and coconuts.

In 1987, New Caledonian voters chose by referendum to remain within the French Republic. There were clashes between French and Melanesians (Kanaks) in 1988. An agreement Apr. 21, 1998, between France and rival New Caledonian factions specified a 15- to 20-year period of "shared sovereignty." The French constitution was amended, July 6, to allow the territory a gradual increase in autonomy; New Caledonian voters approved the plan Nov. 8, 1998, by a 72% majority.

Gabon
Gabonese Republic

People: Population: 1,608,321. **Age distrib.:** <15: 42.2%; 65+: 3.9%. **Pop. density:** 16.2 per sq mi, 6.2 per sq km. **Urban:** 86.2%. **Ethnic groups:** Bantu tribes (incl. Fang, Bapounou, Nzebi, Obamba). **Principal languages:** French (official), Fang, Myene, Nzebi, Bapounou/Eschira, Bandjabi. **Chief religions:** Christian 55%-75%, animist.

Geography: Total area: 103,347 sq mi, 267,667 sq km; **Land area:** 99,486 sq mi, 257,667 sq km. **Location:** On Atlantic coast of W central Africa. **Neighbors:** Equatorial Guinea, Cameroon on N; Congo on E and S. **Topography:** Heavily forested, consisting of coastal lowlands; plateaus in N, E, and S; mountains in N, SE, and center. The Ogooue R. system covers most of Gabon. **Capital:** Libreville, 686,356.

Government: Type: Republic. **Head of state:** Pres. Ali Bongo Ondimba; b. Feb. 9, 1959; in office: Oct. 16, 2009. **Head of gov.:** Prime Min. Raymond Ndong Sima; b. Jan. 23, 1955; in office: Feb. 27, 2012. **Local divisions:** 9 provinces. **Defense budget:** $263 mil. **Active troops:** 4,700.

Economy: Industries: petroleum extraction and refining; manganese, gold; chemicals, ship repair, food and beverages. **Chief crops:** cocoa, coffee, sugar, palm oil, rubber. **Natural resources:** petroleum, nat. gas, diamonds, niobium, manganese, uranium, gold, timber, iron ore, hydropower. **Crude oil reserves:** 2 bil bbls. **Arable land:** 1.3%. **Livestock:** cattle: 36,500; chickens: 3.2 mil; goats: 92,000; pigs: 215,000; sheep: 196,000. **Fish catch:** 32,160 metric tons. **Electricity prod.:** 1.6 bil kWh. **Labor force:** agric. 60%, industry 15%, services 25%.

Finance: Monetary unit: CFA BEAC Franc (XAF) (Sept. 2012: 519.73 = $1 U.S.). **GDP:** $24.9 bil; **per capita GDP:** $16,400; **GDP growth:** 5.8%. **Imports:** $3.2 bil; France 32.9%, China 8.4%, U.S. 6.3%, Belgium 5.8%, Cameroon 4.3%. **Exports:** $10.9 bil; U.S. 40.9%, Australia 9.1%, Malaysia 8.6%, Japan 5.9%, China 5%, Spain 4.8%. **Tourism:** NA. **Budget:** $4.4 bil. **Total reserves less gold:** $2.2 bil. **Gold** (2008): 12,837 oz t. **CPI change:** 1.3%.

Transport: Railways: 403 mi. **Civil aviation:** 578.5 mil pass.-mi; 14 airports. **Chief ports:** Gamba, Libreville, Lucinda, Owendo, Port-Gentil.

Communications: TV sets: 161 per 1,000 pop. **Radios:** 217 per 1,000 pop. **Telephone lines:** 2 per 100 pop. **Internet:** 8%.

Health: Life expect.: 51.7 male; 52.9 female. **Births:** 35.0 (per 1,000 pop.). **Deaths:** 13.1 (per 1,000 pop.). **Natural inc.:** 2.19% **Infant mortality:** 49.0 (per 1,000 live births). **HIV rate:** 5.2%.

Education: Compulsory: ages 6-16. **Literacy:** 88.4%.

Major intl. organizations: UN (FAO, IBRD, ILO, IMF, WHO), AU, WTO.

Embassy: 2034 20th St. NW 20009; 797-1000.

Website: www.gouvernement.ga or www.state.gov/p/af/ci/gb/

France established control over the region in the second half of the 19th cent. Gabon became independent Aug. 17, 1960. Backed by France, Pres. Albert-Bernard Bongo (later Omar Bongo Ondimba) ruled the country 1967-2009, greatly enriching himself and his family. A multiparty political system was introduced in 1990; a new constitution was enacted Mar. 14, 1991. Bongo's reelection victories in 1993, 1998, and 2003 were faulted by international observers. After he died June 8, 2009, his son Ali Bongo Ondimba, Gabon's defense minister 1999-2009, ran for the presidency. He claimed victory in a disputed election Aug. 30 and took office Oct. 16, 2009.

Gabon is one of the most prosperous African countries, thanks to abundant natural resources, foreign private investment, and government development programs.

The Gambia
Republic of The Gambia

People: Population: 1,840,454. **Age distrib.:** <15: 39.6%; 65+: 3.2%. **Pop. density:** 476.7 per sq mi, 184 per sq km. **Urban:** 57.3%. Mandinka 42%, Fula 18%, Wolof 16%, Jola 10%, Serahuli 9%. **Principal languages:** English (official), Mandinka, Wolof, Fula, other indigenous vernaculars. **Chief religions:** Muslim 90%, Christian 8%, indigenous beliefs 2%.

Geography: Total area: 4,361 sq mi, 11,295 sq km; **Land area:** 3,861 sq mi, 10,000 sq km. **Location:** On Atlantic coast near W tip of Africa. **Neighbors:** Surrounded on 3 sides by Senegal. **Topography:** A narrow strip of land on each side of lower Gambia R. **Capital:** Banjul, 506,277.

Government: Type: Republic. **Head of state and gov.:** Pres. Yahya Jammeh; b. May 25, 1965; in office: July 22, 1994. **Local divisions:** 5 divisions, 1 city. **Defense budget** (2010): $7 mil. **Active troops:** 800.

Economy: Industries: peanuts, fish, and hides proc.; tourism; beverages; agric. machinery assembly. **Chief crops:** rice, millet, sorghum, peanuts, corn, sesame, cassava, palm kernels. **Natural resources:** fish, clay, silica sand, titanium, tin, zircon. **Arable land:** 40.0%. **Livestock:** cattle: 425,000; chickens: 850,000; goats: 352,000; pigs: 28,500; sheep: 251,000. **Fish catch:** 46,449 metric tons. **Electricity prod.:** 240 mil kWh. **Labor force:** agric. 75%, industry 19%, services 6%.

Finance: Monetary unit: Dalasi (GMD) (Sept. 2012: 30.73 = $1 U.S.). **GDP:** $3.5 bil; **per capita GDP:** $2,000; **GDP growth:** 3.3%. **Imports:** $327 mil; China 29.2%, Brazil 10.1%, Senegal 8.7%, India 5.5%, Netherlands 4.1%, Turkey 4%. **Exports:** $103.9 mil; China 41.8%, India 20.8%, France 10.4%, UK 6.3%. **Tourism:** $32 mil. **Budget:** $220.6 mil. **Total reserves less gold:** $223.2 mil. **CPI change:** 4.8%.

Transport: Civil aviation: 1 airport. **Chief port:** Banjul.

Communications: TV Sets: 14 per 1,000 pop. Radios: 147 per 1,000 pop. **Telephone lines:** 2.8 per 100 pop. **Internet:** 10.9%.

Health: Life expect.: 61.5 male; 66.2 female. **Births:** 33.4 (per 1,000 pop.). **Deaths:** 7.5 (per 1,000 pop.). **Natural inc.:** 2.59% **Infant mortality:** 69.6 (per 1,000 live births). **HIV rate:** 2%.

Education: Compulsory: ages 7-12. **Literacy:** 50%.

Major intl. organizations: UN (FAO, IBRD, ILO, IMF, WHO), AU, the Commonwealth, WTO.

Embassy: 1156 15th St. NW 20005; 785-1399.

Website: www.gambia.gm

The peoples of The Gambia were at one time associated with the West African empires of Ghana, Mali, and Songhai. The area became Britain's first African possession in 1588.

Independence came Feb. 18, 1965; republic status within the Commonwealth was achieved in 1970. The country suffered from severe famine in the 1970s. Senegambia, a confederation with Senegal, lasted from 1982 to 1989.

On July 22, 1994, after 24 years in power, Pres. Dawda K. Jawara was deposed in a bloodless coup by a military officer, Yahya Jammeh. Jammeh barred political activity, detained potential opponents, and governed by decree. Despite a nominal return to constitutional government in 1996, Jammeh has retained a tight grip on power. Security forces suppressed an alleged coup plot by army officers Mar. 2006. Pres. Jammeh won a fourth 5-year term Nov. 24, 2011. With per capita GDP of $2,000 in 2011, Gambia is one of the world's poorest countries.

Georgia

People: Population: 4,570,934. **Age distrib.:** <15: 15.5%; 65+: 16.1%. **Pop. density:** 169.9 per sq mi, 65.6 per sq km. **Urban:** 52.8%. **Ethnic groups:** Georgian 84%, Azeri 7%, Armenian 6%, Russian 2%. **Principal languages:** Georgian (official), Russian, Armenian, Azeri, Abkhaz (official in Abkhazia). **Chief religions:** Orthodox Christian (official) 84%, Muslim 10%, Armenian-Gregorian 4%.

Geography: Total area: 26,911 sq mi, 69,700 sq km; **Land area:** 26,911 sq mi, 69,700 sq km. **Location:** SW Asia, on E coast of Black Sea. **Neighbors:** Russia on N and NE, Turkey and Armenia on S, Azerbaijan on SE. **Topography:** Separated from Russia on NE by main range of Caucasus Mts. **Capital:** Tbilisi, 1,120,690.

Government: Type: Republic. **Head of state:** Pres. Mikhail Saakashvili; b. Dec. 21, 1967; in office: Jan. 25, 2004. **Head of gov.:** Prime Min. Ivane "Vano" Merabishvili; b. Apr. 15, 1968; in office: June 30, 2012. **Local divisions:** 53 rayons, 9 cities, and 2 autonomous republics. **Defense budget:** $395 mil. **Active troops:** 20,655.

Economy: Industries: steel, machine tools, elec. appliances, mining, chemicals, wood prods., wine. **Chief crops:** citrus, grapes, tea, hazelnuts, vegetables. **Natural resources:** timber, hydropower, manganese, iron ore, copper, minor coal and oil deposits. **Crude oil reserves:** 35 mil bbls. **Arable land:** 6.4%. **Livestock:** cattle: 1.01 mil; chickens: 6.2 mil; goats: 71,500; pigs: 135,200; sheep: 602,300. **Fish catch:** 31,064 metric tons. **Electricity prod.:** 8.4 bil kWh. **Labor force:** agric. 55.6%, industry 8.9%, services 35.5%.

Finance: Monetary unit: Lari (GEL) (Sept. 2012: 1.66 = $1 U.S.). **GDP:** $24.9 bil; **per capita GDP:** $5,600; **GDP growth:** 7%. **Imports:** $7.1 bil; Turkey 17.8%, Ukraine 10%, Azerbaijan 8.3%, China 7.6%, Germany 6.9%, Russia 5.7%. **Exports:** $2.2 bil; Azerbaijan 17.5%, Turkey 10.5%, Armenia 10%, Kazakhstan 7.3%, Ukraine 6.2%, U.S. 5.5%, Canada 5.2%, Bulgaria 4.7%. **Tourism:** $936 mil. **Budget:** $4.7 bil. **Total reserves less gold:** $2.8 bil. **CPI change:** 8.5%.

Transport: Railways: 1,002 mi. Civil aviation: 369.1 mil pass.-mi; 18 airports. **Chief ports:** Batumi, Poti.

Communications: TV sets: 450 per 1,000 pop. **Radios:** 542 per 1,000 pop. **Telephone lines:** 31 per 100 pop. **Daily newspaper circ.:** 3.9 per 1,000 pop. **Internet:** 36.6%.

Health: Life expect.: 74.0 male; 81.0 female. **Births:** 10.8 (per 1,000 pop.). **Deaths:** 10.1 (per 1,000 pop.). **Natural inc.:** 0.07% **Infant mortality:** 14.7 (per 1,000 live births). **HIV rate:** 0.1%.

Education: Compulsory: ages 6-15. **Literacy:** 99.7%.

Major intl. organizations: UN (FAO, IBRD, ILO, IMF, WHO), CIS, OSCE, WTO.

Embassy: 2209 Massachusetts Ave. NW 20008; 387-2390.

Website: www.government.gov.ge

The region, which contained the ancient kingdoms of Colchis and Iberia, was Christianized in the 4th cent. and conquered by Arabs in the 8th cent. Annexed by Russia in 1801, Georgia was forcibly incorporated into the USSR in 1922.

Georgia declared independence Apr. 9, 1991, and became an independent country when the Soviet Union disbanded Dec. 26. After a power struggle, former Soviet Foreign Min. Eduard A. Shevardnadze became president. He survived several coup attempts and won reelection in 1995 and 2000. Parliamentary elections Nov. 2, 2003, denounced as fraudulent by opposition groups and international observers, sparked massive antigovernment protests, causing Shevardnadze to resign Nov. 23. Opposition leader Mikhail Saakashvili won the Jan. 4, 2004, presidential election. He survived an apparent assassination attempt along with U.S. Pres. George W. Bush in Tbilisi May 10, 2005; suppressed an alleged coup plot Sept. 6, 2006; and cracked down violently on antigovernment protests and imposed a state of emergency, Nov. 7-16, 2007. He called early elections, Jan. 5, 2008, which he won.

Since the country gained independence, secessionist movements in the enclaves of South Ossetia and Abkhazia, supported by Russia, have rejected the Tbilisi government. Open warfare between Georgia and Russia erupted when Saakashvili sent troops Aug. 7, 2008, to suppress insurgent activity in Tskhinvali, the South Ossetian capital. Russia retaliated Aug. 8-9 by dispatching its forces to South Ossetia and Abkhazia and attacking key Georgian cities. A cease-fire signed Aug. 15-16 called for withdrawal of Russian forces from Georgia proper, but allowed thousands of Russian troops to remain in the breakaway regions. On Aug. 26, 2008, Russia formally recognized their independence, a step protested by the U.S. and Georgia's other Western allies. International donors Oct. 22 pledged $4.55 bil in reconstruction aid, including about $1.5 bil from EU members and $1 bil from the U.S. Abkhzia's pro-Russian Pres. Sergei Bagapsh died May 29, 2011; his vice president, Aleksandr Ankvab, was elected to succeed him Aug. 26. Citing voting irregularities, the supreme court Nov. 29, 2011, invalidated the results of the South Ossetian presidential election two days earlier. Pro-Russian candidate Leonid Tibilov won a runoff vote Apr. 8, 2012, in the elections that followed.

Germany
Federal Republic of Germany

People: Population: 81,305,856. **Age distrib.:** <15: 13.2%; 65+: 20.7%. **Pop. density:** 604 per sq mi, 233.2 per sq km. **Urban:** 73.9%. **Ethnic groups:** German 92%, Turkish 2%, other (incl. Greek, Italian, Polish, Russian, Serbo-Croatian, Spanish) 6%. **Principal language:** German. **Chief religions:** Protestant 34%, Roman Catholic 34%, Muslim 4%, unaffiliated or other 28%.

Geography: Total area: 137,847 sq mi, 357,022 sq km; **Land area:** 134,623 sq mi, 348,672 sq km. **Location:** In central Europe. **Neighbors:** Denmark on N; Netherlands, Belgium, Luxembourg, France on W; Switzerland, Austria on S; Czech Rep., Poland on E. **Topography:** Germany is flat in N, hilly in center and W, and mountainous in Bavaria in the S. Chief rivers are Elbe, Weser, Ems, Rhine, and Main, all flowing toward North Sea, and Danube, flowing toward Black Sea. **Capital:** Berlin, 3,462,410. **Cities (urban aggl.):** Hamburg, 1,796,029; Munich, 1,364,324; Cologne, 1,005,901.

Government: Type: Federal republic. **Head of state:** Pres. Christian Wulff; b. June 19, 1959; in office: June 30, 2010. **Head of gov.:** Chancellor Angela Merkel; b. July 17, 1954; in office: Nov. 22, 2005. **Local divisions:** 16 laender (states). **Defense budget:** $44.2 bil. **Active troops:** 251,465.

Economy: Industries: among the world's largest and most technologically advanced producers of iron, steel, coal, cement, chemicals, machinery, vehicles, machine tools, electronics, food and beverages, shipbuilding, textiles. **Chief crops:** potatoes, wheat, barley, sugar beets, fruits, cabbages. **Natural resources:** coal, lignite, nat. gas, iron ore, copper, nickel, uranium, potash, salt, constr. materials, timber. **Crude oil reserves:** 276 mil bbls. **Arable land:** 34.3%. **Livestock:** cattle: 12.8 mil; chickens: 114.1 mil; goats: 149,936; pigs: 26.5 mil; sheep: 2.1 mil. **Fish catch:** 263,465 metric tons. **Electricity prod.** (2010): 576.8 bil kWh. **Labor force:** agric. 1.6%, industry 24.6%, services 73.8%.

Finance: Monetary unit: Euro (EUR) (Sept. 2012: 0.79 = $1 U.S.). **GDP:** $3.1 tril; **per capita GDP:** $38,400; **GDP growth:** 3.1%. **Imports:** $1.2 tril; China 9.7%, Netherlands 8.4%, France 7.6%, U.S. 5.7%, Italy 5.2%, UK 4.7%, Belgium 4.2%, Austria 4.1%, Switzerland 4.1%. **Exports:** $1.4 tril; France 9.4%, U.S. 6.8%, Netherlands 6.6%, UK 6.2%, Italy 6.2%, China 5.7%, Austria 5.5%, Belgium 4.7%, Switzerland 4.4%. **Tourism:** $38.8 bil. **Budget:** $1.6 tril. **Total reserves less gold:** $66.9 bil. **Gold:** 109.2 mil oz t. **CPI change:** 2.3%.

Transport: Railways: 26,086 mi. **Motor vehicles:** 545.4 vehicles per 1,000 pop. Civil aviation: 127.6 bil pass.-mi; 322 airports. **Chief ports:** Bremen, Bremerhaven, Duisburg, Hamburg, Karlsruhe, Lubeck, Neuss-Dusseldorf, Rostock, Wilhemshaven.

Communications: TV sets: 675 per 1,000 pop. **Radios:** 558 per 1,000 pop. **Telephone lines:** 63.1 per 100 pop. **Daily newspaper circ.:** 267.5 per 1,000 pop. **Internet:** 83%.

Health: Life expect.: 77.9 male; 82.6 female. **Births:** 8.3 (per 1,000 pop.). **Deaths:** 11.0 (per 1,000 pop.). **Natural inc.:** −0.27% **Infant mortality:** 3.5 (per 1,000 live births). **HIV rate:** 0.1%.

Education: Compulsory: ages 6-18. **Literacy:** 99%.

Major intl. organizations: UN and all of its specialized agencies, EU, NATO, OECD, OSCE, WTO.

Embassy: 4645 Reservoir Rd. NW 20007; 298-4000.

Website: www.deutschland.de

Germany is a central European nation originally composed of numerous states, with a common language and traditions, that were united in one country in 1871. Germany was split into 2 countries from the end of WWII until reunification in 1990.

History and government. Julius Caesar defeated Germanic tribes, 55 and 53 BCE, but Roman expansion north of the Rhine was stopped in 9 CE. Charlemagne, ruler of the Franks, consoli-dated Saxon, Bavarian, Rhenish, Frankish, and other lands; after him the eastern part became the German Empire. The Thirty Years' War, 1618-48, split Germany into small principalities and kingdoms.

Otto von Bismarck, Prussian chancellor, formed the North German Confederation, 1867.

In 1870 Bismarck maneuvered Napoleon III into declaring war. After the quick defeat of France, Bismarck formed the **German Empire** and on Jan. 18, 1871, in Versailles, proclaimed King Wilhelm I of Prussia German emperor (Deutscher kaiser).

The German Empire reached its peak before WWI in 1914, with 208,780 sq mi, plus overseas colonies. After losing the war in 1918, Germany ceded Alsace-Lorraine to France, West Prussia and Posen (Poznan) province to Poland, and part of Schleswig to Denmark. It lost all colonies and the ports of Memel and Danzig.

Republic of Germany, 1919-33, adopted the Weimar constitution; met reparation payments and elected Friedrich Ebert and Gen. Paul von Hindenburg presidents.

Third Reich, 1933-45, Adolf Hitler led the National Socialist German Workers' (Nazi) party after WWI. Pres. von Hindenburg named Hitler chancellor Jan. 30, 1933; on Aug. 3, 1934, the day after Hindenburg's death, the cabinet joined the offices of president and chancellor and made Hitler *fuehrer* (leader). Hitler abolished freedom of speech and assembly, and began a long series of persecutions climaxed by the murder of millions of Jews and others.

He repudiated the Versailles treaty and reparations agreements, remilitarized the Rhineland (1936), and annexed Austria (Anschluss, 1938). At Munich he made an agreement with Neville Chamberlain, British prime minister, which permitted Germany to annex part of Czechoslovakia. He signed a nonaggression treaty with the USSR, 1939, and declared war on Poland Sept. 1, 1939, precipitating WWII. With total defeat near, Hitler committed suicide in Berlin Apr. 1945. The victorious Allies voided all acts and annexations of Hitler's Reich.

Division of Germany. Germany was sectioned into 4 zones of occupation, administered by the Allied Powers (U.S., USSR, UK, and France). The USSR took control of many E German states. The territory E of the so-called Oder-Neisse line was assigned to, and later annexed by, Poland. The USSR annexed Northern East Prussia (now Kaliningrad). Greater Berlin, within but not part of the Soviet zone, was administered by the 4 occupying powers under the Allied Command. In 1948 the USSR withdrew, established its single command in East Berlin, and cut off supplies. The Western Allies utilized a gigantic airlift to bring food to West Berlin, 1948-49.

In 1949, two separate German states were established. In May the zones administered by the Western Allies became West Germany; in Oct. the Soviet sector became East Germany. West Berlin was considered a West German enclave, a status the Soviet bloc disputed.

East Germany. The German Democratic Republic (East Germany) was proclaimed in the Soviet sector of Berlin Oct. 7, 1949. It was declared fully sovereign in 1954, but Soviet troops remained.

Coincident with the entrance of West Germany into the European defense community in 1952, the East German government decreed a prohibited zone 3 mi deep along its 600-mi border with West Germany and cut Berlin's telephone system in two. Berlin was further divided by erection of a fortified wall in 1961, after over 3 mil East Germans had fled to the West. The oppressive Communist regime maintained control through the state security police, known as the Stasi.

By the early 1970s, the economy of East Germany was highly industrialized, and the nation was credited with the highest standard of living among Warsaw Pact countries. Growth slowed in the late 1970s, because of shortages of natural resources and labor, and a huge debt. Comparison with the lifestyle in the West caused many young people to emigrate.

In the late 1980s the government firmly resisted following the USSR's policy of openness (*glasnost*), but was faced with nationwide demonstrations demanding reform. Pres. Erich Honecker, in office since 1976, was forced to resign Oct. 18, 1989. On Nov. 9, the East German government announced its decision to open the border with the West, signaling the end of the Berlin Wall. On Aug. 23, 1990, the East German parliament agreed to unify with West Germany; this occurred Oct. 3.

West Germany. The Federal Republic of Germany (West Germany) was proclaimed May 23, 1949, in Bonn. The occupying powers, the U.S., Britain, and France, restored civil status, Sept. 21. The Western Allies ended the state of war with Germany in 1951, while the USSR did so in 1955. The powers lifted controls, and the republic became fully independent May 5, 1955.

Dr. Konrad Adenauer, a Christian Democrat, was made chancellor Sept. 15, 1949, and reelected 1953, 1957, 1961. Willy Brandt, heading a coalition of Social Democrats and Free Democrats, became chancellor Oct. 21, 1969, and pursued a policy of *Ostpolitik*, or rapprochement with East Germany and the USSR. Brandt resigned May 1974 after a spy scandal. Terrorist acts on German soil in the 1970s included activities of the Baader-Meinhof gang and the murder of Israeli athletes by Palestinian commandos at the Olympic Games in Munich, Sept. 5, 1972.

Helmut Kohl became chancellor in 1982 and led Christian Democrats to victory in 1983 and 1987. In 1990, under Kohl's leadership, West Germany moved rapidly to reunite with East Germany.

A New Era. In May 1990, NATO ministers adopted a package of proposals on reunification, including making the united Germany a full member of NATO and the barring of the new Germany from having its own nuclear, chemical, or biological weapons. The merger of the 2 Germanys took place Oct. 3, and the first all-German elections since 1932 were held Dec. 2, with West German Chancellor Helmut Kohl confirmed as leader of the unified nation. Eastern Germany received over $1 tril in public and private funds from western Germany between 1990 and 1995. In 1991, Berlin again became Germany's official capital; the Bundestag (parliament) and parts of the federal executive were relocated from Bonn to Berlin in 1999.

Unemployment hit a postwar high of 12.6% in Jan. 1998. The 16-year Kohl era ended with the defeat of the Christian Democrats in parliamentary elections Sept. 27; Gerhard Schröder, of the Social Democratic Party, became chancellor. Germany supplied troops for coalition military operations in Afghanistan (2001).

The Christian Democrats, led by Angela Merkel, won a razor-thin plurality in the parliamentary elections of Sept. 18, 2005, and after prolonged negotiations she became chancellor Nov. 22, heading a "grand coalition" that included the Socialists.

Responding to the global recession, the government passed a 50 bil euro economic stimulus plan in early 2009. The German economy shrank 5% in 2009 but rebounded in 2010-11.

Merkel led a center-right coalition to victory in national elections Sept. 27, 2009. Christian Wulff, the Christian Democratic leader of Lower Saxony, became federal president June 30, 2010. After an earthquake and tsunami in Japan caused a nuclear disaster, the Merkel government said May 30, 2011, that it would close Germany's 17 nuclear power plants by 2022. Merkel and French Pres. Sarkozy led the international response to the European debt crisis—first signaled by Greece in late 2009, followed by Ireland, Portugal, Italy, and Spain—which required stern austerity measures in return for aid. But Sarkozy's 2012 ouster and new recessions in several austerity-bound countries cast doubt on Germany's strategy in resolving the euro-zone crisis. Merkel's party performed badly, May 13, 2012, in state parliamentary elections.

Helgoland, an island of 130 acres in the North Sea, was taken from Denmark by a British Naval Force in 1807 and later ceded to Germany to become part of Schleswig-Holstein province in return for rights in East Africa. The heavily fortified island was surrendered to UK, May 23, 1945, demilitarized in 1947, and returned to West Germany, Mar. 1, 1952. It is a free port.

Ghana
Republic of Ghana

People: Population: 24,652,402. **Age distrib.:** <15: 38.9%; 65+: 4%. **Pop. density:** 280.6 per sq mi, 108.3 per sq km. **Urban:** 51.9%. **Ethnic groups:** Akan 45%, Mole-Dagbon 15%, Ewe 12%, Ga-Dangme 7%, Guan 4%, Gurma 4%, Grusi 3%, Mande-Busanga 1%. **Principal languages:** Asante, Ewe, Fante, English (official). **Chief religions:** Christian 69% (Pentecostal/Charismatic 24%, Protestant 19%, Catholic 15%), Muslim 16%, traditional 9%, none 6%.

Geography: Total area: 92,098 sq mi, 238,533 sq km; **Land area:** 87,851 sq mi, 227,533 sq km. **Location:** On S coast of W Africa. **Neighbors:** Côte d'Ivoire on W, Burkina Faso on N, Togo on E. **Topography:** Mostly low fertile plains and scrubland, cut by rivers and by the artificial Lake Volta. **Capital:** Accra, 2,573,220. **Cities (urban aggl.):** Kumasi, 2,019,350.

Government: Type: Republic. **Head of state and gov.:** Pres. John Dramani Mahama; b. Nov. 29, 1958; in office: July 24, 2012. **Local divisions:** 10 regions. **Defense budget:** $128 mil. **Active troops:** 15,500.

Economy: Industries: mining, lumbering, light mfg., aluminum smelting, food proc., cement, small comm. shipbuilding. **Chief crops:** cocoa, rice, cassava, peanuts, corn, shea nuts, bananas. **Natural resources:** gold, timber, industrial diamonds, bauxite, manganese, fish, rubber, hydropower, petroleum, silver, salt, limestone. **Crude oil reserves:** 660 mil bbls. **Arable land:** 19.3%. **Livestock:** cattle: 1.5 mil; chickens: 47.8 mil; goats: 4.9 mil; pigs: 536,000; sheep: 3.8 mil. **Fish catch:** 361,405 metric tons.

Electricity prod.: 8.8 bil kWh. **Labor force:** agric. 56%, industry 15%, services 29%.

Finance: Monetary unit: Cedi (GHS) (Sept. 2012: 1.93 = $1 U.S.). **GDP:** $75.9 bil; **per capita GDP:** $3,100; **GDP growth:** 13.6%. **Imports:** $15.3 bil; China 20.5%, Nigeria 12.4%, U.S. 7.8%, India 5.1%, Netherlands 5.1%, UK 4.2%. **Exports:** $12.8 bil; France 19.5%, Netherlands 10.4%, U.S. 8.8%, Italy 8.3%, UK 4.8%. **Tourism:** $620 mil. **Budget:** $10.4 bil. **Total reserves less gold:** $5.5 bil. **Gold:** 281,000 oz t. **CPI change:** 8.7%.

Transport: Railways: 588 mi. **Motor vehicles:** 7.3 vehicles per 1,000 pop. **Civil aviation:** 225.6 mil pass.-mi; 7 airports. **Chief ports:** Takoradi, Tema.

Communications: TV sets: 52 per 1,000 pop. **Radios:** 133 per 1,000 pop. **Telephone lines:** 1.1 per 100 pop. **Internet:** 14.1%.

Health: Life expect.: 62.6 male; 67.2 female. **Births:** 32.0 (per 1,000 pop.). **Deaths:** 7.7 (per 1,000 pop.). **Natural inc.:** 2.43% **Infant mortality:** 40.9 (per 1,000 live births). **HIV rate:** 1.8%.

Education: Compulsory: ages 6-15. **Literacy:** 67.3%.

Major intl. organizations: UN and all of its specialized agencies, AU, the Commonwealth, WTO.

Embassy: 3512 International Dr. NW 20008; 686-4520.

Website: www.ghana.gov.gh

Named for an African empire along the Niger River, 400-1240 CE, Ghana was ruled by Britain for 113 years as the Gold Coast. The UN in 1956 approved merger with the British Togoland trust territory. Independence came Mar. 6, 1957, and republic status within the Commonwealth in 1960.

Pres. Kwame Nkrumah built hospitals and schools, promoted development projects like the Volta R. hydroelectric and aluminum plants, but ran the country into debt, jailed opponents, and was accused of corruption. A 1964 referendum gave Nkrumah dictatorial powers and set up a one-party socialist state. Nkrumah was overthrown in 1966 by a police-army coup. Elections were held in 1969, but 4 further coups occurred in 1972, 1978, 1979, and 1981. The 1979 and 1981 coups, led by Flight Lieut. Jerry Rawlings, were followed by suspension of the constitution and banning of political parties. A new constitution, allowing multiparty politics, was approved in Apr. 1992.

In Feb. 1993 more than 1,000 people were killed in ethnic clashes in northern Ghana. Rawlings won the Dec. 7, 1996, presidential election. Kofi Annan, a career UN diplomat from Ghana, served as UN secretary general, 1997-2006.

Opposition leader John Agyekum Kufuor won a runoff vote Dec. 28, 2000, and was sworn in Jan. 7, 2001, marking Ghana's first peaceful transfer of power from one elected president to another. He was reelected Dec. 7, 2004. John Atta Mills, a tax law expert who lost presidential elections in 2000 and 2004, defeated the ruling party candidate, Nana Akufo-Addo, in a runoff election Dec. 28, 2008. A major offshore oil and gas find was announced June 2007; the Jubilee field, estimated to hold recoverable reserves of 1.5 bil barrels, began production Dec. 15, 2010. Mills died July 24, 2012; Vice-Pres. John Dramani Mahama replaced him.

Greece
Hellenic Republic

People: Population: 10,767,827. **Age distrib.:** <15: 14.2%; 65+: 19.8%. **Pop. density:** 213.5 per sq mi, 82.4 per sq km. **Urban:** 61.4%. **Ethnic groups:** Greek (citizenship) 93%, other (foreign citizenship) 7%. (Greece does not collect ethnicity data.) **Principal language:** Greek (official). **Chief religions:** Greek Orthodox (official) 98%, Muslim 1%.

Geography: Total area: 50,949 sq mi, 131,957 sq km; **Land area:** 50,443 sq mi, 130,647 sq km. **Location:** Occupies S end of Balkan Peninsula in SE Europe. **Neighbors:** Albania, Macedonia, Bulgaria on N; Turkey on E. **Topography:** About three-quarters is nonarable, with mountains in all areas. Pindus Mts. run through the country N to S. The heavily indented coastline is 9,385 mi long. Of over 2,000 islands, only 169 are inhabited, among them Crete, Rhodes, Milos, Kerkira (Corfu), Chios, Lesbos, Samos, Euboea, Delos, Mykonos. **Capital:** Athens, 3,413,990. **Cities (urban aggl.):** Thessaloniki, 883,017.

Government: Type: Parliamentary republic. **Head of state:** Pres. Karolos Papoulias; b. June 4, 1929; in office: Mar. 12, 2005. **Head of gov.:** Prime Min. Antonis Samaras; b. May 23, 1951; in office: June 20, 2012. **Local divisions:** 13 regions comprising 51 prefectures. **Defense budget:** $6.83 bil. **Active troops:** 145,647.

Economy: Industries: tourism, food and tobacco proc., textiles, chemicals, metal prods., mining, petroleum. **Chief crops:** wheat, corn, barley, sugar beets, olives, tomatoes, wine grapes, tobacco, potatoes. **Natural resources:** lignite, petroleum, iron ore, bauxite, lead, zinc, nickel, magnesite, marble, salt, hydropower potential. **Crude oil reserves:** 10 mil bbls. **Arable land:** 19.8%. **Livestock:** cattle: 624,800; chickens: 31.8 mil; goats: 4.9 mil; pigs: 950,000; sheep: 9 mil. **Fish catch:** 196,493 metric tons. **Electricity prod.:** (2010): 57.1 bil kWh. **Labor force:** agric. 12.4%, industry 22.4%, services 65.1%.

Finance: Monetary unit: Euro (EUR) (Sept. 2012: 0.79 = $1 U.S.). **GDP:** $298.1 bil; **per capita GDP:** $26,600; **GDP growth:** −6.9%. **Imports:** $66 bil; Germany 10.7%, Italy 9.3%, China 7.1%, Netherlands 5.5%, France 5.1%, Austria 4.5%, Russia 4.2%,

Czech Republic 4.1%. **Exports:** $28.2 bil; Italy 9.6%, Germany 8%, UK 6.5%, Italy 6.2%, Bulgaria 5.6%, U.S. 5.1%, China 5.1%, Switzerland 4.7%, Belgium 4.7%, Poland 4.4%. **Tourism:** $14.6 bil. **Budget:** $158.6 bil. **Total reserves less gold:** $1.2 bil. **Gold:** 3.6 mil oz t. **CPI change:** 3.3%.

Transport: Railways: 1,583 mi. **Motor vehicles:** 601.8 vehicles per 1,000 pop. **Civil aviation:** 4.7 bil pass.-mi; 67 airports. **Chief ports:** Agioi Theodoroi, Aspropyrgos, Pachi, Piraeus, Thessaloníki.

Communications: TV sets: 556 per 1,000 pop. **Radios:** 464 per 1,000 pop. **Telephone lines:** 49.9 per 100 pop. **Internet:** 53%.

Health: Life expect.: 77.5 male; 82.8 female. **Births:** 9.1 (per 1,000 pop.). **Deaths:** 10.8 (per 1,000 pop.). **Natural inc.:** −0.17% **Infant mortality:** 4.9 (per 1,000 live births). **HIV rate:** 0.1%.

Education: Compulsory: ages 6-14. **Literacy:** 97.2%.

Major intl. organizations: UN (FAO, IBRD, ILO, IMF, WHO), EU, NATO, OECD, OSCE, WTO.

Embassy: 2217 Massachusetts Ave. NW 20008; 939-1306.

Website: www.primeminister.gov.gr

The achievements of ancient Greece in art, architecture, science, mathematics, philosophy, drama, literature, and democracy became legacies for succeeding ages. Greece reached the height of its glory and power, particularly in the Athenian city-state, in the 5th cent. BCE. Greece fell under Roman rule in the 2nd and 1st centuries BCE. In the 4th cent. CE it became part of the Byzantine Empire and, after the fall of Constantinople to the Turks in 1453, part of the Ottoman Empire.

Greece won its war of independence from Turkey 1821-29, and became a kingdom. A republic was established 1924; the monarchy was restored, 1935. In Oct. 1940, Greece rejected an ultimatum from Italy, but the country was defeated and occupied by Germans, Italians, and Bulgarians. By the end of 1944 the invaders withdrew. Communist resistance forces were overcome by Royalist and British troops. A plebiscite restored the monarchy.

Communists waged guerrilla war 1947-49 against the government but were defeated with the aid of the U.S. A period of reconstruction and rapid development followed, mainly with conservative governments under Premier Constantine Karamanlis. The Center Union, led by George Papandreou, won elections in 1963 and 1964, but King Constantine forced Papandreou to resign. A period of political maneuvers ended with Col. George Papadopoulos's military takeover Apr. 21, 1967. King Constantine tried to reverse the consolidation of the harsh dictatorship Dec. 13, 1967, but failed and fled to Italy. Papadopoulos was ousted Nov. 25, 1973.

Greek army officers serving in the National Guard of Cyprus staged a coup on the island July 15, 1974. Turkey invaded Cyprus a week later, precipitating the collapse of the Greek junta. Democratic government returned, and in 1975 the monarchy was abolished.

The 1981 electoral victory of the Panhellenic Socialist Movement (Pasok) of Andreas Papandreou substantially changed Greece's internal and external policies. A scandal centered on George Koskokas, a banker and publisher, led to the arrest or investigation of leading Socialists, implicated Papandreou, and contributed to the defeat of the Socialists at the polls in 1989. Papandreou, who was acquitted Jan. 1992 of corruption charges, led the Socialists to a comeback victory in general elections Oct. 10, 1993.

Costas Simitis replaced the ailing Papandreou as prime minister, Jan. 18, 1996. Simitis led the Socialists to victory in the Sept. 22, 1996, election.

An earthquake shook Athens Sept. 7, 1999, killing at least 143 people and leaving more than 60,000 homeless. The Socialists retained power by a narrow margin in the elections of Apr. 9, 2000. Police in 2002 cracked down on the November 17 terrorist movement, blamed for 23 killings since the mid-1970s.

The conservative New Democracy Party won parliamentary elections, Mar. 7, 2004, and Konstantinos (Costas) Karamanlis became prime minister. Rampant wildfires, Aug. 2007, left at least 65 people dead and caused over $1.6 bil in damage. On Jan. 23-25, 2008, Karamanlis became the first Greek government leader in 49 years to pay an official visit to Turkey.

Beset by scandals and an ailing economy, Karamanlis called early elections for Oct. 4, 2009, won by Pasok under the leadership of the U.S.-born George A. Papandreou, whose father and grandfather had headed previous Greek governments. The IMF and the 16 eurozone countries agreed May 2, 2010, on a 110 bil euro ($146 bil) loan package to prevent Greece from defaulting; in return, Greek leaders implemented an austerity plan. With default again impending, eurozone leaders agreed July 21, 2011, on another Greek bailout package, for 109 bil euros ($157 bil). The conservative, pro-bailout Antonis Samaras became prime min. of a coalition government, June 20, 2012.

Grenada

People: Population: 109,011. **Age distrib.:** <15: 25%; 65+: 9.1%. **Pop. density:** 820.7 per sq mi, 316.9 per sq km. **Urban:** 39.1%. **Ethnic groups:** black 82%, mixed black and European 13%, European and East Indian 5%. **Principal languages:** English (official), French patois. **Chief religions:** Roman Catholic 53%, Anglican 14%, other Protestant 33%.

Geography: Total area: 133 sq mi, 344 sq km; **Land area:** 133 sq mi, 344 sq km. **Location:** In Caribbean, 90 mi N of Venezuela.

Neighbors: Venezuela, Trinidad and Tobago to S; St. Vincent and the Grenadines to N. **Topography:** Main island is mountainous; country includes Carriacou and Petit Martinique isls. **Capital:** St. George's, 41,054.

Government: Type: Parliamentary democracy. **Head of state:** Queen Elizabeth II, represented by Gov.-Gen. Sir Carlyle Glean; b. Feb. 11, 1932; in office: Nov. 27, 2008. **Head of gov.:** Prime Min. Tillman Thomas; b. June 13, 1945; in office: July 9, 2008. **Local divisions:** 6 parishes, 1 dependency. **Defense budget:** NA. **Active troops:** No regular military forces.

Economy: Industries: food and beverages, textiles, light assembly operations, tourism, constr. **Chief crops:** bananas, cocoa, nutmeg, mace, citrus, avocados, root crops, sugarcane, corn, vegetables. **Natural resources:** timber, tropical fruit. **Arable land:** 7.4%. **Livestock:** cattle: 4,450; chickens: 270,000; goats: 7,200; pigs: 3,000; sheep: 13,200. **Fish catch:** 2,452 metric tons. **Electricity prod.** (2010): 201.4 mil kWh. **Labor force:** agric. 11%, industry 20%, services 69%.

Finance: Monetary unit: East Caribbean Dollar (XCD) (Sept. 2012: 2.70 = $1 U.S.). **GDP:** $1.5 bil; **per capita GDP:** $14,100; **GDP growth:** 1.1%. **Imports** (2010): $284.4 mil; Trinidad and Tobago 43.4%, U.S. 19.1%. **Exports** (2009): $38.7 mil; St. Lucia 19.9%, Antigua and Barbuda 13.5%, St. Kitts and Nevis 12.2%, Dominica 12.1%, U.S. 10.2%. **Tourism:** $104 mil. **Budget** (2009): $215.9 mil. **Total reserves less gold:** $120.7 mil. **CPI change:** 3.03%.

Transport: Civil aviation: 3 airports. **Chief port:** Saint George's.
Communications: TV sets: 383 per 1,000 pop. **Radios:** 567 per 1,000 pop. **Telephone lines** (2010): 27.2 per 100 pop. **Internet** (2010): 33.5%.
Health: Life expect.: 70.8 male; 76.1 female. **Births:** 16.8 (per 1,000 pop.). **Deaths:** 8.0 (per 1,000 pop.). **Natural inc.:** 0.88% **Infant mortality:** 11.1 (per 1,000 live births). **HIV rate:** NA.
Education: Compulsory: ages 5-16. **Literacy:** NA.
Major intl. organizations: UN (FAO, IBRD, ILO, IMF, WHO), Caricom, the Commonwealth, OAS, OECS, WTO.
Embassy: 1701 New Hampshire Ave. NW 20009; 265-2561.
Website: www.gov.gd

Columbus sighted Grenada in 1498. The first European settlers were French, 1650. The island was held alternately by France and England until final British occupation, 1784. Grenada became fully independent Feb. 7, 1974, during a general strike.

On Oct. 14, 1983, a military coup ousted Prime Min. Maurice Bishop, who was put under house arrest, later freed by supporters, rearrested, and, finally, on Oct. 19, executed. U.S. forces, with a token force from 6 area nations, invaded Grenada, Oct. 25. Resistance from the Grenadian army and Cuban advisors was quickly overcome, and U.S. troops left Grenada in June 1985.

Hurricane Ivan slammed into Grenada, Sept. 7, 2004, killing 39 people and damaging an estimated 90% of the buildings on the island. Tillman Thomas of the National Democratic Congress became prime minister after parliamentary elections July 8, 2008.

Guatemala
Republic of Guatemala

People: Population: 14,099,032. **Age distrib.:** <15: 37.4%; 65+: 4%. **Pop. density:** 340.8 per sq mi, 131.6 per sq km. **Urban:** 49.8%. **Ethnic groups:** mestizo (mixed Amerindian-Spanish) & European 59%, K'iche 9%, Kaqchikel 8%, Mam 8%, Q'eqchi 6%, other Mayan 9%. **Principal languages:** Spanish (official), Amerindian langs. (23 officially recognized). **Chief religions:** Roman Catholic, Protestant, indigenous Mayan beliefs.
Geography: Total area: 42,042 sq mi, 108,889 sq km; **Land area:** 41,374 sq mi, 107,159 sq km. **Location:** In Central America. **Neighbors:** Mexico on N and W, El Salvador on S, Honduras and Belize on E. **Topography:** The central highland and mountain areas are bordered by the narrow Pacific coast and lowlands and fertile river valleys on the Caribbean. Numerous volcanoes in S, more than half a dozen over 11,000 ft. **Capital:** Guatemala City, 1,168,420.
Government: Type: Republic. **Head of state and gov.:** Pres. Otto Fernando Perez Molina; b. Dec. 1, 1950; in office: Jan. 14, 2012. **Local divisions:** 22 departments. **Defense budget:** $196 mil. **Active troops:** 15,212.
Economy: Industries: sugar, textiles and clothing, furniture, chemicals, petroleum, metals, rubber, tourism. **Chief crops:** sugarcane, corn, bananas, coffee, beans, cardamom. **Natural resources:** petroleum, nickel, rare woods, fish, chicle, hydropower. **Crude oil reserves:** 83.1 mil bbls. **Arable land:** 14.0%. **Livestock:** cattle: 3.1 mil; chickens: 32.1 mil; goats: 128,000; pigs: 2.7 mil; sheep: 600,000. **Fish catch:** 44,651 metric tons. **Electricity prod.:** 7.2 bil kWh. **Labor force:** agric. 38%, industry 14%, services 48%.
Finance: Monetary unit: Quetzal (GTQ) (Sept. 2012: 7.96 = $1 U.S.). **GDP:** $75.7 bil; **per capita GDP:** $5,100; **GDP growth:** 3.8%. **Imports:** $16.6 bil; U.S. 41.5%, Mexico 10.5%, China 8.4%, El Salvador 4.6%. **Exports:** $10.5 bil; U.S. 38%, El Salvador 10.6%, Honduras 6.9%, Mexico 4.8%. **Tourism:** $1.4 bil. **Budget:** $6.9 bil. **Total reserves less gold:** $5.8 bil. **Gold:** 221,600 oz t. **CPI change:** 6.2%.

Transport: Railways: 206 mi. **Motor vehicles:** 22.6 vehicles per 1,000 pop. **Civil aviation:** 15 airports. **Chief ports:** Puerto Quetzal, Santo Tomas de Castilla.
Communications: TV sets: 163 per 1,000 pop. **Radios:** 80 per 1,000 pop. **Telephone lines:** 11 per 100 pop. **Internet:** 11.7%.
Health: Life expect.: 69.3 male; 73.1 female. **Births:** 26.5 (per 1,000 pop.). **Deaths:** 4.9 (per 1,000 pop.) **Natural inc.:** 2.16% **Infant mortality:** 25.2 (per 1,000 live births). **HIV rate:** 0.8%.
Education: Compulsory: ages 5-15. **Literacy:** 75.2%.
Major intl. organizations: UN (FAO, IBRD, ILO, IMF, WHO), OAS, WTO.
Embassy: 2220 R St. NW 20008; 745-4952.
Website: www.guatemala.gob.gt

A Mayan Indian empire flourished in what is today Guatemala for over 1,000 years before Spaniards came. Guatemala was a Spanish colony 1524-1821. A republic was established in 1839.

The U.S. intervened in Guatemala in 1954 when the Central Intelligence Agency engineered the overthrow of elected Pres. Jacobo Arbenz Guzmán, a left-wing reformer. Since then, the country has experienced a variety of military and civilian governments and periods of insurgency, repression, paramilitary violence, and civil war. After military coups in 1982 and 1983, the nation returned to civilian rule in 1986.

On Sept. 19, 1996, the Guatemalan government and leftist rebels approved a peace accord; the final agreement was signed Dec. 29. During more than 35 years of armed conflict, some 200,000 people were killed or "disappeared" (and are presumed dead); most of these casualties were attributed to the government and its paramilitary allies. U.S. Pres. Bill Clinton, on a visit to Guatemala Mar. 10, 1999, apologized for aid the U.S. had given to forces which he said "engaged in violence and widespread repression."

Drought and weak export prices during 2001-02 worsened the plight of Guatemala's poor, who make up 80% of the population. Floods and mudslides from Tropical Storm Stan, Oct. 2005, killed at least 669 people; another 844 were missing and presumed dead.

After a campaign marred by violence, Álvaro Colom Caballeros, a businessman who pledged to fight poverty, won a presidential runoff election Nov. 4, 2007, and took office Jan. 14, 2008. Floods and landslides from Tropical Storm Agatha, which hit Guatemala May 29, 2010, killed more than 170 people. With Pres. Colom and his relatives constitutionally barred from running in the Sept. 2011 presidential election, his wife, Sandra Torres de Colom, declared her candidacy Mar. 8 and filed for divorce 3 days later, saying she was "getting married to the Guatemalan people"; her bid was blocked by the courts. Former Gen. Otto Pérez Molina won a runoff election Nov. 6, and took office, Jan. 14, 2012. Drug trafficking, arms smuggling, police corruption, and one of the world's highest homicide rates pose threats to national stability.

Guinea
Republic of Guinea

People: Population: 10,884,958. **Age distrib.:** <15: 42.4%; 65+: 3.5%. **Pop. density:** 114.7 per sq mi, 44.3 per sq km. **Urban:** 35.4%. **Ethnic groups:** Peuhl 40%, Malinke 30%, Soussou 20%, smaller ethnic groups 10%. **Principal languages:** French (official), ethnic group-specific langs. **Chief religions:** Muslim 85%, Christian 8%, indigenous beliefs 7%.
Geography: Total area: 94,926 sq mi, 245,857 sq km; **Land area:** 94,872 sq mi, 245,717 sq km. **Location:** On Atlantic coast of W Africa. **Neighbors:** Guinea-Bissau, Senegal, Mali on N; Côte d'Ivoire on E; Liberia, Sierra Leone on S. **Topography:** A narrow coastal belt leads to mountainous middle region, source of the Gambia, Senegal, and Niger rivers. Upper Guinea, farther inland, is cooler upland. The SE is forested. **Capital:** Conakry, 1,786,300.
Government: Type: Republic. **Head of state:** Interim Pres. Alpha Condé; b. Mar. 4, 1938; in office: Dec. 21, 2010. **Head of gov.:** Prime Min. Mohamed Said Fofana; b. 1952; in office: Dec. 24 2010. **Local divisions:** 33 prefectures, 1 special zone. **Defense budget** (2010): $48 mil. **Active troops:** 12,300.
Economy: Industries: bauxite, gold, diamonds, iron; alumina refining; light mfg.; agric. proc. **Chief crops:** rice, coffee, pineapples, palm kernels, cassava, bananas, sweet potatoes. **Natural resources:** bauxite, iron ore, diamonds, gold, uranium, hydropower, fish, salt. **Arable land:** 11.6%. **Livestock:** cattle: 4.9 mil; chickens: 22.5 mil; goats: 1.9 mil; pigs: 95,187; sheep: 1.6 mil. **Fish catch:** 109,869 metric tons. **Electricity prod.:** 955 mil kWh. **Labor force:** agric. 76%, industry and services 24%.
Finance: Monetary unit: Franc (GNF) (Sept. 2012: 6,980.40 = $1 U.S.). **GDP:** $11.6 bil; **per capita GDP:** $1,100; **GDP growth:** 3.6%. **Imports:** $1.8 bil; China 13.4%, Netherlands 8.2%, U.S. 5.4%, France 4%. **Exports:** $1.6 bil; Chile 24.4%, Spain 9.1%, India 7.9%, Russia 7.4%, Germany 5.1%, Ireland 5%, U.S. 4.9%, Ukraine 4.4%. **Tourism:** $2 mil. **Budget:** $1.2 bil. **Total reserves less gold:** NA. **Gold:** 7,107 oz t. **CPI change:** 21.4%.
Transport: Railways: 736 mi. **Civil aviation:** 4 airports. **Chief ports:** Conakry, Kamsar.
Communications: TV sets: 18 per 1,000 pop. **Radios:** 81 per 1,000 pop. **Telephone lines:** 0.2 per 100 pop. **Internet:** 1.3%.

Health: Life expect.: 57.1 male; 60.2 female. **Births:** 36.6 (per 1,000 pop.). **Deaths:** 10.2 (per 1,000 pop.). **Natural inc.:** 2.64% **Infant mortality:** 59.0 (per 1,000 live births). **HIV rate:** 1.3%.

Education: Compulsory: ages 7-16. **Literacy:** 41%.

Major intl. organizations: UN and most of its specialized agencies, AU, WTO.

Embassy: 2112 Leroy Pl. NW 20008; 906-4300.

Website: www.guinee.gov.gn or www.state.gov/p/af/ci/gv/

Guinea, a French colony, attained independence Oct. 2, 1958. Sékou Touré, Guinea's first president (1958-84), turned to Communist nations for support and set up a one-party state. Thousands of opponents were jailed and tortured, and many were killed in the 1970s, after an unsuccessful Portuguese invasion.

The military took control in a bloodless coup after the Mar. 1984 death of Touré. A new constitution was approved in 1991, but movement toward democracy was slow. When presidential elections were finally held, in Dec. 1993, the incumbent, Gen. Lansana Conté, was the official winner; outside monitors called the elections flawed. Conté suppressed an army mutiny in Conakry, Feb. 2-3, 1996, and won reelection in Dec. 1998. Fighting in early 2001 along the border with Liberia and Sierra Leone created a refugee crisis in Guinea; voluntary repatriation of more than 51,000 Liberian refugees was largely completed in 2007.

Major opposition parties boycotted the presidential election Dec. 21, 2003, in which the ailing Conté won 95.6% of the vote. More than 120 died in Jan.-Feb. 2007 strikes and protests that pressured Conté to name a new prime min. from a union-leader approved list; protests followed his ouster by Conté in May 2008. After Conté's death Dec. 22, 2008, a military junta took power, calling itself the National Council for Democracy and Development. More than 150 people were reportedly killed Sept. 28, 2009, when Guinean troops fired into a crowd of about 50,000 antigovernment protesters in Conakry. After an assassination attempt Dec. 3, 2009, by a former aide left Pres. Moussa Dadis Camara seriously wounded, Vice Pres. Sékouba Konaté became interim head of state. Presidential elections June-Nov. 2010 brought a civilian government headed by Alpha Condé to power Dec. 21. He survived an assassination attempt, July 19, 2011, but was criticized for delaying expected parliamentary elections.

Guinea-Bissau
Republic of Guinea-Bissau

People: Population: 1,628,603. **Age distrib.:** <15: 40.2%; 65+: 3.2%. **Pop. density:** 150 per sq mi, 57.9 per sq km. **Urban:** 43.9%. **Ethnic groups:** African 99% (incl. Balanta 30%, Fula 20%, Manjaca 14%, Mandinga 13%, Papel 7%). **Principal languages:** Portuguese (official), Crioulo, African langs. **Chief religions:** Muslim 50%, indigenous beliefs 40%, Christian 10%.

Geography: Total area: 13,948 sq mi, 36,125 sq km; **Land area:** 10,857 sq mi, 28,120 sq km. **Location:** On Atlantic coast of W Africa. **Neighbors:** Senegal on N, Guinea on E and S. **Topography:** A swampy coastal plain covers most of country; to E is a low savanna region. **Capital:** Bissau, 422,811.

Government: Type: Republic. **Head of state:** Pres. Manuel Serifo Nhamadjo; b. 1958; in office: May 11, 2012. **Head of gov.:** Prime Min. Rui Duarte Barros; in office: May 16, 2012. **Local divisions:** 9 regions. **Defense budget:** $20 mil. **Active troops:** 4,458.

Economy: Industries: agric. prods. proc., beer, soft drinks. **Chief crops:** rice, corn, beans, cassava, cashew nuts, peanuts, palm kernels, cotton. **Natural resources:** fish, timber, phosphates, bauxite, clay, granite, limestone, unexploited deposits of petroleum. **Arable land:** 10.7%. **Livestock:** cattle: 641,500; chickens: 2 mil; goats: 440,510; pigs: 418,900; sheep: 453,760. **Fish catch:** 6,800 metric tons. **Electricity prod.:** 65 mil kWh. **Labor force:** agric. 82%, industry and services 18%.

Finance: Monetary unit: CFA BCEAO Franc (XOF) (Sept. 2012: 519.73 = $1 U.S.). **GDP:** $1.95 bil; **per capita GDP:** $1,200; **GDP growth:** 5.3%. **Imports:** $327.6 mil; Portugal 28.3%, Senegal 15.6%, China 4.7%. **Exports:** $244.6 mil; India 41.5%, Nigeria 33.9%, Brazil 8.7%, Togo 7.9%. **Tourism:** $13 mil. **Budget:** $202.8 mil. **Total reserves less gold:** $220 mil. **CPI change:** 5.05%.

Transport: Civil aviation: 2 airports. **Chief ports:** Bissau, Buba, Cacheu, Farim.

Communications: TV sets: 39 per 1,000 pop. **Radios:** 41 per 1,000 pop. **Telephone lines** (2010): 0.3 per 100 pop. **Internet:** 2.7%.

Health: Life expect.: 47.2 male; 51.1 female. **Births:** 34.7 (per 1,000 pop.). **Deaths:** 15.0 (per 1,000 pop.). **Natural inc.:** 1.97% **Infant mortality:** 94.4 (per 1,000 live births). **HIV rate:** 2.5%.

Education: Compulsory: ages 6-11. **Literacy:** 54.2%.

Major intl. organizations: UN (FAO, IBRD, ILO, IMF, WHO), AU, WTO.

Permanent UN Mission: 800 Second Ave., Ste. 400F, New York, NY 10017; (917) 770-5598.

Website: www.state.gov/p/af/ci/pu/

Portuguese mariners explored the area in the mid-15th cent.; the slave trade flourished in the 17th and 18th centuries, and colonization began in the 19th. Independence came Sept. 10, 1974, ending 13 years of guerrilla warfare against the Portuguese regime.

A Nov. 1980 coup gave army chief João Bernardo Vieira absolute power. Vieira eventually initiated political liberalization; multiparty elections were held July 3, 1994. An army uprising June 7, 1998, triggered a civil war, with Senegal and Guinea aiding the Vieira regime. After a peace accord signed on Nov. 2 broke down, rebel troops ousted Vieira on May 7, 1999.

Elections 1999-2000 brought a return to civilian rule, but top military officers staged a coup Sept. 14, 2003. Vieira won a presidential runoff election, July 24, 2005, and returned to power Oct. 1. Gen. Batista Tagme Na Waie, the nation's defense chief, was killed by a bomb Mar. 1, 2009; less than a day later, a group of soldiers murdered Vieira in his presidential palace. Political violence continued as the June 28, 2009, presidential election approached; the ruling party candidate, Malam Bacai Sanhá, won a runoff vote July 26. He died Jan. 9, 2012. A military coup Apr. 12, 2012, derailed a runoff election scheduled for Apr. 29. The military appointed Manuel Serifo Nhamadjo to serve as pres. of a transitional government.

Guyana
Co-operative Republic of Guyana

People: Population: 741,908. **Age distrib.:** <15: 31.1%; 65+: 4.9%. **Pop. density:** 9.8 per sq mi, 3.8 per sq km. **Urban:** 28.4%. **Ethnic groups:** East Indian 44%, black (African) 30%, mixed 17%, Amerindian 9%. **Principal languages:** English, Amerindian dialects, Creole, Caribbean Hindustani, Urdu. **Chief religions:** Protestant 31% (Pentecostal 17%, Anglican 7%, Seventh-Day Adventist 5%, Methodist 2%), Hindu 28%, Roman Catholic 8%, Muslim 7%, Anglican 7%, Seventh-Day Adventist 5%, Methodist 2%, Jehovah's Witnesses 1%, other Christian 18%, none 4%.

Geography: Total area: 83,000 sq mi, 214,969 sq km; **Land area:** 76,004 sq mi, 196,849 sq km. **Location:** On N coast of S. America. **Neighbors:** Venezuela on W, Brazil on S, Suriname on E. **Topography:** Dense tropical forests cover much of land, although flat coastal area up to 40 mi wide, where 90% of the population lives, provides rich alluvial soil for agriculture. A grassy savanna divides the 2 zones. **Capital:** Georgetown, 127,150.

Government: Type: Republic. **Head of state:** Pres. Donald Rabrindranath Ramotar; b. Oct. 22, 1950; in office: Dec. 3, 2011. **Head of gov.:** Prime Min. Samuel Hinds; b. Dec. 27, 1943; in office: Dec. 22, 1997. **Local divisions:** 10 regions. **Defense budget:** $30 mil. **Active troops:** 1,100.

Economy: Industries: bauxite, sugar, rice milling, timber, textiles, gold mining. **Chief crops:** sugarcane, rice, edible oils. **Natural resources:** bauxite, gold, diamonds, timber, shrimp, fish. **Arable land:** 2.1%. **Livestock:** cattle: 110,000; chickens: 21.4 mil; goats: 79,000; pigs: 13,500; sheep: 130,000. **Fish catch:** 45,674 metric tons. **Electricity prod.:** 817 mil kWh. **Labor force:** NA.

Finance: Monetary unit: Dollar (GYD) (Sept. 2012: 202.47 = $1 U.S.). **GDP:** $5.9 bil; **per capita GDP:** $7,600; **GDP growth:** 4.2%. **Imports:** $1.5 bil; U.S. 23.1%, Trinidad and Tobago 21.7%, China 9%, Cuba 6%. **Exports:** $1.2 bil; Canada 29%, U.S. 28.6%, UK 4.9%, Trinidad and Tobago 4.3%, Jamaica 4.3%. **Tourism:** $80 mil. **Budget:** $707.5 mil. **Total reserves less gold:** $801.8 mil. **CPI change:** 4.98%.

Transport: Motor vehicles: 62.1 vehicles per 1,000 pop. **Civil aviation:** 11 airports. **Chief port:** Georgetown.

Communications: TV sets: 167 per 1,000 pop. **Radios:** 571 per 1,000 pop. **Telephone lines:** 20.2 per 100 pop. **Internet:** 32%.

Health: Life expect.: 63.6 male; 71.4 female. **Births:** 16.7 (per 1,000 pop.). **Deaths:** 7.2 (per 1,000 pop.). **Natural inc.:** 0.95% **Infant mortality:** 35.6 (per 1,000 live births). **HIV rate:** 1.2%.

Education: Compulsory: ages 6-14. **Literacy:** NA.

Major intl. organizations: UN (FAO, IBRD, ILO, IMF, WHO), Caricom, the Commonwealth, OAS, WTO.

Embassy: 2490 Tracy Pl. NW 20008; 265-6900.

Website: www.gina.gov.gy

Guyana became a Dutch possession in the 17th cent., but sovereignty passed to Britain in 1815. Indentured servants from India soon outnumbered African slaves. Guyana became independent May 26, 1966.

The Port Kaituma ambush of U.S. Rep. Leo J. Ryan and others investigating mistreatment of American followers of the Rev. Jim Jones's People's Temple cult triggered a mass suicide-execution of 911 cultists at Jonestown in the jungle, Nov. 18, 1978.

The People's National Congress, the party in power since Guyana became independent, was voted out of office with the election of Cheddi Jagan in Oct. 1992. When Pres. Jagan died Mar. 6, 1997, Prime Min. Samuel Hinds succeeded him. Jagan's widow, Janet, became prime min. Mar. 17. She won the presidency in a disputed election Dec. 15. She resigned because of ill health Aug. 11, 1999, and was succeeded by Bharrat Jagdeo, then 35, who became the youngest head of state in the Americas. He won reelection Mar. 19, 2001, and Aug. 28, 2006.

Floods from torrential rains, Jan. 2005, affected about 40% of the population. Gunmen in Georgetown killed Agric. Min. Satyadeow Sawh and two members of his family, Apr. 22, 2006. Donald Ramotar, the candidate of Jagdeo's party, was elected president Nov. 28, 2011.

Haiti
Republic of Haiti

People: Population: 9,801,664. **Age distrib.:** <15: 35.3%; 65+: 4%. **Pop. density:** 921.1 per sq mi, 355.6 per sq km. **Urban:** 53.4%. **Ethnic groups:** black 95%, mulatto and white 5%. **Principal languages:** French, Creole (both official). **Chief religions:** Roman Catholic 80%, Protestant 16% (Baptist 10%, Pentecostal 4%), roughly half of pop. practices voodoo.

Geography: Total area: 10,714 sq mi, 27,750 sq km; **Land area:** 10,641 sq mi, 27,560 sq km. **Location:** In Caribbean, occupies W third of isl. of Hispaniola. **Neighbors:** Dominican Republic on E, Cuba to W. **Topography:** About two-thirds is mountainous. Much of rest is semiarid. Coastal areas are warm and moist. **Capital:** Port-au-Prince, 2,207,110.

Government: Type: Republic. **Head of state:** Pres. Michel Martelly; b. Feb. 12, 1961; in office: May 14, 2011. **Head of gov.:** Prime Min. Laurent Lamothe; b. Aug. 14, 1972; in office: May 16, 2012. **Local divisions:** 9 departments. **Defense budget:** NA. **Active troops:** No active armed forces. UN mission MINUSTAH in country.

Economy: Industries: textiles, sugar refining, flour milling, cement, light assembly of imported parts. **Chief crops:** coffee, mangoes, sugarcane, rice, corn, sorghum. **Natural resources:** bauxite, copper, calcium carbonate, gold, marble, hydropower. **Arable land:** 38.1%. **Livestock:** cattle: 1.5 mil; chickens: 5.6 mil; goats: 1.9 mil; pigs: 1 mil; sheep: 153,500. **Fish catch:** 8,510 metric tons. **Electricity prod.:** 688 mil kWh. **Labor force:** agric 38.1%, industry 11.5%, services 50.4%.

Finance: Monetary unit: Gourde (HTG) (Sept. 2012: 42.45 = $1 U.S.). **GDP:** $12.5 bil; **per capita GDP:** $1,300; **GDP growth:** 5.6%. **Imports:** $3.4 bil; Dominican Republic 31.9%, U.S. 25.3%, Netherlands Antilles 8.7%, China 7.2%. **Exports:** $721.3 mil; U.S. 83.3%. **Tourism:** $167 mil. **Budget:** $1.7 bil. **Total reserves less gold:** $1.2 bil. **Gold:** 1,308 oz t. **CPI change:** 8.4%.

Transport: Motor vehicles: 7.2 vehicles per 1,000 pop. **Civil aviation:** 4 airports. **Chief ports:** Cap-Haïtien, Gonaïves Jacmel, Port-au-Prince.

Communications: TV sets: 104 per 1,000 pop. **Radios:** 170 per 1,000 pop. **Telephone lines** (2010): 0.5 per 100 pop. **Internet** (2010): 8.4%.

Health: Life expect.: 61.2 male; 63.9 female. **Births:** 23.9 (per 1,000 pop.). **Deaths:** 8.1 (per 1,000 pop.). **Natural inc.:** 1.58% **Infant mortality:** 52.4 (per 1,000 live births). **HIV rate:** 1.9%.

Education: Compulsory: ages 6-14. **Literacy:** 48.7%.

Major intl. organizations: UN and most of its specialized agencies, Caricom, OAS, WTO.

Embassy: 2311 Massachusetts Ave. NW 20008; 332-4090.

Website: www.parlementhaitien.ht or www.haiti.org

Haiti, visited by Columbus in 1492 and a French colony from 1697, attained its independence, 1804, following a rebellion led by former slave Toussaint L'Ouverture. After a period of political violence, the U.S. occupied the country 1915-34.

François Duvalier, known as Papa Doc, was elected president in Sept. 1957; in 1964 he was named president for life. Upon his death in 1971, he was succeeded by his son, Jean Claude Duvalier, known as Baby Doc. Following weeks of unrest, Jean Claude fled Haiti aboard a U.S. Air Force jet Feb. 7, 1986. His departure ended the Duvalier family's brutal 28-year dictatorship, but political violence, government corruption, poverty, AIDS and other health problems, and deteriorating environmental quality have continued to plague Haiti.

Father Jean-Bertrand Aristide was elected president Dec. 1990, but in Sept. 1991, he was arrested by the military and expelled from the country. Some 35,000 Haitian refugees were intercepted by the U.S. Coast Guard as they tried to enter the U.S., 1991-92. Most were returned to Haiti. There was a new upsurge of refugees starting in late 1993.

The UN authorized, July 31, 1994, an invasion of Haiti by a multinational force. With U.S. troops already en route, a full-scale invasion was averted, Sept. 18, when military leaders agreed to step down. Aristide returned to Haiti and was restored to office Oct. 15. A UN peacekeeping force exercised responsibility in Haiti from Mar. 31, 1995, to Nov. 30, 1997. Aristide transferred power to his elected successor, René Préval, on Feb. 7, 1996.

At least 140 people died and over 160,000 were left homeless when Hurricane Georges struck Haiti Sept. 22, 1998. Aristide won the presidency Nov. 26, 2000, in an election boycotted by opposition groups. An armed uprising in early 2004 and pressure from France and the U.S. toppled Aristide, who went into exile Feb. 29. A U.S.-led contingent, sent in after the upheaval, yielded authority June 1 to a UN stabilization force (MINUSTAH).

Flooding in late May 2004 killed more than 1,000 people, and more than 2,400 were killed in Tropical Storm Jeanne in Sept. Presidential elections Feb. 7, 2006, restored Préval to power.

Skyrocketing prices for food imports sparked riots and mass protests in Apr. 2008. A succession of hurricanes and tropical storms (Fay, Gustav, Hanna, Ike), Aug.-Sept. 2008, left more than 550 Haitians dead and up to 1 mil homeless. A school collapse near Port-au-Prince Nov. 7, 2008, killed 91 students and teachers.

An earthquake Jan. 12, 2010, near Port-au-Prince caused cataclysmic damage: more than 220,000 people (including nearly 100 UN peacekeepers) were killed, at least 300,000 were injured, and many more were left homeless. With the central government paralyzed and the presidential palace and parliament building in ruins, the U.S. and other countries mounted a massive relief effort. Nearly 600,000 Haitians were still living in displacement camps 18 months later.

After the first round of presidential balloting Nov. 28, 2010, Michel Martelly, an entertainer popularly known as Sweet Micky, was declared ineligible for the 2nd round. Violent protests from his supporters, allegations of electoral fraud from international observers, and diplomatic pressure from the U.S. and other donor countries gained him a place in the runoff Mar. 20, 2011, which he won. Parliament twice blocked his nominee for prime minister before approving his third choice, Garry Conille, a physician and development expert. Conille resigned Feb. 24, 2012, and was replaced by Laurent Lamothe May 16, 2012. MINUSTAH uniformed personnel numbered about 10,000 in mid-2012.

Honduras
Republic of Honduras

People: Population: 8,296,693. **Age distrib.:** <15: 36.1%; 65+: 3.8%. **Pop. density:** 192 per sq mi, 74.2 per sq km. **Urban:** 52.2%. **Ethnic groups:** mestizo (mixed Amerindian & European) 90%, Amerindian 7%, black 2%, white 1%. **Principal languages:** Spanish (official), Amerindian dialects. **Chief religions:** Roman Catholic 97%, Protestant 3%.

Geography: Total area: 43,278 sq mi, 112,090 sq km; **Land area:** 43,201 sq mi, 111,890 sq km. **Location:** In Central America. **Neighbors:** Guatemala on W; El Salvador, Nicaragua on S. **Topography:** Caribbean coast is 500 mi long. Pacific coast, on Gulf of Fonseca, is 40 mi long. Country is mountainous, with wide fertile valleys and rich forests. **Capital:** Tegucigalpa, 1,088,470.

Government: Type: Republic. **Head of state and gov.:** Pres. Porfirio (Pepe) Lobo; b. Dec. 22, 1947; in office: Jan. 27, 2010. **Local divisions:** 18 departments. **Defense budget:** $140 mil. **Active troops:** 12,000.

Economy: Industries: sugar, coffee, woven and knit apparel, wood prods., cigars. **Chief crops:** bananas, coffee, citrus, corn, African palm. **Natural resources:** timber, gold, silver, copper, lead, zinc, iron ore, antimony, coal, fish, hydropower. **Arable land:** 9.1%. **Livestock:** cattle: 2.7 mil; chickens: 40.6 mil; goats: 24,500; pigs: 469,635; sheep: 15,000. **Fish catch:** 38,616 metric tons. **Electricity prod.:** 6.3 bil kWh. **Labor force:** agric. 39.2%, industry 20.9%, services 39.8%.

Finance: Monetary unit: Lempira (HNL) (Sept. 2012: 19.57 = $1 U.S.). **GDP:** $36.2 bil; **per capita GDP:** $4,400; **GDP growth:** 3.6%. **Imports:** $10.3 bil; U.S. 49.8%, Guatemala 8.2%, Mexico 5%, El Salvador 4.9%. **Exports:** $7.2 bil; U.S. 86%. **Tourism:** $701 mil. **Budget:** $3.7 bil. **Total reserves less gold:** $2.7 bil. **Gold:** 21,400 oz t. **CPI change:** 6.8%.

Transport: Railways: 47 mi. **Motor vehicles:** 15.9 vehicles per 1,000 pop. **Civil aviation:** 13 airports. **Chief ports:** La Ceiba, Puerto Cortes, San Lorenzo, Tela.

Communications: TV sets: 176 per 1,000 pop. **Radios:** 1,698 per 1,000 pop. **Telephone lines:** 7.9 per 100 pop. **Internet:** 15.9%.

Health: Life expect.: 69.0 male; 72.5 female. **Births:** 24.7 (per 1,000 pop.). **Deaths:** 5.1 (per 1,000 pop.). **Natural inc.:** 1.96% **Infant mortality:** 19.9 (per 1,000 live births). **HIV rate:** 0.8%.

Education: Compulsory: ages 6-11. **Literacy:** 84.8%.

Major intl. organizations: UN (FAO, IBRD, ILO, IMF, WHO), OAS, WTO.

Embassy: 3007 Tilden St. NW 20008; 966-7702.

Website: www.gob.hn

Mayan civilization flourished in Honduras in the 1st millennium CE. Columbus arrived in 1502. Honduras became independent after freeing itself from Spain, 1821, and from the Fed. of Central America, 1838.

Gen. Oswaldo Lopez Arellano, president for most of the period 1963-75 by virtue of one election and two coups, was ousted by the army in 1975 over charges of pervasive bribery by United Brands Co. of the U.S. An elected civilian government took power in 1982. Some 3,200 U.S. troops were sent to Honduras after the Honduran border was violated by Nicaraguan forces, Mar. 1988.

Already one of the poorest countries in the Western Hemisphere, Honduras was devastated in late Oct. 1998 by Hurricane Mitch, which killed at least 5,600 people and caused more than $850 mil in damage to crops and livestock.

Ricardo Maduro, a businessman who pledged to crack down on crime, won the presidency Nov. 25, 2001. He was succeeded by Manuel Zelaya Rosales of the opposition Liberal Party, who won the presidential election held Nov. 27, 2005. Seeking constitutional changes in his final year in office that may have allowed him to run for a second term, Zelaya lost a political struggle with the Honduran congress and supreme court; he was ousted by the military June 28, 2009. The U.S. and OAS refused to recognize his successor, congressional leader Roberto Micheletti Bain. Porfirio (Pepe) Lobo, a conservative landowner, defeated Liberal Party nominee Elvin Santos in the Nov. 29, 2009, presidential election, and took office Jan. 27, 2010, resolving the constitutional crisis. Honduras has diversified its economy, once dominated by banana and coffe exports, by expanding its textile industry.

Hungary
Republic of Hungary

People: Population: 9,958,453. **Age distrib.:** <15: 14.9%; 65+: 17.1%. **Pop. density:** 287.8 per sq mi, 111.1 per sq km. **Urban:** 69.5%. **Ethnic groups:** Hungarian 92%, Roma 2%. **Principal language:** Hungarian. **Chief religions:** Roman Catholic 52%, Calvinist 16%, Lutheran 3%, Greek Catholic 3%, unaffiliated 15%.

Geography: Total area: 35,918 sq mi, 93,028 sq km; **Land area:** 34,598 sq mi, 89,608 sq km. **Location:** In E central Europe. **Neighbors:** Slovakia, Ukraine on N; Austria on W; Slovenia, Serbia, Croatia on S; Romania on E. **Topography:** The Danube R. forms Slovak border in NW, then swings S to bisect the country. Eastern half of Hungary is mainly a great fertile plain, the Alfold; the W and N are hilly. **Capital:** Budapest, 1,736,720.

Government: Type: Parliamentary democracy. **Head of state:** Pres. János Áder; b. May 9, 1959; in office: May 10, 2012. **Head of gov.:** Prime Min. Viktor Orbán; b. May 31, 1963; in office: May 29, 2010. **Local divisions:** 19 counties, 20 urban counties, 1 capital. **Defense budget:** $1.4 bil. **Active troops:** 22,587.

Economy: Industries: mining, metallurgy, constr. materials, processed foods, textiles, chemicals (espec. pharmaceuticals), motor vehicles. **Chief crops:** wheat, corn, sunflower seeds, potatoes, sugar beets. **Natural resources:** bauxite, coal, nat. gas, fertile soils. **Crude oil reserves:** 31.7 mil bbls. **Arable land:** 50.6%. **Livestock:** cattle: 700,000; chickens: 32.1 mil; goats: 58,000; pigs: 3.2 mil; sheep: 1.2 mil. **Fish catch:** 20,461 metric tons. **Electricity prod.** (2010): 35.3 bil kWh. **Labor force:** agric. 4.7%, industry 30.9%, services 64.4%.

Finance: Monetary unit: Forint (HUF) (Sept. 2012: 225.97 = $1 U.S.). **GDP:** $198.1 bil; **per capita GDP:** $19,800; **GDP growth:** 1.7%. **Imports:** $93.9 bil; Germany 24.7%, Russia 8.6%, China 8.4%, Austria 6.2%, Slovakia 4.9%, Poland 4.7%, Netherlands 4.4%, Italy 4.3%. **Exports:** $103.1 bil; Germany 25.1%, Romania 5.7%, Austria 5.4%, Slovakia 5.4%, Italy 5%, France 4.8%, UK 4.6%. **Tourism:** $5.6 bil. **Budget:** $68.2 bil. **Total reserves less gold:** $48.7 bil. **Gold:** 98,900 oz t. **CPI change:** 3.96%.

Transport: Railways: 5,006 mi. **Motor vehicles:** 344.8 vehicles per 1,000 pop. **Civil aviation:** 2.4 bil pass.-mi; 20 airports. **Chief ports:** Baja, Budapest, Csepel, Dunaujvaros, Gyor-Gonyu, Mohacs. **Communications: TV sets:** 572 per 1,000 pop. **Radios:** 473 per 1,000 pop. **Telephone lines:** 29.4 per 100 pop. **Daily newspaper circ.:** 217 per 1,000 pop. **Internet:** 59%.

Health: Life expect.: 71.3 male; 79.0 female. **Births:** 9.5 (per 1,000 pop.). **Deaths:** 12.7 (per 1,000 pop.). **Natural inc.:** –0.32%. **Infant mortality:** 5.2 (per 1,000 live births). **HIV rate:** <0.1%.

Education: Compulsory: ages 7-16. **Literacy:** 99%.

Major intl. organizations: UN (FAO, IBRD, ILO, IMF, WHO), EU, NATO, OECD, OSCE, WTO.

Embassy: 3910 Shoemaker St. NW 20008; 362-6730.

Website: www.hungary.hu

Earliest settlers, chiefly Slav and Germanic, were overrun by Magyars from the east. Stephen I (997-1038) was made king by Pope Sylvester II in 1000 CE. The country suffered repeated Turkish invasions in the 15th-17th cent. After the Turks were defeated, 1686-97, Austria dominated, but Hungary obtained concessions, and regained internal independence in 1867, under a dual monarchy with the emperor of Austria. Defeated with the Central Powers in 1918, Hungary lost Transylvania to Romania, Croatia and Bacska to Yugoslavia, and Slovakia and Carpatho-Ruthenia to Czechoslovakia. All had large Hungarian minorities. A republic under Michael Karolyi and a Bolshevist revolt under Bela Kun were followed by a vote for a monarchy in 1920 with Admiral Nicholas Horthy as regent.

Hungary joined Germany in WWII, and was allowed to annex most of its lost territories. Russian troops captured the country, 1944-45. By terms of an armistice with the Allied powers Hungary agreed to give up territory acquired by the 1938 dismemberment of Czechoslovakia and to return to its borders of 1937.

A republic was declared Feb. 1, 1946. In 1947 a hard-line Communist, pro-Soviet government was installed. Demonstrations against Communist rule developed into open revolt in 1956. Soviet forces launched a massive attack Nov. 4 against Budapest. About 200,000 persons fled the country. Thousands were arrested and executed.

Hungarian troops participated in the 1968 Warsaw Pact invasion of Czechoslovakia. Major economic reforms were launched early in 1968, switching from a central planning system to one based on market forces and profit.

In 1989 Parliament legalized freedom of assembly and association as Hungary shifted away from Communism. In Oct. the Communist Party was formally dissolved. The last Soviet troops left June 19, 1991. Hungary became a full member of NATO Mar. 12, 1999, and of the EU May 1, 2004.

The IMF, EU, and World Bank agreed Oct. 28, 2008, to extend $25.1 bil to rescue Hungary's economy, which was battered by the global financial crisis. With the nation still reeling from recession, the center-right Fidesz party ousted the Socialists in parliamentary elections Apr. 11-25, 2010. Parliament, dominated by Fidesz, approved Apr. 18, 2011, a fiscally and socially conservative constitution that drew criticism from the EU; the law went into force Jan. 1, 2012.

Iceland
Republic of Iceland

People: Population: 313,183. **Age distrib.:** <15: 20%; 65+: 12.9%. **Pop. density:** 8.1 per sq mi, 3.1 per sq km. **Urban:** 93.7%. **Ethnic groups:** Homogeneous mixture of Norse & Celt descendants 94%, pop. of foreign origin 6%. **Principal languages:** Icelandic, English, Nordic langs., German. **Chief religions:** Lutheran Church of Iceland (official) 81%, Roman Catholic 3%, Reykjavik Free Church 2%, Hafnarfjorour Free Church 2%.

Geography: Total area: 39,769 sq mi, 103,000 sq km; **Land area:** 38,707 sq mi, 100,250 sq km. **Location:** Isl. at N end of Atlantic O. **Neighbors:** Nearest is Greenland (Den.) to W. **Topography:** Recent volcanic origin. Three-quarters of surface is wasteland: glaciers, lakes, a lava desert. There are geysers and hot springs, and the climate is moderated by the Gulf Stream. **Capital:** Reykjavík, 206,297.

Government: Type: Constitutional republic. **Head of state:** Pres. Olafur Ragnar Grímsson; b. May 14, 1943; in office: Aug. 1, 1996. **Head of gov.:** Prime Min. Jóhanna Sigurdardóttir; b. Oct. 4, 1942; in office: Feb. 1. 2009. **Local divisions:** 23 counties, 14 independent towns. **Defense budget:** NA. **Active troops:** No regular military forces. Operates coast guard; relies on NATO allies for air defense.

Economy: Industries: fish proc., aluminum smelting, ferrosilicon prod., geothermal power, hydropower, tourism. **Chief crops:** potatoes, green vegetables. **Natural resources:** fish, hydropower, geothermal power, diatomite. **Arable land:** 0.1%. **Livestock:** cattle: 73,781; chickens: 218,000; goats: 729; pigs: 40,016; sheep: 479,841. **Fish catch:** 1.1 mil metric tons. **Electricity prod.** (2010): 16.8 bil kWh. **Labor force:** agric. 4.8%, industry 22.2%, services 73%.

Finance: Monetary unit: Krona (ISK) (Sept. 2012: 122.78 = $1 U.S.). **GDP:** $12.6 bil; **per capita GDP:** $38,500; **GDP growth:** 3.1%. **Imports:** $4.5 bil; Norway 16%, U.S. 10.9%, Germany 7.9%, Netherlands 7.4%, China 6.3%, Denmark 6.2%, Brazil 5.8%, UK 5.2%. **Exports:** $5.3 bil; Netherlands 32.5%, Germany 15.1%, UK 9%, Norway 4.4%. **Tourism:** $707 mil. **Budget:** $6.5 bil. **Total reserves less gold:** $8.5 bil. **Gold:** 63,800 oz t. **CPI change:** 4%.

Transport: Motor vehicles: 781.9 vehicles per 1,000 pop. **Civil aviation:** 2.3 bil pass.-mi; 6 airports. **Chief ports:** Grundartangi, Hafnarfjordur, Reykjavík.

Communications: TV sets: 505 per 1,000 pop. **Radios:** 1,077 per 1,000 pop. **Telephone lines:** 58.4 per 100 pop. **Daily newspaper circ.:** 551.6 per 1,000 pop. **Internet:** 95%.

Health: Life expect.: 78.8 male; 83.3 female. **Births:** 13.2 (per 1,000 pop.). **Deaths:** 7.0 (per 1,000 pop.). **Natural inc.:** 0.62%. **Infant mortality:** 3.2 (per 1,000 live births). **HIV rate:** 0.3%.

Education: Compulsory: ages 6-16. **Literacy:** 99%.

Major intl. organizations: UN (FAO, IBRD, ILO, IMF, WHO), EFTA, NATO, OECD, OSCE, WTO.

Embassy: 1156 15th St. NW, Ste. 1200, 20005; 265-6653.

Website: www.iceland.is

Iceland was an independent republic from 930 to 1262, when it joined with Norway. Its language has maintained its purity for 1,000 years. The Althing, or assembly, established in 930, is the world's oldest surviving parliament. Danish rule lasted 1380-1918; the last ties with the Danish crown were severed in 1941.

A 55-year U.S. military presence in Iceland ended with the closure of the Keflavík naval air station in Sept. 2006. Iceland's banking system and currency collapsed amid the global financial crisis in Oct. 2008. More than $10 bil in loans from the IMF and European governments restored financial stability; austerity measures were imposed, and the nation entered a deep recession. Political unrest sparked by soaring inflation and unemployment led to the installation Feb. 1, 2009, of a center-left government, which swept to victory in elections Apr. 25. Parliament July 16 approved a plan for Iceland to seek EU membership. A major eruption Apr. 14, 2010, of the Eyjafjallajökull volcano disrupted European air traffic, affecting about 10 mil passengers and 100,000 flights during the next 6 days. The economy has stabilized under the new government; unemployment rates fell to 4.8% July 2012.

India
Republic of India

People: Population: 1,205,073,612. **Age distrib.:** <15: 29.3%; 65+: 5.6%. **Pop. density:** 1,049.8 per sq mi, 405.3 per sq km. **Urban:** 31.3%. **Ethnic groups:** Indo-Aryan 72%, Dravidian 25%, Mongoloid and other 3%. **Principal languages:** Hindi (most widely spoken and primary tongue); 14 other official langs. (Bengali, Telugu, Marathi, Tamil, Urdu, Gujarati, Malayalam, Kannada, Oriya, Punjabi, Assamese, Kashmiri, Sindhi, Sanskrit); English (crucial for national, political, commercial communication); Hindustani (popular variant of Hindi/Urdu widely spoken throughout N). **Chief religions:** Hindu 81%, Muslim 13%, Christian 2%, Sikh 2%.

Geography: Total area: 1,269,219 sq mi, 3,287,263 sq km; **Land area:** 1,147,956 sq mi, 2,973,193 sq km. **Location:** Occupies most of Indian subcontinent in S Asia. **Neighbors:** Pakistan on W; China, Nepal, Bhutan on N; Myanmar, Bangladesh on E. **Topography:**

The Himalaya Mts., highest in world, stretch across India's northern borders. Below, the Ganges Plain is wide, fertile, and among the most densely populated regions of the world. Area below includes Deccan Peninsula. Close to one quarter of area is forested. The climate varies from tropical heat in S to near-Arctic cold in N. Rajasthan Desert is NW; NE Assam Hills get 400 in. of rain a year.

Capital: New Delhi, 22,653,600 (figure for Delhi urban aggl.). **Cities (urban aggl.):** Mumbai (Bombay), 19,743,613; Kolkata (Calcutta), 14,402,345; Chennai (Madras), 8,784,447; Bangalore, 8,614,328; Hyderabad, 7,837,054; Ahmadabad, 6,424,953; Pune, 5,100,205.

Government: Type: Federal republic. **Head of state:** Pres. Pranab Mukherjee; b. Dec. 11, 1935; in office: July 22, 2012. **Head of gov.:** Prime Min. Manmohan Singh; b. Sept. 26, 1932; in office: May 22, 2004. **Local divisions:** 28 states, 6 union territories, 1 national capital territory. **Defense budget:** $31.9 bil. **Active troops:** 1,325,000.

Economy: Industries: textiles, chemicals, food proc., steel, transp. equip., cement, mining, petroleum, machinery, software, pharmaceuticals. **Chief crops:** rice, wheat, oilseed, cotton, jute, tea, sugarcane, lentils, onions, potatoes. **Natural resources:** coal (world's fourth-largest reserves), iron ore, manganese, mica, bauxite, rare earth elements, titanium ore, chromite, nat. gas, diamonds, petroleum, limestone. **Crude oil reserves:** 8.9 bil bbls. **Arable land:** 53.1%. **Livestock:** cattle: 210.2 mil; chickens: 773.9 mil; goats: 154 mil; pigs: 9.6 mil; sheep: 74 mil. **Fish catch:** 9.3 mil metric tons. **Electricity prod.:** (2010): 880 bil kWh. **Labor force:** agric. 52%, industry 14%; services 34%.

Finance: Monetary unit: Rupee (INR) (Sept. 2012: 55.91 = $1 U.S.). **GDP:** $4.5 tril. **Per capita GDP:** $3,700; **GDP growth:** 7.2%. **Imports:** $461.4 bil; China 12.1%, UAE 8.3%, Saudi Arabia 5.8%, U.S. 5.1%, Switzerland 4.7%. **Exports:** $299.4 bil; UAE 13%, U.S. 11.4%, China 6.3%, Singapore 5.3%. **Tourism:** $17.5 bil. **Budget:** $308.8 bil. **Total reserves less gold:** $271.3 bil. **Gold:** 17.9 mil oz t. **CPI change:** 8.9%.

Transport: Railways: 39,752 mi. **Motor vehicles:** 14.4 vehicles per 1,000 pop. **Civil aviation:** 53.3 bil pass.-mi; 251 airports. **Chief ports:** Chennai, Jawaharal Nehru, Kandla, Kolkata, Mumbai, Sikka, Vishakhapatnam.

Communications: TV sets: 137 per 1,000 pop. **Radios:** 120 per 1,000 pop. **Telephone lines:** 2.6 per 100 pop. **Daily newspaper circ.:** 70.9 per 1,000 pop. **Internet:** 10.1%.

Health: Life expect.: 66.1 male; 68.3 female. **Births:** 20.6 (per 1,000 pop.). **Deaths:** 7.4 (per 1,000 pop.). **Natural inc.:** 1.32% **Infant mortality:** 46.1 (per 1,000 live births). **HIV rate:** 0.3%.

Education: Compulsory: ages 6-14. **Literacy:** 62.8%.

Major intl. organizations: UN (FAO, IBRD, ILO, IMF, WHO), the Commonwealth, WTO.

Embassy: 2107 Massachusetts Ave. NW 20008; 939-7000.

Website: www.india.gov.in

India has one of the oldest civilizations in the world. Excavations trace the Indus Valley civilization back for at least 5,000 years. Paintings in the mountain caves of Ajanta, richly carved temples, the Taj Mahal in Agra, and the Kutab Minar in Delhi are among treasured relics of the past.

Aryan tribes, speaking Sanskrit, invaded from the northwest around 1500 BCE. Asoka ruled most of the Indian subcontinent in the 3rd cent. BCE, and established Buddhism. But Hinduism revived and eventually predominated. Under the Guptas, 4th-6th cent. CE, science, literature, and the arts enjoyed a golden age.

Arab invaders established a Muslim foothold in the west in the 8th cent., and Turkish Muslims gained control of North India by 1200. The Mughal emperors ruled 1526-1857.

Vasco da Gama established Portuguese trading posts 1498-1503. The Dutch followed. The British East India Co. sent Capt. William Hawkins, 1609, to get concessions from the Mughal emperor for spices and textiles. Operating as the East India Co. the British gained control of most of India. The British parliament assumed political direction; under Lord Bentinck, 1828-35, rule by rajahs was curbed. After the Sepoy troops mutinied, 1857-58, the British supported the native rulers.

Nationalism grew after WWI. The Indian National Congress and the Muslim League demanded constitutional reform. A leader emerged in Mohandas K. Gandhi (called Mahatma, or Great Soul), b. Oct. 2, 1869, assassinated Jan. 30, 1948. He advocated self-rule, nonviolence, and an end to caste discrimination against "untouchables." In 1930 he launched a program of civil disobedience, boycotting British goods and rejecting taxes without representation.

In 1935 Britain gave India a constitution providing a bicameral federal congress. Muhammad Ali Jinnah, head of the Muslim League, sought creation of a Muslim nation, Pakistan.

The British government partitioned British India into the dominions of India and Pakistan. India became a member of the UN in 1945, a self-governing member of the Commonwealth in 1947, and a democratic republic, Jan. 26, 1950. More than 12 mil Hindu and Muslim refugees crossed the India-Pakistan borders in 1947; about 200,000 were killed in communal fighting.

After Pakistan troops began attacks on Bengali separatists in East Pakistan, Mar. 25, 1971, some 10 mil refugees fled to India. India and Pakistan went to war Dec. 3, 1971, on both the east and west fronts. Pakistan troops in the east surrendered Dec. 16; Pakistan agreed to a cease-fire in the west Dec. 17.

Indira Gandhi, India's prime minister since Jan. 1966, invoked emergency powers in June 1975. Thousands of opponents were arrested and press censorship imposed. These and other actions, including population control through forced vasectomies, were widely resented. Opposition parties, united in the Janata coalition, won the 1977 elections.

Gandhi became prime minister for the second time, Jan. 14, 1980. She was assassinated by 2 of her Sikh bodyguards Oct. 31, 1984, in response to the government suppression of a Sikh uprising in Punjab in June 1984, which included an assault on the Golden Temple at Amritsar, the holiest Sikh shrine. Widespread rioting followed the assassination; thousands of Sikhs were killed and some 50,000 left homeless. Rajiv, Indira Gandhi's son, replaced her as prime minister. A gas leak at a Union Carbide chemical plant in Bhopal, in Dec. 1984, eventually killed some 14,000 people.

Many died in religious, ethnic, and political conflicts during the late 1980s and early '90s. To suppress the Sikh insurgency in Punjab, Indian government troops attacked the Golden Temple again in 1988. Rajiv Gandhi was swept from office in 1989 amid charges of incompetence and corruption and assassinated May 21, 1991, while campaigning to regain power. Nationwide riots followed the destruction of a 16th-cent. mosque by Hindu militants in Dec. 1992. Ethnic clashes in Assam, in northwest India, killed thousands in Feb. 1993. Bombs jolted Mumbai and Kolkata, Mar. 12-19, killing over 300.

India's first lowest-caste president, K. R. Narayanan, took office July 25, 1997. India conducted a series of nuclear tests in mid-May 1998, raising tensions with Pakistan. A cyclone hit the state of Orissa, East India, on Oct. 29, 1999, leaving some 10,000 people dead. A powerful earthquake in Gujarat state, Jan. 26, 2001, claimed more than 20,000 lives.

India blamed Pakistani-sponsored terrorist groups for an Oct. 1, 2001, suicide attack on the state legislature in Jammu and Kashmir (see below), in which at least 40 people died, and a Dec. 13 assault on the Indian parliament in New Delhi that left 13 people dead. Hindu-Muslim clashes in Gujarat Feb. 27-Mar. 11, 2002, claimed more than 700 lives. A. P. J. Abdul Kalam, a Muslim scientist who spearheaded India's nuclear weapons program, became president July 25.

Led by Rajiv Gandhi's Italian-born widow, Sonia, the Congress Party won the most seats in parliamentary elections Apr.-May 2004. When Hindu nationalists objected to her candidacy, she chose not to become prime minister, and Manmohan Singh, a Sikh economist, took office instead.

The Indian Ocean tsunami of Dec. 26, 2004, left more than 10,700 people dead, some 5,600 missing, and over 647,000 displaced. Islamic extremists were suspected in 7 bombings in Mumbai, July 11, 2006, that killed more than 200 on commuter trains. Pratibha Patil took office July 25, 2007, as India's first female president. Monsoon floods, July-Sept. 2007, killed more than 2,600 people. The next year, monsoon floods killed more than 2,200. At least 224 died in a stampede Sept. 30, 2008, at a Hindu temple in Jodhpur. The unmanned Chandrayaan-1, India's first lunar survey mission, was launched into space Oct. 22, 2008.

Ten Pakistanis linked to the militant group Lashkar-e-Taiba stormed luxury hotels, a railway station, a Jewish center, and other sites in Mumbai, Nov. 26, 2008; by the time Indian army commandos took control 3 days later, the attackers had slaughtered 163 people. Nine of the terrorists were also killed; convicted of murder and of waging war against India, the lone surviving gunman, Ajmal Kasab, received a death sentence May 6, 2010.

In parliamentary elections Apr. 16-May 13, 2009, Prime Min. Manmohan Singh's United Progressive Alliance, headed by the Congress party, gained a resounding victory. A triple bombing in Mumbai July 13, 2011, killed 26 people and injured about 140; 11 were killed when a bomb exploded Sept. 7 outside the High Court in New Delhi. Electricity blackouts July 30-31, 2012, left 670 mil people without power.

Development of high-tech industries has propelled rapid economic growth since the 1990s; nearly 200 mil people have emerged from extreme poverty, although distribution of wealth remains highly uneven.

Sikkim, bordered by Tibet, Bhutan, and Nepal, formerly British protected, became a protectorate of India in 1950. Area, 2,740 sq mi; pop. (2011 census): 607,688; capital: Gangtok. In Sept. 1974, India's parliament voted to make Sikkim an associate Indian state, absorbing it into India.

Kashmir is a predominantly Muslim region in the NW that borders India, Pakistan, Afghanistan, and China. Originally a Hindu kingdom, Muslim rule began in 1341; after almost 200 years under the Mughals, the area was incorporated into British India in 1846. Fighting broke out in the region between India and Pakistan in 1947 following independence from Britain. A cease-fire was negotiated by the UN Jan. 1, 1949; it gave Pakistan control of one-third of the area as Azad Kashmir, in the west and northwest, and India the remaining two-thirds, as the Indian state of Jammu and Kashmir. Area: 85,806 sq mi; pop. (2011 census): 12,548,926; capitals: Srinagar (summer) and Jammu (winter). Fighting in the area resumed during the 1965 and 1971 wars with Pakistan. China occupied about 14,000 sq mi in the Ladakh district after a war with India in 1962.

In the 1990s, India's decision to impose central government rule triggered clashes between Indian army troops and separatist fighters. India charged Pakistan with aiding the separatists; fighting was especially heavy in May-June 1999.

A cease-fire between Indian and Pakistani troops along the line of control took effect Nov. 25, 2003, but fighting between Indian forces and Islamic militants continued. Estimates of conflict-related deaths since 1989 range from 40,000 to over 80,000. A powerful earthquake Oct. 8, 2005, killed about 80,000 and left up to 3 mil homeless in Pakistani-held Kashmir and northern Pakistan.

France, 1952-54, peacefully yielded to India its 5 colonies, former French India: Pondicherry, Karikal, Mahe, and Yanaon were merged to become Pondicherry, now **Puducherry**, area 185 sq mi; pop. (2011 census): 1,244,464; the colony of Chandernagor was incorporated into the state of **West Bengal**.

Indonesia
Republic of Indonesia

People: Population: 248,645,008. **Age distrib.:** <15: 27%; 65+: 6.4%. **Pop. density:** 355.5 per sq mi, 137.3 per sq km. **Urban:** 50.7%. **Ethnic groups:** Javanese 41%, Sundanese 15%, Madurese 3%, Minangkabau 3%, Betawi 2%, Bugis 2%, Banten 2%, Banjar 2%. **Principal languages:** Bahasa Indonesia (official; modified form of Malay), English, Dutch, local dialects (Javanese most widely spoken). **Chief religions:** Muslim 86%, Protestant 6%, Roman Catholic 3%, Hindu 2%.

Geography: Total area: 735,358 sq mi, 1,904,569 sq km; **Land area:** 699,451 sq mi, 1,811,569 sq km. **Location:** Archipelago SE of Asian mainland along the Equator. **Neighbors:** Malaysia on N, Papua New Guinea on E, Timor-Leste on S. **Topography:** Indonesia comprises over 13,500 islands (6,000 inhabited), including Java (one of the most densely populated areas in the world with over 2,000 persons per sq mi), Sumatra, Kalimantan (most of Borneo), Sulawesi (Celebes), and West Irian (Irian Jaya, the W half of New Guinea). Also: Bangka, Billiton, Madura, Bali, Timor. The mountains and plateaus on the major islands have a cooler climate than the tropical lowlands. **Capital:** Jakarta, 9,769,010. **Cities (urban aggl.):** Surabaya, 2,787,165; Bandung, 2,429,144; Medan, 2,117,531; Semarang, 1,573,420; Palembang, 1,454,881; Ujung Pandang, 1,386,855; Batam, 1,034,429.

Government: Type: Republic. **Head of state and gov.:** Pres. Susilo Bambang Yudhoyono; b. Sept. 9, 1949; in office: Oct. 20, 2004. **Local divisions:** 30 provinces, 2 special regions, 1 capital district. **Defense budget:** $5.42 bil. **Active troops:** 302,000.

Economy: Industries: petroleum and nat. gas, textiles, apparel, footwear, mining, cement, chemical fertilizers, plywood, rubber, food, tourism. **Chief crops:** rice, cassava, peanuts, rubber, cocoa, coffee, palm oil, copra. **Natural resources:** petroleum, tin, nat. gas, nickel, timber, bauxite, copper, coal, gold, silver. **Crude oil reserves:** 3.9 bil bbls. **Arable land:** 13.0%. **Livestock:** cattle: 13.6 mil; chickens: 1.6 bil; goats: 16.8 mil; pigs: 7.2 mil; sheep: 10.9 mil. **Fish catch:** 11.7 mil metric tons. **Electricity prod.** (2010): 156 bil kWh. **Labor force:** agric. 38.3%, industry 12.8%, services 48.9%.

Finance: Monetary unit: Rupiah (IDR) (Sept. 2012: 9,564.04 = $1 U.S.). **GDP:** $1.1 tril; **per capita GDP:** $4,700; **GDP growth:** 6.5%. **Exports:** $166.1 bil; China 14.8%, Singapore 14.6%, Japan 11%, South Korea 7.3%, U.S. 6.1%, Thailand 5.9%, Malaysia 5.9%. **Exports:** $201.5 bil; Japan 16.6%, China 11.3%, Singapore 9.1%, U.S. 8.1%, South Korea 8.1%, India 6.6%, Malaysia 5.4%. **Tourism:** $7.95 bil. **Budget:** $144.1 bil. **Total reserves less gold:** $106.5 bil. **Gold:** 2.4 mil oz t. **CPI change:** 5.4%.

Transport: Railways: 3,133 mi. **Motor vehicles:** 76.1 vehicles per 1,000 pop. **Civil aviation:** 19.8 bil pass.-mi; 185 airports. **Chief ports:** Banjarmasin, Belawan, Kotabaru, Krueg Geukueh, Palembang, Panjang, Sungai Pakning, Tanjung Perak, Tanjung Priok.

Communications: TV sets: 161 per 1,000 pop. **Radios:** 157 per 1,000 pop. **Telephone lines:** 15.9 per 100 pop. **Internet:** 18%.

Health: Life expect.: 69.1 male; 74.3 female. **Births:** 17.7 (per 1,000 pop.). **Deaths:** 6.3 (per 1,000 pop.). **Natural inc.:** 1.15% **Infant mortality:** 27.0 (per 1,000 live births). **HIV rate:** 0.2%.

Education: Compulsory: ages 7-15. **Literacy:** 92.6%.

Major intl. organizations: UN and all of its specialized agencies, APEC, ASEAN, WTO.

Embassy: 2020 Massachusetts Ave. NW 20036; 775-5200.
Website: www.indonesia.go.id

Hindu and Buddhist civilization from India reached Indonesia nearly 2,000 years ago, taking root especially in Java. Islam spread along the maritime trade routes in the 15th cent., and became predominant by the 16th cent. The Dutch replaced the Portuguese as the area's most important European trade power in the 17th cent., securing territorial control over Java by 1750. The outer islands were subdued in the early 20th cent.

Following Japanese occupation, 1942-45, nationalists led by Sukarno and Hatta declared independence. The Netherlands ceded sovereignty Dec. 27, 1949. A republic was declared, Aug. 17, 1950, with Sukarno as president. West Irian, on New Guinea, remained under Dutch control but was transferred by the UN to Indonesia in 1963.

Sukarno suspended parliament in 1960 and was named president for life in 1963. He made close alliances with Communist governments. In Sept. 1965 an attempted coup was successfully put down, but Sukarno was forced to cede power to the army, led by Gen. Suharto, who became acting president in 1967 and ruled Indonesia for the next 31 years. The regime blamed the coup on the Communist Party; more than 300,000 alleged Communists were killed in army-initiated massacres.

Parliament reelected Suharto to a seventh consecutive 5-year term Mar. 10, 1998, as a severe economic downturn focused public anger on nepotism, cronyism, and corruption in the Suharto regime. Price increases in May sparked mass protests and then mob violence in Jakarta and other cities, claiming some 500 lives. Suharto resigned May 21 and was succeeded by his vice president, Bacharuddin Jusuf Habibie. Abdurrahman Wahid, leader of Indonesia's largest Muslim organization, was elected president Oct. 20, 1999. In Aug. 2000, under pressure from the legislature, he agreed to share power with Vice Pres. Megawati Sukarnoputri, the daughter of the late Pres. Sukarno. Charging Wahid with incompetence and corruption, the legislature ousted him July 23, 2001, and Megawati became Indonesia's first woman president.

Clashes between Muslims and Christians in the Maluku (Molucca) Isls., 1999-2002, claimed about 5,000 lives. Ethnic violence in Kalimantan, Borneo, killed more than 400 in Feb. 2001. East Timor, a former Portuguese colony that Indonesia invaded in Dec. 1975 and controlled until Oct. 1999, became a fully independent country May 20, 2002, as Timor-Leste. Separatists in Aceh, NW Sumatra, fought against government troops during the 1980s and '90s; peace accords were announced in Dec. 2002. The deal unraveled, July 2005, and the last of 24,000 Indonesian troops pulled out of Aceh, Dec. 29, 2005.

Investigators blamed the Islamic terrorist group Jemaah Islamiyah, an al-Qaeda affiliate, for bombings that killed 202 people, mostly foreign tourists, at nightclubs in Bali, Oct. 12, 2002, and 12 people at a Marriott hotel in Jakarta, Aug. 5, 2003. A car bomb attack outside the Australian embassy in Jakarta, Sept. 9, 2004, killed 9 people. Susilo Bambang Yudhoyono, a retired general, defeated Megawati Sept. 20, 2004, in a direct presidential runoff vote.

A massive earthquake off northwest Sumatra, Dec. 26, 2004, triggered tsunamis that wreaked havoc in the Indian Ocean region. The death toll in Indonesia alone exceeded 125,000, not counting almost 40,000 missing. Another large quake off northwest Sumatra, Mar. 28, 2005, left at least 1,300 dead. On Java in 2006, an earthquake May 27 killed 5,800; a tsunami July 17 claimed at least 650 lives.

Two leaders of the Jemaah Islamiyah terror network were arrested in June 2007. Faced with falling oil production, Indonesia left OPEC in 2008. Pres. Yudhoyono won a second 5-year term July 8, 2009. Suicide bombings at two Jakarta hotels July 17 left 9 people dead. Police confirmed Sept. 17 that Noordin Muhammad Top, suspected of plotting the Jakarta attacks and other terrorist bombings, had been killed in a shootout.

Padang, Sumatra, was hit Sept. 30, 2009, by a powerful earthquake, which also triggered mudslides in the region; at least 1,115 people were killed. On Oct. 25, 2010, a 7.7-magnitude earthquake in the Mentawai Islands, off the western coast of Sumatra, triggered a tsunami that killed at least 500 people; that same day, Mt. Merapi, a volcano near Yogyakarta in central Java, began a series of major eruptions that claimed at least 228 lives and displaced 430,500.

Eight-thousand miners at Freeport's Grasberg copper and gold mines on Batam went on strike Sept. 15, 2011, demanding higher wages; they won a 37% pay raise and ended the strike Dec. 17.

Iran
Islamic Republic of Iran

People: Population: 78,868,711. **Age distrib.:** <15: 23.9%; 65+: 5.1%. **Pop. density:** 133.4 per sq mi, 51.5 per sq km. **Urban:** 69.1%. **Ethnic groups:** Persian 51%, Azeri 24%, Gilaki and Mazandarani 8%, Kurd 7%, Arab 3%, Lur 2%, Baloch 2%, Turkmen 2%. **Principal languages:** Persian and Persian dialects (official), Turkic and Turkic dialects, Kurdish, Luri, Balochi, Arabic, Turkish. **Chief religions:** Muslim (official) 98% (Shia 89%, Sunni 9%), other (incl. Zoroastrian, Jewish, Christian, Baha'i) 2%.

Geography: Total area: 636,372 sq mi, 1,648,195 sq km; **Land area:** 591,352 sq mi, 1,531,595 sq km. **Location:** Between the Middle East and S Asia. **Neighbors:** Turkey, Iraq on W; Armenia, Azerbaijan, Turkmenistan on N; Afghanistan, Pakistan on E. **Topography:** Interior highlands and plains surrounded by high mountains, up to 18,000 ft. Large salt deserts cover much of area, but there are many oases and forest areas. Most of population inhabits N and NW. **Capital:** Tehran, 7,304,150. **Cities (urban aggl.):** Mashhad, 2,713,344; Esfahan, 1,780,640; Karaj, 1,635,215; Tabriz, 1,509,091; Shiraz, 1,321,380; Ahvaz, 1,082,148; Qom, 1,064,658.

Government: Type: Islamic republic. **Religious head:** Ayatollah Sayyed Ali Khamenei; b. July 17, 1939; in office: June 4, 1989. **Head of state and gov.:** Pres. Mahmoud Ahmadinejad; b. Oct. 28, 1956;

in office: Aug. 3, 2005. **Local divisions:** 28 provinces. **Defense budget:** $12 bil. **Active troops:** 523,000.

Economy: Industries: petroleum, petrochemicals, fertilizers, caustic soda, textiles, cement and other constr. materials, food proc. (sugar refining and vegetable oil prod.), metal fabrication, armaments. **Chief crops:** wheat, rice, other grains, sugar beets, sugarcane, fruits, nuts, cotton. **Natural resources:** petroleum, nat. gas, coal, chromium, copper, iron ore, lead, manganese, zinc, sulfur. **Crude oil reserves:** 151.2 bil bbls. **Arable land:** 10.6%. **Livestock:** cattle: 8.5 mil; chickens: 507 mil; goats: 25.7 mil; sheep: 54 mil. **Fish catch:** 663,684 metric tons. **Electricity prod.** (2010): 213.7 bil kWh. **Labor force:** agric. 25%, industry 31%, services 45%.

Finance: Monetary unit: Rial (IRR) (Sept. 2012: 12,278.20 = $1 U.S.). **GDP:** $1.003 tril; **per capita GDP:** $13,200; **GDP growth:** 2%. **Imports:** $76.1 bil; UAE 30.6%, China 17.2%, South Korea 8.4%, Germany 4.8%, Turkey 4.2%. **Exports:** $131.8 bil; China 21%, India 9.3%, Japan 8.9%, Turkey 8.7%, South Korea 7.9%, Italy 5.2%. **Tourism:** $2.7 bil. **Budget:** $92.6 bil. **CPI change:** 20.6%.

Transport: Railways: 5,246 mi. **Motor vehicles:** 50.8 vehicles per 1,000 pop. **Civil aviation:** 8 bil pass.-mi; 136 airports. **Chief ports:** Assaluyeh, Bandar Abbas, Bandar-e-Eman Khomeyni.

Communications: TV sets: 170 per 1,000 pop. **Radios:** 734 per 1,000 pop. **Telephone lines:** 37.1 per 100 pop. **Internet:** 21%.

Health: Life expect.: 68.8 male; 71.9 female. **Births:** 18.5 (per 1,000 pop.). **Deaths:** 5.9 (per 1,000 pop.). **Natural inc.:** 1.26% **Infant mortality:** 41.1 (per 1,000 live births). **HIV rate:** 0.2%.

Education: Compulsory: ages 6-13. **Literacy:** 85%.

Major intl. organizations: UN (FAO, IBRD, ILO, IMF, WHO), OPEC, WTO (observer).

Iranian Interests Section: 2209 Wisconsin Ave. NW 20007; 965-4990.

Website: www.president.ir

Iran, formerly known as Persia, has been settled for thousands of years. Ancestors of the Iranians came from the east during the second millennium BCE; they were an Indo-European group related to the Aryans of India. In 549 BCE Cyrus the Great united the Medes and Persians in the Persian Empire; he conquered Babylonia in 538 BCE, and restored Jerusalem to the Jews. Alexander the Great conquered Persia in 333 BCE, but Persians regained independence in the next century under the Parthians, themselves succeeded by Sassanian Persians in 226 CE. Arabs brought Islam to Persia in the 7th cent., replacing the indigenous Zoroastrian faith. After Persian political and cultural autonomy was reasserted in the 9th cent., arts and sciences flourished.

Turks and Mongols ruled Persia in turn from the 11th cent. to 1502, when Ismael I established the Iranian Safavid dynasty and made Shiite Islam the official religion. The dynasty lasted until 1722. The British and Russian empires vied for influence in the 19th cent.; Afghanistan was severed from Iran by Britain in 1857.

Reza Khan, a military officer, became prime min., 1923, and shah in 1925. He began modernization, curbed foreign influence, and officially changed the country's name from Persia to Iran in 1935. Fearing the shah's Axis sympathies, British and Soviet troops forced him to abdicate, 1941; he was succeeded by his son, Mohammad Reza Pahlavi. The U.S. Central Intelligence Agency had a major role in the ouster, 1953, of Prime Min. Muhammad Mossadegh, who had nationalized the oil industry.

With U.S. backing, the shah brought economic and social change to Iran (White Revolution), but repression of opposition groups grew severe. Violent protests in 1978 eventually forced the shah to depart, Jan. 16, 1979. Shiite leader Ayatollah Ruhollah Khomeini, exiled by the shah in 1963, returned to Tehran, Feb. 1. Pro-Khomeini forces defeated government troops, Feb 11. Khomeini established an Islamic theocracy.

Iranian militants seized the U.S. embassy in Tehran Nov. 4, 1979, and took hostages, including 62 Americans. Despite international condemnations and U.S. efforts, including an abortive Apr. 1980 rescue attempt, the crisis continued. The U.S. broke diplomatic relations with Iran, Apr. 7. The shah died in Egypt, July 27. The hostage drama ended Jan. 20, 1981, when an accord, involving the release of frozen Iranian assets, was reached.

A dispute over the Shatt al-Arab waterway situated between Iran and Iraq led to a long and costly war between the 2 countries, 1980-88, killing hundreds of thousands of people. In Nov. 1986 it became known that the U.S., which had generally sided with Iraq during the war, had secretly shipped arms to Iran to gain that country's help in obtaining the release of U.S. hostages held in Lebanon. The revelation sparked a major scandal in the U.S. A U.S. Navy warship shot down an Iranian airliner, July 3, 1988, after mistaking it for an F-14 fighter jet; all 290 aboard died.

An earthquake struck northern Iran June 21, 1990, killing more than 45,000 and leaving 400,000 homeless. Some 1 mil Kurdish refugees fled from Iraq to Iran following the Persian Gulf War of 1991. To curb Iran's alleged support for international terrorism, the U.S. in 1996 authorized sanctions on foreign companies that invest there.

Mohammad Khatami, a moderate Shiite Muslim cleric, was elected president on May 23, 1997. During the next three years,

hard-line Islamists clashed, sometimes violently, with reformers, who won a majority in parliamentary elections Feb. 18 and May 5, 2000. Inviting rapprochement with Iran, the U.S. eased some sanctions Mar. 18. Khatami was reelected June 8, 2001, but continued to face resistance from religious conservatives.

The U.S.-led war in Iraq, beginning Mar. 2003, contributed to a new period of instability in Iran. An earthquake Dec. 26 in Bam, southeast Iran, killed about 26,000 people. After the Guardian Council, dominated by religious conservatives, disqualified some 2,400 reformist candidates, hard-liners won legislative elections Feb. 20, 2004.

The mayor of Tehran, Mahmoud Ahmadinejad, a religious conservative, defeated former Pres. Hashemi Rafsanjani in a runoff election June 24, 2005, and took office Aug. 3. The Bush administration accused Iran of seeking to build nuclear weapons, aiding Shiite militias in Iraq, and supplying rockets to Hezbollah fighters in Lebanon for use against Israel.

Seeking to halt Iran's uranium-enrichment program, which could be used for either military or civilian purposes, the UN Security Council imposed sanctions, Dec. 23, 2006, and toughened them, Mar. 24, 2007. After the Guardian Council disqualified about 1,700 reformist candidates, conservative allies of Ahmadinejad won parliamentary elections Mar.-Apr. 2008. Further talks on nuclear enrichment ended in deadlock July 20, and the U.S. imposed additional sanctions Sept. 10, 2008.

After a hard-fought campaign, Ahmadinejad won the June 12, 2009, presidential election. His main opponent, former Prime Min. Mir Hussein Moussavi claimed the official count, which gave Ahmadinejad more than 62% of the total vote, was fraudulent. Huge protests by Moussavi supporters in Tehran and other major cities were crushed. Tensions with the U.S. and European governments were heightened in late Sept. 2009 by disclosures that Iran had been secretly enriching uranium at an underground site near Qom, and by Iranian tests of medium-range missiles capable of reaching Israel or U.S. and European bases in the Persian Gulf region. In direct talks Oct. 1 with the U.S. and other world powers, Iran agreed to allow international inspection of the Qom site and other nuclear safeguards.

The UN and U.S. toughened sanctions, June-July 2010, but did not object when loading of uranium fuel began in Aug. at Iran's Bushehr nuclear power plant, built and supervised by Russia. Iran blamed Israel, the U.S., and other Western powers for carrying out cyber attacks against the country's nuclear facilities and for assassinating Iranian scientists. On Dec. 21, 2010, the U.S. announced new sanctions targeting companies linked to Iran's nuclear program. The Bushehr plant began generating electricity for the national power grid in Sept. 2011. Iran further advanced its nuclear program, announcing Jan. 8, 2012, that it was enriching uranium at its underground Fordo nuclear facility; more international sanctions followed. Iran sentenced Amir Mirzaei Hekmati, an American citizen and former Marine arrested in Aug. 2011, to death for being a spy Jan. 9, 2012, a charge the U.S. government denied.

Iraq
Republic of Iraq

People: Population: 31,129,225. **Age distrib.:** <15: 37.6%; 65+: 3.1%. **Pop. density:** 184.3 per sq mi, 71.2 per sq km. **Urban:** 66.5%. **Ethnic groups:** Arab 75%-80%; Kurdish 15%-20%; Turkoman, Assyrian, or other 5%. **Principal languages:** Arabic (official), Kurdish (official in Kurdish regions), Turkoman, Assyrian (Neo-Aramaic), Armenian. **Chief religions:** Muslim 97% (Shia 60%-65%, Sunni 32%-37%), Christian or other 3%.

Geography: Total area: 169,235 sq mi, 438,317 sq km; **Land area:** 168,868 sq mi, 437,367 sq km. **Location:** In Middle East, occupying most of historic Mesopotamia. **Neighbors:** Jordan, Syria on W; Turkey on N; Iran on E; Kuwait, Saudi Arabia on S. **Topography:** Mostly an alluvial plain, including the Tigris and Euphrates rivers, descending from mountains in N to desert in SW. Persian Gulf region is marshland. **Capital:** Baghdad, 6,035,580. **Cities (urban aggl.):** Mosul, 1,493,527; Erbil, 1,038,978; Basra, 942,170.

Government: Type: In transition. **Head of state:** Pres. Jalal Talabani; b. 1933; in office: Apr. 7, 2005. **Head of gov.:** Prime Min. Nouri Kamel al-Maliki; b. 1950; in office: May 20, 2006. **Local divisions:** 18 governorates (3 in Kurdish Autonomous Region). **Defense budget:** $4.79 bil. **Active troops:** 271,400.

Economy: Industries: petroleum, chemicals, textiles, leather, constr. materials, food proc., fertilizer, metal fabrication/proc. **Chief crops:** wheat, barley, rice, vegetables, dates, cotton. **Natural resources:** petroleum, nat. gas, phosphates, sulfur. **Arable land:** 10.4%. **Crude oil reserves:** 143.1 bil bbls. **Livestock:** cattle: 1.6 mil; chickens: 29 mil; goats: 1.5 mil; sheep: 7.8 mil. **Fish catch:** 46,040 metric tons. **Electricity prod.:** 40.8 bil kWh. **Labor force:** agric. 21.6%, industry 18.7%, services 59.8%.

Finance: Monetary unit: Dinar (IQD) (Sept. 2012: 1,163.40 = $1 U.S.). **GDP:** $129.3 bil; **per capita GDP:** $3,900; **GDP growth:** 9.9%. **Imports:** $53.9 bil; Turkey 25%, Syria 18.1%, China 11.5%, U.S. 7.3%, South Korea 4.6%. **Exports:** $82.8 bil; U.S. 23.3%, India 19.2%, China 14%, South Korea 12.2%, Japan 5%, Netherlands

4.5%. **Tourism:** $168 mil. **Budget:** $82.6 bil. **Total reserves less gold:** $60.7 bil. **Gold:** 188,600 oz t. **CPI change** (2009-10): 2.9%.

Transport: Railways: 1,412 mi. **Motor vehicles:** 35.7 vehicles per 1,000 pop. **Civil aviation:** 75 airports. **Chief ports:** Al Basrah, Khawr az Zubayr, Umm Qasr.

Communications: TV sets: 82 per 1,000 pop. **Radios:** 211 per 1,000 pop. **Telephone lines:** 5.5 per 100 pop. **Internet:** 5%.

Health: Life expect.: 69.4 male; 72.4 female. **Births:** 28.2 (per 1,000 pop.). **Deaths:** 4.7 (per 1,000 pop.). **Natural inc.:** 2.35% **Infant mortality:** 40.3 (per 1,000 live births). **HIV rate:** NA.

Education: Compulsory: ages 6-11. **Literacy:** 78.2%.

Major intl. organizations: UN (FAO, IBRD, ILO, IMF, WHO), AL, OPEC, WTO (observer).

Iraqi Interests Section: 1801 P St. NW 20036; 483-7500.

Website: www.cabinet.iq

The Tigris-Euphrates valley, formerly called Mesopotamia, was the site of one of the earliest civilizations in the world. Mesopotamia ceased to be a separate entity after Persian, Greek, and Arab conquests. The Arabs founded Baghdad, from where the caliph ruled a vast Islamic empire in the 8th and 9th cent. Mongol and Turkish conquests led to a decline in the region's population, economy, cultural life, and irrigation system.

Britain secured a League of Nations mandate over Iraq after WWI. Independence under a king came in 1932. Rebellious army officers killed King Faisal II, July 14, 1958, and established a leftist, pan-Arab republic, which pursued close ties with the USSR. Successive regimes were increasingly dominated by the Baath Arab Socialist Party. A Baath leader, Saddam Hussein, became president of Iraq, July 16, 1979. After purging his enemies, he ruled as a dictator for more than 2 decades, repressing Iraq's Kurds and Shiites and launching disastrous wars against 2 neighboring nations, Iran and Kuwait. Hussein sought weapons of mass destruction; Israeli planes destroyed a nuclear reactor near Baghdad June 7, 1981, claiming it could be used to produce nuclear weapons.

After skirmishing intermittently for 10 months over the sovereignty of the disputed Shatt al-Arab waterway that divides the two countries, Iraq and Iran entered into open warfare on Sept. 22, 1980. Iran repulsed early Iraqi advances, producing a long and costly stalemate; hundreds of thousands of Iraqis lost their lives during the 8-year conflict. Hussein used poison gas against Iraqi Kurds in 1988, killing more than 5,000 people in Halabja, the first mass use of poison gas against civilians since the Holocaust.

Iraq invaded Kuwait Aug. 2, 1990. Backed by the UN, a U.S.-led coalition launched air and missile attacks on Iraq, Jan. 16, 1991, and began a ground attack to retake Kuwait Feb. 23. Iraqi forces showed little resistance and were defeated in 4 days. Some 175,000 Iraqis were taken prisoner, and Iraqi casualties were estimated at over 85,000. As part of the cease-fire agreement, Iraq agreed to scrap all poison gas and germ weapons and allow UN observers to inspect the sites. UN trade sanctions would remain in effect until Iraq complied with all terms.

Iraqi cooperation with UN weapons inspection teams was intermittent throughout the 1990s. Standoffs over inspections led to diplomatic crises 1997-98, culminating in intensive U.S. and British aerial bombardment of Iraqi military targets, Dec. 16-19, 1998. After 2 years of sporadic activity, U.S. and British warplanes struck sites near Baghdad Feb. 16, 2001.

Despite opposition from some countries, including France, Germany, and Russia, a U.S.-led coalition launched an invasion of Iraq Mar. 19, 2003. By Apr. 6 the British controlled Basra and other areas in the south, and the U.S. entered Baghdad Apr. 7. Hussein disappeared, the Iraqi government collapsed, and most of Iraq's armed forces dissolved into the civilian population. On May 1, Pres. Bush declared the end of major combat. Searches failed to find chemical, biological, or nuclear weapons that the U.S. and other countries claimed Iraq had stockpiled.

The U.S. initially governed Iraq through a Coalition Provisional Authority, headed by L. Paul Bremer, which was unable to maintain order in the weeks following Hussein's fall. Reconstruction efforts were hampered by guerrilla attacks from Baath remnants, Islamic extremists, and others. Bombings at UN headquarters in Baghdad, Aug. 19 and Sept. 22, 2003, led the UN to scale back its presence in Iraq. Coalition forces succeeded in neutralizing many leaders of the former regime. U.S. troops killed two of Hussein's sons, Uday and Qusay, July 22, 2003, in Mosul. Saddam Hussein was captured in an underground hideout Dec. 13, 2003; tried and convicted for committing crimes against humanity in the 1980s, he was executed Dec. 30, 2006.

Photographs released in Apr. 2004 showed instances of physical abuse and sexual humiliation of Iraqi inmates by U.S. military personnel at Baghdad's Abu Ghraib prison in 2003. The images sparked widespread condemnation and U.S. criminal proceedings against some individuals.

On June 28, 2004, U.S. authorities transferred sovereignty to a transitional Iraqi government. Despite threats by insurgents, an estimated 8 mil people in Iraq, mostly Shiites and Kurds, cast ballots Jan. 30, 2005, for a 275-member transitional national assembly. On Apr. 6, the assembly elected Jalal al-Talabani, a Kurd, as president; Ibrahim al-Jaafari, a Shiite, became prime minister. Insurgents launched new waves of attacks. Rumors of a suicide bomber set

off a stampede by Shiite pilgrims in northern Baghdad Aug. 31, killing close to 1,000 people. The U.S. blamed Jordanian militant Abu Musab al-Zarqawi, leader of al-Qaeda in Iraq, for directing a series of kidnappings, beheadings, and suicide bombings. He was killed by a U.S. air strike, June 7, 2006.

Legislative elections were held Dec. 15, 2005, and official results announced Jan. 20, 2006, but political wrangling delayed installation of a new government, headed by Shiite leader Nouri Kamel al-Maliki, until May 20. Meanwhile, a bomb Feb. 22 that destroyed the dome of Samarra's Golden Mosque, a Shiite shrine, intensified sectarian violence between Sunnis and Shiites, much of it in Baghdad. The Iraqi civilian death toll averaged more than 2,800 per month in 2006.

In early 2007, Lt. Gen. David H. Petraeus became the top U.S. military commander in Iraq; a "surge" elevated U.S. troop strength from 132,000 in Jan. to 171,000 in Oct. U.S. troop deaths in 2007 totaled 899 (the highest for any year since the war began), but military and civilian casualties dropped steadily from mid-2007 through 2008. Contributing to the reduction in violence were a cease-fire by Shiite militias and a shift by Sunni clan leaders against al-Qaeda in Iraq.

Parliament approved, Nov. 27, 2008, a status-of-forces agreement calling for the U.S. to withdraw its troops from Iraqi cities and towns by June 30, 2009, and for all U.S. forces to leave Iraq by Dec. 31, 2011. Legislative elections Mar. 7, 2010, brought gains by the Iraqiya coalition headed by former Prime Min. Iyad Allawi, a Shiite who had campaigned as a secularist to win widespread Sunni support. On Aug. 31, Pres. Barack Obama formally declared an end to the U.S. combat role, and Operation Iraqi Freedom was succeeded by Operation New Dawn. More than 9 months of political deadlock ended when Prime Min. Maliki was sworn in for a second term Dec. 21, heading a unity government that included Shiite, Sunni, and Kurdish factions. Civilian casualties, which had averaged more than 2,800 per month in 2006, declined to about 200 per month during 2010.

U.S. troops completed their withdrawal from Iraq Dec. 15, 2011. From Mar. 2003 through Dec. 2011, operations in Iraq cost the lives of more than 4,486 U.S. service members; another 32,000 were wounded. British troop losses totaled 179; other allies, 139. More than 115,000 Iraqi civilians and over 10,000 police and security forces were killed. U.S. budgeted costs of the Iraq war exceeded $820 bil for the 2003-12 period.

Tensions manifested between Sunnis and Shiites after the U.S. departure. The Sunni-backed Iraqiya began a 6-week boycott of parliament Dec. 17, 2011, and accused Prime Min. Maliki of not sharing power. Maliki issued an arrest warrant for Sunni Vice Pres. Tariq al-Hashemi, Dec. 19, 2011, for terrorism. The Sunni insurgent group al-Qaeda in Iraq has been blamed for ongoing violence, including coordinated attacks in more than a dozen cities that killed at least 100 people July 23, 2012, and another series of attacks that killed at least 70, Aug. 16.

Ireland

People: Population: 4,722,028. **Age distrib.:** <15: 21.3%; 65+: 11.9%. **Pop. density:** 177.5 per sq mi, 68.6 per sq km. **Urban:** 62.2%. **Ethnic groups:** Irish 87%, other white 8%, Asian 1%, black 1%, mixed 1%. **Principal languages:** English (official; generally used), Irish (Gaelic or Gaeilge) (official; spoken mainly on W coast). **Chief religions:** Roman Catholic 87%, Church of Ireland 3%, other Christian 2%, none 4%.

Geography: Total area: 27,133 sq mi, 70,273 sq km; **Land area:** 26,596 sq mi, 68,883 sq km. **Location:** In Atlantic O. just W of Great Britain. **Neighbors:** United Kingdom (Northern Ireland) on E. **Topography:** Consists of a central plateau surrounded by isolated groups of hills and mountains. Coastline is heavily indented by the Atlantic O. **Capital:** Dublin, 1,120,870.

Government: Type: Parliamentary republic. **Head of state:** Pres. Mary McAleese; b. June 27, 1951; in office: Nov. 11, 1997. **Head of gov.:** Prime Min. Enda Kenny; b. Apr. 24, 1951; in office: Mar. 9, 2011. **Local divisions:** 26 counties. **Defense budget:** $1.31 bil. **Active troops:** 9,650.

Economy: Industries: pharmaceuticals, chemicals, computer hardware and software, food prods., beverages and brewing. **Chief crops:** barley, potatoes, wheat. **Natural resources:** nat. gas, peat, copper, lead, zinc, silver, barite, gypsum, limestone, dolomite. **Arable land:** 15.8%. **Livestock:** cattle: 6.6 mil; chickens: 13.8 mil; goats: 10,100; pigs: 1.5 mil; sheep: 4.6 mil. **Fish catch:** 394,632 metric tons. **Electricity prod.** (2010): 26.5 bil kWh. **Labor force:** agric. 5%, industry 19%, services 76%.

Finance: Monetary unit: Euro (EUR) (Sept. 2012: 0.79 = $1 U.S.). **GDP:** $183.9 bil; **per capita GDP:** $40,100; **GDP growth:** 0.7%. **Imports:** $68 bil; UK 39.8%, U.S. 13%, Germany 7.8%, Netherlands 5.8%. **Exports:** $118.7 bil; U.S. 22.3%, UK 16.2%, Belgium 15.3%, Germany 7.1%, France 5.7%, Switzerland 4.2%. **Tourism:** $4.6 bil. **Budget:** $97.9 bil. **Total reserves less gold:** $1.4 bil. **Gold:** 193,000 oz t. **CPI change:** 2.6%.

Transport: Railways: 2,011 mi. **Motor vehicles:** 498.7 vehicles per 1,000 pop. **Civil aviation:** 54.4 bil pass.-mi; 16 airports. **Chief ports:** Cork, Dublin, Shannon Foynes, Waterford.

Communications: TV sets: 715 per 1,000 pop. **Radios:** 695 per 1,000 pop. **Telephone lines:** 45.2 per 100 pop. **Daily newspaper circ.:** 182.4 per 1,000 pop. **Internet:** 76.8%.

Health: Life expect.: 78.1 male; 82.7 female. **Births:** 15.8 (per 1,000 pop.). **Deaths:** 6.4 (per 1,000 pop.). **Natural inc.:** 0.94% **Infant mortality:** 3.8 (per 1,000 live births). **HIV rate:** 0.2%.

Education: Compulsory: ages 6-15. **Literacy:** 99%.

Major intl. organizations: UN (FAO, IBRD, ILO, IMF, WHO), EU, OECD, OSCE, WTO.

Embassy: 2234 Massachusetts Ave. NW 20008; 462-3939.

Website: www.gov.ie

Celtic tribes invaded the islands about the 4th cent. BCE; their Gaelic culture and literature flourished in the 5th cent. CE, the same century in which St. Patrick converted the Irish to Christianity. Invasions by Norsemen began in the 8th cent., ended with defeat of the Danes by the Irish King Brian Boru in 1014. English invasions started in the 12th cent.; for over 700 years the Anglo-Irish struggle continued with bitter rebellions and savage repressions.

The Easter Monday Rebellion in 1916 failed but was followed by guerrilla warfare and harsh reprisals by British troops called the "Black and Tans." The Dail Eireann (Irish parliament) reaffirmed independence in Jan. 1919. The British offered dominion status to Ulster (6 counties) and southern Ireland (26 counties) Dec. 1921. The constitution of the Irish Free State, a British dominion, was adopted Dec. 11, 1922. Northern Ireland remained part of the United Kingdom (see United Kingdom—Northern Ireland).

A new constitution adopted by plebiscite came into operation Dec. 29, 1937. It declared the name of the state Eire in the Irish language (Ireland in the English) and declared it a sovereign democratic state. On Dec. 21, 1948, the country was declared a republic rather than a dominion and withdrew from the Commonwealth. The British Parliament recognized both actions, 1949, but the 6 northeastern counties remained in the UK.

Irish governments have favored peaceful unification of all Ireland and cooperated with Britain against terrorist groups. After negotiators in Northern Ireland approved a peace settlement on Good Friday, Apr. 10, 1998, voters in the Irish Republic endorsed the accord, on May 22, and the Irish gave up their constitution's territorial claims on the north.

Expansion of educational opportunities and foreign investment in high-tech industries in the 1990s boosted Ireland's prosperity. Ireland's first woman president, Mary Robinson, resigned Sept. 12, 1997, to become UN high commissioner for human rights, 1997-2002. She was succeeded as president by Mary McAleese, a law professor from Northern Ireland and the first northerner to hold the office. Implicated in a corruption inquiry, Prime Min. Bertie Ahern announced his resignation Apr. 2, 2008, after 11 years in power; the Dail Eireann May 7 chose Finance Min. Brian Cowen to succeed him.

In referendums June 12, 2008, and Oct. 2, 2009, Irish voters first rejected and then approved the Lisbon Treaty, a plan to revamp the EU. Responding to a growing scandal over abusive Catholic clergy, Pope Benedict XVI issued a public apology to victims and their families Mar. 20, 2010, and launched an official church investigation May 31 of Irish dioceses, seminaries, and religious orders.

To aid Ireland's ailing banks and prevent default after a 2008-10 financial crisis, finance ministers from EU member countries approved Nov. 28, 2010, an 85 bil euro ($115 bil) emergency loan package that obligated Ireland to impose unpopular austerity measures. Fianna Fáil, the party that had dominated Irish politics since the 1930s, suffered a crushing defeat in elections Feb. 25, 2011, and Enda Kenny, leader of the opposition Fine Gael and a critic of the bailout, became prime minister. Ireland voted May 31, 2012, to ratify the 2012 European Fiscal Compact, which 25 of the 27 EU countries signed Mar. 2, 2012. The treaty imposes rules on signatories to protect the fiscal security of the EU.

Israel
State of Israel

People: Population: 7,590,758. **Age distrib.:** <15: 27.5%; 65+: 10.3%. **Pop. density:** 967 per sq mi, 373.4 per sq km. **Urban:** 91.9%. **Ethnic groups:** Jewish 76% (Israel-born 67%, Europe/American-born 23%, Africa-born 6%, Asia-born 4%), non-Jewish (mostly Arab) 24%. **Principal languages:** Hebrew, Arabic (both official); English (most common foreign lang.). **Chief religions:** Jewish 76%, Muslim 17%, Christian 2%, Druze 2%.

Geography: Total area: 8,019 sq mi, 20,770 sq km; **Land area:** 7,849 sq mi, 20,330 sq km. **Location:** Middle East, on E end of Mediterranean Sea. **Neighbors:** Lebanon on N; Syria, West Bank, Jordan on E; Gaza Strip, Egypt on W. **Topography:** The Mediterranean coastal plain is fertile and well-watered. In the center is the Judean Plateau. A triangular-shaped semi-desert region, the Negev, extends from S of Beersheba to an apex at head of the Gulf of Aqaba. The E border drops sharply into the Jordan Rift Valley, including Lake Tiberias (Sea of Galilee) and the Dead Sea, which is c. 1,300 ft below sea level, lowest point on Earth's surface. **Capital:** Jerusalem, 790,719. **Cities (urban aggl.):** Tel Aviv-Jaffa, 3,381,429; Haifa, 1,053,937.

Government: Type: Parliamentary democracy. **Head of state:** Pres. Shimon Peres; b. Aug. 1923; in office: July 15, 2007. **Head of gov.:** Prime Min. Benjamin Netanyahu; b. Oct. 21, 1949; in office; Mar. 31, 2009. **Local divisions:** 6 districts. **Defense budget:** $15.3 bil. **Active troops:** 176,500.

Economy: Industries: high-tech prods. (incl. aviation, communications computer-aided design and manufactures, medical electronics, fiber optics) wood and paper prods., potash and phosphates, food, beverages, tobacco. **Chief crops:** citrus, vegetables, cotton. **Natural resources:** timber, potash, copper ore, nat. gas, phosphate rock, magnesium bromide, clays, sand. **Crude oil reserves:** 11.8 mil bbls. **Arable land:** 14.1%. **Livestock:** cattle: 430,000; chickens: 42.6 mil; goats: 100,000; pigs: 223,500; sheep: 445,000. **Fish catch:** 22,188 metric tons. **Electricity prod.** (2010): 53.6 bil kWh. **Labor force:** agric. 2%, industry 16%, services 82%.

Finance: Monetary unit: Shekel (ILS) (Sept. 2012: 4.03 = $1 U.S.). **GDP:** $238.2 bil; **per capita GDP:** $31,400; **GDP growth:** 4.7%. **Imports:** $71.9 bil; U.S. 11.8%, China 7.4%, Germany 6.2%, Belgium 6.1%, Switzerland 5.4%, Italy 4.2%. **Exports:** $62.9 bil; U.S. 28.8%, Hong Kong 7.9%, Belgium 5.6%, UK 5%, India 4.5%, China 4%. **Tourism:** $4.8 bil. **Budget:** $74.8 bil. **Total reserves less gold:** $74.9 bil. **CPI change:** 3.5%.

Transport: Railways: 606 mi. **Motor vehicles:** 324.7 vehicles per 1,000 pop. **Civil aviation:** 10.7 bil pass.-mi; 29 airports. **Chief ports:** Ashdod, Elat, Hadera, Haifa.

Communications: TV sets: 340 per 1,000 pop. **Radios:** 540 per 1,000 pop. **Telephone lines:** 46.3 per 100 pop. **Internet:** 70%.

Health: Life expect.: 78.9 male; 83.4 female. **Births:** 19.0 (per 1,000 pop.). **Deaths:** 5.5 (per 1,000 pop.). **Natural inc.:** 1.35% **Infant mortality:** 4.1 (per 1,000 live births). **HIV rate:** 0.2%.

Education: Compulsory: ages 5-15. **Literacy:** 91.8%.

Major intl. organizations: UN (FAO, IBRD, ILO, IMF, WHO), OECD, WTO.

Embassy: 3514 International Dr. NW 20008; 364-5500.

Website: www.gov.il

Occupying the southwest corner of the ancient Fertile Crescent, Israel contains some of the oldest known evidence of agriculture and of primitive town life. The Hebrews probably arrived early in the 2nd millennium BCE. Under King David and his successors (c. 1000 BCE-597 BCE), Judaism was developed and secured. After conquest by Babylonians, Persians, and Greeks, an independent Jewish kingdom was revived, 168 BCE, but Rome took over in the next century, suppressed Jewish revolts in 70 CE and 135 CE, and renamed Judea Palestine, after the earlier coastal inhabitants, the Philistines.

Arab invaders conquered Palestine in 636. The Arabic language and Islam prevailed within a few centuries, but a Jewish minority remained. The land was ruled from the 11th cent. as a part of non-Arab empires by Seljuks, Mamluks, and Ottomans (with a Crusader interval, 1098-1291).

After four centuries of Ottoman rule, the land was taken in 1917 by Britain, which pledged in the Balfour Declaration to support a Jewish homeland there. In 1920 a British Palestine Mandate was recognized; in 1922 the land east of the Jordan was detached.

Jewish immigration, begun in the late 19th cent., swelled in the 1930s with refugees from the Nazis; heavy Arab immigration from Syria and Lebanon also occurred. Arab opposition to Jewish immigration turned violent in 1920, 1921, 1929, and 1936. The UN General Assembly voted in 1947 to partition Palestine into an Arab and a Jewish state. Britain withdrew in May 1948.

Israel was declared independent May 14, 1948; Arabs rejected partition. Egypt, Jordan, Syria, Lebanon, Iraq, and Saudi Arabia invaded but failed to destroy the Jewish state, which gained territory. Separate armistices with the Arab nations were signed in 1949; Jordan occupied the West Bank, Egypt occupied Gaza. Neither granted Palestinian autonomy.

After persistent terrorist raids, Israel invaded Egypt's Sinai, Oct. 29, 1956, aided briefly by British and French forces. A UN cease-fire was arranged Nov. 6.

An uneasy truce between Israel and the Arab countries lasted until 1967, when Egypt reoccupied the Gaza Strip and closed the Gulf of Aqaba to Israeli shipping. In a 6-day war that started June 5, the Israelis took the Gaza Strip, occupied the Sinai Peninsula to the Suez Canal, and captured East Jerusalem, Syria's Golan Heights, and Jordan's West Bank. Together, the West Bank and Gaza comprise the Palestinian territories, now represented by the Palestinian Authority (see below).

Egypt and Syria attacked Israel, Oct. 6, 1973 (on Yom Kippur, the most solemn day on the Jewish calendar). Israel counterattacked, driving the Syrians back, and crossed the Suez Canal. A cease-fire took effect Oct. 24 and a UN peacekeeping force went to the area. Under a disengagement agreement signed Jan. 18, 1974, Israel withdrew from the canal's west bank. Israeli forces raided Entebbe, Uganda, July 3, 1976, and rescued 103 hostages who had been seized by Arab and German terrorists.

Israel's prime ministers, including David Ben-Gurion, Golda Meir, and Yitzhak Rabin, pursued a moderate socialist program, 1948-77. In 1977, the conservative opposition, led by Menachem Begin, was voted into office for the first time. Egypt's Pres. Anwar al-Sadat visited Jerusalem Nov. 1977, and on Mar. 26, 1979, Egypt and Israel signed a formal peace treaty, ending 30 years of war. Israel returned the Sinai to Egypt in 1982.

On June 7, 1981, Israeli jets destroyed an Iraqi atomic reactor near Baghdad that, Israel claimed, would have enabled Iraq to manufacture nuclear weapons. Israeli forces invaded Lebanon, June 6, 1982, to destroy Palestine Liberation Organization (PLO) strongholds. After massive Israeli bombing of West Beirut, the PLO agreed to evacuate the city. Israeli troops entered West Beirut after newly elected Lebanese Pres. Bashir Gemayel was assassinated on Sept. 14. Israel drew widespread condemnation when Lebanese Christian forces, Sept. 16, entered two West Beirut refugee camps and slaughtered hundreds of Palestinians.

In 1989, violence escalated over the Israeli military occupation of the West Bank and Gaza Strip. In a series of uprisings known as the first intifada, Palestinian protesters defied Israeli troops, who forcibly retaliated. During the Persian Gulf War, 1991, Iraq fired Scud missiles at Israel. The Labor Party of Yitzhak Rabin won parliamentary elections, June 23, 1992.

Ongoing peace talks led to historic agreements between Israel and the PLO, Sept. 1993. The PLO recognized Israel's right to exist; Israel recognized the PLO as the Palestinians' representative. The two sides then signed, Sept. 13, an agreement for limited Palestinian self-rule in the West Bank and Gaza. Israel and Jordan signed, July 25, 1994, in Washington, DC, a declaration ending their 46-year state of war.

Arab and Jewish extremists repeatedly challenged the peace process. On Nov. 4, 1995, an Orthodox Jewish Israeli assassinated Rabin as he left a peace rally in Tel Aviv. Support for Rabin's succes-sor, Shimon Peres, was shaken by a series of suicide bombings and rocket attacks against Israel by Islamic militants. Emphasizing security issues, the candidate of the conservative Likud bloc, Benjamin Netanyahu, was elected prime minister on May 29, 1996.

Under an interim accord brokered by Pres. Bill Clinton and signed by Netanyahu and PLO leader Yasir Arafat at the White House, Oct. 23, 1998, Israel yielded more West Bank territory to the Palestinians, in exchange for new security guarantees. Full implementation did not begin until Sept. 1999. In the interim, Netanyahu lost to the Labor candidate, Ehud Barak, in the May 17, 1999, election.

Israel pulled virtually all its troops out of southern Lebanon by May 24, 2000. Marathon summit talks in the U.S. between Barak and Arafat, July 11-25, failed. A second intifada began in late Sept. in Israel and the Palestinian territories. Barak called new elections for prime minister but lost Feb. 6, 2001, to Ariel Sharon, a hardliner. The bloodshed intensified during the summer, as Palestinian suicide bombers launched attacks on Israeli civilians and Israel struck at Palestinian-controlled territory and carried out an assassination campaign against suspected terrorists.

Israel launched a major West Bank offensive Mar. 29, 2002, 2 days after a suicide bomber killed 26 Israeli Jews at a Passover celebration in Netanya. Fighting was particularly fierce at the Jenin refugee camp, where 23 Israeli troops and at least 50 Palestinians were killed. A U.S.-sponsored "road map" to Middle East peace, unveiled Apr. 30, 2003, made little headway, as violence flared between Israel and Hamas militants in Gaza.

Sharon's decision to pull all Israeli settlers and troops out of Gaza, approved by the cabinet Feb. 20, 2005, led to a realignment in Israeli politics. When right-wing Likud members opposed the plan, Sharon and Deputy Prime Min. Ehud Olmert broke with them and formed the centrist Kadima Party. Sharon suffered a massive stroke Jan. 4, 2006. With Sharon incapacitated, Olmert became prime minister, led Kadima to victory in Mar. 28 elections, and formed a broad coalition government.

Clashes in mid-2006 along the Gaza and Lebanon borders rapidly escalated into full-scale war. Israeli air and ground forces hit hard in Gaza, but the fiercest fighting raged on the northern front. By Aug. 14, when a UN-sponsored cease-fire took hold, the estimated death toll from the war included nearly 1,150 Lebanese, almost 200 Gaza Palestinians, and 150 Israelis. Olmert, criticized for leadership failures during the 2006 war and targeted in multiple corruption inquiries, announced July 30, 2008, that he would resign. Foreign Min. Tzipi Livni won a hard-fought party primary Sept. 17. Unable to form a stable government, she called early elections for Feb. 10, 2009. After a campaign overshadowed by a 3-week war between Israel and Hamas in Gaza, both Kadima and Likud fell far short of a majority. On Mar. 31, Netanyahu became prime minister for a second time.

Israel's relations with allies were strained when senior Hamas commander Mahmoud al-Mabhouh was killed Jan. 2010 in Dubai, allegedly by agents of the Israeli spy agency Mossad who entered the UAE carrying false European and Australian passports. Further criticism greeted the Israeli government's announcement, during a Mar. 9 visit by U.S. Vice Pres. Joe Biden, that it would proceed with construction of 1,600 homes in Ramat Shlomo (a Jewish settlement in mostly Arab East Jerusalem), and the killing by Israeli commandos of 9 pro-Palestinian activists in clashes May 31 on board the *Mavi Marmara*, part of a flotilla that was seeking to break Israel's blockade of Gaza.

"Arab Spring" uprisings in 2011, which toppled the Mubarak government in neighboring Egypt and shook other Middle Eastern regimes, unsettled Israeli policy in the region. In a cross-border clash that raised tensions between Israel and Egypt, militants Aug. 18, 2011, killed 8 Israelis (6 civilians, 2 soldiers), and retaliatory fire by Israel killed at least 7 of the attackers along with at least 3 Egyptian security officers and, according to some reports, several civilians. Israel evacuated its diplomats from Egypt after thousands of protesters stormed the Israeli embassy in Cairo Sept. 9. Mass protests within Israel July-Sept. 2011 focused on social and economic inequality and the rising cost of living.

Tensions between Iran and Israel have grown over Iran's nuclear program, which Israel sees as an existential threat. Prime Min. Netanyahu met in the U.S. with Pres. Barack Obama Mar. 5-6, 2012; both nations pledged to use force against Iran if necessary, though the U.S. urged continued diplomacy and tighter sanctions.

Palestinian Territories

The Palestinian territories comprise the Gaza Strip, often called Gaza, and the West Bank, both occupied by Israel in 1967. Since 1996 the Palestinian Authority has been responsible for civil government in the territories. Elected president Jan. 20, 1996, PLO leader Yasir Arafat headed the Palestinian Authority until his death Nov. 11, 2004. Mahmoud Abbas (also called Abu Mazen), who had succeeded Arafat as PLO chairman and leader of the Fatah faction, was elected president Jan. 9, 2005. A victory by Hamas militants in legislative elections Jan. 25, 2006, led to a power struggle with Abbas, who favored a negotiated settlement with Israel. In bitter fighting, Hamas ousted Fatah from Gaza, June 2007, but Abbas retained power in the West Bank. From Sept. 2000, when the second intifada began, through the end of 2008, the Israeli-Palestinian conflict claimed the lives of more than 1,060 Israelis and at least 4,900 Palestinians; nearly 600 Palestinians were killed by other Palestinians in factional fighting. Fatah and Hamas declared Apr. 27, 2011, that they had reached a reconciliation agreement and announced Feb. 6, 2012, that Abbas would lead an interim unity government, though the reconciliation agreement's goal of holding elections in Palestine by May 2012 was not reached. In a speech Sept. 23, 2011, to the UN General Assembly, Abbas sought full UN membership of an independent Palestinian state; the U.S. and Israel opposed the request.

The **Gaza Strip** extends northeast from the Sinai Peninsula for 25 mi (40 km), with the Mediterranean Sea to the west and Israel to the east. The Palestinian Authority is responsible for civil government. Nearly all the inhabitants are Palestinian Arabs, more than 35% of whom live in refugee camps. Pop. (2012 est.): 1,710,257. Area: 139 sq mi, 360 sq km.

Israel captured Gaza from Egypt in the 1967 war. It remained under Israeli occupation until May 1994, when the Israeli Defense Forces withdrew. Agreements between Israel and the PLO in 1993 and 1994 provided for interim self-rule in Gaza, but Israel retained control over security. Israel forcibly evacuated all 9,000 Jewish settlers from Gaza by Aug. 22, 2005, and the last remaining Israeli soldiers pulled out Sept. 12. Israel established a fortified barrier on its Gaza border to block Palestinian infiltrators.

After the Hamas takeover, Israel declared Gaza a "hostile entity," Sept. 19, 2007, and intensified military and economic pressures. Hamas thwarted an Israeli blockade, Jan. 2008, blowing up part of the border wall between Gaza and Egypt. Retaliating for Hamas rocket and mortar attacks, Israel launched an aerial assault and ground offensive in Gaza, Dec. 27, 2008-Jan. 18, 2009. A UN report issued Sept. 15, 2009, found evidence of war crimes committed by both sides. After the *Mavi Marmara* incident, Israel June 2010 eased some restrictions on the flow of goods to Gaza. Egypt lifted the blockade along its Gaza border May 28, 2011.

The **West Bank** is located west of the Jordan R. and Dead Sea, bounded by Jordan on the east and by Israel on the north, west, and south. The Palestinian Authority administers several major cities, but Israel retains control over much land, including Jewish settlements. Population (2011 est.): 2,568,555. Area: 2,263 sq mi.

Israel captured the West Bank from Jordan in the 1967 war. An accord between Israel and the PLO expanding Palestinian self-rule in the West Bank was signed Sept. 28, 1995. Later agreements gave Palestinians full or shared control of 40% of West Bank territory.

In June 2002 the Israeli government began building a controversial security barrier in the West Bank to restrict Palestinian access to Israel and reduce infiltration by suicide bombers. In a nonbinding ruling, July 9, 2004, the World Court said the barrier violated international law. Israel has continued to allow the expansion of Jewish settlements on the West Bank, despite U.S. government calls for a settlement freeze; by mid-2011, an estimated 320,000 Jewish settlers were living in the West Bank (not including East Jerusalem, which Israel annexed in 1967).

Italy
Italian Republic

People: Population: 61,261,254. **Age distrib.:** <15: 13.8%; 65+: 20.5%. **Pop. density:** 539.4 per sq mi, 208.3 per sq km. **Urban:** 68.4%. **Ethnic groups:** Italian (incl. small clusters of German-, French-, and Slovene-Italians in N; Albanian- and Greek-Italians in S). **Principal languages:** Italian (official), German, French, Slovene. **Chief religions:** Christian 80% (predominantly Roman Catholic), Atheists and Agnostics 20%.

Geography: Total area: 116,348 sq mi, 301,340 sq km; **Land area:** 113,568 sq mi, 294,140 sq km. **Location:** In S Europe, jutting into Mediterranean Sea. **Neighbors:** France on W; Switzerland, Austria on N; Slovenia on E; San Marino, Vatican City. **Topography:** Occupies long boot-shaped peninsula, extending SE from the Alps into Mediterranean, with islands of Sicily and Sardinia offshore. The alluvial Po Valley drains most of N. Rest of the country is rugged and mountainous, except for intermittent coastal plains, like the Campania, S of Rome. Apennine Mts. run down through center of peninsula. **Capital:** Rome, 3,298,300. **Cities (urban aggl.):** Milan, 2,909,180; Naples, 2,372,526; Turin, 1,612,882.

Government: Type: Republic. **Head of state:** Pres. Giorgio Napolitano; b. June 29, 1925; in office: May 15, 2006. **Head of gov.:** Prime Min. Mario Monti; b. Mar. 19, 1943; in office: Nov. 16, 2011. **Local divisions:** 20 regions divided into 103 provinces. **Defense budget:** $21 bil. **Active troops:** 184,532.

Economy: Industries: tourism, machinery, iron and steel, chemicals, food proc., textiles, motor vehicles, clothing, footwear, ceramics. **Chief crops:** fruits, vegetables, grapes, potatoes, sugar beets, soybeans, grain, olives. **Natural resources:** coal, mercury, zinc, potash, marble, barite, asbestos, pumice, fluorspar, feldspar, pyrite (sulfur), nat. gas and crude oil reserves, fish. **Crude oil reserves:** 523.2 mil bbls. **Arable land:** 23.4%. **Livestock:** cattle: 6.1 mil; chickens: 130 mil; goats: 961,000; pigs: 9.2 mil; sheep: 8 mil. **Fish catch:** 388,997 metric tons. **Electricity prod.** (2010): 279 bil kWh. **Labor force:** agric. 3.9%, industry 28.3%, services 67.8%.

Finance: Monetary unit: Euro (EUR) (Sept. 2012: 0.79 = $1 U.S.). **GDP:** $1.9 tril; **per capita GDP:** $30,900; **GDP growth:** 0.4%. **Imports:** $556.4 bil; Germany 16.5%, France 8.9%, China 7.7%, Netherlands 5.5%, Spain 4.7%. **Exports:** $523.9 bil; Germany 13.3%, France 11.8%, U.S. 5.9%, Spain 5.4%, Switzerland 5.4%, UK 4.7%. **Tourism:** $43 bil. **Budget:** $1.1 tril. **Total reserves less gold:** $49.2 bil. **Gold:** 78.8 mil oz t. **CPI change:** 2.7%.

Transport: Railways: 12,586 mi. **Motor vehicles:** 683.5 vehicles per 1,000 pop. **Civil aviation:** 24.7 bil pass.-mi; 99 airports. **Chief ports:** Augusta, Cagliari, Genoa, Livorno, Sarroch, Taranto, Trieste, Venice.

Communications: TV sets: 492 per 1,000 pop. **Radios:** 878 per 1,000 pop. **Telephone lines:** 34.6 per 100 pop. **Daily newspaper circ.:** 137.1 per 1,000 pop. **Internet:** 56.8%.

Health: Life expect.: 79.2 male; 84.6 female. **Births:** 9.1 (per 1,000 pop.). **Deaths:** 9.9 (per 1,000 pop.). **Natural inc.:** −0.09% (per 1,000 pop.). **Infant mortality:** 3.4 (per 1,000 live births). **HIV rate:** 0.3%.

Education: Compulsory: ages 6-14. **Literacy:** 98.9%.

Major intl. organizations: UN and all of its specialized agencies, EU, NATO, OECD, OSCE, WTO.

Embassy: 3000 Whitehaven St. NW 20008; 612-4400.

Website: www.quirinale.it

Rome emerged as the major power in Italy after 500 BCE, dominating the Etruscans to the north and Greeks to the south. Under the Empire, which lasted until the 5th cent. CE, Rome ruled most of Western Europe, the Balkans, the Middle East, and North Africa. After Rome fell, Italy became a patchwork of kingdoms, principalities, and city-states until reunified, 1870.

The Fascist leader Benito Mussolini came to power, 1922, and aligned Italy with Nazi Germany in WWII. After Fascism was overthrown in 1943, Italy declared war on Germany and Japan and contributed to the Allied victory. It surrendered conquered lands and lost its colonies. Mussolini was killed by partisans Apr. 28, 1945. Victor Emmanuel III abdicated May 9, 1946; his son Humbert II was king until June 10, when Italy became a republic after a referendum, June 2-3. In the postwar decades, Italy had a succession of short-lived governments.

Christian Democratic leader and former prime min. Aldo Moro was abducted and murdered in 1978 by Red Brigade terrorists. The wave of left-wing political violence, including other kidnappings and assassinations, continued into the 1980s.

In the early 1990s, scandals implicated some of Italy's most prominent politicians. In Mar. 1994 voting, under reformed election rules, right-wing parties won a majority, dislodging Italy's long-powerful Christian Democratic Party. Italy led a 7,000-member peacekeeping force in Albania, Apr.-Aug. 1997, and contributed 2,000 troops to the NATO-led security force (KFOR) that entered Kosovo in June 1999.

Supporters of Silvio Berlusconi, a multibillionaire media magnate, won the parliamentary elections of May 13, 2001. Berlusconi, a close ally of the U.S., backed American-led military operations in Afghanistan (2001) and Iraq (2003). As of mid-2012, 3,800 Italian troops continued to serve with the NATO mission in Afghanistan.

A coalition of center-left parties led by Romano Prodi scored a narrow win over Berlusconi in parliamentary voting; Berlusconi returned at the head of a center-right coalition after elections Apr. 13-14, 2008. An earthquake in the Abruzzo region of central Italy Apr. 6, 2009, battered the town of L'Aquila, killing more than 300 people. Sluggish economic growth and rising public debt (equal to about 120% of annual GDP in mid-2011) raised investors' concerns about Italy's financial stability. Berlusconi resigned

Nov. 12, 2011, and Mario Monti, an economist, took office as his replacement Nov. 16. Italy's economic problems worsened and its public debt reached nearly 2 tril euros ($2.5 tril) by Aug. 30, 2012. Italy was expected to seek a bailout as of Sept. 2012.

The luxury cruise ship *Costa Concordia* ran into a reef off the coast of Italy Jan. 13, 2012, killing 32 people.

Sicily, 9,927 sq mi, pop. (2010 est.) 5,050,486, is an island 180 by 120 mi, seat of a region that embraces the island of Pantelleria, 32 sq mi, and the Lipari group, 44 sq mi, including two active volcanoes: Vulcano, 1,637 ft, and Stromboli, 3,038 ft. From prehistoric times Sicily has been settled by various peoples; a Greek state had its capital at Syracuse. Rome took Sicily from Carthage 215 BCE. Mt. Etna, an 11,053-ft active volcano, is its tallest peak.

Sardinia, 9,301 sq mi, pop. (2010 est.) 1,675,411, lies in the Mediterranean, 115 mi W of Italy and 7½ mi S of Corsica. It is 160 mi long, 68 mi wide, and mountainous, with mining of coal, zinc, lead, copper. In 1720 Sardinia was added to the possessions of the Dukes of Savoy in Piedmont and Savoy to form the Kingdom of Sardinia. Giuseppe Garibaldi is buried on the nearby isle of Caprera. **Elba,** 86 sq mi, lies 6 mi W of Tuscany. Napoleon I lived in exile on Elba 1814-15.

Jamaica

People: Population: 2,889,187. **Age distrib.:** <15: 29.5%; 65+: 7.7%. **Pop. density:** 690.9 per sq mi, 266.8 per sq km. **Urban:** 52%. **Ethnic groups:** black 91%, mixed 6%. **Principal languages:** English, English patois. **Chief religions:** Protestant 63%, Roman Catholic 3%, none 21%.

Geography: Total area: 4,244 sq mi, 10,991 sq km; **Land area:** 4,182 sq mi, 10,831 sq km. **Location:** In W Indies. **Neighbors:** Nearest are Cuba to N, Haiti to E. **Topography:** Four-fifths of country covered by mountains. **Capital:** Kingston, 571,110.

Government: Type: Constitutional monarchy with parliamentary system based on UK model. **Head of state:** Queen Elizabeth II, represented by Sir Patrick Allen; b. Feb. 7, 1951; in office: Feb. 26, 2009. **Head of gov.:** Prime Min. Portia Simpson-Miller; b. Dec. 12, 1945; in office: Jan. 5, 2012. **Local divisions:** 14 parishes. **Defense budget:** $104 mil. **Active troops:** 2,830.

Economy: Industries: tourism, bauxite/alumina, agric. proc., light manufactures, rum, cement, metal, paper, chem. prods., telecom. **Chief crops:** sugarcane, bananas, coffee, citrus, yams. **Natural resources:** bauxite, gypsum, limestone. **Arable land:** 11.1%. **Livestock:** cattle: 168,000; chickens: 14.1 mil; goats: 440,000; pigs: 223,500; sheep: 1,900. **Fish catch:** 19,490 metric tons. **Electricity prod.:** 5.2 bil kWh. **Labor force:** agric. 17%, industry 19%, services 64%.

Finance: Monetary unit: Dollar (JMD) (Sept. 2012: 89.20 = $1 U.S.). **GDP:** $25.1 bil; **per capita GDP:** $9,100; **GDP growth:** 1.5%. **Imports:** $6.3 bil; U.S. 33.9%, Venezuela 15.5%, Trinidad and Tobago 14.6%, China 6.6%. **Exports:** $1.6 bil; U.S. 37%, Canada 18.1%, Netherlands 7.3%, UK 5.4%, Norway 4.3%. **Tourism:** $2.01 bil. **Budget:** $4.7 bil. **Total reserves less gold:** $2.3 bil. **CPI change:** 7.5%.

Transport: Motor vehicles: 60.2 vehicles per 1,000 pop. **Civil aviation:** 1.8 bil pass.-mi; 12 airports. **Chief ports:** Kingston, Montego Bay, Port Antonio, Port Esquivel, Port Kaiser, Port Rhoades (Discovery Bay), Rocky Point.

Communications: TV sets: 382 per 1,000 pop. **Radios:** 23 per 1,000 pop. **Telephone lines:** 9.9 per 100 pop. **Internet:** 31.5%.

Health: Life expect.: 71.8 male; 75.2 female. **Births:** 18.9 (per 1,000 pop.). **Deaths:** 6.6 (per 1,000 pop.). **Natural inc.:** 1.23%. **Infant mortality:** 14.3 (per 1,000 live births). **HIV rate:** 1.7%.

Education: Compulsory: ages 6-11. **Literacy:** 86.6%.

Major intl. organizations: UN (FAO, IBRD, ILO, IMF, WHO), Caricom, the Commonwealth, OAS, WTO.

Embassy: 1520 New Hampshire Ave. NW 20036; 452-0660.

Website: www.jis.gov.jm

Jamaica was visited by Columbus, 1494, and ruled by Spain (under whom Arawak Indians died out) until seized by Britain, 1655. Jamaica won independence Aug. 6, 1962. The island's rich musical innovations include ska and reggae. Rastafarianism is an influential religious movement.

In 1974 Jamaica sought an increase in taxes paid by U.S. and Canadian bauxite mines. The socialist government acquired 50% ownership of the companies' Jamaican interests in 1976, and was reelected that year. Rudimentary welfare state measures were passed. Relations with the U.S. improved in the 1980s when Jamaican politics entered a more conservative phase. Violence between government forces and West Kingston slum residents claimed at least 20 lives July 7-10, 2001.

At least 17 died when Hurricane Ivan hit southern Jamaica Sept. 10-11, 2004. Portia Simpson-Miller, leader of the People's National Party, became Jamaica's first female prime minister, Mar. 30, 2006. The opposition Jamaica Labour Party (JLP) won the parliamentary elections of Sept. 3, 2007. While trying to arrest an alleged gang leader, Christopher (Dudus) Coke, police and soldiers clashed with residents in the Tivoli Gardens section of Kingston in May 2010, leaving 76 people dead. Coke surrendered June 22, 2010, and was extradited to the U.S.; he pleaded guilty to racketeering charges Aug. 31, 2011. Prime Min. Bruce Golding resigned Oct. 23,

2011. The People's National Party won a landslide victory Dec. 29, 2011; Portia Simpson-Miller again became prime min. Jan. 5, 2012.

Japan

People: Population: 127,368,088. **Age distrib.:** <15: 13.5%; 65+: 23.9%. **Pop. density:** 905.1 per sq mi, 349.4 per sq km. **Urban:** 91.3%. **Ethnic groups:** Japanese 98.5%, Korean 0.5%. **Principal language:** Japanese. **Chief religions:** Shintoism 84%, Buddhism 71% (many people observe together); Christian 2%.

Geography: Total area: 145,914 sq mi, 377,915 sq km; **Land area:** 140,728 sq mi, 364,485 sq km. **Location:** Archipelago off E coast of Asia. **Neighbors:** Russia to N, S. Korea to W. **Topography:** Consists of 4 main islands: Honshu ("mainland"), 87,805 sq mi; Hokkaido, 30,144 sq mi; Kyushu, 14,114 sq mi; and Shikoku, 7,049 sq mi. The coast, deeply indented, measures 16,654 mi. The northern islands are continuation of the Sakhalin Mts. The Kunlun range of China continues into southern islands, the ranges meeting in Japanese Alps. In a vast transverse fissure crossing Honshu E-W rises a group of volcanoes, mostly extinct or inactive, including 12,388 ft. Mt. Fuji (Fujiyama) near Tokyo. **Capital:** Tokyo, 37,217,400. **Cities (urban aggl.):** Osaka-Kobe, 11,494,433; Nagoya, 3,328,296; Fukuoka-Kitakyushu, 2,868,051; Sapporo, 2,741,771; Sendai, 2,427,794; Hiroshima, 2,119,150; Kyoto, 1,804,215.

Government: Type: Constitutional monarchy with parliamentary democracy. **Head of state:** Emperor Akihito; b. Dec. 23, 1933; in office: Jan. 7, 1989. **Head of gov.:** Prime Min. Yoshihiko Noda; b. May 20, 1957; in office: Sept. 2, 2011. **Local divisions:** 47 prefectures. **Defense budget:** $58.4 bil. **Active troops:** 247,746.

Economy: Industries: among world's largest and technologically advanced producers of motor vehicles, electronic equip., machine tools, steel and nonferrous metals, ships, chemicals, textiles, processed foods. **Chief crops:** rice, sugar beets, vegetables, fruits. **Natural resources:** negligible mineral resources, fish. **Crude oil reserves:** 44.1 mil bbls. **Arable land:** 11.8%. **Livestock:** cattle: 4.4 mil; chickens: 286 mil; goats: 15,000; pigs: 9.8 mil; sheep: 12,000. **Fish catch:** 5.3 mil metric tons. **Electricity prod.** (2010): 1.01 tril kWh. **Labor force:** agric. 3.9%, industry 26.2%, services 69.8%.

Finance: Monetary unit: Yen (JPY) (Sept. 2012: 78.32 = $1 U.S.). **GDP:** $4.5 tril; **per capita GDP:** $35,200; **GDP growth:** –0.7%. **Imports:** $808.4 bil; China 21.5%, U.S. 8.9%, Australia 6.6%, Saudi Arabia 5.9%, UAE 5%, South Korea 4.7%. **Exports:** $788 bil; China 19.7%, U.S. 15.5%, South Korea 8%, Hong Kong 5.2%, Thailand 4.6%. **Tourism:** $11 bil. **Budget:** $2.5 tril. **Total reserves less gold:** $1.3 tril. **Gold:** 24.6 mil oz t. **CPI change:** –0.3%.

Transport: Railways: 16,890 mi. **Motor vehicles:** 580.8 vehicles per 1,000 pop. **Civil aviation:** 79.4 bil pass.-mi; 143 airports. **Chief ports:** Chiba, Kawasaki, Kobe, Mizushima, Moji, Nagoya, Osaka, Tokyo, Tomakomai, Yokohama.

Communications: TV sets: 842 per 1,000 pop. **Radios:** 955 per 1,000 pop. **Telephone lines:** 51.1 per 100 pop. **Daily newspaper circ.:** 551.2 per 1,000 pop. **Internet:** 79.5%.

Health: Life expect.: 80.6 male; 87.4 female. **Births:** 8.4 (per 1,000 pop.). **Deaths:** 9.2 (per 1,000 pop.). **Natural inc.:** –0.08% **Infant mortality:** 2.2 (per 1,000 live births). **HIV rate:** <0.1%.

Education: Compulsory: ages 6-14. **Literacy:** 99%.

Major intl. organizations: UN and all its specialized agencies, APEC, OECD, WTO.

Embassy: 2520 Massachusetts Ave. NW 20008; 238-6700.

Website: www.kantei.go.jp

According to Japanese legend, the empire was founded by Emperor Jimmu, 660 BCE, but earliest records of a unified Japan date from 1,000 years later. Chinese influence was strong in the formation of Japanese civilization. Buddhism was introduced before the 6th cent. CE.

A feudal system, with locally powerful noble families and their samurai warrior retainers, dominated from 1192. Central power was held by successive families of shoguns (military dictators), 1192-1867, until recovered by Emperor Meiji, 1868. The Portuguese and Dutch had minor trade with Japan in the 16th and 17th centuries; U.S. Commodore Matthew C. Perry opened the country to U.S. trade in a treaty ratified 1854. Industrialization was begun in the late 19th cent. Japan fought China, 1894-95, gaining Taiwan. After war with Russia, 1904-05, Russia ceded the southern half of Sakhalin. Japan annexed Korea, 1910.

In WWI Japan ousted Germany from Shandong in China and took over German Pacific islands. Japan took Manchuria in 1931 and launched full-scale war in China in 1937. Japan launched war against the U.S. by attacking Pearl Harbor Dec. 7, 1941. The U.S. dropped atomic bombs on Hiroshima, Aug. 6, and Nagasaki, Aug. 9, 1945. Japan surrendered Aug. 14, 1945.

In a new constitution adopted May 3, 1947, Japan renounced the right to wage war; the emperor gave up claims to divinity; the Diet became the sole lawmaking authority. The U.S. and 48 other non-Communist nations signed a peace treaty and the U.S. a bilateral defense agreement with Japan, in San Francisco Sept. 8, 1951, restoring Japan's sovereignty as of Apr. 28, 1952.

Rebuilding after WWII, Japan emerged as one of the most powerful economies in the world. The U.S. and Western Europe criticized

Japan for its import policies, which allowed Japan to accumulate huge trade surpluses.

On June 26, 1968, the U.S. returned control of the Bonin Isls., Volcano Isls. (including Iwo Jima), and Marcus Isls to Japan. On May 15, 1972, the U.S. returned Okinawa, the other Ryukyu Isls., and the Daito Isls., but the U.S. continued to maintain military bases on Okinawa. An agreement reached Apr. 26, 2012, would reduce the number of U.S. Marines stationed on Okinawa from 19,000 to 10,000.

The Liberal Democratic Party (LDP) governed Japan from the mid-1950s through early 1990s. On June 29, 1994, Tomiichi Murayama became Japan's first Socialist premier since 1947-48. An earthquake in the Kobe area in Jan. 1995 claimed more than 5,000 lives. With the country mired in a lengthy recession, the LDP regained power in 1996 and led Japan until 2009.

For the first time since WWII, Japan sent troops to an overseas warzone, when about 600 noncombatant troops served in Iraq Feb. 2004-July 2006. The worldwide recession of 2008-09 hit Japan hard, prompting a series of economic stimulus plans; the largest, unveiled Apr. 10, 2009, called for more than $150 bil in spending and tax measures. The LDP suffered a crushing defeat in parliamentary elections Aug. 30, 2009, and Yukio Hatoyama of the opposition Democratic Party of Japan (DPJ) became prime min. His public support soon plummeted, and he was replaced June 8, 2010, by former Finance Min. Naoto Kan.

A magnitude 9.0 earthquake and tsunami in the Pacific Ocean off Japan's east coast Mar. 11, 2011, killed more than 15,800 people with another 2,800 still listed as missing (as of Aug. 2012). Inundated by the tsunami, the Fukushima Daiichi nuclear power plant experienced meltdowns at three of the plant's six nuclear reactors, spewing radiation over a large area. Criticized for his response to the catastrophe, Prime Min. Naoto Kan submitted his resignation Aug. 26, 2011, and was succeeded by Finance Min. Yoshihiko Noda. Following Fukushima Daiichi meltdowns, Japan began shutting down nuclear reactors and promised to keep them closed until each passed stress tests. The last of the reactors was shut down May 5, 2012, and the first was restarted July 1.

Jordan
Hashemite Kingdom of Jordan

People: Population: 6,508,887. **Age distrib.:** <15: 34.9%; 65+: 4.9%. **Pop. density:** 189.8 per sq mi, 73.3 per sq km. **Urban:** 82.7%. **Ethnic groups:** Arab 98%, Circassian 1%, Armenian 1%. **Principal languages:** Arabic (official), English widely understood among upper and middle classes. **Chief religions:** Sunni Muslim (official) 92%, Christian 6% (majority Greek Orthodox).

Geography: Total area: 34,495 sq mi, 89,342 sq km; **Land area:** 34,287 sq mi, 88,802 sq km. **Location:** In Middle East. **Neighbors:** Israel, West Bank on W; Saudi Arabia on S; Iraq on E; Syria on N. **Topography:** About 88% is arid. Fertile areas are in W. Only port is on short Aqaba Gulf coast. Country shares Dead Sea (about 1,300 ft below sea level) with Israel. **Capital:** Amman, 1,178,650.

Government: Type: Constitutional monarchy. **Head of state:** King Abdullah II; b. Jan. 30, 1962; in office: Feb. 7, 1999. **Head of gov.:** Prime Min. Fayez al-Tarawneh; b. 1949; in office: May 2, 2012. **Local divisions:** 12 governorates. **Defense budget:** $1.36 bil. **Active troops:** 100,500.

Economy: Industries: clothing, fertilizers, potash, phosphate mining, pharmaceuticals, petroleum refining, cement, inorganic chemicals, light mfg., tourism. **Chief crops:** citrus, tomatoes, cucumbers, olives, strawberries, stone fruits. **Natural resources:** phosphates, potash, shale oil. **Crude oil reserves:** 1 mil bbls. **Arable land:** 2.3%. **Livestock:** cattle: 65,390; chickens: 25 mil; goats: 751,730; sheep: 2.2 mil. **Fish catch:** 1,027 metric tons. **Electricity prod.:** 13.4 bil kWh. **Labor force:** agric. 2.7%, industry 20%, services 77.4%.

Finance: Monetary unit: Dinar (JOD) (Sept. 2012: 0.71 = $1 U.S.). **GDP:** $37.4 bil; **per capita GDP:** $6,000; **GDP growth:** 2.5%. **Imports:** $16.2 bil; Saudi Arabia 22.4%, China 10.6%, U.S. 6.2%, Italy 5.1%, Germany 4.2%, Egypt 4.1%. **Exports:** $8 bil; Iraq 15.3%, U.S. 14.7%, India 12.5%, Saudi Arabia 9.6%, Lebanon 4.4%. **Tourism:** $3 bil. **Budget:** $9.6 bil. **Total reserves less gold:** $11.5 bil. **Gold:** 410,000 oz t. **CPI change:** 4.4%.

Transport: Railways: 315 mi. **Motor vehicles:** 84.1 vehicles per 1,000 pop. **Civil aviation:** 4 bil pass.-mi; 16 airports. **Chief port:** Al Aqabah.

Communications: TV sets: 207 per 1,000 pop. **Radios:** 361 per 1,000 pop. **Telephone lines:** 7.4 per 100 pop. **Internet:** 34.9%.

Health: Life expect.: 78.8 male; 81.6 female. **Births:** 26.5 (per 1,000 pop.). **Deaths:** 2.7 (per 1,000 pop.). **Natural inc.:** 2.38% **Infant mortality:** 15.8 (per 1,000 live births). **HIV rate:** NA.

Education: Compulsory: ages 6-15. **Literacy:** 92.6%.

Major intl. organizations: UN (FAO, IBRD, ILO, IMF, WHO), AL, WTO.

Embassy: 3504 International Dr. NW 20008; 966-2664.

Website: www.kinghussein.gov.jo

From ancient times to 1922 the lands to the east of the Jordan R. were culturally and politically united with the lands to the

W. Arabs conquered the area in the 7th cent.; the Ottomans took control in the 16th. Britain's 1920 Palestine Mandate covered both sides of the Jordan. In 1921, Abdullah, son of the ruler of Hejaz in Arabia, was installed by Britain as emir of an autonomous Transjordan, covering two-thirds of Palestine. An independent kingdom was proclaimed, 1946.

During the 1948 Arab-Israeli war, the West Bank and East Jerusalem were added to the kingdom, which changed its name to Jordan. These territories were lost to Israel in 1967, which swelled the number of Arab refugees on the East Bank.

Jordan and Israel officially agreed, July 25, 1994, to end their state of war; a peace treaty was signed Oct. 26. King Hussein died Feb. 7, 1999, ending a nearly 47-year reign; his eldest son assumed the throne as Abdullah II. According to government estimates, at least 450,000 refugees from the Iraq war were living in Jordan at the beginning of 2011. Abdullah II responded to 3 weeks of "Arab Spring" protests by replacing his prime min. in early Feb 2011. Low-level protests persisted, and he appointed two more prime min. over the next 15 months.

Kazakhstan
Republic of Kazakhstan

People: Population: 17,522,010. **Age distrib.:** <15: 24.4%; 65+: 6.7%. **Pop. density:** 16.8 per sq mi, 6.5 per sq km. **Urban:** 53.6%. **Ethnic groups:** Kazakh (Qazaq) 63%, Russian 24%, Uzbek 3%, Ukrainian 2%, Uighur 1%, Tatar 1%, German 1%. **Principal languages:** Kazakh (Qazaq; state lang.), Russian (official; used in everyday business). **Chief religions:** Muslim 47%, Russian Orthodox 44%, Protestant 2%.

Geography: Total area: 1,052,090 sq mi, 2,724,900 sq km; **Land area:** 1,042,360 sq mi, 2,699,700 sq km. **Location:** In Central Asia. **Neighbors:** Russia on N; China on E; Kyrgyzstan, Uzbekistan, Turkmenistan on S; Caspian Sea on W. **Topography:** Extends from lower reaches of Volga in Europe to Altay Mts. on Chinese border. **Capital:** Astana, 664,086. **Cities (urban aggl.):** Almaty, 1,426,277.

Government: Type: Republic. **Head of state:** Pres. Nursultan A. Nazarbayev; b. July 6, 1940; in office: Apr. 24, 1990. **Head of gov.:** Prime Min. Karim Masimov; b. June 15, 1965; in office: Jan. 10, 2007. **Local divisions:** 14 oblystar, 3 cities. **Defense budget:** $1.74 bil. **Active troops:** 49,000.

Economy: Industries: oil, coal, iron ore, manganese, chromite, lead, zinc, copper, titanium, bauxite, gold, silver, phosphates, sulfur, uranium, iron and steel; tractors and other agric. machinery, elec. motors, constr. materials. **Chief crops:** grain (mostly spring wheat), cotton. **Natural resources:** petroleum, nat. gas, coal, iron ore, manganese, chrome ore, nickel, cobalt, copper, molybdenum, lead, zinc, bauxite, gold, uranium. **Crude oil reserves:** 30 bil bbls. **Arable land:** 8.7%. **Livestock:** cattle: 6.1 mil; chickens: 32.5 mil; goats: 2.7 mil; pigs: 1.3 mil; sheep: 14.7 mil. **Fish catch:** 43,177 metric tons. **Electricity prod.** (2010): 77.2 bil kWh. **Labor force:** agric. 25.9%, industry 11.9%, services 62.2%.

Finance: Monetary unit: Tenge (KZT) (Sept. 2012: 149.37 = $1 U.S.). **GDP:** $219.6 bil; **per capita GDP:** $13,200; **GDP growth:** 7.5%. **Imports:** $42.1 bil; China 30.2%, Russia 20%, Germany 7.4%, Ukraine 5%. **Exports:** $88.9 bil; China 21.7%, France 9.4%, Germany 8.3%, Russia 5.3%, Italy 5.2%, Canada 4.5%, Romania 4.5%. **Tourism:** $1.2 bil. **Budget:** $40.5 bil. **Total reserves less gold:** $25.2 bil. **Gold:** 2.6 mil oz t. **CPI change:** 8.3%.

Transport: Railways: 9,370 mi. **Civil aviation:** 1.6 bil pass.-mi; 64 airports. **Chief ports:** Aqtau, Atyrau, Oskemen.

Communications: TV sets: 497 per 1,000 pop. **Radios:** 215 per 1,000 pop. **Telephone lines:** 26.2 per 100 pop. **Internet:** 45%.

Health: Life expect.: 64.3 male; 74.6 female. **Births:** 20.4 (per 1,000 pop.). **Deaths:** 8.5 (per 1,000 pop.). **Natural inc.:** 1.19%. **Infant mortality:** 23.1 (per 1,000 live births). **HIV rate:** 0.1%.

Education: Compulsory: ages 6-17. **Literacy:** 99.7%.

Major intl. organizations: UN (FAO, IBRD, ILO, IMF, WHO), CIS, OSCE, WTO (observer).

Embassy: 1401 16th St. NW 20036; 232-5488.

Website: www.government.kz

The region came under the Mongols' rule in the 13th cent. and gradually came under Russian rule, 1730-1853. It was admitted to the USSR as a constituent republic in 1936.

Kazakhstan declared independence Dec. 16, 1991. It became an independent state when the Soviet Union dissolved Dec. 26, 1991. The Communist Party chief, Nursultan Nazarbayev, was elected president unopposed. He encouraged Western investment in the oil industry, boosting the economy. Dissent was suppressed, and much of the nation's oil wealth was controlled by Nazarbayev's family and aides.

Kazakhstan agreed, Feb. 14, 1994, to dismantle nuclear missiles. Private land ownership was legalized Dec. 26, 1995. Astana (formerly Akmola) became the nation's new capital, June 9, 1998. Reelected in 1999 and 2005, Pres. Nazarbayev was authorized to run for an unlimited number of terms under a constitutional amendment passed by parliament May 18, 2007; he claimed more than

95% of the vote in a presidential election Apr. 3, 2011, deemed flawed by international election monitors. Nazarbayev's Nur Otan party won 81% of the vote in parliamentary elections, Jan. 15, 2012. International election monitors also faulted that election, despite its introduction of two new parties into the formerly one-party parliament.

Kenya
Republic of Kenya

People: Population: 43,013,341. **Age distrib.:** <15: 42.5%; 65+: 2.7%. **Pop. density:** 195.7 per sq mi, 75.6 per sq km. **Urban:** 24%. **Ethnic groups:** Kikuyu 22%, Luhya 14%, Luo 13%, Kalenjin 12%, Kamba 11%, Kisii 6%, Meru 6%, other African 15%. **Principal languages:** English, Kiswahili (both official); numerous indigenous langs. **Chief religions:** Protestant 45%, Roman Catholic 33%, Muslim 10%, indigenous beliefs 10%.

Geography: Total area: 224,081 sq mi, 580,367 sq km; **Land area:** 219,746 sq mi, 569,140 sq km. **Location:** E Africa, on coast of Indian O. **Neighbors:** Uganda on W, Tanzania on S, Somalia on E, Ethiopia on N, Sudan on NW. **Topography:** The northern three-fifths of Kenya is arid. To S, a low coastal area and a plateau varying 3,000-10,000 ft. The Great Rift Valley enters the country N-S, flanked by high mountains. **Capital:** Nairobi, 3,363,130. **Cities (urban aggl.):** Mombasa, 971,523.

Government: Type: Republic. **Head of state:** Pres. Mwai Kibaki; b. Nov. 15, 1931; in office: Dec. 30, 2002. **Head of gov.:** Prime Min. Raila Odinga; b. Jan. 7, 1945; in office: Apr. 17, 2008. **Local divisions:** 47 counties. **Defense budget:** $622 mil. **Active troops:** 24,120.

Economy: Industries: small-scale consumer goods (plastic, furniture, batteries, textiles, clothing, soap, cigarettes, flour), agric. prods., horticulture, oil refining, aluminum, steel, lead, cement. **Chief crops:** tea, coffee, corn, wheat, sugarcane, fruits, vegetables. **Natural resources:** limestone, soda ash, salt, gems, fluorspar, zinc, diatomite, gypsum, wildlife, hydropower. **Arable land:** 9.5%. **Livestock:** cattle: 17.9 mil; chickens: 30.4 mil; goats: 13.3 mil; pigs: 347,400; sheep: 9.9 mil. **Fish catch:** 155,439 metric tons. **Electricity prod.:** 6.6 bil kWh. **Labor force:** agric. 75%, industry and services 25%.

Finance: Monetary unit: Shilling (KES) (Sept. 2012: 84.28 = $1 U.S.). **GDP:** $72.3 bil; **per capita GDP:** $1,800; **GDP growth:** 5%. **Imports:** $13.5 bil; China 14.8%, India 14%, UAE 10.1%, South Africa 7.8%, Saudi Arabia 7.1%. **Exports:** $5.8 bil; Uganda 10%, Tanzania 9.7%, Netherlands 8.5%, UK 8.2%, U.S. 6.2%, Dem. Rep. of the Congo 4.2%. **Tourism:** $884 mil. **Budget:** $8.4 bil. **Total reserves less gold:** $4.3 bil. **Gold:** 500 oz t. **CPI change:** 14%.

Transport: Railways: 1,284 mi. **Motor vehicles:** 11.1 vehicles per 1,000 pop. **Civil aviation:** 4.9 bil pass.-mi; 15 airports. **Chief ports:** Kisumu, Mombasa.

Communications: TV sets: 46 per 1,000 pop. **Radios:** 89 per 1,000 pop. **Telephone lines:** 0.7 per 100 pop. **Internet:** 28%.

Health: Life expect.: 61.6 male; 64.6 female. **Births:** 31.9 (per 1,000 pop.). **Deaths:** 7.3 (per 1,000 pop.). **Natural inc.:** 2.47%. **Infant mortality:** 43.6 (per 1,000 live births). **HIV rate:** 6.3%.

Education: Compulsory: ages 6-13. **Literacy:** 87.4%.

Major intl. organizations: UN and all of its specialized agencies, AU, the Commonwealth, WTO.

Embassy: 2249 R St. NW 20008; 387-6101.

Website: www.primeminister.go.ke

Arab colonies exported spices and slaves from the Kenya coast as early as the 8th cent. Britain obtained control in the 19th cent. Kenya won independence Dec. 12, 1963, four years after the end of the violent Mau Mau uprising. Jomo Kenyatta, the country's leader since independence, died Aug. 22, 1978. He was succeeded by his vice president, Daniel arap Moi.

During the first half of the 1990s, Kenya suffered widespread unemployment and high inflation. Tribal clashes in the western provinces claimed thousands of lives and left tens of thousands homeless. Pres. Moi won a 3rd term in Dec. 1992 elections, which were marred by violence and fraud. He was reelected Dec. 29, 1997, in an election plagued by irregularities. A truck bomb explosion at the U.S. embassy in Nairobi, Aug. 7, 1998, killed more than 200 people and injured about 5,000. The U.S. blamed the attack and a near-simultaneous embassy bombing in Tanzania on al-Qaeda.

Constitutionally barred from seeking another term, Pres. Moi was succeeded Dec. 30, 2002, by Mwai Kibaki, the candidate of the opposition Democratic Party. After a disputed election Dec. 27, 2007, that drew criticism from European and Kenyan monitors, Kenya's Electoral Commission declared Kibaki the winner over challenger Raila Odinga. Weeks of factional violence followed, leaving some 1,500 people dead and and 600,000 displaced. Under a Feb. 28, 2008, power-sharing deal mediated by former UN Sec. Gen. Kofi Annan, Kibaki remained president and Odinga took the newly created post of prime minister. A new constitution curtailing presidential powers, establishing a senate, and reforming regional government won approval in a referendum Aug. 4, 2010. The Intl. Criminal Court Jan. 23, 2012, charged four with crimes against humanity for their roles in the postelection violence. Two of those charged, Deputy Prime Min. Uhuru Kenyatta and former

Education Min. William Ruto were expected to be candidates in the upcoming 2013 presidential election. More than 479,000 Somali refugees were living in Kenya as of Jan. 1, 2012.

Kiribati
Republic of Kiribati

People: Population: 101,998. **Age distrib.:** <15: 33.1%; 65+: 3.8%. **Pop. density:** 325.7 per sq mi, 125.8 per sq km. **Urban:** 43.9%. **Ethnic groups:** Micronesian 99%. **Principal languages:** I-Kiribati, English (official). **Chief religions:** Roman Catholic 55%, Protestant 36%, Mormon 3%, Baha'i 2%, Seventh-Day Adventist 2%.

Geography: Total area: 313 sq mi, 811 sq km; **Land area:** 313 sq mi, 811 sq km. **Location:** 33 Micronesian islands (the Gilbert, Line, and Phoenix groups) in mid-Pacific scattered in a 2-mil sq mi chain around the point where the International Date Line formerly cut the Equator. In 1997 the Date Line was moved to follow Kiribati's E border. **Neighbors:** Nearest are Nauru to SW, Tuvalu and Tokelau Isls. to S. **Topography:** Except Banaba (Ocean) Isl., all are low-lying, with soil of coral sand and rock fragments, subject to erratic rainfall. **Capital:** Bairiki, 44,385 (figure for South Tarawa Isl.).

Government: Type: Republic. **Head of state and gov.:** Pres. Anote Tong; b. June 11, 1952; in office: July 10, 2003. **Local divisions:** 3 units, 6 districts. **Defense budget:** NA. **Active troops:** No regular military forces. Australia and New Zealand provide defense assistance.

Economy: Industries: fishing, handicrafts. **Chief crops:** copra, taro, breadfruit, sweet potatoes, vegetables. **Natural resources:** phosphate (production discontinued in 1979). **Arable land:** 2.5%. **Livestock:** chickens: 570,000; pigs: 12,600. **Fish catch:** 49,355 metric tons. **Electricity prod.:** 21 mil kWh. **Labor force:** agric. 2.7%, industry 32%, services 65.3%.

Finance: Monetary unit: Australian Dollar (AUD) (Sept. 2012: 0.98 = $1 U.S.). **GDP:** $606.7 mil; **per capita GDP:** $5,800; **GDP growth:** 1.8%. **Imports** (2004): $62 mil. **Exports** (2004): $17 mil. **Tourism:** NA. **Budget** (FY05): $59.7 mil.

Transport: Civil aviation: 4 airports. **Chief ports:** Betio, English Harbor.

Communications: TV sets: 41 per 1,000 pop. **Radios:** 830 per 1,000 pop. **Telephone lines:** 8.4 per 100 pop. **Internet:** 10%.

Health: Life expect.: 62.4 male; 67.3 female. **Births:** 22.5 (per 1,000 pop.). **Deaths:** 7.3 (per 1,000 pop.). **Natural inc.:** 1.51% **Infant mortality:** 37.7 (per 1,000 live births). **HIV rate:** NA.

Education: Compulsory: ages 6-14. **Literacy:** NA.

Major intl. organizations: UN (FAO, IBRD, ILO, IMF, WHO), the Commonwealth.

Honorary Consulate: 95 Nakolo Pl., Rm. 265, Honolulu, HI 96819; (808) 834-6775.

Website: www.parliament.gov.ki

A British protectorate since 1892, the Gilbert and Ellice Islands colony was completed with the inclusion of the Phoenix Islands, 1937. Tarawa Atoll was the scene of some of the bloodiest fighting in the Pacific during WWII.

Self-rule was granted 1971; the Ellice Islands separated from the colony in 1975 and became independent Tuvalu, 1978. Kiribati (pronounced *Kiribass*) independence was attained July 12, 1979. Under a treaty of friendship the U.S. relinquished its claims to several Line and Phoenix islands. Kiribati was admitted to the UN Sept. 14, 1999. Pres. Anote Tong won reelection Oct. 17, 2007. Kiribati's land area is shrinking as a result of rising sea levels, and Tong announced Mar. 7, 2012, negotiations with Fiji to buy 5,000 acres of land on which the nation's population could relocate.

Korea, North
Democratic People's Republic of Korea

People: Population: 24,589,122. **Age distrib.:** <15: 22%; 65+: 9.3%. **Pop. density:** 528.9 per sq mi, 204.2 per sq km. **Urban:** 60.3%. **Ethnic group:** Racially homogeneous; small Chinese community and few ethnic Japanese. **Principal language:** Korean. **Chief religions:** traditionally Buddhist and Confucianist, some Christian; autonomous religious activities almost nonexistent.

Geography: Total area: 46,540 sq mi, 120,538 sq km; **Land area:** 46,490 sq mi, 120,408 sq km. **Location:** In northern E Asia. **Neighbors:** China and Russia on N, S. Korea on S. **Topography:** Mountains and hills cover nearly all the country, with narrow valleys and small plains in between. N and E coasts are most rugged areas. **Capital:** P'yongyang, 2,842,570.

Government: Type: Communist state. **Head of state:** Kim Jong Un; b. Jan. 8, 1983; officially assumed post Dec. 17, 2011. **Head of gov.:** Prem. Choe Yong Rim; b. Nov. 20, 1930; in office: June 7, 2010. **Local divisions:** 9 provinces, 4 special cities. **Defense budget:** NA. **Active troops:** 1,190,000.

Economy: Industries: military prods.; machine building, elec. power, chemicals; mining, metallurgy; textiles, food proc. **Chief crops:** rice, corn, potatoes, soybeans. **Natural resources:** coal, lead, tungsten, zinc, graphite, magnesite, iron ore, copper, gold, pyrites, salt, fluorspar, hydropower. **Arable land:** 22.0%. **Livestock:** cattle: 577,000; chickens: 14.9 mil; goats: 3.6 mil; pigs: 2.2 mil; sheep: 166,000. **Fish catch:** 713,350 metric tons. **Electricity prod.:** 20.5 bil kWh. **Labor force:** agric. 35%, industry and services 65%.

Finance: Monetary unit: Won (KPW) (Sept. 2012: 130.08 = $1 U.S.). **GDP:** $40 bil (country does not publish reliable national income accounts data; figure derived from OECD study); **per capita GDP:** $1,800; **GDP growth** (2009): 4%. **Imports** (2010): $3.5 bil; China 64.5%, South Korea 24.6%, Russia 2.4%. **Exports** (2010): $2.6 bil; China 46.5%, South Korea 40.8%, Bangladesh 1.4%. **Tourism:** NA. **Budget** (2007): $3.3 bil.

Transport: Railways: 3,257 mi. **Civil aviation:** 25.5 mil pass.-mi; 39 airports. **Chief ports:** Chongjin, Haeju, Hungnam, Nampo, Senbong, Sonbong, Songnim, Wonsan.

Communications: TV sets: 172 per 1,000 pop. **Radios:** 157 per 1,000 pop. **Telephone lines:** 4.8 per 100 pop. **Internet:** NA.

Health: Life expect.: 65.3 male; 73.2 female. **Births:** 14.5 (per 1,000 pop.). **Deaths:** 9.1 (per 1,000 pop.). **Natural inc.:** 0.54% **Infant mortality:** 26.2 (per 1,000 live births). **HIV rate:** NA.

Education: Compulsory: ages 6-16. **Literacy:** 100%.

Major intl. organizations: UN (FAO, WHO).

Permanent UN mission: 820 Second Ave., 13th Fl., New York, NY 10017; (212) 972-3105.

Website: www.korea-dpr.com

The Democratic People's Republic of Korea was founded May 1, 1948, in the zone occupied by Russia after WWII. Its armies tried to conquer the south, 1950. After three years of fighting, with Chinese and U.S. intervention, a cease-fire was proclaimed.

For the next four decades, a hard-line Communist regime headed by Kim Il Sung kept tight control over the nation's political, economic, and cultural life. The nation used its abundant mineral and hydroelectric resources to develop its military strength and heavy industry. By the early 1990s, North Korea was widely believed to be developing nuclear weapons. The U.S. and North Korea signed an agreement, Oct. 21, 1994, providing for phased dismantling of North Korea's nuclear development program in return for U.S. energy aid and improved ties with the U.S.

Kim Il Sung died July 8, 1994. He was succeeded by his son, Kim Jong Il. Defections by high officials, a deteriorating economy, and severe food shortages plagued North Korea in the late 1990s. A first-ever summit conference in P'yongyang between North and South Korean leaders, June 13-15, 2000, marked an improvement in relations between the two nations. North Korea and Japan agreed to normalize relations in a Sept. 2002 summit.

Pres. George W. Bush, in a speech Jan. 31, 2002, declared North Korea, along with Iraq and Iran, part of an "axis of evil." In Oct. 2002, North Korea admitted to pursuing a secret nuclear weapons program, in violation of past agreements. The U.S. insisted that North Korea end its nuclear weapons program, while P'yongyang demanded a nonaggression treaty and economic aid from the U.S. During 2003-09, as 6-nation talks sponsored by China sought to resolve the nuclear dispute, North Korea followed a zigzag course, alternately stopping and resuming its nuclear program in order to win concessions from the U.S.

In Apr.-May 2009, North Korea suspended participation in the 6-nation talks, expelled IAEA inspectors, tested multiple missiles, and exploded a nuclear device underground. The UN Security Council June 12 toughened sanctions on North Korean. Tensions between North and South Korea increased after the sinking Mar. 26, 2010, of the South Korean warship *Cheonan* killed 46 sailors; a South Korean panel including international investigators concluded May 20 that the *Cheonan* had been torpedoed by a North Korean submarine. Visits to P'yongyang by former presidents Bill Clinton, Aug. 2009, and Jimmy Carter, Aug. 2010, gained the release of several detained Americans. A North Korean artillery barrage killed 2 South Korean marines and 2 civilians on Yeonpyeong Isl. Nov. 23, 2010. Kim Jong Il died Dec. 17, 2011, and was succeeded by his son Kim Jong Un.

Korea, South
Republic of Korea

People: Population: 48,860,500. **Age distrib.:** <15: 15.1%; 65+: 11.9%. **Pop. density:** 1,305.7 per sq mi, 504.1 per sq km. **Urban:** 83.2%. **Ethnic group:** Homogeneous, except for some Chinese. **Principal languages:** Korean, English widely taught in school. **Chief religions:** Christian 26% (Protestant 20%, Roman Catholic 7%), Buddhist 23%, none 49%.

Geography: Total area: 38,502 sq mi, 99,720 sq km; **Land area:** 37,421 sq mi, 96,920 sq km. **Location:** In northern E Asia. **Neighbors:** North Korea on N. **Topography:** Mountainous, with a rugged E coast. W and S coasts are deeply indented, with many islands and harbors. **Capital:** Seoul, 9,735,860. **Cities (urban aggl.):** Busan, 3,372,181; Incheon, 2,622,113; Daegu, 2,446,516; Daejon, 1,538,091; Gwangju, 1,502,963; Suweon, 1,159,232; Ulsan, 1,100,053.

Government: Type: Republic. **Head of state:** Pres. Lee Myung Bak; b. Dec. 19, 1941; in office: Feb. 25, 2008. **Head of gov.:** Prime Min. Kim Hwang Sik; b. Aug. 9, 1948; in office: Oct. 1, 2010. **Local divisions:** 9 provinces, 7 special cities. **Defense budget:** $28.5 bil. **Active troops:** 655,000.

Economy: Industries: electronics, telecom., auto prod., chemicals, shipbuilding, steel. **Chief crops:** rice, root crops, barley, vegetables, fruits. **Natural resources:** coal, tungsten, graphite, molybdenum, lead, hydropower potential. **Arable land:** 16.4%. **Livestock:** cattle: 3.4 mil; chickens: 149.2 mil; goats: 243,520; pigs: 9.9 mil; sheep: 3,000. **Fish catch:** 3.1 mil metric tons. **Electricity prod.** (2010): 450.1 bil kWh. **Labor force:** agric. 6.4%, industry 24.2%, services 69.4%.

Finance: Monetary unit: Won (KRW) (Sept. 2012: 1,135.53 = $1 U.S.). **GDP:** $1.6 tril; **per capita GDP:** $32,100; **GDP growth:** 3.6%. **Imports:** $524.4 bil; China 16.5%, Japan 13%, U.S. 8.5%, Saudi Arabia 7.1%, Australia 5%. **Exports:** $556.5 bil; China 24.4%, U.S. 10.1%, Japan 7.1%. **Tourism:** $12.3 bil. **Budget:** $242 bil. **Total reserves less gold:** $304.3 bil. **Gold:** 1.8 mil oz t. **CPI change:** 4%.

Transport: Railways: 2,101 mi. **Motor vehicles:** 357.2 vehicles per 1,000 pop. **Civil aviation:** 51.1 bil pass.-mi; 71 airports. **Chief ports:** Busan, Incheon, Pohang, Ulsan, Yeosu.

Communications: TV sets: 424 per 1,000 pop. **Radios:** 1,037 per 1,000 pop. **Telephone lines:** 60.9 per 100 pop. **Internet:** 83.8%.

Health: Life expect.: 76.1 male; 82.7 female. **Births:** 8.4 (per 1,000 pop.). **Deaths:** 6.4 (per 1,000 pop.). **Natural inc.:** 0.20%. **Infant mortality:** 4.1 (per 1,000 live births). **HIV rate:** <0.1%.

Education: Compulsory: ages 6-14. **Literacy:** NA.

Major intl. organizations: UN (FAO, IBRD, ILO, IMF, WHO), APEC, OECD, WTO.

Embassy: 2320 Massachusetts Ave. NW 20008; 939-5663. **Website:** www.korea.net

Korea, once called the Hermit Kingdom, has a recorded history since the 1st cent. BCE. It was united in a kingdom under the Silla Dynasty, 668 CE. It was at times associated with the Chinese empire; the treaty that concluded the Sino-Japanese war of 1894-95 recognized Korea's complete independence. In 1910 Japan forcibly annexed Korea as Chosun.

At the Potsdam conference, July 1945, the 38th parallel was designated as the line dividing Soviet and U.S. occupation zones. Russian troops entered Korea Aug. 10, 1945; U.S. troops entered Sept. 8, 1945.

The South Koreans formed the Republic of Korea in May 1948 with Seoul as the capital. Dr. Syngman Rhee was chosen president. A separate, Communist regime was formed in the north; its army attacked the south in June 1950, initiating the Korean War. UN troops, under U.S. command, supported South Korea in the war, which ended in an armistice (July 1953) leaving Korea divided by a demilitarized zone (DMZ) along the 38th parallel.

Rhee's authoritarian rule became increasingly unpopular, and a movement spearheaded by college students forced his resignation Apr. 26, 1960. In an army coup May 16, 1961, Gen. Park Chung Hee became chairman of a ruling junta. He was elected president, 1963; a 1972 referendum allowed him to be reelected for an unlimited series of 6-year terms. Park was assassinated by the chief of the Korean CIA, Oct. 26, 1979.

In May 1980, Gen. Chun Doo Hwan, head of military intelligence, ordered the brutal suppression of pro-democracy demonstrations in Kwangju. On July 1, 1987, following weeks of antigovernment protests, some of them violent, Chun agreed to democratic reforms. In Dec., Roh Tae Woo, a longtime ally of Chun's, was elected president. In 1990, the nation's three largest political parties merged; some 100,000 students protested the merger as undemocratic.

Pres. Kim Young Sam took office in 1993. Convicted of mutiny, treason, and corruption, Chun was sentenced to death by a Seoul court, Aug. 26, 1996, for his role in the 1979 coup and 1980 Kwangju massacre; Roh received a 22½ year prison sentence.

The collapse in Jan. 1997 of the Hanbo steel firm triggered a series of corruption scandals. With currency and stock values plummeting, the nation averted default by agreeing, Dec. 4, on a $57-bil bailout from the IMF. Kim Dae Jung, a longtime dissident, won the presidential election Dec. 18. Chun and Roh were released and pardoned Dec. 22, 1997.

At a summit meeting in P'yongyang, June 13-15, 2000, Pres. Kim Dae Jung and North Korean leader Kim Jong Il agreed to work for reconciliation and eventual reunification of their two countries. On Oct. 13, 2000, Kim Dae Jung was named the winner of the Nobel Peace Prize. Roh Moo Hyun won a presidential election Dec. 19, 2002.

A subway fire in Taegu, Feb. 18, 2003, killed 198 people; the arsonist received a life term, and 8 subway officials received prison sentences for negligence. Typhoon Maemi battered Pusan and other areas Sept. 12-13, 2003, leaving about 130 people dead.

The National Assembly, Mar. 12, 2004, impeached Pres. Roh Moo Hyun for violating political neutrality and urging voters to support the Uri Party; the Constitutional Court May 14 restored Roh to office. The IAEA Sept. 2 said South Korea had acknowledged having secretly processed a small amount of uranium to near

weapons-grade level in 2000, violating the Nuclear Non-Proliferation Treaty and a bilateral accord with N. Korea.

Ban Ki-Moon, South Korea's foreign minister, 2004-06, took office as UN secretary-general Jan. 1, 2007. Lee Myung Bak, a former construction executive and Seoul mayor nicknamed "The Bulldozer," won the presidential election Dec. 19. Former Pres. Roh Moo Hyun, under investigation for corruption, committed suicide May 23, 2009.

As of mid-2012, South Korea had 350 troops serving in Afghanistan, and the U.S. had about 28,500 troops stationed in South Korea. Tensions between South Korea and Japan came to the fore after Pres. Lee Myung-bak, Aug. 10, visited Dokdo, a group of small islands that South Korea administers but Japan claims.

Kosovo
Republic of Kosovo

People: Population: 1,836,529. **Age distrib.:** <15: 26.9%; 65+: 6.8%. **Pop. density:** 436.9 per sq mi, 168.7 per sq km. **Urban:** NA. **Ethnic groups:** Albanian 92%, other (incl. Serb, Bosniak, Gorani, Roma, Turk, Ashkali, Egyptian) 8%. **Principal languages:** Albanian, Serbian (both official); Bosnian; Turkish; Roma. **Chief religions:** Muslim, Serbian Orthodox, Roman Catholic.

Geography: Total area: 4,203 sq mi, 10,887 sq km. **Land area:** 4,203 sq mi, 10,887 sq km. **Location:** SE Europe between Serbia and Macedonia. **Neighbors:** Serbia on N, Montenegro on NW, Albania on SW, Macedonia on SE. **Topography:** Low flood basins surrounded by several high mountain ranges. **Capital:** Pristina.

Government: Type: Republic. **Head of state:** Pres. Atifete Jahjaga; b. Apr. 20, 1975; in office: Apr. 7, 2011. **Head of gov.:** Prime Min. Hashim Thaçi; b. Apr. 24, 1968; in office: Jan. 9, 2008. **Local divisions:** 30 municipalities. **Defense budget/active troops:** NA.

Economy: Industries: mineral mining, constr. materials, base metals, leather, machinery, appliances, foodstuffs and beverages, textiles. **Chief crops:** wheat, corn, berries, potatoes, peppers. **Natural resources:** nickel, lead, zinc, magnesium, lignite, kaolin, chrome, bauxite. **Arable land:** NA. **Labor force:** agric. 23.6%.

Finance: Monetary unit: Euro (EUR) (Sept. 2012: 0.79 = $1 U.S.). **GDP:** $13 bil; **per capita GDP:** $6,500; **GDP growth:** 5%. **Imports:** $3.3 bil. **Exports:** $419 mil. **Tourism:** NA. **Budget:** $2.1 bil. **Total reserves less gold:** $741.5 mil.

Transport: Railways: 267 mi. **Civil aviation:** 4 airports. **Communications:** NA.

Health: Life expect.: 68.4 male; 72.7 female. **Births:** 18.0 (per 1,000 pop.). **Deaths:** 7.0 (per 1,000 pop.). **Natural inc.:** 1.09%. **Infant mortality:** 40.7 (per 1,000 live births). **HIV rate:** NA.

Education: NA. **Literacy:** NA.

Major intl. organizations: UN (IBRD, IMF).

Embassy: 900 19th St. NW, Ste. 400, 20006; 380-3581. **Website:** www.rks-gov.net

Kosovo was part of the Roman and Byzantine empires before Serbs, a Slavic people, took control in the Middle Ages. After Ottoman Turks defeated Serb forces, 1389, Kosovo's population became predominantly Muslim and Kosovar (ethnic Albanian). Serbia regained control in the First Balkan War (1912-13). Kosovo entered the Kingdom of Serbs, Croats, and Slovenes as part of Serbia after World War I and became an autonomous province of Serbia, a constituent republic of Yugoslavia, after World War II.

Revoking provincial autonomy, Serbia began ruling Kosovo by force in 1989. Albanian secessionists proclaimed an independent Republic of Kosovo in July 1990. As Yugoslavia collapsed, the republics of Serbia (incl. Kosovo) and Montenegro proclaimed a new Federal Republic of Yugoslavia, 1992, under Pres. Slobodan Milosevic. Guerrilla attacks by the Kosovo Liberation Army in 1997 brought a ferocious counteroffensive by Serbian authorities.

Fearful that the Serbs were employing "ethnic cleansing" tactics, as they had in Bosnia, the U.S. and its NATO allies pressured the Yugoslav government to end hostilities. When Milosevic refused, NATO launched an air war against Yugoslavia, Mar.-June 1999; the Serbs retaliated by terrorizing the Kosovars. Hundreds of thousands fled, mostly to Albania and Macedonia. A 50,000-member multinational force (KFOR) entered Kosovo in June, and most refugees returned by Sept. 1, 1999.

From June 1999, Kosovo was administered by a UN mission (UNMIK). Kosovar and Serbian negotiators were unable to reach agreement on the status of the region, and Kosovo declared independence, Feb. 17, 2008. The U.S. and most European allies immediately recognized the new country, but Serbia and Russia refused. In a nonbinding ruling, the World Court held July 22, 2010, that Kosovo's independence declaration was legal. As of Aug. 2012, KFOR had about 5,600 troops in Kosovo. Kosovo and Serbia entered negotiations meant to normalize their relations Mar. 8, 2011, but last held talks Feb. 22-23, 2012.

Kuwait
State of Kuwait

People: Population: 2,646,314. **Age distrib.:** <15: 25.7%; 65+: 2.1%. **Pop. density:** 384.7 per sq mi, 148.5 per sq km. **Urban:**

98.3%. **Ethnic groups:** Kuwaiti 45%, other Arab 35%, South Asian 9%, Iranian 4%. **Principal languages:** Arabic (official), English widely spoken. **Chief religions:** Muslim (official) 85% (Sunni 70%, Shia 30%), other (incl. Christian, Hindu, Parsi) 15%.

Geography: Total area: 6,880 sq mi, 17,818 sq km; **Land area:** 6,880 sq mi, 17,818 sq km. **Location:** In Middle East, at N end of Persian Gulf. **Neighbors:** Iraq on N, Saudi Arabia on S. **Topography:** Flat, very dry, and extremely hot. **Capital:** Kuwait City, 2,406,410.

Government: Type: Constitutional monarchy. **Head of state:** Emir Sheikh Sabah al-Ahmad al-Jabir as-Sabah; b. June 6, 1929; in office: Jan. 29, 2006. **Head of gov.:** Prime Min. Sheikh Jaber al-Mubarak al-Hamad al-Sabah; b. Jan. 5, 1942; in office: Nov. 30, 2011. **Local divisions:** 5 governorates. **Defense budget:** $4.05 bil. **Active troops:** 15,500.

Economy: Industries: petroleum, petrochemicals, cement, shipbuilding and repair, water desalination, food proc., constr. materials. **Chief crops:** NA. **Natural resources:** petroleum, fish, shrimp, nat. gas. **Crude oil reserves:** 104 bil bbls. (half of Neutral Zone reserves). **Arable land:** 0.6%. **Livestock:** cattle: 31,500; chickens: 33.8 mil; goats: 145,000; sheep: 900,000. **Fish catch:** 4,360 metric tons. **Electricity prod.** (2010): 51.3 bil kWh. **Labor force:** NA.

Finance: Monetary unit: Dinar (KWD) (Sept. 2012: 0.28 = $1 U.S.). **GDP:** $155.5 bil; **per capita GDP:** $42,200; **GDP growth:** 8.2%. **Imports:** $22 bil; U.S. 11.9%, India 10%, China 9.3%, Saudi Arabia 8%, South Korea 6.3%, Japan 5.9%, Germany 4.8%, UAE 4.1%. **Exports:** $104.3 bil; South Korea 18.3%, Japan 14.2%, India 13.4%, China 9.9%, U.S. 8.7%. **Tourism:** $199 mil. **Budget:** $58.1 bil. **Total reserves less gold:** $25.8 bil. **Gold:** 2.5 mil oz t. **CPI change:** 4.7%.

Transport: Motor vehicles: 466.9 vehicles per 1,000 pop. **Civil aviation:** 4.8 bil pass.-mi; 4 airports. **Chief ports:** Ash Shuaybah, Ash Shuwaykh, Az Zawr, Mina Abd Allah, Mina al Ahmadi.

Communications: TV sets: 399 per 1,000 pop. **Radios:** 572 per 1,000 pop. **Telephone lines** (2010): 20.7 per 100 pop. **Internet:** 74.2%.

Health: Life expect.: 76.1 male; 78.5 female. **Births:** 21.0 (per 1,000 pop.). **Deaths:** 2.1 (per 1,000 pop.). **Natural inc.:** 1.88% **Infant mortality:** 7.9 (per 1,000 live births). **HIV rate:** NA.

Education: Compulsory: ages 6-14. **Literacy:** 93.9%.

Major intl. organizations: UN (FAO, IBRD, ILO, IMF, WHO), AL, OPEC, WTO.

Embassy: 2940 Tilden St. NW 20008; 966-0702.

Website: www.da.gov.kw

Kuwait is ruled by the Sabah dynasty, founded 1759. Britain ran foreign relations and defense from 1899 until independence in 1961. Nearly half the population is non-Kuwaiti, including many Palestinians, and cannot vote.

Oil is the fiscal mainstay, providing most of Kuwait's income. Oil pays for free medical care, education, and social security. There are no taxes, except customs duties.

Kuwait was attacked and overrun by Iraqi forces Aug. 2, 1990. In Operation Desert Storm a U.S.-led coalition, with authorization from the UN Security Council, began bombing Iraq and Iraqi forces in Kuwait, Jan. 1991, then launched a ground assault Feb. 23. By Feb. 27, Iraqi forces were routed and Kuwait liberated.

Political rights were extended to women, May 16, 2005; the first female cabinet member was appointed June 12. Kuwait enacted a $5.2 bil program Mar. 26, 2009, to bail out banks and investment companies battered by the global financial crisis. The moderate Jaber al-Mubarak al-Hamad al-Sabah was reappointed prime min. July 5, 2012, after resigning in response to a June 2012 ruling of the Constitutional Court that declared unconstitutional the Feb. 2011 elections that brought him to power.

Kyrgyzstan
Kyrgyz Republic

People: Population: 5,496,737. **Age distrib.:** <15: 29.6%; 65+: 4.9%. **Pop. density:** 74.2 per sq mi, 28.7 per sq km. **Urban:** 35.3%. **Ethnic groups:** Kyrgyz 65%, Uzbek 14%, Russian 13%, Dungan 1%, Ukrainian 1%, Uighur 1%. **Principal languages:** Kyrgyz (official), Uzbek, Russian (official), Dungun. **Chief religions:** Muslim 75%, Russian Orthodox 20%.

Geography: Total area: 77,202 sq mi, 199,951 sq km; **Land area:** 74,055 sq mi, 191,801 sq km. **Location:** In Central Asia. **Neigh-bors:** Kazakhstan on N, China on E, Uzbekistan on W, Tajikistan on S. **Topography:** Landlocked country nearly covered by Tien Shan and Pamir Mts.; avg. elevation 9,020 ft. A large lake, Issyk-Kul, in NE is 1 mi above sea level. **Capital:** Bishkek, 838,606.

Government: Type: Parliamentary republic. **Head of state:** Pres. Almazbek Sharshenovich Atambayev; b. Sept. 17, 1956; in office: Dec. 1, 2011. Head of gov.: Prime Min. Jantoro Satybaldiev; b. Jan. 6, 1956; in office: Sept. 5, 2012. **Local divisions:** 7 oblasts and Bishkek. **Defense budget:** $33 mil. **Active troops:** 10,900.

Economy: Industries: small machinery, textiles, food proc., cement, shoes, sawn logs, refrigerators, furniture, elec. motors. **Chief crops:** tobacco, cotton, potatoes, vegetables, grapes, fruits and berries. **Natural resources:** hydropower, gold, rare earth metals, coal, oil, nat. gas, nepheline, mercury, bismuth, lead, zinc. **Crude oil reserves:** 40 mil bbls. **Arable land:** 6.7%. **Livestock:** cattle: 1.3 mil; chickens: 4.4 mil; goats: 933,713; pigs: 61,315; sheep: 3.9 mil. **Fish catch:** 346 metric tons. **Electricity prod.:** 10.9 bil kWh. **Labor force:** agric. 48%, industry 12.5%, services 39.5%.

Finance: Monetary unit: Som (KGS) (Sept. 2012: 47.24 = $1 U.S.). **GDP:** $13.3 bil; **per capita GDP:** $2,400; **GDP growth:** 5.7%. **Imports:** $3.9 bil; China 59.8%, Russia 13.9%, Kazakhstan 5.2%. **Exports:** $2.3 bil; Uzbekistan 25.4%, Russia 22.2%, Kazakhstan 20.1%, China 7.8%, UAE 5.5%, Afghanistan 5%, Turkey 4.2%. **Tourism:** $284 mil. **Budget:** $2 bil. **Total reserves less gold:** $1.7 bil. **Gold:** 83,888 oz t. **CPI change:** 16.5%.

Transport: Railways: 292 mi. **Civil aviation:** 361.6 mil pass.-mi; 18 airports. **Chief port:** Balykchy.

Communications: TV sets: 224 per 1,000 pop. **Radios:** 110 per 1,000 pop. **Telephone lines:** 8.9 per 100 pop. **Daily newspaper circ.:** 0.96 per 1,000 pop. **Internet:** 20%.

Health: Life expect.: 65.3 male; 73.9 female. **Births:** 23.9 (per 1,000 pop.). **Deaths:** 6.9 (per 1,000 pop.) **Natural inc.:** 1.70% **Infant mortality:** 30.8 (per 1,000 live births). **HIV rate:** 0.3%.

Education: Compulsory: ages 7-15. **Literacy:** 99.2%.

Major intl. organizations: UN (FAO, IBRD, ILO, WHO), CIS, OSCE, WTO.

Embassy: 2360 Massachusetts Ave. NW 20008; 338-5141.

Website: www.president.kg

The region was inhabited around the 13th cent. by the Kyrgyz. It was annexed to Russia, 1864, and became a constituent republic of the USSR in 1936. Kyrgyzstan declared independence Aug. 31, 1991. It became an independent state when the USSR disbanded Dec. 26, 1991.

In power since 1990, Pres. Askar Akayev won a third 5-year term in the Oct. 29, 2000, election. Fraud by Akayev loyalists in parliamentary elections Feb.-Mar. 2005 sparked protests. Akayev fled the country, Mar. 24, and formally resigned, Apr. 4. His interim successor, former Prime Min. Kurmanbek Bakiyev, a leader of the "tulip revolution," won the July 10, 2005, presidential vote.

Pres. Bakiyev again won presidential elections July 23, 2009, but monitors reported numerous irregularities. He was ousted by opposition parties Apr. 7, 2010, after clashes between protesters and government security forces left at least 85 people dead; an interim government was led by former Foreign Min. Roza Otunbayeva. Fighting in mid-June between majority Kyrgyz and minority Uzbeks in the southern cities of Osh and Jalalabad claimed up to 2,000 lives. A June 27, 2010, referendum on a new constitution received overwhelming approval. Elections Oct. 10, 2010 brought 5 parties to the parliament and Omurbek Babanov became prime min. of a coalition government. Almazbek Atambayev won the presidential election Oct. 30, 2011, and took office Dec. 1. Babanov's coalition broke up Aug. 22, 2012; the formation of a new coalition was agreed upon Sept. 3, two days afer Babanov resigned, and Jantoro Satybaldiev was sworn in as prime min. on Sept. 5.

Laos
Lao People's Democratic Republic

People: Population: 6,586,266. **Age distrib.:** <15: 36.1%; 65+: 3.7%. **Pop. density:** 73.9 per sq mi, 28.5 per sq km. **Urban:** 34.3%. **Ethnic groups:** Lao 55%, Khmou 11%, Hmong 8%, other (100+ minor ethnic groups) 26%. **Principal languages:** Lao (official), French, English, various ethnic langs. **Chief religions:** Buddhist 67%, Christian 2%.

Geography: Total area: 91,429 sq mi, 236,800 sq km; **Land area:** 89,112 sq mi, 230,800 sq km. **Location:** In Indochina Peninsula in SE Asia. **Neighbors:** Myanmar, China on N; Vietnam on E; Cambodia on S; Thailand on W. **Topography:** Landlocked, dominated by jungle. High mountains along E border are source of the E-W rivers slicing across the country to the Mekong R., which defines most of W border. **Capital:** Vientiane, 810,054.

Government: Type: Communist. **Head of state:** Pres. Choummaly Sayasone; b. Mar. 6, 1936; in office: June 8, 2006. **Head of gov.:** Prime Min. Thongsing Thammavong; b. 1944; in office: Dec. 23, 2010. **Local divisions:** 16 provinces, 1 municipality, 1 special zone. **Defense budget:** NA. **Active troops:** 29,100.

Economy: Industries: mining, timber, elec. power, agric. proc., rubber, constr., garments, cement, tourism. **Chief crops:** sweet potatoes, vegetables, corn, coffee, sugarcane, tobacco, cotton, tea, peanuts, rice. **Natural resources:** timber, hydropower, gypsum, tin, gold, gems. **Arable land:** 5.9%. **Livestock:** cattle: 1.5 mil; chickens: 25.1 mil; goats: 367,000; pigs: 2.8 mil. **Fish catch:** 113,000 metric tons. **Electricity prod.:** 3.7 bil kWh. **Labor force:** agric. 75.1%.

Finance: Monetary unit: Kip (LAK) (Sept. 2012: 8,004.14 = $1 U.S.). **GDP:** $17.7 bil; **per capita GDP:** $2,700; **GDP growth:** 8.3%. **Imports:** $2.3 bil; Thailand 65.9%, China 11.3%, Vietnam 5.3%. **Exports:** $2.1 bil; Thailand 34.8%, China 24.6%, Vietnam 10%. 4.1%. **Tourism:** $406 mil. **Budget:** $2 bil. **Total reserves less gold** (2010): $703.4 mil. **Gold** (2010): 285,429 oz t. **CPI change:** 7.6%.

Transport: Civil aviation: 82.6 mil pass.-mi; 9 airports.

Communications: TV sets: 57 per 1,000 pop. **Radios:** 148 per 1,000 pop. **Telephone lines:** 1.7 per 100 pop. **Daily newspaper circ.:** 2.6 per 1,000 pop. **Internet:** 9%.

Health: Life expect.: 60.9 male; 64.8 female. **Births:** 25.7 (per 1,000 pop.). **Deaths:** 8.0 (per 1,000 pop.). **Natural inc.:** 1.77% **Infant mortality:** 57.8 (per 1,000 live births). **HIV rate:** 0.2%.

Education: Compulsory: ages 6-10. **Literacy:** 72.7%.

Major intl. organizations: UN (FAO, IBRD, ILO, IMF, WHO), ASEAN, WTO (observer).

Embassy: 2222 S St. NW 20008; 332-6416.

Website: www.laopdr.gov.la

Laos became a French protectorate in 1893, but regained independence as a constitutional monarchy July 19, 1949.

Conflicts among neutralist, Communist, and conservative factions created a chaotic political situation. Armed conflict increased after 1960.

The three factions formed a coalition government in June 1962, with neutralist Prince Souvanna Phouma as premier. A 14-nation conference in Geneva signed agreements, 1962, guaranteeing independence. By 1964 the Pathet Lao had withdrawn from the coalition, and, with aid from North Vietnamese troops, renewed sporadic attacks. U.S. planes bombed the Ho Chi Minh trail, a supply line from North Vietnam to Communist forces in Laos and South Vietnam.

In 1970 the U.S. stepped up air support and military aid. After Pathet Lao military gains, Souvanna Phouma, May 1975, ordered government troops to cease fighting; the Pathet Lao took control. The Lao People's Democratic Republic was proclaimed Dec. 3, 1975.

From the mid-1970s through the 1980s, Laos relied on Vietnam for military and financial aid. After easing its finance laws in 1988, Laos attracted substantial foreign investment from Thailand, China, Vietnam, the U.S., and other nations. Laos was admitted to ASEAN on July 23, 1997. The U.S. Congress, Nov. 19, 2004, approved normalization of trade with Laos. To spur further investment, Laos opened its first stock exchange Jan. 11, 2011, in Vientiane.

Latvia
Republic of Latvia

People: Population: 2,191,580. **Age distrib.:** <15: 13.7%; 65+: 17%. **Pop. density:** 91.2 per sq mi, 35.2 per sq km. **Urban:** 67.7%. **Ethnic groups:** Latvian 59%, Russian 28%, Belarusian 4%, Ukrainian 3%, Polish 2%, Lithuanian 1%. **Principal languages:** Latvian (official), Russian, Lithuanian. **Chief religions:** Lutheran 20%, Orthodox 15%.

Geography: Total area: 24,938 sq mi, 64,589 sq km; **Land area:** 24,034 sq mi, 62,249 sq km. **Location:** E Europe, on Baltic Sea. **Neighbors:** Estonia on N; Lithuania, Belarus on S; Russia on E. **Topography:** Lowland with numerous lakes, marshes, and peat bogs. Principal river, W. Dvina (Daugava), rises in Russia. Glacial hills in E. **Capital:** Riga, 701,135.

Government: Type: Republic. **Head of state:** Pres. Andris Berzins; b. Dec. 10, 1944; in office: July 8, 2011. **Head of gov.:** Prime Min. Valdis Dombrovskis; b. Aug. 5, 1971; in office: Mar. 12, 2009. **Local divisions:** 26 counties, 7 municipalities. **Defense budget:** $292 mil. **Active troops:** 4,600.

Economy: Industries: processed foods, processed wood prods., textiles, processed metals, pharmaceuticals, railroad cars, synthetic fibers, electronics. **Chief crops:** grain, rapeseed, potatoes, vegetables. **Natural resources:** peat, limestone, dolomite, amber, hydropower, timber. **Arable land:** 18.8%. **Livestock:** cattle: 378,200; chickens: 4.1 mil; goats: 13,200; pigs: 376,500; sheep: 70,700. **Fish catch:** 165,368 metric tons. **Electricity prod.** (2010): 6.5 bil kWh. **Labor force:** agric. 8.8%, industry 24%, services 67.2%.

Finance: Monetary unit: Lat (LVL) (Sept. 2012: 0.55 = $1 U.S.). **GDP:** $35.4 bil; **per capita GDP:** $15,900; **GDP growth:** 5.5%. **Imports:** $14.8 bil; Lithuania 17.8%, Germany 11.8%, Russia 8.4%, Poland 7.5%, Estonia 7.1%, Finland 4.5%, Italy 4.3%. **Exports:** $12 bil; Russia 17.7%, Lithuania 16.5%, Estonia 12.9%, Germany 7.9%, Sweden 5.6%, Poland 5.5%. **Tourism:** $771 mil. **Budget:** $11.1 bil. **Total reserves less gold:** $6 bil. **Gold:** 248,700 oz t. **CPI change:** 4.4%.

Transport: Railways: 1,391 mi. **Motor vehicles:** 463.5 vehicles per 1,000 pop. **Civil aviation:** 904.7 mil pass.-mi; 19 airports. **Chief ports:** Riga, Ventspils.

Communications: TV sets: 855 per 1,000 pop. **Radios:** 700 per 1,000 pop. **Telephone lines:** 23 per 100 pop. **Daily newspaper circ.:** 154.1 per 1,000 pop. **Internet:** 71.7%.

Health: Life expect.: 67.8 male; 78.3 female. **Births:** 10.0 (per 1,000 pop.). **Deaths:** 13.6 (per 1,000 pop.). **Natural inc.:** −0.36% **Infant mortality:** 8.2 (per 1,000 live births). **HIV rate:** 0.7%.

Education: Compulsory: ages 7-15. **Literacy:** 99.8%.

Major intl. organizations: UN (FAO, IBRD, ILO, IMF, WHO), EU, NATO, OSCE, WTO.

Embassy: 2306 Massachusetts Ave. NW 20008; 328-2840.

Website: www.li.lv

Prior to 1918, Latvia was occupied by the Russians and Germans. It was an independent republic, 1918-39. The Aug. 1939

Soviet-German agreement assigned Latvia to the Soviet sphere of influence. It was officially absorbed by the USSR on Aug. 5, 1940. It was overrun by the German army in 1941, but retaken in 1945.

During an abortive Soviet coup, Latvia declared independence, Aug. 21, 1991. The last Russian troops in Latvia withdrew by Aug. 31, 1994. Responding to international pressure, Latvian voters on Oct. 3, 1998, eased citizenship laws that had discriminated against some 500,000 ethnic Russians. Latvia joined the EU and NATO in 2004.

Hit hard by recession, Latvia reached agreement Dec. 2008 on a $10.4 bil emergency loan from the EU, IMF, World Bank, and Nordic countries. Angered by the prolonged economic downturn and by the growing influence of wealthy oligarchs over Latvian politics, voters in a July 23, 2011, referendum approved a proposal to dissolve parliament. Prime Min. Valdis Dombrovskis's Unity Party came in third in Sept. 17, 2011, elections but Dombrovskis remained prime min.

Lebanon
Lebanese Republic

People: Population: 4,140,289. **Age distrib.:** <15: 22.5%; 65+: 9.2%. **Pop. density:** 1,048.2 per sq mi, 404.7 per sq km. **Urban:** 87.2%. **Ethnic groups:** Arab 95%, Armenian 4%; many Christian Lebanese do not identify as Arab but prefer to be called Phoenician. **Principal languages:** Arabic (official), French, English, Armenian. **Chief religions:** Muslim 60%, Christian 39%.

Geography: Total area: 4,015 sq mi, 10,400 sq km; **Land area:** 3,950 sq mi, 10,230 sq km. **Location:** In Middle East, on E end of Mediterranean Sea. **Neighbors:** Syria on N, Israel on S. **Topography:** There is a narrow coastal strip, and 2 mountain ranges running N-S enclosing the fertile Beqaa Valley. The Litani R. runs S through the valley, turning W to empty into Mediterranean. **Capital:** Beirut, 2,022,350.

Government: Type: Republic. **Head of state:** Pres. Michel Suleiman; b. Nov. 21, 1948; in office: May 25, 2008. **Head of gov.:** Prime Min. Najib Mikati; b. Nov. 24, 1955; in office: June 13, 2011. **Local divisions:** 6 governorates. **Defense budget:** $1.11 bil. **Active troops:** 59,100.

Economy: Industries: banking, tourism, food proc., wine, jewelry, cement, textiles, mineral and chem. prods., wood and furniture prods. **Chief crops:** citrus, grapes, tomatoes, apples, vegetables, potatoes, olives, tobacco. **Natural resources:** limestone, iron ore, salt, water (surplus in a water-deficit region). **Arable land:** 14.2%. **Livestock:** cattle: 77,000; chickens: 37.5 mil; goats: 450,000; pigs: 9,500; sheep: 335,000. **Fish catch:** 4,614 metric tons. **Electricity prod.:** 13 bil kWh. **Labor force:** NA.

Finance: Monetary unit: Pound (LBP) (Sept. 2012: 1,502.83 = $1 U.S.). **GDP:** $62.2 bil; **per capita GDP:** $15,700; **GDP growth:** 1.5%. **Imports:** $19.9 bil; U.S. 10.3%, Italy 9.5%, France 8.9%, China 8.3%, Germany 5.2%, Turkey 4.1%. **Exports:** $5.5 bil; UAE 11.6%, South Africa 9.3%, Iraq 7.4%, Saudi Arabia 6.8%, Turkey 6.2%, Syria 6%, Egypt 5.4%, Switzerland 4.9%. **Tourism:** $8.01 bil. **Budget:** $11.7 bil. **Total reserves less gold:** $33.7 bil. **Gold:** 9.2 mil oz t. **CPI change** (2009-10): 4%.

Transport: Railways: 249 mi (unusable because of damage from fighting). **Motor vehicles:** 131.5 vehicles per 1,000 pop. **Civil aviation:** 1.7 bil pass.-mi; 5 airports. **Chief ports:** Beirut, Tripoli.

Communications: TV sets: 387 per 1,000 pop. **Radios:** 75 per 1,000 pop. **Telephone lines:** 21.1 per 100 pop. **Daily newspaper circ.:** 54.2 per 1,000 pop. **Internet:** 52%.

Health: Life expect.: 73.7 male; 76.9 female. **Births:** 14.9 (per 1,000 pop.). **Deaths:** 6.6 (per 1,000 pop.) **Natural inc.:** 0.83% **Infant mortality:** 15.3 (per 1,000 live births). **HIV rate:** 0.1%.

Education: Compulsory: ages 6-15. **Literacy:** 89.6%.

Major intl. organizations: UN (FAO, IBRD, ILO, IMF, WHO), AL, WTO (observer).

Embassy: 2560 28th St. NW 20008; 939-6300.

Website: www.presidency.gov.lb

Formed from five former Turkish Empire districts, Lebanon became independent Sept. 1, 1920, administered under French mandate 1920-41. French troops withdrew in 1946.

Under the 1943 National Covenant, all public positions were divided among the various religious communities, with Christians in the majority. By the 1970s, Muslims became the majority and demanded a larger political and economic role.

U.S. Marines intervened, May-Oct. 1958, during a Syrian-aided revolt. Continued raids against Israeli civilians, 1970-75, brought Israeli retaliation in southern Lebanon.

An estimated 60,000 were killed in a 1975-76 civil war. Palestinian units and leftist Muslims fought against Maronite militia (the Phalange) and other Christians. Several Arab countries provided support to various factions, while Israel aided Christian forces. Syria, which intervened in 1976 to fight Palestinian groups, largely policed a cease-fire.

Israeli forces invaded Lebanon June 6, 1982, attacking strongholds of the Palestine Liberation Organization (PLO). Israeli and Syrian forces engaged in the Bekaa Valley. On Aug. 21, the PLO evacuated west Beirut after massive Israeli bombings. Israeli troops entered west Beirut following the Sept. 14 assassination of newly elected Lebanese Pres. Bashir Gemayel. On Sept. 16, 1982, Lebanese Christian troops entered the Sabra and Shatila refugee camps and massacred hundreds of Palestinian civilians. An agreement May 17, 1983, between Lebanon, Israel, and the U.S. (but not Syria) provided for the withdrawal of Israeli troops; at least 30,000 Syrian troops remained in Lebanon, and Israel held onto a "security zone" in the south.

In 1983, terrorist bombings became a way of life in Beirut. Some 50 people were killed in an explosion at the U.S. Embassy, Apr. 18; 241 U.S. service members and 58 French soldiers died in separate Islamist suicide attacks, Oct. 23. The 1980s witnessed kidnappings of U.S., British, French, and Soviet citizens by Islamic militants. All hostages were released by 1992.

A treaty signed May 22, 1991, between Lebanon and Syria recognized Lebanon as a separate state for the first time since 1943.

Israeli forces conducted air raids and artillery strikes against guerrilla bases and villages in southern Lebanon, causing over 200,000 to flee their homes July 25-29, 1993. Some 500,000 civilians fled their homes in Apr. 1996 when Israel struck suspected guerrilla bases in the south. The economy revived in the 1990s, but Syria continued to dominate Lebanon's political affairs. Israel withdrew virtually all its troops from S Lebanon by May 24, 2000, leaving Hezbollah, an Iranian-backed guerrilla group, in control of much of the region.

Rafik al-Hariri, a former prime minister (1992-98, 2000-04), was killed by a truck bomb, Feb. 14, 2005. Many Lebanese blamed Syria. As anti-Syrian protests mounted, Syrian troops left Lebanon (some intelligence agents may have remained). An anti-Syrian bloc won parliamentary elections held, May and June. A new cabinet, installed July 19, 2005, was headed by Fouad Siniora, a friend and aide to Hariri, and included a Hezbollah member.

A rocket attack and border raid by Hezbollah, July 12, 2006, in which 3 Israeli soldiers were killed and 2 captured, triggered a massive escalation of hostilities. Hezbollah, led by Sheikh Hassan Nasrallah, bombarded northern Israel with nearly 4,000 rockets, while Israeli air and ground forces assaulted suspected Hezbollah strongholds in southern Lebanon and southern Beirut. By Aug. 14, 2006, when a UN-sponsored cease-fire took hold, the war dead included nearly 1,150 Lebanese. To enforce the truce, thousands of Lebanese troops moved into southern Lebanon, and the small UN force already in Lebanon (UNIFIL) was expanded.

At an international conference in Paris, Jan. 25, 2007, donor countries pledged more than $7.6 bil in reconstruction aid. After more than three months of fighting in which over 400 people died, Lebanese forces Sept. 2 defeated Islamic militants at the Nahr al-Bared Palestinian refugee camp north of Tripoli. A power-sharing accord May 21, 2008, between the Siniora government and Hezbollah eased factional violence and paved the way for Army Chief Gen. Michel Suleiman to become president, ending an 18-month stalemate.

A pro-Western coalition, the March 14 Movement, led by Saad Hariri (son of the slain former prime minister), won a parliamentary majority in elections June 7, 2009. A 5-month impasse ended with the installation of Prime Min. Hariri and his cabinet (including Hezbollah) Nov. 9, 2009. After that government collapsed in Jan. 2011, a 5-month deadlock culminated in the installation June 13 of a cabinet dominated by Hezbollah and headed by Prime Min. Najib Mikati, a telecommunications billionaire. UNIFIL had about 12,000 uniformed personnel in Lebanon in mid-2012. The Syrian civil war spilled over into Lebanon in 2012, most dramatically in Tripoli, where Sunni Muslims and Alawite Muslims took part in firefights Aug. 21-26, 2012, that left at least 17 dead.

Lesotho
Kingdom of Lesotho

People: Population: 1,930,493. **Age distrib.:** <15: 33.4%; 65+: 5.4%. **Pop. density:** 164.7 per sq mi, 63.6 per sq km. **Urban:** 27.6%. **Ethnic groups:** Sotho 99.7%. **Principal languages:** Sesotho, English (both official); Zulu; Xhosa. **Chief religions:** Christian 80%, indigenous beliefs 20%.

Geography: Total area: 11,720 sq mi, 30,355 sq km; **Land area:** 11,720 sq mi, 30,355 sq km. **Location:** In southern Africa. **Neighbors:** Completely surrounded by Republic of South Africa. **Topography:** Landlocked and mountainous, altitudes from 5,000 to 11,000 ft. **Capital:** Maseru, 238,553.

Government: Type: Modified constitutional monarchy. **Head of state:** King Letsie III; b. July 17, 1963; in office: Feb. 7, 1996. **Head of gov.:** Prime Min. Thomas Motsoahae Thabane; b. 1939; in office: June 8, 2012. **Local divisions:** 10 districts. **Defense budget:** $48 mil. **Active troops:** 2,000.

Economy: Industries: food, beverages, textiles, apparel assembly, handicrafts, constr., tourism. **Chief crops:** corn, wheat, pulses, sorghum, barley. **Natural resources:** water, diamonds, sand, clay, building stone. **Arable land:** 11.0%. **Livestock:** cattle: 626,343; chickens: 502,000; goats: 875,184; pigs: 83,976; sheep: 1.2 mil. **Fish catch:** 345 metric tons. **Electricity prod.:** 200 mil kWh. **Labor force:** agric. 86% (subsistence), industry and services 14%. Approx. 35% of active male wage earners work in South Africa.

Finance: Monetary unit: Loti (LSL) (Sept. 2012: 8.39 = $1 U.S.). **GDP:** $3.9 bil; **per capita GDP:** $2,000; **GDP growth:** 4.2%. **Imports:** $2.3 bil; South Korea 26.9%, China 23.1%, Taiwan 22.1%, Hong Kong 6.6%, U.S. 4.4%. **Exports:** $1 bil; U.S. 58.4%, Belgium 34%, Canada 3.7%. **Tourism:** $34 mil. **Budget:** $1.6 bil. **CPI change:** 5.02%.

Transport: Civil aviation: 3 airports.

Communications: TV sets: 44 per 1,000 pop. **Radios:** 121 per 1,000 pop. **Telephone lines:** 1.6 per 100 pop. **Internet:** 4.2%.

Health: Life expect.: 51.8 male; 52.0 female. **Births:** 26.7 (per 1,000 pop.). **Deaths:** 15.2 (per 1,000 pop.). **Natural inc.:** 1.15% **Infant mortality:** 53.4 (per 1,000 live births). **HIV rate:** 23.6%.

Education: Compulsory ages: NA. **Literacy:** 89.6%.

Major intl. organizations: UN (FAO, IBRD, ILO, IMF, WHO), AU, the Commonwealth, WTO.

Embassy: 2511 Massachusetts Ave. NW 20008; 797-5533.

Website: www.gov.ls

Lesotho (once called Basutoland) became a British protectorate in 1868 when Chief Moshesh sought protection against the Boers. Independence came Oct. 4, 1966. Most of Lesotho's GNP is provided by citizens working in South Africa. Livestock raising is a major industry; diamonds are the chief export.

In Mar. 1990, King Moshoeshoe was exiled by the military government. Letsie III became king Nov. 12. In Mar. 1993, Ntsu Mokhehle, a civilian, was elected prime minister, ending 23 years of military rule. After a series of violent disturbances, the king dismissed the Mokhehle government Aug. 17, 1994; constitutional rule was restored Sept. 14.

Letsie abdicated and Moshoeshoe was reinstated Jan. 25, 1995. Moshoeshoe died in an automobile accident, Jan. 15, 1996. Letsie was reinstated Feb. 7, 1996. South Africa and Botswana sent troops Sept. 22, 1998, to help suppress violent antigovernment protests. After parliamentary elections May 26, 2012, the left-leaning Thomas Motsoahae Thabane became the first new prime min. since 1998.

According to UN estimates, more than 20% of the population between the ages of 15 and 49 has HIV/AIDS. Cultivation of marijuana for smuggling to South Africa is a significant source of income.

Liberia
Republic of Liberia

People: Population: 3,887,886. **Age distrib.:** <15: 44.1%; 65+: 3%. **Pop. density:** 104.5 per sq mi, 40.4 per sq km. **Urban:** 48.2%. **Ethnic groups:** Kpelle 20%, Bassa 13%, Gio 8%, Mano 8%, Kru 6%, Lorma 5%, Kissi 5%, Gola 4%. **Principal languages:** English (official), about 20 ethnic langs. **Chief religions:** Christian 86%, Muslim 12%.

Geography: Total area: 43,000 sq mi, 111,369 sq km; **Land area:** 37,189 sq mi, 96,320 sq km. **Location:** On SW coast of W Africa. **Neighbors:** Sierra Leone on W, Guinea on N, Côte d'Ivoire on E. **Topography:** Marshy Atlantic coastline rises to low mountains and plateaus in forested interior; 6 major rivers flow in parallel courses to the ocean. **Capital:** Monrovia, 750,376.

Government: Type: Republic. **Head of state and gov.:** Pres. Ellen Johnson-Sirleaf; b. Oct. 29, 1938; in office: Jan. 16, 2006. **Local divisions:** 15 counties. **Defense budget** (2010): $8 mil. **Active troops:** 2,050.

Economy: Industries: rubber and palm oil proc., timber, diamonds. **Chief crops:** rubber, coffee, cocoa, rice, cassava, palm oil, sugarcane, bananas. **Natural resources:** iron ore, timber, diamonds, gold, hydropower. **Arable land:** 4.2%. **Livestock:** cattle: 39,500; chickens: 6.8 mil; goats: 338,300; pigs: 265,300; sheep: 263,750. **Fish catch:** 8,020 metric tons. **Electricity prod.:** 335 mil kWh. **Labor force:** agric. 70%, industry 8%, services 22%.

Finance: Monetary unit: Dollar (LRD) (Sept. 2012: 73.90 = $1 U.S.). **GDP:** $1.8 bil; **per capita GDP:** $500; **GDP growth:** 6.4%. **Imports** $755.9 mil; South Korea 42.4%, China 28.6%, Japan 18.9%. **Exports** $422.6 mil; South Africa 29.9%, U.S. 15.7%, Spain 7.6%, Côte d'Ivoire 4.9%, Germany 4.2%, Japan 4.1%, China 4%. **Tourism:** $12 mil. **Budget:** $441.4 mil. **Total reserves less gold** (2009): $372.5 mil. **Gold** (2009): 372.5 mil oz t. **CPI change:** 8.5%.

Transport: Railways: 267 mi. **Motor vehicles:** 14.3 vehicles per 1,000 pop. **Civil aviation:** 2 airports. **Chief ports:** Buchanan, Monrovia.

Communications: TV sets: 26 per 1,000 pop. **Radios:** 318 per 1,000 pop. **Telephone lines:** 0.08 per 100 pop. **Internet:** 3%.

Health: Life expect.: 55.8 male; 59.0 female. **Births:** 36.5 (per 1,000 pop.). **Deaths:** 10.4 (per 1,000 pop.). **Natural inc.:** 2.61% **Infant mortality:** 72.7 (per 1,000 live births). **HIV rate:** 1.5%.

Education: Compulsory ages: NA. **Literacy:** 60.8%.

Major intl. organizations: UN and most of its specialized agencies, AU, WTO (observer).

Embassy: 5201 16th St. NW 20011; 723-0437.

Website: www.emansion.gov.lr

Liberia was founded in 1822 by freed black slaves from the U.S. who settled at Monrovia with the aid of colonization societies. It became a republic July 26, 1847, with a constitution modeled on that of the U.S. Descendants of freed slaves dominated politics for much of the 19th and 20th cents.

Under Pres. William V. S. Tubman, Liberia was a founding member of the UN in 1945. Tubman died in 1971 and was succeeded by his vice president, William R. Tolbert Jr. Charging rampant corruption, an Army Redemption Council of enlisted men staged a bloody predawn coup, Apr. 12, 1980, killing Pres. Tolbert and installing Sgt. Samuel Doe, an indigenous African, as head of state. In 1985, Doe was chosen president in a disputed election.

A civil war began Dec. 1989. In Sept. 1990, Pres. Doe was executed. Despite the introduction of peacekeeping forces from several countries, the conflict intensified. Factional fighting devastated Monrovia in Apr. 1996. Ruth Perry became modern Africa's first female head of state Sept. 3, 1996, leading a transitional government. By then, the civil war had claimed more than 150,000 lives.

Former rebel leader Charles Taylor was elected president July 19, 1997, in Liberia's first national election in 12 years. The UN imposed sanctions May 4, 2001, to punish Liberia for aiding the Revolutionary United Front (RUF) insurgency in Sierra Leone. Taylor declared a state of emergency Feb. 8, 2002, after Liberian rebels launched raids near Monrovia.

A UN-sponsored war crimes tribunal indicted Taylor June 4, 2003, for his role in the conflict in Sierra Leone. With rebels again threatening Monrovia, Taylor resigned Aug. 11 and went into exile. The UN authorized a 15,000-member peacekeeping force (UNMIL) Sept. 19 to help stabilize the nation. A businessman, Charles Gyude Bryant, was sworn in Oct. 14 to head a power-sharing interim government. Ellen Johnson-Sirleaf won a presidential run-off election Nov. 8, 2005. Johnson-Sirleaf won the presidential election Oct. 11, 2011, 4 days after sharing the Nobel Peace Prize with 2 other women. Captured Mar. 29, 2006, while trying to flee Nigeria, Charles Taylor's trial at The Hague began June 4, 2007, but was plagued by delays. Taylor was convicted of 11 counts of aiding and abetting war crimes and crimes against humanity, Apr. 26, 2012, and sentenced to 50 years in prison May 30.

UNMIL had about 8,900 uniformed personnel in Liberia in mid-2012.

Libya
Libyan Republic

People: Population: 5,613,380. **Age distrib.:** <15: 27.7%; 65+: 3.9%. **Pop. density:** 8.3 per sq mi, 3.2 per sq km. **Urban:** 77.7%. **Ethnic groups:** Berber and Arab 97%, other (incl. Greek, Maltese, Italian, Egyptian, Pakistani, Turk, Indian, Tunisian) 3%. **Principal languages:** Arabic (official), Italian, English all widely understood in major cities. **Chief religion:** Sunni Muslim (official) 97%.

Geography: Total area: 679,362 sq mi, 1,759,540 sq km; **Land area:** 679,362 sq mi, 1,759,540 sq km. **Location:** On Mediterranean coast of N Africa. **Neighbors:** Tunisia, Algeria on W; Niger, Chad on S; Sudan, Egypt on E. **Topography:** Desert and semidesert regions cover 92% of land, with low mountains in N, higher mountains in S, and a narrow coastal zone. **Capital:** Tripoli (Tarabulus), 1,126,950.

Government: Type: In transition. **Head of state:** Chairman, Libyan Interim National Council, Mustafa Mohammed Abdul Jalil; b. 1952; in office: Aug. 23, 2011 (de facto). **Head of gov.:** Interim Prime Min. Abdel-Rahim al-Keeb; b. 1950; in office: Oct. 23, 2011 (de facto). **Local divisions:** 25 municipalities. **Defense budget:** NA. **Active troops:** In transition.

Economy: Industries: petroleum, petrochemicals, aluminum, iron and steel, food proc., textiles, handicrafts, cement. **Chief crops:** wheat, barley, olives, dates, citrus, vegetables, peanuts, soybeans. **Natural resources:** petroleum, nat. gas, gypsum. **Crude oil reserves:** 47.1 bil bbls. **Arable land:** 1.0%. **Livestock:** cattle: 195,000; chickens: 33 mil; goats: 2.7 mil; sheep: 7 mil. **Fish catch:** 50,246 metric tons. **Electricity prod.:** 28.6 bil kWh. **Labor force:** agric. 17%, industry 23%, services 59%.

Finance: Monetary unit: Dinar (LYD) (Sept. 2012: 1.26 = $1 U.S.). **GDP:** $38 bil; **per capita GDP** (2010 est.): $14,100; **GDP growth:** NA. **Imports:** $10.3 bil; Egypt 15.5%, Tunisia 11.9%, Turkey 8.1%, China 7.8%, Italy 7.5%, Syria 4.6%, France 4.4%, Germany 4.3%. **Exports:** $16.5 bil; Italy 21.5%, Germany 13.5%, France 13.4%, China 10.1%, Spain 4.9%, Tunisia 4.6%, India 4.3%. **Tourism:** $60 mil. **Budget:** $32 bil. **Total reserves less gold:** $104.8 bil. **Gold:** 3.8 mil oz t. **CPI change** (2009-10): 2.5%.

Transport: Motor vehicles: 133 vehicles per 1,000 pop. **Civil aviation:** 945.1 mil pass.-mi; 64 airports. **Chief ports:** Az Zawiyah, Marsa al Burayqah, Ra's Lanuf, Tripoli.

Communications: TV sets: 147 per 1,000 pop. **Radios:** 270 per 1,000 pop. **Telephone lines:** 15.6 per 100 pop. **Internet:** 17%.

Health: Life expect.: 74.0 male; 77.3 female. **Births:** 19.0 (per 1,000 pop.). **Deaths:** 3.6 (per 1,000 pop.). **Natural inc.:** 1.55% **Infant mortality:** 12.7 (per 1,000 live births). **HIV rate:** NA.

Education: Compulsory: ages 6-14. **Literacy:** 89.2%.

Major intl. organizations: UN (FAO, IBRD, ILO, IMF, WHO), AL, AU, OPEC, WTO (observer).

Embassy: 2600 Virginia Ave. NW, Ste. 705, 20037; 944-9601.

Website: www.libyausaembassy.com

First settled by Berbers, Libya was ruled in succession by Carthage, Rome, the Vandals, and the Ottomans. Italy ruled from 1912, and Britain and France after WWII. Libya became an independent constitutional monarchy Jan. 2, 1952. In 1969 a junta led by Col. Muammar al-Qaddafi seized power.

Qaddafi ruled as a dictator, suppressing domestic dissent and engaging in armed conflicts with neighboring Egypt and Chad. During the 1980s, Libya was accused of aiding terrorists and violent revolutionary groups. The U.S. charged Qaddafi with ordering the Apr. 5, 1986, bombing of a West Berlin discotheque, which killed 3, including a U.S. serviceman. In response, the U.S. sent war-planes to attack what it called "terrorist-related targets" in Libya, Apr. 14, including Qaddafi's barracks.

Libyan agents were accused of planting bombs that blew up Pan Am Flight 103 over Lockerbie, Scotland, killing 270 people Dec. 21, 1988, and UTA Flight 772 over Niger, killing 170 people Sept. 19, 1989. The UN imposed sanctions, Apr. 15, 1992, for Libya's failure to cooperate in the Lockerbie and UTA cases.

Libya agreed in 2003 to renounce terrorism and settle compensation cases for the families of the Lockerbie and UTA bombing victims. The UN lifted sanctions, Sept. 12, 2003. Secret talks with the U.S. and UK led to Libya's announcement Dec. 19 that it would stop developing nuclear, chemical, and biological weapons and long-range missiles. The U.S. ended most economic sanctions Apr. 23, 2004, and restored full diplomatic relations May 15, 2006. Abdel Basset Ali al-Megrahi, a former Libyan agent sentenced to life in prison in 2001 for his role in the Lockerbie bombing, was freed by Scottish authorities on humanitarian grounds Aug. 20, 2009; he received a jubilant welcome in Libya.

"Arab Spring" rebels gained control Feb. 2011 of much of Libya's eastern region, while Qaddafi held power in western Libya. Qaddafi launched a ferocious counteroffensive, but with diplomatic backing from the Arab League and the UN Security Council, NATO forces led by France, UK, and U.S. imposed an arms embargo and no-fly zone against Qaddafi. With aid from NATO, the rebels took control of Tripoli Aug. 23, 2011, and began governing through the Libyan Interim National Council. Rebels killed Qaddafi Oct. 20, 2011. The moderate National Forces Alliance, led by former interim prime min. Mahmoud Jibril, won July 7, 2012, elections.

Liechtenstein
Principality of Liechtenstein

People: Population: 36,713. **Age distrib.:** <15: 16%; 65+: 14.9%. **Pop. density:** 594.3 per sq mi, 229.5 per sq km. **Urban:** 14.4%. **Ethnic groups:** Liechtensteiner 66%. **Principal languages:** German (official), Alemannic dialect. **Chief religions:** Roman Catholic (official) 76%, Protestant 7%.

Geography: Total area: 62 sq mi, 160 sq km; **Land area:** 62 sq mi, 160 sq km. **Location:** Central Europe, in Alps. **Neighbors:** Switzerland on W, Austria on E. **Topography:** Rhine Valley occupies one-third of country, Alps cover the rest. **Capital:** Vaduz, 5,225.

Government: Type: Hereditary constitutional monarchy. **Head of state:** Prince Hans-Adam II; b. Feb. 14, 1945; in office: Nov. 13, 1989. **Head of gov.:** Klaus Tschütscher; b. July 8, 1967; in office: Mar. 25, 2009. **Local divisions:** 11 communes. **Defense budget:** NA. **Active troops:** No regular military forces.

Economy: Industries: electronics, metal mfg., dental prods., ceramics, pharmaceuticals, food prods., precision instruments, tourism, optical instruments. **Chief crops:** wheat, barley, corn, potatoes. **Natural resources:** hydroelectric potential. **Arable land:** 21.9%. **Livestock:** cattle: 6,100; goats: 460; pigs: 1,820; sheep: 4,000. **Labor force:** agric. 0.8%, industry 41.3%, services 56%.

Finance: Monetary unit: Swiss Franc (CHF) (Sept. 2012: 0.95 = $1 U.S.). **GDP** (2009): $5 bil; **per capita GDP** (2008 est.): $141,100; **GDP growth** (2009): –0.5%. **Imports** (2009): $1.7 bil. **Exports** (2009): $2.8 bil. **Tourism:** NA. **Budget** (2008): $820 mil.

Transport: Railways: 6 mi.

Communications: TV sets: 540 per 1,000 pop. **Radios:** 662 per 1,000 pop. **Telephone lines:** 54 per 100 pop. **Daily newspaper circ.:** 513.6 per 1,000 pop. **Internet:** 85%.

Health: Life expect.: 79.4 male; 84.2 female. **Births:** 10.8 (per 1,000 pop.). **Deaths:** 6.8 (per 1,000 pop.). **Natural inc.:** 0.40% **Infant mortality:** 4.4 (per 1,000 live births). **HIV rate:** NA.

Education: Compulsory: ages 6-14. **Literacy:** 100%.

Major intl. organizations: EFTA, OSCE, WTO.

Embassy: 2900 K St. NW, Ste. 602B, 20007; 331-0590.

Website: www.liechtenstein.li

Liechtenstein became sovereign in 1806. It is united with Switzerland by a customs and monetary union. Nearly half of all workers commute daily from Austria, Switzerland, and Germany.

On Aug. 15, 2004, Prince Hans-Adam II assigned day-to-day responsibilities for running the tiny country to his son, Crown Prince Alois. Long regarded as a tax haven, Liechtenstein has recently agreed to ease banking secrecy laws that had impeded international tax fraud investigations. A referendum to abolish the prince's power to veto referendums was defeated July 1, 2012.

Lithuania
Republic of Lithuania

People: Population: 3,525,761. **Age distrib.:** <15: 13.7%; 65+: 16.6%. **Pop. density:** 145.7 per sq mi, 56.3 per sq km. **Urban:** 67.1%. **Ethnic groups:** Lithuanian 84%, Polish 6%, Russian 5%, Belarusian 1%. **Principal languages:** Lithuanian (official), Russian, Polish. **Chief religions:** Roman Catholic 79%, Russian Orthodox 4%, Protestant (incl. Lutheran, Evangelical Christian Baptist) 2%, none 10%.

Geography: Total area: 25,212 sq mi, 65,300 sq km; **Land area:** 24,201 sq mi, 62,680 sq km. **Location:** In E Europe, on SE coast of Baltic. **Neighbors:** Latvia on N; Belarus on E, S; Poland, Russia on W. **Topography:** Lowland with hills in W and S; fertile soil; many small lakes and rivers, with marshes espec. in N and W. **Capital:** Vilnius, 545,607.

Government: Type: Republic. **Head of state:** Pres. Dalia Grybauskaite; b. Mar. 1, 1956; in office: July 12, 2009. **Head of gov.:** Prime Min. Andrius Kubilius; b. Dec. 8, 1956; in office: Dec. 9, 2008. **Local divisions:** 10 provinces. **Defense budget:** $425 mil. **Active troops:** 10,640.

Economy: Industries: machine tools, elec. motors, TVs, refrigerators and freezers, petroleum refining, shipbuilding, furniture making, textiles, food proc. **Chief crops:** grain, potatoes, sugar beets, flax, vegetables. **Natural resources:** peat, amber. **Crude oil reserves:** 12 mil bbls. **Arable land:** 32.8%. **Livestock:** cattle: 759,400; chickens: 9 mil; goats: 14,700; pigs: 928,200; sheep: 52,500. **Fish catch:** 153,042 metric tons. **Electricity prod.:** 13.5 bil kWh. **Labor force:** agric. 14%, industry 29.1%, services 56.9%.

Finance: Monetary unit: Litas (LTL) (Sept. 2012: 2.74 = $1 U.S.). **GDP:** $62.4 bil; **per capita GDP:** $19,100; **GDP growth:** 5.9%. **Imports:** $30.8 bil; Russia 33%, Germany 9.8%, Poland 9.2%, Latvia 6.7%, Netherlands 5%. **Exports:** $28.7 bil; Russia 16.7%, Latvia 10.4%, Germany 9.5%, Poland 7.1%, Estonia 6.8%, Netherlands 6.2%, Belarus 5.2%, UK 4.2%, France 4.2%. **Tourism:** $1.4 bil. **Budget:** $16.3 bil. **Total reserves less gold:** $7.9 bil. **Gold:** 187,000 oz t. **CPI change:** 4.1%.

Transport: Railways: 1,098 mi. **Civil aviation:** 577.9 mil pass.-mi; 26 airports. **Chief port:** Klaipeda.

Communications: TV sets: 518 per 1,000 pop. **Radios:** 525 per 1,000 pop. **Telephone lines:** 21.9 per 100 pop. **Daily newspaper circ.:** 107.8 per 1,000 pop. **Internet:** 65.1%.

Health: Life expect.: 70.7 male; 80.7 female. **Births:** 9.3 (per 1,000 pop.). **Deaths:** 11.4 (per 1,000 pop.). **Natural inc.:** −0.21% **Infant mortality:** 6.2 (per 1,000 live births). **HIV rate:** 0.1%.

Education: Compulsory: ages 7-15. **Literacy:** 99.7%.

Major intl. organizations: UN (FAO, IBRD, ILO, IMF, WHO), EU, NATO, OSCE, WTO.

Embassy: 4590 MacArthur Blvd. NW, Ste. 200, 20007; 234-5860.

Website: www.lrvk.lt

Lithuania was occupied by the German army, 1914-18. It was annexed by the Soviet Russian army, but the Soviets were overthrown, 1919. In 1939 the Soviet-German treaty assigned most of Lithuania to the Soviet sphere of influence. Lithuania was annexed by the USSR Aug. 3, 1940.

Lithuania declared its independence from the Soviet Union Mar. 11, 1990. During an abortive Soviet coup in Aug., Western nations recognized Lithuania's independence, which was ratified by the Soviet Union Sept. 1991. The country became a full member of NATO and the EU in 2004. A plummeting economy spurred popular discontent and brought a rightward shift in parliamentary and presidential elections, 2008-09. In mid-2012, Lithuania had 200 troops serving with the NATO mission (ISAF) in Afghanistan. Parliamentary elections were scheduled for Oct. 14, 2012.

Luxembourg
Grand Duchy of Luxembourg

People: Population: 509,074. **Age distrib.:** <15: 18.1%; 65+: 15.1%. **Pop. density:** 509.9 per sq mi, 196.9 per sq km. **Urban:** 85.4%. **Ethnic groups:** Luxembourger 63%, Portuguese 13%, French 5%, Italian 4%, German 2%, other EU 7%. **Principal languages:** Luxembourgish (national); German, French (both administrative). **Chief religions:** Roman Catholic 87%, other (incl. Protestant, Jewish, Muslim) 13%.

Geography: Total area: 998 sq mi, 2,586 sq km; **Land area:** 998 sq mi, 2,586 sq km. **Location:** In W Europe. **Neighbors:** Belgium on W, France on S, Germany on E. **Topography:** Heavy forests (Ardennes) cover N. S is a low, open plateau. **Capital:** Luxembourg, 94,478.

Government: Type: Constitutional monarchy. **Head of state:** Grand Duke Henri; b. Apr. 16, 1955; in office: Oct. 7, 2000. **Head of gov.:** Prime Min. Jean-Claude Juncker; b. Dec. 9, 1954; in office: Jan. 20, 1995. **Local divisions:** 3 districts. **Defense budget:** $281 mil. **Active troops:** 900.

Economy: Industries: banking and financial services, iron and steel, information tech., telecom., cargo transp., food proc., chemicals, metal prods., engineering, tires, glass, aluminum, tourism.

Chief crops: grapes, barley, oats, potatoes, wheat, fruits. **Natural resources:** iron ore (no longer exploited). **Arable land:** 23.9%. **Livestock:** cattle: 198,892; chickens: 90,000; goats: 5,084; pigs: 83,774; sheep: 9,084. **Electricity prod.** (2010): 2.5 bil kWh. **Labor force:** agric. 2.2%, industry 17.2%, services 80.6%.

Finance: Monetary unit: Euro (EUR) (Sept. 2012: 0.79 = $1 U.S.). **GDP:** $41.8 bil; **per capita GDP:** $81,100; **GDP growth:** 1%. **Imports:** $26.3 bil; Belgium 30.3%, Germany 26%, France 10.8%, China 6.9%, Netherlands 5.8%, U.S. 5.2%. **Exports:** $19.9 bil; Germany 22.2%, France 15.6%, Belgium 13.2%, UK 7.3%, Italy 5.4%, Switzerland 4.3%, Netherlands 4.1%. **Tourism:** $4.5 bil. **Budget:** $25.5 bil. **Total reserves less gold:** $900.5 mil. **Gold:** 72,000 oz t. **CPI change:** 3.4%.

Transport: Railways: 171 mi. **Motor vehicles:** 753.4 vehicles per 1,000 pop. **Civil aviation:** 255.4 mil pass.-mi; 1 airport. **Chief port:** Mertert.

Communications: TV sets: 605 per 1,000 pop. **Radios:** 683 per 1,000 pop. **Telephone lines:** 54.1 per 100 pop. **Daily newspaper circ.** (2004): 254.5 per 1,000 pop. **Internet:** 90.9%.

Health: Life expect.: 76.5 male; 83.2 female. **Births:** 11.7 (per 1,000 pop.). **Deaths:** 8.5 (per 1,000 pop.). **Natural inc.:** 0.32% **Infant mortality:** 4.4 (per 1,000 live births). **HIV rate:** 0.3%.

Education: Compulsory: ages 6-15. **Literacy:** 100%.

Major intl. organizations: UN (FAO, IBRD, ILO, IMF, WHO), EU, NATO, OECD, OSCE, WTO.

Embassy: 2200 Massachusetts Ave. NW 20008; 265-4171.

Website: www.gouvernement.lu

Luxembourg, founded about 963, was ruled by Burgundy, Spain, Austria, and France from 1448 to 1815. It left the Germanic Confederation in 1866. Overrun by Germany in two world wars, Luxembourg ended its neutrality in 1948, when a customs union with Belgium and Netherlands was adopted.

Luxembourg was one of the six founding members (1951) of what became the European Union. Prime Min. Jean-Claude Juncker is the EU's longest-serving head of government.

Macedonia
Former Yugoslav Republic of Macedonia

People: Population: 2,082,370. **Age distrib.:** <15: 18.2%; 65+: 11.8%. **Pop. density:** 212.1 per sq mi, 81.9 per sq km. **Urban:** 59.3%. **Ethnic groups:** Macedonian 64%, Albanian 25%, Turkish 4%, Roma 3%, Serb 2%. **Principal languages:** Macedonian, Albanian (both official); Turkish; Roma; Serbian. **Chief religions:** Macedonian Orthodox 65%, Muslim 33%.

Geography: Total area: 9,928 sq mi, 25,713 sq km; **Land area:** 9,820 sq mi, 25,433 sq km. **Location:** In SE Europe. **Neighbors:** Bulgaria on E, Greece on S, Albania on W, Serbia on N. **Topography:** Macedonia is a landlocked, mostly mountainous country, with deep river valleys, 3 large lakes; country is bisected by Vardar R. **Capital:** Skopje, 499,026.

Government: Type: Republic. **Head of state:** Pres. Gjorge Ivanov; b. May 2, 1960; in office: May 12, 2009. **Head of gov.:** Prime Min. Nikola Gruevski; b. Aug. 31, 1970; in office: Aug. 27, 2006. **Local divisions:** 123 municipalities. **Defense budget:** $137 mil. **Active troops:** 8,000.

Economy: Industries: food proc., beverages, textiles, chemicals, iron, steel, cement, energy, pharmaceuticals. **Chief crops:** grapes, tobacco, vegetables, fruits. **Natural resources:** iron ore, copper, lead, zinc, chromite, manganese, nickel, tungsten, gold, silver, asbestos. **Arable land:** 16.7%. **Livestock:** cattle: 259,887; chickens: 2 mil; goats: 94,016; pigs: 190,552; sheep: 778,404. **Fish catch:** 1,817 metric tons. **Electricity prod.:** 6.5 bil kWh. **Labor force:** agric. 19.9%, industry 22.1%, services 58%.

Finance: Monetary unit: Denar (MKD) (Sept. 2012: 48.78 = $1 U.S.). **GDP:** $21.6 bil (figure might not reflect country's large informal sector); **per capita GDP:** $10,500; **GDP growth:** 3%. **Imports:** $7 bil; Germany 13.1%, Greece 13.1%, Bulgaria 11.1%, UK 7.9%, Turkey 5.4%, Italy 5.4%. **Exports:** $4.3 bil; Germany 28.5%, Italy 7.3%, Bulgaria 5.4%, Greece 5%. **Tourism:** $239 mil. **Budget:** $3.4 bil. **Total reserves less gold:** $2.3 bil. **Gold:** 219,453 oz t. **CPI change:** 3.9%.

Transport: Railways: 434 mi. **Civil aviation:** 54.1 mil pass.-mi; 10 airports.

Communications: TV sets: 296 per 1,000 pop. **Radios:** 207 per 1,000 pop. **Telephone lines:** 20 per 100 pop. **Daily newspaper circ.:** 88.8 per 1,000 pop. **Internet:** 56.7%.

Health: Life expect.: 72.8 male; 78.1 female. **Births:** 11.8 (per 1,000 pop.). **Deaths:** 9.0 (per 1,000 pop.). **Natural inc.:** 0.29% **Infant mortality:** 8.3 (per 1,000 live births). **HIV rate:** NA.

Education: Compulsory: ages 7-14. **Literacy:** 97.3%.

Major intl. organizations: UN (FAO, IBRD, ILO, IMF, WHO) OSCE, WTO.

Embassy: 2129 Wyoming Ave. NW 20008; 667-0501.

Website: www.vlada.mk

Muslim Turks ruled Macedonia from 1389 to 1912. In 1913, the area was incorporated into Serbia, which in 1918 became part of the Kingdom of Serbs, Croats, and Slovenes (later Yugoslavia). In 1946, Macedonia became a constituent republic of Yugoslavia.

Macedonia declared its independence Sept. 8, 1991, and was admitted to the UN in 1993. Greece, which objected to Macedonia's use of what it considered a Hellenic name and symbols, imposed a trade blockade on the landlocked nation; the 2 countries agreed to normalize relations Sept. 13, 1995.

By the end of NATO's air war against Yugoslavia, Mar.-June 1999, Macedonia had a Kosovar refugee population of more than 250,000; over 90% had been repatriated by Sept. 1. Boris Trajkovski, candidate of the ruling center-right coalition, won a presidential runoff vote Nov. 14.

Ethnic Albanian guerrillas launched an offensive Mar. 2001 in NW Macedonia. An accord signed Aug. 13 paved the way for the introduction of a NATO peacekeeping force. A law broadening the rights of ethnic Albanians was enacted Jan. 24, 2002. A 320-member EU force replaced the NATO peacekeepers, Mar.-Dec. 2003.

After Trajkovski died in a plane crash Feb. 26, 2004, Prime Min. Branko Crvenkovski won a presidential runoff vote Apr. 28. Prime Min. Nikola Gruevski's governing coalition retained power after parliamentary elections June 1, 2008, and June 5, 2011. Gjorge Ivanov won a presidential runoff vote Apr. 5, 2009, and took office May 12. Greece has blocked Macedonia's bid to join NATO because of the dispute over Macedonia's name.

Madagascar
Republic of Madagascar

People: Population: 22,005,222. **Age distrib.:** <15: 41.4%; 65+: 3.1%. **Pop. density:** 98 per sq mi, 37.8 per sq km. **Urban:** 32.6%. **Ethnic groups:** Malayo-Indonesian (Merina and related Betsileo), Cotiers (mixed African, Malayo-Indonesian, and Arab), French, Indian, Creole, Comoran. **Principal languages:** French, Malagasy (both official); English. **Chief religions:** indigenous beliefs 52%, Christian 41%, Muslim 7%.

Geography: Total area: 226,658 sq mi, 587,041 sq km; **Land area:** 224,534 sq mi, 581,540 sq km. **Location:** In Indian O., off SE coast of Africa. **Neighbors:** Comoro Isls. to NW, Mozambique to W. **Topography:** Humid coastal strip in E, fertile valleys in mountainous center plateau region, and a wider coastal strip on W. **Capital:** Antananarivo, 1,986,710.

Government: Type: In transition. **Head of state:** Pres. Andry Rajoelina; b. May 30, 1974; in office: Mar. 17, 2009. **Head of gov.:** Prime Min. Albert Camille Vital; b. July 18, 1952; in office: Dec. 20, 2009. **Local divisions:** 6 provinces. **Defense budget:** $71 mil. **Active troops:** 13,500.

Economy: Industries: meat proc., seafood, soap, breweries, tanneries, sugar, textiles, glassware, cement, auto assembly plant, paper, petroleum, tourism. **Chief crops:** coffee, vanilla, sugarcane, cloves, cocoa, rice, cassava, beans, bananas, peanuts. **Natural resources:** graphite, chromite, coal, bauxite, rare earth elements, salt, quartz, tar sands, semiprec. stones, mica, fish, hydropower. **Arable land:** 5.1%. **Livestock:** cattle: 9.9 mil; chickens: 26.5 mil; goats: 1.3 mil; pigs: 1.4 mil; sheep: 730,000. **Fish catch:** 140,522 metric tons. **Electricity prod.:** 1.4 bil kWh. **Labor force:** NA.

Finance: Monetary unit: Ariary (MGA) (Sept. 2012: 2,232.08 = $1 U.S.). **GDP:** $20.7 bil; **per capita GDP:** $900; **GDP growth:** 0.5%. **Imports:** $3.7 bil; China 17.4%, France 13.2%, South Africa 6.7%, Singapore 4.9%, Bahrain 4.8%, Mauritius 4.6%, Kuwait 4.5%. **Exports:** $1.4 bil; France 23.4%, Indonesia 15.8%, Singapore 6.8%, China 5.9%, Germany 5.7%, U.S. 5.2%, Canada 4%. **Tourism:** $321 mil. **Budget:** $1.7 bil. **Total reserves less gold:** $1.3 bil. **CPI change:** 9.5%.

Transport: Railways: 531 mi. **Motor vehicles:** 6.3 vehicles per 1,000 pop. **Civil aviation:** 508.9 mil pass.-mi; 26 airports. **Chief ports:** Antsiranana, Mahajanga, Toamasina, Toliara.

Communications: TV sets: 37 per 1,000 pop. **Radios:** 268 per 1,000 pop. **Telephone lines:** 0.7 per 100 pop. **Internet:** 1.9%.

Health: Life expect.: 63.1 male; 65.9 female. **Births:** 34.0 (per 1,000 pop.). **Deaths:** 7.3 (per 1,000 pop.). **Natural inc.:** 2.68%. **Infant mortality:** 47.4 (per 1,000 live births). **HIV rate:** 0.2%.

Education: Compulsory: ages 6-14. **Literacy:** 64.5%.

Major intl. organizations: UN (FAO, IBRD, ILO, IMF, WHO), AU, WTO.

Embassy: 2374 Massachusetts Ave. NW 20008; 265-5525.

Website: www.madagascar-presidency.gov.mg

Madagascar was settled 2,000 years ago by Malayan-Indonesian people, whose descendants still predominate. A unified kingdom ruled in the 18th and 19th cent. The island became a French protectorate, 1885, and a colony 1896. Independence came June 26, 1960.

Discontent with inflation and French domination led to a coup in 1972. The new regime nationalized French-owned financial interests, closed French bases and a U.S. space-tracking station, and obtained Chinese aid. The government conducted a program of arrests, expulsion of foreigners, and repression of strikes, 1979.

In 1990, Madagascar ended a ban on multiparty politics that had been in place since 1975. Albert Zafy was elected president in 1993, ending the 17-year rule of Adm. Didier Ratsiraka. After Zafy was impeached by the legislature, Madagascar's constitutional

court removed him from office, Sept. 5, 1996. A cholera epidemic, then cyclones in Feb. and Apr. 2000, claimed 1,600 lives.

Marc Ravalomanana won a power struggle with Ratsiraka that followed a disputed presidential election Dec. 16, 2001; he was reelected with a 55% majority Dec. 3, 2006. Cyclone Ivan hit Feb. 17, 2008, killing at least 83 people and leaving 145,000 homeless. A power struggle between Ravalomanana and Antananarivo Mayor Andry Rajoelina, backed by the military, culminated in Rajoelina's installation as head of a transitional regime, Mar. 17, 2009. The African Union suspended Madagascar and pushed for a power-sharing arrangement, but accords signed in Aug. and Nov. 2009 were abrogated by Rajoelina. The transitional government suppressed a coup attempt launched by dissident military officers Nov. 17, 2010, the same day voters approved a new constitution that would allow Rajoelina to hold power indefinitely.

Malawi
Republic of Malawi

People: Population: 16,323,044. **Age distrib.:** <15: 44.9%; 65+: 2.7%. **Pop. density:** 449.4 per sq mi, 173.5 per sq km. **Urban:** 15.7%. **Ethnic groups:** Chewa 33%, Lomwe 18%, Yao 14%, Ngoni 12%, Tumbuka 9%, Nyanja 6%, Sena 4%, Tonga 2%, Ngonde 1%. **Principal languages:** Chichewa (official), Chinyanja, Chiyao, Chitumbuka, Chisena, Chilomwe, Chitonga. **Chief religions:** Christian 83%, Muslim 13%, none 3%.

Geography: Total area: 45,747 sq mi, 118,484 sq km; **Land area:** 36,324 sq mi, 94,080 sq km. **Location:** In SE Africa. **Neighbors:** Zambia on W, Mozambique on S and E, Tanzania on N. **Topography:** Malawi stretches 560 mi N-S along Lake Malawi (Lake Nyasa), most of which belongs to Malawi. High plateaus and mountains line the Rift Valley the length of the nation. **Capital:** Lilongwe, 771,503.

Government: Type: Republic. **Head of state and gov.:** Pres. Joyce Banda; b. Apr. 12, 1950; in office: Apr. 7, 2012. **Local divisions:** 3 regions, 26 districts. **Defense budget:** NA. **Active troops:** 5,300.

Economy: Industries: tobacco, tea, sugar, sawmill prods., cement, consumer goods. **Chief crops:** tobacco, sugarcane, cotton, tea, corn, potatoes, cassava, sorghum, pulses, groundnuts. **Natural resources:** limestone, hydropower, uranium, coal, bauxite. **Arable land:** 38.2%. **Livestock:** cattle: 1.1 mil; chickens: 16 mil; goats: 3.9 mil; pigs: 1.9 mil; sheep: 214,230. **Fish catch:** 101,462 metric tons. **Electricity prod.:** 1.7 bil kWh. **Labor force:** agric. 90%, industry and services 10%.

Finance: Monetary unit: Kwacha (MWK) (Sept. 2012: 269.70 = $1 U.S.). **GDP:** $14.1 bil; **per capita GDP:** $900; **GDP growth:** 5.5%. **Imports:** $1.7 bil; South Africa 41.1%, India 8.4%, Zambia 8.1%, China 7.6%, Tanzania 4.9%, U.S. 4.4%. **Exports:** $911.5 mil; Canada 12.3%, South Africa 9%, Zimbabwe 8.9%, Germany 8.7%, U.S. 6%, Russia 6%, UK 4.1%, China 4.1%. **Tourism:** $47 mil. **Budget:** $1.8 bil. **Total reserves less gold:** $197.4 mil. **Gold:** 12,800 oz t. **CPI change:** 7.6%.

Transport: Railways: 495 mi. **Motor vehicles:** 2 vehicles per 1,000 pop. **Civil aviation:** 124.3 mil pass.-mi; 7 airports. **Chief ports:** Chilumba, Chipoka, Monkey Bay, Nkhata Bay, Nkhotakota.

Communications: TV sets: 11 per 1,000 pop. **Radios:** 3 per 1,000 pop. **Telephone lines:** 1.1 per 100 pop. **Internet:** 3.3%.

Health: Life expect.: 51.5 male; 53.1 female. **Births:** 40.4 (per 1,000 pop.). **Deaths:** 12.8 (per 1,000 pop.). **Natural inc.:** 2.76% **Infant mortality:** 79.0 (per 1,000 live births). **HIV rate:** 11%.

Education: Compulsory: ages 6-13. **Literacy:** 74.8%.

Major intl. organizations: UN (FAO, IBRD, ILO, IMF, WHO), AU, the Commonwealth, WTO.

Embassy: 1029 Vermont Ave. NW, Ste. 1000, 20005; 721-0270.

Website: www.malawi.gov.mw

Bantus came to the land in the 16th cent., Arab slavers in the 19th. The area became the British protectorate Nyasaland in 1891. It became independent July 6, 1964, and a republic in 1966.

After three decades as a one-party state under Pres. Hastings Kamuzu Banda, Malawi adopted a new constitution and, in multiparty elections held May 17, 1994, chose a new leader, Bakili Muluzi.

Bingu wa Mutharika, candidate of the ruling United Democratic Front, won a disputed presidential election May 20, 2004. In an ongoing power struggle, an effort by his former political allies to impeach him was halted by Malawi's Constitutional Court, Oct. 26, 2005. Mutharika won reelection May 19, 2009. Clashes between police and antigovernment protesters July 2011 left at least 19 people dead. Joyce Banda became Malawi's first female president after the death of Bingu wa Mutharika Apr. 5, 2012.

Malaysia

People: Population: 29,179,952. **Age distrib.:** <15: 29.4%; 65+: 5.1%. **Pop. density:** 230 per sq mi, 88.8 per sq km. **Urban:** 72.8%. **Ethnic groups:** Malay 50%, Chinese 24%, indigenous 11%, Indian 7%. **Principal languages:** Bahasa Malaysia (official), English, Chinese dialects, Tamil, Telugu, Malayalam, Panjabi, Thai. **Chief religions:** Muslim (official) 60%; Buddhist 19%; Christian

9%; Hindu 6%; Confucianism, Taoism, other traditional Chinese religions 3%.

Geography: Total area: 127,355 sq mi, 329,847 sq km; **Land area:** 126,895 sq mi, 328,657 sq km. **Location:** On SE tip of Asia, plus N coast of the island of Borneo. **Neighbors:** Thailand, Brunei on N; Indonesia on S. **Topography:** Most of W Malaysia is covered by tropical jungle, including the central mountain range that runs N-S through the peninsula. W coast is marshy, the E coast, sandy. E Malaysia has a wide, swampy coastal plain, with interior jungles and mountains. **Capital:** Kuala Lumpur (financial), 1,555,910; Putrajaya (admin.). **Cities (urban aggl.):** Klang, 1,189,777; Johore Bahru, 1,045,005.

Government: Type: Constitutional monarchy. **Head of state:** Paramount Ruler Tuanku Abdul Halim Mu'adzam Shah; b. Nov. 28, 1927; in office: Apr. 11, 2012. **Head of gov.:** Prime Min. Najib Razak; b. July 23, 1953; in office: Apr. 3, 2009. **Local divisions:** 13 states, 3 federal territories. **Defense budget:** $4.54 bil. **Active troops:** 109,000.

Economy: Industries: rubber and palm oil proc. and mfg., light mfg., pharmaceuticals, medical tech., electronics, tin mining and smelting, logging, timber proc. **Chief crops:** rubber, palm oil, cocoa, rice, coconuts, pepper. **Natural resources:** tin, petroleum, timber, copper, iron ore, nat. gas, bauxite. **Crude oil reserves:** 4 bil bbls. **Arable land:** 5.5%. **Livestock:** cattle: 909,810; chickens: 225.8 mil; goats: 537,670; pigs: 1.7 mil; sheep: 128,070. **Fish catch:** 2.02 mil metric tons. **Electricity prod.** (2010): 112 bil kWh. **Labor force:** agric. 13%, industry 36%, services 51%.

Finance: Monetary unit: Ringgit (MYR) (Sept. 2012: 3.12 = $1 U.S.). **GDP:** $453 bil; **per capita GDP:** $15,800; **GDP growth:** 5.1%. **Imports:** $177.1 bil; Singapore 20.5%, China 13.7%, Japan 10%, U.S. 7.9%, Thailand 6%, Indonesia 5.6%. **Exports:** $225.6 bil; China 17.9%, Singapore 12.8%, Japan 10.6%, U.S. 8.6%, Thailand 4.4%, Hong Kong 4.1%. **Tourism:** $18.3 bil. **Budget:** $73.8 bil. **Total reserves less gold:** $131.8 bil. **Gold:** 1.2 mil oz t. **CPI change:** 3.2%.

Transport: Railways: 1,149 mi. **Motor vehicles:** 345.3 vehicles per 1,000 pop. **Civil aviation:** 28.3 bil pass.-mi; 39 airports. **Chief ports:** Bintulu, George Town (Penang), Johor Bahru, Port Kelang, Tanjung Pelepas.

Communications: TV sets: 224 per 1,000 pop. **Radios:** 425 per 1,000 pop. **Telephone lines:** 14.7 per 100 pop. **Daily newspaper circ.:** 109.3 per 1,000 pop. **Internet:** 61%.

Health: Life expect.: 71.3 male; 77.0 female. **Births:** 20.7 (per 1,000 pop.). **Deaths:** 5.0 (per 1,000 pop.). **Natural inc.:** 1.58%. **Infant mortality:** 14.6 (per 1,000 live births). **HIV rate:** 0.5%.

Education: Compulsory: ages 6-11. **Literacy:** 93.1%.

Major intl. organizations: UN (FAO, IBRD, ILO, IMF, WHO), APEC, ASEAN, the Commonwealth, WTO.

Embassy: 3516 International Ct. NW 20008; 572-9700.

Website: www.malaysia.gov.my

European traders appeared in the 16th cent.; Britain established control in 1867. Malaysia was created Sept. 16, 1963. It included Malaya (which gained independence in 1957 after the suppression of Communist rebels), plus the formerly British Singapore, Sabah (N Borneo), and Sarawak (NW Borneo). Singapore was separated in 1965, in order to end tensions between Chinese, the majority in Singapore, and Malays in control of the Malaysian government.

A monarch is elected by a council of hereditary rulers of the Malayan states every five years.

Abundant natural resources have bolstered prosperity, and foreign investment has aided industrialization and trade. Work on a federal administrative center at Putrajaya, south of Kuala Lumpur, was completed in 1999; it is linked by rail with Kuala Lumpur's city center and international airport and with Cyberjaya, a hub for high-tech manufacturing and research.

Mahathir bin Mohamad dominated Malaysian politics as prime minister, 1981-2003. His successor, Abdullah Ahmad Badawi, took office Oct. 31, 2003, and led his National Front coalition to a resounding win in parliamentary elections Mar. 21, 2004. The Indian Ocean tsunami of Dec. 26, 2004, left at least 68 people dead in Malaysia. Recession and scandals plagued Malaysia as National Front leader Najib Razak took office as prime min. Apr. 3, 2009. Tuanku Abdul Halim Mu'adzam Shah, Oct. 14, 2011, was chosen to serve as the paramount ruler for a second 5-year term, more than 30 years after his first (1970-75).

Maldives
Republic of Maldives

People: Population: 394,451. **Age distrib.:** <15: 21.2%; 65+: 4.1%. **Pop. density:** 3,428.3 per sq mi, 1,323.7 per sq km. **Urban:** 41.2%. **Ethnic groups:** South Indian, Sinhalese, Arab. **Principal languages:** Dhivehi (official), English spoken by most govt. officials. **Chief religion:** Sunni Muslim (official).

Geography: Total area: 115 sq mi, 298 sq km; **Land area:** 115 sq mi, 298 sq km. **Location:** In Indian O., SW of India. **Neighbors:** Nearest is India on N. **Topography:** 19 atolls with 1,190 islands, 198 inhabited. None of the islands are over 5 sq mi in area, and all are nearly flat. **Capital:** Male, 131,777.

Government: Type: Republic. **Head of state and gov.:** Pres. Mohamed Waheed Hassan Maniku; b. Jan. 3, 1953; in office: Feb. 7, 2012. **Local divisions:** 19 atolls and Male capital atoll. **Defense budget/active troops:** NA.

Economy: Industries: tourism, fish proc., shipping, boat building, coconut proc., garments, woven mats, rope, handicrafts, coral and sand mining. **Chief crops:** coconuts, corn, sweet potatoes. **Natural resources:** fish. **Arable land:** 13.3%. **Fish catch:** 94,953 metric tons. **Electricity prod.:** 300 mil kWh. **Labor force:** agric. 11%, industry 23%, services 65%.

Finance: Monetary unit: Rufiyaa (MVR) (Sept. 2012: 15.30 = $1 U.S.). **GDP:** $2.9 bil; **per capita GDP:** $8,800; **GDP growth:** 7.4%. **Imports** (2009): $967 mil; Singapore 23.1%, UAE 17.9%, India 8.9%, China 7.1%, Malaysia 6.6%, Sri Lanka 5.3%, Thailand 4.9%. **Exports** (2009): $163 mil; France 16.9%, Thailand 16.5%, India 15.2%, UK 9.1%, Sri Lanka 8.9%, Italy 7.3%, Philippines 4.4%, Germany 4.2%. **Tourism:** $714 mil. **Budget** (2010): $758 mil. **Total reserves less gold:** $348.7 mil. **CPI change:** 11.3%.

Transport: Civil aviation: 28 mil pass.-mi; 4 airports. **Chief port:** Male.

Communications: TV sets: 131 per 1,000 pop. **Radios:** 131 per 1,000 pop. **Telephone lines:** 7.5 per 100 pop. **Internet:** 34%.

Health: Life expect.: 72.4 male; 77.1 female. **Births:** 15.1 (per 1,000 pop.). **Deaths:** 3.8 (per 1,000 pop.) **Natural inc.:** 1.14% **Infant mortality:** 26.5 (per 1,000 live births). **HIV rate:** <0.1%.

Education: Compulsory: ages 6-12. **Literacy:** 98.4%.

Major intl. organizations: UN (FAO, IBRD, IMF, WHO), the Commonwealth, WTO.

Embassy: 800 2nd Ave., Ste. 400E, New York, NY 10017; (212) 599-6194.

Website: www.presidencymaldives.gov.mv

A British protectorate since 1887, the nation achieved independence July 26, 1965; long a sultanate, the Maldives became a republic in 1968. Tourism and fishing are the most important sectors of the economy. Rising sea levels threaten the country, which comprises at least 1,200 small, low-lying coral islands.

The Indian Ocean tsunami of Dec. 26, 2004, killed at least 82 people and displaced more than 21,600 in the Maldives. Pres. Maumoon Abdul Gayoom, in office 1978-2008, lost a runoff vote Oct. 29, 2008, to pro-democracy leader and former political prisoner Mohamed (Anni) Nasheed. Following protests over the arrest of a judge, Nasheed resigned Feb. 7, 2012, and Vice Pres. Mohamed Waheed Hassan Maniku took office. Nasheed later claimed a gun was pointed at his head while he resigned, but an international-backed commission ruled, Aug. 29, that he voluntarily resigned.

Mali
Republic of Mali

People: Population: 15,494,466. **Age distrib.:** <15: 47.8%; 65+: 3%. **Pop. density:** 32.9 per sq mi, 12.7 per sq km. **Urban:** 34.9%. **Ethnic groups:** Mande (Bambara, Malinke, Soninke) 50%, Peul 17%, Voltaic 12%, Songhai 6%, Tuareg and Moor 10%. **Principal languages:** French (official), Bambara, numerous African langs. **Chief religions:** Muslim 90%, Christian 1%, indigenous beliefs 9%.

Geography: Total area: 478,841 sq mi, 1,240,192 sq km; **Land area:** 471,118 sq mi, 1,220,190 sq km. **Location:** In interior of W Africa. **Neighbors:** Mauritania, Senegal on W; Guinea, Côte d'Ivoire, Burkina Faso on S; Niger on E; Algeria on N. **Topography:** Landlocked grassy plain in upper basins of the Senegal and Niger rivers, extending N into the Sahara. **Capital:** Bamako, 2,036,520.

Government: Type: Republic. **Head of state:** Pres. Dioncounda Traoré; b. Feb. 23, 1942; in office: Apr. 12, 2012. **Head of gov.:** Prime Min. Cheick Modibo Diarra; b. 1952; in office: Apr. 17, 2012. **Local divisions:** 8 regions, 1 capital district. **Defense budget** (2010): $204 mil. **Active troops:** 7,350.

Economy: Industries: food proc., constr., phosphate and gold mining. **Chief crops:** cotton, millet, rice, corn, vegetables, peanuts. **Natural resources:** gold, phosphates, kaolin, salt, limestone, uranium, gypsum, granite, hydropower. **Arable land:** 5.2%. **Livestock:** cattle: 9.2 mil; chickens: 36.8 mil; goats: 16.5 mil; pigs: 75,089; sheep: 11.9 mil. **Fish catch:** 102,083 metric tons. **Electricity prod.:** 520 mil kWh. **Labor force:** agric. 80%, industry and services 20%.

Finance: Monetary unit: CFA BCEAO Franc (XOF) (Sept. 2012: 519.73 = $1 U.S.). **GDP:** $18.1 bil; **per capita GDP:** $1,100; **GDP growth:** 2.7%. **Imports:** $2.5 bil; Senegal 15%, France 11.7%, China 8.2%, Côte d'Ivoire 6.3%. **Exports:** $2.3 bil; China 33%, South Korea 15.2%, Indonesia 12.8%, Thailand 6.6%, Bangladesh 5.3%. **Tourism:** $205 mil. **Budget:** $2.6 bil. **Total reserves less gold:** $1.4 bil. **CPI change:** 2.9%.

Transport: Railways: 368 mi. **Motor vehicles:** 1.7 vehicles per 1,000 pop. **Civil aviation:** 8 airports. **Chief port:** Koulikoro.

Communications: TV sets: 49 per 1,000 pop. **Radios:** 132 per 1,000 pop. **Telephone lines:** 0.7 per 100 pop. **Internet:** 2%.

Health: Life expect.: 52.4 male; 56.0 female. **Births:** 46.6 (per 1,000 pop.). **Deaths:** 13.9 (per 1,000 pop.). **Natural inc.:** 3.27% **Infant mortality:** 108.7 (per 1,000 live births). **HIV rate:** 1%.
Education: Compulsory: ages 7-15. **Literacy:** 31.1%.
Major intl. organizations: UN and most of its specialized agencies, AU, WTO.
Embassy: 2130 R St. NW 20008; 332-2249.
Website: www.primature.gov.ml

Until the 15th cent. the area was part of the great Mali Empire. Timbuktu (Tombouctou) was a center of Islamic study. French rule was secured, 1898. The Sudanese Rep. and Senegal became independent as the Mali Federation June 20, 1960, but Senegal withdrew, and the Sudanese Rep. was renamed Mali.

A socialist regime led, 1960-68, by Pres. Modibo Keita, was toppled by a coup. Famine struck in 1973-74, killing as many as 100,000 people. Drought conditions returned in the 1980s.

The military, Mar. 26, 1991, overthrew the government of Pres. Moussa Traoré, who had ruled since 1968. Oumar Konare, a coup leader, was elected president, Apr. 26, 1992. The government and a Tuareg rebel group signed a peace accord June 1994. Twice condemned to death for crimes committed in office, Traoré had his sentences commuted to life imprisonment Dec. 1997 and Sept. 1999; he was pardoned May 2002.

Amadou Toumani Touré, who led the 1991 coup, was elected president May 12, 2002, and reelected Apr. 29, 2007. Mali's first female prime minister, Cissé Mariam Kaïdama Sidibé, took office Apr. 3, 2011. Amadou Sanogo, an army captain, staged a coup Mar. 22, 2012, and brokered a deal to transfer power Apr. 12, 2012, to an interim government led by Pres. Dioncounda Traoré and Prime Min. Cheick Modibo Diarra. The coup enabled Islamic rebels to seize control of the country's north.

Malta
Republic of Malta

People: Population: 409,836. **Age distrib.:** <15: 15.4%; 65+: 16.5%. **Pop. density:** 3,359.1 per sq mi, 1,296.9 per sq km. **Urban:** 94.8%. **Ethnic groups:** Maltese (descendants of ancient Carthaginians and Phoenicians with strong Italian, other Mediterranean elements). **Principal languages:** Maltese, English (both official). **Chief religion:** Roman Catholic (official) 98%.
Geography: Total area: 122 sq mi, 316 sq km; **Land area:** 122 sq mi, 316 sq km. **Location:** In center of Mediterranean Sea. **Neighbors:** Nearest is Italy on N. **Topography:** Isl. of Malta is 95 sq mi; other islands in the group: Gozo, 26 sq mi; Comino, 1 sq mi. Coastline is heavily indented. Low hills cover the interior. **Capital:** Valletta, 198,256.
Government: Type: Parliamentary democracy. **Head of state:** Pres. George Abela; b. Apr. 22, 1948; in office: Apr. 4, 2009. **Head of gov.:** Prime Min. Lawrence Gonzi; b. July 1, 1953; in office: Mar. 23, 2004. **Local divisions:** 3 regions comprising 67 local councils. **Defense budget:** $60 mil. **Active troops:** 1,954.
Economy: Industries: tourism, electronics, shipbuilding and repair, constr., food and beverages, pharmaceuticals, footwear, clothing, tobacco, aviation services. **Chief crops:** potatoes, cauliflower, grapes, wheat, barley, tomatoes, citrus, cut flowers, green peppers. **Natural resources:** limestone, salt. **Arable land:** 25.0%. **Livestock:** cattle: 14,954; chickens: 1.2 mil; goats: 5,110; pigs: 70,583; sheep: 12,379. **Fish catch:** 4,752 metric tons. **Electricity prod.:** 2 bil kWh. **Labor force:** agric. 1.5%, industry 24.7%, services 73.9%.
Finance: Monetary unit: Euro (EUR) (Sept. 2012: 0.79 = $1 U.S.). **GDP:** $10.9 bil; **per capita GDP:** $25,800; **GDP growth:** 2.1%. **Imports:** $7.3 bil; Italy 31.8%, France 8.6%, UK 8%, Germany 6.9%. **Exports:** $5.2 bil; Germany 14.8%, France 9.3%, Italy 6.9%, UK 6.9%. **Tourism:** $1.3 bil. **Budget:** $3.4 bil. **Total reserves less gold:** $499.8 mil. **Gold:** 10,000 oz t. **CPI change:** 2.7%.
Transport: Motor vehicles: 681.3 vehicles per 1,000 pop. **Civil aviation:** 2 bil pass.-mi; 1 airport. **Chief ports:** Marsaxlokk (Malta Freeport), Valletta.
Communications: TV sets: 554 per 1,000 pop. **Radios:** 664 per 1,000 pop. **Telephone lines:** 54.9 per 100 pop. **Internet:** 69.2%.
Health: Life expect.: 77.6 male; 82.3 female. **Births:** 10.3 (per 1,000 pop.). **Deaths:** 8.7 (per 1,000 pop.). **Natural inc.:** 0.16% **Infant mortality:** 3.7 (per 1,000 live births). **HIV rate:** 0.1%.
Education: Compulsory: ages 5-15. **Literacy:** 92.4%.
Major intl. organizations: UN (FAO, IBRD, ILO, IMF, WHO), the Commonwealth, EU, OSCE, WTO.
Embassy: 2017 Connecticut Ave. NW 20008; 462-3611.
Website: www.gov.mt

Malta was ruled by Phoenicians, Romans, Arabs, Normans, the Knights of Malta, France, and Britain (since 1814). It became independent Sept. 21, 1964. Malta became a republic in 1974. The withdrawal of the last British sailors, Apr. 1, 1979, ended 179 years of British military presence on the island.

From 1971 to 1987 and again from 1996 to 1998, Malta was governed by the socialist Labour Party; the Nationalist Party, which pressed for Malta's entry into the EU, held office 1987-96 and won parliamentary elections in 1998, 2003, and 2008. Malta became a full member of the EU May 1, 2004.

Marshall Islands
Republic of the Marshall Islands

People: Population: 68,480. **Age distrib.:** <15: 37.8%; 65+: 3.1%. **Pop. density:** 979.9 per sq mi, 378.3 per sq km. **Urban:** 71.8%. **Ethnic groups:** Marshallese 92%, mixed Marshallese 6%. **Principal languages:** Marshallese, English (both official). **Chief religions:** Protestant 55%, Assembly of God 26%, Roman Catholic 8%, Bukot nan Jesus 3%, Mormon 2%, other Christian 4%, none 2%.
Geography: Total area: 70 sq mi, 181 sq km; **Land area:** 70 sq mi, 181 sq km. **Location:** In N Pacific Ocean; composed of two 800-mi-long parallel chains of coral atolls. **Neighbors:** Nearest are Micronesia to W, Nauru and Kiribati to S. **Topography:** Marshall Islands are low coral limestone and sand islands. **Capital:** Majuro, 31,018.
Government: Type: Republic in free association with the U.S. **Head of state and gov.:** Pres. Christopher J. Loeak; b. Nov. 11, 1952; in office: Jan. 17, 2012. **Local divisions:** 33 municipalities. **Defense budget:** NA. **Active troops:** No regular military forces. Defense is responsibility of U.S.
Economy: Industries: copra, tuna proc., tourism, craft items. **Chief crops:** coconuts, tomatoes, melons, taro, breadfruit, fruits. **Natural resources:** coconut prods., marine prods., deep-seabed minerals. **Arable land:** 11.1%. **Fish catch:** 59,730 metric tons. **Labor force:** agric. 21.4%, industry 20.9%, services 57.7%.
Finance: Monetary unit: U.S. Dollar (USD). **GDP (2008 est.):** $133.5 mil; **per capita GDP (2008 est.):** $2,500; **GDP growth (2008):** –0.3%. **Imports (2008):** $79.4 mil. **Exports (2008):** $19.4 mil. **Tourism:** $3 mil. **Budget:** NA.
Transport: Civil aviation: 0.6 mil pass.-mi; 4 airports. **Chief port:** Majuro.
Communications: Telephone lines (2010): 8.1 per 100 pop. **Internet (2009):** 3.6%.
Health: Life expect.: 69.9 male; 74.3 female. **Births:** 28.1 (per 1,000 pop.). **Deaths:** 4.3 (per 1,000 pop.). **Natural inc.:** 2.38% **Infant mortality:** 22.9 (per 1,000 live births). **HIV rate:** NA.
Education: Compulsory: ages 6-13. **Literacy:** NA.
Major intl. organizations: UN (FAO, IBRD, IMF, WHO).
Embassy: 2433 Massachusetts Ave. NW 20008; 234-5414.
Website: www.rmigovernment.org

The Marshall Islands were a German possession until WWI and were administered by Japan between the World Wars. After WWII, they were administered by the U.S. as part of the UN Trust Territory of the Pacific Islands. During 1946-58, Bikini and Enewetak atolls were used as test sites for U.S. nuclear weapons, including the hydrogen bomb.

The Compact of Free Association, ratified by the U.S. on Oct. 21, 1986, gave the islands their independence. In the compact, the U.S. agreed to provide financial aid to the islands, maintain their defense, and compensate victims of nuclear testing; it was renewed Dec. 2003. The Marshall Islands joined the UN Sept. 17, 1991. Amata Kabua, the islands' first and only president since 1979, died Dec. 19, 1996. His cousin Imata Kabua, elected president Jan. 13, 1997, was succeeded by Kessai Note on Jan. 10, 2000; Litokwa Tomeing, Jan. 14, 2008; Jurelang Zedkaia, Nov. 2, 2009; and Christopher J. Loeak, Jan. 17, 2012.

Mauritania
Islamic Republic of Mauritania

People: Population: 3,359,185. **Age distrib.:** <15: 40.1%; 65+: 3.5%. **Pop. density:** 8.4 per sq mi, 3.3 per sq km. **Urban:** 41.5%. **Ethnic groups:** mixed Moor/black 40%, Moor 30%, black 30%. **Principal languages:** Arabic (official and national); Pulaar, Soninke, Wolof (all national); French; Hassaniya. **Chief religion:** Muslim (official) 100%.
Geography: Total area: 397,955 sq mi, 1,030,700 sq km; **Land area:** 397,955 sq mi, 1,030,700 sq km. **Location:** In NW Africa. **Neighbors:** Western Sahara on N; Algeria, Mali on E; Senegal on S. **Topography:** Fertile Senegal R. valley in the S gives way to a wide central region of sandy plains and scrub trees. N is arid and extends into the Sahara. **Capital:** Nouakchott, 786,226.
Government: Type: Republic. **Head of state:** Pres. Mohamed Ould Abdel Aziz; b. Dec. 20, 1956; in office: Aug. 5. 2009. **Head of gov.:** Prime Min. Moulaye Ould Mohamed Laghdaf; b. 1957; in office: Aug. 14, 2008. **Local divisions:** 12 regions, 1 capital district. **Defense budget:** NA. **Active troops:** 15,870.
Economy: Industries: fish proc.; oil prod.; iron ore, gold, copper mining. **Chief crops:** dates, millet, sorghum, rice, corn. **Natural resources:** iron ore, gypsum, copper, phosphate, diamonds, gold, oil, fish. **Crude oil reserves:** 20 mil bbls. **Arable land:** 0.4%. **Livestock:** cattle: 1.7 mil; chickens: 4.3 mil; goats: 5.5 mil; sheep: 8.9 mil. **Fish catch:** 276,238 metric tons. **Electricity prod.:** 474 mil kWh. **Labor force:** agric. 50%, industry 10%, services 40%.

Finance: Monetary unit: Ouguiya (MRO) (Sept. 2012: 299.20 = $1 U.S.). **GDP:** $7.2 bil; **per capita GDP:** $2,200; **GDP growth:** 3.6%. **Imports:** $2.9 bil; China 12.6%, Netherlands 9.1%, France 8.8%, U.S. 7.9%, Spain 5.9%, Germany 5.5%, Brazil 5.2%, Belgium 4.4%. **Exports:** $2.8 bil; China 46.6%, Italy 8.8%, France 8.1%, Côte d'Ivoire 5.1%, Spain 4.6%, Japan 4.5%, Belgium 4.3%, Netherlands 4%. **Tourism:** NA. **Budget:** $1.4 bil. **Total reserves less gold:** $484.7 mil. **Gold:** 11,500 oz t. **CPI change:** 5.7%.

Transport: Railways: 452 mi. **Motor vehicles:** 7.2 vehicles per 1,000 pop. **Civil aviation:** 39.8 mil pass.-mi; 10 airports. **Chief ports:** Nouadhibou, Nouakchott.

Communications: TV sets: 46 per 1,000 pop. **Radios:** 384 per 1,000 pop. **Telephone lines:** 2 per 100 pop. **Internet:** 4.5%.

Health: Life expect.: 59.3 male; 63.8 female. **Births:** 32.8 (per 1,000 pop.). **Deaths:** 8.7 (per 1,000 pop.). **Natural inc.:** 2.41% **Infant mortality:** 58.9 (per 1,000 live births). **HIV rate:** 0.7%.

Education: Compulsory: ages 6-14. **Literacy:** 58%.

Major intl. organizations: UN (FAO, IBRD, ILO, IMF, WHO), AL, AU, WTO.

Embassy: 2129 Leroy Pl. NW 20008; 232-5700.

Website: www.mauritania.mr

A French protectorate from 1903, Mauritania became independent Nov. 28, 1960. It annexed the south of former Spanish Sahara (now Western Sahara) in 1976 but renounced its claim to the region after signing a peace treaty with the Saharan guerrillas of the Polisario Front, 1979.

Maaouiya Ould Sid Ahmed Taya took power in a military coup in 1984. Taya, a U.S. ally, was toppled in a bloodless coup, Aug. 3, 2005. During Jan.-June 2006, up to 10,000 people tried to emigrate in handmade boats from Mauritania to Spain's Canary Islands; more than 1,700 died. Civilian rule was restored, 2006-07, but a military coup, Aug. 6, 2008, toppled the elected government. The coup leader, Gen. Mohamed Ould Abdel Aziz, won a disputed presidential election July 18, 2009. Security concerns, including a rising threat from al-Qaeda in the Islamic Maghreb, led the U.S. Peace Corps to pull its volunteers out of Mauritania in Aug. 2009.

Major oil finds have recently been developed. Although slavery has been repeatedly abolished, most recently in 1981, thousands of Mauritanians continued to live under conditions of servitude; legislation mandating prison terms for slaveholders was enacted Aug. 8, 2007. Parliamentary elections scheduled for Mar. 31, 2012 were called off due to conflicts between Pres. Aziz and opposition parties.

Mauritius
Republic of Mauritius

People: Population: 1,313,095. **Age distrib.:** <15: 21.6%; 65+: 7.7%. **Pop. density:** 1,675.3 per sq mi, 646.8 per sq km. **Urban:** 41.8%. **Ethnic groups:** Indo-Mauritian 68%, Creole 27%, Sino-Mauritian 3%, Franco-Mauritian 2%. **Principal languages:** Creole, Bhojpuri, French, English (official). **Chief religions:** Hindu 48%, Roman Catholic 24%, Muslim 17%, other Christian 9%.

Geography: Total area: 788 sq mi, 2,040 sq km; **Land area:** 784 sq mi, 2,030 sq km. **Location:** In Indian O., 500 mi E of Madagascar. **Neighbors:** Nearest is Madagascar to W. **Topography:** A volcanic island nearly surrounded by coral reefs. A central plateau is encircled by mountain peaks. **Capital:** Port Louis, 150,697.

Government: Type: Republic. **Head of state:** Pres. Rajkeswur Kailash Purryag; b. Dec. 12, 1947; in office: July 21, 2012. **Head of gov.:** Prime Min. Navinchandra Ramgoolam; b. July 14, 1947; in office: July 5, 2005. **Local divisions:** 9 districts, 3 dependencies. **Defense budget:** $10 mil. **Active troops:** No regular military forces. 2,000 paramilitary only.

Economy: Industries: food proc. (largely sugar milling), textiles, clothing, mining, chemicals, metal prods. **Chief crops:** sugarcane, tea, corn, potatoes, bananas, pulses. **Natural resources:** fish. **Arable land:** 42.9%. **Livestock:** cattle: 7,491; chickens: 13.7 mil; goats: 27,819; pigs: 22,327; sheep: 20,200. **Fish catch:** 8,354 metric tons. **Electricity prod.:** 2.9 bil kWh. **Labor force:** agric. and fishing 9%; constr. and industry 30%; transp. and communication 7%; trade, restaurants, hotels 22%; finance 6%; other services 25%.

Finance: Monetary unit: Rupee (MUR) (Sept. 2012: 30.70 = $1 U.S.). **GDP:** $19.5 bil; **per capita GDP:** $15,100; **GDP growth:** 4.1%. **Imports:** $5.2 bil; India 25.6%, China 11.5%, France 9.4%, South Africa 7.3%, Singapore 5.9%. **Exports:** $2.6 bil; UK 19.7%, France 17.1%, U.S. 11.5%, Italy 8.8%, South Africa 7.3%, Spain 6.8%, Madagascar 6.5%. **Tourism:** $1.5 bil. **Budget:** $2.8 bil. **Total reserves less gold:** $2.6 bil. **Gold:** 125,780 oz t. **CPI change:** 6.5%.

Transport: Motor vehicles: 160.8 vehicles per 1,000 pop. **Civil aviation:** 3.5 bil pass.-mi; 2 airports. **Chief port:** Port Louis.

Communications: TV sets: 370 per 1,000 pop. **Radios:** 78 per 1,000 pop. **Telephone lines:** 28.7 per 100 pop. **Daily newspaper circ.:** 77.2 per 1,000 pop. **Internet:** 35%.

Health: Life expect.: 71.3 male; 78.4 female. **Births:** 13.8 (per 1,000 pop.). **Deaths:** 6.7 (per 1,000 pop.). **Natural inc.:** 0.71% **Infant mortality:** 11.2 (per 1,000 live births). **HIV rate:** 1%.

Education: Compulsory: ages 5-16. **Literacy:** 88.5%.

Major intl. organizations: UN and all of its specialized agencies, AU, the Commonwealth, WTO.

Embassy: 4301 Connecticut Ave. NW, Ste. 441, 20008; 244-1491.

Website: www.gov.mu

Mauritius was uninhabited when settled in 1638 by the Dutch, who introduced sugarcane. France took over in 1721, bringing African slaves. Britain ruled from 1810 to Mar. 12, 1968, bringing Indian workers for the sugar plantations.

Mauritius formally severed its association with the British crown Mar. 12, 1992. Since 2006, Mauritius has topped the Ibrahim Index of African Governance as the best governed African country.

Mexico
United Mexican States

People: Population: 114,975,406. **Age distrib.:** <15: 27.8%; 65+: 6.7%. **Pop. density:** 153.2 per sq mi, 59.1 per sq km. **Urban:** 78.1%. **Ethnic groups:** mestizo (Amerindian-Spanish) 60%, Amerindian or predominantly Amerindian 30%, white 9%. **Principal languages:** Spanish, indigenous langs. (incl. various Mayan, Nahuatl, and others). **Chief religions:** Roman Catholic 77%, Protestant 5%, none 3%.

Geography: Total area: 758,449 sq mi, 1,964,375 sq km; **Land area:** 750,561 sq mi, 1,943,945 sq km. **Location:** In southern N. America. **Neighbors:** U.S. on N, Guatemala and Belize on S. **Topography:** The Sierra Madre Occidental Mts. run NW-SE near the west coast; the Sierra Madre Oriental Mts. run near Gulf of Mexico. They join S of Mexico City. Between the 2 ranges lies the dry central plateau, 5,000 to 8,000 ft alt., rising toward the S, with temperate vegetation. Coastal lowlands are tropical. About 45% of land is arid. **Capital:** Mexico City, 20,445,800. **Cities (urban aggl.):** Guadalajara, 4,524,669; Monterrey, 4,213,328; Puebla, 2,334,514; Tijuana, 1,819,831; Toluca de Lerdo, 1,747,849; León de los Aldamas, 1,652,641; Ciudad Juárez, 1,337,558; Torreón, 1,241,961; Querétaro, 1,143,102; San Luis Potosí, 1,061,040; Mérida, 1,040,229.

Government: Type: Federal republic. **Head of state and gov.:** Pres. Felipe de Jesús Calderón Hinojosa; b. Aug. 18, 1962; in office: Dec. 1, 2006. **Local divisions:** 31 states, 1 federal district. **Defense budget:** $5.15 bil. **Active troops:** 280,250.

Economy: Industries: food and beverages, tobacco, chemicals, iron and steel, petroleum, mining, textiles, clothing, motor vehicles, consumer durables, tourism. **Chief crops:** corn, wheat, soybeans, rice, beans, cotton, coffee, fruits, tomatoes. **Natural resources:** petroleum, silver, copper, gold, lead, zinc, nat. gas, timber. **Crude oil reserves:** 10.2 bil bbls. **Arable land:** 12.9%. **Livestock:** cattle: 32.6 mil; chickens: 506.3 mil; goats: 9 mil; pigs: 15.4 mil; sheep: 8.1 mil. **Fish catch:** 1.7 mil metric tons. **Electricity prod.:** (2010): 254.4 bil kWh. **Labor force:** agric. 13.7%, industry 23.4%, services 62.9%.

Finance: Monetary unit: Peso (MXN) (Sept. 2012: 13.11 = $1 U.S.). **GDP:** $1.7 tril; **per capita GDP:** $14,800; **GDP growth:** 4%. **Imports:** $350.8 bil; U.S. 62.2%, China 7.5%. **Exports:** $349.7 bil; U.S. 71.7%, Canada 7.4%. **Tourism:** $11.7 bil. **Budget:** $292.2 bil. **Total reserves less gold:** $144 bil. **Gold:** 3.4 mil oz t. **CPI change:** 3.4%.

Transport: Railways: 10,666 mi. **Motor vehicles:** 267.1 vehicles per 1,000 pop. **Civil aviation:** 17.4 bil pass.-mi; 249 airports. **Chief ports:** Altamira, Coatzacoalcos, Lazaro Cardenas, Manzanillo, Salina Cruz, Veracruz.

Communications: TV sets: 274 per 1,000 pop. **Radios:** 324 per 1,000 pop. **Telephone lines:** 17.2 per 100 pop. **Internet:** 36.2%.

Health: Life expect.: 73.8 male; 79.6 female. **Births:** 18.9 (per 1,000 pop.). **Deaths:** 4.9 (per 1,000 pop.). **Natural inc.:** 1.40% **Infant mortality:** 16.8 (per 1,000 live births). **HIV rate:** 0.3%.

Education: Compulsory: ages 4-14. **Literacy:** 93.1%.

Major intl. organizations: UN (FAO, IBRD, ILO, IMF, WHO), APEC, NAFTA, OAS, OECD, WTO.

Embassy: 1911 Pennsylvania Ave. NW 20006; 728-1600.

Website: www.presidencia.gob.mx

Mexico was the site of advanced civilizations. The Mayans, an agricultural people, moved up from Yucatan, built huge stone pyramids, and invented a calendar. The Toltecs were overcome by the Aztecs, who founded Tenochtitlan 1325 CE, now Mexico City. Hernán Cortés, Spanish conquistador, destroyed the Aztec empire, 1519-21. After 3 centuries of Spanish rule the people revolted, under Fr. Miguel Hidalgo y Costilla, 1810, Fr. Morelos y Pavón, 1812, and Gen. Agustín Iturbide, who made himself emperor as Agustín I, 1822. A republic was declared in 1823.

Mexican territory extended into the present American Southwest and California. Texas established a republic in 1836, and Mexico lost lands north of the Rio Grande during the U.S.-Mexican War, 1846-48.

The French supported an Austrian archduke on the throne of Mexico as Maximilian I, 1864-67. He was deposed in an uprising led by Benito Juárez. Dictatorial rule by Porfirio Díaz, president 1877-80, 1884-1911, led to a period of rebellion and factional fighting. A new constitution, Feb. 5, 1917, brought reform.

The Institutional Revolutionary Party (PRI) dominated politics from 1929 until the late 1990s. Radical opposition, including some guerrilla activity, was contained by strong measures. Some gains in agriculture, industry, and social services were achieved, but much of the work force remained jobless or underemployed. Although prospects brightened with the discovery of vast oil reserves, inflation and a drop in world oil prices aggravated Mexico's economic problems in the 1980s. Mexico reached agreement with the U.S. and Canada on the North American Free Trade Agreement (NAFTA) Aug. 12, 1992; it took effect Jan. 1, 1994.

Guerrillas of the Zapatista National Liberation Army (EZLN) launched an uprising, Jan. 1, 1994, in southern Mexico. A tentative peace accord was reached Mar. 2. The presidential candidate of the governing PRI, Luis Donaldo Colosio Murrieta, was assassinated at a political rally in Tijuana, Mar. 23. The new PRI candidate, Ernesto Zedillo Ponce de León, won election Aug. 21 and was inaugurated Dec. 1, 1994.

An austerity plan and pledges of aid from the U.S. saved Mexico's currency from collapse in early 1995. Popular Revolutionary Army guerrillas launched coordinated attacks on government targets in Aug. 1996. In elections July 6, 1997, the PRI failed to win a congressional majority for the first time since 1929.

In the July 2, 2000, presidential election, the PRI lost for the first time in over 7 decades; the winner, Vicente Fox Quesada of the National Action Party (PAN), took office Dec. 1, 2000.

Results of the July 2, 2006, presidential vote gave the PAN candidate, conservative Felipe Calderón Hinojosa, a slim margin over former Mexico City mayor Andrés Manuel López Obrador, nominee of the leftist Democratic Revolutionary Party. Claiming vote fraud, López Obrador and his supporters held massive protests, but Calderón was declared the winner and took office Dec. 1, 2006. Despite a government crackdown on drug cartels, drug-related violence intensified, including an arson attack on a Monterrey casino Aug. 25, 2011, that killed 52 people, mostly women; the cumulative death toll in the drug war exceeded 47,500, Dec. 2006-Sept. 2012. Enrique Pena Nieto (PRI) won July 1, 2012, presidential elections. His opponent, Andrés Manuel López Obrador, challenged the results, but the Federal Electoral Tribunal dismissed Obrador's case. Nieto was expected to take office in Dec. 2012.

Micronesia
Federated States of Micronesia

People: Population: 106,487. **Age distrib.:** <15: 33%; 65+: 3.1%. **Pop. density:** 392.9 per sq mi, 151.7 per sq km. **Urban:** 22.6%. **Ethnic groups:** Chuukese 49%, Pohnpeian 24%, Kosraean 6%, Yapese 5%, Yap outer islands 5%, Asian 2%, Polynesian 2%. **Principal languages:** English (official & common), Chuukese, Kosrean, Pohnpeian, Yapese, Ulithian, Woleaian, Nukuoro, Kapingamarangi. **Chief religions:** Roman Catholic 53%, Protestant 42%.

Geography: Total area: 271 sq mi, 702 sq km; **Land area:** 271 sq mi, 702 sq km. **Location:** Consists of 607 islands in W Pacific Ocean. **Topography:** Includes both high mountainous islands and low coral atolls; volcanic outcroppings on Pohnpei, Kosrae, and Truk. Climate is tropical. **Capital:** Palikir, 6,696.

Government: Type: Republic in free association with U.S. **Head of state and gov.:** Pres. Emanuel (Manny) Mori; b. Dec. 25, 1948; in office: May 11, 2007. **Local divisions:** 4 states. **Defense budget:** NA. **Active troops:** No regular military forces. Defense is responsibility of U.S.

Economy: Industries: tourism, constr., fish proc., specialized aquaculture, craft items. **Chief crops:** black pepper, tropical fruits and vegetables, coconuts, bananas, cassava, kava, citrus, betel nuts, sweet potatoes. **Natural resources:** timber, marine prods., deep-seabed minerals, phosphate. **Arable land:** 2.9%. **Livestock:** cattle: 14,000; chickens: 190,000; goats: 4,100; pigs: 33,000. **Fish catch:** 31,021 metric tons. **Labor force:** agric. 0.9%, industry 34.4%, services 64.7% (two-thirds govt. employees).

Finance: Monetary unit: U.S. dollar (USD). **GDP** (2008 est.): $238.1 mil (supplemented by grant aid, averaging perhaps $100 mil annually); **per capita GDP** (2008 est.): $2,200; **GDP growth** (2005): 0.3%. **Imports** (2004): $132.7 mil. **Exports** (2004): $14 mil. **Tourism:** $25 mil. **Budget** (FY07 est.): $152.7 mil. **Total reserves less gold:** $75.1 mil. **CPI change:** NA.

Transport: Civil aviation: 6 airports. **Chief port:** Colonia.

Communications: TV sets: 27 per 1,000 pop. **Radios:** 47 per 1,000 pop. **Telephone lines** (2010): 7.6 per 100 pop. **Internet** (2010): 20%.

Health: Life expect.: 69.8 male; 73.9 female. **Births:** 21.9 (per 1,000 pop.). **Deaths:** 4.3 (per 1,000 pop.). **Natural inc.:** 1.75%. **Infant mortality:** 23.5 (per 1,000 live births). **HIV rate:** NA.

Education: Compulsory: ages 6-13. **Literacy:** NA.

Major intl. organizations: UN (FAO, IBRD, IMF, WHO).

Embassy: 1725 N St. NW 20036; 223-4383.

Website: micronesia.fm

The Federated States of Micronesia, formerly known as the Caroline Islands, was ruled successively by Spain, Germany, Japan, and the U.S. The nation gained independence under a compact of free association with the U.S., Nov. 1986, and was admitted to the UN, Sept. 17, 1991. Micronesian officials have repeatedly warned of the dangers to their country of rising sea levels linked to global climate change.

Moldova
Republic of Moldova

People: Population: 3,656,843. **Age distrib.:** <15: 17.5%; 65+: 10.6%. **Pop. density:** 288 per sq mi, 111.2 per sq km. **Urban:** 47.7%. **Ethnic groups:** Moldovan/Romanian 78%, Ukrainian 8%, Russian 6%, Gagauz 4%, Bulgarian 2%. **Principal languages:** Moldovan (official; virtually same as Romanian), Russian, Gagauz. **Chief religions:** Eastern Orthodox 98%, Jewish 1.5%.

Geography: Total area: 13,070 sq mi, 33,851 sq km; **Land area:** 12,699 sq mi, 32,891 sq km. **Location:** In E Europe. **Neighbors:** Romania on W; Ukraine on N, E, and S. **Topography:** Country is landlocked; mainly hilly plains, with steppelands in S near Black Sea. **Capital:** Chişinău, 676,787.

Government: Type: Republic. **Head of state:** Pres. Nicolae Timofti; b. Dec. 22, 1948; in office: Mar. 23, 2012 (acting). **Head of gov.:** Prime Min. Vladimir Filat; b. May 6, 1969; in office: Sept. 25, 2009. **Local divisions:** 9 counties, 1 municipality, 1 autonomous territory. **Defense budget:** $38 mil. **Active troops:** 5,354.

Economy: Industries: sugar, vegetable oil, food proc., agric. machinery, foundry equip, refrigerators and freezers. **Chief crops:** vegetables, fruits, grapes, grain, sugar beets, sunflower seeds, tobacco. **Natural resources:** lignite, phosphorites, gypsum, limestone. **Arable land:** 55.2%. **Livestock:** cattle: 221,622; chickens: 22.3 mil; goats: 111,155; pigs: 337,142; sheep: 803,747. **Fish catch:** 10,003 metric tons. **Electricity prod.:** 3.4 bil kWh. **Labor force:** agric. 27.5%, industry 12.7%, services 59.8%.

Finance: Monetary unit: Leu (MDL) (Sept. 2012: 12.42 = $1 U.S.). **GDP:** $12.2 bil; **per capita GDP:** $3,400; **GDP growth:** 6.4%. **Imports:** $5.1 bil; Italy 6.7%, Ukraine 12.3%, Romania 11.1%, China 7.7%, Germany 7.7%, Turkey 7.1%. **Exports:** $2.3 bil; Italy 9.7%, Ukraine 6.9%, Germany 5%, UK 4.6%. **Tourism:** $194 mil. **Budget:** $2.7 bil. **Total reserves less gold:** $1.96 bil. **Gold:** 227 oz t. **CPI change:** 7.6%.

Transport: Railways: 739 mi. **Civil aviation:** 330.6 mil pass.-mi; 5 airports.

Communications: TV sets: 310 per 1,000 pop. **Radios:** 39 per 1,000 pop. **Telephone lines:** 33.3 per 100 pop. **Internet:** 38%.

Health: Life expect.: 65.6 male; 73.6 female. **Births:** 12.5 (per 1,000 pop.). **Deaths:** 12.6 (per 1,000 pop.). **Natural inc.:** −0.01% **Infant mortality:** 13.7 (per 1,000 live births). **HIV rate:** 0.4%.

Education: Compulsory: ages 7-15. **Literacy:** 98.5%.

Major intl. organizations: UN (FAO, IBRD, ILO, IMF, WHO), CIS, OSCE, WTO.

Embassy: 2101 S St. NW 20008; 667-1130.

Website: www.moldova.md

In 1918, Romania annexed all of Bessarabia that Russia had acquired from Turkey in 1812 by the Treaty of Bucharest. In 1924, the Soviet Union established the Moldavian Autonomous Soviet Socialist Republic on the eastern bank of the Dniester. It was merged with the Romanian-speaking districts of Bessarabia in 1940 to form the Moldavian SSR.

During WWII, Romania, allied with Germany, occupied the area. It was recaptured by the USSR in 1944. Moldova declared independence Aug. 27, 1991. It became an independent state when the USSR disbanded Dec. 26, 1991.

Fighting erupted Mar. 1992 in the Trans-Dniester region between Moldovan security forces and Slavic separatists—ethnic Russians and ethnic Ukrainians—who feared Moldova would merge with neighboring Romania. In a plebiscite on Mar. 6, 1994, voters in Moldova supported independence, without unification with Romania.

Defying the Moldovan government, voters in the breakaway Trans-Dniester region held legislative elections and approved a separatist constitution Dec. 24, 1995. A peace accord with Trans-Dniester separatists was signed in Moscow May 8, 1997. In a referendum Sept. 17, 2006, Trans-Dniester voters overwhelmingly supported independence from Moldova and eventual union with Russia. The Communists gained legislative majorities in 2001 and 2005 but were outpolled by a fragile coalition of pro-Western parties in 2009 and 2010. When a deadlocked parliament failed to agree on a president, a constitutional referendum providing for direct presidential elections was held Sept. 5, 2010. Although 88% of voters supported it, the measure failed to pass because of insufficient turnout. The pro-Western Nicolae Timofti became president Mar. 23, 2012.

Monaco
Principality of Monaco

People: Population: 30,510. **Age distrib.:** <15: 12.1%; 65+: 27.8%. **Pop. density:** 39,510.3 per sq mi, 15,255 per sq km. **Urban:** 100%. **Ethnic groups:** French 47%, Monegasque 16%, Italian 16%. **Principal languages:** French (official), English, Italian, Monegasque. **Chief religion:** Roman Catholic (official) 90%.

Geography: Total area: 0.77 sq mi, 2 sq km; **Land area:** 0.77 sq mi, 2 sq km. **Location:** On NW Mediterranean coast. **Neighbors:** France to W, N, E. **Topography:** Monaco-Ville sits atop a high promontory, the rest of the principality rises from the port up the hillside. **Capital:** Monaco, 35,427.

Government: Type: Constitutional monarchy. **Head of state:** Prince Albert II; b. Mar. 14, 1958; in office: Apr. 6, 2005. **Head of gov.:** Min. of State Michel Roger; b. Mar. 9, 1949; in office: Mar. 29, 2010. **Local divisions:** 4 quarters. **Defense budget:** NA. **Active troops:** No regular military forces. Defense is responsibility of France.

Economy: Industries: tourism, constr., small-scale industrial and consumer prods. **Chief crops:** none. **Natural resources:** none. **Arable land:** None. **Fish catch:** 1 metric ton. **Labor force:** NA.

Finance: Monetary unit: Euro (EUR) (Sept. 2012: 0.79 = $1 U.S.). **GDP** (2010 est.): $5.5 bil; **per capita GDP** (2009 est.): $63,400; **GDP growth** (2010): 2.5%. **Imports** (2010): $882.6 mil. **Exports** (2010): $711 mil. (Full customs integration with France. Also participates in EU market system through customs union with France). **Tourism:** NA. **Budget** (2010): $1.1 bil.

Transport: Civil aviation: 1.9 mil pass.-mi; 1 heliport. **Chief port:** Monaco.

Communications: TV sets: 758 per 1,000 pop. **Telephone lines:** 96.4 per 100 pop. **Internet** (2010): 75%.

Health: Life expect.: 85.7 male; 93.8 female. **Births:** 6.9 (per 1,000 pop.). **Deaths:** 8.5 (per 1,000 pop.) **Natural inc.:** –0.17% **Infant mortality:** 1.8 (per 1,000 live births). **HIV rate:** NA.

Education: Compulsory: ages 6-16. **Literacy:** 99%.

Major intl. organizations: UN (FAO, WHO), OSCE.

Embassy: 2314 Wyoming Ave. NW 20008; 234-1530.

Website: www.gouv.mc

An independent principality for over 300 years, Monaco has belonged to the House of Grimaldi since 1297, except during the French Revolution. It was placed under the protectorate of Sardinia in 1815, and under France, 1861. The Prince of Monaco was an absolute ruler until the 1911 constitution. Monaco was admitted to the UN on May 28, 1993.

Monaco is noted for its mild climate, magnificent scenery, and elegant casinos. Prince Rainier III, who ruled Monaco from 1949 and turned it into one of Europe's top tourist spots, died Apr. 6, 2005, and was succeeded by his son, Albert II.

Mongolia

People: Population: 3,179,997. **Age distrib.:** <15: 27.1%; 65+: 4%. **Pop. density:** 5.3 per sq mi, 2 per sq km. **Urban:** 68.5%. **Ethnic groups:** Mongol (mostly Khalkha) 95%, Turkic (mostly Kazakh) 5%. **Principal languages:** Khalkha Mongol, Turkic, Russian. **Chief religions:** Buddhist Lamaist 50%, Shamanist and Christian 6%, Muslim 4%, none 40%.

Geography: Total area: 603,909 sq mi, 1,564,116 sq km; **Land area:** 599,831 sq mi, 1,553,556 sq km. **Location:** In E Central Asia. **Neighbors:** Russia on N, China on E, W, and S. **Topography:** Mostly a high plateau with mountains, salt lakes, and vast grasslands. Arid lands in S are part of the Gobi Desert. **Capital:** Ulaanbaatar, 1,183,910.

Government: Type: Republic. **Head of state:** Pres. Tsakhiagiin Elbegdorj; b. Mar. 30, 1963; in office: June 18, 2009. **Head of gov.:** Prime. Min. Norov Altankhuyag; b. Jan. 20, 1958; in office: Aug. 9, 2012. **Local divisions:** 18 provinces, 3 municipalities. **Defense budget:** NA. **Active troops:** 10,000.

Economy: Industries: constr. and constr. materials, mining, oil, food and beverages, animal prods. proc., cashmere and natural fiber mfg. **Chief crops:** wheat, barley, vegetables, forage crops. **Natural resources:** oil, coal, copper, molybdenum, tungsten, phosphates, tin, nickel, zinc, fluorspar, gold, silver, iron. **Arable land:** 0.6%. **Livestock:** cattle: 2.2 mil; chickens: 426,000; goats: 13.9 mil; pigs: 24,842; sheep: 14.5 mil. **Fish catch:** 90 metric tons. **Electricity prod.** (2010): 4.1 bil kWh. **Labor force:** agric. 33.5%, industry 11.5%, services 55%.

Finance: Monetary unit: Tughrik (MNT) (Sept. 2012: 1,367.02 = $1 U.S.). **GDP:** $13.4 bil; **per capita GDP:** $4,800; **GDP growth:** 17.3%. **Imports:** $6.5 bil; China 30.7%, Russia 24.5%, U.S. 8.1%, Japan 7.4%, South Korea 5.5%. **Exports:** $4.8 bil; China 92.1%, Russia 2%, Canada 1.9%. **Tourism:** $218 mil. **Budget:** $3.5 bil. **Total reserves less gold:** $2.3 bil. **Gold:** 112,769 oz t. **CPI change:** 9.5%.

Transport: Railways: 1,186 mi (partly owned by Russian State Railway). **Civil aviation:** 379 mil pass.-mi; 15 airports.

Communications: TV sets: 88 per 1,000 pop. **Radios:** 328 per 1,000 pop. **Telephone lines:** 6.7 per 100 pop. **Daily newspaper circ.:** 19.6 per 1,000 pop. **Internet:** 20%.

Health: Life expect.: 66.2 male; 71.2 female. **Births:** 20.7 (per 1,000 pop.). **Deaths:** 6.0 (per 1,000 pop.). **Natural inc.:** 1.47% **Infant mortality:** 36.0 (per 1,000 live births). **HIV rate:** <0.1%.

Education: Compulsory: ages 7-15. **Literacy:** 97.4%.

Major intl. organizations: UN (FAO, IBRD, ILO, IMF, WHO), WTO.

Embassy: 2833 M St. NW 20007; 333-7117.

Website: www.pmis.gov.mn

One of the world's oldest countries, Mongolia reached the zenith of its power in the 13th cent. when Genghis Khan and his successors conquered all of China and extended their influence as far west as Hungary and Poland. In later centuries, the empire dissolved and Mongolia became a province of China.

With the advent of the 1911 Chinese revolution, Mongolia, with Russian backing, declared its independence. A Communist regime was established July 11, 1921. In 1990, the Mongolian Communist Party yielded its monopoly on power. A new constitution took effect Feb. 12, 1992.

Mongolia sent more than 100 troops to U.S.-led operations in Afghanistan (2001); they remained in Afghanistan as of Aug. 2012. Riots followed parliamentary elections June 29, 2008, won by the ruling Mongolian People's Revolutionary Party (MPRP). In presidential voting May 24, 2009, former Prime Min. Tsakhiagiin Elbergdorj (1998, 2004-06), the Democratic Party candidate, defeated the MPRP's incumbent Pres. Nambaryn Enkhbayar. A June 28, 2012, legislative election gave the Democratic Party the most seats in parliament, and Norov Altankhuyag became prime min. Aug. 9. Exploitation of vast mineral resources is expected to boost Mongolia's GDP at annual rates of more than 14% from 2013 to 2015.

Montenegro

People: Population: 657,394. **Age distrib.:** <15: 15.4%; 65+: 13.6%. **Pop. density:** 126.6 per sq mi, 48.9 per sq km. **Urban:** 63.3%. **Ethnic groups:** Montenegrin 43%, Serbian 32%, Bosniak 8%, Albanian 5%, other (Muslim, Croat, Roma) 12%. **Principal languages:** Serbian, Montenegrin (official), Bosnian, Albanian. **Chief religions:** Orthodox 74%, Muslim 18%, Catholic 4%, atheist 1%.

Geography: Total area: 5,333 sq mi, 13,812 sq km; **Land area:** 5,194 sq mi, 13,452 sq km. **Location:** On Balkan Peninsula in SE Europe. **Neighbors:** Bosnia and Herzegovina on N and W; Serbia on E; Albania on SE; Adriatic Sea on SW; Croatia on W. **Topography:** Most terrain is rugged and mountainous, with few arable regions, mostly along the Zeta R.; narrow coastline is highly indented. **Capital:** Podgorica, 156,418.

Government: Type: Republic. **Head of state:** Pres. Filip Vujanovic; b. Sept. 1, 1954; in office: May 22, 2003. **Head of gov.:** Prime. Min. Igor Luksic; b. June 14, 1976; in office: Dec. 29, 2010. **Local divisions:** 21 municipalities. **Defense budget:** $54 mil. **Active troops:** 2,984.

Economy: Industries: steelmaking, aluminum, agric. proc., consumer goods, tourism. **Chief crops:** tobacco, potatoes, citrus, olives, grapes. **Natural resources:** bauxite, hydroelectricity. **Arable land:** 12.9%. **Livestock:** cattle: 118,833; chickens: 601,000; pigs: 11,533; sheep: 220,653. **Fish catch:** 1,935 metric tons. **Electricity prod.:** 2.6 bil kWh. **Labor force:** agric. 6.3%, industry 20.9%, services 72.8%.

Finance: Monetary unit: Euro (EUR) (Sept. 2012: 0.79 = $1 U.S.). **GDP:** $7.2 bil; **per capita GDP:** $11,700; **GDP growth:** 2.5%. **Imports:** $2.5 bil; Serbia 28.4%, Greece 7.9%, Bosnia and Herzegovina 7.6%. **Exports:** $640 mil; Serbia 17.5%, Hungary 16.9%, Croatia 10.1%. **Tourism:** $777 mil. **Budget:** $1.9 bil. **Total reserves less gold:** $392.7 mil. **CPI change:** 3.2%.

Transport: Railways: 155 mi. **Civil aviation:** 5 airports. **Chief port:** Bar.

Communications: Telephone lines (2010): 26.8 per 100 pop. **Internet:** 40%.

Health: Life expect.: 75.0 male; 81.1 female. **Births:** 10.9 (per 1,000 pop.). **Deaths:** 9.0 (per 1,000 pop.). **Natural inc.:** 0.19% **Infant mortality:** 9.3 (per 1,000 live births). **HIV rate:** NA.

Education: Compulsory: ages 6-14. **Literacy:** 98.4%.

Major intl. organizations: UN (FAO, ILO, WHO), OSCE, WTO (observer).

Embassy: 1610 New Hampshire Ave. NW 20009; 234-6108.

Website: www.gov.me

Part of the medieval Serbian Kingdom, Montenegro preserved its autonomy for centuries because of its mountainous terrain. After WWI, it was part of the Kingdom of Serbs, Croats, and Slovenes, later renamed Yugoslavia. Italian forces occupied parts of Montenegro during WWII. In 1945, with the establishment of a federal Yugoslavia under Communist rule, Montenegro became one of 6 constituent republics.

In Apr. 1992, after 4 other republics had declared independence, Montenegro and Serbia reconstituted themselves as the Federal Republic of Yugoslavia. Because of its ties with Serbia, Montenegro was a target of NATO air strikes during the Kosovo war, Mar.-June 1999. The republic sought closer ties with the West, however, and worked to reduce its political and economic dependence on Serbia. A referendum on independence passed May 21, 2006, with barely more than the 55% majority required. Montenegro declared independence June 3, 2006, and was admitted as a UN member June 28. It applied Dec. 15, 2008, to join the EU. Early elections were expected to be held Oct. 14, 2012.

Morocco
Kingdom of Morocco

People: Population: 32,309,239. **Age distrib.:** <15: 27.4%; 65+: 6.2%. **Pop. density:** 187.5 per sq mi, 72.4 per sq km.

Urban: 57%. **Ethnic groups:** Arab-Berber 99%. **Principal languages:** Arabic (official), Berber dialects, French (lang. of business, govt., diplomacy). **Chief religions:** Muslim (official) 99%, Christian 1%.

Geography: Total area: 172,414 sq mi, 446,550 sq km; **Land area:** 172,317 sq mi, 446,300 sq km. **Location:** On NW coast of Africa. **Neighbors:** Western Sahara on S, Algeria on E, Spain on N. **Topography:** Consists of 5 natural regions: mountain ranges (Riff in the N, Middle Atlas, Upper Atlas, and Anti-Atlas); rich plains in W; alluvial plains in SW; well-cultivated plateaus in the center; a pre-Sahara arid zone extending from SE. **Capital:** Rabat, 1,842,850. **Cities (urban aggl.):** Casablanca (Dar-el-Beida), 3,046,040; Fès, 1,087,516.

Government: Type: Constitutional monarchy. **Head of state:** King Mohammed VI; b. Aug. 21, 1963; in office: July 23, 1999. **Head of gov.:** Prime Min. Abdelilah Benkirane; b. Apr. 4, 1954; in office: Nov. 29, 2011. **Local divisions:** 16 regions. **Defense budget:** $3.34 bil. **Active troops:** 195,800.

Economy: Industries: phosphate rock mining and proc., food proc., leather goods, textiles, constr., energy, tourism. **Chief crops:** barley, wheat, citrus, grapes, vegetables, olives. **Natural resources:** phosphates, iron ore, manganese, lead, zinc, fish, salt. **Crude oil reserves:** 680,000 bbls. **Arable land:** 18.0%. **Livestock:** cattle: 2.9 mil; chickens: 170 mil; goats: 5.7 mil; pigs: 8,500; sheep: 18 mil. **Fish catch:** 1.1 mil metric tons. **Electricity prod.:** 20.1 bil kWh. **Labor force:** agric. 44.6%, industry 19.8%, services 35.5%.

Finance: Monetary unit: Dirham (MAD) (Sept. 2012: 8.74 = $1 U.S.). **GDP:** $164.7 bil; **per capita GDP:** $5,100; **GDP growth:** 4.3%. **Imports:** $40.4 bil; France 15.4%, Spain 14.4%, China 7.7%, U.S. 7.3%, Saudi Arabia 6.1%, Italy 5.1%, Germany 4.8%. **Exports:** $21 bil; Spain 18.6%, France 16.9%, Brazil 6%, U.S. 4.8%, India 4.5%. **Tourism:** $7.3 bil. **Budget:** $31.4 bil. **Total reserves less gold:** $19.5 bil. **Gold:** 708,800 oz t. **CPI change:** 0.9%.

Transport: Railways: 1,284 mi. **Motor vehicles:** 58.8 vehicles per 1,000 pop. **Civil aviation:** 6 bil pass.-mi; 31 airports. **Chief ports:** Casablanca, Jorf Lasfar, Mohammedia, Safi, Tangier.

Communications: TV sets: 174 per 1,000 pop. **Radios:** 246 per 1,000 pop. **Telephone lines:** 11.1 per 100 pop. **Daily newspaper circ.:** 11.7 per 1,000 pop. **Internet:** 51%.

Health: Life expect.: 73.0 male; 79.3 female. **Births:** 19.0 (per 1,000 pop.). **Deaths:** 4.8 (per 1,000 pop.). **Natural inc.:** 1.42%. **Infant mortality:** 26.5 (per 1,000 live births). **HIV rate:** 0.1%.

Education: Compulsory: ages 6-15. **Literacy:** 56.1%.

Major intl. organizations: UN (FAO, IBRD, ILO, IMF, WHO), AL, WTO.

Embassy: 1601 21st St. NW 20009; 462-7979.

Website: www.maroc.ma

Berbers were the original inhabitants of the region, followed by Carthaginians and Romans. Arabs conquered it in 683. In the 11th and 12th cent., a Berber empire ruled all NW Africa and most of Spain from Morocco.

Part of Morocco came under Spanish rule in the 19th cent.; France controlled the rest in the early 20th. Tribal uprisings lasted from 1911 to 1933. Independence was achieved Mar. 2, 1956. Tangier, an internationalized seaport, was incorporated into Morocco, 1956. Ifni, a Spanish enclave, was ceded in 1969. Morocco annexed the disputed territory of Western Sahara during the second half of the 1970s.

King Hassan II assumed the throne in 1961, reigning until his death on July 23, 1999; he was succeeded by his eldest son. A bicameral legislature was established in 1997.

Five terrorist attacks in Casablanca May 16, 2003, left 45 people dead, including 12 suicide bombers; the government blamed Salafia Jihadia, an al-Qaeda-linked group. An earthquake Feb. 24, 2004, killed at least 629 people near al-Hoceima, northern coastal Morocco. Following a series of suicide bombings in 2007, the government stepped up its campaign against militant Islamists. Following "Arab Spring" street demonstrations Feb.-Mar. 2011, the monarchy implemented modest constitutional reforms.

Western Sahara

Western Sahara, formerly the protectorate of Spanish Sahara, is bounded on the N by Morocco, the NE by Algeria, the E and S by Mauritania, and the W by the Atlantic Ocean. Phosphates are the major resource. Pop. (2012 est.): 522,928; area: 102,703 sq mi; capital: Laayoune (El Aaiún).

Spain withdrew from its protectorate in Feb. 1976. On Apr. 14, 1976, Morocco annexed over 70,000 sq mi, with the remainder annexed by Mauritania. The Polisario Front guerrilla movement, which proclaimed the region independent Feb. 27, launched attacks with Algerian support. After Mauritania signed a treaty with Polisario Aug. 5, 1979, Morocco occupied Mauritania's portion of Western Sahara.

After years of bitter fighting, Morocco controlled the main urban areas, but Polisario guerrillas moved freely in the vast, sparsely populated deserts. The two sides implemented a cease-fire in 1991, when a UN peacekeeping force (MINURSO) was established with a mandate to prepare for a referendum on self-determination as early as 1992; in mid-2012, MINURSO had about 219 uniformed personnel in Western Sahara, but a referendum had still not been held.

Mozambique
Republic of Mozambique

People: Population: 23,515,934. **Age distrib.:** <15: 45.7%; 65+: 3%. **Pop. density:** 77.5 per sq mi, 29.9 per sq km. **Urban:** 31.2%. **Ethnic groups:** African (Makhuwa, Tsonga, Lomwe, Sena, others) 99.7%. **Principal languages:** Emakhuwa, Portuguese (official), Xichangana, Cisena, Elomwe, Echuwabo, other Mozambican langs. **Chief religions:** Catholic 28%, Protestant 28% (Zionist Christian 16%, Evangelical Pentecostal 11%), Muslim 18%, none 19%.

Geography: Total area: 308,642 sq mi, 799,380 sq km; **Land area:** 303,623 sq mi, 786,380 sq km. **Location:** On SE coast of Africa. **Neighbors:** Tanzania on N; Malawi, Zambia, Zimbabwe on W; South Africa, Swaziland on S. **Topography:** Coastal lowlands comprise nearly half the country with plateaus rising in steps to the mountains along W border. **Capital:** Maputo, 1,150,030. **Cities (urban aggl.):** Matola, 793,486.

Government: Type: Republic. **Head of state:** Pres. Armando Guebuza; b. Jan. 20, 1943; in office: Feb. 2, 2005. **Head of gov.:** Prime Min. Aires Ali; b. Dec. 6, 1955; in office: Jan. 16, 2010. **Local divisions:** 10 provinces and Maputo municipality. **Defense budget** (2010): $61 mil. **Active troops:** 11,200.

Economy: Industries: food, beverages, chemicals, aluminum, petroleum prods., textiles, cement, glass, asbestos, tobacco. **Chief crops:** cotton, cashew nuts, sugarcane, tea, cassava, corn, coconuts, sisal, citrus and tropical fruits, potatoes, sunflowers. **Natural resources:** coal, titanium, nat. gas, hydropower, tantalum, graphite. **Arable land:** 6.4%. **Livestock:** cattle: 1.3 mil; chickens: 19 mil; goats: 4.8 mil; pigs: 1.4 mil; sheep: 200,000. **Fish catch:** 152,198 metric tons. **Electricity prod.:** 16.8 bil kWh. **Labor force:** agric. 81%, industry 6%, services 13%.

Finance: Monetary unit: Metical (MZN) (Sept. 2012: 28.62 = $1 U.S.). **GDP:** $24.2 bil; **per capita GDP:** $1,100; **GDP growth:** 7.1%. **Imports:** $4 bil; South Africa 22.1%, China 12.4%, India 9.1%, U.S. 8%, Australia 7.4%, Portugal 5.4%. **Exports:** $2.6 bil; Belgium 17.8%, South Africa 17.4%, Italy 13.9%, Spain 10%, China 7.7%. **Tourism:** $197 mil. **Budget:** $4.2 bil. **Total reserves less gold:** $2.5 bil. **Gold:** 80,189 oz t. **CPI change:** 10.4%.

Transport: Railways: 2,975 mi. **Motor vehicles:** 3 vehicles per 1,000 pop. **Civil aviation:** 343 mil pass.-mi; 21 airports. **Chief ports:** Beira, Maputo, Nacala.

Communications: TV sets: 21 per 1,000 pop. **Radios:** 63 per 1,000 pop. **Telephone lines:** 0.4 per 100 pop. **Daily newspaper circ.:** 2.7 per 1,000 pop. **Internet:** 4.3%.

Health: Life expect.: 51.3 male; 52.8 female. **Births:** 39.3 (per 1,000 pop.). **Deaths:** 12.8 (per 1,000 pop.). **Natural inc.:** 2.66% **Infant mortality:** 76.9 (per 1,000 live births). **HIV rate:** 11.5%.

Education: Compulsory: ages 6-12. **Literacy:** 56.1%.

Major intl. organizations: UN (FAO, IBRD, ILO, IMF, WHO), AU, the Commonwealth, WTO.

Embassy: 1525 New Hampshire Ave. NW 20036; 293-7146.

Website: www.mozambique.mz

The first Portuguese post on the Mozambique coast was established in 1505, on the trade route to the East. Mozambique became independent June 25, 1975, after a 10-year war against the Portuguese. The 1974 revolution in Portugal paved the way for an orderly transfer of power to Frelimo (Front for the Liberation of Mozambique).

The Frelimo government, headed by Pres. Samora Machel, a former guerrilla commander, gradually transitioned to a Communist system. Most of the country's whites emigrated. In the 1980s, severe drought and civil war caused famine and heavy loss of life. Pres. Machel was killed in a plane crash just inside the South African border, Oct. 19, 1986. Frelimo formally abandoned Marxist-Leninism in 1989, and a new constitution, effective Nov. 30, 1990, established multiparty elections and a free-market economy.

On Oct. 4, 1992, a peace agreement ended hostilities between the government and the Mozambique National Resistance (MNR). Repatriation of 1.7 mil Mozambican refugees ended June 1995. In Mar. 1999 the heaviest floods in four decades left nearly 200,000 people stranded, and worse flooding in Feb.-Mar. 2000 claimed more than 600 lives and devastated the economy.

Frelimo retained its hold under Pres. Joaquim Chissano (in office 1986-2005) and his successor, Pres. Armando Guebuza, elected Dec. 1-2, 2004. Flooding of the Zambezi River basin, followed by Cyclone Favio, killed at least 45 people in Feb. 2007. Another flood crisis, Jan.-Mar. 2008, claimed some 700 lives and displaced 650,000 people. Despite robust economic growth during 2000-11, poverty remains widespread. Guebuza won reelection Oct. 28, 2009. According to Aug. 1, 2012, estimates, 70 tril cubic feet of crude oil reserves were discovered off Mozambique's coast, 2011-12.

SCIENCE

Last Chance The rare transit of Venus across the face of the Sun June 5-6, 2012, was visible from every continent; the next will not be seen until 2117.

Under the Sea Filmmaker James Cameron completed the world's first solo dive to Challenger Deep, the lowest point in the Mariana Trench, in *Deepsea Challenger*, a specially engineered submersible Mar. 25, 2012.

Last Trip The retired space shuttles found their new homes in 2012; *Discovery* was placed on view at the National Air and Space Museum in Washington, DC.

View From Mars NASA's *Curiosity* rover landed safely on Mars in an ingenious feat of engineering Aug. 6, 2012; it returned images and data from the Red Planet for analysis.

"God Particle" Research efforts at Switzerland's Large Hadron Collider paid dividends July 4, 2012, when scientists there announced the discovery of the elusive Higgs boson, a long-theorized particle.

SPORTS

Greatest Olympian U.S. swimmer Michael Phelps set the record Aug. 4, 2012, for most career Olympic medals with 22 (18 gold).

Leaps and Bounds U.S. gymnast Gabrielle Douglas claimed the women's individual all-around competition gold medal Aug. 2, 2012.

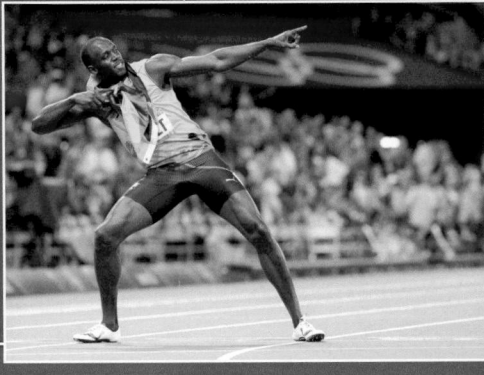

Double-Double Jamaican sprinter Usain Bolt continued his dominance Aug. 9, 2012, becoming the first athlete ever to win the Olympic 100- and 200-meter events at two consecutive Summer Games.

Blade Runner South African sprinter Oscar Pistorius became the first double-amputee runner to compete on artificial legs at the Summer Olympic Games Aug. 4, 2012.

Baylor Dominates Brittney Griner (right) led the undefeated Baylor Bears to victory over the Notre Dame Fighting Irish to claim the Women's Div. I NCAA title Apr. 3, 2012.

Tidal Crush Alabama's defense shut out the LSU Tigers in the BCS championship title game Jan. 9, 2012.

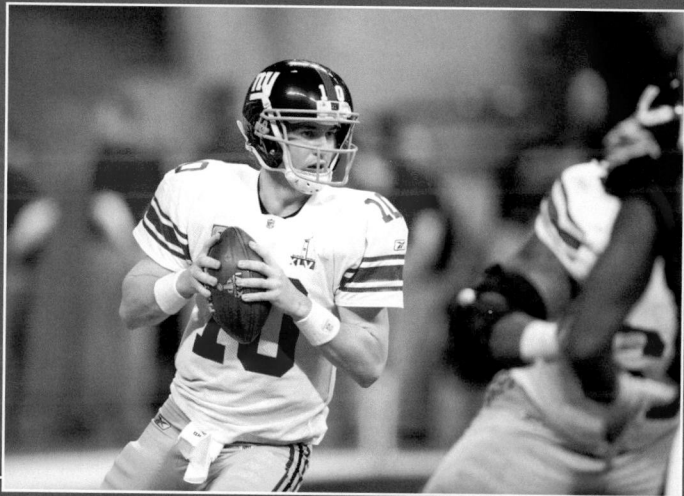

Déjà Vu Eli Manning and the NY Giants came from behind to win Super Bowl XLVI Feb. 5, 2012, over the New England Patriots.

"Fate" Accompli LeBron James and the Miami Heat defeated the Oklahoma City Thunder for the NBA Championship June 21, 2012.

Triple-Crown Tiger Detroit's Miguel Cabrera Oct. 3, 2012, became the first Major League Baseball player since 1967 to lead the league in batting average, home runs, and runs batted in.

SPORTS

Tiger Triumph With a tournament win July 1, 2012, Tiger Woods claimed his 74th PGA Tour victory, surpassing the record set by the legendary Jack Nicklaus.

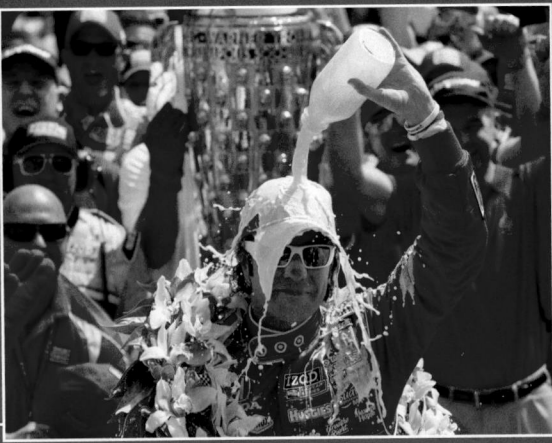

Indy Win Dario Franchitti sped away with his third Indianapolis 500 victory May 27, 2012.

Kings Crowned The L.A. Kings beat the New Jersey Devils June 11, 2012, to claim the first Stanley Cup Finals victory in the Kings' 45-year history.

Double Take The UK's Andy Murray and American Serena Williams doubled up on wins in 2012; each claimed the Olympic singles gold medal in Aug. and went on to win the U.S. Open in Sept.

PEOPLE

Lance's Loss
Seven-time Tour de France champion Lance Armstrong quit his fight against charges of doping Aug. 23, 2012; in accordance with World Anti-Doping Code, he was stripped of all seven Tour titles.

Welcome to the Club
Augusta National Golf Club, host to the Masters golf tournament, announced Aug. 20, 2012, that financier Darla Moore and former Sec. of State Condoleezza Rice would become the first female members in the club's 80-year history.

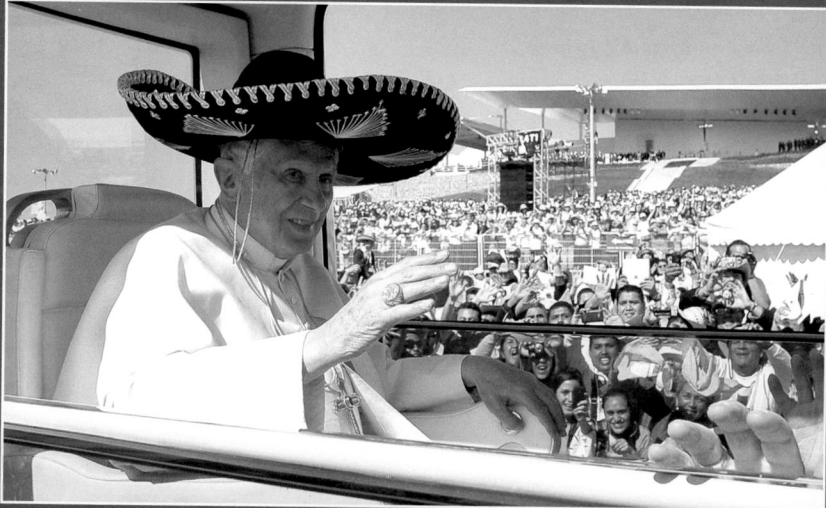

Hola, Papa
Pope Benedict XVI visited Mexico and Cuba Mar. 23-28, 2012.

Summitt Departs
After 38 years, Tennessee's Pat Summitt, the winningest basketball coach in NCAA history, announced her retirement Apr. 18, 2012; she was diagnosed with early onset Alzheimer's disease.

"TomKat" No More
Katie Holmes and Tom Cruise reached a divorce settlement July 9, 2012, after six years of marriage.

ARTS

Surprise Bestseller E. L. James's *Fifty Shades of Grey* camped out on top of bestseller lists in 2012; the book was the first in a trilogy of erotic fiction.

Oscar Honors Silent film *The Artist* won the Oscar for best picture Feb. 26, 2012; star Jean Dujardin was named best actor.

Fab Four Blake Shelton, Christina Aguilera, Cee Lo Green, and Adam Levine served as mentors on NBC's high-rated singing competition show *The Voice*.

Home Run Showtime's *Homeland* won the Emmy award for best drama Sept. 23, 2012; costars Claire Danes and Damian Lewis claimed best actress and best actor.

Neil Armstrong
AUG. 5, 1930-AUG. 25, 2012

Ernest Borgnine
JAN. 24, 1917-JULY 8, 2012

Ray Bradbury
AUG. 22, 1920-JUNE 5, 2012

Helen Gurley Brown
FEB. 18, 1922-AUG. 13, 2012

Gary Carter
APR. 8, 1954-FEB. 16, 2012

Dick Clark
NOV. 30, 1929-APR. 18, 2012

Phyllis Diller
JULY 17, 1917-AUG. 20, 2012

Nora Ephron
MAY 19, 1941-JUNE 26, 2012

Andy Griffith
JUNE 1, 1926-JULY 3, 2012

Marvin Hamlisch
JUNE 2, 1944-AUG. 6, 2012

Sherman Hemsley
FEB. 1, 1938-JULY 24, 2012

Christopher Hitchens
APR. 13, 1949-DEC. 15, 2011

Whitney Houston
AUG. 9, 1963-FEB. 11, 2012

Etta James
JAN. 25, 1938-JAN. 20, 2012

George McGovern
JULY 19, 1922-OCT. 21, 2012

Russell Means
NOV. 10, 1939-OCT. 22, 2012

Sally Ride
MAY 26, 1951-JULY 23, 2012

Maurice Sendak
JUNE 10, 1928-MAY 8, 2012

Donna Summer
DEC. 31, 1948-MAY 17, 2012

Gore Vidal
OCT. 3, 1925-JULY 31, 2012

Mike Wallace
MAY 9, 1918-APR. 7, 2012

Kitty Wells
AUG. 30, 1919-JULY 16, 2012

Andy Williams
DEC. 3, 1927-SEPT. 25, 2012

Adam Yauch
AUG. 5, 1964-MAY 4, 2012

Myanmar (*formerly* Burma)
Republic of the Union of Myanmar

People: Population: 54,584,650. **Age distrib.:** <15: 27.1%; 65+: 5.1%. **Pop. density:** 216.3 per sq mi, 83.5 per sq km. **Urban:** 32.6%. **Ethnic groups:** Burman 68%, Shan 9%, Karen 7%, Rakhine 4%, Chinese 3%, Indian 2%, Mon 2%. **Principal languages:** Burmese (official), ethnic minority langs. **Chief religions:** Buddhist 89%, Christian 4%, Muslim 4%, animist 1%.

Geography: Total area: 261,228 sq mi, 676,578 sq km; **Land area:** 252,321 sq mi, 653,508 sq km. **Location:** Between S and SE Asia, on Bay of Bengal. **Neighbors:** Bangladesh, India on W; China, Laos, Thailand on E. **Topography:** Mountains surround Myanmar on W, N, and E, and dense forests cover much of the nation. N-S rivers provide habitable valleys and communications, especially the Irrawaddy, navigable for 900 mi. Country has a tropical monsoon climate. **Capital:** Nay Pyi Taw, 1,059,530. **Cities (urban aggl.):** Yangon, 4,456,592; Mandalay, 1,063,103.

Government: Type: Presidential republic dominated by the military. **Head of state and gov.:** Pres. Thein Sein; b. Apr. 20, 1945; in office: Mar. 30, 2011. **Local divisions:** 7 states, 7 divisions. **Defense budget:** $2.04 bil. **Active troops:** 406,000.

Economy: Industries: agric. proc.; wood and wood prods.; copper, tin, tungsten, iron; cement, constr. materials; pharmaceuticals. **Chief crops:** rice, pulses, beans, sesame, groundnuts, sugarcane. **Natural resources:** petroleum, timber, tin, antimony, zinc, copper, tungsten, lead, coal, marble, limestone, prec. stones, nat. gas, hydropower. **Crude oil reserves:** 50 mil bbls. **Arable land:** 16.9%. **Livestock:** cattle: 13 mil; chickens: 125 mil; goats: 2.8 mil; pigs: 7.9 mil; sheep: 535,000. **Fish catch:** 3.9 mil metric tons. **Electricity prod.:** 5.7 bil kWh. **Labor force:** agric. 70%, industry 7%, services 23%.

Finance: Monetary unit: Kyat (MMK) (Sept. 2012: 870.00 = $1 U.S.) (official; black market rate may vary widely). **GDP:** $83.7 bil; **per capita GDP:** $1,300; **GDP growth:** 5.5%. **Imports:** $6 bil (grossly underestimated due to value of consumer goods, diesel fuel, and other products smuggled in from Thailand, China, Malaysia, India); China 39.2%, Thailand 22.9%, Singapore 9.8%, South Korea 5.4%, Japan 4.1%. **Exports:** $8.2 bil (official export figure grossly underestimated due to value of timber, gems, narcotics, rice, and other products smuggled to Thailand, China, Bangladesh); Thailand 37.1%, China 19%, India 12.3%, Japan 6.7%. **Tourism:** $73 mil. **Budget:** $4.3 bil. **Total reserves less gold:** $7 bil. **Gold:** 233,700 oz t. **CPI change:** 5.02%.

Transport: Railways: 3,126 mi. **Motor vehicles:** 0.5 vehicles per 1,000 pop. **Civil aviation:** 913.4 mil pass.-mi; 36 airports. **Chief ports:** Moulmein, Rangoon (Yangon), Sittwe.

Communications: TV sets: 7 per 1,000 pop. **Radios:** 203 per 1,000 pop. **Telephone lines:** 1.1 per 100 pop. **Internet:** 1%.

Health: Life expect.: 62.9 male; 67.7 female. **Births:** 19.1 (per 1,000 pop.). **Deaths:** 8.1 (per 1,000 pop.). **Natural inc.:** 1.10%. **Infant mortality:** 47.7 (per 1,000 live births). **HIV rate:** 0.6%.

Education: Compulsory: ages 5-9. **Literacy:** 92.3%.

Major intl. organizations: UN (FAO, IBRD, ILO, IMF, WHO), ASEAN, WTO.

Embassy: 2300 S St. NW 20008; 332-3344.

Website: www.mofa.gov.mm

The Burmese arrived from Tibet before the 9th cent., displacing earlier cultures, and a Buddhist monarchy was established by the 11th cent. Burma was conquered by the Mongol dynasty of China in 1272, then ruled by Shans as a Chinese tributary, until the 16th cent. Britain subjugated Burma in three wars, 1824-84, and ruled the country as part of India until 1937, when Burma became self-governing. Independence outside the Commonwealth was achieved Jan. 4, 1948.

Gen. Ne Win dominated politics from 1962 to 1988, first as military ruler, then as constitutional president. His regime drove Indians from the civil service and Chinese from commerce. Economic socialization was advanced, isolation from foreign countries enforced. In 1987 Burma, once the richest nation in SE Asia, was granted less-developed status by the UN.

Ne Win resigned July 1988, following antigovernment riots. In Sept., the military seized power, under Gen. Saw Maung. In 1989 the country's name was changed to Myanmar.

The first free multiparty elections in 30 years took place May 27, 1990, with the main opposition party winning a decisive victory, but the military refused to hand over power. A key opposition leader, Aung San Suu Kyi, awarded the Nobel Peace Prize in 1991, was held under house arrest, 1989-95, 2000-02, and 2003-10. Because of the regime's poor human rights record and continued harassment of Aung San Suu Kyi and her supporters, the U.S. imposed sanctions. The Indian Ocean tsunami of Dec. 26, 2004, killed at least 61 people in Myanmar.

Public anger over soaring fuel costs in Aug. 2007 triggered new challenges to the military regime. In late Sept., thousands of Buddhist monks led mass protests in Yangon; security forces cracked down by raiding monasteries, arresting monks, and firing on demonstrators. On Sept. 25, 2007, the U.S. announced tougher sanctions. Cyclone Nargis, May 2-3, 2008, left at least 84,537 people dead, with an estimated 53,836 missing.

Parliamentary elections Nov. 7, 2010, dominated by the military, led to the dissolution of the ruling State Peace and Development Council and an initially nominal return to civilian government, Mar. 30, 2011. The National League for Democracy (NLD), led by Aung San Suu Kyi, won 43 of 45 parliamentary seats in an Apr. 1, 2012, by election, and Suu Kyi traveled to Oslo, Norway, to accept her 1991 Nobel Peace Prize June 16. The EU, Apr. 23, and U.S., May 17, 2012, suspended most of its sanctions against Myanmar to recognize the steps it was taking toward democracy. Myanmar's government announced Aug. 28, 2012, that more than 2,000 names had been removed from the country's notorious blacklist of those banned from entering or leaving the country.

Namibia
Republic of Namibia

People: Population: 2,165,828. **Age distrib.:** <15: 33.4%; 65+: 4.2%. **Pop. density:** 6.8 per sq mi, 2.6 per sq km. **Urban:** 38.4%. **Ethnic groups:** black 88%, white 6%, mixed 7%; about 50% of pop. belong to Ovambo tribe. **Principal languages:** English (official), Afrikaans (common), German, indigenous langs. (incl. Oshivambo, Herero, Nama). **Chief religions:** Christian 80%-90%, indigenous beliefs 10%-20%.

Geography: Total area: 318,261 sq mi, 824,292 sq km; **Land area:** 317,874 sq mi, 823,290 sq km. **Location:** In southern Africa on coast of Atlantic O. **Neighbors:** Angola on N; Botswana, Zambia on E; South Africa on S. **Topography:** Three distinct regions incl. Namib Desert along the Atlantic coast, a mountainous central plateau with woodland savanna, and Kalahari Desert in E. True forests found in NE. There are 4 rivers, but little other surface water. **Capital:** Windhoek, 380,103.

Government: Type: Republic. **Head of state:** Pres. Hifikepunye Pohamba; b. Aug. 18, 1935; in office: Mar. 21, 2005. **Head of gov.:** Prime Min. Nahas Angula; b. Aug. 22, 1943; in office: Mar. 21, 2005. **Local divisions:** 13 regions. **Defense budget:** $421 mil. **Active troops:** 9,200.

Economy: Industries: meatpacking, fish proc., dairy prods., mining. **Chief crops:** millet, sorghum, peanuts, grapes. **Natural resources:** diamonds, copper, uranium, gold, silver, lead, tin, lithium, cadmium, tungsten, zinc, salt, hydropower, fish. **Arable land:** 1.0%. **Livestock:** cattle: 2.4 mil; chickens: 5.1 mil; goats: 2.1 mil; pigs: 65,000; sheep: 2.8 mil. **Fish catch:** 370,675 metric tons. **Electricity prod.** (2010): 1.3 bil kWh. **Labor force:** agric. 16.3%, industry 22.4%, services 61.3% (formal sector only). About half of population unemployed. About two-thirds of rural population rely on subsistence agric.

Finance: Monetary unit: Dollar (NAD) (Sept. 2012: 8.39 = $1 U.S.). **GDP:** $15.9 bil; **per capita GDP:** $7,500; **GDP growth:** 3.6%. **Imports:** $5.3 bil. **Exports:** $4.4 bil. **Tourism:** $517 mil. **Budget:** $4.9 bil. **Total reserves less gold:** $1.8 bil. **CPI change:** 5.05%.

Transport: Railways: 1,632 mi. **Motor vehicles:** 82.4 vehicles per 1,000 pop. **Civil aviation:** 1 bil pass.-mi; 19 airports. **Chief ports:** Luderitz, Walvis Bay.

Communications: TV sets: 78 per 1,000 pop. **Radios:** 62 per 1,000 pop. **Telephone lines:** 6 per 100 pop. **Daily newspaper circ.:** 28.0 per 1,000 pop. **Internet:** 12%.

Health: Life expect.: 52.5 male; 51.9 female. **Births:** 21.1 (per 1,000 pop.). **Deaths:** 13.1 (per 1,000 pop.). **Natural inc.:** 0.80%. **Infant mortality:** 45.6 (per 1,000 live births). **HIV rate:** 13.1%.

Education: Compulsory: ages 7-16. **Literacy:** 88.8%.

Major intl. organizations: UN (FAO, IBRD, ILO, IMF, WHO), AU, the Commonwealth, WTO.

Embassy: 1605 New Hampshire Ave. NW 20009; 986-0540.

Website: www.grnnet.gov.na

Namibia was declared a German protectorate in 1890 and officially called South-West Africa. South Africa seized the territory in 1915 during WWI; the League of Nations gave South Africa a mandate over the territory in 1920. In 1966, the Marxist South-West Africa People's Organization (SWAPO) launched a guerrilla war for independence. The UN General Assembly named the area Namibia in 1968.

After many years of guerrilla warfare, South Africa, Angola, and Cuba signed a U.S.-mediated agreement Dec. 22, 1988, to end South African administration of Namibia and provide for a cease-fire and transition to independence, in accordance with a 1978 UN plan. A separate accord between Cuba and Angola provided for a phased withdrawal of Cuban troops from Namibia. A constitution providing for multiparty government was adopted Feb. 9, 1990, and Namibia gained independence Mar. 21.

Walvis Bay, the principal deepwater port, had been turned over to South African administration in 1922. It remained in South African hands after independence, but South Africa turned control of the port back to Namibia, as of Mar. 1, 1994. Separatist violence flared in the Caprivi Strip in the late 1990s. In 2009, severe flooding in northern Namibia claimed more than 100 lives. SWAPO, the leading political group since independence, dominated the general election held Nov. 27-28, 2009.

Nauru
Republic of Nauru

People: Population: 9,378. **Age distrib.:** <15: 32.7%; 65+: 1.7%. **Pop. density:** 1,156.6 per sq mi, 446.6 per sq km. **Urban:** 100%.

Ethnic groups: Nauruan 58%, other Pacific Islander 26%, Chinese 8%, European 8%. **Principal languages:** Nauruan (official; English widely understood, spoken, used for most govt. and commercial purposes). **Chief religions:** Protestant 46% (Nauru Congregational 35%, Nauru Independent Church 10%), Roman Catholic 33%, none 5%.

Geography: Total area: 8.1 sq mi, 21 sq km; **Land area:** 8.1 sq mi, 21 sq km. **Location:** In W Pacific O. just S of Equator. **Neighbors:** Nearest is Kiribati to E. **Topography:** Mostly a plateau bearing high-grade phosphate deposits, surrounded by a sandy shore and coral reef in concentric rings. **Capital:** Nauru, 10,308.

Government: Type: Republic. **Head of state and gov.:** Pres. Sprent Dabwido; b. Sept. 16, 1972; in office: Nov. 15, 2011. **Local divisions:** 14 districts. **Defense budget:** NA. **Active troops:** No regular military forces. Defense is responsibility of Australia.

Economy: Industries: phosphate mining, offshore banking, coconut prods. **Chief crops:** coconuts. **Natural resources:** phosphates, fish. **Arable land:** None. **Livestock:** chickens: 5,000; pigs: 3,000. **Fish catch:** 200 metric tons. **Electricity prod.:** 33 mil kWh. **Labor force:** mining phosphates, public administration, education, transportation.

Finance: Monetary unit: Australian Dollar (AUD) (Sept. 2012: 0.98 = $1 U.S.). **GDP** (2005 est.): $60 mil; **per capita GDP** (2005 est.): $5,000; **GDP growth:** NA. **Imports** (2004): $20 mil. **Exports** (2005): $64,000. **Tourism:** NA. **Budget** (2005): $13.5 mil.

Transport: Civil aviation: 220 mil pass.-mi; 1 airport. **Chief port:** Nauru.

Communications: TV sets: 1 per 1,000 pop. **Radios:** 618 per 1,000 pop. **Telephone lines** (2009): 18.6 per 100 pop. **Internet** (2010): 6%.

Health: Life expect.: 61.6 male; 69.1 female. **Births:** 27.1 (per 1,000 pop.). **Deaths:** 6.0 (per 1,000 pop.). **Natural inc.:** 2.11%. **Infant mortality:** 8.5 (per 1,000 live births). **HIV rate:** NA.

Education: Compulsory: ages 6-16. **Literacy:** NA.

Major intl. organizations: UN (FAO, WHO), the Commonwealth.

Permanent UN mission: 800 2nd Ave., Ste. 400A, New York, NY 10017; (212) 937-0074.

Website: www.mofa.gov.nr

The British discovered the island in 1798, but it was annexed to the German Empire in 1886. After WWI, Australia administered Nauru under a League of Nations mandate. During WWII the Japanese occupied the island. In 1947 Nauru was made a UN trust territory, administered by Australia. It became an independent republic Jan. 31, 1968, and was admitted to the UN Sept. 14, 1999.

Phosphate exports provided Nauru with per capita revenues that were among the highest in the Third World. Phosphate reserves, however, are nearly depleted, and environmental damage from strip-mining has been severe. Lax banking practices have made Nauru a haven for money laundering. Nauru defaulted on a loan payment for its real estate holdings in Australia and was virtually bankrupt by 2004, when financial reforms were implemented. Rising seas linked to global climate change have eroded the nation's coastline.

Nepal
Federal Democratic Republic of Nepal

People: Population: 29,890,686. **Age distrib.:** <15: 33.5%; 65+: 4.4%. **Pop. density:** 540 per sq mi, 208.5 per sq km. **Urban:** 17%. **Ethnic groups:** Chhettri 16%, Brahman-Hill 13%, Magar 7%, Tharu 7%, Tamang 6%, Newar 5%, Muslim 4%, Kami 4%, Yadav 4%. **Principal languages:** Nepali (official), Maithali, Bhojpuri, Tharu (Dagaura/Rana), Tamang, Newar, Magar, Awadhi, English spoken by many in govt. and business. **Chief religions:** Hindu 81%, Buddhist 11%, Muslim 4%, Kirant 4%.

Geography: Total area: 56,827 sq mi, 147,181 sq km; **Land area:** 55,348 sq mi, 143,351 sq km. **Location:** Astride the Himalaya Mts. **Neighbors:** China on N, India on S. **Topography:** The Himalayas stretch across the N, the hill country with its fertile valleys extends across the center, while S border region is part of the flat, subtropical Ganges Plain. **Capital:** Kathmandu, 1,014,570.

Government: Type: Republic. **Head of state:** Pres. Ram Baran Yadav; b. Feb. 4, 1948; in office: July 23, 2008. **Head of gov.:** Prime Min. Baburam Bhattarai; b. June 18, 1954; in office: Aug. 29, 2011. **Local divisions:** 5 regions subdivided into 14 zones. **Defense budget:** $261 mil. **Active troops:** 95,753.

Economy: Industries: tourism, carpets, textiles; small rice, jute, sugar, and oilseed mills; cigarettes, cement, and brick prod. **Chief crops:** pulses, rice, corn, wheat, sugarcane, jute, root crops. **Natural resources:** quartz, water, timber, hydropower, lignite, copper, cobalt, iron ore. **Arable land:** 16.7%. **Livestock:** cattle: 7.2 mil; chickens: 25.8 mil; goats: 8.8 mil; pigs: 1.1 mil; sheep: 801,371. **Fish catch:** 49,730 metric tons. **Electricity prod.:** 3.1 bil kWh. **Labor force:** agric. 75%, industry 7%, services 18%.

Finance: Monetary unit: Rupee (NPR). (Sept. 2012: 88.68 = $1 U.S.) **GDP:** $38.3 bil; **per capita GDP:** $1,300; **GDP growth:** 3.5%. **Imports:** $5.4 bil; India 54.4%, China 27.5%. **Exports:** $896 mil; India 59.2%, U.S. 9.2%, Germany 5.2%. **Tourism:** $386 mil. **Budget** (FY11): $5.3 bil. **Total reserves less gold:** $3.6 bil. **CPI change:** 9.5%.

Transport: Railways: 37 mi. **Civil aviation:** 533.1 mil pass.-mi; 11 airports.

Communications: TV sets: 21 per 1,000 pop. **Radios:** 37 per 1,000 pop. **Telephone lines:** 2.8 per 100 pop. **Internet:** 9%.

Health: Life expect.: 65.3 male; 67.8 female. **Births:** 21.9 (per 1,000 pop.). **Deaths:** 6.8 (per 1,000 pop.). **Natural inc.:** 1.51%. **Infant mortality:** 43.1 (per 1,000 live births). **HIV rate:** 0.4%.

Education: NA. **Literacy:** 60.3%.

Major intl. organizations: UN (FAO, IBRD, ILO, IMF, WHO), WTO.

Embassy: 2131 Leroy Pl. NW 20008; 667-4550.

Website: www.nepalgov.gov.np

Nepal was originally a group of petty principalities, the inhabitants of one of which, the Gurkhas, became dominant about 1769. In 1951 King Tribhubana Bir Bikram, member of the Shah family, ended the system of rule by hereditary premiers of the Ranas family, who had kept the kings virtual prisoners, and established a cabinet system of government. Polygamy, child marriage, and the caste system were officially abolished in 1963. Political parties were legalized in 1990.

Nine members of Nepal's royal family, including King Birendra and Queen Aishwarya, died in a massacre on June 1, 2001. An official inquiry blamed the carnage on a 10th family member, Crown Prince Dipendra, who reportedly shot himself that night and died 3 days later, allowing Birendra's brother Gyanendra Bir Bikram Shah Dev to take the throne.

Citing the government's failure to stop a Maoist insurgency, King Gyanendra assumed absolute authority, Feb. 1, 2005. After weeks of pro-democracy demonstrations, in which police killed at least 12 protesters, the king agreed, Apr. 24, 2006, to reinstate parliament, which had not met for four years. A new government, led by Prime Min. Girija Prasad Koirala, signed a peace accord with Maoist rebels Nov. 21, 2006, ending a decade-long civil war that claimed 13,000 lives.

Under a draft constitution that made Koirala acting head of state, Maoists joined an interim parliament Jan. 15, 2007, and entered the cabinet Apr. 1. The king was stripped of most powers. A constituent assembly voted May 28, 2008, to abolish the monarchy and make Nepal a republic. After months of political wrangling, Maoist leader Pushpa Kamal Dahal, popularly known as Prachanda, became prime min. Aug. 18. On May 3, 2009, Prachanda moved to fire Nepal's army chief, who had refused orders to integrate some 19,000 former Maoist rebels into the armed forces; when Pres. Ram Baran Yadav countermanded the firing, Prachanda resigned May 4. After two more short-lived governments, Baburam Bhattarai, also a Maoist, was sworn as prime min. Aug. 29, 2011.

Netherlands
Kingdom of the Netherlands

People: Population: 16,730,632. **Age distrib.:** <15: 17.2%; 65+: 16.6%. **Pop. density:** 1,278.5 per sq mi, 493.6 per sq km. **Urban:** 83.2%. **Ethnic groups:** Dutch 80%, EU 5%, Indonesian 2%, Turkish 2%, Surinamese 2%, Moroccan 2%. **Principal languages:** Dutch, Frisian (both official). **Chief religions:** Roman Catholic 30%, Protestant 20% (Dutch Reformed 11%, Calvinist 6%), Muslim 6%, none 42%.

Geography: Total area: 16,040 sq mi, 41,543 sq km; **Land area:** 13,086 sq mi, 33,893 sq km. **Location:** In NW Europe on North Sea. **Neighbors:** Germany on E, Belgium on S. **Topography:** Land is flat, an average alt. of 37 ft above sea level, with much land below sea level reclaimed and protected by some 1,500 mi of dikes. Since 1920 the government has been draining the IJsselmeer, formerly the Zuiderzee. **Capital:** Amsterdam, 1,055,610; s-Gravenhage (The Hague) (seat), 635,023. **Cities (urban aggl.):** Rotterdam, 1,013,700.

Government: Type: Parliamentary democracy under a constitutional monarch. **Head of state:** Queen Beatrix; b. Jan. 31, 1938; in office: Apr. 30, 1980. **Head of gov.:** Prime Min: Mark Rutte; b. Feb. 14, 1967; in office: Oct. 14, 2010. **Local divisions:** 12 provinces. **Defense budget:** $11.7 bil. **Active troops:** 37,368.

Economy: Industries: agroindustries, metal and engineering prods., elec. machinery and equip., chemicals, petroleum, constr., microelectronics, fishing. **Chief crops:** grains, potatoes, sugar beets, fruits, vegetables. **Natural resources:** nat. gas, petroleum, peat, limestone, salt, sand and gravel. **Crude oil reserves:** 287.4 mil bbls. **Arable land:** 31.3%. **Livestock:** cattle: 4 mil; chickens: 101.2 mil; goats: 352,830; pigs: 12.3 mil; sheep: 1.1 mil. **Fish catch:** 456,302 metric tons. **Electricity prod.** (2010): 108 bil kWh. **Labor force:** agric. 2%, industry 18%, services 80%.

Finance: Monetary unit: Euro (EUR) (Sept. 2012: 0.79 = $1 U.S.). **GDP:** $713.1 bil; **per capita GDP:** $42,700; **GDP growth:** 1.3%. **Imports:** $493.1 bil; Germany 14.6%, China 11.9%, Belgium 8.7%, UK 6.1%, Russia 6%, U.S. 5.9%, France 4.1%. **Exports:** $551.8 bil; Germany 26.2%, Belgium 14.1%, France 9.3%, UK 7.7%, Italy 4.8%. **Tourism:** $14.4 bil. **Budget:** $420.4 bil. **Total reserves less gold:** $20.3 bil. **Gold:** 19.7 mil oz t. **CPI change:** 2.3%.

Transport: Railways: 1,799 mi. **Motor vehicles:** 533.6 vehicles per 1,000 pop. **Civil aviation:** 56 bil pass.-mi (incl. airlines based in territories and dependencies); 20 airports. **Chief ports:** Amsterdam, Ijmuiden, Moerdijk, Rotterdam, Terneuzen, Vlissingen.

Communications: TV sets: 767 per 1,000 pop. **Radios:** 978 per 1,000 pop. **Telephone lines:** 42.8 per 100 pop. **Daily newspaper circ.:** 307.5 per 1,000 pop. **Internet:** 92.3%.

Health: Life expect.: 78.8 male; 83.1 female. **Births:** 10.9 (per 1,000 pop.). **Deaths:** 8.4 (per 1,000 pop.). **Natural inc.:** 0.25%. **Infant mortality:** 3.7 (per 1,000 live births). **HIV rate:** 0.2%.

Education: Compulsory: ages 5-17. **Literacy:** 99%.

Major intl. organizations: UN and all of its specialized agencies, EU, NATO, OECD, OSCE, WTO.

Embassy: 4200 Linnean Ave. NW 20008; 877-DUTCHHELP.

Website: www.government.nl

Julius Caesar conquered the region in 55 BCE, when it was inhabited by Celtic and Germanic tribes. After the empire of Charlemagne fell apart, the Netherlands (Holland, Belgium, Flanders) split among counts, dukes, and bishops, passed to Burgundy and thence to Spain. William the Silent, prince of Orange, led a confederation of the northern provinces, called Estates, in the Union of Utrecht, 1579; in 1581 they repudiated allegiance to Spain. The rise of the Dutch republic to naval, economic, and artistic eminence came in the 17th cent.

After a period of French hegemony, 1795-1813, the Congress of Vienna in 1815 formed a kingdom of the Netherlands, including Belgium, under William I. In 1830, the Belgians seceded and formed a separate kingdom.

The Netherlands maintained its neutrality in WWI, but was invaded and occupied by Germany, 1940-45. In 1949, after several years of fighting, the Netherlands granted independence to Indonesia.

The murder May 6, 2002, of right-wing populist leader Pim Fortuyn, 9 days before legislative elections, marked the first political assassination in modern Dutch history. The killing of filmmaker Theo van Gogh, Nov. 2, 2004, by an Islamic extremist shocked many Dutch. On Apr. 30, 2009, the national Queen's Day holiday, a Dutch motorist in Apeldoorn aimed his car at an open-topped bus carrying Queen Beatrix and other royal family members; they were unhurt, but 7 bystanders died, as did the driver. The anti-Islamic, right-wing Freedom Party, headed by Geert Wilders, gained in parliamentary elections June 9, 2010. Prime Min. Mark Rutte and his cabinet resigned Apr. 23, 2012, after failing to pass a budget in line with EU requirements. Rutte's government nonetheless remained in a caretaker capacity, and his pro-business Liberal party won a majority of seats in parliamentary elections held Sept. 12, 2012.

Netherlands Dependencies

The **Netherlands Antilles** consists of two island groups in the West Indies. **Curaçao** and **Bonaire** are near the coast of Venezuela; **Sint Eustatius**, **Saba**, and the southern part of **Sint Maarten** are southeast of Puerto Rico. The northern two-thirds of St. Maarten was formerly part of French Guadeloupe and is now an overseas territorial collectivity; the French call the island Saint Martin. Total area of the two groups is 371 sq mi, incl. Bonaire (111), Curaçao (171), St. Eustatius (8), Saba (5), St. Maarten (13). St. Maarten suffered extensive damage from Hurricane Luis, Sept. 1995. Total pop. of the Netherlands Antilles (2010 est.) was 228,693. Willemstad, on Curaçao, is the capital. The principal industry is the refining of crude oil from Venezuela. Tourism is also an important industry, as is shipbuilding. Constitutional changes effective Oct. 10, 2010, dissolved the Netherlands Antilles as a political entity and elevated Curaçao and St. Maarten to the status of "autonomous countries" within the Kingdom of the Netherlands. Bonaire, St. Eustatius, and Saba were classified as special municipalities.

Aruba, about 26 mi west of Curaçao, was separated from the Netherlands Antilles on Jan. 1, 1986; it is an autonomous component of the Netherlands, with a status similar to Curaçao and St. Maarten. Area: 69 sq mi; pop. (2011 est.): 106,113; capital: Oranjestad. Chief industries are oil refining and tourism. **Website:** www.kabga.aw

New Zealand

People: Population: 4,327,944. **Age distrib.:** <15: 20.2%; 65+: 13.6%. **Pop. density:** 41.9 per sq mi, 16.2 per sq km. **Urban:** 86.2%. **Ethnic groups:** European 57%, Asian 8%, Maori 7%, Pacific Islander 5%, mixed 10%. **Principal languages:** English, Maori (both official); Samoan; French; Hindi; Yue; Northern Chinese; NZ, sign language (official). **Chief religions:** Protestant 39% (Anglican 14%, Presbyterian, Congregational, Reformed 10%; Christian [no denomination specified] 5%; Methodist 3%; Pentecostal 2%; other Christian 4%); Roman Catholic 13%, Maori Christian 2%, Hindu 2%, none 32%.

Geography: Total area: 103,363 sq mi, 267,710 sq km; **Land area:** 103,363 sq mi, 267,710 sq km. **Location:** In SW Pacific O. **Neighbors:** Nearest are Australia on W, Fiji and Tonga on N. **Topography:** Each of the 2 main islands (North and South Isls.) is mainly hilly and mountainous. The E coasts consist of fertile plains, especially the broad Canterbury Plains on South Isl. A volcanic plateau is in center of North Isl. South Isl. has glaciers and 15 peaks over 10,000 ft. **Capital:** Wellington, 410,410. **Cities (urban aggl.):** Auckland, 1,451,955.

Government: Type: Parliamentary democracy. **Head of state:** Queen Elizabeth II, represented by Gov.-Gen. Sir Jeremiah (Jerry) Mateparae; b. Nov. 14, 1954; in office: Aug. 31, 2011. **Head of gov.:** Prime Min. John Key; b. Aug. 9, 1961; in office: Nov. 19, 2008. **Local divisions:** 16 regions. **Defense budget:** $2.14 bil. **Active troops:** 9,673.

Economy: Industries: food proc., wood and paper prods., textiles, machinery, transp. equip., banking and insurance, tourism, mining. **Chief crops:** wheat, barley, potatoes, pulses, fruits, vegetables. **Natural resources:** nat. gas, iron ore, sand, coal, timber,

hydropower, gold, limestone. **Crude oil reserves:** 96.1 mil bbls. **Arable land:** 1.8%. **Livestock:** cattle: 9.9 mil; chickens: 13.5 mil; goats: 95,281; pigs: 335,114; sheep: 32.6 mil. **Fish catch:** 547,232 metric tons. **Electricity prod.** (2010): 43.4 bil kWh. **Labor force:** agric. 7%, industry 19%, services 74%.

Finance: Monetary unit: Dollar (NZD) (Sept. 2012: 1.26 = $1 U.S.). **GDP:** $123.8 bil; **per capita GDP:** $28,000; **GDP growth:** 1.4%. **Imports:** $35.5 bil; China 16.1%, Australia 15.9%, U.S. 10.4%, Japan 6.3%, Singapore 4.6%, Germany 4.3%. **Exports:** $37.5 bil; Australia 22.2%, China 12.5%, U.S. 8.5%, Japan 7.1%. **Tourism:** $5.5 bil. **Budget:** $74.7 bil. **Total reserves less gold:** $17 bil. **CPI change:** 4.4%.

Transport: Railways: 2,565 mi. **Motor vehicles:** 729.4 vehicles per 1,000 pop. **Civil aviation:** 16.1 bil pass.-mi; 39 airports. **Chief ports:** Auckland, Lyttelton, Manukau Harbor, Marsden Point, Tauranga, Wellington.

Communications: TV sets: 615 per 1,000 pop. **Radios:** 1,006 per 1,000 pop. **Telephone lines:** 42.6 per 100 pop. **Daily newspaper circ.:** 182.5 per 1,000 pop. **Internet:** 86%.

Health: Life expect.: 78.7 male; 82.8 female. **Births:** 13.6 (per 1,000 pop.). **Deaths:** 7.2 (per 1,000 pop.). **Natural inc.:** 0.64%. **Infant mortality:** 4.7 (per 1,000 live births). **HIV rate:** 0.1%.

Education: Compulsory: ages 5-16. **Literacy:** 99%.

Major intl. organizations: UN (FAO, IBRD, ILO, IMF, WHO), APEC, the Commonwealth, OECD, WTO.

Embassy: 37 Observatory Cir. NW 20008; 328-4800.

Website: newzealand.govt.nz

The Maori, a Polynesian group from the eastern Pacific, reached New Zealand before and during the 14th cent. The first European to sight New Zealand was Dutch navigator Abel Janszoon Tasman. The Maori refused to allow him to land. British Capt. James Cook explored the coasts, 1769-70.

British sovereignty was proclaimed and Maori land rights were recognized in the Treaty of Waitangi, 1840, with organized settlement beginning in the same year. Representative institutions were granted in 1853. The Maori wars, or New Zealand Wars, ended in 1870 with British victory. The colony became a dominion in 1907 and gained full independence in 1947. It is a member of the Commonwealth. The Maori make up about 15% of the population; 7 of 122 members of the House of Representatives are directly elected from Maori constituencies, but Maori may also run in other districts.

A progressive tradition in politics dates back to the 19th cent., when New Zealand was known for social experimentation; much of the nation's economy has been deregulated since the 1980s. Jenny Shipley of the National Party became the nation's first female prime min., Dec. 8, 1997. The Labour Party, led by Helen Clark, won general elections, Nov. 27, 1999, and July 27, 2002. New Zealand supplied small troop contingents to coalition forces in Iraq and Afghanistan.

The legislature legalized prostitution June 2003. In July, New Zealand contributed troops to the Australian-led force in the Solomon Islands. A measure establishing a supreme court and ending appeals to the UK Privy Council passed Oct. 14. A major settlement of Maori land claims dating from the 19th cent. was signed June 25, 2008. With the country in recession, Clark called new elections Nov. 8, which were won by the National Party, led by John Key.

A South Island earthquake Sept. 3, 2010, caused property damage estimated at $2.7 bil. An explosion Nov. 19 at the Pike River coal mine on South Island claimed the lives of 29 men. Another Christchurch quake, Feb. 22, 2011, killed 181 people and caused damage estimated at $11 bil to the central business district. Key's handling of these disasters bolstered his party's popularity, and it was returned to power in elections Nov. 26, 2011.

New Zealand comprises **North Island**, 43,911 sq mi; **South Island**, 58,084 sq mi; **Stewart Island**, 649 sq mi; **Chatham Isls.**, 373 sq mi; and several groups of smaller islands.

In 1965, the **Cook Islands** (2012 est. pop.: 10,777; area: 91 sq mi), halfway between New Zealand and Hawaii, became self-governing. New Zealand retains responsibility for defense and foreign affairs. **Niue** attained the same status in 1974; it lies 400 mi W (2012 est. pop.: 1,269; area: 100 sq mi). Cyclone Heta devastated Niue Jan. 6, 2004. **Tokelau** (2012 est. pop.: 1,368; area: 4 sq mi) comprises three atolls 300 mi N of Samoa. Two referendums on Tokelau self-government, held Feb. 13-15, 2006, and Oct. 20-24, 2007, failed to gain the required two-third majority.

Ross Dependency, administered by New Zealand since 1923, comprises 160,000 sq mi of Antarctic territory.

Nicaragua
Republic of Nicaragua

People: Population: 5,727,707. **Age distrib.:** <15: 30.8%; 65+: 4.6%. **Pop. density:** 123.6 per sq mi, 47.7 per sq km. **Urban:** 57.5%. **Ethnic groups:** mestizo (mixed Amerindian and white) 69%, white 17%, black 9%, Amerindian 5%. **Principal languages:** Spanish (official), Miskito, English and indigenous langs. on Atlantic coast. **Chief religions:** Roman Catholic 59%, Protestant 23% (Evangelical 22%, Moravian 2%), none 16%.

Geography: Total area: 50,336 sq mi, 130,370 sq km; **Land area:** 46,328 sq mi, 119,990 sq km. **Location:** In Central America. **Neighbors:** Honduras on N, Costa Rica on S. **Topography:** Both

Caribbean and Pacific coasts are over 200 mi long. Cordillera Mts., with many volcanic peaks, run NW-SE through middle of the country. Between this and a volcanic range to the E lie Lakes Managua and Nicaragua. **Capital:** Managua, 969,698.

Government: Type: Republic. **Head of state and gov.:** Pres. Daniel Ortega Saavedra; b. Nov. 11, 1945; in office: Jan. 10, 2007. **Local divisions:** 15 departments, 2 autonomous regions. **Defense budget:** $53 mil. **Active troops:** 12,000.

Economy: Industries: food proc., chemicals, machinery and metal prods., knit and woven apparel, petroleum refining and distrib., beverages, footwear, wood. **Chief crops:** coffee, bananas, sugarcane, cotton, rice, corn, tobacco, sesame, soya, beans. **Natural resources:** gold, silver, copper, tungsten, lead, zinc, timber, fish. **Arable land:** 15.8%. **Livestock:** cattle: 3.6 mil; chickens: 18 mil; goats: 7,100; pigs: 480,000; sheep: 6,300. **Fish catch:** 54,395 metric tons. **Electricity prod.** (2010): 3.6 bil kWh. **Labor force:** agric. 28%, industry 19%, services 53%.

Finance: Monetary unit: Cordoba (NIO) (Sept. 2012: 23.75 = $1 U.S.). **GDP:** $19.1 bil; **per capita GDP:** $3,200; **GDP growth:** 4.7%. **Imports:** $6.5 bil; U.S. 22%, Venezuela 14.5%, Costa Rica 9%, China 8.8%, Guatemala 8.3%, Mexico 7.2%, El Salvador 5.6%, South Korea 4.1%. **Exports:** $4 bil; U.S. 60.2%, Canada 8.3%, El Salvador 4.6%. **Tourism:** $377 mil. **Budget:** $1.6 bil. **Total reserves less gold:** $1.9 bil. **CPI change:** 8.1%.

Transport: Motor vehicles: 33.9 vehicles per 1,000 pop. **Civil aviation:** 11 airports. **Chief ports:** Bluefields, Corinto.

Communications: TV sets: 129 per 1,000 pop. **Radios:** 273 per 1,000 pop. **Telephone lines:** 4.9 per 100 pop. **Internet:** 10.6%.

Health: Life expect.: 70.1 male; 74.4 female. **Births:** 19.1 (per 1,000 pop.). **Deaths:** 5.0 (per 1,000 pop.). **Natural inc.:** 1.41%. **Infant mortality:** 21.9 (per 1,000 live births). **HIV rate:** 0.2%.

Education: Compulsory: ages 6-11. **Literacy:** 78%.

Major intl. organizations: UN and most of its specialized agencies, OAS, WTO.

Embassy: 1627 New Hampshire Ave. NW 20009; 939-6570. **Website:** www.presidencia.gob.ni

Nicaragua, inhabited by various Indian tribes, was conquered by Spain in 1552. After gaining independence from Spain, 1821, Nicaragua was united for a short period with Mexico, then with the United Provinces of Central America, finally becoming an independent republic, 1838. U.S. Marines occupied the country at times in the early 20th cent., the last time from 1926 to 1933.

Gen. Anastasio Somoza Debayle held the presidency 1967-72, 1974-79. Martial law was imposed in Dec. 1974, after officials were kidnapped by the Marxist Sandinista guerrillas. Nationwide antigovernment strikes touched off a civil war, 1978, which ended when Somoza fled Nicaragua and the Sandinistas took control of Managua, July 1979. Somoza was assassinated in Paraguay, Sept. 17, 1980.

Relations with the U.S. were strained as a result of Nicaragua's aid to leftist guerrillas in El Salvador and U.S. backing of anti-Sandinista contra guerrilla groups. In 1983 the contras launched a major offensive; the Sandinistas imposed rule by decree. In 1985 the U.S. House rejected Pres. Reagan's request for military aid to the contras. The subsequent diversion of funds to the contras from the proceeds of a secret arms sale to Iran caused a major scandal in the U.S.

In a stunning upset, Violeta Barrios de Chamorro defeated Sandinista leader Daniel Ortega Saavedra in national elections, Feb. 25, 1990. The conservative Arnoldo Alemán Lacayo defeated Ortega in the presidential election of Oct. 20, 1996. Up to 2,000 people died Oct. 30, 1998, in a mudslide caused by rains from Hurricane Mitch.

Drought and a drop in coffee prices plunged Nicaragua into an economic crisis in 2001. Enrique Bolaños Geyer, a conservative businessman, won the presidency that year. Convicted Dec. 7, 2003, on corruption charges, former Pres. Alemán was fined $10 mil and received a 20-year sentence, which he was allowed to serve under house arrest. Ortega won the presidential election of Nov. 5, 2006. After taking office Jan. 10, 2007, he irritated the U.S. by cultivating ties with Venezuela and Iran, which offered aid to the financially hard-pressed country. He was reelected Nov. 6, 2011.

Niger
Republic of Niger

People: Population: 16,344,687. **Age distrib.:** <15: 50.1%; 65+: 2.6%. **Pop. density:** 33.4 per sq mi, 12.9 per sq km. **Urban:** 17.8%. **Ethnic groups:** Haoussa 55%, Djerma Sonrai 21%, Tuareg 9%, Peuhl 9%, Kanouri Manga 5%. **Principal languages:** French (official), Hausa, Djerma. **Chief religions:** Muslim 80%, other (incl. indigenous beliefs, Christian) 20%.

Geography: Total area: 489,191 sq mi, 1,267,000 sq km; **Land area:** 489,076 sq mi, 1,266,700 sq km. **Location:** In interior of N Africa. **Neighbors:** Libya, Algeria on N; Mali, Burkina Faso on W; Benin, Nigeria on S; Chad on E. **Topography:** Mostly arid desert and mountains. A narrow savanna in S and Niger R. basin in the SW contain most of the population. **Capital:** Niamey, 1,297,160.

Government: Type: Republic. **Head of state:** Pres. Mahamadou Issoufou; b. 1952; in office: Apr. 7, 2011. **Head of gov.:** Prime Min. Brigi Rafini; b. Apr. 7, 1953; in office: Apr. 7, 2011. **Local divisions:** 7 departments, 1 capital district. **Defense budget** (2010): $46 mil. **Active troops:** 5,300.

Economy: Industries: uranium mining, cement, brick, soap, textiles, food proc., chemicals, slaughterhouses. **Chief crops:** cowpeas, cotton, peanuts, millet, sorghum, cassava, rice. **Natural resources:** uranium, coal, iron ore, tin, phosphates, gold, molybdenum, gypsum, salt, petroleum. **Arable land:** 11.8%. **Livestock:** cattle: 9.8 mil; chickens: 17.1 mil; goats: 13.7 mil; pigs: 40,000; sheep: 10.9 mil. **Fish catch:** 29,954 metric tons. **Electricity prod.:** 210 mil kWh. **Labor force:** agric. 90%, industry 6%, services 4%.

Finance: Monetary unit: CFA BCEAO Franc (XOF) (Sept. 2012: 519.73 = $1 U.S.). **GDP:** $11.8 bil; **per capita GDP:** $800; **GDP growth:** 2.3%. **Imports:** $2 bil; France 15.8%, China 9.8%, Nigeria 9%, French Polynesia 8.5%, Belgium 6.9%, India 5%, Togo 4.8%. **Exports:** $1.2 bil; U.S. 49.1%, Nigeria 29.3%, Russia 10.3%, Ghana 4.1%. **Tourism:** $79 mil. **Budget:** $1.4 bil. **Total reserves less gold:** $673 mil. **CPI change:** 2.9%.

Transport: Motor vehicles: 7.8 vehicles per 1,000 pop. **Civil aviation:** 10 airports.

Communications: TV sets: 12 per 1,000 pop. **Radios:** 235 per 1,000 pop. **Telephone lines:** 0.6 per 100 pop. **Daily newspaper circ.:** 0.2 per 1,000 pop. **Internet:** 1.3%.

Health: Life expect.: 52.8 male; 55.1 female. **Births:** 47.6 (per 1,000 pop.). **Deaths:** 13.4 (per 1,000 pop.). **Natural inc.:** 3.42%. **Infant mortality:** 89.7 (per 1,000 live births). **HIV rate:** 0.8%.

Education: Compulsory: ages 7-12. **Literacy:** 28.7%.

Major intl. organizations: UN (FAO, IBRD, ILO, IMF, WHO), AU, WTO

Embassy: 2204 R St. NW 20008; 483-4224. **Website:** www.gouv.ne

Niger was part of ancient and medieval African empires. European explorers reached the area in the late 18th cent. The French colony of Niger was established 1900-22, after the defeat of Tuareg fighters, who had invaded the area from the north a century before. The country became independent Aug. 3, 1960.

In 1993, Niger held its first free and open elections since independence; an opposition leader, Mahamane Ousmane, won the presidency. A peace accord Apr. 24, 1995, ended a Tuareg rebellion that began in 1990. A coup, Jan. 27, 1996, followed by a disputed presidential election in July, left the military in control of Niger. On Apr. 9, 1999, Gen. Ibrahim Bare Mainassara, Niger's president since 1996, was assassinated, apparently by members of his security team. Elections were held Oct. 17 and Nov. 24, 1999, under a new constitution, approved by referendum July 18, that restored civilian rule.

One of the world's poorest countries, Niger experienced severe food shortages in 2005 after locusts and drought ruined the grain harvest. A resurgence of Tuareg rebel activity in June 2007 brought a major government counteroffensive. Popularly elected in 1999 and 2004, Pres. Mamadou Tandja invoked emergency powers in 2009, seeking to remain in office for a third 5-year term; he was overthrown by a military junta Feb. 18, 2010. Civilian rule returned following Jan.-Mar. 2011 elections. Increased terrorist activity in countries surrounding Niger, particularly Mali, since the fall of Muammar al-Qaddafi's government in Libya led the U.S. and EU to send anti-terrorist experts to train Niger's forces to fight al-Qaeda-affiliated militants in 2012.

Nigeria
Federal Republic of Nigeria

People: Population: 170,123,740. **Age distrib.:** <15: 43.9%; 65+: 3%. **Pop. density:** 483.8 per sq mi, 186.8 per sq km. **Urban:** 49.6%. **Ethnic groups:** 250+ ethnic groups: Hausa and Fulani 29%, Yoruba 21%, Igbo (Ibo) 18%, Ijaw 10%, Kanuri 4%, Ibibio 4%, Tiv 3% most populous, politically influential groups. **Principal languages:** English (official), Hausa, Yoruba, Igbo (Ibo), Fulani, 500+ indigenous langs. **Chief religions:** Muslim 50%, Christian 40%, indigenous beliefs 10%.

Geography: Total area: 356,669 sq mi, 923,768 sq km; **Land area:** 351,649 sq mi, 910,768 sq km. **Location:** On S coast of W Africa. **Neighbors:** Benin on W, Niger on N, Chad and Cameroon on E. **Topography:** 4 E-W regions divide Nigeria: a coastal mangrove swamp 10-60 mi wide, a tropical rain forest 50-100 mi wide, a plateau of savanna and open woodland, and semi-desert in N. **Capital:** Abuja, 2,152,770. **Cities (urban aggl.):** Lagos, 11,223,041; Kano, 3,374,598; Ibadan, 2,948,530; Port Harcourt, 1,894,164; Kaduna, 1,523,505; Benin City, 1,358,874; Ogbomosho, 1,074,953.

Government: Type: Federal republic. **Head of state and gov.:** Pres. Goodluck Jonathan; b. Nov. 20, 1957; in office: May 6, 2010 (acting from Feb. 9). **Local divisions:** 36 states, 1 capital territory. **Defense budget:** $2.23 bil. **Active troops:** 80,000.

Economy: Industries: crude oil, coal, tin, columbite; rubber prods., wood; hides and skins, textiles, cement and other constr. materials, food prods. **Chief crops:** cocoa, peanuts, cotton, palm oil, corn, rice, sorghum, millet, cassava, yams, rubber. **Natural resources:** nat. gas, petroleum, tin, iron ore, coal, limestone, niobium, lead, zinc. **Crude oil reserves:** 37.2 bil bbls. **Arable land:** 37.3%. **Livestock:** cattle: 16 mil; chickens: 192.3 mil; goats: 56.5 mil; pigs: 7.5 mil; sheep: 35.5 mil. **Fish catch:** 817,516 metric tons. **Electricity prod.:** 18.8 bil kWh. **Labor force:** agric. 70%, industry 10%, services 20%.

Finance: Monetary unit: Naira (NGN) (Sept. 2012: 158.40 = $1 U.S.). **GDP:** $418.7 bil; **per capita GDP:** $2,600; **GDP growth:** 7.2%. **Imports:** $69.5 bil; China 17.5%, U.S. 9.1%, Netherlands 4.9%, India 4.7%, South Korea 4.7%. **Exports:** $103.9 bil; U.S. 28.9%, India 12%, Brazil 7.8%, Spain 7.1%, France 4.9%, Netherlands 4.2%.

Tourism: $601 mil. **Budget:** $31.1 bil. **Total reserves less gold:** $35.2 bil. **Gold:** 687,000 oz t. **CPI change:** 10.8%.

Transport: Railways: 2,178 mi. **Motor vehicles:** 8.3 vehicles per 1,000 pop. **Civil aviation:** 1.2 bil pass.-mi; 40 airports. **Chief ports:** Calabar, Lagos.

Communications: TV sets: 67 per 1,000 pop. **Radios:** 602 per 1,000 pop. **Telephone lines:** 0.4 per 100 pop. **Internet:** 28.4%.

Health: Life expect.: 49.0 male; 55.3 female. **Births:** 39.2 (per 1,000 pop.). **Deaths:** 13.5 (per 1,000 pop.). **Natural inc.:** 2.58%. **Infant mortality:** 74.4 (per 1,000 live births). **HIV rate:** 3.6%.

Education: Compulsory: ages 6-14. **Literacy:** 61.3%.

Major intl. organizations: UN (FAO, IBRD, ILO, IMF, WHO), AU, the Commonwealth, OPEC, WTO.

Embassy: 3519 International Ct. NW 20008; 986-8400.

Website: www.nigeria.gov.ng

Early cultures in Nigeria date back to at least 700 BCE. From the 12th to the 14th cent., more advanced cultures developed in the Yoruba area, at Ife, and in the north, where Muslim influence prevailed. Portuguese and British slavers appeared in the 15th-16th cent. Britain seized Lagos, 1861, and gradually extended control inland until 1900. Nigeria became independent Oct. 1, 1960, and a republic Oct. 1, 1963.

On May 30, 1967, the Eastern Region seceded, proclaiming itself the Republic of Biafra, plunging the country into civil war. Casualties in the war were estimated at over 1 mil, including many Biafrans (mostly Ibos) who died of starvation despite international efforts to provide relief. The secessionists, after steadily losing ground, capitulated Jan. 12, 1970.

Nigeria emerged as one of the world's leading oil exporters in the 1970s, but much of the revenue has been squandered through corruption and mismanagement. Oil spills have polluted much of the Niger Delta region, and rebel activities there have been extensive.

After 13 years of military rule, the nation made a peaceful return to civilian government, Oct. 1979. Military rule resumed, Dec. 31, 1983; a second coup came in 1985. Headed by Gen. Ibrahim Babangida, the military regime held elections June 12, 1993, but annulled the vote June 23 when it appeared that Moshood Abiola would win. Riots followed and many were killed. Babangida resigned and appointed a civilian to head an interim government, Aug. 26, but that government was ousted Nov. 17 in a coup led by Gen. Sani Abacha. On June 11, 1994, Abiola declared himself president; he was jailed June 23.

Abacha's brutal rule ended June 8, 1998, when he died of an apparent heart attack. Abiola died in prison July 7, as Abacha's successor, Gen. Abdulsalam Abubakar, was reportedly preparing to free him. Abiola's death sparked riots in Lagos and other cities; on July 20, Abubakar promised elections and a return to civilian rule. Olusegun Obasanjo (a former military ruler) won the presidential vote Feb. 27, 1999, Nigeria's first civilian government in 15 years.

An oil fire that exploded from a ruptured pipeline in southern Nigeria, Oct. 17, 1998, killed at least 700 people who were scavenging for fuel. The imposition of strict Islamic law in northern states led to clashes, Jan.-Mar. 2000, in which at least 800 people died. Fighting between Muslims and Christians Sept. 7-12, 2001, and Oct. 13-14, 2001, claimed an estimated 600 lives; another 200 people died when soldiers went on a rampage in SE Nigeria Oct. 22-24, 2001.

At least 1,000 people were killed Jan. 27, 2002, when an army weapons depot in Lagos exploded. Controversy over Nigeria's plans to host a Miss World pageant sparked sectarian riots in Kaduna, Nov. 20-24, 2002, leaving more than 200 people dead. Christian militia members massacred about 630 Muslims at Yelwa, central Nigeria, May 2, 2004. Obasanjo's chosen successor, Umaru Musa Yar'Adua, won a presidential election, Apr. 21, 2007, marred by violence and described as "not credible" by international monitors. After prolonged illness, for which he sought treatment in Saudi Arabia, Yar'Adua died May 5, 2010, and was succeeded by Vice Pres. Goodluck Jonathan, a southern Christian. After he won reelection Apr. 16, 2011, over Muhammadu Buhari, a northern-based Muslim, riots in 12 northern provinces left more than 800 people dead. Boko Haram, a radical Islamist sect in NE Nigeria founded in 2001, aims to transform Nigeria into an Islamist state and has been blamed for more than 1,100 deaths since 2009.

Norway
Kingdom of Norway

People: Population: 4,707,270. **Age distrib.:** <15: 17.7%; 65+: 16.4%. **Pop. density:** 40.1 per sq mi, 15.5 per sq km. **Urban:** 79.4%. **Ethnic groups:** Norwegian (incl. Sami) 94%, other European 4%. **Principal languages:** Bokmal Norwegian, Nynorsk Norwegian (both official); Sami (official in 6 municipalities). **Chief religions:** Church of Norway (Evangelical Lutheran official) 86%, other Christian 2%, Muslim 2%.

Geography: Total area: 125,021 sq mi, 323,802 sq km; **Land area:** 117,484 sq mi, 304,282 sq km. **Location:** W part of Scandinavian peninsula in NW Europe (extends farther N than any European land). **Neighbors:** Sweden, Finland, Russia on E. **Topography:** Highly indented coast is lined with tens of thousands of islands. Mountains and plateaus cover most of the country, which is only 25% forested. **Capital:** Oslo, 915,386.

Government: Type: Hereditary constitutional monarchy. **Head of state:** King Harald V; b. Feb. 21, 1937; in office: Jan. 17, 1991. **Head of gov.:** Prime Min. Jens Stoltenberg; b. Mar. 16, 1959; in office: Oct. 17, 2005. **Local divisions:** 19 provinces. **Defense budget:** $6.43 bil. **Active troops:** 24,450.

Economy: Industries: petroleum and gas, food proc., ship-building, pulp and paper prods., metals, chemicals, timber, mining, textiles, fishing. **Chief crops:** barley, wheat, potatoes. **Natural resources:** petroleum, nat. gas, iron ore, copper, lead, zinc, titanium, pyrites, nickel, fish, timber, hydropower. **Crude oil reserves:** 5.3 bil bbls. **Arable land:** 2.7%. **Livestock:** cattle: 874,535; chickens: 3.9 mil; goats: 67,491; pigs: 850,383; sheep: 2.3 mil. **Fish catch:** 3.7 mil metric tons. **Electricity prod.** (2010): 122.2 bil kWh. **Labor force:** agric. 2.9%, industry 21.1%, services 76%.

Finance: Monetary unit: Krone (NOK) (Sept. 2012: 5.82 = $1 U.S.). **GDP:** $269.3 bil; **per capita GDP:** $54,200; **GDP growth:** 1.7%. **Imports:** $88.5 bil; Sweden 13.4%, Germany 12%, China 9%, Denmark 6.3%, UK 5.6%, U.S. 5.4%, Netherlands 4.2%. **Exports:** $162.4 bil; UK 27.2%, Netherlands 11.6%, Germany 11.1%, France 7.2%, Sweden 6.5%, U.S. 5.6%. **Tourism:** $5.3 bil. **Budget:** $209.5 bil. **Total reserves less gold:** $49.4 bil. **CPI change:** 1.3%.

Transport: Railways: 2,590 mi. **Motor vehicles:** 601 vehicles per 1,000 pop. **Civil aviation:** 5.5 bil pass.-mi; 67 airports. **Chief ports:** Bergen, Haugesund, Maaloy, Mongstad, Narvik, Sture.

Communications: TV sets: 1,554 per 1,000 pop. **Radios:** 913 per 1,000 pop. **Telephone lines:** 42.7 per 100 pop. **Daily newspaper circ.:** 516 per 1,000 pop. **Internet:** 94%.

Health: Life expect.: 77.7 male; 83.1 female. **Births:** 10.8 (per 1,000 pop.). **Deaths:** 9.2 (per 1,000 pop.). **Natural inc.:** 0.16%. **Infant mortality:** 3.5 (per 1,000 live births). **HIV rate:** 0.1%.

Education: Compulsory: ages 6-16. **Literacy:** 100%.

Major intl. organizations: UN and all of its specialized agencies, EFTA, NATO, OECD, OSCE, WTO.

Embassy: 2720 34th St. NW 20008; 333-6000.

Website: www.norway.no

The first ruler of Norway was Harald the Fairhaired, who came to power in 872 CE. Between 800 and 1000, Norway's Vikings raided and occupied widely dispersed parts of Europe.

The country was united with Denmark, 1381-1814, and with Sweden, 1814-1905. In 1905, the country became independent with Prince Charles of Denmark as king.

Norway remained neutral during WWI. Germany attacked Norway Apr. 9, 1940, and held it until liberation May 8, 1945. The country abandoned its neutrality after the war, and joined NATO. In a referendum Nov. 28, 1994, Norwegian voters rejected European Union membership.

Abundant hydroelectric resources provided the base for industrialization, giving Norway one of the highest living standards in the world. The country is a leading producer and exporter of crude oil, with extensive reserves in the North Sea.

A center-left bloc headed by Labor Party leader Jens Stoltenberg won parliamentary elections Sept. 12, 2005, and remained in power after elections Sept. 13-14, 2009. A right-wing extremist, Anders Behring Breivik, confessed to carrying out mass killings July 22, 2011, in which he killed 8 people with a car bomb near government buildings in central Oslo, and murdered another 69 at an island camp sponsored by the Labor Party's youth wing. He was declared sane and sentenced Aug. 24, 2012, to 21 years in prison, the maximum sentence in Norway. As of mid-2012, 550 Norwegian soldiers were serving with the NATO command in Afghanistan. Two hundred solders were scheduled to withdraw in Oct. 2012.

Svalbard is a group of mountainous islands in the Arctic O., area 23,956 sq mi, pop. (2012 est.) 1,970. The largest, Spitsbergen (formerly called West Spitsbergen), 15,060 sq mi, seat of the governor, is about 370 mi N of Norway. By a treaty signed in Paris, 1920, major European powers recognized the sovereignty of Norway, which incorporated it in 1925.

Jan Mayen, area 146 sq mi, is a volcanic island located about 565 mi W-NW of Norway; it was annexed in 1929.

Oman
Sultanate of Oman

People: Population: 3,090,150. **Age distrib.:** <15: 30.8%; 65+: 3.2%. **Pop. density:** 25.9 per sq mi, 10 per sq km. **Urban:** 73.4%. **Ethnic groups:** Arab, Baluchi, South Asian (Indian, Pakistani, Sri Lankan, Bangladeshi), African. **Principal languages:** Arabic (official), English, Baluchi, Urdu, Indian dialects. **Chief religions:** Ibadhi Muslim (official) 75%, other (incl. Sunni Muslim, Shia Muslim, Hindu) 25%.

Geography: Total area: 119,499 sq mi, 309,500 sq km; **Land area:** 119,499 sq mi, 309,500 sq km. **Location:** On SE coast of Arabian peninsula. **Neighbors:** United Arab Emirates, Saudi Arabia, Yemen on W. **Topography:** A narrow coastal plain up to 10 mi wide, a range of barren mountains reaching 9,900 ft, and a wide, stony, mostly waterless plateau, avg. alt. 1,000 ft. Also, an exclave at the tip of the Musandam peninsula controls access to the Persian Gulf. **Capital:** Muscat, 743,029.

Government: Type: Absolute monarchy. **Head of state and gov.:** Sultan Qabus bin Said; b. Nov. 18, 1940; in office: July 23, 1970 (also prime min. since Jan. 2, 1972). **Local divisions:** 6 regions and 2 governorates. **Defense budget:** $4.27 bil. **Active troops:** 42,600.

Economy: Industries: crude oil prod. and refining, nat. and liquefied nat. gas prod., constr., cement, copper, steel, chemicals, optic fiber. **Chief crops:** dates, limes, bananas, alfalfa, vegetables. **Natural resources:** petroleum, copper, asbestos, marble, limestone, chromium, gypsum, nat. gas. **Crude oil reserves:** 5.5 bil bbls. **Arable land:** 0.3%. **Livestock:** cattle: 332,780; chickens: 4.2 mil; goats: 1.7 mil; sheep: 388,590. **Fish catch:** 164,054 metric tons. **Electricity prod.** (2010): 18.6 bil kWh. **Labor force:** NA.

Finance: Monetary unit: Rial (OMR) (Sept. 2012: 0.38 = $1 U.S.). **GDP:** $82.8 bil; **per capita GDP:** $26,900; **GDP growth:** 5.5%. **Imports:** $21.4 bil; UAE 27.8%, Japan 12%, U.S. 6.1%, India 5.3%, China 4.3%, Saudi Arabia 4.1%, Germany 4%. **Exports:** $45.9 bil; China 30.5%, South Korea 11%, UAE 10.6%, Japan 10.5%, India 10.1%, Thailand 5.4%, U.S. 4.7%. **Tourism:** $775 mil. **Budget:** $22.5 bil. **Total reserves less gold:** $14.4 bil. **Gold:** 600 oz t. **CPI change:** 4.1%.

Transport: Motor vehicles: 149.5 vehicles per 1,000 pop. **Civil aviation:** 2.7 bil pass.-mi; 12 airports. **Chief ports:** Mina' Qabus, Salalah, Suhar.

Communications: TV sets: 620 per 1,000 pop. **Radios:** 72 per 1,000 pop. **Telephone lines:** 10.1 per 100 pop. **Internet:** 68%.

Health: Life expect.: 72.6 male; 76.4 female. **Births:** 24.3 (per 1,000 pop.). **Deaths:** 3.4 (per 1,000 pop.). **Natural inc.:** 2.09%. **Infant mortality:** 15.0 (per 1,000 live births). **HIV rate:** 0.1%.

Education: NA. **Literacy:** 86.6%.

Major intl. organizations: UN (FAO, IBRD, ILO, IMF, WHO), AL, WTO.

Embassy: 2535 Belmont Rd. NW 20008; 387-1980.

Website: www.omanet.om

Oman was originally called Muscat and Oman. A long history of rule by other lands, including Portugal in the 16th cent., ended with the ouster of the Persians in 1744. By the early 19th cent., Muscat and Oman controlled much of the Persian and Pakistan coasts.

British influence was confirmed in a 1951 treaty, and Britain helped suppress an uprising by traditionally rebellious interior tribes against control by Muscat in the 1950s.

On July 23, 1970, Sultan Said bin Taimur was overthrown by his son, Sultan Qabus bin Said, who changed the nation's name to Sultanate of Oman. Petroleum and natural gas are major sources of income. Oman has strong military and economic ties to the U.S. but also has favorable relations with Iran. Sultan Qabus shuffled his cabinet after "Arab Spring" protests Feb. 2011 and expanded the powers of the Majlis al-Shura, the lower house of parliament, Oct. 20, 2011.

Pakistan
Islamic Republic of Pakistan

People: Population: 190,291,129. **Age distrib.:** <15: 34.7%; 65+: 4.2%. **Pop. density:** 639.3 per sq mi, 246.9 per sq km. **Urban:** 36.2%. **Ethnic groups:** Punjabi 45%, Pashtun (Pathan) 15%, Sindhi 14%, Sariaki 8%, Muhajir 8%, Balochi 4%. **Principal languages:** Punjabi, Sindhi, Siraiki, Pashtu, Urdu (official), Balochi, Hindko, Brahui, English (official; lingua franca of elite, most govt. ministries), Burushaski. **Chief religion:** Muslim (official) 95% (Sunni 75%, Shia 20%), other (incl. Christian, Hindu) 5%.

Geography: Total area: 307,374 sq mi, 796,095 sq km; **Land area:** 297,637 sq mi, 770,875 sq km. **Location:** In W part of South Asia. **Neighbors:** Iran on W, Afghanistan and China on N, India on E. **Topography:** The Indus R. rises in the Hindu Kush and Himalaya Mts. in the N (highest is K2, or Godwin Austen, 28,250 ft, 2nd highest in world), then flows over 1,000 mi through fertile valley and empties into Arabian Sea. Thar Desert, Eastern Plains flank Indus Valley. **Capital:** Islamabad, 918,854. **Cities (urban aggl.):** Karachi, 13,876,254; Lahore, 7,565,722; Faisalabad, 3,038,200; Rawalpindi, 2,164,316; Multan, 1,774,636; Gujranwala, 1,767,370; Hyderabad, 1,700,769; Peshawar, 1,522,703.

Government: Type: Republic. **Head of state:** Pres. Asif Ali Zardari; b. July 26, 1955; in office: Sept. 9, 2008. **Head of gov.:** Prime Min. Raja Pervaiz Ashraf; b. Dec. 29, 1950; in office: June 22, 2012. **Local divisions:** 4 provinces and 1 capital territory, plus federally administered tribal areas. **Defense budget:** $5.16 bil. **Active troops:** 642,000.

Economy: Industries: textiles and apparel, food proc., pharmaceuticals, constr. materials, paper prods., fertilizer, shrimp. **Chief crops:** cotton, wheat, rice, sugarcane, fruits, vegetables. **Natural resources:** nat. gas, limited petroleum, poor quality coal, iron ore, copper, salt, limestone. **Crude oil reserves:** 280.7 mil bbls. **Arable land:** 26.5%. **Livestock:** cattle: 34.3 mil; chickens: 321 mil; goats: 59.9 mil; sheep: 27.8 mil. **Fish catch:** 593,365 metric tons. **Electricity prod.** (2010): 88.2 bil kWh. **Labor force:** agric. 45%, industry 20.1%, services 34.9%.

Finance: Monetary unit: Rupee (PKR) (Sept. 2012: 94.75 = $1 U.S.). **GDP:** $494.8 bil; **per capita GDP:** $2,800; **GDP growth:** 2.4%. **Imports:** $35.8 bil; China 17.9%, Saudi Arabia 11.2%, UAE 11.1%, Kuwait 5.8%, Malaysia 5.7%, India 4.9%, U.S. 4.3%. **Exports:** $25.4 bil; U.S. 14.3%, UAE 7.7%, Afghanistan 7.6%, China 7.6%, Germany 5%, UK 4.1%. **Tourism:** $358 mil. **Budget:** $40.2 bil. **Total reserves less gold:** $14.5 bil. **Gold:** 2.1 mil oz t. **CPI change:** 11.9%.

Transport: Railways: 4,841 mi. **Motor vehicles:** 12 vehicles per 1,000 pop. **Civil aviation:** 8.1 bil pass.-mi; 107 airports. **Chief ports:** Karachi, Port Muhammad Bin Qasim.

Communications: TV sets: 81 per 1,000 pop. **Radios:** 83 per 1,000 pop. **Telephone lines:** 3.2 per 100 pop. **Daily newspaper circ.:** 50.3 per 1,000 pop. **Internet:** 9%.

Health: Life expect.: 64.5 male; 68.3 female. **Births:** 24.3 (per 1,000 pop.). **Deaths:** 6.8 (per 1,000 pop.). **Natural inc.:** 1.75%. **Infant mortality:** 61.3 (per 1,000 live births). **HIV rate:** 0.1%.

Education: Compulsory: ages 5-9. **Literacy:** 54.9%.

Major intl. organizations: UN (FAO, IBRD, ILO, IMF, WHO), the Commonwealth, WTO.

Embassy: 3517 International Ct. NW 20008; 243-6500.

Website: www.pakistan.gov.pk

Pakistan shares the 5,000-year history of the India-Pakistan subcontinent. At present-day Harappa and Mohenjo Daro, the Indus Valley Civilization, with large cities and elaborate irrigation systems, flourished c. 4,000-2,500 BCE. Aryan invaders from the northwest conquered the region around 1,500 BCE, forging the Vedic civilization that dominated the region for over a thousand years. The first Arab invasion, 712 CE, introduced Islam. Present-day Pakistan and India were part of the Mughal empire from 1526 to 1857. Muslim power faded by the end of the 19th cent. as the British gained control.

Muhammad Ali Jinnah (1876-1948) was the principal architect of Pakistan. When the British withdrew Aug. 14, 1947, the Islamic majority areas of India acquired self-government as Pakistan, with dominion status in the Commonwealth. Pakistan was divided into two sections, West Pakistan and East Pakistan. The two areas were nearly 1,000 mi apart on opposite sides of India. Kashmir, a predominantly Muslim region divided between Pakistan and India, has remained a source of conflict between the two countries.

The Awami League, which had sought regional autonomy for East Pakistan for several years, won a majority in Dec. 1970 elections to a constituent assembly. On Mar. 1, 1971, Pakistan's military-dominated government postponed the assembly. Rioting and strikes broke out in the East. On Mar. 25, 1971, government troops attacked the East. The Easterners, aided by India, proclaimed the independent nation of Bangladesh. In months of widespread fighting, thousands were killed. Some 10 mil Easterners fled to India. Full-scale war between India and Pakistan had spread to both the East and West fronts by Dec. 3. Pakistan troops in the East surrendered Dec. 16; Pakistan agreed to a cease-fire in the West Dec. 17. On July 3, 1972, Pakistan and India signed a pact agreeing to withdraw troops from their borders and resolve problems peacefully.

Zulfikar Ali Bhutto, leader of the Pakistan People's Party, which had won the most West Pakistan votes in Dec. 1970 elections, became president, Dec. 20, 1971. Bhutto was overthrown in a military coup July 1977. Convicted of complicity in a 1974 political murder, he was executed Apr. 4, 1979. Millions of Afghan refugees flooded into Pakistan after the USSR invaded Afghanistan Dec. 1979; during 2002-10, some 3.6 mil refugees were repatriated, but 1.7 mil remained.

Pres. Mohammad Zia ul-Haq was killed when his plane exploded in Aug. 1988. Following Nov. elections, Benazir Bhutto, daughter of Zulfikar Ali Bhutto, was named prime min., becoming the first woman leader of a Muslim nation. She was accused of corruption and dismissed by the president, Aug. 1990. Bhutto returned to power Oct. 1993 but was dismissed again, Nov. 1996, amid further corruption charges. Responding to nuclear weapons tests by India, Pakistan conducted its own tests in 1998; the U.S. imposed economic sanctions on both countries.

Growing conflict between Prime Min. Nawaz Sharif and the military climaxed in his firing, Oct. 12, 1999, of army chief Gen. Pervez Musharraf, whose supporters staged a bloodless coup. Musharraf assumed the presidency June 20, 2001. Following the Sept. 11, 2001, terrorist attacks on the U.S., Pres. Musharraf, Sept. 19, pledged cooperation with the U.S. in fighting Taliban and al-Qaeda militants within Pakistan's tribal areas and in neighboring Afghanistan. In return, the U.S. waived its 1998 sanctions and offered Pakistan financial aid and debt relief. A referendum Apr. 30, 2002, extended Musharraf's rule for 5 years; many observers called the vote rigged.

Accused of selling atomic secrets to Iran, Libya, and North Korea, Pakistan's top nuclear scientist, Abdul Qadeer Khan, made a televised apology, Feb. 4, 2004, and described his actions as unauthorized. He received a pardon from Musharraf Feb. 5. An earthquake that rocked Pakistan and the Pakistani-held region of Kashmir Oct. 8, 2005, killed about 80,000 people.

Musharraf's grip weakened in 2007, as his efforts to oust Pakistan's chief justice sparked mass protests by pro-democracy demonstrators. He retained the presidency in an electoral-college vote Oct. 6, 2007, after his main opponents boycotted the election. More than 140 people died Oct. 18 when suicide bombers struck a convoy carrying Benazir Bhutto from the Karachi airport after more than eight years in exile. Musharraf imposed emergency rule Nov. 3 and suspended the constitution, while Pakistan's supreme court debated the constitutionality of his reelection. Musharraf gave up his army post Nov. 25, was sworn in as civilian president the next day, and lifted emergency rule Dec. 16. Bhutto was assassinated Dec. 27, 2007, after a rally in Rawalpindi.

Headed by Bhutto's widower, Asif Ali Zardari, the Pakistan Peoples Party led in parliamentary elections Feb. 18, 2008. Musharraf resigned Aug. 18 under threat of impeachment, and Zardari became president Sept. 9. Meanwhile, the security situation continued to deteriorate, as U.S. and Pakistani forces clashed with the Taliban near the Afghan border, and Islamists executed new suicide attacks. The government announced Feb. 16, 2009, a truce conceding de facto control of the strategic Swat Valley to the Taliban, but in May, government forces launched an offensive that reclaimed most of the region; the fighting displaced nearly 2 mil civilians. Catastrophic floods and monsoon rains, July-Aug. 2010, inundated one-fifth of Pakistan, leaving more than 1,750 people dead and displacing up to 20 mil.

From 2003 to Oct. 2012, terrorist attacks, sectarian clashes, and armed conflict between Islamic insurgents and government forces killed more than 14,000 civilians. In Karachi alone, ethnic violence claimed about 1,000 lives during 2011. Extremists targeted proponents of religious tolerance, including Punjab's provincial Gov. Salman Taseer, who was assassinated Jan. 4, 2011, and Shahbaz Bhatti, the only Christian in the federal cabinet, who was killed Mar. 2.

A decade-long international manhunt came to an end shortly after midnight May 2, 2011, when U.S. commandos killed al-Qaeda leader Osama bin Laden at his fortified compound in Abbottabad. The raid, carried out by helicopter from Jalalabad, Afghanistan, was launched without prior warning to Pakistani authorities. The operation led to tensions between the U.S. and Pakistan, which grew worse after a U.S. airstrike killed 24 Pakistani soldiers, Nov. 2011. In response, Pakistan closed ground supply routes into Afghanistan until July 3, 2012.

Palau
Republic of Palau

People: Population: 21,032. **Age distrib.:** <15: 21%; 65+: 6.6%. **Pop. density:** 118.7 per sq mi, 45.8 per sq km. **Urban:** 84.2%. **Ethnic groups:** Palauan (Micronesian with Malayan and Melanesian) 70%, Filipino 15%, Chinese 5%, other Asian 2%, white 2%, Carolinian 1%, other Micronesian 1%. **Principal languages:** Palauan (official on most islands); Filipino; English; Chinese; Carolinian; Japanese; Sonsorolese, Tobi, Angaur (all also official in certain states). **Chief religions:** Roman Catholic 42%, Protestant 23%, Modekngei 9%, Seventh-Day Adventist 5%, unspecified or none 16%.

Geography: Total area: 177 sq mi, 459 sq km; **Land area:** 177 sq mi, 459 sq km. **Location:** Archipelago (26 islands, more than 300 islets) in W Pacific Ocean, about 530 mi SE of the Philippines. **Neighbors:** Micronesia to E, Indonesia to S. **Topography:** A mountainous main island and low coral atolls, usually fringed with large barrier reefs. **Capital:** Melekeok, 638.

Government: Type: Republic in free association with the U.S. **Head of state and gov.:** Pres. Johnson Toribiong; b. July 22, 1946; in office: Jan. 15, 2009. **Local divisions:** 16 states. **Defense budget:** NA. **Active troops:** No regular military forces. Defense is responsibility of U.S.

Economy: Industries: tourism, craft items, constr., garment making. **Chief crops:** coconuts, copra, cassava, sweet potatoes. **Natural resources:** forests, minerals (espec. gold), marine prods., deep-seabed minerals. **Arable land:** 2.2%. **Fish catch:** 1,012 metric tons. **Labor force:** agric. 20%.

Finance: Monetary unit: U.S. Dollar (USD). **GDP** (2008 est.): $164 mil (incl. U.S. subsidy); **per capita GDP** (2008 est.): $8,100; **GDP growth** (2005): 5.5%. **Imports** (2004): $107.3 mil. **Exports** (2004): $5.9 mil. **Tourism:** $124 mil. **Budget** (2008): $99.5 mil.

Transport: Civil aviation: 1 airport. **Chief port:** Koror.

Communications: TV sets: 98 per 1,000 pop. **Telephone lines:** 33.6 per 100 pop. **Internet** (2004): 27%.

Health: Life expect.: 68.9 male; 75.4 female. **Births:** 10.8 (per 1,000 pop.). **Deaths:** 7.9 (per 1,000 pop.). **Natural inc.:** 0.29%. **Infant mortality:** 12.1 (per 1,000 live births). **HIV rate:** NA.

Education: Compulsory: ages 6-14. **Literacy:** 91.9%.

Major intl. organizations: UN (FAO, IBRD, ILO, IMF, WHO).

Embassy: 1700 Pennsylvania Ave. NW, Ste. 400, 20006; 452-6814.

Website: www.palaugov.net

Spain acquired the Palau Islands, 1886, and sold them to Germany, 1899. Japan seized them in 1914. American forces occupied the islands in 1944; in 1947, they became part of the U.S.-administered UN Trust Territory of the Pacific Islands. In 1981 Palau became an autonomous republic; the republic ratified a compact of free association with the U.S. in 1993 and became an independent nation, Oct. 1, 1994. On Nov. 1, 2009, the government of Pres. Johnson Toribiong accepted resettlement of six Uighur (Chinese Muslim) detainees who had been held by the U.S. at Guantánamo Bay, Cuba, since 2001. Threatened by climate change, the island nation is pushing the UN court to formulate an advisory opinion on the relevance to the issue of climate change of international laws forbidding nations to act in ways within their own jurisdictions that damage other nations.

Panama
Republic of Panama

People: Population: 3,510,045. **Age distrib.:** <15: 28.1%; 65+: 7.4%. **Pop. density:** 122.3 per sq mi, 47.2 per sq km. **Urban:** 75.3%. **Ethnic groups:** mestizo (mixed Amerindian and white) 70%, Amerindian and mixed (West Indian) 14%, white 10%, Amerindian 6%. **Principal languages:** Spanish (official), English. **Chief religions:** Roman Catholic 85%, Protestant 15%.

Geography: Total area: 29,120 sq mi, 75,420 sq km; **Land area:** 28,703 sq mi, 74,340 sq km. **Location:** in Central America. **Neighbors:** Costa Rica on W, Colombia on E. **Topography:** 2 mountain ranges run the length of the isthmus. Tropical rain forests cover the Caribbean coast and E Panama. **Capital:** Panama City, 1,426,110.

Government: Type: Republic. **Head of state and gov.:** Pres. Ricardo Martinelli Berrocal; b. Mar. 11, 1952; in office: July 1, 2009. **Local divisions:** 9 provinces, 5 territories. **Defense budget:** $481

mil. **Active troops:** No regular military forces. 12,000 paramilitary only.

Economy: Industries: constr., brewing, cement and other constr. materials, sugar milling. **Chief crops:** bananas, rice, corn, coffee, sugarcane, vegetables. **Natural resources:** copper, mahogany forests, shrimp, hydropower. **Arable land:** 7.4%. **Livestock:** cattle: 1.6 mil; chickens: 17.3 mil; goats: 6,300; pigs: 276,400. **Fish catch:** 169,736 metric tons. **Electricity prod.:** 6.7 bil kWh. **Labor force:** agric. 17%, industry 18.6%, services 64.4%.

Finance: Monetary unit: Balboa (PAB) (Sept. 2012: 1.00 = $1 U.S.). **GDP:** $51.3 bil; **per capita GDP:** $14,300; **GDP growth:** 10.6%. **Imports:** $23 bil; Japan 23.9%, China 23.5%, Singapore 18.4%, U.S. 13.3%, South Korea 6.1%. **Exports:** $17 bil. (Imports and exports incl. the Colón Free Zone.). **Tourism:** $1.9 bil. **Budget:** $8.5 bil. **Total reserves less gold:** $2.3 bil. **CPI change:** 5.9%.

Transport: Railways: 47 mi. **Motor vehicles:** 138.7 vehicles per 1,000 pop. **Civil aviation:** 5.2 bil pass.-mi; 55 airports. **Chief ports:** Balboa, Colon, Cristobal.

Communications: TV sets: 219 per 1,000 pop. **Radios:** 293 per 1,000 pop. **Telephone lines:** 15.2 per 100 pop. **Daily newspaper circ.:** 65.1 per 1,000 pop. **Internet:** 42.7%.

Health: Life expect.: 75.2 male; 80.9 female. **Births:** 19.2 (per 1,000 pop.). **Deaths:** 4.7 (per 1,000 pop.). **Natural inc.:** 1.45%. **Infant mortality:** 11.3 (per 1,000 live births). **HIV rate:** 0.9%.

Education: Compulsory: ages 6-14. **Literacy:** 94.1%.

Major intl. organizations: UN (FAO, IBRD, ILO, IMF, WHO), OAS, WTO.

Embassy: 2862 McGill Ter. NW 20008; 483-1407.

Website: www.presidencia.gob.pa

The coast of Panama was sighted by Rodrigo de Bastidas, sailing with Columbus for Spain in 1501, and was visited by Columbus in 1502. Vasco Núñez de Balboa crossed the isthmus and "discovered" the Pacific Ocean, Sept. 13, 1513. Spanish colonies were ravaged by Francis Drake, 1572-95, and Henry Morgan, 1668-71. Morgan destroyed the old city of Panama, which was founded in 1519. Freed from Spain, Panama joined Colombia in 1821.

Panama declared independence from Colombia Nov. 3, 1903. Panama granted use, occupation, and control of the Canal Zone to the U.S. Feb. 26, 1904. In 1978, a new treaty provided for a gradual takeover by Panama of the canal, and withdrawal of U.S. troops, to be completed before the end of the century.

Pres. Eric Arturo Delvalle was ousted by the National Assembly, Feb. 26, 1988, after he tried to fire the head of the Panama Defense Forces, Gen. Manuel Antonio Noriega, who was under U.S. federal indictment on drug charges. U.S. troops invaded Panama Dec. 20, 1989, and Noriega surrendered Jan. 3, 1990.

The U.S. handed over control of the Panama Canal to Panama Dec. 31, 1999. A $5.3-bil plan to widen the canal was approved by national referendum Oct. 22, 2006; construction on the 7-year project began Sept. 3, 2007. Ricardo Martinelli Berrocal, a conservative supermarket magnate, was elected president May 3, 2009, and took office July 1. After two decades in a U.S. prison, Noriega was extradited to France Apr. 26, 2010, where he was convicted of money laundering July 7 and received a 7-year sentence. France extradited him to Panama, Dec. 11, 2011, to serve a 20-year sentence for human rights violations he had committed as president.

Papua New Guinea
Independent State of Papua New Guinea

People: Population: 6,310,129. **Age distrib.:** <15: 35.9%; 65+: 3.7%. **Pop. density:** 36.1 per sq mi, 13.9 per sq km. **Urban:** 12.5%. **Ethnic groups:** Melanesian, Papuan, Negrito, Micronesian, Polynesian. **Principal languages:** Tok Pisin, English, Hiri Motu (all official); some 860 indigenous langs. spoken. **Chief religions:** Protestant 69% (Evangelical Lutheran 20%, United Church 12%, Seventh-Day Adventist 10%, Pentecostal 9%, Evangelical Alliance 5%, Anglican 3%, Baptist 3%), Roman Catholic 27%.

Geography: Total area: 178,704 sq mi, 462,840 sq km; **Land area:** 174,850 sq mi, 452,860 sq km. **Location:** SE Asia, occupying E half of island of New Guinea and about 600 nearby islands. **Neighbors:** Indonesia on W, Australia on S. **Topography:** Thickly forested mts. cover much of center of the country, with lowlands along the coasts. Included are some islands of Bismarck and Solomon groups, such as Admiralty Isls., New Ireland, New Britain, and Bougainville. **Capital:** Port Moresby, 342,904.

Government: Type: Parliamentary democracy. **Head of state:** Queen Elizabeth II, represented by Gov.-Gen. Sir Michael Ogio; b. July 7, 1942; in office: Feb. 25, 2011 (acting from Dec, 20, 2010). **Head of gov.:** Prime Min. Peter O'Neill; b. Feb. 13, 1965; in office: Aug. 2, 2011. **Local divisions:** 20 provinces. **Defense budget:** $60 mil. **Active troops:** 3,100.

Economy: Industries: copra crushing, palm oil proc., plywood prod., wood chip prod., mining, crude oil prod., petroleum refining. **Chief crops:** coffee, cocoa, copra, palm kernels, tea, sugar, rubber, sweet potatoes. **Natural resources:** gold, copper, silver, nat. gas, timber, oil, fisheries. **Crude oil reserves:** 182 mil bbls. **Arable land:** 0.6%. **Livestock:** cattle: 94,000; chickens: 4 mil; goats: 3,000; pigs: 1.8 mil; sheep: 7,000. **Fish catch:** 226,372 metric tons. **Electricity prod.:** 3.3 bil kWh. **Labor force:** agric. 85%.

Finance: Monetary unit: Kina (PGK) (Sept. 2012: 2.13 = $1 U.S.). **GDP:** $17.1 bil; **per capita GDP:** $2,600; **GDP growth:** 8.9%.

Imports: $6.1 bil; Australia 38.5%, Singapore 14.7%, China 7.3%, Malaysia 5.5%, Japan 5.2%, Indonesia 4.9%, U.S. 4.9%. **Exports:** $6.7 bil; Australia 31.2%, Japan 7.1%, China 6.1%. **Tourism:** $2 mil. **Budget:** $4.2 bil. **Total reserves less gold:** $4.2 bil. **Gold:** 63,000 oz t. **CPI change:** 8.4%.

Transport: Motor vehicles: 22 vehicles per 1,000 pop. **Civil aviation:** 452.4 mil pass.-mi; 20 airports. **Chief ports:** Kimbe, Lae, Madang, Rabaul, Wewak.

Communications: TV sets: 24 per 1,000 pop. **Radios:** 191 per 1,000 pop. **Telephone lines:** 1.9 per 100 pop. **Daily newspaper circ.:** 8.6 per 1,000 pop. **Internet:** 2%.

Health: Life expect.: 64.2 male; 68.8 female. **Births:** 25.9 (per 1,000 pop.). **Deaths:** 6.6 (per 1,000 pop.). **Natural inc.:** 1.94%. **Infant mortality:** 42.1 (per 1,000 live births). **HIV rate:** 0.9%.

Education: NA. **Literacy:** 60.6%.

Major intl. organizations: UN (FAO, IBRD, ILO, IMF, WHO), APEC, the Commonwealth, WTO.

Embassy: 1779 Massachusetts Ave. NW, Ste. 805, 20036; 745-3680.

Website: www.pm.gov.pg

Human remains have been found in the interior of New Guinea dating back at least 10,000 years and possibly much earlier. Europeans visited in the 15th cent., but colonization did not begin until the 19th cent., when the Dutch took control of the island's western half (now part of Indonesia). The southern half of eastern New Guinea was claimed by Britain in 1884 and transferred to Australia in 1905. The northern half was claimed by Germany in 1884, but captured in WWI by Australia, which received a League of Nations mandate and later a UN trusteeship. The two territories were administered jointly after 1949; gained self-government Dec. 1, 1973; and became independent Sept. 16, 1975.

Secessionist rebels clashed with government forces on Bougainville beginning in 1988; a truce signed Oct. 10, 1997, ended the fighting, which had claimed some 20,000 lives. A tsunami killed at least 3,000 July 17, 1998. A Bougainville autonomy agreement was signed Aug. 30, 2001. Sir Michael Somare, the nation's first prime min. (1975-80, 1982-85), regained the office in 2002 and was reelected by parliament Aug. 13, 2007. After serving a two-week suspension Apr. 2011 for filing improper financial reports, the elderly Somare took indefinite medical leave; parliament, Aug. 2, elected a permanent replacement, Prime Min. Peter O'Neill. The supreme court ruled that election illegal Dec. 12, 2011, and ordered that Somare be returned to office. O'Neill refused to step aside, beginning a chaotic period in which two prime ministers, two cabinets, and two governors-general claimed legitimacy. The crisis came to an end after elections, from which O'Neill emerged, Aug. 3, 2012, as the prime min.

The country has extensive energy resources; a proposed pipeline would transport natural gas to Queensland, Australia.

Paraguay
Republic of Paraguay

People: Population: 6,541,591. **Age distrib.:** <15: 27.6%; 65+: 6.3%. **Pop. density:** 42.6 per sq mi, 16.5 per sq km. **Urban:** 61.9%. **Ethnic groups:** mestizo (mixed Spanish and Amerindian) 95%. **Principal languages:** Spanish, Guaraní (both official). **Chief religions:** Roman Catholic 90%, Protestant 6%.

Geography: Total area: 157,048 sq mi, 406,752 sq km; **Land area:** 153,399 sq mi, 397,302 sq km. **Location:** Landlocked country in central S. America. **Neighbors:** Bolivia on N, Argentina on S, Brazil on E. **Topography:** Paraguay R. bisects the country. To E are fertile plains, wooded slopes, grasslands. To W is the Gran Chaco plain, with marshes and scrub trees. Extreme W is arid. **Capital:** Asunción, 2,139,490.

Government: Type: Republic. **Head of state and gov.:** Pres. Luis Federico Franco Gomez; b. July 23, 1962; in office: June 22, 2012. **Local divisions:** 17 departments and capital city. **Defense budget:** $248 mil. **Active troops:** 10,650.

Economy: Industries: sugar, cement, textiles, beverages, wood prods., steel. **Chief crops:** cotton, sugarcane, soybeans, corn, wheat, tobacco, cassava, fruits, vegetables. **Natural resources:** hydropower, timber, iron ore, manganese, limestone. **Arable land:** 9.6%. **Livestock:** cattle: 12.3 mil; chickens: 20 mil; goats: 135,000; pigs: 1.2 mil; sheep: 400,000. **Fish catch:** 4,657 metric tons. **Electricity prod.:** 54.4 bil kWh. **Labor force:** agric. 26.5%, industry 18.5%, services 55%.

Finance: Monetary unit: Guarani (PYG) (Sept. 2012: 4,412.32 = $1 U.S.). **GDP:** $35.8 bil; **per capita GDP:** $5,500; **GDP growth:** 3.8%. **Imports:** $12.1 bil; Brazil 27.4%, China 16.9%, U.S. 15%, Argentina 14.8%, Chile 4.4%. **Exports:** $10.3 bil; Uruguay 15.4%, Brazil 11.7%, Argentina 10.4%, Chile 8.5%, Russia 6.7%, Netherlands 5.6%, Germany 4.4%, Italy 4%. **Tourism:** $241 mil. **Budget:** $4.4 bil. **Total reserves less gold:** $4.95 bil. **Gold:** 21,220 oz t. **CPI change:** 8.3%.

Transport: Railways: 22 mi. **Motor vehicles:** 29.7 vehicles per 1,000 pop. **Civil aviation:** 311.9 mil pass.-mi; 15 airports. **Chief ports:** Asunción, Encarnación, San Antonio, Villeta.

Communications: TV sets: 262 per 1,000 pop. **Radios:** 182 per 1,000 pop. **Telephone lines:** 5.6 per 100 pop. **Internet:** 23.9%.

Health: Life expect.: 73.8 male; 79.1 female. **Births:** 17.2 (per 1,000 pop.). **Deaths:** 4.6 (per 1,000 pop.). **Natural inc.:** 1.26%. **Infant mortality:** 22.2 (per 1,000 live births). **HIV rate:** 0.3%.

Education: Compulsory: ages 6-14. **Literacy:** 93.9%.

Major intl. organizations: UN (FAO, IBRD, ILO, IMF, WHO), OAS, WTO.

Embassy: 2400 Massachusetts Ave. NW 20008; 483-6960.

Website: www.embaparusa.gov.py

Guaraní Indians inhabited Paraguay before Europeans came. Visited by Sebastian Cabot in 1527 and settled as a Spanish possession in 1535, Paraguay gained independence from Spain in 1811. It lost half its population and much of its territory to Brazil, Uruguay, and Argentina in the War of the Triple Alliance, 1865-70. Large areas were won from Bolivia in the Chaco War, 1932-35. Gen. Alfredo Stroessner, a military strongman, held the presidency 1954-89, until his ouster in a military coup.

Although the country returned to civilian rule in 1993, the next 6 years were marked by a protracted power struggle involving a popular military leader, Gen. Lino César Oviedo. Accused of insubordination, he surrendered Dec. 12, 1997, but was freed Aug. 18, 1998, following the inauguration of Pres. Raúl Cubas Grau, Oviedo's successor as Colorado Party nominee. The assassination of Vice Pres. Luis María Argaña, Mar. 23, 1999, was widely attributed to Cubas and triggered protests and an impeachment vote; Cubas resigned Mar. 28 and was succeeded by Senate leader Luis Angel González Macchi. An attempted military coup was suppressed May 18, 2000.

Mass protests over the depressed economy led to the proclamation of a state of emergency July 15, 2002. Nicanor Duarte Frutos of the Colorado Party won the presidency, Apr. 27, 2003.

Paraguayan authorities blamed a leftist group, Patria Libre, for the Sept. 2004 kidnapping and subsequent murder of Cecilia Cubas, daughter of former Pres. Cubas. Fernando Lugo, a former Catholic cleric known as the "bishop of the poor," won a presidential election Apr. 20, 2008, ending over 6 decades of Colorado rule. On June 22, 2012, Lugo was removed from office after his handling of a dispute between landless peasants and police left 17 dead June 15. Federico Franco, Lugo's vice president, was sworn into office. Elections were scheduled for Apr. 21, 2013.

Peru
Republic of Peru

People: Population: 29,549,517. **Age distrib.:** <15: 28.1%; 65+: 6.5%. **Pop. density:** 59.8 per sq mi, 23.1 per sq km. **Urban:** 77.3%. **Ethnic groups:** Amerindian 45%; mestizo (mixed Amerindian and white) 37%; white 15%; black, Japanese, Chinese, and other 3%. **Principal languages:** Spanish, Quechua (both official); Aymara; Ashaninka; other native langs. (incl. large number of minor Amazonian langs.). **Chief religions:** Roman Catholic 81%, Evangelical 13%.

Geography: Total area: 496,225 sq mi, 1,285,216 sq km; **Land area:** 494,209 sq mi, 1,279,996 sq km. **Location:** On Pacific coast of S. America. **Neighbors:** Ecuador, Colombia on N; Brazil, Bolivia on E; Chile on S. **Topography:** An arid coastal strip, 10-100 mi wide, supports much of the population thanks to widespread irrigation. The Andes cover 27% of land area. The uplands are well-watered, as are the eastern slopes reaching the Amazon basin, which covers half the country. **Capital:** Lima, 9,129,790. **Cities (urban aggl.):** Arequipa, 803,902.

Government: Type: Republic. **Head of state:** Pres. Ollanta Humala Tasso; b. June 27, 1962; in office: July 28, 2011. **Head of gov.:** Prime Min. Juan Federico Jimenez; b. Aug. 5, 1964; in office: July 23, 2012. **Local divisions:** 12 regions, 24 departments, 1 constitutional province. **Defense budget:** $1.82 bil. **Active troops:** 115,000.

Economy: Industries: mining and refining of minerals; steel, metal fabrication; petroleum extraction and refining, nat. gas and nat. gas liquefaction; fishing and fish proc., cement, glass, textiles, clothing, food proc. **Chief crops:** asparagus, coffee, cocoa, cotton, sugarcane, rice, potatoes, corn, plantains, grapes, oranges and other fruits, coca, tomatoes, barley, medicinal plants. **Natural resources:** copper, silver, gold, petroleum, timber, fish, iron ore, coal, phosphate, potash, hydropower, nat. gas. **Crude oil reserves:** 582 mil bbls. **Arable land:** 2.9%. **Livestock:** cattle: 5.5 mil; chickens: 130.8 mil; goats: 2 mil; pigs: 3.3 mil; sheep: 14.2 mil. **Fish catch:** 4.4 mil metric tons. **Electricity prod.** (2010): 32.5 bil kWh. **Labor force:** agric. 0.7%, industry 23.8%, services 75.5%.

Finance: Monetary unit: Nuevo Sol (PEN) (Sept. 2012: 2.61 = $1 U.S.). **GDP:** $305.8 bil; **per capita GDP:** $10,200; **GDP growth:** 6.9%. **Imports:** $37 bil; U.S. 24.7%, China 13.8%, Brazil 6.7%, Chile 6%, Ecuador 4.4%, South Korea 4.1%. **Exports:** $46.3 bil; China 18.4%, U.S. 15.3%, Canada 11.5%, Japan 5.6%, Spain 5.4%, Chile 4.8%, South Korea 4.6%, Germany 4.1%. **Tourism:** $2.4 bil. **Budget:** $32.6 bil. **Total reserves less gold:** $47.2 bil. **Gold:** 1.1 mil oz t. **CPI change:** 3.4%.

Transport: Railways: 1,184 mi. **Motor vehicles:** 51 vehicles per 1,000 pop. **Civil aviation:** 5.8 bil pass.-mi; 58 airports. **Chief ports:** Callao, Iquitos, Matarani, Paita, Pucallpa, Yurimaguas.

Communications: TV sets: 201 per 1,000 pop. **Radios:** 269 per 1,000 pop. **Telephone lines:** 11.1 per 100 pop. **Internet:** 36.5%.

Health: Life expect.: 70.8 male; 74.8 female. **Births:** 19.1 (per 1,000 pop.). **Deaths:** 6.0 (per 1,000 pop.). **Natural inc.:** 1.32%. **Infant mortality:** 21.5 (per 1,000 live births). **HIV rate:** 0.4%.

Education: Compulsory: ages 3-16. **Literacy:** 89.6%.

Major intl. organizations: UN and all of its specialized agencies, APEC, OAS, WTO.

Embassy: 1700 Massachusetts Ave. NW 20036; 833-9860.

Website: www.peru.gob.pe

The powerful Inca empire had its seat at Cuzco in the Andes and covered much of S. America. A civil war had weakened the empire when Francisco Pizarro, Spanish conquistador, began raiding Peru for its wealth, 1532. In 1533 he executed the Inca ruler, Atahualpa, and enslaved the people.

Lima was the seat of Spanish viceroys until the Argentine liberator, José de San Martin, captured it in 1821; Spanish forces were ultimately routed by Simón Bolívar, 1824. For much of the 19th cent., the country was governed by military leaders. Chile defeated Peru in the War of the Pacific, 1879-83. The first half of the 20th cent. was dominated by rivalry between right-wing groups (allied with the military) and the leftist APRA party.

Peru returned to democratic leadership in 1980 but was plagued by economic problems and by leftist Shining Path (Sendero Luminoso) guerrillas. Conflict between guerrillas and government troops, 1980-2000, killed more than 69,000 people, mostly Andean Indians.

Elected president in June 1990, Alberto Fujimori, the son of Japanese immigrants, dissolved the National Congress, suspended parts of the constitution, and initiated press censorship, Apr. 5, 1992. The leader of Shining Path was captured Sept. 12. Fujimori won reelection Apr. 9, 1995, but his repressive antiterrorism tactics drew international criticism.

Fujimori's path to a 3rd term was cleared when his lone remaining challenger withdrew, charging electoral fraud, six days before a runoff vote on May 28, 2000. Scandals involving his top aide and intelligence chief, Vladimiro Montesinos, led Fujimori to resign Nov. 20; instead of accepting his resignation, Congress ousted him as "morally unfit." Montesinos was captured in Venezuela June 23, 2001; extradited to Peru, he was convicted in a series of criminal trials. Fujimori was arrested in Chile, Nov. 7, 2005, and extradited to Peru, Sept. 22, 2007. He was convicted in three separate proceedings, 2007-09, on charges that included complicity in a paramilitary death squad's killing at least 25 people, 1991-92.

Alan García, whose first term as president, 1985-90, ended with the country facing hyperinflation and guerrilla war, won a presidential runoff June 4, 2006. An earthquake rocked SW coastal Peru, Aug. 15, 2007, killing more than 500 people. In a presidential runoff election June 5, 2011, Ollanta Humala Tasso, a leftist former military officer, defeated Peruvian legislator Keiko Fujimori Higuchi, the daughter of jailed former Pres. Fujimori.

Philippines
Republic of the Philippines

People: Population: 103,775,002. **Age distrib.:** <15: 34.3%; 65+: 4.3%. **Pop. density:** 901.4 per sq mi, 348 per sq km. **Urban:** 48.8%. **Ethnic groups:** Tagalog 28%, Cebuano 13%, Ilocano 9%, Bisaya/Binisaya 8%, Hiligaynon Ilonggo 8%, Bikol 6%, Waray 3%. **Principal languages:** Filipino, English (both official); 8 major dialects. **Chief religions:** Roman Catholic 81%, Muslim 5%, Evangelical 3%, Iglesia ni Kristo 2%, Aglipayan 2%, other Christian 5%.

Geography: Total area: 115,831 sq mi, 300,000 sq km; **Land area:** 115,124 sq mi, 298,170 sq km. **Location:** An archipelago off SE coast of Asia. **Neighbors:** Nearest are Malaysia, Indonesia on S; Taiwan on N. **Topography:** The country consists of some 7,100 islands stretching 1,100 mi N-S. About 95% of area and population are on 11 largest islands, which are mountainous, except for the heavily indented coastlines and central plain on Luzon. **Capital:** Manila, 11,861,600. **Cities (urban aggl.):** Davao, 1,564,651.

Government: Type: Republic. **Head of state and gov.:** Pres. Benigno (NoyNoy) Aquino III; b. Feb. 8, 1960; in office: June 30, 2010. **Local divisions:** 79 provinces. **Defense budget:** $2.34 bil. **Active troops:** 125,000.

Economy: Industries: electronics assembly, garments, footwear, pharmaceuticals, chemicals, wood prods., food proc., petroleum refining, fishing. **Chief crops:** sugarcane, coconuts, rice, corn, bananas, cassava, pineapples, mangoes. **Natural resources:** timber, petroleum, nickel, cobalt, silver, gold, salt, copper. **Crude oil reserves:** 138.5 mil bbls. **Arable land:** 18.1%. **Livestock:** cattle: 2.6 mil; chickens: 159 mil; goats: 4.2 mil; pigs: 13.4 mil; sheep: 30,000. **Fish catch:** 5.2 mil metric tons. **Electricity prod.** (2010): 64.2 bil kWh. **Labor force:** agric. 33%, industry 15%, services 52%.

Finance: Monetary unit: Peso (PHP) (Sept. 2012: 41.96 = $1 U.S.). **GDP:** $395.4 bil; **per capita GDP:** $4,100; **GDP growth:** 3.7%. **Imports:** $62.7 bil; China 14.6%, Japan 12.3%, U.S. 9.4%, South Korea 8.4%, Singapore 8%, Thailand 5.6%, Indonesia 4.1%. **Exports:** $47.2 bil; China 21.3%, Japan 14.1%, U.S. 13.9%, Singapore 8.9%, Hong Kong 7.5%, South Korea 4.7%. **Tourism:** $3.2 bil. **Budget:** $36 bil. **Total reserves less gold:** $67.3 bil. **Gold:** 5.1 mil oz t. **CPI change:** 4.6%.

Transport: Railways: 618 mi. **Motor vehicles:** 30.5 vehicles per 1,000 pop. **Civil aviation:** 11.3 bil pass.-mi; 83 airports. **Chief ports:** Batangas, Cagayan de Oro, Cebu, Davao, Liman, Manila.

Communications: TV sets: 194 per 1,000 pop. **Radios:** 735 per 1,000 pop. **Telephone lines:** 7.2 per 100 pop. **Daily newspaper circ.:** 78.6 per 1,000 pop. **Internet:** 29%.

Health: Life expect.: 69.0 male; 75.0 female. **Births:** 25.0 (per 1,000 pop.). **Deaths:** 5.0 (per 1,000 pop.). **Natural inc.:** 2.00%. **Infant mortality:** 18.8 (per 1,000 live births). **HIV rate:** <0.1%.

Education: Compulsory: ages 6-11. **Literacy:** 95.4%.

Major intl. organizations: UN (FAO, IBRD, ILO, IMF, WHO), APEC, ASEAN, WTO.

Embassy: 1600 Massachusetts Ave. NW 20036; 467-9300.

Website: www.gov.ph

Originally inhabited by Malay peoples, the archipelago was visited by Magellan, 1521. The Spanish founded Manila, 1571. The islands, named for King Philip II of Spain, were ceded by Spain to the U.S. for $20 mil, 1898, following the Spanish-American War. U.S. troops suppressed a guerrilla uprising in a brutal 6-year war, 1899-1905. Japan attacked the Philippines Dec. 8, 1941, and occupied the islands during WWII. Independence was proclaimed, July 4, 1946. A republic was established.

The repressive and corrupt regime of Pres. Ferdinand Marcos and his wife, Imelda, ruled the Philippines 1965-86. The assassination of prominent opposition leader Benigno S. Aquino Jr., Aug. 21, 1983, sparked demonstrations calling for Marcos's resignation. Amid allegations of widespread election fraud, Marcos was declared the victor, Feb. 16, 1986, over Corazon Aquino, widow of the slain opposition leader. Mass protests and international pressure forced Marcos to flee the country Feb. 25, and Corazon Aquino became president.

Her government was plagued by a weak economy, widespread poverty, Communist and Muslim insurgencies, and lukewarm military support. Rebel troops seized military bases and TV stations and bombed the presidential palace, Dec. 1, 1989. Government forces, with U.S. air support, defeated the attempted coup. Aquino endorsed Fidel Ramos in the May 1992 presidential election, which he won. The U.S. vacated the Subic Bay Naval Station in late 1992, ending its long military presence in the Philippines. The government signed a cease-fire agreement, Jan. 30, 1994, with Muslim separatist guerrillas, but some rebels refused to abide by the accord. A new treaty providing for expansion and development of an autonomous Muslim region on Mindanao was signed Sept. 2, 1996, formally ending a rebellion that had claimed more than 120,000 lives since 1972.

Running as a populist, Joseph (Erap) Estrada, a former movie actor, won the presidential election, May 11, 1998. Charged with bribery and corruption, he was impeached Nov. 13, 2000. When the Supreme Court ruled the presidency vacant Jan. 20, 2001, Vice Pres. Gloria Macapagal Arroyo became president.

As part of the war on terrorism, the U.S. assisted Filipino troops in combating Abu Sayyaf, an Islamic guerrilla group. Pres. Arroyo won reelection May 10, 2004. Flooding and mudslides from tropical storms, Nov.-Dec. 2004, left at least 1,060 people dead. Former Pres. Estrada was convicted, Sept. 12, 2007, of taking more than $85 mil in bribes and kickbacks while in office; he received a pardon from Pres. Arroyo, Oct. 25. Typhoon Fengshen, June 21-22, 2008, left at least 557 people dead and destroyed more than 90,000 homes; at least 700 more people died when the ferry *Princess of the Stars* capsized and ran aground in the storm. Tropical storms Sept.-Oct. 2009 claimed more than 900 lives and affected over 9 mil people. Benigno (NoyNoy) Aquino III, the son of former Pres. Corazon Aquino (who died Aug. 1, 2009), defeated Estrada in the presidential election of May 10, 2010, and was sworn in June 30.

Poland
Republic of Poland

People: Population: 38,415,284. **Age distrib.:** <15: 14.6%; 65+: 14%. **Pop. density:** 327 per sq mi, 126.3 per sq km. **Urban:** 60.9%. **Ethnic groups:** Polish 97%. **Principal language:** Polish (official). **Chief religions:** Roman Catholic 90%, Eastern Orthodox 1%.

Geography: Total area: 120,728 sq mi, 312,685 sq km; **Land area:** 117,474 sq mi, 304,255 sq km. **Location:** On Baltic Sea in E central Europe. **Neighbors:** Germany on W; Czech Rep., Slovakia on S; Lithuania, Belarus, Ukraine on E; Russia on N. **Topography:** Mostly lowlands forming part of the Northern European Plain. The Carpathian Mts. along S border rise to 8,200 ft. **Capital:** Warsaw, 1,723,260. **Cities (urban aggl.):** Kraków, 756,047.

Government: Type: Republic. **Head of state:** Pres. Bronislaw Komorowski; b. June 4, 1952; in office: Aug. 6, 2010. **Head of gov.:** Prime Min. Donald Tusk; b. Apr. 22, 1957; in office: Nov. 16, 2007. **Local divisions:** 16 provinces. **Defense budget:** $9.43 bil. **Active troops:** 100,000.

Economy: Industries: machine building, iron and steel, coal mining, chemicals, shipbuilding, food proc., glass, beverages, textiles. **Chief crops:** potatoes, fruits, vegetables, wheat. **Natural resources:** coal, sulfur, copper, nat. gas, silver, lead, salt, amber. **Crude oil reserves:** 155 mil bbls. **Arable land:** 41.2%. **Livestock:** cattle: 5.7 mil; chickens: 117.8 mil; goats: 122,123; pigs: 14.9 mil; sheep: 258,262. **Fish catch:** 220,478 metric tons. **Electricity prod.** (2010): 147.5 bil kWh. **Labor force:** agric. 17.4%, industry 29.2%, services 53.4%.

Finance: Monetary unit: Zloty (PLN) (Sept. 2012: 3.32 = $1 U.S.). **GDP:** $781.5 bil; **per capita GDP:** $20,600; **GDP growth:** 4.4%. **Imports:** $208 bil; Germany 28.7%, Russia 10.3%, Netherlands 5.9%, Italy 5.4%, China 5.3%, France 4.4%, Czech Republic 4.3%. **Exports:** $193.9 bil; Germany 27%, UK 6.6%, Czech

Republic 6.4%, France 6.3%, Italy 5.6%, Netherlands 4.5%, Russia 4.2%. **Tourism:** $10.7 bil. **Budget:** $100.6 bil. **Total reserves less gold:** $92.6 bil. **Gold:** 3.3 mil oz t. **CPI change:** 4.2%.

Transport: Railways: 12,072 mi. **Motor vehicles:** 503.8 vehicles per 1,000 pop. **Civil aviation:** 4.5 bil pass.-mi; 86 airports. **Chief ports:** Gdansk, Gdynia, Swinoujscie, Szczecin.

Communications: TV sets: 408 per 1,000 pop. **Radios:** 297 per 1,000 pop. **Telephone lines:** 18.1 per 100 pop. **Daily newspaper circ.:** 113.6 per 1,000 pop. **Internet:** 64.9%.

Health: Life expect.: 72.3 male; 80.4 female. **Births:** 10.0 (per 1,000 pop.). **Deaths:** 10.2 (per 1,000 pop.). **Natural inc.:** −0.03%. **Infant mortality:** 6.4 (per 1,000 live births). **HIV rate:** 0.1%.

Education: Compulsory: ages 7-15. **Literacy:** 99.5%.

Major intl. organizations: UN (FAO, IBRD, ILO, IMF, WHO), EU, NATO, OECD, OSCE, WTO.

Embassy: 2640 16th St. NW 20009; 234-3800.

Website: www.poland.gov.pl

Slavic tribes in the area were converted to Latin Christianity in the 10th cent. Poland was a great power from the 14th to the 17th cent. In three partitions (1772, 1793, 1795) it was apportioned among Prussia, Russia, and Austria. Overrun by the Austro-German armies in WWI, it declared its independence on Nov. 11, 1918, and was recognized as independent by the Treaty of Versailles, June 28, 1919. Large territories to the east were taken in a war with Russia, 1921.

Germany and the USSR invaded Poland Sept. 1939 and divided the country. During the war, Nazis killed some 6 mil Polish citizens, half of them Jews. In compensation for 69,860 sq mi ceded to the USSR when the war ended, Poland received approx. 40,000 sq mi of German territory east of the Oder-Neisse line comprising Silesia, Pomerania, West Prussia, and part of East Prussia. Communists, who aligned themselves with the USSR, dominated the 1947 election.

In 12 years of rule by Stalinists, large estates were abolished, industries nationalized, schools secularized, and Roman Catholic prelates jailed. Farm production fell off. Harsh working conditions caused a riot in Poznan, June 28-29, 1956. A new Politburo, committed to a more independent Polish Communism, was named Oct. 1956, with Wladyslaw Gomulka as first secretary of the party. Collectivization of farms was ended. Gomulka agreed to permit religious liberty and religious publications, provided the church kept out of politics.

In Dec. 1970 workers in port cities rioted because of price rises and new incentive wage rules. On Dec. 20 Gomulka resigned as party leader; he was succeeded by Edward Gierek. The rules were dropped and price rises revoked.

After two months of labor turmoil crippled the country, the Polish government, Aug. 30, 1980, met the demands of striking workers at the Lenin Shipyard, Gdansk. Government concessions included the right to form independent trade unions and the right to strike. By 1981, 9.5 mil workers had joined the independent trade union (Solidarity). As Solidarity's demands grew bolder, the government, spurred by fear of Soviet intervention, imposed martial law Dec. 13. Lech Walesa and other Solidarity leaders were arrested.

On Apr. 5, 1989, an accord was reached between the government and opposition factions on political and economic reforms, including free elections. Candidates endorsed by Solidarity swept the parliamentary elections, June 4. Lech Walesa became president Dec. 22, 1990.

A radical economic program designed to transform the economy into a free-market system led to inflation and unemployment. In Sept. 1993, former Communists and other leftists won a majority in the lower house of Parliament. A former Communist, Aleksander Kwasniewski, defeated Walesa in the 1995 presidential election and was reelected five years later. A new constitution was approved by referendum May 25, 1997. Poland became a full member of NATO, Mar. 12, 1999, and entered the European Union May 1, 2004.

Lech Kaczynski, the conservative mayor of Warsaw, won a presidential runoff election Oct. 23, 2005. In July 2006 he appointed his identical twin brother Jaroslaw as prime min. Poland's governing coalition fell apart in 2007, and the center-right Civic Platform party, led by Donald Tusk, won parliamentary elections Oct. 21. Pres. Lech Kaczynski, his wife Maria, and many senior Polish government officials were among the 96 passengers and crew members killed in a plane crash Apr. 10, 2010, near Smolensk, in western Russia. Parliament Speaker Bronislaw Komorowski, an ally of Prime Min. Tusk, became acting president after the crash; he won a full term July 4 by defeating Kaczynski's brother Jaroslaw in a runoff election.

Nearly 2,500 Polish troops were serving in Afghanistan as of mid-2012.

Portugal
Portuguese Republic

People: Population: 10,781,459. **Age distrib.:** <15: 16.1%; 65+: 18.1%. **Pop. density:** 305.3 per sq mi, 117.9 per sq km. **Urban:** 61.1%. **Ethnic groups:** homogeneous Mediterranean stock; East Europeans have immigrated since 1990. **Principal languages:** Portuguese, Mirandese (both official). **Chief religion:** Roman Catholic 85%, other Christian 2%, none 4%.

Geography: Total area: 35,556 sq mi, 92,090 sq km; **Land area:** 35,317 sq mi, 91,470 sq km. **Location:** At SW extreme of Europe. **Neighbors:** Spain on N, E. **Topography:** Portugal N of Tajus R.,

which bisects country NE-SW, is mountainous, cool and rainy. To the S there are drier, rolling plains, and a warm climate. **Capital:** Lisbon, 2,843,410. **Cities (urban aggl.):** Porto, 1,366,940.

Government: Type: Republic. **Head of state:** Pres. Aníbal Cavaco Silva; b. July 15, 1939; in office: Mar. 9, 2006. **Head of gov.:** Prime Min. Pedro Passos Coelho; b. July 24,1964; in office: June 21, 2011. **Local divisions:** 18 districts, 2 autonomous regions. **Defense budget:** $2.83 bil. **Active troops:** 42,634.

Economy: Industries: textiles, clothing, footwear, wood and cork, paper, chemicals, auto-parts mfg., base metals, dairy prods., wine and other foods, porcelain and ceramics, glassware, tech., telecom. **Chief crops:** grain, potatoes, tomatoes, olives, grapes. **Natural resources:** fish, forests (cork), iron ore, copper, zinc, tin, tungsten, silver, gold, uranium, marble, clay, gypsum, salt, hydropower. **Arable land:** 12.3%. **Livestock:** cattle: 1.4 mil; chickens: 40 mil; goats: 444,000; pigs: 2.3 mil; sheep: 2.9 mil. **Fish catch:** 226,632 metric tons. **Electricity prod.** (2010): 50.3 bil kWh. **Labor force:** agric. 11.7%, industry 28.5%, services 59.8%.

Finance: Monetary unit: Euro (EUR) (Sept. 2012: 0.79 = $1 U.S.). **GDP:** $252.2 bil; **per capita GDP:** $23,700; **GDP growth:** −1.5%. **Imports:** $77.3 bil; Spain 31.7%, Germany 12.4%, France 6.9%, Italy 5.4%, Netherlands 4.8%. **Exports:** $55.8 bil; Spain 25.1%, Germany 13.7%, France 12.1%, Angola 5.5%, UK 5.1%. **Tourism:** $11.3 bil. **Budget:** $120.2 bil. **Total reserves less gold:** $1.97 bil. **Gold:** 12.3 mil oz t. **CPI change:** 3.7%.

Transport: Railways: 2,062 mi. **Motor vehicles:** 542.5 vehicles per 1,000 pop. **Civil aviation:** 14.2 bil pass.-mi; 43 airports. **Chief ports:** Leixoes, Lisbon, Setubal, Sines.

Communications: TV sets: 425 per 1,000 pop. **Radios:** 299 per 1,000 pop. **Telephone lines:** 42.3 per 100 pop. **Internet:** 55.3%.

Health: Life expect.: 75.5 male; 82.2 female. **Births:** 9.8 (per 1,000 pop.). **Deaths:** 10.9 (per 1,000 pop.). **Natural inc.:** −0.11%. **Infant mortality:** 4.6 (per 1,000 live births). **HIV rate:** 0.6%.

Education: Compulsory: ages 6-14. **Literacy:** 95.2%.

Major intl. organizations: UN (FAO, IBRD, ILO, IMF, WHO), EU, NATO, OECD, OSCE, WTO.

Embassy: 2012 Massachusetts Ave. NW 20036; 350-5400.

Website: www.portugal.gov.pt

Portugal, an independent state since the 12th cent., was a kingdom until a 1910 revolution drove out King Manoel II and a republic was proclaimed. Beginning in 1932, Prim. Antonio de Oliveira Salazar headed a repressive government. Illness forced his retirement in Sept. 1968.

On Apr. 25, 1974, a military junta led by Gen. Antonio de Spinola seized the government; Spinola became president. The new government granted independence to Guinea-Bissau, Mozambique, Cape Verde Islands, Angola, and São Tomé and Príncipe. Portugal returned Macao to China on Dec. 20, 1999.

With the economy lagging, opposition Socialists, led by Jóse Sócrates, gained a parliamentary majority in 2005 and held onto a plurality in 2009. The conservative Aníbal Cavaco Silva, a former prime min., 1985-95, defeated two Socialist candidates to win the Jan. 2006 presidential election and was reelected five years later. After Portugal was forced to negotiate a $116 bil bailout package from international lenders to avert default, voters delivered a parliamentary election victory, June 5, 2011, to the center-right Social Democratic Party, headed by Pedro Passos Coelho.

Azores Isls., in the Atlantic, 740 mi W of Portugal, have an area of 868 sq mi and a pop. (2011 est.) of 246,102. A 1951 agreement gave the U.S. rights to use defense facilities in the Azores. The **Madeira Isls.**, 350 mi off the NW coast of Africa, have an area of 306 sq mi and a pop. (2011 est.) of 267,785. Both groups were offered partial autonomy in 1976.

Qatar
State of Qatar

People: Population: 1,951,591. **Age distrib.:** <15: 12.5%; 65+: 0.8%. **Pop. density:** 436.3 per sq mi, 168.4 per sq km. **Urban:** 98.8%. **Ethnic groups:** Arab 40%, Indian 18%,Pakistani 18%, Iranian 10%. **Principal languages:** Arabic (official), English commonly used as second lang. **Chief religions:** Muslim 78%, Christian 9%.

Geography: Total area: 4,473 sq mi, 11,586 sq km; **Land area:** 4,473 sq mi, 11,586 sq km. **Location:** Middle East, occupying peninsula on W coast of Persian Gulf. **Neighbors:** Saudi Arabia on S. **Topography:** Mostly flat desert with some limestone ridges; vegetation of any kind is scarce. **Capital:** Ad-Dawhah (Doha), 567,051.

Government: Type: Traditional monarchy. **Head of state:** Emir Sheikh Hamad bin Khalifa al-Thani; b. 1952; in office: June 27, 1995. **Head of gov.:** Prime Min. Sheikh Hamad bin Jassim bin Jabr al-Thani; b. 1959; in office: Apr. 3, 2007. **Local divisions:** 9 municipalities. **Defense budget:** NA. **Active troops:** 11,800.

Economy: Industries: liquefied nat. gas, crude oil prod. and refining, ammonia, fertilizers, petrochemicals, steel reinforcing bars, cement, commercial ship repair. **Chief crops:** fruits, vegetables. **Natural resources:** petroleum, nat. gas, fish. **Crude oil reserves:** 25.4 bil bbls. **Arable land:** 1%. **Livestock:** cattle: 8,000; chickens: 4.9 mil; goats: 145,000; sheep: 150,000. **Fish catch:** 13,796 metric tons. **Electricity prod.** (2010): 22.3 bil kWh. **Labor force:** NA.

Finance: Monetary unit: Riyal (QAR) (Sept. 2012: 3.64 = $1 U.S.). **GDP:** $184.3 bil; **per capita GDP:** $104,300; **GDP growth:** 18.8%. **Imports:** $23.1 bil; U.S. 12.9%, UAE 12.5%, Saudi Arabia 9.4%, UK 6.2%, China 5.5%, Germany 5.2%, Japan 4.7%, France

4.6%, Italy 4.5%. **Exports:** $107 bil; Japan 26.6%, South Korea 18.3%, India 8.1%, Singapore 6.6%, UK 6.5%, China 4.1%. **Tourism:** $1.2 bil. **Budget:** $51.2 bil. **Total reserves less gold:** $16.2 bil. **Gold:** 399,100 oz t. **CPI change:** 1.9%.

Transport: Motor vehicles: 341.5 vehicles per 1,000 pop. **Civil aviation:** 25.1 bil pass.-mi; 4 airports. **Chief ports:** Doha, Mesaieed, Ra's Laffan.

Communications: TV sets: 405 per 1,000 pop. **Radios:** 468 per 1,000 pop. **Telephone lines:** 16.4 per 100 pop. **Internet:** 86.2%.

Health: Life expect.: 76.1 male; 80.1 female. **Births:** 10.2 (per 1,000 pop.). **Deaths:** 1.6 (per 1,000 pop.). **Natural inc.:** 0.87%. **Infant mortality:** 6.8 (per 1,000 live births). **HIV rate:** <0.1%.

Education: Compulsory: ages 6-17. **Literacy:** 96.3%.

Major intl. organizations: UN (FAO, IBRD, ILO, IMF, WHO), AL, OPEC, WTO.

Embassy: 2555 M St. NW 20037; 274-1600.

Website: portal.www.gov.qa

Qatar was under Bahrain's control until the Ottoman Turks took power, 1872 to 1915. In a treaty signed 1916, Qatar gave Great Britain responsibility for its defense and foreign relations. After Britain announced it would remove its military forces from the Persian Gulf area by the end of 1971, Qatar sought a federation with other British-protected states in the area; this failed and Qatar declared itself independent, Sept. 1, 1971. Crown Prince Hamad bin Khalifa al-Thani ousted his father, Emir Khalifa bin Hamad al-Thani, June 27, 1995. In municipal elections held Mar. 8, 1999, women participated for the first time as candidates and voters.

Qatar, one of the world's leading exporters of liquefied natural gas, has experienced rapid economic growth in recent years. Military ties with the U.S. have been expanding; Camp As-Sayliyah, a base near Doha, served as a command center for the U.S.-led invasion of Iraq, Mar. 2003. The influential Arab news network Al-Jazeera is based in Qatar. Qatar will host the World Cup soccer tournament in 2022.

Romania

People: Population: 21,848,504. **Age distrib.:** <15: 14.8%; 65+: 14.9%. **Pop. density:** 246.1 per sq mi, 95 per sq km. **Urban:** 52.8%. **Ethnic groups:** Romanian 90%, Hungarian 7%, Roma 3%. **Principal languages:** Romanian (official), Hungarian, Romany. **Chief religions:** Eastern Orthodox 87%, Protestant 8%, Roman Catholic 5%.

Geography: Total area: 92,043 sq mi, 238,391 sq km; **Land area:** 88,761 sq mi, 229,891 sq km. **Location:** SE Europe, on the Black Sea. **Neighbors:** Moldova on E, Ukraine on N, Hungary and Serbia on W, Bulgaria on S. **Topography:** The Carpathian Mts. encase the N-central Transylvanian plateau. There are wide plains S and E of the mountains, through which flow the lower reaches of the rivers of Danube system. **Capital:** Bucharest, 1,936,600.

Government: Type: Republic. **Head of state:** Pres. Traian Basescu; b. Nov. 4, 1951; in office: Dec. 20, 2004. **Head of gov.:** Prime Min. Victor-Viorel Ponta; b. Sept. 20, 1972; in office: May 7, 2012. **Local divisions:** 41 counties and Bucharest. **Defense budget:** $2.67 bil. **Active troops:** 73,900.

Economy: Industries: elec. machinery and equip., textiles and footwear, light machinery, auto assembly, mining, timber, constr. materials. **Chief crops:** wheat, corn, barley, sugar beets, sunflower seeds, potatoes, grapes. **Natural resources:** petroleum (reserves declining), timber, nat. gas, coal, iron ore, salt, hydropower. **Crude oil reserves:** 600 mil bbls. **Arable land:** 38.2%. **Livestock:** cattle: 2.5 mil; chickens: 83.8 mil; goats: 917,300; pigs: 5.8 mil; sheep: 9.1 mil. **Fish catch:** 11,669 metric tons. **Electricity prod.:** (2010): 57.3 bil kWh. **Labor force:** agric. 30%, industry 20.2%, services 49.8%.

Finance: Monetary unit: New Leu (RON) (Sept. 2012: 3.55 = $1 U.S.). **GDP:** $270.6 bil; **per capita GDP:** $12,600; **GDP growth:** 2.5%. **Imports:** $73.1 bil; Germany 17.2%, Italy 11.4%, Hungary 8.8%, France 5.8%, China 4.6%, Kazakhstan 4.2%, Austria 4%. **Exports:** $62.7 bil; Germany 18.9%, Italy 13.1%, France 7.6%, Turkey 6.2%, Hungary 5.7%. **Tourism:** $1.4 bil. **Budget:** $67.4 bil. **Total reserves less gold:** $42.9 bil. **Gold:** 3.3 mil oz t. **CPI change:** 5.8%.

Transport: Railways: 6,701 mi. **Motor vehicles:** 224.8 vehicles per 1,000 pop. **Civil aviation:** 2.5 bil pass.-mi; 26 airports. **Chief ports:** Braila, Constanta, Galati, Mancanului, Midia, Tulcea.

Communications: TV sets: 885 per 1,000 pop. **Radios:** 143 per 1,000 pop. **Telephone lines:** 21.9 per 100 pop. **Daily newspaper circ.:** 70.3 per 1,000 pop. **Internet:** 44%.

Health: Life expect.: 70.8 male; 77.9 female. **Births:** 9.5 (per 1,000 pop.). **Deaths:** 11.8 (per 1,000 pop.). **Natural inc.:** −0.24%. **Infant mortality:** 10.7 (per 1,000 live births). **HIV rate:** 0.1%.

Education: Compulsory: ages 7-14. **Literacy:** 97.7%.

Major intl. organizations: UN (FAO, IBRD, ILO, IMF, WHO), NATO, OSCE, WTO.

Embassy: 1607 23rd St. NW 20008; 332-4846.

Website: www.gov.ro

Romania's earliest known people merged with invading Proto-Thracians, preceding by centuries the Dacians. The Dacian kingdom was occupied by Rome, 106-271 CE; people and language were Romanized. The principalities of Wallachia and Moldavia, dominated by Turkey, were united in 1859, became Romania in 1861, and gained recognition as an independent kingdom, 1881.

After WWI, Romania acquired Bessarabia, Bukovina, Transylvania, and Banat. In 1940 it ceded Bessarabia and Northern Bukovina to the USSR, part of southern Dobrudja to Bulgaria, and northern Transylvania to Hungary. In 1941, Prem. Marshal Ion Antonescu led Romania in support of Germany against the USSR. In 1944 he was overthrown, and Romania joined the Allies. After occupation by Soviet troops, a People's Republic was proclaimed, Dec. 30, 1947.

On Aug. 22, 1965, a new constitution proclaimed Romania a socialist republic. Pres. Nicolae Ceausescu maintained an independent course in foreign affairs, but his domestic policies were repressive. All industry was state-owned, and state farms and cooperatives owned almost all arable land. Ceausescu's security forces fired on antigovernment demonstrators, Dec. 1989, killing hundreds, but when the army sided with the protesters, his regime fell. Charged with genocide and abuse of power, Ceausescu and his wife were executed Dec. 25, 1989.

A new constitution providing for a multiparty system took effect Dec. 8, 1991. Many of Romania's state-owned companies were privatized in 1996. Romania became a full NATO member in 2004 and entered the European Union Jan. 1, 2007. The IMF and other donors agreed to provide a $27 bil loan Mar. 25, 2009, to rescue the country from the global recession. Romania, a firm U.S. ally, pulled its remaining troops out of Iraq July 2009. About 1,800 Romanian soldiers were serving with NATO-led forces in Afghanistan in mid-2012. After Victor-Viorel Ponta became prime min. May 7, 2012, he accused Pres. Traian Basescu of abusing his authority, and parliament voted to impeach him July 6, 2012, making Crin Antonescu acting pres. An impeachment referendum was held July 29, 2012; more than 87% of those who went to the polls voted for impeachment. The country's Supreme Court later overturned the result, deeming it unconstitutional because less than 50% of eligible voters had participated.

Russia
Russian Federation

People: Population: 142,517,670. **Age distrib.:** <15: 15.7%; 65+: 13%. **Pop. density:** 22.5 per sq mi, 8.7 per sq km. **Urban:** 73.8%. **Ethnic groups:** Russian 80%, Tatar 4%, Ukrainian 2%, Bashkir 1%, Chuvash 1%. **Principal languages:** Russian (official), many minor langs. **Chief religions:** Russian Orthodox 15%-20%, Muslim 10%-15%, other Christian 2%.

Geography: Total area: 6,601,668 sq mi, 17,098,242 sq km; **Land area:** 6,323,482 sq mi, 16,377,742 sq km, more than 76% of total area of the former USSR and the largest country in the world. **Location:** Stretches from E Europe across N Asia to the Pacific O. **Neighbors:** Finland, Norway, Estonia, Latvia, Belarus, Ukraine on W; Georgia, Azerbaijan, Kazakhstan, China, Mongolia, N. Korea on S; Kaliningrad exclave bordered by Poland on the S, Lithuania on the N and E. **Topography:** Every type of climate except distinctly tropical. The European portion is a low plain, grassy in S, wooded in N, with Ural Mts. on E, and Caucasus Mts. on S. Urals stretch N-S for 2,500 mi. The Asiatic portion is a vast plain, with mountains on S and in E; tundra covers extreme N, with forest belt below; plains, marshes are in W, desert in SW. **Capital:** Moscow, 11,620,600. **Cities (urban aggl.):** Saint Petersburg, 4,865,720; Novosibirsk, 1,478,053; Yekaterinburg, 1,355,296; Nizhniy Novgorod, 1,245,351; Samara, 1,165,506; Omsk, 1,155,804; Kazan, 1,147,068; Chelyabinsk, 1,135,042; Rostov-on-Don, 1,091,669; Ufa, 1,064,087; Volgograd, 1,021,950.

Government: Type: Federal republic. **Head of state:** Pres. Vladimir Putin; b. Oct. 7, 1952; in office: May 7, 2012. **Head of gov.:** Prime Min. Dmitri Medvedev; b. Sept. 14, 1965; in office: May 8, 2012. **Local divisions:** 7 federal districts incl. 49 provinces, 21 autonomous republics, 6 territories, 1 autonomous region, 10 autonomous districts, 2 federal cities. **Defense budget:** $52.7 bil. **Active troops:** 956,000.

Economy: Industries: mining and extractive industries producing coal, oil, gas, chemicals, metals; machine building; defense (incl. radar, missile prod.); transp. equip.; communications equip.; agric. machinery, constr. equip.; elec. power generating and transmitting equip.; medical and scientific instruments; consumer durables, textiles. **Chief crops:** grain, sugar beets, sunflower seeds, vegetables, fruits. **Natural resources:** oil, nat. gas, coal, minerals, rare earth elements, timber (climate, terrain, and distance are obstacles to exploitation of resources). **Crude oil reserve:** 60 bil bbls. **Arable land:** 7.4%. **Livestock:** cattle: 20.7 mil; chickens: 390.5 mil; goats: 2.1 mil; pigs: 17.2 mil; sheep: 19.8 mil. **Fish catch:** 4.2 mil metric tons. **Electricity prod.:** (2010): 982.3 bil kWh. **Labor force:** agric. 9.8%, industry 27.5%, services 62.7%.

Finance: Monetary unit: Ruble (RUB) (Sept. 2012: 32.26 = $1 U.S.). **GDP:** $2.4 tril; **per capita GDP:** $17,000; **GDP growth:** 4.3%. **Imports:** $322.5 bil; China 15.6%, Germany 10%, Ukraine 6.6%, Italy 4.3%. **Exports:** $520.9 bil; Netherlands 12.3%, China 6.5%, Italy 5.6%, Germany 4.6%, Poland 4.3%. **Tourism:** $11.4 bil. **Budget:** $376.2 bil. **Total reserves less gold:** $453.9 bil. **Gold:** 28.4 mil oz t. **CPI change:** 8.4%.

Transport: Railways: 54,157 mi. **Motor vehicles:** 282.1 vehicles per 1,000 pop. **Civil aviation:** 52.1 bil pass.-mi; 593 airports. **Chief ports:** Kaliningrad, Kavkaz, Nakhodka, Novorossiysk, Primorsk, Saint Petersburg, Vostochny.

Communications: TV sets: 546 per 1,000 pop. **Radios:** 416 per 1,000 pop. **Telephone lines:** 30.9 per 100 pop. **Daily newspaper circ.:** 91.8 per 1,000 pop. **Internet:** 49%.

Health: Life expect.: 63.7 male; 75.7 female. **Births:** 12.3 (per 1,000 pop.). **Deaths:** 14.1 (per 1,000 pop.). **Natural inc.:** −0.18%. **Infant mortality:** 7.3 (per 1,000 live births). **HIV rate:** 1%.

Education: Compulsory: ages 6-15. **Literacy:** 99.6%.

Major intl. organizations: UN (FAO, IBRD, ILO, IMF, WHO), APEC, CIS, OSCE, WTO (observer).

Embassy: 2650 Wisconsin Ave. NW 20007; 298-5700.

Website: www.gov.ru or kremlin.ru

Slavic tribes began migrating into Russia from the W in the 5th cent. The first Russian state, centered in Novgorod and Kiev, was founded by Scandinavian chieftains in the 9th cent. In the 13th cent., Mongols overran the country. It recovered under the grand dukes and princes of Muscovy, or Moscow, and by 1480 freed itself from the Mongols. Ivan the Terrible was proclaimed Tsar, 1547. Peter the Great (1682-1725) extended the domain and, in 1721, founded the Russian empire. Western ideas and the beginnings of modernization spread through the Russian empire in the 19th and early 20th cent., but political evolution failed to keep pace.

Military reverses in the 1905 war with Japan and in WWI led to the breakdown of the Tsarist regime. The 1917 Revolution began in Mar. with a series of sporadic strikes for higher wages by factory workers. A provisional democratic government under Prince Georgi Lvov was established but was followed in May by a second provisional government, under Alexander Kerensky. Vladimir Ilyich Lenin, Nov. 7, overthrew the Kerensky government and the freely elected Constituent Assembly in a Communist coup.

Soviet Union

Lenin's death Jan. 21, 1924, led to an internal power struggle won by Joseph Stalin. His brutal tactics, including purge trials, mass executions, and exile of many to work camps, resulted in millions of deaths.

Germany and the USSR signed a non-aggression pact Aug. 1939; Germany launched a massive invasion of the Soviet Union, June 1941. Russian winter counterthrusts, 1941-42 and 1942-43, and heroic resistance to the siege of Leningrad (now St. Petersburg) stopped the German advance. Russians drove the Germans from Eastern Europe and the Balkans in the next two years.

After WWII, Communists took over in countries throughout the region, extending the Soviet sphere of influence. The USSR and the U.S., the world's leading nuclear superpowers, faced off against each other as cold war rivals. After Stalin died, Mar. 5, 1953, Nikita Khrushchev gained power and denounced Stalin, 1956, beginning "de-Stalinization."

Under Khrushchev the open antagonism of Poles and Hungarians toward Moscow's domination was suppressed in 1956. He aided the Cuban revolution under Fidel Castro but withdrew Soviet missiles from Cuba during a confrontation with U.S. Pres. Kennedy, Sept.-Oct. 1962. Khrushchev was deposed, Oct. 1964, and replaced by Leonid I. Brezhnev. In Aug. 1968 Soviet forces invaded Czechoslovakia, crushing liberalization there.

Massive Soviet military aid to North Vietnam in the late 1960s and early 1970s helped assure Communist victories throughout Indochina. In Dec. 1979, Soviet forces entered Afghanistan to support a pro-Soviet regime against U.S.-supported Muslim resistance fighters. In Apr. 1988, the Soviets agreed to withdraw their troops, ending a futile 8-year war.

Mikhail Gorbachev was chosen gen. sec. of the Communist Party, Mar. 1985. In 1987 he initiated a program of political and economic reforms, through openness (*glasnost*) and restructuring (*perestroika*). Gorbachev faced economic problems as well as ethnic and nationalist unrest in the republics. A coup by Communist hardliners Aug. 1991 was foiled with help from Russian Republic Pres. Boris Yeltsin. On Aug. 24, Gorbachev resigned as leader of the Communist Party. Several republics declared their independence, including Russia, Ukraine, and Kazakhstan. On Aug. 29, the Soviet Parliament voted to suspend all activities of the Communist Party.

The Soviet Union officially broke up Dec. 26, 1991, ending the 74-year domination of the Communist Party.

Russian Federation

Under Pres. Yeltsin, Russia took steps toward privatization, which caused inflation and a severe economic downturn. In June 1992, Yeltsin and U.S. Pres. George H. W. Bush agreed to massive arms reductions. Yeltsin prevailed in a power struggle with the Congress of People's Deputies, which was dominated by former Communists, and in a referendum Dec. 12, 1993, a new constitution was approved. In Dec. 1994 Russia sent troops into the breakaway republic of Chechnya. A peace accord was signed with Chechen rebels Aug. 31, 1996, temporarily ending the conflict. On May 27, 1997, Yeltsin signed a "founding act," increasing cooperation with NATO and paving the way for NATO to admit Eastern European nations.

Russia's economic crisis deepened in the late 1990s, heightening tensions between parliament and Pres. Yeltsin, who had been reelected in 1996. Russia moved forcibly in Aug. 1999 to suppress Islamic rebels in Dagestan; the conflict reignited the war in neighboring Chechnya, where Russia launched a full-scale assault. Yeltsin unexpectedly resigned Dec. 31, 1999, naming Prime Min. Vladimir Putin as his interim successor. Putin won presidential elections Mar. 26, 2000. Putin's allies won legislative elections, Dec. 7, 2003, and the president was reelected Mar. 14, 2004; international election monitors cited flaws on both occasions.

A bomb in Grozny, May 9, 2004, killed Chechnya's pro-Moscow president, Akhmad Kadyrov. In another terrorist act linked to the Chechnya conflict, two passenger planes exploded in midair after taking off from Moscow Aug. 24, killing 90 people. Chechen rebels, Sept. 1, 2004, seized control of a school in Beslan, North Ossetia, taking more than 1,100 hostages. Russian troops stormed the school Sept. 3; more than 330 people died, including 186 children. Putin cited the terrorist threat Sept. 13 in proposing a government overhaul that tightened his control over parliament and regional officeholders. Russian forces killed Chechen rebel leader Aslan Maskhadov, Mar. 8, 2005, and Chechen guerrilla leader Shamil Basayev, who had organized the terrorist attack at Beslan, July 10, 2006.

Constitutionally barred from seeking another term, Pres. Putin backed his protégé Dmitri Medvedev, who won the presidential election Mar. 2, 2008; after taking office May 7 Medvedev named Putin as prime min. A long-simmering conflict with Georgia erupted into open warfare Aug. 7-16. Russia dispatched troops to support secessionists in the enclaves of South Ossetia and Abkhazia and launched assaults on strategic Georgian cities; a cease-fire left thousands of Russian troops in the breakaway regions, which Pres. Medvedev recognized as independent, Aug. 26, 2008.

An economic boom fueled by oil and gas sales came to a halt in late 2008. The global financial crisis and a drop in oil prices led to turmoil on Russian financial markets, which were closed Sept. 17-18 as the government put together a $130-bil emergency rescue plan. As the crisis deepened, the government loaned banks $37 bil Oct. 7 and began buying shares to prop up the Russian stock exchange.

Russia declared, Apr. 16, 2009, that it had ended counterterrorism operations in Chechnya; from June through Aug., there was an upsurge of insurgent violence in Chechnya and neighboring Dagestan and Ingushetia. Female suicide bombers from Dagestan struck two Moscow subway stations Mar. 29, 2010, killing 40 people. A bombing at a Moscow airport Jan. 24, 2011, killed 37.

During a visit to Russia July 6-7, 2009, U.S. Pres. Obama met with Pres. Medvedev and Prime Min. Putin. Repairing relations strained since the 2008 Georgia war, Russia and the U.S. agreed to reduce nuclear stockpiles and increase military cooperation. Medvedev and Obama Apr. 8, 2010, signed a nuclear arms reduction treaty known as New START, which was ratified by the U.S. Senate Dec. 22, 2010. Medvedev announced Sept. 24, 2011, that Putin would run for president in elections Mar. 2012, with Medvedev then serving as his prime min. Parliamentary elections were held Dec. 3, 2011, with Putin's party, United Russia, failing to garner 50% of the vote, despite alleged fraud, and getting just over 50% of the seats in the Duma. Tens of thousands marched through Moscow, Dec 10 and Dec. 24, calling for Putin's resignation. After a quiet Jan., an estimated 120,000 people protested in Moscow during a sanctioned event, Feb. 4. Unsanctioned protests followed, including the performance of a "punk prayer" at Christ the Savior Cathedral in Moscow, Feb. 21, by members of Pussy Riot, a punk collective formed to protest Putin's presidential candidacy. Putin nonetheless won 64% of the vote in the Mar. 4, 2012, election, though there were again claims of fraud. Two members of Pussy Riot, Nadezhda Tolokonnikova and Maria Alekhina, were jailed Mar. 4, 2012, and a third, Yekaterina Samutsevich, Mar. 15. They were convicted of hooliganism and sentenced to two years in jail Aug. 17, 2012, despite international criticism.

Rwanda
Republic of Rwanda

People: Population: 11,689,696. **Age distrib.:** <15: 42.6%; 65+: 2.4%. **Pop. density:** 1,227.3 per sq mi, 473.9 per sq km. **Urban:** 19.1%. **Ethnic groups:** Hutu (Bantu) 84%, Tutsi (Hamitic) 15%, Twa (Pygmy) 1%. **Principal languages:** Kinyarwanda (universal Bantu vernacular), French, English (all official); Swahili used in commercial centers. **Chief religions:** Roman Catholic 57%, Protestant 26%, Adventist 11%, Muslim 5%, none 2%.

Geography: Total area: 10,169 sq mi, 26,338 sq km; **Land area:** 9,524 sq mi, 24,668 sq km. **Location:** In E central Africa. **Neighbors:** Uganda on N, Congo (formerly Zaire) on W, Burundi on S, Tanzania on E. **Topography:** Grassy uplands and hills cover most of country, with chain of volcanoes in the NW. The source of the Nile R. has been located in headwaters of the Kagera (Akagera) R., SW of Kigali. **Capital:** Kigali, 1,003,570.

Government: Type: Republic. **Head of state:** Pres. Paul Kagame; b. Oct. 23, 1957; in office: Apr. 22, 2000 (de facto from Mar. 24). **Head of gov.:** Prime Min. Pierre Damien Habumuremyi; b. Feb. 21, 1961; in office: Oct. 7, 2011. **Local divisions:** 12 prefectures subdivided into 155 communes. **Defense budget:** $73 mil. **Active troops:** 33,000.

Economy: Industries: cement; agric. prods.; small-scale beverages, soap, furniture, shoes, plastic goods, textiles, cigarettes. **Chief crops:** coffee, tea, pyrethrum (insecticide made from chrysanthemums), bananas, beans, sorghum, potatoes. **Natural resources:** gold, tin ore, tungsten ore, methane, hydropower. **Arable land:** 52.7%. **Livestock:** cattle: 1.3 mil; chickens: 3.5 mil; goats: 2.7 mil; pigs: 684,708; sheep: 743,201. **Fish catch:** 9,678 metric tons. **Electricity prod.:** 240 mil kWh. **Labor force:** agric. 90%, industry and services 10%.

Finance: Monetary unit: Franc (RWF) (Sept. 2012: 607.42 = $1 U.S.). **GDP:** $13.9 bil; **per capita GDP:** $1,400; **GDP growth:** 8.8%. **Imports:** $1.4 bil; Kenya 18.1%, Uganda 16.4%, U.S. 10.4%, UAE 8.8%, China 5.7%, Tanzania 5.3%. **Exports:** $372.9 mil; Kenya

30.1%, China 13.5%, Dem. Rep. of the Congo 12%, Malaysia 8.8%, U.S. 5.6%, Swaziland 4.8%. **Tourism:** $202 mil. **Budget:** $1.6 bil. **Total reserves less gold:** $1.1 bil. **CPI change:** 5.7%.

Transport: Civil aviation: 4 airports. **Chief ports:** Cyangugu, Gisenyi, Kibuye.

Communications: TV sets: 8 per 1,000 pop. Radios: 854 per 1,000 pop. **Telephone lines:** 0.4 per 100 pop. **Internet:** 7%.

Health: Life expect.: 57.0 male; 60.0 female. **Births:** 36.1 (per 1,000 pop.). **Deaths:** 9.6 (per 1,000 pop.). **Natural inc.:** 2.65%. **Infant mortality:** 62.5 (per 1,000 live births). **HIV rate:** 2.9%.

Education: Compulsory: ages 7-15. **Literacy:** 71.1%.

Major intl. organizations: UN (FAO, IBRD, ILO, IMF, WHO), AU, the Commonwealth, WTO.

Embassy: 1714 New Hampshire Ave. NW 20009; 232-2882.

Website: www.gov.rw

For centuries, the Tutsi dominated the Hutu (90% of the population). A civil war broke out in 1959 and Tutsi power was ended. Many Tutsi went into exile. Rwanda, which had been part of the Belgian UN trusteeship of Rwanda-Urundi, became independent July 1, 1962.

In 1963 Tutsi exiles unsuccessfully attempted to regain power; a large-scale massacre of Tutsi followed. Hutu rivalries led to a bloodless coup July 1973 in which Hutu army officer Juvénal Habyarimana took power. After another invasion and coup attempt by Tutsi exiles in 1990, a multiparty democracy was established.

Renewed ethnic strife led to an Aug. 1993 peace accord between the government and rebels of the Tutsi-led Rwandan Patriotic Front (RPF). But after Habyarimana and Burundi Pres. Cyprien Ntaryamira were killed Apr. 6, 1994, in a suspicious plane crash, violence broke out. More than 1 mil may have died in massacres, mostly of Tutsi by Hutu militias, and in civil warfare as the RPF sought power. About 2 mil Tutsi and Hutu fled to camps in Zaire (now Dem. Rep. of the Congo) and other countries; many died of disease. French troops under a UN mandate moved into SW Rwanda June 23 to establish a safe zone. The RPF claimed victory, installing a government led by a moderate Hutu president in July. French troops pulled out Aug. 22. A UN peacekeeping mission ended Mar. 8, 1996. The Rwandan government and a UN-sponsored tribunal in Tanzania continued to gather evidence of crimes against humanity. More than 1 mil refugees, mostly Hutu, returned to Rwanda in Nov. and Dec. 1996.

Firing squads in Rwanda on Apr. 24, 1998, executed 22 people convicted of genocide. Former Prime Min. Jean Kambanda pleaded guilty May 1 before the UN tribunal and received a life sentence Sept. 4, 1998. RPF leader Maj. Gen. Paul Kagame became Rwanda's first Tutsi president Apr. 22, 2000.

Rwandans approved a new constitution, May 26, 2003; reelected Pres. Kagame, Aug. 25; and chose a new parliament, Sept. 29-30. Former Pres. Bizimungu was sentenced to 15 years for embezzlement, June 2004 but was pardoned by Kagame and released, Apr. 6, 2007. Rwanda cut diplomatic ties with France Nov. 24, 2006, after a French judge linked Kagame and his close aides to the 1994 deaths of Habyarimana and Ntaryamira, but restored relations with France, Nov. 2009, when Rwanda also joined the Commonwealth.

Accused of being one of the architects of the 1994 genocide, Col. Theoneste Bagosora was convicted and sentenced to life in prison by the UN tribunal Dec. 18, 2008. A Rwandan court handed out a life sentence, Jan. 20, 2009, to former Justice Min. Agnes Ntamabyariro for her role in inciting the massacres. Up to 4,000 Rwandan troops fought that month alongside Congolese forces against Hutu militias in E Congo. After a campaign criticized as repressive by human rights groups, Pres. Kagame won reelection Aug. 9, 2010

Rwanda has experienced steady economic growth in recent years. The U.S. has funded efforts to train the Rwandan military and control HIV/AIDS and malaria.

Saint Kitts and Nevis
Federation of Saint Kitts and Nevis

People: Population: 50,726. **Age distrib.:** <15: 22.3%; 65+: 7.7%. **Pop. density:** 503.4 per sq mi, 194.4 per sq km. **Urban:** 32%. **Ethnic group:** predominantly black; some British, Portuguese, Lebanese. **Principal language:** English (official). **Chief religions:** Anglican, other Protestant, Roman Catholic.

Geography: Total area: 101 sq mi, 261 sq km; **Land area:** 101 sq mi, 261 sq km. **Location:** In N part of the Leeward group of Lesser Antilles in E Caribbean Sea. **Neighbors:** Antigua and Barbuda to E. **Topography:** St. Kitts has forested volcanic slopes; Nevis rises from beaches to central peak. Climate is tropical moderated by sea breezes. **Capital:** Basseterre, 12,496.

Government: Type: Constitutional monarchy. **Head of state:** Queen Elizabeth II, represented by Gov.-Gen. Sir Cuthbert M. Sebastian; b. Oct. 22, 1921; in office: Jan. 1, 1996. **Head of gov.:** Prime Min. Denzil Douglas; b. Jan. 14, 1953; in office: July 7, 1995. **Local div.:** 14 parishes. **Defense budget:** NA. **Active troops:** Relies on Regional Security System headquartered in Barbados for national defense.

Economy: Industries: tourism, cotton, salt, copra, clothing, footwear, beverages. **Chief crops:** sugarcane, rice, yams, vegetables, bananas. **Arable land:** 15.4%. **Livestock:** cattle: 7,000; chickens: 80,000; goats: 9,000; pigs: 6,000; sheep: 7,000. **Fish catch:** 21,099 metric tons. **Electricity prod.:** 135 mil kWh. **Labor force:** NA.

Finance: Monetary unit: East Caribbean Dollar (XCD) (Sept. 2012: 2.70 = $1 U.S.). **GDP:** $886.2 mil; **per capita GDP:** $15,800;

GDP growth: –2%. **Imports:** $315.7 mil; U.S. 37.3%, Trinidad and Tobago 20.4%, Barbados 4.8%. **Exports:** $58.6 mil; U.S. 57.8%, Canada 9.8%, Russia 5.2%, Germany 4.2%. **Tourism:** $92 mil. **Budget:** $222.2 mil. **Total reserves less gold:** $244.3 mil. **CPI change:** 5.9%.

Transport: Railways: 31 mi. **Civil aviation:** 2 airports. **Chief ports:** Basseterre, Charlestown.

Communications: TV sets: 312 per 1,000 pop. **Radios:** 697 per 1,000 pop. **Telephone lines** (2010): 37.8 per 100 pop. **Internet** (2010): 76%.

Health: Life expect.: 72.5 male; 77.3 female. **Births:** 13.9 (per 1,000 pop.). **Deaths:** 7.1 (per 1,000 pop.). **Natural inc.:** 0.68%. **Infant mortality:** 9.4 (per 1,000 live births). **HIV rate:** NA.

Education: Compulsory: ages 5-16. **Literacy:** NA.

Major intl. organizations: UN (FAO, IBRD, ILO, IMF, WHO), Caricom, the Commonwealth, OAS, OECS, WTO.

Embassy: 3216 New Mexico Ave. NW 20016; 686-2636.

Website: www.gov.kn

St. Kitts (formerly St. Christopher; known by indigenous peoples as Liamuiga) and Nevis were reached and named by Columbus in 1493. They were settled by Britain in 1623, but ownership was disputed with France until 1713. They were part of the Leeward Islands Federation, 1871-1956, and the Federation of the West Indies, 1958-62. The colony achieved self-government as an Associated State of the UK in 1967, becoming independent, Sept. 19, 1983, and the smallest independent nation in the Western Hemisphere. A secession referendum on Nevis, Aug. 10, 1998, fell short of the two-thirds majority required.

Saint Lucia

People: Population: 162,178. **Age distrib.:** <15: 22.2%; 65+: 9.9%. **Pop. density:** 693.1 per sq mi, 267.6 per sq km. **Urban:** 17.5%. **Ethnic groups:** black 83%, mixed 12%, East Indian 2%. **Principal languages:** English (official), French patois. **Chief religions:** Roman Catholic 68%, Protestant 18% (Seventh-Day Adventist 9%, Pentecostal 6%, Anglican 2%, Evangelical 2%), other Christian 5%, Rastafarian 2%, none 5%.

Geography: Total area: 238 sq mi, 616 sq km; **Land area:** 234 sq mi, 606 sq km. **Location:** In E Caribbean, 2nd largest of Windward Isls. **Neighbors:** Martinique to N, St. Vincent to S. **Topography:** Mountainous, volcanic in origin; Soufriere, a volcanic crater, in S. Wooded mountains run N-S to Mt. Gimie, 3,145 ft, with streams through fertile valleys. **Capital:** Castries, 20,645.

Government: Type: Constitutional monarchy. **Head of state:** Queen Elizabeth II, represented by Gov.-Gen. Dame Calliopa Pearlette Louisy; b. June 8, 1946; in office: Sept. 17, 1997. **Head of gov.:** Prime Min. Kenny Davis Anthony; b. Jan. 8, 1951; in office: Nov. 30, 2011. **Local divisions:** 11 quarters. **Defense budget:** NA. **Active troops:** No regular military forces.

Economy: Industries: tourism, clothing, electronic components assembly, beverages, corrugated cardboard boxes, lime proc., coconut proc. **Chief crops:** bananas, coconuts, vegetables, citrus, root crops, cocoa. **Natural resources:** forests, beaches, pumice, mineral springs, geothermal potential. **Arable land:** 4.9%. **Livestock:** cattle: 11,000; chickens: 450,000; goats: 9,500; pigs: 20,000; sheep: 10,000. **Fish catch:** 1,851 metric tons. **Electricity prod.** (2010): 358 mil kWh. **Labor force:** agric. 21.7%; industry 24.7%; services 53.6%.

Finance: Monetary unit: East Caribbean Dollar (XCD) (Sept. 2012: 2.70 = $1 U.S.). **GDP:** $2.1 bil; **per capita GDP:** $12,800; **GDP growth:** 0.2%. **Imports:** $545.9 mil; Brazil 78.8%, U.S. 8.4%, Trinidad and Tobago 5.1%. **Exports:** $198.6 mil; Colombia 21%, U.S. 14.9%, Peru 8.5%, Antigua and Barbuda 8.1%, Dominica 7.9%, Barbados 7.1%, Trinidad and Tobago 6.6%, UK 5.6%, Grenada 5.4%. **Tourism:** $296 mil. **Budget** (2010): $393.3 mil. **Total reserves less gold:** $213.4 mil. **CPI change:** 2.8%.

Transport: Civil aviation: 2 airports. **Chief ports:** Castries, Culde-Sac, Vieux-Fort.

Communications: TV sets: 341 per 1,000 pop. **Radios:** 193 per 1,000 pop. **Telephone lines:** 20.4 per 100 pop. **Internet:** 42%.

Health: Life expect.: 74.3 male; 79.9 female. **Births:** 14.4 (per 1,000 pop.). **Deaths:** 7.1 (per 1,000 pop.). **Natural inc.:** 0.73%. **Infant mortality:** 12.4 (per 1,000 live births). **HIV rate:** NA.

Education: Compulsory: ages 5-14. **Literacy:** NA.

Major intl. organizations: UN (FAO, IBRD, ILO, IMF, WHO), Caricom, the Commonwealth, OAS, OECS, WTO.

Embassy: 3216 New Mexico Ave. NW 20016; 364-6792.

Website: www.stlucia.gov.lc

St. Lucia was ceded to Britain by France at the Treaty of Paris, 1814. Self-government was granted with the West Indies Act, 1967. Independence was attained Feb. 22, 1979.

Saint Vincent and the Grenadines

People: Population: 103,537. **Age distrib.:** <15: 24%; 65+: 8.2%. **Pop. density:** 689.4 per sq mi, 266.2 per sq km. **Urban:** 49.3%. **Ethnic groups:** black 66%, mixed 19%, East Indian 6%, European 4%, Carib Amerindian 2%. **Principal languages:** English, French patois. **Chief religions:** Protestant 75% (Anglican 47%, Methodist 28%), Roman Catholic 13%, other (incl. Hindu, Seventh-Day Adventist, other Protestant) 12%.

Geography: Total area: 150 sq mi, 389 sq km; **Land area:** 150 sq mi, 389 sq km. **Location:** In E Caribbean, St. Vincent (133 sq mi) and the northern islets of the Grenadines form a part of Windward chain. **Neighbors:** St. Lucia to N, Barbados to E, Grenada to S. **Topography:** St. Vincent is volcanic, with a ridge of thickly wooded mountains running its length. **Capital:** Kingstown, 30,863.

Government: Type: Constitutional monarchy. **Head of state:** Queen Elizabeth II, represented by Sir Frederick Ballantyne; b. July 5, 1936; in office: Sept. 2, 2002. **Head of gov.:** Prime Min. Ralph Gonsalves; b. Aug. 8, 1946; in office: Mar. 29, 2001. **Local divisions:** 6 parishes. **Defense budget:** NA. **Active troops:** Relies on Regional Security System headquartered in Barbados for national defense.

Economy: Industries: tourism, food proc., cement, furniture, clothing, starch. **Chief crops:** bananas, coconuts, sweet potatoes, spices. **Natural resources:** hydropower. **Arable land:** 12.8%. **Livestock:** cattle: 5,200; chickens: 250,000; goats: 7,500; pigs: 9,300; sheep: 13,500. **Fish catch:** 65,626 metric tons. **Electricity prod.:** 132 mil kWh. **Labor force:** agric. 26%, industry 17%, services 57%.

Finance: Monetary unit: East Caribbean Dollar (XCD) (Sept. 2012: 2.70 = $1 U.S.). **GDP:** $1.3 bil; **per capita GDP:** $11,600; **GDP growth:** −0.4%. **Imports:** $348 mil; Singapore 25.4%, Trinidad and Tobago 17.9%, U.S. 12.8%, China 12.5%, Norway 7.6%. **Exports:** $64.4 mil; Trinidad and Tobago 12.1%, Austria 12%, St. Lucia 10.7%, France 9.6%, Turkey 9%, Barbados 8.9%, Dominica 7%, Grenada 6.7%, Antigua and Barbuda 6.1%. **Tourism:** $92 mil. **Budget:** $259.3 mil. **Total reserves less gold:** $89.6 mil. **CPI change:** 3.95%.

Transport: Civil aviation: 5 airports. **Chief port:** Kingstown.

Communications: TV sets: 341 per 1,000 pop. **Radios:** 1,025 per 1,000 pop. **Telephone lines:** 20.8 per 100 pop. **Internet:** 43%.

Health: Life expect.: 72.5 male; 76.4 female. **Births:** 14.4 (per 1,000 pop.). **Deaths:** 7.0 (per 1,000 pop.). **Natural inc.:** 0.73%. **Infant mortality:** 13.9 (per 1,000 live births). **HIV rate:** NA.

Education: Compulsory: ages 5-16. **Literacy:** NA.

Major intl. organizations: UN (FAO, IBRD, ILO, IMF, WHO), Caricom, the Commonwealth, OAS, OECS, WTO.

Embassy: 3216 New Mexico Ave. NW 20016; 364-6730.

Website: www.gov.vc

Columbus landed on St. Vincent on Jan. 22, 1498 (St. Vincent's Day). Britain and France both laid claim to the island in the 17th and 18th cent.; the Treaty of Versailles, 1783, finally ceded it to Britain. Associated State status was granted 1969; independence was attained Oct. 27, 1979.

Samoa (*formerly* Western Samoa)
Independent State of Samoa

People: Population: 194,320. **Age distrib.:** <15: 34.7%; 65+: 5.3%. **Pop. density:** 178.4 per sq mi, 68.9 per sq km. **Urban:** 19.9%. **Ethnic groups:** Samoan 93%, Euronesians (mixed European, Polynesian) 7%. **Principal languages:** Samoan (Polynesian) (official), English. **Chief religions:** Protestant 60% (Congregationalist 35%, Methodist 15%, Assembly of God 7%, Seventh-Day Adventist 4%), Roman Catholic 20%, Mormon 13%.

Geography: Total area: 1,093 sq mi, 2,831 sq km; **Land area:** 1,089 sq mi, 2,821 sq km. **Location:** In S Pacific O. **Neighbors:** Nearest are Fiji to SW, Tonga to S. **Topography:** Main islands, Savaii (659 sq mi) and Upolu (432 sq mi), both ruggedly mountainous, and small islands Manono and Apolima. **Capital:** Apia, 36,513.

Government: Type: Constitutional monarchy. **Head of state:** Tuiatua Tupua Tamasese Efi; b. Mar. 1, 1938; in office: June 20, 2007. **Head of gov.:** Prime Min. Tuilaepa Sailele Malielegaoi; b. Apr. 14, 1945; in office: Nov. 23, 1998. **Local divisions:** 11 districts. **Defense budget:** NA. **Active troops:** No regular military forces. Informal defense ties with New Zealand.

Economy: Industries: food proc., building materials, auto parts. **Chief crops:** coconuts, bananas, taro, yams, coffee, cocoa. **Natural resources:** forests, fish, hydropower. **Arable land:** 8.8%. **Livestock:** cattle: 30,000; chickens: 620,000; pigs: 202,000. **Fish catch:** 13,005 metric tons. **Electricity prod.** 104 mil kWh. **Labor force:** NA.

Finance: Monetary unit: Tala (WST) (Sept. 2012: 2.33 = $1 U.S.). **GDP:** $1.1 bil; **per capita GDP:** $6,000; **GDP growth:** 2.1%. **Imports** (2010): $280 mil; New Zealand 24%, Fiji 17.2%, Singapore 15.4%, China 8.5%, Japan 8.2%, Australia 6.7%, U.S. 5.3%. **Exports** (2010): $35.5 mil; American Samoa 50%, Australia 23.6%. **Tourism:** $124 mil. **Budget:** $302.1 mil. **Total reserves less gold:** $166.8 mil. **CPI change:** 5.2%.

Transport: Civil aviation: 224.9 mil pass.-mi; 1 airport. **Chief port:** Apia.

Communications: TV sets: 122 per 1,000 pop. **Radios:** 312 per 1,000 pop. **Telephone lines** (2010): 19.3 per 100 pop. **Internet** (2010): 7%.

Health: Life expect.: 69.8 male; 75.7 female. **Births:** 22.1 (per 1,000 pop.). **Deaths:** 5.3 (per 1,000 pop.). **Natural inc.:** 1.68%. **Infant mortality:** 21.9 (per 1,000 live births). **HIV rate:** NA.

Education: Compulsory: ages 5-12. **Literacy:** 98.8%.

Major intl. organizations: UN (FAO, IBRD, ILO, IMF, WHO), the Commonwealth, WTO (observer).

Embassy: 800 Second Ave., Ste. 400J, New York, NY 10017; (212) 599-6196.

Website: www.govt.ws

Samoa (formerly known as Western Samoa to distinguish it from American Samoa, a small U.S. territory) was a German colony,

1899 to 1914, when New Zealand landed troops and took over. It became a New Zealand mandate under the League of Nations and, in 1945, a New Zealand UN Trusteeship.

An elected local government took office in Oct. 1959, and the country became fully independent Jan. 1, 1962. Malietoa Tanumafili II, Samoa's head of state since independence, died May 11, 2007, and was succeeded by Tuiatua Tupua Tamasese Efi. At the end of the day on Dec. 29, 2011, Samoa moved to the western side of the Intl. Date Line, to simplify trade with Australia and New Zealand. Samoa is now 3 hours ahead of eastern Australia rather than 21 hours behind.

San Marino
Republic of San Marino

People: Population: 32,140. **Age distrib.:** <15: 16.4%; 65+: 18.2%. **Pop. density:** 1,364.6 per sq mi, 526.9 per sq km. **Urban:** 94.1%. **Ethnic groups:** Sammarinese, Italian. **Principal language:** Italian. **Chief religion:** Roman Catholic.

Geography: Total area: 24 sq mi, 61 sq km; **Land area:** 24 sq mi, 61 sq km. **Location:** In N central Italy near Adriatic coast. **Neighbors:** Completely surrounded by Italy. **Topography:** The country lies on slopes of Mt. Titano. **Capital:** San Marino, 4,280.

Government: Type: Republic. **Heads of state and gov.:** Two co-regents appt. every 6 months. **Local divisions:** 9 castelli. **Defense budget:** NA. **Active troops:** No regular military forces. Defense is responsibility of Italy.

Economy: Industries: tourism, banking, textiles, electronics, ceramics, cement, wine. **Chief crops:** wheat, grapes, corn, olives. **Natural resources:** building stone. **Arable land:** 16.7%. **Labor force:** agric. 0.2%, industry 36.3%, services 63.5%.

Finance: Monetary unit: Euro (EUR) (Sept. 2012: 0.79 = $1 U.S.). **GDP:** $1.1 bil; **per capita GDP** (2009): $36,200; **GDP growth:** 0.8%. **Imports** (2010): $2.1 bil. **Exports** (2010): $2.5 bil. **Total reserves less gold:** $341.9 mil. **Tourism:** NA. **Budget** (2009): $940.4 mil. **Total reserves less gold:** $341.9 mil.

Transport: NA.

Communications: TV sets: 792 per 1,000 pop. **Radios:** 1,322 per 1,000 pop. **Telephone lines:** 58.9 per 100 pop. **Internet:** 49.6%.

Health: Life expect.: 80.6 male; 85.8 female. **Births:** 8.9 (per 1,000 pop.). **Deaths:** 8.1 (per 1,000 pop.). **Natural inc.:** 0.08%. **Infant mortality:** 4.7 (per 1,000 live births). **HIV rate:** NA.

Education: Compulsory: ages 6-16. **Literacy:** NA.

Major intl. organizations: UN (FAO, IBRD, ILO, IMF, WHO), OSCE.

Honorary Consulate: 1899 L St. NW, Ste. 500, 20036; 223-3517.

Website: www.visitsanmarino.com or www.consigliograndee generale.sm

San Marino claims to be the oldest state in Europe and to have been founded in the 4th cent. It has had a treaty of friendship with Italy since 1862. A Communist-led coalition ruled 1947-57; a similar coalition ruled 1978-86. The Pact for San Marino, a center-right coalition, won parliamentary elections Nov. 9, 2008.

São Tomé and Príncipe
Democratic Republic of São Tomé and Príncipe

People: Population: 183,176. **Age distrib.:** <15: 44.4%; 65+: 3.1%. **Pop. density:** 492.1 per sq mi, 190 per sq km. **Urban:** 62.7%. **Ethnic groups:** mestico, angolares (descendants of Angolan slaves), forros (descendants of freed slaves), servicais (contract laborers fr. Angola, Mozambique, Cape Verde), tongas (children of servicais born in country), Europeans (primarily Portuguese). **Principal language:** Portuguese (official). **Chief religions:** Catholic 70%, Evangelical 3%, New Apostolic 2%, Adventist 2%, none 19%.

Geography: Total area: 372 sq mi, 964 sq km; **Land area:** 372 sq mi, 964 sq km. **Location:** In Gulf of Guinea about 125 mi off W central Africa. **Neighbors:** Gabon, Equatorial Guinea to E. **Topography:** São Tomé and Príncipe islands, part of an extinct volcano chain, are both covered by lush forests and croplands. **Capital:** São Tomé, 63,952.

Government: Type: Republic. **Head of state:** Pres. Manuel Pinto da Costa; b. Aug. 5, 1937; in office: Sept. 3, 2011. **Head of gov.:** Prime Min. Patrice Trovoada; b. Mar. 18, 1962; in office: Aug. 14, 2010. **Local divisions:** 2 provinces. **Defense budget/active troops:** NA.

Economy: Industries: light constr., textiles, soap, beer, fish proc., timber. **Chief crops:** cocoa, coconuts, palm kernels, copra, cinnamon, pepper, coffee, bananas, papayas, beans. **Natural resources:** fish, hydropower. **Arable land:** 10.4%. **Livestock:** cattle: 5,000; chickens: 430,000; goats: 5,500; pigs: 2,850; sheep: 3,200. **Fish catch:** 4,650 metric tons. **Electricity prod.:** 32 mil kWh. **Labor force:** Pop. mainly engaged in subsistence agric. and fishing; shortage of skilled workers.

Finance: Monetary unit: Dobra (STD) (Sept. 2012: 19,927.00 = $1 U.S.). **GDP:** $383.9 mil; **per capita GDP:** $2,300; **GDP growth:** 4.9%. **Imports:** $112.1 mil; Portugal 55.3%, Malaysia 14.3%, U.S. 5.2%, Gabon 4%. **Exports:** $12.5 mil; Netherlands 24%, Belgium 22.5%, Egypt 19.1%, U.S. 7.1%. **Tourism:** $9 mil. **Budget:** $117.9 mil. **Total reserves less gold:** $51.5 mil. **CPI change:** 11.9%.

Transport: Civil aviation: 12.4 mil pass.-mi; 2 airports. **Chief port:** São Tomé.

Communications: TV sets: 127 per 1,000 pop. **Radios:** 106 per 1,000 pop. **Telephone lines:** 4.7 per 1,000 pop. **Internet:** 20.2%.

Health: Life expect.: 62.3 male; 64.7 female. **Births:** 37.0 (per 1,000 pop.). **Deaths:** 7.9 (per 1,000 pop.). **Natural inc.:** 2.91%. **Infant mortality:** 51.8 (per 1,000 live births). **HIV rate:** NA.

Education: Compulsory: ages 6-16. **Literacy:** 89.2%.

Major intl. organizations: UN (FAO, IBRD, ILO, IMF, WHO), AU, WTO (observer).

Permanent UN mission: 460 Park Ave., 11th Fl., New York, NY 10022; (212) 317-0533.

Website: www.gov.st

The Portuguese discovered the islands in 1471 and brought the first settlers—convicts and exiled Jews. Sugar planting was replaced by the slave trade as the chief economic activity until coffee and cocoa were introduced in the 19th cent.

Portugal agreed, 1974, to turn the colony over to the Gabon-based Movement for the Liberation of São Tomé and Príncipe; and its East German-trained leader, Manuel Pinto da Costa became its first president. Independence came July 12, 1975. Democratic reforms were instituted in 1987. In 1991, Miguel Trovoada won the first free presidential election. A military coup that ousted Trovoada Aug. 15, 1995, was reversed a week later after Angolan mediation. Trovoada defeated Pinto da Costa in a presidential runoff election, July 21, 1996.

Fradique de Menezes, a wealthy cocoa exporter, beat Pinto da Costa in July 29, 2001, presidential elections. The government was ousted in a military coup July 16, 2003, but was restored to power a week later and reelected July 30, 2006. After the opposition Independent Democratic Action party won parliamentary elections Aug. 1, 2010, Patrice Trovoada (son of the former president) was chosen to head the new government. Pinto da Costa returned to power after a presidential run-off vote Aug. 7, 2011. The country, long one of the world's poorest, has sought to develop oil deposits in the Gulf of Guinea.

Saudi Arabia
Kingdom of Saudi Arabia

People: Population: 26,534,504. **Age distrib.:** <15: 28.8%; 65+: 3%. **Pop. density:** 32 per sq mi, 12.3 per sq km. **Urban:** 82.3%. **Ethnic groups:** Arab 90%, Afro-Asian 10%. **Principal language:** Arabic (official). **Chief religion:** Muslim (official) 100%.

Geography: Total area: 830,000 sq mi, 2,149,690 sq km; **Land area:** 830,000 sq mi, 2,149,690 sq km. **Location:** Occupies most of Arabian Peninsula in Mid-East. **Neighbors:** Kuwait, Iraq, Jordan on N; Yemen, Oman on S; United Arab Emirates, Qatar on E. **Topography:** Bordered by Red Sea on W. The highlands on W, up to 9,000 ft, slope as arid, barren desert to the Persian Gulf on E. **Capital:** Riyadh, 5,450,820. **Cities (urban aggl.):** Jiddah, 3,578,315; Mecca, 1,590,505; Medina, 1,142,292.

Government: Type: Monarchy with council of ministers. **Head of state and gov.:** King Abdullah bin Abdul Aziz; b. Aug. 1, 1924; in office: Aug. 1, 2005. **Local divisions:** 13 provinces. **Defense budget:** $46.2 bil. **Active troops:** 233,500.

Economy: Industries: crude oil prod., petroleum refining, basic petrochemicals, ammonia, industrial gases, caustic soda, cement, fertilizer, plastics, metals, commercial ship repair, commercial aircraft repair. **Chief crops:** wheat, barley, tomatoes, melons, dates, citrus. **Natural resources:** petroleum, nat. gas, iron ore, gold, copper. **Crude oil reserves:** 267 bil bbls (incl. half of Neutral Zone reserves). **Arable land:** 1.5%. **Livestock:** cattle: 421,000; chickens: 146 mil; goats: 4.5 mil; sheep: 5.9 mil. **Fish catch:** 91,516 metric tons. **Electricity prod.** (2010): 212.3 bil kWh. **Labor force:** agric. 6.7%, industry 21.4%, services 71.9%.

Finance: Monetary unit: Riyal (SAR) (Sept. 2012: 3.75 = $1 U.S.). **GDP:** $691.5 bil; **per capita GDP:** $24,500; **GDP growth:** 6.8%. **Imports:** $117.4 bil; China 12.8%, U.S. 11.9%, Germany 7.1%, South Korea 6%, Japan 5.6%, India 5.3%, Italy 4.1%. **Exports:** $359.9 bil; Japan 13.9%, China 13.7%, U.S. 13.4%, South Korea 10.2%, India 7.2%, Singapore 4.9%. **Tourism:** $8.5 bil. **Budget:** $214.3 bil. **Total reserves less gold:** $540.7 bil. **Gold:** 10.4 mil oz t. **CPI change:** 5.01%.

Transport: Railways: 856 mi. **Motor vehicles:** 210 vehicles per 1,000 pop. **Civil aviation:** 18 bil pass.-mi; 80 airports. **Chief ports:** Ad Dammam, Al Jubayl, Jeddah, Yanbu al Bahr.

Communications: TV sets: 275 per 1,000 pop. **Radios:** 317 per 1,000 pop. **Telephone lines:** 16.5 per 100 pop. **Internet:** 47.5%.

Health: Life expect.: 72.4 male; 76.4 female. **Births:** 19.2 (per 1,000 pop.). **Deaths:** 3.3 (per 1,000 pop.). **Natural inc.:** 1.59%. **Infant mortality:** 15.6 (per 1,000 live births). **HIV rate:** NA.

Education: Compulsory: ages 6-11. **Literacy:** 86.6%.

Major intl. organizations: UN (FAO, IBRD, ILO, IMF, WHO), AL, OPEC, WTO.

Embassy: 601 New Hampshire Ave. NW 20037; 342-3800.

Website: www.saudi.gov.sa

Before Muhammad, Arabia was divided among numerous warring tribes and small kingdoms. Muhammad united it in the early 7th cent. His successors conquered the entire Near East and North Africa, bringing Islam and the Arabic language. But Arabia soon returned to its former status.

Nejd, in central Arabia, long an independent state and center of the Wahhabi sect, fell under Turkish rule in the 18th cent. Ibn Saud, founder of the Saudi dynasty, overthrew the Turks, 1913. He

captured Hasa, a Turkish province in eastern Arabia, also 1913; the Hejaz region in western Arabia, 1925; and most of Asir, in SW Arabia, by 1926. The discovery of oil in the 1930s transformed the nation.

The Hejaz contains the holy cities of Islam—Medina, where the Mosque of the Prophet enshrines the tomb of Muhammad, and Mecca, his birthplace. An estimated 3 mil Muslims make pilgrimage to Mecca annually.

Ibn Saud reigned until his death, Nov. 1953. Subsequent kings have been his sons. The king exercises authority with a Council of Ministers. The Islamic religious code is the law of the land. Alcohol and public entertainments are restricted; women have an inferior legal status.

Saudi Arabia has often allied itself with the U.S. and other Western nations, and billions of dollars of advanced arms have been purchased from Britain, France, and the U.S. Western support for Israel has often strained relations. Saudi units fought against Israel in the 1948 and 1973 Arab-Israeli wars. Beginning with the 1967 Arab-Israeli war, Saudi Arabia gave Egypt large annual financial gifts; aid was later extended to Syria, Jordan, and Palestinian groups.

King Faisal played a leading role in the 1973-74 Arab oil embargo against the U.S. and other nations. Crown Prince Khalid was proclaimed king, Mar. 25, 1975, after the assassination of Faisal. Fahd became king, June 13, 1982, following Khalid's death.

After Iraq invaded Kuwait, Aug. 2, 1990, Saudi Arabia accepted the Kuwait royal family and more than 400,000 Kuwaiti refugees. King Fahd invited Western and Arab troops to deploy on Saudi soil before and during the 1991 Persian Gulf War.

The presence of 15 Saudis among the 19 al-Qaeda hijackers who carried out the Sept. 11, 2001, attacks on the U.S. raised tensions between the U.S. and Saudi governments. Some blamed the Saudi government for allowing Muslim extremism to flourish in Saudi Arabia. Policy differences over the Israeli-Palestinian dispute and Iraq (where Saudi jihadists supported the Sunni cause) were further irritants. The U.S. completed a pullout of its combat forces from Saudi Arabia, Sept. 2003.

Alarmed at guerrilla attacks that killed more than 100 people, mostly foreigners, in Saudi Arabia, 2003-04, the Saudis stepped up antiterrorist activities in cooperation with the U.S. Islamist candidates on a "golden list" circulated by conservative clerics fared well in Feb.-Apr. 2005, municipal council elections, the country's first since 1963; women were barred from voting.

King Fahd died Aug. 1, 2005. His half-brother, Abdullah, who had in effect ruled the Kingdom since Fahd suffered a stroke in Nov. 1995, succeeded him.

Hoping to contain the wave of "Arab Spring" uprisings that had challenged or toppled other entrenched regimes in North Africa and the Middle East in 2011, Saudi Arabia led a Gulf Cooperation Council force that entered Bahrain Mar. 14 to suppress protests. The Saudis also took steps to aid monarchies in Jordan and Morocco, and sent $4 bil to assist the military council that assumed power in Egypt after Pres. Hosni Mubarak was ousted. King Abdullah announced Sept. 25, 2011, that women would have the right to vote and run for office by 2015 and allowed the nation's women athletes to compete in the 2012 Olympics for the first time.

Senegal
Republic of Senegal

People: Population: 12,969,606. **Age distrib.:** <15: 43%; 65+: 2.9%. **Pop. density:** 174.5 per sq mi, 67.4 per sq km. **Urban:** 42.5%. **Ethnic groups:** Wolof 43%, Pular 24%, Serer 15%, Jola 4%, Mandinka 3%, Soninke 1%, European and Lebanese 1%. **Principal languages:** French (official), Wolof, Pulaar, Jola, Mandinka. **Chief religions:** Muslim 94%, Christian 5% (mostly Roman Catholic), indigenous beliefs 1%.

Geography: Total area: 75,955 sq mi, 196,722 sq km; **Land area:** 74,336 sq mi, 192,530 sq km. **Location:** At W extreme of Africa. **Neighbors:** Mauritania on N, Mali on E, Guinea and Guinea-Bissau on S; surrounds Gambia on three sides. **Topography:** Low rolling plains cover most of Senegal, rising somewhat in SE. Swamp and jungles are in SW. **Capital:** Dakar, 3,035,470.

Government: Type: Republic. **Head of state:** Pres. Macky Sall; b. Dec. 11, 1961; in office: Apr. 2, 2012. **Head of gov.:** Prime Min. Abdoul Mbaye; b. Apr. 13, 1953; in office: Apr. 3, 2012. **Local divisions:** 11 regions. **Defense budget** (2010): $196 mil. **Active troops:** 13,620.

Economy: Industries: agric. and fish proc., phosphate mining, fertilizer prod., petroleum refining, mining, constr. materials, ship constr. and repair. **Chief crops:** peanuts, millet, corn, sorghum, rice, cotton, tomatoes, green vegetables. **Natural resources:** fish, phosphates, iron ore. **Arable land:** 20%. **Livestock:** cattle: 3.3 mil; chickens: 46.3 mil; goats: 4.8 mil; pigs: 346,681; sheep: 5.6 mil. **Fish catch:** 409,658 metric tons. **Electricity prod.:** 2.6 bil kWh. **Labor force:** agric. 77.5%, industry and services 22.5%.

Finance: Monetary unit: CFA BCEAO Franc (XOF) (Sept. 2012: 519.73 = $1 U.S.). **GDP:** $25.5 bil; **per capita GDP:** $1,900; **GDP growth:** 2.6%. **Imports:** $5.4 bil; France 17.5%, China 10%, UK 8.8%, Nigeria 8.7%, Netherlands 6%, U.S. 5%. **Exports:** $2.4 bil; Mali 22.6%, India 9.2%, France 4.8%, Italy 4.4%. **Tourism:** $453 mil. **Budget:** $4.3 bil. **Total reserves less gold:** $1.9 bil. **CPI change:** 3.4%.

Transport: Railways: 563 mi. **Civil aviation:** 612.1 mil pass.-mi;
9 airports. **Chief port:** Dakar.

Communications: TV sets: 44 per 1,000 pop. **Radios:** 536 per
1,000 pop. **Telephone lines:** 2.7 per 100 pop. **Daily newspaper
circ.:** 8.7 per 1,000 pop. **Internet:** 17.5%.

Health: Life expect.: 58.2 male; 62.2 female. **Births:** 36.2 (per
1,000 pop.). **Deaths:** 9.1 (per 1,000 pop.). **Natural inc.:** 2.71%.
Infant mortality: 55.2 (per 1,000 live births). **HIV rate:** 0.9%.

Education: Compulsory: ages 6-15. **Literacy:** 49.7%.

Major intl. organizations: UN and all of its specialized agencies,
AU, WTO.

Embassy: 2112 Wyoming Ave. NW 20008; 234-0540.

Website: www.gouv.sn

Portuguese settlers arrived in the 15th cent., but French control
grew from the 17th cent. The last independent Muslim state was subdued in 1893. Senegal became an independent republic Aug. 20,
1960, but French political and economic influence remained strong.
Senegambia, a loose confederation of Senegal and The Gambia,
was established in 1982 but dissolved seven years later.

Forty years of Socialist Party rule ended when Abdoulaye Wade,
leader of the Senegalese Democratic Party, won a presidential
runoff election, Mar. 19, 2000. A Senegalese ferry capsized off the
coast of The Gambia Sept. 26, 2002, killing at least 1,863 people.
A peace accord signed Dec. 30, 2004, with separatists in Cassa-
mance Province, S Senegal, sought to end a 22-year insurgency.
Pres. Wade was reelected Feb. 25, 2007, but lost his bid for a third
term Mar. 26, 2012, to Macky Sall, his former prime min., who
was elected president with about two-thirds of the vote in a runoff election.

Serbia

Republic of Serbia

People: Population: 7,276,604. **Age distrib.:** <15: 14.9%; 65+:
16.6%. **Pop. density:** 243.3 per sq mi, 93.9 per sq km. **Urban:**
56.4% (incl. Kosovo). **Ethnic groups:** Serb 83%, Hungarian 4%,
Bosniak 2%, Romany 1%, Yugoslav 1%. **Principal languages:** Serbian (official), Hungarian, Bosniak, Romany. **Chief religions:** Serbian Orthodox 85%, Catholic 6%, Muslim 3%, Protestant 1%.

Geography: Total area: 29,913 sq mi, 77,474 sq km; **Land area:**
29,913 sq mi, 77,474 sq km. **Location:** On Balkan Peninsula in SE
Europe. **Neighbors:** Croatia, Bosnia and Herzegovina on W; Hungary on N; Romania, Bulgaria on E; Montenegro, Albania, Macedonia on S. **Topography:** Terrain varies widely, with fertile plains
drained by Danube and other rivers in N, limestone basins in E,
ancient mountains and hills in SE, and very high coastline in Montenegro along SW. **Capital:** Belgrade, 1,135,080.

Government: Type: Republic. **Head of state:** Pres. Tomislav
Nikolić; b. Feb. 15, 1952; in office: May 31, 2012. **Head of gov.:**
Prime Min. Ivica Dačić; b. Jan. 1, 1956; in office: July 27, 2012. **Local
divisions:** 1 republic with 1 autonomous province. **Defense budget:** $975 mil. **Active troops:** 28,184.

Economy: Industries: base metals, furniture, food proc.,
machinery, chemicals, sugar, tires, clothes, pharmaceuticals. **Chief
crops:** wheat, maize, sugar beets, sunflowers, raspberries. **Natural
resources:** oil, gas, coal, iron ore, copper, zinc, antimony, chromite,
gold, silver, magnesium, pyrite, limestone, marble, salt. **Crude oil
reserves:** 77.5 mil bbls. **Arable land:** 37.7%. **Livestock:** cattle:
938,038; chickens: 19.7 mil; goats: 128,733; pigs: 3.5 mil; sheep:
1.5 mil. **Fish catch:** 12,960 metric tons. **Electricity prod.:** 35.4 bil
kWh. **Labor force:** agric. 21.9%, industry 19.5%, services 58.6%.

Finance: Monetary unit: Dinar (RSD) (Sept. 2012: 93.84 = $1
U.S.). **GDP:** $79.9 bil; **per capita GDP:** $10,800; **GDP growth:**
1.8%. **Imports:** $19.5 bil; Russia 12.8%, Germany 10.6%, Italy
8.5%, China 7.2%, Hungary 4.6%. **Exports:** $11.8 bil; Germany
11.3%, Bosnia and Herzegovina 11.2%, Montenegro 7.6%, Romania 6.3%, Russia 5.4%, Macedonia 4.9%, Slovenia 4.4%. **Tourism:**
$992 mil. **Budget:** $19.6 bil. **Total reserves less gold:** $14.9 bil.
Gold: 461,041 oz t. **CPI change:** 11.1%.

Transport: Railways: 2,100 mi. **Civil aviation:** 588.4 mil pass.-
mi; 11 airports.

Communications: TV sets: 248 per 1,000 pop. **Telephone
lines:** 37.3 per 100 pop. **Internet:** 42.2%.

Health: Life expect.: 71.7 male; 77.6 female. **Births:** 9.2 (per
1,000 pop.). **Deaths:** 13.8 (per 1,000 pop.). **Natural inc.:** −0.46%.
Infant mortality: 6.4 (per 1,000 live births). **HIV rate:** 0.1%.

Education: Compulsory: ages 7-14. **Literacy:** 97.9%.

Major intl. organizations: UN (FAO, IBRD, ILO, IMF, WHO),
OSCE, WTO (observer).

Embassy: 2134 Kalorama Rd. NW 20008; 332-0333.

Website: www.srbija.gov.rs

Serbia was a vassal principality of Turkey from 1389 to 1878,
when the Treaty of Berlin established it as an independent kingdom.
After the Balkan wars, Serbia annexed Old Serbia and Macedonia,
1913.

When the Austro-Hungarian empire collapsed after WWI, the
Kingdom of Serbs, Croats, and Slovenes—Yugoslavia after 1929—
was formed from the provinces of Croatia, Dalmatia, Bosnia,
Herzegovina, Slovenia, Vojvodina, and the independent state of
Montenegro.

Nazi Germany invaded in 1941. After the Nazis were driven out in
1945, Yugoslavia became a federal republic, headed by Josip Broz,

a Communist, known as Marshal Tito. He rejected Stalin's policy of
dictating to all Communist nations and accepted economic and military aid from the West. Pres. Tito died May 4, 1980. Yugoslavia held
together for a decade, then broke apart. During 1991-95, Serbia,
under Pres. Slobodan Milosevic, supported ethnic Serb fighters as
war raged in Croatia and in Bosnia and Herzegovina, which had
declared independence. The republics of Serbia and Montenegro
proclaimed a new Federal Republic of Yugoslavia, Apr. 17, 1992.
The UN imposed sanctions on the newly reconstituted Yugoslavia to
end the bloodshed in Bosnia.

A peace agreement initialed in Dayton, OH, Nov. 21, 1995, was
signed in Paris, Dec. 14, by Milosevic and leaders of Bosnia and
Croatia. In May 1996, a UN tribunal in the Netherlands began trying
suspected war criminals from the former Yugoslavia. Mass protests
erupted when Milosevic refused to accept opposition victories in
local elections, Nov. 17; non-Communist governments took office in
Belgrade and other cities, Feb. 1997. Barred from running for a third
term as Serbian president, Milosevic had himself inaugurated as
president of Yugoslavia, July 23, 1997.

Efforts by Serbia to suppress a secessionist movement in Kosovo
led in Mar.-June 1999 to a war with the U.S. and its NATO allies; they
accused Milosevic of pursuing a policy of ethnic cleansing against
the predominantly Muslim Kosovars (ethnic Albanians). NATO stationed a multinational force in Kosovo, which was placed under UN
administration.

Defeated in a presidential election Sept. 24, 2000, by opposition
leader Vojislav Kostunica, Milosevic initially refused to accept the
result. Mass demonstrations forced him to resign, Oct. 6. Kostunica
was sworn in the next day. Charged with corruption and abuse of
power, Milosevic surrendered to Serbian authorities Apr. 1, 2001.
He was extradited June 28 to The Hague, Netherlands, where a
UN tribunal had indicted him for war crimes. His trial began Feb. 12,
2002. He was found dead in his prison cell Mar. 11, 2006, before a
verdict was reached.

A pact to reconstitute Yugoslavia as a new union of Serbia and
Montenegro took effect Feb. 4, 2003. Zoran Djindjic, premier of the
Republic of Serbia, was assassinated Mar. 12 in Belgrade, triggering a roundup of more than 4,500 people associated with organized
crime and the Milosevic regime. Serbia's union with Montenegro
disintegrated in 2006. Montenegrins voted for separation in a referendum May 21 and became an independent republic June 3.

After years of fruitless negotiations, Kosovo declared independence from Serbia Feb. 17, 2008; the U.S. and most European allies
immediately recognized the new country; Serbia and Russia did not.
Following parliamentary elections Serbia May 11, a pro-Western
government under Mirko Cvetkovic took office July 7. Serbia, seeking EU membership, met a requirement of European leaders July 21,
2008, by arresting former Bosnian Serb leader Radovan Karadzic,
who was extradited to the International Criminal Court in The
Hague, Netherlands, on charges of genocide and crimes against
humanity; the prosecution rested its case in May, and Karadzic was
set to begin his defense Oct. 16, 2012. Serbia's parliament passed
a resolution Mar. 31, 2010, apologizing for the 1995 massacre of
thousands of Muslims by Bosnian Serbs at Srebrenica; in a further
effort to deal with wartime atrocities, Serbian prosecutors, Sept. 11,
2010, indicted 9 former members of the Jackals paramilitary unit for
allegedly killing 43 ethnic Albanian civilians during the 1999 Kosovo
conflict. Ratko Mladic, the former Bosnian Serb military commander
accused of directing the 1995 massacre of 8,000 Bosnian Muslims
in Srebrenica, was arrested in Serbia May 26, 2011, and sent to
The Hague. He went on trial in 2012. Serbia attained EU candidate
status, Mar. 2012, but not a start date for negotiations. Ivica Dačić,
once a spokesman for Milosevic, became prime min. of a coalition
government, July 26, 2012.

Vojvodina is a nominally autonomous province in northern
Serbia (8,304 sq mi), with a pop. (2011 est.) of 1,916,889, mostly
Serbian. The capital is Novi Sad.

Seychelles

Republic of Seychelles

People: Population: 90,024. **Age distrib.:** <15: 21.4%; 65+:
7.2%. **Pop. density:** 512.4 per sq mi, 197.9 per sq km. **Urban:**
53.6%. **Ethnic groups:** mixed French, African, Indian, Chinese,
Arab. **Principal languages:** Creole, English (official). **Chief religions:** Roman Catholic 82%, Protestant 8% (Anglican 6%, Seventh-Day Adventist 1%), other Christian 3%, Hindu 2%, Muslim 1%.

Geography: Total area: 176 sq mi, 455 sq km; **Land area:** 176
sq mi, 455 sq km. **Location:** In Indian O. 700 mi NE of Madagascar. **Neighbors:** Nearest are Madagascar on SW, Somalia on NW.
Topography: A group of 86 islands, about half of them composed of
coral, the other half granite, the latter predominantly mountainous.
Capital: Victoria, 26,609.

Government: Type: Republic. **Head of state and gov.:** Pres.
James Michel, b. Aug. 18, 1944; in office: Apr. 14, 2004. **Local divisions:** 23 districts. **Defense budget:** $22 mil. **Active troops:** 200.

Economy: Industries: fishing, tourism, coconuts and vanilla
proc., coir (coconut fiber) rope, boat building, printing, furniture.
Chief crops: coconuts, cinnamon, vanilla, sweet potatoes, cassava,
copra, bananas. **Natural resources:** fish, cinnamon trees. **Arable
land:** 2.2%. **Livestock:** cattle: 350; chickens: 551,000; goats: 5,300;
pigs: 5,363. **Fish catch:** 87,408 metric tons. **Electricity prod.:** 245

Finance: Monetary unit: Rupee (SCR) (Sept. 2012: 12.93 = $1 U.S.). **GDP:** $2.3 bil; **per capita GDP:** $25,000; **GDP growth:** 4.9%. **Imports:** $873.5 mil; Saudi Arabia 23.1%, South Africa 8.1%, Spain 8%, France 5.6%. **Exports:** $495.1 mil; France 25.7%, UK 20.4%, Japan 10.6%, Italy 9.7%. **Tourism:** $291 mil. **Budget:** $380.3 mil. **Total reserves less gold:** $252.3 mil. **CPI change:** 2.6%.

Transport: Civil aviation: 887.3 mil pass.-mi; 7 airports. **Chief port:** Victoria.

Communications: TV sets: 278 per 1,000 pop. **Radios:** 278 per 1,000 pop. **Telephone lines:** 32.1 per 100 pop. **Internet:** 43.2%.

Health: Life expect.: 69.1 male; 78.5 female. **Births:** 15.1 (per 1,000 pop.). **Deaths:** 6.9 (per 1,000 pop.). **Natural inc.:** 0.82%. **Infant mortality:** 11.4 (per 1,000 live births). **HIV rate:** NA.

Education: Compulsory: ages 6-16. **Literacy:** 91.8%.

Major intl. organizations: UN (FAO, IBRD, ILO, IMF, WHO), AU, the Commonwealth, WTO (observer).

Embassy: 800 Second Ave., Ste. 400C, New York, NY 10017; (212) 972-1785.

Website: www.egov.sc

The islands were occupied by France in 1768 and seized by Britain in 1794. Ruled as part of Mauritius from 1814, Seychelles became a separate colony in 1903 and declared independence June 29, 1976. The first president was ousted in a coup a year later by socialist leader France Albert René. A new constitution, approved June 1993, provided for a multiparty state. After nearly 27 years in power, Pres. René resigned Apr. 14, 2004, and Vice Pres. James Michel succeeded him. Michel won a 5-year term in elections July 28-30, 2006, and was reelected May 19-21, 2011.

Sierra Leone
Republic of Sierra Leone

People: Population: 5,485,998. **Age distrib.:** <15: 41.9%; 65+: 3.7%. **Pop. density:** 198.4 per sq mi, 76.6 per sq km. **Urban:** 39.2%. **Ethnic groups:** Temne 35%, Mende 31%, Limba 8%, Kono 5%, Kriole (descendants of freed Jamaican slaves) 2%, Mandingo 2%, Loko 2%, other (incl. Liberian refugees and small numbers of Europeans, Lebanese, Pakistanis, Indians) 15%. **Principal languages:** English (official), Mende (principal vernacular in S), Temne (principal vernacular in N), Krio (English-based Creole, a lingua franca). **Chief religions:** Muslim 60%, indigenous beliefs 30%, Christian 10%.

Geography: Total area: 27,699 sq mi, 71,740 sq km; **Land area:** 27,653 sq mi, 71,620 sq km. **Location:** On W coast of W Africa. **Neighbors:** Guinea on N and E, Liberia on S. **Topography:** The heavily-indented, 210-mi coastline has mangrove swamps. Behind are wooded hills, rising to a plateau and mountains in E. **Capital:** Freetown, 940,683.

Government: Type: Republic. **Head of state and gov.:** Pres. Ernest Bai Koroma; b. Oct. 2, 1953; in office: Sept. 17, 2007. **Local divisions:** 3 provinces, 1 area. **Defense budget:** $13 mil. **Active troops:** 10,500.

Economy: Industries: diamond mining, small-scale mfg. (beverages, textiles), petroleum refining, small commercial ship repair. **Chief crops:** rice, coffee, cocoa, palm kernels, palm oil, peanuts. **Natural resources:** diamonds, titanium ore, bauxite, iron ore, gold, chromite. **Arable land:** 15.1%. **Livestock:** cattle: 517,000; chickens: 9.5 mil; goats: 803,000; pigs: 47,364; sheep: 682,000. **Fish catch:** 200,040 metric tons. **Electricity prod.:** 120 mil kWh. **Labor force:** NA.

Finance: Monetary unit: Leone (SLL) (Sept. 2012: 4,340.40 = $1 U.S.). **GDP:** $5.2 bil; **per capita GDP:** $900; **GDP growth:** 5.3%. **Imports:** $1.3 bil; China 16.2%, South Africa 10.9%, U.S. 7.4%, UK 7.2%, India 5.1%, Malaysia 4.3%. **Exports:** $472.3 mil; Belgium 28.9%, Romania 12.6%, Netherlands 9.2%, China 7.3%, U.S. 6.9%, Turkey 6%, UK 5.8%. **Tourism:** $26 mil. **Budget:** $589.7 mil. **Total reserves less gold:** $439.1 mil. **CPI change:** 16.2%.

Transport: Motor vehicles: 5.9 vehicles per 1,000 pop. **Civil aviation:** 66.5 mil pass.-mi; 1 airport. **Chief ports:** Freetown, Pepel.

Communications: TV sets: 13 per 1,000 pop. **Radios:** 132 per 1,000 pop. **Telephone lines** (2010): 0.2 per 100 pop. **Internet** (2009): 0.3%.

Health: Life expect.: 54.1 male; 59.1 female. **Births:** 38.1 (per 1,000 pop.). **Deaths:** 11.5 (per 1,000 pop.). **Natural inc.:** 2.66%. **Infant mortality:** 76.6 (per 1,000 live births). **HIV rate:** 1.6%.

Education: Compulsory: ages 6-11. **Literacy:** 42.1%.

Major intl. organizations: UN (FAO, IBRD, ILO, IMF, WHO), AU, the Commonwealth, WTO.

Embassy: 1701 19th St. NW 20009; 939-9261.

Website: www.statehouse.gov.sl

The British founded Freetown, 1787, as a haven for freed slaves. Full independence arrived Apr. 27, 1961. A one-party state was established by referendum in 1978.

Mutinous soldiers ousted Pres. Joseph Momoh, Apr. 30, 1992. A coup, Jan. 16, 1996, paved the way for multiparty elections and a return to civilian rule. A peace accord, signed Nov. 30 with the Revolutionary United Front (RUF), brought a temporary halt to a civil war that had claimed over 10,000 lives in five years.

A coup on May 25, 1997, was met with international opposition. Armed intervention by Nigeria restored Pres. Ahmad Tejan Kabbah to power on Mar. 10, 1998, but RUF rebels (who funded their operations through illicit diamond sales) mounted a gue-

rilla counteroffensive, killing thousands of civilians and mutilating thousands more. The Kabbah government signed a power-sharing agreement with the RUF, July 7, 1999. A UN mission (UNAMSIL) was established in Oct. to help maintain the agreement. The accord collapsed in early May 2000, as RUF guerrillas took more than 500 UN peacekeepers hostage. Rebel leader Foday Sankoh was captured in Freetown, May 17. The hostages were freed by the end of May, and 233 more UN personnel behind rebel lines were rescued July 15.

A UN-sponsored disarmament program in 2001 reduced the level of violence. On Jan. 16, 2002, the government and the UN agreed to create the Sierra Leone Special Court to try war crimes that had occurred after Nov. 1996. Government and rebel leaders declared an official end to the war Jan. 18; more than 50,000 people had died in the conflict. Kabbah won the May 14 presidential election. The next election was scheduled for Nov. 17, 2012.

Sankoh, an indicted war criminal, died in UN custody, July 29, 2003. UNAMSIL, which ended Dec. 31, 2005, was succeeded by UNIOSIL, a UN mission intended to strengthen political institutions. Opposition leader Ernest Bai Koroma won a presidential runoff vote, Sept. 8, 2007. Under an anti-corruption law signed Sept. 2, 2008, Koroma became Sierra Leone's first head of state to declare all his assets. Three former RUF leaders were convicted of war crimes, Feb. 25, 2009.

Singapore
Republic of Singapore

People: Population: 5,353,494. **Age distrib.:** <15: 14%; 65+: 7.8%. **Pop. density:** 20,182.7 per sq mi, 7,792.6 per sq km. **Urban:** 100%. **Ethnic groups:** Chinese 77%, Malay 14%, Indian 8%. **Principal languages:** Mandarin, English, Malay (all official); Hokkien; Cantonese; Teochew; Tamil (official). **Chief religions:** Buddhist 43%, Muslim 15%, Taoist 9%, Catholic 5%, Hindu 4%, other Christian 10%, none 15%.

Geography: Total area: 269 sq mi, 697 sq km; **Land area:** 265 sq mi, 687 sq km. **Location:** Off tip of Malayan Peninsula in SE Asia. **Neighbors:** Nearest are Malaysia on N, Indonesia on S. **Topography:** Singapore is a flat, formerly swampy island. The nation includes 40 nearby islets. **Capital:** Singapore, 5,187,930.

Government: Type: Republic. **Head of state:** Pres. Tony Tan Keng Yam; b. Feb, 7, 1940; in office: Sept. 1, 2011. **Head of gov.:** Prime Min. Lee Hsien Loong; b. Feb. 10, 1952; in office: Aug. 12, 2004. **Defense budget:** $9.66 bil. **Active troops:** 72,500.

Economy: Industries: electronics, chemicals, financial services, oil drilling equip., petroleum refining, rubber proc. and rubber prods., processed food and beverages, ship repair, offshore platform constr. **Chief crops:** orchids, vegetables. **Natural resources:** fish. **Arable land:** 0.7%. **Livestock:** cattle: 200; chickens: 3.3 mil; goats: 670; pigs: 270,000. **Fish catch:** 5,231 metric tons. **Electricity prod.** (2010): 42.7 bil kWh. **Labor force:** agric. 0.1%, industry 19.6%, services 80.3%.

Finance: Monetary unit: Dollar (SGD) (Sept. 2012: 1.25 = $1 U.S.). **GDP:** $318.9 bil; **per capita GDP:** $60,500; **GDP growth:** 4.9%. **Imports:** $366.3 bil; Malaysia 10.7%, U.S. 10.7%, China 10.4%, Japan 7.2%, South Korea 5.9%, Taiwan 5.9%. **Exports:** $414.8 bil; Malaysia 12.2%, Hong Kong 11%, China 10.4%, Indonesia 10.4%, U.S. 5.4%, Japan 4.5%. **Tourism:** $18 bil. **Budget:** $37.2 bil (incl. both operational and development expenditures). **Total reserves less gold:** $237.7 bil. **Gold:** 4.1 mil oz t. **CPI change:** 5.2%.

Transport: Motor vehicles: 164.3 vehicles per 1,000 pop. **Civil aviation:** 52.5 bil pass.-mi; 9 airports. **Chief port:** Singapore.

Communications: TV sets: 213 per 1,000 pop. **Radios:** 689 per 1,000 pop. **Telephone lines:** 38.9 per 100 pop. **Daily newspaper circ.:** 360.8 per 1,000 pop. **Internet:** 75%.

Health: Life expect.: 81.5 male; 86.2 female. **Births:** 7.7 (per 1,000 pop.). **Deaths:** 3.4 (per 1,000 pop.). **Natural inc.:** 0.43%. **Infant mortality:** 2.7 (per 1,000 live births). **HIV rate:** 0.1%.

Education: Compulsory: ages 6-11. **Literacy:** 95.9%.

Major intl. organizations: UN (IBRD, ILO, IMF, WHO), APEC, ASEAN, the Commonwealth, WTO.

Embassy: 3501 International Pl. NW 20008; 537-3100.

Website: www.gov.sg

Founded in 1819 by Sir Thomas Stamford Raffles, Singapore was a British colony until 1959, when it became autonomous within the Commonwealth. On Sept. 16, 1963, it joined with Malaya, Sarawak, and Sabah to form the Federation of Malaysia. Tensions between Malayans, dominant in the federation, and ethnic Chinese, dominant in Singapore, led to an accord under which Singapore became a separate nation, Aug. 9, 1965.

Singapore is one of the world's largest ports and a major center of manufacturing, banking, and commerce. Standards in health, education, and housing are generally high. A free trade pact with the U.S. took effect Jan. 1, 2004.

Singapore has had only three prime mins.: Lee Kuan Yew, 1959-90; Goh Chok Tong, 1990-2004; and Lee Kuan Yew's son, Lee Hsien Loong, who took office, Aug. 12, 2004. The government, dominated by the People's Action Party (PAP), has taken strong actions to keep order and suppress dissent. Singapore's export-dependent economy was hit hard by the global downturn in 2008 but rebounded during 2009-11. Opposition parties mounted a vigorous challenge to the PAP in 2011 elections.

Slovakia
Slovak Republic

People: Population: 5,483,088. **Age distrib.:** <15: 15.6%; 65+: 13.1%. **Pop. density:** 295.2 per sq mi, 114 per sq km. **Urban:** 54.7%. **Ethnic groups:** Slovak 86%, Hungarian 10%, Roma 2%, Ruthenian/Ukrainian 1%. **Principal languages:** Slovak (official), Hungarian, Roma, Ukrainian. **Chief religions:** Roman Catholic 69%, Protestant 11%, Greek Catholic 4%, none 13%.

Geography: Total area: 18,933 sq mi, 49,035 sq km; **Land area:** 18,573 sq mi, 48,105 sq km. **Location:** In E central Europe. **Neighbors:** Poland on N, Hungary on S, Austria and Czech Rep. on W, Ukraine on E. **Topography:** Carpathian Mts. in N, fertile Danube plane in S. **Capital:** Bratislava, 433,540.

Government: Type: Republic. **Head of state:** Pres. Ivan Gasparovic; b. Mar. 27, 1941; in office: June 15, 2004. **Head of gov.:** Prime Min. Robert Fico; b. Sept. 15, 1964; in office: Apr. 4, 2012. **Local divisions:** 8 departments. **Defense budget:** $1.07 bil. **Active troops:** 15,799.

Economy: Industries: metal and metal prods.; food and beverages; electricity, gas, coke, oil, nuclear fuel; chemicals and manmade fibers; machinery; paper and printing. **Chief crops:** grains, potatoes, sugar beets, hops, fruits. **Natural resources:** brown coal and lignite, iron ore, copper, manganese ore, salt. **Crude oil reserves:** 9 mil bbls. **Arable land:** 28.7%. **Livestock:** cattle: 471,965; chickens: 12.5 mil; goats: 35,300; pigs: 687,260; sheep: 376,978. **Fish catch:** 2,295 metric tons. **Electricity prod.:** (2010) 26.1 bil kWh. **Labor force:** agric. 3.5%, industry 27%, services 69.4%.

Finance: Monetary unit: Euro (EUR) (Sept. 2012: 0.79 = $1 U.S.). **GDP:** $128.5 bil; **per capita GDP:** $23,600; **GDP growth:** 3.3%. **Imports:** $72 bil; Germany 19.2%, Czech Republic 18.5%, Russia 11.4%, Hungary 7%, Poland 5.5%, Austria 4.6%, Italy 4.1%, China 4%. **Exports:** $86.7 bil; Germany 21.4%, Czech Republic 15.2%, Poland 7.9%, Hungary 7.8%, Austria 7.5%, France 6.7%, Italy 5.3%. **Tourism:** $2.4 bil. **Budget:** $37.8 bil. **Total reserves less gold:** $853.3 mil. **Gold:** 1.02 mil oz t. **CPI change:** 3.9%.

Transport: Railways: 2,251 mi. **Motor vehicles:** 350.3 vehicles per 1,000 pop. **Civil aviation:** 2.1 bil pass.-mi; 19 airports. **Chief ports:** Bratislava, Komarno.

Communications: TV sets: 437 per 1,000 pop. **Radios:** 964 per 1,000 pop. **Telephone lines:** 19.3 per 100 pop. **Daily newspaper circ.:** 125.7 per 1,000 pop. **Internet:** 74.4%.

Health: Life expect.: 72.1 male; 80.1 female. **Births:** 10.4 (per 1,000 pop.). **Deaths:** 9.6 (per 1,000 pop.). **Natural inc.:** 0.07%. **Infant mortality:** 6.5 (per 1,000 live births). **HIV rate:** <0.1%.

Education: Compulsory: ages 6-14. **Literacy:** NA.

Major intl. organizations: UN (FAO, IBRD, ILO, IMF, WHO), EU, NATO, OECD, OSCE, WTO.

Embassy: 3523 International Ct. NW 20008; 237-1054.

Website: www.government.gov.sk

Slovakia was originally settled by Illyrian, Celtic, and Germanic tribes and was incorporated into Great Moravia in the 9th cent. It became part of Hungary in the 11th cent. Overrun by Czech Hussites in the 15th cent., it was restored to Hungarian rule in 1526. The Slovaks disassociated themselves from Hungary after WWI and joined the Czechs of Bohemia to form the Republic of Czechoslovakia, Oct. 28, 1918.

Germany invaded Czechoslovakia, 1939, and declared Slovakia independent. Slovakia rejoined Czechoslovakia in 1945. Czechoslovakia split into two separate states—the Czech Republic and Slovakia—on Jan. 1, 1993.

Slovakia attained full membership in the EU and NATO in 2004. The country adopted the euro currency as scheduled on Jan. 1, 2009, but its economy, which had been one of Europe's fastest growing, was battered by the global recession. Pres. Ivan Gasparovic won a second 5-year term in a runoff election Apr. 4, 2009. A coalition of right-leaning parties led by Iveta Radicová, who became Slovakia's first female prime min., took power after the parliamentary elections of June 12, 2010. That coalition fell apart, and in early elections, Mar. 10, 2012, Robert Fico's social-democratic party, Smer (Direction), won 83 seats, in the first time in Slovakia's post-communist history a single party held a majority. Fico became prime min. Apr. 4, 2012.

Slovenia
Republic of Slovenia

People: Population: 1,996,617. **Age distrib.:** <15: 13.4%; 65+: 17.1%. **Pop. density:** 256.6 per sq mi, 99.1 per sq km. **Urban:** 49.9%. **Ethnic groups:** Slovene 83%, Serb 2%, Croat 2%, Bosniak 1%. **Principal languages:** Slovenian; Serbo-Croatian; Italian, Hungarian (both official in some municipalities). **Chief religions:** Catholic 58%, Muslim 2%, Orthodox 2%, none 10%.

Geography: Total area: 7,827 sq mi, 20,273 sq km; **Land area:** 7,780 sq mi, 20,151 sq km. **Location:** In SE Europe. **Neighbors:** Italy on W, Austria on N, Hungary on NE, Croatia on SE, S. **Topography:** Mostly hilly; 42% forested. **Capital:** Ljubljana, 272,897.

Government: Type: Republic. **Head of state:** Pres. Danilo Türk; b. Feb. 19, 1952; in office: Dec. 22, 2007. **Head of gov.:** Prime Min. Janez Jansa; b. Sept. 17, 1958; in office: Jan. 28, 2012. **Local divisions:** 183 municipalities, 11 urban municipalities. **Defense budget:** $578 mil. **Active troops:** 7,600.

Economy: Industries: ferrous metallurgy and aluminum prods., lead and zinc smelting, electronics (incl. military), automobiles, elec.

power equip., wood prods., textiles, chemicals, machine tools. **Chief crops:** potatoes, hops, wheat, sugar beets, corn, grapes. **Natural resources:** lignite coal, lead, zinc, building stone, hydropower, forests. **Arable land:** 8.7%. **Livestock:** cattle: 472,878; chickens: 2.9 mil; goats: 29,896; pigs: 415,230; sheep: 138,108. **Fish catch:** 1,717 metric tons. **Electricity prod.:** (2010): 15.6 bil kWh. **Labor force:** agric. 2.2%, industry 35%, services 62.8%.

Finance: Monetary unit: Euro (EUR) (Sept. 2012: 0.79 = $1 U.S.). **GDP:** $58.6 bil; **per capita GDP:** $29,000; **GDP growth:** −0.2%. **Imports:** $30.6 bil; Germany 16.4%, Italy 15.9%, Austria 10.2%, Croatia 4.5%, France 4.1%, China 4.1%. **Exports:** $28.8 bil; Germany 19.9%, Italy 11.9%, Austria 7.7%, Croatia 6.4%, France 5.7%, Hungary 4%. **Tourism:** $2.7 bil. **Budget:** $23.5 bil. **Total reserves less gold:** $830.7 mil. **Gold:** 102,000 oz t. **CPI change:** 1.8%.

Transport: Railways: 763 mi. **Motor vehicles:** 569.8 vehicles per 1,000 pop. **Civil aviation:** 541.8 mil pass.-mi; 7 airports. **Chief port:** Koper.

Communications: TV sets: 371 per 1,000 pop. **Radios:** 409 per 1,000 pop. **Telephone lines:** 42.9 per 100 pop. **Daily newspaper circ.:** 172.8 per 1,000 pop. **Internet:** 72%.

Health: Life expect.: 73.8 male; 81.4 female. **Births:** 8.8 (per 1,000 pop.). **Deaths:** 11.0 (per 1,000 pop.). **Natural inc.:** −0.22%. **Infant mortality:** 4.1 (per 1,000 live births). **HIV rate:** <0.1%.

Education: Compulsory: ages 6-14. **Literacy:** 99.7%.

Major intl. organizations: UN (FAO, IBRD, ILO, IMF, WHO), EU, NATO, OECD, OSCE, WTO.

Embassy: 2410 California St. NW 20008; 386-6601.

Website: e-uprava.gov.si

The Slovenes settled in their current territory during the 6th to the 8th cent. They fell under German domination in the 9th cent. Modern Slovenian political history began after 1848 when the Slovenes, divided among several Austrian provinces, began their struggle for unification. In 1918 a majority of Slovenes became part of the Kingdom of Serbs, Croats, and Slovenes, later renamed Yugoslavia.

Slovenia declared independence June 25, 1991; joined the UN May 22, 1992; and attained full membership in the EU and NATO in 2004. Slovenia adopted the euro currency Jan. 1, 2007. On Mar. 5, 2008, it became the first former Yugoslav republic to recognize Kosovo's independence from Serbia. A center-left coalition took office following legislative elections Sept. 21, 2008. New elections were called for Dec. 4, 2011, and Janez Jansa's Positive Slovenia party won a majority of parliamentary seats, forming a five-party coalition government that allowed Jansa to become prime min., Jan. 28, 2012.

Solomon Islands

People: Population: 584,578. **Age distrib.:** <15: 37.3%; 65+: 3.9%. **Pop. density:** 54.1 per sq mi, 20.9 per sq km. **Urban:** 20.5%. **Ethnic groups:** Melanesian 95%, Polynesian 3%, Micronesian 1%. **Principal languages:** Melanesian pidgin (lingua franca in much of country), English (official, but only spoken by 1%-2% of pop.), 120 indigenous languages. **Chief religions:** Protestant 74% (Church of Melanesia 33%, South Seas Evangelical 17%, Seventh-Day Adventist 11%, United Church 10%, Christian Fellowship Church 2%), Roman Catholic 19%, other Christian 4%.

Geography: Total area: 11,157 sq mi, 28,896 sq km; **Land area:** 10,805 sq mi, 27,986 sq km. **Location:** Melanesian Archipelago in W Pacific O. **Neighbors:** Nearest is Papua New Guinea to W. **Topography:** 10 large volcanic, rugged islands; 4 groups of smaller ones. **Capital:** Honiara, 67,610.

Government: Type: Parliamentary democracy. **Head of state:** Queen Elizabeth II, represented by Gov.-Gen. Sir Frank Ofagioro Kabui; in office: July 7, 2009. **Head of gov.:** Prime Min. Gordon Darcy Lilo; b. Aug. 28, 1965; in office: Nov. 16, 2011. **Local divisions:** 9 provinces and Honiara. **Defense budget:** NA. **Active troops:** No regular military forces.

Economy: Industries: fish (tuna), mining, timber. **Chief crops:** cocoa beans, coconuts, palm kernels, rice, potatoes, vegetables, fruits. **Natural resources:** fish, forests, gold, bauxite, phosphates, lead, zinc, nickel. **Arable land:** 0.6%. **Livestock:** cattle: 14,500; chickens: 235,000; pigs: 54,000. **Fish catch:** 43,198 metric tons. **Electricity prod.:** 82 mil kWh. **Labor force:** agric. 75%, industry 5%, services 20%.

Finance: Monetary unit: Dollar (SBD) (Sept. 2012: 7.09 = $1 U.S.). **GDP:** $1.7 bil; **per capita GDP:** $3,200; **GDP growth:** 9.3%. **Imports** (2010): $360.3 mil; Australia 27.3%, Singapore 26.4%, China 6.5%, Malaysia 5.1%, New Zealand 5.1%. **Exports** (2010): $226.5 mil; China 54%, Australia 12.5%, Thailand 4.6%. **Tourism:** $53 mil. **Budget:** $261.7 mil. **Total reserves less gold:** $412.3 mil. **CPI change:** 4.1%.

Transport: Civil aviation: 49.7 mil pass.-mi; 1 airport. **Chief ports:** Honiara, Viru Harbor.

Communications: TV sets: 12 per 1,000 pop. **Radios:** 65 per 1,000 pop. **Telephone lines:** 1.5 per 100 pop. **Daily newspaper circ.:** 10.8 per 1,000 pop. **Internet:** 6%.

Health: Life expect.: 71.8 male; 77.1 female. **Births:** 27.5 (per 1,000 pop.). **Deaths:** 3.9 (per 1,000 pop.). **Natural inc.:** 2.36%. **Infant mortality:** 17.3 (per 1,000 live births). **HIV rate:** NA.

Education: NA. **Literary:** 76.6%.

Major intl. organizations: UN (FAO, IBRD, ILO, IMF, WHO), the Commonwealth, WTO.

Embassy: 800 Second Ave., Ste. 400L, New York, NY 10017; (212) 599-6192.

Website: www.pmc.gov.sb

The Solomon Isls. were sighted 1568 by an expedition from Peru. Britain established a protectorate in the 1890s over most of the group, inhabited by Melanesians. The islands saw major WWII battles. They achieved self-government, Jan. 2, 1976, and formal independence, July 7, 1978.

A coup attempt, June 5, 2000, sparked factional fighting in Honiara. Lawlessness became widespread over the next three years. To restore order, a 2,225-member intervention force, led by Australia and authorized by the Pacific Isls. Forum, began arriving in Honiara, July 24, 2003; nearly all foreign troops were removed by mid-2005.

Following elections Apr. 5, 2006, parliament's choice of Snyder Rini as prime min. led to two days of rioting in Honiara over alleged influence-buying by the ethnic Chinese business community. Rini resigned Apr. 26, 2006, rather than face a no-confidence vote. Prime Min. Danny Philip, who was elected Aug. 25, 2010, dismissed finance min. Gordon Darcy Lilo and was forced to resign when a number of MPs abandoned the government in protest. The parliament then elected Lilo prime min., Nov. 16, 2011.

Somalia

People: Population: 10,085,638. **Age distrib.:** <15: 44.5%; 65+: 2.4%. **Pop. density:** 41.6 per sq mi, 16.1 per sq km. **Urban:** 37.7%. **Ethnic groups:** Somali 85%, Bantu and other non-Somali 15%. **Principal languages:** Somali (official), Arabic, Italian, English. **Chief religion:** Sunni Muslim (official).

Geography: Total area: 246,201 sq mi, 637,657 sq km; **Land area:** 242,216 sq mi, 627,337 sq km. **Location:** Occupies eastern horn of Africa. **Neighbors:** Djibouti, Ethiopia, Kenya on W. **Topography:** The coastline extends for 1,700 mi. Hills cover the N; center and S are flat. **Capital:** Mogadishu, 1,554,260.

Government: Type: In transition. **Head of state:** Pres. Sheikh Sharif Sheikh Ahmed; b. July 25, 1964; in office: Jan. 31, 2009. **Head of gov.:** Abdiweli Mohamed Ali; in office: June 28, 2011 (acting from June 19). **Local divisions:** 18 regions. **Defense budget:** NA. **Active troops:** No national armed forces since 1991. Transitional govt. has attempted to establish armed forces.

Economy: Industries: few light industries incl. sugar refining, textiles, wireless communication. **Chief crops:** bananas, sorghum, corn, coconuts, rice, sugarcane, mangoes, sesame seeds, beans. **Natural resources:** uranium, iron ore, reserves, tin, gypsum, bauxite, copper, salt, nat. gas, likely oil. **Arable land:** 1.6%. **Livestock:** cattle: 4.8 mil; chickens: 3.4 mil; goats: 11.4 mil; pigs: 4,200; sheep: 11.8 mil. **Fish catch:** 30,000 metric tons. **Electricity prod.:** 315 mil kWh. **Labor force:** agric. 71%, industry and services 29%.

Finance: Monetary unit: Shilling (SOS) (Sept. 2012: 1,624.42 = $1 U.S.). **GDP** (2010 est.): $5.9 bil; **per capita GDP** (2010 est.): $600; **GDP growth** (2010): 2.6%. **Imports** (2010): $1.3 bil; Djibouti 27.8%, India 13.7%, Kenya 7.3%, Pakistan 6.6%, China 6.4%, Oman 5%, UAE 4.9%, Yemen 4.5%. **Exports** (2010): $515.8 mil; UAE 50.7%, Yemen 19%, Oman 12.8%. **Tourism:** NA. **Budget:** NA.

Transport: Civil aviation: 7 airports. **Chief ports:** Berbera, Kismaayo.

Communications: TV sets: 26 per 1,000 pop. **Radios:** 242 per 1,000 pop. **Telephone lines** (2010): 1.1 per 100 pop. **Internet:** 1.3%.

Health: Life expect.: 48.9 male; 52.8 female. **Births:** 42.1 (per 1,000 pop.). **Deaths:** 14.6 (per 1,000 pop.). **Natural inc.:** 2.76%. **Infant mortality:** 103.7 (per 1,000 live births). **HIV rate:** 0.7%.

Education: NA. **Literacy:** NA.

Major intl. organizations: UN (FAO, IBRD, ILO, IMF, WHO), AL, AU.

Permanent UN mission: 425 E. 61st St., Ste. 702, New York, NY, 10021; (212) 688-9410. (Embassy ceased operation in U.S. in 1991.)

Website: www.state.gov/p/af/ci/so/

British Somaliland (present-day North Somalia) was formed in the 19th cent., as was Italian Somaliland (now central and South Somalia). Italy lost its African colonies in WWII. British Somaliland gained independence, June 26, 1960, and by prearrangement, merged, July 1, with the UN Trust Territory of Somalia to create the independent Somali Republic.

On Oct. 15, 1969, Somalia's first civilian president, Abdirashid Ali Sharmarke, was assassinated. Six days later, Maj. Gen. Muhammad Siad Barre led a military coup. In 1970, he declared the country a socialist state—the Somali Democratic Republic.

Somalia has laid claim to Ogaden, the huge eastern region of Ethiopia, peopled mostly by Somalis. Some 11,000 Cuban troops with Soviet arms defeated Somali army troops and ethnic Somali rebels in Ethiopia, 1978. As many as 1.5 mil refugees entered Somalia. Guerrilla fighting in Ogaden continued until 1988, when a peace agreement was reached with Ethiopia.

After a month of fighting in Mogadishu between pro-government soldiers and the rebel United Somali Congress, Siad Barre fled the capital, Jan. 1991. Fighting between rival factions caused 40,000 casualties, 1991-92, and by mid-1992 the civil war, drought, and banditry combined to produce a famine that threatened some 1.5 mil people.

In Dec. 1992 the UN accepted a U.S. offer of troops to safeguard food delivery. The UN took control of the multinational relief effort from the U.S. May 4, 1993. While the operation helped alleviate the

famine, there were significant U.S. and other casualties; a failed mission Oct. 3-4 left 18 U.S. troops and more than 500 Somalis dead. The U.S. withdrew its peacekeeping forces Mar. 25, 1994.

When the last UN troops pulled out, Mar. 3, 1995, Mogadishu had no functioning central government; armed factions controlled different regions. By 1999 a joint police force was operating in the capital, but much of the country, especially southern Somalia, faced continued violence and food shortages. After political and factional leaders signed a peace deal Jan. 29, 2004, a transitional parliament, Somalia's first legislature in 13 years, was inaugurated Aug. 22. Meeting in Nairobi, Kenya, the parliament chose Abdullahi Yusuf Ahmed as president; he was sworn in Oct. 14.

Because Mogadishu was held by his rivals, Pres. Yusuf moved, July 26, 2005, to make his transitional capital at Jowhar; an interim parliament convened Feb. 26, 2006, at Baidoa. On June 5, an Islamist militia took over Mogadishu, defeating U.S.-backed secular warlords. The Islamists, calling themselves the Supreme Islamic Courts Council, held much of the central and southern regions. Pres. Yusuf escaped assassination, Sept. 18, 2006.

With aid from Ethiopian troops, transitional govt. forces recaptured Mogadishu in Dec. 2006. The UN Security Council authorized, Feb. 20, 2007, an African Union peacekeeping mission to Somalia (AMISOM). An upsurge of fighting in Mogadishu, Feb.-Apr., killed hundreds of people and caused 350,000 to flee. Bombings and kidnappings escalated in 2007-08, as a series of cease-fires failed; the increasing violence forced international aid workers to pull out, worsening a humanitarian crisis. Many of the attacks on transitional authorities and their allies were blamed on al-Shabaab, an al-Qaeda ally.

After Pres. Yusuf resigned Dec. 29, 2008, the transitional parliament, meeting in Djibouti Jan. 31, 2009, elected a moderate Islamist, Sheikh Sharif Sheikh Ahmed; by then, Ethiopia had completely withdrawn its troops from Somalia. Meanwhile, pirates intensified their operations in coastal waters in 2009, carrying out more than 200 attacks off the Horn of Africa. Activities by pirates and Islamist insurgents continued in 2010-11, disrupting efforts to relieve a famine that by mid-2011 threatened an estimated 3.7 mil Somalis. Pressured by the 9,000-member AMISOM force, al-Shabaab pulled out of Mogadishu, Aug. 6, 2011, but continued to control much of southern Somalia. Despite the continuing violence, Somali leaders met in Feb. 2012 for a second Somali national consultative constitutional conference in Garowe, Somalia, and signed Feb. 18 the Garowe II Principles, which established the conditions to install a caretaker government, which was sworn in Aug. 20.

South Africa
Republic of South Africa

People: Population: 48,810,427. **Age distrib.:** <15: 28.4%; 65+: 5.9%. **Pop. density:** 104.1 per sq mi, 40.2 per sq km. **Urban:** 62%. **Ethnic groups:** black African 79%, white 10%, colored 9%, Indian/Asian 3%. **Principal languages:** IsiZulu, IsiXhosa, Afrikaans, Sepedi, English, Setswana, Sesotho, Xitsonga, isiNdebele, Tshivenda, siSwati (all official). **Chief religions:** Protestant 37% (Zionist Christian 11%, Pentecostal/Charismatic 8%, Methodist 7%, Dutch Reformed 7%, Anglican 4%), Catholic 7%, Muslim 2%, other Christian 36%, none 15%.

Geography: Total area: 470,693 sq mi, 1,219,090 sq km; **Land area:** 468,909 sq mi, 1,214,470 sq km. **Location:** At southern extreme of Africa. **Neighbors:** Namibia, Botswana, Zimbabwe on N; Mozambique, Swaziland on E; surrounds Lesotho. **Topography:** Large interior plateau reaches close to the country's 1,739-mi coastline. There are few major rivers or lakes; rainfall sparse in W, more plentiful in E. **Capital:** Pretoria (admin.), 1,500,960; Cape Town (legislative), 3,562,470; Bloemfontein (judicial), 467,778. **Cities (urban aggl.):** Johannesburg, 3,843,760; Ekurhuleni (East Rand), 3,356,754; Durban, 3,012,423; Vereeniging, 1,200,177; Port Elizabeth, 1,118,923.

Government: Type: Republic. **Head of state and gov.:** Pres. Jacob Zuma; b. Apr. 12, 1942; in office: May 9, 2009. **Local divisions:** 9 provinces. **Defense budget:** $4.29 bil. **Active troops:** 62,082.

Economy: Industries: mining (world's largest producer of platinum, gold, chromium), auto assembly, metalworking, machinery, textiles, iron and steel, chemicals, fertilizer, foodstuffs. **Chief crops:** corn, wheat, sugarcane, fruits, vegetables. **Natural resources:** gold, chromium, antimony, coal, iron ore, manganese, nickel, phosphates, tin, rare earth elements, uranium, gem diamonds, platinum, copper, vanadium, salt, nat. gas. **Crude oil reserves:** 15 mil bbls. **Arable land:** 11.8%. **Livestock:** cattle: 13.7 mil; chickens: 160 mil; goats: 6.3 mil; pigs: 1.6 mil; sheep: 24.5 mil. **Fish catch:** 642,075 metric tons. **Electricity prod.:** 232.1 bil kWh. **Labor force:** agric. 9%, industry 26%, services 65%.

Finance: Monetary unit: Rand (ZAR) (Sept. 2012: 8.39 = $1 U.S.). **GDP:** $562.2 bil; **per capita GDP:** $11,100; **GDP growth:** 3.1%. **Imports:** $102.6 bil; China 13.3%, Germany 10.4%, U.S. 7.2%, Saudi Arabia 5.4%, Iran 4.4%, Japan 4.3%, UK 4.2%. **Exports:** $104.5 bil; China 15.8%, U.S. 9.5%, Japan 8.2%, India 8%, Germany 6.9%, UK 4%. **Tourism:** $9.5 bil. **Budget:** $118.3 bil. **Total reserves less gold:** $42.6 bil. **Gold:** 4.02 mil oz t. **CPI change:** 5%.

Transport: Railways: 12,547 mi. **Motor vehicles:** 159.5 vehicles per 1,000 pop. **Civil aviation:** 16.7 bil pass.-mi; 145 airports. **Chief ports:** Cape Town, Durban, Port Elizabeth, Richards Bay, Saldanha Bay.

Communications: TV sets: 195 per 1,000 pop. **Radios:** 443 per 1,000 pop. **Telephone lines:** 8.2 per 100 pop. **Daily newspaper circ.:** 29.6 per 1,000 pop. **Internet:** 21%.

Health: Life expect.: 50.3 male; 48.5 female. **Births:** 19.3 (per 1,000 pop.). **Deaths:** 17.2 (per 1,000 pop.). **Natural inc.:** 0.21%. **Infant mortality:** 42.7 (per 1,000 live births). **HIV rate:** 17.8%.

Education: Compulsory: ages 7-15. **Literacy:** 88.7%.

Major intl. organizations: UN (FAO, IBRD, ILO, IMF, WHO), AU, the Commonwealth, WTO.

Embassy: 3051 Massachusetts Ave. NW 20008; 232-4400.

Website: www.gov.za

Bushmen and KhoiKhoi were the original inhabitants. Bantus, including Zulu, Xhosa, Swazi, and Sotho, occupied the area from northeastern to southern South Africa before the 17th cent.

The Dutch settled the Cape of Good Hope area, beginning in the 17th cent. Britain seized the Cape,1806. Many Dutch trekked north and founded two republics, Transvaal and Orange Free State. Diamonds were discovered, 1867, and gold, 1886. The Dutch (Boers) resented encroachments by the British and others; the Anglo-Boer War followed, 1899-1902. Britain won and created, May 31, 1910, the Union of South Africa, incorporating two British colonies (Cape and Natal) with Transvaal and Orange Free State. After a referendum, the Union became the Republic of South Africa, May 31, 1961, and withdrew from the Commonwealth.

With the election of Daniel Malan's National Party in 1948, the policy of separate development of the races, or apartheid, became official. Under apartheid, blacks were severely restricted to certain occupations, and paid lower wages than whites for similar work. Only whites could vote or run for public office. Persons of Asian Indian ancestry and those of mixed race ("coloureds") had limited political rights. In 1959 the government passed acts providing for the eventual creation of several Bantu nations, or Bantustans.

Protests against apartheid were suppressed. At Sharpeville on Mar. 21, 1960, government troops killed 69 black protesters. At least 600 persons, mostly Bantus, were killed in 1976 anti-apartheid riots. In 1981, South Africa launched military operations in Angola and Mozambique to combat guerrilla groups.

In 1986, Nobel Peace Prize winner Bishop Desmond Tutu called for Western nations to apply sanctions against South Africa to force an end to apartheid. Pres. P. W. Botha announced in Apr. the end to the nation's system of racial pass laws and offered blacks an advisory role in government. On May 19, South Africa attacked three neighboring countries—Zimbabwe, Botswana, Zambia—striking at guerrilla strongholds of the African National Congress (ANC). A nationwide state of emergency was declared June 12, giving almost unlimited power to the security forces.

Some 2 mil South African black workers staged a strike, June 6-8, 1988. Pres. Botha, head of the government since 1978, resigned Aug. 14, 1989, and was replaced by F. W. de Klerk. In 1990 the government lifted its ban on the ANC. Anti-apartheid leader Nelson Mandela was freed Feb. 11 after more than 27 years in prison. In Feb. 1991, Pres. de Klerk pledged to end apartheid laws.

In 1993 negotiators agreed on basic principles for a new democratic constitution. South Africa's partially self-governing black territories, or "homelands," were incorporated into a national system of 9 provinces. The ANC won elections Apr. 26-29, 1994, making Mandela president. The Inkatha Freedom Party won control of the legislature in a mainly Zulu province. By then, fighting between the ANC and Inkatha (aided, during the apartheid era, by South African defense forces) had killed more than 14,000 people in the Zulu region.

In 1995, Mandela appointed a truth commission, led by Desmond Tutu, to document human rights abuses under apartheid. A post-apartheid constitution became law Dec. 10, 1996. The ANC won elections, June 2, 1999, and ANC leader Thabo Mbeki became president. South Africa, Nov. 30, 2006, became the first African country to legalize same-sex marriage.

After Mbeki's former deputy president, Jacob Zuma, defeated him in a power struggle for the ANC leadership, Mbeki resigned his presidency, Sept. 21, 2008. Corruption charges against Zuma were dropped Apr. 6, 2009, and he became president after Apr. 22, 2009, elections. Demanding better wages, 3,000 miners walked off the job in a wildcat strike at a Lonmin platinum mine near Marikana, 40 mi NW of Johannesburg, Aug. 10, 2012. Subsequent protests left at least 10 dead, including two guards and two police officers, before police officers opened fire on protesters Aug. 16, killing 34 and wounding 78, in an incident that some saw as comparable to apartheid-era brutality.

South Sudan
Republic of South Sudan

People: Population: 10,625,176. **Age distrib.:** <15: 46.5%; 65+: 2.2%. **Pop. density:** 42.7 per sq mi, 16.5 per sq km (calc. using total area). **Urban:** 18%. **Ethnic groups:** Dinka, Kakwa, Bari, Azande, Shilluk, Kuku, Murle, Mandari, Didinga, Ndogo, Bviri, Lndi, Anuak, Bongo, Lango, Dungotona, Acholi. **Principal languages:** English, Arabic (incl. Juba, Sudanese variants) (both official); Dinka; Nuer; Bari; Zande; Shilluk. **Chief religions:** animist, Christian.

Geography: Total area: 248,777 sq mi, 644,329 sq km. **Location:** In NE Africa. **Neighbors:** Sudan on N, Uganda and Kenya on S, Ethiopia on E. **Topography:** The White Nile R. flows N through the center of the country. The river feeds the Sudd, a swampy area

occupying more than 15% of the country's center; it is one of the world's largest wetlands. **Capital:** Juba, 268,597.

Government: Type: Republic. **Head of state and gov.:** Salva Kiir Mayardit; b. 1951; in office: July 9, 2011. **Local divisions:** 10 states. **Defense budget:** NA. **Active troops:** 140,000.

Economy: Industries: industry and infrastructure severely underdeveloped. **Chief crops:** sorghum, maize, rice, millet, wheat, gum arabic, sugarcane, fruits, sweet potatoes, sunflower, cotton, sesame, cassava, beans, peanuts. **Natural resources:** petroleum; fertile soils; ecotourism, hydroelectricity potential. **Labor force:** Vast majority of pop. relies on subsistence agriculture.

Finance: Monetary unit: South Sudanese Pound (SSP) (Aug. 2012: 2.85 = $1 U.S.).

Transport: Railways: 147 mi (reported to be in disrepair). **Civil aviation:** 3 airports.

Health: Life expect.: 58.2 male; 61.1 female. **Births:** 39.4 (per 1,000 pop.). **Deaths:** 9.0 (per 1,000 pop.). **Natural inc.:** 3.04%. **Infant mortality:** 71.8 (per 1,000 live births).

Major intl. organizations: UN.

Embassy: 1233 20th St. NW, Ste. 602, 20036; 293-7940.

Website: www.goss.org

South Sudan was a region of the Republic of the Sudan when that country became independent in 1956. Northerners (mostly Arab Muslims) had the dominant role, while southerners (mostly black Africans who practiced Christianity or traditional religions) were marginalized. Southern Anya Nya rebels waged war against the north, 1955-72, until an agreement reached in Addis Ababa, Ethiopia, offered regional self-government for the south. Oil was discovered in the southern region in 1978.

Civil war broke out again in 1983, with southern rebels led by the Sudan People's Liberation Movement (SPLM). Fighting and related famine cost an estimated 2 mil lives and displaced millions of southerners. A peace accord was signed in 2005. A power-sharing agreement offered autonomy for southern Sudan and allowed for an independence referendum.

Nearly 4 mil southern Sudanese voted in the referendum, Jan. 9-15, 2011; almost 99% supporting secession. The UN Security Council, July 8, authorized a peacekeeping mission (UNMISS) with up to 7,900 uniformed personnel. South Sudan attained full independence, July 9, 2011, and was admitted to the UN, July 14. Issues regarding the border with Sudan remained unresolved in Aug. 2012, but a 4-year interim deal on the division of oil revenues was reached Aug. 4. South Sudan also faced challenges of poverty, underdevelopment, and factional conflict.

Spain
Kingdom of Spain

People: Population: 47,042,984. **Age distrib.:** <15: 15.3%; 65+: 17.3%. **Pop. density:** 244.2 per sq mi, 94.3 per sq km. **Urban:** 77.4%. **Ethnic groups:** mixed Mediterranean and Nordic. **Principal languages:** Castilian Spanish (official); Catalan, Galician, Basque (all official regionally). **Chief religion:** Roman Catholic 94%.

Geography: Total area: 195,124 sq mi, 505,370 sq km; **Land area:** 192,657 sq mi, 498,980 sq km. **Location:** In SW Europe. **Neighbors:** Portugal on W; France, Andorra on N; Morocco to S. **Topography:** The interior is a high, arid plateau broken by mountain ranges and river valleys. The NW is heavily watered, the S has lowlands and a Medit. climate. **Capital:** Madrid, 6,574,450. **Cities (urban aggl.):** Barcelona, 5,569,950.

Government: Type: Constitutional monarchy. **Head of state:** King Juan Carlos I de Borbon y Borbon; b. Jan. 5, 1938; in office: Nov. 22, 1975. **Head of gov.:** Prime Min. Mariano Rajoy; b. Mar. 27, 1955; in office: Dec., 20, 2011. **Local divisions:** 17 autonomous communities and two autonomous cities. **Defense budget:** $15.3 bil. **Active troops:** 143,006.

Economy: Industries: textiles and apparel (incl. footwear), food and beverages, metals and metal manufactures, chemicals, shipbuilding, automobiles, machine tools, tourism, clay and refractory prods., pharmaceuticals. **Chief crops:** grain, vegetables, olives, wine grapes, sugar beets, citrus. **Natural resources:** coal, lignite, iron ore, copper, lead, zinc, uranium, tungsten, mercury, pyrites, magnesite, fluorspar, gypsum, sepiolite, kaolin, potash, hydropower. **Crude oil reserves:** 150 mil bbls. **Arable land:** 25.1%. **Livestock:** cattle: 6.1 mil; chickens: 138 mil; goats: 2.9 mil; pigs: 25.3 mil; sheep: 18.6 mil. **Fish catch:** 1.2 mil metric tons. **Electricity prod.** (2010): 279.6 bil kWh. **Labor force:** agric. 4.2%, industry 24%, services 71.7%.

Finance: Monetary unit: Euro (EUR) (Sept. 2012: 0.79 = $1 U.S.). **GDP:** $1.4 tril; **per capita GDP:** $31,000; **GDP growth:** 0.7%. **Imports:** $363.1 bil; Germany 12.6%, France 11.5%, Italy 6.9%, China 6%, Netherlands 5%, UK 4.3%, Portugal 4%. **Exports:** $303.6 bil; France 18.2%, Germany 10.4%, Portugal 8.1%, Italy 8.1%, UK 6.5%. **Tourism:** $59.9 bil. **Budget:** $672.1 bil. **Total reserves less gold:** $32.8 bil. **Gold:** 9.1 mil oz t. **CPI change:** 3.2%.

Transport: Railways: 9,503 mi. **Motor vehicles:** 596.9 vehicles per 1,000 pop. **Civil aviation:** 49.8 bil pass.-mi; 98 airports. **Chief ports:** Algeciras, Barcelona, Bilbao, Cartagena, Huelva, Tarragona, Valencia.

Communications: TV sets: 556 per 1,000 pop. **Radios:** 327 per 1,000 pop. **Telephone lines:** 42.3 per 100 pop. **Daily newspaper circ.:** 144.5 per 1,000 pop. **Internet:** 67.6%.

Health: Life expect.: 78.3 male; 84.5 female. **Births:** 10.4 (per 1,000 pop.). **Deaths:** 8.9 (per 1,000 pop.). **Natural inc.:** 0.15%. **Infant mortality:** 3.4 (per 1,000 live births). **HIV rate:** 0.4%. **Education:** Compulsory: ages 6-16. **Literacy:** 97.7%.

Major intl. organizations: UN and all of its specialized agencies, EU, NATO, OECD, OSCE, WTO.

Embassy: 2375 Pennsylvania Ave. NW 20037; 452-0100.

Website: www.lamoncloa.gob.es

Settled by Iberians, Basques, and Celts, Spain was successively ruled (wholly or in part) by Carthage, Rome, and the Visigoths. Muslims invaded Iberia from N Africa in 711. Reconquest of the peninsula by Christians from the N laid the foundations of modern Spain. In 1469 the kingdoms of Aragon and Castile were united by the marriage of Ferdinand II and Isabella I. Moorish rule ended with the fall of Granada, 1492, the year Spain's large Jewish community was expelled.

Spain established a colonial empire after Columbus's 1492 "discovery" of America. Cortés conquered Mexico, and Pizarro conquered Peru. Spain also controlled the Netherlands and parts of Italy and Germany. Spain lost its American colonies in the early 19th cent. and Cuba, the Philippines, and Puerto Rico during the Spanish-American War, 1898.

Primo de Rivera became dictator, 1923. King Alfonso XIII revoked the dictatorship, 1930, but was forced into exile in 1931. A republic was proclaimed, which disestablished the church, curtailed its privileges, and secularized education. A Popular Front of socialists, Communists, republicans, and anarchists governed, 1936-39.

Army officers under Francisco Franco revolted, 1936. Italy and Germany supported Franco, while the USSR, France, and Mexico supported the republic. Some 500,000 to 1 mil died before the war's end, Mar. 28, 1939. Franco was named *caudillo*, leader of the nation. Spain was officially neutral in WWII, but its cordial relations with fascist countries prompted its exclusion from the UN until 1955.

In July 1969, Franco and the Cortes (Parliament) designated Prince Juan Carlos future king and chief of state. After Franco's death, Nov. 20, 1975, Juan Carlos became king. In free elections, June 1977, moderates and democratic socialists won the most votes.

The king thwarted a 1981 coup attempt by right-wing military officers. The Socialist Workers' Party, under Felipe González Márquez, won four consecutive general elections between 1982 and 1993 but lost to a coalition of conservative and regional parties, 1996. Conservative Prime Min. José María Aznar, who won a parliamentary majority in the 2000 election, openly supporting the U.S.-led invasion of Iraq, Mar. 2003, against Spanish public opinion.

Islamic extremists bombed four commuter trains in central Madrid, Mar. 11, 2004, killing 191 people. The opposition Socialist Workers Party won elections three days later, and Socialist leader José Luis Rodríguez Zapatero, who became prime min. Apr. 17, fulfilled a campaign pledge to remove all 1,300 Spanish troops from Iraq. Spain legalized same-sex marriage, July 3, 2005.

Prime Min. Zapatero won a 2nd term in elections Mar. 9, 2008. As the financial crisis spread worldwide, Spain's banking, building, and tourism industries suffered; in May 2010, as the budget deficit mounted and unemployment surged above 20%, the government introduced austerity measures to reassure international lenders. Mariano Rajoy's conservative Popular Party won elections Nov. 20, 2011, and Rajoy became prime min. Dec. 20. Spain requested $125.5 bil bailout from the EU for its ailing banks, June 25, 2012; the request was approved on the condition that Spain establish a "bad bank" for troubled assets.

Catalonia and the **Basque country** were granted autonomy, Jan. 1980, following overwhelming approval in home-rule referendums. But Basque extremists pushed for independence. The Basque separatist group ETA carried out bombings that have killed about 830 since 1968. ETA declared a permanent cease-fire effective Mar. 24, 2006, after which the Spanish govt. agreed to formal peace talks. Negotiations broke down after ETA exploded a car bomb at the Madrid airport, Dec. 30, 2006, killing two; Basque militants formally rescinded the truce, June 5, 2007, but reinstated it Sept. 5, 2010. In Catalonia, voters approved a plan for expanded home-rule, June 18, 2006.

The **Balearic Isls.** in the W Mediterranean, 1,927 sq mi, are a province of Spain; they include **Majorca** (Mallorca; capital Palma de Mallorca), **Minorca**, **Cabrera**, **Ibiza**, and **Formentera**. The **Canary Isls.**, 2,807 sq mi, in the Atlantic W of Morocco, form two provinces, and include the islands of Tenerife, Palma, Gomera, Hierro, Grand Canary, Fuerteventura, and Lanzarote; Las Palmas and Santa Cruz are thriving ports. More than 1,700 people died trying to get from Mauritania to the Canary Islands in rickety boats, Jan.-June 2006.

Ceuta and Melilla, small Spanish enclaves on Morocco's Mediterranean coast, gained limited autonomy in Sept. 1994. Spain has sought the return of Gibraltar, in British hands since 1704.

Sri Lanka
Democratic Socialist Republic of Sri Lanka

People: Population: 21,481,334. **Age distrib.:** <15: 24.9%; 65+: 8.1%. **Pop. density:** 860.8 per sq mi, 332.4 per sq km. **Urban:** 15.1%. **Ethnic groups:** Sinhalese 74%, Sri Lankan Moors 7%, Indian Tamil 5%, Sri Lankan Tamil 4%. **Principal languages:** Sinhala (official and national), Tamil (national), English commonly used in govt. **Chief religions:** Buddhist (official) 69%, Muslim 8%, Hindu 7%, Christian 6%.

Geography: Total area: 25,332 sq mi, 65,610 sq km; **Land area:** 24,954 sq mi, 64,630 sq km. **Location:** In Indian O. off SE coast of India. **Neighbors:** India on NW. **Topography:** Coastal area and N half are flat; S-central area is hilly and mountainous. **Capital:** Sri Jayewardenepura Kotte (admin., legis.), 125,515; Colombo (commercial), 693,470.

Government: Type: Republic. **Head of state:** Pres. Mahinda Rajapaksa; b. Nov. 18, 1945; in office: Nov. 19, 2005. **Head of gov.:** Dissanayake Mudiyanselage (Di Mu) Jayaratne; b. June 7, 1931; in office: Apr. 21, 2010. **Local divisions:** 9 provinces with 25 districts. **Defense budget:** $1.97 bil. **Active troops:** 160,900.

Economy: Industries: rubber, tea, coconuts, tobacco and other agric. commodities proc.; telecom., insurance, banking; tourism, shipping; clothing, textiles; cement, petroleum refining. **Chief crops:** rice, sugarcane, grains, pulses, oilseed, spices, vegetables, fruits, tea, rubber, coconuts. **Natural resources:** limestone, graphite, mineral sands, gems, phosphates, clay, hydropower. **Arable land:** 19.1%. **Livestock:** cattle: 1.2 mil; chickens: 14 mil; goats: 373,465; pigs: 83,785; sheep: 7,910. **Fish catch:** 445,526 metric tons. **Electricity prod.:** 9.5 bil kWh. **Labor force:** agric. 32.7%, industry 24.2%, services 43.1%.

Finance: Monetary unit: Rupee (LKR) (Sept. 2012: 132.32 = $1 U.S.). **GDP:** $118 bil; **per capita GDP:** $5,700; **GDP growth:** 8.2%. **Imports:** $20 bil; India 26%, China 15.9%, Singapore 7.1%, Iran 6.2%, Japan 5%. **Exports:** $10.2 bil; U.S. 20.1%, UK 9.3%, India 6.3%, Italy 5.1%, Germany 5%, Belgium 4.5%. **Tourism:** $830 mil. **Budget:** $12.6 bil. **Total reserves less gold:** $6.2 bil. **Gold:** 320,884 oz t. **CPI change:** 6.7%.

Transport: Railways: 900 mi. **Motor vehicles:** 36.5 vehicles per 1,000 pop. **Civil aviation:** 4.8 bil pass.-mi; 14 airports. **Chief port:** Colombo.

Communications: TV sets: 118 per 1,000 pop. **Radios:** 200 per 1,000 pop. **Telephone lines:** 17.2 per 100 pop. **Daily newspaper circ.:** 26.1 per 1,000 pop. **Internet:** 15%.

Health: Life expect.: 72.4 male; 79.6 female. **Births:** 17.0 (per 1,000 pop.). **Deaths:** 6.0 (per 1,000 pop.). **Natural inc.:** 1.11%. **Infant mortality:** 9.5 (per 1,000 live births). **HIV rate:** <0.1%. **Education:** Compulsory: ages 5-13. **Literacy:** 91.2%.

Major intl. organizations: UN (FAO, IBRD, ILO, IMF, WHO), the Commonwealth, WTO.

Embassy: 2148 Wyoming Ave. NW 20008; 483-4025.

Website: www.priu.gov.lk

The island was known to the ancient world as Taprobane (Greek for copper-colored) and later as Serendip (from Arabic). Colonists from N India subdued the indigenous Veddahs about 543 BCE; their descendants, the Buddhist Sinhalese, still form most of the population. Hindu descendants of Tamil immigrants from S India account for about one-fifth of the population.

Parts were occupied by the Portuguese in 1505 and the Dutch in 1658. The British seized the island in 1796. It became an independent member of the Commonwealth as Ceylon in 1948 and changed to Sri Lanka May 22, 1972.

Prime Min. Solomon W. R. D. Bandaranaike was assassinated Sept. 25, 1959. His widow, Mrs. Sirimavo Bandaranaike, served as prime min. 1960-65, 1970-77, 1994-2000. In 1971 the nation endured economic problems and terrorist activities by ultra-leftists, thousands of whom were executed. Massive land reform and nationalization of foreign-owned plantations took place in the mid-1970s.

Tensions between Sinhalese and Tamil separatists erupted into violence in the early 1980s. More than 60,000 died in the civil war, which continued for two decades; another 20,000, mostly young Tamils, "disappeared" after government security forces took them into custody.

Pres. Ranasinghe Premadasa was assassinated May 1, 1993, by a Tamil rebel. Mrs. Bandaranaike's daughter, Chandrika Bandaranaike Kumaratunga, became prime min. after Aug. 16, 1994, general elections. Elected president Nov. 9, Kumaratunga appointed her mother prime min. Kumaratunga, who was injured in a suicide bomb attack at a campaign rally Dec. 18, 1999, won a second 6-year term three days later. In failing health, Mrs. Bandaranaike resigned Aug. 10 and died Oct. 10, 2000.

A truce accord intended to bring an end to the civil war was signed Feb. 22, 2002. The Indian Ocean tsunami of Dec. 26, 2004, left more than 31,100 dead.

Prime Min. Mahinda Rajapaksa of the United People's Freedom Alliance won the Nov. 17, 2005, presidential election. A resurgence of fighting by govt. forces, paramilitary groups, and Tamil rebels beginning in Dec. 2005 claimed thousands more lives during the next three years. The army launched a fierce offensive, eventually trapping the rebels in a small patch of territory in the northeast; an estimated 7,000 noncombatants were killed between Jan. 20 and May 7, 2009. On May 18-19, Tamil leader Vellupillai Prabhakaran was killed, and Pres. Rajapaksa formally declared victory. He won reelection Jan. 26, 2010.

Sudan
Republic of the Sudan

(Unless otherwise noted, Sudan's data still includes South Sudan, which became independent July 9, 2011.)

People: Population: 34,206,710. **Age distrib.:** <15: 42%; 65+: 3.3%. **Pop. density:** 47.6 per sq mi, 18.4 per sq km (calc. using total area). **Urban:** 33.2%. **Ethnic groups:** Sudanese Arab 70%, Fur,

Beja, Nuba, Fallata. **Principal languages:** Arabic, English (both official); Nubian; Ta Bedawie; Fur. **Chief religions:** Sunni Muslim, small Christian minority.

Geography: Total area: 718,723 sq mi, 1,861,484 sq km; **Land area:** NA. **Location:** At E end of Sahara desert zone. **Neighbors:** Egypt on N; Libya, Chad, Central African Republic on W; Congo, Uganda, Kenya on S; Ethiopia, Eritrea on E. **Topography:** The N consists of Libyan Desert in W, and the mountainous Nubia Desert in E, with narrow Nile valley between. Center contains large, fertile, rainy areas with fields, pasture, and forest. The S has rich soil, heavy rain. **Capital:** Khartoum, 4,632,310.

Government: Type: Republic with strong military influence. **Head of state and gov.:** Pres. Gen. Omar Hassan Ahmad Al-Bashir; b. Jan. 1, 1944; in office: June 30, 1989. **Local divisions:** 26 states. **Defense budget:** NA. **Active troops:** 109,300.

Economy: Industries: oil, cotton ginning, textiles, cement, edible oils, sugar, soap distilling, shoes, petroleum refining, pharmaceuticals, armaments. **Chief crops:** cotton, groundnuts sorghum, millet, wheat, sugarcane, cassava, mangoes, papayas, bananas, sweet potatoes, sesame. **Natural resources:** petroleum; small reserves of iron ore, copper, chromium ore, zinc, tungsten, mica, silver, gold; hydropower. **Crude oil reserves:** 5 bil bbls. **Arable land:** 8.5%. **Livestock:** cattle: 41.8 mil; chickens: 43.3 mil; goats: 43.4 mil; sheep: 52.1 mil. **Fish catch:** 73,908 metric tons. **Electricity prod.:** 6.5 bil kWh. **Labor force:** agric. 80%, industry 7%, services 13%.

Finance: Monetary unit: Pound (SDG) (Sept. 2012: 4.43 = $1 U.S.). **GDP:** $90.2 bil; **per capita GDP:** $2,800; **GDP growth:** –3.9%. **Imports:** $8.1 bil; China 20.2%, Saudi Arabia 9.1%, UAE 6.7%, Egypt 6.6%, India 6.3%, Germany 4.3%. **Exports:** $8.8 bil; China 68.1%, Japan 14.3%, India 5.6%. **Tourism:** $94 mil. **Budget:** $11.9 bil. **Total reserves less gold:** $192.5 mil. **CPI change** (2009-10): 13%.

Transport: Railways: 3,715 mi. **Motor vehicles:** 2.2 vehicles per 1,000 pop. **Civil aviation:** 690.3 mil; pass.-mi; 15 airports. **Chief port:** Port Sudan.

Communications: TV sets: 370 per 1,000 pop. **Radios:** 172 per 1,000 pop. **Telephone lines:** 1.1 per 100 pop. **Internet:** 19%.

Health: Life expect.: 60.6 male; 64.7 female. **Births:** 31.7 (per 1,000 pop.). **Deaths:** 8.3 (per 1,000 pop.). **Natural inc.:** 2.34%. **Infant mortality:** 55.6 (per 1,000 live births). **HIV rate:** 1.1%.

Education: Compulsory: ages 6-13. **Literacy:** 71.1%.

Major intl. organizations: UN (FAO, IBRD, ILO, IMF, WHO), AL, AU, WTO (observer).

Embassy: 2210 Massachusetts Ave. NW 20008; 338-8565.

Website: www.presidency.gov.sd or www.state.gov/p/af/ci/su/

Northern Sudan, ancient Nubia, was settled by Egyptians in antiquity. The population was converted to Coptic Christianity in the 6th cent. Arab conquests brought Islam to the area in the 15th cent. In the 1820s, Egypt took over Sudan, defeating the last of the earlier empires, including the Fung. In the 1880s, Muhammad Ahmad, who called himself the Mahdi (leader of the faithful), and his followers, the dervishes, led a revolution. An Anglo-Egyptian force crushed the Mahdi's successors, 1898.

Sudan gained independence Jan. 1, 1956. In 1969, a Revolutionary Council took power, led by authoritarian Pres. Gaafar al-Nimeiry. He was overthrown, Apr. 6, 1985. Sudan held its first democratic parliamentary elections in 18 years in 1986. Brig. Omar Hassan Ahmad al-Bashir staged a bloodless military coup, toppling the elected government, June 30, 1989. He took the title of president in 1993.

During 1955-72 and 1983-2005, rebels in the south (populated largely by black Christians and followers of traditional religions) took up arms against government domination by northern Sudan, mostly Arab-Muslim. War and related famine cost an estimated 2 mil lives. An accord to end the rebellion was signed Jan. 9, 2005.

A rebellion in the Darfur region of western Sudan caused a new crisis, 2003-11. Marauding Arab militias, the *janjaweed*, reportedly acting in collusion with Sudanese government troops, looted and burned homes in Darfur and killed many African villagers. The African Union sent more than 7,000 peacekeepers, but fighting continued. Rebel and militia activities in Sudan and Chad led to border clashes and further attacks on civilians. By Sept. 2009 the Darfur war had killed about 300,000 people and displaced another 2.7 mil. The UN Security Council voted July 31, 2007, to deploy a joint UN-African Union force of up to 26,000 peacekeepers (UNMIS). The mission was succeeded by UNMISS upon South Sudan's independence, July 2011.

On Mar. 4, 2009, the International Criminal Court in The Hague, Netherlands, issued a warrant for Pres. Bashir's arrest on charges of war crimes and other crimes against humanity in Darfur. On July 12, 2010, the Court issued another warrant for Bashir's arrest for genocide, the first time it had ever accused a head of state of genocide. Bashir defied the calls for his arrest, and in Apr. 2010 won a new 5-year term in elections from which his main challengers dropped out, alleging fraud.

After southern Sudanese voted overwhelmingly for secession, Jan. 9-15, 2011, South Sudan attained full independence July 9. Differences over the border between Sudan and South Sudan remained unresolved in Aug. 2012, though a 4-year interim deal on the division of oil revenues, which the two countries almost went to war over, was reached Aug. 6.

Suriname
Republic of Suriname

People: Population: 560,157. **Age distrib.:** <15: 27.5%; 65+: 5.6%. **Pop. density:** 9.3 per sq mi, 3.6 per sq km. **Urban:** 69.7%.

Ethnic groups: Hindustani (known locally as East Indian) 37%, Creole 31%, Javanese 15%, Maroon (descendants of escaped slaves) 10%, Amerindian 2%, Chinese 2%, white 1%. **Principal languages:** Dutch (official), English widely spoken, Sranang Tongo (Surinamese), Caribbean Hindustani, Javanese. **Chief religions:** Hindu 27%, Protestant 25% (predominantly Moravian), Roman Catholic 23%, Muslim 20%, indigenous beliefs 5%.

Geography: Total area: 63,251 sq mi, 163,820 sq km; **Land area:** 60,232 sq mi, 156,000 sq km. **Location:** On N shore of S. America. **Neighbors:** Guyana on W, Brazil on S, French Guiana on E. **Topography:** A flat Atlantic coast, where dikes permit agriculture. Inland is forest belt; to S, largely unexplored hills cover 75% of country. **Capital:** Paramaribo, 277,802.

Government: Type: Republic. **Head of state and gov.:** Pres. Désiré (Dési) Delano Bouterse; b. Oct. 13, 1945; in office: Aug. 12, 2010. **Local divisions:** 10 districts. **Defense budget** (2010): $49.2 mil. **Active troops:** 1,840.

Economy: Industries: mining, alumina prod., oil, lumber, food proc., fishing. **Chief crops:** paddy rice, bananas, palm kernels, coconuts, plantains, peanuts. **Natural resources:** timber, hydropower, fish, kaolin, shrimp, bauxite, gold, small amounts of nickel, copper, platinum, iron ore. **Crude oil reserves:** 72 mil bbls. **Arable land:** 0.4%. **Livestock:** cattle: 58,150; chickens: 6.8 mil; goats: 5,650; pigs: 32,125; sheep: 6,900. **Fish catch:** 34,473 metric tons. **Electricity prod.:** 1.6 bil kWh. **Labor force:** agric. 8%, industry 14%, services 78%.

Finance: Monetary unit: Dollar (SRD) (Sept. 2012: 3.27 = $1 U.S.). **GDP:** $5.1 bil; **per capita GDP:** $9,600; **GDP growth:** 4.5%. **Imports:** $1.4 bil; U.S. 26.2%, Netherlands 15.7%, UAE 8.6%, China 8.2%, Antigua and Barbuda 7.4%, Netherlands Antilles 5.5%, Brazil 4.4%, Japan 4.1%. **Exports:** $1.6 bil; U.S. 24.1%, Canada 19.5%, Belgium 17.2%, UAE 8.9%, Norway 6.2%, Guyana 4.8%, France 4.1%. **Tourism:** $61 mil. **Budget** (2010): $939.7 mil. **Total reserves less gold:** $706.3 mil. **Gold:** 70,881 oz t. **CPI change:** 17.7%.

Transport: Motor vehicles: 228.7 vehicles per 1,000 pop. **Civil aviation:** 1.1 bil pass.-mi; 5 airports. **Chief ports:** Paramaribo, Wageningen.

Communications: TV sets: 266 per 1,000 pop. **Radios:** 711 per 1,000 pop. **Telephone lines:** 16.2 per 100 pop. **Daily newspaper circ.:** 80.1 per 1,000 pop. **Internet:** 32%.

Health: Life expect.: 68.8 male; 73.6 female. **Births:** 17.4 (per 1,000 pop.). **Deaths:** 6.2 (per 1,000 pop.). **Natural inc.:** 1.13%. **Infant mortality:** 28.9 (per 1,000 live births). **HIV rate:** 1%.

Education: Compulsory: ages 7-12. **Literacy:** 94.7%.

Major intl. organizations: UN (FAO, IBRD, ILO, IMF, WHO), Caricom, OAS, WTO.

Embassy: 4301 Connecticut Ave. NW, Ste. 460, 20008; 244-7488.

Website: www.gov.sr or www.surinameembassy.org

The Netherlands acquired Suriname in 1667 from Britain, in exchange for New Netherlands (New York). The 1954 Dutch constitution raised the colony to a level of equality with the Netherlands and the Netherlands Antilles. Independence was granted Nov. 25, 1975. Some 40% of the population (mostly East Indians, who opposed independence) immigrated to the Netherlands in the months before independence.

Military coups and political intrigues have dominated Suriname's history since 1980. Désiré (Dési) Bouterse, who masterminded coups in 1982 and 1990, was elected president by parliament, July 19, 2010; as he took office Aug. 12, he was facing trial in Suriname on charges of having executed 15 political opponents in 1982, and he had been convicted in absentia in the Netherlands, 1999, for drug trafficking. The U.S. State Dept. has labeled Suriname a transshipment point for cocaine trafficking, a reputation Suriname sought to rid itself of by signing the UN-supported Container Control Programme (CCP), Aug. 23, 2012, to insure the better inspection of shipping containers in its ports.

Swaziland
Kingdom of Swaziland

People: Population: 1,386,914. **Age distrib.:** <15: 37.4%; 65+: 3.7%. **Pop. density:** 208.8 per sq mi, 80.6 per sq km. **Urban:** 21.2%.

Ethnic groups: African 97%, European 3%. **Principal languages:** English used in govt., siSwati (both official). **Chief religions:** Zionist 40%, Roman Catholic 20%, Muslim 10%, other (incl. Anglican, Baha'i, Methodist, Mormon, Jewish) 30%.

Geography: Total area: 6,704 sq mi, 17,364 sq km; **Land area:** 6,643 sq mi, 17,204 sq km. **Location:** In southern Africa, near Indian O. coast. **Neighbors:** South Africa on N, W, S; Mozambique on E. **Topography:** Descends W-E in broad belts, becoming more arid in low veld region, then rising to plateau in E. **Capital:** Mbabane (admin.), 65,536; Lobamba (legislative).

Government: Type: Constitutional monarchy. **Head of state:** King Mswati III; b. Apr. 19, 1968; in office: Apr. 25, 1986. **Head of gov.:** Prime Min. Barnabas Sibusiso Dlamini; b. May 15, 1942; in office: Oct. 23, 2008. **Local divisions:** 4 districts. **Defense budget/active troops:** NA.

Economy: Industries: coal, wood pulp, sugar, soft drink concentrates, textiles and apparel. **Chief crops:** sugarcane, cotton, corn, tobacco, rice, citrus, pineapples, sorghum, peanuts. **Natural resources:** asbestos, coal, clay, cassiterite, hydropower, forests, small gold and diamond deposits, quarry stone, talc. **Arable land:** 10.2%. **Livestock:** cattle: 620,000; chickens: 3.5 mil; goats: 276,000; pigs: 32,000; sheep: 34,500. **Fish catch:** 279 metric tons. **Electricity prod.:** 450 mil kWh. **Labor force:** agric. 70%.

Finance: Monetary unit: Lilangeni (SZL) (Sept. 2012: 8.39 = $1 U.S.). **GDP:** $6.3 bil; **per capita GDP:** $5,400; **GDP growth:** 0.3%. **Imports:** $2.1 bil. **Exports:** $2 bil. **Tourism:** $51 mil. **Budget:** $1.5 bil. **Total reserves less gold:** $600.5 mil. **CPI change:** 6.1%.

Transport: Railways: 187 mi. **Civil aviation:** 2 airports.

Communications: TV sets: 37 per 1,000 pop. **Radios:** 362 per 1,000 pop. **Telephone lines:** 4.4 per 100 pop. **Daily newspaper circ.:** 24.2 per 1,000 pop. **Internet:** 18.1%.

Health: Life expect.: 49.8 male; 49.1 female. **Births:** 26.2 (per 1,000 pop.). **Deaths:** 14.2 (per 1,000 pop.). **Natural inc.:** 1.20%. **Infant mortality:** 59.6 (per 1,000 live births). **HIV rate:** 25.9%.

Education: Compulsory: ages 6-12. **Literacy:** 87.4%.

Major intl. organizations: UN (FAO, IBRD, ILO, IMF, WHO), the Commonwealth, WTO.

Embassy: 1712 New Hampshire Ave. NW 20009; 234-5002.

Website: www.gov.sz

The royal house of Swaziland, one of Africa's last ruling dynasties, traces back 400 years. The Zulus drove the Swazis, a Bantu people, to Swaziland from lands to the N, 1820. Britain and Transvaal (later part of South Africa) later guaranteed their autonomy, and Britain assumed control after 1903. Independence came Sept. 6, 1968. In 1973, the king repealed the constitution and assumed full powers.

A new constitution banning political parties took effect Oct. 13, 1978. Under a revised constitution effective Feb. 8, 2006, nonpartisan parliamentary elections were held Sept. 19, 2008. The AIDS crisis and the huge gap between rich and poor have fueled student and labor unrest in recent years. An attempt was made to unite various Swazi pro-democracy groups under the banner of the People's United Democratic Movement (PUDEMO), the largest opposition group in the country, at a conference in Johannesburg, South Africa, Aug. 20, 2012, but the proposal was rejected.

Sweden
Kingdom of Sweden

People: Population: 9,103,788. **Age distrib.:** <15: 15.4%; 65+: 20.2%. **Pop. density:** 57.5 per sq mi, 22.2 per sq km. **Urban:** 85.2%. **Ethnic groups:** Swedes; foreign-born or immigrant Finns, Yugoslavs, Danes, Norwegians, Greeks, Turks. **Principal language:** Swedish (official). **Chief religions:** Lutheran 87%, other (incl. Roman Catholic, Orthodox, Baptist, Muslim, Jewish, Buddhist) 13%.

Geography: Total area: 173,860 sq mi, 450,295 sq km; **Land area:** 158,431 sq mi, 410,335 sq km. **Location:** On Scandinavian Peninsula in N Europe. **Neighbors:** Norway on W, Denmark on S (across Kattegat), Finland on E. **Topography:** Mountains along NW border cover 25% of Sweden, flat or rolling terrain covers central and southern areas, which include several large lakes. **Capital:** Stockholm, 1,385,200.

Government: Type: Constitutional monarchy. **Head of state:** King Carl XVI Gustaf; b. Apr. 30, 1946; in office: Sept. 19, 1973. **Head of gov.:** Prime Min. Fredrik Reinfeldt; b. Aug. 4, 1965; in office: Oct. 5, 2006. **Local divisions:** 21 counties. **Defense budget:** $6.21 bil. **Active troops:** 20,363.

Economy: Industries: iron and steel, precision equip. (bearings, radio and phone parts, armaments), wood pulp and paper prods., processed foods, motor vehicles. **Chief crops:** barley, wheat, sugar beets. **Natural resources:** iron ore, copper, lead, zinc, gold, silver, tungsten, uranium, arsenic, feldspar, timber, hydropower. **Arable land:** 6.4%. **Livestock:** cattle: 1.5 mil; chickens: 7.7 mil; pigs: 1.5 mil; sheep: 564,900. **Fish catch:** 222,679 metric tons. **Electricity prod.:** (2010): 147.8 bil kWh. **Labor force:** agric. 1.1%, industry 28.2%, services 70.7%.

Finance: Monetary unit: Krona (SEK) (Sept. 2012: 6.71 = $1 U.S.). **GDP:** $386.6 bil; **per capita GDP:** $40,900; **GDP growth:** 4%. **Imports:** $179.6 bil; Germany 18.4%, Denmark 8.2%, Norway 7.8%, Netherlands 6.1%, UK 5.9%, Russia 5.7%, Finland 5.3%, China 4.7%, France 4.6%. **Exports:** $192.9 bil; Germany 10.5%, Norway 9.3%, UK 7.4%, Denmark 6.5%, Finland 6.5%, U.S. 5.5%, Netherlands 5.2%, France 4.9%, Belgium 4.8%. **Tourism:** $13.9 bil. **Budget:** $277.1 bil. **Total reserves less gold:** $44 bil. **Gold:** 4.04 mil oz t. **CPI change:** 2.96%.

Transport: Railways: 7,228 mi. **Motor vehicles:** 533 vehicles per 1,000 pop. **Civil aviation:** 5.6 bil pass.-mi; 149 airports. **Chief ports:** Brofjorden, Göteborg, Helsingborg, Karlshamn, Lulea, Malmö, Stockholm, Trelleborg, Visby.

Communications: TV sets: 551 per 1,000 pop. **Radios:** 931 per 1,000 pop. **Telephone lines:** 48.7 per 100 pop. **Daily newspaper circ.:** 480.6 per 1,000 pop. **Internet:** 91%.

Health: Life expect.: 78.9 male; 83.6 female. **Births:** 10.2 (per 1,000 pop.). **Deaths:** 10.2 (per 1,000 pop.). **Natural inc.:** 0%. **Infant mortality:** 2.7 (per 1,000 live births). **HIV rate:** 0.1%.

Education: Compulsory: ages 7-16. **Literacy:** 99%.

Major intl. organizations: UN and all of its specialized agencies, EU, OECD, OSCE, WTO.

Embassy: 2900 K St. NW 20007; 467-2600.

Website: www.sweden.se

The Swedes have lived in present-day Sweden for at least 5,000 years, longer than nearly any other European people have lived in their present-day homelands. Gothic tribes from Sweden played a major role in the disintegration of the Roman Empire. Other Swedes helped create the first Russian state in the 9th cent.

The Swedes were Christianized from the 11th cent., and a strong centralized monarchy developed. A parliament, the Riksdag, was first called in 1435, the earliest European parliament with all classes of society represented.

Swedish independence from Danish rule (dating from 1397) was secured by Gustavus I in a revolt, 1521-23; he built up the government and military and established the Lutheran Church. In the 17th cent. Sweden was a major European power, gaining most of the Baltic seacoast. The Napoleonic wars, 1799-1815, in which Sweden acquired Norway (it became independent 1905), were the last in which Sweden participated. Armed neutrality was maintained in both world wars.

Social Democrats have governed Sweden for most of the period since World War II. Prime Min. Olof Palme was shot to death in Stockholm, Feb. 28, 1986. Accused of murdering Palme, Christer Pettersson was found guilty in 1988 and sentenced to life in prison. His conviction was overturned on appeal the following year.

Swedish voters approved membership in the European Union Nov. 13, 1994, and Sweden entered the EU, Jan. 1, 1995.

A center-right alliance led by Fredrik Reinfeldt defeated the Social Democrats in the elections of Sept. 17, 2006. Parliament voted Apr. 1, 2009, to legalize same-sex marriage. The global recession of 2008-09 led to a decline in Swedish exports, especially cars and trucks, but the economy began recovering in mid-2009. Reinfeldt's center-right bloc won a renewed mandate in parliamentary elections Sept. 19, 2010.

Switzerland
Swiss Confederation

People: Population: 7,925,517. **Age distrib.:** <15: 15.2%; 65+: 17.1%. **Pop. density:** 513.2 per sq mi, 198.2 per sq km. **Urban:** 73.7%. **Ethnic groups:** German 65%, French 18%, Italian 10%, Romansch 1%. **Principal languages:** German, French, Italian, Romansch (all official); Serbo-Croatian; Albanian; Portuguese; Spanish; English. **Chief religions:** Roman Catholic 42%, Protestant 35%, Muslim 4%, Orthodox 2%, none 11%.

Geography: Total area: 15,937 sq mi, 41,277 sq km; **Land area:** 15,443 sq mi, 39,997 sq km. **Location:** In Alps Mts. in central Europe. **Neighbors:** France on W; Italy on S; Liechtenstein, Austria on E; Germany on N. **Topography:** The Alps cover 60% of land area; the Jura, near France, 10%. Running between, NE-SW, are midlands, 30%. **Capital:** Bern, 353,462. **Cities (urban aggl.):** Zürich, 1,194,176.

Government: Type: Federal republic. **Head of state and gov.:** 7-member Federal Council with a president chosen on a rotating basis to a nonrenewable 1-year term. Eveline Widmer-Schlumpf, b. Mar. 16, 1956, in office Jan. 1, 2012. **Local divisions:** 20 full cantons, 6 half cantons. **Defense budget:** $5.48 bil. **Active troops:** 25,287.

Economy: Industries: machinery, chemicals, watches, textiles, precision instruments, tourism, banking, insurance. **Chief crops:** grains, fruits, vegetables. **Natural resources:** hydropower potential, timber, salt. **Arable land:** 10.2%. **Livestock:** cattle: 1.6 mil; chickens: 8.9 mil; pigs: 86,987; sheep: 434,083. **Fish catch:** 2,909 metric tons. **Electricity prod.:** (2010): 64 bil kWh. **Labor force:** agric. 3.4%, industry 23.4%, services 73.2%.

Finance: Monetary unit: Franc (CHF) (Sept. 2012: 0.95 = $1 U.S.). **GDP:** $344.2 bil; **per capita GDP:** $43,900; **GDP growth:** 1.9%. **Imports:** $294.1 bil; Germany 32.4%, Italy 10.4%, France 8.6%, U.S. 5%, Netherlands 4.4%, Austria 4.3%. **Exports:** $312.5 bil; Germany 20.2%, U.S. 10.3%, Italy 7.7%, France 7.1%, UK 4.8%, China 4.3%. **Tourism:** $17.6 bil. **Budget:** $214.5 bil. **Total reserves less gold:** $279.4 bil. **Gold:** 33.4 mil oz t. **CPI change:** 0.2%.

Transport: Railways: 3,030 mi. **Motor vehicles:** 577.1 vehicles per 1,000 pop. **Civil aviation:** 18.4 bil pass.-mi; 41 airports. **Chief port:** Basel.

Communications: TV sets: 594 per 1,000 pop. **Radios:** 1,004 per 1,000 pop. **Telephone lines:** 60.8 per 100 pop. **Daily newspaper circ.:** 420 per 1,000 pop. **Internet:** 85.2%.

Health: Life expect.: 79.9 male; 84.6 female. **Births:** 10.4 (per 1,000 pop.). **Deaths:** 8.1 (per 1,000 pop.). **Natural inc.:** 0.24%. **Infant mortality:** 3.9 (per 1,000 live births). **HIV rate:** 0.4%.

Education: Compulsory: ages 7-15. **Literacy:** 99%.

Major intl. organizations: UN and most of its specialized agencies, EFTA, OECD, OSCE, WTO.

Embassy: 2900 Cathedral Ave. NW 20008; 745-7900.

Website: www.ch.ch

Switzerland, the former Roman province of Helvetia, traces its modern history to 1291, when three cantons created a defensive league. Other cantons were subsequently admitted to the Swiss Confederation, which obtained its independence from the Holy Roman Empire through the Peace of Westphalia (1648). The cantons were joined under a federal constitution in 1848.

Switzerland has maintained an armed neutrality since 1815 and has not been involved in a foreign war since 1515. It is the seat of many UN and other international agencies but only became a full UN member on Sept. 10, 2002.

Switzerland is a world banking center. Stung by charges that assets seized by the Nazis and deposited in Swiss banks in WWII had not been properly returned, the government announced, Mar. 5, 1997, a $4.7 bil fund to compensate victims of the Holocaust and other catastrophes. Swiss banks agreed Aug. 12, 1998, to pay $1.25 bil in reparations. Abortion was decriminalized by a June 2, 2002, referendum. In referendums June 5 and Sept. 25, 2005, voters backed plans harmonizing travel, asylum, law enforcement, and labor policies with the EU; more rights for same-sex couples were also endorsed June 5.

The Swiss government responded to an international financial crisis in Oct. 2008 by bailing out the troubled banking giant UBS. Bowing to pressure from U.S. tax authorities, UBS agreed, Jan. 2009, to close some 19,000 hidden offshore accounts, and pledged Aug. 19 to disclose data on the accounts of over 4,400 U.S. clients. In a referendum Nov. 29, 2009, that reflected rising anti-Muslim sentiment, voters approved a constitutional ban on construction of new minarets on mosques. In Sept. 2011, Switzerland put a 1.20 Swiss franc per Euro cap on its currency, a strategy that seems to have enabled the economy to grow in 2012.

Syria
Syrian Arab Republic

People: Population: 22,530,746. **Age distrib.:** <15: 34.6%; 65+: 3.8%. **Pop. density:** 317.8 per sq mi, 122.7 per sq km. **Urban:** 56.1%. **Ethnic groups:** Arab 90%; Kurds, Armenians, and other 10%. **Principal languages:** Arabic (official), Kurdish, Armenian, Aramaic, Circassian widely understood. **Chief religions:** Sunni Muslim 74% (Islam official), other Muslim (incl. Alawite, Druze) 16%, Christian 10%.

Geography: Total area: 71,498 sq mi, 185,180 sq km; **Land area:** 70,900 sq mi, 183,630 sq km. **Location:** Middle East, at E end of Medit. Sea. **Neighbors:** Lebanon, Israel on W; Jordan on S; Iraq on E; Turkey on N. **Topography:** Syria has a short Medit. coastline, then stretches E and S with fertile lowlands and plains, alternating with mountains and large desert areas. **Capital:** Dimashq (Damascus), 2,649,860. **Cities (urban aggl.):** Halab (Aleppo), 3,163,759; Hims (Homs), 1,369,287.

Government: Type: Republic (under military regime). **Head of state:** Pres. Bashar al-Assad; b. Sept. 11, 1965; in office: July 17, 2000. **Head of gov.:** Prime Min. Adel Safar; b. 1953; in office: Apr. 14, 2011. **Local divisions:** 14 provinces. **Defense budget:** $2.06 bil. **Active troops:** 295,000.

Economy: Industries: petroleum, textiles, food proc., beverages, tobacco, phosphate rock mining, cement. **Chief crops:** wheat, barley, cotton, lentils, chickpeas, olives, sugar beets. **Natural resources:** petroleum, phosphates, chrome and manganese ores, asphalt, iron ore, rock salt, marble, gypsum, hydropower. **Crude oil reserves:** 2.5 bil bbls. **Arable land:** 25.4%. **Livestock:** cattle: 1 mil; chickens: 25.4 mil; goats: 2.1 mil; sheep: 15.5 mil. **Fish catch:** 15,245 metric tons. **Electricity prod.:** 40.9 bil kWh. **Labor force:** agric. 17%, industry 16%, services 67%.

Finance: Monetary unit: Pound (SYP) (Sept. 2012: 66.82 = $1 U.S.). **GDP:** $107.6 bil; **per capita GDP:** $5,100; **GDP growth:** –2%. **Imports:** $12.9 bil; Saudi Arabia 14.5%, China 10.1%, UAE 7.1%, Turkey 6.7%, Iran 5.3%, Italy 5%, Russia 4.5%, Iraq 4.3%. **Exports:** $8.1 bil; Iraq 38.8%, Italy 7.9%, Germany 7.1%, Saudi Arabia 6.5%, Kuwait 4.2%. **Tourism:** $6.2 bil. **Budget:** $17.9 bil. **Total reserves less gold** (2010): $19.5 bil. **Gold** (2010): 830,000 oz t. **CPI change:** 4.8%.

Transport: Railways: 1,275 mi. **Motor vehicles:** 27.3 vehicles per 1,000 pop. **Civil aviation:** 1.6 bil pass.-mi; 29 airports. **Chief ports:** Baniyas, Latakia, Tartus.

Communications: TV sets: 192 per 1,000 pop. **Radios:** 267 per 1,000 pop. **Telephone lines:** 20.9 per 100 pop. **Internet:** 22.5%.

Health: Life expect.: 72.5 male; 77.5 female. **Births:** 23.5 (per 1,000 pop.). **Deaths:** 3.7 (per 1,000 pop.). **Natural inc.:** 1.99%. **Infant mortality:** 15.1 (per 1,000 live births). **HIV rate:** NA.

Education: Compulsory: ages 6-14. **Literacy:** 83.4%.

Major intl. organizations: UN (FAO, IBRD, ILO, IMF, WHO), AL, WTO (observer).

Embassy: 2215 Wyoming Ave. NW 20008; 232-6313.

Website: parliament.sy

Syria was the center of the Seleucid empire but later was absorbed into the Roman and Arab empires. Ottoman rule prevailed for four cents., until the end of WWI.

The state of Syria was formed from former Turkish districts, separated by the Treaty of Sevres, 1920, and divided into the states of Syria and Greater Lebanon. Both were administered under a French League of Nations mandate, 1920-41. Syria was proclaimed a republic by the occupying French Sept. 16, 1941, and gained independence Apr. 17, 1946. Syria joined the Arab invasion of Israel in 1948.

Syria joined Egypt Feb. 1958 in the United Arab Republic but seceded Sept. 1961. The Socialist Baath party and military leaders seized power, Mar. 1963. The Baath, a pan-Arab organization, became the only legal party. The Alawite minority has dominated the government.

In the Arab-Israeli war of June 1967, Israel seized and occupied the Golan Heights, from which Syria had shelled Israeli settlements. On Oct. 6, 1973, Syria participated with Egypt in an attack on Israel, but failed to recapture the Golan Heights. Syrian troops entered

Lebanon in 1976, during the Lebanese civil war, and remained a strong presence in the country. They fought Palestinian guerrillas and, later, Christian militiamen. Syria sided with Iran during the Iran-Iraq war, 1980-88.

Thousands died in the city of Hama Feb. 1982 when government forces crushed a Muslim Brotherhood uprising. Following Israel's invasion of Lebanon, June 6, 1982, Israeli planes destroyed 17 Syrian antiaircraft missile batteries in the Bekaa Valley, June 9. Some 25 Syrian planes were downed during the engagement. Israel and Syria agreed to a cease-fire June 11. Syria's alleged role in promoting international terrorism led to strained relations with the U.S. and Great Britain.

Syria condemned the Aug. 1990 Iraqi invasion of Kuwait and sent troops to help Allied forces in the Gulf War. In 1991, Syria accepted U.S. proposals for the terms of an Arab-Israeli peace conference. Syria subsequently participated in negotiations with Israel. Little progress was made.

Hafez al-Assad, president of Syria since 1971, died June 10, 2000, and was succeeded by his son Bashar al-Assad. Following the U.S.-led invasion of Iraq, Mar. 2003, hundreds of thousands of Iraqi refugees flooded into Syria. The U.S. pressured Syria to rein in extremists and deny safe haven to fugitive Iraqi leaders. Israeli planes hit an alleged terrorist camp near Damascus Oct. 4, 2003. The U.S. imposed limited sanctions on Syria, May 11, 2004.

The killing of former Lebanese Prime Min. Rafik al-Hariri by a truck bomb in Beirut, Feb. 14, 2005, was a catalyst for massive anti-Syrian protests in Lebanon. Syria denied responsibility for the blast but pulled nearly all its troops out of Lebanon by Apr. 26; some Syrian intelligence agents may have remained. Syria aided Hezbollah fighters in their conflict with Israel. When Israeli armed forces struck Lebanon, July-Aug. 2006, in an effort to cripple Hezbollah, about 180,000 Lebanese found temporary refuge in Syria.

In an uncontested referendum, May 27, 2007, Syrian voters confirmed Pres. Bashar al-Assad for another 7-year term. On Sept. 6, Israel bombed a secret site in N Syria where the Israelis believed Syria and North Korea were developing a nuclear facility; both countries denied the claim. Beginning Mar. 2011, the Baathist government faced its most serious challenge in decades, as "Arab Spring" protesters staged mass demonstrations in many cities. The Assad regime used troops and tanks to enforce control, but the conflict escalated into outright rebellion. Assad escalated his attacks on the opposition, and the International Committee of the Red Cross declared the conflict a civil war, July 15, 2012. The designation means that the rules of war under the Geneva Convention apply, and acknowledges that the conflict has spread throughout the nation and that the armed opposition forces have achieved a level of unity, though no single group has emerged as a viable alternative to Assad. The civilian death toll, according to Syria's opposition Local Coordinating Committee, was more than 23,000 as of Sept. 2012, while 1.2 mil had been displaced, the UN said.

Taiwan

People: Population: 23,234,936. **Age distrib.:** <15: 14.7%; 65+: 11.3%. **Pop. density:** 1,865.4 per sq mi, 720.2 per sq km. **Urban:** NA. **Ethnic groups:** Taiwanese (incl. Hakka) 84%, mainland Chinese 14%, indigenous 2%. **Principal languages:** Mandarin Chinese (official), Taiwanese (Min), Hakka dialects. **Chief religions:** mixture of Buddhist and Taoist 93%, Christian 5%.

Geography: Total area: 13,892 sq mi, 35,980 sq km; **Land area:** 12,456 sq mi, 32,260 sq km. **Location:** Off SE coast of China, between E and S China seas. **Neighbors:** Nearest is China to NW. **Topography:** A mountain range forms backbone of island; the eastern half is very steep and craggy, western slope is flat, fertile, and well cultivated. **Capital:** Taipei, 2,657,180. **Cities (urban aggl.):** Kaohsiung, 1,516,443; Taichung, 1,156,696.

Government: Type: Democracy. **Head of state:** Pres. Ma Ying-jeou; b. July 13, 1950; in office: May 20, 2008. **Head of gov.:** Prime Min. Sean C. Chen; b. Oct. 13, 1949; in office: Feb. 6, 2012. **Local divisions:** 16 counties, 5 municipalities, 2 special municipalities (Taipei, Kaohsiung). **Defense budget:** $9.9 bil. **Active troops:** 290,000.

Economy: Industries: electronics, communications and info. tech. prods., petroleum refining, armaments, chemicals, textiles, iron and steel, machinery, cement, food proc., vehicles, consumer prods., pharmaceuticals. **Chief crops:** rice, vegetables, fruits, tea, flowers. **Natural resources:** small deposits of coal, nat. gas, limestone, marble, asbestos. **Crude oil reserves:** 2.4 mil bbls. **Arable land:** 24%. **Fish catch:** 1.2 mil metric tons. **Electricity prod.:** 213.2 bil kWh. **Labor force:** agric. 5.2%, industry 35.9%, services 58.8%.

Finance: Monetary unit: New Dollar (TWD) (Sept. 2012: 29.89 = $1 U.S.). **GDP:** $887.3 bil; **per capita GDP:** $38,200; **GDP growth:** 4%. **Imports:** $279.4 bil; Japan 20.7%, China 14.2%, U.S. 10%, South Korea 6.4%, Saudi Arabia 4.7%. **Exports:** $307.1 bil; China 28.1%, Hong Kong 13.8%, U.S. 11.5%, Japan 6.6%, Singapore 4.4%. **Tourism:** $11 bil. **Budget:** $90.7 bil.

Transport: Railways: 982 mi. **Motor vehicles:** 294.4 vehicles per 1,000 pop. **Civil aviation:** 37 airports. **Chief ports:** Chilung, Hualian, Kaohsiung, Taichung.

Communications: TV sets: 444 per 1,000 pop. **Radios:** 178 per 1,000 pop. **Telephone lines:** 72.7 per 100 pop. **Internet:** 72%.

Health: Life expect.: 76.4 male; 82.9 female. **Births:** 8.7 (per 1,000 pop.). **Deaths:** 6.7 (per 1,000 pop.). **Natural inc.:** 0.20%. **Infant mortality:** 4.6 (per 1,000 live births). **HIV rate:** NA.
Education: Compulsory: ages 6-14. **Literacy:** 96.1%.
Major intl. organizations: APEC, WTO.
Taipei Economic and Cultural Representative Office: 4201 Wisconsin Ave. NW 20016; 895-1800.
Website: www.taiwan.gov.tw

Large-scale Chinese immigration began in the 17th cent. The island came under mainland control after an interval of Dutch rule, 1620-62. Japan ruled Taiwan (also called Formosa), 1895-1945. The Kuomintang (Chinese nationalist govt.) fled to Taiwan in 1949 and established the Republic of China under Chiang Kai-shek, who ruled until his death in 1975. The U.S. provided military aid to deter a Communist invasion.

In 1971, the UN expelled Taiwan from its seat and recognized the mainland government. The U.S. recognized the People's Republic, Dec. 15, 1978, and severed ties with Taiwan. However, the U.S. and Taiwan have continued a strong trading relationship and maintain contact via quasi-official agencies.

Land reform, government planning, U.S. aid and investment, and free universal education brought advances in industry, agriculture, and living standards. In 1987 martial law was lifted after 38 years, and in 1991 the 43-year period of emergency rule ended. Taiwan held its first direct presidential election Mar. 23, 1996. An earthquake on Sept. 21, 1999, killed more than 2,300 people.

Five decades of Nationalist Party rule ended when Chen Shui-bian, leader of the pro-independence Democratic Progressive Party, won the presidential election, Mar. 18, 2000. Chen was wounded in an apparent assassination attempt Mar. 19, 2004, one day before he won a second term as president. Promising increased cooperation with China, Taipei Mayor Ma Ying-jeou won the presidential election, Mar. 22, 2008.

Former Pres. Chen Shui-bian was convicted of corruption and sentenced to life in prison, Sept. 11, 2009. Flooding and mudslides from Typhoon Morakot, Aug. 7-9, left at least 700 people dead or missing; criticism of the government's disaster response led to a cabinet shake-up a month later. Former Pres. Lee Teng-hui, who introduced democratic reforms 1988-2000, was indicted June 30, 2011, for allegedly embezzling $7.8 mil while in office.

Since 1949, the People's Republic has considered Taiwan a rebel province of the mainland; until 1991, Taiwan claimed to be the sole government of both. In 2003, China replaced the U.S. as Taiwan's leading trade partner. China has warned that any Taiwan move toward independence could provoke military action.

The **Penghu Isls.** (Pescadores), 49 sq mi, pop. (2011 est.) 96,597, lie between Taiwan and the mainland. **Kinmen**, fmr. Quemoy, pop. (2011 est.) 99,691, and **Matsu**, pop. (2011 est.) 10,106, lie just off the mainland.

Tajikistan
Republic of Tajikistan

People: Population: 7,768,385. **Age distrib.:** <15: 33.7%; 65+: 3.3%. **Pop. density:** 142.2 per sq mi, 54.9 per sq km. **Urban:** 26.5%. **Ethnic groups:** Tajik 80%, Uzbek 15%, Russian 1%, Kyrgyz 1%. **Principal languages:** Tajik (official), Russian widely used in govt. and business. **Chief religion:** Sunni Muslim 85%, Shia Muslim 5%.

Geography:Total area: 55,251 sq mi, 143,100 sq km; **Land area:** 54,637 sq mi, 141,510 sq km. **Location:** Central Asia. **Neighbors:** Uzbekistan on N and W, Kyrgyzstan on N, China on E, Afghanistan on S. **Topography:** Mountainous region that contains the Pamirs, Trans-Alai mountain system. **Capital:** Dushanbe, 738,883.

Government: Type: Republic. **Head of state:** Pres. Imomali Rakhmon; b. Oct. 5, 1952; in office: Nov. 6, 1994. **Head of gov.:** Prime Min. Akil Akilov; b. Feb. 2, 1944; in office: Dec. 20, 1999. **Local divisions:** 2 viloyats, 1 autonomous viloyat. **Defense budget:** $72 mil. **Active troops:** 8,800.

Economy: Industries: aluminum, cement, vegetable oil. **Chief crops:** cotton, grain, fruits, grapes, vegetables. **Natural resources:** hydropower, petroleum, uranium, mercury, brown coal, lead, zinc, antimony, tungsten, silver, gold. **Crude oil reserves:** 12 mil bbls. **Arable land:** 5.3%. **Livestock:** cattle: 1.9 mil; chickens: 3.9 mil; goats: 1.6 mil; pigs: 418; sheep: 2.6 mil. **Fish catch:** 677 metric tons. **Electricity prod.:** 15.9 bil kWh. **Labor force:** agric. 49.8%, industry 12.8%, services 37.4%.

Finance: Monetary unit: Somoni (TJS) (Sept. 2012: 4.76 = $1 U.S.). **GDP:** $16.4 bil; **per capita GDP:** $2,100; **GDP growth:** 7.4%. **Imports:** $3.2 bil; China 45.7%, Russia 16.4%, Kazakhstan 6.8%, U.S. 4.1%. **Exports:** $1.2 bil; Turkey 30.2%, Russia 8.3%, Iran 7%, China 6.7%, South Korea 6.7%, Afghanistan 6%, Italy 5.2%. **Tourism:** NA. **Budget:** $1.8 bil. **Total reserves less gold:** $289.3 mil. **Gold:** 150,000 oz t. **CPI change:** 12.4%.

Transport: Railways: 423 mi. **Civil aviation:** 1.1 bil pass.-mi; 17 airports.
Communications: TV sets: 386 per 1,000 pop. **Radios:** 398 per 1,000 pop. **Telephone lines:** 5.5 per 100 pop. **Internet:** 13%.
Health: Life expect.: 63.3 male; 69.6 female. **Births:** 25.9 (per 1,000 pop.). **Deaths:** 6.5 (per 1,000 pop.). **Natural inc.:** 1.94%. **Infant mortality:** 37.3 (per 1,000 live births). **HIV rate:** 0.2%.
Education: Compulsory: ages 7-15. **Literacy:** 99.7%.
Major International Organizations: UN (FAO, IBRD, ILO, IMF, WHO), CIS, OSCE, WTO (observer).

Embassy: 1005 New Hampshire Ave. NW 20037; 223-6090.
Website: www.parlament.tj

Societies were settled in the region from about 3000 BCE. Invaders have included Iranians, Arabs (who converted the population to Islam), Mongols, Uzbeks, Afghans, and Russians. The USSR gained control 1918-25, making the region a part of the Uzbek SSR until the Tajik SSR was proclaimed, 1929.

Tajikistan declared independence Sept. 9, 1991. Factional fighting led to the installation of a pro-Communist regime, Jan. 1993. A new constitution establishing a presidential system was approved by referendum Nov. 6, 1994.

Clashes between Muslim rebels and troops loyal to the government (and supported by Russia) claimed an estimated 55,000 lives by mid-1997, despite a series of peace accords. Constitutional changes including legalization of Islamic political parties were approved by referendum Sept. 26, 1999. Pres. Imomali Rakhmonov won a Nov. 6 election called a farce by human-rights observers. Voters approved, June 22, 2003, constitutional changes giving Rakhmonov the right to serve as president until 2020. Leading opposition groups boycotted the election of Nov. 6, 2006, again won by Rakhmonov. He changed his name to Rakhmon in 2007 after a decree banned Slavic name endings and other Soviet-era practices.

Poverty and corruption are widespread. Much of the nation's income is supplied by international donors and by remittances from young Tajiks working in Russia and Kazakhstan.

Tanzania
United Republic of Tanzania

People: Population: 46,912,768. **Age distrib.:** <15: 45%; 65+: 2.9%. **Pop. density:** 137.2 per sq mi, 53 per sq km. **Urban:** 26.7%. **Ethnic groups:** African 99% (Bantu 95%, 130+ tribes); other 1%. **Principal languages:** Kiswahili/Swahili, English primary lang. of commerce, admin., higher ed. (both official); Arabic widely spoken in Zanzibar; local langs. **Chief religions:** Christian 30%, Muslim 35%, indigenous beliefs 35%; 99%+ Muslim on Zanzibar.

Geography: Total area: 365,755 sq mi, 947,300 sq km; **Land area:** 342,009 sq mi, 885,800 sq km. **Location:** On coast of E Africa. **Neighbors:** Kenya, Uganda on N; Rwanda, Burundi, Congo on W; Zambia, Malawi, Mozambique on S. **Topography:** Hot, arid central plateau, surrounded by lake region in W, temperate highlands in N and S, the coastal plains. Mt. Kilimanjaro, 19,340 ft, is highest in Africa. **Capital:** Dodoma, 226,139 (planned new capital: legis. and National Assembly currently meet here); Dar es Salaam, 3,588,180 (exec. branch).

Government: Type: Republic. **Head of state and gov.:** Pres. Jakaya Mrisho Kikwete; b. Oct. 7, 1950; in office: Dec. 21, 2005. **Local divisions:** 25 regions. **Defense budget:** $226 mil. **Active troops:** 27,000.

Economy: Industries: agric. proc.; diamond, gold, iron mining; salt, soda ash; cement, oil refining, shoes, apparel. **Chief crops:** coffee, sisal, tea, cotton, pyrethrum (insecticide made from chrysanthemums), cashews, tobacco, cloves, corn, wheat. **Natural resources:** hydropower, tin, phosphates, iron ore, coal, diamonds, gems, gold, nat. gas, nickel. **Arable land:** 11.3%. **Livestock:** cattle: 19.2 mil; chickens: 33.5 mil; goats: 12.9 mil; pigs: 495,000; sheep: 4.2 mil. **Fish catch:** 350,436 metric tons. **Electricity prod.:** 4.5 bil kWh. **Labor force:** agric. 80%, industry and services 20%.

Finance: Monetary unit: Shilling (TZS) (Sept. 2012: 1,569.52 = $1 U.S.). **GDP:** $64.7 bil; **per capita GDP:** $1,500; **GDP growth:** 6.7%. **Imports:** $8.7 bil; India 19.8%, China 17%, South Africa 6.5%, Kenya 5.8%, UAE 4.6%. **Exports:** $5.4 bil; China 14.2%, India 9.9%, Japan 7.7%, Germany 6.7%, UAE 4.5%. **Tourism:** $1.5 bil. **Budget:** $6.1 bil. **Total reserves less gold:** $3.7 bil. **CPI change:** 12.7%.

Transport: Railways: 2,292 mi. **Motor vehicles:** 1.9 vehicles per 1,000 pop. **Civil aviation:** 245.4 mil pass.-mi; 11 airports. **Chief ports:** Dar es Salaam, Zanzibar.
Communications: TV sets: 41 per 1,000 pop. **Radios:** 352 per 1,000 pop. **Telephone lines:** 0.4 per 100 pop. **Daily newspaper circ.:** 1.6 per 1,000 pop. **Internet:** 12%.
Health: Life expect.: 59.0 male; 61.6 female. **Births:** 37.7 (per 1,000 pop.). **Deaths:** 8.6 (per 1,000 pop.). **Natural inc.:** 2.91%. **Infant mortality:** 46.5 (per 1,000 live births). **HIV rate:** 5.6%.
Education: Compulsory: ages 7-13. **Literacy:** 73.2%.
Major intl. organizations: UN and all of its specialized agencies, AU, the Commonwealth, WTO.
Embassy: 2139 R St. NW 20008; 939-6125.
Website: www.tanzania.go.tz

The Republic of Tanganyika in E Africa and the island Republic of Zanzibar, off Tanganyika's coast, both of which had recently gained independence, joined to form the United Republic of Tanzania, Apr. 26, 1964. Zanzibar retains internal self-government.

Until resigning as president in 1985, Julius K. Nyerere, a former Tanganyikan independence leader, dominated Tanzania's single-party government, which emphasized government planning and control of the economy. In 1992 the constitution was amended to establish a multiparty system. Privatization of the economy was undertaken in the 1990s.

A bomb at the U.S. embassy in Dar es Salaam, Aug. 7, 1998, killed 11 people and injured at least 70 others. The U.S. blamed the attack and a near-simultaneous embassy bombing in Kenya on Islamic terrorists associated with Osama bin Laden.

President since 1995, Benjamin Mkapa was reelected Oct. 29, 2000.Jakaya Mrisho Kikwete of the ruling Chama Cha Mapinduzi (Party of the Revolution) won the Dec. 14, 2005, presidential election; he was reelected to a second 5-year term Oct. 31, 2010. Discovery of offshore natural gas in 2011-12 increased the country's total recoverable gas reserves to as much as 28.7 tril cubic ft.

Tanganyika. Arab colonization and slaving began in the 8th cent. CE; Portuguese sailors explored the coast around 1500. Other Europeans followed.

In 1885 Germany established German East Africa, of which Tanganyika formed the bulk. It became a League of Nations mandate and, after 1946, a UN trust territory, both under Britain. It became independent, Dec. 9, 1961, and a republic within the Commonwealth a year later.

Zanzibar, the Isle of Cloves, lies 23 mi off mainland Tanzania; area 640 sq mi and pop. (2002) 622,459. The island of **Pemba**, 25 mi to the NE, area 380 sq mi and pop. (2002) 362,166 is included in the administration.

Chief industry is cloves and clove oil production, of which Zanzibar and Pemba produce most of the world's supply.

Zanzibar was for centuries the center for Arab slave traders. Portugal ruled the region for two centuries until ousted by Arabs around 1700. Zanzibar became a British Protectorate in 1890; independence came Dec. 10, 1963. Revolutionary forces overthrew the Sultan, Jan. 12, 1964. The new government ousted Western diplomats and newsmen, slaughtered thousands of Arabs, and nationalized farms. Union with Tanganyika followed.

Thailand
Kingdom of Thailand

People: Population: 67,091,089. **Age distrib.:** <15: 19.5%; 65+: 9.5%. **Pop. density:** 340.1 per sq mi, 131.3 per sq km. **Urban:** 34.1%. **Ethnic groups:** Thai 75%, Chinese 14%. **Principal languages:** Thai, English secondary lang. of elite, ethnic and regional dialects. **Chief religions:** Buddhist (official) 95%, Muslim 5%.

Geography: Total area: 198,117 sq mi, 513,120 sq km; **Land area:** 197,256 sq mi, 510,890 sq km. **Location:** On Indochinese and Malayan peninsulas in SE Asia. **Neighbors:** Myanmar on W and N, Laos on N, Cambodia on E, Malaysia on S. **Topography:** A plateau dominates NE third of Thailand, dropping to the fertile alluvial valley of Chao Phraya R. in center. Forested mountains are in N, with narrow fertile valleys. The S peninsula region is covered by rain forests. **Capital:** Krung Thep (Bangkok), 8,426,080. **Cities (urban aggl.):** Samut Prakan, 1,211,568.

Government: Type: Constitutional monarchy. **Head of state:** King Bhumibol Adulyadej; b. Dec. 5, 1927; in office: June 9, 1946. **Head of gov.:** Prime Min. Yingluck Shinawatra; b. June 21, 1967; in office: Aug. 8, 2011. **Local divisions:** 76 provinces. **Defense budget:** $5.52 bil. **Active troops:** 305,860.

Economy: Industries: tourism, textiles and garments, agric. proc., beverages, tobacco, cement, light mfg. (jewelry, elec. appliances, computers and parts, integrated circuits, furniture); world's second-largest tungsten producer and third-largest tin producer. **Chief crops:** rice, cassava, rubber, corn, sugarcane, coconuts, soybeans. **Natural resources:** tin, rubber, nat. gas, tungsten, tantalum, timber, lead, fish, gypsum, lignite, fluorite. **Crude oil reserves:** 442 mil bbls. **Arable land:** 29.9%. **Livestock:** cattle: 6.5 mil; chickens: 231.9 mil; goats: 380,277; pigs: 7.6 mil; sheep: 43,139. **Fish catch:** 3.1 mil metric tons. **Electricity prod.** (2010): 147.9 bil kWh. **Labor force:** agric. 40.7%, industry 13.2%, services 46.1%.

Finance: Monetary unit: Baht (THB) (Sept. 2012: 31.26 = $1 U.S.). **GDP:** $609.8 bil; **per capita GDP:** $9,500; **GDP growth:** 0.1%. **Imports:** $196.3 bil; Japan 18.5%, China 13.4%, UAE 6.3%, U.S. 5.9%, Malaysia 5.4%, South Korea 4%. **Exports:** $221.6 bil; China 12%, Japan 10.5%, U.S. 9.6%, Hong Kong 7.2%, Malaysia 5.4%, Singapore 5%, Indonesia 4.4%. **Tourism:** $26.3 bil. **Budget:** $70.3 bil. **Total reserves less gold:** $167.4 bil. **Gold:** 4.9 mil oz t. **CPI change:** 3.8%.

Transport: Railways: 2,530 mi. **Motor vehicles:** 154.4 vehicles per 1,000 pop. **Civil aviation:** 33.2 bil pass.-mi; 63 airports. **Chief ports:** Bangkok, Laem Chabang, Map Ta Phut, Prachuap Port, Si Racha.

Communication: TV sets: 285 per 1,000 pop. **Radios:** 229 per 1,000 pop. **Telephone lines:** 9.7 per 100 pop. **Internet:** 23.7%.

Health: Life expect.: 71.5 male; 76.3 female. **Births:** 12.8 (per 1,000 pop.). **Deaths:** 7.4 (per 1,000 pop.). **Natural inc.:** 0.54%. **Infant mortality:** 15.9 (per 1,000 live births). **HIV rate:** 1.3%.

Education: Compulsory: ages 6-14. **Literacy:** 93.5%.

Major intl. organizations: UN (FAO, IBRD, ILO, IMF, WHO), APEC, ASEAN, WTO.

Embassy: 1024 Wisconsin Ave. NW, Ste. 401, 20007; 944-3600. **Website:** www.thaigov.go.th

Thais began migrating from southern China during the 11th cent. and established a unified Thai kingdom, 1350. Known as Siam until 1939, Thailand is the only country in SE Asia never colonized by Europeans. King Mongkut and his son King Chulalongkorn, ruling successively from 1851 to 1910, modernized the country and signed trade treaties with Britain and France. A bloodless revolution in 1932 limited the monarchy. Thailand was an ally of Japan during WWII and of the U.S. during the postwar period. For decades, the military had a dominant role in governing the country.

A downturn in the economy forced Thailand to seek more than $15 bil in emergency international loans, Aug. 1997. A new constitution won legislative approval Sept. 27. By the end of the 1990s, according to UN estimates, more than 750,000 people in Thailand had HIV/AIDS; a nationwide prevention campaign has reduced the number of new infections.

Following elections in Jan. 2001, Thaksin Shinawatra, a wealthy former telecommunications executive, became prime min. The Indian Ocean tsunami of Dec. 26, 2004, left more than 5,400 people dead in Thailand.

Elections Feb. 6, 2005, gave Thaksin's party a huge majority in parliament. Facing rising opposition and accused of benefiting improperly from the sale of his family's telecom business, Thaksin called snap elections for Apr. 2, 2006, three years ahead of schedule; the vote, which many parties boycotted, was later ruled unconstitutional. A military junta took power in a bloodless coup Sept. 19.

Thaksin supporters won elections Dec. 23, 2007, and Samak Sundaravej became prime min. after civilian rule was restored Jan. 22, 2008. After a series of antigovernment protests paralyzed Bangkok, Prime Min. Samak imposed emergency rule Sept. 2; Thailand's Constitutional Court ousted him a week later, ostensibly for getting paid to host TV cooking shows while he held public office. Thaksin's brother-in-law Somchai Wongsawat became prime min. Sept. 18, but a Constitutional Court ruling, Dec. 2, barred him from politics and dissolved his People Power Party because of electoral fraud.

Mass protests by Thaksin supporters, known as Red Shirts, led the government to declare a state of emergency in Bangkok, Apr. 12-14, 2009. Meanwhile, about 60,000 security forces in southern Thailand suppressed a Muslim insurgency; from Jan. 2004 to Sept. 2009, more than 3,500 people, mostly civilians, died in the fighting.

On Feb. 26, 2010, Thailand's Supreme Court ordered the seizure of about $1.4 bil of Thaksin's family assets. Thaksin supporters staged mass rallies in Bangkok, and on Apr. 7 a group of Red Shirts stormed the parliament building, leading the government to impose emergency rule in the capital. After the Red Shirts began to build a fortified compound in the heart of Bangkok's business district, a crackdown by Thai security forces May 14-19, 2010, left at least 54 people dead and some 470 injured. After parliamentary elections July 3, 2011, Thaksin's sister, Yingluck Shinawatra, took office as Thailand's first female prime min. Monsoon season brought floods that began July 25, 2011, covered two-thirds of the country by Oct. 12, did not fully recede until Jan. 16, 2012, and cost the country an estimated 1.4 tril bhat ($45.7 bil).

Timor-Leste
(East Timor)
Democratic Republic of Timor-Leste

People: Population: 1,143,667. **Age distrib.:** <15: 43%; 65+: 3.5%. **Pop. density:** 199.1 per sq mi, 76.9 per sq km. **Urban:** 28.3%. **Ethnic groups:** Austronesian (Malayo-Polynesian), Papuan, small Chinese minority. **Principal languages:** Tetum, Portuguese (both official); Indonesian; English; about 16 indigenous langs. (incl. Tetum, Galole, Mambae, Kemak). **Chief religions:** Roman Catholic 98%, Muslim 1%, Protestant 1%.

Geography: Total area: 5,743 sq mi, 14,874 sq km. **Land area:** 5,743 sq mi, 14,874 sq km. **Location:** E half of Timor Isl. in SW Pacific O. **Neighbors:** Indonesia (West Timor) on W. **Topography:** Terrain is rugged, rising to 9,721 ft at Mt. Ramelau. **Capital:** Dili, 180,224.

Government: Type: Republic. **Head of state:** Taur Matan Ruak; b. Oct. 10, 1956; in office: May 20, 2012. **Head of gov.:** Prime Min. Kay Rala Xanana Gusmão; b. June 20, 1946; in office: Aug. 8, 2007. **Local divisions:** 13 districts. **Defense budget:** $5.85 mil **Active troops:** 1,332.

Economy: Industries: printing, soap mfg., handicrafts, woven cloth. **Chief crops:** coffee, rice, corn, cassava, sweet potatoes, soybeans. **Natural resources:** gold, petroleum, nat. gas, manganese, marble. **Arable land:** 11.1%. **Livestock:** cattle: 152,854; chickens: 800,000; goats: 144,342; pigs: 415,315; sheep: 43,166. **Fish catch:** 4,677 metric tons. **Labor force:** agric. 64%, industry 10%, services 26%.

Finance: Monetary unit: U.S. Dollar (USD). **GDP:** $9.6 bil; **per capita GDP:** $8,800; **GDP growth** 10.6%. **Imports:** $689 mil. **Exports:** $18 mil (excl. oil). **Tourism:** $21 mil. **Budget:** $1.3 bil. **Total reserves less gold:** $461.6 mil. **CPI change:** 13.5%.

Transport: Civil aviation: 2 airports. **Chief port:** Dili.

Communication: Telephone lines: 0.3 per 100 pop. **Internet:** 0.9%.

Health: Life expect.: 65.3 male; 68.3 female. **Births:** 35.2 (per 1,000 pop.). **Deaths:** 6.4 (per 1,000 pop.). **Natural inc.:** 2.88%. **Infant mortality:** 41.4 (per 1,000 live births). **HIV rate:** NA.

Education: Compulsory: ages 6-14. **Literacy:** 58.3%.

Major intl. organizations: UN (FAO, IBRD, ILO, IMF, WHO).

Embassy: 4201 Connecticut Ave. NW 20008; 966-3202.

Website: www.timor-leste.gov.tl

The collapse of Portuguese rule in East Timor led to an outbreak of factional fighting, Aug. 1975 and an invasion by Indonesia in Dec. Indonesia annexed East Timor as a 27th province in 1976. In over two decades more than 200,000 Timorese died as a result of civil war, famine, and persecution by Indonesian authorities. In a referendum held Aug. 30, 1999, under UN auspices, Timorese voted overwhelmingly for independence. Pro-Indonesian militias then went on a rampage, terrorizing the population. Under pressure, the government allowed entrance of an international peacekeeping force in Sept.; a UN interim administration formally took command Oct. 26, 1999.

Pro-independence forces won elections for a constituent assembly Aug. 30, 2001. Xanana Gusmão, a former guerrilla leader, won the presidential election Apr. 14, 2002. As Timor-Leste, the territory became independent May 20 and entered the UN Sept. 27. Australia and other nations sent peacekeepers to suppress a wave of gang violence that engulfed Dili in May 2006.

José Ramos-Horta, a Nobel laureate, won a presidential run-off vote May 9, 2007. After inconclusive parliamentary elections June 30, Ramos-Horta ended a political deadlock by choosing Gusmão as prime min. The Gusmão-supported independent candidate Taur Matan Ruak won a runoff election to become president, May 20, 2012. Gusmão's party won a majority of seats in the parliamentary election, July 7, and he became prime min. of a coalition government, Aug. 8.

Togo
Togolese Republic

People: Population: 6,961,049. **Age distrib.:** <15: 40.8%; 65+: 3.2%. **Pop. density:** 331.5 per sq mi, 128 per sq km. **Urban:** 38%. **Ethnic groups:** African (37 tribes; Ewe, Mina, Kabre largest). **Principal languages:** French (official and lang. of commerce), Ewe and Mina (in S), Kabye and Dagomba (in N). **Chief religions:** indigenous beliefs 51%, Christian 29%, Muslim 20%.

Geography: Total area: 21,925 sq mi, 56,785 sq km; **Land area:** 20,998 sq mi, 54,385 sq km. **Location:** On S coast of W Africa. **Neighbors:** Ghana on W, Burkina Faso on N, Benin on E. **Topography:** A range of hills running SW-NE splits Togo into 2 savanna plains regions. **Capital:** Lomé, 1,523,930.

Government: Type: Republic. **Head of state:** Pres. Faure Gnassingbé; b. June 6, 1966; in office: May 4, 2005. **Head of gov.:** Prime Min. Gilbert Fossoun Houngbo; b. Feb. 4, 1961; in office: Sept. 8, 2008. **Local divisions:** 5 regions. **Defense budget:** $58 mil. **Active troops:** 8,550.

Economy: Industries: phosphate mining, agric. proc., cement, handicrafts, textiles, beverages. **Chief crops:** coffee, cocoa, cotton, yams, cassava, corn, beans, rice. **Natural resources:** phosphates, limestone, marble. **Arable land:** 40.4%. **Livestock:** cattle: 309,411; chickens: 21.7 mil; goats: 1.9 mil; pigs: 643,630; sheep: 2.1 mil. **Fish catch:** 27,635 metric tons. **Electricity prod.:** 123 mil kWh. **Labor force:** agric. 65%, industry 5%, services 30%.

Finance: Monetary unit: CFA BCEAO Franc (XOF) (Sept. 2012: 519.73 = $1 U.S.). **GDP:** $6.5 bil; **per capita GDP:** $900; **GDP growth:** 4.1%. **Imports:** $1.5 bil; China 35.5%, France 9.4%, Belgium 8.6%, U.S. 5.6%, UK 5.1%. **Exports:** $910.8 mil; China 11.3%, Burkina Faso 8.7%, Benin 8.6%, Niger 6.6%, Germany 6%, India 5.5%, Ghana 5%, Indonesia 4.9%. **Tourism:** $66 mil. **Budget:** $938.2 mil. **Total reserves less gold:** $774.3 mil. **CPI change:** 3.6%.

Transport: Railways: 353 mil. **Motor vehicles:** 24.2 vehicles per 1,000 pop. **Civil aviation:** 2 airports. **Chief ports:** Kpeme, Lomé. **Communications: TV sets:** 26 per 1,000 pop. **Radios:** 669 per 1,000 pop. **Telephone lines:** 3.9 per 100 pop. **Internet:** 3.5%.

Health: Life expect.: 60.6 male; 65.8 female. **Births:** 35.3 (per 1,000 pop.). **Deaths:** 7.8 (per 1,000 pop.). **Natural inc.:** 2.75%. **Infant mortality:** 49.9 (per 1,000 live births). **HIV rate:** 3.2%.

Education: Compulsory: ages 6-15. **Literacy:** 57.1%.

Major intl. organizations: UN (FAO, IBRD, ILO, IMF, WHO), AU, WTO.

Embassy: 2208 Massachusetts Ave. NW 20008; 234-4212.

Website: www.assemblee-nationale.tg or www.state.gov/p/af/ci/to/

Togoland was administered by Germany and then by France and Britain. The French sector became the republic of Togo Apr. 27, 1960. In office since 1967, Pres. Gnassingbé Eyadéma was Africa's longest-serving head of state until his death Feb. 5, 2005. His son, Faure Gnassingbé, was installed as president, but African leaders pressured Togo to hold an election, which Gnassingbé won Apr. 24. Opposition parties disputed the result, and protests led to violent clashes in Lomé.

After a shootout at his home Apr. 12, 2009, former Defense Min. Kpatcha Gnassingbé, the president's brother, sought refuge Apr. 15 at the U.S. embassy in Lomé; denied asylum, he was arrested by Togolese authorities and accused of plotting a coup. Pres. Gnassingbé won reelection Mar. 4, 2010, to a second 5-year term. Weeks of antigovernment protest led to the resignation of Prime Min. Gilbert Fossoun Houngbo, July 13, 2012, and a new government was formed under Prime Min. Kwesi Seleagodzi Ahoomey-Zunu. Legislative elections were expected to be held Oct. 2012.

Tonga
Kingdom of Tonga

People: Population: 106,146. **Age distrib.:** <15: 36.7%; 65+: 6.1%. **Pop. density:** 383.4 per sq mi, 148 per sq km. **Urban:** 23.4%. **Ethnic groups:** Polynesian, European. **Principal languages:** Tongan, English (both official). **Chief religion:** Christian (mostly Free Wesleyan Church).

Geography: Total area: 288 sq mi, 747 sq km; **Land area:** 277 sq mi, 717 sq km. **Location:** In western S Pacific O. **Neighbors:** Nearest are Fiji to W, Samoa to NE. **Topography:** Tonga comprises 170 volcanic and coral islands, 36 inhabited. **Capital:** Nuku'alofa, 24,500.

Government: Type: Constitutional monarchy. **Head of state:** King Tupou VI; b. July 12, 1959; in office: Mar. 18, 2012. **Head of gov.:** Prime Min. Tu'ivakano; b. Jan. 15, 1952; in office: Dec, 22, 2010. **Local divisions:** 3 island groups. **Defense budget/active troops:** NA.

Economy: Industries: tourism, constr., fishing. **Chief crops:** squash, coconuts, copra, bananas, vanilla beans, cocoa, coffee, ginger, black pepper. **Natural resources:** fish. **Arable land:** 22.2%. **Livestock:** cattle: 11,300; chickens: 330,000; goats: 12,600; pigs: 81,200. **Fish catch:** 2,151 metric tons. **Electricity prod.:** 41 mil kWh. **Labor force:** agric. 31.8%, industry 30.6%, services 37.6%.

Finance: Monetary unit: Pa'anga (TOP) (Sept. 2012: 1.77 = $1 U.S.). **GDP:** $772.8 mil; **per capita GDP:** $7,400; **GDP growth:** 1.5%. **Imports:** $139.6 mil; Fiji 35.4%, New Zealand 24%, U.S. 10.1%, China 7%. **Exports:** $8.4 mil; Hong Kong 19.9%, Japan 14.6%, U.S. 10.6%, South Korea 10.1%, Fiji 8.9%, New Zealand 8.6%, Samoa 7.5%, Brazil 5.3%, American Samoa 4.7%. **Tourism:** $31 mil. **Budget:** $117.6 mil. **Total reserves less gold:** $143.3 mil. **CPI change:** 6.6%.

Transport: Civil aviation: 11.8 mil pass.-mi; 1 airport. **Chief ports:** Neiafu, Nuku'alofa, Pangai.

Communications: TV sets: 49 per 1,000 pop. **Radios:** 662 per 1,000 pop. **Telephone lines:** 28.7 per 100 pop. **Internet:** 25%.

Health: Life expect.: 74.0 male; 76.8 female. **Births:** 24.7 (per 1,000 pop). **Deaths:** 4.9 (per 1,000 pop.). **Natural inc.:** 1.98%. **Infant mortality:** 13.2 (per 1,000 live births). **HIV rate:** NA.

Education: Compulsory: ages 6-14. **Literacy:** 99%.

Major intl. organizations: UN (FAO, IBRD, ILO, IMF, WHO), the Commonwealth, WTO.

Embassy: 250 E. 51st St., New York, NY 10022; (917) 369-1025.

Website: pmo.gov.to

The islands were first visited by the Dutch in the early 17th cent. A series of civil wars ended, 1845, with establishment of the Tupou dynasty. In 1900 Tonga became a British protectorate. On June 4, 1970, Tonga became independent and a member of the Commonwealth. It joined the UN on Sept. 14, 1999. George Tupou VI became king Mar. 18, 2012, following the death of his brother, George Tupou V, who had reigned since 2006. Tupou V introduced democratic reforms to Tonga, and elections, Nov. 2010, gave the country its first democratically elected parliament, which took the monarch's executive powers. The role of the monarch was reduced to that of an advisor.

Trinidad and Tobago
Republic of Trinidad and Tobago

People: Population: 1,226,383. **Age distrib.:** <15: 19.5%; 65+: 8.7%. **Pop. density:** 619.4 per sq mi, 239.2 per sq km. **Urban:** 13.7%. **Ethnic groups:** Indian (South Asian) 40%, African 38%, mixed 21%. **Principal languages:** English (official), Caribbean Hindustani, French, Spanish, Chinese. **Chief religions:** Roman Catholic 26%, Protestant 26% (Anglican 8%, Baptist 7%, Pentecostal 7%, Seventh-Day Adventist 4%), Hindu 23%, Muslim 6%, other Christian 6%, none 2%.

Geography: Total area: 1,980 sq mi, 5,128 sq km; **Land area:** 1,980 sq mi, 5,128 sq km. **Location:** In Caribbean, off E coast of Venezuela. **Neighbors:** Nearest is Venezuela to SW. **Topography:** Three low mountain ranges cross Trinidad E-W, with a well-watered plain between N and central ranges. Parts of E and W coasts are swamps. Tobago, 116 sq mi, lies 20 mi NE. **Capital:** Port of Spain, 65,839.

Government: Type: Parliamentary democracy. **Head of state:** Pres. George Maxwell Richards; b. Dec. 1, 1931; in office: Mar. 17, 2003. **Head of gov.:** Prime Min. Kamla Persad-Bissessar; b. Apr. 22, 1952; in office: May 26, 2010. **Local div.:** 8 counties, 3 municipalities, 1 ward. **Defense budget:** $172 mil. **Active troops:** 4,063.

Economy: Industries: petroleum and petroleum prods., liquefied nat. gas, methanol, ammonia, urea, steel prods., beverages, food proc. **Chief crops:** cocoa, rice, citrus, coffee, vegetables. **Natural resources:** petroleum, nat. gas, asphalt. **Crude oil reserves:** 728.3 mil bbls. **Arable land:** 4.9%. **Livestock:** cattle: 32,500; chickens: 32 mil; goats: 62,170; pigs: 48,000; sheep: 3,800. **Fish catch:** 13,944 metric tons. **Electricity prod.:** 7.3 bil kWh. **Labor force:** agric. 3.8%; mfg., mining, and quarrying 12.8%; constr. and utilities 20.4%; services 62.9%.

Finance: Monetary unit: Dollar (TTD) (Sept. 2012: 6.10 = $1 U.S.). **GDP:** $26.9 bil; **per capita GDP:** $20,300; **GDP growth:** –1.3%. **Imports:** $8.9 bil; U.S. 32.7%, Brazil 10.7%, Russia 6.2%, Gabon 5.7%, Canada 5.1%, China 4.2%. **Exports:** $14.6 bil; U.S. 43.7%, Spain 5.1%, South Korea 4.8%, Jamaica 4.7%. **Tourism:** $393 mil. **Budget:** $8.1 bil. **Total reserves less gold:** $10.4 bil. **Gold:** 61,740 oz t. **CPI change:** 5.1%.

Transport: Motor vehicles: 291.1 vehicles per 1,000 pop. **Civil aviation:** 1.9 bil pass.-mi; 2 airports. **Chief ports:** Point Lisas, Port of Spain, Scarborough.

Communications: TV sets: 355 per 1,000 pop. **Radios:** 535 per 1,000 pop. **Telephone lines:** 21.7 per 100 pop. **Daily newspaper circ.:** 149.1 per 1,000 pop. **Internet:** 55.2%.

Health: Life expect.: 68.8 male; 74.6 female. **Births:** 14.3 (per 1,000 pop.). **Deaths:** 8.4 (per 1,000 pop.). **Natural inc.:** 0.59%. **Infant mortality:** 26.7 (per 1,000 live births). **HIV rate:** 1.5%.

Education: Compulsory: ages 6-11. **Literacy:** 98.8%.

Major intl. organizations: UN (FAO, IBRD, ILO, IMF, WHO), Caricom, the Commonwealth, OAS, WTO.
Embassy: 1708 Massachusetts Ave. NW 20036; 467-6490.
Website: www.ttconnect.gov.tt

Columbus sighted Trinidad in 1498. A British possession since 1802, Trinidad and Tobago won independence Aug. 31, 1962. It became a republic in 1976.

The nation, among the most prosperous in the Caribbean, refines and exports Middle Eastern oil. Oil production increased after offshore finds.

In July 1990, some 120 Muslim extremists captured the Parliament building and TV station and took about 50 hostages, including Prime Min. Arthur N. R. Robinson, who was beaten, shot in the legs, and tied to explosives. After a 6-day siege, the rebels surrendered.

Basdeo Panday, in office 1995-2001, was the nation's first prime min. of East Indian ancestry. The country's first female prime min., Kamla Persad-Bissessar, leader of the People's Partnership coalition, took office May 26, 2010.

Tunisia
Tunisian Republic

People: Population: 10,732,900. **Age distrib.:** <15: 23.1%; 65+: 7.6%. **Pop. density:** 178.9 per sq mi, 69.1 per sq km. **Urban:** 66.3%. **Ethnic groups:** Arab 98%, European 1%, Jewish and other 1%. **Principal languages:** Arabic (official), French used in commerce. **Chief religions:** Muslim (official) 98%, Christian 1%, Jewish and other 1%.

Geography: Total area: 63,170 sq mi, 163,610 sq km; **Land area:** 59,985 sq mi, 155,360 sq km. **Location:** On N coast of Africa. **Neighbors:** Algeria on W, Libya on E. **Topography:** The N is wooded and fertile. The central coastal plains are given to grazing and orchards. The S is arid, approaching Sahara Desert. **Capital:** Tunis, 790,205.

Government: Type: In transition. **Head of state:** Moncef Marzouki; b. July 7, 1945; in office: Dec. 13, 2011 (interim). **Head of gov.:** Prime Min. Hamadi Jebali; b. Jan. 12, 1949; in office: Dec. 14, 2011. **Local divisions:** 24 governorates. **Defense budget:** NA. **Active troops:** 35,800.

Economy: Industries: petroleum, mining, tourism, textiles, footwear, agribusiness. **Chief crops:** olives, olive oil, grain, tomatoes, citrus fruits, sugar beets, dates, almonds. **Natural resources:** petroleum, phosphates, iron ore, lead, zinc, salt. **Crude oil reserves:** 425 mil bbls. **Arable land:** 17.4%. **Livestock:** cattle: 670,900; chickens: 80 mil; goats: 1.3 mil; pigs: 6,000; sheep: 7.2 mil. **Fish catch:** 103,187 metric tons. **Electricity prod.:** 14.8 bil kWh. **Labor force:** agric. 18.3%, industry 31.9%, services 49.8%.

Finance: Monetary unit: Dinar (TND) (Sept. 2012: 1.59 = $1 U.S.). **GDP:** $102.3 bil; **per capita GDP:** $9,600; **GDP growth:** –0.8%. **Imports:** $23.6 bil; France 21%, Italy 17.5%, Germany 8.8%, Spain 4.9%, China 4.7%, Russia 4.5%. **Exports:** $17.7 bil; France 29.4%, Italy 19.2%, Germany 10.3%, Libya 6.6%. **Tourism:** $1.8 bil. **Budget:** $12.8 bil. **Total reserves less gold** (2010): $9.5 bil. **Gold:** 217,000 oz t. **CPI change:** 3.6%.

Transport: Railways: 1,345 mi. **Motor vehicles:** 94.3 vehicles per 1,000 pop. **Civil aviation:** 2 bil pass.-mi; 15 airports. **Chief ports:** Bizerte, Gabes, Rades, Sfax, Skhira.

Communications: TV sets: 225 per 1,000 pop. **Radios:** 158 per 1,000 pop. **Telephone lines:** 11.5 per 100 pop. **Daily newspaper circ.:** 22.7 per 1,000 pop. **Internet:** 39.1%.

Health: Life expect.: 73.2 male; 77.4 female. **Births:** 17.3 (per 1,000 pop.). **Deaths:** 5.9 (per 1,000 pop.). **Natural inc.:** 1.14%. **Infant mortality:** 25.0 (per 1,000 live births). **HIV rate:** <0.1%.

Education: Compulsory: ages 6-16. **Literacy:** 77.6%.
Major intl. organizations: UN (FAO, IBRD, ILO, IMF, WHO), AL, AU, WTO.
Embassy: 1515 Massachusetts Ave. NW 20005; 862-1850.
Website: www.tunisie.gov.tn

Site of ancient Carthage and a former Barbary state under the suzerainty of Turkey, Tunisia became a protectorate of France, May 12, 1881. The nation became independent Mar. 20, 1956, and ended the monarchy the following year. Habib Bourguiba, an independence leader, served as president until 1987, when he was deposed by his prime min., Zine el-Abidine Ben Ali, who then won five presidential elections, 1989-2009, all tightly controlled.

"Arab Spring" protests, which began Dec. 2010 in the town of Sidi Bouzid, succeeded in ousting Ben Ali, Jan. 14, 2011, and Parliament Speaker Fouad Mebazaa became interim president. Subsequent protests also forced the removal of holdover Prime Min. Mohamed Ghannouchi. Elections for a constituent assembly were held Oct. 23, 2011, and the newly elected assembly appointed Moncef Marzouki of the secular center-left Congress for the Republic party as interim president. He took office, Dec. 13, 2011, but real power lies with Prime Min. Hamadi Jebali, an Islamist politician who leads the moderate Ennahda party, the winner of Oct. 23, 2011, elections. That government was expected to hold power until a constitution is ratified and elections held.

Turkey
Republic of Turkey

People: Population: 79,749,461. **Age distrib.:** <15: 26.2%; 65+: 6.4%. **Pop. density:** 268.4 per sq mi, 103.6 per sq km. **Urban:** 71.5%. **Ethnic groups:** Turkish 70%-75%, Kurdish 18%. **Principal languages:** Turkish (official), Kurdish, other minority languages. **Chief religion:** Muslim (mostly Sunni) 99.8%.

Geography: Total area: 302,535 sq mi, 783,562 sq km; **Land area:** 297,157 sq mi, 769,632 sq km. **Location:** Occupies Asia Minor, stretches into continental Europe; borders on Medit. and Black seas. **Neighbors:** Bulgaria, Greece on W; Georgia, Armenia on N; Iran on E; Iraq, Syria on S. **Topography:** Central Turkey has wide plateaus, with hot, dry summers and cold winters. High mountains ring the interior on all but W, with more than 20 peaks over 10,000 ft. Rolling plains are in W; mild, fertile coastal plains are in S, W. **Capital:** Ankara, 4,193,850. **Cities (urban aggl.):** Istanbul, 11,253,297; Izmir, 2,927,468; Bursa, 1,712,985; Adana, 1,467,504; Gaziantep, 1,197,537; Konya, 1,056,582.

Government: Type: Republic. **Head of state:** Pres. Abdullah Gül; b. Oct. 29, 1950; in office: Aug. 28, 2007. **Head of gov.:** Prime Min. Recep Tayyip Erdogan; b. Feb. 26, 1954; in office: Mar. 14, 2003. **Local divisions:** 81 provinces. **Defense budget:** $10.3 bil. **Active troops:** 510,600.

Economy: Industries: textiles, food proc., autos, electronics, mining, steel, petroleum, constr., lumber, paper. **Chief crops:** tobacco, cotton, grain, olives, sugar beets, hazelnuts, pulse, citrus. **Natural resources:** coal, iron ore, copper, chromium, antimony, mercury, gold, barite, borate, strontium, emery, feldspar, limestone, magnesite. **Crude oil reserves:** 270.4 mil bbls. **Arable land:** 27.7%. **Livestock:** cattle: 10.7 mil; chickens: 230 mil; goats: 5.1 mil; pigs: 1,896; sheep: 21.8 mil. **Fish catch:** 653,660 metric tons. **Electricity prod.** (2010): 201.2 bil kWh. **Labor force:** agric. 25.5%, industry 26.2%, services 48.4%.

Finance: Monetary unit: Lira (TRY) (Sept. 2012: 1.82 = $1 U.S.). **GDP:** $1.1 tril; **per capita GDP:** $14,700; **GDP growth:** 8.5%. **Imports:** $232.9 bil; Russia 9.9%, Germany 9.5%, China 9%, U.S. 6.7%, Italy 5.6%, Iran 5.2%. **Exports:** $143.5 bil; Germany 10.3%, Iraq 6.2%, UK 6%, Italy 5.8%, France 5%, Russia 4.4%. **Tourism:** $23 bil. **Budget:** $187.1 bil. **Total reserves less gold:** $78.3 bil. **Gold:** 6.3 mil oz t. **CPI change:** 6.5%.

Transport: Railways: 5,405 mi. **Motor vehicles:** 138.2 vehicles per 1,000 pop. **Civil aviation:** 30.8 bil pass.-mi; 89 airports. **Chief ports:** Aliaga, Diliskelesi, Eregli, Izmir, Izmit.

Communications: TV sets: 428 per 1,000 pop. **Radios:** 283 per 1,000 pop. **Telephone lines:** 20.7 per 100 pop. **Internet:** 42.1%.

Health: Life expect.: 70.9 male; 74.8 female. **Births:** 17.6 (per 1,000 pop.). **Deaths:** 6.1 (per 1,000 pop.). **Natural inc.:** 1.15%. **Infant mortality:** 23.1 (per 1,000 live births). **HIV rate:** <0.1%.

Education: Compulsory: ages 6-14. **Literacy:** 90.8%.
Major intl. organizations: UN (FAO, IBRD, ILO, IMF, WHO), NATO, OECD, OSCE, WTO.
Embassy: 2525 Massachusetts Ave. NW 20008; 612-6700.
Website: www.tccb.gov.tr

Ancient inhabitants of Turkey were among the world's first agriculturalists. Such civilizations as the Hittite, Phrygian, and Lydian flourished in Asiatic Turkey (Asia Minor), as did much of Greek civilization. After the fall of Rome in the 5th cent., Constantinople (now Istanbul) was the capital of the Byzantine Empire for 1,000 years. It fell in 1453 to Ottoman Turks, who ruled a vast empire for over 400 years.

Just before WWI, Turkey, or the Ottoman Empire, ruled what is now Syria, Lebanon, Iraq, Jordan, Israel, Saudi Arabia, Yemen, and islands in the Aegean Sea. Turkey joined Germany and Austria in WWI, and its defeat resulted in the loss of territory and the fall of the sultanate. A secular republic was established Oct. 29, 1923. The first pres., Mustafa Kemal (later Kemal Ataturk), led Turkey until his death in 1938.

Turkey kept neutral during most of WWII. The country became a full member of NATO in 1952 and remained a Western ally despite domestic political instability. Military coups overthrew civilian governments in 1960 and 1980. Turkey invaded nearby Cyprus July 20, 1974, to prevent that country from uniting with Greece, and Cyprus was divided into Greek and Turkish zones.

In recent decades, Turkish governments have contended with Kurdish separatism and Islamic militants. Turkey was a member of the U.S.-led force that ousted Iraq from Kuwait, 1991. Millions of Kurdish refugees fled to Turkey's border after the war. Turkish offensives against the Kurds caused heavy casualties among guerrillas and civilians. Kurdish militants raided Turkish diplomatic missions in some 25 Western European cities, June 24, 1993.

Tansu Ciller became Turkey's first woman prime min. July 5, 1993. The Islamic Welfare Party gained strength in the 1990s but was unable to form a government until June 1996, when a coalition with Ciller's True Path Party was formed. The pro-Islamic government resigned June 18, 1997, under pressure from the military, which stepped up its campaign against Islamic fundamentalism in 1998.

Kurdish rebel leader Abdullah Öcalan was captured Feb. 15, 1999; convicted of terrorism June 29, he was sentenced to death by a Turkish security court. His organization, the Kurdistan Workers' Party, announced Aug. 5, 1999, that it would abandon its 14-year-old insurgency.

Earthquakes in Apr. and Nov. 1999 killed over 17,000 people. The IMF announced $7.5 bil in emergency loans Dec. 6, 2000, to help Turkey cope with a severe financial crisis. The death penalty was abolished Aug. 3, 2002, and Öcalan's sentence was commuted to life in prison Oct. 3. The Islamic Justice and Development Party (AKP) led by Recep Tayyip Erdogan won elections Nov. 3.

During the U.S.-led invasion of Iraq, Mar.-Apr. 2003, Turkey refused to allow coalition forces to launch attacks on N Iraq from Turkish soil. Suicide bombings by Islamic extremists, Nov. 15-20, 2003, killed 58 people and wounded more than 750 in Istanbul.

Erdogan's party scored a landslide win in national elections, July 22, 2007. Parliament, Aug. 28, chose an Islamic politician, Abdullah Gül, as president. An effort by secularists to ban the ruling AKP failed by one vote in Turkey's Constitutional Court, July 30, 2008, but the justices cut the party's public funding in half and warned it to restrain Islamic influence on state institutions. Turkish voters, Sept. 12, 2010, gave resounding approval to constitutional changes favored by the Islamic government, including a provision that would expand membership of the Constitutional Court.

The AKP gained a third consecutive general election victory June 12, 2011, amid its government's ongoing struggle with the military. Dozens of military officers, including some retired generals, were detained for allegedly plotting to seize power; after the nation's four top military commanders resigned en masse, July 29, 2011. Pres Gül appointed their replacements Aug. 4, breaking with a tradition that had allowed the military to promote its own leaders.

Turkey has long sought to become a full member of the European Union, but the EU has deferred talks on accession until economic, human rights, and immigration issues are resolved. As Turkey has strengthened its ties with Islamic countries, relations with Israel, a former ally, have soured.

Throughout the 2011-12 Syrian crisis, Turkey became a haven for refugees, the Syrian Free Army, and the opposition group the Syrian National Council. Despite opposing intervention from Western countries early in the conflict, Turkey had begun exploring the idea of establishing a no-fly zone over Syria with U.S. Sec. of State Hillary Clinton, during her Aug. 11, 2012, visit to Istanbul.

Turkmenistan

People: Population: 5,054,828. **Age distrib.:** <15: 27.1%; 65+: 4.1%. **Pop. density:** 27.9 per sq mi, 10.8 per sq km. **Urban:** 48.7%. **Ethnic groups:** Turkmen 85%, Uzbek 5%, Russian 4%. **Principal languages:** Turkmen (official), Russian, Uzbek. **Chief religions:** Muslim 89%, Eastern Orthodox 9%.

Geography: Total area: 188,456 sq mi, 488,100 sq km; **Land area:** 181,441 sq mi, 469,930 sq km. **Location:** Central Asia bordering Caspian Sea. **Neighbors:** Kazakhstan on N; Uzbekistan on N and E; Afghanistan, Iran on S. **Topography:** The Kara Kum Desert occupies 80% of the area. Bordered on W by Caspian Sea. **Capital:** Ashgabat, 683,260.

Government: Type: Republic with authoritarian rule. **Head of state and gov.:** Pres. Gurbanguly Berdymukhammedov; b. June 29, 1957; in office: Feb. 14, 2007 (acting from Dec. 21, 2006). **Local divisions:** 5 regions. **Defense budget** (2010): $198 mil. **Active troops:** 22,000.

Economy: Industries: nat. gas, oil, petroleum prods., textiles, food proc. **Chief crops:** cotton, grain. **Natural resources:** petroleum, nat. gas, sulfur, salt. **Crude oil reserves:** 600 mil bbls. **Arable land:** 3.9%. **Livestock:** cattle: 2.2 mil; chickens: 15 mil; goats: 2.8 mil; pigs: 30,000; sheep: 13.5 mil. **Fish catch:** 15,017 metric tons. **Electricity prod.:** 15 bil kWh. **Labor force:** agric. 48.2%, industry 14%, services 37.8%.

Finance: Monetary unit: Manat (TMT) (Sept. 2012: 2.85 = $1 U.S.). **GDP:** $43.9 bil; **per capita GDP:** $7,900; **GDP growth:** 14.7%. **Imports:** $9.6 bil; Turkey 21.1%, Russia 14.1%, China 11.1%, UAE 8%, Germany 5.8%. **Exports:** $14.8 bil; China 59%, Turkey 4.9%, Italy 4.6%, UAE 4.3%. **Tourism:** NA. **Budget:** $4.1 bil.

Transport: Railways: 1,852 mi. **Civil aviation:** 1.2 bil pass.-mi; 21 airports. **Chief port:** Turkmenbasy.

Communications: TV sets: 190 per 1,000 pop. **Radios:** 155 per 1,000 pop. **Telephone lines:** 10.7 per 100 pop. **Daily newspaper circ.:** 9.4 per 1,000 pop. **Internet:** 5%.

Health: Life expect.: 65.9 male; 72.0 female. **Births:** 19.6 (per 1,000 pop.). **Deaths:** 6.2 (per 1,000 pop.). **Natural inc.:** 1.33%. **Infant mortality:** 40.9 (per 1,000 live births). **HIV rate:** NA.

Education: Compulsory: ages 7-15. **Literacy:** 99.6%.

Major intl. organizations: UN (FAO, IBRD, ILO, IMF, WHO), CIS, OSCE.

Embassy: 2207 Massachusetts Ave. NW 20008; 588-1500.

Website: www.turkmenistan.gov.tm

The region has been inhabited by Turkic tribes since the 10th cent. It became part of Russian Turkestan in 1881, and a constituent republic of the USSR in 1925. Turkmenistan declared independence Oct. 27, 1991, and became an independent state when the USSR disbanded Dec. 26, 1991.

Extensive oil and gas reserves place Turkmenistan in a favorable economic position. Political power centered around the former Communist Party apparatus, and authoritarian Pres. Saparmurad Niyazov (also known as Turkmenbashi) became the object of a personality cult. Niyazov died Dec. 21, 2006, and was succeeded by Gurbanguly Berdymukhammedov; he won the presidential election of Feb. 11, 2007, considered neither free nor fair by international observers. In a gesture toward democracy not likely to threaten Berdymukhamedov's grip on power, the country's one party system officially ended Aug. 21, 2012, permitting a second political party,

the Party of Industrialists and Entrepreneurs of Turkmenistan, to be founded.

Tuvalu

People: Population: 10,619. **Age distrib.:** <15: 30.2%; 65+: 5.3%. **Pop. density:** 1,057.8 per sq mi, 408.4 per sq km. **Urban:** 50.6%. **Ethnic group:** Polynesian 96%, Micronesian 4%. **Principal languages:** Tuvaluan, English (both official); Samoan; Kiribati. **Chief religions:** Protestant 98% (Church of Tuvalu [Congregationalist] 97%, Seventh-Day Adventist 1%), Baha'i 1%.

Geography: Total area: 10 sq mi, 26 sq km; **Land area:** 10 sq mi, 26 sq km. **Location:** 9 islands forming NW-SE chain 360 mi long in SW Pacific O. **Neighbors:** Nearest are Kiribati to N, Fiji to S. **Topography:** The islands are all low-lying atolls, nowhere rising more than 15 ft above sea level, composed of coral reefs. **Capital:** Funafuti, 4,979.

Government: Type: Constitutional monarchy, with a parliamentary democracy. **Head of state:** Queen Elizabeth II, represented by Gov.-Gen. Sir Iakoba Italeli; b. 1936; in office: Apr. 16, 2010. **Head of gov.:** Prime Min. Willy Telavi; b. July 7, 1958; in office: Dec. 24, 2010. **Defense budget:** NA. **Active troops:** No regular military forces.

Economy: Industries: fishing, tourism, copra. **Chief crops:** coconuts. **Natural resources:** fish. **Arable land:** none. **Livestock:** chickens: 45,000; pigs: 13,600. **Fish catch:** 11,324 metric tons. **Labor force:** Pop. makes living mainly through exploitation of the sea, reefs, and atolls and from wages sent home by those abroad (mostly phosphate industry workers and sailors).

Finance: Monetary unit: Dollar (TVD) (Sept. 2012: 0.98 = $1 U.S.). **GDP:** $37.5 mil; **per capita GDP** (2010 est.): $3,400; **GDP growth:** 0.4%. **Imports** (2005): $12.9 mil. **Exports** (2004): $1 mil. **Tourism:** NA. **Budget** (2006): $23.1 mil.

Transport: Civil aviation: 1 airport (unpaved runway). **Chief port:** Funafuti.

Communications: TV sets: 9 per 1,000 pop. **Telephone lines:** 14.7 per 100 pop. **Internet:** 30%.

Health: Life expect.: 63.0 male; 67.3 female. **Births:** 23.4 (per 1,000 pop.). **Deaths:** 9.1 (per 1,000 pop.). **Natural inc.:** 1.42%. **Infant mortality:** 33.6 (per 1,000 live births). **HIV rate:** NA.

Education: Compulsory: ages 7-14. **Literacy:** NA.

Major intl. organizations: UN (FAO, ILO, WHO), the Commonwealth.

Permanent UN Mission: 800 Second Ave., Ste. 400D, New York, NY 10017; (212) 490-0534.

Website: www.timelesstuvalu.com

The Ellice Islands separated from the British Gilbert and Ellice Islands Colony in 1975 and became Tuvalu; independence came Oct. 1, 1978. In 2000, Tuvalu joined the United Nations. A major drought since Nov. 2010 obliged the government to declare a state of emergency Sept. 28, 2011. Rising sea levels due to climate change are threatening to submerge the tiny island nation.

Uganda
Republic of Uganda

People: Population: 33,640,833. **Age distrib.:** <15: 49.1%; 65+: 2.1%. **Pop. density:** 442.1 per sq mi, 170.7 per sq km. **Urban:** 15.6%. **Ethnic groups:** Baganda 17%, Banyakole 10%, Basoga 8%, Bakiga 7%, Iteso 6%, Langi 6%, Acholi 5%, Bagisu 5%, Lugbara 4%, Bunyoro 3%. **Principal languages:** English (official), Ganda or Luganda and other Niger-Congo langs., Nilo-Saharan langs., Swahili, Arabic. **Chief religions:** Roman Catholic 42%, Protestant 42% (Anglican 36%, Pentecostal 5%, Seventh-Day Adventist 2%), Muslim 12%.

Geography: Total area: 93,065 sq mi, 241,038 sq km; **Land area:** 76,101 sq mi, 197,100 sq km. **Location:** In E Central Africa. **Neighbors:** Sudan on N, Congo (formerly Zaire) on W, Rwanda and Tanzania on S, Kenya on E. **Topography:** Most of Uganda is a high plateau 3,000-6,000 ft high, with high Ruwenzori range in W (Mt. Margherita 16,763 ft), volcanoes in SW; NE is arid, W and SW rainy. Lakes Victoria, Edward, Albert form much of borders. **Capital:** Kampala, 1,659,480.

Government: Type: Republic. **Head of state and gov.:** Pres. Yoweri Kaguta Museveni; b. Aug. 15, 1944; in office: Jan. 29, 1986. **Local divisions:** 56 districts. **Defense budget:** $189 mil. **Active troops:** 45,000.

Economy: Industries: sugar, brewing, tobacco, cotton textiles, cement, steel prod. **Chief crops:** coffee, tea, cotton, tobacco, cassava, potatoes, corn, millet, pulses, cut flowers. **Natural resources:** copper, cobalt, hydropower, limestone, salt, gold. **Crude oil reserves:** 1 bil bbls. **Livestock:** cattle: 7.7 mil; chickens: 34.7 mil; goats: 9 mil; pigs: 2.3 mil; sheep: 1.8 mil. **Fish catch:** 508,805 metric tons. **Electricity prod.:** 2.4 bil kWh. **Labor force:** agric. 82%, industry 5%, services 13%.

Finance: Monetary unit: Shilling (UGX) (Sept. 2012: 2,518.04 = $1 U.S.). **GDP:** $47 bil; **per capita GDP:** $1,300; **GDP growth:** 6.7%. **Imports:** $5.1 bil; Kenya 15.3%, UAE 14.4%, India 9.5%, China 9.5%, South Africa 5.6%, Japan 4.5%. **Exports:** $2.6 bil; Sudan 15%, Kenya 10%, Rwanda 8.3%, UAE 7.8%, Dem. Rep. of the Congo 7.6%, Netherlands 6%, Germany 5.7%. **Tourism:** $784 mil. **Budget:** $3.4 bil. **Total reserves less gold:** $2.6 bil. **CPI change:** 18.7%.

Transport: Railways: 773 mi. **Motor vehicles:** 3.2 vehicles per 1,000 pop. **Civil aviation:** 213.8 mil pass.-mi; 5 airports. **Chief ports:** Entebbe, Jinja, Port Bell.

Communications: TV sets: 22 per 1,000 pop. **Radios:** 888 per 1,000 pop. **Telephone lines:** 1.4 per 100 pop. **Internet:** 13%.

Health: Life expect.: 52.2 male; 54.8 female. **Births:** 45.8 (per 1,000 pop.). **Deaths:** 11.6 (per 1,000 pop.). **Natural inc.:** 3.42%. **Infant mortality:** 64.2 (per 1,000 live births). **HIV rate:** 6.5%.

Education: Compulsory: ages 6-12. **Literacy:** 73.2%.

Major intl. organizations: UN (FAO, IBRD, ILO, IMF, WHO), AU, the Commonwealth, WTO.

Embassy: 5911 16th St. NW 20011; 726-7100.

Website: www.statehouse.go.ug

Britain obtained a protectorate over Uganda in 1894. The country became independent Oct. 9, 1962, and a republic within the Commonwealth a year later. In 1967, the traditional kingdoms, including the powerful Buganda state, were abolished.

Gen. Idi Amin seized power from Prime Min. Milton Obote in 1971. During his 8-year dictatorship, he was responsible for the deaths of up to 300,000 of his opponents. In 1972 he expelled nearly all of Uganda's 45,000 Asians. Tanzanian troops and Ugandan exiles and rebels ousted Amin, Apr. 11, 1979.

Obote held the presidency from Dec. 1980 until his ouster in a military coup July 27, 1985. Guerrilla war and rampant human rights abuses plagued Uganda under Obote's regime.

Conditions improved after Yoweri Museveni took power in Jan. 1986. In 1993 the Buganda and other traditional monarchies were restored for ceremonial purposes. Uganda helped Laurent Kabila seize power in the Dem. Rep. of the Congo (formerly Zaire) in 1997 but sent troops in 1998 to aid insurgents seeking his ouster. A withdrawal accord was signed Sept. 6, 2002.

Pres. Museveni won reelection Mar. 12, 2001, and Feb. 23, 2006; opponents disputed the latter result, citing allegedly trumped-up charges of treason, terrorism, and rape lodged against Museveni's main rival, Kizza Besigye. Museveni again defeated Besigye in a presidential election Feb. 18, 2011, described as flawed by European observers.

An insurgency in N Uganda has killed more than 100,000 people and forced about 2 mil to flee. The Lord's Resistance Army (LRA), a rebel group, has fought the Museveni govt. since 1986 and has abducted some 30,000 children to serve as soldiers and sex slaves. Peace talks brokered by Sudan began July 2006; as talks continued through 2007, the violence diminished. A cease-fire accord was signed Feb. 23, 2008, but Ugandan and Congolese troops (with aid from the U.S.) launched a new offensive against the LRA in late 2008. Suicide bombings July 11, 2010, killed 76 people as they watched a World Cup soccer match on outdoor video screens in Kampala. Rising food and fuel prices spurred protests in 2011 against Museveni's regime. Al-Shabaab, a Somali al-Qaeda-linked Islamist group, claimed responsibility.

An online campaign to capture the LRA's leader, Joseph Kony, was boosted by the film *Kony 2012*, which went viral, gaining over 100 mil views by Mar. 2012; Kony remains at large.

Ukraine

People: Population: 44,854,065. **Age distrib.:** <15: 13.8%; 65+: 15.5%. **Pop. density:** 200.5 per sq mi, 77.4 per sq km. **Urban:** 68.9%. **Ethnic groups:** Ukrainian 78%, Russian 17%. **Principal languages:** Ukrainian (official), Russian. **Chief religions:** Ukrainian Orthodox (Kiev patriarchate) 50%, Ukrainian Orthodox (Moscow patriarchate) 26%, Ukrainian Greek Catholic 8%, Ukrainian Autocephalous Orthodox 7%, Roman Catholic 2%, Protestant 2%.

Geography: Total area: 233,032 sq mi, 603,550 sq km; **Land area:** 223,681 sq mi, 579,330 sq km. **Location:** In E Europe. **Neighbors:** Belarus on N; Russia on NE and E; Moldova and Romania on SW; Hungary, Slovakia, and Poland on W. **Topography:** Part of the E European plain. Mountainous areas include the Carpathians in the SW and Crimean chain in the S. Arable black soil constitutes a large part of the country. **Capital:** Kiev, 2,829,300. **Cities (urban aggl.):** Kharkiv, 1,450,522; Odesa, 1,009,979.

Government: Type: Republic. **Head of state:** Pres. Viktor Yanukovych; b. July 9, 1950; in office: Feb. 25, 2010. **Head of gov.:** Prime Min. Mykola Azarov; b. Dec. 17, 1947; in office: Mar. 11, 2010. **Local divisions:** 24 oblasts, 2 municipalities, 1 autonomous republic. **Defense budget:** $1.1 bil. **Active troops:** 129,925.

Economy: Industries: coal, elec. power, metals, machinery and transp. equip., chemicals, food proc. **Chief crops:** grain, sugar beets, sunflower seeds, vegetables. **Natural resources:** iron ore, coal, manganese, nat. gas, petroleum, salt, sulfur, graphite, titanium, magnesium, kaolin, nickel, mercury, timber. **Crude oil reserves:** 395 mil bbls. **Arable land:** 56.1%. **Livestock:** cattle: 4.8 mil; chickens: 172.6 mil; goats: 635,500; pigs: 7.6 mil; sheep: 1.2 mil. **Fish catch:** 209,128 metric tons. **Electricity prod.:** 164.5 bil kWh. **Labor force:** agric. 15.8%, industry 18.5%, services 65.7%.

Finance: Monetary unit: Hryvna (UAH) (Sept. 2012: 8.10 = $1 U.S.). **GDP:** $333.7 bil; **per capita GDP:** $7,300; **GDP growth:** 5.2%. **Imports:** $83.2 bil; Russia 30.8%, Germany 9.1%, China 8.9%, Poland 5.3%, Belarus 5%. **Exports:** $69.4 bil; Russia 27.3%, Turkey 5.9%, Italy 4.7%. **Tourism:** $4.3 bil. **Budget:** $56.4 bil (planned and consolidated). **Total reserves less gold:** $30.4 bil. **Gold:** 901,000 oz t. **CPI change:** 7.96%.

Transport: Railways: 13,474 mi. **Motor vehicles:** 201.8 vehicles per 1,000 pop. **Civil aviation:** 3.7 bil pass.-mi; 179 airports. **Chief ports:** Feodosiya, Illichivsk, Mariupol, Mykolayiv, Odesa, Yuzhnyy.

Communications: TV sets: 433 per 1,000 pop. **Radios:** 283 per 1,000 pop. **Telephone lines:** 28.1 per 100 pop. **Daily newspaper circ.:** 131 per 1,000 pop. **Internet:** 30.6%.

Health: Life expect.: 63.1 male; 74.8 female. **Births:** 9.6 (per 1,000 pop.). **Deaths:** 15.8 (per 1,000 pop.). **Natural inc.:** −0.62%. **Infant mortality:** 8.4 (per 1,000 live births). **HIV rate:** 1.1%.

Education: Compulsory: ages 6-17. **Literacy:** 99.7%.

Major intl. organizations: UN (FAO, IBRD, ILO, IMF, WHO), CIS, OSCE, WTO.

Embassy: 3350 M St. NW 20007; 333-0606.

Website: www.kmu.gov.ua

Ukrainians' Slavic ancestors inhabited the region well before the 1st cent. CE. In the 9th cent., the princes of Kiev established a strong state called Kievan Rus, which included much of present-day Ukraine. Internal conflicts led to the disintegration of the Ukrainian state by the 13th cent. Mongol rule was supplanted by Poland and Lithuania in the 14th and 15th cent. The N Black Sea coast and Crimea came under Turkish control in 1478. Ukrainian Cossacks, starting in the late 16th cent., rebelled against the occupiers of Ukraine: Russia, Poland, and Turkey.

An independent Ukrainian National Republic was proclaimed on Jan. 22, 1918. But in 1921, Ukraine's neighbors occupied and divided Ukrainian territory. In 1922, Ukraine became a constituent republic of the USSR. In 1932-33, the Soviet government engineered a famine in eastern Ukraine, and 6-7 mil Ukrainians died. During WWII the Ukrainian nationalist underground fought Nazi and Soviet forces. Over 5 mil Ukrainians died in the war. The reoccupation of Ukraine by Soviet troops in 1944 brought a renewed wave of repression.

The world's worst nuclear power plant disaster occurred in Chernobyl, Ukraine, in Apr. 1986; many thousands were killed or disabled as a result of the radiation leak. The plant was shut down Dec. 15, 2000.

Ukrainian independence was restored, Dec. 1991, with the Soviet Union's dissolution. In the post-Soviet period Ukraine's economy deteriorated. Following a 1994 accord with Russia and the U.S., Ukraine's large nuclear arsenal was transferred to Russia for destruction.

President since 1994, Leonid Kuchma attempted to engineer the election in 2004 of his handpicked successor, Prime Min. Viktor Yanukovych, also favored by Russia. The main challenger, Viktor Yushchenko, a former prime min., was poisoned in Sept. with dioxin, but continued to campaign. Official results of a runoff vote Nov. 21 showed a win for Yanukovych. Yushchenko supporters, calling the election fraudulent, staged massive protests (the "orange revolution"), and the vote was annulled. An election rerun Dec. 26 gave the victory to Yushchenko.

Yushchenko's Our Ukraine party fared poorly in parliamentary elections Mar. 26, 2006, and the resurgent Yanukovych returned as prime min. Aug. 4. The two rivals then engaged in a year-long political struggle.

Following elections Sept. 30, 2007, Yulia Tymoshenko, a former Orange Revolution ally of Yushchenko, became prime min. Dec. 18. Yanukovych defeated Tymoshenko in a presidential runoff election Feb. 7, 2010. The installation of a pro-Russian government in Ukraine led to a rapid improvement in relations with Moscow. In what her supporters and some international observers viewed as a politically motivated prosecution, former Prime Min. Tymoshenko went on trial June 24, 2011, for abusing her powers as prime min. She was convicted and sentenced to seven years in jail Oct. 11, 2011, and faces tax-evasion and embezzlement charges. In protest, the EU halted agreements with the Ukraine. Ignoring international pressure to do so, Yanukovych has refused to secure Tymoshenko's release.

United Arab Emirates

People: Population: 5,314,317. **Age distrib.:** <15: 20.5%; 65+: 0.9%. **Pop. density:** 164.6 per sq mi, 63.6 per sq km. **Urban:** 84.4%. **Ethnic groups:** Emirati 19%, other Arab and Iranian 23%, South Asian 50%, other expatriates (incl. Westerners and E Asians) 8%. (Less than 20% are UAE citizens.) **Principal languages:** Arabic (official), Persian, English, Hindi, Urdu. **Chief religions:** Muslim (official) 96% (Shia 16%), other (incl. Christian, Hindu) 4%.

Geography: Total area: 32,278 sq mi, 83,600 sq km; **Land area:** 32,278 sq mi, 83,600 sq km. **Location:** Middle East, on S shore of the Persian Gulf. **Neighbors:** Saudi Arabia on W and S, Oman on E. **Topography:** A barren, flat coastal plain gives way to uninhabited sand dunes on S. Hajar Mts. on E. **Capital:** Abu Dhabi, 942,193. **Cities (urban aggl.):** Dubai, 1,978,377.

Government: Type: Federation of emirates. **Head of state:** Pres. Sheikh Khalifa ibn Zaid an-Nahayan; b. 1948; in office: Nov. 3, 2004. **Head of gov.:** Prime Min. Sheikh Muhammad ibn Rashid al-Maktum; b. 1949; in office: Jan. 5, 2006. **Local divisions:** 7 autonomous emirates: Abu Dhabi, Ajman, Dubai, Fujaira, Ras al-Khaimah, Sharjah, Umm al-Qaiwain. **Defense budget:** $9.32 bil. **Active troops:** 51,000.

Economy: Industries: petroleum and petrochemicals, fishing, aluminum, cement, fertilizers, commercial ship repair, constr.

materials. **Chief crops:** dates, vegetables, watermelons. **Natural resources:** petroleum, nat. gas. **Crude oil reserves:** 97.8 bil bbls. **Arable land:** 0.8%. **Livestock:** cattle: 68,500; chickens: 18 mil; goats: 1.9 mil; sheep: 1.3 mil. **Fish catch:** 79,610 metric tons. **Electricity prod.** (2010): 83.3 bil kWh. **Labor force:** agric. 7%, industry 15%, services 78%.

Finance: Monetary unit: Dirham (AED) (Sept. 2012: 3.67 = $1 U.S.). **GDP:** $262.1 bil; **per capita GDP:** $48,800; **GDP growth:** 4.9%. **Imports:** $185.6 bil; India 19.8%, China 13.9%, U.S. 8.2%, Germany 4.6%. **Exports:** $252.6 bil; Japan 16.1%, India 14%, Iran 10.9%, South Korea 5.5%, Thailand 5.4%, Singapore 4.4%. **Tourism:** $9.2 bil. **Budget:** $95.5 bil. **Total reserves less gold:** $37.3 bil.

Transport: Motor vehicles: 86.6 vehicles per 1,000 pop. **Civil aviation:** 89.4 bil pass.-mi; 25 airports. **Chief ports:** Al Fujayrah, Khawr Fakkan, Mina' Jabal Ali, Mina' Rashid, Mina' Saqr. **Communications: TV sets:** 197 per 1,000 pop. **Radios:** 1,455 per 1,000 pop. **Telephone lines:** 23.1 per 100 pop. **Internet:** 70%. **Health: Life expect.:** 74.1 male; 79.4 female. **Births:** 15.8 (per 1,000 pop.). **Deaths:** 2.0 (per 1,000 pop.). **Natural inc.:** 1.37%. **Infant mortality:** 11.6 (per 1,000 live births). **HIV rate:** NA. **Education:** Compulsory: ages 6-14. **Literacy:** 90%. **Major intl. organizations:** UN (FAO, IBRD, ILO, IMF, WHO), AL, OPEC, WTO. **Embassy:** 3522 International Ct. NW, Ste. 400, 20008; 243-2400. **Website:** www.government.ae

The 7 "Trucial Sheikdoms" gave Britain control of defense and foreign relations in the 19th cent. They merged to become an independent state Dec. 2, 1971. Oil revenues have made the UAE one of the world's wealthiest countries. Foreigners make up more than 80% of the population and nearly all the private work force.

International banking, investment, and construction boomed during the late 1990s and early 2000s; holdings of Abu Dhabi's largest government-sponsored investment fund were estimated at $550 bil in Oct. 2008. But the global recession grounded Dubai's high-flying economy. On Mar. 25, 2010, Dubai's government was forced to extend up to $9.5 bil in loans to help its state-controlled investment company, Dubai World, avoid default.

United Kingdom
United Kingdom of Great Britain and Northern Ireland

People: Population: 63,047,162. **Age distrib.:** <15: 17.3%; 65+: 16.9%. **Pop. density:** 675 per sq mi, 260.6 per sq km. **Urban:** 79.6%. **Ethnic groups:** white 92% (English 84%, Scottish 9%, Welsh 5%, N Irish 3%), black 2%, Indian 2%, Pakistani 1%, mixed 1%. **Principal languages:** English; Scots, Scottish Gaelic, Welsh, Irish, Cornish (all recognized regional langs.). **Chief religions:** Christian 72%, Muslim 3%.

Geography: Total area: 94,058 sq mi, 243,610 sq km; **Land area:** 93,410 sq mi, 241,930 sq km. **Location:** Off NW coast of Europe, across English Channel, Strait of Dover, North Sea. **Neighbors:** Ireland to W, France to SE. **Topography:** England is mostly rolling land, rising to Uplands of southern Scotland. Lowlands are in center of Scotland, granite Highlands are in N. Coast is heavily indented, especially on W. British Isles have milder climate than N Europe due to Gulf Stream and ample rainfall. Severn, 220 mi, and Thames, 215 mi, are longest rivers. **Capital:** London, 9,005,300. **Cities (urban aggl.):** Birmingham, 2,271,900; Manchester, 2,212,558; West Yorkshire, 1,624,543; Glasgow, 1,137,321.

Government: Type: Constitutional monarchy. **Head of state:** Queen Elizabeth II; b. Apr. 21, 1926; in office: Feb. 6, 1952. **Head of gov.:** Prime Min. David Cameron; b. Oct. 9, 1966; in office: May 11, 2010. **Local divisions:** 467 local authorities, including England 387; Wales: 22; Scotland: 32; Northern Ireland: 26. **Defense budget:** $63.7 bil. **Active troops:** 174,030.

Economy: Industries: machine tools, elec. power equip., automation equip., railroad equip., shipbuilding, aircraft, motor vehicles and parts, electronics and communications equip., metals, chemicals, coal, petroleum, paper and paper prods. **Chief crops:** cereals, oilseed, potatoes, vegetables. **Natural resources:** coal, petroleum, nat. gas, iron ore, lead, zinc, gold, tin, limestone, salt, clay, chalk, gypsum, potash, silica sand, slate. **Crude oil reserves:** 2.8 bil bbls. **Arable land:** 25%. **Livestock:** cattle: 10.1 mil; chickens: 164 mil; goats: 84,500; pigs: 4.5 mil; sheep: 31.1 mil. **Fish catch:** 813,746 metric tons. **Electricity prod.** (2010): 352.7 bil kWh. **Labor force:** agric. 1.4%, industry 18.2%, services 80.4%.

Finance: Monetary unit: Pound (GBP) (Sept. 2012: 0.63 = $1 U.S.). **GDP:** $2.3 tril; **per capita GDP:** $36,600; **GDP growth:** 0.7%. **Imports:** $639.5 bil; Germany 13.2%, China 8.7%, Netherlands 7.5%, U.S. 6.1%, France 6%, Norway 5%, Belgium 5%. **Exports:** $479.7 bil; Germany 11.6%, U.S. 10.6%, Netherlands 8.4%, France 7.8%, Ireland 6.4%, Belgium 5.7%. **Tourism:** $35.9 bil. **Budget:** $1.2 tril. **Total reserves less gold:** $79.3 bil. **Gold:** 10 mil oz t. **CPI change:** 4.5%.

Transport: Railways: 10,224 mi. **Motor vehicles:** 568 vehicles per 1,000 pop. **Civil aviation:** 143.3 bil pass.-mi; 272 airports. **Chief ports:** Dover, Felixstowe, Immingham, Liverpool, London, Southampton, Teesport.

Communications: TV sets: 1,105 per 1,000 pop. **Radios:** 2,059 per 1,000 pop. **Telephone lines:** 53.2 per 100 pop. **Daily newspaper circ.:** 289.8 per 1,000 pop. **Internet:** 82%. **Health: Life expect.:** 78.1 male; 82.4 female. **Births:** 12.3 (per 1,000 pop.). **Deaths:** 9.3 (per 1,000 pop.). **Natural inc.:** 0.29%. **Infant mortality:** 4.6 (per 1,000 live births). **HIV rate:** 0.2%. **Education:** Compulsory: ages 5-16. **Literacy:** 99%. **Major intl. organizations:** UN and all of its specialized agencies, the Commonwealth, EU, NATO, OECD, OSCE, WTO. **Embassy:** 3100 Massachusetts Ave. NW 20008; 588-6500. **Website:** www.direct.gov.uk

The United Kingdom of Great Britain and Northern Ireland comprises England, Wales, Scotland, and Northern Ireland.

Queen and Royal Family. The ruling sovereign is Elizabeth II of the House of Windsor, b. Apr. 21, 1926, elder daughter of King George VI. She succeeded to the throne Feb. 6, 1952, and was crowned June 2, 1953. She was married Nov. 20, 1947, to Lt. Philip Mountbatten, b. June 10, 1921, former Prince of Greece. He was created Duke of Edinburgh, and given the title H.R.H., Nov. 19, 1947; he was named Prince of the United Kingdom and Northern Ireland Feb. 22, 1957. Prince Charles Philip Arthur George, b. Nov. 14, 1948, is the Prince of Wales and heir apparent. His first son, William Philip Arthur Louis, b. June 21, 1982, is second in line to the throne.

Parliament is the legislative body for the UK, with certain powers over dependent units. It consists of two houses: The **House of Commons** has 650 members, elected by direct ballot and divided as follows: England, 533; Wales, 40; Scotland, 59; Northern Ireland, 18. Following a drastic reduction in 1999 in the number of hereditary peerages, the **House of Lords** (Oct. 2011) comprised 826 members: 92 hereditary peers, 710 life peers, and 24 archbishops and bishops of the Church of England.

Resources and Industries. Great Britain's major occupations are manufacturing and trade. Metals and metal-using industries contribute more than 50% of exports. Of about 60 mil acres of land in England, Wales, and Scotland, 46 mil are farmed, of which 17 mil are arable, the rest pastures. Large oil and gas fields have been found in the North Sea. Commercial oil production began in 1975. There are large deposits of coal.

Britain imports all of its cotton, rubber, sulphur, about 80% of its wool, half of its food and iron ore, also certain amounts of paper, tobacco, chemicals. Manufactured goods made from these basic materials have been exported since the industrial age began. Main exports are machinery, chemicals, textiles, clothing, autos and trucks, iron and steel, locomotives, ships, jet aircraft, farm machinery, drugs, radio, TV, radar and navigation equipment, scientific instruments, arms, whisky.

Religion and Education. The Church of England is Protestant Episcopal. The queen is its temporal head, with rights of appointments to archbishoprics, bishoprics, and other offices. There are two provinces, Canterbury and York, each headed by an archbishop. The most famous church is Westminster Abbey (1050-1760), site of coronations, tombs of Elizabeth I, Mary, Queen of Scots, kings, poets, and of the Unknown Warrior.

The most celebrated British universities are Oxford and Cambridge, each dating to the 13th cent. There are about 70 other universities.

History. Recent research indicates that Britain was separated from the European continent at least 200,000 years ago by a catastrophic flood that created the English Channel. Migrants across the Channel included the Celts, who arrived 2,500 to 3,000 years ago. Their language survives in Welsh and Gaelic enclaves.

England was added to the Roman Empire in 43 CE. After the withdrawal of Roman legions in 410, waves of Jutes, Angles, and Saxons arrived from German lands. They contended with Danish raiders for control from the 8th through 11th cent. The last successful invasion was by French speaking Normans in 1066, who united the country with their dominions in France.

Opposition by nobles to royal authority forced King John to agree to the Magna Carta in 1215, a guarantee of rights and the rule of law. In the ensuing decades, the foundations of the parliamentary system were laid.

English dynastic claims to large parts of France led to the Hundred Years War, 1338-1453, and the defeat of England. A long civil war, the War of the Roses, lasted 1455-85, and ended with the establishment of the Tudor monarchy. The economy prospered over long periods of domestic peace unmatched in continental Europe. The Church of England separated from the authority of the pope, 1534.

During the reign of Queen Elizabeth I, 1558-1603, England became a major naval power, leading to the founding of colonies in the new world and the expansion of trade with Europe and the Orient. Scotland and England shared a single monarch after James VI of Scotland was crowned James I of England in 1603.

A struggle between Parliament and the Stuart kings led to a civil war, 1642-49, and the establishment of a republic under the Puritan Oliver Cromwell. The monarchy was restored in 1660, but the "Glorious Revolution" of 1688 confirmed the sovereignty of Parliament: a Bill of Rights was granted 1689. Scotland was united with England after the ratification of the Articles of Union of Scotland and England, May 1707.

In the 18th cent., parliamentary rule was strengthened. Technological and entrepreneurial innovations led to the Industrial Revolution. The 13 N American colonies were lost but replaced by growing empires in Canada and India. Britain's role in the defeat of Napoleon, 1815, strengthened its position as the leading world power.

The extension of the franchise in 1832 and 1867, the formation of trade unions, and the development of universal public education were among the drastic social changes that accompanied the spread of industrialization and urbanization in the 19th cent. Large parts of Africa and Asia were added to the empire during the reign of Queen Victoria, 1837-1901.

Though victorious in WWI, Britain suffered huge casualties and economic dislocation. Ireland became independent in 1921, and independence movements became active in India and other colonies. The country suffered major bombing damage in WWII but rallied by Prime Min. Winston Churchill, held out against Germany until Allied victory was achieved, 1945.

Industrial growth continued in the postwar period, but Britain lost its leadership position to other powers. Labour governments passed socialist programs nationalizing some basic industries and expanding social security. Prime Min. Margaret Thatcher's Conservative governments, 1979-90, revived the role of private enterprise. Her Conservative successor, John Major, held power 1990-97. The UK sent military forces to the Persian Gulf War, 1991. The Channel Tunnel linking Britain to the Continent was opened May 6, 1994.

On May 1, 1997, the Labour Party swept into power, making Tony Blair, 43, Britain's youngest prime min. since 1812. Diana, Princess of Wales, died in a car crash in Paris, Aug. 31. Britain played a leading role in the NATO air war against Yugoslavia, Mar.-June 1999, and contributed 12,000 troops to the multinational security force in Kosovo (KFOR).

After the Sept. 11 attacks on the U.S., Britain took an important role in the U.S.-led war against terrorism. The UK participated in the bombing of Afghanistan that began Oct. 7, 2001; 9,500 UK troops were serving in Afghanistan as of Sept. 2012, with more than 427 fatalities since the war started. Overcoming dissent within his own cabinet, Blair, who had won a landslide election victory June 7, 2001, committed British troops to the U.S.-led invasion of Iraq, Mar.-Apr. 2003. UK forces, which numbered 46,000 at the height of combat operations, almost entirely pulled out by mid-2009;179 had died.

In elections May 5, 2005, Blair became the first Labour prime min. to win three consecutive terms. Suicide bombings on three London underground trains and a bus, July 7, 2005, left 56 people dead and hundreds injured; police identified the bombers as four British Muslim men (three of Pakistani origin).

Blair stepped down June 27, 2007, and was succeeded by Gordon Brown. Failed car bombings in London, June 29, 2007, and at Glasgow Airport in Scotland, June 30, led to the arrest in Britain of seven suspects, mostly foreign-born medical workers. Responding Oct. 13, 2008, to the worldwide financial crisis, Prime Min. Brown initiated a plan to partially nationalize three of Britain's largest banks and support them with a capital infusion of up to $63 bil.

In the wake of Britain's deepest recession since WWII, voters rejected Brown and the Labour Party in parliamentary elections May 6, 2010. Conservatives and Liberal Democrats formed the first coalition government in 70 years, with Conservative leader David Cameron becoming prime min. and Liberal Democratic leader Nick Clegg deputy prime min. Cameron responded to the country's fiscal crisis with austerity measures meant to reign in the country's debt and announced, before the UK's successful hosting of the Olympics, July 27-Aug. 12, 2012, that the original 5-year austerity plan will likely need to be expanded for another five years.

Wales

The Principality of Wales in western Britain has an area of 8,019 sq mi and a population (2011 est.) of 3,060,000. Cardiff is the capital, pop. (2010 est., city proper) 341,054.

Less than 20% of Wales residents speak English and Welsh; about 32,000 speak Welsh solely. A 1979 referendum rejected, 4-1, the creation of an elected Welsh assembly; a similar proposal passed by a thin margin on Sept. 18, 1997. Elections for the 60-seat assembly were held in 1997, 2003, 2007, and 2011.

Early Anglo-Saxon invaders drove Celtic peoples into the mountains of Wales, terming them Waelise (Welsh, or foreign). There they developed a distinct nationality. Members of the ruling house of Gwynedd in the 13th cent. fought England but were crushed, 1283. Edward of Caernarvon, son of Edward I of England, was created Prince of Wales, 1301.

Scotland

Scotland, a kingdom now united with England and Wales in Great Britain, occupies the northern 37% of the main British island, and the Hebrides, Orkney, Shetland, and smaller islands. Length 275 mi, breadth approx. 150 mi, area 30,414 sq mi, pop. (2010 est.) 5,222,100.

The Lowlands, a belt of land approx. 60 mi wide from the Firth of Clyde to the Firth of Forth, divide the farming region of the Southern Uplands from the granite Highlands of the N; they contain 75% of the population and most of the industry. The Highlands, famous for hunting and fishing, have been opened to industry by many hydroelectric power stations.

Edinburgh, pop. (2010 est., city proper) 486,120, is the capital. Glasgow, pop. (2010 est., city proper) 592,820, is Britain's greatest industrial center. It is a shipbuilding complex on the Clyde and an ocean port. Aberdeen, pop. (2010 est.) 217,120, NE of Edinburgh, is a major port, center of granite industry, fish-processing, and North Sea oil exploration. Dundee, pop. (2010 est.) 144,290, NE of Edinburgh, is an industrial and fish-processing center. About 90,000 persons speak Gaelic as well as English.

History. Scotland was called Caledonia by the Romans who battled early Celtic tribes and occupied southern areas from the 1st to the 4th cent. Missionaries from Britain introduced Christianity in the 4th cent.; St. Columba, an Irish monk, converted most of Scotland in the 6th cent.

The Kingdom of Scotland was founded in 1018. William Wallace and Robert Bruce both defeated English armies 1297 and 1314, respectively.

In 1603, James VI of Scotland, son of Mary, Queen of Scots, succeeded to the throne of England as James I, and effected the Union of the Crowns. In 1707 Scotland received representation in the British Parliament, resulting from the union of former separate Parliaments. Its executive in the British cabinet is the Secretary of State for Scotland. The growing Scottish National Party urges independence. A 1979 referendum on the creation of an elected Scottish assembly was defeated, but a proposal to create a regional legislature with limited taxing authority passed by a landslide Sept. 11, 1997. Elections for the 129-seat parliament were held 1999, 2003, 2007, and 2011; in the 2011 vote, Scottish Nationalist candidates won a majority.

Memorials of Robert Burns, Sir Walter Scott, John Knox, and Mary, Queen of Scots, draw many tourists, as do the beauties of the Trossachs, Loch Katrine, Loch Lomond, and abbey ruins.

Industries. Engineering products are the most important industry, with growing emphasis on office machinery, autos, electronics, and other consumer goods. Oil has been discovered offshore in the North Sea, stimulating on-shore support industries.

Scotland produces fine woolens, worsteds, tweeds, silks, fine linens, and jute. It is known for its special breeds of cattle and sheep. Fisheries have large hauls of herring, cod, whiting. Whisky is a major export.

The Hebrides are a group of about 500 islands, 100 inhabited, off the W coast. The **Inner Hebrides** include Skye, Mull, and Iona, the last famous for the arrival of St. Columba, 563 CE. The **Outer Hebrides** include Lewis and Harris. Industries include sheep raising and weaving. The **Orkney Isls.**, c. 90, are to the NE. The capital is Kirkwall, on Pomona Isl. Fish curing, sheep raising, and weaving are occupations. NE of the Orkneys are the 200 **Shetland Isls.**, 24 inhabited, home of Shetland ponies. The Orkneys and Shetlands are centers for the North Sea oil industry.

Northern Ireland

Northern Ireland was constituted in 1920 from 6 of the 9 counties of Ulster, the NE corner of Ireland. Area 5,452 sq mi, pop. (2011 est.) 1,810,900. Capital and chief industrial center, Belfast, pop. (2010 est., city proper) 268,745.

Industries. Shipbuilding, including large tankers, has long been an important industry, centered in Belfast, the largest port. Linen manufacture is also important, along with apparel, rope, and twine. Growing diversification has added engineering products, synthetic fibers, and electronics. There are large numbers of cattle, hogs, and sheep. Potatoes, poultry, and dairy foods are also produced.

Government and History. An act of the British Parliament, 1920, divided Northern from Southern Ireland, each with a parliament and government. When Ireland became a dominion, 1921, and later a republic, Northern Ireland chose to remain a part of the United Kingdom. It elects 18 members to the House of Commons.

During 1968-69, large demonstrations were conducted by Roman Catholics who charged they were discriminated against in voting rights, housing, and employment. The Catholics, a minority comprising about a third of the population, demanded abolition of property qualifications for voting in local elections. Violence and terrorism intensified, involving branches of the Irish Republican Army (outlawed in the Irish Republic), Protestant groups, police, and British troops. Between 1969 and 2001 more than 3,500 were killed in sectarian violence in Northern Ireland, Ireland, England, and elsewhere. For most of this period, the Northern Ireland parliament was suspended, and Britain imposed direct rule.

A settlement reached on Good Friday, Apr. 10, 1998, provided for restoration of home rule and election of a 108-member assembly with safeguards for minority rights. Both Ireland and Great Britain agreed to give up their constitutional claims on Northern Ireland. The accord was approved May 22 by voters in Northern Ireland and the Irish Republic, and elections to the assembly were held June 25. IRA dissidents seeking to derail the agreement were responsible for a bomb at Omagh Aug. 15 that killed 29 people and injured over 330.

London transferred authority to a Northern Ireland power-sharing government Dec. 2, 1999. Delays in IRA disarmament led to several suspensions of self-government. The IRA stated July 28, 2005, that it had renounced violence and ordered all units to disarm. In response, the British began reducing their military presence in the region. On Sept. 26, an international monitoring group reported that the IRA had apparently scrapped its entire arsenal. The Northern Ireland legislature, suspended for 3½ years, reconvened May 15, 2006. Elections were held in 2007 and 2011. **Website:** www.northern ireland.gov.uk

Religion and Education. Northern Ireland is about 58% Protestant, 42% Roman Catholic. Education is compulsory between the ages of 5 and 16 years.

Channel Islands

The Channel Islands, area 75 sq mi, off the NW coast of France, the only parts of the one-time Dukedom of Normandy belonging to England, are Jersey, Guernsey and the dependencies of Guernsey—Alderney, Brechou, Great Sark, Little Sark, Herm, Jethou, and Lihou. **Jersey,** area 45 sq mi, pop. (2011 est.) 94,161, and **Guernsey,** area 30 sq mi, pop. (2011 est.) 65,068, have separate legal existences and lieutenant governors named by the Crown. The islands were the only British soil occupied by German troops in WWII.

Websites: www.gov.je; www.gov.gg

Isle of Man

The Isle of Man, area 221 sq mi, pop. (2011 est.) 84,655, is in the Irish Sea, 20 mi from Scotland, 30 mi from Cumberland. It is rich in lead and iron. The island has its own laws and a lieutenant governor appointed by the Crown. The Tynwald (legislature) consists of the Legislative Council, partly elected, and House of Keys, elected. Capital: Douglas. Farming, tourism, and fishing (kippers, scallops) are chief occupations. Man is famous for the Manx tailless cat. **Website:** www.gov.im

Gibraltar

Gibraltar, a dependency on the S coast of Spain, guards the entrance to the Mediterranean. The Rock of Gibraltar has been in British possession since 1704. It is 2.5 mi long, 0.75 of a mi wide, and 1,396 ft in height, with a total area of 2.5 sq mi (6.5 sq km); a narrow isthmus connects it with the mainland. Pop. (2011 est.) 28,956. **Website:** www.gibraltar.gov.gi

Gibraltar has historically been an object of contention between Britain and Spain. In 1967, residents voted with near unanimity to remain under British rule. A new constitution, May 30, 1969, increased Gibraltarian control of domestic affairs (the UK continues to handle defense and internal security matters). Following a 1984 agreement between Britain and Spain, the border, closed by Spain in 1969, was fully reopened in Feb. 1985. A UN General Assembly resolution requested Britain to end Gibraltar's colonial status by Oct. 1, 1996. A plan for the UK and Spain to share sovereignty was rejected by Gibraltar voters, Nov. 7, 2002. Residents approved a new constitution Nov. 30, 2006.

British West Indies

Swinging in a vast arc from the coast of Venezuela NE, then N and NW toward Puerto Rico are the Leeward Islands, forming a coral and volcanic barrier sheltering the Caribbean from the open Atlantic. Many of the islands are self-governing British possessions. Universal suffrage was instituted 1951-54; ministerial systems were set up 1956-60.

The **Leeward Isls.** still associated with the UK are **Montserrat,** area 39 sq mi, pop. (2011 est.) 5,140, capital Plymouth; the **British Virgin Isls.,** 58 sq mi, pop. (2011 est.) 30,391, capital Road Town; and **Anguilla,** the most northerly of Leeward Islands, 35 sq mi, pop. (2011 est.) 15,094, capital The Valley. Montserrat has been devastated by the Soufrière Hills volcano, which began erupting July 18, 1995.

The three **Cayman Isls.,** a dependency, lie S of Cuba, NW of Jamaica. Pop. (2011 est.) 51,384, most of it on Grand Cayman. It is a free port; in the 1970s Grand Cayman became a tax-free refuge for foreign funds and branches of many Western banks were opened there. Total area 102 sq mi, capital George Town.

The **Turks and Caicos Isls.** are a dependency at the SE end of the Bahama Islands. Of about 30 islands, only 6 are inhabited; area 366 sq mi, pop. (2011 est.) 44,819; capital Grand Turk. Salt, shellfish, and conch shells are the main exports.

Bermuda

Bermuda is a British dependency governed by a royal governor and an assembly, dating from 1620, the oldest legislative body among British dependencies. Capital is Hamilton. **Website:** www.gov.bm

It is a group of about 150 small islands of coral formation, 20 inhabited, comprising 21 sq mi in the western Atlantic, 580 mi E of N. Carolina. Pop. (2011 est.) 68,679 (about 55% of African descent). Pop. density is high.

Tourism is the major industry. Bermuda is also a haven for the offshore insurance industry. Exports include petroleum products, medicine. In a referendum Aug. 15, 1995, voters rejected independence by nearly a 3-to-1 majority.

Hurricane Fabian, the most potent storm to reach Bermuda in 50 years, struck Sept. 5, 2003; four people were missing and presumed dead, and damage was estimated at over $300 mil.

South Atlantic

The **Falkland Isls.,** a dependency, lie 300 mi E of the Strait of Magellan at the southern end of S. America.

The Falklands, or Islas Malvinas, include 2 large islands and about 200 smaller ones, area 4,700 sq mi, pop. (2008 est.) 3,140, capital Stanley. The licensing of foreign fishing vessels has become the major source of revenue. Sheep-grazing is a main industry; wool is the principal export. There are indications of large oil and gas deposits. The islands are also claimed by Argentina, though 97% of inhabitants are of British origin. Argentina invaded the islands Apr. 2, 1982. The British responded by sending a task force to the area, landing their main force on the Falklands, May 21, and forcing an Argentine surrender at Port Stanley, June 14. A pact resuming commercial air service with Argentina was signed July 14, 1999. **Website:** www.falklands.gov.fk

British Antarctic Territory, S of 60° S lat., formerly a dependency of the Falkland Isls., was made a separate colony in 1962 and includes the South Shetland Isls., the South Orkneys, and the Antarctic Peninsula. A chain of meteorological stations is maintained.

South Georgia and the **South Sandwich Isls.,** formerly administered by the Falklands Isls., became a separate dependency in 1985. Total area of 1,507 sq mi. South Georgia, with no permanent population, is about 800 mi SE of the Falklands; the South Sandwich Isls. are uninhabited, about 470 mi SE of South Georgia.

St. Helena, an island 1,200 mi off the W coast of Africa and 1,800 mi E of S. America, 47 sq mi and pop. (2011 est.) 7,700. Flax, lace, and rope-making are the chief industries. After Napoleon Bonaparte was defeated at Waterloo the Allies exiled him to St. Helena, where he lived from Oct. 16, 1815, to his death, May 5, 1821. Capital is Jamestown. **Website:** www.sainthelena.gov.sh

Tristan da Cunha is the principal island in a group of islands of volcanic origin, total area 38 sq mi, halfway between the Cape of Good Hope and S. America. A volcanic peak 6,760 ft high erupted in 1961. The 262 inhabitants were removed to England, but most returned in 1963. The islands are dependencies of St. Helena. Pop. (2010 est.): 265.

Ascension is an island of volcanic origin, 34 sq mi in area, 700 mi NW of St. Helena, through which it is administered. It is a communications relay center for Britain, and has a U.S. satellite tracking center. Pop. (2010) was 884, half of them communications workers. The island is noted for sea turtles. **Website:** www.ascension-island. gov.ac.

British Indian Ocean Territory

Formed Nov. 1965, embracing islands formerly dependencies of Mauritius or Seychelles: the Chagos Archipelago (including Diego Garcia), Aldabra, Farquhar, and Des Roches. The latter three were transferred to Seychelles, which became independent in 1976. Total area 21,004 sq mi, land area 23 sq mi. No permanent civilian population remains; the UK and the U.S. maintain a military presence.

Pacific Ocean

Pitcairn Isl. is in the Pacific, halfway between S. America and Australia. The island was discovered in 1767 by Philip Carteret but was not inhabited until 23 years later when the mutineers of the *Bounty* landed there. The 2011 pop. was 48. It is a British dependency and is administered by a British High Commissioner in New Zealand and a local Council. The uninhabited islands of Henderson, Ducie, and Oeno are in the Pitcairn group, area 18 sq mi. **Website:** www.government.pn

United States
United States of America

People: Population: 313,847,465. 50 states and DC. (Note: U.S. pop. figures may differ elsewhere in *The World Almanac*.) **Age distrib.:** <15: 20%; 65+: 13.5%. **Pop. density:** 88.9 per sq mi, 34.3 per sq km. **Urban:** 82.4%. **Ethnic groups:** white 80%, black 13%, Asian 4%, Amerindian and Alaska native 1%. (Hispanic, any race 15%.) **Principal languages:** English, Spanish, other Indo-European, Asian and Pacific Island, Hawaiian (official in Hawaii). **Chief religions:** Protestant 51%, Roman Catholic 24%, Mormon 2%, Jewish 2%, other Christian 2%, unaffiliated 12%, none 4%.

Geography: Total area: 3,794,100 sq mi, 9,826,675 sq km; **Land area:** 3,537,455 sq mi, 9,161,966 sq km. (Area is for 50 states and DC only.) **Topography:** Vast central plain, mountains in W, hills and low mountains in E. **Capital:** Washington, DC, 4,705,070.

Government: Federal republic, strong democratic tradition. **Head of state and gov.:** Pres. Barack Obama; b. Aug. 4, 1961; in office: Jan. 20, 2009. **Local divisions:** 50 states and Dist. of Columbia. **Defense budget:** $739.3 bil. **Active troops:** 1,569,417.

Economy: Industries: second largest industrial output in world; petroleum, steel, motor vehicles, aerospace, telecom., chemicals, electronics, food proc., consumer goods, lumber, mining. **Chief**

crops: wheat, corn, other grains, fruits, vegetables, cotton. **Natural resources:** coal, copper, lead, molybdenum, phosphates, rare earth elements, uranium, bauxite, gold, iron, mercury, nickel, potash, silver, tungsten, zinc, petroleum, nat. gas, timber. **Crude oil reserves** (2009): 20.7 bil bbls. **Arable land:** 17.8%. **Livestock:** cattle: 93.9 mil; chickens: 2.1 bil; goats: 3 mil; pigs: 64.9 mil; sheep: 5.6 mil. **Fish catch:** 4.9 mil metric tons. **Electricity prod.** (2010): 4.1 tril kWh. **Labor force** (excl. unemployed): farming, forestry, fishing 0.7%; mfg., extraction, transp., crafts 20.3%; managerial, professional, technical 37.3%; sales and office 24.2%; other services 17.6%.

Finance: Monetary unit: Dollar (USD). **GDP:** $15.3 tril; **per capita GDP:** $49,000; **GDP growth:** 1.7%. **Imports:** $2.2 tril; China 18.4%, Canada 14.2%, Mexico 11.7%, Japan 5.8%, Germany 4.4%. **Exports:** $1.5 tril; Canada 19%, Mexico 13.3%, China 7%, Japan 4.5%. **Tourism:** $116.3 bil. **Budget:** $3.6 tril (excl. social benefits of approx. $2.3 tril). **Total reserves less gold:** $136.9 bil. **Gold:** 261.5 mil oz t. **CPI change:** 3.2%.

Transport: Railways: 139,679 mi. **Motor vehicles:** 809.3 vehicles per 1,000 pop. **Civil aviation:** 762.8 bil pass.-mi (incl. airlines based in territories and dependencies); (2010) 5,194 airports.

Communications: TV sets: 844 per 1,000 pop. **Radios:** 145 per 1,000 pop. **Telephone lines:** 47.9 per 100 pop. **Daily newspaper circ.:** 193.2 per 1,000 pop. **Internet:** 77.9%.

Health: Life expect.: 76.1 male; 81.1 female. **Births:** 13.7 (per 1,000 pop.). **Deaths:** 8.4 (per 1,000 pop.). **Natural inc.:** 0.53%. **Infant mortality:** 6.0 (per 1,000 live births). **HIV rate:** 0.6%.

Education: Compulsory: ages 6-17. **Literacy:** 99%.

Major intl. organizations: UN (FAO, IBRD, ILO, IMF, WHO), APEC, NAFTA, NATO, OAS, OECD, OSCE, WTO.

Website: www.usa.gov

See also U.S. History chapter; Chronology of the Year's Events.

Uruguay
Oriental Republic of Uruguay

People: Population: 3,316,328. **Age distrib.:** <15: 21.8%; 65+: 13.8%. **Pop. density:** 49.1 per sq mi, 18.9 per sq km. **Urban:** 92.5%. **Ethnic groups:** white 88%, mestizo 8%, black 4%. **Principal languages:** Spanish (official), Portunol, Brazilero. **Chief religions:** Roman Catholic 47%, non-Catholic Christian 11%, nondenominational 23%, atheist or agnostic 17%.

Geography: Total area: 68,037 sq mi, 176,215 sq km; **Land area:** 67,574 sq mi, 175,015 sq km. **Location:** In southern S. America, on Atlantic O. **Neighbors:** Argentina on W, Brazil on N. **Topography:** Uruguay is composed of rolling, grassy plains and hills, well watered by rivers flowing W to Uruguay R. **Capital:** Montevideo, 1,671,570.

Government: Type: Republic. **Head of state and gov.:** Pres. José (Pepe) Mujica; b. May 20, 1935; in office: Mar. 1, 2010. **Local divisions:** 19 departments. **Defense budget:** $478 mil. **Active troops:** 24,621.

Economy: Industries: food proc., elec. machinery, transp. equip., petroleum prods., textiles, chemicals, beverages. **Chief crops:** soybeans, cellulose, rice, wheat. **Natural resources:** hydropower, minor minerals, fish. **Arable land:** 10.7%. **Livestock:** cattle: 11.8 mil; chickens: 15 mil; goats: 16,700; pigs: 210,000; sheep: 7.7 mil. **Fish catch:** 74,238 metric tons. **Electricity prod.:** 7.8 bil kWh. **Labor force:** agric. 13%, industry 14%, services 73%.

Finance: Monetary unit: Peso (UYU) (Sept. 2012: 21.58 = $1 U.S.). **GDP:** $51.6 bil; **per capita GDP:** $15,300; **GDP growth:** 5.7%. **Imports:** $10.4 bil; Brazil 16%, China 14.7%, Argentina 13.2%, U.S. 9.2%, Paraguay 7%, Venezuela 6.6%. **Exports:** $9.3 bil; Brazil 19.4%, China 14.2%, Argentina 6.8%, Germany 6%, Venezuela 4.3%. **Tourism:** $2.2 bil. **Budget:** $14 bil. **Total reserves less gold:** $10.3 bil. **Gold:** 8,444 oz t. **CPI change:** 8.1%.

Transport: Railways: 1,020 mi. **Motor vehicles:** 222.7 vehicles per 1,000 pop. **Civil aviation:** 610.2 mil pass.-mi; 11 airports. **Chief port:** Montevideo.

Communications: TV sets: 381 per 1,000 pop. **Radios:** 603 per 1,000 pop. **Telephone lines:** 28.6 per 100 pop. **Internet:** 51.4%.

Health: Life expect.: 73.3 male; 79.7 female. **Births:** 13.4 (per 1,000 pop.). **Deaths:** 9.6 (per 1,000 pop.). **Natural inc.:** 0.39%. **Infant mortality:** 9.4 (per 1,000 live births). **HIV rate:** 0.5%.

Education: Compulsory: ages 6-14. **Literacy:** 98.1%.

Major intl. organizations: UN (FAO, IBRD, ILO, IMF, WHO), OAS, WTO.

Embassy: 1913 I St. NW 20006; 331-1313.

Website: portal.gub.uy

Spanish settlers began to supplant the indigenous Charrua Indians in 1624. Portuguese from Brazil arrived later, but Uruguay was attached to the Spanish Viceroyalty of Rio de la Plata in the 18th cent. Rebels fought against Spain beginning in 1810. An independent republic was declared Aug. 25, 1825. To suppress Tupamaro guerrilla activities, a repressive military regime took power in 1973. Constitutional government was restored in 1985.

Uruguay's standard of living remains one of the highest in S. America, and political and labor conditions now rank among the freest. José (Pepe) Mujica, a former guerrilla who transformed his Marxist Tupamaro movement into a mainstream political party, won a presidential runoff election Nov. 29, 2009, and took office Mar. 1, 2010.

Uzbekistan
Republic of Uzbekistan

People: Population: 28,394,180. **Age distrib.:** <15: 25.8%; 65+: 4.7%. **Pop. density:** 172.9 per sq mi, 66.7 per sq km. **Urban:** 36.2%. **Ethnic groups:** Uzbek 80%, Russian 6%, Tajik 5%, Kazakh 3%, Karakalpak 3%, Tatar 2%. **Principal languages:** Uzbek (official), Russian, Tajik. **Chief religions:** Muslim (mostly Sunni) 88%, Eastern Orthodox 9%.

Geography: Total area: 172,742 sq mi, 447,400 sq km; **Land area:** 164,248 sq mi, 425,400 sq km. **Location:** Central Asia. **Neighbors:** Kazakhstan on N and W; Kyrgyzstan, Tajikistan on E; Afghanistan, Turkmenistan on S. **Topography:** Mostly plains and desert. **Capital:** Tashkent, 2,226,580.

Government: Type: Republic with authoritarian rule. **Head of state:** Pres. Islam A. Karimov; b. Jan. 30, 1938; in office: Mar. 24, 1990. **Head of gov.:** Prime Min. Shavkat Mirziyaev; b. 1957; in office: Dec. 11, 2003. **Local divisions:** 12 regions, 1 autonomous republic, 1 city. **Defense budget** (2010): $1.42 bil. **Active troops:** 67,000.

Economy: Industries: textiles, food proc., machine building, metallurgy, mining, hydrocarbon extraction, chemicals. **Chief crops:** cotton, vegetables, fruits, grain. **Natural resources:** nat. gas, petroleum, coal, gold, uranium, silver, copper, lead, zinc, tungsten, molybdenum. **Crude oil reserves:** 594 mil bbls. **Arable land:** 10.1%. **Livestock:** cattle: 8.5 mil; chickens: 34.8 mil; goats: 2.3 mil; pigs: 92,000; sheep: 12.2 mil. **Fish catch:** 10,732 metric tons. **Electricity prod.** 47.4 bil kWh. **Labor force:** agric. 44%, industry 20%, services 36%.

Finance: Monetary unit: Som (UZS) (Sept. 2012: 1,953.00 = $1 U.S.). **GDP:** $96.5 bil; **per capita GDP:** $3,300; **GDP growth:** 8.3%. **Imports:** $8.5 bil; Russia 21.4%, South Korea 19.1%, China 15.1%, Germany 7.4%, Kazakhstan 5.6%. **Exports:** $12.6 bil; Russia 20.9%, Turkey 17.1%, China 14.7%, Kazakhstan 10.3%, Bangladesh 8.7%. **Tourism:** $121 mil. **Budget:** $14.8 bil.

Transport: Railways: 2,265 mi. **Civil aviation:** 3 bil pass.-mi; 33 airports. **Chief port:** Termiz.

Communications: TV sets: 226 per 1,000 pop. **Radios:** 456 per 1,000 pop. **Telephone lines:** 6.9 per 100 pop. **Internet:** 30.2%.

Health: Life expect.: 69.7 male; 76.0 female. **Births:** 17.3 (per 1,000 pop.). **Deaths:** 5.3 (per 1,000 pop.). **Natural inc.:** 1.20%. **Infant mortality:** 21.2 (per 1,000 live births). **HIV rate:** 0.1%.

Education: Compulsory: ages 7-19. **Literacy:** 99.4%.

Major intl. organizations: UN (FAO, IBRD, ILO, IMF, WHO), CIS, OSCE, WTO (observer).

Embassy: 1746 Massachusetts Ave. NW 20036; 887-5300.

Website: www.gov.uz

The region was overrun by the Mongols under Genghis Khan in 1220. In the 14th cent., Uzbekistan became the center of a native Timurid empire. In later centuries Muslim feudal states emerged. Russian military conquest began in the 19th cent. Uzbek SSR became a Soviet republic in 1925.

Uzbekistan gained independence when the Soviet Union disbanded Dec. 26, 1991, and has been led by the authoritarian government of a former Communist, Islam A. Karimov.

Attacks by Islamic militants, Mar.-July 2004, killed more than 50 people. In June 2004, Russia's OAO Lukoil signed a $1 bil deal to develop Uzbekistan's natural gas fields. Militants bombed the U.S. and Israeli embassies in Tashkent, July 30.

After armed dissidents at Andizhan, east Uzbekistan, attacked government buildings and freed hundreds of prisoners, May 12-13, 2005, Uzbek security forces opened fire on rebels and unarmed demonstrators, killing many. Karimov then launched a general crackdown on human rights activists. Irritated by U.S. human rights pressures, Karimov ordered the U.S. to vacate an airbase used to support operations in Afghanistan; the U.S. pullout was completed Nov. 21. Meeting in Moscow a week earlier, Karimov and Russian Pres. Vladimir Putin signed a military cooperation agreement.

Karimov remained in office following the formal expiration of his presidential term Jan. 22, 2007; despite a 2-term limit under the constitution, he ran for a third term Dec. 23 and won with an 88.1% majority. Sanctions imposed by the EU on Uzbek officials after the 2005 Andizhan shootings were lifted Oct. 13, 2008.

When Pakistan closed its supply route to Afghanistan in Nov. 2011-July 2012, much of the non-lethal cargo that was moved into the warzone through the Northern Distribution Network came through Uzbekistan.

Vanuatu
Republic of Vanuatu

People: Population: 256,155. **Age distrib.:** <15: 38.4%; 65+: 3.5%. **Pop. density:** 54.4 per sq mi, 21 per sq km. **Urban:** 24.9%. **Ethnic groups:** Ni-Vanuatu 99%. **Principal languages:** Local langs. (100+); creole (Bislama), English, French (all official). **Chief religions:** Protestant 56% (Presbyterian 31%, Anglican 13%, Seventh-Day Adventist 11%), Roman Catholic 13%, indigenous beliefs 6%, other Christian 14%.

Geography: Total area: 4,706 sq mi, 12,189 sq km; **Land area:** 4,706 sq mi, 12,189 sq km. **Location:** SW Pacific, 1,200 mi. NE of Brisbane, Australia. **Neighbors:** Fiji to E, Solomon Isls. to NW. **Topography:** Dense forest with narrow coastal strips of cultivated land. **Capital:** Port Vila, 47,061.

Government: Type: Republic. **Head of state:** Pres. Iolu Johnson Abil; b. 1942; in office: Sept. 2, 2009. **Head of gov.:** Prime Min. Sato Kilman; in office: June 26, 2011. **Local divisions:** 6 provinces. **Defense budget:** NA. **Active troops:** No regular military forces.

Economy: Industries: food and fish freezing, wood proc., meat canning. **Chief crops:** copra, coconuts, cocoa, coffee, taro, yams, fruits, vegetables. **Natural resources:** manganese, forests, fish. **Arable land:** 1.6%. **Livestock:** cattle: 160,000; chickens: 810,000; goats: 20,000; pigs: 90,000. **Fish catch:** 97,936 metric tons. **Electricity prod.:** 55 mil kWh. **Labor force:** agric. 65%, industry 5%, services 30%.

Finance: Monetary unit: Vatu (VUV) (Sept. 2012: 91.81 = $1 U.S.). **GDP:** $1.2 bil; **per capita GDP:** $5,000; **GDP growth:** 3.3%. **Imports** (2006): $156 mil; China 26.7%, Singapore 21.2%, Australia 13.5%, New Zealand 7.2%, Fiji 6.6%, Japan 5%. **Exports** (2006): $40 mil; Thailand 56.7%, Japan 21.4%. **Tourism:** NA. **Budget:** $192.4 mil. **Total reserves less gold:** $173.8 mil. **CPI change:** 0.9%.

Transport: Motor vehicles: 64.6 vehicles per 1,000 pop. **Civil aviation:** 141.1 mil pass.-mi; 3 airports. **Chief port:** Port-Vila.

Communications: TV sets: 13 per 1,000 pop. **Radios:** 344 per 1,000 pop. **Telephone lines** (2010): 2.1 per 100 pop. **Daily newspaper circ.:** 14.3 per 1,000 pop. **Internet** (2010): 8%.

Health: Life expect.: 70.5 male; 73.6 female. **Births:** 27.0 (per 1,000 pop.). **Deaths:** 4.3 (per 1,000 pop.). **Natural inc.:** 2.28%. **Infant mortality:** 17.9 (per 1,000 live births). **HIV rate:** NA.

Education: Compulsory: ages 6-12. **Literacy:** 82.6%.

Major intl. organizations: UN (FAO, IBRD, ILO, IMF, WHO), the Commonwealth, WTO.

Permanent UN mission: 800 Second Ave., Ste. 400B, New York, NY 10017; (212) 661-4323.

Website: www.governmentofvanuatu.gov.vu

The Anglo-French condominium of the New Hebrides, administered jointly by France and Great Britain since 1906, became the independent Republic of Vanuatu on July 30, 1980. Vanuatu is located in the Ring of Fire, a zone where earthquakes and volcanic eruptions are frequent. The nation joined the World Trade Organization Aug. 24, 2012.

Vatican City (The Holy See)

People: Population: 836. **Pop. density:** 4,921 per sq mi, 1,900 per sq km. **Urban:** 100%. **Ethnic groups:** Italian, Swiss, other. **Principal languages:** Italian, Latin, French, various others. **Chief religion:** Roman Catholic.

Geography: Total area: 0.17 sq mi, 0.44 sq km; **Land area:** 0.17 sq mi, 0.44 sq km. **Location:** In Rome, Italy. **Neighbors:** Completely surrounded by Italy. **Capital:** Vatican City, 459.

Economy: Industries: printing; coins, medals, postage stamps prod.; mosaics and staff uniforms; worldwide banking and financial activities. **Labor force:** Essentially services with small amount of industry; nearly all dignitaries, priests, nuns, guards, and approx. 3,000 lay workers live outside the Vatican.

Finance: Monetary unit: Euro (EUR) (Sept. 2012: 0.79 = $1 U.S.). **Budget** (2010): $313 mil.

Apostolic Nunciature: 3339 Massachusetts Ave. NW 20008; 333-7121.

Website: www.vatican.va

The popes for many centuries, with brief interruptions, held temporal sovereignty over mid-Italy (the so-called Papal States), comprising an area of some 16,000 sq mi, with a population in the 19th cent. of more than 3 mil. This territory was incorporated in the new Kingdom of Italy (1861), the sovereignty of the pope being confined to the palaces of the Vatican and the Lateran in Rome and the villa of Castel Gandolfo, by an Italian law, May 13, 1871.

A Treaty of Conciliation, a concordat, and a financial convention were signed Feb. 11, 1929, by Cardinal Gasparri and Premier Mussolini. The documents established the independent state of Vatican City and gave the Roman Catholic Church special status in Italy. The treaty (Lateran Agreement) was made part of the Constitution of Italy (Article 7) in 1947. Italy and the Vatican signed an agreement in 1984 on revisions of the concordat; the accord eliminated Roman Catholicism as the state religion and ended required religious education in Italian schools.

Vatican City includes the Basilica of Saint Peter, the Vatican Palace and Museum covering over 13 acres, the Vatican gardens, and neighboring buildings between Viale Vaticano and the church. Thirteen buildings in Rome, outside the boundaries, enjoy extraterritorial rights; these buildings house congregations or officers necessary for the administration of the Holy See.

The legal system is based on the code of canon law, the apostolic constitutions, and laws especially promulgated for the Vatican City by the pope. The Secretariat of State represents the Holy See in its diplomatic relations.

The present sovereign of the State of Vatican City is Pope Benedict XVI, born Joseph Ratzinger in Marktl am Inn, Germany, Apr. 16, 1927, elected Apr. 19, 2005.

Venezuela
Bolivarian Republic of Venezuela

People: Population: 28,047,938. **Age distrib.:** <15: 29%; 65+: 5.6%. **Pop. density:** 82.4 per sq mi, 31.8 per sq km. **Urban:** 93.5%. **Ethnic groups:** Spanish, Italian, Portuguese, Arab, German, African, indigenous. **Principal languages:** Spanish (official), indigenous dialects. **Chief religions:** Roman Catholic (nominally) 96%, Protestant 2%.

Geography: Total area: 352,144 sq mi, 912,050 sq km; **Land area:** 340,561 sq mi, 882,050 sq km. **Location:** On Carib. coast of S. America. **Neighbors:** Colombia on W, Brazil on S, Guyana on E. **Topography:** Flat coastal plain and Orinoco Delta are bordered by Andes Mts. and hills. Plains, called llanos, extend between mountains and Orinoco. Guiana Highlands and plains are S of Orinoco, which stretches 1,600 mi and drains 80% of country. **Capital:** Caracas, 3,241,580. **Cities (urban aggl.):** Maracaibo, 2,309,557; Valencia, 1,865,721; Barquisimeto, 1,245,226; Maracay, 1,114,872.

Government: Type: Federal republic. **Head of state and gov.:** Pres. Hugo Rafael Chávez Frías; b. July 28, 1954; in office: Feb. 2, 1999. **Local divisions:** 23 states, 1 federal district (Caracas), 1 federal dependency (72 islands). **Defense budget:** $2.38 bil. **Active troops:** 115,000.

Economy: Industries: petroleum, constr. materials, food proc., textiles, iron ore mining, steel, aluminum, motor vehicle assembly, chem. prods. **Chief crops:** corn, sorghum, sugarcane, rice, bananas, vegetables, coffee. **Natural resources:** petroleum, nat. gas, iron ore, gold, bauxite, other minerals, hydropower, diamonds. **Crude oil reserves:** 211.2 bil bbls. **Arable land:** 3.1%. **Livestock:** cattle: 16.9 mil; chickens: 115 mil; goats: 1.4 mil; pigs: 3.3 mil; sheep: 550,000. **Fish catch:** 292,817 metric tons. **Electricity prod.:** (2010): 105.6 bil kWh. **Labor force:** agric. 7.3%, industry 21.8%, services 70.9%.

Finance: Monetary unit: Bolivar Fuerte (VEF) (Sept. 2012: 4.30 = $1 U.S.). **GDP:** $378.9 bil; **per capita GDP:** $12,700; **GDP growth:** 4.2%. **Imports:** $46.4 bil; U.S. 28.8%, China 15.2%, Brazil 10.7%. **Exports:** $92.6 bil; U.S. 39.9%, China 10.5%, India 6%. **Tourism:** $739 mil. **Budget:** $106.1 bil. **Total reserves less gold:** $9.9 bil. **Gold:** 11.8 mil oz t. **CPI change:** 27.1%.

Transport: Railways: 501 mi. **Motor vehicles:** 115.6 vehicles per 1,000 pop. **Civil aviation:** 1.6 mil pass.-mi; 128 airports. **Chief ports:** La Guaira, Maracaibo, Puerto Cabello, Punta Cardon.

Communications: TV sets: 208 per 1,000 pop. **Radios:** 291 per 1,000 pop. **Telephone lines:** 24.9 per 100 pop. **Daily newspaper circ.:** 93.3 per 1,000 pop. **Internet:** 40.2%.

Health: Life expect.: 71.0 male; 77.3 female. **Births:** 19.9 (per 1,000 pop.). **Deaths:** 5.2 (per 1,000 pop.). **Natural inc.:** 1.47%. **Infant mortality:** 20.2 (per 1,000 live births). **HIV rate:** NA.

Education: Compulsory: ages 3-16. **Literacy:** 95.5%.

Major intl. organizations: UN (FAO, IBRD, ILO, IMF, WHO), OAS, OPEC, WTO.

Embassy: 1099 30th St. NW 20007; 342-2214.

Website: www.presidencia.gob.ve or venezuela-us.org

Columbus first set foot on the South American continent on the peninsula of Paria, Aug. 1498. Alonso de Ojeda, 1499, was the first European to see Lake Maracaibo. He called the land Venezuela, or Little Venice, because the Indians had houses on stilts. Spanish colonialists dominated Venezuela until Simón Bolívar's victory near Carabobo in June 1821. The republic was formed after secession from the Colombian Federation in 1830. Military strongmen ruled Venezuela for much of its history. Since 1959, the country has had democratically elected governments.

Oil accounts for more than 75% of export earnings and about half of government revenues. The government, Jan. 1, 1976, nationalized the oil industry. Attempts to reduce dependence on the hydrocarbon sector have met with limited success. The country has large reserves of natural gas; a large new gas find in the Gulf of Venezuela was announced Sept. 2009.

An attempted coup by midlevel military officers was thwarted by loyalist troops Feb. 4, 1992. A second coup attempt was thwarted in Nov. Pres. Carlos Andrés Pérez was removed from office on corruption charges, May 1993, and convicted, May 1996, of mismanaging a $17 mil secret government fund.

A 1992 coup leader, Hugo Chávez, who ran as a populist, was elected president Dec. 6, 1998. Voters on Dec. 15, 1999, approved a new constitution greatly increasing his powers.

Popular among the poor, Chávez alienated middle- and upper-class Venezuelans with his program of economic and political reform, and his foreign policy antagonized the U.S. Gunfire erupted at a mass protest Apr. 11, 2002, in Caracas, killing at least 17 people. Chávez was forced to relinquish power, but when an interim government issued decrees suspending democratic institutions, Chávez loyalists rebelled; the coup fell apart, and the president reclaimed his office Apr. 14. Opponents of Chávez organized strikes and recall efforts, 2003-04, but failed to oust him.

Chávez countered U.S. attempts to isolate him diplomatically and militarily by solidifying ties with Latin American leftist leaders and with Iran and Russia. With the economy surging, he won Dec. 3, 2006, presidential election. On Jan. 31, 2007, the legislature granted him the power to rule by decree. Venezuelan voters approved constitutional changes abolishing presidential term limits Feb. 15, 2009. Chávez traveled repeatedly to Cuba for cancer treatments 2011-12 and won a tough reelection challenge Oct. 7, 2012.

Vietnam
Socialist Republic of Vietnam

People: Population: 91,519,289. **Age distrib.:** <15: 24.9%; 65+: 5.5%. **Pop. density:** 764.5 per sq mi, 295.2 per sq km. **Urban:** 31%. **Ethnic groups:** Kinh (Viet) 86%, Tay 2%, Thai 2%, Muong 2%, Khmer 2%, Mong 1%, Nung 1%. **Principal languages:** Vietnamese (official), English increasingly favored as second lang., French, Chinese, Khmer, mountain area langs. (Mon-Khmer, Malayo-Polynesian). **Chief religions:** Buddhist 9%, Catholic 7%, Hoa Hao 2%, Cao Dai 1%, none 81%.

Geography: Total area: 127,881 sq mi, 331,210 sq km; **Land area:** 119,719 sq mi, 310,070 sq km. **Location:** SE Asia, on E coast of Indochinese Peninsula. **Neighbors:** China on N; Laos, Cambodia on W. **Topography:** Vietnam is long and narrow, with 1,400-mi coast. About 22% of country is readily arable, including densely settled Red R. valley in N, narrow coastal plains in center, and the wide, often marshy Mekong R. Delta in S. The rest consists of semi-arid plateaus and barren mountains, with some stretches of tropical rain forest. **Capital:** Hà Noi, 2,955,130. **Cities (urban aggl.):** Ho Chi Minh City, 6,405,447; Can Tho, 1,004,067.

Government: Type: Communist. **Head of state:** Pres. Truong Tan Sang; b. Jan. 21, 1949; in office: July 25, 2011. **Head of gov.:** Prime Min. Nguyen Tan Dung; b. Nov. 17, 1949; in office: June 27, 2006. **Local divisions:** 58 provinces, 3 cities, 1 capital region. **Defense budget:** $2.66 bil. **Active troops:** 482,000.

Economy: Industries: food proc., garments, shoes, machine-building, mining, coal, steel, cement, chemical fertilizer. **Chief crops:** paddy rice, coffee, rubber, cotton, tea, pepper, soybeans, cashews, sugarcane, peanuts, bananas. **Natural resources:** phosphates, coal, manganese, rare earth elements, bauxite, chromate, offshore oil and gas deposits, timber, hydropower. **Crude oil reserves:** 4.4 bil bbls. **Arable land:** 20.3%. **Livestock:** cattle: 5.9 mil; chickens: 218.2 mil; goats: 1.3 mil; pigs: 27.4 mil. **Fish catch:** 5.1 mil metric tons. **Electricity prod.:** 79.7 bil kWh. **Labor force:** agric. 48%, industry 22.4%, services 29.6%.

Finance: Monetary unit: Dong (VND) (Sept. 2012: 20,839.04 = $1 U.S.). **GDP:** $303.8 bil; **per capita GDP:** $3,400; **GDP growth:** 5.9%. **Imports:** $97.8 bil; China 22%, South Korea 13.2%, Japan 10.4%, Taiwan 8.6%, Thailand 6.4%, Singapore 6.4%. **Exports:** $95.3 bil; U.S. 18%, China 11%, Japan 11%, Germany 3.7%. **Tourism:** $5.6 bil. **Budget:** $35.7 bil. **Total reserves less gold:** $13.5 bil. **CPI change:** 18.7%.

Transport: Railways: 1,635 mi. **Motor vehicles:** 3.8 vehicles per 1,000 pop. **Civil aviation:** 10.2 bil pass.-mi; 37 airports. **Chief ports:** Cam Pha Port, Da Nang, Hai Phong, Ho Chi Minh City, Phu My, Quy Nhon.

Communications: TV sets: 208 per 1,000 pop. **Radios:** 109 per 1,000 pop. **Telephone lines:** 11.5 per 100 pop. **Internet:** 35.1%.

Health: Life expect.: 70.0 male; 75.2 female. **Births:** 16.8 (per 1,000 pop.). **Deaths:** 6.0 (per 1,000 pop.). **Natural inc.:** 1.09%. **Infant mortality:** 20.2 (per 1,000 live births). **HIV rate:** 0.4%.

Education: Compulsory: ages 6-14. **Literacy:** 93.2%.

Major intl. organizations: UN (FAO, IBRD, ILO, IMF, WHO), APEC, ASEAN, WTO.

Embassy: 1233 20th St. NW, Ste. 400, 20036; 861-0737.

Website: www.na.gov.vn

Settled by Viets from central China, Vietnam was held by China, 111 BCE-939 CE, and was a vassal state during subsequent periods. Conquest by France began in 1858 and ended in 1884 with the protectorates of Tonkin and Annam in the N and the colony of Cochin-China in the S.

Japan occupied Vietnam in 1940. A number of groups formed the Vietminh (Independence) League, headed by Ho Chi Minh, the Communist guerrilla leader. In Aug. 1945 the Vietminh forced out Bao Dai, former emperor of Annam, head of a Japan-sponsored regime. France, seeking to reestablish colonial control, battled Communist and nationalist forces, 1946-54, and was defeated, May 8, 1954.

Separate states formed in N. and S. Vietnam, with Communists under Ho Chi Minh (backed by Russia and China) controlling N. Vietnam and a non-Communist government (backed by the U.S.) controlling S. Vietnam. N. Vietnam aided Vietcong guerrillas who sought to take over S. Vietnam. U.S. troops defended S. Vietnam and launched massive bombing raids against N. Vietnam and border areas of Laos and Cambodia. Casualties of the war were as follows—combat deaths: U.S. 47,369; S. Vietnam more than 200,000; other allied forces 5,225. Total U.S. fatalities numbered more than 58,000. Vietnamese civilian casualties were more than 1 mil. The war displaced more than 6.5 mil in S. Vietnam.

A never-implemented cease-fire agreement was signed in Paris Jan. 27, 1973, by the U.S., N. and S. Vietnam, and the Vietcong. S. Vietnam surrendered Apr. 30, 1975. N. Vietnam assumed control. The country was officially reunited July 2, 1976.

Conditions in the region remained unstable after the Vietnam War. Heavy fighting with Cambodia took place, 1977-80. China cut off economic aid when 140,000 ethnic Chinese left Vietnam, fleeing discrimination. Reacting to Vietnam's 1979 invasion of Cambodia, China attacked four Vietnamese border provinces, Feb. 1979.

Vietnam announced reforms aimed at reducing central control of the economy in 1987. Citing Hanoi's cooperation in returning remains of U.S. soldiers killed in the Vietnam War, the U.S. ended, Feb. 3, 1994, a 19-year-old U.S. embargo on trade with Vietnam. The U.S. extended full diplomatic recognition to Vietnam July 11, 1995. The U.S. has become Vietnam's top export market, with total annual trade over $15 bil between the two countries. The U.S. began cleaning up the herbicide Agent Orange that the U.S. used to clear forests during the Vietnam War, Aug. 9, 2012.

Yemen
Republic of Yemen

People: Population: 24,771,809. **Age distrib.:** <15: 42.5%; 65+: 2.6%. **Pop. density:** 121.5 per sq mi, 46.9 per sq km. **Urban:** 32.3%. **Ethnic groups:** predominantly Arab; Afro-Arab, South Asian, European. **Principal language:** Arabic (official). **Chief religion:** Muslim (official, incl. Sunni, Shia).

Geography: Total area: 203,850 sq mi, 527,968 sq km; **Land area:** 203,850 sq mi, 527,968 sq km. **Location:** Middle East, on S coast of the Arabian Peninsula. **Neighbors:** Saudi Arabia on N, Oman on E. **Topography:** A sandy coastal strip leads to well-watered fertile mountains in interior. **Capital:** Sana'a, 2,418,680. **Cities (urban aggl.):** Aden, 783,608.

Government: Type: In transition. **Head of state:** Pres. Abd al-Rab Mansur al-Hadi; b. Sept. 9, 1950; in office: Feb. 25, 2012. **Head of gov.:** Prime Min. Muhammad Salim Ba Sindwah; b. 1935; in office: Nov. 27, 2011. **Local divisions:** 19 governorates and capital region. **Defense budget:** $2.04 bil. **Active troops:** 66,700.

Economy: Industries: crude oil prod. and petroleum refining, small-scale prod. of cotton textiles and leather goods, food proc., handicrafts. **Chief crops:** grains, fruits, vegetables, pulses, qat, coffee, cotton. **Natural resources:** petroleum; fish; rock salt; marble; small deposits of coal, gold, lead, nickel, copper. **Crude oil reserves:** 3 bil bbls. **Arable land:** 2.2%. **Livestock:** cattle: 1.6 mil; chickens: 60 mil; goats: 9 mil; sheep: 9.2 mil. **Fish catch:** 191,100 metric tons. **Electricity prod.:** 6.3 bil kWh. **Labor force:** Most people employed in agric. and herding; services, constr., industry, and commerce account for less than one-fourth of labor force.

Finance: Monetary unit: Rial (YER) (Sept. 2012: 214.59 = $1 U.S.). **GDP:** $58.7 bil; **per capita GDP:** $2,300; **GDP growth:** –10.5%. **Imports:** $8.3 bil; UAE 18.5%, China 11.6%, Saudi Arabia 8.7%, Kuwait 6.5%, India 6.4%, France 4.6%, U.S. 4.1%. **Exports:** $7.6 bil; China 27.3%, Thailand 12.4%, India 10.9%, South Korea 9.8%, Japan 5.6%, U.S. 5.4%, South Africa 4.5%, UAE 4.3%. **Tourism:** $622 mil. **Budget:** $10.6 bil. **Total reserves less gold:** $4.4 bil. **Gold:** 50,000 oz t. **CPI change:** 16.4%.

Transport: Motor vehicles: 28.1 vehicles per 1,000 pop. **Civil aviation:** 1.9 bil pass.-mi; 17 airports. **Chief ports:** Aden, Al Hudaydah, Al Mukalla.

Communications: TV sets: 344 per 1,000 pop. **Radios:** 64 per 1,000 pop. **Telephone lines:** 4.3 per 100 pop. **Daily newspaper circ.:** 4.1 per 1,000 pop. **Internet:** 14.9%.

Health: Life expect.: 62.1 male; 66.3 female. **Births:** 32.6 (per 1,000 pop.). **Deaths:** 6.8 (per 1,000 pop.). **Natural inc.:** 2.58%. **Infant mortality:** 53.5 (per 1,000 live births). **HIV rate:** NA.

Education: Compulsory: ages 6-14. **Literacy:** 63.9%.

Major intl. organizations: UN (FAO, IBRD, ILO, IMF, WHO), AL, WTO (observer).

Embassy: 2319 Wyoming Ave. NW 20008; 965-4760.

Website: www.yemen.gov.ye or www.yemenembassy.org

Yemen's territory once was part of the ancient biblical Kingdom of Sheba, or Saba. Yemen became independent in 1918, after centuries of Ottoman Turkish rule.

Imam Yahya ibn Muhammad ruled, 1904-48, and after his assassination was succeeded by his son, Imam Ahmed, 1948-62. Army officers headed by Brig. Gen. Abdullah al-Salal declared the country to be the Yemen Arab Republic, Sept. 1962. Ahmed's heir, the Imam Mohamad al-Badr, fled to the mountains where tribesmen joined royalist forces, aided by the Saudi monarchy. Fighting between royalists and republicans killed about 150,000 people until hostilities ended in 1970.

Meanwhile, South Yemen, formed from the British colony of Aden and the British protectorate of South Arabia, became independent Nov. 1967. A Marxist state and a Soviet ally, it took the name People's Democratic Republic of Yemen in 1970. More than 300,000 Yemenis fled from the S to the N after independence, contributing to two decades of hostility between the two states.

The two countries were formally united May 21, 1990, but regional clan-based rivalries led to full-scale civil war in 1994. Secessionists declared a breakaway state in South Yemen, May 21, 1994, but northern troops captured the former southern capital of Aden in July. A new constitution was approved Sept. 28.

Yemen, the ancestral home of Osama bin Laden, has been caught in a crossfire between the U.S. and Islamic extremists. While on a refueling stop in Aden, Oct. 12, 2000, the destroyer U.S.S. Cole was bombed, leaving 17 Americans dead and more than three dozen injured; the U.S. government blamed the attack on terrorists associated with bin Laden.

Clashes beginning in June 2004 between Yemeni government forces and Shiite rebels led by an anti-U.S. cleric, Hussein al-Houthi, left more than 200 people dead. The government announced Sept. 10 that Yemeni troops had killed al-Houthi. Incumbent Pres. Ali Abdullah Saleh was reelected Sept. 20, 2006.

During 2007-10, Shiite rebels in the northwest, secessionists in the south, al-Qaeda militants in the east, and pirates in coastal waters challenged Yemeni government authority. Emboldened by the success of "Arab Spring" protests in Tunisia and Egypt in early 2011, mass demonstrations in Yemeni cities demanded Pres. Saleh's resignation, and the U.S. and Gulf Arab nations also pressed him to depart. Saleh was severely wounded June 3 in a rocket attack on the presidential compound in Sana'a'. Vice Pres. Abd al-Rab Mansur al-Hadi served as acting president June 4-Sept. 23, 2011, while Saleh received extended medical treatment in Saudi Arabia. After a 2-year manhunt, Anwar al-Awlaki, an American citizen and radical Muslim cleric linked to several plots against the U.S., was killed Sept. 30, 2011, by a U.S. missile in northern Yemen. Saleh ceded power Nov. 23, 2011, remaining in office in name only. Al-Hadi served as the acting president. He officially became president in uncontested elections, Feb. 25, 2012, but has failed to stabilize the country, allowing al-Qaeda to strengthen its foothold.

Zambia
Republic of Zambia

People: Population: 13,817,479. **Age distrib.:** <15: 46.3%; 65+: 2.4%. **Pop. density:** 48.1 per sq mi, 18.6 per sq km. **Urban:** 39.2%. **Ethnic groups:** African 99.5%. **Principal languages:** Bemba, Nyanja, Tonga, Lozi, Lunda, Kaonde, Luvale, English (all official); Chewa; Nsenga; Tumbuka; Lala. **Chief religions:** Christian 50%-75%, Muslim and Hindu 24%-49%, indigenous beliefs 1%.

Geography: Total area: 290,587 sq mi, 752,618 sq km; **Land area:** 287,028 sq mi, 743,398 sq km. **Location:** In S central Africa. **Neighbors:** Congo on N; Tanzania, Malawi, Mozambique on E; Zimbabwe, Namibia on S; Angola on W. **Topography:** Mostly high plateau covered with thick forests and drained by several important rivers, including the Zambezi. **Capital:** Lusaka, 1,802,470.

Government: Type: Republic. **Head of state and gov.:** Pres. Michael Sata; b. 1937; in office: Sept. 23, 2011. **Local divisions:** 9 provinces. **Defense budget:** $291 mil. **Active troops:** 15,100.

Economy: Industries: copper mining and proc., constr., foodstuffs, beverages, chemicals, textiles, fertilizer, horticulture. **Chief crops:** corn, sorghum, rice, peanuts, sunflower seeds, vegetables, flowers, tobacco, cotton, sugarcane, cassava, coffee. **Natural resources:** copper, cobalt, zinc, lead, coal, emeralds, gold, silver, uranium, hydropower. **Arable land:** 4.5%. **Livestock:** cattle: 3 mil; chickens: 35 mil; goats: 2.2 mil; pigs: 500,000; sheep: 220,000. **Fish catch:** 86,686 metric tons. **Electricity prod.:** 10.2 bil kWh. **Labor force:** agric. 85%, industry 6%, services 9%.

Finance: Monetary unit: Kwacha (ZMK) (Sept. 2012: 5,030.40 = $1 U.S.). **GDP:** $22.2 bil; **per capita GDP:** $1,600; **GDP growth:** 6.6%. **Imports:** $6.4 bil; South Africa 33.4%, Dem. Rep. of the Congo 21.9%, China 10.6%, Kuwait 6.3%. **Exports:** $9.2 bil; China 34.8%, Switzerland 18.3%, South Africa 11.7%, Dem. Rep. of the Congo 5.4%, South Korea 4.4%. **Tourism:** $125 mil. **Budget:** $4.4 bil. **Total reserves less gold:** $2.3 bil. **CPI change:** 6.4%.

Transport: Railways: 1,340 mi (incl. part of Tanzania-Zambia Railway Authority). **Motor vehicles:** 20.7 vehicles per 1,000 pop. **Civil aviation:** 12.4 mil pass.-mi; 8 airports. **Chief port:** Mpulungu.

Communications: TV sets: 64 per 1,000 pop. **Radios:** 145 per 1,000 pop. **Telephone lines:** 0.6 per 100 pop. **Daily newspaper circ.:** 4.9 per 1,000 pop. **Internet:** 11.5%.

Health: Life expect.: 49.6 male; 52.8 female. **Births:** 43.1 (per 1,000 pop.). **Deaths:** 13.4 (per 1,000 pop.). **Natural inc.:** 2.97%. **Infant mortality:** 70.6 (per 1,000 live births). **HIV rate:** 13.5%.

Education: Compulsory: ages 7-13. **Literacy:** 71.2%.

Major intl. organizations: UN (FAO, IBRD, ILO, IMF, WHO), AU, the Commonwealth, WTO.

Embassy: 2419 Massachusetts Ave. NW 20008; 265-9717.

Website: www.statehouse.gov.zm

Ruled by the British as Northern Rhodesia, the country became the independent republic of Zambia within the Commonwealth Oct. 24, 1964. Independence leader Kenneth Kaunda governed as president, 1964-91. A Zambian government corporation in 1970 took over 51% of two foreign-owned copper-mining companies. Privately-held land and other enterprises were nationalized in 1975. In the 1980s and 1990s lowered copper prices hurt the economy and severe drought caused famine.

Food riots erupted in June 1990. Elections held Oct. 1991 brought an end to Kaunda's one-party rule. The new government sought to sell state enterprises, including the copper industry. Pres. Frederick Chiluba won reelection Nov. 18, 1996. A coup attempt was suppressed Oct. 28, 1997.

Unable to change the constitution to allow himself a third term, Chiluba endorsed Levy Patrick Mwanawasa, who won a disputed election Dec. 27, 2001. Food shortages threatened more than 2 mil Zambians in 2002; the government refused to distribute shipments of U.S. grain because it was genetically modified. In a hard-fought election, Sept. 28, 2006, Mwanawasa won a second term. Accused of embezzling state funds as president, Chiluba was ordered to

pay $58 mil by a British court, June 7, 2007; he was acquitted by a Zambian court, Aug. 17, 2009, of misusing $500,000 in public money.

Pres. Mwanawasa suffered a stroke June 29, 2008, and died Aug. 19. Vice-Pres. Rupiah Banda became acting pres. He won the presidency by a narrow margin in an election Oct. 30, 2008, but lost to opposition leader Michael Sata Sept. 20, 2011.

The country has made progress in treating HIV/AIDS, which afflicts nearly 1 mil adults in Zambia.

Zimbabwe
Republic of Zimbabwe

People: Population: 12,619,600. **Age distrib.:** <15: 40.6%; 65+: 3.7%. **Pop. density:** 84.5 per sq mi, 32.6 per sq km. **Urban:** 38.6%. **Ethnic groups:** African 98% (Shona 82%, Ndebele 14%), mixed and Asian 1%. **Principal languages:** English (official), Shona, Sindebele, minor tribal dialects. **Chief religions:** syncretic (Christian and indigenous beliefs) 50%, Christian 25%, indigenous beliefs 24%, Muslim and other 1%.

Geography: Total area: 150,872 sq mi, 390,757 sq km; **Land area:** 149,362 sq mi, 386,847 sq km. **Location:** In southern Africa. **Neighbors:** Zambia on N, Botswana on W, South Africa on S, Mozambique on E. **Topography:** High plateau country, rising to mountains on E border, sloping down on other borders. **Capital:** Harare, 1,541,570.

Government: Type: In transition. **Head of state.:** Pres. Robert Gabriel Mugabe; b. Feb. 21, 1924; in office: Dec. 31, 1987. **Head of gov.:** Prime Min. Morgan Tsvangirai; b. Mar. 10, 1952; in office: Feb. 11, 2009. **Local divisions:** 8 provinces, 2 cities. **Defense budget:** $195 mil. **Active troops:** 29,000.

Economy: Industries: mining, steel, wood prods., cement, chemicals, fertilizer, clothing and footwear, foodstuffs. **Chief crops:** corn, cotton, tobacco, wheat, coffee, sugarcane, peanuts. **Natural resources:** coal, chromium ore, asbestos, gold, nickel, copper, iron ore, vanadium, lithium, tin, platinum group metals. **Arable land:** 10.8%. **Livestock:** cattle: 5 mil; chickens: 33 mil; goats: 2.7 mil; pigs: 635,000; sheep: 375,000. **Fish catch:** 13,202 metric tons. **Electricity prod.:** 7.6 bil kWh. **Labor force:** agric. 66%, industry 10%, services 24%.

Finance: Monetary unit: The U.S. dollar and South African rand have been in use since the Zimbabwean dollar (ZWD) stopped circulating in 2009; the Zimbabwe dollar is hence essentially worthless. **GDP:** $6.2 bil; **per capita GDP:** $500; **GDP growth:** 9.3%. **Imports:** $4.4 bil; South Africa 53.9%, China 9.4%. **Exports:** $2.9 bil; China 18.1%, Dem. Rep. of the Congo 12.5%, South Africa 11.3%, Botswana 11.2%, Italy 6.5%. **Tourism:** $634 mil. **Budget:** NA. **Total reserves less gold:** NA. **CPI change (2006-07):** 24,411%.

Transport: Railways: 2,129 mi. **Motor vehicles:** 40.6 vehicles per 1,000 pop. **Civil aviation:** 436.8 mil pass.-mi; 17 airports. **Chief ports:** Binga, Kariba.

Communications: TV sets: 71 per 1,000 pop. **Radios:** 135 per 1,000 pop. **Telephone lines:** 2.8 per 100 pop. **Internet:** 15.7%.

Health: Life expect.: 52.0 male; 51.7 female. **Births:** 32.2 (per 1,000 pop.). **Deaths:** 12.4 (per 1,000 pop.). **Natural inc.:** 1.98%. **Infant mortality:** 28.2 (per 1,000 live births). **HIV rate:** 14.3%.

Education: Compulsory: ages 6-12. **Literacy:** 92.2%.

Major intl. organizations: UN (FAO, IBRD, ILO, IMF, WHO), AU, WTO.

Embassy: 1608 New Hampshire Ave. NW 20009; 332-7100.

Website: www.zim.gov.zw

Britain took over the area as Southern Rhodesia in 1923 from the British South Africa Co. (which, under Cecil Rhodes, had conquered it by 1897) and granted internal self-government. A 1961 constitution restricted voting to keep whites in power.

On Nov. 11, 1965, Prime Min. Ian D. Smith unilaterally declared independence. Britain termed the act illegal and demanded that the country (known as Rhodesia until 1980) enfranchise the black African majority. The UN imposed sanctions and, in May 1968, a trade embargo, as black nationalists launched guerrilla attacks.

After the country held its first universal-franchise election, Apr. 21, 1979, all parties accepted a cease-fire, Dec. 5. The country changed its name to Zimbabwe upon independence, Apr. 18, 1980. Robert Mugabe, the nation's first prime min., became executive president in 1987.

From the late 1990s, Mugabe's rule became increasingly repressive. A land redistribution campaign triggered violent attacks in Apr. 2000 against some white farmers. (Whites made up less than 1% of the population but held 70% of the land.) Mugabe, relying on fraud and intimidation, international observers claimed, won the Mar. 9-11, 2002, presidential election. The EU, the U.S., and the Commonwealth imposed sanctions on the Mugabe regime. In May 2005, Mugabe launched Operation Murambatsvina ("Drive out rubbish"), razing shanty dwellings and illegal street markets in urban areas and leaving some 700,000 people homeless. During 2006-08, inflation soared to a yearly rate of more than 100,000%.

Mugabe clung to power after a widely discredited presidential election, Mar. 29, 2008, and June 27 runoff vote. A power-sharing deal was reached Sept. 15, 2008, and after prolonged negotiations, opposition leader Morgan Tsvangirai was sworn in as prime min., Feb. 11, 2009.

SPORTS

Sports Highlights, 2012

Alabama defeated LSU in the **BCS National Championship Game**, 21-0, in New Orleans, Jan. 9, avenging a 9-6 loss to the Tigers earlier in the season. It was the sixth straight championship for the Southeastern Conference and the first time two teams from the same conference met in the title game. The NY Giants defeated the New England Patriots 21-17 in **Super Bowl XLVI** at Lucas Oil Stadium in Indianapolis, IN, Feb. 5. The game was a rematch of Super Bowl XLII in 2008, when the Giants spoiled New England's bid for an undefeated season with a 17-14 win. Giants quarterback Eli Manning won the MVP award, just as he had four years earlier.

The Univ. of Kentucky won its eighth **NCAA men's basketball championship** Apr. 2, defeating the Univ. of Kansas in the final, 67-59, in New Orleans. The Wildcats started a lineup composed exclusively of freshmen and sophomores, all of whom left for the NBA draft at season's end. Defensive standout Anthony Davis, one of Kentucky's three freshman starters, was named most outstanding player. Led by senior center Brittney Griner, Baylor Univ. completed an undefeated 40-0 season with an 80-61 win over Notre Dame in the finals of the **NCAA women's basketball championship** Apr. 3 in Denver. Griner scored 26 points and had 13 rebounds in the final and was chosen the Final Four's most outstanding player.

American Bubba Watson literally came out of the trees to win his first **Masters Championship** in Augusta, GA, Apr. 8. The 33-year-old finished the final round tied with South Africa's Louis Oosthuizen. After both players missed birdie putts on the first playoff hole, Watson hooked what he called "a crazy shot" from the woods onto the green, then putted to win the green jacket. Webb Simpson, another relatively unheralded American, hit four birdies in the final round to capture the **U.S. Open** at San Francisco's Olympic Club June 17. The 26-year-old Simpson began the day four strokes behind leader and 2010 champion Graeme McDowell, who missed a birdie putt on the 18th hole that would have forced an 18-hole playoff. Australian Adam Scott was on his way July 22 to his first major win at the **British Open Championship**, at Royal Lytham & St. Annes Golf Club, England. But he gave up a six-stroke lead to South Africa's Ernie Els, who birdied four of the last nine holes for the victory. Northern Ireland's Rory McIlroy echoed his command performance at the 2011 U.S. Open with another eight-stroke victory at the **PGA Championship** Aug. 12 at the Ocean Course, Kiawah Island, SC.

Thoroughbred racing seemed like it might have its first triple crown winner since Affirmed in 1978, when I'll Have Another won both the **Kentucky Derby** May 5 and the **Preakness Stakes** in Baltimore two weeks later. But a leg injury forced the 4-5 favorite into retirement a day before the **Belmont Stakes** in New York June 9, and the race was won by Union Rags.

The L.A. Kings won their first **Stanley Cup** championship since the franchise debuted in the National Hockey League in 1967. The Kings soundly defeated the New Jersey Devils 6-1 in the sixth game in Los Angeles, June 11. Goalie Jonathan Quick, who allowed just seven goals in the finals, took the Conn Smythe Trophy for the most valuable player in the playoffs. The joy was short-lived, however, as NHL owners locked out players before the start of the 2012-13 season.

Led by NBA regular season and Finals MVP LeBron James, point guard Dwyane Wade, and forward Chris Bosh, the Miami Heat defeated the Oklahoma City Thunder in five games to capture the **NBA Championship**. It was the first title for Bosh and James, both of whom joined Miami as free agents in 2010.

American swimmer Michael Phelps became the most decorated Olympian in history at the **Summer Olympics** July 27-Aug. 12 in London, England. His 2012 tally of four gold and two silver medals brought his career total to 18 golds and a record 22 medals overall. The United States won the greatest number of medals (104) and gold medals (46) of any country. Women were responsible for more than half of the U.S. medal haul (58) and nearly two-thirds (29) of the gold medals. Gabrielle "Gabby" Douglas won the individual all-around gymnastics gold and powered the U.S. to the team gold. China (38 gold medals, 88 total) placed second in the medal count, while host country Great Britain captured a surprising 29 gold medals and 65 medals overall. Jamaica's Usain Bolt retained the title of world's fastest man by repeating his 2008 gold-medal-winning performances in the 100 meters, 200 meters, and 4x100 meter relay. For the first time, all represented nations sent women to compete as part of their Olympic delegations.

Major League Baseball added a second wild-card berth to each league in 2012, which kept more teams in the hunt for the postseason into Oct. St. Louis and Texas, who met in the World Series a year earlier, each claimed wild card berths, along with Atlanta and Baltimore. They joined National League division champs Washington, Cincinnati, and San Francisco, and American League division winners New York, Detroit, and Oakland, which overcame a 13-game deficit to win the AL West.

Pitching continued to demonstrate its importance with seven no-hitters in 2012. Three pitchers threw perfect games: Philip Humber of the Chicago White Sox (Apr. 21), San Francisco's Matt Cain (June 13), and Seattle's Felix Hernandez (Aug. 15). But performance-enhancing drugs continued to cast a long shadow over the game. San Francisco outfielder Melky Cabrera had been on track to finish with the National League's highest batting average before he was suspended for the final 45 games of the season for failing a drug test. Detroit's Miguel Cabrera became the 15th player in history, and the first since Carl Yastrzemski in 1967, to win baseball's triple crown. Cabrera led the American League in home runs (44), runs batted in (139), and batting average (.330).

Serbia's Novak Djokovic won his third straight Grand Slam over Spain's Rafael Nadal by outlasting him in an epic five-hour, 53-minute, five-set final in the **Australian Open** (Jan. 29). But Nadal got his revenge at the **French Open** (June 11), defeating Djokovic in four sets. Nadal's seven French Open crowns are the most in Roland Garros history. Roger Federer of Switzerland dispelled whispers that he was too old to win a major by beating Scotland's Andy Murray at **Wimbledon** (July 8). The 30-year-old became the oldest man to win a major since Arthur Ashe in 1975. Murray, who won the singles gold at the Olympic Games just weeks before, became the first British man to win a Grand Slam since Fred Perry in 1936, defeating Djokovic in a **U.S. Open** final delayed a day by rain (Sept. 10).

Victoria Azarenka became the first woman from Belarus ever to win a Grand Slam championship with a 6-3, 6-0 drubbing of Russia's Maria Sharapova at the **Australian Open** (Jan. 28). Sharapova rebounded to win the **French Open** (June 9), dispatching Italy's Sara Errani in straight sets. Thirty-year-old Serena Williams showed no signs of slowing down as she defeated Poland's Agnieszka Radwanska in three sets at **Wimbledon** (July 7), won Olympic gold in London in singles and doubles, then defeated Azarenka in three sets at the **U.S. Open** (Sept. 9).

College Football: At Last, a Playoff System

The NCAA's major football conference commissioners and a committee of university presidents and chancellors agreed June 20, 2012, to implement a playoff system to determine a national champion after the 2014 season. Under this new system, four teams chosen by a committee—similar to the one that selects the entrants in the NCAA basketball tournament—will meet in a three-game playoff. Two semifinal games will take place Dec. 31 or Jan. 1, and will rotate among six existing bowl sites over a 12-year period. The national championship will be played at a neutral site on the first Monday at least six days after the semifinals. The first championship game will be held Jan. 12, 2015. The new playoff system will end the controversial experiment known as the Bowl Championship Series (BCS), in which the site of the championship game rotated among the Rose, Fiesta, Sugar, and Orange Bowls. From 1999 to 2006, the national championship game replaced one of the four bowls; since 2007, the title game has been played as an additional contest at the same site, approximately a week after the bowl game.

When it was adopted in 1998, the system was heralded as a breakthrough way to settle the national championship on the playing field. For the previous 62 years, college football had selected a champion based on press polls of sportswriters and coaches. Disagreement between the polls led to co-champions 10 times. Even when polls settled on a single champion, their pick wasn't necessarily definitive. Because so many conferences had contractual agreements to meet in certain bowl games, top teams often failed to play one another.

While the BCS insured that the top two teams squared off, it continued to rely on a frequently changing mix of polls and computer rankings to determine who those top two teams were. There was criticism anytime three or more teams could legitimately claim to rank in the top two, especially when their records were equivalent.

The new playoff system won't satisfy every critic. The NCAA has yet to reveal its criteria for choosing the four playoff teams, though officials have intimated that it will involve some combination of record, schedule strength, head-to-head results, and conference championship games. Also in question is whether more than one team from a single conference could appear in the playoffs.

World Almanac Editors' Picks: Greatest College Football Games

In the days before national TV broadcasts and ESPN, college football was a largely regional sport, with few national observers qualified to compare games fluently. This chronological list is thus chosen from contests over the last 50 years.

The Perfect Game

Nebraska 35, Oklahoma 31: Nov. 25, 1971, Norman, OK

Both teams were 10-0 coming into this Thanksgiving Day contest. The defending national champion Nebraska Cornhuskers were ranked no. 1 and riding a 20-game winning streak, and the Oklahoma Sooners were no. 2. Despite trailing by 11 points twice, Oklahoma took a 31-28 fourth quarter lead on a touchdown pass from Jack Mildren to Jon Harrison. But Nebraska responded with a time-consuming scoring drive of their own. Dave Kindred, sportswriter for the *Louisville Courier-Journal*, summed up the contest as follows: "They can quit playing now, they have played the perfect game." ABC broadcast the contest to 55 million people nationally, at that time the largest audience ever for a college football game.

The Chicken Soup Game

Notre Dame 35, Houston 34: Jan. 1, 1979, Dallas, TX

The worst Dallas ice storm in 30 years made for challenging conditions in the 1979 Cotton Bowl, and hypothermia challenged Notre Dame quarterback Joe Montana. The Fighting Irish had jumped out to a 12-0 lead, but Houston countered with 34 unanswered points. Montana remained in the locker room after halftime, trying to elevate his body temperature with chicken soup. He returned to the field with 7:37 remaining and rallied Notre Dame to two touchdown drives, the last one on an 8-yard pass to Kris Haines with time expiring. Montana's performance has been known as the "Chicken Soup Game" ever since.

The Play

California 25, Stanford 20: Nov. 20, 1982, Berkeley, CA

When Stanford took a 20-19 lead with four seconds remaining, everybody assumed the game was over. That included the Cardinal band, which marched onto the field to celebrate their school's triumph over the archrival Golden Bears before the end of the ensuing kickoff return. The Cal return team lateraled the ball five times in a last-ditch attempt to keep the play alive, and somehow managed to avoid the Stanford defenders and oncoming musicians en route to the end zone. The bizarre sequence has been known henceforth simply as "The Play."

Hail Flutie

Boston College 47, Miami 45: Nov. 23, 1984, Miami, FL

Billed as a shootout between superstar quarterbacks, Miami's Bernie Kosar and Boston's Doug Flutie, this Friday-after-Thanksgiving classic did not disappoint. Both quarterbacks consistently marched their offenses down the field, amassing a combined 1,273 yards. Miami scored with 28 seconds left to take a 45-41 lead. But with six seconds remaining, Flutie, the eventual Heisman Trophy winner, scrambled out of the pocket before unloading a Hail Mary pass into the wind. It fell into the hands of his roommate, Gerard Phelan, 63 yards downfield and a yard deep into the end zone, for the winning touchdown.

Wide Left

Florida State 18, Nebraska 16: Jan. 1, 1994, Miami, FL

Fortune smiled on the 1994 Orange Bowl with an on-field meeting between the country's two top-ranked teams. Despite a loss to Notre Dame, the Seminoles were heavily favored over the undefeated Cornhuskers. The kickers for both teams figured prominently in this defensive battle, and Scott Bentley's 22-yard field goal gave Florida State the lead with 21 seconds remaining. Nebraska drove to the Seminole 28-yard line with one second remaining, but kicker Byron Bennett's 45-yard attempt was wide left. Florida State coach Bobby Bowden, whose 1991 and 1992 teams had been plagued by missed field goals, finally won his first national title.

Late Flag

Ohio State 31, Miami 24 (2 OT): Jan. 3, 2003, Tempe, AZ

The first BCS title game to go into overtime wasn't without controversy. The defending champion Hurricanes were riding a 34-game unbeaten streak and were heavily favored over the also-undefeated Buckeyes. Ohio State slowed Miami's offense to 369 yards, dueling to a 17-17 tie at the end of regulation. Miami appeared to claim victory in the first overtime after batting down Ohio State's fourth-down pass. But a late pass interference call gave the Buckeyes a second TD chance, which they converted. In the second OT, Ohio State scored again and its defense stopped Miami at the 1-yard line.

The Vince Young Show

Texas 41, USC 38: Jan. 4, 2006, Pasadena, CA

This game had everything: two undefeated teams—with freewheeling offenses featuring the top three finishers in the Heisman Trophy voting—clashing with a national championship on the line in the biggest bowl game of them all, the Rose Bowl. And the game was as good as the hype, with six lead changes throughout and 32 points scored in the fourth quarter. Texas quarterback Vince Young almost singlehandedly defeated offense put up by USC quarterback Matt Leinart and then-Heisman-winning tailback Reggie Bush. Young threw for 267 yards and rushed for 200, including runs of 17 and 8 yards for the Longhorns' final two touchdowns.

A Bag of Tricks

Boise State 43, Oklahoma 42: Jan. 1, 2007, Glendale, AZ

The Broncos went 13-0 in the Western Athletic Conference but didn't convince the BCS they belonged in the national title game. Boise State changed many minds after the thrilling 2007 Fiesta Bowl, however. Boise State led early 14-0, but with 1:02 remaining in the game, they trailed 35-28. On fourth-and-18, the Broncos scored on a 50-yard hook-and-lateral for the tie. The Sooners struck first in overtime, but Boise State again countered with a fourth-down touchdown pass. Rather than kick the extra point, Broncos coach Chris Petersen called a Statue of Liberty play to notch the winning two-point conversion. Boise State tailback Ian Johnson proposed to his girlfriend in the stands just moments after he scored the winning points.

OLYMPIC GAMES

General Olympic Information

The modern Olympic Games, first held in Athens, Greece, in 1896, were the result of efforts by Baron Pierre de Coubertin, a French educator, to promote interest in education and culture and to foster better international understanding through love of athletics. His inspiration was the ancient Greek Olympic Games, most notable of the four Panhellenic celebrations. The games were combined patriotic, religious, and athletic festivals held every four years. The first such recorded festival was held in 776 BCE, when the Greeks began to keep their calendar by "Olympiads," or four-year spans between the games.

Baron de Coubertin enlisted 14 nations to send athletes to the first modern Olympics in 1896; now athletes from more than 200 nations and territories compete in the Summer Olympics. The Winter Olympic Games were started in 1924.

Symbol: Five rings or circles, linked to represent the sporting friendship of all peoples. They also symbolize five geographic areas—Europe, Asia, Africa, Australia, and America. Each ring is a different color—blue, yellow, black, green, and red—which, with the color white, represent the colors of the world's flags.

Flag: The five-ring symbol on a plain white background.

Creed: "The most important thing in the Olympic Games is not to win but to take part, just as the most important thing in life is not the triumph but the struggle. The essential thing is not to have conquered but to have fought well."

Motto: "Citius, Altius, Fortius." Latin meaning "swifter, higher, stronger."

Oath: "In the name of all the competitors I promise that we shall take part in these Olympic Games, respecting and abiding by the rules which govern them, committing ourselves to a sport without doping and without drugs, in the true spirit of sportsmanship, for the glory of sport and the honor of our teams."

Flame: The modern version of the flame was adopted in 1936. The torch used to kindle it is first lit by the sun's rays at Olympia, Greece, then carried to the site of the Games by relays of runners. Ships and planes are used when necessary.

Winter Olympic Games Sites, 1924-2018

1924 Chamonix, France	1956 Cortina d'Ampezzo, Italy	1980 Lake Placid, NY, U.S.	2006 Turin, Italy
1928 St. Moritz, Switzerland		1984 Sarajevo, Yugoslavia	2010 Vancouver, BC, Canada
1932 Lake Placid, NY, U.S.	1960 Squaw Valley, CA, U.S.	1988 Calgary, AB, Canada	
1936 Garmisch-Partenkirchen, Germany	1964 Innsbruck, Austria	1992 Albertville, France	2014 Sochi, Russia
	1968 Grenoble, France	1994 Lillehammer, Norway	2018 PyeongChang, South Korea
1948 St. Moritz, Switzerland	1972 Sapporo, Japan	1998 Nagano, Japan	
1952 Oslo, Norway	1976 Innsbruck, Austria	2002 Salt Lake City, UT, U.S.	

Summer Olympic Games Sites, 1896-2016

1896 Athens, Greece	1928 Amsterdam, Netherlands	1964 Tokyo, Japan	1992 Barcelona, Spain
1900 Paris, France	1932 Los Angeles, CA, U.S.	1968 Mexico City, Mexico	1996 Atlanta, GA, U.S.
1904 St. Louis, MO, U.S.	1936 Berlin, Germany	1972 Munich, W. Germany	2000 Sydney, Australia
1906 Athens, Greece*	1948 London, England, UK	1976 Montreal, QC, Canada	2004 Athens, Greece
1908 London, England, UK	1952 Helsinki, Finland	1980 Moscow, USSR	2008 Beijing, China
1912 Stockholm, Sweden	1956 Melbourne, Australia	1984 Los Angeles, CA, U.S.	2012 London, England, UK
1920 Antwerp, Belgium	1960 Rome, Italy	1988 Seoul, South Korea	2016 Rio de Janeiro, Brazil
1924 Paris, France			

*Games not recognized by International Olympic Committee. **Note:** Games VI (1916), XII (1940), and XIII (1944) were not celebrated.

2012 Summer Olympic Games

London, England, UK, July 27-Aug. 12, 2012

London welcomed more than 11,000 athletes from 204 nations and territories at the Summer Olympic Games, July 27-Aug. 12, 2012. The XXX Summer Olympiad marked the first time in history that each nation or territory's delegation included women athletes.

The United States was ahead of all countries with 46 gold medals and 104 overall. Michael Phelps, who starred at the 2008 Beijing Olympics, led a U.S. swim team that dominated with 16 gold medals and 31 overall. Phelps topped all athletes at the Summer Games with six medals and became the all-time most decorated Olympian with 22 career medals. Fellow U.S. swimmers Missy Franklin, Ryan Lochte, and Allison Schmitt each collected five medals. A team of NBA stars carried the U.S. to basketball gold, topping Spain, 107-100, in the men's final. The gold medal-winning U.S. women's basketball team extended its Olympic winning streak to 41 games with an 86-50 win over France. In women's soccer, Carli Lloyd scored both goals as the U.S. defeated Japan, 2-1, to capture the gold medal, avenging the U.S. loss to Japan in the 2011 World Cup final. For the first time since 1996, U.S. women won the gymnastics team all-around gold, and Americans Gabrielle "Gabby" Douglas and Aly Raisman captured individual gold medals.

London hosted the Olympic Games for the third time and Britain's competitors recorded the country's best performance in over a century. British athletes won 65 medals overall, including 12 in cycling competitions. Among the British gold medalists were track and field stars Mo Farah (men's 5,000-m and 10,000-m) and Jessica Ennis (heptathlon), while Andy Murray earned tennis gold when he defeated Switzerland's Roger Federer in the final in straight sets. Jamaica's Usain Bolt, another star from Beijing 2008, electrified the London games. Bolt won gold in both the men's 100-m and 200-m sprints, as he did in Beijing, and was part of the team that won the 4x100-m relay in world-record time (36.84 seconds). South Africa's Oscar Pistorius became the first double-amputee to compete in the Olympics, reaching the semifinals in the men's track and field 400-m race and running in the 4x400-m relay.

Controversy ensued Aug. 1, 2012, when eight badminton players were kicked out of the Games. They had tried to purposely lose July 31 matches of the round-robin format in order to gain a more advantageous pairing in the knockout round. The players represented China, South Korea, and Indonesia.

2012 Summer Olympic Games Final Medal Standings

Country	G	S	B	T	Country	G	S	B	T	Country	G	S	B	T
United States	46	29	29	104	Ukraine...........	6	5	9	20	Kenya............	2	4	5	11
China............	38	27	23	88	Canada...........	1	5	12	18	Czech Republic	4	3	3	10
Russia............	24	26	32	82	Hungary..........	8	4	5	17	Azerbaijan	2	2	6	10
Great Britain	29	17	19	65	Spain	3	10	4	17	Poland	2	2	6	10
Germany..........	11	19	14	44	Brazil............	3	5	9	17	Romania..........	2	5	2	9
Japan............	7	14	17	38	Cuba............	5	3	6	14	Denmark..........	2	4	3	9
Australia..........	7	16	12	35	Kazakhstan.......	7	1	5	13	Sweden	1	4	3	8
France...........	11	11	12	34	New Zealand	6	2	5	13	Colombia	1	3	4	8
South Korea	13	8	7	28	Iran	4	5	3	12	Ethiopia	3	1	3	7
Italy.............	8	9	11	28	Jamaica	4	4	4	12	Georgia...........	1	3	3	7
Netherlands	6	6	8	20	Belarus	2	5	5	12	Mexico	1	3	3	7

Country	G	S	B	T
North Korea	4	0	2	6
South Africa	3	2	1	6
Croatia	3	1	2	6
India	0	2	4	6
Turkey	2	2	1	5
Lithuania	2	1	2	5
Ireland	1	1	3	5
Mongolia	0	2	3	5
Switzerland	2	2	0	4
Norway	2	1	1	4
Argentina	1	1	2	4
Serbia	1	1	2	4
Slovenia	1	1	2	4
Trinidad and Tobago	1	0	3	4
Uzbekistan	1	0	3	4
Slovakia	0	1	3	4
Tunisia	1	1	1	3
Thailand	0	2	1	3

Country	G	S	B	T
Armenia	0	1	2	3
Belgium	0	1	2	3
Finland	0	1	2	3
Dominican Republic	1	1	0	2
Latvia	1	0	1	2
Egypt	0	2	0	2
Bulgaria	0	1	1	2
Estonia	0	1	1	2
Indonesia	0	1	1	2
Malaysia	0	1	1	2
Puerto Rico	0	1	1	2
Taiwan	0	1	1	2
Greece	0	0	2	2
Moldova	0	0	2	2
Qatar	0	0	2	2
Singapore	0	0	2	2
Algeria	1	0	0	1

Country	G	S	B	T
The Bahamas	1	0	0	1
Grenada	1	0	0	1
Uganda	1	0	0	1
Venezuela	1	0	0	1
Botswana	0	1	0	1
Cyprus	0	1	0	1
Gabon	0	1	0	1
Guatemala	0	1	0	1
Montenegro	0	1	0	1
Portugal	0	1	0	1
Afghanistan	0	0	1	1
Bahrain	0	0	1	1
Hong Kong	0	0	1	1
Kuwait	0	0	1	1
Morocco	0	0	1	1
Saudi Arabia	0	0	1	1
Tajikistan	0	0	1	1

2012 Summer Olympic Medal Winners

Archery

Men's Team: G-Italy, S-U.S., B-South Korea.
Women's Team: G-South Korea, S-China, B-Japan.
Men's Individual: G-Oh Jin-Hyek, South Korea; S-Takaharu Furukawa, Japan; B-Dai Xiaoxiang, China.
Women's Individual: G-Ki Bo-Bae, South Korea; S-Aída Román, Mexico; B-Mariana Avitia, Mexico.

Badminton

Men's Singles: G-Lin Dan, China; S-Lee Chong Wei, Malaysia; B-Chen Long, China.
Men's Doubles: G-Cai Yun & Fu Haifeng, China; S-Mathias Boe & Carsten Mogensen, Denmark; B-Jeong Jae-Seong & Lee Yong-Dae, South Korea.
Women's Singles: G-Li Xuerui, China; S-Wang Yihan, China; B-Saina Nehwal, Indonesia.
Women's Doubles G-Tian Qing & Zhao Yunlei, China; S-Mizuki Fujii & Reika Kakiiwa, Japan; B-Valeriya Sorokina & Nina Vislova, Russia.
Mixed Doubles: G-Zhang Nan & Zhao Yunlei, China; S-Xu Chen & Ma Jin, China; B-Joachim Fischer Nielsen & Christinna Pedersen, Denmark.

Basketball

Men: G-U.S., S-Spain, B-Russia.
Women: G-U.S., S-France, B-Australia.

Beach Volleyball

Men: G-Julius Brink & Jonas Reckermann, Germany; S-Alison Cerutti & Emanuel, Brazil; B-Mārtiņš Pļaviņš & Jānis Šmēdiņš, Latvia.
Women: G-Kerri Walsh & Misty May-Treanor, U.S.; S-April Ross & Jen Kessy, U.S.; B-Juliana Silva & Larissa Franca, Brazil.

Boxing
Men

Light-Flyweight (49 kg/108 lbs): G-Zou Shiming, China; S-Kaeo Pongprayoon, Thailand; B-Paddy Barnes, Ireland; B-David Ayrapetyan, Russia.
Flyweight (52 kg/114 lbs): G-Robeisy Ramírez, Cuba; S-Nyambayaryn Tögstsogt, Mongolia; B-Misha Aloyan, Russia; B-Michael Conlan, Ireland.
Bantamweight (56 kg/123 lbs): G-Luke Campbell, Great Britain; S-John Joe Nevin, Ireland; B-Lazaro Alvárez, Cuba; B-Satoshi Shimizu, Japan.
Lightweight (60 kg/132 lbs): G-Vasyl Lomachenko, Ukraine; S-Han Sun-Cheol, South Korea; B-Yasnier Toledo, Cuba; B-Evaldas Petrauskas, Lithuania.
Light-Welterweight (64 kg/141 lbs): G-Rosniel Iglesias, Cuba; S-Denys Berinchyk, Ukraine; B-Vincenzo Mangiacapre, Italy; B-Uranchimegiin Mönkh-Erdene, Mongolia.
Welterweight (69 kg/152 lbs): G-Serik Sapiyev, Kazakhstan; S-Fred Evans, Great Britain; B-Taras Shelestyuk, Ukraine; B-Andrey Zamkovoy, Russia.
Middleweight (75 kg/165 lbs): G-Ryota Murata, Japan; S-Esquiva Florentino, Brazil; B-Anthony Ogogo, Great Britain; B-Abbos Atayev, Uzbekistan.
Light-Heavyweight (81 kg/178 lbs): G-Yegor Mekhontsev, Russia; S-Adilbek Niyazymbetov, Kazakhstan; B-Yamaguchi Florentino, Brazil; B-Oleksandr Gvozdyk, Ukraine.

Heavyweight (91 kg/201 lbs): G-Oleksandr Usik, Ukraine; S-Clemente Russo, Italy; B-Tervel Pulev, Bulgaria; B-Teymur Mammadov, Azerbaijan.
Super-Heavyweight (91+ kg/201+ lbs): G-Anthony Joshua, Great Britain; S-Roberto Cammarelle, Italy; B-Magomedrasul Medzhidov, Azerbaijan; B-Ivan Dychko, Kazakhstan.

Women

Flyweight (51 kg/112 lbs): G-Nicola Adams, Great Britain; S-Ren Cancan, China; B-Marlen Esparza, U.S.; B-Chungneijang Mery Kom Hmangte, India.
Lightweight, (60 kg/132 lbs): G-Katie Taylor, Ireland; S-Sofya Ochigava, Russia; B-Mavzuna Chorieva, Tajikistan; B-Adriana Araújo, Brazil.
Middleweight (75 kg/165 lbs): G-Claressa Shields, U.S.; S-Nadezhda Torlopova, Russia; B-Marina Volnova, Kazakhstan; B-Li Jinzi, China.

Canoe/Kayak—Flatwater
Men

Canoe Single (200m): G-Yuriy Cheban, Ukraine; S-Jevgenijus Šuklinas, Lithuania; B-Ivan Shtyl, Russia.
Canoe Single (1,000m): G-Sebastian Brendel, Germany; S-David Cal, Spain; B-Mark Oldershaw, Canada.
Canoe Double (1,000m): G-Peter Kretschmer & Kurt Kuschela, Germany; S-Andrey Bogdanovich & Aleksandr Bogdanovich, Belarus; B-Aleksey Korovashkov & Ilya Pervukhin, Russia.
Kayak Single (200m): G-Ed McKeever, Great Britain; S-Saúl Craviotto, Spain; B-Mark de Jonge, Canada.
Kayak Double (200m): G-Yury Postrigay & Aleksandr Dyachenko, Russia; S-Roman Petrushenko & Vadim Makhnyov, Belarus; B-Liam Heath & Jon Schofield, Great Britain.
Kayak Single (1,000m): G-Eirik Verås Larsen, Norway; S-Adam Van Koeverden, Canada; B-Max Hoff, Germany.
Kayak Double (1,000m): G-Rudolf Dombi & Roland Kökény, Hungary; S-Fernando Pimenta & Emanuel Silva, Portugal; B-Martin Hollstein & Andreas Ihle, Germany.
Kayak Four (1,000m): G-Australia, S-Hungary, B-Czech Republic.

Women

Kayak Single (200m): G-Lisa Carrington, New Zealand; S-Inna Osypenko-Radomska, Ukraine; B-Natasa Douchev-Janics, Hungary.
Kayak Single (500m): G-Danuta Kozák, Hungary; S-Inna Osypenko-Radomska, Ukraine; B-Bridgitte Hartley, South Africa.
Kayak Double (500m): G-Franziska Weber & Tina Dietze, Germany; S-Katalin Kovács & Natasa Douchev-Janics; B-Karolina Naja & Beata Mikołajczyk, Poland.
Kayak Four (500m): G-Hungary, S-Germany, B-Belarus.

Canoe/Kayak—Slalom

Men's Canoe Single (Slalom): G-Tony Estanguet, France; S-Sideris Tasiadis, Germany; B-Michal Martikán, Slovakia.
Men's Canoe Double (Slalom): G-Tim Baillie & Etienne Stott, Great Britain; S-David Florence & Richard Hounslow, Great Britain; B-Pavol Hochschorner & Peter Hochschorner, Slovakia.
Men's Kayak (Slalom): G-Daniele Molmenti, Italy; S-Vavřinec Hradílek, Czech Republic; B-Hannes Aigner, Germany.
Women's Kayak (Slalom): G-Emilie Fer, France; S-Jessica Fox, Australia; B-Maialen Chourraut, Spain.

Cycling—BMX

Men: G-Māris Štrombergs, Latvia; S-Sam Willoughby, Australia; B-Carlos Oquendo, Colombia.
Women: G-Mariana Pajón, Colombia; S-Sarah Walker, New Zealand; B-Laura Smulders, Netherlands.

Cycling—Mountain Bike

Men's Cross Country: G-Jaroslav Kulhavý, Czech Republic; S-Nino Schurter, Switzerland; B-Marco Aurelio Fontana, Italy.
Women's Cross Country: G-Julie Bresset, France; S-Sabine Spitz, Germany; B-Georgia Gould, U.S.

Cycling—Road

Men's Road Race: G-Aleksandr Vinokurov, Kazakhstan; S-Rigoberto Urán, Colombia; B-Alexander Kristoff, Norway.
Men's Individual Time Trial: G-Bradley Wiggins, Great Britain; S-Tony Martin, Germany; B-Chris Froome, Great Britain.
Women's Road Race: G-Marianne Vos, Netherlands; S-Elizabeth Armitstead, Great Britain; B-Olga Zabelinskaya, Russia.
Women's Individual Time Trial: G-Kristin Armstrong, U.S.; S-Judith Arndt, Germany; B-Olga Zabelinskaya, Russia.

Cycling—Track
Men

Team Sprint: G-Great Britain, S-France, B-Germany.
Team Pursuit: G-Great Britain, S-Australia, B-New Zealand.
Sprint: G-Jason Kenny, Great Britain; S-Grégory Baugé, France; B-Shane Perkins, Australia.
Keirin: G-Chris Hoy, Great Britain; S-Maximilian Levy, Germany; B-Simon van Velthooven, New Zealand; B-Teun Mulder, Netherlands.
Omnium: G-Lasse Norman Hansen, Denmark; S-Bryan Coquard, France; B-Ed Clancy, Great Britain.

Women

Team Sprint: G-Germany, S-China, B-Australia.
Team Pursuit: G-Great Britain, S-U.S., B-Canada.
Sprint: G-Anna Meares, Australia; S-Vicki Pendleton, Great Britain; B-Guo Shuang, China.
Keirin: G-Vicki Pendleton, Great Britain; S-Guo Shuang, China; B-Lee Wai Sze, Hong Kong, China.
Omnium: G-Laura Trott, Great Britain; S-Sarah Hammer, U.S.; B-Annette Edmondson, Australia.

Diving
Men

Platform: G-David Boudia, U.S.; S-Qiu Bo, China; B-Tom Daley, Great Britain.
Springboard: G-Ilya Zakharov, Russia; S-Qin Kai, China; B-He Chong, China.
Synchronized Platform: G-Cao Yuan & Zhang Yanquan, China; S-Iván García & Germán Sánchez, Mexico; B-David Boudia & Nick McCrory, U.S.
Synchronized Springboard: G-Luo Yutong & Qin Kai, China; S-Yevgeny Kuznetsov & Ilya Zakharov, Russia; B-Troy Dumais & Kristian Ipsen, U.S.

Women

Platform: G-Chen Ruolin, China; S-Brittany Broben, Australia; B-Pandelela Pamg, Malaysia.
Springboard: G-Wu Minxia, China; S-He Zi, China; B-Laura Sánchez, Mexico.
Synchronized Platform: G-Chen Ruolin & Wang Hao, China; S-Paola Espinosa & Alejandra Orozco, Mexico; B-Meaghan Benfeito & Roseline Filion, Canada.
Synchronized Springboard: G-He Zi & Wu Minxia, China; S-Kelci Bryant & Abby Johnston, U.S.; B-Jennifer Abel & Emilie Heymans, Canada.

Equestrian

Individual Dressage: G-Charlotte Dujardin, Great Britain; S-Adelinde Cornelissen, Netherlands; B-Laura Bechtolsheimer, Great Britain.
Team Dressage: G-Great Britain, S-Germany, B-Netherlands.
Three-Day Event, Individual, Mixed: G-Michael Jung, Germany; S-Sara Algotsson, Sweden; B-Sandra Auffarth, Germany.
Three-Day Event, Team, Mixed: G-Germany, S-Great Britain, B-New Zealand.

Individual Jumping: G-Steve Guerdat, Switzerland; S-Gerco Schröder, Netherlands; B-Cian O'Connor, Ireland.
Team Jumping: G-Great Britain, S-Netherlands, B-Saudi Arabia.

Fencing
Men

Épée, Individual: G-Rubén Limardo, Venezuela; S-Bartosz Piasecki, Norway; B-Jeong Jin-Seon, South Korea.
Foil, Individual: G-Lei Sheng, China; S-Alaaeldin Abouelkassem, Egypt; B-Choi Byeong-Cheol, South Korea.
Sabre, Individual: G-Áron Szilágyi, Hungary; S-Diego Occhiuzzi, Italy; B-Nikolay Kovalyov, Russia.
Foil, Team: G-Italy, S-Japan, B-Germany.
Sabre, Team: G-South Korea, S-Romania, B-Italy.

Women

Épée, Individual: G-Yana Shemiakina, Ukraine; S-Britta Heidemann, Germany; B-Sun Yujie, China.
Foil, Individual: G-Elisa di Francisca, Italy; S-Arianna Errigo, Italy; B-Valentina Vezzali, Italy.
Sabre, Individual: G-Kim Ji-Yeon, South Korea; S-Sofiya Velikaya, Russia; B-Olha Kharlan, Ukraine.
Foil, Team: G-Italy, S-Russia, B-South Korea.
Épée, Team: G-China, S-South Korea, B-U.S.

Field Hockey

Men: G-Germany, S-Netherlands, B-Australia.
Women: G-Netherlands, S-Argentina, B-Great Britain.

Gymnastics—Artistic
Men

Floor Exercise: G-Zou Kai, China; S-Kohei Uchimura, Japan; B-Denis Ablyazin, Russia.
Horizontal Bar: G-Epke Zonderland, Netherlands; S-Fabian Hambüchen, Germany; B-Zou Kai, China.
Individual All-Around: G-Kohei Uchimura, Japan; S-Marcel Nguyen, Germany; B-Danell Leyva, U.S.
Parallel Bars: G-Feng Zhe, China; S-Marcel Nguyen, Germany; B-Hamilton Sabot, France.
Pommel Horse: G-Krisztián Berki, Hungary; S-Louis Smith, Great Britain; B-Max Whitlock, Great Britain.
Rings: G-Arthur Zanetti, Brazil; S-Chen Yibing, China; B-Matteo Morandi, Italy.
Team Competition: G-China, S-Japan, B-Great Britain.
Vault: G-Yang Hak-Seon, South Korea; S-Denis Ablyazin, Russia; B-Igor Radivilov, Ukraine.

Women

Balance Beam: G-Deng Linlin, China; S-Sui Lu, China; B-Aly Raisman, U.S.
Floor Exercise: G-Aly Raisman, U.S.; S-Cătălina Ponor, Romania; B-Aliya Mustafina, Russia.
Individual All-Around: G-Gabby Douglas, U.S.; S-Viktoriya Komova, Russia; B-Aliya Mustafina, Russia.
Team Competition: G-U.S., S-Russia, B-Romania.
Uneven Bars: G-Aliya Mustafina, Russia; S-He Kexin, China; B-Beth Tweddle, Great Britain.
Vault: G-Sandra Izbaşa, Romania; S-McKayla Maroney, U.S.; B-Mariya Paseka, Russia.

Gymnastics—Rhythmic

Group All-Around: G-Russia, S-Belarus, B-Italy.
Individual All-Around: G-Yevgeniya Kanayeva, Russia; S-Dariya Dmitriyeva, Russia; B-Lyubov Cherkashina, Belarus.

Gymnastics—Trampoline

Men: G-Dong Dong, China; S-Dmitry Ushakov, Russia; B-Lu Chunlong, China.
Women: G-Rosie MacLennan, Canada; S-Huang Shanshan, China; B-He Wenna, China.

Handball

Men: G-France, S-Sweden, B-Croatia.
Women: G-Norway, S-Montenegro, B-Spain.

Judo
Men

60 kg/132 lbs: G-Arsen Galstyan, Russia; S-Hiroaki Hiraoka, Japan; B-Felipe Kitadai, Brazil; B-Rishod Sobirov, Uzbekistan.
66 kg/145 lbs: G-Lasha Shavdatuashvili, Georgia; S-Miklós Ungvári, Hungary; B-Masashi Ebinuma, Japan; B-Jo Jun-Ho, South Korea.

73 kg/161 lbs: G-Mansur Isayev, Russia; S-Riki Nakaya, Japan; B-Saynjargalyn Nyam-Ochir, Mongolia; B-Ugo Legrand, France.

81 kg/178 lbs: G-Kim Jae-Beom, South Korea; S-Ole Bischof, Germany; B-Ivan Nifontov, Russia; B-Antoine Valois-Fortier, Canada.

90 kg/198 lbs: G-Song Dae-Nam, South Korea; S-Asley González, Cuba; B-Ilias Iliadis, Greece; B-Masashi Nishiyama, Japan.

100 kg/220 lbs: G-Tagir Khaybulayev, Russia; S-Naidangiin Tüvshinbayar, Mongolia; B-Dimitri Peters, Germany; B-Henk Grol, Netherlands.

100+ kg/220+ lbs: G-Teddy Riner, France; S-Aleksandr Mikhaylin, Russia; B-Andreas Tölzer, Germany; B-Rafael da Silva, Brazil.

Women

48 kg/106 lbs: G-Sarah Menezes, Brazil; S-Alina Dumitru, Romania; B-Charline Van Snick, Belgium; B-Éva Csernoviczki, Hungary.

52 kg/114 lbs: G-An Kum-Ae, North Korea; S-Yanet Bermoy, Cuba; B-Rosalba Forciniti, Italy; B-Priscilla Gneto, France.

57 kg/125 lbs: G-Kaori Matsumoto, Japan; S-Corina Căprioriu, Romania; B-Marti Malloy, U.S.; B-Automne Pavia, France.

63 kg/139 lbs: G-Urška Žolnir, Slovenia; S-Xu Lili, China; B-Yoshie Ueno, Japan; B-Gevrise Emane, France.

70 kg/154 lbs: G-Lucie Décosse, France; S-Kerstin Thiele, Germany; B-Yuri Alvear, Colombia; B-Edith Bosch, Netherlands.

78 kg/172 lbs: G-Kayla Harrison, U.S.; S-Gemma Gibbons, Great Britain; B-Audrey Tcheumeo, France; B-Mayra Silva, Brazil.

78+ kg/172+ lbs: G-Idalys Ortíz, Cuba; S-Mika Sugimoto, Japan; B-Karina Bryant, Great Britain; B-Tong Wen, China.

Modern Pentathlon

Men: G-David Svoboda, Czech Republic; S-Cao Zhongrong, China; B-Ádám Marosi, Hungary.

Women: G-Laura Asadauskaitė, Lithuania; S-Samantha Murray, Great Britain; B-Yane Marques, Brazil.

Rowing
Men

Single Sculls: G-Mahe Drysdale, New Zealand; S-Ondřej Synek, Czech Republic; B-Alan Campbell, Great Britain.

Pairs: G-Eric Murray & Hamish Bond, New Zealand; S-Germain Chardin & Dorian Mortelette, France; B-George Nash & Will Satch, Great Britain.

Double Sculls: G-Nathan Cohen & Joseph Sullivan, New Zealand; S-Alessio Sartori & Romano Battisti, Italy; B-Luka Špik & Iztok Čop, Slovenia.

Lightweight Double Sculls: G-Mads Rasmussen & Rasmus Quist, Denmark; S-Zac Purchase & Mark Hunter, Great Britain; B-Storm Uru & Peter Taylor, New Zealand.

Four: G-Great Britain, S-Australia, B-U.S.

Lightweight Four: G-South Africa, S-Great Britain, B-Denmark.

Quadruple Sculls: G-Germany, S-Croatia, B-Australia.

Eight: G-Germany, S-Canada, B-Great Britain.

Women

Single Sculls: G-Miroslava Knapková, Czech Republic; S-Fie Udby Erichsen, Denmark; B-Kim Crow, Australia.

Pairs: G-Helen Glover & Heather Stanning, Great Britain; S-Kate Hornsey & Sarah Tait, Australia; B-Juliette Haigh & Rebecca Scown, New Zealand.

Double Sculls: G-Anna Bebington & Katherine Grainger, Great Britain; S-Kim Crow & Brooke Pratley, Australia; B-Magdalena Fularczyk & Julia Michalska, Poland.

Lightweight Double Sculls: G-Kat Copeland & Sophie Hosking, Great Britain; S-Xu Dongxiang & Huang Wenyi, China; B-Khristina Giazitzidou & Alexandra Tsiavou, Greece.

Quadruple Sculls: G-Ukraine, S-Germany, B-U.S.

Eight: G-U.S., S-Canada, B-Netherlands.

Sailing
Men

RS-X: G-Dorian van Rijsselberge, Netherlands; S-Nick Dempsey, Great Britain; B-Przemysław Miarczyński, Poland.

Laser: G-Tom Slingsby, Australia; S-Pavlos Kontides, Cyprus; B-Rasmus Myrgren, Sweden.

Two Person Dinghy (470): G-Mathew Belcher & Malcolm Page, Australia; S-Stuart Bithell & Luke Patience, Great Britain; B-Lucas Calabrese & Juan de la Fuente, Argentina.

Two Person Keelboat (Star): G-Max Salminen & Fredrik Lööf, Sweden; S-Iain Percy & Andrew Simpson, Great Britain; B-Bruno Prada & Robert Scheidt, Brazil.

49er: G-Iain Jensen & Nathan Outteridge, Australia; S-Peter Burling & Blair Tuke, New Zealand; B-Peter Ørsted Lang & Allan Nørregaard, Denmark.

Finn: G-Ben Ainslie, Great Britain; S-Jonas Høgh Christensen, Denmark; B-Jonathan Lobert, France.

Women

RS-X: G-Marina Alabau, Spain; S-Tuuli Petäjä, Finland; B-Zofia Noceti-Klepacka, Poland.

Laser Radial: G-Xu Lijia, China; S-Marit Bouwmeester, Netherlands; B-Evi Van Acker, Belgium.

Two Person Dinghy (470): G-Jo Aleh & Olivia Powrie, New Zealand; S-Saskia Clark & Hannah Mills, Great Britain; B-Lobke Berkhout & Lisa Westerhof, Netherlands.

Elliott 6m: G-Spain, S-Australia, B-Finland.

Shooting
Men

Skeet: G-Vincent Hancock, U.S.; S-Anders Golding, Denmark; B-Nasser Al-Attiya, Qatar.

Double Trap: G-Peter Robert Russell Wilson, Great Britain; S-Håkan Dahlby, Sweden; B-Vasily Mosin, Russia.

Trap: G-Giovanni Cernogoraz, Croatia; S-Massimo Fabbrizi, Italy; B-Fehaid Al-Deehani, Kuwait.

10-m Air Pistol: G-Jin Jong-Oh, South Korea; S-Luca Tesconi, Italy; B-Andrija Zlatić, Serbia.

10-m Air Rifle: G-Alin Moldoveanu, Romania; S-Niccolò Campriani, Italy; B-Gagan Narang, India.

25-m Rapid-Fire Pistol: G-Leuris Pupo, Cuba; S-Vijay Kumar, India; B-Ding Feng, China.

50-m Free Pistol: G-Jin Jong-Oh, South Korea; S-Choi Yeong-Rae, South Korea; B-Wang Zhiwei, China.

50-m Small-Bore Rifle, Prone: G-Sergey Martynov, Belarus; S-Lionel Cox, Belgium; B-Rajmond Debevec, Slovenia.

50-m Small-Bore Rifle, Three Positions: G-Niccolò Campriani, Italy; S-Kim Jong-Hyeon, South Korea; B-Matt Emmons, U.S.

Women

Skeet: G-Kim Rhode, U.S.; S-Wei Ning, China; B-Danka Barteková, Slovakia.

Trap: G-Jessica Rossi, Italy; S-Zuzana Štefečeková, Slovakia; B-Delphine Racinet, France.

10-m Air Pistol: G-Guo Wenjun, China; S-Celine Goberville, France; B-Olena Kostevych, Ukraine.

10-m Air Rifle: G-Yi Siling, China; S-Sylwia Bogacka, Poland; B-Yu Dan, China.

25-m Sporting Pistol: G-Kim Jang-Mi, South Korea; S-Chen Ying, China; B-Olena Kostevych, Ukraine.

50-m Small-Bore Rifle, Three Positions: G-Jamie (Beyerle) Gray, U.S.; S-Ivana Maksimović, Serbia; B-Adéla Sýkorová, Czech Republic.

Soccer

Men: G-Mexico, S-Brazil, B-South Korea.

Women: G-U.S., S-Japan, B-Canada.

Swimming
Men

100-m Backstroke: G-Matt Grevers, U.S.; S-Nick Thoman, U.S.; B-Ryosuke Irie, Japan.

200-m Backstroke: G-Tyler Clary, U.S.; S-Ryosuke Irie, Japan; B-Ryan Lochte, U.S.

100-m Breaststroke: G-Cameron van der Burgh, South Africa; S-Christian Sprenger, Australia; B-Brendan Hansen, U.S.

200-m Breaststroke: G-Dániel Gyurta, Hungary; S-Michael Jamieson, Great Britain; B-Ryo Tateishi, Japan.

100-m Butterfly: G-Michael Phelps, U.S.; S-Chad le Clos, South Africa; S-Yevgeny Korotyshkin, Russia.

200-m Butterfly: G-Chad le Clos, South Africa; S-Michael Phelps, U.S.; B-Takeshi Matsuda, Japan.

50-m Freestyle: G-Florent Manaudou, France; S-Cullen Jones, U.S.; B-César Cielo Filho, Brazil.

100-m Freestyle: G-Nathan Adrian, U.S.; S-James Magnussen, Australia; B-Brent Hayden, Canada.
200-m Freestyle: G-Yannick Agnel, France; S-Park Tae-Hwan, South Korea; S-Sun Yang, China.
400-m Freestyle: G-Sun Yang, China; S-Park Tae-Hwan, South Korea; B-Peter Vanderkaay, U.S.
1,500-m Freestyle: G-Sun Yang, China; S-Ryan Cochrane, Canada; B-Oussama Mellouli, Tunisia.
200-m Individual Medley: G-Michael Phelps, U.S.; S-Ryan Lochte, U.S.; B-László Cseh Jr., Hungary.
400-m Individual Medley: G-Ryan Lochte, U.S.; S-Thiago Pereira, Brazil; B-Kosuke Hagino, Japan.
4×100-m Freestyle Relay: G-France, S-U.S., B-Russia.
4×200-m Freestyle Relay: G-U.S., S-France, B-China.
4×100-m Medley Relay: G-U.S., S-Japan, B-Australia.
10-km Marathon: G-Oussama Mellouli, Tunisia; S-Thomas Lurz, Germany; B-Richard Weinberger, Canada.

Women
100-m Backstroke: G-Missy Franklin, U.S.; S-Emily Seebohm, Australia; B-Aya Terakawa, Japan.
200-m Backstroke: G-Missy Franklin, U.S.; S-Anastasiya Zuyeva, Russia; B-Elizabeth Beisel, U.S.
100-m Breaststroke: G-Rūta Meilutytė, Lithuania; S-Rebecca Soni, U.S.; B-Satomi Suzuki, Japan.
200-m Breaststroke: G-Rebecca Soni, U.S.; S-Satomi Suzuki, Japan; B-Yuliya Yefimova, Russia.
100-m Butterfly: G-Dana Vollmer, U.S.; S-Lu Ying, China; B-Alicia Coutts, Australia.
200-m Butterfly: G-Jiao Liuyang, China; S-Mireia Belmonte, Spain; B-Natsumi Hoshi, Japan.
50-m Freestyle: G-Ranomi Kromowidjojo, Netherlands; S-Aleksandra Gerasimenya, Belarus; B-Marleen Veldhuis, Netherlands.
100-m Freestyle: G-Ranomi Kromowidjojo, Netherlands; S-Aleksandra Gerasimenya, Belarus; B-Tang Yi, China.
200-m Freestyle: G-Allison Schmitt, U.S.; S-Camille Muffat, France; B-Bronte Barratt, Australia.
400-m Freestyle: G-Camille Muffat, France; S-Allison Schmitt, U.S.; B-Becky Adlington, Great Britain.
800-m Freestyle: G-Katie Ledecky, U.S.; S-Mireia Belmonte, Spain; B-Becky Adlington, Great Britain.
200-m Individual Medley: G-Ye Shiwen, China; S-Alicia Coutts, Australia; B-Caitlin Leverenz, U.S.
400-m Individual Medley: G-Ye Shiwen, China; S-Elizabeth Beisel, U.S.; B-Li Xuanxu, China.
4×100-m Freestyle Relay: G-Australia, S-Netherlands, B-U.S.
4×200-m Freestyle Relay: G-U.S., S-Australia, B-France.
4×100-m Medley Relay: G-U.S., S-Australia, B-Japan.
10-km Marathon: G-Éva Risztov, Hungary; S-Haley Anderson, U.S.; B-Martina Grimaldi, Italy.

Synchronized Swimming
Duet: G-Nataliya Ishchenko & Svetlana Romashina, Russia; S-Ona Carbonell & Andrea Fuentes, Spain; B-Huang Xuechen & Liu Ou, China.
Team: G-Russia, S-China, B-Spain.

Table Tennis
Men's Singles: G-Zhang Jike, China; S-Wang Hao, China; B-Dmitrij Ovtcharov, Germany.
Men's Team: G-China, S-South Korea, B-Germany.
Women's Singles: G-Li Xiaoxia, China; S-Ding Ning, China; B-Feng Tian Wei, Singapore.
Women's Team: G-China, S-Japan, B-Singapore.

Taekwondo
Men
58 kg/128 lbs: G-Joel González, Spain; S-Lee Dae-Hun, South Korea; B-Oscar Muñoz, Colombia; B-Aleksey Denisenko, Russia.
68 kg/150 lbs: G-Servet Tazegül, Turkey; S-Mohammad Bagheri Motamed, Iran; B-Rohullah Nikpai, Afghanistan; B-Terrence Jennings, U.S.
80 kg/176 lbs: G-Sebastian Crismanich, Argentina; S-Nicolás García, Spain; B-Lutalo Muhammad, Great Britain; B-Mauro Sarmiento, Italy.
80+ kg/176+ lbs: G-Carlo Molfetta, Italy; S-Anthony Obame, Gabon; B-Liu Xiaobo, China; B-Robelis Despaigne, Cuba.

Women
49 kg/108 lbs: G-Wu Jingyu, China; S-Brigitte Yagüe, Spain; B-Lucija Zaninović, Croatia; B-Chanatip Sonkham, Thailand.
57 kg/126 lbs: G-Jade Jones, Great Britain; S-Hou Yuzhuo, China; B-Marlene Harnois, France; B-Tseng Li-Cheng, Taiwan.
67 kg/148 lbs: G-Hwang Gyeong-Seon, South Korea; S-Nur Tatar, Turkey; B-Paige McPherson, U.S.; B-Helena Fromm, Germany.
67+ kg/148+ lbs: G-Milica Mandić, Serbia; S-Anne-Caroline Graffe, France; B-Anastasiya Baryshnikova, Russia; B-María Espinoza, Mexico.

Tennis
Men's Singles: G-Andy Murray, Great Britain; S-Roger Federer, Switzerland; B-Juan Martín del Potro, Argentina.
Men's Doubles: G-Mike Bryan & Bob Bryan, U.S.; S-Jo-Wilfried Tsonga & Michaël Llodra, France; B-Julien Benneteau & Richard Gasquet, France.
Women's Singles: G-Serena Williams, U.S.; S-Maria Sharapova, Russia; B-Victoria Azarenka, Belarus.
Women's Doubles: G-Serena Williams & Venus Williams, U.S.; S-Andrea Hlaváčková & Lucie Hradecká, Czech Republic; B-Nadia Petrova & Maria Kirilenko, Russia.
Mixed Doubles: G-Victoria Azarenka & Max Mirnyi, Belarus; S-Andy Murray & Laura Robson, Great Britain; B-Mike Bryan & Lisa Raymond, U.S.

Track and Field
Men
100-m Run: G-Usain Bolt, Jamaica; S-Yohan Blake, Jamaica; B-Justin Gatlin, U.S.
200-m Run: G-Usain Bolt, Jamaica; S-Yohan Blake, Jamaica; B-Warren Weir, Jamaica.
400-m Run: G-Kirani James, Grenada; S-Luguelin Santos, Dominican Republic; B-Lalonde Gordon, Trinidad & Tobago.
800-m Run: G-David Rudisha, Kenya; S-Nijel Amos, Botswana; B-Timothy Kitum, Kenya.
1,500-m Run: G-Taoufik Makhloufi, Algeria; S-Leo Manzano, U.S.; B-Abdalaati Iguider, Morocco.
3,000-m Steeplechase: G-Ezekiel Kemboi, Kenya; S-Mahiedine Mekhissi-Benabbad, France; B-Abel Mutai, Kenya.
5,000-m Run: G-Mo Farah, Great Britain; S-Dejen Gebremeskel, Ethiopia; B-Thomas Pkemei Longosiwa, Kenya.
10,000-m Run: G-Mo Farah, Great Britain; S-Galen Rupp, U.S.; B-Tariku Bekele, Ethiopia.
Marathon: G-Stephen Kiprotich, Uganda; S-Abel Kirui, Kenya; B-Wilson Kipsang Kiprotich, Kenya.
4x100-m Relay: G-Jamaica, S-U.S., B-Trinidad & Tobago.
4x400-m Relay: G-The Bahamas, S-U.S., B-Trinidad & Tobago.
20-km Walk: G-Chen Ding, China; S-Erick Barrondo, Guatemala; B-Wang Zhen, China.
50-km Walk: G-Sergey Kirdyapkin, Russia; S-Jared Tallent, Australia; B-Si Tianfeng, China.
110-m Hurdles: G-Aries Merritt, U.S.; S-Jason Richardson, U.S.; B-Hansle Parchment, Jamaica.
400-m Hurdles: G-Félix Sánchez, Dominican Republic; S-Michael Tinsley, U.S.; B-Javier Culson, Puerto Rico.
Decathlon: G-Ashton Eaton, U.S.; S-Trey Hardee, U.S.; B-Leonel Suárez, Cuba.
Discus Throw: G-Robert Harting, Germany; S-Ehsan Haddadi, Iran; B-Gerd Kanter, Estonia.
Hammer Throw: G-Krisztián Pars, Hungary; S-Primož Kozmus, Slovenia; B-Koji Murofushi, Japan.
High Jump: G-Ivan Ukhov, Russia; S-Erik Kynard, U.S.; B-Mutaz Essa Barshim, Qatar; B-Derek Drouin, Canada; B-Robbie Grabarz, Great Britain.
Javelin Throw: G-Keshorn Walcott, Trinidad & Tobago; S-Oleksandr Pyatnytsya, Ukraine; B-Antti Ruuskanen, Finland.
Long Jump: G-Greg Rutherford, Great Britain; S-Mitchell Watt, Australia; B-Will Claye, U.S.
Pole Vault: G-Renaud Lavillenie, France; S-Björn Otto, Germany; B-Raphael Holzdeppe, Germany.
Shot Put: G-Tomasz Majewski, Poland; S-David Storl, Germany; B-Reese Hoffa, U.S.
Triple Jump: G-Christian Taylor, U.S.; S-Will Claye, U.S.; B-Fabrizio Donato, Italy.

Women

100-m Run: G-Shelly-Ann Fraser, Jamaica; S-Carmelita Jeter, U.S.; B-Veronica Campbell-Brown, Jamaica.

200-m Run: G-Allyson Felix, U.S.; S-Shelly-Ann Fraser, Jamaica; B-Carmelita Jeter, U.S.

400-m Run: G-Sanya Richards-Ross, U.S.; S-Christine Ohuruogu, Great Britain; B-DeeDee Trotter, U.S.

800-m Run: G-Mariya Savinova, Russia; S-Caster Semenya, South Africa; B-Yekaterina Poistogova, Russia.

1,500-m Run: G-Asli Çakir, Turkey; S-Gamze Bulut, Turkey; B-Maryam Jamal, Bahrain.

3,000-m Steeplechase: G-Yuliya Zaripova, Russia; S-Habiba Ghribi, Tunisia; B-Sofia Assefa, Ethiopia.

5,000-m Run: G-Meseret Defar, Ethiopia; S-Vivian Cheruiyot, Kenya; B-Tirunesh Dibaba, Ethiopia.

10,000-m Run: G-Tirunesh Dibaba, Ethiopia; S-Sally Jepkosgei Kipyego, Kenya; B-Vivian Cheruiyot, Kenya.

Marathon: G-Tiki Gelana, Ethiopia; S-Priscah Jeptoo, Kenya; B-Tatyana Petrova, Russia.

4x100-m Relay: G-U.S., S-Jamaica, B-Ukraine.

4x400-m Relay: G-U.S., S-Russia, B-Jamaica.

20-km Walk: G-Yelena Lashmanova, Russia; S-Olga Kaniskina, Russia; B-Qieyang Shenjie, China.

100-m Hurdles: G-Sally McLellan Pearson, Australia; S-Dawn Harper, U.S.; B-Kellie Wells, U.S.

400-m Hurdles: G-Nataliya Antyukh, Russia; S-Lashinda Demus, U.S.; B-Zuzana Hejnová, Czech Republic.

Discus Throw: G-Sandra Perković, Croatia; S-Darya Pishchalnikova, Russia; B-Li Yanfeng, China.

Hammer Throw: G-Tatyana Lysenko, Russia; S-Anita Wtodarczyk, Poland; B-Betty Heidler, Germany.

Heptathlon: G-Jessica Ennis, Great Britain; S-Lilli Schwarzkopf, Germany; B-Tatyana Chernova, Russia.

High Jump: G-Anna Chicherova, Russia; S-Brigetta Barrett, U.S.; B-Svetlana Shkolina, Russia.

Javelin Throw: G-Barbora Špotáková, Czech Republic; S-Christina Obergföll, Germany; B-Linda Stahl, Germany.

Long Jump: G-Brittney Reese, U.S.; S-Yelena Sokolova, Russia; B-Janay DeLoach, U.S.

Pole Vault: G-Jenn Stuczynski-Suhr, U.S.; S-Yarisley Silva, Cuba; B-Yelena Isinbayeva, Russia.

Shot Put: G-Valerie Adams, New Zealand; S-Yevgeniya Kolodko, Russia; B-Gong Lijiao, China. (Belarus's Nadzeya Ostapchuk was stripped of the gold medal after testing positive for steroids.)

Triple Jump: G-Olga Rypakova, Kazakhstan; S-Caterine Ibargüen, Colombia; B-Olha Saladukha, Ukraine.

Triathlon

Men: G-Alistair Brownlee, Great Britain; S-Francisco Gómez, Spain; B-Jonathan Brownlee, Great Britain.

Women: G-Nicola Spirig, Switzerland; S-Lisa Nordén, Sweden; B-Erin Densham, Australia.

Volleyball

Men: G-Russia, S-Brazil, B-Italy.

Women: G-Brazil, S-U.S., B-Japan.

Water Polo

Men: G-Croatia, S-Italy, B-Serbia.

Women: G-U.S., S-Spain, B-Australia.

Weightlifting
Men

56 kg/123 lbs: G-Om Yun Chol, North Korea; S-Wu Jingbiao, China; B-Valentin Xristov, Azerbaijan.

62 kg/137 lbs: G-Kim Un Guk, North Korea; S-Oscar Figueroa, Colombia; B-Eko Irawan, Indonesia.

69 kg/152 lbs: G-Lin Qingfeng, China; S-Triyatno, Indonesia; B-Răzvan Martin, Romania.

77 kg/170 lbs: G-Lu Xiaojun, China; S-Lu Haojie, China; B-Iván Cambar, Cuba.

85 kg/187 lbs: G-Adrian Zieliński, Poland; S-Apti Aukhadov, Russia; B-Kianoush Rostami, Iran.

94 kg/207 lbs: G-Ilya Ilyin, Kazakhstan; S-Aleksandr Ivanov, Russia; B-Anatolii Cîrîcu, Moldova.

105 kg/231 lbs: G-Oleksiy Torokhtiy, Ukraine; S-Navab Nasirshelal, Iran; B-Bartłomiej Bonk, Poland.

105+ kg/231+ lbs: G-Behdad Salimikordasiabi, Iran; S-Sajjad Anoushiravani Hamlabad, Iran; B-Ruslan Albegov, Russia.

Women

48 kg/106 lbs: G-Wang Mingjuan, China; S-Hiromi Miyake, Japan; B-Ryang Chun Hwa, North Korea.

53 kg/117 lbs: G-Zulfiya Chinshanlo, Kazakhstan; S-Hsu Shu-Ching, Taiwan; B-Cristina Iovu, Moldova.

58 kg/128 lbs: G-Li Xueying, China; S-Pimsiri Sirikaew, Thailand; B-Yuliya Kalina, Ukraine.

63 kg/139 lbs: G-Maiya Maneza, Kazakhstan; S-Svetlana Tsarukayeva, Russia; B-Christine Girard, Canada.

69 kg/152 lbs: G-Rim Jong Sim, North Korea; S-Roxana Cocoş, Romania; B-Marina Shkermankova, Belarus.

75 kg/165 lbs: G-Svetlana Podobedova, Kazakhstan; S-Nataliya Zabolotnaya, Russia; B-Irina Kulesha, Belarus.

75+ kg/165+ lbs: G-Zhou Lulu, China; S-Tatyana Kashirina, Russia; B-Hripsime Khurshudyan, Armenia.

Wrestling
Men

Freestyle 55 kg/121 lbs: G-Dzhamal Otarsultanov, Russia; S-Vladimer Khinchegashvili, Georgia; B-Yang Kyong-Il, North Korea; B-Shinichi Yumoto, Japan.

Freestyle 60 kg/132 lbs: G-Toğrul Asgarov, Azerbaijan; S-Besik Kudukhov, Russia; B-Yogeshwar Dutt, India; B-Coleman Scott, U.S.

Freestyle 66 kg/145.5 lbs: G-Tatsuhiro Yonemitsu, Japan; S-Sushil Kumar, India; B-Livan López, Cuba; B-Akzhurek Tanatarov, Kazakhstan.

Freestyle 74 kg/163 lbs: G-Jordan Burroughs, U.S.; S-Sadegh Saeed Goudarzi, Iran; B-Soslan Tigiyev, Uzbekistan; B-Denis Tsargush, Russia.

Freestyle 84 kg/185 lbs: G-Sarif Sarifov, Azerbaijan; S-Jaime Espinal, Puerto Rico; B-Dato Marsagishvili, Georgia; B-Ehsan Naser Lashgari, Iran.

Freestyle 96 kg/211.5 lbs: G-Jake Varner, U.S.; S-Valerii Andriitsev, Ukraine; B-Xetaq Qazyumov, Azerbaijan; B-Giorgi Gogshelidze, Georgia.

Freestyle 120 kg/264.5 lbs: G-Artur Taymazov, Uzbekistan; S-Davit Modzmanashvili, Georgia; B-Bilyal Makhov, Russia; B-Komeil Ghasemi, Iran.

Greco-Roman 55 kg/121 lbs: G-Hamid Soryan, Iran; S-Rövsan Bayramov, Azerbaijan; B-Mingiyan Semyonov, Russia; B-Péter Módos, Hungary.

Greco-Roman 60 kg/132 lbs: G-Omid Haji Noroozi, Iran; S-Revaz Lashkhi, Georgia; B-Zaur Kuramagomedov, Russia; B-Ryutaro Matsumoto, Japan.

Greco-Roman 66 kg/145.5 lbs: G-Kim Hyeon-Woo, South Korea; S-Tamás Lőrincz, Hungary; B-Steeve Guénot, France; B-Manuchar Tskhadaia, Georgia.

Greco-Roman 74 kg/163 lbs: G-Roman Vlasov, Russia; S-Arsen Julfalakyan, Armenia; B-Aleksandras Kazakevičius, Lithuania; B-Emin Ahmadov, Azerbaijan.

Greco-Roman 84 kg/185 lbs: G-Alan Khugayev, Russia; S-Karam Gaber, Egypt; B-Damian Janikowski, Poland; B-Daniyal Gadzhiyev, Kazakhstan.

Greco-Roman 96 kg/211.5 lbs: G-Ghasem Rezaei, Iran; S-Rustam Totrov, Russia; B-Jimmy Lidberg, Sweden; B-Artur Aleksanyan, Armenia.

Greco-Roman 120 kg/264.5 lbs: G-Mijaín López, Cuba; S-Heiki Nabi, Estonia; B-Riza Kayaalp, Turkey; B-Johan Eurén, Sweden.

Women

Freestyle 48 kg/105.5 lbs: G-Hitomi Obara, Japan; S-Mariya Stadnik, Azerbaijan; B-Carol Huynh, Canada; B-Clarissa Chun, U.S.

Freestyle 55 kg/121 lbs: G-Saori Yoshida, Japan; S-Tonya Verbeek, Canada; B-Jackeline Rentería, Colombia; B-Yuliya Ratkeviç, Azerbaijan.

Freestyle 63 kg/138.5 lbs: G-Kaori Icho, Japan; S-Jing Ruixue, China; B-Lyubov Volosova, Russia; B-Soronzonboldyn Battsetseg, Mongolia.

Freestyle 72 kg/158.5 lbs: G-Nataliya Vorobyova, Russia; S-Stanka Zlateva, Bulgaria; B-Gyuzel Manyurova, Kazakhstan; B-Maider Unda, Spain.

Summer Olympic Games Champions, 1896-2012

*Olympic record; (w) wind-aided

The 1980 games were boycotted by 62 nations, including the U.S. The 1984 games were boycotted by the USSR and most Eastern bloc nations. East and West Germany competed separately, 1968-88. The 1992 Unified Team consisted of 12 former Soviet republics. The 1992 Independent Olympic Participants (I.O.P.) were from Serbia, Montenegro, and Macedonia.

Not all sports are listed here, and many events are omitted, even within listed sports, particularly if the event has not been held in more recent Games.

Baseball (Men)

1992	Cuba, Taiwan, Japan	2000	United States, Cuba, S. Korea	2008	S. Korea, Cuba, United States
1996	Cuba, Japan, United States	2004	Cuba, Australia, Japan		

Boxing—Men

Weight class limits have changed many times since the first Olympic boxing events were held in 1904. The limits shown were used in the 2012 Olympic Games.

Lt. Flyweight (49 kg/108 lbs)
1968	Francisco Rodriguez, Venezuela
1972	Gyorgy Gedo, Hungary
1976	Jorge Hernandez, Cuba
1980	Shamil Sabyrov, USSR
1984	Paul Gonzalez, United States
1988	Ivailo Hristov, Bulgaria
1992	Rogelio Marcelo, Cuba
1996	Daniel Petrov, Bulgaria
2000	Brahim Asloum, France
2004	Yan Bhartelemy Varela, Cuba
2008	Zou Shiming, China
2012	Zou Shiming, China

Flyweight (52 kg/114 lbs)
1904	George Finnegan, United States
1920	Frank Di Gennara, United States
1924	Fidel LaBarba, United States
1928	Antal Kocsis, Hungary
1932	Istvan Enekes, Hungary
1936	Willi Kaiser, Germany
1948	Pascual Perez, Argentina
1952	Nathan Brooks, United States
1956	Terence Spinks, Great Britain
1960	Gyula Török, Hungary
1964	Fernando Atzori, Italy
1968	Ricardo Delgado, Mexico
1972	Georgi Kostadinov, Bulgaria
1976	Leo Randolph, United States
1980	Peter Lesov, Bulgaria
1984	Steve McCrory, United States
1988	Kim Kwang Sun, S. Korea
1992	Choi Chol-Su, N. Korea
1996	Maikro Romero, Cuba
2000	Wijan Ponlid, Thailand
2004	Yuriorkis Gamboa Toledano, Cuba
2008	Somjit Jongjohor, Thailand
2012	Robeisy Ramírez, Cuba

Bantamweight (56 kg/123 lbs)
1904	Oliver Kirk, United States
1908	A. Henry Thomas, Great Britain
1920	Clarence Walker, South Africa
1924	William Smith, South Africa
1928	Vittorio Tamagnini, Italy
1932	Horace Gwynne, Canada
1936	Ulderico Sergo, Italy
1948	Tibor Csik, Hungary
1952	Pentti Hamalainen, Finland
1956	Wolfgang Behrendt, E. Germany
1960	Oleg Grigoryev, USSR
1964	Takao Sakurai, Japan
1968	Valery Sokolov, USSR
1972	Orlando Martinez, Cuba
1976	Yong-Jo Gu, N. Korea
1980	Juan Hernandez, Cuba
1984	Maurizio Stecca, Italy
1988	Kennedy McKinney, United States
1992	Joel Casamayor, Cuba
1996	Istvan Kovacs, Hungary
2000	Guillermo Rigondeaux, Cuba
2004	Guillermo Rigondeaux, Cuba
2008	Badar-Uugan Enkhbat, Mongolia
2012	Luke Campbell, Great Britain

Featherweight (57 kg/125 lbs)
1904	Oliver Kirk, United States
1908	Richard Gunn, Great Britain
1920	Paul Fritsch, France
1924	John Fields, United States
1928	Lambertus van Klaveren, Netherlands

(Featherweight continued / second column)
1932	Carmelo Robledo, Argentina
1936	Oscar Casanovas, Argentina
1948	Ernesto Formenti, Italy
1952	Jan Zachara, Czechoslovakia
1956	Vladimir Safronov, USSR
1960	Francesco Musso, Italy
1964	Stanislav Stephashkin, USSR
1968	Antonio Roldan, Mexico
1972	Boris Kousnetsov, USSR
1976	Angel Herrera, Cuba
1980	Rudi Fink, E. Germany
1984	Meldrick Taylor, United States
1988	Giovanni Parisi, Italy
1992	Andreas Tews, Germany
1996	Somluck Kamsing, Thailand
2000	Bekzat Sattarkhanov, Kazakhstan
2004	Alexei Tichtchenko, Russia
2008	Vasyl Lomachenko, Ukraine

Lightweight (60 kg/132 lbs)
1904	Harry Spanger, United States
1908	Frederick Grace, Great Britain
1920	Samuel Mosberg, United States
1924	Hans Nielsen, Denmark
1928	Carlo Orlandi, Italy
1932	Lawrence Stevens, South Africa
1936	Imre Harangi, Hungary
1948	Gerald Dreyer, South Africa
1952	Aureliano Bolognesi, Italy
1956	Richard McTaggart, Great Britain
1960	Kazimierz Pazdzior, Poland
1964	Jozef Grudzien, Poland
1968	Ronald Harris, United States
1972	Jan Szczepanski, Poland
1976	Howard Davis, United States
1980	Angel Herrera, Cuba
1984	Pernell Whitaker, United States
1988	Andreas Zülow, E. Germany
1992	Oscar De La Hoya, United States
1996	Hocine Soltani, Algeria
2000	Mario Kindelan, Cuba
2004	Mario Kindelan, Cuba
2008	Alexey Tishchenko, Russia
2012	Vasyl Lomachenko, Ukraine

Lt. Welterweight (64 kg/141 lbs)
1952	Charles Adkins, United States
1956	Vladimir Yengibaryan, USSR
1960	Bohumil Nemecek, Czechoslovakia
1964	Jerzy Kulej, Poland
1968	Jerzy Kulej, Poland
1972	Ray Seales, United States
1976	Ray Leonard, United States
1980	Patrizio Oliva, Italy
1984	Jerry Page, United States
1988	Viatcheslav Janovski, USSR
1992	Hector Vinent, Cuba
1996	Hector Vinent, Cuba
2000	Mahamadkadyz Abdullaev, Uzbekistan
2004	Manus Boonjumnong, Thailand
2008	Felix Diaz, Dominican Republic
2012	Rosniel Iglesias, Cuba

Welterweight (69 kg/152 lbs)
1904	Albert Young, United States
1920	Albert Schneider, Canada
1924	Jean Delarge, Belgium
1928	Edward Morgan, New Zealand
1932	Edward Flynn, United States
1936	Sten Suvio, Finland
1948	Julius Torma, Czechoslovakia
1952	Zygmunt Chychia, Poland
1956	Nicolae Linca, Romania

1960	Giovanni Benvenuti, Italy
1964	Marian Kasprzyk, Poland
1968	Manfred Wolke, E. Germany
1972	Emilio Correa, Cuba
1976	Jochen Bachfeld, E. Germany
1980	Andres Aldama, Cuba
1984	Mark Breland, United States
1988	Robert Wangila, Kenya
1992	Michael Carruth, Ireland
1996	Oleg Saitov, Russia
2000	Oleg Saitov, Russia
2004	Artayev Bakhtiyar, Kazakhstan
2008	Bakhyt Sarsekbayev, Kazakhstan
2012	Serik Sapiyev, Kazakhstan

Lt. Middleweight (71 kg/156 lbs)
1952	Laszlo Papp, Hungary
1956	Laszlo Papp, Hungary
1960	Wilbert McClure, United States
1964	Boris Lagutin, USSR
1968	Boris Lagutin, USSR
1972	Dieter Kottysch, W. Germany
1976	Jerzy Rybicki, Poland
1980	Armando Martinez, Cuba
1984	Frank Tate, United States
1988	Park Si Hun, S. Korea
1992	Juan Lemus, Cuba
1996	David Reid, United States
2000	Yermakhan Ibraimov, Kazakhstan

Middleweight (75 kg/165 lbs)
1904	Charles Mayer, United States
1908	John Douglas, Great Britain
1920	Harry Mallin, Great Britain
1924	Harry Mallin, Great Britain
1928	Piero Toscani, Italy
1932	Carmen Barth, United States
1936	Jean Despeaux, France
1948	Laszlo Papp, Hungary
1952	Floyd Patterson, United States
1956	Gennady Schatkov, USSR
1960	Edward Crook, United States
1964	Valery Popenchenko, USSR
1968	Christopher Finnegan, Great Britain
1972	Vyacheslav Lemechev, USSR
1976	Michael Spinks, United States
1980	Jose Gomez, Cuba
1984	Joon-Sup Shin, S. Korea
1988	Henry Maske, E. Germany
1992	Ariel Hernandez, Cuba
1996	Ariel Hernandez, Cuba
2000	Jorge Gutierrez, Cuba
2004	Gaydarbek Gaydarbekov, Russia
2008	James Degale, Great Britain
2012	Ryota Murata, Japan

Lt. Heavyweight (81 kg/178 lbs)
1920	Edward Eagan, United States
1924	Harry Mitchell, Great Britain
1928	Victor Avendaño, Argentina
1932	David Carstens, South Africa
1936	Roger Michelot, France
1948	George Hunter, South Africa
1952	Norvel Lee, United States
1956	James Boyd, United States
1960	Cassius Clay, United States
1964	Cosimo Pinto, Italy
1968	Dan Poznyak, USSR
1972	Mate Parlov, Yugoslavia
1976	Leon Spinks, United States
1980	Slobodan Kacar, Yugoslavia
1984	Anton Josipovic, Yugoslavia
1988	Andrew Maynard, United States

Lt. Heavyweight (81 kg/178 lbs)
1992 Torsten May, Germany
1996 Vassili Jirov, Kazakhstan
2000 Alexander Lebziak, Russia
2004 Andre Ward, United States
2008 Zhang Xiaoping, China
2012 Yegor Mekhontsev, Russia

Heavyweight (91 kg/201 lbs)
1984 Henry Tillman, United States
1988 Ray Mercer, United States
1992 Felix Savon, Cuba
1996 Felix Savon, Cuba
2000 Felix Savon, Cuba
2004 Odlanier Solis Fonte, Cuba
2008 Rakhim Chakhkiev, Russia
2012 Oleksandr Usik, Ukraine

Super Heavyweight (91+ kg/201+ lbs)
(known as heavyweight, 1904-80)
1904 Samuel Berger, United States
1908 Albert Oldham, Great Britain
1920 Ronald Rawson, Great Britain
1924 Otto von Porat, Norway
1928 Arturo Rodriguez Jurado, Argentina
1932 Santiago Lovell, Argentina
1936 Herbert Runge, Germany
1948 Rafael Iglesias, Argentina
1952 H. Edward Sanders, United States
1956 T. Peter Rademacher, United States

1960 Franco De Piccoli, Italy
1964 Joe Frazier, United States
1968 George Foreman, United States
1972 Teofilo Stevenson, Cuba
1976 Teofilo Stevenson, Cuba
1980 Teofilo Stevenson, Cuba
1984 Tyrell Biggs, United States
1988 Lennox Lewis, Canada
1992 Roberto Balado, Cuba
1996 Vladimir Klitchko, Ukraine
2000 Audley Harrison, Great Britain
2004 Alexander Povetkin, Russia
2008 Roberto Cammarelle, Italy
2012 Anthony Joshua, Great Britain

Boxing—Women

Flyweight (51 kg/112 lbs)
2012 Nicola Adams, Great Britain

Lightweight (60 kg/132 lbs)
2012 Katie Taylor, Ireland

Middleweight (75 kg/165 lbs)
2012 Claressa Shields, United States

Gymnastics—Men

Floor Exercise
1932 István Pelle, Hungary
1936 Georges Miez, Switzerland
1948 Ferenc Pataki, Hungary
1952 William Thoresson, Sweden
1956 Valentin Muratov, USSR
1960 Nobuyuki Aihara, Japan
1964 Franco Menichelli, Italy
1968 Sawao Kato, Japan
1972 Nikolay Andrianov, USSR
1976 Nikolay Andrianov, USSR
1980 Roland Brückner, E. Germany
1984 Li Ning, China
1988 Serguei Kharikov, USSR
1992 Xiaosahuang Li, China
1996 Ioannis Melissanidis, Greece
2000 Igors Vihrovs, Latvia
2004 Kyle Shewfelt, Canada
2008 Zou Kai, China
2012 Zou Kai, China

Horizontal Bar
1896 Hermann Weingärtner, Germany
1904 Anton Heida, United States;
     Edward Hennig, United States (tie)
1924 Leon Stukelj, Yugoslavia
1928 Georges Miez, Switzerland
1932 Dallas Denver Bixler, United States
1936 Aleksanteri Saarvala, Finland
1948 Josef Stadler, Switzerland
1952 Jakob "Jack" Günthard, Switzerland
1956 Takashi Ono, Japan
1960 Takashi Ono, Japan
1964 Boris Shakhlin, USSR
1968 Mikhail Voronin, USSR;
     Akinori Nakayama, Japan (tie)
1972 Mitsuo Tsukahara, Japan
1976 Mitsuo Tsukahara, Japan
1980 Stoyan Deltchev, Bulgaria
1984 Shinji Morisue, Japan
1988 Valeri Lioukine, USSR;
     Vladimir Artemov, USSR (tie)
1992 Trent Dimas, United States
1996 Andreas Wecker, Germany
2000 Alexei Nemov, Russia
2004 Igor Cassina, Italy
2008 Zou Kai, China
2012 Epke Zonderland, Netherlands

Individual All-Around
1900 Gustave Sandras, France
1904 Julius Lenhart, United States
1908 G. Alberto Braglia, Italy
1912 G. Alberto Braglia, Italy
1920 Giorgio Zampori, Italy
1924 Leon Stukelj, Yugoslavia
1928 Georges Miez, Switzerland
1932 Romeo Neri, Italy
1936 Karl-Alfred Schwarzmann, Germany
1948 Veikko Huhtanen, Finland
1952 Viktor Ivanovich Chukarin, USSR
1956 Viktor Ivanovich Chukarin, USSR
1960 Boris Shakhlin, USSR
1964 Yukio Endo, Japan
1968 Sawao Kato, Japan
1972 Sawao Kato, Japan
1976 Nikolay Andrianov, USSR
1980 Aleksandr Dityatin, USSR
1984 Koji Gushiken, Japan
1988 Vladimir Artemov, USSR

Individual All-Around
1992 Vitaly Scherbo, Unified Team (Belarus)
1996 Li Xiaosahuang, China
2000 Alexei Nemov, Russia
2004 Paul Hamm, United States
2008 Yang Wei, China
2012 Kohei Uchimura, Japan

Parallel Bars
1896 Alfred Flatow, Germany
1904 George Eyser, United States
1924 August Güttinger, Switzerland
1928 Ladislav Vacha, Czechoslovakia
1932 Romeo Neri, Italy
1936 Konrad Frey, Germany
1948 Michael Reusch, Switzerland
1952 Hans Eugster, Switzerland
1956 Viktor Ivanovich Chukarin, USSR
1960 Boris Shakhlin, USSR
1964 Yukio Endo, Japan
1968 Akinori Nakayama, Japan
1972 Sawao Kato, Japan
1976 Sawao Kato, Japan
1980 Aleksandr Tkachev, USSR
1984 Barthold Wayne Conner, United States
1988 Vladimir Artemov, USSR
1992 Vitaly Scherbo, Unified Team (Belarus)
1996 Roustam Sharipov, Ukraine
2000 Li Xiaopeng, China
2004 Valeri Goncharov, Ukraine
2008 Li Xiaopeng, China
2012 Feng Zhe, China

Pommel Horse
1896 Louis Zutter, Switzerland
1904 Anton Heida, United States
1924 Josef Wilhelm, Switzerland
1928 Hermann Hänggi, Switzerland
1932 István Pelle, Hungary
1936 Konrad Frey, Germany
1948 Heikki Savolainen, Finland;
     Paavo Johannes Aaltonen, Finland;
     Veikko Huhtanen, Finland (tie)
1952 Viktor Ivanovich Chukarin, USSR
1956 Boris Shakhlin, USSR
1960 Eugen Georg Oskar Ekman, Finland;
     Boris Shakhlin, USSR (tie)
1964 Miroslav Cerar, Yugoslavia
1968 Miroslav Cerar, Yugoslavia
1972 Viktor Klimenko, USSR
1976 Zoltan Magyar, Hungary
1980 Zoltan Magyar, Hungary
1984 Li Ning, China; Peter Glen Vidmar, United States (tie)
1988 Zsolt Borkai, Hungary;
     Dmitri Bilozerchev, USSR;
     Lubomir Geraskov, Bulgaria (tie)
1992 Pae Gil-Su, North Korea; Vitaly Scherbo, Unified Team (Belarus) (tie)
1996 Li Donghua, Switzerland
2000 Marius Daniel Urzica, Romania
2004 Teng Haibin, China
2008 Xiao Qin, China
2012 Krisztián Berki, Hungary

Rings
1896 Ioannis Mitropoulos, Greece
1904 Hermann Glass, United States
1924 Francesco Martino, Italy
1928 Leon Stukelj, Yugoslavia
1932 George Julius Gulack, United States
1936 Alois Hudec, Czechoslovakia
1948 Karl Frei, Switzerland
1952 Grant Shaginyan, USSR
1956 Albert Azaryan, USSR
1960 Albert Azaryan, USSR
1964 Takuji Hayata, Japan
1968 Akinori Nakayama, Japan
1972 Akinori Nakayama, Japan
1976 Nikolay Andrianov, USSR
1980 Aleksandr Dityatin, USSR
1984 Li Ning, China;
     Koji Gushiken, Japan (tie)
1988 Holger Behrendt, E. Germany;
     Dmitri Bilozerchev, USSR (tie)
1992 Vitaly Scherbo, Unified Team (Belarus)
1996 Juri Chechi, Italy
2000 Szilveszter Csollany, Hungary
2004 Dimosthenis Tampakos, Greece
2008 Chen Yibing, China
2012 Arthur Zanetti, Brazil

Team Competition
1904 United States, United States, United States
1908 Sweden, Norway, Finland
1912 Italy, Hungary, Great Britain
1920 Italy, Belgium, France
1924 Italy, France, Switzerland
1928 Switzerland, Czechoslovakia, Yugoslavia
1932 Italy, United States, Finland
1936 Germany, Switzerland, Finland
1948 Finland, Switzerland, Hungary
1952 USSR, Switzerland, Finland
1956 USSR, Japan, Finland
1960 Japan, USSR, Italy
1964 Japan, USSR, Unified Team of Germany
1968 Japan, USSR, E. Germany
1972 Japan, USSR, E. Germany
1976 Japan, USSR, E. Germany
1980 USSR, E. Germany, Hungary
1984 United States, China, Japan
1988 USSR, E. Germany, Japan
1992 Unified Team, China, Japan
1996 Russia, China, Ukraine
2000 China, Ukraine, Russia
2004 Japan, United States, Romania
2008 China, Japan, United States
2012 China, Japan, Great Britain

Trampoline
2000 Alexander Moskalenko, Russia
2004 Yuri Nikitin, Ukraine
2008 Lu Chunlong, China
2012 Dong Dong, China

Vault
1896 Carl Schumann, Germany
1904 George Eyser, United States;
     Anton Heida, United States (tie)
1924 Frank Kriz, United States

Vault

1928	Eugen Mack, Switzerland
1932	Savino Guglielmetti, Italy
1936	Karl-Alfred Schwarzmann, Germany
1948	Paavo Johannes Aaltonen, Finland
1952	Viktor Ivanovich Chukarin, USSR
1956	Helmut Bantz, Unified Team of Germany;
	Valentin Muratov, USSR (tie)

Vault

1960	Takashi Ono, Japan;
	Boris Shakhlin, USSR (tie)
1964	Haruhiro Yamashita, Japan
1968	Mikhail Voronin, USSR
1972	Klaus Köste, E. Germany
1976	Nikolay Andrianov, USSR
1980	Nikolay Andrianov, USSR
1984	Lou Yun, China

Vault

1988	Lou Yun, China
1992	Vitaly Scherbo, Unified Team (Belarus)
1996	Alexei Nemov, Russia
2000	Gervasio Deferr, Spain
2004	Gervasio Deferr, Spain
2008	Leszek Blanik, Poland
2012	Yang Hak-Seon, South Korea

Gymnastics—Women

Balance Beam

1952	Nina Bocharova, USSR
1956	Agnes Keleti, Hungary
1960	Eva Vechtova-Bosakova, Czechoslovakia
1964	Vera Caslavska, Czechoslovakia
1968	Natalya Kuchinskaya, USSR
1972	Olga Korbut, USSR
1976	Nadia Comaneci, Romania
1980	Nadia Comaneci, Romania
1984	Ecaterina Szabo, Romania; Simona Pauca, Romania (tie)
1988	Daniela Silivas, Romania
1992	Tatiana Lyssenko, Unified Team (Ukraine)
1996	Shannon Miller, United States
2000	Liu Xuan, China
2004	Catalina Ponor, Romania
2008	Shawn Johnson, United States
2012	Deng Linlin, China

Floor Exercise

1952	Agnes Keleti, Hungary
1956	Agnes Keleti, Hungary; Larisa Latynina, USSR (tie)
1960	Larisa Latynina, USSR
1964	Larisa Latynina, USSR
1968	Vera Caslavska, Czechoslovakia; Larisa Petrik, USSR (tie)
1972	Olga Korbut, USSR
1976	Nelli Kim, USSR
1980	Nelli Kim, USSR; Nadia Comaneci, Romania (tie)
1984	Ecaterina Szabo, Romania
1988	Daniela Silivas, Romania
1992	Lavinia Corina Milosovici, Romania
1996	Lilia Podkopayeva, Ukraine
2000	Elena Zamolodchikova, Russia
2004	Catalina Ponor, Romania
2008	Sandra Izbasa, Romania
2012	Aly Raisman, United States

Individual All-Around

1952	Mariya Gorokhovskaya, USSR
1956	Larisa Latynina, USSR
1960	Larisa Latynina, USSR
1964	Vera Caslavska, Czechoslovakia
1968	Vera Caslavska, Czechoslovakia
1972	Lyudmila Turischeva, USSR
1976	Nadia Comaneci, Romania
1980	Elena Davydova, USSR
1984	Mary-Lou Retton, United States
1988	Elena Shushunova, USSR
1992	Tatiana Goutsou, Unified Team
1996	Lilia Podkopayeva, Ukraine
2000	Simona Amanar, Romania
2004	Carly Patterson, United States
2008	Nastia Liukin, United States
2012	Gabby Douglas, United States

Team Competition

1928	Netherlands, Italy, Great Britain
1936	Germany, Czechoslovakia, Hungary
1948	Czechoslovakia, Hungary, United States
1952	USSR, Hungary, Czechoslovakia
1956	USSR, Hungary, Romania
1960	USSR, Czechoslovakia, Romania
1964	USSR, Czechoslovakia, Japan
1968	USSR, Czechoslovakia, E. Germany
1972	USSR, E. Germany, Hungary
1976	USSR, Romania, E. Germany
1980	USSR, Romania, E. Germany
1984	Romania, United States, China
1988	USSR, Romania, E. Germany
1992	Unified Team, Romania, United States
1996	United States, Russia, Romania
2000	Romania, Russia, United States
2004	Romania, United States, Russia
2008	China, United States, Romania
2012	United States, Russia, Romania

Trampoline

2000	Irina Karavaeva, Russia
2004	Anna Dogonadze, Germany
2008	He Wenna, China
2012	Rosie MacLennan, Canada

Uneven Bars

1952	Margit Korondi, Hungary
1956	Agnes Keleti, Hungary
1960	Polina Astakhova, USSR
1964	Polina Astakhova, USSR
1968	Vera Caslavska, Czechoslovakia
1972	Karin Janz, E. Germany
1976	Nadia Comaneci, Romania
1980	Maxi Gnauck, E. Germany
1984	Julianne Lyn McNamara, United States; Yan-Hong Ma, China (tie)
1988	Daniela Silivas, Romania
1992	Lu Li, China
1996	Svetlana Khorkina, Russia
2000	Svetlana Khorkina, Russia
2004	Emilie LePennec, France
2008	He Kexin, China
2012	Aliya Mustafina, Russia

Vault

1952	Ekaterina Kalinchuk, USSR
1956	Larisa Latynina, USSR
1960	Margarita Nikolaeva, USSR
1964	Vera Caslavska, Czechoslovakia
1968	Vera Caslavska, Czechoslovakia
1972	Karin Janz, E. Germany
1976	Nelli Kim, USSR
1980	Natalia Shaposhnikova, USSR
1984	Ecaterina Szabo, Romania
1988	Svetlana Boginskaya, USSR
1992	Henrietta Onodi, Hungary; Lavinia Corina Milosovici, Romania (tie)
1996	Simona Amanar, Romania
2000	Elena Zamolodchikova, Russia
2004	Monica Rosu, Romania
2008	Hong Un Jong, N. Korea
2012	Sandra Izbaşa, Romania

Soccer

Men

1900	Great Britain, France, Belgium
1904	Canada, United States, United States
1908	Great Britain, Denmark, Netherlands
1912	Great Britain, Denmark, Netherlands
1920	Belgium, Spain, Netherlands
1924	Uruguay, Switzerland, Sweden
1928	Uruguay, Argentina, Italy
1936	Italy, Austria, Norway
1948	Sweden, Yugoslavia, Denmark
1952	Hungary, Yugoslavia, Sweden
1956	USSR, Yugoslavia, Bulgaria

Men

1960	Yugoslavia, Denmark, Hungary
1964	Hungary, Czechoslovakia, Unified Team of Germany
1968	Hungary, Bulgaria, Japan
1972	Poland; Hungary; USSR, E. Germany (tie for bronze)
1976	E. Germany, Poland, USSR
1980	Czechoslovakia, E. Germany, USSR
1984	France, Brazil, Yugoslavia
1988	USSR, Brazil, W. Germany
1992	Spain, Poland, Ghana

Men

1996	Nigeria, Argentina, Brazil
2000	Cameroon, Spain, Chile
2004	Argentina, Paraguay, Italy
2008	Argentina, Nigeria, Brazil
2012	Mexico, Brazil, South Korea

Women

1996	United States, China, Norway
2000	Norway, United States, Germany
2004	United States, Brazil, Germany
2008	United States, Brazil, Germany
2012	United States, Japan, Canada

Swimming and Diving—Men

50-Meter Freestyle

Year		Time
1988	Matt Biondi, United States	0:22.14
1992	Aleksandr Popov, Unified Team	0:21.91
1996	Aleksandr Popov, Russia	0:22.13
2000	Anthony Ervin, United States	0:21.98
	Gary Hall Jr., United States (tie)	0:21.98
2004	Gary Hall Jr., United States	0:21.93
2008	Cesar Cielo Filho, Brazil	0:21.30*
2012	Florent Manaudou, France	0:21.34

100-Meter Freestyle

Year		Time
1896	Alfred Hajos, Hungary	1:22.2
1904	Zoltan de Halmay, Hungary (100 yds)	1:02.8
1908	Charles Daniels, United States	1:05.6
1912	Duke P. Kahanamoku, United States	1:03.4
1920	Duke P. Kahanamoku, United States	1:01.4
1924	Johnny Weissmuller, United States	0:59.0
1928	Johnny Weissmuller, United States	0:58.6
1932	Yasuji Miyazaki, Japan	0:58.2
1936	Ferenc Csik, Hungary	0:57.6
1948	Wally Ris, United States	0:57.3
1952	Clark Scholes, United States	0:57.4

Year		Time
1956	Jon Henricks, Australia	0:55.4
1960	John Devitt, Australia	0:55.2
1964	Don Schollander, United States	0:53.4
1968	Mike Wenden, Australia	0:52.2
1972	Mark Spitz, United States	0:51.22
1976	Jim Montgomery, United States	0:49.99
1980	Jorg Woithe, E. Germany	0:50.40
1984	Ambrose "Rowdy" Gaines, United States	0:49.80
1988	Matt Biondi, United States	0:48.63
1992	Aleksandr Popov, Unified Team	0:49.02
1996	Aleksandr Popov, Russia	0:48.74
2000	Pieter van den Hoogenband, Netherlands	0:48.30
2004	Pieter van den Hoogenband, Netherlands	0:48.17
2008	Alain Bernard, France	0:47:21
2012	Nathan Adrian, United States	0:47.52

200-Meter Freestyle

Year		Time
1968	Mike Wenden, Australia	1:55.2
1972	Mark Spitz, United States	1:52.78
1976	Bruce Furniss, United States	1:50.29
1980	Sergei Kopliakov, USSR	1:49.81
1984	Michael Gross, W. Germany	1:47.44

200-Meter Freestyle

Year	Champion	Time
1988	Duncan Armstrong, Australia	1:47.25
1992	Yevgeny Sadovyi, Unified Team	1:46.70
1996	Danyon Loader, New Zealand	1:47.63
2000	Pieter van den Hoogenband, Netherlands	1:45.35
2004	Ian Thorpe, Australia	1:44.71
2008	Michael Phelps, United States	1:42.96*
2012	Yannick Agnel, France	1:43.14

400-Meter Freestyle

Year	Champion	Time
1904	C. M. Daniels, United States (440 yds)	6:16.2
1908	Henry Taylor, Great Britain	5:36.8
1912	George Hodgson, Canada	5:24.4
1920	Norman Ross, United States	5:26.8
1924	Johnny Weissmuller, United States	5:04.2
1928	Albert Zorilla, Argentina	5:01.6
1932	Clarence Crabbe, United States	4:48.4
1936	Jack Medica, United States	4:44.5
1948	William Smith, United States	4:41.0
1952	Jean Boiteux, France	4:30.7
1956	Murray Rose, Australia	4:27.3
1960	Murray Rose, Australia	4:18.3
1964	Don Schollander, United States	4:12.2
1968	Mike Burton, United States	4:09.0
1972	Brad Cooper, Australia	4:00.27
1976	Brian Goodell, United States	3:51.93
1980	Vladimir Salnikov, USSR	3:51.31
1984	George DiCarlo, United States	3:51.23
1988	Ewe Dassler, E. Germany	3:46.95
1992	Yevgeny Sadovyi, Unified Team	3:45.00
1996	Danyon Loader, New Zealand	3:47.97
2000	Ian Thorpe, Australia	3:40.59
2004	Ian Thorpe, Australia	3:43.10
2008	Park Taehwan, S. Korea	3:41.86
2012	Sun Yang, China	3:40.14*

1,500-Meter Freestyle

Year	Champion	Time
1908	Henry Taylor, Great Britain	22:48.4
1912	George Hodgson, Canada	22:00.0
1920	Norman Ross, United States	22:23.2
1924	Johnny Charlton, Australia	20:06.6
1928	Arne Borg, Sweden	19:51.8
1932	Kusuo Kitamura, Japan	19:12.4
1936	Noboru Terada, Japan	19:13.7
1948	James McLane, United States	19:18.5
1952	Ford Konno, United States	18:30.3
1956	Murray Rose, Australia	17:58.9
1960	Jon Konrads, Australia	17:19.6
1964	Robert Windle, Australia	17:01.7
1968	Mike Burton, United States	16:38.9
1972	Mike Burton, United States	15:52.58
1976	Brian Goodell, United States	15:02.40
1980	Vladimir Salnikov, USSR	14:58.27
1984	Michael O'Brien, United States	15:05.20
1988	Vladimir Salnikov, USSR	15:00.40
1992	Kieren Perkins, Australia	14:43.48
1996	Kieren Perkins, Australia	14:56.40
2000	Grant Hackett, Australia	14:48.33
2004	Grant Hackett, Australia	14:43.40
2008	Oussama Mellouli, Tunisia	14:40.84
2012	Sun Yang, China	14:31.02*

100-Meter Backstroke

Year	Champion	Time
1904	Walter Brack, Germany (100 yds)	1:16.8
1908	Arno Bieberstein, Germany	1:24.6
1912	Harry Hebner, United States	1:21.2
1920	Warren Kealoha, United States	1:15.2
1924	Warren Kealoha, United States	1:13.2
1928	George Kojac, United States	1:08.2
1932	Masaji Kiyokawa, Japan	1:08.6
1936	Adolph Kiefer, United States	1:05.9
1948	Allen Stack, United States	1:06.4
1952	Yoshi Oyakawa, United States	1:05.4
1956	David Thiele, Australia	1:02.2
1960	David Thiele, Australia	1:01.9
1968	Roland Matthes, E. Germany	0:58.7
1972	Roland Matthes, E. Germany	0:56.58
1976	John Naber, United States	0:55.49
1980	Bengt Baron, Sweden	0:56.33
1984	Rick Carey, United States	0:55.79
1988	Daichi Suzuki, Japan	0:55.05
1992	Mark Tewksbury, Canada	0:53.98
1996	Jeff Rouse, United States	0:54.10
2000	Lenny Krayzelburg, United States	0:53.72
2004	Aaron Peirsol, United States	0:54.06
2008	Aaron Peirsol, United States	0:52.54
2012	Matt Grevers, United States	0:52.16*

200-Meter Backstroke

Year	Champion	Time
1964	Jed Graef, United States	2:10.3
1968	Roland Matthes, E. Germany	2:09.6
1972	Roland Matthes, E. Germany	2:02.82
1976	John Naber, United States	1:59.19
1980	Sandor Wladar, Hungary	2:01.93
1984	Rick Carey, United States	2:00.23
1988	Igor Polianski, USSR	1:59.37

200-Meter Backstroke

Year	Champion	Time
1992	Martin Lopez-Zubero, Spain	1:58.47
1996	Brad Bridgewater, United States	1:58.54
2000	Lenny Krayzelburg, United States	1:56.76
2004	Aaron Peirsol, United States	1:54.95
2008	Ryan Lochte, United States	1:53.94
2012	Tyler Clary, United States	1:53.41*

100-Meter Breaststroke

Year	Champion	Time
1968	Don McKenzie, United States	1:07.79
1972	Nobutaka Taguchi, Japan	1:04.94
1976	John Hencken, United States	1:03.11
1980	Duncan Goodhew, Great Britain	1:03.44
1984	Steve Lundquist, United States	1:01.65
1988	Adrian Moorhouse, Great Britain	1:02.04
1992	Nelson Diebel, United States	1:01.50
1996	Fred Deburghgraeve, Belgium	1:00.60
2000	Domenico Fioravanti, Italy	1:00.46
2004	Kosuke Kitajima, Japan	1:00.08
2008	Kosuke Kitajima, Japan	0:58.91
2012	Cameron van der Burgh, South Africa	0:58.46*

200-Meter Breaststroke

Year	Champion	Time
1908	Frederick Holman, Great Britain	3:09.2
1912	Walter Bathe, Germany	3:01.8
1920	Haken Malmroth, Sweden	3:04.4
1924	Robert Skelton, United States	2:56.6
1928	Yoshiyuki Tsuruta, Japan	2:48.8
1932	Yoshiyuki Tsuruta, Japan	2:45.4
1936	Tetsuo Hamuro, Japan	2:41.5
1948	Joseph Verdeur, United States	2:39.3
1952	John Davies, Australia	2:34.4
1956	Masaru Furukawa, Japan	2:34.7
1960	William Mulliken, United States	2:37.4
1964	Ian O'Brien, Australia	2:27.8
1968	Felipe Munoz, Mexico	2:28.7
1972	John Hencken, United States	2:21.55
1976	David Wilkie, Great Britain	2:15.11
1980	Robertas Zhulpa, USSR	2:15.85
1984	Victor Davis, Canada	2:13.34
1988	Jozsef Szabo, Hungary	2:13.52
1992	Mike Barrowman, United States	2:10.16
1996	Norbert Rozsa, Hungary	2:12.57
2000	Domenico Fioravanti, Italy	2:10.87
2004	Kosuke Kitajima, Japan	2:09.44
2008	Kosuke Kitajima, Japan	2:07.64
2012	Dániel Gyurta, Hungary	2:07.28*

100-Meter Butterfly

Year	Champion	Time
1968	Doug Russell, United States	0:55.9
1972	Mark Spitz, United States	0:54.27
1976	Matt Vogel, United States	0:54.35
1980	Par Arvidsson, Sweden	0:54.92
1984	Michael Gross, W. Germany	0:53.08
1988	Anthony Nesty, Suriname	0:53.00
1992	Pablo Morales, United States	0:53.32
1996	Denis Pankratov, Russia	0:52.27
2000	Lars Froelander, Sweden	0:52.00
2004	Michael Phelps, United States	0:51.25
2008	Michael Phelps, United States	0:50.58*
2012	Michael Phelps, United States	0:51.21

200-Meter Butterfly

Year	Champion	Time
1956	William Yorzyk, United States	2:19.3
1960	Michael Troy, United States	2:12.8
1964	Kevin J. Berry, Australia	2:06.6
1968	Carl Robie, United States	2:08.7
1972	Mark Spitz, United States	2:00.70
1976	Mike Bruner, United States	1:59.23
1980	Sergei Fesenko, USSR	1:59.76
1984	Jon Sieben, Australia	1:57.04
1988	Michael Gross, W. Germany	1:56.94
1992	Mel Stewart, United States	1:56.26
1996	Denis Pankratov, Russia	1:56.51
2000	Tom Malchow, United States	1:55.35
2004	Michael Phelps, United States	1:54.04
2008	Michael Phelps, United States	1:52.03*
2012	Chad le Clos, South Africa	1:52.96

200-Meter Individual Medley

Year	Champion	Time
1968	Charles Hickcox, United States	2:12.0
1972	Gunnar Larsson, Sweden	2:07.17
1984	Alex Baumann, Canada	2:01.42
1988	Tamas Darnyi, Hungary	2:00.17
1992	Tamas Darnyi, Hungary	2:00.76
1996	Attila Czene, Hungary	1:59.91
2000	Massimiliano Rosolino, Italy	1:58.98
2004	Michael Phelps, United States	1:57.14
2008	Michael Phelps, United States	1:54.23*
2012	Michael Phelps, United States	1:54.27

400-Meter Individual Medley

Year	Champion	Time
1964	Dick Roth, United States	4:45.4
1968	Charles Hickcox, United States	4:48.4
1972	Gunnar Larsson, Sweden	4:31.98
1976	Rod Strachan, United States	4:23.68

400-Meter Individual Medley	Time
1980 Aleksandr Sidorenko, USSR	4:22.89
1984 Alex Baumann, Canada	4:17.41
1988 Tamas Darnyi, Hungary	4:14.75
1992 Tamas Darnyi, Hungary	4:14.23
1996 Tom Dolan, United States	4:14.90
2000 Tom Dolan, United States	4:11.76
2004 Michael Phelps, United States	4:08.26
2008 Michael Phelps, United States	4:03.84*
2012 Ryan Lochte, United States	4:05.18

4x100-Meter Freestyle Relay	Time
1964 United States	3:31.2
1968 United States	3:31.7
1972 United States	3:26.42
1984 United States	3:19.03
1988 United States	3:16.53
1992 United States	3:16.74
1996 United States	3:15.41
2000 Australia	3:13.67
2004 South Africa	3:13.17
2008 United States	3:08.24*
2012 France	3:09.93

4x200-Meter Freestyle Relay	Time
1908 Great Britain	10:55.6
1912 Australasia	10:11.6
1920 United States	10:04.4
1924 United States	9:53.4
1928 United States	9:36.2
1932 Japan	8:58.4
1936 Japan	8:51.5
1948 United States	8:46.0
1952 United States	8:31.1
1956 Australia	8:23.6
1960 United States	8:10.2
1964 United States	7:52.1
1968 United States	7:52.33
1972 United States	7:35.78
1976 United States	7:23.22
1980 USSR	7:23.50
1984 United States	7:15.69
1988 United States	7:12.51
1992 Unified Team	7:11.95
1996 United States	7:14.84
2000 Australia	7:07.05
2004 United States	7:07.33
2008 United States	6:58.56*
2012 United States	6:59.70

4x100-Meter Medley Relay	Time
1960 United States	4:05.4
1964 United States	3:58.4
1968 United States	3:54.9
1972 United States	3:48.16
1976 United States	3:42.22
1980 Australia	3:45.70
1984 United States	3:39.30
1988 United States	3:36.93
1992 United States	3:36.93
1996 United States	3:34.84
2000 United States	3:33.73
2004 United States	3:30.68
2008 United States	3:29.34*
2012 United States	3:29.35

10-Kilometer Marathon	Time
2008 Maarten van der Weijden, Netherlands	1:51:51.6
2012 Oussama Mellouli, Tunisia	1:49:55.1

Platform Diving	Points
1904 Dr. G. E. Sheldon, United States	112.75
1908 Hjalmar Johansson, Sweden	183.75
1912 Erik Adlerz, Sweden	73.94
1920 Clarence Pinkston, United States	100.67
1924 Albert White, United States	97.46
1928 Pete Desjardins, United States	98.74
1932 Harold Smith, United States	124.80
1936 Marshall Wayne, United States	113.58
1948 Sammy Lee, United States	130.05
1952 Sammy Lee, United States	156.28
1956 Joaquin Capilla, Mexico	152.44
1960 Robert Webster, United States	165.56
1964 Robert Webster, United States	148.58
1968 Klaus Dibiasi, Italy	164.18
1972 Klaus Dibiasi, Italy	504.12
1976 Klaus Dibiasi, Italy	600.51
1980 Falk Hoffmann, E. Germany	835.65
1984 Greg Louganis, United States	710.91
1988 Greg Louganis, United States	638.61
1992 Sun Shuwei, China	677.31
1996 Dmitri Sautin, Russia	692.34
2000 Tian Liang, China	724.53
2004 Hu Jia, China	748.08
2008 Matthew Mitcham, Australia	537.95
2012 David Boudia, United States	568.65

Springboard Diving	Points
1908 Albert Zurner, Germany	85.50
1912 Paul Guenther, Germany	79.23
1920 Louis Kuehn, United States	675.40
1924 Albert White, United States	97.46
1928 Pete Desjardins, United States	185.04
1932 Michael Galitzen, United States	161.38
1936 Richard Degener, United States	163.57
1948 Bruce Harlan, United States	163.64
1952 David Browning, United States	205.29
1956 Robert Clotworthy, United States	159.56
1960 Gary Tobian, United States	170.00
1964 Kenneth Sitzberger, United States	159.90
1968 Bernie Wrightson, United States	170.15
1972 Vladimir Vasin, USSR	594.09
1976 Phil Boggs, United States	619.52
1980 Aleksandr Portnov, USSR	905.02
1984 Greg Louganis, United States	754.41
1988 Greg Louganis, United States	730.80
1992 Mark Lenzi, United States	676.53
1996 Xiong Ni, China	701.46
2000 Xiong Ni, China	708.72
2004 Peng Bo, China	787.30
2008 He Chong, China	572.90
2012 Ilya Zakharov, Russia	555.90

Synchronized Platform	Points
2004 Tian Liang and Yang Jinghui, China	383.88
2008 Lin Yue and Huo Liang, China	468.18
2012 Cao Yuan and Zhang Yanquan, China	486.78

Synchronized Springboard	Points
2004 Nikolaos Siranidis and Thomas Bimis, Greece	353.34
2008 Wang Feng and Qin Kai, China	469.08
2012 Luo Yutong and Qin Kai, China	477.00

Swimming and Diving—Women

50-Meter Freestyle	Time
1988 Kristin Otto, E. Germany	0:25.49
1992 Yang Wenyi, China	0:24.76
1996 Amy Van Dyken, United States	0:24.87
2000 Inge de Bruijn, Netherlands	0:24.32
2004 Inge de Bruijn, Netherlands	0:24.58
2008 Britta Steffen, Germany	0:24.06
2012 Ranomi Kromowidjojo, Netherlands	0:24.05*

100-Meter Freestyle	Time
1912 Fanny Durack, Australia	1:22.2
1920 Ethelda Bleibtrey, United States	1:13.6
1924 Ethel Lackie, United States	1:12.4
1928 Albina Osipowich, United States	1:11.0
1932 Helene Madison, United States	1:06.8
1936 Hendrika Mastenbroek, Holland	1:05.9
1948 Greta Andersen, Denmark	1:06.3
1952 Katalin Szoke, Hungary	1:06.8
1956 Dawn Fraser, Australia	1:02.0
1960 Dawn Fraser, Australia	1:01.2
1964 Dawn Fraser, Australia	0:59.5
1968 Jan Henne, United States	1:00.0
1972 Sandra Neilson, United States	0:58.59
1976 Kornelia Ender, E. Germany	0:55.65
1980 Barbara Krause, E. Germany	0:54.79
1984 Carrie Steinseifer, United States	0:55.92
Nancy Hogshead, United States (tie)	0:55.92

100-Meter Freestyle	Time
1988 Kristin Otto, E. Germany	0:54.93
1992 Zhuang Yong, China	0:54.64
1996 Li Jingyi, China	0:54.50
2000 Inge de Bruijn, Netherlands	0:53.83
2004 Jodie Henry, Australia	0:53.84
2008 Britta Steffen, Germany	0:53.12
2012 Ranomi Kromowidjojo, Netherlands	0:53.00*

200-Meter Freestyle	Time
1968 Debbie Meyer, United States	2:10.5
1972 Shane Gould, Australia	2:03.56
1976 Kornelia Ender, E. Germany	1:59.26
1980 Barbara Krause, E. Germany	1:58.33
1984 Mary Wayte, United States	1:59.23
1988 Heike Friedrich, E. Germany	1:57.65
1992 Nicole Haislett, United States	1:57.90
1996 Claudia Poll, Costa Rica	1:58.16
2000 Susan O'Neill, Australia	1:58.24
2004 Camelia Potec, Romania	1:58.03
2008 Federica Pellegrini, Italy	1:54.82
2012 Allison Schmitt, United States	1:53.61*

400-Meter Freestyle	Time
1924 Martha Norelius, United States	6:02.2
1928 Martha Norelius, United States	5:42.8
1932 Helene Madison, United States	5:28.5

400-Meter Freestyle

Year	Champion	Time
1936	Hendrika Mastenbroek, Netherlands	5:26.4
1948	Ann Curtis, United States	5:17.8
1952	Valerie Gyenge, Hungary	5:12.1
1956	Lorraine Crapp, Australia	4:54.6
1960	Susan Chris von Saltza, United States	4:50.6
1964	Virginia Duenkel, United States	4:43.3
1968	Debbie Meyer, United States	4:31.8
1972	Shane Gould, Australia	4:19.44
1976	Petra Thuemer, E. Germany	4:09.89
1980	Ines Diers, E. Germany	4:08.76
1984	Tiffany Cohen, United States	4:07.10
1988	Janet Evans, United States	4:03.85
1992	Dagmar Hase, Germany	4:07.18
1996	Michelle Smith, Ireland	4:07.25
2000	Brooke Bennett, United States	4:05.80
2004	Laure Manaudou, France	4:05.34
2008	Rebecca Adlington, Great Britain	4:03.22
2012	Camille Muffat, France	4:01.45*

800-Meter Freestyle

Year	Champion	Time
1968	Debbie Meyer, United States	9:24.0
1972	Keena Rothhammer, United States	8:53.68
1976	Petra Thuemer, E. Germany	8:37.14
1980	Michelle Ford, Australia	8:28.90
1984	Tiffany Cohen, United States	8:24.95
1988	Janet Evans, United States	8:20.20
1992	Janet Evans, United States	8:25.52
1996	Brooke Bennett, United States	8:27.89
2000	Brooke Bennett, United States	8:19.67
2004	Ai Shibata, Japan	8:24.54
2008	Rebecca Adlington, Great Britain	8:14.10*
2012	Katie Ledecky, United States	8:14.63

100-Meter Backstroke

Year	Champion	Time
1924	Sybil Bauer, United States	1:23.2
1928	Marie Braun, Netherlands	1:22.0
1932	Eleanor Holm, United States	1:19.4
1936	Dina Senff, Netherlands	1:18.9
1948	Karen Harup, Denmark	1:14.4
1952	Joan Harrison, South Africa	1:14.3
1956	Judy Grinham, Great Britain	1:12.9
1960	Lynn Burke, United States	1:09.3
1964	Cathy Ferguson, United States	1:07.7
1968	Kaye Hall, United States	1:06.2
1972	Melissa Belote, United States	1:05.78
1976	Ulrike Richter, E. Germany	1:01.83
1980	Rica Reinisch, E. Germany	1:00.86
1984	Theresa Andrews, United States	1:02.55
1988	Kristin Otto, E. Germany	1:00.89
1992	Krisztina Egerszegi, Hungary	1:00.68
1996	Beth Botsford, United States	1:01.19
2000	Diana Mocanu, Romania	1:00.21
2004	Natalie Coughlin, United States	1:00.37
2008	Natalie Coughlin, United States	0:58.96
2012	Missy Franklin, United States	0:58.33

200-Meter Backstroke

Year	Champion	Time
1968	Pokey Watson, United States	2:24.8
1972	Melissa Belote, United States	2:19.19
1976	Ulrike Richter, E. Germany	2:13.43
1980	Rica Reinisch, E. Germany	2:11.77
1984	Jolanda De Rover, Netherlands	2:12.38
1988	Krisztina Egerszegi, Hungary	2:09.29
1992	Krisztina Egerszegi, Hungary	2:07.06
1996	Krisztina Egerszegi, Hungary	2:07.83
2000	Diana Mocanu, Romania	2:08.16
2004	Kirsty Coventry, Zimbabwe	2:09.19
2008	Kirsty Coventry, Zimbabwe	2:05.24
2012	Missy Franklin, United States	2:04.06*

100-Meter Breaststroke

Year	Champion	Time
1968	Djurdjica Bjedov, Yugoslavia	1:15.8
1972	Cathy Carr, United States	1:13.58
1976	Hannelore Anke, E. Germany	1:11.16
1980	Ute Geweniger, E. Germany	1:10.22
1984	Petra Van Staveren, Netherlands	1:09.88
1988	Tania Dangalakova, Bulgaria	1:07.95
1992	Elena Roudkovskaia, Unified Team	1:08.00
1996	Penny Heyns, South Africa	1:07.73
2000	Megan Quann, United States	1:07.05
2004	Luo Xuejuan, China	1:06.64
2008	Leisel Jones, Australia	1:05.17*
2012	Rūta Meilutytė, Lithuania	1:05.47

200-Meter Breaststroke

Year	Champion	Time
1924	Lucy Morton, Great Britain	3:33.2
1928	Hilde Schrader, Germany	3:12.6
1932	Clare Dennis, Australia	3:06.3
1936	Hideko Maehata, Japan	3:03.6
1948	Nelly Van Vliet, Netherlands	2:57.2
1952	Eva Szekely, Hungary	2:51.7
1956	Ursula Happe, Germany	2:53.1
1960	Anita Lonsbrough, Great Britain	2:49.5

200-Meter Breaststroke

Year	Champion	Time
1964	Galina Prozumenschikova, USSR	2:46.4
1968	Sharon Wichman, United States	2:44.4
1972	Beverly Whitfield, Australia	2:41.71
1976	Marina Koshevaia, USSR	2:33.35
1980	Lina Kachushite, USSR	2:29.54
1984	Anne Ottenbrite, Canada	2:30.38
1988	Silke Hoerner, E. Germany	2:26.71
1992	Kyoko Iwasaki, Japan	2:26.65
1996	Penny Heyns, South Africa	2:25.41
2000	Agnes Kovacs, Hungary	2:24.35
2004	Amanda Beard, United States	2:23.37
2008	Rebecca Soni, United States	2:20.22
2012	Rebecca Soni, United States	2:19.59*

100-Meter Butterfly

Year	Champion	Time
1956	Shelley Mann, United States	1:11.0
1960	Carolyn Schuler, United States	1:09.5
1964	Sharon Stouder, United States	1:04.7
1968	Lynn McClements, Australia	1:05.5
1972	Mayumi Aoki, Japan	1:03.34
1976	Kornelia Ender, E. Germany	1:00.13
1980	Caren Metschuck, E. Germany	1:00.42
1984	Mary T. Meagher, United States	0:59.26
1988	Kristin Otto, E. Germany	0:59.00
1992	Qian Hong, China	0:58.62
1996	Amy Van Dyken, United States	0:59.13
2000	Inge de Bruijn, Netherlands	0:56.61
2004	Petria Thomas, Australia	0:57.72
2008	Lisbeth Trickett, Australia	0:56.73
2012	Dana Vollmer, United States	0:55.98*

200-Meter Butterfly

Year	Champion	Time
1968	Ada Kok, Netherlands	2:24.7
1972	Karen Moe, United States	2:15.57
1976	Andrea Pollack, E. Germany	2:11.41
1980	Ines Geissler, E. Germany	2:10.44
1984	Mary T. Meagher, United States	2:06.90
1988	Kathleen Nord, E. Germany	2:09.51
1992	Summer Sanders, United States	2:08.67
1996	Susan O'Neill, Australia	2:07.76
2000	Misty Hyman, United States	2:05.88
2004	Otylia Jedrzejczak, Poland	2:06.05
2008	Liu Zige, China	2:04.18
2012	Jiao Liuyang, China	2:04.06*

200-Meter Individual Medley

Year	Champion	Time
1968	Claudia Kolb, United States	2:24.7
1972	Shane Gould, Australia	2:23.07
1984	Tracy Caulkins, United States	2:12.64
1988	Daniela Hunger, E. Germany	2:12.59
1992	Lin Li, China	2:11.65
1996	Michelle Smith, Ireland	2:13.93
2000	Yana Klochkova, Ukraine	2:10.68
2004	Yana Klochkova, Ukraine	2:11.14
2008	Stephanie Rice, Australia	2:08.45
2012	Ye Shiwen, China	2:07.57*

400-Meter Individual Medley

Year	Champion	Time
1964	Donna de Varona, United States	5:18.7
1968	Claudia Kolb, United States	5:08.5
1972	Gail Neall, Australia	5:02.97
1976	Ulrike Tauber, E. Germany	4:42.77
1980	Petra Schneider, E. Germany	4:36.29
1984	Tracy Caulkins, United States	4:39.24
1988	Janet Evans, United States	4:37.76
1992	Krisztina Egerszegi, Hungary	4:36.54
1996	Michelle Smith, Ireland	4:39.18
2000	Yana Klochkova, Ukraine	4:33.59
2004	Yana Klochkova, Ukraine	4:34.83
2008	Stephanie Rice, Australia	4:29.45
2012	Ye Shiwen, China	4:28.43*

4x100-Meter Freestyle Relay

Year	Champion	Time
1912	Great Britain	5:52.8
1920	United States	5:11.6
1924	United States	4:58.8
1928	United States	4:47.6
1932	United States	4:38.0
1936	Netherlands	4:36.0
1948	United States	4:29.2
1952	Hungary	4:24.4
1956	Australia	4:17.1
1960	United States	4:08.9
1964	United States	4:03.8
1968	United States	4:02.5
1972	United States	3:55.19
1976	United States	3:44.82
1980	East Germany	3:42.71
1984	United States	3:43.43
1988	East Germany	3:40.63
1992	United States	3:39.46
1996	United States	3:39.29

4x100-Meter Freestyle Relay

		Time
2000	United States	3:36.61
2004	Australia	3:35.94
2008	Netherlands	3:33.76
2012	Australia	3:33.15*

4x200-Meter Freestyle Relay

		Time
1996	United States	7:59.87
2000	United States	7:57.80
2004	United States	7:53.42
2008	Australia	7:44.31
2012	United States	7:42.92*

4x100-Meter Medley Relay

		Time
1960	United States	4:41.1
1964	United States	4:33.9
1968	United States	4:28.3
1972	United States	4:20.75
1976	East Germany	4:07.95
1980	East Germany	4:06.67
1984	United States	4:08.34
1988	East Germany	4:03.74
1992	United States	4:02.54
1996	United States	4:02.88
2000	United States	3:58.30
2004	Australia	3:57.32
2008	Australia	3:52.69
2012	United States	3:52.05*

10-Kilometer Marathon

		Time
2008	Larisa Ilchenko, Russia	1:59:27.7
2012	Éva Risztov, Hungary	1:57:38.2

Platform Diving

		Points
1912	Greta Johansson, Sweden	39.90
1920	Stefani Fryland-Clausen, Denmark	34.60
1924	Caroline Smith, United States	33.20
1928	Elizabeth B. Pinkston, United States	31.60
1932	Dorothy Poynton, United States	40.26
1936	Dorothy Poynton Hill, United States	33.93
1948	Victoria M. Draves, United States	68.87
1952	Patricia McCormick, United States	79.37
1956	Patricia McCormick, United States	84.85
1960	Ingrid Kramer, Germany	91.28
1964	Lesley Bush, United States	99.80
1968	Milena Duchkova, Czechoslovakia	109.59
1972	Ulrika Knape, Sweden	390.00

Platform Diving

		Points
1976	Elena Vaytsekhouskaya, USSR	406.59
1980	Martina Jaschke, E. Germany	596.25
1984	Zhou Jihong, China	435.51
1988	Xu Yanmei, China	445.20
1992	Fu Mingxia, China	461.43
1996	Fu Mingxia, China	521.58
2000	Laura Wilkinson, United States	543.75
2004	Chantelle Newbery, Australia	590.31
2008	Chen Ruolin, China	447.70
2012	Chen Ruolin, China	422.30

Springboard Diving

		Points
1920	Aileen Riggin, United States	539.90
1924	Elizabeth Becker, United States	474.50
1928	Helen Meany, United States	78.62
1932	Georgia Coleman United States	87.52
1936	Marjorie Gestring, United States	89.27
1948	Victoria M. Draves, United States	108.74
1952	Patricia McCormick, United States	147.30
1956	Patricia McCormick, United States	142.36
1960	Ingrid Kramer, Germany	155.81
1964	Ingrid Engel-Kramer, Germany	145.00
1968	Sue Gossick, United States	150.77
1972	Micki King, United States	450.03
1976	Jenni Chandler, United States	506.19
1980	Irina Kalinina, USSR	725.91
1984	Sylvie Bernier, Canada	530.70
1988	Gao Min, China	580.23
1992	Gao Min, China	572.40
1996	Fu Mingxia, China	547.68
2000	Fu Mingxia, China	609.42
2004	Guo Jingjing, China	633.15
2008	Guo Jingjing, China	415.35
2012	Wu Minxia, China	414.00

Synchronized Platform

		Points
2004	Lao Lishi and Li Ting, China	352.14
2008	Wang Xin and Chen Ruolin, China	363.54
2012	Chen Ruolin and Wang Hao, China	368.40

Synchronized Springboard

		Points
2004	Wu Minxia and Guo Jingjing, China	336.90
2008	Guo Jingjing and Wu Minxia, China	343.50
2012	He Zi and Wu Minxia, China	346.20

Tennis

Men's Singles

1896	John Boland, Great Britain
1900	Hugh Lawrence Doherty, Great Britain
1904	Beals Coleman Wright, United States
1908	Josiah George Ritchie, Great Britain
1912	Charles Lyndhurst Winslow, South Africa
1920	Louis Raymond, South Africa
1924	Vincent Richards, United States
1988	Miloslav Mecir, Czechoslovakia
1992	Marc Rosset, Switzerland
1996	Andre Agassi, United States
2000	Eugueni Kafelnikov, Russia
2004	Nicolas Massu, Chile
2008	Rafael Nadal, Spain
2012	Andy Murray, Great Britain

Men's Doubles

1896	John Boland, Great Britain & Friedrick Traun, Germany
1900	Hugh Lawrence Doherty & Reginald Frank Doherty, Great Britain
1904	Edgar Welch Leonard & Beals Coleman Wright, United States
1908	George Whiteside Hillyard & Reginald Frank Doherty, Great Britain
1912	Harry Austin Kitson & Charles Lyndhurst Winslow, South Africa
1920	Oswald Graham Noel Turnbull & Maxwell Woosnam, Great Britain
1924	Vincent Richards & Francis Townsend Hunter, United States
1988	Kenneth Flach & Robert A. Seguso, United States
1992	Boris Franz Becker & Michael Stich, Germany
1996	Mark Woodforde & Todd Woodbridge, Australia

Men's Doubles

2000	Sebastien Lareau & Daniel Nestor, Canada
2004	Fernando Gonzales & Nicolas Massu, Chile
2008	Roger Federer & Stanislas Wawrinka, Switzerland
2012	Mike Bryan & Bob Bryan, United States

Women's Singles

1900	Charlotte Cooper, Great Britain
1908	Dorothy Katherine Chambers, Great Britain
1912	Marguerite Broquedis, France
1920	Suzanne Lenglen, France
1924	Helen Wills, United States
1988	Steffi Graf, W. Germany
1992	Jennifer Capriati, United States
1996	Lindsay Davenport, United States
2000	Venus Williams, United States
2004	Justine Henin-Hardenne, Belgium
2008	Elena Dementieva, Russia
2012	Serena Williams, United States

Women's Doubles

1920	Winifred Margaret McNair & Kathleen McKane, Great Britain
1924	Hazel Virginia Wightman & Helen Wills, United States
1988	Pamela Howard Shriver & Zina Garrison, United States
1992	Gigi Fernandez & Mary Joe Fernandez, United States
1996	Gigi Fernandez & Mary Joe Fernandez, United States
2000	Venus Williams & Serena Williams, United States
2004	Ting Li & Tian Tian Sun, China
2008	Serena Williams & Venus Williams, United States
2012	Serena Williams & Venus Williams, United States

Mixed Doubles

2012	Victoria Azarenka & Max Mirnyi, Belarus

Track and Field—Men

100-Meter Run

		Time
1896	Thomas Burke, United States	12.0s
1900	Francis W. Jarvis, United States	11.0s
1904	Archie Hahn, United States	11.0s
1908	Reginald Walker, South Africa	10.8s
1912	Ralph Craig, United States	10.8s
1920	Charles Paddock, United States	10.8s
1924	Harold Abrahams, Great Britain	10.6s
1928	Percy Williams, Canada	10.8s
1932	Eddie Tolan, United States	10.3s

100-Meter Run

		Time
1936	Jesse Owens, United States	10.3s
1948	Harrison Dillard, United States	10.3s
1952	Lindy Remigino, United States	10.4s
1956	Bobby Morrow, United States	10.5s
1960	Armin Hary, Germany	10.2s
1964	Bob Hayes, United States	10.0s
1968	Jim Hines, United States	9.95s
1972	Valery Borzov, USSR	10.14s
1976	Hasely Crawford, Trinidad	10.06s

100-Meter Run

Year	Athlete	Time
1980	Allan Wells, Great Britain	10.25s
1984	Carl Lewis, United States	9.99s
1988	Carl Lewis, United States	9.92s
1992	Linford Christie, Great Britain	9.96s
1996	Donovan Bailey, Canada	9.84s
2000	Maurice Greene, United States	9.87s
2004	Justin Gatlin, United States	9.85s
2008	Usain Bolt, Jamaica	9.69s
2012	Usain Bolt, Jamaica	9.63s*

200-Meter Run

Year	Athlete	Time
1900	Walter Tewksbury, United States	22.2s
1904	Archie Hahn, United States	21.6s
1908	Robert Kerr, Canada	22.6s
1912	Ralph Craig, United States	21.7s
1920	Allan Woodring, United States	22.0s
1924	Jackson Scholz, United States	21.6s
1928	Percy Williams, Canada	21.8s
1932	Eddie Tolan, United States	21.2s
1936	Jesse Owens, United States	20.7s
1948	Mel Patton, United States	21.1s
1952	Andrew Stanfield, United States	20.7s
1956	Bobby Morrow, United States	20.6s
1960	Livio Berruti, Italy	20.5s
1964	Henry Carr, United States	20.3s
1968	Tommie Smith, United States	19.83s
1972	Valeri Borzov, USSR	20.00s
1976	Donald Quarrie, Jamaica	20.23s
1980	Pietro Mennea, Italy	20.19s
1984	Carl Lewis, United States	19.80s
1988	Joe DeLoach, United States	19.75s
1992	Mike Marsh, United States	20.01s
1996	Michael Johnson, United States	19.32s
2000	Konstantinos Kenteris, Greece	20.09s
2004	Shawn Crawford, United States	19.79s
2008	Usain Bolt, Jamaica	19.30s*
2012	Usain Bolt, Jamaica	19.32s

400-Meter Run

Year	Athlete	Time
1896	Thomas Burke, United States	54.2s
1900	Maxey Long, United States	49.4s
1904	Harry Hillman, United States	49.2s
1908	Wyndham Halswelle, Gr. Brit., walkover	50.0s
1912	Charles Reidpath, United States	48.2s
1920	Bevil Rudd, South Africa	49.6s
1924	Eric Liddell, Great Britain	47.6s
1928	Ray Barbuti, United States	47.8s
1932	William Carr, United States	46.2s
1936	Archie Williams, United States	46.5s
1948	Arthur Wint, Jamaica	46.2s
1952	George Rhoden, Jamaica	45.9s
1956	Charles Jenkins, United States	46.7s
1960	Otis Davis, United States	44.9s
1964	Michael Larrabee, United States	45.1s
1968	Lee Evans, United States	43.86s
1972	Vincent Matthews, United States	44.66s
1976	Alberto Juantorena, Cuba	44.26s
1980	Viktor Markin, USSR	44.60s
1984	Alonzo Babers, United States	44.27s
1988	Steven Lewis, United States	43.87s
1992	Quincy Watts, United States	43.50s
1996	Michael Johnson, United States	43.49s*
2000	Michael Johnson, United States	43.84s
2004	Jeremy Wariner, United States	44.00s
2008	LaShawn Merritt, United States	43.75s
2012	Kirani James, Grenada	43.94s

800-Meter Run

Year	Athlete	Time
1896	Edwin Flack, Australia	2m. 11s
1900	Alfred Tysoe, Great Britain	2m. 01.2s
1904	James Lightbody, United States	1m. 56s
1908	Mel Sheppard, United States	1m. 52.8s
1912	James Meredith, United States	1m. 51.9s
1920	Albert Hill, Great Britain	1m. 53.4s
1924	Douglas Lowe, Great Britain	1m. 52.4s
1928	Douglas Lowe, Great Britain	1m. 51.8s
1932	Thomas Hampson, Great Britain	1m. 49.8s
1936	John Woodruff, United States	1m. 52.9s
1948	Mal Whitfield, United States	1m. 49.2s
1952	Mal Whitfield, United States	1m. 49.2s
1956	Thomas Courtney, United States	1m. 47.7s
1960	Peter Snell, New Zealand	1m. 46.3s
1964	Peter Snell, New Zealand	1m. 45.1s
1968	Ralph Doubell, Australia	1m. 44.3s
1972	Dave Wottle, United States	1m. 45.9s
1976	Alberto Juantorena, Cuba	1m. 43.50s
1980	Steve Ovett, Great Britain	1m. 45.40s
1984	Joaquim Cruz, Brazil	1m. 43.00s
1988	Paul Ereng, Kenya	1m. 43.45s
1992	William Tanui, Kenya	1m. 43.66s
1996	Vebjoern Rodal, Norway	1m. 42.58s
2000	Nils Schumann, Germany	1m. 45.08s
2004	Yuriy Borzakovskiy, Russia	1m. 44.45s
2008	Wilfred Bungei, Kenya	1m. 44.65s
2012	David Rudisha, Kenya	1m. 40.91s*

1,500-Meter Run

Year	Athlete	Time
1896	Edwin Flack, Australia	4m. 33.2s
1900	Charles Bennett, Great Britain	4m. 06.2s
1904	James Lightbody, United States	4m. 05.4s
1908	Mel Sheppard, United States	4m. 03.4s
1912	Arnold Jackson, Great Britain	3m. 56.8s
1920	Albert Hill, Great Britain	4m. 01.8s
1924	Paavo Nurmi, Finland	3m. 53.6s
1928	Harry Larva, Finland	3m. 53.2s
1932	Luigi Beccali, Italy	3m. 51.2s
1936	Jack Lovelock, New Zealand	3m. 47.8s
1948	Henri Eriksson, Sweden	3m. 49.8s
1952	Joseph Barthel, Luxembourg	3m. 45.2s
1956	Ron Delany, Ireland	3m. 41.2s
1960	Herb Elliott, Australia	3m. 35.6s
1964	Peter Snell, New Zealand	3m. 38.1s
1968	Kipchoge Keino, Kenya	3m. 34.9s
1972	Pekka Vasala, Finland	3m. 36.3s
1976	John Walker, New Zealand	3m. 39.17s
1980	Sebastian Coe, Great Britain	3m. 38.4s
1984	Sebastian Coe, Great Britain	3m. 32.53s
1988	Peter Rono, Kenya	3m. 35.96s
1992	Fermin Cacho Ruiz, Spain	3m. 40.12s
1996	Noureddine Morceli, Algeria	3m. 35.78s
2000	Noah Ngeny, Kenya	3m. 32.07s*
2004	Hicham el-Guerrouj, Morocco	3m. 34.18s
2008	Rashid Ramzi, Bahrain (a)	3m. 32.94s
2012	Taoufik Makhloufi, Algeria	3m. 34.08s

(a) Stripped of medal in 2009 for doping.

3,000-Meter Steeplechase

Year	Athlete	Time
1920	Percy Hodge, Great Britain	10m. 0.4s
1924	Willie Ritola, Finland	9m. 33.6s
1928	Toivo Loukola, Finland	9m. 21.8s
1932	Volmari Iso-Hollo, Finland (about 3,450 m; extra lap by error)	10m. 33.4s
1936	Volmari Iso-Hollo, Finland	9m. 3.8s
1948	Thore Sjoestrand, Sweden	9m. 4.6s
1952	Horace Ashenfelter, United States	8m. 45.4s
1956	Chris Brasher, Great Britain	8m. 41.2s
1960	Zdzislaw Krzyszkowiak, Poland	8m. 34.2s
1964	Gaston Roelants, Belgium	8m. 30.8s
1968	Amos Biwott, Kenya	8m. 51s
1972	Kipchoge Keino, Kenya	8m. 23.6s
1976	Anders Garderud, Sweden	8m. 08.2s
1980	Bronislaw Malinowski, Poland	8m. 09.7s
1984	Julius Korir, Kenya	8m. 11.8s
1988	Julius Kariuki, Kenya	8m. 05.51s*
1992	Matthew Birir, Kenya	8m. 08.84s
1996	Joseph Keter, Kenya	8m. 07.12s
2000	Reuben Kosgei, Kenya	8m. 21.43s
2004	Ezekiel Kemboi, Kenya	8m. 05.81s
2008	Brimin Kiprop Kirpruto, Kenya	8m. 10.34s
2012	Ezekiel Kemboi, Kenya	8m. 18.56s

5,000-Meter Run

Year	Athlete	Time
1912	Hannes Kolehmainen, Finland	14m. 36.6s
1920	Joseph Guillemot, France	14m. 55.6s
1924	Paavo Nurmi, Finland	14m. 31.2s
1928	Willie Ritola, Finland	14m. 38s
1932	Lauri Lehtinen, Finland	14m. 30s
1936	Gunnar Hockert, Finland	14m. 22.2s
1948	Gaston Reiff, Belgium	14m. 17.6s
1952	Emil Zatopek, Czechoslovakia	14m. 06.6s
1956	Vladimir Kuts, USSR	13m. 39.6s
1960	Murray Halberg, New Zealand	13m. 43.4s
1964	Bob Schul, United States	13m. 48.8s
1968	Mohamed Gammoudi, Tunisia	14m. 05.0s
1972	Lasse Viren, Finland	13m. 26.4s
1976	Lasse Viren, Finland	13m. 24.76s
1980	Miruts Yifter, Ethiopia	13m. 21.0s
1984	Said Aouita, Morocco	13m. 05.59s
1988	John Ngugi, Kenya	13m. 11.70s
1992	Dieter Baumann, Germany	13m. 12.52s
1996	Venuste Niyongabo, Burundi	13m. 07.96s
2000	Millon Wolde, Ethiopia	13m. 35.49s
2004	Hicham el-Guerrouj, Morocco	13m. 14.39s
2008	Kenenisa Bekele, Ethiopia	12m. 57.82s*
2012	Mo Farah, Great Britain	13m. 41.66s

10,000-Meter Run

Year	Athlete	Time
1912	Hannes Kolehmainen, Finland	31m. 20.8s
1920	Paavo Nurmi, Finland	31m. 45.8s
1924	Willie Ritola, Finland	30m. 23.2s
1928	Paavo Nurmi, Finland	30m. 18.8s
1932	Janusz Kusocinski, Poland	30m. 11.4s
1936	Ilmari Salminen, Finland	30m. 15.4s
1948	Emil Zatopek, Czechoslovakia	29m. 59.6s
1952	Emil Zatopek, Czechoslovakia	29m. 17.0s
1956	Vladimir Kuts, USSR	28m. 45.6s
1960	Pyotr Bolotnikov, USSR	28m. 32.2s
1964	Billy Mills, United States	28m. 24.4s
1968	Naftali Temu, Kenya	29m. 27.4s
1972	Lasse Viren, Finland	27m. 38.4s
1976	Lasse Viren, Finland	27m. 40.4s

10,000-Meter Run		Time
1980	Miruts Yifter, Ethiopia	27m. 42.7s
1984	Alberto Cova, Italy	27m. 47.54s
1988	Brahim Boutaib, Morocco	27m. 21.46s
1992	Khalid Skah, Morocco	27m. 46.70s
1996	Haile Gebrselassie, Ethiopia	27m. 07.34s
2000	Haile Gebrselassie, Ethiopia	27m. 18.20s
2004	Kenenisa Bekele, Ethiopia	27m. 05.10s
2008	Kenenisa Bekele, Ethiopia	27m. 01.17s*
2012	Mo Farah, Great Britain	27m. 30.42s

Marathon		Time
1896	Spiridon Loues, Greece	2h. 58m. 50s
1900	Michel Theato, France	2h. 59m. 45s
1904	Thomas Hicks, United States	3h. 28m. 63s
1908	John J. Hayes, United States	2h. 55m. 18.4s
1912	Kenneth McArthur, South Africa	2h. 36m. 54.8s
1920	Hannes Kolehmainen, Finland	2h. 32m. 35.8s
1924	Albin Stenroos, Finland	2h. 41m. 22.6s
1928	A. B. El Ouafi, France	2h. 32m. 57s
1932	Juan Zabala, Argentina	2h. 31m. 36s
1936	Kee-chung Sohn, Japan (Korean who competed under Japanese name Kitei Son)	2h. 29m. 19.2s
1948	Delfo Cabrera, Argentina	2h. 34m. 51.6s
1952	Emil Zatopek, Czechoslovakia	2h. 23m. 03.2s
1956	Alain Mimoun, France	2h. 25m.
1960	Abebe Bikila, Ethiopia	2h. 15m. 16.2s
1964	Abebe Bikila, Ethiopia	2h. 12m. 11.2s
1968	Mamo Wolde, Ethiopia	2h. 20m. 26.4s
1972	Frank Shorter, United States	2h. 12m. 19.8s
1976	Waldemar Cierpinski, E. Germany	2h. 09m. 55s
1980	Waldemar Cierpinski, E. Germany	2h. 11m. 03s
1984	Carlos Lopes, Portugal	2h. 09m. 21s
1988	Gelindo Bordin, Italy	2h. 10m. 32s
1992	Hwang Young-Cho, S. Korea	2h. 13m. 23s
1996	Josia Thugwane, South Africa	2h. 12m. 36s
2000	Gezahgne Abera, Ethiopia	2h. 10m. 11s
2004	Stefano Baldino, Italy	2h. 10m. 55s
2008	Samuel Kamau Wansiru, Kenya	2h. 06m. 32s*
2012	Stephen Kiprotich, Uganda	2h. 08m. 01s

4x100-Meter Relay		Time
1912	Great Britain	42.4s
1920	United States	42.2s
1924	United States	41.0s
1928	United States	41.0s
1932	United States	40.0s
1936	United States	39.8s
1948	United States	40.6s
1952	United States	40.1s
1956	United States	39.5s
1960	Germany (U.S. disqualified)	39.5s
1964	United States	39.0s
1968	United States	38.24s
1972	United States	38.19s
1976	United States	38.33s
1980	USSR	38.26s
1984	United States	37.83s
1988	USSR (U.S. disqualified)	38.19s
1992	United States	37.40s
1996	Canada	37.69s
2000	United States	37.61s
2004	Great Britain	38.07s
2008	Jamaica	37.10s
2012	Jamaica	36.84s*

4x400-Meter Relay		Time
1908	United States	3m. 29.4s
1912	United States	3m. 16.6s
1920	Great Britain	3m. 22.2s
1924	United States	3m. 16s
1928	United States	3m. 14.2s
1932	United States	3m. 08.2s
1936	Great Britain	3m. 09s
1948	United States	3m. 10.4s
1952	Jamaica	3m. 03.9s
1956	United States	3m. 04.8s
1960	United States	3m. 02.2s
1964	United States	3m. 00.7s
1968	United States	2m. 56.16s
1972	Kenya	2m. 59.8s
1976	United States	2m. 58.65s
1980	USSR	3m. 01.1s
1984	United States	2m. 57.91s
1988	United States	2m. 56.16s
1992	United States	2m. 55.74s
1996	United States	2m. 55.99s
2000	Nigeria (a)	2m. 58.68
2004	United States	2m. 55.91s
2008	United States	2m. 55.39s*
2012	The Bahamas	2m. 56.72s

(a) The International Olympic Committee stripped the 2000 U.S. relay team of their medals in Aug. 2008 after one of the team's members, Antonio Pettigrew, admitted to doping; the medal was reallocated to the second place Nigerian team in July 2012.

20-Kilometer Walk		Time
1956	Leonid Spirin, USSR	1h. 31m. 27.4s
1960	Vladimir Golubnichy, USSR	1h. 33m. 7.2s
1964	Kenneth Mathews, Great Britain	1h. 29m. 34.0s
1968	Vladimir Golubnichy, USSR	1h. 33m. 58.4s
1972	Peter Frenkel, E. Germany	1h. 26m. 42.4s
1976	Daniel Bautista, Mexico	1h. 24m. 40.6s
1980	Maurizio Damilano, Italy	1h. 23m. 35.5s
1984	Ernesto Canto, Mexico	1h. 23m. 13.0s
1988	Josef Pribilinec, Czechoslovakia	1h. 19m. 57.0s
1992	Daniel Plaza Montero, Spain	1h. 21m. 45.0s
1996	Jefferson Perez, Ecuador	1h. 20m. 07s
2000	Robert Korzeniowski, Poland	1h. 18m. 59.0s
2004	Ivano Brugnetti, Italy	1h. 19m. 40s
2008	Valeriy Borchin, Russia	1h. 19m. 01s
2012	Chen Ding, China	1h. 18m. 46s*

50-Kilometer Walk		Time
1932	Thomas W. Green, Great Britain	4h. 50m. 10s
1936	Harold Whitlock, Great Britain	4h. 30m. 41.4s
1948	John Ljunggren, Sweden	4h. 41m. 52s
1952	Giuseppe Dordoni, Italy	4h. 28m. 07.8s
1956	Norman Read, New Zealand	4h. 30m. 42.8s
1960	Donald Thompson, Great Britain	4h. 25m. 30s
1964	Abdon Pamich, Italy	4h. 11m. 12.4s
1968	Christoph Hohne, E. Germany	4h. 20m. 13.6s
1972	Bern Kannenberg, W. Germany	3h. 56m. 11.6s
1980	Hartwig Gauder, E. Germany	3h. 49m. 24.0s
1984	Raul Gonzalez, Mexico	3h. 47m. 26.0s
1988	Vyacheslav Ivanenko, USSR	3h. 38m. 29.0s
1992	Andrei Perlov, Unified Team	3h. 50m. 13.0s
1996	Robert Korzeniowski, Poland	3h. 43m. 30s
2000	Robert Korzeniowski, Poland	3h. 42m. 22s
2004	Robert Korzeniowski, Poland	3h. 38m. 46s
2008	Alex Schwazer, Italy	3h. 37m. 09s
2012	Sergey Kirdyapkin, Russia	3h. 35m. 59s*

110-Meter Hurdles		Time
1896	Thomas Curtis, United States	17.6s
1900	Alvin Kraenzlein, United States	15.4s
1904	Frederick Schule, United States	16.0s
1908	Forrest Smithson, United States	15.0s
1912	Frederick Kelly, United States	15.1s
1920	Earl Thomson, Canada	14.8s
1924	Daniel Kinsey, United States	15.0s
1928	Sydney Atkinson, South Africa	14.8s
1932	George Saling, United States	14.6s
1936	Forrest Towns, United States	14.2s
1948	William Porter, United States	13.9s
1952	Harrison Dillard, United States	13.7s
1956	Lee Calhoun, United States	13.5s
1960	Lee Calhoun, United States	13.8s
1964	Hayes Jones, United States	13.6s
1968	Willie Davenport, United States	13.33s
1972	Rod Milburn, United States	13.24s
1976	Guy Drut, France	13.30s
1980	Thomas Munkelt, E. Germany	13.39s
1984	Roger Kingdom, United States	13.20s
1988	Roger Kingdom, United States	12.98s
1992	Mark McKoy, Canada	13.12s
1996	Allen Johnson, United States	12.95s
2000	Anier Garcia, Cuba	13.00s
2004	Liu Xiang, China	12.91s*
2008	Dayron Robles, Cuba	12.93s
2012	Aries Merritt, United States	12.92s

400-Meter Hurdles		Time
1900	J. W. B. Tewksbury, United States	57.6s
1904	Harry Hillman, United States	53.0s
1908	Charles Bacon, United States	55.0s
1920	Frank Loomis, United States	54.0s
1924	F. Morgan Taylor, United States	52.6s
1928	Lord Burghley, Great Britain	53.4s
1932	Robert Tisdall, Ireland	51.7s
1936	Glenn Hardin, United States	52.4s
1948	Roy Cochran, United States	51.1s
1952	Charles Moore, United States	50.8s
1956	Glenn Davis, United States	50.1s
1960	Glenn Davis, United States	49.3s
1964	Rex Cawley, United States	49.6s
1968	Dave Hemery, Great Britain	48.12s
1972	John Akii-Bua, Uganda	47.82s
1976	Edwin Moses, United States	47.64s
1980	Volker Beck, E. Germany	48.70s
1984	Edwin Moses, United States	47.75s
1988	Andre Phillips, United States	47.19s
1992	Kevin Young, United States	46.78s
1996	Derrick Adkins, United States	47.54s
2000	Angelo Taylor, United States	47.50s
2004	Félix Sánchez, Dominican Republic	47.63s
2008	Angelo Taylor, United States	47.25s
2012	Félix Sánchez, Dominican Republic	47.63s

Discus Throw		Dist.
1896	Robert Garrett, United States	29.15m (95' 7")
1900	Rudolf Bauer, Hungary	36.04m (118' 3")

Discus Throw

Year	Champion	Dist.	
1904	Martin Sheridan, United States	39.28m	(128' 10")
1908	Martin Sheridan, United States	40.89m	(134' 1")
1912	Armas Taipale, Finland	45.21m	(148' 3")
1920	Elmer Niklander, Finland	44.68m	(146' 7")
1924	Clarence Houser, United States	46.15m	(151' 4")
1928	Clarence Houser, United States	47.32m	(155' 3")
1932	John Anderson, United States	49.49m	(162' 4")
1936	Ken Carpenter, United States	50.48m	(165' 7")
1948	Adolfo Consolini, Italy	52.78m	(173' 2")
1952	Sim Iness, United States	55.03m	(180' 6")
1956	Al Oerter, United States	56.36m	(184' 11")
1960	Al Oerter, United States	59.18m	(194' 2")
1964	Al Oerter, United States	61.00m	(200' 1")
1968	Al Oerter, United States	64.78m	(212' 6")
1972	Ludvik Danek, Czechoslovakia	64.40m	(211' 3")
1976	Mac Wilkins, United States	67.50m	(221' 5")
1980	Viktor Rashchupkin, USSR	66.64m	(218' 8")
1984	Rolf Dannenberg, W. Germany	66.60m	(218' 6")
1988	Jurgen Schult, E. Germany	68.82m	(225' 9")
1992	Romas Ubartas, Lithuania	65.12m	(213' 8")
1996	Lars Riedel, Germany	69.40m	(227' 8")
2000	Virgilijus Alekna, Lithuania	69.30m	(227' 4")
2004	Virgilijus Alekna, Lithuania	69.89m	(228' 9¾")*
2008	Gerd Kanter, Estonia	68.82m	(225' 9½")
2012	Robert Harting, Germany	68.27m	(224')

Hammer Throw

Year	Champion	Dist.	
1900	John Flanagan, United States	49.73m	(163' 1")
1904	John Flanagan, United States	51.22m	(168' 0")
1908	John Flanagan, United States	51.92m	(170' 4")
1912	Matt McGrath, United States	54.74m	(179' 7")
1920	Pat Ryan, United States	52.86m	(173' 5")
1924	Fred Tootell, United States	53.28m	(174' 10")
1928	Patrick O'Callaghan, Ireland	51.38m	(168' 7")
1932	Patrick O'Callaghan, Ireland	53.92m	(176' 11")
1936	Karl Hein, Germany	56.48m	(185' 4")
1948	Imre Németh, Hungary	56.06m	(183' 11")
1952	József Csérmák, Hungary	60.34m	(197' 11")
1956	Harold Connolly, United States	63.18m	(207' 3")
1960	Vasily Rudenkov, USSR	67.10m	(202' 0")
1964	Romuald Klim, USSR	69.74m	(228' 10")
1968	Gyula Zsivótsky, Hungary	73.36m	(240' 8")
1972	Anatoly Bondarchuk, USSR	75.50m	(247' 8")
1976	Yuri Syedykh, USSR	77.52m	(254' 4")
1980	Yuri Syedykh, USSR	81.80m	(268' 4")
1984	Juha Tiainen, Finland	78.08m	(256' 2")
1988	Sergei Litvinov, USSR	84.80m	(278' 2")*
1992	Andrey Abduvaliyev, Unified Team	82.54m	(270' 9")
1996	Balázs Kiss, Hungary	81.24m	(266' 6")
2000	Szymon Ziolkowski, Poland	80.02m	(262' 6")
2004	Koji Murofushi, Japan	82.91m	(272')
2008	Primoz Kozmus, Slovenia	82.02m	(269' 1")
2012	Krisztián Pars, Hungary	80.59m	(264' 5")

High Jump

Year	Champion	Height	
1896	Ellery Clark, United States	1.81m	(5' 11¼")
1900	Irving Baxter, United States	1.90m	(6' 2¾")
1904	Samuel Jones, United States	1.80m	(5' 11")
1908	Harry Porter, United States	1.90m	(6' 2¾")
1912	Alma Richards, United States	1.93m	(6' 4")
1920	Richmond Landon, United States	1.93m	(6' 4")
1924	Harold Osborn, United States	1.98m	(6' 6")
1928	Robert W. King, United States	1.94m	(6' 4¼")
1932	Duncan McNaughton, Canada	1.97m	(6' 5½")
1936	Cornelius Johnson, United States	2.03m	(6' 8")
1948	John L. Winter, Australia	1.98m	(6' 6")
1952	Walter Davis, United States	2.04m	(6' 8¼")
1956	Charles Dumas, United States	2.12m	(6' 11½")
1960	Robert Shavlakadze, USSR	2.16m	(7' 1")
1964	Valery Brumel, USSR	2.18m	(7' 1¾")
1968	Dick Fosbury, United States	2.24m	(7' 4¼")
1972	Jüri Tarmak, USSR	2.23m	(7' 3¾")
1976	Jacek Wszola, Poland	2.25m	(7' 4½")
1980	Gerd Wessig, E. Germany	2.36m	(7' 8¾")
1984	Dietmar Mögenburg, W. Germany	2.35m	(7' 8½")
1988	Hennady Avdeyenko, USSR	2.38m	(7' 9¾")
1992	Javier Sotomayor Sanabria, Cuba	2.34m	(7' 8")
1996	Charles Austin, United States	2.39m	(7' 10")*
2000	Sergey Kliugin, Russia	2.35m	(7' 8½")
2004	Stefen Holm, Sweden	2.36m	(7' 8¾")
2008	Andrey Silnov, Russia	2.36m	(7' 8¾")
2012	Ivan Úkhov, Russia	2.38m	(7' 9¾")

Javelin Throw

Year	Champion	Dist.	
1908	Erik Lemming, Sweden	54.82m	(179' 10")
1912	Erik Lemming, Sweden	60.64m	(198' 11")
1920	Jonni Myyrä, Finland	64.78m	(215' 10")
1924	Jonni Myyrä, Finland	62.96m	(206' 7")
1928	Eric Lundkvist, Sweden	66.60m	(218' 6")
1932	Matti Järvinen, Finland	72.70m	(238' 6")
1936	Gerhard Stöck, Germany	71.84m	(235' 8")
1948	Kai Tapio Rautavaara, Finland	69.76m	(228' 11")
1952	Cy Young, United States	73.78m	(242' 1")
1956	Egil Danielsen, Norway	85.70m	(281' 2")

Javelin Throw

Year	Champion	Dist.	
1960	Viktor Tsibulenko, USSR	84.64m	(277' 8")
1964	Pauli Nevala, Finland	82.66m	(271' 2")
1968	Janis Lusis, USSR	90.10m	(295' 7")
1972	Klaus Wolfermann, W. Germany	90.48m	(296' 10")
1976	Miklós Németh, Hungary	94.58m	(310' 4")
1980	Dainis Kula, USSR	91.20m	(299' 2")
1984	Arto Härkönen, Finland	86.76m	(284' 8")
1988	Tapio Korjus, Finland	84.28m	(276' 6")
1992	Jan Zelezny, Czechoslovakia	89.66m	(294' 2")
1996	Jan Zelezny, Czech Republic	88.16m	(289' 3")
2000	Jan Zelezny, Czech Republic	90.17m	(295' 9½")
2004	Andreas Thorkildsen, Norway	86.50m	(283' 10")
2008	Andreas Thorkildsen, Norway	90.57m	(297' 1¾")
2012	Keshorn Walcott, Trinidad & Tobago	84.58m	(277' 6")

Note: New records were kept after javelin was modified in 1986.

Long Jump

Year	Champion	Dist.	
1896	Ellery Clark, United States	6.35m	(20' 10")
1900	Alvin Kraenzlein, United States	7.18m	(23' 6¾")
1904	Meyer Prinstein, United States	7.34m	(24' 1")
1908	Frank Irons, United States	7.48m	(24' 6½")
1912	Albert Gutterson, United States	7.60m	(24' 11¼")
1920	William Petterssen, Sweden	7.15m	(23' 5½")
1924	William DeHart Hubbard, U.S.	7.44m	(24' 5")
1928	Edward B. Hamm, United States	7.73m	(25' 4½")
1932	Edward Gordon, United States	7.64m	(25' ¾")
1936	Jesse Owens, United States	8.06m	(26' 5½")
1948	Willie Steele, United States	7.82m	(25' 8")
1952	Jerome Biffle, United States	7.57m	(24' 10")
1956	Gregory Bell, United States	7.83m	(25' 8¼")
1960	Ralph Boston, United States	8.12m	(26' 7¾")
1964	Lynn Davies, Great Britain	8.07m	(26' 5¾")
1968	Bob Beamon, United States	8.90m	(29' 2½")*
1972	Randy Williams, United States	8.24m	(27' ½")
1976	Arnie Robinson, United States	8.35m	(27' 4¾")
1980	Lutz Dombrowski, E. Germany	8.54m	(28' ¼")
1984	Carl Lewis, United States	8.54m	(28' ¼")
1988	Carl Lewis, United States	8.72m	(28' 7½")
1992	Carl Lewis, United States	8.67m	(28' 5½")
1996	Carl Lewis, United States	8.50m	(27' 10¾")
2000	Ivan Pedroso, Cuba	8.55m	(28' ¾")
2004	Dwight Phillips, United States	8.59m	(28' 2¼")
2008	Irving Jahir Saladino Aranda, Panama	8.34m	(27' 4¼")
2012	Greg Rutherford, Great Britain	8.31m	(27' 3¼")

Pole Vault

Year	Champion	Height	
1896	William Welles Hoyt, United States	3.30m	(10' 10")
1900	Irving Baxter, United States	3.30m	(10' 10")
1904	Charles Dvorak, United States	3.50m	(11' 6")
1908	Edward Cooke Jr., United States	3.71m	(12' 2")
	A. C. Gilbert, United States (tie)	3.71m	(12' 2")
1920	Frank Foss, United States	4.09m	(13' 5")
1924	Lee Barnes, United States	3.95m	(12' 11½")
1928	Sabin W. Carr, United States	4.20m	(13' 9¼")
1932	William Miller, United States	4.31m	(14' 1¾")
1936	Earle Meadows, United States	4.35m	(14' 3¼")
1948	Guinn Smith, United States	4.30m	(14' 1¼")
1952	Robert Richards, United States	4.55m	(14' 11¼")
1956	Robert Richards, United States	4.56m	(14' 11½")
1960	Don Bragg, United States	4.70m	(15' 5")
1964	Fred Hansen, United States	5.10m	(16' 8¾")
1968	Bob Seagren, United States	5.40m	(17' 8½")
1972	Wolfgang Nordwig, E. Germany	5.50m	(18' ½")
1976	Tadeusz Slusarski, Poland	5.50m	(18' ½")
1980	Wladyslaw Kozakiewicz, Poland	5.78m	(18' 11½")
1984	Pierre Quinon, France	5.75m	(18' 10¼")
1988	Sergei Bubka, USSR	5.90m	(19' 4¼")
1992	Maksim Tarasov, Unified Team	5.80m	(19' ¼")
1996	Jean Galfione, France	5.92m	(19' 5")
2000	Nick Hysong, United States	5.90m	(19' 4¼")
2004	Timothy Mack, United States	5.95m	(19' 6¼")
2008	Steve Hooker, Australia	5.96m	(19' 6¾")
2012	Renaud Lavillenie, France	5.97m	(19' 7")*

Shot Put

Year	Champion	Dist.	
1896	Robert Garrett, United States	11.22m	(36' 9¾")
1900	Richard Sheldon, United States	14.10m	(46' 3¼")
1904	Ralph Rose, United States	14.81m	(48' 7")
1908	Ralph Rose, United States	14.21m	(46' 7½")
1912	Pat McDonald, United States	15.34m	(50' 4")
1920	Ville Pörhölä, Finland	14.81m	(48' 7¼")
1924	L. Clarence Houser, United States	14.99m	(49' 2¼")
1928	John Kuck, United States	15.87m	(52' ¾")
1932	Leo Sexton, United States	16.00m	(52' 6")
1936	Hans Woellke, Germany	16.20m	(53' 1¾")
1948	Wilbur Thompson, United States	17.12m	(56' 2")
1952	W. Parry O'Brien, United States	17.41m	(57' 1½")
1956	W. Parry O'Brien, United States	18.57m	(60' 11¼")
1960	William Nieder, United States	19.68m	(64' 6¾")
1964	Dallas Long, United States	20.33m	(66' 8½")
1968	Randy Matson, United States	20.54m	(67' 4¾")
1972	Wladyslaw Komar, Poland	21.18m	(69' 6")

Shot Put

		Dist.	
1976	Udo Beyer, E. Germany	21.05m	(69' ¾")
1980	Vladimir Kyselyov, USSR	21.35m	(70' ½")
1984	Alessandro Andrei, Italy	21.26m	(69' 9")
1988	Ulf Timmermann, E. Germany	22.47m	(73' 8¾")*
1992	Michael Stulce, United States	21.70m	(71' 2½")
1996	Randy Barnes, United States	21.62m	(70' 11¼")
2000	Arsi Harju, Finland	21.29m	(69' 10¼")
2004	Yuriy Bilonog, Ukraine	21.16m	(69' 5¼")
2008	Tomasz Majewski, Poland	21.51m	(70' 6¾")
2012	Tomasz Majewski, Poland	21.89m	(71' 9¾")

Triple Jump

		Dist.	
1896	James Connolly, United States	13.71m	(44' 11¾")
1900	Meyer Prinstein, United States	14.47m	(47' 5¾")
1904	Meyer Prinstein, United States	14.35m	(47' 1")
1908	Timothy Ahearne, G.B.-Ireland	14.92m	(48' 11½")
1912	Gustaf Lindblom, Sweden	14.76m	(48' 5")
1920	Vilho Tuulos, Finland	14.50m	(47' 7")
1924	Anthony Winter, Australia	15.52m	(50' 11")
1928	Mikio Oda, Japan	15.21m	(49' 11")
1932	Chuhei Nambu, Japan	15.72m	(51' 7")
1936	Naoto Tajima, Japan	16.00m	(52' 6")
1948	Arne Ahman, Sweden	15.40m	(50' 6¼")
1952	Adhemar Ferreira da Silva, Brazil	16.22m	(53' 2¾")
1956	Adhemar Ferreira da Silva, Brazil	16.35m	(53' 7¾")
1960	Jozef Schmidt, Poland	16.81m	(55' 1½")
1964	Jozef Schmidt, Poland	16.85m	(55' 3½")
1968	Viktor Saneyev, USSR	17.39m	(57' ¾")
1972	Viktor Saneyev, USSR	17.35m	(56' 11¼")
1976	Viktor Saneyev, USSR	17.29m	(56' 8¾")
1980	Jaak Uudmae, USSR	17.35m	(56' 11")
1984	Al Joyner, United States	17.26m	(56' 7½")
1988	Khristo Markov, Bulgaria	17.61m	(57' 9½")
1992	Mike Conley, United States	18.17m	(59' 7½")(w)
1996	Kenny Harrison, United States	18.09m	(59' 4¼")*
2000	Jonathan Edwards, Britain	17.71m	(58' 1¼")

Triple Jump

		Dist.	
2004	Christian Olsson, Sweden	17.79m	(58' 4½")
2008	Nelson Evora, Portugal	17.67m	(57' 11¾")
2012	Christian Taylor, United States	17.81m	(58' 5¼")

Decathlon (not held 1908)

		Points
1904	Thomas Kiely, Ireland	6,036
1912	Hugo Wieslander, Sweden (a)	7,724.49
1920	Helge Lovland, Norway	6,804.35
1924	Harold Osborn, United States	7,710.77
1928	Paavo Yrjola, Finland	8,053.29
1932	James Bausch, United States	8,462.23
1936	Glenn Morris, United States	7,900
1948	Robert Mathias, United States	7,139
1952	Robert Mathias, United States	7,887
1956	Milton Campbell, United States	7,937
1960	Rafer Johnson, United States	8,392
1964	Willi Holdorf, Germany (b)	7,887
1968	Bill Toomey, United States	8,193
1972	Nikolai Avilov, USSR	8,454
1976	Bruce Jenner, United States	8,617
1980	Daley Thompson, Great Britain	8,495
1984	Daley Thompson, Great Britain (c)	8,798
1988	Christian Schenk, E. Germany	8,488
1992	Robert Zmelik, Czechoslovakia	8,611
1996	Dan O'Brien, United States	8,824
2000	Erki Nool, Estonia	8,641
2004	Roman Sebrle, Czech Republic	8,893*
2008	Bryan Clay, United States	8,791
2012	Ashton Eaton, United States	8,869

(a) Jim Thorpe of the U.S. won the 1912 decathlon with 8,413 pts. but was disqualified and had to return his medals because he had played pro baseball prior to the Olympics. The IOC in 1982 posthumously restored his decathlon and pentathlon golds. (b) Former point systems used prior to 1964. (c) Scoring change effective Apr. 1985; Thompson's readjusted score is 8,847 pts.

Track and Field—Women

100-Meter Run

		Time
1928	Elizabeth Robinson, United States	12.2s
1932	Stella Walsh, Poland (a)	11.9s
1936	Helen Stephens, United States	11.5s
1948	Francina Blankers-Koen, Netherlands	11.9s
1952	Marjorie Jackson, Australia	11.5s
1956	Betty Cuthbert, Australia	11.5s
1960	Wilma Rudolph, United States	11.0s
1964	Wyomia Tyus, United States	11.4s
1968	Wyomia Tyus, United States	11.08s
1972	Renate Stecher, E. Germany	11.07s
1976	Annegret Richter, W. Germany	11.08s
1980	Lyudmila Kondratyeva, USSR	11.06s
1984	Evelyn Ashford, United States	10.97s
1988	Florence Griffith-Joyner, United States	10.54s*
1992	Gail Devers, United States	10.82s
1996	Gail Devers, United States	10.94s
2000	No winner (b)	NA
2004	Yuliya Nesterenko, Belarus	10.93s
2008	Shelly-Ann Fraser, Jamaica	10.78s
2012	Shelly-Ann Fraser, Jamaica	10.75s

(a) A 1980 autopsy determined that Walsh was a man. (b) Marion Jones, U.S., was stripped of her gold medal in 2007 due to doping; the IOC declined to award the medal to the runner-up, who was also suspected of using performance-enhancing drugs.

200-Meter Run

		Time
1948	Francina Blankers-Koen, Netherlands	24.4s
1952	Marjorie Jackson, Australia	23.7s
1956	Betty Cuthbert, Australia	23.4s
1960	Wilma Rudolph, United States	24.0s
1964	Edith McGuire, United States	23.0s
1968	Irena Szewinska, Poland	22.5s
1972	Renate Stecher, E. Germany	22.40s
1976	Barbel Eckert, E. Germany	22.37s
1980	Barbel Wockel, E. Germany	22.03s
1984	Valerie Brisco-Hooks, United States	21.81s
1988	Florence Griffith-Joyner, United States	21.34s*
1992	Gwen Torrence, United States	21.81s
1996	Marie-Jose Perec, France	22.12s
2000	Pauline Davis-Thompson, The Bahamas (a)	21.84s
2004	Veronica Campbell, Jamaica	22.05s
2008	Veronica Campbell-Brown, Jamaica	21.74s
2012	Allyson Felix, United States	21.88s

(a) Originally won by Marion Jones, U.S., who was stripped of the gold in 2007 due to doping.

400-Meter Run

		Time
1964	Betty Cuthbert, Australia	52.0s
1968	Colette Besson, France	52.0s
1972	Monika Zehrt, E. Germany	51.08s
1976	Irena Szewinska, Poland	49.29s
1980	Marita Koch, E. Germany	48.88s

400-Meter Run

		Time
1984	Valerie Brisco-Hooks, United States	48.83s
1988	Olga Bryzgina, USSR	48.65s
1992	Marie-Jose Perec, France	48.83s
1996	Marie-Jose Perec, France	48.25s*
2000	Cathy Freeman, Australia	49.11s
2004	Tonique Williams-Darling, The Bahamas	49.41s
2008	Christine Ohuruogu, Great Britain	49.62s
2012	Sanya Richards-Ross, United States	49.55s

800-Meter Run

		Time
1928	Lina Radke, Germany	2m. 16.8s
1960	Ludmila Shevtsova, USSR	2m. 04.3s
1964	Ann Packer, Great Britain	2m. 01.1s
1968	Madeline Manning, United States	2m. 00.9s
1972	Hildegard Falck, W. Germany	1m. 58.6s
1976	Tatyana Kazankina, USSR	1m. 54.94s
1980	Nadezhda Olizarenko, USSR	1m. 53.43s*
1984	Doina Melinte, Romania	1m. 57.60s
1988	Sigrun Wodars, E. Germany	1m. 56.10s
1992	Ellen Van Langen, Netherlands	1m. 55.54s
1996	Svetlana Masterkova, Russia	1m. 57.73s
2000	Maria Mutola, Mozambique	1m. 56.15s
2004	Kelly Holmes, Great Britain	1m. 56.38s
2008	Pamela Jelimo, Kenya	1m. 54.87s
2012	Mariya Savinova, Russia	1m. 56.19s

1,500-Meter Run

		Time
1972	Lyudmila Bragina, USSR	4m. 01.4s
1976	Tatyana Kazankina, USSR	4m. 05.48s
1980	Tatyana Kazankina, USSR	3m. 56.6s
1984	Gabriella Dorio, Italy	4m. 03.25s
1988	Paula Ivan, Romania	3m. 53.96s*
1992	Hassiba Boulmerka, Algeria	3m. 55.30s
1996	Svetlana Masterkova, Russia	4m. 00.83s
2000	Nouria Benida Merah, Algeria	4m. 05.10s
2004	Kelly Holmes, Great Britain	3m. 57.90s
2008	Nancy Jebet Langat, Kenya	4m. 00.23s
2012	Asli Çakir, Turkey	4m. 10.23s

3,000-Meter Run

		Time
1984	Maricica Puica, Romania	8m. 35.96s
1988	Tatyana Samolenko, USSR	8m. 26.53s*
1992	Elena Romanova, Unified Team	8m. 46.04s

3,000-Meter Steeplechase

		Time
2008	Gulnara Galkina-Samitova, Russia	8m. 58.81s*
2012	Yuliya Zaripova, Russia	9m. 06.72s

5,000-Meter Run

		Time
1996	Wang Junxia, China	14m. 59.88s
2000	Gabriela Szabo, Romania	14m. 40.79s*
2004	Meseret Defar, Ethiopia	14m. 45.65s
2008	Tirunesh Dibaba, Ethiopia	15m. 41.40s
2012	Meseret Defar, Ethiopia	15m. 04.25s

10,000-Meter Run

Year	Champion	Time
1988	Olga Boldarenko, USSR	31m. 44.69s
1992	Derartu Tulu, Ethiopia	31m. 06.02s
1996	Fernanda Ribeiro, Portugal	31m. 01.63s
2000	Derartu Tulu, Ethiopia	30m. 17.49s
2004	Xing Huina, China	30m. 24.36s
2008	Tirunesh Dibaba, Ethiopia	29m. 54.66s*
2012	Tirunesh Dibaba, Ethiopia	30m. 20.75s

Marathon

Year	Champion	Time
1984	Joan Benoit, United States	2h. 24m. 52s
1988	Rosa Mota, Portugal	2h. 25m. 40s
1992	Valentina Yegorova, Unified Team	2h. 32m. 41s
1996	Fatuma Roba, Ethiopia	2h. 26m. 05s
2000	Naoko Takahashi, Japan	2h. 23m. 14s
2004	Mizuki Noguchi, Japan	2h. 26m. 20s
2008	Constantina Tomescu, Romania	2h. 26m. 44s
2012	Tiki Gelana, Ethiopia	2h. 23m. 07s*

4x100-Meter Relay

Year	Champion	Time
1928	Canada	48.4s
1932	United States	46.9s
1936	United States	46.9s
1948	Netherlands	47.5s
1952	United States	45.9s
1956	Australia	44.5s
1960	United States	44.5s
1964	Poland	43.6s
1968	United States	42.88s
1972	West Germany	42.81s
1976	East Germany	42.55s
1980	East Germany	41.60s
1984	United States	41.65s
1988	United States	41.98s
1992	United States	42.11s
1996	United States	41.95s
2000	The Bahamas	41.95s
2004	Jamaica	41.73s
2008	Russia	42.31s
2012	United States	40.82s*

4x400-Meter Relay

Year	Champion	Time
1972	East Germany	3m. 23s
1976	East Germany	3m. 19.23s
1980	USSR	3m. 20.02s
1984	United States	3m. 18.29s
1988	USSR	3m. 15.17s*
1992	Unified Team	3m. 20.20s
1996	United States	3m. 20.91s
2000	United States (a)	3m. 22.62s
2004	United States (b)	3m. 19.01s
2008	United States	3m. 18.54s
2012	United States	3m. 16.87s

(a) Due to team member Marion Jones's doping, the U.S. was stripped of the victory in 2008, but Jones's teammates won an appeal in 2010 to have their medals restored. (b) U.S. team member Crystal Cox was stripped of her gold medal in 2012 due to doping.

10-Kilometer Walk

Year	Champion	Time
1992	Chen Yueling, China	44m. 32s
1996	Elena Nikolayeva, Russia	41m. 49s*

20-Kilometer Walk

Year	Champion	Time
2000	Wang Liping, China	1h. 29m. 05s
2004	Athanasia Tsoumeleka, Greece	1h. 29m. 12s
2008	Olga Kaniskina, Russia	1h. 26m. 31s
2012	Yelena Lashmanova, Russia	1h. 25m. 02s*

100-Meter Hurdles

Year	Champion	Time
1972	Annelie Ehrhardt, E. Germany	12.59s
1976	Johanna Schaller, E. Germany	12.77s
1980	Vera Komisova, USSR	12.56s
1984	Benita Brown-Fitzgerald, United States	12.84s
1988	Jordanka Donkova, Bulgaria	12.38s
1992	Paraskevi Patoulidou, Greece	12.64s
1996	Ludmila Enquist, Sweden	12.58s
2000	Olga Shishigina, Kazakhstan	12.65s
2004	Joanna Hayes, United States	12.37s
2008	Dawn Harper, United States	12.54s
2012	Sally McLellan Pearson, Australia	12.35s*

400-Meter Hurdles

Year	Champion	Time
1984	Nawal el Moutawakil, Morocco	54.61s
1988	Debra Flintoff-King, Australia	53.17s
1992	Sally Gunnell, Great Britain	53.23s
1996	Deon Hemmings, Jamaica	52.82s
2000	Irina Privalova, Russia	53.02s
2004	Fani Halkia, Greece	52.82s
2008	Melaine Walker, Jamaica	52.64s*
2012	Nataliya Antyukh, Russia	52.70s

Discus Throw

Year	Champion	Dist.	
1928	Halina Konopacka, Poland	39.62m	(130' 0")
1932	Lillian Copeland, United States	40.58m	(133' 2")
1936	Gisela Mauermayer, Germany	47.62m	(156' 3")

Discus Throw

Year	Champion	Dist.	
1948	Micheline Ostermeyer, France	41.92m	(137' 6")
1952	Nina Ponomareva, USSR	51.42m	(168' 8")
1956	Olga Fikotová, Czechoslovakia	53.68m	(176' 1")
1960	Nina Ponomareva, USSR	55.10m	(180' 9")
1964	Tamara Press, USSR	57.26m	(187' 10")
1968	Lia Manoliu, Romania	58.28m	(191' 2")
1972	Faina Melnik, USSR	66.62m	(218' 7")
1976	Evelin Jahl, E. Germany	69.00m	(226' 4")
1980	Evelin Jahl, E. Germany	69.96m	(229' 6")
1984	Ria Stalman, Netherlands	65.36m	(214' 5")
1988	Martina Hellmann, E. Germany	72.30m	(237' 2")*
1992	Maritza Martén Garcia, Cuba	70.06m	(229' 10")
1996	Ilke Wyludda, Germany	69.66m	(228' 6")
2000	Ellina Zvereva, Belarus	68.40m	(224' 5")
2004	Natalya Sadova, Russia	67.02m	(219' 8¾")
2008	Stephanie Brown Trafton, United States	64.74m	(212' 4¾")
2012	Sandra Perkoviç, Croatia	69.11m	(226' 9")

Hammer Throw

Year	Champion	Dist.	
2000	Kamila Skolimowska, Poland	71.16m	(233' 5¾")
2004	Olga Kuzenkova, Russia	75.02m	(246' 1")
2008	Aksana Miankova, Belarus	76.34m	(250' 5½")*
2012	Tatyana Lysenko, Russia	78.18m	(256' 6")

High Jump

Year	Champion	Height	
1928	Ethel Catherwood, Canada	1.59m	(5' 2½")
1932	Jean Shiley, United States	1.65m	(5' 5")
1936	Ibolya Csák, Hungary	1.60m	(5' 3")
1948	Alice Coachman, United States	1.68m	(5' 6")
1952	Esther Brand, South Africa	1.67m	(5' 5¾")
1956	Mildred L. McDaniel, United States	1.76m	(5' 9¼")
1960	Iolanda Balas, Romania	1.85m	(6' ¾")
1964	Iolanda Balas, Romania	1.90m	(6' 2¾")
1968	Miloslava Resková, Czech.	1.82m	(5' 11½")
1972	Ulrike Meyfarth, W. Germany	1.92m	(6' 3½")
1976	Rosemarie Ackermann, E. Germany	1.93m	(6' 4")
1980	Sara Simeoni, Italy	1.97m	(6' 5½")
1984	Ulrike Meyfarth, W. Germany	2.02m	(6' 7½")
1988	Louise Ritter, United States	2.03m	(6' 8")
1992	Heike Henkel, Germany	2.02m	(6' 7½")
1996	Stefka Kostadinova, Bulgaria	2.05m	(6' 8¾")
2000	Yelena Yelesina, Russia	2.01m	(6' 7")
2004	Yelena Slesarenko, Russia	2.06m	(6' 9")*
2008	Tia Hellebaut, Belgium	2.05m	(6' 8¾")
2012	Anna Chicherova, Russia	2.05m	(6' 8¾")

Javelin Throw

Year	Champion	Dist.	
1932	"Babe" Didrikson, United States	43.68m	(143' 4")
1936	Tilly Fleischer, Germany	45.18m	(148' 3")
1948	Herma Bauma, Austria	45.56m	(149' 6")
1952	Dana Zátopková, Czechoslovakia	50.46m	(165' 7")
1956	Inese Jaunzeme, USSR	53.86m	(176' 8")
1960	Elvira Ozolina, USSR	55.98m	(183' 8")
1964	Mihaela Penes, Romania	60.54m	(198' 7")
1968	Angéla Németh, Hungary	60.36m	(198' 0")
1972	Ruth Fuchs, E. Germany	63.88m	(209' 7")
1976	Ruth Fuchs, E. Germany	65.94m	(216' 4")
1980	Maria Colón Ruenes, Cuba	68.40m	(224' 5")
1984	Tessa Sanderson, Great Britain	69.56m	(228' 2")
1988	Petra Felke, E. Germany	74.68m	(245' 0")
1992	Silke Renke, Germany	68.34m	(224' 2")
1996	Heli Rantanen, Finland	67.94m	(222' 11")
2000	Trine Hattestad, Norway	68.91m	(226' 1")
2004	Osleidys Menendez, Cuba	71.53m	(234' 8")*
2008	Barbora Špotáková, Czech Republic	71.42m	(234' ¾")
2012	Barbora Špotáková, Czech Republic	69.55m	(228' 2¼")

Note: New records were kept after javelin was modified in 1999.

Long Jump

Year	Champion	Dist.	
1948	Olga Gyarmati, Hungary	5.69m	(18' 8")
1952	Yvette Williams, New Zealand	6.24m	(20' 5¼")
1956	Elzbieta Krzeskinska, Poland	6.35m	(20' 10")
1960	Vira Krepkina, USSR	6.37m	(20' 10¾")
1964	Mary Rand, Great Britain	6.76m	(22' 2¼")
1968	Viorica Viscopoleanu, Romania	6.82m	(22' 4½")
1972	Heidemarie Rosendahl, W. Ger.	6.78m	(22' 3")
1976	Angela Voigt, E. Germany	6.72m	(22' ¾")
1980	Tatyana Kolpakova, USSR	7.06m	(23' 2")
1984	Anisoara Cusmir-Stanciu, Rom.	6.96m	(22' 10")
1988	Jackie Joyner-Kersee, United States	7.40m	(24' 3½")*
1992	Heike Drechsler, Germany	7.14m	(23' 5¼")
1996	Chioma Ajunwa, Nigeria	7.12m	(23' 4¼")
2000	Heike Drechsler, Germany	6.99m	(22' 11¼")
2004	Tatyana Lebedeva, Russia	7.07m	(23' 2½")
2008	Maurren Higa Maggi, Brazil	7.04m	(23' 1¼")
2012	Brittney Reese, United States	7.12m	(23' 4¼")

Pole Vault

Year	Champion	Height	
2000	Stacy Dragila, United States	4.60m	(15' 1")
2004	Elena Isinbaeva, Russia	4.91m	(16' 1⅓")
2008	Elena Isinbaeva, Russia	5.05m	(16' 6¾")
2012	Jenn Stuczynski-Suhr, United States	4.75m	(15' 7")

Shot Put	Dist.	
1948 Micheline Ostermeyer, France	13.75m	(45' 1½")
1952 Galina Zybina, USSR	15.28m	(50' 1½")
1956 Tamara Tyshkyevich, USSR	16.59m	(54' 5¼")
1960 Tamara Press, USSR	17.32m	(56' 10")
1964 Tamara Press, USSR	18.14m	(59' 6¼")
1968 Margitta Gummel, E. Germany	19.61m	(64' 4")
1972 Nadezhda Chizova, USSR	21.03m	(69' 0")
1976 Ivanka Khristova, Bulgaria	21.16m	(69' 5¼")
1980 Ilona Slupianek, E. Germany	22.41m	(73' 6¼")*
1984 Claudia Losch, W. Germany	20.49m	(67' 2¼")
1988 Natalya Lisovskaya, USSR	22.24m	(72' 11¾")
1992 Svetlana Krivelyova, Unified Team.	21.06m	(69' 1¼")
1996 Astrid Kumbernuss, Germany	20.56m	(67' 5½")
2000 Yanina Karolchik, Belarus	20.56m	(67' 5½")
2004 Yumileidi Cumba Jay, Cuba	19.59m	(64' 3¼")
2008 Valerie Vili, New Zealand	20.56m	(67' 5½")
2012 Valerie Adams, New Zealand	20.70m	(67' 11")

Triple Jump	Dist.	
1996 Inessa Kravets, Ukraine	15.33m	(50' 3½")
2000 Tereza Marinova, Bulgaria	15.20m	(49' 10½")
2004 Francoise Mbango Etone, Cameroon	15.30m	(50' 2¼")
2008 Francoise Mbango Etone, Cameroon	15.39m	(50' 6")*
2012 Olga Rypakova, Kazakhstan	14.98m	(49' 1¾")

Heptathlon	Points
1984 Glynis Nunn, Australia	6,390
1988 Jackie Joyner-Kersee, United States	7,291*
1992 Jackie Joyner-Kersee, United States	7,044
1996 Ghada Shouaa, Syria	6,780
2000 Denise Lewis, Great Britain	6,584
2004 Carolina Kluft, Sweden	6,952
2008 Nataliia Dobrynska, Ukraine	6,733
2012 Jessica Ennis, Great Britain	6,955

2010 Winter Olympic Games
Vancouver, BC, Canada, Feb. 12-28, 2010

More than 2,600 athletes from 82 nations met in Vancouver, BC, Canada, to compete in 86 events in the XXI Olympic Winter Games Feb. 12-28, 2010. Host nation Canada set the record for most gold medals won by a nation at a single Winter Olympics, with 14. Two of Canada's gold medals came in women's and men's hockey, the latter determined by a climactic 3-2 overtime win over the U.S. The U.S. led the overall medal count with 37. Opening ceremonies held Feb. 12 were subdued by the death of luger Nodar Kumaritashvili of Georgia, who was killed during a training run earlier that day.

Despite a well-publicized injury, U.S. alpine skier Lindsey Vonn became the first American woman to win an Olympic gold medal in the downhill event Feb. 17; Vonn also won the bronze medal in the super-G event Feb. 20. U.S. snowboarder Shaun White won his second men's halfpipe gold Feb. 17. Figure skater Evan Lysacek Feb. 18 won the first U.S. gold medal in the men's event since 1988, defeating defending Olympic champion Yevgeny Plushenko of Russia. The women's figure skating medal was awarded to South Korean Kim Yu-Na. Speedskater Apolo Ohno won one silver and two bronze medals, setting a record for a U.S. Winter Olympian with a career total of eight. One new medal event, ski cross, debuted at the Vancouver games, with the event's first gold medals awarded to Switzerland's Michael Schmid and Canada's Ashleigh McIvor.

2010 Final Medal Standings

Country	Gold	Silver	Bronze	Total	Country	Gold	Silver	Bronze	Total
United States	9	15	13	37	Italy	1	1	3	5
Germany	10	13	7	30	Japan	0	3	2	5
Canada	14	7	5	26	Finland	0	1	4	5
Norway	9	8	6	23	Australia	2	1	0	3
Austria	4	6	6	16	Belarus	1	1	1	3
Russia	3	5	7	15	Slovakia	1	1	1	3
South Korea	6	6	2	14	Croatia	0	2	1	3
China	5	2	4	11	Slovenia	0	2	1	3
Sweden	5	2	4	11	Latvia	0	2	0	2
France	2	3	6	11	Great Britain	1	0	0	1
Switzerland	6	0	3	9	Estonia	0	1	0	1
Netherlands	4	1	3	8	Kazakhstan	0	1	0	1
Czech Republic	2	0	4	6					
Poland	1	3	2	6	**Total**	**86**	**87**	**85**	**258**

Winter Olympic Games Champions, 1924-2010
In 1992, the Unified Team represented the former Soviet republics of Russia, Ukraine, Belarus, Kazakhstan, and Uzbekistan.

Alpine Skiing

Men's Downhill	Time
1948 Henri Oreiller, France	2:55.0
1952 Zeno Colo, Italy	2:30.8
1956 Toni Sailer, Austria	2:52.2
1960 Jean Vuarnet, France	2:06.0
1964 Egon Zimmermann, Austria	2:18.16
1968 Jean-Claude Killy, France	1:59.85
1972 Bernhard Russi, Switzerland	1:51.43
1976 Franz Klammer, Austria	1:45.73
1980 Leonhard Stock, Austria	1:45.50
1984 Bill Johnson, United States	1:45.49
1988 Pirmin Zurbriggen, Switzerland	1:59.63
1992 Patrick Ortlieb, Austria	1:50.37
1994 Tommy Moe, United States	1:45.75
1998 Jean-Luc Cretier, France	1:50.11
2002 Fritz Strobl, Austria	1:39.13
2006 Antoine Deneriaz, France	1:48.80
2010 Didier Defago, Switzerland	1:54.31

Men's Giant Slalom	Time
1952 Stein Eriksen, Norway	2:25.0
1956 Toni Sailer, Austria	3:00.1
1960 Roger Staub, Switzerland	1:48.3
1964 Francois Bonlieu, France	1:46.71
1968 Jean-Claude Killy, France	3:29.28
1972 Gustavo Thoeni, Italy	3:09.62
1976 Heini Hemmi, Switzerland	3:26.97
1980 Ingemar Stenmark, Sweden	2:40.74
1984 Max Julen, Switzerland	2:41.18
1988 Alberto Tomba, Italy	2:06.37

Men's Giant Slalom	Time
1992 Alberto Tomba, Italy	2:06.98
1994 Markus Wasmeier, Germany	2:52.46
1998 Hermann Maier, Austria	2:38.51
2002 Stephan Eberharter, Austria	2:23.28
2006 Benjamin Raich, Austria	2:35.00
2010 Carlo Janka, Switzerland	2:37.83

Men's Slalom	Time
1948 Edi Reinalter, Switzerland	2:10.3
1952 Othmar Schneider, Austria	2:00.0
1956 Toni Sailer, Austria	3:14.7
1960 Ernst Hinterseer, Austria	2:08.9
1964 Josef Stiegler, Austria	2:11.13
1968 Jean-Claude Killy, France	1:39.73
1972 Francisco Fernandez-Ochoa, Spain	1:49.27
1976 Piero Gros, Italy	2:03.29
1980 Ingemar Stenmark, Sweden	1:44.26
1984 Phil Mahre, United States	1:39.41
1988 Alberto Tomba, Italy	1:39.47
1992 Finn Christian Jagge, Norway	1:44.39
1994 Thomas Stangassinger, Austria	2:02.02
1998 Hans-Petter Buraas, Norway	1:49.31
2002 Jean-Pierre Vidal, France	1:41.06
2006 Benjamin Raich, Austria	1:43.14
2010 Giuliano Razzoli, Italy	1:39.32

Men's Super Combined	Time
1936 Franz-Pfnuer, Germany	99.25 (pts.)
1948 Henri Oreiller, France	3.27 (pts.)
1988 Hubert Strolz, Austria	36.55 (pts.)
1992 Josef Polig, Italy	14.58 (pts.)
1994 Lasse Kjus, Norway	3:17.53

Men's Super Combined

		Time
1998	Mario Reiter, Austria	3:08.06
2002	Kjetil Andre Aamodt, Norway	3:17.56
2006	Ted Ligety, United States	3:09.35
2010	Bode Miller, United States	2:44.92

Note: In 2010, a one-day super combined event replaced the traditional two-day combined event.

Men's Super Giant Slalom

		Time
1988	Franck Piccard, France	1:39.66
1992	Kjetil-Andre Aamodt, Norway	1:13.04
1994	Markus Wasmeier, Germany	1:32.53
1998	Hermann Maier, Austria	1:34.82
2002	Kjetil Andre Aamodt, Norway	1:21.58
2006	Kjetil Andre Aamodt, Norway	1:30.65
2010	Aksel Lund Svindal, Norway	1:30.34

Women's Downhill

		Time
1948	Hedi Schlunegger, Switzerland	2:28.3
1952	Trude Beiser-Jochum, Austria	1:47.1
1956	Madeleine Berthod, Switzerland	1:40.7
1960	Heidi Biebl, Germany	1:37.6
1964	Christl Haas, Austria	1:55.39
1968	Olga Pall, Austria	1:40.87
1972	Marie-Theres Nadig, Switzerland	1:36.68
1976	Rosi Mittermaier, W. Germany	1:46.16
1980	Annemarie Moser-Proell, Austria	1:37.52
1984	Michela Figini, Switzerland	1:13.36
1988	Marina Kiehl, W. Germany	1:25.86
1992	Kerrin Lee-Gartner, Canada	1:52.55
1994	Katja Seizinger, Germany	1:35.93
1998	Katja Seizinger, Germany	1:28.89
2002	Carole Montillet, France	1:39.56
2006	Michaela Dorfmeister, Austria	1:56.49
2010	Lindsey Vonn, United States	1:44.19

Women's Giant Slalom

		Time
1952	Andrea Mead Lawrence, United States	2:06.8
1956	Ossi Reichert, Germany	1:56.5
1960	Yvonne Ruegg, Switzerland	1:39.9
1964	Marielle Goitschel, France	1:52.24
1968	Nancy Greene, Canada	1:51.97
1972	Marie-Theres Nadig, Switzerland	1:29.90
1976	Kathy Kreiner, Canada	1:29.13
1980	Hanni Wenzel, Liechtenstein (2 runs)	2:41.66
1984	Debbie Armstrong, United States	2:20.98
1988	Vreni Schneider, Switzerland	2:06.49
1992	Pernilla Wiberg, Sweden	2:12.74
1994	Deborah Compagnoni, Italy	2:30.97
1998	Deborah Compagnoni, Italy	2:50.59
2002	Janica Kostelic, Croatia	2:30.01
2006	Julia Mancuso, United States	2:09.19
2010	Viktoria Rebensburg, Germany	2:27.11

Women's Slalom

		Time
1948	Gretchen Fraser, United States	1:57.2
1952	Andrea Mead Lawrence, United States	2:10.6
1956	Renee Colliard, Switzerland	1:52.3
1960	Anne Heggtveit, Canada	1:49.6
1964	Christine Goitschel, France	1:29.86
1968	Marielle Goitschel, France	1:25.86
1972	Barbara Ann Cochran, United States	1:31.24
1976	Rosi Mittermaier, W. Germany	1:30.54
1980	Hanni Wenzel, Liechtenstein	1:25.09
1984	Paoletta Magoni, Italy	1:36.47
1988	Vreni Schneider, Switzerland	1:36.69
1992	Petra Kronberger, Austria	1:32.68
1994	Vreni Schneider, Switzerland	1:56.01
1998	Hilde Gerg, Germany	1:32.40
2002	Janica Kostelic, Croatia	1:46.10
2006	Anja Paerson, Sweden	1:29.04
2010	Maria Riesch, Germany	1:42.89

Women's Super Combined

		Time
1936	Christl Cranz, Germany	97.06 (pts.)
1948	Trude Beiser-Jochum, Austria	6.58 (pts.)
1988	Anita Wachter, Austria	29.25 (pts.)
1992	Petra Kronberger, Austria	2.55 (pts.)
1994	Pernilla Wiberg, Sweden	3:05.16
1998	Katja Seizinger, Germany	2:40.74
2002	Janica Kostelic, Croatia	2:43.28
2006	Janica Kostelic, Croatia	2:51.08
2010	Maria Riesch, Germany	2:09.14

Note: In 2010, a one-day super combined event replaced the traditional two-day combined event.

Women's Super Giant Slalom

		Time
1988	Sigrid Wolf, Austria	1:19.03
1992	Deborah Compagnoni, Italy	1:21.22
1994	Diann Roffe (Steinrotter), United States	1:22.15
1998	Picabo Street, United States	1:18.02
2002	Daniela Ceccarelli, Italy	1:13.59
2006	Michaela Dorfmeister, Austria	1:32.47
2010	Andrea Fischbacher, Austria	1:20.14

Biathlon

Men's 10-Kilometer Sprint

		Time
1980	Frank Ullrich, E. Germany	32:10.69
1984	Eirik Kvalfoss, Norway	30:53.80
1988	Frank-Peter Roetsch, E. Germany	25:08.10
1992	Mark Kirchner, Germany	26:02.30
1994	Serguei Tchepikov, Russia	28:07.00
1998	Ole Einar Bjoerndalen, Norway	27:16.20
2002	Ole Einar Bjoerndalen, Norway	24:51.30
2006	Sven Fischer, Germany	26:11.6
2010	Vincent Jay, France	24:07.8

Men's 12.5-Kilometer Pursuit

		Time
2002	Ole Einar Bjoerndalen, Norway	32:34.6
2006	Vincent Defrasne, France	35:20.2
2010	Bjorn Ferry, Sweden	33:38.4

Men's 15-Kilometer Mass Start

		Time
2006	Michael Greis, Germany	47:20.0
2010	Evgeny Ustyugov, Russia	35.35.7

Men's 20-Kilometer Individual

		Time
1960	Klas Lestander, Sweden	1:33:21.6
1964	Vladimir Melanin, USSR	1:20:26.8
1968	Magnar Solberg, Norway	1:13:45.9
1972	Magnar Solberg, Norway	1:15:55.50
1976	Nikolai Kruglov, USSR	1:14:12.26
1980	Anatoly Aljabiev, USSR	1:08:16.31
1984	Peter Angerer, W. Germany	1:11:52.7
1988	Frank-Peter Roetsch, E. Germany	0:56:33.33
1992	Yevgeny Redkine, Unified Team	0:57:34.4
1994	Serguei Tarasov, Russia	0:57:25.3
1998	Halvard Hanevold, Norway	0:56:16.4
2002	Ole Einar Bjoerndalen, Norway	0:51:03.03
2006	Michael Greis, Germany	0:54:23.0
2010	Emil Hegle Svendsen, Norway	0:48:22.5

Men's 4x7.5-Kilometer Relay

		Time
1968	USSR, Norway, Sweden (40 km)	2:13:02.4
1972	USSR, Finland, E. Germany (40 km)	1:51:44.92
1976	USSR, Finland, E. Germany (40 km)	1:57:55.64
1980	USSR, E. Germany, W. Germany	1:34:03.27
1984	USSR, Norway, W. Germany	1:38:51.70
1988	USSR, W. Germany, Italy	1:22:30.00
1992	Germany, Unified Team, Sweden	1:24:43.50
1994	Germany, Russia, France	1:30:22.1
1998	Germany, Norway, Russia	1:19:43.3
2002	Norway, Germany, France	1:23:42.3
2006	Germany, Russia, France	1:21:51.5
2010	Norway, Austria, Russia	1:21:38.1

Women's 7.5-Kilometer Sprint

		Time
1992	Anfissa Restsova, Unified Team	24:29.2
1994	Myriam Bedard, Canada	26:08.8
1998	Galina Koukleva, Russia	23:08.0
2002	Kati Wilhelm, Germany	20:41.4
2006	Florence Baverel-Robert, France	22:31.4
2010	Anastazia Kuzmina, Slovakia	19:55.6

Women's 10-Kilometer Pursuit

		Time
2002	Olga Pyleva, Russia	31:07.7
2006	Kati Wilhelm, Germany	36:43.6
2010	Magdalena Neuner, Germany	30:16.0

Women's 12.5-Kilometer Mass Start

		Time
2006	Anna Carin Olofsson, Sweden	40:36.5
2010	Magdalena Neuner, Germany	35:19.6

Women's 15-Kilometer Individual

		Time
1992	Antje Misersky, Germany	51:47.2
1994	Myriam Bedard, Canada	52:06.6
1998	Ekaterina Dafovska, Bulgaria	54:52.0
2002	Andrea Henkel, Germany	47:30.0
2006	Svetlana Ishmouratova, Russia	49:24.1
2010	Tora Berger, Norway	40:52.8

Women's 4x6-Kilometer Relay

		Time
1992	France, Germany, Unified Team (22.5 km)	1:15:55.6
1994	Russia, Germany, France (30 km)	1:47:19.5
1998	Germany, Russia, Norway (30 km)	1:40:13.6
2002	Germany, Norway, Russia (30 km)	1:27:55.0
2006	Russia, Germany, France	1:16:12.5
2010	Russia, France, Germany	1:09:36.3

Bobsledding

(Driver in parentheses.)

2-Man Bobsled

		Time
1932	United States (Hubert Stevens)	8:14.74
1936	United States (Ivan Brown)	5:29.29

2-Man Bobsled

		Time
1948	Switzerland (Felix Endrich)	5:29.20
1952	Germany (Andreas Ostler)	5:24.54
1956	Italy (Dalla Costa)	5:30.14
1964	Great Britain (Anthony Nash)	4:21.90
1968	Italy (Eugenio Monti)	4:41.54
1972	W. Germany (Wolfgang Zimmerer)	4:57.07
1976	E. Germany (Meinhard Nehmer)	3:44.42
1980	Switzerland (Erich Schaerer)	4:09.36
1984	E. Germany (Wolfgang Hoppe)	3:25.56
1988	USSR (Janis Kipours)	3:54.19
1992	Switzerland (Gustav Weber)	4:03.26
1994	Switzerland (Gustav Weber)	3:30.81
1998	Canada (Pierre Lueders)	3:37.24
	Italy (Guenther Huber) (tie)	3:37.24
2002	Germany II (Christoph Langen)	3:10.11
2006	Germany (Andre Lange)	3:43.38
2010	Germany (Andre Lange)	3:26.65

4-Man Bobsled

		Time
1924	Switzerland (Eduard Scherrer)	5:45.54
1928	United States (William Fiske) (5-man)	3:20.50
1932	United States (William Fiske)	7:53.68
1936	Switzerland (Pierre Musy)	5:19.85
1948	United States (Francis Tyler)	5:20.10
1952	Germany (Andreas Ostler)	5:07.84
1956	Switzerland (Franz Kapus)	5:10.44
1964	Canada (Victor Emery)	4:14.46
1968	Italy (Eugenio Monti) (2 races)	2:17.39
1972	Switzerland (Jean Wicki)	4:43.07
1976	E. Germany (Meinhard Nehmer)	3:40.43
1980	E. Germany (Meinhard Nehmer)	3:59.92
1984	E. Germany (Wolfgang Hoppe)	3:20.22
1988	Switzerland (Ekkehard Fasser)	3:47.51
1992	Austria (Ingo Appelt)	3:53.90
1994	Germany (Wolfgang Hoppe)	3:27.28
1998	Germany II (Christoph Langen)	2:39.41
2002	Germany II (Andre Lange)	3:07.51
2006	Germany (Andre Lange)	3:40.42
2010	United States (Steven Holcomb)	3:24.46

2-Woman Bobsled

		Time
2002	United States II (Jill Bakken)	1:37.76
2006	Germany (Sandra Kiriasis)	3:49.98
2010	Canada (Kaillie Humphries)	3:32.28

Cross-Country Skiing

Men's Individual Sprint Classic

		Time
2002	Tor Arne Hetland, Norway (1.5 km)	2:56.9
2006	Bjoern Lind, Sweden (1.3 km)	2:26.5
2010	Nikita Kriukov, Russia	3:36.3

Men's 10 Kilometers

		Time
1992	Vegard Ulvang, Norway	27:36.0
1994	Bjoern Daehlie, Norway	24:20.1
1998	Bjoern Daehlie, Norway	27:24.5
2002	Thomas Alsgaard, Norway	49:48.9
	Frode Estil, Norway (tie) (a)	49:48.9

(a) Awarded gold after Johann Muehlegg of Spain was stripped of gold for a drug offense.

Men's 15-Kilometer Free

		Time
1924	Thorleif Haug, Norway	1:14:31
1928	Johan Grottumsbraaten, Norway	1:37:01
1932	Sven Utterstrom, Sweden	1:23:07
1936	Erik-August Larsson, Sweden	1:14:38
1948	Martin Lundstrom, Sweden	1:13:50
1952	Hallgeir Brenden, Norway	1:01:34
1956	Hallgeir Brenden, Norway	0:49:39.0
1960	Haakon Brusveen, Norway	0:51:55.5
1964	Eero Maentyranta, Finland	0:50:54.1
1968	Harald Groenningen, Norway	0:47:54.2
1972	Sven-Ake Lundback, Sweden	0:45:28.24
1976	Nikolai Balukov, USSR	0:43:58.47
1980	Thomas Wassberg, Sweden	0:41:57.63
1984	Gunde Svan, Sweden	0:41:25.6
1988	Mikhail Deviatiarov, USSR	0:41:18.9
1992	Bjoern Daehlie, Norway	0:38:01.9
1994	Bjoern Daehlie, Norway	0:35:48.8
1998	Thomas Alsgaard, Norway	1:07:01.7
2002	Andrus Veerpalu, Estonia	0:37:07.4
2006	Andrus Veerpalu, Estonia	0:38:01.3
2010	Dario Cologna, Switzerland	0:33:36.3

Note: Approx. 18-km course 1924-52.

Men's 30-Kilometer Pursuit

		Time
1956	Veikko Hakulinen, Finland	1:44:06.0
1964	Eero Maentyranta, Finland	1:30:50.7
1968	Franco Nones, Italy	1:35:39.2
1972	Vyacheslav Vedenine, USSR	1:36:31.15
1976	Sergei Saveliev, USSR	1:30:29.38
1980	Nikolai Zimyatov, USSR	1:27:02.80

Men's 30-Kilometer Pursuit

		Time
1984	Nikolai Zimyatov, USSR	1:28:56.3
1988	Aleksei Prokourorov, USSR	1:24:26.3
1992	Vegard Ulvang, Norway	1:22:27.8
1994	Thomas Alsgaard, Norway	1:12:26.4
1998	Mika Myllylae, Finland	1:33:55.8
2002	Christian Hoffmann, Austria (a)	1:11:31.0
2006	Eugeni Dementiev, Russia	1:17:00.8
2010	Marcus Hellner, Sweden	1:15:11.4

(a) Awarded gold after Johann Muehlegg of Spain was stripped of gold for a drug offense.

Men's 50-Kilometer Mass Start Classic

		Time
1924	Thorleif Haug, Norway	3:44:32.0
1928	Per Erik Hedlund, Sweden	4:52:03.0
1932	Veli Saarinen, Finland	4:28:00.0
1936	Elis Wiklund, Sweden	3:30:11.0
1948	Nils Karlsson, Sweden	3:47:48.0
1952	Veikko Hakulinen, Finland	3:33:33.0
1956	Sixten Jernberg, Sweden	2:50:27.0
1960	Kalevi Hamalainen, Finland	2:59:06.3
1964	Sixten Jernberg, Sweden	2:43:52.6
1968	Ole Ellefsaeter, Norway	2:28:45.8
1972	Paal Tyldum, Norway	2:43:14.75
1976	Ivar Formo, Norway	2:37:30.05
1980	Nikolai Zimyatov, USSR	2:27:24.60
1984	Thomas Wassberg, Sweden	2:15:55.8
1988	Gunde Svan, Sweden	2:04:30.9
1992	Bjoern Daehlie, Norway	2:03:41.5
1994	Vladimir Smirnov, Kazakhstan	2:07:20.3
1998	Bjoern Daehlie, Norway	2:05:08.2
2002	Mikhail Ivanov, Russia	2:06:20.8
2006	Giorgio di Centa, Italy	2:06:11.8
2010	Petter Northug, Norway	2:05:35.5

Men's 4x10-Kilometer Relay

		Time
1936	Finland, Norway, Sweden	2:41:33.0
1948	Sweden, Finland, Norway	2:32:08.0
1952	Finland, Norway, Sweden	2:20:16.0
1956	USSR, Finland, Sweden	2:15:30.0
1960	Finland, Norway, USSR	2:18:45.6
1964	Sweden, Finland, USSR	2:18:34.6
1968	Norway, Sweden, Finland	2:08:33.5
1972	USSR, Norway, Switzerland	2:04:47.94
1976	Finland, Norway, USSR	2:07:59.72
1980	USSR, Norway, Finland	1:57:03.46
1984	Sweden, USSR, Finland	1:55:06.30
1988	Sweden, USSR, Czechoslovakia	1:43:58.60
1992	Norway, Italy, Finland	1:39:26.00
1994	Italy, Norway, Finland	1:41:15.00
1998	Norway, Italy, Finland	1:40:55.70
2002	Norway, Italy, Germany	1:32:45.5
2006	Italy, Germany, Sweden	1:43:45.7
2010	Sweden, Norway, Czech Republic	1:45:05.4

Men's Team Sprint

		Time
2006	Bjoern Lind & Thobias Fredriksson, Sweden	17:02.9
2010	Oeystein Pettersen & Petter Northug, Norway	19:01.0

Women's Individual Sprint Classic

		Time
2002	Julia Tchepalova, Russia (1.5 km)	3:10.6
2006	Chandra Crawford, Canada (1.1 km)	2:12.3
2010	Marit Bjoergen, Norway	3:39.2

Women's 5 Kilometers

		Time
1964	Claudia Boyarskikh, USSR	17:50.5
1968	Toini Gustafsson, Sweden	16:45.2
1972	Galina Koulacova, USSR	17:00.50
1976	Helena Takalo, Finland	15:48.69
1980	Raisa Smetanina, USSR	15:06.92
1984	Marja-Liisa Haemaelainen, Finland	17:04.0
1988	Marjo Matikainen, Finland	15:04.0
1992	Marjut Lukkarinen, Finland	14:13.8
1994	Ljubov Egorova, Russia	14:08.8
1998	Larissa Lazutina, Russia	17:37.9
2002	Beckie Scott, Canada (a)	25:09.9

(a) Awarded gold after Olga Danilova of Russia was stripped of gold and Larissa Lazutina of Russia was stripped of silver for drug offenses.

Women's 10-Kilometer Free

		Time
1952	Lydia Wideman, Finland	41:40.0
1956	Lyubov Kosyreva, USSR	38:11.0
1960	Maria Gusakova, USSR	39:46.6
1964	Claudia Boyarskikh, USSR	40:24.3
1968	Toini Gustafsson, Sweden	36:46.5
1972	Galina Koulacova, USSR	34:17.82
1976	Raisa Smetanina, USSR	30:13.41
1980	Barbara Petzold, E. Germany	30:31.54
1984	Marja-Liisa Haemaelainen, Finland	31:44.2
1988	Vida Ventsene, USSR	30:08.3
1992	Lyubov Egorova, Unified Team	25:53.7

Women's 10-Kilometer Free

		Time
1994	Lyubov Egorova, Russia	27:30.1
1998	Larissa Lazutina, Russia	46.06.9
2002	Bente Skari, Norway	28:05.6
2006	Kristina Smigun, Estonia	27:51.4
2010	Charlotte Kalla, Sweden	24:58.4

Women's 15-Kilometer Pursuit

		Time
1992	Lyubov Egorova, Unified Team	42:20.8
1994	Manuela Di Centa, Italy	39:44.5
1998	Olga Danilova, Russia	46:55.4
2002	Stefania Belmondo, Italy	39:54.4
2006	Kristina Smigun, Estonia	42:48.7
2010	Marit Bjoergen, Norway	39:58.1

Women's 30-Kilometer Mass Start Classic

		Time
1992	Stefania Belmondo, Italy	1:22:30.1
1994	Manuela Di Centa, Italy	1:25:41.6
1998	Julija Tchepalova, Russia	1:22:01.5
2002	Gabriella Paruzzi, Italy	1:30:57.1
2006	Katerina Neumannova, Czech Republic	1:22:25.4
2010	Justyna Kowalczyk, Poland	1:30:33.7

Women's 4x5-Kilometer Relay

		Time
1956	Finland, USSR, Sweden (15 km)	1:09:01.0
1960	Sweden, USSR, Finland (15 km)	1:04:21.4
1964	USSR, Sweden, Finland (15 km)	0:59:20.2
1968	Norway, Sweden, USSR (15 km)	0:57:30.0
1972	USSR, Finland, Norway (15 km)	0:48:46.15
1976	USSR, Finland, E. Germany	1:07:49.75
1980	E. Germany, USSR, Norway	1:02:11.1
1984	Norway, Czechoslovakia, Finland	1:06:49.7
1988	USSR, Norway, Finland	0:59:51.1
1992	United Team, Norway, Italy	0:59:34.8
1994	Russia, Norway, Italy	0:57:12.5
1998	Russia, Norway, Italy	0:55:13.5
2002	Germany, Norway, Switzerland	0:49:30.6
2006	Russia, Germany, Italy	0:54:47.7
2010	Norway, Germany, Finland	0:55:19.5

Women's Team Sprint

		Time
2006	Lina Andersson & Anna Dahlberg, Sweden	16:36.9
2010	Evi Sachenbacher-Stehle & Claudia Nystad, Germany	18:03.7

Curling

Men

1998	Switzerland, Canada, Norway
2002	Norway, Canada, Switzerland
2006	Canada, Finland, United States
2010	Canada, Norway, Switzerland

Women

1998	Canada, Denmark, Sweden
2002	Britain, Switzerland, Canada
2006	Sweden, Switzerland, Canada
2010	Sweden, Canada, China

Figure Skating

Men's Singles

1908[1]	Ulrich Salchow, Sweden
1920[1]	Gillis Grafstrom, Sweden
1924	Gillis Grafstrom, Sweden
1928	Gillis Grafstrom, Sweden
1932	Karl Schaefer, Austria
1936	Karl Schaefer, Austria
1948	Richard Button, United States
1952	Richard Button, United States
1956	Hayes Alan Jenkins, United States
1960	David W. Jenkins, United States
1964	Manfred Schnelldorfer, Germany
1968	Wolfgang Schwartz, Austria
1972	Ondrej Nepela, Czechoslovakia
1976	John Curry, Great Britain
1980	Robin Cousins, Great Britain
1984	Scott Hamilton, United States
1988	Brian Boitano, United States
1992	Viktor Petrenko, Unified Team
1994	Aleksei Urmanov, Russia
1998	Ilya Kulik, Russia
2002	Alexei Yagudin, Russia
2006	Yevgeny Plushenko, Russia
2010	Evan Lysacek, United States

(1) Event held during Summer Olympic Games.

Women's Singles

1908[1]	Madge Syers, Great Britain
1920[1]	Magda Julin-Mauroy, Sweden
1924	Herma von Szabo-Planck, Austria

Women's Singles

1928	Sonja Henie, Norway
1932	Sonja Henie, Norway
1936	Sonja Henie, Norway
1948	Barbara Ann Scott, Canada
1952	Jeanette Altwegg, Great Britan
1956	Tenley Albright, United States
1960	Carol Heiss, United States
1964	Sjoukje Dijkstra, Netherlands
1968	Peggy Fleming, United States
1972	Beatrix Schuba, Austria
1976	Dorothy Hamill, United States
1980	Anett Poetzsch, E. Germany
1984	Katarina Witt, E. Germany
1988	Katarina Witt, E. Germany
1992	Kristi Yamaguchi, United States
1994	Oksana Baiul, Ukraine
1998	Tara Lipinski, United States
2002	Sarah Hughes, United States
2006	Shizuka Arakawa, Japan
2010	Kim Yu-Na, South Korea

(1) Event held during Summer Olympic Games.

Pairs

1908[1]	Anna Hubler & Heinrich Burger, Germany
1920[1]	Ludovika & Walter Jakobsson, Finland
1924	Helene Engelman & Alfred Berger, Austria
1928	Andree Joly & Pierre Brunet, France
1932	Andree Joly & Pierre Brunet, France
1936	Maxi Herber & Ernst Baier, Germany
1948	Micheline Lannoy & Pierre Baugniet, Belgium
1952	Ria & Paul Falk, Germany
1956	Elisabeth Schwartz & Kurt Oppelt, Austria
1964	Ludmila Beloussova & Oleg Protopopov, USSR
1968	Ludmila Beloussova & Oleg Protopopov, USSR
1972	Irina Rodnina & Alexei Ulanov, USSR
1976	Irina Rodnina & Aleksandr Zaitzev, USSR
1980	Irina Rodnina & Aleksandr Zaitzev, USSR
1984	Elena Valova & Oleg Vassiliev, USSR
1988	Ekaterina Gordeeva & Sergei Grinkov, USSR
1992	Natalia Mishkutienok & Artur Dimitriev, Unified Team
1994	Ekaterina Gordeeva & Sergei Grinkov, Russia
1998	Oksana Kazakova & Artur Dmitriev, Russia
2002	Elena Berezhnaya & Anton Sikharulidze, Russia; Jamie Sale & David Pelletier, Canada (tie)
2006	Tatyana Totmianina & Maxim Marinin, Russia
2010	Shen Xue & Zhao Hongbo, China

(1) Event held during Summer Olympic Games.

Ice Dancing

1976	Ludmila Pakhomova & Aleksandr Gorshckov, USSR
1980	Natalya Linichuk & Gennadi Karponosov, USSR
1984	Jayne Torvill & Christopher Dean, Great Britain
1988	Natalia Bestemianova & Andrei Bukin, USSR
1992	Marina Klimova & Sergei Ponomarenko, Unified Team
1994	Pasha Grishuk & Evgeny Platov, Russia
1998	Pasha Grishuk & Evgeny Platov, Russia
2002	Marina Anissina & Gwendal Peizerat, France
2006	Tatyana Navka & Roman Kostomarov, Russia
2010	Tessa Virtue & Scott Moir, Canada

Freestyle Skiing

Men's Aerials

		Points
1994	Andreas Schoenbaechler, Switzerland	234.67
1998	Eric Bergoust, United States	255.64
2002	Ales Valenta, Czech Republic	257.02
2006	Xiaopeng Han, China	250.77
2010	Alexei Grishin, Belarus	248.41

Men's Moguls

		Points
1992	Edgar Grospiron, France	25.81
1994	Jean-Luc Brassard, Canada	27.24
1998	Jonny Moseley, United States	26.93
2002	Janne Lahtela, Finland	27.97
2006	Dale Begg-Smith, Australia	26.77
2010	Alexandre Bilodeau, Canada	26.75

Men's Ski Cross

2010	Michael Schmid, Switzerland

Women's Aerials

		Points
1994	Lina Tcherjazova, Uzbekistan	166.84
1998	Nikki Stone, United States	193.00
2002	Alisa Camplin, Australia	193.47
2006	Evelyne Leu, Switzerland	202.55
2010	Lydia Lassila, Australia	214.74

Women's Moguls

		Points
1992	Donna Weinbrecht, United States	23.69
1994	Stine Lise Hattestad, Norway	25.97

Women's Moguls	Points
1998 Tae Satoya, Japan	25.06
2002 Kari Traa, Norway	25.94
2006 Jennifer Heil, Canada	26.50
2010 Hannah Kearney, United States	26.63

Women's Ski Cross

2010   Ashleigh McIvor, Canada

Ice Hockey

Men

1920[1]	Canada, United States, Czechoslovakia
1924	Canada, United States, Great Britain
1928	Canada, Sweden, Switzerland
1932	Canada, United States, Germany
1936	Great Britain, Canada, United States
1948	Canada, Czechoslovakia, Switzerland
1952	Canada, United States, Sweden
1956	USSR, United States, Canada
1960	United States, Canada, USSR
1964	USSR, Sweden, Czechoslovakia
1968	USSR, Czechoslovakia, Canada
1972	USSR, United States, Czechoslovakia
1976	USSR, Czechoslovakia, W. Germany
1980	United States, USSR, Sweden
1984	USSR, Czechoslovakia, Sweden
1988	USSR, Finland, Sweden
1992	Unified Team, Canada, Czechoslovakia
1994	Sweden, Canada, Finland
1998	Czech Republic, Russia, Finland
2002	Canada, United States, Russia
2006	Sweden, Finland, Czech Republic
2010	Canada, United States, Finland

Women

1998	United States, Canada, Finland
2002	Canada, United States, Sweden
2006	Canada, Sweden, United States
2010	Canada, United States, Finland

(1) Event held during Summer Olympic Games.

Luge

Men's Singles	Time
1964 Thomas Keohler, E. Germany	3:27.77
1968 Manfred Schmid, Austria	2:52.48
1972 Wolfgang Scheidel, E. Germany	3:27.58
1976 Detlef Guenther, E. Germany	3:27.688
1980 Bernhard Glass, E. Germany	2:54.796
1984 Paul Hildgartner, Italy	3:04.258
1988 Jens Mueller, E. Germany	3:05.548
1992 Georg Hackl, Germany	3:02.363
1994 Georg Hackl, Germany	3:21.571
1998 Georg Hackl, Germany	3:18.436
2002 Armin Zoeggeler, Italy	2:57.941
2006 Armin Zoeggeler, Italy	3:26.088
2010 Felix Loch, Germany	3:13.085

Men's Doubles	Time
1964 Austria	1:41.62
1968 E. Germany	1:35.85
1972 Italy, E. Germany (tie)	1:28.35
1976 E. Germany	1:25.604
1980 E. Germany	1:19.331
1984 W. Germany	1:23.620
1988 E. Germany	1:31.940
1992 Germany	1:32.053
1994 Italy	1:36.720
1998 Germany	1:41.105
2002 Germany	1:26.082
2006 Austria	1:34.497
2010 Austria	1:22.705

Women's Singles	Time
1964 Ortun Enderlein, Germany	3:24.67
1968 Erica Lechner, Italy	2:28.66
1972 Anna M. Muller, E. Germany	2:59.18
1976 Margit Schumann, E. Germany	2:50.621
1980 Vera Zozulya, USSR	2:36.537
1984 Steffi Martin, E. Germany	2:46.570
1988 Steffi Walter, E. Germany	3:03.973
1992 Doris Neuner, Austria	3:06.696
1994 Gerda Weissensteiner, Italy	3:15.517
1998 Silke Kraushaar, Germany	3:23.779
2002 Sylke Otto, Germany	2:52.464

Women's Singles	Time
2006 Sylke Otto, Germany	3:07.979
2010 Tatjana Huefner, Germany	2:46.524

Nordic Combined

Men's 7.5-Kilometer Nordic Combined

2002	Samppa Lajunen, Finland
2006	Felix Gottwald, Austria

Men's 15-Kilometer Nordic Combined

1924	Thorleif Haug, Norway
1928	Johan Grottumsbraaten, Norway
1932	Johan Grottumsbraaten, Norway
1936	Oddbjorn Hagen, Norway
1948	Heikki Hasu, Finland
1952	Simon Slattvik, Norway
1956	Sverre Stenersen, Norway
1960	Georg Thoma, W. Germany
1964	Tormod Knutsen, Norway
1968	Franz Keller, W. Germany
1972	Ulrich Wehling, E. Germany
1976	Ulrich Wehling, E. Germany
1980	Ulrich Wehling, E. Germany
1984	Tom Sandberg, Norway
1988	Hippolyt Kempf, Switzerland
1992	Fabrice Guy, France
1994	Fred Barre Lundberg, Norway
1998	Bjarte Engen Vik, Norway
2002	Samppa Lajunen, Finland
2006	Georg Hettich, Germany

Men's 10-Kilometer Large Hill

2010   Bill Demong, United States

Men's 10-Kilometer Normal Hill

2010   Jason Lamy Chappuis, France

4x5-Kilometer Relay

1988	W. Germany, Switzerland, Austria
1992	Japan, Norway, Austria
1994	Japan, Norway, Switzerland
1998	Norway, Finland, France
2002	Finland, Germany, Austria
2006	Austria, Germany, Finland
2010	Austria, United States, Germany

Skeleton

Men		Time
1928	Jennison Heaton, United States	3:01.8
1948	Nino Bibbia, Italy	5:23.2
2002	Jim Shea, United States	1:41.96
2006	Duff Gibson, Canada	1:55.88
2010	Jon Montgomery, Canada	3:29.73

Women		Time
2002	Tristan Gale, United States	1:45.11
2006	Maya Pedersen, Switzerland	1:59.83
2010	Amy Williams, Great Britain	3:35.64

Ski Jumping

Normal Hill		Points
1964	Veikko Kankkonen, Finland	229.9
1968	Jiri Raska, Czechoslovakia	216.5
1972	Yukio Kasaya, Japan	244.2
1976	Hans-Georg Aschenbach, E. Germany	252.0
1980	Toni Innauer, Austria	266.3
1984	Jens Weissflog, E. Germany	215.2
1988	Matti Nykaenen, Finland	230.5
1992	Ernst Vettori, Austria	222.8
1994	Espen Bredesen, Norway	282.0
1998	Jani Soininen, Finland	234.5
2002	Simon Ammann, Switzerland	269.0
2006	Lars Bystoel, Norway	266.5
2010	Simon Ammann, Switzerland	276.5

Large Hill		Points
1924	Jacob Tullin Thams, Norway	18.960
1928	Alfred Andersen, Norway	19.208
1932	Birger Ruud, Norway	228.1
1936	Birger Ruud, Norway	232.0
1948	Petter Hugsted, Norway	228.1
1952	Arnfinn Bergmann, Norway	226.0
1956	Antti Hyvarinen, Finland	227.0

Large Hill	Points
1960 Helmut Recknagel, E. Germany	227.2
1964 Toralf Engan, Norway	230.7
1968 Vladimir Beloussov, USSR	231.3
1972 Wojciech Fortuna, Poland	219.9
1976 Karl Schnabl, Austria	234.8
1980 Jouko Tormanen, Finland	271.0
1984 Matti Nykaenen, Finland	231.2
1988 Matti Nykaenen, Finland	224.0
1992 Toni Nieminen, Finland	239.5
1994 Jens Weissflog, Germany	274.5
1998 Kazuyoshi Funaki, Japan	272.3
2002 Simon Ammann, Switzerland	281.4
2006 Thomas Morgenstern, Austria	276.9
2010 Simon Ammann, Switzerland	283.6

Team Large Hill	Points
1988 Finland, Yugoslavia, Norway	634.4
1992 Finland, Austria, Czechoslovakia	644.4
1994 Germany, Japan, Austria	970.1
1998 Japan, Germany, Austria	933.0
2002 Germany, Finland, Slovenia	974.1
2006 Austria, Finland, Norway	984.0
2010 Austria, Germany, Norway	1,107.9

Snowboarding

Men's Halfpipe	Points
1998 Gian Simmen, Switzerland	85.2
2002 Ross Powers, United States	46.1
2006 Shaun White, United States	46.8
2010 Shaun White, United States	48.4

Men's Parallel Giant Slalom
1998 Ross Rebagliati, Canada
2002 Philipp Schoch, Switzerland
2006 Philipp Schoch, Switzerland
2010 Jasey Jay Anderson, Canada
Note: In 2002, the Giant Slalom became the Parallel Giant Slalom.

Men's Snowboard Cross
2006 Seth Wescott, United States
2010 Seth Wescott, United States

Women's Halfpipe	Points
1998 Nicola Thost, Germany	74.6
2002 Kelly Clark, United States	47.9

Women's Halfpipe	Points
2006 Hannah Teter, United States	46.4
2010 Torah Bright, Australia	45.0

Women's Parallel Giant Slalom
1998 Karine Ruby, France
2002 Isabelle Blanc, France
2006 Daniela Meuli, Switzerland
2010 Nicolien Sauerbreij, Netherlands
Note: In 2002, the Giant Slalom became the Parallel Giant Slalom.

Women's Snowboard Cross
2006 Tanja Frieden, Switzerland
2010 Maelle Ricker, Canada

Speed Skating
*Olympic record

Men's 500 Meters	Time
1924 Charles Jewtraw, United States	0:44.0
1928 Thunberg, Finland; Evensen, Norway (tie)	0:43.4
1932 John A. Shea, United States	0:43.4
1936 Ivar Ballangrud, Norway	0:43.4
1948 Finn Helgesen, Norway	0:43.1
1952 Kenneth Henry, United States	0:43.2
1956 Evgeniy Grishin, USSR	0:40.2
1960 Evgeniy Grishin, USSR	0:40.2
1964 Terry McDermott, United States	0:40.1
1968 Erhard Keller, W. Germany	0:40.3
1972 Erhard Keller, W. Germany	0:39.44
1976 Evgeny Kulikov, USSR	0:39.17
1980 Eric Heiden, United States	0:38.03
1984 Sergei Fokichev, USSR	0:38.19
1988 Uwe-Jens Mey, E. Germany	0:36.45
1992 Uwe-Jens Mey, Germany	0:37.14
1994 Aleksandr Golubev, Russia	0:36.33
1998 Hiroyasu Shimizu, Japan	0:35.59

Men's 500 Meters	Time
2002 Casey FitzRandolph, United States	0:34.42*
2006 Joey Cheek, United States	0:34.82
2010 Mo Tae-Bum, S. Korea	0:34.906

Men's 1,000 Meters	Time
1976 Peter Mueller, United States	1:19.32
1980 Eric Heiden, United States	1:15.18
1984 Gaetan Boucher, Canada	1:15.80
1988 Nikolai Guiliaev, USSR	1:13.03
1992 Olaf Zinke, Germany	1:14.85
1994 Dan Jansen, United States	1:12.43
1998 Ids Postma, Netherlands	1:10.64
2002 Gerard van Velde, Netherlands	1:07.18*
2006 Shani Davis, United States	1:08.89
2010 Shani Davis, United States	1:08.94

Men's 1,500 Meters	Time
1924 Clas Thunberg, Finland	2:20.8
1928 Clas Thunberg, Finland	2:21.1
1932 John A. Shea, United States	2:57.5
1936 Charles Mathiesen, Norway	2:19.2
1948 Sverre Farstad, Norway	2:17.6
1952 Hjalmar Andersen, Norway	2:20.4
1956 Grishin, USSR; Mikhailov, USSR (tie)	2:08.6
1960 Aas, Norway; Grishin, USSR (tie)	2:10.4
1964 Ants Anston, USSR	2:10.3
1968 Cornetis Verkerk, Netherlands	2:03.4
1972 Ard Schenk, Netherlands	2:02.96
1976 Jan Egil Storholt, Norway	1:59.38
1980 Eric Heiden, United States	1:55.44
1984 Gaetan Boucher, Canada	1:58.36
1988 Andre Hoffmann, E. Germany	1:52.06
1992 Johann Koss, Norway	1:54.81
1994 Johann Koss, Norway	1:51.29
1998 Aadne Sondral, Norway	1:47.87
2002 Derek Parra, United States	1:43.95*
2006 Enrico Fabris, Italy	1:45.97
2010 Mark Tuitert, Netherlands	1:45.57

Men's 5,000 Meters	Time
1924 Clas Thunberg, Finland	8:39.0
1928 Ivar Ballangrud, Norway	8:50.5
1932 Irving Jaffee, United States	9:40.8
1936 Ivar Ballangrud, Norway	8:19.6
1948 Reidar Liaklev, Norway	8:29.4
1952 Hjalmar Andersen, Norway	8:10.6
1956 Boris Shilkov, USSR	7:48.7
1960 Viktor Kosichkin, USSR	7:51.3
1964 Knut Johannesen, Norway	7:38.4
1968 F. Anton Maier, Norway	7:22.4
1972 Ard Schenk, Netherlands	7:23.61
1976 Sten Stensen, Norway	7:24.48
1980 Eric Heiden, United States	7:02.29
1984 Tomas Gustafson, Sweden	7:12.28
1988 Tomas Gustafson, Sweden	6:44.63
1992 Geir Karlstad, Norway	6:59.97
1994 Johann Koss, Norway	6:34.96
1998 Gianni Romme, Netherlands	6:22.20
2002 Jochem Uytdehaage, Netherlands	6:14.66
2006 Chad Hedrick, United States	6:14.68
2010 Sven Kramer, Netherlands	6:14.60*

Men's 10,000 Meters	Time
1924 Julius Skutnabb, Finland	18:04.8
1928 Event not held because of thawing of ice	
1932 Irving Jaffee, United States	19:13.6
1936 Ivar Ballangrud, Norway	17:24.3
1948 Ake Seyffarth, Sweden	17:26.3
1952 Hjalmar Andersen, Norway	16:45.8
1956 Sigvard Ericsson, Sweden	16:35.9
1960 Knut Johannesen, Norway	15:46.6
1964 Jonny Nilsson, Sweden	15:50.1
1968 Jonny Hoeglin, Sweden	15:23.6
1972 Ard Schenk, Netherlands	15:01.35
1976 Piet Kleine, Netherlands	14:50.59
1980 Eric Heiden, United States	14:28.13
1984 Igor Malkov, USSR	14:39.90
1988 Tomas Gustafson, Sweden	13:48.20
1992 Bart Veldkamp, Netherlands	14:12.12
1994 Johann Koss, Norway	13:30.55
1998 Gianni Romme, Netherlands	13:15.33
2002 Jochem Uytdehaage, Netherlands	12:58.92
2006 Bob de Jong, Netherlands	13:01.57
2010 Lee Seung-Hoon, S. Korea	12:58.55*

Men's Team Pursuit	Time
2006 Italy, Canada, Netherlands 3:44.46	
2010 Canada, United States, Netherlands. 3:41.37	

Women's 500 Meters	Time
1960 Helga Haase, Germany 0:45.9	
1964 Lydia Skoblikova, USSR 0:45.0	
1968 Ludmila Titova, USSR 0:46.1	
1972 Anne Henning, United States 0:43.33	
1976 Sheila Young, United States 0:42.76	
1980 Karin Enke, E. Germany. 0:41.78	
1984 Christa Rothenburger, E. Germany 0:41.02	
1988 Bonnie Blair, United States 0:39.10	
1992 Bonnie Blair, United States 0:40.33	
1994 Bonnie Blair, United States 0:39.25	
1998 Catriona Le May-Doan, Canada. 0:38.21	
2002 Catriona Le May Doan, Canada. 0:37.30*	
2006 Svetlana Zhurova, Russia 0:38.23	
2010 Lee Sang-Hwa, S. Korea 0:37.850	

Women's 1,000 Meters	Time
1960 Klara Guseva, USSR 1:34.1	
1964 Lydia Skoblikova, USSR 1:33.2	
1968 Carolina Geijssen, Netherlands 1:32.6	
1972 Monika Pflug, W. Germany 1:31.40	
1976 Tatiana Averina, USSR 1:28.43	
1980 Natalya Petruseva, USSR 1:24.10	
1984 Karin Enke, E. Germany. 1:21.61	
1988 Christa Rothenburger, E. Germany 1:17.65	
1992 Bonnie Blair, United States 1:21.90	
1994 Bonnie Blair, United States 1:18.74	
1998 Marianne Timmer, Netherlands 1:16.51	
2002 Chris Witty, United States 1:13.83*	
2006 Marianne Timmer, Netherlands 1:16.05	
2010 Christine Nesbitt, Canada 1:16.56	

Women's 1,500 Meters	Time
1960 Lydia Skoblikova, USSR 2:52.2	
1964 Lydia Skoblikova, USSR 2:22.6	
1968 Kaija Mustonen, Finland. 2:22.4	
1972 Dianne Holum, United States 2:20.85	
1976 Galina Stepanskaya, USSR 2:16.58	
1980 Anne Borckink, Netherlands. 2:10.95	
1984 Karin Enke, E. Germany. 2:03.42	
1988 Yvonne van Gennip, Netherlands 2:00.68	
1992 Jacqueline Boerner, Germany 2:05.87	
1994 Emese Hunyady, Austria 2:02.19	
1998 Marianne Timmer, Netherlands 1:57.58	
2002 Anni Friesinger, Germany 1:54.02*	
2006 Cindy Klassen, Canada 1:55.27	
2010 Ireen Wust, Netherlands. 1:56.89	

Women's 3,000 Meters	Time
1960 Lydia Skoblikova, USSR. 5:14.3	
1964 Lydia Skoblikova, USSR. 5:14.9	
1968 Johanna Schut, Netherlands. 4:56.2	
1972 Christina Baas-Kaiser, Netherlands 4:52.14	
1976 Tatiana Averina, USSR. 4:45.19	
1980 Bjoerg Eva Jensen, Norway 4:32.13	
1984 Andrea Schoene, E. Germany 4:24.79	
1988 Yvonne van Gennip, Netherlands. 4:11.94	
1992 Gunda Niemann, Germany. 4:19.90	
1994 Svetlana Bazhanova, Russia 4:17.43	
1998 Gunda Niemann-Stirnemann, Germany 4:07.29	
2002 Claudia Pechstein, Germany 3:57.70*	
2006 Ireen Wust, Netherlands. 4:02.43	
2010 Martina Sablikova, Czech Republic 4:02.53	

Women's 5,000 Meters	Time
1988 Yvonne van Gennip, Netherlands 7:14.13	
1992 Gunda Niemann, Germany. 7:31.57	
1994 Claudia Pechstein, Germany 7:14.37	
1998 Claudia Pechstein, Germany 6:59.61	
2002 Claudia Pechstein, Germany 6:46.91*	
2006 Clara Hughes, Canada 6:59.07	
2010 Martina Sablikova, Czech Republic 6:50.91	

Women's Team Pursuit	Time
2006 Germany, Canada, Russia 3:01.25	
2010 Germany, Japan, Poland 3:02.82	

Speed Skating (Short Track)
*Olympic record

Men's 500 Meters	Time
1998 Takafumi Nishitani, Japan. 0:42.862	
2002 Marc Gagnon, Canada 0:41.802	
2006 Apolo Anton Ohno, United States 0:41.935	
2010 Charles Hamelin, Canada. 0:40.981	

Men's 1,000 Meters	Time
1992 Kim Ki-Hoon, S. Korea 1:30.76	
1994 Kim Ki-Hoon, S. Korea 1:34.57	
1998 Dong-Sung Kim, S. Korea. 1:32.375	
2002 Steven Bradbury, Australia 1:29.109	
2006 Hyun-Soo Ahn, S. Korea. 1:26.739	
2010 Lee Jung-Su, S. Korea 1:23.747*	

Men's 1,500 Meters	Time
2002 Apolo Anton Ohno, United States 2:18.541	
2006 Hyun-Soo Ahn, S. Korea. 2:25.341	
2010 Lee Jung-Su, S. Korea 2:17.611	

Men's 5,000-Meter Relay	Time
1992 S. Korea, Canada, Japan 7:14.02	
1994 Italy, United States, Australia 7:11.74	
1998 Canada, S. Korea, China 7:06.075	
2002 Canada, Italy, China 6:51.579	
2006 S. Korea, Canada, United States 6:43.376*	
2010 Canada, S. Korea, United States 6:44.224	

Women's 500 Meters	Time
1992 Cathy Turner, United States 0:47.04	
1994 Cathy Turner, United States 0:45.98	
1998 Annie Perreault, Canada. 0:46.568	
2002 Yang Yang (A), China. 0:44.187	
2006 Meng Wang, China 0:44.345	
2010 Wang Meng, China 0:43.048	

Women's 1,000 Meters	Time
1998 Chun Lee-Kyung, S. Korea. 1:42.776	
2002 Yang Yang (A), China. 1:36.391	
2006 Sun-Yu Jin, S. Korea 1:32.859	
2010 Wang Meng, China 1:29.213	

Women's 1,500 Meters	Time
2002 Gi-Hyun Ko, S. Korea 2:31.581	
2006 Sun-Yu Jin, S. Korea 2:23.494	
2010 Zhou Yang, China. 2:16.993*	

Women's 3,000-Meter Relay	Time
1992 Canada, United States, Unified Team. 4:36.62	
1994 S. Korea, Canada, United States 4:26.64	
1998 S. Korea, China, Canada 4:16.26	
2002 S. Korea, China, Canada 4:12.793	
2006 S. Korea, Canada, Italy. 4:17.040	
2010 China, Canada, United States 4:06.610*	

Paralympic Games

More than 4,250 athletes from a record 164 countries met at the XIV Paralympic Summer Games, held Aug. 29-Sept. 9, 2012, in London, England, UK. A total of 503 gold medals were awarded in 20 sports. China claimed 231 medals, nearly twice as many as host country Great Britain, which collected 120 medals. Russia finished third with 102 medals, just ahead of the U.S., in fourth with 98.

The first Olympic Games for athletes with disabilities were held in Rome after the 1960 Summer Olympics; use of the name "paralympic" began at the 1964 games in Tokyo. The Paralympics are held by the Olympic host country in the same year and usually the same city and venue or venues. A goal of the Paralympics is to provide elite competition for athletes with functional disabilities that prevent their involvement in the Olympics. In 1976, the first Winter Paralympics were held, in Ornskoldsvik, Sweden.

The X Paralympic Winter Games were held Mar. 12-21, 2010, in Vancouver, BC, Canada. More than 500 athletes from 44 nations competed in five sports. Russia dominated the total medal count with 38, while Germany won the most gold medals, with 13.

COLLEGE SPORTS

COLLEGE BASKETBALL

2012 Men's NCAA Tournament: Kentucky Conquers Kansas

The Univ. of Kentucky Wildcats defeated the Univ. of Kansas Jayhawks, 67-59, in New Orleans, LA, to claim the NCAA Men's Division I national basketball title Apr. 2, 2012. Sophomore Doron Lamb led the Wildcats with 22 points, but freshman Anthony Davis was named the tournament's most outstanding player. This was the first national championship for head coach John Calipari, who had been to the Final Four four times with three different schools without claiming the title. Kentucky, a perennial basketball powerhouse, claimed its eighth national title and its first championship since 1998.

NCAA Division I Basketball Champions, 1943-2012

Year	Champion	Coach	Final opponent	Score	Most outstanding player	Site
1943	Wyoming	Everett Shelton	Georgetown	46-34	Ken Sailors, Wyoming	New York, NY
1944	Utah	Vadal Peterson	Dartmouth	42-40[1]	Arnold Ferrin, Utah	New York, NY
1945	Oklahoma St.[2]	Henry Iba	NYU	49-45	Bob Kurland, Oklahoma St.	New York, NY
1946	Oklahoma St.[2]	Henry Iba	North Carolina	43-40	Bob Kurland, Oklahoma St.	New York, NY
1947	Holy Cross	Alvin Julian	Oklahoma	58-47	George Kaftan, Holy Cross	New York, NY
1948	Kentucky	Adolph Rupp	Baylor	58-42	Alex Groza, Kentucky	New York, NY
1949	Kentucky	Adolph Rupp	Oklahoma St.	46-36	Alex Groza, Kentucky	Seattle, WA
1950	CCNY	Nat Holman	Bradley	71-68	Irwin Dambrot, CCNY	New York, NY
1951	Kentucky	Adolph Rupp	Kansas St.	68-58	Bill Spivey, Kentucky	Minneapolis, MN
1952	Kansas	Forrest Allen	St. John's	80-63	Clyde Lovellette, Kansas	Seattle, WA
1953	Indiana	Branch McCracken	Kansas	69-68	B. H. Born, Kansas	Kansas City, MO
1954	La Salle	Kenneth Loeffler	Bradley	92-76	Tom Gola, La Salle	Kansas City, MO
1955	San Francisco	Phil Woolpert	La Salle	77-63	Bill Russell, San Francisco	Kansas City, MO
1956	San Francisco	Phil Woolpert	Iowa	83-71	Hal Lear, Temple	Evanston, IL
1957	North Carolina	Frank McGuire	Kansas	54-53[1]	Wilt Chamberlain, Kansas	Kansas City, MO
1958	Kentucky	Adolph Rupp	Seattle	84-72	Elgin Baylor, Seattle	Louisville, KY
1959	California	Pete Newell	West Virginia	71-70	Jerry West, West Virginia	Louisville, KY
1960	Ohio St.	Fred Taylor	California	75-55	Jerry Lucas, Ohio St.	San Francisco, CA
1961	Cincinnati	Edwin Jucker	Ohio St.	70-65[1]	Jerry Lucas, Ohio St.	Kansas City, MO
1962	Cincinnati	Edwin Jucker	Ohio St.	71-59	Paul Hogue, Cincinnati	Louisville, KY
1963	Loyola (IL)	George Ireland	Cincinnati	60-58[1]	Art Heyman, Duke	Louisville, KY
1964	UCLA	John Wooden	Duke	98-83	Walt Hazzard, UCLA	Kansas City, MO
1965	UCLA	John Wooden	Michigan	91-80	Bill Bradley, Princeton	Portland, OR
1966	Texas-El Paso[3]	Don Haskins	Kentucky	72-65	Jerry Chambers, Utah	College Park, MD
1967	UCLA	John Wooden	Dayton	79-64	Lew Alcindor, UCLA	Louisville, KY
1968	UCLA	John Wooden	North Carolina	78-55	Lew Alcindor, UCLA	Los Angeles, CA
1969	UCLA	John Wooden	Purdue	92-72	Lew Alcindor, UCLA	Louisville, KY
1970	UCLA	John Wooden	Jacksonville	80-69	Sidney Wicks, UCLA	College Park, MD
1971	UCLA	John Wooden	Villanova*	68-62	Howard Porter, Villanova*	Houston, TX
1972	UCLA	John Wooden	Florida St.	81-76	Bill Walton, UCLA	Los Angeles, CA
1973	UCLA	John Wooden	Memphis[4]	87-66	Bill Walton, UCLA	St. Louis, MO
1974	North Carolina St.	Norm Sloan	Marquette	76-64	David Thompson, NC St.	Greensboro, NC
1975	UCLA	John Wooden	Kentucky	92-85	Richard Washington, UCLA	San Diego, CA
1976	Indiana	Bob Knight	Michigan	86-68	Kent Benson, Indiana	Philadelphia, PA
1977	Marquette	Al McGuire	North Carolina	67-59	Butch Lee, Marquette	Atlanta, GA
1978	Kentucky	Joe Hall	Duke	94-88	Jack Givens, Kentucky	St. Louis, MO
1979	Michigan St.	Jud Heathcote	Indiana St.	75-64	Magic Johnson, Michigan St.	Salt Lake City, UT
1980	Louisville	Denny Crum	UCLA*	59-54	Darrell Griffith, Louisville	Indianapolis, IN
1981	Indiana	Bob Knight	North Carolina	63-50	Isiah Thomas, Indiana	Philadelphia, PA
1982	North Carolina	Dean Smith	Georgetown	63-62	James Worthy, N. Carolina	New Orleans, LA
1983	North Carolina St.	Jim Valvano	Houston	54-52	Hakeem Olajuwon, Houston	Albuquerque, NM
1984	Georgetown	John Thompson	Houston	84-75	Patrick Ewing, Georgetown	Seattle, WA
1985	Villanova	Rollie Massimino	Georgetown	66-64	Ed Pinckney, Villanova	Lexington, KY
1986	Louisville	Denny Crum	Duke	72-69	Pervis Ellison, Louisville	Dallas, TX
1987	Indiana	Bob Knight	Syracuse	74-73	Keith Smart, Indiana	New Orleans, LA
1988	Kansas	Larry Brown	Oklahoma	83-79	Danny Manning, Kansas	Kansas City, MO
1989	Michigan	Steve Fisher	Seton Hall	80-79[1]	Glen Rice, Michigan	Seattle, WA
1990	UNLV	Jerry Tarkanian	Duke	103-73	Anderson Hunt, UNLV	Denver, CO
1991	Duke	Mike Krzyzewski	Kansas	72-65	Christian Laettner, Duke	Indianapolis, IN
1992	Duke	Mike Krzyzewski	Michigan	71-51	Bobby Hurley, Duke	Minneapolis, MN
1993	North Carolina	Dean Smith	Michigan	77-71	Donald Williams, N. Carolina	New Orleans, LA
1994	Arkansas	Nolan Richardson	Duke	76-72	Corliss Williamson, Arkansas	Charlotte, NC
1995	UCLA	Jim Harrick	Arkansas	89-78	Ed O'Bannon, UCLA	Seattle, WA
1996	Kentucky	Rick Pitino	Syracuse	76-67	Tony Delk, Kentucky	E. Rutherford, NJ
1997	Arizona	Lute Olson	Kentucky	84-79[1]	Miles Simon, Arizona	Indianapolis, IN
1998	Kentucky	Tubby Smith	Utah	78-69	Jeff Sheppard, Kentucky	San Antonio, TX
1999	Connecticut	Jim Calhoun	Duke	77-74	Richard Hamilton, Connecticut	St. Petersburg, FL
2000	Michigan St.	Tom Izzo	Florida	89-76	Mateen Cleaves, Michigan St.	Indianapolis, IN
2001	Duke	Mike Krzyzewski	Arizona	82-72	Shane Battier, Duke	Minneapolis, MN
2002	Maryland	Gary Williams	Indiana	64-52	Juan Dixon, Maryland	Atlanta, GA
2003	Syracuse	Jim Boeheim	Kansas	81-78	Carmelo Anthony, Syracuse	New Orleans, LA
2004	Connecticut	Jim Calhoun	Georgia Tech	82-73	Emeka Okafor, Connecticut	San Antonio, TX
2005	North Carolina	Roy Williams	Illinois	75-70	Sean May, North Carolina	St. Louis, MO
2006	Florida	Billy Donovan	UCLA	73-57	Joakim Noah, Florida	Indianapolis, IN
2007	Florida	Billy Donovan	Ohio St.	84-75	Corey Brewer, Florida	Atlanta, GA
2008	Kansas	Bill Self	Memphis	75-68[1]	Mario Chalmers, Kansas	San Antonio, TX
2009	North Carolina	Roy Williams	Michigan St.	89-72	Wayne Ellington, North Carolina	Detroit, MI
2010	Duke	Mike Krzyzewski	Butler	61-59	Kyle Singler, Duke	Indianapolis, IN
2011	Connecticut	Jim Calhoun	Butler	53-41	Kemba Walker, Connecticut	Houston, TX
2012	Kentucky	John Calipari	Kansas	67-59	Anthony Davis, Kentucky	New Orleans, LA

*Declared ineligible after the tournament. (1) Overtime. (2) Then known as Oklahoma A&M. (3) Then known as Texas Western. (4) Then known as Memphis State.

2012 Men's NCAA Basketball Tournament

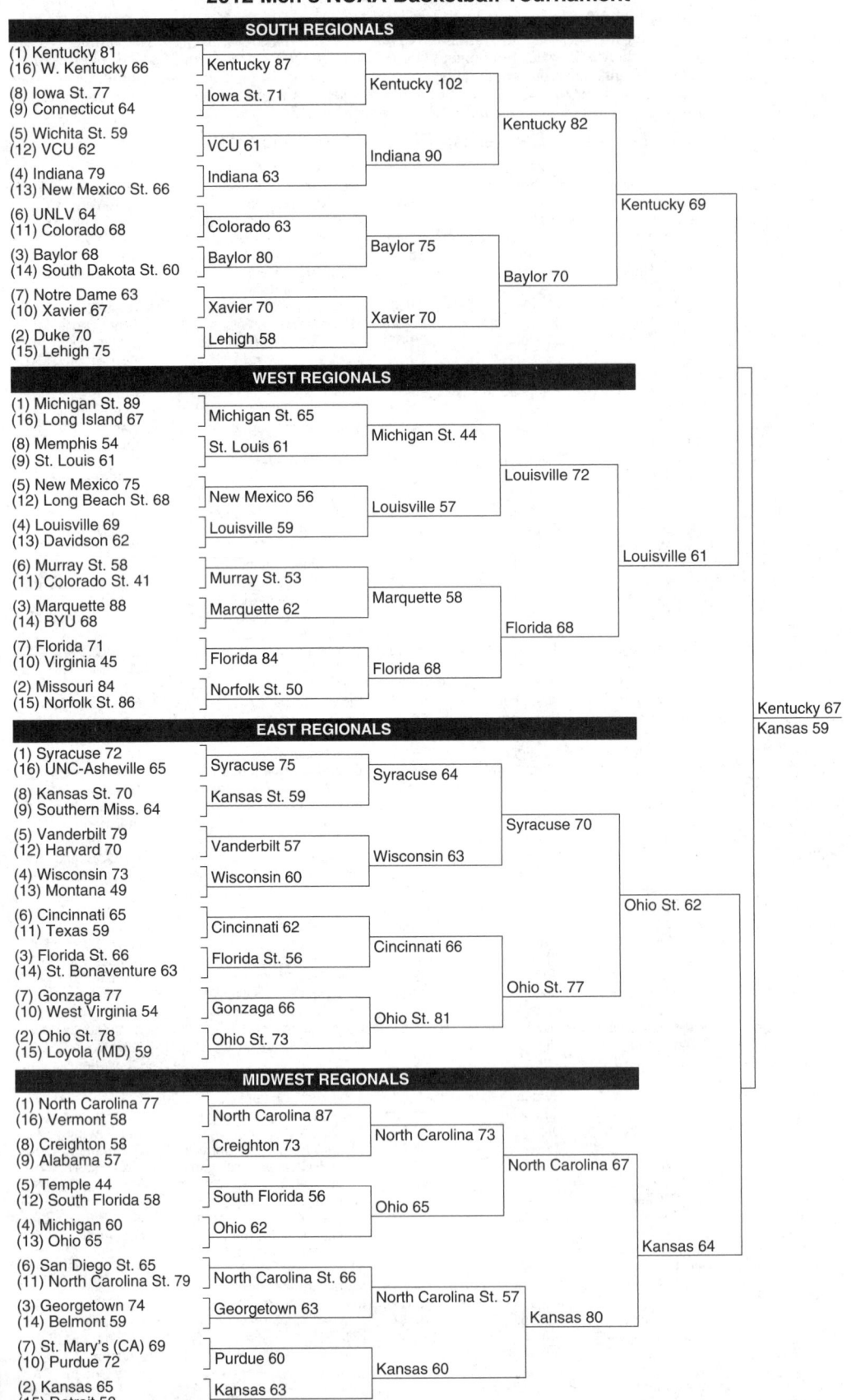

SOUTH REGIONALS

(1) Kentucky 81 / (16) W. Kentucky 66 — Kentucky 87
(8) Iowa St. 77 / (9) Connecticut 64 — Iowa St. 71
Kentucky 102
(5) Wichita St. 59 / (12) VCU 62 — VCU 61
(4) Indiana 79 / (13) New Mexico St. 66 — Indiana 63
Indiana 90
Kentucky 82
(6) UNLV 64 / (11) Colorado 68 — Colorado 63
(3) Baylor 68 / (14) South Dakota St. 60 — Baylor 80
Baylor 75
(7) Notre Dame 63 / (10) Xavier 67 — Xavier 70
(2) Duke 70 / (15) Lehigh 75 — Lehigh 58
Xavier 70
Baylor 70
Kentucky 69

WEST REGIONALS

(1) Michigan St. 89 / (16) Long Island 67 — Michigan St. 65
(8) Memphis 54 / (9) St. Louis 61 — St. Louis 61
Michigan St. 44
(5) New Mexico 75 / (12) Long Beach St. 68 — New Mexico 56
(4) Louisville 69 / (13) Davidson 62 — Louisville 59
Louisville 57
Louisville 72
(6) Murray St. 58 / (11) Colorado St. 41 — Murray St. 53
(3) Marquette 88 / (14) BYU 68 — Marquette 62
Marquette 58
(7) Florida 71 / (10) Virginia 45 — Florida 84
(2) Missouri 84 / (15) Norfolk St. 86 — Norfolk St. 50
Florida 68
Florida 68
Louisville 61

EAST REGIONALS

(1) Syracuse 72 / (16) UNC-Asheville 65 — Syracuse 75
(8) Kansas St. 70 / (9) Southern Miss. 64 — Kansas St. 59
Syracuse 64
(5) Vanderbilt 79 / (12) Harvard 70 — Vanderbilt 57
(4) Wisconsin 73 / (13) Montana 49 — Wisconsin 60
Wisconsin 63
Syracuse 70
(6) Cincinnati 65 / (11) Texas 59 — Cincinnati 62
(3) Florida St. 66 / (14) St. Bonaventure 63 — Florida St. 56
Cincinnati 66
(7) Gonzaga 77 / (10) West Virginia 54 — Gonzaga 66
(2) Ohio St. 78 / (15) Loyola (MD) 59 — Ohio St. 73
Ohio St. 81
Ohio St. 77
Ohio St. 62

MIDWEST REGIONALS

(1) North Carolina 77 / (16) Vermont 58 — North Carolina 87
(8) Creighton 58 / (9) Alabama 57 — Creighton 73
North Carolina 73
(5) Temple 44 / (12) South Florida 58 — South Florida 56
(4) Michigan 60 / (13) Ohio 65 — Ohio 62
Ohio 65
North Carolina 67
(6) San Diego St. 65 / (11) North Carolina St. 79 — North Carolina St. 66
(3) Georgetown 74 / (14) Belmont 59 — Georgetown 63
North Carolina St. 57
(7) St. Mary's (CA) 69 / (10) Purdue 72 — Purdue 60
(2) Kansas 65 / (15) Detroit 50 — Kansas 63
Kansas 60
Kansas 80
Kansas 64

Kentucky 67
Kansas 59

All-Time Winningest Division I College Basketball Teams

Team	Yrs.	Won	Lost	Pct.	Team	Yrs.	Won	Lost	Pct.	Team	Yrs.	Won	Lost	Pct.
Kentucky	109	2,090	649	0.763	W. Kentucky . .	93	1,655	828	0.667	Utah	104	1,670	918	0.645
N. Carolina. . . .	102	2,065	734	0.738	Louisville	98	1,662	864	0.658	Missouri State	100	1,564	870	0.643
Kansas.	114	2,070	806	0.720	St. John's (NY)	105	1,737	915	0.655	Murray State . .	87	1,480	825	0.642
UNLV	54	1,133	456	0.713	Illinois.	107	1,667	897	0.650	Connecticut. . .	109	1,569	878	0.641
Duke	107	1,971	834	0.703	Notre Dame . . .	107	1,723	939	0.647	Arkansas.	89	1,537	867	0.639
Syracuse	111	1,844	822	0.692	Temple.	116	1,790	982	0.646	VCU	42	791	446	0.639
UCLA.	93	1,728	769	0.692	Arizona	107	1,618	892	0.645	Indiana	112	1,690	959	0.638

Note: Through 2011-12 season; winningest teams by percentage.

National Invitation Tournament Champions, 1938-2012

The National Invitation Tournament (NIT), first played in 1938, is the oldest U.S. basketball tournament. The first National Collegiate Athletic Association (NCAA) national championship tournament was played one year later. In Aug. 2005, the NCAA agreed to purchase the NIT from the five New York City-area colleges that had run the NIT.

Year	Champion	Year	Champion	Year	Champion	Year	Champion	Year	Champion
1938	Temple	1953	Seton Hall	1968	Dayton	1983	Fresno State	1998	Minnesota
1939	Long Island Univ.	1954	Holy Cross	1969	Temple	1984	Michigan	1999	California
1940	Colorado	1955	Duquesne	1970	Marquette	1985	UCLA	2000	Wake Forest
1941	Long Island Univ.	1956	Louisville	1971	North Carolina	1986	Ohio State	2001	Tulsa
1942	West Virginia	1957	Bradley	1972	Maryland	1987	Southern Miss.	2002	Memphis
1943	St. John's (NY)	1958	Xavier (OH)	1973	Virginia Tech	1988	Connecticut	2003	St. John's (NY)
1944	St. John's (NY)	1959	St. John's (NY)	1974	Purdue	1989	St. John's (NY)	2004	Michigan
1945	DePaul	1960	Bradley	1975	Princeton	1990	Vanderbilt	2005	South Carolina
1946	Kentucky	1961	Providence	1976	Kentucky	1991	Stanford	2006	South Carolina
1947	Utah	1962	Dayton	1977	St. Bonaventure	1992	Virginia	2007	West Virginia
1948	St. Louis	1963	Providence	1978	Texas	1993	Minnesota	2008	Ohio State
1949	San Francisco	1964	Bradley	1979	Indiana	1994	Villanova	2009	Penn State
1950	CCNY	1965	St. John's (NY)	1980	Virginia	1995	Virginia Tech	2010	Dayton
1951	Brigham Young	1966	Brigham Young	1981	Tulsa	1996	Nebraska	2011	Wichita State
1952	La Salle	1967	Southern Illinois	1982	Bradley	1997	Michigan	2012	Stanford

John R. Wooden Award, 1977-2012

Awarded to the nation's outstanding men's college basketball player by the Los Angeles Athletic Club since 1977; awarded under the same name to women since 2004.

Year	Player, school	Year	Player, school	Year	Player, school
1977	Marques Johnson, UCLA	1993	Calbert Cheaney, Indiana	2006	(M) J. J. Redick, Duke
1978	Phil Ford, North Carolina	1994	Glenn Robinson, Purdue		(W) Seimone Augustus, LSU
1979	Larry Bird, Indiana State	1995	Ed O'Bannon, UCLA	2007	(M) Kevin Durant, Texas
1980	Darrell Griffith, Louisville	1996	Marcus Camby, Massachusetts		(W) Candace Parker, Tennessee
1981	Danny Ainge, Brigham Young	1997	Tim Duncan, Wake Forest	2008	(M) Tyler Hansbrough, N. Carolina
1982	Ralph Sampson, Virginia	1998	Antawn Jamison, North Carolina		(W) Candace Parker, Tennessee
1983	Ralph Sampson, Virginia	1999	Elton Brand, Duke	2009	(M) Blake Griffin, Oklahoma
1984	Michael Jordan, North Carolina	2000	Kenyon Martin, Cincinnati		(W) Maya Moore, Connecticut
1985	Chris Mullin, St. John's (NY)	2001	Shane Battier, Duke	2010	(M) Evan Turner, Ohio State
1986	Walter Berry, St. John's (NY)	2002	Jay Williams, Duke		(W) Tina Charles, Connecticut
1987	David Robinson, Navy	2003	T. J. Ford, Texas	2011	(M) Jimmer Fredette, Brigham Young
1988	Danny Manning, Kansas	2004	(M) Jameer Nelson, St. Joseph's		(W) Maya Moore, Connecticut
1989	Sean Elliott, Arizona		(W) Alana Beard, Duke	2012	(M) Anthony Davis, Kentucky
1990	Lionel Simmons, La Salle	2005	(M) Andrew Bogut, Utah		(W) Brittney Griner, Baylor
1991	Larry Johnson, UNLV		(W) Seimone Augustus, LSU		
1992	Christian Laettner, Duke				

Most Coaching Victories in the NCAA Basketball Tournament

Coach, school(s), first/latest appearance	Wins	Tournaments	Championships
Mike Krzyzewski, Duke, 1984/2012	79	28	4
Dean Smith, North Carolina, 1967/1997	65	27	2
Roy Williams; Kansas, North Carolina; 1990/2012	61	22	2
Jim Calhoun; Northeastern, Connecticut; 1981/2012	49	23	3
Jim Boeheim; Syracuse, 1977/2012	48	29	1
John Wooden, UCLA, 1950/1975	47	16	10
Lute Olson; Iowa, Arizona; 1979/2007	46	27	1
Bob Knight; Indiana, Texas Tech; 1973/2007	45	28	3
Denny Crum, Louisville, 1972/2000	42	23	2
Rick Pitino; Boston, Providence, Kentucky, Louisville; 1983/2012	42	18	1

Note: Through 2012 tournament. Coaches active in 2011-12 season in **bold**. Some records adjusted for vacated victories.

Wade Trophy, 1978-2012

Awarded by the National Assn. for Girls and Women in Sport and the Women's Basketball Coaches Assn. (WBCA) for character, leadership, and player performance.

Year	Player, school	Year	Player, school	Year	Player, school
1978	Carol Blazejowski, Montclair St.	1990	Jennifer Azzi, Stanford	2002	Sue Bird, Connecticut
1979	Nancy Lieberman, Old Dominion	1991	Daedra Charles, Tennessee	2003	Diana Taurasi, Connecticut
1980	Nancy Lieberman, Old Dominion	1992	Susan Robinson, Penn St.	2004	Alana Beard, Duke
1981	Lynette Woodard, Kansas	1993	Karen Jennings, Nebraska	2005	Seimone Augustus, LSU
1982	Pam Kelly, Louisiana Tech	1994	Carol Ann Shudlick, Minnesota	2006	Seimone Augustus, LSU
1983	LaTaunya Pollard, Long Beach St.	1995	Rebecca Lobo, Connecticut	2007	Candace Parker, Tennessee
1984	Janice Lawrence, Louisiana Tech	1996	Jennifer Rizzotti, Connecticut	2008	Candice Wiggins, Stanford
1985	Cheryl Miller, USC	1997	DeLisha Milton, Florida	2009	Maya Moore, Connecticut
1986	Kamie Ethridge, Texas	1998	Ticha Penicheiro, Old Dominion	2010	Maya Moore, Connecticut
1987	Shelly Pennefeather, Villanova	1999	Stephanie White-McCarty, Purdue	2011	Maya Moore, Connecticut
1988	Teresa Weatherspoon, Louisiana Tech	2000	Edwina Brown, Texas	2012	Brittney Griner, Baylor
1989	Clarissa Davis, Texas	2001	Jackie Stiles, SW Missouri St.		

2012 Women's NCAA Basketball Tournament

DES MOINES REGIONAL

(1) Baylor 81
(16) UC Santa Barbara 40
— Baylor 76

(8) Ohio St. 65
(9) Florida 70
— Florida 57

Baylor 83

(5) Georgetown 61
(12) Fresno St. 56
— Georgetown 64

(4) Georgia Tech 76
(13) Sacred Heart 50
— Georgia Tech 76

Georgia Tech 68

Baylor 77

(6) Nebraska 49
(11) Kansas 57
— Kansas 70

(3) Delaware 73
(14) Arkansas-Little Rock 42
— Delaware 64

Kansas 73

Baylor 59

(7) DePaul 59
(10) Brigham Young 55
— DePaul 48

(2) Tennessee 72
(15) Tennessee-Martin 49
— Tennessee 63

Tennessee 84

Tennessee 58

FRESNO REGIONAL

(1) Stanford 73
(16) Hampton 51
— Stanford 72

(8) West Virginia 68
(9) Texas 55
— West Virginia 55

Stanford 76

(5) South Carolina 80
(12) East Michigan 48
— South Carolina 72

(4) Purdue 83
(13) South Dakota St. 68
— Purdue 61

South Carolina 60

Stanford 81

(6) Oklahoma 88
(11) Michigan 67
— Oklahoma 70

(3) St. John's (NY) 69
(14) Creighton 67
— St. John's (NY) 74

St. John's (NY) 47

Stanford 47

(7) Vanderbilt 60
(10) Mid. Tennessee St. 46
— Vanderbilt 80

(2) Duke 82
(15) Samford 47
— Duke 96

Duke 74

Duke 69

KINGSTON REGIONAL

(1) Connecticut 83
(16) Prairie View A&M 47
— Connecticut 72

(8) Kansas St. 67
(9) Princeton 64
— Kansas St. 26

Connecticut 77

(5) LSU 64
(12) San Diego St. 56
— LSU 80

(4) Penn State 85
(13) Texas-El Paso 77
— Penn State 90

Penn State 59

Connecticut 80

(6) Rutgers 73
(11) Gonzaga 86
— Gonzaga 65

(3) Miami (FL) 70
(14) Idaho St. 41
— Miami (FL) 54

Gonzaga 62

Connecticut 75

(7) Green Bay 71
(10) Iowa St. 57
— Green Bay 62

(2) Kentucky 68
(15) McNeese St. 62
— Kentucky 65

Kentucky 79

Kentucky 65

RALEIGH REGIONAL

(1) Notre Dame 74
(16) Liberty 43
— Notre Dame 73

(8) California 84
(9) Iowa 74
— California 62

Notre Dame 79

(5) St. Bonaventure 72
(12) Florida Gulf Coast 65
— St. Bonaventure 66

(4) Georgia 70
(13) Marist 76
— Marist 63

St. Bonaventure 35

Notre Dame 80

(6) Arkansas 72
(11) Dayton 55
— Arkansas 59

(3) Texas A&M 69
(14) Albany (NY) 47
— Texas A&M 61

Texas A&M 74

Notre Dame 83

(7) Louisville 67
(10) Michigan St. 55
— Louisville 68

(2) Maryland 59
(15) Navy 44
— Maryland 72

Maryland 81

Maryland 49

Baylor 80
Notre Dame 61

2012 Women's NCAA Tournament: Baylor Caps Undefeated Season With Title

The Baylor Univ. Lady Bears Apr. 3, 2012, defeated the Notre Dame Fighting Irish in an 80-61 blowout in Denver, CO, to claim the Women's Division I basketball title. Baylor's title win capped the NCAA's first-ever undefeated, 40-0 season. Baylor star Brittney Griner dominated the Irish with 26 points, 13 rebounds, and 5 blocks; she was named the tournament's most outstanding player.

NCAA Division I Women's Basketball Champions, 1982-2012

Year	Champion	Coach	Final opponent	Score	Most outstanding player	Site
1982	Louisiana Tech	Sonja Hogg	Cheyney	76-62	Janice Lawrence, La. Tech	Norfolk, VA
1983	USC	Linda Sharp	Louisiana Tech	69-67	Cheryl Miller, USC	Norfolk, VA
1984	USC	Linda Sharp	Tennessee	72-61	Cheryl Miller, USC	Los Angeles, CA
1985	Old Dominion	Marianne Stanley	Georgia	70-65	Tracy Claxton, Old Dominion	Austin, TX
1986	Texas	Jody Conradt	USC	97-81	Clarissa Davis, Texas	Lexington, KY
1987	Tennessee	Pat Summitt	Louisiana Tech	67-44	Tonya Edwards, Tennessee	Austin, TX
1988	Louisiana Tech	Leon Barmore	Auburn	56-54	Erica Westbrooks, La. Tech	Tacoma, WA
1989	Tennessee	Pat Summitt	Auburn	76-60	Bridgette Gordon, Tennessee	Tacoma, WA
1990	Stanford	Tara VanDerveer	Auburn	88-81	Jennifer Azzi, Stanford	Knoxville, TN
1991	Tennessee	Pat Summitt	Virginia	70-67 (OT)	Dawn Staley, Virginia	New Orleans, LA
1992	Stanford	Tara VanDerveer	W. Kentucky	78-62	Molly Goodenbour, Stanford	Los Angeles, CA
1993	Texas Tech	Marsha Sharp	Ohio St.	84-82	Sheryl Swoopes, Texas Tech	Atlanta, GA
1994	North Carolina	Sylvia Hatchell	Louisiana Tech	60-59	Charlotte Smith, North Carolina	Richmond, VA
1995	Connecticut	Geno Auriemma	Tennessee	70-64	Rebecca Lobo, Connecticut	Minneapolis, MN
1996	Tennessee	Pat Summitt	Georgia	83-65	Michelle Marciniak, Tennessee	Charlotte, NC
1997	Tennessee	Pat Summitt	Old Dominion	68-59	Chamique Holdsclaw, Tennessee	Cincinnati, OH
1998	Tennessee	Pat Summitt	Louisiana Tech	93-75	Chamique Holdsclaw, Tennessee	Kansas City, MO
1999	Purdue	Carolyn Peck	Duke	62-45	Ukari Figgs, Purdue	San Jose, CA
2000	Connecticut	Geno Auriemma	Tennessee	71-52	Shea Ralph, Connecticut	Philadelphia, PA
2001	Notre Dame	Muffet McGraw	Purdue	68-66	Ruth Riley, Notre Dame	St. Louis, MO
2002	Connecticut	Geno Auriemma	Oklahoma	82-70	Swin Cash, Connecticut	San Antonio, TX
2003	Connecticut	Geno Auriemma	Tennessee	73-68	Diana Taurasi, Connecticut	Atlanta, GA
2004	Connecticut	Geno Auriemma	Tennessee	70-61	Diana Taurasi, Connecticut	New Orleans, LA
2005	Baylor	Kim Mulkey-Robertson	Michigan State	84-62	Sophia Young, Baylor	Indianapolis, IN
2006	Maryland	Brenda Frese	Duke	78-75 (OT)	Laura Harper, Maryland	Boston, MA
2007	Tennessee	Pat Summitt	Rutgers	59-46	Candace Parker, Tennessee	Cleveland, OH
2008	Tennessee	Pat Summitt	Stanford	64-48	Candace Parker, Tennessee	Tampa Bay, FL
2009	Connecticut	Geno Auriemma	Louisville	76-54	Tina Charles, Connecticut	St. Louis, MO
2010	Connecticut	Geno Auriemma	Stanford	53-47	Maya Moore, Connecticut	San Antonio, TX
2011	Texas A&M	Gary Blair	Notre Dame	76-70	Danielle Adams, Texas A&M	Indianapolis, IN
2012	Baylor	Kim Mulkey	Notre Dame	80-61	Brittney Griner, Baylor	Denver, CO

COLLEGE FOOTBALL

2011 BCS Championship: Alabama Crushes LSU

The Alabama Univ. Crimson Tide demolished the top-ranked Louisiana State Univ. Tigers in a 21-0 clash of defenses in New Orleans, LA, to win the Bowl Championship Series (BCS) national title game Jan. 9, 2012. With the win, 'Bama avenged a regular-season loss to LSU, which became the first team to be shut out in a BCS championship game. The Crimson Tide's Jeremy Shelley scored a BCS-record 5 field goals, but the team's defense, which held the Tigers' offense under 100 offensive yards, was credited with the win.

National College Football Champions, 1936-2011

The official champion, as determined by the BCS National Championship game (BCS No. 1 vs. BCS No. 2), is listed starting 2006. For years preceding 2006, the unofficial champion, as selected by the AP poll of writers and USA Today/ESPN (until 1991, UPI; 1991-96, USA Today/CNN) poll of coaches, is listed. Where the polls disagreed, both teams are listed with AP winner first. The AP poll started in 1936, the UPI poll in 1950.

Year	Champion(s)	Year	Champion(s)	Year	Champion(s)	Year	Champion(s)	Year	Champion(s)
1936	Minnesota	1952	Michigan St.	1967	USC	1982	Penn St.	1997	Mich./Nebraska
1937	Pittsburgh	1953	Maryland	1968	Ohio St.	1983	Miami (FL)	1998	Tennessee
1938	Texas Christian	1954	Ohio St./UCLA	1969	Texas	1984	Brigham Young	1999	Florida St.
1939	Texas A&M	1955	Oklahoma	1970	Nebraska/Texas	1985	Oklahoma	2000	Oklahoma
1940	Minnesota	1956	Oklahoma	1971	Nebraska	1986	Penn St.	2001	Miami (FL)
1941	Minnesota	1957	Auburn/Ohio St.	1972	USC	1987	Miami (FL)	2002	Ohio St.
1942	Ohio St.	1958	Louisiana St. (LSU)	1973	Notre Dame/Alabama	1988	Notre Dame	2003	LSU/USC
1943	Notre Dame	1959	Syracuse	1974	Oklahoma/USC	1989	Miami (FL)	2004	USC[1]
1944	Army	1960	Minnesota	1975	Oklahoma	1990	Colorado/GA Tech	2005	Texas
1945	Army	1961	Alabama	1976	Pittsburgh	1991	Miami (FL)/Washington	2006	Florida
1946	Notre Dame	1962	USC	1977	Notre Dame	1992	Alabama	2007	LSU
1947	Notre Dame	1963	Texas	1978	Alabama/USC	1993	Florida St.	2008	Florida
1948	Michigan	1964	Alabama	1979	Alabama	1994	Nebraska	2009	Alabama
1949	Notre Dame	1965	Alabama/Mich. St.	1980	Georgia	1995	Nebraska	2010	Auburn
1950	Oklahoma	1966	Notre Dame	1981	Clemson	1996	Florida	2011	Alabama
1951	Tennessee								

(1) The Bowl Championship Series' Presidential Oversight Committee vacated USC's 2004 championship due to rules violations.

2011 Final Standings

Bowl Championship Series		Associated Press Poll		USA Today Poll	
Rank, team	**Rank, team**	**Rank, team**	**Rank, team**	**Rank, team**	**Rank, team**
1. LSU	14. Oklahoma	1. Alabama	14. TCU	1. Alabama	14. Houston
2. Alabama	15. Clemson	2. LSU	15. Kansas St.	2. LSU	15. Oklahoma
3. Oklahoma St.	16. Georgia	3. Oklahoma St.	16. Oklahoma	3. Oklahoma St.	16. Kansas St.
4. Stanford	17. Michigan St.	4. Oregon	17. West Virginia	4. Oregon	17. Virginia Tech
5. Oregon	18. TCU	5. Arkansas	18. Houston	5. Arkansas	18. West Virginia
6. Arkansas	19. Houston	6. USC	19. Georgia	6. Boise St.	19. Southern Miss.
7. Boise St.	20. Nebraska	7. Stanford	20. Southern Miss.	7. Stanford	20. Georgia
8. Kansas St.	21. Southern Miss.	8. Boise St.	21. Virginia Tech	8. South Carolina	21. Cincinnati
9. South Carolina	22. Penn St.	9. South Carolina	22. Clemson	9. Michigan	22. Clemson
10. Wisconsin	23. West Virginia	10. Wisconsin	23. Florida St.	10. Michigan St.	23. Florida St.
11. Virginia Tech	24. Texas	11. Michigan St.	24. Nebraska	11. Wisconsin	24. Nebraska
12. Baylor	25. Auburn	12. Michigan	25. Cincinnati	12. Baylor	25. BYU
13. Michigan		13. Baylor		13. TCU	

Note: BCS ranking is as of Dec. 4, 2011, prior to bowl games. Final AP and USA Today polls are as of Jan. 10, 2012 (after all bowl games).

Annual Results of Major Bowl Games

Dates indicate years the game was played; bowl games are generally played in late Dec. or early Jan.

Rose Bowl Results, 1935-2012

(Played in Pasadena, CA, unless otherwise noted; first played in 1902.)

1935	Alabama 29, Stanford 13	1961	Washington 17, Minnesota 7
1936	Stanford 7, SMU 0	1962	Minnesota 21, UCLA 3
1937	Pittsburgh 21, Washington 0	1963	USC 42, Wisconsin 37
1938	California 13, Alabama 0	1964	Illinois 17, Washington 7
1939	USC 7, Duke 3	1965	Michigan 34, Oregon St. 7
1940	USC 14, Tennessee 0	1966	UCLA 14, Michigan St. 12
1941	Stanford 21, Nebraska 13	1967	Purdue 14, USC 13
1942*	Oregon St. 20, Duke 16	1968	USC 14, Indiana 3
1943	Georgia 9, UCLA 0	1969	Ohio St. 27, USC 16
1944	USC 29, Washington 0	1970	USC 10, Michigan 3
1945	USC 25, Tennessee 0	1971	Stanford 27, Ohio St. 17
1946	Alabama 34, USC 14	1972	Stanford 13, Michigan 12
1947	Illinois 45, UCLA 14	1973	USC 42, Ohio St. 17
1948	Michigan 49, USC 0	1974	Ohio St. 42, USC 21
1949	Northwestern 20, California 14	1975	USC 18, Ohio St. 17
1950	Ohio St. 17, California 14	1976	UCLA 23, Ohio St. 10
1951	Michigan 14, California 6	1977	USC 14, Michigan 6
1952	Illinois 40, Stanford 7	1978	Washington 27, Michigan 20
1953	USC 7, Wisconsin 0	1979	USC 17, Michigan 10
1954	Michigan St. 28, UCLA 20	1980	USC 17, Ohio St. 16
1955	Ohio St. 20, USC 7	1981	Michigan 23, Washington 6
1956	Michigan St. 17, UCLA 14	1982	Washington 28, Iowa 0
1957	Iowa 35, Oregon St. 19	1983	UCLA 24, Michigan 14
1958	Ohio St. 10, Oregon 7	1984	UCLA 45, Illinois 9
1959	Iowa 38, California 12	1985	USC 20, Ohio St. 17
1960	Washington 44, Wisconsin 8	1986	UCLA 45, Iowa 28

1987	Arizona St. 22, Michigan 15
1988	Michigan St. 20, USC 17
1989	Michigan 22, USC 14
1990	USC 17, Michigan 10
1991	Washington 46, Iowa 34
1992	Washington 34, Michigan 14
1993	Michigan 38, Washington 31
1994	Wisconsin 21, UCLA 16
1995	Penn St. 38, Oregon 20
1996	USC 41, Northwestern 32
1997	Ohio St. 20, Arizona St. 17
1998	Michigan 21, Washington St. 16
1999	Wisconsin 38, UCLA 31
2000	Wisconsin 17, Stanford 9
2001	Washington 34, Purdue 24
2002	Miami (FL) 37, Nebraska 14
2003	Oklahoma 34, Washington St. 14
2004	USC 28, Michigan 14
2005	Texas 38, Michigan 37
2006	Texas 41, USC 38
2007	USC 32, Michigan 18
2008	USC 49, Illinois 17
2009	USC 38, Penn St. 24
2010	Ohio St. 26, Oregon 17
2011	TCU 21, Wisconsin 19
2012	Oregon 45, Wisconsin 38

*Played in Durham, NC.

Orange Bowl Results, 1935-2012

(Played in Miami or Miami Gardens, FL, since 1935.)

1935	(Jan.) Bucknell 26, Miami (FL) 0	1961	Missouri 21, Navy 14
1936	Catholic U. 20, Mississippi 19	1962	LSU 25, Colorado 7
1937	Duquesne 13, Mississippi St. 12	1963	Alabama 17, Oklahoma 0
1938	Auburn 6, Michigan St. 0	1964	Nebraska 13, Auburn 7
1939	Tennessee 17, Oklahoma 0	1965	Texas 21, Alabama 17
1940	Georgia Tech 21, Missouri 7	1966	Alabama 39, Nebraska 28
1941	Mississippi St. 14, Georgetown 7	1967	Florida 27, Georgia Tech 12
1942	Georgia 40, TCU 26	1968	Oklahoma 26, Tennessee 24
1943	Alabama 37, Boston Coll. 21	1969	Penn St. 15, Kansas 14
1944	LSU 19, Texas A&M 14	1970	Penn St. 10, Missouri 3
1945	Tulsa 26, Georgia Tech 12	1971	Nebraska 17, LSU 12
1946	Miami (FL) 13, Holy Cross 6	1972	Nebraska 38, Alabama 6
1947	Rice 8, Tennessee 0	1973	Nebraska 40, Notre Dame 6
1948	Georgia Tech 20, Kansas 14	1974	Penn St. 16, LSU 9
1949	Texas 41, Georgia 28	1975	Notre Dame 13, Alabama 11
1950	Santa Clara 21, Kentucky 13	1976	Oklahoma 14, Michigan 6
1951	Clemson 15, Miami (FL) 14	1977	Ohio St. 27, Colorado 10
1952	Georgia Tech 17, Baylor 14	1978	Arkansas 31, Oklahoma 6
1953	Alabama 61, Syracuse 6	1979	Oklahoma 31, Nebraska 24
1954	Oklahoma 7, Maryland 0	1980	Oklahoma 24, Florida St. 7
1955	Duke 34, Nebraska 7	1981	Oklahoma 18, Florida St. 17
1956	Oklahoma 20, Maryland 6	1982	Clemson 22, Nebraska 15
1957	Colorado 27, Clemson 21	1983	Nebraska 21, LSU 20
1958	Oklahoma 48, Duke 21	1984	Miami (FL) 31, Nebraska 30
1959	Oklahoma 21, Syracuse 6	1985	Washington 28, Oklahoma 17
1960	Georgia 14, Missouri 0	1986	Oklahoma 25, Penn St. 10

1987	Oklahoma 42, Arkansas 8
1988	Miami (FL) 20, Oklahoma 14
1989	Miami (FL) 23, Nebraska 3
1990	Notre Dame 21, Colorado 6
1991	Colorado 10, Notre Dame 9
1992	Miami (FL) 22, Nebraska 0
1993	Florida St. 27, Nebraska 14
1994	Florida St. 18, Nebraska 16
1995	Nebraska 24, Miami (FL) 17
1996	Florida St. 31, Notre Dame 26
1996	(Dec.) Nebraska 41, Virginia Tech 21
1998	Nebraska 42, Tennessee 17
1999	Florida 31, Syracuse 10
2000	Michigan 35, Alabama 34 (OT)
2001	Oklahoma 13, Florida St. 2
2002	Florida 56, Maryland 23
2003	USC 38, Iowa 17
2004	Miami (FL) 16, Florida St. 14
2005	USC 55, Oklahoma 19
2006	Penn St. 26, Florida St. 23 (3 OT)[1]
2007	Louisville 24, Wake Forest 13
2008	Kansas 24, Virginia Tech 21
2009	Virginia Tech 20, Cincinnati 7
2010	Iowa 24, Georgia Tech 14
2011	Stanford 40, Virginia Tech 12
2012	West Virginia 70, Clemson 33

(1) The NCAA vacated all of Penn State's 1998-2011 victories July 23, 2012, due to a child sexual abuse scandal at the school.

Sugar Bowl Results, 1935-2012

(Played in New Orleans, LA, unless otherwise noted.)

1935	(Jan.) Tulane 20, Temple 14	1961	Mississippi 14, Rice 6
1936	TCU 3, LSU 2	1962	Alabama 10, Arkansas 3
1937	Santa Clara 21, LSU 14	1963	Mississippi 17, Arkansas 13
1938	Santa Clara 6, LSU 0	1964	Alabama 12, Mississippi 7
1939	TCU 15, Carnegie Tech 7	1965	LSU 13, Syracuse 10
1940	Texas A&M 14, Tulane 13	1966	Missouri 20, Florida 18
1941	Boston Coll. 19, Tennessee 13	1967	Alabama 34, Nebraska 7
1942	Fordham 2, Missouri 0	1968	LSU 20, Wyoming 13
1943	Tennessee 14, Tulsa 7	1969	Arkansas 16, Georgia 2
1944	Georgia Tech 20, Tulsa 18	1970	Mississippi 27, Arkansas 22
1945	Duke 29, Alabama 26	1971	Tennessee 34, Air Force 13
1946	Oklahoma A&M 33, St. Mary's 13	1972	Oklahoma 40, Auburn 22
1947	Georgia 20, N. Carolina 10	1972	(Dec.) Oklahoma 14, Penn St. 0
1948	Texas 27, Alabama 7	1973	(Dec.) Notre Dame 24, Alabama 23
1949	Oklahoma 14, N. Carolina 6	1974	(Dec.) Nebraska 13, Florida 10
1950	Oklahoma 35, LSU 0	1975	(Dec.) Alabama 13, Penn St. 6
1951	Kentucky 13, Oklahoma 7	1977	Pittsburgh 27, Georgia 3
1952	Maryland 28, Tennessee 13	1978	Alabama 35, Ohio St. 6
1953	Georgia Tech 24, Mississippi 7	1979	Alabama 14, Penn St. 7
1954	Georgia Tech 42, West Virginia 19	1980	Alabama 24, Arkansas 9
1955	Navy 21, Mississippi 0	1981	Georgia 17, Notre Dame 10
1956	Georgia Tech 7, Pittsburgh 0	1982	Pittsburgh 24, Georgia 20
1957	Baylor 13, Tennessee 7	1983	Penn St. 27, Georgia 23
1958	Mississippi 39, Texas 7	1984	Auburn 9, Michigan 7
1959	LSU 7, Clemson 0	1985	Nebraska 28, LSU 10
1960	Mississippi 21, LSU 0	1986	Tennessee 35, Miami (FL) 7

1987	Nebraska 30, LSU 15
1988	Syracuse 16, Auburn 16
1989	Florida St. 13, Auburn 7
1990	Miami (FL) 33, Alabama 25
1991	Tennessee 23, Virginia 22
1992	Notre Dame 39, Florida 28
1993	Alabama 34, Miami (FL) 13
1994	Florida 41, West Virginia 7
1995	Florida St. 23, Florida 17
1995	(Dec.) Virginia Tech 28, Texas 10
1997	Florida 52, Florida St. 20
1998	Florida St. 31, Ohio St. 14
1999	Ohio St. 24, Texas A&M 14
2000	Florida St. 46, Virginia Tech 29
2001	Miami (FL) 37, Florida 20
2002	LSU 47, Illinois 34
2003	Georgia 26, Florida St. 13
2004	LSU 21, Oklahoma 14
2005	Auburn 16, Virginia Tech 13
2006*	West Virginia 38, Georgia 35
2007	LSU 41, Notre Dame 14
2008	Georgia 41, Hawaii 10
2009	Utah 31, Alabama 17
2010	Florida 51, Cincinnati 24
2011	Ohio St. 31, Arkansas 26
2012	Michigan 23, Virginia Tech 20

*Played in Atlanta, GA.

Other Bowl Results, Dec. 2011-Jan. 2012

Alamo Bowl, San Antonio, TX: Baylor 67, Washington 56
Armed Forces Bowl, Ft. Worth, TX: BYU 24, Tulsa 21
BBVA Compass Bowl, Birmingham, AL: SMU 28, Pittsburgh 6
Beef 'O' Brady's Bowl, St. Petersburg, FL: Marshall 20, Florida Intl. 10
Belk Bowl, Charlotte, NC: North Carolina St. 31, Louisville 24
Capital One Bowl, Orlando, FL: South Carolina 30, Nebraska 13
Champs Sports Bowl, Orlando, FL: Florida St. 18, Notre Dame 14
Chick-fil-A Bowl, Atlanta, GA: Auburn 43, Virginia 24
Cotton Bowl, Arlington, TX: Arkansas 29, Kansas St. 16
Fiesta Bowl, Glendale, AZ: Oklahoma St. 41, Stanford 38 (OT)
Gator Bowl, Jacksonville, FL: Florida 24, Ohio St. 17

GoDaddy.com Bowl, Mobile, AL: N. Illinois 38, Arkansas St. 20
Hawaii Bowl, Honolulu, HI: Southern Miss. 24, Nevada 17
Holiday Bowl, San Diego, CA: Texas 21, California 10
Idaho Potato Bowl, Boise, ID: Ohio 24, Utah St. 23
Independence Bowl, Shreveport, LA: Missouri 41, North Carolina 24
Insight Bowl, Tempe, AZ: Oklahoma 31, Iowa 14
Kraft Fight Hunger Bowl, San Francisco, CA: Illinois 20, UCLA 14
Liberty Bowl, Memphis, TN: Cincinnati 31, Vanderbilt 24
Little Caesars Bowl, Detroit, MI: Purdue 37, W. Michigan 32
MAACO Las Vegas Bowl, Las Vegas, NV: Boise St. 56, Arizona St. 24

Meineke Car Care Bowl of Texas, Houston, TX: Texas A&M 33, Northwestern 22
Military Bowl, Washington, DC: Toledo 42, Air Force 41
Music City Bowl, Nashville, TN: Mississippi 23, Wake Forest 17
New Mexico Bowl, Albuquerque, NM: Temple 37, Wyoming 15
New Orleans Bowl, New Orleans, LA: LA-Lafayette 32, San Diego St. 30
Outback Bowl, Tampa, FL: Michigan St. 33, Georgia 30 (3 OT)
Pinstripe Bowl, Bronx, NY: Rutgers 27, Iowa St. 13
Poinsettia Bowl, San Diego, CA: TCU 31, Louisiana Tech 24
Sun Bowl, El Paso, TX: Utah 30, Georgia Tech 27 (OT)
TicketCity Bowl, Dallas, TX: Houston 30, Penn St. 14

All-Time NCAA Bowl Subdivision (FBS) Statistical Leaders

Career Rushing Yards

Player, team	Yrs.	Carries	Yds.	Avg.
Ron Dayne, Wisconsin	1996-99	1,115	6,397	5.74
Ricky Williams, Texas	1995-98	1,011	6,279	6.21
Tony Dorsett, Pittsburgh	1973-76	1,074	6,082	5.66
DeAngelo Williams, Memphis	2002-05	969	6,026	6.22
Charles White, USC	1976-79	1,023	5,598	5.47

Career Passing Yards

Player, team	Yrs.	Comp./att.	Yds.
Case Keenum, Houston	2007-11	1,546/2,229	19,217
Timmy Chang, Hawaii	2000-04	1,388/2,436	17,072
Graham Harrell, Texas Tech	2005-08	1,403/2,010	15,793
Ty Detmer, BYU	1988-91	958/1,530	15,031
Kellen Moore, Boise St.	2008-11	1,157/1,658	14,667

Career Rushing Yards/Game (min. 2,500 yds.)

Player, team	Yrs.	Carries	Yds.	Avg./game
Ed Marinaro, Cornell	1969-71	918	4,715	174.6
O. J. Simpson, USC	1967-68	621	3,214	164.4
Herschel Walker, Georgia . . .	1980-82	994	5,259	159.4
Garrett Wolfe, N. Illinois. . . .	2004-06	807	5,164	156.5
LeShon Johnson, N. Illinois . .	1992-93	592	3,314	150.6

Career Receiving Yards

Player, team	Yrs.	Rec.	Yds.	Avg.
Trevor Insley, Nevada	1996-99	298	5,005	16.8
Ryan Broyles, Oklahoma	2008-11	349	4,586	13.1
Marcus Harris, Wyoming. . . .	1993-96	259	4,518	17.4
Rashaun Woods, Oklahoma St.	2000-03	293	4,414	15.1
Ryan Yarborough, Wyoming	1990-93	229	4,357	19.0

Note: As of end of 2011 season. Prior to 2002, postseason games were not included in NCAA final football statistics or records. All postseason games were included for the 2002 season and thereafter. Career rushing yards per game rankings do not include active players.

All-Time Bowl Subdivision (FBS) Team Won-Lost Records

Team	Years	Won	Lost	Tied	Pct.	Total	Team	Years	Won	Lost	Tied	Pct.	Total
Michigan	132	895	310	36	0.736	1,241	Florida St.[1].	65	473	235	17	0.664	725
Notre Dame.	123	853	300	42	0.731	1,195	Penn St.[2].	125	715	361	41	0.658	1,117
Boise St. (1996). . .	44	377	146	2	0.720	525	LSU	118	733	390	47	0.647	1,170
Oklahoma	117	821	307	53	0.718	1,181	Georgia	118	747	400	54	0.644	1,201
Texas.	119	858	330	33	0.716	1,221	Miami-FL	86	574	326	19	0.635	919
Ohio St.[1]	122	824	316	53	0.713	1,206	Auburn.	119	711	405	47	0.632	1,163
Alabama[1].	117	814	320	43	0.710	1,177	Florida	105	669	385	40	0.630	1,094
USC[1]	119	779	314	54	0.703	1,147	Miami-OH	123	664	402	44	0.618	1,110
Nebraska.	122	846	349	40	0.701	1,235	Washington	122	670	418	50	0.611	1,138
Tennessee	115	794	347	53	0.687	1,194	South Fla. (2000)..	15	108	69	0	0.610	177

Note: As of end of 2011 season. Includes records as senior college only. Bowl and playoff games are included, and each tie game is computed as half won and half lost. Teams listed with years in parentheses indicates reclassification to Bowl Subdivision (FBS), formerly Division I-A. The year in parentheses is the first year of FBS membership. Tiebreaker rule began with 1996 season. (1) Record adjusted by action of the NCAA Committee on Infractions. (2) Does not include 111 Penn St. 1998-2011 victories, which the NCAA vacated July 23, 2012, due to a child sexual abuse scandal at the school.

Heisman Trophy Winners, 1935-2011

Awarded annually to the nation's outstanding college football player by the Downtown Athletic Club.

Year	Winner, school, position	Year	Winner, school, position	Year	Winner, school, position
1935	Jay Berwanger, Chicago, HB	1961	Ernest Davis, Syracuse, HB	1987	Tim Brown, Notre Dame, WR
1936	Larry Kelley, Yale, E	1962	Terry Baker, Oregon St., QB	1988	Barry Sanders, Oklahoma St., RB
1937	Clinton Frank, Yale, HB	1963	Roger Staubach, Navy, QB	1989	Andre Ware, Houston, QB
1938	David O'Brien, Texas Christian, QB	1964	John Huarte, Notre Dame, QB	1990	Ty Detmer, BYU, QB
1939	Nile Kinnick, Iowa, HB	1965	Mike Garrett, USC, HB	1991	Desmond Howard, Michigan, WR
1940	Tom Harmon, Michigan, HB	1966	Steve Spurrier, Florida, QB	1992	Gino Torretta, Miami (FL), QB
1941	Bruce Smith, Minnesota, HB	1967	Gary Beban, UCLA, QB	1993	Charlie Ward, Florida St., QB
1942	Frank Sinkwich, Georgia, HB	1968	O. J. Simpson, USC, RB	1994	Rashaan Salaam, Colorado, RB
1943	Angelo Bertelli, Notre Dame, QB	1969	Steve Owens, Oklahoma, RB	1995	Eddie George, Ohio St., RB
1944	Leslie Horvath, Ohio St., QB	1970	Jim Plunkett, Stanford, QB	1996	Danny Wuerffel, Florida, QB
1945	Felix Blanchard, Army, FB	1971	Pat Sullivan, Auburn, QB	1997	Charles Woodson, Michigan, CB
1946	Glenn Davis, Army, HB	1972	Johnny Rodgers, Nebraska, RB-WR	1998	Ricky Williams, Texas, RB
1947	John Lujack, Notre Dame, QB	1973	John Cappelletti, Penn St., RB	1999	Ron Dayne, Wisconsin, RB
1948	Doak Walker, SMU, HB	1974	Archie Griffin, Ohio St., RB	2000	Chris Weinke, Florida St., QB
1949	Leon Hart, Notre Dame, E	1975	Archie Griffin, Ohio St., RB	2001	Eric Crouch, Nebraska, QB
1950	Vic Janowicz, Ohio St., HB	1976	Tony Dorsett, Pittsburgh, RB	2002	Carson Palmer, USC, QB
1951	Richard Kazmaier, Princeton, HB	1977	Earl Campbell, Texas, RB	2003	Jason White, Oklahoma, QB
1952	Billy Vessels, Oklahoma, HB	1978	Billy Sims, Oklahoma, RB	2004	Matt Leinart, USC, QB
1953	John Lattner, Notre Dame, HB	1979	Charles White, USC, RB	2005	Reggie Bush, USC, RB[1]
1954	Alan Ameche, Wisconsin, FB	1980	George Rogers, S. Carolina, RB	2006	Troy Smith, Ohio State, QB
1955	Howard Cassady, Ohio St., HB	1981	Marcus Allen, USC, RB	2007	Tim Tebow, Florida, QB
1956	Paul Hornung, Notre Dame, QB	1982	Herschel Walker, Georgia, RB	2008	Sam Bradford, Oklahoma, QB
1957	John Crow, Texas A&M, HB	1983	Mike Rozier, Nebraska, RB	2009	Mark Ingram, Alabama, RB
1958	Pete Dawkins, Army, HB	1984	Doug Flutie, Boston College, QB	2010	Cam Newton, Auburn, QB
1959	Billy Cannon, LSU, HB	1985	Bo Jackson, Auburn, RB	2011	Robert Griffin III, Baylor, QB
1960	Joe Bellino, Navy, HB	1986	Vinny Testaverde, Miami (FL), QB		

(1) Bush forfeited the trophy voluntarily Sept. 14, 2010, following revelations of NCAA rules violations while Bush was at USC.

All-Time Bowl Subdivision (FBS) Coaching Victories

Bobby Bowden	377	Bo Schembechler	234	Jim Sweeney	200	John Heisman 186
Paul "Bear" Bryant	323	Hayden Fry	232	Dana X. Bible	198	Johnny Majors 185
Glenn "Pop" Warner	319	Jim Tressel	229	Fielding Yost	198	Darrell Royal 184
Amos Alonzo Stagg	314	**Chris Ault**	226	Dan McGugin	197	Dick Tomey 183
Joe Paterno	298[1]	**Mack Brown**	227	**Steve Spurrier**	197	Gil Dobie 180
LaVell Edwards	257	Jess Neely	207	Howard Jones	194	Jackie Sherrill 180
Tom Osborne	255	Warren Woodson	203	John Cooper	192	Carl Snavely 180
Frank Beamer	251	Don Nehlen	202	John Vaught	190	Jerry Claiborne 179
Lou Holtz	249	Eddie Anderson	201	George Welsh	188	Carmen Cozza 179
Woody Hayes	238	Vince Dooley	201	Dennis Franchione	187	Ben Schwartzwalder 178

Note: Coaches active in 2011 shown in bold. Total victories through Jan. 10, 2012, including bowl games; coaches must have at least 10 seasons coaching BCS schools to be eligible. (1) Does not include Paterno's 111 victories at Penn St. 1998-2011, which were vacated by the NCAA July 23, 2012, because of a child sexual abuse scandal at the school.

College Football Coach of the Year, 1935-2011

The Coach of the Year has been selected by the American Football Coaches Assn. (AFCA) since 1935 as well as the Football Writers Assn. of America (FWAA) since 1957. When polls disagree, both winners are indicated.

1935 Lynn Waldorf, Northwestern
1936 Dick Harlow, Harvard
1937 Edward Mylin, Lafayette
1938 Bill Kern, Carnegie Tech
1939 Eddie Anderson, Iowa
1940 Clark Shaughnessy, Stanford
1941 Frank Leahy, Notre Dame
1942 Bill Alexander, Georgia Tech
1943 Amos Alonzo Stagg, Pacific (CA)
1944 Carroll Widdoes, Ohio St.
1945 Bo McMillin, Indiana
1946 Earl "Red" Blaik, Army
1947 Fritz Crisler, Michigan
1948 Bennie Oosterbaan, Michigan
1949 Bud Wilkinson, Oklahoma
1950 Charlie Caldwell, Princeton
1951 Chuck Taylor, Stanford
1952 Biggie Munn, Michigan St.
1953 Jim Tatum, Maryland
1954 Henry "Red" Sanders, UCLA
1955 Duffy Daugherty, Michigan St.
1956 Bowden Wyatt, Tennessee
1957 Woody Hayes, Ohio St.
1958 Paul Dietzel, LSU
1959 Ben Schwartzwalder, Syracuse
1960 Murray Warmath, Minnesota
1961 Paul "Bear" Bryant, Alabama (AFCA); Darrell Royal, Texas (FWAA)
1962 John McKay, USC
1963 Darrell Royal, Texas
1964 Ara Parseghian, Notre Dame, & Frank Broyles, Arkansas (AFCA); Ara Parseghian (FWAA)
1965 Tommy Prothro, UCLA (AFCA); Duffy Daugherty, Mich. St. (FWAA)

1966 Tom Cahill, Army
1967 John Pont, Indiana
1968 Joe Paterno, Penn St. (AFCA); Woody Hayes, Ohio St. (FWAA)
1969 Bo Schembechler, Michigan
1970 Charles McClendon, LSU, & Darrell Royal, Texas (AFCA); Alex Agase, Northwestern (FWAA)
1971 Paul "Bear" Bryant, Alabama (AFCA); Bob Devaney, Nebraska (FWAA)
1972 John McKay, USC
1973 Paul "Bear" Bryant, Alabama (AFCA); Johnny Majors, Pittsburgh (FWAA)
1974 Grant Teaff, Baylor
1975 Frank Kush, Arizona St. (AFCA); Woody Hayes, Ohio St. (FWAA)
1976 Johnny Majors, Pittsburgh
1977 Don James, Washington (AFCA); Lou Holtz, Arkansas (FWAA)
1978 Joe Paterno, Penn St.
1979 Earle Bruce, Ohio St.
1980 Vince Dooley, Georgia
1981 Danny Ford, Clemson
1982 Joe Paterno, Penn St.
1983 Ken Hatfield, Air Force (AFCA); Howard Schnellenberger, Miami (FL) (FWAA)
1984 LaVell Edwards, Brigham Young
1985 Fisher De Berry, Air Force
1986 Joe Paterno, Penn St.
1987 Dick MacPherson, Syracuse
1988 Don Nehlen, W. Virginia (AFCA); Lou Holtz, Notre Dame (FWAA)
1989 Bill McCartney, Colorado

1990 Bobby Ross, Georgia Tech
1991 Don James, Washington
1992 Gene Stallings, Alabama
1993 Barry Alvarez, Wisconsin (AFCA); Terry Bowden, Auburn (FWAA)
1994 Tom Osborne, Nebraska (AFCA); Rich Brooks, Oregon (FWAA)
1995 Gary Barnett, Northwestern
1996 Bruce Snyder, Arizona St.
1997 Mike Price, Washington St.
1998 Phillip Fulmer, Tennessee
1999 Frank Beamer, Virginia Tech
2000 Bob Stoops, Oklahoma
2001 Larry Coker, Miami (FL), & Ralph Friedgen, Maryland (AFCA); Ralph Friedgen, Maryland (FWAA)
2002 Jim Tressel, Ohio St.
2003 Pete Carroll, USC (AFCA); Nick Saban, LSU (FWAA)
2004 Tommy Tuberville, Auburn (AFCA); Urban Meyer, Utah (FWAA)
2005 Joe Paterno, Penn St. (AFCA); Charlie Weis, Notre Dame (FWAA)
2006 Jim Grobe, Wake Forest (AFCA); Greg Schiano, Rutgers (FWAA)
2007 Mark Mangino, Kansas
2008 Kyle Whittingham, Utah (AFCA); Nick Saban, Alabama (FWAA)
2009 Gary Patterson, TCU
2010 Chip Kelly, Oregon
2011 Les Miles, LSU (AFCA); Mike Gundy, Oklahoma St. (FWAA)

NCAA Div. I-A (FBS) Football Conference Champions, 1980-2011

Atlantic Coast
1980 North Carolina
1981 Clemson
1982 Clemson
1983 Maryland
1984 Maryland
1985 Maryland
1986 Clemson
1987 Clemson
1988 Clemson
1989 Virginia, Duke
1990 Georgia Tech
1991 Clemson
1992 Florida St.
1993 Florida St.
1994 Florida St.
1995 Virginia, Florida St.
1996 Florida St.
1997 Florida St.
1998 Florida St., Georgia Tech
1999 Florida St.
2000 Florida St.
2001 Maryland
2002 Florida St.
2003 Florida St.
2004 Virginia Tech
2005 Florida St.
2006 Wake Forest
2007 Virginia Tech
2008 Virginia Tech
2009 Georgia Tech
2010 Virginia Tech
2011 Clemson

Big East
1991 Miami (FL), Syracuse
1992 Miami (FL)

1993 West Virginia
1994 Miami (FL)
1995 Virginia Tech, Miami (FL)
1996 Virginia Tech, Miami (FL), Syracuse
1997 Syracuse
1998 Syracuse
1999 Virginia Tech
2000 Miami (FL)
2001 Miami (FL)
2002 Miami (FL)
2003 Miami (FL), West Virginia
2004 Boston Coll., Pittsburgh, Syracuse, West Virginia
2005 West Virginia
2006 Louisville
2007 Connecticut, West Virginia
2008 Cincinnati
2009 Cincinnati
2010 Connecticut, Pittsburgh, West Virginia
2011 Cincinnati, Louisville, West Virginia

Big Ten
1980 Michigan
1981 Iowa, Ohio St.
1982 Michigan
1983 Illinois
1984 Ohio St.
1985 Iowa
1986 Michigan, Ohio St.

1987 Michigan St.
1988 Michigan
1989 Michigan
1990 Iowa, Illinois, Mich., Michigan St.
1991 Michigan
1992 Michigan
1993 Ohio St., Wisconsin
1994 Penn St.
1995 Northwestern
1996 Northwestern, Ohio St.
1997 Michigan
1998 Michigan, Ohio St., Wisconsin
1999 Wisconsin
2000 Michigan, Northwestern, Purdue
2001 Illinois
2002 Iowa, Ohio St.
2003 Michigan
2004 Iowa, Michigan
2005 Ohio St., Penn St.[1]
2006 Ohio St.
2007 Ohio St.
2008 Ohio St., Penn St.[1]
2009 Ohio St.
2010 Michigan St., Ohio St., Wisconsin
2011 Wisconsin

Big 12
1996 Texas
1997 Nebraska
1998 Texas A&M
1999 Nebraska
2000 Oklahoma

2001 Colorado
2002 Oklahoma
2003 Kansas St.
2004 Oklahoma
2005 Texas
2006 Oklahoma
2007 Oklahoma
2008 Oklahoma
2009 Texas
2010 Oklahoma
2011 Oklahoma St.

Conference USA
1996 Houston, Southern Miss.
1997 Southern Miss.
1998 Tulane
1999 Southern Miss.
2000 Louisville
2001 Louisville
2002 Cincinnati, TCU
2003 Southern Miss.
2004 Louisville
2005 Tulsa
2006 Houston
2007 Central Florida
2008 East Carolina
2009 East Carolina
2010 Central Florida
2011 Southern Miss.

Mid-American Athletic
1980 Central Michigan
1981 Toledo
1982 Bowling Green
1983 Northern Illinois
1984 Toledo
1985 Bowling Green
1986 Miami (OH)
1987 E. Michigan

1988 W. Michigan
1989 Ball St.
1990 Central Michigan
1991 Bowling Green
1992 Bowling Green
1993 Ball St.
1994 Central Michigan
1995 Toledo
1996 Ball St.
1997 Marshall
1998 Marshall
1999 Marshall
2000 Marshall
2001 Toledo
2002 Marshall
2003 Miami (OH)
2004 Toledo
2005 Akron
2006 Central Michigan
2007 Central Michigan
2008 Buffalo
2009 Central Michigan
2010 Miami (OH)
2011 Northern Illinois

Mountain West
1999 BYU, Colorado St., Utah
2000 Colorado St.
2001 BYU
2002 Colorado St.
2003 Utah
2004 Utah
2005 TCU
2006 BYU, TCU
2007 BYU
2008 Utah
2009 TCU
2010 TCU
2011 TCU

Pac-12
1980 Washington
1981 Washington
1982 UCLA
1983 UCLA
1984 USC
1985 UCLA
1986 Arizona St.
1987 UCLA, USC
1988 USC
1989 USC
1990 Washington
1991 Washington
1992 Stanford, Washington
1993 Arizona, UCLA, USC
1994 Oregon
1995 USC, Washington
1996 Arizona St.
1997 UCLA, Washington St.
1998 UCLA
1999 Stanford
2000 Oregon, Oregon St., Washington

2001 Oregon
2002 USC, Washington St.
2003 USC
2004 USC
2005 USC
2006 California, USC
2007 Arizona St., USC
2008 USC
2009 Oregon
2010 Oregon
2011 Oregon

Southeastern
1980 Georgia
1981 Alabama, Georgia
1982 Georgia
1983 Auburn
1984 Florida (title vacated)
1985 Tennessee
1986 LSU
1987 Auburn
1988 Auburn, LSU
1989 Ala., Auburn, Tenn.
1990 Tennessee
1991 Florida
1992 Alabama

1993 Florida
1994 Florida
1995 Florida
1996 Florida
1997 Tennessee
1998 Tennessee
1999 Alabama
2000 Florida
2001 LSU
2002 Georgia
2003 LSU
2004 Auburn
2005 Georgia
2006 Florida
2007 LSU
2008 Florida
2009 Alabama
2010 Auburn
2011 LSU

Sun Belt
2001 Middle Tenn. St., North Texas
2002 North Texas
2003 North Texas
2004 North Texas

2005 Arkansas St., LA-Lafayette, LA-Monroe
2006 Middle Tenn. St., Troy
2007 Florida Atlantic, Troy
2008 Troy
2009 Troy
2010 Florida Intl., Troy
2011 Arkansas St.

Western Athletic
1980 Brigham Young (BYU)
1981 BYU
1982 BYU
1983 BYU
1984 BYU
1985 Air Force, BYU
1986 San Diego St.
1987 Wyoming
1988 Wyoming
1989 BYU
1990 BYU
1991 BYU

1992 BYU, Fresno St., Hawaii
1993 BYU, Fresno St., Wyoming
1994 Colorado St.
1995 Air Force, BYU, Colorado St., Utah
1996 BYU
1997 Colorado St.
1998 Air Force
1999 Fresno St., Hawaii, TCU
2000 TCU, UTEP
2001 Louisiana Tech
2002 Boise St.
2003 Boise St.
2004 Boise St.
2005 Boise St., Nevada
2006 Boise St.
2007 Hawaii
2008 Boise St.
2009 Boise St.
2010 Boise St., Hawaii, Nevada
2011 Louisiana Tech

(1) On July 23, 2012, the NCAA vacated all of Penn State's football victories between 1998 and 2011 due to a child sexual abuse scandal at the school.

NCAA Div. I-AA (FCS) Football Conference Champions, 1990-2011

Big Sky
1990 Nevada
1991 Nevada
1992 Eastern Wash., Idaho
1993 Montana
1994 Boise St.
1995 Montana
1996 Montana
1997 Eastern Wash.
1998 Montana
1999 Montana
2000 Montana
2001 Montana
2002 Idaho St., Montana, Montana St.
2003 Montana, Montana St., No. Arizona
2004 Eastern Wash., Montana
2005 Eastern Wash., Montana, Montana St.
2006 Montana
2007 Montana
2008 Montana, Weber St.
2009 Montana
2010 Eastern Wash., Montana St.
2011 Montana, Montana St.

Big South
2002 Gardner-Webb
2003 Gardner-Webb
2004 Coastal Carolina
2005 Charleston Southern, Coastal Carolina
2006 Coastal Carolina
2007 Liberty
2008 Liberty
2009 Liberty, Stony Brook
2010 Coastal Carolina, Liberty, Stony Brook
2011 Stony Brook

Colonial Athletic Association
2007 Massachusetts, Richmond
2008 James Madison
2009 Richmond, Villanova
2010 Delaware, William & Mary
2011 Towson

Great West
2004 Cal. Poly
2005 Cal. Poly, UC Davis
2006 North Dakota St.
2007 South Dakota St.
2008 Cal. Poly
2009 UC Davis
2010 Southern Utah
2011 Cal Poly, North Dakota

Ivy League
1990 Cornell, Dartmouth
1991 Dartmouth
1992 Dartmouth, Princeton
1993 Pennsylvania
1994 Pennsylvania
1995 Princeton
1996 Dartmouth
1997 Harvard
1998 Pennsylvania
1999 Brown, Yale
2000 Pennsylvania
2001 Harvard
2002 Pennsylvania
2003 Pennsylvania
2004 Harvard
2005 Brown
2006 Princeton, Yale
2007 Harvard
2008 Harvard, Brown
2009 Pennsylvania
2010 Pennsylvania
2011 Harvard

Mid-Eastern Athletic
1990 Florida A&M
1991 North Carolina A&T
1992 North Carolina A&T
1993 Howard
1994 South Carolina St.
1995 Florida A&M
1996 Florida A&M
1997 Hampton
1998 Florida A&M, Hampton
1999 North Carolina A&T
2000 Florida A&M
2001 Florida A&M
2002 Bethune-Cookman
2003 North Carolina A&T
2004 Hampton, South Carolina St.
2005 Hampton
2006 Hampton
2007 Delaware St.
2008 South Carolina St.
2009 South Carolina St.
2010 Bethune-Cookman, Florida A&M, South Carolina St.
2011 Norfolk St.

Missouri Valley
1990 Northern Iowa
1991 Northern Iowa
1992 Northern Iowa
1993 Northern Iowa
1994 Northern Iowa
1995 Eastern Illinois, Northern Iowa
1996 Northern Iowa
1997 Western Illinois
1998 Western Illinois
1999 Illinois St.
2000 Western Illinois

2001 Northern Iowa
2002 W. Illinois, W. Kentucky
2003 N. Iowa, S. Illinois
2004 Southern Illinois
2005 N. Iowa, S. Illinois, Youngstown St.
2006 Youngstown St.
2007 Northern Iowa
2008 N. Iowa, S. Illinois
2009 Southern Illinois
2010 Northern Iowa
2011 North Dakota St., Northern Iowa

Northeast
1996 Monmouth, Robert Morris
1997 Robert Morris
1998 Monmouth, Robert Morris
1999 Robert Morris
2000 Robert Morris
2001 Sacred Heart
2002 Albany
2003 Albany, Monmouth
2004 Central Conn. St., Monmouth
2005 Central Conn. St., Stony Brook
2006 Monmouth
2007 Albany
2008 Albany
2009 Central Conn. St.
2010 Central Conn. St., Robert Morris
2011 Albany, Duquesne

Ohio Valley
1990 E. Kentucky, Middle Tenn. St.
1991 Eastern Kentucky
1992 Middle Tenn. St.
1993 Eastern Kentucky
1994 Eastern Kentucky
1995 Murray St.
1996 Murray St.
1997 Eastern Kentucky
1998 Tennessee St.
1999 Tennessee St.
2000 Western Kentucky
2001 Eastern Illinois
2002 Eastern Illinois, Murray St.
2003 Jacksonville St.
2004 Jacksonville St.
2005 Eastern Illinois
2006 Eastern Illinois, Tenn.-Martin
2007 Eastern Kentucky
2008 Eastern Kentucky
2009 Eastern Kentucky
2010 SE Missouri St.
2011 Eastern Kentucky, Jacksonville St., Tennessee Tech

Patriot
1990 Holy Cross
1991 Holy Cross
1992 Lafayette
1993 Lehigh
1994 Lafayette
1995 Lehigh
1996 Bucknell
1997 Colgate
1998 Lehigh
1999 Colgate, Lehigh
2000 Lehigh
2001 Lehigh
2002 Colgate, Fordham
2003 Colgate
2004 Lafayette, Lehigh
2005 Colgate, Lafayette
2006 Colgate, Lafayette, Lehigh
2007 Fordham
2008 Colgate
2009 Holy Cross
2010 Lehigh
2011 Lehigh

Pioneer
1993 Dayton
1994 Butler, Dayton
1995 Drake
1996 Dayton
1997 Dayton
1998 Drake
1999 Dayton
2000 Dayton, Drake, Valparaiso
2001 Dayton
2002 Dayton
2003 Valparaiso
2004 Drake
2005 San Diego
2006 San Diego
2007 Dayton, San Diego
2008 Jacksonville
2009 Butler, Dayton
2010 Dayton, Jacksonville
2011 Drake, San Diego

Southern
1990 Furman
1991 Appalachian St.
1992 Citadel
1993 Georgia Southern
1994 Marshall
1995 Appalachian St.
1996 Marshall
1997 Georgia Southern
1998 Georgia Southern
1999 Appalachian St., Furman, Georgia Southern
2000 Georgia Southern
2001 Furman, Southern
2002 Georgia Southern
2003 Wofford

2004 Furman, Georgia Southern
2005 Appalachian St.
2006 Appalachian St.
2007 Appalachian St., Wofford
2008 Appalachian St.
2009 Appalachian St.
2010 Appalachian St., Wofford
2011 Georgia Southern

Southland
1990 La.-Monroe
1991 McNeese St.
1992 La.-Monroe
1993 McNeese St.
1994 North Texas
1995 McNeese St.
1996 Troy St.
1997 McNeese St., Northwestern St.
1998 Northwestern St.
1999 Stephen F. Austin, Troy
2000 Troy
2001 McNeese St., Sam Houston St.
2002 McNeese St.
2003 McNeese St.
2004 Northwestern St., Sam Houston St.
2005 Nicholls St., Texas St.
2006 McNeese St.
2007 McNeese St.
2008 Texas St.
2009 McNeese St., Stephen F. Austin
2010 Stephen F. Austin
2011 Sam Houston St.

Southwestern Athletic
1990 Jackson St.
1991 Alabama St.
1992 Alcorn St.
1993 Southern
1994 Alcorn St., Grambling St.
1995 Jackson St.
1996 Jackson St.
1997 Southern
1998 Southern
1999 Southern
2000 Grambling St.
2001 Grambling St.
2002 Grambling St.
2003 Southern
2004 Alabama St.
2005 Grambling St.
2006 Alabama A&M
2007 Jackson St.
2008 Grambling St.
2009 Prairie View A&M
2010 Texas Southern
2011 Grambling St.

Note: Missouri Valley Conference was known as Gateway Football Conference, 1992-2007, and as Gateway Collegiate Athletic Conference, 1985-91.

Selected NCAA Division I Teams

(Conferences and coaches listed are as of Aug. 2012)

Team	Nickname	Team colors	Conference	Basketball coach	Football coach
Air Force	Falcons	Blue & silver	Mountain West	Dave Pilipovich	Troy Calhoun
Akron	Zips	Blue & gold	Mid-American	Keith Dambrot	Terry Bowden
Alabama	Crimson Tide	Crimson & white	Southeastern	Anthony Grant	Nick Saban
Appalachian State*	Mountaineers	Black & gold	Southern	Jason Capel	Jerry Moore
Arizona	Wildcats	Cardinal & navy	Pac-12	Sean Miller	Rich Rodriguez
Arizona State	Sun Devils	Maroon & gold	Pac-12	Herb Sendek	Todd Graham
Arkansas	Razorbacks	Cardinal & white	Southeastern	Mike Anderson	John L. Smith
Arkansas State	Red Wolves	Scarlet & black	Sun Belt	John Brady	Gus Malzahn
Army	Black Knights	Black, gold, & gray	Independent#	Zach Spiker	Rich Ellerson
Auburn	Tigers	Burnt orange & navy	Southeastern	Tony Barbee	Gene Chizik
Ball State	Cardinals	Cardinal & white	Mid-American	Billy Taylor	Pete Lembo
Baylor	Bears	Green & gold	Big 12	Scott Drew	Art Briles
Boise State	Broncos	Blue & orange	Mountain West	Leon Rice	Chris Petersen
Boston College	Eagles	Maroon & gold	Atlantic Coast	Steve Donahue	Frank Spaziani
Bowling Green	Falcons	Orange & brown	Mid-American	Louis Orr	Dave Clawson
Brigham Young (BYU)	Cougars	Dark blue & white	Independent#	Dave Rose	Bronco Mendenhall
Brown*	Bears	Brown, cardinal, & white	Ivy League	Mike Martin	Phil Estes
California	Golden Bears	Blue & gold	Pac-12	Mike Montgomery	Jeff Tedford
Central Michigan	Chippewas	Maroon & gold	Mid-American	Keno Davis	Dan Enos
Cincinnati	Bearcats	Red & black	Big East	Mick Cronin	Butch Jones
Citadel*	Bulldogs	Citadel blue & white	Southern	Chuck Driesell	Kevin Higgins
Clemson	Tigers	Burnt orange & purple	Atlantic Coast	Brad Brownell	Dabo Swinney
Colgate*	Raiders	Maroon & white	Patriot League	Matt Langel	Dick Biddle
Colorado	Buffaloes	Silver, gold, & black	Pac-12	Tad Boyle	Jon Embree
Colorado State	Rams	Green & gold	Mountain West	Larry Eustachy	Jim McElwain
Columbia*	Lions	Columbia blue & white	Ivy League	Kyle Smith	Pete Mangurian
Connecticut	Huskies	Blue & white	Big East	Jim Calhoun	Paul Pasqualoni
Cornell*	Big Red	Carnelian & white	Ivy League	Bill Courtney	Kent Austin
Dartmouth*	Big Green	Dartmouth green & white	Ivy League	Paul Cormier	Buddy Teevens
Delaware*	Fightin' Blue Hens	Blue & gold	Colonial Athletic	Monté Ross	K. C. Keeler
Duke	Blue Devils	Duke blue & white	Atlantic Coast	Mike Krzyzewski	David Cutcliffe
East Carolina	Pirates	Purple & gold	Conference USA	Jeff Lebo	Ruffin McNeill
Eastern Illinois*	Panthers	Blue & gray	Ohio Valley	Jay Spoonhur	Dino Babers
Eastern Kentucky*	Colonels	Maroon & white	Ohio Valley	Jeff Neubauer	Dean Hood
Eastern Michigan	Eagles	Green & white	Mid-American	Rob Murphy	Ron English
Eastern Washington*	Eagles	Red & white	Big Sky	Jim Hayford	Beau Baldwin
Florida	Gators	Orange & blue	Southeastern	Billy Donovan	Will Muschamp
Florida A&M*	Rattlers	Orange & green	Mid-Eastern Athletic	Clemon Johnson	Joe Taylor
Florida State	Seminoles	Garnet & gold	Atlantic Coast	Leonard Hamilton	Jimbo Fisher
Fresno State	Bulldogs	Red & blue	Mountain West	Rodney Terry	Tim DeRuyter
Furman*	Paladins	Purple & white	Southern	Jeff Jackson	Bruce Fowler
Georgia	Bulldogs	Red & black	Southeastern	Mark Fox	Mark Richt
Georgia Southern*	Eagles	Blue & white	Southern	Charlton Young	Jeff Monken
Georgia Tech	Yellow Jackets	Old gold & white	Atlantic Coast	Brian Gregory	Paul Johnson
Harvard*	Crimson	Crimson, black, & white	Ivy League	Tommy Amaker	Tim Murphy
Hawaii	Warriors	Green, black, white, silver	Mountain West#	Gib Arnold	Norm Chow
Holy Cross*	Crusaders	Royal purple	Patriot League	Milan Brown	Tom Gilmore
Houston	Cougars	Scarlet & white	Conference USA	James Dickey	Tony Levine
Howard*	Bison	Blue & white	Mid-Eastern Athletic	Kevin Nickelberry	Gary Harrell
Idaho	Vandals	Silver & gold	Western Athletic	Don Verlin	Robb Akey
Illinois	Fighting Illini	Orange & blue	Big Ten	John Groce	Tim Beckman
Illinois State*	Redbirds	Red & white	Missouri Valley	Dan Miller	Brock Spack
Indiana	Hoosiers	Cream & crimson	Big Ten	Tom Crean	Kevin Wilson
Indiana State*	Sycamores	Blue & white	Missouri Valley	Greg Lansing	Trent Miles
Iowa	Hawkeyes	Old gold & black	Big Ten	Fran McCaffery	Kirk Ferentz
Iowa State	Cyclones	Cardinal & gold	Big 12	Fred Hoiberg	Paul Rhoads
Jackson State*	Tigers	Blue & white	Southwestern Athletic	Tevester Anderson	Rick Comegy
James Madison*	Dukes	Purple & gold	Colonial Athletic	Matt Brady	Mickey Matthews
Kansas	Jayhawks	Crimson & blue	Big 12	Bill Self	Charlie Weis
Kansas State	Wildcats	Purple & white	Big 12	Bruce Weber	Bill Snyder
Kent State	Golden Flashes	Navy blue & gold	Mid-American	Rob Senderoff	Darrell Hazell
Kentucky	Wildcats	Blue & white	Southeastern	John Calipari	Joker Phillips
Lafayette*	Leopards	Maroon & white	Patriot League	Fran O'Hanlon	Frank Tavani
Lehigh*	Mountain Hawks	Brown & white	Patriot League	Brett Reed	Andy Coen
Liberty*	Flames	Red, white, & blue	Big South	Dale Layer	Turner Gill
Louisiana State (LSU)	Fighting Tigers	Purple & gold	Southeastern	Johnny Jones	Les Miles
Louisiana Tech	Bulldogs	Red & blue	Western Athletic	Michael White	Sonny Dykes
Louisiana-Lafayette	Ragin' Cajuns	Vermilion & white	Sun Belt	Bob Marlin	Mark Hudspeth
Louisiana-Monroe	Warhawks	Maroon & gold	Sun Belt	Keith Richard	Todd Berry
Louisville	Cardinals	Red & black	Big East	Rick Pitino	Charlie Strong
Maine*	Black Bears	Blue & white	Colonial Athletic#	Ted Woodward	Jack Cosgrove
Marshall	Thundering Herd	Kelly green & white	Conference USA	Tom Herrion	Doc Holliday
Maryland	Terrapins	Red, white, black, gold	Atlantic Coast	Mark Turgeon	Randy Edsall
Massachusetts*	Minutemen	Maroon & white	Mid-American#	Derek Kellogg	Charley Molnar
Memphis	Tigers	Blue & gray	Conference USA	Josh Pastner	Justin Fuente
Miami (Florida)	Hurricanes	Orange & green	Atlantic Coast	Jim Larranaga	Al Golden
Miami (Ohio)	RedHawks	Red & white	Mid-American	John Cooper	Don Treadwell
Michigan	Wolverines	Maize & blue	Big Ten	John Beilein	Brady Hoke
Michigan State	Spartans	Green & white	Big Ten	Tom Izzo	Mark Dantonio
Mid. Tennessee State	Blue Raiders	Royal blue & white	Sun Belt	Kermit Davis	Rick Stockstill
Minnesota	Golden Gophers	Maroon & gold	Big Ten	Tubby Smith	Jerry Kill
Mississippi	Rebels	Cardinal red & navy	Southeastern	Andy Kennedy	Hugh Freeze
Mississippi State	Bulldogs	Maroon & white	Southeastern	Rick Ray	Dan Mullen
Missouri	Tigers	Old gold & black	Southeastern	Frank Haith	Gary Pinkel

Team	Nickname	Team colors	Conference	Basketball coach	Football coach
Montana*	Grizzlies	Maroon & silver	Big Sky	Wayne Tinkle	Mick Delaney
Montana State*	Bobcats	Blue & gold	Big Sky	Brad Huse	Rob Ash
Morgan State*	Bears	Blue & orange	Mid-Eastern Athletic	Todd Bozeman	Donald Hill-Eley
Murray State*	Racers	Navy & gold	Ohio Valley	Steve Prohm	Chris Hatcher
Navy	Midshipmen	Navy & gold	Independent#	Ed DeChellis	Ken Niumatalolo
Nebraska	Cornhuskers	Scarlet & cream	Big Ten	Tim Miles	Bo Pelini
Nevada	Wolf Pack	Cobalt blue & silver	Mountain West	David Carter	Chris Ault
Nevada-Las Vegas (UNLV)	Rebels	Scarlet & gray	Mountain West	Dave Rice	Bobby Hauck
New Hampshire*	Wildcats	Blue & white	Colonial Athletic#	Bill Herrion	Sean McDonnell
New Mexico	Lobos	Cherry & silver	Mountain West	Steve Alford	Bob Davie
New Mexico State	Aggies	Crimson & white	Western Athletic	Marvin Menzies	DeWayne Walker
Nicholls State*	Colonels	Red & gray	Southland	J. P. Piper	Charlie Stubbs
North Carolina	Tar Heels	Carolina blue & white	Atlantic Coast	Roy Williams	Larry Fedora
North Carolina State	Wolfpack	Red & white	Atlantic Coast	Mark Gottfried	Tom O'Brien
North Texas	Mean Green	Green & white	Sun Belt	Tony Benford	Dan McCarney
Northern Illinois	Huskies	Cardinal & black	Mid-American	Mark Montgomery	Dave Doeren
Northern Iowa*	Panthers	Purple & gold	Missouri Valley	Ben Jacobson	Mark Farley
Northwestern	Wildcats	Purple & white	Big Ten	Bill Carmody	Pat Fitzgerald
Northwestern State*	Demons	Purple, white, & orange	Southland	Mike McConathy	Bradley Dale Peveto
Notre Dame	Fighting Irish	Gold & blue	Independent#	Mike Brey	Brian Kelly
Ohio	Bobcats	Hunter green & white	Mid-American	Jim Christian	Frank Solich
Ohio State	Buckeyes	Scarlet & gray	Big Ten	Thad Matta	Urban Meyer
Oklahoma	Sooners	Crimson & cream	Big 12	Lon Kruger	Bob Stoops
Oklahoma State	Cowboys	Orange & black	Big 12	Travis Ford	Mike Gundy
Oregon	Ducks	Green & yellow	Pac-12	Dana Altman	Chip Kelly
Oregon State	Beavers	Orange & black	Pac-12	Craig Robinson	Mike Riley
Penn State	Nittany Lions	Blue & white	Big Ten	Patrick Chambers	Bill O'Brien
Pennsylvania*	Quakers	Red & blue	Ivy League	Jerome Allen	Al Bagnoli
Pittsburgh	Panthers	Blue & gold	Big East	Jamie Dixon	Paul Chryst
Princeton*	Tigers	Orange & black	Ivy League	Mitch Henderson	Bob Surace
Purdue	Boilermakers	Old gold & black	Big Ten	Matt Painter	Danny Hope
Rhode Island*	Rams	Keaney blue, dark blue, white	Colonial Athletic#	Dan Hurley	Joe Trainer
Rice	Owls	Blue & gray	Conference USA	Ben Braun	David Bailiff
Richmond*	Spiders	Red & blue	Colonial Athletic#	Chris Mooney	Danny Rocco
Rutgers	Scarlet Knights	Scarlet	Big East	Mike Rice	Kyle Flood
Sam Houston State*	Bearkats	Orange & white	Southland	Jason Hooten	Willie Fritz
San Diego State	Aztecs	Scarlet & black	Mountain West	Steve Fisher	Rocky Long
San Jose State	Spartans	Gold, white, & blue	Western Athletic	George Nessman	Mike MacIntyre
SE Missouri State*	Redhawks	Red, white, & black	Ohio Valley	Dickey Nutt	Tony Samuel
South Carolina	Gamecocks	Garnet & black	Southeastern	Frank Martin	Steve Spurrier
South Carolina State*	Bulldogs	Garnet & blue	Mid-Eastern Athletic	Tim Carter	Oliver Pough
South Florida	Bulls	Green & gold	Big East	Stan Heath	Skip Holtz
Southern California (USC)	Trojans	Cardinal & gold	Pac-12	Kevin O'Neill	Lane Kiffin
Southern Illinois*	Salukis	Maroon & white	Missouri Valley	Barry Hinson	Dale Lennon
Southern Methodist (SMU)	Mustangs	Crimson & blue	Conference USA	Larry Brown	June Jones
Southern Mississippi	Golden Eagles	Black & gold	Conference USA	Donnie Tyndall	Ellis Johnson
Stanford	Cardinal	Cardinal & white	Pac-12	Johnny Dawkins	David Shaw
Stephen F. Austin*	Lumberjacks	Purple & white	Southland	Danny Kaspar	J. C. Harper
Syracuse	Orange	Orange	Big East[1]	Jim Boeheim	Doug Marrone
Temple	Owls	Cherry & white	Mid-American#	Fran Dunphy	Steve Addazio
Tennessee	Volunteers	Orange & white	Southeastern	Cuonzo Martin	Derek Dooley
Tennessee State*	Tigers	Reflex blue & white	Ohio Valley	Travis Williams	Rod Reed
Tennessee Tech*	Golden Eagles	Purple & gold	Ohio Valley	Steve Payne	Watson Brown
Texas	Longhorns	Burnt orange & white	Big 12	Rick Barnes	Mack Brown
Texas A&M	Aggies	Maroon & white	Big 12	Billy Kennedy	Kevin Sumlin
Texas Christian (TCU)	Horned Frogs	Purple & white	Big 12	Trent Johnson	Gary Patterson
Texas Southern*	Tigers	Maroon & gray	Southwestern Athletic	Mike Davis	Darrell Asberry
Texas State*	Bobcats	Maroon & gold	Western Athletic[1]	Doug Davalos	Dennis Franchione
Texas Tech	Red Raiders	Scarlet & black	Big 12	Billy Gillispie	Tommy Tuberville
Toledo	Rockets	Midnight blue & gold	Mid-American	Tod Kowalczyk	Matt Campbell
Troy	Trojans	Cardinal, black, & silver	Sun Belt	Don Maestri	Larry Blakeney
Tulane	Green Wave	Olive green & sky blue	Conference USA	Ed Conroy	Curtis Johnson
Tulsa	Golden Hurricane	Blue, gold, & crimson	Conference USA	Danny Manning	Bill Blankenship
UCLA	Bruins	Blue & gold	Pac-12	Ben Howland	Jim Mora Jr.
Utah	Utes	Crimson & white	Pac-12	Larry Krystkowiak	Kyle Whittingham
Utah State	Aggies	Navy blue & white	Western Athletic	Stew Morrill	Gary Andersen
UTEP (Texas-El Paso)	Miners	Orange, blue, & silver	Conference USA	Tim Floyd	Mike Price
Vanderbilt	Commodores	Black & gold	Southeastern	Kevin Stallings	James Franklin
Villanova*	Wildcats	Blue & white	Colonial Athletic#	Jay Wright	Andy Talley
Virginia	Cavaliers	Orange & blue	Atlantic Coast	Tony Bennett	Mike London
Virginia Tech	Hokies	Burnt orange & maroon	Atlantic Coast	James Johnson	Frank Beamer
Wake Forest	Demon Deacons	Old gold & black	Atlantic Coast	Jeff Bzdelik	Jim Grobe
Washington	Huskies	Purple & gold	Pac-12	Lorenzo Romar	Steve Sarkisian
Washington State	Cougars	Crimson & gray	Pac-12	Ken Bone	Mike Leach
Weber State*	Wildcats	Royal purple & white	Big Sky	Randy Rahe	Jody Sears
West Virginia	Mountaineers	Old gold & blue	Big East	Bob Huggins	Dana Holgorsen
Western Illinois*	Leathernecks	Purple & gold	Missouri Valley#	Jim Molinari	Mark Hendrickson
Western Kentucky	Hilltoppers	Red & white	Sun Belt	Ray Harper	Willie Taggart
Western Michigan	Broncos	Brown & gold	Mid-American	Steve Hawkins	Bill Cubit
William & Mary*	Tribe	Green, gold, & silver	Colonial Athletic	Tony Shaver	Jimmye Laycock
Wisconsin	Badgers	Cardinal & white	Big Ten	Bo Ryan	Bret Bielema
Wyoming	Cowboys	Brown & gold	Mountain West	Larry Shyatt	Dave Christensen
Yale*	Bulldogs, Elis	Yale blue & white	Ivy League	James Jones	Tony Reno
Youngstown State*	Penguins	Red & white	Missouri Valley#	Jerry Slocum	Eric Wolford

* = Football Championship Subdivision (FCS) team (formerly known as I-AA). # = Team competes in conference listed in football but not basketball. (1) Team is expected to change conferences on July 1, 2013. Syracuse: Atlantic Coast; Texas State: Sun Belt.

NCAA Men's Baseball Division I Champions, 1947-2012

Year	Champion	Year	Champion	Year	Champion	Year	Champion	Year	Champion
1947	California	1960	Minnesota	1974	USC	1987	Stanford	2000	LSU
1948	Southern California	1961	USC	1975	Texas	1988	Stanford	2001	Miami (FL)
		1962	Michigan	1976	Arizona	1989	Wichita St.	2002	Texas
1949	Texas	1963	USC	1977	Arizona St.	1990	Georgia	2003	Rice
1950	Texas	1964	Minnesota	1978	USC	1991	LSU	2004	Cal. St.-Fullerton
1951	Oklahoma	1965	Arizona St.	1979	Cal. St.-Fullerton	1992	Pepperdine	2005	Texas
1952	Holy Cross	1966	Ohio St.	1980	Arizona	1993	LSU	2006	Oregon St.
1953	Michigan	1967	Arizona St.	1981	Arizona St.	1994	Oklahoma	2007	Oregon St.
1954	Missouri	1968	USC	1982	Miami (FL)	1995	Cal. St.-Fullerton	2008	Fresno St.
1955	Wake Forest	1969	Arizona St.	1983	Texas	1996	LSU	2009	LSU
1956	Minnesota	1970	USC	1984	Cal. St.-Fullerton	1997	LSU	2010	South Carolina
1957	California	1971	USC	1985	Miami (FL)	1998	USC	2011	South Carolina
1958	USC	1972	USC	1986	Arizona	1999	Miami (FL)	2012	Arizona
1959	Oklahoma St.	1973	USC						

NCAA Women's Softball Division I Champions, 1982-2012

Year	Champion	Year	Champion	Year	Champion	Year	Champion	Year	Champion
1982	UCLA	1989	UCLA	1995	UCLA	2001	Arizona	2007	Arizona
1983	Texas A&M	1990	UCLA	1996	Arizona	2002	California	2008	Arizona St.
1984	UCLA	1991	Arizona	1997	Arizona	2003	UCLA	2009	Washington
1985	UCLA	1992	UCLA	1998	Fresno St.	2004	UCLA	2010	UCLA
1986	Cal. St.-Fullerton	1993	Arizona	1999	UCLA	2005	Michigan	2011	Arizona St.
1987	Texas A&M	1994	Arizona	2000	Oklahoma	2006	Arizona	2012	Alabama
1988	UCLA								

NCAA Men's Hockey Division I Champions, 1948-2012

Year	Champion	Year	Champion	Year	Champion	Year	Champion	Year	Champion
1948	Michigan	1961	Denver	1974	Minnesota	1987	North Dakota	2000	North Dakota
1949	Boston College	1962	Michigan Tech	1975	Michigan Tech	1988	Lake Superior St.	2001	Boston College
1950	Colorado College	1963	North Dakota	1976	Minnesota	1989	Harvard	2002	Minnesota
1951	Michigan	1964	Michigan	1977	Wisconsin	1990	Wisconsin	2003	Minnesota
1952	Michigan	1965	Michigan Tech	1978	Boston Univ.	1991	North Dakota	2004	Denver
1953	Michigan	1966	Michigan State	1979	Minnesota	1992	Lake Superior St.	2005	Denver
1954	Rensselaer	1967	Cornell	1980	North Dakota	1993	Maine	2006	Wisconsin
1955	Michigan	1968	Denver	1981	Wisconsin	1994	Lake Superior St.	2007	Michigan St.
1956	Michigan	1969	Denver	1982	North Dakota	1995	Boston Univ.	2008	Boston College
1957	Colorado College	1970	Cornell	1983	Wisconsin	1996	Michigan	2009	Boston Univ.
1958	Denver	1971	Boston Univ.	1984	Bowling Green	1997	North Dakota	2010	Boston College
1959	North Dakota	1972	Boston Univ.	1985	Rensselaer	1998	Michigan	2011	Minnesota-Duluth
1960	Denver	1973	Wisconsin	1986	Michigan St.	1999	Maine	2012	Boston College

NCAA Women's Hockey Champions, 2001-12

Year	Champion	Year	Champion	Year	Champion	Year	Champion	Year	Champion
2001	Minnesota-Duluth	2004	Minnesota	2007	Wisconsin	2009	Wisconsin	2011	Wisconsin
2002	Minnesota-Duluth	2005	Minnesota	2008	Minnesota-Duluth	2010	Minnesota-Duluth	2012	Minnesota
2003	Minnesota-Duluth	2006	Wisconsin						

NCAA Division I Lacrosse Champions, 1982-2012

Year[1]	Men	Women	Year[1]	Men	Women	Year[1]	Men	Women
1982	North Carolina	Massachusetts	1993	Syracuse	Virginia	2003	Virginia	Princeton
1983	Syracuse	Delaware	1994	Princeton	Princeton	2004	Syracuse	Virginia
1984	Johns Hopkins	Temple	1995	Syracuse	Maryland	2005	Johns Hopkins	Northwestern
1985	Johns Hopkins	New Hampshire	1996	Princeton	Maryland	2006	Virginia	Northwestern
1986	North Carolina	Maryland	1997	Princeton	Maryland	2007	Johns Hopkins	Northwestern
1987	Johns Hopkins	Penn St.	1998	Princeton	Maryland	2008	Syracuse	Northwestern
1988	Syracuse	Temple	1999	Virginia	Maryland	2009	Syracuse	Northwestern
1989	Syracuse	Penn St.	2000	Syracuse	Maryland	2010	Duke	Maryland
1990	Vacated	Harvard	2001	Princeton	Maryland	2011	Virginia	Northwestern
1991	North Carolina	Virginia	2002	Syracuse	Princeton	2012	Loyola (MD)	Northwestern
1992	Princeton	Maryland						

(1) NCAA Championships began in 1971 for men, in 1982 for women.

NCAA Division I Soccer Champions, 1982-2011

Year[1]	Men	Women	Year[1]	Men	Women	Year[1]	Men	Women
1982	Indiana	North Carolina	1992	Virginia	North Carolina	2002	UCLA	Portland
1983	Indiana	North Carolina	1993	Virginia	North Carolina	2003	Indiana	North Carolina
1984	Clemson	North Carolina	1994	Virginia	North Carolina	2004	Indiana	Notre Dame
1985	UCLA	George Mason	1995	Wisconsin	Notre Dame	2005	Maryland	Portland
1986	Duke	North Carolina	1996	St. John's (NY)	North Carolina	2006	UC Santa Barbara	North Carolina
1987	Clemson	North Carolina	1997	UCLA	North Carolina	2007	Wake Forest	USC
1988	Indiana	North Carolina	1998	Indiana	Florida	2008	Maryland	North Carolina
1989	Santa Clara/ Virginia (tie)	North Carolina	1999	Indiana	North Carolina	2009	Virginia	North Carolina
			2000	Connecticut	North Carolina	2010	Akron	Notre Dame
1990	UCLA	North Carolina	2001	North Carolina	Santa Clara	2011	North Carolina	Stanford
1991	Virginia	North Carolina						

(1) NCAA Championships began in 1959 for men, in 1982 for women.

NCAA Division I Wrestling Champions, 1964-2012

Year	Champion	Year	Champion	Year	Champion	Year	Champion	Year	Champion
1964	Oklahoma St.	1974	Oklahoma	1984	Iowa	1994	Oklahoma St.	2004	Oklahoma St.
1965	Iowa St.	1975	Iowa	1985	Iowa	1995	Iowa	2005	Oklahoma St.
1966	Oklahoma St.	1976	Iowa	1986	Iowa	1996	Iowa	2006	Oklahoma St.
1967	Michigan St.	1977	Iowa St.	1987	Iowa St.	1997	Iowa	2007	Minnesota
1968	Oklahoma St.	1978	Iowa	1988	Arizona St.	1998	Iowa	2008	Iowa
1969	Iowa St.	1979	Iowa	1989	Oklahoma St.	1999	Iowa	2009	Iowa
1970	Iowa St.	1980	Iowa	1990	Oklahoma St.	2000	Iowa	2010	Iowa
1971	Oklahoma St.	1981	Iowa	1991	Iowa	2001	Minnesota	2011	Penn St.
1972	Iowa St.	1982	Iowa	1992	Iowa	2002	Minnesota	2012	Penn St.
1973	Iowa St.	1983	Iowa	1993	Iowa	2003	Oklahoma St.		

FOOTBALL

NFL 2011: Owners and Players Agree to 10-Year Deal

National Football League owners and player representatives agreed to a new 10-year collective bargaining agreement on July 25, 2011, ending a 132-day lockout and ushering in an explosive season. A record-tying six NFL teams won 12 or more games in 2011, but the 9-7 New York Giants won the NFC East on the season's final day and went on to win their second Super Bowl title in five years over the New England Patriots Feb. 5, 2012, at Lucas Oil Stadium in Indianapolis, IN.

Giants quarterback Eli Manning passed for a regular season career-high 4,933 yards, but three other QBs surpassed the 5,000-yard mark in another banner year for NFL signal-callers. New Orleans Saints QB Drew Brees set an NFL single-season record with 5,476 passing yards and broke league records for completions (468), completion percentage (71.2%), and 300-yard passing games (13). New England Patriots QB Tom Brady passed for 5,235 yards, and QB Matthew Stafford led the resurgent Detroit Lions with 5,038 yards. Carolina QB Cam Newton set NFL rookie records with a 4,051-yard season and 422 passing yards in his debut game (a Week 1 loss to Arizona). Another Week 1 highlight included an NFL record-tying 63-yard field goal by Oakland's Sebastian Janikowski in a Monday Night Football win over Denver on Sept. 12, 2011.

The New York Giants reached the Super Bowl with playoff wins over Atlanta, Green Bay, and San Francisco (20-17 in overtime in the conference title game). The Packers earned the NFC's top playoff seed and NFC North title with a 15-1 record, their only loss coming against Kansas City in Week 15. Green Bay led the league with 560 points, one of a record three franchises with over 500 points in the 2011 season (New Orleans 547, New England 513).

In the AFC, the Houston Texans won their first AFC South crown and earned their first-ever playoff win by defeating Cincinnati, 31-10, in the AFC wild-card round. Denver won the AFC West with the help of QB Tim Tebow, who led game-winning drives in the fourth quarter or overtime six times in his first 11 starts. Denver followed up with a stunning 29-23 overtime wild-card playoff win over Pittsburgh. Tom Brady tied a postseason record with six TD passes as the Patriots ended Denver's season with a 45-10 victory in the AFC divisional playoffs.

NFL Final Standings, 2011
(playoff seeding in parentheses)

AMERICAN FOOTBALL CONFERENCE

East Division	W	L	T	Pct	Pts	Opp	Div
New England (1)	13	3	0	.813	513	342	5-1
NY Jets	8	8	0	.500	377	363	3-3
Miami	6	10	0	.375	329	313	3-3
Buffalo	6	10	0	.375	372	434	1-5

North Division	W	L	T	Pct	Pts	Opp	Div
Baltimore (2)	12	4	0	.750	378	266	6-0
*Pittsburgh (5)	12	4	0	.750	325	227	4-2
*Cincinnati (6)	9	7	0	.563	344	323	2-4
Cleveland	4	12	0	.250	218	307	0-6

South Division	W	L	T	Pct	Pts	Opp	Div
Houston (3)	10	6	0	.625	381	278	4-2
Tennessee	9	7	0	.563	325	317	3-3
Jacksonville	5	11	0	.313	243	329	3-3
Indianapolis	2	14	0	.125	243	430	2-4

West Division	W	L	T	Pct	Pts	Opp	Div
Denver (4)	8	8	0	.500	309	390	3-3
San Diego	8	8	0	.500	406	377	3-3
Oakland	8	8	0	.500	359	433	3-3
Kansas City	7	9	0	.438	212	338	3-3

NATIONAL FOOTBALL CONFERENCE

East Division	W	L	T	Pct	Pts	Opp	Div
NY Giants (4)	9	7	0	.563	394	400	3-3
Philadelphia	8	8	0	.500	396	328	5-1
Dallas	8	8	0	.500	369	347	2-4
Washington	5	11	0	.313	288	367	2-4

North Division	W	L	T	Pct	Pts	Opp	Div
Green Bay (1)	15	1	0	.938	560	359	6-0
*Detroit (6)	10	6	0	.625	474	387	3-3
Chicago	8	8	0	.500	353	341	3-3
Minnesota	3	13	0	.188	340	449	0-6

South Division	W	L	T	Pct	Pts	Opp	Div
New Orleans (3)	13	3	0	.813	547	339	5-1
*Atlanta (5)	10	6	0	.625	402	350	3-3
Carolina	6	10	0	.375	406	429	2-4
Tampa Bay	4	12	0	.250	287	494	2-4

West Division	W	L	T	Pct	Pts	Opp	Div
San Francisco (2)	13	3	0	.813	380	229	5-1
Arizona	8	8	0	.500	312	348	4-2
Seattle	7	9	0	.438	321	315	3-3
St. Louis	2	14	0	.125	193	407	0-6

* = Wild card qualifier for playoffs. **Note:** Baltimore finished ahead of Pittsburgh based on head-to-head win percentage; Denver won the AFC West over Oakland and San Diego based on best win percentage in common games; Cincinnati earned a wild card playoff berth over Tennessee based on head-to-head win percentage. San Francisco finished ahead of New Orleans in overall NFC playoff rank based on best win percentage in conference games; Atlanta finished ahead of Detroit in the NFC wild card seeding based on head-to-head win percentage.

Playoffs and Postseason, 2011

AFC Wild Card Playoff Games: Houston 31, Cincinnati 10; Denver 29, Pittsburgh 23 (OT)
NFC Wild Card Playoff Games: New Orleans 45, Detroit 28; NY Giants 24, Atlanta 2
AFC Divisional Playoff Games: New England 45, Denver 10; Baltimore 20, Houston 13
NFC Divisional Playoff Games: San Francisco 36, New Orleans 32; NY Giants 37, Green Bay 20

AFC Championship Game: New England 23, Baltimore 20
NFC Championship Game: NY Giants 20, San Francisco 17 (OT)
Super Bowl XLVI at Lucas Oil Stadium, Indianapolis, IN: NY Giants 21, New England 17
AFC-NFC Pro Bowl at Aloha Stadium, Honolulu, HI: AFC 59, NFC 41

NFL Individual Leaders: American Football Conference, 2011
(* = rookie)

PASSING	Att	Comp	Pct comp	Yds	Yds/att	Long	TD	Pct TD	Int	Rating
Tom Brady, New England	611	401	65.6	5,235	8.6	99T	39	6.4	12	105.6
Matt Schaub, Houston	292	178	61.0	2,479	8.5	80T	15	5.1	6	96.8
Ben Roethlisberger, Pittsburgh	513	324	63.2	4,077	7.9	95T	21	4.1	14	90.1
Philip Rivers, San Diego	582	366	62.9	4,624	7.9	58	27	4.6	20	88.7
Matt Moore, Miami	347	210	60.5	2,497	7.2	65T	16	4.6	9	87.1
Matt Hasselbeck, Tennessee	518	319	61.6	3,571	6.9	80T	18	3.5	14	82.4
Joe Flacco, Baltimore	542	312	57.6	3,610	6.7	74T	20	3.7	12	80.9
Carson Palmer, Oakland	328	199	60.7	2,753	8.4	78	13	4.0	16	80.5
*Andy Dalton, Cincinnati	516	300	58.1	3,398	6.6	84	20	3.9	13	80.4
Ryan Fitzpatrick, Buffalo	569	353	62.0	3,832	6.7	60T	24	4.2	23	79.1
Mark Sanchez, NY Jets	543	308	56.7	3,474	6.4	74	26	4.8	18	78.2
Matt Cassel, Kansas City	269	160	59.5	1,713	6.4	52T	10	3.7	9	76.6
Colt McCoy, Cleveland	463	265	57.2	2,733	5.9	56	14	3.0	11	74.6
Tim Tebow, Denver	271	126	46.5	1,729	6.4	56T	12	4.4	6	72.9
Curtis Painter, Indianapolis	243	132	54.3	1,541	6.3	87T	6	2.5	9	66.6

RUSHING YARDS	Yds	Att	Avg	Long	TD
Maurice Jones-Drew, Jacksonville	1,606	343	4.7	56	8
Ray Rice, Baltimore	1,364	291	4.7	70T	12
Arian Foster, Houston........	1,224	278	4.4	43	10
Willis McGahee, Denver......	1,199	249	4.8	60T	4
Ryan Mathews, San Diego.....	1,091	222	4.9	39	6
Reggie Bush, Miami	1,086	216	5.0	76T	6
Cedric Benson, Cincinnati	1,067	273	3.9	42	6
Shonn Greene, NY Jets	1,054	253	4.2	31	6
Chris Johnson, Tennessee.....	1,047	262	4.0	48T	4
Michael Bush, Oakland........	977	256	3.8	44	7

RECEPTIONS	Rec	Yds	Avg	Long	TD
Wes Welker, New England	122	1,569	12.9	99T	9
Rob Gronkowski, New England	90	1,327	14.7	52T	17
Dwayne Bowe, Kansas City	81	1,159	14.3	52T	5
Brandon Marshall, Miami	81	1,214	15.0	65T	6
Aaron Hernandez, New England	79	910	11.5	46	7
Steve Johnson, Buffalo........	76	1,004	13.2	55	7
Ray Rice, Baltimore	76	704	9.3	52	3
Reggie Wayne, Indianapolis....	75	960	12.8	56T	4
Nate Washington, Tennessee...	74	1,023	13.8	57	7
Mike Wallace, Pittsburgh.......	72	1,193	16.6	95T	8

SCORING—KICKERS	PAT	FG	Long	Pts
Stephen Gostkowski, New England	59/59	28/33	50	143
Neil Rackers, Houston	39/40	32/38	54	135
Mike Nugent, Cincinnati	33/34	33/38	49	132
Sebastian Janikowski, Oakland	36/36	31/35	63	129
Billy Cundiff, Baltimore	38/38	28/37	51	122
Nick Novak, San Diego........	41/42	27/34	53	122

SCORING—NON-KICKERS	TD	Rush	Rec	2-Pt	Pts
Rob Gronkowski, New England (TE).....................	18	1	17	0	108
Ray Rice, Baltimore (RB)	15	12	3	0	90
Arian Foster, Houston (RB).....	12	10	2	0	72
BenJarvus Green-Ellis, New England (RB)	11	11	0	0	66
Maurice Jones-Drew, Jacksonville (RB)	11	8	3	0	66
Mike Tolbert, San Diego (RB)...	10	8	2	0	60

INTERCEPTIONS	No.	Yds	Avg	Long	TD
Kyle Arrington, New England ...	7	92	13.1	28	0
Eric Weddle, San Diego	7	89	12.7	26	0
Matt Giordano, Oakland	5	130	26.0	62	0
Lardarius Webb, Baltimore	5	81	16.2	73T	1
Jason Allen, Houston	4	34	8.5	34	0
Brandon Carr, Kansas City.....	4	17	4.3	14	0
Antonio Cromartie, NY Jets	4	105	26.3	42	0
Vontae Davis, Miami	4	60	15.0	28	0
Brandon Flowers, Kansas City ..	4	95	23.8	58T	1
David Harris, NY Jets	4	55	13.8	35T	1
Johnathan Joseph, Houston....	4	40	10.0	29	0
Reggie Nelson, Cincinnati	4	115	28.8	75T	1
Darrelle Revis, NY Jets........	4	184	46.0	100T	1
Stanford Routt, Oakland	4	7	1.8	3	0
George Wilson, Buffalo........	4	26	6.5	12	0

KICKOFF RETURNS	No.	Yds	Avg	Long	TD
Joe McKnight, NY Jets	34	1,073	31.6	107T	1
Richard Goodman, San Diego ..	34	936	27.5	105T	1
Antonio Brown, Pittsburgh	27	737	27.3	52	0
Josh Cribbs, Cleveland........	39	974	25.0	63	0
Clyde Gates, Miami	34	843	24.8	77	0
Deji Karim, Jacksonville	27	652	24.1	37	0

PUNTING	No.	Yds	Long	Avg
Shane Lechler, Oakland	78	3,960	80	50.8
Brandon Fields, Miami	78	3,810	70	48.8
Brian Moorman, Buffalo	72	3,472	66	48.2
Mike Scifres, San Diego	47	2,234	71	47.5
Britton Colquitt, Denver.......	101	4,783	66	47.4
Pat McAfee, Indianapolis	88	4,098	64	46.6

PUNT RETURNS	No.	Yds	Avg	Long	TD
Javier Arenas, Kansas City.....	32	410	12.8	37	0
Davone Bess, Miami..........	37	442	11.9	25	0
Josh Cribbs, Cleveland........	34	388	11.4	84T	1
Jeremy Kerley, NY Jets.......	29	317	10.9	53	0
Antonio Brown, Pittsburgh	30	325	10.8	60T	1
Marc Mariani, Tennessee......	46	490	10.7	79T	1

SACKS: Terrell Suggs, Baltimore, 14; Tamba Hali, Kansas City, 12; Connor Barwin, Houston, 11.5; *Von Miller, Denver, 11.5; Antwan Barnes, San Diego, 11; Mark Anderson, New England, 10; Andre Carter, New England, 10; Elvis Dumervil, Denver, 9.5; Robert Mathis, Indianapolis, 9.5; James Harrison, Pittsburgh, 9; LaMarr Woodley, Pittsburgh, 9; Dwight Freeney, Indianapolis, 8.5; *Jabaal Sheard, Cleveland, 8.5; Cameron Wake, Miami, 8.5; Jeremy Mincey, Jacksonville, 8.

NFL Individual Leaders: National Football Conference, 2011

(* = rookie)

PASSING	Att	Comp	Pct comp	Yds	Yds/att	Long	TD	Pct TD	Int	Rating
Aaron Rodgers, Green Bay.............	502	343	68.3	4,643	9.2	93T	45	9.0	6	122.5
Drew Brees, New Orleans	657	468	71.2	5,476	8.3	79T	46	7.0	14	110.6
Tony Romo, Dallas	522	346	66.3	4,184	8.0	77	31	5.9	10	102.5
Matthew Stafford, Detroit	663	421	63.5	5,038	7.6	73T	41	6.2	16	97.2
Eli Manning, NY Giants	589	359	61.0	4,933	8.4	99T	29	4.9	16	92.9
Matt Ryan, Atlanta	566	347	61.3	4,177	7.4	80T	29	5.1	12	92.2
Alex Smith, San Francisco	445	273	61.3	3,144	7.1	56T	17	3.8	5	90.7
Jay Cutler, Chicago..................	314	182	58.0	2,319	7.4	56T	13	4.1	7	85.7
Michael Vick, Philadelphia	423	253	59.8	3,303	7.8	73	18	4.3	14	84.9
*Cam Newton, Carolina	517	310	60.0	4,051	7.8	91T	21	4.1	17	84.5
Kevin Kolb, Arizona..................	253	146	57.7	1,955	7.7	73T	9	3.6	8	81.1
Tarvaris Jackson, Seattle	450	271	60.2	3,091	6.9	61T	14	3.1	13	79.2
Josh Freeman, Tampa Bay.............	551	346	62.8	3,592	6.5	65T	16	2.9	22	74.6
Rex Grossman, Washington.............	458	265	57.9	3,151	6.9	51	16	3.5	20	72.4
Sam Bradford, St. Louis	357	191	53.5	2,164	6.1	68	6	1.7	6	70.5
*Christian Ponder, Minnesota............	291	158	54.3	1,853	6.4	72	13	4.5	13	70.1

RUSHING YARDS	Yds	Att	Avg	Long	TD
Michael Turner, Atlanta	1,340	301	4.5	81T	11
LeSean McCoy, Philadelphia ...	1,309	273	4.8	60	17
Frank Gore, San Francisco.....	1,211	282	4.3	55	8
Marshawn Lynch, Seattle	1,204	285	4.2	47	12
Steven Jackson, St. Louis	1,145	260	4.4	47T	5
Beanie Wells, Arizona.........	1,047	245	4.3	71	10
Matt Forte, Chicago	997	203	4.9	46	3
Adrian Peterson, Minnesota	970	208	4.7	54	12
*DeMarco Murray, Dallas	897	164	5.5	91T	2
DeAngelo Williams, Carolina	836	155	5.4	74T	2

RECEPTIONS	Rec	Yds	Avg	Long	TD
Roddy White, Atlanta	100	1,296	13.0	43	8
Jimmy Graham, New Orleans ...	99	1,310	13.2	59	11
Calvin Johnson, Detroit.........	96	1,681	17.5	73T	16
Percy Harvin, Minnesota.......	87	967	11.1	52T	6
Darren Sproles, New Orleans ...	86	710	8.3	39	7
Brandon Pettigrew, Detroit	83	777	9.4	27	5
Victor Cruz, NY Giants	82	1,536	18.7	99T	9
Marques Colston, New Orleans ..	80	1,143	14.3	50	8
Larry Fitzgerald, Arizona........	80	1,411	17.6	73T	8
Tony Gonzalez, Atlanta.........	80	875	10.9	30	7

SCORING—KICKERS	PAT	FG	Long	Pts
David Akers, San Francisco	34/34	44/52	55	166
John Kasay, New Orleans.	63/63	28/34	53	147
Mason Crosby, Green Bay	68/69	24/28	58	140
*Dan Bailey, Dallas	39/39	32/37	51	135
Matt Bryant, Atlanta	45/45	27/29	51·	126
Jason Hanson, Detroit	54/54	24/29	51	126

SCORING—NON-KICKERS	TD	Rush	Rec	2-Pt	Pts
LeSean McCoy, Philadelphia (RB)	20	17	3	0	120
Calvin Johnson, Detroit (WR)	16	0	16	0	96
Jordy Nelson, Green Bay (WR) . .	15	0	15	0	90
*Cam Newton, Carolina (QB)	14	14	0	0	84
Marshawn Lynch, Seattle (RB) . . .	13	12	1	0	78
Adrian Peterson, Minnesota (RB)	13	12	1	0	78

INTERCEPTIONS	No.	Yds	Avg	Long	TD
Charles Woodson, Green Bay . . .	7	63	9.0	30T	1
Brandon Browner, Seattle.	6	220	36.7	94T	2
Dashon Goldson, San Francisco	6	53	8.8	21	0
Carlos Rogers, San Francisco . . .	6	106	17.7	31T	1
Corey Webster, NY Giants	6	71	11.8	25	0
Chris Houston, Detroit	5	225	45.0	100T	1
Charlie Peprah, Green Bay.	5	147	29.4	76	1

KICKOFF RETURNS	No.	Yds	Avg	Long	TD
*Randall Cobb, Green Bay	34	941	27.7	108T	1
Ted Ginn, San Francisco	29	800	27.6	102T	1
Darren Sproles, New Orleans. . . .	40	1,089	27.2	92	0

KICKOFF RETURNS	No.	Yds	Avg	Long	TD
Sammie Stroughter, Tampa Bay . .	20	540	27.0	78	0
Kealoha Pilares, Carolina	23	590	25.7	101T	1
Jerious Norwood, St. Louis.	24	611	25.5	47	0

PUNTING	No.	Yds	Long	Avg
Andy Lee, San Francisco	78	3,970	68	50.9
Thomas Morstead, New Orleans	46	2,224	64	48.3
Jon Ryan, Seattle	95	4,431	77	46.6
Chris Kluwe, Minnesota	77	3,517	60	45.7
Steve Weatherford, NY Giants . . .	82	3,745	62	45.7
Tim Masthay, Green Bay	55	2,506	71	45.6

PUNT RETURNS	No.	Yds	Avg	Long	TD
Devin Hester, Chicago	28	454	16.2	82T	2
*Patrick Peterson, Arizona	44	699	15.9	99T	4
Ted Ginn, San Francisco	38	466	12.3	55T	1
*Randall Cobb, Green Bay	26	295	11.3	80T	1
Leon Washington, Seattle.	41	464	11.3	37	0
Darren Sproles, New Orleans. . . .	29	294	10.1	72T	1

SACKS: Jared Allen, Minnesota, 22; DeMarcus Ware, Dallas, 19.5; Jason Babin, Philadelphia, 18; Jason Pierre-Paul, NY Giants, 16.5; *Aldon Smith, San Francisco, 14; Chris Long, St. Louis, 13; Cliff Avril, Detroit, 11; Chris Clemons, Seattle, 11; Trent Cole, Philadelphia, 11; Julius Peppers, Chicago, 11; John Abraham, Atlanta, 9.5; Charles Johnson, Carolina, 9; Brian Orakpo, Washington, 9; Osi Umenyiora, NY Giants, 9; Calais Campbell, Arizona, 8; Brian Robison, Minnesota, 8; Kyle Vanden Bosch, Detroit, 8.

Super Bowl XLVI: NY Giants 21, New England 17

The New York Giants beat the New England Patriots in Super Bowl XLVI for the franchise's fourth Super Bowl title and eighth overall NFL championship. Eli Manning passed for 296 yards and directed a late fourth-quarter scoring drive that ended when Ahmad Bradshaw scored from six yards out with 57 seconds remaining. The score capped an 88-yard drive that began with a spectacular 38-yard pass completion to wide receiver Mario Manningham along the Patriots' sideline.

Manning completed five of six passes for 74 yards on the go-ahead drive. The eight-year veteran completed 30 of 40 passes, including a Super Bowl-record nine consecutive completions at the start of a game, to earn the Pete Rozelle Trophy as Super Bowl XLVI Most Valuable Player. Manning is the fifth player in league history to win multiple Super Bowl MVPs, having earned the award following another win over the Patriots in Super Bowl XLII.

Patriots QB Tom Brady passed for 276 yards and a pair of touchdowns in New England's loss. Brady directed a 96-yard touchdown drive, tying the record for the longest in Super Bowl history, and the Patriots went into halftime leading 10-9. New England extended its lead to 17-9 in the third quarter when Brady hit Aaron Hernandez on a 12-yard pass that capped an eight-play, 79-yard drive. The Giants, who have trailed at halftime in each of their Super Bowl victories, cut the lead to 17-15 on a pair of Lawrence Tynes field goals in the third quarter prior to the late-game surge.

The Giants' 65-year-old head coach, Tom Coughlin, became the oldest winning head coach in Super Bowl history. Brady set a Super Bowl record with 16 consecutive completions over the second and third quarters and established Super Bowl career records for passing yards (1,277), passes (197), and completions (127).

Quarters

Team	1	2	3	4	Total
NY Giants	9	0	6	6	21
New England	0	10	7	0	17

Scoring

NY Giants: Intentional grounding penalty on Tom Brady enforced in end zone for a safety
NY Giants: Victor Cruz, 2-yard pass from Eli Manning (Lawrence Tynes PAT)
New England: Stephen Gostkowski, 29-yard field goal
New England: Danny Woodhead, 4-yard pass from Tom Brady (Stephen Gostkowski PAT)
New England: Aaron Hernandez, 12-yard pass from Tom Brady (Stephen Gostkowski PAT)
NY Giants: Lawrence Tynes, 38-yard field goal
NY Giants: Lawrence Tynes, 33-yard field goal
NY Giants: Ahmad Bradshaw, 6-yard run (run failed)

Individual Statistics

Rushing
NY Giants: Bradshaw, 17-72; Jacobs, 9-37; Ware, 1-6; Manning, 1-minus-1.
New England: Green-Ellis, 10-44; Welker, 2-21; Woodhead, 7-18.

Passing
NY Giants: Manning, 30-40, 296 yards, 1 TD, 0 int.
New England: Brady, 27-41, 276 yards, 2 TD, 1 int.

Receiving

NY Giants: Nicks, 10-109; Manningham, 5-73; Pascoe, 4-33; Cruz, 4-25; Bradshaw, 2-19; Hynoski, 2-19; Ballard, 1-1; Ware, 1-8.
New England: Hernandez, 8-67; Welker, 7-60; Woodhead, 4-42; Branch, 3-45; Gronkowski, 2-26; Green-Ellis, 2-15; Ochocinco, 1-21.

Team Statistics

	Giants	Patriots
First downs	26	21
Total net yards	396	349
Rushes-yards	28-114	19-83
Passing yards, net	282	266
Punt returns-yards	1-10	0-0
Kickoff returns-yards.	4-75	3-73
Interception returns-yards.	1-0	0-0
Field goals made-attempts	2-2	1-1
Att-comp-int	40-30-0	41-27-1
Sacked-yards lost	3-14	2-10
Punts-average	4-40.8	3-41.0
Fumbles-lost	2-0	0-0
Penalties-yards.	4-24	5-28
Time of possession.	37:05	22:55

Total attendance: 68,658   **Game length:** 3:23

Super Bowl Sites, 2013-15

No.	Site	Date	No.	Site	Date
XLVII	Louisiana Superdome, New Orleans, LA . .	Feb. 3, 2013	XLIX	Univ. of Phoenix Stadium, Glendale, AZ . . .	Feb. 2015
XLVIII	New Meadowlands Stadium, East Rutherford, NJ	Feb. 2, 2014			

Super Bowl Results, 1967-2012

No.	Year	Winner	Opponent	Winning coach	Site
I	1967	*Green Bay Packers, 35	Kansas City Chiefs, 10	Vince Lombardi	Memorial Coliseum, Los Angeles, CA
II	1968	Green Bay Packers, 33	*Oakland Raiders, 14	Vince Lombardi	Orange Bowl, Miami, FL
III	1969	*NY Jets, 16	Baltimore Colts, 7	Weeb Ewbank	Orange Bowl, Miami, FL
IV	1970	Kansas City Chiefs, 23	*Minnesota Vikings, 7	Hank Stram	Tulane Stadium, New Orleans, LA
V	1971	Baltimore Colts, 16	*Dallas Cowboys, 13	Don McCafferty	Orange Bowl, Miami, FL
VI	1972	Dallas Cowboys, 24	*Miami Dolphins, 3	Tom Landry	Tulane Stadium, New Orleans, LA
VII	1973	*Miami Dolphins, 14	Washington Redskins, 7	Don Shula	Memorial Coliseum, Los Angeles, CA
VIII	1974	*Miami Dolphins, 24	Minnesota Vikings, 7	Don Shula	Rice Stadium, Houston, TX
IX	1975	*Pittsburgh Steelers, 16	Minnesota Vikings, 6	Chuck Noll	Tulane Stadium, New Orleans, LA
X	1976	Pittsburgh Steelers, 21	*Dallas Cowboys, 17	Chuck Noll	Orange Bowl, Miami, FL
XI	1977	*Oakland Raiders, 32	Minnesota Vikings, 14	John Madden	Rose Bowl, Pasadena, CA
XII	1978	*Dallas Cowboys, 27	Denver Broncos, 10	Tom Landry	Superdome, New Orleans, LA
XIII	1979	Pittsburgh Steelers, 35	*Dallas Cowboys, 31	Chuck Noll	Orange Bowl, Miami, FL
XIV	1980	Pittsburgh Steelers, 31	*L.A. Rams, 19	Chuck Noll	Rose Bowl, Pasadena, CA
XV	1981	Oakland Raiders, 27	*Philadelphia Eagles, 10	Tom Flores	Superdome, New Orleans, LA
XVI	1982	*San Francisco 49ers, 26	Cincinnati Bengals, 21	Bill Walsh	Silverdome, Pontiac, MI
XVII	1983	Washington Redskins, 27	*Miami Dolphins, 17	Joe Gibbs	Rose Bowl, Pasadena, CA
XVIII	1984	*L.A. Raiders, 38	Washington Redskins, 9	Tom Flores	Tampa Stadium, Tampa, FL
XIX	1985	*San Francisco 49ers, 38	Miami Dolphins, 16	Bill Walsh	Stanford Stadium, Stanford, CA
XX	1986	*Chicago Bears, 46	New England Patriots, 10	Mike Ditka	Superdome, New Orleans, LA
XXI	1987	NY Giants, 39	*Denver Broncos, 20	Bill Parcells	Rose Bowl, Pasadena, CA
XXII	1988	*Washington Redskins, 42	Denver Broncos, 10	Joe Gibbs	Jack Murphy Stadium, San Diego, CA
XXIII	1989	*San Francisco 49ers, 20	Cincinnati Bengals, 16	Bill Walsh	Joe Robbie Stadium, Miami, FL
XXIV	1990	San Francisco 49ers, 55	*Denver Broncos, 10	George Seifert	Superdome, New Orleans, LA
XXV	1991	NY Giants, 20	*Buffalo Bills, 19	Bill Parcells	Tampa Stadium, Tampa, FL
XXVI	1992	*Washington Redskins, 37	Buffalo Bills, 24	Joe Gibbs	Metrodome, Minneapolis, MN
XXVII	1993	Dallas Cowboys, 52	*Buffalo Bills, 17	Jimmy Johnson	Rose Bowl, Pasadena, CA
XXVIII	1994	*Dallas Cowboys, 30	Buffalo Bills, 13	Jimmy Johnson	Georgia Dome, Atlanta, GA
XXIX	1995	*San Francisco 49ers, 49	San Diego Chargers, 26	George Seifert	Joe Robbie Stadium, Miami, FL
XXX	1996	*Dallas Cowboys, 27	Pittsburgh Steelers, 17	Barry Switzer	Sun Devil Stadium, Tempe, AZ
XXXI	1997	Green Bay Packers, 35	*New England Patriots, 21	Mike Holmgren	Superdome, New Orleans, LA
XXXII	1998	Denver Broncos, 31	*Green Bay Packers, 24	Mike Shanahan	Qualcomm Stadium, San Diego, CA
XXXIII	1999	Denver Broncos, 34	*Atlanta Falcons, 19	Mike Shanahan	Pro Player Stadium, Miami, FL
XXXIV	2000	*St. Louis Rams, 23	Tennessee Titans, 16	Dick Vermeil	Georgia Dome, Atlanta, GA
XXXV	2001	Baltimore Ravens, 34	*NY Giants, 7	Brian Billick	Raymond James Stadium, Tampa, FL
XXXVI	2002	New England Patriots, 20	*St. Louis Rams, 17	Bill Belichick	Superdome, New Orleans, LA
XXXVII	2003	*Tampa Bay Buccaneers, 48	Oakland Raiders, 21	Jon Gruden	Qualcomm Stadium, San Diego, CA
XXXVIII	2004	New England Patriots, 32	*Carolina Panthers, 29	Bill Belichick	Reliant Stadium, Houston, TX
XXXIX	2005	New England Patriots, 24	*Philadelphia Eagles, 21	Bill Belichick	Alltel Stadium, Jacksonville, FL
XL	2006	Pittsburgh Steelers, 21	*Seattle Seahawks, 10	Bill Cowher	Ford Field, Detroit, MI
XLI	2007	Indianapolis Colts, 29	*Chicago Bears, 17	Tony Dungy	Dolphin Stadium, Miami, FL
XLII	2008	*NY Giants, 17	New England Patriots, 14	Tom Coughlin	Univ. of Phoenix Stadium, Glendale, AZ
XLIII	2009	Pittsburgh Steelers, 27	*Arizona Cardinals, 23	Mike Tomlin	Raymond James Stadium, Tampa, FL
XLIV	2010	*New Orleans Saints, 31	Indianapolis Colts, 17	Sean Payton	Sun Life Stadium, Miami Gardens, FL
XLV	2011	*Green Bay Packers, 31	Pittsburgh Steelers, 25	Mike McCarthy	Cowboys Stadium, Arlington, TX
XLVI	2012	NY Giants, 21	*New England Patriots, 17	Tom Coughlin	Lucas Oil Stadium, Indianapolis, IN

*Team that won the coin toss. All teams that won the toss elected to receive, except the 2009 Cardinals, 2011 Packers, and 2012 Patriots, who deferred their choice to receive in the second half.

Super Bowl Single-Game Statistical Leaders

Passing Yards

	Year	Att/comp	Yds	TD
Kurt Warner, Rams	2000	45/24	414	2
Kurt Warner, Cardinals	2009	43/31	377	3
Kurt Warner, Rams	2002	44/28	365	1
Donovon McNabb, Eagles. . .	2005	51/30	357	3
Joe Montana, 49ers	1989	36/23	357	2

Receiving Yards

	Year	Rec	Yds	TD
Jerry Rice, 49ers	1989	11	215	1
Ricky Sanders, Redskins. . . .	1988	9	193	2
Isaac Bruce, Rams	2000	6	162	1

Rushing Yards

	Year	Att	Yds	TD
Timmy Smith, Redskins	1988	22	204	2
Marcus Allen, Raiders	1984	20	191	2
John Riggins, Redskins	1983	38	166	1

Passing Touchdowns

	Year	Att/comp	Yds	TD
Steve Young, 49ers	1995	36/24	325	6
Joe Montana, 49ers.	1990	29/22	297	5
Troy Aikman, Cowboys	1993	30/22	273	4
Doug Williams, Redskins. . . .	1988	29/18	340	4
Terry Bradshaw, Steelers . . .	1979	30/17	318	4

Scoring

	Year	Pts	
Terrell Davis, Broncos	1998	18	3 TDs
Jerry Rice, 49ers	1995	18	3 TDs
Ricky Watters, 49ers	1995	18	3 TDs
Jerry Rice, 49ers	1990	18	3 TDs
Roger Craig, 49ers	1985	18	3 TDs
Don Chandler, Packers	1968	15	4 FG, 3 PATs

Super Bowl MVPs, 1967-2012

Year	Most valuable player, team	Year	Most valuable player, team	Year	Most valuable player, team
1967	Bart Starr, Green Bay	1983	John Riggins, Washington	1998	Terrell Davis, Denver
1968	Bart Starr, Green Bay	1984	Marcus Allen, L.A. Raiders	1999	John Elway, Denver
1969	Joe Namath, NY Jets	1985	Joe Montana, San Francisco	2000	Kurt Warner, St. Louis
1970	Len Dawson, Kansas City	1986	Richard Dent, Chicago	2001	Ray Lewis, Baltimore
1971	Chuck Howley, Dallas	1987	Phil Simms, NY Giants	2002	Tom Brady, New England
1972	Roger Staubach, Dallas	1988	Doug Williams, Washington	2003	Dexter Jackson, Tampa Bay
1973	Jake Scott, Miami	1989	Jerry Rice, San Francisco	2004	Tom Brady, New England
1974	Larry Csonka, Miami	1990	Joe Montana, San Francisco	2005	Deion Branch, New England
1975	Franco Harris, Pittsburgh	1991	Ottis Anderson, NY Giants	2006	Hines Ward, Pittsburgh
1976	Lynn Swann, Pittsburgh	1992	Mark Rypien, Washington	2007	Peyton Manning, Indianapolis
1977	Fred Biletnikoff, Oakland	1993	Troy Aikman, Dallas	2008	Eli Manning, NY Giants
1978	Randy White, Harvey Martin; Dallas	1994	Emmitt Smith, Dallas	2009	Santonio Holmes, Pittsburgh
1979	Terry Bradshaw, Pittsburgh	1995	Steve Young, San Francisco	2010	Drew Brees, New Orleans
1980	Terry Bradshaw, Pittsburgh	1996	Larry Brown, Dallas	2011	Aaron Rodgers, Green Bay
1981	Jim Plunkett, Oakland	1997	Desmond Howard, Green Bay	2012	Eli Manning, NY Giants
1982	Joe Montana, San Francisco				

First-Round Selections in the 2012 NFL Draft

Team	Player	Pos.	College	Team	Player	Pos.	College
1. Indianapolis Colts	Andrew Luck	QB	Stanford	19. Chicago Bears	Shea McClellin	DE	Boise State
2. Washington Redskins[1]	Robert Griffin III	QB	Baylor	20. Tennessee Titans	Kendall Wright	WR	Baylor
3. Cleveland Browns[2]	Trent Richardson	RB	Alabama	21. New England Patriots[11]	Chandler Jones	DE	Syracuse
4. Minnesota Vikings[3]	Matt Kalil	OT	USC	22. Cleveland Browns[12]	Brandon Weeden	QB	Okla. St
5. Jacksonville Jaguars[4]	Justin Blackmon	WR	Okla. St	23. Detroit Lions	Riley Reiff	OT	Iowa
6. Dallas Cowboys[5]	Morris Claiborne	CB	LSU	24. Pittsburgh Steelers	David DeCastro	G	Stanford
7. Tampa Bay Buccaneers[6]	Mark Barron	S	Alabama	25. New England Patriots[13]	Dont'a Hightower	LB	Alabama
8. Miami Dolphins	Ryan Tannehill	QB	Texas A&M	26. Houston Texans	Whitney Mercilus	DE	Illinois
9. Carolina Panthers	Luke Kuechly	LB	Boston Coll.	27. Cincinnati Bengals[14]	Kevin Zeitler	G	Wisconsin
10. Buffalo Bills	Stephon Gilmore	CB	South Carolina	28. Green Bay Packers	Nick Perry	DE	USC
11. Kansas City Chiefs	Dontari Poe	DT	Memphis	29. Minnesota Vikings[15]	Harrison Smith	S	Notre Dame
12. Philadelphia Eagles[7]	Fletcher Cox	DT	Miss. St.	30. San Francisco 49ers	A. J. Jenkins	WR	Illinois
13. Arizona Cardinals	Michael Floyd	WR	Notre Dame	31. Tampa Bay Buccaneers[16]	Doug Martin	RB	Boise State
14. St. Louis Rams[8]	Michael Brockers	DT	LSU	32. NY Giants	David Wilson	RB	Virginia Tech
15. Seattle Seahawks[9]	Bruce Irvin	DE	West Virginia				
16. NY Jets	Quinton Coples	DE	North Carolina				
17. Cincinnati Bengals[10]	Dre Kirkpatrick	CB	Alabama				
18. San Diego Chargers	Melvin Ingram	DE	South Carolina				

(1) From St. Louis. (2) From Minnesota. (3) From Cleveland. (4) From Tampa Bay. (5) From Washington through St. Louis. (6) From Jacksonville. (7) From Seattle. (8) From Dallas. (9) From Philadelphia. (10) From Oakland. (11) From Cincinnati. (12) From Atlanta. (13) From Denver. (14) From New Orleans through New England. (15) From Baltimore. (16) From New England through Denver.

Number One NFL Draft Choices, 1936-2012

Year	Team	Player, pos., college	Year	Team	Player, pos., college
1936	Philadelphia	Jay Berwanger, HB, Chicago	1975	Atlanta	Steve Bartkowski, QB, California
1937	Philadelphia	Sam Francis, FB, Nebraska	1976	Tampa Bay	Lee Roy Selmon, DE, Oklahoma
1938	Cleveland Rams	Corbett Davis, FB, Indiana	1977	Tampa Bay	Ricky Bell, RB, USC
1939	Chicago Cards	Ki Aldrich, C, TCU	1978	Houston	Earl Campbell, RB, Texas
1940	Chicago Cards	George Cafego, HB, Tennessee	1979	Buffalo	Tom Cousineau, LB, Ohio St.
1941	Chicago Bears	Tom Harmon, HB, Michigan	1980	Detroit	Billy Sims, RB, Oklahoma
1942	Pittsburgh	Bill Dudley, HB, Virginia	1981	New Orleans	George Rogers, RB, S. Carolina
1943	Detroit	Frank Sinkwich, HB, Georgia	1982	New England	Kenneth Sims, DT, Texas
1944	Boston Yanks	Angelo Bertelli, QB, Notre Dame	1983	Baltimore Colts	John Elway, QB, Stanford
1945	Chicago Cards	Charley Trippi, HB, Georgia	1984	New England	Irving Fryar, WR, Nebraska
1946	Boston Yanks	Frank Dancewicz, QB, Notre Dame	1985	Buffalo	Bruce Smith, DE, Virginia Tech
1947	Chicago Bears	Bob Fenimore, HB, Oklahoma St.	1986	Tampa Bay	Bo Jackson, RB, Auburn
1948	Washington	Harry Gilmer, QB, Alabama	1987	Tampa Bay	Vinny Testaverde, QB, Miami (FL)
1949	Philadelphia	Chuck Bednarik, C, Pennsylvania	1988	Atlanta	Aundray Bruce, LB, Auburn
1950	Detroit	Leon Hart, E, Notre Dame	1989	Dallas	Troy Aikman, QB, UCLA
1951	NY Giants	Kyle Rote, HB, SMU	1990	Indianapolis	Jeff George, QB, Illinois
1952	L.A. Rams	Bill Wade, QB, Vanderbilt	1991	Dallas	Russell Maryland, DL, Miami (FL)
1953	San Francisco	Harry Babcock, E, Georgia	1992	Indianapolis	Steve Emtman, DL, Washington
1954	Cleveland	Bobby Garrett, QB, Stanford	1993	New England	Drew Bledsoe, QB, Washington St.
1955	Baltimore Colts	George Shaw, QB, Oregon	1994	Cincinnati	Dan Wilkinson, DT, Ohio St.
1956	Pittsburgh	Gary Glick, DB, Colorado State	1995	Cincinnati	Ki-Jana Carter, RB, Penn State
1957	Green Bay	Paul Hornung, QB, Notre Dame	1996	NY Jets	Keyshawn Johnson, WR, USC
1958	Chicago Cards	King Hill, QB, Rice	1997	St. Louis	Orlando Pace, T, Ohio St.
1959	Green Bay	Randy Duncan, QB, Iowa	1998	Indianapolis	Peyton Manning, QB, Tennessee
1960	L.A. Rams	Billy Cannon, HB, LSU	1999	Cleveland	Tim Couch, QB, Kentucky
1961	Minnesota	Tommy Mason, HB, Tulane	2000	Cleveland	Courtney Brown, DE, Penn State
1962	Washington	Ernie Davis, HB, Syracuse	2001	Atlanta	Michael Vick, QB, Virginia Tech
1963	L.A. Rams	Terry Baker, QB, Oregon St.	2002	Houston	David Carr, QB, Fresno St.
1964	San Francisco	Dave Parks, E, Texas Tech	2003	Cincinnati	Carson Palmer, QB, USC
1965	NY Giants	Tucker Frederickson, HB, Auburn	2004	San Diego	Eli Manning, QB, Mississippi
1966	Atlanta	Tommy Nobis, LB, Texas	2005	San Francisco	Alex D. Smith, QB, Utah
1967	Baltimore Colts	Bubba Smith, DT, Michigan St.	2006	Houston	Mario Williams, DE, NC State
1968	Minnesota	Ron Yary, T, USC	2007	Oakland	JaMarcus Russell, QB, LSU
1969	Buffalo	O. J. Simpson, RB, USC	2008	Miami	Jake Long, OT, Michigan
1970	Pittsburgh	Terry Bradshaw, QB, LA Tech	2009	Detroit	Matthew Stafford, QB, Georgia
1971	New England	Jim Plunkett, QB, Stanford	2010	St. Louis	Sam Bradford, QB, Oklahoma
1972	Buffalo	Walt Patulski, DE, Notre Dame	2011	Carolina	Cam Newton, QB, Auburn
1973	Houston	John Matuszak, DE, Tampa	2012	Indianapolis	Andrew Luck, QB, Stanford
1974	Dallas	Ed "Too Tall" Jones, DE, Tenn. St.			

American Football League Champions, 1960-69

Year	Eastern (W-L-T)	Western (W-L-T)	Championship
1960	Houston Oilers (10-4-0)	L.A. Chargers (10-4-0)	Houston 24, L.A. 16
1961	Houston Oilers (10-3-1)	San Diego Chargers (12-2-0)	Houston 10, San Diego 3
1962	Houston Oilers (11-3-0)	Dallas Texans (11-3-0)	Dallas 20, Houston 17 (2 OT)
1963	Boston Patriots (7-6-1)[1]	San Diego Chargers (11-3-0)	San Diego 51, Boston 10
1964	Buffalo Bills (12-2-0)	San Diego Chargers (8-5-1)	Buffalo 20, San Diego 7
1965	Buffalo Bills (10-3-1)	San Diego Chargers (9-2-3)	Buffalo 23, San Diego 0
1966	Buffalo Bills (9-4-1)	Kansas City Chiefs (11-2-1)	Kansas City 31, Buffalo 7
1967	Houston Oilers (9-4-1)	Oakland Raiders (13-1-0)	Oakland 40, Houston 7
1968	NY Jets (11-3-0)	Oakland Raiders (12-2-0)[2]	NY 27, Oakland 23
1969	NY Jets (10-4-0)	Oakland Raiders (12-1-1)	Kansas City 17, Oakland 7[3]

(1) Defeated Buffalo Bills in divisional playoff. (2) Defeated Kansas City Chiefs in divisional playoff. (3) Kansas City Chiefs defeated NY Jets, and Oakland Raiders defeated Houston Oilers in divisional playoffs.

National Football League Champions, 1933-69

Year	East (W-L-T)	West (W-L-T)	Championship
1933	NY Giants (11-3-0)	Chicago Bears (10-2-1)	Chicago Bears 23, NY 21
1934	NY Giants (8-5-0)	Chicago Bears (13-0-0)	NY 30, Chicago Bears 13
1935	NY Giants (9-3-0)	Detroit Lions (7-3-2)	Detroit 26, NY 7
1936	Boston Redskins (7-5-0)	Green Bay Packers (10-1-1)	Green Bay 21, Boston 6
1937	Washington Redskins (8-3-0)	Chicago Bears (9-1-1)	Washington 28, Chicago Bears 21
1938	NY Giants (8-2-1)	Green Bay Packers (8-3-0)	NY 23, Green Bay 17
1939	NY Giants (9-1-1)	Green Bay Packers (9-2-0)	Green Bay 27, NY 0
1940	Washington Redskins (9-2-0)	Chicago Bears (8-3-0)	Chicago Bears 73, Washington 0
1941	NY Giants (8-3-0)	Chicago Bears (10-1-1)[1]	Chicago Bears 37, NY 9
1942	Washington Redskins (10-1-1)	Chicago Bears (11-0-0)	Washington 14, Chicago Bears 6
1943	Washington Redskins (6-3-1)	Chicago Bears (8-1-1)	Chicago Bears, 41, Washington 21
1944	NY Giants (8-1-1)	Green Bay Packers (8-2-0)	Green Bay 14, NY 7
1945	Washington Redskins (8-2-0)	Cleveland Rams (9-1-0)	Cleveland 15, Washington 14
1946	NY Giants (7-3-1)	Chicago Bears (8-2-1)	Chicago Bears 24, NY 14
1947	Philadelphia Eagles (8-4-0)[1]	Chicago Cardinals (9-3-0)	Chicago Cardinals 28, Philadelphia 21
1948	Philadelphia Eagles (9-2-1)	Chicago Cardinals (11-1-0)	Philadelphia 7, Chicago Cardinals 0
1949	Philadelphia Eagles (11-1-0)	L.A. Rams (8-2-2)	Philadelphia 14, L.A. 0
1950	Cleveland Browns (10-2-0)[1]	L.A. Rams (9-3-0)[1]	Cleveland 30, L.A. 28
1951	Cleveland Browns (11-1-0)	L.A. Rams (8-4-0)	L.A. 24, Cleveland 17
1952	Cleveland Browns (8-4-0)	Detroit Lions (9-3-0)[1]	Detroit 17, Cleveland 7
1953	Cleveland Browns (11-1-0)	Detroit Lions (10-2-0)	Detroit 17, Cleveland 16
1954	Cleveland Browns (9-3-0)	Detroit Lions (9-2-1)	Cleveland 56, Detroit 10
1955	Cleveland Browns (9-2-1)	L.A. Rams (8-3-1)	Cleveland 38, L.A. 14
1956	NY Giants (8-3-1)	Chicago Bears (9-2-1)	NY 47, Chicago Bears 7
1957	Cleveland Browns (9-2-1)	Detroit Lions (8-4-0)[1]	Detroit 59, Cleveland 14
1958	NY Giants (9-3-0)[1]	Baltimore Colts (9-3-0)	Baltimore 23, NY 17[2]
1959	NY Giants (10-2-0)	Baltimore Colts (9-3-0)	Baltimore 31, NY 16
1960	Philadelphia Eagles (10-2-0)	Green Bay Packers (8-4-0)	Philadelphia 17, Green Bay 13
1961	NY Giants (10-3-1)	Green Bay Packers (11-3-0)	Green Bay 37, NY 0
1962	NY Giants (12-2-0)	Green Bay Packers (13-1-0)	Green Bay 16, NY 7
1963	NY Giants (11-3-0)	Chicago Bears (11-1-2)	Chicago 14, NY 10
1964	Cleveland Browns (10-3-1)	Baltimore Colts (12-2-0)	Cleveland 27, Baltimore 0
1965	Cleveland Browns (11-3-0)	Green Bay Packers (10-3-1)[1]	Green Bay 23, Cleveland 12
1966	Dallas Cowboys (10-3-1)	Green Bay Packers (12-2-0)	Green Bay 34, Dallas 27
1967	Dallas Cowboys (9-5-0)	Green Bay Packers (9-4-1)	Green Bay 21, Dallas 17
1968	Cleveland Browns (10-4-0)	Baltimore Colts (13-1-0)	Baltimore 34, Cleveland 0
1969	Cleveland Browns (10-3-1)	Minnesota Vikings (12-2-0)	Minnesota 27, Cleveland 7

(1) Won divisional playoff. (2) Won at 8:15 of sudden death overtime period.

NFL Divisional Champions and Wild Cards, 1970-95

The American Football League and National Football League officially merged in 1966. At the beginning of the 1970 season, the two leagues became the AFC and NFC conferences in the new NFL. Regular-season (W-L-T) records are in parentheses.

AMERICAN FOOTBALL CONFERENCE

Year	Eastern	Central	Western	Wild card
1970	Baltimore Colts (11-2-1)	Cincinnati Bengals (8-6-0)	Oakland Raiders (8-4-2)	Miami Dolphins (10-4-0)
1971	Miami Dolphins (10-3-1)	Cleveland Browns (9-5-0)	Kansas City Chiefs (10-3-1)	Baltimore Colts (10-4-0)
1972	Miami Dolphins (14-0-0)	Pittsburgh Steelers (11-3-0)	Oakland Raiders (10-3-1)	Cleveland Browns (10-4-0)
1973	Miami Dolphins (12-2-0)	Cincinnati Bengals (10-4-0)	Oakland Raiders (9-4-1)	Cincinnati Bengals (10-4-0)
1974	Miami Dolphins (11-3-0)	Pittsburgh Steelers (10-3-1)	Oakland Raiders (12-2-0)	Buffalo Bills (9-5-0)
1975	Baltimore Colts (10-4-0)	Pittsburgh Steelers (12-2-0)	Oakland Raiders (11-3-0)	Cincinnati Bengals (11-3-0)
1976	Baltimore Colts (11-3-0)	Pittsburgh Steelers (10-4-0)	Oakland Raiders (13-1-0)	New England Patriots (11-3-0)
1977	Baltimore Colts (10-4-0)	Pittsburgh Steelers (9-5-0)	Denver Broncos (12-2-0)	Oakland Raiders (11-3-0)
1978	New England Patriots (11-5-0)	Pittsburgh Steelers (14-2-0)	Denver Broncos (10-6-0)	Houston Oilers (10-6-0) Miami Dolphins (11-5-0)
1979	Miami Dolphins (10-6-0)	Pittsburgh Steelers (12-4-0)	San Diego Chargers (12-4-0)	Houston Oilers (11-5-0) Denver Broncos (10-6-0)
1980	Buffalo Bills (11-5-0)	Cleveland Browns (11-5-0)	San Diego Chargers (11-5-0)	Houston Oilers (11-5-0) Oakland Raiders (11-5-0)
1981	Miami Dolphins (11-4-1)	Cincinnati Bengals (12-4-0)	San Diego Chargers (10-6-0)	Buffalo Bills (10-6-0) NY Jets (10-5-1)
1982	Strike abbreviated season. See note.			
1983	Miami Dolphins (12-4-0)	Pittsburgh Steelers (10-6-0)	L.A. Raiders (12-4-0)	Denver Broncos (9-7-0) Seattle Seahawks (9-7-0)
1984	Miami Dolphins (14-2-0)	Pittsburgh Steelers (9-7-0)	Denver Broncos (13-3-0)	L.A. Raiders (11-5-0) Seattle Seahawks (12-4-0)
1985	Miami Dolphins (12-4-0)	Cleveland Browns (8-8-0)	L.A. Raiders (12-4-0)	New England Patriots (11-5-0) NY Jets (11-5-0)

AMERICAN FOOTBALL CONFERENCE

Year	Eastern	Central	Western	Wild card
1986	New England Patriots (11-5-0)	Cleveland Browns (12-4-0)	Denver Broncos (11-5-0)	Kansas City Chiefs (10-6-0) NY Jets (10-6-0)
1987	Indianapolis Colts (9-6-0)	Cleveland Browns (10-5-0)	Buffalo Bills (12-4-0)	Houston Oilers (9-6-0) Seattle Seahawks (9-6-0)
1988	Buffalo Bills (12-4-0)	Cincinnati Bengals (12-4-0)	Seattle Seahawks (9-7-0)	Cleveland Browns (10-6-0) Houston Oilers (10-6-0)
1989	Buffalo Bills (9-7-0)	Cleveland Browns (9-6-1)	Denver Broncos (11-5-0)	Houston Oilers (9-7-0) Pittsburgh Steelers (9-7-0)
1990	Buffalo Bills (13-3-0)	Cincinnati Bengals (9-7-0)	L.A. Raiders (12-4-0)	Houston Oilers (9-7-0) Kansas City Chiefs (11-5-0) Miami Dolphins (12-4-0)
1991	Buffalo Bills (13-3-0)	Houston Oilers (11-5-0)	Denver Broncos (12-4-0)	Kansas City Chiefs (11-5-0) Miami Dolphins (12-4-0) NY Jets (8-8-0)
1992	Miami Dolphins (11-5-0)	Pittsburgh Steelers (11-5-0)	San Diego Chargers (11-5-0)	Buffalo Bills (11-5-0) Houston Oilers (10-6-0) Kansas City Chiefs (10-6-0)
1993	Buffalo Bills (12-4-0)	Houston Oilers (12-4-0)	Kansas City Chiefs (11-5-0)	Denver Broncos (9-7-0) L.A. Raiders (10-6-0) Pittsburgh Steelers (9-7-0)
1994	Miami Dolphins (10-6-0)	Pittsburgh Steelers (12-4-0)	San Diego Chargers (11-5-0)	Cleveland Browns (11-5-0) Kansas City Chiefs (9-7-0) New England Patriots (10-6-0)
1995	Buffalo Bills (10-6-0)	Pittsburgh Steelers (11-5-0)	Kansas City Chiefs (13-3-0)	Miami Dolphins (9-7-0) Indianapolis Colts (9-7-0) San Diego Chargers (9-7-0)

NATIONAL FOOTBALL CONFERENCE

Year	Eastern	Central	Western	Wild card
1970	Dallas Cowboys (10-4-0)	Minnesota Vikings (12-2-0)	San Francisco 49ers (10-3-1)	Detroit Lions (10-4-0)
1971	Dallas Cowboys (11-3-0)	Minnesota Vikings (11-3-0)	San Francisco 49ers (9-5-0)	Washington Redskins (9-4-1)
1972	Washington Redskins (11-3-0)	Green Bay Packers (10-4-0)	San Francisco 49ers (8-5-1)	Dallas Cowboys (10-4-0)
1973	Dallas Cowboys (10-4-0)	Minnesota Vikings (12-2-0)	L.A. Rams (12-2-0)	Washington Redskins (10-4-0)
1974	St. Louis Cardinals (10-4-0)	Minnesota Vikings (10-4-0)	L.A. Rams (10-4-0)	Washington Redskins (10-4-0)
1975	St. Louis Cardinals (11-3-0)	Minnesota Vikings (12-2-0)	L.A. Rams (12-2-0)	Dallas Cowboys (10-4-0)
1976	Dallas Cowboys (11-3-0)	Minnesota Vikings (11-2-1)	L.A. Rams (10-3-1)	Washington Redskins (10-4-0)
1977	Dallas Cowboys (12-2-0)	Minnesota Vikings (9-5-0)	L.A. Rams (10-4-0)	Chicago Bears (9-5-0)
1978	Dallas Cowboys (12-4-0)	Minnesota Vikings (8-7-1)	L.A. Rams (12-4-0)	Atlanta Falcons (9-7-0) Philadelphia Eagles (9-7-0)
1979	Dallas Cowboys (11-5-0)	Tampa Bay Buccaneers (10-6-0)	L.A. Rams (9-7-0)	Chicago Bears (10-6-0) Philadelphia Eagles (11-5-0)
1980	Philadelphia Eagles (12-4-0)	Minnesota Vikings (9-7-0)	Atlanta Falcons (12-4-0)	Dallas Cowboys (12-4-0) L.A. Rams (11-5-0)
1981	Dallas Cowboys (12-4-0)	Tampa Bay Buccaneers (9-7-0)	San Francisco 49ers (13-3-0)	NY Giants (9-7-0) Philadelphia Eagles (10-6-0)
1982	Strike abbreviated season. See note.			
1983	Washington Redskins (14-2-0)	Detroit Lions (9-7-0)	San Francisco 49ers (10-6-0)	Dallas Cowboys (12-4-0) L.A. Rams (9-7-0)
1984	Washington Redskins (11-5-0)	Chicago Bears (10-6-0)	San Francisco 49ers (15-1-0)	L.A. Rams (10-6-0) NY Giants (9-7-0)
1985	Dallas Cowboys (10-6-0)	Chicago Bears (15-1-0)	L.A. Rams (11-5-0)	NY Giants (10-6-0) San Francisco 49ers (10-6-0)
1986	NY Giants (14-2-0)	Chicago Bears (14-2-0)	San Francisco 49ers (10-5-1)	L.A. Rams (10-6-0) Washington Redskins (12-4-0)
1987	Washington Redskins (11-4-0)	Chicago Bears (11-4-0)	San Francisco 49ers (13-2-0)	Minnesota Vikings (8-7-0) New Orleans Saints (12-3-0)
1988	Philadelphia Eagles (10-6-0)	Chicago Bears (12-4-0)	San Francisco 49ers (10-6-0)	L.A. Rams (10-6-0) Minnesota Vikings (11-5-0)
1989	NY Giants (12-4-0)	Minnesota Vikings (10-6-0)	San Francisco 49ers (14-2-0)	L.A. Rams (11-5-0) Philadelphia Eagles (11-5-0)
1990	NY Giants (13-3-0)	Chicago Bears (11-5-0)	San Francisco 49ers (14-2-0)	New Orleans Saints (8-8-0) Philadelphia Eagles (10-6-0) Washington Redskins (10-6-0)
1991	Washington Redskins (14-2-0)	Detroit Lions (12-4-0)	New Orleans Saints (11-5-0)	Atlanta Falcons (10-6-0) Chicago Bears (11-5-0) Dallas Cowboys (11-5-0)
1992	Dallas Cowboys (13-3-0)	Minnesota Vikings (11-5-0)	San Francisco 49ers (14-2-0)	New Orleans Saints (12-4-0) Philadelphia Eagles (11-5-0) Washington Redskins (9-7-0)
1993	Dallas Cowboys (12-4-0)	Detroit Lions (10-6-0)	San Francisco 49ers (10-6-0)	Green Bay Packers (9-7-0) Minnesota Vikings (9-7-0) NY Giants (11-5-0)
1994	Dallas Cowboys (12-4-0)	Minnesota Vikings (10-6-0)	San Francisco 49ers (13-3-0)	Chicago Bears (9-7-0) Detroit Lions (9-7-0) Green Bay Packers (9-7-0)
1995	Dallas Cowboys (12-4-0)	Green Bay Packers (11-5-0)	San Francisco 49ers (11-5-0)	Philadelphia Eagles (10-6-0) Detroit Lions (10-6-0) Atlanta Falcons (9-7-0)

Note: A strike shortened the 1982 season from 16 to 9 games. The top eight teams in each conference played in a tournament to determine the conference champion. AFC—Miami Dolphins, New England Patriots, L.A. Raiders, Cleveland Browns, NY Jets, Cincinnati Bengals, San Diego Chargers, Pittsburgh Steelers. NFC—Washington Redskins, Detroit Lions, Green Bay Packers, St. Louis Cardinals, Dallas Cowboys, Tampa Bay Buccaneers, Minnesota Vikings, Atlanta Falcons.

NFL Playoff Results, 1996-2011

Year	Conference	Division	Winner (W-L-T)	Playoffs[1]	Year
1996	American	Eastern	New England Patriots (11-5-0)	Jacksonville* 30, Denver 27	1996
		Central	Pittsburgh Steelers (10-6-0)	New England 28, Pittsburgh 3	
		Western	Denver Broncos (13-3-0)	New England 20, Jacksonville* 6	
	National	Eastern	Dallas Cowboys (10-6-0)	Green Bay 35, San Francisco* 14	
		Central	Green Bay Packers (13-3-0)	Carolina 26, Dallas 17	
		Western	Carolina Panthers (12-4-0)	Green Bay 30, Carolina 13	
1997	American	Eastern	New England Patriots (10-6-0)	Pittsburgh 7, New England 6	1997
		Central	Pittsburgh Steelers (11-5-0)	Denver* 14, Kansas City 10	
		Western	Kansas City Chiefs (13-3-0)	Denver* 24, Pittsburgh 21	
	National	Eastern	NY Giants (10-5-1)	San Francisco 38, Minnesota* 22	
		Central	Green Bay Packers (13-3-0)	Green Bay 21, Tampa Bay* 7	
		Western	San Francisco 49ers (13-3-0)	Green Bay 23, San Francisco 10	
1998	American	Eastern	NY Jets (12-4-0)	Denver 38, Miami* 3	1998
		Central	Jacksonville Jaguars (11-5-0)	NY Jets 34, Jacksonville 24	
		Western	Denver Broncos (14-2-0)	Denver 23, NY Jets 10	
	National	Eastern	Dallas Cowboys (10-6-0)	Atlanta 20, San Francisco* 18	
		Central	Minnesota Vikings (15-1-0)	Minnesota 41, Arizona* 21	
		Western	Atlanta Falcons (14-2-0)	Atlanta 30, Minnesota 27 (OT)	
1999	American	Eastern	Indianapolis Colts (13-3-0)	Jacksonville 62, Miami* 7	1999
		Central	Jacksonville Jaguars (14-2-0)	Tennessee* 19, Indianapolis 16	
		Western	Seattle Seahawks (9-7-0)	Tennessee* 33, Jacksonville 14	
	National	Eastern	Washington Redskins (10-6-0)	Tampa Bay 14, Washington 13	
		Central	Tampa Bay Buccaneers (11-5-0)	St. Louis 49, Minnesota* 37	
		Western	St. Louis Rams (13-3-0)	St. Louis 11, Tampa Bay 6	
2000	American	Eastern	Miami Dolphins (11-5-0)	Oakland 27, Miami 0	2000
		Central	Tennessee Titans (13-3-0)	Baltimore* 24, Tennessee 10	
		Western	Oakland Raiders (12-4-0)	Baltimore* 16, Oakland 3	
	National	Eastern	NY Giants (12-4-0)	Minnesota 34, New Orleans 16	
		Central	Minnesota Vikings (11-5-0)	NY Giants 20, Philadelphia* 10	
		Western	New Orleans Saints (10-6-0)	NY Giants 41, Minnesota 0	
2001	American	Eastern	New England Patriots (11-5-0)	New England 16, Oakland 13	2001
		Central	Pittsburgh Steelers (13-3-0)	Pittsburgh 27, Baltimore 10	
		Western	Oakland Raiders (10-6-0)	New England 24, Pittsburgh 17	
	National	Eastern	Philadelphia Eagles (11-5-0)	Philadelphia 33, Chicago 19	
		Central	Chicago Bears (13-3-0)	St. Louis 45, Green Bay* 17	
		Western	St. Louis Rams (14-2-0)	St. Louis 29, Philadelphia 24	
2002	American	East	NY Jets (9-7-0)		2002
		North	Pittsburgh Steelers (10-5-1)	Oakland 30, NY Jets 10	
		South	Tennessee Titans (11-5-0)	Tennessee 34, Pittsburgh 31	
		West	Oakland Raiders (11-5-0)	Oakland 41, Tennessee 24	
	National	East	Philadelphia Eagles (12-4-0)		
		North	Green Bay Packers (12-4-0)	Philadelphia 20, Atlanta* 6	
		South	Tampa Bay Buccaneers (12-4-0)	Tampa Bay 31, San Francisco 6	
		West	San Francisco 49ers (10-6-0)	Tampa Bay 27, Philadelphia 10	
2003	American	East	New England Patriots (14-2-0)		2003
		North	Baltimore Ravens (10-6-0)	Indianapolis 38, Kansas City 31	
		South	Indianapolis Colts (12-4-0)	New England 17, Tennessee* 14	
		West	Kansas City Chiefs (13-3-0)	New England 24, Indianapolis 14	
	National	East	Philadelphia Eagles (12-4-0)		
		North	Green Bay Packers (10-6-0)	Carolina 29, St. Louis 23	
		South	Carolina Panthers (11-5-0)	Philadelphia 20, Green Bay 17	
		West	St. Louis Rams (12-4-0)	Carolina 14, Philadelphia 3	
2004	American	East	New England Patriots (14-2-0)		2004
		North	Pittsburgh Steelers (15-1-0)	Pittsburgh 20, NY Jets* 17 (OT)	
		South	Indianapolis Colts (12-4-0)	New England 20, Indianapolis 3	
		West	San Diego Chargers (12-4-0)	New England 41, Pittsburgh 27	
	National	East	Philadelphia Eagles (13-3-0)		
		North	Green Bay Packers (10-6-0)	Atlanta 47, St. Louis* 17	
		South	Atlanta Falcons (11-5-0)	Philadelphia 27, Minnesota* 14	
		West	Seattle Seahawks (9-7-0)	Philadelphia 27, Atlanta 10	
2005	American	East	New England Patriots (10-6-0)		2005
		North	Cincinnati Bengals (11-5-0)	Denver 27, New England 13	
		South	Indianapolis Colts (14-2-0)	Pittsburgh* 21, Indianapolis 18	
		West	Denver Broncos (13-3-0)	Pittsburgh* 34, Denver 17	
	National	East	NY Giants (11-5-0)		
		North	Chicago Bears (11-5-0)	Seattle 20, Washington* 10	
		South	Tampa Bay Buccaneers (11-5-0)	Carolina* 29, Chicago 21	
		West	Seattle Seahawks (13-3-0)	Seattle 34, Carolina* 14	
2006	American	East	New England Patriots (12-4-0)		2006
		North	Baltimore Ravens (13-3-0)	Indianapolis 15, Baltimore 6	
		South	Indianapolis Colts (12-4-0)	New England 24, San Diego 21	
		West	San Diego Chargers (14-2-0)	Indianapolis 38, New England 34	
	National	East	Philadelphia Eagles (10-6-0)		
		North	Chicago Bears (13-3-0)	New Orleans 27, Philadelphia 24	
		South	New Orleans Saints (10-6-0)	Chicago 27, Seattle 24 (OT)	
		West	Seattle Seahawks (9-7-0)	Chicago 39, New Orleans 14	

Year	Conference	Division	Winner (W-L-T)	Playoffs[1]	Year
2007	American	East	New England Patriots (16-0-0)		2007
		North	Pittsburgh Steelers (10-6-0)	New England 31, Jacksonville* 20	
		South	Indianapolis Colts (13-3-0)	San Diego 28, Indianapolis 24	
		West	San Diego Chargers (11-5-0)	New England 21, San Diego 12	
	National	East	Dallas Cowboys (13-3-0)		
		North	Green Bay Packers (13-3-0)	Green Bay 42, Seattle 20	
		South	Tampa Bay Buccaneers (9-7-0)	NY Giants* 21, Dallas 17	
		West	Seattle Seahawks (10-6-0)	NY Giants* 22, Green Bay 20	
2008	American	East	Miami Dolphins (11-5-0)		2008
		North	Pittsburgh Steelers (12-4-0)	Baltimore* 13, Tennessee 10	
		South	Tennessee Titans (13-3-0)	Pittsburgh 35, San Diego 24	
		West	San Diego Chargers (8-8-0)	Pittsburgh 23, Baltimore* 14	
	National	East	NY Giants (12-4-0)		
		North	Minnesota Vikings (10-6-0)	Arizona 33, Carolina 13	
		South	Carolina Panthers (12-4-0)	Philadelphia* 23, NY Giants 11	
		West	Arizona Cardinals (9-7-0)	Arizona 32, Philadelphia* 25	
2009	American	East	New England Patriots (10-6-0)		2009
		North	Cincinnati Bengals (10-6-0)	Indianapolis 20, Baltimore 3	
		South	Indianapolis Colts (14-2-0)	NY Jets* 17, San Diego 14	
		West	San Diego Chargers (13-3-0)	Indianapolis 30, NY Jets* 17	
	National	East	Dallas Cowboys (11-5-0)		
		North	Minnesota Vikings (12-4-0)	New Orleans 45, Arizona 14	
		South	New Orleans Saints (13-3-0)	Minnesota 34, Dallas 3	
		West	Arizona Cardinals (10-6-0)	New Orleans 31, Minnesota 28 (OT)	
2010	American	East	New England Patriots (14-2-0)		2010
		North	Pittsburgh Steelers (12-4-0)	Pittsburgh 31, Baltimore* 24	
		South	Indianapolis Colts (10-6-0)	NY Jets* 28, New England 21	
		West	Kansas City Chiefs (10-6-0)	Pittsburgh 24, NY Jets* 19	
	National	East	Philadelphia Eagles (10-6-0)		
		North	Chicago Bears (11-5-0)	Green Bay* 48, Atlanta 21	
		South	Atlanta Falcons (13-3-0)	Chicago 35, Seattle 24	
		West	Seattle Seahawks (7-9-0)	Green Bay* 21, Chicago 14	
2011	American	East	New England Patriots (13-3-0)		2011
		North	Baltimore Ravens (12-4-0)	New England 45, Denver 10	
		South	Houston Texans (10-6-0)	Baltimore 20, Houston 13	
		West	Denver Broncos (8-8-0)	New England 23, Baltimore 20	
	National	East	NY Giants (9-7-0)		
		North	Green Bay Packers (15-1-0)	San Francisco 36, New Orleans 32	
		South	New Orleans (13-3-0)	NY Giants 37, Green Bay 20	
		West	San Francisco (13-3-0)	NY Giants 20, San Francisco 17 (OT)	

*Wild card team. (1) Only the final conference playoff rounds are shown.

American Football Conference Leaders, 1960-2011

(American Football League, 1960-69)

Passing (based on QB rating points)						Receptions			
Player, team	Att	Comp	YG	TD	Year	Player, team	Rec	YG	TD
Jack Kemp, L.A. Chargers	406	211	3,018	20	1960	Lionel Taylor, Denver	92	1,235	12
George Blanda, Houston	362	187	3,330	36	1961	Lionel Taylor, Denver	100	1,176	4
Len Dawson, Dallas Texans	310	189	2,759	29	1962	Lionel Taylor, Denver	77	908	4
Tobin Rote, San Diego	286	170	2,510	20	1963	Lionel Taylor, Denver	78	1,101	10
Len Dawson, Kansas City	354	199	2,879	30	1964	Charley Hennigan, Houston	101	1,546	8
John Hadl, San Diego	348	174	2,798	20	1965	Lionel Taylor, Denver	85	1,131	6
Len Dawson, Kansas City	284	159	2,527	26	1966	Lance Alworth, San Diego	73	1,383	13
Daryle Lamonica, Oakland	425	220	3,228	30	1967	George Sauer, NY Jets	75	1,189	6
Len Dawson, Kansas City	224	131	2,109	17	1968	Lance Alworth, San Diego	68	1,312	10
Greg Cook, Cincinnati	197	106	1,854	15	1969	Lance Alworth, San Diego	64	1,003	4
Daryle Lamonica, Oakland	356	179	2,516	22	1970	Marlin Briscoe, Buffalo	57	1,036	8
Bob Griese, Miami	263	145	2,089	19	1971	Fred Biletnikoff, Oakland	61	929	9
Earl Morrall, Miami	150	83	1,360	11	1972	Fred Biletnikoff, Oakland	58	802	7
Ken Stabler, Oakland	260	163	1,997	14	1973	Fred Willis, Houston	57	371	1
Ken Anderson, Cincinnati	328	213	2,667	18	1974	Lydell Mitchell, Baltimore Colts	72	544	2
Ken Anderson, Cincinnati	377	228	3,169	21	1975	Reggie Rucker, Cleveland	60	770	3
						Lydell Mitchell, Baltimore Colts	60	554	4
Ken Stabler, Oakland	291	194	2,737	27	1976	MacArthur Lane, Kansas City	66	686	1
Bob Griese, Miami	307	180	2,252	22	1977	Lydell Mitchell, Baltimore Colts	71	620	4
Terry Bradshaw, Pittsburgh	368	207	2,915	28	1978	Steve Largent, Seattle	71	1,168	8
Dan Fouts, San Diego	530	332	4,082	24	1979	Joe Washington, Baltimore Colts	82	750	3
Brian Sipe, Cleveland	554	337	4,132	30	1980	Kellen Winslow, San Diego	89	1,290	9
Ken Anderson, Cincinnati	479	300	3,754	29	1981	Kellen Winslow, San Diego	88	1,075	10
Ken Anderson, Cincinnati	309	218	2,495	12	1982	Kellen Winslow, San Diego	54	721	6
Dan Marino, Miami	296	173	2,210	20	1983	Todd Christensen, L.A. Raiders	92	1,247	12
Dan Marino, Miami	564	362	5,084	48	1984	Ozzie Newsome, Cleveland	89	1,001	5
Ken O'Brien, NY Jets	488	297	3,888	25	1985	Lionel James, San Diego	86	1,027	6
Dan Marino, Miami	623	378	4,746	44	1986	Todd Christensen, L.A. Raiders	95	1,153	8
Bernie Kosar, Cleveland	389	241	3,033	22	1987	Al Toon, NY Jets	68	976	5
Boomer Esiason, Cincinnati	388	223	3,572	28	1988	Al Toon, NY Jets	93	1,067	5
Boomer Esiason, Cincinnati	455	258	3,525	28	1989	Andre Reed, Buffalo	88	1,312	9
Jim Kelly, Buffalo	346	219	2,829	24	1990	Haywood Jeffires, Houston	74	1,048	8
						Drew Hill, Houston	74	1,019	5

Passing (based on QB rating points)

Player, team	Att	Comp	YG	TD	Year
Jim Kelly, Buffalo	474	304	3,844	33	1991
Warren Moon, Houston	346	224	2,521	18	1992
John Elway, Denver	551	348	4,030	25	1993
Dan Marino, Miami	615	385	4,453	30	1994
Jim Harbaugh, Indianapolis	314	200	2,575	17	1995
John Elway, Denver	466	287	3,328	26	1996
Mark Brunell, Jacksonville	435	264	3,281	18	1997
Vinny Testaverde, NY Jets	421	259	3,256	29	1998
Peyton Manning, Indianapolis	533	331	4,135	26	1999
Brian Griese, Denver	336	216	2,688	19	2000
Rich Gannon, Oakland	549	361	3,828	27	2001
Chad Pennington, NY Jets	399	275	3,120	22	2002
Steve McNair, Tennessee	400	250	3,215	24	2003
Peyton Manning, Indianapolis	497	336	4,557	49	2004
Peyton Manning, Indianapolis	453	305	3,747	28	2005
Peyton Manning, Indianapolis	557	362	4,397	31	2006
Tom Brady, New England	578	398	4,806	50	2007
Philip Rivers, San Diego	478	312	4,009	34	2008
Philip Rivers, San Diego	486	317	4,254	28	2009
Tom Brady, New England	492	324	3,900	36	2010
Tom Brady, New England	611	401	5,235	39	2011

Receptions

Player, team	Rec	YG	TD	Year
Haywood Jeffires, Houston	100	1,181	7	1991
Haywood Jeffires, Houston	90	913	9	1992
Reggie Langhorne, Indianapolis	85	1,038	3	1993
Ben Coates, New England	96	1,174	7	1994
Carl Pickens, Cincinnati	99	1,234	17	1995
Carl Pickens, Cincinnati	100	1,180	12	1996
Tim Brown, Oakland	104	1,408	5	1997
O. J. McDuffie, Miami	90	1,050	7	1998
Jimmy Smith, Jacksonville	116	1,636	6	1999
Marvin Harrison, Indianapolis	102	1,413	14	2000
Rod Smith, Denver	113	1,343	11	2001
Marvin Harrison, Indianapolis	143	1,722	11	2002
LaDainian Tomlinson, San Diego	100	725	4	2003
Tony Gonzalez, Kansas City	102	1,258	7	2004
Chad Johnson, Cincinnati	97	1,432	9	2005
Andre Johnson, Houston	103	1,147	5	2006
Wes Welker, New England	112	1,175	8	2007
Andre Johnson, Houston	115	1,575	8	2008
Wes Walker, New England	123	1,348	4	2009
Reggie Wayne, Indianapolis	111	1,355	6	2010
Wes Welker, New England	122	1,569	9	2011

Scoring

Player, team	TD	PAT	FG	Pts	Year
Gene Mingo, Denver	6	33	18	123	1960
Gino Cappelletti, Boston	8	48	17	147	1961
Gene Mingo, Denver	4	32	27	137	1962
Gino Cappelletti, Boston	2	35	22	113	1963
Gino Cappelletti, Boston	7	36	25	155	1964
Gino Cappelletti, Boston	9	27	17	132	1965
Gino Cappelletti, Boston	6	35	16	119	1966
George Blanda, Oakland	0	56	20	116	1967
Jim Turner, NY Jets	0	43	34	145	1968
Jim Turner, NY Jets	0	33	32	129	1969
Jan Stenerud, Kansas City	0	26	30	116	1970
Garo Yepremian, Miami	0	33	28	117	1971
Bobby Howfield, NY Jets	0	40	27	121	1972
Roy Gerela, Pittsburgh	0	36	29	123	1973
Roy Gerela, Pittsburgh	0	33	20	93	1974
O. J. Simpson, Buffalo	23	0	0	138	1975
Toni Linhart, Baltimore Colts	0	49	20	109	1976
Errol Mann, Oakland	0	39	20	99	1977
Pat Leahy, NY Jets	0	41	22	107	1978
John Smith, New England	0	46	23	115	1979
John Smith, New England	0	51	26	129	1980
Jim Breech, Cincinnati	0	49	22	115	1981
Nick Lowery, Kansas City	0	37	26	115	
Marcus Allen, L.A. Raiders	14	0	0	84	1982
Gary Anderson, Pittsburgh	0	38	27	119	1983
Gary Anderson, Pittsburgh	0	45	24	117	1984
Gary Anderson, Pittsburgh	0	40	33	139	1985
Tony Franklin, New England	0	44	32	140	1986
Jim Breech, Cincinnati	0	25	24	97	1987
Scott Norwood, Buffalo	0	33	32	129	1988
David Treadwell, Denver	0	39	27	120	1989
Nick Lowery, Kansas City	0	37	34	139	1990
Pete Stoyanovich, Miami	0	28	31	121	1991
Pete Stoyanovich, Miami	0	34	30	124	1992
Jeff Jaeger, L.A. Raiders	0	27	35	132	1993
John Carney, San Diego	0	33	34	135	1994
Norm Johnson, Pittsburgh	0	39	34	141	1995
Cary Blanchard, Indianapolis	0	27	36	135	1996
Mike Hollis, Jacksonville	0	41	31	134	1997
Steve Christie, Buffalo	0	41	33	140	1998
Mike Vanderjagt, Indianapolis	0	43	34	145	1999
Matt Stover, Baltimore	0	30	35	135	2000
Mike Vanderjagt, Indianapolis	0	41	28	125	2001
Priest Holmes, Kansas City	24	0	0	144	2002
Priest Holmes, Kansas City	27	0	0	162	2003
Adam Vinatieri, New England	0	48	31	141	2004
Shayne Graham, Cincinnati	0	47	28	131	2005
LaDainian Tomlinson, San Diego	31	0	0	186	2006
Randy Moss, New England	23	0	0	138	2007
Stephen Gostkowski, New England	0	40	36	148	2008
Nate Kaeding, San Diego	0	50	32	146	2009
Sebastian Janikowski, Oakland	0	43	33	142	2010
Stephen Gostkowski, New England	0	59	28	143	2011

Rushing

Player, team	Yds	Att	TD	Year
Abner Haynes, Dallas Texans	875	156	9	1960
Billy Cannon, Houston	948	200	6	1961
Cookie Gilchrist, Buffalo	1,096	214	13	1962
Clem Daniels, Oakland	1,099	215	3	1963
Cookie Gilchrist, Buffalo	981	230	6	1964
Paul Lowe, San Diego	1,121	222	7	1965
Jim Nance, Boston	1,458	299	11	1966
Jim Nance, Boston	1,216	269	7	1967
Paul Robinson, Cincinnati	1,023	238	8	1968
Dickie Post, San Diego	873	182	6	1969
Floyd Little, Denver	901	209	3	1970
Floyd Little, Denver	1,133	284	6	1971
O. J. Simpson, Buffalo	1,251	292	6	1972
O. J. Simpson, Buffalo	2,003	332	12	1973
Otis Armstrong, Denver	1,407	263	9	1974
O. J. Simpson, Buffalo	1,817	329	16	1975
O. J. Simpson, Buffalo	1,503	290	8	1976
Mark van Eeghen, Oakland	1,273	324	7	1977
Earl Campbell, Houston	1,450	302	13	1978
Earl Campbell, Houston	1,697	368	19	1979
Earl Campbell, Houston	1,934	373	13	1980
Earl Campbell, Houston	1,376	361	10	1981
Freeman McNeil, NY Jets	786	151	6	1982
Curt Warner, Seattle	1,449	335	13	1983
Earnest Jackson, San Diego	1,179	296	8	1984
Marcus Allen, L.A. Raiders	1,759	380	11	1985
Curt Warner, Seattle	1,481	319	13	1986
Eric Dickerson, L.A. Rams-Ind.	1,288*	283	6	1987
Eric Dickerson, Indianapolis	1,659	388	14	1988
Christian Okoye, Kansas City	1,480	370	12	1989
Thurman Thomas, Buffalo	1,297	271	11	1990
Thurman Thomas, Buffalo	1,407	288	7	1991
Barry Foster, Pittsburgh	1,690	390	11	1992
Thurman Thomas, Buffalo	1,315	355	6	1993
Chris Warren, Seattle	1,545	333	9	1994
Curtis Martin, New England	1,487	368	14	1995
Terrell Davis, Denver	1,538	345	13	1996
Terrell Davis, Denver	1,750	369	15	1997
Terrell Davis, Denver	2,008	392	21	1998
Edgerrin James, Indianapolis	1,553	369	13	1999
Edgerrin James, Indianapolis	1,709	387	13	2000
Priest Holmes, Kansas City	1,555	327	8	2001
Ricky Williams, Miami	1,853	383	16	2002
Jamal Lewis, Baltimore	2,066	387	14	2003
Curtis Martin, NY Jets	1,697	371	12	2004
Larry Johnson, Kansas City	1,750	336	20	2005
LaDainian Tomlinson, San Diego	1,815	348	28	2006
LaDainian Tomlinson, San Diego	1,474	315	15	2007
Thomas Jones, NY Jets	1,312	290	14	2008
Chris Johnson, Tennessee	2,006	358	14	2009
Arian Foster, Houston	1,616	327	16	2010
Maurice Jones-Drew, Jacksonville	1,606	343	8	2011

*Includes 277 yards after being traded to NFC; 1,011 yards led AFC.

National Football Conference Leaders, 1960-2011

(National Football League, 1960-69)

Passing (based on QB rating points) / Receptions

Player, team	Att	Comp	YG	TD	Year	Player, team	Rec	YG	TD
Milt Plum, Cleveland	250	151	2,297	21	1960	Raymond Berry, Baltimore Colts	74	1,298	10
Milt Plum, Cleveland	302	177	2,416	18	1961	Jim Phillips, L.A. Rams	78	1,092	5
Bart Starr, Green Bay	285	178	2,438	12	1962	Bobby Mitchell, Washington	72	1,384	11
Y. A. Tittle, NY Giants	367	221	3,145	36	1963	Bobby Joe Conrad, St. Louis Cardinals	73	967	10
Bart Starr, Green Bay	272	163	2,144	15	1964	Johnny Morris, Chicago	93	1,200	10
Rudy Bukich, Chicago	312	176	2,641	20	1965	Dave Parks, San Francisco	80	1,344	12
Bart Starr, Green Bay	251	156	2,257	14	1966	Charley Taylor, Washington	72	1,119	12
Sonny Jurgensen, Washington	508	288	3,747	31	1967	Charley Taylor, Washington	70	990	9
Earl Morrall, Baltimore Colts	317	182	2,909	26	1968	Clifton McNeil, San Francisco	71	994	7
Sonny Jurgensen, Washington	442	274	3,102	22	1969	Dan Abramowicz, New Orleans	73	1,015	7
John Brodie, San Francisco	378	223	2,941	24	1970	Dick Gordon, Chicago	71	1,026	13
Roger Staubach, Dallas	211	126	1,882	15	1971	Bob Tucker, NY Giants	59	791	4
Norm Snead, NY Giants	325	196	2,307	17	1972	Harold Jackson, Philadelphia	62	1,048	4
Roger Staubach, Dallas	286	179	2,428	23	1973	Harold Carmichael, Philadelphia	67	1,116	9
Sonny Jurgensen, Washington	167	107	1,185	11	1974	Charles Young, Philadelphia	63	696	3
Fran Tarkenton, Minnesota	425	273	2,994	25	1975	Chuck Foreman, Minnesota	73	691	9
James Harris, L.A. Rams	158	91	1,460	8	1976	Drew Pearson, Dallas	58	806	6
Roger Staubach, Dallas	361	210	2,620	18	1977	Ahmad Rashad, Minnesota	51	681	2
Roger Staubach, Dallas	413	231	3,190	25	1978	Rickey Young, Minnesota	88	704	5
Roger Staubach, Dallas	461	267	3,586	27	1979	Ahmad Rashad, Minnesota	80	1,156	9
Ron Jaworski, Philadelphia	451	257	3,529	27	1980	Earl Cooper, San Francisco	83	567	4
Joe Montana, San Francisco	488	311	3,565	19	1981	Dwight Clark, San Francisco	85	1,105	4
Joe Thiesmann, Washington	252	161	2,033	13	1982	Dwight Clark, San Francisco	60	913	5
Steve Bartkowski, Atlanta	432	274	3,167	22	1983	Roy Green, St. Louis Cardinals	78	1,227	14
						Charlie Brown, Washington	78	1,225	8
						Earnest Gray, NY Giants	78	1,139	5
Joe Montana, San Francisco	432	279	3,630	28	1984	Art Monk, Washington	106	1,372	7
Joe Montana, San Francisco	494	303	3,653	27	1985	Roger Craig, San Francisco	92	1,016	6
Tommy Kramer, Minnesota	372	208	3,000	24	1986	Jerry Rice, San Francisco	86	1,570	15
Joe Montana, San Francisco	398	266	3,054	31	1987	J. T. Smith, St. Louis Cardinals	91	1,117	8
Wade Wilson, Minnesota	332	204	2,746	15	1988	Henry Ellard, L.A. Rams	86	1,414	10
Joe Montana, San Francisco	386	271	3,521	26	1989	Sterling Sharpe, Green Bay	90	1,423	12
Phil Simms, NY Giants	311	184	2,284	15	1990	Jerry Rice, San Francisco	100	1,502	13
Steve Young, San Francisco	279	180	2,517	17	1991	Michael Irvin, Dallas	93	1,523	8
Steve Young, San Francisco	402	268	3,465	25	1992	Sterling Sharpe, Green Bay	108	1,461	13
Steve Young, San Francisco	462	314	4,023	29	1993	Sterling Sharpe, Green Bay	112	1,274	11
Steve Young, San Francisco	461	324	3,969	35	1994	Cris Carter, Minnesota	122	1,256	7
Brett Favre, Green Bay	570	359	4,413	38	1995	Herman Moore, Detroit	123	1,686	14
Steve Young, San Francisco	316	214	2,410	14	1996	Jerry Rice, San Francisco	108	1,254	8
Steve Young, San Francisco	356	241	3,029	19	1997	Herman Moore, Detroit	104	1,293	8
Randall Cunningham, Minnesota	425	259	3,704	34	1998	Frank Sanders, Arizona	89	1,145	3
Kurt Warner, St. Louis	499	325	4,353	41	1999	Muhsin Muhammad, Carolina	96	1,253	8
Trent Green, St. Louis	240	145	2,063	16	2000	Muhsin Muhammad, Carolina	102	1,183	6
Kurt Warner, St. Louis	546	375	4,830	36	2001	Keyshawn Johnson, Tampa Bay	106	1,266	1
Brad Johnson, Tampa Bay	451	281	3,049	22	2002	Randy Moss, Minnesota	106	1,347	7
Daunte Culpepper, Minnesota	454	295	3,479	25	2003	Torry Holt, St. Louis	117	1,696	12
Daunte Culpepper, Minnesota	548	379	4,717	39	2004	Joe Horn, New Orleans	94	1,399	11
						Torry Holt, St. Louis	94	1,372	10
Matt Hasselbeck, Seattle	449	294	3,459	24	2005	Steve Smith, Carolina	103	1,563	12
						Larry Fitzgerald, Arizona	103	1,409	10
Drew Brees, New Orleans	554	356	4,418	26	2006	Mike Furrey, Detroit	98	1,086	6
Tony Romo, Dallas	520	335	4,211	36	2007	Larry Fitzgerald, Arizona	100	1,409	10
Kurt Warner, Arizona	598	401	4,583	30	2008	Larry Fitzgerald, Arizona	96	1,431	12
Drew Brees, New Orleans	514	363	4,388	34	2009	Steve Smith, NY Giants	107	1,220	7
Aaron Rodgers, Green Bay	475	312	3,922	28	2010	Roddy White, Atlanta	115	1,389	10
Aaron Rodgers, Green Bay	502	343	4,643	45	2011	Roddy White, Atlanta	100	1,296	8

Scoring / Rushing

Player, team	TD	PAT	FG	Pts	Year	Player, team	Yds	Att	TD
Paul Hornung, Green Bay	15	41	15	176	1960	Jim Brown, Cleveland	1,257	215	9
Paul Hornung, Green Bay	10	41	15	146	1961	Jim Brown, Cleveland	1,408	305	8
Jim Taylor, Green Bay	19	0	0	114	1962	Jim Taylor, Green Bay	1,474	272	19
Don Chandler, NY Giants	0	52	18	106	1963	Jim Brown, Cleveland	1,863	291	12
Lenny Moore, Baltimore Colts	20	0	0	120	1964	Jim Brown, Cleveland	1,446	280	7
Gale Sayers, Chicago	22	0	0	132	1965	Jim Brown, Cleveland	1,544	289	17
Bruce Gossett, L.A. Rams	0	29	28	113	1966	Gale Sayers, Chicago	1,231	229	8
Jim Bakken, St. Louis Cardinals	0	36	27	117	1967	Leroy Kelly, Cleveland	1,205	235	11
Leroy Kelly, Cleveland	20	0	0	120	1968	Leroy Kelly, Cleveland	1,239	248	16
Fred Cox, Minnesota	0	43	26	121	1969	Gale Sayers, Chicago	1,032	236	8
Fred Cox, Minnesota	0	35	30	125	1970	Larry Brown, Washington	1,125	237	5
Curt Knight, Washington	0	27	29	114	1971	John Brockington, Green Bay	1,105	216	4
Chester Marcol, Green Bay	0	29	33	128	1972	Larry Brown, Washington	1,216	285	8
David Ray, L.A. Rams	0	40	30	130	1973	John Brockington, Green Bay	1,144	265	3

Scoring

Player, team	TD	PAT	FG	Pts
Chester Marcol, Green Bay	0	19	25	94
Chuck Foreman, Minnesota	22	0	0	132
Mark Moseley, Washington	0	31	22	97
Walter Payton, Chicago	16	0	0	96
Frank Corral, L.A. Rams	0	31	29	118
Mark Moseley, Washington	0	39	25	114
Ed Murray, Detroit	0	35	27	116
Ed Murray, Detroit	0	46	25	121
Rafael Septien, Dallas	0	40	27	121
Wendell Tyler, L.A. Rams	13	0	0	78
Mark Moseley, Washington	0	62	33	161
Ray Wersching, San Francisco	0	56	25	131
Kevin Butler, Chicago	0	51	31	144
Kevin Butler, Chicago	0	36	28	120
Jerry Rice, San Francisco	23	0	0	138
Mike Cofer, San Francisco	0	40	27	121
Mike Cofer, San Francisco	0	49	29	136
Chip Lohmiller, Washington	0	41	30	131
Chip Lohmiller, Washington	0	56	31	149
Morten Andersen, New Orleans	0	33	29	120
Chip Lohmiller, Washington	0	30	30	120
Jason Hanson, Detroit	0	28	34	130
Fuad Reveiz, Minnesota	0	30	34	132
Emmitt Smith, Dallas	22	0	0	132
Emmitt Smith, Dallas	25	0	0	150
John Kasay, Carolina	0	34	37	145
Richie Cunningham, Dallas	0	24	34	126
Gary Anderson, Minnesota	0	59	35	164
Jeff Wilkins, St. Louis	0	64	20	124
Marshall Faulk, St. Louis	26	0	0	156
Marshall Faulk, St. Louis	21	0	0	128
Jay Feely, Atlanta	0	42	32	138
Jeff Wilkins, St. Louis	0	46	39	163
David Akers, Philadelphia	0	41	27	122
Shaun Alexander, Seattle	28	0	0	168
Robbie Gould, Chicago	0	47	32	143
Mason Crosby, Green Bay	0	48	31	141
David Akers, Philadelphia	0	45	33	144
David Akers, Philadelphia	0	43	32	139
David Akers, Philadelphia	0	47	32	143
David Akers, San Francisco	0	34	44	166

Rushing

Year	Player, team	Yds	Att	TD
1974	Lawrence McCutcheon, L.A. Rams	1,109	236	3
1975	Jim Otis, St. Louis Cardinals	1,076	269	5
1976	Walter Payton, Chicago	1,390	311	13
1977	Walter Payton, Chicago	1,852	339	14
1978	Walter Payton, Chicago	1,395	333	11
1979	Walter Payton, Chicago	1,610	369	14
1980	Walter Payton, Chicago	1,460	317	6
1981	George Rogers, New Orleans	1,674	378	13
1982	Tony Dorsett, Dallas	745	177	5
1983	Eric Dickerson, L.A. Rams	1,808	390	18
1984	Eric Dickerson, L.A. Rams	2,105	379	14
1985	Gerald Riggs, Atlanta	1,719	397	10
1986	Eric Dickerson, L.A. Rams	1,821	404	11
1987	Charles White, L.A. Rams	1,374	324	11
1988	Herschel Walker, Dallas	1,514	361	5
1989	Barry Sanders, Detroit	1,470	280	14
1990	Barry Sanders, Detroit	1,304	255	13
1991	Emmitt Smith, Dallas	1,563	365	12
1992	Emmitt Smith, Dallas	1,713	373	18
1993	Emmitt Smith, Dallas	1,486	283	9
1994	Barry Sanders, Detroit	1,883	331	7
1995	Emmitt Smith, Dallas	1,773	377	25
1996	Barry Sanders, Detroit	1,553	307	11
1997	Barry Sanders, Detroit	2,053	335	11
1998	Jamal Anderson, Atlanta	1,846	410	14
1999	Stephen Davis, Washington	1,405	290	17
2000	Robert Smith, Minnesota	1,521	295	7
2001	Stephen Davis, Washington	1,432	356	5
2002	Deuce McAllister, New Orleans	1,388	325	13
2003	Ahman Green, Green Bay	1,883	355	15
2004	Shaun Alexander, Seattle	1,696	353	16
2005	Shaun Alexander, Seattle	1,880	370	27
2006	Frank Gore, San Francisco	1,695	312	8
2007	Adrian Peterson, Minnesota	1,341	238	12
2008	Adrian Peterson, Minnesota	1,760	363	10
2009	Steven Jackson, St. Louis	1,416	324	4
2010	Michael Turner, Atlanta	1,371	334	12
2011	Michael Turner, Atlanta	1,340	301	11

NFL MVP and Rookies of the Year, 1957-2011

The Most Valuable Player, Offensive Rookie of the Year, and Defensive Rookie of the Year are a few of the many awards given out annually by the Associated Press according to the results of balloting by a nationwide panel of media. Many other organizations give out annual awards honoring the NFL's best players.

Year	NFL Most Valuable Player Award	Offensive Rookie of the Year	Defensive Rookie of the Year
1957	Jim Brown, Cleveland	NA	NA
1958	Jim Brown, Cleveland	NA	NA
1959	Charley Conerly, NY Giants	NA	NA
1960	Norm Van Brocklin, Philadelphia	NA	NA
1961	Paul Hornung, Green Bay	NA	NA
1962	Jim Taylor, Green Bay	NA	NA
1963	Y. A. Tittle, NY Giants	NA	NA
1964	Johnny Unitas, Baltimore	NA	NA
1965	Jim Brown, Cleveland	NA	NA
1966	Bart Starr, Green Bay	NA	NA
1967	Johnny Unitas, Baltimore	Mel Farr, Detroit	Lem Barney, Detroit
1968	Earl Morrall, Baltimore	Earl McCullouch, Detroit	Claude Humphrey, Atlanta
1969	Roman Gabriel, Los Angeles	Calvin Hill, Dallas	Joe Greene, Pittsburgh
1970	John Brodie, San Francisco	Dennis Shaw, Buffalo	Bruce Taylor, San Francisco
1971	Alan Page, Minnesota	John Brockington, Green Bay	Isiah Robertson, Los Angeles
1972	Larry Brown, Washington	Franco Harris, Pittsburgh	Willie Buchanon, Green Bay
1973	O. J. Simpson, Buffalo	Chuck Foreman, Minnesota	Wally Chambers, Chicago
1974	Ken Stabler, Oakland	Don Woods, San Diego	Jack Lambert, Pittsburgh
1975	Fran Tarkenton, Minnesota	Mike Thomas, Washington	Robert Brazile, Houston
1976	Bert Jones, Baltimore	Sammy White, Minnesota	Mike Haynes, New England
1977	Walter Payton, Chicago	Tony Dorsett, Dallas	A. J. Duhe, Miami
1978	Terry Bradshaw, Pittsburgh	Earl Campbell, Houston	Al Baker, Detroit
1979	Earl Campbell, Houston	Ottis Anderson, St. Louis	Jim Haslett, Buffalo
1980	Brian Sipe, Cleveland	Billy Sims, Detroit	Buddy Curry, Atlanta; Al Richardson, Atlanta
1981	Ken Anderson, Cincinnati	George Rogers, New Orleans	Lawrence Taylor, NY Giants
1982	Mark Moseley, Washington	Marcus Allen, Los Angeles	Chip Banks, Cleveland

Year	NFL Most Valuable Player Award	Offensive Rookie of the Year	Defensive Rookie of the Year
1983	Joe Theismann, Washington	Eric Dickerson, Los Angeles	Vernon Maxwell, Baltimore
1984	Dan Marino, Miami	Louis Lipps, Pittsburgh	Bill Maas, Kansas City
1985	Marcus Allen, Los Angeles	Eddie Brown, Cincinnati	Duane Bickett, Indianapolis
1986	Lawrence Taylor, NY Giants	Rueben Mayes, New Orleans	Leslie O'Neal, San Diego
1987	John Elway, Denver	Troy Stradford, Miami	Shane Conlan, Buffalo
1988	Boomer Esiason, Cincinnati	John Stephens, New England	Erik McMillan, NY Jets
1989	Joe Montana, San Francisco	Barry Sanders, Detroit	Derrick Thomas, Kansas City
1990	Joe Montana, San Francisco	Emmitt Smith, Dallas	Mark Carrier, Chicago
1991	Thurman Thomas, Buffalo	Leonard Russell, New England	Mike Croel, Denver
1992	Steve Young, San Francisco	Carl Pickens, Cincinnati	Dale Carter, Kansas City
1993	Emmitt Smith, Dallas	Jerome Bettis, Los Angeles	Dana Stubblefield, San Francisco
1994	Steve Young, San Francisco	Marshall Faulk, Indianapolis	Tim Bowens, Miami
1995	Brett Favre, Green Bay	Curtis Martin, New England	Hugh Douglas, NY Jets
1996	Brett Favre, Green Bay	Eddie George, Houston	Simeon Rice, Arizona
1997	Brett Favre, Green Bay; Barry Sanders, Detroit	Warrick Dunn, Tampa Bay	Peter Boulware, Baltimore
1998	Terrell Davis, Denver	Randy Moss, Minnesota	Charles Woodson, Oakland
1999	Kurt Warner, St. Louis	Edgerrin James, Indianapolis	Jevon Kearse, Tennessee
2000	Marshall Faulk, St. Louis	Mike Anderson, Denver	Brian Urlacher, Chicago
2001	Kurt Warner, St. Louis	Anthony Thomas, Chicago	Kendrell Bell, Pittsburgh
2002	Rich Gannon, Oakland	Clinton Portis, Denver	Julius Peppers, Carolina
2003	Peyton Manning, Indianapolis; Steve McNair, Tennessee	Anquan Boldin, Arizona	Terrell Suggs, Baltimore
2004	Peyton Manning, Indianapolis	Ben Roethlisberger, Pittsburgh	Jonathan Vilma, NY Jets
2005	Shaun Alexander, Seattle	Cadillac Williams, Tampa Bay	Shawne Merriman, San Diego
2006	LaDainian Tomlinson, San Diego	Vince Young, Tennessee	DeMeco Ryans, Houston
2007	Tom Brady, New England	Adrian Peterson, Minnesota	Patrick Willis, San Francisco
2008	Peyton Manning, Indianapolis	Matt Ryan, Atlanta	Jerod Mayo, New England
2009	Peyton Manning, Indianapolis	Percy Harvin, Minnesota	Brian Cushing, Houston
2010	Tom Brady, New England	Sam Bradford, St. Louis	Ndamukong Suh, Detroit
2011	Aaron Rodgers, Green Bay	Cam Newton, Carolina	Von Miller, Denver

All-Time Professional (NFL and AFL) Football Records

(at end of 2011 season; * = active in 2011; (a) includes AFL statistics; ** = 2-pt conversions scored)

Leading Lifetime Scorers

Player	Yrs	TD	PAT	FG	Total
Morten Andersen	25	0	849	565	2,544
Gary Anderson	23	0	820	538	2,434
John Carney	23	0	628	478	2,062
Jason Hanson*	20	0	627	463	2,016
Matt Stover	19	0	591	471	2,004
George Blanda (a) . . .	26	9	942	335	2,002
Jason Elam.	17	0	675	436	1,983
John Kasay*	20	0	587	461	1,970
Adam Vinatieri*	16	0	589**	387	1,752
Norm Johnson	18	0	638	366	1,736
Nick Lowery	18	0	562	383	1,711
Jan Stenerud (a).	19	0	580	373	1,699
Ryan Longwell*	15	0	604	361	1,687
Eddie Murray	19	0	538	352	1,594
Al Del Greco	17	0	543	347	1,584
Olindo Mare*	15	0	480	350	1,530
David Akers*	14	0	477	338	1,491
Steve Christie	15	0	468	336	1,476
Pat Leahy	18	0	558	304	1,470
Jim Turner (a)	16	1	521	304	1,439

Leading Lifetime Touchdown Scorers

Player	Yrs	Rush	Rec	Ret	TD
Jerry Rice	20	10	197	1	208
Emmitt Smith	15	164	11	0	175
LaDainian Tomlinson* . .	11	145	17	0	162
Terrell Owens	15	3	153	0	156
Randy Moss*	13	0	153	1	154
Marcus Allen	16	123	21	1	145
Marshall Faulk	12	100	36	0	136
Cris Carter	16	0	130	1	131
Marvin Harrison	13	0	128	0	128
Jim Brown.	9	106	20	0	126
Walter Payton	13	110	15	0	125
John Riggins.	14	104	12	0	116
Lenny Moore.	12	63	48	2	113
Shaun Alexander	10	100	12	0	112
Barry Sanders.	10	99	10	0	109
Tim Brown.	17	1	100	4	105
Don Hutson.	11	3	99	3	105
Steve Largent	14	1	100	0	101
Franco Harris	13	91	9	0	100
Curtis Martin.	11	90	10	0	100

Points, season: 186, LaDainian Tomlinson, San Diego Chargers, 2006 (31 TDs).
Points, game: 40, Ernie Nevers, Chicago Cardinals vs. Chicago Bears, Nov. 28, 1929 (6 TDs, 4 PATs).
Touchdowns, season: 31, LaDainian Tomlinson, San Diego Chargers, 2006.
Touchdowns, game: 6, Ernie Nevers, Chicago Cardinals vs. Chicago Bears, Nov. 28, 1929 (6 rushing); Dub Jones, Cleveland Browns vs. Chicago Bears, Nov. 25, 1951 (4 rushing, 2 pass receptions); Gale Sayers, Chicago Bears vs. San Francisco 49ers, Dec. 12, 1965 (4 rushing, 1 pass reception, 1 punt return).
Points after TD, season: 74, Stephen Gostkowski, New England Patriots, 2007.
Consecutive points after TD: 422, Matt Stover, Baltimore Ravens-Indianapolis Colts, 1996-2009.
Field goals, career: 565, Morten Andersen, New Orleans Saints-Atlanta Falcons-NY Giants-Kansas City Chiefs-Minnesota Vikings-Atlanta Falcons, 1982-2007.
Field goals, season: 44, David Akers, San Francisco 49ers, 2011.
Field goals, game: 8, Rob Bironas, Tennessee Titans vs. Houston Texans, Oct. 21, 2007.
Longest field goal: 63 yards, Tom Dempsey, New Orleans Saints vs. Detroit Lions, Nov. 8, 1970; Jason Elam, Denver Broncos vs. Jacksonville Jaguars, Oct. 25, 1998.

Defensive Records

Interceptions, career: 81, Paul Krause, Washington Redskins-Minnesota Vikings, 1964-79.
Interceptions, season: 14, Dick "Night Train" Lane, L.A. Rams, 1952.
Touchdowns, career: 12, Rod Woodson, Pittsburgh Steelers-San Francisco 49ers-Baltimore Ravens-Oakland Raiders, 1987-2003.
Touchdowns, season: 4, Ken Houston, Houston Oilers, 1971; Jim Kearney, Kansas City Chiefs, 1972; Eric Allen, Philadelphia Eagles, 1993.
Sacks, career (since 1982): 200, Bruce Smith, Buffalo Bills-Washington Redskins, 1985-2003.
Sacks, season (since 1982): 22.5, Michael Strahan, NY Giants, 2001.

Leading Lifetime Rushers

(ranked by rushing yards; * = active in 2011)

Player	Yrs	Att	Yds	Avg	Long	TD	Player	Yrs	Att	Yds	Avg	Long	TD
Emmitt Smith	15	4,409	18,355	4.2	75	164	Edgerrin James	11	3,028	12,246	4.0	72	80
Walter Payton	13	3,838	16,726	4.4	76	110	Marcus Allen.	16	3,022	12,243	4.1	61	123
Barry Sanders.	10	3,062	15,269	5.0	85	99	Franco Harris	13	2,949	12,120	4.1	75	91
Curtis Martin.	11	3,518	14,101	4.0	70	90	Thurman Thomas	13	2,877	12,074	4.2	80	65
LaDainian Tomlinson*	11	3,174	13,684	4.3	85	145	Fred Taylor	13	2,534	11,695	4.6	80	66
Jerome Bettis	13	3,479	13,662	3.9	71	91	John Riggins.	14	2,916	11,352	3.9	66	104
Eric Dickerson.	11	2,996	13,259	4.4	85	90	Corey Dillon	10	2,618	11,241	4.3	96	82
Tony Dorsett	12	2,936	12,739	4.3	99	77	O. J. Simpson	11	2,404	11,236	4.7	94	61
Jim Brown.	9	2,359	12,312	5.2	80	106	Warrick Dunn	12	2,669	10,967	4.1	90	49
Marshall Faulk	12	2,836	12,279	4.3	71	100	Ricky Watters	10	2,622	10,643	4.1	57	78

Yards gained, season: 2,105, Eric Dickerson, L.A. Rams, 1984.
Yards gained, game: 296, Adrian Peterson, Minnesota Vikings vs. San Diego Chargers, Nov. 4, 2007.
Rushing TDs, career: 164, Emmitt Smith, Dallas Cowboys-Arizona Cardinals, 1990-2004.
Rushing TDs, season: 28, LaDainian Tomlinson, San Diego Chargers, 2006.
Rushing TDs, game: 6, Ernie Nevers, Chicago Cardinals vs. Chicago Bears, Nov. 28, 1929.
Rushing attempts, game: 45, Jamie Morris, Washington Redskins vs. Cincinnati Bengals, Dec. 17, 1988 (OT).
Longest run from scrimmage: 99 yards, Tony Dorsett, Dallas Cowboys vs. Minnesota Vikings, Jan. 3, 1983 (TD).

Leading Lifetime Receivers

(ranked by number of receptions; * = active in 2011)

Player	Yrs	No.	Yds	Avg	Long	TD	Player	Yrs	No.	Yds	Avg	Long	TD
Jerry Rice	20	1,549	22,895	14.8	96	197	Derrick Mason*	15	943	12,061	12.8	79	66
Tony Gonzalez*	15	1,149	13,338	11.6	73	95	Art Monk	16	940	12,721	13.5	79	68
Marvin Harrison.	13	1,102	14,580	13.2	80	128	Torry Holt	11	920	13,382	14.5	85	74
Cris Carter	16	1,101	13,899	12.6	80	130	Keenan McCardell. . . .	16	883	11,373	12.9	76	63
Tim Brown	17	1,094	14,934	13.7	80	100	Jimmy Smith	12	862	12,287	14.3	75	67
Terrell Owens.	15	1,078	15,934	14.8	98	153	Reggie Wayne*	11	862	11,708	13.6	71	73
Isaac Bruce	16	1,024	15,208	14.9	80	91	Muhsin Muhammad . .	14	860	11,438	13.3	72	62
Hines Ward*	14	1,000	12,083	12.1	85	85	Irving Fryar	17	851	12,785	15.0	80	84
Randy Moss*	13	954	14,858	15.6	82	153	Rod Smith	12	849	11,389	13.4	85	68
Andre Reed	16	951	13,198	13.9	83	87	Larry Centers.	14	827	6,797	8.2	54	28

Yards gained, career: 22,895, Jerry Rice, San Francisco 49ers-Oakland Raiders-Seattle Seahawks, 1985-2004.
Yards gained, season: 1,848, Jerry Rice, San Francisco 49ers, 1995.
Yards gained, game: 336, Willie "Flipper" Anderson, L.A. Rams vs. New Orleans Saints, Nov. 26, 1989 (OT).
Pass receptions, season: 143, Marvin Harrison, Indianapolis Colts, 2002.
Pass receptions, game: 21, Brandon Marshall, Denver Broncos vs. Indianapolis Colts, Dec. 13, 2009 (200 yards).
Touchdown receptions, career: 197, Jerry Rice, San Francisco 49ers-Oakland Raiders-Seattle Seahawks, 1985-2004.
Touchdown receptions, season: 23, Randy Moss, New England Patriots, 2007.
Touchdown receptions, game: 5, Bob Shaw, Chicago Cardinals vs. Baltimore Colts, Oct. 2, 1950; Kellen Winslow, San Diego Chargers vs. Oakland Raiders, Nov. 22, 1981; Jerry Rice, San Francisco 49ers vs. Atlanta Falcons, Oct. 14, 1990.

Leading Lifetime Passers

(minimum 1,500 attempts; ranked by quarterback rating points; * = active in 2011)

Player	Yrs	Att	Comp	Yds	TD	Int	Pts[1]	Player	Yrs	Att	Comp	Yds	TD	Int	Pts[1]
Aaron Rodgers* . . .	7	2,113	1,381	17,366	132	38	104.1	Ben Roethlisberger*	8	3,313	2,090	26,579	165	100	92.1
Tony Romo*	8	2,592	1,672	20,834	149	72	96.9	Chad Pennington . .	11	2,471	1,632	17,823	102	64	90.1
Steve Young	15	4,149	2,667	33,124	232	107	96.8	Matt Ryan*	4	2,022	1,232	14,238	95	46	88.4
Tom Brady*	12	5,321	3,397	39,979	300	115	96.4	Daunte Culpepper	11	3,199	2,016	24,153	149	106	87.8
Philip Rivers*	8	3,037	1,930	24,285	163	78	95.5	Jeff Garcia	11	3,676	2,264	25,537	161	83	87.5
Peyton Manning* . .	13	7,210	4,682	54,828	399	198	94.9	Dan Marino.	17	8,358	4,967	61,361	420	252	86.4
Drew Brees*	11	5,479	3,613	40,742	281	146	94.0	Carson Palmer* . . .	8	3,545	2,223	25,447	167	116	86.3
Kurt Warner	12	4,070	2,666	32,344	208	128	93.7	Trent Green.	11	3,740	2,266	28,475	162	114	86.0
Joe Montana.	15	5,391	3,409	40,551	273	139	92.3	Brett Favre	20	10,169	6,300	71,838	508	336	86.0
Matt Schaub*	8	2,279	1,466	17,936	98	58	92.2	Joe Flacco*	4	1,958	1,190	13,816	80	46	86.0

(1) Rating points based on performances in the following categories: percentage of completions, percentage of touchdown passes, percentage of interceptions, and average gain per pass attempt.

Most yards gained, career: 71,838, Brett Favre, Atlanta Falcons-Green Bay Packers-NY Jets-Minnesota Vikings, 1991-2010.
Most yards gained, season: 5,476, Drew Brees, New Orleans, 2011.
Most yards gained, game: 554, Norm Van Brocklin, L.A. Rams vs. NY Yanks, Sept. 28, 1951 (27 completions in 41 attempts).
Most touchdowns passing, career: 508, Brett Favre, Atlanta Falcons-Green Bay Packers-NY Jets-Minnesota Vikings, 1991-2010.
Most touchdowns passing, season: 50, Tom Brady, New England Patriots, 2007.
Most touchdowns passing, game: 7, Sid Luckman, Chicago Bears vs. NY Giants, Nov. 14, 1943; Adrian Burk, Philadelphia Eagles vs. Washington Redskins, Oct. 17, 1954; George Blanda, Houston Oilers vs. NY Titans, Nov. 19, 1961; Y. A. Tittle, NY Giants vs. Washington Redskins, Oct. 28, 1962; Joe Kapp, Minnesota Vikings vs. Baltimore Colts, Sept. 28, 1969.
Most passes completed, career: 6,300, Brett Favre, Atlanta Falcons-Green Bay Packers-NY Jets-Minnesota Vikings, 1991-2010.
Most passes completed, season: 468, Drew Brees, New Orleans Saints, 2011.
Most passes completed, game: 45, Drew Bledsoe, New England Patriots vs. Minnesota Vikings, Nov. 13, 1994 (OT).

NFL Stadiums, 2011

(G = Grass, S = Synthetic, A = AstroPlay, D = DD Grassmaster (grass), F = FieldTurf, N = Natural grass,
SS = Sportfield Softtop, SM = Sportexe Momentum)

Team: stadium, location, surface (year built)	Capacity[1]	Team: stadium, location, surface (year built)	Capacity[1]
Bears: Soldier Field[2], Chicago, IL, N (1924)	61,500	**Giants:** MetLife Stadium[7], E. Rutherford, NJ, F (2010)	82,500
Bengals: Paul Brown Stadium, Cincinnati, OH, S (2000)	65,535	**Jaguars:** EverBank Field[8], Jacksonville, FL, G (1995)	67,246
Bills: Ralph Wilson Stadium, Orchard Park, NY, A (1973)	73,079	**Jets:** MetLife Stadium[7], E. Rutherford, NJ, F (2010)	82,500
Broncos: Sports Authority Field at Mile High[3], Denver, CO, D (2001)	76,125	**Lions:** Ford Field, Detroit, MI, F (2002)	65,000
Browns: Cleveland Browns Stadium, Cleveland, OH, G (1999)	73,200	**Packers:** Lambeau Field[9], Green Bay, WI, D (1957)	73,142
Buccaneers: Raymond James Stadium, Tampa, FL, G (1998)	65,890	**Panthers:** Bank of America Stadium[10], Charlotte, NC, G (1996)	73,778
Cardinals: University of Phoenix Stadium, Glendale, AZ, G (2006)	63,400	**Patriots:** Gillette Stadium, Foxborough, MA, F (2002)	68,756
Chargers: Qualcomm Stadium[4], San Diego, CA, G (1967)	71,500	**Raiders:** O.co Coliseum[11], Oakland, CA, G (1966)	63,132
Chiefs: Arrowhead Stadium, Kansas City, MO, G (1972)	76,416	**Rams:** Edward Jones Dome at America's Center[12], St. Louis, MO, F (1995)	66,000
Colts: Lucas Oil Stadium, Indianapolis, IN, F (2008)	63,000	**Ravens:** M&T Bank Stadium[13], Baltimore, MD, SM (1998)	71,008
Cowboys: Cowboys Stadium, Arlington, TX, SS (2009)	100,000	**Redskins:** FedExField[14], Landover, MD, N (1997)	91,704
Dolphins: Sun Life Stadium[5], Miami Gardens, FL, G (1987)	75,540	**Saints:** Mercedes-Benz Superdome[15], New Orleans, LA, S (1975)	70,000
Eagles: Lincoln Financial Field, Philadelphia, PA, N (2003)	69,144	**Seahawks:** CenturyLink Field[16], Seattle, WA, F (2002)	67,000
Falcons: Georgia Dome, Atlanta, GA, F (1992)	71,250	**Steelers:** Heinz Field, Pittsburgh, PA, D (2001)	65,050
49ers: Candlestick Park[6], San Francisco, CA, N (1960)	69,900	**Texans:** Reliant Stadium, Houston, TX, G (2002)	71,054
		Titans: LP Field[17], Nashville, TN, N (1999)	69,143
		Vikings: Mall of America Field at Hubert H. Humphrey Metrodome[18], Minneapolis, MN, F (1982)	64,111

(1) As of the start of the 2011 season. (2) Renovation in 2002 replaced interior of stadium. (3) Formerly INVESCO Field at Mile High (2001-11). (4) Formerly San Diego Stadium (1967-80); San Diego Jack Murphy Stadium (1981-97). (5) Formerly Joe Robbie Stadium (1987-96); Pro Player Stadium (1996-2005); Land Shark Stadium (2009). (6) Formerly Candlestick Park (1960-94); 3Com Park at Candlestick Point (1995-2004). (7) Formerly New Meadowlands Stadium (2010-11). (8) Formerly ALLTEL Stadium (1997-2007); Jacksonville Municipal Stadium (1946-97, 2007-09). (9) Formerly City Stadium (1957-65). Renovation completed in 2003 added 11,625 seats. (10) Formerly Ericsson Stadium (1996-2003). (11) Formerly Oakland-Alameda County Coliseum (1966-98); Network Associates Coliseum (1998-2004); McAfee Stadium (2004-08); Oakland Coliseum (2008-11). (12) Formerly Trans World Dome (1995-2001). (13) Formerly PSINet Stadium (1998-2002); Ravens Stadium (2002-03). (14) Formerly Jack Kent Cooke Stadium (1997-99). (15) Formerly Louisiana Superdome (1975-2011). (16) Formerly Seahawks Stadium (2002-04); Qwest Field (2004-11). (17) Formerly Adelphia Coliseum (1999-2002). (18) Formerly Hubert H. Humphrey Metrodome (1982-2009).

National Football League Franchise Origins

(Founding year, league. Home stadium location; subsequent history.)

Arizona Cardinals: 1920, American Professional Football Association (APFA)[1]. Chicago, 1920-59; St. Louis, 1960-87; Tempe, AZ, 1988-2005; Glendale, AZ, 2006-present.

Atlanta Falcons: 1966, NFL. Atlanta, 1966-present.

Baltimore Ravens: 1996, NFL. Baltimore, 1996-present.

Buffalo Bills: 1960, American Football League (AFL)[2]. Buffalo, 1960-72; Orchard Park, NY, 1973-present.

Carolina Panthers: 1995, NFL. Clemson, SC, 1995; Charlotte, NC, 1996-present.

Chicago Bears: 1920, APFA. Decatur, IL, 1920; Chicago, 1921-present.

Cincinnati Bengals: 1968, AFL. Cincinnati, 1968-present.

Cleveland Browns: 1946, All-America Football Conference (AAFC)[3]. Cleveland, 1946-95; 1999-present.

Dallas Cowboys: 1960, NFL. Dallas, 1960-70; Irving, TX, 1971-2008; Arlington, TX, 2009-present.

Denver Broncos: 1960, AFL. Denver, 1960-present.

Detroit Lions: 1930, NFL. Portsmouth, OH, 1930-33; Detroit, 1934-74; Pontiac, MI, 1975-2001; Detroit, 2002-present.

Green Bay Packers: 1921, APFA. Green Bay, WI, 1921-present.

Houston Texans: 2002, NFL. Houston, 2002-present.

Indianapolis Colts: 1953, NFL. Baltimore, 1953-83; Indianapolis, 1984-present.

Jacksonville Jaguars: 1995, NFL. Jacksonville, FL, 1995-present.

Kansas City Chiefs: 1960, AFL. Dallas, 1960-62; Kansas City, MO, 1963-present.

Miami Dolphins: 1966, AFL. Miami, 1966-2002; Miami Gardens, FL, 2003-present.

Minnesota Vikings: 1961, NFL. Bloomington, MN, 1961-81; Minneapolis, 1982-present.

New England Patriots: 1960, AFL. Boston, 1960-70; Foxborough, MA, 1971-present.

New Orleans Saints: 1967, NFL. New Orleans, 1967-2004; Baton Rouge and San Antonio, 2005; New Orleans, 2006-present.

NY Giants: 1925, NFL. New York, NY, 1925-73, 1975; New Haven, CT, 1973-74; E. Rutherford, NJ, 1976-present.

NY Jets: 1960, AFL. NY, 1960-83; E. Rutherford, NJ, 1984-present.

Oakland Raiders: 1960, AFL. San Francisco, 1960-61; Oakland, CA, 1962-81; Los Angeles, 1982-94; Oakland, CA, 1995-present.

Philadelphia Eagles: 1933, NFL. Philadelphia, 1933-present.

Pittsburgh Steelers: 1933, NFL. Pittsburgh, 1933-present.

St. Louis Rams: 1937, NFL. Cleveland, 1936-45; Los Angeles, 1946-79; Anaheim, CA, 1980-94; St. Louis, 1995-present.

San Diego Chargers: 1960, AFL. Los Angeles, 1960; San Diego, 1961-present.

Seattle Seahawks: 1976, NFL. Seattle, 1976-present.

San Francisco 49ers: 1946, AAFC. San Francisco, 1946-present.

Tampa Bay Buccaneers: 1976, NFL. Tampa, 1976-present.

Tennessee Titans: 1960, AFL. Houston, 1969-96; Memphis, 1997; Nashville, 1998-present.

Washington Redskins: 1932, NFL. Boston, 1932-36; Washington, DC, 1937-96; Landover, MD, 1997-present.

(1) The American Professional Football Association (APFA) was formed in 1920 to standardize the rules of professional football. In 1922, the name was changed to the National Football League (NFL). (2) The most successful of four leagues called the American Football League or AFL (1926; 1936-37; 1940-41; 1960-69). Congress approved an NFL/AFL merger in 1966. Baltimore, Cleveland, and Pittsburgh agreed to join the 10 incoming AFL teams to form the American Football Conference. The NFL began play in 1970 with 26 teams. (3) The All-America Football Conference, 1946-49. In 1950, three of its teams joined the NFL (Baltimore, Cleveland, and San Francisco). The Baltimore franchise failed, but the NFL awarded the city a second one, also called the Colts, in 1953.

All-Time NFL Coaching Victories

(at end of 2011 season; ranked by overall career wins; * = active in 2011)

Coach	Team	Yrs	W	L	T	Pct	W	L	T	Pct
				Regular Season				Overall		
Don Shula	Colts, Dolphins	33	328	156	6	.677	347	173	6	.666
George Halas	Bears	40	318	148	31	.682	324	151	31	.682
Tom Landry	Cowboys	29	250	162	6	.607	270	178	6	.603
Earl "Curly" Lambeau	Packers, Chi. Cardinals, Redskins	33	226	132	22	.631	229	134	22	.631
Chuck Noll	Steelers	23	193	148	1	.566	209	156	1	.572
Marty Schottenheimer	Browns, Chiefs, Redskins, Chargers	21	200	126	1	.613	205	139	1	.596
Dan Reeves	Broncos, Giants, Falcons	23	190	165	2	.535	201	174	2	.536
Chuck Knox	Rams, Bills, Seahawks	22	186	147	1	.558	193	158	1	.550
Bill Belichick*	Browns, Patriots	17	175	97	0	.643	192	104	0	.649
Bill Parcells	Giants, Patriots, Jets, Cowboys	19	172	130	1	.569	183	138	1	.570
Mike Holmgren	Packers, Seahawks	17	161	111	0	.592	174	122	0	.588
Joe Gibbs	Redskins	21	154	94	0	.621	171	101	0	.629
Paul Brown	Browns, Bengals	21	166	100	6	.624	170	108	6	.612
Bud Grant	Vikings	18	158	96	5	.621	168	108	5	.608
Bill Cowher	Steelers	15	149	90	1	.623	161	99	1	.619
Mike Shanahan*	Raiders, Broncos, Redskins	18	157	119	0	.569	165	124	0	.571
Marv Levy	Chiefs, Bills	17	143	112	0	.561	154	120	0	.562
Steve Owen	Giants	23	151	100	17	.602	153	108	17	.586
Tom Coughlin*	Jaguars, Giants	16	142	114	0	.557	154	121	0	.560
Tony Dungy	Buccaneers, Colts	13	139	69	0	.668	148	79	0	.652

Pro Football Hall of Fame, Canton, OH

(Asterisk indicates member elected in Feb. 2012 and inducted Aug. 4, 2012.)

Herb Adderley
Troy Aikman
George Allen
Marcus Allen
Lance Alworth
Doug Atkins
Morris "Red" Badgro
Lem Barney
Cliff Battles
Sammy Baugh
Chuck Bednarik
Bert Bell
Bobby Bell
Raymond Berry
Elvin Bethea
Charles Bidwill
Fred Biletnikoff
George Blanda
Mel Blount
Terry Bradshaw
Bob Brown
Jim Brown
Paul Brown
Roosevelt Brown
Willie Brown
Buck Buchanan
Nick Buoniconti
Dick Butkus
*Jack Butler
Earl Campbell
Tony Canadeo
Joe Carr
Harry Carson
Dave Casper
Guy Chamberlin
Jack Christiansen
Earl "Dutch" Clark
George Connor
Jim Conzelman
Lou Creekmur
Larry Csonka
Al Davis
Willie Davis
*Dermontti Dawson
Len Dawson
Fred Dean
Joe DeLamielleure
Richard Dent
Eric Dickerson
Dan Dierdorf
Mike Ditka
*Chris Doleman
Art Donovan
Tony Dorsett
John "Paddy" Driscoll
Bill Dudley

Glen "Turk" Edwards
Carl Eller
John Elway
Weeb Ewbank
Marshall Faulk
Tom Fears
Jim Finks
Ray Flaherty
Len Ford
Dr. Daniel Fortmann
Dan Fouts
Benny Friedman
Frank Gatski
Bill George
Joe Gibbs
Frank Gifford
Sid Gillman
Otto Graham
Red Grange
Bud Grant
Darrell Green
Joe Greene
Forrest Gregg
Bob Griese
Russ Grimm
Lou Groza
Joe Guyon
George Halas
Jack Ham
Dan Hampton
Chris Hanburger
John Hannah
Franco Harris
Bob Hayes
Mike Haynes
Ed Healey
Mel Hein
Ted Hendricks
Wilbur "Pete" Henry
Arnold Herber
Bill Hewitt
Gene Hickerson
Clarke Hinkle
Elroy "Crazylegs" Hirsch
Paul Hornung
Ken Houston
Cal Hubbard
Sam Huff
Lamar Hunt
Don Hutson
Michael Irvin
Rickey Jackson
Jimmy Johnson
John Henry Johnson
Charlie Joiner
David "Deacon" Jones

Stan Jones
Henry Jordan
Sonny Jurgensen
Jim Kelly
Leroy Kelly
*Cortez Kennedy
Walt Kiesling
Frank "Bruiser" Kinard
Paul Krause
Earl "Curly" Lambeau
Jack Lambert
Tom Landry
Dick "Night Train" Lane
Jim Langer
Willie Lanier
Steve Largent
Yale Lary
Dante Lavelli
Bobby Layne
Dick LeBeau
Alphonse "Tuffy" Leemans
Marv Levy
Bob Lilly
Floyd Little
Larry Little
James Lofton
Vince Lombardi
Howie Long
Roy "Link" Lyman
Tom Mack
John Mackey
John Madden
Tim Mara
Wellington Mara
Gino Marchetti
Dan Marino
George Preston Marshall
*Curtis Martin
Bruce Mathews
Ollie Matson
Don Maynard
George McAfee
Mike McCormack
Randall McDaniel
Tommy McDonald
Hugh McElhenny
Johnny "Blood" McNally
Mike Michalske
Wayne Millner
Bobby Mitchell
Ron Mix
Art Monk

Joe Montana
Warren Moon
Lenny Moore
Marion Motley
Mike Munchak
Anthony Muñoz
George Musso
Bronko Nagurski
Joe Namath
Earle "Greasy" Neale
Ernie Nevers
Ozzie Newsome
Ray Nitschke
Chuck Noll
Leo Nomellini
Merlin Olsen
Jim Otto
Steve Owen
Alan Page
Clarence "Ace" Parker
Jim Parker
Walter Payton
Joe Perry
Pete Pihos
Fritz Pollard
John Randle
Hugh "Shorty" Ray
Dan Reeves
Mel Renfro
Jerry Rice
Les Richter
John Riggins
Jim Ringo
*Willie Roaf
Andy Robustelli
Art Rooney
Dan Rooney
Pete Rozelle
Ed Sabol
Bob St. Clair
Barry Sanders
Charlie Sanders
Deion Sanders
Gale Sayers
Joe Schmidt
Tex Schramm
Lee Roy Selmon
Shannon Sharpe
Billy Shaw
Art Shell
Don Shula
O. J. Simpson
Mike Singletary
Jackie Slater
Bruce Smith
Emmitt Smith

Jackie Smith
John Stallworth
Bart Starr
Roger Staubach
Ernie Stautner
Jan Stenerud
Dwight Stephenson
Hank Stram
Ken Strong
Joe Stydahar
Lynn Swann
Fran Tarkenton
Charley Taylor
Jim Taylor
Lawrence "LT" Taylor
Derrick Thomas
Emmitt Thomas
Thurman Thomas
Jim Thorpe
Andre Tippett
Y. A. Tittle
George Trafton
Charley Trippi
Emlen Tunnell
Clyde "Bulldog" Turner
Johnny Unitas
Gene Upshaw
Norm Van Brocklin
Steve Van Buren
Doak Walker
Bill Walsh
Paul Warfield
Bob Waterfield
Mike Webster
Roger Wehrli
Arnie Weinmeister
Randy White
Reggie White
Dave Wilcox
Bill Willis
Larry Wilson
Ralph Wilson Jr.
Kellen Winslow
Alex Wojciechowicz
Willie Wood
Rod Woodson
Rayfield Wright
Ron Yary
Steve Young
Jack Youngblood
Gary Zimmerman

BASEBALL

American League

American League Wild Card Game: The Baltimore Orioles, in their first postseason game since 1997, defeated the two-time defending American League champion Texas Rangers, 5-1, in the inaugural AL Wild Card playoff game Oct. 5, 2012, in Arlington, Texas.

American League Division Series (ALDS)

NY Yankees defeated Baltimore, 3 games to 2.

New York's CC Sabathia struck out nine in a 3-1 victory in Game 5 on Oct. 12, 2012, at Yankee Stadium, ending Baltimore's playoff run. Earlier in Game 3 on Oct. 10 in the Bronx, Raul Ibanez pinch-hit for Alex Rodriguez and homered to tie the game in the bottom of the ninth, then homered again for the game-winner in the 12th.

American League Division Series (ALDS)

Detroit defeated Oakland, 3 games to 2.

Detroit's Justin Verlander won both of his starts against the AL West champs, including a four-hit, 6-0 series-clinching shutout in Game 5 on Oct. 11, 2012, in Oakland. The A's forced a fifth and deciding game with a dramatic 4-3 victory in Game 4, Oct. 10 in Oakland, when a single by Coco Crisp drove home Seth Smith with the winning run in the bottom of the ninth.

American League Championship Series (ALCS)

Detroit defeated NY Yankees, 4 games to 0.

New York batted .157 in the series and scored just six runs, four of them in a 6-4, 12-inning loss to Detroit in the opener on Oct. 13, 2012, at Yankee Stadium. Justin Verlander won his third game of the playoffs in a 2-1 victory in Game 3 on Oct. 16 at Detroit's Comerica Park. The Tigers hit four home runs in an 8-1, Game 4 clincher on Oct. 17. Tigers DH Delmon Young won ALCS MVP, hitting .353 with six RBI.

National League

National League Wild Card Game: The defending champion St. Louis Cardinals defeated the Atlanta Braves, 6-3, in the inaugural NL Wild Card playoff game at Turner Field in Atlanta on Oct. 5, 2012. Atlanta played the game under protest due to a disputed infield fly call in the bottom of the eighth that negated a potential rally.

National League Division Series (NLDS)

St. Louis defeated Washington, 3 games to 2.

The Cardinals scored a total of 29 runs in three wins against the upstart Nationals, none more dramatic than the four they notched in the ninth inning of Game 5 on Oct. 12, 2012, at Nationals Park in Washington, DC. The Nationals took a 6-0 lead after three innings and led, 7-5, in the ninth, when Cardinals second baseman Daniel Descalso singled home two runs with the bases loaded and two outs, and shortstop Pete Kozma followed with another two-run single that proved to be the difference in St. Louis's 9-7 victory.

National League Division Series (NLDS)

San Francisco defeated Cincinnati, 3 games to 2.

The Giants lost the first two games of the series, but Buster Posey's grand slam capped a 6-run fifth inning in Game 5 and the Giants held on for a 6-4 win on Oct. 11, 2012, at Great American Ball Park in Cincinnati, to advance to their second NL Championship series in three years.

National League Championship Series (NLCS)

San Francisco defeated St. Louis, 4 games to 3.

Another comeback lifted San Francisco to its second World Series in three years. The Cardinals took a three-games-to-one lead in the series following an 8-3 win in Game 4 on Oct. 18, 2012, at Busch Stadium in St. Louis, but the Giants won the next two and forced a seventh game. On Oct. 22 in San Francisco, a 5-run outburst in the third carried the Giants to a 9-0 victory. Giants' second baseman Marco Scutaro tied an LCS record with 14 hits and batted .500 to earn NLCS MVP honors.

World Series, 2012
San Francisco Defeated Detroit, 4 games to 0.

San Francisco ended its 2012 championship season on a seven-game winning streak, including four straight wins in the World Series over the American League champion Detroit Tigers. San Francisco completed the Series sweep on Oct. 28 at Comerica Park when Marco Scutaro's RBI single scored Ryan Theriot with the go-ahead run in the 10th inning for a 4-3 win. Sergio Romo struck out Miguel Cabrera to end the game in the 10th for his third save of the series. Cabrera gave the Tigers their first lead of the series with a two-run homer in the third off Matt Cain. The Giants, more specifically Pablo Sandoval, set the tone in Game 1 Oct. 24 in San Francisco. The Giants' third baseman hit three home runs in the 8-3 San Francisco victory, joining Babe Ruth (twice), Reggie Jackson, and Albert Pujols as the only players to hit three homers in a World Series game. Sandoval batted .500 with 4 RBI and was voted World Series MVP. Giants' pitching shut down the Tigers' offense in the next two games. Madison Bumgarner pitched seven strong innings in a two-hit, 2-0 shutout in Game 2 on Oct. 25. Ryan Vogelsong, Tim Lincecum, and Romo limited Detroit to five hits in a 2-0 win in Game 3. The victory marks the third straight World Series win for a National League club and the seventh in Giants' history.

Game 1
Wednesday, Oct. 24 at AT&T Park, San Francisco, CA

	1	2	3	4	5	6	7	8	9	R	H	E	
Detroit Tigers	0	0	0	0	0	1	0	0	2	3	8	0	**Winning pitcher:** Barry Zito
San Francisco Giants	1	0	3	1	1	0	2	0	X	8	11	0	**Losing pitcher:** Justin Verlander **Attendance:** 42,855

Game 2
Thursday, Oct. 25 at AT&T Park, San Francisco, CA

	1	2	3	4	5	6	7	8	9	R	H	E	
Detroit Tigers	0	0	0	0	0	0	0	0	0	0	2	0	**Winning pitcher:** Madison Bumgarner
San Francisco Giants	0	0	0	0	0	0	1	1	X	2	5	0	**Losing pitcher:** Doug Fister **Save:** Sergio Romo **Attendance:** 42,982

Game 3
Saturday, Oct. 27 at Comerica Park, Detroit, MI

	1	2	3	4	5	6	7	8	9	R	H	E	
San Francisco Giants	0	2	0	0	0	0	0	0	0	2	7	1	**Winning pitcher:** Ryan Vogelsong
Detroit Tigers	0	0	0	0	0	0	0	0	0	0	5	1	**Losing pitcher:** Anibal Sanchez **Save:** Sergio Romo **Attendance:** 42,262

Game 4
Sunday, Oct. 28 at Comerica Park, Detroit, MI

	1	2	3	4	5	6	7	8	9	10	R	H	E	
San Francisco Giants	0	1	0	0	0	2	0	0	0	1	4	9	0	**Winning pitcher:** Santiago Casilla
Detroit Tigers	0	0	2	0	0	1	0	0	0	0	3	5	0	**Losing pitcher:** Phil Coke **Save:** Sergio Romo **Attendance:** 42,152

Major League Baseball, 2012: No-Hitters Abound

The San Francisco Giants' second World Series title in three years shared the stage with many MLB highlights in 2012. Detroit third baseman Miguel Cabrera won baseball's Triple Crown by leading the American League with 44 home runs, 139 RBI, and a .330 batting average. The All-Star was baseball's first Triple Crown winner since Boston's Carl Yastrzemski in 1967. Rookie center fielder Mike Trout of the L.A. Angels hit .326 with 30 home runs in his debut season, and he became the first major leaguer ever to hit 30 home runs, steal 45 bases, and score 125 runs in a single season. San Francisco catcher Buster Posey led the National League with a .336 batting average, and 38-year-old shortstop Derek Jeter led the majors with 216 hits. Posey was the first catcher since Ernie Lombardi in 1942 to lead the NL in hitting.

There were seven no-hitters in 2012, tying the single-season mark set in 1990 and 1991. Philip Humber of the Chicago White Sox began the historic run with a perfect game against the Seattle Mariners on Apr. 21, and L.A. Angels right-hander Jered Weaver pitched a no-hitter over Minnesota on May 2. Johan Santana pitched the first no-hitter in NY Mets' franchise history when he beat St. Louis, 8-0, in New York on June 1. A week later on June 8, Kevin Millwood and five Mariner relievers combined on a 1-0 no-hitter against the L.A. Dodgers in Seattle. Matt Cain fired a perfect game in the Giants' 10-0 win over Houston June 13. The Mariners' Felix Hernandez pitched the season's third perfect game, a 1-0 win over Tampa Bay Aug. 15 in Seattle. Cincinnati's Homer Bailey ended the pitching highlight reel when he no-hit the Pirates, 1-0, in Pittsburgh on Sept. 28. Elsewhere, knuckleballer R. A. Dickey won 20 games for the Mets and in June became the first major leaguer to pitch back-to-back one-hitters since 1988. Toronto's Fernando Rodney had 48 saves and a 0.60 earned run average, a record low ERA for a reliever with at least 50 innings in one season.

Baseball's best record in 2012 belonged to the NL East champion Washington Nationals (98-64). Nationals left-hander Gio Gonzalez led the majors with 21 wins and Stephen Strasburg won 15 games, despite not pitching after Sept. 7 due to an innings limit imposed on the right-hander after he underwent Tommy John elbow surgery in 2010. The Oakland Athletics were 13 games out of first on June 30, but went 57-26 the rest of the way and won the AL West on the season's final day, one game ahead of the Texas Rangers. The NY Yankees hit a single-season franchise record 245 home runs en route to their 13th AL East crown in 17 years. Miguel Cabrera's offense and Justin Verlander's 17 wins, MLB-high 239 strikeouts, and 2.64 ERA (second-best in AL) led Detroit to its second straight AL Central title. Johnny Cueto won 19 games to help Cincinnati capture the NL Central Division. San Francisco won the NL West, overcoming a blow to its offense when outfielder Melky Cabrera was suspended for 50 games on Aug. 15 for failing a doping test. Cabrera, who won the All-Star Game MVP award in the NL's 8-0 win over the AL All-Stars in July, was leading the NL with a .346 batting average at the time of his suspension but announced he would withdraw himself from consideration for the NL batting title (eventually won by teammate Posey).

National League Final Standings, 2012

(* = wild card team)

Eastern Division

	W	L	Pct.	GB	Home	Road	vs. East	vs. Central	vs. West	vs. AL
Washington.........	98	64	.605	—	50-31	48-33	42-30	29-13	17-13	10-8
Atlanta*............	94	68	.580	4	48-33	46-35	46-26	19-19	21-13	8-10
Philadelphia	81	81	.500	17	40-41	41-40	33-39	24-16	19-16	5-10
NY Mets	74	88	.457	24	36-45	38-43	32-40	17-22	17-19	8-7
Miami	69	93	.426	29	38-43	31-50	27-45	18-20	19-15	5-13

Central Division

	W	L	Pct.	GB	Home	Road	vs. East	vs. Central	vs. West	vs. AL
Cincinnati*	97	65	.599	—	50-31	47-34	19-15	49-30	22-12	7-8
St. Louis*	88	74	.543	9	50-31	38-43	14-20	45-32	21-15	8-7
Milwaukee..........	83	79	.512	14	49-32	34-47	15-19	45-34	17-17	6-9
Pittsburgh	79	83	.488	18	45-36	34-47	17-14	39-42	13-19	10-8
Chicago Cubs.......	61	101	.377	36	38-43	23-58	13-19	31-50	12-22	5-10
Houston	55	107	.340	42	35-46	20-61	12-20	29-50	8-28	6-9

Western Division

	W	L	Pct.	GB	Home	Road	vs. East	vs. Central	vs. West	vs. AL
San Francisco.......	94	68	.580	—	48-33	46-35	15-19	27-14	45-27	7-8
L.A. Dodgers........	86	76	.531	8	45-36	41-40	20-12	25-18	35-37	6-9
Arizona............	81	81	.500	13	41-40	40-41	14-20	20-21	38-34	9-6
San Diego..........	76	86	.469	18	42-39	34-47	12-20	22-21	34-38	8-7
Colorado...........	64	98	.395	30	35-46	29-52	15-22	19-19	28-44	2-13

American League Final Standings, 2012

(* = wild card team)

Eastern Division

	W	L	Pct.	GB	Home	Road	vs. East	vs. Central	vs. West	vs. NL
NY Yankees	95	67	.586	—	51-30	44-37	41-31	21-16	20-15	13-5
Baltimore*..........	93	69	.574	2	47-34	46-35	43-29	23-15	16-18	11-7
Tampa Bay	90	72	.556	5	46-35	44-37	41-31	16-18	24-14	9-9
Toronto	73	89	.451	22	41-40	32-49	29-43	21-16	14-21	9-9
Boston	69	93	.426	26	34-47	35-46	26-46	24-16	8-24	11-7

Central Division

	W	L	Pct.	GB	Home	Road	vs. East	vs. Central	vs. West	vs. NL
Detroit.............	88	74	.543	—	50-31	38-43	21-18	43-29	13-20	11-7
Chicago White Sox...	85	77	.525	3	45-36	40-41	19-21	37-35	20-12	9-9
Kansas City	72	90	.444	16	37-44	35-46	16-21	34-38	14-21	8-10
Cleveland	68	94	.420	20	37-44	31-50	14-22	31-41	15-21	8-10
Minnesota..........	66	96	.407	22	31-50	35-46	11-23	35-37	11-27	9-9

Western Division

	W	L	Pct.	GB	Home	Road	vs. East	vs. Central	vs. West	vs. NL
Oakland	94	68	.580	—	50-31	44-37	28-18	23-18	33-24	10-8
Texas*.............	93	69	.574	1	50-31	43-38	24-16	28-19	27-30	14-4
L.A. Angels	89	73	.549	5	46-35	43-38	22-20	25-20	30-27	12-6
Seattle	75	87	.463	19	40-41	35-46	18-28	25-16	24-33	8-10

National League Statistics, 2012

Individual statistics. Players recording fewer than 150 at-bats (batters) or fewer than 70 innings or 10 saves (pitchers) are not listed here. * = changed teams within NL during season; entry includes statistics for more than one team. # = changed teams to or from AL during season; entry includes only NL statistics. Team batting and pitching statistics include players not shown separately.

Team Batting

Team	AVG	AB	R	H	HR	RBI
Colorado Rockies	.274	5,577	758	1,526	166	716
St. Louis Cardinals	.271	5,622	765	1,526	159	732
San Francisco Giants	.269	5,558	718	1,495	103	675
Washington Nationals	.261	5,615	731	1,468	194	688
Milwaukee Brewers	.259	5,557	776	1,442	202	741
Arizona Diamondbacks	.259	5,462	734	1,416	165	710
Philadelphia Phillies	.255	5,544	684	1,414	158	659
Los Angeles Dodgers	.252	5,438	637	1,369	116	607
Cincinnati Reds	.251	5,477	669	1,377	172	636
New York Mets	.249	5,450	650	1,357	139	625
Atlanta Braves	.247	5,425	700	1,341	149	660
San Diego Padres	.247	5,422	651	1,339	121	610
Miami Marlins	.244	5,437	609	1,327	137	576
Pittsburgh Pirates	.243	5,412	651	1,313	170	620
Chicago Cubs	.240	5,411	613	1,297	137	570
Houston Astros	.236	5,407	583	1,276	146	545

Team Pitching

Team	ERA	IP	H	BB	SO	SV
Washington Nationals	3.33	1,468.1	1,296	497	1,325	51
Los Angeles Dodgers	3.34	1,449.2	1,277	539	1,276	40
Cincinnati Reds	3.34	1,453	1,356	427	1,248	56
Atlanta Braves	3.42	1,445.1	1,310	464	1,232	47
San Francisco Giants	3.68	1,451	1,361	489	1,237	53
St. Louis Cardinals	3.71	1,462.2	1,420	436	1,218	42
Philadelphia Phillies	3.83	1,451.1	1,387	409	1,385	42
Pittsburgh Pirates	3.86	1,433.1	1,357	490	1,192	45
Arizona Diamondbacks	3.93	1,433.2	1,432	417	1,200	39
San Diego Padres	4.01	1,434.2	1,356	539	1,205	43
New York Mets	4.09	1,434	1,368	488	1,240	36
Miami Marlins	4.09	1,440.2	1,448	495	1,113	38
Milwaukee Brewers	4.22	1,453.2	1,458	525	1,402	44
Chicago Cubs	4.51	1,413.2	1,399	573	1,128	28
Houston Astros	4.56	1,423.1	1,493	540	1,170	31
Colorado Rockies	5.22	1,422	1,637	566	1,144	36

Arizona Diamondbacks

Batters	AVG	AB	R	H	HR	RBI	SO	SB
Willie Bloomquist	.302	324	47	98	0	23	55	7
Aaron Hill	.302	609	93	184	26	85	86	14
Miguel Montero	.286	486	65	139	15	88	130	0
Paul Goldschmidt	.286	514	82	147	20	82	130	18
Chris Johnson*	.281	488	48	137	15	76	132	5
Justin Upton	.280	554	107	155	17	67	121	18
Gerardo Parra	.273	385	58	105	7	36	77	15
Jason Kubel	.253	506	75	128	30	90	151	1
Ryan Roberts#	.250	252	28	63	6	34	45	6
John McDonald	.249	197	16	49	6	22	33	0
Chris Young	.231	325	36	75	14	41	79	8
Cody Ransom*	.220	246	29	54	11	42	109	0

Pitchers	ERA	W	L	IP	H	BB	SO	SV
J. J. Putz	2.82	1	5	54.1	45	11	65	32
Wade Miley	3.33	16	11	194.2	193	37	144	0
Josh Collmenter	3.69	5	3	90.1	92	22	80	0
Trevor Cahill	3.78	13	12	200	184	74	156	0
Ian Kennedy	4.02	15	12	208.1	216	55	187	0
Joe Saunders#	4.22	6	10	130	146	31	89	0
Patrick Corbin	4.54	6	8	107	117	25	86	1

Manager: Kirk Gibson

Atlanta Braves

Batters	AVG	AB	R	H	HR	RBI	SO	SB
Martin Prado	.301	617	81	186	10	70	69	17
Reed Johnson*	.290	269	30	78	3	20	61	2
Andrelton Simmons	.289	166	17	48	3	19	21	1
Chipper Jones	.287	387	58	111	14	62	51	1
Michael Bourn	.274	624	96	171	9	57	155	42
Jason Heyward	.269	587	93	158	27	82	152	21
Freddie Freeman	.259	540	91	140	23	94	129	2
David Ross	.256	176	18	45	9	23	60	1
Jeff Baker*#	.248	153	17	38	4	21	38	4
Tyler Pastornicky	.243	169	21	41	2	13	32	2
Juan Francisco	.234	192	17	45	9	32	70	1
Brian McCann	.230	439	44	101	20	67	76	3
Dan Uggla	.220	523	86	115	19	78	168	4
Paul Janish	.186	167	18	31	0	9	30	1

Pitchers	ERA	W	L	IP	H	BB	SO	SV
Craig Kimbrel	1.01	3	1	62.2	27	14	116	42
Kris Medlen	1.57	10	1	138	103	23	120	1
Brandon Beachy	2.00	5	5	81	49	29	68	0
Paul Maholm*	3.67	13	11	189	178	53	140	0
Tim Hudson	3.62	16	7	179	168	48	102	0
Cristhian Martinez	3.91	5	4	73.2	80	19	65	1
Mike Minor	4.12	11	10	179.1	151	56	145	0
Randall Delgado	4.37	4	9	92.2	89	42	76	0
Tommy Hanson	4.48	13	10	174.2	183	71	161	0

Manager: Fredi Gonzalez

Chicago Cubs

Batters	AVG	AB	R	H	HR	RBI	SO	SB
Reed Johnson*	.290	269	30	78	3	20	61	2
Anthony Rizzo	.285	337	44	96	15	48	62	3
Starlin Castro	.283	646	78	183	14	78	100	25
Welington Castillo	.265	170	16	45	5	22	51	0
Tony Campana	.264	174	26	46	0	5	43	30
David DeJesus	.263	506	76	133	9	50	89	7
Alfonso Soriano	.262	561	68	147	32	108	153	6
Bryan LaHair	.259	340	42	88	16	40	124	4
Darwin Barney	.254	548	73	139	7	44	58	6
Jeff Baker*#	.248	153	17	38	4	21	38	4
Luis Valbuena	.219	265	26	58	4	28	55	0
Joe Mather	.209	225	18	47	5	19	46	5
Ian Stewart	.201	179	16	36	5	17	46	0
Steve Clevenger	.201	199	16	40	1	16	39	0
Geovany Soto#	.199	176	26	35	6	14	35	0

Pitchers	ERA	W	L	IP	H	BB	SO	SV
Ryan Dempster#	2.25	5	5	104	81	27	83	0
Carlos Marmol	3.42	3	3	55.1	40	45	72	20
Shawn Camp	3.59	3	6	77.2	79	21	54	2
Paul Maholm*	3.67	13	11	189	178	53	140	0
Jeff Samardzija	3.81	9	13	174.2	157	56	180	0
Matt Garza	3.91	5	7	103.2	90	32	96	0
Travis Wood	4.27	6	13	156	133	54	119	0
Chris Volstad	6.31	3	12	111.1	137	43	61	0

Manager: Dale Sveum

Cincinnati Reds

Batters	AVG	AB	R	H	HR	RBI	SO	SB
Joey Votto	.337	374	59	126	14	56	85	5
Brandon Phillips	.281	580	86	163	18	77	79	15
Ryan Ludwick	.275	422	53	116	26	80	97	0
Ryan Hanigan	.274	317	25	87	2	24	37	0
Todd Frazier	.273	422	55	115	19	67	103	3
Chris Heisey	.265	347	44	92	7	31	81	6
Jay Bruce	.252	560	89	141	34	99	155	9
Zack Cozart	.246	561	72	138	15	35	113	4
Scott Rolen	.245	294	26	72	8	39	62	2
Drew Stubbs	.213	493	75	105	14	40	166	30
Devin Mesoraco	.212	165	17	35	5	14	33	1
Wilson Valdez	.206	194	15	40	0	15	36	3
Miguel Cairo	.187	150	9	28	1	13	20	4

Pitchers	ERA	W	L	IP	H	BB	SO	SV
Aroldis Chapman	1.51	5	5	71.2	35	23	122	38
Johnny Cueto	2.78	19	9	217	205	49	170	0
Mat Latos	3.48	14	4	209.1	179	64	185	0
Homer Bailey	3.68	13	10	208	206	52	168	0
Bronson Arroyo	3.74	12	10	202	209	35	129	0
Mike Leake	4.58	8	9	179	201	41	116	0

Manager: Dusty Baker

Colorado Rockies

Batters	AVG	AB	R	H	HR	RBI	SO	SB
Eric Young	.316	174	36	55	4	15	31	14
Jordan Pacheco	.309	475	51	147	5	54	61	7
Marco Scutaro*	.306	620	87	190	7	74	49	9
Carlos Gonzalez	.303	518	89	157	22	85	115	20
Chris Nelson	.301	345	45	104	9	53	84	2
Dexter Fowler	.300	454	72	136	13	53	128	12
DJ LeMahieu	.297	229	26	68	2	22	42	1
Tyler Colvin	.290	420	62	122	18	72	117	7
Troy Tulowitzki	.287	181	33	52	8	27	19	2
Josh Rutledge	.274	277	37	76	8	37	54	7
Wilin Rosario	.270	396	67	107	28	71	99	4
Jonathan Herrera	.262	225	29	59	3	12	39	4
Michael Cuddyer	.260	358	53	93	16	58	78	8
Todd Helton	.238	240	31	57	7	37	44	1
Ramon Hernandez	.217	184	16	40	5	28	32	0

Pitchers	ERA	W	L	IP	H	BB	SO	SV
Rafael Betancourt	2.81	1	4	57.2	53	12	57	31
Josh Roenicke	3.25	4	2	88.2	85	43	54	1
Matt Belisle	3.71	3	8	80	91	18	69	3
Adam Ottavino	4.56	5	1	79	76	34	81	0
Drew Pomeranz	4.93	2	9	96.2	97	46	83	0
Alex White	5.51	2	9	98	114	51	64	0
Jeff Francis	5.58	6	7	113	145	22	76	0
Christian Friedrich	6.17	5	8	84.2	102	30	74	0
Jeremy Guthrie#	6.35	3	9	90.2	122	31	45	0

Manager: Jim Tracy

Houston Astros

Batters	AVG	AB	R	H	HR	RBI	SO	SB
José Altuve	.290	576	80	167	7	37	74	33
Chris Johnson*	.281	488	48	137	15	76	132	5
Carlos Lee*	.264	550	53	145	9	77	49	3
Scott Moore	.259	201	23	52	9	26	56	0
Jason Castro	.257	257	29	66	6	29	61	0
Brett Wallace	.253	229	24	58	9	24	73	0
Jed Lowrie	.244	340	43	83	16	42	65	2
J. D. Martinez	.241	395	34	95	11	55	96	0
Marwin Gonzalez	.234	205	21	48	2	12	29	3
Tyler Greene*	.230	305	34	70	11	30	95	12
Justin Maxwell	.229	315	46	72	18	53	114	9
Jordan Schafer	.211	313	40	66	4	23	106	27
Brian Bogusevic	.203	355	39	72	7	28	96	15
Matt Downs	.202	178	15	36	8	16	38	2
Chris Snyder	.176	221	23	39	7	24	70	0

Pitchers	ERA	W	L	IP	H	BB	SO	SV
Wilton Lopez	2.17	6	3	66.1	61	8	54	10
Brett Myers#	3.52	0	4	30.2	35	6	20	19
Lucas Harrell	3.76	11	11	193.2	185	78	140	0
Wandy Rodriguez*	3.76	12	13	205.2	205	56	139	0
Bud Norris	4.65	7	13	168.1	165	66	165	0
J. A. Happ#	4.83	7	9	104.1	112	39	98	0
Jordan Lyles	5.09	5	12	141.1	159	42	99	0
Dallas Keuchel	5.27	3	8	85.1	93	39	38	0
Fernando Rodriguez	5.37	2	10	70.1	68	34	78	0

Managers: Brad Mills, Tony DeFrancesco

Los Angeles Dodgers

Batters	AVG	AB	R	H	HR	RBI	SO	SB
Matt Kemp	.303	403	74	122	23	69	103	9
Luis Cruz	.297	283	26	84	6	40	34	2
Andre Ethier	.284	556	79	158	20	89	124	2
Jerry Hairston	.273	238	19	65	4	26	27	1
A. J. Ellis	.270	423	44	114	13	52	107	0
Adam Kennedy	.262	168	22	44	2	16	33	1
Mark Ellis	.258	415	52	107	7	31	70	5
Hanley Ramirez*	.257	604	79	155	24	92	132	21
Shane Victorino*	.255	595	72	152	11	55	80	39
James Loney#	.254	334	32	85	4	33	39	0
Elian Herrera	.251	187	26	47	1	17	50	4
Bobby Abreu#	.246	195	28	48	3	19	51	6
Juan Rivera	.244	312	30	76	9	47	35	1
Tony Gwynn	.232	259	29	60	0	17	52	13
Dee Gordon	.228	303	38	69	1	17	62	32
Juan Uribe	.191	162	15	31	2	17	37	0

Pitchers	ERA	W	L	IP	H	BB	SO	SV
Kenley Jansen	2.35	5	3	65	33	22	99	25
Clayton Kershaw	2.53	14	9	227.2	170	63	229	0
Ronald Belisario	2.54	8	1	71	47	29	69	1
Josh Lindblom*	3.55	3	5	71	61	35	70	1
Chad Billingsley	3.55	10	9	149.2	148	45	128	0
Aaron Harang	3.61	10	10	179.2	167	85	131	0

Pitchers	ERA	W	L	IP	H	BB	SO	SV
Chris Capuano	3.72	12	12	198.1	188	54	162	0
Nathan Eovaldi*	4.30	4	13	119.1	133	47	78	0
Joe Blanton*	4.71	10	13	191	207	34	166	0

Manager: Don Mattingly

Miami Marlins

Batters	AVG	AB	R	H	HR	RBI	SO	SB
Justin Ruggiano	.313	288	38	90	13	36	84	14
Donovan Solano	.295	285	29	84	2	28	58	7
Giancarlo Stanton	.290	449	75	130	37	86	143	6
Omar Infante#	.287	328	42	94	8	33	42	10
Jose Reyes	.287	642	86	184	11	57	56	40
Greg Dobbs	.285	319	26	91	5	39	53	4
Carlos Lee*	.264	550	53	145	9	77	49	3
Emilio Bonifacio	.258	244	30	63	1	11	52	30
Hanley Ramirez*	.257	604	79	155	24	92	132	21
Logan Morrison	.230	296	30	68	11	36	58	1
Gaby Sanchez*	.217	299	30	65	7	30	56	1
Bryan Petersen	.195	241	29	47	0	17	58	8
Gorkys Hernandez*	.192	156	18	30	3	13	42	7
John Buck	.192	343	29	66	12	41	103	0

Pitchers	ERA	W	L	IP	H	BB	SO	SV
Steve Cishek	2.69	5	2	63.2	54	29	68	15
Mark Buehrle	3.74	13	13	202.1	197	40	125	0
Josh Johnson	3.81	8	14	191.1	180	65	165	0
Anibal Sanchez#	3.94	5	7	121	119	33	110	0
Nathan Eovaldi*	4.30	4	13	119.1	133	47	78	0
Ricky Nolasco	4.48	12	13	191	214	47	125	0
Carlos Zambrano	4.49	7	10	132.1	123	75	95	0
Heath Bell	5.09	4	5	63.2	70	29	59	19

Manager: Ozzie Guillen

Milwaukee Brewers

Batters	AVG	AB	R	H	HR	RBI	SO	SB
Jonathan Lucroy	.320	316	46	101	12	58	44	4
Ryan Braun	.319	598	108	191	41	112	128	30
Aramis Ramirez	.300	570	92	171	27	105	82	9
Norichika Aoki	.288	520	81	150	10	50	55	30
Corey Hart	.270	562	91	152	30	83	151	5
Martin Maldonado	.266	233	22	62	8	30	56	1
Carlos Gomez	.260	415	72	108	19	51	98	37
Travis Ishikawa	.257	152	19	39	4	30	42	0
Cesar Izturis*	.241	166	13	40	2	11	13	1
Nyjer Morgan	.239	289	44	69	3	16	63	12
Rickie Weeks	.230	588	85	135	21	63	169	16
Cody Ransom*	.220	246	29	54	11	42	109	0

Pitchers	ERA	W	L	IP	H	BB	SO	SV
Zack Greinke#	3.44	9	3	123	120	28	122	0
Marco Estrada	3.64	5	7	138.1	129	29	143	0
Yovani Gallardo	3.66	16	9	204	185	81	204	0
Shaun Marcum	3.70	7	4	124	116	41	109	0
Mike Fiers	3.74	9	10	127.2	125	36	135	0
Francisco Rodriguez	4.38	2	7	72	65	31	72	3
John Axford	4.67	5	8	69.1	61	39	93	35
Randy Wolf#	5.69	3	10	142.1	179	45	96	0

Manager: Ron Roenicke

New York Mets

Batters	AVG	AB	R	H	HR	RBI	SO	SB
David Wright	.306	581	91	178	21	93	112	15
Daniel Murphy	.291	571	62	166	6	65	82	10
Ruben Tejada	.289	464	53	134	1	25	73	4
Justin Turner	.269	171	20	46	2	19	24	1
Scott Hairston	.263	377	52	99	20	57	83	8
Mike Baxter	.263	179	26	47	3	17	45	5
Ronny Cedeno	.259	166	18	43	4	22	35	0
Kirk Nieuwenhuis	.252	282	40	71	7	28	98	4
Jordany Valdespin	.241	191	28	46	8	26	44	10
Lucas Duda	.239	401	43	96	15	57	120	1
Josh Thole	.234	321	24	75	1	21	50	0
Andres Torres	.230	374	47	86	3	35	90	13
Ike Davis	.227	519	66	118	32	90	141	0
Jason Bay	.165	194	21	32	8	20	58	5

Pitchers	ERA	W	L	IP	H	BB	SO	SV
R. A. Dickey	2.73	20	6	233.2	192	54	230	0
Jon Niese	3.40	13	9	190.1	174	49	155	0
Dillon Gee	4.10	6	7	109.2	108	29	97	0
Chris Young	4.15	4	9	115	119	36	80	0
Johan Santana	4.85	6	9	117	117	39	111	0
Jeremy Hefner	5.09	4	7	93.2	110	18	62	0
Frank Francisco	5.53	1	3	42.1	47	21	47	23

Manager: Terry Collins

Philadelphia Phillies

Batters	AVG	AB	R	H	HR	RBI	SO	SB
Kevin Frandsen.....	.338	195	24	66	2	14	18	0
Carlos Ruiz........	.325	372	56	121	16	68	50	4
Juan Pierre.......	.307	394	59	121	1	25	27	37
Nate Schierholtz* ..	.257	241	20	62	6	21	46	3
Placido Polanco	.257	303	28	78	2	19	25	0
Chase Utley	.256	301	48	77	11	45	43	11
Shane Victorino*...	.255	595	72	152	11	55	80	39
Hunter Pence*	.253	617	87	156	24	104	145	5
Jimmy Rollins	.250	632	102	158	23	68	96	30
John Mayberry	.245	441	53	108	14	46	111	1
Domonic Brown	.235	187	21	44	5	26	34	0
Ty Wigginton	.235	315	40	74	11	43	81	1
Freddy Galvis	.226	190	14	43	3	24	29	0
Ryan Howard	.219	260	28	57	14	56	99	0

Pitchers	ERA	W	L	IP	H	BB	SO	SV
Jonathan Papelbon..	2.44	5	6	70	56	18	92	38
Cole Hamels.......	3.05	17	6	215.1	190	52	216	0
Cliff Lee	3.16	6	9	211	207	28	207	0
Kyle Kendrick	3.90	11	12	159.1	154	49	116	0
Vance Worley	4.20	6	9	133	154	47	107	0
Roy Halladay	4.49	11	8	156.1	155	36	132	0
Joe Blanton*......	4.71	10	13	191	207	34	166	0
Josh Lindblom*.....	3.55	3	5	71	61	35	70	1

Manager: Charlie Manuel

Pittsburgh Pirates

Batters	AVG	AB	R	H	HR	RBI	SO	SB
Andrew McCutchen..	.327	593	107	194	31	96	132	20
Neil Walker	.280	472	62	132	14	69	104	7
Garrett Jones	.274	475	68	130	27	86	103	2
Starling Marte......	.257	167	18	43	5	17	50	12
Pedro Alvarez	.244	525	64	128	30	85	180	1
Jose Tabata	.243	333	43	81	3	16	58	0
Alex Presley	.237	346	46	82	10	25	72	9
Michael McKenry ...	.233	240	25	56	12	39	73	0
Josh Harrison	.233	249	34	58	3	16	37	7
Casey McGehee#...	.230	265	27	61	8	35	60	1
Clint Barmes.......	.229	455	34	104	8	45	106	0
Gaby Sanchez*.....	.217	299	30	65	7	30	56	1
Rod Barajas	.206	321	29	66	11	31	69	0
Gorkys Hernandez*	.192	156	18	30	3	13	42	7

Pitchers	ERA	W	L	IP	H	BB	SO	SV
Joel Hanrahan	2.72	5	2	59.2	40	36	67	36
Jared Hughes......	2.85	2	2	75.2	65	22	50	2
A. J. Burnett......	3.51	16	10	202.1	189	62	180	0
Wandy Rodriguez*..	3.76	12	13	205.2	205	56	139	0
Chris Resop.......	3.91	1	4	73.2	81	24	46	1
Jeff Karstens.......	3.97	5	4	90.2	89	15	66	0
Kevin Correia	4.21	12	11	171	176	46	89	0
James McDonald ...	4.21	12	8	171	147	69	151	0
Erik Bedard........	5.01	7	14	125.2	129	56	118	0

Manager: Clint Hurdle

San Diego Padres

Batters	AVG	AB	R	H	HR	RBI	SO	SB
Yasmani Grandal ...	.297	192	28	57	8	36	39	0
Chris Denorfia......	.293	348	56	102	8	36	52	13
Chase Headley.....	.286	604	95	173	31	115	157	17
Yonder Alonso......	.273	549	47	150	9	62	101	3
Logan Forsythe	.273	315	45	86	6	26	57	8
Will Venable	.264	417	62	110	9	45	94	24
Carlos Quentin	.261	284	44	74	16	46	41	0
Jesus Guzman	.247	287	32	71	9	48	71	3
Everth Cabrera	.246	398	49	98	2	24	110	44
Cameron Maybin	.243	507	67	123	8	45	110	26
Alexi Amarista#.....	.240	275	35	66	5	32	42	8
John Baker	.238	193	17	46	0	14	41	2
Nick Hundley	.157	204	14	32	3	22	56	0

Pitchers	ERA	W	L	IP	H	BB	SO	SV
Huston Street	1.85	2	1	39	17	11	47	23
Luke Gregerson	2.39	2	0	71.2	57	21	72	9
Eric Stults#........	2.92	8	3	92.1	86	23	51	0
Clayton Richard	3.99	14	14	218.2	228	42	107	0
Jason Marquis#.....	4.04	6	7	93.2	94	28	79	0
Edinson Volquez ...	4.14	11	11	182.2	160	105	174	0
Anthony Bass	4.73	2	8	97	89	39	80	1

Manager: Bud Black

San Francisco Giants

Batters	AVG	AB	R	H	HR	RBI	SO	SB
Melky Cabrera	.346	459	84	159	11	60	63	13
Buster Posey	.336	530	78	178	24	103	96	1
Marco Scutaro*....	.306	620	87	190	7	74	49	9
Angel Pagan	.288	605	95	174	8	56	97	29
Pablo Sandoval....	.283	396	59	112	12	63	59	1
Hector Sanchez ...	.280	218	22	61	3	34	52	0
Brandon Belt......	.275	411	47	113	7	56	106	12
Ryan Theriot......	.270	352	45	95	0	28	47	13
Joaquin Arias	.270	319	30	86	5	34	44	5
Nate Schierholtz*..	.257	241	20	62	6	21	46	3
Hunter Pence*	.253	617	87	156	24	104	145	5
Brandon Crawford..	.248	435	44	108	4	45	95	1
Gregor Blanco	.244	393	56	96	5	34	104	26
Xavier Nady*......	.184	152	12	28	4	13	37	1

Pitchers	ERA	W	L	IP	H	BB	SO	SV
Sergio Romo......	1.79	4	2	55.1	37	10	63	14
Matt Cain	2.79	16	5	219.1	177	51	193	0
Santiago Casilla ...	2.84	7	6	63.1	55	22	55	25
Ryan Vogelsong ...	3.37	14	9	189.2	171	62	158	0
Madison Bumgarner	3.37	16	11	208.1	183	49	191	0
Barry Zito	4.15	15	8	184.1	186	70	114	0
Tim Lincecum.....	5.18	10	15	186	183	90	190	0

Manager: Bruce Bochy

St. Louis Cardinals

Batters	AVG	AB	R	H	HR	RBI	SO	SB
Yadier Molina	.315	505	65	159	22	76	55	12
Allen Craig	.307	469	76	144	22	92	89	2
Jon Jay	.305	443	70	135	4	40	71	19
Matt Holliday......	.295	599	95	177	27	102	132	4
Matt Carpenter	.294	296	44	87	6	46	63	1
David Freese......	.293	501	70	147	20	79	122	3
Skip Schumaker ...	.276	272	37	75	1	28	50	1
Carlos Beltran.....	.269	547	83	147	32	97	124	13
Rafael Furcal......	.264	477	69	126	5	49	57	12
Shane Robinson ...	.253	166	20	42	3	16	32	1
Tyler Greene*	.230	305	34	70	11	30	95	12
Daniel Descalso ...	.227	374	41	85	4	26	83	6

Pitchers	ERA	W	L	IP	H	BB	SO	SV
Mitchell Boggs	2.21	4	1	73.1	56	21	58	0
Jason Motte	2.75	4	5	72	49	17	86	42
Kyle Lohse	2.86	16	3	211	192	38	143	0
Joe Kelly.........	3.53	5	7	107	112	36	75	0
Lance Lynn.......	3.78	18	7	176	168	64	180	0
Jaime Garcia	3.92	7	7	121.2	136	30	98	0
Adam Wainwright ..	3.94	14	13	198.2	196	52	184	0
Jake Westbrook ...	3.97	13	11	174.2	191	52	106	0

Manager: Mike Matheny

Washington Nationals

Batters	AVG	AB	R	H	HR	RBI	SO	SB
Jayson Werth	.300	300	42	90	5	31	57	8
Ian Desmond	.292	513	72	150	25	73	113	21
Roger Bernadina ..	.291	227	25	66	5	25	53	15
Michael Morse	.291	406	53	118	18	62	97	0
Ryan Zimmerman..	.282	578	93	163	25	95	116	5
Steve Lombardozzi	.273	384	40	105	3	27	46	5
Adam LaRoche....	.271	571	76	155	33	100	138	1
Bryce Harper	.270	533	98	144	22	59	120	18
Tyler Moore.......	.263	156	20	41	10	29	46	3
Danny Espinosa ...	.247	594	82	147	17	56	189	20
Cesar Izturis*......	.241	166	13	40	2	11	13	1
Rick Ankiel........	.228	158	15	36	5	15	59	1
Jesus Flores	.213	277	22	59	6	26	59	1
Xavier Nady*......	.184	152	12	28	4	13	37	1

Pitchers	ERA	W	L	IP	H	BB	SO	SV
Craig Stammen	2.34	6	1	88.1	70	36	87	1
Tom Gorzelanny ...	2.88	4	2	72	65	30	62	1
Gio Gonzalez	2.89	21	8	199.1	149	76	207	0
Jordan Zimmermann	2.94	12	8	195.2	186	43	153	0
Stephen Strasburg..	3.16	15	6	159.1	136	48	197	0
Ross Detwiler.....	3.40	10	8	164.1	149	52	105	0
Tyler Clippard	3.72	2	6	72.2	55	29	84	32
Edwin Jackson	4.03	10	11	189.2	173	58	168	0

Manager: Davey Johnson

American League Statistics, 2012

Individual statistics. Players recording fewer than 150 at-bats (batters) or fewer than 70 innings or 10 saves (pitchers) are not listed here. * = changed teams within AL during season; entry includes statistics for more than one team. # = changed teams to or from NL during season; entry includes only AL statistics. Team batting and pitching statistics include players not shown separately.

Team Batting

Team	AVG	AB	R	H	HR	RBI
Los Angeles Angels	.274	5,536	767	1,518	187	732
Texas Rangers	.273	5,590	808	1,526	200	780
Detroit Tigers	.268	5,476	726	1,467	163	698
Kansas City Royals..	.265	5,636	676	1,492	131	643
New York Yankees...	.265	5,524	804	1,462	245	774
Boston Red Sox	.260	5,604	734	1,459	165	695
Minnesota Twins....	.260	5,562	701	1,448	131	667
Chicago White Sox ..	.255	5,518	748	1,409	211	726
Cleveland Indians...	.251	5,525	667	1,385	136	635
Baltimore Orioles ...	.247	5,560	712	1,375	214	677
Toronto Blue Jays ...	.245	5,487	716	1,346	198	677
Tampa Bay Rays....	.240	5,398	697	1,293	175	665
Oakland Athletics ...	.238	5,527	713	1,315	195	676
Seattle Mariners	.234	5,494	619	1,285	149	584

Team Pitching

Team	ERA	IP	H	BB	SO	SV
Tampa Bay Rays....	3.19	1,459.2	1,233	469	1,383	50
Oakland Athletics ...	3.48	1,470	1,360	462	1,136	47
Detroit Tigers	3.75	1,430.2	1,409	438	1,318	40
Seattle Mariners	3.76	1,456.2	1,359	449	1,166	43
New York Yankees...	3.85	1,445.1	1,401	431	1,318	51
Baltimore Orioles ...	3.90	1,483	1,433	481	1,177	55
Texas Rangers	3.99	1,442	1,378	446	1,286	43
Los Angeles Angels	4.02	1,433.1	1,339	483	1,157	38
Chicago White Sox ..	4.02	1,445.2	1,365	503	1,246	37
Kansas City Royals..	4.30	1,451.1	1,504	542	1,177	44
Toronto Blue Jays ...	4.64	1,443.2	1,439	574	1,142	29
Boston Red Sox	4.70	1,443	1,449	529	1,176	35
Minnesota Twins....	4.77	1,438.2	1,536	465	943	35
Cleveland Indians...	4.78	1,442	1,503	543	1,086	43

Baltimore Orioles

Batters	AVG	AB	R	H	HR	RBI	SO	SB
Nick Markakis	.298	420	59	125	13	54	51	1
Adam Jones........	.287	648	103	186	32	82	126	16
Chris Davis	.270	515	75	139	33	85	169	2
Nate McLouth#.....	.268	209	35	56	7	18	43	12
Manny Machado	.262	191	24	50	7	26	38	2
Wilson Betemit	.261	341	41	89	12	40	103	0
Matt Wieters	.249	526	67	131	23	83	112	3
J. J. Hardy	.238	663	85	158	22	68	106	0
Mark Reynolds	.221	457	65	101	23	69	159	1
Ryan Flaherty	.216	153	15	33	6	19	43	1
Robert Andino	.211	384	41	81	7	28	100	5
Endy Chavez	.203	158	15	32	2	12	24	3

Pitchers	ERA	W	L	IP	H	BB	SO	SV
Jim Johnson	2.49	2	1	68.2	55	15	41	51
Luis Ayala	2.64	5	5	75	81	14	51	1
Chris Tillman	2.93	9	3	86	66	24	66	0
Miguel Gonzalez	3.25	9	4	105.1	92	35	77	0
Jason Hammel	3.43	8	6	118	104	42	113	0
Wei-Yin Chen	4.02	12	11	192.2	186	57	154	0
Brian Matusz......	4.87	6	10	98	112	41	81	0
Tommy Hunter......	5.45	7	8	133.2	161	27	77	0
Jake Arrieta........	6.20	3	9	114.2	122	35	109	0

Manager: Buck Showalter

Chicago White Sox

Batters	AVG	AB	R	H	HR	RBI	SO	SB
Alex Rios	.304	605	93	184	25	91	92	23
Paul Konerko	.298	533	66	159	26	75	83	0
Alejandro De Aza ...	.281	524	81	147	9	50	109	26
A. J. Pierzynski	.278	479	68	133	27	77	78	0
Alexei Ramirez	.265	593	59	157	9	73	77	20
Dewayne Wise*.....	.259	224	31	58	8	30	52	19
Dayan Viciedo......	.255	505	64	129	25	78	120	0
Jose Lopez*.......	.246	236	18	58	4	28	41	0
Kevin Youkilis*.....	.235	438	72	103	19	60	108	0
Gordon Beckham ...	.234	525	62	123	16	60	89	5
Adam Dunn........	.204	539	87	110	41	96	222	2
Brent Lillibridge*....	.195	190	25	37	3	10	71	13

Pitchers	ERA	W	L	IP	H	BB	SO	SV
Nate Jones	2.39	8	0	71.2	67	32	65	0
Chris Sale.........	3.05	17	8	192	167	51	192	0
Hector Santiago	3.33	4	1	70.1	54	40	79	4
Jake Peavy........	3.37	11	12	219	191	49	194	0
Jose Quintana	3.76	6	6	136.1	142	42	81	0
Gavin Floyd........	4.29	12	11	168	166	63	144	0
Addison Reed......	4.75	3	2	55	57	18	54	29
Francisco Liriano*...	5.34	6	12	156.2	143	97	167	0
Philip Humber......	6.44	5	5	102	113	44	85	0

Manager: Robin Ventura

Boston Red Sox

Batters	AVG	AB	R	H	HR	RBI	SO	SB
David Ortiz	.318	324	65	103	23	60	51	0
Scott Podsednik ...	.302	199	19	60	1	12	35	8
Adrian Gonzalez#...	.300	484	63	145	15	86	81	0
Pedro Ciriaco	.293	259	33	76	2	19	47	16
Dustin Pedroia	.290	563	81	163	15	65	60	20
Will Middlebrooks ...	.288	267	34	77	15	54	70	4
Jacoby Ellsbury	.271	303	43	82	4	26	43	14
Cody Ross	.267	476	70	127	22	81	129	2
Ryan Sweeney	.260	204	22	53	0	16	43	0
Mike Aviles	.250	512	57	128	13	60	77	14
Daniel Nava	.243	267	38	65	6	33	63	3
Kevin Youkilis*......	.235	438	72	103	19	60	108	0
Jarrod Saltalamacchia	.222	405	55	90	25	59	139	0
Brent Lillibridge*....	.195	190	25	37	3	10	71	13
Danny Valencia*....	.188	154	14	29	3	21	38	0
Ryan Lavarnway....	.157	153	11	24	2	12	41	0

Pitchers	ERA	W	L	IP	H	BB	SO	SV
Franklin Morales	3.77	3	4	76.1	64	30	76	1
Clay Buchholz......	4.56	11	8	189.1	187	64	129	0
Jon Lester	4.82	9	14	205.1	216	68	166	0
Felix Doubront	4.86	11	10	161	162	71	167	0
Josh Beckett#......	5.23	5	11	127.1	131	38	94	0
Alfredo Aceves	5.36	2	10	84	80	31	75	25
Aaron Cook........	5.65	4	11	94	117	21	20	0

Manager: Bobby Valentine

Cleveland Indians

Batters	AVG	AB	R	H	HR	RBI	SO	SB
Michael Brantley....	.288	552	63	159	6	60	56	12
Shin-Soo Choo.....	.283	598	88	169	16	67	150	21
Asdrubal Cabrera ...	.270	555	70	150	16	68	99	9
Jason Kipnis	.257	591	86	152	14	76	109	31
Carlos Santana.....	.252	507	72	128	18	76	101	3
Jose Lopez*	.246	236	18	58	4	28	41	0
Jack Hannahan.....	.244	287	23	70	4	29	63	0
Casey Kotchman ...	.229	463	46	106	12	55	49	3
Travis Hafner	.228	219	23	50	12	34	47	0
Lou Marson........	.226	195	27	44	0	13	44	4
Johnny Damon	.222	207	25	46	4	19	27	4
Shelley Duncan	.203	232	29	47	11	31	59	1
Brent Lillibridge*....	.195	190	25	37	3	10	71	13

Pitchers	ERA	W	L	IP	H	BB	SO	SV
Vinnie Pestano	2.57	3	3	70	53	24	76	2
Chris Perez........	3.59	0	4	57.2	49	16	59	39
Zach McAllister.....	4.24	6	8	125.1	133	38	110	0
Justin Masterson....	4.93	11	15	206.1	212	88	159	0
Ubaldo Jimenez	5.40	9	17	176.2	190	95	143	0
Derek Lowe*.......	5.11	9	11	142.2	180	51	55	1
Jeanmar Gomez	5.96	5	8	90.2	95	34	47	0
Josh Tomlin........	6.36	5	8	103.1	126	25	56	0

Managers: Manny Acta, Sandy Alomar Jr.

Detroit Tigers

Batters	AVG	AB	R	H	HR	RBI	SO	SB
Miguel Cabrera	.330	622	109	205	44	139	98	4
Andy Dirks	.322	314	56	101	8	35	53	1
Prince Fielder	.313	581	83	182	30	108	84	1
Austin Jackson	.300	543	103	163	16	66	134	12
Gerald Laird	.282	174	24	49	2	11	21	0
Delmon Young	.267	574	54	153	18	74	112	0
Quintin Berry	.258	291	44	75	2	29	80	21
Omar Infante#	.257	226	27	58	4	20	23	7
Alex Avila	.243	367	42	89	9	48	104	2
Brennan Boesch	.240	470	52	113	12	54	104	6
Jhonny Peralta	.239	531	58	127	13	63	105	1
Brandon Inge*	.218	303	33	66	12	54	91	0
Ramon Santiago	.206	228	19	47	2	17	39	1
Ryan Raburn	.171	205	14	35	1	12	53	1

Pitchers	ERA	W	L	IP	H	BB	SO	SV
Justin Verlander	2.64	17	8	238.1	192	60	239	0
Doug Fister	3.45	10	10	161.2	156	37	137	0
Joaquin Benoit	3.68	5	3	71	59	22	84	2
Anibal Sanchez#	3.74	4	6	74.2	81	15	57	0
Max Scherzer	3.74	16	7	187.2	179	60	231	0
Jose Valverde	3.78	3	4	69	59	27	48	35
Drew Smyly	3.99	4	3	99.1	93	33	94	0
Rick Porcello	4.59	10	12	176.1	226	44	107	0

Manager: Jim Leyland

Kansas City Royals

Batters	AVG	AB	R	H	HR	RBI	SO	SB
Billy Butler	.313	614	72	192	29	107	111	2
Salvador Perez	.301	289	38	87	11	39	27	0
Alex Gordon	.294	642	93	189	14	72	140	10
Alcides Escobar	.293	605	68	177	5	52	100	35
Chris Getz	.275	189	22	52	0	17	17	9
Lorenzo Cain	.266	222	27	59	7	31	56	10
Jarrod Dyson	.260	292	52	76	0	9	56	30
Mike Moustakas	.242	563	69	136	20	73	124	5
Johnny Giavotella	.238	181	21	43	1	15	35	3
Brayan Pena	.236	212	16	50	2	25	24	0
Jeff Francoeur	.235	561	58	132	16	49	119	4
Eric Hosmer	.232	535	65	124	14	60	95	16
Yuniesky Betancourt	.228	215	21	49	7	36	25	0

Pitchers	ERA	W	L	IP	H	BB	SO	SV
Jonathan Broxton#	2.27	1	2	35.2	36	14	25	23
Kelvin Herrera	2.35	4	3	84.1	79	21	77	3
Greg Holland	2.96	7	4	67	58	34	91	16
Jeremy Guthrie#	3.16	5	3	91	84	19	56	0
Luis Mendoza	4.23	8	10	166	176	59	104	0
Bruce Chen	5.07	11	14	191.2	215	47	140	0
Will Smith	5.32	6	9	89.2	111	33	59	0
Luke Hochevar	5.73	8	16	185.1	202	61	144	0

Manager: Ned Yost

Los Angeles Angels

Batters	AVG	AB	R	H	HR	RBI	SO	SB
Mike Trout	.326	559	129	182	30	83	139	49
Torii Hunter	.313	534	81	167	16	92	133	9
Erick Aybar	.290	517	67	150	8	45	61	20
Howard Kendrick	.287	550	57	158	8	67	115	14
Albert Pujols	.285	607	85	173	30	105	76	8
Kendrys Morales	.273	484	61	132	22	73	116	0
Mark Trumbo	.268	544	66	146	32	95	153	4
Maicer Izturis	.256	289	35	74	2	20	38	17
Alberto Callaspo	.252	457	55	115	10	53	59	4
Chris Iannetta	.240	221	27	53	9	26	60	1
Vernon Wells	.230	243	36	56	11	29	35	3
Peter Bourjos	.220	168	27	37	3	19	44	3
Bobby Wilson	.211	171	19	36	3	13	33	0

Pitchers	ERA	W	L	IP	H	BB	SO	SV
Ernesto Frieri#	2.32	4	2	54.1	26	26	80	23
Jered Weaver	2.81	20	5	188.2	147	45	142	0
Zack Greinke#	3.53	6	2	89.1	80	26	78	0
C. J. Wilson	3.83	13	10	202.1	181	91	173	0
Dan Haren	4.33	12	13	176.2	190	38	142	0
Jerome Williams	4.58	6	8	137.2	139	35	98	1
Garrett Richards	4.69	4	3	71	77	34	47	1
Ervin Santana	5.16	9	13	178	165	61	133	0

Manager: Mike Scioscia

Minnesota Twins

Batters	AVG	AB	R	H	HR	RBI	SO	SB
Joe Mauer	.319	545	81	174	10	85	88	8
Ben Revere	.294	511	70	150	0	32	54	40
Denard Span	.283	516	71	146	4	41	62	17
Ryan Doumit	.275	484	56	133	18	75	98	0
Jamey Carroll	.268	470	65	126	1	40	65	9
Justin Morneau	.267	505	63	135	19	77	102	1
Josh Willingham	.260	519	85	135	35	110	141	3
Darin Mastroianni	.252	163	22	41	3	17	45	21
Alexi Casilla	.241	299	33	72	1	30	52	21
Trevor Plouffe	.235	422	56	99	24	55	92	1
Brian Dozier	.234	316	33	74	6	33	58	9
Chris Parmelee	.229	192	18	44	5	20	52	0
Danny Valencia*	.188	154	14	29	3	21	38	0

Pitchers	ERA	W	L	IP	H	BB	SO	SV
Glen Perkins	2.56	3	1	70.1	57	16	78	16
Alex Burnett	3.52	4	4	71.2	71	26	36	0
Scott Diamond	3.54	12	9	173	184	31	90	0
Matt Capps	3.68	1	4	29.1	28	4	18	14
Cole De Vries	4.11	5	5	87.2	88	18	58	0
Samuel Deduno	4.44	6	5	79	69	53	57	0
Anthony Swarzak	5.03	3	6	96.2	106	31	62	0
Brian Duensing	5.12	4	12	109	126	27	69	0
Francisco Liriano*	5.34	6	12	156.2	143	97	167	0
Liam Hendriks	5.59	1	8	85.1	106	26	50	0
Nick Blackburn	7.39	4	9	98.2	143	26	42	0

Manager: Ron Gardenhire

New York Yankees

Batters	AVG	AB	R	H	HR	RBI	SO	SB
Derek Jeter	.316	683	99	216	15	58	90	9
Robinson Cano	.313	627	105	196	33	94	96	3
Ichiro Suzuki*	.283	629	77	178	9	55	61	29
Eric Chavez	.281	278	36	78	16	37	59	0
Alex Rodriguez	.272	463	74	126	18	57	116	13
Nick Swisher	.272	537	75	146	24	93	141	2
Dewayne Wise*	.259	224	31	58	8	30	52	19
Mark Teixeira	.251	451	66	113	24	84	83	2
Jayson Nix	.243	177	24	43	4	18	53	6
Raul Ibanez	.240	384	50	92	19	62	67	3
Curtis Granderson	.232	596	102	138	43	106	195	10
Russell Martin	.211	422	50	89	21	53	95	6
Andruw Jones	.197	233	27	46	14	34	71	0

Pitchers	ERA	W	L	IP	H	BB	SO	SV
Rafael Soriano	2.26	2	1	67.2	55	24	69	42
Andy Pettitte	2.87	5	4	75.1	65	21	69	0
Derek Lowe*	5.11	9	11	142.2	180	51	55	1
Hiroki Kuroda	3.32	16	11	219.2	205	51	167	0
David Phelps	3.34	4	4	99.2	81	38	96	0
CC Sabathia	3.38	15	6	200	184	44	197	0
Phil Hughes	4.23	16	13	191.1	196	46	165	0
Ivan Nova	5.02	12	8	170.1	194	56	153	0
Freddy Garcia	5.20	7	6	107.1	112	35	89	0

Manager: Joe Girardi

Oakland Athletics

Batters	AVG	AB	R	H	HR	RBI	SO	SB
Yoenis Cespedes	.292	487	70	142	23	82	102	16
Brandon Moss	.291	265	48	77	21	52	90	1
Jonny Gomes	.262	279	46	73	18	47	104	3
Coco Crisp	.259	455	68	118	11	46	64	39
Stephen Drew#	.250	152	21	38	5	16	41	1
Josh Reddick	.242	611	85	148	32	85	151	11
Josh Donaldson	.241	274	34	66	9	33	61	4
Seth Smith	.240	383	55	92	14	52	98	2
Chris Carter	.239	218	38	52	16	39	83	0
Jemile Weeks	.221	444	54	98	2	20	70	16
Brandon Inge*.......	.218	303	33	66	12	54	91	0
Kurt Suzuki#.......	.218	262	19	57	1	18	53	1
Cliff Pennington......	.215	418	50	90	6	28	90	15
Derek Norris	.201	209	19	42	7	34	66	5

Pitchers	ERA	W	L	IP	H	BB	SO	SV
Ryan Cook	2.09	6	2	73.1	42	27	80	14
Grant Balfour	2.53	3	2	74.2	41	28	72	24
A. J. Griffin	3.06	7	1	82.1	74	19	64	0
Brandon McCarthy ...	3.24	8	6	111	115	24	73	0
Bartolo Colon	3.43	10	9	152.1	161	23	91	0
Jarrod Parker	3.47	13	8	181.1	166	63	140	0
Tommy Milone	3.74	13	10	190	207	36	137	0
Travis Blackley#	3.86	6	4	102.2	91	30	69	0
Tyson Ross	6.50	2	11	73.1	96	37	46	0

Manager: Bob Melvin

Seattle Mariners

Batters	AVG	AB	R	H	HR	RBI	SO	SB
Ichiro Suzuki*	.283	629	77	178	9	55	61	29
John Jaso	.276	294	41	81	10	50	51	5
Jesus Montero	.260	515	46	134	15	62	99	0
Franklin Gutierrez	.260	150	18	39	4	17	31	3
Kyle Seager	.259	594	62	154	20	86	110	13
Michael Saunders....	.247	507	71	125	19	57	132	21
Eric Thames*	.232	271	27	63	9	25	87	1
Casper Wells	.228	285	42	65	10	36	80	3
Dustin Ackley	.226	607	84	137	12	50	124	13
Miguel Olivo	.222	315	27	70	12	29	85	3
Justin Smoak	.217	483	49	105	19	51	111	1
Mike Carp	.213	164	17	35	5	20	46	1
Brendan Ryan.......	.194	407	42	79	3	31	98	11
Chone Figgins	.181	166	18	30	2	11	48	4

Pitchers	ERA	W	L	IP	H	BB	SO	SV
Tom Wilhelmsen	2.50	4	3	79.1	59	29	87	29
Felix Hernandez	3.06	13	9	232	209	56	223	0
Hisashi Iwakuma	3.16	9	5	125.1	117	43	101	2
Jason Vargas	3.85	14	11	217.1	201	55	141	0
Kevin Millwood	4.25	6	12	161	168	56	107	0
Blake Beavan	4.43	11	11	152.1	168	24	67	0
Hector Noesi........	5.82	2	12	106.2	107	39	68	0

Manager: Eric Wedge

Tampa Bay Rays

Batters	AVG	AB	R	H	HR	RBI	SO	SB
Jeff Keppinger.......	.325	385	46	125	9	40	31	1
Evan Longoria	.289	273	39	79	17	55	61	2
Ben Zobrist........	.270	560	88	151	20	74	103	14
B. J. Upton	.246	573	79	141	28	78	169	31
Desmond Jennings...	.246	505	85	124	13	47	120	31
Elliot Johnson.......	.242	297	32	72	6	33	84	18
Matt Joyce........	.241	399	55	96	17	59	102	4
Luke Scott.........	.229	314	35	72	14	55	80	5
Jose Molina	.223	251	27	56	8	32	60	3

Batters	AVG	AB	R	H	HR	RBI	SO	SB
Jose Lobaton	.222	167	16	37	2	20	46	0
Ryan Roberts#	.214	187	23	40	6	18	47	4
Sean Rodriguez	.213	301	36	64	6	32	75	5
Carlos Pena	.197	497	72	98	19	61	182	2

Pitchers	ERA	W	L	IP	H	BB	SO	SV
Fernando Rodney ...	0.60	2	2	74.2	43	15	76	48
Wade Davis	2.43	3	0	70.1	48	29	87	0
David Price........	2.56	20	5	211	173	59	205	0
Jeremy Hellickson ..	3.10	10	11	177	163	59	124	0
James Shields	3.52	15	10	227.2	208	58	223	0
Matt Moore........	3.81	11	11	177.1	158	81	175	0
Alex Cobb.........	4.03	11	9	136.1	130	40	106	0

Manager: Joe Maddon

Texas Rangers

Batters	AVG	AB	R	H	HR	RBI	SO	SB
Adrian Beltre.......	.321	604	95	194	36	102	82	1
Craig Gentry	.304	240	31	73	1	26	41	13
David Murphy	.304	457	65	139	15	61	74	10
Elvis Andrus	.286	629	85	180	3	62	96	21
Josh Hamilton......	.285	562	103	160	43	128	162	7
Michael Young......	.277	611	79	169	8	67	70	2
Mitch Moreland.....	.275	327	41	90	15	50	71	1
Nelson Cruz	.260	585	86	152	24	90	140	8
Ian Kinsler........	.256	655	105	168	19	72	90	21
Yorvit Torrealba*# ...	.233	189	19	44	4	14	38	1
Mike Napoli........	.227	352	53	80	24	56	125	1

Pitchers	ERA	W	L	IP	H	BB	SO	SV
Joe Nathan........	2.80	3	5	64.1	55	13	78	37
Matt Harrison	3.29	18	11	213.1	210	59	133	0
Colby Lewis	3.43	6	6	105	99	14	93	0
Yu Darvish	3.90	16	9	191.1	156	89	221	0
Derek Holland......	4.67	12	7	175.1	162	52	145	0
Scott Feldman.....	5.09	6	11	123.2	139	32	96	0

Manager: Ron Washington

Toronto Blue Jays

Batters	AVG	AB	R	H	HR	RBI	SO	SB
Edwin Encarnacion..	.280	542	93	152	42	110	94	13
Brett Lawrie........	.273	494	73	135	11	48	86	13
Rajai Davis	.257	447	64	115	8	43	102	46
Adam Lind	.255	321	28	82	11	45	61	0
Yunel Escobar......	.253	558	58	141	9	51	70	5
Jose Bautista	.241	332	64	80	27	65	63	5
Omar Vizquel	.235	153	13	36	0	7	17	3
J. P. Arencibia	.233	347	45	81	18	56	108	1
Yorvit Torrealba*# ...	.233	189	19	44	4	14	38	1
Eric Thames*	.232	271	27	63	9	25	87	1
Kelly Johnson......	.225	507	61	114	16	55	159	14
Colby Rasmus	.223	565	75	126	23	75	149	4
Anthony Gose......	.223	166	25	37	1	11	59	15
Jeff Mathis	.218	211	25	46	8	27	68	1

Pitchers	ERA	W	L	IP	H	BB	SO	SV
Casey Janssen.....	2.54	1	1	63.2	44	11	67	22
Brandon Morrow....	2.96	10	7	124.2	98	41	108	0
Carlos Villanueva ...	4.16	7	7	125.1	113	46	122	0
Aaron Laffey	4.56	4	6	100.2	100	37	48	0
Kyle Drabek	4.67	4	7	71.1	67	47	47	0
Henderson Alvarez ..	4.85	9	14	187.1	216	54	79	0
Ricky Romero	5.77	9	14	181	198	105	124	0

Manager: John Farrell

Major League Leaders, 2012

National League

Batting Average: Buster Posey, San Francisco, .336; Andrew McCutchen, Pittsburgh, .327; Ryan Braun, Milwaukee, .319; Yadier Molina, St. Louis, .315; Jordan Pacheco, Colorado, .309.

Runs Scored: Ryan Braun, Milwaukee, 108; Andrew McCutchen, Pittsburgh, 107; Justin Upton, Arizona, 107; Jimmy Rollins, Philadelphia, 102; Bryce Harper, Washington, 98.

Runs Batted In: Chase Headley, San Diego, 115; Ryan Braun, Milwaukee, 112; Alfonso Soriano, Chicago Cubs, 108; Aramis Ramirez, Milwaukee, 105; Hunter Pence, Philadelphia/San Francisco, 104.

Hits: Andrew McCutchen, Pittsburgh, 194; Ryan Braun, Milwaukee, 191; Marco Scutaro, Colorado/San Francisco, 190; Martin Prado, Atlanta, 186; Aaron Hill, Arizona, 184; Jose Reyes, Miami, 184.

Doubles: Aramis Ramirez, Milwaukee, 50; Aaron Hill, Arizona, 44; Joey Votto, Cincinnati, 44; Paul Goldschmidt, Arizona, 43; Martin Prado, Atlanta, 42.

Triples: Angel Pagan, San Francisco, 15; Starlin Castro, Chicago Cubs, 12; Jose Reyes, Miami, 12; Dexter Fowler, Colorado, 11; Michael Bourn, Atlanta, 10; Melky Cabrera, San Francisco, 10; Tyler Colvin, Colorado, 10.

Home Runs: Ryan Braun, Milwaukee, 41; Giancarlo Stanton, Miami, 37; Jay Bruce, Cincinnati, 34; Adam LaRoche, Washington, 33; Carlos Beltran, St. Louis, 32; Ike Davis, NY Mets, 32; Alfonso Soriano, Chicago Cubs, 32.

Stolen Bases: Everth Cabrera, San Diego, 44; Michael Bourn, Atlanta, 42; Jose Reyes, Miami, 40; Shane Victorino, Philadelphia/L.A. Dodgers, 39; Carlos Gomez, Milwaukee, 37; Juan Pierre, Philadelphia, 37.

Pitching Wins: Gio Gonzalez, Washington, 21-8; R. A. Dickey, NY Mets, 20-6; Johnny Cueto, Cincinnati, 19-9; Lance Lynn, St. Louis, 18-7; Cole Hamels, Philadelphia, 17-6.

Earned Run Average: Clayton Kershaw, L.A. Dodgers, 2.53; R. A. Dickey, NY Mets, 2.73; Johnny Cueto, Cincinnati, 2.78; Matt Cain, San Francisco, 2.79; Kyle Lohse, St. Louis, 2.86.

Strikeouts: R. A. Dickey, NY Mets, 230; Clayton Kershaw, L.A. Dodgers, 229; Cole Hamels, Philadelphia, 216; Gio Gonzalez, Washington, 207; Cliff Lee, Philadelphia, 207.

Saves: Craig Kimbrel, Atlanta, 42; Jason Motte, St. Louis, 42; Aroldis Chapman, Cincinnati, 38; Jonathan Papelbon, Philadelphia, 38; Joel Hanrahan, Pittsburgh, 36.

American League

Batting Average: Miguel Cabrera, Detroit, .330; Mike Trout, L.A. Angels, .326; Adrian Beltre, Texas, .321; Joe Mauer, Minnesota, .319; Derek Jeter, NY Yankees, .316.

Runs Scored: Mike Trout, L.A. Angels, 129; Miguel Cabrera, Detroit, 109; Ian Kinsler, Texas, 105; Robinson Cano, NY Yankees, 105; Josh Hamilton, Texas, 103; Austin Jackson, Detroit, 103; Adam Jones, Baltimore, 103.

Runs Batted In: Miguel Cabrera, Detroit, 139; Josh Hamilton, Texas, 128; Edwin Encarnacion, Toronto, 110; Josh Willingham, Minnesota, 110; Prince Fielder, Detroit, 108.

Hits: Derek Jeter, NY Yankees, 216; Miguel Cabrera, Detroit, 205; Robinson Cano, NY Yankees, 196; Adrian Beltre, Texas, 194; Billy Butler, Kansas City, 192.

Doubles: Alex Gordon, Kansas City, 51; Albert Pujols, L.A. Angels, 50; Robinson Cano, NY Yankees, 48; Nelson Cruz, Texas, 45; Shin-Soo Choo, Cleveland, 43.

Triples: Austin Jackson, Detroit, 10; Elvis Andrus, Texas, 9; Alex Rios, Chicago White Sox, 8; Mike Trout, L.A. Angels, 8; Jemile Weeks, Oakland, 8.

Home Runs: Miguel Cabrera, Detroit, 44; Curtis Granderson, NY Yankees, 43; Josh Hamilton, Texas, 43; Edwin Encarnacion, Toronto, 42; Adam Dunn, Chicago White Sox, 41.

Stolen Bases: Mike Trout, L.A. Angels, 49; Rajai Davis, Toronto, 46; Ben Revere, Minnesota, 40; Coco Crisp, Oakland, 39; Alcides Escobar, Kansas City, 35.

Pitching Wins: Jered Weaver, L.A. Angels, 20-5; David Price, Tampa Bay, 20-5; Matt Harrison, Texas, 18-11; Justin Verlander, Detroit, 17-8; Chris Sale, Chicago White Sox, 17-8.

Earned Run Average: David Price, Tampa Bay, 2.56; Justin Verlander, Detroit, 2.64; Jered Weaver, L.A. Angels, 2.81; Chris Sale, Chicago White Sox, 3.05; Felix Hernandez, Seattle, 3.06.

Strikeouts: Justin Verlander, Detroit, 239; Max Scherzer, Detroit, 231; Felix Hernandez, Seattle, 223; James Shields, Tampa Bay, 223; Yu Darvish, Texas, 221.

Saves: Jim Johnson, Baltimore, 51; Fernando Rodney, Tampa Bay, 48; Rafael Soriano, NY Yankees, 42; Chris Perez, Cleveland, 39; Joe Nathan, Texas, 37.

All-Time Major League Single-Season Leaders

Source: www.mlb.com; * = Active in 2012 season; records for "modern" era beginning in 1901

Home Runs

Barry Bonds (2001)	73
Mark McGwire (1998)	70
Sammy Sosa (1998)	66
Mark McGwire (1999)	65
Sammy Sosa (2001)	64

Runs Scored

Babe Ruth (1921)	177
Lou Gehrig (1936)	167
Lou Gehrig (1931)	163
Babe Ruth (1928)	163
Chuck Klein (1930)	158
Babe Ruth (1920, 1927)	158

Hits

Ichiro Suzuki* (2004)	262
George Sisler (1920)	257
Lefty O'Doul (1929)	254
Bill Terry (1930)	254
Al Simmons (1925)	253
Rogers Hornsby (1922)	250
Chuck Klein (1930)	250

Runs Batted In

Hack Wilson (1930)	191
Lou Gehrig (1931)	184
Hank Greenberg (1937)	183
Jimmie Foxx (1938)	175
Lou Gehrig (1927)	175

Batting Average

Nap Lajoie (1901)	.426
Rogers Hornsby (1924)	.424
George Sisler (1922)	.420
Ty Cobb (1911)	.420
Ty Cobb (1912)	.410

Stolen Bases

Rickey Henderson (1982)	130
Lou Brock (1974)	118
Vince Coleman (1985)	110
Vince Coleman (1987)	109
Rickey Henderson (1983)	108

Walks (Batter)

Barry Bonds (2004)	232
Barry Bonds (2002)	198
Barry Bonds (2001)	177
Babe Ruth (1923)	170
Mark McGwire (1998)	162
Ted Williams (1947, 1949)	162

Strikeouts (Batter)

Mark Reynolds* (2009)	223
Adam Dunn* (2012)	222
Mark Reynolds* (2010)	211
Drew Stubbs* (2011)	205
Mark Reynolds* (2008)	204
Adam Dunn* (2010)	199
Ryan Howard* (2007, 2008)	199

Earned Run Average

Dutch Leonard (1914)	0.96
Mordecai "Three Finger" Brown (1906)	1.04
Bob Gibson (1968)	1.12
Christy Mathewson (1909)	1.14
Walter Johnson (1913)	1.14

Wins

Jack Chesbro (1904)	41
Ed Walsh (1908)	40
Christy Mathewson (1908)	37
Walter Johnson (1913)	36
Joe McGinnity (1904)	35

Strikeouts

Nolan Ryan (1973)	383
Sandy Koufax (1965)	382
Randy Johnson (2001)	372
Nolan Ryan (1974)	367
Randy Johnson (1999)	364

Saves

Francisco Rodriguez* (2008)	62
Bobby Thigpen (1990)	57
Eric Gagne (2003)	55
John Smoltz (2002)	55
Trevor Hoffman (1998)	53
Randy Myers (1993)	53
Mariano Rivera* (2004)	53

All-Time Major League Leaders

Source: www.mlb.com; * = Active in 2012 season; career records for players in "modern" era beginning in 1901 may include some statistics from preceding years.

Games		At Bats		Runs Batted In		Runs	
Pete Rose	3,562	Pete Rose	14,053	Hank Aaron	2,297	Rickey Henderson	2,295
Carl Yastrzemski	3,308	Hank Aaron	12,364	Babe Ruth	2,213	Ty Cobb	2,246
Hank Aaron	3,298	Carl Yastrzemski	11,988	Barry Bonds	1,996	Barry Bonds	2,227
Rickey Henderson	3,081	Cal Ripken Jr.	11,551	Lou Gehrig	1,995	Hank Aaron	2,174
Ty Cobb	3,035	Ty Cobb	11,429	Stan Musial	1,951	Babe Ruth	2,174
Eddie Murray	3,026	Eddie Murray	11,336	Alex Rodriguez*	1,950	Pete Rose	2,165
Stan Musial	3,026	Robin Yount	11,008	Ty Cobb	1,938	Willie Mays	2,062
Cal Ripken Jr.	3,001	Dave Winfield	11,003	Jimmie Foxx	1,922	Stan Musial	1,949
Willie Mays	2,992	Stan Musial	10,972	Eddie Murray	1,917	Alex Rodriguez*	1,898
Barry Bonds	2,986	Rickey Henderson	10,961	Willie Mays	1,903	Lou Gehrig	1,888

Stolen Bases		Triples		Batting Average		Walks (Batter)	
Rickey Henderson	1,406	Sam Crawford	309	Ty Cobb	.367	Barry Bonds	2,558
Lou Brock	938	Ty Cobb	297	Rogers Hornsby	.358	Rickey Henderson	2,190
Billy Hamilton	912	Honus Wagner	252	Joe Jackson	.356	Babe Ruth	2,062
Ty Cobb	892	Tris Speaker	222	Ed Delahanty	.346	Ted Williams	2,019
Tim Raines	808	Jake Beckley	221	Tris Speaker	.345	Joe Morgan	1,865
Vince Coleman	752	Fred Clarke	220	Ted Williams	.344	Carl Yastrzemski	1,845
Eddie Collins	745	Roger Connor	218	Billy Hamilton	.344	Jim Thome*	1,747
Max Carey	738	Dan Brouthers	196	Dan Brouthers	.342	Mickey Mantle	1,733
Honus Wagner	722	Joe Kelley	194	Babe Ruth	.342	Mel Ott	1,708
Arlie Latham	707	Paul Waner	191	Harry Heilmann	.342	Frank Thomas	1,667

Strikeouts		Saves		Shutouts		Losses	
Nolan Ryan	5,714	Mariano Rivera*	608	Walter Johnson	110	Cy Young	316
Randy Johnson	4,875	Trevor Hoffman	601	Grover Alexander	90	Nolan Ryan	292
Roger Clemens	4,672	Lee Smith	478	Christy Mathewson	79	Walter Johnson	279
Steve Carlton	4,136	John Franco	424	Cy Young	76	Phil Niekro	274
Bert Blyleven	3,701	Billy Wagner	422	Eddie Plank	69	Gaylord Perry	265
Tom Seaver	3,640	Dennis Eckersley	390	Warren Spahn	63	Don Sutton	256
Don Sutton	3,574	Jeff Reardon	367	Nolan Ryan	61	Jack Powell	254
Gaylord Perry	3,534	Troy Percival	358	Tom Seaver	61	Eppa Rixey	251
Walter Johnson	3,508	Randy Myers	347	Bert Blyleven	60	Bert Blyleven	250
Greg Maddux	3,371	Rollie Fingers	341	Don Sutton	58		

All-Time Home Run Leaders

Source: www.mlb.com; * = Active in 2012 season

Player	HR	Player	HR	Player	HR	Player	HR
Barry Bonds	762	Mike Schmidt	548	Albert Pujols*	475	Jason Giambi*	429
Hank Aaron	755	Mickey Mantle	536	Willie Stargell	475	Mike Piazza	427
Babe Ruth	714	Jimmie Foxx	534	Carlos Delgado	473	Billy Williams	426
Willie Mays	660	Willie McCovey	521	Chipper Jones*	468	Paul Konerko*	422
Alex Rodriguez*	647	Frank Thomas	521	Dave Winfield	465	Darrell Evans	414
Ken Griffey Jr.	630	Ted Williams	521	Jose Canseco	462	Duke Snider	407
Jim Thome*	612	Ernie Banks	512	Carl Yastrzemski	452	Adam Dunn*	406
Sammy Sosa	609	Eddie Mathews	512	Jeff Bagwell	449	David Ortiz*	401
Frank Robinson	586	Mel Ott	511	Vladimir Guerrero	449	Andres Galarraga	399
Mark McGwire	583	Gary Sheffield	509	Dave Kingman	442	Al Kaline	399
Harmon Killebrew	573	Eddie Murray	504	Andre Dawson	438	Dale Murphy	398
Rafael Palmeiro	569	Lou Gehrig	493	Juan Gonzalez	434	Joe Carter	396
Reggie Jackson	563	Fred McGriff	493	Andruw Jones*	434	Jim Edmonds	393
Manny Ramirez	555	Stan Musial	475	Cal Ripken Jr.	431	Graig Nettles	390

Players With 3,000 Major League Hits

Source: www.mlb.com; * = Active in 2012 season

Player	Hits	Player	Hits	Player	Hits	Player	Hits
Pete Rose	4,256	Paul Molitor	3,319	George Brett	3,154	Rod Carew	3,053
Ty Cobb	4,191	Eddie Collins	3,314	Paul Waner	3,152	Lou Brock	3,023
Hank Aaron	3,771	Derek Jeter*	3,304	Robin Yount	3,142	Rafael Palmeiro	3,020
Stan Musial	3,630	Willie Mays	3,283	Tony Gwynn	3,141	Cap Anson	3,011
Tris Speaker	3,515	Eddie Murray	3,255	Dave Winfield	3,110	Wade Boggs	3,010
Honus Wagner	3,430	Nap Lajoie	3,252	Craig Biggio	3,060	Al Kaline	3,007
Carl Yastrzemski	3,419	Cal Ripken Jr.	3,184	Rickey Henderson	3,055	Roberto Clemente	3,000

50 Home Run Club

Only Mark McGwire and Barry Bonds hit 70 or more home runs in a season. Five players—including Babe Ruth and Roger Maris—hit 60 or more, a feat Sammy Sosa accomplished for the third time in 2001. Those five are at the pinnacle of a select group of players to have hit 50 or more homers in a season. The following list shows each time a player achieved this mark.

HR	Player, team	Year	HR	Player, team	Year
73	Barry Bonds, San Francisco Giants	2001	54	David Ortiz, Boston Red Sox	2006
70	Mark McGwire, St. Louis Cardinals	1998	54	Alex Rodriguez, NY Yankees	2007
66	Sammy Sosa, Chicago Cubs	1998	54	Babe Ruth, NY Yankees	1920
65	Mark McGwire, St. Louis Cardinals	1999	54	Babe Ruth, NY Yankees	1928
64	Sammy Sosa, Chicago Cubs	2001	52	George Foster, Cincinnati Reds	1977
63	Sammy Sosa, Chicago Cubs	1999	52	Mickey Mantle, NY Yankees	1956
61	Roger Maris, NY Yankees	1961	52	Willie Mays, San Francisco Giants	1965
60	Babe Ruth, NY Yankees	1927	52	Mark McGwire, Oakland A's	1996
59	Babe Ruth, NY Yankees	1921	52	Alex Rodriguez, Texas Rangers	2001
58	Jimmie Foxx, Philadelphia Athletics	1932	52	Jim Thome, Cleveland Indians	2002
58	Hank Greenberg, Detroit Tigers	1938	51	Cecil Fielder, Detroit Tigers	1990
58	Ryan Howard, Philadelphia Phillies	2006	51	Andruw Jones, Atlanta Braves	2005
58	Mark McGwire, Oakland A's/St. Louis Cardinals	1997	51	Ralph Kiner, Pittsburgh Pirates	1947
57	Luis Gonzalez, Arizona Diamondbacks	2001	51	Willie Mays, NY Giants	1955
57	Alex Rodriguez, Texas Rangers	2002	51	Johnny Mize, NY Giants	1947
56	Ken Griffey Jr., Seattle Mariners	1997	50	Brady Anderson, Baltimore Orioles	1996
56	Ken Griffey Jr., Seattle Mariners	1998	50	Albert Belle, Cleveland Indians	1995
56	Hack Wilson, Chicago Cubs	1930	50	Prince Fielder, Milwaukee Brewers	2007
54	Jose Bautista, Toronto Blue Jays	2010	50	Jimmie Foxx, Boston Red Sox	1938
54	Ralph Kiner, Pittsburgh Pirates	1949	50	Sammy Sosa, Chicago Cubs	2000
54	Mickey Mantle, NY Yankees	1961	50	Greg Vaughn, San Diego Padres	1998

Pitchers With 300 Major League Wins

Source: www.mlb.com

Pitcher	Wins	Pitcher	Wins	Pitcher	Wins	Pitcher	Wins
Cy Young	511	Kid Nichols	361	Eddie Plank	326	Charley Radbourn	309
Walter Johnson	417	Greg Maddux	355	Nolan Ryan	324	Mickey Welch	307
Grover Alexander	373	Roger Clemens	354	Don Sutton	324	Tom Glavine	305
Christy Mathewson	373	Tim Keefe	342	Phil Niekro	318	Randy Johnson	303
Warren Spahn	363	Steve Carlton	329	Gaylord Perry	314	Lefty Grove	300
Pud Galvin	361	John Clarkson	328	Tom Seaver	311	Early Wynn	300

Official Major League Perfect Games Since 1901

Date	Pitcher	Teams	Date	Pitcher	Teams
5/5/1904	Cy Young	Boston 3 vs. Phil. 0 (AL)	9/16/1988	Tom Browning	Cincinnati 1 vs. L.A. 0 (NL)
10/2/1908	Addie Joss	Clev. 1 vs. Chicago 0 (AL)	5/17/1998	David Wells	NY 4 vs. Minn. 0 (AL)
4/30/1922	Charlie Robertson	Chicago 2 vs. Detroit 0 (AL)	7/18/1999	David Cone	NY 6 vs. Montréal 0 (AL)
10/8/1956	Don Larsen	NY 2 (AL) vs. Brooklyn 0* (NL)	5/18/2004	Randy Johnson	Arizona 2 vs. Atlanta 0 (NL)
6/21/1964	Jim Bunning	Phil. 6 vs. NY 0 (NL)	7/23/2009	Mark Buehrle	Chicago 5 vs. Tampa Bay 0 (AL)
9/9/1965	Sandy Koufax	L.A. 1 vs. Chicago 0 (NL)	5/9/2010	Dallas Braden	Oakland 4 vs. Tampa Bay 0 (AL)
5/8/1968	Jim "Catfish" Hunter	Oakland 4 vs. Minn. 0 (AL)	5/29/2010	Roy Halladay	Phil. 1 vs. Florida 0 (NL)
5/15/1981	Len Barker	Clev. 3 vs. Toronto 0 (AL)	4/21/2012	Philip Humber	Chicago 4 vs. Seattle 0 (AL)
9/30/1984	Mike Witt	California 1 vs. Texas 0 (AL)	6/13/2012	Matt Cain	San Fran. 10 vs. Houston 0 (NL)
7/28/1991	Dennis Martinez	Montréal 2 vs. L.A. 0 (NL)	8/15/2012	Felix Hernandez	Seattle 1 vs. Tampa Bay 0 (AL)
7/28/1994	Kenny Rogers	Texas 4 vs. California 0 (AL)			

* = World Series game. **Note:** Two pre-1901 National League pitchers are also credited with perfect games. Within one week in 1880, Lee Richmond (June 12, Worcester 1, Cleveland 0) and John "Monte" Ward (June 17, Providence 5, Buffalo 0), each threw a perfect game.

Most Career Major League No-Hitters

No.	Pitcher
7	Nolan Ryan
4	Sandy Koufax
3	Larry Corcoran, Bob Feller, Cy Young

No.	Pitcher
2	Mark Buehrle, Jim Bunning, Steve Busby, Carl Erskine, Bob Forsch, Pud Galvin, Roy Halladay, Ken Holtzman, Randy Johnson, Addie Joss, Dutch Leonard, Jim Maloney, Christy Mathewson, Hideo Nomo, Allie Reynolds, Frank Smith, Warren Spahn, Bill Stoneman, Virgil Trucks, Johnny Vander Meer, Justin Verlander, Ed Walsh, Don Wilson

Home Run Leaders, by Season, 1901-2012

* = All-time single-season record for league since beginning of "modern" era in 1901

	National League			American League	
Year	Player, team	HR	Year	Player, team	HR
1901	Sam Crawford, Cincinnati	16	1901	Napoleon Lajoie, Philadelphia	14
1902	Thomas Leach, Pittsburgh	6	1902	Socks Seybold, Philadelphia	16
1903	James Sheckard, Brooklyn	9	1903	Buck Freeman, Boston	13
1904	Harry Lumley, Brooklyn	9	1904	Harry Davis, Philadelphia	10
1905	Fred Odwell, Cincinnati	9	1905	Harry Davis, Philadelphia	8
1906	Timothy Jordan, Brooklyn	12	1906	Harry Davis, Philadelphia	12
1907	David Brain, Boston	10	1907	Harry Davis, Philadelphia	8
1908	Timothy Jordan, Brooklyn	12	1908	Sam Crawford, Detroit	7
1909	Red Murray, New York	7	1909	Ty Cobb, Detroit	9
1910	Fred Beck, Boston; Frank Schulte, Chicago	10	1910	Jake Stahl, Boston	10
1911	Frank Schulte, Chicago	21	1911	J. Franklin Baker, Philadelphia	11
1912	Henry Zimmerman, Chicago	14	1912	J. Franklin Baker, Phil.; Tris Speaker, Boston	10
1913	Gavvy Cravath, Philadelphia	19	1913	J. Franklin Baker, Philadelphia	12
1914	Gavvy Cravath, Philadelphia	19	1914	J. Franklin Baker, Philadelphia	9
1915	Gavvy Cravath, Philadelphia	24	1915	Robert Roth, Chicago-Cleveland	7
1916	Dave Robertson, NY; Fred "Cy" Williams, Chi.	12	1916	Wally Pipp, New York	12
1917	Gavvy Cravath, Phil.; Dave Robertson, NY	12	1917	Wally Pipp, New York	9
1918	Gavvy Cravath, Philadelphia	8	1918	Babe Ruth, Boston; Tilly Walker, Philadelphia	11
1919	Gavvy Cravath, Philadelphia	12	1919	Babe Ruth, Boston	29
1920	Cy Williams, Philadelphia	15	1920	Babe Ruth, New York	54
1921	George Kelly, New York	23	1921	Babe Ruth, New York	59
1922	Rogers Hornsby, St. Louis	42	1922	Ken Williams, St. Louis	39
1923	Cy Williams, Philadelphia	41	1923	Babe Ruth, New York	41

National League			American League		
Year	**Player, team**	**HR**	**Year**	**Player, team**	**HR**
1924	Jacques Fournier, Brooklyn	27	1924	Babe Ruth, New York	46
1925	Rogers Hornsby, St. Louis	39	1925	Bob Meusel, New York	33
1926	Hack Wilson, Chicago	21	1926	Babe Ruth, New York	47
1927	Hack Wilson, Chicago; Cy Williams, Philadelphia	30	1927	Babe Ruth, New York	60
1928	Hack Wilson, Chicago; Jim Bottomley, St. Louis	31	1928	Babe Ruth, New York	54
1929	Chuck Klein, Philadelphia	43	1929	Babe Ruth, New York	46
1930	Hack Wilson, Chicago	56	1930	Babe Ruth, New York	49
1931	Chuck Klein, Philadelphia	31	1931	Lou Gehrig, New York; Babe Ruth, New York	46
1932	Chuck Klein, Philadelphia; Mel Ott, New York	38	1932	Jimmie Foxx, Philadelphia	58
1933	Chuck Klein, Philadelphia	28	1933	Jimmie Foxx, Philadelphia	48
1934	Rip Collins, St. Louis; Mel Ott, New York	35	1934	Lou Gehrig, New York	49
1935	Walter Berger, Boston	34	1935	Jimmie Foxx, Phil.; Hank Greenberg, Detroit	36
1936	Mel Ott, New York	33	1936	Lou Gehrig, New York	49
1937	Joe Medwick, St. Louis; Mel Ott, New York	31	1937	Joe DiMaggio, New York	46
1938	Mel Ott, New York	36	1938	Hank Greenberg, Detroit	58
1939	John Mize, St. Louis	28	1939	Jimmie Foxx, Boston	35
1940	John Mize, St. Louis	43	1940	Hank Greenberg, Detroit	41
1941	Dolph Camilli, Brooklyn	34	1941	Ted Williams, Boston	37
1942	Mel Ott, New York	30	1942	Ted Williams, Boston	36
1943	Bill Nicholson, Chicago	29	1943	Rudy York, Detroit	34
1944	Bill Nicholson, Chicago	33	1944	Nick Etten, New York	22
1945	Tommy Holmes, Boston	28	1945	Vern Stephens, St. Louis	24
1946	Ralph Kiner, Pittsburgh	23	1946	Hank Greenberg, Detroit	44
1947	Ralph Kiner, Pittsburgh; John Mize, New York	51	1947	Ted Williams, Boston	32
1948	Ralph Kiner, Pittsburgh; John Mize, New York	40	1948	Joe DiMaggio, New York	39
1949	Ralph Kiner, Pittsburgh	54	1949	Ted Williams, Boston	43
1950	Ralph Kiner, Pittsburgh	47	1950	Al Rosen, Cleveland	37
1951	Ralph Kiner, Pittsburgh	42	1951	Gus Zernial, Chicago-Philadelphia	33
1952	Ralph Kiner, Pittsburgh; Hank Sauer, Chicago	37	1952	Larry Doby, Cleveland	32
1953	Ed Mathews, Milwaukee	47	1953	Al Rosen, Cleveland	43
1954	Ted Kluszewski, Cincinnati	49	1954	Larry Doby, Cleveland	32
1955	Willie Mays, New York	51	1955	Mickey Mantle, New York	37
1956	Duke Snider, Brooklyn	43	1956	Mickey Mantle, New York	52
1957	Hank Aaron, Milwaukee	44	1957	Roy Sievers, Washington	42
1958	Ernie Banks, Chicago	47	1958	Mickey Mantle, New York	42
1959	Ed Mathews, Milwaukee	46	1959	Rocky Colavito, Clev.; Harmon Killebrew, Wash.	42
1960	Ernie Banks, Chicago	41	1960	Mickey Mantle, New York	40
1961	Orlando Cepeda, San Francisco	46	1961	Roger Maris, New York	61*
1962	Willie Mays, San Francisco	49	1962	Harmon Killebrew, Minnesota	48
1963	Hank Aaron, Milwaukee; Willie McCovey, S.F.	44	1963	Harmon Killebrew, Minnesota	45
1964	Willie Mays, San Francisco	47	1964	Harmon Killebrew, Minnesota	49
1965	Willie Mays, San Francisco	52	1965	Tony Conigliaro, Boston	32
1966	Hank Aaron, Atlanta	44	1966	Frank Robinson, Baltimore	49
1967	Hank Aaron, Atlanta	39	1967	Harmon Killebrew, Minn.; Carl Yastrzemski, Boston	44
1968	Willie McCovey, San Francisco	36	1968	Frank Howard, Washington	44
1969	Willie McCovey, San Francisco	45	1969	Harmon Killebrew, Minnesota	49
1970	Johnny Bench, Cincinnati	45	1970	Frank Howard, Washington	44
1971	Willie Stargell, Pittsburgh	48	1971	Bill Melton, Chicago	33
1972	Johnny Bench, Cincinnati	40	1972	Dick Allen, Chicago	37
1973	Willie Stargell, Pittsburgh	44	1973	Reggie Jackson, Oakland	32
1974	Mike Schmidt, Philadelphia	36	1974	Dick Allen, Chicago	32
1975	Mike Schmidt, Philadelphia	38	1975	Reggie Jackson, Oak.; George Scott, Milw.	36
1976	Mike Schmidt, Philadelphia	38	1976	Graig Nettles, New York	32
1977	George Foster, Cincinnati	52	1977	Jim Rice, Boston	39
1978	George Foster, Cincinnati	40	1978	Jim Rice, Boston	46
1979	Dave Kingman, Chicago	48	1979	Gorman Thomas, Milwaukee	45
1980	Mike Schmidt, Philadelphia	48	1980	Reggie Jackson, New York; Ben Oglivie, Milw.	41
1981	Mike Schmidt, Philadelphia	31	1981	Tony Armas, Oakland; Dwight Evans, Boston; Bobby Grich, Cal.; Eddie Murray, Baltimore	22
1982	Dave Kingman, New York	37	1982	Gorman Thomas, Milw.; Reggie Jackson, Cal.	39
1983	Mike Schmidt, Philadelphia	40	1983	Jim Rice, Boston	39
1984	Dale Murphy, Atlanta; Mike Schmidt, Philadelphia	36	1984	Tony Armas, Boston	43
1985	Dale Murphy, Atlanta	37	1985	Darrell Evans, Detroit	40
1986	Mike Schmidt, Philadelphia	37	1986	Jesse Barfield, Toronto	40
1987	Andre Dawson, Chicago	49	1987	Mark McGwire, Oakland	49
1988	Darryl Strawberry, New York	39	1988	Jose Canseco, Oakland	42
1989	Kevin Mitchell, San Francisco	47	1989	Fred McGriff, Toronto	36
1990	Ryne Sandberg, Chicago	40	1990	Cecil Fielder, Detroit	51
1991	Howard Johnson, New York	38	1991	Jose Canseco, Oakland; Cecil Fielder, Detroit	44
1992	Fred McGriff, San Diego	35	1992	Juan Gonzalez, Texas	43
1993	Barry Bonds, San Francisco	46	1993	Juan Gonzalez, Texas	46
1994	Matt Williams, San Francisco	43	1994	Ken Griffey Jr., Seattle	40
1995	Dante Bichette, Colorado	40	1995	Albert Belle, Cleveland	50
1996	Andres Galarraga, Colorado	47	1996	Mark McGwire, Oakland	52
1997[1]	Larry Walker, Colorado	49	1997[1]	Ken Griffey Jr., Seattle	56
1998	Mark McGwire, St. Louis	70	1998	Ken Griffey Jr., Seattle	56
1999	Mark McGwire, St. Louis	65	1999	Ken Griffey Jr., Seattle	48
2000	Sammy Sosa, Chicago	50	2000	Troy Glaus, Anaheim	47
2001	Barry Bonds, San Francisco	73*	2001	Alex Rodriguez, Texas	52
2002	Sammy Sosa, Chicago	49	2002	Alex Rodriguez, Texas	57
2003	Jim Thome, Philadelphia	47	2003	Alex Rodriguez, Texas	47
2004	Adrian Beltre, Los Angeles	48	2004	Manny Ramirez, Boston	43
2005	Andruw Jones, Atlanta	51	2005	Alex Rodriguez, New York	48
2006	Ryan Howard, Philadelphia	58	2006	David Ortiz, Boston	54
2007	Prince Fielder, Milwaukee	50	2007	Alex Rodriguez, New York	54
2008	Ryan Howard, Philadelphia	48	2008	Miguel Cabrera, Detroit	37
2009	Albert Pujols, St. Louis	47	2009	Carlos Pena, Tampa Bay; Mark Teixeira, New York	39
2010	Albert Pujols, St. Louis	42	2010	Jose Bautista, Toronto	54
2011	Matt Kemp, Los Angeles	39	2011	Jose Bautista, Toronto	43
2012	Ryan Braun, Milwaukee	41	2012	Miguel Cabrera, Detroit	44

(1) In 1997, Mark McGwire hit 58 home runs, 34 with the Oakland Athletics (AL) and 24 with the St. Louis Cardinals (NL).

Runs Batted In Leaders, by Season, 1907-2012

* = All-time single-season record for league since beginning of "modern" era in 1901

National League			American League		
Year	Player, team	RBI	Year	Player, team	RBI
1907	Sherwood Magee, Philadelphia	85	1907	Ty Cobb, Detroit	119
1908	Honus Wagner, Pittsburgh	109	1908	Ty Cobb, Detroit	108
1909	Honus Wagner, Pittsburgh	100	1909	Ty Cobb, Detroit	107
1910	Sherwood Magee, Philadelphia	123	1910	Sam Crawford, Detroit	120
1911	Frank Schulte, Chicago	121	1911	Ty Cobb, Detroit	127
1912	Henry Zimmerman, Chicago	103	1912	J. Franklin Baker, Philadelphia	133
1913	Gavvy Cravath, Philadelphia	128	1913	J. Franklin Baker, Philadelphia	126
1914	Sherwood Magee, Philadelphia	103	1914	Sam Crawford, Detroit	104
1915	Gavvy Cravath, Philadelphia	115	1915	Sam Crawford, Detroit; Robert Veach, Detroit	112
1916	Henry Zimmerman, Chicago-New York	83	1916	Del Pratt, St. Louis	103
1917	Henry Zimmerman, New York	102	1917	Robert Veach, Detroit	103
1918	Sherwood Magee, Philadelphia	76	1918	Robert Veach, Detroit	78
1919	Hi Myers, Boston	73	1919	Babe Ruth, Boston	114
1920	George Kelly, NY; Rogers Hornsby, St. Louis	94	1920	Babe Ruth, New York	137
1921	Rogers Hornsby, St. Louis	126	1921	Babe Ruth, New York	171
1922	Rogers Hornsby, St. Louis	152	1922	Ken Williams, St. Louis	155
1923	Emil Meusel, New York	125	1923	Babe Ruth, New York	131
1924	George Kelly, New York	136	1924	Goose Goslin, Washington	129
1925	Rogers Hornsby, St. Louis	143	1925	Bob Meusel, New York	138
1926	Jim Bottomley, St. Louis	120	1926	Babe Ruth, New York	146
1927	Paul Waner, Pittsburgh	131	1927	Lou Gehrig, New York	175
1928	Jim Bottomley, St. Louis	136	1928	Babe Ruth, New York; Lou Gehrig, New York	142
1929	Hack Wilson, Chicago	159	1929	Al Simmons, Philadelphia	157
1930	Hack Wilson, Chicago	191*	1930	Lou Gehrig, New York	174
1931	Chuck Klein, Philadelphia	121	1931	Lou Gehrig, New York	184*
1932	Don Hurst, Philadelphia	143	1932	Jimmie Foxx, Philadelphia	169
1933	Chuck Klein, Philadelphia	120	1933	Jimmie Foxx, Philadelphia	163
1934	Mel Ott, New York	135	1934	Lou Gehrig, New York	165
1935	Walter Berger, Boston	130	1935	Hank Greenberg, Detroit	170
1936	Joe Medwick, St. Louis	138	1936	Hal Trosky, Cleveland	162
1937	Joe Medwick, St. Louis	154	1937	Hank Greenberg, Detroit	183
1938	Joe Medwick, St. Louis	122	1938	Jimmie Foxx, Boston	175
1939	Frank McCormick, Cincinnati	128	1939	Ted Williams, Boston	145
1940	John Mize, St. Louis	137	1940	Hank Greenberg, Detroit	150
1941	Dolph Camilli, Brooklyn	120	1941	Joe DiMaggio, New York	125
1942	John Mize, New York	110	1942	Ted Williams, Boston	137
1943	Bill Nicholson, Chicago	128	1943	Rudy York, Detroit	118
1944	Bill Nicholson, Chicago	122	1944	Vern Stephens, St. Louis	109
1945	Dixie Walker, Brooklyn	124	1945	Nick Etten, New York	111
1946	Enos Slaughter, St. Louis	130	1946	Hank Greenberg, Detroit	127
1947	John Mize, New York	138	1947	Ted Williams, Boston	114
1948	Stan Musial, St. Louis	131	1948	Joe DiMaggio, New York	155
1949	Ralph Kiner, Pittsburgh	127	1949	Ted Williams, Boston; Vern Stephens, Boston	159
1950	Del Ennis, Philadelphia	126	1950	Walt Dropo, Boston; Vern Stephens, Boston	144
1951	Monte Irvin, New York	121	1951	Gus Zernial, Chicago-Philadelphia	129
1952	Hank Sauer, Chicago	121	1952	Al Rosen, Cleveland	105
1953	Roy Campanella, Brooklyn	142	1953	Al Rosen, Cleveland	145
1954	Ted Kluszewski, Cincinnati	141	1954	Larry Doby, Cleveland	126
1955	Duke Snider, Brooklyn	136	1955	Ray Boone, Detroit; Jackie Jensen, Boston	116
1956	Stan Musial, St. Louis	109	1956	Mickey Mantle, New York	130
1957	Hank Aaron, Milwaukee	132	1957	Roy Sievers, Washington	114
1958	Ernie Banks, Chicago	129	1958	Jackie Jensen, Boston	122
1959	Ernie Banks, Chicago	143	1959	Jackie Jensen, Boston	112
1960	Hank Aaron, Milwaukee	126	1960	Roger Maris, New York	112
1961	Orlando Cepeda, San Francisco	142	1961	Roger Maris, New York	142
1962	Tommy Davis, Los Angeles	153	1962	Harmon Killebrew, Minnesota	126
1963	Hank Aaron, Milwaukee	130	1963	Dick Stuart, Boston	118
1964	Ken Boyer, St. Louis	119	1964	Brooks Robinson, Baltimore	118
1965	Deron Johnson, Cincinnati	130	1965	Rocky Colavito, Cleveland	108
1966	Hank Aaron, Atlanta	127	1966	Frank Robinson, Baltimore	122
1967	Orlando Cepeda, St. Louis	111	1967	Carl Yastrzemski, Boston	121
1968	Willie McCovey, San Francisco	105	1968	Ken Harrelson, Boston	109
1969	Willie McCovey, San Francisco	126	1969	Harmon Killebrew, Minnesota	140
1970	Johnny Bench, Cincinnati	148	1970	Frank Howard, Washington	126
1971	Joe Torre, St. Louis	137	1971	Harmon Killebrew, Minnesota	119
1972	Johnny Bench, Cincinnati	125	1972	Dick Allen, Chicago	113
1973	Willie Stargell, Pittsburgh	119	1973	Reggie Jackson, Oakland	117
1974	Johnny Bench, Cincinnati	129	1974	Jeff Burroughs, Texas	118
1975	Greg Luzinski, Philadelphia	120	1975	George Scott, Milwaukee	109
1976	George Foster, Cincinnati	121	1976	Lee May, Baltimore	109
1977	George Foster, Cincinnati	149	1977	Larry Hisle, Minnesota	119
1978	George Foster, Cincinnati	120	1978	Jim Rice, Boston	139
1979	Dave Winfield, San Diego	118	1979	Don Baylor, California	139
1980	Mike Schmidt, Philadelphia	121	1980	Cecil Cooper, Milwaukee	122
1981	Mike Schmidt, Philadelphia	91	1981	Eddie Murray, Baltimore	78
1982	Dale Murphy, Atlanta; Al Oliver, Montréal	109	1982	Hal McRae, Kansas City	133
1983	Dale Murphy, Atlanta	121	1983	Cecil Cooper, Milwaukee; Jim Rice, Boston	126
1984	Gary Carter, Montréal; Mike Schmidt, Phil.	106	1984	Tony Armas, Boston	123
1985	Dave Parker, Cincinnati	125	1985	Don Mattingly, New York	145
1986	Mike Schmidt, Philadelphia	119	1986	Joe Carter, Cleveland	121
1987	Andre Dawson, Chicago	137	1987	George Bell, Toronto	134
1988	Will Clark, San Francisco	109	1988	Jose Canseco, Oakland	124
1989	Kevin Mitchell, San Francisco	125	1989	Ruben Sierra, Texas	119
1990	Matt Williams, San Francisco	122	1990	Cecil Fielder, Detroit	132

National League			American League		
Year	Player, team	RBI	Year	Player, team	RBI
1991	Howard Johnson, New York	117	1991	Cecil Fielder, Detroit	133
1992	Darren Daulton, Philadelphia	109	1992	Cecil Fielder, Detroit	124
1993	Barry Bonds, San Francisco	123	1993	Albert Belle, Cleveland	129
1994	Jeff Bagwell, Houston	116	1994	Kirby Puckett, Minnesota	112
1995	Dante Bichette, Colorado	128	1995	Albert Belle, Cleveland; Mo Vaughn, Boston	126
1996	Andres Galarraga, Colorado	150	1996	Albert Belle, Cleveland	148
1997	Andres Galarraga, Colorado	140	1997	Ken Griffey Jr., Seattle	147
1998	Sammy Sosa, Chicago	158	1998	Juan Gonzalez, Texas	157
1999	Mark McGwire, St. Louis	147	1999	Manny Ramirez, Cleveland	165
2000	Todd Helton, Colorado	147	2000	Edgar Martinez, Seattle	145
2001	Sammy Sosa, Chicago	160	2001	Bret Boone, Seattle	141
2002	Lance Berkman, Houston	128	2002	Alex Rodriguez, Texas	142
2003	Preston Wilson, Colorado	141	2003	Carlos Delgado, Toronto	145
2004	Vinny Castilla, Colorado	131	2004	Miguel Tejada, Baltimore	150
2005	Andruw Jones, Atlanta	128	2005	David Ortiz, Boston	148
2006	Ryan Howard, Philadelphia	149	2006	David Ortiz, Boston	137
2007	Matt Holliday, Colorado	137	2007	Alex Rodriguez, New York	156
2008	Ryan Howard, Philadelphia	146	2008	Josh Hamilton, Texas	130
2009	Prince Fielder, Milwaukee; Ryan Howard, Phil.	141	2009	Mark Teixeira, New York	122
2010	Albert Pujols, St. Louis	118	2010	Miguel Cabrera, Detroit	126
2011	Matt Kemp, Los Angeles	126	2011	Curtis Granderson, New York	119
2012	Chase Headley, San Diego	115	2012	Miguel Cabrera, Detroit	139

Batting Champions, by Season, 1901-2012

* = All-time single-season record for league since beginning of "modern" era in 1901

National League			American League		
Year	Player, team	AVG	Year	Player, team	AVG
1901	Jesse C. Burkett, St. Louis	.382	1901[1]	Napoleon Lajoie, Philadelphia	.426*
1902	Clarence Beaumont, Pittsburgh	.357	1902	Ed Delahanty, Washington	.376
1903	Honus Wagner, Pittsburgh	.355	1903	Napoleon Lajoie, Cleveland	.355
1904	Honus Wagner, Pittsburgh	.349	1904	Napoleon Lajoie, Cleveland	.381
1905	James Seymour, Cincinnati	.377	1905	Elmer Flick, Cleveland	.306
1906	Honus Wagner, Pittsburgh	.339	1906	George Stone, St. Louis	.358
1907	Honus Wagner, Pittsburgh	.350	1907	Ty Cobb, Detroit	.350
1908	Honus Wagner, Pittsburgh	.354	1908	Ty Cobb, Detroit	.324
1909	Honus Wagner, Pittsburgh	.339	1909	Ty Cobb, Detroit	.377
1910	Sherwood Magee, Philadelphia	.331	1910[2]	Ty Cobb, Detroit	.385
1911	Honus Wagner, Pittsburgh	.334	1911	Ty Cobb, Detroit	.420
1912	Henry Zimmerman, Chicago	.372	1912	Ty Cobb, Detroit	.410
1913	Jacob Daubert, Brooklyn	.350	1913	Ty Cobb, Detroit	.390
1914	Jacob Daubert, Brooklyn	.329	1914	Ty Cobb, Detroit	.368
1915	Larry Doyle, New York	.320	1915	Ty Cobb, Detroit	.369
1916	Hal Chase, Cincinnati	.339	1916	Tris Speaker, Cleveland	.386
1917	Edd Roush, Cincinnati	.341	1917	Ty Cobb, Detroit	.383
1918	Zach Wheat, Brooklyn	.335	1918	Ty Cobb, Detroit	.382
1919	Edd Roush, Cincinnati	.321	1919	Ty Cobb, Detroit	.384
1920	Rogers Hornsby, St. Louis	.370	1920	George Sisler, St. Louis	.407
1921	Rogers Hornsby, St. Louis	.397	1921	Harry Heilmann, Detroit	.394
1922	Rogers Hornsby, St. Louis	.401	1922	George Sisler, St. Louis	.420
1923	Rogers Hornsby, St. Louis	.384	1923	Harry Heilmann, Detroit	.403
1924	Rogers Hornsby, St. Louis	.424*	1924	Babe Ruth, New York	.378
1925	Rogers Hornsby, St. Louis	.403	1925	Harry Heilmann, Detroit	.393
1926	Eugene Hargrave, Cincinnati	.353	1926	Henry Manush, Detroit	.378
1927	Paul Waner, Pittsburgh	.380	1927	Harry Heilmann, Detroit	.398
1928	Rogers Hornsby, Boston	.387	1928	Goose Goslin, Washington	.379
1929	Lefty O'Doul, Philadelphia	.398	1929	Lew Fonseca, Cleveland	.369
1930	Bill Terry, New York	.401	1930	Al Simmons, Philadelphia	.381
1931	Chick Hafey, St. Louis	.349	1931	Al Simmons, Philadelphia	.390
1932	Lefty O'Doul, Brooklyn	.368	1932	Dale Alexander, Detroit-Boston	.367
1933	Chuck Klein, Philadelphia	.368	1933	Jimmie Foxx, Philadelphia	.356
1934	Paul Waner, Pittsburgh	.362	1934	Lou Gehrig, New York	.363
1935	Arky Vaughan, Pittsburgh	.385	1935	Buddy Myer, Washington	.349
1936	Paul Waner, Pittsburgh	.373	1936	Luke Appling, Chicago	.388
1937	Joe Medwick, St. Louis	.374	1937	Charlie Gehringer, Detroit	.371
1938	Ernie Lombardi, Cincinnati	.342	1938	Jimmie Foxx, Boston	.349
1939	John Mize, St. Louis	.349	1939	Joe DiMaggio, New York	.381
1940	Debs Garms, Pittsburgh	.355	1940	Joe DiMaggio, New York	.352
1941	Pete Reiser, Brooklyn	.343	1941	Ted Williams, Boston	.406
1942	Ernie Lombardi, Boston	.330	1942	Ted Williams, Boston	.356
1943	Stan Musial, St. Louis	.357	1943	Luke Appling, Chicago	.328
1944	Dixie Walker, Brooklyn	.357	1944	Lou Boudreau, Cleveland	.327
1945	Phil Cavarretta, Chicago	.355	1945	George Stirnweiss, New York	.309
1946	Stan Musial, St. Louis	.365	1946	Mickey Vernon, Washington	.353
1947	Harry Walker, St. Louis-Phil.	.363	1947	Ted Williams, Boston	.343
1948	Stan Musial, St. Louis	.376	1948	Ted Williams, Boston	.369
1949	Jackie Robinson, Brooklyn	.342	1949	George Kell, Detroit	.343
1950	Stan Musial, St. Louis	.346	1950	Billy Goodman, Boston	.354
1951	Stan Musial, St. Louis	.355	1951	Ferris Fain, Philadelphia	.344
1952	Stan Musial, St. Louis	.336	1952	Ferris Fain, Philadelphia	.327
1953	Carl Furillo, Brooklyn	.344	1953	Mickey Vernon, Washington	.337
1954	Willie Mays, New York	.345	1954	Roberto Avila, Cleveland	.341
1955	Richie Ashburn, Philadelphia	.338	1955	Al Kaline, Detroit	.340
1956	Hank Aaron, Milwaukee	.328	1956	Mickey Mantle, New York	.353
1957	Stan Musial, St. Louis	.351	1957	Ted Williams, Boston	.388
1958	Richie Ashburn, Philadelphia	.350	1958	Ted Williams, Boston	.328
1959	Hank Aaron, Milwaukee	.355	1959	Harvey Kuenn, Detroit	.353
1960	Dick Groat, Pittsburgh	.325	1960	Pete Runnels, Boston	.320
1961	Roberto Clemente, Pittsburgh	.351	1961	Norm Cash, Detroit	.361
1962	Tommy Davis, Los Angeles	.346	1962	Pete Runnels, Boston	.326

Year	National League Player, team	AVG	Year	American League Player, team	AVG
1963	Tommy Davis, Los Angeles	.326	1963	Carl Yastrzemski, Boston	.321
1964	Roberto Clemente, Pittsburgh	.339	1964	Tony Oliva, Minnesota	.323
1965	Roberto Clemente, Pittsburgh	.329	1965	Tony Oliva, Minnesota	.321
1966	Matty Alou, Pittsburgh	.342	1966	Frank Robinson, Baltimore	.316
1967	Roberto Clemente, Pittsburgh	.357	1967	Carl Yastrzemski, Boston	.326
1968	Pete Rose, Cincinnati	.335	1968	Carl Yastrzemski, Boston	.301
1969	Pete Rose, Cincinnati	.348	1969	Rod Carew, Minnesota	.332
1970	Rico Carty, Atlanta	.366	1970	Alex Johnson, California	.329
1971	Joe Torre, St. Louis	.363	1971	Tony Oliva, Minnesota	.337
1972	Billy Williams, Chicago	.333	1972	Rod Carew, Minnesota	.318
1973	Pete Rose, Cincinnati	.338	1973	Rod Carew, Minnesota	.350
1974	Ralph Garr, Atlanta	.353	1974	Rod Carew, Minnesota	.364
1975	Bill Madlock, Chicago	.354	1975	Rod Carew, Minnesota	.359
1976	Bill Madlock, Chicago	.339	1976	George Brett, Kansas City	.333
1977	Dave Parker, Pittsburgh	.338	1977	Rod Carew, Minnesota	.388
1978	Dave Parker, Pittsburgh	.334	1978	Rod Carew, Minnesota	.333
1979	Keith Hernandez, St. Louis	.344	1979	Fred Lynn, Boston	.333
1980	Bill Buckner, Chicago	.324	1980	George Brett, Kansas City	.390
1981	Bill Madlock, Pittsburgh	.341	1981	Carney Lansford, Boston	.336
1982	Al Oliver, Montréal	.331	1982	Willie Wilson, Kansas City	.332
1983	Bill Madlock, Pittsburgh	.323	1983	Wade Boggs, Boston	.361
1984	Tony Gwynn, San Diego	.351	1984	Don Mattingly, New York	.343
1985	Willie McGee, St. Louis	.353	1985	Wade Boggs, Boston	.368
1986	Tim Raines, Montréal	.334	1986	Wade Boggs, Boston	.357
1987	Tony Gwynn, San Diego	.370	1987	Wade Boggs, Boston	.363
1988	Tony Gwynn, San Diego	.313	1988	Wade Boggs, Boston	.366
1989	Tony Gwynn, San Diego	.336	1989	Kirby Puckett, Minnesota	.339
1990	Willie McGee, St. Louis	.335	1990	George Brett, Kansas City	.329
1991	Terry Pendleton, Atlanta	.319	1991	Julio Franco, Texas	.341
1992	Gary Sheffield, San Diego	.330	1992	Edgar Martinez, Seattle	.343
1993	Andres Galarraga, Colorado	.370	1993	John Olerud, Toronto	.363
1994	Tony Gwynn, San Diego	.394	1994	Paul O'Neill, New York	.359
1995	Tony Gwynn, San Diego	.368	1995	Edgar Martinez, Seattle	.356
1996	Tony Gwynn, San Diego	.353	1996	Alex Rodriguez, Seattle	.358
1997	Tony Gwynn, San Diego	.372	1997	Frank Thomas, Chicago	.347
1998	Larry Walker, Colorado	.363	1998	Bernie Williams, New York	.339
1999	Larry Walker, Colorado	.379	1999	Nomar Garciaparra, Boston	.357
2000	Todd Helton, Colorado	.372	2000	Nomar Garciaparra, Boston	.372
2001	Larry Walker, Colorado	.350	2001	Ichiro Suzuki, Seattle	.350
2002	Barry Bonds, San Francisco	.370	2002	Manny Ramirez, Boston	.349
2003	Albert Pujols, St. Louis	.359	2003	Bill Mueller, Boston	.326
2004	Barry Bonds, San Francisco	.362	2004	Ichiro Suzuki, Seattle	.372
2005	Derrek Lee, Chicago	.335	2005	Michael Young, Texas	.331
2006	Freddy Sanchez, Pittsburgh	.344	2006	Joe Mauer, Minnesota	.347
2007	Matt Holliday, Colorado	.340	2007	Magglio Ordonez, Detroit	.363
2008	Chipper Jones, Atlanta	.364	2008	Joe Mauer, Minnesota	.328
2009	Hanley Ramirez, Florida	.342	2009	Joe Mauer, Minnesota	.365
2010	Carlos Gonzalez, Colorado	.336	2010	Josh Hamilton, Texas	.359
2011	Jose Reyes, New York	.377	2011	Miguel Cabrera, Detroit	.344
2012	Buster Posey, San Francisco	.336	2012	Miguel Cabrera, Detroit	.330

(1) Napoleon Lajoie's 1901 batting average varies in historical records from .421 to .426. (2) Some baseball researchers have concluded that Ty Cobb actually hit .382 in 1910 while Napoleon Lajoie, Cleveland, hit .383.

Earned Run Average Leaders, by Season, 1977-2012

Year	National League Pitcher, team	G	IP	ERA	Year	American League Pitcher, team	G	IP	ERA
1977	John Candelaria, Pittsburgh	33	230.2	2.34	1977	Frank Tanana, California	31	241.1	2.54
1978	Craig Swan, New York	29	207.1	2.43	1978	Ron Guidry, New York	35	273.2	1.74
1979	J. R. Richard, Houston	38	292.1	2.71	1979	Ron Guidry, New York	33	236.1	2.78
1980	Don Sutton, Los Angeles	32	212.1	2.21	1980	Rudy May, New York	41	175.1	2.47
1981	Nolan Ryan, Houston	21	149	1.69	1981	Sammy Stewart, Baltimore	29	112.1	2.32
1982	Steve Rogers, Montréal	35	277	2.40	1982	Rick Sutcliffe, Cleveland	34	216	2.96
1983	Atlee Hammaker, San Francisco	23	172.1	2.25	1983	Rick Honeycutt, Texas	25	174.2	2.42
1984	Alejandro Pena, Los Angeles	28	199.1	2.48	1984	Mike Boddicker, Baltimore	34	261.1	2.79
1985	Dwight Gooden, New York	35	276.2	1.53	1985	Dave Stieb, Toronto	36	265	2.48
1986	Mike Scott, Houston	37	275.1	2.22	1986	Roger Clemens, Boston	33	254	2.48
1987	Nolan Ryan, Houston	34	211.2	2.76	1987	Jimmy Key, Toronto	36	261	2.76
1988	Joe Magrane, St. Louis	24	165.1	2.18	1988	Allan Anderson, Minnesota	30	202.1	2.45
1989	Scott Garrelts, San Francisco	30	193.1	2.28	1989	Bret Saberhagen, Kansas City	36	262.1	2.16
1990	Danny Darwin, Houston	48	162.2	2.21	1990	Roger Clemens, Boston	31	228.1	1.93
1991	Dennis Martinez, Montréal	31	222	2.39	1991	Roger Clemens, Boston	35	271.1	2.62
1992	Bill Swift, San Francisco	30	164.2	2.08	1992	Roger Clemens, Boston	32	246.2	2.41
1993	Greg Maddux, Atlanta	36	267	2.36	1993	Kevin Appier, Kansas City	34	238.2	2.56
1994	Greg Maddux, Atlanta	25	202	1.56	1994	Steve Ontiveros, Oakland	27	115.1	2.65
1995	Greg Maddux, Atlanta	28	209.2	1.63	1995	Randy Johnson, Seattle	30	214.1	2.48
1996	Kevin Brown, Florida	32	233	1.89	1996	Juan Guzman, Toronto	27	187.2	2.93
1997	Pedro Martinez, Montréal	31	241.1	1.90	1997	Roger Clemens, Toronto	34	264	2.05
1998	Greg Maddux, Atlanta	34	251	2.22	1998	Roger Clemens, Toronto	33	234.2	2.65
1999	Randy Johnson, Arizona	35	271.2	2.48	1999	Pedro Martinez, Boston	31	213.1	2.07
2000	Kevin Brown, Los Angeles	33	230	2.58	2000	Pedro Martinez, Boston	29	217	1.74
2001	Randy Johnson, Arizona	35	249.2	2.49	2001	Freddy Garcia, Seattle	34	238.2	3.05
2002	Randy Johnson, Arizona	35	260	2.32	2002	Pedro Martinez, Boston	30	199.1	2.26
2003	Jason Schmidt, San Francisco	29	207.2	2.34	2003	Pedro Martinez, Boston	29	186.2	2.22
2004	Jake Peavy, San Diego	27	166.1	2.27	2004	Johan Santana, Minnesota	34	228	2.61
2005	Roger Clemens, Houston	32	211.1	1.87	2005	Kevin Millwood, Cleveland	30	192	2.86
2006	Roy Oswalt, Houston	33	220.2	2.98	2006	Johan Santana, Minnesota	34	233.2	2.77
2007	Jake Peavy, San Diego	34	223.1	2.54	2007	John Lackey, Los Angeles	33	224	3.01
2008	Johan Santana, New York	34	234.1	2.53	2008	Cliff Lee, Cleveland	31	223.1	2.54
2009	Chris Carpenter, St. Louis	28	192.2	2.24	2009	Zack Greinke, Kansas City	33	229.1	2.16
2010	Josh Johnson, Florida	28	183.2	2.30	2010	Felix Hernandez, Seattle	34	249.2	2.27
2011	Clayton Kershaw, Los Angeles	33	233.1	2.28	2011	Justin Verlander, Detroit	34	251	2.40
2012	Clayton Kershaw, Los Angeles	33	227.2	2.53	2012	David Price, Tampa Bay	31	211	2.56

Note: ERA is computed by multiplying earned runs allowed by 9, then dividing by innings pitched.

Strikeout Leaders, by Season, 1901-2012

* = All-time single-season record for league since beginning of "modern" era in 1901

	National League			American League	
Year	**Pitcher, team**	**SO**	**Year**	**Pitcher, team**	**SO**
1901	Noodles Hahn, Cincinnati	239	1901	Cy Young, Boston	158
1902	Vic Willis, Boston	225	1902	Rube Waddell, Philadelphia	210
1903	Christy Mathewson, New York	267	1903	Rube Waddell, Philadelphia	302
1904	Christy Mathewson, New York	212	1904	Rube Waddell, Philadelphia	349
1905	Christy Mathewson, New York	206	1905	Rube Waddell, Philadelphia	287
1906	Fred Beebe, Chicago-St. Louis	171	1906	Rube Waddell, Philadelphia	196
1907	Christy Mathewson, New York	178	1907	Rube Waddell, Philadelphia	232
1908	Christy Mathewson, New York	259	1908	Ed Walsh, Chicago	269
1909	Orval Overall, Chicago	205	1909	Frank Smith, Chicago	177
1910	Earl Moore, Philadelphia	185	1910	Walter Johnson, Washington	313
1911	Rube Marquard, New York	237	1911	Ed Walsh, Chicago	255
1912	Grover Alexander, Philadelphia	195	1912	Walter Johnson, Washington	303
1913	Tom Seaton, Philadelphia	168	1913	Walter Johnson, Washington	243
1914	Grover Alexander, Philadelphia	214	1914	Walter Johnson, Washington	225
1915	Grover Alexander, Philadelphia	241	1915	Walter Johnson, Washington	203
1916	Grover Alexander, Philadelphia	167	1916	Walter Johnson, Washington	228
1917	Grover Alexander, Philadelphia	200	1917	Walter Johnson, Washington	188
1918	Hippo Vaughn, Chicago	148	1918	Walter Johnson, Washington	162
1919	Hippo Vaughn, Chicago	141	1919	Walter Johnson, Washington	147
1920	Grover Alexander, Chicago	173	1920	Stan Coveleski, Cleveland	133
1921	Burleigh Grimes, Brooklyn	136	1921	Walter Johnson, Washington	143
1922	Dazzy Vance, Brooklyn	134	1922	Urban Shocker, St. Louis	149
1923	Dazzy Vance, Brooklyn	197	1923	Walter Johnson, Washington	130
1924	Dazzy Vance, Brooklyn	262	1924	Walter Johnson, Washington	158
1925	Dazzy Vance, Brooklyn	221	1925	Lefty Grove, Philadelphia	116
1926	Dazzy Vance, Brooklyn	140	1926	Lefty Grove, Philadelphia	194
1927	Dazzy Vance, Brooklyn	184	1927	Lefty Grove, Philadelphia	174
1928	Dazzy Vance, Brooklyn	200	1928	Lefty Grove, Philadelphia	183
1929	Pat Malone, Chicago	166	1929	Lefty Grove, Philadelphia	170
1930	Bill Hallahan, St. Louis	177	1930	Lefty Grove, Philadelphia	209
1931	Bill Hallahan, St. Louis	159	1931	Lefty Grove, Philadelphia	175
1932	Dizzy Dean, St. Louis	191	1932	Red Ruffing, New York	190
1933	Dizzy Dean, St. Louis	199	1933	Lefty Gomez, New York	163
1934	Dizzy Dean, St. Louis	195	1934	Lefty Gomez, New York	158
1935	Dizzy Dean, St. Louis	190	1935	Tommy Bridges, Detroit	163
1936	Van Lingle Mungo, Brooklyn	238	1936	Tommy Bridges, Detroit	175
1937	Carl Hubbell, New York	159	1937	Lefty Gomez, New York	194
1938	Clay Bryant, Chicago	135	1938	Bob Feller, Cleveland	240
1939	Claude Passeau, Philadelphia-Chicago	137	1939	Bob Feller, Cleveland	246
	Bucky Walters, Cincinnati	137			
1940	Kirby Higbe, Philadelphia	137	1940	Bob Feller, Cleveland	261
1941	John Vander Meer, Cincinnati	202	1941	Bob Feller, Cleveland	260
1942	John Vander Meer, Cincinnati	186	1942	Tex Hughson, Boston	113
				Bobo Newsom, Washington	113
1943	John Vander Meer, Cincinnati	174	1943	Allie Reynolds, Cleveland	151
1944	Bill Voiselle, New York	161	1944	Hal Newhouser, Detroit	187
1945	Preacher Roe, Pittsburgh	148	1945	Hal Newhouser, Detroit	212
1946	Johnny Schmitz, Cincinnati	135	1946	Bob Feller, Cleveland	348
1947	Ewell Blackwell, Cincinnati	193	1947	Bob Feller, Cleveland	196
1948	Harry Brecheen, St. Louis	149	1948	Bob Feller, Cleveland	164
1949	Warren Spahn, Boston	151	1949	Virgil Trucks, Detroit	153
1950	Warren Spahn, Boston	191	1950	Bob Lemon, Cleveland	170
1951	Warren Spahn, Boston	164	1951	Vic Raschi, New York	164
	Don Newcombe, Brooklyn	164			
1952	Warren Spahn, Boston	183	1952	Allie Reynolds, New York	160
1953	Robin Roberts, Philadelphia	198	1953	Billy Pierce, Chicago	186
1954	Robin Roberts, Philadelphia	185	1954	Bob Turley, Baltimore	185
1955	Sam Jones, Chicago	198	1955	Herb Score, Cleveland	245
1956	Sam Jones, Chicago	176	1956	Herb Score, Cleveland	263
1957	Jack Sanford, Philadelphia	188	1957	Early Wynn, Cleveland	184
1958	Sam Jones, St. Louis	225	1958	Early Wynn, Chicago	179
1959	Don Drysdale, Los Angeles	242	1959	Jim Bunning, Detroit	201
1960	Don Drysdale, Los Angeles	246	1960	Jim Bunning, Detroit	201
1961	Sandy Koufax, Los Angeles	269	1961	Camilo Pascual, Minnesota	221
1962	Don Drysdale, Los Angeles	232	1962	Camilo Pascual, Minnesota	206
1963	Sandy Koufax, Los Angeles	306	1963	Camilo Pascual, Minnesota	202
1964	Bob Veale, Pittsburgh	250	1964	Al Downing, New York	217
1965	Sandy Koufax, Los Angeles	382*	1965	Sam McDowell, Cleveland	325
1966	Sandy Koufax, Los Angeles	317	1966	Sam McDowell, Cleveland	225
1967	Jim Bunning, Philadelphia	253	1967	Jim Lonborg, Boston	246
1968	Bob Gibson, St. Louis	268	1968	Sam McDowell, Cleveland	283
1969	Ferguson Jenkins, Chicago	273	1969	Sam McDowell, Cleveland	279
1970	Tom Seaver, New York	283	1970	Sam McDowell, Cleveland	304
1971	Tom Seaver, New York	289	1971	Mickey Lolich, Detroit	308
1972	Steve Carlton, Philadelphia	310	1972	Nolan Ryan, California	329
1973	Tom Seaver, New York	251	1973	Nolan Ryan, California	383*
1974	Steve Carlton, Philadelphia	240	1974	Nolan Ryan, California	367
1975	Tom Seaver, New York	243	1975	Frank Tanana, California	269
1976	Tom Seaver, New York	235	1976	Nolan Ryan, California	327
1977	Phil Niekro, Atlanta	262	1977	Nolan Ryan, California	341
1978	J. R. Richard, Houston	303	1978	Nolan Ryan, California	260
1979	J. R. Richard, Houston	313	1979	Nolan Ryan, California	223
1980	Steve Carlton, Philadelphia	286	1980	Len Barker, Cleveland	187
1981	Fernando Valenzuela, Los Angeles	180	1981	Len Barker, Cleveland	127
1982	Steve Carlton, Philadelphia	286	1982	Floyd Bannister, Seattle	209
1983	Steve Carlton, Philadelphia	275	1983	Jack Morris, Detroit	232
1984	Dwight Gooden, New York	276	1984	Mark Langston, Seattle	204
1985	Dwight Gooden, New York	268	1985	Bert Blyleven, Cleveland-Minnesota	206
1986	Mike Scott, Houston	306	1986	Mark Langston, Seattle	245
1987	Nolan Ryan, Houston	270	1987	Mark Langston, Seattle	262
1988	Nolan Ryan, Houston	228	1988	Roger Clemens, Boston	291
1989	Jose DeLeon, St. Louis	201	1989	Nolan Ryan, Texas	301
1990	David Cone, New York	233	1990	Nolan Ryan, Texas	232

National League			American League		
Year	Pitcher, team	SO	Year	Pitcher, team	SO
1991	David Cone, New York	241	1991	Roger Clemens, Boston	241
1992	John Smoltz, Atlanta	215	1992	Randy Johnson, Seattle	241
1993	Jose Rijo, Cincinnati	227	1993	Randy Johnson, Seattle	308
1994	Andy Benes, San Diego	189	1994	Randy Johnson, Seattle	204
1995	Hideo Nomo, Los Angeles	236	1995	Randy Johnson, Seattle	294
1996	John Smoltz, Atlanta	276	1996	Roger Clemens, Boston	257
1997	Curt Schilling, Philadelphia	319	1997	Roger Clemens, Toronto	292
1998	Curt Schilling, Philadelphia	300	1998	Roger Clemens, Toronto	271
1999	Randy Johnson, Arizona	364	1999	Pedro Martinez, Boston	313
2000	Randy Johnson, Arizona	347	2000	Pedro Martinez, Boston	284
2001	Randy Johnson, Arizona	372	2001	Hideo Nomo, Boston	220
2002	Randy Johnson, Arizona	334	2002	Pedro Martinez, Boston	239
2003	Kerry Wood, Chicago	266	2003	Esteban Loaiza, Chicago	207
2004	Randy Johnson, Arizona	290	2004	Johan Santana, Minnesota	265
2005	Jake Peavy, San Diego	216	2005	Johan Santana, Minnesota	238
2006	Aaron Harang, Cincinnati	216	2006	Johan Santana, Minnesota	245
2007	Jake Peavy, San Diego	240	2007	Scott Kazmir, Tampa Bay	239
2008	Tim Lincecum, San Francisco	265	2008	A. J. Burnett, Toronto	231
2009	Tim Lincecum, San Francisco	261	2009	Justin Verlander, Detroit	269
2010	Tim Lincecum, San Francisco	231	2010	Jered Weaver, Los Angeles	233
2011	Clayton Kershaw, Los Angeles	248	2011	Justin Verlander, Detroit	250
2012	R. A. Dickey, New York	230	2012	Justin Verlander, Detroit	239

Victory Leaders, by Season, 1901-2012

* = All-time single-season record for league since beginning of "modern" era in 1901

National League			American League		
Year	Pitcher, team	Wins	Year	Pitcher, team	Wins
1901	Bill Donavan, Brooklyn	25	1901	Cy Young, Boston	33
1902	Jack Chesbro, Pittsburgh	28	1902	Cy Young, Boston	32
1903	Joe McGinnity, New York	31	1903	Cy Young, Boston	28
1904	Joe McGinnity, New York	35	1904	Jack Chesbro, New York	41*
1905	Christy Mathewson, New York	31	1905	Rube Waddell, Philadelphia	27
1906	Joe McGinnity, New York	27	1906	Al Orth, New York	27
1907	Christy Mathewson, New York	24	1907	Addie Joss, Cleveland; Doc White, Chicago	27
1908	Christy Mathewson, New York	37*	1908	Ed Walsh, Chicago	40
1909	Mordecai Brown, Chicago	27	1909	George Mullin, Detroit	29
1910	Christy Mathewson, New York	27	1910	Jack Coombs, Philadelphia	31
1911	Grover Alexander, Chicago	28	1911	Jack Coombs, Philadelphia	28
1912	Larry Cheney, Chicago; Rube Marquard, New York	26	1912	Joe Wood, Boston	34
1913	Tom Seaton, Philadelphia	27	1913	Walter Johnson, Washington	36
1914	Grover Alexander, Philadelphia	27	1914	Walter Johnson, Washington	28
1915	Grover Alexander, Philadelphia	31	1915	Walter Johnson, Washington	27
1916	Grover Alexander, Philadelphia	33	1916	Walter Johnson, Washington	25
1917	Grover Alexander, Philadelphia	30	1917	Eddie Cicotte, Chicago	28
1918	Hippo Vaughn, Chicago	22	1918	Walter Johnson, Washington	23
1919	Jesse Barnes, New York	25	1919	Eddie Cicotte, Chicago	29
1920	Grover Alexander, Philadelphia	27	1920	Jim Bagby, Cleveland	31
1921	Wilbur Cooper, Pitt.; Burleigh Grimes, Brooklyn	22	1921	Carl Mays, New York; Urban Shocker, St. Louis	27
1922	Eppa Rixey, Cincinnati	25	1922	Eddie Rommel, Philadelphia	27
1923	Dolf Luque, Cincinnati	27	1923	George Uhle, Cleveland	26
1924	Dazzy Vance, Brooklyn	28	1924	Walter Johnson, Washington	23
1925	Dazzy Vance, Brooklyn	22	1925	Ted Lyons, Chicago; Eddie Rommel, Philadelphia	21
1926	Pete Donohue, Cincinnati; Remy Kremer, Pitt.; Lee Meadows, Pitt.; Flint Rhem, St. Louis	20	1926	George Uhle, Cleveland	27
1927	Charlie Root, Chicago	26	1927	Waite Hoyt, New York; Ted Lyons, Chicago	22
1928	Burleigh Grimes, Pittsburgh; Larry Benton, NY	25	1928	Lefty Grove, Philadelphia; George Pipgras, NY	24
1929	Pat Malone, Chicago	22	1929	George Earnshaw, Philadelphia	24
1930	Pat Malone, Chicago; Remy Kremer, Pitt.	20	1930	Lefty Grove, Philadelphia	28
1931	Jumbo Elliott, Phil.; Bill Hallahan, St. Louis; Heine Meine, Pittsburgh	19	1931	Lefty Grove, Philadelphia	31
1932	Lon Warneke, Chicago	22	1932	Alvin Crowder, Washington	26
1933	Carl Hubbell, New York	23	1933	Alvin Crowder, Wash.; Lefty Grove, Phila.	24
1934	Dizzy Dean, St. Louis	30	1934	Lefty Gomez, New York	26
1935	Dizzy Dean, St. Louis	28	1935	Wes Ferrell, Boston	25
1936	Carl Hubbell, New York	26	1936	Tommy Bridges, Detroit	23
1937	Carl Hubbell, New York	22	1937	Lefty Gomez, New York	21
1938	Bill Lee, Chicago	22	1938	Red Ruffing, New York	21
1939	Bucky Walters, Cincinnati	27	1939	Bob Feller, Cleveland	24
1940	Bucky Walters, Cincinnati	22	1940	Bob Feller, Cleveland	27
1941	Kirby Higbe, Brooklyn; Whit Wyatt, Brooklyn	22	1941	Bob Feller, Cleveland	25
1942	Mort Cooper, St. Louis	22	1942	Tex Hughson, Boston	22
1943	Mort Cooper, St. Louis; Elmer Riddle, Cincinnati; Rip Sewell, Pittsburgh	21	1943	Spurgeon "Spud" Chandler, New York; Dizzy Trout, Detroit	20
1944	Bucky Walters, Cincinnati	23	1944	Hal Newhouser, Detroit	29
1945	Red Barrett, Boston-St. Louis	23	1945	Hal Newhouser, Detroit	25
1946	Howie Pollet, St. Louis	21	1946	Bob Feller, Cleveland; Hal Newhouser, Detroit	26
1947	Ewell Blackwell, Cincinnati	22	1947	Bob Feller, Cleveland	20
1948	Johnny Sain, Boston	24	1948	Hal Newhouser, Detroit	21
1949	Warren Spahn, Boston	21	1949	Mel Parnell, Boston	25
1950	Warren Spahn, Boston	21	1950	Bob Lemon, Cleveland	23
1951	Larry Jansen, New York; Sal Maglie, New York	23	1951	Bob Feller, Cleveland	22
1952	Robin Roberts, Philadelphia	28	1952	Bobby Shantz, Philadelphia	24
1953	Robin Roberts, Phil.; Warren Spahn, Milwaukee	23	1953	Bob Porterfield, Washington	22
1954	Robin Roberts, Philadelphia	23	1954	Bob Lemon, Early Wynn, Cleveland	23
1955	Robin Roberts, Philadelphia	23	1955	Whitey Ford, New York; Bob Lemon, Cleveland; Frank Sullivan, Boston	
1956	Don Newcombe, Brooklyn	27	1956	Frank Lary, Detroit	21
1957	Warren Spahn, Milwaukee	21	1957	Jim Bunning, Detroit; Billy Pierce, Chicago	20
1958	Bob Friend, Pitt.; Warren Spahn, Milwaukee	22	1958	Bob Turley, New York	21
1959	Lew Burdette, Warren Spahn, Milwaukee; Sam Jones, NY Giants	21	1959	Early Wynn, Chicago	22
1960	Ernie Broglio, St. Louis; Warren Spahn, Milwaukee	21	1960	Chuck Estrada, Baltimore; Jim Perry, Cleveland	18
1961	Joey Jay, Cincinnati; Warren Spahn, Milwaukee	21	1961	Whitey Ford, New York	25
1962	Don Drysdale, Los Angeles	25	1962	Ralph Terry, New York	23
1963	Sandy Koufax, L.A.; Juan Marichal, San Francisco	25	1963	Whitey Ford, New York	24

	National League			American League	
Year	Pitcher, team	Wins	Year	Pitcher, team	Wins
1964	Larry Jackson, Chicago	24	1964	Dean Chance, Los Angeles; Gary Peters, Chicago	20
1965	Sandy Koufax, Los Angeles	26	1965	Jim "Mudcat" Grant, Minnesota	21
1966	Sandy Koufax, Los Angeles	27	1966	Jim Kaat, Minnesota	25
1967	Mike McCormick, San Francisco	22	1967	Jim Lonborg, Boston; Earl Wilson, Detroit	22
1968	Juan Marichal, San Francisco	26	1968	Denny McLain, Detroit	31
1969	Tom Seaver, New York	25	1969	Denny McLain, Detroit	24
1970	Bob Gibson, St. Louis; Gaylord Perry, San Francisco	23	1970	Mike Cuellar, Dave McNally, Baltimore; Jim Perry, Minnesota	24
1971	Ferguson Jenkins, Chicago	24	1971	Mickey Lolich, Detroit	25
1972	Steve Carlton, Philadelphia	27	1972	Gaylord Perry, Cleveland; Wilbur Wood, Chicago	24
1973	Ron Bryant, San Francisco	24	1973	Wilbur Wood, Chicago	24
1974	Andy Messersmith, L.A.; Phil Niekro, Atlanta	20	1974	Jim "Catfish" Hunter, Oak.; Ferguson Jenkins, Tex.	25
1975	Tom Seaver, New York	22	1975	Jim "Catfish" Hunter, NY; Jim Palmer, Baltimore	23
1976	Randy Jones, San Diego	22	1976	Jim Palmer, Baltimore	22
1977	Steve Carlton, Philadelphia	23	1977	Dave Goltz, Minnesota; Dennis Leonard, Kansas City; Jim Palmer, Baltimore	20
1978	Gaylord Perry, San Diego	21	1978	Ron Guidry, New York	25
1979	Joe Niekro, Houston; Phil Niekro, Atlanta	21	1979	Mike Flanagan, Baltimore	23
1980	Steve Carlton, Philadelphia	24	1980	Steve Stone, Baltimore	25
1981	Tom Seaver, Cincinnati	14	1981	Dennis Martinez, Balt.; Steve McCatty, Oakland; Jack Morris, Detroit; Pete Vuckovich, Milwaukee	14
1982	Steve Carlton, Philadelphia	23	1982	LaMarr Hoyt, Chicago	19
1983	John Denny, Philadelphia	19	1983	LaMarr Hoyt, Chicago	24
1984	Joaquin Andujar, St. Louis	20	1984	Mike Boddicker, Baltimore	20
1985	Dwight Gooden, New York	24	1985	Ron Guidry, New York	22
1986	Fernando Valenzuela, Los Angeles	21	1986	Roger Clemens, Boston	24
1987	Rick Sutcliffe, Chicago	18	1987	Roger Clemens, Boston; Dave Stewart, Oakland	20
1988	Orel Hershiser, L.A.; Danny Jackson, Cincinnati	23	1988	Frank Viola, Minnesota	24
1989	Mike Scott, Houston	20	1989	Bret Saberhagen, Kansas City	23
1990	Doug Drabek, Pittsburgh	22	1990	Bob Welch, Oakland	27
1991	Tom Glavine, Atlanta; John Smiley, Pittsburgh	20	1991	Scott Erickson, Minnesota; Bill Gullickson, Detroit	20
1992	Tom Glavine, Atlanta; Greg Maddux, Chicago	20	1992	Kevin Brown, Texas; Jack Morris, Toronto	21
1993	John Burkett, San Francisco; Tom Glavine, Atlanta	22	1993	Jack McDowell, Chicago	22
1994	Ken Hill, Montréal; Greg Maddux, Atlanta	16	1994	Jimmy Key, New York	17
1995	Greg Maddux, Atlanta	19	1995	Mike Mussina, Baltimore	19
1996	John Smoltz, Atlanta	24	1996	Andy Pettitte, New York	21
1997	Denny Neagle, Atlanta	20	1997	Roger Clemens, Toronto	21
1998	Tom Glavine, Atlanta	20	1998	Roger Clemens, Toronto; David Cone, New York; Rick Helling, Texas	20
1999	Mike Hampton, Houston	22	1999	Pedro Martinez, Boston	23
2000	Tom Glavine, Atlanta	21	2000	Tim Hudson, Oakland; David Wells, Toronto	20
2001	Matt Morris, St. Louis; Curt Schilling, Arizona	22	2001	Mark Mulder, Oakland	21
2002	Randy Johnson, Arizona	24	2002	Barry Zito, Oakland	23
2003	Russ Ortiz, Atlanta	21	2003	Roy Halladay, Toronto	22
2004	Roy Oswalt, Houston	20	2004	Curt Schilling, Boston	21
2005	Dontrelle Willis, Florida	22	2005	Bartolo Colon, Los Angeles	21
2006	Aaron Harang, Cincinnati; Derek Lowe, L.A.; Brad Penny, L.A.; John Smoltz, Atlanta; Brandon Webb, Arizona; Carlos Zambrano, Chicago	16	2006	Johan Santana, Minnesota; Chien-Ming Wang, New York	19
2007	Jake Peavy, San Diego	19	2007	Josh Beckett, Boston	20
2008	Brandon Webb, Arizona	22	2008	Cliff Lee, Cleveland	22
2009	Adam Wainwright, St. Louis	19	2009	Felix Hernandez, Seattle; CC Sabathia, New York; Justin Verlander, Detroit	19
2010	Roy Halladay, Philadelphia	21	2010	CC Sabathia, New York	21
2011	Ian Kennedy, Arizona; Clayton Kershaw, L.A.	21	2011	Justin Verlander, Detroit	24
2012	Gio Gonzalez, Washington	21	2012	David Price, Tampa Bay; Jered Weaver, L.A.	20

Cy Young Award Winners, 1956-2011

Year	Pitcher, team	Year	Pitcher, team	Year	Pitcher, team
1956	Don Newcombe, Brooklyn	1978	(NL) Gaylord Perry, San Diego	1995	(NL) Greg Maddux, Atlanta
1957	Warren Spahn, Milwaukee		(AL) Ron Guidry, NY		(AL) Randy Johnson, Seattle
1958	Bob Turley, NY	1979	(NL) Bruce Sutter, Chicago	1996	(NL) John Smoltz, Atlanta
1959	Early Wynn, Chicago		(AL) Mike Flanagan, Baltimore		(AL) Pat Hentgen, Toronto
1960	Vernon Law, Pittsburgh	1980	(NL) Steve Carlton, Philadelphia	1997	(NL) Pedro Martinez, Montréal
1961	Whitey Ford, NY		(AL) Steve Stone, Baltimore		(AL) Roger Clemens, Toronto
1962	Don Drysdale, L.A.	1981	(NL) Fernando Valenzuela, L.A.	1998	(NL) Tom Glavine, Atlanta
1963	Sandy Koufax, L.A.		(AL) Rollie Fingers, Milwaukee		(AL) Roger Clemens, Toronto
1964	Dean Chance, L.A.	1982	(NL) Steve Carlton, Philadelphia	1999	(NL) Randy Johnson, Arizona
1965	Sandy Koufax, L.A.		(AL) Pete Vuckovich, Milwaukee		(AL) Pedro Martinez, Boston
1966	Sandy Koufax, L.A.	1983	(NL) John Denny, Philadelphia	2000	(NL) Randy Johnson, Arizona
1967	(NL) Mike McCormick, San Francisco		(AL) LaMarr Hoyt, Chicago		(AL) Pedro Martinez, Boston
	(AL) Jim Lonborg, Boston	1984	(NL) Rick Sutcliffe, Chicago	2001	(NL) Randy Johnson, Arizona
1968	(NL) Bob Gibson, St. Louis		(AL) Willie Hernandez, Detroit		(AL) Roger Clemens, NY
	(AL) Denny McLain, Detroit	1985	(NL) Dwight Gooden, NY	2002	(NL) Randy Johnson, Arizona
1969	(NL) Tom Seaver, NY		(AL) Bret Saberhagen, Kansas City		(AL) Barry Zito, Oakland
	(AL) (tie) Denny McLain, Detroit; Mike Cuellar, Baltimore	1986	(NL) Mike Scott, Houston	2003	(NL) Eric Gagne, L.A.
			(AL) Roger Clemens, Boston		(AL) Roy Halladay, Toronto
1970	(NL) Bob Gibson, St. Louis	1987	(NL) Steve Bedrosian, Philadelphia	2004	(NL) Roger Clemens, Houston
	(AL) Jim Perry, Minnesota				(AL) Johan Santana, Minnesota
1971	(NL) Ferguson Jenkins, Chicago		(AL) Roger Clemens, Boston	2005	(NL) Chris Carpenter, St. Louis
	(AL) Vida Blue, Oakland	1988	(NL) Orel Hershiser, L.A.		(AL) Bartolo Colon, L.A.
1972	(NL) Steve Carlton, Philadelphia		(AL) Frank Viola, Minnesota	2006	(NL) Brandon Webb, Arizona
	(AL) Gaylord Perry, Cleveland	1989	(NL) Mark Davis, San Diego		(AL) Johan Santana, Minnesota
1973	(NL) Tom Seaver, NY		(AL) Bret Saberhagen, Kansas City	2007	(NL) Jake Peavy, San Diego
	(AL) Jim Palmer, Baltimore	1990	(NL) Doug Drabek, Pittsburgh		(AL) CC Sabathia, Cleveland
1974	(NL) Mike Marshall, L.A.		(AL) Bob Welch, Oakland	2008	(NL) Tim Lincecum, San Francisco
	(AL) Jim "Catfish" Hunter, Oakland	1991	(NL) Tom Glavine, Atlanta		(AL) Cliff Lee, Cleveland
			(AL) Roger Clemens, Boston	2009	(NL) Tim Lincecum, San Francisco
1975	(NL) Tom Seaver, NY	1992	(NL) Greg Maddux, Chicago		(AL) Zack Greinke, Kansas City
	(AL) Jim Palmer, Baltimore		(AL) Dennis Eckersley, Oakland	2010	(NL) Roy Halladay, Philadelphia
1976	(NL) Randy Jones, San Diego	1993	(NL) Greg Maddux, Atlanta		(AL) Felix Hernandez, Seattle
	(AL) Jim Palmer, Baltimore		(AL) Jack McDowell, Chicago	2011	(NL) Clayton Kershaw, L.A.
1977	(NL) Steve Carlton, Philadelphia	1994	(NL) Greg Maddux, Atlanta		(AL) Justin Verlander, Detroit
	(AL) Sparky Lyle, NY		(AL) David Cone, Kansas City		

Most Valuable Players, 1931-2011

As selected by the Baseball Writers' Assn. of America. Prior to 1931, MVP honors were named by various sources.

National League

Year	Player, team	Year	Player, team	Year	Player, team
1931	Frank Frisch, St. Louis	1959	Ernie Banks, Chicago	1985	Willie McGee, St. Louis
1932	Chuck Klein, Philadelphia	1960	Dick Groat, Pittsburgh	1986	Mike Schmidt, Philadelphia
1933	Carl Hubbell, New York	1961	Frank Robinson, Cincinnati	1987	Andre Dawson, Chicago
1934	Dizzy Dean, St. Louis	1962	Maury Wills, Los Angeles	1988	Kirk Gibson, Los Angeles
1935	Gabby Hartnett, Chicago	1963	Sandy Koufax, Los Angeles	1989	Kevin Mitchell, San Francisco
1936	Carl Hubbell, New York	1964	Ken Boyer, St. Louis	1990	Barry Bonds, Pittsburgh
1937	Joe Medwick, St. Louis	1965	Willie Mays, San Francisco	1991	Terry Pendleton, Atlanta
1938	Ernie Lombardi, Cincinnati	1966	Roberto Clemente, Pittsburgh	1992	Barry Bonds, Pittsburgh
1939	Bucky Walters, Cincinnati	1967	Orlando Cepeda, St. Louis	1993	Barry Bonds, San Francisco
1940	Frank McCormick, Cincinnati	1968	Bob Gibson, St. Louis	1994	Jeff Bagwell, Houston
1941	Dolph Camilli, Brooklyn	1969	Willie McCovey, San Francisco	1995	Barry Larkin, Cincinnati
1942	Mort Cooper, St. Louis	1970	Johnny Bench, Cincinnati	1996	Ken Caminiti, San Diego
1943	Stan Musial, St. Louis	1971	Joe Torre, St. Louis	1997	Larry Walker, Colorado
1944	Martin Marion, St. Louis	1972	Johnny Bench, Cincinnati	1998	Sammy Sosa, Chicago
1945	Phil Cavarretta, Chicago	1973	Pete Rose, Cincinnati	1999	Chipper Jones, Atlanta
1946	Stan Musial, St. Louis	1974	Steve Garvey, Los Angeles	2000	Jeff Kent, San Francisco
1947	Bob Elliott, Boston	1975	Joe Morgan, Cincinnati	2001	Barry Bonds, San Francisco
1948	Stan Musial, St. Louis	1976	Joe Morgan, Cincinnati	2002	Barry Bonds, San Francisco
1949	Jackie Robinson, Brooklyn	1977	George Foster, Cincinnati	2003	Barry Bonds, San Francisco
1950	Jim Konstanty, Philadelphia	1978	Dave Parker, Pittsburgh	2004	Barry Bonds, San Francisco
1951	Roy Campanella, Brooklyn	1979	(tie) Keith Hernandez, St. Louis;	2005	Albert Pujols, St. Louis
1952	Hank Sauer, Chicago		Willie Stargell, Pittsburgh	2006	Ryan Howard, Philadelphia
1953	Roy Campanella, Brooklyn	1980	Mike Schmidt, Philadelphia	2007	Jimmy Rollins, Philadelphia
1954	Willie Mays, New York	1981	Mike Schmidt, Philadelphia	2008	Albert Pujols, St. Louis
1955	Roy Campanella, Brooklyn	1982	Dale Murphy, Atlanta	2009	Albert Pujols, St. Louis
1956	Don Newcombe, Brooklyn	1983	Dale Murphy, Atlanta	2010	Joey Votto, Cincinnati
1957	Hank Aaron, Milwaukee	1984	Ryne Sandberg, Chicago	2011	Ryan Braun, Milwaukee
1958	Ernie Banks, Chicago				

American League

Year	Player, team	Year	Player, team	Year	Player, team
1931	Lefty Grove, Philadelphia	1958	Jackie Jensen, Boston	1985	Don Mattingly, New York
1932	Jimmie Foxx, Philadelphia	1959	Nellie Fox, Chicago	1986	Roger Clemens, Boston
1933	Jimmie Foxx, Philadelphia	1960	Roger Maris, New York	1987	George Bell, Toronto
1934	Mickey Cochrane, Detroit	1961	Roger Maris, New York	1988	Jose Canseco, Oakland
1935	Hank Greenberg, Detroit	1962	Mickey Mantle, New York	1989	Robin Yount, Milwaukee
1936	Lou Gehrig, New York	1963	Elston Howard, New York	1990	Rickey Henderson, Oakland
1937	Charlie Gehringer, Detroit	1964	Brooks Robinson, Baltimore	1991	Cal Ripken Jr., Baltimore
1938	Jimmie Foxx, Boston	1965	Zoilo Versalles, Minnesota	1992	Dennis Eckersley, Oakland
1939	Joe DiMaggio, New York	1966	Frank Robinson, Baltimore	1993	Frank Thomas, Chicago
1940	Hank Greenberg, Detroit	1967	Carl Yastrzemski, Boston	1994	Frank Thomas, Chicago
1941	Joe DiMaggio, New York	1968	Denny McLain, Detroit	1995	Mo Vaughn, Boston
1942	Joe Gordon, New York	1969	Harmon Killebrew, Minnesota	1996	Juan Gonzalez, Texas
1943	Spurgeon "Spud" Chandler,	1970	John "Boog" Powell, Baltimore	1997	Ken Griffey Jr., Seattle
	New York	1971	Vida Blue, Oakland	1998	Juan Gonzalez, Texas
1944	Hal Newhouser, Detroit	1972	Dick Allen, Chicago	1999	Ivan Rodriguez, Texas
1945	Hal Newhouser, Detroit	1973	Reggie Jackson, Oakland	2000	Jason Giambi, Oakland
1946	Ted Williams, Boston	1974	Jeff Burroughs, Texas	2001	Ichiro Suzuki, Seattle
1947	Joe DiMaggio, New York	1975	Fred Lynn, Boston	2002	Miguel Tejada, Oakland
1948	Lou Boudreau, Cleveland	1976	Thurman Munson, New York	2003	Alex Rodriguez, Texas
1949	Ted Williams, Boston	1977	Rod Carew, Minnesota	2004	Vladimir Guerrero, Anaheim
1950	Phil Rizzuto, New York	1978	Jim Rice, Boston	2005	Alex Rodriguez, New York
1951	Yogi Berra, New York	1979	Don Baylor, California	2006	Justin Morneau, Minnesota
1952	Bobby Shantz, Philadelphia	1980	George Brett, Kansas City	2007	Alex Rodriguez, New York
1953	Al Rosen, Cleveland	1981	Rollie Fingers, Milwaukee	2008	Dustin Pedroia, Boston
1954	Yogi Berra, New York	1982	Robin Yount, Milwaukee	2009	Joe Mauer, Minnesota
1955	Yogi Berra, New York	1983	Cal Ripken Jr., Baltimore	2010	Josh Hamilton, Texas
1956	Mickey Mantle, New York	1984	Willie Hernandez, Detroit	2011	Justin Verlander, Detroit
1957	Mickey Mantle, New York				

Rookie of the Year, 1949-2011

(as selected by the Baseball Writers' Assn. of America)

1947—Combined selection—Jackie Robinson, Brooklyn, 1B; 1948—Combined selection—Alvin Dark, Boston (NL), SS.

National League

Year	Player, team, position	Year	Player, team, position	Year	Player, team, position
1949	Don Newcombe, Brooklyn, P	1971	Earl Williams, Atlanta, C	1992	Eric Karros, L.A., 1B
1950	Sam Jethroe, Boston, OF	1972	Jon Matlack, NY, P	1993	Mike Piazza, L.A., C
1951	Willie Mays, NY, OF	1973	Gary Matthews, San Francisco, OF	1994	Raul Mondesi, L.A., OF
1952	Joe Black, Brooklyn, P	1974	Bake McBride, St. Louis, OF	1995	Hideo Nomo, L.A., P
1953	Jim Gilliam, Brooklyn, 2B	1975	John Montefusco, San Francisco, P	1996	Todd Hollandsworth, L.A., OF
1954	Wally Moon, St. Louis, OF	1976	(tie) Butch Metzger, San Diego, P;	1997	Scott Rolen, Philadelphia, 3B
1955	Bill Virdon, St. Louis, OF		Pat Zachry, Cincinnati, P	1998	Kerry Wood, Chicago, P
1956	Frank Robinson, Cincinnati, OF	1977	Andre Dawson, Montréal, OF	1999	Scott Williamson, Cincinnati, P
1957	Jack Sanford, Philadelphia, P	1978	Bob Horner, Atlanta, 3B	2000	Rafael Furcal, Atlanta, SS
1958	Orlando Cepeda, San Francisco, 1B	1979	Rick Sutcliffe, L.A., P	2001	Albert Pujols, St. Louis, OF
1959	Willie McCovey, San Francisco, 1B	1980	Steve Howe, L.A., P	2002	Jason Jennings, Colorado, P
1960	Frank Howard, L.A., OF	1981	Fernando Valenzuela, L.A., P	2003	Dontrelle Willis, Florida, P
1961	Billy Williams, Chicago, OF	1982	Steve Sax, L.A., 2B	2004	Jason Bay, Pittsburgh, OF
1962	Ken Hubbs, Chicago, 2B	1983	Darryl Strawberry, NY, OF	2005	Ryan Howard, Philadelphia, 1B
1963	Pete Rose, Cincinnati, 2B	1984	Dwight Gooden, NY, P	2006	Hanley Ramirez, Florida, SS
1964	Richie Allen, Philadelphia, 3B	1985	Vince Coleman, St. Louis, OF	2007	Ryan Braun, Milwaukee, OF
1965	Jim Lefebvre, L.A., 2B	1986	Todd Worrell, St. Louis, P	2008	Geovany Soto, Chicago, C
1966	Tommy Helms, Cincinnati, 2B	1987	Benito Santiago, San Diego, C	2009	Chris Coghlan, Florida, OF
1967	Tom Seaver, NY, P	1988	Chris Sabo, Cincinnati, 3B	2010	Buster Posey, San Francisco, C
1968	Johnny Bench, Cincinnati, C	1989	Jerome Walton, Chicago, OF	2011	Craig Kimbrel, Atlanta, P
1969	Ted Sizemore, L.A., 2B	1990	Dave Justice, Atlanta, 1B		
1970	Carl Morton, Montréal, P	1991	Jeff Bagwell, Houston, 1B		

American League

Year	Player, team, position	Year	Player, team, position	Year	Player, team, position
1949	Roy Sievers, St. Louis, OF	1971	Chris Chambliss, Cleveland, 1B	1991	Chuck Knoblauch, Minnesota, 2B
1950	Walt Dropo, Boston, 1B	1972	Carlton Fisk, Boston, C	1992	Pat Listach, Milwaukee, SS
1951	Gil McDougald, NY, 3B	1973	Al Bumbry, Baltimore, OF	1993	Tim Salmon, California, OF
1952	Harry Byrd, Philadelphia, P	1974	Mike Hargrove, Texas, 1B	1994	Bob Hamelin, Kansas City, DH
1953	Harvey Kuenn, Detroit, SS	1975	Fred Lynn, Boston, OF	1995	Marty Cordova, Minnesota, OF
1954	Bob Grim, NY, P	1976	Mark Fidrych, Detroit, P	1996	Derek Jeter, NY, SS
1955	Herb Score, Cleveland, P	1977	Eddie Murray, Baltimore, DH	1997	Nomar Garciaparra, Boston, SS
1956	Luis Aparicio, Chicago, SS	1978	Lou Whitaker, Detroit, 2B	1998	Ben Grieve, Oakland, OF
1957	Tony Kubek, NY, IF-OF	1979	(tie) John Castino, Minnesota, 3B;	1999	Carlos Beltran, Kansas City, OF
1958	Albie Pearson, Washington, OF		Alfredo Griffin, Toronto, SS	2000	Kazuhiro Sasaki, Seattle, P
1959	Bob Allison, Washington, OF	1980	Joe Charboneau, Cleveland, OF	2001	Ichiro Suzuki, Seattle, OF
1960	Ron Hansen, Baltimore, SS	1981	Dave Righetti, NY, P	2002	Eric Hinske, Toronto, 3B
1961	Don Schwall, Boston, P	1982	Cal Ripken Jr., Baltimore, SS	2003	Angel Berroa, Kansas City, SS
1962	Tom Tresh, NY, IF-OF	1983	Ron Kittle, Chicago, OF	2004	Bobby Crosby, Oakland, SS
1963	Gary Peters, Chicago, P	1984	Alvin Davis, Seattle, 1B	2005	Huston Street, Oakland, P
1964	Tony Oliva, Minnesota, OF	1985	Ozzie Guillen, Chicago, SS	2006	Justin Verlander, Detroit, P
1965	Curt Blefary, Baltimore, OF	1986	Jose Canseco, Oakland, OF	2007	Dustin Pedroia, Boston, 2B
1966	Tommie Agee, Chicago, OF	1987	Mark McGwire, Oakland, 1B	2008	Evan Longoria, Tampa Bay, 3B
1967	Rod Carew, Minnesota, 2B	1988	Walt Weiss, Oakland, SS	2009	Andrew Bailey, Oakland, P
1968	Stan Bahnsen, NY, P	1989	Gregg Olson, Baltimore, P	2010	Neftali Feliz, Texas, P
1969	Lou Piniella, Kansas City, OF	1990	Sandy Alomar Jr., Cleveland, C	2011	Jeremy Hellickson, Tampa Bay, P
1970	Thurman Munson, NY, C				

Major League Pennant Winners, 1901-75

	National League						American League				
Year	Winner	Won	Lost	Pct	Manager	Year	Winner	Won	Lost	Pct	Manager
1901	Pittsburgh	90	49	.647	Clarke	1901	Chicago	83	53	.610	Griffith
1902	Pittsburgh	103	36	.741	Clarke	1902	Philadelphia	83	53	.610	Mack
1903	Pittsburgh	91	49	.650	Clarke	1903	Boston	91	47	.659	Collins
1904	New York	106	47	.693	McGraw	1904	Boston	95	59	.617	Collins
1905	New York	105	48	.686	McGraw	1905	Philadelphia	92	56	.622	Mack
1906	Chicago	116	36	.763	Chance	1906	Chicago	93	58	.616	Jones
1907	Chicago	107	45	.704	Chance	1907	Detroit	92	58	.613	Jennings
1908	Chicago	99	55	.643	Chance	1908	Detroit	90	63	.588	Jennings
1909	Pittsburgh	110	42	.724	Clarke	1909	Detroit	98	54	.645	Jennings
1910	Chicago	104	50	.675	Chance	1910	Philadelphia	102	48	.680	Mack
1911	New York	99	54	.647	McGraw	1911	Philadelphia	101	50	.669	Mack
1912	New York	103	48	.682	McGraw	1912	Boston	105	47	.691	Stahl
1913	New York	101	51	.664	McGraw	1913	Philadelphia	96	57	.627	Mack
1914	Boston	94	59	.614	Stallings	1914	Philadelphia	99	53	.651	Mack
1915	Philadelphia	90	62	.592	Moran	1915	Boston	101	50	.669	Carrigan
1916	Brooklyn	94	60	.610	Robinson	1916	Boston	91	63	.591	Carrigan
1917	New York	98	56	.636	McGraw	1917	Chicago	100	54	.649	Rowland
1918	Chicago	84	45	.651	Mitchell	1918	Boston	75	51	.595	Barrow
1919	Cincinnati	96	44	.686	Moran	1919	Chicago	88	52	.629	Gleason
1920	Brooklyn	93	61	.604	Robinson	1920	Cleveland	98	56	.636	Speaker
1921	New York	94	59	.614	McGraw	1921	New York	98	55	.641	Huggins
1922	New York	93	61	.604	McGraw	1922	New York	94	60	.610	Huggins
1923	New York	95	58	.621	McGraw	1923	New York	98	54	.645	Huggins
1924	New York	93	60	.608	McGraw	1924	Washington	92	62	.597	Harris
1925	Pittsburgh	95	58	.621	McKechnie	1925	Washington	96	55	.636	Harris
1926	St. Louis	89	65	.578	Hornsby	1926	New York	91	63	.591	Huggins
1927	Pittsburgh	94	60	.610	Bush	1927	New York	110	44	.714	Huggins
1928	St. Louis	95	59	.617	McKechnie	1928	New York	101	53	.656	Huggins
1929	Chicago	98	54	.645	McCarthy	1929	Philadelphia	104	46	.693	Mack
1930	St. Louis	92	62	.597	Street	1930	Philadelphia	102	52	.662	Mack
1931	St. Louis	101	53	.656	Street	1931	Philadelphia	107	45	.704	Mack
1932	Chicago	90	64	.584	Hornsby, Grimm	1932	New York	107	47	.695	McCarthy
1933	New York	91	61	.599	Terry	1933	Washington	99	53	.651	Cronin
1934	St. Louis	95	58	.621	Frisch	1934	Detroit	101	53	.656	Cochrane
1935	Chicago	100	54	.649	Grimm	1935	Detroit	93	58	.616	Cochrane
1936	New York	92	62	.597	Terry	1936	New York	102	51	.667	McCarthy
1937	New York	95	57	.625	Terry	1937	New York	102	52	.662	McCarthy
1938	Chicago	89	63	.586	Grimm, Hartnett	1938	New York	99	53	.651	McCarthy
1939	Cincinnati	97	57	.630	McKechnie	1939	New York	106	45	.702	McCarthy
1940	Cincinnati	100	53	.654	McKechnie	1940	Detroit	90	64	.584	Baker
1941	Brooklyn	100	54	.649	Durocher	1941	New York	101	53	.656	McCarthy
1942	St. Louis	106	48	.688	Southworth	1942	New York	103	51	.669	McCarthy
1943	St. Louis	105	49	.682	Southworth	1943	New York	98	56	.636	McCarthy
1944	St. Louis	105	49	.682	Southworth	1944	St. Louis	89	65	.578	Sewell
1945	Chicago	98	56	.636	Grimm	1945	Detroit	88	65	.575	O'Neill
1946	St. Louis	98	58	.628	Dyer	1946	Boston	104	50	.675	Cronin
1947	Brooklyn	94	60	.610	Shotton	1947	New York	97	57	.630	Harris
1948	Boston	91	62	.595	Southworth	1948	Cleveland	97	58	.626	Boudreau
1949	Brooklyn	97	57	.630	Shotton	1949	New York	97	57	.630	Stengel
1950	Philadelphia	91	63	.591	Sawyer	1950	New York	98	56	.636	Stengel
1951	New York	98	59	.624	Durocher	1951	New York	98	56	.636	Stengel
1952	Brooklyn	96	57	.627	Dressen	1952	New York	95	59	.617	Stengel
1953	Brooklyn	105	49	.682	Dressen	1953	New York	99	52	.656	Stengel
1954	New York	97	57	.630	Durocher	1954	Cleveland	111	43	.721	Lopez
1955	Brooklyn	98	55	.641	Alston	1955	New York	96	58	.623	Stengel
1956	Brooklyn	93	61	.604	Alston	1956	New York	97	57	.630	Stengel
1957	Milwaukee	95	59	.617	Haney	1957	New York	98	56	.636	Stengel
1958	Milwaukee	92	62	.597	Haney	1958	New York	92	62	.597	Stengel
1959	Los Angeles	88	68	.564	Alston	1959	Chicago	94	60	.610	Lopez
1960	Pittsburgh	95	59	.617	Murtaugh	1960	New York	97	57	.630	Stengel
1961	Cincinnati	93	61	.604	Hutchinson	1961	New York	109	53	.673	Houk
1962	San Francisco	103	62	.624	Dark	1962	New York	96	66	.593	Houk
1963	Los Angeles	99	63	.611	Alston	1963	New York	104	57	.646	Houk
1964	St. Louis	93	69	.574	Keane	1964	New York	99	63	.611	Berra

National League

Year	Winner	Won	Lost	Pct	Manager
1965	Los Angeles	97	65	.599	Alston
1966	Los Angeles	95	67	.586	Alston
1967	St. Louis	101	60	.627	Schoendienst
1968	St. Louis	97	65	.599	Schoendienst
1969	NY Mets	100	62	.617	Hodges
1970	Cincinnati	102	60	.630	Anderson
1971	Pittsburgh	97	65	.599	Murtaugh
1972	Cincinnati	95	59	.617	Anderson
1973	NY Mets	82	79	.509	Berra
1974	Los Angeles	102	60	.630	Alston
1975	Cincinnati	108	54	.667	Anderson

American League

Year	Winner	Won	Lost	Pct	Manager
1965	Minnesota	102	60	.630	Mele
1966	Baltimore	97	63	.606	Bauer
1967	Boston	92	70	.568	Williams
1968	Detroit	103	59	.636	Smith
1969	Baltimore	109	53	.673	Weaver
1970	Baltimore	108	54	.667	Weaver
1971	Baltimore	101	57	.639	Weaver
1972	Oakland	93	62	.600	Williams
1973	Oakland	94	68	.580	Williams
1974	Oakland	90	72	.556	Dark
1975	Boston	95	65	.594	Johnson

Major League Pennant Winners, 1976-2012

National League

Year	East Winner	W	L	Pct	Manager	West Winner	W	L	Pct	Manager	Pennant winner
1976	Philadelphia	101	61	.623	Ozark	Cincinnati	102	60	.630	Anderson	Cincinnati
1977	Philadelphia	101	61	.623	Ozark	Los Angeles	98	64	.605	Lasorda	Los Angeles
1978	Philadelphia	90	72	.556	Ozark	Los Angeles	95	67	.586	Lasorda	Los Angeles
1979	Pittsburgh	98	64	.605	Tanner	Cincinnati	90	71	.559	McNamara	Pittsburgh
1980	Philadelphia	91	71	.562	Green	Houston	93	70	.571	Virdon	Philadelphia
1981(a)	Philadelphia	34	21	.618	Green	Los Angeles	36	21	.632	Lasorda	(c)
1981(b)	Montréal	30	23	.566	Williams, Fanning	Houston	33	20	.623	Virdon	Los Angeles
1982	St. Louis	92	70	.568	Herzog	Atlanta	89	73	.549	Torre	St. Louis
1983	Philadelphia	90	72	.556	Corrales, Owens	Los Angeles	91	71	.562	Lasorda	Philadelphia
1984	Chicago	96	65	.596	Frey	San Diego	92	70	.568	Williams	San Diego
1985	St. Louis	101	61	.623	Herzog	Los Angeles	95	67	.586	Lasorda	St. Louis
1986	NY Mets	108	54	.667	Johnson	Houston	96	66	.593	Lanier	New York
1987	St. Louis	95	67	.586	Herzog	San Francisco	90	72	.556	Craig	St. Louis
1988	NY Mets	100	60	.625	Johnson	Los Angeles	94	67	.584	Lasorda	Los Angeles
1989	Chicago	93	69	.571	Zimmer	San Francisco	92	70	.568	Craig	San Francisco
1990	Pittsburgh	95	67	.586	Leyland	Cincinnati	91	71	.562	Piniella	Cincinnati
1991	Pittsburgh	98	64	.605	Leyland	Atlanta	94	68	.580	Cox	Atlanta
1992	Pittsburgh	96	66	.593	Leyland	Atlanta	98	64	.605	Cox	Atlanta
1993	Philadelphia	97	65	.599	Fregosi	Atlanta	104	58	.642	Cox	Philadelphia

Year	Division	Winner	W	L	Pct	Manager	Playoffs	Pennant winner
1994(d)	East	Montréal	74	40	.649	Alou	—	—
	Central	Cincinnati	66	48	.579	Johnson		
	West	Los Angeles	58	56	.509	Lasorda		
1995	East	Atlanta	90	54	.625	Cox	Atlanta 3, Colorado* 1	Atlanta
	Central	Cincinnati	85	59	.590	Johnson	Cincinnati 3, Los Angeles 0	
	West	Los Angeles	78	66	.542	Lasorda	Atlanta 4, Cincinnati 0	
1996	East	Atlanta	96	66	.593	Cox	Atlanta 3, Los Angeles* 0	Atlanta
	Central	St. Louis	88	74	.543	La Russa	St. Louis 3, San Diego 0	
	West	San Diego	91	71	.562	Bochy	Atlanta 4, St. Louis 3	
1997	East	Atlanta	101	61	.623	Cox	Atlanta 3, Houston 0	Florida*
	Central	Houston	84	78	.519	Dierker	Florida* 3, San Francisco 0	(Leyland)
	West	San Francisco	90	72	.556	Baker	Florida* 4, Atlanta 2	
1998	East	Atlanta	106	56	.654	Cox	Atlanta 3, Chicago* 0	San Diego
	Central	Houston	102	60	.630	Dierker	San Diego 3, Houston 1	
	West	San Diego	98	64	.605	Bochy	San Diego 4, Atlanta 2	
1999	East	Atlanta	103	59	.636	Cox	Atlanta 3, Houston 1	Atlanta
	Central	Houston	97	65	.599	Dierker	New York* 3, Arizona 1	
	West	Arizona	100	62	.617	Showalter	Atlanta 4, New York* 2	
2000	East	Atlanta	95	67	.586	Cox	St. Louis 3, Atlanta 0	New York*
	Central	St. Louis	95	67	.586	La Russa	New York* 3, San Francisco 1	(Valentine)
	West	San Francisco	97	65	.599	Baker	New York* 4, St. Louis 1	
2001	East	Atlanta	88	74	.543	Cox	Atlanta 3, Houston 0	Arizona
	Central	Houston	93	69	.574	Dierker	Arizona 3, St. Louis* 2	
	West	Arizona	92	70	.568	Brenly	Arizona 4, Atlanta 1	
2002	East	Atlanta	101	59	.631	Cox	St. Louis 3, Arizona 0	San Francisco*
	Central	St. Louis	97	65	.599	La Russa	San Francisco* 3, Atlanta 2	(Baker)
	West	Arizona	98	64	.605	Brenly	San Francisco* 4, St. Louis 1	
2003	East	Atlanta	101	61	.623	Cox	Chicago 3, Atlanta 2	Florida*
	Central	Chicago	88	74	.543	Baker	Florida* 3, San Francisco 1	(McKeon)
	West	San Francisco	100	61	.621	Alou	Florida* 4, Chicago 3	
2004	East	Atlanta	96	66	.593	Cox	Houston* 3, Atlanta 2	St. Louis
	Central	St. Louis	105	57	.648	La Russa	St. Louis 3, Dodgers 1	
	West	Los Angeles	93	69	.594	Tracy	St. Louis 4, Houston* 3	
2005	East	Atlanta	90	72	.556	Cox	St. Louis 3, San Diego 0	Houston*
	Central	St. Louis	100	62	.617	La Russa	Houston* 3, Atlanta 1	(Garner)
	West	San Diego	82	80	.506	Bochy	Houston* 4, St. Louis 2	
2006	East	New York	97	65	.599	Randolph	New York, Los Angeles* 0	St. Louis
	Central	St. Louis	83	78	.516	La Russa	St. Louis 3, San Diego 1	
	West	San Diego	88	74	.543	Bochy	St. Louis 4, New York 3	
2007	East	Philadelphia	89	73	.549	Manuel	Colorado* 3, Philadelphia 0	Colorado*
	Central	Chicago	85	77	.525	Piniella	Arizona 3, Chicago 0	(Hurdle)
	West	Arizona	90	72	.556	Melvin	Colorado* 4, Arizona 0	
2008	East	Philadelphia	92	70	.568	Manuel	Philadelphia 3, Milwaukee* 1	Philadelphia
	Central	Chicago	97	64	.602	Piniella	Los Angeles 3, Chicago 0	
	West	Los Angeles	84	78	.519	Torre	Philadelphia 4, Los Angeles 1	
2009	East	Philadelphia	93	69	.574	Manuel	Philadelphia 3, Colorado* 1	Philadelphia
	Central	St. Louis	91	71	.562	La Russa	Los Angeles 3, St. Louis 0	
	West	Los Angeles	95	67	.586	Torre	Philadelphia 4, Los Angeles 1	
2010	East	Philadelphia	97	65	.599	Manuel	San Francisco 3, Atlanta* 1	San Francisco
	Central	Cincinnati	91	71	.562	Baker	Philadelphia 3, Cincinnati 0	
	West	San Francisco	92	70	.568	Bochy	San Francisco 4, Philadelphia 2	
2011	East	Philadelphia	102	60	.630	Manuel	Milwaukee 3, Arizona 2	St. Louis*
	Central	Milwaukee	96	66	.593	Roenicke	St. Louis* 3, Philadelphia 2	(La Russa)
	West	Arizona	94	68	.580	Gibson	St. Louis* 4, Milwaukee 2	
2012	East	Washington	98	64	.605	Johnson	#St. Louis* 6, Atlanta* 3	San Francisco
	Central	Cincinnati	97	65	.599	Baker	St. Louis* 3, Washington 2	
	West	San Francisco	94	68	.580	Bochy	San Francisco 3, Cincinnati 2	
							San Francisco 4, St. Louis* 3	

American League

Year	East Winner	W	L	Pct	Manager	West Winner	W	L	Pct	Manager	Pennant winner
1976	New York	97	62	.610	Martin	Kansas City	90	72	.556	Herzog	New York
1977	New York	100	62	.617	Martin	Kansas City	102	60	.630	Herzog	New York
1978	New York	100	63	.613	Martin, Lemon	Kansas City	92	70	.568	Herzog	New York
1979	Baltimore	102	57	.642	Weaver	California	88	74	.543	Fregosi	Baltimore
1980	New York	103	59	.636	Howser	Kansas City	97	65	.599	Frey	Kansas City
1981(a)	New York	34	22	.607	Michael	Oakland	37	23	.617	Martin	(c)
1981(b)	Milwaukee	31	22	.585	Rodgers	Kansas City	30	23	.566	Frey, Howser	New York
1982	Milwaukee	95	67	.586	Rodgers, Kuenn	California	93	69	.574	Mauch	Milwaukee
1983	Baltimore	98	64	.605	Altobelli	Chicago	99	63	.611	La Russa	Baltimore
1984	Detroit	104	58	.642	Anderson	Kansas City	84	78	.519	Howser	Detroit
1985	Toronto	99	62	.615	Cox	Kansas City	91	71	.562	Howser	Kansas City
1986	Boston	95	66	.590	McNamara	California	92	70	.568	Mauch	Boston
1987	Detroit	98	64	.605	Anderson	Minnesota	85	77	.525	Kelly	Minnesota
1988	Boston	89	73	.549	McNamara, Morgan	Oakland	104	58	.642	La Russa	Oakland
1989	Toronto	89	73	.549	Williams, Gaston	Oakland	99	63	.611	La Russa	Oakland
1990	Boston	88	74	.543	Morgan	Oakland	103	59	.636	La Russa	Oakland
1991	Toronto	91	71	.562	Gaston	Minnesota	95	67	.586	Kelly	Minnesota
1992	Toronto	96	66	.593	Gaston	Oakland	96	66	.593	La Russa	Toronto
1993	Toronto	95	67	.586	Gaston	Chicago	94	68	.580	Lamont	Toronto

Year	Division	Winner	W	L	Pct	Manager	Playoffs	Pennant winner
1994(d)	East	New York	70	43	.619	Showalter	—	—
	Central	Chicago	67	46	.593	Lamont		
	West	Texas	52	62	.456	Kennedy		
1995	East	Boston	86	58	.597	Kennedy	Cleveland 3, Boston 0	Cleveland
	Central	Cleveland	100	44	.694	Hargrove	Seattle 3, New York* 2	
	West	Seattle	79	66	.545	Piniella	Cleveland 4, Seattle 2	
1996	East	New York	92	70	.568	Torre	Baltimore* 3, Cleveland 1	New York
	Central	Cleveland	99	62	.615	Hargrove	New York 3, Texas 1	
	West	Texas	90	72	.556	Oates	New York 4, Baltimore* 1	
1997	East	Baltimore	98	64	.605	Johnson	Baltimore 3, Seattle 1	Cleveland
	Central	Cleveland	86	75	.534	Hargrove	Cleveland 3, New York* 2	
	West	Seattle	90	72	.556	Piniella	Cleveland 4, Baltimore 2	
1998	East	New York	114	48	.704	Torre	New York 3, Texas 0	New York
	Central	Cleveland	89	73	.549	Hargrove	Cleveland 3, Boston* 1	
	West	Texas	88	74	.543	Oates	New York 4, Cleveland 2	
1999	East	New York	98	64	.605	Torre	New York 3, Texas 0	New York
	Central	Cleveland	97	65	.599	Hargrove	Boston* 3, Cleveland 2	
	West	Texas	95	67	.586	Oates	New York 4, Boston* 1	
2000	East	New York	87	74	.540	Torre	New York 3, Oakland 2	New York
	Central	Chicago	95	67	.586	Manuel	Seattle* 3, Chicago 0	
	West	Oakland	91	70	.565	Howe	New York 4, Seattle* 2	
2001	East	New York	95	65	.594	Torre	Seattle 3, Cleveland 2	New York
	Central	Cleveland	91	71	.562	Manuel	New York 3, Oakland* 2	
	West	Seattle	116	46	.716	Piniella	New York 4, Seattle 1	
2002	East	New York	103	58	.640	Torre	Anaheim* 3, New York 1	Anaheim* (Scioscia)
	Central	Minnesota	94	67	.584	Gardenhire	Minnesota 3, Oakland 2	
	West	Oakland	103	59	.636	Howe	Anaheim* 4, Minnesota 1	
2003	East	New York	101	61	.623	Torre	New York 3, Minnesota 1	New York
	Central	Minnesota	90	72	.556	Gardenhire	Boston* 3, Oakland 2	
	West	Oakland	96	66	.593	Macha	New York 4, Boston* 3	
2004	East	New York	101	61	.623	Torre	New York 3, Minnesota 1	Boston* (Francona)
	Central	Minnesota	92	70	.568	Gardenhire	Boston* 3, Anaheim 0	
	West	Anaheim	92	70	.568	Scioscia	Boston* 4, New York 3	
2005	East	New York	95	67	.586	Torre	Chicago 3, Boston* 0	Chicago
	Central	Chicago	99	63	.611	Guillen	Los Angeles 3, New York 2	
	West	Los Angeles	95	67	.586	Scioscia	Chicago 4, Los Angeles 1	
2006	East	New York	97	65	.599	Torre	Oakland 3, Minnesota 0	Detroit* (Leyland)
	Central	Minnesota	96	66	.593	Gardenhire	Detroit* 3, New York 1	
	West	Oakland	93	69	.574	Macha	Detroit* 4, Oakland 0	
2007	East	Boston	96	66	.593	Francona	Boston 3, Los Angeles 0	Boston
	Central	Cleveland	96	66	.593	Wedge	Cleveland 3, New York* 1	
	West	Los Angeles	94	68	.580	Scioscia	Boston 4, Cleveland 3	
2008	East	Tampa Bay	97	65	.599	Maddon	Tampa Bay 3, Chicago 1	Tampa Bay
	Central	Chicago	89	74	.546	Guillen	Boston* 3, Los Angeles 1	
	West	Los Angeles	100	62	.617	Scioscia	Tampa Bay 4, Boston* 3	
2009	East	New York	103	59	.636	Girardi	New York 3, Minnesota 0	New York
	Central	Minnesota	87	76	.534	Gardenhire	Los Angeles 3, Boston* 0	
	West	Los Angeles	97	65	.599	Scioscia	New York 4, Los Angeles 2	
2010	East	Tampa Bay	96	66	.593	Maddon	New York* 3, Minnesota 0	Texas
	Central	Minnesota	94	68	.580	Gardenhire	Texas 3, Tampa Bay 2	
	West	Texas	90	72	.556	Washington	Texas 4, New York* 2	
2011	East	New York	97	65	.599	Girardi	Detroit 3, New York 2	Texas
	Central	Detroit	95	67	.586	Leyland	Texas 3, Tampa Bay* 1	
	West	Texas	96	66	.593	Washington	Texas 4, Detroit 2	
2012	East	New York	95	67	.586	Girardi	#Baltimore* 5, Texas* 1	Detroit
	Central	Detroit	88	74	.543	Leyland	New York 3, Baltimore* 2	
	West	Oakland	94	68	.580	Melvin	Detroit 3, Oakland 2	
							Detroit 4, New York 0	

*Wild card team. If pennant winner is wild card team, manager's name is given in parentheses. #Single-game wild card playoff (debuted in 2012). (a) First half. (b) Second half. (c) Montréal, L.A., NY Yankees, and Oakland won the divisional playoffs. (d) In Aug. 1994, a players' strike began that caused the cancellation of the remainder of the season, the playoffs, and the World Series. Teams listed as division "winners" for 1994 were leading their divisions at the time of the strike.

Rawlings Gold Glove Awards, 2012

National League		American League	
Mark Buehrle, Miami, P	Jimmy Rollins, Philadelphia, SS	Jeremy Hellickson, Tampa Bay, and	Adrian Beltre, Texas, 3B
Yadier Molina, St. Louis, C	Carlos Gonzalez, Colorado, LF	Jake Peavy, Chicago White Sox, P	J. J. Hardy, Baltimore, SS
Adam LaRoche, Washington, 1B	Andrew McCutchen, Pittsburgh, CF	Matt Wieters, Baltimore, C	Alex Gordon, Kansas City, LF
Darwin Barney, Chicago Cubs, 2B	Jason Heyward, Atlanta, RF	Mark Teixeira, NY Yankees, 1B	Adam Jones, Baltimore, CF
Chase Headley, San Diego, 3B		Robinson Cano, NY Yankees, 2B	Josh Reddick, Oakland, RF

World Series Results, 1903-2012

1903	Boston AL 5, Pittsburgh NL 3	1940	Cincinnati NL 4, Detroit AL 3	1977	New York AL 4, Los Angeles NL 2
1904	No series	1941	New York AL 4, Brooklyn NL 1	1978	New York AL 4, Los Angeles NL 2
1905	New York NL 4, Philadelphia AL 1	1942	St. Louis NL 4, New York AL 1	1979	Pittsburgh NL 4, Baltimore AL 3
1906	Chicago AL 4, Chicago NL 2	1943	New York AL 4, St. Louis NL 1	1980	Philadelphia NL 4, Kansas City AL 2
1907	Chicago NL 4, Detroit AL 0, 1 tie	1944	St. Louis NL 4, St. Louis AL 2	1981	Los Angeles NL 4, New York AL 2
1908	Chicago NL 4, Detroit AL 1	1945	Detroit AL 4, Chicago NL 3	1982	St. Louis NL 4, Milwaukee AL 3
1909	Pittsburgh NL 4, Detroit AL 3	1946	St. Louis NL 4, Boston AL 3	1983	Baltimore AL 4, Philadelphia NL 1
1910	Philadelphia AL 4, Chicago NL 1	1947	New York AL 4, Brooklyn NL 3	1984	Detroit AL 4, San Diego NL 1
1911	Philadelphia AL 4, New York NL 2	1948	Cleveland AL 4, Boston NL 2	1985	Kansas City AL 4, St. Louis NL 3
1912	Boston AL 4, New York NL 3, 1 tie	1949	New York AL 4, Brooklyn NL 1	1986	New York NL 4, Boston AL 3
1913	Philadelphia AL 4, New York NL 1	1950	New York AL 4, Philadelphia NL 0	1987	Minnesota AL 4, St. Louis NL 3
1914	Boston NL 4, Philadelphia AL 0	1951	New York AL 4, New York NL 2	1988	Los Angeles NL 4, Oakland AL 1
1915	Boston AL 4, Philadelphia NL 1	1952	New York AL 4, Brooklyn NL 3	1989	Oakland AL 4, San Francisco NL 0
1916	Boston AL 4, Brooklyn NL 1	1953	New York AL 4, Brooklyn NL 2	1990	Cincinnati NL 4, Oakland AL 0
1917	Chicago AL 4, New York NL 2	1954	New York NL 4, Cleveland AL 0	1991	Minnesota AL 4, Atlanta NL 3
1918	Boston AL 4, Chicago NL 2	1955	Brooklyn NL 4, New York AL 3	1992	Toronto AL 4, Atlanta NL 2
1919	Cincinnati NL 5, Chicago AL 3	1956	New York AL 4, Brooklyn NL 3	1993	Toronto AL 4, Philadelphia NL 2
1920	Cleveland AL 5, Brooklyn NL 2	1957	Milwaukee NL 4, New York AL 3	1994	No series due to strike
1921	New York NL 5, New York AL 3	1958	New York AL 4, Milwaukee NL 3	1995	Atlanta NL 4, Cleveland AL 2
1922	New York NL 4, New York AL 0, 1 tie	1959	Los Angeles NL 4, Chicago AL 2	1996	New York AL 4, Atlanta NL 2
1923	New York AL 4, New York NL 2	1960	Pittsburgh NL 4, New York AL 3	1997	Florida NL 4, Cleveland AL 3
1924	Washington AL 4, New York NL 3	1961	New York AL 4, Cincinnati NL 1	1998	New York AL 4, San Diego NL 0
1925	Pittsburgh NL 4, Washington AL 3	1962	New York AL 4, San Francisco NL 3	1999	New York AL 4, Atlanta NL 0
1926	St. Louis NL 4, New York AL 3	1963	Los Angeles NL 4, New York AL 0	2000	New York AL 4, New York NL 1
1927	New York AL 4, Pittsburgh NL 0	1964	St. Louis NL 4, New York AL 3	2001	Arizona NL 4, New York AL 3
1928	New York AL 4, St. Louis NL 0	1965	Los Angeles NL 4, Minnesota AL 3	2002	Anaheim AL 4, San Francisco NL 3
1929	Philadelphia AL 4, Chicago NL 1	1966	Baltimore AL 4, Los Angeles NL 0	2003	Florida NL 4, New York AL 2
1930	Philadelphia AL 4, St. Louis NL 2	1967	St. Louis NL 4, Boston AL 3	2004	Boston AL 4, St. Louis NL 0
1931	St. Louis NL 4, Philadelphia AL 3	1968	Detroit AL 4, St. Louis NL 3	2005	Chicago AL 4, Houston NL 0
1932	New York AL 4, Chicago NL 0	1969	New York NL 4, Baltimore AL 1	2006	St. Louis NL 4, Detroit AL 1
1933	New York NL 4, Washington AL 1	1970	Baltimore AL 4, Cincinnati NL 1	2007	Boston AL 4, Colorado NL 0
1934	St. Louis NL 4, Detroit AL 3	1971	Pittsburgh NL 4, Baltimore AL 3	2008	Philadelphia NL 4, Tampa Bay AL 1
1935	Detroit AL 4, Chicago NL 2	1972	Oakland AL 4, Cincinnati NL 3	2009	New York AL 4, Philadelphia NL 2
1936	New York AL 4, New York NL 2	1973	Oakland AL 4, New York NL 3	2010	San Francisco NL 4, Texas AL 1
1937	New York AL 4, New York NL 1	1974	Oakland AL 4, Los Angeles NL 1	2011	St. Louis NL 4, Texas AL 3
1938	New York AL 4, Chicago NL 0	1975	Cincinnati NL 4, Boston AL 3	2012	San Francisco NL 4, Detroit AL 0
1939	New York AL 4, Cincinnati NL 0	1976	Cincinnati NL 4, New York AL 0		

World Series Most Valuable Player, 1955-2012

Year	Player, position, team	Year	Player, position, team	Year	Player, position, team
1955	Johnny Podres, P, Brooklyn	1975	Pete Rose, 3B, Cincinnati	1993	Paul Molitor, DH, Toronto
1956	Don Larsen, P, NY (AL)	1976	Johnny Bench, C, Cincinnati	1994	No series due to strike
1957	Lew Burdette, P, Milwaukee (NL)	1977	Reggie Jackson, OF, NY (AL)	1995	Tom Glavine, P, Atlanta
1958	Bob Turley, P, NY (AL)	1978	Bucky Dent, SS, NY (AL)	1996	John Wetteland, P, NY (AL)
1959	Larry Sherry, P, Los Angeles (NL)	1979	Willie Stargell, 1B, Pittsburgh	1997	Livan Hernandez, P, Florida
1960[1]	Bobby Richardson, 2B, NY (AL)	1980	Mike Schmidt, 3B, Philadelphia	1998	Scott Brosius, 3B, NY (AL)
1961	Whitey Ford, P, NY (AL)	1981	Ron Cey, 3B, Los Angeles (NL);	1999	Mariano Rivera, P, NY (AL)
1962	Ralph Terry, P, NY (AL)		Pedro Guerrero, OF, Los Angeles;	2000	Derek Jeter, SS, NY (AL)
1963	Sandy Koufax, P, Los Angeles (NL)		Steve Yeager, C, Los Angeles	2001	Curt Schilling, P, Arizona;
1964	Bob Gibson, P, St. Louis	1982	Darrell Porter, C, St. Louis		Randy Johnson, P, Arizona
1965	Sandy Koufax, P, Los Angeles (NL)	1983	Rick Dempsey, C, Baltimore	2002	Troy Glaus, 3B, Anaheim
1966	Frank Robinson, OF, Baltimore	1984	Alan Trammell, SS, Detroit	2003	Josh Beckett, P, Florida
1967	Bob Gibson, P, St. Louis	1985	Bret Saberhagen, P, Kansas City	2004	Manny Ramirez, OF, Boston
1968	Mickey Lolich, P, Detroit	1986	Ray Knight, 3B, NY (NL)	2005	Jermaine Dye, OF, Chicago (AL)
1969	Donn Clendenon, 1B, NY (NL)	1987	Frank Viola, P, Minnesota	2006	David Eckstein, SS, St. Louis
1970	Brooks Robinson, 3B, Baltimore	1988	Orel Hershiser, P, Los Angeles (NL)	2007	Mike Lowell, 3B, Boston
1971	Roberto Clemente, OF, Pittsburgh	1989	Dave Stewart, P, Oakland	2008	Cole Hamels, P, Philadelphia
1972	Gene Tenace, C, Oakland	1990	Jose Rijo, P, Cincinnati	2009	Hideki Matsui, DH, NY (AL)
1973	Reggie Jackson, OF, Oakland	1991	Jack Morris, P, Minnesota	2010	Edgar Renteria, SS, San Francisco
1974	Rollie Fingers, P, Oakland	1992	Pat Borders, C, Toronto	2011	David Freese, 3B, St. Louis
				2012	Pablo Sandoval, 3B, San Francisco

(1) Richardson won the MVP although Pittsburgh beat New York.

World Series Won-Lost Records, by Franchise

Since beginning of "modern" era in 1901. Figures represent overall Series wins, not individual games.

Team	Wins	Losses	Team	Wins	Losses
New York Yankees	27	13	Toronto Blue Jays	2	0
St. Louis Cardinals	11	7	New York Mets	2	2
Philadelphia/Kansas City/Oakland A's	9	5	Cleveland Indians	2	3
Boston Red Sox	7	4	Philadelphia Phillies	2	5
New York/San Francisco Giants	7	12	Chicago Cubs	2	8
Brooklyn/Los Angeles Dodgers	6	12	L.A./California/Anaheim/L.A. Angels	1	0
Pittsburgh Pirates	5	2	Arizona Diamondbacks	1	0
Cincinnati Reds	5	4	Kansas City Royals	1	1
Detroit Tigers	4	7	Houston Astros	0	1
Chicago White Sox	3	2	Seattle Pilots/Milwaukee Brewers	0	1
Washington Senators/Minnesota Twins	3	3	Tampa Bay Rays	0	1
St. Louis Browns/Baltimore Orioles	3	4	Colorado Rockies	0	1
Boston/Milwaukee/Atlanta Braves	3	6	San Diego Padres	0	2
Florida Marlins	2	0	Texas Rangers	0	2

All-Time World Series Career Leaders
(through 2012)
Batting Leaders

Batter (min. 50 PA)	Hits	AB	AVG	Batter (min. 50 PA)	Hits	AB	AVG
1. Johnny "Pepper" Martin	23	55	.418	6. Marquis Grissom	30	77	.390
2. Paul Molitor	23	55	.418	7. Thurman Munson	25	67	.373
3. Lance Berkman	16	39	.410	8. George Brett	19	51	.373
4. Hal McRae	18	45	.400	9. Hank Aaron	20	55	.364
5. Lou Brock	34	87	.391	10. Frank "Home Run" Baker	33	91	.363

Games Played

Yogi Berra	75
Mickey Mantle	65
Elston Howard	54
Hank Bauer	53
Gil McDougald	53
Phil Rizzuto	52
Joe DiMaggio	51
Frankie Frisch	50
Pee Wee Reese	44
Roger Maris	41
Babe Ruth	41

Runs Batted In

Mickey Mantle	40
Yogi Berra	39
Lou Gehrig	35
Babe Ruth	33
Joe DiMaggio	30
Bill Skowron	29
Duke Snider	26
Hank Bauer	24
Bill Dickey	24
Reggie Jackson	24
Gil McDougald	24

Hits

Yogi Berra	71
Mickey Mantle	59
Frankie Frisch	58
Joe DiMaggio	54
Derek Jeter	50
Hank Bauer	46
Pee Wee Reese	46
Gil McDougald	45
Phil Rizzuto	45
Lou Gehrig	43

Home Runs

Mickey Mantle	18
Babe Ruth	15
Yogi Berra	12
Duke Snider	11
Lou Gehrig	10
Reggie Jackson	10
Joe DiMaggio	8
Frank Robinson	8
Bill Skowron	8
Hank Bauer	7
Goose Goslin	7
Gil McDougald	7
Chase Utley	7

Runs

Mickey Mantle	42
Yogi Berra	41
Babe Ruth	37
Derek Jeter	32
Lou Gehrig	30
Joe DiMaggio	27
Roger Maris	26
Elston Howard	25
Gil McDougald	23
Jackie Robinson	22

Stolen Bases

Lou Brock	14
Eddie Collins	14
Frank Chance	10
Dave Lopes	10
Phil Rizzuto	10
Frankie Frisch	9
Kenny Lofton	9
Honus Wagner	9
Johnny Evers	8
Roberto Alomar	7
Rickey Henderson	7
Pepper Martin	7
Joe Morgan	7
Joe Tinker	7

Pitching Leaders

Games Pitched

Mariano Rivera	24
Whitey Ford	22
Mike Stanton	20
Rollie Fingers	16
Jeff Nelson	16
Allie Reynolds	15
Bob Turley	15
Clay Carroll	14
Clem Labine	13
Andy Pettitte	13
Mark Wohlers	13
Waite Hoyt	12
Catfish Hunter	12
Art Nehf	12

Wins

Whitey Ford	10
Bob Gibson	7
Allie Reynolds	7
Red Ruffing	7
Chief Bender	6
Lefty Gomez	6
Waite Hoyt	6
Three Finger Brown	5
Jack Coombs	5
Catfish Hunter	5
Christy Mathewson	5
Herb Pennock	5
Andy Pettitte	5
Vic Raschi	5

Strikeouts

Whitey Ford	94
Bob Gibson	92
Allie Reynolds	62
Sandy Koufax	61
Red Ruffing	61
Chief Bender	59
George Earnshaw	56
Andy Pettitte	56
John Smoltz	52
Roger Clemens	49
Waite Hoyt	49
Christy Mathewson	48
Bob Turley	46

Saves

Mariano Rivera	11
Rollie Fingers	6
Johnny Murphy	4
Robb Nen	4
Allie Reynolds	4
John Wetteland	4
Roy Face	3
Neftali Feliz	3
Firpo Marberry	3
Will McEnaney	3
Tug McGraw	3
Jonathan Papelbon	3
Herb Pennock	3
Troy Percival	3
Sergio Romo	3
Kent Tekulve	3
Todd Worrell	3

All-Star Baseball Games, 1933-2012

Year	Winner, score	Host team	Year	Winner, score	Host team	Year	Winner, score	Host team
1933*	American, 4-2	Chicago (AL)	1960*	National, 5-3	Kansas City	1985	National, 6-1	Minnesota
1934*	American, 9-7	New York (NL)	1960*	National, 6-0	New York (AL)	1986	American, 3-2	Houston
1935*	American, 4-1	Cleveland	1961*	National, 5-4[3]	San Francisco	1987	National, 2-0[5]	Oakland
1936*	National, 4-3	Boston (NL)	1961*	Called—rain, 1-1	Boston	1988	American, 2-1	Cincinnati
1937*	American, 8-3	Washington	1962*	National, 3-1[3]	Washington	1989	American, 5-3	California
1938*	National, 4-1	Cincinnati	1962*	American, 9-4	Chicago (NL)	1990	American, 2-0	Chicago (NL)
1939*	American, 3-1	New York (AL)	1963*	National, 5-3	Cleveland	1991	American, 4-2	Toronto
1940*	National, 4-0	St. Louis (NL)	1964*	National, 7-4	New York (NL)	1992	American, 13-6	San Diego
1941*	American, 7-5	Detroit	1965*	National, 6-5	Minnesota	1993	American, 9-3	Baltimore
1942	American, 3-1	New York (NL)	1966*	National, 2-1[3]	St. Louis	1994	National, 8-7[3]	Pittsburgh
1943	American, 5-3	Philadelphia (AL)	1967*	National, 2-1[4]	California	1995	National, 3-2	Texas
1944	National, 7-1	Pittsburgh	1968	National, 1-0	Houston	1996	National, 6-0	Philadelphia
1945	Not played		1969*	National, 9-3	Washington	1997	American, 3-1	Cleveland
1946*	American, 12-0	Boston (AL)	1970	National, 5-4[2]	Cincinnati	1998	American, 13-8	Colorado
1947*	American, 2-1	Chicago (NL)	1971	American, 6-4	Detroit	1999	American, 4-1	Boston
1948*	American, 5-2	St. Louis (AL)	1972	National, 4-3[3]	Atlanta	2000	American, 6-3	Atlanta
1949*	American, 11-7	Brooklyn	1973	National, 7-1	Kansas City	2001	American, 4-1	Seattle
1950*	National, 4-3[1]	Chicago (AL)	1974	National, 7-2	Pittsburgh	2002	Tie, 7-7[6]	Milwaukee
1951*	National, 8-3	Detroit	1975	National, 6-3	Milwaukee	2003	American, 7-6[7]	Chicago (AL)
1952*	National, 3-2	Philadelphia (NL)	1976	National, 7-1	Philadelphia	2004	American, 9-4	Houston
1953*	National, 5-1	Cincinnati	1977	National, 7-5	New York (AL)	2005	American, 7-5	Detroit
1954*	American, 11-9	Cleveland	1978	National, 7-3	San Diego	2006	American, 3-2	Pittsburgh
1955*	National, 6-5[2]	Milwaukee	1979	National, 7-6	Seattle	2007	American, 5-4	San Francisco
1956*	National, 7-3	Washington	1980	National, 4-2	Los Angeles (NL)	2008	American, 4-3[4]	New York (AL)
1957*	American, 6-5	St. Louis	1981	National, 5-4	Cleveland	2009	American, 4-3	St. Louis
1958*	American, 4-3	Baltimore	1982	National, 4-1	Montréal	2010	National, 3-1	Los Angeles (AL)
1959*	National, 5-4	Pittsburgh	1983	American, 13-3	Chicago (AL)	2011	National, 5-1	Arizona
1959*	American, 5-3	Los Angeles (NL)	1984	National, 3-1	San Francisco	2012	National, 8-0	Kansas City

*Day game. (1) 14 innings. (2) 12 innings. (3) 10 innings. (4) 15 innings. (5) 13 innings. (6) Commissioner's decision—game called in the 11th inning when both teams ran out of pitchers. (7) Under rule change beginning in 2003, league winning All-Star game earned World Series home-field advantage.

Baseball Stadiums

National League

Team	Stadium (year opened)	Surface	Distances (ft)			Seating capacity[1]
			LF	Center	RF	
Arizona Diamondbacks	Chase Field (1998)	Grass	330	407	335	48,635
Atlanta Braves	Turner Field (1997)	Grass	335	400	330	49,481
Chicago Cubs	Wrigley Field (1914)	Grass	355	400	353	41,159
Cincinnati Reds	Great American Ball Park (2003)	Grass	328	404	325	42,319
Colorado Rockies	Coors Field (1995)	Grass	347	415	350	50,398
Houston Astros	Minute Maid Park at Union Station (2000)	Grass	315	435	326	40,963
Los Angeles Dodgers	Dodger Stadium (1962)	Grass	330	395	330	56,000
Miami Marlins	Marlins Park (2012)	Grass	344	418	335	37,442
Milwaukee Brewers	Miller Park (2001)	Grass	344	400	345	41,900
New York Mets	Citi Field (2009)	Grass	335	408	330	41,800
Philadelphia Phillies	Citizens Bank Park (2004)	Grass	329	401	330	43,651
Pittsburgh Pirates	PNC Park at North Shore (2001)	Grass	325	399	320	38,362
St. Louis Cardinals	Busch Stadium (2006)	Grass	336	400	335	43,975
San Diego Padres	Petco Park (2004)	Grass	336	396	322	42,691
San Francisco Giants	AT&T Park (2000)	Grass	339	399	309	41,915
Washington Nationals	Nationals Park (2008)	Grass	336	402	335	41,525

American League

Team	Stadium (year opened)	Surface	LF	Center	RF	Seating capacity[1]
Baltimore Orioles	Oriole Park at Camden Yards (1992)	Grass	333	400	318	45,971
Boston Red Sox	Fenway Park (1912)	Grass	310	390	302	37,067[2]
Chicago White Sox	U.S. Cellular Field (1991)	Grass	330	400	335	40,615
Cleveland Indians	Progressive Field (1994)	Grass	325	405	325	43,429
Detroit Tigers	Comerica Park (2000)	Grass	345	420	330	41,255
Kansas City Royals	Kauffman Stadium (1973)	Grass	330	410	330	37,903
Los Angeles Angels	Angel Stadium of Anaheim (1966)	Grass	333	404	333	45,987
Minnesota Twins	Target Field (2010)	Grass	339	404	328	39,500
New York Yankees	Yankee Stadium (2009)	Grass	318	408	314	50,329
Oakland Athletics	Oakland Alameda County Coliseum (1968)	Grass	330	400	330	35,067
Seattle Mariners	Safeco Field (1999)	Grass	331	405	326	47,860
Tampa Bay Rays	Tropicana Field (1990)	Astroturf	315	404	322	34,078
Texas Rangers	Rangers Ballpark in Arlington (1994)	Grass	332	400	325	48,194
Toronto Blue Jays	Rogers Centre (1989)	Turf	328	400	328	49,278

(1) As of 2012 season. (2) For day games; night game capacity is 37,495.

Major League Franchise Shifts and Additions

1953: Boston Braves (NL) became Milwaukee Braves.
1954: St. Louis Browns (AL) became Baltimore Orioles.
1955: Philadelphia Athletics (AL) became Kansas City Athletics.
1958: New York Giants (NL) became San Francisco Giants.
1958: Brooklyn Dodgers (NL) became L.A. Dodgers.
1961: Washington Senators (AL) became Minnesota Twins.
1961: L.A. Angels (renamed California Angels in 1965 and Anaheim Angels in 1997) enfranchised by the American League.
1961: Washington Senators enfranchised by the American League (a new team, replacing the former Washington club, whose franchise was moved to Minneapolis-St. Paul).
1962: Houston Colt .45's (renamed the Houston Astros in 1965) enfranchised by the National League.
1962: New York Mets enfranchised by the National League.
1966: Milwaukee Braves (NL) became Atlanta Braves.
1968: Kansas City Athletics (AL) became Oakland Athletics.

1969: Kansas City Royals and Seattle Pilots enfranchised by the American League; Montréal Expos and San Diego Padres enfranchised by the National League.
1970: Seattle Pilots (AL) became Milwaukee Brewers.
1971: Washington Senators (AL) became Texas Rangers (Dallas-Fort Worth area).
1977: Toronto Blue Jays and Seattle Mariners enfranchised by the American League.
1993: Colorado Rockies (Denver) and Florida Marlins (renamed Miami Marlins in 2012) enfranchised by the National League.
1998: Tampa Bay Devil Rays (renamed Tampa Bay Rays in 2007) began play in the American League; Arizona Diamondbacks (Phoenix) began play in the National League (both teams enfranchised in 1995). Milwaukee Brewers moved from the AL to the NL.
2005: Montréal Expos (NL) became Washington Nationals; Anaheim Angels became Los Angeles Angels of Anaheim.

Little League World Series, 1947-2012

The Little League World Series is played annually in Williamsport, PA.

Year	Winning team; opponent	Score	Year	Winning team; opponent	Score
1947	Williamsport, PA; Lock Haven, PA	16-7	1980	Taiwan; Tampa, FL	4-3
1948	Lock Haven, PA; St. Petersburg, FL	6-5	1981	Taiwan; Tampa, FL	4-2
1949	Hammonton, NJ; Pensacola, FL	5-0	1982	Kirkland, WA; Taiwan	6-0
1950	Houston, TX; Bridgeport, CT	2-1	1983	Marietta, GA; Dominican Republic	3-1
1951	Stamford, CT; Austin, TX	3-0	1984	South Korea; Altamonte Springs, FL	6-2
1952	Norwalk, CT; Monongahela, PA	4-3	1985	South Korea; Mexico	7-1
1953	Birmingham, AL; Schenectady, NY	1-0	1986	Taiwan; Tucson, AZ	12-0
1954	Schenectady, NY; Colton, CA	7-5	1987	Taiwan; Irvine, CA	21-1
1955	Morrisville, PA; Merchantville, NJ	4-3	1988	Taiwan; Pearl City, HI	10-0
1956	Roswell, NM; Delaware, NJ	3-1	1989	Trumbull, CT; Chinese Taipei	5-2
1957	Mexico; La Mesa, CA	4-0	1990	Taiwan; Shippensburg, PA	9-0
1958	Mexico; Kankakee, IL	10-1	1991	Taiwan; Danville, CA	11-0
1959	Hamtramck, MI; Auburn, CA	12-0	1992	Long Beach, CA; Philippines	6-0[1]
1960	Levittown, PA; Ft. Worth, TX	5-0	1993	Long Beach, CA; Panama	3-2
1961	El Cajon, CA; El Campo, TX	4-2	1994	Venezuela; Northridge, CA	4-3
1962	San Jose, CA; Kankakee, IL	3-0	1995	Taiwan; Spring, TX	17-3
1963	Granada Hills, CA; Stratford, CT	2-1	1996	Taiwan; Cranston, RI	13-3
1964	Staten Island, NY; Mexico	4-0	1997	Mexico; Mission Viejo, CA	5-4
1965	Windsor Locks, CT; Ontario, Canada	3-1	1998	Toms River, NJ; Japan	12-9
1966	Houston, TX; W. New York, NJ	8-2	1999	Japan; Phenix City, AL	5-0
1967	Tokyo, Japan; Chicago, IL	4-1	2000	Venezuela; Bellaire, TX	3-2
1968	Osaka, Japan; Richmond, VA	1-0	2001	Japan; Apopka, FL	2-1
1969	Taiwan; Santa Clara, CA	5-0	2002	Louisville, KY; Japan	1-0
1970	Wayne, NJ; Campbell, CA	2-0	2003	Tokyo, Japan; East Boynton Beach, FL	10-1
1971	Taiwan; Gary, IN	12-3	2004	Curaçao; Conejo Valley of Thousand Oaks, CA	5-2
1972	Taiwan; Hammond, IN	6-0	2005	Ewa Beach, HI; Curaçao, Neth. Antilles	7-6
1973	Taiwan; Tucson, AZ	12-0	2006	Columbus, GA; Kawaguchi City, Japan	2-1
1974	Taiwan; Red Bluff, CA	12-1	2007	Macon, GA; Tokyo, Japan	3-2
1975	Lakewood, NJ; Tampa, FL	4-3	2008	Waipahu, HI; Mexico	12-3
1976	Tokyo, Japan; Campbell, CA	10-3	2009	Chula Vista, CA; Taiwan	6-3
1977	Taiwan; El Cajon, CA	7-2	2010	Tokyo, Japan; Waipahu, HI	4-1
1978	Taiwan; Danville, CA	11-1	2011	Huntington Beach, CA; Hamamatsu, Japan	2-1
1979	Taiwan; Campbell, CA	2-1	2012	Tokyo, Japan; Goodlettsville, TN	12-2

(1) Philippines won 15-4 but was disqualified for using ineligible players. Long Beach was awarded title by forfeit 6-0 (1 run per inning).

Manager of the Year, 1983-2011

1983	(NL) Tommy Lasorda, L.A.	1993	(NL) Dusty Baker, San Francisco	2002	(NL) Tony La Russa, St. Louis
	(AL) Tony La Russa, Chicago		(AL) Gene Lamont, Chicago		(AL) Mike Scioscia, Anaheim
1984	(NL) Jim Frey, Chicago	1994	(NL) Felipe Alou, Montréal	2003	(NL) Jack McKeon, Florida
	(AL) Sparky Anderson, Detroit		(AL) Buck Showalter, NY		(AL) Tony Pena, Kansas City
1985	(NL) Whitey Herzog, St. Louis	1995	(NL) Don Baylor, Colorado	2004	(NL) Bobby Cox, Atlanta
	(AL) Bobby Cox, Toronto		(AL) Lou Piniella, Seattle		(AL) Buck Showalter, Texas
1986	(NL) Hal Lanier, Houston	1996	(NL) Bruce Bochy, San Diego	2005	(NL) Bobby Cox, Atlanta
	(AL) John McNamara, Boston		(AL) (tie) Joe Torre, NY;		(AL) Ozzie Guillen, Chicago
1987	(NL) Buck Rodgers, Montréal		Johnny Oates, Texas	2006	(NL) Joe Girardi, Florida
	(AL) Sparky Anderson, Detroit	1997	(NL) Dusty Baker, San Francisco		(AL) Jim Leyland, Detroit
1988	(NL) Tommy Lasorda, L.A.		(AL) Davey Johnson, Baltimore	2007	(NL) Bob Melvin, Arizona
	(AL) Tony La Russa, Oakland	1998	(NL) Larry Dierker, Houston		(AL) Eric Wedge, Cleveland
1989	(NL) Don Zimmer, Chicago		(AL) Joe Torre, NY	2008	(NL) Lou Piniella, Chicago
	(AL) Frank Robinson, Baltimore	1999	(NL) Jack McKeon, Cincinnati		(AL) Joe Maddon, Tampa Bay
1990	(NL) Jim Leyland, Pittsburgh		(AL) Jimy Williams, Boston	2009	(NL) Jim Tracy, Colorado
	(AL) Jeff Torborg, Chicago	2000	(NL) Dusty Baker, San		(AL) Mike Scioscia, L.A.
1991	(NL) Bobby Cox, Atlanta		Francisco	2010	(NL) Bud Black, San Diego
	(AL) Tom Kelly, Minnesota		(AL) Jerry Manuel, Chicago		(AL) Ron Gardenhire, Minnesota
1992	(NL) Jim Leyland, Pittsburgh	2001	(NL) Larry Bowa, Philadelphia	2011	(NL) Kirk Gibson, Arizona
	(AL) Tony La Russa, Oakland		(AL) Lou Piniella, Seattle		(AL) Joe Maddon, Tampa Bay

National Baseball Hall of Fame and Museum, Cooperstown, NY

Player must generally be retired for five complete seasons before being eligible for induction. Four players—Babe Ruth (1936), Lou Gehrig (1939), Joe DiMaggio (1955), and Roberto Clemente (1973)—were inducted less than five years after retirement or, in Clemente's case, death. # = Players chosen in first year of Hall of Fame eligibility or under special circumstances earlier. * = 2012 inductee.

#Aaron, Hank "The Hammer"	Connor, Roger	Hartnett, Gabby	Mathews, Eddie	Selee, Frank
Alexander, Grover Cleveland "Old Pete"	Cooper, Andy	Harvey, Doug	Mathewson, Christy[1]	Sewell, Joe
	Coveleski, Stan	Heilmann, Harry	#Mays, Willie	Simmons, Al
Alomar, Roberto	Crawford, Sam	#Henderson, Rickey	Mazeroski, Bill	Sisler, George
Alston, Walt	Cronin, Joe	Herman, Billy	McCarthy, Joe	Slaughter, Enos
Anderson, George "Sparky"	Cummings, W. A. "Candy"	Herzog, Whitey	McCarthy, Thomas	Smith, Hilton
Anson, Cap	Cuyler, Hazen "Kiki"	Hill, Pete	#McCovey, Willie	#Smith, Ozzie
Aparicio, Luis	Dandridge, Ray	Hooper, Harry	McGinnity, Joe	Snider, Duke
Appling, Luke	Davis, George "Gorgeous"	Hornsby, Rogers	McGowan, Bill	Southworth, Billy
Ashburn, Richie	Dawson, Andre	Hoyt, Waite	McGraw, John	#Spahn, Warren
Averill, Earl	Day, Leon	Hubbard, Cal	McKechnie, Bill	Spalding, Albert
Baker, Frank "Home Run"	Dean, Jay Hanna "Dizzy"	Hubbell, Carl	McPhee, John "Bid"	Speaker, Tris
Bancroft, Dave	Delahanty, Ed	Huggins, Miller	Medwick, Joe	#Stargell, Willie
#Banks, Ernie	Dickey, Bill	Hulbert, William	Mendez, Jose	Stearnes, Norman "Turkey"
Barlick, Al	Dihigo, Martín	Hunter, James "Catfish"	Miller, Jon	
Barrow, Edward G.	DiMaggio, Joe	Irvin, Monte	Mize, Johnny	Stengel, Casey
Beckley, Jake	#Doby, Larry	#Jackson, Reggie	#Molitor, Paul	Sutter, Bruce
Bell, James "Cool Papa"	Doerr, Bobby	Jackson, Travis	#Morgan, Joe	Suttles, George "Mule"
#Bench, Johnny	Dreyfuss, Barney	Jenkins, Ferguson	#Murray, Eddie	Sutton, Don
Bender, Charles "Chief"	Drysdale, Don	Jennings, Hugh	#Musial, Stan	Taylor, Ben
Berra, Lawrence "Yogi"	Duffy, Hugh	Johnson, Byron "Ban"	Newhouser, Hal	Terry, Bill
Blyleven, Bert	Durocher, Leo	Johnson, Walter[1]	Nichols, Kid	Thompson, Sam
#Boggs, Wade	#Eckersley, Dennis	Johnson, William "Judy"	Niekro, Phil	Tinker, Joe
Bottomley, Jim	Evans, Billy	Joss, Addie	O'Malley, Walter	Torriente, Cristobal
Boudreau, Lou	Evers, John	#Kaline, Al	O'Rourke, James	Traynor, Harold J. "Pie"
Bresnahan, Roger	Ewing, Buck	Keefe, Timothy	Ott, Mel	Vance, Arthur "Dazzy"
#Brett, George	Faber, Urban "Red"	Keeler, William	Paige, Satchel	Vaughan, Joseph "Arky"
#Brock, Lou	#Feller, Bob	Kell, George	#Palmer, Jim	Veeck, Bill
Brouthers, Dan	Ferrell, Rick	Kelley, Joe	Pennock, Herb	Waddell, Rube
Brown, Mordecai "Three Finger"	Fingers, Rollie	Kelly, George	Perez, Tony	Wagner, Honus[1]
	Fisk, Carlton	Kelly, King	Perry, Gaylord	Wallace, Roderick "Bobby"
Brown, Ray	Flick, Elmer H.	Killebrew, Harmon	Peters, Nick	
Brown, Willard	Ford, Whitey	Kiner, Ralph	Plank, Ed	Walsh, Ed
Bulkeley, Morgan C.	Foster, Andrew "Rube"	Klein, Chuck	Pompez, Alex	Waner, Lloyd
Bunning, Jim	Foster, Bill	Klem, Bill	Posey, Cum(berland)	Waner, Paul
Burkett, Jesse C.	Fox, Nellie	#Koufax, Sandy	#Puckett, Kirby	Ward, John
Campanella, Roy	Foxx, Jimmie	Kubek, Tony	Radbourn, Charlie	Weaver, Earl
#Carew, Rod	Frick, Ford	Kuhn, Bowie	Reese, Pee Wee	Weiss, George
Carey, Max	Frisch, Frank	Lajoie, Napoleon	Rice, Jim	Welch, Mickey
#Carlton, Steve	Galvin, James "Pud"	Landis, Kenesaw M.	Rice, Sam	Wells, Willie
Carter, Gary	#Gehrig, Lou	*Larkin, Barry	Rickey, Branch	Wheat, Zach
Cartwright, Alexander	Gehringer, Charles	Lasorda, Tom	#Ripken, Cal, Jr.	White, Sol
Cepeda, Orlando	#Gibson, Bob	Lazzeri, Tony	Rixey, Eppa	Wilhelm, Hoyt
Chadwick, Henry	Gibson, Josh	Lemon, Bob	Rizzuto, Phil "Scooter"	Wilkinson, J. L.
Chance, Frank	Giles, Warren	Leonard, Buck	Roberts, Robin	Williams, Billy
Chandler, Albert "Happy"	Gillick, Pat	Lindstrom, Fred	#Robinson, Brooks	Williams, Dick
Charleston, Oscar	Gomez, Lefty	Lloyd, Pop	#Robinson, Frank	Williams, Joe "Smokey Joe"
Chesbro, John	Gordon, Joe	Lombardi, Ernie	#Robinson, Jackie	
Chylak, Nestor	Goslin, Leon "Goose"	Lopez, Al	Robinson, Wilbert	#Williams, Ted
Clarke, Fred	Gossage, Rich	Lyons, Ted	Rogan, Joe "Bullet"	Willis, Vic
Clarkson, John	Grant, Frank	Mack, Connie	Roush, Edd	Wilson, Hack
#Clemente, Roberto	Greenberg, Hank	Mackey, James "Biz"	Ruffing, Red	Wilson, Jud
Cobb, Ty[1]	Griffith, Clark	MacPhail, Larry	Rusie, Amos	#Winfield, Dave
Cochrane, Mickey	Grimes, Burleigh	MacPhail, Lee	#Ruth, Babe[1]	Wright, George
Collins, Eddie	Grove, Lefty	Madden, Bill	#Ryan, Nolan	Wright, Harry
Collins, James	#Gwynn, Tony	Manley, Effa	Sandberg, Ryne	Wynn, Early
Combs, Earle	Hafey, Charles "Chick"	#Mantle, Mickey	*Santo, Ron	#Yastrzemski, Carl
Comiskey, Charles A.	Haines, Jesee	Manush, Henry	Santop, Louis	Yawkey, Tom
Conlan, John "Jocko"	Hamilton, Billy	Maranville, Walter "Rabbit"	Schalk, Ray	Young, Cy
Connolly, Thomas H.	Hanlon, Ned	Marichal, Juan	#Schmidt, Mike	Youngs, Ross
	Harridge, Will	Marquard, Rube	Schoendienst, Red	#Yount, Robin
	Harris, Bucky		#Seaver, Tom	

(1) Player inducted in 1936, the year the Hall of Fame began.

BASKETBALL

Miami Heat Win 2012 NBA Title After Shortened Season

LeBron James and Dwyane Wade led the Miami Heat to the NBA Championship over the Oklahoma City Thunder with a hard-fought, four games to one victory in the NBA Finals. The superstar James, who grabbed headlines when he signed with Miami in 2010, averaged 28.6 points per game (PPG) and was named the Finals MVP. He also recorded a triple-double in the decisive Game 5 June 21, 2012, at American Airlines Arena in Miami, FL, with 26 points, 11 rebounds, and 13 assists.

Oklahoma City's 23-year-old forward Kevin Durant, who topped all scorers in the Finals with 30.6 PPG, poured in 36 in the Thunder's 105-94 win in the Finals opener June 12, 2012, at Chesapeake Energy Arena in Oklahoma City. But the Heat then reeled off four straight wins for the second league title in franchise history.

The Thunder advanced to the Finals after a four-game win streak in the Western Conference championship that erased a two-game lead by the top-seeded San Antonio Spurs in their best-of-seven matchup. And Miami faced elimination against the Boston Celtics in the Eastern Conference series, but James's 45-point Game 6 on June 7, 2012, at TD Garden in Boston powered a 98-79 Heat victory that tied the series, and the Heat captured Game 7 two days later in Miami.

Oklahoma's Durant led the league in scoring (28.0 PPG) for the third straight year and was runner-up in the regular-season MVP voting, while LeBron James won his third regular-season MVP award. One of the more ignominious stories of the NBA season was the Charlotte Bobcats, who set a league record for lowest winning percentage at .106 (7-59) and ended the season with a 23-game losing streak.

The NBA began an abbreviated, 66-game regular season on Dec. 25, 2011, following contentious labor negotiations. The league had announced a lockout July 1, 2011, when the collective bargaining agreement between team owners and players expired. NBA Commissioner David Stern announced Oct. 28, 2011, that all games would be called off through Nov. After nearly five months of negotiations, owners and players agreed to a new deal Nov. 26, which was ratified Dec. 8, 2011.

Final Standings, 2011-12

(playoff seeding in parentheses)

Eastern Conference

Atlantic Division	W	L	PCT	GB
Boston (4)	39	27	.591	—
New York (7)	36	30	.545	3
Philadelphia (8)	35	31	.530	4
Toronto	23	43	.348	16
New Jersey	22	44	.333	17

Central Division	W	L	PCT	GB
Chicago (1)	50	16	.758	—
Indiana (3)	42	24	.636	8
Milwaukee	31	35	.470	19
Detroit	25	41	.379	25
Cleveland	21	45	.318	29

Southeast Division	W	L	PCT	GB
Miami (2)	46	20	.697	—
Atlanta (5)	40	26	.606	6
Orlando (6)	37	29	.561	9
Washington	20	46	.303	26
Charlotte	7	59	.106	39

Western Conference

Northwest Division	W	L	PCT	GB
Oklahoma City (2)	47	19	.712	—
Denver (6)	38	28	.576	9
Utah (8)	36	30	.545	11
Portland	28	38	.424	19
Minnesota	26	40	.394	21

Pacific Division	W	L	PCT	GB
L.A. Lakers (3)	41	25	.621	—
L.A. Clippers (5)	40	26	.606	1
Phoenix	33	33	.500	8
Golden State	23	43	.348	18
Sacramento	22	44	.333	19

Southwest Division	W	L	PCT	GB
San Antonio (1)	50	16	.758	—
Memphis (4)	41	25	.621	9
Dallas (7)	36	30	.545	14
Houston	34	32	.515	16
New Orleans	21	45	.318	29

Note: Dallas earned the no. 7 seed in the West over Utah due to a better head-to-head record (3-1).

NBA Playoff Results, 2012

Eastern Conference
Philadelphia defeated Chicago, 4 games to 2
Miami defeated New York, 4 games to 1
Indiana defeated Orlando, 4 games to 1
Boston defeated Atlanta, 4 games to 2
Miami defeated Indiana, 4 games to 2
Boston defeated Philadelphia, 4 games to 3
Miami defeated Boston, 4 games to 3

Western Conference
San Antonio defeated Utah, 4 games to 0
Oklahoma City defeated Dallas, 4 games to 0
L.A. Lakers defeated Denver, 4 games to 3
L.A. Clippers defeated Memphis, 4 games to 3
San Antonio defeated L.A. Clippers, 4 games to 0
Oklahoma City defeated L.A. Lakers, 4 games to 1
Oklahoma City defeated San Antonio, 4 games to 2

Championship
Miami defeated Oklahoma City, 4 games to 1 (94-105, 100-96, 91-85, 104-98, 121-106)

NBA Regular Season Individual Highs, 2011-12

Minutes, game: 57, Gordon Hayward, Utah v. Atlanta, Mar. 25 (4 OT)
Points, game: 57, Deron Williams, New Jersey v. Charlotte, Mar. 4
Field goals, game: 19, Kevin Durant, Oklahoma City v. Denver, Feb. 19
Field goal attempts, game: 34, Kevin Durant, Oklahoma City v. L.A. Lakers, Apr. 22
3-pointers, game: 9, Nicolas Batum, Portland v. Denver, Feb. 4; Ben Gordon, Detroit v. Denver, Mar. 21; Jason Richardson, Orlando v. Milwaukee, Feb. 11.
3-pt. attempts, game: 15, Nicolas Batum, Portland v. Denver, Feb. 4; Randy Foye, L.A. Clippers v. Dallas, Apr. 2.
Free throws, game: 21, Dwight Howard, Orlando v. Golden State, Jan. 12; Deron Williams, New Jersey v. Charlotte, Mar. 4
Free throw attempts, game: 39, Dwight Howard, Orlando v. Golden State, Jan. 12

Rebounds, game: 30, Andrew Bynum, L.A. Lakers v. San Antonio, Apr. 11
Assists, game: 20, Rajon Rondo, Boston v. New York, Mar. 4; Rajon Rondo, Boston v. Atlanta, Apr. 11; Deron Williams, New Jersey v. Golden State, Mar. 30
Steals, game: 8, Tony Allen, Memphis v. Cleveland, Apr. 23; Ty Lawson, Denver v. Portland, Dec. 29; Paul Millsap, Utah v. Minnesota, Mar. 15; Chris Paul, L.A. Clippers v. New Orleans, Apr. 22.
Blocks, game: 11, Serge Ibaka, Oklahoma City v. Denver, Feb. 19
Minutes played, season: 2,546, Kevin Durant, Oklahoma City
Off. rebounds, season: 265, DeMarcus Cousins, Sacramento
Def. rebounds, season: 585, Dwight Howard, Orlando
Personal fouls, season: 257, DeMarcus Cousins, Sacramento

NBA Finals MVP, 1969-2012

1969	Jerry West, L.A. Lakers	1983	Moses Malone, Philadelphia
1970	Willis Reed, New York	1984	Larry Bird, Boston
1971	Lew Alcindor (Kareem Abdul-	1985	Kareem Abdul-Jabbar, L.A. Lakers
	Jabbar), Milwaukee	1986	Larry Bird, Boston
1972	Wilt Chamberlain, L.A. Lakers	1987	Magic Johnson, L.A. Lakers
1973	Willis Reed, New York	1988	James Worthy, L.A. Lakers
1974	John Havlicek, Boston	1989	Joe Dumars, Detroit
1975	Rick Barry, Golden State	1990	Isiah Thomas, Detroit
1976	JoJo White, Boston	1991	Michael Jordan, Chicago
1977	Bill Walton, Portland	1992	Michael Jordan, Chicago
1978	Wes Unseld, Washington	1993	Michael Jordan, Chicago
1979	Dennis Johnson, Seattle	1994	Hakeem Olajuwon, Houston
1980	Magic Johnson, L.A. Lakers	1995	Hakeem Olajuwon, Houston
1981	Cedric Maxwell, Boston	1996	Michael Jordan, Chicago
1982	Magic Johnson, L.A. Lakers	1997	Michael Jordan, Chicago

1998	Michael Jordan, Chicago
1999	Tim Duncan, San Antonio
2000	Shaquille O'Neal, L.A. Lakers
2001	Shaquille O'Neal, L.A. Lakers
2002	Shaquille O'Neal, L.A. Lakers
2003	Tim Duncan, San Antonio
2004	Chauncey Billups, Detroit
2005	Tim Duncan, San Antonio
2006	Dwyane Wade, Miami
2007	Tony Parker, San Antonio
2008	Paul Pierce, Boston
2009	Kobe Bryant, L.A. Lakers
2010	Kobe Bryant, L.A. Lakers
2011	Dirk Nowitzki, Dallas
2012	LeBron James, Miami

NBA Finals All-Time Statistical Leaders

(At the end of the 2012 NBA Finals. * = Active in 2011-12 season. Minimum 10 games played.)

Scoring average leader	GP	FG	FT	PTS	AVG	Scoring average leader	GP	FG	FT	PTS	AVG
Rick Barry	10	138	87	363	36.3	*Dwyane Wade	17	164	140	480	28.2
Michael Jordan	35	438	258	1176	33.6	Hakeem Olajuwon	17	187	91	467	27.5
Jerry West	55	612	455	1677	30.5	Elgin Baylor	44	442	227	1161	26.4
Shaquille O'Neal	30	349	185	865	28.8	Julius Erving	22	216	128	561	25.5
Bob Pettit	25	241	227	709	28.4	*Kobe Bryant	37	333	223	937	25.3

Games played		Rebounds		Assists	
Bill Russell	70	Bill Russell	1,718	Magic Johnson	584
Sam Jones	64	Wilt Chamberlain	862	Bob Cousy	400
Kareem Abdul-Jabbar	56	Elgin Baylor	593	Bill Russell	315
Jerry West	55	Kareem Abdul-Jabbar	507	Jerry West	306
Tom Heinsohn	52	Tom Heinsohn	473	Dennis Johnson	228

NBA Scoring Leaders, 1947-2012

Year	Player, team	PTS	AVG	Year	Player, team	PTS	AVG
1947	Joe Fulks, Philadelphia	1,389	23.2	1980	George Gervin, San Antonio	2,585	33.1
1948	Max Zaslofsky, Chicago	1,007	21.0	1981	Adrian Dantley, Utah	2,452	30.7
1949	George Mikan, Minneapolis	1,698	28.3	1982	George Gervin, San Antonio	2,551	32.3
1950	George Mikan, Minneapolis	1,865	27.4	1983	Alex English, Denver	2,326	28.4
1951	George Mikan, Minneapolis	1,932	28.4	1984	Adrian Dantley, Utah	2,418	30.6
1952	Paul Arizin, Philadelphia	1,674	25.4	1985	Bernard King, New York	1,809	32.9
1953	Neil Johnston, Philadelphia	1,564	22.3	1986	Dominique Wilkins, Atlanta	2,366	30.3
1954	Neil Johnston, Philadelphia	1,759	24.4	1987	Michael Jordan, Chicago	3,041	37.1
1955	Neil Johnston, Philadelphia	1,631	22.7	1988	Michael Jordan, Chicago	2,868	35.0
1956	Bob Pettit, St. Louis	1,849	25.7	1989	Michael Jordan, Chicago	2,633	32.5
1957	Paul Arizin, Philadelphia	1,817	25.6	1990	Michael Jordan, Chicago	2,753	33.6
1958	George Yardley, Detroit	2,001	27.8	1991	Michael Jordan, Chicago	2,580	31.5
1959	Bob Pettit, St. Louis	2,105	29.2	1992	Michael Jordan, Chicago	2,404	30.1
1960	Wilt Chamberlain, Philadelphia	2,707	37.9	1993	Michael Jordan, Chicago	2,541	32.6
1961	Wilt Chamberlain, Philadelphia	3,033	38.4	1994	David Robinson, San Antonio	2,383	29.8
1962	Wilt Chamberlain, Philadelphia	4,029	50.4	1995	Shaquille O'Neal, Orlando	2,315	29.3
1963	Wilt Chamberlain, San Francisco	3,586	44.8	1996	Michael Jordan, Chicago	2,465	30.4
1964	Wilt Chamberlain, San Francisco	2,948	36.5	1997	Michael Jordan, Chicago	2,431	29.6
1965	Wilt Chamberlain, San Francisco, Phil.	2,534	34.7	1998	Michael Jordan, Chicago	2,357	28.7
1966	Wilt Chamberlain, Philadelphia	2,649	33.5	1999	Allen Iverson, Philadelphia	1,284	26.8
1967	Rick Barry, San Francisco	2,775	35.6	2000	Shaquille O'Neal, L.A. Lakers	2,344	29.7
1968	Dave Bing, Detroit	2,142	27.1	2001	Allen Iverson, Philadelphia	2,207	31.1
1969	Elvin Hayes, San Diego	2,327	28.4	2002	Allen Iverson, Philadelphia	1,883	31.4
1970	Jerry West, L.A. Lakers	2,309	31.2	2003	Tracy McGrady, Orlando	2,407	32.1
1971	Lew Alcindor (Abdul-Jabbar), Milwaukee	2,596	31.7	2004	Tracy McGrady, Orlando	1,878	28.0
1972	Kareem Abdul-Jabbar, Milwaukee	2,822	34.8	2005	Allen Iverson, Philadelphia	2,302	30.7
1973	Nate Archibald, Kansas City-Omaha	2,719	34.0	2006	Kobe Bryant, L.A. Lakers	2,832	35.4
1974	Bob McAdoo, Buffalo	2,261	30.6	2007	Kobe Bryant, L.A. Lakers	2,430	31.6
1975	Bob McAdoo, Buffalo	2,831	34.5	2008	LeBron James, Cleveland	2,250	30.0
1976	Bob McAdoo, Buffalo	2,427	31.1	2009	Dwyane Wade, Miami	2,386	30.2
1977	Pete Maravich, New Orleans	2,273	31.1	2010	Kevin Durant, Oklahoma City	2,472	30.1
1978	George Gervin, San Antonio	2,232	27.2	2011	Kevin Durant, Oklahoma City	2,161	27.7
1979	George Gervin, San Antonio	2,365	29.6	2012	Kevin Durant, Oklahoma City	1,850	28.0

NBA Most Valuable Player, 1956-2012

Year	Player, team	Year	Player, team	Year	Player, team
1956	Bob Pettit, St. Louis	1967	Wilt Chamberlain, Philadelphia	1978	Bill Walton, Portland
1957	Bob Cousy, Boston	1968	Wilt Chamberlain, Philadelphia	1979	Moses Malone, Houston
1958	Bill Russell, Boston	1969	Wes Unseld, Baltimore	1980	Kareem Abdul-Jabbar, L.A. Lakers
1959	Bob Pettit, St. Louis	1970	Willis Reed, New York	1981	Julius Erving, Philadelphia
1960	Wilt Chamberlain, Philadelphia	1971	Lew Alcindor (Abdul-Jabbar), Milw.	1982	Moses Malone, Houston
1961	Bill Russell, Boston	1972	Kareem Abdul-Jabbar, Milwaukee	1983	Moses Malone, Philadelphia
1962	Bill Russell, Boston	1973	Dave Cowens, Boston	1984	Larry Bird, Boston
1963	Bill Russell, Boston	1974	Kareem Abdul-Jabbar, Milwaukee	1985	Larry Bird, Boston
1964	Oscar Robertson, Cincinnati	1975	Bob McAdoo, Buffalo	1986	Larry Bird, Boston
1965	Bill Russell, Boston	1976	Kareem Abdul-Jabbar, L.A. Lakers	1987	Magic Johnson, L.A. Lakers
1966	Wilt Chamberlain, Philadelphia	1977	Kareem Abdul-Jabbar, L.A. Lakers	1988	Michael Jordan, Chicago

Year	Player, team	Year	Player, team	Year	Player, team
1989	Magic Johnson, L.A. Lakers	1997	Karl Malone, Utah	2005	Steve Nash, Phoenix
1990	Magic Johnson, L.A. Lakers	1998	Michael Jordan, Chicago	2006	Steve Nash, Phoenix
1991	Michael Jordan, Chicago	1999	Karl Malone, Utah	2007	Dirk Nowitzki, Dallas
1992	Michael Jordan, Chicago	2000	Shaquille O'Neal, L.A. Lakers	2008	Kobe Bryant, L.A. Lakers
1993	Charles Barkley, Phoenix	2001	Allen Iverson, Philadelphia	2009	LeBron James, Cleveland
1994	Hakeem Olajuwon, Houston	2002	Tim Duncan, San Antonio	2010	LeBron James, Cleveland
1995	David Robinson, San Antonio	2003	Tim Duncan, San Antonio	2011	Derrick Rose, Chicago
1996	Michael Jordan, Chicago	2004	Kevin Garnett, Minnesota	2012	LeBron James, Miami

NBA Champions, 1947-2012

Year	Eastern Conference	Western Conference	Champion	Coach	Opponent
1947	Washington Capitols	Chicago Stags	Philadelphia	Ed Gottlieb	Chicago
1948	Philadelphia Warriors	St. Louis Bombers	Baltimore	Buddy Jeannette	Philadelphia
1949	Washington Capitols	Rochester	Minneapolis	John Kundla	Washington
1950	Syracuse	Minneapolis	Minneapolis	John Kundla	Syracuse
1951	Philadelphia Warriors	Minneapolis	Rochester	Lester Harrison	New York
1952	Syracuse	Rochester	Minneapolis	John Kundla	New York
1953	New York	Minneapolis	Minneapolis	John Kundla	New York
1954	New York	Minneapolis	Minneapolis	John Kundla	Syracuse
1955	Syracuse	Ft. Wayne	Syracuse	Al Cervi	Ft. Wayne
1956	Philadelphia Warriors	Ft. Wayne	Philadelphia	George Senesky	Ft. Wayne
1957	Boston	St. Louis	Boston	Red Auerbach	St. Louis
1958	Boston	St. Louis	St. Louis	Alex Hannum	Boston
1959	Boston	St. Louis	Boston	Red Auerbach	Minneapolis
1960	Boston	St. Louis	Boston	Red Auerbach	St. Louis
1961	Boston	St. Louis	Boston	Red Auerbach	St. Louis
1962	Boston	L.A. Lakers	Boston	Red Auerbach	L.A. Lakers
1963	Boston	L.A. Lakers	Boston	Red Auerbach	L.A. Lakers
1964	Boston	San Francisco	Boston	Red Auerbach	San Francisco
1965	Boston	L.A. Lakers	Boston	Red Auerbach	L.A. Lakers
1966	Philadelphia	L.A. Lakers	Boston	Red Auerbach	L.A. Lakers
1967	Philadelphia	San Francisco	Philadelphia	Alex Hannum	San Francisco
1968	Philadelphia	St. Louis	Boston	Bill Russell	L.A. Lakers
1969	Baltimore	L.A. Lakers	Boston	Bill Russell	L.A. Lakers
1970	New York	Atlanta	New York	Red Holzman	L.A. Lakers

Year	Atlantic	Central	Midwest	Pacific	Champion	Coach	Opponent
1971	New York	Baltimore	Milwaukee	L.A. Lakers	Milwaukee	Larry Costello	Baltimore
1972	Boston	Baltimore	Milwaukee	L.A. Lakers	L.A. Lakers	Bill Sharman	New York
1973	Boston	Baltimore	Milwaukee	L.A. Lakers	New York	Red Holzman	L.A. Lakers
1974	Boston	Capital	Milwaukee	L.A. Lakers	Boston	Tom Heinsohn	Milwaukee
1975	Boston	Washington	Chicago	Golden State	Golden State	Al Attles	Washington
1976	Boston	Cleveland	Milwaukee	Golden State	Boston	Tom Heinsohn	Phoenix
1977	Philadelphia	Houston	Denver	L.A. Lakers	Portland	Jack Ramsay	Philadelphia
1978	Philadelphia	San Antonio	Denver	Portland	Washington	Dick Motta	Seattle
1979	Washington	San Antonio	Kansas City	Seattle	Seattle	Len Wilkens	Washington
1980	Boston	Atlanta	Milwaukee	L.A. Lakers	L.A. Lakers	Paul Westhead	Philadelphia
1981	Boston	Milwaukee	San Antonio	Phoenix	Boston	Bill Fitch	Houston
1982	Boston	Milwaukee	San Antonio	L.A. Lakers	L.A. Lakers	Pat Riley	Philadelphia
1983	Philadelphia	Milwaukee	San Antonio	L.A. Lakers	Philadelphia	Billy Cunningham	L.A. Lakers
1984	Boston	Milwaukee	Utah	L.A. Lakers	Boston	K. C. Jones	L.A. Lakers
1985	Boston	Milwaukee	Denver	L.A. Lakers	L.A. Lakers	Pat Riley	Boston
1986	Boston	Milwaukee	Houston	L.A. Lakers	Boston	K. C. Jones	Houston
1987	Boston	Atlanta	Dallas	L.A. Lakers	L.A. Lakers	Pat Riley	Boston
1988	Boston	Detroit	Denver	L.A. Lakers	L.A. Lakers	Pat Riley	Detroit
1989	New York	Detroit	Utah	L.A. Lakers	Detroit	Chuck Daly	L.A. Lakers
1990	Philadelphia	Detroit	San Antonio	L.A. Lakers	Detroit	Chuck Daly	Portland
1991	Boston	Chicago	San Antonio	Portland	Chicago	Phil Jackson	L.A. Lakers
1992	Boston	Chicago	Utah	Portland	Chicago	Phil Jackson	Portland
1993	New York	Chicago	Houston	Phoenix	Chicago	Phil Jackson	Phoenix
1994	New York	Atlanta	Houston	Seattle	Houston	Rudy Tomjanovich	New York
1995	Orlando	Indiana	San Antonio	Phoenix	Houston	Rudy Tomjanovich	Orlando
1996	Orlando	Chicago	San Antonio	Seattle	Chicago	Phil Jackson	Seattle
1997	Miami	Chicago	Utah	Seattle	Chicago	Phil Jackson	Utah
1998	Miami	Chicago	Utah	L.A. Lakers	Chicago	Phil Jackson	Utah
1999	Miami	Indiana	San Antonio	Portland	San Antonio	Gregg Popovich	New York
2000	Miami	Indiana	Utah	L.A. Lakers	L.A. Lakers	Phil Jackson	Indiana
2001	Philadelphia	Milwaukee	San Antonio	L.A. Lakers	L.A. Lakers	Phil Jackson	Philadelphia
2002	New Jersey	Detroit	San Antonio	Sacramento	L.A. Lakers	Phil Jackson	New Jersey
2003	New Jersey	Detroit	San Antonio	Sacramento	San Antonio	Gregg Popovich	New Jersey
2004	New Jersey	Indiana	Minnesota	L.A. Lakers	Detroit	Larry Brown	L.A. Lakers

Year	Atlantic	Central	Southeast	Northwest	Pacific	Southwest	Champion	Coach	Opponent
2005	Boston	Detroit	Miami	Seattle	Phoenix	San Antonio	San Antonio	Gregg Popovich	Detroit
2006	New Jersey	Detroit	Miami	Denver	Phoenix	San Antonio	Miami	Pat Riley	Dallas
2007	Toronto	Detroit	Miami	Utah	Phoenix	Dallas	San Antonio	Gregg Popovich	Cleveland
2008	Boston	Detroit	Orlando	Utah	L.A. Lakers	New Orleans	Boston	Glenn "Doc" Rivers	L.A. Lakers
2009	Boston	Cleveland	Orlando	Denver	L.A. Lakers	San Antonio	L.A. Lakers	Phil Jackson	Orlando
2010	Boston	Cleveland	Orlando	Denver	L.A. Lakers	Dallas	L.A. Lakers	Phil Jackson	Boston
2011	Boston	Chicago	Miami	OK City	L.A. Lakers	San Antonio	Dallas	Rick Carlisle	Miami
2012	Boston	Chicago	Miami	OK City	L.A. Lakers	San Antonio	Miami	Erik Spoelstra	OK City

All-NBA and All-Defensive Teams, 2011-12

All-NBA Team		Position	All-Defensive Team	
First Team	Second Team		First Team	Second Team
LeBron James, Miami	Kevin Love, Minnesota	Forward	LeBron James, Miami	Kevin Garnett, Boston
Kevin Durant, Oklahoma City	Blake Griffin, L.A. Clippers	Forward	Serge Ibaka, Oklahoma City	Luol Deng, Chicago
Dwight Howard, Orlando	Andrew Bynum, L.A. Lakers	Center	Dwight Howard, Orlando	Tyson Chandler, New York
Kobe Bryant, L.A. Lakers	Tony Parker, San Antonio	Guard	Chris Paul, L.A. Clippers	Rajon Rondo, Boston
Chris Paul, L.A. Clippers	Russell Westbrook, Oklahoma City	Guard	Tony Allen, Memphis	Kobe Bryant, L.A. Lakers

NBA Coach of the Year, 1963-2012

Year	Coach, team	Year	Coach, team	Year	Coach, team
1963	Harry Gallatin, St. Louis	1980	Bill Fitch, Boston	1997	Pat Riley, Miami
1964	Alex Hannum, San Francisco	1981	Jack McKinney, Indiana	1998	Larry Bird, Indiana
1965	Red Auerbach, Boston	1982	Gene Shue, Washington	1999	Mike Dunleavy, Portland
1966	Dolph Schayes, Philadelphia	1983	Don Nelson, Milwaukee	2000	Glenn "Doc" Rivers, Orlando
1967	Johnny Kerr, Chicago	1984	Frank Layden, Utah	2001	Larry Brown, Philadelphia
1968	Richie Guerin, St. Louis	1985	Don Nelson, Milwaukee	2002	Rick Carlisle, Detroit
1969	Gene Shue, Baltimore	1986	Mike Fratello, Atlanta	2003	Gregg Popovich, San Antonio
1970	Red Holzman, New York	1987	Mike Schuler, Portland	2004	Hubie Brown, Memphis
1971	Dick Motta, Chicago	1988	Doug Moe, Denver	2005	Mike D'Antoni, Phoenix
1972	Bill Sharman, L.A. Lakers	1989	Cotton Fitzsimmons, Phoenix	2006	Avery Johnson, Dallas
1973	Tom Heinsohn, Boston	1990	Pat Riley, L.A. Lakers	2007	Sam Mitchell, Toronto
1974	Ray Scott, Detroit	1991	Don Chaney, Houston	2008	Byron Scott, New Orleans
1975	Phil Johnson, Kansas City-Omaha	1992	Don Nelson, Golden State	2009	Mike Brown, Cleveland
1976	Bill Fitch, Cleveland	1993	Pat Riley, New York	2010	Scott Brooks, Oklahoma City
1977	Tom Nissalke, Houston	1994	Lenny Wilkens, Atlanta	2011	Tom Thibodeau, Chicago
1978	Hubie Brown, Atlanta	1995	Del Harris, L.A. Lakers	2012	Gregg Popovich, San Antonio
1979	Cotton Fitzsimmons, Kansas City	1996	Phil Jackson, Chicago		

NBA Statistical Leaders, 2011-12

(* = rookie)

Scoring Average
(Minimum 57 games or 1,127 points)

Player, team	GP	FG	FT	PTS	AVG
Kevin Durant, Oklahoma City	66	643	431	1,850	28.0
Kobe Bryant, L.A. Lakers	58	574	381	1,616	27.9
LeBron James, Miami	62	621	387	1,683	27.1
Kevin Love, Minnesota	55	474	379	1,432	26.0
Russell Westbrook, Oklahoma City	66	578	340	1,558	23.6
Carmelo Anthony, New York	55	441	295	1,245	22.6
LaMarcus Aldridge, Portland	55	483	223	1,191	21.7
Dirk Nowitzki, Dallas	62	473	318	1,342	21.6
Deron Williams, New Jersey	55	391	257	1,154	21.0
Blake Griffin, L.A. Clippers	66	561	244	1,368	20.7

Rebounds per Game
(Minimum 57 games or 644 rebounds)

Player, team	GP	OFF	DEF	TOT	AVG
Dwight Howard, Orlando	54	200	585	785	14.5
Kevin Love, Minnesota	55	226	508	734	13.3
Andrew Bynum, L.A. Lakers	60	192	517	709	11.8
DeMarcus Cousins, Sacramento	64	265	438	703	11.0
Kris Humphries, New Jersey	62	233	448	681	11.0
Blake Griffin, L.A. Clippers	66	218	499	717	10.9
Pau Gasol, L.A. Lakers	65	183	495	678	10.4
Marcin Gortat, Phoenix	66	185	474	659	10.0
Tyson Chandler, New York	62	212	400	612	9.9
Joakim Noah, Chicago	64	242	387	629	9.8

3-Point Field Goal Percentage
(Minimum 45 3-point field goals made)

Player, team	3-FGM	3-FGA	PCT
Steve Novak, New York	133	282	.472
Stephen Curry, Golden State	55	121	.455
Ersan Ilyasova, Milwaukee	51	112	.455
Ray Allen, Boston	106	234	.453
Mike Miller, Miami	53	117	.453
Brandon Rush, Golden State	99	219	.452
Willie Green, Atlanta	50	113	.442
Jordan Farmar, New Jersey	55	125	.440
Danny Green, San Antonio	102	234	.436
Kyle Korver, Chicago	118	271	.435

Assists per Game
(Minimum 57 games or 322 assists)

Player, team	GP	AST	APG
Rajon Rondo, Boston	53	620	11.7
Steve Nash, Phoenix	62	664	10.7
Chris Paul, L.A. Clippers	60	543	9.1
Jose Calderon, Toronto	53	468	8.8
Deron Williams, New Jersey	55	481	8.7
*Ricky Rubio, Minnesota	41	336	8.2
John Wall, Washington	66	530	8.0
Tony Parker, San Antonio	60	463	7.7
Andre Miller, Denver	66	441	6.7
Ty Lawson, Denver	61	401	6.6

Field Goal Percentage
(Minimum 241 field goals made)

Player, team	FGM	FGA	PCT
Tyson Chandler, New York	241	355	.679
Dwight Howard, Orlando	416	726	.573
Nikola Pekovic, Minnesota	256	454	.564
Andrew Bynum, L.A. Lakers	444	796	.558
JaVale McGee, Denver-Washington	307	552	.556
Marcin Gortat, Phoenix	427	769	.555
Blake Griffin, L.A. Clippers	561	1,022	.549
Serge Ibaka, Oklahoma City	262	490	.535
DeJuan Blair, San Antonio	269	504	.534
Carlos Boozer, Chicago	448	842	.532
Steve Nash, Phoenix	295	555	.532

Steals per Game
(Minimum 57 games or 101 steals)

Player, team	GP	STL	AVG
Chris Paul, L.A. Clippers	60	152	2.53
Mike Conley, Memphis	62	136	2.19
LeBron James, Miami	62	115	1.85
Paul Millsap, Utah	64	118	1.84
Tony Allen, Memphis	58	104	1.79
Andre Iguodala, Philadelphia	62	107	1.73
*Iman Shumpert, New York	59	101	1.71
Russell Westbrook, Oklahoma City	66	112	1.70
Paul George, Indiana	66	108	1.64
Jeff Teague, Atlanta	66	106	1.61

Free Throw Percentage
(Minimum 101 free throws made)

Player, team	FTM	FTA	PCT
Jamal Crawford, Portland	191	206	.927
J.J. Redick, Orlando	143	157	.911
Dirk Nowitzki, Dallas	318	355	.896
Kevin Martin, Houston	160	179	.894
Steve Nash, Phoenix	127	142	.894
Luke Ridnour, Minnesota	106	119	.891
Ryan Anderson, Orlando	150	171	.877
D.J. Augustin, Charlotte	105	120	.875
Andrea Bargnani, Toronto	151	173	.873
Danny Granger, Indiana	254	291	.873

Blocked Shots per Game
(Minimum 57 games or 80 blocked shots)

Player, team	GP	BLK	AVG
Serge Ibaka, Oklahoma City	66	241	3.65
JaVale McGee, Denver-Washington	61	132	2.16
Dwight Howard, Orlando	54	116	2.15
DeAndre Jordan, L.A. Clippers	66	135	2.05
Roy Hibbert, Indiana	65	128	1.97
Andrew Bynum, L.A. Lakers	60	116	1.93
Marc Gasol, Memphis	65	121	1.86
*Bismack Biyombo, Charlotte	63	115	1.83
Josh Smith, Atlanta	66	115	1.74
Samuel Dalembert, Houston	65	111	1.71

NBA Defensive Player of the Year, 1983-2012

1983	Sidney Moncrief, Milwaukee	1994	Hakeem Olajuwon, Houston	2003	Ben Wallace, Detroit
1984	Sidney Moncrief, Milwaukee	1995	Dikembe Mutombo, Denver	2004	Ron Artest, Indiana
1985	Mark Eaton, Utah	1996	Gary Payton, Seattle	2005	Ben Wallace, Detroit
1986	Alvin Robertson, San Antonio	1997	Dikembe Mutombo, Atlanta	2006	Ben Wallace, Detroit
1987	Michael Cooper, L.A. Lakers	1998	Dikembe Mutombo, Atlanta	2007	Marcus Camby, Denver
1988	Michael Jordan, Chicago	1999	Alonzo Mourning, Miami	2008	Kevin Garnett, Boston
1989	Mark Eaton, Utah	2000	Alonzo Mourning, Miami	2009	Dwight Howard, Orlando
1990	Dennis Rodman, Detroit	2001	Dikembe Mutombo, Philadelphia-Atlanta	2010	Dwight Howard, Orlando
1991	Dennis Rodman, Detroit			2011	Dwight Howard, Orlando
1992	David Robinson, San Antonio	2002	Ben Wallace, Detroit	2012	Tyson Chandler, New York
1993	Hakeem Olajuwon, Houston				

NBA Rookie of the Year, 1953-2012

1953 Don Meineke, Ft. Wayne	1973 Bob McAdoo, Buffalo	1994 Chris Webber, Golden State
1954 Ray Felix, Baltimore	1974 Ernie DiGregorio, Buffalo	1995 Grant Hill, Detroit;
1955 Bob Pettit, Milwaukee	1975 Keith Wilkes, Golden State	Jason Kidd, Dallas
1956 Maurice Stokes, Rochester	1976 Alvan Adams, Phoenix	1996 Damon Stoudamire, Toronto
1957 Tom Heinsohn, Boston	1977 Adrian Dantley, Buffalo	1997 Allen Iverson, Philadelphia
1958 Woody Sauldsberry, Philadelphia	1978 Walter Davis, Phoenix	1998 Tim Duncan, San Antonio
1959 Elgin Baylor, Minneapolis	1979 Phil Ford, Kansas City	1999 Vince Carter, Toronto
1960 Wilt Chamberlain, Philadelphia	1980 Larry Bird, Boston	2000 Elton Brand, Chicago;
1961 Oscar Robertson, Cincinnati	1981 Darrell Griffith, Utah	Steve Francis, Houston
1962 Walt Bellamy, Chicago	1982 Buck Williams, New Jersey	2001 Mike Miller, Orlando
1963 Terry Dischinger, Chicago	1983 Terry Cummings, San Diego	2002 Pau Gasol, Memphis
1964 Jerry Lucas, Cincinnati	1984 Ralph Sampson, Houston	2003 Amar'e Stoudemire, Phoenix
1965 Willis Reed, New York	1985 Michael Jordan, Chicago	2004 LeBron James, Cleveland
1966 Rick Barry, San Francisco	1986 Patrick Ewing, New York	2005 Emeka Okafor, Charlotte
1967 Dave Bing, Detroit	1987 Chuck Person, Indiana	2006 Chris Paul, New Or./Okla. City
1968 Earl Monroe, Baltimore	1988 Mark Jackson, New York	2007 Brandon Roy, Portland
1969 Wes Unseld, Baltimore	1989 Mitch Richmond, Golden State	2008 Kevin Durant, Seattle
1970 Lew Alcindor (Abdul-Jabbar), Milw.	1990 David Robinson, San Antonio	2009 Derrick Rose, Chicago
1971 Dave Cowens, Boston;	1991 Derrick Coleman, New Jersey	2010 Tyreke Evans, Sacramento
Geoff Petrie, Portland	1992 Larry Johnson, Charlotte	2011 Blake Griffin, L.A. Clippers
1972 Sidney Wicks, Portland	1993 Shaquille O'Neal, Orlando	2012 Kyrie Irving, Cleveland

NBA Sixth Man Award, 1983-2012

1983 Bobby Jones, Philadelphia	1993 Clifford Robinson, Portland	2003 Bobby Jackson, Sacramento
1984 Kevin McHale, Boston	1994 Dell Curry, Charlotte	2004 Antawn Jamison, Dallas
1985 Kevin McHale, Boston	1995 Anthony Mason, New York	2005 Ben Gordon, Chicago
1986 Bill Walton, Boston	1996 Toni Kukoc, Chicago	2006 Mike Miller, Memphis
1987 Ricky Pierce, Milwaukee	1997 John Starks, New York	2007 Leandro Barbosa, Phoenix
1988 Roy Tarpley, Dallas	1998 Danny Manning, Phoenix	2008 Manu Ginobili, San Antonio
1989 Eddie Johnson, Phoenix	1999 Darrell Armstrong, Orlando	2009 Jason Terry, Dallas
1990 Ricky Pierce, Milwaukee	2000 Rodney Rogers, Phoenix	2010 Jamal Crawford, Atlanta
1991 Detlef Schrempf, Indiana	2001 Aaron McKie, Philadelphia	2011 Lamar Odom, L.A. Lakers
1992 Detlef Schrempf, Indiana	2002 Corliss Williamson, Detroit	2012 James Harden, Oklahoma City

NBA Player Draft First-Round Picks, 2012
(June 28, 2012)

Team	Player, position, college/team	Team	Player, position, college/team
1. New Orleans	Anthony Davis, Forward, Kentucky	17. Dallas	Tyler Zeller, Forward, North Carolina[6]
2. Charlotte	Michael Kidd-Gilchrist, Forward, Kentucky	18. Houston[7]	Terrence Jones, Forward, Kentucky
3. Washington	Bradley Beal, Guard, Florida	19. Orlando	Andrew Nicholson, Forward, St. Bonaventure
4. Cleveland	Dion Waiters, Guard, Syracuse	20. Denver	Evan Fournier, Guard, Poitiers Basket 86
5. Sacramento	Thomas Robinson, Forward, Kansas		(France)
6. Portland[1]	Damian Lillard, Guard, Weber State	21. Boston	Jared Sullinger, Forward, Ohio State
7. Golden State	Harrison Barnes, Forward, North Carolina	22. Boston[8]	Fab Melo, Center, Syracuse
8. Toronto	Terrence Ross, Guard, Washington	23. Atlanta	John Jenkins, Guard, Vanderbilt
9. Detroit	Andre Drummond, Forward, Connecticut	24. Cleveland[9]	Jared Cunningham, Guard, Oregon State[10]
10. New Orleans[2]	Austin Rivers, Guard, Duke	25. Memphis	Tony Wroten Jr., Guard, Washington
11. Portland	Meyers Leonard, Center, Illinois	26. Indiana	Miles Plumlee, Forward, Duke
12. Houston[3]	Jeremy Lamb, Guard, Connecticut	27. Miami	Arnett Moultrie, Forward, Mississippi State[11]
13. Phoenix	Kendall Marshall, Guard, North Carolina	28. Oklahoma City	Perry Jones III, Forward, Baylor
14. Milwaukee[4]	John Henson, Forward, North Carolina	29. Chicago	Marquis Teague, Guard, Kentucky
15. Philadelphia	Maurice Harkless, Forward, St. John's (NY)	30. Golden State[12]	Festus Ezeli, Center, Vanderbilt
16. Houston[5]	Royce White, Forward, Iowa State		

(1) From Brooklyn. (2) From Minnesota via L.A. Clippers. (3) From Milwaukee. (4) From Houston. (5) From New York. (6) Rights traded to Cleveland. (7) From Minnesota via Utah. (8) From L.A. Clippers via Oklahoma City. (9) From L.A. Lakers. (10) Rights traded to Dallas. (11) Rights traded to Philadelphia. (12) From San Antonio.

Number-One First-Round NBA Draft Picks, 1966-2012

Year	Team	Player, college/team	Year	Team	Player, college/team
1966	New York	Cazzie Russell, Michigan	1990	New Jersey	Derrick Coleman, Syracuse
1967	Detroit	Jimmy Walker, Providence	1991	Charlotte	Larry Johnson, UNLV
1968	San Diego	Elvin Hayes, Houston	1992	Orlando	Shaquille O'Neal, LSU
1969	Milwaukee	Lew Alcindor (Kareem Abdul-Jabbar), UCLA	1993	Orlando	Chris Webber[2], Michigan
1970	Detroit	Bob Lanier, St. Bonaventure	1994	Milwaukee	Glenn Robinson, Purdue
1971	Cleveland	Austin Carr, Notre Dame	1995	Golden State	Joe Smith, Maryland
1972	Portland	LaRue Martin, Loyola-Chicago	1996	Philadelphia	Allen Iverson, Georgetown
1973	Philadelphia	Doug Collins, Illinois State	1997	San Antonio	Tim Duncan, Wake Forest
1974	Portland	Bill Walton, UCLA	1998	L.A. Clippers	Michael Olowokandi, Pacific (CA)
1975	Atlanta	David Thompson[1], NC State	1999	Chicago	Elton Brand, Duke
1976	Houston	John Lucas, Maryland	2000	New Jersey	Kenyon Martin, Cincinnati
1977	Milwaukee	Kent Benson, Indiana	2001	Washington	Kwame Brown, Glynn Academy (HS)
1978	Portland	Mychal Thompson, Minnesota	2002	Houston	Yao Ming, Shanghai Sharks (China)
1979	L.A. Lakers	Earvin "Magic" Johnson, Michigan State	2003	Cleveland	LeBron James, St. Vincent-St. Mary (HS)
1980	Golden State	Joe Barry Carroll, Purdue	2004	Orlando	Dwight Howard, Southwest Atlanta
1981	Dallas	Mark Aguirre, DePaul			Christian Academy (HS)
1982	L.A. Lakers	James Worthy, North Carolina	2005	Milwaukee	Andrew Bogut, Utah
1983	Houston	Ralph Sampson, Virginia	2006	Toronto	Andrea Bargnani, Benetton Treviso (Italy)
1984	Houston	Hakeem Olajuwon, Houston	2007	Portland	Greg Oden, Ohio State
1985	New York	Patrick Ewing, Georgetown	2008	Chicago	Derrick Rose, Memphis
1986	Cleveland	Brad Daugherty, North Carolina	2009	L.A. Clippers	Blake Griffin, Oklahoma
1987	San Antonio	David Robinson, Navy	2010	Washington	John Wall, Kentucky
1988	L.A. Clippers	Danny Manning, Kansas	2011	Cleveland	Kyrie Irving, Duke
1989	Sacramento	Pervis Ellison, Louisville	2012	New Orleans	Anthony Davis, Kentucky

HS = High school. (1) Signed with Denver of the American Basketball Association. (2) Traded to Golden State for rights to Anfernee Hardaway and three future first-round draft choices.

All-Time NBA Statistical Leaders

(At the end of the 2011-12 season. * = Active in 2011-12 season.)

Scoring Average
(Minimum 400 games or 10,000 points)

	GP	PTS	AVG
Michael Jordan	1,072	32,292	30.1
Wilt Chamberlain	1,045	31,419	30.1
*LeBron James	689	19,045	27.6
Elgin Baylor	846	23,149	27.4
Jerry West	932	25,192	27.0
Allen Iverson	914	24,368	26.7
Bob Pettit	792	20,880	26.4
George Gervin	791	20,708	26.2
Oscar Robertson	1,040	26,710	25.7
*Kobe Bryant	1,161	29,484	25.4

Field Goal Percentage
(Minimum 2,000 field goals made)

	FGM	FGA	PCT
Artis Gilmore	5,732	9,570	.599
Shaquille O'Neal	11,330	19,457	.582
Mark West	2,528	4,356	.580
*Tyson Chandler	2,287	3,956	.578
*Dwight Howard	4,034	6,988	.577
Steve Johnson	2,841	4,965	.572
Darryl Dawkins	3,477	6,079	.572
James Donaldson	3,105	5,442	.571
Bo Outlaw	2,005	3,534	.567
Jeff Ruland	2,105	3,734	.564

Free Throw Percentage
(Minimum 1,200 free throws made)

	FTM	FTA	PCT
*Steve Nash	2,931	3,244	.904
Mark Price	2,135	2,362	.904
Rick Barry	3,818	4,243	.900
Peja Stojakovic	2,237	2,500	.895
*Ray Allen	4,153	4,646	.894
*Chauncey Billups	4,441	4,969	.894
Calvin Murphy	3,445	3,864	.892
Scott Skiles	1,548	1,741	.889
Reggie Miller	6,237	7,026	.888
Larry Bird	3,960	4,471	.886

3-Point Field Goal Percentage
(Minimum 250 3-point field goals made)

	3-FGM	3-FGA	PCT
Steve Kerr	726	1,599	.454
Hubert Davis	728	1,651	.441
*Stephen Curry	372	843	.441
Drazen Petrovic	255	583	.437
*Steve Novak	347	795	.436
*Jason Kapono	457	1,054	.434
Tim Legler	260	603	.431
*Steve Nash	1,620	3,785	.428
*Anthony Morrow	442	1,037	.426
B.J. Armstrong	436	1,026	.425

Minutes Played

Kareem Abdul-Jabbar	57,446
Karl Malone	54,852
Elvin Hayes	50,000
*Jason Kidd	48,068
Wilt Chamberlain	47,859
John Stockton	47,764
Reggie Miller	47,619
Gary Payton	47,117
John Havlicek	46,471
*Kevin Garnett	45,779

Field Goals Attempted

Kareem Abdul-Jabbar	28,307
Karl Malone	26,210
Michael Jordan	24,537
Elvin Hayes	24,272
John Havlicek	23,930
Wilt Chamberlain	23,497
*Kobe Bryant	22,706
Dominique Wilkins	21,589
Alex English	21,036
Hakeem Olajuwon	20,991

Points

Kareem Abdul-Jabbar	38,387
Karl Malone	36,928
Michael Jordan	32,292
Wilt Chamberlain	31,419
*Kobe Bryant	29,484
Shaquille O'Neal	28,596
Moses Malone	27,409
Elvin Hayes	27,313
Hakeem Olajuwon	26,946
Oscar Robertson	26,710

Games Played

Robert Parish	1,611
Kareem Abdul-Jabbar	1,560
John Stockton	1,504
Karl Malone	1,476
Kevin Willis	1,424
Reggie Miller	1,389
Clifford Robinson	1,380
Gary Payton	1,335
Moses Malone	1,329
*Jason Kidd	1,315

Field Goals Made

Kareem Abdul-Jabbar	15,837
Karl Malone	13,528
Wilt Chamberlain	12,681
Michael Jordan	12,192
*Shaquille O'Neal	11,330
Elvin Hayes	10,976
Hakeem Olajuwon	10,749
Alex English	10,659
John Havlicek	10,513
*Kobe Bryant	10,286

Rebounds

Wilt Chamberlain	23,924
Bill Russell	21,620
Kareem Abdul-Jabbar	17,440
Elvin Hayes	16,279
Moses Malone	16,212
Karl Malone	14,968
Robert Parish	14,715
Nate Thurmond	14,464
Walt Bellamy	14,241
Wes Unseld	13,769

Personal Fouls

Kareem Abdul-Jabbar	4,657
Karl Malone	4,578
Robert Parish	4,443
Charles Oakley	4,421
Hakeem Olajuwon	4,383
Buck Williams	4,267
Elvin Hayes	4,193
Clifford Robinson	4,176
Kevin Willis	4,172
Shaquille O'Neal	4,146
Otis Thorpe	4,146

3-Point Field Goals Attempted

*Ray Allen	6,788
Reggie Miller	6,486
*Jason Kidd	5,376
*Jason Terry	4,706
*Chauncey Billups	4,587
*Paul Pierce	4,546
*Kobe Bryant	4,472
Peja Stojakovic	4,392
*Rashard Lewis	4,360
Tim Hardaway	4,345

Assists

John Stockton	15,806
*Jason Kidd	11,842
Mark Jackson	10,334
Magic Johnson	10,141
*Steve Nash	9,916
Oscar Robertson	9,887
Isiah Thomas	9,061
Gary Payton	8,966
Rod Strickland	7,987
*Andre Miller	7,472

Blocks

Hakeem Olajuwon	3,830
Dikembe Mutombo	3,289
Kareem Abdul-Jabbar	3,189
Mark Eaton	3,064
David Robinson	2,954
Patrick Ewing	2,894
Shaquille O'Neal	2,732
Tree Rollins	2,542
*Tim Duncan	2,469
Robert Parish	2,361

3-Point Field Goals Made

*Ray Allen	2,718
Reggie Miller	2,560
*Jason Kidd	1,874
*Jason Terry	1,788
*Chauncey Billups	1,783
*Peja Stojakovic	1,760
Dale Ellis	1,719
*Rashard Lewis	1,690
*Paul Pierce	1,678
*Steve Nash	1,620

Steals

John Stockton	3,265
*Jason Kidd	2,559
Michael Jordan	2,514
Gary Payton	2,445
Maurice Cheeks	2,310
Scottie Pippen	2,307
Clyde Drexler	2,207
Hakeem Olajuwon	2,162
Alvin Robertson	2,112
Karl Malone	2,085

All-Time NBA Regular Season Coaching Victories

(At the end of the 2011-12 season, ranked by wins. * = Active in 2011-12 season.)

Coach	W	L	PCT	Coach	W	L	PCT	Coach	W	L	PCT
Don Nelson	1,335	1,063	.557	Bill Fitch	944	1,106	.460	John MacLeod	707	657	.518
Lenny Wilkens	1,332	1,155	.536	Red Auerbach	938	479	.662	Red Holzman	696	604	.535
Jerry Sloan	1,221	803	.603	Dick Motta	935	1,017	.479	Mike Fratello	667	548	.549
Pat Riley	1,210	694	.636	Jack Ramsay	864	783	.525	Chuck Daly	638	437	.593
Phil Jackson	1,155	485	.704	*Gregg Popovich	847	399	.680	*Flip Saunders	638	526	.548
Larry Brown	1,098	904	.548	Cotton Fitzsimmons	832	775	.518	Doug Moe	628	529	.543
*George Karl	1,074	731	.595	Gene Shue	784	861	.477	Mike Dunleavy	613	716	.461
*Rick Adelman	971	656	.597								

Naismith Memorial Basketball Hall of Fame

(Located in Springfield, MA. * = 2012 inductee. ** = Enshrined as both a player and coach.)

Players
Abdul-Jabbar, Kareem
Archibald, Nate
Arizin, Paul
Barkley, Charles
Barlow, Thomas
Barry, Rick
Baylor, Elgin
Beckman, John
Bellamy, Walt
Belov, Sergei
Bing, Dave
Bird, Larry
Blazejowski, Carol
Borgmann, Bennie
Bradley, Bill
Brennan, Joseph
Cervi, Al
Chamberlain, Wilt
Cooper, Charles
Cooper, Cynthia
Cosic, Kresimir
Cousy, Bob
Cowens, Dave
Crawford, Joan
Cunningham, Billy
Curry, Denise
Dalipagic, Drazen
*Daniels, Mel
Dantley, Adrian
Davies, Bob
DeBernardi, Forrest
DeBusschere, Dave
Dehnert, Henry "Dutch"
Donovan, Anne
Drexler, Clyde
Dumars, Joe
Edwards, Teresa
Endacott, Paul
English, Alex
Erving, Julius
Ewing, Patrick
Foster, Bud
Frazier, Walt
Friedman, Max
Fulks, Joe
Gale, Lauren
Gallatin, Harry
Gates, William "Pop"
Gervin, George
Gilmore, Artis
Gola, Tom
Goodrich, Gail
Greer, Hal
Gruenig, Robert "Ace"
Hagan, Cliff
Hanson, Victor
Harris-Stewart, Lusia

Havlicek, John
Hawkins, Cornelius "Connie"
Hayes, Elvin
Haynes, Marques
Heinsohn, Tom
Holman, Nat
Houbregs, Bob
Howell, Bailey
Hyatt, Chuck
Issel, Dan
Jeannette, Harry "Buddy"
Johnson, Dennis
Johnson, Earvin "Magic"
Johnson, Gus
Johnson, William "Satch"
Johnston, Neil
Jones, K. C.
Jones, Sam
Jordan, Michael
Krause, Ed "Moose"
Kurland, Bob
Lanier, Bob
Lapchick, Joe
Lieberman, Nancy
Lovellette, Clyde
Lucas, Jerry
Luisetti, Angelo "Hank"
Macauley, Ed
Malone, Karl
Malone, Moses
Maravich, Pete
Marcari, Hortencia
Martin, Slater
McAdoo, Bob
*McClain, Katrina
McCracken, Emmett "Branch"
McCracken, Jack
McDermott, Bobby
McGuire, Dick
McHale, Kevin
Meneghin, Dino
Meyers, Ann
Mikan, George
Mikkelsen, Vern
Miller, Cheryl
*Miller, Reggie
Monroe, Earl
Mullin, Chris
Murphy, Calvin
Murphy, Charles "Stretch"
Olajuwon, Hakeem
Page, Harlan "Pat"
Parish, Robert
Pereira, Maciel "Ubiratan"

Petrovic, Drazen
Pettit, Bob
Phillip, Andy
Pippen, Scottie
Pollard, Jim
Ramsay, Frank
Reed, Willis
Risen, Arnie
Robertson, Oscar
Robinson, David
Rodman, Dennis
Roosma, John
Russell, Bill
Russell, John "Honey"
Sabonis, Arvydas
Sanders, Tom "Satch"
*Sampson, Ralph
Schayes, Adolph
Schmidt, Ernest
Schommer, John
Sedran, Barney
Semjonova, Uljana
**Sharman, Bill
Stockton, John
Steinmetz, Chris
Stokes, Maurice
Tatum, Reece "Goose"
Thomas, Isiah
Thompson, David
Thompson, John
Thurmond, Nate
Twyman, Jack
Unseld, Wes
Vandivier, Robert "Fuzzy"
Wachter, Ed
*Walker, Chet
Walton, Bill
Wanzer, Bobby
West, Jerry
White, Nera
**Wilkens, Lenny
*Wilkes, Jamaal
Wilkins, Dominique
Woodard, Lynette
**Wooden, John
Worthy, James
Yardley, George

Coaches
*Alexeeva, Lidia
Allen, Forrest C. "Phog"
Anderson, Harold
Auerbach, Arnold "Red"
Auriemma, Geno
Barmore, Leon
Barry, Justin "Sam"

Blood, Ernest
Boeheim, Jim
Brown, Larry
Calhoun, Jim
Cann, Howard
Carlson, Clifford
Carnesecca, Lou
Carnevale, Ben
Carril, Pete
Case, Everett
Chancellor, Van
Chaney, John
Conradt, Jody
Crum, Denzil "Denny"
Daly, Chuck
Dean, Everett
Diaz-Miguel, Antonio
Diddle, Edgar
Drake, Bruce
Ferrandiz, Pedro
Gaines, Clarence
Gamba, Sandro
Gardner, James "Jack"
Gill, Amory "Slats"
Gomelsky, Aleksandr
Gunter, Sue
Hannum, Alex
Harshman, Marv
Haskins, Don
Hickey, Edgar
Hobson, Howard
Holzman, William "Red"
Hurley, Bob, Sr.
Iba, Hank
Jackson, Phil
Julian, Alvin
Keaney, Frank
Keogan, George
Knight, Bob
Krzyzewski, Mike
Kundla, John
Lambert, Ward
Litwack, Harry
Loeffler, Kenneth
Lonborg, Arthur "Dutch"
Magee, Herb
McCutchan, Arad
McGuire, Al
McGuire, Frank
McLendon, John
Meanwell, Dr. Walter
Meyer, Ray
Miller, Ralph
Moore, Billie
*Nelson, Don
Newell, Pete
Nikolic, Aleksandar

Novosel, Mirko
Olson, Robert "Lute"
Ramsay, John "Jack"
Riley, Pat
Rubini, Cesare
Rupp, Adolph
Rush, Cathy
Sachs, Leonard
**Sharman, Bill
Shelton, Everett
Sloan, Jerry
Smith, Dean
Stringer, C. Vivian
Summitt, Pat
Taylor, Fred
Thompson, John
VanDerveer, Tara
Wade, Margaret
Watts, Stan
**Wilkens, Lenny
Williams, Roy
Winter, Tex
**Wooden, John
Woolpert, Phil
Wootten, Morgan
Yow, Kay

Teams
1960 USA Men's Olympic team
1992 USA Basketball "Dream Team"
*All American Red Heads
Buffalo Germans First Team
Harlem Globetrotters
New York Renaissance
Original Celtics
Texas Western

Referees
Enright, James
Hepbron, George
Hoyt, George
Kennedy, Matthew
Leith, Lloyd
Mihalik, Zigmund "Red"
*Nichols, Hank
Nucatola, John
Quigley, Ernest
Rudolph, Marvin "Mendy"
Shirley, J. Dallas
Strom, Earl
Tobey, David
Walsh, David

Contributors
Abbott, Senda
Berenson
*Barksdale, Don
Bee, Clair
Biasone, Danny
Brown, Hubert "Hubie"
Brown, Walter
Bunn, John
Buss, Jerry
Colangelo, Jerry
Davidson, Bill
Douglas, Bob
Duer, Al
Embry, Wayne
Fagan, Cliff
Fisher, Harry
Fleisher, Larry
Gavitt, David
Gottlieb, Edward
Gulick, Dr. Luther
Harrison, Lester
Hearn, Francis "Chick"
Hepp, Dr. Ferenc
Hickox, Edward
Hinkle, Tony
Irish, Edward "Ned"
Jones, R. William
Kennedy, Walter
*Knight, Phil
Lemon, Meadowlark
Liston, Emil
Lloyd, Earl
Mokray, Bill
Morgan, Ralph
Morgenweck, Frank
Naismith, Dr. James
Newton, C. M.
O'Brien, John
O'Brien, Larry
Olsen, Harold
Podoloff, Maurice
Porter, Henry V.
Reid, William
Ripley, Elmer
St. John, Lynn
Saperstein, Abe
Schabinger, Arthur
Stagg, Alonzo
Stankovic, Boris
Steitz, Edward
Taylor, Chuck
Teague, Bertha
Tower, Oswald
Trester, Arthur
Wells, Clifford
Wilke, Lou
Zollner, Fred

NBA Home Courts

Team	Name (year built)	Capacity[1]	Team	Name (year built)	Capacity[1]
Atlanta	Philips Arena (1999)	18,729	Milwaukee	Bradley Center (1988)	18,717
Boston	TD Garden[2] (1995)	18,624	Minnesota	Target Center (1990)	19,356
Charlotte	Time Warner Cable Arena (2005)	19,077	New Jersey	Prudential Center (2007)	18,711
Chicago	United Center (1994)	20,917	New Orleans[5]	New Orleans Arena (1999)	17,188
Cleveland	Quicken Loans Arena (1994)	20,562	New York	Madison Square Garden (IV) (1968)	19,763
Dallas	American Airlines Center (2001)	19,200	Oklahoma City	Chesapeake Energy Arena[6] (2002)	18,203
Denver	Pepsi Center (1999)	19,155	Orlando	Amway Center[7] (2010)	18,846
Detroit	The Palace of Auburn Hills (1988)	22,076	Philadelphia	Wells Fargo Center[8] (1996)	20,328
Golden State	ORACLE Arena[3] (1966)	19,596	Phoenix	US Airways Center[9] (1992)	18,422
Houston	Toyota Center (2003)	18,043	Portland	The Rose Garden (1995)	20,796
Indiana	Bankers Life Fieldhouse[4] (1999)	18,165	Sacramento	Power Balance Pavilion[10] (1988)	17,317
L.A. Clippers	STAPLES Center (1999)	19,060	San Antonio	AT&T Center[11] (2002)	18,581
L.A. Lakers	STAPLES Center (1999)	18,997	Toronto	Air Canada Centre (1999)	19,800
Memphis	FedExForum (2004)	18,119	Utah	EnergySolutions Arena[12] (1991)	19,911
Miami	AmericanAirlines Arena (1999)	19,600	Washington	Verizon Center[13] (1997)	20,278

Note: The New Jersey Nets became the Brooklyn Nets Apr. 30, 2012; their home court is the Barclays Center in Brooklyn, NY. (1) At the end of the 2011-12 season. (2) Fleet Center (1995-2005). (3) Oakland Coliseum Arena (1966-96); Arena in Oakland (1997-2006). (4) Conseco Fieldhouse (1999-2011). (5) Because of damage to New Orleans Arena due to Hurricane Katrina, the Hornets played 35 games in the Ford Center in Oklahoma City, OK, 3 games in New Orleans Arena, and 3 games at other locations during the 2005-06 season. In 2006-07, the Hornets played 35 games at the Ford Center and 6 games in New Orleans Arena. They played 2007-08 home games in New Orleans Arena. (6) Ford Center (2008-11). The Seattle SuperSonics relocated to Oklahoma City prior to the 2008-09 season. (7) Orlando Arena (1989-2000); TD Waterhouse Centre (2000-06); Amway Arena (2006-10). (8) CoreStates Center (1996-98); First Union Center (1998-2003). (9) America West Arena (1992-2006). (10) ARCO Arena (1988-2011). (11) SBC Center (2002-06). (12) Delta Center (1991-2006). (13) MCI Center (1997-2006).

WOMEN'S NATIONAL BASKETBALL ASSOCIATION

Indiana Wins First WNBA Title

The Indiana Fever won their first-ever WNBA title by beating the defending-champion Minnesota Lynx, three games to one, in the WNBA Finals. Tamika Catchings scored 25 points in an 87-78 victory over the Lynx in the deciding Game 4 on Oct. 21, 2012, at Bankers Life Fieldhouse in Indianapolis. Catchings earned WNBA Finals MVP, capping a year that included Olympic gold medals for Catchings and 11 other WNBA stars at the 2012 London Olympics (the league took a one-month hiatus).

WNBA Final Standings, 2012

(playoff seeding in parentheses; conference winner automatically gets top seed)

Eastern Conference	W	L	Pct	GB	Western Conference	W	L	Pct	GB
Connecticut Sun (1)	25	9	.735	—	Minnesota Lynx (1)	27	7	.794	—
Indiana Fever (2)	22	12	.647	3	Los Angeles Sparks (2)	24	10	.706	3
Atlanta Dream (3)	19	15	.559	6	San Antonio Silver Stars (3)	21	13	.618	6
New York Liberty (4)	15	19	.441	10	Seattle Storm (4)	16	18	.471	11
Chicago Sky	14	20	.412	11	Tulsa Shock	9	25	.265	18
Washington Mystics	5	29	.147	20	Phoenix Mercury	7	27	.206	20

WNBA Playoffs, 2012

Eastern Conference
(1) Connecticut defeated (4) New York, 2 games to 0
(2) Indiana defeated (3) Atlanta, 2 games to 1
(2) Indiana defeated (1) Connecticut, 2 games to 1

Western Conference
(1) Minnesota defeated (4) Seattle, 2 games to 1
(2) Los Angeles defeated (3) San Antonio, 2 games to 0
(1) Minnesota defeated (2) Los Angeles, 2 games to 0

WNBA Championship, 2012

Indiana defeated Minnesota, 3 games to 1 (76-70, 71-83, 76-59, 87-78) in the best-of-five series.

All-WNBA Teams, 2012

First team	Position	Second team	Position
Candace Parker, Los Angeles	Forward	Maya Moore, Minnesota	Forward
Tamika Catchings, Indiana	Forward	Sophia Young, San Antonio	Forward
Tina Charles, Connecticut	Center	Sylvia Fowles, Chicago	Center
Cappie Pondexter, New York	Guard	Kristi Toliver, Los Angeles	Guard
Seimone Augustus, Minnesota	Guard	Lindsay Whalen, Minnesota	Guard

WNBA Statistical Leaders, 2012

Minutes played: 1,161, Cappie Pondexter, New York
Total points: 695, Cappie Pondexter, New York
Points per game: 21.4, Angel McCoughtry, Atlanta
Field goal pct.: .638, Sylvia Fowles, Chicago
3-pt field goal pct.: .531, Temeka Johnson, Tulsa

Free throw pct.: .935, Kara Lawson, Connecticut
Rebounds: 345, Tina Charles, Connecticut
Assists: 178, Lindsay Whalen, Minnesota
Steals: 82, Sancho Lyttle, Atlanta
Blocked shots: 76, Candace Parker, Los Angeles

WNBA Champions, 1997-2012

Year	Regular Season Eastern Conference	Western Conference	Playoffs Champion	Coach	Opponent
1997	Houston Comets	Phoenix Mercury	Houston	Van Chancellor	New York
1998	Cleveland Rockers	Houston Comets	Houston	Van Chancellor	Phoenix
1999	New York Liberty	Houston Comets	Houston	Van Chancellor	New York
2000	New York Liberty	Los Angeles Sparks	Houston	Van Chancellor	New York
2001	Cleveland Rockers	Los Angeles Sparks	Los Angeles	Michael Cooper	Charlotte
2002	New York Liberty	Los Angeles Sparks	Los Angeles	Michael Cooper	New York
2003	Detroit Shock	Los Angeles Sparks	Detroit	Bill Laimbeer	Los Angeles
2004	Connecticut Sun	Los Angeles Sparks	Seattle	Anne Donovan	Connecticut
2005	Connecticut Sun	Sacramento Monarchs	Sacramento	John Whisenant	Connecticut
2006	Connecticut Sun	Sacramento Monarchs	Detroit	Bill Laimbeer	Sacramento
2007	Detroit Shock	Phoenix Mercury	Phoenix	Paul Westhead	Detroit
2008	Detroit Shock	San Antonio Silver Stars	Detroit	Bill Laimbeer	San Antonio
2009	Indiana Fever	Phoenix Mercury	Phoenix	Corey Gaines	Indiana
2010	Washington Mystics	Seattle Storm	Seattle	Brian Agler	Atlanta
2011	Indiana Fever	Minnesota Lynx	Minnesota	Cheryl Reeve	Atlanta
2012	Connecticut Sun	Minnesota Lynx	Indiana	Lin Dunn	Minnesota

WNBA Scoring Leaders, 1997-2012

(average points per game; 10 games minimum)

Year	Leader, team	Pts	Avg	Year	Leader, team	Pts	Avg	Year	Leader, team	Pts	Avg
1997	Cynthia Cooper, Houston	621	22.2	2002	Chamique Holdsclaw, Washington	397	19.9	2007	Lauren Jackson, Seattle	739	23.8
1998	Cynthia Cooper, Houston	680	22.7					2008	Diana Taurasi, Phoenix	820	24.1
1999	Cynthia Cooper, Houston	686	22.1	2003	Lauren Jackson, Seattle	698	21.2	2009	Diana Taurasi, Phoenix	631	20.4
2000	Sheryl Swoopes, Houston	643	20.7	2004	Lauren Jackson, Seattle	634	20.5	2010	Diana Taurasi, Phoenix	702	22.6
2001	Katie Smith, Minnesota	739	23.1	2005	Sheryl Swoopes, Houston	614	18.6	2011	Diana Taurasi, Phoenix	692	21.6
				2006	Diana Taurasi, Phoenix	860	25.3	2012	Angel McCoughtry, Atlanta	514	21.4

WNBA Finals MVP

Year	Player, team
1997	Cynthia Cooper, Houston
1998	Cynthia Cooper, Houston
1999	Cynthia Cooper, Houston
2000	Cynthia Cooper, Houston
2001	Lisa Leslie, Los Angeles
2002	Lisa Leslie, Los Angeles
2003	Ruth Riley, Detroit
2004	Betty Lennox, Seattle
2005	Yolanda Griffith, Sacramento
2006	Deanna Nolan, Detroit
2007	Cappie Pondexter, Phoenix
2008	Katie Smith, Detroit
2009	Diana Taurasi, Phoenix
2010	Lauren Jackson, Seattle
2011	Seimone Augustus, Minnesota
2012	Tamika Catchings, Indiana

WNBA Most Valuable Player

Year	Player, team
1997	Cynthia Cooper, Houston
1998	Cynthia Cooper, Houston
1999	Yolanda Griffith, Sacramento
2000	Sheryl Swoopes, Houston
2001	Lisa Leslie, Los Angeles
2002	Sheryl Swoopes, Houston
2003	Lauren Jackson, Seattle
2004	Lisa Leslie, Los Angeles
2005	Sheryl Swoopes, Houston
2006	Lisa Leslie, Los Angeles
2007	Lauren Jackson, Seattle
2008	Candace Parker, Los Angeles
2009	Diana Taurasi, Phoenix
2010	Lauren Jackson, Seattle
2011	Tamika Catchings, Indiana
2012	Tina Charles, Connecticut

WNBA Rookie of the Year

Year	Player, team
1997	No award
1998	Tracy Reid, Charlotte
1999	Chamique Holdsclaw, Washington
2000	Betty Lennox, Minnesota
2001	Jackie Stiles, Portland
2002	Tamika Catchings, Indiana
2003	Cheryl Ford, Detroit
2004	Diana Taurasi, Phoenix
2005	Temeka Johnson, Washington
2006	Seimone Augustus, Minnesota
2007	Armintie Price, Chicago
2008	Candace Parker, Los Angeles
2009	Angel McCoughtry, Atlanta
2010	Tina Charles, Connecticut
2011	Maya Moore, Minnesota
2012	Nneka Ogwumike, Los Angeles

HOCKEY

Los Angeles Kings Claim First Stanley Cup Crown

The Los Angeles Kings captured the first championship in the franchise's 45-year history, topping the New Jersey Devils, four games to two, in the 2012 Stanley Cup Finals. Los Angeles scored three power play goals in less than four minutes en route to a 6-1 win over the Devils in the deciding Game 6, June 11, 2012, at STAPLES Center in Los Angeles. The Kings tied a league record of 10 consecutive road playoff wins in a single postseason. The team was led by three different head coaches in 2011-12 en route to the title (Terry Murray, interim coach John Stevens, and Darryl Sutter). Kings goaltender Jonathan Quick recorded a .946 save percentage in the postseason and won the Conn Smythe Trophy as playoff MVP.

The eighth-seeded Kings beat the top three seeds in the Western Conference playoffs, including the Vancouver Canucks in five games in the first round. The Canucks had won their second straight Presidents' Trophy, for best overall record in the regular season, with 111 points. In the regular season, the Detroit Red Wings set a new record with a 23-game home winning streak.

Tampa Bay's Steven Stamkos led the NHL with 60 goals. Edmonton Oiler Sam Gagner became the 11th player in NHL history to record eight points in a game Feb. 2, 2012 (an 8-4 victory over the Chicago Blackhawks). Teammates Sidney Crosby and Evgeni Malkin made headlines for the Pittsburgh Penguins. Crosby returned to the ice Nov. 21, 2011, after missing 61 games due to a concussion, but the former league MVP was back on the shelf in Dec. after a recurrence of concussion-like symptoms and played just 22 games. Malkin had a league-high 109 points and captured the Art Ross Trophy, as well as awards for league MVP and best player as voted by his peers.

Final NHL Standings, 2011-12

Playoff seeding in parentheses; division winners automatically seeded 1, 2, or 3. Standings were determined by total points, then by the greater number of games won, excluding games won in a shootout. This figure is reflected in the ROW column (regulation + OT wins). Teams tied at the end of regulation time are each awarded one point. An additional point is awarded to the overtime or shootout winner.

Eastern Conference

Atlantic Division	W	L	OT	GF	GA	PTS	ROW
New York Rangers (1)	51	24	7	226	187	109	47
Pittsburgh Penguins (4)	51	25	6	282	221	108	42
Philadelphia Flyers (5)	47	26	9	264	232	103	43
New Jersey Devils (6)	48	28	6	228	209	102	36
New York Islanders	34	37	11	203	255	79	27

Northeast Division	W	L	OT	GF	GA	PTS	ROW
Boston Bruins (2)	49	29	4	269	202	102	40
Ottawa Senators (8)	41	31	10	249	240	92	35
Buffalo Sabres	39	32	11	218	230	89	32
Toronto Maple Leafs	35	37	10	231	264	80	31
Montréal Canadiens	31	35	16	212	226	78	26

Southeast Division	W	L	OT	GF	GA	PTS	ROW
Florida Panthers (3)	38	26	18	203	227	94	32
Washington Capitals (7)	42	32	8	222	230	92	38
Tampa Bay Lightning	38	36	8	235	281	84	35
Winnipeg Jets	37	35	10	225	246	84	33
Carolina Hurricanes	33	33	16	213	243	82	32

Western Conference

Central Division	W	L	OT	GF	GA	PTS	ROW
St. Louis Blues (2)	49	22	11	210	165	109	45
Nashville Predators (4)	48	26	8	237	210	104	43
Detroit Red Wings (5)	48	28	6	248	203	102	39
Chicago Blackhawks (6)	45	26	11	248	238	101	38
Columbus Blue Jackets	29	46	7	202	262	65	25

Northwest Division	W	L	OT	GF	GA	PTS	ROW
Vancouver Canucks (1)	51	22	9	249	198	111	43
Calgary Flames	37	29	16	202	226	90	34
Colorado Avalanche	41	35	6	208	220	88	32
Minnesota Wild	35	36	11	177	226	81	24
Edmonton Oilers	32	40	10	212	239	74	27

Pacific Division	W	L	OT	GF	GA	PTS	ROW
Phoenix Coyotes (3)	42	27	13	216	204	97	36
San Jose Sharks (7)	43	29	10	228	210	96	34
Los Angeles Kings (8)	40	27	15	194	179	95	34
Dallas Stars	42	35	5	211	222	89	35
Anaheim Ducks	34	36	12	204	231	80	31

Stanley Cup Playoff Results, 2012

Eastern Conference
NY Rangers defeated Ottawa, 4-3
Washington defeated Boston, 4-3
New Jersey defeated Florida, 4-3
Philadelphia defeated Pittsburgh, 4-2
NY Rangers defeated Washington, 4-3
New Jersey defeated Philadelphia, 4-1
New Jersey defeated NY Rangers, 4-2

Western Conference
Los Angeles defeated Vancouver, 4-1
St. Louis defeated San Jose, 4-1
Phoenix defeated Chicago, 4-2
Nashville defeated Detroit, 4-1
Los Angeles defeated St. Louis, 4-0
Phoenix defeated Nashville, 4-1
Los Angeles defeated Phoenix, 4-1

Stanley Cup Final
Los Angeles defeated New Jersey, 4-2 (2-1 [OT], 2-1 [OT], 4-0, 1-3, 1-2, 6-1)

Stanley Cup Champions, 1927-2012

Year	Champion	Coach	Final opponent
1927	Ottawa	Dave Gill	Boston
1928	NY Rangers	Lester Patrick	Montréal Maroons
1929	Boston	Cy Denneny	NY Rangers
1930	Montréal Canadiens	Cecil Hart	Boston
1931	Montréal Canadiens	Cecil Hart	Chicago
1932	Toronto	Dick Irvin	NY Rangers
1933	NY Rangers	Lester Patrick	Toronto
1934	Chicago	Tommy Gorman	Detroit
1935	Montréal Maroons	Tommy Gorman	Toronto
1936	Detroit	Jack Adams	Toronto
1937	Detroit	Jack Adams	NY Rangers
1938	Chicago	Bill Stewart	Toronto
1939	Boston	Art Ross	Toronto
1940	NY Rangers	Frank Boucher	Toronto
1941	Boston	Cooney Weiland	Detroit
1942	Toronto	Hap Day	Detroit
1943	Detroit	Jack Adams	Boston
1944	Montréal	Dick Irvin	Chicago
1945	Toronto	Hap Day	Detroit
1946	Montréal	Dick Irvin	Boston
1947	Toronto	Hap Day	Montréal
1948	Toronto	Hap Day	Detroit
1949	Toronto	Hap Day	Detroit
1950	Detroit	Tommy Ivan	NY Rangers
1951	Toronto	Joe Primeau	Montréal
1952	Detroit	Tommy Ivan	Montréal
1953	Montréal	Dick Irvin	Boston
1954	Detroit	Tommy Ivan	Montréal
1955	Detroit	Jimmy Skinner	Montréal
1956	Montréal	Toe Blake	Detroit
1957	Montréal	Toe Blake	Boston
1958	Montréal	Toe Blake	Boston
1959	Montréal	Toe Blake	Toronto
1960	Montréal	Toe Blake	Toronto
1961	Chicago	Rudy Pilous	Detroit
1962	Toronto	Punch Imlach	Chicago
1963	Toronto	Punch Imlach	Detroit
1964	Toronto	Punch Imlach	Detroit
1965	Montréal	Toe Blake	Chicago
1966	Montréal	Toe Blake	Detroit
1967	Toronto	Punch Imlach	Montréal
1968	Montréal	Toe Blake	St. Louis
1969	Montréal	Claude Ruel	St. Louis
1970	Boston	Harry Sinden	St. Louis
1971	Montréal	Al MacNeil	Chicago
1972	Boston	Tom Johnson	NY Rangers
1973	Montréal	Scotty Bowman	Chicago
1974	Philadelphia	Fred Shero	Boston
1975	Philadelphia	Fred Shero	Buffalo
1976	Montréal	Scotty Bowman	Philadelphia
1977	Montréal	Scotty Bowman	Boston

Year	Champion	Coach	Final opponent	Year	Champion	Coach	Final opponent
1978	Montréal	Scotty Bowman	Boston	1996	Colorado	Marc Crawford	Florida
1979	Montréal	Scotty Bowman	NY Rangers	1997	Detroit	Scotty Bowman	Philadelphia
1980	NY Islanders	Al Arbour	Philadelphia	1998	Detroit	Scotty Bowman	Washington
1981	NY Islanders	Al Arbour	Minnesota	1999	Dallas	Ken Hitchcock	Buffalo
1982	NY Islanders	Al Arbour	Vancouver	2000	New Jersey	Larry Robinson	Dallas
1983	NY Islanders	Al Arbour	Edmonton	2001	Colorado	Bob Hartley	New Jersey
1984	Edmonton	Glen Sather	NY Islanders	2002	Detroit	Scotty Bowman	Carolina
1985	Edmonton	Glen Sather	Philadelphia	2003	New Jersey	Pat Burns	Anaheim
1986	Montréal	Jean Perron	Calgary	2004	Tampa Bay	John Tortorella	Calgary
1987	Edmonton	Glen Sather	Philadelphia	2005	No competition (labor dispute; season cancelled)		
1988	Edmonton	Glen Sather	Boston	2006	Carolina	Peter Laviolette	Edmonton
1989	Calgary	Terry Crisp	Montréal	2007	Anaheim	Randy Carlyle	Ottawa
1990	Edmonton	John Muckler	Boston	2008	Detroit	Mike Babcock	Pittsburgh
1991	Pittsburgh	Bob Johnson	Minnesota	2009	Pittsburgh	Dan Bylsma	Detroit
1992	Pittsburgh	Scotty Bowman	Chicago	2010	Chicago	Joel Quenneville	Philadelphia
1993	Montréal	Jacques Demers	Los Angeles	2011	Boston	Claude Julien	Vancouver
1994	NY Rangers	Mike Keenan	Vancouver	2012	Los Angeles	Darryl Sutter	New Jersey
1995	New Jersey	Jacques Lemaire	Detroit				

Most NHL Goals in a Season

Player	Team	Season	Goals	Player	Team	Season	Goals
Wayne Gretzky	Edmonton	1981-82	92	Jari Kurri	Edmonton	1984-85	71
Wayne Gretzky	Edmonton	1983-84	87	Mario Lemieux	Pittsburgh	1987-88	70
Brett Hull	St. Louis	1990-91	86	Bernie Nicholls	Los Angeles	1988-89	70
Mario Lemieux	Pittsburgh	1988-89	85	Brett Hull	St. Louis	1991-92	70
Phil Esposito	Boston	1970-71	76	Mike Bossy	NY Islanders	1978-79	69
Alexander Mogilny	Buffalo	1992-93	76	Mario Lemieux	Pittsburgh	1992-93	69
Teemu Selanne	Winnipeg	1992-93	76	Mario Lemieux	Pittsburgh	1995-96	69
Wayne Gretzky	Edmonton	1984-85	73	Phil Esposito	Boston	1973-74	68
Brett Hull	St. Louis	1989-90	72	Mike Bossy	NY Islanders	1980-81	68
Wayne Gretzky	Edmonton	1982-83	71	Jari Kurri	Edmonton	1985-86	68

All-Time Regular Season Leading Scorers

(Through end of 2011-12 season. * = Active in 2011-12 season.)

Player	Goals	Assists	Points	Player	Goals	Assists	Points	Player	Goals	Assists	Points
Wayne Gretzky	894	1,963	2,857	*Jaromir Jagr	665	988	1,653	Bryan Trottier	524	901	1,425
Mark Messier	694	1,193	1,887	Joe Sakic	625	1,016	1,641	Adam Oates	341	1,079	1,420
Gordie Howe	801	1,049	1,850	Phil Esposito	717	873	1,590	Doug Gilmour	450	964	1,414
Ron Francis	549	1,249	1,798	Ray Bourque	410	1,169	1,579	Dale Hawerchuk	518	891	1,409
Marcel Dionne	731	1,040	1,771	Mark Recchi	577	956	1,533	*Teemu Selanne	663	743	1,406
Steve Yzerman	692	1,063	1,755	Paul Coffey	396	1,135	1,531	Jari Kurri	601	797	1,398
Mario Lemieux	690	1,033	1,723	Stan Mikita	541	926	1,467	Luc Robitaille	668	726	1,394

Hart Memorial Trophy (MVP), 1927-2012

Year	Player, team	Year	Player, team	Year	Player, team
1927	Herb Gardiner, Montréal Canadiens	1956	Jean Beliveau, Montréal	1984	Wayne Gretzky, Edmonton
1928	Howie Morenz, Montréal Canadiens	1957	Gordie Howe, Detroit	1985	Wayne Gretzky, Edmonton
1929	Roy Worters, NY Americans	1958	Gordie Howe, Detroit	1986	Wayne Gretzky, Edmonton
1930	Nels Stewart, Montréal Maroons	1959	Andy Bathgate, NY Rangers	1987	Wayne Gretzky, Edmonton
1931	Howie Morenz, Montréal Canadiens	1960	Gordie Howe, Detroit	1988	Mario Lemieux, Pittsburgh
1932	Howie Morenz, Montréal Canadiens	1961	Bernie Geoffrion, Montréal	1989	Wayne Gretzky, Los Angeles
1933	Eddie Shore, Boston	1962	Jacques Plante, Montréal	1990	Mark Messier, Edmonton
1934	Aurel Joliat, Montréal Canadiens	1963	Gordie Howe, Detroit	1991	Brett Hull, St. Louis
1935	Eddie Shore, Boston	1964	Jean Beliveau, Montréal	1992	Mark Messier, NY Rangers
1936	Eddie Shore, Boston	1965	Bobby Hull, Chicago	1993	Mario Lemieux, Pittsburgh
1937	Babe Siebert, Montréal Canadiens	1966	Bobby Hull, Chicago	1994	Sergei Fedorov, Detroit
1938	Eddie Shore, Boston	1967	Stan Mikita, Chicago	1995	Eric Lindros, Philadelphia
1939	Toe Blake, Montréal	1968	Stan Mikita, Chicago	1996	Mario Lemieux, Pittsburgh
1940	Ebbie Goodfellow, Detroit	1969	Phil Esposito, Boston	1997	Dominik Hasek, Buffalo
1941	Bill Cowley, Boston	1970	Bobby Orr, Boston	1998	Dominik Hasek, Buffalo
1942	Tom Anderson, Brooklyn Americans	1971	Bobby Orr, Boston	1999	Jaromir Jagr, Pittsburgh
1943	Bill Cowley, Boston	1972	Bobby Orr, Boston	2000	Chris Pronger, St. Louis
1944	Babe Pratt, Toronto	1973	Bobby Clarke, Philadelphia	2001	Joe Sakic, Colorado
1945	Elmer Lach, Montréal	1974	Phil Esposito, Boston	2002	Jose Theodore, Montréal
1946	Max Bentley, Chicago	1975	Bobby Clarke, Philadelphia	2003	Peter Forsberg, Colorado
1947	Maurice Richard, Montréal	1976	Bobby Clarke, Philadelphia	2004	Martin St. Louis, Tampa Bay
1948	Buddy O'Connor, NY Rangers	1977	Guy Lafleur, Montréal	2006	Joe Thornton, San Jose
1949	Sid Abel, Detroit	1978	Guy Lafleur, Montréal	2007	Sidney Crosby, Pittsburgh
1950	Chuck Rayner, NY Rangers	1979	Bryan Trottier, NY Islanders	2008	Alexander Ovechkin, Washington
1951	Milt Schmidt, Boston	1980	Wayne Gretzky, Edmonton	2009	Alexander Ovechkin, Washington
1952	Gordie Howe, Detroit	1981	Wayne Gretzky, Edmonton	2010	Henrik Sedin, Vancouver
1953	Gordie Howe, Detroit	1982	Wayne Gretzky, Edmonton	2011	Corey Perry, Anaheim
1954	Al Rollins, Chicago	1983	Wayne Gretzky, Edmonton	2012	Evgeni Malkin, Pittsburgh
1955	Ted Kennedy, Toronto				

Conn Smythe Trophy (MVP in Playoffs), 1965-2012

Year	Player, team	Year	Player, team	Year	Player, team
1965	Jean Beliveau, Montréal	1976	Reggie Leach, Philadelphia	1987	Ron Hextall, Philadelphia
1966	Roger Crozier, Detroit	1977	Guy Lafleur, Montréal	1988	Wayne Gretzky, Edmonton
1967	Dave Keon, Toronto	1978	Larry Robinson, Montréal	1989	Al MacInnis, Calgary
1968	Glenn Hall, St. Louis	1979	Bob Gainey, Montréal	1990	Bill Ranford, Edmonton
1969	Serge Savard, Montréal	1980	Bryan Trottier, NY Islanders	1991	Mario Lemieux, Pittsburgh
1970	Bobby Orr, Boston	1981	Butch Goring, NY Islanders	1992	Mario Lemieux, Pittsburgh
1971	Ken Dryden, Montréal	1982	Mike Bossy, NY Islanders	1993	Patrick Roy, Montréal
1972	Bobby Orr, Boston	1983	Billy Smith, NY Islanders	1994	Brian Leetch, NY Rangers
1973	Yvan Cournoyer, Montréal	1984	Mark Messier, Edmonton	1995	Claude Lemieux, New Jersey
1974	Bernie Parent, Philadelphia	1985	Wayne Gretzky, Edmonton	1996	Joe Sakic, Colorado
1975	Bernie Parent, Philadelphia	1986	Patrick Roy, Montréal	1997	Mike Vernon, Detroit

Year	Player, team	Year	Player, team	Year	Player, team
1998	Steve Yzerman, Detroit	2003	Jean-Sebastien Giguere, Anaheim	2009	Evgeni Malkin, Pittsburgh
1999	Joe Nieuwendyk, Dallas	2004	Brad Richards, Tampa Bay	2010	Jonathan Toews, Chicago
2000	Scott Stevens, New Jersey	2006	Cam Ward, Carolina	2011	Tim Thomas, Boston
2001	Patrick Roy, Colorado	2007	Scott Niedermayer, Anaheim	2012	Jonathan Quick, Los Angeles
2002	Nicklas Lidstrom, Detroit	2008	Henrik Zetterberg, Detroit		

Calder Memorial Trophy (Rookie of the Year), 1933-2012

Year	Player, team	Year	Player, team	Year	Player, team
1933	Carl Voss, Detroit	1960	Bill Hay, Chicago	1986	Gary Suter, Calgary
1934	Russ Blinco, Montréal Maroons	1961	Dave Keon, Toronto	1987	Luc Robitaille, Los Angeles
1935	Dave Schriner, NY Americans	1962	Bobby Rousseau, Montréal	1988	Joe Nieuwendyk, Calgary
1936	Mike Karakas, Chicago	1963	Kent Douglas, Toronto	1989	Brian Leetch, NY Rangers
1937	Syl Apps, Toronto	1964	Jacques Laperriere, Montréal	1990	Sergei Makarov, Calgary
1938	Cully Dahlstrom, Chicago	1965	Roger Crozier, Detroit	1991	Ed Belfour, Chicago
1939	Frank Brimsek, Boston	1966	Brit Selby, Toronto	1992	Pavel Bure, Vancouver
1940	Kilby MacDonald, NY Rangers	1967	Bobby Orr, Boston	1993	Teemu Selanne, Winnipeg
1941	John Quilty, Montréal	1968	Derek Sanderson, Boston	1994	Martin Brodeur, New Jersey
1942	Grant Warwick, NY Rangers	1969	Danny Grant, Minnesota	1995	Peter Forsberg, Quebec
1943	Gaye Stewart, Toronto	1970	Tony Esposito, Chicago	1996	Daniel Alfredsson, Ottawa
1944	Gus Bodnar, Toronto	1971	Gilbert Perreault, Buffalo	1997	Bryan Berard, NY Islanders
1945	Frank McCool, Toronto	1972	Ken Dryden, Montréal	1998	Sergei Samsonov, Boston
1946	Edgar Laprade, NY Rangers	1973	Steve Vickers, NY Rangers	1999	Chris Drury, Colorado
1947	Howie Meeker, Toronto	1974	Denis Potvin, NY Islanders	2000	Scott Gomez, New Jersey
1948	Jim McFadden, Detroit	1975	Eric Vail, Atlanta	2001	Evgeni Nabokov, San Jose
1949	Pentti Lund, NY Rangers	1976	Bryan Trottier, NY Islanders	2002	Dany Heatley, Atlanta
1950	Jack Gelineau, Boston	1977	Willi Plett, Atlanta	2003	Barret Jackman, St. Louis
1951	Terry Sawchuk, Detroit	1978	Mike Bossy, NY Islanders	2004	Andrew Raycroft, Boston
1952	Bernie Geoffrion, Montréal	1979	Bobby Smith, Minnesota	2006	Alexander Ovechkin, Washington
1953	Gump Worsley, NY Rangers	1980	Ray Bourque, Boston	2007	Evgeni Malkin, Pittsburgh
1954	Camille Henry, NY Rangers	1981	Peter Stastny, Quebec	2008	Patrick Kane, Chicago
1955	Ed Litzenberger, Chicago	1982	Dale Hawerchuk, Winnipeg	2009	Steve Mason, Columbus
1956	Glenn Hall, Detroit	1983	Steve Larmer, Chicago	2010	Tyler Myers, Buffalo
1957	Larry Regan, Boston	1984	Tom Barrasso, Buffalo	2011	Jeff Skinner, Carolina
1958	Frank Mahovlich, Toronto	1985	Mario Lemieux, Pittsburgh	2012	Gabriel Landeskog, Colorado
1959	Ralph Backstrom, Montréal				

Lady Byng Memorial Trophy (Most Gentlemanly Player), 1925-2012

Year	Player, team	Year	Player, team	Year	Player, team
1925	Frank Nighbor, Ottawa	1954	Red Kelly, Detroit	1983	Mike Bossy, NY Islanders
1926	Frank Nighbor, Ottawa	1955	Sid Smith, Toronto	1984	Mike Bossy, NY Islanders
1927	Billy Burch, NY Americans	1956	Earl Reibel, Detroit	1985	Jari Kurri, Edmonton
1928	Frank Boucher, NY Rangers	1957	Andy Hebenton, NY Rangers	1986	Mike Bossy, NY Islanders
1929	Frank Boucher, NY Rangers	1958	Camille Henry, NY Rangers	1987	Joe Mullen, Calgary
1930	Frank Boucher, NY Rangers	1959	Alex Delvecchio, Detroit	1988	Mats Naslund, Montréal
1931	Frank Boucher, NY Rangers	1960	Don McKenney, Boston	1989	Joe Mullen, Calgary
1932	Joe Primeau, Toronto	1961	Red Kelly, Toronto	1990	Brett Hull, St. Louis
1933	Frank Boucher, NY Rangers	1962	Dave Keon, Toronto	1991	Wayne Gretzky, Los Angeles
1934	Frank Boucher, NY Rangers	1963	Dave Keon, Toronto	1992	Wayne Gretzky, Los Angeles
1935	Frank Boucher, NY Rangers	1964	Ken Wharram, Chicago	1993	Pierre Turgeon, NY Islanders
1936	Doc Romnes, Chicago	1965	Bobby Hull, Chicago	1994	Wayne Gretzky, Los Angeles
1937	Marty Barry, Detroit	1966	Alex Delvecchio, Detroit	1995	Ron Francis, Pittsburgh
1938	Gordie Drillon, Toronto	1967	Stan Mikita, Chicago	1996	Paul Kariya, Anaheim
1939	Clint Smith, NY Rangers	1968	Stan Mikita, Chicago	1997	Paul Kariya, Anaheim
1940	Bobby Bauer, Boston	1969	Alex Delvecchio, Detroit	1998	Ron Francis, Pittsburgh
1941	Bobby Bauer, Boston	1970	Phil Goyette, St. Louis	1999	Wayne Gretzky, NY Rangers
1942	Syl Apps, Toronto	1971	John Bucyk, Boston	2000	Pavol Demitra, St. Louis
1943	Max Bentley, Chicago	1972	Jean Ratelle, NY Rangers	2001	Joe Sakic, Colorado
1944	Clint Smith, Chicago	1973	Gil Perreault, Buffalo	2002	Ron Francis, Carolina
1945	Bill Mosienko, Chicago	1974	John Bucyk, Boston	2003	Alexander Mogilny, Toronto
1946	Toe Blake, Montréal	1975	Marcel Dionne, Detroit	2004	Brad Richards, Tampa Bay
1947	Bobby Bauer, Boston	1976	Jean Ratelle, NYR-Boston	2006	Pavel Datsyuk, Detroit
1948	Buddy O'Connor, NY Rangers	1977	Marcel Dionne, Los Angeles	2007	Pavel Datsyuk, Detroit
1949	Bill Quackenbush, Detroit	1978	Butch Goring, Los Angeles	2008	Pavel Datsyuk, Detroit
1950	Edgar Laprade, NY Rangers	1979	Bob MacMillan, Atlanta	2009	Pavel Datsyuk, Detroit
1951	Red Kelly, Detroit	1980	Wayne Gretzky, Edmonton	2010	Martin St. Louis, Tampa Bay
1952	Sid Smith, Toronto	1981	Rick Kehoe, Pittsburgh	2011	Martin St. Louis, Tampa Bay
1953	Red Kelly, Detroit	1982	Rick Middleton, Boston	2012	Brian Campbell, Florida

James Norris Memorial Trophy (Outstanding Defenseman), 1954-2012

Year	Player, team	Year	Player, team	Year	Player, team
1954	Red Kelly, Detroit	1974	Bobby Orr, Boston	1993	Chris Chelios, Chicago
1955	Doug Harvey, Montréal	1975	Bobby Orr, Boston	1994	Ray Bourque, Boston
1956	Doug Harvey, Montréal	1976	Denis Potvin, NY Islanders	1995	Paul Coffey, Detroit
1957	Doug Harvey, Montréal	1977	Larry Robinson, Montréal	1996	Chris Chelios, Chicago
1958	Doug Harvey, Montréal	1978	Denis Potvin, NY Islanders	1997	Brian Leetch, NY Rangers
1959	Tom Johnson, Montréal	1979	Denis Potvin, NY Islanders	1998	Rob Blake, Los Angeles
1960	Doug Harvey, Montréal	1980	Larry Robinson, Montréal	1999	Al MacInnis, St. Louis
1961	Doug Harvey, Montréal	1981	Randy Carlyle, Pittsburgh	2000	Chris Pronger, St. Louis
1962	Doug Harvey, NY Rangers	1982	Doug Wilson, Chicago	2001	Nicklas Lidstrom, Detroit
1963	Pierre Pilote, Chicago	1983	Rod Langway, Washington	2002	Nicklas Lidstrom, Detroit
1964	Pierre Pilote, Chicago	1984	Rod Langway, Washington	2003	Nicklas Lidstrom, Detroit
1965	Pierre Pilote, Chicago	1985	Paul Coffey, Edmonton	2004	Scott Niedermayer, New Jersey
1966	Jacques Laperriere, Montréal	1986	Paul Coffey, Edmonton	2006	Nicklas Lidstrom, Detroit
1967	Harry Howell, NY Rangers	1987	Ray Bourque, Boston	2007	Nicklas Lidstrom, Detroit
1968	Bobby Orr, Boston	1988	Ray Bourque, Boston	2008	Nicklas Lidstrom, Detroit
1969	Bobby Orr, Boston	1989	Chris Chelios, Montréal	2009	Zdeno Chara, Boston
1970	Bobby Orr, Boston	1990	Ray Bourque, Boston	2010	Duncan Keith, Chicago
1971	Bobby Orr, Boston	1991	Ray Bourque, Boston	2011	Nicklas Lidstrom, Detroit
1972	Bobby Orr, Boston	1992	Brian Leetch, NY Rangers	2012	Erik Karlsson, Ottawa
1973	Bobby Orr, Boston				

Art Ross Trophy (Leading Points Scorer), 1927-2012

Trophy first awarded in 1948. Prior years list NHL scoring leader.

Year	Player, team	Year	Player, team	Year	Player, team
1927	Bill Cook, NY Rangers	1956	Jean Beliveau, Montréal	1984	Wayne Gretzky, Edmonton
1928	Howie Morenz, Montréal Canadiens	1957	Gordie Howe, Detroit	1985	Wayne Gretzky, Edmonton
1929	Ace Bailey, Toronto	1958	Dickie Moore, Montréal	1986	Wayne Gretzky, Edmonton
1930	Cooney Weiland, Boston	1959	Dickie Moore, Montréal	1987	Wayne Gretzky, Edmonton
1931	Howie Morenz, Montréal Canadiens	1960	Bobby Hull, Chicago	1988	Mario Lemieux, Pittsburgh
1932	Harvey Jackson, Toronto	1961	Bernie Geoffrion, Montréal	1989	Mario Lemieux, Pittsburgh
1933	Bill Cook, NY Rangers	1962	Bobby Hull, Chicago	1990	Wayne Gretzky, Los Angeles
1934	Charlie Conacher, Toronto	1963	Gordie Howe, Detroit	1991	Wayne Gretzky, Los Angeles
1935	Charlie Conacher, Toronto	1964	Stan Mikita, Chicago	1992	Mario Lemieux, Pittsburgh
1936	Dave Schriner, NY Americans	1965	Stan Mikita, Chicago	1993	Mario Lemieux, Pittsburgh
1937	Dave Schriner, NY Americans	1966	Bobby Hull, Chicago	1994	Wayne Gretzky, Los Angeles
1938	Gordie Drillon, Toronto	1967	Stan Mikita, Chicago	1995	Jaromir Jagr, Pittsburgh
1939	Toe Blake, Montréal	1968	Stan Mikita, Chicago	1996	Mario Lemieux, Pittsburgh
1940	Milt Schmidt, Boston	1969	Phil Esposito, Boston	1997	Mario Lemieux, Pittsburgh
1941	Bill Cowley, Boston	1970	Bobby Orr, Boston	1998	Jaromir Jagr, Pittsburgh
1942	Bryan Hextall, NY Rangers	1971	Phil Esposito, Boston	1999	Jaromir Jagr, Pittsburgh
1943	Doug Bentley, Chicago	1972	Phil Esposito, Boston	2000	Jaromir Jagr, Pittsburgh
1944	Herbie Cain, Boston	1973	Phil Esposito, Boston	2001	Jaromir Jagr, Pittsburgh
1945	Elmer Lach, Montréal	1974	Phil Esposito, Boston	2002	Jarome Iginla, Calgary
1946	Max Bentley, Chicago	1975	Bobby Orr, Boston	2003	Peter Forsberg, Colorado
1947	Max Bentley, Chicago	1976	Guy Lafleur, Montréal	2004	Martin St. Louis, Tampa Bay
1948	Elmer Lach, Montréal	1977	Guy Lafleur, Montréal	2006	Joe Thornton, San Jose
1949	Roy Conacher, Chicago	1978	Guy Lafleur, Montréal	2007	Sidney Crosby, Pittsburgh
1950	Ted Lindsay, Detroit	1979	Bryan Trottier, NY Islanders	2008	Alexander Ovechkin, Washington
1951	Gordie Howe, Detroit	1980	Marcel Dionne, Los Angeles	2009	Evgeni Malkin, Pittsburgh
1952	Gordie Howe, Detroit	1981	Wayne Gretzky, Edmonton	2010	Henrik Sedin, Vancouver
1953	Gordie Howe, Detroit	1982	Wayne Gretzky, Edmonton	2011	Daniel Sedin, Vancouver
1954	Gordie Howe, Detroit	1983	Wayne Gretzky, Edmonton	2012	Evgeni Malkin, Pittsburgh
1955	Bernie Geoffrion, Montréal				

Vezina Trophy (Outstanding Goalie), 1927-2012

Before 1982, awarded to the goalie or goalies who played a minimum of 25 games for the team that allowed the fewest goals; since 1982, awarded to the most outstanding goalie, as determined by a vote of NHL general managers.

Year	Player, team	Year	Player, team	Year	Player, team
1927	George Hainsworth, Montréal Canadiens	1954	Harry Lumley, Toronto	1983	Pete Peeters, Boston
1928	George Hainsworth, Montréal Canadiens	1955	Terry Sawchuk, Detroit	1984	Tom Barrasso, Buffalo
1929	George Hainsworth, Montréal Canadiens	1956	Jacques Plante, Montréal	1985	Pelle Lindbergh, Philadelphia
1930	Tiny Thompson, Boston	1957	Jacques Plante, Montréal	1986	John Vanbiesbrouck, NY Rangers
1931	Roy Worters, NY Americans	1958	Jacques Plante, Montréal	1987	Ron Hextall, Philadelphia
1932	Charlie Gardiner, Chicago	1959	Jacques Plante, Montréal	1988	Grant Fuhr, Edmonton
1933	Tiny Thompson, Boston	1960	Jacques Plante, Montréal	1989	Patrick Roy, Montréal
1934	Charlie Gardiner, Chicago	1961	Johnny Bower, Toronto	1990	Patrick Roy, Montréal
1935	Lorne Chabot, Chicago	1962	Jacques Plante, Montréal	1991	Ed Belfour, Chicago
1936	Tiny Thompson, Boston	1963	Glenn Hall, Chicago	1992	Patrick Roy, Montréal
1937	Normie Smith, Detroit	1964	Charlie Hodge, Montréal	1993	Ed Belfour, Chicago
1938	Tiny Thompson, Boston	1965	Sawchuk, Bower; Toronto	1994	Dominik Hasek, Buffalo
1939	Frank Brimsek, Boston	1966	Worsley, Hodge; Montréal	1995	Dominik Hasek, Buffalo
1940	Dave Kerr, NY Rangers	1967	Hall, DeJordy; Chicago	1996	Jim Carey, Washington
1941	Turk Broda, Toronto	1968	Worsley, Vachon; Montréal	1997	Dominik Hasek, Buffalo
1942	Frank Brimsek, Boston	1969	Hall, Plante; St. Louis	1998	Dominik Hasek, Buffalo
1943	Johnny Mowers, Detroit	1970	Tony Esposito, Chicago	1999	Dominik Hasek, Buffalo
1944	Bill Durnan, Montréal	1971	Giacomin, Villemure; NY Rangers	2000	Olaf Kolzig, Washington
1945	Bill Durnan, Montréal	1972	Esposito, Smith; Chicago	2001	Dominik Hasek, Buffalo
1946	Bill Durnan, Montréal	1973	Ken Dryden, Montréal	2002	Jose Theodore, Montréal
1947	Bill Durnan, Montréal	1974	Bernie Parent, Philadelphia; Tony Esposito, Chicago	2003	Martin Brodeur, New Jersey
1948	Turk Broda, Toronto	1975	Bernie Parent, Philadelphia	2004	Martin Brodeur, New Jersey
1949	Bill Durnan, Montréal	1976	Ken Dryden, Montréal	2006	Miikka Kiprusoff, Calgary
1950	Bill Durnan, Montréal	1977	Dryden, Larocque; Montréal	2007	Martin Brodeur, New Jersey
1951	Al Rollins, Toronto	1978	Dryden, Larocque; Montréal	2008	Martin Brodeur, New Jersey
1952	Terry Sawchuk, Detroit	1979	Dryden, Larocque; Montréal	2009	Tim Thomas, Boston
1953	Terry Sawchuk, Detroit	1980	Sauve, Edwards; Buffalo	2010	Ryan Miller, Buffalo
		1981	Sevigny, Larocque, Herron; Montréal	2011	Tim Thomas, Boston
		1982	Bill Smith, NY Islanders	2012	Henrik Lundqvist, NY Rangers

NHL Home Ice

Team	Name (built)	Capacity[1]	Team	Name (built)	Capacity[1]
Anaheim	Honda Center[2] (1993)	17,174	New Jersey	Prudential Center (2007)	17,625
Boston	TD Garden[3] (1995)	17,565	NY Islanders	Nassau Veterans Memorial Coliseum (1972)	16,234
Buffalo	First Niagara Center[4] (1996)	18,690	NY Rangers	Madison Square Garden (1968)	18,200
Calgary	Scotiabank Saddledome[5] (1983)	19,289	Ottawa	Scotiabank Place[11] (1996)	19,153
Carolina	PNC Arena[6] (1999)	18,680	Philadelphia	Wells Fargo Center[12] (1996)	19,537
Chicago	United Center (1994)	19,717	Phoenix	Jobing.com Arena[13] (2003)	17,125
Colorado	Pepsi Center (1999)	18,007	Pittsburgh	CONSOL Energy Center (2010)	18,387
Columbus	Nationwide Arena (2000)	18,144	St. Louis	Scottrade Center[14] (1994)	19,150
Dallas	American Airlines Center (2001)	18,532	San Jose	HP Pavilion at San Jose[15] (1993)	17,562
Detroit	Joe Louis Arena (1979)	20,066	Tampa Bay	Tampa Bay Times Forum[16] (1996)	19,500
Edmonton	Rexall Place[7] (1974)	16,839	Toronto	Air Canada Centre (1999)	18,819
Florida	BankAtlantic Center[8] (1998)	19,250	Vancouver	Rogers Arena[17] (1995)	18,890
Los Angeles	STAPLES Center (1999)	18,118	Washington	Verizon Center[18] (1997)	18,506
Minnesota	Xcel Energy Center (2000)	18,064	Winnipeg	MTS Centre (2004)	15,015
Montréal	Le Centre Bell[9] (1996)	21,273			
Nashville	Bridgestone Arena[10] (1997)	17,113			

(1) At the end of the 2011-12 season. (2) The Arrowhead Pond of Anaheim, 1993-2006. (3) FleetCenter, 1995-2005; TD Banknorth Garden, 2005-09. (4) Marine Midland Arena, 1996-99; HSBC Arena, 1999-2011. (5) Olympic Saddledome, 1983-96; Canadian Airlines Saddledome, 1996-2000; Pengrowth Saddledome, 2000-10. (6) Raleigh Entertainment and Sports Arena, 1999-2002; RBC Center, 2002-11. (7) Northlands Col., 1974-79; Edmonton Col., 1979-98; Skyreach Centre, 1998-2003. (8) National Car Rental Center, 1998-2002; Office Depot Center, 2002-05. (9) Le Centre Molson, 1996-2002. (10) Nashville Arena, 1997-99; Gaylord Entertainment Center, 1999-2007; Sommet Center, 2007-10. (11) Corel Centre, 1996-2006. (12) CoreStates Center, 1996-98; First Union Center, 1998-2003; Wachovia Center, 2003-10. (13) Glendale Arena, 2003-06. (14) Kiel Center, 1994-2000; Savvis Center, 2000-06. (15) San Jose Arena, 1993-2001; Compaq Center, 2001-02. (16) Ice Palace, 1996-2002; St. Pete Times Forum, 2002-12. (17) General Motors Place, 1995-2010. (18) MCI Center, 1997-2006.

Hockey Hall of Fame

(Located in Toronto, ON, Canada. * = 2012 inductee.)

Players

Abel, Sid
Adams, Jack
Anderson, Glenn
Apps, Syl
Armstrong, George
Bailey, Irvine "Ace"
Bain, Dan
Baker, Hobey
Barber, Bill
Barry, Marty
Bathgate, Andy
Bauer, Bobby
Belfour, Ed
Beliveau, Jean
Benedict, Clint
Bentley, Doug
Bentley, Max
Blake, Hector "Toe"
Boivin, Leo
Boon, Dickie
Bossy, Mike
Bouchard, Butch
Boucher, Frank
Boucher, George
Bourque, Ray
Bower, Johnny
Bowie, Russell "Dubbie"
Brimsek, Frank
Broadbent, Harry L. "Punch"
Broda, Turk
Bucyk, John
Burch, Billy
*Bure, Pavel
Cameron, Harry
Cheevers, Gerry
Ciccarelli, Dino
Clancy, King
Clapper, Aubrey "Dit"
Clarke, Bobby
Cleghorn, Sprague
Coffey, Paul
Colville, Neil
Conacher, Charlie
Conacher, Lionel
Conacher, Roy
Connell, Alex
Cook, Bill
Cook, Frederick "Bun"
Coulter, Art
Cournoyer, Yvan
Cowley, Bill
Crawford, Rusty
Darragh, Jack
Davidson, Scotty
Day, Clarence "Hap"
Delvecchio, Alex
Denneny, Cy
Dionne, Marcel
Drillon, Gordie
Drinkwater, Graham
Dryden, Ken
Duff, Terrance "Dick"
Dumart, Woody
Dunderdale, Tommy
Durnan, Bill
Dutton, Mervyn "Red"
Dye, Babe
Esposito, Phil
Esposito, Tony
Farrel, Arthur
Federko, Bernie
Fetisov, Viacheslav
Flaman, Fernie
Foyston, Frank
Francis, Ron

Fredrickson, Frank
Fuhr, Grant
Gadsby, Bill
Gainey, Bob
Gardiner, Chuck
Gardiner, Herb
Gardiner, Jimmy
Gartner, Mike
Geoffrion, Bernie
Gerard, Eddie
Giacomin, Eddie
Gilbert, Rod
Gillies, Clark
Gilmour, Billy
Gilmour, Doug
Goheen, Frank "Moose"
Goodfellow, Ebbie
Goulet, Michel
Granato, Cammi
Grant, Mike
Green, Wilfred "Shorty"
Gretzky, Wayne
Griffis, Si
Hainsworth, George
Hall, Glenn
Hall, Joe
Harvey, Doug
Hawerchuk, Dale
Hay, George
Hern, Riley
Hextall, Bryan
Holmes, Hap
Hooper, Tom
Horner, Red
Horton, Tim
Howe, Gordie
Howe, Mark
Howe, Syd
Howell, Harry
Hull, Bobby
Hull, Brett
Hutton, John "Bouse"
Hyland, Harry
Irvin, Dick
Jackson, Harvey "Busher"
James, Angela
Johnson, Ching
Johnson, Ernie
Johnson, Tom
Joliat, Aurel
Keats, Duke
Kelly, Red
Kennedy, Ted
Keon, Dave
Kharlamov, Valeri
Kurri, Jari
Lach, Elmer
Lafleur, Guy
LaFontaine, Pat
Lalonde, Newsy
Langway, Rod
Laperriere, Jacques
Lapointe, Guy
Laprade, Edgar
Larionov, Igor
Laviolette, Jack
Leetch, Brian
Lehman, Hughie
Lemaire, Jacques
Lemieux, Mario
LeSueur, Percy
Lewis, Herbie
Lindsay, Ted
Lumley, Harry
MacInnis, Al
MacKay, Mickey
Mahovlich, Frank
Malone, Joe

Mantha, Sylvio
Marshall, Jack
Maxwell, Fred
McDonald, Lanny
McGee, Frank
McGimsie, Billy
McNamara, George
Messier, Mark
Mikita, Stan
Moore, Dickie
Moran, Paddy
Morenz, Howie
Mosienko, Bill
Mullen, Joe
Murphy, Larry
Neely, Cam
Nieuwendyk, Joe
Nighbor, Frank
Noble, Reg
*Oates, Adam
O'Connor, Buddy
Oliver, Harry
Olmstead, Bert
Orr, Bobby
Parent, Bernie
Park, Brad
Patrick, Lester
Patrick, Lynn
Perreault, Gilbert
Phillips, Tom
Pilote, Pierre
Pitre, Didier
Plante, Jacques
Potvin, Denis
Pratt, Babe
Primeau, Joe
Pronovost, Marcel
Pulford, Bob
Pulford, Harvey
Quackenbush, Bill
Rankin, Frank
Ratelle, Jean
Rayner, Chuck
Reardon, Kenny
Richard, Henri
Richard, Maurice
Richardson, George
Roberts, Gordie
Robinson, Larry
Robitaille, Luc
Ross, Art
Roy, Patrick
Russel, Blair
Russell, Ernie
Ruttan, Jack
*Sakic, Joe
Salming, Börje
Savard, Denis
Savard, Serge
Sawchuk, Terry
Scanlan, Fred
Schmidt, Milt
Schriner, Sweeney
Seibert, Earl
Seibert, Oliver
Shore, Eddie
Shutt, Steve
Siebert, Babe
Simpson, Joe "Bullet"
Sittler, Darryl
Smith, Alf
Smith, Billy
Smith, Clint
Smith, Hooley
Smith, Tommy
Stanley, Allan
Stanley, Barney

Stastny, Peter
Stevens, Ronald Scott
Stewart, Jack
Stewart, Nels
Stuart, Bruce
Stuart, Hod
*Sundin, Mats
Taylor, Frederick "Cyclone"
Thompson, Cecil "Tiny"
Tretiak, Vladislav
Trihey, Harry
Trottier, Bryan
Ullman, Norm
Vezina, Georges
Walker, Jack
Walsh, Marty
Watson, Harry "Moose"
Watson, Harry Percival
Weiland, Cooney
Westwick, Harry
Whitcroft, Fred
Wilson, Gordon Allan "Phat"
Worsley, Gump
Worters, Roy
Yzerman, Steve

Builders

Adams, Charles
Adams, Weston
Ahearn, Frank
Ahearn, John "Bunny"
Allan, Sir Montagu
Allen, Keith
Arbour, Al
Ballard, Harold
Bauer, Father David
Bickell, J. P.
Bowman, Scotty
Brooks, Herbert
Brown, George
Brown, Walter
Buckland, Frank
Bush, Walter, Jr.
Butterfield, Jack
Calder, Frank
Campbell, Angus
Campbell, Clarence
Cattarinich, Joseph
Chynoweth, Ed
Costello, Murray
Dandurand, Leo
Devellano, Jim
Dilio, Frank
Dudley, George
Dunn, James
Fletcher, Cliff
Francis, Emile
Gibson, Jack
Gorman, Tommy
Gregory, Jim
Griffiths, Frank
Hanley, Bill
Hay, Charles
Hendy, Jim
Hewitt, Foster
Hewitt, William
Hotchkiss, Harley
Hume, Fred
Ilitch, Mike
Imlach, Harry "Punch"
Ivan, Tommy
Jennings, William
Johnson, Bob
Juckes, Gordon
Kilpatrick, John
Kilrea, Brian

Knox, Seymour
Lamoriello, Lou
Leader, Al
LeBel, Robert
Lockhart, Thomas
Loicq, Paul
Mariucci, John
Mathers, Frank
McLaughlin, Frederic
Milford, Jake
Molson, Sen. Hartland
Morrison, Ian "Scotty"
Murray, Athol "Père"
Neilson, Roger
Nelson, Francis
Norris, Bruce
Norris, James
Norris, James, Sr.
Northey, William
O'Brien, J. Ambrose
O'Neill, Brian Francis
Page, Frederick
Patrick, Craig
Patrick, Frank
Pickard, Allan
Pilous, Rudy
Poile, Bud
Pollock, Sam
Raymond, Sen. Donat
Robertson, John Ross
Robinson, Claude
Ross, Phillip
Sabetzki, Gunther
Sather, Glen
Seaman, Daryl "Doc"
Selke, Frank
Sinden, Harry
Smith, Frank
Smythe, Conn
Snider, Ed
Stanley, Lord (of Preston)
Sutherland, Capt. James T.
Tarasov, Anatoli
Torrey, Bill
Turner, Lloyd
Tutt, William
Voss, Carl
Waghorne, Fred
Wirtz, Arthur
Wirtz, Bill
Ziegler, John A., Jr.

Referees and Linesmen

Armstrong, Neil
Ashley, John
Chadwick, Bill
D'Amico, John
Elliott, Edwin "Chaucer"
Hayes, George
Hewiston, Bobby
Ion, Mickey
Pavelich, Matt
Rodden, Mike
Scapinello, Ray
Smeaton, Cooper
Storey, Red
Udvari, Frank
Van Hellemond, Andy

SOCCER

Major League Soccer, 2011

David Beckham and Landon Donovan carried the Los Angeles Galaxy to the 2011 Major League Soccer (MLS) Cup title over the Houston Dynamo Nov. 20, 2011, at the Home Depot Center in Carson, CA. Donovan scored the lone goal in the 72nd minute in LA's 1-0 win. The Galaxy were undefeated at home (12-0-5) and led MLS with 19 wins, 67 points, and 28 goals allowed on the way to the team's third championship. Houston defeated first-place Sporting Kansas City in the Eastern Conference title game, 2-0, on Nov. 6 to earn its third MLS Cup appearance. Sporting KC had won just one of its first 10 games, all on the road, but lost only three matches after its new home, Livestrong Sporting Park, opened June 9, 2011.

The newest MLS teams found success at the turnstiles, if not the standings, as the league adjusted its regular season schedule from 30 to 34 games. The Portland (OR) Timbers sold out all 17 home games in their inaugural season. Despite a last-place finish, the Vancouver Whitecaps averaged 20,406 fans, third best in the league. The Seattle Sounders broke their own league-best record for average home attendance (38,495).

The league's best players met the UK's Manchester United at the MLS All-Star Game July 27, 2011, at Red Bull Arena in Harrison, NJ, but the MLS proved to be no match and lost 4-0.

Major League Soccer (MLS) Cup, 1996-2011

Year	Winner	Final opponent	Score	Site	MVP
1996	DC United	Los Angeles Galaxy	3-2 (OT)	Foxborough, MA	Marco Etcheverry
1997	DC United	Colorado Rapids	2-1	Washington, DC	Jaime Moreno
1998	Chicago Fire	DC United	2-0	Pasadena, CA	Peter Nowak
1999	DC United	Los Angeles Galaxy	2-0	Foxborough, MA	Ben Olsen
2000	Kansas City Wizards	Chicago Fire	1-0	Washington, DC	Tony Meola
2001	San Jose Earthquakes	Los Angeles Galaxy	2-1 (OT)	Columbus, OH	Dwayne De Rosario
2002	Los Angeles Galaxy	New England Revolution	1-0 (OT)	Foxborough, MA	Carlos Ruiz
2003	San Jose Earthquakes	Chicago Fire	4-2	Carson, CA	Landon Donovan
2004	DC United	Kansas City Wizards	3-2	Carson, CA	Alecko Eskandarian
2005	Los Angeles Galaxy	New England Revolution	1-0 (OT)	Frisco, TX	Guillermo Ramírez
2006	Houston Dynamo	New England Revolution	1-1 (4-3)*	Frisco, TX	Brian Ching
2007	Houston Dynamo	New England Revolution	2-1	Washington, DC	Dwayne De Rosario
2008	Columbus Crew	New York Red Bulls	3-1	Carson, CA	Guillermo Barros Schelotto
2009	Real Salt Lake	Los Angeles Galaxy	1-1 (5-4)*	Seattle, WA	Nick Rimando
2010	Colorado Rapids	FC Dallas	2-1	Toronto, ON, Canada	Conor Casey
2011	Los Angeles Galaxy	Houston Dynamo	1-0	Carson, CA	Landon Donovan

* = Match decided in penalty kicks (shootout score in parentheses). OT = Overtime.

Major League Soccer Final Standings, 2011

(Does not include playoff games.)

Eastern Conference	W	L	T	PTS	GF	GA	GD	Western Conference	W	L	T	PTS	GF	GA	GD
Sporting Kansas City	13	9	12	51	50	40	10	Los Angeles Galaxy	19	5	10	67	48	28	20
Houston Dynamo . . .	12	9	13	49	45	41	4	Seattle Sounders FC	18	7	9	63	56	37	19
Philadelphia Union . .	11	8	15	48	44	36	8	Real Salt Lake	15	11	8	53	44	36	8
Columbus Crew	13	13	8	47	43	44	−1	FC Dallas	15	12	7	52	42	39	3
New York Red Bulls	10	8	16	46	50	44	6	Colorado Rapids. . . .	12	9	13	49	44	41	3
Chicago Fire	9	9	16	43	46	45	1	Portland Timbers . . .	11	14	9	42	40	48	−8
DC United	9	13	12	39	49	52	−3	San Jose Earthquakes	8	12	14	38	40	45	−5
Toronto FC	6	13	15	33	36	59	−23	Chivas USA	8	14	12	36	41	43	−2
New England Revolution	5	16	13	28	38	58	−20	Vancouver Whitecaps FC	6	18	10	28	35	55	−20

Major League Soccer Scoring Leaders, 2011

Player	Club	GP	Goals	Player	Club	GP	Goals
Dwayne De Rosario	DC United.	33	16	Camilo	Vancouver	32	12
Chris Wondolowski.	San Jose.	30	16	Dominic Oduro	Chicago	34	12
Thierry Henry	New York	26	14	Sebastien Le Toux	Philadelphia	34	11
Andres Mendoza	Columbus	29	13	Brek Shea.	FC Dallas	31	11
Fredy Montero	Seattle	30	12	Alvaro Saborio	Real Salt Lake	23	11
Landon Donovan	Los Angeles	23	12	Charlie Davies	DC United.	26	11

Selected European Soccer League Champions, 1950-2012

Season	England: Premier League[1]	Spain: La Liga	Italy: Serie A	Germany: Bundesliga[2]
1949-50	Portsmouth FC	Atlético Madrid	Juventus	VfB Stuttgart
1950-51	Tottenham Hotspur	Atlético Madrid	AC Milan	Kaiserslautern
1951-52	Manchester United	FC Barcelona	Juventus	VfB Stuttgart
1952-53	Arsenal	FC Barcelona	Inter Milan	Kaiserslautern
1953-54	Wolverhampton Wanderers	Real Madrid	Inter Milan	Hannoverscher SV 96
1954-55	Chelsea	Real Madrid	AC Milan	Rot-Weiss Essen
1955-56	Manchester United	Athletic Bilbao	Fiorentina	Borussia Dortmund
1956-57	Manchester United	Real Madrid	AC Milan	Borussia Dortmund
1957-58	Wolverhampton Wanderers	Real Madrid	Juventus	Schalke 04
1958-59	Wolverhampton Wanderers	FC Barcelona	AC Milan	Eintracht Frankfurt
1959-60	Burnley FC	FC Barcelona	Juventus	Hamburg SV
1960-61	Tottenham Hotspur	Real Madrid	Juventus	FC Nuremberg
1961-62	Ipswich Town	Real Madrid	AC Milan	Cologne
1962-63	Everton	Real Madrid	Inter Milan	Borussia Dortmund
1963-64	Liverpool	Real Madrid	Bologna	FC Cologne
1964-65	Manchester United	Real Madrid	Inter Milan	Werder Bremen
1965-66	Liverpool	Atlético Madrid	Inter Milan	TSV 1860 Munich

Season	England: Premier League[1]	Spain: La Liga	Italy: Serie A	Germany: Bundesliga[2]
1966-67	Manchester United	Real Madrid	Juventus	Eintracht Braunschweig
1967-68	Manchester City	Real Madrid	AC Milan	FC Nuremberg
1968-69	Leeds United	Real Madrid	Fiorentina	Bayern Munich
1969-70	Everton	Atlético Madrid	Cagliari	Borussia Mönchengladbach
1970-71	Arsenal	Valencia	Inter Milan	Borussia Mönchengladbach
1971-72	Derby County	Real Madrid	Juventus	Bayern Munich
1972-73	Liverpool	Atlético Madrid	Juventus	Bayern Munich
1973-74	Leeds United	FC Barcelona	Lazio	Bayern Munich
1974-75	Derby County	Real Madrid	Juventus	Borussia Mönchengladbach
1975-76	Liverpool	Real Madrid	Torino	Borussia Mönchengladbach
1976-77	Liverpool	Atlético Madrid	Juventus	Borussia Mönchengladbach
1977-78	Nottingham Forest	Real Madrid	Juventus	FC Cologne
1978-79	Liverpool	Real Madrid	AC Milan	Hamburg SV
1979-80	Liverpool	Real Madrid	Inter Milan	Bayern Munich
1980-81	Aston Villa	Real Sociedad	Juventus	Bayern Munich
1981-82	Liverpool	Real Sociedad	Juventus	Hamburg SV
1982-83	Liverpool	Athletic Bilbao	AS Roma	Hamburg SV
1983-84	Liverpool	Athletic Bilbao	Juventus	VfB Stuttgart
1984-85	Everton	FC Barcelona	Verona	Bayern Munich
1985-86	Liverpool	Real Madrid	Juventus	Bayern Munich
1986-87	Everton	Real Madrid	Napoli	Bayern Munich
1987-88	Liverpool	Real Madrid	AC Milan	Werder Bremen
1988-89	Arsenal	Real Madrid	Inter Milan	Bayern Munich
1989-90	Liverpool	Real Madrid	Napoli	Bayern Munich
1990-91	Arsenal	FC Barcelona	Sampdoria	FC Kaiserslautern
1991-92	Leeds United	FC Barcelona	AC Milan	VfB Stuttgart
1992-93	Manchester United	FC Barcelona	AC Milan	Werder Bremen
1993-94	Manchester United	FC Barcelona	AC Milan	Bayern Munich
1994-95	Blackburn Rovers	Real Madrid	Juventus	Borussia Dortmund
1995-96	Manchester United	Atlético Madrid	AC Milan	Borussia Dortmund
1996-97	Manchester United	Real Madrid	Juventus	Bayern Munich
1997-98	Arsenal	FC Barcelona	Juventus	FC Kaiserslautern
1998-99	Manchester United	FC Barcelona	AC Milan	Bayern Munich
1999-2000	Manchester United	Deportivo Coruña	Lazio	Bayern Munich
2000-01	Manchester United	Real Madrid	AS Roma	Bayern Munich
2001-02	Arsenal	Valencia	Juventus	Borussia Dortmund
2002-03	Manchester United	Real Madrid	Juventus	Bayern Munich
2003-04	Arsenal	Valencia	AC Milan	Werder Bremen
2004-05	Chelsea	FC Barcelona	None[3]	Bayern Munich
2005-06	Chelsea	FC Barcelona	Inter Milan	Bayern Munich
2006-07	Manchester United	Real Madrid	Inter Milan	VfB Stuttgart
2007-08	Manchester United	Real Madrid	Inter Milan	Bayern Munich
2008-09	Manchester United	FC Barcelona	Inter Milan	VfL Wolfsburg
2009-10	Chelsea	FC Barcelona	Inter Milan	Bayern Munich
2010-11	Manchester United	FC Barcelona	AC Milan	Borussia Dortmund
2011-12	Manchester City	Real Madrid	Juventus	Borussia Dortmund

(1) Football League champions are listed prior to 1992, when the Premier League formed. (2) Regional champions are listed prior to 1963, when National Bundesliga formed. (3) Juventus was stripped of the title because of match-fixing.

UEFA Champions League, 1956-2012

Year	Winner	Final opponent	Score
1956	Real Madrid	Reims	4-3
1957	Real Madrid	Fiorentina	2-0
1958	Real Madrid	AC Milan	3-2#
1959	Real Madrid	Reims	2-0
1960	Real Madrid	Eintracht	7-3
1961	Benfica	Barcelona	3-2
1962	Benfica	Real Madrid	5-3
1963	AC Milan	Benfica	2-1
1964	Inter Milan	Real Madrid	3-1
1965	Inter Milan	Benfica	1-0
1966	Real Madrid	Partizan	2-1
1967	Celtic	Inter Milan	2-1
1968	Manchester United	Benfica	4-1#
1969	AC Milan	Ajax	4-1
1970	Feyenoord	Celtic	2-1#
1971	Ajax	Panathinaikos	2-0
1972	Ajax	Inter Milan	2-0
1973	Ajax	Juventus	1-0
1974	Bayern Munich	Atlético	5-1[1]
1975	Bayern Munich	Leeds	2-0
1976	Bayern Munich	St-Etienne	1-0
1977	Liverpool	Mönchengladbach	3-1
1978	Liverpool	Club Brugge	1-0
1979	Nottingham Forest	Malmö	1-0
1980	Nottingham Forest	Hamburg	1-0
1981	Liverpool	Real Madrid	1-0
1982	Aston Villa	Bayern Munich	1-0
1983	Hamburg	Juventus	1-0
1984	Liverpool	Roma	1-1 (4-2)*

Year	Winner	Final opponent	Score
1985	Juventus	Liverpool	1-0
1986	Steaua	Barcelona	0-0 (2-0)*
1987	Porto	Bayern Munich	2-1
1988	PSV	Benfica	0-0 (6-5)*
1989	AC Milan	Steaua	4-0
1990	AC Milan	Benfica	1-0
1991	Crvena Zvezda	Marseille	0-0 (5-3)*
1992	Barcelona	Sampdoria	1-0#
1993	Marseille	AC Milan	1-0
1994	AC Milan	Barcelona	4-0
1995	Ajax	AC Milan	1-0
1996	Juventus	Ajax	1-1 (4-2)*
1997	Dortmund	Juventus	3-1
1998	Real Madrid	Juventus	1-0
1999	Manchester United	Bayern Munich	2-1
2000	Real Madrid	Valencia	3-0
2001	Bayern Munich	Valencia	1-1 (5-4)*
2002	Real Madrid	Leverkusen	2-1
2003	AC Milan	Juventus	0-0 (3-2)*
2004	Porto	Monaco	3-0
2005	Liverpool	AC Milan	3-3 (3-2)*
2006	Barcelona	Arsenal	2-1
2007	AC Milan	Liverpool	2-1
2008	Manchester United	Chelsea	1-1 (6-5)*
2009	Barcelona	Manchester United	2-0
2010	Inter Milan	Bayern Munich	2-0
2011	Barcelona	Manchester United	3-1
2012	Chelsea	Bayern Munich	1-1 (4-3)*

* = Match decided in penalty kicks (shootout score in parentheses). # = Match decided in extra time. (1) Aggregate score. First game 1-1; second, 4-0.

UEFA European Football Championships, 1960-2012

The final rounds of the 2012 UEFA European Championships were jointly hosted by Poland and Ukraine and opened June 8, 2012, in Warsaw and Wroclawa, Poland, with the final match at Olympic Stadium in Kiev, Ukraine, on July 1, 2012.

Year	Winner	Final opponent	Score	Site	Year	Winner	Final opponent	Score	Site
1960	USSR	Yugoslavia	2-1#	France	1988	Netherlands	USSR	2-0	W. Germany
1964	Spain	USSR	2-1	Spain	1992	Denmark	Germany	2-0	Sweden
1968	Italy	Yugoslavia	2-0	Italy	1996	Germany	Czech Rep.	2-1#	England
1972	W. Germany	USSR	3-0	Belgium	2000	France	Italy	2-1#	Belgium/Neth.
1976	Czechoslovakia	W. Germany	2-2 (5-3)*	Yugoslavia	2004	Greece	Portugal	1-0	Portugal
1980	W. Germany	Belgium	2-1	Italy	2008	Spain	Germany	1-0	Austria
1984	France	Spain	2-0	France	2012	Spain	Italy	4-0	Ukraine

* = Match decided in penalty kicks (shootout score in parentheses). # = Match decided in extra time.

Japan Beats U.S. to Claim 2011 Women's World Cup Championship

Japan earned a stunning championship win at the 2011 Women's World Cup, defeating the United States, 3-1, on penalty kicks July 17, 2011, in Frankfurt, Germany. The win capped a determined effort by Japan, which made its first-ever appearance in the final of a major international tournament. Japan's Homare Sawa scored the game-tying goal in extra time, after the U.S.'s Abby Wambach scored on a header for a 2-1 lead in the 104th minute. Sawa, playing in her fifth World Cup tournament, won both the Golden Ball as the best player of the tournament and the Golden Boot with a tournament-leading five goals. The underdog Japanese squad, known as the Nadeshiko, defeated Germany, the tournament host and two-time defending champion, 1-0, in extra time in a quarterfinal match on July 9, 2011, in Wolfsburg.

The U.S. enjoyed a dramatic quarterfinal triumph July 10, 2011, beating Brazil, 5-3, on penalty kicks in Dresden. Wambach converted a header into the net off a pass from Megan Rapinoe deep into injury time of the second overtime period for a 2-2 tie. Wambach and Rapinoe then scored two of the U.S.'s five successful penalty kicks and goalkeeper Hope Solo saved one of four attempts in the shootout with Brazil. The U.S. team then advanced to its first World Cup Final since 1999 with a 3-1 win over France in Mönchengladbach on July 13, 2011. France dropped a 2-1 decision to Sweden in the match for third place July 16, 2011, in Sinsheim.

Women's World Cup, 1991-2011

Year	Winner	Final opponent	Score	Site	Third place
1991	U.S.	Norway	2-1	China	Germany
1995	Norway	Germany	2-0	Sweden	U.S.
1999	U.S.	China	0-0 (5-4)*	Pasadena, CA	Brazil
2003	Germany	Sweden	2-1#	Carson, CA	U.S.
2007	Germany	Brazil	2-0	China	U.S.
2011	Japan	U.S.	2-2 (3-1)*	Germany	Sweden

* = Match decided in penalty kicks (shootout score in parentheses). # = Match decided in extra time.

Spain Defeats the Netherlands for 2010 Men's World Cup Title

Amid the drone of vuvuzelas, Spain earned its first-ever FIFA World Cup soccer championship with a 1-0 victory over the Netherlands July 11, 2010, in Johannesburg, South Africa. Andrés Iniesta scored in the 116th minute as Spain became the first country to be crowned World Cup champion after losing its first tournament match. Spain goalkeeper Iker Casillas allowed just two goals and was named winner of the Golden Glove award as the tournament's top goaltender.

The Netherlands fell for the third time in a World Cup championship match. The Orange lost the 1974 and 1978 World Cup finals, and now have more wins in World Cup matches (19) than any other nation without a title. Germany took third place with a 3-2 win over Uruguay in the consolation match. Uruguay's Diego Forlán was named Best Player and Thomas Müller of Germany won the Golden Boot for most goals.

Men's World Cup, 1930-2010

Year	Winner	Final opponent	Score	Site	Year	Winner	Final opponent	Score	Site
1930	Uruguay	Argentina	4-2	Uruguay	1978	Argentina	Netherlands	3-1#	Argentina
1934	Italy	Czechoslovakia	2-1#	Italy	1982	Italy	W. Germany	3-1	Spain
1938	Italy	Hungary	4-2	France	1986	Argentina	W. Germany	3-2	Mexico
1950	Uruguay	Brazil	2-1	Brazil	1990	W. Germany	Argentina	1-0	Italy
1954	W. Germany	Hungary	3-2	Switzerland	1994	Brazil	Italy	0-0 (3-2)*	U.S.
1958	Brazil	Sweden	5-2	Sweden	1998	France	Brazil	3-0	France
1962	Brazil	Czechoslovakia	3-1	Chile	2002	Brazil	Germany	2-0	Japan/S. Korea
1966	England	W. Germany	4-2#	England	2006	Italy	France	1-1 (5-3)*	Germany
1970	Brazil	Italy	4-1	Mexico	2010	Spain	Netherlands	1-0#	South Africa
1974	W. Germany	Netherlands	2-1	W. Germany					

* = Match decided on penalty kicks (shootout score in parentheses). # = Match decided in extra time.

FIFA Confederations Cup, South Africa, 2009

The U.S. men's soccer team created much excitement at the Confederations Cup tournament in South Africa in June 2009. In one of the greatest upset victories in U.S. men's soccer history, Jozy Altidore and Clint Dempsey each scored to support a solid effort in goal by Tim Howard as the United States beat Spain, 2-0, in the semifinals of the tournament at Bloemfontein, South Africa. Spain entered the match as the world's top-ranked team, boasting 15 consecutive victories and a 35-match unbeaten streak. The United States eventually lost to Brazil, 3-2, in the tournament final, the first-ever U.S. appearance in a FIFA tournament championship match. Dempsey and Landon Donovan scored to give the U.S. a 2-0 halftime lead, but Brazil responded with three unanswered second-half goals for its second straight Confederations Cup victory and third overall. The 2013 Confederations Cup is scheduled to be held June 15-30 in Brazil.

FIFA Confederations Cup Winners, 1997-2009

Year	Winner	Final opponent	Score	Third place	Fourth place	Site
1997	Brazil	Australia	6-0	Czech Republic	Uruguay	Saudi Arabia
1999	Mexico	Brazil	4-3	U.S.	Saudi Arabia	Mexico
2001	France	Japan	1-0	Australia	Brazil	S. Korea/Japan
2003	France	Cameroon	1-0	Turkey	Colombia	France
2005	Brazil	Argentina	4-1	Germany	Mexico	Germany
2009	Brazil	U.S.	3-2	Spain	South Africa	South Africa

GOLF

Men's All-Time Major Professional Championship Leaders
Through Sept. 2012. * = Active PGA player in 2012. (a) = Amateur.

Player	Masters	U.S. Open	British Open	PGA	Total
Jack Nicklaus	1963, '65-'66, '72, '75, '86	1962, '67, '72, '80	1966, '70, '78	1963, '71, '73, '75, '80	18
Tiger Woods*	1997, 2001-02, '05	2000, '02, '08	2000, '05-'06	1999-2000, '06-'07	14
Walter Hagen	—	1914, '19	1922, '24, '28-'29	1921, '24-'27	11
Ben Hogan	1951, '53	1948, '50-'51, '53	1953	1946, '48	9
Gary Player	1961, '74, '78	1965	1959, '68, '74	1962, '72	9
Tom Watson	1977, '81	1982	1975, '77, '80, '82-'83	—	8
Bobby Jones (a)	—	1923, '26, '29-'30	1926-27, '30	—	7
Arnold Palmer	1958, '60, '62, '64	1960	1961-62	—	7
Gene Sarazen	1935	1922, '32	1932	1922-23, '33	7
Sam Snead	1949, '52, '54	—	1946	1942, '49, '51	7
Harry Vardon	—	1900	1896, '98-'99, 1903, '11, '14	—	7
Nick Faldo	1989-90, '96	—	1987, '90, '92	—	6
Lee Trevino	—	1968, '71	1971-72	1974, '84	6

Professional Golfers' Association Leading Money Winners, 1946-2011

Year	Player	Earnings	Year	Player	Earnings	Year	Player	Earnings
1946	Ben Hogan	$42,556	1968	Billy Casper	$205,168	1990	Greg Norman	$1,165,477
1947	Jimmy Demaret	27,936	1969	Frank Beard	175,223	1991	Corey Pavin	979,430
1948	Ben Hogan	36,812	1970	Lee Trevino	157,037	1992	Fred Couples	1,344,188
1949	Sam Snead	31,593	1971	Jack Nicklaus	244,490	1993	Nick Price	1,478,557
1950	Sam Snead	35,758	1972	Jack Nicklaus	320,542	1994	Nick Price	1,499,927
1951	Lloyd Mangrum	26,088	1973	Jack Nicklaus	308,362	1995	Greg Norman	1,654,959
1952	Julius Boros	37,032	1974	Johnny Miller	353,201	1996	Tom Lehman	1,780,159
1953	Lew Worsham	34,002	1975	Jack Nicklaus	323,149	1997	Tiger Woods	2,066,833
1954	Bob Toski	65,819	1976	Jack Nicklaus	266,438	1998	David Duval	2,591,031
1955	Julius Boros	65,121	1977	Tom Watson	310,653	1999	Tiger Woods	6,616,585
1956	Ted Kroll	72,835	1978	Tom Watson	362,429	2000	Tiger Woods	9,188,321
1957	Dick Mayer	65,835	1979	Tom Watson	462,636	2001	Tiger Woods	5,687,777
1958	Arnold Palmer	42,407	1980	Tom Watson	530,808	2002	Tiger Woods	6,912,625
1959	Art Wall Jr.	53,167	1981	Tom Kite	375,699	2003	Vijay Singh	7,573,907
1960	Arnold Palmer	75,262	1982	Craig Stadler	446,462	2004	Vijay Singh	10,905,166
1961	Gary Player	64,540	1983	Hal Sutton	426,668	2005	Tiger Woods	10,628,024
1962	Arnold Palmer	81,448	1984	Tom Watson	476,260	2006	Tiger Woods	9,941,563
1963	Arnold Palmer	128,230	1985	Curtis Strange	542,321	2007	Tiger Woods	10,867,052
1964	Jack Nicklaus	113,284	1986	Greg Norman	653,296	2008	Vijay Singh	6,601,094
1965	Jack Nicklaus	140,752	1987	Curtis Strange	925,941	2009	Tiger Woods	10,508,163
1966	Billy Casper	121,944	1988	Curtis Strange	1,147,644	2010	Matt Kuchar	4,910,477
1967	Jack Nicklaus	188,988	1989	Tom Kite	1,395,278	2011	Luke Donald	6,683,214

Masters Golf Tournament Winners, 1940-2012
First contested in 1934 as Augusta National Invitation Tournament; not played, 1943-45.

Year	Winner	Year	Winner	Year	Winner	Year	Winner	Year	Winner
1940	Jimmy Demaret	1958	Arnold Palmer	1973	Tommy Aaron	1988	Sandy Lyle	2000	Vijay Singh
1941	Craig Wood	1959	Art Wall Jr.	1974	Gary Player	1989	Nick Faldo	2001	Tiger Woods
1942	Byron Nelson	1960	Arnold Palmer	1975	Jack Nicklaus	1990	Nick Faldo	2002	Tiger Woods
1946	Herman Keiser	1961	Gary Player	1976	Ray Floyd	1991	Ian Woosnam	2003	Mike Weir
1947	Jimmy Demaret	1962	Arnold Palmer	1977	Tom Watson	1992	Fred Couples	2004	Phil Mickelson
1948	Claude Harmon	1963	Jack Nicklaus	1978	Gary Player	1993	Bernhard Langer	2005	Tiger Woods
1949	Sam Snead	1964	Arnold Palmer	1979	Fuzzy Zoeller	1994	José María Olazábal	2006	Phil Mickelson
1950	Jimmy Demaret	1965	Jack Nicklaus	1980	Seve Ballesteros	1995	Ben Crenshaw	2007	Zach Johnson
1951	Ben Hogan	1966	Jack Nicklaus	1981	Tom Watson	1996	Nick Faldo	2008	Trevor Immelman
1952	Sam Snead	1967	Gay Brewer Jr.	1982	Craig Stadler	1997	Tiger Woods	2009	Angel Cabrera
1953	Ben Hogan	1968	Bob Goalby	1983	Seve Ballesteros	1998	Mark O'Meara	2010	Phil Mickelson
1954	Sam Snead	1969	George Archer	1984	Ben Crenshaw	1999	José María Olazábal	2011	Charl Schwartzel
1955	Cary Middlecoff	1970	Billy Casper	1985	Bernhard Langer			2012	Bubba Watson
1956	Jack Burke	1971	Charles Coody	1986	Jack Nicklaus				
1957	Doug Ford	1972	Jack Nicklaus	1987	Larry Mize				

U.S. Open Winners, 1940-2012
First contested in 1895; not played, 1942-45.

Year	Winner	Year	Winner	Year	Winner	Year	Winner	Year	Winner
1940	Lawson Little	1958	Tommy Bolt	1972	Jack Nicklaus	1986	Ray Floyd	2000	Tiger Woods
1941	Craig Wood	1959	Billy Casper	1973	Johnny Miller	1987	Scott Simpson	2001	Retief Goosen
1946	Lloyd Mangrum	1960	Arnold Palmer	1974	Hale Irwin	1988	Curtis Strange	2002	Tiger Woods
1947	Lew Worsham	1961	Gene Littler	1975	Lou Graham	1989	Curtis Strange	2003	Jim Furyk
1948	Ben Hogan	1962	Jack Nicklaus	1976	Jerry Pate	1990	Hale Irwin	2004	Retief Goosen
1949	Cary Middlecoff	1963	Julius Boros	1977	Hubert Green	1991	Payne Stewart	2005	Michael Campbell
1950	Ben Hogan	1964	Ken Venturi	1978	Andy North	1992	Tom Kite	2006	Geoff Ogilvy
1951	Ben Hogan	1965	Gary Player	1979	Hale Irwin	1993	Lee Janzen	2007	Angel Cabrera
1952	Julius Boros	1966	Billy Casper	1980	Jack Nicklaus	1994	Ernie Els	2008	Tiger Woods
1953	Ben Hogan	1967	Jack Nicklaus	1981	David Graham	1995	Corey Pavin	2009	Lucas Glover
1954	Ed Furgol	1968	Lee Trevino	1982	Tom Watson	1996	Steve Jones	2010	Graeme McDowell
1955	Jack Fleck	1969	Orville Moody	1983	Larry Nelson	1997	Ernie Els	2011	Rory McIlroy
1956	Cary Middlecoff	1970	Tony Jacklin	1984	Fuzzy Zoeller	1998	Lee Janzen	2012	Webb Simpson
1957	Dick Mayer	1971	Lee Trevino	1985	Andy North	1999	Payne Stewart		

British Open Winners, 1946-2012
First contested in 1860; not played, 1940-45.

Year	Winner	Year	Winner	Year	Winner	Year	Winner	Year	Winner
1946	Sam Snead	1960	Kel Nagle	1973	Tom Weiskopf	1987	Nick Faldo	2000	Tiger Woods
1947	Fred Daly	1961	Arnold Palmer	1974	Gary Player	1988	Seve Ballesteros	2001	David Duval
1948	Henry Cotton	1962	Arnold Palmer	1975	Tom Watson	1989	Mark Calcavecchia	2002	Ernie Els
1949	Bobby Locke	1963	Bob Charles	1976	Johnny Miller	1990	Nick Faldo	2003	Ben Curtis
1950	Bobby Locke	1964	Tony Lema	1977	Tom Watson	1991	Ian Baker-Finch	2004	Todd Hamilton
1951	Max Faulkner	1965	Peter Thomson	1978	Jack Nicklaus	1992	Nick Faldo	2005	Tiger Woods
1952	Bobby Locke	1966	Jack Nicklaus	1979	Seve Ballesteros	1993	Greg Norman	2006	Tiger Woods
1953	Ben Hogan	1967	Roberto de	1980	Tom Watson	1994	Nick Price	2007	Padraig Harrington
1954	Peter Thomson		Vicenzo	1981	Bill Rogers	1995	John Daly	2008	Padraig Harrington
1955	Peter Thomson	1968	Gary Player	1982	Tom Watson	1996	Tom Lehman	2009	Stewart Cink
1956	Peter Thomson	1969	Tony Jacklin	1983	Tom Watson	1997	Justin Leonard	2010	Louis Oosthuizen
1957	Bobby Locke	1970	Jack Nicklaus	1984	Seve Ballesteros	1998	Mark O'Meara	2011	Darren Clarke
1958	Peter Thomson	1971	Lee Trevino	1985	Sandy Lyle	1999	Paul Lawrie	2012	Ernie Els
1959	Gary Player	1972	Lee Trevino	1986	Greg Norman				

PGA Championship Winners, 1940-2012
First contested in 1916; not played, 1943.

Year	Winner	Year	Winner	Year	Winner	Year	Winner	Year	Winner
1940	Byron Nelson	1956	Jack Burke	1971	Jack Nicklaus	1985	Hubert Green	1999	Tiger Woods
1941	Victor Ghezzi	1957	Lionel Hebert	1972	Gary Player	1986	Bob Tway	2000	Tiger Woods
1942	Sam Snead	1958	Dow Finsterwald	1973	Jack Nicklaus	1987	Larry Nelson	2001	David Toms
1944	Bob Hamilton	1959	Bob Rosburg	1974	Lee Trevino	1988	Jeff Sluman	2002	Rich Beem
1945	Byron Nelson	1960	Jay Hebert	1975	Jack Nicklaus	1989	Payne Stewart	2003	Shaun Micheel
1946	Ben Hogan	1961	Jerry Barber	1976	Dave Stockton	1990	Wayne Grady	2004	Vijay Singh
1947	Jim Ferrier	1962	Gary Player	1977	Lanny Wadkins	1991	John Daly	2005	Phil Mickelson
1948	Ben Hogan	1963	Jack Nicklaus	1978	John Mahaffey	1992	Nick Price	2006	Tiger Woods
1949	Sam Snead	1964	Bob Nichols	1979	David Graham	1993	Paul Azinger	2007	Tiger Woods
1950	Chandler Harper	1965	Dave Marr	1980	Jack Nicklaus	1994	Nick Price	2008	Padraig Harrington
1951	Sam Snead	1966	Al Geiberger	1981	Larry Nelson	1995	Steve Elkington	2009	Y.E.Yang
1952	James Turnesa	1967	Don January	1982	Ray Floyd	1996	Mark Brooks	2010	Martin Kaymer
1953	Walter Burkemo	1968	Julius Boros	1983	Hal Sutton	1997	Davis Love III	2011	Keegan Bradley
1954	Melvin Harbert	1969	Ray Floyd	1984	Lee Trevino	1998	Vijay Singh	2012	Rory McIlroy
1955	Doug Ford	1970	Dave Stockton						

FedEx Cup, 2007-12
The FedEx Cup, a season-long, $10-mil competition with points awarded by finishing rank in each tournament, divides the PGA Tour into a regular season lasting 33 weeks, combined with a 4-week-long playoff that ends with the Tour Championship at East Lake Golf Club in Atlanta, GA.

Year	Winner	Year	Winner	Year	Winner	Year	Winner	Year	Winner
2007	Tiger Woods	2009	Tiger Woods	2010	Jim Furyk	2011	Bill Haas	2012	Brandt Snedeker
2008	Vijay Singh								

Women's All-Time Major Professional Championship Leaders
Through Oct. 2012. * = Active in 2012 LPGA season.

Player	Kraft Nabisco[1]	LPGA	U.S. Women's Open	Women's British Open[2]	Titleholders[3]	Western Open[4]	Total
Patty Berg	—	—	1946	—	1937-39, '48, '53, '55, '57	1941, '43, '48, '51, '55, '57-'58	15
Mickey Wright	—	1958, '60-'61, '63	1958-59, '61, '64	—	1961-62	1962-63, '66	13
Louise Suggs	—	1957	1949, '52	—	1946, '54, '56, '59	1946-47, '49, '53	11
Annika Sorenstam	2001-02, '05	2003-05	1995-96, 2006	2003	—	—	10
Babe Zaharias	—	—	1948, '50, '54	—	1947, '50, '52	1940, '44-'45, '50	10
Betsy Rawls	—	1959, '69	1951, '53, '57, '60	—	—	1952, '59	8
Juli Inkster*	1984, '89	1999-2000	1999, 2002	1984	—	—	7
Karrie Webb*	2000, '06	2001	2000-01	1999, 2002	—	—	7
Pat Bradley	1986	1986	1981	1980, '85-'86	—	—	6
Betsy King	1987, '90, '97	1992	1989-90	—	—	—	6
Patty Sheehan	1996	1983-84, '93	1992, '94	—	—	—	6
Kathy Whitworth	—	1967, '71, '75	—	—	1965-66	1967	6

(1) Formerly the Nabisco Dinah Shore (1982-99) and the Nabisco Championship (2000-01); designated major in 1983. (2) In 2001, the British Open replaced the du Maurier Classic as the LPGA's fourth major; wins in column prior to 2001 are for the du Maurier (1983-2000) or Peter Jackson Classic (1979-82). (3) Titleholders Championship was a major from 1937 to 1972. (4) Western Open was a major from 1930 to 1967.

Ladies Professional Golf Association Leading Money Winners, 1954-2011

Year	Player	Earnings	Year	Player	Earnings	Year	Player	Earnings
1954	Patty Berg	$16,011	1974	JoAnne Carner	$87,094	1993	Betsy King	$595,992
1955	Patty Berg	16,492	1975	Sandra Palmer	76,374	1994	Laura Davies	687,201
1956	Marlene Hagge	20,235	1976	Judy Rankin	150,734	1995	Annika Sorenstam	666,533
1957	Patty Berg	16,272	1977	Judy Rankin	122,890	1996	Karrie Webb	1,002,000
1958	Beverly Hanson	12,639	1978	Nancy Lopez	189,813	1997	Annika Sorenstam	1,236,789
1959	Betsy Rawls	26,774	1979	Nancy Lopez	197,489	1998	Annika Sorenstam	1,092,748
1960	Louise Suggs	16,892	1980	Beth Daniel	231,000	1999	Karrie Webb	1,591,959
1961	Mickey Wright	22,236	1981	Beth Daniel	206,977	2000	Karrie Webb	1,876,853
1962	Mickey Wright	21,641	1982	JoAnne Carner	310,399	2001	Annika Sorenstam	2,105,868
1963	Mickey Wright	31,269	1983	JoAnne Carner	291,404	2002	Annika Sorenstam	2,863,904
1964	Mickey Wright	29,800	1984	Betsy King	266,771	2003	Annika Sorenstam	2,029,506
1965	Kathy Whitworth	28,658	1985	Nancy Lopez	416,472	2004	Annika Sorenstam	2,544,707
1966	Kathy Whitworth	33,517	1986	Pat Bradley	492,021	2005	Annika Sorenstam	2,588,240
1967	Kathy Whitworth	32,937	1987	Ayako Okamoto	466,034	2006	Lorena Ochoa	2,592,872
1968	Kathy Whitworth	48,379	1988	Sherri Turner	350,851	2007	Lorena Ochoa	4,364,994
1969	Carol Mann	49,152	1989	Betsy King	654,132	2008	Lorena Ochoa	2,763,193
1970	Kathy Whitworth	30,235	1990	Beth Daniel	863,578	2009	Jiyai Shin	1,807,334
1971	Kathy Whitworth	41,181	1991	Pat Bradley	763,118	2010	Na Yeon Choi	1,871,166
1972	Kathy Whitworth	65,063	1992	Dottie Mochrie	693,335	2011	Yani Tseng	2,921,713
1973	Kathy Whitworth	82,864						

Kraft Nabisco Championship Winners, 1983-2012

Formerly the Colgate Dinah Shore (1972-81), the Nabisco Dinah Shore (1982-99), and the Nabisco Championship (2000-01). Designated as a major championship in 1983.

Year	Winner	Year	Winner	Year	Winner	Year	Winner	Year	Winner
1983	Amy Alcott	1990	Betsy King	1996	Patty Sheehan	2002	Annika Sorenstam	2007	Morgan Pressel
1984	Juli Inkster	1991	Amy Alcott	1997	Betsy King	2003	Patricia Meunier-	2008	Lorena Ochoa
1985	Alice Miller	1992	Dottie Pepper	1998	Pat Hurst		Lebouc	2009	Brittany Lincicome
1986	Pat Bradley	1993	Helen Alfredsson	1999	Dottie Pepper	2004	Grace Park	2010	Yani Tseng
1987	Betsy King	1994	Donna Andrews	2000	Karrie Webb	2005	Annika Sorenstam	2011	Stacy Lewis
1988	Amy Alcott	1995	Nanci Bowen	2001	Annika Sorenstam	2006	Karrie Webb	2012	Sun Young Yoo
1989	Juli Inkster								

LPGA Championship Winners, 1955-2012

Year	Winner	Year	Winner	Year	Winner	Year	Winner	Year	Winner
1955	Beverly Hanson	1967	Kathy Whitworth	1979	Donna Caponi	1991	Meg Mallon	2002	Se Ri Pak
1956	Marlene Hagge	1968	Sandra Post	1980	Sally Little	1992	Betsy King	2003	Annika Sorenstam
1957	Louise Suggs	1969	Betsy Rawls	1981	Donna Caponi	1993	Patty Sheehan	2004	Annika Sorenstam
1958	Mickey Wright	1970	Shirley Englehorn	1982	Jan Stephenson	1994	Laura Davies	2005	Annika Sorenstam
1959	Betsy Rawls	1971	Kathy Whitworth	1983	Patty Sheehan	1995	Kelly Robbins	2006	Se Ri Pak
1960	Mickey Wright	1972	Kathy Ahern	1984	Patty Sheehan	1996	Laura Davies	2007	Suzann Pettersen
1961	Mickey Wright	1973	Mary Mills	1985	Nancy Lopez	1997	Christa Johnson	2008	Yani Tseng
1962	Judy Kimball	1974	Sandra Haynie	1986	Pat Bradley	1998	Se Ri Pak	2009	Anna Nordqvist
1963	Mickey Wright	1975	Kathy Whitworth	1987	Jane Geddes	1999	Juli Inkster	2010	Cristie Kerr
1964	Mary Mills	1976	Betty Burfeindt	1988	Sherri Turner	2000	Juli Inkster	2011	Yani Tseng
1965	Sandra Haynie	1977	Chako Higuchi	1989	Nancy Lopez	2001	Karrie Webb	2012	Shanshan Feng
1966	Gloria Ehret	1978	Nancy Lopez	1990	Beth Daniel				

U.S. Women's Open Winners, 1946-2012

Year	Winner	Year	Winner	Year	Winner	Year	Winner	Year	Winner
1946	Patty Berg	1961	Mickey Wright	1973	Susie Maxwell	1986	Jane Geddes	2000	Karrie Webb
1947	Betty Jameson	1962	Murle Lindstrom		Berning	1987	Laura Davies	2001	Karrie Webb
1948	Babe Zaharias	1963	Mary Mills	1974	Sandra Haynie	1988	Liselotte Neumann	2002	Juli Inkster
1949	Louise Suggs	1964	Mickey Wright	1975	Sandra Palmer	1989	Betsy King	2003	Hilary Lunke
1950	Babe Zaharias	1965	Carol Mann	1976	JoAnne Carner	1990	Betsy King	2004	Meg Mallon
1951	Betsy Rawls	1966	Sandra Spuzich	1977	Hollis Stacy	1991	Meg Mallon	2005	Birdie Kim
1952	Louise Suggs	1967	Catherine Lacoste	1978	Hollis Stacy	1992	Patty Sheehan	2006	Annika Sorenstam
1953	Betsy Rawls		(amateur)	1979	Jerilyn Britz	1993	Lauri Merten	2007	Cristie Kerr
1954	Babe Zaharias	1968	Susie Maxwell	1980	Amy Alcott	1994	Patty Sheehan	2008	Inbee Park
1955	Fay Crocker		Berning	1981	Pat Bradley	1995	Annika Sorenstam	2009	Eun-Hee Ji
1956	Kathy Cornelius	1969	Donna Caponi	1982	Janet Alex	1996	Annika Sorenstam	2010	Paula Creamer
1957	Betsy Rawls	1970	Donna Caponi	1983	Jan Stephenson	1997	Alison Nicholas	2011	So Yeon Ryu
1958	Mickey Wright	1971	JoAnne Carner	1984	Hollis Stacy	1998	Se Ri Pak	2012	Na Yeon Choi
1959	Mickey Wright	1972	Susie Maxwell	1985	Kathy Baker	1999	Juli Inkster		
1960	Betsy Rawls		Berning						

Women's British Open Winners, 1979-2012

First held as the Ladies' British Open in 1976; became the LPGA's fourth major championship in 2001, replacing the du Maurier Classic. Winners listed are for the du Maurier Classic (1983-2000) and the Peter Jackson Classic (1979-82).

Year	Winner	Year	Winner	Year	Winner	Year	Winner	Year	Winner
1979	Amy Alcott	1986	Pat Bradley	1993	Brandie Burton	2000	Meg Mallon	2007	Lorena Ochoa
1980	Pat Bradley	1987	Jody Rosenthal	1994	Martha Nause	2001	Se Ri Pak	2008	Jiyai Shin
1981	Jan Stephenson	1988	Sally Little	1995	Jenny Lidback	2002	Karrie Webb	2009	Catriona Matthew
1982	Sandra Haynie	1989	Tammie Green	1996	Laura Davies	2003	Annika Sorenstam	2010	Yani Tseng
1983	Hollis Stacy	1990	Cathy Johnston	1997	Colleen Walker	2004	Karen Stupples	2011	Yani Tseng
1984	Juli Inkster	1991	Nancy Scranton	1998	Brandie Burton	2005	Jeong Jang	2012	Jiyai Shin
1985	Pat Bradley	1992	Sherri Steinhauer	1999	Karrie Webb	2006	Sherri Steinhauer		

Ryder Cup, 1927-2012

Europe earned a dramatic come-from-behind victory at the 39th Ryder Cup, held Sept. 28-30, 2012, at Medinah Country Club in Medinah, IL. The European team trailed by 4 points after the first two rounds as the U.S. squad tried to regain the Cup for the first time since 2008. But Europe outscored the U.S. 8½ to 3½ in the last round for a 14½-13½ overall victory. The Ryder Cup began as a biennial team competition between pro male golfers from the U.S. and Great Britain. The British team was expanded in 1973 to include players from Ireland and in 1979 from the rest of Europe. The Ryder Cup moved to even years after being postponed following the terrorist attacks of Sept. 11, 2001.

Year	Winner, score	Year	Winner, score	Year	Winner, score	Year	Winner, score
1927	U.S., 9½-2½	1953	U.S., 6½-5½	1973	U.S., 19-13	1993	U.S., 15-13
1929	Britain-Ireland, 7-5	1955	U.S., 8-4	1975	U.S., 21-11	1995	Europe, 14½-13½
1931	U.S., 9-3	1957	Britain-Ireland, 7½-4½	1977	U.S., 12½-7½	1997	Europe, 14½-13½
1933	Britain, 6½-5½	1959	U.S., 8½-3½	1979	U.S., 17-11	1999	U.S., 14½-13½
1935	U.S., 9-3	1961	U.S., 14½-9½	1981	U.S., 18½-9½	2002	Europe, 15½-12½
1937	U.S., 8-4	1963	U.S., 23-9	1983	U.S., 14½-13½	2004	Europe, 18½-9½
1939-45	Not played	1965	U.S., 19½-12½	1985	Europe, 16½-11½	2006	Europe, 18½-9½
1947	U.S., 11-1	1967	U.S., 23½-8½	1987	Europe, 15-13	2008	U.S., 16½-11½
1949	U.S., 7-5	1969	Draw, 16-16	1989	Draw, 14-14	2010	Europe, 14½-13½
1951	U.S., 9½-2½	1971	U.S., 18½-13½	1991	U.S., 14½-13½	2012	Europe, 14½-13½

Solheim Cup, 1990-2012

The Solheim Cup began in 1990 as a biennial team competition between pro women golfers from the U.S. and Europe. Competition moved to odd years in 2003 to alternate with the Ryder Cup.

Year	Winner, score	Year	Winner, score	Year	Winner, score	Year	Winner, score
1990	U.S., 11½-4½	1996	U.S., 17-11	2002	U.S., 15½-12½	2007	U.S., 16-12
1992	Europe, 11½-6½	1998	U.S., 16-12	2003	Europe, 17½-10½	2009	U.S., 16-12
1994	U.S., 13-7	2000	Europe, 14½-11½	2005	U.S., 15½-12½	2011	Europe, 15-13

TENNIS

Australian Open Singles Champions, 1969-2012

First contested 1905 for men, 1922 for women. Became an Open Championship in 1969. Two tournaments held in 1977 in Jan. and Dec. No tournament held in 1986.

Men's Singles

Year	Champion	Final opponent
1969	Rod Laver	Andres Gimeno
1970	Arthur Ashe	Dick Crealy
1971	Ken Rosewall	Arthur Ashe
1972	Ken Rosewall	Mal Anderson
1973	John Newcombe	Onny Parun
1974	Jimmy Connors	Phil Dent
1975	John Newcombe	Jimmy Connors
1976	Mark Edmondson	John Newcombe
1977	Roscoe Tanner	Guillermo Vilas
	Vitas Gerulaitis	John Lloyd
1978	Guillermo Vilas	John Marks
1979	Guillermo Vilas	John Sadri
1980	Brian Teacher	Kim Warwick
1981	Johan Kriek	Steve Denton
1982	Johan Kriek	Steve Denton
1983	Mats Wilander	Ivan Lendl
1984	Mats Wilander	Kevin Curren
1985	Stefan Edberg	Mats Wilander
1987	Stefan Edberg	Pat Cash
1988	Mats Wilander	Pat Cash
1989	Ivan Lendl	Miloslav Mecir
1990	Ivan Lendl	Stefan Edberg
1991	Boris Becker	Ivan Lendl
1992	Jim Courier	Stefan Edberg
1993	Jim Courier	Stefan Edberg
1994	Pete Sampras	Todd Martin
1995	Andre Agassi	Pete Sampras
1996	Boris Becker	Michael Chang
1997	Pete Sampras	Carlos Moya
1998	Petr Korda	Marcelo Rios
1999	Yevgeny Kafelnikov	Thomas Enqvist
2000	Andre Agassi	Yevgeny Kafelnikov
2001	Andre Agassi	Arnaud Clement
2002	Thomas Johansson	Marat Safin
2003	Andre Agassi	Rainer Schuettler
2004	Roger Federer	Marat Safin
2005	Marat Safin	Lleyton Hewitt
2006	Roger Federer	Marcos Baghdatis
2007	Roger Federer	Fernando Gonzalez
2008	Novak Djokovic	Jo-Wilfried Tsonga
2009	Rafael Nadal	Roger Federer
2010	Roger Federer	Andy Murray
2011	Novak Djokovic	Andy Murray
2012	Novak Djokovic	Rafael Nadal

Women's Singles

Year	Champion	Final opponent
1969	Margaret Smith Court	Billie Jean King
1970	Margaret Smith Court	Kerry Melville Reid
1971	Margaret Smith Court	Evonne Goolagong
1972	Virginia Wade	Evonne Goolagong
1973	Margaret Smith Court	Evonne Goolagong
1974	Evonne Goolagong	Chris Evert
1975	Evonne Goolagong	Martina Navratilova
1976	Evonne Goolagong Cawley	Renata Tomanova
1977	Kerry Reid	Dianne Balestrat
	Evonne Goolagong Cawley	Helen Gourlay
1978	Chris O'Neill	Betsy Nagelsen
1979	Barbara Jordan	Sharon Walsh
1980	Hana Mandlikova	Wendy Turnbull
1981	Martina Navratilova	Chris Evert Lloyd
1982	Chris Evert Lloyd	Martina Navratilova
1983	Martina Navratilova	Kathy Jordan
1984	Chris Evert Lloyd	Helena Sukova
1985	Martina Navratilova	Chris Evert Lloyd
1987	Hana Mandlikova	Martina Navratilova
1988	Steffi Graf	Chris Evert
1989	Steffi Graf	Helena Sukova
1990	Steffi Graf	Mary Joe Fernandez
1991	Monica Seles	Jana Novotna
1992	Monica Seles	Mary Joe Fernandez
1993	Monica Seles	Steffi Graf
1994	Steffi Graf	Arantxa Sánchez Vicario
1995	Mary Pierce	Arantxa Sánchez Vicario
1996	Monica Seles	Anke Huber
1997	Martina Hingis	Mary Pierce
1998	Martina Hingis	Conchita Martínez
1999	Martina Hingis	Amelie Mauresmo
2000	Lindsay Davenport	Martina Hingis
2001	Jennifer Capriati	Martina Hingis
2002	Jennifer Capriati	Martina Hingis
2003	Serena Williams	Venus Williams
2004	Justine Henin	Kim Clijsters
2005	Serena Williams	Lindsay Davenport
2006	Amelie Mauresmo	Justine Henin
2007	Serena Williams	Maria Sharapova
2008	Maria Sharapova	Ana Ivanovic
2009	Serena Williams	Dinara Safina
2010	Serena Williams	Justine Henin
2011	Kim Clijsters	Li Na
2012	Victoria Azarenka	Maria Sharapova

French Open (Roland Garros) Singles Champions, 1968-2012

First contested 1891 for men, 1897 for women. Became an Open Championship in 1968.

Men's Singles

Year	Champion	Final opponent
1968	Ken Rosewall	Rod Laver
1969	Rod Laver	Ken Rosewall
1970	Jan Kodes	Zeljko Franulovic
1971	Jan Kodes	Ilie Nastase
1972	Andres Gimeno	Patrick Proisy
1973	Ilie Nastase	Nikki Pilic
1974	Björn Borg	Manuel Orantes
1975	Björn Borg	Guillermo Vilas
1976	Adriano Panatta	Harold Solomon
1977	Guillermo Vilas	Brian Gottfried
1978	Björn Borg	Guillermo Vilas
1979	Björn Borg	Victor Pecci
1980	Björn Borg	Vitas Gerulaitis
1981	Björn Borg	Ivan Lendl
1982	Mats Wilander	Guillermo Vilas
1983	Yannick Noah	Mats Wilander
1984	Ivan Lendl	John McEnroe
1985	Mats Wilander	Ivan Lendl
1986	Ivan Lendl	Mikael Pernfors
1987	Ivan Lendl	Mats Wilander
1988	Mats Wilander	Henri Leconte
1989	Michael Chang	Stefan Edberg
1990	Andres Gomez	Andre Agassi
1991	Jim Courier	Andre Agassi
1992	Jim Courier	Petr Korda
1993	Sergi Bruguera	Jim Courier
1994	Sergi Bruguera	Alberto Berasategui
1995	Thomas Muster	Michael Chang
1996	Yevgeny Kafelnikov	Michael Stich
1997	Gustavo Kuerten	Sergei Bruguera
1998	Carlos Moya	Alex Corretja
1999	Andre Agassi	Andrei Medvedev
2000	Gustavo Kuerten	Magnus Norman
2001	Gustavo Kuerten	Alex Corretja
2002	Albert Costa	Juan Carlos Ferrero
2003	Juan Carlos Ferrero	Martin Verkerk
2004	Gaston Gaudio	Guillermo Coria
2005	Rafael Nadal	Mariano Puerta
2006	Rafael Nadal	Roger Federer
2007	Rafael Nadal	Roger Federer
2008	Rafael Nadal	Roger Federer
2009	Roger Federer	Robin Soderling
2010	Rafael Nadal	Robin Soderling
2011	Rafael Nadal	Roger Federer
2012	Rafael Nadal	Novak Djokovic

Women's Singles

Year	Champion	Final opponent
1968	Nancy Richey	Ann Jones
1969	Margaret Smith Court	Ann Jones
1970	Margaret Smith Court	Helga Niessen
1971	Evonne Goolagong	Helen Gourlay
1972	Billie Jean King	Evonne Goolagong
1973	Margaret Smith Court	Chris Evert
1974	Chris Evert	Olga Morozova
1975	Chris Evert	Martina Navratilova
1976	Sue Barker	Renata Tomanova
1977	Mima Jausovec	Florenza Mihai
1978	Virginia Ruzici	Mima Jausovec
1979	Chris Evert Lloyd	Wendy Turnbull
1980	Chris Evert Lloyd	Virginia Ruzici
1981	Hana Mandlikova	Sylvia Hanika
1982	Martina Navratilova	Andrea Jaeger
1983	Chris Evert Lloyd	Mima Jausovec
1984	Martina Navratilova	Chris Evert Lloyd
1985	Chris Evert Lloyd	Martina Navratilova
1986	Chris Evert Lloyd	Martina Navratilova

Year	Champion	Final opponent	Year	Champion	Final opponent
1987	Steffi Graf	Martina Navratilova	2000	Mary Pierce	Conchita Martínez
1988	Steffi Graf	Natalia Zvereva	2001	Jennifer Capriati	Kim Clijsters
1989	Arantxa Sánchez Vicario	Steffi Graf	2002	Serena Williams	Venus Williams
1990	Monica Seles	Steffi Graf	2003	Justine Henin	Kim Clijsters
1991	Monica Seles	Arantxa Sánchez Vicario	2004	Anastasia Myskina	Elena Dementieva
1992	Monica Seles	Steffi Graf	2005	Justine Henin	Mary Pierce
1993	Steffi Graf	Mary Joe Fernandez	2006	Justine Henin	Svetlana Kuznetsova
1994	Arantxa Sánchez Vicario	Mary Pierce	2007	Justine Henin	Ana Ivanovic
1995	Steffi Graf	Arantxa Sánchez Vicario	2008	Ana Ivanovic	Dinara Safina
1996	Steffi Graf	Arantxa Sánchez Vicario	2009	Svetlana Kuznetsova	Dinara Safina
1997	Iva Majoli	Martina Hingis	2010	Francesca Schiavone	Samantha Stosur
1998	Arantxa Sánchez Vicario	Monica Seles	2011	Li Na	Francesca Schiavone
1999	Steffi Graf	Martina Hingis	2012	Maria Sharapova	Sara Errani

Wimbledon Champions, 1925-2012

First contested 1877 for men, 1884 for women. Became an Open Championship in 1968. Not held 1940-45.

Men's Singles

Year	Champion	Final opponent
1925	René Lacoste	Jean Borotra
1926	Jean Borotra	Howard Kinsey
1927	Henri Cochet	Jean Borotra
1928	René Lacoste	Henri Cochet
1929	Henri Cochet	Jean Borotra
1930	Bill Tilden	Wilmer Allison
1931	Sidney B. Wood	Francis X. Shields
1932	Ellsworth Vines	Henry Austin
1933	Jack Crawford	Ellsworth Vines
1934	Fred Perry	Jack Crawford
1935	Fred Perry	Gottfried von Cramm
1936	Fred Perry	Gottfried von Cramm
1937	Donald Budge	Gottfried von Cramm
1938	Donald Budge	Henry Austin
1939	Bobby Riggs	Elwood Cooke
1946	Yvon Petra	Geoff E. Brown
1947	Jack Kramer	Tom P. Brown
1948	Bob Falkenburg	John Bromwich
1949	Ted Schroeder	Jaroslav Drobny
1950	Budge Patty	Frank Sedgman
1951	Dick Savitt	Ken McGregor
1952	Frank Sedgman	Jaroslav Drobny
1953	Vic Seixas	Kurt Nielsen
1954	Jaroslav Drobny	Ken Rosewall
1955	Tony Trabert	Kurt Nielsen
1956	Lew Hoad	Ken Rosewall
1957	Lew Hoad	Ashley Cooper
1958	Ashley Cooper	Neale Fraser
1959	Alex Olmedo	Rod Laver
1960	Neale Fraser	Rod Laver
1961	Rod Laver	Chuck McKinley
1962	Rod Laver	Martin Mulligan
1963	Chuck McKinley	Fred Stolle
1964	Roy Emerson	Fred Stolle
1965	Roy Emerson	Fred Stolle
1966	Manuel Santana	Dennis Ralston
1967	John Newcombe	Wilhelm Bungert
1968	Rod Laver	Tony Roche
1969	Rod Laver	John Newcombe
1970	John Newcombe	Ken Rosewall
1971	John Newcombe	Stan Smith
1972	Stan Smith	Ilie Nastase
1973	Jan Kodes	Alex Metreveli
1974	Jimmy Connors	Ken Rosewall
1975	Arthur Ashe	Jimmy Connors
1976	Björn Borg	Ilie Nastase
1977	Björn Borg	Jimmy Connors
1978	Björn Borg	Jimmy Connors
1979	Björn Borg	Roscoe Tanner
1980	Björn Borg	John McEnroe
1981	John McEnroe	Björn Borg
1982	Jimmy Connors	John McEnroe
1983	John McEnroe	Chris Lewis
1984	John McEnroe	Jimmy Connors
1985	Boris Becker	Kevin Curren
1986	Boris Becker	Ivan Lendl
1987	Pat Cash	Ivan Lendl
1988	Stefan Edberg	Boris Becker
1989	Boris Becker	Stefan Edberg
1990	Stefan Edberg	Boris Becker
1991	Michael Stich	Boris Becker
1992	Andre Agassi	Goran Ivanisevic
1993	Pete Sampras	Jim Courier
1994	Pete Sampras	Goran Ivanisevic
1995	Pete Sampras	Boris Becker
1996	Richard Krajicek	MaliVai "Mai" Washington

Year	Champion	Final opponent
1997	Pete Sampras	Cedric Pioline
1998	Pete Sampras	Goran Ivanisevic
1999	Pete Sampras	Andre Agassi
2000	Pete Sampras	Patrick Rafter
2001	Goran Ivanisevic	Patrick Rafter
2002	Lleyton Hewitt	David Nalbandian
2003	Roger Federer	Mark Philippoussis
2004	Roger Federer	Andy Roddick
2005	Roger Federer	Andy Roddick
2006	Roger Federer	Rafael Nadal
2007	Roger Federer	Rafael Nadal
2008	Rafael Nadal	Roger Federer
2009	Roger Federer	Andy Roddick
2010	Rafael Nadal	Tomas Berdych
2011	Novak Djokovic	Rafael Nadal
2012	Roger Federer	Andy Murray

Women's Singles

Year	Champion	Final opponent
1925	Suzanne Lenglen	Joan Fry
1926	Kathleen McKane Godfree	Lili de Alvarez
1927	Helen Wills	Lili de Alvarez
1928	Helen Wills	Lili de Alvarez
1929	Helen Wills	Helen Jacobs
1930	Helen Wills Moody	Elizabeth Ryan
1931	Cilly Aussem	Hilde Kranwinkel
1932	Helen Wills Moody	Helen Jacobs
1933	Helen Wills Moody	Dorothy Round
1934	Dorothy Round	Helen Jacobs
1935	Helen Wills Moody	Helen Jacobs
1936	Helen Jacobs	Hilde Kranwinkel Sperling
1937	Dorothy Round	Jadwiga Jedrzejowska
1938	Helen Wills Moody	Helen Jacobs
1939	Alice Marble	Kay Stammers
1946	Pauline Betz	Louise Brough
1947	Margaret Osborne	Doris Hart
1948	Louise Brough	Doris Hart
1949	Louise Brough	Margaret Osborne duPont
1950	Louise Brough	Margaret Osborne duPont
1951	Doris Hart	Shirley Fry
1952	Maureen Connolly	Louise Brough
1953	Maureen Connolly	Doris Hart
1954	Maureen Connolly	Louise Brough
1955	Louise Brough	Beverly Fleitz
1956	Shirley Fry	Angela Buxton
1957	Althea Gibson	Darlene Hard
1958	Althea Gibson	Angela Mortimer
1959	Maria Bueno	Darlene Hard
1960	Maria Bueno	Sandra Reynolds
1961	Angela Mortimer	Christine Truman
1962	Karen Hantze-Susman	Vera Sukova
1963	Margaret Smith	Billie Jean Moffitt
1964	Maria Bueno	Margaret Smith
1965	Margaret Smith	Maria Bueno
1966	Billie Jean King	Maria Bueno
1967	Billie Jean King	Ann Haydon Jones
1968	Billie Jean King	Judy Tegart
1969	Ann Haydon Jones	Billie Jean King
1970	Margaret Smith Court	Billie Jean King
1971	Evonne Goolagong	Margaret Smith Court
1972	Billie Jean King	Evonne Goolagong
1973	Billie Jean King	Chris Evert
1974	Chris Evert	Olga Morozova
1975	Billie Jean King	Evonne Goolagong Cawley
1976	Chris Evert	Evonne Goolagong Cawley

Year	Champion	Final opponent	Year	Champion	Final opponent
1977	Virginia Wade	Betty Stove	1995	Steffi Graf	Arantxa Sánchez Vicario
1978	Martina Navratilova	Chris Evert	1996	Steffi Graf	Arantxa Sánchez Vicario
1979	Martina Navratilova	Chris Evert Lloyd	1997	Martina Hingis	Jana Novotna
1980	Evonne Goolagong Cawley	Chris Evert Lloyd	1998	Jana Novotna	Nathalie Tauziat
			1999	Lindsay Davenport	Steffi Graf
1981	Chris Evert Lloyd	Hana Mandlikova	2000	Venus Williams	Lindsay Davenport
1982	Martina Navratilova	Chris Evert Lloyd	2001	Venus Williams	Justine Henin
1983	Martina Navratilova	Andrea Jaeger	2002	Serena Williams	Venus Williams
1984	Martina Navratilova	Chris Evert Lloyd	2003	Serena Williams	Venus Williams
1985	Martina Navratilova	Chris Evert Lloyd	2004	Maria Sharapova	Serena Williams
1986	Martina Navratilova	Hana Mandlikova	2005	Venus Williams	Lindsay Davenport
1987	Martina Navratilova	Steffi Graf	2006	Amelie Mauresmo	Justine Henin
1988	Steffi Graf	Martina Navratilova	2007	Venus Williams	Marion Bartoli
1989	Steffi Graf	Martina Navratilova	2008	Venus Williams	Serena Williams
1990	Martina Navratilova	Zina Garrison	2009	Serena Williams	Venus Williams
1991	Steffi Graf	Gabriela Sabatini	2010	Serena Williams	Vera Zvonareva
1992	Steffi Graf	Monica Seles	2011	Petra Kvitova	Maria Sharapova
1993	Steffi Graf	Jana Novotna	2012	Serena Williams	Agnieszka Radwanska
1994	Conchita Martínez	Martina Navratilova			

U.S. Open Champions, 1925-2012

First contested 1881 for men, 1887 for women. Became an Open Championship in 1968.

Men's Singles

Year	Champion	Final opponent
1925	Bill Tilden	William Johnston
1926	René Lacoste	Jean Borotra
1927	René Lacoste	Bill Tilden
1928	Henri Cochet	Francis Hunter
1929	Bill Tilden	Francis Hunter
1930	John Doeg	Francis Shields
1931	Ellsworth Vines	George Lott
1932	Ellsworth Vines	Henri Cochet
1933	Fred Perry	John Crawford
1934	Fred Perry	Wilmer Allison
1935	Wilmer Allison	Sidney Wood
1936	Fred Perry	Don Budge
1937	Don Budge	Gottfried von Cramm
1938	Don Budge	C. Gene Mako
1939	Robert Riggs	S. Welby Van Horn
1940	Don McNeill	Robert Riggs
1941	Robert Riggs	F. L. Kovacs
1942	F. R. Schroeder Jr.	Frank Parker
1943	Joseph Hunt	Jack Kramer
1944	Frank Parker	William Talbert
1945	Frank Parker	William Talbert
1946	Jack Kramer	Thomas Brown Jr.
1947	Jack Kramer	Frank Parker
1948	Pancho Gonzales	Eric Sturgess
1949	Pancho Gonzales	F. R. Schroeder Jr.
1950	Arthur Larsen	Herbert Flam
1951	Frank Sedgman	E. Victor Seixas Jr.
1952	Frank Sedgman	Gardnar Mulloy
1953	Tony Trabert	E. Victor Seixas Jr.
1954	E. Victor Seixas Jr.	Rex Hartwig
1955	Tony Trabert	Ken Rosewall
1956	Ken Rosewall	Lewis Hoad
1957	Malcolm Anderson	Ashley Cooper
1958	Ashley Cooper	Malcolm Anderson
1959	Neale A. Fraser	Alejandro Olmedo
1960	Neale A. Fraser	Rod Laver
1961	Roy Emerson	Rod Laver
1962	Rod Laver	Roy Emerson
1963	Rafael Osuna	F. A. Froehling III
1964	Roy Emerson	Fred Stolle
1965	Manuel Santana	Cliff Drysdale
1966	Fred Stolle	John Newcombe
1967	John Newcombe	Clark Graebner
1968	Arthur Ashe	Tom Okker
1969	Rod Laver	Tony Roche
1970	Ken Rosewall	Tony Roche
1971	Stan Smith	Jan Kodes
1972	Ilie Nastase	Arthur Ashe
1973	John Newcombe	Jan Kodes
1974	Jimmy Connors	Ken Rosewall
1975	Manuel Orantes	Jimmy Connors
1976	Jimmy Connors	Björn Borg
1977	Guillermo Vilas	Jimmy Connors
1978	Jimmy Connors	Björn Borg
1979	John McEnroe	Vitas Gerulaitis
1980	John McEnroe	Björn Borg
1981	John McEnroe	Björn Borg
1982	Jimmy Connors	Ivan Lendl
1983	Jimmy Connors	Ivan Lendl
1984	John McEnroe	Ivan Lendl
1985	Ivan Lendl	John McEnroe
1986	Ivan Lendl	Miloslav Mecir
1987	Ivan Lendl	Mats Wilander
1988	Mats Wilander	Ivan Lendl
1989	Boris Becker	Ivan Lendl
1990	Pete Sampras	Andre Agassi
1991	Stefan Edberg	Jim Courier
1992	Stefan Edberg	Pete Sampras
1993	Pete Sampras	Cedric Pioline
1994	Andre Agassi	Michael Stich
1995	Pete Sampras	Andre Agassi
1996	Pete Sampras	Michael Chang
1997	Patrick Rafter	Greg Rusedski
1998	Patrick Rafter	Mark Philippoussis
1999	Andre Agassi	Todd Martin
2000	Marat Safin	Pete Sampras
2001	Lleyton Hewitt	Pete Sampras
2002	Pete Sampras	Andre Agassi
2003	Andy Roddick	Juan Carlos Ferrero
2004	Roger Federer	Lleyton Hewitt
2005	Roger Federer	Andre Agassi
2006	Roger Federer	Andy Roddick
2007	Roger Federer	Novak Djokovic
2008	Roger Federer	Andy Murray
2009	Juan Martin del Potro	Roger Federer
2010	Rafael Nadal	Novak Djokovic
2011	Novak Djokovic	Rafael Nadal
2012	Andy Murray	Novak Djokovic

Women's Singles

Year	Champion	Final opponent
1925	Helen Wills	Kathleen McKane
1926	Molla B. Mallory	Elizabeth Ryan
1927	Helen Wills	Betty Nuthall
1928	Helen Wills	Helen Jacobs
1929	Helen Wills	Phoebe Holcroft-Watson
1930	Betty Nuthall	L. A. Harper
1931	Helen Wills Moody	E. B. Whittingstall
1932	Helen Jacobs	Carolin A. Babcock
1933	Helen Jacobs	Helen Wills Moody
1934	Helen Jacobs	Sarah H. Palfrey
1935	Helen Jacobs	Sarah Palfrey Fabyan
1936	Alice Marble	Helen Jacobs
1937	Anita Lizana	Jadwiga Jedrzejowska
1938	Alice Marble	Nancye Wynne
1939	Alice Marble	Helen Jacobs
1940	Alice Marble	Helen Jacobs
1941	Sarah Palfrey Cooke	Pauline Betz
1942	Pauline Betz	Louise Brough
1943	Pauline Betz	Louise Brough
1944	Pauline Betz	Margaret Osborne
1945	Sarah Palfrey Cooke	Pauline Betz
1946	Pauline Betz	Patricia Canning
1947	Louise Brough	Margaret Osborne
1948	Margaret Osborne duPont	Louise Brough
1949	Margaret Osborne duPont	Doris Hart
1950	Margaret Osborne duPont	Doris Hart
1951	Maureen Connolly	Shirley Fry
1952	Maureen Connolly	Doris Hart
1953	Maureen Connolly	Doris Hart
1954	Doris Hart	Louise Brough
1955	Doris Hart	Patricia Ward
1956	Shirley Fry	Althea Gibson
1957	Althea Gibson	Louise Brough
1958	Althea Gibson	Darlene Hard

Year	Champion	Final opponent	Year	Champion	Final opponent
1959	Maria Bueno	Christine Truman	1985	Hana Mandlikova	Martina Navratilova
1960	Darlene Hard	Maria Bueno	1986	Martina Navratilova	Helena Sukova
1961	Darlene Hard	Ann Haydon	1987	Martina Navratilova	Steffi Graf
1962	Margaret Smith	Darlene Hard	1988	Steffi Graf	Gabriela Sabatini
1963	Maria Bueno	Margaret Smith	1989	Steffi Graf	Martina Navratilova
1964	Maria Bueno	Carole Graebner	1990	Gabriela Sabatini	Steffi Graf
1965	Margaret Smith	Billie Jean Moffitt	1991	Monica Seles	Martina Navratilova
1966	Maria Bueno	Nancy Richey	1992	Monica Seles	Arantxa Sánchez Vicario
1967	Billie Jean King	Ann Haydon Jones	1993	Steffi Graf	Helena Sukova
1968	Virginia Wade	Billie Jean King	1994	Arantxa Sánchez Vicario	Steffi Graf
1969	Margaret Smith Court	Nancy Richey	1995	Steffi Graf	Monica Seles
1970	Margaret Smith Court	Rosemary Casals	1996	Steffi Graf	Monica Seles
1971	Billie Jean King	Rosemary Casals	1997	Martina Hingis	Venus Williams
1972	Billie Jean King	Kerry Melville	1998	Lindsay Davenport	Martina Hingis
1973	Margaret Smith Court	Evonne Goolagong	1999	Serena Williams	Martina Hingis
1974	Billie Jean King	Evonne Goolagong	2000	Venus Williams	Lindsay Davenport
1975	Chris Evert	Evonne Goolagong Cawley	2001	Venus Williams	Serena Williams
			2002	Serena Williams	Venus Williams
1976	Chris Evert	Evonne Goolagong Cawley	2003	Justine Henin	Kim Clijsters
			2004	Svetlana Kuznetsova	Elena Dementieva
1977	Chris Evert	Wendy Turnbull	2005	Kim Clijsters	Mary Pierce
1978	Chris Evert	Pam Shriver	2006	Maria Sharapova	Justine Henin
1979	Tracy Austin	Chris Evert Lloyd	2007	Justine Henin	Svetlana Kuznetsova
1980	Chris Evert Lloyd	Hana Mandlikova	2008	Serena Williams	Jelena Jankovic
1981	Tracy Austin	Martina Navratilova	2009	Kim Clijsters	Caroline Wozniacki
1982	Chris Evert Lloyd	Hana Mandlikova	2010	Kim Clijsters	Vera Zvonareva
1983	Martina Navratilova	Chris Evert Lloyd	2011	Samantha Stosur	Serena Williams
1984	Martina Navratilova	Chris Evert Lloyd	2012	Serena Williams	Victoria Azarenka

Davis Cup, 1950-2011

The Davis Cup began in 1900 as a competition between the U.S. and Great Britain and later expanded to other countries.

Year	Result	Year	Result	Year	Result
1950	Australia 4, U.S. 1	1971	U.S. 3, Romania 2	1992	U.S. 3, Switzerland 1
1951	Australia 3, U.S. 2	1972	U.S. 3, Romania 2	1993	Germany 4, Australia 1
1952	Australia 4, U.S. 1	1973	Australia 5, U.S. 0	1994	Sweden 4, Russia 1
1953	Australia 3, U.S. 2	1974	South Africa (default by India)	1995	U.S. 3, Russia 2
1954	U.S. 3, Australia 2	1975	Sweden 3, Czechoslovakia 2	1996	France 3, Sweden 2
1955	Australia 5, U.S. 0	1976	Italy 4, Chile 1	1997	Sweden 5, U.S. 0
1956	Australia 5, U.S. 0	1977	Australia 3, Italy 1	1998	Sweden 4, Italy 1
1957	Australia 3, U.S. 2	1978	U.S. 4, Great Britain 1	1999	Australia 3, France 2
1958	U.S. 3, Australia 2	1979	U.S. 5, Italy 0	2000	Spain 3, Australia 1
1959	Australia 3, U.S. 2	1980	Czechoslovakia 4, Italy 1	2001	France 3, Australia 2
1960	Australia 4, Italy 1	1981	U.S. 3, Argentina 1	2002	Russia 3, France 2
1961	Australia 5, Italy 0	1982	U.S. 4, France, 1	2003	Australia 3, Spain 1
1962	Australia 5, Mexico 0	1983	Australia 3, Sweden 2	2004	Spain 3, U.S. 2
1963	U.S. 3, Australia 2	1984	Sweden 4, U.S. 1	2005	Croatia 3, Slovakia 2
1964	Australia 3, U.S. 2	1985	Sweden 3, W. Germany 2	2006	Russia 3, Argentina 2
1965	Australia 4, Spain 1	1986	Australia 3, Sweden 2	2007	U.S. 4, Russia 1
1966	Australia 4, India 1	1987	Sweden 5, India 0	2008	Spain 3, Argentina 1
1967	Australia 4, Spain 1	1988	W. Germany 4, Sweden 1	2009	Spain 5, Czech Republic 0
1968	U.S. 4, Australia 1	1989	W. Germany 3, Sweden 2	2010	Serbia 3, France 2
1969	U.S. 5, Romania 0	1990	U.S. 3, Australia 2	2011	Spain 3, Argentina 1
1970	U.S. 5, W. Germany 0	1991	France 3, U.S. 1		

Note: The challenge round format, which guaranteed the previous year's winner a spot in the finals at home, was eliminated in 1972.

All-Time Grand Slam Singles Titles Leaders

Men	Australian Open	French Open[1]	Wimbledon	U.S. Open	Total
Roger Federer	2004, '06-'07, '10	2009	2003-07, '09, '12	2004-08	17
Pete Sampras	1994, '97	—	1993-95, 1997-2000	1990, '93, '95-'96, 2002	14
Roy Emerson	1961, '63-'67	1963, '67	1964-65	1961, '64	12
Björn Borg	—	1974-75, '78-'81	1976-80	—	11
Rod Laver	1960, '62, '69	1962, '69	1961-62, '68-'69	1962, '69	11
Rafael Nadal	2009	2005-08, '10-'12	2008, '10	2010	11
Bill Tilden	—	—	1920-21, '30	1920-25, '29	10
Andre Agassi	1995, 2000, '01, '03	1999	1992	1994, '99	8
Jimmy Connors	1974	—	1974, '82	1974, '76, '78, '82-'83	8
Ivan Lendl	1989-90	1984, '86-'87	—	1985-87	8
Fred Perry	1934	1935	1934-36	1933-34, '36	8
Ken Rosewall	1953, '55, '71-'72	1953, '68	—	1956, '70	8

Women	Australian Open	French Open[1]	Wimbledon	U.S. Open	Total
Margaret Smith Court	1960-66, '69-'71, '73	1962, '64, '69-'70, '73	1963, '65, '70	1962, '65, '69-'70, '73	24
Steffi Graf	1988-90, '94	1987-88, '93, '95-'96, '99	1988-89, '91-'93, '95-'96	1988-89, '93, '95-'96	22
Helen Wills Moody	—	1928-30, '32	1927-30, '32-'33, '35, '38	1923-25, '27-'29, '31	19
Chris Evert	1982, '84	1974-75, '79-'80, '83, '85-'86	1974, '76, '81	1975-78, '80, '82	18
Martina Navratilova	1981, '83, '85	1982, '84	1978-79, '82-'87, '90	1983-84, '86-'87	18
Serena Williams	2003, '05, '07, '09-'10	2002	2002-03, '09-'10, '12	1999, 2002, '08, '12	15
Billie Jean King	1968	1972	1966-68, '72-'73, '75	1967, '71-'72, '74	12
Suzanne Lenglen	—	1920-23, '25-'26	1919-23, '25	—	12
Maureen Connolly	1953	1953-54	1952-54	1951-53	9
Monica Seles	1991-93, '96	1990-92	—	1991-92	9

Note: Players active in 2012 are in bold. (1) Prior to 1925, French Open entry was limited to members of French clubs.

AUTO RACING

Indianapolis 500 Winners, 1911-2012

At Indianapolis Motor Speedway in Indianapolis, IN. Not held 1917-18, 1942-45. * = Race record.

Year	Driver(s), car[1]	Avg. mph	Year	Driver(s), car[1]	Avg. mph
1911	Ray Harroun, Marmon	74.602	1965	Jim Clark, Lotus-Ford	150.686
1912	Joe Dawson, National	78.719	1966	Graham Hill, Lola-Ford	144.317
1913	Jules Goux, Peugeot	75.933	1967	A. J. Foyt, Coyote-Ford	151.207
1914	Rene Thomas, Delage	82.474	1968	Bobby Unser, Eagle-Offy	152.882
1915	Ralph DePalma, Mercedes	89.840	1969	Mario Andretti, Hawk-Ford	156.867
1916	Dario Resta, Peugeot	84.001	1970	Al Unser, P.J. Colt-Ford	155.749
1919	Howdy Wilcox, Peugeot	88.050	1971	Al Unser, P.J. Colt-Ford	157.735
1920	Gaston Chevrolet, Frontenac	88.618	1972	Mark Donohue, McLaren-Offy	162.962
1921	Tommy Milton, Frontenac	89.621	1973	Gordon Johncock, Eagle-Offy	159.036
1922	Jimmy Murphy, Duesenberg-Miller	94.484	1974	Johnny Rutherford, McLaren-Offy	158.589
1923	Tommy Milton, Miller	90.954	1975	Bobby Unser, Eagle-Offy	149.213
1924	L. L. Corum/Joe Boyer, Duesenberg	98.234	1976	Johnny Rutherford, McLaren-Offy	148.725
1925	Peter DePaolo, Duesenberg	101.127	1977	A. J. Foyt, Coyote-Foyt	161.331
1926	Frank Lockhart, Miller	95.904	1978	Al Unser, Lola-Cosworth	161.363
1927	George Souders, Duesenberg	97.545	1979	Rick Mears, Penske-Cosworth	158.899
1928	Louie Meyer, Miller	99.482	1980	Johnny Rutherford, Chaparral-Cosworth	142.862
1929	Ray Keech, Miller	97.585	1981	Bobby Unser, Penske-Cosworth	139.084
1930	Billy Arnold, Summers-Miller	100.448	1982	Gordon Johncock, Wildcat-Cosworth	162.029
1931	Louis Schneider, Stevens-Miller	96.629	1983	Tom Sneva, March-Cosworth	162.117
1932	Fred Frame, Wetteroth-Miller	104.144	1984	Rick Mears, March-Cosworth	163.612
1933	Louie Meyer, Miller	104.162	1985	Danny Sullivan, March-Cosworth	152.982
1934	Bill Cummings, Miller	104.863	1986	Bobby Rahal, March-Cosworth	170.722
1935	Kelly Petillo, Wetteroth-Offy	106.240	1987	Al Unser, March-Cosworth	162.175
1936	Louie Meyer, Stevens-Miller	109.069	1988	Rick Mears, Penske-Chevy Indy V8	144.809
1937	Wilbur Shaw, Shaw-Offy	113.580	1989	Emerson Fittipaldi, Penske-Chevy Indy V8	167.581
1938	Floyd Roberts, Wetteroth-Miller	117.200	1990	Arie Luyendyk, Lola-Chevy Indy V8	185.981*
1939	Wilbur Shaw, Maserati	115.035	1991	Rick Mears, Penske-Chevy Indy V8	176.457
1940	Wilbur Shaw, Maserati	114.277	1992	Al Unser Jr., Galmer-Chevy Indy V8A	134.477
1941	Floyd Davis/Mauri Rose, Wetteroth-Offy	115.117	1993	Emerson Fittipaldi, Penske-Chevy Indy V8C	157.207
1946	George Robson, Adams-Sparks	114.820	1994	Al Unser Jr., Penske-Mercedes Benz	160.872
1947	Mauri Rose, Deidt-Offy	116.338	1995	Jacques Villeneuve, Reynard-Ford Cosworth XB	153.616
1948	Mauri Rose, Deidt-Offy	119.814	1996	Buddy Lazier, Reynard-Ford Cosworth	147.956
1949	Bill Holland, Deidt-Offy	121.327	1997	Arie Luyendyk, G Force-Aurora	145.827
1950	Johnnie Parsons, Kurtis-Offy	124.002	1998	Eddie Cheever, Dallara-Aurora	145.155
1951	Lee Wallard, Kurtis-Offy	126.244	1999	Kenny Brack, Dallara-Aurora	153.176
1952	Troy Ruttman, Kuzma-Offy	128.922	2000	Juan Montoya, G Force-Oldsmobile	167.607
1953	Bill Vukovich, KK500A-Offy	127.740	2001	Helio Castroneves, Reynard-Honda	141.574
1954	Bill Vukovich, KK500A-Offy	130.840	2002	Helio Castroneves, Reynard-Honda	166.499
1955	Bob Sweikert, KK500C-Offy	128.213	2003	Gil de Ferran, G Force-Toyota	156.291
1956	Pat Flaherty, Watson-Offy	128.490	2004	Buddy Rice, G Force-Honda	138.518
1957	Sam Hanks, Salih-Offy	135.601	2005	Dan Wheldon, Dallara-Honda	157.603
1958	Jimmy Bryan, Salih-Offy	133.791	2006	Sam Hornish Jr., Dallara-Honda	157.085
1959	Rodger Ward, Watson-Offy	135.857	2007	Dario Franchitti, Dallara-Honda	151.774
1960	Jim Rathmann, Watson-Offy	138.767	2008	Scott Dixon, Dallara-Honda	143.567
1961	A. J. Foyt, Trevis-Offy	139.130	2009	Helio Castroneves, Dallara-Honda	150.318
1962	Rodger Ward, Watson-Offy	140.293	2010	Dario Franchitti, Dallara-Honda	161.623
1963	Parnelli Jones, Watson-Offy	143.137	2011	Dan Wheldon, Dallara-Honda	170.265
1964	A. J. Foyt, Watson-Offy	147.350	2012	Dario Franchitti, Dallara-Honda	167.734

Note: The race was less than 500 mi in the following years: 1916 (300 mi), 1926 (400 mi), 1950 (345 mi), 1973 (332.5 mi), 1975 (435 mi), 1976 (255 mi), 2004 (450 mi), 2007 (415 mi). (1) Chassis-engine.

IndyCar Series Champions, 1996-2011

A breakaway group of Championship Auto Racing Teams (CART) drivers began the Indy Racing League (IRL) in 1994; it awarded its first championship in 1996. Known as IndyCar Series since 2003, IRL announced it would officially change its name to IndyCar as of Jan. 1, 2011. Merged with Champ Car World Series, 2008.

Year	Driver	Year	Driver	Year	Driver	Year	Driver	Year	Driver
1996	Scott Sharp; Buzz Calkins (tie)	1999	Greg Ray	2003	Scott Dixon	2006	Sam Hornish Jr.	2009	Dario Franchitti
		2000	Buddy Lazier	2004	Tony Kanaan	2007	Dario Franchitti	2010	Dario Franchitti
1997	Tony Stewart	2001	Sam Hornish Jr.	2005	Dan Wheldon	2008	Scott Dixon	2011	Dario Franchitti
1998	Kenny Brack	2002	Sam Hornish Jr.						

Champ Car World Series Vanderbilt Cup Winners, 1959-2007

U.S. Auto Club champions, 1959-78; Championship Auto Racing Teams (CART) champions, 1979-2003; Champ Car World Series champions, 2004-07. The Vanderbilt Cup became the series championship trophy in 2000. Merged with Indy Racing League, 2008.

Year	Driver	Year	Driver	Year	Driver	Year	Driver	Year	Driver
1959	Rodger Ward	1969	Mario Andretti	1979	Rick Mears	1989	Emerson Fittipaldi	1999	Juan Montoya
1960	A. J. Foyt	1970	Al Unser	1980	Johnny Rutherford	1990	Al Unser Jr.	2000	Gil de Ferran
1961	A. J. Foyt	1971	Joe Leonard	1981	Rick Mears	1991	Michael Andretti	2001	Gil de Ferran
1962	Rodger Ward	1972	Joe Leonard	1982	Rick Mears	1992	Bobby Rahal	2002	Cristiano da Matta
1963	A. J. Foyt	1973	Roger McCluskey	1983	Al Unser	1993	Nigel Mansell	2003	Paul Tracy
1964	A. J. Foyt	1974	Bobby Unser	1984	Mario Andretti	1994	Al Unser Jr.	2004	Sébastien Bourdais
1965	Mario Andretti	1975	A. J. Foyt	1985	Al Unser	1995	Jacques Villeneuve	2005	Sébastien Bourdais
1966	Mario Andretti	1976	Gordon Johncock	1986	Bobby Rahal	1996	Jimmy Vasser	2006	Sébastien Bourdais
1967	A. J. Foyt	1977	Tom Sneva	1987	Bobby Rahal	1997	Alex Zanardi	2007	Sébastien Bourdais
1968	Bobby Unser	1978	Tom Sneva	1988	Danny Sullivan	1998	Alex Zanardi		

NASCAR Sprint Cup Champions, 1949-2011

Known as Strictly Stock, 1949; Grand National, 1950-70; Winston Cup, 1971-2003; and Sprint Cup, 2004-present.

Year	Driver	Year	Driver	Year	Driver	Year	Driver	Year	Driver
1949	Red Byron	1962	Joe Weatherly	1975	Richard Petty	1988	Bill Elliott	2000	Bobby Labonte
1950	Bill Rexford	1963	Joe Weatherly	1976	Cale Yarborough	1989	Rusty Wallace	2001	Jeff Gordon
1951	Herb Thomas	1964	Richard Petty	1977	Cale Yarborough	1990	Dale Earnhardt	2002	Tony Stewart
1952	Tim Flock	1965	Ned Jarrett	1978	Cale Yarborough	1991	Dale Earnhardt	2003	Matt Kenseth
1953	Herb Thomas	1966	David Pearson	1979	Richard Petty	1992	Alan Kulwicki	2004	Kurt Busch
1954	Lee Petty	1967	Richard Petty	1980	Dale Earnhardt	1993	Dale Earnhardt	2005	Tony Stewart
1955	Tim Flock	1968	David Pearson	1981	Darrell Waltrip	1994	Dale Earnhardt	2006	Jimmie Johnson
1956	Buck Baker	1969	David Pearson	1982	Darrell Waltrip	1995	Jeff Gordon	2007	Jimmie Johnson
1957	Buck Baker	1970	Bobby Isaac	1983	Bobby Allison	1996	Terry Labonte	2008	Jimmie Johnson
1958	Lee Petty	1971	Richard Petty	1984	Terry Labonte	1997	Jeff Gordon	2009	Jimmie Johnson
1959	Lee Petty	1972	Richard Petty	1985	Darrell Waltrip	1998	Jeff Gordon	2010	Jimmie Johnson
1960	Rex White	1973	Benny Parsons	1986	Dale Earnhardt	1999	Dale Jarrett	2011	Tony Stewart
1961	Ned Jarrett	1974	Richard Petty	1987	Dale Earnhardt				

NASCAR Sprint Cup Rookie of the Year, 1958-2011

Year	Driver	Year	Driver	Year	Driver	Year	Driver	Year	Driver
1958	Shorty Rollins	1969	Dick Brooks	1980	Jody Riley	1991	Bobby Hamilton	2002	Ryan Newman
1959	Richard Petty	1970	Bill Dennis	1981	Ron Bouchard	1992	Jimmy Hensley	2003	Jamie McMurray
1960	David Pearson	1971	Walter Ballard	1982	Geoff Bodine	1993	Jeff Gordon	2004	Kasey Kahne
1961	Woodie Wilson	1972	Larry Smith	1983	Sterling Marlin	1994	Jeff Burton	2005	Kyle Busch
1962	Tom Cox	1973	Lennie Pond	1984	Rusty Wallace	1995	Ricky Craven	2006	Denny Hamlin
1963	Billy Wade	1974	Earl Ross	1985	Ken Schrader	1996	Johnny Benson	2007	Juan Montoya
1964	Doug Cooper	1975	Bruce Hill	1986	Alan Kulwicki	1997	Mike Skinner	2008	Regan Smith
1965	Sam McQuagg	1976	Skip Manning	1987	Davey Allison	1998	Kenny Irwin	2009	Joey Logano
1966	James Hylton	1977	Ricky Rudd	1988	Ken Bouchard	1999	Tony Stewart	2010	Kevin Conway
1967	Donnie Allison	1978	Ronnie Thomas	1989	Dick Trickle	2000	Matt Kenseth	2011	Andy Lally
1968	Pete Hamilton	1979	Dale Earnhardt	1990	Rob Moroso	2001	Kevin Harvick		

Daytona 500 Winners, 1959-2012

At Daytona International Speedway in Daytona Beach, FL.

Year	Driver, car	Avg. mph	Year	Driver, car	Avg. mph	Year	Driver, car	Avg. mph
1959	Lee Petty, Oldsmobile	135.521	1978	Bobby Allison, Ford	159.730	1996	Dale Jarrett, Ford	154.308
1960	Junior Johnson, Chevrolet	124.740	1979	Richard Petty, Oldsmobile	143.977	1997	Jeff Gordon, Chevrolet	148.295
1961	Marvin Panch, Pontiac	149.601	1980	Buddy Baker, Oldsmobile	177.602	1998	Dale Earnhardt, Chevrolet	172.712
1962	Fireball Roberts, Pontiac	152.529	1981	Richard Petty, Buick	169.651	1999	Jeff Gordon, Chevrolet	161.551
1963	Tiny Lund, Ford	151.566	1982	Bobby Allison, Buick	153.991	2000	Dale Jarrett, Ford	155.669
1964	Richard Petty, Plymouth	154.334	1983	Cale Yarborough, Pontiac	155.979	2001	Michael Waltrip, Chevrolet	161.783
1965	Fred Lorenzen, Ford	141.539	1984	Cale Yarborough,		2002	Ward Burton, Dodge	142.971
1966	Richard Petty, Plymouth	160.627		Chevrolet	150.994	2003	Michael Waltrip, Chevrolet	133.870
1967	Mario Andretti, Ford	146.926	1985	Bill Elliott, Ford	172.265	2004	Dale Earnhardt Jr.,	
1968	Cale Yarborough, Mercury	143.251	1986	Geoff Bodine, Chevrolet	148.124		Chevrolet	156.345
1969	LeeRoy Yarbrough, Ford	157.950	1987	Bill Elliott, Ford	176.263	2005	Jeff Gordon, Chevrolet	135.173
1970	Pete Hamilton, Plymouth	149.601	1988	Bobby Allison, Buick	137.531	2006	Jimmie Johnson, Chevrolet	142.667
1971	Richard Petty, Plymouth	144.456	1989	Darrell Waltrip, Chevrolet	148.466	2007	Kevin Harvick, Chevrolet	149.335
1972	A. J. Foyt, Mercury	161.550	1990	Derrike Cope, Chevrolet	165.761	2008	Ryan Newman, Dodge	152.672
1973	Richard Petty, Dodge	157.205	1991	Ernie Irvan, Chevrolet	148.148	2009	Matt Kenseth, Ford	132.816
1974	Richard Petty, Dodge	140.894	1992	Davey Allison, Ford	160.256	2010	Jamie McMurray,	
1975	Benny Parsons, Chevrolet	153.649	1993	Dale Jarrett, Chevrolet	154.972		Chevrolet	137.284
1976	David Pearson, Mercury	152.181	1994	Sterling Marlin, Chevrolet	156.931	2011	Trevor Bayne, Ford	130.326
1977	Cale Yarborough,		1995	Sterling Marlin, Chevrolet	141.710	2012	Matt Kenseth, Ford	140.256
	Chevrolet	153.218						

Note: The race was less than 500 mi in the following years: 1965 (322.5 mi), 1966 (495 mi), 1974 (450 mi), 2003 (272.5 mi).

Coca-Cola 600 Winners, 1960-2012

At Charlotte Motor Speedway in Concord, NC. Known as the World 600, 1960-85. * = Rain-shortened.

Year	Driver, car	Avg. mph	Year	Driver, car	Avg. mph	Year	Driver, car	Avg. mph
1960	Joe Lee Johnson,		1978	Darrell Waltrip, Chevrolet	138.355	1996	Dale Jarrett, Ford	147.581
	Chevrolet	107.735	1979	Darrell Waltrip, Chevrolet	136.674	1997	Jeff Gordon, Chevrolet	136.745*
1961	David Pearson, Pontiac	111.633	1980	Benny Parsons,		1998	Jeff Gordon, Chevrolet	136.424
1962	Nelson Stacy, Ford	125.552		Chevrolet	119.265	1999	Jeff Burton, Ford	151.367
1963	Fred Lorenzen, Ford	132.418	1981	Bobby Allison, Buick	129.326	2000	Matt Kenseth, Ford	142.640
1964	Jim Paschal, Plymouth	125.772	1982	Neil Bonnett, Ford	130.058	2001	Jeff Burton, Ford	138.107
1965	Fred Lorenzen, Ford	121.772	1983	Neil Bonnett, Chevrolet	140.707	2002	Mark Martin, Ford	137.729
1966	Marvin Panch, Plymouth	135.042	1984	Bobby Allison, Buick	129.233	2003	Jimmie Johnson,	
1967	Jim Paschal, Plymouth	135.832	1985	Darrell Waltrip, Chevrolet	141.807		Chevrolet	126.198*
1968	Buddy Baker, Dodge	104.207*	1986	Dale Earnhardt,		2004	Jimmie Johnson,	
1969	LeeRoy Yarbrough,			Chevrolet	140.406		Chevrolet	142.763
	Mercury	134.361	1987	Kyle Petty, Ford	131.483	2005	Jimmie Johnson,	
1970	Donnie Allison, Ford	129.680	1988	Darrell Waltrip, Chevrolet	124.460		Chevrolet	114.698
1971	Bobby Allison, Mercury	140.422	1989	Darrell Waltrip, Chevrolet	144.077	2006	Kasey Kahne, Dodge	128.840
1972	Buddy Baker, Dodge	142.255	1990	Rusty Wallace, Pontiac	137.650	2007	Casey Mears, Chevrolet	130.222
1973	Buddy Baker, Dodge	134.890	1991	Davey Allison, Ford	138.951	2008	Kasey Kahne, Dodge	135.722
1974	David Pearson, Mercury	135.720	1992	Dale Earnhardt, Chevrolet	132.980	2009	David Reutimann, Toyota	120.899*
1975	Richard Petty, Dodge	145.327	1993	Dale Earnhardt, Chevrolet	145.504	2010	Kurt Busch, Dodge	144.966
1976	David Pearson, Mercury	137.352	1994	Jeff Gordon, Chevrolet	139.445	2011	Kevin Harvick, Chevrolet	132.414
1977	Richard Petty, Dodge	137.676	1995	Bobby Labonte, Chevrolet	151.952	2012	Kasey Kahne, Chevrolet	155.687

Brickyard 400 Winners, 1994-2012

At Indianapolis Motor Speedway in Indianapolis, IN.

Year	Driver, car	Avg. mph	Year	Driver, car	Avg. mph	Year	Driver, car	Avg. mph
1994	Jeff Gordon, Chevrolet	131.977	2001	Jeff Gordon, Chevrolet	130.790	2007	Tony Stewart, Chevrolet	117.379
1995	Dale Earnhardt, Chevrolet	155.206	2002	Bill Elliott, Dodge	125.033	2008	Jimmie Johnson, Chevrolet	115.117
1996	Dale Jarrett, Ford	139.508	2003	Kevin Harvick, Chevrolet	134.554	2009	Jimmie Johnson, Chevrolet	145.882
1997	Ricky Rudd, Ford	130.814	2004	Jeff Gordon, Chevrolet	115.037	2010	Jamie McMurray, Chevrolet	136.054
1998	Jeff Gordon, Chevrolet	126.772	2005	Tony Stewart, Chevrolet	118.782	2011	Paul Menard, Chevrolet	140.762
1999	Dale Jarrett, Ford	148.194	2006	Jimmie Johnson, Chevrolet	137.182	2012	Jimmie Johnson, Chevrolet	137.680
2000	Bobby Labonte, Pontiac	155.912						

Irwin Tools Night Race Winners, 1961-2012

At Bristol Motor Speedway in Bristol, TN. Known as the Volunteer 500, 1961-75, '78-'79; Volunteer 400, 1976-77; Busch 500, 1980-90; Bud 500, 1991-93; Goody's 500, 1994-99; goracing.com 500, 2000; and Sharpie 500, 2001-09. * = Rain-shortened.

Year	Driver, car	Avg. mph	Year	Driver, car	Avg. mph	Year	Driver, car	Avg. mph
1961	Jack Smith, Pontiac	68.373	1979	Darrell Waltrip, Chevrolet	91.493	1997	Dale Jarrett, Ford	80.013
1962	Bobby Johns, Pontiac	73.397	1980	Cale Yarborough, Chevrolet	86.973	1998	Mark Martin, Ford	86.949
1963	Fred Lorenzen, Ford	74.844	1981	Darrell Waltrip, Buick	84.723	1999	Dale Earnhardt, Chevrolet	91.276
1964	Fred Lorenzen, Ford	78.044	1982	Darrell Waltrip, Buick	94.318	2000	Rusty Wallace, Ford	85.394
1965	Ned Jarrett, Ford	61.826	1983	Darrell Waltrip, Chevrolet	89.430*	2001	Tony Stewart, Pontiac	85.106
1966	Paul Goldsmith, Plymouth	77.963	1984	Terry Labonte, Chevrolet	85.365	2002	Jeff Gordon, Chevrolet	77.097
1967	Richard Petty, Plymouth	78.705	1985	Dale Earnhardt, Chevrolet	81.388	2003	Kurt Busch, Ford	77.421
1968	David Pearson, Ford	76.310	1986	Darrell Waltrip, Chevrolet	86.934	2004	Dale Earnhardt Jr.,	
1969	David Pearson, Ford	79.737	1987	Dale Earnhardt, Chevrolet	90.373		Chevrolet	88.538
1970	Bobby Allison, Dodge	84.880	1988	Dale Earnhardt, Chevrolet	78.775	2005	Matt Kenseth, Ford	84.678
1971	Charlie Glotzbach,		1989	Darrell Waltrip, Chevrolet	85.554	2006	Matt Kenseth, Ford	90.025
	Chevrolet	101.074	1990	Ernie Irvan, Chevrolet	91.782	2007	Carl Edwards, Ford	89.006
1972	Bobby Allison, Chevrolet	92.735	1991	Alan Kulwicki, Ford	82.028	2008	Carl Edwards, Ford	91.581
1973	Benny Parsons, Chevrolet	91.342	1992	Darrell Waltrip, Chevrolet	91.198	2009	Kyle Busch, Toyota	84.820
1974	Cale Yarborough, Chevrolet	75.430	1993	Mark Martin, Ford	88.172	2010	Kyle Busch, Toyota	99.071
1975	Richard Petty, Dodge	97.016	1994	Rusty Wallace, Ford	91.363	2011	Brad Keselowski, Dodge	96.753
1976	Cale Yarborough, Chevrolet	99.175	1995	Terry Labonte, Chevrolet	81.979	2012	Denny Hamlin, Toyota	84.402
1977	Cale Yarborough, Chevrolet	79.726	1996	Rusty Wallace, Ford	91.267			
1978	Cale Yarborough, Oldsmobile	88.628						

NASCAR Sprint All-Star Race Winners, 1985-2012

At Charlotte Motor Speedway in Concord, NC. Known as The Winston, 1985-93, 1997-2003; The Winston Select, 1994-96; and Nextel All-Star Challenge, 2004-07.

Year	Driver, car	Year	Driver, car	Year	Driver, car
1985	Darrell Waltrip, Chevrolet	1995	Jeff Gordon, Chevrolet	2004	Matt Kenseth, Ford
1986	Bill Elliott, Ford	1996	Michael Waltrip, Ford	2005	Mark Martin, Ford
1987	Dale Earnhardt, Chevrolet	1997	Jeff Gordon, Chevrolet	2006	Jimmie Johnson, Chevrolet
1988	Terry Labonte, Chevrolet	1998	Mark Martin, Ford	2007	Kevin Harvick, Chevrolet
1989	Rusty Wallace, Ford	1999	Terry Labonte, Chevrolet	2008	Kasey Kahne, Dodge
1990	Dale Earnhardt, Chevrolet	2000	Dale Earnhardt Jr., Chevrolet	2009	Tony Stewart, Chevrolet
1991	Davey Allison, Ford	2001	Jeff Gordon, Chevrolet	2010	Kurt Busch, Dodge
1992	Davey Allison, Ford	2002	Ryan Newman, Ford	2011	Carl Edwards, Ford
1993	Dale Earnhardt, Chevrolet	2003	Jimmie Johnson, Chevrolet	2012	Jimmie Johnson, Chevrolet
1994	Geoffrey Bodine, Ford				

Formula One World Grand Prix Champions, 1950-2011

Year	Driver, country	Year	Driver, country	Year	Driver, country
1950	Giuseppe "Nino" Farina, Italy	1971	Jackie Stewart, Scotland, UK	1991	Ayrton Senna, Brazil
1951	Juan Manuel Fangio, Argentina	1972	Emerson Fittipaldi, Brazil	1992	Nigel Mansell, England, UK
1952	Alberto Ascari, Italy	1973	Jackie Stewart, Scotland, UK	1993	Alain Prost, France
1953	Alberto Ascari, Italy	1974	Emerson Fittipaldi, Brazil	1994	Michael Schumacher, Germany
1954	Juan Manuel Fangio, Argentina	1975	Niki Lauda, Austria	1995	Michael Schumacher, Germany
1955	Juan Manuel Fangio, Argentina	1976	James Hunt, England, UK	1996	Damon Hill, England, UK
1956	Juan Manuel Fangio, Argentina	1977	Niki Lauda, Austria	1997	Jacques Villeneuve, Canada
1957	Juan Manuel Fangio, Argentina	1978	Mario Andretti, United States	1998	Mika Hakkinen, Finland
1958	Mike Hawthorn, England, UK	1979	Jody Scheckter, South Africa	1999	Mika Hakkinen, Finland
1959	Jack Brabham, Australia	1980	Alan Jones, Australia	2000	Michael Schumacher, Germany
1960	Jack Brabham, Australia	1981	Nelson Piquet, Brazil	2001	Michael Schumacher, Germany
1961	Phil Hill, United States	1982	Keke Rosberg, Finland	2002	Michael Schumacher, Germany
1962	Graham Hill, England, UK	1983	Nelson Piquet, Brazil	2003	Michael Schumacher, Germany
1963	Jim Clark, Scotland, UK	1984	Niki Lauda, Austria	2004	Michael Schumacher, Germany
1964	John Surtees, England, UK	1985	Alain Prost, France	2005	Fernando Alonso, Spain
1965	Jim Clark, Scotland, UK	1986	Alain Prost, France	2006	Fernando Alonso, Spain
1966	Jack Brabham, Australia	1987	Nelson Piquet, Brazil	2007	Kimi Raikkonen, Finland
1967	Denis Hulme, New Zealand	1988	Ayrton Senna, Brazil	2008	Lewis Hamilton, England, UK
1968	Graham Hill, England, UK	1989	Alain Prost, France	2009	Jenson Button, England, UK
1969	Jackie Stewart, Scotland, UK	1990	Ayrton Senna, Brazil	2010	Sebastian Vettel, Germany
1970	Jochen Rindt, Austria	1990	Ayrton Senna, Brazil	2011	Sebastian Vettel, Germany

24 Hours of Le Mans Race, 2012

In the first-ever Le Mans hybrid victory, Audi won the 80th running of the 24 Hours of Le Mans auto race June 17, 2012. Defending champions Marcel Fassler of Switzerland, André Lotterer of Germany, and Benoit Treluyer of France drove an Audi R18 e-tron Quattro to victory, completing 378 laps in 24 hours. It was Audi's eighth top finish in the last nine years at Circuit de la Sarthe in Le Mans, France. The winning trio was one lap better than the Audi No. 2 car, also a hybrid, driven by Italy's Rinaldo Capello, Denmark's Tom Kristensen, and Great Britain's Allan McNish. The German company swept the podium as its Audi No. 4 car, driven by Marco Bonanomi of Italy, Oliver Jarvis of Great Britain, and Mike Rockenfeller of Germany, placed third. Only 35 out of 56 cars that started the endurance race, which was first held in 1923, finished.

BOXING

There are many boxing governing bodies, including the World Boxing Assn. (WBA; known as the National Boxing Assn. [NBA] until 1962), World Boxing Council (WBC), International Boxing Fed. (IBF), World Boxing Org., U.S. Boxing Assn., N. American Boxing Fed., and European Boxing Union. All have their own champions and divisions.

Boxing Champions by Class

Class (weight limit)	WBA Champion	WBC Champion	IBF Champion
Heavyweight (none)	Wladimir Klitschko, Ukraine[1] Alexander Povetkin, Russia	Vitali Klitschko, Ukraine	Wladimir Klitschko, Ukraine
Cruiserweight (200 lbs)	Guillermo Jones, Panama Denis Lebedev, Russia[2]	Krzysztof Wlodarczyk, Poland	Yoan Pablo Hernández, Cuba
Light Heavyweight (175 lbs)	Beibut Shumenov, Kazakhstan	Chad Dawson, U.S.	Tavoris Cloud, U.S.
Super Middleweight (168 lbs)	Andre Ward, U.S.[1] Brian Magee, UK	Andre Ward, U.S.	Carl Froch, UK
Middleweight (160 lbs)	Daniel Geale, Australia[1] Gennady Golovkin, Kazakhstan	Sergio Martínez, Argentina	Daniel Geale, Australia
Super Welterweight/ Jr. Middleweight (154 lbs)	Floyd Mayweather Jr., U.S.[1] Austin Trout, U.S.	Saúl Álvarez, Mexico	Cornelius Bundrage, U.S.
Welterweight (147 lbs)	Paulie Malignaggi, U.S. Diego Chaves, Argentina[2]	Floyd Mayweather Jr., U.S. Robert Guerrero, U.S.[2]	Randall Bailey, U.S.
Super Lightweight/ Jr. Welterweight (140 lbs)	Danny García, U.S.[1] Pablo César Cano, Mexico[2]	Danny García, U.S. Lucas Matthysse, Argentina[2]	Lamont Peterson, U.S.
Lightweight (135 lbs)	Vacant Richard Abril, Cuba[2]	Antonio DeMarco, Mexico	Miguel Vázquez, Mexico
Super Featherweight/ Jr. Lightweight (130 lbs)	Takashi Uchiyama, Japan Bryan Vázquez, Costa Rica[2]	Takahiro Ao, Japan	Juan Carlos Salgado, Mexico
Featherweight (126 lbs)	Chris John, Indonesia[1] Celestino Caballero, Panama	Daniel Ponce de León, Mexico	Billy Dib, Australia
Super Bantamweight/ Jr. Featherweight (122 lbs)	Guillermo Rigondeaux, Cuba	Abner Mares, Mexico	Nonito Donaire, Philippines
Bantamweight (118 lbs)	Anselmo Moreno, Panama[1] Koki Kameda, Japan Hugo Ruiz, Mexico[2]	Shinsuke Yamanaka, Japan	Leo Santa Cruz, Mexico
Super Flyweight/ Jr. Bantamweight (115 lbs)	Tepparith Singwancha, Thailand Liborio Solís, Venezuela[2]	Yota Sato, Japan	Juan Carlos Sánchez Jr., Mexico
Flyweight (112 lbs)	Hernán Márquez, Mexico Juan Carlos Reveco, Argentina[2]	Toshiyuki Igarashi, Japan	Moruti Mthalane, South Africa
Jr. Flyweight (108 lbs)	Román González, Nicaragua Alberto Rossel, Peru[2]	Kompayak Porpramook, Thailand	Johnriel Casimero, Philippines
Strawweight/ Mini Flyweight (105 lbs)	Kazuto Ioka, Japan Jesús Silvestre, Mexico[2]	Vacant	Mario Rodríguez, Mexico

Note: As of Sept. 22, 2012. (1) Super champion. (2) Interim champion.

Ring Champions by Years

* = Abandoned the title or was stripped of it; IBF champions listed only for heavyweight division; International Boxing Hall of Fame inductees in *italics*.

Heavyweights

1882-92	*John L. Sullivan*[1]	1978	Leon Spinks (WBC*/WBA)[5]; *Ken Norton* (WBC)	1994-95	Oliver McCall (WBC); *George Foreman* (WBA*/IBF*)
1892-97	*James J. Corbett*[2]				
1897-99	*Bob Fitzsimmons*	1978-79	*Muhammad Ali* (WBA*)	1995	Frans Botha (IBF*)
1899-1905	*James J. Jeffries*[3]	1978-83	*Larry Holmes* (WBC*)[6]	1995-96	Bruce Seldon (WBA); Frank Bruno (WBC)
1905-06	Marvin Hart	1979-80	John Tate (WBA)		
1906-08	*Tommy Burns*	1980-82	Mike Weaver (WBA)	1996	*Mike Tyson* (WBC*/WBA)
1908-15	*Jack Johnson*	1982-83	Michael Dokes (WBA)	1996-97	Michael Moorer (IBF)
1915-19	*Jess Willard*	1983-84	Gerrie Coetzee (WBA)	1996-99	Evander Holyfield (WBA/IBF)
1919-26	*Jack Dempsey*	1983-85	Larry Holmes (IBF)[6]	1997-2001	*Lennox Lewis* (WBC)
1926-28	*Gene Tunney**	1984	Tim Witherspoon (WBC)	1999-2001	*Lennox Lewis* (WBA*/WBC/IBF)
1928-30	Vacant	1984-85	Greg Page (WBA)	2000-01	Evander Holyfield (WBA)
1930-32	*Max Schmeling*	1984-86	Pinklon Thomas (WBC)	2001-03	John Ruiz (WBA)
1932-33	*Jack Sharkey*	1985-86	Tony Tubbs (WBA)	2001	Hasim Rahman (WBC/IBF)
1933-34	Primo Carnera	1985-87	*Michael Spinks* (IBF*)	2001-02	*Lennox Lewis* (IBF*)
1934-35	*Max Baer*	1986	Tim Witherspoon (WBA); Trevor Berbick (WBC)	2001-04	*Lennox Lewis* (WBC)
1935-37	*James J. Braddock*			2002-06	Chris Byrd (IBF)
1937-49	*Joe Louis**	1986-87	*Mike Tyson* (WBC); James "Bonecrusher" Smith (WBA)	2003	Roy Jones Jr. (WBA*)
1949-51	*Ezzard Charles*			2004-05	John Ruiz (WBA)[7]; Vitali Klitschko (WBC*)
1951-52	*Joe Walcott*	1987	Tony Tucker (IBF)		
1952-56	*Rocky Marciano**	1987-90	*Mike Tyson* (WBA/WBC/IBF)	2005-06	Hasim Rahman (WBC)
1956-59	*Floyd Patterson*	1990	James "Buster" Douglas (WBA/WBC/IBF)	2005-07	Nicolay Valuev (WBA)
1959-60	*Ingemar Johansson*			2006-08	Oleg Maskaev (WBC)
1960-62	*Floyd Patterson*	1990-92	Evander Holyfield (WBA/WBC/IBF)	2006-	Wladimir Klitschko (IBF)
1962-64	*Sonny Liston*			2007-08	Ruslan Chagaev (WBA)
1964-67	*Cassius Clay (Muhammad Ali)*[4]	1992-93	Riddick Bowe (WBA/WBC*/IBF)	2008	Samuel Peter (WBC)
		1992-94	*Lennox Lewis* (WBC)	2008-09	Nikolai Valuev (WBA)
1970-73	*Joe Frazier*	1993-94	Evander Holyfield (WBA/IBF)	2009-	Vitali Klitschko (WBC)
1973-74	*George Foreman*	1994	Michael Moorer (WBA/IBF)	2009-11	David Haye (WBA)
1974-78	*Muhammad Ali*			2011-	Wladimir Klitschko (WBA)

(1) London Prize Ring (bare-knuckle champion). (2) First Marquis of Queensberry champion. (3) Jeffries vacated title (1905), designated Marvin Hart and Jack Root as logical contenders. Hart def. Root in 12 rounds (1905); in turn was def. by Tommy Burns (1906), who claimed the title. Jack Johnson def. Burns (1908) and was recognized as champ. Johnson won the title by defeating Jeffries in the latter's attempted comeback (1910). (4) Title declared vacant by the WBA and others in 1967 after Ali refused military induction for religious reasons during the Vietnam War. Joe Frazier recognized as champ by six states, Mexico, and S. America. Jimmy Ellis declared champ by the WBA. Frazier KOd Ellis, Feb. 16, 1970. (5) After Spinks def. Ali, the WBC recognized Ken Norton as champ. Ali def. Spinks in 1978 rematch for WBA title, retired in 1979. (6) Holmes relinquished WBC title in Dec. 1983 to fight as champ of the new IBF. (7) James Toney def. Ruiz Apr. 30, 2005, to claim the title, but it was rescinded when Toney tested positive for steroids.

Light Heavyweights

Year	Champion
1903	Jack Root; George Gardner
1903-05	Bob Fitzsimmons
1905-12	Philadelphia Jack O'Brien*
1912-16	Jack Dillon
1916-20	Battling Levinsky
1920-22	George Carpentier
1922-23	Battling Siki
1923-25	Mike McTigue
1925-26	Paul Berlenbach
1926-27	Jack Delaney*
1927-29	Tommy Loughran*
1930-34	Maxie Rosenbloom
1934-35	Bob Olin
1935-39	John Henry Lewis*
1939	Melio Bettina
1939-41	Billy Conn*
1941	Anton Christoforidis (won NBA title)
1941-48	Gus Lesnevich; Freddie Mills
1948-50	Freddie Mills
1950-52	Joey Maxim
1952-62	Archie Moore
1962-63	Harold Johnson
1963-65	Willie Pastrano
1965-66	Jose Torres
1966-68	Dick Tiger
1968-74	Bob Foster*
1974-77	John Conteh (WBC)
1974-78	Victor Galindez (WBA)
1977-78	Miguel Cuello (WBC)
1978	Mate Parlov (WBC)
1978-79	Mike Rossman (WBA); Marvin Johnson (WBC)
1979-81	Matthew Saad Muhammad (WBC)
1979-80	Marvin Johnson (WBA)
1980-81	Eddie Mustafa Muhammad (WBA)
1981-83	Michael Spinks (WBA); Dwight Muhammed-Qawi Braxton (WBC)
1983-85	Michael Spinks*
1985-86	J. B. Williamson (WBC)
1986-87	Marvin Johnson (WBA); Dennis Andries (WBC)
1987	Leslie Stewart (WBA)
1987-91	Virgil Hill (WBA)
1987	Thomas Hearns (WBC*)
1987-88	Don Lalonde (WBC)
1988	Sugar Ray Leonard (WBC*)
1989	Dennis Andries (WBC)
1989-90	Jeff Harding (WBC)
1990-91	Dennis Andries (WBC)
1991-94	Jeff Harding (WBC)
1991-92	Thomas Hearns (WBA)
1992	Iran Barkley (WBA*)
1992-97	Virgil Hill (WBA)
1994-95	Mike McCallum (WBC)
1995-96	Fabrice Tiozzo (WBC*)
1996-97	Roy Jones Jr. (WBC)
1997	Montell Griffin (WBC); Roy Jones Jr. (WBC); Darius Michalczewski (WBA*)
1997-98	Lou Del Valle (WBA)
1998-2003	Roy Jones Jr. (WBA*/WBC*)
2003	Mehdi Sahnoune (WBA); Antonio Tarver (WBC)
2003-04	Roy Jones Jr. (WBA/WBC*)
2004	Antonio Tarver (WBA)
2004-06	Fabrice Tiozzo (WBA)
2005-07	Tomasz Adamek (WBC)
2006-07	Silvio Branco (WBA)
2007-08	Chad Dawson (WBC); Stipe Drews (WBA)
2008	Hugo Hernan Garay (WBA); Adrian Diaconu (WBC)
2009-10	Gabriel Campillo (WBA)
2009-11	Jean Pascal (WBC)
2010-	Beibut Shumenov (WBA)
2011-12	Bernard Hopkins (WBC)
2012	Chad Dawson (WBC)

Middleweights

Year	Champion
1884-91	Jack "Nonpareil" Dempsey
1891-97	Bob Fitzsimmons*
1897-1907	Tommy Ryan*
1907-08	Stanley Ketchel; Billy Papke
1908-10	Stanley Ketchel
1911-13	Vacant
1913	Frank Klaus; George Chip
1914-17	Al McCoy
1917-20	Mike O'Dowd
1920-23	Johnny Wilson
1923-26	Harry Greb
1926-31	Theodore "Tiger" Flowers; Mickey Walker
1931-32	William "Gorilla" Jones (NBA)
1932-37	Marcel Thil
1938	Al Hostak (NBA); Solly Krieger (NBA)
1939-40	Al Hostak (NBA)
1941-47	Tony Zale
1947-48	Rocky Graziano
1948	Tony Zale; Marcel Cerdan
1949-51	Jake LaMotta
1951	"Sugar" Ray Robinson; Randy Turpin; "Sugar" Ray Robinson*
1953-55	Carl "Bobo" Olson
1955-57	"Sugar" Ray Robinson
1957	Gene Fullmer; "Sugar" Ray Robinson
1957-58	Carmen Basilio
1958	"Sugar" Ray Robinson
1959	Gene Fullmer (NBA); "Sugar" Ray Robinson (NY)
1960	Gene Fullmer (NBA); Paul Pender (NY/MA)
1961	Gene Fullmer (NBA); Terry Downes (NY/MA/Europe)
1962	Gene Fullmer; Dick Tiger (NBA); Paul Pender (NY/MA*)
1963	Dick Tiger (universal)
1963-65	Joey Giardello
1965-66	Dick Tiger
1966-67	Emile Griffith
1967	Nino Benvenuti
1967-68	Emile Griffith
1968-70	Nino Benvenuti
1970-77	Carlos Monzon*
1977-78	Rodrigo Valdez
1978-79	Hugo Corro
1979-80	Vito Antuofermo
1980	Alan Minter
1980-87	"Marvelous" Marvin Hagler
1987	Sugar Ray Leonard (WBC*)
1987-89	Sumbu Kalambay (WBA)
1987-88	Thomas Hearns (WBC)
1988-89	Iran Barkley (WBC)
1989-90	Roberto Duran (WBC*)
1989-91	Mike McCallum (WBA)
1990-93	Julian Jackson (WBC)
1992-93	Reggie Johnson (WBA)
1993-95	Gerald McClellan (WBC*)
1993-94	John David Jackson (WBA)
1994-97	Jorge Castro (WBA)
1995	Julian Jackson (WBC)
1995-96	Quincy Taylor (WBC); Shinji Takehara (WBA)
1996-98	Keith Holmes (WBC)
1996-97	William Joppy (WBA)
1997	Julio Cesar Green (WBA)
1998-2001	William Joppy (WBA)
1998-99	Hassine Cherifi (WBC)
1999-2001	Keith Holmes (WBC)
2001	Felix Trinidad (WBA)
2001-05	Bernard Hopkins (WBC/WBA)
2005-06	Jermain Taylor (WBA)
2005-07	Jermain Taylor (WBC)
2006-07	Javier Castillejo (WBA)[1]
2007-12	Felix Sturm (WBA)
2007-10	Kelly Pavlik (WBC)
2009-11	Sebastian Zbik (WBC)
2010	Sergio Martínez (WBC)
2011-12	Julio Cesar Chavez Jr. (WBC)
2012	Daniel Geale (WBA); Sergio Martínez (WBC)

(1) Castillejo lost title to Mariano Carrera Dec. 2, 2006, but regained it Feb. 23, 2007, after Carrera tested positive for steroids.

Welterweights

Year	Champion
1892-94	"Mysterious" Billy Smith
1894-96	Tommy Ryan
1896	Kid McCoy*
1900	Rube Ferns; Matty Matthews
1901	Rube Ferns
1901-04	Joe Walcott
1904-06	Dixie Kid; Joe Walcott; William "Honey" Mellody
1907-11	Mike Sullivan
1911-15	Vacant
1915-19	Ted Lewis
1919-22	Jack Britton
1922-26	Mickey Walker
1926	Pete Latzo
1927-29	Joe Dundee
1929	Jackie Fields
1930	Jack Thompson; Tommy Freeman
1931	Tommy Freeman; Jack Thompson; Lou Brouillard
1932	Jackie Fields
1933	Young Corbett III; Jimmy McLarnin
1934	Barney Ross; Jimmy McLarnin
1935-38	Barney Ross
1938-40	Henry Armstrong
1940-41	Fritzie Zivic
1941-46	Fred Cochrane
1946	Marty Servo*
1946-51	Ray Robinson*[1]
1951	Johnny Bratton (NBA)
1951-54	Kid Gavilan
1954-55	Johnny Saxton
1955	Tony De Marco
1955-56	Carmen Basilio
1956	Johnny Saxton
1956-57	Carmen Basilio*
1958	Virgil Akins
1958-60	Don Jordan
1960-61	Benny Paret
1961	Emile Griffith
1961-62	Benny Paret
1962-63	Emile Griffith
1963	Luis Rodriguez
1963-66	Emile Griffith*
1966-69	Curtis Cokes
1969-70	Jose Napoles
1970-71	Billy Backus
1971-75	Jose Napoles
1975-76	John Stracey (WBC); Angel Espada (WBA)
1976-79	Carlos Palomino (WBC)
1976-80	Jose "Pepino" Cuevas (WBA)
1979	Wilfred Benitez (WBC)
1979-80	Sugar Ray Leonard (WBC)
1980	Roberto Duran (WBC)
1980-81	Thomas Hearns (WBA)
1980-82	Sugar Ray Leonard*
1983-85	Donald Curry (WBA); Milton McCrory (WBC)
1985-86	Donald Curry
1986-87	Lloyd Honeyghan (WBC)
1987	Mark Breland (WBA)
1987-88	Marlon Starling (WBA); Jorge Vaca (WBC)
1988-89	Thomas Hearns (WBA); Lloyd Honeyghan (WBC)
1989-90	Marlon Starling (WBC); Mark Breland (WBA)
1990-91	Maurice Blocker (WBC); Aaron Davis (WBA)
1991	Simon Brown (WBC)
1991-92	Meldrick Taylor (WBA)
1991-93	Buddy McGirt (WBC)
1992-94	Crisanto Espana (WBA)

1993-97	Pernell Whitaker (WBC)	2002-03	Vernon Forrest (WBC)	2008	Antonio Margarito (WBA)
1994-98	Ike Quartey (WBA*)	2003	Ricardo Mayorga (WBA/WBC)	2008-11	Andre Berto (WBC)
1997-99	Oscar De La Hoya (WBC*)	2003-05	Cory Spinks (WBA/WBC)	2009	Shane Mosley (WBA)
1998	James Page (WBA*)	2005-06	Zab Judah (WBA/WBC)	2009-12	Vyacheslav Senchenko (WBA)
1999-00	Felix Trinidad (WBC*)	2006	Ricky Hatton (WBA);	2011-12	Victor Ortiz (WBC)
2000	Oscar De La Hoya (WBC*)		Carlos Baldomir (WBC)	2011-	Floyd Mayweather Jr. (WBC)
2000-02	Shane Mosley (WBC)	2006-08	Floyd Mayweather Jr. (WBC);	2012	Paulie Malignaggi (WBA)
2001-02	Andrew Lewis (WBA)		Miguel Cotto (WBA)		
2002	Ricardo Mayorga (WBA)				

(1) Robinson gained the title by defeating Tommy Bell in an elimination agreed to by the New York Commission and the National Boxing Association. Both claimed Robinson waived his title when he won the middleweight crown from LaMotta in 1951.

Lightweights

1896-99	Kid Lavigne	1965-68	Carlos Ortiz	1990-92	Pernell Whitaker*
1899-02	Frank Erne	1968-69	Teo Cruz	1992	Joey Gamache (WBA)
1902-08	Joe Gans	1969-70	Mando Ramos	1992-96	Miguel Angel Gonzalez (WBC*)
1908-10	Oscar "Battling" Nelson	1970	Ismael Laguna	1992-93	Tony Lopez (WBA)
1910-12	Ad Wolgast	1970-72	Ken Buchanan (WBA)	1993	Dingaan Thobela (WBA)
1912-14	Willie Ritchie	1971-72	Pedro Carrasco (WBC)	1993-98	Orzubek Nazarov (WBA)
1914-17	Freddie Welsh	1972-79	Roberto Duran (WBA*)	1996-97	Jean-Baptiste Mendy (WBC)
1917-25	Benny Leonard*	1972	Mando Ramos (WBC);	1997-98	Steve Johnston (WBC)
1925	Jimmy Goodrich;		Chango Carmona (WBC)	1998-99	Jean-Baptiste Mendy (WBA);
	Rocky Kansas	1972-74	Rodolfo Gonzalez (WBC)		Cesar Bazan (WBC)
1926-30	Sammy Mandell	1974-76	Ishimatsu Suzuki (WBC)	1999	Julian Lorcy (WBA);
1930	Al Singer; Tony Canzoneri	1976-78	Esteban De Jesus (WBC)		Stefano Zoff (WBA)
1930-33	Tony Canzoneri	1979-81	Jim Watt (WBC)	1999-2000	Gilberto Serrano (WBA);
1933-35	Barney Ross*	1979-80	Ernesto Espana (WBA)		Steve Johnston (WBC)
1935-36	Tony Canzoneri	1980-81	Hilmer Kenty (WBA)	2000-01	Takanori Hatakeyama (WBA)
1936-38	Lou Ambers	1981	Sean O'Grady (WBA);	2000-02	Jose Luis Castillo (WBC)
1938	Henry Armstrong		Claude Noel (WBA)	2001	Julien Lorcy (WBA)
1939	Lou Ambers	1981-83	Alexis Arguello (WBC*)	2001-02	Raul Balbi (WBA)
1940	Lew Jenkins	1981-82	Arturo Frias (WBA)	2002-03	Leonard Dorin (WBA)
1941-43	Sammy Angott	1982-84	Ray Mancini (WBA)	2002-04	Floyd Mayweather Jr. (WBC)
1944	Sammy Angott (NBA);	1983-84	Edwin Rosario (WBC)	2004	Lakva Sim (WBA)
	J. Zurita (NBA)	1984-86	Livingstone Bramble (WBA)	2004-05	Jose Luis Castillo (WBC)
1945-51	Ike Williams (NBA; later	1984-85	Jose Luis Ramirez (WBC)	2004-08	Juan Diaz (WBA)
	universal)	1985-86	Hector "Macho" Camacho	2005-06	Diego Corrales (WBC)
1951-52	James Carter		(WBC)	2006	Joel Casamayor (WBC)
1952	Lauro Salas; James Carter	1986-87	Edwin Rosario (WBA)	2006-08	David Diaz (WBC)
1953-54	James Carter	1987-88	Julio Cesar Chavez (WBA);	2008	Nate Campbell (WBA);
1954	Paddy De Marco; James Carter		Jose Luis Ramirez (WBC)		Manny Pacquiao (WBC)
1955	James Carter; Bud Smith	1988-89	Julio Cesar Chavez (WBA/	2009-	John Manuel Marquez
1956	Bud Smith; Joe Brown		WBC)		(WBA)
1956-62	Joe Brown	1989-90	Edwin Rosario (WBA);	2009-10	Edwin Valero (WBC)
1962-65	Carlos Ortiz		Pernell Whitaker (WBC)	2010-11	Humberto Soto (WBC*)
1965	Ismael Laguna	1990	Juan Nazario (WBA)	2011-	Antonio DeMarco (WBC)

Featherweights

1892-1900	George Dixon (disputed)	1968-71	Shozo Saijyo (WBA)	1991-93	Park Yung Kyun (WBA);
1900-01	Terry McGovern;	1969-70	Johnny Famechon (WBC)		Paul Hodkinson (WBC)
	Young Corbett II*	1970	Vicente Salvidar (WBC)	1993	Goyo Vargas (WBC)
1901-12	Abe Attell	1970-72	Kuniaki Shibata (WBC)	1993-95	Kevin Kelley (WBC)
1912-23	Johnny Kilbane	1971-72	Antonio Gomez (WBA)	1993-96	Eloy Rojas (WBA)
1923	Eugene Criqui;	1972	Clemente Sanchez (WBC*)	1995	Alejandro Gonzalez (WBC)
	Johnny Dundee	1972-74	Ernesto Marcel (WBA*)	1995-96	Manuel Medina (WBC)
1923-25	Johnny Dundee*	1972-73	Jose Legra (WBC)	1995-99	Luisito Espinosa (WBC)
1925-27	Kid Kaplan*	1973-74	Eder Jofre (WBC*)	1996-97	Wilfredo Vasquez (WBA*)
1927-28	Benny Bass; Tony Canzoneri	1974	Ruben Olivares (WBA)	1998	Freddie Norwood (WBA)
1928-29	Andre Routis	1974-75	Bobby Chacon (WBC)	1998-99	Antonio Ceremeno (WBA)
1929-32	Battling Battalino*	1974-76	Alexis Arguello (WBA*)	1999	Cesar Soto (WBC);
1932-34	Tommy Paul (NBA)	1975	Ruben Olivares (WBC)		Naseem Hamed (WBC*);
1933-36	Freddie Miller	1975-76	David Kotey (WBC)		Freddie Norwood (WBA)
1936-37	Petey Sarron	1976-80	Danny "Little Red"	2000-01	Guty Espadas (WBC)
1937-38	Henry Armstrong*		Lopez (WBC)	2000-03	Derrick Gainer (WBA)
1938-40	Joey Archibald	1977	Rafael Ortega (WBA)	2001-04	Erik Morales (WBC)[1]
1940-41	Harry Jeffra	1977-78	Cecilio Lastra (WBA)	2003-06	Juan Manuel Marquez (WBA)
1942-48	Willie Pep	1978-85	Eusebio Pedroza (WBA)	2004-06	In-Jin Chi (WBC)
1948-49	Sandy Saddler	1980-82	Salvador Sanchez (WBC)	2006-	Chris John (WBA)
1949-50	Willie Pep	1982-84	Juan LaPorte (WBC)	2006	Takashi Koshimoto (WBC)
1950-57	Sandy Saddler*	1984	Wilfredo Gomez (WBC)	2006	Rodolfo Lopez (WBC)
1957-59	Hogan "Kid" Bassey	1984-88	Azumah Nelson (WBC)	2006-07	In-Jin Chi (WBC)
1959-63	Davey Moore	1985-86	Barry McGuigan (WBA)	2007-08	Jorge Linares (WBC)
1963-64	Ultiminio "Sugar" Ramos	1986-87	Steve Cruz (WBA)	2008	Oscar Larios (WBC)
1964-67	Vicente Saldivar*	1987-91	Antonio Esparragoza (WBA)	2009-10	Elio Rojas (WBC)
1968	Paul Rojas (WBA)	1988-90	Jeff Fenech (WBC*)	2010-11	Hozumi Hasegawa (WBC)
1968-69	Jose Legra (WBC)	1990-91	Marcos Villasana (WBC)	2012	Daniel Ponce de León (WBC)

(1) Marco Antonio Barrera won unan. decision over Morales, June 22, 2002, but refused WBC title. Morales regained WBC title with unan. decision over Paulie Ayala, Nov. 16, 2002. Morales moved up to Jr. Lightweight div. in 2004.

International Boxing Hall of Fame Inductees, 2012

Source: International Boxing Hall of Fame, 1 Hall of Fame Dr., Canastota, NY 13032. www.ibhof.com

Modern	Thomas Hearns, 61-5-1 (48 KO)	Mark Johnson, 44-5, 1 NC (28 KO)	Cocoa Kid, 176-56-10, 2 NC (48 KO)	
Old-Timer	Newsboy Brown, 57-13-5, 14 ND (11 KO)	Leo Houck, 158-9-11, 34 ND (21 KO)	Jake Kilrain, 18-6-12, 1 ND (3 KO)	
Pioneer	James Wharton			
Non-participant	Hugh D. McIntosh, promoter	Rip Valenti, promoter	Freddie Roach, trainer	Michael Buffer, ring announcer
Observer	Al Bernstein, broadcaster	Michael Katz, journalist		

Title-Changing Heavyweight Championship Bouts, 1889-2011

1889: July 8, John L. Sullivan def. Jake Kilrain, 75, Richburg, MS.

1892: Sept. 7, James J. Corbett def. John L. Sullivan, 21, New Orleans.

1897: Mar. 17, Bob Fitzsimmons def. James J. Corbett, 14, Carson City, NV.

1899: June 9, James J. Jeffries def. Bob Fitzsimmons, 11, Coney Island, NY. (Jeffries retired as champion in 1905.)

1905: July 3, Marvin Hart KOd Jack Root, 12, Reno, NV. (Jeffries refereed, gave title to Hart. Jack O'Brien also claimed the title.)

1906: Feb. 23, Tommy Burns def. Marvin Hart, 20, Los Angeles.

1908: Dec. 26, Jack Johnson KOd Tommy Burns, 14, Sydney, Australia. (Police halted contest.)

1915: Apr. 5, Jess Willard KOd Jack Johnson, 26, Havana, Cuba.

1919: July 4, Jack Dempsey KOd Jess Willard, Toledo, OH. (Willard failed to answer bell for 4th round.)

1926: Sept. 23, Gene Tunney def. Jack Dempsey, 10, Philadelphia. (Tunney retired as champion in 1928.)

1930: June 12, Max Schmeling def. Jack Sharkey, 4, New York City. (Resulted in the election of a successor to Gene Tunney.)

1932: June 21, Jack Sharkey def. Max Schmeling, 15, NYC.

1933: June 29, Primo Carnera KOd Jack Sharkey, 6, NYC.

1934: June 14, Max Baer KOd Primo Carnera, 11, NYC.

1935: June 13, James J. Braddock def. Max Baer, 15, NYC.

1937: June 22, Joe Louis KOd James J. Braddock, 8, Chicago. (Louis retired as champion in 1949.)

1949: June 22, Ezzard Charles def. Joe Walcott, 15, Chicago; NBA recognition only.

1951: July 18, Joe Walcott KOd Ezzard Charles, 7, Pittsburgh.

1952: Sept. 23, Rocky Marciano KOd Joe Walcott, 13, Philadelphia. (Marciano retired as champion in 1956.)

1956: Nov. 30, Floyd Patterson KOd Archie Moore, 5, Chicago.

1959: June 26, Ingemar Johansson KOd Floyd Patterson, 3, NYC.

1960: June 20, Floyd Patterson KOd Ingemar Johansson, 5, NYC.

1962: Sept. 25, Sonny Liston KOd Floyd Patterson, 1, Chicago.

1964: Feb. 25, Cassius Clay (Muhammad Ali) KOd Sonny Liston, 7, Miami Beach, FL. (In 1967, Ali was stripped of his title by the WBA and others for refusing military service.)

1970: Feb. 16, Joe Frazier KOd Jimmy Ellis, 5, NYC. (Frazier def. Ali in 15 rounds, Mar. 8, 1971, in NYC.)

1973: Jan. 22, George Foreman KOd Joe Frazier, 2, Jamaica.

1974: Oct. 30, Muhammad Ali KOd George Foreman, 8, Kinshasa, Zaire.

1978: Feb. 15, Leon Spinks def. Muhammad Ali, 15, Las Vegas. (WBC recognized Ken Norton as champion after Spinks refused to fight him before his rematch with Ali); June 9, (WBC) Larry Holmes def. Ken Norton, 15, Las Vegas; Sept. 15, (WBA) Muhammad Ali def. Leon Spinks, 15, New Orleans. (Ali retired as champion in 1979.)

1979: Oct. 20, (WBA) John Tate def. Gerrie Coetzee, 15, Pretoria, South Africa.

1980: Mar. 31, (WBA) Mike Weaver KOd John Tate, 15, Knoxville, TN.

1982: Dec. 10, (WBA) Michael Dokes KOd Mike Weaver, 1, Las Vegas.

1983: Sept. 23, (WBA) Gerrie Coetzee KOd Michael Dokes, 10, Richfield, OH; in Dec., Larry Holmes relinquished the WBC title and was named champion of the newly formed IBF.

1984: Mar. 9, (WBC) Tim Witherspoon def. Greg Page, 12, Las Vegas; Aug. 31, (WBC) Pinklon Thomas def. Tim Witherspoon, 12, Las Vegas; Dec. 2, (WBA) Greg Page KOd Gerrie Coetzee, 8, Sun City, Bophuthatswana, South Africa.

1985: Apr. 29, (WBA) Tony Tubbs def. Greg Page, 15, Buffalo, NY; Sept. 21, (IBF) Michael Spinks def. Larry Holmes, 15, Las Vegas. (Spinks relinquished title in Feb. 1987.)

1986: Jan. 17, (WBA) Tim Witherspoon def. Tony Tubbs, 15, Atlanta, GA; Mar. 23, (WBC) Trevor Berbick def. Pinklon Thomas, 12, Miami; Nov. 22, (WBC) Mike Tyson KOd Trevor Berbick, 2, Las Vegas; Dec. 12, (WBA) James "Bonecrusher" Smith KOd Tim Witherspoon, 1, NYC.

1987: Mar. 7, (WBA/WBC) Mike Tyson def. James "Bonecrusher" Smith, 12, Las Vegas; May 30, (IBF) Tony Tucker KOd James "Buster" Douglas, 10, Las Vegas; Aug. 1, (WBA/WBC/IBF) Mike Tyson def. Tony Tucker, 12, Las Vegas. (Tyson became undisputed champion.)

1990: Feb. 11, (WBA/WBC/IBF) James "Buster" Douglas KOd Mike Tyson, 10, Tokyo, Japan; Oct. 25, (WBA/WBC/IBF) Evander Holyfield KOd James "Buster" Douglas, 3, Las Vegas.

1992: Nov. 13, (WBA/WBC/IBF) Riddick Bowe def. Evander Holyfield, 12, Las Vegas. (Lennox Lewis was later named WBC champion when Bowe refused to fight him.)

1993: Nov. 6, (WBA/IBF) Evander Holyfield def. Riddick Bowe, 12, Las Vegas.

1994: Apr. 22, (WBA/IBF) Michael Moorer def. Evander Holyfield, 12, Las Vegas; Sept. 24, (WBC) Oliver McCall KOd Lennox Lewis, 2, London, Eng.; Nov. 5, (WBA/IBF) George Foreman KOd Michael Moorer, 10, Las Vegas. (In Mar. 1995, Foreman was stripped of the WBA title; he relinquished the IBF title in June.)

1995: Sept. 2, (WBC) Frank Bruno def. Oliver McCall, 12, London, Eng.; Dec. 9, (IBF) Frans Botha def. Axel Schulz, 12, Las Vegas. (Botha was subsequently stripped of title after testing positive for a steroid.)

1996: Mar. 16, (WBC) Mike Tyson KOd Frank Bruno, 3, Las Vegas; June 22, (IBF) Michael Moorer def. Axel Schulz, 12, Dortmund, Germany; Sept. 7, (WBA/IBF) Mike Tyson KOd Bruce Seldon, 1, Las Vegas (Tyson was subsequently stripped of WBC title); Nov. 9, (WBA) Evander Holyfield KOd Mike Tyson, 11, Las Vegas.

1997: Feb. 7, (WBC) Lennox Lewis KOd Oliver McCall, 5, Las Vegas; Nov. 8, (IBF) Evander Holyfield def. Michael Moorer, 8, Las Vegas.

1999: Nov. 13, (WBA/WBC/IBF) Lennox Lewis def. Evander Holyfield, 12, Las Vegas. (Lewis became undisputed champion. In Apr. 2000, Lewis was stripped of his WBA title.)

2000: Aug. 12, (WBA) Evander Holyfield def. John Ruiz, 12, Las Vegas.

2001: Mar. 3, (WBA) John Ruiz def. Evander Holyfield, 12, Las Vegas; Apr. 21, (WBC/IBF) Hasim Rahman KOd Lennox Lewis, 5, Brakpan, South Africa; Nov. 17, (WBC, IBF) Lennox Lewis KOd Hasim Rahman, 4, Las Vegas.

2002: Dec. 14, (IBF) Chris Byrd def. Evander Holyfield, 12, Atlantic City, NJ.

2003: Mar. 1, (WBA) Roy Jones Jr. def. John Ruiz, 12, Las Vegas.

2004: Feb. 20, (WBA) Ruiz gained title when Roy Jones Jr. relinquished it; Apr. 24, (WBC) Vitali Klitschko TKOd Corrie Sanders, 8, Los Angeles, to win title vacated when champ Lennox Lewis retired in Feb.

2005: Apr. 30, (WBA) James Toney def. John Ruiz, 12, NYC (Toney tested positive for steroids; title returned to Ruiz); Nov. 9, (WBC) Hasim Rahman gained title when Vitali Klitschko retired; Dec. 17, (WBA) Nikolai Valuev def. John Ruiz, 12, Berlin, Germany.

2006: Aug. 12, (WBC) Oleg Maskaev TKOd Hasim Rahman, 12, Las Vegas; Apr. 22, (IBF) Wladimir Klitschko TKOd Chris Byrd, 7, Mannheim, Germany.

2007: Apr. 14, (WBA) Ruslan Chagaev def. Nicolay Valuev, 12, Stuttgart, Germany.

2008: Mar. 8, (WBC) Samuel Peter TKOd Oleg Maskaev, 6, Cancun, Mexico; Aug. 30, (WBA) Nikolai Valuev def. John Ruiz, 12, Berlin, Germany; Oct. 11, (WBC) Vitali Klitschko TKOd Samuel Peter, 8, Berlin, Germany; Dec. 13, (IBF) Wladimir Klitschko TKOd Hasim Rahman, 7, Mannheim, Germany; Dec. 20, (WBA) Nikolai Valuev def. Evander Holyfield, 12, Zurich, Switzerland.

2009: Mar. 21, (WBC) Vitali Klitschko TKOd Juan Carlos Gomez, 9, Stuttgart, Germany; June 20, (IBF) Wladimir Klitschko TKOd Ruslan Chagaev, 10, Gelsenkirchen, Germany; Nov. 7, (WBA) David Haye def. Nikolai Valuev, 12, Nuremberg, Germany.

2011: July 2, (WBA) Wladimir Klitschko def. David Haye, 12, Hamburg, Germany.

THOROUGHBRED RACING

Triple Crown Winners

The Kentucky Derby, Preakness Stakes, and Belmont Stakes make up the Triple Crown. Since 1920, colts have carried 126 lbs in Triple Crown events; fillies, 121 lbs.

Year	Horse	Jockey	Trainer	Year	Horse	Jockey	Trainer
1919	Sir Barton	J. Loftus	H. G. Bedwell	1946	Assault	W. Mehrtens	M. Hirsch
1930	Gallant Fox	E. Sande	J. Fitzsimmons	1948	Citation	E. Arcaro	H. A. Jones
1935	Omaha	W. Sanders	J. Fitzsimmons	1973	Secretariat	R. Turcotte	L. Laurin
1937	War Admiral	C. Kurtsinger	G. Conway	1977	Seattle Slew	J. Cruguet	W. H. Turner Jr.
1941	Whirlaway	E. Arcaro	B. A. Jones	1978	Affirmed	S. Cauthen	L. S. Barrera
1943	Count Fleet	J. Longden	G. D. Cameron				

Kentucky Derby, 1875-2012

Churchill Downs, Louisville, KY; inaug. 1875. Distance: 1-1/4 mi; 1-1/2 mi until 1896. 3-year-olds. Best time: 1:59 2/5, Secretariat (1973); 2012 time: 2:01 4/5.

Year	Winner	Jockey	Year	Winner	Jockey	Year	Winner	Jockey
1875	Aristides	O. Lewis	1921	Behave Yourself	C. Thompson	1967	Proud Clarion	R. Ussery
1876	Vagrant	R. Swim	1922	Morvich	A. Johnson	1968	Dancer's Image[2]	R. Ussery
1877	Baden Baden	W. Walker	1923	Zev	E. Sande	1969	Majestic Prince	W. Hartack
1878	Day Star	J. Carter	1924	Black Gold	J. D. Mooney	1970	Dust Commander	M. Manganello
1879	Lord Murphy	C. Schauer	1925	Flying Ebony	E. Sande	1971	Canonero II	G. Avila
1880	Fonso	G. Lewis	1926	Bubbling Over	A. Johnson	1972	Riva Ridge	R. Turcotte
1881	Hindoo	J. McLaughlin	1927	Whiskery	L. McAtee	1973	Secretariat	R. Turcotte
1882	Apollo	B. Hurd	1928	Reigh Count	C. Lang	1974	Cannonade	A. Cordero
1883	Leonatus	W. Donohue	1929	Clyde Van Dusen	L. McAtee	1975	Foolish Pleasure	J. Vasquez
1884	Buchanan	I. Murphy	1930	Gallant Fox	E. Sande	1976	Bold Forbes	A. Cordero
1885	Joe Cotton	E. Henderson	1931	Twenty Grand	C. Kurtsinger	1977	Seattle Slew	J. Cruguet
1886	Ben Ali	P. Duffy	1932	Burgoo King	E. James	1978	Affirmed	S. Cauthen
1887	Montrose	I. Lewis	1933	Brokers Tip	D. Meade	1979	Spectacular Bid	R. Franklin
1888	Macbeth II	G. Covington	1934	Cavalcade	M. Garner	1980	Genuine Risk[1]	J. Vasquez
1889	Spokane	T. Kiley	1935	Omaha	W. Saunders	1981	Pleasant Colony	J. Velasquez
1890	Riley	I. Murphy	1936	Bold Venture	I. Hanford	1982	Gato del Sol	E. Delahoussaye
1891	Kingman	I. Murphy	1937	War Admiral	C. Kurtsinger	1983	Sunny's Halo	E. Delahoussaye
1892	Azra	A. Clayton	1938	Lawrin	E. Arcaro	1984	Swale	L. Pincay
1893	Lookout	E. Kunze	1939	Johnstown	J. Stout	1985	Spend a Buck	A. Cordero
1894	Chant	F. Goodale	1940	Gallahadion	C. Bierman	1986	Ferdinand	W. Shoemaker
1895	Halma	J. Perkins	1941	Whirlaway	E. Arcaro	1987	Alysheba	C. McCarron
1896	Ben Brush	W. Simms	1942	Shut Out	W. D. Wright	1988	Winning Colors[1]	G. Stevens
1897	Typhoon II	F. Garner	1943	Count Fleet	J. Longden	1989	Sunday Silence	P. Valenzuela
1898	Plaudit	W. Simms	1944	Pensive	C. McCreary	1990	Unbridled	C. Perret
1899	Manuel	F. Taral	1945	Hoop, Jr.	E. Arcaro	1991	Strike the Gold	C. Antley
1900	Lieut. Gibson	J. Boland	1946	Assault	W. Mehrtens	1992	Lil E. Tee	P. Day
1901	His Eminence	J. Winkfield	1947	Jet Pilot	E. Guerin	1993	Sea Hero	J. Bailey
1902	Alan-a-Dale	J. Winkfield	1948	Citation	E. Arcaro	1994	Go for Gin	C. McCarron
1903	Judge Himes	H. Booker	1949	Ponder	S. Brooks	1995	Thunder Gulch	G. Stevens
1904	Elwood	F. Prior	1950	Middleground	W. Boland	1996	Grindstone	J. Bailey
1905	Agile	J. Martin	1951	Count Turf	C. McCreary	1997	Silver Charm	G. Stevens
1906	Sir Huon	R. Troxler	1952	Hill Gail	E. Arcaro	1998	Real Quiet	K. Desormeaux
1907	Pink Star	A. Minder	1953	Dark Star	H. Moreno	1999	Charismatic	C. Antley
1908	Stone Street	A. Pickens	1954	Determine	R. York	2000	Fusaichi Pegasus	K. Desormeaux
1909	Wintergreen	V. Powers	1955	Swaps	W. Shoemaker	2001	Monarchos	J. Chavez
1910	Donau	F. Herbert	1956	Needles	D. Erb	2002	War Emblem	V. Espinoza
1911	Meridian	G. Archibald	1957	Iron Liege	W. Hartack	2003	Funny Cide	J. Santos
1912	Worth	C. H. Shilling	1958	Tim Tam	I. Valenzuela	2004	Smarty Jones	S. Elliot
1913	Donerail	R. Goose	1959	Tomy Lee	W. Shoemaker	2005	Giacomo	M. Smith
1914	Old Rosebud	J. McCabe	1960	Venetian Way	W. Hartack	2006	Barbaro	E. Prado
1915	Regret[1]	J. Notter	1961	Carry Back	J. Sellers	2007	Street Sense	C. Borel
1916	George Smith	J. Loftus	1962	Decidedly	W. Hartack	2008	Big Brown	K. Desormeaux
1917	Omar Khayyam	C. Borel	1963	Chateaugay	B. Baeza	2009	Mine That Bird	C. Borel
1918	Exterminator	W. Knapp	1964	Northern Dancer	W. Hartack	2010	Super Saver	C. Borel
1919	Sir Barton	J. Loftus	1965	Lucky Debonair	W. Shoemaker	2011	Animal Kingdom	J. Velazquez
1920	Paul Jones	T. Rice	1966	Kauai King	D. Brumfield	2012	I'll Have Another	M. Gutierrez

Only two jockeys have won the Kentucky Derby five times: Eddie Arcaro (1938, 1941, 1945, 1948, 1952) and Bill Hartack (1957, 1960, 1962, 1964, 1969). Willie Shoemaker won four times (1955, 1959, 1965, 1986). Six jockeys won three times: Isaac Murphy (1884, 1890, 1891); Earle Sande (1923, 1925, 1930); Angel Cordero (1974, 1976, 1985); Gary Stevens (1988, 1995, 1997); Kent Desormeaux (1998, 2000, 2008); and Calvin Borel (2007, 2009, 2010). (1) Regret, Genuine Risk, and Winning Colors are the only fillies to have won the Derby. (2) Dancer's Image was disqualified from purse money after tests disclosed that he had run with a painkilling drug, phenylbutazone, in his system. All wagers were paid on Dancer's Image. Forward Pass was awarded first place money.

Fastest Winning Times for the Kentucky Derby

(Kentucky Derby times are measured in fifths of a second according to tradition.)

Time	Horse	Jockey	Year	Time	Horse	Jockey	Year
1 min., 59 2/5 s.	Secretariat	Ron Turcotte	1973	2 min., 1 1/5 s.	Thunder Gulch	Gary Stevens	1995
1 min., 59 4/5 s.	Monarchos	Jorge Chavez	2001		Affirmed	Steve Cauthen	1978
2 min.,	Northern Dancer	Bill Hartack	1964		Lucky Debonair	Bill Shoemaker	1965
2 min., 1/5 s.	Spend a Buck	Angel Cordero Jr.	1985	2 min., 1 2/5 s.	Whirlaway	Eddie Arcaro	1941
2 min., 2/5 s.	Decidedly	Bill Hartack	1962		Barbaro	Edgar Prado	2006
2 min., 3/5 s.	Proud Clarion	Robert Ussery	1967	2 min., 1 3/5 s.	Bold Forbes	Angel Cordero Jr.	1976
2 min., 1 s.	Funny Cide	Jose Santos	2003		Hill Gail	Eddie Arcaro	1952
	War Emblem	Victor Espinoza	2002		Middleground	William Boland	1950
	Fusaichi Pegasus	Kent Desormeaux	2000				
	Grindstone	Jerry Bailey	1996				

Preakness Stakes, 1873-2012

Pimlico Race Course, Baltimore, MD; inaug. 1873. Distance: 1-3/16 mi. 3-year-olds. * = Horses ran in two divisions. Best time: 1:53 2/5, Tank's Prospect (1985), Louis Quatorze (1996), and Curlin (2007); 2012 time: 1:55.90.

Year	Winner	Jockey	Year	Winner	Jockey	Year	Winner	Jockey
1873	Survivor	G. Barbee	1922	Pillory	L. Morris	1968	Forward Pass	I. Valenzuela
1874	Culpepper	M. Donohue	1923	Vigil	B. Marinelli	1969	Majestic Prince	W. Hartack
1875	Tom Ochiltree	L. Hughes	1924	Nellie Morse	J. Merimee	1970	Personality	E. Belmonte
1876	Shirley	G. Barbee	1925	Coventry	C. Kummer	1971	Canonero II	G. Avila
1877	Cloverbrook	C. Holloway	1926	Display	J. Malben	1972	Bee Bee Bee	E. Nelson
1878	Duke of Magenta	C. Holloway	1927	Bostonian	A. Abel	1973	Secretariat	R. Turcotte
1879	Harold	L. Hughes	1928	Victorian	R. Workman	1974	Little Current	M. Rivera
1880	Grenada	L. Hughes	1929	Dr. Freeland	L. Schaefer	1975	Master Derby	D. McHargue
1881	Saunterer	W. Costello	1930	Gallant Fox	E. Sande	1976	Elocutionist	J. Lively
1882	Vanguard	W. Costello	1931	Mate	G. Ellis	1977	Seattle Slew	J. Cruguet
1883	Jacobus	G. Barbee	1932	Burgoo King	E. James	1978	Affirmed	S. Cauthen
1884	Knight of Ellerslie	S. H. Fisher	1933	Head Play	C. Kurtsinger	1979	Spectacular Bid	R. Franklin
1885	Tecumseh	J. McLaughlin	1934	High Quest	R. Jones	1980	Codex	A. Cordero
1886	The Bard	S. H. Fisher	1935	Omaha	W. Saunders	1981	Pleasant Colony	J. Velasquez
1887	Dunboyne	W. Donohue	1936	Bold Venture	G. Woolf	1982	Aloma's Ruler	J. Kaenel
1888	Refund	F. Littlefield	1937	War Admiral	C. Kurtsinger	1983	Deputed	
1889	Buddhist	G. Anderson	1938	Dauber	M. Peters		Testamony	D. Miller
1890	Montague	W. Martin	1939	Challedon	G. Seabo	1984	Gate Dancer	A. Cordero
1894	Assignee	F. Taral	1940	Bimelech	F. A. Smith	1985	Tank's Prospect	P. Day
1895	Belmar	F. Taral	1941	Whirlaway	E. Arcaro	1986	Snow Chief	A. Solis
1896	Margrave	H. Griffin	1942	Alsab	B. James	1987	Alysheba	C. McCarron
1897	Paul Kauvar	C. Thorpe	1943	Count Fleet	J. Longden	1988	Risen Star	E. Delahoussaye
1898	Sly Fox	W. Simms	1944	Pensive	C. McCreary	1989	Sunday Silence	P. Valenzuela
1899	Half Time	R. Clawson	1945	Polynesian	W. D. Wright	1990	Summer Squall	P. Day
1900	Hindus	H. Spencer	1946	Assault	W. Mehrtens	1991	Hansel	J. Bailey
1901	The Parader	F. Landry	1947	Faultless	D. Dodson	1992	Pine Bluff	C. McCarron
1902	Old England	L. Jackson	1948	Citation	E. Arcaro	1993	Prairie Bayou	M. Smith
1903	Flocarline	W. Gannon	1949	Capot	T. Atkinson	1994	Tabasco Cat	P. Day
1904	Bryn Mawr	E. Hildebrand	1950	Hill Prince	E. Arcaro	1995	Timber Country	P. Day
1905	Cairngorm	W. Davis	1951	Bold	E. Arcaro	1996	Louis Quatorze	P. Day
1906	Whimsical	W. Miller	1952	Blue Man	C. McCreary	1997	Silver Charm	G. Stevens
1907	Don Enrique	G. Mountain	1953	Native Dancer	E. Guerin	1998	Real Quiet	K. Desormeaux
1908	Royal Tourist	E. Dugan	1954	Hasty Road	J. Adams	1999	Charismatic	C. Antley
1909	Effendi	W. Doyle	1955	Nashua	E. Arcaro	2000	Red Bullet	J. Bailey
1910	Layminster	R. Estep	1956	Fabius	W. Hartack	2001	Point Given	G. Stevens
1911	Watervale	E. Dugan	1957	Bold Ruler	E. Arcaro	2002	War Emblem	V. Espinoza
1912	Colonel Holloway	C. Turner	1958	Tim Tam	I. Valenzuela	2003	Funny Cide	J. Santos
1913	Buskin	J. Butwell	1959	Royal Orbit	W. Harmatz	2004	Smarty Jones	S. Elliot
1914	Holiday	A. Schuttinger	1960	Bally Ache	R. Ussery	2005	Afleet Alex	J. Rose
1915	Rhine Maiden	D. Hoffman	1961	Carry Back	J. Sellers	2006	Bernardini	J. Castellano
1916	Damrosch	L. McAtee	1962	Greek Money	J. L. Rotz	2007	Curlin	R. Albarado
1917	Kalitan	E. Haynes	1963	Candy Spots	W. Shoemaker	2008	Big Brown	K. Desormeaux
1918*	War Cloud	J. Loftus	1964	Northern Dancer	W. Hartack	2009	Rachel Alexandra	C. Borel
	Jack Hare Jr.	C. Peak	1965	Tom Rolfe	R. Turcotte	2010	Lookin At Lucky	M. Garcia
1919	Sir Barton	J. Loftus	1966	Kauai King	D. Brumfield	2011	Shackleford	J. Castanon
1920	Man o' War	C. Kummer	1967	Damascus	W. Shoemaker	2012	I'll Have Another	M. Gutierrez
1921	Broomspun	F. Coltiletti						

Belmont Stakes, 1867-2012

Belmont Park, Elmont, NY; inaug. 1867. Distance: 1-1/2 mi. 3-year-olds. Best time: 2:24, Secretariat (1973); 2012 time: 2:30.42.

Year	Winner	Jockey	Year	Winner	Jockey	Year	Winner	Jockey
1867	Ruthless	J. Gilpatrick	1902	Masterman	J. Bullman	1939	Johnstown	J. Stout
1868	General Duke	R. Swim	1903	Africander	J. Bullman	1940	Bimelech	F. A. Smith
1869	Fenian	C. Miller	1904	Delhi	G. Odom	1941	Whirlaway	E. Arcaro
1870	Kingfisher	W. Dick	1905	Tanya	E. Hildebrand	1942	Shut Out	E. Arcaro
1871	Harry Bassett	W. Miller	1906	Burgomaster	L. Lyne	1943	Count Fleet	J. Longden
1872	Joe Daniels	R. Rowe	1907	Peter Pan	G. Mountain	1944	Bounding Home	G. L. Smith
1873	Springbok	J. Rowe	1908	Colin	J. Notter	1945	Pavot	E. Arcaro
1874	Saxon	G. Barbee	1909	Joe Madden	E. Dugan	1946	Assault	W. Mehrtens
1875	Calvin	R. Swim	1910	Sweep	J. Butwell	1947	Phalanx	R. Donoso
1876	Algerine	W. Donohue	1913	Prince Eugene	R. Troxler	1948	Citation	E. Arcaro
1877	Cloverbrook	C. Holloway	1914	Luke McLuke	M. Buxton	1949	Capot	T. Atkinson
1878	Duke of Magenta	L. Hughes	1915	The Finn	G. Byrne	1950	Middleground	W. Boland
1879	Spendthrift	S. Evans	1916	Friar Rock	E. Haynes	1951	Counterpoint	D. Gorman
1880	Grenada	L. Hughes	1917	Hourless	J. Butwell	1952	One Count	E. Arcaro
1881	Saunterer	T. Costello	1918	Johren	F. Robinson	1953	Native Dancer	E. Guerin
1882	Forester	J. McLaughlin	1919	Sir Barton	J. Loftus	1954	High Gun	E. Guerin
1883	George Kinney	J. McLaughlin	1920	Man o' War	C. Kummer	1955	Nashua	E. Arcaro
1884	Panique	J. McLaughlin	1921	Grey Lag	E. Sande	1956	Needles	D. Erb
1885	Tyrant	P. Duffy	1922	Pillory	C. H. Miller	1957	Gallant Man	W. Shoemaker
1886	Inspector	B. J. McLaughlin	1923	Zev	E. Sande	1958	Cavan	P. Anderson
1887	Hanover	J. McLaughlin	1924	Mad Play	E. Sande	1959	Sword Dancer	W. Shoemaker
1888	Sir Dixon	J. McLaughlin	1925	American Flag	A. Johnson	1960	Celtic Ash	W. Hartack
1889	Eric	W. Hayward	1926	Crusader	A. Johnson	1961	Sherluck	B. Baeza
1890	Burlington	S. Barnes	1927	Chance Shot	E. Sande	1962	Jaipur	W. Shoemaker
1891	Foxford	E. Garrison	1928	Vito	C. Kummer	1963	Chateaugay	B. Baeza
1892	Patron	W. Hayward	1929	Blue Larkspur	M. Garner	1964	Quadrangle	M. Ycaza
1893	Comanche	W. Simms	1930	Gallant Fox	E. Sande	1965	Hail to All	J. Sellers
1894	Henry of Navarre	W. Simms	1931	Twenty Grand	C. Kurtsinger	1966	Amberoid	W. Boland
1895	Belmar	F. Taral	1932	Faireno	T. Malley	1967	Damascus	W. Shoemaker
1896	Hastings	H. Griffin	1933	Hurryoff	M. Garner	1968	Stage Door Johnny	H. Gustines
1897	Scottish Chieftain	J. Scherrer	1934	Peace Chance	W. D. Wright	1969	Arts and Letters	B. Baeza
1898	Bowling Brook	F. Littlefield	1935	Omaha	W. Saunders	1970	High Echelon	J. L. Rotz
1899	Jean Bereaud	R. R. Clawson	1936	Granville	J. Stout	1971	Pass Catcher	W. Blum
1900	Ildrim	N. Turner	1937	War Admiral	C. Kurtsinger	1972	Riva Ridge	R. Turcotte
1901	Commando	H. Spencer	1938	Pasteurized	J. Stout	1973	Secretariat	R. Turcotte

Year	Winner	Jockey	Year	Winner	Jockey	Year	Winner	Jockey
1974	Little Current	M. Rivera	1987	Bet Twice	C. Perret	2000	Commendable	P. Day
1975	Avatar	W. Shoemaker	1988	Risen Star	E. Delahoussaye	2001	Point Given	G. Stevens
1976	Bold Forbes	A. Cordero	1989	Easy Goer	P. Day	2002	Sarava	E. Prado
1977	Seattle Slew	J. Cruguet	1990	Go and Go	M. Kinane	2003	Empire Maker	J. Bailey
1978	Affirmed	S. Cauthen	1991	Hansel	J. Bailey	2004	Birdstone	E. Prado
1979	Coastal	R. Hernandez	1992	A.P. Indy	E. Delahoussaye	2005	Afleet Alex	J. Rose
1980	Temperence Hill	E. Maple	1993	Colonial Affair	J. Krone	2006	Jazil	F. Jara
1981	Summing	G. Martens	1994	Tabasco Cat	P. Day	2007	Rags to Riches	J. Velazquez
1982	Conquistador Cielo	L. Pincay	1995	Thunder Gulch	G. Stevens	2008	Da' Tara	A. Garcia
1983	Caveat	L. Pincay	1996	Editor's Note	R. Douglas	2009	Summer Bird	K. Desormeaux
1984	Swale	L. Pincay	1997	Touch Gold	C. McCarron	2010	Drosselmeyer	M. Smith
1985	Creme Fraiche	E. Maple	1998	Victory Gallop	G. Stevens	2011	Ruler On Ice	J. Valdivia Jr.
1986	Danzig Connection	C. McCarron	1999	Lemon Drop Kid	J. Santos	2012	Union Rags	J. Velazquez

Annual Leading Jockey by Earnings, 1957-2011

(Total earnings for all horses that jockey raced in year listed; does not reflect what jockey earned.)

Year	Jockey	Earnings	Year	Jockey	Earnings	Year	Jockey	Earnings
1957	Bill Hartack	$3,060,501	1976	Angel Cordero Jr.	$4,709,500	1994	Mike Smith	$15,979,820
1958	Willie Shoemaker	2,961,693	1977	Steve Cauthen	6,151,750	1995	Jerry Bailey	16,311,876
1959	Willie Shoemaker	2,843,133	1978	Darrel McHargue	6,029,885	1996	Jerry Bailey	19,465,376
1960	Willie Shoemaker	2,123,961	1979	Laffit Pincay Jr.	8,193,535	1997	Jerry Bailey	18,320,743
1961	Willie Shoemaker	2,690,819	1980	Chris McCarron	7,663,300	1998	Gary Stevens	19,622,855
1962	Willie Shoemaker	2,916,844	1981	Chris McCarron	8,397,604	1999	Pat Day	18,092,845
1963	Willie Shoemaker	2,526,925	1982	Angel Cordero Jr.	9,483,590	2000	Pat Day	17,479,838
1964	Willie Shoemaker	2,649,553	1983	Angel Cordero Jr.	10,116,697	2001	Jerry D. Bailey	22,597,720
1965	Braulio Baeza	2,582,702	1984	Chris McCarron	12,045,813	2002	Jerry D. Bailey	19,271,814
1966	Braulio Baeza	2,951,022	1985	Laffit Pincay Jr.	13,353,299	2003	Jerry D. Bailey	23,354,960
1967	Braulio Baeza	3,088,888	1986	Jose Santos	11,329,297	2004	John R. Velazquez	22,220,261
1968	Braulio Baeza	2,835,108	1987	Jose Santos	12,375,433	2005	John R. Velazquez	20,799,923
1969	Jorge Velasquez	2,542,315	1988	Jose Santos	14,877,298	2006	Garrett K. Gomez	20,122,592
1970	Laffit Pincay Jr.	2,626,526	1989	Jose Santos	13,838,389	2007	Garrett K. Gomez	22,800,074
1971	Laffit Pincay Jr.	3,784,377	1990	Gary Stevens	13,881,198	2008	Garrett K. Gomez	23,344,351
1972	Laffit Pincay Jr.	3,225,827	1991	Chris McCarron	14,441,083	2009	Garrett K. Gomez	18,536,105
1973	Laffit Pincay Jr.	4,093,492	1992	Kent Desormeaux	14,193,006	2010	Ramon A. Dominguez	16,911,880
1974	Laffit Pincay Jr.	4,251,060	1993	Mike Smith	14,024,815	2011	Ramon A. Dominguez	20,267,032
1975	Braulio Baeza	3,695,198						

Breeders' Cup World Thoroughbred Championships, 1984-2012

The Breeders' Cup began in 1984 and through 2006, consisted of seven races at one track on one day. In 2007, it expanded to two days, and three new races debuted: the Filly and Mare Sprint, won in 2012 by Groupie Doll (jockey: R. Maragh); the Juvenile Turf, won in 2012 by George Vancouver (R. Moore); and the Dirt Mile, won in 2012 by Tapizar (C. Nakatani). In 2008, a "Ladies' Day" for fillies and several more races debuted: Turf Sprint, won in 2012 by Mizdirection (M. Smith); Marathon, won in 2012 by Calidoscopio (A. Gryder); and Juvenile Fillies Turf, won in 2012 by Flotilla (C. Lemaire). In 2011, the Juvenile Sprint debuted, won in 2012 by Hightail (R. Maragh).

Classic

Distance: 1-1/4 mi.

Year	Horse	Jockey	Year	Horse	Jockey	Year	Horse	Jockey
1984	Wild Again	P. Day	1994	Concern	J. Bailey	2004	Ghostzapper	J. Castellano
1985	Proud Truth	J. Velasquez	1995	Cigar	J. Bailey	2005	Saint Liam	J. Bailey
1986	Skywalker	L. Pincay Jr.	1996	Alphabet Soup	C. McCarron	2006	Invasor	F. Jara
1987	Ferdinand	W. Shoemaker	1997	Skip Away	M. Smith	2007	Curlin	R. Albarado
1988	Alysheba	C. McCarron	1998	Awesome Again	P. Day	2008	Raven's Pass	F. Dettori
1989	Sunday Silence	C. McCarron	1999	Cat Thief	P. Day	2009	Zenyatta	M. Smith
1990	Unbridled	P. Day	2000	Tiznow	C. McCarron	2010	Blame	G. Gomez
1991	Black Tie Affair	J. Bailey	2001	Tiznow	C. McCarron	2011	Drosselmeyer	M. Smith
1992	A.P. Indy	E. Delahoussaye	2002	Volponi	J. Santos	2012	Fort Larned	B. Hernandez
1993	Arcangues	J. Bailey	2003	Pleasantly Perfect	A. Solis			

Juvenile

Distance: 1 mi, 1984-85, 1987; 1-1/16 mi, 1986 and since 1988.

Year	Horse	Jockey	Year	Horse	Jockey	Year	Horse	Jockey
1984	Chief's Crown	D. MacBeth	1994	Timber Country	P. Day	2004	Wilko	F. Dettori
1985	Tasso	L. Pincay Jr.	1995	Unbridled's Song	M. Smith	2005	Stevie Wonderboy	G. Gomez
1986	Capote	L. Pincay Jr.	1996	Boston Harbor	J. Bailey	2006	Street Sense	C. Borel
1987	Success Express	J. Santos	1997	Favorite Trick	P. Day	2007	War Pass	C. Velasquez
1988	Is It True	L. Pincay Jr.	1998	Answer Lively	J. Bailey	2008	Midshipman	G. Gomez
1989	Rhythm	C. Perret	1999	Anees	G. Stevens	2009	Vale of York	A. Ajtebi
1990	Fly So Free	J. Santos	2000	Macho Uno	J. Bailey	2010	Uncle Mo	J. Velazquez
1991	Arazi	P. Valenzuela	2001	Johannesburg	M. Kinane	2011	Hansen	R. Dominguez
1992	Gilded Time	C. McCarron	2002	Vindication	M. Smith	2012	Shanghai Bobby	R. Napravnik
1993	Brocco	G. Stevens	2003	Action This Day	D. Flores			

Juvenile Fillies

Distance: 1 mi, 1984-85, 1987; 1-1/16 mi, 1986 and since 1988. Outstandingly won the 1984 race by disqualification.

Year	Horse	Jockey	Year	Horse	Jockey	Year	Horse	Jockey
1984	Outstandingly	W. Guerra	1994	Flanders	P. Day	2004	Sweet Catomine	C. Nakatani
1985	Twilight Ridge	J. Velasquez	1995	My Flag	J. Bailey	2005	Folklore	E. Prado
1986	Brave Raj	P. Valenzuela	1996	Storm Song	C. Perret	2006	Dreaming of Anna	R. Douglas
1987	Epitome	P. Day	1997	Countess Diana	S. Sellers	2007	Indian Blessing	C. Nakatani
1988	Open Mind	A. Cordero Jr.	1998	Silverbulletday	G. Stevens	2008	Stardom Bound	M. Smith
1989	Go for Wand	R. Romero	1999	Cash Run	J. Bailey	2009	She Be Wild	J. Leparoux
1990	Meadow Star	J. Santos	2000	Caressing	J. Velazquez	2010	Awesome Feather	J. Sanchez
1991	Pleasant Stage	E. Delahoussaye	2001	Tempera	D. Flores	2011	My Miss Aurelia	C. Nakatani
1992	Eliza	P. Valenzuela	2002	Storm Flag Flying	J. Velazquez	2012	Beholder	G. Gomez
1993	Phone Chatter	L. Pincay Jr.	2003	Halfbridled	J. Krone			

Sprint

Distance: 6 furlongs.

Year	Horse	Jockey	Year	Horse	Jockey	Year	Horse	Jockey
1984	Eillo	C. Perret	1994	Cherokee Run	M. Smith	2004	Speightstown	J. Velazquez
1985	Precisionist	C. McCarron	1995	Desert Stormer	K. Desormeaux	2005	Silver Train	E. Prado
1986	Smile	J. Vasquez	1996	Lit De Justice	C. Nakatani	2006	Thor's Echo	C. Nakatani
1987	Very Subtle	P. Valenzuela	1997	Elmhurst	C. Nakatani	2007	Midnight Lute	G. Gomez
1988	Gulch	A. Cordero Jr.	1998	Reraise	C. Nakatani	2008	Midnight Lute	G. Gomez
1989	Dancing Spree	A. Cordero Jr.	1999	Artax	J. Chaves	2009	Dancing in Silks	J. Rosario
1990	Safely Kept	C. Perret	2000	Kona Gold	A. Solis	2010	Big Drama	E. Coa
1991	Sheikh Albadou	P. Eddery	2001	Squirtle Squirt	J. Bailey	2011	Amazombie	M. Smith
1992	Thirty Slews	E. Delahoussaye	2002	Orientate	J. Bailey	2012	Trinniberg	W. Martinez
1993	Cardmania	E. Delahoussaye	2003	Cajun Beat	C. Velasquez			

Mile

Year	Horse	Jockey	Year	Horse	Jockey	Year	Horse	Jockey
1984	Royal Heroine	F. Toro	1994	Barathea	L. Dettori	2004	Singletary	D. Flores
1985	Cozzene	W. Guerra	1995	Ridgewood Pearl	J. Murtagh	2005	Artie Schiller	G. Gomez
1986	Last Tycoon	Y. St.-Martin	1996	Da Hoss	G. Stevens	2006	Miesque's Approval	E. Castro
1987	Miesque	F. Head	1997	Spinning World	C. Asmussen	2007	Kip Deville	C. Velasquez
1988	Miesque	F. Head	1998	Da Hoss	J. Velazquez	2008	Goldikova	O. Peslier
1989	Steinlen	J. Santos	1999	Silic	C. Nakatani	2009	Goldikova	O. Peslier
1990	Royal Academy	L. Piggott	2000	War Chant	G. Stevens	2010	Goldikova	O. Peslier
1991	Opening Verse	P. Valenzuela	2001	Val Royal	J. Valdivia Jr.	2011	Court Vision	R. Albarado
1992	Lure	M. Smith	2002	Domedriver	T. Thulliez	2012	Wise Dan	J. Velazquez
1993	Lure	M. Smith	2003	Six Perfections	J. Bailey			

Filly and Mare Turf

Distance: 1-3/8 mi, 1999-2000, 2004, 2006-07; 1-1/4 mi, 2001-03, 2005, and since 2008.

Year	Horse	Jockey	Year	Horse	Jockey	Year	Horse	Jockey
1999	Soaring Softly	J. Bailey	2004	Ouija Board	K. Fallon	2009	Midday	T. Queally
2000	Perfect Sting	J. Bailey	2005	Intercontinental	R. Bejarano	2010	Shared Account	E. Prado
2001	Banks Hill	O. Peslier	2006	Ouija Board (GB)	F. Dettori	2011	Perfect Shirl	J. Velazquez
2002	Starine	J. Velazquez	2007	Lahudood	A. Garcia	2012	Zagora	J. Castellano
2003	Islington	K. Fallon	2008	Forever Together	J. Leparoux			

Ladies' Classic

Distance: 1-1/4 mi, 1984-87; 1-1/8 mi, since 1988. Race known as Distaff, 1984-2007.

Year	Horse	Jockey	Year	Horse	Jockey	Year	Horse	Jockey
1984	Princess Rooney	E. Delahoussaye	1994	One Dreamer	G. Stevens	2004	Ashado	J. Velazquez
1985	Life's Magic	A. Cordero Jr.	1995	Inside Information	M. Smith	2005	Pleasant Home	C. Velasquez
1986	Lady's Secret	P. Day	1996	Jewel Princess	C. Nakatani	2006	Round Pond	E. Prado
1987	Sacahuista	R. Romero	1997	Ajina	M. Smith	2007	Ginger Punch	R. Bejarano
1988	Personal Ensign	R. Romero	1998	Escena	G. Stevens	2008	Zenyatta	M. Smith
1989	Bayakoa	L. Pincay Jr.	1999	Beautiful Pleasure	J. Chaves	2009	Life Is Sweet	G. Gomez
1990	Bayakoa	L. Pincay Jr.	2000	Spain	V. Espinoza	2010	Unrivaled Belle	K. Desormeaux
1991	Dance Smartly	P. Day	2001	Unbridled Elaine	P. Day	2011	Royal Delta	J. Lezcano
1992	Paseana	C. McCarron	2002	Azeri	M. Smith	2012	Royal Delta	M. Smith
1993	Hollywood Wildcat	E. Delahoussaye	2003	Adoration	P. Valenzuela			

Turf

Distance: 1-1/2 mi.

Year	Horse	Jockey	Year	Horse	Jockey	Year	Horse	Jockey
1984	Lashkari	Y. St.-Martin	1993	Kotashaan	K. Desormeaux	2003	(tie) High Chaparral	M. Kinane
1985	Pebbles	P. Eddery	1994	Tikkanen	M. Smith		Johar	A. Solis
1986	Manila	J. Santos	1995	Northern Spur	C. McCarron	2004	Better Talk Now	R. Dominguez
1987	Theatrical	P. Day	1996	Pilsudski	W. Swinburn	2005	Shirocco	C. Soumillon
1988	Great Communicator	R. Sibille	1997	Chief Bearhart	J. Santos	2006	Red Rocks	F. Dettori
			1998	Buck's Boy	S. Sellers	2007	English Channel	J. Velasquez
1989	Prized	E. Delahoussaye	1999	Daylami	L. Dettori	2008	Conduit	R. Moore
1990	In The Wings	G. Stevens	2000	Kalanisi	J. Murtagh	2009	Conduit	R. Moore
1991	Miss Alleged	E. Legrix	2001	Fantastic Light	L. Dettori	2010	Dangerous Midge	F. Dettori
1992	Fraise	P. Valenzuela	2002	High Chaparral	M. Kinane	2011	St Nicholas Abbey	J. O'Brien
1993	Kotashaan	K. Desormeaux				2012	Little Mike	R. Dominguez

Eclipse Awards

The Eclipse Awards, honoring the Horse of the Year and other champions of the sport, began in 1971 and are sponsored by the *Daily Racing Form*, the National Thoroughbred Racing Association, and the National Turf Writers Assn. Prior to 1971, the *DRF* (1936-70) and the NTRA (1950-70) issued separate selections for Horse of the Year.

Eclipse Awards, 2011

Horse of the Year: Havre de Grace
2-year-old male: Hansen
2-year-old female: My Miss Aurelia
3-year-old male: Animal Kingdom
3-year-old female: Royal Delta
Older male (4-year-old+): Acclamation

Older female (4-year-old+): Havre de Grace
Male sprinter: Amazombie
Female sprinter: Musical Romance
Male turf horse: Cape Blanco
Female turf horse: Stacelita

Steeplechase horse: Black Jack Blues
Trainer: Bill Mott
Jockey: Ramon Dominguez
Apprentice jockey: Kyle Frey
Breeder: Adena Springs
Owner: Ken and Sarah Ramsey

Horse of the Year, 1936-2011

Year	Horse	Year	Horse	Year	Horse	Year	Horse
1936	Granville	1949	Capot	1960	Kelso	1971	Ack Ack
1937	War Admiral	1950	Hill Prince	1961	Kelso	1972	Secretariat
1938	Seabiscuit	1951	Counterpoint	1962	Kelso	1973	Secretariat
1939	Challedon	1952	One Count (DRF); Native Dancer (TRA)	1963	Kelso	1974	Forego
1940	Challedon			1964	Kelso	1975	Forego
1941	Whirlaway	1953	Tom Fool	1965	Roman Brother (DRF); Moccasin (TRA)	1976	Forego
1942	Whirlaway	1954	Native Dancer			1977	Seattle Slew
1943	Count Fleet	1955	Nashua	1966	Buckpasser	1978	Affirmed
1944	Twilight Tear	1956	Swaps	1967	Damascus	1979	Affirmed
1945	Busher	1957	Bold Ruler (DRF); Dedicate (TRA)	1968	Dr. Fager	1980	Spectacular Bid
1946	Assault			1969	Arts and Letters	1981	John Henry
1947	Armed	1958	Round Table	1970	Fort Marcy (DRF); Personality (TRA)	1982	Conquistador Cielo
1948	Citation	1959	Sword Dancer			1983	All Along

Year	Horse	Year	Horse	Year	Horse	Year	Horse
1984	John Henry	1991	Black Tie Affair	1998	Skip Away	2005	Saint Liam
1985	Spend A Buck	1992	A.P. Indy	1999	Charismatic	2006	Invasor
1986	Lady's Secret	1993	Kotashaan	2000	Tiznow	2007	Curlin
1987	Ferdinand	1994	Holy Bull	2001	Point Given	2008	Curlin
1988	Alysheba	1995	Cigar	2002	Azeri	2009	Rachel Alexandra
1989	Sunday Silence	1996	Cigar	2003	Mineshaft	2010	Zenyatta
1990	Criminal Type	1997	Favorite Trick	2004	Ghostzapper	2011	Havre de Grace

HARNESS RACING
Harness Horse of the Year, 1947-2011
(Chosen by the U.S. Trotting Assn. and the U.S. Harness Writers Assn.)

Year	Horse	Year	Horse	Year	Horse	Year	Horse
1947	Victory Song	1964	Bret Hanover	1980	Niatross	1996	Continental Victory
1948	Rodney	1965	Bret Hanover	1981	Fan Hanover	1997	Malabar Man
1949	Good Time	1966	Bret Hanover	1982	Cam Fella	1998	Moni Maker
1950	Proximity	1967	Nevele Pride	1983	Cam Fella	1999	Moni Maker
1951	Pronto Don	1968	Nevele Pride	1984	Fancy Crown	2000	Gallo Blue Chip
1952	Good Time	1969	Nevele Pride	1985	Nihilator	2001	Bunny Lake
1953	Hi Lo's Forbes	1970	Fresh Yankee	1986	Forrest Skipper	2002	Real Desire
1954	Stenographer	1971	Albatross	1987	Mack Lobell	2003	No Pan Intended
1955	Scott Frost	1972	Albatross	1988	Mack Lobell	2004	Rainbow Blue
1956	Scott Frost	1973	Sir Dalrae	1989	Matt's Scooter	2005	Rocknroll Hanover
1957	Torpid	1974	Delmonica Hanover	1990	Beach Towel	2006	Glidemaster
1958	Emily's Pride	1975	Savoir	1991	Precious Bunny	2007	Donato Hanover
1959	Bye Bye Byrd	1976	Keystone Ore	1992	Artsplace	2008	Somebeachsomewhere
1960	Adios Butler	1977	Green Speed	1993	Staying Together	2009	Muscle Hill
1961	Adios Butler	1978	Abercrombie	1994	Cam's Card Shark	2010	Rock and Roll Heaven
1962	Su Mac Lad	1979	Niatross	1995	CR Kay Suzie	2011	San Pail
1963	Speedy Scot						

The Hambletonian (3-year-old trotters), 1965-2012

Year	Horse	Driver	Year	Horse	Driver
1965	Egyptian Candor	Del Cameron	1989	Park Avenue Joe	Ron Waples
1966	Kerry Way	Frank Ervin	1990	Harmonious	John Campbell
1967	Speedy Streak	Del Cameron	1991	Giant Victory	Jack Moiseyev
1968	Nevele Pride	Stanley Dancer	1992	Alf Palema	Mickey McNicholl
1969	Lindy's Pride	Howard Beissinger	1993	American Winner	Ron Pierce
1970	Timothy T	John Simpson Sr.	1994	Victory Dream	Michel Lachance
1971	Speedy Crown	Howard Beissinger	1995	Tagliabue	John Campbell
1972	Super Bowl	Stanley Dancer	1996	Continental Victory	Michel Lachance
1973	Flirth	Ralph Baldwin	1997	Malabar Man	Malvern Burroughs
1974	Christopher T	Bill Haughton	1998	Muscles Yankee	John Campbell
1975	Bonefish	Stanley Dancer	1999	Self Possessed	Mike Lachance
1976	Steve Lobell	Bill Haughton	2000	Yankee Paco	Trevor Ritchie
1977	Green Speed	Bill Haughton	2001	Scarlet Knight	Stefan Melander
1978	Speedy Somolli	Howard Beissinger	2002	Chip Chip Hooray	Eric Ledford
1979	Legend Hanover	George Sholty	2003	Amigo Hall	Mike Lachance
1980	Burgomeister	Bill Haughton	2004	Windsong's Legacy	Trond Smedshammer
1981	Shiaway St. Pat	Ray Remmen	2005	Vivid Photo	Roger Hammer
1982	Speed Bowl	Tommy Haughton	2006	Glidemaster	John Campbell
1983	Duenna	Stanley Dancer	2007	Donato Hanover	Ron Pierce
1984	Historic Freight	Ben Webster	2008	Deweycheatumnhowe	Ray Schnittker
1985	Prakas	Bill O'Donnell	2009	Muscle Hill	Brian Sears
1986	Nuclear Kosmos	Ulf Thoresen	2010	Muscle Massive	Ron Pierce
1987	Mack Lobell	John Campbell	2011	Broad Bahn	George Brennan
1988	Armbro Goal	John Campbell	2012	Market Share	Tim Tetrick

BOWLING
Professional Bowlers Association
PBA Tournament of Champions, 1965-2012

Year	Winner	Year	Winner	Year	Winner	Year	Winner
1965	Billy Hardwick	1977	Mike Berlin	1988	Mark Williams	2000	Jason Couch
1966	Wayne Zahn	1978	Earl Anthony	1989	Del Ballard Jr.	2002	Jason Couch
1967	Jim Stefanich	1979	George Pappas	1990	Dave Ferraro	2003	Patrick Healey Jr.
1968	Dave Davis	1980	Wayne Webb	1991	David Ozio	2005	Steve Jaros
1969	Jim Godman	1981	Steve Cook	1992	Marc McDowell	2006	Chris Barnes
1970	Don Johnson	1982	Mike Durbin	1993	George Branham III	2007	Tommy Jones
1971	Johnny Petraglia	1983	Joe Berardi	1994	Norm Duke	2008	Michael Haugen Jr.
1972	Mike Durbin	1984	Mike Durbin	1996	Dave D'Entremont	2009	Patrick Allen
1973	Jim Godman	1985	Mark Williams	1997	John Gant	2010	Kelly Kulick
1974	Earl Anthony	1986	Marshall Holman	1998	Bryan Goebel	2011	Mika Koivuniemi
1975	Dave Davis	1987	Pete Weber	1999	Jason Couch	2012	Sean Rash
1976	Marshall Holman						

Note: No tournament held in 2001 or 2004.

PBA Hall of Fame Performance Inductees

Bill Allen	Don Carter	Dave Ferraro	David Ozio	Jim Stefanich
Earl Anthony	Paul Colwell	Jim Godman	George Pappas	Brian Voss
Mike Aulby	Steve Cook	Billy Hardwick	Randy Pedersen	Wayne Webb
Del Ballard Jr.	Jason Couch	Marshall Holman	Johnny Petraglia	Dick Weber
Joe Berardi	Dave Davis	Tommy Hudson	Dick Ritger	Pete Weber
Ray Bluth	Gary Dickinson	Dave Husted	Mark Roth	Billy Welu
Parker Bohn III	Norm Duke	Don Johnson	Carmen Salvino	Mark Williams
Roy Buckley	Mike Durbin	Larry Laub	Harry Smith	Walter Ray Williams Jr.
Nelson Burton Jr.	Buzz Fazio	Amleto Monacelli	Dave Soutar	Wayne Zahn

PBA Leading Money Winners, 1962-2012

Total winnings from tournaments only. After 2000, year shown is year the PBA season ended.

Year	Bowler	Amount	Year	Bowler	Amount	Year	Bowler	Amount
1962	Don Carter	$49,972	1979	Mark Roth	$124,517	1996	Walter Ray Williams Jr.	$241,330
1963	Dick Weber	46,333	1980	Wayne Webb	116,700	1997	Walter Ray Williams Jr.	240,544
1964	Bob Strampe	33,592	1981	Earl Anthony	164,735	1998	Walter Ray Williams Jr.	238,225
1965	Dick Weber	47,674	1982	Earl Anthony	134,760	1999	Parker Bohn III	240,912
1966	Wayne Zahn	54,720	1983	Earl Anthony	135,605	2000	Norm Duke	143,325
1967	Dave Davis	54,165	1984	Mark Roth	158,712	2002	Parker Bohn III	245,200
1968	Jim Stefanich	67,377	1985	Mike Aulby	201,200	2003	Walter Ray Williams Jr.	419,700
1969	Billy Hardwick	64,160	1986	Walter Ray Williams Jr.	145,550	2004	Mika Koivuniemi	238,590
1970	Mike McGrath	52,049	1987	Pete Weber	175,491	2005	Patrick Allen	350,740
1971	Johnny Petraglia	85,065	1988	Brian Voss	225,485	2006	Tommy Jones	301,700
1972	Don Johnson	56,648	1989	Mike Aulby	298,237	2007	Doug Kent	200,530
1973	Don McCune	69,000	1990	Amleto Monacelli	204,775	2008	Norm Duke	176,855
1974	Earl Anthony	99,585	1991	David Ozio	225,585	2009	Norm Duke	199,130
1975	Earl Anthony	107,585	1992	Marc McDowell	174,215	2010	Walter Ray Williams Jr.	152,670
1976	Earl Anthony	110,833	1993	Walter Ray Williams Jr.	296,370	2011	Mika Koivuniemi	333,040
1977	Mark Roth	105,583	1994	Norm Duke	273,753	2012	Sean Rash	140,250
1978	Mark Roth	134,500	1995	Mike Aulby	219,792			

Leading PBA Averages by Year, 1962-2012

Year	Bowler	Average	Year	Bowler	Average	Year	Bowler	Average
1962	Don Carter	212.84	1979	Mark Roth	221.66	1996	Walter Ray Williams Jr.	225.37
1963	Billy Hardwick	210.34	1980	Earl Anthony	218.53	1997	Walter Ray Williams Jr.	222.00
1964	Ray Bluth	210.51	1981	Mark Roth	216.69	1998	Walter Ray Williams Jr.	226.13
1965	Dick Weber	211.89	1982	Marshall Holman	212.84	1999	Parker Bohn III	228.04
1966	Wayne Zahn	208.66	1983	Earl Anthony	216.64	2000	Chris Barnes	220.93
1967	Wayne Zahn	212.34	1984	Marshall Holman	213.91	2002	Parker Bohn III	221.54
1968	Jim Stefanich	211.89	1985	Mark Baker	213.71	2003	Walter Ray Williams Jr.	224.94
1969	Bill Hardwick	212.95	1986	John Gant	214.37	2004	Mika Koivuniemi	222.73
1970	Nelson Burton Jr.	214.90	1987	Marshall Holman	216.80	2005	Walter Ray Williams Jr.	227.07
1971	Don Johnson	213.97	1988	Mark Roth	218.03	2006	Norm Duke	224.29
1972	Don Johnson	215.29	1989	Pete Weber	215.43	2007	Norm Duke	228.47
1973	Earl Anthony	215.79	1990	Amleto Monacelli	218.15	2008	Walter Ray Williams Jr.	228.34
1974	Earl Anthony	219.39	1991	Norm Duke	218.20	2009	Wes Malott	222.98
1975	Earl Anthony	219.06	1992	Dave Ferraro	219.70	2010	Walter Ray Williams Jr.	222.92
1976	Mark Roth	215.97	1993	Walter Ray Williams Jr.	222.98	2011	Mika Koivuniemi	222.50
1977	Mark Roth	218.17	1994	Norm Duke	222.83	2012	Sean Rash	228.13
1978	Mark Roth	219.83	1995	Mike Aulby	225.49			

United States Bowling Congress

Formed Jan. 1, 2005, from a merger of the American Bowling Congress (ABC), Women's International Bowling Congress, the Young American Bowling Alliance, and USA Bowling. Before 2006, certified games and champions are for ABC only.

Men's Career 300 Games
(as of July 31, 2012)

Rank	Bowler, hometown	Games
1.	Fero Williams, Falkfield, OH	135
2.	Andrew Neuer, Lewisburg, PA	131
3.	Jim Hosier, Wayne, NJ	130
4.	Gordon Childers, Benton, AR	126
5.	Jim Tomek, Camp Hill, PA	118
6.	Stephen Aiello, North Haledon, NJ	114
	Chris Hayward, Toledo, OH	114
8.	John Delp, Sinking Spring, PA	110
9.	Frank Massengale Jr., Hixson, TN	108
10.	Jack Kurent, Luzerne, PA	106

Women's Career 300 Games
(as of July 31, 2012)

Rank	Bowler, hometown	Games
1.	Teri Haefke, Austintown, OH	41
2.	Tammy Jones, Decatur, IL	39
3.	Altramese Webb, Detroit, MI	37
	Jodi Musto, Schenectady, NY	37
5.	Tish Johnson, Colorado Springs, CO	33
6.	Shannon Pluhowsky, Dayton, OH	32
	Jodi Woessner, Oregon, OH	32
8.	Alisia Kellow, Louisville, KY	31
	Barb Staub, Cedar Rapids, IA	31
10.	Marianne DiRupo, Succasunna, NJ	30

USBC Masters Tournament Champions, 1980-2012

Year	Winner, hometown	Year	Winner, hometown	Year	Winner, hometown
1980	Neil Burton, St. Louis, MO	1992	Ken Johnson, N. Richmond Hills, TX	2003	Bryon Smith, Roseburg, OR
1981	Randy Lightfoot, St. Charles, MO	1993	Norm Duke, Oklahoma City, OK	2004	Walter Ray Williams Jr., FL (Jan.);
1982	Joe Berardi, Brooklyn, NY	1994	Steve Fehr, Cincinnati, OH		Danny Wiseman, MD (Oct.)
1983	Mike Lastowski, Havre de Grace, MD	1995	Mike Aulby, Indianapolis, IN	2005	Mike Scroggins, Amarillo, TX
1984	Earl Anthony, Dublin, CA	1996	Ernie Schlegel, Vancouver, WA	2006	Doug Kent, Newark, NY
1985	Steve Wunderlich, St. Louis, MO	1997	Jason Queen, Decatur, IL	2007	Sean Rash, Wichita, KS
1986	Mark Fahy, Chicago, IL	1998	Mike Aulby, Indianapolis, IN	2008	No tournament
1987	Rick Steelsmith, Wichita, KS	1999	Brian Boghosian, Middletown, CT	2009	John Nolen, Waterford, MI
1988	Del Ballard Jr., Richardson, TX	2000	Mika Koivuniemi, Finland	2010	Walter Ray Williams Jr., Ocala, FL
1989	Mike Aulby, Indianapolis, IN	2001	Parker Bohn III, Jackson, NJ	2011	Tom Hess, Urbandale, IA
1990	Chris Warren, Dallas, TX	2002	Brett Wolfe, Reno, NV	2012	Mike Fagan, Dallas, TX
1991	Doug Kent, Canandaigua, NY				

USBC Open Champions, 2012

Regular Singles: Henry Teetz III, West Allis, WI
Regular Doubles: Matt McNiel, Prior Lake, MN, and Charles Vashaw, Deephaven, MN
Regular All-Events: Matt McNiel, Prior Lake, MN
Regular Team: Nicholas J's Pro Shop 2, La Crosse, WI
Team All-Events: S&B Pro Shop 1, Clinton Township, MI

USBC Queens and Women's Champions, 2012

According to the new format introduced in 2010, USBC women's champions are selected from an all-handicap format with three divisions: Diamond (180 and higher with handicap based on 100% of 220), Ruby (150-179 with handicap based on 100% of 180), and Sapphire (149 and below with handicap based on 100% of 150). Overall champions (scratch) also are crowned.

Queens Tournament: Diandra Asbaty, Chicago, IL

Scratch Singles: Pam Pancoast, Lomita, CA

Scratch Doubles: Lindsay Baker, Brigham City, UT, and Elysia Current, Ephrata, PA

Scratch All-Events: Lindsay Baker, Brigham City, UT

Scratch Team: Coefficient of Friction, Palo Alto, CA

Diamond Singles: Lashon Henderson, Elgin, IL

Diamond Doubles: Corina Grasso, Fort Collins, CO, and Megan Hill, Eastlake, OH; and Lindsay Baker, Brigham City, UT, and Elysia Current, Ephrata, PA

Diamond All-Events: Joyce Biondo, Carpentersville, IL

Diamond Team: Some Strike It Hot, Albuquerque, NM

World Chess Champions, 1886-2012

Source: U.S. Chess Federation, International Chess Federation (FIDE)
Official world champions since the title was first used, as of Oct. 1, 2012.

1886-94	Wilhelm Steinitz, Austria	1972-75	Bobby Fischer, U.S.[2]
1894-1921	Emanuel Lasker, Germany	1975-85	Anatoly Karpov, USSR
1921-27	Jose R. Capablanca, Cuba	1985-2000	Garry Kasparov, USSR/Russia[3]
1927-35	Alexander Alekhine, France	1993-99	Anatoly Karpov, Russia (FIDE)[3]
1935-37	Max Euwe, Netherlands	1999-2000	Alexander Khalifman, Russia (FIDE)
1937-46	Alexander Alekhine, France[1]	2000-02	Viswanathan Anand, India (FIDE)
1948-57	Mikhail Botvinnik, USSR	2000-06	Vladimir Kramnik, Russia (classical)[4,5]
1957-58	Vassily Smyslov, USSR	2002-04	Ruslan Ponomariov, Ukraine (FIDE)
1958-59	Mikhail Botvinnik, USSR	2004-05	Rustam Kasimdzhanov, Uzbekistan (FIDE)
1960-61	Mikhail Tal, USSR	2005-06	Veselin Topalov, Bulgaria (FIDE)
1961-63	Mikhail Botvinnik, USSR	2006-07	Vladimir Kramnik, Russia[5]
1963-69	Tigran Petrosian, USSR	2007-	Viswanathan Anand, India
1969-72	Boris Spassky, USSR		

(1) After Alekhine died in 1946, the title was vacant until 1948, when Botvinnik won the first world championship event sanctioned by FIDE. (2) Defaulted championship after refusing to accept FIDE rules for a championship match, Apr. 1975. (3) Kasparov broke with FIDE, Feb. 26, 1993. FIDE stripped Kasparov of his FIDE title Mar. 23. Kasparov defeated Nigel Short (UK) in a world championship match played Sept.-Oct. 1993 under the auspices of the Professional Chess Association (PCA), a new organization the two had founded. FIDE held a championship match between Anatoly Karpov (Russia) and Jan Timman (Netherlands), which Karpov won in Nov. 1993. The PCA folded in 1995, but Kasparov was still considered the "classical" world champion. (4) In Nov. 2000, Kramnik defeated Garry Kasparov (Russia) for the classical world championship title in London. (5) Kramnik, the classical world champion since 2000, and Veselin Topalov, FIDE champion since 2005, met at a world chess championship match in Elista, Russia, to compete for a unified championship, which Kramnik won Oct. 13, 2006.

U.S. and World Figure Skating Champions, 1952-2012

U.S. Champions			World Champions	
Men, country	Women, country	Year	Men, country	Women, country
Dick Button	Tenley Albright	1952	Dick Button, U.S.	Jacqueline du Bief, France
Hayes Jenkins	Tenley Albright	1953	Hayes Jenkins, U.S.	Tenley Albright, U.S.
Hayes Jenkins	Tenley Albright	1954	Hayes Jenkins, U.S.	Gundi Busch, W. Germany
Hayes Jenkins	Tenley Albright	1955	Hayes Jenkins, U.S.	Tenley Albright, U.S.
Hayes Jenkins	Tenley Albright	1956	Hayes Jenkins, U.S.	Carol Heiss, U.S.
Dave Jenkins	Carol Heiss	1957	Dave Jenkins, U.S.	Carol Heiss, U.S.
Dave Jenkins	Carol Heiss	1958	Dave Jenkins, U.S.	Carol Heiss, U.S.
Dave Jenkins	Carol Heiss	1959	Dave Jenkins, U.S.	Carol Heiss, U.S.
Dave Jenkins	Carol Heiss	1960	Alain Giletti, France	Carol Heiss, U.S.
Bradley Lord	Laurence Owen	1961	None	None
Monty Hoyt	Barbara Roles Pursley	1962	Don Jackson, Canada	Sjoukje Dijkstra, Netherlands
Tommy Litz	Lorraine Hanlon	1963	Don McPherson, Canada	Sjoukje Dijkstra, Netherlands
Scott Allen	Peggy Fleming	1964	Manfred Schnelldorfer, W. Germany	Sjoukje Dijkstra, Netherlands
Gary Visconti	Peggy Fleming	1965	Alain Calmat, France	Petra Burka, Canada
Scott Allen	Peggy Fleming	1966	Emmerich Danzer, Austria	Peggy Fleming, U.S.
Gary Visconti	Peggy Fleming	1967	Emmerich Danzer, Austria	Peggy Fleming, U.S.
Tim Wood	Peggy Fleming	1968	Emmerich Danzer, Austria	Peggy Fleming, U.S.
Tim Wood	Janet Lynn	1969	Tim Wood, U.S.	Gabriele Seyfert, E. Germany
Tim Wood	Janet Lynn	1970	Tim Wood, U.S.	Gabriele Seyfert, E. Germany
John Misha Petkevich	Janet Lynn	1971	Ondrej Nepela, Czechoslovakia	Beatrix Schuba, Austria
Ken Shelley	Janet Lynn	1972	Ondrej Nepela, Czechoslovakia	Beatrix Schuba, Austria
Gordon McKellen Jr.	Janet Lynn	1973	Ondrej Nepela, Czechoslovakia	Karen Magnussen, Canada
Gordon McKellen Jr.	Dorothy Hamill	1974	Jan Hoffmann, E. Germany	Christine Errath, E. Germany
Gordon McKellen Jr.	Dorothy Hamill	1975	Sergei Volkov, USSR	Dianne de Leeuw, Neth.-U.S.
Terry Kubicka	Dorothy Hamill	1976	John Curry, UK	Dorothy Hamill, U.S.
Charles Tickner	Linda Fratianne	1977	Vladimir Kovalev, USSR	Linda Fratianne, U.S.
Charles Tickner	Linda Fratianne	1978	Charles Tickner, U.S.	Anett Poetzsch, E. Germany
Charles Tickner	Linda Fratianne	1979	Vladimir Kovalev, USSR	Linda Fratianne, U.S.
Charles Tickner	Linda Fratianne	1980	Jan Hoffmann, E. Germany	Anett Poetzsch, E. Germany
Scott Hamilton	Elaine Zayak	1981	Scott Hamilton, U.S.	Denise Biellmann, Switzerland
Scott Hamilton	Rosalynn Sumners	1982	Scott Hamilton, U.S.	Elaine Zayak, U.S.
Scott Hamilton	Rosalynn Sumners	1983	Scott Hamilton, U.S.	Rosalynn Sumners, U.S.
Scott Hamilton	Rosalynn Sumners	1984	Scott Hamilton, U.S.	Katarina Witt, E. Germany
Brian Boitano	Tiffany Chin	1985	Aleksandr Fadeev, USSR	Katarina Witt, E. Germany
Brian Boitano	Debi Thomas	1986	Brian Boitano, U.S.	Debi Thomas, U.S.
Brian Boitano	Jill Trenary	1987	Brian Orser, Canada	Katarina Witt, E. Germany
Brian Boitano	Debi Thomas	1988	Brian Boitano, U.S.	Katarina Witt, E. Germany
Christopher Bowman	Jill Trenary	1989	Kurt Browning, Canada	Midori Ito, Japan
Todd Eldredge	Jill Trenary	1990	Kurt Browning, Canada	Jill Trenary, U.S.
Todd Eldredge	Tonya Harding	1991	Kurt Browning, Canada	Kristi Yamaguchi, U.S.

U.S. Champions			World Champions	
Men	**Women**	**Year**	**Men, country**	**Women, country**
Christopher Bowman	Kristi Yamaguchi	1992	Viktor Petrenko, Ukraine	Kristi Yamaguchi, U.S.
Scott Davis	Nancy Kerrigan	1993	Kurt Browning, Canada	Oksana Baiul, Ukraine
Scott Davis	Vacant[1]	1994	Elvis Stojko, Canada	Yuka Sato, Japan
Todd Eldredge	Nicole Bobek	1995	Elvis Stojko, Canada	Chen Lu, China
Rudy Galindo	Michelle Kwan	1996	Todd Eldredge, U.S.	Michelle Kwan, U.S.
Todd Eldredge	Tara Lipinski	1997	Elvis Stojko, Canada	Tara Lipinski, U.S.
Todd Eldredge	Michelle Kwan	1998	Alexei Yagudin, Russia	Michelle Kwan, U.S.
Michael Weiss	Michelle Kwan	1999	Alexei Yagudin, Russia	Maria Butyrskaya, Russia
Michael Weiss	Michelle Kwan	2000	Alexei Yagudin, Russia	Michelle Kwan, U.S.
Timothy Goebel	Michelle Kwan	2001	Yevgeny Plushenko, Russia	Michelle Kwan, U.S.
Todd Eldredge	Michelle Kwan	2002	Alexei Yagudin, Russia	Irina Slutskaya, Russia
Michael Weiss	Michelle Kwan	2003	Yevgeny Plushenko, Russia	Michelle Kwan, U.S.
Johnny Weir	Michelle Kwan	2004	Yevgeny Plushenko, Russia	Shizuka Arakawa, Japan
Johnny Weir	Michelle Kwan	2005	Stephane Lambiel, Switzerland	Irina Slutskaya, Russia
Johnny Weir	Sasha Cohen	2006	Stephane Lambiel, Switzerland	Kimmie Meissner, U.S.
Evan Lysacek	Kimmie Meissner	2007	Brian Joubert, France	Miki Ando, Japan
Evan Lysacek	Mirai Nagasu	2008	Jeffrey Buttle, Canada	Mao Asada, Japan
Jeremy Abbott	Alissa Czisny	2009	Evan Lysacek, U.S.	Yu-Na Kim, South Korea
Jeremy Abbott	Rachael Flatt	2010	Daisuke Takahashi, Japan	Mao Asada, Japan
Ryan Bradley	Alissa Czisny	2011	Patrick Chan, Canada	Miki Ando, Japan
Jeremy Abbott	Ashley Wagner	2012	Patrick Chan, Canada	Carolina Kostner, Italy

(1) Tonya Harding was stripped of the title for her involvement in an attack on rival Nancy Kerrigan.

Alpine Skiing World Cup Champions, 1967-2012

Year	Men's champion, country	Year	Men's champion, country	Year	Women's champion, country
1967	Jean Claude Killy, France	1998	Hermann Maier, Austria	1981	Marie-Theres Nadig, Switzerland
1968	Jean Claude Killy, France	1999	Lasse Kjus, Norway	1982	Erika Hess, Switzerland
1969	Karl Schranz, Austria	2000	Hermann Maier, Austria	1983	Tamara McKinney, U.S.
1970	Karl Schranz, Austria	2001	Hermann Maier, Austria	1984	Erika Hess, Switzerland
1971	Gustavo Thoeni, Italy	2002	Stephan Eberharter, Austria	1985	Michela Figini, Switzerland
1972	Gustavo Thoeni, Italy	2003	Stephan Eberharter, Austria	1986	Maria Walliser, Switzerland
1973	Gustavo Thoeni, Italy	2004	Hermann Maier, Austria	1987	Maria Walliser, Switzerland
1974	Piero Gros, Italy	2005	Bode Miller, U.S.	1988	Michela Figini, Switzerland
1975	Gustavo Thoeni, Italy	2006	Benjamin Raich, Austria	1989	Vreni Schneider, Switzerland
1976	Ingemar Stenmark, Sweden	2007	Aksel Lund Svindal, Norway	1990	Petra Kronberger, Austria
1977	Ingemar Stenmark, Sweden	2008	Bode Miller, U.S.	1991	Petra Kronberger, Austria
1978	Ingemar Stenmark, Sweden	2009	Aksel Lund Svindal, Norway	1992	Petra Kronberger, Austria
1979	Peter Luescher, Switzerland	2010	Carlo Janka, Switzerland	1993	Anita Wachter, Austria
1980	Andreas Wenzel, Liechtenstein	2011	Ivica Kostelic, Croatia	1994	Vreni Schneider, Switzerland
1981	Phil Mahre, U.S.	2012	Marcel Hirscher, Austria	1995	Vreni Schneider, Switzerland
1982	Phil Mahre, U.S.			1996	Katja Seizinger, Germany
1983	Phil Mahre, U.S.	**Year**	**Women's champion, country**	1997	Pernilla Wiberg, Sweden
1984	Pirmin Zurbriggen, Switzerland	1967	Nancy Greene, Canada	1998	Katja Seizinger, Germany
1985	Marc Girardelli, Luxembourg	1968	Nancy Greene, Canada	1999	Alexandra Meissnitzer, Austria
1986	Marc Girardelli, Luxembourg	1969	Gertrud Gabl, Austria	2000	Renate Goetschl, Austria
1987	Pirmin Zurbriggen, Switzerland	1970	Michele Jacot, France	2001	Janica Kostelic, Croatia
1988	Pirmin Zurbriggen, Switzerland	1971	Annemarie Proell, Austria	2002	Michaela Dorfmeister, Austria
1989	Marc Girardelli, Luxembourg	1972	Annemarie Proell, Austria	2003	Janica Kostelic, Croatia
1990	Pirmin Zurbriggen, Switzerland	1973	Annemarie Proell, Austria	2004	Anja Paerson, Sweden
1991	Marc Girardelli, Luxembourg	1974	Annemarie Proell, Austria	2005	Anja Paerson, Sweden
1992	Paul Accola, Switzerland	1975	Annemarie Proell, Austria	2006	Janica Kostelic, Croatia
1993	Marc Girardelli, Luxembourg	1976	Rose Mittermaier, W. Germany	2007	Nicole Hosp, Austria
1994	Kjetil Andre Aamodt, Norway	1977	Lise-Marie Morerod, Switzerland	2008	Lindsey Vonn, U.S.
1995	Alberto Tomba, Italy	1978	Hanni Wenzel, Liechtenstein	2009	Lindsey Vonn, U.S.
1996	Lasse Kjus, Norway	1979	Annemarie Proell Moser, Austria	2010	Lindsey Vonn, U.S.
1997	Luc Alphand, France	1980	Hanni Wenzel, Liechtenstein	2011	Maria Höfl-Riesch, Germany
				2012	Lindsey Vonn, U.S.

Tour de France, 2012

The UK's Bradley Wiggins July 22, 2012, became the first British rider ever to win the Tour de France in the 99th edition of cycling's premier race. The 2,173-mile (3,497-km) Tour de France began June 30 with Cadel Evans defending his title. Just a few days before the Olympic Games would open in London, Wiggins finished the race in 87 hr., 34 min., 47 sec.

Alberto Contador of Spain was found guilty of doping Feb. 6, 2012, by the Court of Arbitration for Sport. Contador had tested positive for a banned substance during the 2010 Tour. Contador was stripped of his 2010 Tour win and suspended from competition for two years. Seven-time Tour champion Lance Armstrong, cycling's most high-profile U.S. athlete, announced Aug. 23, 2012, that he would stop fighting the doping charges brought against him by the U.S. Anti-Doping Agency (USADA). Armstrong did not admit to doping though the USADA had eyewitness testimony from former Armstrong teammates. The 41-year-old Armstrong was barred from competitive sports and lost his unprecedented seven Tour de France titles and any other victories, titles, and awards claimed since Aug. 1998.

Tour de France Winners, 1980-2012

Year	Winner, country	Year	Winner, country	Year	Winner, country
1980	Zoop Zoetemelk, Netherlands	1991	Miguel Indurain, Spain	2002	Vacant[1]
1981	Bernard Hinault, France	1992	Miguel Indurain, Spain	2003	Vacant[1]
1982	Bernard Hinault, France	1993	Miguel Indurain, Spain	2004	Vacant[1]
1983	Laurent Fignon, France	1994	Miguel Indurain, Spain	2005	Vacant[1]
1984	Laurent Fignon, France	1995	Miguel Indurain, Spain	2006	Oscar Pereiro, Spain[2]
1985	Bernard Hinault, France	1996	Bjarne Riis, Denmark	2007	Alberto Contador, Spain
1986	Greg LeMond, U.S.	1997	Jan Ullrich, Germany	2008	Carlos Sastre, Spain
1987	Stephen Roche, Ireland	1998	Marco Pantani, Italy	2009	Alberto Contador, Spain
1988	Pedro Delgado, Spain	1999	Vacant[1]	2010	Andy Schleck, Luxembourg[3]
1989	Greg LeMond, U.S.	2000	Vacant[1]	2011	Cadel Evans, Australia
1990	Greg LeMond, U.S.	2001	Vacant[1]	2012	Bradley Wiggins, UK

(1) Lance Armstrong, U.S., was stripped of his seven Tour titles Oct. 22, 2012, in accordance with World Anti-Doping Code; Armstrong dropped his fight against doping charges Aug. 23, 2012. (2) Floyd Landis, U.S., was stripped of the 2006 title, Sept. 20, 2007, for doping. Landis lost a final appeal of the ruling June 30, 2008. (3) Alberto Contador, Spain, was stripped of the 2010 title, Feb. 6, 2012, for doping.

World Swimming Records

Long course (50 m), as of Oct. 2012. All times in minutes:seconds.

Men's Records

Freestyle

Distance	Record	Holder	Nationality	Location	Date
50 meters	0:20.91	César Cielo Filho	Brazil	São Paulo, Brazil	Dec. 18, 2009
100 meters	0:46.91	César Cielo Filho	Brazil	Rome, Italy	July 30, 2009
200 meters	1:42.00	Paul Biedermann	Germany	Rome, Italy	July 28, 2009
400 meters	3:40.07	Paul Biedermann	Germany	Rome, Italy	July 26, 2009
800 meters	7:32.12	Zhang Lin	China	Rome, Italy	July 29, 2009
1,500 meters	14:34.14	Yang Sun	China	Shanghai, China	July 31, 2011

Backstroke

Distance	Record	Holder	Nationality	Location	Date
50 meters	0:24.04	Liam Tancock	UK	Rome, Italy	Aug. 2, 2009
100 meters	0:51.94	Aaron Peirsol	U.S.	Indianapolis, IN	July 7, 2009
200 meters	1:51.92	Aaron Peirsol	U.S.	Rome, Italy	July 31, 2009

Breaststroke

Distance	Record	Holder	Nationality	Location	Date
50 meters	0:26.67	Cameron van der Burgh	South Africa	Rome, Italy	July 29, 2009
100 meters	0:58.46	Cameron van der Burgh	South Africa	London, England, UK	July 29, 2012
200 meters	2:07.28	Daniel Gyurta	Hungary	London, England, UK	Aug. 1, 2012

Butterfly

Distance	Record	Holder	Nationality	Location	Date
50 meters	0:22.43	Rafael Muñoz	Spain	Malaga, Spain	Apr. 5, 2009
100 meters	0:49.82	Michael Phelps	U.S.	Rome, Italy	Aug. 1, 2009
200 meters	1:51.51	Michael Phelps	U.S.	Rome, Italy	July 29, 2009

Individual medley

Distance	Record	Holder	Nationality	Location	Date
200 meters	1:54.00	Ryan Lochte	U.S.	Shanghai, China	July 28, 2011
400 meters	4:03.84	Michael Phelps	U.S.	Beijing, China	Aug. 10, 2008

Freestyle relay

Distance	Record	Holder	Nationality	Location	Date
400 m (4×100)	3:08.24	Phelps, Weber-Gale, Jones, Lezak	U.S.	Beijing, China	Aug. 11, 2008
800 m (4×200)	6:58.55	Phelps, Berens, Walters, Lochte	U.S.	Rome, Italy	July 31, 2009

Medley relay

Distance	Record	Holder	Nationality	Location	Date
400 m (4×100)	3:27.28	Peirsol, Shanteau, Phelps, Walters	U.S.	Rome, Italy	Aug. 2, 2009

Women's Records

Freestyle

Distance	Record	Holder	Nationality	Location	Date
50 meters	0:23.73	Britta Steffen	Germany	Rome, Italy	Aug. 2, 2009
100 meters	0:52.07	Britta Steffen	Germany	Rome, Italy	July 31, 2009
200 meters	1:52.98	Federica Pellegrini	Italy	Rome, Italy	July 29, 2009
400 meters	3:59.15	Federica Pellegrini	Italy	Rome, Italy	July 26, 2009
800 meters	8:14.10	Rebecca Adlington	UK	Beijing, China	Aug. 16, 2008
1,500 meters	15:42.54	Kate Ziegler	U.S.	Mission Viejo, CA	June 17, 2007

Backstroke

Distance	Record	Holder	Nationality	Location	Date
50 meters	0:27.06	Zhao Jing	China	Rome, Italy	July 30, 2009
100 meters	0:58.12	Gemma Spofforth	UK	Rome, Italy	July 28, 2009
200 meters	2:04.81	Kirsty Coventry	Zimbabwe	Rome, Italy	Aug. 1, 2009

Breaststroke

Distance	Record	Holder	Nationality	Location	Date
50 meters	0:29.80	Jessica Hardy	U.S.	Federal Way, WA	Aug. 7, 2009
100 meters	1:04.45	Jessica Hardy	U.S.	Federal Way, WA	Aug. 7, 2009
200 meters	2:19.59	Rebecca Soni	U.S.	London, England, UK	Aug. 2, 2012

Butterfly

Distance	Record	Holder	Nationality	Location	Date
50 meters	0:25.07	Therese Alshammar	Sweden	Rome, Italy	July 31, 2009
100 meters	0:55.98	Dana Vollmer	U.S.	London, England, UK	July 29, 2012
200 meters	2:01.81	Liu Zige	China	Jinan, China	Oct. 21, 2009

Individual medley

Distance	Record	Holder	Nationality	Location	Date
200 meters	2:06.15	Ariana Kukors	U.S.	Rome, Italy	July 27, 2009
400 meters	4:28.43	Ye Shiwen	China	London, England, UK	July 28, 2012

Freestyle relay

Distance	Record	Holder	Nationality	Location	Date
400 m (4×100)	3:31.72	Dekker, Kromowidjojo, Heemskerk, Veldhuis	Netherlands	Rome, Italy	July 26, 2009
800 m (4×200)	7:42.08	Yang, Zhu, Liu, Pang	China	Rome, Italy	July 30, 2009

Medley relay

Distance	Record	Holder	Nationality	Location	Date
400 m (4×100)	3:52.19	Zhao, Chen, Jiao, Li	China	Rome, Italy	Aug. 1, 2009

World Track and Field Outdoor Records

As of Oct. 1, 2012.

The International Association of Athletics Federations (IAAF), the world body of track and field, recognizes only records in metric distances, except for the mile. * = Record pending ratification.

Men's Records

Running

Event	Record	Holder	Nationality	Location	Date
100 meters	9.58 s.	Usain Bolt	Jamaica	Berlin, Germany	Aug. 16, 2009
200 meters	19.19 s.	Usain Bolt	Jamaica	Berlin, Germany	Aug. 20, 2009
400 meters	43.18 s.	Michael Johnson	U.S.	Seville, Spain	Aug. 26, 1999
800 meters	1 min., 40.91 s.*	David Lekuta Rudisha	Kenya	London, England, UK	Aug. 9, 2012
1,000 meters	2 min., 11.96 s.	Noah Ngeny	Kenya	Rieti, Italy	Sept. 5, 1999
1,500 meters	3 min., 26.00 s.	Hicham El Guerrouj	Morocco	Rome, Italy	July 14, 1998
1 mile	3 min., 43.13 s.	Hicham El Guerrouj	Morocco	Rome, Italy	July 7, 1999
2,000 meters	4 min., 44.79 s.	Hicham El Guerrouj	Morocco	Berlin, Germany	Sept. 7, 1999
3,000 meters	7 min., 20.67 s.	Daniel Komen	Kenya	Rieti, Italy	Sept. 1, 1996
3,000-meter stpl.	7 min., 53.63 s.	Saif Saaeed Shaheen	Qatar	Brussels, Belgium	Sept. 3, 2004
5,000 meters	12 min., 37.35 s.	Kenenisa Bekele	Ethiopia	Hengelo, Netherlands	May 31, 2004
10,000 meters	26 min., 17.53 s.	Kenenisa Bekele	Ethiopia	Brussels, Belgium	Aug. 26, 2005
20,000 meters	56 min., 26.00 s.	Haile Gebrselassie	Ethiopia	Ostrava, Czech Rep.	June 27, 2007
25,000 meters	1 hr., 12 min., 25.4 s.	Moses Cheruiyot Mosop	Kenya	Eugene, OR	June 3, 2011
Marathon	2 hr., 3 min., 38 s.*	Patrick Makau Musyoki	Kenya	Berlin, Germany	Sept. 25, 2011
110-meter hurdles	12.80 s.	Aries Merritt	U.S.	Brussels, Belgium	Sept. 7, 2012
400-meter hurdles	46.78 s.	Kevin Young	U.S.	Barcelona, Spain	Aug. 6, 1992
400 m (4×100)	36.84 s.*	(Carter, Frater, Blake, Bolt)	Jamaica	London, England, UK	Aug. 11, 2012
800 m (4×200)	1 min., 18.68 s.	(Marsh, Burrell, Heard, Lewis)	U.S.	Walnut, CA	Apr. 17, 1994
1,600 m (4×400)	2 min., 54.29 s.[1]	(Valmon, Watts, Reynolds, Johnson)	U.S.	Stuttgart, Germany	Aug. 22, 1993
3,200 m (4×800)	7 min., 2.43 s.	(Mutua, Yiampoy, Kombich, Bungei)	Kenya	Brussels, Belgium	Aug. 25, 2006

(1) IAAF voted in Aug. 2008 to revoke a world record set by the U.S. team in 1998; one of the team's members, Antonio Pettigrew, admitted to doping in May 2008.

Field Events

Event	Record	Holder	Nationality	Location	Date
High jump	2.45 m (8' ½")	Javier Sotomayor	Cuba	Salamanca, Spain	July 27, 1993
Long jump	8.95 m (29' 4½")	Mike Powell	U.S.	Tokyo, Japan	Aug. 30, 1991
Triple jump	18.29 m (60' ¼")	Jonathan Edwards	UK	Göteborg, Sweden	Aug. 7, 1995
Pole vault	6.14 m (20' 1¾")	Sergey Bubka	Ukraine	Sestriere, Italy	July 31, 1994
Shot put	23.12 m (75' 10¼")	Randy Barnes	U.S.	Westwood, CA	May 20, 1990
Discus	74.08 m (243' 0")	Jürgen Schult	E. Germany	Neubrandenburg, E. Germany	June 6, 1986
Hammer	86.74 m (284' 7")	Yuriy Sedykh	USSR	Stuttgart, W. Germany	Aug. 30, 1986
Javelin	98.48 m (323' 1")	Jan Zelezný	Czech Rep.	Stuttgart, W. Germany	May 25, 1996
Decathlon	9,039 pts.	Ashton Eaton	U.S.	Eugene, OR	June 23, 2012

Women's Records

Running

Event	Record	Holder	Nationality	Location	Date
100 meters	10.49 s.	Florence Griffith-Joyner	U.S.	Indianapolis, IN	July 16, 1988
200 meters	21.34 s.	Florence Griffith-Joyner	U.S.	Seoul, S. Korea	Sept. 29, 1988
400 meters	47.60 s.	Marita Koch	E. Germany	Canberra, Australia	Oct. 6, 1985
800 meters	1 min., 53.28 s.	Jarmila Kratochvílová	Czechoslovakia	Munich, W. Germany	July 26, 1983
1,000 meters	2 min., 28.98 s.	Svetlana Masterkova	Russia	Brussels, Belgium	Aug. 23, 1996
1,500 meters	3 min., 50.46 s.	Qu Yunxia	China	Beijing, China	Sept. 11, 1993
1 mile	4 min., 12.56 s.	Svetlana Masterkova	Russia	Zürich, Switzerland	Aug. 14, 1996
2,000 meters	5 min., 25.36 s.	Sonia O'Sullivan	Ireland	Edinburgh, Scotland, UK	July 8, 1994
3,000 meters	8 min., 6.11 s.	Wang Junxia	China	Beijing, China	Sept. 13, 1993
3,000-meter stpl.	8 min., 58.81 s.	Gulnara Galkina-Samitova	Russia	Beijing, China	Aug. 17, 2008
5,000 meters	14 min., 11.15 s.	Tirunesh Dibaba	Ethiopia	Oslo, Norway	June 6, 2008
10,000 meters	29 min., 31.78 s.	Wang Junxia	China	Beijing, China	Sept. 8, 1993
20,000 meters	1 h., 5 min., 26.6 s.	Tegla Loroupe	Kenya	Borgholzhausen, Germany	Sept. 3, 2000
30,000 meters	1 h., 45 min., 50.0 s.	Tegla Loroupe	Kenya	Warstein, Germany	June 6, 2003
Marathon	2 h., 15 min., 25.0 s.	Paula Radcliffe	UK	London, England, UK	Apr. 13, 2003
100-meter hurdles	12.21 s.	Yordanka Donkova	Bulgaria	Stara Zagora, Bulgaria	Aug. 20, 1988
400-meter hurdles	52.34 s.	Yuliya Pechenkina	Russia	Tula, Russia	Aug. 8, 2003
400 m (4×100)	40.82 s.*	(Madison, Felix, Knight, Jeter)	U.S.	London, England, UK	Aug. 10, 2012
800 m (4×200)	1 min., 27.46 s.	(Jenkins, Colander, Perry, Jones)	U.S.	Philadelphia, PA	Apr. 29, 2000
1,600 m (4×400)	3 min., 15.17 s.	(Ledovskaya, Nazarova, Pinigina, Bryzgina)	USSR	Seoul, S. Korea	Oct. 1, 1988
3,200 m (4×800)	7 min., 50.17 s.	(Olizarenko, Gurina, Borisova, Podyalovskaya)	USSR	Moscow, USSR	Aug. 5, 1984

Field Events

Event	Record	Holder	Nationality	Location	Date
High jump	2.09 m (6' 10¼")	Stefka Kostadinova	Bulgaria	Rome, Italy	Aug. 30, 1987
Long jump	7.52 m (24' 8¼")	Galina Chistyakova	USSR	Leningrad, Russia	June 11, 1988
Triple jump	15.50 m (50' 10¼")	Inessa Kravets	Ukraine	Göteborg, Sweden	Aug. 10, 1995
Pole vault	5.06 m (16' 7¾")	Yelena Isinbaeva	Russia	Zürich, Switzerland	Aug. 28, 2009
Shot put	22.63 m (74' 3")	Natalya Lisovskaya	USSR	Moscow, Russia	June 7, 1987
Discus	76.80 m (252' 0")	Gabriele Reinsch	E. Germany	Neubrandenburg, E. Germany	July 9, 1988
Hammer	79.42 m (260' 4½")	Betty Heidler	Germany	Halle, Germany	May 21, 2011
Javelin	72.28 m (237' 1¾")	Barbora Spotáková	Czech Rep.	Stuttgart, Germany	Sept. 13, 2008
Heptathlon	7,291 pts.	Jackie Joyner-Kersee	U.S.	Seoul, S. Korea	Sept. 24, 1988

2012 Iditarod Trail Sled Dog Race

Dallas Seavey won the 40th annual Iditarod Trail Sled Dog Race from Anchorage to Nome, AK, Mar. 13, 2012, capturing the $50,400 prize and a new pick-up truck. The 25-year-old Seavey finished the 1,112-mile course along the northern route to Nome in 9 days, 4 hr., 29 min., and 26 sec., to become the youngest Iditarod champion in the race's history. The 2013 race was scheduled to begin Mar. 1 in Anchorage and follow the 1,131-mile southern route to Nome.

Westminster Kennel Club Best-In-Show Dogs, 1990-2012

Year	Best-In-Show	Breed	Owner(s)
1990	Ch. Wendessa Crown Prince	Pekingese	Ed Jenner
1991	Ch. Whisperwind on a Carousel	Poodle	Joan and Frederick Hartsock
1992	Ch. Registry's Lonesome Dove	Fox Terrier	Marion and Sam Lawrence
1993	Ch. Salilyn's Condor	English Springer Spaniel	Donna and Roger Herzig
1994	Ch. Chidley Willum	Norwich Terrier	Ruth Cooper, Patricia Lussier
1995	Ch. Gaelforce Post Script	Scottish Terrier	Dr. Vandra Huber, Dr. Joe Kinnarney
1996	Ch. Clussexx Country Sunrise	Clumber Spaniel	Judith and Richard Zaleski
1997	Ch. Parsifal Di Casa Netzer	Standard Schnauzer	Rita Holloway, Gabrio Del Torre
1998	Ch. Fairewood Frolic	Norwich Terrier	Sandina Kennels
1999	Ch. Loteki Supernatural Being	Papillon	John Oulton
2000	Ch. Salilyn 'N Erin's Shameless	English Springer Spaniel	Carl Blain, Fran Sunseri, Julia Gasow
2001	Ch. Special Times Just Right	Bichon Frise	Cecilia Ruggles, E. McDonald, F. Werneck
2002	Ch. Surrey Spice Girl	Poodle (Miniature)	Ron L. and Barbara Scott
2003	Ch. Torum's Scarf Michael	Kerry Blue Terrier	Marilu Hanson
2004	Ch. Darbydale's All Rise Pouchcove	Newfoundland	Peggy Helming, Carol A. Bernard Bergmann
2005	Ch. Kan-Point's VJK Autumn Roses	German Shorthaired Pointer	Linda & Richard Stark, Carol Cronk, Valerie Nunes-Atkinson
2006	Ch. Rocky Top's Sundance Kid	Bull Terrier (colored)	Barbara Bishop, W. F. Poole, N. Shepherd, R. P. Poole
2007	Ch. Felicity's Diamond Jim	English Springer Spaniel	Teresa and Allen Patton, Ruth Dehmel, D. Hadsall
2008	Ch. K-Run's Park Me In First	Beagle (15 in.)	Caroline Dowell, Eddie Dziuk, Jon Woodring, Kathy Weichert
2009	Ch. Clussexx Three D Grinchy Glee	Sussex Spaniel	Cecilia Ruggles, Beth Dowd, Scott Sommer
2010	Ch. Roundtown Mercedes Of Maryscot	Scottish Terrier	Amelia Musser
2011	Ch. Foxcliffe Hickory Wind	Scottish Deerhound	Sally Sweatt, Cecilia L. Dove, R. Scott Dove
2012	Ch. Palacegarden Malachy	Pekingese	Iris Love, S. Middlebrooks, D. Fitzpatrick

MARATHONS
World Marathon Majors

Five of the world's leading marathons (Berlin, Boston, Chicago, London, and New York) agreed Jan. 23, 2006, to form a series called the World Marathon Majors. Marathon runners are awarded points relative to their finish in each race in the series and in Olympic and the Intl. Assn. of Athletics Federations World Championships marathons. The male and female runners with the most points at the end of each two-year cycle win $500,000. The 2010-11 World Marathon Majors series winners were Emmanuel Mutai, Kenya, and Liliya Shobukhova, Russia.

Boston Marathon Winners, 1972-2012
All times in hour:minute:second format. * = Course record.

Men's winner, country	Time	Year	Women's winner, country	Time
Olavi Suomalainen, Finland	2:15:39	1972	Nina Kuscsik, U.S.	3:10:26
Jon Anderson, U.S.	2:16:03	1973	Jacqueline Hansen, U.S.	3:05:59
Neil Cusack, Ireland	2:13:39	1974	Michiko Gorman, U.S.	2:47:11
Bill Rodgers, U.S.	2:09:55	1975	Liane Winter, West Germany	2:42:24
Jack Fultz, U.S.	2:20:19	1976	Kim Merritt, U.S.	2:47:10
Jerome Drayton, Canada	2:14:46	1977	Michiko Gorman, U.S.	2:48:33
Bill Rodgers, U.S.	2:10:13	1978	Gayle S. Barron, U.S.	2:44:52
Bill Rodgers, U.S.	2:09:27	1979	Joan Benoit, U.S.	2:35:15
Bill Rodgers, U.S.	2:12:11	1980	Jacqueline Gareau, Canada	2:34:28
Toshihiko Seko, Japan	2:09:26	1981	Allison Roe, New Zealand	2:26:46
Alberto Salazar, U.S.	2:08:52	1982	Charlotte Teske, West Germany	2:29:33
Greg Meyer, U.S.	2:09:00	1983	Joan Benoit, U.S.	2:22:43
Geoff Smith, England, UK	2:10:34	1984	Lorraine Moller, New Zealand	2:29:28
Geoff Smith, England, UK	2:14:05	1985	Lisa Larsen Weidenbach, U.S.	2:34:06
Robert de Castella, Australia	2:07:51	1986	Ingrid Kristiansen, Norway	2:24:55
Toshihiko Seko, Japan	2:11:50	1987	Rosa Mota, Portugal	2:25:21
Ibrahim Hussein, Kenya	2:08:43	1988	Rosa Mota, Portugal	2:24:30
Abebe Mekonnen, Ethiopia	2:09:06	1989	Ingrid Kristiansen, Norway	2:24:33
Gelindo Bordin, Italy	2:08:19	1990	Rosa Mota, Portugal	2:25:24
Ibrahim Hussein, Kenya	2:11:06	1991	Wanda Panfil, Poland	2:24:18
Ibrahim Hussein, Kenya	2:08:14	1992	Olga Markova, Russia	2:23:43
Cosmas Ndeti, Kenya	2:09:33	1993	Olga Markova, Russia	2:25:27
Cosmas Ndeti, Kenya	2:07:15	1994	Uta Pippig, Germany	2:21:45
Cosmas Ndeti, Kenya	2:09:22	1995	Uta Pippig, Germany	2:25:11
Moses Tanui, Kenya	2:09:15	1996	Uta Pippig, Germany	2:27:12
Lameck Aguta, Kenya	2:10:34	1997	Fatuma Roba, Ethiopia	2:26:23
Moses Tanui, Kenya	2:07:34	1998	Fatuma Roba, Ethiopia	2:23:21
Joseh Chebet, Kenya	2:09:52	1999	Fatuma Roba, Ethiopia	2:23:25
Elijah Lagat, Kenya	2:09:47	2000	Catherine Ndereba, Kenya	2:26:11
Lee Bong-ju, South Korea	2:09:43	2001	Catherine Ndereba, Kenya	2:23:53
Rodgers Rop, Kenya	2:09:02	2002	Margaret Okayo, Kenya	2:20:43*
Robert Kipkoech Cheruiyot, Kenya	2:10:11	2003	Svetlana Zakharova, Russia	2:25:20
Timothy Cherigat, Kenya	2:10:37	2004	Catherine Ndereba, Kenya	2:24:27
Hailu Negussie, Ethiopia	2:11:45	2005	Catherine Ndereba, Kenya	2:25:13
Robert Kipkoech Cheruiyot, Kenya	2:07:14	2006	Rita Jeptoo, Kenya	2:23:38
Robert Kipkoech Cheruiyot, Kenya	2:14:13	2007	Lidiya Grigoryeva, Russia	2:29:18
Robert Kipkoech Cheruiyot, Kenya	2:07:46	2008	Dire Tune, Ethiopia	2:25:25
Deriba Merga, Ethiopia	2:08:42	2009	Salina Kosgei, Kenya	2:32:16
Robert Kiprono Cheruiyot, Kenya	2:05:52	2010	Teyba Erkesso, Ethiopia	2:26:11
Geoffrey Mutai, Kenya	2:03:02*	2011	Caroline Kilel, Kenya	2:22:36
Wesley Korir, Kenya	2:12:40	2012	Sharon Cherop, Kenya	2:31:50

Boston Marathon Winners, 1897-1971

The first Boston Marathon was held in 1897. Women were officially accepted into the race in 1972.

Year	Winner, state/country	Time	Year	Winner, state/country	Time
1897	John J. McDermott, New York	2:55:10	1935	John A. Kelley, Massachusetts	2:32:07
1898	Ronald J. MacDonald, Canada	2:42:00	1936	Ellison M. Brown, Rhode Island	2:33:40
1899	Lawrence Brignolia, Massachusetts	2:54:38	1937	Walter Young, Canada	2:33:20
1900	John Caffery, Canada	2:39:44	1938	Leslie S. Pawson, Rhode Island	2:35:34
1901	John Caffery, Canada	2:29:23	1939	Ellison M. Brown, Rhode Island	2:28:51
1902	Sammy Mellor, New York	2:43:12	1940	Gerard Cote, Canada	2:28:28
1903	John Lorden , Massachusetts	2:41:29	1941	Leslie S. Pawson, Rhode Island	2:30:38
1904	Michael Spring, New York	2:38:04	1942	Joe Smith, Massachusetts	2:26:51
1905	Frederick Lorz, New York	2:38:25	1943	Gerard Cote, Canada	2:28:25
1906	Tim Ford, Massachusetts	2:45:45	1944	Gerard Cote, Canada	2:31:50
1907	Thomas Longboat, Canada	2:24:24	1945	John A. Kelley, Massachusetts	2:30:40
1908	Thomas Morrissey, New York	2:25:43	1946	Stylianos Kyriakides, Greece	2:29:27
1909	Henri Renaud, New Hampshire	2:53:36	1947	Yun Bok Suh, Korea	2:25:39
1910	Fred Cameron, Canada	2:28:52	1948	Gerard Cote, Canada	2:31:02
1911	Clarence DeMar, Massachusetts	2:21:39	1949	Karl Leandersson, Sweden	2:31:50
1912	Michael Ryan, New York	2:21:18	1950	Kee Yong Ham, Korea	2:32:39
1913	Fritz Carlson, Minnesota	2:25:14	1951	Shigeki Tanaka, Japan	2:27:45
1914	James Duffy, Canada	2:25:14	1952	Doroteo Flores, Guatamela	2:31:53
1915	Edouard Fabre, Canada	2:31:41	1953	Keizo Yamada, Japan	2:18:51
1916	Arthur Roth, Massachusetts	2:27:16	1954	Veikko Karvonen, Finland	2:20:39
1917	Bill Kennedy, New York	2:28:37	1955	Hideo Hamamura, Japan	2:18:22
1918	Military relay, Camp Devens	2:29:53	1956	Antti Viskari, Finland	2:14:14
1919	Carl Linder, Massachusetts	2:29:13	1957	John J. Kelley, Connecticut	2:20:05
1920	Peter Trivoulides, New York	2:29:31	1958	Franjo Mihalic, Yugoslavia	2:25:54
1921	Frank Zuna, New York	2:18:57	1959	Eino Oksanen, Finland	2:22:42
1922	Clarence DeMar, Massachusetts	2:18:10	1960	Paavo Kotila, Finland	2:20:54
1923	Clarence DeMar, Massachusetts	2:23:47	1961	Eino Oksanen, Finland	2:23:39
1924	Clarence DeMar, Massachusetts	2:29:40	1962	Eino Oksanen, Finland	2:23:48
1925	Charles Mellor, Illinois	2:33:00	1963	Aurele Vandendriessche, Belgium	2:18:58
1926	John C. Miles, Canada	2:25:40	1964	Aurele Vandendriessche, Belgium	2:19:59
1927	Clarence DeMar, Massachusetts	2:40:22	1965	Morio Shigematsu, Japan	2:16:33
1928	Clarence DeMar, Massachusetts	2:37:07	1966	Kenji Kemihara, Japan	2:17:11
1929	John C. Miles, Canada	2:33:08	1967	David McKenzie, New Zealand	2:15:45
1930	Clarence DeMar, Massachusetts	2:34:48	1968	Amby Burfoot, Connecticut	2:22:17
1931	James P. Henigan, Massachusetts	2:46:45	1969	Yoshiaki Unetani, Japan	2:13:49
1932	Paul DeBruyn, Germany	2:33:36	1970	Ron Hill, England, UK	2:10:30
1933	Leslie S. Pawson, Rhode Island	2:31:01	1971	Alvaro Mejia, Colombia	2:18:45
1934	Dave Komonen, Canada	2:32:53			

New York City Marathon Winners, 1970-2011

All times in hour:minute:second format. * = Course record.

Men's winner, country	Time	Year	Women's winner, country	Time
Gary Muhrcke, U.S.	2:31:38	1970	No finisher	—
Norman Higgins, U.S.	2:22:54	1971	Beth Bonner, U.S.	2:55:22
Sheldon Karlin, U.S.	2:27:52	1972	Nina Kuscsik, U.S.	3:08:41
Tom Fleming, U.S.	2:19:25	1973	Nina Kuscsik, U.S.	2:57:07
Norbert Sander, U.S.	2:26:30	1974	Katherine Switzer, U.S.	3:07:29
Tom Fleming, U.S.	2:19:27	1975	Kim Merritt, U.S.	2:46:14
Bill Rodgers, U.S.	2:10:10	1976	Miki Gorman, U.S.	2:39:11
Bill Rodgers, U.S.	2:11:28	1977	Miki Gorman, U.S.	2:43:10
Bill Rodgers, U.S.	2:12:12	1978	Grete Waitz, Norway	2:32:30
Bill Rodgers, U.S.	2:11:42	1979	Grete Waitz, Norway	2:27:33
Alberto Salazar, U.S.	2:09:41	1980	Grete Waitz, Norway	2:25:42
Alberto Salazar, U.S.	2:08:13	1981	Allison Roe, New Zealand	2:25:29
Alberto Salazar, U.S.	2:09:29	1982	Grete Waitz, Norway	2:27:14
Rod Dixon, New Zealand	2:08:59	1983	Grete Waitz, Norway	2:27:00
Orlando Pizzolato, Italy	2:14:53	1984	Grete Waitz, Norway	2:29:30
Orlando Pizzolato, Italy	2:11:34	1985	Grete Waitz, Norway	2:28:34
Gianni Poli, Italy	2:11:06	1986	Grete Waitz, Norway	2:28:06
Ibrahim Hussein, Kenya	2:11:01	1987	Priscilla Welch, England, UK	2:30:17
Steve Jones, Wales, UK	2:08:20	1988	Grete Waitz, Norway	2:28:07
Juma Ikangaa, Tanzania	2:08:01	1989	Ingrid Kristiansen, Norway	2:25:30
Douglas Wakiihuri, Kenya	2:12:39	1990	Wanda Panfil, Poland	2:30:45
Salvador Garcia, Mexico	2:09:28	1991	Liz McColgan, Scotland, UK	2:27:32
Willie Mtolo, South Africa	2:09:29	1992	Lisa Ondieki, Australia	2:24:40
Andres Espinosa, Mexico	2:10:04	1993	Uta Pippig, Germany	2:26:24
German Silva, Mexico	2:11:21	1994	Tegla Loroupe, Kenya	2:27:37
German Silva, Mexico	2:11:00	1995	Tegla Loroupe, Kenya	2:28:06
Giacomo Leone, Italy	2:09:54	1996	Anuta Catuna, Romania	2:28:43
John Kagwe, Kenya	2:08:12	1997	F. Rochat-Moser, Switzerland	2:28:43
John Kagwe, Kenya	2:08:45	1998	Franca Fiacconi, Italy	2:25:17
Joseph Chebet, Kenya	2:09:14	1999	Adriana Fernandez, Mexico	2:25:06
Abdelkhader El Mouaziz, Morocco	2:10:09	2000	Ludmila Petrova, Russia	2:25:45
Tesfaye Jifar, Ethiopia	2:07:43	2001	Margaret Okayo, Kenya	2:24:21
Rodgers Rop, Kenya	2:08:07	2002	Joyce Chepchumba, Kenya	2:25:56
Martin Lel, Kenya	2:10:30	2003	Margaret Okayo, Kenya	2:22:31*
Hendrik Ramaala, South Africa	2:09:28	2004	Paula Radcliffe, England, UK	2:23:10
Paul Tergat, Kenya	2:09:30	2005	Jelena Prokopcuka, Latvia	2:24:41
Marilson Gomes dos Santos, Brazil	2:09:58	2006	Jelena Prokopcuka, Latvia	2:25:05
Martin Lel, Kenya	2:09:04	2007	Paula Radcliffe, England, UK	2:23:09
Marilson Gomes dos Santos, Brazil	2:08:43	2008	Paula Radcliffe, England, UK	2:23:56
Meb Keflezighi, U.S.	2:09:15	2009	Derartu Tulu, Ethiopia	2:28:52
Gebre Gebrmariam, Ethiopia	2:08:14	2010	Edna Kiplagat, Kenya	2:28:20
Geoffrey Mutai, Kenya	2:05:06*	2011	Firehiwot Dado, Ethiopia	2:23:15

Other Marathon Results, 2012

Los Angeles Marathon: Mar. 18. Men: Simon Njoroge, Kenya, 2:12:12. Women: Fatuma Sado, Ethiopia, 2:25:39.

Paris Marathon: Apr. 15. Men: Stanley Biwott, Kenya, 2:05:12. Women: Tirfe Beyene, Ethiopia, 2:21:40.

Rotterdam Marathon: Apr. 15. Men: Yemane Adhane, Ethiopia, 2:04:48. Women: Tiki Gelana, Ethiopia, 2:18:58.

London Marathon: Apr. 22. Men: Wilson Kipsang, Kenya, 2:04:44. Women: Mary Keitany, Kenya, 2:18:37.

Berlin Marathon: Sept. 30. Men: Geoffrey Mutai, Kenya, 2:04:15. Women: Aberu Kebede, Ethiopia, 2:20:30.

Chicago Marathon: Oct. 7. Men: Tsegaye Kebede, Ethiopia, 2:04:38. Women: Atsede Baysa, Ethiopia, 2:22:03.

Ironman Triathlon World Championships, 1978-2012

All times in hour:minute:second format. * = Course record. The Ironman Triathlon World Championship—a 2.4-mile ocean swim, 112-mile bike ride, and 26.2-mile run—is held annually in Kailua-Kona, Hawaii.

Men's winner, country	Time	Year	Women's winner, country	Time
Gordon Haller, U.S.	11:46:58	1978	No finisher	—
Tom Warren, U.S.	11:15:56	1979	Lyn Lemaire, U.S.	12:55:00
Dave Scott, U.S.	9:24:33	1980	Robin Beck, U.S.	11:21:24
John Howard, U.S.	9:38:29	1981	Linda Sweeney, U.S.	12:00:32
Dave Scott, U.S.	9:08:23	1982	Julie Leach, U.S.	10:54:08
Dave Scott, U.S.	9:05:57	1983	Sylviane Puntous, Canada	10:43:36
Dave Scott, U.S	8:54:20	1984	Sylvanie Puntous, Canada	10:25:13
Scott Tinley, U.S.	8:50:54	1985	Joanne Ernst, U.S.	10:25:22
Dave Scott, U.S.	8:28:37	1986	Paula Newby-Fraser, Zimbabwe	9:49:14
Dave Scott, U.S.	8:34:13	1987	Erin Baker, New Zealand	9:35:25
Scott Molina, U.S.	8:31:00	1988	Paula Newby-Fraser, Zimbabwe	9:01:01
Mark Allen, U.S.	8:09:15	1989	Paula Newby-Fraser, Zimbabwe	9:00:56
Mark Allen, U.S.	8:28:17	1990	Erin Baker, New Zealand	9:13:42
Mark Allen, U.S.	8:18:32	1991	Paula Newby-Fraser, Zimbabwe	9:07:52
Mark Allen, U.S.	8:09:08	1992	Paula Newby-Fraser, Zimbabwe	8:55:28
Mark Allen, U.S.	8:07:45	1993	Paula Newby-Fraser, Zimbabwe	8:58:23
Greg Welch, Australia	8:20:27	1994	Paula Newby-Fraser, Zimbabwe	9:20:14
Mark Allen, U.S.	8:20:34	1995	Karen Smyers, U.S.	9:16:46
Luc Van Lierde, Belgium	8:04:08	1996	Paula Newby-Fraser, Zimbabwe	9:06:49
Thomas Hellriegel, Germany	8:33:01	1997	Heather Fuhr, Canada	9:31:43
Peter Reid, Canada	8:24:20	1998	Natascha Badmann, Switzerland	9:24:16
Luc Van Lierde, Belgium	8:17:17	1999	Lori Bowden, U.S.	9:13:02
Peter Reid, Canada	8:21:01	2000	Natascha Badmann, Switzerland	9:26:16
Timothy Deboom, U.S.	8:31:18	2001	Natascha Badmann, Switzerland	9:28:37
Timothy Deboom, U.S.	8:29:56	2002	Natascha Badmann, Switzerland	9:07:54
Peter Reid, Canada	8:22:35	2003	Lori Bowden, Canada	9:11:55
Normann Stadler, Germany	8:33:29	2004	Natascha Badmann, Switzerland[1]	9:50:04
Faris al-Sultan, Germany	8:14:17	2005	Natascha Badmann, Switzerland	9:09:30
Normann Stadler, Germany	8:11:56	2006	Michellie Jones, U.S.	9:18:31
Chris McCormack, Australia	8:15:34	2007	Chrissie Wellington, UK	9:08:45
Craig Alexander, Australia	8:17:45	2008	Chrissie Wellington, UK	9:06:23
Craig Alexander, Australia	8:20:21	2009	Chrissie Wellington, UK	8:54:02*
Chris McCormack, Australia	8:10:37	2010	Mirinda Carfrae, Australia	8:58:36
Craig Alexander, Australia	8:03:56*	2011	Chrissie Wellington, UK	8:55:08
Pete Jacobs, Australia	8:18:37	2012	Leanda Cave, U.S.	9:15:54

(1) First-place finisher Nina Kraft, Germany, admitted to using performance-enhancing drugs and was disqualified, Nov. 15, 2004.

James E. Sullivan Memorial Trophy Winners, 1930-2011

The James E. Sullivan Memorial Trophy, named after the former president of the Amateur Athletic Union (AAU) and inaugurated in 1930, is awarded annually by the AAU to the athlete who "by his or her performance, example, and influence as an amateur, has done the most during the year to advance the cause of sportsmanship."

Year Winner	Sport	Year Winner	Sport	Year Winner	Sport
1930 Bobby Jones	Golf	1961 Wilma Rudolph Ward	Track	1990 John Smith	Wrestling
1931 Barney Berlinger	Track	1962 James Beatty	Track	1991 Mike Powell	Track
1932 Jim Bausch	Track	1963 John Pennel	Track	1992 Bonnie Blair	Speed
1933 Glenn Cunningham	Track	1964 Don Schollander	Swimming		skating
1934 Bill Bonthron	Track	1965 Bill Bradley	Basketball	1993 Charlie Ward	Football,
1935 Lawson Little	Golf	1966 Jim Ryun	Track		basketball
1936 Glenn Morris	Track	1967 Randy Matson	Track	1994 Dan Jansen	Speed
1937 Don Budge	Tennis	1968 Debbie Meyer	Swimming		skating
1938 Don Lash	Track	1969 Bill Toomey	Track	1995 Bruce Baumgartner	Wrestling
1939 Joe Burk	Rowing	1970 John Kinsella	Swimming	1996 Michael Johnson	Track
1940 Greg Rice	Track	1971 Mark Spitz	Swimming	1997 Peyton Manning	Football
1941 Leslie MacMitchell	Track	1972 Frank Shorter	Track	1998 Chamique Holdsclaw	Basketball
1942 Cornelius Warmerdam	Track	1973 Bill Walton	Basketball	1999 Coco Miller and	
1943 Gilbert Dodds	Track	1974 Rick Wohlhutter	Track		Kelly Miller	Basketball
1944 Ann Curtis	Swimming	1975 Tim Shaw	Swimming	2000 Rulon Gardner	Wrestling
1945 Doc Blanchard	Football	1976 Bruce Jenner	Track	2001 Michelle Kwan	Figure
1946 Arnold Tucker	Football	1977 John Naber	Swimming		skating
1947 John Kelly Jr.	Rowing	1978 Tracy Caulkins	Swimming	2002 Sarah Hughes	Figure
1948 Robert Mathias	Track	1979 Kurt Thomas	Gymnastics		skating
1949 Dick Button	Skating	1980 Eric Heiden	Speed	2003 Michael Phelps	Swimming
1950 Fred Wilt	Track		skating	2004 Paul Hamm	Gymnastics
1951 Rev. Robert Richards	Track	1981 Carl Lewis	Track	2005 J. J. Redick	Basketball
1952 Horace Ashenfelter	Track	1982 Mary Decker	Track	2006 Jessica Long	Swimming
1953 Dr. Sammy Lee	Diving	1983 Edwin Moses	Track		(paralympics)
1954 Mal Whitfield	Track	1984 Greg Louganis	Diving	2007 Tim Tebow	Football
1955 Harrison Dillard	Track	1985 Joan Benoit		2008 Shawn Johnson	Gymnastics
1956 Patricia McCormick	Diving	Samuelson	Marathon	2009 Amy Palmiero-	Ultra-
1957 Bobby Joe Morrow	Track	1986 Jackie Joyner-Kersee	Track	Winters	marathon
1958 Glenn Davis	Track	1987 Jim Abbott	Baseball	2010 Evan Lysacek	Figure
1959 Parry O'Brien	Track	1988 Florence Griffith Joyner	Track		skating
1960 Rafer Johnson	Track	1989 Janet Evans	Swimming	2011 Andrew Rodriguez	Football

America's Cup Yacht Race, 2010

Competition for the America's Cup grew out of the first contest to establish a world yachting championship, one of the carnival features of the London Exposition of 1851. The race covered a 60-mile course around the Isle of Wight. The prize was a cup worth about $500, donated by the Royal Yacht Squadron of England, known as America's Cup because it was first won by the U.S. yacht *America*.

America's Cup Yacht Race, 1851-2010

Prior to 1983, all yachts are American unless otherwise noted.

Year	Result
1851	America
1870	Magic defeated Cambria, England (1-0)
1871	Columbia (first three races) and Sappho (last two races) defeated Livonia, England (4-1)
1876	Madeline defeated Countess of Dufferin, Canada (2-0)
1881	Mischief defeated Atalanta, Canada (2-0)
1885	Puritan defeated Genesta, England (2-0)
1886	Mayflower defeated Galatea, England (2-0)
1887	Volunteer defeated Thistle, Scotland (2-0)
1893	Vigilant defeated Valkyrie II, England (3-0)
1895	Defender defeated Valkyrie III, England (3-0)
1899	Columbia defeated Shamrock, England (3-0)
1901	Columbia defeated Shamrock II, England (3-0)
1903	Reliance defeated Shamrock III, England (3-0)
1920	Resolute defeated Shamrock IV, England (3-2)
1930	Enterprise defeated Shamrock V, England (4-0)
1934	Rainbow defeated Endeavour, England (4-2)
1937	Ranger defeated Endeavour II, England (4-0)
1958	Columbia defeated Sceptre, England (4-0)
1962	Weatherly defeated Gretel, Australia (4-1)
1964	Constellation defeated Sovereign, England (4-0)
1967	Intrepid defeated Dame Pattie, Australia (4-0)
1970	Intrepid defeated Gretel II, Australia (4-1)
1974	Courageous defeated Southern Cross, Australia (4-0)
1977	Courageous defeated Australia, Australia (4-0)
1980	Freedom defeated Australia, Australia (4-1)
1983	Australia II, Australia, defeated Liberty, U.S. (4-3)
1987	Stars & Stripes, U.S., defeated Kookaburra III, Australia (4-0)
1988	Stars & Stripes, U.S., defeated New Zealand, NZ (2-0)
1992	America[3], U.S., defeated Il Moro di Venezia, Italy (4-1)
1995	Black Magic 1, NZ, defeated Young America, U.S. (5-0)
2000	New Zealand, NZ, defeated Luna Rossa, Italy (5-0)
2003	Alinghi, Switzerland, defeated Team New Zealand, NZ (5-0)
2007	Alinghi, Switzerland, defeated Emirates Team New Zealand, NZ (5-2)
2010	USA-17, U.S., defeated Alinghi 5, Switzerland (2-0)

Rifle and Pistol Championships, 2012

Source: National Rifle Association

NRA Bianchi Cup National Action Pistol Championship

Action Pistol: Doug Koenig, Alburtis, PA, 1920-182x
Woman Action Pistol: Julie Golob, Glasgow, MT, 1907-144x
Junior Action Pistol: Tiffany Piper, Auckland, New Zealand, 1879-143x

National Outdoor Rifle and Pistol Championships

Smallbore Rifle Prone: Cpt. Christopher R. Abalo, Ft. Mitchell, AL, 4792-352x
Civilian Smallbore Rifle Prone: Reya L. Kempley, Carson City, NV, 4790-363x
Woman Smallbore Rifle Prone: Reya L. Kempley, Carson City, NV, 4790-363x
Smallbore Rifle NRA 3-Position: Tarl Kempley, Carson City, NV, 2295-108x
Civilian Smallbore Rifle NRA 3-Position: Tarl Kempley, Carson City, NV, 2295-108x
Woman Smallbore Rifle NRA 3-Position: Kirsten Weiss, Cornwall, PA, 2287-96x
High Power Rifle: Carl R. Bernosky, Ashland, PA, 2391-141x
Civilian High Power Rifle: Carl R. Bernosky, Ashland, PA, 2391-141x
Woman High Power Rifle: Sgt. Sherri J. Gallagher, U.S. Army, Ft. Benning, GA, 2390-131x
High Power Rifle Long Range: David Luckman, Great Britain, 1246-74x
Woman High Power Rifle Long Range: Michelle M. Gallagher, Phoenix, AZ, 1243-75x
Pistol: Brian H. Zins, Girard, OH, 2649-142x
Civilian Pistol: Brian H. Zins, Girard, OH, 2649-142x
Woman Pistol: Judy Tant, East Lansing, MI, 2560-89x

National Indoor Rifle and Pistol Championships

Smallbore Rifle Conventional Position: Lisette Grunwell-Lacey, Old Lyme, CT, 799-76x
Woman Smallbore Rifle Conventional Position: Denise Martin, Chewelah, WA, 794-66x
Smallbore Rifle NRA Metric Position: Lisette Grunwell-Lacey, Old Lyme, CT, 1168
Woman Smallbore Rifle NRA Metric Position: Alyssa Gestl, Palmyra, PA, 1150
International Smallbore Rifle: Ryan Anderson, Wasilla, AK, 1162
Woman International Smallbore Rifle: Anna Hjelmevoll, Fairbanks, AK, 1145
Air Rifle: Lisette Grunwell-Lacey, Old Lyme, CT, 590
Woman Air Rifle: Anna Hjelmevoll, Fairbanks, AK, 586
Conventional Pistol: John Zurek, Tucson, AZ, 893-44x
Woman Conventional Pistol: Karen Pizzitola, Ellington, CT, 857-23x
International Free Pistol: Nick Mowrer, Ramsay, MT, 555
Woman International Free Pistol: Liz David, Mountain View, CA, 445
International Standard Pistol: David Lange, Glen Rock, NJ, 566
Woman International Standard Pistol: Kathy Chatterton, Glen Rock, NJ: 539
Air Pistol: Travis Jorgenson, Vergas, MN, 581
Woman Air Pistol: Darian Shenk, Annville, PA, 557

Pro Rodeo Cowboys Association All-Around Champions, 1977-2011

Year	Winner, hometown	Earnings	Year	Winner, hometown	Earnings
1977	Tom Ferguson, Miami, OK	$76,730	1995	Joe Beaver, Huntsville, TX	$141,753
1978	Tom Ferguson, Miami, OK	103,734	1996	Joe Beaver, Huntsville, TX	166,103
1979	Tom Ferguson, Miami, OK	96,272	1997	Dan Mortensen, Manhattan, MT	184,559
1980	Paul Tierney, Rapid City, SD	105,568	1998	Ty Murray, Stephenville, TX	264,673
1981	Jimmie Cooper, Monument, NM	105,862	1999	Fred Whitfield, Hockley, TX	217,819
1982	Chris Lybbert, Coyote, CA	123,709	2000	Joe Beaver, Huntsville, TX	225,396
1983	Roy Cooper, Durant, OK	153,391	2001	Cody Ohl, Stephensville, TX	296,419
1984	Dee Pickett, Caldwell, ID	122,618	2002	Trevor Brazile, Anson, TX	273,997
1985	Lewis Feild, Elk Ridge, UT	130,347	2003	Trevor Brazile, Anson, TX	294,839
1986	Lewis Feild, Elk Ridge, UT	166,042	2004	Trevor Brazile, Decatur, TX	253,170
1987	Lewis Feild, Elk Ridge, UT	144,335	2005	Ryan Jarrett, Summerville, GA	263,665
1988	Dave Appleton, Arlington, TX	121,546	2006	Trevor Brazile, Decatur, TX	329,924
1989	Ty Murray, Odessa, TX	134,806	2007	Trevor Brazile, Decatur, TX	425,115
1990	Ty Murray, Stephenville, TX	213,772	2008	Trevor Brazile, Decatur, TX	419,868
1991	Ty Murray, Stephenville, TX	244,230	2009	Trevor Brazile, Decatur, TX	346,779
1992	Ty Murray, Stephenville, TX	225,992	2010	Trevor Brazile, Decatur, TX	507,921
1993	Ty Murray, Stephenville, TX	297,896	2011	Trevor Brazile, Decatur, TX	337,601
1994	Ty Murray, Stephenville, TX	246,170			

GENERAL INDEX

Note: Page numbers in **boldface** indicate key reference. Page numbers in *italics* indicate photo or illustration captions.

QUICK REFERENCE INDEX

For complete index, see pages 979-1007.

GERMANNA COMM COLLEGE LOCUST GROVE VA

3 7218 000 211 966

Ref.
AY
67
°N5
W7
2013

GERMANNA COMMUNITY COLLEGE
GERMANNA CENTER FOR ADVANCED TECHNOLOGY
18121 TECHNOLOGY DRIVE
CULPEPER, VA 22701

For Reference

Not to be taken from this room